Stanley Gibbons SIMPLIFIED CATALOGUE

Stamps of the World

1998 Edition

An illustrated and priced three-volume guide to the postage stamps of the whole world, excluding changes of paper, perforation, shade and watermark

VOLUME 2

FOREIGN COUNTRIES K–Z

STANLEY GIBBONS LTD
London and Ringwood

By Appointment to
Her Majesty the Queen
Stanley Gibbons Limited
London
Philatelists

63rd Edition

Published in Great Britain by
Stanley Gibbons Ltd
Publications Editorial, Sales Office and Distribution Centre
5, Parkside, Christchurch Road,
Ringwood, Hampshire BH24 3SH
Telephone 01425 472363

ISBN: 085259-431-3

Published as Stanley Gibbons Simplified Stamp Catalogue from 1934 to 1970, renamed Stamps of the World in 1971, and produced in two (1982–88) or three (from 1989) volumes as Stanley Gibbons Simplified Catalogue of Stamps of the World.
This volume published October 1997

S.G. ITEM No. 2882 (98)

Printed in Great Britain by Bemrose Security Printing, London & Derby

Stanley Gibbons
SIMPLIFIED CATALOGUE
Stamps of the World

This popular catalogue is a straightforward three-volume listing of the stamps that have been issued everywhere in the world since the very first–Great Britain's famous Penny Black in 1840.

This edition continues the three-volume format. Volume 1 (Foreign countries A-J) appears in September, Volume 2 (Foreign countries K–Z) in October, and Volume 3 covering Commonwealth countries in November.

Readers are reminded that the Catalogue Supplements, published in each issue of **Gibbons Stamp Monthly,** can be used to update the listings in **Stamps of the World** as well as our twenty-two part standard catalogue. To make the supplement even more useful the Type numbers given to the illustrations are the same in the Stamps of the World as in the standard catalogues. The first Catalogue Supplement to this Volume appeared in the August 1997 issue of **Gibbons Stamp Monthly.**

Gibbons Stamp Monthly can be obtained through newsagents or on postal subscription from Stanley Gibbons Publications, 5, Parkside, Christchurch Road, Ringwood, Hants BH24 3SH.

The catalogue has many important features:

- As an indication of current values virtually every stamp is priced. Thousands of alterations have been made since the last edition.
- By being set out on a simplified basis that excludes changes of paper, perforation, shade, watermark, gum or printer's and date imprints it is particularly easy to use. (For its exact scope see "Information for users" pages following.)
- The thousands of illustrations and helpful descriptions of stamp designs make it of maximum appeal to collectors with thematic interests.
- Its catalogue numbers are the world-recognised Stanley Gibbons numbers throughout.
- Helpful introductory notes for the collector are included, backed by much historical, geographical and currency information.
- A very detailed index gives instant location of countries in this volume, and a cross-reference to those included in other volumes.

Over 4,328 stamps and 1,168 new illustrations have been added to the listings in this volume. Last year's three-volume edition contained over 330,490 stamps and 79,375 illustrations.

The listings in this edition are based on the standard catalogues: Part 1 (British Commonwealth) (1998 edition), Part 2 (Austria & Hungary) (5th edition), Part 3 (Balkans) (3rd edition), Part 4 (Benelux) (4th edition), Part 5 (Czechoslovakia & Poland) (5th edition), Part 6 (France) (4th edition), Part 7 (Germany) (5th edition), Part 8 (Italy & Switzerland) (5th edition), Part 9 (Portugal & Spain) (4th edition), Part 10 (Russia) (4th edition), Part 11 (Scandinavia) (4th edition), Part 12 (Africa since Independence A-E) (2nd edition), Part 13 (Africa since Independence F-M) (1st edition), Part 14 (Africa since Independence N-Z) (1st edition), Part 15 (Central America) (2nd edition), Part 16 (Central Asia) (3rd edition), Part 17 (China) (5th edition), Part 18 (Japan & Korea) (4th edition), Part 19 (Middle East) (5th edition), Part 20 (South America) (3rd edition), Part 21 (South-East Asia) (3rd edition), and Part 22 (United States) (4th edition).

Important price revisions made specially for this edition include Luxembourg, Monaco, Netherlands, Netherlands Indies, Netherland New Guinea, Rwanda, Surinam, Sweden and Tunisia.

Stanley Gibbons Stamp Catalogue
Complete List of Parts

1 British Commonwealth
(Annual in two volumes)

Foreign Countries

2 Austria & Hungary (5th edition, 1994)
Austria · Bosnia & Herzegovina · U.N. (Vienna) · Hungary

3 Balkans (3rd edition, 1987)
Albania · Bulgaria · Greece & Islands · Rumania · Yugoslavia

4 Benelux (4th edition, 1993)
Belgium & Colonies · Netherlands & Colonies · Luxembourg

5 Czechoslovakia & Poland (5th edition, 1994)
Czechoslovakia · Bohemia & Moravia · Slovakia · Poland

6 France (4th edition, 1993)
France · Colonies · Post Offices · Andorra · Monaco

7 Germany (5th edition, 1996)
Germany · States · Colonies · Post Offices

8 Italy & Switzerland (5th edition, 1997)
Italy & Colonies · Fiume · San Marino · Vatican City · Trieste · Liechtenstein · Switzerland · U.N. (Geneva)

9 Portugal & Spain (4th edition, 1996)
Andorra · Portugal & Colonies · Spain & Colonies

10 Russia (4th edition, 1991)
Russia · Baltic States · Mongolia · Tuva

11 Scandinavia (4th edition, 1994)
Aland Islands · Denmark · Faroe Islands · Finland · Greenland · Iceland · Norway · Sweden

12 Africa since Independence A-E (2nd edition, 1983)
Algeria · Angola · Benin · Bophuthatswana · Burundi · Cameroun · Cape Verde · Central African Republic · Chad · Comoro Islands · Congo · Djibouti · Equatorial Guinea · Ethiopia

13 Africa since Independence F-M (1st edition, 1981)
Gabon · Guinea · Guinea-Bissau · Ivory Coast · Liberia · Libya · Malagasy Republic · Mali · Mauritania · Morocco · Mozambique

14 Africa since Independence N-Z (1st edition, 1981)
Niger Republic · Rwanda · St. Thomas & Prince · Senegal · Somalia · Sudan · Togo · Transkei · Tunisia · Upper Volta · Venda · Zaire

15 Central America (2nd edition, 1984)
Costa Rica · Cuba · Dominican Republic · El Salvador · Guatemala · Haiti · Honduras · Mexico · Nicaragua · Panama

16 Central Asia (3rd edition, 1992)
Afghanistan · Iran · Turkey

17 China (5th edition, 1995)
China · Taiwan · Tibet · Foreign P.O.s

18 Japan & Korea (4th edition, 1997)
Japan · Ryukyus · Korean Empire · South Korea · North Korea

19 Middle East (5th edition, 1996)
Bahrain · Egypt · Iraq · Israel · Jordan · Kuwait · Lebanon · Oman · Qatar · Saudi Arabia · Syria · U.A.E. · Yemen

20 South America (3rd edition, 1989)
Argentina · Bolivia · Brazil · Chile · Colombia · Ecuador · Paraguay · Peru · Surinam · Uruguay · Venezuela

21 South-East Asia (3rd edition, 1995)
Bhutan · Burma · Indonesia · Kampuchea · Laos · Myanmar · Nepal · Philippines · Thailand · Vietnam

22 United States (4th edition, 1994)
U.S. & Possessions · Canal Zone · Marshall Islands · Micronesia · Palau · U.N. (New York, Geneva, Vienna)

Thematic Catalogues

Stanley Gibbons Catalogues for use with **Stamps of the World**

Collect Aircraft on Stamps (1st edition, 1994)

Collect Birds on Stamps (4th edition, 1996)

Collect Butterflies and Other Insects on Stamps (1st edition, 1991)

Collect Chess on Stamps (out of stock)

Collect Fungi on Stamps (2nd edition, 1997)

Collect Mammals on Stamps (out of print)

Collect Railways on Stamps (new edition in preparation)

Collect Shells on Stamps (1st edition, 1995)

Collect Ships on Stamps (2nd edition, 1993)

Information for users

Aim

The aim of this catalogue is to provide a straightforward illustrated and priced guide to the postage stamps of the whole world to help to enjoy the greatest hobby of the present day.

Arrangement

The catalogue lists countries in alphabetical order and there is a complete index at the end of each volume. For ease of reference country names are also printed at the head of each page.

Within each country, postage stamps are listed first. They are followed by separate sections for such other categories as postage due stamps, parcel post stamps, express stamps, official stamps, etc.

All catalogue lists are set out according to dates of issue of the stamps, starting from the earliest and working through to the most recent. New issues received too late for inclusion in the main lists will be found as "Addenda" at the end of each volume.

Scope of the Catalogue

The *Simplified Catalogue of Stamps of the World* contains listings of postage stamps only. Apart from the ordinary definitive, commemorative and airmail stamps of each country – which appear first in each list – there are sections for the following where appropriate:

- postage due stamps
- parcel post stamps
- official stamps
- express and special delivery stamps
- charity and compulsory tax stamps
- newspaper and journal stamps
- printed matter stamps
- registration stamps
- acknowledgement of receipt stamps
- late fee and too late stamps
- military post stamps
- recorded message stamps
- personal delivery stamps

We receive numerous enquiries from collectors about other items which do not fall within the categories set out above and which consequently do not appear in the catalogue lists. It may be helpful, therefore, to summarise the other kinds of stamp that exist but which we deliberately exclude from this postage stamp catalogue.

We do *not* list the following:

Fiscal or revenue stamps: stamps used solely in collecting taxes or fees for non-postal purposes. Examples would be stamps which pay a tax on a receipt, represent the stamp duty on a contract or frank a customs document. Common inscriptions found include: Documentary, Proprietary, Inter. Revenue, Contract Note.

Local stamps: postage stamps whose validity and use are limited in area, say to a single town or city, though in some cases they provided, with official sanction, services in parts of countries not covered by the respective government.

Local carriage labels and Private local issues: many labels exist ostensibly to cover the cost of ferrying mail from one of Great Britain's offshore islands to the nearest mainland post office. They are not recognised as valid for national or international mail. Examples: Calf of Man, Davaar, Herm, Lundy, Pabay, Stroma. Items from some other places have only the status of tourist souvenir labels.

Telegraph stamps: stamps intended solely for the prepayment of telegraphic communication.

Bogus or "phantom" stamps: labels from mythical places or non-existent administrations. Examples in the classical period were Sedang, Counani, Clipperton Island and in modern times Thomond and Monte Bello Islands. Numerous labels have also appeared since the War from dissident groups as propaganda for their claims without authority from the home governments. Common examples are labels for "Free Albania", "Free Rumania", and "Free Croatia" and numerous issues for Nagaland, Indonesia and the South Moluccas ("Republik Maluku Selatan").

Railway letter fee stamps: special stamps issued by railway companies for the conveyance of letters by rail. Example: Talyllyn Railway. Similar services are now offered by some bus companies and the labels they issue likewise do not qualify for inclusion in the catalogue.

Perfins ("perforated initials"): numerous postage stamps may be found with initial letters or designs punctured through them by tiny holes. These are applied by private and public concerns as a precaution against theft and do not qualify for separate mention.

Information for users

Labels: innumerable items exist resembling stamps but – as they do not prepay postage – they are classified as labels. The commonest categories are:

– propaganda and publicity labels: designed to further a cause or campaign;

– exhibition labels: particularly souvenirs from philatelic events;

– testing labels: stamp-size labels used in testing stamp-vending machines;

– Post Office training school stamps: British stamps overprinted with two thick vertical bars or SCHOOL SPECIMEN are produced by the Post Office for training purposes;

– seals and stickers: numerous charities produce stamp-like labels, particularly at Christmas and Easter, as a means of raising funds and these have no postal validity.

Cut-outs: items of postal stationery, such as envelopes, cards and wrappers, often have stamps impressed or imprinted on them. They may usually be cut out and affixed to envelopes, etc., for postal use if desired, but such items are not listed in this catalogue.

Collectors wanting further information about exact definitions are referred to *Philatelic Terms Illustrated,* published by Stanley Gibbons and containing many illustrations in colour (third edition price £7.50 plus £3 postage and packing).

There is also a priced listing of the postal fiscals of Great Britain in our Part 1 *(British Commonwealth)* Catalogue and in Volume 1 of the *Great Britain Specialised* Catalogue (5th and later editions)

Although, as stated, none of the above qualify for inclusion in this postage stamp catalogue, this does not imply that they are of no interest to certain collectors. Indeed, in the 1950s a group was formed in Great Britain called the 'Cinderella Stamp Club', whose object is the study of all those stamps which Stanley Gibbons do *not* list in their catalogues.

Catalogue Numbers

Stanley Gibbons catalogue numbers are recognised universally and any individual stamp can be identified by quoting a catalogue number (the one at the left of the column) prefixed by the name of the country and the letters "S.G.". Do not confuse the catalogue number with the type numbers which refer to illustrations.

Prices

Prices in the left-hand column are for unused stamps and those in the right-hand column for used. Prices are given in pence and pounds:

100 pence (p) = 1 pound (£1).

Prices are shown as follows:

10 means 10p (10 pence);
1.75 means £1.75 (1 pound and 75 pence);
For £100 and above, prices are in whole pounds.

Our prices are for stamps in fine average condition, and in issues where condition varies we may ask more for the superb and less for the sub-standard.

The minimum catalogue price quoted is 10p. For individual stamps prices between 10p. and 30p. are provided as a guide for catalogue users. The lowest price *charged* for individual stamps purchased from Stanley Gibbons is 30p.

The prices quoted are generally for the cheapest variety of stamps but it is worth noting that differences of watermark, perforation, or other details, outside the scope of this catalogue, may often increase the value of the stamp.

Prices quoted for mint issues are for single examples. Those in *se-tenant* pairs, strips, blocks or sheets may be worth more.

Where prices are not given in either column it is either because the stamps are not known to exist in that particular condition, or, more usually, because there is no reliable information as to value.

All prices are subject to change without prior notice and we give no guarantee to supply all stamps priced. Prices quoted for albums, publications, etc. advertised in this catalogue are also subject to change without prior notice.

Due to different production methods it is sometimes possible for new editions of Parts 2 to 22 to appear showing revised prices which are not included in that year's *Stamps of the World.*

Unused Stamps

In the case of stamps from *Great Britain* and the *Commonwealth,* prices for unused stamps of Queen Victoria to King George V are for lightly hinged examples; unused prices of King Edward VIII to Queen Elizabeth II issues are for unmounted mint. The prices of unused *Foreign* stamps are for lightly hinged examples for those issued before 1946, thereafter for examples unmounted mint.

Used Stamps

Prices for used stamps generally refer to postally used examples, though for certain issues it is for cancelled-to-order.

Information for users

Guarantee

All stamps supplied by us are guaranteed originals in the following terms:

If not as described, and returned by the purchaser, we undertake to refund the price paid to us in the original transaction. If any stamp is certified as genuine by the Expert Committee of the Royal Philatelic Society, London, or by B.P.A. Expertising Ltd., the purchaser shall not be entitled to make any claim against us for any error, omission or mistake in such certificate.

Consumers' statutory rights are not affected by the above guarantee.

Currency

At the beginning of each country brief details give the currencies in which the values of the stamps are expressed. The dates, where given, are those of earliest stamp issues in the particular currency. Where the currency is obvious, e.g. where the colony has the same currency as the mother country, no details are given.

Illustrations

Illustrations of surcharges and overprints, which are shown and not described, are actual size; stamp illustrations are reduced to $\frac{3}{4}$ linear, *unless otherwise stated.*

"Key-Types"

A number of standard designs occur so frequently in the stamps of the French, German, Portuguese and Spanish colonies that it would be a waste of space to repeat them. Instead these are all illustrated on page xii together with the descriptive names and letters by which they are referred to in the lists.

Type Numbers

These are bold figures found below each illustration. References to "Type **6**", for example, in the lists of a country should therefore be understood to refer to the illustration below which the number **"6"** appears. These type numbers are also given in the second column of figures alongside each list of stamps, thus indicating clearly the design of each stamp. In the case of Key-Types – see above – letters take the place of the type numbers.

Where an issue comprises stamps of similar design, represented in this catalogue by one illustration, the corresponding type numbers should be taken as indicating this general design.

Where there are blanks in the type number column it means that the type of the corresponding stamps is that shown by the last number above in the type column of the same issue.

A dash (–) in the type column means that no illustration of the stamp is shown.

Where type numbers refer to stamps of another country, e.g. where stamps of one country are overprinted for use in another, this is always made clear in the text.

Stamp Designs

Brief descriptions of the subjects of the stamp designs are given either below or beside the illustrations, at the foot of the list of the issue concerned, or in the actual lists. Where a particular subject, e.g. the portrait of a well-known monarch, recurs frequently the description is not repeated, nor are obvious designs described.

Generally, the unillustrated designs are in the same shape and size as the one illustrated, except where otherwise indicated.

Surcharges and Overprints

Surcharges and overprints are usually described in the headings to the issues concerned. Where the actual wording of a surcharge or overprint is given it is shown in bold type.

Some stamps are described as being "Surcharged in words", e.g. **TWO CENTS,** and others "Surcharged in figures and words", e.g. **20 CENTS,** although of course many surcharges are in foreign languages and combinations of words and figures are numerous. There are often bars, etc., obliterating old values or inscriptions but in general these are only mentioned where it is necessary to avoid confusion.

No attention is paid in this catalogue to colours of overprints and surcharges so that stamps with the same overprint in different colours are not listed separately.

Numbers in brackets after the descriptions of overprinted or surcharged stamps are the catalogue numbers of the overprinted stamps.

Note – the words "inscribed" or "inscription" always refer to wording incorporated in the design of a stamp and not surcharges or overprints.

Coloured Papers

Where stamps are printed on coloured paper the description is given as e.g. '3'4c. black on blue" – a stamp printed in black on blue paper. No attention is paid in this catalogue to differences in the texture of paper, e.g. laid, wove.

Watermarks

Stamps having different watermarks, but otherwise the same, are not listed separately. No reference is therefore made to watermarks in this volume.

Stamp Colours

Colour names are only required for the identification of stamps, therefore they have been made as simple as possible. Thus "scarlet", "vermilion", "carmine" are all usually called red. Qualifying colour names have been introduced only where necessary for the sake of clearness.

Where stamps are printed in two or more colours the central portion of the design is in the first colour given, unless otherwise stated.

Perforations

All stamps are perforated unless otherwise stated. No distinction is made between the various gauges of perforation but early stamp issues which exist both imperforated and perforated are usually listed separately.

Where a heading states "Imperf or perf" or "Perf or rouletted" this does not necessarily mean that all values of the issue are found in both conditions.

Dates of Issue

The date given at the head of each issue is that of the appearance of the earliest stamp in the series. As stamps of the same design or issue are usually grouped together a list of King George VI stamps, for example, headed "1938" may include stamps issued from 1938 to the end of the reign.

Se-tenant Pairs

Many modern issues are printed in sheets containing different designs or face values. Such pairs, blocks, strips or sheets are described as being "se-tenant" and are outside the scope of this catalgoue, although reference to them may occur in instances where they form a composite design.

Miniature Sheets

These are outside the scope of this catalogue but are listed in all other Stanley Gibbons catalogues.

"Appendix" Countries

We regret that since 1968, it has been necessary to establish an Appendix (at the end of each country as appropriate) to which numerous stamps have had to be consigned. Several countries imagine that by issuing huge quantities of unnecessary stamps they will have a ready source of income from stamp collectors – and particulary from the less-experienced ones. Stanley Gibbons refuse to encourage this exploitation of the hobby and we do not stock the stamps concerned.

Two kinds of stamp are therefore given the briefest of mentions in the Appendix, purely for the sake of record. Administrations issuing stamps greatly in excess of true postal needs have the offending issues placed there. Likewise it contains stamps which have not fulfilled all the normal conditions for full catalogue listing.

These conditions are that the stamps must be issued by a legitimate postal authority, recognised by the government concerned, and are adhesives, valid for proper postal use in the class of service for which they are inscribed. Stamps, with the exception of such categories as postage dues and officials, must be available to the general public at face value with no artificial restrictions being imposed on their distribution.

The publishers of this catalogue have observed, with concern, the proliferation of "artificial" stamp-issuing territories. On several occasions this has resulted in separately inscribed issues for various component parts of otherwise united states or territories.

Stanley Gibbons Publications have decided that where such circumstances occur, they will not, in the future, list these items in the SG catalogue without first satisfying themselves that the stamps represent a genuine political, historical or postal division within the country concerned. Any such issues which do not fulfil this stipulation will be recorded in the Catalogue Appendix only.

Stamps in the Appendix are kept under review in the light of any newly acquired information about them. If we are satisfied that a stamp qualifies for proper listing in the body of the catalogue it is moved there.

"Undesirable Issues"

The rules governing many competitive exhibitions - including the Melville Competition - are set by the Fédération Internationale de Philatelie and stipulate a downgrading of marks for stamps classed as "undesirable issues".

This catalogue can be taken as a guide to status. All stamps in the main listings and Addenda are acceptable. Stamps in the Appendix should not be entered for competition as these are the "undesirable issues".

Information for users

Particular care is advised with Aden Protectorate States, Ajman, Bhutan, Chad, Fujeira, Khor Fakkan, Manama, Ras al Khaima, Sharjah, Umm al Qiwain and Yemen. Totally bogus stamps exist (as explained in Appendix notes) and these are to be avoided also for competition. As distinct from "undesirable stamps" certain categories are not covered in this catalogue purely by reason of its scope (see page v). Consult the particular competition rules to see if such are admissible even though not listed by us.

Where to Look for More Detailed Listings

The present work deliberately omits details of paper, perforation, shade and watermark. But as you become more absorbed in stamp collecting and wish to get greater enjoyment from the hobby you may well want to study these matters.

All the information you require about any particular postage stamp will be found in the main Stanley Gibbons Catalogues.

Commonwealth countries in Volume 3 are covered by the Part 1 (British Commonwealth) Catalogue published annually in two volumes.

For foreign countries you can easily find which catalogue to consult by looking at the country headings in the present book.

To the right of each country name are code letters specifying which volume of our main catalogues contains that country's listing.

The code letters are as follows:

Pt. 2 Part 2
Pt. 3 Part 3 etc.

(See page iv for complete list of Parts.)

So, for example, if you want to know more about Chinese stamps than is contained in the *Simplified Catalogue of Stamps of the World* the reference to

CHINA Pt.17

guides you to the Gibbons Part 17 *(China)* Catalogue listing for the details you require.

New editions of Part 2 to 22 appear at irregular intervals.

Correspondence

Whilst we welcome information and suggestions we must ask correspondents to include the cost of postage for the return of any stamps submitted plus registration where appropriate. Letters should be addressed to The Catalogue Editor at Ringwood.

Where information is solicited purely for the benefit of the enquirer we regret we cannot undertake to reply unless stamps or reply coupons are sent to cover postage.

Identification of Stamps

We regret we do not give opinions as to the genuineness of stamps, nor do we identify stamps or number them by our Catalogue.

Users of this catalogue are referred to our companion booklet entitled *Stamp Collecting – How to Identify Stamps*. It explains how to look up stamps in this catalogue, contains a full checklist of stamp inscriptions and gives help in dealing with unfamiliar scripts. It is available from Stanley Gibbons at £2.95, postage extra.

Stanley Gibbons would like to complement your collection

At Stanley Gibbons we offer a range of services which are designed to complement your collection.

Our modern stamp shop, the largest in Europe, together with our rare stamp department has one of the most comprehensive stocks of Great Britain in the world, so whether you are a beginner or an experienced philatelist you are certain to find something to suit your special requirements.

Alternatively through our Mail Order services you can control the growth of your collection from the comfort of your own home. Our Postal Sales Department regularly sends out mailings of Special Offers. We can also help with your wants lists–so why not ask us for those elusive items?

And don't forget Stanley Gibbons Auctions which holds regular sales each year. Come along in person or send in a written bid for the items you require. For details of current subscription rates for Auction catalogues write to Stanley Gibbons Auctions, 399 Strand, London WC2R 0LX.

Why not take advantage of the many services we have to offer? Visit our premises in the Strand or, for more information, write to the appropriate address on page x.

Stanley Gibbons Holdings Plc Addresses

Stanley Gibbons Limited, Stanley Gibbons Auctions

399 Strand, London WC2R 0LX
Telephone 0171 8368444 Fax 0171 8367342 for all departments.

Auction Room and Specialist Stamp Departments. Open Monday–Friday 9.30 a.m. to 5 p.m.
Shop. Open Monday–Friday 8.30 a.m. to 6 p.m. and Saturday 10 a.m. to 4 p.m.

Fraser's

Autographs, photographs, letters and documents
399 Strand, London WC2R 0LX
Telephone 0171 8368444 Fax 0171 8367342
Monday–Friday 9 a.m. to 5.30 p.m. and Saturday 10 a.m. to 4 p.m.

Stanley Gibbons Publications

5 Parkside, Christchurch Road, Ringwood, Hants BH24 3SH
Telephone 01425 472363 (24 hour answerphone service)
Fax 01425 470247.
E-mail: info@stangib.demon.co.uk.

Publications Showroom (at above address). Open Monday–Friday 9.00 a.m. to 3 p.m.
Publications Mail Order. FREEPHONE 0800 611622. Monday–Friday 8.30 a.m. to 5 p.m.
Trade Desk 01425 478776
Monday–Friday 8.30 a.m. to 5 p.m.

Urch Harris & Co.

1 Denmark Avenue, Bristol BS1 5HD.
Telephone 0117 9349333 Fax 0117 9273037
Monday–Friday 8.30 a.m. to 5 p.m.

Stanley Gibbons Publications Overseas Representation

Stanley Gibbons Publications are represented overseas by the following sole distributors (*), distributors (**) or licensees (***).

Australia*
Lighthouse Philatelics (Aust) Pty. Ltd., P.O. Box 763, Strawberry Hills, New South Wales, 2012 Australia.

Stanley Gibbons (Australia) Pty. Ltd.***
P.O. Box 863J, Melbourne 3001, Australia.

Belgium and Luxembourg **
Davo c/o Philac, Rue du Midi 48, Bruxelles, 1000 Belgium.

Canada*
Lighthouse Publications (Canada) Ltd., 255 Duke Street, Montreal, Quebec, Canada H3C 2M2.

Denmark**
Davo c/o Lindner Falzlos, Gl Randersvej 28, 8450 Hammel, Denmark.

Finland**
Davo c/o Suomen Postimerkkeily Ludvingkatu 5 SF-00130 Helsinki, Finland.

France*
Davo France (Casteilla), 10 Rue Leon Foucault 78184 St. Quentin Yvelines, Cesex, France.

Germany and Austria*
Leuchtturm Albenverlag, Paul Koch KG AM Spakenberg 45, Postfach 1340, D-2054 Geesthacht, Germany.

Hong Kong**
Po-on Stamp Service, G.P.O. Box 2498, Hong Kong.

Israel**
Capital Stamps, P.O. Box 3769, Jerusalem 91036, Israel.

Italy*
Secrian Srl, Via Pantelleria 2, 1-20156, Milan, Italy.

Japan**
Japan Philatelic Co. Ltd., P.O. Box 2, Suginami-Minami, Tokyo, Japan.

Netherlands*
Davo Publications, P.O. Box 411, 7400 AK Deventer, Netherlands.

New Zealand***
Stanley Gibbons (New Zealand) Ltd., P.O. Box 80, Wellington, New Zealand.

Norway**
Davo Norge A/S, P.O. Box 738, Sentrum, N-0105, Oslo, Norway.

Singapore***
Stanley Gibbons (Singapore) Pte Ltd., Raffles City P.O. Box 1689, Singapore 9117.

South Africa**
Republic Coin and Stamp Accessories (Pty) Ltd., P.O. Box 11199, Johannesburg, RSA 2000.

Sweden*
Chr Winther Soerensen AB, Box 43, S-310 Knaered, Sweden.

Switzerland**
Phila Service, Burgstrasse 160, CH 4125, Riehen, Switzerland.

West Indies/Caribbean**
Hugh Dunphy, P.O. Box 413, Kingston 10, Jamaica, West Indies.

Abbreviations

Anniv.	denotes	Anniversary
Assn.	"	Association
Bis.	"	Bistre
Bl.	"	Blue
Bldg.	"	Building
Blk.	"	Black
Br.	"	British *or* Bridge
Brn.	"	Brown
B.W.I.	"	British West Indies
C.A.R.I.F.T.A.	"	Caribbean Free Trade Area
Cent.	"	Centenary
Chest.	"	Chestnut
Choc.	"	Chocolate
Clar.	"	Claret
Coll.	"	College
Commem.	"	Commemoration
Conf.	"	Conference
Diag.	"	Diagonally
E.C.A.F.E.	"	Economic Commission for Asia and Far East
Emer.	"	Emerald
E.P.T. Conference	"	European Postal and Telecommunications Conference
Exn.	"	Exhibition
F.A.O.	"	Food and Agriculture Organization
Fig.	"	Figure
G.A.T.T.	"	General Agreement on Tariffs and Trade
G.B.	"	Great Britain
Gen.	"	General
Govt.	"	Government
Grn.	"	Green
Horiz.	"	Horizontal
H.Q.	"	Headquarters
Imperf.	"	Imperforate
Inaug.	"	Inauguration
Ind.	"	Indigo
Inscr.	"	Inscribed *or* inscription
Int.	"	International
I.A.T.A.	"	International Air Transport Association
I.C.A.O.	"	International Civil Aviation Organization
I.C.Y.	"	International Co-operation Year
I.G.Y.	"	International Geophysical Year
I.L.O.	"	International Labour Office (or later, Organization)
I.M.C.O.	"	Inter-Governmental Maritime Consultative Organization
I.T.U.	"	International Telecommunication Union
Is.	"	Islands
Lav.	"	Lavender
Mar.	"	Maroon
mm.	"	Millimetres
Mult.	"	Multicoloured
Mve.	denotes	Mauve
Nat.	"	National
N.A.T.O.	"	North Atlantic Treaty Organization
O.D.E.C.A	"	Organization of Central American States
Ol.	"	Olive
Optd.	"	Overprinted
Orge *or* oran.	"	Orange
P.A.T.A.	"	Pacific Area Travel Association
Perf.	"	Perforated
Post.	"	Postage
Pres.	"	President
P.U.	"	Postal Union
Pur.	"	Purple
R.	"	River
R.S.A.	"	Republic of South Africa
Roul.	"	Rouletted
Sep.	"	Sepia
S.E.A.T.O.	"	South East Asia Treaty Organization
Surch.	"	Surcharged
T.	"	Type
T.U.C.	"	Trades Union Congress
Turq.	"	Turquoise
Ultram.	"	Ultramarine
U.N.E.S.C.O.	"	United Nations Educational, Scientific & Cultural Organization
U.N.I.C.E.F.	"	United Nations Children's Fund
U.N.O.	"	United Nations Organization
U.N.R.W.A.	"	United Nations Relief and Works Agency for Palestine Refugees in the Near East
U.N.T.E.A.	"	United Nations Temporary Executive Authority
U.N.R.R.A.	"	United Nations Relief and Rehabilitation Administration
U.P.U.	"	Universal Postal Union
Verm.	"	Vermilion
Vert.	"	Vertical
Vio.	"	Violet
W.F.T.U.	"	World Federation of Trade Unions
W.H.O.	"	World Health Organization
Yell.	"	Yellow

Arabic Numerals

As in the case of European figures, the details of the Arabic numerals vary in different stamp designs, but they should be readily recognised with the aid of this illustration:

٠	١	٢	٣	٤
0	1	2	3	4
٥	٦	٧	٨	٩
5	6	7	8	9

Key-types

(see note on page vii)

French Group

A. "Blanc."

B. "Mouchon."

C. "Merson."

D. "Tablet."

E.

F.

G.

H.

"International Colonial Exhibition"

I. "Faidherbe."

J. "Palms."

K. "Balay."

L. "Natives."

M. "Figure."

German Group

N. "Yacht."

O. "Yacht."

Spanish Group

X. "Alfonso XII."

Y. "Baby."

Z. "Curly Head"

Portuguese Group

P. "Crown."

Q. "Embossed."

R. "Figures."

S. "Carlos."

T. "Manoel."

U. "Ceres."

V. "Newspaper."

W. "Due."

KEEP THIS CATALOGUE UP TO DATE EACH MONTH WITH . . .

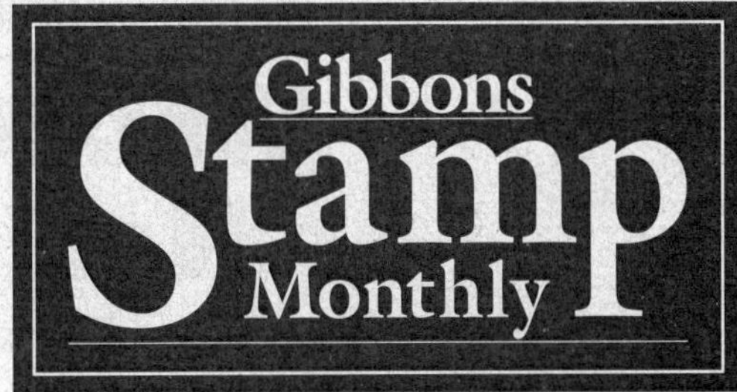

...the only magazine containing the Stanley Gibbons catalogue supplement

- Exceptional value for money with 50% more editorial than other magazines
- Authoritatively written by active stamp collectors
- Read by thousands of subscribers in over 80 countries worldwide
- Covers all areas of philately including Commonwealth, GB, Foreign, Thematics and Postal History
- The essential accessory for all collectors from beginners to specialists
- Contains a comprehensive round up of latest news and opinion from around the world
- Regular features devoted to new issues, first day covers, varieties, Machins, books, auctions and fairs
- Includes the unique Stanley Gibbons catalogue supplement
- Exclusive British Stamps and GB specialised catalogue supplement
- Monthly competition and frequent free gifts

SUBSCRIBE AND RECEIVE

- The next 12 issues delivered direct to your door
- Each issue at the current cover price
- FREE P&P anywhere in the UK
- FREE 10% Stanley Gibbons discount voucher
- Exclusive offers every month

For a free sample copy and subscription details phone **+44 (0)1425 472363** today or write to:

Gibbons Stamp Monthly
5 Parkside, Christchurch Road, Ringwood,
Hampshire BH24 3SH England
Facsimile: +44 (0)1425 470247
e.mail sales@stangib.demon.co.uk

KAMPUCHEA Pt. 21

Following the fall of the Khmer Rouge government, which had terminated the Khmer Republic, the People's Republic of Kampuchea was proclaimed on 10 January 1979.
Kampuchea was renamed Cambodia in 1989.

100 cents = 1 riel.

105 Soldiers with Flag and Independence Monument, Phnom Penh
106 Moscow Kremlin and Globe

1980. Multicoloured. Without gum.
402 0.1 r. Type **105** 1·90 1·90
403 0.2 r. Khmer people and flag 3·75 3·75
404 0.5 r. Fisherman pulling in nets 5·00 5·00
405 1 r. Armed forces and Kampuchean flag 8·25 8·25

1982. 60th Anniv of U.S.S.R. Multicoloured.
406 50 c. Type **106** 15 10
407 1 r. Industrial complex and map of U.S.S.R. 30 10

107 Arms of Kampuchea

1983. 4th Anniv of People's Republic of Kampuchea. Multicoloured.
408 50 c. Type **107** 25 10
409 1 r. Open book illustrating national flag and arms (horiz) 50 15
410 3 r. Stylized figures and map 1·40 40

108 Runner with Olympic Torch
109 Orange Tiger

1983. Olympic Games, Los Angeles (1984) (1st issue). Multicoloured.
412 20 c. Type **108** 10 10
413 50 c. Javelin throwing 15 10
414 80 c. Pole vaulting 20 10
415 1 r. Discus throwing 35 15
416 1 r. 50 Relay (horiz) 50 20
417 2 r. Swimming (horiz) 85 30
418 3 r. Basketball 1·25 45
See also Nos. 526/32.

1983. Butterflies. Multicoloured.
420 20 c. Type **109** 15 10
421 50 c. "Euploea althaea" 20 15
422 80 c. "Byasa polyeuctes" (horiz) 40 20
423 1 r. "Stichophthalma howqua" (horiz) 70 25
424 1 r. 50 Leaf butterfly 1·25 45
425 2 r. Blue argus 1·75 60
426 3 r. Lemon migrant 2·75 80

110 Srah Srang

1983. Khmer Culture. Multicoloured.
427 20 c. Type **110** 10 10
428 50 c. Bakong 15 10
429 80 c. Ta Som (vert) 25 10
430 1 r. North gate, Angkor Thom (vert) 40 15
431 1 r. 50 Kennora (winged figures) (vert) 70 25
432 2 r. Apsara (carved figures), Angkor (vert) 75 25
433 3 r. Banteai Srei (goddess), Tevoda (vert) 1·25 40

111 Dancers with Castanets

1983. Folklore. Multicoloured.
434 50 c. Type **111** 25 10
435 1 r. Dancers with grass headdresses 55 20
436 3 r. Dancers with scarves 1·25 40

112 Detail of Fresco

1983. 500th Birth Anniv of Raphael (artist).
438 **112** 20 c. multicoloured 10 10
439 – 50 c. multicoloured 15 10
440 – 80 c. multicoloured 25 10
441 – 1 r. multicoloured 50 15
442 – 1 r. 50 multicoloured 85 25
443 – 2 r. multicoloured 1·10 25
444 – 3 r. multicoloured 1·40 40
DESIGNS: Nos. 439/44, different details of frescoes by Raphael.

113 Montgolfier Balloon
114 Cobra

1983. Bicentenary of Manned Flight. Mult.
446 20 c. Type **113** 10 15
447 30 c. "La Ville d'Orleans", 1870 20 10
448 50 c. Charles's hydrogen balloon 30 15
449 1 r. Blanchard and Jeffries crossing Channel, 1785 50 20
450 1 r. 50 Salomon Andree's balloon flight over Arctic 85 35
451 2 r. Auguste Piccard's stratosphere balloon "F.N.R.S." 90 40
452 3 r. Hot-air balloon race 1·50 50

1983. Reptiles. Multicoloured.
454 20 c. Crested lizard (horiz) 15 10
455 30 c. Type **114** 20 10
456 80 c. Trionyx turtle (horiz) 25 10
457 1 r. Chameleon 45 15
458 1 r. 50 Boa constrictor 75 25
459 2 r. Crocodile (horiz) 90 25
460 3 r. Turtle (horiz) 1·40 40

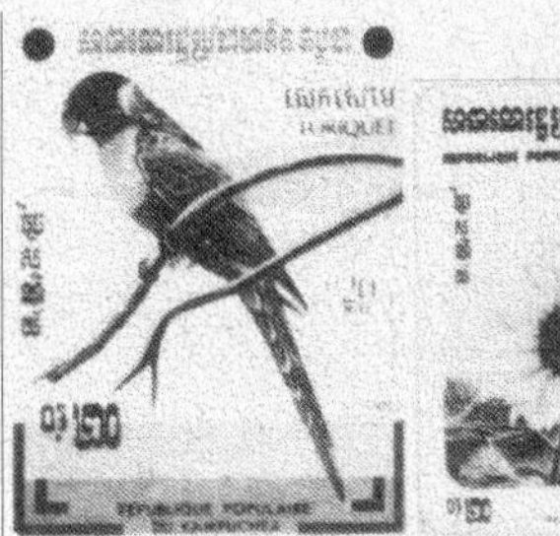

115 Rainbow Lory
116 Sunflower

1983. Birds. Multicoloured.
461 20 c. Type **115** 20 10
462 50 c. Barn swallow 30 15
463 80 c. Golden eagle (horiz) 50 25
464 1 r. Griffon vulture (horiz) 85 40
465 1 r. 50 Javanese collared dove (horiz) 1·25 55
466 2 r. Magpie 1·60 70
467 3 r. Great Indian hornbill 2·50 1·10

1983. Flowers. Multicoloured.
468 20 c. Type **116** 10 10
469 50 c. "Caprifoliaceae" 15 10
470 80 c. "Bougainvillea" 25 10
471 1 r. "Ranunculaceae" 40 15
472 1 r. 50 "Nyctagynaceae" 75 25
473 2 r. Cockscomb 90 25
474 3 r. Roses 1·40 40

117 Luge

1983. Winter Olympic Games, Sarajevo (1984) (1st issue). Multicoloured.
475 1 r. Type **117** 40 15
476 2 r. Biathlon 90 25
477 4 r. Ski-jumping 1·75 50
478 5 r. Two-man bobsleigh 1·90 60
479 7 r. Ice hockey 2·75 85
See also Nos. 496/502.

118 "Cyprinidae"

1983. Fishes. Multicoloured.
481 20 c. Type **118** 15 10
482 50 c. Trout 20 10
483 80 c. Catfish 25 10
484 1 r. Moray eel 50 15
485 1 r. 50 "Cyprinidae" (different) 90 25
486 2 r. "Cyprinidae" (different) 1·00 25
487 3 r. "Cyprinidae" (different) 1·40 40

119 Factory and Gearwheel

1983. Festival of Rebirth. Multicoloured.
488 50 c. Type **119** 20 10
489 1 r. Tractor and cow (horiz) 35 15
490 3 r. Bulk carrier, diesel locomotive, car and bridge 2·50 60

120 Red Cross and Sailing Ship

1984. 5th Anniv of Liberation. Multicoloured.
492 50 c. Type **120** 20 10
493 1 r. Three soldiers, flags and temple 35 15
494 3 r. Crowd surrounding temple 1·00 35

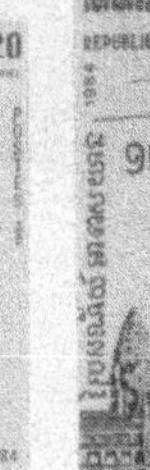

121 Speed Skating
122 Ilyushin Il-62M Jet over Angkor Vat

1984. Winter Olympic Games, Sarajevo (2nd issue). Multicoloured.
496 20 c. Type **121** 10 10
497 50 c. Ice hockey 15 10
498 80 c. Skiing 20 10
499 1 r. Ski jumping 50 15
500 1 r. 50 Skiing (different) 75 25
501 2 r. Cross-country skiing 90 25
502 3 r. Ice skating (pairs) 1·25 40

1984. Air.
504 **122** 5 r. multicoloured 2·50 75
505 10 r. multicoloured 4·75 1·50
506 15 r. multicoloured 7·25 2·25
507 25 r. multicoloured 12·25 3·75
For design as Type **122** but inscribed "R.P. DU KAMPUCHEA", see Nos. 695/8.

123 Cattle Egret
124 Doves and Globe

1984. Birds. Multicoloured.
508 10 c. Type **123** 15 10
509 40 c. Black-headed shrike 40 25
510 80 c. Slaty-headed parakeet 75 35
511 1 r. Golden-fronted leafbird 1·10 35
512 1 r. 20 Red-winged crested cuckoo 1·25 40
513 2 r. Grey wagtail 2·10 85
514 2 r. 50 Forest wagtail 2·50 95

1984. International Peace in South-East Asia Forum, Phnom Penh. Mult, background colour given.
515 **124** 50 c. green 20 10
516 1 r. blue 40 15
517 3 r. violet 1·25 35

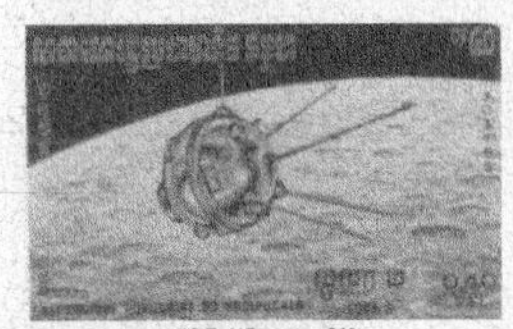

125 "Luna 2"

1984. Space Research. Multicoloured.
518 10 c. "Luna 1" 10 10
519 40 c. Type **125** 15 10
520 80 c. "Luna 3" 25 10
521 1 r. "Soyuz 6" and cosmonauts (vert) 40 15
522 1 r. 20 "Soyuz 7" and cosmonauts (vert) 65 20
523 2 r. "Soyuz 8" and cosmonauts (vert) 75 25
524 2 r. 50 Book, rocket and S. P. Korolev (Russian spaceship designer) (vert) 1·25 40

126 Throwing the Discus

1984. Olympic Games, Los Angeles (2nd issue). Multicoloured.

526 20 c. Type **126** 10 10
527 50 c. Long jumping 15 10
528 80 c. Hurdling 25 10
529 1 r. Relay 50 15
530 1 r. 50 Pole vaulting 75 25
531 2 r. Throwing the javelin 90 25
532 3 r. High jumping 1·25 40

128 Coyote

1984. Dog Family. Multicoloured.

535 10 c. Type **128** 10 10
536 40 c. Dingo 15 10
537 80 c. Hunting dog 25 10
538 1 r. Golden jackal 45 15
539 1 r. 20 Red fox 75 20
540 2 r. Maned wolf (vert) 1·25 25
541 2 r. 50 Wolf 1·75 40

129 French "BB-1002" Type Diesel, 1966

1984. Railway Locomotives. Multicoloured.

542 10 c. Type **129** 10 10
543 40 c. French "BB-1052" type diesel, 1966 15 10
544 80 c. Franco-Belgian steam locomotive, 1945 25 15
545 1 r. Franco-Belgian "231-505" type steam, 1929 45 20
546 1 r. 20 German "803" type railcar, 1968 75 25
547 2 r. French "BDE-405" type diesel, 1957 1·10 35
548 2 r. 50 French "DS-01" type diesel railcar, 1929 1·60 50

130 Magnolia

1984. Flowers. Multicoloured.

549 10 c. Type **130** 10 10
550 40 c. "Plumeria" sp. 15 10
551 80 c. "Himenoballis" sp. 25 15
552 1 r. "Peltophorum roxburghii" 45 20
553 1 r. 20 "Couroupita guianensis" 70 25
554 2 r. "Lagerstroemia" sp. 1·10 30
555 2 r. 50 "Thevetia perubiana" 1·75 50

131 Mercedes Benz

1984. Cars. Multicoloured.

556 20 c. Type **131** 10 10
557 50 c. Bugatti 15 10
558 80 c. Alfa Romeo 35 15
559 1 r. Franklin 50 20
560 1 r. 50 Hispano-Suiza 85 25
561 2 r. Rolls Royce 1·25 30
562 3 r. Tatra 1·50 50

132 Sra Lai (Rattle)

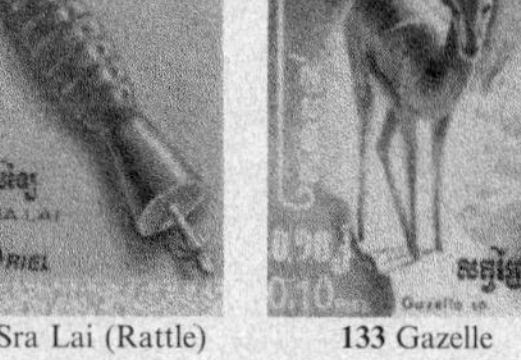

133 Gazelle

1984. Musical Instruments. Multicoloured.

564 10 c. Type **132** 10 10
565 40 c. Skor drum (horiz) 15 10
566 80 c. Skor drums (different) 35 15
567 1 r. Thro khmer (stringed instrument) (horiz) 40 20
568 1 r. 20 Raneat ek (xylophone) (horiz) 70 25
569 2 r. Raneat kong (bells) (horiz) 75 30
570 2 r. 50 Thro khe (stringed instrument) (horiz) 1·25 50

1984. Mammals. Multicoloured.

571 10 c. Type **133** 10 10
572 40 c. Roe deer 15 10
573 80 c. Hare (horiz) 25 15
574 1 r. Red deer 50 20
575 1 r. 20 Indian elephant 75 30
576 2 r. Genet (horiz) 90 40
577 2 r. 50 Kouprey (horiz) 1·25 60

134 "Madonna and Child"

136 Footballers

135 Bullock Cart

1984. 450th Death Anniv of Correggio (artist). Multicoloured.

578 20 c. Type **134** 10 10
579 50 c. Detail showing man striking monk 15 10
580 80 c. "Madonna and Child" (different) 25 15
581 1 r. "Madonna and Child" (different) 40 20
582 1 r. 50 "Mystical Marriage of St. Catherine" 70 30
583 2 r. "Pieta" 75 40
584 3 r. Detail showing man descending ladder 1·25 60

1985. National Festival (6th Anniv of People's Republic). Multicoloured.

586 50 c. Type **135** 40 10
587 1 r. Horse-drawn passenger cart 65 25
588 3 r. Elephants 1·60 50

1985. World Cup Football Championship, Mexico (1986) (1st issue). Designs showing footballers.

590 **136** 20 c. multicoloured 10 10
591 – 50 c. multicoloured 25 10
592 – 80 c. multicoloured 45 15
593 – 1 r. multicoloured (horiz) 55 25
594 – 1 r. 50 multicoloured (horiz) 80 35
595 – 2 r. multicoloured 1·00 45
596 – 3 r. multicoloured 1·60 70

See also Nos. 680/6.

137 Eska-Mofa Motor Cycle, 1939

1985. Centenary of Motor Cycle. Multicoloured.

598 20 c. Type **137** 10 10
599 50 c. Wanderer, 1939 25 10
600 80 c. Premier, 1929 45 15
601 1 r. Ardie, 1939 55 25
602 1 r. 50 Jawa, 1932 80 35
603 2 r. Simson, 1983 1·00 45
604 3 r. "CZ 125", 1984 1·60 70

138 Glistening Ink Cap

1985. Fungi. Multicoloured.

606 20 c. "Gymnophilus spectabilis" (horiz) 15 10
607 50 c. Type **138** 40 15
608 80 c. Panther cap 70 20
609 1 r. Fairy cake mushroom 90 35
610 1 r. 50 Fly agaric 1·40 45
611 2 r. Shaggy ink cap 1·60 60
612 3 r. Caesar's mushroom 2·75 95

139 "Sputnik 1"

1985. Space Exploration. Multicoloured.

613 20 c. Type **139** 10 10
614 50 c. Rocket on transporter and Yury Gagarin (first man in space) 25 10
615 80 c. "Vostok 6" and Valentina Tereshkova (first woman in space) 45 15
616 1 r. Space walker 55 25
617 1 r. 50 "Salyut"–"Soyuz" link 80 35
618 2 r. "Lunokhod 1" (lunar vehicle) 1·00 45
619 3 r. "Venera" (Venus probe) 1·60 70

140 Absara Dancer

140a Captured Nazi Standards, Red Square, Moscow

1985. Traditional Dances. Multicoloured.

621 50 c. Absara group (horiz) 35 10
622 1 r. Tepmonorom dance (horiz) 70 25
623 3 r. Type **140** 1·75 75

1985. 40th Anniv of End of Second World War. Multicoloured.

623a 50 c. Rejoicing soldiers in Berlin 30 10
623b 1 r. Type **140a** 55 25
623c 3 r. Tank battle 1·75 75

141 Tortoiseshell Cat

142 "Black Dragon" Lily

1985. Domestic Cats. Multicoloured.

624 20 c. Type **141** 10 10
625 50 c. Tortoiseshell (different) 25 10
626 80 c. Tabby 45 15
627 1 r. Long-haired Siamese 60 25
628 1 t. 50 Sealpoint Siamese 1·00 35
629 2 r. Grey cat 1·25 45
630 3 r. Black cat 2·00 70

1985. Flowers. Multicoloured.

631 20 c. Type **142** 10 10
632 50 c. "Iris delavayi" 25 10
633 80 c. "Crocus aureus" 45 15
634 1 r. "Cyclamen persicum" 60 25
635 1 r. 50 Fairy primrose 90 35
636 2 r. Pansy "Ullswater" 1·10 45
637 3 r. "Crocus purpureus grandiflorus" 1·75 70

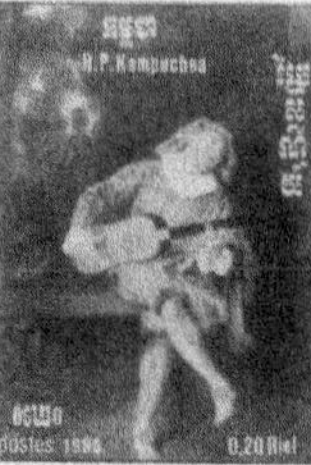

143 "Per Italiani" (Antoine Watteau)

144 Lenin and Arms

1987. International Music Year. Multicoloured.

638 20 c. Type **143** 10 10
639 50 c. "St. Cecilia" (Carlos Saraceni) 25 10
640 80 c. "Still Life with Violin" (Jean Baptiste Oudry) (horiz) 45 15
641 1 r. "Three Musicians" (Fernand Leger) 55 25
642 1 r. 50 Orchestra 80 35
643 2 r. "St. Cecilia" (Bartholomeo Schedoni) 1·00 45
644 3 r. "Harlequin with Violin" (Christian Caillard) 1·60 70

1985. 115th Birth Anniv of Lenin. Multicoloured.

646 1 r. Type **144** 60 25
647 3 r. Lenin on balcony and map 1·60 70

145 Saffron-cowled Blackbird

1985. "Argentina '85" International Stamp Exhibition, Buenos Aires. Birds. Multicoloured.

648 20 c. Type **145** 15 10
649 50 c. Saffron finch (vert) 30 15
650 80 c. Blue and yellow tanager (vert) 50 20
651 1 r. Scarlet-headed blackbird 70 25
652 1 r. 50 Amazon kingfisher (vert) 1·40 35
653 2 r. Toco toucan (vert) 1·90 45
654 3 r. Rufous-bellied thrush 2·50 70

146 River Launch, Cambodia, 1942

1985. Water Craft. Multicoloured.

655 10 c. Type **146** 15 10
656 40 c. River launch, Cambodia, 1948 25 15
657 80 c. Tug, Japan, 1913 45 20
658 1 r. Dredger, Holland 65 25
659 1 r. 20 Tug, U.S.A. 1·10 35
660 2 r. River freighter 1·50 45
661 2 r. 50 River tanker, Panama 2·00 70

147 "The Flood" (Michelangelo)

148 Son Ngoc Minh

1985. "Italia '85" International Stamp Exhibition, Rome. Paintings. Multicoloured.

662 20 r. Type **147** 10 10
663 50 r. "The Virgin of St. Marguerite" (Mazzola) 25 10
664 80 r. "The Martyrdom of St. Peter" (Zampieri Domenichino) 45 15
665 1 r. "Allegory of Spring" (detail) (Sandro Botticelli) 55 25
666 1 r. 50 "The Sacrifice of Abraham" (Caliari) 80 35
667 2 r. "The Meeting of Joachim and Anne" (Giotto) 1·00 45
668 3 r. "Bacchus" (Michel Angelo Carravaggio) 1·60 70

1985. Festival of Rebirth.

670 **148** 50 c. multicoloured 15 10
671 1 r. multicoloured 40 15
672 3 r. multicoloured 1·10 45

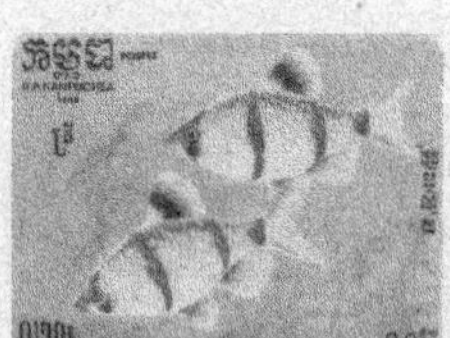

149 Damsel Barbs

1985. Fishes. Multicoloured.
673 20 c. Type **149** 10 10
674 50 c. "Ophiocephalus micropeltes" 25 10
675 80 c. Goldfish 45 15
676 1 r. Pearl gourami 55 25
677 1 r. 50 Black-banded barbs 80 35
678 2 r. Siamese fighting fish 1·00 45
679 3 r. "Datnioides microlepis" 1·60 70

150 Footballers

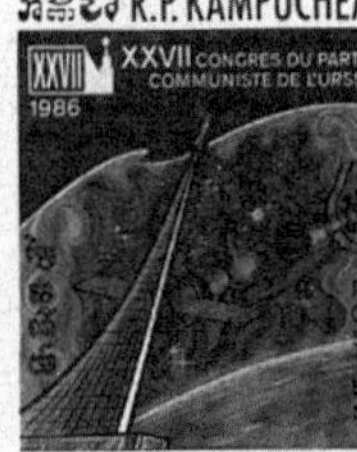
152 "Mir" Space Station and Spacecraft

151 Cob

1986. World Cup Football Championship, Mexico (2nd issue).
680 **150** 20 c. multicoloured 10 10
681 – 50 c. multicoloured 25 10
682 – 80 c. multicoloured 45 15
683 – 1 r. multicoloured 55 25
684 – 1 r. 50 multicoloured 80 35
685 – 2 r. multicoloured 1·00 45
686 – 3 r. multicoloured 1·60 70
DESIGNS: 50 c. to 3 r. Various footballing scenes.

1986. Horses. Multicoloured.
688 20 c. Type **151** 10 10
689 50 c. Arab 25 10
690 80 c. Australian pony 45 15
691 1 r. Appaloosa 55 25
692 1 r. 50 Quarter horse 80 35
693 2 r. Vladimir heavy draught horse 1·00 45
694 3 r. Andalusian 1·60 70

1986. 27th Russian Communist Party Congress. Multicoloured.
694a 50 c. Type **152** 25 10
694b 1 r. Lenin 55 25
694c 5 r. Statue and launch of space rocket 2·50 1·00

1986. Air. As Nos. 504/7 but inscr "R.P. DU KAMPUCHEA".
695 **122** 5 r. multicoloured 2·75 95
696 10 r. multicoloured 5·75 1·60
697 15 r. multicoloured 8·50 2·50
698 25 r. multicoloured 15·00 4·25

153 Edaphosaurus
(⅔-size illustration)

1986. Prehistoric Animals. Multicoloured.
699 20 c. Type **153** 10 10
700 50 c. Sauroctonus 25 10
701 80 c. Mastodonsaurus 45 15
702 1 r. Rhamphorhynchus (vert) 60 25
703 1 r. 50 "Brachiosaurus brancai" (vert) 90 35
704 2 r. "Tarbosaurus bataar" (vert) 1·10 45
705 3 r. Indricotherium (vert) 1·75 70

154 "Luna 16"

1986. 25th Anniv of First Man in Space. Multicoloured.
706 10 c. Type **154** 10 10
707 40 c. "Luna 3" 25 10
708 80 c. "Vostok" 45 15
709 1 r. Cosmonaut Leonov on space walk 55 25
710 1 r. 20 "Apollo" and "Soyuz" preparing to dock 80 35
711 2 r. "Soyuz" docking with "Salyut" space station 1·00 45
712 2 r. 50 Yury Gagarin (first man in space) and spacecraft 1·60 75

155 Baksei Chmkrong Temple, 920

1986. Khmer Culture. Multicoloured.
713 20 c. Type **155** 10 10
714 50 c. Buddha's head 25 10
715 80 c. Prea Vihear monastery, Dangrek 45 15
716 1 r. Fan with design of man and woman 55 25
717 1 r. 50 Fan with design of men fighting 80 35
718 2 r. Fan with design of dancer 1·00 45
719 3 r. Fan with design of dragon-drawn chariot 1·60 70

156 Tricar, 1885

1986. Centenary (1985) of Motor Car. Mercedes Benz Models. Multicoloured.
720 20 c. Type **156** 10 10
721 50 c. Limousine, 1935 25 10
722 80 c. Open tourer, 1907 45 15
723 1 r. Light touring car, 1920 55 25
724 1 r. 50 Cabriolet, 1932 80 35
725 2 r. "SKK" tourer, 1938 1·00 45
726 3 r. "190", 1985 1·60 70

157 Orange Tiger

159 Solar System, Copernicus, Galileo and Tycho Brahe (astronomers)

158 English Kogge of Richard II's Reign

1986. Butterflies. Multicoloured.
727 20 c. Type **157** 15 10
728 50 c. Five-bar swallowtail 35 15
729 80 c. Chequered swallowtail 65 20
730 1 r. Chestnut tiger 75 35
731 1 r. 50 "Idea blanchardi" 1·10 45
732 2 r. Common mormon 1·40 60
733 3 r. "Dabasa payeni" 2·25 95

1986. Medieval Ships.
734 20 c. Type **158** 10 10
735 50 c. Kogge 25 10
736 80 c. Knarr 45 15
737 1 r. Galley 55 25
738 1 r. 50 Norman ship 80 35
739 2 r. Mediterranean usciere 1·10 45
740 3 r. French kogge 1·75 70

1986. Appearance of Halley's Comet. Multicoloured.
741 10 c. Type **159** 10 10
742 20 c. "Nativity" (Giotto) and comet from Bayeux Tapestry 10 10
743 50 c. Comet, 1910, and Mt. Palomar observatory, U.S.A. 25 10
744 80 c. Edmond Halley and "Planet A" space probe 45 15
745 1 r. 20 Diagram of comet's trajectory and "Giotto" space probe 60 25
746 1 r. 50 "Vega" space probe and camera 80 35
747 2 r. Thermal pictures of comet 1·00 45

160 Ruy Lopez

1986. "Stockholmia 86" International Stamp Exhibition. Chess. Multicoloured.
749 20 c. Type **160** 10 10
750 50 c. Francois-Andre Philidor 25 10
751 80 c. Karl Anderssen and Houses of Parliament, London 45 15
752 1 r. Wilhelm Steinitz and Charles Bridge, Prague 60 25
753 1 r. 50 Emanuel Lasker and medieval knight 90 35
754 2 r. Jose Raul Capablanca and Morro Castle, Cuba 1·10 45
755 3 r. Aleksandr Alekhine 1·75 70

161 "Parodia maassii"

162 Bananas

1986. Cacti. Multicoloured.
757 20 c. Type **161** 10 10
758 50 c. "Rebutia marsoneri" 25 10
759 80 c. "Melocactus evae" 45 15
760 1 r. "Gymnocalycium valnicekianum" 55 25
761 1 r. 50 "Discocactus silichromus" 80 35
762 2 r. "Neochilenia simulans" 1·00 45
763 3 r. "Weingartia chiquichuquensis" 1·60 70

1986. Fruit. Multicoloured.
764 10 c. Type **162** 10 10
765 40 c. Papaya 20 10
766 80 c. Mangoes 45 15
767 1 r. Breadfruit 55 35
768 1 r. 20 Lychees 60 25
769 2 r. Pineapple 1·00 45
770 2 r. 50 Grapefruit (horiz) 1·40 55

163 Concorde
(⅔-size illustration)

1986. Aircraft. Multicoloured.
771 20 c. Type **163** (wrongly inscr "Concord") 10 10
772 50 c. Douglas DC-10 25 10
773 80 c. Boeing 747SP 45 15
774 1 r. Ilyushin Il-62M 55 25
775 1 r. 50 Ilyushin Il-86 80 35
776 2 r. Antonov An-24 (wrongly inscr "AN-124") 1·10 45
777 3 r. Airbus Industrie A300 1·75 70

164 Elephant and Silver Containers on Tray

1986. Festival of Rebirth. Silverware. Mult.
778 50 c. Type **164** 25 10
779 1 r. Tureen 55 20
780 3 r. Dish on stand 1·60 45

165 Kouprey

1986. Endangered Animals. Cattle. Mult.
781 20 c. Type **165** 10 10
782 20 c. Gaur 10 10
783 80 c. Bateng cow and calf 45 15
784 1 r. 50 Asiatic water buffalo 90 30

166 Tou Samuth (revolutionary)

1987. National Festival. 8th Anniv of People's Republic.
785 **166** 50 c. multicoloured 20 10
786 1 r. multicoloured 40 15
787 3 r. multicoloured 1·10 35

167 Biathlon

1987. Winter Olympic Games, Calgary (1988) (1st issue). Multicoloured.
788 20 c. Type **167** 10 10
789 50 c. Figure skating 25 10
790 80 c. Speed skating 45 15
791 1 r. Ice hockey 55 25
792 1 r. 50 Two-man luge 80 35
793 2 r. Two-man bobsleigh 1·00 45
794 3 r. Cross-country skiing 1·60 70
See also Nos. 864/70.

168 Weightlifting

1987. Olympic Games, Seoul (1988) (1st issue). Designs showing ancient Greek and modern athletes. Multicoloured.
796 20 c. Type **168** 10 10
797 50 c. Archery (horiz) 25 10
798 80 c. Fencing (horiz) 45 15
799 1 r. Gymnastics 55 25
800 1 r. 50 Throwing the discus (horiz) 80 35
801 2 r. Throwing the javelin 1·00 45
802 3 r. Hurdling 1·60 70
See also Nos. 875/81.

169 Papillon

1987. Dogs. Multicoloured.
804 20 c. Type **169** 10 10
805 50 c. Greyhound 25 10
806 80 c. Great dane 45 15
807 1 r. Dobermann 55 25
808 1 r. 50 Samoyed 80 35
809 2 r. Borzoi 1·00 45
810 3 r. Rough collie 1·60 70

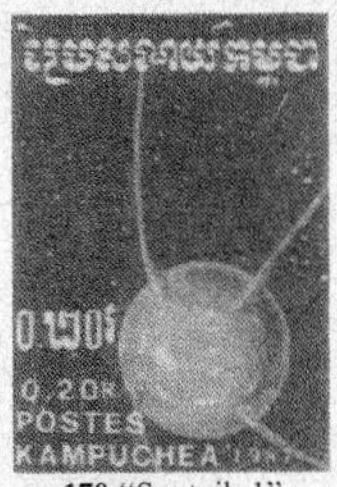
170 "Sputnik 1"

171 Flask

1987. Space Exploration. Multicoloured.
811 20 c. Type **170** 10 10
812 50 c. "Soyuz 10" 25 10
813 80 c. "Proton" 45 15
814 1 r. "Vostok 1" 55 25
815 1 r. 50 "Elektron 2" 80 35
816 2 r. "Kosmos" 1·00 45
817 3 r. "Luna 2" 1·60 70

1987. Metalwork. Multicoloured.

819	50 c. Type **171**	20	10
820	1 r. Repousse box (horiz)	50	25
821	1 r. 50 Teapot and cups on tray (horiz)	75	35
822	3 r. Ornamental sword	1·50	70

172 Carmine Bee Eater

1987. "Capex'87" International Stamp Exhibition, Toronto. Birds. Multicoloured.

823	20 c. Type **172**	10	10
824	50 c. Hoopoe (vert)	25	10
825	80 c. South African crowned crane (vert)	45	15
826	1 r. Barn owl (vert)	55	25
827	1 r. 50 Grey-headed kingfisher (vert)	80	35
828	2 r. Red-whiskered bulbul	1·00	45
829	3 r. Purple heron (vert)	1·60	70

173 Horatio Phillip's "Multiplane" Model, 1893

1987. Experimental Aircraft Designs. Mult.

831	20 c. Type **173**	10	10
832	50 c. John Stringfellow's steam-powered model, 1848	25	10
833	80 c. Thomas Moy's model "Aerial Steamer", 1875	45	15
834	1 r. Leonardo da Vinci's "ornithopter", 1490	55	25
835	1 r. 50 Sir George Cayley's "convertiplane", 1843	80	35
836	2 r. Sir Hiram Maxim's "Flying Test Rig", 1894	1·00	45
837	3 r. William Henson's "Aerial Steam Carriage", 1842	1·60	70

174 Giant Tortoise

1987. Reptiles. Multicoloured.

839	20 c. Type **174**	10	10
840	50 c. African spiny-tailed lizard	25	10
841	80 c. Iguana	45	15
842	1 r. Coast horned lizard	55	25
843	1 r. 50 Northern chuckwalla	80	35
844	2 r. Glass lizard	1·00	45
845	3 r. Common garter snake	1·60	70

175 Kamov Ka-15

1987. "Hafnia 87" International Stamp Exhibition, Copenhagen. Helicopters. Multicoloured.

846	20 c. Type **175**	10	10
847	50 c. Kamov Ka-18	25	10
848	80 c. Westland Lynx	45	15
849	1 r. Sud Aviation Gazelle	55	25
850	1 r. 50 Sud Aviation SA 330E Puma	80	35
851	2 r. Boeing-Vertol CH-47 Chinook	1·00	45
852	3 r. Boeing UTTAS	1·60	70

176 Revolutionaries

178 Earth Station Dish Aerial

177 Magirus-Deutz No. 21

1987. 70th Anniv of Russian October Revolution. Multicoloured.

853a	2 r. Revolutionaries on street corner (horiz)	95	40
853b	3 r. Type **176**	1·25	50
853c	5 r. Lenin receiving ticker-tape message (horiz)	2·50	1·00

1987. Fire Engines. Multicoloured.

854	20 c. Type **177**	10	10
855	50 c. "SIL-131" rescue vehicle	25	10
856	80 c. "Cas-25" fire pump	45	15
857	1 r. Sirmac Saab "424"	60	25
858	1 r. 50 Rosenbaum-Falcon	85	35
859	2 r. Tatra "815-PRZ"	1·10	45
860	3 r. Chubbfire "C-44-20"	1·60	70

1987. Telecommunications. Multicoloured.

861	50 c. Type **178**	10	10
862	1 r. Technological building with radio microwave aerial (27 × 44 mm)	55	25
863	3 r. Intersputnik programme earth station (44 × 27 mm)	1·60	70

179 Speed Skating

1988. Winter Olympic Games, Calgary (2nd issue). Multicoloured.

864	20 c. Type **179**	10	10
865	50 c. Ice hockey	25	10
866	80 c. Slalom	45	15
867	1 r. Ski jumping	55	25
868	1 r. 50 Biathlon	80	35
869	2 r. Ice dancing	1·00	45
870	3 r. Cross-country skiing	1·60	70

180 Irrigation Canal Bed

1988. Irrigation Projects. Multicoloured.

872	50 c. Type **180**	10	10
873	1 r. Dam construction	50	20
874	3 r. Dam and bridge	1·50	65

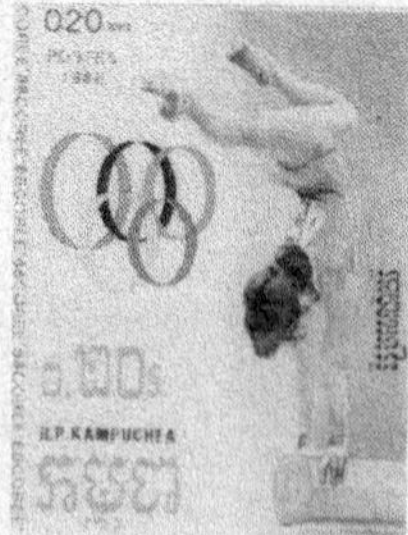

181 Beam Exercise

1988. Olympic Games, Seoul (2nd issue). Women's Gymnastics. Multicoloured.

875	20 c. Type **181**	10	10
876	50 c. Bar exercise (horiz)	25	10
877	80 c. Ribbon exercise	45	15
878	1 r. Hoop exercise	55	25
879	1 r. 50 Baton exercise	80	35
880	2 r. Ball exercise (horiz)	1·00	45
881	3 r. Floor exercise (horiz)	1·60	70

182 Abyssinian

1988. "Juvalux 88" 9th Youth Philately Exhibition, Luxembourg. Cats. Multicoloured.

883	20 c. White long-haired (horiz)	10	10
884	50 c. Type **182**	25	10
885	80 c. Ginger and white long-haired	45	15
886	1 r. Tortoiseshell queen and kitten (horiz)	55	25
887	1 r. 50 Brown cat	80	35
888	2 r. Black long-haired cat	1·00	45
889	3 r. Grey cat	1·60	70

183 "Emerald Seas" (liner)

1988. "Essen 88" International Stamp Fair. Ships. Multicoloured.

891	20 c. Type **183**	10	10
892	50 c. Car ferry	20	10
893	80 c. Freighter	35	10
894	1 r. "Kosmonavt Yury Gagarin" (research ship)	50	15
895	1 r. 50 Tanker	55	20
896	2 r. Hydrofoil	75	30
897	3 r. Hovercraft	1·25	35

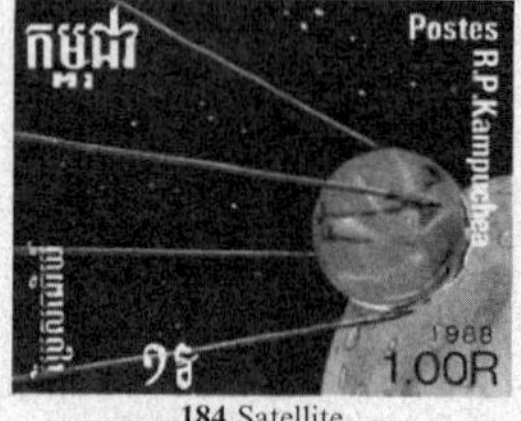

184 Satellite

1988. Space Exploration. Designs showing different satellites.

899	– 20 c. multicoloured (vert)	10	10
900	– 50 c. multicoloured (vert)	20	10
901	– 80 c. multicoloured (vert)	35	10
902	**184** 1 r. multicoloured	50	15
903	– 1 r. 50 multicoloured	55	20
904	– 2 r. multicoloured	75	30
905	– 3 r. multicoloured	1·25	35

185 "Xiphophorus helleri"

1988. "Finlandia 88" International Stamp Exhibition, Helsinki. Tropical Fish. Multicoloured.

907	20 c. Type **185**	10	10
908	50 c. Head- and tail-light tetra	20	10
909	80 c. Paradise fish	35	10
910	1 r. Goldfish	50	15
911	1 r. 50 Tetra	55	20
912	2 r. "Corynopoma riisei"	75	30
913	3 r. Sailfin molly	1·25	35

186 Flowery Helicostyla

188 "Cattleya aclandiae"

187 Seven-spotted Ladybird

1988. Sea Shells. Multicoloured.

915	20 c. Type **186**	10	10
916	50 c. Changing helicostyla	20	10
917	80 c. Shining helicostyla	35	10
918	1 r. Marinduque helicostyla	50	15
919	1 r. 50 Siren chlorena	55	20
920	2 r. Miraculous helicostyla	75	30
921	3 r. "Helicostyla limansauensis"	1·25	35

1988. Insects. Multicoloured.

922	20 c. Type **187**	10	10
923	50 c. "Zonabride geminata" (blister beetle)	20	10
924	80 c. "Carabus auronitens" (ground beetle)	35	10
925	1 r. Honey bee	50	15
926	1 r. 50 Praying mantis	55	20
927	2 r. Dragonfly	75	30
928	3 r. Soft-winged flower beetle	1·25	35

1988. Orchids. Multicoloured.

929	20 c. Type **188**	10	10
930	50 c. "Odontoglossum" "Royal Sovereign"	20	10
931	80 c. "Cattleya labiata"	35	10
932	1 r. Bee orchid	50	15
933	1 r. 50 "Laelia anceps"	55	20
934	2 r. "Laelia pumila"	75	30
935	3 r. "Stanhopea tigrina" (horiz)	1·25	35

189 Egyptian Banded Cobra

190 Walking Dance

1988. Reptiles. Multicoloured.

936	20 c. Type **189**	10	10
937	50 c. Common iguana	20	10
938	80 c. Long-nosed vine snake (horiz)	35	10
939	1 r. Common box turtle (horiz)	50	15
940	1 r. 50 Iguana (horiz)	55	20
941	2 r. Viper (horiz)	75	30
942	3 r. Common cobra	1·25	35

1988. Festival of Rebirth. Khmer Culture. Multicoloured.

943	50 c. Type **190**	20	10
944	1 r. Peacock dance (horiz)	50	15
945	3 r. Kantere dance (horiz)	1·25	35

191 Bridge

1989. Multicoloured.

946	50 c. Type **191**	25	10
947	1 r. More distant view of bridge	50	20
948	3 r. Closer view of bridge	1·60	65

192 Cement Works

1989. National Festival. 10th Anniv of People's Republic of Kampuchea. Multicoloured.

949	3 r. Bayon Earth Station (horiz)	20	10
950	12 r. Electricity generating station 4 (horiz)	75	30
951	30 r. Type **192**	2·10	85

193 Footballers

1989. World Cup Football Championship, Italy (1990).

952 **193** 2 r. multicoloured 10 10
953 – 3 r. multicoloured 20 10
954 – 5 r. multicoloured 30 10
955 – 10 r. multicoloured . . . 65 25
956 – 15 r. multicoloured . . . 1·00 40
957 – 20 r. multicoloured . . . 1·25 50
958 – 35 r. multicoloured . . . 2·40 95
DESIGNS: 3 r. to 35 r. Various footballing scenes.

194 Train

1989. Trains.

960 **194** 2 r. multicoloured 10 10
961 – 3 r. multicoloured 20 10
962 – 5 r. multicoloured 30 10
963 – 10 r. multicoloured . . . 65 25
964 – 15 r. multicoloured . . . 1·00 40
965 – 20 r. multicoloured . . . 1·25 50
966 – 35 r. multicoloured . . . 2·40 95
DESIGNS: 3 r. to 35 r. Various trains.

195 Fidel Castro

196 Scarlet Macaw

1989. 30th Anniv of Cuban Revolution.

968 **195** 12 r. multicoloured . . . 90 40

1989. Parrots. Multicoloured.

969 20 c. Type **196** 10 10
970 80 c. Sulphur-crested cockatoo 10 10
971 3 r. Rose-ringed parakeet . . 25 10
972 6 r. Blue and yellow macaw . 50 15
973 10 r. Cape parrot 90 30
974 15 r. Blue-fronted amazon . . 1·40 45
975 25 r. White-capped parrot (horiz) 2·10 70

197 Skiing

1989. Winter Olympic Games, Albertville (1992). Multicoloured.

977 2 r. Type **197** 10 10
978 3 r. Biathlon 20 10
979 5 r. Cross-country skiing . . . 30 10
980 10 r. Ski jumping 65 25
981 15 r. Speed skating . . . . . 1·00 40
982 20 r. Ice hockey . . . . 1·25 50
983 35 r. Two-man bobsleighing . 2·40 95

198 "Nymphaea capensis" (pink)

1989. Water Lilies. Multicoloured.

985 20 c. Type **198** 10 10
986 80 c. "Nymphaea capensis" (mauve) 10 10
987 3 r. "Nymphaea lotus dentata" 25 10
988 6 r. "Dir. Geo. T. Moore" . . 50 15
989 10 r. "Sunrise" 90 30
990 15 r. "Escarboncle" . . . . . 1·40 45
991 25 r. "Cladstoniana" . . . . . 2·10 70

199 Wrestling

1989. Olympic Games, Barcelona (1992). Multicoloured.

993 2 r. Type **199** 10 10
994 3 r. Gymnastics (vert) 20 10
995 5 r. Putting the shot 30 10
996 10 r. Running (vert) 65 25
997 15 r. Fencing . . . . 1·00 40
998 20 r. Canoeing (vert) . . . . 1·40 50
999 35 r. Hurdling (vert) . . . . 2·40 95

200 Downy Boletus

1989. Fungi. Multicoloured.

1001 20 c. Type **200** 10 10
1002 80 c. Red-staining inocybe . 10 10
1003 3 r. Honey fungus 35 15
1004 6 r. Field mushroom 70 25
1005 10 r. Brown roll-rim . . . . 1·25 45
1006 15 r. Shaggy ink cap . . . . 1·90 65
1007 25 r. Parasol mushroom . . 3·00 1·00

201 Shire Horse

1989. Horses. Multicoloured.

1008 2 r. Type **201** 10 10
1009 3 r. Brabant 20 10
1010 5 r. Boulonais 30 10
1011 10 r. Breton 65 25
1012 15 r. Vladimir heavy draught horse . . . . 1·00 40
1013 20 r. Italian heavy draught horse . . . . 1·25 50
1014 35 r. Freiberger . . . . . . 2·40 95

KATANGA Pt. 14

The following stamps were issued by Mr. Tshombe's Government for independent Katanga. In 1963 Katanga was reunited with the Central Government of Congo.

1960. Various stamps of Belgian Congo optd **KATANGA** and bar or surch also. (a) Masks issue of 1948.

1 1 f. 50 on 1 f. 25 mauve and blue 50 20
2 3 f. 50 on 2 f. 50 green & brown 50 25
3 20 f. purple and red . . . . . 1·75 90
4 50 f. black and brown . . . . 4·00 3·25
5 100 f. black and red . . . . . 30·00 22·00

(b) Flowers issue of 1952. Flowers in natural colours; colours given are of backgrounds and inscriptions.

6 10 c. yellow and purple . . . 10 10
7 15 c. green and red 10 10
8 20 c. grey and green 15 15
9 25 c. orange and green 15 15
10 40 c. salmon and green 15 15
11 50 c. turquoise and red 20 20
12 60 c. purple and green 15 15
13 75 c. grey and lake 20 20
14 1 f. lemon and red 25 25
15 2 f. buff and olive 30 30
16 3 f. pink and green 40 35
17 4 f. lavender and sepia 60 50
18 5 f. green and purple 60 50
19 6 f. 50 lilac and red 60 45
20 7 f. brown and green 80 70
21 8 f. yellow and green 80 70
22 10 f. olive and purple . . . . 11·50 9·00

(c) Wild animals issue of 1959.

23 10 c. brown, sepia and blue . . 15 10
24 20 c. blue and red 15 10
25 40 c. brown and blue 15 10
26 50 c. multicoloured 15 10
27 1 f. black, green and brown . . 5·25 3·25
28 1 f. 50 black and yellow . . . 8·75 6·00
29 2 f. black, brown and red . . . 40 10
30 3 f. black, purple and slate . . 3·25 2·50
31 5 f. brown, green and sepia . . 60 25
32 6 f. 50 brown, yellow and blue 75 25
33 8 f. bistre, violet and brown . 1·10 35
34 10 f. multicoloured . . . . . 1·60 50

(d) Madonna.

35 **102** 50 c. brown, ochre & chest 15 15
36 1 f. brown, violet and blue 15 15
37 2 f. brown, blue and slate 20 20

(e) African Technical Co-operation Commission. Inscr in French or Flemish.

38 **103** 3 f. salmon and slate . . . 7·00 7·00
39 3 f. 50 on 3 f. sal & slate . 2·10 2·10

1960. Independence. Independence issue of Congo optd **11 JUILLET DE L'ETAT DU KATANGA**.

40 **106** 20 c. bistre 10 10
41 50 c. red 10 10
42 1 f. green 10 10
43 1 f. 50 brown 10 10
44 2 f. mauve 10 10
45 3 f. 50 violet 15 10

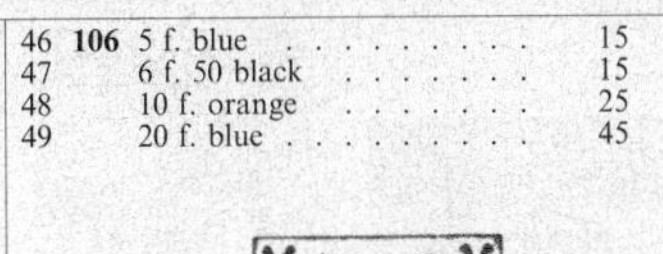

46 **106** 5 f. blue 15 10
47 6 f. 50 black 15 10
48 10 f. orange 25 20
49 20 f. blue 45 30

5

1961. Katanga Art.

50 **5** 10 c. green 10 10
51 20 c. violet 10 10
52 50 c. blue 10 10
53 1 f. 50 green 10 10
54 2 f. brown 10 10
55 – 3 f. 50 blue 10 10
56 – 5 f. turquoise 10 10
57 – 6 f. brown 10 10
58 – 6 f. 50 blue 10 10
59 – 8 f. purple 15 10
60 – 10 f. brown 15 10
61 – 20 f. myrtle 25 20
62 – 50 f. brown 50 40
63 – 100 f. turquoise 85 70
DESIGNS: 3 f. 50 to 8 f. "Preparing food"; 10 f. to 100 f. "Family circle".

6 Pres. Tshombe

1961. 1st Anniv of Independence. Portrait in brown.

64 **6** 6 f. 50 + 5 f. red, green & gold 1·25 1·00
65 8 f. + 5 f. red, green and gold 1·25 1·00
66 10 f. + 5 f. red, green and gold 1·25 1·00

7 "Tree"

8 Early Aircraft, Train and Safari

1961. Katanga International Fair. Vert symbolic designs as T **7**.

67 **7** 50 c. red, green and black . . 10 10
68 – 1 f. black and blue 10 10
69 – 2 f. 50 black and yellow . . . 15 15
70 **7** 3 f. 50 red, brown and black . 15 15
71 – 5 f. black and violet 25 25
72 – 6 f. 50 black and yellow . . . 30 30

1961. Air.

73 **8** 3 f. 50 multicoloured . . . . 3·00 3·00
74 – 6 f. 50 multicoloured . . . . 1·10 1·10
75 **8** 8 f. multicoloured . . . . . 3·25 3·00
76 – 10 f. multicoloured . . . . . 2·10 1·10
DESIGNS: 6 f. 50, 10 f. Tail of Boeing 707.

9 Gendarme in armoured Vehicle

1962. Katanga Gendarmerie.

77 **9** 6 f. multicoloured . . . . . 2·25 2·25
78 8 f. multicoloured 35 35
79 10 f. multicoloured 45 45

POSTAGE DUE STAMPS

1960. Postage Due stamps of Belgian Congo handstamped **KATANGA**. (a) On Nos. D 270/4.

D50 **D 86** 10 c. olive 80 80
D51 20 c. blue 80 80
D52 50 c. green . . . . . . 1·00 1·00
D53 1 f. brown . . . . . .
D54 2 f. orange . . . . . .

(b) On Nos. D 330/6.

D55 **D 99** 10 c. brown . . . . . 3·25 3·25
D56 20 c. purple . . . . . 3·25 3·25
D57 50 c. green . . . . . 3·25 3·25
D58 1 f. blue . . . . . . 1·00 1·00
D59 2 f. red . . . . . . 2·00 2·00
D60 4 f. violet . . . . . 2·75 2·75
D61 6 f. blue . . . . . . 3·25 3·25

KAZAKHSTAN Pt. 10

Formerly a constituent republic of the Soviet Union, Kazakhstan declared its independence on 16 December 1991.

1992. 100 kopeks = 1 rouble.
1994. 100 Tyin (ty.) = 1 tenge (t.).

1 "Golden Warrior" (**2**)

1992. "Golden Warrior" (from 5th-century B.C. tomb).

1 **1** 50 k. multicoloured . . . . . 1·00 50

1992. Nos. 6079/80 of Russia optd as T **2**, in Cyrillic (2, 4) or English (3, 5).

2 12 k. purple . . . . 6·00 3·00
3 12 k. purple . . . . 6·00 3·00
4 13 k. violet . . . . 6·00 3·00
5 13 k. violet . . . . 6·00 3·00

(**3**)

4 Saiga

1992. Russian–French Space Flight. Nos. 5940/1 and 6073 of Russia surch as T **3**.

6 30 k. on 2 k. brown . . . . . . 1·25 60
7 75 k. on 3 k. green . . . . . . 1·25 60
8 1 r. on 1 k. brown . . . . . . 1·25 60

1992.

9 **4** 75 k. multicoloured 50 25

5 "Turksib" (E. K. Kasteev)

1992. Kazakh Art.

10 **5** 1 r. multicoloured 40 20

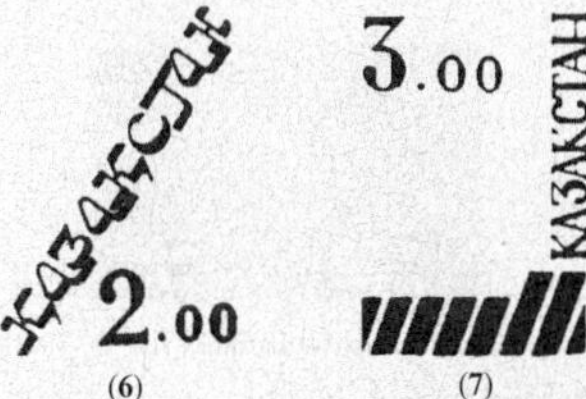

(**6**) (**7**)

(**8**)

9 National Flag and Arms

1992. Various stamps of Russia surch as T **6** (11/12), **7** (13/14) or **8** (15/16).

11 1 r. 50 on 1 k. brown (No. 5940) 50 25
12 2 r. on 2 k. brown (No. 6073) 50 25
13 3 r. on 6 k. blue (No. 4673) . . 65 35
14 5 r. on 6 k. blue (No. 4673) . . 1·10 55
15 10 r. on 1 k. brown (No. 5940) 2·00 1·00
16 24 r. 50 on 1 k. brown (No. 5940) 3·00 1·50

1992. Republic Day.

17 **9** 5 r. multicoloured 10 10

10 Rocket Launch

11 National Flag

1993.

18 **10** 1 r. green 15 10
19 3 r. red 15 10
20 10 r. bistre 15 10
21 25 r. violet 50 25
22 **11** 50 r. yellow, blue and deep blue 1·00 50
See also Nos. 45 etc.

12 Buran and Earth

1993. Space Mail.
23 **12** 100 r. multicoloured . . . . 2·50 1·25

13 Cock

1993. New Year. Year of the Cock.
24 **13** 60 r. black, red and yellow . 75 40

14 Space Station

1993. Cosmonauts Day.
25 **14** 90 r. multicoloured . . . . . 2·00 1·00

15 Nazarbaev and Flag on Map

1993. President Nursultan Nazarbaev (1st series).
26 **15** 50 r. multicoloured 75 40
See also No. 28.

16 Kalkaman

1993. 325th Birth Anniv of Bukar Zhyrau Kalkaman (poet).
27 **16** 15 r. multicoloured 35 20

17 Arms, Flag on Map and Nazarbaev

1993. President Nursultan Nazarbaev (2nd series).
28 **17** 100 r. multicoloured . . . . 1·00 50

18 Desert Dormouse

1993. Mammals. Multicoloured.
29 5 r. Type **18** 10 10
30 10 r. Porcupine 20 10
31 15 r. Marbled polecat 25 15
32 20 r. Asiatic wild ass 40 20
33 25 r. Mouflon 45 25
34 30 r. Cheetah 50 25

19 Ice Hockey **20** Skiers

1994. Winter Olympic Games, Lillehammer, Norway (1st issue). Multicoloured.
35 15 t. Type **19** 25 15
36 25 t. Skiing 45 25
37 90 t. Ski jumping . . . . 1·60 80
38 150 t. Speed skating . . . . . 2·75 1·40

1994. Winter Olympic Games, Lillehammer, Norway (2nd issue). Multicoloured.
39 2 t. Type **20** 35 20
40 6 t. 80 Vladimir Smirnov (Kazakh skier) . . . . 1·00 50

21 Dog **22** Smirnov

1994. New Year. Year of the Dog.
41 **21** 30 t. black, blue and green . 55 30

1994. Vladimir Smirnov, Winter Olympic Games Medals Winner. As No. 40 but face value changed and with additional inscription in Kazakh.
42 **22** 12 t. multicoloured . . . . 2·00 1·00

23 Launch of "Soyuz TM16" at Baikonur

1994. Cosmonautics Day.
43 **23** 2 t. multicoloured 75 40

1994.

45 **10** 15 ty. blue 10 10
76 20 ty. orange 10 10
77 25 ty. yellow 10 10
78 50 ty. grey 10 10
46 80 ty. purple 10 10
79 1 t. green 10 10
80 2 t. blue 10 10
81 4 t. mauve 10 10
82 6 t. green 10 10
83 12 t. mauve 20 10

25 Mt. Abay

1994. "Asia Dauysy" International Music Festival, Almaty. Multicoloured.
47 10 t. Type **25** 50 25
48 15 t. Medeo Ice Stadium, Almaty 85 45
Almaty is the former Alma-Ata.

26 Horsfield's Tortoises

1994. Reptiles. Multicoloured.
49 1 t. Type **26** 10 10
50 1 t. 20 Toad-headed agamas . . 10 10
51 2 t. Halys vipers 25 15
52 3 t. Turkestan plate-tailed geckos 35 20
53 5 t. Steppe agamas 50 25
54 7 t. Glass lizards 75 40

27 National Arms

1994. Republic Day.
56 **27** 2 t. multicoloured 25 15

28 "Why does the Swallow have a Forked Tail?"

1994. Children's Fund. Kazakh Children's Films. Multicoloured.
57 1 t. + 30 ty. Type **28** 10 10
58 1 t. + 30 ty. "The Calf and Hare seek a Better Life" 10 10
59 1 t. + 30 ty. Asses ("The Lame Kulan") 10 10

29 Entelodon

1994. Prehistoric Animals. Multicoloured.
60 1 t. Type **29** 10 10
61 1 t. 20 Saurolophus 10 10
62 2 t. Plesiosaurus 25 15
63 3 t. "Sordes pilosus" 35 20
64 5 t. Mosasaurus 50 25
65 7 t. "Megaloceros giganteum" . 75 40

1995. Nos. 45/6 surch.
67 **24** 1 t. on 15 ty. blue 10 10
68 2 t. on 15 ty. blue 10 10
69 3 t. on 80 ty. purple 10 10
70 4 t. on 80 ty. purple 10 10
71 6 t. on 80 ty. purple 10 10
72 8 t. on 80 ty. purple 15 15
73 12 t. on 80 ty. purple 20 20
74 20 t. on 80 ty. purple 35 35

31 Pig **32** Kunanbaev

1994. New Year. Year of the Pig.
75 **31** 10 t. blue, black and light blue 15 10

1995. 150th Birth Anniv of Abai Kunanbaev (writer). Multicoloured.
86 4 t. Type **32** 25 15
87 9 t. Kunanbaev holding pen and book 60 30

33 Flight Path of Satellite

1995. Cosmonautics Day. Multicoloured.
88 2 t. Type **33** 15 10
89 10 t. Yury Malenchenko, Talgat Musabaev and Ulf Merbold (cosmonauts) 75 40

34 Manshuk Mametova and Battle Scene

1995. 50th Anniv of End of Second World War. Multicoloured.
90 1 t. Type **34** 10 10
91 3 t. Aliya Moldafulova and tank 10 10
92 5 t. Wheat field, dove and eternal flame 25 15

35 "Spring" (S. Membeev)

1995. Paintings. Multicoloured.
93 4 t. Type **35** 10 10
94 9 t. "Mountains" (Zh. Shardenov) 15 10
95 15 t. "Kulash Baiseitova in role of Kyz Zhibek" (G. Ismailova) (vert) 25 15
96 28 t. "Kokpar" (K. Telzhanov) 50 25

1995. "Asia Dauysy" International Music Festival, Almaty. Nos. 47/8 optd **KAZAKSTAN '95 1995.**
97 10 t. multicoloured 15 10
98 15 t. multicoloured 25 15

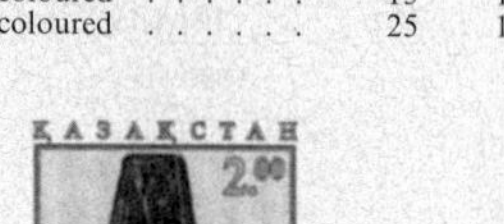
37 Dauletkerei

1995. 175th Birth Anniv of Dauletkerei (composer and poet).
99 **37** 2 t. multicoloured 10 10
100 28 t. multicoloured 50 25

38 Gandhi, Temple and Spinning Wheel

1995. 125th Birth Anniv (1994) of Mahatma Gandhi.
101 **38** 9 t. red and black 15 10
102 22 t. red and black 40 20

39 Anniversary Emblem **40** Cathedral

1995. 50th Anniv of U.N.O.
103 **39** 10 t. gold and blue 20 10
104 36 t. gold and blue 65 35

1995. Buildings in Almaty.
105 **40** 1 t. green 10 10
106 – 2 t. blue 10 10
107 – 3 t. red 10 10
108 – 48 t. brown 85 45
DESIGNS: 2 t. Culture Palace; 3 t. Opera and Ballet House; 48 t. Theatre.
See also Nos. 124/5.

41 White-tailed Sea Eagle

1995. Birds of Prey. Multicoloured.
109 1 t. Type **41** 10 10
110 3 t. Osprey 10 10
111 5 t. Lammergeier 10 10
112 6 t. Himalayan griffon 10 10
113 30 t. Saker falcon 55 30
114 50 t. Golden eagle 90 45

42 Rat and Lunar Cycle

43 Earth

1996. Chinese New Year. Year of the Rat.
115 **42** 25 t. red, black and lilac . 45 25

1996. Cosmonauts Day. Multicoloured.
116 6 t. Type **43** 10 10
117 15 t. Yury Gagarin 25 15
118 20 t. "Alpha" space station . 35 20

45 Cycling

1996. Olympic Games, Atlanta. Multicoloured.

120	4 t. Type **45**	10	10
121	6 t. Wrestling	10	10
122	30 t. Boxing	55	30

1996. As T **40** but smaller, size 24 x 19 mm.

124	1 t. green	10	10
125	6 t. green	10	10

DESIGNS: 1 t. Circus; 6 t. Academy of Sciences (50th anniv).

KHMER REPUBLIC Pt. 21

Cambodia was renamed Khmer Republic on 9th October 1970.

Following the fall of the Khmer Republic, the People's Republic of Kampuchea was proclaimed on 10 January 1979.

100 cents = 1 riel.

78 "Attack"

1971. Defence of Khmer Territory.

285	78	1 r. multicoloured	10	10
286		3 r. multicoloured	20	10
287		10 r. multicoloured	50	20

79 "World Races" and U.N. Emblem

1971. Racial Equality Year.

288	79	3 r. multicoloured	10	10
289		7 r. multicoloured	35	15
290		8 r. multicoloured	55	25

80 General Post Office, Phnom Penh

1971.

291	80	3 r. multicoloured	20	15
292		9 r. multicoloured	40	20
293		10 r. multicoloured	50	30

81 Global Emblem

1971. World Telecommunications Day.

294	81	3 r. multicoloured	10	10
295		4 r. multicoloured	20	10
296	–	7 r. multicoloured	30	15
297	–	8 r. red, black and orange	40	20

DESIGN: 7, 8 r. I.T.U. emblem.

82 Indian Coral Bean

1971. Wild Flowers. Multicoloured.

298	2 r. Type **82**	25	20
299	3 r. Orchid tree	35	25
300	6 r. Flame-of-the-forest	70	30
301	10 r. Malayan crape myrtle (vert)	90	50

83 Arms of the Republic

84 Monument and Flag

1971. 1st Anniv of Republic.

302	83	3 r. bistre and green	15	10
303	84	3 r. multicoloured	10	10
304		4 r. multicoloured	20	10
305	83	8 r. bistre and orange	25	15
306		10 r. bistre and brown	50	20
307	84	10 r. multicoloured	50	25

85 U.N.I.C.E.F. Emblem

86 Book Year Emblem

1971. 25th Anniv of U.N.I.C.E.F.

309	85	3 r. purple	20	10
310		5 r. blue	25	15
311		9 r. red and violet	45	30

1972. International Book Year.

312	86	3 r. green, purple & blue	15	10
313		8 r. blue, green and purple	25	15
314		9 r. bistre, blue and green	45	20

87 Lion of St. Mark's

1972. U.N.E.S.C.O. "Save Venice" Campaign.

316	87	3 r. brown, buff and purple	20	10
317	–	5 r. brown, buff and green	35	20
318	–	10 r. brown, blue & green	65	20

DESIGNS—HORIZ: 5 r. St. Mark's Basilica. VERT: 10 r. Bridge of Sighs.

88 U.N. Emblem

89 Dancing Apsaras (relief), Angkor

1972. 25th Anniv of Economic Commission for Asia and the Far East (C.E.A.E.O.)

320	88	3 r. red	15	10
321		6 r. blue	20	15
322		9 r. red	35	20

1972.

324	89	1 r. brown	10	10
325		3 r. violet	15	10
326		7 r. purple	25	15
327		8 r. brown	30	15
328		9 r. green	40	20
329		10 r. blue	55	20
330		12 r. purple	70	25
331		14 r. blue	85	40

90 "UIT" on TV Screen

91 Conference Emblem

1972. World Telecommunications Day.

332	90	3 r. black, blue and yellow	15	10
333		9 r. black, blue and mauve	35	15
334		14 r. black, blue and brown	55	25

1972. United Nations Environmental Conservation Conference, Stockholm.

335	91	3 r. green, brown and violet	15	10
336		12 r. violet and green	40	20
337		15 r. green and violet	55	35

92 Javan Rhinoceros

94 Hoisting Flag

1972. Wild Animals.

339	92	3 r. black, red and violet	25	10
340	–	4 r. violet, bistre and purple	35	10
341	–	6 r. brown, green and blue	60	20
342	–	7 r. ochre, green and brown	60	20
343	–	8 r. black, green and blue	85	20
344	–	10 r. black, blue and green	1·25	30

DESIGNS: 4 r. Mainland serow; 6 r. Thamin; 7 r. Banteng; 8 r. Water buffalo; 10 r. Gaur.

1972. Olympic Games, Munich. Nos. 164 of Cambodia and 302, 306 and 336/7 of Khmer Republic optd **XXe JEUX OLYMPIQUES MUNICH 1972**, Olympic rings and emblem.

345	83	3 r. bistre and green	25	20
346		10 r. bistre and brown	60	50
347	–	12 r. green and brown	1·50	50
348	91	12 r. violet and green	70	50
349		15 r. green and violet	75	50

1972. 2nd Anniv of Republic.

350	94	3 r. multicoloured	10	10
351		5 r. multicoloured	15	10
352		9 r. multicoloured	35	20

1972. Red Cross Aid for War Victims. No. 164 of Cambodia and 302, 306 and 336/7 of Khmer Republic surch **SECOURS AUX VICTIMES DE GUERRE**, red cross and value.

353	83	3 r. + 2 r. bistre & green	20	20
354		10 r. + 6 r. bistre & brown	45	45
355	–	12 r. + 7 r. green & brown	1·75	55
356	91	12 r. + 7 r. violet & green	55	55
357		15 r. + 8 r. green & violet	1·00	1·00

96 Garuda

97 Crest and Temple

1973. Air.

358	96	3 r. red	10	15
359		30 r. blue	1·40	70
360		50 r. lilac	2·50	1·40
361		100 r. green	4·00	2·25

1973. New Constitution.

362	97	3 r. multicoloured	10	10
363		12 r. multicoloured	15	15
364		14 r. multicoloured	35	20

98 Apsara

99 Interpol Emblem

1972. Angkor Sculptures.

366	98	3 r. black	10	10
367	–	8 r. blue	15	10
368	–	10 r. brown	35	20

DESIGNS: 8 r. Devata (12th century); 10 f. Devata (10th century).

1973. 50th Anniv of International Criminal Police Organization (Interpol).

370	99	3 r. green and turquoise	10	10
371		7 r. green and red	20	15
372		10 r. green and brown	30	20

100 Marshal Lon Nol

1973. Honouring Marshal Lon Nol, 1st President of Republic.

374	100	3 r. black, brown & green	10	10
375		8 r. black, brown and green	20	15
376		14 r. black, brown and agate	20	15

102 Copernicus and Space Rocket

1974. 500th Birth Anniv of Nicolas Copernicus (astronomer). Multicoloured.

382	1 r. Type **102** (postage)	10	10
383	5 r. Copernicus and "Mariner II"	10	10
384	10 r. Copernicus and "Apollo"	25	15
385	25 r. Copernicus and "Telstar"	70	35
386	50 r. Copernicus and space-walker	1·25	70
387	100 r. Copernicus and spaceship landing on Moon	3·00	1·50
388	150 r. Copernicus, and Moon-landing craft leaving "Apollo"	4·25	2·75
389	200 r. Copernicus and "Skylab III" (air)	5·25	2·75
390	250 r. Copernicus and Concorde	7·50	3·75

1974. 4th Anniv of Republic. Various stamps optd **4E ANNIVERSAIRE DE LA REPUBLIQUE.**

391	78	10 r. multicoloured	70	50
392	77	50 r. on 3 r. multicoloured	1·75	1·40
393	94	100 r. on 5 r. multicoloured	3·75	3·25

No. 392 is additionally optd **REPUBLIQUE KHMERE** in French and Cambodian.

104 Xylophone

1975. Unissued stamps of Cambodia showing musical instruments, surch **REPUBLIQUE KHMERE** in French and Cambodian and new value. Multicoloured.

394	5 r. on 8 r. Type **104**
395	20 r. on 1 r. So (two-stringed violin)
396	160 r. on 7 r. Khoung vong (bronze gongs)
397	180 r. on 14 r. Two drums
398	235 r. on 12 r. Barrel-shaped drum
399	500 r. on 9 r. Xylophone (different)
400	1000 r. on 10 r. Boat-shaped xylophone
401	2000 r. on 3 r. Twenty-stringed guitar on legs

Set of 8 £130

POSTAGE DUE STAMPS

D 101 Frieze, Angkor Vat

1974.

D378	D 101	2 r. brown	15	15
D379		6 r. green	25	25
D380		8 r. red	30	30
D381		10 r. blue	35	35

APPENDIX

The following stamps have either been issued in excess of postal needs or have not been available to the public in reasonable quantities at face value. Such stamps may later be given full listing if there is evidence of regular postal use.

1972.

Moon Landing of "Apollo 16". Embossed on gold foil. Air 900 r. x 2.

Visit of Pres. Nixon to China. Embossed on gold foil. Air 900 r. x 2.

Olympic Games, Munich. Embossed on gold foil. Air 900 r. x 2.

1973.

Gold Medal Winners, Munich Olympics. Embossed on gold foil. Air 900 r. x 2.

World Cup Football Championships, West Germany (1974). Embossed on gold foil. Air 900 r. x 4.

1974.

Pres. Kennedy and "Apollo 11". Embossed on gold foil. Air 1100 r. x 2.

500th Birth Anniv of Nicolas Copernicus (astronomer). Embossed on gold foil. Air 1200 r.

Centenary of U.P.U. (1st issue). Postage 10, 60 r.; Air 700 r.; 1200 r. embossed on gold foil.

1975.

Olympic Games, Montreal (1976). Postage 5, 10, 15, 25 r.; Air 50, 100, 150, 200, 250 r.; 1200 r. embossed on gold foil.

World Cup Football Championships, West Germany (1974). Postage 1, 5, 10, 25 r.; Air 50, 100, 150, 200, 250 r.; 1200 r. embossed on gold foil.

Centenary of U.P.U. (2nd issue). Postage 15, 20, 70, 160, 180, 235 r.; Air 500, 1000, 2000 r.; 2000 r. embossed on gold foil.

KHOR FAKKAN Pt. 19

From 1965 various issues were produced for this dependency, some being overprinted on, or in the same designs as, issues for Sharjah.

APPENDIX

The following stamps have either been issued in excess of postal needs or have not been available to the public in reasonable quantities at face value. Such stamps may later be given full listing if there is evidence of regular postal use.

1965.

Views. Nos. 75/80 of Sharjah optd. Air 10, 20, 30, 40, 75, 100 n.p.

Boy and Girl Scouts. Nos. 74 and 89 of Sharjah optd. 2, 2 r.

Birds. Nos. 101/6 of Sharjah optd. Air 30, 40, 75, 150 n.p., 2, 3 r.

Olympic Games, Tokyo 1964. Nos. 95/7 of Sharjah optd. 40, 50 n.p. 2 r.

New York World's Fair. Nos. 81/3 of Sharjah optd. Air 20, 40 n.p. 1 r.

Pres. Kennedy Commem. Nos. 98/100 of Sharjah optd. Air 40, 60, 100 n.p.

Centenary of I.T.U. Postage 1, 2, 3, 4, 5, 50 n.p., 1 r., 120 n.p.

Pan-Arab Games, Cairo. 50 p. × 5.

1966.

International Co-operation Year. 50 n.p. × 8.

Churchill Commemoration. 2, 3, 4, 5 r.

Roses. 20, 35, 60, 80 n.p., 1 r., 125 n.p.

Fish. 1, 2, 3, 4, 5, 15, 20, 30, 40, 50, 75 n.p., 1, 2, 3, 4, 5, 10 r.

Int. Stamp Exhibition, Washington D.C. (SIPEX). 80, 120 n.p., 2 r.

New Currency Surcharges in Rials and Piastres.

(a) 1965 I.T.U. Centenary issue. 10 p. on 50 n.p., 16 p. on 120 n.p., 1 r. on 1 r.

(b) Churchill issue. 1 r. on 2 r., 2 r. on 3 r., 3 r. on 4 r., 4 r. on 5 r.

(c) Roses issue. 1 p. on 20 n.p., 2 p. on 35 n.p., 4 p. on 60 n.p., 6 p. on 80 n.p., 10 p. on 125 n.p., 12 p. on 1 r.

New Currency Surcharges in Dirhams and Riyals.

(a) 1965 Pan-Arab Games issue. 20 d. on 50 p. × 5.

(b) Fish issue. 1 d. on 1 n.p., 2 d. on 2 n.p., 3 d. on 3 n.p., 4 d. on 4 n.p., 5 d. on 5 n.p., 15 d. on 15 n.p., 20 d. on 20 n.p., 30 d. on 30 n.p., 40 d. on 40 n.p., 50 d. on 50 n.p., 75 d. on 75 n.p., 1 r. on 1 r., 2 r. on 2 r., 3 r. on 3 r., 4 r. on 4 r., 5 r. on 5 r., 10 r. on 10 r.

3rd Death Anniv of Pres. J. Kennedy. Optd on Int. Stamp Exhibition, Washington issue. 80 d. on 80 n.p., 120 d. on 120 n.p., 2 r. on 2 r.

World Football Cup Championship, England. ½r. × 7.

1967.

4th Death Anniv of Pres. J. Kennedy. Optd on 1966 Int. Stamp Exhibition issue. 80 d. on 80 n.p., 120 d. on 120 n.p., 2 r. on 2 r.

1968.

Famous Paintings. Optd on Sharjah. Postage 1, 2, 3, 4, 5, 30, 40, 60, 75 d.; Air 1, 2, 3, 4, 5 r.

Winter Olympic Games, Grenoble. Optd on Sharjah. Postage 1, 2, 3, 4, 5 d.; Air 1, 2, 3 r.

Previous Olympic Games. Optd on Sharjah. Air 25, 50, 75 d., 1 r. 50, 3, 4 r.

Olympic Games, Mexico. Optd on Sharjah. 10, 20, 30 d., 2, 2 r. 40, 5 r.

1969.

12th World Jamboree. Optd on 1968 issue of Sharjah. Postage 1, 2, 3, 4, 5, 10 d.; Air 30, 50, 60 d., 1 r. 50.

Martyrs of Liberty. Optd on 1968 issue of Sharjah. Air 35 d. × 4, 60 d. × 4, 1 r. × 4.

Sportsmen and Women. Optd on 1968 issue of Sharjah. Postage 20, 30, 40, 60 d., 1 r. 50, 2 r. 50; Air 35, 50 d., 1, 2, 3 r. 25, 4, 4 r.

A number of issues on gold or silver foil also exist, but it is understood that these were mainly for presentation purposes, although valid for postage.

In common with the other states of the United Arab Emirates the Khor Fakkan stamp contract was terminated on 1 August 1972, and any further new issues released after that date were unauthorised.

KIAUTSCHOU (KIAOCHOW) Pt. 7

A port in Shantung, China, leased by Germany from China in 1898. It was occupied by Japan in 1914, but reverted to China in 1922.

1900. 100 pfennige = 1 mark.
1905. 100 cents = 1 dollar (Chinese).

1900. No. 9 of German Post Offices in China surch **5 Pfg**.

3		5 pf. on 10 pf. red	48·00	50·00

1901. "Yacht" key-types inscr "KIAUTSCHOU".

11	N	3 pf. brown	2·00	2·00
12		5 pf. green	2·40	1·00
13		10 pf. red	4·25	1·75
14		20 pf. blue	10·00	8·75
15		25 pf. black & red on yell	22·00	32·00
16		30 pf. black & orge on buff	22·00	27·00
17		40 pf. black and red	24·00	29·00
18		50 pf. black & pur on buff	25·00	29·00
19		80 pf. black & red on pink	48·00	70·00
20	O	1 m. red	85·00	£140
21		2 m. blue	£130	£150
22		3 m. black	£110	£275
23		5 m. red and black	£400	£800

1905. Chinese currency. "Yacht" key-types inscr "KIAUTSCHOU".

34	N	1 c. brown	85	1·25
35		2 c. green	1·00	1·00
36		4 c. red	1·25	75
37		10 c. blue	1·00	1·10
38		20 c. black and red	1·50	18·00
39		40 c. black and red on pink	2·50	55·00
40	O	½ d. red	6·00	75·00
41		1 d. blue	7·50	65·00
42		1½ d. black	8·50	£150
43		2½ d. red and black	40·00	£450

KIONGA Pt. 9

Part of German E. Africa, occupied by the Portuguese during the 1914/18 war, and now incorporated in Mozambique.

1916. "King Carlos" key-type of Lourenco Marques optd **REPUBLICA** and surch **KIONGA** and new value.

1	S	½ c. on 100 r. blue on blue	5·50	5·00
2		1 c. on 100 r. blue on blue	5·50	5·00
3		2½c. on 100 r. blue on blue	5·50	5·00
4		5 c. on 100 r. blue on blue	5·50	5·00

KOREA Pt. 18

A peninsula to the S. of Manchuria in E. Asia. Formerly an empire under Chinese suzeraintv, it was annexed by Japan in 1910 and used Japanese stamps. After the defeat of Japan in 1945, Russian and United States Military administrations were set up in Korea to the north and south of the 38th Parallel respectively; in 1948 South Korea and North Korea became independent republics.

KOREAN EMPIRE

1884. 100 mon = 1 tempo.
1895. 5 poon = 1 cheun.
1900. 10 re (or rin) = 1 cheun; 100 cheun = 1 weun.

1

3 Korean Flag

(4)

1894.

1	1	5 m. pink	34·00	£4000
2	–	10 m. blue	7·50	£2500

DESIGN: 10 m. Central motif as in Type **1** but different frame and inscribed "CORGAN POST POST".

1895.

7	3	5 p. green	14·00	12·00
8		10 p. blue	18·00	10·00
9		25 p. red	14·00	16·00
10a		50 p. lilac	12·00	6·50

1897. Optd with T **4**.

12	3	5 p. green	20·00	15·00
13		10 p. blue	24·00	20·00
14		25 p. red	30·00	24·00
16		50 p. lilac	30·00	20·00

1899. Surch in Korean characters.

17	3	1 (p.) on 5 p. green (No. 7)	£1200	£750
20		1 (p.) on 5 p. green (No. 12)	£250	£200
18		1 (p.) on 25 p. red (No. 9)	£150	75·00
21		1 (p.) on 25 p. red (No. 14)	50·00	32·00

6

7 National Emblems

8

1900. T **6**, **7** (2 ch.), **8** (2 ch.) and similar designs.

22a	2 r. grey	75	1·50
23	1 ch. green	5·50	4·00
24	2 ch. blue (T **7**)	35·00	38·00
25	2 ch. blue (T **8**)	8·00	7·00
26	3 ch. orange	7·50	7·50
27	4 ch. red	10·00	9·00
28	5 ch. pink	10·00	10·00
29	6 ch. blue	12·00	11·00
30	10 ch. purple	18·00	16·00
31a	15 ch. purple	30·00	25·00
32	20 ch. red	50·00	38·00
33	50 ch. green and pink	£200	£140
34	1 wn. multicoloured	£300	£200
35	2 wn. green and purple	£500	£250

9 Imperial Crown

17 Falcon, Sceptre and Orb

1902. 40th Anniv of Emperor's Accession as King.

36	9	3 ch. orange	32·00	25·00

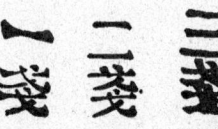

(10) (11) (12) (16)

Types **10** to **12** are in two parts, the horizontal strokes (one, two or three) representing the value figures and the bottom part being the character for "cheun".

Some variation can be found in these woodblock overprints.

1902.

(a) Surch as Types **10** to **12**.

37	3	1 ch. on 25 p. red (No. 9)	8·50	6·50
38		1 ch. on 25 p. red (No. 14)	45·00	45·00
39		2 ch. on 25 p. red (No. 9)	8·50	7·00
40		1 ch. on 25 p. red (No. 14)	42·00	40·00
42		2 ch. on 50 p. lilac (No 10a)	—	£350
43		3 ch. on 25 p. red (No. 9)	42·00	90·00
44		3 ch. on 25 p. red (No. 14)		
46		3 ch. on 50 p. lilac (No. 10a)	8·00	10·00
47		3 ch. on 50 p. lilac (No. 16)	12·00	12·00

(b) Surch as T **16** (Japanese "sen" character) and strokes.

49	3	3 ch. on 50 p. lilac	£650	£500

1903.

50	17	2 r. grey	50	75
51		1 ch. purple	4·50	4·50
52		2 ch. green	4·50	4·50
53		3 ch. orange	5·50	5·50
54		4 ch. pink	6·50	6·00
55		5 ch. brown	9·00	8·00
56		6 ch. lilac	9·00	8·50
57		10 ch. blue	12·00	10·00
58		15 ch. red on yellow	22·00	22·00
59		20 ch. purple on yellow	30·00	32·00
60		50 ch. red on green	90·00	95·00
61		1 wn. lilac on lilac	£150	£160
62		2 wn. purple on orange	£250	£250

SOUTH KOREA

1946. 100 cheun = 1 weun.
1953. 100 weun = 1 hwan.
1962. 100 chon = 1 won.

A. UNITED STATES MILITARY GOVERNMENT

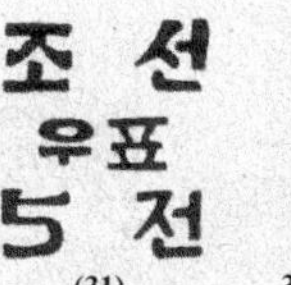

(31)

33 National Emblem

1946. Stamps of Japan surch as T **31**.

69	5 ch. on 5 s. purple (No. 396)	7·00	7·00
70	5 ch. on 14 s. red & brn (No. 324)	1·50	1·75
71	10 ch. on 40 s. purple (No. 407)	1·50	1·50
72	20 ch. on 6 s. blue (No. 397)	1·50	1·25
73	30 ch. on 27 s. red (No. 404)	1·50	1·25
74	5 w. on 17 s. violet (No. 402)	6·50	5·50

1946. Liberation from Japanese Rule.

75	–	3 ch. orange	75	65
76	–	5 ch. green	75	55
77	–	10 ch. red	75	45
78	–	20 ch. blue	75	45
79	33	50 ch. purple	1·10	80
80		1 w. brown	1·40	70

DESIGN: 3 ch. to 20 ch. Family and flag.

34 Dove of Peace and Map of Korea

1946. 1st Anniv of Liberation.

81	34	50 ch. violet	5·00	2·75

35 U.S. and Korean Flags

36 Kyongju Observatory

39 Golden Crown of Silla

40 Admiral Li Sun Sin

1946. Resumption of Postal Service between Korea and U.S.A.

82	35	10 w. red	6·00	4·00

1946.

83	36	50 ch. blue	75	45
84	–	1 w. brown	1·25	60
85	–	2 w. blue	1·50	40
86	39	5 w. mauve	14·00	6·00
87	40	10 w. green	14·00	7·00

DESIGNS—As Type **36**: 1 w. Hibiscus; 2 w. Map of Korea.

41 Korean Alphabet

42 Li Jun, patriot

44 16th-century "Turtle" Ship

45 Letters Surrounding Globe

1946. 500th Anniv of Creation of Korean Alphabet.

88	41	50 ch. blue	3·50	2·00

1947.

89	42	5 w. green	8·50	3·00
90	–	10 w. blue	8·50	3·00
91	–	20 w. red	3·00	65
92	44	50 w. brown	40·00	10·00

DESIGNS: 10 w. Admiral Li Sun Sin; 20 w. Independence Arch, Seoul.

1947. Resumption of Int Postal Service.

93	45	10 w. blue	12·00	5·00

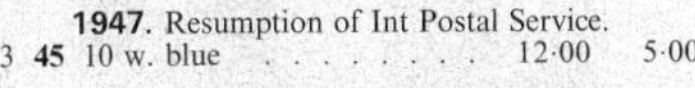

46 Douglas DC-4 Airliner

1947. Air. Inauguration of Air Mail Service.

94	46	50 w. red	6·00	2·50
126		150 w. blue	1·00	90
127		150 w. green	8·00	4·00

47 Hand and Ballot Slip

48 Casting Votes

1948. South Korea Election.
95 47 2 w. orange 10·00 7·00
96 5 w. mauve 10·00 6·00
97 10 w. violet 20·00 8·00
98 48 20 w. red 30·00 16·00
99 50 w. blue 28·00 17·00

49 Korean Flag and Laurel Wreath

1948. Olympic Games.
100 49 5 w. green 65·00 35·00
101 – 10 w. violet 25·00 14·00
DESIGN—VERT: 10 w. Runner with torch

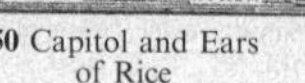
50 Capitol and Ears of Rice
51 Korean Family

1948. Meeting of First National Assembly.
102 50 4 w. brown 16·00 8·00

1948. Promulgation of Constitution.
103 51 4 w. green 45·00 16·00
104 – 10 w. brown 32·00 10·00
DESIGN—HORIZ: 10 w. Flag of Korea.

52 Dr. Syngman Rhee (First President)
53 Hibiscus

1948. Election of First President.
105 52 5 w. blue 60·00 25·00

B. REPUBLIC OF KOREA

1948. Proclamation of Republic.
106 – 4 w. blue 30·00 18·00
107 53 5 w. mauve 26·00 16·00
DESIGN: 4 w. Dove and olive branch.

54 Li Jun
55 Kyongju Observatory

1948.
108 54 4 w. red 40 20
109 55 14 w. blue 40 25

56 Doves and U.N. Emblem

57 Citizen and Date

1949. Arrival of U.N. Commission.
110 56 10 w. blue 30·00 14·00

1949. National Census.
111 57 15 w. violet 30·00 14·00

58 Children and Plant

1949. 20th Anniv of Children's Day.
112 58 15 w. violet 15·00 7·00

59 Hibiscus
60 Map of Korea and Magpies

61 Dove and Globe
62 Admiral Li Sun Sin

1949.
113 – 1 w. red 3·00 1·50
114 – 2 w. grey 1·50 60
115 – 5 w. green 7·50 2·25
116 – 10 w. green 3·00 60
117 59 15 w. red 45 20
118 – 20 w. brown 45 20
119 – 30 w. green 50 20
120 – 50 w. blue 45 20
121 60 65 w. blue 2·00 60
122 – 100 w. green 50 20
123 61 200 w. green 60 35
124 – 400 w. brown 60 40
125 62 500 w. blue 60 45
DESIGNS—AS TYPE 59: 1 w. Postman; 2 w. Worker and factory; 5 w. Harvesting rice; 10 w. Manchurian cranes; 20 w. Diamond Mountains; 30 w. Ginseng plant; 50 w. South Gate, Seoul; 100 w. Tabo Pogoda, Kyongju. AS TYPE 61: 400 w. Diamond Mountains.

63 Symbol and Phoenix

64 Steam Train

1949. 1st Anniv of Independence.
128 63 15 w. blue 18·00 7·50

1949. 50th Anniv of Korean Railways.
129 64 15 w. blue 40·00 22·00

65 Korean Flag

66 Post-horse Warrant

1949. 75th Anniv of U.P.U.
130 65 15 w. multicoloured 12·00 8·00

1950. 50th Anniv of Membership of U.P.U.
131 66 15 w. green 15·00 6·00
132 65 w. brown 10·00 3·50

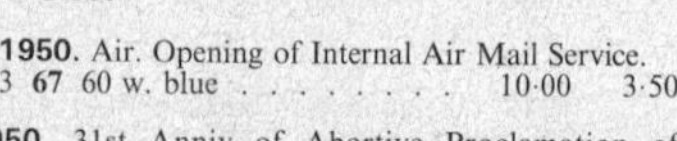
67 Douglas DC-2 Airplane and Globe
68 Demonstrators
69 Capitol, Seoul

1950. Air. Opening of Internal Air Mail Service.
133 67 60 w. blue 10·00 3·50

1950. 31st Anniv of Abortive Proclamation of Independence.
134 68 15 w. green 14·00 6·00
135 65 w. violet 6·00 2·50

1950. 2nd South Korean Election.
136 69 30 w. multicoloured 8·00 3·00

70 Dr. Syngman Rhee

71 Flag and Mountains

1950. Unification of Korea.
137 70 100 w. blue 2·50 1·00
138 71 100 w. green 3·50 1·00
139 – 200 w. green 2·00 75
DESIGN—35 × 24 mm: 200 w. Map of Korea and flags of U.N. and Korea.

73 Manchurian Crane

76 Post-horse Warrant

77 Fairy (8th cent painting)

1951. Perf or roul.
140 73 5 w. brown 2·75 60
181 – 20 w. violet 1·00 30
187 – 50 w. green 2·00 30
183 76 100 w. blue 1·25 25
193 77 1000 w. green 2·25 40
DESIGNS—HORIZ: 20 w. Astrological Tiger (ancient painting); 50 w. Dove and Korean flag.

1951. Surch with new value.
145 54 100 w. on 4 w. red 2·75 75
146 59 200 w. on 15 w. red 4·50 2·00
147 54 300 w. on 4 w. red 1·50 1·00
156 – 300 w. on 10 w. green (116) 10·00 2·00
149 55 300 w. on 14 w. blue 2·25 75
150 59 300 w. on 15 w. red 1·75 75
151 – 300 w. on 20 w. brown (118) 2·50 85
152 – 300 w. on 30 w. green (119) 2·00 75
153 – 300 w. on 50 w. blue (120) 2·00 80
154 60 300 w. on 65 w. blue 4·50 1·60
155 – 300 w. on 100 w. green (122) 2·25 75

80 Statue of Liberty and Flags

1951. Participation in Korean War. Flags in national colours. A. As Type 80 in green. B. As Type 80 but showing U.N. Emblem and doves in blue.

		A	B
158	500 w. Australia	6·00	6·00
159	500 w. Belgium	6·00	6·00
160	500 w. Britain	6·00	6·00
161	500 w. Canada	6·00	6·00
162	500 w. Colombia	6·00	6·00
163	500 w. Denmark	12·00	15·00
164	500 w. Ethiopia	6·00	6·00
165	500 w. France	6·00	6·00
166	500 w. Greece	6·00	6·00
167	500 w. India	10·00	10·00
168	500 w. Italy (with crown)	15·00	15·00
169	500 w. Italy (without crown)	7·00	7·00
170	500 w. Luxembourg	10·00	10·00
171	500 w. Netherlands	6·00	6·00
172	500 w. New Zealand	6·00	6·00
173	500 w. Norway	10·00	10·00
174	500 w. Philippines	6·00	6·00
175	500 w. Sweden	6·00	6·00
176	500 w. Thailand	6·00	6·00
177	500 w. Turkey	6·00	6·00
178	500 w. Union of S. Africa	6·00	6·00
179	500 w. U.S.A.	5·00	5·00

The prices are the same for unused or used.

1951. Air. No. 126 surch **500 WON**.
180 46 500 w. on 150 w. blue 2·50 75

82 Buddha of Sokkuram

83 Pulguksa Temple, Kyongju

84 Monument to King Muryol, Kyongju
85 Shrine of Admiral Li Sun Sin, Tongyong

1952. Inscr "KOREA".
184 82 200 w. red 1·00 25
185 83 300 w. green 80 25
191 84 500 w. red 2·00 40
192 500 w. blue 10·00 50·00
194 85 2000 w. blue 1·50 40
See also Nos. 200/1 and 205.

86 President Syngman Rhee

1952. President's Election to 2nd Term of Office.
195 86 1000 w. green 2·00 70

87 Douglas DC-3 over Freighter

1952. Air.
196 87 1200 w. brown 1·10 40
197 1800 w. blue 1·10 40
198 4200 w. violet 1·10 35
For stamps in new currency, see Nos. 210/12.

88 Tree-planting

89 Monument to King Muryol, Kyongju

91 Pagoda Park, Seoul
92 Sika Deer

93 Sika Deer

1953. New currency. With character "hwan" after figure of value.
244 88 1 h. blue 25 10
200 84 2 h. blue 50 10
201 5 h. green 60 10
202 89 5 h. green 50 10
203 88 10 h. green 1·00 10
204 – 10 h. brown 2·50 10
205 85 20 h. brown 3·25 10
206 91 30 h. blue 1·00 10
242 92 100 h. brown 7·50 30
243 91 200 h. violet 3·50 25
208 93 500 h. orange 28·00 1·60
209 1000 h. brown 60·00 3·00
DESIGN: No. 204, "Metopta rectifasciata" (moth) and Korean flag.
For designs without character after figure of value, see 1955 issue (No. 273 etc).

1953. Air. Colours changed and new Currency.
210 87 12 h. blue 1·25 35
211 18 h. violet 1·50 40
212 42 h. green 1·75 50

94 Field Hospital

1953. Red Cross Fund. Crosses in red.
213 94 10 h. + 5 h. green 5·00 1·50
214 – 10 h. + 5 h. blue 5·00 1·50
DESIGN—VERT: No. 214, Nurses supporting wounded soldier.

95 Y.M.C.A. Badge and Map

96 Douglas DC-6 over East Gate, Seoul

1953. 50th Anniv of Korean Young Men's Christian Association.
215 95 10 h. red and black 2·00 70

1954. Air.

216	96	25 h. brown	1·60	40
217		35 h. purple	2·25	40
218		38 h. green	2·25	40
219		58 h. blue	2·50	40
258		70 h. green	3·50	30
220		71 h. blue	3·25	40
259		110 h. brown	3·25	30
260		205 h. mauve	3·75	30

98 Tokto Island

99 Erosion Control

1954.

221	–	2 h. purple	1·00	15
222	–	5 h. blue	80	15
223	98	10 h. green	1·25	15

DESIGN: 2 h., 5 h. Rocks off Tokto Is.

1954. 4th World Forestry Congress, Dehru Dun.

224	99	10 h. light green and green	1·00	15
225		19 h. light green and green	1·00	15

100 Presidents Syngman Rhee and Eisenhower

101 "Rebirth of Industry"

1954. Korea–United States Mutual Defence Treaty.

226	100	10 h. blue	1·75	40
227		19 h. brown	1·25	40
228		71 h. green	2·50	85

1955. Reconstruction.

229	101	10 h. brown	2·50	15
230		15 h. violet	2·25	15
231		20 h. blue	2·25	15
232		50 h. mauve	3·00	25
269		50 h. red	5·00	15

102 Rotary Emblem

103 Pres. Syngman Rhee

1955. 50th Anniv of Rotary International.

236	102	20 h. violet	2·50	85
237		25 h. green	1·25	45
238		71 h. purple	1·50	50

1955. 80th Birthday of President.

239	103	20 h. blue	3·25	1·00

104 Independence Arch, Seoul

1955. 10th Anniv of Liberation.

240	104	40 h. green	2·00	70
241		100 h. brown	2·00	1·00

105 Hibiscus

106 King Sejong

107 Kyongju Observatory

1955. Without character after figure of value.

273	88	2 h. blue	25	10
309	89	4 h. blue	60	10
310		5 h. green	60	10
247	105	10 h. mauve	1·00	10
277	–	10 h. green	75	10
248	106	20 h. purple	2·50	10
279	105	20 h. mauve	60	15
280	–	30 h. violet	75	15
281	106	40 h. purple	85	15
249	107	50 h. violet	2·75	10
315	–	55 h. purple	2·00	10
250	92	100 h. purple	12·00	10
284	107	100 h. violet	2·75	15
285	92	200 h. purple	3·25	15
286	91	400 h. violet	32·00	35
251	93	500 h. brown	28·00	40
288		1000 h. brown	50·00	2·25

DESIGNS—HORIZ: No. 277, South Gate, Seoul; 280, Tiger. VERT: No. 315, Haegumgang (cliff face).

108 Runners and Torch

109 U.N. Emblem

1955. 36th National Athletic Meeting.

252	108	20 h. purple	3·00	1·00
253		55 h. green	3·00	1·00

1955. 10th Anniv of U.N.

254	109	20 h. green	2·25	60
255		55 h. blue	2·25	60

110 Admiral Li Sun Sin and 16th-century "Turtle" Ship

1955. 10th Anniv of Korean Navy.

256	110	20 h. blue	3·00	1·50

111 Admiration Pagoda

112 Pres. Syngman Rhee

1956. 81st Birthday of President.

257	111	20 h. green	3·00	1·00

1956. President's Election to Third Term of Office.

261	112	20 h. brown	16·00	5·00
262		55 h. blue	7·50	3·00

113 Torch and Olympic Rings

114 Central P.O., Seoul

1956. Olympic Games.

263	113	20 h. brown	3·00	80
264		55 h. green	3·00	80

1956. Stamp Day. Inscr "4289.12.4".

265	114	20 h. turquoise	3·00	55
266	–	50 h. red	3·75	1·00
267	–	55 h. green	1·50	55

DESIGNS—VERT: 50 h. Stamp of 1884. HORIZ: 55 h. Man leading post-pony.

119 I.T.U. Emblem and Radio Mast

120 Korean Scout and Badge

1957. 5th Anniv of Korea's Admission to I.T.U.

290	119	40 h. blue	1·50	60
291		55 h. green	1·50	60

1957. 50th Anniv of Boy Scout Movement.

293	120	40 h. purple	1·75	60
294		55 h. purple	1·75	60

1957. Flood Relief Fund. As No. 281 but Korean inscr and premium added and colour changed.

299		40 h. + 10 h. green	2·50	50

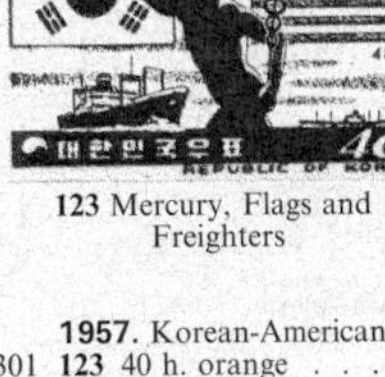
123 Mercury, Flags and Freighters

124 Star of Bethlehem and Pine Cone

1957. Korean-American Friendship Treaty.

301	123	40 h. orange	1·25	60
302		205 h. green	1·60	80

1957. Christmas and New Year Issue.

304	124	15 h. brown, green & orange	2·50	50
305	–	25 h. green, red & yellow	2·50	30
306	–	30 h. blue, green & yellow	4·25	1·25

DESIGNS: 25 h. Christmas tree and tassels; 30 h. Christmas tree and dog by window.

125 Winged Letter

126 Korean Children regarding future

1958. Postal Week.

321	125	40 h. blue and red	80	25

1958. 10th Anniv of Republic of Korea.

323	126	20 h. grey	80	25
324	–	40 h. red	1·25	25

DESIGN—HORIZ: 40 h. Hibiscus flowers forming figure "10".

127 U.N.E.S.C.O. Headquarters, Paris

128 Children flying Kites

1958. Inaug of U.N.E.S.C.O. Building, Paris.

326	127	40 h. orange and green	1·00	25

1958. Christmas and New Year.

330	128	15 h. green	1·00	30
331	–	25 h. red, yellow and blue	1·00	30
332	–	30 h. red, blue and yellow	2·00	50

DESIGNS—VERT: 25 h. Christmas tree, tassels and wicker basket (cooking sieve); 30 h. Children in traditional festive costume.

129 Rejoicing Crowds in Pagoda Park, Flag and Torch

1959. 40th Anniv of Abortive Proclamation of Independence.

334	129	40 h. purple and brown	1·00	25

130 Marines going Ashore from Landing-craft

1959. 10th Anniv of Korean Marine Corps.

336	130	40 h. green	1·00	25

131

1959. 10th Anniv of Korea's Admission to W.H.O.

339	131	40 h. purple and pink	1·00	25

132 Diesel Train

1959. 60th Anniv of Korean Railways.

341	132	40 h. sepia and brown	1·75	75

133 Runners in Relay Race

1959. 40th Korean National Games.

343	133	40 h. brown and blue	1·00	25

134 Red Cross and Korea

1959. Red Cross. Inscr "1959 4292".

345	134	40 h. red and green	1·00	25
346	–	55 h. red and mauve	1·00	25

DESIGN: 55 h. Red Cross on Globe.

135 Korean Postal Flags Old and New

136 Mice in Korean Costume and New Year Emblem

1959. 75th Anniv of Korean Postal Service.

348	135	40 h. red and blue	1·00	25

1959. Christmas and New Year.

350	136	15 h. pink, blue and grey	1·00	15
351	–	25 h. red, green and blue	80	15
352	–	30 h. red, black & mauve	1·40	15

DESIGNS: 25 h. Carol singers; 30 h. Crane.

137 U.P.U. Monument

138 Honey Bee and Clover

1960. 60th Anniv of Admission of Korea to U.P.U.

354	137	40 h. brown and blue	1·10	50

1960. Children's Savings Campaign.

356	138	10 h. yellow, brown & green	75	10
357	–	20 h. brown, blue & pink	1·25	10

DESIGN: 20 h. Snail and Korean money-bag.

For these stamps in new currency, see Nos. 452 etc.

139 "Uprooted Tree"

140 Pres. Eisenhower

1960. World Refugee Year.

358	139	40 h. red, blue and green	80	10

1960. Visit of President Eisenhower of United States.

360	140	40 h. blue, red and green	3·00	80

141 Schoolchildren

1960. 75th Anniv of Educational System.

362	141	40 h. purple, brown & green	1·00	25

142 Assembly 143 "Liberation"

1960. Inauguration of House of Councillors.
364 **142** 40 h. blue . . . . 1·00 25

1960. 15th Anniv of Liberation.
366 **143** 40 h. red, blue and brown 1·00 25

144 Weightlifting

145 Barn Swallow and Insulators

1960. Olympic Games.
368 **144** 20 h. brown, flesh & turq . 1·00 35
369 – 40 h. brown, blue & turq . 1·00 35
DESIGN: 40 h. South Gate, Seoul.

1960. 75th Anniv of Korean Telegraph Service.
371 **145** 40 h. violet, grey and blue 1·10 60

146 "Rebirth of Republic"

147 "Torch of Culture"

1960. Establishment of New Government.
373 **146** 40 h. green, blue & orange 1·00 25

1960. Cultural Month.
376 **147** 40 h. yellow, lt blue & bl . 1·00 25

148 U.N. Flag

149 U.N. Emblem and Gravestones

1960. 15th Anniv of U.N.
378 **148** 40 h. blue, green & mauve 1·00 25

1960. Establishment of U.N. Memorial Cemetery.
380 **149** 40 h. brown and orange . 1·00 25

150 "National Stocktaking"

151 Festival Stocking

1960 Census of Population and Resources.
382 **150** 40 h. red, drab and blue . 1·00 25

1960. Christmas and New Year Issue.
384 – 15 h. brown, yellow & grey 50 15
385 **151** 25 h. red, green and blue . 40 10
386 – 30 h. red, yellow and blue 75 15
DESIGNS: 15 h. Ox's head; 30 h. Girl bowing in New Year's greeting.

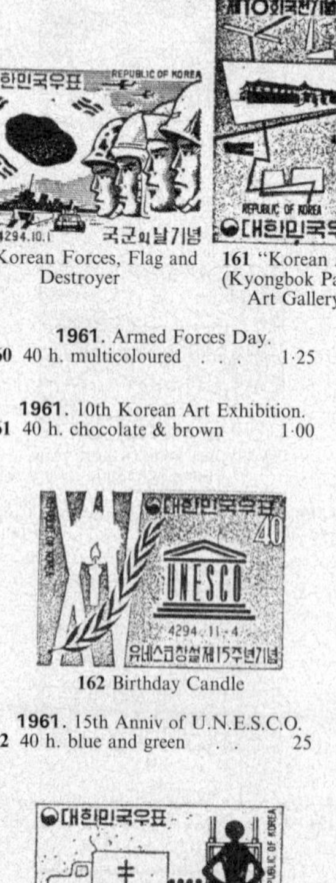

152 Wind-sock and Ancient Rain-gauge

1961. World Meteorological Day.
388 **152** 40 h. ultramarine and blue 1·00 25

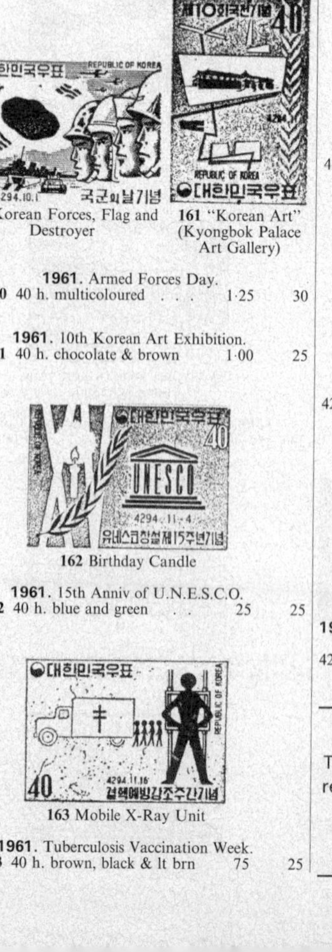

153 Family, Sun and Globe

1961. World Health Day.
390 **153** 40 h. brown and orange . 1·00 25

154 Students' Demonstration

155 Workers and Conference Emblem

1961. 1st Anniv of April Revolution (Overthrow of Pres. Syngman Rhee).
392 **154** 40 h. green, red and blue 1·00 30

1961. Int Community Development Conf, Seoul.
394 **155** 40 h. green 80 25

156 Girl Guide, Camp and Badge

157 Soldier's Grave

1961. 15th Anniv of Korean Girl Guide Movement.
396 **156** 40 h. green . . . . 1·00 25

1961. Memorial Day.
398 **157** 40 h. black and drab . . 1·00 30

158 Soldier with Torch

159 "Three Liberations"

1961. Revolution of 16 May (Seizure of Power by Gen. Pak Chung Hi).
400 **158** 40 h. brown and yellow . 1·00 30

1961. Liberation Day.
402 **159** 40 h. multicoloured . . . 1·00 30

160 Korean Forces, Flag and Destroyer

161 "Korean Art" (Kyongbok Palace Art Gallery)

1961. Armed Forces Day.
404 **160** 40 h. multicoloured . . . 1·25 30

1961. 10th Korean Art Exhibition.
406 **161** 40 h. chocolate & brown 1·00 25

162 Birthday Candle

1961. 15th Anniv of U.N.E.S.C.O.
408 **162** 40 h. blue and green . . 25 25

163 Mobile X-Ray Unit

1961. Tuberculosis Vaccination Week.
410 **163** 40 h. brown, black & lt brn 75 25

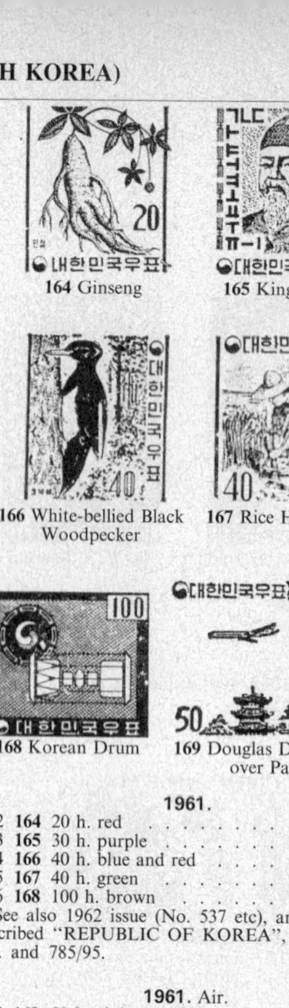

164 Ginseng

165 King Sejong

166 White-bellied Black Woodpecker

167 Rice Harvester

168 Korean Drum

169 Douglas DC-8 Jetliner over Pagoda

1961.
412 **164** 20 h. red 80 10
413 **165** 30 h. purple 80 10
414 **166** 40 h. blue and red . . . . 3·75 50
415 **167** 40 h. green . . . . 1·10 10
416 **168** 100 h. brown . . . . . . 1·75 10
See also 1962 issue (No. 537 etc), and for stamps inscribed "REPUBLIC OF KOREA", see Nos. 641 etc. and 785/95.

1961. Air.
417 **169** 50 h. violet and blue . . . 5·00 70
418 – 100 h. brown and blue . . 5·00 35
419 – 200 h. brown and blue . . 12·00 55
420 – 400 h. green and blue . . . 6·00 35
DESIGNS—Plane over: 100 h. West Gate, Suwon; 200 h. Gateway and wall of Toksu Palace, Seoul; 400 h. Pavilion, Kyongbok Palace, Seoul.
See also Nos. 454 etc.

170 I.T.U. Emblem as Satellite

1962. 10th Anniv of Admission to I.T.U.
421 **170** 40 h. red and blue . . . . 1·25 40

171 Triga Mark II Reactor

1962. 1st Korean Atomic Reactor.
423 **171** 40 h. green, drab and blue 1·00 25

172 Mosquito and Emblem

1962. Malaria Eradication.
424 **172** 40 h. red and green . . . 50 25

173 Girl and Y.W.C.A. Emblem

1962. 40th Anniv of Korean Young Women's Christian Association.
426 **173** 40 h. blue and orange . . 1·00 30

MINIMUM PRICE

The minimum price quoted is 10p which represents a handling charge rather than a basis for valuing common stamps. For further notes about prices, see introductory pages.

174 Emblem of Asian Film Producers' Federation

175 Soldiers crossing Han River Bridge

1962. 9th Asian Film Festival, Seoul.
427 **174** 40 h. violet, red & turquoise 1·25 25

1962. 1st Anniv of 16th May Revolution.
428 – 30 h. green and brown . . 1·50 50
429 **175** 40 h. brown, green & turq 1·50 50
430 – 200 h. yellow, red & blue 11·00 3·00
DESIGNS—HORIZ: 30 h. "Industrial Progress" (men moving cogwheel up slope); 200 h. "Egg" containing Korean badge and industrial skyline.

176 20-oared "Turtle" Ship

1962. 370th Anniv of Hansan Naval Victory over Japanese.
433 **176** 2 w. blue and light blue . 1·50 70
434 – 4 w. black, violet & turq . 2·75 1·00
DESIGN: 4 w. 16-oared "turtle" ship.

177 Chindo Dog

178 "Hanabusaya asiatica"

179 Statue of Goddess Mikuk Besal

213 Longhorn Beetle

180 Farmers' Dance

181 12th-century Wine-jug

214 Factory, Fishes and Corn

182 Mison

183 13th-century Printing-block and Impression used for "Tripitaka Koreana"

191 Sika Deer

192 Bell of King Kyongdok

215 Bodhisatva, Sokkuram Shrine

216 Tile, Silla Dynasty **217** "Azure Dragon", Koguryo period

1962. New Currency.
537 **177** 20 ch. brown 25 10
436 **178** 40 ch. blue 30 10
785 – 40 ch. green 40 10
539 **179** 50 ch. brown 30 10
540 **213** 60 ch. brown 40 10
541 **180** 1 w. blue . . . . 1·00 10
542 **179** 1 w. 50 grey 30 10
543 **164** 2 w. red . . . . 1·25 10
472 **165** 3 w. purple . . . . . . 2·25 10
545 **167** 4 w. green 30 10
442 **181** 5 w. blue . . . . 3·50 10
547 **214** 7 w. mauve . . . . . . 1·10 10
548 **168** 10 w. brown . . . . . . 2·00 10
549 **182** 20 w. mauve . . . . . . 3·00 10
550 **183** 40 w. purple . . . . . . 4·50 10
551 **191** 50 w. brown . . . . . . 6·00 15
552 **192** 100 w. green . . . . . . 15·00 20
553 **215** 200 w. dp green and green 5·00 10
554 **216** 300 w. green and brown . 10·00 10
555 **217** 500 w. blue and lt blue . 7·00 10
DESIGN—18 × 72 mm: No. 785, motif as Type **178** but inscriptions differently arranged.
See also Nos. 607, 609 and 641/9.

184 Scout Badge and Korean Flag **185** Mackerel, Trawler and Nets

1962. 40th Anniv of Korean Scout Movement.
446 **184** 4 w. brown, red and blue 80 25
447 4 w. green, red and blue 80 25

1962. 10th Indo-Pacific Fishery Council Meeting, Seoul.
449 **185** 4 w. ultramarine and blue 1·00 25

186 I.C.A.O. Emblem

1962. 10th Anniv of Korea's Entry into I.C.A.O.
450 **186** 4 w. blue and brown . . . 1·00 25

1962. Children's Savings Campaign. As Nos. 356/7 but new currency.
452 1 w. yellow, brown and green 3·25 10
453 2 w. brown, blue and pink . . 8·25 65

1962. Air. New Currency.
454 **169** 5 w. blue and violet . . . 12·50 2·40
512 – 10 w. brown and green (As No. 418) . . . . 2·75 30
513 – 20 w. brown and green (As No. 419) . . . . . . 3·50 35
563 **169** 39 w. drab and blue . . . 4·75 35
514 – 40 w. green and blue (As No. 420) . . . . . . 4·00 50
564 – 64 w. green and blue (As No. 418) . . . . . . 2·10 25
565 78 w. blue and green (As No. 419) . . . . . . 3·00 30
566 – 112 w. green and blue (As No. 420) . . . . . . 3·00 30

187 Electric Power Plant

1962. Inauguration of 1st Korean Economic Five Year Plan.
458 **187** 4 w. violet and orange . . 1·25 40
459 – 4 w. ultramarine and blue 1·25 40
DESIGN: No. 459, Irrigation Dam.
See also Nos. 482/3, 528/9, 593/4 and 634/5.

188 Campaign Emblem

1963. Freedom from Hunger.
460 **188** 4 w. green, buff and blue 75 25

189 Globe and Letters

1963. 1st Anniv of Asian-Oceanic Postal Union.
462 **189** 4 w. purple, green & blue 90 25

190 Centenary Emblem and Map

1963. Centenary of Red Cross.
464 **190** 4 w. red, grey and blue . 90 25
465 4 w. red, grey and orange 90 25

1963. Flood Relief. As No. 545, but new colour and inscr with premium.
479 4 w. + 1 w. blue . . . . . . 1·50 45

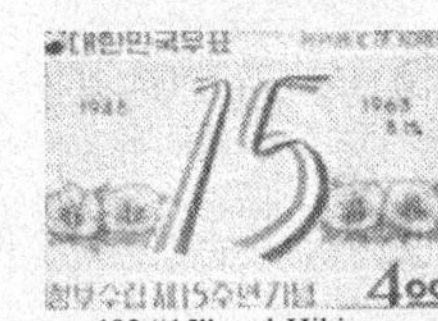

193 "15" and Hibiscus

1963. 15th Anniv of Republic.
480 **193** 4 w. red, violet and blue . 1·40 30

194 Nurse and Emblem

1963. 15th Anniv of Korean Army Nursing Corps.
481 **194** 4 w. black, turquoise & grn 1·00 25

1963. Five Year Plan. Dated "1963". As T **187**.
482 4 w. violet and blue 90 25
483 4 w. chocolate and brown . . 1·10 50
DESIGNS: No. 482, Cement Factory, Mun'gyong, and bag of cement. 483; Miner and coal train, Samch'ok region.

195 Rock Temples of Abu Simbel **196**

1963. Nubian Monuments Preservation.
484 **195** 3 w. green and drab . . . 2·25 40
485 **196** 4 w. green and drab . . . 2·25 40
Nos. 484/5 were issued together, se-tenant, forming a composite design.

197 Rugby Football and Athlete **198** Nurse and Motor Clinic

1963. 44th National Games.
487 **197** 4 w. green, brown & blue 1·00 25

1963. 10th Anniv of Korean Tuberculosis Prevention Society.
488 **198** 4 w. blue and red . . . . 1·00 25

199 Eleanor Roosevelt **200** U.N. Headquarters

1963. 15th Anniv of Declaration of Human Rights.
489 **199** 3 w. brown and blue . . . 80 25
490 – 4 w. blue, green and buff 80 25
DESIGN: 4 w. Freedom torch and globe.

1963. 15th Anniv of U.N. Recognition of Korea.
492 **200** 4 w. green, blue and black 1·00 25

201 Pres. Pak Chong Hi and Capitol **202** "Tai-Keum" (Bamboo Flute)

1963. Inaug of President Pak Chong Hi.
494 **201** 4 w. blue, turquoise & blk 11·00 3·50

1963. Musical Instruments and Players. As T **202**.
495 4 w. green, brown and drab . . 2·25 60
496 4 w. black, blue and light blue 2·25 60
497 4 w. green, mauve and pink . . 2·25 60
498 4 w. brown, violet and grey . . 2·25 60
499 4 w. blue, brown and pink . . 2·25 60
500 4 w. turquoise, black and blue 2·25 60
501 4 w. violet, bistre and yellow 2·25 60
502 4 w. blue, brown and mauve 2·25 60
503 4 w. black, blue and purple . . 2·25 60
504 4 w. black, brown and pink . . 2·25 60
MUSICAL INSTRUMENTS (and players)—VERT: No. 495, Type **202**; 496, "Wul-keum" (banjo); 497, "Tang-piri" (flageolet); 498, "Na-bal" (trumpet); 499, "Hyang-pipa" (lute); 500, "Pyenkyeng" jade chimes; 501, "Taipyeng-so" (clarinet); 502, "Chang-ko" (double-ended drum). HORIZ: No. 503, "Wa-kong-hu" (harp); 504, "Kaya-ko" (zither).

203 Symbols of Metric System **204** "U.N.E.S.C.O."

1964. Introduction of Metric System in Korea.
505 **203** 4 w. multicoloured 90 25

1964. 10th Anniv of Korean U.N.E.S.C.O. Committee.
506 **204** 4 w. ultramarine, red & bl 90 25

205 Symbols of Industry and Census

1964. National Industrial Census (1963).
507 **205** 4 w. brown, black & grey 1·10 50

206 Y.M.C.A. Emblem and Profile of Young Man

1964. 50th Anniv of Korean Young Men's Christian Association.
508 **206** 4 w. red, blue and green 75 25

207 Fair Emblem, Ginseng Root and Freighter

1964. New York World's Fair.
509 **207** 40 w. brown, green & yellow 1·75 40
510 – 100 w. ultramarine, brown & blue . . . . 9·00 1·50
DESIGN: 100 w. Korean pavilion at Fair.

208 Secret Garden

1964. Background in light blue.
517 **208** 1 w. green 60 20
518 – 2 w. green . . . . 1·00 25
519 – 3 w. green . . . . 1·00 25
520 – 4 w. green . . . . 1·50 30
521 – 5 w. violet . . . . 2·00 30
522 – 6 w. blue . . . . 2·00 40
523 – 7 w. brown . . . . 2·40 40
524 – 8 w. brown . . . . 2·50 40
525 – 9 w. violet . . . . 2·50 40
526 – 10 w. green . . . . 2·75 45
DESIGNS: 2 w. Whahong Gate; 3 w. Uisang Pavilion; 4 w. Mt. Songni; 5 w. Paekma River; 6 w. Anab Pond; 7 w. Choksok Pavilion; 8 w. Kwanghan Pavilion; 9 w. Whaom Temple; 10 w. Chonjeyon Falls.

1964. Five Year Plan. Dated "1964". As T **187**.
528 4 w. black and blue . . . . . 1·25 30
529 4 w. blue and yellow . . . . 1·00 30
DESIGNS: No. 528, Trawlers and fish; 529, Oil refinery and barrels.

209 Wheel and Globe

1964. Colombo Plan Day.
530 **209** 4 w. lt brown, brn & grn 70 25

210 "Helping Hand"

1964. 15th Anniv of Korea's Admission to W.H.O.
532 **210** 4 w. black, green and light green 50 25

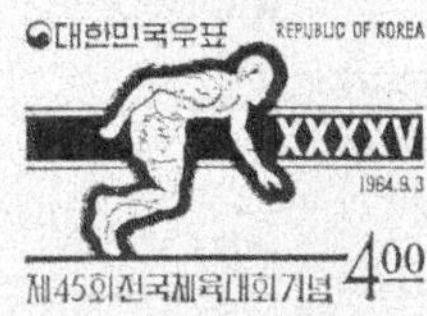

211 Running

1964. 45th National Games, Inchon.
534 **211** 4 w. pink, green & purple 1·00 25

212 U.P.U. Monument, Berne, and Ribbons

1964. 90th Anniv of U.P.U.
535 **212** 4 w. brown, blue and pink 75 25

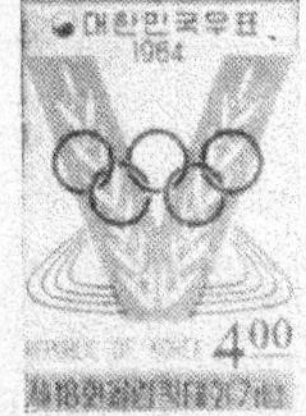

218 Federation Emblem **219** Olympic "V" Emblem

1964. 5th Meeting of Int Federation of Asian and Western Pacific Contractors' Assns
536 **218** 4 w. green, light green and brown 75 25

1964. Olympic Games, Tokyo.
557 **219** 4 w. blue, turquoise & brn 1·50 60
558 – 4 w. mauve, blue & green 1·50 60
559 – 4 w. brown, ultram & blue 1·50 60
560 – 4 w. red, brown and blue 1·50 60
561 – 4 w. brown, purple and blue 1·50 60
DESIGNS—HORIZ: No. 558, Running; 559, Rowing; 560, Horse-jumping; 561, Gymnastics.

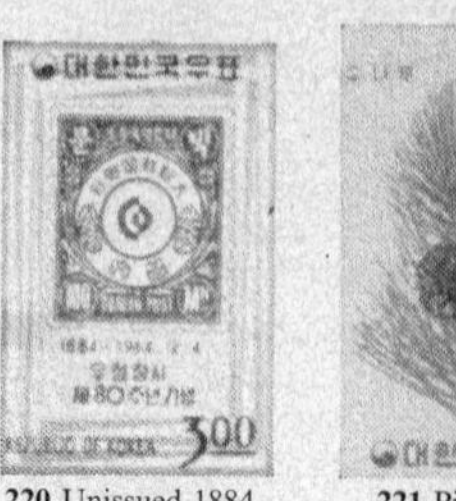
220 Unissued 1884 100 m. Stamp

221 Pine Cone

1964. 80th Anniv of Korean Postal Services.
567 **220** 3 w. blue, violet & mauve 1·00 40
568 – 4 w. black, violet & green 1·60 60
DESIGNS: 4 w. Hong Yong Sik, 1st Korean Postmaster-general.

1965. Korean Plants. Plants multicoloured, background colours given.
571 **221** 4 w. green 1·25 40
572 – 4 w. brown (Plum blossom) 1·25 40
573 – 4 w. blue (Forsythia) 1·25 40
574 – 4 w. green (Azalea) 1·25 40
575 – 4 w. pink (Lilac) 1·25 40
576 – 4 w. grey (Wild rose) 1·25 40
577 – 4 w. green (Balsam) 1·25 40
578 – 4 w. grey (Hibiscus) 1·25 40
579 – 4 w. flesh (Crepe myrtle) 1·25 40
580 – 4 w. blue (Ullung chrysanthemum) 1·25 40
581 – 4 w. buff (Paulownia, tree) 1·25 40
582 – 4 w. blue (Bamboo) 1·25 40

222 Folk Dancing

1965. Pacific Area Travel Assn Conf, Seoul.
584 **222** 4 w. violet, brown & green 1·00 25

223 Flag and Doves

1965. Military Aid for Vietnam.
586 **223** 4 w. brown, blue & yellow 60 50

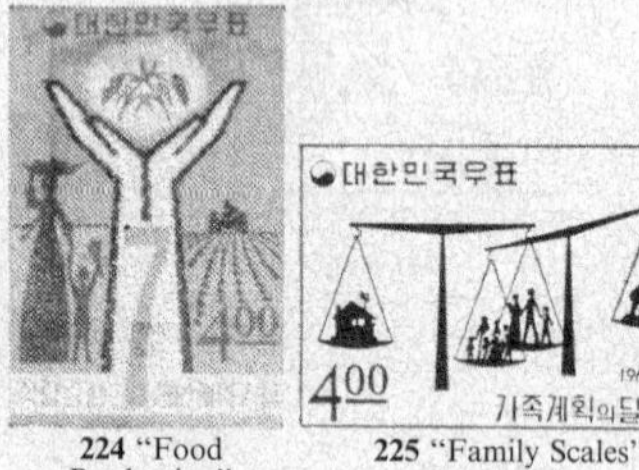
224 "Food Production"
225 "Family Scales"

1965. Agricultural Seven Year Plan.
588 **224** 4 w. brown, green & black 50 25

1965. Family Planning Month.
589 **225** 4 w. green, drab & lt green 65 25

226 I.T.U. Emblem and Symbols

1965. Centenary of I.T.U.
591 **226** 4 w. black, red and blue 65 20

1965. Five Year Plan. Dated "1965". As T **187**.
593 4 w. blue and pink 1·00 25
594 4 w. sepia and brown 80 25
DESIGNS: No. 593, "Korea" (freighter) at quayside and crates; 594, Fertiliser plant and wheat.

227 Flags of Australia, Belgium, Great Britain, Canada and Colombia

1965. 15th Anniv of Outbreak of Korean War.
595 **227** 4 w. multicoloured 1·00 40
596 – 4 w. multicoloured 1·00 40
597 – 4 w. multicoloured 1·00 40
598 – 4 w. multicoloured 1·00 40
599 – 10 w. multicoloured 2·50 60
DESIGNS—U.N. Emblem and flags of: No. 596, Denmark, Ethiopia, France, Greece and India; 597, Italy, Luxembourg, Netherlands, New Zealand and Norway; 598, Philippines, Sweden, Thailand, Turkey and South Africa; 599, General MacArthur and flags of Korea, U.N. and U.S.A.

228 Flag and Sky-writing ("20")

229 Ants and Leaf

1965. 20th Anniv of Liberation.
601 **228** 4 w. red, violet and blue 65 25
602 – 10 w. red, blue and violet 1·10 40
DESIGN: 10 w. South Gate and fireworks.

1965. Savings Campaign.
603 **229** 4 w. brown, ochre & green 50 25

230 Hoisting Flag

231 Radio Aerial

1965. 15th Anniv of Recapture of Seoul.
604 **230** 3 w. green, blue & orange 1·10 35

1965. 80th Anniv of Korean Telecommunications.
605 **231** 3 w. green, black and blue 60 25
606 – 10 w. black, blue & yellow 1·00 35
DESIGN: 10 w. Telegraphist of 1885.

1965. Flood Relief. As No. 545 (1962 issue), but colour changed and inscr with premium.
607 4 w. + 2 w. blue 1·00 30

232 Pole Vaulting

1965. National Athletic Meeting, Kwangju.
608 **232** 3 w. multicoloured 1·00 40

1965. Aid for Children. As No. 545 (1962 issue), but colour changed and inscr with premium.
609 4 w. + 2 w. purple 1·10 30

233 I.C.Y. Emblem

1965. International Co-operation Year and 20th Anniv of United Nations.
610 **233** 3 w. red, green & dp green 50 25
611 – 10 w. ultramarine, grn & bl 1·10 25
DESIGN—VERT: 10 w. U.N. flag and headquarters, New York.

234 Child posting Letter

235 Children with Toboggan

1965. 10th Communications Day.
613 **234** 3 w. multicoloured 1·00 25
614 – 10 w. red, blue and green 1·60 30
DESIGN: 10 w. Airmail envelope and telephone receiver.

1965. Christmas and New Year.
615 **235** 3 w. blue, red and green 60 25
616 – 4 w. blue, red & green 75 25
DESIGN: 4 w. Boy and girl in traditional costume.

236 Freedom House

1966. Opening of Freedom House, Panmunjom.
618 **236** 7 w. black, emer & grn 1·00 40
619 39 w. black, lilac & green 4·25 60

237 Mandarins

1966. Korean Birds. Multicoloured.
621 3 w. Type **237** 1·75 1·00
622 5 w. Manchurian crane 1·90 1·00
623 7 w. Ring-necked pheasant 2·40 1·00

238 Pine Forest

239 Printing Press and Pen

1966. Reafforestation Campaign.
625 **238** 7 w. brown, green and light green 70 15

1966. 10th Newspaper Day.
626 **239** 7 w. purple, yellow & green 60 15

240 Curfew Bell and Young Koreans

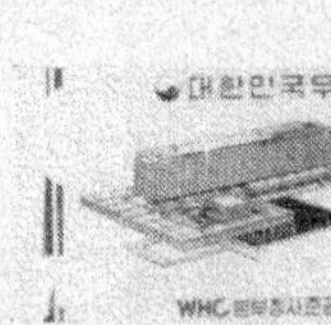
241 W.H.O. Building

1966. Youth Guidance Month.
627 **240** 7 w. orange, green & blue 60 15

1966. Inauguration of W.H.O. Headquarters, Geneva.
628 **241** 7 w. black, blue & yellow 1·00 40
629 39 w. red, grey and yellow 4·00 1·00

242 Pres. Pak, Handclasp and Flags

1966. Pres. Pak Chung Hi's State Tour of South-East Asia.
631 **242** 7 w. multicoloured 3·00 1·00

243 Girl Scout and Flag

1966. 20th Anniv of Korean Girl Scouts.
632 **243** 7 w. black, green & yellow 1·00 20

244 Student and Ehwa Women's University

1966. 80th Anniv of Korean Women's Education.
633 **244** 7 w. multicoloured 65 20

1966. 5-Year Plan. Dated "1966". As T **187**.
634 7 w. ultramarine and blue 1·50 60
635 7 w. black and yellow 1·00 30
DESIGNS: No. 634, Map and transport; 635, Radar aerials and telephone.

246 Alaska Pollack

1966. Korean Fishes. Multicoloured.
637 3 w. Type **246** 1·00 40
638 5 w. Manchurian trout 1·00 40
639 7 w. Yellow corvina 1·40 40

247 Incense-burner

249 Buddha, Kwanchok Temple

1966. As previous issues (some redrawn) and new designs, all inscr "REPUBLIC OF KOREA".
641 **213** 60 ch. green 20 10
642 **180** 1 w. green 1·10 10
643 **164** 2 w. green 15 10
644 **165** 3 w. brown 15 10
645 **181** 5 w. blue 2·00 10
646 **214** 7 w. blue 1·75 10
789 **168** 10 w. blue (22 × 18 mm) 3·50 10
647 **247** 13 w. blue 1·90 10
709 **182** 20 w. green and light green 6·00 10
710 **183** 40 w. green and olive 7·00 10
793 40 w. blue and pink (18 × 22 mm) 6·50 10
711 **191** 50 w. brown and bistre 5·75 10
648 – 60 w. green 2·25 10
649 **249** 80 w. green 2·25 10
DESIGN—As Type **247**: 60 w. 12th-century porcelain vessel.

250 Children and Hemispheres

1966. 15th Assembly of World Conf of Teaching Profession (WCOTP), Seoul.
650 **250** 7 w. violet, brown & blue 45 15

251 Factory within Pouch

1966. Savings Campaign.
652 **251** 7 w. multicoloured 45 15

252 People on Map of Korea

1966. National Census.
653 **252** 7 w. multicoloured 45 15

253 "Lucida lateralis"

1966. Insects. Multicoloured.
654 3 w. Type **253** 90 50
655 5 w. "Hexacentrus japonicus" (grasshopper) 90 50
656 7 w. "Sericinus montela" (butterfly) 1·00 50

254 C.I.S.M. Emblem and "Round Table" Meeting

1966. 21st General Assembly of International Military Sports Council (C.I.S.M.), Seoul.
658 **254** 7 w. multicoloured 50 15

255 Soldiers and Flags

1966. 1st Anniv of Korean Troops in Vietnam.
660 **255** 7 w. multicoloured . . . . 3·00 90

256 Wrestling

1966. 47th Athletic Meeting, Seoul.
661 **256** 7 w. multicoloured . . . . 2·00 45

257 Lions Emblem and Map

1966. 5th Orient and South-East Asian Lions Convention, Seoul.
662 **257** 7 w. multicoloured 50 15

258 University Emblem, "20" and Shields

1966. 20th Anniv of Seoul University.
664 **258** 7 w. multicoloured 40 15

259 A.P.A.C.L. Emblem

1966. 12th Conference of Asian People's Anti-Communist League (A.P.A.C.L.), Seoul.
665 **259** 7 w. multicoloured 50 25

260 Presidents Pak and Johnson　**261** U.N.E.S.C.O. Symbols and Emblem

1966. President Johnson's Visit to Korea.
667 **260** 7 w. multicoloured . . . . 1·00 25
668 83 w. multicoloured . . . . 5·00 70

1966. 20th Anniv of U.N.E.S.C.O.
670 **261** 7 w. multicoloured 55 20

1966. Hurricane Relief. As No. 646 but colour changed and premium added.
672 **214** 7 w. + 2 w. red . . . . . 1·10 15

262 "Lucky Bag"　**263** Eurasian Badger

1966. Christmas and New Year. Multicoloured.
673 5 w. Type **262** 45 15
674 7 w. Sheep (vert) 45 15

1966. Korean Fauna. Multicoloured.
676 3 w. Type **263** . . . . 1·25 25
677 5 w. Asiatic black bear . . . . 1·25 25
678 7 w. Tiger . . . . 1·50 25

264 "Syncom" Satellite　**265** Presidents Pak and Lubke

1967. 15th Anniv of Korea's Admission to I.T.U.
680 **264** 7 w. multicoloured . . . 70 30

1967. Visit of Pres. Lubke of West Germany to Korea.
682 **265** 7 w. multicoloured . . . 2·00 80

266 Coin, Factories and Houses　**267** Okwangdae Mask

1967. 1st Anniv of Korean Revenue Office.
684 **266** 7 w. sepia and green . . . 50 25

1967. Folklore. Multicoloured.
685 4 w. Type **267** . . . . . . 1·00 25
686 5 w. Sandi mask (horiz) . . . 1·00 25
687 7 w. Mafoe mask . . . . . . 1·00 25

268 J.C.I. Emblem and Pavilion　**269** Map Emblem

1967. International Junior Chamber of Commerce Conference, Seoul.
689 **268** 7 w. multicoloured . . . 50 25

1967. 5th Asian Pacific Dental Congress, Seoul.
691 **269** 7 w. multicoloured . . . 55 25

270 Korean Pavilion　**271** Worker and Soldier

1967. World Fair, Montreal.
693 **270** 7 w. black, red and yellow 1·00 35
694 83 w. black, red and blue 6·50 70

1967. Veterans' Day.
696 **271** 7 w. multicoloured . . . 50 25

272 Railway Wheel and Rail　**273** Sword Dance

1967. 2nd Five Year Plan. Dated "1967".
697 **272** 7 w. black, yellow & brn 1·00 45
698 – 7 w. orange, brown & blk 1·00 30
DESIGN: No. 698, Nut and bolt.
See also 773/4, 833/4, 895/6 and 981/2.

1967. Folklore. Multicoloured.
699 4 w. Type **273** 85 25
700 5 w. Peace dance (vert) . . . 85 25
701 7 w. Buddhist dance (vert) . . 1·10 25

274 Soldier and Family　**275** President Pak and Phoenix

1967. Fund for Korean Troops Serving in Vietnam.
703 **274** 7 w. + 3 w. black & purple 1·00 15

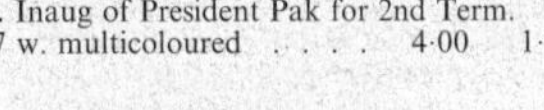
1967. Inaug of President Pak for 2nd Term.
704 **275** 7 w. multicoloured . . . . 4·00 1·00

276 Scout, Badge and Camp

1967. 3rd Korean Scout Jamboree. Multicoloured.
706 7 w. Type **276** . . . . 1·00 30
707 20 w. Scout badge, bridge and tent . . . . 2·50 50

280 Girls on Swing

1967. Folklore. Multicoloured.
712 4 w. Type **280** . . . . 1·00 25
713 5 w. Girls on seesaw (vert) . . 1·00 25
714 7 w. Girls dancing (vert) . . . 1·40 25

281 Freedom Centre　**282** Boxing

1967. 1st World Anti-Communist League Conference, Taipei. Multicoloured.
716 5 w. Type **281** 50 25
717 7 w. Hand grasping chain (vert) 50 25

1967. National Athletic Meeting, Seoul. Mult.
719 5 w. Type **282** . . . . 1·10 25
720 7 w. Basketball . . . . 1·10 25

283 Students' Memorial, Kwangjoo　**284** Decade Emblem

1967. Students' Day.
721 **283** 7 w. multicoloured 50 25

1967. International Hydrological Decade.
722 **284** 7 w. multicoloured 50 25

285 Children spinning Top　**286** Playing Shuttlecock

1967. Christmas and New Year.
723 **285** 5 w. blue, red and pink . . 50 15
724 – 7 w. brown, blue & bistre 50 15
DESIGN: 7 w. Monkey and Signs of the Zodiac.

1967. Folklore. Multicoloured.
726 4 w. Type **286** 90 25
727 5 w. "Dalmaji" (horiz) 90 25
728 7 w. Archery . . . . 1·25 25

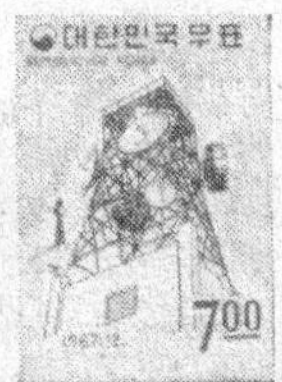
287 Microwave Transmitter

1967. Inauguration of Microwave Telecommunications Service.
730 **287** 7 w. black, green and blue 50 25

288 Carving, King Songdok's Bell　**289** 5th–6th century Earrings　**290** Korean Flag

1968.
732 **288** 1 w. brown and yellow . . 25 10
733 **289** 5 w. yellow and green . . 1·25 10
734 **290** 7 w. red and blue 70 10
787 7 w. blue * 45 10
788 7 w. blue * 30 10
790 10 w. blue* 60 10
Nos. 788 and 790 have their face values shown as "7" or "10" only, omitting the noughts shown on Nos. 734 and 788.
For designs similar to Type **290** see Nos. 771, 780 and 827.

291 W.H.O. Emblem　**292** E.A.T.A. Emblem and Korean Motif

1968. 20th Anniv of W.H.O.
735 **291** 7 w. multicoloured . . . 55 25

1968. 2nd East Asia Travel Association Conference, Seoul.
737 **292** 7 w. multicoloured . . . 50 25

293 C.A.C.C.I. Emblem, Korean Doorknocker and Factories

1968. 2nd Conference of Confederation of Asian Chambers of Commerce and Industry (C.A.C.C.I.), Seoul.
739 **293** 7 w. multicoloured . . . 50 25

294 Pres. Pak and Emperor Haile Selassie

1968. Visit of Emperor of Ethiopia.
741 **294** 7 w. multicoloured . . . 2·00 75

295 Post-bag

1968. Postman's Day. Multicoloured.
743 5 w. Type **295** . . . . 1·10 45
744 7 w. Postman 50 25

296 Atomic and Development Symbols

1968. Promotion of Science and Technology.
745 **296** 7 w. blue, green and red 50 25

297 Kyung Hi University and Conference Emblem

1968. 2nd Conf of Int Assn of University Presidents.
746 **297** 7 w. multicoloured . . . 50 25

298 "Liberation"

1968. Liberation of Suppressed Peoples' Campaign.
748 **298** 7 w. multicoloured 50 25

299 Reservist **300** Stylised Peacock

1968. Army Reservists' Fund.
749 **299** 7 w. + 3 w. black & green 1·50 30

1968. 20th Anniv of Republic.
750 **300** 7 w. multicoloured 60 25

301 Fair Entrance **302** Assembly Emblem

1968. 1st Korean Trade Fair, Seoul.
751 **301** 7 w. multicoloured 50 25

1968. 3rd General Assembly of Asian Pharmaceutical Association Federation.
752 **302** 7 w. multicoloured 50 25

303 Scout Badge **304** Soldier and Battle Scene

1968. 6th Far East Scout Conference, Seoul.
753 **303** 7 w. multicoloured . . . . 1·25 25

1968. 20th Anniv of Korean Armed Forces.
754 **304** 7 w. orange and green . . 2·00 40
755 – 7 w. blue and light blue . . 2·00 40
756 – 7 w. blue and orange . . . 2·00 40
757 – 7 w. light blue and blue . . 2·00 40
758 – 7 w. green and orange . . 2·00 40
DESIGNS: No. 755, Sailor and naval guns; 756, Servicemen and flags; 757, Airman and jet fighters; 758, Marine and landings.

305 Colombo Plan Emblem and Globe

1968. 19th Meeting of Colombo Plan Consultative Committee, Seoul.
759 **305** 7 w. multicoloured 50 15

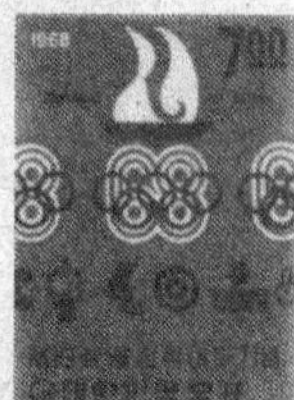
306 (I) Olympic Emblems **307** (II)

1968. Olympic Games, Mexico. Multicoloured.
760 7 w. Type **306** . . . . 2·00 60
761 7 w. Type **307** . . . . 2·00 60
762 7 w. Cycling (I) . . . . 2·00 60
763 7 w. Cycling (II) . . . . 2·00 60
764 7 w. Boxing (I) . . . . 2·00 60
765 7 w. Boxing (II) . . . . 2·00 60
766 7 w. Wrestling (I) . . . . . . 2·00 60
767 7 w. Wrestling (II) . . . . . . 2·00 60

The two types of each design may be identified by the position of the country name at the foot of the design–ranged right in types I, and left in types II. On three of the designs (excluding "Cycling") the figures of value are on left and right respectively. Types I and II of each design were issued together horizontally se-tenant within the sheets of 50 stamps.

308 Statue of Woman **309** Coin and Symbols

1968. 60th Anniv of Women's Secondary Education.
769 **308** 7 w. multicoloured . . . 50 20

1968. National Wealth Survey.
770 **309** 7 w. multicoloured . . . 50 20

1968. Disaster Relief Fund. As No. 734, but with additional inscr and premium added.
771 **290** 7 w. + 3 w. red and blue 5·00 50
The face value on No. 771 is expressed as "7 00 + 3 00", see also No. 827.

310 Shin Eui Ju Memorial **311** Demonstrators

1968. Anniv of Student Uprising, Shin Eui Ju (1945).
772 **310** 7 w. multicoloured . . . 50 20

1968. 2nd Five Year Plan. As T **272**. Dated "1968". Multicoloured.
773 7 w. Express motorway 60 25
774 7 w. "Clover-leaf" road junction 60 25

1968. Human Rights Year.
775 **311** 7 w. multicoloured . . . 50 20

312 Christmas Lanterns **314** Korean House and UN Emblems

1968. Christmas and New Year. Multicoloured.
776 5 w. Type **312** 75 10
777 7 w. Cockerel 75 10

1968. 20th Anniv of South Korea's Admission to U.N.
779 **314** 7 w. multicoloured . . . 50 20

1969. Military Helicopter Fund. As No. 734 but colours changed and inscr with premium added.
780 **290** 7 w. + 3 w. red, bl & grn 1·25 40

315 Torch and Monument, Pagoda Park, Seoul **316** Hyun Choong Sa and "Turtle" Ships

1969. 50th Anniv of Samil (Independence) Movement.
781 **315** 7 w. multicoloured . . . 60 25

1969. Dedication of Rebuilt Hyun Choong Sa (Shrine of Admiral Li Sun Sin).
782 **316** 7 w. multicoloured . . . 80 25

317 President Pak and Yang di-Pertuan Agong **318** Stone Temple Lamp

1969. Visit of Yang di-Pertuan Agong (Malaysian Head-of-State).
783 **317** 7 w. multicoloured . . . 2·00 75

1969.
786 **318** 5 w. purple 50 10
791 – 20 w. green . . . . 1·50 10
792 – 30 w. green . . . . 2·25 10
794 – 40 w. mauve and blue . . 1·75 10
795 – 100 w. brown and purple 28·00 10
DESIGNS—As Type **318**. VERT: 20 w. Wine jug. 40 w. Porcelain Jar, Yi Dynasty; 100 w. Seated Buddha (bronze). HORIZ: 30 w. "Duck" vase.

323 "Red Cross" between Faces **324** "Building the Nation's Economy"

1969. 50th Anniv of League of Red Cross Societies.
796 **323** 7 w. multicoloured 85 20

1969. "Second Economy Drive".
798 **324** 7 w. multicoloured 40 15

325 Presidents Pak and Nguyen van Thieu

1969. Visit of President Nguyen van Thieu of South Vietnam.
799 **325** 7 w. multicoloured . . . . 2·00 65

326 Reafforestation and Flooded Fields **327** Ignition of Second-stage Rocket

1969. Flood and Drought Damage Prevention Campaign. Multicoloured.
801 7 w. Type **326** 60 25
802 7 w. Withered and flourishing plants 60 25

1969. First Man on the Moon.
803 **327** 10 w. blue, black and red 1·50 50
804 – 10 w. blue, black and red 1·50 50
805 – 20 w. multicoloured . . . 1·50 50
806 – 20 w. multicoloured . . . 1·50 50
807 – 40 w. blue, red and black 1·50 50
DESIGNS: No. 804, Separation of modules from rocket; No. 805, Diagram of lunar orbit; No. 806, Astronauts on Moon; No. 807, Splashdown of "Apollo 11".

328 Stepmother admonishing Kongji **332** Steam Locomotive of 1899

1969. Korean Fairy Tales (1st series). "Kongji and Patji". Multicoloured.
809 5 w. Type **328** 65 25
810 7 w. Kongji and sparrows . . 75 25
811 10 w. Kongji and ox . . . . 1·10 40
812 20 w. Kongji in sedan-chair . . 1·25 40
See also Nos. 828/31, 839/42, 844/7 and 853/6.

1969. 70th Anniv of Korean Railways. Multicoloured.
814 7 w. Type **332** . . . . 1·50 50
815 7 w. Early steam and modern diesel locomotives . . . . . 1·50 50

333 Northrop F-5A Freedom Jet Fighters **334** Game of Cha-jun

1969. 20th Anniv of Korean Air Force. Multicoloured.
816 10 w. Type **333** . . . . 1·25 25
817 10 w. McDonnell-Douglas F-4D Phantom II jet fighter . . . 1·25 25

1969. 10th Korean Traditional Arts Contest, Taegu.
818 **334** 7 w. multicoloured 60 15

335 Molecule and Institute Building **336** Presidents Pak and Hamani

1969. Completion of Korean Institute of Science and Technology.
819 **335** 7 w. multicoloured . . . 60 15

1969. Visit of President Hamani of Niger Republic.
820 **336** 7 w. multicoloured . . . 1·25 40

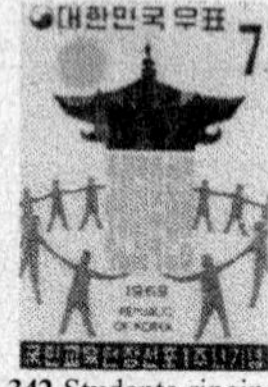
337 Football **342** Students ringing "Education"

1969. 50th Anniv of National Athletic Meeting. Multicoloured.
822 10 w. Type **337** . . . . 1·10 40
823 10 w. Volleyball . . . . 1·10 40
824 10 w. Korean wrestling . . . 1·10 40
825 10 w. Fencing . . . . 1·10 40
826 10 w. Taekwondo (karate) . . 1·10 40
Nos. 824/6 are horiz.

1969. Searchlight Fund. As T **290** but with additional inscri and premium. Face value expressed as "7 + 3".
827 7 w. + 3 w. red and blue . . 80 25

1969. Korean Fairy Tales (2nd series). "The Hare's Liver". As T **328**. Multicoloured.
828 5 w. Princess and Doctors . . 65 30
829 7 w. Hare arriving at Palace . 70 30
830 10 w. Preparing to remove the Hare's liver . . . . 1·10 40
831 20 w. Escape of the Hare . . 1·25 40

1969. 2nd Five-year Plan. As T **272**. Dated "1969". Multicoloured.
833 7 w. "Agriculture and Fisheries" 75 40
834 7 w. Industrial emblems . . . 50 15

1969. 1st Anniv of National Education Charter.
835 **342** 7 w. multicoloured . . . 50 15

343 Toy Dogs **344** Woman with Letter and U.P.U. Monument, Berne

1969. Lunar New Year ("Year of the Dog"). Multicoloured.
836 5 w. Type **343** 60 25
837 7 w. Candle and lattice doorway 60 25

1970. 70th Anniv of Korea's Admission to U.P.U.
838 **344** 10 w. multicoloured . . . . 3·00 70

1970. Korean Fairy Tales (3rd series). "The Sun and the Moon". As T **328**. Multicoloured.
839 5 w. Mother meets the tiger . 65 25
840 7 w. Tiger in disguise 70 25
841 10 w. Children chased up a tree 1·10 40
842 20 w. Children escape to Heaven 1·25 40

1970. Korean Fairy Tales (4th series). "The Woodcutter and the Fairy". As T **328**. Mult.
844 10 w. Woodcutter hiding Fairy's dress . . . . 1·10 40
845 10 w. Fairy as Woodcutter's Wife 1·10 40
846 10 w. Fairy and children fly to Heaven . . . . 1·10 40
847 10 w. Happy reunion . . . . 1·10 40

353 I.E.Y. Emblem on Open Book **354** Seated Buddha and Korean Pavilion

1970. International Education Year.
849 **353** 10 w. multicoloured . . . 3·00 70

1970. "EXPO 70" World Fair, Osaka, Japan.
850 **354** 10 w. multicoloured . . . 2·25 60

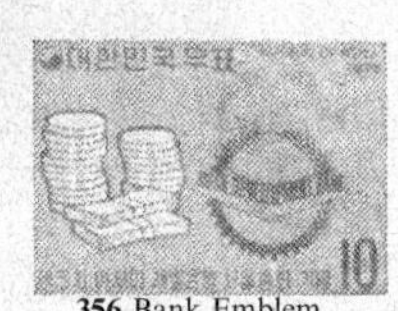

355 "4-11" Club Emblem
356 Bank Emblem and Cash

1970. 15th "4-11" Club (young farmers' organization) Central Contest, Suwon.

851 **355** 10 w. multicoloured . . . 80 30

1970. 3rd General Meeting of Asian Development Bank, Seoul.

852 **356** 10 w. multicoloured . . . 80 30

1970. Korean Fairy Tales (5th series). "Heungbu and Nolbu". As T **328**. Multicoloured.

853 10 w. Heungbu tending swallow 1·00 25
854 10 w. Heungbu finds treasure in pumpkin . . . . 1·00 25
855 10 w. Nolbu with pumpkin . . 1·00 25
856 10 w. Nolbu chased by devil 1·00 25

361 Royal Palanquin (Yi dynasty)
362 New Headquarters Building

1970. Early Korean Transport.

858 **361** 10 w. multicoloured . . . 1·00 25
859 – 10 w. multicoloured . . . 1·00 40
860 – 10 w. multicoloured . . . 1·00 25
861 – 10 w. black, stone and blue 1·25 25

DESIGNS—HORIZ: No. 859, Tramcar, 1899; 860, Emperor Sunjong's cadillac, 1903; 861, An Chang Nam's Nieuport 28 biplane, 1922.

1970. Opening of New U.P.U. Headquarters Building, Berne.

862 **362** 10 w. multicoloured . . . 70 30

363 Dish Aerial and Hemispheres

1970. Inauguration of Satellite Communications Station, Kum San.

863 **363** 10 w. multicoloured . . . 1·10 30

364 "PEN" and Quill Pen
366 Postal Code Symbol

365 Section of Motorway

1970. 37th International P.E.N. (literary organization) Congress, Seoul.

864 **364** 10 w. multicoloured . . . 70 25

1970. Opening of Seoul–Pusan Motorway.

865 **365** 10 w. multicoloured . . . 1·25 30

1970. Introduction of Postal Codes.

866 **366** 10 w. multicoloured . . . 60 25

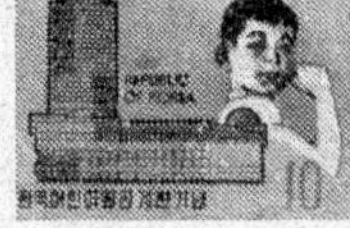

367 Parcel Sorting Area
368 Children's Hall and Boy

1970. Inauguration of Postal Mechanization.

867 **367** 10 w. multicoloured . . . 60 25

1970. Opening of Children's Hall, Seoul.

869 **368** 10 w. multicoloured . . . 60 30

369 "Mountain and River" (Yi In Moon)

1970. Korean Paintings of Yi Dynasty (1st series). Multicoloured.

870 10 w. Type **369** . . . . 1·25 30
871 10 w. "Jongyangsa Temple" (Chong Son) . . . . 1·25 30
872 10 w. "Mountain and River by Moonlight" (Kim Doo Ryang) (vert) . . . . 1·25 30

See also Nos. 887/89, 897/899, 947/52, 956/8 and 961/5.

370 P.T.T.I. Emblem
371 WAC and Corps Badge

1970. Councillors' Meeting, Asian Chapter of Postal, Telegraph and Telephone International (Post Office Trade Union Federation).

874 **370** 10 w. multicoloured . . . 55 25

1970. 20th Anniv of Korean Women's Army Corps.

875 **371** 10 w. multicoloured . . . 60 25

372 Pres. Pak and Flag

1970.

876 **372** 10 w. multicoloured . . . 3·00 55
877 – 10 w. black, green & blue 2·75 50

DESIGN—VERT: No. 877, Pres. Pak and industrial complex.

373 Presidents Pak and Sanchez Hernandez

1970. Visit of Pres. Sanchez Hernandez of El Salvador.

878 **373** 10 w. multicoloured . . . 2·00 60

374 "People and Houses"

1970. National Census.

880 **374** 10 w. multicoloured . . . 90 25

375 Diving

1970. 51st National Athletic Games, Seoul.

881 10 w. Type **375** . . . . 1·40 50
882 10 w. Hockey . . . . 1·40 50
883 10 w. Baseball . . . . 1·40 50

376 Police Badge and Activities
377 Bell and Globe

1970. National Police Day.

885 **376** 10 w. multicoloured . . . 1·00 30

1970. 25th Anniv of United Nations.

886 **377** 10 w. multicoloured . . . 75 30

1970. Korean Paintings of the Yi Dynasty (2nd series). Vert designs at T **369**, showing animals. Multicoloured.

887 30 w. "Fierce Tiger" (Shim Sa Yung) . . . . 1·75 45
888 30 w. "Cats and Sparrows" (Pyun Sang Byuk) . . . . . 1·75 45
889 30 w. "Dog with Puppies" (Yi Am) . . . . 1·75 45

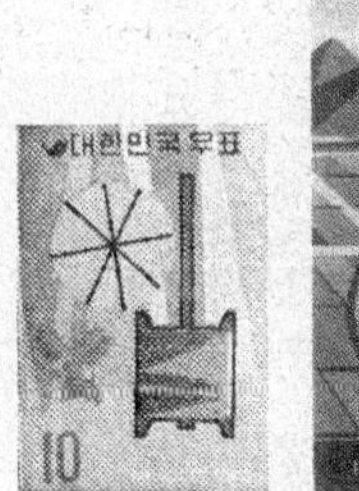

378 Kite and Reel
380 Fields ("Food Production")

379 Quotation and Emblems on Globe

1970. Lunar New Year ("Year of the Pig"). Multicoloured.

891 10 w. Type **378** 65 20
892 10 w. Toy pig 65 20

1970. 15th Communications Day.

894 **379** 10 w. multicoloured . . . 65 30

1970. 2nd Five Year Plan. At T **272**. Dated "1970". Multicoloured.

895 10 w. "Port Development" . . 50 20
896 10 w. "House Construction" . 50 20

1970. Korean Paintings of the Yi Dynasty (3rd series). Vert designs as T **369**. Multicoloured.

897 10 w. "Chokpyokdo" (river cliff) (Kim Hong Do) . . . . . . 1·75 30
898 10 w. "Hen and Chicks" (Pyn Sang Byuk) . . . . 1·75 30
899 10 w. "The Flute-player" (Shin Yun Bok) . . . . 1·75 30

1971. Economic Development (1st series). Mult.

901 10 w. Type **380** 65 30
902 10 w. Dam ("Electric Power") (horiz) 65 30
903 10 w. Map on crate ("Exports") (horiz) 65 30

See also Nos. 905/7 and 910/12.

381 Coal-mining
382 Globe, Torch and Spider

1971. Economic Development (2nd series). Mult.

905 10 w. Type **381** 60 20
906 10 w. Cement works (vert) . . 60 20
907 10 w. Fertilizer plant 60 20

1971. Anti-Espionage Month.

909 **382** 10 w. multicoloured . . . 70 20

383 Motorway Junction
384 Reservist and Badge

1971. Economic Develepment (3rd series). Mult.

910 10 w. Type **383** 60 20
911 10 w. Scales ("Gross National Income") (horiz) 60 20
912 10 w. Bee and coins ("Increased Savings") (horiz) 60 20

1971. 3rd Home Reserve Forces Day.

914 **384** 10 w. multicoloured . . . 1·00 30

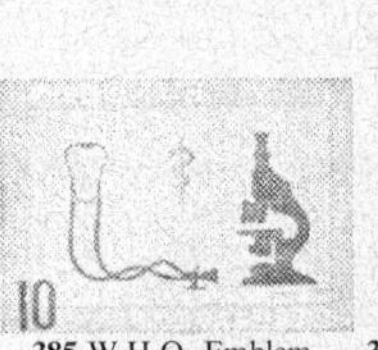

385 W.H.O. Emblem, Stethoscope and Microscope
386 Underground Train

1971. 20th World Health Day.

915 **385** 10 w. multicoloured . . . 50 30

1971. Construction of Seoul Underground Railway System.

916 **386** 10 w. multicoloured . . . 1·10 20

387 Footballer
388 Veteran and Association Flag

1971. 1st Asian Soccer Games, Seoul.

917 **387** 10 w. multicoloured . . . 1·40 40

1971. 20th Korean Veterans' Day.

918 **388** 10 w. multicoloured . . . 50 20

389 Girl Scouts
390 Torch and Economic Symbols

1971. 25th Anniv of Korean Girl Scouts Federation.

919 **389** 10 w. multicoloured . . . 55 20

1971. 10th Anniv of May 16th Revolution.

920 **390** 10 w. multicoloured . . . 50 20

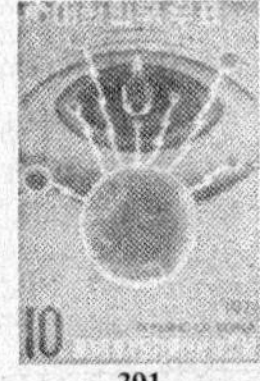

391 "Telecommunications"
392 F.A.O. Emblem

1971. 3rd World Telecommunications Day.

921 **391** 10 w. multicoloured . . . 50 20

1971. "The Work of the United Nations Organization".

922 – 10 w. mauve, black & grn 1·50 50
923 **392** 10 w. blue, black & mauve 1·50 50
924 – 10 w. multicoloured . . . 1·50 50
925 – 10 w. blue, black & mauve 1·50 50
926 – 10 w. mauve, black & grn 1·50 50
927 – 10 w. blue, black & mauve 1·50 50
928 – 10 w. mauve, black & blue 1·50 50
929 – 10 w. black, green & mauve 1·50 50
930 – 10 w. mauve, black & blue 1·50 50
931 – 10 w. blue, black & mauve 1·50 50
932 – 10 w. mauve, black & blue 1·50 50
933 – 10 w. black, mauve & grn 1·50 50
934 – 10 w. mauve, blue & black 1·50 50
935 – 10 w. black, mauve & grn 1·50 50
936 – 10 w. mauve, black & blue 1·50 50
937 – 10 w. blue, black & mauve 1·50 50

938 – 10 w. mauve, black & blue 1·50 50
939 – 10 w. black, mauve & grn 1·50 50
940 – 10 w. mauve, black & blue 1·50 50
941 – 10 w. blue, black & mauve 1·50 50
942 – 10 w. mauve, black & grn 1·50 50
943 – 10 w. black, blue & mauve 1·50 50
944 – 10 w. multicoloured . . . 1·50 50
945 – 10 w. black, blue & mauve 1·50 50
946 – 10 w. black, mauve & grn 1·50 50

EMBLEMS: No. 992, I.L.O.; No. 924, General Assembly and New York Headquarters; No. 925, U.N.E.S.C.O.; No. 926, W.H.O.; No. 927, World Bank; No. 928, International Development Association; No 929, Security Council; No. 930, International Finance Corporation; No. 931, International Monetary Fund; No. 932, International Civil Aviation Organization; No. 933, Economic and Social Council; No. 934, South Korean flag; No. 935, Trusteeship Council; No. 936, U.P.U.; No. 937, I.T.U.; No. 938, World Meteorological Organization; No. 939, Int Court of Justice; No. 940, I.M.C.O.; No. 941, U.N.I.C.E.F.; No. 942, International Atomic Energy Agency; No. 943, United Nations Industrial Development Organization; No. 944, United Nations Commission for the Unification and Rehabilitation of Korea; No. 945, United Nations Development Programme; No. 946, United Nations Conference on Trade and Development.

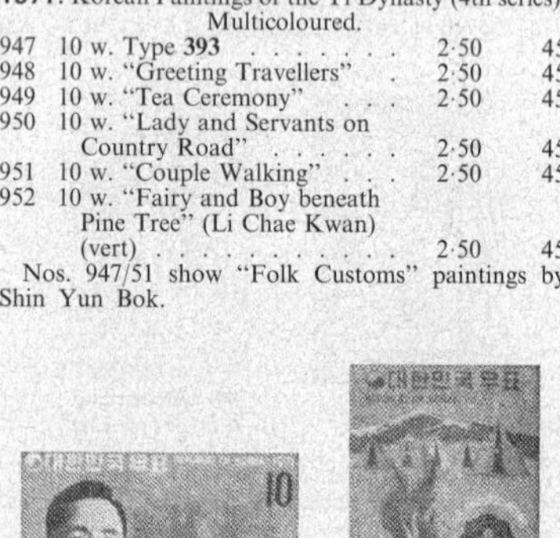

393 "Boating" (Shin Yun Bok)

1971. Korean Paintings of the Yi Dynasty (4th series). Multicoloured.
947 10 w. Type **393** . . . . 2·50 45
948 10 w. "Greeting Travellers" . 2·50 45
949 10 w. "Tea Ceremony" . . 2·50 45
950 10 w. "Lady and Servants on Country Road" . . . . . . 2·50 45
951 10 w. "Couple Walking" . . . 2·50 45
952 10 w. "Fairy and Boy beneath Pine Tree" (Li Chae Kwan) (vert) . . . . 2·50 45
Nos. 947/51 show "Folk Customs" paintings by Shin Yun Bok.

394 Pres. Pak, Emblem and Motorway **395** Campfire and Badge

1971. Re-election of Pres. Pak for 3rd Term.
954 **394** 10 w. multicoloured . . . 2·00 1·00

1971. Korean Paintings of the Yi Dynasty (5th series). As T **393**. Multicoloured.
956 10 w. "Chasing the Cat" (Kim Deuk Shin) . . . . 1·75 50
957 10 w. "Valley Family" (Li Chae Kwan) (vert) . . . . . . 1·75 50
958 10 w. "Man Reading" (Li Chae Kwan) (vert) . . . . . . 1·75 50

1971. 13th World Scout Jamboree, Asagiri, Japan.
960 **395** 10 w. multicoloured . . . 55 20

1971. Korean Paintings of the Yi Dynasty (6th series). As T **393** but vert. Multicoloured.
961 10 w. "Classroom" . . . . . 2·00 60
962 10 w. "Wrestling Match" . . 2·00 60
963 10 w. "Dancer with Musicians" 2·00 60
964 10 w. "Weavers" . . . . . . 2·00 60
965 10 w. "Drawing Water at the Well" . . . . 2·00 60
Nos. 961/5 depict genre paintings by Kim Hong Do.

396 Cogwheel and Asian Map

1971. 3rd Asian Labour Minister's Conference, Seoul.
967 **396** 10 w. multicoloured . . . 50 20

397 Judo

1971. 52nd National Athletic Meeting, Seoul. Multicoloured.
969 10 w. Type **397** . . . . 1·25 40
970 10 w. Archery . . . . 1·25 40

398 Korean Symbol on Palette

1971. 20th National Fine Art Exhibition.
972 **398** 10 w. multicoloured . . . 50 20

399 Doctor and Globe **400** Emblems and "Vocational Skills"

1971. 7th Congress of Medical Associations from Asia and Oceania.
973 **399** 10 w. multicoloured . . . 55 20

1971. 2nd National Vocational Skill Contest for High School Students.
974 **400** 10 w. multicoloured . . . 50 20

401 Callipers and "K" Emblem

1971. 10th Anniv of Industrial Standardisation.
976 **401** 10 w. multicoloured . . . 50 20

402 Fairy Tale Rats **403** Emblem and Hangul Alphabet

1971. Lunar New Year ("Year of the Rat"). Multicoloured.
977 10 w. Type **402** 60 20
978 10 w. Flying crane 65 20

1971. 50th Anniv of Hangul Hakhoe (Korean Language Research Society).
980 **403** 10 w. multicoloured . . . 50 20

1971. 2nd Five Year Plan. As T **272**. Dated "1971". Multicoloured.
981 10 w. Atomic power plant . . 60 20
982 10 w. Hydro-electric power project 65 20

404 Korean Red Cross Building on Map **405** Globe and Open Book

1971. South-North Korean Red Cross Conference, Panmunjom.
983 **404** 10 w. multicoloured . . . 1·00 30

1971. International Book Year.
985 **405** 10 w. multicoloured . . . 60 20

406 "Intelsat 4" and Korean Earth Station **407** Speed Skating

1971. 20th Anniv of Korea's Membership of I.T.U.
987 **406** 10 w. multicoloured . . . 50 20

1972. Winter Olympic Games, Sapporo, Japan. Multicoloured.
988 10 w. Type **407** . . . . . . 1·00 30
989 10 w. Figure-skating . . . . 1·00 30

408 Forestry Map **410** E.C.A.F.E. Emblem and Industrial Symbols

409 Scarab Beetles and Emblem

1972. "Trees for Unity" Campaign.
991 **408** 10 w. multicoloured . . . 50 20

1972. 20th Anniv of Korean Junior Chamber of Commerce.
992 **409** 10 w. multicoloured . . . 70 20

1972. 25th Anniv of U.N. Economic Commission for Asia and the Far East.
993 **410** 10 w. multicoloured . . . 55 20

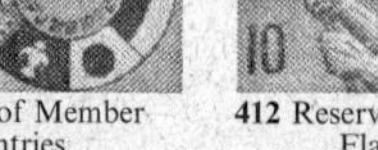

411 Flags of Member Countries **412** Reserve Forces' Flag

1972. 10th Anniv of Asian and Oceanic Postal Union.
994 **411** 10 w. multicoloured . . . 50 20

1972. Home Reserve Forces Day.
995 **412** 10 w. multicoloured . . . 1·00 30

413 Emblem and "Terias harina" **414** Rural Activities

1972. 50th Anniv of Korean Young Women's Christian Association.
996 **413** 10 w. multicoloured . . . 1·40 30

1972. "New Community" (rural development) Movement.
997 **414** 10 w. multicoloured . . . 50 20

415 "Anti-Espionage" and Korean Flag **416** Children with Balloons

1972. Anti-Espionage Month.
998 **415** 10 w. multicoloured . . . 50 20

1972. 50th Children's Day.
999 **416** 10 w. multicoloured . . . 50 20

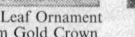

417 Leaf Ornament from Gold Crown **419** Kalkot, Koje Island, Hanryo Straits Park

418 Lake Paengnokdam, Mt. Halla Park

1972. Treasures from King Munyong's Tomb. Multicoloured.
1000 10 w. Type **417** 60 20
1001 10 w. Gold earrings (horiz) 65 20

1972. National Parks (1st series).
1002 **418** 10 w. multicoloured . . 50 20
1003 **419** 10 w. multicoloured . . 50 20
See also Nos. 1018/19 and 1026/7.

420 Marguerite and Conference Emblem **421** Gwanghwa Gate and National Flags

1972. U.N. Environmental Conservation Conference, Stockholm.
1004 **420** 10 w. multicoloured . . 45 20

1972. 7th Asian and Pacific Council (ASPAC) Ministerial Meeting, Seoul.
1006 **421** 10 w. multicoloured . . 60 25

422 Pasture ("Development of Rural Economy") **423** "Love Pin"

1972. 3rd Five Year Plan. Dated "1972". Multicoloured.
1007 10 w. Type **422** 60 25
1008 10 w. Foundry ladle ("Heavy Industries") 60 25
1009 10 w. Crate and Globe ("Increased Exports") . . 60 25

1972. Disaster Relief Fund.
1010 **423** 10 w. + 5 w. red & blue 75 20

424 Judo **425** Family Reunion through Red Cross

1972. Olympic Games, Munich. Multicoloured.
1011 20 w. Type **424** 75 20
1012 20 w. Weightlifting 75 20
1013 20 w. Wrestling 75 20
1014 20 w. Boxing 75 20

1972. 1st Plenary Meeting of South-North Korean Red Cross Conference, Pyongyang.
1016 **425** 10 w. multicoloured . . 1·25 35

426 Bulkuk Temple, Kyongju Park **428** Conference Emblem within "5"

427 Statue and Bopju Temple, Mt. Sokri Park

1972. National Parks (2nd series).
1018 **426** 10 w. multicoloured . . 60 20
1019 **427** 10 w. multicoloured . . 60 20

1972. 5th Asian Judicial Conference, Seoul.
1020 **428** 10 w. multicoloured . . 55 20

429 Lions Badge between Korean Emblems

1972. 11th Orient and South-East Asian Lions Convention, Seoul.
1021 **429** 10 w. multicoloured . . . 50 20

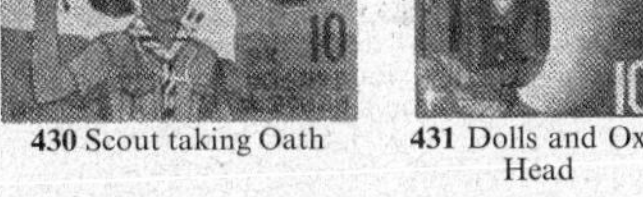

430 Scout taking Oath **431** Dolls and Ox's Head

1972. 50th Anniv of Korean Boy Scouts Movement.
1022 **430** 10 w. multicoloured . . . 85 25

1972. Lunar New Year ("Year of the Ox"). Multicoloured.
1023 10 w. Type **431** 60 20
1024 10 w. Revellers in balloon . . 60 20

432 Temple, Mt. Naejang Park **433** Madeungryong Pass, Mt. Sorak Park

1972. National Parks. (3rd series).
1026 **432** 10 w. multicoloured . . . 55 20
1027 **433** 10 w. multicoloured . . . 55 20

434 President Pak, Flag and "Development"

1972. Re-election of President Pak.
1028 **434** 10 w. multicoloured . . . 2·00 65

435 National Central Museum, Kyongbok Palace **437** Korean Family

436 Temple, Mt. Sorak

1973. Korean Tourist Attractions (1st series).
1030 **435** 10 w. multicoloured . . . 50 15
1031 **436** 10 w. multicoloured . . . 50 15
See also Nos. 1042/3, 1048/9, 1057/8 and 1075/6.

1973. Korean Unification Campaign.
1032 **437** 10 w. multicoloured . . . 50 15

438 "V" Sign and Flags **439** Construction Workers and Cogwheel

1973. Return of Korean Forces from South Vietnam.
1033 **438** 10 w. multicoloured . . . 60 20

1973. 10th Workers' Day.
1034 **439** 10 w. multicoloured . . . 50 15

440 W.M.O. Emblem and Satellite **442** Wonsam Costume (woman's ceremonial)

1973. Centenary of World Meteorological Organization.
1035 **440** 10 w. multicoloured . . 50 15

1973. Korean Court Costumes of the Yi Dynasty (1st series). Multicoloured. Background colours given.
1037 – 10 w. orange . . . . . 1·10 30
1038 **442** 10 w. orange . . . . . 1·10 30
DESIGN: No. 1037, Kujangbok (king's ceremonial costume);
See also Nos. 1045/6, 1053/4, 1060/1 and 1078/9.

443 Nurse with Lamp **444** Reservists and Flag

1973. 50th Anniv of Korean Nurses' Association.
1040 **443** 10 w. multicoloured . . 65 15

1973. Home Reserve Forces Day.
1041 **444** 10 w. multicoloured . . 75 30

445 Palmi Island **446** Sain-am Rock, Mt. Dokjol

1973. Korean Tourist Attractions (2nd series).
1042 **445** 10 w. multicoloured . . 60 15
1043 **446** 10 w. multicoloured . . 60 15

447 Table Tennis Player

1973. Victory of South Korean Women's Team in World Table Tennis Championships, Sarajevo.
1044 **447** 10 w. multicoloured . . 1·25 30

1973. Korean Court Costumes of the Yi Dynasty (2nd series). As T **442**. Mult. Background colours given.
1045 10 w. purple 80 15
1046 10 w. green 80 15
DESIGNS: No. 1045, Konryongpo (king's costume); No. 1046, Jokui (queen's ceremonial costume).

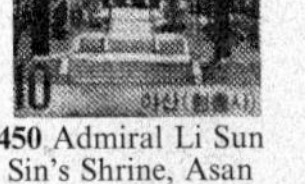

450 Admiral Li Sun Sin's Shrine, Asan **451** Limestone Cavern, Kusan-ni

1973. Korean Tourist Attractions (3rd series).
1048 **450** 10 w. multicoloured . . 50 10
1049 **451** 10 w. multicoloured . . 50 10

452 Children's Choir

1973. 20th Anniv of World Vision Int.
1050 **452** 10 w. multicoloured . . . 75 25

453 Love Pin and "Disasters"

1973. Disaster Relief Fund.
1051 **453** 10 w. + 5 w. mult . . . 45 15

454 Steel Converter **457** Table Tennis Bat and Ball

1973. Inauguration of Pohang Steel Works.
1052 **454** 10 w. multicoloured . . . 50 15

1973. Korean Court Costumes of the Yi Dynasty (3rd series). As T **442**. Mult. Background colours given.
1053 10 w. blue . . . . 1·25 15
1054 10 w. pink . . . . 1·25 15
DESIGNS: No. 1053, Kangsapo (crown prince's) costume; No. 1054, Tangui (princess's) costume.

1973. Table Tennis Gymnasium Construction Fund.
1056 **457** 10 w. + 5 w. mve & grn 75 20

458 Namhae Suspension Bridge **459** Hongdo Island

1973. Korean Tourist Attractions (4th series).
1057 **458** 10 w. multicoloured . . . 55 10
1058 **459** 10 w. multicoloured . . . 55 10

460 Interpol and Korean Police Emblems

1973. 50th Anniv of International Criminal Police Organization (Interpol).
1059 **460** 10 w. multicoloured . . . 65 10

1973. Korean Court Costumes of the Yi Dynasty (4th series). As T **442**. Mult. Background colours given.
1060 10 w. yellow 75 10
1061 10 w. blue 75 10
DESIGNS: No. 1060, Kumkwanchobok (court official's) costume; 1061, Hwalot (queen's wedding) costume.

465 Manchurian Cranes **466** Sommal Lily **467** Motorway and Farm

1973.
1063 – 1 w. brown 40 10
1063a – 3 w. black and blue . . 50 15
1064 – 5 w. brown 10 10
1064a – 6 w. turquoise and green 30 10
1065 **465** 10 w. ultramarine & blue 75 15
1066 **466** 10 w. red, black & green 50 10
1067 **467** 10 w. green and red . . 50 10
1068 – 30 w. brown and yellow 65 10
1068a – 50 w. green and brown 50 10
1068b – 60 w. brown and yellow 50 10
1068c – 80 w. black and brown 75 10
1069 – 100 w. yellow & brown 11·00 40
1069a – 100 w. red . . . . . . 1·00 15
1069b – 200 w. brown and pink 1·40 20
1069c – 300 w. red and lilac . . 2·00 25
1069d – 500 w. multicoloured . . 10·00 30
1069e – 500 w. purple & brown 3·25 25
1069f – 1000 w. green . . . . . 6·50 60

DESIGNS—VERT: 1 w. Mask of old man; 5 w. Siberian chipmunk; 6 w. Lily; 30 w. Honey bee; 50 w. Pot with lid; 60 w. Jar; 100 w. (No. 1069) Gold Crown, Silla dynasty; 100 w. (No. 1069a) Admiral Yi Soon Shin; 300 w. Pobjusa Temple; 500 w. (No. 1069d) Gold Crown; 500 w. (No. 1069e) Carved dragon (tile, Backje Dynasty). LARGER 24 × 33 mm: 100 w. Flying deities (relief from bronze bell, Sangweon Temple). HORIZ: 3 w. Magpie; 80 w. Ceramic horseman; 200 w. Muryangsujeon Hall, Busok Temple.
For designs similar to Type **465** but with frame, see Type **703**.

470 Tennis

1973. 54th National Athletic Meeting, Pusan. Multicoloured.
1070 10 w. Type **470** 65 15
1071 10 w. Hurdling 65 15

471 Children with Stamp Albums

1973. Philatelic Week.
1072 **471** 10 w. multicoloured . . 40 10

472 Soyang River Dam

1973. Inauguration of Soyang River Dam.
1074 **472** 10 w. multicoloured . . 40 10

473 Mt. Mai, Chinan **474** Tangerine Grove, Cheju Island

1973. Korean Tourist Attractions (5th series).
1075 **473** 10 w. multicoloured . . 50 10
1076 **474** 10 w. multicoloured . . 50 10

475 Match, Cigarette and Flames **478** Tiger and Candles

1973. 10th Fire Prevention Day.
1077 **475** 10 w. multicoloured . . . 40 10

1973. Korean Court Costumes of the Yi Dynasty (5th series). As T **442**. Mult. Back-ground colours given.
1078 10 w. orange 75 10
1079 10 w. pink 75 10
DESIGNS: No. 1078, Pyongsangbok (official's wife) costume; 1079, Kokunbok (military officer's) costume.

1973. Lunar New Year ("Year of the Tiger"). Multicoloured.
1081 10 w. Type **478** 50 10
1082 10 w. Decorated top 50 10

479 Korean Girl and Flame Emblem

1973. 25th Anniv of Declaration of Human Rights.
1084 **479** 10 w. multicoloured . . 40 10

480 Boeing 747-200 Jetliner and Polar Zone

1973. Air.
1085 **480** 110 w. blue and pink . . 2·75 30
1086 – 135 w. red and green . . 2·75 30
1087 – 145 w. red and blue . . . 2·75 30
1088 – 180 w. yellow and lilac . 2·75 30
DESIGNS—Boeing 747-200 jetliner and postal zones on map; 135 w. South-east Asia; 145 w. India, Australasia and North America; 180 w. Europe, Africa and South America.

481 "Komunko" (zither)

1974. Traditional Musical Instruments (1st series). Multicoloured. Background colours given.
1089 **481** 10 w. blue 75 10
1090 – 30 w. orange 85 40
DESIGN: 30 w. "Nagak" (trumpet triton).
See also Nos. 1098/9, 1108/9, 1117/18 and 1132/3.

483 Apricots

485 Reservist and Factory

1974. Fruits (1st series). Multicoloured.
1092 10 w. Type **483** 30 10
1093 30 w. Strawberries 60 15
See also Nos. 1104/5, 111/2, 1120/1 and 1143/4.

1974. Home Reserve Forces Day.
1095 **485** 10 w. multicoloured . . . 30 10

486 W.P.Y. Emblem

489 Mail Train and Communications Emblem

1974. World Population Year.
1096 **486** 10 w. multicoloured . . . 25 10

1974. Traditional Musical Instruments (2nd series). As T **481**. Multicoloured. Background colours given.
1098 10 w. blue 60 10
1099 30 w. green . . . . 1·25 15
DESIGNS: 10 w. "Tchouk"; 30 w. "Eu".

1974. Communications Day.
1101 **489** 10 w. multicoloured . . . 75 15

490 C.A.F.E.A.-I.C.C. Emblem on Globe

491 Port Installations

1974. 22nd Session of International Chamber of Commerce's Commission on Asian and Far Eastern Affairs, Seoul.
1102 **490** 10 w. multicoloured . . . 30 10

1974. Inaug of New Port Facilities, Inchon.
1103 **491** 10 w. multicoloured . . . 40 10

1974. Fruits (2nd series). As T **483**. Mult.
1104 10 w. Peaches 40 10
1105 30 w. Grapes 60 15

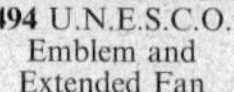
494 U.N.E.S.C.O. Emblem and Extended Fan

499 Cross and Emblems

1974. 20th Anniv of South Korean U.N.E.S.C.O. Commission.
1107 **494** 10 w. multicoloured . . . 30 10

1974. Traditional Musical Instruments (3rd series). As T **481**. Multicoloured. Background colours given.
1108 10 w. orange 65 10
1109 30 w. pink . . . . 1·25 15
DESIGNS: 10 w. "A-chaing" (stringed instrument); 30 w. "Kyobang-ko" (drum).

1974. Fruits (3rd series). As T **483**. Multicoloured.
1111 10 w. Pears 40 10
1112 30 w. Apples 60 15

1974. "Explo 74" 2nd International Training Congress on Evangelism. Multicoloured.
1114 10 w. Type **499** 30 10
1115 10 w. Emblem and Korean map on Globe 30 10

501 Underground Train

1974. Opening of Seoul Underground Railway.
1116 **501** 10 w. multicoloured . . 85 10

1974. Traditional Musical Instruments (4th series). As T **481**. Multicoloured. Background colours given.
1117 10 w. blue 65 10
1118 30 w. pink . . . . 1·10 15
DESIGNS: No. 1117, So ("Pan pipes"); No. 1118, Haikem (Two-stringed fiddle).

1974. Fruits (4th series). As T **483**. Multicoloured.
1120 10 w. Cherries 40 10
1121 30 w. Persimmons 60 10

506 Rifle Shooting

1974. 55th National Athletic Meeting, Seoul. Multicoloured.
1123 10 w. Type **506** 30 10
1124 30 w. Rowing 80 10

508 U.P.U. Emblem

509 Symbols of Member Countries

1974. Centenary of U.P.U.
1125 **508** 10 w. multicoloured (postage) 30 10
1126 110 w. multicoloured (air) 1·25 50

1974. 1st World Conference of People-to-People International.
1128 **509** 10 w. multicoloured . . 30 10

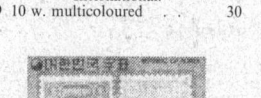

510 Korean Stamps of 1884

1974. Philatelic Week and 90th Anniv of First Korean Stamps.
1129 **510** 10 w. multicoloured . . 40 10

511 Taekwondo Contestants

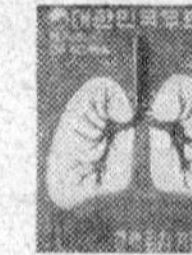
514 Lungs

1974. 1st Asian Taekwondo Championships, Seoul.
1131 **511** 10 w. multicoloured . . 40 10

1974. Traditional Musical Instruments (5th series). As T **481**. Multicoloured. Background colours given.
1132 10 w. pink 40 10
1133 30 w. ochre 60 15
DESIGNS: 10 w. Pak (clappers); 30 w. Pyenchong (chimes).

1974. Tuberculosis Control Fund.
1135 **514** 10 w. + 5 w. red & green 40 10

515 Presidents Pak and Ford

516 Yook Young Soo (wife of Pres. Pak)

1974. State Visit of President Ford of United States.
1136 **515** 10 w. multicoloured . . . 55 20

1974. Yook Young Soo Memorial Issue.
1138 **516** 10 w. green 50 15
1139 10 w. orange 50 15
1140 10 w. violet 50 15
1141 10 w. blue 50 15

1974. Fruits (5th series). As T **483**. Multicoloured.
1143 10 w. Tangerines 40 10
1144 30 w. Chestnuts 50 15

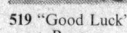

519 "Good Luck" Purse

521 U.P.U. Emblem and "75"

1974. Lunar New Year ("Year of the Rabbit"). Multicoloured.
1146 10 w. Type **519** 40 10
1147 10 w. Toy rabbits 40 10

1975. 75th Anniv of Korea's Membership of U.P.U. Multicoloured.
1149 10 w. Type **521** 30 10
1150 10 w. U.P.U. emblem and paper dart 30 10

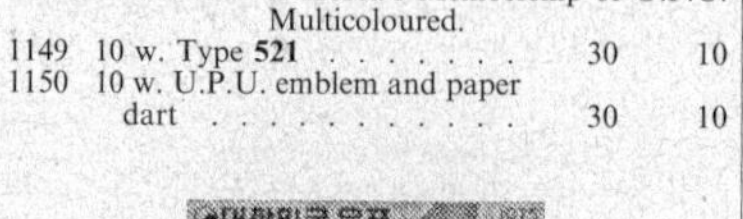

523 Dove with "Good Luck" Card

1975. Inauguration of National Welfare Insurance System.
1151 **523** 10 w. multicoloured . . . 20 10

524 Dr. Schweitzer, Map and Syringe

525 Salpuli Dancer

1975. Birth Centenary of Dr. Albert Schweitzer.
1152 **524** 10 w. bistre 50 15
1153 10 w. mauve 50 15
1154 10 w. orange 50 15
1155 10 w. green 50 15

1975. Korean Folk Dances (1st series). Multicoloured, background colour given.
1156 **525** 10 w. green 40 10
1157 – 10 w. blue 40 10
DESIGN: No. 1157, Exorcism in dance.
See also Nos. 1168/9, 1175/6, 1193/4 and 1208/9.

527 Globe and Rotary Emblem

1975. 70th Anniv of Rotary International.
1159 **527** 10 w. multicoloured . . . 25 10

528 Women and I.W.Y. Emblem

1975. International Women's Year.
1160 **528** 10 w. multicoloured . . . 25 10

529 Violets

531 Saemaeul Township

1975. Flowers (1st series). Multicoloured.
1161 10 w. Type **529** 40 10
1162 10 w. Anemones 40 10
See also Nos. 1171/2, 1184/5, 1199/1200 and 1213/4.

1975. National Afforestation Campaign. Multicoloured.
1163 10 w. Type **531** 50 10
1164 10 w. Lake and trees 50 10
1165 10 w. "Green" forest 50 10
1166 10 w. Felling timber 50 10
Nos. 1163/6 were issued together, se-tenant, forming a composite design.

535 H.R.F. Emblem on Map of Korea

536 Butterfly Dance

1975. Homeland Reserve Forces Day.
1167 **535** 10 w. multicoloured . . 40 10

1975. Folk Dances (2nd series). Multicoloured, background colour given.
1168 **536** 10 w. green 45 10
1169 – 10 w. yellow 45 10
DESIGN: No. 1169, Victory dance.

538 Rhododendron

540 Metric Symbols

1975. Flowers (2nd series). Multicoloured.
1171 10 w. Type **538** 40 10
1172 10 w. Clematis 40 10

1975. Centenary of Metric Convention.
1173 **540** 10 w. multicoloured . . 25 10

541 Soldier and Incense Pot

542 Mokjoong Dance

1975. 20th Memorial Day.
1174 **541** 10 w. multicoloured . . 25 10

1975. Folk Dances (3rd series). Multicoloured.
1175 **542** 10 w. blue 45 10
1176 – 10 w. pink 45 10
DESIGN: No. 1176, Malttungi dancer.

544 Flags of South Korea, U.N. and U.S

1975. 25th Anniv of Korean War. Multicoloured.
1178 10 w. Type **544** 45 10
1179 10 w. Flags of Ethiopia, France, Greece, Canada and South Africa 45 10

1180 10 w. Flags of Luxembourg, Australia, U.K., Colombia and Turkey 45 10
1181 10 w. Flags of Netherlands, Belgium, Philippines, New Zealand and Thailand . . 45 10

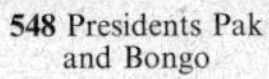

548 Presidents Pak and Bongo   549 Iris

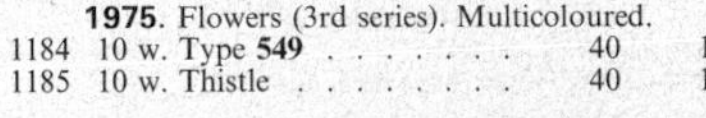

1975. State Visit of President Bongo of Gabon.
1182 **548** 10 w. multicoloured . . . 40 10

1975. Flowers (3rd series). Multicoloured.
1184 10 w. Type **549** 40 10
1185 10 w. Thistle 40 10

551 Scout Scarf   552 Freedom Flame

1975. "Nordjamb 75" World Scout Jamboree, Norway. Multicoloured.
1186 10 w. Type **551** 40 10
1187 10 w. Scout oath 40 10
1188 10 w. Scout camp 40 10
1189 10 w. Axe and rope 40 10
1190 10 w. Camp fire 40 10

1975. 30th Anniv of Liberation. Multicoloured.
1191 20 w. Type **552** 45 10
1192 20 w. Balloon emblems . . . 45 10

554 Drum Dance   556 Taekwondo Contestant

1975. Folk Dances (4th series). Multicoloured, background colour given.
1193 **554** 20 w. yellow 60 10
1194 – 20 w. orange 60 10
DESIGN: No. 1194, Bara dance.

1975. 2nd World Taekwondo Championships, Seoul.
1196 **556** 20 w. multicoloured . . . 30 10

557 Assembly Hall

1975. Completion of National Assembly Hall.
1197 **557** 20 w. multicoloured . . . 30 10

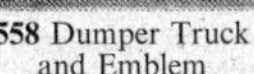

558 Dumper Truck and Emblem   559 Broad-bell Flower

1975. Contractors' Association Convention, Seoul.
1198 **558** 20 w. multicoloured . . . 40 10

1975. Flowers (4th series). Multicoloured.
1199 20 w. Type **559** 45 10
1200 20 w. Bush clover 45 10

561 Morse Key and Dish Aerial

1975. 90th Anniv of Korean Telecommunications.
1201 **561** 20 w. black, orge & pur 35 10

562 Yeongweol Caves   564 Flag and Missiles

1975. International Tourism Day. Multicoloured.
1202 20 w. Type **562** 30 10
1203 20 w. Mount Sorak 30 10

1975. Korean Armed Forces Day.
1204 **564** 20 w. multicoloured . . 25 10

565 "Gymnastics"   567 "Kangaroo" Collector

1975. 56th National Athletic Meeting. Multicoloured.
1205 20 w. Type **565** 25 10
1206 20 w. "Handball" 25 10

1975. Philatelic Week.
1207 **567** 20 w. multicoloured . . 30 10

568 Sogo Dance   570 U.N. Emblem and Handclasps

1975. Folk Dances (5th series). Multicoloured, background colour given.
1208 **568** 20 w. blue 45 10
1209 – 20 w. yellow 55 10
DESIGN: No. 1209, Bupo Nori dance.

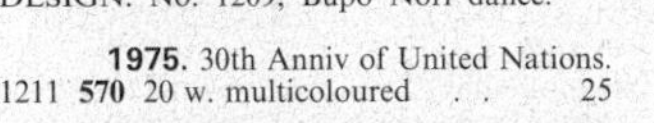

1975. 30th Anniv of United Nations.
1211 **570** 20 w. multicoloured . . 25 10

571 Red Cross and Emblems   572 Camellia

1975. 70th Anniv of Korean Red Cross.
1212 **571** 20 w. multicoloured . . 35 10

1975. Flowers (5th series). Multicoloured.
1213 20 w. Type **572** 50 10
1214 20 w. Gentian 50 10

574 Union Emblem   575 Children Playing

1975. 10th Anniv of Asian Parliamentary Union.
1215 **574** 20 w. multicoloured . . 30 10

1975. Lunar New Year. Multicoloured.
1216 20 w. Type **575** 30 10
1217 20 w. Dragon ("Year of the Dragon") 30 10

577 Electric Train

1975. Opening of Cross-country Electric Railway.
1219 **577** 20 w. multicoloured . . . 50 10

578 "Dilipa fenestra"

1976. Butterflies (1st series). Multicoloured, background colour given.
1220 **578** 20 w. red 65 10
1221 – 20 w. blue 65 10
DESIGN: No. 1221, "Luehdorfia puziloi".
See also Nos. 1226/7, 1246/7, 1254/5 and 1264/5.

580 Institute Emblem and Science Emblems   581 Japanese White-necked Crane

1976. 10th Anniv of Korean Institute of Science and Technology.
1222 **580** 20 w. multicoloured . . . 25 10

1976. Birds (1st series). Multicoloured.
1223 20 w. Type **581** 75 25
1224 20 w. Great bustard 75 25
See also Nos. 1243/4, 1251/2, 1257/8 and 1266/7.

583 Globe and Telephones

1976. Telephone Centenary.
1225 **583** 20 w. multicoloured . . . 20 10

584 "Papilio xuthus"

1976. Butterflies (2nd series). Multicoloured, background colour given.
1226 **584** 20 w. yellow 65 10
1227 – 20 w. green 65 10
DESIGN: No. 1227, "Parnassius bremeri".

586 "National Development"   587 Eye and People

1976. Homeland Reserve Forces Day.
1228 **586** 20 w. multicoloured . . . 30 10

1976. World Health Day. Prevention of Blindness.
1229 **587** 20 w. multicoloured . . . 30 10

588 Pres. Pak and Flag   589 Ruins of Moenjodaro

1976. 6th Anniv of Saemaul Movement (community self-help programme). Multicoloured.
1230 20 w. Type **588** 45 15
1231 20 w. People ("Intellectual edification") 45 15
1232 20 w. Village ("Welfare") . . 45 15
1233 20 w. Produce and fields ("Production") 45 15
1234 20 w. Produce and factory ("Increase of Income") . . 45 15

1976. Moenjodaro (Pakistan) Preservation Campaign.
1235 **589** 20 w. multicoloured . . 40 10

590 U.S. Flags of 1776 and 1976   591 Camp Scene on Emblem

1976. Bicentenary of American Revolution. Each black, blue and red.
1236 100 w. Type **590** . . . . . . 1·60 45
1237 100 w. Statue of Liberty . . 1·60 45
1238 100 w. Map of United States 1·60 45
1239 100 w. Liberty Bell . . . . . 1·60 45
1240 100 w. American astronaut . 1·60 45

1976. 30th Anniv of Korean Girl Scouts Federation.
1242 **591** 20 w. multicoloured . . 60 10

592 Blue-winged Pitta   594 Buddha and Temple

1976. Birds (2nd series). Multicoloured.
1243 20 w. Type **592** 80 25
1244 20 w. White-bellied black woodpecker 80 25

1976. U.N.E.S.C.O. Campaign for Preservation of Borobudur Temple (in Indonesia).
1245 **594** 20 w. multicoloured . . 25 10

595 Eastern Pale Clouded Yellow

1976. Butterflies (3rd series). Multicoloured, background colour given.
1246 **595** 20 w. olive 55 10
1247 – 20 w. violet 55 10
DESIGN: No. 1247, Chinese windmill.

597 Protected Family   598 Volleyball

1976. National Life Insurance.
1248 **597** 20 w. multicoloured . . 30 10

1976. Olympic Games, Montreal. Multicoloured.
1249 20 w. Type **598** 35 10
1250 20 w. Boxing 35 10

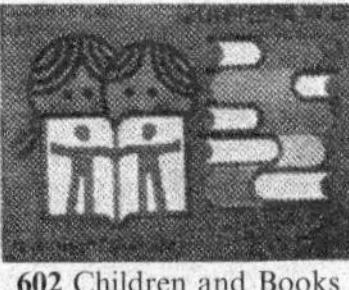

600 Black Wood Pigeon   602 Children and Books

1976. Birds (3rd series). Multicoloured.
1251 20 w. Type **600** 80 25
1252 20 w. Oystercatcher 80 25

1976. Books for Children.
1253 **602** 20 w. multicoloured . . 25 10

603 "Hestina assimilis"

1976. Butterflies (4th series). Multicoloured, background colour given.

1254 **603** 20 w. brown 55 10
1255 – 20 w. drab 55 10

DESIGN: No. 1255, Blue triangle.

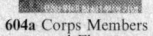

604a Corps Members and Flag **605** Black-faced Spoonbill

1976. 1st Anniv of Korean Civil Defence Corps.

1256 **604a** 20 w. multicoloured 30 10

1976. Birds (4th series). Multicoloured.

1257 20 w. Type **605** 75 25
1258 20 w. Black stork 75 25

607 Chamsungdan, Mani Mountain

1976. International Tourism Day. Multicoloured.

1259 20 w. Type **607** 40 10
1260 20 w. Ilchumun Gate, Tongdosa 40 10

609 Cadet and Parade **610** "Musa basjoo" (flower arrangement, Cheong Jo the Great)

1976. 30th Anniv of Korean Military Academy.

1261 **609** 20 w. multicoloured 25 10

1976. Philatelic Week.

1262 **610** 20 w. black, red and drab 25 10

611 Yellow-legged Tortoiseshell **613** European Black Vulture

1976. Butterflies (5th series). Multicoloured, background colour given.

1264 **611** 20 w. light green 55 10
1265 – 20 w. purple 55 10

DESIGN: No. 1265, "Fabriciana nerippe".

1976. Birds (5th series). Multicoloured.

1266 20 w. Type **613** 2·75 1·25
1267 20 w. Whistling Swan 2·75 1·25

615 Snake (bas-relief, Kim Yu Shin's tomb) **619** Dish Aerial

617 "Training Technicians"

1976. Lunar New Year (Year of the Snake). Multicoloured.

1268 20 w. Type **615** 30 10
1269 20 w. Door knocker with Manchurian cranes 30 10

1977. 4th Five Year Economic Development Plan. Multicoloured.

1271 20 w. Type **617** 40 10
1272 20 w. Tanker ("Heavy Industries") 50 10

1977. 25th Anniv of Korea's I.T.U. Membership.

1273 **619** 20 w. multicoloured 30 10

620 Korean Broadcasting Centre **621** Jar with Grape Design

1977. 50th Anniv of Broadcasting in Korea.

1274 **620** 20 w. multicoloured 35 10

1977. Korean Ceramics (1st series). Multicoloured, background colours given.

1275 20 w. Type **621** (brown) 75 10
1276 20 w. Celadon vase (grey) 75 10

See also Nos. 1285/6, 1287/8, 1290/1 and 1300/1.

623 "Two-children" Family **624** Reserve Soldier

1977. Family Planning.

1277 **623** 20 w. green, turq & orge 30 10

1977. 9th Homeland Reserve Forces Day.

1278 **624** 20 w. multicoloured 35 10

625 Diagram of Brain **626** Medical Book and Equipment

1977. 10th Anniv of Science Day.

1279 **625** 20 w. multicoloured 25 10

1977. 35th International Military Medicine Meeting.

1280 **626** 20 w. multicoloured 45 10

627 Child with Flowers **628** Veterans' Flag and Emblem

1977. 20th Anniv of Children's Charter.

1281 **627** 20 w. multicoloured 25 10

1977. 25th Anniv of Korean Veterans' Day.

1282 **628** 20 w. multicoloured 40 10

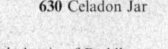

629 Statue of Buddha, Sokkulam Grotto **630** Celadon Jar

1977. 2600th Birth Anniv of Buddha.

1283 **629** 20 w. green and brown 40 10

1977. Korean Ceramics (2nd series). Multicoloured, background colours given.

1285 20 w. Type **630** (pink) 45 10
1286 20 w. Porcelain vase (blue) (vert) 45 10

632 "Buddha" Celadon Wine Jar

1977. Korean Ceramics (3rd series). Multicoloured, background colours given.

1287 20 w. Type **632** (mauve) 45 10
1288 20 w. Celadon vase (pale blue) 45 10

(634)

635 Celadon Vase, Black Koryo Ware

1977. Flood Relief. No. 791 surch with T **634**.

1289 20 w. + 10 w. green 1·25 40

1977. Korean Ceramics (4th series). Multicoloured, background colours given.

1290 20 w. Type **635** (stone) 45 10
1291 20 w. White porcelain bowl (green) (horiz) 45 10

637 Ulleung-do Island **639** Servicemen

1977. World Tourism Day. Multicoloured.

1292 20 w. Type **637** 30 10
1293 20 w. Haeundae Beach 30 10

1977. Armed Forces Day.

1294 **639** 20 w. multicoloured 20 10

640 **641**

"Mount Inwang Clearing-up after the Rain" (detail from drawing by Chung Seon)

1977. Philatelic Week.

1295 **640** 20 w. multicoloured 40 10
1296 **641** 20 w. multicoloured 40 10

Nos. 1294/5 were issued together, se-tenant, forming a composite design.

642 Rotary Emblem and Koryo Dynasty Bronze Bell **643** South Korean Flag over Everest

1977. 50th Anniv of Korean Rotary Club.

1298 **642** 20 w. multicoloured 50 10

1977. South Korean Conquest of Mount Everest.

1299 **643** 20 w. multicoloured 50 10

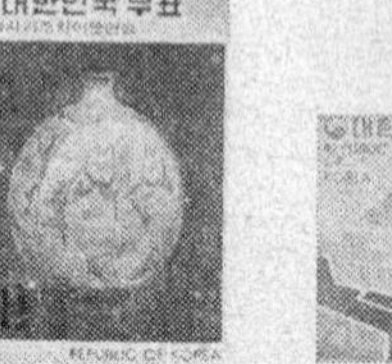

644 Punch'ong Bottle **646** Hands preserving Nature

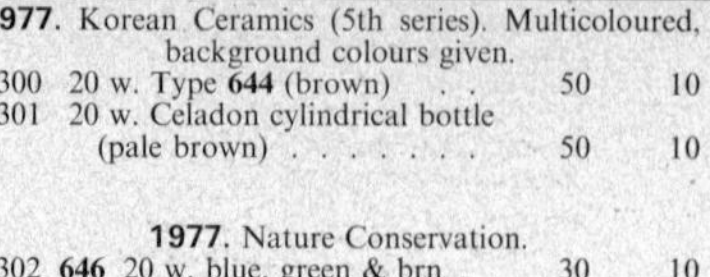

1977. Korean Ceramics (5th series). Multicoloured, background colours given.

1300 20 w. Type **644** (brown) 50 10
1301 20 w. Celadon cylindrical bottle (pale brown) 50 10

1977. Nature Conservation.

1302 **646** 20 w. blue, green & brn 30 10

647 Children with Kites **649** Clay Pigeon Shooting

1977. Lunar New Year ("Year of the Horse"). Multicoloured.

1303 20 w. Type **647** 30 10
1304 20 w. Horse (bas-relief, Kim Yu Shin's tomb) 30 10

1977. 42nd World Shooting Championships, Seoul. Multicoloured.

1306 20 w. Type **649** 35 10
1307 20 w. Air pistol shooting 35 10
1308 20 w. Air rifle shooting 35 10

652 Korean Airlines Boeing 747-200

1977. 25th Anniv of Korean Membership of I.C.A.O.

1310 **652** 20 w. multicoloured 45 10

653 "Exports"

1977. Korean Exports.

1311 **653** 20 w. multicoloured 35 10

654 Ships and World Map

1978. National Maritime Day.

1312 **654** 20 w. multicoloured 30 10

655 Three-storey Pagoda, Hwaom Temple **656** Seven-storey Pagoda, T'app'yong-ri

1978. Stone Pagodas (1st series).

1313 **655** 20 w. multicoloured 35 10
1314 **656** 20 w. multicoloured 35 10

See also Nos. 1319/20, 1322/5 and 1340/1.

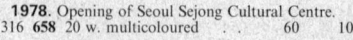

657 Ants with Coins **658** Seoul Sejong Cultural Centre, Hahoe Mask and Violin

1978. Savings Encouragement.

1315 **657** 20 w. multicoloured 30 10

1978. Opening of Seoul Sejong Cultural Centre.

1316 **658** 20 w. multicoloured 60 10

659 Standard Bearer

660 Pigeon and Young

1978. 10th Homeland Reserve Forces Day.
1317 **659** 20 w. multicoloured . . . 25 10

1978. Family Planning.
1318 **660** 20 w. black and green . . 35 10

661 Pagoda, Punhwang Temple

662 Pagoda, Miruk Temple

1978. Stone Pagodas (2nd series).
1319 **661** 20 w. multicoloured . . . 35 10
1320 **662** 20 w. multicoloured . . . 35 10

663 National Assembly

1978. 30th Anniv of National Assembly.
1321 **663** 20 w. multicoloured . . . 25 10

664 Tabo Pagoda, Pulguk Temple

665 Three-storey Pagoda, Pulguk Temple

1978. Stone Pagodas (3rd series).
1322 **664** 20 w. multicoloured . . . 35 10
1323 **665** 20 w. multicoloured . . . 35 10

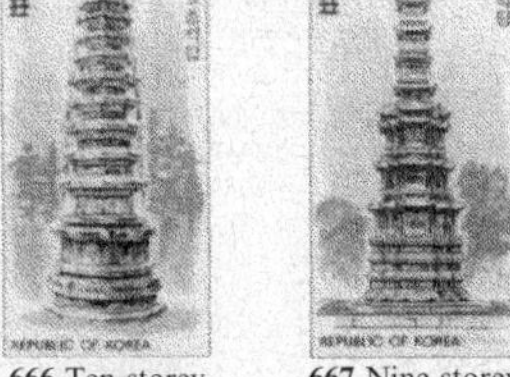
666 Ten-storey Pagoda, Kyongch'on Temple

667 Nine-storey Octagonal Pagoda, Wolchong Temple

1978. Stone Pagodas (4th series).
1324 **666** 20 w. multicoloured . . . 45 10
1325 **667** 20 w. multicoloured . . . 45 10

668 Emblem and Hands with Tools

669 Crater Lake, Mt. Baeguda and Bell of Joy

1978. 24th International Youth Skill Olympics, Pusan.
1326 **668** 20 w. multicoloured . . . 25 10

1978. 30th Anniv of Republic of Korea.
1328 **669** 20 w. multicoloured . . . 25 10

670 Army Nursing Officer

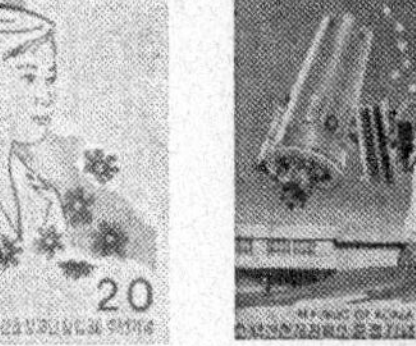
671 Sobaeksan Observatory and Telescope

1978. 30th Anniv of Army Nursing Corps.
1329 **670** 20 w. multicoloured . . 25 10

1978. Opening of Sobaeksan Observatory.
1330 **671** 20 w. multicoloured . . 40 10

672 Kyonghoeru Pavilion, Kyonbok Palace

673 Baeg-do Island

1978. World Tourism Day.
1331 **672** 20 w. multicoloured . . 30 10
1332 **673** 20 w. multicoloured . . 30 10

674 Customs Officers and Flag

1978. Centenary of Custom House.
1333 **674** 20 w. multicoloured . . 25 10

675 Armed Forces

676 Earthenware Figures, Silla Dynasty

1978. 30th Anniv of Korean Armed Forces.
1334 **675** 20 w. multicoloured . . 30 10

1978. Culture Month.
1335 **676** 20 w. black and green . 25 10

677 Painting of a Lady (Shin Yoon-bok)

678 Young Men and Y.M.C.A. Emblem

1978. Philatelic Week.
1336 **677** 20 w. multicoloured . . 35 10

1978. 75th Anniv of Korean Y.M.C.A.
1338 **678** 20 w. multicoloured . . 25 10

679 Hand smothering Fire

1978. Fire Prevention Campaign.
1339 **679** 20 w. multicoloured . . 25 10

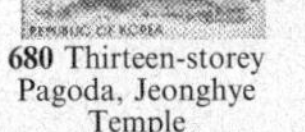
680 Thirteen-storey Pagoda, Jeonghye Temple

681 Three-storey Pagoda, Jinjeon Temple

1978. Stone Pagodas (5th series).
1340 **680** 20 w. multicoloured . . . 30 10
1341 **681** 20 w. multicoloured . . . 30 10

682 Snow Scene

684 People within Hibiscus

1978. Lunar New Year ("Year of the Sheep"). Multicoloured.
1342 20 w. Type **682** 30 10
1343 20 w. Sheep (bas-relief, Kim Yu Shin's tomb) 30 10

1978. 10th Anniv of National Education Charter.
1345 **684** 20 w. multicoloured . . . 25 10

685 President Pak

1978. Re-election of President Pak.
1346 **685** 20 w. multicoloured . . . 40 10

686 Golden Mandarinfish

687 Lace Bark Pine

1979. Nature Conservation.
1348 **686** 20 w. multicoloured . . . 35 10
1349 **687** 20 w. multicoloured . . . 35 10

688 Samil Monument

689 Worker and Bulldozer

1979. 60th Anniv of Samil Independence Movement.
1350 **688** 20 w. multicoloured . . . 25 10

1979. Labour Day.
1351 **689** 20 w. multicoloured . . . 25 10

690 Tabo Pagoda, Pulgak Temple

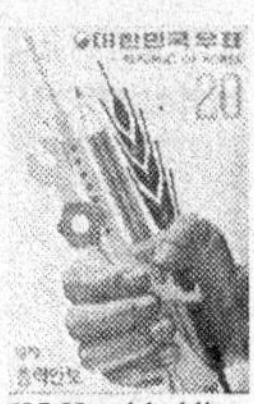
695 Hand holding Symbols of Security

1979. Korean Art. Multicoloured.
1352 20 w. Type **690** 25 10
1353 20 w. Gilt-bronze Maitreya 25 10
1354 20 w. Gold crown of Silla . . 25 10
1355 20 w. Celadon vase 25 10
1356 60 w. "Tano Day Activities" (silk screen) (50 × 33 mm) 45 10

1979. Strengthening National Security.
1358 **695** 20 w. multicoloured . . . 25 10

696 Pulguk Temple and P.A.T.A. Emblem

1979. 28th Pacific Area Travel Association Conference, Seoul.
1359 **696** 20 w. multicoloured . . 25 10

697 Presidents Pak and Senghor

1979. Visit of President Senghor of Senegal.
1360 **697** 20 w. multicoloured . . 25 10

698 Basketball

699 Children playing

1979. 8th World Women's Basketball Championships, Seoul.
1362 **698** 20 w. multicoloured . . 40 10

1979. International Year of the Child.
1363 **699** 20 w. multicoloured . . 30 10

700 Children on Swing

1979. Family Planning.
1364 **700** 20 w. multicoloured . . 30 10

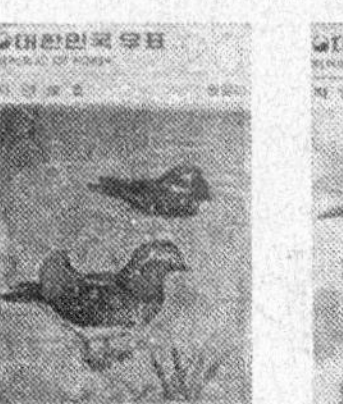
701 Mandarins

702 "Neofinettia falcata" (orchid)

1979. Nature Conservation.
1365 **701** 20 w. multicoloured . . 60 15
1366 **702** 20 w. multicoloured . . 40 10

703 Manchurian Cranes

1979.
1367 **703** 10 w. black and green 50 15
1368 – 15 w. dp green & green 15 10
1369 – 20 w. bistre, black & blue 20 10
1370 – 30 w. multicoloured . . 25 10
1371 – 40 w. multicoloured . . 30 10
1372 – 50 w. brown, red & orge 20 10
1373 – 60 w. grey, purple & mve 30 10
1374 – 70 w. multicoloured . . 50 10
1375 – 80 w. yellow, blk & red 60 10
1376 – 90 w. buff, green and orange 75 10
1377 – 100 w. purple & mauve 45 10
1377a – 100 w. black 45 10
1378 – 150 w. black, bistre and blue 50 10
1379 – 200 w. brown and green 1·10 10
1380 – 300 w. blue . . . . . . 2·00 20
1381 – 400 w. green, brown and deep green . . . . . 2·25 20
1381a – 400 w. blue, ochre, brown and grey . . . . . 3·00 30
1382 – 450 w. brown . . . . . 1·60 40
1383 – 500 w. dp green & green 2·00 40
1383a – 550 w. black . . . . . 2·00 50
1384 – 600 w. multicoloured . 2·25 1·00
1385 – 700 w. multicoloured . 3·25 40
1386 – 800 w. multicoloured . 2·40 50
1387 – 1000 w. lt brown & brn 3·25 40
1388 – 1000 w. lt brown & brn 3·25 40
1389 – 5000 w. multicoloured . 18·00 4·00

DESIGNS:—As T **703**: HORIZ: 15 w. Mt. Sorak; 50 w. Earthenware model of wagon; 90 w. Paikryung Island; 1000 w. Duck earthenware vessels (1387 facing right; 1388 facing left). VERT: 20 w. Tolharubang (stone grandfather); 30 w. National flag; 40 w. "Hibiscus syriacus"; 60 w. Porcelain jar, Yi Dynasty; 70 w. Kyongju Observatory; 80 w. Mounted warrior (pottery vessel); 100 w. (1377) Ryu Kwan Soon; 100 w. (1377a) Chung Yak Yong (writer); 150 w. Porcelain jar, Chosun Dynasty; 200 w. Ahn Joong Geun; 300 w. Ahn Chang Ho; 400 w. Koryo celadon incense burner; 450, 550 w. Kim Ku (organizer of Korean Independence Party); 500 w. Brick with mountain landscape; 600 w. Hong Yung Sik (postal reformer); 700 w. Duck (lid of incense burner). 29×41 mm: 800 w. Dragon's head flagpole finial; 5000 w. Tiger.

See also No. 1065.

725 People suffering from Traffic Pollution

1979. Environmental Protection.
1390 **725** 20 w. brown and green . . 30 10

726 Common Goral **727** "Convallaria leiskei" Miquel

1979. Nature Conservation.
1391 **726** 20 w. multicoloured . . . 40 10
1392 **727** 20 w. multicoloured . . . 40 10

728 Presidents Pak and Carter

1979. Visit of President Carter of United States.
1393 **728** 20 w. multicoloured . . . 20 10

729 Exhibition Building and Emblem

1979. Opening of Korea Exhibition Centre.
1395 **729** 20 w. multicoloured . . . 20 10

730 Boeing 747-200 Jetliner and Globe

1979. 10th Anniv of Korean Air Lines.
1396 **730** 20 w. multicoloured . . . 30 10

731 "The Courtesans' Sword Dance" (Shin Yun-bok)

1979. United States "5000 Years of Korean Art" Exhibition (1st issue).
1397 **731** 60 w. multicoloured . . . 60 15
See also Nos. 1402/3, 1406/7, 1420/1, 1426/7, 1433/4, 1441/2 and 1457/8.

732 Mount Mai, North Cholla Province **733** Dragon's Head Rock, Cheju Island

1979. World Tourism Day.
1399 **732** 20 w. multicoloured . . . 25 10
1400 **733** 20 w. multicoloured . . . 25 10

734 Heart, Donors and Blood Drop

1979. Blood Donors.
1401 **734** 20 w. red and green . . 50 10

735 White Porcelain Jar with Grape Design **736** Mounted Warrior (pottery vessel)

1979. "5000 Years of Korean Art" Exhibition (2nd issue).
1402 **735** 20 w. multicoloured . . 40 10
1403 **736** 20 w. multicoloured . . 40 10

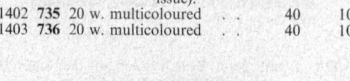

737 "Moon Travel" (Park Chung Jae)

1979. Philatelic Week.
1404 **737** 20 w. multicoloured . . 20 10

738 Hahoe Mask **739** Golden Amitabha with Halo

1979. "5000 Years of Korean Art" Exhibition (3rd issue).
1406 **738** 20 w. multicoloured . . 40 10
1407 **739** 20 w. multicoloured . . 40 10

740 Rain Frog **741** Asian Polypody

1979. Nature Conservation.
1408 **740** 20 w. multicoloured . . 45 10
1409 **741** 20 w. multicoloured . . 45 10

742 Monkey (bas-relief, Kim Yun Shin's tomb) **743** Children playing Yut

1979. Lunar New Year ("Year of the Monkey").
1410 **742** 20 w. multicoloured . . 20 10
1411 **743** 20 w. multicoloured . . 20 10

744 President Choi Kyu Hah

1979. Presidential Inauguration.
1413 **744** 20 w. multicoloured . . 30 10

745 Firefly **746** Meesun Tree

1980. Nature Conservation (5th series).
1415 **745** 30 w. multicoloured . . . 45 10
1416 **746** 30 w. multicoloured . . . 45 10

747 President Pak **748** Earthenware Kettle

749 "Landscape" (Kim Hong Do)

1980. President Pak Commemoration.
1417 **747** 30 w. red 25 10
1418 30 w. purple 25 10

1980. Exhibition "5000 Years of Korean Art" (4th issue).
1420 **748** 30 w. multicoloured . . . 40 10
1421 **749** 60 w. multicoloured . . . 55 10

750 "Lotus" . **751** "Magpie and Tiger"

1980. Folk Paintings (1st series).
1423 **750** 30 w. multicoloured . . . 45 20
1424 **751** 60 w. multicoloured . . . 1·25 40
See also Nos. 1429/31, 1437/40 and 1453/6.

752 Merchant Ships

1980. Korean Merchant Navy.
1425 **752** 30 w. multicoloured . . . 30 10

753 "Heavenly Horse" (tomb painting) **754** Banner Staff with Dragonhead Finial

1980. Exhibition "5000 Years of Korean Art" (5th series).
1426 **753** 30 w. multicoloured . . . 40 10
1427 **754** 30 w. multicoloured . . . 40 10

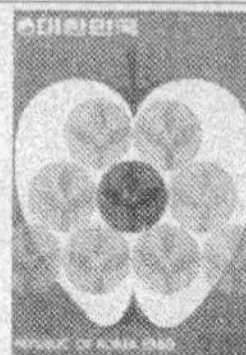

755 "Fruition"

1980. 10th Anniv of Saemaul Movement (community self-help programme).
1428 **755** 30 w. multicoloured . . 25 10

756 "Red Phoenix"

757/8 "Sun and Moon over Mt. Konryun" (½-size illustration)

1980. Folk Paintings (2nd series).
1429 **756** 30 w. multicoloured . . 30 10
1430 **757** 60 w. multicoloured . . 50 40
1431 **758** 60 w. multicoloured . . 50 40
Nos. 1430/1 were issued together, se-tenant, forming a composite design.

759 "Man on a Horse" (mural, Koguryo period) **760** "Tiger" (granite sculpture)

1980. Exhibition "5000 Years of Korean Art" (6th issue).
1433 **759** 30 w. multicoloured . . 40 10
1434 **760** 30 w. multicoloured . . 40 10

761 U.N. Flag and Rifle **762** "Venus de Milo" and Contestants

1980. 30th Anniv of Intervention of U.N. Forces in Korean War.
1435 **761** 30 w. multicoloured . . 30 10

1980. "Miss Universe" Beauty Contest, Seoul.
1436 **762** 30 w. multicoloured . . 30 10

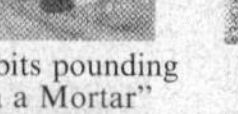

763 "Rabbits pounding Grain in a Mortar" **764** "Dragon in Cloud"

1980. Folk Paintings (3rd series).
1437 **763** 30 w. multicoloured . . . 40 10
1438 **764** 30 w. multicoloured . . 40 10

765 "Pine Tree"

766 "Flowers and Manchurian Cranes" (detail, folding screen)

1980. Folk Paintings (4th series).

1439 **765** 30 w. multicoloured . . . 40 10
1440 **766** 30 w. multicoloured . . . 75 20

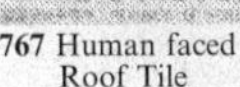

767 Human faced Roof Tile

768 "White Tiger" (mural)

1980. Exhibition "5000 Years of Korean Art" (7th issue).

1441 **767** 30 w. multicoloured . . . 30 10
1442 **768** 30 w. multicoloured . . . 30 10

769 Football

770 President Chun Doo Hwan

1980. 10th President's Cup Football Tournament.

1443 **769** 30 w. multicoloured . . . 30 10

1980. Presidential Inauguration.

1444 **770** 30 w. multicoloured . . . 25 10

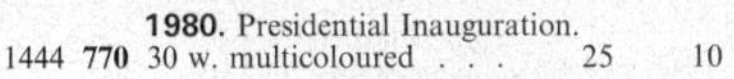

771 Woman Soldier and Emblem

1980. 30th Anniv of Women's Army Corps.

1446 **771** 30 w. multicoloured . . . 25 10

772 River Baegma

773 Three Peaks of Dodam

1980. World Tourism Day.

1447 **772** 30 w. pink and purple . . 30 10
1448 **773** 30 w. yellow, green & bl 30 10

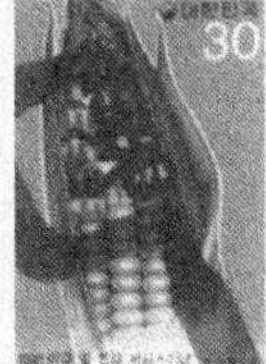

774 Corn-cob and Micrometer

775 Tree

1980. Population and Housing Census.

1449 **774** 30 w. multicoloured . . . 30 10

1980. 75th Anniv of Korean Red Cross.

1450 **775** 30 w. multicoloured . . . 35 10

776 "Angels delivering Mail" (Kim Ki Chul)

1980. Philatelic Week.

1451 **776** 30 w. multicoloured . . 25 10

777 "Ten Long-life Symbols"

781 Deva King (sculpture)

1980. Folk Paintings (5th series). Multicoloured.

1453 30 w. Type **777** 30 10
1454 30 w. "Herb of eternal youth" and deer 30 10
1455 30 w. Pine and deer eating herb 30 10
1456 30 w. Pine, water and rock . . 30 10

Nos. 1453/6 were issued together, se-tenant, forming a composite design.

1980. Exhibition "5000 Years of Korean Art" (8th series).

1457 **781** 30 w. black 40 10
1458 30 w. red 40 10

782 Cable Ship and Cross-section of Cable

1980. Inauguration of Korea-Japan Submarine Cable.

1459 **782** 30 w. multicoloured . . 35 10

783 Cock (bas-relief Kim Yu Shin's tomb)

784 Cranes

1980. Lunar New Year ("Year of the Cock").

1460 **783** 30 w. multicoloured . . 30 10
1461 **784** 30 w. multicoloured . . 30 10

785 President Chun Doo Hwan and Factory within "Hibiscus syriacus"

1981. Presidential Inauguration.

1463 **785** 30 w. multicoloured . . 25 10

786 "Korea Sun" (tanker)

787 "Asia Yukho" (freighter)

1981. Ships (1st series).

1465 **786** 30 w. multicoloured . . 45 10
1466 **787** 90 w. multicoloured . . 80 20

See also Nos. 1470/1, 1482/5 and 1501/2.

788 National Assembly Building

1981. Inaugural Session of 11th National Assembly.

1467 **788** 30 w. brown and gold . . 30 10

789 Symbols of Disability and I.Y.D.P. Emblem

790 Disabled Person in Wheelchair at Foot of Steps

1981. International Year of Disabled Persons.

1468 **789** 30 w. multicoloured . . . 30 10
1469 **790** 90 w. multicoloured . . . 60 35

791 "Satum" (bulk-carrier)

792 "Hanjin Seoul" (container ship)

1981. Ships (2nd series).

1470 **791** 30 w. deep purple, purple and blue 45 10
1471 **792** 90 w. grey, blue and red 80 20

793 Council Emblem on Ribbon

1981. Advisory Council on Peaceful Unification Policy.

1472 **793** 40 w. multicoloured . . . 30 10

794 "Clean Rivers and Air"

795 White Storks visiting Breeding Grounds

1981. World Environment Day.

1473 **794** 30 w. multicoloured . . . 30 10
1474 **795** 90 w. multicoloured . . . 70 20

796 Presidents Chun and Suharto of Indonesia

1981. Presidential Visit to A.S.E.A.N. Countries. Multicoloured.

1475 40 w. Type **796** 50 10
1476 40 w. Pres. Chun and Sultan of Malaysia 50 10
1477 40 w. Handshake and flags of South Korea and Singapore 50 10
1478 40 w. Pres. Chun and King of Thailand 50 10
1479 40 w. Presidents Chun and Marcos of Philippines . . . 50 10
1480 40 w. Pres. Chun and flags of Korea, Singapore, Malaysia and Philippines (39 × 43 mm) 50 10

802 "Chung Ryong No. 3" (tug)

803 "Soo Gong No. 71" (trawler)

1981. Ships (3rd series).

1482 **802** 40 w. multicoloured . . 55 10
1483 **803** 100 w. multicoloured . . 85 20

804 "Al Debaran" (log carrier)

805 "Hyundai No. 1" (car carrier)

1981. Ships (4th series).

1484 **804** 40 w. multicoloured . . 55 10
1485 **805** 100 w. multicoloured . . 85 20

806 Korean with Flag and Dates on Graph

812 W.H.O. Emblem and Citizens

807 Glider

1981. 36th Anniv of Liberation.

1486 **806** 40 w. multicoloured . . 30 10

1981. 3rd Model Aeronautic Competition. Multicoloured.

1487 10 w. Type **807** 40 10
1488 20 w. Elastic-powered airplane 40 10
1489 40 w. Line-controlled airplane 40 15
1490 50 w. Radio-controlled airplane 60 20
1491 80 w. Radio-controlled helicopter 75 30

1981. 32nd Session of W.H.O. Regional Committee for the Western Pacific, Seoul.

1492 **812** 40 w. multicoloured . . 30 10

813 Seoul Communications Tower

814 Ulreung Island

1981. World Tourism Day.

1493 **813** 40 w. multicoloured . . 30 10
1494 **814** 40 w. multicoloured . . 30 10

815 Cycling

816 Swimming

1981. 62nd National Sports Meeting, Seoul.

1495 **815** 40 w. multicoloured . . 35 10
1496 **816** 40 w. multicoloured . . 35 10

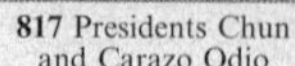

817 Presidents Chun and Carazo Odio

818 Hand holding Plate with F.A.O. Emblem

1981. Visit of President Carazo Odio of Costa Rica.
1497 **817** 40 w. multicoloured . . . 30 10

1981. World Food Day.
1498 **818** 40 w. multicoloured . . . 30 10

819 Airliner and Clouds

820 South Gate of Seoul and Olympic Rings

1981. National Aviation Day.
1499 **819** 40 w. orange, brown and silver 40 10

1981. Choice of Seoul as 1988 Olympic Host City.
1500 **820** 40 w. multicoloured . . . 30 10

821 "Stolt Hawk" (chemical carrier)

822 Passenger Ferry

1981. Ships (5th series).
1501 **821** 40 w. black 55 10
1502 **822** 100 w. blue 85 20

823 "Hang-gliding" (Kim Kyung Jun)

1981. Philatelic Week.
1503 **823** 40 w. multicoloured . . . 30 10

824 Camellia and Dog

825 Children flying Kite

1981. Lunar New Year ("Year of the Dog").
1505 **824** 40 w. multicoloured . . . 30 10
1506 **825** 40 w. multicoloured . . . 30 10

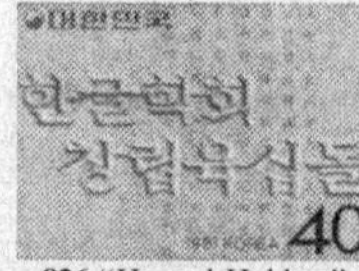

826 "Hangul Hakhoe"

1981. 60th Anniv of Hangul Hakhoe (Korean Language Society).
1508 **826** 40 w. multicoloured . . . 35 10

INDEX

Countries can be quickly located by referring to the index at the end of this volume.

827 Telephone and Dish Aerial

828 Scout Emblem and Logs forming "75"

1982. Inauguration of Korea Telecommunication Authority.
1509 **827** 60 w. multicoloured . . 40 10

1982. 75th Anniv of Boy Scout Movement.
1510 **828** 60 w. multicoloured . . 60 10

829 Young Woman

830 Dividers and World Map

1982. 60th Anniv of Korean Young Women's Christian Association.
1511 **829** 60 w. multicoloured . . 35 10

1982. Centenary of International Polar Year.
1512 **830** 60 w. multicoloured . . 50 10

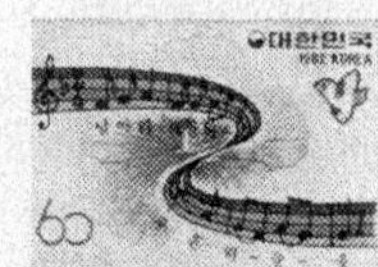

831 Music and "Hibiscus syriacus"

1982. Children's Day.
1513 **831** 60 w. multicoloured . . 40 10

832 President Chun and Samuel Doe

1982. Visit of Samuel Doe (Liberian Head of State).
1514 **832** 60 w. multicoloured . . 35 10

833 Centenary Emblem

1982. Centenary of Korea–United States Friendship Treaty.
1516 **833** 60 w. multicoloured . . 30 10
1517 – 60 w. multicoloured . . 30 10
DESIGN: No. 1517, Statue of Liberty and Seoul South Gate.

835 Presidents Chun and Mobutu

1982. Visit of President Mobutu of Zaire.
1519 **835** 60 w. multicoloured . . 30 10

836 "Territorial Expansion by Kwanggaeto the Great" (Lee Chong Sang)

837 "General Euljimunduck's Great Victory at Salsoo" (Park Kak Soon)

1982. Documentary Paintings (1st series).
1521 **836** 60 w. multicoloured . . . 40 10
1522 **837** 60 w. multicoloured . . . 40 10
See also Nos. 1523/4, 1537/8 and 1548/9.

838 "Shilla's Repulse of Invading Tang Army" (Oh Seung Woo)

839 "General Kang Kam Chan's Great Victory at Kyiju" (Lee Yong Hwan)

1982. Documentary Paintings (2nd series).
1523 **838** 60 w. multicoloured . . . 40 10
1524 **839** 60 w. multicoloured . . . 40 10

840 Convention Emblem and Globe

841 Presidents Chun and Moi of Kenya

1982. 55th International Y's Men's Club Convention, Seoul.
1525 **840** 60 w. multicoloured . . . 20 10

1982. Presidential Visits to Africa and Canada. Multicoloured.
1526 60 w. Type **841** 35 10
1527 60 w. Presidents Chun and Shagari of Nigeria 35 10
1528 60 w. Presidents Chun and Bongo of Gabon 35 10
1529 60 w. Presidents Chun and Diouf of Senegal 35 10
1530 60 w. Flags of South Korea and Canada 35 10

846 National Flag

1982. Centenary of National Flag.
1532 **846** 60 w. multicoloured . . . 40 10

847 Emblem and Player

1982. 2nd Seoul Table Tennis Championships.
1534 **847** 60 w. multicoloured . . . 40 10

848 Baseball Player

1982. 27th World Baseball Championship Series, Seoul.
1535 **848** 60 w. brown 40 10

849 Exhibition Centre

1982. Seoul International Trade Fair.
1536 **849** 60 w. multicoloured . . 30 10

850 "Admiral Yi Sun Sin's Great Victory at Hansan" (Kim Hyung Ku)

851 "General Kim Chwa Jin's Chungsanri Battle" (Sohn Soo Kwang)

1982. Documentary Paintings (3rd series).
1537 **850** 60 w. multicoloured . . 50 10
1538 **851** 60 w. multicoloured . . 35 10

852 "Miners reading Consolatory Letters" (Um Soon Keun)

1982. Philatelic Week.
1539 **852** 60 w. multicoloured . . 30 10

853 Presidents Chung and Suharto

1982. Visit of President Suharto of Indonesia.
1541 **853** 60 w. multicoloured . . 30 10

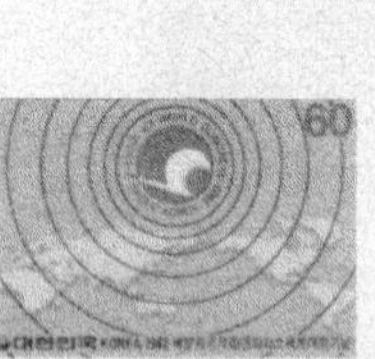

854 J.C.I. Emblem over World Map

855 "Intelsat 5" and "4-A" orbiting Globe

1982. 37th Junior Chamber International World Congress, Seoul.
1543 **854** 60 w. multicoloured . . 30 10

1982. Second U.N. Conference on the Exploration and Peaceful Uses of Outer Space, Vienna.
1544 **855** 60 w. multicoloured . . 30 10

856 Pig (bas-relief, Kim Yu Shin's tomb)

1982. Lunar New Year ("Year of the Pig").
1545 60 w. Type **856** 35 10
1546 60 w. Magpies and Korean moneybag 40 10

858 "General Kwon Yul's Great Victory at Haengju" (Oh Seung Woo)

859 "Kim Chong Suh's Exploitation of Yukin" (Kim Tae)

1982. Documentary Paintings (4th series).
1548 **858** 60 w. multicoloured . . . 40 10
1549 **859** 60 w. multicoloured . . . 40 10

860 Flags of South Korea and Turkey

861 Hand writing Letter

1982. Visit of President Evran of Turkey.
1550 **860** 60 w. multicoloured . . . 35 10

1982. Letter Writing Campaign.
1552 **861** 60 w. multicoloured . . . 30 10

862 Emblem, Airliner, Container Ship and Cranes

863 Hyundai "Pony 2"

1983. International Customs Day.
1553 **862** 60 w. multicoloured . . . 50 15

1983. Korean-made Vehicles (1st series). Multicoloured.
1554 60 w. Type **863** 50 10
1555 60 w. Keohwa Jeep 50 10
See also Nos. 1558/9, 1564/5, 1572/3 and 1576/7.

865 President Chun and Sultan of Malaysia

1983. Visit of Sultan of Malaysia.
1556 **865** 60 w. multicoloured . . . 30 10

866 Daewoo "Maepsy" **867** Kia "Bongo" Minibus

1983. Korean-made Vehicles (2nd series).
1558 **866** 60 w. multicoloured . . . 50 10
1559 **867** 60 w. multicoloured . . . 50 10

868 Former General Bureau of Postal Administration

869 Central Post Office, Seoul

1983. "Philakorea 84" International Stamp Exhibition, Seoul. Centenary of Korean Postal Service (1st series).
1560 **868** 60 w. multicoloured . . 30 10
1561 **869** 60 w. multicoloured . . 30 10
See also Nos. 1566/7, 1574/5 and 1603/6.

870 Old Village Schoolroom

1983. Teachers' Day.
1562 **870** 60 w. multicoloured . . 35 10

871 Asia Motor Co. Bus **872** Kia "Super Titan" Truck

1983. Korean-made Vehicles (3rd series).
1564 **871** 60 w. multicoloured . . 45 10
1565 **872** 60 w. multicoloured . . 45 10

873 Early Postman

1983. "Philakorea 84" International Stamp Exhibition, Seoul. Centenary of Korean Postal Service (2nd series).
1566 **873** 70 w. multicoloured . . 40 10
1567 – 70 w. multicoloured . . 40 10
DESIGN: No. 1567, Modern postman on motor-cycle.

875 "Communications in Outer Space" (Chun Ja Eun)

1983. World Communications Year.
1568 **875** 70 w. multicoloured . . 35 10

876 Whooper Swans at Sunrise

1983. Inaug of Communications Insurance.
1570 **876** 70 w. multicoloured . . 60 15

877 Emblems of Science and Engineering

1983. Korean Symposium on Science and Technology, Seoul.
1571 **877** 70 w. multicoloured . . . 35 10

878 Daewoo Dump Truck

879 Hyundai Cargo Lorry

1983. Korean-made Vehicles (4th series).
1572 **878** 70 w. multicoloured . . . 45 10
1573 **879** 70 w. multicoloured . . . 45 10

880 Mail carried by Horse

1983. "Philakorea 84" International Stamp Exhibition, Seoul. Centenary of Korean Postal Service (3rd series). Multicoloured.
1574 70 w. Type **880** 35 10
1575 70 w. Mail truck and Douglas DC-8-60 Super Sixty jetliner 40 10

882 Dong-A Concrete Mixer Truck

883 Dong-A Tanker

1983. Korean-made Vehicles (5th series).
1576 **882** 70 w. multicoloured . . . 50 10
1577 **883** 70 w. multicoloured . . . 50 10

884 President Chun and King Hussein

885 Woman with Fan

1983. Visit of King Hussein of Jordan.
1578 **884** 70 w. multicoloured . . . 35 10

1983. 53rd American Society of Travel Agents World Congress, Seoul.
1580 **885** 70 w. multicoloured . . . 35 10

886 I.P.U. Emblem and Flags

1983. 70th Inter-Parliamentary Union Conference, Seoul.
1581 **886** 70 w. multicoloured . . . 35 10

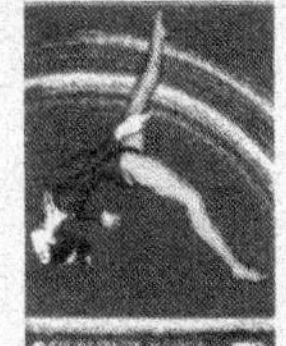

887 Gymnastics **888** Football

1983. 64th National Sports Meeting, Inchon.
1583 **887** 70 w. multicoloured . . 40 10
1584 **888** 70 w. multicoloured . . 40 10

889 Presidents Chun and U San Yu of Burma

894 Rain Drops containing Symbols of Industry, Light and Food

1983. Presidential Visits. Multicoloured.
1585 70 w. Type **889** 60 50
1586 70 w. Presidents Chun and Giani Zail Singh of India 60 50
1587 70 w. Presidents Chun and Jayewardene of Sri Lanka 60 50
1588 70 w. Flags of South Korea and Australia 60 50
1589 70 w. Flags of South Korea and New Zealand 60 50

1983. Development of Water Resources and 10th Anniv of Soyang-gang Dam.
1591 **894** 70 w. multicoloured . . 35 10

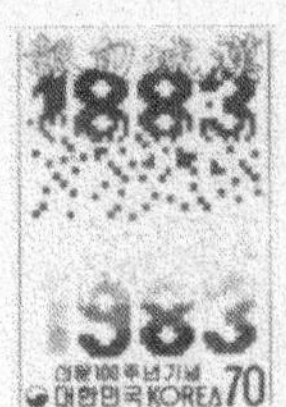

895 Centenary Dates

896 Tree with Lungs and Cross of Lorraine

1983. Centenary of 1st Korean Newspaper "Hansong Sunbo".
1592 **895** 70 w. multicoloured . . 35 10

1983. 30th Anniv of Korean National Tuberculosis Association.
1593 **896** 70 w. multicoloured . . 35 10

897 Presidents Chun and Reagan

898 Child collecting Stamps

1983. Visit of President Reagan of United States of America.
1594 **897** 70 w. multicoloured . . 35 10

1983. Philatelic Week.
1596 **898** 70 w. multicoloured . . 35 10

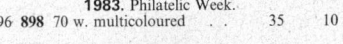

899 Rat (bas-relief, Kim Yu Shin's tomb)

1983. Lunar New Year ("Year of the Rat"). Multicoloured.
1598 70 w. Type **899** 35 10
1599 70 w. Manchurian cranes and pine 45 10

901 Bicentenary Emblem
902 5 m. and 10 m. Stamps, 1884

1984. Bicentenary of Catholic Church in Korea.
1601 **901** 70 w. red, violet & silver 35 10

1984. "Philakorea 84" International Stamp Exhibition, Seoul. Centenary of Korean Postal Service (4th series). Multicoloured.
1603 70 w. Type **902** 40 10
1604 70 w. 5000 w. stamp, 1983 . 40 10

904 Old Postal Emblem and Post Box

1984. "Philakorea 84" International Stamp Exhibition, Seoul. Centenary of Korean Postal Service (5th series). Multicoloured.
1605 70 w. Type **904** 40 10
1606 70 w. Modern postal emblem and post box 40 10

906 President Chun and Sultan

1984. Visit of Sultan of Brunei.
1607 **906** 70 w. multicoloured . . . 40 10

907 President Chun and Sheikh Khalifa

1984. Visit of Sheikh Khalifa of Qatar.
1609 **907** 70 w. multicoloured . . . 35 10

908 Child posting Letter

1984. Centenary of Korean Postal Administration. Multicoloured.
1611 70 w. Type **908** 35 10
1612 70 w. Postman in city 35 10

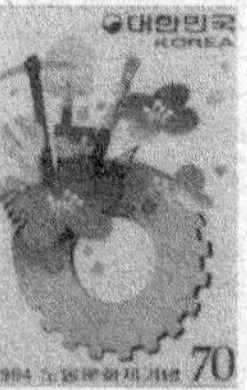

910 Pope John Paul II
911 Cogwheel, Worker's Tools and Flowers

1984. Visit of Pope John Paul II.
1614 **910** 70 w. black 35 10
1615 70 w. multicoloured . . . 35 10

1984. Labour Festival.
1617 **911** 70 w. multicoloured . . 30 10

912 Globe, Jetliner, Container Ship and Emblem
913 Map and Flags of S. Korea and Sri Lanka

1984. 63rd/64th Sessions of Customs Co-operation Council, Seoul.
1618 **912** 70 w. multicoloured . . 65 15

1984. Visit of President Jayewardene of Sri Lanka.
1619 **913** 70 w. multicoloured . . 35 10

914 Symbols and Punctuation Marks
915 Expressway

1984. 14th Asian Advertising Congress, Seoul.
1621 **914** 70 w. multicoloured . . 35 10

1984. Opening of 88 Olympic Expressway.
1622 **915** 70 w. multicoloured . . 35 10

916 Laurel, "Victory" and Olympic Rings
917 A.B.U. Emblem and Microphone

1984. 90th Anniv of International Olympic Committee.
1623 **916** 70 w. multicoloured . . 35 10

1984. 20th Anniv of Asia-Pacific Broadcasting Union.
1624 **917** 70 w. multicoloured . . 35 10

918 Flags of S. Korea and Senegal

1984. Visit of President Abdou Diouf of Senegal.
1625 **918** 70 w. multicoloured . . 35 10

919 Archery
921 Crucifixion

1984. Olympic Games, Los Angeles. Multicoloured.
1627 70 w. Type **919** 40 10
1628 440 w. Fencing . . . . . . 1·60 35

1984. Centenary of Korean Protestant Church. Multicoloured.
1629 70 w. Type **921** 40 10
1630 70 w. Cross, vine and dove . 40 10

923 Man carrying Silk-covered Lantern

1984. Folk Customs (1st series). "Wedding" (Kim Kyo Man). Multicoloured.
1632 70 w. Type **923** 40 10
1633 70 w. Bridegroom on horse 40 10
1634 70 w. Man playing clarinet . 40 10
1635 70 w. Bride in sedan chair (51 × 35 mm) 40 10
See also Nos. 1657/8, 1683/4, 1734/8, 1808/11, 1840/3, 1858/61 and 1915/18.

927 Pres. Chun and Mt. Fuji

1984. Pres. Chun's Visit to Japan.
1637 **927** 70 w. multicoloured . . . 40 10

928 Flags of S. Korea and Gambia

1984. Visit of President Sir Dawada Kairaba Jawara of Gambia.
1639 **928** 70 w. multicoloured . . . 40 10

929 Symbols of International Trade
930 Namsan Tower and National Flags

1984. "Sitra '84" International Trade Fair, Seoul.
1641 **929** 70 w. multicoloured . . . 40 10

1984. Visit of President El Hadj Omar Bongo of Gabon.
1642 **930** 70 w. multicoloured . . . 40 10

931 Badminton
932 Magnifying Glass and Exhibition Emblem

1984. 65th National Sports Meeting, Taegu. Multicoloured.
1644 70 w. Type **931** 40 10
1645 70 w. Wrestling 40 10

1984. "Philakorea 1984" International Stamp Exhibition, Seoul. Multicoloured.
1646 70 w. Type **932** 40 10
1647 70 w. South Gate, Seoul, and stamps (horiz) 40 10

934 Presidents Chun and Gayoom

1984. Visit of President Maumoon Abdul Gayoom of the Maldives.
1650 **934** 70 w. multicoloured . . . 40 10

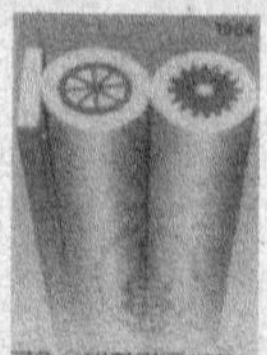

935 "100" and Industrial Symbols

1984. Centenary of Korean Chamber of Commerce and Industry.
1652 **935** 70 w. multicoloured . . . 40 10

936 Children playing Jaegi-chagi
937 Ox (bas-relief, Kim Yu Shin's tomb)

1984. Lunar New Year ("Year of the Ox").
1653 **936** 70 w. multicoloured . . 40 10
1654 **937** 70 w. multicoloured . . 40 10

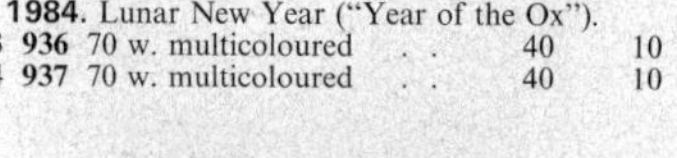

938 I.Y.Y. Emblem

1985. International Youth Year.
1656 **938** 70 w. multicoloured . . 40 10

939 Pounding Rice for New Year Rice Cake
940 Welcoming Year's First Full Moon

1985. Folk Customs (2nd series).
1657 **939** 70 w. multicoloured . . 40 10
1658 **940** 70 w. multicoloured . . 40 10

941 Seoul Olympic Emblem

1985. Olympic Games, Seoul (1988) (1st issue). Multicoloured.
1659 70 w. + 30 w. Type **941** . . 45 20
1660 70 w. + 30 w. Hodori (mascot) 45 20
See also Nos. 1673/4, 1678/8, 1694/5, 1703/10, 1747/50, 1752/5, 1784/7, 1814/17, 1826/7, 1835/6 and 1844/7.

943 "Still Life with Doll" (Lee Chong Woo)

944 "Rocky Mountain in Early Spring Morning" (Ahn Jung Shik)

1985. Modern Art (1st series).
1662 **943** 70 w. multicoloured . . 40 10
1663 **944** 70 w. multicoloured . . 40 10
See also Nos. 1680/1, 1757/60, 1791/4 and 1875/8.

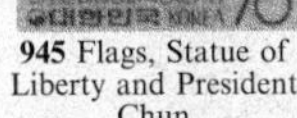

945 Flags, Statue of Liberty and President Chun

946 Flags, Seoul South Gate and National Flower

1985. Presidential Visit to United States.
1664 **945** 70 w. multicoloured . . . 40 10

1985. Visit of President Mohammed Zia-ul-Haq of Pakistan.
1666 **946** 70 w. multicoloured . . . 40 10

947 Underwood Hall

1985. Centenary of Yonsei University.
1668 **947** 70 w. black, buff & green 40 10

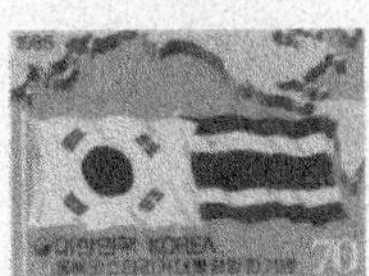

948 Flags and Map

1985. Visit of President Luis Alberto Monge of Costa Rica.
1669 **948** 70 w. multicoloured . . . 40 10

949 Silver Carp

950 Sailfish

1985. Fishes (1st series).
1671 **949** 70 w. multicoloured . . . 50 10
1672 **950** 70 w. multicoloured . . . 50 10
See also Nos. 1730/3, 1797/1800, 1881/4, 1903/6 and 1951/4.

951 Rowing

952 National Flags

1985. Olympic Games, Seoul (1988) (2nd issue). Multicoloured.
1673 70 w. + 30 w. Type **951** . . 45 30
1674 70 w. + 30 w. Hurdling . . 45 30

1985. Visit of President Hussain Muhammed Ershad of Bangladesh.
1676 **952** 70 w. multicoloured . . . 40 10

953 National Flags

1985. Visit of President Joao Bernardo Vieira of Guinea-Bissau.
1678 **953** 70 w. multicoloured . . . 40 10

954 "Spring Day on the Farm" (Huh Paik Ryun)

955 "The Exorcist" (Kim Chung Hyun)

1985. Modern Art (2nd issue).
1680 **954** 70 w. multicoloured . . 40 10
1681 **955** 70 w. multicoloured . . 40 10

956 Heavenly Lake, Paekdu and National Flower

1985. 40th Anniv of Liberation.
1682 **956** 70 w. multicoloured . . 40 10

957 Wrestling

958 Janggi

1985. Folk Customs (3rd series).
1683 **957** 70 w. multicoloured . . 40 10
1684 **958** 70 w. multicoloured . . 40 10

959 "The Spring of My Home" (Lee Won Su and Hong Nan Pa)

960 "A Leaf Boat" (Park Hong Keun and Yun Yong Ha)

1985. Korean Music (1st series).
1685 **959** 70 w. multicoloured . . 45 10
1686 **960** 70 w. multicoloured . . 45 10
See also Nos. 1728/9, 1776/7, 1854/5, 1862/3, 1893/4, 1935/6, 1996/7 and 2064/5.

1985. Olympic Games, Seoul (1988) (3rd issue). As T **951**. Multicoloured.
1687 70 w. + 30 w. Basketball . 45 20
1688 70 w. + 30 w. Boxing . . . 45 20

961 Satellite, "100" and Dish Aerial

962 Meetings Emblem

1985. Centenary of First Korean Telegraph Service.
1690 **961** 70 w. multicoloured . . 40 10

1985. World Bank and International Monetary Fund Meetings, Seoul.
1691 **962** 70 w. multicoloured . . 40 10

963 U.N. Emblem and Doves

964 Red Cross and Hands (detail "Creation of Adam", Michelangelo)

1985. 40th Anniv of U.N.O.
1692 **963** 70 w. multicoloured . . . 40 10

1985. 80th Anniv of Korea Red Cross.
1693 **964** 70 w. black, red and blue 45 10

1985. Olympic Games, Seoul (1988) (4th issue). As T **951**. Multicoloured.
1694 70 w. + 30 w. Cycling . . . 40 20
1695 70 w. + 30 w. Canoeing . . 40 20

965 Cancelled Stamp on Envelope

966 Tiger (bas-relief, Kim Yu Shin's tomb)

1985. Philatelic Week.
1697 **965** 70 w. multicoloured . . . 40 10

1985. Lunar New Year ("Year of the Tiger").
1698 **966** 70 w. multicoloured . . . 40 10

967 Mount Fuji and Boeing 747 Jetliner

1985. 20th Anniv of Korea-Japan Treaty on Basic Relations.
1699 **967** 70 w. mult (postage) . . . 45 10
1700 370 w. multicoloured (air) 1·50 50

968 Doves and Globe

970 Pres. Chun, Big Ben and Korean and British Flags

1986. International Peace Year.
1701 **968** 70 w. multicoloured . . . 35 10
1702 400 w. multicoloured . . 1·75 40

1986. Olympic Games, Seoul (1988) (5th series). As T **951**. Multicoloured.
1703 70 w. + 30 w. Show jumping (postage) 40 20
1704 70 w. + 30 w. Fencing . . . 40 20
1705 70 w. + 30 w. Football . . . 40 20
1706 70 w. + 30 w. Gymnastics . . 40 20
1707 370 w. + 100 w. As No. 1703 (air) . . . . 1·60 70
1708 400 w. + 100 w. As No. 1704 1·75 70
1709 440 w. + 100 w. As No. 1705 1·90 70
1710 470 w. + 100 w. As No. 1706 2·00 70

1986. Presidential Visit to Europe. Multicoloured.
1711 70 w. Type **970** 40 10
1712 70 w. Pres. Chun, Eiffel Tower and Korean and French flags 40 10
1713 70 w. Pres. Chun, Belgian Parliament and Korean and Belgian flags 40 10
1714 70 w. Pres. Chun, Cologne Cathedral and Korean and West German flags 40 10

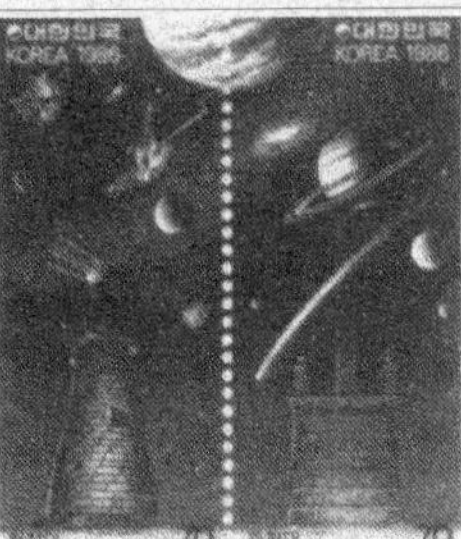

974 Kyongju Observatory

975 Kwanchon Observatory

1986. Science (1st series). Appearance of Halley's Comet.
1716 **974** 70 w. multicoloured . . 30 10
1717 **975** 70 w. multicoloured . . 30 10
See also Nos. 1781/2, 1833/4, 1864/5 and 1898/9.

976 General Assembly Emblem

977 Swallowtail and Flowers

1986. 5th Association of National Olympic Committees General Assembly, Seoul.
1718 **976** 70 w. multicoloured . . 45 10

1986. "Ameripex '86" International Stamp Exhibition, Chicago. Multicoloured.
1719 70 w. Type **977** . . . . . . 2·00 75
1720 370 w. "Papilio bianor" . . 2·00 75
1721 400 w. Swallowtails . . . . 2·00 75
1722 440 w. Swallowtail and frog 2·00 75
1723 450 w. Swallowtail . . . . 2·00 75
1724 470 w. "Papilio bianor" . . 2·00 75
Nos. 1719/24 were printed together, se-tenant, forming a composite design.

983 Male and Female Symbols in Balance

1986. Centenary of Korean Women's Education.
1725 **983** 70 w. multicoloured . . 35 10

984 National Flags

1986. Visit of President Andre Kolingba of Central African Republic.
1726 **984** 70 w. multicoloured . . 35 10

985 "Half Moon" (Yun Keuk Young)

986 "Let's Go and Pick the Moon" (Yun Seok Jung and Park Tae Hyun)

1986. Korean Music (2nd series).
1728 **985** 70 w. multicoloured . . 35 10
1729 **986** 70 w. multicoloured . . 35 10

987 Eoreumchi

988 Sweetfish

989 Sardine

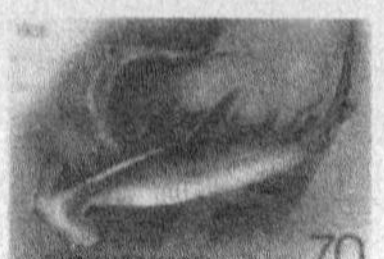

990 Hammerhead Sharks

1986. Fishes (2nd series).

1730	**987**	70 w. multicoloured . . .	50	10
1731	**988**	70 w. multicoloured . . .	50	10
1732	**989**	70 w. multicoloured . . .	50	10
1733	**990**	70 w. multicoloured . . .	50	10

991 Flag Carrier and Gong Player

996 Child

1986. Folk Customs (4th series). Farm Music. Multicoloured.

1734	70 w. Type **991**	30	10
1735	70 w. Drummer and piper . .	30	10
1736	70 w. Drummer and gong player	30	10
1737	70 w. Men with ribbons . . .	30	10
1738	70 w. Man and woman with child	30	10

Nos. 1734/8 were printed together, se-tenant, forming a composite design.

1986. Family Planning.

1739	**996**	80 w. multicoloured . . .	40	10

997 Bridge and "63" Building

1986. Completion of Han River Development. Multicoloured.

1740	30 w. Type **997**	40	10
1741	60 w. Buildings and excursion boat	40	10
1742	80 w. Rowing boat and Seoul Tower	40	10

Nos. 1740/2 were printed together, se-tenant, forming a composite design.

1000 Emblem

1004 Boy fishing for Stamp

1002 "5", Delegates and Juan Antonio Samaranch (President of International Olympic Committee)

1986. 10th Asian Games, Seoul. Multicoloured.

1743	80 w. Type **1000**	40	10
1744	80 w. Firework display . . .	40	10

1986. 5th Anniv of Choice of Seoul as 1988 Olympic Games Host City.

1746	**1002**	80 w. multicoloured . .	45	10

1986. Olympic Games, Seoul (1988) (6th issue). As T **951**. Multicoloured.

1747	80 w. + 50 w. Weightlifting (postage)	1·25	60
1748	80 w. + 50 w. Handball . . .	1·25	60
1749	370 w. + 100 w. As No. 1747 (air)	1·75	75
1750	400 w. + 100 w. As No. 1748	1·90	75

1986. Olympic Games, Seoul (1988) (7th issue). As T **951**. Multicoloured.

1752	80 w. + 50 w. Judo (postage)	1·10	60
1753	80 w. + 50 w. Hockey	1·10	60
1754	440 w. + 100 w. As No. 1752 (air)	1·75	70
1755	470 w. + 100 w. As No. 1753	1·90	70

1986. Philatelic Week.

1756	**1004**	80 w. multicoloured . .	40	10

1005 "Chunhyang-do" (Kim Un Ho)

1006 "Flowers" (Lee Sang Bum)

1007 "Portrait of a Friend" (Ku Bon Wung)

1008 "Woman in a Ski Suit" (Son Ung Seng)

1986. Modern Art (3rd series).

1757	**1005**	80 w. multicoloured . .	40	10
1758	**1006**	80 w. multicoloured . .	40	10
1759	**1007**	80 w. multicoloured . .	40	10
1760	**1008**	80 w. multicoloured . .	40	10

1009 Rabbit

1010 Eastern Broad-billed Roller

1986. Lunar New Year ("Year of the Rabbit").

1761	**1009**	80 w. multicoloured . .	35	10

1986. Birds. Multicoloured.

1762	80 w. Type **1010**	90	30
1763	80 w. Japanese waxwing . .	90	30
1764	80 w. Black-naped oriole . .	90	30
1765	80 w. Black-capped kingfisher	90	30
1766	80 w. Hoopoe	90	30

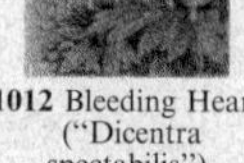

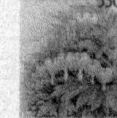

1011 Siberian Tiger

1012 Bleeding Heart ("Dicentra spectabilis")

1987. Endangered Animals. Multicoloured.

1767	80 w. Type **1011**	50	10
1768	80 w. Leopard cat	50	10
1769	80 w. Red fox	50	10
1770	80 w. Wild boar	50	10

1987. Flowers. Multicoloured.

1771	550 w. Type **1012**	1·50	25
1772	550 w. Diamond bluebell ("Hanabusaya asiatica") . .	1·50	25
1773	550 w. "Erythronium japonicum"	1·50	25
1774	550 w. Pinks ("Dianthus chinensis")	1·50	25
1775	550 w. "Chrysanthemum zawadskii"	1·50	25

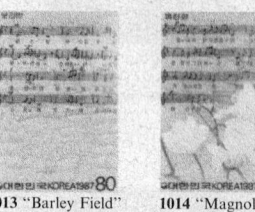

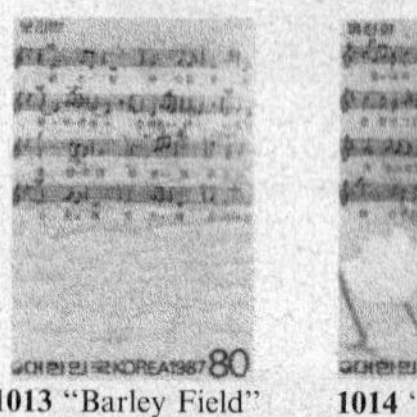

1013 "Barley Field" (Park Wha Mok and Yun Yong Ha)

1014 "Magnolia" (Cho Young Shik and Kim Dong Jin)

1987. Korean Music (3rd series).

1776	**1013**	80 w. multicoloured . .	40	10
1777	**1014**	80 w. multicoloured . .	40	10

1015 National Flags and Korean National Flower

1987. Visit of President Ahmed Abdallah Abderemane of Comoros.

1778	**1015**	80 w. multicoloured . .	35	10

1016 "100", Light Bulb and Hyang Woen Jeong

1987. Centenary of Electric Light in Korea.

1780	**1016**	80 w. multicoloured . .	35	10

1017 Punggi Wind Observatory

1019 Globes, Crane and Ship

1987. Science (2nd series).

1781	**1017**	80 w. dp brown & brown	40	10
1782	–	80 w. brown & dp brown	40	10

DESIGN: No. 1782, Rain gauge.

1987. 15th International Association of Ports and Harbours General Session, Seoul.

1783	**1019**	80 w. multicoloured . .	40	10

1987. Olympic Games, Seoul (1988) (8th issue). As T **951**. Multicoloured.

1784	80 w. + 50 w. Wrestling . .	80	25
1785	80 w. + 50 w. Tennis	80	25
1786	80 w. + 50 w. Diving	80	25
1787	80 w. + 50 w. Show jumping	80	25

1020 Flags and Doves

1987. Visit of President U San Yu of Burma.

1789	**1020**	80 w. multicoloured . .	40	10

1021 "Valley of Peach Blossoms" (Pyen Kwan Sik)

1022 "Rural Landscape" (Lee Yong Wu)

1023 "Man" (Lee Ma Dong)

1024 "Woman with Water Jar on Head", (sculpture Yun Hyo Chung)

1987. Modern Art (4th series).

1791	**1021**	80 w. multicoloured . .	35	10
1792	**1022**	80 w. multicoloured . .	35	10
1793	**1023**	80 w. multicoloured . .	35	10
1794	**1024**	80 w. multicoloured . .	35	10

1025 Map and Digital Key Pad

1987. Completion of Automatic Telephone Network (1795) and Communications for Information Year (1796).

1795	80 w. Type **1025**	35	10
1796	80 w. Emblem	35	10

1027 Pilchards

1028 Eel

1029 Barbel

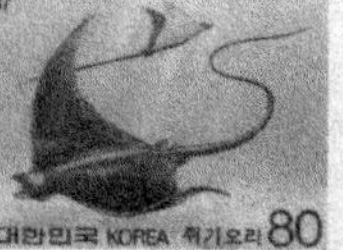

1030 Ray

1987. Fishes (3rd series).
1797 **1027** 80 w. multicoloured . . 50 15
1798 **1028** 80 w. multicoloured . . 50 15
1799 **1029** 80 w. multicoloured . . 50 15
1800 **1030** 80 w. multicoloured . . 50 15

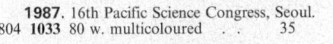

1031 Statue of Indomitable Koreans (detail) and Flags

1033 Map and Pen within Profile

1987. Opening of Independence Hall. Mult.
1801 80 w. Type **1031** 35 10
1802 80 w. Monument of the Nation and aerial view of Hall . . 35 10

1987. 16th Pacific Science Congress, Seoul.
1804 **1033** 80 w. multicoloured . . 35 10

1034 Flags and Seoul South Gate

1987. Visit of President Virgilio Barco of Colombia.
1806 **1034** 80 w. multicoloured . . 40 10

1035/1038 Festivities ($\frac{1}{2}$-size illustration)

1987. Folk Customs (5th series). Harvest Moon Day.
1808 **1035** 80 w. multicoloured . . 35 10
1809 **1036** 80 w. multicoloured . . 35 10
1810 **1037** 80 w. multicoloured . . 35 10
1811 **1038** 80 w. multicoloured . . 35 10
Nos. 1808/11 were issued together, se-tenant, forming a composite design.

1039 Telephone Dials forming Number

1040 Service Flags and Servicemen

1987. Installation of over 10,000,000 Telephone Lines.
1812 **1039** 80 w. multicoloured . . 40 10

1987. Armed Forces Day.
1813 **1040** 80 w. multicoloured . . 40 10

1987. Olympic Games, Seoul (1988) (9th issue). As T **951**. Multicoloured.
1814 80 w. + 50 w. Table tennis 70 20
1815 80 w. + 50 w. Shooting . . . 70 20
1816 80 w. + 50 w. Archery . . . 70 20
1817 80 w. + 50 w. Volleyball . . 70 20

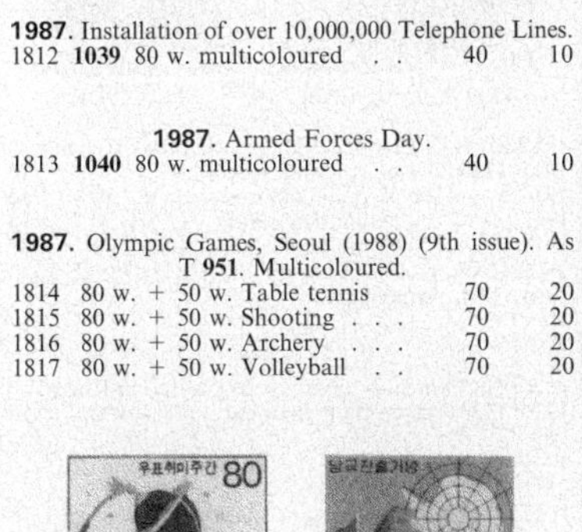

1041 Stamps around Child playing Trumpet

1042 Korean Scientist and Map

1987. Philatelic Week.
1819 **1041** 80 w. multicoloured . . 35 10

1987. 1st Anniv of South Korea's Signing of Antarctic Treaty.
1820 **1042** 80 w. multicoloured . . 1·25 30

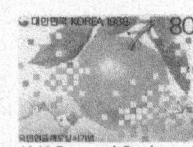

1043 Dragon

1044 Scattered Sections of Apple

1987. Lunar New Year ("Year of the Dragon").
1821 **1043** 80 w. multicoloured . . 35 10

1988. Compulsory Pension Programme.
1822 **1044** 80 w. multicoloured . . 30 10

1045 Base and Gentoo Penguins

1046 Flag, Olympic Stadium and President Roh Tae Woo

1988. Completion of Antarctic Base.
1823 **1045** 80 w. multicoloured . . 90 30

1988. Presidential Inauguration.
1824 **1046** 80 w. multicoloured . . 30 10

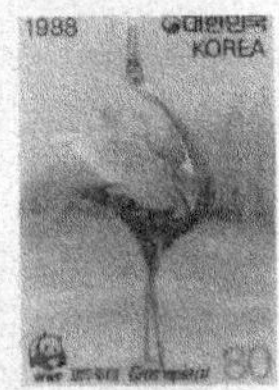

1047 Yachting

1049 Crane

1988. Olympic Games, Seoul (1988) (10th issue). Multicoloured.
1826 80 w. + 20 w. Type **1047** . 35 20
1827 80 w. + 20 w. Taekwondo . 35 20

1988. Japanese White-necked Crane. Mult.
1829 80 w. Type **1049** 75 45
1830 80 w. Crane taking off . . . 75 45
1831 80 w. Crane with wings spread 75 45
1832 80 w. Two cranes in flight . 75 45

1053 Water Clock

1055 Torch Carrier

1988. Science (3rd series). Multicoloured.
1833 80 w. Type **1053** 30 10
1834 80 w. Sundial 30 10
Nos. 1833/4 were issued together, se-tenant, forming a composite design.

1988. Olympic Games, Seoul (1988) (11th issue). Multicoloured.
1835 80 w. + 20 w. Type **1055** . 35 20
1836 80 w. + 20 w. Stadium . . 35 20

1057 Globe and Red Cross as Candle

1058 Computer Terminal

1988. 125th Anniv of International Red Cross.
1838 **1057** 80 w. multicoloured . . 30 10

1988. 1st Anniv of National Use of Telepress.
1839 **1058** 80 w. multicoloured . . 30 10

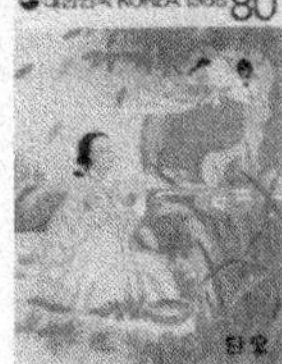

1059 Woman sitting by Pool and Woman on Swing

1063 Olympic Flag and Pierre de Coubertin (founder of modern Games)

1988. Folk Customs (6th series). Tano Day. Multicoloured.
1840 80 w. Type **1059** 65 35
1841 80 w. Women dressing their hair 65 35
1842 80 w. Woman on swing and boy smelling flowers 65 35
1843 80 w. Boys wrestling 65 35
Nos. 1840/3 were issued together, se-tenant, forming a composite design.

1988. Olympic Games, Seoul (1988) (12th issue). Multicoloured.
1844 80 w. Type **1063** 30 10
1845 80 w. Olympic monument . . 30 10
1846 80 w. View of Seoul (vert) 30 10
1847 80 w. Women in Korean costume (vert) 30 10

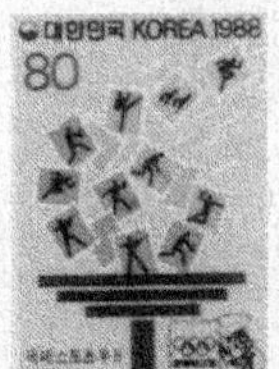

1067 Stamps forming Torch Flame

1068 Pouring Molten Metal from Crucible

1988. "Olymphilex '88" Olympic Stamps Exhibition, Seoul.
1849 **1067** 80 w. multicoloured . . 30 10

1988. 22nd International Iron and Steel Institute Conference, Seoul.
1851 **1068** 80 w. multicoloured . . 30 10

1069 Gomdoori (mascot)

1988. Paralympic Games, Seoul.
1852 80 w. Type **1069** 30 10
1853 80 w. Archery 30 10

1071 "Homesick" (Lee Eun Sang and Kim Dong Jin)

1072 "The Pioneer" (Yoon Hae Young and Cho Doo Nam)

1988. Korean Music (4th series).
1854 **1071** 80 w. multicoloured . . 35 10
1855 **1072** 80 w. multicoloured . . 35 10

1073 Girls on See-saw

1074 Dancers

1988. Lunar New Year ("Year of the Snake").
1856 **1073** 80 w. multicoloured . . 25 10

1989. Folk Customs (7th series). Mask Dance. Multicoloured.
1858 80 w. Type **1074** 25 10
1859 80 w. Dancer with fans . . . 25 10
1860 80 w. Dancer holding branch 25 10
1861 80 w. Dancer with "Lion" . . 25 10
Nos. 1858/61 were issued together, se-tenant, forming a composite design.

1079 "Arirang"

1080 "Doraji-taryong"

1989. Korean Music (5th series).
1862 **1079** 80 w. multicoloured . . 25 10
1863 **1080** 80 w. multicoloured . . 25 10

1081 Wooden Type Printing

1082 Metal Type Printing

1989. Science (4th series).
1864 **1081** 80 w. brn, bis & stone 25 10
1865 **1082** 80 w. brn, bis & stone 25 10
Nos. 1864/5 were issued together, se-tenant, forming a composite design.

1083 Teeth, Globe, Pencil and Book

1084 Hand with Stick in Heart

1989. 14th Asian–Pacific Dental Congress.
1866 **1083** 80 w. multicoloured . . 25 10

1989. Respect for the Elderly.
1867 **1084** 80 w. multicoloured . . 25 10

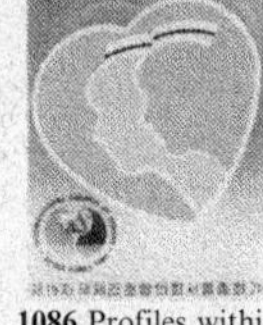

1085 Emblem

1086 Profiles within Heart

1989. Rotary Int Convention, Seoul.
1868 **1085** 80 w. multicoloured . . 25 10

1989. 19th International Council of Nurses Congress, Seoul.
1869 **1086** 80 w. multicoloured . . 25 10

1087 "Communication"

1088 "Longevity"

1989. National Information Technology Month.
1870 **1087** 80 w. multicoloured . . 25 10

1989. World Environment Day.
1871 **1088** 80 w. multicoloured . . 30 10

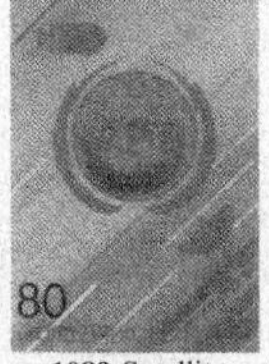

1089 Satellite, Globe and Dish Aerial

1090 "Liberty guiding the People" (detail, Eugene Delacroix)

1989. 10th Anniv of Asia–Pacific Telecommunity.
1872 **1089** 80 w. multicoloured . . 25 10

1989. Bicentenary of French Revolution.
1873 **1090** 80 w. multicoloured . . 25 10

1091 Apple and Flask

1989. 5th Asian and Oceanic Biochemists Federation Congress, Seoul.
1874 **1091** 80 w. multicoloured . . 25 10

1092 "White Ox" (Lee Joong Sub)

1093 "Street Stall" (Park Lae Hyun)

1094 "Little Girl" (Lee Bong Sang)

1095 "Autumn Scene" (Oh Ji Ho)

1989. Modern Art (5th series).
1875 **1092** 80 w. multicoloured . . 30 10
1876 **1093** 80 w. multicoloured . . 30 10
1877 **1094** 80 w. multicoloured . . 30 10
1878 **1095** 80 w. multicoloured . . 30 10

1096 Hunting Scene

1097 Goddess of Law and Ancient Law Code

1989. Seoul Olympics Commemorative Festival and World Sports Festival for Ethnic Koreans.
1879 **1096** 80 w. multicoloured . . 25 10

1989. 1st Anniv of Constitutional Court.
1880 **1097** 80 w. multicoloured . . 25 10

1098 Japanese Parrot Fish

1099 Spined Loach

1100 Torrent Catfish

1101 Pinecone Fish

1989. Fishes (4th series).
1881 **1098** 80 w. multicoloured . . 50 10
1881 **1099** 80 w. multicoloured . . 50 10
1882 **1100** 80 w. multicoloured . . 50 10
1883 **1101** 80 w. multicoloured . . 50 10

1102 Emblem

1989. 44th International Eucharistic Congress, Seoul.
1885 **1102** 80 w. multicoloured . . 25 10

1103 Control Tower and Boeing 747 Jetliner

1989. 29th International Civil Airports Association World Congress, Seoul.
1886 **1103** 80 w. multicoloured . . 35 10

1104 Scissors cutting Burning Banner

1105 Lantern

1989. Fire Precautions Month.
1887 **1104** 80 w. multicoloured . . 25 10

1989. Philatelic Week.
1888 **1105** 80 w. multicoloured . . 25 10

1106 Cranes

1107 New Year Custom

1989. Lunar New Year ("Year of the Horse").
1890 **1106** 80 w. multicoloured . . 25 10
1891 **1107** 80 w. multicoloured . . 25 10

1108 "Pakyon Fall"

1109 "Chonan Samgori"

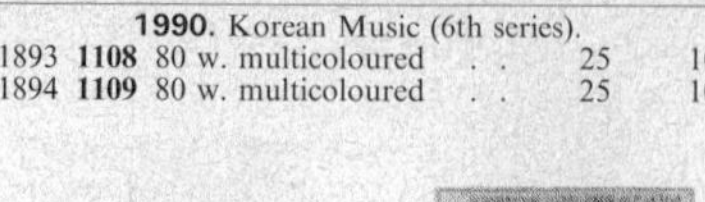
1990. Korean Music (6th series).
1893 **1108** 80 w. multicoloured . . 25 10
1894 **1109** 80 w. multicoloured . . 25 10

1110 Clouds, Umbrella and Satellite

1111 Child with Rose

1990. World Meteorological Day.
1895 **1110** 80 w. multicoloured . . 25 10

1990. 40th Anniv of U.N.I.C.E.F. Work in Korea.
1896 **1111** 80 w. multicoloured . . 25 10

1112 Cable, Fish and Route Map

1990. Completion of Cheju Island–Kohung Optical Submarine Cable.
1897 **1112** 80 w. multicoloured . . 25 10

1113 Gilt-bronze Maitreya

1114 Spear and Dagger Moulds

1990. Science (5th series). Metallurgy.
1898 **1113** 100 w. multicoloured . . 30 15
1899 **1114** 100 w. multicoloured . . 30 15
Nos. 1898/9 were issued together, se-tenant, forming the composite design illustrated.

1115 Housing and "20"

1990. 20th Anniv of Saemaul Movement (community self-help programme).
1900 **1115** 100 w. multicoloured . . 30 15

1116 Youths

1117 Butterfly Net catching Pollution

1990. Youth Month.
1901 **1116** 100 w. multicoloured . . 30 15

1990. World Environmental Day.
1902 **1117** 100 w. multicoloured . . 30 15

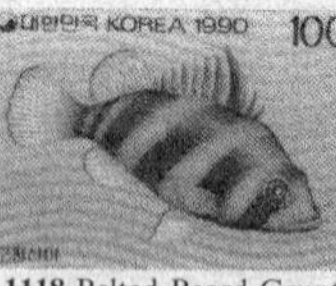
1118 Belted Beard Grunt

1119 Puffer

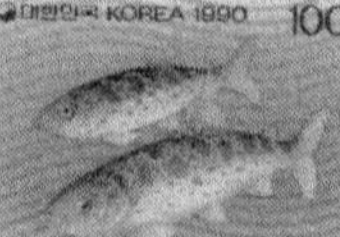
1120 Salmon Trout

1121 Butterling

1990. Fishes (5th series).
1903 **1118** 100 w. multicoloured . 50 15
1904 **1119** 100 w. multicoloured . 50 15
1905 **1120** 100 w. multicoloured . 50 15
1906 **1121** 100 w. multicoloured . 50 15

1122 Automatic Sorting Machines

1123 Bandaged Teddy Bear in Hospital Bed

1990. Opening of Seoul Mail Centre.
1907 **1122** 100 w. multicoloured . 30 15

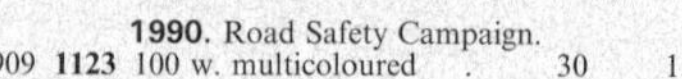
1990. Road Safety Campaign.
1909 **1123** 100 w. multicoloured . 30 15

1124 Campfire

1125 Lily

1990. 8th Korean Boy Scouts Jamboree, Kosong.
1910 **1124** 100 w. multicoloured . 30 15

1990. Wild Flowers (1st series). Multicoloured.
1911 370 w. Type **1125** . . . . . 1·25 60
1912 400 w. Asters . . . . 1·40 60
1913 440 w. Pheasant's eye . . . . 1·25 60
1914 470 w. Scabious . . . . . . 1·90 60
See also Nos. 1956/9, 1992/5, 2082/5, 2133/6, 2162/5 and 2191/4.

1129 Washing Wool

1133 Church

1990. Folk Customs (8th series). Hand Weaving.
1915 **1129** 100 w. red, yellow & blk 30 15
1916 – 100 w. multicoloured . 30 15
1917 – 100 w. multicoloured . 30 15
1918 – 100 w. multicoloured . 30 15
DESIGNS: No. 1916, Spinning; 1917, Dyeing spun yarn; 1918, Weaving.

1990. Centenary of Anglican Church in Korea.
1919 **1133** 100 w. multicoloured . 30 15

1134 Top of Tower

1135 Peas in Pod

1990. 10th Anniv of Seoul Communications Tower.
1920 **1134** 100 w. black, blue & red 30 15

1990. Census.
1921 **1135** 100 w. multicoloured . 30 15

1136 "40" and U.N. Emblem
1137 Inlaid Case with Mirror

1990. 40th Anniv of U.N. Development Programme.
1922 **1136** 100 w. multicoloured . . 30 15

1990. Philatelic Week.
1923 **1137** 100 w. multicoloured . . 30 15

1138 Children feeding Ram
1140 Mascot

1990. Lunar New Year ("Year of the Sheep"). Multicoloured.
1925 100 w. Type **1138** 30 15
1926 100 w. Crane flying above mountains 30 15

1990. "Expo '93" World's Fair, Taejon (1st issue). Multicoloured.
1928 100 w. Type **1140** 30 20
1929 440 w. Yin and Yang (exhibition emblem) . . . 1·25 60
See also Nos. 1932/3, 2000/1 and 2058/61.

1142 Books and Emblem
1143 Earth

1991. 30th Anniv of Saemaul Minlibrary.
1931 **1142** 100 w. multicoloured . . 30 15

1991. "Expo '93" World's Fair, Taejon (2nd issue). Multicoloured.
1932 100 w. Type **1143** 30 15
1933 100 w. Expo Tower 30 15

1145 "In a Flower Garden" (Uh Hyo Sun and Kwon Kil Sang)
1146 "Way to the Orchard" (Park Hwa Mok and Kim Kong Sun)

1991. Korean Music (7th series).
1935 **1145** 100 w. multicoloured . . 30 15
1936 **1146** 100 w. multicoloured . . 30 15

1147 Moth
1148 Beetle

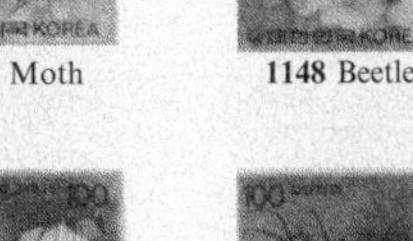

1149 Butterfly
1150 Beetle

1151 Cicada
1152 Water Beetle

1153 Hornet
1154 Ladybirds

1155 Dragonfly
1156 Grasshopper

1991. Insects.
1937 **1147** 100 w. multicoloured . 40 15
1938 **1148** 100 w. multicoloured . 40 15
1939 **1149** 100 w. multicoloured . 40 15
1940 **1150** 100 w. multicoloured . 40 15
1941 **1151** 100 w. multicoloured . 40 15
1942 **1152** 100 w. multicoloured . 40 15
1943 **1153** 100 w. multicoloured . 40 15
1944 **1154** 100 w. multicoloured . 40 15
1945 **1155** 100 w. multicoloured . 40 15
1946 **1156** 100 w. multicoloured . 40 15

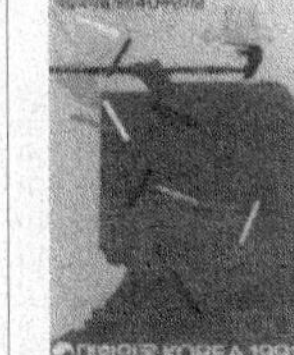

1157 Flautist and Centre
1158 Flag and Provisional Government Building

1991. 40th Anniv of Korean Traditional Performing Arts Centre.
1947 **1157** 100 w. multicoloured . 30 15

1991. 72nd Anniv of Establishment of Korean Provisional Government in Shanghai.
1948 **1158** 100 w. multicoloured . 30 15

1159 Urban Landscape and Emblem

1991. Employment for Disabled People.
1949 **1159** 100 w. multicoloured . 30 15

1160 Bouquet

1991. Teachers' Day.
1950 **1160** 100 w. multicoloured . 30 15

1161 "Microphysogobio longidorsalis"

1162 "Gnathopogon majimae"

1163 "Therapon oxyrhynchus"

1164 "Psettina ijimae"

1991. Fishes (6th series).
1951 **1161** 100 w. multicoloured . . 35 20
1952 **1162** 100 w. multicoloured . . 35 20
1953 **1163** 100 w. multicoloured . . 35 20
1954 **1164** 100 w. multicoloured . . 35 20

1165 Animals waiting to Board Bus
1166 "Aerides japonicum"

1991. "Waiting One's Turn" Campaign.
1955 **1165** 100 w. multicoloured . . 30 15

1991. Wild Flowers (2nd series). Mult.
1956 100 w. Type **1166** 35 15
1957 100 w. "Heloniopsis orientalis" 35 15
1958 370 w. "Aquilegia buergeriana" 90 40
1959 440 w. "Gentiana zollingeri" 1·25 40

1167 Scout with Semaphore Flags
1168 "Y.M.C.A."

1991. 17th World Scout Jamboree.
1960 **1167** 100 w. multicoloured . . 30 10

1991. Young Men's Christian Association World Assembly, Seoul.
1962 **1168** 100 w. multicoloured . . 25 10

1169 Rusted Train and Family Members Reunited
1170 Globe, Rainbow, Dove and U.N. Emblem

1991. "North–South Reunification".
1963 **1169** 100 w. multicoloured . . 25 10

1991. Admission of South Korea to United Nations Organization.
1964 **1170** 100 w. multicoloured . . 25 10

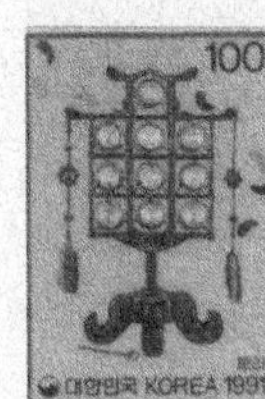
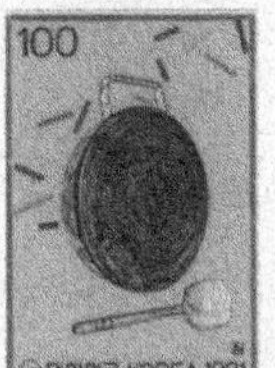

1171 Unra
1172 Jing

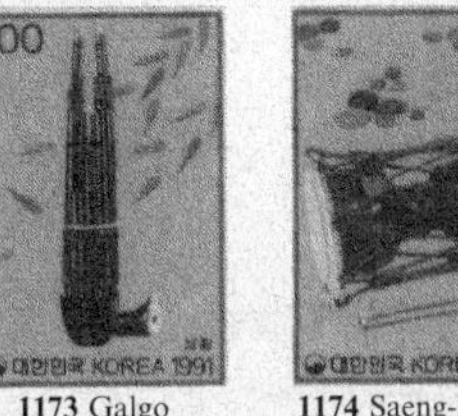

1173 Galgo
1174 Saeng-hwang

1991. Traditional Musical Instruments (1st series).
1965 **1171** 100 w. multicoloured . . 40 20
1966 **1172** 100 w. multicoloured . . 40 20
1967 **1173** 100 w. multicoloured . . 40 20
1968 **1174** 100 w. multicoloured . . 40 20
See also Nos. 1981/4.

1175 Film and Theatrical Masks
1176 Globe and Satellite

1991. Culture Month.
1969 **1175** 100 w. multicoloured . 25 10

1991. "Telecom 91" International Telecommunications Exhibition, Geneva.
1970 **1176** 100 w. multicoloured . 25 10

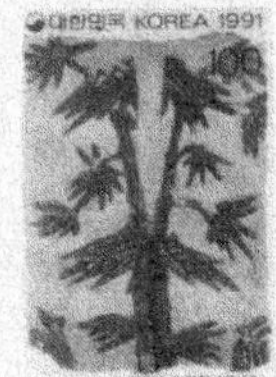

1177 Hexagonals
1178 Bamboo

1179 Geometric
1180 Tree

1991. Korean Beauty (1st series). Kottams (patterns on walls) from Jakyung Hall, Kyungbok Palace.
1971 **1177** 100 w. multicoloured . 55 25
1972 **1178** 100 w. multicoloured . 55 25
1973 **1179** 100 w. multicoloured . 55 25
1974 **1180** 100 w. multicoloured . 55 25
See also Nos. 2006/9, 2068/71, 2103/6 and 2157/60.

1181 Light Bulb turning off Switch
1182 "Longevity"

1991. Energy Saving Campaign.
1975 **1181** 100 w. multicoloured . 25 10

1991. Lunar New Year ("Year of the Monkey"). Multicoloured.
1976 100 w. Type **1182** 25 10
1977 100 w. Flying kites 25 10

1184 Stamps

1991. Philatelic Week.
1979 **1184** 100 w. multicoloured . 25 10

1185 Yonggo
1186 Chwago

1187 Kkwaenggwari
1188 T'ukchong

1992. Traditional Musical Instruments (2nd series).
1981 **1185** 100 w. multicoloured . 40 15
1982 **1186** 100 w. multicoloured . 40 15
1983 **1187** 100 w. multicoloured . 40 15
1984 **1188** 100 w. multicoloured . 40 15

1189 White Hibiscus **1191** Satellite

1992. "Hibiscus syriacus" (national flower). Multicoloured.
1985 100 w. Type **1189** 45 25
1986 100 w. Pink hibiscus 45 25

1992. Science Day.
1987 **1191** 100 w. multicoloured . . 25 10

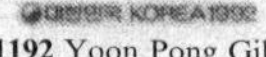

1192 Yoon Pong Gil **1193** Children and Heart

1992. 60th Death Anniv of Yoon Pong Gil (independence fighter).
1988 **1192** 100 w. multicoloured . . 25 10

1992. Child Protection.
1989 **1193** 100 w. multicoloured . . 30 10

1194 Japanese Warship attacking Korean Settlement **1195** Farmer

1992. 400th Anniv of Start of Im-Jin War.
1990 **1194** 100 w. multicoloured . . 25 10

1992. 60th International Fertilizer Industry Association Conference, Seoul.
1991 **1195** 100 w. multicoloured . . 25 10

1992. Wild Flowers (3rd series). As T **1166**. Multicoloured.
1992 100 w. "Lychnis wilfordii" . 30 10
1993 100 w. "Lycoris radiata" . . 30 10
1994 370 w. "Commelina communis" 1·00 45
1995 440 w. "Calanthe striata" . . 1·00 45

1196 "Longing for Mt. Keumkang" (Han Sang Ok and Choi Young Shurp) **1197** "The Swing" (Kim Mal Bong and Geum Su Hyeon)

1992. Korean Music (8th series).
1996 **1196** 100 w. multicoloured . . 30 10
1997 **1197** 100 w. multicoloured . . 30 10

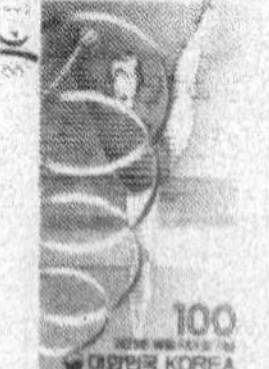

1198 Gymnastics **1199** Stylized View of Exhibition

1992. Olympic Games, Barcelona. Multicoloured.
1998 100 w. Type **1198** 30 10
1999 100 w. Pole vaulting 30 10

1992. "Expo '93" World's Fair, Taejon (3rd issue). Multicoloured.
2000 100 w. Type **1199** 25 10
2001 100 w. "Expo 93" 25 10

1201 Korea Exhibition Centre and South Gate, Seoul

1992. 21st Universal Postal Union Congress, Seoul (1st issue). Multicoloured.
2003 100 w. Type **1201** 25 10
2004 100 w. Tolharubang (stone grandfather), Cheju . . . 25 10
See also Nos. 2075/6, 2088 and 2112/15.

1203 Woven Pattern **1204** Fruit and Flower Decorations

1205 Carved Decorations **1206** Coral, Butterfly and Pine Resin Decorations

1992. Korean Beauty (2nd series). Maedeups (tassels).
2006 **1203** 100 w. multicoloured . 40 15
2007 **1204** 100 w. multicoloured . 40 15
2008 **1205** 100 w. multicoloured . 40 15
2009 **1206** 100 w. multicoloured . 40 15

1207 Lee Pong Chang **1208** Hwang Young Jo (Barcelona, 1992)

1992. 60th Death Anniv of Lee Pong Chang (independence fighter).
2010 **1207** 100 w. brown & orange 30 10

1992. Korean Winners of Olympic Marathon. Multicoloured.
2011 100 w. Type **1208** 30 15
2012 100 w. Shon Kee Chung (Berlin, 1936) 30 15

1209 Sails on Map of Americas **1210** Heads and Speech Balloon

1992. 500th Anniv of Discovery of America by Columbus.
2014 **1209** 100 w. multicoloured . 25 10

1992. Campaign for Purification of Language.
2015 **1210** 100 w. multicoloured . 30 10

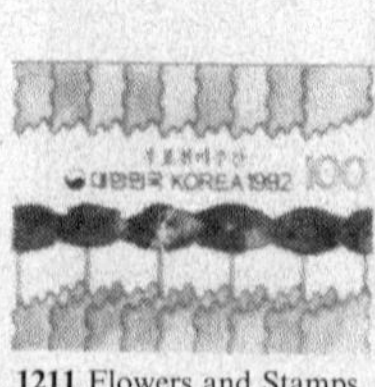

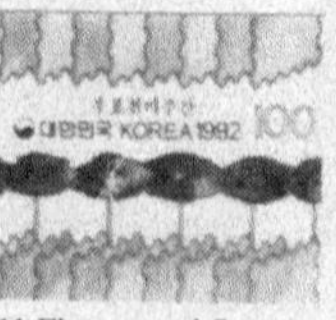

1211 Flowers and Stamps **1212** Cockerels in Snow-covered Yard

1992. Philatelic Week.
2016 **1211** 100 w. multicoloured . 25 10

1992. Lunar New Year ("Year of the Cock"). Mult.
2018 100 w. Type **1212** 25 10
2019 100 w. Flying kites 25 10

1214 Emblem, Globe and Woman holding Bowl

1992. International Nutrition Conference, Rome.
2021 **1214** 100 w. multicoloured . . 25 10

1215 View of Centre and Logo

1993. Inauguration of Seoul Arts Centre's Opera House.
2022 **1215** 110 w. multicoloured . . 30 15

1216 Pres. Kim Young Sam, Flag and Mt. Paekdu Lake **1217** National Flag

1993. Inauguration of 14th President.
2023 **1216** 110 w. multicoloured . . 40 15

1993. Multicoloured.
2025 10 w. Type **1217** 10 10
2026 20 w. White stork 10 10
2027 30 w. White magnolia . . . 10 10
2028 40 w. Korean white pine . . 10 10
2029 60 w. Squirrel 10 10
2030 70 w. Chinese lanterns (plant) 10 10
2031 90 w. Scops owl 15 10
2032 110 w. "Hibiscus syriacus" (plant) 25 10
2033 120 w. As 110 w. 15 10
2034 130 w. Narcissi 20 10
2035 150 w. Painted porcelain jar . 25 10
2036 160 w. Pine tree (horiz) . . . 30 10
2037 180 w. Little tern (horiz) . . 30 10
2038 200 w. Turtle (horiz) 30 10
2038a 210 w. As 180 w. 35 10
2039 300 w. Sky lark (horiz) . . . 45 15
2040 370 w. Drum and drum dance (horiz) 65 15
2041 400 w. Celadon cockerel water dropper (horiz) 65 15
2042 420 w. As 370 w. 65 15
2043 440 w. Haho'i mask and Ssirum wrestlers (horiz) 80 15
2044 480 w. As 440 w. 75 15
2045 500 w. Celadon pomegranate water dropper 80 15
2046 700 w. Gilt-bronze Bongnae-san incense burner (23 × 34 mm) . . . . 1·10 25
2046a 710 w. King Sejong and alphabet . . . . 1·25 25
2047 900 w. Gilt-bronze buddha triad (23 × 34 mm) . . . 1·60 30
2048 910 w. As 710 w. . . . . . 1·60 30
2049 930 w. Celadon pitcher (blue background) (23 × 31 mm) 1·50 25
2049a 930 w. As No. 2049 (brown background) . . . . 1·60 25
2050 1050 w. As 930 w. . . . . . 1·60 40

1243 Student and Computer **1244** Emblem and Map

1993. Korean Student Inventions Exhibition.
2051 **1243** 110 w. mauve and silver 25 10

1993. International Human Rights Conference, Vienna, Austria.
2052 **1244** 110 w. multicoloured . . 25 10

1245 Hand scooping Globe from Water **1246** Matsu-take Mushroom ("Tricholoma matsutake")

1993. "Water is Life".
2053 **1245** 110 w. multicoloured . . 25 10

1993. Fungi (1st series). Multicoloured.
2054 110 w. Type **1246** 30 10
2055 110 w. "Ganoderma lucidum" 30 10
2056 110 w. "Lentinula edodes" . . 30 10
2057 110 w. Oyster fungus ("Pleurotus ostreatus") . . 30 10
See also Nos. 2095/8, 2146/9 and 2207/10.

1247 Government Pavilion **1248** International Pavilion and Mascot

1249 Recycling Art Pavilion **1250** Telecom Pavilion

1993. "Expo '93" World's Fair, Taejon (4th issue).
2058 **1247** 110 w. multicoloured . 25 10
2059 **1248** 110 w. multicoloured . 25 10
2060 **1249** 110 w. multicoloured . 25 10
2061 **1250** 110 w. multicoloured . 25 10

1251 Emblems

1993. 19th Congress of International Society of Orthopaedic and Trauma Surgery.
2063 **1251** 110 w. multicoloured . 25 10

1252 "O Dol Ddo Gi" (Cheju Island folk song) **1253** "Ong He Ya" (barley threshing song)

1993. Korean Music (9th series).
2064 **1252** 110 w. multicoloured . 25 10
2065 **1253** 110 w. multicoloured . 25 10

1254 Janggu Drum Dance **1255** Emblem

1993. "Visit Korea" Year (1994) (1st issue).
2066 **1254** 110 w. multicoloured . 25 10
2067 **1255** 110 w. multicoloured . 25 10
See also Nos. 2086/7.

1256 "Twin Tigers" (military officials, 1st to 3rd rank) **1260** Campaign Emblem

1993. Korean Beauty (3rd series). Hyoongbae (embroidered insignia of the Chosun dynasty). Multicoloured.
2068 110 w. Type **1256** 25 10
2069 110 w. "Single Crane" (civil officials, 4th to 9th rank) . 25 10
2070 110 w. "Twin Cranes" (civil officials, 1st to 3rd rank) . 25 10
2071 110 w. "Dragon" (King) . . 25 10

1993. Anti-litter Campaign.
2072 **1260** 110 w. multicoloured . 25 10

HAVE YOU READ THE NOTES AT THE BEGINNING OF THIS CATALOGUE?
These often provide the answers to the enquiries we receive.

1261 "Eggplant and Oriental Long-nosed Locust" (Shin Saim Dang)
1262 "Weaving"

1993. Philatelic Week.
2073 **1261** 110 w. multicoloured . . 25 10

1993. 21st U.P.U. Congress, Seoul (2nd issue). Paintings by Kim Hong Do. Multicoloured.
2075 110 w. Type **1262** 25 10
2076 110 w. "Musicians and a Dancer" (vert) 25 10

1263 Ribbon and Globe as "30", Freighter and Ilyushin Il-86 Airliner

1993. 30th Trade Day.
2078 **1263** 110 w. multicoloured . . 25 10

1264 Sapsaree and Kite

1993. Lunar New Year ("Year of the Dog"). Multicoloured.
2079 110 w. Type **1264** 25 10
2080 110 w. Puppy with New Year's Greetings bow 25 10

1993. Wild Flowers (4th series). As T **1166**.
2082 110 w. "Weigela hortensis" . 25 10
2083 110 w. "Iris ruthenica" . . 25 10
2084 110 w. "Aceriphyllum rossii" . 25 10
2085 110 w. Marsh marigold ("Caltha palustris") 25 10

1266 Flautist on Cloud
1267 T'alch'um Mask Dance

1994. "Visit Korea" Year (2nd issue).
2086 **1266** 110 w. multicoloured . . 25 10
2087 **1267** 110 w. multicoloured . . 25 10

1268 Map'ae, Horse, Envelope and Emblem
1269 Monument

1994. 21st U.P.U. Congress, Seoul (3rd issue).
2088 **1268** 300 w. multicoloured . . 55 15
The map'ae was a token which gave authority to impress post horses.

1994. 75th Anniv of Samil (Independence) Movement.
2090 **1269** 110 w. multicoloured . . 25 10

1270 Great Purple ("Sasakia charonda")

1994. Protection of Wildlife and Plants (1st series). Multicoloured.
2091 110 w. Type **1270** (butterfly) . 25 10
2092 110 w. "Allomyrina dichotoma" (beetle) 25 10
See also Nos. 2143/4 and 2186/7.

1271 Family of Mandarins

1994. International Year of the Family.
2094 **1271** 110 w. multicoloured . 25 10

1994. Fungi (2nd series). As T **1246**. Multicoloured.
2095 110 w. Common morel ("Morchella esculenta") . 25 10
2096 110 w. "Gomphus floccosus" 25 10
2097 110 w. "Cortinarius purpurascens" 25 10
2098 110 w. "Oudemansiella platyphylla" 25 10

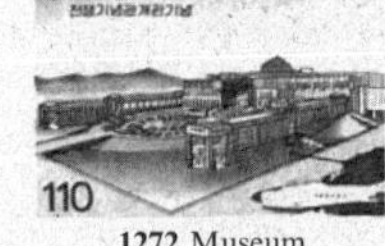

1272 Museum

1994. Inauguration of War Memorial Museum, Yongsan (Seoul).
2100 **1272** 110 w. multicoloured . 20 10

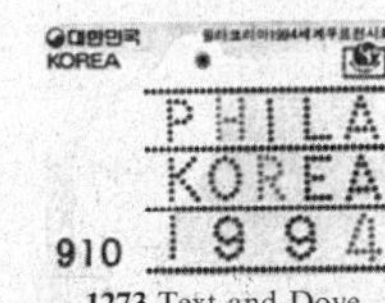

1273 Text and Dove

1994. "Philakorea 1994" International Stamp Exhibition, Seoul (1st issue).
2101 **1273** 910 w. multicoloured . 2·00 40
See also Nos. 2107/9.

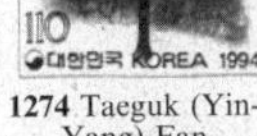

1274 Taeguk (Yin-Yang) Fan
1275 Crane Fan

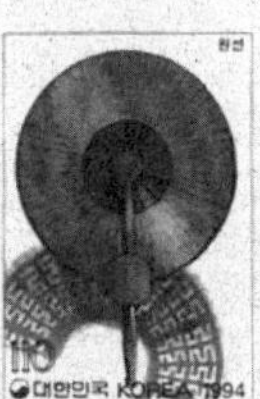

1276 Pearl Fan
1277 Wheel Fan

1994. Korean Beauty (4th series). Fans.
2103 **1274** 110 w. multicoloured . 25 10
2104 **1275** 110 w. multicoloured . 25 10
2105 **1276** 110 w. multicoloured . 25 10
2106 **1277** 110 w. multicoloured . 25 10

1278 "Wintry Days" (Kim Chong Hui)
1282 "Sword Dance" (Sin Yun Bok)

1994. "Philakorea 1994" International Stamp Exhibition, Seoul (2nd issue). Multicoloured.
2107 130 w. Type **1278** 25 10
2108 130 w. "Grape" (Choe Sok Hwan) 25 10
2109 130 w. "Riverside Scene" (Kim Duk Sin) 25 10

1994. 21st U.P.U. Congress, Seoul (4th issue). Mult.
2112 130 w. Type **1282** 25 10
2113 130 w. "Book Shelves" (detail of folk painting showing stamps) 25 10
2114 130 w. Congress emblem . . 25 10
2115 130 w. Hong Yung Sik (postal reformer) and Heinrich von Stephan (founder of U.P.U.) (horiz) 65 10

1283 Old Map
1284 Mail Van

1994. 600th Anniv of Adoption of Seoul as Capital of Korea (1st issue).
2118 **1283** 130 w. multicoloured . . 25 10
See also No. 2139.

1994. Transport. Multicoloured.
2121 300 w. Type **1284** 45 15
2122 330 w. Airplane 50 15
2123 390 w. Airplane (different) . . 65 15
2124 400 w. As 330 w. 65 15
2126 540 w. Train 85 15
2127 560 w. As 330 w. 90 15
2130 1190 w. River cruiser . . . . 1·90 25
2131 1300 w. As 330 w. . . . . . 2·00 40

1994. Wild Flowers (5th series). As T **1166**. Multicoloured.
2133 130 w. "Gentiana jamesii" . . 25 10
2134 130 w. "Geranium eriostemon var. megalanthum" 25 10
2135 130 w. "Leontopodium japonicum" 25 10
2136 130 w. "Lycoris aurea" . . . 25 10

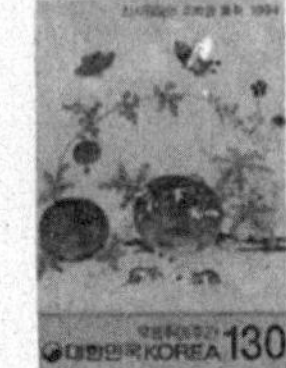

1285 "Water Melon and Field Mice" (detail of folding screen, Shin Saimdang)
1286 "600"

1994. Philatelic Week.
2137 **1285** 130 w. multicoloured . . 25 10

1994. 600th Anniv of Seoul as Capital (2nd issue).
2139 **1286** 130 w. multicoloured . . 25 10

1287 Pigs travelling in Snow

1994. Lunar New Year ("Year of the Pig"). Multicoloured.
2140 130 w. Type **1287** 25 10
2141 130 w. Family in forest . . . 25 10

1995. Protection of Wildlife and Plants (2nd series). Multicoloured.
2143 130 w. Plancy's green pond frog ("Rana plancyi") 25 10
2144 130 w. Common toad ("Bufo bufo") 25 10

1995. Fungi (3rd series). As T **1246**. Multicoloured.
2146 130 w. Shaggy ink caps ("Coprinus comatus") . . . 25 10
2147 130 w. Chicken mushroom ("Laetiporus sulphureus") . 25 10
2148 130 w. "Lentinus lepideus" . 25 10
2149 130 w. Cracked green russula ("Russula virescens") . . . 25 10

1290 Spheres around Reactor
1291 Scales of Justice

1995. Completion of Hanaro Research Reactor.
2151 **1290** 130 w. multicoloured . . 25 10

1995. Centenary of Judicial System.
2152 **1291** 130 w. multicoloured . . 25 10

MINIMUM PRICE

The minimum price quoted is 10p which represents a handling charge rather than a basis for valuing common stamps. For further notes about prices, see introductory pages.

1292 Tiger

1995. Centenary of Law Education.
2153 **1292** 130 w. multicoloured . 25 10

1293 Dooly the Little Dinosaur (Kim Soo Jeung)

1294 Kochuboo (Kim Yong Hwan)

1995. Cartoons (1st series). Multicoloured.
2154 **1293** 130 w. multicoloured . 25 10
2155 **1294** 440 w. multicoloured . 65 15
See also Nos. 2196/7.

1295 Gate of Eternal Youth, Changdokkung Palace
1296 Fish Water Gate, Chuhamru Pavilion, Changdokkung Palace

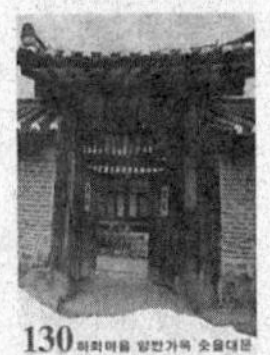

1297 Pomosa Temple Gate, Pusan City
1298 Yangban Residence Gate, Hahoe Village

1995. Korean Beauty (5th series). Gates.
2157 **1295** 130 w. multicoloured . 25 10
2158 **1296** 130 w. multicoloured . 25 10
2159 **1297** 130 w. multicoloured . 25 10
2160 **1298** 130 w. multicoloured . 25 10

1299 Lion and Emblem

1995. 78th Convention of Lions Clubs International.
2161 **1299** 130 w. multicoloured . 25 10

1995. Wild Flowers (6th series). As T **1166**. Multicoloured.
2162 130 w. "Halenia corniculata" 25 10
2163 130 w. "Erythronium japonicum" 25 10
2164 130 w. "Iris odaesanensis" . 25 10
2165 130 w. "Leontice microrrhyncha" 25 10

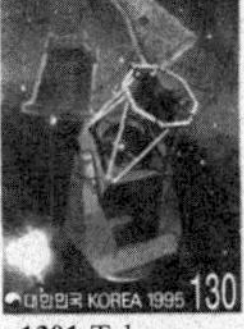

1300 National Flag
1301 Telescope

1995. 50th Anniv of Liberation. Multicoloured.
2166 130 w. Type **1300** 25 10
2167 440 w. Anniversary emblem (96 × 19 mm) 65 15

1995. Inauguration of Mt. Bohyun Optical Astronomy Observatory.
2169 **1301** 130 w. multicoloured . 25 10

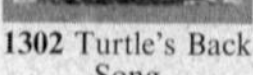

1302 Turtle's Back Song

1303 Song from "Standards of Musical Science"

1995. Literature (1st series).
2170 **1302** 130 w. multicoloured . 25 10
2171 **1303** 130 w. multicoloured . 25 10
See also Nos. 2212/13.

1304 "50 Th" incorporating Man with Wheat

1995. 50th Anniv of F.A.O.
2172 **1304** 150 w. black and violet 25 10

1305 Open Bible

1306 Families in Houses

1995. Centenary of Korean Bible Society.
2174 **1305** 150 w. multicoloured . 25 10

1995. Population and Housing Census.
2175 **1306** 150 w. multicoloured . 25 10

1307 Dove of Flags

1995. 50th Anniv of United Nations Organization.
2176 **1307** 150 w. multicoloured . 25 10

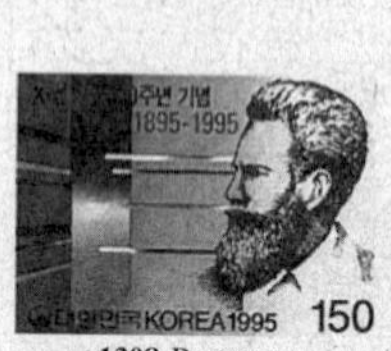

1308 Rontgen

1309 "Water Pepper and Mantis" (detail of folding screen, Shin Saim Dang)

1995. Centenary of Discovery of X-Rays by Wilhelm Rontgen.
2177 **1308** 150 w. multicoloured . 25 10

1995. Philatelic Week.
2178 **1309** 150 w. multicoloured . 25 10

1310 Rat and Snowman

1312 Miroku Bosatsu, Koryu Temple, Kyoto

1995. Lunar New Year ("Year of the Rat"). Multicoloured.
2180 150 w. Type **1310** 25 10
2181 150 w. Cranes and pine trees (horiz) 25 10

1995. 30th Anniv of Resumption of Korea–Japan Diplomatic Relations.
2183 **1312** 420 w. multicoloured . 65 15

1313 Cable Route

1314 "30" and Molecule

1996. Inauguration of Korea–China Submarine Cable.
2184 **1313** 420 w. multicoloured . 65 15

1996. 30th Anniv of Korea Institute of Science and Technology.
2185 **1314** 150 w. multicoloured . 25 10

1996. Protection of Wildlife and Plants (3rd series). As T **1270.** Multicoloured.
2186 150 w. Black pond turtle ("Geoclemys reevesii") . . 25 10
2187 150 w. Ground skink ("Scincella laterale") 25 10

1315 Satellite and Launching Pad

1996. Launch of "Mugunghwa 2" Telecommunications Satellite.
2189 **1315** 150 w. multicoloured . 25 10

1316 So Chae P'il (founder) and Leader from First Issue

1996. Centenary of "Tongnip Shinmun" (first independent newspaper).
2190 **1316** 150 w. multicoloured . 25 10

1996. Wild Flowers (7th series). As T **1166.** Multicoloured.
2191 150 w. "Cypripedium macranthum" 25 10
2192 150 w. "Trilium tschonoskii" 25 10
2193 150 w. "Viola variegata" . . 25 10
2194 150 w. "Hypericum ascyron" 25 10

1317 Anniversary Emblem and Cadets

1996. 50th Anniv of Korean Military Academy.
2195 **1317** 150 w. multicoloured . 25 10

1318 Gobau (Kim Song Hwan)

1319 Battle between Kkach'i and Caesarius (Lee Hyun Se) (from film "Armageddon")

1996. Cartoons (2nd series).
2196 **1318** 150 w. multicoloured . 25 10
2197 **1319** 150 w. multicoloured . 25 10

1320 Anniversary Emblem

1321 Globe and Congress Emblem

1996. 50th Anniv of Korean Girl Scouts.
2199 **1320** 150 w. multicoloured . 25 10

1996. 35th World Congress of International Advertising Association, Seoul.
2200 **1321** 150 w. multicoloured . 25 10

1322 Syringes and Drugs

1996. International Anti-drug Day.
2201 **1322** 150 w. multicoloured . . 25 10

1323 Skater

1324 Torch Bearer

1996. World University Students' Games, Muju and Chonju. Multicoloured.
2202 150 w. Type **1323** 25 10
2203 150 w. Games emblem (vert) . 25 10

1996. Olympic Games, Atlanta. Multicoloured.
2204 150 w. Type **1324** 25 10
2205 150 w. Games emblem . . . 25 10

1996. Fungi (4th series). As T **1246.** Multicoloured.
2207 150 w. "Amanita inaurata" . 25 10
2208 150 w. "Paxillus atrotomentosus" 25 10
2209 150 w. "Rhodophyllus crassipes" 25 10
2210 150 w. "Sarcodon imbricatum" 25 10

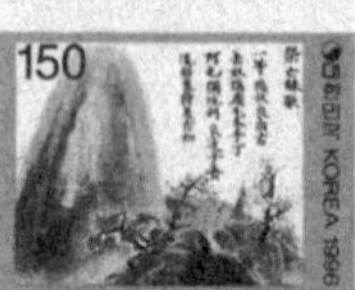

1327 Requiem for a Deceased Sister

1328 Ode to Knight Kip'a

1996. Literature (2nd series).
2212 **1327** 150 w. multicoloured . . 25 10
2213 **1328** 150 w. multicoloured . . 25 10

1329 Alphabet

1330 Castle

1996. 550th Anniv of Han-Gul (Korean alphabet created by King Sejong).
2215 **1329** 150 w. black and grey . 25 10

1996. Bicentenary of Suwon Castle.
2217 **1330** 400 w. multicoloured . . 60 15

1331 Front Gate, University Flag and Emblem

1996. 50th Anniv of Seoul National University.
2218 **1331** 150 w. multicoloured . . 25 10

C. NORTH KOREAN OCCUPATION.

(**1** "Democratic People's Republic of Korea")

1950. Nos. 116 and 118/19, optd with Type **1**.
1 10 w. green . . . . 45·00
2 20 w. brown . . . . 12·50
3 30 w. green . . . . 15·00

NORTH KOREA

100 cheun = 1 won.

GUM. All stamps of North Korea up to No. N1506 are without gum, except where otherwise stated.

A. RUSSIAN OCCUPATION

1 Hibiscus 2 Diamond Mountains

1946. Perf, roul or imperf.

N1 **1** 20 ch. red . . . . 55·00 38·00
N2 **2** 50 ch. green . . . . 17·00 15·00
N4b 50 ch. red . . . . 10·00 10·00
N5b 50 ch. violet . . . . 10·00 12·00

4 Gen. Kim Il Sung and Flag 5 Peasants

1946. 1st Anniv of Liberation from Japan.

N6 **4** 50 ch. brown £190 £190

1947. Perf, roul or imperf.

N 7 **5** 1 wn. green . . . . 5·00 4·00
N 8 1 wn. violet . . . . 15·00 10·00
N 9 1 wn. blue on buff . . . . 5·50 4·50
N10 1 wn. blue . . . . 3·25 2·50

6 7 8

1948. 2nd Anniv of Labour Law.

N11 **6** 50 ch. blue £225 £180

1948. 3rd Anniv of Liberation from Japan.

N12 **7** 50 ch. red . . . . — £325

1948. Promulgation of Constitution.

N13 **8** 50 ch. blue and red . . . . £160 40·00

B. KOREAN PEOPLE'S DEMOCRATIC REPUBLIC

9 North Korean Flag 10

1948. Establishment of People's Republic. Roul.

N16 **9** 25 ch. violet . . . . 3·50 3·50
N17 50 ch. blue . . . . 6·00 6·00

1949. Roul or perf.

N18 **10** 6 wn. red and blue . . . . 2·00 2·00

11 Kim Il Sung University, Pyongyang 12 North Korean Flags

11a Kim Il Sung University, Pyongyang

1949. Roul.

N19 **11** 1 wn. violet . . . . . . 45·00 20·00
N20 **11a** 1 wn. blue . . . . 45·00 20·00

1949. 4th Anniv of Liberation from Japan. Roul or perf.

N22 **12** 1 wn. red, green and blue 35·00 14·00

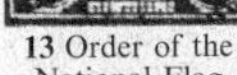

13 Order of the National Flag 14 Liberation Monument, Pyongyang

15 Soldier and Flags 16 Peasant and Worker

17 Tractor 18 Capitol, Seoul

1950. Perf, roul or imperf. Various sizes.

N24 **13** 1 wn. green (A) . . . . . 4·00 1·00
N25 1 wn. orange (A) . . . . . — 25·00
N26 1 wn. orange (B) . . . . 17·00 12·00
N27 1 wn. green (C) . . . . . 4·00 1·25
N28 1 wn. olive (D) . . . . . 7·00 4·50

SIZES: (A) $23\frac{1}{4} \times 37\frac{1}{2}$ mm. (B) $20 \times 32\frac{1}{2}$ mm. (C) $22 \times 35\frac{1}{2}$ mm. (D) $22\frac{1}{2} \times 36\frac{1}{2}$ mm.

1950. 5th Anniv of Liberation from Japan. Roul, perf or imperf. Various sizes.

N29 **14** 1 wn. red, indigo and blue 1·25 90
N30 1 wn. orange . . . . . . 7·00 5·00
N31 **15** 2 wn. black, blue red . . 1·25 90
N32 **16** 6 wn. green (A) . . . . . 1·75 1·25
N36 6 wn. red (B) . . . . . 12·50 11·00
N33 **17** 10 wn. brown (C) . . . . 2·50 2·00
N37 10 wn. brown (D) . . . . 18·00 13·50

SIZES: (A) 20×30 mm. (B) 22×33 mm. (C) 20×28 mm. (D) 22×30 mm.

1950. Capture of Seoul by North Korean Forces. Roul.

N38 **18** 1 wn. red, blue and green 40·00 32·00

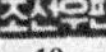

19 20 Kim Gi Ok and Aeroplane

1951. Order of Admiral Li Sun Sin. Imperf or perf.

N39 **19** 6 wn. orange . . . . . . 6·50 5·00

1951. Air Force Hero Kim Gi Ok. Imperf.

N40 **20** 1 wn. blue . . . . 8·00 3·00

21 Russian and North Korean Flags 22 Kim Ki U (hero) 23 N. Korean and Chinese Soldiers

1951. 6th Anniv of Liberation from Japan. Roul or perf.

N41 **21** 1 wn. blue . . . . 3·50 2·50
N42 1 wn. red . . . . 3·50 2·50
N43 **22** 1 wn. blue . . . . 3·50 2·50
N44 1 wn. red . . . . 3·75 2·50
N45 **23** 2 wn. blue . . . . 6·50 5·00
N46 2 wn. red . . . . 10·00 7·50

All values exist on buff and on white paper.

24 Order of Soldier's Honour 25 26 Woman Partisan, Li Su Dok

1951. Imperf or perf.

N47 **24** 40 wn. red . . . . 9·00 4·50

1951. Co-operation of Chinese People's Volunteers. Imperf or perf.

N49 **25** 10 wn. blue . . . . 5·00 3·25

1952. Partisan Heroes. Imperf or perf.

N50 **26** 70 wn. brown . . . . . . 4·00 1·00

27 28 Gen. P'eng Teh-huai 29 Munition Worker

1952. Peace Propaganda. Imperf or perf.

N51 **27** 20 wn. blue, green & red 6·00 2·00

1952. Honouring Commander of Chinese People's Volunteers. Imperf.

N52 **28** 10 wn. purple . . . . . . 8·00 4·00

1952. Labour Day. Imperf or perf.

N53 **29** 10 wn. red . . . . 17·00 17·00

30 31 32

1952. 6th Anniv of Labour Law. Imperf or perf.

N54a **30** 10 wn. blue . . . . 11·00 11·00

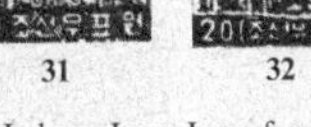

1952. Anti-U.S. Imperialism Day. Imperf or perf.

N55 **31** 10 wn. red . . . . 13·00 13·00

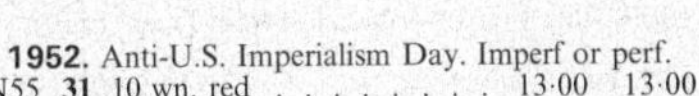

1952. North Korean and Chinese Friendship. Imperf or perf.

N56b **32** 20 wn. deep blue . . . . 9·00 9·00

33 34

1952. 7th Anniv of Liberation from Japan. Imperf or perf.

N57 **33** 10 wn. red . . . . 10·00 10·00
N58 **34** 10 wn. red . . . . 12·00 12·00

35

1952. Int Youth Day. With gum. Imperf or perf.

N59 **35** 10 wn. green . . . . 8·00 8·00

36 37

1953. 5th Anniv of People's Army. Imperf or perf.

N60 **36** 10 wn. red . . . . 12·50 12·50
N61 **37** 40 wn. purple . . . . . . 12·50 12·50

38 39

1953. Int Women's Day. With gum. Imperf or perf.

N62 **38** 10 wn. red . . . . 10·00 8·00
N63 **39** 40 wn. green . . . . 10·00 8·00

40 41

1953. Labour Day. Imperf or perf.

N64 **40** 10 wn. green . . . . . . 7·50 7·50
N65 **41** 40 wn. orange . . . . . . 7·50 7·50

42 43

1953. Anti-U.S. Imperialism Day. With gum. Imperf or perf.

N66 **42** 10 wn. turquoise . . . . 15·00 13·00
N67 **43** 40 wn. red . . . . 15·00 13·00

44 45

1953. 4th World Youth Festival, Bucharest. With gum. Imperf or perf.

N68 **44** 10 wn. blue and green . . 4·00 3·25
N69 **45** 20 wn. green and pink . . 4·00 3·25

46 47

1953. Armistice and Victory Issue. With gum. Imperf or perf.

N70a **46** 10 wn. brown & yellow 38·00 32·00

1953. 8th Anniv of Liberation from Japan. Imperf.

N71 **47** 10 wn. red . . . . £120 90·00

48 49 Liberation Monument, Pyongyang

1953. 5th Anniv of People's Republic. Imperf or perf.

N72 **48** 10 wn. blue and red . . . 11·00 11·00

1953. With gum. Imperf or perf.

N73 **49** 10 wn. slate . . . . 3·75 3·50

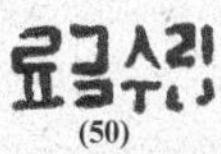

(50) (51)

1954. No. N18 optd "Fee Collected" in Korean characters, T **50**.

N74 **10** 6 wn. red and blue . . . £150 £150

1954. Nos. N18 and N39 surch with T **51**.

N75 **10** 5 wn. on 6 wn. red & blue 12·00 12·00
N76 **19** 5 wn. on 6 wn. orange . . 55·00 45·00

52 53

1954. Post-war Economic Reconstruction. With gum. Imperf or perf.
N77 **52** 10 wn. blue . . . . 15·00 9·00

1954. 6th Anniv of People's Army. With gum. Imperf or perf.
N78 **53** 10 wn. red . . . . 13·00 10·00

54 55

1954. Int Women's Day. With gum. Imperf or perf.
N79 **54** 10 wn. red . . . . 5·50 5·50

1954. Labour Day. With gum. Imperf or perf.
N80 **55** 10 wn. red . . . . 6·00 6·00

56

57 Taedong Gate, Pyongyang

1954. Anti-U.S. Imperialism Day. With gum. Imperf or perf.
N81 **56** 10 wn. red . . . . 17·00 15·00

1954. Imperf or perf.
N82 **57** 5 wn. lake . . . . 2·00 75
N83 5 wn. brown . . . . 2·00 75

58

59 Soldier

1954. National Young Activists' Conf. With gum. Imperf or perf.
N84 **58** 10 wn. red, blue and slate 3·00 3·00

1954. 9th Anniv of Liberation from Japan. With gum. Imperf or perf.
N85 **59** 10 wn. red . . . . 6·00 6·00

60 North Korean Flag

61 Hwanghae Iron Works

62 Hwanghae Iron Works and Workers

194. 6th Anniv of People's Republic. With gum. Imperf or perf.
N86 **60** 10 wn. blue and red . . . 5·00 5·00

1954. Economic Reconstruction. Imperf or perf.
N87 **61** 10 wn. blue . . . . 4·50 50
N88 **62** 10 wn. brown . . . . . . 4·50 50

63

64

1955. 7th Anniv of People's Army. With gum. Imperf or perf.
N89 **63** 10 wn. red . . . . 4·50 3·50

1955. Int. Women's Day. With gum. Imperf or perf.
N90 **64** 10 wn. deep blue . . . . . 5·00 3·50

65

66

1955. Labour Day. With gum. Imperf or perf.
N91 **65** 10 wn. green . . . . . . 3·25 3·25
N92 **66** 10 wn. red . . . . 3·25 3·25

67 Admiral Li Sun Sin

68

1955. Imperf or perf.
N93 **67** 1 wn. blue on green . . . 1·25 20
N94 2 wn. red on buff . . . . 1·75 25
N95 2 wn. red . . . . 3·00 50

1955. 9th Anniv of Labour Law. With gum. Imperf or perf.
N96 **68** 10 wn. red . . . . 3·50 2·50

69 Liberation Monument and Flags

1955. 10th Anniv of Liberation from Japan. Imperf or perf.
N97 **69** 10 wn. green . . . . . . 2·00 1·50
N98 10 wn. red, blue and brown ($29\frac{1}{2}\times42\frac{1}{2}$ mm) . . . . 1·25 1·00

70

71

1955. Soviet Union Friendship Month. Imperf or perf.
N 99 **70** 10 wn. red . . . . 1·50 1·00
N100 10 wn. red and blue . . 2·25 1·50
N101 **71** 20 wn. red and slate . . 3·25 2·50
N102 20 wn. red and blue . . 1·50 1·25
SIZES: No. N99, $22\times32\frac{1}{2}$ mm; N100, $29\frac{1}{2}\times43$ mm; N101, $18\frac{1}{2}\times32$ mm; N102, 25×43 mm.

72 Son Rock

73

1956. Haegumgang Maritime Park. Imperf or perf.
N103 **72** 10 wn. blue on blue . . . 3·00 1·75

1956. 8th Anniv of People's Army. Imperf or perf.
N104 **73** 10 wn. red on green . . . 5·50 5·50

74

1956. Labour Day. Imperf or perf.
N105 **74** 10 wn. blue . . . . 4·50 2·75

75 Machinist

76 Taedong Gate, Pyongyang

77 Woman Harvester

78 Moranbong Theatre, Pyongyang

1956. Imperf or perf.
N106 **75** 1 wn. brown . . . . . . 1·25 60
N107 **76** 2 wn. blue 90 60
N108 **77** 10 wn. red 90 60
N109 **78** 40 wn. green . . . . . . 8·00 3·50

79 Miner

80 Boy Bugler and Girl Drummer

1956. 10th Anniv of Labour Law. Imperf or perf.
N110 **79** 10 wn. brown . . . . . . 2·50 1·00

1956. 10th Anniv of Children's Union. Imperf or perf.
N111 **80** 10 wn. brown . . . . . . 4·00 2·75

81 Workers

82 Industrial Plant

1956. 10th Anniv of Sex Equality Law. Imperf or perf.
N112 **81** 10 wn. brown . . . . . . 2·00 1·40

1956. 10th Anniv of Nationalization of Industry. Imperf or perf.
N113 **82** 10 wn. brown . . . . . . 38·00 16·00

83 Liberation Tower

84 Kim Il Sung University

1956. 11th Anniv of Liberation from Japan. Imperf or perf.
N114 **83** 10 wn. red . . . . 3·00 1·25

1956. 10th Anniv of Kim Il Sung University. Imperf or perf.
N115 **84** 10 wn. brown . . . . . . 2·50 1·75

85 Boy and Girl 86 Pak Ji Won

1956. 4th Democratic Youth League Congress. Imperf or perf.
N116 **85** 10 wn. brown . . . . . . 2·50 1·50

1957. 220th Birth Anniv of Pak Ji Won "Yonam", (statesman). Imperf or perf.
N117 **86** 10 wn. blue . . . . 1·50 90

87 Tabo Pagoda, Pulguksa

88 Ulmil Pavilion, Pyongyang

89 Furnaceman

1957. Imperf, perf or roul.
N118 **87** 5 wn. blue . . . . 1·00 75
N119 **88** 40 wn. green . . . . . . 2·00 1·25

1957. Production and Economy Campaign. With or without gum. Imperf or perf.
N121 **89** 10 wn. blue . . . . 2·50 1·25

90 Furnaceman

91 Voters and Polling Booth

1957. 2nd General Election. Imperf or perf.
N122 **90** 1 wn. orange 75 30
N123 2 wn. brown 75 30
N124 **91** 10 wn. red . . . . 3·75 1·25

92 Ryongwangjong, Pyongyang

93 Lenin and Flags

94 Kim Il Sung at Pochonbo

95 Lenin

96 Pouring Steel

1957. 1530th Anniv of Pyongyang. Imperf or perf.
N125 **92** 10 wn. green . . . . . . 1·00 25

1957. 40th Anniv of Russian Revolution. Imperf or perf.
N126 **93** 10 wn. green 75 40
N127 **94** 10 wn. red 75 40
N128 **95** 10 wn. blue 75 40
N129 **96** 10 wn. orange . . . . . 2·00 40
No. N126 exists with gum.

97 Congress Emblem

98 Liberation Monument, Spassky Tower and Flags

1957. 4th World Trade Unions Federation Congress, Leipzig. Imperf (with or without gum) or perf.
N130 **97** 10 wn. blue and green . 1·25 50

1957. Russian Friendship Month. Imperf or perf.
N131 **98** 10 wn. green . . . . . . 1·75 50

99 Weighing a Baby

100 Bandaging a Hand

1957. Red Cross. Imperf, perf or roul.
N132 **99** 1 wn. red . . . . 6·00 1·00
N133 2 wn. red . . . . 6·00 1·00
N134 **100** 10 wn. red . . . . . . 15·00 2·75
No. N133 exists with or without gum.

101 Koryo Celadon Jug (12th century)

102 Koryo Incense-burner (12th century)

1958. Korean Antiquities. Imperf (with or without gum) or perf.
N135 **101** 10 wn. blue . . . . . . 4·50 75
N136 **102** 10 wn. green . . . . . 4·50 75

103 Woljong Temple Pagoda

104 Soldier

1958. With gum (5 wn.), without gum (10 wn.). Imperf or perf.
N137 **103** 5 wn. green . . . . . . 1·00 50
N138 10 wn. blue . . . . . . 1·50 75

1958. 10th Anniv of People's Army. No gum (No. N139) with or without gum (No. N140). Imperf or perf.
N139 **104** 10 wn. blue . . . . . . 1·75 50
N140 – 10 wn. red . . . . . . 4·50 65
DESIGN—HORIZ: (37½ × 26 mm.): No. N140, Soldier, flag and Hwanghae Iron Works.

106 Lisunov Li-2 Airliner over Pyongyang

1958. Air. Imperf or perf.
N141 **106** 20 wn. blue . . . . . . 5·50 1·00

107 Sputniks

108 Sputnik encircling Globe

1958. I.G.Y. Inscr "1957-1958". Imperf or perf.
N142 **107** 10 wn. slate 45 10
N143 **108** 20 wn. slate 45 10
N144 – 40 wn. slate . . . . . . 1·75 30
N145 **107** 70 wn. slate 50 20
DESIGN—HORIZ: 40 wn. Sputnik over Pyongyang Observatory.
Nos. N142/4 exist with or without gum.

109 Furnaceman

110 Hwanghae Iron Works

1958. Young Socialist Constructors' Congress, Pyongyang. Imperf or perf.
N146 **109** 10 wn. blue . . . . . . 2·75 50

1958. Opening of Hwanghae Iron Works. Imperf or perf.
N147 **110** 10 wn. blue . . . . . . 4·25 65

111 Commemorative Badge

112 Federation Emblem

1958. Farewell to Chinese People's Volunteers (1st issue). Imperf or perf.
N148 **111** 10 wn. purple and blue 1·50 40
See also No. N158.

1958. 4th International Women's Federation Democratic Congress. Imperf or perf.
N149 **112** 10 wn. blue . . . . . . 1·00 35

113 Conference Emblem

1958. 1st World Young Workers' Trade Union Federation Conference, Prague. Imperf or perf.
N150 **113** 10 wn. brown & green 1·75 35

114 Flats, East Ward, Pyongyang

115 Workers' Flats, Pyongyang

1958. Rehousing Progress. Imperf or perf.
N151 **114** 10 wn. blue . . . . . . 2·00 50
N152 **115** 10 wn. green . . . . . 2·00 50

117 Pyongyang Railway Station

119 Textile Worker

1958. 10th Anniv of Korean People's Republic. Imperf or perf.
N153 – 10 wn. green . . . . . 3·00 50
N154 **117** 10 wn. green . . . . . 9·50 1·50
N155 – 10 wn. brown and buff 1·50 50
N156 **119** 10 wn. brown . . . . . 7·50 1·75
N157 – 10 wn. brown . . . . . 6·50 1·00
DESIGNS—HORIZ: No. N153, Hungnam Fertiliser Plant; N157, Yongp'ung Dam, Pyongyang. VERT: No. N155, Arms of People's Republic.

121 Volunteer and Troop Train

122 Transplanting Rice

1958. Farewell to Chinese People's Volunteers (2nd issue). Imperf or perf.
N158 **121** 10 wn. sepia . . . . . 24·00 8·00

1958. Imperf or perf.
N159 **122** 10 wn. sepia 75 15

123 Winged Horse of Chollima

124 N. Korean and Chinese Flags

1958. National Production Executives' Meeting, Pyongyang. With or without gum. Imperf or perf.
N160 **123** 10 wn. red . . . . . . 1·60 30

1958. North Koreanen Chinese Friendship Month. With or without gum. Imperf or perf.
N161 **124** 10 wn. red, blue & green 1·25 30

125 Farm Workers

126 Gen. Ulji Mun Dok

1959. National Co-operative Farming Congress, Pyongyang. With or without gum. Imperf or perf.
N162 **125** 10 wn. blue 90 25

1959. With gum. Imperf or perf.
N163 **126** 10 wn. red and yellow . 2·00 50
See also Nos. N165/7 and N216/19.

127 Women with Banner

128 Rocket and Moon

1959. National Conference of Women Socialist Constructors, Pyongyang. With or without gum.
N164 **127** 10 ch. brown and red . . 75 30

1959. Revalued currency. Portraits as T **126**. Imperf (with or without gum) or perf (with gum).
N165 – 2 ch. blue on green . . . 60 10
N166 – 5 ch. purple on buff . . 70 10
N167 **126** 10 ch. red on cream . . 85 10
PORTRAITS: 2 ch. General Kang Gam Chan; 5 ch. General Chon Bong Jun.

1959. Launch of Soviet Moon Rocket. With or without gum. Imperf or perf.
N168 **128** 2 ch. purple on buff . . 1·00 25
N169 10 ch. blue on green . . 1·25 35

129 "Irrigation"

130 Inscribed Tree at Partisan H.Q., Chongbong

131 Kim Il Sung Statue

132 Mt. Paekdu

1959. Land Irrigation Project. Imperf or perf.
N170 **129** 10 ch. multicoloured . . 3·75 65

1959. Partisan Successes against Japanese 1937–39. With gum (No. N172) or no gum (others). Perf (N172) or imperf or perf (others).
N171 **130** 5 ch. multicoloured . . . 2·75 45
N172 **131** 10 ch. blue & turquoise 1·00 10
N173 **132** 10 ch. violet . . . . . . 2·25 40

133 "Flying Horse" Tractor

1959. "Great Perspectives" (1st issue: Development of Industrial Mechanisation). With or without gum. Perf, roul or imperf.
N174 **133** 1 ch. red, olive and green 65 10
N175 – 2 ch. multicoloured . . 3·25 75
N176 – 2 ch. red, pink and violet 60 10
N177 – 5 ch. orange, brown and ochre 60 15
N178 – 10 ch. blue, green & brn 70 15
N179 – 10 ch. grn, lt grn & brn 1·50 25
DESIGNS: No. N175, Electric shunting locomotive; N176, "Red Star 58" bulldozer; N177, "Flying Horse" excavator; N178, "SU-50" universal lathe; N179, "Victory 58" lorry.
See also Nos. N189a/200 and N275/79.

134 Armistice Building, Panmunjom

135 Protest Meeting

136 "Hoisting link between N. and S. Korea"

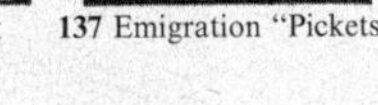
137 Emigration "Pickets"

1959. Campaign for Withdrawal of U.S. Forces from S. Korea. With gum. Perf (20 ch.) or imperf or perf (others).
N180 **134** 10 ch. blue & ultramarine 55 20
N181 **135** 20 ch. deep blue & blue 75 30
N182 **136** 70 ch. brown, cream and purple . . . . . . 12·00 6·00

1959. Campaign Against Emigration of South Koreans. With gum.
N183 **137** 20 ch. brown and sepia 3·50 1·00

138 Korean Type of "1234"

139 Books breaking Chains

140 Emblems of Peace, Labour and Letters

141 Korean Alphabet of 1443

1959. International Book Exibition, Leipzig. With gum (No. N184, N186) or no gum (others).
N184 **138** 5 ch. sepia . . . . . . 15·00 5·00
N185 **139** 5 ch. red and green . . 4·50 1·50
N186 **140** 10 ch. blue . . . . . . 4·50 1·50
N187 **141** 10 ch. violet and blue . 7·00 2·50

142 Pig Farm

143 Rotary Cement Kiln

1959. Animal Husbandry. With gum (5 ch.) or no gum (2 ch.).
N188 – 2 ch. brown, grn & buff 55 15
N189 **142** 5 ch. cream, blue & brn 75 20
DESIGN—HORIZ: 2 ch. Cow-girl with Cattle.

1959. "Great Perspectives" (2nd issue: Production Targets). With gum (Nos. N190 and N192) or no gum (others). Perf (N197/8 and N200), perf or imperf (others).
N189a **143** 1 ch. cinnamon, brn & bl 25 10
N190 – 2 ch. multicoloured . . 50 10
N191 – 5 ch. multicoloured . . 90 25
N192 – 10 ch. multicoloured . 1·10 35
N193 – 10 ch. purple, yell & bl 50 10
N194 – 10 ch. yellow, grn & red 75 10
N195 – 10 ch. multicoloured . 50 10
N196 – 10 ch. blue, light blue and green 60 10
N197 – 10 ch. multicoloured . 50 10
N198 – 10 ch. green, buff and brown 75 10
N199 – 10 ch. brown & orange 50 10
N200 – 10 ch. multicoloured . 95 15
DESIGNS–VERT: No. N190, Electric power lines and dam; N191, Loading fertilizers into truck. HORIZ: No. N192, Factory, electric power lines and dam; N193, Harvesting; N194, Sugar-beet, factory and pieces of sugar; N195, Steel furnace; N196, Trawlers; N197, Pig-iron workers; N198, Coal miners; N199, Girl picking apples; N200, Textile worker.

144 Sika Deer

145 Congress Emblem

1959. Game Preservation. No gum (5 ch.), with gum (10 ch.).
N201 – 5 ch. multicoloured . . 1·50 20
N202 – 5 ch. yellow, brown & bl 1·50 10
N203 – 5 ch. sepia, green & brn 1·50 10
N204 – 5 ch. brown, black & blue 1·50 10
N205 **144** 10 ch. multicoloured . 1·50 25
N206 – 10 ch. red, brown and green on cream . . . 4·50 65
DESIGNS—HORIZ: No. N201, Chinese water deer; N202, Siberian weasel; N203, Steppe polecat; N204, European otter; N206, Ring-necked pheasant.

1960. 3rd Korean Trade Unions Federation Congress. With gum.
N207 **145** 5 ch. multicoloured . . 45 20

146 "Chungnyon-ho" (freighter)

1959. Transport. With gum.

N208 – 5 ch. purple . . . . . . 6·75 75
N209 **146** 10 ch. green . . . . . . 2·25 60
DESIGN: 5 ch. Electric train.

147 Soldier, Tractor and Plough

148 Knife Dance

1960. 12th Anniv of Korean People's Army. With gum.

N210 **147** 5 ch. violet and blue . . 35·00 28·00

1960. Korean National Dances. Multicoloured.

N211 5 ch. Type **148** . . . . . . 3·00 20
N212 5 ch. Drum dance . . . . . 3·00 20
N213 10 ch. Farmers' dance . . . 3·00 25

149 Women of Three Races

150 Kim Jong Ho (geographer)

1960. 50th Anniv of Int Women's Day. With gum.

N214 **149** 5 ch. mauve and blue . 90 15
N215 – 10 ch. green and orange 90 25
DESIGN—VERT: 10 ch. Woman operating lathe.

1960. Korean Celebrities. With gum.

N216 **150** 1 ch. grey and green . . 75 10
N217 – 2 ch. blue and yellow . . 90 10
N218 – 5 ch. blue and yellow . . 3·00 20
N219 – 10 ch. brown and ochre 85 10
PORTRAITS: 2 ch. Kim Hong Do (painter); 5 ch. Pak Yon (musician); 10 ch. Chong Da San (scholar).

151 Grapes

152 Lenin

1960. Wild Fruits. Fruits in natural colours. With or without gum (N221/2), with gum (others).

N220 5 ch. olive and turquoise . . 80 15
N221 5 ch. drab and blue 80 15
N222 5 ch. olive and blue 80 15
N223 10 ch. olive and orange . . 1·10 20
N224 10 ch. green and pink . . . 1·10 20
FRUITS: No. N220, T **151**; N221, Fruit of "Actinidia arguta planch"; N222, Pine-cone; N223, Hawthorn berries; N224, Horse-chestnut.

1960. 90th Birth Anniv of Lenin. With gum.

N225 **152** 10 ch. purple 55 15

153 Koreans and American Soldier (caricature)

154 Arch of Triumph Square, Pyongyang

1960. Campaign Day for Withdrawal of U.S. Forces from South Korea. With gum.

N226 **153** 10 ch. blue . . . . . . 3·25 40

1960. Views of Pyongyang.

N227 **154** 10 ch. green 60 10
N228 – 20 ch. slate 90 20
N229 – 40 ch. green . . . . . . 2·00 35
N230 – 70 ch. green . . . . . . 2·75 45
N231 – 1 wn. blue . . . . . . 4·00 70
VIEWS OF PYONGYANG: 20 ch. River Taedong promenade; 40 ch. Youth Street; 70 ch. People's Army Street; 1 wn. Sungri Street.

155 Russian Flag on Moon (14.9.59)

156 "Mirror Rock"

1960. Russian Cosmic Rocket Flights. With gum (5 ch.) or no gum (10 ch.).

N232 – 5 ch. turquoise . . . . 1·75 1·10
N233 **155** 10 ch. multicoloured . 1·75 75
DESIGN: 5 ch. "Lunik 3" approaching Moon (4.10.59).

1960. Diamond Mountains Scenery (1st issue). Multicoloured.

N234 5 ch. Type **156** . . . . . . 1·00 10
N235 5 ch. Devil-faced Rock . . 1·00 10
N236 10 ch. Dancing Dragon Bridge (horiz) . . . . 3·00 25
N237 10 ch. Nine Dragon Falls . 3·50 25
N238 10 ch. Mt. Diamond on the Sea (horiz) 90 10
See also Nos. N569/72, N599/601 and N1180/4.

157 Lily

158 Guerrillas in the Snow

1960. Flowers. Multicoloured. With gum (N242), with or without gum (others).

N239 5 ch. Type **157** 75 15
N240 5 ch. Rhododendron . . . 75 15
N241 10 ch. Hibiscus . . . . . . 1·25 20
N242 10 ch. Blue campanula . . 1·25 20
N243 10 ch. Mauve campanula . 1·25 20

1960. Revolutionary Leadership of Kim Il Sung.

N244 **158** 5 ch. red 45 10
N245 – 10 ch. blue 70 10
N246 – 10 ch. red 70 10
N247 – 10 ch. blue 70 10
N248 – 10 ch. red 70 10
DESIGNS: No. N245, Kim Il Sung talks to guerrillas; N246, Kim Il Sung at Pochonbo; N247, Kim Il Sung on bank of Amnok River; N248, Kim Il Sung returns to Pyongyang.

159 Korean and Soviet Flags

160 "North Korean–Soviet Friendship"

1960. 15th Anniv of Liberation from Japan.

N249 **159** 10 ch. red, blue & brown 60 15

1960. North Korean–Soviet Friendship Month.

N250 **160** 10 ch. lake on cream . 35 15

161 Okryu Bridge, Pyongyang

1960. Pyongyang Buildings.

N251 **161** 10 ch. blue . . . . . . 2·00 20
N252 – 10 ch. violet . . . . . 1·25 15
N253 – 10 ch. green 50 10
DESIGNS: No. N252, Grand Theatre, Pyongyang; N253, Okryu Restaurant.

162 Tokro River Dam

1960. Inauguration of Tokro River Hydro-electric Power Station. With gum.

N254 **162** 5 ch. blue 70 10

163

164 Quayside Welcome

1960. 15th Anniv of World Federation of Trade Unions.

N255 **163** 10 ch. light blue, ultram and blue 25 10

1960. Repatriation of Korean Nationals from Japan.

N256 **164** 10 ch. purple . . . . . 2·50 35

165 Lenin and Workers

166 Football

1960. Korea–Soviet Friendship. With gum.

N257 **165** 10 ch. brown and flesh 35 15

1960. Liberation Day Sports Meeting, Pyongyang. Multicoloured.

N258 5 ch. Running (vert) 60 10
N259 5 ch. Weightlifting (vert) . . 60 10
N260 5 ch. Cycling (vert) . . . . 2·25 15
N261 5 ch. Gymnastics (vert) . . . 60 10
N262 5 ch. Type **166** . . . . . . 1·10 15
N263 10 ch. Swimming 60 10
N264 10 ch. Moranbong Stadium, Pyongyang 60 10

167 Friendship Monument, Pyongyang

168 Federation Emblem

1960. 10th Anniv of Entry of Chinese Volunteers into Korean War. With gum.

N265 – 5 ch. mauve 30 10
N266 **167** 10 ch. blue 30 10
DESIGN—HORIZ: 5 ch. Chinese and Korean soldiers celebrating.

1960. 15th Anniv of World Democratic Youth Federation.

N267 **168** 10 ch. multicoloured . . 30 10

169 White-backed Woodpecker

170 Korean Wrestling

1960. Birds.

N268 **169** 2 ch. multicoloured . . 3·25 10
N268a – 5 ch. multicoloured . . 3·75 25
N269 – 5 ch. brown, yell & bl 6·00 60
N270 – 10 ch. yellow, brn & grn 3·75 45
DESIGNS—HORIZ: 5 ch. (N268a), Mandarins; 10 ch. Black-naped oriole. VERT: 5 ch. (N269), Scops owl.

1960. Sports and Games. Multicoloured.

N271 5 ch. Type **170** 45 10
N272 5 ch. Riding on swing (vert) 45 10
N273 5 ch. Archery . . . . 2·00 30
N274 10 ch. Jumping on see-saw (vert) 45 10

171 Cogwheel and Corn ("Mechanization of Rural Economy")

172 Cultivated Ginseng

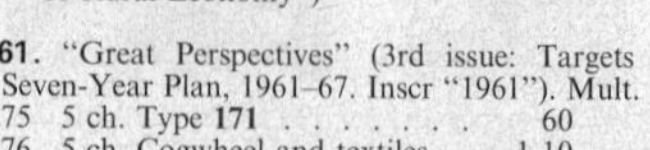

1961. "Great Perspectives" (3rd issue: Targets of Seven-Year Plan, 1961–67. Inscr "1961"). Mult.

N275 5 ch. Type **171** 60 10
N276 5 ch. Cogwheel and textiles 1·10 10

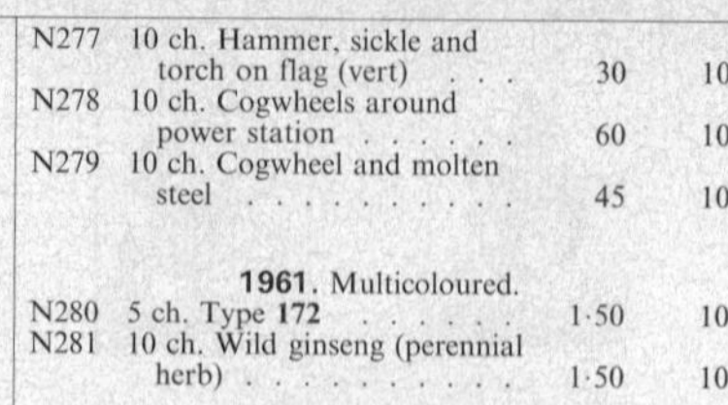

N277 10 ch. Hammer, sickle and torch on flag (vert) . . . 30 10
N278 10 ch. Cogwheels around power station 60 10
N279 10 ch. Cogwheel and molten steel 45 10

1961. Multicoloured.

N280 5 ch. Type **172** . . . . . . 1·50 10
N281 10 ch. Wild ginseng (perennial herb) . . . . 1·50 10

173 Aldehyde Shop

1961. Construction of Vinalon Factory. With gum.

N282 **173** 5 ch. red and yellow . . 60 10
N283 – 10 ch. green and yellow 1·10 10
N284 – 10 ch. blue and yellow 1·10 10
N285 – 20 ch. purple and yellow 1·25 15
DESIGNS: No. N283, Glacial acetic acid shop; N284, Polymerization and saponification shop; N285, Spinning shop.
See also Nos. N338/41.

174 Construction Work

175 Museum Building

1961. Construction of Children's Palace, Pyongyang. With gum.

N286 **174** 2 ch. red on yellow . . 35 15

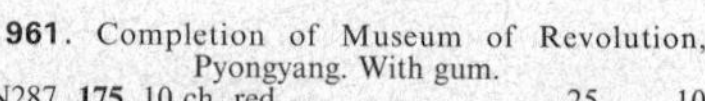

1961. Completion of Museum of Revolution, Pyongyang. With gum.

N287 **175** 10 ch. red 25 10

176 Cosmic Rocket

177 Wheat Harvester

1961. Launching of Soviet Venus Rocket.

N288 **176** 10 ch. red, yellow & blue 60 15

1961. Agricultural Mechanisation. With gum.

N289 – 5 ch. violet 50 10
N290 – 5 ch. green 50 10
N291 **177** 5 ch. green 50 10
N292 – 10 ch. blue 60 10
N293 – 10 ch. purple 60 10
DESIGNS: No. N289, Tractor-plough; N290, Disc-harrow; N292, Maize-harvester; N293, Tractors.

178

179 Agriculture

1961. Opening of Training Institute.

N294 **178** 10 ch. brown on buff . 25 10

1961. 15th Anniv of Land Reform Law. With gum.

N295 **179** 10 ch. green on yellow 45 15

180

181 Mackerel

1961. 15th Anniv of National Programme. With gum.

N296 **180** 10 ch. purple & yellow 20 10

1961. Marine Life.

N297 **181** 5 ch. multicoloured . . 90 10
N298 – 5 ch. black and blue . . 2·00 25
N299 – 10 ch. blue, black & lt bl 2·50 25
N300 – 10 ch. multicoloured . . 90 10
N301 – 10 ch. brown, yell & grn 90 10
DESIGNS: No. N298, Common dolphin; N299, Whale sp; N300, Tunny; N301, Pollack.

182 Tractor-crane **183** Tree-planting

1961. With gum.

N302 **182** 1 ch. brown 65 10
N303 – 2 ch. brown 65 10
N304 – 5 ch. green 90 10
N305 – 10 ch. violet 90 20

DESIGNS—HORIZ: 2 ch. Heavy-duty lorry; 5 ch. Eight-metres turning lathe. VERT: 10 ch. 3000-ton press.

See also Nos. N378/9c.

1961. Re-afforestation Campaign. With gum.

N306 **183** 10 ch. green . . . . . . 1·00 25

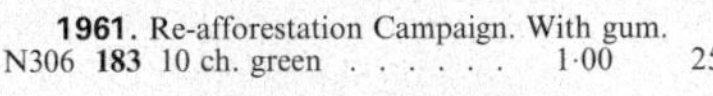

184 "Peaceful Unification" Banner

1961. Propaganda for Peaceful Reunification of Korea.

N307 **184** 10 ch. multicoloured . . 6·50 1·50

185 Pioneers visiting Battlefield

1961. 15th Anniv of Children's Union. Mult.

N308 5 ch. Pioneers bathing . . . 40 10
N309 10 ch. Pioneer bugler . . . 1·25 20
N310 10 ch. Type **185** 40 10

186 "Labour Law" **187** Apples

1961. 15th Anniv of Labour Law. With gum.

N311 **186** 10 ch. blue on yellow . . 45 20

1961. Fruit. Multicoloured.

N312 5 ch. Peaches 75 10
N313 5 ch. Plums 75 10
N314 5 ch. Type **187** 75 10
N315 10 ch. Persimmons 75 10
N316 10 ch. Pears 75 10

188 Yury Gagarin and "Vostok 1"

1961. World's First Manned Space Flight.

N317 **188** 10 ch. ultramarine & bl 35 10
N318 10 ch. violet and blue . 35 10

189 Power Station

1961. 15th Anniv of Nationalization of Industries Law. With gum.

N319 **189** 10 ch. brown . . . . . 4·50 60

190 Women at Work **191** Children planting Tree

1961. 15th Anniv of Sex Equality Law. With gum.

N320 **190** 10 ch. red 35 10

1961. Children. Multicoloured.

N321 5 ch. Type **191** 60 10
N322 5 ch. Reading book 30 10
N323 10 ch. Playing with ball . . 30 10
N324 10 ch. Building a house . . 30 10
N325 10 ch. Waving flag 30 10

192 Poultry and Stock-breeding **193** Soldiers on March (statue)

1961. Improvement in Living Standards. Mult.

N326 5 ch. Type **192** 60 10
N327 10 ch. Fabrics and textile factory . . . . 1·10 10
N328 10 ch. Trawler and fish (horiz) 1·00 20
N329 10 ch. Grain-harvesting (horiz) 50 10

1961. 25th Anniv of Fatherland Restoration Association. With gum.

N330 – 10 ch. violet 40 10
N331 – 10 ch. violet 25 10
N332 **193** 10 ch. blue and buff . . 25 10

DESIGNS—Marshal Kim Il Sung; No. N330, Seated under tree; N331, Working at desk.

194 Party Emblem and Members **195** Miner

1961. 4th Korean Workers' Party Congress, Pyongyang. With gum.

N333 **194** 10 ch. green 20 10
N334 – 10 ch. purple 20 10
N335 – 10 ch. red 20 10

DESIGNS—VERT: No. N334, "Chollima" statue, Pyongyang. HORIZ: No. N335, Marshal Kim Il Sung.

1961. Miners' Day. With gum.

N336 **195** 10 ch. brown . . . . . 1·75 60

196 Pak in Ro **197** Aldehyde Shop

1961. 400th Birth Anniv of Pak in Ro (poet).

N337 **196** 10 ch. indigo on blue . 45 15

1961. Completion of Vinalon Factory. With gum.

N338 **197** 5 ch. red and yellow . . 60 10
N339 – 10 ch. brown & yellow 90 10
N340 – 10 ch. blue and yellow 90 10
N341 – 20 ch. purple & yellow 1·40 20

DESIGNS: No. N339, Glacial-acetic shop; N340, Polymerization and saponification shop; N341, Spinning shop.

198 Korean and Chinese Flags **199** Basketball

1961. North Korean Friendship Treaties with China and the U.S.S.R.

N342 – 10 ch. multicoloured . 40 10
N343 **198** 10 ch. red, blue & yellow 40 10

DESIGN: No. N342, Korean and Soviet flags.

1961. Physical Culture Day. With gum.

N344 – 2 ch. grey 50 10
N345 – 5 ch. blue 75 10
N346 **199** 10 ch. blue 75 10
N347 – 10 ch. blue 75 10
N348 – 10 ch. purple 75 10
N349 – 20 ch. purple 50 10

DESIGNS: 2 ch. Table tennis; 5 ch. Flying model glider; 10 ch. (N347) Rowing; 10 ch. (N348) High jumping; 20 ch. Sports emblem.

(200) **201** General Rock

1961. Centenary of Publication of Map "Taidong Yu Jido" by Kim Jung Ho. No. N216 surch with T **200**.

N350 **150** 5 ch. on 1 ch. grey and green . . . . 35·00 24·00

1961. Mt. Chilbo Scenery. With gum.

N351 **201** 5 ch. blue 65 10
N352 – 5 ch. brown 65 10
N353 – 10 ch. violet . . . . . 1·25 20
N354 – 10 ch. blue . . . . . . 1·25 20
N355 – 10 ch. blue . . . . . . 1·25 20

DESIGNS—HORIZ: No. N352, Chonbul Peak; N354, Tiled House Rock; N355, Rainbow Rock. VERT: No. N353, Mansa Peak.

202 "Agriculture and Industry" **203** Winged Horse and Congress Emblem

1961. With gum.

N356 **202** 10 ch. green 35 10

1961. 5th World Federation of Trade Unions Congress, Moscow. With gum.

N357 **203** 10 ch. blue, purple & vio 25 10

204 "Red Banner" Class Electric Locomotive **205** Ice Hockey

1961. Railway Electrification. With gum.

N358 **204** 10 ch. violet and yellow . 4·00 1·60

1961. Winter Sports. With gum.

N359 – 10 ch. brown and green . 60 10
N360 – 10 ch. brown and green . 60 10
N361 **205** 10 ch. brown and blue . 60 10
N362 – 10 ch. brown and blue . 60 10

DESIGNS: No. N359, Figure skating; N360, Speed skating; N362, Skiing.

206 Grain Harvest **207** Tiger

1962. "Six Heights" of Production Targets (1st series). Inscr "1962". With gum.

N363 – 5 ch. red, violet and grey 30 10
N364 – 5 ch. brown and grey . 1·75 30
N365 **206** 10 ch. yellow, black & bl 30 10
N366 – 10 ch. red, yellow & blue 90 10
N367 – 10 ch. black and blue . 75 15
N368 – 10 ch. yellow, brn & blue 30 10

DESIGNS: No. N363, Ladle and molten steel; N364, Coal trucks; N366, Fabrics and mill; N367, Trawler and catch; N368, Construction of flats.

See also Nos. N440/5.

1962. Animals.

N369 **207** 2 ch. multicoloured . . . 1·75 15
N370 – 2 ch. brown and green 1·25 10
N371 – 5 ch. yellow and green 1·25 10
N372 – 10 ch. brown and green 1·50 15

ANIMALS—HORIZ: 2 ch. (N370), Racoon-dog; 5 ch. Chinese ferret-badger; 10 ch. Asiatic black bear.

208 Kayagum Player **209** "Leuhdorfia puziloi"

1962. Musical Instruments and Players (1st series). Multicoloured.

N373 10 ch. Type **208** . . . . . . 1·75 20
N374 10 ch. Man playing haegum (two-stringed bowed instrument) . . . . 1·75 20
N375 10 ch. Woman playing wolgum (banjo) . . . . 1·75 20
N376 10 ch. Man playing chotdae (flute) . . . . 1·75 20
N377 10 ch. Woman playing wagonghu (harp) . . . . 1·75 20

See also Nos. N473/7.

1962. As T **182**. Inscr "1962". With gum (Nos. N379 and 379b), no gum (others).

N378 5 ch. green 50 10
N379 10 ch. blue 75 15
N379a 10 ch. brown . . . . . . - 3·75
N379b 5 wn. brown . . . . . . 9·50 3·00
N379c 10 wn. purple . . . . . . 11·50 6·00

DESIGNS—VERT: 5 ch. Hydraulic press; 10 ch. (2), Three-ton hammer; 10 wn. Tunnel drill. HORIZ: 5 wn. Hobbing machine.

See also Nos. N415/22, N513/15 and 573.

1962. Butterflies. Multicoloured.

N380 5 ch. Type **209** . . . . . . 2·25 15
N381 10 ch. "Sericinus telamon" (purple background) . . . 2·25 15
N382 10 ch. Keeled apollo (lilac background) . . . . . . 2·25 15
N383 10 ch. Peacock (green background) . . . . . . 2·25 15

210 G. S. Titov and "Vostok 2"

1962. 2nd Soviet Manned Space Flight.

N384 **210** 10 ch. multicoloured . . 45 15

211 Marshal Kim Il Sung and (inset) addressing Workers

1962. Marshal Kim Il Sung's 50th Birthday. With gum.

N385 **211** 10 ch. red 45 15
N386 – 10 ch. green 45 15
N387 – 10 ch. blue 45 10

DESIGN: No. 387, Kim Il Sung in fur hat and (inset) inspecting battle-front.

212 Kim Chaek **214** Black-faced Spoonbill

213 Mother with Children

1962. Korean Revolutionaries (1st series). With gum.

N388 **212** 10 ch. sepia 35 10
N389 – 10 ch. blue 35 10
N390 – 10 ch. red 35 10
N391 – 10 ch. purple 35 10
N392 – 10 ch. green 35 10
N393 – 10 ch. blue 35 10
N394 – 10 ch. brown 35 10

PORTRAITS: No. N389, Kang Gon; N390, An Gil; N391, Ryu Gyong Su; N392/3, Kim Jong Suk; N394, Choe Chun Guk.

See also Nos. N478/82 and N733/5.

1962. National Mothers' Meeting, Pyongyang.

N395 **213** 10 ch. multicoloured . . 30 10

1962. Birds. Inscr "1962". Multicoloured.
N396 5 ch. Type **214** . . . . . . 1·25 15
N397 5 ch. Brown hawk owl . . . 4·25 15
N398 10 ch. Eastern broad-billed roller . . . . 2·40 35
N399 10 ch. Black paradise flycatcher . . . . 2·40 35
N400 20 ch. Whistling swan . . . 3·00 65

215 Victory Flame **216** Croaker

1962. 25th Anniv of Battle of Pochonbo.
N401 **215** 10 ch. multicoloured . . 55 10

1962. Fishes. Multicoloured.
N402 5 ch. Type **216** . . . . . . 1·10 10
N403 5 ch. Hairtail . . . . 1·10 10
N404 10 ch. Gizzard shad (head pointing to right) . . . . 1·40 15
N405 10 ch. Japanese sea bass (blue background) . . . . . 1·40 15
N406 10 ch. Japanese croaker (green background) . . . . . . 1·40 15

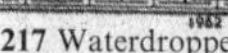

217 Waterdropper **218** Radial Drill

1962. Antiques. With gum.
N407 – 4 ch. black and blue . . 1·00 10
N408 **217** 5 ch. black and ochre . . 1·00 10
N409 A 10 ch. black and green . 1·25 10
N410 B 10 ch. black and orange 1·25 10
N411 C 10 ch. black and purple 1·25 10
N412 D 10 ch. black and brown 1·25 10
N413 E 10 ch. black and yellow 1·25 10
N414 – 40 ch. black and grey . 3·50 35

DESIGNS—VERT: 4 ch. Brush pot; 40 ch. Porcelain decanter. HORIZ: A, Inkstand; B, Brushstand; C, Turtle paperweight; D, Inkstone; E, Document case.

1962. Double frame-line. With gum.
N415 – 2 ch. green 25 10
N415a – 2 ch. brown . . . . . — 3·75
N416 – 4 ch. blue . . . . . . 1·50 10
N417 **218** 5 ch. blue 35 10
N418 – 5 ch. purple 35 10
N419 – 10 ch. purple 40 10
N420 – 40 ch. blue . . . . . . 3·50 20
N421 – 90 ch. blue . . . . . . 1·40 30
N422 – 1 wn. brown . . . . . 4·50 50

DESIGNS—VERT: 2 ch. Vertical milling machine; 5 ch. (N418), Hydraulic hammer; 1 wn. Spindle drill. HORIZ: 4 ch. "Victory April 15" motor-car; 10 ch. All-purpose excavator; 40 ch. Trolley-bus; 90 ch. Planning machine.

See also Nos. N513/15 and N573.

219 Chong Da San **220** Voter

1962. Birth Bicentenary of Chong Da San (philosopher).
N423 **219** 10 ch. purple 35 10

1962. Election of Deputies to National Assembly. Multicoloured.
N424 10 ch. Type **220** 80 10
N425 10 ch. Family going to poll 80 10

221 Pyongyang

1962. 1535th Anniv of Pyongyang. With gum.
N426 **221** 10 ch. black and blue . 65 10

222 Globe and "Vostok 3" and "4" **223** Spiraea

1962. 1st "Team" Manned Space Flight.
N427 **222** 10 ch. indigo, blue & red 60 20

1962. Korean Plants. Plants in natural colours; frame and inscr colours given.
N428 **223** 5 ch. lt green and green 1·10 10
N429 – 10 ch. green and red . . 1·10 10
N430 – 10 ch. blue and purple 1·10 10
N431 – 10 ch. green and olive . 1·10 10

PLANTS: No. N429, Ginseng; N430, Campanula; N431, "Rheumcoreanum makai (Polyonaceae)".

224 "Uibang Ryuchui" **225** Science Academy

1962. 485th Anniv of Publication of "Uibang Ryuchui" (medical encyclopaedia).
N432 **224** 10 ch. multicoloured . 3·50 30

1962. 10th Anniv of Korean Science Academy.
N433 **225** 10 ch. blue & turquoise 1·00 10

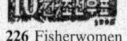

226 Fisherwomen **227** European Mink

1962.
N434 **226** 10 ch. blue 70 10

1962. Animals.
N435 **227** 4 ch. brown and green 70 10
N436 – 5 ch. blue, drab & green 70 10
N437 – 10 ch. blue and yellow 90 10
N438 – 10 ch. sepia & turquoise 90 10
N439 – 20 ch. brown and blue 1·50 15

ANIMALS—HORIZ: No. N436, Chinese hare. VERT: No. N437, Eurasian red squirrel; N438, Common goral; N439, Siberian chipmunk.

228 Harvesting

1963. "Six Heights" of Production Targets (2nd issue). Inscr "1963". Multicoloured.
N440 5 ch. Miner 70 20
N441 10 ch. Type **228** 40 10
N442 10 ch. Furnaceman 30 10
N443 10 ch. Construction worker 30 10
N444 10 ch. Textiles loom operator 65 10
N445 40 ch. Fisherman and trawler 1·75 40

229 Soldier **230** Peony

1963. 15th Anniv of Korean People's Army. With gum.
N446 – 5 ch. brown 50 10
N447 **229** 10 ch. red 60 10
N448 – 10 ch. blue 85 10

DESIGNS: 5 ch. Airman; 10 ch. Sailor.

1963. Korean Flowers. Multicoloured.
N449 5 ch. Type **230** 45 10
N450 10 ch. Rugosa rose 75 10
N451 10 ch. Azalea 75 10
N452 20 ch. Campion 75 10
N453 40 ch. Orchid . . . . . . 2·25 35

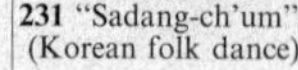

231 "Sadang-ch'um" (Korean folk dance) **232** Revolutionaries

1963. International Music and Dancing Contest, Pyongyang. Multicoloured.
N454 10 ch. Type **231** . . . . . 1·75 15
N455 10 ch. Dancer with fan . . . 1·75 15

1963. 3rd Anniv of South Korean Rising of April, 1960.
N456 **232** 10 ch. multicoloured . . 40 15

233 Karl Marx **234** Children in Chemistry Class

1963. 145th Birth Anniv of Karl Marx. With gum.
N457 **233** 10 ch. blue 30 10

1963. Child Care and Amenities. Multicoloured.
N458 2 ch. Type **234** 80 20
N459 5 ch. Children running . . . 70 15
N460 10 ch. Boy conducting choir 1·75 20
N461 10 ch. Girl chasing butterfly 3·50 25

235 Armed Koreans and American Soldier (caricature)

1963. Campaign Month for Withdrawal of U.S. Forces from South Korea.
N462 **235** 10 ch. multicoloured . . 45 10

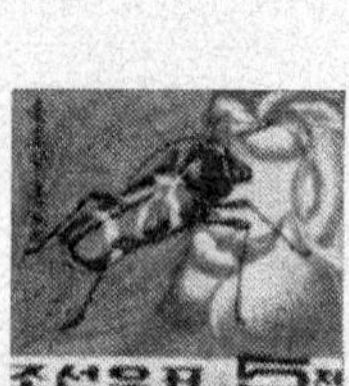

236 "Cyrtoclytus capra" **237** Soldier with Flag

1963. Korean Beetles. Multicoloured designs. Colours of beetles given.
N463 5 ch. Type **236** 65 10
N464 10 ch. multicoloured 95 10
N465 10 ch. red and blue 95 10
N466 10 ch. indigo, blue & purple 95 10

BEETLES: No. N464, "Cicindela chinensis" (tiger beetle); N465, "Purpuricenus lituratus"; N466, "Agapanthia pilicornis".

1963. 10th Anniv of Victory in Korean War.
N467 **237** 10 ch. multicoloured . . 50 10

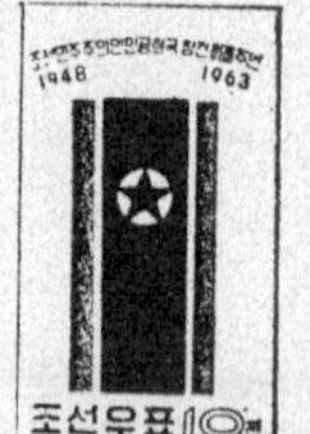

238 North Korean Flag **239** Namdae Gate, Kaesong

1963. 15th Anniv of People's Republic. Mult.
N468 10 ch. Type **238** 30 10
N469 10 ch. North Korean Badge . 30 10

1963. Ancient Korean Buildings (1st series). With gum.
N470 **239** 5 ch. black 20 10
N471 – 10 ch. blue 40 10
N472 – 10 ch. brown 40 10

BUILDINGS: No. N471, Taedong Gate, Pyongyang; N472, Potong Gate, Pyongyang.

See also Nos. N537/8.

240 Ajaeng (bowed zither) **241** Nurse with Children

1963. Musical Instruments and Players (2nd series). Multicoloured. Nos. N473 and N476 with gum.
N473 3 ch. Type **240** . . . . . . 1·25 15
N474 5 ch. Pyongyon (jade chimes) 1·25 15
N475 10 ch. Saenap (brass bowl) 1·50 15
N476 10 ch. Rogo (drums in frame) 1·50 15
N477 10 ch. Piri ("wooden pipe") 1·50 15

1963. Korean Revolutionaries (2nd issue). As T **212**. With gum.
N478 5 ch. brown 25 10
N479 5 ch. purple 25 10
N480 10 ch. rose 30 10
N481 10 ch. slate 30 10
N482 10 ch. dull purple 30 10

PORTRAITS: No. N478, Kwon Yong Byok; N479, Ma Dong Hui; N480, Li Je Sun; N481, Pak Dal; N482, Kim Yong Bom.

1963. Child Welfare. Multicoloured.
N483 10 ch. Type **241** 30 10
N484 10 ch. Children in playground 30 10

242 Hwajang Hall **243** Furnaceman

1963. Mount Myohyang Resort. Multicoloured.
N485 5 ch. Type **242** 35 10
N486 10 c. Mountain stream and chalet 75 10
N487 10 ch. Kwanum Pavilion and stone pagoda 65 10
N488 10 ch. Rope bridge across river 1·75 15

Nos. N487/8 are horiz.

1963. Seven Year Plan. With gum.
N489 **243** 5 ch. red 20 10
N490 – 10 ch. grey . . . . . 1·50 20
N491 – 10 ch. red . . . . . 1·50 20
N492 – 10 ch. lilac 85 10

DESIGNS—VERT: No. N490, Construction workers. HORIZ: No. N491, Power technicians; N492, Miners.

244 Children hoeing

1963. "Hung Bo" (fairytale). Multicoloured.
N493 5 ch. Type **244** 30 10
N494 10 ch. Tying up broken leg of swallow 90 10
N495 10 ch. Barn swallow dropping gourd seed 90 10
N496 10 ch. Sawing through giant gourd 50 10
N497 10 ch. Treasure inside gourd 50 10

245 Marksman

1963. Marksmanship. Multicoloured.
N498 5 ch. Type **245** 30 10
N499 10 ch. Marksman with small-bore rifle 55 10
N500 10 ch. Marksman with standard rifle 55 10

246 Sinuiju Chemical Fibre Factory **248** Korean Alphabet

247 Strikers

1964. Chemical Fibres Factories. With gum.

No.	Type	Description	Unused	Used
N501	246	10 ch. slate	75	10
N052	–	10 ch. purple	75	10

DESIGN: No. N502, Chongjin Chemical Fibre Factory.

1964. 35th Anniv of Wonsan General Strike. With gum.

No.	Type	Description	Unused	Used
N503	247	10 ch. brown	60	10

1964. 520th Anniv of Korean Alphabet.

No.	Type	Description	Unused	Used
N504	248	10 ch. green, buff & brn	60	20

249 Lenin

250 Whale-catcher

1964. 40th Death Anniv of Lenin. With gum.

No.	Type	Description	Unused	Used
N505	249	10 ch. red	30	10

1964. Fishing Industry. Multicoloured.

No.	Type	Description	Unused	Used
N506		5 ch. Type 250	40	10
N507		5 ch. Trawler No. 051	40	10
N508		10 ch. Trawler No. 397	85	20
N509		10 ch. Trawler No. 738	85	20

251 Insurgents

1964. 45th Anniv of Rising of 1st March. With gum.

No.	Type	Description	Unused	Used
N510	251	10 ch. purple	30	10

252 Warring Peasants

1964. 70th Anniv of Kabo Peasants' War. With gum.

No.	Type	Description	Unused	Used
N511	252	10 ch. purple	30	10

253 Students' Palace, Pyongyang

254 "Changbaek" Excavator

1964. With gum.

No.	Type	Description	Unused	Used
N512	253	10 ch. green	30	10

1964. Single frame-line. Dated "1964" or "1965" (No. N573). With gum.

No.	Type	Description	Unused	Used
N513	–	5 ch. violet	60	10
N514	254	10 ch. green	90	10
N515	–	10 ch. blue	90	10
N573	–	10 ch. violet	75	20

DESIGNS—VERT: 5 ch. 200 Metre drill; 10 ch. (N573) "Horning 500" machine. HORIZ: 10 ch. (N515) 400 h.p. Diesel engine.

255 "On the March"

1964. 5th Korean Democratic Youth League Congress, Pyongyang.

No.	Type	Description	Unused	Used
N516	255	10 ch. multicoloured	30	10

256 Electric Train

1964. Inauguration of Pyongyang–Sinuiju Electric Railway.

No.	Type	Description	Unused	Used
N517	256	10 ch. multicoloured	2·50	20

257 Rejoicing in Chongsan-ri Village

1964. Popular Movement at Chongsan-ri. With gum.

No.	Type	Description	Unused	Used
N517a	257	5 ch. brown		

258 Drum Dance

259 "For the Sake of the Fatherland"

1964. Korean Dances.

No.	Type	Description	Unused	Used
N518	258	2 ch. mauve, buff & blk	1·50	15
N519	–	5 ch. red, black & yellow	1·75	15
N520	–	10 ch. multicoloured	2·00	15

DESIGNS: 5 ch. "Ecstasy" (solo); 10 ch. Tabor.

1964. Li Su Bok Commemorative. With gum.

No.	Type	Description	Unused	Used
N521	259	5 ch. red	20	10

260 Nampo Smelting Works

1964. With gum.

No.	Type	Description	Unused	Used
N522	260	5 ch. green	2·50	10
N523	–	10 ch. slate	2·75	20

DESIGN: 10 ch. Hwanghae iron works.

261 Torch, Chollima Statue and Cogwheel

1964. Asian Economic Seminar, Pyongyang. Multicoloured.

No.	Type	Description	Unused	Used
N524		5 ch. Type 261	25	10
N525		10 ch. Flags, statue and cogwheel	30	10

262 Korean People and Statue of Kang Ho Yong (war hero)

1964. Struggle for Reunification of Korea.

No.	Type	Description	Unused	Used
N526	262	10 ch. multicoloured	45	10

263 Hawk Fowl

1964. Domestic Poultry. Multicoloured.

No.	Type	Description	Unused	Used
N527		2 ch. Type 263	35	10
N528		4 ch. White fowl	35	10
N529		5 ch. Ryongyon fowl	55	10
N530		5 ch. Black fowl	55	10
N531		40 ch. Helmet guineafowl	2·00	60

264 Skiing

1964. Winter Olympic Games, Innsbruck.

No.	Type	Description	Unused	Used
N532	264	5 ch. red, blue and buff	50	10
N533	–	10 ch. blue, green & buff	75	10
N534	–	10 ch. blue, red & buff	75	10

DESIGNS: No. N533, Ice skating; N534, Skiing (slalom).

265 "Tobolsk" (passenger ship) and Flags

266 Tonggun Pavilion Uiju

1964. 5th Anniv of Agreement for Repatriation of Koreans in Japan.

No.	Type	Description	Unused	Used
N535	265	10 ch. red, blue & lt blue	1·10	20
N536	–	30 ch. multicoloured	1·10	15

DESIGN: 30 ch. Return of repatriates.

1964. Ancient Korean Buildings (2nd series). With gum.

No.	Type	Description	Unused	Used
N537	266	5 ch. purple	20	10
N538	–	10 ch. green	30	10

DESIGN: 10 ch. Inpang Pavilion, Kanggye City.

267 Cycling

268 Burning of the "General Sherman"

1964. Olympic Games, Tokyo.

No.	Type	Description	Unused	Used
N539	–	2 ch. brown and blue	25	10
N540	267	5 ch. brown and green	75	10
N541	–	10 ch. orange and blue	35	10
N542	–	10 ch. orange and green	35	10
N543	–	40 ch. brown and blue	60	35

DESIGNS—HORIZ: 2 ch. Rifle-shooting; 10 ch. blue, Running. VERT: 10 ch. green, Wrestling; 40 ch. Volleyball.

1964. The "General Sherman" Incident, 1866. With gum.

No.	Type	Description	Unused	Used
N544	268	30 ch. brown	2·00	30

269 Organizing Guerrillas

1964. Guerrilla Operations in the 1930's against the Japanese. With gum.

No.	Type	Description	Unused	Used
N545	269	2 ch. violet	25	10
N546	–	5 ch. blue	35	10
N547	–	10 ch. black	45	10

DESIGNS: 5 ch. Kim Il Sung addressing guerrillas; 10 ch. Battle scene at Xiaowangqing.

270 Students attacking

271 Weightlifting

1964. Kwangju Students Rising, 1929. With gum.

No.	Type	Description	Unused	Used
N548	270	10 ch. violet	1·60	15

1964. "GANEFO" Athletic Games, Djakarta, Indonesia (1963). Multicoloured.

No.	Type	Description	Unused	Used
N549		2 ch. Type 271	25	10
N550		5 ch. Athlete breasting tape	30	10
N551		5 ch. Boxing	30	10
N552		10 ch. Football	75	15
N553		10 ch. Globe Emblem	30	15

Nos. N551/3 are horiz.

272 Lynx

273 Vietnamese Attack

1964. Animals. With gum.

No.	Type	Description	Unused	Used
N554		2 ch. sepia (Type 272)	60	10
N555		5 ch. sepia (Leopard cat)	1·50	10
N556		10 ch. brown (Leopard)	2·00	10
N557		10 ch. sepia (Yellow-throated marten)	2·00	10

1964. Support for People of Vietnam.

No.	Type	Description	Unused	Used
N558	273	10 ch. multicoloured	30	10

274 Prof. Kim Bong Han and Emblems

1964. Kyongrak Biological Systems.

No.	Type	Description	Unused	Used
N559	274	2 ch. purple and olive	65	10
N560	–	5 ch. green, orange & bl	90	10
N561	–	10 ch. red, yellow & blue	1·25	10

DESIGNS—33 × $23\frac{1}{2}$ mm: 5 ch. "Bonghan" duct; 10 ch. "Bonghan" corpuscle. Each include emblems as in Type 274.

275 Farmers, Tractor and Lorry

1964. Agrarian Programme. Multicoloured.

No.	Type	Description	Unused	Used
N562		5 ch. Type 275	20	10
N563		10 ch. Peasants with scroll and book	30	10
N564		10 ch. Peasants, one writing in book	30	10

276 Chung Jin gets a Pistol

277 Girl with Korean Products

1964. The Struggle to capture Japanese Arms. With gum.

No.	Type	Description	Unused	Used
N565	276	4 ch. brown	25	10

1964. Economic 7 Year Plan. Multicoloured. With gum (5 ch.) or no gum (others).

No.	Type	Description	Unused	Used
N566		5 ch. Type 277	40	10
N567		10 ch. Farm girl	40	10
N568		10 ch. Couple on winged horse ($23\frac{1}{2}$ × $23\frac{1}{2}$ mm)	25	10

278 Three Fairies Rock

280 Soldiers Advancing, Fusong

1964. Diamond Mountains Scenery (2nd issue). Inscr "1964". Multicoloured. Without gum (2, 4 ch.) or with gum (others).

No.	Type	Description	Unused	Used
N569		2 ch. Type 278	75	10
N570		4 ch. Ryonju Falls	2·75	10
N571		10 ch. The Ten Thousand Rocks, Manmulsang	75	10
N572		10 ch. Chinju Falls	2·75	10

1965. Guerrilla Operations against the Japanese, 1934–40. With gum.

No.	Type	Description	Unused	Used
N574	280	10 ch. violet	30	10
N575	–	10 ch. violet	30	10
N576	–	10 ch. green	30	10

DESIGNS: No. N575, Soldiers descending hill, Hongqihe; N576, Soldiers attacking hill post, Luozigou.

281 Tuman River

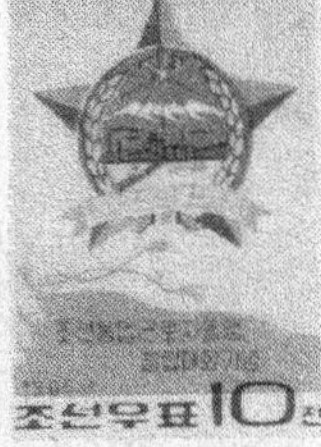
282 Union Badge

1965. Korean Rivers. Multicoloured.

No.	Type	Description	Unused	Used
N577		2 ch. Type 281	45	10
N578		5 ch. Taedong (vert)	1·50	15
N579		10 ch. Amnok	60	10

1965. 1st Congress of Landworkers' Union, Pyongyang. With gum.

No.	Type	Description	Unused	Used
N580	282	10 ch. multicoloured	30	10

283 Furnacemen and Workers

1965. 10 Major Tasks of 7 Year Plan. With gum.
N581 **283** 10 ch. multicoloured . . 30 10

284 Miners' Strike, Sinhung Colliery

1965. 35th Anniv of Strikes and Peasants' Revolt. With gum.
N582 **284** 10 ch. olive . . . . . . 1·25 15
N583 – 10 ch. brown . . . . . 1·50 15
N584 – 40 ch. purple . . . . . 1·00 15
DESIGNS: 10 ch. Strikers at Pyongyang Rubber Factory; 40ch. Revolt of Tanchon peasants.

285 Embankment Construction — 286 Hand holding Torch

1965. Sunhwa River Works. With gum.
N585 **285** 10 ch. multicoloured . . 30 10

1965. 5th Anniv of South Korean Rising of April 19th. Multicoloured. With gum.
N586 10 ch. Type **286** 20 10
N587 40 ch. Student-hero, Kim Chio 45 20

287 Power Station under Construction

1965. Construction of Thermal Power Station, Pyongyang. With gum.
N588 **287** 5 ch. brown and blue . . 25 10

288 African and Asian

1965. 10th Anniv of 1st Afro-Asian Conference, Bandung. With gum.
N589 **288** 10 ch. multicoloured . . 30 10

289 Rejoicing of Koreans

1965. 10th Anniv of General Assn of Koreans in Japan. With gum.
N590 **289** 10 ch. blue and red . . 25 10
N591 – 40 ch. indigo, blue & red 45 15
DESIGN: 40 ch. Patriot and flag.

290 Workers in Battle — 291 "Victory 64" 10-ton Lorry

1965. 2nd Afro-Asian Conf, Algiers. With gum.
N592 **290** 10 ch. black, yellow & red 75 10
N593 – 40 ch. black, yellow & red 1·25 25
DESIGN: 40 ch. Korean and African soldiers.
The Algiers Conference did not take place.

1965. With gum.
N594 **291** 10 ch. green . . . . . 1·25 20

292 Kim Chang Gol

1965. War Heroes (1st series). With gum.
N595 **292** 10 ch. green 30 10
N596 – 10 ch. brown 30 10
N597 – 40 ch. purple 75 20
PORTRAITS: No. N596, Cho Gun Sil and machine-gun; N597, An Hak Ryong and machine-gun.
See also Nos. N781/3 and N842/3.

293 Marx and Lenin

1965. Postal Ministers' Congress, Peking. With gum.
N598 **293** 10 ch. black, yell & red 1·50 15

294 Lake Samil

1965. Diamond Mountains Scenery (3rd issue). Multicoloured. With gum.
N599 2 ch. Type **294** 60 10
N600 5 ch. Chipson Peak . . . . 1·00 10
N601 10 ch. Kwanum Falls . . . 2·75 25

295 Amnok River, Kusimuldong

1965. Scenes of Japanese War. With gum.
N602 **295** 5 ch. green and blue . . 35 10
N603 – 10 ch. turquoise & blue 60 10
DESIGN: 10 ch. Lake Samji.

296 Footballer and Games' Emblem — 297 Workers and Map

1965. "GANEFO" Football Games, Pyongyang. Multicoloured. With gum.
N604 10 ch. Type **296** 90 10
N605 10 ch. Games emblem and Moranbong Stadium . . 90 10

1965. 20th Anniv of Liberation from Japan. With gum.
N606 **297** 10 ch. multicoloured . 30 10

298 Engels — 299 Pole Vaulting

1965. 145th Birth Anniv of Engels. With gum.
N607 **298** 10 ch. brown 30 10

1965. Sports. Multicoloured. With gum.
N608 2 ch. Type **299** 35 10
N609 4 ch. Throwing the javelin 1·50 20
N610 10 ch. Throwing the discus 40 10
N611 10 ch. High jumping (horiz) 40 10
N612 10 ch. Putting the shot (horiz) 40 10

301 Korean Fighters

1965. 20th Anniv of Korean Workers' Party. Each black, yellow and red. With gum.
N613 10 ch. Type **301** 45 10
N614 10 ch. Party emblem 45 10
N615 10 ch. Lenin and Marx . . . 45 10
N616 10 ch. Workers marching . . 45 10
N617 10 ch. Fighters 45 10
N618 40 ch. Workers 45 10
Nos. N613/8 each have a red banner in the background and were issued together in blocks of 6 (3×2), forming a composite design, within the sheet.

302 Kim Chaek Iron Works — 303 Grass carp

1965. With gum.
N620 **302** 10 ch. purple . . . . . 3·50 10
N621 – 10 ch. brown . . . . . 3·50 10
DESIGN: No. 621, Chongjin Steel Works.

1965. Freshwater Fish. Multicoloured. With gum.
N622 2 ch. Rainbow trout 50 10
N623 4 ch. Dolly Varden trout . . 65 10
N624 10 ch. Brown trout (surfacing water) . . . . 1·40 15
N625 10 ch. Carp diving (date at left) 1·40 15
N626 10 ch. Type **303** . . . . . . 1·40 15
N627 40 ch. Crucian carp . . . . 2·25 30

304 Building House — 305 Children in Workshop

1965. Kim Hong Do's Drawings. With gum.
N628 2 ch. green (Type **304**) . . . 45 10
N629 4 ch. purple (Weaving) . . . 90 10
N630 10 ch. brown (Wrestling) . . 80 10
N631 10 ch. blue (School class) . . 80 10
N632 10 ch. red (Dancing) . . . 1·25 10
N633 10 ch. violet (Blacksmiths) 1·10 10

1965. Life at Pyongyang Children's and Students' Palace. Multicoloured. With gum.
N634 2 ch. Type **305** 20 10
N635 4 ch. Boxing 20 10
N636 10 ch. Chemistry 75 10
N637 10 ch. Playing violin and accordion 75 10

306 Whale-catcher

1965. Korean Fishing Boats. With gum.
N638 **306** 10 ch. blue . . . . . . 1·25 20
N639 – 10 ch. green . . . . . . 1·25 20
DESIGN: No. 639, Fishing fleet service vessel.

307 Great Tit — 308 Silkworm Moth ("Bombyx mori") and Cocoon

1965. Korean Birds. Inscr "1965". Multicoloured. With gum.
N640 4 ch. Black-capped kingfisher (vert) . . . . 1·75 10
N641 10 ch. Type **307** . . . . . . 2·40 25
N642 10 ch. Pied wagtail (facing left) 2·40 25
N643 10 ch. Azure-winged magpie (facing right) . . . . . . 2·40 25
N644 40 ch. Black-tailed hawfinch 5·50 85

1965. Korean Sericulture. With gum.
N645 **308** 2 ch. green . . . . . . 5·00 20
N646 – 10 ch. brown . . . . . 5·00 30
N647 – 10 ch. purple . . . . . 5·00 30
MOTHS AND COCOONS: No. N646, Ailathus silk moth ("Samia cynthia"); N647, Chinese oak silk moth ("Antheraea pernyi").

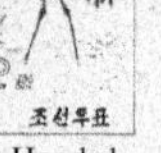
309 Hooded Crane — 310 Japanese Common Squid

1965. Wading Birds. With gum.
N648 **309** 2 ch. brown . . . . . . 3·00 10
N649 – 10 ch. blue . . . . . . 3·25 30
N650 – 10 ch. purple . . . . . 3·25 30
N651 – 40 ch. green . . . . . . 6·00 70
BIRDS: No. N649, Japanese white-necked crane; N650, Manchurian crane; N651, Grey heron.

1965. Korean Molluscs. Multicoloured. With gum.
N652 5 ch. Type **310** . . . . . . 1·25 10
N653 10 ch. Giant Pacific octopus 1·75 10

311 Spotbill Duck

1965. Korean Ducks. Multicoloured. With gum.
N654 2 ch. Type **311** . . . . . . 2·40 10
N655 4 ch. Ruddy shelduck . . . 2·40 15
N656 10 ch. Mallard . . . . 3·50 35
N657 40 ch. Baikal teal . . . . . 5·00 85

312 Circus Theatre, Pyongyang — 313 "Marvel of Peru" ("Mirabilis jalapa")

1965. Korean Circus. With gum except No. N661.
N658 **312** 2 ch. blue, black & brn 50 10
N659 – 10 ch. blue, red & black 1·25 10
N660 – 10 ch. red, black & green 1·25 10
N661 – 10 ch. orange, sepia & grn 1·25 10
N662 – 10 ch. red, yellow & turq 1·25 10
DESIGNS—VERT: No. N659, Trapeze artistes; N660, Performer with hoops on seesaw; N661, Tightrope dancers; N662, Performer with revolving cap on stick.

1965. Korean Flowers. Multicoloured. With gum except No. N663.
N663 4 ch. Type **313** . . . . . . 1·00 10
N664 10 ch. Peony . . . . 1·40 10
N665 10 ch. Moss rose . . . . . . 1·40 10
N666 10 ch. Magnolia . . . . . . 1·40 10

314 "Finn" Class Yacht — 315 Cuban, Korean and African

1965. Yachts. Multicoloured. With gum.
N667 2 ch. Type **314** 55 20
N668 10 ch. "5.5m" class 85 30
N669 10 ch. "Dragon" class . . . 85 30
N670 40 ch. "Star" class . . . . . 1·75 60

1966. African-Asian and Latin American Friendship Conference, Havana. With gum.
N671 **315** 10 ch. multicoloured . . 30 10

316 Hosta **317** Farmer and Wife

1966. Wild Flowers. Mult. With gum. (a) 1st series.
N672 2 ch. Type **316** 40 10
N673 4 ch. Dandelion 40 10
N674 10 ch. Pink convolvulus . . 60 10
N675 10 ch. Lily-of-the-valley . . 60 10
N676 40 ch. Catalpa blossom . . 1·75 20

(b) 2nd series.
N677 2 ch. Polyanthus 40 10
N678 4 ch. Lychnis 40 10
N679 10 ch. Adonis 60 10
N680 10 ch. Orange lily 60 10
N681 90 ch. Rhododendron . . . 2·75 30

1966. 20th Anniv of Land Reform Law. With gum.
N682 **317** 10 ch. multicoloured . . 20 10

318 Troops advancing, Dashahe **319** Silla Bowl

1966. Paintings of Guerrilla Battles, 1937–39. With gum, except No. N684.
N683 **318** 10 ch. red 30 10
N684 – 10 ch. turquoise 30 10
N685 – 10 ch. purple 30 10
DESIGNS AND BATTLES: No. N684, Troops firing from trees, Taehongdan; N685, Troops on hillside, Jiansanfeng.

1966. Art Treasures of Silla Dynasty. With gum.
N686 **319** 2 ch. ochre . . . . . . 1·25 10
N687 – 5 ch. black . . . . . . 1·25 10
N688 – 10 ch. violet . . . . . . 1·25 10
DESIGNS: 5 ch. Earthenware jug. 10 ch. Censer.

320 Hands holding Torch, Rifle and Hammer **321** Torch and Patriots

1966. 80th Anniv of Labour Day. With gum.
N689 **320** 10 ch. multicoloured . . 30 10

1966. 30th Anniv of Association for Restoration of Fatherland.
N690 **321** 10 ch. red and yellow . 30 10

322 Harvester

1966. Aid for Agriculture. Multicoloured.
N691 5 ch. Type **322** 25 10
N692 10 ch. Labourer 35 10

323 Young Pioneers

1966. 20th Anniv of Korean Children's Union. Without gum.
N693 **323** 10 ch. multicoloured . . 30 10

324 Kangson Steel Works

1966. Korean Industries. With gum.
N694 **324** 10 ch. grey . . . . . . 3·50 15
N695 – 10 ch. red (Pongung Chemical Works) . . 3·50 15

325 Saury

1966. Korean Fishes. With gum except Nos. 699/700.
N696 **325** 2 ch. blue, green & pur 50 10
N697 – 5 ch. purple, green & brn 65 10
N698 – 10 ch. blue, buff & green 1·00 20
N699 – 10 ch. purple and green 1·00 20
N700 – 40 ch. green, buff & blue 2·50 35
FISHES: 5 ch. Cod; 10 ch. (N698), Salmon, (N699), "Pleurogrammus azonus"; 40 ch. "Pink" salmon.

326 Professor Kim Bong Han

1966. Kyungrak Biological System. With gum.
N701 **326** 2 ch. blue, green & yell 45 10
N702 – 4 ch. multicoloured . . 45 10
N703 – 5 ch. multicoloured . . 45 10
N704 – 10 ch. multicoloured . . 45 10
N705 – 10 ch. multicoloured . . 45 10
N706 – 10 ch. multicoloured . . 45 10
N707 – 15 ch. multicoloured . . 45 10
N708 – 40 ch. multicoloured . . 45 10
DESIGNS: No. N704, Kyongrak Institute; N708, Figure of Man; N702/3, 705/7, Diagram of system.
Nos. N701/8 were issued together, se-tenant, forming a composite design.

327 Leonov in Space ("Voskhod 2")

1966. Cosmonauts Day. Multicoloured.
N710 5 ch. Type **327** 20 10
N711 10 ch. "Luna 9" 55 10
N712 40 ch. "Luna 10" . . . . . 1·10 20

328 Footballers

1966. World Cup Football Championship. Mult.
N713 10 ch. Type **328** . . . . . 1·25 25
N714 10 ch. Jules Rimet Cup, football and boots . . . 1·25 25
N715 10 ch. Goalkeeper saving goal (vert) . . . . 1·25 25

329 Defence of Seoul

1966. Korean War of 1950–53. With gum.
N716 **329** 10 ch. green 35 10
N717 – 10 ch. purple 35 10
N718 – 10 ch. purple 35 10
DESIGNS: No. N717, Battle on Mt. Napal; N718, Battle for Height 1211.

330 Women in Industry

1966. 20th Anniv of Sex Equality Law.
N719 **330** 10 ch. multicoloured . 30 10

331 Industrial Workers **332** Water-jar Dance

1966. 20th Anniv of Industrial Nationalization.
N720 **331** 10 ch. multicoloured . . 90 10

1966. Korean Dances. Multicoloured. 5 ch., 40 ch. with or without gum; others without.
N721 5 ch. Type **332** 90 10
N722 10 ch. Bell dance . . . . . . 1·60 15
N723 10 ch. "Dancer in a Mural Painting" . . . . 1·60 15
N724 15 ch. Sword dance . . . . 1·60 20
N725 40 ch. Gold Cymbal dance 3·00 30

333 Korean attacking U.S. Soldier **334** Yakovlev Yak-12M Crop-spraying

1966. Korean Reunification Campaign. With gum.
N726 **333** 10 ch. green 60 10
N727 – 10 ch. purple 60 10
N728 – 10 ch. lilac . . . . 3·75 45
DESIGNS: No. N727, Korean with young child; N728, Korean with shovel, industrial scene and electric train.

1966. Industrial Uses of Aircraft. With gum except 2 ch. and 5 ch.
N729 **334** 2 ch. green and purple 40 10
N730 – 5 ch. brown and green 5·50 20
N731 – 10 ch. brown and blue 1·25 10
N732 – 40 ch. brown and blue 1·25 10
DESIGNS: 5 ch. Yakovlev Yak-18U (forest-fire observation); 10 ch. Lisunov Li-2 (geological survey); 40 ch. Lisunov Li-2 (detection of fish shoals).

1966. Korean Revolutionaries (3rd issue). As T **212**. With gum.
N733 10 ch. violet (O Jung Hub)
N734 10 ch. green (Kim Gyong Sok)
N735 10 ch. blue (Li Dong Gol)

335 Kim Il Sung University

1966. 20th Anniv of Kim Il Sung University. With gum.
N736 **335** 10 ch. violet 50 10

336 Judo **337** Hoopoe

1966. Ganefo Games, Phnom-Penh.
N737 **336** 5 ch. black, green & bl 45 10
N738 – 10 ch. black, green and deep green 45 10
N739 – 10 ch. black and red . . 45 10
DESIGNS: No. N738, Basketball; N739, Table tennis.

1966. Korean Birds. Multicoloured. Inscr "1966".
N740 2 ch. Common rosefinch . . 1·40 10
N741 5 ch. Type **337** . . . . 1·60 15
N742 10 ch. Black-breasted thrush (blue background) . . . . 1·90 25
N743 10 ch. Crested lark (green background) . . . . 1·90 25
N744 40 ch. White-bellied black woodpecker . . . . 4·25 70
The 2 ch. and 10 ch. (both) are horiz.

338 Building Construction

1966. "Increased Production with Economy". Multicoloured. Without gum (40 ch.) or with gum (others).
N745 5 ch. Type **338** 25 10
N746 10 ch. Furnaceman and graph 45 10
N747 10 ch. Machine-tool production 45 10
N748 40 ch. Miners and pit-head 1·40 15

339 Parachuting

1966. National Defence Sports. With gum.
N749 **339** 2 ch. brown 75 10
N750 – 5 ch. red 55 10
N751 – 10 ch. blue . . . . . . 2·75 30
N752 – 40 ch. green . . . . . . 1·60 20
DESIGNS: 5 ch. Show jumping; 10 ch. Motor cycle racing; 40 ch. Radio receiving and transmitting competition.

340 "Samil Wolgan" (Association Magazine) **341** Red Deer

1966. 30th Anniv of "Samil Wolgan" Magazine.
N753 **340** 10 ch. multicoloured . . 90 15

1966. Korean Deer. Multicoloured.
N754 2 ch. Type **341** 20 10
N755 5 ch. Sika deer 35 10
N756 10 ch. Indian muntjac (erect) 70 10
N757 10 ch. Reindeer (grazing) . 70 10
N758 70 ch. Fallow deer . . . . . 2·50 25

342 Blueberries **343** Onpo Rest Home

1966. Wild Fruit. Multicoloured.
N759 2 ch. Type **342** 40 10
N760 5 ch. Wild pears 60 10
N761 10 ch. Wild raspberries . . 75 10
N762 10 ch. Schizandra 75 10
N763 10 ch. Wild plums 75 10
N764 40 ch. Jujube . . . . 2·00 15

1966. Korean Rest Homes. With gum.
N765 **343** 2 ch. violet 25 10
N766 – 5 ch. turquoise 35 10
N767 – 10 ch. green 50 10
N768 – 40 ch. black 80 20
REST HOMES: 5 ch. Mt. Myohyang; 10 ch. Songdowon; 40 ch. Hongwon.

344 Soldier

1967. 19th Anniv of Army Day. Without gum.
N769 **344** 10 ch. green, yell & red 25 10

345 Sow

1967. Domestic Animals. Multicoloured. Without gum. 40 ch. also with gum.
N770 5 ch. Type **345** 25 10
N771 10 ch. Goat 35 10
N772 40 ch. Ox 85 25

346 Battle Scene

1967. 30th Anniv of Battle of Pochonbo. With gum.
N773 **346** 10 ch. orange, red & grn . . 50 10

347 Students

1967. Compulsory Technical Education for Nine Years.
N774 **347** 10 ch. multicoloured . . 25 10

348 Table Tennis Player

1967. 29th International Table Tennis Championships, Pyongyang. Designs showing players in action. 5 ch. with or without gum.
N775 **348** 5 ch. multicoloured . . 40 10
N776 – 10 ch. multicoloured . . 70 10
N777 – 40 ch. multicoloured . . 1·10 15

349 Anti-aircraft Defences

1967. Paintings of Guerrilla War against the Japanese. With gum.
N778 **349** 10 ch. blue 35 10
N779 – 10 ch. purple . . . . . 3·00 25
N780 – 10 ch. violet 35 10
PAINTINGS: No. N779, Blowing-up railway bridge; N780, People helping guerrillas in Wangyugou.

1967. War Heroes (2nd series). As T **292**. Designs showing portraits and combat scenes. With gum.
N781 10 ch. slate 40 10
N782 10 ch. violet 40 10
N783 10 ch. blue 75 10
PORTRAITS: No. N781, Li Dae Hun and grenade-throwing; N782, Choe Jong Un and soldiers charging; N783, Kim Hwa Ryong and air dog-fighter aircraft.

350 Workers

1967. Labour Day.
N784 **350** 10 ch. multicoloured . . 25 10

351 Card Game

1967. Korean Children. Multicoloured.
N785 5 ch. Type **351** 85 10
N786 10 ch. Children modelling tractor 45 10
N787 40 ch. Children playing with ball 90 20

MINIMUM PRICE

The minimum price quoted is 10p which represents a handling charge rather than a basis for valuing common stamps. For further notes about prices, see introductory pages.

352 Victory Monument

1967. Unveiling of Battle of Ponchonbo Monument.
N788 **352** 10 ch. multicoloured . 30 10

353 Attacking Tank

354 "Polygonatum japonicum"

1967. Monuments to War of 1950–53. 2 ch. with or without gum.
N789 **353** 2 ch. green & turquoise 20 10
N790 – 5 ch. sepia and green . 85 10
N791 – 10 ch. brown and buff 30 10
N792 – 40 ch. brown and blue 60 15
MONUMENTS: 5 ch. Soldier-musicians; 10 ch. Soldier; 40 ch. Soldier with children.

1967. Medicinal Plants. Multicoloured; background colour of 10 ch. values given to aid identification. Nos. 793/5 and 797 with or without gum.
N793 2 ch. Type **354** 90 10
N794 5 ch. "Hibiscus manihot" . 90 10
N795 10 ch. "Scutellaria baicalensis" (turquoise) . . . . 1·10 10
N796 10 ch. "Pulsatilla koreana" (blue) . . . . 1·10 10
N797 10 ch. "Rehmannian glutinosa" (yellow) . . . 1·10 10
N798 40 ch. "Tanacetum boreale" 3·00 35

355 Servicemen

1967. People's Army. Multicoloured. 5 ch. with or without gum.
N799 5 ch. Type **355** 20 10
N800 10 ch. Soldier and farmer . 25 10
N801 10 ch. Officer decorating soldier 25 10

356 Freighter "Chollima"

1967. With gum.
N802 **356** 10 ch. green . . . . . 1·10 10

357 "Reclamation of Tideland"

1967. "Heroic Struggle of the Chollima Riders". Paintings. Without gum (5 ch.) or with gum (others).
N803 – 5 ch. brown 40 10
N804 **357** 10 ch. grey 55 10
N805 – 10 ch. green 85 10
DESIGNS—VERT: 5 ch. "Drilling Rock Precipice"; 10 ch. (N805), "Felling Trees".

358 "Erimaculus isenbeckii"

1967. Crabs. Multicoloured.
N806 2 ch. Type **358** 75 15
N807 5 ch. "Neptunus trituberculatus" 95 15
N808 10 ch. "Paralithodes camtschatica" . . . . . . 1·40 15
N809 40 ch. "Chionoecetes opilio" 2·25 40

359 Electric Train and Hand switching points

1967. Propaganda for Reunification of Korea.
N810 **359** 10 ch. multicoloured . . 2·25 40

360 Tongrim Waterfall

361 Chollima Flying Horse and Banners

1967. Korean Waterfalls. 2 ch. with or without gum. Multicoloured.
N811 2 ch. Type **360** . . . . 2·75 15
N812 10 ch. Sanju waterfall, Mt. Myohyang . . . . 3·25 20
N813 40 ch. Sambang waterfall, Mt. Chonak . . . . 5·00 45

1967. "The Revolutionary Surge Upwards". Various designs incorporating the Chollima Flying Horse.
N814 – 5 ch. blue . . . . 1·40 20
N815 – 10 ch. red 25 10
N816 – 10 ch. green 25 10
N817 – 10 ch. lilac 25 10
N817 **361** 10 ch. red 20 10
DESIGNS—HORIZ: 5 ch. Ship, diesel train and lorry (Transport); N815, Bulldozers (Building construction); N816, Tractors (Rural development); N817, Heavy presses (Machine-building industry).

362 Lenin

1967. 50th Anniv of Russian October Revolution.
N819 **362** 10 ch. brown, yell & red 25 10

363 Voters and Banner

1967. Korean Elections. Multicoloured.
N820 10 ch. Type **363** 35 10
N821 10 ch. Woman casting vote (vert) 35 10

364 European Black Vulture

1967. Birds of Prey. Multicoloured. With gum.
N822 2 ch. Type **364** . . . . . 2·10 35
N823 10 ch. Booted eagle (horiz) 4·00 50
N824 40 ch. White-bellied sea eagle 5·00 80

365 Chongjin

1967. North Korean Cities. With gum.
N825 **365** 5 ch. green 70 10
N826 – 10 ch. lilac 70 10
N827 – 10 ch. violet 70 10
DESIGNS: No. N826, Humhung; N827, Sinuiju.

366 Soldier brandishing Red Book

1967. "Let us carry out the Decisions of the Workers' Party Conference!". Multicoloured.
N828 10 ch. Type **366** 25 10
N829 10 ch. Militiaman holding bayonet 25 10
N830 10 ch. Foundryman and bayonet 25 10

367 Whaler firing Harpoon

1967. With gum.
N831 **367** 10 ch. blue . . . . 1·60 25

368 Airman, Soldier and Sailor

1968. 20th Anniv of People's Army. Mult. With gum.
N832 10 ch. Type **368** 30 10
N833 10 ch. Soldier below attack in snow 30 10
N834 10 ch. Soldier below massed ranks 30 10
N835 10 ch. Soldier holding flag 30 10
N836 10 ch. Soldier holding book 30 10
N837 10 ch. Soldiers and armed workers with flag 30 10
N838 10 ch. Furnaceman and soldier 30 10
N839 10 ch. Soldier saluting . . . 30 10
N840 10 ch. Charging soldiers . . 30 10
N841 10 ch. Soldier, sailor and airman below flag 30 10

1968. War Heroes (3rd series). As T **292**. With gum.
N842 10 ch. violet 25 10
N843 10 ch. purple 25 10
PORTRAITS: No. N842, Han Gye Ryol firing Bren gun; N843, Li Su Bok charging up hill.

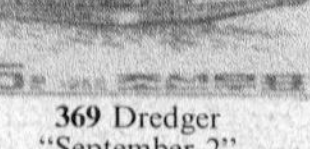
369 Dredger "September 2"

370 Ten-storey Flats, East Pyongyang

371 Palace of Students and Children, Kaesong

1968. With gum.
N844 **369** 5 ch. green 75 10
N845 **370** 10 ch. blue 30 10
N846 **371** 10 ch. blue 30 10

372 Marshal Kim Il Sung

1968. Marshal Kim Il Sung's 56th Birthday. With gum.
N847 **372** 40 ch. multicoloured . . 65 40

373 Kim Il Sung with Mother

1968. Childhood of Kim Il Sung. Multicoloured.
N848 10 ch. Type **373** 35 10
N849 10 ch. Kim Il Sung with his father 35 10
N850 10 ch. Setting out from home, aged 13 . . . . 35 10
N851 10 ch. Birthplace at Mangyongdae 35 10
N852 10 ch. Mangyong Hill . . . 35 10

374 Matsu-take Mushroom

1968. Mushrooms. With gum.
N853 **374** 5 ch. brown and green . 4·00 25
N854 – 10 ch. ochre, brn & grn 5·75 35
N855 – 10 ch. brown and green 5·75 35
DESIGNS: No. N854, Black mushroom; N855, Cultivated mushroom.

375 Leaping Horseman

1968. 20th Anniv of Korean People's Democratic Republic. Multicoloured. With gum.
N856 10 ch. Type **375** . . . . . . 1·10 10
N857 10 ch. Four servicemen . . . 1·10 10
N858 10 ch. Soldier with bayonet . 1·10 10
N859 10 ch. Advancing with banners 1·10 10
N860 10 ch. Statue . . . . 1·10 10
N861 10 ch. Korean flag . . . . . 1·10 10
N862 10 ch. Soldier and peasant with flag . . . . 1·10 10
N863 10 ch. Machine-gunner with flag . . . . 1·10 10

376 Domestic Products

377 Proclaiming the Ten Points

1968. Development of Light Industries. Multicoloured. With gum.
N864 2 ch. Type **376** 25 10
N865 5 ch. Textiles . . . . 1·00 10
N866 10 ch. Tinned produce . . 40 10

1968. Kim Il Sung's Ten Point Political Programme. Multicoloured.
N867 2 ch. Type **377** 15 10
N868 5 ch. Soldier and artisan (horiz) 20 10

378 Livestock

1968. Development of Agriculture. Mult. With gum.
N869 5 ch. Type **378** 25 10
N870 10 ch. Fruit-growing . . . 25 10
N871 10 ch. Wheat-harvesting . . 25 10

379 Yesso Scallop

1968. Shellfish. Multicoloured. With gum.
N872 5 ch. Type **379** 90 10
N873 5 ch. Meretrix chione (venus clam) 90 10
N874 10 ch. "Modiolus hanleyi" (mussel) . . . . 1·50 20

380 Kim Il Sung at Head of Columns

1967. Battle of Pochonbo Monument. Detail of Monument. Multicoloured.
N875 10 ch. Type **380** 25 10
N876 10 ch. Head of right-hand column 25 10
N877 10 ch. Tail of right-hand column 25 10
N878 10 ch. Head of left-hand column 25 10
N879 10 ch. Tail of left-hand column 25 10
N880 10 ch. Centre of right-hand column 25 10
N881 10 ch. Centre of left-hand column 25 10
SIZES—HORIZ: Nos. N876/8, 43 × 28 mm. 880/1, 56 × 28 mm.
The centrepiece of the Monument is flanked by two columns of soldiers, headed by Kim Il Sung.

381 Museum of the Revolution, Pochonbo

382 Grand Theatre, Pyongyang

1968.
N883 **381** 2 ch. green 20 10
N884 **382** 10 ch. brown 65 10

383 Irrigation

1969. Rural Development. Multicoloured.
N885 3 ch. Type **383** 20 10
N886 5 ch. Agricultural mechanisation 20 10
N887 10 ch. Electrification 40 10
N888 40 ch. Applying fertilisers and spraying trees 60 10

384 Grey Rabbits

1969. Rabbits. Mult. With or without gum.
N889 2 ch. Type **384** 45 10
N890 10 ch. Black rabbits 45 10
N891 10 ch. Brown rabbits 45 10
N892 10 ch. White rabbits 45 10
N893 40 ch. Doe and young . . . 1·40 15

385 "Age and Youth"

1969. Public Health Service.
N894 **385** 2 ch. brown and blue . . 35 10
N895 – 10 ch. blue and red . . . 75 10
N896 – 40 ch. green and yellow 1·50 20
DESIGNS: 10 ch. Nurse with syringe; 40 ch. Auscultation by woman doctor.

386 Sowing Rice Seed

1969. Agricultural Mechanisation.
N897 **386** 10 ch. green 55 10
N898 – 10 ch. orange 55 10
N899 – 10 ch. black 55 10
N900 – 10 ch. brown 55 10
DESIGNS: No. N898, Rice harvester; N899, Weed-spraying machine; N900, Threshing machine.

387 Ponghwa

1969. Revolutionary Historical Sites. Multicoloured.
N901 10 ch. Type **387** 25 10
N902 10 ch. Mangyongdae, birthplace of Kim Il Sung 25 10

388 Kim crosses into Manchuria, 1926, aged 13

1969. Kim Il Sung in Manchuria. Multicoloured. No. N907 with gum.
N903 10 ch. Type **388** 40 10
N904 10 ch. Leading strike of Yuwen Middle School boys, 1927 40 10
N905 10 ch. Leading anti-Japanese demonstration in Kirin, 1928 40 10
N906 10 ch. Presiding at meeting of Young Communist League, 1930 . . . . 40 10
N907 10 ch. Meeting of young revolutionaries 40 10

389 Birthplace at Chilgol

1969. Commemoration of Mrs. Kang Ban Sok, mother of Kim Il Sung. Multicoloured.
N908 10 ch. Type **389** 30 10
N909 10 ch. With members of Women's Association . . 30 10
N910 10 ch. Resisting Japanese police . . . . 2·50 40

390 Pegaebong Bivouac

1969. Bivouac Sites in the Guerrilla War against the Japanese. Multicoloured.
N911 5 ch. Type **390** 20 10
N912 10 ch. Mupo site (horiz) . . 30 10
N913 10 ch. Chongbong site . . . 30 10
N914 40 ch. Konchang site (horiz) 1·00 20

391 Chollima Statue

392 Museum of the Revolution, Pyongyang

1969.
N915 **391** 10 ch. blue 25 10
N916 **392** 10 ch. green 25 10

393 Mangyong Chickens

395 Statue of Marshal Kim Il Sung

394 Marshal Kim Il Sung and Children

1969. Korean Poultry.
N917 **393** 10 ch. blue 45 10
N918 – 10 ch. violet . . . . . 1·25 15
DESIGN: No. N918, Kwangpo ducks.

1969. Kim Il Sung's Educational System. Mult.
N919 2 ch. Type **394** 25 10
N920 10 ch. Worker with books . 25 10
N921 40 ch. Students with books 50 20

1969. Memorials on Pochonbo Battlefield. Inscr "1937.6.4". Multicoloured.
N922 5 ch. Machine-gun post . . 25 10
N923 10 ch. Type **395** 25 10
N924 10 ch. "Aspen-tree" monument 25 10
N925 10 ch. Glade Konjang Hill 25 10

396 Teaching at Myongsin School

1969. Commemoration of Kim Hyong Jik, father of Kim Il Sung. Multicoloured.
N926 10 ch. Type **396** 30 10
N927 10 ch. Secret meeting with Korean National Association members . . 30 10

397 Relay Runner

1969. 20th Anniv of Sports Day.
N928 **397** 10 ch. multicoloured . . 35 10

398 President Nixon attacked by Pens

1969. Anti-U.S. Imperialism Journalists' Conference, Pyongyang.
N929 **398** 10 ch. multicoloured . . 35 10

399 Fighters and Battle

1969. Implementation of Ten-Point Programme of Kim Il Sung. Multicoloured.
N930 5 ch. Type **399** (Reunification of Korea) 30 10
N931 10 ch. Workers upholding slogan (vert) 30 10

400 Bayonet Attack over U.S. Flag

1969. Anti-American Campaign.
N932 **400** 10 ch. multicoloured . . 35 10

401 Armed Workers

1969. Struggle for the Reunification of Korea. Multicoloured.
N933 10 ch. Workers stabbing U.S. soldier (vert) 20 10
N934 10 ch. Kim Il Sung and crowd with flags (vert) 20 10
N935 50 ch. Type **401** 50 20

402 Yellowtail

1969. Korean Fishes. Multicoloured.
N936 5 ch. Type **402** 60 10
N937 10 ch. Dace 90 10
N938 40 ch. Mullet . . . . 1·75 25

403 Freighter "Taesungsan"

1969.
N939 **403** 10 ch. purple 75 10

405 Dahwangwai (1935)

1970. Guerrilla Conference Places.
N940 **405** 2 ch. blue and green . . 25 10
N941 – 5 ch. brown and green 25 10
N942 – 10 ch. lt green and green 25 10
DESIGNS: 5 ch. Yaoyinggou (barn) (1935); 10 ch. Xiaohaerbaling (tent) (1940).

406 Lake Chon

407 Vietnamese Soldier and Furnaceman

1970. Mt. Paekdu, Home of Revolution (1st issue). Inscr "1970".
N943 **406** 10 ch. black, brn & grn 40 10
N944 – 10 ch. black, grn & yell 40 10
N945 – 10 ch. purple, bl & yell 40 10
N946 – 10 ch. black, blue and pink 40 10
DESIGNS: No. N944, Piryu Peak; N945, Pyongsa (Soldier) Peak; N946, Changgun (General) Peak.
See also Nos. 979/81.

1970. Help for the Vietnamese People.
N947 **407** 10 ch. green, brn & red 20 10

408 Receiving his Father's Revolvers from his Mother

1970. Revolutionary Career of Kim Il Sung. Multicoloured.
N948 10 ch. Type **408** 65 20
N949 10 ch. Receiving smuggled weapons from his mother 65 20
N950 10 ch. Talking to farm workers 65 20
N951 10 ch. At Kalun meeting, 1930 65 20

409 Lenin

410 March of Koreans

1970. Birth Centenary of Lenin.
N952 **409** 10 ch. brn & cinnamon 30 10
N953 – 10 ch. brown and green 30 10
DESIGN: No. N953, Lenin making a speech.

1970. 15th Anniv of Association of Koreans in Japan.
N954 **410** 10 ch. red 20 10
N955 10 ch. purple 20 10

411 Uniformed Factory Worker

412 Students and Newspapers

1970. Workers' Militia.
N956 **411** 10 ch. green, brn & mve 20 10
N957 – 10 ch. green, brown & bl 20 10
DESIGN—HORIZ: No. N957, Militiaman saluting.

1970. Peasant Education. Multicoloured.
N958 2 ch. Type **412** 35 10
N959 5 ch. Peasant with book . . 20 10
N960 10 ch. Students in class . . 20 10

413 "Electricity Flows"

1970. Commemoration of Army Electrical Engineers.
N961 **413** 10 ch. brown 40 10

414 Soldier with Rifle

1970. Campaign Month for Withdrawal of U.S. Troops from South Korea.
N962 **414** 5 ch. violet 15 10
N963 – 10 ch. purple 30 10
DESIGN: 10 ch. Soldier and partisan.

415 Rebel wielding Weapons

1970. Struggle in South Korea against U.S. Imperialism.
N964 **415** 10 ch. violet 20 10

416 Labourer ("Fertilisers")

417 Railway Guard

1970. Encouragement of Increased Productivity.
N965 **416** 10 ch. green, pink & brn 40 10
N966 – 10 ch. green, red & brn . 70 10
N967 – 10 ch. blue, green & brn 40 10
N968 – 10 ch. bistre, brn & grn 40 10
N969 – 10 ch. violet, grn & brn 50 10
DESIGNS: No. N966, Furnaceman ("Steel"); N967, Operative ("Machines"); N968, Labourer ("Building Construction"); N969, Miner ("Mining").

1970. "Speed the Transport System".
N970 **417** 10 ch. blue, orge & grn 1·25 15

418 Agriculture

1970. Executive Decisions of the Workers' Party Congress. Designs embodying book.
N971 **418** 5 ch. red 20 10
N972 – 10 ch. green . . . . . 1·10 15
N973 – 40 ch. green . . . . . 1·10 15
DESIGNS: 10 ch. Industry; 40 ch. The Armed Forces.

419 Chollima Statue and Workers' Party Banner

421 Emblem of League

1970. 25th Anniv of Korean Workers' Party.
N974 **419** 10 ch. red, brown & buff 20 10

1971. 25th Anniv of League of Socialist Working Youth.
N976 **421** 10 ch. red, brown & blue 20 10

422 Log Cabin, Nanhutou

1971. 35th Anniv of Nanhutou Guerrilla Conference.
N977 **422** 10 ch. multicoloured . . 20 10

423 Tractor Driver

1971. 25th Anniv of Land Reform Law.
N978 **423** 2 ch. red, green & black 20 10

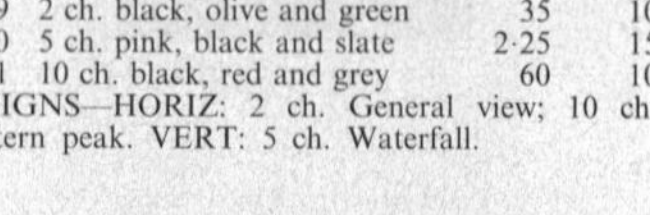

1971. Mt. Paekdu, Home of Revolution (2nd issue). As T **406** but inscr "1971".
N979 2 ch. black, olive and green 35 10
N980 5 ch. pink, black and slate 2·25 15
N981 10 ch. black, red and grey 60 10
DESIGNS—HORIZ: 2 ch. General view; 10 ch. Western peak. VERT: 5 ch. Waterfall.

424 Popyong Museum

1971. Museum of the Revolution.
N982 **424** 10 ch. brown and yellow 20 10
N983 – 10 ch. blue and orange 20 10
N984 – 10 ch. green and orange 20 10
DESIGNS: No. N983, Mangyongdae Museum; N984, Chunggang Museum.

425 Miner

1971. Six Year Plan for Coal Industry.
N985 **425** 10 ch. multicoloured . . 40 10

426 Kim Il Sung

1971. Founding of Anti-Japanese Guerrilla Army. Multicoloured.
N986 10 ch. Type **426** 35 10
N987 10 ch. Kim Il Sung founding Anti-Japanese Guerrilla Army 35 10
N988 10 ch. Kim Il Sung addressing the people 35 10
N989 10 ch. Kim Il Sung and members of Children's Corps 35 10
Nos. N987/9 are horiz.

428 Hands holding Hammer and Rifle

1971. 85th Anniv of Labour Day.
N990 **428** 1 w. red, brown & buff 2·25 40

429 Soldiers and Map

430 Monument

1971. 35th Anniv of Association for Restoration of Fatherland.
N991 **429** 10 ch. red, buff & black 35 10

1971. Battlefields in Musan Area, May 1939. Multicoloured.
N992 5 ch. Type **430** 15 10
N993 10 ch. Machine guns in perspex cases (horiz) 20 10
N994 40 ch. Huts among birch trees (horiz) 55 15

431 Koreans Marching

432 Flame Emblem

1971. Solidarity of Koreans in Japan.
N995 **431** 10 ch. brown 20 10

1971. 25th Anniv of Korean Childrens' Union.
N996 **432** 10 ch. red, yellow and blue 20 10

433 Marchers and Banners

434 Foundryman

1971. 6th Congress of League of Socialist Working Youth.
N997 **433** 5 ch. red, buff and black 10 10
N998 – 10 ch. red, green & black 20 10
DESIGN: 10 c. Marchers and banner under globe.

1971. 25th Anniv of Labour Law.
N999 **434** 5 ch. black, purple & buff 20 10

435 Young Women

1971. 25th Anniv of Sex Equality Law.
N1000 **435** 5 ch. multicoloured . . 20 10

436 Schoolchildren

1971. 15th Anniv of Compulsory Primary Education.
N1001 **436** 10 ch. multicoloured . 35 10

437 Choe Yong Do and Combat Scene

1971. Heroes of the Revolutionary Struggle in South Korea.
N1002 **437** 5 ch. black and green 25 10
N1003 – 10 ch. red and brown 25 10
N1004 – 10 ch. black and red 25 10
DESIGNS: No. N1003, Revolutionary with book; N1004, Kim Jong Tae and scene of triumph.

438 Two Foundrymen

1971. 25th Anniv of Nationalization of Industry Law.
N1005 **438** 5 ch. black, grn & brn 1·50 10

HAVE YOU READ THE NOTES AT THE BEGINNING OF THIS CATALOGUE?
These often provide the answers to the enquiries we receive.

439 Struggle in Korea

1971. The Anti-Imperialist and Anti-U.S. Imperialist Struggles.
N1006 **439** 10 ch. red, black and brown 25 10
N1007 – 10 ch. brown, black and blue 35 10
N1008 – 10 ch. red, black and pink 50 10
N1009 – 10 ch. black, olive and green 25 10
N1010 – 10 ch. orange, black and red 50 10
N1011 – 40 ch. green, black and pink 50 15
DESIGNS: No. N1007, Struggle in Vietnam; N1008, Soldier with rifle and airplane marked "EC"; N1009, Struggle in Africa; N1010, Cuban soldier and Central America; N1011, Bayonetting U.S. soldier.

440 Kim Il Sung University

1971. 25th Anniv of Kim Il Sung University.
N1012 **440** 10 ch. grey, red & yellow 20 10

441 Iron-ore Ladle (Mining)

1971. Tasks of Six Year Plan. Multicoloured.
N1013 10 ch. Type **441** . . . . . 1·50 15
N1014 10 ch. Workers and text . 30 10
N1015 10 ch. Railway track (Transport) . . . . . . 1·50 15
N1016 10 ch. Hand and wrench (Industry) 30 10
N1017 10 ch. Mechanical scoop (Construction) . . . . . 1·50 15
N1018 10 ch. Manufactured goods (Trade) 30 10
N1019 10 ch. Crate on hoists (Exports) 25 10
N1020 10 ch. Lathe (Heavy Industries) . . . . . . 1·50 15
N1021 10 ch. Freighter (Shipping) 60 10
N1022 10 ch. Household equipment (Light Industries) . . . 25 10
N1023 10 ch. Corncob and wheat (Agriculture) 40 10

442 Technicians

1971. Cultural Revolution. Multicoloured.
N1024 2 ch. Type **442** 20 10
N1025 5 ch. Mechanic 25 10
N1026 10 ch. Schoolchildren . . 30 10
N1027 10 ch. Chemist 50 10
N1028 10 ch. Composer at piano 85 15

443 Workers with Red Books

1971. Ideological Revolution. Multicoloured.
N1029 10 ch. Type **443** 20 10
N1030 10 ch. Workers reading book 20 10
N1031 10 ch. Workers' lecture . . 20 10
N1032 10 ch. Worker and pneumatic drill 20 10

444 Korean Family

1971. Improvement in Living Standards.
N1033 **444** 10 ch. multicoloured . . 15 10

445 Furnaceman

1971. Implementation of Decisions of Fifth Workers' Party Conference.
N1034 **445** 10 ch. multicoloured . . 1·00 10

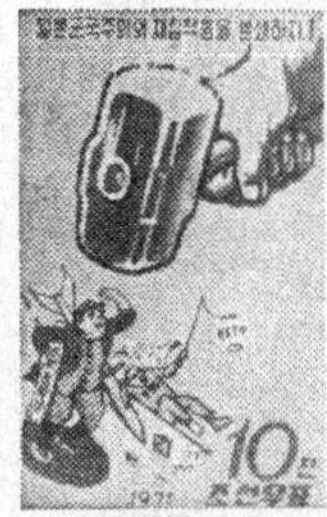
446

447 6000-ton Press

1971. Solidarity with South Korean Revolutionaries.
N1036 **446** 10 ch. brown, blue and black 30 10
N1037 – 10 ch. brown, flesh and red 30 10
N1038 – 10 ch. multicoloured . . 30 10
N1039 – 10 ch. multicoloured . . 30 10
DESIGNS—VERT: No. N1037, U.S. soldier attacked by poster boards; N1038, Hands holding rifles aloft. HORIZ: No. N1039, Men advancing with rifles.

1971.
N1040 **447** 2 ch. brown 70 10
N1041 – 5 ch. blue 90 15
N1042 – 10 ch. green . . . . . 1·10 10
N1043 – 10 ch. green . . . . . 1·10 10
DESIGNS: No. N1041, Refrigerated freighter "Ponghwasan"; N1042, 300 h.p. bulldozer; N1043, "Sungrisan" lorry.

448 Title-page and Militants

1971. 35th Anniv of "Samil Wolgan" Magazine.
N1044 **448** 10 ch. red, green & blk 45 10

452 Poultry Chicks

1972. Poultry Breeding.
N1051 **452** 5 ch. yellow, black and brown 25 10
N1052 – 10 ch. orange, bistre and brown 35 10
N1053 – 40 ch. blue, orange and deep blue 55 15
DESIGNS: 10 ch. Chickens and battery egg house; 40 ch. Eggs and fowls suspended from hooks.

453 Scene from "Village Shrine"

1972. Films of Guerrilla War.
N1054 **453** 10 ch. grey and green 60 10
N1055 – 10 ch. blue, pur & orge 60 10
N1056 – 10 ch. purple, bl & yell 60 10
DESIGNS: No. N1055, Patriot with pistol ("A Sea of Blood"); N1056, Guerrilla using bayonet ("The Lot of a Self-Defence Corps Member").

454 Kim Il Sung acknowledging Greetings

1972. Kim Il Sung's 60th Birthday. Scenes in the life of Kim Il Sung, dated "1912–1972". Mult.
N1057 5 ch. Type **454** 20 10
N1058 5 ch. In campaign H.Q. . . 20 10
N1059 5 ch. Military conference (horiz) 20 10
N1060 10 ch. In wheatfield (horiz) 30 10
N1061 10 ch. Directing construction (horiz) . . . . 2·00 40
N1062 10 ch. Talking to foundry workers (horiz) 20 10
N1063 10 ch. Aboard whaler (horiz) 55 10
N1064 10 ch. Visiting a hospital (horiz) 75 10
N1065 10 ch. Viewing orchard (horiz) 20 10
N1066 10 ch. With survey party on Haeju–Hasong railway line (horiz) . . . . 2·00 40
N1067 10 ch. Meeting female workers at silk factory (horiz) . . . . 1·00 15
N1068 10 ch. Village conference (horiz) 20 10
N1069 10 ch. Touring chicken factory (horiz) 35 10
N1070 40 ch. Relaxing with children 45 20
N1071 1 wn. Giant portrait and marchers 70 40

455 Bugler sounding "Charge".

1972. 40th Anniv of Guerrilla Army.
N1073 **455** 10 ch. multicoloured . 45 10

456 Pavilion of Ryongpo

1972. Historic Sites of the 1950–53 War. Mult.
N1074 2 ch. Type **456** 15 10
N1075 5 ch. Houses at Onjong . . 15 10
N1076 10 ch. Headquarters, Kosanjin 15 10
N1077 40 ch. Victory Museum, Chonsung-dong 30 10

457 Volleyball

1972. Olympic Games, Munich. Multicoloured.
N1078 2 ch. Type **457** 25 10
N1079 5 ch. Boxing (horiz) . . . 35 10
N1080 10 ch. Judo 40 10
N1081 10 ch. Wrestling (horiz) . . 40 10
N1082 40 ch. Rifle-shooting . . . 95 20

458 Chollima Street, Pyongyang

1971. Chollima Street, Pyongyang.

N1083 5 ch. orange and black 1·60 15
N1084 **458** 10 ch. yellow and black 60 15
N1085 10 ch. green and black 60 15

DESIGNS: No. N1083, Bridge and skyscraper blocks; N1085, Another view looking up street.

459 Dredger

1972. Development of Natural Resources. Multicoloured.

N1086 5 ch. Type **459** 35 10
N1087 10 ch. Forestry 50 10
N1088 40 ch. Reclaiming land from the sea 60 15

460 Ferrous Industry

1972. Tasks of the Six-Year Plan. The Metallurgical Industry. Inscr "1971–1976". Multicoloured.

N1089 10 ch. Type **460** . . . . . 1·40 10
N1090 10 ch. Non-ferrous Industry 40 10

461 Iron Ore Industry

1972. Tasks of the Six-Year Plan. The Mining Industry. Inscr "1971–1976". Multicoloured.

N1091 10 ch. Type **461** 40 10
N1092 10 ch. Coal mining industry 1·50 15

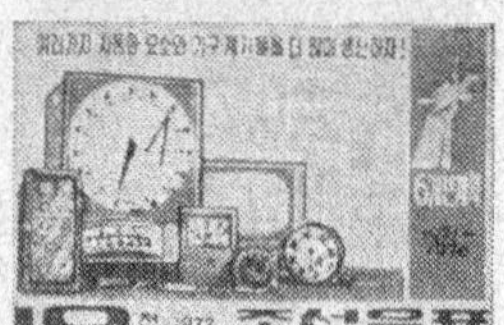

462 Electronic and Automation Industry

1972. Tasks of the Six-Year Plan. The Engineering Industry. Inscr "1971–1976". Multicoloured.

N1093 10 ch. Type **462** 60 10
N1094 10 ch. Single-purpose machines 40 10
N1095 10 ch. Machine tools . . . 40 10

463 Clearing Virgin Soil

1972. Tasks of the Six-Year Plan. Rural Economy. Multicoloured.

N1096 10 ch. Type **463** 45 10
N1097 10 ch. Irrigation 45 10
N1098 10 ch. Harvesting 45 10

464 Automation

1972. Tasks of the Six-Year Plan. Inscr "1971–1976". Multicoloured.

N1099 10 ch. Type **464** 90 10
N1100 10 ch. Agricultural mechanisation 50 10
N1101 10 ch. Lightening of house-hold chores 50 10

465 Chemical Fibres and Materials

1972. Tasks of the Six-Year Plan. The Chemical Industry. Inscr "1971–1976". Multicoloured.

N1102 10 ch. Type **465** 60 10
N1103 10 ch. Fertilisers, insecticides and weed killers 60 10

466 Textiles

1972. Tasks of the Six-Year Plan. Consumer Goods. Inscr "1971–1976". Multicoloured.

N1104 10 ch. Type **466** 65 10
N1105 10 ch. Kitchen ware and overalls 45 10
N1106 10 ch. Household goods . 45 10

467 Fish, Fruit and Vegetables

1972. Tasks of the Six-Year Plan. The Food Industry. Multicoloured.

N1107 10 ch. Type **467** 65 10
N1108 10 ch. Tinned foods . . . 65 10
N1109 10 ch. Food packaging . . 65 10

468 Electrifying Railway Lines

1972. Tasks of the Six-Year Plan. Transport. Inscr "1971–1976". Multicoloured.

N1110 10 ch. Type **468** 45 10
N1111 10 ch. Laying new railway track 45 10
N1112 10 ch. Freighters 40 10

469 Soldier with Shell

1972. North Korean Armed Forces. Multicoloured.

N1113 10 ch. Type **469** 35 10
N1114 10 ch. Marine 35 10
N1115 10 ch. Air Force pilot . . 35 10

470 "Revolution of 19 April 1960"

1972. The Struggle for Reunification of Korea. Multicoloured.

N1116 10 ch. Type **470** 15 10
N1117 10 ch. Marchers with banner 15 10
N1118 10 ch. Insurgents with red banner 15 10
N1119 10 ch. Attacking U.S. and South Korean soldiers . 15 10
N1120 10 ch. Workers with posters 15 10
N1121 10 ch. Workers acclaiming revolution . . . . 3·50 40
N1122 10 ch. Workers and manifesto 15 10

471 Single-spindle Automatic Lathe

1972. Machine Tools.

N1123 **471** 5 ch. green and purple 25 10
N1124 – 10 ch. blue and green 35 10
N1125 – 40 ch. green & brown 80 15

DESIGNS—HORIZ: 10 ch. "Kusong-3" lathe; VERT: 40 ch. 2,000 ton crank press.

472 Casting Vote

1972. National Elections. Multicoloured.

N1126 10 ch. Type **472** 25 10
N1127 10 ch. Election campaigner 25 10

475 Soldier

1973. 25th Anniv of Founding of Korean People's Army. Multicoloured.

N1130 5 ch. Type **475** 20 10
N1131 10 ch. Sailor 30 10
N1132 40 ch. Airman 70 25

476 Wrestling Site

1973. Scenes of Kim Il Sung's Childhood, Mangyongdae. Multicoloured.

N1133 2 ch. Type **476** 15 10
N1134 5 ch. Warship rock 15 10
N1135 10 ch. Swinging site (vert) 20 10
N1136 10 ch. Sliding rock 20 10
N1137 40 ch. Fishing site 60 15

477 Monument to Socialist Revolution and Construction, Mansu Hill

1973. Museum of the Korean Revolution.

N1138 **477** 10 ch. multicoloured . . 25 10
N1139 – 10 ch. multicoloured . . 25 10
N1140 – 40 ch. multicoloured . . 50 15
N1141 – 3 wn. green and yellow 2·50 60

DESIGNS—As Type **477**: 10 ch. (N1139) Similar monument but men in military clothes; 40 ch. Statue of Kim Il Sung. HORIZ—60 × 29 mm: 3 wn. Museum building.

478 Karajibong Camp

1973. Secret Camps by Tuman-Gang in Guerrilla War, 1932. Multicoloured.

N1142 10 ch. Type **478** 15 10
N1143 10 ch. Soksaegol Camp . . 15 10

479

1973. Menace of Japanese Influence in South Korea.

N1144 **479** 10 ch. multicoloured . 20 10

480 Wrecked U.S. Tanks

1973. Five-point Programme for Reunification of Korea. Multicoloured.

N1145 2 ch. Type **480** 40 10
N1146 5 ch. Electric train and crane lifting tractor . . . . . 2·50 15
N1147 10 ch. Leaflets falling on crowd 20 10
N1148 10 ch. Hand holding leaflet and map of Korea . . . 40 10
N1149 40 ch. Banner and globe . 60 20

481 Lorries **482** Volleyball

1973. Lorries and Tractors. Multicoloured.

N1150 10 ch. Type **481** 35 10
N1151 10 ch. Tractors and earth-moving machine 35 10

1973. Socialist Countries' Junior Women's Volleyball Games, Pyongyang.

N1152 **482** 10 ch. multicoloured . 30 10

483 Battlefield

1973. 20th Anniv of Victory in Korean War.

N1153 **483** 10 ch. green, purple and black 20 10
N1154 – 10 ch. brown, blue and black 20 10

DESIGN: 10 ch. Urban fighting.

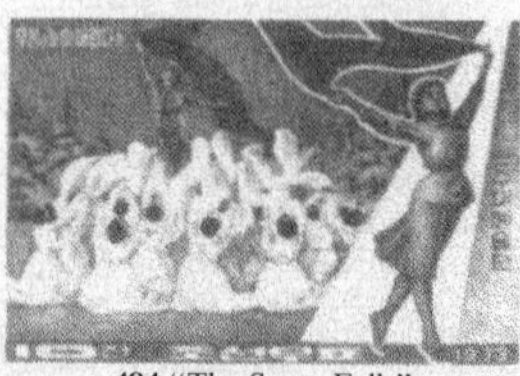

484 "The Snow Falls"

1973. Mansudae Art Troupe. Dances. Multicoloured.

N1155 10 ch. Type **484** 50 10
N1156 25 ch. "A Bumper Harvest of Apples" . . . . 1·10 25
N1157 40 ch. "Azalea of the Fatherland" . . . . . . 1·40 30

485 Schoolchildren

1973. Ten Years Compulsory Secondary Education.

N1158 **485** 10 ch. multicoloured . 25 10

486 "Fervour in the Revolution"

1973. The Works of Kim Il Sung (1st series).

N1159 **486** 10 ch. brown, red and yellow 15 10
N1160 – 10 ch. brown, green and yellow 15 10
N1161 – 10 ch. lake, brown and yellow 15 10

DESIGNS: No. N1160, Selected works; N1161, "Strengthen the Socialist System".

See also Nos. N1217/18.

487 Celebrating Republic

1973. 25th Anniv of People's Republic. Multicoloured.

N1162 5 ch. Type **487** 10 10
N1163 10 ch. Fighting in Korean War 10 10
N1164 40 ch. Peace and reconstruction . . . . . 1·60 40

488 Pobwang Peak

1973. Mt. Myohyang. Multicoloured.

N1165 2 ch. Type **488** 25 10
N1166 5 ch. Inhodae Pavilion . . 35 10
N1167 10 ch. Taeha Falls (vert) . 1·75 30
N1168 40 ch. Rongyon Falls (vert) 2·50 30

489 Party Memorial Building

1973. Party Memorial Building.

N1169 **489** 1 wn. brown, grey and buff . . . . 1·25 30

490 Football and Handball

1973. National People's Sports Meeting. Mult.

N1170 2 ch. Type **490** 50 10
N1171 5 ch. High jumper and woman sprinter 25 10
N1172 10 ch. Skaters and skiers . 40 10
N1173 10 ch. Wrestling and swinging 30 10
N1174 40 ch. Parachutist and motor cyclists . . . . 2·75 25

491 Weightlifting

492 Chongryu Cliff

1973. Junior Weightlifting Championships of Socialist Countries.

N1175 **491** 10 ch. blue, brown and green 25 10

1973. Scenery of Moran Hill, Pyongyang. Multicoloured.

N1176 2 ch. Type **492** 70 15
N1177 5 ch. Moran Waterfall . . 2·75 40
N1178 10 ch. Pubyok Pavilion . . 75 10
N1179 40 ch. Ulmil Pavilion . . . 90 15

493 Rainbow Bridge **494** Magnolia Flower

1973. Diamond Mountains Scenery (4th issue). Multicoloured.

N1180 2 ch. Type **493** . . . . . 1·25 15
N1181 5 ch. Suspension footbridge, Okryudong (horiz) . . . 1·25 15
N1182 10 ch. Chonnyo Peak . . 65 10
N1183 10 ch. Chilchung Rock and Sonji Peak (horiz) . . . 65 10
N1184 40 ch. Sujong and Pari Peaks (horiz) 75 15

1973.

N1185 **494** 10 ch. multicoloured . 40 10

495 S. Korean Revolutionaries

1973. South Korean Revolution. Multicoloured

N1186 10 ch. Type **495** 15 10
N1187 10 ch. Marching revolutionaries 15 10

496 Cock sees Butterflies

1973. Scenes from "Cock Chasing Butterflies". Fairy Tale. Multicoloured.

N1188 2 ch. Type **496** . . . . . . 1·25 10
N1189 5 ch. Butterflies discuss how to repel cock . . . . . 1·25 10
N1190 10 ch. Cock chasing butterflies with basket . 1·75 15
N1191 10 ch. Cock chasing butterfly up cliff . . . . 1·75 20
N1192 40 ch. Cock chasing butterflies over cliff . . 2·00 25
N1193 90 ch. Cock falls into sea and butterflies escape . . . 2·50 30

497 Yonpung

1973. Historical Sites of War and Revolution (40 ch.). Multicoloured.

N1196 2 ch. Type **497** 10 10
N1197 5 ch. Hyangha 10 10
N1198 10 ch. Changgol 15 10
N1199 40 ch. Paeksong 55 10

498 Science Library, Kim Il Sung University

1973. New Buildings in Pyongyang.

N1200 **498** 2 ch. violet 50 10
N1201 – 5 ch. green 15 10
N1202 – 10 ch. brown 25 10
N1203 – 40 ch. brown and buff . 55 15
N1204 – 90 ch. buff 95 30

DESIGNS—HORIZ: 10 ch. Victory Museum; 40 ch. People's Palace of Culture; 90 ch. Indoor stadium. VERT: 5 ch. Building No. 2, Kim Il Sung University.

499 Red Book

1973. Socialist Constitution of North Korea. Multicoloured.

N1205 10 ch. Type **499** 15 10
N1206 10 ch. Marchers with red book and banners 15 10
N1207 10 ch. Marchers with red book and emblem 15 10

500 Oriental Great Reed Warbler

1973. Korean Songbirds. Multicoloured.

N1208 5 ch. Type **500** . . . . . . 1·60 25
N1209 10 ch. Grey starling (facing right) . . . . 2·25 45
N1210 10 ch. Daurian starling (facing left) . . . . 2·25 45

503 Chollima Statue

1974. The Works of Kim Il Sung (2nd series). Multicoloured.

N1217 10 ch. Type **503** 65 10
N1218 10 ch. Bayonets threatening U.S. soldier 15 10

504 Train in Station

1974. Opening of Pyongyang Metro. Multicoloured.

N1219 10 ch. Type **504** 45 10
N1220 10 ch. Escalators 45 10
N1221 10 ch. Station Hall 45 10

505 Capital Construction Front

1974. Five Fronts of Socialist Construction. Multicoloured.

N1222 10 ch. Type **505** 15 10
N1223 10 ch. Agricultural front . . 25 10
N1224 10 ch. Transport front . . . 1·25 15
N1225 10 ch. Fisheries front . . . 75 15
N1226 10 ch. Industrial front (vert) 25 10

506 Marchers with Banners

1974. 10th Anniv of Publication of "Theses on the Socialist Rural Question in Our Country". Multicoloured.

N1227 10 ch. Type **506** 15 10
N1228 10 ch. Book and rejoicing crowd 15 10
N1229 10 ch. Tractor & banners . 15 10

Nos. 1227/9 were issued together, se-tenant, forming a composite design.

507 Manure Spreader

1974. Farm Machinery.

N1230 **507** 2 ch. green, black & red 40 10
N1231 – 5 ch. red, black & blue 40 10
N1232 – 10 ch. red, black & grn 40 10

DESIGNS: 5 ch. "Progress" tractor; 10 ch. "Mount Taedoksan" tractor.

508 Archery (Grenoble)

1974. North Korean Victories at International Sports Meetings. Multicoloured.

N1233 2 ch. Type **508** 90 15
N1234 5 ch. Gymnastics (Varna) 15 10
N1235 10 ch. Boxing (Bucharest) 25 10
N1236 20 ch. Volleyball (Pyongyang) 15 10
N1237 30 ch. Rifle shooting (Sofia) 45 10
N1238 40 ch. Judo (Tbilisi) . . . 65 15
N1239 60 ch. Model aircraft flying (Vienna) (horiz) . . . . 1·10 20
N1240 1 wn. 50 Table tennis (Peking) (horiz) . . . . 2·00 30

509 Book and Rejoicing Crowd

1974. The First Country with No Taxes.

N1241 **509** 10 ch. multicoloured . 20 10

510 Drawing up Programme in Woods

1974. Kim Il Sung during the Anti-Japanese Struggle. Multicoloured.

N1242 10 ch. Type **510** 25 10
N1243 10 ch. Giving directions to Pak Dal 25 10
N1244 10 ch. Presiding over Nanhutou Conference . 25 10
N1245 10 ch. Supervising creation of strongpoint 25 10

511 Sun Hui loses her Sight

1974. Scenes from "The Flower Girl" (revolutionary opera). Multicoloured.

N1246 2 ch. Type **511** 65 10
N1247 5 ch. Death of Ggot Bun's mother 65 10
N1248 10 ch. Ggot Bun throws boiling water at landlord 1·40 10
N1249 40 ch. Ggot Bun joins revolutionaries . . . . . 1·75 15

MINIMUM PRICE

The minimum price quoted is 10p which represents a handling charge rather than a basis for valuing common stamps. For further notes about prices, see introductory pages.

512 Leopard Cat

1974. 15th Anniv of Pyongyang Zoo. Multicoloured.

N1251	2 ch. Type **512**	50	10
N1252	5 ch. Lynx	50	10
N1253	10 ch. Red fox	50	10
N1254	10 ch. Wild boar	50	10
N1255	20 ch. Dhole	50	15
N1256	40 ch. Brown bear	60	25
N1257	60 ch. Leopard	1·00	25
N1258	70 ch. Tiger	1·40	30
N1259	90 ch. Lion	1·75	35

513 "Rosa acucularis lindly"

1974. Roses. Multicoloured.

N1261	2 ch. Type **513**	40	10
N1262	5 ch. Yellow sweet briar	45	10
N1263	10 ch. Pink aromatic rose	55	10
N1264	10 ch. Aronia sweet briar (yellow centres)	55	10
N1265	40 ch. Multi-petal sweet briar	1·40	10

515 Weigela

1974. Flowering Plants of Mt. Paekdu. Mult.

N1267	2 ch. Type **515**	40	10
N1268	5 ch. Amaryllis	40	10
N1269	10 ch. Red lily	40	10
N1270	20 ch. Orange lily	55	10
N1271	40 ch. Azalea	75	10
N1272	60 ch. Yellow lily	1·25	10

516 Postwoman and Construction Site

1974. Cent of U.P.U. and Admission of North Korea to Union. Multicoloured.

N1273	10 ch. Type **516**	1·25	15
N1274	25 ch. Chollima monument	10	10
N1275	40 ch. Globe and Antonov An-12 transport planes	90	15

517 Common Pond Frog

1974. Amphibians. Multicoloured.

N1276	2 ch. Type **517**	90	10
N1277	5 ch. Oriental fire-bellied toad	1·10	10
N1278	10 ch. Bullfrog	1·25	15
N1279	40 ch. Common toad	1·75	25

518 "Women of Namgang Village"

1974. Korean Paintings. Multicoloured.

N1281	2 ch. Type **518**	50	10
N1282	5 ch. "An Old Man on the Rakdong River" (60 × 49 mm)	60	10
N1283	10 ch. "Morning in the Naekumgang" (bridge)	1·25	10
N1284	20 ch. "Mt. Kumgang" (60 × 49 mm)	1·10	15

519 "Elektron 1" and "Elektron 2", 1964

1974. Cosmonauts Day. Multicoloured.

N1286	10 ch. Type **519**	15	10
N1287	20 ch. "Proton 1", 1965	25	10
N1288	30 ch. "Venera 3", 1966	40	10
N1289	40 ch. "Venera 5" and "Venera 6", 1969	50	10

521 Antonov An-2 Biplane

1974. Civil Aviation. Multicoloured

N1292	2 ch. Type **521**	55	10
N1293	5 ch. Lisunov Li-2	55	10
N1294	10 ch. Ilyushin Il-14P	75	10
N1295	40 ch. Antonov An-24	1·00	35
N1296	60 ch. Ilyushin Il-18	1·75	50

522 "Rhododendron redowskianum"

1974. Plants of Mt. Paekdu. Multicoloured.

N1298	2 ch. Type **522**	35	10
N1299	5 ch. "Dryas octopetala"	35	10
N1300	10 ch. "Potentilla fruticosa"	40	10
N1301	20 ch. "Papaver somniferum"	50	10
N1302	40 ch. "Phyllodoce caerulea"	70	20
N1303	60 ch. "Oxytropis anertii"	1·25	40

523 "Sobaek River in the Morning"

1974. Modern Korean Paintings (1st series). Multicoloured.

N1304	10 ch. Type **523**	60	10
N1305	20 ch. "Combatants of Mt. Laohei" (60 × 40 mm)	65	10
N1306	30 ch. "Spring in the Fields"	75	15
N1307	40 ch. "Tideland Night"	2·75	30
N1308	60 ch. "Daughter" (60 × 54 mm)	90	40

See also Nos. N1361/5, N1386/96 and N1485/9.

525 Log cabin, Unha Village

1974. Historic Sites of the Revolution. Multicoloured.

N1310	5 ch. Munmyong	10	10
N1311	10 ch. Type **525**	10	10

526 Sesame

1974. Oil-producing Plants. Multicoloured.

N1312	2 ch. Type **526**	65	10
N1313	5 ch. "Perilla frutescens"	70	10
N1314	10 ch. Sunflower	80	10
N1315	40 ch. Castor bean	1·10	40

527 Kim Il Sung as Guerrilla Leader

1974. Kim Il Sung. Multicoloured.

N1316	10 ch. Type **527**	20	10
N1317	10 ch. Commander of the People's Army (52 × 35 mm)	20	10
N1318	10 ch. "The commander is also a son of the people" (52 × 35 mm)	20	10
N1319	10 ch. Negotiating with the Chinese anti-Japanese unit (52 × 35 mm)	20	10

528

1974. Grand Monument on Mansu Hill. Mult.

N1320	10 ch. Type **528**	15	10
N1321	10 ch. As T **528** but men in civilian clothes	15	10
N1322	10 ch. As T **528** but men facing left	15	10
N1323	10 ch. As No. N1322 but men in civilian clothes	15	10

529 Factory Ship "Chilbosan"

1974. Deep-sea Fishing. Multicoloured.

N1324	2 ch. Type **529**	70	25
N1325	5 ch. Trawler support ship "Paekdusan"	70	25
N1326	10 ch. Freighter "Moranbong"	70	25
N1327	20 ch. Whale-catcher	70	25
N1328	30 ch. Trawler	70	25
N1329	40 ch. Stern trawler	70	25

539 Kim Il Sung crosses River Agrok

1975. 50th Anniv of Kim Il Sung's crossing of River Agrok.

N1349	**539** 10 ch. multicoloured	25	10

540 Pak Yong Sun "World Table Tennis Queen"

1975. Pak Yong Sun, Winner of 33rd World Table Tennis Championships, Calcutta.

N1350	**540** 10 ch. multicoloured	50	10

541 Common Zebra

1975. Pyongyang Zoo. Multicoloured.

N1352	10 ch. Type **541**	30	10
N1353	10 ch. African buffalo	30	10
N1354	20 ch. Giant panda (horiz)	80	10
N1355	25 ch. Bactrian camel	70	15
N1356	30 ch. Indian elephant	1·25	20

542 "Blue Dragon"

1975. 7th-century Mural Paintings from Koguryo Tombs, Kangso.

N1357	10 ch. Type **542**	65	10
N1358	15 ch. "White Tiger"	85	10
N1359	25 ch. "Red Phoenix" (vert)	1·00	10
N1360	40 ch. "Snake-turtle"	1·40	25

543 "Spring in the Guerrilla Base" (1968)

1975. Modern Korean Paintings (2nd series). Anti-Japanese struggle. Multicoloured.

N1361	10 ch. Type **543**	35	10
N1362	10 ch. "Revolutionary Army landing at Unggi" (1969)	35	10
N1363	15 ch. "Sewing Team Members" (1961)	55	10
N1364	20 ch. "Girl Watering Horse" (1969)	1·00	15
N1365	30 ch. "Kim Jong Suk giving Guidance to Children's Corps" (1970)	80	20

544 Cosmonaut

1975. Cosmonauts' Day. Multicoloured.

N1366 10 ch. Type **544** 15 10

N1367 30 ch. "Lunokhod" moon vehicle (horiz) 40 10

N1368 40 ch. "Soyuz" spacecraft and "Salyut" space laboratory (horiz) 55 15

546 The Beacon lit at Pochonbo, 1937

1975. Kim Il Sung during the Guerrilla War against the Japanese. Multicoloured.

N1370 10 ch. Type **546** 25 10

N1371 10 ch. "A Bowl of Parched-rice Powder", 1938 . . . 25 10

N1372 10 ch. Guiding the Nanpaizi meeting, November, 1938 25 10

N1373 10 ch. Welcoming helper . 25 10

N1374 10 ch. Lecturing the guerrillas 25 10

N1375 15 ch. Advancing into the homeland, May 1939 . . 35 10

N1376 25 ch. By Lake Samji, May 1939 . . . . 45 10

N1377 30 ch. At Sinsadong, May 1939 . . . . 55 10

N1378 40 ch. Xiaohaerbaling meeting, 1940 . . . . . 65 15

547 Vase of Flowers and Kim Il Sung's Birthplace

1975. Kim Il Sung's 63rd Birthday. Multicoloured.

N1379 10 ch. Type **547** 10 10

N1379a 40 ch. Kim Il Sung's birthplace, Mangyongdae 35 10

548 South Korean Insurgent

1975. 15th Anniv of April 19th Rising.

N1380 **548** 10 ch. multicoloured . 15 10

549 "Kingfisher at a Lotus Pond"

1975. Paintings of Li Dynasty. Multicoloured.

N1381 5 ch. Type **549** . . . . . 1·40 10

N1382 10 ch. "Crabs" 85 10

N1383 15 ch. "Rose of Sharon" . 1·25 15

N1384 25 ch. "Lotus and Water Cock" . . . . 1·75 30

N1385 30 ch. "Tree Peony and Red Junglefowl" . . . . . . 2·75 30

1975. Modern Korean Paintings (3rd series). Fatherland Liberation War. Dated designs as T **543**. Multicoloured.

N1386 5 ch. "On the Advance Southward" (1966) (vert) 20 10

N1387 10 ch. "The Assigned Post" (girl sentry) (1968) (vert) 25 10

N1388 15 ch. "The Heroism of Li Su Bok" (1965) 30 10

N1389 25 ch. "Retaliation" (woman machine-gunner) (1970) . 50 20

N1390 30 ch. "The awaited Troops" (1970) 60 20

1975. Modern Korean Paintings (4th series). Socialist Construction. As T **543**. Multicoloured.

N1391 10 ch. "Pine Tree" (1966) (vert) 70 10

N1392 10 ch. "The Blue Signal Lamp" (1960) (vert) . . 2·50 10

N1393 15 ch. "A Night of Snowfall" (1963) 75 10

N1394 20 ch. "Smelters" (1968) . 85 15

N1395 25 ch. "Tideland Reclamation" (1961) . . 85 15

N1396 30 ch. "Mount Paekgum" (1966) 85 20

550 Flag and Building

552 "Feet first" entry (man)

1975. 20th Anniv of "Chongryon" Association of Koreans in Japan.

N1397 **550** 10 ch. multicoloured . 15 10

N1398 3 wn. multicoloured . 2·50 55

1975. Diving. Multicoloured.

N1400 10 ch. Type **552** 15 10

N1401 25 ch. Piked somersault (man) 40 10

N1402 40 ch. "Head first" entry (woman) 85 15

553

1975. Campaign against U.S. Imperialism.

N1403 **553** 10 ch. multicoloured . 15 10

554 Memorial Fish

1975. Fresh-water Fish. Multicoloured.

N1404 10 ch. Type **554** 40 10

N1405 10 ch. Whitefish (fish swimming to right) . . . 40 10

N1406 15 ch. "Opsanichthys bidens" 60 10

N1407 25 ch. Naere . . . . 1·00 15

N1408 30 ch. Catfish (fish swimming to right) . . . . 1·25 20

N1409 30 ch. Snakehead (fish swimming to left) . . . 1·25 20

555

1975. 10th Socialist Countries' Football Tournament, Pyongyang.

N1410 **555** 5 ch. multicoloured . . 25 10

N1411 – 10 ch. multicoloured . . 25 10

N1412 – 15 ch. multicoloured . . 30 10

N1413 – 20 ch. multicoloured . . 40 15

N1414 – 50 ch. multicoloured . . 75 35

DESIGNS: 10 ch. to 50 ch. Various footballers.

556 Blue and Yellow Macaw

557 Flats

1975. Birds. Multicoloured.

N1416 10 ch. Type **556** . . . . . . 1·25 15

N1417 15 ch. Sulphur-crested cockatoo . . . . 1·50 20

N1418 20 ch. Blyth's parakeet . . 1·90 30

N1419 25 ch. Rainbow lory . . . . 2·25 35

N1420 30 ch. Budgerigar . . . . . 2·50 40

1975. New Buildings in Pyongyang. Multicoloured.

N1421 90 ch. Saesallim (formerly Sarguson) St. . . . . . . 1·50 40

N1422 1 wn. Type **557** . . . . . . 1·75 45

N1423 2 wn. Potonggang Hotel . . 2·75 60

558 White Peach Blossom

559 Sejongbong

1975. Blossoms of Flowering Trees. Multicoloured.

N1424 10 ch. Type **558** 30 10

N1425 15 ch. Red peach blossom 30 10

N1426 20 ch. Red plum blossom 45 15

N1427 25 ch. Apricot blossom . . 60 15

N1428 30 ch. Cherry blossom . . . 85 20

1975. Landscapes in the Diamond Mountains. Multicoloured.

N1429 5 ch. Type **559** 40 10

N1430 10 ch. Chonsondae 65 10

N1431 15 ch. Pisamun 85 10

N1432 25 ch. Manmulsang . . . . 1·10 20

N1433 30 ch. Chaehabong . . . . 1·25 20

560 Azalea

1975. Flowers of the Azalea Family. Multicoloured.

N1434 5 ch. Type **560** 35 10

N1435 10 ch. White azalea 35 10

N1436 15 ch. Wild rhododendron 50 10

N1437 20 ch. White rhododendron 50 15

N1438 25 ch. Rhododendron 65 15

N1439 30 ch. Yellow rhododendron 90 20

561 Gliders

1975. Training for National Defence. Mult.

N1440 5 ch. Type **561** 45 10

N1441 5 ch. Radio-controlled model airplane 45 10

N1442 10 ch. "Free fall parachutist" (vert) 60 10

N1443 10 ch. Parachutist landing on target (vert) 60 10

N1444 20 ch. Parachutist with bouquet of flowers (vert) 95 15

HAVE YOU READ THE NOTES AT THE BEGINNING OF THIS CATALOGUE?

These often provide the answers to the enquiries we receive.

562 Wild Apple

1975. Fruit Tree Blossom. Multicoloured.

N1446 10 ch. Type **562** 30 10

N1447 15 ch. Wild pear 30 10

N1448 20 ch. Hawthorn 40 15

N1449 25 ch. Chinese quince . . . 55 20

N1450 30 ch. Flowering quince . . 65 20

563 Torch of Juche

1975. 30th Anniv of Korean Workers' Party. Multicoloured.

N1451 2 ch. "Victory" and American graves 10 10

N1452 2 ch. Sunrise over Mt. Paekdu-san 10 10

N1453 5 ch. Type **563** 10 10

N1454 5 ch. Chollima Statue and sunset over Pyongyang 10 10

N1455 10 ch. Korean with Red Book 10 10

N1456 10 ch. Chollima Statue . . 10 10

N1457 25 ch. Crowds and burning building 35 10

N1458 70 ch. Flowers and map of Korea 95 15

564 Welcoming Crowd

1975. 30th Anniv of Kim Il Sung's Return to Pyongyang.

N1460 **564** 20 ch. multicoloured . 25 15

565 Workers holding "Juche" Torch

1975. 30th Anniv of "Rodong Simmun" (Journal of the Central Committee of the Worker's Party.)

N1461 **565** 10 ch. multicoloured . 50 10

566 Hyonmu Gate

1975. Ancient Wall-Gates of Pyongyang. Multicoloured.

N1463 10 ch. Type **566** 10 10

N1464 10 ch. Taedong Gate . . . 10 10

N1465 15 ch. Potong Gate 20 10

N1466 20 ch. Chongum Gate . . 35 15

N1467 30 ch. Chilsong Gate (vert) 45 25

567

1975. Views of Mt. Chilbo.

N1468 567 10 ch. multicoloured . 40 10
N1469 – 10 ch. multicoloured . 40 10
N1470 – 15 ch. multicoloured . 65 10
N1471 – 20 ch. multicoloured . 75 15
N1472 – 30 ch. multicoloured . 85 20

DESIGNS: Nos. N1468/72, Various views.

568 Right-hand Section of Monument

1975. Historic Site of Revolution in Wangjaesan. Multicoloured.

N1473 10 ch. Type **568** 10 10
N1474 15 ch. Left-hand section of monument 20 10
N1475 25 ch. Centre section of monument 30 15
N1476 30 ch. Centre section, close up 40 20

No. N1475 is 38 × 60 mm and No. N1476, 60 × 38 mm.

569 Marchers with Flags

1976. 30th Anniv of Korean League of Socialist Working Youth. Multicoloured.

N1477 2 ch. Flags and Emblem . . 15 10
N1478 70 ch. Type **569** 90 40

570 Geese

1976. Ducks and Geese. Multicoloured.

N1479 10 ch. Type **570** 40 10
N1480 20 ch. "Perennial" duck . . 90 10
N1481 40 ch. Kwangpo duck . . . 1·60 20

571 "Oath"

1976. Korean Peoples Army (sculptural works). Multicoloured.

N1482 5 ch. Type **571** 10 10
N1483 10 ch. "Union of Officers with Men" (horiz) 15 10
N1484 10 ch. "This Flag to the Height" 15 10

572 "Rural Road at Evening"

1976. Modern Korean Paintings (5th series). Social Welfare. Multicoloured.

N1485 10 ch. Type **572** 45 10
N1486 15 ch. "Passing on Technique" (1970) . . . 55 10
N1487 25 ch. "Mother (and Child)" (1965) 70 15
N1488 30 ch. "Medical Examination at School" (1970) (horiz) 1·25 15
N1489 40 ch. "Lady Doctor of Village" (1970) (horiz) . 1·50 20

573 Worker holding Text of Law

1976. 30th Anniv of Agrarian Reform Law.

N1490 573 10 ch. multicoloured . 20 10

574 Telephones and Satellite

1976. Centenary of First Telephone Call. Multicoloured. With or without gum.

N1491 2 ch. Type **574** 40 10
N1492 5 ch. Satellite and antenna 40 10
N1493 10 ch. Satellite and telecommunications systems 40 10
N1494 15 ch. Telephone and linesman . . . . 1·10 10
N1495 25 ch. Satellite and map of receiving stations . . . 1·50 15
N1496 40 ch. Satellite and cable-laying barge . . . . . . 1·75 20

575 Cosmos

1976. Flowers. Multicoloured.

N1498 5 ch. Type **575** 25 10
N1499 10 ch. Dahlia 25 10
N1500 20 ch. Zinnia 45 15
N1501 40 ch. China aster 70 25

576 Fruit and Products

1976. Pukchong Meeting of Korean Workers' Party Presidium. Multicoloured.

N1502 5 ch. Type **576** 65 10
N1503 10 ch. Fruit and orchard scene 65 10

577 "Pulgunji" Type Electric Locomotive

1976. Railway Locomotives. Multicoloured.

N1504 5 ch. Type **577** 40 10
N1505 10 ch. "Chaju" type underground train . . . 75 10
N1506 15 ch. "Saebyol" type diesel locomotive 90 15

GUM. All the following stamps were issued with gum, except where otherwise stated.

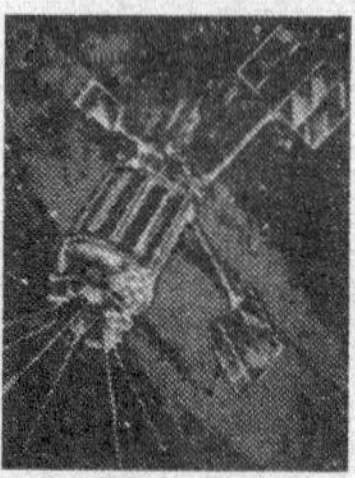

578 Satellite

1976. Space Flight. With or without gum.

N1507 578 2 ch. multicoloured . . 15 10
N1508 – 5 ch. multicoloured . . 15 10
N1509 – 10 ch. multicoloured . . 20 10
N1510 – 15 ch. multicoloured . . 30 10
N1511 – 25 ch. multicoloured . . 45 15
N1512 – 40 ch. multicoloured . . 70 20

DESIGNS: 5 ch. to 40 ch. Various satellites and space craft.

579 Kim Il Sung beside Car

1976. Kim Il Sung's 64th Birthday.

N1514 579 10 ch. multicoloured . . 40 10

580 Bat and Ribbon

1976. 3rd Asian Table Tennis Championships. Multicoloured. Without gum.

N1516 5 ch. Type **580** 25 10
N1517 10 ch. Three women players with flowers 25 10
N1518 20 ch. Player defending . . 45 10
N1519 25 ch. Player making attacking shot 75 15

581 Kim Il Sung announcing Establishment of Association

1976. 40th Anniv of Association for the Restoration of the Fatherland. Without gum.

N1521 581 10 ch. multicoloured . 10 10

582 Golden Pheasant

1976. Pheasants. Multicoloured. With or without gum.

N1522 2 ch. Type **582** 75 10
N1523 5 ch. Lady Amherst's pheasant 80 10
N1524 10 ch. Silver pheasant . . 95 15
N1525 15 ch. Reeves's pheasant . 1·10 25
N1526 25 ch. Temminck's tragopan 1·40 40
N1527 40 ch. Ringed-necked pheasant (albino) . . . . 1·75 65

583 Monument and Map of River

585 Bronze Medal (Hockey, Pakistan)

584 Running

1976. Potong River Monument. Without gum.

N1529 583 10 ch. brown & green 20 10

1976. Olympic Games, Montreal. Multicoloured.

N1530 2 ch. Type **584** 20 10
N1531 5 ch. Diving 20 10
N1532 10 ch. Judo 20 10
N1533 15 ch. Gymnastics 30 10
N1534 25 ch. Gymnastics 70 15
N1535 40 ch. Fencing . . . . . . 2·75 20

1976. Olympic Medal Winners (1st issue). Multicoloured.

N1537 2 ch. Type **585** 75 10
N1538 5 ch. Bronze medal (shooting, Rudolf Dollinger) . . . 25 10
N1539 10 ch. Silver medal (boxing, Li Byong Uk) 25 15
N1540 15 ch. Silver medal (cycling, Daniel Morelon) . . . . 2·00 15
N1541 25 ch. Gold medal (marathon, Waldemar Cierpinski) . 90 20
N1542 40 ch. Gold medal (boxing, Ku Yong Jo) . . . . . 1·10 25

586 Boxing (Ku Yong Jo)

1976. Olympic Medal Winners (2nd issue). Multicoloured.

N1544 2 ch. Type **586** 25 10
N1545 5 ch. Gymnastics (Nadia Comaneci) 25 10
N1546 10 ch. Pole vaulting (Tadeusz Slusarki) 25 10
N1547 15 ch. Hurdling (Guy Drut) 30 10
N1548 20 ch. Cycling (Bernt Johansson) . . . . . . 2·50 15
N1549 40 ch. Football (East Germany) . . . . 1·50 20

587 U.P.U. Headquarters, Berne

1976. International Festivities. Multicoloured.

N1551	2 ch. Type **587**	40	10
N1552	5 ch. Footballers (World Cup)	40	10
N1553	10 ch. Olympic Stadium	40	10
N1554	15 ch. Olympic Village	40	10
N1555	25 ch. Junk and satellite	70	20
N1556	40 ch. Satellites	75	20

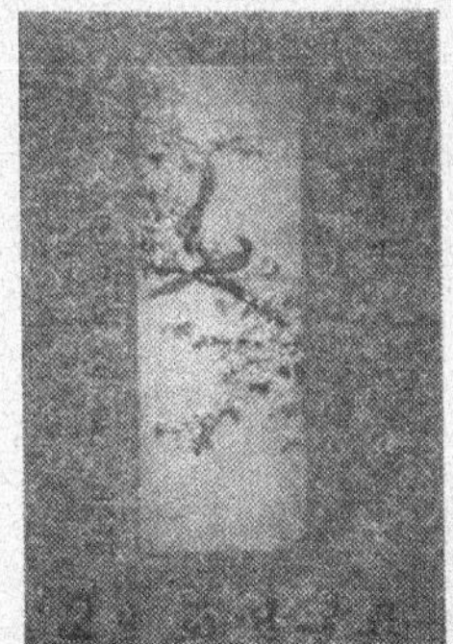
588 Azure-winged Magpies

1976. Embroidery. Multicoloured. With or without gum.

N1558	2 ch. Type **588**	1·25	15
N1559	5 ch. White magpie	90	15
N1560	10 ch. Roe deer	30	10
N1561	15 ch. Black-naped oriole and magnolias	1·40	15
N1562	25 ch. Fairy with flute (horiz)	70	15
N1563	40 ch. Tiger	1·60	40

589 Roman "5" and Flame

1976. 5th Non-aligned States' Summit Conference, Colombo. Without gum.

N1565	**589** 10 ch. multicoloured	10	10

590 Trophy and Certificate

1976. World Model Plane Championships (1975). Multicoloured. Without gum.

N1566	5 ch. Type **590**	20	10
N1567	10 ch. Trophy and medals	30	10
N1568	20 ch. Model airplane and emblem	45	10
N1569	40 ch. Model glider and medals	75	15

591 "Pulgungi" Type Diesel Shunting Locomotive

1976. Locomotives. Multicoloured.

N1570	2 ch. Type **591**	40	10
N1571	5 ch. "Saebyol" type diesel locomotive	55	10
N1572	10 ch. "Saebyol" type diesel shunting locomotive	65	10
N1573	15 ch. Electric locomotive	75	10
N1574	25 ch. "Kumsung" type diesel locomotive	95	15
N1575	40 ch. "Pulgungi" type electric locomotive	1·10	20

592 House of Culture

1976. House of Culture. Without gum.

N1577	**592** 10 ch. brown and black	15	10

593 Kim Il Sung visiting Tosongrang

1976. Revolutionary Activities of Kim Il Sung. Multicoloured.

N1578	2 ch. Type **593**	20	10
N1579	5 ch. Kim Il Sung visits pheasants	20	10
N1580	10 ch. Kim Il Sung on hilltop	25	10
N1581	15 ch. Kim Il Sung giving house to farmhand	30	10
N1582	25 ch. Kim Il Sung near front line	70	10
N1583	40 ch. Kim Il Sung walking in rain	70	15

594 Kim Il Sung with Union Members

1976. 50th Anniv of Down-with-Imperialism Union. Without gum.

N1585	**594** 20 ch. multicoloured	35	15

604 Searchlights and Kim Il Sung's Birthplace

605 Spring Costume

1977. New Year. Without gum.

N1589	**604** 10 ch. multicoloured	10	10

1977. National Costumes of Li Dynasty. Mult.

N1590	10 ch. Type **605** (postage)	45	10
N1591	15 ch. Summer costume	60	10
N1592	20 ch. Autumn costume	70	15
N1593	40 ch. Winter costume (air)	1·10	20

606 Two Deva Kings (Koguryo Dynasty)

1977. Korean Cultural Relics. Multicoloured.

N1594	2 ch. Type **606** (postage)	40	10
N1595	5 ch. Gold-copper decoration, Koguryo Dynasty	40	10
N1596	10 ch. Copper Buddha, Koryo Dynasty	60	10
N1597	15 ch. Gold-copper Buddha, Paekje Dynasty	70	10
N1598	25 ch. Gold crown, Koguryo Dynasty	85	15
N1599	40 ch. Gold-copper sun decoration, Koguryo Dynasty (horiz)	1·00	20
N1600	50 ch. Gold crown, Silla Dynasty (air)	1·10	35

607 Worker with Five-point Programme

1977. Five-point Programme for Remaking Nature. Without gum.

N1601	**607** 10 ch. multicoloured	20	10

608 Pine Branch and Map of Korea

1977. 60th Anniv of Korean National Association. Without gum.

N1602	**608** 10 ch. multicoloured	35	10

609 Championship Emblem and Trophy

1977. 34th World Table Tennis Championships. Multicoloured. Without gum.

N1603	10 ch. Type **609** (postage)	20	10
N1604	15 ch. Pak Yong Sun	30	10
N1605	20 ch. Pak Yong Sun with trophy	50	15
N1606	40 ch. Pak Yong Ok and Yang Ying (air)	95	20

610 Kim Il Sung founds Guerrilla Army at Mingyuegou

1977. Kim Il Sung's 65th Birthday. Multicoloured.

N1607	2 ch. Type **610**	10	10
N1608	5 ch. In command of army	10	10
N1609	10 ch. Visiting steel workers in Kangson	25	10
N1610	15 ch. Before battle	20	10
N1611	25 ch. In schoolroom	25	10
N1612	40 ch. Viewing bumper harvest	35	10

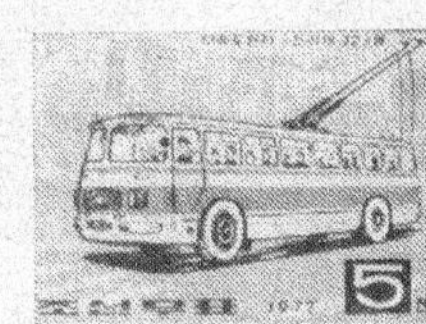
611 "Chollima 72" Trolleybus

1977. Trolleybuses. Without gum.

N1614	**611** 5 ch. blue, lilac & black	1·00	10
N1615	– 10 ch. red, green & blk	1·00	10

DESIGN: 10 ch. "Chollima 74" trolleybus.

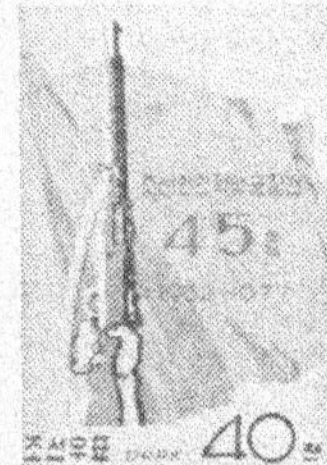
612 Red Flag and Hand holding Rifle

1977. 45th Anniv of Korean People's Revolutionary Army. Without gum.

N1616	**612** 40 ch. red, yellow & blk	50	20

613 Proclamation and Watchtower

1977. 40th Anniv of Pochonbo Battle. Without gum.

N1617	**613** 10 ch. multicoloured	10	10

614 Koryo White Ware Teapot

1977. Korean Porcelain. Multicoloured.

N1618	10 ch. Type **614** (postage)	50	10
N1619	15 ch. White vase, Li Dynasty	70	10
N1620	20 ch. Celadon vase, Koryo Dynasty	85	10
N1621	40 ch. Celadon vase with lotus decoration, Koryo Dynasty (air)	1·25	15

615 Postal Transport

1977. Postal Services. Multicoloured. Without gum.

N1623	2 ch. Type **615**	1·00	15
N1624	10 ch. Postwoman delivering letter	40	10
N1625	30 ch. Mil Mi-8 helicopter	1·00	30
N1626	40 ch. Ilyushin Il-18 airliner and world map	1·10	30

616 "Rapala arata"

1977. Butterflies and Dragonflies. Multicoloured.

N1627	2 ch. Type **616** (postage)	50	10
N1628	5 ch. "Colias aurora"	70	10
N1629	10 ch. Poplar admiral	90	10
N1630	15 ch. "Anax partherope" (dragonfly)	1·25	10
N1631	25 ch. "Sympetrum pedemontanum" (dragonfly)	1·60	10
N1632	50 ch. "Papilio maackii" (air)	1·90	20

617 Grey Cat

618

1977. Cats. Multicoloured.

N1634	2 ch. Type **617**	1·10	10
N1635	10 ch. Black and white cat	1·40	15
N1636	25 ch. Ginger cat	2·40	20

1977. Dogs. Multicoloured.

N1638	5 ch. Type **618** (postage)	75	10
N1639	15 ch. Chow	1·00	10
N1640	50 ch. Pungsang dog (air)	1·60	15

619 Kim Il Sung and President Tito

1977. Visit of President Tito.

N1642 **619** 10 ch. multicoloured . 10 10
N1643 15 ch. multicoloured . 15 10
N1644 20 ch. multicoloured . 20 10
N1645 40 vh. multicoloured . 25 10

620 Girl and Symbols of Education

1977. 5th Anniv of 11-year Compulsory Education. Without gum.

N1646 **620** 10 ch. multicoloured . 10 10

621 Chinese Mactra **622** Students and "Theses"

1977. Shellfish and Fish. Multicoloured.

N1647 2 ch. Type **621** (postage) . 35 10
N1648 5 ch. Bladder moon 50 10
N1649 10 ch. "Arca inflata" . . . 70 10
N1650 25 ch. Thomas's rapa whelk 1·00 25
N1651 50 ch. Thomas's rapa whelk (air) . . . . 1·60 45

1977. Kim Il Sung's "Theses on Socialist Education". Multicoloured. Without gum.

N1653 10 ch. Type **622** 10 10
N1654 20 ch. Students, crowd and text 15 10

623 "Juche" Torch **624** Jubilant Crowd

1977. Seminar on the Juche Idea. Multicoloured. Without gum.

N1655 2 ch. Type **623** 10 10
N1656 5 ch. Crowd and red book 10 10
N1657 10 ch. Chollima Statue and flags 10 10
N1658 15 ch. Handclasp and red flag on world map 10 10
N1659 25 ch. Map of Korea and anti-U.S. slogans 15 10
N1660 40 ch. Crowd and Mt. Paekdu-san 20 10

1977. Election of Deputies to Supreme People's Assembly. Without gum.

N1662 **624** 10 ch. multicoloured . 10 10

625 Footballers

1977. World Cup Football Championship, Argentina. Without gum.

N1663 **625** 10 ch. multicoloured . 75 15
N1664 – 15 ch. multicoloured . 1·10 20
N1665 – 40 ch. multicoloured . 1·75 25
DESIGNS: 15, 40 ch. Different football scenes.

626 Kim Il Sung with Rejoicing Crowds

1977. Re-election of Kim Il Sung. Without gum.

N1667 **626** 10 ch. multicoloured . 20 10

627 Chollima Statue and Symbols of Communication

1977. 20th Anniv of Socialist Countries' Communication Organization. Without gum.

N1668 **627** 10 ch. multicoloured . 20 10

638 Chollima Statue and City Skyline

1978. New Year. Without gum.

N1687 **638** 10 ch. multicoloured . 20 10

639 Skater in 19th-century Costume **640** Post-rider and "Horse-ticket"

1978. Winter Olympic Games, Sapporo and Innsbruck. Multicoloured.

N1688 2 ch. Type **639** (postage) . 40 10
N1699 5 ch. Skier 40 10
N1690 10 ch. Woman skater . . . 40 10
N1691 15 ch. Hunter on skis . . 50 10
N1692 20 ch. Woman (in 19th-century costume) on skis 50 10
N1693 25 ch. Viking with long-bow 2·40 15
N1694 40 ch. Skier (air) . . . . . 1·40 15

1978. Postal Progress. Multicoloured.

N1696 2 ch. Type **640** (postage) . 25 10
N1697 5 ch. Postman on motor cycle 1·50 10
N1698 10 ch. Electric train and post-van . . . . 1·50 15
N1699 15 ch. Mail steamer and Mil Mi-8 helicopter 85 15
N1700 25 ch. Tupolev Tu-154 jetliner and satellite 75 15
N1701 40 ch. Dove and U.P.U. headquarters (air) . . . 50 15

641 Self-portrait **643** Show Jumping

642 "Chungsong" Tractor

1978. 400th Birth Anniv of Rubens.

N1703 **641** 2 ch. multicoloured . . 25 10
N1704 5 ch. multicoloured . . 25 10
N1705 40 ch. multicoloured . . 1·50 20

1978. Farm Machines. Without gum.

N1707 **642** 10 ch. red and black . . 45 10
N1708 – 10 ch. brown and black 45 10
DESIGN: No. N1708, Sprayer.

1978. Olympic Games, Moscow (1980). Equestrian Events. Multicoloured.

N1709 2 ch. Type **643** 25 10
N1710 5 ch. Jumping bar 35 10
N1711 10 ch. Cross-country . . . 45 10
N1712 15 ch. Dressage 50 10
N1713 25 ch. Water splash 75 15
N1714 40 ch. Dressage (different) 1·25 15

644 Soldier

1978. Korean People's Army Day. Multicoloured. Without gum.

N1716 5 ch. Type **644** 10 10
N1717 10 ch. Servicemen saluting 10 10

645 "Mangyongbong" (Freighter)

1978. Korean Ships. Multicoloured.

N1718 2 ch. Type **645** (postage) . . 1·75 45
N1719 5 ch. "Hyoksin" (freighter) 35 15
N1720 10 ch. "Chongchongang" (gas carrier) 35 15
N1721 30 ch. "Sonbong" (tanker) 60 20
N1722 50 ch. "Taedonggang" (freighter) (air) . . . . . 1·10 40

646 Uruguayan Footballer

1978. World Cup Football Championship Winners. Multicoloured.

N1724 5 ch. Type **646** (postage) . . 40 10
N1725 10 ch. Italian player 40 10
N1726 15 ch. West German player 40 10
N1727 25 ch. Brazilian player . . 40 10
N1728 40 ch. English player . . . 75 10
N1729 50 ch. Hands holding World Cup (vert) (air) . . . . . 1·25 15

647 Footballers (1930 Winners, Uruguay)

1978. History of World Cup Football Championship. Multicoloured.

N1731 20 ch. Type **647** (postage) 75 15
N1732 20 ch. Italy, 1934 . . . . . 75 15
N1733 20 ch. France, 1938 . . . . 75 15
N1734 20 ch. Brazil, 1950 . . . . 75 15
N1735 20 ch. Switzerland, 1954 . 75 15
N1736 20 ch. Sweden, 1958 . . . 75 15
N1737 20 ch. Chile, 1962 . . . . 75 15
N1738 20 ch. England, 1966 . . . 75 15
N1739 20 ch. Mexico, 1970 . . . 75 15
N1740 20 ch. West Germany, 1974 75 15
N1741 20 ch. Argentina, 1978 . . 75 15
N1742 50 ch. Footballers and emblem (air) 75 15

648 "Sea of Blood" (opera)

1978. Art from the Period of Anti-Japanese Struggle. Multicoloured.

N1744 10 ch. Type **648** 25 10
N1745 15 ch. Floral kerchief embroidered with map of Korea 35 10
N1746 20 ch. "Tansimjul" (maypole dance) 50 15

649 Red Flag and "7", Electricity and Coal

1978. Second 7 Year Plan. Multicoloured. Without gum.

N1748 5 ch. Type **649** 25 10
N1749 10 ch. Steel and non-ferrous metal 30 10
N1750 15 ch. Engineering and chemical fertilizer . . . 35 10
N1751 30 ch. Cement and fishing 55 10
N1752 50 ch. Grain and tideland reclamation 75 10

650 Gymnastics (Alfred Flatow)

1978. Olympic Games History and Medal-winners. Multicoloured.

N1753 20 ch. Type **650** 60 15
N1754 20 ch. Runners (Michel Theato) 60 15
N1755 20 ch. Runners (Wyndham Halswelle) 60 15
N1756 20 ch. Rowing (William Kinnear) 60 15
N1757 20 ch. Fencing (Paul Anspach) . . . . 1·25 25
N1758 20 ch. Runners (Ugo Frigerio) 60 15
N1759 20 ch. Runners (Ahmed El Quafi) 60 15
N1760 20 ch. Cycling (Robert Charpentier) . . . . . . 1·50 35
N1761 20 ch. Gymnastics (Josep Stalder) 60 15
N1762 20 ch. Boxing (Lazio Papp) 85 20
N1763 20 ch. Runners (Ronald Delany) 60 15
N1764 20 ch. High jump (Jolanda Balas) 60 15
N1765 20 ch. High jump (Valery Brumel) 60 15
N1766 20 ch. Gymnastics (Vera Caslavska) 60 15
N1767 20 ch. Rifle shooting (Li Ho Jun) 60 15

651 Douglas DC-8-63 and Comte Gentleman

1978. Airplanes. Multicoloured.

N1769 2 ch. Type **651** 55 10
N1770 10 ch. Ilyushin Il-62M and Avia BH-25 . . . . . . 70 10
N1771 15 ch. Douglas DC-8-63 and Savoia Marchetti S-71 80 10
N1772 20 ch. Tupolev Tu-144 and Kalinin K-5 . . . . . . 95 10
N1773 25 ch. Tupolev Tu-154 and Antonov An-2 biplane . 95 10
N1774 30 ch. Ilyushin Il-18 . . . 95 10
N1775 40 ch. Concorde and Wibault 283 trimotor . . . . . . 2·00 40

652 White-bellied Black Woodpecker and Map — **653** Demonstrators and Korean Map

1978. White-bellied Black Woodpecker Preservation. Multicoloured.

N1777 5 ch. Type **652** 85 10
N1778 10 ch. Woodpecker and eggs 1·00 15
N1779 15 ch. Woodpecker feeding young . . . . 1·25 25
N1780 25 ch. Woodpecker feeding young (different) . . . . 1·60 40
N1781 50 ch. Adult woodpecker on tree trunk . . . . 2·50 80

1978. 30th Anniv of Democratic People's Republic of Korea. Multicoloured. Without gum.

N1783 10 ch. Type **653** 10 10
N1784 10 ch. Flag and soldiers . . 10 10
N1785 10 ch. Flag and "Juche" . . 10 10
N1786 10 ch. Red Flag 10 10
N1787 10 ch. Chollima Statue and city skyline 10 10
N1788 10 ch. "Juche" torch and men of three races 10 10

654 Cat and Pup — **668** Red Flag and Pine Branch

655 Footballers

1978. Animal Paintings by Li Am. Multicoloured.

N1789 10 ch. Type **654** . . . . . 2·25 30
N1790 15 ch. Cat up a tree . . . . 2·25 30
N1791 40 ch. Wild geese . . . . . 2·25 30

1978. Argentina's Victory in World Cup Football Championship. Without gum.

N1792 **655** 10 ch. multicoloured. 65 10
N1793 – 15 ch. multicoloured . 75 15
N1794 – 25 ch. multicoloured . 90 20
DESIGNS: 15, 25 ch. Different football scenes.

1979. New Year. Without gum.

N1812 **668** 10 ch. multicoloured . 15 10

669 Kim Il Sung with Children's Corps Members, Maanshan

1979. International Year of the Child (1st issue). Multicoloured.

(a) Paintings of Kim Il Sung and children.

N1813 5 ch. Type **669** 15 10
N1814 10 ch. Kim Il Sung and Children's Corps members in classroom 25 10
N1815 15 ch. New Year gathering 30 10
N1816 20 ch. Kim Il Sung and children in snow 45 10
N1817 30 ch. Kim Il Sung examines children's schoolbooks (vert) 50 10

(b) Designs showing children

N1818 10 ch. Tug-of-war 15 10
N1819 15 ch. Dance "Growing up Fast" 40 15
N1820 20 ch. Children of many races and globe 40 10
N1821 25 ch. Children singing . . 65 15
N1822 30 ch. Children in toy spaceships 40 10
See also Nos. N1907/17.

670 Rose

1979. Roses. Multicoloured.

N1824 1 wn. Red rose . . . . .
N1825 3 wn. White rose . . . . .
N1826 5 wn. Type **670** . . . . .
N1827 10 wn. Deep pink rose . .
See also Nos. N1837/42.

671 Warriors on Horseback — **672** Red Guard and Industrial Skyline

1979. "The Story of Two Generals". Multicoloured. Without gum.

N1828 5 ch. Type **671** 20 10
N1829 10 ch. Farm labourer blowing feather 30 10
N1830 10 ch. Generals fighting on foot 30 10
N1831 10 ch. Generals on horseback 30 10

1979. 20th Anniv of Worker-Peasant Red Guards. Without gum.

N1832 **672** 10 ch. multicoloured . 15 10

673 Clement-Bayard Airship "Fleurus"

1979. Airships. Multicoloured. Without gum.

N1833 10 ch. Type **673** . . . . . 1·00 15
N1834 20 ch. N.1 "Norge" . . . 1·00 15

674 Crowd of Demonstrators

1979. 60th Anniv of 1st March Popular Uprising. Without gum.

N1836 **674** 10 ch. blue and red . . 15 10

1979. Roses. As Nos. N1824/7. Multicoloured.

N1837 5 ch. Type **670** (postage) . . 25 10
N1838 10 ch. As No. N1827 . . . 30 10
N1839 15 ch. As No. N1824 . . . 35 10
N1840 20 ch. Yellow rose 45 10
N1841 30 ch. As No. 1825 . . . . 60 10
N1842 50 ch. Deep pink rose (different) (air) 80 15

675 Table Tennis Trophy — **676** Marchers with Red Flag

1979. 35th World Table Tennis Championship, Pyongyang. Multicoloured. With or without gum.

N1843 5 ch. Type **675** 15 10
N1844 10 ch. Women's doubles . . 15 10
N1845 15 ch. Women's singles . . 25 10
N1846 20 ch. Men's doubles . . . 40 10
N1847 30 ch. Men's singles 60 10

1979. Socialist Construction under Banner of Juche Idea. Multicoloured. Without gum.

N1849 5 ch. Type **676** 10 10
N1850 10 ch. Map of Korea . . . 10 10
N1851 10 ch. Juche torch 10 10

677 Badge — **678** Emblem, Satellite orbiting Globe and Aerials

1979. Order of Honour of the Three Revolutions. Without gum.

N1852 **677** 10 ch. blue 10 10

1979. World Telecommunications Day. Without gum.

N1853 **678** 10 ch. multicoloured . . 25 10

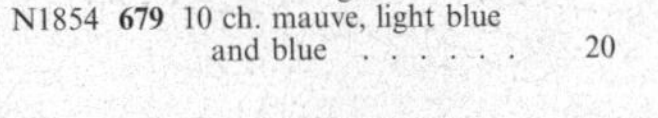

679 Advancing Soldiers and Monument

1979. 40th Anniv of Battle in Musan Area. Without gum.

N1854 **679** 10 ch. mauve, light blue and blue 20 10

680 Exhibition Entrance

1979. International Friendship Exhibition. Without gum.

N1855 **680** 10 ch. multicoloured . . 10 10

681 "Peonies"

1979. 450th Death Anniv (1978) of Albrecht Durer (artist) (1st issue). Multicoloured.

N1856 15 ch. Type **681** 60 20
N1857 20 ch. "Columbines" . . . 1·10 20
N1858 25 ch. "A Great Tuft of Grass" . . . . 1·10 20
N1859 30 ch. "Wing of a Bird" . 1·60 40
See also No. 2012.

682 Fencing

1979. Olympic Games, Moscow (2nd issue). Multicoloured. With gum (10, 40 ch. only).

N1861 5 ch. Type **682** . . . . . . 1·25 10
N1862 10 ch. Gymnastics 30 10
N1863 20 ch. Yachting 60 15
N1864 30 ch. Athletics 50 15
N1865 40 ch. Weightlifting . . . 50 15

683 Hunting

1979. Horse-riding (people of Koguryo Dynasty). Multicoloured.

N1867 5 ch. Type **683** 65 10
N1868 10 ch. Archery contest . . 65 10
N1869 15 ch. Man beating drum on horseback 25 10
N1870 20 ch. Man blowing horn 25 10
N1871 30 ch. Man and horse, armoured with chainmail 25 10
N1872 50 ch. Hawking (air) . . . 2·00 15

684 Judo — **685** Warrior's Costume

1979. Olympic Games, Moscow (3rd issue). Multicoloured. With gum (5, 15, 20, 30 ch. only).

N1873 5 ch. Type **684** 30 10
N1874 10 ch. Volleyball 30 10
N1875 15 ch. Cycling . . . . . . 1·25 25
N1876 20 ch. Basketball 50 15
N1877 25 ch. Canoeing 50 15
N1878 30 ch. Boxing 75 25
N1879 40 ch. Shooting 70 20

1979. Warrior Costumes of Li Dynasty.

N1881 **685** 5 ch. multicoloured . . 20 10
N1882 – 10 ch. multicoloured 20 10
N1883 – 15 ch. multicoloured 30 10
N1884 – 20 ch. multicoloured 45 10
N1885 – 30 ch. multicoloured 60 10
N1886 – 50 ch. multicoloured (air) 90 15
DESIGNS: 10 ch. to 50 ch. Different costumes.

686 Wrestling — **687** Monument

1979. Olympic Games, Moscow (4th issue). Multicoloured.

N1887 10 ch. Type **686** 25 10
N1888 15 ch. Handball 30 10
N1889 20 ch. Archery . . . . . . 1·60 25
N1890 25 ch. Hockey . . . . . . 1·60 45
N1891 30 ch. Rowing 75 15
N1892 40 ch. Football . . . . . 1·50 25

1979. Chongbong Monument. Without gum.

N1894 **687** 10 ch. multicoloured . 20 10

688 Bottle-feeding Fawn

1979. Sika Deer. Multicoloured.

N1895	5 ch. Type **688** (postage)	20	10
N1896	10 ch. Doe and fawn	20	10
N1897	15 ch. Stag drinking from stream	20	15
N1898	20 ch. Stag	25	15
N1899	30 ch. Stag and doe	35	25
N1900	50 ch. Antlers and deer (air)	50	35

689 Moscovy Ducks

1979. Central Zoo, Pyongyang. Multicoloured.

N1901	5 ch. Type **689** (postage)	25	10
N1902	10 ch. Ostrich	50	10
N1903	15 ch. Common turkey	70	15
N1904	20 ch. Dalmatian pelican	80	20
N1905	30 ch. Vulturine guinea-fowl	95	30
N1906	50 ch. Mandarins (air)	1·50	45

690 Girl with Model Viking Ship

1979. International Year of the Child (2nd issue). Multicoloured.

N1907	20 ch. Type **690**	1·00	20
N1908	20 ch. Boys with model steam railway locomotive	2·50	85
N1909	20 ch. Boy with model biplane	1·25	20
N1910	20 ch. Boy with model spaceman	80	20
N1911	30 ch. Boy with model speedboat	1·50	30
N1912	30 ch. Boy sitting astride toy electric train	2·50	85
N1913	30 ch. Boy and model airplane	1·60	30
N1914	30 ch. Boy and flying spaceman	1·00	30

691 Footballers

1979. International Year of the Child (3rd issue). Multicoloured.

N1916	20 ch. Type **691**	1·00	20
N1917	30 ch. Footballers (different)	1·50	30

692 Devil Stinger

1979. Marine Life. Multicoloured.

N1919	20 ch. Type **692**	75	10
N1920	30 ch. "Sebastes schlegeli" (fish)	1·00	20
N1921	50 ch. Northern sealion	1·60	30

693 Cross-country Skiing (Sergei Saveliev)

1979. Winter Olympic Games, Lake Placid. Multicoloured.

N1922	10 ch. Figure skating (Irina Rodnina and Aleksandr Zaitsev) (horiz)	40	15
N1923	20 ch. Ice hockey (Russian team) (horiz)	65	20
N1924	30 ch. Ladies 5 km relay (horiz)	1·10	25
N1925	40 ch. Type **693**	1·25	30
N1926	50 ch. Ladies' speed skating (Tatiana Averina)	1·50	35

694 The honey Bee collecting Nectar

1979. The Honey Bee. Multicoloured.

N1928	20 ch. Type **694**	1·25	10
N1929	30 ch. Bee and flowers	1·50	15
N1930	50 ch. Bee hovering over flower	1·75	25

695 Kim Jong Suk's Birthplace, Heoryong

1979. Historic Revolutionary Sites.

N1931	**695** 10 ch. multicoloured	15	10
N1932	– 10 ch. brown, blue & blk	15	10

DESIGN: No. N1932, Sinpa Revolutionary Museum.

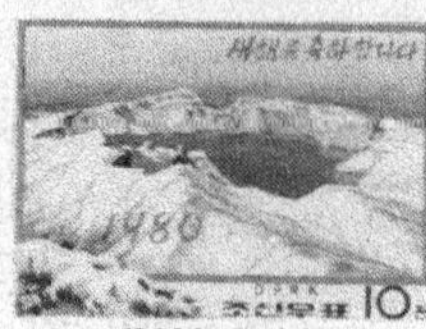
696 Mt. Paekdu

1980. New Year.

N1933	**696** 10 ch. multicoloured	55	10

697 Student and Books

1980. Studying.

N1934	**697** 10 ch. multicoloured	25	10

698 Conveyor Belt

1980. Unryul Mine Conveyor Belt.

N1935	**698** 10 ch. multicoloured	55	10

699 Children of Three Races

1980. International Day of the Child. Multicoloured.

N1936	10 ch. Type **699**	30	10
N1937	10 ch. Girl dancing to accordion	50	10
N1938	10 ch. Children in fairground airplane	40	10
N1939	10 ch. Children as astronauts	30	10
N1940	10 ch. Children on tricycles	1·25	30
N1941	10 ch. Children with toy train	1·75	45
N1942	10 ch. "His loving care for the children, future of the fatherland" ($59\frac{1}{2} \times 38$ mm)	30	10

700 Monument

1980. Chongsan-ri Historic Site. Multicoloured.

N1944	5 ch. Type **700**	10	10
N1945	10 ch. Meeting place of the General Membership	15	10

701 Monument

1980. Monument marking Kim Jong Suk's Return.

N1946	**701** 10 ch. multicoloured	15	10

702 Vasco Nunez de Balboa

1980. Conquerors of the Earth. Multicoloured.

N1947	10 ch. Type **702**	50	10
N1948	20 ch. Francisco de Orellana	75	20
N1949	30 ch. Haroun Tazieff	1·00	35
N1950	40 ch. Edmund Hillary and Sherpa Tenzing	1·50	45

703 Museum

1980. Ryongpo Revolutionary Museum.

N1952	**703** 10 ch. blue and black	20	10

704 Rowland Hill and Stamps

1980. Death Centenary (1979) of Sir Rowland Hill. Multicoloured.

N1953	30 ch. Type **704**	3·25	75
N1954	50 ch. Rowland Hill and stamps (different)	3·25	75

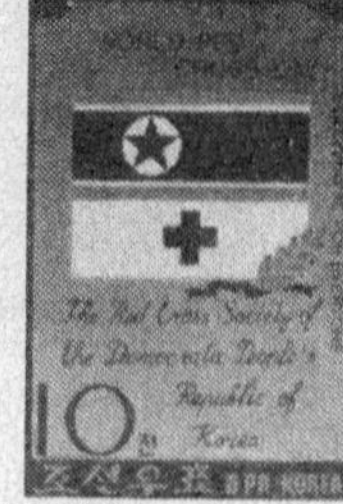
705 North Korean Red Cross Flag

1980. World Red Cross Day. Multicoloured.

N1955	10 ch. Type **705**	70	20
N1956	10 ch. Henri Dunant (founder)	70	20
N1957	10 ch. Nurse and child	70	20
N1958	10 ch. Polikarpov Po-2 biplane and ship	1·00	25
N1959	10 ch. Mil Mi-4 helicopter	1·00	25
N1960	10 ch. Children playing at nurses	70	20
N1961	10 ch. Red Cross Map over Korea and forms of transport	2·50	60

706 Fernando Magellan

1980. Conquerors of the Sea. Multicoloured.

N1963	10 ch. Type **706**	1·50	25
N1964	20 ch. Fridtjof Nansen	1·50	25
N1965	30 ch. Auguste and Jacques Piccard	2·00	25
N1966	40 ch. Jacques-Yves Cousteau	2·25	55

707 Korean Stamps and Penny Black

1980. "London 1980" International Stamp Exhibition. Multicoloured.

N1968	10 ch. Type **707** (postage)	2·00	40
N1969	20 ch. Korean cover and British Guiana 1 c. black and red	2·00	30
N1970	30 ch. Early Korean stamp and modern cover	1·50	25
N1971	50 ch. Korean stamps	2·50	35
N1972	40 ch. Korean stamp and miniature sheet (air)	1·60	35

708 Wright Brothers

1980. Conquerors of Sky and Space. Multicoloured.

N1974	10 ch. Type **708**	60	15
N1975	20 ch. Louis Bleriot	90	25
N1976	30 ch. Anthony Fokker	1·25	40
N1977	40 ch. Secondo Campini and Sir Frank Whittle	1·75	45

709 Space Station on Planet
710 Flag and Banners

1980. Conquerors of the Universe. Multicoloured.

N1979	10 ch. Orbiting space station	20	10
N1980	20 ch. Type **709**	25	20
N1981	30 ch. Prehistoric animals and spaceships	90	35
N1982	40 ch. Prehistoric animals and birds and spaceship	1·10	45

1980. 25th Anniv of General Association of Korean Residents in Japan (Chongryon).

N1984	**710** 10 ch. multicoloured	20	10

711 Hospital

1980. Pyongyang Maternity Hospital.

N1985	**711** 10 ch. blue, pur & blk	45	15

712 Health Centre

1980. Changgangwon Health Centre, Pyongyang.

N1986	**712** 2 ch. black and blue	25	10

713 Hand holding Rifle
714 Workers' Hostel, Samjiyon

1980. 50th Anniv of Revolutionary Army.

N1987	**713** 10 ch. multicoloured	25	10

1980.

N1988	**714**	10 ch. brown, bl & blk	30	10
N1989	–	10 ch. black and green	50	20
N1990	–	10 ch. black and red	50	20
N1991	–	10 ch. black and yellow	50	20
N1992	–	10 ch. multicoloured	30	10
N1993	–	10 ch. multicoloured	30	10
N1994	–	10 ch. multicoloured	1·00	35
N1995	–	10 ch. green and black	75	25
N1996	–	10 ch. grey, blue & blk	3·50	60
N1997	–	10 ch. multicoloured	4·00	60

DESIGNS: No. N1989, "Taedonggang" rice transplanter; N1990, "Chongsan-ri" rice harvester; N1991, Maize harvester; N1992, Revolutionary building, Songmun-ri; N1993, Revolutionary building, Samhwa; N1994, Sundial of 1438; N1995, 16th-century "turtle" ship; N1996, Pungsan dog; N1997, Japanese quail.

715 Party Emblem

1980. 6th Korean Workers' Party Congress. Multicoloured.

N1998	10 ch. Type **715**	15	10
N1999	10 ch. Students and Laurel leaf on globe	15	10
N2000	10 ch. Group with accordion	45	15
N2001	10 ch. Group with banner, microscope, book and trophy	25	10
N2002	10 ch. Worker with book and flag	75	25
N2003	10 ch. Worker with spanner and flag	75	25
N2004	10 ch. Marchers with torch and flags	15	10
N2005	10 ch. Emblem, marchers and map	20	10

716 Dribbling Ball

1980. World Cup Football Championship, 1978–1982. Multicoloured.

N2007	20 ch. Type **716**	2·50	60
N2008	30 ch. Tackle	3·00	80

717 Irina Rodnina and Aleksandr Zaitsev

1980. Winter Olympic Gold Medal Winners.

N2010	**717** 20 ch. multicoloured	4·00	1·75

718 "Soldier with Horse"
719 Kepler, Astrolabe and Satellites

1980. 450th Death Anniv (1978) of Albrecht Durer (artist) (2nd issue).

N2012	**718** 20 ch. multicoloured	5·00	1·50

1980. 350th Death Anniv of Johannes Kepler (astronomer).

N2014	**719** 20 ch. multicoloured	2·50	90

720 German 1 m. and Russian 30 k. Zeppelin Stamps

1980. 3rd International Stamp Fair, Essen. Mult.

N2016	10 ch. Type **720**	85	25
N2017	20 ch. German 2 m. and Russian 35 k. Zeppelin stamps	1·75	45
N2018	30 ch. German 4 m. and Russian 1 r. Zeppelin stamps	2·50	65

721 Shooting (Aleksandr Melentev)

1980. Olympic Medal Winners. Multicoloured.

N2020	10 ch. Type **721**	30	15
N2021	20 ch. Cycling (Robert Dill-Bundi)	3·25	75
N2022	25 ch. Gymnastics (Stoyan Deltchev)	50	25
N2023	30 ch. Wrestling (Chang Se Hong and Li Ho Pyong)	50	25
N2024	35 ch. Weightlifting (Ho Bong Chol)	50	25
N2025	40 ch. Running (Marita Koch)	50	30
N2026	50 ch. Modern Pentathlon (Anatoli Starostin)	70	35

722 Tito
723 Convair CV 340 Airliner

1980. President Tito of Yugoslavia Commemoration.

N2028	**722** 20 ch. multicoloured	30	10

1980. 25th Anniv of First Post-War Flight of Lufthansa.

N2029	**723** 20 ch. multicoloured	4·00	1·75

724 "The Rocket"

1980. 150th Anniv of Liverpool–Manchester Railway.

N2031	**724** 20 ch. multicoloured	5·00	1·75

725 Steam and Electric Locomotives

1980. Centenary of First Electric Train.

N2033	**725** 20 ch. multicoloured	5·00	1·75

726 Hammarskjold

1980. 75th Birth Anniv of Dag Hammarskjold (Former Secretary General of United Nations).

N2035	**726** 20 ch. multicoloured	2·50	1·25

727 Bobby Fischer and Boris Spassky

1980. World Chess Championship, Merano.

N2037	**727** 20 ch. multicoloured	5·50	1·75

728 Stolz

1980. Birth Centenary of Robert Stolz (composer).

N2039	**728** 20 ch. multicoloured	2·50	75

729 Chollima Statue
730 Russian Fairy Tale

1981. New Year. Without gum.

N2041	**729** 10 ch. multicoloured	25	10

1981. International Year of the Child (1979) (4th issue). Fairy Tales. Multicoloured.

N2042	10 ch. Type **730**	1·10	30
N2043	10 ch. Icelandic tale	1·10	30
N2044	10 ch. Swedish tale	1·10	30
N2045	10 ch. Irish tale	1·10	30
N2046	10 ch. Italian tale	1·10	30
N2047	10 ch. Japanese tale	1·10	30
N2048	10 ch. German tale	1·10	30

731 Changgwang Street

1981. Changgwang Street, Pyongyang.

N2050	**731** 10 ch. multicoloured	35	10

732 Footballers

1981. World Cup Football Championship, Spain (1982) (1st issue). Multicoloured.

N2051	10 ch. Type **732**	2·25	45
N2052	20 ch. Hitting ball past defender	2·25	45
N2053	30 ch. Disputing possession of ball	2·25	45

See also Nos. N2055/9 and N2201/6.

733 Map, Emblem and World Cup

1981. World Cup Football Championship, Spain (1982) (2nd issue). Multicoloured.

N2055	10 ch. Type **733**	1·50	30
N2056	15 ch. Footballers	1·50	30
N2057	20 ch. Heading ball	1·50	30
N2058	25 ch. Footballers (different)	1·50	30
N2059	30 ch. Footballers (different)	1·50	30

734 Workers with Book and Marchers with Banner

1981. Implementation of Decision of the 6th Koreans' Party Congress. Multicoloured.

N2061	2 ch. Type **734**	10	10
N2062	10 ch. Worker with book	10	10
N2063	10 ch. Workers and industrial plant	25	10
N2064	10 ch. Electricity and coal (horiz)	1·25	25
N2065	10 ch. Steel and non-ferrous metals (horiz)	25	10

N2066 10 ch. Cement and fertilizers (horiz) 25 10
N2067 30 ch. Fishing and fabrics (horiz) 25 10
N2068 40 ch. Grain and harbour (horiz) 25 10
N2069 70 ch. Clasped hands . . . 20 10
N2070 1 w. Hand holding torch . 30 15

735 Footballers

1981. Gold Cup Football Championship, Uruguay.
N2071 735 20 ch. multicoloured . 2·25 75

736 Dornier Do-X Flying Boat

1981. "Naposta '81" International Stamp Exhibition, Stuttgart. Multicoloured.
N2073 10 ch. Type 736 . . . . . 2·50 50
N2074 20 ch. Airship LZ-120 "Bodensee" . . . . . . 2·50 50
N2075 30 ch. "Gotz von Berlichingen" . . . . . 1·25 40

737 Telecommunications Equipment

1981. World Telecommunications Day.
N2077 737 10 ch. multicoloured . 1·75 20

738 "Iris pseudacorus"

1981. Flowers. Multicoloured.
N2078 10 ch. Type 738 . . . . . 75 15
N2079 20 ch. "Iris pallasii" . . . 1·00 20
N2080 30 ch. "Gladiolus gandavensis" . . . . . . 1·40 30

739 Austrian "WIPA 1981" and Rudolf Kirchschlager Stamps

1981. "WIPA 1981" International Stamp Exhibition, Vienna. Multicoloured.
N2081 20 ch. Type 739 . . . . . 1·90 60
N2082 30 ch. Austrian Maria Theresa and Franz Joseph stamps . . . . 2·50 80

MORE DETAILED LISTS
are given in the Stanley Gibbons Catalogues referred to in the country headings. For lists of current volumes see introduction

740 Rings Exercise

741 Armed Workers

1981. Centenary of International Gymnastic Federation. Multicoloured.
N2084 10 ch. Type 740 . . . . . 35 20
N2085 15 ch. Horse exercise . . . 45 20
N2086 20 ch. Backwards somersault 70 20
N2087 25 ch. Floor exercise . . . 80 25
N2088 30 ch. Exercise with hoop 95 25

1981. 50th Anniv of Mingyuehgou Meeting.
N2090 741 10 ch. multicoloured . 20 10

742 Farm Building, Sukchon

1981. 20th Anniv of Agricultural Guidance System and Taean Work System.
N2091 742 10 ch. green, black and gold 20 10
N2092 – 10 ch. blue, black and gold 20 10
DESIGN: No. N2092, Taean Revolutionary Museum.

743 Woman and Banner

1981. 55th Anniv of Formation of Women's Anti-Japanese Association.
N2093 743 5 wn. multicoloured . 2·75 75

743a Scene from Opera

1981. 10th Anniv of "Sea of Blood" (opera).
N2094 743a 10 wn. multicoloured

744 Joan of Arc

1981. 550th Death Anniv of Joan of Arc. Multicoloured.
N2095 10 ch. Type 744 . . . . . 2·00 50
N2096 10 ch. Archangel Michael 2·25 50
N2097 70 ch. Joan of Arc in armour 2·25 50

745 Torch, Mountains and Flag

1981. 55th Anniv of Down with Imperialism Union.
N2099 745 1 wn. 50 multicoloured 40 20

746 "Young Girl by the Window"

1981. 375th Birth Anniv of Rembrandt (artist). Multicoloured.
N2100 10 ch. Type 746 . . . . . . 55 25
N2101 20 ch. "Rembrandt's Mother" 1·25 45
N2102 30 ch. "Saskia van Uylenburgh" . . . . . . 1·75 70
N2103 40 ch. "Pallas Athene" . . 2·25 90

747 Emblem and Banners over Pyongyang

1981. Symposium of Non-Aligned Countries on Food Self-Sufficiency, Pyongyang. Multicoloured.
N2105 10 ch. Type 747 . . . . . . 20 10
N2106 50 ch. Harvesting 50 10
N2107 90 ch. Factories, tractors and marchers with banner . . 70 15

748 St. Paul's Cathedral

1981. Wedding of Prince of Wales (1st issue). Multicoloured.
N2108 10 ch. Type 748 . . . . . . 1·40 35
N2109 20 ch. Great Britain Prince of Wales Investiture Stamp 1·40 35
N2110 30 ch. Lady Diana Spencer 1·40 35
N2111 40 ch. Prince Charles in military uniform . . . . 1·40 35
See also Nos. N2120/3.

749 "Four Philosophers" (detail)

1981. Paintings by Rubens. Multicoloured.
N2113 10 ch. Type 749 . . . . . . 40 20
N2114 15 ch. "Portrait of Helena Fourment" 60 25
N2115 20 ch. "Portrait of Isabella Brandt" 90 25
N2116 25 ch. "Education of Maria de Medici" . . . . 1·10 30
N2117 30 ch. "Helena Fourment and her Child" . . . . 1·40 35
N2118 40 ch. "Helena Fourment in her Wedding Dress" . . . 1·75 40

750 Royal Couple

1981. Wedding of Prince of Wales (2nd issue). Multicoloured.
N2120 10 ch. Type 750 . . . . . 1·75 45
N2121 20 ch. Couple on balcony after wedding . . . . . 1·75 45
N2122 30 ch. Couple outside St. Paul's Cathedral . . . . 1·75 45
N2123 70 ch. Full-length wedding portrait of couple . . . 1·75 45

751 Rowland Hill and Stamps

1981. "Philatokyo '81" International Stamp Exhibition. Multicoloured.
N2125 10 ch. Korean 2 ch. Seminar on Juche Idea stamp (41 × 29 mm) 75 20
N2126 10 ch. Korean 10 and 70 ch. stamps (41 × 29 mm) . . 2·00 75
N2127 10 ch. Type 751 . . . . . 2·00 75
N2128 20 ch. Korean Fairy Tale stamps . . . . 1·75 40
N2129 30 ch. Japanese stamps . . 3·00 90

752 League Members and Flag

1981. Seventh League of Socialist Working Youth Congress, Pyongyang.
N2131 752 10 ch. multicoloured . 20 10
N2132 80 ch. multicoloured . 60 10

753 Government Palace, Sofia, Bulgarian Arms and Khan Asparuch

1981. 1300th Anniv of Bulgarian State.
N2133 753 10 ch. multicoloured . 25 10

754 Dimitrov

1981. Birth Centenary of Georgi Dimitrov (Bulgarian statesman).
N2134 754 10 ch. multicoloured . 25 10

755 Emblem, Boeing 747-200, City Hall and Mercedes "500"

1981. "Philatelia '81" International Stamp Fair, Frankfurt-am-Main.

N2135 **755** 20 ch. multicoloured . 2·25 35

756 Concorde, Airship "Graf Zeppelin" and Count Ferdinand von Zeppelin

1981. "Philexfrance 82" International Stamp Exhibition, Paris. Multicoloured. (a) As T **756**.

N2136 10 ch. Type **756** . . . . . 2·75 40
N2137 20 ch. Concorde, Breguet Provence airliner and Santos-Dumont's biplane "14 bis" . . . . 3·25 75
N2138 30 ch. "Mona Lisa" (Leonardo da Vinci) and stamps . . . . 1·75 30

(b) Size 32 × 53 mm.

N2140 10 ch. Hotel des Invalides, Paris . . . . 1·00 45
N2141 20 ch. President Mitterrand of France . . . . 1·00 45
N2142 30 ch. International Friendship Exhibition building . . . . 1·00 45
N2143 70 ch. Kim Il Sung . . . . 1·00 45

757 Rising Sun

758 Emblem and Flags

1982. New Year.

N2144 **757** 10 ch. multicoloured . 30 10

1982. "Prospering Korea". Multicoloured.

N2145 2 ch. Type **758** 15 10
N2146 10 ch. Industry 25 10
N2147 10 ch. Agriculture 25 10
N2148 10 ch. Mining 45 10
N2149 10 ch. Arts 25 10
N2150 10 ch. Al Islet lighthouse, Uam-ri . . . . 2·50 40
N2151 40 ch. Buildings 50 15

759 "The Hair-do"

1982. Birth Centenary of Pablo Picasso (artist). Multicoloured.

N2152 10 ch. Type **759** 75 20
N2153 10 ch. "Paulo on a donkey" 1·75 35
N2154 20 ch. "Woman Leaning on Arm" 90 25
N2155 20 ch. "Harlequin" . . . . 1·75 35
N2156 25 ch. "Child with Pigeon" 1·90 50
N2157 25 ch. "Reading a Letter" 1·75 35
N2158 35 ch. "Portrait of Gertrude Stein" . . . . 1·50 30
N2159 35 ch. "Harlequin" (different) 1·75 35
N2160 80 ch. "Minotaur" . . . . 1·75 35
N2161 90 ch. "Mother with Child" 1·75 35

760 Fireworks over Pyongyang

1982. Kim Il Sung's 70th Birthday. Multicoloured.

N2163 10 ch. Kim Il Sung's birthplace, Mangyongdae 20 10
N2164 10 ch. Type **760** 20 10
N2165 10 ch. "The Day will dawn on downtrodden Korea" . 20 10
N2166 10 ch. Signalling start of Pochonbo Battle 20 10
N2167 10 ch. Kim Il Sung starting Potong River project . . 20 10
N2168 10 ch. Embracing bereaved children 20 10
N2169 10 ch. Kim Il Sung as Supreme Commander . 20 10
N2170 10 ch. "On the Road of Advance" 20 10
N2171 10 ch. Kim Il Sung kindling flame of Chollima Movement, Kansong Steel Plant 75 25
N2172 10 ch. Kim Il Sung talking to peasants 20 10
N2173 10 ch. Kim Il Sung fixing site of reservoir 30 10
N2174 20 ch. Kim Il Sung visiting Komdok Valley 75 25
N2175 20 ch. Kim Il Sung visiting Red Flag Company . . 20 10
N2176 20 ch. Kim Il Sung teaching Juche farming methods 20 10
N2177 20 ch. Kim Il Sung visiting iron works 35 10
N2178 20 ch. Kim Il Sung talking with smelters 35 10
N2179 20 ch. Kim Il Sung at chemical plant 45 10
N2180 20 ch. Kim Il Sung with fishermen 40 10

Nos. 2165/80 are horiz designs.

761 Soldier saluting

1982. 50th Anniv of People's Army.

N2182 **761** 10 ch. multicoloured . 25 10

762 "The Bagpiper" (Durer)

763 Surveyors

1982. 4th Essen International Stamp Fair.

N2183 **762** 30 ch. multicoloured . 3·75 40

1982. Implementation of Four Nature-remaking Tasks.

N2184 **763** 10 ch. multicoloured . 45 10

764 Princess as Baby

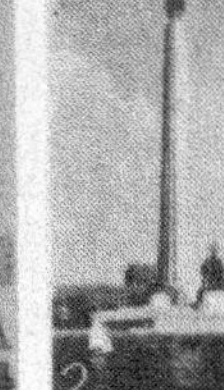

765 Tower of the Juche Idea Pyongyang

1982. 21st Birthday of Princess of Wales.

N2185 **764** 10 ch. multicoloured . 30 20
N2186 – 20 ch. multicoloured . 65 35
N2187 – 30 ch. multicoloured . 75 45
N2188 – 50 ch. multicoloured . 1·00 40
N2189 – 60 ch. multicoloured . . 1·00 40
N2190 – 70 ch. multicoloured . . 1·00 40
N2191 – 80 ch. multicoloured . . 1·00 40

DESIGNS: 20 to 80 ch. Princess at various ages.

1982.

2193 **765** 2 wn. multicoloured . . . 1·25 30
2194 – 3 wn. orange and black . 1·75 40

DESIGN: (26 × 38 mm) 3 wn. Arch of Triumph.

766 Tiger

1982. Tigers.

N2195 **766** 20 ch. multicoloured . . 1·25 35
N2196 – 30 ch. multicoloured . . 1·90 35
N2197 – 30 ch. mult (horiz) . . 2·75 45
N2198 – 40 ch. mult (horiz) . . 2·75 45
N2199 – 80 ch. mult (horiz) . . 2·75 45

DESIGNS: 30 to 80 ch. Tigers.

767 Group 1 Countries

1982. World Cup Football Championship, Spain (3rd issue). Multicoloured.

N2201 10 ch. Type **767** 45 20
N2202 20 ch. Group 2 countries . 1·00 25
N2203 30 ch. Group 3 countries . 1·40 30
N2204 40 ch. Group 4 countries . 1·75 40
N2205 50 ch. Group 5 countries . 2·00 50
N2206 60 ch. Group 6 countries . 2·25 50

768 Rocket Launch **769** Charlotte von Stein

1982. The Universe. Multicoloured.

N2208 10 ch. Type **768** . . . . . . 1·00 40
N2209 20 ch. Spaceship over globe 1·00 40
N2210 80 ch. Spaceship between globe and moon . . . . 1·25 40

1982. 150th Death Anniv of Johann von Goethe (writer). Multicoloured.

N2212 10 ch. Type **769** 50 25
N2213 10 ch. Goethe's mother . . 1·50 45
N2214 20 ch. Goethe's sister . . . 75 30
N2215 20 ch. Angelika Kauffmann 1·50 45
N2216 25 ch. Charlotte Buff . . . 90 35
N2217 25 ch. Anna Amalia . . . . 1·50 45
N2218 35 ch. Lili Schonemann . . 1·25 40
N2219 35 ch. Charlotte von Lengefeld . . . . 1·50 45
N2220 80 ch. Goethe . . . . 1·60 45

770 Player holding aloft World Cup

1982. World Cup Football Championship Results. Multicoloured.

N2222 20 ch. Type **770** . . . . . . 1·25 30
N2223 30 ch. Group of players with World Cup . . . . 1·75 50
N2224 30 ch. Type **770** . . . . . . 2·50 65
N2225 40 ch. As No. N2203 . . . 2·50 65
N2226 80 ch. King Juan Carlos of Spain and two players with World Cup . . . . 2·50 65

771 Princess and Prince William of Wales

1982. 1st Wedding Anniv of Prince and Princess of Wales.

N2228 **771** 30 ch. multicoloured . 2·75 90

772 Royal Couple with Prince William

1982. Birth of Prince William of Wales. Multicoloured.

N2230 10 ch. Couple with Prince William (different) . . . 75 25
N2231 10 ch. Princess of Wales holding bouquet . . . . 1·50 75
N2232 20 ch. Couple with Prince William (different) . . . 90 30
N2233 20 ch. Prince Charles carrying baby, and Princess of Wales 1·50 75
N2234 30 ch. Type **772** . . . . . 1·00 40
N2235 30 ch. Prince Charles carrying baby, and Princess of Wales (different) . . . . 1·50 75
N2236 40 ch. Princess with baby 1·40 45
N2237 40 ch. Prince and Princess of Wales (horiz) . . . . . 2·40 95
N2238 50 ch. Princess with baby (different) . . . . 1·75 50
N2239 50 ch. Prince and Princess of Wales in evening dress (horiz) . . . . 2·40 95
N2240 80 ch. Couple with Prince William (different) . . . 1·50 75
N2241 80 ch. Prince Charles holding baby, and Princess of Wales (horiz) . . . . 2·40 95

773 Airship "Nulli Secundus II", 1908

1982. Bicentenary of Manned Flight (1st issue). Multicoloured.

N2243 10 ch. Type **773** . . . . . 1·25 40
N2244 10 ch. Pauley and Durs Egg's dirigible balloon "The Dolphin", 1818 . . . . 2·50 60
N2245 20 ch. Tissandier Brothers' airship, 1883 . . . . . . 1·50 50
N2246 20 ch. Guyton de Morveau's balloon with oars, 1784 2·50 60
N2247 30 ch. Parseval airship PL-VII, 1912 . . . . 2·00 60
N2248 30 ch. Sir George Cayley's airship design, 1837 . . 2·50 60
N2249 40 ch. Count Lennox's balloon "Eagle", 1834 . 2·25 60
N2250 40 ch. Camille Vert's balloon "Poisson Volant", 1859 . 2·50 60
N2251 80 ch. Dupuy de Lome's airship, 1872 . . . . . . 2·50 60

774 "Utopic Balloon Post" (Balthasar Antoine Dunker)

1982. Bicentenary of Manned Flight (2nd issue). Multicoloured.

N2253	10 ch. Type **774**	1·50	40
N2254	10 ch. Montgolfier balloon at Versailles, 1783	3·00	60
N2255	20 ch. "... and they fly into heaven and have no wings ..."	2·00	50
N2256	20 ch. Montgolfier Brothers' balloon, 1783	3·00	60
N2257	30 ch. Pierre Testu-Brissy's balloon ascent on horseback, 1798	2·50	60
N2258	30 ch. Charles's hydrogen balloon landing at Nesle, 1783	3·00	60
N2259	40 ch. Gaston Tissandier's test flight of "Zenith", 1875	3·00	60
N2260	40 ch. Blanchard and Jeffries' balloon flight over English Channel, 1785	3·00	60
N2261	80 ch. Henri Giffard's balloon "Le Grand Ballon Captif" at World Fair, 1878	3·00	60

775 Turtle with Scroll

1982. Tale of the Hare. Multicoloured.

N2263	10 ch. Type **775**	90	15
N2264	20 ch. Hare riding on turtle	1·25	20
N2265	30 ch. Hare and turtle before Dragon King	1·50	30
N2266	40 ch. Hare back on land	2·00	40

776 Flag, Red Book and City

777 Tower of Juche Idea

1982. 10th Anniv of Socialist Constitution.

N2267 **776** 10 ch. multicoloured . 25 10

1983. New Year.

N2268 **777** 10 ch. multicoloured . 15 10

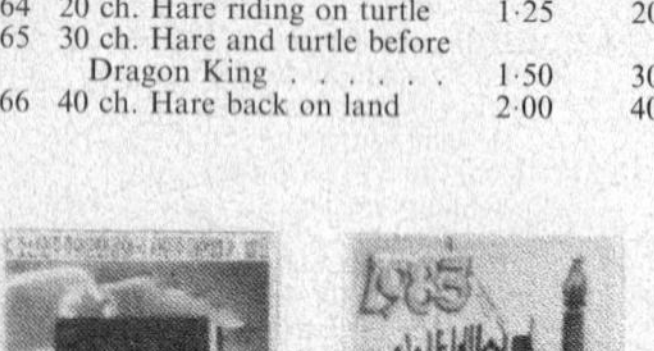

778 Children reading "Saenal"

1983. 55th Anniv of "Saenal" Newspaper.

N2269 **778** 10 ch. multicoloured . 50 10

779 "Man in Oriental Costume"

1983. Paintings by Rembrandt. Multicoloured.

N2270	10 ch. Type **779**	60	20
N2271	10 ch. "Child with dead Peacocks" (detail)	2·00	40
N2272	20 ch. "The Noble Slav"	1·25	30
N2273	20 ch. "Old Man in Fur Hat"	2·00	40
N2274	30 ch. "Dr. Tulp's Anatomy Lesson" (detail)	3·25	50
N2275	30 ch. "Portrait of a fashionable Couple"	2·00	40
N2276	40 ch. "Two Scholars disputing"	1·50	35
N2277	40 ch. "Woman with Child"	2·00	40
N2278	80 ch. "Woman holding an Ostrich Feather Fan"	2·00	40

780 Airships "Gross Basenach II" and "Graf Zepplin" over Cologne

1983. "Luposta" International Air Mail Exhibition, Cologne. Multicoloured.

N2280	30 ch. Type **780**	3·00	90
N2281	40 ch. Parsevel airship PL-II over Cologne	3·00	90

781 Banner and Monument

1983. 50th Anniv of Wangjaesan Meeting.

N2283 **781** 10 ch. multicoloured . 20 10

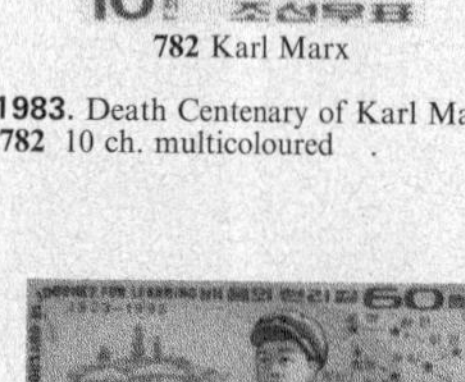

782 Karl Marx

1983. Death Centenary of Karl Marx.

N2284 **782** 10 ch. multicoloured . 50 25

783 Scholar, Marchers and Map of Journey

1983. 60th Anniv of Thousand-ri Journey for Learning.

N2285 **783** 10 ch. multicoloured . 1·00 10

784 "Madonna of the Goldfinch"

1983. 500th Birth Anniv of Raphael. Multicoloured.

N2286	10 ch. Type **784**	1·50	40
N2287	20 ch. "The School of Athens" (detail)	1·50	40
N2288	30 ch. "Madonna of the Grand Duke"	1·75	45
N2289	50 ch. "Madonna of the Chair"	1·90	45
N2290	50 ch. "Madonna of the Lamb"	1·50	50
N2291	80 ch. "The Beautiful Gardener"	1·50	50

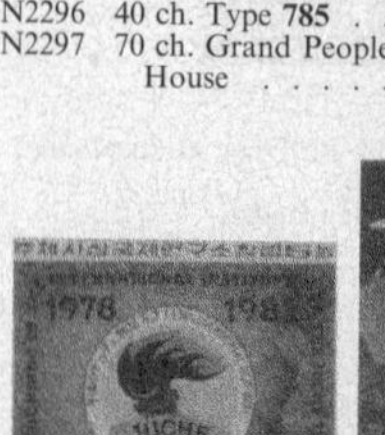

785 Department Store No. 1

1983. Pyongyang Buildings. Multicoloured.

N2293	2 ch. Chongryu Restaurant	20	10
N2294	10 ch. Part of Munsu Street	30	10
N2295	10 ch. Ice Rink	40	10
N2296	40 ch. Type **785**	60	15
N2297	70 ch. Grand People's Study House	75	25

786 Emblem and Crowd

788 Satellite, Masts and Dish Aerial

787 Judo

1983. 5th Anniv of International Institute of Juche Idea.

N2298 **786** 10 ch. multicoloured . . 15 10

1983. Olympic Games, Los Angeles (1st issue). Multicoloured.

N2299	20 ch. Type **787**	65	40
N2300	20 ch. Wrestling	1·25	40
N2301	30 ch. Judo (different) (value in gold)	65	40
N2302	30 ch. Judo (different) (value in black)	1·25	40
N2303	40 ch. Boxing	65	40
N2304	40 ch. Li Ho Jun (1972 shooting gold medalist)	1·25	40
N2305	50 ch. Weightlifting	65	40
N2306	50 ch. Wrestling (different)	1·25	40
N2307	80 ch. Boxing (different)	1·25	40

See also Nos. N2359/64.

1983. World Communications Year (1st issue).

N2309 **788** 10 ch. multicoloured . . 1·50 20

See also Nos. N2349/53.

789 Emblem, Giant Panda and Stamp

1983. "Tembal 83" International Thematic Stamp Exhibition, Basel. Multicoloured.

N2310	20 ch. Type **789**	1·75	35
N2311	30 ch. Emblem, flag and Basel Town Post stamp	1·90	35

790 "Colourful Cow" (kogge), 1402

1983. Old Ships. Multicoloured.

N2312	20 ch. Type **790**	1·10	45
N2313	20 ch. "Turtle" ship, 1592	2·50	75
N2314	35 ch. "Great Harry" (warship), 1555	1·50	55
N2315	35 ch. Admiral Li Sun Sin and "turtle" ship	2·50	75
N2316	50 ch. "Eagle of Lubeck" (galleon), 1567	2·10	70
N2317	50 ch. "Merkur" (full-rigged sailing ship), 1847	2·50	75
N2318	80 ch. "Herzogin Elisabeth" (cadet ship)	2·50	75

791 "Locomotion", 1825

1983. Railway Locomotives. Multicoloured.

N2320	20 ch. Type **791**	1·50	60
N2321	20 ch. "Drache", 1848	4·50	1·00
N2322	35 ch. "Der Adler", 1835	2·00	80
N2323	35 ch. Korean steam locomotive, 1853	4·50	1·00
N2324	50 ch. "Austria", 1837	3·25	80
N2325	50 ch. Bristol and Exeter Railway steam locomotive, 1853	4·50	1·00
N2326	80 ch. Caledonian Railway locomotive, 1859	4·50	1·00

792 Map, Hand and Weapons

1983. 10th Anniv of Publication of Five-point Policy for Korea's Reunification.

N2328 **792** 10 ch. multicoloured . 25 10

793 Emblem, Tower of Juche Idea and Fireworks

1983. World Conference on Journalists against Imperialism and for Friendship and Peace, Pyongyang. Multicoloured.

N2329	10 ch. Type **793**	20	10
N2330	40 ch. Emblem and rainbow and clasped hands	40	15
N2331	70 ch. Emblem, map and hand with raised forefinger	50	20

794 Worker and Banners

1983. "Let's Create the Speed of the 80s".

N2332 **794** 10 ch. multicoloured . 25 10

795 Soldier and Rejoicing Crowd

1983. 30th Anniv of Victory in Liberation War.

N2333 **795** 10 ch. multicoloured . 25 10

796 "Gorch Fock" (cadet barque) and Korean 1978 2 ch. Stamp

1983. "Bangkok 1983" International Stamp Exhibition.

N2334 **796** 40 ch. multicoloured . 3·00 1·25

797 Skiing

1983. Winter Olympic Games, Sarajevo (1984). Multicoloured.

N2336 10 ch. Type **797** 55 25
N2337 20 ch. Figure skating (vert) 2·00 45
N2338 30 ch. Skating (pair) . . . 1·60 55
N2339 50 ch. Ski jumping . . . . 1·60 55
N2340 50 ch. Ice hockey (vert) . . 2·00 45
N2341 80 ch. Speed skating (vert) 2·00 45

798 Workers and Soldier with Books

1983. 35th Anniv of Korean People's Democratic Republic.

N2343 **798** 10 ch. multicoloured . 35 10

799 Archery

800 Girls holding Hands

1983. Folk Games. Multicoloured.

N2344 10 ch. Type **799** . . . . . 2·50 40
N2345 10 ch. Flying kites 65 20
N2346 40 ch. See-sawing 65 20
N2347 40 ch. Swinging 65 20

1983. Korean–Chinese Friendship.

N2348 **800** 10 ch. multicoloured . 50 10

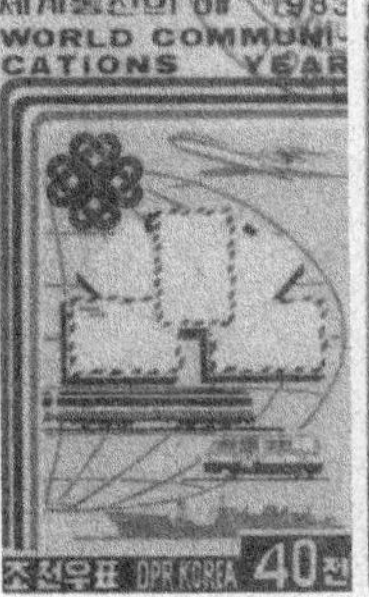

801 Envelopes and Forms of Transport

802 Portrait

1983. World Communications Year (2nd issue). Multicoloured.

N2349 30 ch. Mail van, motorcyclist and hand holding magazines . . . . . 4·75 90
N2350 30 ch. Satellite, globe and dish aerial . . . . 1·25 40
N2351 40 ch. Type **801** . . . . . 4·75 1·10
N2352 40 ch. Television cameraman 1·25 40
N2353 80 ch. Telephone and aerial 1·25 40

1983. Paintings by Rubens. Multicoloured.

N2355 40 ch. Type **802** . . . . . 1·40 60
N2356 40 ch. Portrait (different) (horiz) . . . . 1·75 75
N2357 80 ch. "The Sentencing of Midas" (horiz) . . . . . 1·75 75

803 Sprinting

1983. Olympic Games, Los Angeles (2nd issue). Multicoloured.

N2359 10 ch. Type **803** 75 20
N2360 20 ch. Show jumping . . . 1·75 45
N2361 30 ch. Cycling . . . . . . 3·00 55
N2362 50 ch. Handball . . . . . 2·00 60
N2363 50 ch. Fencing . . . . . 1·75 45
N2364 80 ch. Gymnastics . . . . 1·75 45

804 "St. Catherine"

805 Kimilsungflower

804a Cat

1983. 450th Death Anniv (1984) of Antonio Correggio (artist). Multicoloured.

N2366 20 ch. Type **804** . . . . . 1·75 60
N2367 20 ch. "Morning" (detail) 2·50 75
N2368 35 ch. "Madonna" . . . . 1·75 60
N2369 35 ch. "Morning" (different) 2·50 75
N2370 50 ch. "Madonna with St. John" . . . . 1·75 60
N2371 50 ch. "St. Catherine" (different) . . . . 2·50 75
N2372 80 ch. "Madonna and Child" 2·50 75

1983. Cats. Multicoloured, frame colour given.

N2373a **804a** 10 ch. green . . . . 1·10 10
N2373b – 10 ch. gold . . . . 1·10 10
N2373c – 10 ch. blue . . . . 1·10 10
N2373d – 10 ch. red . . . . . 1·10 10
N2373e – 10 ch. silver . . . . 1·10 10

DESIGNS: Different cats' heads.

1983. New Year.

N2374 **805** 10 ch. multicoloured . 65 10

806 Worker and Workers' Party Flag

1984. "Under the Leadership of the Workers' Party". Multicoloured.

N2375 10 ch. Type **806** 25 10
N2376 10 ch. Ore-dressing plant No. 3, Komdok General Mining Enterprise, and Party Flag 40 10

807 Farm Worker, Rice and Maize

1984. 20th Anniv of Publication of "Theses of the Socialist Rural Question in Our Country".

N2377 **807** 10 ch. multicoloured . 25 10

808 Changdok School, Chilgol

1984. Kim Il Sung's 72nd Birthday.

N2378 **808** 5 ch. green, black & bl 25 10
N2379 – 10 ch. multicoloured . 25 10

DESIGN: 10 ch. Birthplace, Mangyongdae, and rejoicing crowd.

809 "Spanish Riding School" (Julius von Blaas)

1984. "Espana 84" International Stamp Exhibition, Madrid. Multicoloured.

N2380 10 ch. Type **809** . . . . . 1·75 50
N2381 20 ch. "Ferdinand of Austria" (Rubens) . . . . 1·75 50

810 "La Donna Velata"

812 Construction Site

811 Map and Second Stage Pumping Station

1984. 500th Birth Anniv (1983) of Raphael (artist). Multicoloured.

N2383 10 ch. "Portrait of Agnolo Doni" . . . . 1·50 50
N2384 20 ch. Type **810** . . . . . 1·50 50
N2385 30 ch. "Portrait of Jeanne d'Aragon" . . . . 1·50 50

1984. 25th Anniv of Kiyang Irrigation System.

N2387 **811** 10 ch. multicoloured . . 50 10

1984. Construction on Five District Fronts.

N2388 **812** 10 ch. red, black & yell 50 10

813 Bobsleighing (East Germany)

1984. Winter Olympic Games Medal Winners. Multicoloured.

N2389 10 ch. Ski jumping (Matti Nykaenen) . . . . 1·75 50
N2390 20 ch. Speed skating (Karin Enke) . . . . 1·50 40
N2391 20 ch. Slalom (Max Julen) 1·75 50
N2392 30 ch. Type **813** . . . . . 1·50 40
N2393 30 ch. Downhill skiing (Maria Walliser) . . . . 1·75 50
N2394 40 ch. Cross-country skiing (Thomas Wassberg) . . . 2·75 60
N2395 80 ch. Cross-country skiing (Marja-Liisa Hamalainen) 2·75 60

814 Type "E" Goods Locomotive

1984. Essen International Stamp Fair. Mult.

N2397 20 ch. Type "202" express locomotive . . . . 4·00 65
N2398 30 ch. Type **814** . . . . . . 4·00 65

815 "Mlle. Fiocre in the Ballet 'La Source' "

1984. 150th Birth Anniv of Edgar Degas (artist). Multicoloured.

N2400 10 ch. Type **815** . . . . . 1·50 25
N2401 20 ch. "The Dance Foyer at the Rue le Peletier Opera" 2·50 25
N2402 30 ch. "Race Meeting" . . 3·75 40

816 Map of Pyongnam Irrigation System and Reservoir

1984. Irrigation Experts Meeting, Pyongyang.

N2404 **816** 2 ch. multicoloured . . 40 10

817 Korean Stamp and Building

818 Crowd and Banners

1984. U.P.U. Congress Stamp Exn, Hamburg.

N2405 **817** 20 ch. multicoloured . 3·00 40

1984. Proposal for Tripartite Talks.

N2407 **818** 10 ch. multicoloured . 40 10

819 Nobel experimenting

1984. 150th Birth Anniv (1983) of Alfred Bernhard Nobel (inventor). Multicoloured.

N2408 20 ch. Type **819** . . . . . 3·00 45
N2409 30 ch. Portrait of Nobel . 3·00 45

820 Drinks, Tinned Food, Clothes and Flats

1984. Improvements of Living Standards.

N2411 **820** 10 ch. multicoloured . 55 10

821 Sunhwa School, Mangyongdae

1984. School of Kim Hyong Jik (Kim Il Sung's Father).

N2412 **821** 10 ch. multicoloured . . 40 10

822 Armed Crowd with Banners

1984. 65th Anniv of Kuandian Conference.

N2413 **822** 10 ch. multicoloured . 40 10

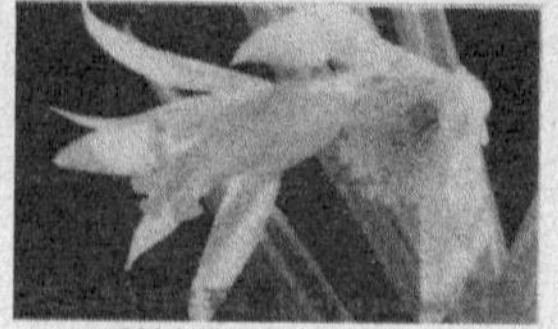

823 "Thunia bracteata"

1984. Flowers. Multicoloured.

N2414 10 ch. "Cattleya loddigesii" . . 75 10
N2415 20 ch. Type **823** . . . . . 1·10 25
N2416 30 ch. "Phalaenopsis amabilis" . . . . 1·50 40

824 Swordfish and Trawler

1984. Fishing Industry. Multicoloured.

N2418 5 ch. Type **824** 75 15
N2419 10 ch. Marlin and trawler . . 1·00 25
N2420 40 ch. "Histiophorus orientalis" and game fishing launch . . . . 2·75 95

825 Revolutionary Museum, Chilgol

1984.

N2421 **825** 10 ch. multicoloured . 40 10

826 Kim Hyok, Cha Gwang Su and Youth

828 Clock Face

827 Inauguration of a French Railway Line, 1860

1984. "Let's All become the Kim Hyoks and Cha Gwang Sus of the '80s".

N2422 **826** 10 ch. multicoloured . 40 10

1984. Centenary (1983) of "Orient Express". Multicoloured.

N2423 10 ch. Type **827** . . . . . 1·25 25
N2424 20 ch. Opening of a British railway line, 1821 . . . 2·50 55
N2425 30 ch. Inauguration of Paris-Rouen line, 1843 . . . . 3·25 85

1984. Centenary of Greenwich Meridian.

N2427 **828** 10 ch. multicoloured. 2·50 1·00

829 Grand Theatre, Hamburg

830 Turning on Machinery

1984.

N2429 **829** 10 ch. blue 40 10

1984. Automation of Industry.

N2430 **830** 40 ch. multicoloured . 60 30

831 "Dragon Angler"

1984. Paintings. Multicoloured.

N2431 10 ch. Type **831** 90 10
N2432 20 ch. "Ox Driver" (Kim Du Ryang) (47 × 35 mm) . . 1·10 25
N2433 30 ch. "Bamboo" (Kim Jin U) (47 × 35 mm) . . . . . 1·60 40

832 Tsiolkovsky

1984. K. E. Tsiolkovsky (space scientist). Mult.

N2435 20 ch. Type **832** 90 25
N2436 30 ch. "Sputnik" orbiting Earth . . . . 1·25 40

833 "Pongdaesan"

1984. Container Ships. Multicoloured.

N2438 10 ch. Type **833** 95 10
N2439 20 ch. "Ryongnamsan" . . 1·10 35
N2440 30 ch. "Rungrado" . . . 1·50 55

834 Caracal

1984. Animals. Multicoloured.

N2442 10 ch. Spotted hyenas . . 60 10
N2443 20 ch. Type **834** 90 25
N2444 30 ch. Black-backed jackals 1·25 40
N2445 40 ch. Foxes . . . . . . 1·60 60

835 Marie Curie

836 Chestnut-eared Aracari

1984. 50th Anniv of Marie Curie (physicist).

N2447 **835** 10 ch. multicoloured . 2·00 25

1984. Birds. Multicoloured.

N2449 10 ch. Hoopoe . . . . . . 1·10 15
N2450 20 ch. South African crowned cranes . . . . 1·50 35
N2451 30 ch. Saddle-bill stork . . 2·00 50
N2452 40 ch. Type **836** . . . . . 2·75 65

837 Cosmonaut

1984. Space Exploration. Multicoloured.

N2454 10 ch. Type **837** 50 10
N2455 20 ch. Cosmonaut on space-walk 75 25
N2456 30 ch. Cosmonaut (different) 1·00 40

838 "Arktika"

1984. Russian Ice-breakers. Multicoloured.

N2458 20 ch. Type **838** . . . . . 1·25 35
N2459 30 ch. "Ermak" . . . . . . 1·75 50

839 Mendeleev

1984. 150th Birth Anniv of Dmitri Mendeleev (chemist).

N2461 **839** 10 ch. multicoloured . . 95 10

840 Kim Il Sung in U.S.S.R.

1984. Kim Il Sung's Visits to Eastern Europe. Multicoloured.

N2463 10 ch. Type **840** 60 10
N2464 10 ch. In Poland 60 10
N2465 10 ch. In German Democratic Republic 60 10
N2466 10 ch. In Czechoslovakia . 60 10
N2467 10 ch. In Hungary 60 10
N2468 10 ch. In Bulgaria 60 10
N2469 10 ch. In Rumania 60 10

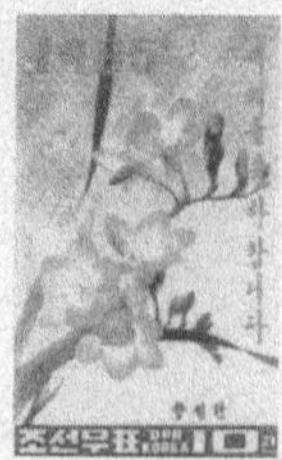

841 Freesia

1985. New Year.

N2471 **841** 10 ch. multicoloured . . 75 10

842 Journey Route, Steam Locomotive and Memorials

1985. 60th Anniv of 1000 ri Journey by Kim Il Sung. Multicoloured.

N2472 5 ch. Type **842** . . . . . . 1·25 10
N2473 10 ch. Boy trumpeter and schoolchildren following route 50 10

Nos. N2472/3 were issued together, se-tenant, forming a composite design.

843 Cugnot's Steam Car, 1769

844 Camp, Mt. Paekdu

1985. History of the Motor Car (1st series). Multicoloured.

N2474 10 ch. Type **843** . . . . . 1·25 10
N2475 15 ch. Goldsworthy Gurney steam omnibus, 1825 . . 1·25 15
N2476 20 ch. Gottlieb Daimler diesel car, 1885 . . . . . . 1·25 25
N2477 25 ch. Benz three-wheeled diesel car, 1886 . . . . 1·40 35
N2478 30 ch. Peugeot diesel car, 1891 1·75 40

See also Nos. N2562/6.

1985. Korean Revolution Headquarters.

N2480 **844** 10 ch. multicoloured . 40 20

845 Taechodo Lighthouse

846 Hedgehog challenges Tiger

1985. Lighthouses. Multicoloured.

N2481 10 ch. Type **845** . . . . . 1·75 10
N2482 20 ch. Sodo . . . . 1·90 30
N2483 30 ch. Pido . . . . 2·25 45
N2484 40 ch. Suundo . . . . . . 2·75 70

1985. "The Hedgehog defeats the Tiger" (fable). Multicoloured.

N2485 10 ch. Type **846** 60 10
N2486 20 ch. Tiger goes to stamp on rolled-up hedgehog . . . 90 25
N2487 30 ch. Hedgehog clings to tiger's nose . . . . . . 1·25 40
N2488 35 ch. Tiger flees . . . . . 1·40 50
N2489 40 ch. Tiger crawls before hedgehog . . . . 1·60 60

847 "Pleurotus cornucopiae"

848 West Germany v. Hungary, 1954

1985. Fungi. Multicoloured.

N2490 10 ch. Type **847** . . . . . 1·10 10
N2491 20 ch. Oyster fungus . . . 1·40 25
N2492 30 ch. "Catathelasma ventricosum" . . . . . 1·90 40

1985. World Cup Football Championship Finals.

N2493 **848** 10 ch. black, buff & brn 60 10
N2494 – 10 ch. multicoloured . . 60 10
N2495 – 20 ch. black, buff & brn 90 25
N2496 – 20 ch. multicoloured . . 90 25
N2497 – 30 ch. black, buff & brn 1·25 40
N2498 – 30 ch. multicoloured . 1·25 40
N2499 – 40 ch. black, buff & brn 1·60 60
N2500 – 40 ch. multicoloured . 1·60 60

DESIGNS—VERT: No. N2496 West Germany v. Netherlands, 1974; N2499, England v. West Germany, 1966. HORIZ: No. N2494, Brazil v. Italy, 1970; N2495, Brazil v. Sweden, 1958; N2497, Brazil v. Czechoslovakia, 1962; N2498, Argentina v. Netherlands, 1968; N2500, Italy v. West Germany, 1982.

MINIMUM PRICE

The minimum price quoted is 10p which represents a handling charge rather than a basis for valuing common stamps. For further notes about prices, see introductory pages.

849 Date and Kim Il Sung's Birthplace
850 Horn Player

1985. 73rd Birthday of Kim Il Sung.

N2502 **849** 10 ch. multicoloured 40 10

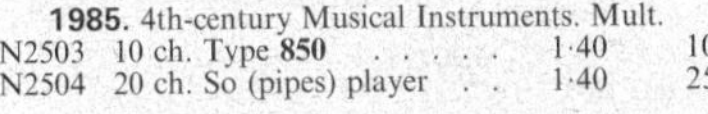

1985. 4th-century Musical Instruments. Mult.

N2503 10 ch. Type **850** 1·40 10
N2504 20 ch. So (pipes) player 1·40 25

851 Chongryon Hall, Tokyo
852 Common Marmoset

1985. 30th Anniv of Chongryon (General Association of Korean Residents in Japan).

N2505 **851** 10 ch. brown 40 10

1985. Mammals. Multicoloured.

N2506 5 ch. Type **852** 85 10
N2507 10 ch. Ring-tailed lemur 85 10

854 Buenos Aires and Argentina 1982 Stamp
855 Dancer and Gymnast

1985. "Argentina '85" International Stamp Exhibition, Buenos Aires. Multicoloured.

N2509 10 ch. Type **854** 75 10
N2510 20 ch. Iguacu Falls and Argentina 1984 and North Korea 1978 stamps (horiz) 2·50 25

1985. 12th World Youth and Students' Festival, Moscow. Multicoloured.

N2512 10 ch. Type **855** 60 10
N2513 20 ch. Spassky Tower, Moscow, and Festival emblem 90 25
N2514 40 ch. Youths of different races 1·60 60

856 Peace Pavilion, Youth Park
857 Liberation Celebrations

1985. Pyongyang Buildings.

N2515 **856** 2 ch. black and green 20 10
N2516 – 40 ch. brown and lt brn 45 20
DESIGN: 40 ch. Multi-storey flats, Chollima Street.

1985. 40th Anniv of Liberation.

N2517 – 5 ch. red, black & blue 20 10
N2518 – 10 ch. multicoloured 40 10
N2519 – 10 ch. brown, blk & grn 40 10
N2520 – 10 ch. multicoloured 40 10
N2521 **857** 10 ch. yellow, blk & red 40 10
N2522 – 10 ch. red, orange & blk 40 10
N2523 – 40 ch. multicoloured 60 20
DESIGNS—HORIZ: No. N2517, Soldiers with rifles and flag; N2518, Crowd with banners and Flame of Juche; N2519, Korean and Soviet soldiers raising arms; N2520, Japanese soldiers laying down weapons; N2523, Students bearing banners. VERT: No. N2522, Liberation Tower, Moran Hill, Pyongyang.

MORE DETAILED LISTS
are given in the Stanley Gibbons Catalogues referred to in the country headings. For lists of current volumes see introduction

858 Halley and Comet

1985. Appearance of Halley's Comet. Multicoloured.

N2525 10 ch. Type **858** 75 10
N2526 20 ch. Diagram of comet's flight and space probe 1·10 25

859 "Camellia japonica"
861 Party Founding Museum

860 "Hunting"

1985. Flowers. Multicoloured.

N2528 10 ch. "Hippeastrum hybridum" 75 10
N2529 20 ch. Type **859** 1·10 25
N2530 30 ch. "Cyclamen persicum" 1·50 40

1985. Koguryo Culture.

N2531 10 ch. "Hero" (vert) 60 10
N2532 15 ch. "Heroine" (vert) 75 15
N2533 20 ch. "Flying Fairy" 90 25
N2534 25 ch. Type **860** 1·10 35

1985. 40th Anniv of Korean Workers' Party. Multicoloured.

N2536 5 ch. Type **861** 20 10
N2537 10 ch. Soldier with gun and workers 40 10
N2538 10 ch. Soldiers and flag 40 10
N2539 40 ch. Statue of worker, peasant and intellectual holding aloft party emblem 60 20

862 Arch of Triumph, Pyongyang
863 Colosseum, Rome, and N. Korea 1975 10 ch. Stamp

1985. 40th Anniv of Kim Il Sung's Return.

N2541 **862** 10 ch. brown and green 40 10

1985. "Italia '85" International Stamp Exhibition, Rome. Multicoloured.

N2542 10 ch. Type **863** 60 10
N2543 20 ch. "The Holy Family" (Raphael) (vert) 90 25
N2544 30 ch. Head of "David" (statue, Michelangelo) (vert) 1·25 40

864 Mercedes Benz Type "300"

1985. South-West German Stamp Fair, Sindelfingen. Multicoloured.

N2546 10 ch. Type **864** 90 10
N2547 15 ch. Mercedes Benz Type "770" 1·25 15
N2548 20 ch. Mercedes Benz "W 150" 1·50 25
N2549 30 ch. Mercedes Type "600" 1·90 40

865 Tackle

1985. World Cup Football Championship, Mexico (1st issue). Multicoloured.

N2551 20 ch. Type **865** 1·10 25
N2552 30 ch. Three players 1·40 40
See also Nos. N2558/9 and N2577/82.

866 Dancers

1985. International Youth Year. Multicoloured.

N2554 10 ch. Type **866** 60 10
N2555 20 ch. Sports activities 90 25
N2556 30 ch. Technology 1·25 40

867 Players

1985. World Cup Football Championship, Mexico (2nd issue). Multicoloured.

N2558 20 ch. Type **867** 1·10 25
N2559 30 ch. Goalkeeper and players 1·40 40

868 Juche Torch
869 Amedee Bollee and Limousine, 1901

1986. New Year.

N2561 **868** 10 ch. multicoloured 40 10

1986. History of the Motor Car (2nd series). Multicoloured.

N2562 10 ch. Type **869** 75 10
N2563 20 ch. Stewart Rolls, Henry Royce and "Silver Ghost", 1906 1·25 25
N2564 25 ch. Giovanni Agnelli and Fiat car, 1912 1·40 35
N2565 30 ch. Ettore Bugatti and "Royal" coupe, 1928 1·60 40
N2566 40 ch. Louis Renault and fiacre, 1906 2·25 60

870 Gary Kasparov
872 Tongdu Rock, Songgan

871 Cemetery Gate

1986. World Chess Championship, Moscow.

N2568 **870** 20 ch. multicoloured 2·25 25

1986. Revolutionary Martyrs' Cemetery, Pyongyang. Multicoloured.

N2570 5 ch. Type **871** 20 10
N2571 10 ch. Bronze sculpture (detail) 55 10

1986. 37th Anniv of Pres. Kim Il Sung's Visit to Songgan Revolutionary Site.

N2572 **872** 10 ch. multicoloured 40 10

873 Buddhist Scriptures Museum

1986. Mt. Myohyang Buildings.

N2573 **873** 10 ch. brown and green 40 10
N2574 – 20 ch. violet and red 50 10
DESIGN: 20 ch. Taeung Hall.

874 "Amphiprion frenatus"

1986. Fishes. Multicoloured.

N2575 10 ch. Pennant coralfish 85 10
N2576 20 ch. Type **874** 1·40 25

875 Footballers and Flags of Italy, Bulgaria and Argentina

1986. World Cup Football Championship, Mexico (3rd issue). Designs showing footballers and flags of participating countries. Multicoloured.

N2577 10 ch. Type **875** 60 10
N2578 20 ch. Mexico, Belgium, Paraguay and Iraq 90 25
N2579 25 ch. France, Canada, U.S.S.R. and Hungary 1·10 35
N2580 30 ch. Brazil, Spain, Algeria and Northern Ireland 1·25 40
N2581 35 ch. West Germany, Uruguay, Scotland and Denmark 1·40 50
N2582 40 ch. Poland, Portugal, Morocco and England 1·60 60

876 Singer, Pianist and Emblem

1986. 4th Spring Friendship Art Festival, Pyongyang.

N2584 **876** 1 wn. multicoloured 1·25 55

877 Daimler "Motorwagen", 1886
878 Mangyong Hill

1986. 60th Anniv of Mercedes-Benz (car manufacturers). Multicoloured.

N2585 10 ch. Type **877** 60 10
N2586 10 ch. Benz "velo", 1894 60 10
N2587 20 ch. Mercedes car, 1901 90 25
N2588 20 ch. Benz limousine, 1909 90 25
N2589 30 ch. Mercedes "tourenwagen", 1914 1·25 40
N2590 30 ch. Mercedes-Benz "170" 6-cylinder, 1931 1·25 40
N2591 40 ch. Mercedes-Benz "380", 1933 1·60 60
N2592 40 ch. Mercedes-Benz "540 K", 1936 1·60 60

1986. 74th Birthday of Kim Il Sung.

N2594 **878** 10 ch. multicoloured 30 10

879 Crowd

1968. 50th Anniv of Association for the Restoration of the Fatherland.

N2595 **879** 10 ch. multicoloured . 30 10

880 Dove carrying Letter 881 "Mona Lisa" (Leonardo da Vinci)

1986. International Peace Year. Multicoloured.

N2596 10 ch. Type **880** 50 10
N2597 20 ch. U.N. Headquarters, New York 80 25
N2598 30 ch. Dove, globe and broken missiles . . . . . 1·10 40

1986.

N2600 **881** 20 ch. multicoloured . 90 25

882 Pink Iris 883 Kim Un Suk

1986. Irises. Multicoloured.

N2601 20 ch. Type **882** . . . . . . 1·10 25
N2602 30 ch. Violet iris . . . . . . 1·40 40

1986. Tennis Players. Multicoloured.

N2604 10 ch. Type **883** (postage) 1·75 35
N2605 20 ch. Ivan Lendl . . . . . 1·75 35
N2606 30 ch. Steffi Graf . . . . . 1·75 35
N2607 50 ch. Boris Becker (air) . . 1·75 35

884 Sulphur crested Cockatoo

1986. "Stampex '86" Stamp Exhibition, Adelaide, Australia.

N2608 **884** 10 ch. multicoloured . 1·50 15

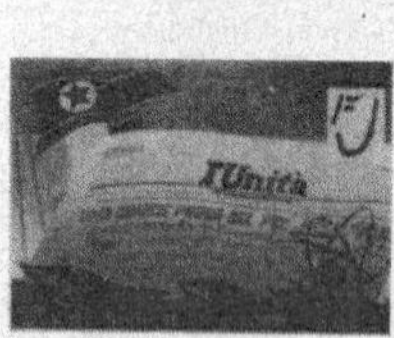
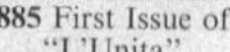
885 First Issue of "L'Unita" 886 "Express II" (icebreaker) and Sweden 1872 20 ore Stamp

1986. National "L'Unita" (Italian Communist Party newspaper) Festival, Milan. Multicoloured.

N2610 10 ch. Type **885** 60 10
N2611 20 ch. Milan Cathedral . . . 90 25
N2612 30 ch. "Pieta" (Michelangelo) (vert) . . . . 1·25 40

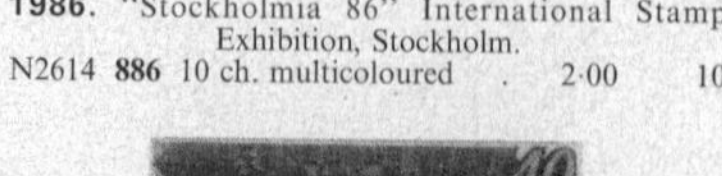

1986. "Stockholmia 86" International Stamp Exhibition, Stockholm.

N2614 **886** 10 ch. multicoloured . . 2·00 10

887 Reprint of First Stamp

1986. 40th Anniv of First North Korean Stamps (1st issue). Multicoloured.

N2616 10 ch. Type **887** (postage) 60 10
N2617 15 ch. Imperforate reprint of first stamp 75 15
N2618 50 ch. 1946 50 ch. violet stamp (air) . . . . 1·75 75

See also Nos. N2619/21.

888 Postal Emblems and 1962 and 1985 Stamps

1986. 40th Anniv of First North Korean Stamps (2nd issue). Multicoloured.

N2619 10 ch. Type **888** (postage) 1·75 25
N2620 15 ch. General Post Office and 1976 and 1978 stamps 90 15
N2621 50 ch. Kim Il Sung, first stamp and reprint (vert) (air) . . . . 1·40 45

1986. World Cup Football Championship Results. Nos. N2577/82 optd **1st: ARG 2nd: FRG 3rd: FRA 4th: BEL.**

N2622 10 ch. multicoloured . . . 80 10
N2623 20 ch. multicoloured . . . 1·10 25
N2624 25 ch. multicoloured . . . 1·40 35
N2625 30 ch. multicoloured . . . 1·50 40
N2626 35 ch. multicoloured . . . 1·60 50
N2627 40 ch. multicoloured . . . 1·90 60

890 Flag and Man with raised Fist 892 Schoolchildren

891 Gift Animals House

1986. 60th Anniv of Down-with-Imperialism Union.

N2629 **890** 10 ch. multicoloured . 30 10

1986. 1st Anniv of Gift Animals House, Central Zoo, Pyongyang.

N2630 **891** 2 wn. multicoloured . 3·00 1·10

1986. 40th Anniv of U.N.E.S.C.O. Multicoloured.

N2631 10 ch. Type **892** 60 10
N2632 50 ch. Anniversary emblem, Grand People's Study House and telecommunications (horiz) 1·50 75

893 Communications Satellite

1986. 15th Anniv of Intersputnik.

N2633 **893** 5 wn. multicoloured . 7·00 3·00

894 Oil tanker leaving Lock

1986. West Sea Barrage.

N2634 **894** 10 ch. multicoloured . 50 10
N2635 – 40 ch. green, black and gold . . . . 1·25 20
N2636 – 1 wn. 20 multicoloured 2·75 60

DESIGNS: 20 ch. Aerial view of dam; 1 wn. 20, Aerial view of lock.

895 Common Morel 896 Machu Picchu, Peru, and N. Korea Taedong Gate Stamp

1986. Minerals and Fungi. Multicoloured.

N2637 10 ch. Lengenbachite (postage) . . . . 1·60 25
N2638 10 ch. Common funnel cap 1·60 25
N2639 15 ch. Rhodochrosite . . . 1·60 25
N2640 15 ch. Type **895** . . . . . . 1·60 25
N2641 50 ch. Annabergite (air) . . 1·60 25
N2642 50 ch. Blue russula . . . . 1·60 25

1986. North Korean Three-dimensional Photographs and Stamps Exhibition, Lima, Peru.

N2643 **896** 10 ch. multicoloured . . 1·25 20

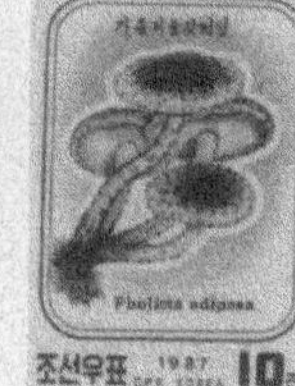
897 Pine Tree 898 "Pholiota adiposa"

1987. New Year. Multicoloured.

N2645 10 ch. Type **897** 75 15
N2646 40 ch. Hare 90 25

1987. Fungi. Multicoloured.

N2647 10 ch. Type **898** . . . . . . 1·25 20
N2648 20 ch. Chanterelle . . . . . 1·50 20
N2649 30 ch. "Boletus impolitus" . . 1·75 30

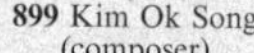
899 Kim Ok Song (composer) 901 East Pyongyang Grand Theatre

1987. Musicians' Death Anniversaries. Mult.

N2651 10 ch. Maurice Ravel (composer, 50th anniv) 1·25 20
N2652 10 ch. Type **899** (22nd anniv) 1·25 20
N2653 20 ch. Giovanni Lully (composer, 300th anniv) 1·25 20
N2654 30 ch. Franz Liszt (composer, centenary (1986)) . . . . 1·25 20
N2655 40 ch. Violins (250th anniv of Antonio Stradivari (violin maker) . . . . 1·25 20
N2656 40 ch. Christoph Gluck (composer, bicent) . . . 1·25 20

1987. Buildings.

N2658 **901** 5 ch. green 35 10
N2659 – 10 ch. brown 45 10
N2660 – 3 wn. blue . . . . . . 3·00 90

DESIGNS—VERT: 10 ch. Pyongyang Koryo Hotel. HORIZ: 3 wn. Rungnado Stadium.

902 "Gorch Fock" (German cadet barque)

1987. Sailing Ships. Multicoloured.

N2661 20 ch. Type **902** (postage) 70 20
N2662 30 ch. "Tovarishch" (Russian cadet barque) (vert) . . 1·00 30
N2663 50 ch. "Belle Poule" (cadet schooner) (vert) (air) . . 1·50 50
N2664 50 ch. "Sagres II" (Portuguese cadet barque) (vert) . . . 1·50 50
N2665 1 wn. Koryo period merchantman . . . . . 3·00 1·00
N2666 1 wn. "Dar Mlodziezy" (Polish cadet full-rigged ship) (vert) . . . . . . 3·00 1·00

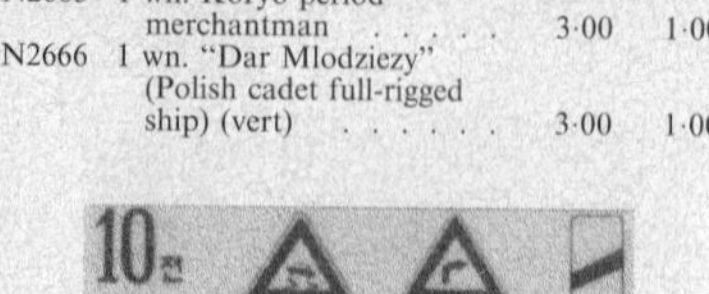

903 Road Signs

1987. Road Safety.

N2667 **903** 10 ch. blue, red and black (postage) . . . . . 1·00 10
N2668 – 10 ch. red and black . 1·00 10
N2669 – 20 ch. blue, red & blk 1·25 20
N2670 – 50 ch. red and black (air) 1·50 50

DESIGNS: Nos. N2668/70, Different road signs.

904 Fire Engine

1987. Fire Engines.

N2671 **904** 10 ch. multicoloured (postage) . . . . . 1·75 25
N2672 – 20 ch. multicoloured . 1·90 25
N2673 – 30 ch. multicoloured . 2·50 30
N2674 – 50 ch. multicoloured (air) 3·25 50

DESIGNS: N2672/4, 20 ch. to 50 ch. Different machines.

905 "Apatura ilia" and Spiraea

1987. Butterflies and Flowers. Multicoloured.

N2675 10 ch. Type **905** 70 10
N2676 10 ch. "Ypthima argus" and fuchsia 70 10
N2677 20 ch. "Neptis philyra" and aquilegia . . . . 1·00 20
N2678 20 ch. "Papilio protenor" and chrysanthemum . . . . 1·00 20
N2679 40 ch. "Parantica sita" and celosia . . . . 1·60 40
N2680 40 ch. "Vanessa indica" and hibiscus . . . . 1·60 40

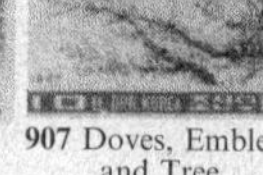
906 Association Monument, Pyongyang 907 Doves, Emblem and Tree

1987. 70th Anniv of Korean National Association (independence movement).

N2681 **906** 10 ch. red, silver & blk 25 10

1987. 5th Spring Friendship Art Festival, Pyongyang.

N2682 **907** 10 ch. multicoloured . 25 10

908 Mangyong Hill 909 Bay

1987. 75th Birthday of Kim Il Sung. Mult.

N2683 10 ch. Type **908** 25 10
N2684 10 ch. Kim Il Sung's birthplace, Mangyongdae (horiz) 25 10
N2685 10 ch. "A Bumper Crop of Pumpkins" (62 × 41 mm) 25 10
N2686 10 ch. "Profound Affection for the Working Class" 25 10

1987. Horses. Multicoloured.

N2687 10 ch. Type **909** 40 10
N2688 10 ch. Bay (different) . . . 40 10
N2689 40 ch. Grey rearing . . . . 1·25 40
N2690 40 ch. Grey on beach . . . 1·25 40

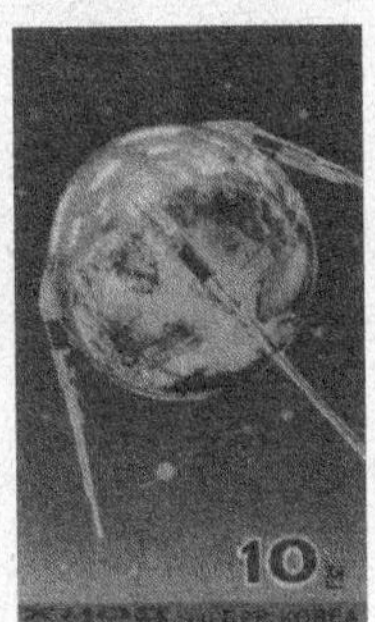

910 "Sputnik 1" (first artificial satellite)

1987. Transport. Multicoloured.

N2691 10 ch. Electric train "Juche" (horiz) 40 10
N2692 10 ch. Electric locomotive "Mangyongdae" (horiz) 40 10
N2693 10 ch. Type **910** (30th anniv of flight) 40 10
N2694 20 ch. Laika (30th anniv of first animal in space) . . 70 20
N2695 20 ch. Tupolev Tu-144 supersonic airliner (horiz) 70 20
N2696 20 ch. Concorde (11th anniv of first commercial flight) (horiz) 70 20
N2697 30 ch. Count Ferdinand von Zeppelin (70th death anniv) and airship LZ-4 (horiz) 1·00 30
N2698 80 ch. Zeppelin and diagrams and drawings of airships (horiz) . . . . 3·00 1·00

911 Musk Ox

1987. "Capex '87" International Stamp Exhibition, Toronto. Multicoloured.

N2699 10 ch. Type **911** 65 10
N2700 40 ch. Jacques Cartier, his ship "Grande Hermine" and ice-breaker (horiz) . 1·75 40
N2701 60 ch. Ice hockey (Winter Olympics, Calgary, 1988) (horiz) . . . . 1·75 60

912 Trapeze Artistes

1987. International Circus Festival, Monaco. Multicoloured.

N2702 10 ch. Type **912** 40 10
N2703 10 ch. "Brave Sailors" (North Korean acrobatic act) (vert) 40 10
N2704 20 ch. Clown and elephant (vert) 70 20
N2705 20 ch. North Korean artiste receiving "Golden Clown" award 70 20
N2706 40 ch. Performing horses and cat act . . . . 2·10 40
N2707 50 ch. Prince Rainier and his children applauding . . . 1·50 50

913 Attack on Watch Tower

1987. 50th Anniv of Battle of Pochonbo.

N2708 **913** 10 ch. brown, black and ochre 25 10

914 Sports

1987. Angol Sports Village.

N2709 **914** 5 ch. brown and gold 15 10
N2710 – 10 ch. blue and gold . 25 10
N2711 – 40 ch. brown and gold 75 25
N2712 – 70 ch. blue and gold . 1·25 40
N2713 – 1 wn. red and gold . . 1·90 60
N2714 – 1 wn. 20 violet . . . . 2·25 70

DESIGNS: Exteriors of—10 ch. Indoor swimming pool; 40 ch. Weightlifting gymnasium; 70 ch. Table tennis gymnasium; 1 wn. Football stadium; 1 wn. 20, Handball gymnasium.

915 Mandarins

1987. Mandarins. Multicoloured.

N2715 20 ch. Type **915** . . . . . 1·10 25
N2716 20 ch. Mandarins on shore 1·10 25
N2717 20 ch. Mandarins on branch 1·10 25
N2718 40 ch. Mandarins in water 1·60 40

916 Exhibition Site and 1987 3 wn. Stamp

1987. "Olymphilex '87" Olympic Stamps Exhibition, Rome.

N2719 **916** 10 ch. multicoloured . 90 10

917 Underground Station and Guard

1987. Railway Uniforms. Multicoloured.

N2721 10 ch. Type **917** 40 10
N2722 10 ch. Underground train and station supervisor . . . 40 10
N2723 20 ch. Guard and train . . 60 10
N2724 30 ch. Guard and train . . 85 20
N2725 40 ch. "Orient Express" guard 1·10 25
N2726 40 ch. German ticket controller and steam train 1.10 25

918 White Stork

920 Victory Column

919 Ice Skating

1987. "Hafnia 87" International Stamp Exhibition, Copenhagen. Multicoloured.

N2727 40 ch. Type **918** . . . . . . 1·75 40
N2728 60 ch. "Danmark" (cadet full-rigged ship) and "Little Mermaid", Copenhagen 1·75 40

1987. Winter Olympic Games, Calgary (1988). Multicoloured.

N2729 40 ch. Type **919** . . . . . . 1·00 30
N2730 40 ch. Ski jumping . . . . 1·00 30
N2731 40 ch. Skiing (value on left) (horiz) . . . . 1·00 30
N2732 40 ch. Skiing (value on right) (horiz) . . . . 1·00 30

1987. 750th Anniv of Berlin and "Philatelia '87" International Stamp Exhibition, Cologne. Mult.

N2734 10 ch. Type **920** 40 10
N2735 20 ch. Reichstag (horiz) . . 70 20
N2736 30 ch. Pfaueninsel Castle . . 1·00 30
N2737 40 ch. Charlottenburg Castle (horiz) . . . . 1·25 40

921 Garros and Bleriot XI

1987. Birth Centenary of Roland Garros (aviator) and Tennis as an Olympic Sport. Multicoloured.

N2739 20 ch. Type **921** . . . . . . 1·50 20
N2740 20 ch. Ivan Lendl (tennis player) . . . . 2·25 20
N2741 40 ch. Steffi Graf (tennis player) . . . . 3·00 40

923 Pyongyang Buildings

1988. New Year. Multicoloured.

N2744 10 ch. Type **923** 20 10
N2745 40 ch. Dragon 75 25

924 Banner and Newspaper

925 Birthplace, Mt. Paekdu

1988. 60th Anniv of "Saenal" Newspaper.

N2746 **924** 10 ch. multicoloured . . 45 10

1988. Kim Jong Il's Birthday.

N2747 **925** 10 ch. multicoloured . . 20 10

926 Henry Dunant (founder)

1988. 125th Anniv of International Red Cross. Multicoloured.

N2749 10 ch. Type **926** 60 10
N2750 20 ch. North Korean Red Cross emblem and map 90 15
N2751 20 ch. International Committee headquarters, Geneva 90 15
N2752 40 ch. Pyongyang Maternity Hospital, doctor and baby 90 25

927 "Santa Maria"

1988. 500th Anniv (1992) of Discovery of America by Christopher Columbus. Multicoloured.

N2754 10 ch. Type **927** . . . . . 1·25 10
N2755 20 ch. "Pinta" . . . . . . 1·25 20
N2756 30 ch. "Nina" . . . . . . 1·25 30

Nos. N2754/6 were issued together, se-tenant, forming a composite design of Columbus's ships leaving Palos.

928 Montgolfier Balloon and Modern Hot-air Balloons

929 Dancers

1988. "Juvalux '88" International Youth Stamp Exhibition, Luxembourg. Multicoloured.

N2758 40 ch. Type **928** 90 25
N2759 60 ch. Early railway locomotive and railway map of Luxembourg, 1900 1·60 35

1988. 6th Spring Friendship Art Festival, Pyongyang. Multicoloured.

N2760 10 ch. Singer (poster) . . . 20 10
N2761 1 wn. 20 Type **929** . . . . 1·90 75

930 Inaugural Congress Emblem

931 Birthplace, Mangyongdae

1988. 10th Anniv of International Institute of the Juche Idea.

N2762 **930** 10 ch. multicoloured . 20 10

1988. 76th Birthday of Kim Il Sung.

N2763 **931** 10 ch. multicoloured . 20 10

932 "Urho" (ice-breaker)

1988. "Finlandia 88" International Stamp Exhibition, Helsinki. Multicoloured.

N2765 40 ch. Type **932** . . . . . 1·40 25
N2766 60 ch. Matti Nykaenen (Olympic Games ski-jumping medallist) . . . 1·10 35

933 Postcard for 1934 Championship

934 Emblem

1988. World Cup Football Championship, Italy (1st issue). Multicoloured.

N2767 10 ch. Football match . . 50 10
N2768 20 ch. Type **933** 85 15
N2769 30 ch. Player tackling (horiz) 1·25 20

See also Nos. N2924/7.

1988. 13th World Youth and Students' Festival, Pyongyang (1st issue). Multicoloured.

N2771 5 ch. Type **934** 10 10
N2772 10 ch. Dancer 40 10
N2773 10 ch. Gymnast and gymnasium, Angol Sports Village 20 10
N2774 10 ch. Map of Korea, globe and doves 30 10
N2775 10 ch. Finger pointing at shattered nuclear rockets 75 10
N2776 1 wn. 20 Three differently coloured hands and dove 2·10 75

See also Nos. N2860/3 and N2879/80.

935 Fairy

936 Mallards

1988. "Eight Fairies of Mt. Kumgang" (tale). Multicoloured.

N2777 10 ch. Type **935** 20 10
N2778 15 ch. Fairy at pool and fairies on rainbow . . . 30 10
N2779 20 ch. Fairy and woodman husband 40 15
N2780 25 ch. Couple with baby . 50 15
N2781 30 ch. Couple with son and daughter 55 20
N2782 35 ch. Family on rainbow 65 20

1988. "Praga '88" International Stamp Exhibition, Prague. Multicoloured.

N2783 20 ch. Type **936** . . . . . 1·10 15
N2784 40 ch. Vladimir Remek (Czechoslovak cosmonaut) 75 25

937 Red Crossbill

1988. Birds. Multicoloured.

N2785 10 ch. Type **937** 55 15
N2786 15 ch. Stonechat 75 20
N2787 20 ch. European nuthatch 1·10 25
N2788 25 ch. Great spotted woodpecker . . . . . . 1·25 30
N2789 30 ch. Common kingfisher 1·50 35
N2790 35 ch. Bohemian waxwing 1·60 45

938 Fair Emblem

1988. 40th International Stamp Fair, Riccione.

N2791 **938** 20 ch. multicoloured . 40 15

939 Emu

1988. Bicentenary of Australian Settlement. Mult.

N2793 10 ch. Type **939** 60 15
N2794 15 ch. Satin bowerbirds . . 85 20
N2795 25 ch. Laughing kookaburra (vert) . . . . 1·40 35

MINIMUM PRICE

The minimum price quoted is 10p which represents a handling charge rather than a basis for valuing common stamps. For further notes about prices, see introductory pages.

940 Floating Crane "5-28"

1988. Ships. Multicoloured.

N2797 10 ch. Type **940** 40 15
N2798 20 ch. Freighter "Hwanggumsan" . . . 60 20
N2799 30 ch. Freighter "Changjasan Chongnyon-ho" 75 25
N2800 40 ch. Liner "Samjiyon" . 1·00 30

941 "Hansa"

1988. 150th Birth Anniv of Count Ferdinand von Zeppelin (airship pioneer). Multicoloured.

N2801 10 ch. Type **941** 35 10
N2802 20 ch. "Schwaben" 55 15
N2803 30 ch. "Viktoria Luise" . 75 20
N2804 40 ch. LZ-3 . . . . 1·00 25

942 Kim Il Sung and Jambyn Batmunkh

944 Tower of Juche Idea

943 Hero and Labour Hero of the D.P.R.K. Medals

1988. Kim Il Sung's Visit to Mongolia.

N2806 **942** 10 ch. multicoloured . 20 10

1988. National Heroes Congress.

N2807 **943** 10 ch. multicoloured . 20 10

1988. 40th Anniv of Democratic Republic. Multicoloured.

N2808 5 ch. Type **944** 10 10
N2809 10 ch. Smelter and industrial buildings 20 10
N2810 10 ch. Soldier and Mt. Paekdu 20 10
N2811 10 ch. Map of Korea and globe 20 10
N2812 10 ch. Hand holding banner, globe and doves 20 10

945 "Sunflowers" (Vincent van Gogh)

946 Emblem

1988. "Filacept 88" Stamp Exhibition, The Hague. Multicoloured.

N2814 40 ch. Type **945** . . . . 1·25 25
N2815 60 ch. "The Chess Game" (Lucas van Leyden) (horiz) 2·25 35

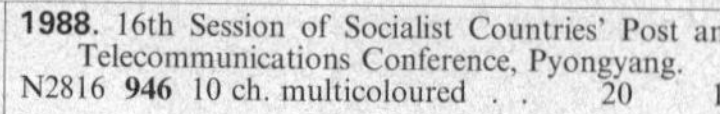

1988. 16th Session of Socialist Countries' Post and Telecommunications Conference, Pyongyang.

N2816 **946** 10 ch. multicoloured . . 20 10

947 Chaju "82" 10-ton Truck

948 "Owl"

1988. Tipper Trucks. Multicoloured.

N2817 20 ch. Type **947** 40 15
N2818 40 ch. Kumsusan-ho 40-ton truck 75 25

1988. Paintings by O Un Byol. Multicoloured.

N2819 10 ch. Type **948** . . . . . . 1·75 20
N2820 15 ch. "Dawn" (red junglefowl) 80 20
N2821 20 ch. "Beautiful Rose received by Kim Il Sung" 60 15
N2822 25 ch. "Sun and Bamboo" 75 15
N2823 30 ch. "Autumn" (fruit tree) 85 20

949 "Chunggi" Type Steam Locomotive No. 35

1988. Railway Locomotives. Multicoloured.

N2824 10 ch. Type **949** 50 10
N2825 20 ch. "Chunggi" type steam locomotive No. 22 . . . 70 15
N2826 30 ch. "Chongiha" type electric locomotive No. 3 80 20
N2827 40 ch. "Chunggi" type steam locomotive No. 307 . . . 1·00 25

950 Pirmen Zurbriggen (downhill skiing)

1988. Winter Olympic Games, Calgary, Medal Winners. Multicoloured.

N2828 10 ch. Type **950** 20 10
N2829 20 ch. Yvonne van Gennip (speed skating) 40 15
N2830 30 ch. Marjo Matikainen (cross-country skiing) . . 55 20
N2831 40 ch. U.S.S.R. (ice hockey) (horiz) 75 25

951 Yury Gagarin

1988. 1st Man and Woman in Space. Mult.

N2833 20 ch. Type **951** 40 15
N2834 40 ch. Valentina Tereshkova 75 25

952 Nehru

953 Chollima Statue

1988. Birth Centenary of Jawaharlal Nehru (Indian statesman) and "India 89" International Stamp Exhibition, New Delhi.

N2835 **952** 20 ch. purple, black and gold 60 15

1989. New Year. Multicoloured.

N2837 10 ch. Type **953** 20 10
N2838 20 ch. "The Dragon Angler" (17th-century painting) 60 15
N2839 40 ch. "Tortoise and Serpent" (Kangso tomb painting) (horiz) 90 25

954 Archery

1989. National Defence Training. Multicoloured.

N2840 10 ch. Type **954** 90 10
N2841 15 ch. Rifle shooting . . . 30 10
N2842 20 ch. Pistol shooting . . . 40 15
N2843 25 ch. Parachuting 50 15
N2844 30 ch. Launching model glider 55 20

955 Dobermann Pinscher

957 Agriculture

1989. Animals presented to Kim Il Sung. Mult.

N2845 10 ch. Type **955** 50 10
N2846 20 ch. Labrador 70 15
N2847 25 ch. German shepherd . 1·00 15
N2848 30 ch. Rough collies (horiz) 1·00 20
N2849 35 ch. Serval (horiz) . . . 1·25 20

1989. 25th Anniv of Publication of "Theses on the Socialist Rural Question in our Country" by Kim Il Sung.

N2852 **957** 10 ch. multicoloured . 40 10

958 The Gypsy and Grapes **959** Korean Girl

1989. Fungi and Fruits. Multicoloured.

N2853 10 ch. Type **958** 50 10
N2854 20 ch. Caesar's mushroom and magnolia vine . . . 80 15
N2855 25 ch. "Lactarius hygrophoides" and "Eleagnus crispa" . . . 1·10 15
N2856 30 ch. "Agaricus placomyces" and Chinese gooseberries 1·25 20
N2857 35 ch. Horse mushroom and "Lycium chinense" . . . 1·50 20
N2858 40 ch. Elegant boletus and "Juglans cordiformis" . 1·75 25

1989. 13th World Youth and Students' Festival, Pyongyang (2nd issue). Multicoloured.

N2860 10 ch. Type **959** 20 10
N2861 20 ch. Children of different races 40 15
N2862 30 ch. Fairy and rainbow 55 20
N2863 40 ch. Young peoples and Tower of Juche Idea . . 45 25

960 "Parnassius eversmanni"

1969. Insects. Multicoloured.
N2864 10 ch. Type **960** 75 15
N2865 15 ch. "Colias heos" . . . 75 15
N2866 20 ch. "Dilipa fenestra" . . 75 15
N2867 25 ch. "Buthus martensis" 75 15
N2868 30 ch. "Trichogramma ostriniae" 75 15
N2869 40 ch. "Damaster constricticollis" 75 15

961 Dancers (poster)

962 Birthplace, Mangyongdae

1989. Spring Friendship Art Festival, Pyongyang.
N2871 **961** 10 ch. multicoloured . 45 10

1989. 77th Birthday of Kim Il Sung.
N2872 **962** 10 ch. multicoloured . 20 10

963 Battle Plan and Monument to the Victory

1989. 50th Anniv of Battle of the Musan Area.
N2873 **963** 10 ch. blue, flesh & red 60 10

964 Modern Dance

1989. Chamo System of Dance Notation. Multicoloured.
N2874 10 ch. Type **964** 45 10
N2875 20 ch. Ballet 55 15
N2876 25 ch. Modern dance (different) 75 15
N2877 30 ch. Traditional dance . . 85 20

965 Hands supporting Torch

966 Victorious Badger

1989. 13th World Youth and Students' Festival, Pyongyang (3rd issue).
N2879 **965** 5 ch. blue 10 10
N2880 – 10 ch. brown 20 10
DESIGN: 10 ch. Youth making speech.

1989. "Badger measures the Height" (cartoon film). Multicoloured.
N2881 10 ch. Cat, bear and badger race to flag pole 80 10
N2882 40 ch. Cat and bear climb pole while badger measures shadow . . . . 1·25 25
N2883 50 ch. Type **966** . . . . . 1·50 30

MINIMUM PRICE

The minimum price quoted is 10p which represents a handling charge rather than a basis for valuing common stamps. For further notes about prices, see introductory pages.

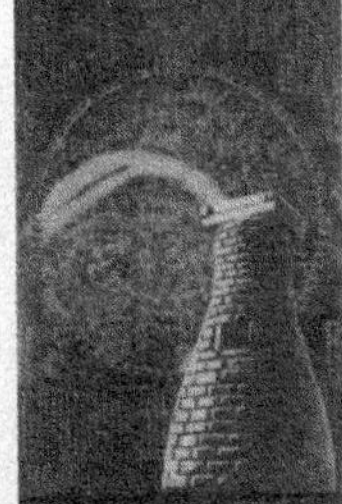

967 Kyongju Observatory and Star Chart

969 Pele (footballer) and 1978 25 ch. Stamp

1989. Astronomy.
N2884 **967** 20 ch. multicoloured . 1·00 15

1989. "Brasiliana 89" International Stamp Exhibition, Rio de Janeiro.
N2887 **969** 40 ch. multicoloured . 1·00 25

970 Nurse and Ambulance

1989. Emergency Services. Multicoloured.
N2888 10 ch. Type **970** 20 10
N2889 20 ch. Surgeon and ambulance 30 15
N2890 30 ch. Fireman and fire engine 2·25 20
N2891 40 ch. Fireman and engine (different) . . . . 2·25 25

971 Kaffir Lily

972 Air Mail Letter and Postal Transport

1989. Plants presented to Kim Il Sung. Mult.
N2892 10 ch. Type **971** 30 10
N2893 15 ch. Tulips 40 10
N2894 20 ch. Flamingo lily . . . 55 15
N2895 25 ch. "Rhododendron obtusum" 70 15
N2896 30 ch. Daffodils 80 20

1989. 150th Anniv of the Penny Black and "Stamp World London 90" International Stamp Exhibition (1st issue). Multicoloured.
N2898 5 ch. Type **972** 35 10
N2899 10 ch. Post box and letters 45 10
N2900 20 ch. Stamps, tweezers and magnifying glass 50 15
N2901 30 ch. First North Korean stamps 65 20
N2902 40 ch. Universal Postal Union emblem and headquarters, Berne 80 25
N2903 50 ch. Sir Rowland Hill and Penny Black . . . . . . 1·10 30
See also No. N2956.

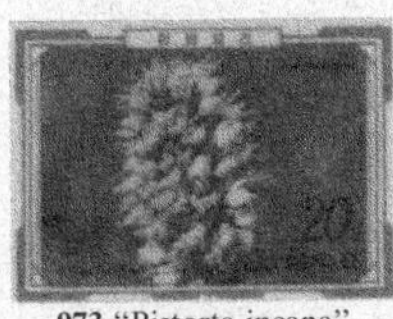

973 "Bistorta incana"

1989. Alpine Flowers. Multicoloured.
N2904 10 ch. "Iris setosa" . . . 40 10
N2905 15 ch. "Aquilegia japonica" 50 10
N2906 20 ch. Type **973** 60 15
N2907 25 ch. "Rodiola elongata" 70 15
N2908 30 ch. "Sanguisorba sitchensis" 75 20

974 Tree, Mt. Paekdu

975 Skipping

1989. Slogan-bearing Trees (1st series). Mult.
N2910 10 ch. Type **974** 20 10
N2911 3 wn. Tree, Oun-dong, Pyongyang . . . . . . 5·50 1·75
N2912 5 wn. Tree, Mt. Kanbaek . 9·50 3·25
See also No. N2931.

1989. Children's Games. Multicoloured.
N2913 10 ch. Type **975** 20 10
N2914 20 ch. Windmill . . . . . 1·25 15
N2915 30 ch. Kite 55 20
N2916 40 ch. Whip and top . . . 75 25

977 Diesel Train and Sinpa Youth Station

1989. Railway Locomotives. Multicoloured.
N2918 10 ch. Type **977** 40 10
N2919 20 ch. "Pulgungi" type electric locomotive . . . 60 15
N2920 25 ch. Diesel locomotive . . 70 15
N2921 30 ch. Diesel locomotive (different) 85 20
N2922 40 ch. Steam locomotive . . 1·00 25
N2923 50 ch. Steam locomotive (different) . . . . . . 1·10 30

978 Players and Map of Italy

1989. World Cup Football Championship, Italy (2nd issue). Multicoloured.
N2924 10 ch. Type **978** 75 10
N2925 20 ch. Free kick 40 15
N2926 30 ch. Goal mouth scrimmage 55 20
N2927 40 ch. Goalkeeper diving for ball 75 25

979 Megellan (navigator) and his Ship "Vitoria"

1989. "Descobrex '89" International Stamp Exhibition, Portugal.
N2928 **979** 30 ch. multicoloured . . 1·25 20

980 Mangyong Hill and Pine Branches

981 Ryukwoli

1990. New Year. Multicoloured.
N2929 10 ch. Type **980** 20 10
N2930 20 ch. Koguryo mounted archers 90 15

1990. Slogan-bearing Trees (2nd series). As T **974**. Multicoloured.
N2931 5 ch. Tree, Mt. Paekdu . . 25 10

1990. Dogs. Multicoloured.
N2932 20 ch. Type **981** . . . . . 1·00 20
N2933 30 ch. Palryuki . . . . . 1·00 20
N2934 40 ch. Komdungi . . . . . 1·00 20
N2935 50 ch. Oulruki . . . . . 1·00 20

982 Birthplace, Mt. Paekdu

983 Stone Instruments and Primitive Man

1990. Birthday of Kim Jong Il.
N2936 **982** 10 ch. brown 20 10

1990. Evolution of Man. Multicoloured.
N2937 10 ch. Type **983** 45 10
N2938 40 ch. Palaeolithic and Neolithic man 90 25

984 Rungna Bridge, Pyongyang

1990. Bridges. Multicoloured.
N2939 10 ch. Type **984** 45 10
N2940 20 ch. Potong bridge, Pyongyang 60 15
N2941 30 ch. Sinuiji-Ryucho Island Bridge 85 20
N2942 40 ch. Chungsongui Bridge, Pyongyang . . . . . . 1·10 25

985 Infantryman

987 Dancers (poster)

986 "Atergatis subdentatus"

1990. Warriors' Costumes. Multicoloured.
N2943 20 ch. Type **985** 40 15
N2944 30 ch. Archer 55 20
N2945 50 ch. Military commander in armour 95 30
N2946 70 ch. Officer's costume, 10th–14th centuries . . . . 1·25 40
Nos. N2943/5 depict costumes from the 3rd century B.C. to the 7th century A.D.

1990. Crabs. Multicoloured.
N2947 20 ch. Type **986** 40 15
N2948 30 ch. "Platylambrus validus" 55 20
N2949 50 ch. "Uca arcuata" . . . 95 30

1990. Spring Friendship Art Festival, Pyongyang.
N2950 **987** 10 ch. multicoloured . 20 10

988 Monument at Road Folk, Mangyongdae

989 "Gymnocalycium sp."

1990. 78th Birthday of Kim Il Sung.
N2951 **988** 10 ch. green and gold 20 10

1990. Cacti. Multicoloured.
N2953 10 ch. Type **989** 40 10
N2954 30 ch. "Pyllocactus hybridus" 75 20
N2955 50 ch. "Epiphyllum truncatum" . . . . . . 1·25 30

990 Exhibition Emblem

991 Congo Peafowl

1990. "Stamp World London 90" International Stamp Exhibition (2nd issue).
N2956 **990** 20 ch. red and black . 40 15

1990. Peafowl. Multicoloured.
N2958 10 ch. Type **991** 50 10
N2959 20 ch. Common peafowl . 1·00 20

992 Dolphin and Submarine

1990. Bio-engineering. Multicoloured.

N2961	10 ch. Type **992**	1·10	25
N2962	20 ch. Bat and dish aerial	1·10	25
N2963	30 ch. Owl and Tupolev Tu-154 jetliner	1·10	30
N2964	40 ch. Squid, rockets and Concorde supersonic jetliner	1·10	25

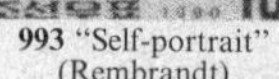

993 "Self-portrait" (Rembrandt) 994 K. H. Rummenigge (footballer)

1990. "Belgica 90" International Stamp Exhibition, Brussels. Multicoloured.

N2965	10 ch. Type **993**	20	10
N2966	20 ch. "Self-portrait" (Raphael)	40	15
N2967	30 ch. "Self-portrait" (Rubens)	55	20

1990. "Dusseldorf '90" International Youth Stamp Exhibition. Multicoloured.

N2968	20 ch. Steffi Graf (tennis player)	85	15
N2969	30 ch. Exhibition emblem	55	20
N2970	70 ch. Type **994**	1·25	40

995 Workers' Stadium, Peking, and Games Mascot

1990. 11th Asian Games, Peking (Nos. N2971/2) and 3rd Asian Winter Games, Samjiyon (N2973). Multicoloured.

N2971	10 ch. Type **995**	20	10
N2972	30 ch. Chollima Statue and sportsmen	55	20
N2973	40 ch. Sportsmen and Games emblem	75	25

996 Ball

1990. West Germany, Winners of World Cup Football Championship. Multicoloured.

N2974	15 ch. Emblem of F.I.F.A. (International Federation of Football Associations)	30	10
N2975	20 ch. Jules Rimet	40	15
N2976	25 ch. Type **996**	50	15
N2977	30 ch. Olympic Stadium, Rome (venue of final)	55	20
N2978	35 ch. Goalkeeper	65	20
N2979	40 ch. Emblem of West German Football Association	75	25

997 Kakapo and Map of New Zealand

1990. "New Zealand 1990" International Stamp Exhibition, Auckland.

N2981	**997** 30 ch. multicoloured	1·25	40

999 Head of Procession

1990. Koguryo Wedding Procession. Mult.

N2983	10 ch. Type **999**	1·00	20
N2984	30 ch. Bridegroom	1·00	20
N2985	50 ch. Bride in carriage	1·00	20
N2986	1 wn. Drummer on horse	1·00	20

Nos. N2983/6 were issued together, se-tenant, forming a composite design.

1000 Marchers descending Mt. Paekdu

1990. Rally for Peace and Reunification of Korea.

N2987	**1000** 10 ch. multicoloured	20	10

1001 Praying Mantis

1990. Insects. Multicoloured.

N2989	20 ch. Type **1001**	40	15
N2990	30 ch. Ladybird	55	20
N2991	40 ch. "Pheropsophus jessoensis"	75	25
N2992	70 ch. "Phyllium siccifolium"	1·25	40

1002 Footballers

1990. North–South Reunification Football Match, Pyongyang. Multicoloured.

N2993	10 ch. Type **1002**	65	10
N2994	20 ch. Footballers (different)	65	15

1003 Concert Emblem 1004 Ox

1990. National Reunification Concert.

N2996	**1003** 10 ch. multicoloured	20	10

1990. Farm Animals.

N2997	**1004** 10 ch. brown & green	20	10
N2998	– 20 ch. lilac & yellow	40	15
N2999	– 30 ch. grey and red	55	20
N3000	– 40 ch. green and yellow	75	25
N3001	– 50 ch. brown and blue	95	30

DESIGNS: 20 ch. Pig; 30 ch. Goat; 40 ch. Sheep; 50 ch. Horse.

1005 Chinese and North Korean Soldiers 1006 Anniversary Emblem

1990. 40th Anniv of Participation of Chinese Volunteers in Korean War. Multicoloured.

N3002	10 ch. Type **1005**	20	10
N3003	20 ch. Populace welcoming volunteers (horiz)	40	15
N3004	30 ch. Rejoicing soldiers and battle scene (horiz)	50	20
N3005	40 ch. Post-war reconstruction (horiz)	60	25

1990. 40th Anniv of United Nations Development Programme.

N3007	**1006** 1 wn. blue, silver & blk	1·90	65

1007 Sturgeon 1008 Sheep

1990. Fishes.

N3008	**1007** 10 ch. brown & green	20	10
N3009	– 20 ch. green and blue	40	15
N3010	– 30 ch. blue and puple	55	20
N3011	– 40 ch. brown and blue	75	25
N3012	– 50 ch. violet and green	95	30

DESIGNS: 20 ch. Sea bream; 30 ch. Flying fish; 40 ch. Fat greenling; 50 ch. Ray.

1990. New Year.

N3013	**1008** 40 ch. multicoloured	75	25

1009 Moorhen 1010 Giant Panda

1990. Birds.

N3014	**1009** 10 ch. blue, grn & blk	45	10
N3015	– 20 ch. brown, bistre and black	70	25
N3016	– 30 ch. green, grey and black	90	35
N3017	– 40 ch. brown, orange and black	1·25	45
N3018	– 50 ch. ochre, brown and black	1·75	55

DESIGNS: 20 ch. Jay; 30 ch. Three-toed woodpecker; 40 ch. Whimbrel; 50 ch. Water rail.

1991. "Phila Nippon '91" International Stamp Exhibition, Tokyo. Multicoloured.

N3019	10 ch. Type **1010**	20	10
N3020	20 ch. Two giant pandas feeding	40	15
N3021	30 ch. Giant panda clambering onto branch	55	20
N3022	40 ch. Giant panda on rock	75	25
N3023	50 ch. Two giant pandas	95	30
N3024	60 ch. Giant panda in tree fork	1·10	35

1011 Changsan

1991. Revolutionary Sites.

N3026	5 ch. Type **1011**	10	10
N3027	10 ch. Oun	20	10

1012 Black-faced Spoonbills 1014 Hedgehog Fungus

1013 "Clossiana angarensis"

1991. Endangered Birds. Multicoloured.

N3028	10 ch. Type **1012**	25	10
N3029	20 ch. Grey herons	50	15
N3030	30 ch. Great egrets	70	25
N3031	40 ch. Manchurian cranes	95	30
N3032	50 ch. Japanese white-necked cranes	1·25	35
N3033	70 ch. White storks	1·75	50

1991. Alpine Butterflies. Multicoloured.

N3034	10 ch. Type **1013**	15	10
N3035	20 ch. "Erebia embla"	30	15
N3036	30 ch. Camberwell beauty	45	20
N3037	40 ch. Comma	60	30
N3038	50 ch. Eastern pale clouded yellow	75	35
N3039	60 ch. "Theela betulae"	90	45

1991. Fungi. Multicoloured.

N3040	10 ch. Type **1014**	15	10
N3041	20 ch. "Phylloporus rhodoxanthus"	35	15
N3042	30 ch. "Calvatia craniiformis"	50	20
N3043	40 ch. Cauliflower clavaria	65	30
N3044	50 ch. "Russula integra"	85	35

1015 Kumchon

1991. Revolutionary Sites. Multicoloured.

N3045	10 ch. Type **1015**	15	10
N3046	40 ch. Samdung	60	30

1016 Dr. Kye Ung Sang (researcher) 1017 Emblem and Venue

1991. Silkworm Research. Multicoloured.

N3047	10 ch. Type **1016**	15	10
N3048	20 ch. Chinese oak silk moth	30	15
N3049	30 ch. "Attacus ricini"	45	20
N3050	40 ch. "Antheraea yamamai"	60	30
N3051	50 ch. Silkworm moth	75	35
N3052	60 ch. "Aetias artemis"	90	45

1991. 9th Spring Friendship Art Festival, Pyongyang.

N3053	**1017** 10 ch. multicoloured	10	10

1018 Emperor Penguins 1020 Map and Kim Jong Ho

1019 People's Palace of Culture (venue)

1991. Antarctic Exploration. Multicoloured.

N3054	10 ch. Type **1018**	30	15
N3055	20 ch. Research station	30	15
N3056	30 ch. Elephant seals	45	20
N3057	40 ch. Research ship	75	30
N3058	50 ch. Southern black-backed gulls	1·25	35

1991. 85th Interparliamentary Union Conference, Pyongyang.

N3060	**1019** 10 ch. dp green, grn & sil	15	10
N3061	– 1 wn. 50 multicoloured	2·25	1·10

DESIGN: 1 wn. 50, Conference emblem and azalea.

1991. 130th Anniv of Publication of Kim Jong Ho's Map "Taidong Yu Jido".

N3062	**1020** 90 ch. black, brn & sil	1·40	70

1021 Cynognathus

1991. Dinosaurs. Multicoloured.

N3063	10 ch. Type **1021**	15	10
N3064	20 ch. Brontosaurus	30	15
N3065	30 ch. Stegosaurus and allosaurus	45	20
N3066	40 ch. Pterosauria	60	30
N3067	50 ch. Ichthyosaurus	75	35

1022 Sprinting

1991. Olympic Games, Barcelona (1992 (1st issue). Multicoloured

N3068	10 ch. Type **1022**	15	10
N3069	10 ch. Hurdling	15	10
N3070	20 ch. Long jumping	30	15
N3071	20 ch. Throwing the discus	30	15
N3072	30 ch. Putting the shot	45	20
N3073	30 ch. Pole vaulting	45	20
N3074	40 ch. High jumping	60	30
N3075	40 ch. Throwing the javelin	60	30

See also Nos. N3142/7.

1023 Cats and Tree Sparrows

1991. Cats. Multicoloured.

N3077	10 ch. Type **1023**	15	10
N3078	20 ch. Cat and rat	30	15
N3079	30 ch. Cat and butterfly	45	20
N3080	40 ch. Cats with ball	60	30
N3081	50 ch. Cat and frog	75	35

1025 Wild Horse

1991. Horses. Multicoloured.

N3083	10 ch. Type **1025**	15	10
N3084	20 ch. Hybrid of wild ass and wild horse	30	15
N3085	30 ch. Przewalski's horse	45	20
N3086	40 ch. Wild ass	60	30
N3087	50 ch. Wild horse (different)	75	35

1026 Pennant Coralfish

1991. Fishes. Multicoloured.

N3088	10 ch. Type **1026** (postage)	15	10
N3089	20 ch. Big-spotted triggerfish	30	15
N3090	30 ch. Anemone fish	45	20
N3091	40 ch. Blue surgeon fish	60	30
N3092	50 ch. Angel fish (air)	75	35

1027 Rhododendrons

1991. Flowers. Multicoloured.

N3094	10 ch. Begonia	15	10
N3095	20 ch. Gerbera	30	15
N3096	30 ch. Type **1027**	45	20
N3097	40 ch. Phalaenopsis	60	30
N3098	50 ch. "Impatiens sultanii"	75	35
N3099	60 ch. Streptocarpus	90	45

Nos. N3097/9 commemorate "CANADA '92" international youth stamp exhibition, Montreal.

1028 Panmunjom

1991.

N3100	**1028** 10 ch. multicoloured	15	10

1029 Magnolia

1030 Players

1991. National Flower.

N3101	**1029** 10 ch. multicoloured	15	10

1991. Women's World Football Championship, China. Multicoloured.

N3102	10 ch. Type **1030**	15	10
N3103	20 ch. Dribbling the ball	30	15
N3104	30 ch. Heading the ball	45	20
N3105	40 ch. Overhead kick	60	30
N3106	50 ch. Tackling	75	35
N3107	60 ch. Goalkeeper	90	45

1031 Squirrel Monkeys

1992. Monkeys. Multicoloured.

N3108	10 ch. Type **1031**	15	10
N3109	20 ch. Pygmy marmosets	30	15
N3110	30 ch. Red-handed tamarins	45	20

1032 Eagle Owl

1992. Birds of Prey. Multicoloured.

N3112	10 ch. Type **1032**	15	10
N3113	20 ch. Common buzzard	30	15
N3114	30 ch. African fish eagle	45	20
N3115	40 ch. Steller's sea eagle	60	30
N3116	50 ch. Golden eagle	75	35

1033 Birthplace, Mt. Paekdu

1992. Birthday of Kim Jong Il. Mt. Paekdu. Multicoloured.

N3118	10 ch. Type **1033**	15	10
N3119	20 ch. Mountain summit	30	15
N3120	30 ch. Lake Chon (crater lake)	45	20
N3121	40 ch. Lake Sarryi	60	30

1034 Service Bus

1992. Transport.

N3123	**1034** 10 ch. multicoloured	15	10
N3124	– 20 ch. multicoloured	30	15
N3125	– 30 ch. multicoloured	45	20
N3126	– 40 ch. multicoloured	60	30
N3127	– 50 ch. multicoloured	75	35
N3128	– 60 ch. multicoloured	90	45

DESIGNS: 20 ch. to 60 ch. Different buses and trams.

1035 Dancers and Emblem

1992. Spring Friendship Art Festival, Pyongyang.

N3129	**1035** 10 ch. multicoloured	15	10

1036 Birthplace, Mangyongdae

1992. 80th Birthday of Kim Il Sung. Revolutionary Sites. Multicoloured.

N3130	10 ch. Type **1036** (postage)	15	10
N3131	10 ch. Party emblem and Turubong monument	15	10
N3132	10 ch. Map and Ssuksom	15	10
N3133	10 ch. Statue of soldier and Tongchang	15	10
N3134	40 ch. Cogwheels and Telan	60	30
N3135	40 ch. Chollima Statue and Kangson	60	30
N3136	1 wn. 20 Monument and West Sea Barrage (air)	1·75	85

1038 Soldiers on Parade

1992. 60th Anniv of People's Army. Multicoloured.

N3139	10 ch. Type **1038**	15	10
N3140	10 ch. Couple greeting soldier	15	10
N3141	10 ch. Army, air force and navy personnel	15	10

1039 Hurdling

1992. Olympic Games, Barcelona (2nd issue). Multicoloured.

N3142	10 ch. Type **1039**	15	10
N3143	20 ch. High jumping	30	15
N3144	30 ch. Putting the shot	45	20
N3145	40 ch. Sprinting	60	30
N3146	50 ch. Long jumping	75	35
N3147	60 ch. Throwing the javelin	90	45

1040 Planting Crops

1992. Evolution of Man. Designs showing life in the New Stone Age (10, 20 ch.) and the Bronze Age (others). Multicoloured.

N3149	10 ch. Type **1040** (postage)	15	10
N3150	20 ch. Family around cooking pot	30	15
N3151	30 ch. Ploughing fields	45	20
N3152	40 ch. Performing domestic chores	60	30
N3153	50 ch. Building a dolmen (air)	75	35

1041 White-bellied Black Woodpecker

1042 Map and Hands holding Text

1992. Birds. Multicoloured.

N3154	10 ch. Type **1041**	15	10
N3155	20 ch. Ring-necked pheasant	30	15
N3156	30 ch. White stork	45	20
N3157	40 ch. Blue-winged pitta	60	30
N3158	50 ch. Pallas's sandgrouse	75	35
N3159	60 ch. Black grouse	90	45

1992. 20th Anniv of Publication of North–South Korea Joint Agreement.

N3161	**1042** 1 wn. 50 multicoloured	90	30

1043 "Bougainvillea spectabilis"

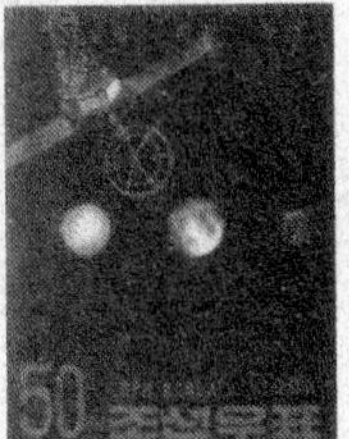
1044 Venus, Earth, Mars and Satellite

1992. Flowers. Multicoloured.

N3163	10 ch. Type **1043**	15	10
N3164	20 ch. "Ixora chinensis"	30	15
N3165	30 ch. "Dendrobium taysuwie"	45	20
N3166	40 ch. "Columnea gloriosa"	60	30
N3167	50 ch. "Crinum"	75	35
N3168	60 ch. "Ranunculus asiaticus"	90	45

1992. The Solar System. Multicoloured.

N3169	50 ch. Type **1044**	75	35
N3170	50 ch. Jupiter	75	35
N3171	50 ch. Saturn	75	35
N3172	50 ch. Uranus	75	35
N3173	50 ch. Neptune and Pluto	75	35

Nos. N3169/73 were issued together, se-tenant, forming a composite design.

1045 Yacht

1046 Moreno Mannini (defender)

1992. "Riccione '92" Stamp Fair. Multicoloured.

N3175	10 ch. Type **1045**	15	10
N3176	20 ch. Sailboard	30	15
N3177	30 ch. Sailing dinghy	45	20
N3178	40 ch. Sailing dinghy (different)	60	30
N3179	50 ch. Yacht (different)	75	35
N3180	60 ch. Fair emblem	90	45

1992. Sampdoria, Italian Football Champion, 1991. Multicoloured.

N3181	20 ch. Type **1046**	30	15
N3182	30 ch. Gianluca Vialli (forward)	45	30
N3183	40 ch. Pietro Vierchowod (defender)	60	30
N3184	50 ch. Fausto Pari (defender)	75	35
N3185	60 ch. Roberto Mancini (forward)	90	45
N3186	1 wn. Paolo Mantovani (club president)	1·50	75

1047 Black-belts warming up

1992. 8th World Taekwondo Championship, Pyongyang. Multicoloured.
N3188 10 ch. Type **1047** 15 10
N3189 30 ch. "Roundhouse" kick 45 30
N3190 50 ch. High kick 75 35
N3191 70 ch. Flying kick . . . . 1·00 50
N3192 90 ch. Black-belt breaking tiles with fist . . . . . . 1·40 70

1048 Common Toad ("Bufo bufo")

1992. Frogs and Toads. Multicoloured.
N3194 40 ch. Type **1048** (postage) 60 30
N3195 40 ch. Moor frog ("Rana arvalis") 60 30
N3196 40 ch. "Rana chosenica" . 60 30
N3197 70 ch. Common pond frog ("Rana nigromaculata") 1·00 50
N3198 70 ch. Japanese tree toad ("Hyla japonica") . . . 1·00 50
N3199 70 ch. "Rana coreana" (air) 1·00 50

1049 "Rhododendron mucronulatum"

1992. World Environment Day. Multicoloured.
N3200 10 ch. Type **1049** (postage) 15 10
N3201 30 ch. Barn swallow . . . 45 20
N3202 40 ch. "Stewartia koreana" (flower) 60 30
N3203 50 ch. "Dictyoptera aurora" (beetle) 75 35
N3204 70 ch. "Metasequoia glyptostroboides" (tree) 1·00 50
N3205 90 ch. Chinese salamander 1·40 70
N3206 1 wn. 20 "Ginkgo biloba" (tree) (air) . . . . . . 1·75 85
N3207 1 wn. 40 Spotted sculpin . 2·10 1·00

1050 Fin Whale ("Balaenoptera physalus")

1992. Whales and Dolphins. Multicoloured.
N3208 50 ch. Type **1050** (postage) . 75 35
N3209 50 ch. Common dolphin ("Delphinus delphis") . . 75 35
N3210 50 ch. Killer Whale ("Orcinus orca") 75 35
N3211 50 ch. Hump-backed whale ("Megaptera nodosa") . 75 35
N3212 50 ch. Bottle-nosed whale ("Berardius bairdii") . . 75 35
N3213 50 ch. Sperm whale ("Physeter catadon") (air) 75 35

1051 Mother and Chicks

1992. New Year. Roosters in various costumes. Multicoloured.
N3214 10 ch. Type **1051** 15 10
N3215 20 ch. Lady 30 15
N3216 30 ch. Warrior 45 20
N3217 40 ch. Courtier 60 30
N3218 50 ch. Queen 75 35
N3219 60 ch. King 90 45

1052 Choe Chol Su (boxing)

1992. Gold Medal Winners at Barcelona Olympics. Multicoloured.
N3221 10 ch. Type **1052** 15 10
N3222 20 ch. Pae Kil Su (gymnastics) 30 15
N3223 50 ch. Ri Hak Son (freestyle wrestling) 75 35
N3224 60 ch. Kim Il (freestyle wrestling) 90 45

1053 Golden Mushroom **1055** League Members and Flag

1054 "Keumkangsania asiatica"

1993. Fungi. Multicoloured.
N3227 10 ch. Type **1053** 15 10
N3228 20 ch. Shaggy caps 30 15
N3229 30 ch. "Ganoderma lucidum" 45 20
N3230 40 ch. Brown mushroom 60 30
N3231 50 ch. "Volvaria bombycina" 75 35
N3232 60 ch. "Sarcodon aspratus" 90 45

1993. Plants. Multicoloured.
N3234 10 ch. Type **1054** 15 10
N3235 20 ch. "Echinosophora koreensis" 30 15
N3236 30 ch. "Abies koreana" . 45 20
N3237 40 ch. "Benzoin angustifolium" 60 30
N3238 50 ch. "Abeliophyllum distichum" 75 35
N3239 60 ch. "Abelia mosanensis" 90 45

1993. 8th League of Socialist Working Youth Congress. Multicoloured.
N3241 10 ch. Type **1055** 15 10
N3242 40 ch. Flame, League emblem and text 60 30

1056 Phophyong Revolutionary Site Tower and March Corps Emblem **1057** Tower of Juche Idea and Grand Monument, Mt. Wangjae

1993. 70th Anniv of 1000-ri Journey for Learning.
N3243 **1056** 10 ch. multicoloured 15 10

1993. 60th Anniv of Wangjaesan Meeting.
N3244 **1057** 5 ch. multicoloured . 10 10

1058 "Kimjomgil" (begonia) **1059** Pilot Fish

1993. 51st Birthday of Kim Jong Il.
N3245 **1058** 10 ch. multicoloured 15 10

1993. Fishes. Multicoloured.
N3247 10 ch. Type **1059** 15 10
N3248 20 ch. Japanese stingray . 30 15
N3249 30 ch. Moonfish 45 20
N3250 40 ch. Coelacanth 60 30
N3251 50 ch. Grouper 70 35

MINIMUM PRICE

The minimum price quoted is 10p which represents a handling charge rather than a basis for valuing common stamps. For further notes about prices, see introductory pages.

1060/1064 "Spring on the Hill" (½-size illustration)

1993. 18th-century Korean Painting.
N3253 **1060** 40 ch. multicoloured . 60 30
N3254 **1061** 40 ch. multicoloured . 60 30
N3255 **1062** 40 ch. multicoloured . 60 30
N3256 **1063** 40 ch. multicoloured . 60 30
N3257 **1064** 40 ch. multicoloured . 60 30
Nos. N3253/7 were issued together, se-tenant, forming the composite design illustrated.

1065 Violinist, Dancers and Emblem

1993. Spring Friendship Art Festival, Pyongyang.
N3258 **1065** 10 ch. multicoloured 15 10

1066 Books

1993. 80th Birthday of Kim Il Sung and Publication of his Reminiscences "With the Century".
N3259 **1066** 10 ch. multicoloured 15 10

1067 Kwangbok Street

1993. Pyongyang. Multicoloured.
N3261 10 ch. Type **1067** 15 10
N3262 20 ch. Chollima Street . . . 30 15
N3263 30 ch. Munsu Street 45 20
N3264 40 ch. Moranbong Street . 60 30
N3265 50 ch. Thongil Street . . . 75 35

1068 "Trichogramma dendrolimi" (fly) **1069** Ri In Mo

1993. Insects. Multicoloured.
N3267 10 ch. Type **1068** 15 10
N3268 20 ch. "Brachymeria obscurata" (fly) 30 15
N3269 30 ch. "Metrioptera brachyptera" (cricket) . . 45 20
N3270 50 ch. European field cricket 75 35
N3271 70 ch. "Geocoris pallidipennis" (beetle) . . 1·00 50
N3272 90 ch. "Cyphonony x dorsalis" (wasp) fighting spider . . . . 1·40 70

1993. Return from Imprisonment of Ri In Mo (war correspondent).
N3273 **1069** 10 ch. multicoloured 15 10

1070 Footballers **1071** Grey-headed Green Woodpecker

1993. World Cup Football Championship, U.S.A.
N3275 **1070** 10 ch. multicoloured 15 10
N3276 – 20 ch. multicoloured 30 15
N3277 – 30 ch. multicoloured 45 20
N3278 – 50 ch. multicoloured 75 35
N3279 – 70 ch. multicoloured 1·00 50
N3280 – 90 ch. multicoloured 1·40 70
DESIGNS: 20 ch. to 90 ch. Various footballing scenes.

1993. Birds. Multicoloured.
N3281 10 ch. Type **1071** 15 10
N3282 20 ch. King bird of paradise 30 15
N3283 30 ch. Lesser bird of paradise 45 20
N3284 40 ch. Paradise whydah . . 60 30
N3285 50 ch. Magnificent bird of paradise 75 35
N3286 60 ch. Greater bird of paradise 90 45
Nos. N3283/4 also commemorate "Indopex '93" international stamp exhibition, Surabaya.

1072 Korean Peninsula and Flag (½-size illustration)

1993. Self-adhesive. Roul.
N3287 **1072** 1 w. 50 multicoloured 90 30
No. N3287 is for any one of the six stamps which together make up the design illustrated. They are peeled from a card backing.

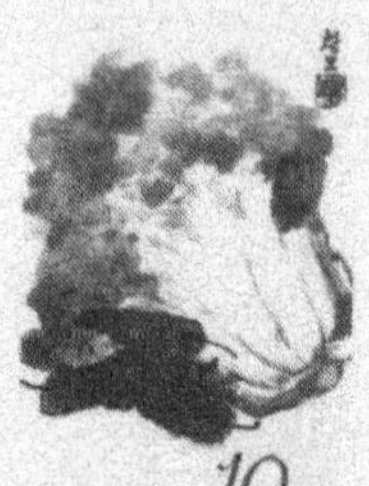

1073 Kim Myong Nam (weightlifting, 1990)

1993. World Champions. Multicoloured.
N3293 10 ch. Type **1073** 15 10
N3294 20 ch. Kim Kwang Suk (gymnastics, 1991) . . . 30 15
N3295 30 ch. Pak Yong Sun (table tennis, 1975, 1977) . . . 45 20
N3296 50 ch. Kim Yong Ok (radio direction-finding, 1990) 75 35
N3297 70 ch. Han Yun Ok (taekwondo, 1987, 1988, 1990) . . . . 1·00 50
N3298 90 ch. Kim Yong Sik (free-style wrestling, 1986, 1989) 1·40 70

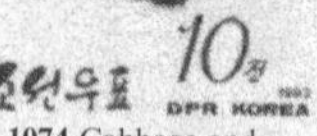

1074 Cabbage and Chilli Peppers **1075** State Arms

1993. Fruits and Vegetables. Multicoloured.
N3299 10 ch. Type **1074** 15 10
N3300 20 ch. Squirrels and horse chestnuts 30 15
N3301 30 ch. Grapes and peach 45 20
N3302 40 ch. Birds and persimmon 60 30
N3303 50 ch. Tomatoes, aubergine and cherries 75 35
N3304 60 ch. Radish, onion and garlic 90 45

1993.
N3305 **1075** 10 ch. red 15 10

1076 Soldiers and Civilians

1993. 40th Anniv of Victory in Liberation War. Multicoloured.
N3306 10 ch. Type **1076** 15 10
N3307 10 ch. Officer and soldier 15 10
N3308 10 ch. Guided missiles on low-loaders on parade . . . 15 10
N3309 10 ch. Anti-aircraft missiles on lorries on parade . . 15 10

N3310	10 ch. Self-propelled missile launchers (tracked vehicles) on parade	15	10
N3311	10 ch. Machine gun emplacement (30×48 mm)	15	10
N3312	10 ch. Soldier holding flag (bronze statue) (30×48 mm)	15	10
N3314	10 ch. Kim Il Sung at strategic policy meeting	15	10
N3315	10 ch. Kim Il Sung directing battle for Height 1211	15	10
N3316	10 ch. Kim Il Sung at munitions factory	15	10
N3317	10 ch. Kim Il Sung with tank commanders	15	10
N3318	10 ch. Kim Il Sung with triumphant soldiers	15	10
N3319	20 ch. Kim Il Sung with artillery unit	30	15
N3320	20 ch. Kim Il Sung encouraging machine gun crew	30	15
N3321	20 ch. Kim Il Sung studying map of Second Front	30	15
N3322	20 ch. Kim Il Sung with airmen	30	15
N3323	20 ch. Musicians ("Alive is art of Korea")	30	15
N3313	40 ch. Soldiers and flags ("Let us become Kim Jims and Ri Su Boks of the 90s") (30×48 mm)	60	30

1077 Choe Yong Do

1078 "Robinia sp."

1993. National Reunification Prize Winners. Multicoloured.

N3325	10 ch. Type **1077**	15	10
N3326	20 ch. Kim Ku	30	15
N3327	30 ch. Hong Myong Hui	45	20
N3328	40 ch. Ryo Un Hyong	60	30
N3329	50 ch. Kim Jong Thae	75	35
N3330	60 ch. Kim Chaek	90	45

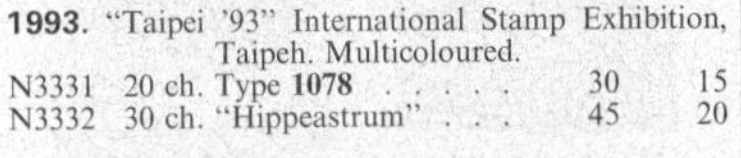

1993. "Taipei '93" International Stamp Exhibition, Taipeh. Multicoloured.

N3331	20 ch. Type **1078**	30	15
N3332	30 ch. "Hippeastrum"	45	20

1079 Newton

1080 King Tongmyong shooting Bow

1993. 350th Birth Anniv (1992) of Sir Isaac Newton (mathematician and scientist). Multicoloured.

N3334	10 ch. Type **1079**	15	10
N3335	20 ch. Apple tree and formula of law of gravitation	30	15
N3336	30 ch. Satellite, reflecting telescope, dish aerial, globe and rocket	45	20
N3337	50 ch. Formula of binomial theorem	75	35
N3338	70 ch. Newton's works and statue	1·00	50

1993. Restoration of King Tongmyong of Koguryo's Tomb. Multicoloured.

N3339	10 ch. Type **1080**	15	10
N3340	20 ch. King Tongmyong saluting crowd	30	15
N3341	30 ch. Restoration monument	45	20
N3342	40 ch. Temple of the Tomb of King Tongmyong (horiz)	60	30
N3343	50 ch. Tomb (horiz)	75	35

1082 "Cyrtopodium andresoni"

1084 Mao Tse-tung at Yanan, 1944

1993. Orchids. Multicoloured.

N3346	10 ch. Type **1082**	15	10
N3347	20 ch. "Cattleya"	30	15
N3348	30 ch. "Cattleya intermedia" "Oculata"	45	20
N3349	40 ch. Potinaria "Maysedo godensia"	60	30
N3350	50 ch. Kim Il Sung flower	75	35

1993. Birth Centenary of Mao Tse-tung. Multicoloured.

N3352	10 ch. Type **1084**	15	10
N3353	20 ch. Seated portrait (Peking, 1960)	30	15
N3354	30 ch. Casting a vote, 1953	45	20
N3355	40 ch. With pupils at Shaoshan Secondary School, 1959	60	30

1085 Phungsan

1086 Purple Hyosong Flower

1994. New Year. Dogs. Multicoloured.

N3358	10 ch. Type **1085**	15	10
N3359	20 ch. Yorkshire terriers	30	15
N3360	30 ch. Gordon setter	45	20
N3361	40 ch. Pomeranian	60	30
N3362	50 ch. Spaniel with pups	75	35

1994. 52nd Birthday of Kim Jong Il. Multicoloured.

N3364	10 ch. Type **1086**	15	10
N3365	40 ch. Yellow hyosong flower	60	30

1087 Red and Black Dragon-eye

1994. Goldfishes. Multicoloured.

N3367	10 ch. Type **1087**	15	10
N3368	30 ch. Red and white bubble-eye	45	20
N3369	50 ch. Red and white long-finned wenyu	75	35
N3370	70 ch. Red and white fringetail	1·00	50

1088 Crowd with Banners

1089 Wheat, Banner and Woman writing

1994. 20th Anniv of Publication of "Programme for Modelling the Whole Society on the Juche Idea" by Kim Jong Il.

N3371	**1088** 20 ch. multicoloured	30	15

1994. 30th Anniv of Publication of "Theses on the Socialist Rural Question in Our Country" by Kim Il Sung. Multicoloured.

N3373	10 ch. Type **1089**	15	10
N3374	10 ch. Electricity generating systems and pylon	15	10
N3375	10 ch. Lush fields, grain and tractor	15	10
N3376	40 ch. Modern housing, books, food crops and laboratory technician	60	30
N3377	40 ch. Revellers	60	30

1090 "Mangyongbong-92" (passenger ship)

1091 National Flag

1994. Ships. Multicoloured.

N3379	20 ch. Type **1090**	30	15
N3380	30 ch. "Osandok" (cargo ship)	45	20
N3381	40 ch. "Ryongaksan" (factory stern trawler)	60	30
N3382	50 ch. Stern trawler	75	35

1994.

N3384	**1091** 10 ch. red and blue	15	10

1092 Birthplace and Magnolia (national flower)

1093 "Chrysosplenium sphaerospermum"

1994. 81st Birthday of Kim Il Sung. Multicoloured.

N3385	10 ch. Type **1092**	15	10
N3386	40 ch. Birthplace, Manyongdae, and Kim Il Sung flower	60	30

1994. Alpine Plants on Mt. Paekdu. Multicoloured.

N3388	10 ch. Type **1093**	15	10
N3389	20 ch. "Campanula cephalotes"	30	15
N3390	40 ch. "Trollius macropetalus"	60	30
N3391	40 ch. "Gentiana algida"	60	30
N3392	50 ch. "Sedum kamtschaticum"	75	35

1094 National Olympic Committee Emblem

1095 Red Cross Launch ("Relief on the Sea")

1994. Centenary of International Olympic Committee. Multicoloured.

N3394	10 ch. Type **1094**	15	10
N3395	20 ch. Pierre de Coubertin (founder)	30	15
N3396	30 ch. Olympic flag and flame	45	20
N3397	50 ch. Emblem of Centennial Olympic Congress, Paris	75	35

1994. 75th Anniv of International Red Cross and Red Crescent Federation. Multicoloured.

N3399	10 ch. Tram, pedestrians on footbridge and traffic lights ("Prevention of Traffic Accident")	15	10
N3400	20 ch. Type **1095**	30	15
N3401	30 ch. Planting tree ("Protection of Environment")	45	20
N3402	40 ch. Dam ("Prevention of Drought Damage")	60	30

1994. No. N3287 surch **160** in circle.

N3403	**1072** 1 wn. 60 on 1 wn. 50 multicoloured	2·10	1·00

1097 Northern Fur Seal

1994. Marine Mammals. Multicoloured.

N3404	10 ch. Type **1097**	15	10
N3405	40 ch. Southern elephant seal	60	30
N3406	60 ch. Southern sealion	90	45

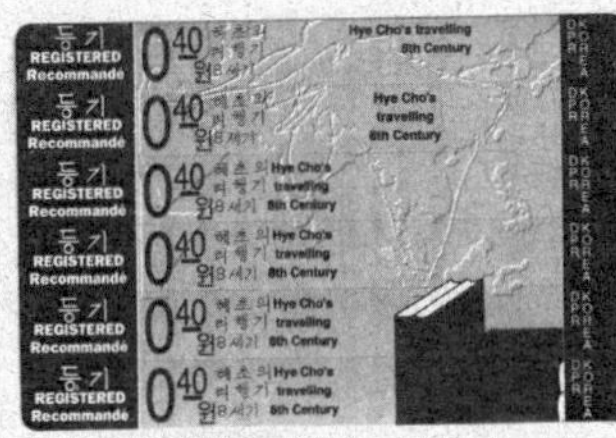
1098 Map of Asia and Books (½-size illustration)

1994. 8th-century Travels of Hye Cho. Self-adhesive. Roul.

N3408	**1098** 40 ch. multicoloured	55	25

No. N3408 is for any one of the six stamps which together make up the design illustrated. They are peeled from a card backing.

MINIMUM PRICE

The minimum price quoted is 10p which represents a handling charge rather than a basis for valuing common stamps. For further notes about prices, see introductory pages.

1099 Tigers (½-size illustration)

1994. Self-adhesive. Roul.

N3409	**1099** 1 wn. 40 multicoloured	1·90	95

No. N3409 is for any one of the six stamps which together make up the design illustrated. They are peeled from a card backing.

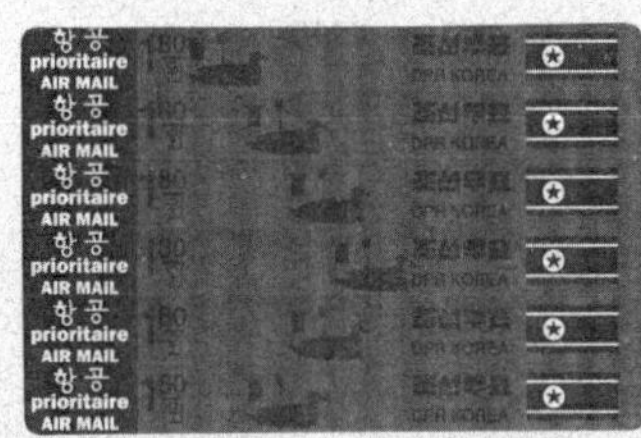
1101 "Turtle" Ships (½-size illustration)

1994. Self-adhesive. Roul.

N3411	**1101** 1 wn. 80 multicoloured	2·40	1·10

No. N3411 is for any one of the six stamps which together make up the design illustrated. They are peeled from a card backing.

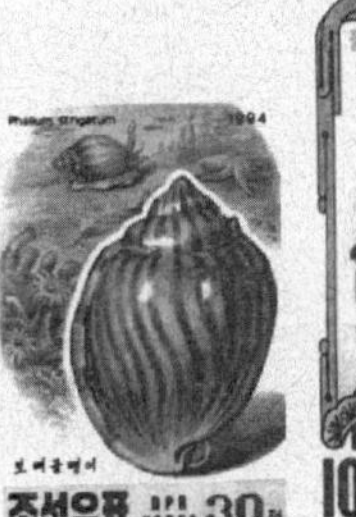
1102 Striped Bonnet

1104 Korean Script and "100"

1103 Trapeze

1994. Molluscs. Multicoloured.

N3412	30 ch. Type **1102**	45	20
N3413	40 ch. Equilateral venus	60	30

1994. Circus Acrobatics. Multicoloured.

N3416	10 ch. Type **1103**	15	10
N3417	20 ch. Reino (Swedish acrobat) performing rope dance	30	15
N3418	30 ch. Seesaw performer	45	20
N3419	40 ch. Unicycle juggler	60	30

1994. Birth Centenary of Kim Hyong Jik (father of Kim Il Sung). Multicoloured.

N3420	**1104** 10 ch. multicoloured	10	10

1105 Jon Pong Jun and Battle Scene

1994. Centenary of Kabo Peasant War.

N3422	**1105** 10 ch. multicoloured	15	10

1107 Workers and Banner

1109 "Acorus calamus"

1108 Onsong Fish

1994. Revolutionary Economic Strategy.
N3424 **1107** 10 ch. multicoloured . 15 10

1994. Fossils. Multicoloured.
N3425 40 ch. Type **1108** 60 30
N3426 40 ch. Metasequoia 60 30
N3427 40 ch. Mammoth teeth . . 60 30
N3428 80 ch. Archaeopteryx . . . 1·25 60

1994. Medicinal Plants. Multicoloured.
N3429 20 ch. Type **1109** 30 15
N3430 30 ch. "Arctium lappa" . . 45 20

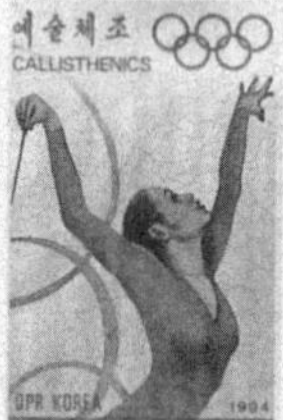

1110 Ribbon Exercise

1111 Chou En-lai at Tianjun, 1919

1994. Callisthenics. Multicoloured.
N3432 10 ch. Type **1110** 15 10
N3433 20 ch. Ball exercise 30 15
N3434 30 ch. Hoop exercise . . . 45 20
N3435 40 ch. Ribbon exercise (different) 60 30
N3436 50 ch. Club exercise 75 35

1994. 96th Birth Anniv of Chou En-lai (Chinese statesman). Multicoloured.
N3437 10 ch. Type **1111** 15 10
N3438 20 ch. Arrival in Northern Shanxi from Long March 30 15
N3439 30 ch. At Conference of Asian and African Countries, Bandung, Indonesia, 1955 45 20
N3440 40 ch. Surrounded by children in Wulumuqi, Xinjiang Province 60 30

1113 Kim Il Sung as Youth, 1927

1994. Kim Il Sung Commemoration (1st issue). (a) As T **1113**. Each red, gold and black.
N3444 40 ch. Type **1113** 60 30
N3445 40 ch. Kim Il Sung and Kim Jong Suk 60 30
N3446 40 ch. Kim Il Sung as young man 60 30
(b) Horiz designs as T **1115**. Each purple, gold and black.
N3447 40 ch. Kim Il Sung making speech, Pyongyang, 1945 60 30
N3448 40 ch. Kim Il Sung sitting at desk 60 30
N3449 40 ch. Kim Il Sung at microphone 60 30
See also Nos. N3459/63.

1114 Player No. 4

1994. World Cup Football Championship, U.S.A. Multicoloured.
N3451 10 ch. Type **1114** 15 10
N3452 20 ch. Player No. 5 . . . . 30 15
N3453 30 ch. Player No. 6 . . . . 45 20
N3454 40 ch. Player No. 7 . . . . 60 30
N3455 1 wn. Player No. 8 . . . . 1·50 75
N3456 1 wn. 50 Player No. 9 . . . 2·25 1·10

1115 Kim Il Sung making Radio Broadcast, 1950

1994. Kim Il Sung Commemoration (2nd issue). (a) Each green, gold and black.
N3458 40 ch. Type **1115** 60 30
N3459 40 ch. Kim Il Sung with four soldiers, 1951 . . . . . . 60 30
N3460 40 ch. Kim Il Sung and crowd of soldiers, 1953 . . . . 60 30
(b) Multicoloured (N3463) or lilac, gold and black (others).
N3461 40 ch. Kim Il Sung with workers at Chongjin Steel Plant, 1959 . . . . 60 30
N3462 40 ch. Kim Il Sung on Onchon Plain 60 30
N3463 40 ch. Kim Il Sung at desk using telephone 60 30

1116 National Flags and Flowers

1117 Ri Myon Sang and Score of "Snow Falls"

1994. Korean–Chinese Friendship.
N3465 **1116** 40 ch. multicoloured 60 30

1994. Composers. Multicoloured.
N3467 50 ch. Type **1117** 75 35
N3468 50 ch. Pak Han Kyu and score of "Nobody Knows" . . 75 35
N3469 50 ch. Ludwig van Beethoven and score of piano sonata No. 14 . . . . 75 35
N3470 50 ch. Wolfgang Amadeus Mozart and score of symphony No. 39 . . . 75 35

1118 National Emblem

1994.
N3471 **1118** 1 wn. green . . . . . 1·50 75
N3472 3 wn. brown . . . . 4·00 2·00

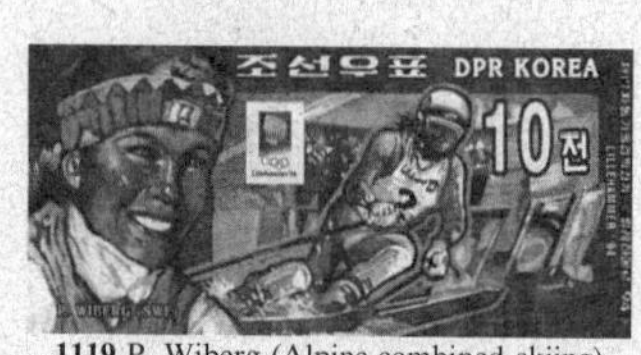

1119 P. Wiberg (Alpine combined skiing)

1994. Winter Olympic Games, Lillehammer, Gold Medal Winners. Multicoloured.
N3473 10 ch. Type **1119** 15 10
N3474 20 ch. D. Compagnoni (slalom) 30 15
N3475 30 ch. O. Baiul (figure skating) 45 20
N3476 40 ch. D. Jansen (speed skating) 60 30
N3477 1 wn. L. Yegorova (cross-country sking) . . . . . 1·50 75
N3478 1 wn. 50 B. Blair (speed skating) . . . . 2·25 1·10

1120 Pig Couple

1121 Pison Waterfalls, Mt. Myohyang

1995. New Year. Year of the Pig. Multicoloured.
N3480 20 ch. Type **1120** 30 15
N3481 40 ch. Pigs carrying bucket and spade 60 30

1995. 20th Anniv of World Tourism Organization. Multicoloured.
N3483 30 ch. Tower of Juche Idea, Pyongyang 45 20
N3484 30 ch. Type **1121** 45 20
N3485 30 ch. Myogilsang (cliff-face carving of Buddha), Mt. Kumgang 45 20

1122 Mangyongdae, Badaogou and Badge

1123 Monument bearing 50th Birthday Ode, Mt. Paekdu

1995. 70th Anniv of 1000-ri (250 mile) Journey by Kim Il Sung to Restore Fatherland.
N3486 **1122** 40 ch. multicoloured . 60 30

1995. 53rd Birthday of Kim Jong Il.
N3487 **1123** 10 ch. multicoloured . 15 10

1124 Reconstruction Monument

1125 Jamaedo Lighthouse

1995. Completion of Reconstruction of King Tangun's Tomb. Multicoloured.
N3489 10 ch. Type **1124** 15 10
N3490 30 ch. Bronze dagger on plinth 45 20
N3491 50 ch. Monument inscribed with exploits of King Tangun 75 15
N3492 70 ch. Gateway (horiz) . . 1·00 50

1995. Lighthouses. Multicoloured.
N3494 20 ch. Type **1125** 30 15
N3495 1 wn. Phido Lighthouse, West Sea Barrage . . . . . . 1·75 85

1126 Cracked Green Russula

1127 Couple planting Tree

1995. Fungi. Multicoloured.
N3496 20 ch. Type **1126** 30 15
N3497 30 ch. "Russula atropurpurea" 45 20

1995. Tree Planting Day.
N3499 **1127** 10 ch. multicoloured . 15 10

1128 Birthplace, Mangyongdae

1995. 82nd Birth Anniv of Kim Il Sung. Multicoloured.
N3500 10 ch. Type **1128** 15 10
N3501 40 ch. Tower of Juche Idea and Kim Il Sung flower (vert) 60 30

1129 Deng Xiaoping waving

1995. 20th Anniv of Kim Il Sung's Visit to China. Multicoloured.
N3503 10 ch. Type **1129** 15 10
N3504 20 ch. Deng Xiaoping of China sitting in armchair (vert) 30 15

1130 Venue

1995. 40th Anniv of Asian–African Conference, Bandung.
N3506 **1130** 10 ch. black, buff and red 15 10
N3507 – 50 ch. brown, gold and black 75 35
DESIGN: 50 ch. Kim Il Sung receiving honorary Doctorate at Indonesia University.

1131 Emblem

1132 Amethyst

1995. International Sports and Cultural Festival for Peace, Pyongyang. Multicoloured.
N3509 20 ch. Type **1131** 30 15
N3510 40 ch. Dancer 60 30
N3511 40 ch. Inoki Kanji (leader of Sports Peace Party of Japan) 60 30

1995. Minerals.
N3513 **1132** 20 ch. multicoloured . 30 15

1133 Tree Sparrow

1134 Ostrea

1995. White Animals. Multicoloured.
N3514 40 ch. Type **1133** 60 30
N3515 40 ch. "Stichopus japonicus" (sea slug) 60 30

1995. Fossils. Multicoloured.
N3516 50 ch. Type **1134** 75 35
N3517 1 wn. Cladophlebis (fern) . . 1·50 75

1135 Chess

1136 National Flag and Korean Hall, Tokyo

1995. Traditional Games. Multicoloured.
N3518 30 ch. Type **1135** 40 20
N3519 60 ch. Taekwondo 90 45
N3520 70 ch. Yut . . . . 1·00 50

1995. 40th Anniv of Association of Koreans in Japan.
N3521 **1136** 1 wn. multicoloured . 1·50 75

1137 Weightlifting

1138 "Russula citrina"

1995. Olympic Games, Atlanta (1996). Multicoloured.
N3522 50 ch. Type **1137** 75 35
N3523 50 ch. Boxing 75 35

1995. Fungi. Multicoloured.
N3525 40 ch. Type **1138** 60 30
N3526 60 ch. Black trumpets . . . 90 45
N3527 80 ch. Shaggy caps . . . 1·25 60

1140 Mt. Paekdu and Revolutionaries

1141 Markswoman

1995. 50th Anniv of Liberation. Multicoloured.
N3529 10 ch. Type **1140** 15 10
N3530 30 ch. Map of Korea and family 45 20
N3531 60 ch. Medal 90 45

1995. 1st Military World Games, Rome.
N3534 **1141** 40 ch. multicoloured . 60 30

1143 Emblem and Banner

1144 Arch of Triumph, Pyongyang

1995. 50th Anniv of Korean Workers' Party. Multicoloured.
N3536 10 ch. Type **1143** 15 10
N3537 20 ch. Statue of worker, peasant and intellectual . 30 15
N3538 30 ch. Party monument . . 45 20

1995. 50th Anniv of Kim Il Sung's Return to Homeland.
N3540 **1144** 10 ch. multicoloured . 15 10

1145 Great Tunny

1147 Guinea Pig

1995. Designs as T **1145**. Each brown and black.
(a) Fishes.
N3541 40 ch. Type **1145** 60 30
N3542 50 ch. Pennant coralfish (with two bands) 75 35
N3543 50 ch. Needlefish 75 35
N3544 60 ch. Bullrout 90 45
N3545 5 wn. Imperial butterfly fish 6·50 3·25

(b) Buildings on Kwangbok Street, Pyongyang.
N3546 60 ch. Circus 90 45
N3547 70 ch. Flats . . . . 1·00 50
N3548 80 ch. Ryanggang Hotel . . 1·25 60
N3549 90 ch. Tower apartment block (vert) . . . . 1·40 70
N3550 1 wn. Sosan Hotel (vert) . . 1·50 75

(c) Machines.
N3551 10 ch. Kamsusan tipper truck 15 10
N3552 20 ch. Bulldozer 30 15
N3553 30 ch. Excavator 45 20
N3554 40 ch. Earth mover (vert) . 60 30
N3555 10 wn. "Chollima 80" tractor (vert) . . . . 13·00 6·50

(d) Animals.
N3556 30 ch. Giraffe (vert) 45 20
N3557 40 ch. Ostrich (vert) 60 30
N3558 60 ch. Bluebuck (vert) . . . 90 45
N3559 70 ch. Bactrian camel . . . 1·00 50
N3560 3 wn. Indian rhinoceros . . 4·25 2·00

(e) Sculptures of Children.
N3561 30 ch. Boy holding bird (vert) 45 20
N3562 40 ch. Boy with goose (vert) 60 30
N3563 60 ch. Girl with geese (vert) 90 45
N3564 70 ch. Boy and girl with football (vert) . . . . . . 1·00 50
N3565 2 wn. Boy and girl arguing over football (vert) . . . 3·00 1·50

1996. Rodents. Multicoloured.
N3567 20 ch. Type **1147** 30 15
N3568 20 ch. Squirrel 30 15
N3569 30 ch. White mouse 45 20

1148 Emblem, Badge and Flag

1149 Restoration Mounument

1996. 50th Anniv of League of Socialist Working Youth.
N3570 **1148** 10 ch. multicoloured . 15 10

1996. Reconstruction of Tomb of King Wanggon. Multicoloured.
N3571 30 ch. Type **1149** 45 20
N3572 40 ch. Entrance gate . . . 60 30
N3573 50 ch. Tomb 75 35

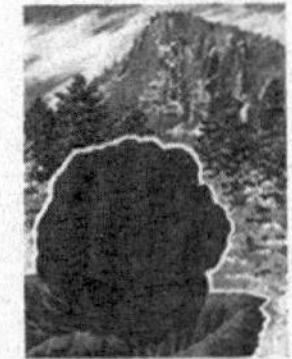
1152 Jong Il Peak and Kim Jong Il Flower

1153 Pairs Skating

1996. 54th Birthday of Kim Jong Il.
N3576 **1152** 10 ch. multicoloured . 15 10

1996. 5th Paektusan Prize Figure Skating Championships. Multicoloured.
N3578 10 ch. Type **1153** 15 10
N3579 20 ch. Pairs skating (different) 30 15
N3580 30 ch. Pairs skating (different) 45 20
N3581 50 ch. Women's individual skating 75 35

1155 Farm Worker

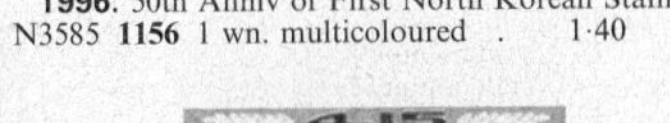
1156 1946 20 ch. Stamp and Tower of Juche Idea

1996. 50th Anniv of Agrarian Reform Law.
N3584 **1155** 10 ch. multicoloured . 15 10

1996. 50th Anniv of First North Korean Stamps.
N3585 **1156** 1 wn. multicoloured . 1·40 70

1158 Birthplace, Mangyongdae

1996. 83rd Birth Anniv of Kim Il Sung.
N3587 **1158** 10 ch. multicoloured . 15 10

1159 Gateway

1996. "China '96" Asian International Stamp Exhibition, Peking. Landmarks in Zhejiang. Multicoloured.
N3589 10 ch. Type **1159** 15 10
N3590 10 ch. Haiyin Pool 15 10

1160 Hopscotch

1161 Association Pamphlets

1996. Children's Games. Multicoloured.
N3592 20 ch. Type **1160** 30 15
N3593 40 ch. Shuttlecock 60 30
N3594 50 ch. Sledging 75 35

1996. 60th Anniv of Association for Restoration of the Fatherland.
N3595 **1161** 10 ch. multicoloured . 15 10

MINIMUM PRICE

The minimum price quoted is 10p which represents a handling charge rather than a basis for valuing common stamps. For further notes about prices, see introductory pages.

1163 Arctic Fox

1164 Boy Saluting

1996. Polar Animals. Multicoloured.
N3597 50 ch. Type **1163** 75 35
N3598 50 ch. Polar bear 75 35
N3599 50 ch. Emperor penguins . . 75 35
N3600 50 ch. Leopard seals 75 35

1996. 50th Anniv of Korean Children's Union.
N3601 **1164** 10 ch. multicoloured . 15 10

1165 Steam Locomotive

1167 Open Book and Characters

1996. Railway Locomotives. Multicoloured.
N3603 50 ch. Type **1165** 75 35
N3604 50 ch. Electric locomotive (green) 75 35
N3605 50 ch. Steam locomotive (different) 75 35
N3606 50 ch. Electric locomotive (red and yellow) 75 35

1996. 760th Anniv of Publication of "Complete Collection of Buddhist Scriptures printed from 80,000 Wooden Blocks".
N3608 **1167** 40 ch. multicoloured . 60 30

1168 Worker using Microphone

1996. 50th Anniv of Labour Law.
N3609 **1168** 50 ch. multicoloured . 75 35

1171 Kumsusan Memorial Palace

1996. 2nd Death Anniv of Kim Il Sung.
N3612 **1171** 10 ch. multicoloured . 15 10

1172 Kim Il Sung meeting Jiang Zemin of China, 1991

1173 Football and Ancient Greek Athletes

1996. 35th Anniv of Korean–Chinese Treaty for Friendship, Co-operation and Mutual Assistance.
N3614 **1172** 10 ch. brown, gold and black 15 10
N3615 – 10 ch. green, gold and black 15 10
DESIGN: 10 ch. Kim Il Sung meeting Pres. Mao Tse-tung of China, 1954.

1996. Centenary of Modern Olympic Games and Olympic Games, Atlanta. Multicoloured.
N3617 50 ch. Type **1173** 70 35
N3618 50 ch. Tennis, Olympic Anthem and 1896 5 l. Greek stamp 70 35
N3619 50 ch. Throwing the hammer and advertisement poster for first modern olympics 70 35
N3620 50 ch. Baseball and Olympic stadium, Atlanta 70 35

1174 Couple

1996. 50th Anniv of Sex Equality Law.
N3621 **1174** 50 ch. multicoloured . 70 35

APPENDIX

The following stamps have either been issued in excess of postal needs or have not been available to the public in reasonable quantities at face value. Such stamps may later be given full listing if there is evidence of regular postal use.

1976.

Olympic Games, Montreal. Three-dimensional stamps showing Olympic events. 5, 10, 15, 20, 25, 40 ch.

1977.

Olympic Games, Montreal. Three-dimensional stamps showing medals. 5, 10, 15, 20, 25, 40 ch.

Olympic Games, Montreal. 1976 Olympic Games issue optd with winners' names. 5, 10, 15, 20, 25, 40 ch.

1979.

XIII Winter Olympic Games, 1980. Nos. N1688/94 optd. 2, 5, 10, 15, 20, 25, 40 ch.

1981.

Nobel Prizes for Medicine. Nos. N1955/61 optd. 7 × 10 ch.

World Cup Football Championship, Spain (1982). Nos. N1731/41 optd. 12 × 20 ch.

World Cup Football Championship, Spain (1982). Three-dimensional stamps. Air 20, 30 ch.

1982.

21st Birthday of Princess of Wales. Nos. N2108/11 and N2120/3 optd. 10, 20, 30, 40 ch; 10, 20, 30, 70 ch.

Birth of Prince William of Wales. Nos. N2185/91 optd. 10, 20, 30, 50, 60, 70, 80 ch.

World Cup Football Championship, Spain, Results. Nos. N2201/6 optd. 10, 20, 30, 40, 50, 60 ch.

Birth of Prince William of Wales. Three-dimensional stamps. 3 × 30 ch.

1983.

XXIII Olympic Games, Los Angeles, 1984. Nos. N2084/8 optd. 10, 15, 20, 25, 30 ch.

1984.

European Royal History. 81 × 10 ch.

KOUANG TCHEOU (KWANGCHOW) Pt. 17

An area and port of S. China, leased by France from China in April 1898. It was returned to China in February 1943.

1906. 100 centimes = 1 franc.
1919. 100 cents = 1 piastre.

Unless otherwise stated the following are optd or surch on stamps of Indo-China.

1906. Surch **Kouang Tcheou-Wan** and value in Chinese.
1 **8** 1 c. olive . . . . 1·50 1·50
2 2 c. red on yellow . . . . . 1·50 1·40
3 4 c. purple on grey . . . . 2·00 1·90
4 5 c. green . . . . 2·00 2·00
5 10 c. red . . . . 2·00 2·00
6 15 c. brown on blue . . . . 5·00 4·75
7 20 c. red on green . . . . . 2·00 2·00
8 25 c. blue . . . . 2·00 2·00
9 30 c. brown on cream . . . 2·50 2·50
10 35 c. black on yellow . . . 3·50 3·25
11 40 c. black on grey . . . . 2·50 2·50
12 50 c. brown on cream . . . 10·00 10·00
13 **D** 75 c. brown on orange . . . 15·00 15·00
14 **8** 1 f. green . . . . 18·00 18·00
15 2 f. brown on yellow . . . . 18·00 18·00
16 **D** 5 f. mauve on lilac £120 £120
17 **8** 10 f. red on green £150 £150

1908. Native types surch **KOUANG-TCHEOU** and value in Chinese.
18 **10** 1 c. black and brown . . . 40 45
19 2 c. black and brown . . . 40 50
20 4 c. black and blue . . . 45 50
21 5 c. black and green . . . 45 45
22 10 c. black and red . . . 45 45
23 15 c. black and violet . . . 1·10 1·10
24 **11** 20 c. black and violet . . . 2·00 2·00
25 25 c. black and blue . . . 2·50 2·50
26 30 c. black and brown . . . 4·25 4·50
27 35 c. black and green . . . 5·75 6·00
28 40 c. black and brown . . . 6·00 6·00
29 50 c. black and red . . . 6·50 6·50
30 **12** 75 c. black and orange . . . 6·50 6·50
31 – 1 f. black and red . . . . . 7·50 7·50
32 – 2 f. black and green . . . . 20·00 20·00
33 – 5 f. black and blue . . . . . 40·00 40·00
34 – 10 f. black and violet . . . 60·00 60·00

1919. Nos. 18/34 surch in figures and words.
35 **10** $\frac{2}{5}$ on 1 c. black and brown 40 45
36 $\frac{4}{5}$ c. on 2 c. black and brown 35 45
37 1$\frac{3}{5}$ c. on 4 c. black and blue 50 55
38 2 c. on 5 c. black and green 55 55
39 4 c. on 10 c. black and red 1·40 85
40 6 c. on 15 c. black & violet 55 45
41 **11** 8 c. on 20 c. black & violet 2·00 1·90
42 10 c. on 25 c. black and blue 5·50 5·00
43 12 c. on 30 c. black & brown 1·10 85
44 14 c. on 35 c. black & green 1·25 1·10
45 16 c. on 40 c. black & brown 90 70
46 20 c. on 50 c. black and red 90 65
47 **12** 30 c. on 75 c. black & orange 3·50 3·50
48 – 40 c. on 1 f. black and red 4·25 4·25
49 – 80 c. on 2 f. black and green 5·00 4·25
50 – 2 p. on 5 f. black and blue 95·00 90·00
51 – 4 p. on 10 f. black & violet 12·00 11·50

1923. Native types optd **KOUANG-TCHEOU** only. (Value in cents and piastres).
52 **10** $\frac{1}{10}$ c. red and grey 15 30
53 $\frac{1}{5}$ c. black and blue 15 30
54 $\frac{2}{5}$ c. black and brown 20 30
55 $\frac{4}{5}$ c. black and red 25 35
56 1 c. black and brown 35 35
57 2 c. black and green 55 55
58 3 c. black and violet 55 55
59 4 c. black and orange . . . 55 55
60 5 c. black and red 55 55
61 **11** 6 c. black and red 70 55
62 7 c. black and green 55 70
63 8 c. black on lilac 90 55
64 9 c. black & yellow on green 90 85
65 10 c. black and blue 85 85
66 11 c. black and violet . . . 85 85
67 12 c. black and brown . . . 85 85
68 15 c. black and orange . . . 1·40 1·40
69 20 c. black and blue on buff 90 85
70 40 c. black and red . . . . 1·75 1·75
71 1 p. black & green on green 4·75 4·75
72 2 p. black & purple on pink 7·50 7·75

1927. Pictorial types optd **KOUANG-TCHEOU**.
73 **22** $\frac{1}{10}$ c. olive 15 30
74 $\frac{1}{5}$ c. yellow 20 30
75 $\frac{2}{5}$ c. blue 25 35
76 $\frac{4}{5}$ c. brown 30 35
77 1 c. orange 40 45
78 2 c. green 55 55
79 3 c. blue 55 55
80 4 c. mauve 55 55
81 5 c. violet 55 55
82 **23** 6 c. red 50 55
83 7 c. brown 50 55
84 8 c. olive 55 55
85 9 c. purple 65 65
86 10 c. blue 65 65
87 11 c. orange 65 70
88 12 c. green 65 65
89 **24** 15 c. brown and red . . . . 1·10 1·10
90 20 c. grey and violet . . . . 1·40 1·40
91 – 25 c. mauve and brown . . 1·40 1·40
92 – 30 c. olive and blue 95 95
93 – 40 c. blue and red 90 85
94 – 50 c. grey and green . . . . 1·00 1·00
95 – 1 p. black, yellow and blue 2·50 2·50
96 – 2 p. blue, orange and red . . 2·75 2·75

1937. 1931 issue optd **KOUANG-TCHEOU**.
98 **33** $\frac{1}{10}$ c. blue 15 30
99 $\frac{1}{5}$ c. lake 20 30
100 $\frac{2}{5}$ c. red 15 30
101 $\frac{1}{2}$ c. brown 15 25
102 $\frac{4}{5}$ c. violet 30 30
103 **33** 1 c. brown 20 30
104 2 c. green 20 30
126 – 3 c. brown 30 30
105 – 3 c. green 50 45
106 – 4 c. blue 55 55
127 – 4 c. green 30 30
128 – 4 c. yellow . . . . 1·00 1·00
107 – 5 c. purple 55 55
129 – 5 c. green 35 35
108 – 6 c. red 35 45
130 – 7 c. black 35 45
131 – 8 c. lake 35 45
132 – 9 c. black on yellow . . . 40 45
109 – 10 c. blue 65 65
133 – 10 c. blue on pink 50 55
110 – 15 c. blue 40 45
134 – 18 c. blue 20 30
111 – 20 c. red 40 45
112 – 21 c. green 40 45
135 – 22 c. green 35 35
113 – 25 c. purple . . . . 1·60 1·60
136 – 25 c. blue 45 45
114 – 30 c. brown 35 45
115 **36** 50 c. brown 55 60
116 60 c. purple 60 60
137 70 c. blue 45 45
117 1 p. green 85 90
118 2 p. red . . . . 1·00 1·00

1939. New York World's Fair. As T **28** of Mauritania.
119 13 c. red 50 55
120 23 c. deep blue and blue . . . 50 55

1939. 150th Anniv of French Revolution. As T **29** of Mauritania.
121 6 c. + 2 c. green . . . . . 3·75 3·75
122 7 c. + 3 c. brown . . . . . 3·75 3·75
123 9 c. + 4 c. orange . . . . . 3·75 3·75
124 13 c. + 10 c. red . . . . . 3·75 3·75
125 23 c. + 20 c. blue . . . . . 3·75 3·75

KUWAIT Pt. 19

An independent Arab Shaikhdom on the N.W. coast of the Persian Gulf with Indian and later British postal administration. On 1st February, 1959, the Kuwait Government assumed responsibility for running its own postal service. In special treaty relations with Great Britain until 19 June 1961 when Kuwait became completely independent.

For stamps issued by Indian and British postal administrations, see Vol. 3.

1958. 100 naye paise = 1 rupee.
1961. 1000 fils = 1 dinar.

20 Shaikh Abdullah 21 Dhow

1958.
131 **20** 5 n.p. green 50 10
132a 10 n.p. red 20 10
133 15 n.p. brown 20 15
134 20 n.p. violet 20 10
135 25 n.p. orange 35 10
136 40 n.p. purple . . . . . . 1·50 55
137 **21** 40 n.p. blue 45 20
138 – 50 n.p. red 40 20
139 – 75 n.p. green 45 30
140 – 1 r. purple 50 35
141 – 2 r. blue and brown . . . 2·50 70
142 – 5 r. green . . . . 4·00 1·50
143 – 10 r. lilac . . . . 13·00 4·50
DESIGNS—HORIZ: As Type **21**: 50 n.p. Oil pipelines; 75 n.p. Shuwaikh Power Station. 36 × 20 mm: 1 r. Oil rig; 2 r. Single-masted dhow; 5 r. Kuwait Mosque; 10 r. Main Square, Kuwait Town.

22 Shaikh Abdullah and Flag

1960. 10th Anniv of Shaikh's Accession.
144 **22** 40 n.p. red and green . . . 35 10
145 60 n.p. red and blue . . . 45 20

1961. As 1958 issue but currency changed and new designs.
146 **20** 1 f. green 15 10
147 2 f. red 15 10
148 4 f. brown 15 10
149 5 f. violet 15 10
150 8 f. red 20 10
151 15 f. purple 25 10
152 – 20 f. green (as No. 142) . . 50 10
153 – 25 f. blue 90 10
154 – 30 f. blue and brown (as No. 141) . . . . 1·25 10
155 – 35 f. black and red 75 40
156 **21** 40 f. blue (32 × 22 mm) . . 1·25 15
157 – 45 f. brown 50 10
158 – 75 f. brown & grn (as No. 141) 2·50 60
159 – 90 f. brown and blue . . . 1·75 35
160 – 100 f. red . . . . 3·25 10
161 **21** 250 f. green (32 × 22 mm) . . 7·00 1·50
162 – 1 d. orange . . . . 10·00 1·50
163 – 3 d. red (as No. 142) . . . 25·00 18·00
NEW DESIGNS—37 × 20 mm: 25, 100 f. Vickers Viscount 700 airliner over South Pier, Mina al Ahmadi; 35, 90 f. Shuwaikh Secondary School; 45 f., 1 d. Wara Hill.

23 Telegraph Pole

1962. 4th Arab Telecommunications Union Conference.
164 **23** 8 f. blue and black 15 10
165 20 f. red and black 35 20

1962. Arab League Week. As T **76** of Libya.
166 20 f. purple 20 10
167 45 f. brown 50 20

25 Mubarakiya School, Shaikh Abdullah and Shaikh Mubarak

1962. Golden Jubilee of Mubarakiya School.
168 **25** 8 f. multicoloured 20 10
169 20 f. multicoloured 50 20

26 National Flag and Crest

1962. National Day.
170 **26** 8 f. multicoloured 10 10
171 20 f. multicoloured 35 20
172 45 f. multicoloured 80 30
173 90 f. multicoloured . . . . 1·25 1·25

1962. Malaria Eradication. As T **26a** of Yemen.
174 4 f. green and turquoise . . . 15 10
175 25 f. grey and green 55 25

28 "Industry and Progress"

1962. Bicentenary of Sabah Dynasty.
176 **28** 8 f. multicoloured 10 10
177 20 f. multicoloured 35 15
178 45 f. multicoloured 75 15
179 75 f. multicoloured . . . . 1·25 50

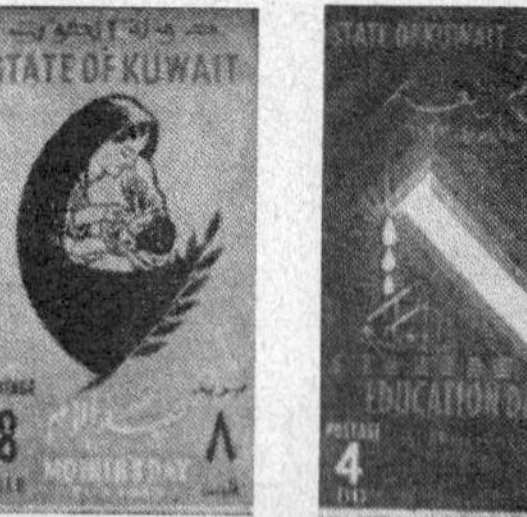

29 Mother and Child 31 "Education from Oil"

30 Campaign Emblem, Palm and Domestic Animals

1963. Mothers' Day. Centres black and green; value black; country name red.
180 **29** 8 f. yellow 10 10
181 20 f. blue 20 15
182 45 f. olive 50 25
183 75 f. grey 80 40

1963. Freedom from Hunger. Design in brown and green. Background colours given.
184 **30** 4 f. blue 10 10
185 8 f. yellow 25 15
186 20 f. lilac 50 25
187 45 f. pink . . . . 1·10 70

1963. Education Day.
188 **31** 4 f. brown, blue and yellow 10 10
189 20 f. green, blue and yellow 50 15
190 45 f. purple, blue and yellow 90 35

32 Shaikh Abdullah and Flags

1963. 2nd Anniv of National Day. Flags in green, black and red; values in black.
191 **32** 4 f. blue 40 30
192 5 f. ochre 60 55
193 20 f. violet . . . . 3·25 2·25
194 50 f. brown . . . . 6·50 3·75

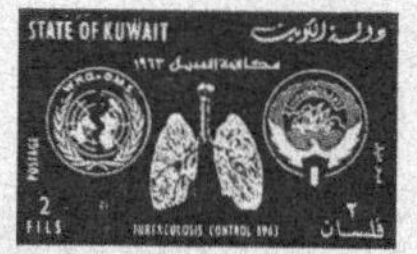

33 Human Lungs, and Emblems of W.H.O. and Kuwait

1963. W.H.O. "Tuberculosis Control" Campaign. Emblem yellow: arms black, green and red.
195 **33** 2 f. black and stone . . . 10 10
196 4 f. black and green . . . 20 10
197 8 f. black and blue 25 10
198 20 f. black and red . . . . 1·00 35

34 Municipal Hall and Scroll

1963. New Constitution. Centres dull purple; Amir red.
199 **34** 4 f. red 15 10
200 8 f. green 20 10
201 20 f. purple 35 10
202 45 f. brown 60 15
203 75 f. violet . . . . 1·25 50
204 90 f. blue . . . . 1·40 75

35 Football

36 Scales of Justice and Globe

1963. Arab Schools Games. Multicoloured.
205 1 f. Type **35** 10 10
206 4 f. Basketball 10 10
207 5 f. Swimming (horiz) . . . 10 10
208 8 f. Running 15 10
209 15 f. Throwing the javelin (horiz) 30 15
210 20 f. Pole vaulting (horiz) . . 40 20
211 35 f. Gymnastics (horiz) . . . 90 35
212 45 f. Gymnastics . . . . . . 1·25 75

1963. 15th Anniv of Declaration of Human Rights.
213 **36** 8 f. black, green & violet . 10 10
214 20 f. black, yellow & grey . 40 20
215 25 f. black, brown and blue 60 30

37 Shaikh Abdullah

38 Rameses II in War Chariot

1964. Multicoloured, frame colours given.
216 **37** 1 f. grey 10 10
217 2 f. blue 10 10
218 4 f. brown 15 10
219 5 f. brown 15 10
220 8 f. brown 25 10
221 10 f. green 25 10
222 15 f. green 35 35
223 20 f. blue 35 10
224 25 f. green 40 10
225 30 f. green 50 10
226 40 f. violet 70 15
227 45 f. violet 85 15
228 50 f. yellow 90 20

229 **37** 70 f. purple . . . . 1·10 25
230 75 f. red . . . . 1·25 35
231 90 f. blue . . . . 1·60 35
232 100 f. lilac . . . . 1·75 40
233 250 f. brown . . . . 5·00 90
234 1 d. purple . . . . 14·00 3·75
Nos. 233/4 are larger 25×30 mm.

1964. Nubian Monuments Preservation.
235 **38** 8 f. purple, blue and buff 15 10
236 20 f. violet, blue & lt blue 40 20
237 30 f. violet, blue & turquoise 55 35

39 Mother and Child

1964. Mother's Day.
238 **39** 8 f. blue, green and grey . . 10 10
239 20 f. blue, green and red . . 25 10
240 30 f. blue, green and bistre 40 20
241 45 f. indigo, green and blue 65 30

40 Nurse giving B.C.G. Vaccine to Patient, and Bones of Chest

41 Dhow and Microscope

1964. World Health Day.
242 **40** 8 f. green and brown . . . 30 10
243 20 f. red and green 85 25

1964. Education Day.
244 **41** 8 f. multicoloured 15 10
245 15 f. multicoloured 30 10
246 20 f. multicoloured 35 15
247 30 f. multicoloured 60 25

42 Dhow and Doves

1964. 3rd Anniv of National Day. Badge in blue, brown, black, red and green.
248 **42** 8 f. black and brown . . . 25 15
249 20 f. black and green . . . 40 25
250 30 f. black and grey 60 35
251 45 f. black and blue 85 55

43 A.P.U. Emblem

44 Hawker Siddeley Comet 4C and Douglas DC-3 Airliners

1964. 10th Anniv of Arab Postal Union's Permanent Office, Cairo.
252 **43** 8 f. brown and blue 25 10
253 20 f. blue and yellow . . . 45 20
254 45 f. brown and green . . . 85 50

1964. Air. 10th Anniv of Kuwait Airways. Sky in blue; aircraft blue, red and black.
255 **44** 20 f. black and bistre . . . 45 25
256 25 f. black and brown . . . 60 30
257 30 f. black and green . . . 70 30
258 45 f. black and brown . . . 1·00 40

45 Conference Emblem

46 Dhow, Doves and Oil-drilling Rig

1965. 1st Arab Journalists' Conference, Kuwait.
259 **45** 8 f. multicoloured 30 10
260 20 f. multicoloured 55 20

1965. 4th Anniv of National Day.
261 **46** 10 f. multicoloured 15 10
262 15 f. multicoloured 35 15
263 20 f. multicoloured 75 20

47 I.C.Y. Emblem

48 Mother and Children

1965. International Co-operation Year.
264 **47** 8 f. black and red 25 10
265 20 f. black and blue . . . 55 25
266 30 f. black and green . . . 1·00 40
The stamps are inscribed "CO-OPERATIVE".

1965. Mothers' Day.
267 **48** 8 f. multicoloured 20 10
268 15 f. multicoloured 40 20
269 20 f. multicoloured 65 25

49 Weather Kite

1965. World Meteorological Day.
270 **49** 4 f. blue and yellow . . . 25 10
271 5 f. blue and orange . . . 25 10
272 20 f. blue and green . . . 1·10 25

50 Census Graph

1965. Population Census.
273 **50** 8 f. black, brown & blue . 20 10
274 20 f. black, pink and green 60 25
275 50 f. black, green and red . 1·40 60

1965. Deir Yassin Massacre. As T **52a** of Yemen.
276 4 f. red and blue 40 20
277 45 f. red and green . . . . . 1·90 65

51 Atomic Symbol and Tower of Shuwaikh Secondary School

1965. Education Day.
278 **51** 4 f. multicoloured 15 10
279 20 f. multicoloured 45 15
280 45 f. multicoloured 80 30

52 I.T.U. Emblem and Symbols

53 Saker Falcon

1965. I.T.U. Centenary.
281 **52** 8 f. red and blue 40 25
282 20 f. red and green 80 40
283 45 f. blue and red . . . . 1·50 70

1965. Reconstitution of Burnt Algiers Library. As T **53a** of Yemen.
284 8 f. green, red and black . . 40 15
285 15 f. red, green and black . . 1·00 20

1965. Centre in brown.
286 **53** 8 f. purple . . . . 1·25 15
287 15 f. green . . . . 1·10 15
288 20 f. blue . . . . 1·75 25
289 25 f. red . . . . 1·90 35
290 30 f. green . . . . 2·25 40
291 45 f. blue . . . . 4·25 60
292 50 f. purple . . . . 5·00 70
293 90 f. red . . . . 8·00 1·40

54 Open Book

55 Shaikh Sabah

1966. Education Day.
294 **54** 8 f. multicoloured 20 10
295 20 f. multicoloured 45 10
296 30 f. multicoloured 85 25

1966.
297 **55** 4 f. multicoloured 15 10
298 5 f. multicoloured 15 10
299 20 f. multicoloured 40 15
300 30 f. multicoloured 55 25
301 40 f. multicoloured 70 35
302 45 f. multicoloured 75 40
303 70 f. multicoloured . . . . 1·75 60
304 90 f. multicoloured . . . . 2·00 80

56 Fishes and Ears of Wheat

1966. Freedom from Hunger.
305 **56** 20 f. multicoloured . . . . 1·00 50
306 45 f. multicoloured . . . . 2·25 95

57 Eagle and Scales of Justice

1966. 5th Anniv of National Day.
307 **57** 20 f. multicoloured 80 30
308 25 f. multicoloured 90 30
309 45 f. multicoloured . . . . 1·60 60

58 Cogwheel and Map of Arab States

59 Mother and Children

1966. Arab Countries Industrial Development Conference, Kuwait.
310 **58** 20 f. green black and blue 50 15
311 50 f. green, black & brown 1·00 45

1966. Mothers' Day.
312 **59** 20 f. multicoloured 50 15
313 45 f. multicoloured . . . . 1·00 30

60 Red Crescent and Emblem of Medicine

61 "Man and his Cities"

1966. 5th Arab Medical Conference, Kuwait.
314 **60** 15 f. red and blue 35 15
315 30 f. red, blue and pink . . 80 40

1966. World Health Day.
316 **61** 8 f. multicoloured 50 15
317 10 f. multicoloured 75 20

62 W.H.O. Building

63 Symbol of Blood Donation

1966. Inaug of W.H.O. Headquarters, Geneva.
318 **62** 5 f. green, blue and red . . 50 10
319 10 f. green, blue & turq . . 90 15

1966. Traffic Day. As T **66** of Yemen.
320 10 f. red, emerald and green 50 10
321 20 f. emerald, red and green 75 25

1966. Blood Bank Day.
322 **63** 4 f. multicoloured 40 10
323 8 f. multicoloured 85 25

64 Shaikh Ahmad and "British Fusilier" (tanker)

1966. 20th Anniv of 1st Crude Oil Shipment.
324 **64** 20 f. multicoloured 60 25
325 45 f. multicoloured . . . . 1·40 55

65 Ministry Building

1966. Inauguration of Ministry of Guidance and Information Building.
326 **65** 4 f. red and brown 20 10
327 5 f. brown and green . . . 20 10
328 8 f. green and violet . . . 30 10
329 20 f. orange and blue . . . 65 20

66 Dhow, Lobster, Fish and Crab

67 U.N. Flag

1966. F.A.O. Near East Countries Fisheries Conference, Kuwait.
330 **66** 4 f. multicoloured 85 25
331 20 f. multicoloured . . . . 1·10 50

1966. U.N. Day.
332 **67** 20 f. multicoloured 75 25
333 45 f. multicoloured . . . . 1·10 50

68 U.N.E.S.C.O. Emblem

69 Ruler and University Shield

1966. 20th Anniv of U.N.E.S.C.O.
334 **68** 20 f. multicoloured 75 60
335 45 f. multicoloured . . . . 1·50 1·25

1966. Opening of Kuwait University.
336 **69** 8 f. multicoloured 25 10
337 10 f. multicoloured 25 15
338 20 f. multicoloured 75 25
339 45 f. multicoloured . . . . 1·50 75

70 Ruler and Heir-Apparent

1966. Appointment of Heir-Apparent.
340 **70** 8 f. multicoloured 25 10
341 20 f. multicoloured 60 30
342 45 f. multicoloured . . . . 1·25 70

71 Scout Badge

72 Symbols of Learning

1966. 30th Anniv of Kuwait Scouts.
343 **71** 4 f. brown and green . . . 50 15
344 20 f. green and brown . . . 1·75 50

1967. Education Day.
345 **72** 10 f. multicoloured 30 15
346 45 f. multicoloured 80 35

73 Fertiliser Plant

1967. Inauguration of Chemical Fertiliser Plant.

347 **73** 8 f. multicoloured 40 15
348 20 f. multicoloured . . . . 1·00 30

74 Ruler, Dove and Olive-branch

1967. 6th Anniv of National Day.

349 **74** 8 f. multicoloured 30 10
350 20 f. multicoloured 80 30

75 Map and Municipality Building

76 Arab Family

1967. 1st Arab Cities Organization Conf, Kuwait.

351 **75** 20 f. multicoloured . . . . 1·00 25
352 30 f. multicoloured . . . . 1·40 60

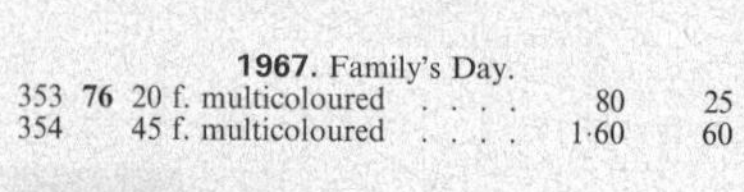

1967. Family's Day.

353 **76** 20 f. multicoloured 80 25
354 45 f. multicoloured . . . . 1·60 60

77 Arab League Emblem

78 Sabah Hospital

1967. Arab Cause Week.

355 **77** 8 f. blue and grey 30 10
356 10 f. green and yellow . . . 60 15

1967. World Health Day.

357 **78** 8 f. multicoloured 85 15
358 20 f. multicoloured . . . . 1·00 40

79 Nubian Statues

1967. Arab Week for Nubian Monuments Preservation.

359 **79** 15 f. green, brown & yellow 60 20
360 20 f. green, purple and blue 90 25

80 Traffic Policeman

1967. Traffic Day.

361 **80** 8 f. multicoloured 80 25
362 20 f. multicoloured . . . . 1·75 65

81 I.T.Y. Emblem

82 "Reaching for Knowledge"

1967. International Tourist Year.

363 **81** 20 f. black, blue & turq . 65 40
364 45 f. black, blue and mauve 1·25 85

1967. "Eliminate Illiteracy" Campaign.

365 **82** 8 f. multicoloured 75 10
366 20 f. multicoloured . . . . 1·50 35

83 Map of Palestine

84 Factory and Cogwheels

1967. U.N. Day.

367 **83** 20 f. red and blue 50 20
368 45 f. red and orange . . . 1·10 50

1967. 3rd Arab Labour Ministers' Conference.

369 **84** 20 f. yellow and red . . . 60 20
370 45 f. yellow and grey . . . 1·40 50

85 Open Book and Kuwaiti Flag

86 Oil Rig and Map

1968. Education Day.

371 **85** 20 f. multicoloured 50 30
372 45 f. multicoloured . . . . 1·25 60

1968. 30th Anniv of Oil Discovery in Greater Burgan Field.

373 **86** 10 f. multicoloured 75 40
374 20 f. multicoloured . . . . 1·25 70

87 Ruler and Sun's Rays

88 Book, Eagle and Sun

1968. 7th Anniv of National Day.

375 **87** 8 f. multicoloured 25 10
376 10 f. multicoloured 25 20
377 15 f. multicoloured 45 25
378 20 f. multicoloured 60 35

1968. Teachers' Day.

379 **88** 8 f. multicoloured 30 10
380 20 f. multicoloured 40 15
381 45 f. multicoloured 75 40

89 Family Picnicking

1968. Family Day.

382 **89** 8 f. multicoloured 20 10
383 10 f. multicoloured 20 10
384 15 f. multicoloured 30 10
385 20 f. multicoloured 45 20

MORE DETAILED LISTS
are given in the Stanley Gibbons Catalogues referred to in the country headings. For lists of current volumes see introduction

90 Ruler, W.H.O. and State Emblems

1968. World Health Day and 20th Anniv of W.H.O.

386 **90** 20 f. multicoloured 60 50
387 45 f. multicoloured . . . . 1·50 1·10

91 Dagger on Deir Yassin, and Scroll

1968. 20th Anniv of Deir Yassin Massacre.

388 **91** 20 f. red and blue 80 25
389 45 f. red and violet . . . . 2·75 50

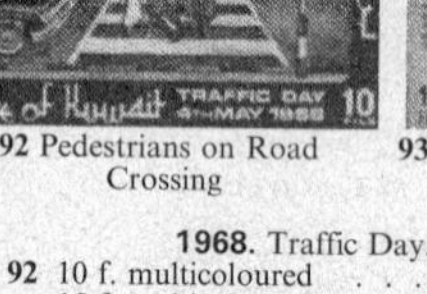

92 Pedestrians on Road Crossing

93 Torch and Map

1968. Traffic Day.

390 **92** 10 f. multicoloured 75 60
391 15 f. multicoloured . . . . 1·25 85
392 20 f. multicoloured . . . . 1·75 1·00

1968. Palestine Day.

393 **93** 10 f. multicoloured 70 10
394 20 f. multicoloured . . . . 1·25 25
395 45 f. multicoloured . . . . 2·50 50

94 Palestine Refugees

1968. Human Rights Year.

396 **94** 20 f. multicoloured 25 15
397 30 f. multicoloured 35 15
398 45 f. multicoloured 65 15
399 90 f. multicoloured . . . . 1·25 45

95 National Museum

96 Man reading Book

1968.

400 **95** 1 f. green and brown . . . 10 10
401 2 f. green and purple . . . 10 10
402 5 f. red and black 15 10
403 8 f. green and brown . . . 20 10
404 10 f. purple and blue . . . 20 10
405 20 f. blue and brown . . . 45 10
406 25 f. orange and blue . . . 55 10
407 30 f. green and blue 70 20
408 45 f. deep purple and purple 1·10 20
409 50 f. red and green . . . . 1·60 45

1968. International Literacy Day.

410 **96** 15 f. multicoloured 30 10
411 20 f. multicoloured 70 15

97 Refugee Children and U.N. Headquarters

1968. United Nations Day.

412 **97** 20 f. multicoloured 30 10
413 30 f. multicoloured 40 20
414 45 f. multicoloured 70 25

98 Chamber of Commerce Building

1968. Inauguration of Kuwait Chamber of Commerce and Industry Building.

415 **98** 10 f. purple and orange . . 25 10
416 15 f. blue and mauve . . . 30 15
417 20 f. green and brown . . 45 15

99 Conference Emblem

1968. 14th Arab Chambers of Commerce, Industry and Agriculture Conference.

418 **99** 10 f. multicoloured 25 10
419 15 f. multicoloured 30 10
420 20 f. multicoloured 40 15
421 30 f. multicoloured 70 30

100 Refinery Plant

101 Holy Koran, Scales and People

1968. Inauguration of Shuaiba Refinery.

422 **100** 10 f. multicoloured . . . 30 15
423 20 f. multicoloured . . . 60 20
424 30 f. multicoloured . . . 95 35
425 45 f. multicoloured . . . 1·75 45

1968. 1,400th Anniv of the Holy Koran.

426 **101** 8 f. multicoloured 30 15
427 20 f. multicoloured . . . 75 40
428 30 f. multicoloured . . . 1·25 60
429 45 f. multicoloured . . . 1·60 85

102 Boeing 707 Airliner

1969. Inauguration of Boeing 707 Aircraft by Kuwait Airways.

430 **102** 10 f. multicoloured . . . 35 20
431 20 f. multicoloured . . . 75 35
432 25 f. multicoloured . . . 1·10 45
433 45 f. multicoloured . . . 2·00 65

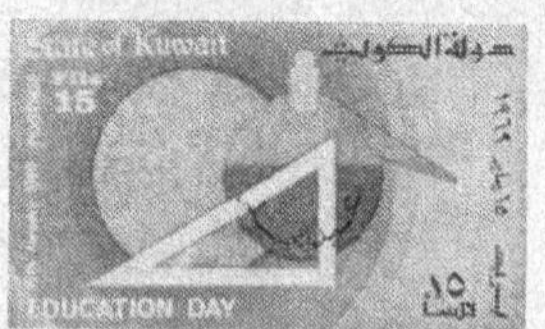

103 Globe and Symbols of Engineering and Science

1969. Education Day.

434 **103** 15 f. multicoloured . . . 35 25
435 20 f. multicoloured . . . 65 30

104 Hilton Hotel

105 Family and Teachers' Society Emblem

1969. Inauguration of Kuwait Hilton Hotel.

436 **104** 10 f. multicoloured . . . 35 15
437 20 f. multicoloured . . . 65 15

1969. Education Week.

438 **105** 10 f. multicoloured . . . 35 15
439 20 f. multicoloured . . . 65 15

106 Flags and Laurel 107 Emblem, Teacher and Class

1969. 8th Anniv of National Day.

440 **106** 15 f. multicoloured . . . 25 15
441 20 f. multicoloured . . . 40 20
442 30 f. multicoloured . . . 60 40

1969. Teachers' Day.

443 **107** 10 f. multicoloured . . . 30 15
444 20 f. multicoloured . . . 55 15

108 Kuwaiti Family

1969. Family Day.

445 **108** 10 f. multicoloured . . . 30 15
446 20 f. multicoloured . . . 55 20

109 Ibn Sina, Nurse with Patient and W.H.O. Emblem **110** Motor-cycle Police

1969. World Health Day.

447 **109** 15 f. multicoloured . . . 70 15
448 20 f. multicoloured . . . 80 20

1969. Traffic Day.

449 **110** 10 f. multicoloured . . . 75 15
450 20 f. multicoloured . . . 2·00 25

111 I.L.O. Emblem

1969. 50th Anniv of I.L.O.

451 **111** 10 f. gold, black and red 30 10
452 20 f. gold, black and green 50 15

112 Tanker "Al Sabahiah"

1969. 4th Anniv of Kuwait Shipping Company.

453 **112** 20 f. multicoloured . . . 90 35
454 45 f. multicoloured . . . 1·90 90

113 Woman writing Letter **114** Amir Shaikh Sabah

1969. International Literacy Day.

455 **113** 10 f. multicoloured . . . 25 10
456 20 f. multicoloured . . . 55 20

1969. Portraits multicoloured; background colours given.

457 **114** 8 f. blue 25 10
458 10 f. pink 25 10
459 15 f. grey 35 15
460 20 f. yellow 40 15
461 25 f. lilac 50 20
462 30 f. orange 70 25
463 45 f. grey 95 35
464 **114** 50 f. green . . . . 1·10 40
465 70 f. blue . . . . 1·25 50
466 75 f. blue . . . . 1·40 55
467 90 f. brown . . . . . . 1·40 70
468 250 f. purple . . . . . . 5·50 2·00
469 500 f. green . . . . . . 10·50 6·50
470 1 d. purple . . . . 17·00 11·00

115 "Appeal to World Conscience" **116** Earth Station

1969. United Nations Day.

471 **115** 10 f. blue, black and green 30 10
472 20 f. blue, black and stone 60 15
473 45 f. blue, black and red 1·00 30

1969. Inauguration of Kuwait Satellite Communications Station. Multicoloured.

474 20 Type **116** 90 20
475 45 f. Dish aerial on Globe (vert) 1·90 50

117 Refugee Family **118** Globe, Symbols and I.E.Y. Emblem

1969. Palestinian Refugee Week.

476 **117** 20 f. multicoloured. . . . 1·40 40
477 45 f. multicoloured . . . 3·00 1·25

1970. International Education Year.

478 **118** 20 f. multicoloured . . . 40 25
479 45 f. multicoloured . . . 1·00 60

119 Shoue

1970. Kuwait Sailing Dhows. Multicoloured.

480 8 f. Type **119** 40 10
481 10 f. Sambuk 40 10
482 15 f. Baggala 60 20
483 20 f. Battela 75 15
484 25 f. Bum 90 25
485 45 f. Baggala . . . . 1·75 55
486 50 f. Dhow-building . . . . 2·00 55

120 Kuwaiti Flag

1970. 9th Anniv of National Day.

487 **120** 15 f. multicoloured . . . 65 15
488 20 f. multicoloured . . . 75 15

121 Young Commando and Dome of the Rock, Jerusalem

1970. Support for Palestinian Commandos. Multicoloured.

489 10 f. Type **121** 50 20
490 20 f. Commando in battle-dress 1·00 40
491 45 f. Woman commando . . 2·50 90

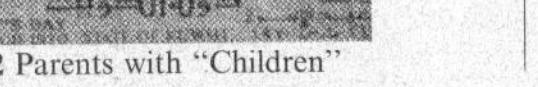

122 Parents with "Children"

1970. Family Day.

492 **122** 20 f. multicoloured 40 15
493 30 f. multicoloured 60 25

123 Arab League Flag, Emblem and Map

1970. 25th Anniv of Arab League.

494 **123** 20 f. brown, green and blue 50 10
495 45 f. violet, green and orange 75 30

124 Census Emblem and Graph

1970. Population Census.

496 **124** 15 f. multicoloured 20 10
497 20 f. multicoloured 50 10
498 30 f. multicoloured 70 20

125 Cancer the Crab in "Pincers" **126** Traffic Lights and Road Signs

1970. World Health Day.

499 **125** 20 f. multicoloured 45 10
500 30 f. multicoloured 65 20

1970. Traffic Day.

501 **126** 20 f. multicoloured . . . . 1·00 45
502 30 f. multicoloured . . . . 1·50 70

127 Red Crescent

1970. International Red Cross and Crescent Day.

503 **127** 10 f. multicoloured 40 15
504 15 f. multicoloured 60 20
505 30 f. multicoloured . . . . 1·50 50

128 New Headquarters Building

1970. Opening of New U.P.U. Headquarters Building, Berne.

506 **128** 20 f. multicoloured 60 20
507 30 f. multicoloured 90 35

129 Amir Shaikh Sabah **130** U.N. Symbols

1970.

508 **129** 20 f. multicoloured 65 20
509 45 f. multicoloured . . . . 1·60 75

1970. 25th Anniv of United Nations.

511 **130** 20 f. multicoloured 40 15
512 45 f. multicoloured 70 30

131 "Medora" (tanker) at Sea Island Jetty

1970. Oil Shipment Facilities, Kuwait.

513 **131** 20 f. multicoloured . . . 90 30
514 45 f. multicoloured . . . 2·10 65

132 Kuwaiti and U.N. Emblems and Hand writing

1970. International Literacy Day.

515 **132** 10 f. multicoloured . . . 70 15
516 15 f. multicoloured . . . 90 15

133 Guards and Badge

1970. First Graduation of National Guards.

517 **133** 10 f. multicoloured . . . 55 15
518 20 f. multicoloured . . . 1·10 20

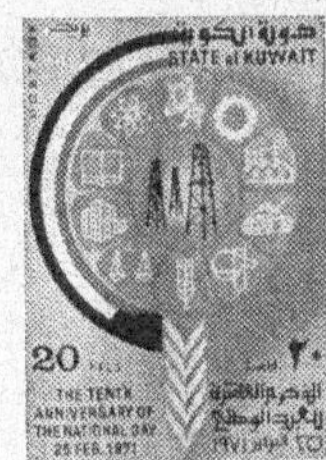

134 Symbols and Flag **136** Map of Palestine on Globe

135 Dr. C. Best and Sir F. Banting (discoverers of insulin) and Syringe

1971. 10th Anniv of National Day.

519 **134** 20 f. multicoloured . . . 70 30
520 30 f. multicoloured . . . 95 45

1971. World Health Day, and 50th Anniv of Discovery of Insulin.

521 **135** 20 f. multicoloured . . . 50 15
522 45 f. multicoloured . . . 1·10 40

1971. Palestine Week.

523 **136** 20 f. multicoloured . . . 1·00 75
524 45 f. multicoloured . . . 2·25 1·50

137 I.T.U. Emblem **138** "Three Races"

1971. World Telecommunications Day.

525 **137** 20 f. black, brown & silver 70 20
526 45 f. black, brown & gold 1·60 60

1971. Racial Equality Year.

527 **138** 15 f. multicoloured . . . 35 20
528 30 f. multicoloured . . . 65 50

139 A.P.U. Emblem

1971. 25th Anniv of Founding of Arab Postal Union at Sofar Conference.
529 **139** 20 f. multicoloured . . . 50 25
530 45 f. multicoloured . . . 1·00 40

140 Book, Pupils, Globes and Pen

1971. International Literacy Day.
531 **140** 25 f. multicoloured . . . 60 20
532 60 f. multicoloured . . . 1·50 60

141 Footballers

1971. Regional Sports Tournament, Kuwait. Multicoloured.
533 20 f. Type **141** 95 35
534 30 f. Footballer blocking attack 1·40 50

142 Emblems of U.N.I.C.E.F. and Kuwait

1971. 25th Anniv of U.N.I.C.E.F.
535 **142** 25 f. multicoloured . . . 40 25
536 60 f. multicoloured . . . 90 50

143 Book Year Emblem

1972. International Book Year.
537 **143** 20 f. black and brown . . 50 30
538 45 f. black and green . . . 1·10 60

144 Crest and Laurel

1972. 11th Anniv of National Day.
539 **144** 20 f. multicoloured . . . 85 50
540 45 f. multicoloured . . . 1·40 85

145 Telecommunications Centre

1972. Inauguration of Telecommunications Centre, Kuwait.
541 **145** 20 f. multicoloured . . . 1·00 40
542 45 f. multicoloured . . . 2·50 1·00

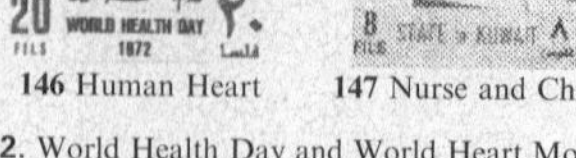
146 Human Heart 147 Nurse and Child

1972. World Health Day and World Heart Month.
543 **146** 20 f. multicoloured . . . 1·25 25
544 45 f. multicoloured . . . 2·75 50

1972. International Red Cross and Crescent Day.
545 **147** 8 f. multicoloured 75 10
546 40 f. multicoloured . . . 2·40 75

148 Football

1972. Olympic Games, Munich. Multicoloured.
547 2 f. Type **148** 10 10
548 4 f. Running 15 10
549 5 f. Swimming 20 10
550 8 f. Gymnastics 30 10
551 10 f. Throwing the discus . . 35 10
552 15 f. Show jumping 45 15
553 20 f. Basketball 50 20
554 25 f. Volleyball 65 30

149 Produce and Fishing Boat 151 Ancient Capitals

150 Bank Emblem

1972. 11th F.A.O. Near East Regional Conference, Kuwait.
555 **149** 5 f. multicoloured 30 30
556 10 f. multicoloured . . . 1·00 75
557 20 f. multicoloured . . . 2·00 1·40

1972. 20th Anniv of National Bank of Kuwait.
558 **150** 10 f. multicoloured . . . 30 15
559 35 f. multicoloured . . . 1·00 70

1972. Archaeological Excavations on Failaka Island. Multicoloured.
560 2 f. Type **151** 10 15
561 5 f. View of excavations . . . 25 10
562 10 f. "Leaf" capital 45 10
563 15 f. Excavated building . . . 95 20

152 Floral Emblem 153 Interpol Emblem

1973. 12th Anniv of National Day.
564 **152** 10 f. multicoloured . . . 30 15
565 20 f. multicoloured . . . 65 45
566 30 f. multicoloured . . . 95 65

1973. 50th Anniv of International Criminal Police Organization (Interpol).
567 **153** 10 f. multicoloured . . . 50 45
568 15 f. multicoloured . . . 1·00 65
569 20 f. multicoloured . . . 1·50 95

154 C.I.S.M. Badge and Flags 155 Airways Building

1973. 25th Anniv of International Military Sports Council (C.I.S.M.).
570 **154** 30 f. multicoloured 65 40
571 40 f. multicoloured . . . . 1·00 50

1973. Opening of Kuwait Airways H.Q. Building.
572 **155** 10 f. multicoloured 35 15
573 15 f. multicoloured 55 25
574 20 f. multicoloured 70 30

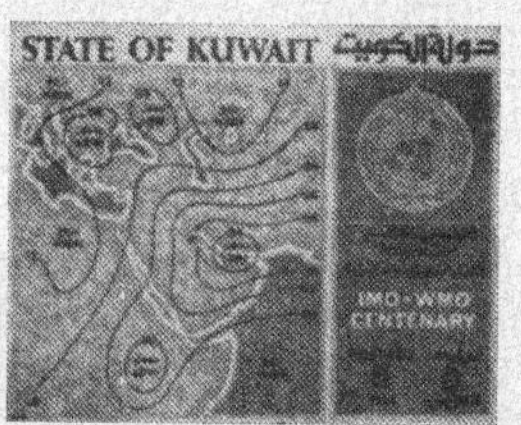
156 Weather Map of Middle East

1973. Centenary of World Meteorological Organization.
575 **156** 5 f. multicoloured 30 10
576 10 f. multicoloured 50 15
577 15 f. multicoloured 85 25

157 Shaikhs Ahmed and Sabah

1973. 50th Anniv of 1st Kuwait Stamp Issue (overprints on India of 1923).
578 **157** 10 f. multicoloured 40 15
579 20 f. multicoloured 75 25
580 70 f. multicoloured . . . . 2·50 1·10

158 Mourning Dove

1973. Birds and Hunting Equipment. Multicoloured.
(a) Size 32 × 32 mm.
581 5 f. Type **158** 50 15
582 5 f. Hoopoe ("Upupa epops") 50 15
583 5 f. Rock dove ("Columba livia") 50 15
584 5 f. Stone-curlew ("Burhinus oedicnemus") . . 50 15
585 8 f. Great grey shrike ("Lanius excubitor") 70 15
586 8 f. Red-backed shrike ("Lanius collurio") 70 15
587 8 f. Black-headed shrike ("Lanius schach") 70 15
588 8 f. Golden oriole ("Orielus chinensis") 70 15
589 10 f. Willow warbler ("Phylloscopus trochilus") . 70 15
590 10 f. Great reed warbler ("Acrocephalus arundinaceus") 70 15
591 10 f. Blackcap ("Sylvia atricapilla") 70 15
592 10 f. Barn swallow ("Hirundo rustica") 70 15
593 15 f. Rock thrush ("Monticola solitarius") . . 1·10 25
594 15 f. Redstart ("Phoenicurus phoenicurus") 1·10 25
595 15 f. Common wheatear ("Oenanthe oenanthe") . . . 1·10 25
596 15 f. Bluethroat ("Luscinia svecica") . . . . 1·10 25
597 20 f. Houbara bustard ("Chlamydotis undulata") . 1·50 30
598 20 f. Pin-tailed sandgrouse ("Pterocles alchata") . . . 1·50 30
599 20 f. Giant wood rail ("Aramides ypecaha") . . . 1·50 30
600 20 f. Spotted crake ("Porzana porzana") . . . . 1·50 30
(b) Size 38 × 38 mm.
601 25 f. American kestrel ("Falco sparverius") . . . . 2·00 35
602 25 f. Great black-backed gull ("Larus marinus") . . . . 2·00 35

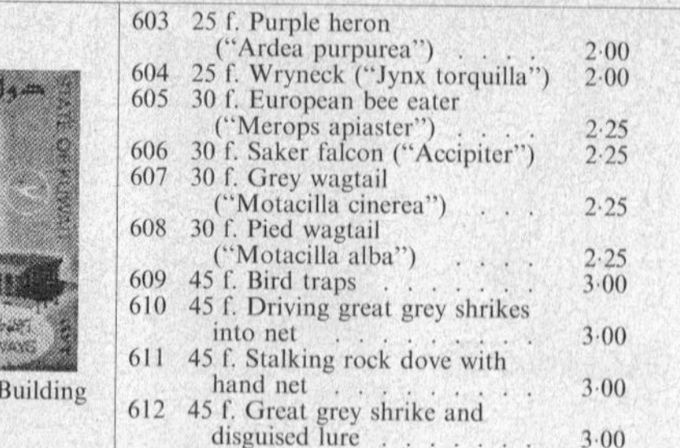
603 25 f. Purple heron ("Ardea purpurea") . . . . 2·00 35
604 25 f. Wryneck ("Jynx torquilla") 2·00 35
605 30 f. European bee eater ("Merops apiaster") . . . . 2·25 45
606 30 f. Saker falcon ("Accipiter") 2·25 45
607 30 f. Grey wagtail ("Motacilla cinerea") . . . 2·25 45
608 30 f. Pied wagtail ("Motacilla alba") . . . . 2·25 45
609 45 f. Bird traps . . . . 3·00 80
610 45 f. Driving great grey shrikes into net . . . . 3·00 80
611 45 f. Stalking rock dove with hand net . . . . 3·00 80
612 45 f. Great grey shrike and disguised lure . . . . . . 3·00 80

159 Flame Emblem 160 Congress Emblem

1973. 25th Anniv of Declaration of Human Rights.
613 **159** 10 f. multicoloured . . . 40 10
614 40 f. multicoloured . . . 1·10 35
615 75 f. multicoloured . . . 1·75 60

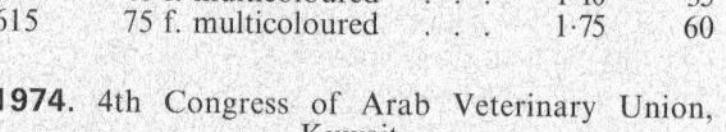
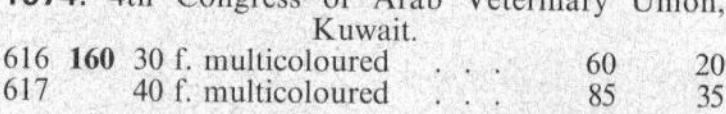
1974. 4th Congress of Arab Veterinary Union, Kuwait.
616 **160** 30 f. multicoloured . . . 60 20
617 40 f. multicoloured . . . 85 35

161 Flag and Wheat Ear Symbol 163 Tournament Emblem

162 A.M.U. Emblem

1974. 13th Anniv of National Day.
618 **161** 20 f. multicoloured . . . 30 10
619 30 f. multicoloured . . . 50 25
620 70 f. multicoloured . . . 1·40 1·00

1974. 12th Conference of Arab Medical Union and 1st Conference of Kuwait Medical Society.
621 **162** 30 f. multicoloured . . . 1·25 30
622 40 f. multicoloured . . . 1·75 80

1974. 3rd Arabian Gulf Trophy Football Tournament, Kuwait.
623 **163** 25 f. multicoloured . . . 80 15
624 45 f. multicoloured . . . 1·75 70

164 Institute Buildings

1974. Inauguration of Kuwait Institute for Scientific Research.
625 **164** 15 f. multicoloured . . . 70 25
626 20 f. multicoloured . . . 1·40 30

165 Emblems of Kuwait, Arab Postal Union and U.P.U.

1974. Centenary of U.P.U.
627 **165** 20 f. multicoloured . . . 25 15
628 30 f. multicoloured . . . 30 30
629 60 f. multicoloured . . . 50 45

166 Symbolic Telephone Dial — **167** Council Emblem and Flags of Member States

1974. World Telecommunications Day.

630 **166** 10 f. multicoloured . . . 30 15
631 30 f. multicoloured . . . 85 40
632 40 f. multicoloured . . . 1·10 55

1974. 17th Anniv of Signing Arab Economic Unity Agreement.

633 **167** 20 f. green, black and red 60 25
634 30 f. red, black and green 70 40

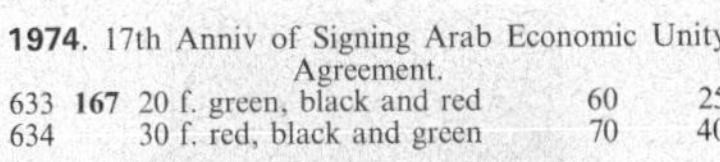

168 "Population Growth"

1974. World Population Year.

635 **168** 30 f. multicoloured . . . 75 30
636 70 f. multicoloured . . . 1·75 70

169 Fund Building

1974. Kuwait Fund for Arab Economic Development.

637 **169** 10 f. multicoloured . . . 45 10
638 20 f. multicoloured . . . 75 25

170 Shuaiba Emblem

1974. 10th Anniv of Shuaiba Industrial Area.

639 **170** 10 f. multicoloured . . . 40 15
640 20 f. multicoloured . . . 1·00 30
641 30 f. multicoloured . . . 1·40 55

171 Arms of Kuwait and "14"

1975. 14th Anniv of National Day.

642 **171** 20 f. multicoloured . . . 40 20
643 70 f. multicoloured . . . 1·25 60
644 75 f. multicoloured . . . 1·60 70

172 Census Symbols

1975. Population Census.

645 **172** 8 f. multicoloured 15 10
646 20 f. multicoloured . . . 35 10
647 30 f. multicoloured . . . 50 25
648 70 f. multicoloured . . . 1·40 75
649 100 f. multicoloured . . . 1·75 1·10

173 I.W.Y. and Kuwait Women's Union Emblems

1975. International Women's Year.

650 **173** 15 f. multicoloured . . . 50 15
651 20 f. multicoloured . . . 60 30
652 30 f. multicoloured . . . 85 45

174 Classroom within Open Book

1975. International Literacy Day.

653 **174** 20 f. multicoloured . . . 50 15
654 30 f. multicoloured . . . 85 45

175 I.S.O. Emblem — **176** U.N. Flag, Rifle and Olive-branch

1975. World Standards Day.

655 **175** 10 f. multicoloured . . . 30 15
656 20 f. multicoloured . . . 55 25

1975. 30th Anniv of U.N.O.

657 **176** 20 f. multicoloured . . . 50 15
658 45 f. multicoloured . . . 1·10 50

177 Shaikh Sabah

1975.

659 **177** 8 f. multicoloured 35 15
660 20 f. multicoloured . . . 60 20
661 30 f. multicoloured . . . 70 30
662 50 f. multicoloured . . . 1·25 50
663 90 f. multicoloured . . . 2·40 85
664 100 f. multicoloured . . . 3·00 1·10

178 Kuwait "Skyline"

1976. 15th Anniv of National Day.

665 **178** 10 f. multicoloured . . . 50 15
666 20 f. multicoloured . . . 90 15

178a Emblem, Microscope and Operation — **179** Early and Modern Telephones

1976. 2nd Annual Conference of Kuwait Medical Association.

667 **178a** 5 f. multicoloured . . . 30 15
668 10 f. multicoloured . . . 60 20
669 30 f. multicoloured . . . 1·90 55

1976. Telephone Centenary.

670 **179** 5 f. black and orange . . 20 15
671 15 f. black and blue . . . 65 15

180 Eye

1976. World Health Day.

672 **180** 10 f. multicoloured . . . 40 15
673 20 f. multicoloured . . . 75 15
674 30 f. multicoloured . . . 1·25 35

181 Red Crescent Emblem

1976. 10th Anniv of Kuwait Red Crescent Society.

675 **181** 20 f. multicoloured 40 15
676 30 f. multicoloured 70 30
677 45 f. multicoloured . . . . 1·25 55
678 75 f. multicoloured . . . . 2·00 1·40

182 Suburb of Manama — **183** Basketball

1976. U.N. Human Settlements Conference.

679 **182** 10 f. multicoloured 35 15
680 20 f. multicoloured 65 15

1976. Olympic Games, Montreal. Multicoloured.

681 4 f. Type **183** 10 10
682 8 f. Running 15 10
683 10 f. Judo 20 10
684 15 f. Handball 30 10
685 20 f. Figure-skating 35 10
686 30 f. Volleyball 55 25
687 45 f. Football 70 35
688 70 f. Swimming . . . . 1·10 85

184 Ethnic Heads and Map of Sri Lanka — **185** Torch, U.N.E.S.C.O. Emblem and Kuwaiti Arms

1976. Non-Aligned Countries' Congress, Colombo.

689 **184** 20 f. multicoloured 35 10
690 30 f. multicoloured 50 30
691 45 f. multicoloured 85 45

1976. 30th Anniv of U.N.E.S.C.O.

692 **185** 20 f. multicoloured 45 10
693 45 f. multicoloured . . . . 1·00 50

186 Pot-throwing — **187** Diseased Knee

1977. Popular Games. Multicoloured.

694 5 f. Type **186** 20 10
695 5 f. Kite-flying 20 10
696 5 f. Balancing sticks 20 10
697 5 f. Spinning tops 20 10
698 10 f. Blind-man's-buff (horiz) 25 15
699 10 f. Rowing (horiz) 25 15
700 10 f. Rolling hoops (horiz) . . 25 15
701 10 f. Rope game (horiz) . . . 25 15
702 15 f. Skipping 50 25
703 15 f. Marbles 50 25
704 15 f. Carting 50 25
705 15 f. Teetotum (tops) 50 25
706 20 f. Halma (horiz) 80 40
707 20 f. Model boating (horiz) . . 80 40
708 20 f. Pot and candle (horiz) . . 80 40
709 20 f. Hide-and-seek (horiz) . . 80 40
710 30 f. Knucklebones 90 50
711 30 f. Hiding the stone 90 50
712 30 f. Hopscotch 90 50
713 30 f. Catch-as-catch-can . . . 90 50
714 40 f. Bowls (horiz) . . . . . 1·60 70
715 40 f. Hockey (horiz) . . . . . 1·60 70
716 40 f. Guessing which hand (horiz) . . . . 1·60 70
717 40 f. Jacks (horiz) . . . . . 1·60 70
718 60 f. Hiding the cake (horiz) . 2·00 1·25
719 60 f. Chess (horiz) . . . . . 2·00 1·25
720 60 f. Story-telling (horiz) . . 2·00 1·25
721 60 f. Treasure hunt (horiz) . . 2·00 1·25
722 70 f. Hobby horses (horiz) . . 2·25 1·40
723 70 f. Hide-and-seek (horiz) . . 2·25 1·40
724 70 f. Catch shadow (horiz) . . 2·25 1·40
725 70 f. Throwing game (horiz) . 2·25 1·40

1977. World Rheumatism Year.

726 **187** 20 f. multicoloured 40 15
727 30 f. multicoloured 60 30
728 45 f. multicoloured 90 45
729 75 f. multicoloured . . . . 1·25 85

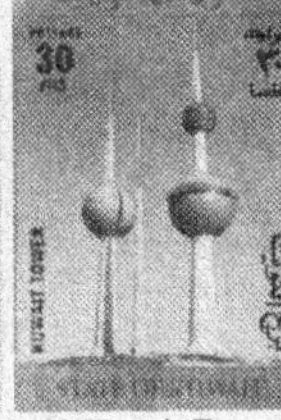

188 Shaikh Sabah — **189** Kuwait Tower

1977. 16th National Day.

730 **188** 10 f. multicoloured . . . 15 10
731 15 f. multicoloured . . . 30 15
732 30 f. multicoloured . . . 65 20
733 80 f. multicoloured . . . 1·40 55

1977. Inauguration of Kuwait Tower.

734 **189** 30 f. multicoloured . . . 75 15
735 80 f. multicoloured . . . 2·00 55

190 A.P.U. Emblem and Flags — **191** Printed Circuit

1977. 25th Anniv of Arab Postal Union.

736 **190** 5 f. multicoloured 20 10
737 15 f. multicoloured . . . 20 10
738 30 f. multicoloured . . . 40 20
739 80 f. multicoloured . . . 1·10 60

1977. World Telecommunications Day.

740 **191** 30 f. orange and brown . . 60 30
741 80 f. orange and green . . 1·50 70

192 Shaikh Sabah — **192a** Aerogramme stamp

1977.

742 **192** 15 f. brown, black & blue 80 35
743 25 f. brown, black & yell . 1·40 35
744 30 f. brown, black & red . 1·75 50
745 80 f. brown, black & lilac 4·00 1·25
746 100 f. brown, black & orge 5·00 1·40
747 150 f. brown, black & blue 9·00 2·25
748 200 f. brown, black & green 10·00 3·25

1977. Aerogramme stamp. Imperf.

748a **192a** 55 f. red and blue . . .

No. 748a was applied before sale to aerogrammes to uprate the imprinted 25 f. stamp. It was not available separately.

193 Championship Emblem

1977. 4th Asian Youth Basketball Championships.

749 **193** 30 f. multicoloured . . . 50 50
750 80 f. multicoloured . . . 1·50 1·00

194 "Popular Dancing" (O. Al-Nakeeb)

1977. Children's Paintings. Multicoloured.

751 15 f. Type **194** 35 20
752 15 f. "Al Deirah" (A. M. al-Onizi) 35 20
753 30 f. "Fishing" (M. al-Jasem) 60 45
754 30 f. "Dugg al-Harees" (B. al-Sa'adooni) (vert) 60 45
755 80 f. "Fraisa Dancing" (M. al-Mojaibel) (vert) . . . 1·50 1·25
756 80 f. "Kuwaiti Girl" (K. Ghazi) (vert) . . . . 1·50 1·25

195 Dome of the Rock and Palestinian Freedom Fighters

1978. Palestinian Freedom Fighters.

757 **195** 30 f. multicoloured . . . 1·25 70
758 80 f. multicoloured . . . 2·40 1·50

196 Dentist treating Patient

1978. 10th Arab Dental Union Congress.

759 **196** 30 f. multicoloured . . . 70 55
760 80 f. multicoloured . . . 1·75 1·10

197 Carrying Water from Dhows

1978. Water Resources. Multicoloured.

761 5 f. Type **197** 25 10
762 5 f. Camel 25 10
763 5 f. Water carrier 25 10
764 5 f. Pushing water in cart . . 25 10
765 10 f. Irrigation with donkey . 35 10
766 10 f. Water troughs in desert . 35 10
767 10 f. Pool by a town 35 10
768 10 f. Watering crops 35 10
769 15 f. Bedouin watering sheep . 50 10
770 15 f. Bedouin women by pool 50 10
771 15 f. Camels watered by pipeline 50 10
772 15 f. Water skins in Bedouin tent 50 10
773 20 f. Oasis with wells 55 10
774 20 f. Washing and drinking at home 55 10
775 20 f. Water urn 55 10
776 20 f. Filling vessels from taps . 55 10
777 25 f. Desalination plant . . . 65 15
778 25 f. Water tanker 65 15
779 25 f. Filling water tankers . . 65 15
780 25 f. Modern water tanks . . 65 15
781 30 f. Catching water during storm (vert) 85 15
782 30 f. Water tank (vert) 85 15
783 30 f. Sheet to catch rain (vert) 85 15
784 30 f. Trees by water tanks (vert) 85 15
785 80 f. Carrying water on donkey (vert) . . . . 2·00 60
786 80 f. Woman carrying water-can (vert) . . . . 2·00 60
787 80 f. Woman with water-skins (vert) . . . . 2·00 60
788 80 f. Tanker delivering water to house (vert) . . . . 2·00 60
789 100 f. Tanker delivering to courtyard tank (vert) . . . 2·75 90
790 100 f. Household cistern (vert) 2·75 90
791 100 f. Filling cistern (vert) . . 2·75 90
792 100 f. Drawing water from well (vert) . . . . 2·75 90

198 Symbols of Development

1978. 17th National Day.

793 **198** 30 f. multicoloured . . . 35 25
794 80 f. multicoloured . . . 1·00 70

199 Face of Smallpox Victim

1978. Global Eradication of Smallpox.

795 **199** 30 f. multicoloured . . . 40 30
796 80 f. multicoloured . . . 1·10 70

INDEX

Countries can be quickly located by referring to the index at the end of this volume.

200 Microwave Antenna

201 Shaikh Jabir

1978. 10th World Telecommunications Day.

797 **200** 30 f. multicoloured . . . 35 25
798 80 f. multicoloured . . . 1·10 70

1978. Portrait in brown; background colour given.

799 **201** 15 f. green 40 15
800 30 f. orange 80 35
801 80 f. purple . . . . . . 1·75 85
802 100 f. green . . . . . . 2·00 1·00
803 130 f. brown . . . . . . 3·25 1·40
804 180 f. violet . . . . . . 4·75 2·00
805 1 d. red . . . . 15·00 9·00
806 4 d. blue . . . . 50·00 22·00

Nos. 805/6 are larger, 24 × 29 mm.

202 Mount Arafat, Pilgrims and Kaaba

1978. Pilgrimage to Mecca.

807 **202** 30 f. multicoloured . . . 50 40
808 80 f. multicoloured . . . 1·40 1·00

203 U.N. and Anti-Apartheid Emblems

1978. International Anti-Apartheid Year.

809 **203** 30 f. multicoloured . . . 40 25
810 80 f. multicoloured . . . 1·00 70
811 180 f. multicoloured . . . 2·10 1·50

204 Refugees

1978. 30th Anniv of Declaration of Human Rights.

812 **204** 30 f. multicoloured . . . 40 30
813 80 f. multicoloured . . . 1·25 75
814 100 f. multicoloured . . . 1·75 1·00

205 Information Centre

1978. Kuwait Information Centre.

815 **205** 5 f. multicoloured 10 10
816 15 f. multicoloured . . . 20 10
817 30 f. multicoloured . . . 35 20
818 80 f. multicoloured . . . 90 60

206 Kindergarten

207 Kuwaiti Flag and Doves

1979. International Year of the Child.

819 **206** 30 f. multicoloured . . . 40 35
820 80 f. multicoloured . . . 1·00 85

1979. 18th National Day.

821 **207** 30 f. multicoloured . . . 40 30
822 80 f. multicoloured . . . 95 75

208 Crops and Greenhouse

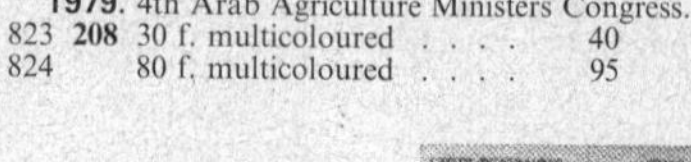

1979. 4th Arab Agriculture Ministers Congress.

823 **208** 30 f. multicoloured 40 25
824 80 f. multicoloured 95 75

209 World Map, Koran and Symbols of Arab Achievements

210 Children flying Kites

1979. The Arabs.

825 **209** 30 f. multicoloured 40 30
826 80 f. multicoloured 95 75

1979. Children's Paintings. Multicoloured.

827 30 f. Type **210** 40 35
828 30 f. Girl and doves 40 35
829 30 f. Crowd and balloons . . . 40 35
830 80 f. Boys smiling (horiz) . . . 1·00 90
831 80 f. Children in landscape (horiz) . . . . 1·00 90
832 80 f. Tug-of-war (horiz) . . . 1·00 90

211 Wave Pattern and Television Screen

212 International Military Sports Council Emblem

1979. World Telecommunications Day.

833 **211** 30 f. multicoloured 35 30
834 80 f. multicoloured 95 85

1979. 29th International Military Football Championship.

835 **212** 30 f. multicoloured 45 25
836 80 f. multicoloured . . . . 1·25 85

213 Child and Industrial Landscape

1979. World Environment Day.

837 **213** 30 f. multicoloured 50 40
838 80 f. multicoloured . . . . 1·40 1·10

214 Children supporting Globe

215 Children with Television

1979. 50th Anniv of International Bureau of Education.

839 **214** 30 f. multicoloured 35 25
840 80 f. multicoloured 85 75
841 130 f. multicoloured . . . 1·40 1·25

1979. 25th Anniv of Kuwaiti Kindergartens. Children's Drawings. Multicoloured.

842 30 f. Type **215** 40 25
843 80 f. Children with flags . . . 1·00 75

216 The Kaaba, Mecca

217 Figure, with Dove and Torch, clothed in Palestinian Flag

1979. Pilgrimage to Mecca.

844 **216** 30 f. multicoloured 40 30
845 80 f. multicoloured . . . . 1·50 85

1979. International Day of Solidarity with Palestinians.

846 **217** 30 f. multicoloured . . . 1·50 65
847 80 f. multicoloured . . . 3·00 1·25

218 Boeing 747 and Douglas DC-3 Airliners

1979. 25th Anniv of Kuwait Airways.

848 **218** 30 f. multicoloured . . . 55 40
849 80 f. multicoloured . . . 1·50 1·25

219 "Pinctada" Shell bearing Map of Kuwait

1980. 19th National Day.

850 **219** 30 f. multicoloured . . . 40 30
851 80 f. multicoloured . . . 1·10 75

220 Graph with Human Figures

1980. Population Census.

852 **220** 30 f. black, silver and blue 50 25
853 80 f. black, gold & orange 1·10 60

221 Campaign Emblem

1980. World Health Day. Anti-Smoking Campaign.

854 **221** 30 f. multicoloured . . . 60 35
855 80 f. multicoloured . . . 1·75 1·10

222 Municipality Building

1980. 50th Anniv of Kuwait Municipality.

856 **222** 15 f. multicoloured . . . 20 10
857 30 f. multicoloured . . . 40 30
858 80 f. multicoloured . . . 1·25 75

223 "The Future"

1980. Children's Imagination of Future Kuwait. Multicoloured.

859 30 f. Type **223** 50 30
860 80 f. Motorways . . . . 1·50 95

224 Hand blotting-out Factory

1980. World Environment Day.

861 **224** 30 f. multicoloured . . . 55 30
862 80 f. multicoloured . . . 1·50 60

225 Volleyball

226 O.P.E.C. Emblem and Globe

1980. Olympic Games, Moscow. Multicoloured.
863 15 f. Type **225** 20 20
864 15 f. Tennis 20 20
865 30 f. Swimming 35 25
866 30 f. Weightlifting 35 25
867 30 f. Basketball 35 25
868 30 f. Judo 35 25
869 80 f. Gymnastics 95 60
870 80 f. Badminton 95 60
871 80 f. Fencing 95 60
872 80 f. Football 95 60

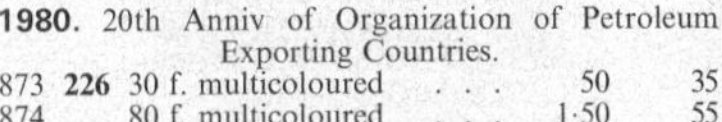

1980. 20th Anniv of Organization of Petroleum Exporting Countries.
873 **226** 30 f. multicoloured 50 35
874 80 f. multicoloured 1·50 55

227 Mosque and Kaaba, Mecca

1980. 1400th Anniv of Hegira.
875 **227** 15 f. multicoloured 25 15
876 30 f. multicoloured 50 30
877 80 f. multicoloured 1·40 85

228 Dome of the Rock

229 Ibn Sina (Avicenna)

1980. International Day of Solidarity with Palestinian People.
878 **228** 30 f. multicoloured 1·00 40
879 80 f. multicoloured 2·50 1·25

1980. Birth Millenary of Ibn Sina (philosopher and physician).
880 **229** 30 f. multicoloured 60 25
881 80 f. multicoloured 1·25 85

230 Islamic Symbols

231 Person in Wheelchair playing Snooker

1981. 1st Islamic Medicine Conference, Kuwait.
882 **230** 30 f. multicoloured 50 30
883 80 f. multicoloured 1·50 85

1981. International Year of Disabled Persons. Multicoloured.
884 30 f. Type **231** 50 30
885 80 f. Girl in wheelchair 1·50 85

232 Symbols of Development and Progress

1981. 20th National Day.
886 **232** 30 f. multicoloured 50 30
887 80 f. multicoloured 1·50 85

233 Emblem of Kuwait Dental Association

234 "Lamp"

1981. 1st Kuwait Dental Association Conference.
888 **233** 30 f. multicoloured 1·00 55
889 80 f. multicoloured 2·50 1·50

1981. World Red Cross and Red Crescent Day.
890 **234** 30 f. multicoloured 90 55
891 80 f. multicoloured 2·50 1·50

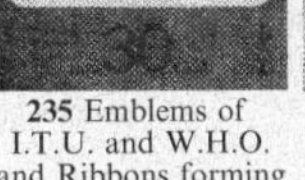
235 Emblems of I.T.U. and W.H.O. and Ribbons forming Caduceus

236 Tanker polluting Sea and Car polluting Atmosphere

1981. World Telecommunications Day.
892 **235** 30 f. multicoloured 70 50
893 70 f. multicoloured 2·25 1·40

1981. World Environment Day.
894 **236** 30 f. multicoloured 75 50
895 80 f. multicoloured 2·40 1·25

237 Sief Palace

1981.
896 **237** 5 f. multicoloured 10 10
897 10 f. multicoloured 10 10
898 15 f. multicoloured 10 10
899 25 f. multicoloured 15 15
900 30 f. multicoloured 20 15
901 40 f. multicoloured 25 15
902 60 f. multicoloured 40 20
903 80 f. multicoloured 50 30
904 100 f. multicoloured 65 45
905 115 f. multicoloured 70 50
906 130 f. multicoloured 80 70
907 150 f. multicoloured 1·10 70
908 180 f. multicoloured 1·25 75
909 250 f. multicoloured 1·50 80
910 500 f. multicoloured 3·25 1·10
911 1 d. multicoloured 6·25 1·50
912 2 d. multicoloured 12·00 2·25
913 3 d. multicoloured 16·00 6·75
914 4 d. multicoloured 25·00 8·50
Nos. 911/14 are larger, 33 × 28 mm and have a different border.

238 Pilgrims

1981. Pilgrimage to Mecca.
915 **238** 30 f. multicoloured 60 50
916 80 f. multicoloured 2·25 1·25

239 Palm Trees, Sheep, Camel, Goat and F.A.O. Emblem

1981. World Food Day.
917 **239** 30 f. multicoloured 65 45
918 80 f. multicoloured 2·00 1·25

240 Television Emblem

241 Blood Circulation Diagram

1981. 20th Anniv of Kuwait Television.
919 **240** 30 f. multicoloured 70 45
920 80 f. multicoloured 2·00 1·25

1982. 1st International Symposium on Pharmacology of Human Blood Vessels.
921 **241** 30 f. multicoloured 1·00 80
922 80 f. multicoloured 2·25 1·10

242 Symbols of Development, Progress and Peace

1982. 21st National Day.
923 **242** 30 f. multicoloured 50 30
924 80 f. multicoloured 1·40 85

243 Emblem of Kuwait Boy Scouts Association on Globe

1982. 75th Anniv of Boy Scout Movement.
925 **243** 30 f. multicoloured 60 40
926 80 f. multicoloured 1·75 1·00

244 Emblem of Arab Pharmacists Union

1982. Arab Pharmacists Day.
927 **244** 30 f. multicoloured 85 60
928 80 f. multicoloured 2·75 1·75

245 Red Crescent, Arab and W.H.O. Emblem

246 A.P.U. Emblem

1982. World Health Day.
929 **245** 30 f. multicoloured 1·00 65
930 80 f. multicoloured 3·00 1·75

1982. 30th Anniv of Arab Postal Union.
931 **246** 30 f. black, orange and green 85 60
932 80 f. black, green and orange 2·75 1·50

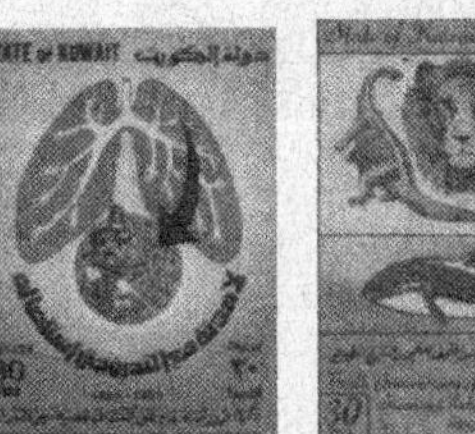
247 Lungs and Microscope

249 Museum Exhibits

248 Crest and Emblems of Kuwait Football Association and Olympic Committee

1982. Centenary of Discovery of Tubercle Bacillus.
933 **247** 30 f. multicoloured 1·00 60
934 80 f. multicoloured 2·75 1·60

1982. World Cup Football Championship, Spain.
935 **248** 30 f. multicoloured 75 40
936 80 f. multicoloured 2·00 1·25

1982. 10th Anniv of Science and Natural History Museum.
937 **249** 30 f. multicoloured 1·50 1·00
938 80 f. multicoloured 4·50 3·00

250 Container Ship

1982. 6th Anniv of United Arab Shipping Company. Multicoloured.
939 30 f. Type **250** 75 35
940 80 f. Freighter 1·75 90

251 Palm Trees

1982. Arab Palm Tree Day.
941 **251** 30 f. multicoloured 50 30
942 80 f. multicoloured 1·50 90

252 Pilgrims

1982. Pilgrimage to Mecca.
943 **252** 15 f. multicoloured 30 20
944 30 f. multicoloured 70 45
945 80 f. multicoloured 1·90 1·25

253 Desert Flower

1983. Desert Plants. Multicoloured; background colours given. (a) Vert designs.
946 10 f. green 10 10
947 10 f. violet 10 10
948 10 f. salmon 10 10
949 10 f. pink (blue flowers) 10 10
950 10 f. bistre 10 10
951 10 f. green 10 10
952 10 f. light orange 10 10
953 10 f. red (poppy) 10 10
954 10 f. brown 10 10
955 10 f. blue 10 10
956 15 f. green 15 15
957 15 f. purple 15 15
958 15 f. blue 15 15
959 15 f. blue (iris) 15 15
960 15 f. olive 15 15
961 15 f. red 15 15
962 15 f. brown 15 15
963 15 f. blue (bellflowers) 15 15
964 15 f. mauve 15 15
965 15 f. pink 15 15
966 30 f. brown 40 25
967 30 f. mauve 40 25
968 30 f. blue 40 25
969 30 f. green 40 25
970 30 f. pink 40 25
971 30 f. blue 40 25
972 30 f. green 40 25
973 30 f. mauve 40 25

974 30 f. bistre 40 25
975 30 f. yellow 40 25

(a) Horiz designs.

976 40 f. red (fungi) 75 35
977 40 f. green (fungi) 75 35
978 40 f. violet 50 35
979 40 f. blue 50 35
980 40 f. grey 50 35
981 40 f. green 50 35
982 40 f. mauve 50 35
983 40 f. brown 50 35
984 40 f. blue 50 35
985 40 f. green (daisies) 50 35
986 80 f. violet 90 70
987 80 f. green 90 70
988 80 f. yellow (yellow flowers) . 90 70
989 80 f. brown (green leaves) . . 90 70
990 80 f. blue 90 70
991 80 f. yellow 90 70
992 80 f. green 90 70
993 80 f. violet (red berries) . . . 90 70
994 80 f. brown (yellow flowers) . 90 70
995 80 f. yellow (red and blue flowers) 90 70

DESIGNS: Various plants.

254 Peace Dove on Map of Kuwait

1983. 22nd National Day.

996 **254** 30 f. multicoloured . . . 60 35
997 80 f. multicoloured . . . 1·50 95

255 I.M.O. Emblem

1983. 25th Anniv of International Maritime Organization.

998 **255** 30 f. multicoloured . . . 35 20
999 80 f. multicoloured . . . 1·00 60

256 Virus and Map of Africa

1983. 3rd International Conference on Impact of Viral Diseases on Development of Middle East and African Countries.

1000 **256** 15 f. multicoloured . . . 30 15
1001 30 f. multicoloured . . . 60 35
1002 80 f. multicoloured . . . 1·50 95

257 Stylized Figures exercising

1983. World Health Day.

1003 **257** 15 f. multicoloured . . . 30 20
1004 30 f. multicoloured . . . 65 45
1005 80 f. multicoloured . . . 1·90 1·25

258 U.P.U., W.C.Y. and I.T.U. Emblems

1983. World Communications Year.

1006 **258** 15 f. multicoloured . . . 35 20
1007 30 f. multicoloured . . . 65 45
1008 80 f. multicoloured . . . 1·60 1·25

259 Map of Kuwait and Dhow

1983. World Environment Day.

1009 **259** 15 f. multicoloured . . . 45 20
1010 30 f. multicoloured . . . 85 45
1011 80 f. multicoloured . . . 2·00 1·25

260 Walls of Jerusalem

1983. World Heritage Convention.

1012 **260** 15 f. multicoloured . . . 35 20
1013 30 f. multicoloured . . . 65 45
1014 80 f. multicoloured . . . 1·60 1·25

261 Pilgrims in Mozdalipha

1983. Pilgrimage to Mecca.

1015 **261** 15 f. multicoloured . . . 35 20
1016 30 f. multicoloured . . . 65 45
1017 80 f. multicoloured . . . 1·60 1·25

262 Arab within Dove

1983. International Day of Solidarity with Palestinian People.

1018 **262** 15 f. multicoloured . . . 35 20
1019 30 f. multicoloured . . . 65 45
1020 80 f. multicoloured . . . 1·60 1·25

263 Kuwait Medical Association and Congress Emblems

1984. 21st Pan-Arab Medical Congress.

1021 **263** 15 f. multicoloured . . . 35 20
1022 30 f. multicoloured . . . 65 45
1023 80 f. multicoloured . . . 1·60 1·25

264 State Arms within Key

1984. Inauguration of New Health Establishments.

1024 **264** 15 f. multicoloured . . . 35 20
1025 30 f. multicoloured . . . 65 45
1026 80 f. multicoloured . . . 1·60 1·25

265 Dove and Globe **266** Symbols of Medicine within Head

1984. 23rd National Day.

1027 **265** 15 f. multicoloured . . . 35 20
1028 30 f. multicoloured . . . 65 45
1029 80 f. multicoloured . . . 1·60 1·25

1984. 2nd International Medical Science Conference.

1030 **266** 15 f. multicoloured . . . 35 20
1031 30 f. multicoloured . . . 65 45
1032 80 f. multicoloured . . . 1·60 1·25

267 Douglas DC-3 Airliner

1984. 30th Anniv of Kuwait Airways Corporation.

1033 **267** 30 f. blue, dp blue & yell 75 60
1034 80 f. blue, dp bl & mve . 2·00 1·10

268 Magazine Covers **269** Family and Emblems

1984. 25th Anniv of "Al-Arabi" (magazine).

1035 **268** 15 f. multicoloured . . . 30 20
1036 30 f. multicoloured . . . 60 35
1037 80 f. multicoloured . . . 1·50 1·00

1984. World Health Day.

1038 **269** 15 f. multicoloured . . . 30 20
1039 30 f. multicoloured . . . 70 40
1040 80 f. multicoloured . . . 1·90 1·10

270 Sudanese Orphan and Village

1984. Hanan Kuwaiti Village, Sudan.

1041 **270** 15 f. multicoloured . . . 35 20
1042 30 f. multicoloured . . . 75 40
1043 80 f. multicoloured . . . 1·90 1·10

271 I.C.A.O., Kuwait Airport and Kuwait Airways Emblems

1984. 40th Anniv of I.C.A.O.

1044 **271** 15 f. multicoloured . . . 35 20
1045 30 f. multicoloured . . . 75 40
1046 80 f. multicoloured . . . 1·90 1·10

272 Map of Arab Countries and Youths

1984. Arab Youth Day.

1047 **272** 30 f. multicoloured . . . 70 40
1048 80 f. multicoloured . . . 1·90 1·10

273 Swimming

1984. Olympic Games, Los Angeles. Multicoloured.

1049 30 f. Type **273** 40 25
1050 30 f. Hurdling 40 25
1051 80 f. Judo 75 60
1052 80 f. Equestrian 75 60

274 Anniversary Emblem, Camera, Airplane, Al-Aujairy Observatory and Wind Tower

1984. 10th Anniv of Science Club.

1053 **274** 15 f. multicoloured . . . 35 15
1054 30 f. multicoloured . . . 85 40
1055 80 f. multicoloured . . . 2·10 1·10

275 Stoning the Devil

1984. Pilgrimage to Mecca.

1056 **275** 30 f. multicoloured . . . 80 40
1057 80 f. multicoloured . . . 1·75 1·10

276 Anniversary Emblem

1984. 20th Anniv of International Telecommunications Satellite Consortium (Intelsat).

1058 **276** 30 f. multicoloured . . . 80 40
1059 80 f. multicoloured . . . 1·75 1·10

277 Council Emblem **278** Hands breaking Star

1984. 5th Supreme Council Session of Gulf Co-operation Council.

1060 **277** 30 f. multicoloured . . . 70 40
1061 80 f. multicoloured . . . 1·75 1·10

1984. International Day of Solidarity with Palestinian People.

1062 **278** 30 f. multicoloured . . . 70 40
1063 80 f. multicoloured . . . 1·75 1·10

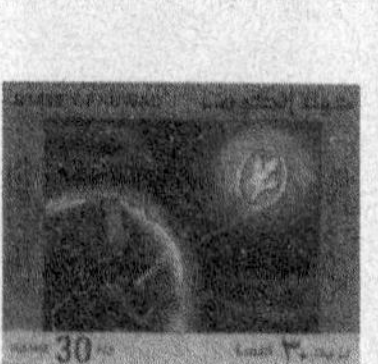

279 Company Emblem as Satellite **280** I.Y.Y. Emblem

1984. 50th Anniv of Kuwait Oil Company.

1064 **279** 30 f. multicoloured . . . 70 40
1965 80 f. multicoloured . . . 1·75 1·10

1985. International Youth Year.

1066 **280** 30 f. multicoloured . . . 40 20
1067 80 f. multicoloured . . . 1·25 75

281 "24", Hand holding Flame and Dove **282** Programme Emblem

1985. 24th National Day.

1068	**281**	30 f. multicoloured . . .	60	30
1069		80 f. multicoloured . . .	1·75	1·10

1985. International Programme for Communications Development.

1070	**282**	30 f. multicoloured . . .	70	40
1071		80 f. multicoloured . . .	1·75	1·10

283 Emblem

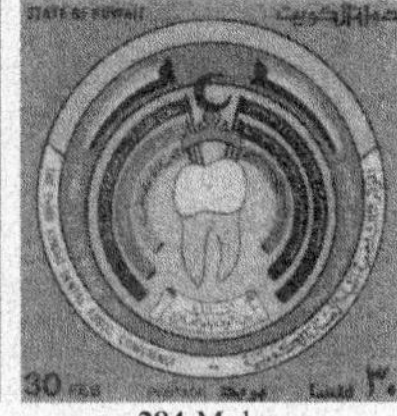

284 Molar

1985. 1st Arab Gulf Social Work Week.

1072	**283**	30 f. multicoloured . . .	70	40
1073		80 f. multicoloured . . .	1·75	1·10

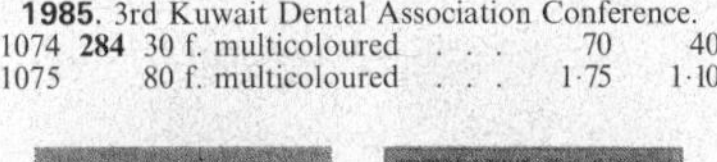

1985. 3rd Kuwait Dental Association Conference.

1074	**284**	30 f. multicoloured . . .	70	40
1075		80 f. multicoloured . . .	1·75	1·10

285 Emblem

286 Globe and Figures

1985. Population Census.

1076	**285**	30 f. multicoloured . . .	85	40
1077		80 f. multicoloured . . .	1·75	1·10

1985. World Health Day.

1078	**286**	30 f. multicoloured . . .	85	40
1079		80 f. multicoloured . . .	1·75	1·10

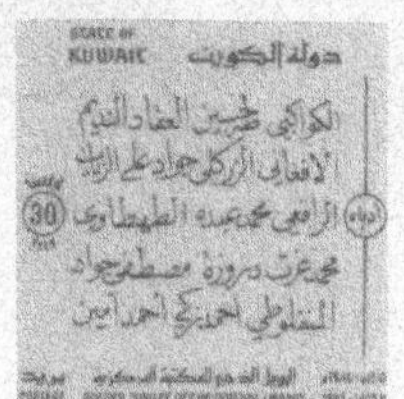

287 Arabic Script

No. 1080

No. 1081

No. 1082

No. 1083

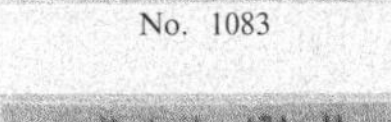

No. 1084

No. 1085

No. 1086

No. 1087

1985. 50th Anniv of Central Library. Square designs showing titles of books and names of authors in Arabic script (first line of text illustrated above).

1080	30 f. gold	1·00	45
1081	30 f. gold	1·00	45
1082	30 f. gold	1·00	45
1083	30 f. gold	1·00	45
1084	80 f. black and gold	2·50	1·00
1085	80 f. black and gold	2·50	1·00
1086	80 f. black and gold	2·50	1·00
1087	80 f. black and gold	2·50	1·00

288 Seascape

1985. World Environment Day.

1088	**288**	30 f. multicoloured . . .	1·50	40
1089		80 f. multicoloured . . .	3·00	1·10

289 Anniversary Emblem

1985. 25th Anniv of Organization of Petroleum Exporting Countries.

1090	**289**	30 f. ultram, bl & mve	85	40
1091		80 f. ultram, bl & brn	1·90	1·10

290 Emblem and Heads

1985. Introduction of Civilian Identity Cards.

1092	**290**	30 f. multicoloured . . .	85	40
1093		80 f. multicoloured . . .	1·90	1·10

291 Flag on Globe within Symbolic Design

1985. International Day of Solidarity with Palestinian People.

1094	**291**	15 f. multicoloured . . .	75	30
1095		30 f. multicoloured . . .	1·40	60
1096		80 f. multicoloured . . .	2·50	1·50

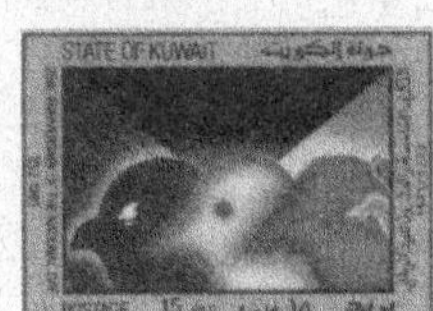

292 Birds

1986. 25th National Day.

1097	**292**	15 f. multicoloured . . .	20	15
1098		30 f. multicoloured . . .	75	35
1099		80 f. multicoloured . . .	2·00	90

293 Emblem

294 W.H.O. Emblem as Flower

1986. 20th Anniv of Kuwait Red Crescent.

1100	**293**	20 f. multicoloured . . .	60	45
1101		25 f. multicoloured . . .	85	70
1102		70 f. multicoloured . . .	2·50	1·90

1986. World Health Day.

1103	**294**	20 f. multicoloured . . .	60	45
1104		25 f. multicoloured . . .	85	70
1105		70 f. multicoloured . . .	2·50	1·90

295 I.P.Y. Emblem

1986. International Peace Year.

1106	**295**	20 f. green, blue & black	50	45
1107		25 f. blue, yellow & black	75	50
1108		70 f. blue, mauve & black	2·25	1·40

296 "Al Mirqab"

1986. 10th Anniv of United Arab Shipping Company. Container Ships. Multicoloured.

1109	20 f. Type **296**	75	45
1110	70 f. "Al Mubarakiah" . . .	3·00	1·90

297 Bank Emblem on Map

1986. 25th Anniv of Gulf Bank.

1111	**297**	20 f. multicoloured . . .	50	30
1112		25 f. multicoloured . . .	75	40
1113		70 f. multicoloured . . .	2·25	1·50

298 Zig-zags and Diamonds

1986. Sadu Art. Multicoloured.

1114	20 f. Type **298**	50	25
1115	70 f. Triangles and symbols	1·60	95
1116	200 f. Stripes and triangles . .	3·75	2·75

299 Dove on Manacled Hand pointing to Map

1986. International Day of Solidarity with Palestinian People.

1117	**299**	20 f. multicoloured . . .	75	50
1118		25 f. multicoloured . . .	1·00	70
1119		70 f. multicoloured . . .	3·00	2·00

300 Conference Emblem

1987. 5th Islamic Summit Conference.

1120	**300**	25 f. multicoloured . . .	60	30
1121		50 f. multicoloured . . .	1·25	70
1122		150 f. multicoloured . . .	3·25	2·00

301 Map in National Colours and Symbols of Development

1987. 26th National Day.

1123	**301**	50 f. multicoloured . . .	1·25	50
1124		150 f. multicoloured . .	3·00	1·50

302 Health Science Centre

1987. 3rd Kuwait International Medical Sciences Conference: Infectious Diseases in Developing Countries.

1125	**302**	25 f. multicoloured . . .	75	25
1126		150 f. multicoloured . .	3·00	1·50

303 Campaign Emblem

1987. World Health Day. Child Immunization Campaign.

1127	**303**	25 f. multicoloured . . .	60	25
1128		50 f. multicoloured . . .	1·00	50
1129		150 f. multicoloured . .	2·40	1·50

304 Jerusalem

1987. "Jerusalem is an Arab City".

1130	**304**	25 f. multicoloured . . .	60	15
1131		50 f. multicoloured . . .	1·00	40
1132		150 f. multicoloured . .	2·40	1·25

305 Pilgrims in Miqat Wadi Mihrim

1987. Pilgrimage to Mecca.

1133	**305**	25 f. multicoloured . . .	50	15
1134		50 f. multicoloured . . .	75	40
1135		150 f. multicoloured . .	2·25	1·00

306 Emblem

308 Project Monument and Site Plan

307 Buoy and Container Ship

1987. Arab Telecommunications Day.

1136	**306**	25 f. multicoloured . . .	50	15
1137		50 f. multicoloured . . .	75	40
1138		150 f. multicoloured . .	2·25	1·00

1987. World Maritime Day.

1139	**307**	25 f. multicoloured . . .	50	20
1140		50 f. multicoloured . . .	75	40
1141		150 f. multicoloured . .	2·25	1·00

1987. Al-Qurain Housing Project.
1142 **308** 25 f. multicoloured . . . 50 15
1143 50 f. multicoloured . . . 75 40
1144 150 f. multicoloured . . 2·25 1·00

309 Unloading Container Ship

1987. 10th Anniv of Ports Public Authority.
1145 **309** 25 f. multicoloured . . . 20 10
1146 50 f. multicoloured . . . 55 25
1147 150 f. multicoloured . . 2·00 85

310 Symbolic Design **311** Emblem

1987. International Day of Solidarity with Palestinian People.
1148 **310** 25 f. multicoloured . . . 20 10
1149 50 f. multicoloured . . . 60 25
1150 150 f. multicoloured . . 2·00 85

1988. 25th Anniv of Women's Cultural and Social Society.
1151 **311** 25 f. multicoloured . . . 20 10
1152 50 f. multicoloured . . . 60 25
1153 150 f. multicoloured . . 2·00 85

312 Emblem **313** Hands holding W.H.O. Emblem

1988. 27th National Day.
1154 **312** 25 f. multicoloured . . . 20 10
1155 50 f. multicoloured . . . 60 25
1156 150 f. multicoloured . . 2·00 85

1988. World Health Day. 40th Anniv of W.H.O.
1157 **313** 25 f. multicoloured . . . 20 10
1158 50 f. multicoloured . . . 60 25
1159 150 f. multicoloured . . 2·00 85

314 Regional Maritime Protection Organization Symbol **315** Society Emblem

1988. 10th Anniv of Kuwait Regional Convention for Protection of Marine Environment.
1160 **314** 35 f. ultram, blue & brn . 25 15
1161 50 f. ultram, blue & grn . 60 25
1162 150 f. ultram, blue & pur 2·00 85

1988. 25th Anniv of Kuwait Teachers' Society.
1163 **315** 25 f. multicoloured . . . 20 10
1164 50 f. multicoloured . . . 60 25
1165 150 f. multicoloured . . 2·00 75

316 Pilgrims at al-Sail al-Kabir Miqat

1988. Pilgrimage to Mecca.
1166 **316** 25 f. multicoloured . . . 20 10
1167 50 f. multicoloured . . . 60 25
1168 150 f. multicoloured . . 2·00 75

317 Gang of Youths lying in wait for Soldiers **318** Ring of Dwellings around Key

1988. Palestinian "Intifida" Movement.
1169 **317** 50 f. multicoloured . . . 75 40
1170 150 f. multicoloured . . 3·00 1·50

1988. Arab Housing Day.
1171 **318** 50 f. multicoloured . . . 50 30
1172 100 f. multicoloured . . 1·00 60
1173 150 f. multicoloured . . 2·00 75

319 Map of Palestine highlighted on Globe **320** Volunteers embracing Globe

1988. International Day of Solidarity with Palestinian People.
1174 **319** 50 f. multicoloured . . . 40 25
1175 100 f. multicoloured . . 1·00 60
1176 150 f. multicoloured . . 2·00 75

1988. International Volunteer Day.
1177 **320** 50 f. multicoloured . . . 50 30
1178 100 f. multicoloured . . 1·00 60
1179 150 f. multicoloured . . 2·00 75

321 Conference, Kuwait Society of Engineers and Arab Engineers Union Emblems

1989. 18th Arab Engineering Conference.
1180 **321** 50 f. multicoloured . . . 50 30
1181 100 f. multicoloured . . 1·00 60
1182 150 f. multicoloured . . 2·00 75

322 Flags as Figures supporting Map **323** Conference Emblem

1989. 28th National Day.
1183 **322** 50 f. multicoloured . . . 50 30
1184 100 f. multicoloured . . 1·00 60
1185 150 f. multicoloured . . 2·00 75

1989. 5th Kuwait Dental Association Conference.
1186 **323** 50 f. multicoloured . . . 50 30
1187 150 f. multicoloured . . 1·00 70
1188 250 f. multicoloured . . 1·75 1·10

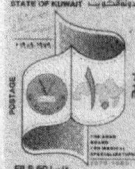

324 Emblems **325** Anniversary Emblem

1989. World Health Day.
1189 **324** 50 f. multicoloured . . . 50 30
1190 150 f. multicoloured . . 1·00 70
1191 250 f. multicoloured . . 1·75 1·10

1989. 10th Anniv of Arab Board for Medical Specializations.
1192 **325** 50 f. multicoloured . . . 50 20
1193 150 f. multicoloured . . 1·00 55
1194 250 f. multicoloured . . 1·75 85

326 Torch, Pen and Flag

1989. 25th Anniv of Kuwait Journalists' Association.
1195 **326** 50 f. multicoloured . . . 40 35
1196 200 f. multicoloured . . . 1·50 1·00
1197 250 f. multicoloured . . . 2·00 1·40

327 Attan'eem Miqat, Mecca

1989. Pilgrimage to Mecca.
1198 **327** 50 f. multicoloured . . . 85 55
1199 150 f. multicoloured . . . 2·75 1·75
1200 200 f. multicoloured . . . 3·50 2·25

328 Al-Qurain Housing Project **329** Tree

1989. Arab Housing Day.
1201 **328** 25 f. multicoloured . . . 45 30
1202 50 f. multicoloured . . . 85 55
1203 150 f. multicoloured . . . 2·75 1·75

1989. Greenery Week.
1204 **329** 25 f. multicoloured . . . 45 30
1205 50 f. multicoloured . . . 85 55
1206 150 f. multicoloured . . . 2·75 1·75

330 Dhow **331** Emblem and Map

1989. Coil Stamps.
1207 **330** 50 f. gold and green . . . 1·25 85
1208 100 f. gold and blue . . . 2·50 1·75
1209 200 f. gold and red . . . 5·00 3·50

1989. 5th Anniv of Gulf Investment Corporation.
1210 **331** 25 f. multicoloured . . . 45 30
1211 50 f. multicoloured . . . 85 55
1212 150 f. multicoloured . . . 2·75 1·75

332 Emblem **333** Zakat House

1989. 1st Anniv of "Declaration of Palestine State".
1213 **332** 50 f. multicoloured . . . 85 55
1214 150 f. multicoloured . . . 2·75 1·75
1215 200 f. multicoloured . . . 3·50 2·25

1989. Orphanage Sponsorship Project.
1216 **333** 25 f. multicoloured . . . 45 30
1217 50 f. multicoloured . . . 85 55
1218 150 f. multicoloured . . . 2·75 1·75

334 Shaikh Sabah al-Salem as-Sabah (former Chief) and Officers **335** Globe and Dove

1989. 50th Anniv (1988) of Kuwait Police.
1219 **334** 25 f. multicoloured . . . 45 30
1220 50 f. multicoloured . . . 85 55
1221 150 f. multicoloured . . 2·75 1·75

1990. 29th National Day.
1222 **335** 25 f. multicoloured . . . 45 30
1223 50 f. multicoloured . . . 85 55
1224 150 f. multicoloured . . 2·75 1·75

336 Earth, Clouds and Weather Balloon

1990. World Meteorological Day.
1225 **336** 50 f. multicoloured . . . 85 55
1226 100 f. multicoloured . . 1·75 1·10
1227 150 f. multicoloured . . 2·75 1·75

337 Map bordered by National Flag **338** Lanner Falcon

1990. World Health Day.
1228 **337** 50 f. multicoloured . . . 85 55
1229 100 f. multicoloured . . 1·75 1·10
1230 150 f. multicoloured . . 2·75 1·75

1990.
1231 **338** 50 f. gold and blue . . . 85 55
1232 100 f. gold and red . . 1·75 1·10
1233 150 f. gold and green . . 2·75 1·75

339 Soldiers carrying Kuwait Flag **340** Dove and Map

1991. Liberation (1st issue).
1234 **339** 25 f. multicoloured . . . 40 25
1235 50 f. multicoloured . . . 80 50
1236 150 f. multicoloured . . 2·40 1·60
See also Nos. 1243/84.

1991. Peace.
1237 **340** 50 f. multicoloured . . . 80 50
1238 100 f. multicoloured . . 1·60 1·00
1239 150 f. multicoloured . . 2·40 1·60

341 Flag, Map, Kuwait Towers and Globe **342** Sweden

1991. Reconstruction.
1240 **341** 50 f. multicoloured . . . 80 50
1241 150 f. multicoloured . . 2·40 1·60
1242 200 f. multicoloured . . 3·00 1·90

1991. Liberation (2nd issue). Each showing a dove coloured with the flag of one of the assisting nations. Multicoloured.
1243 50 f. Type **342** 45 30
1244 50 f. Soviet Union 45 30
1245 50 f. United States of America 45 30

1246 50 f. Kuwait 45 30
1247 50 f. Saudi Arabia 45 30
1248 50 f. United Nations 45 30
1249 50 f. Singapore 45 30
1250 50 f. France 45 30
1251 50 f. Italy 45 30
1252 50 f. Egypt 45 30
1253 50 f. Morocco 45 30
1254 50 f. United Kingdom 45 30
1255 50 f. Philippines 45 30
1256 50 f. United Arab Emirates 45 30
1257 50 f. Syria 45 30
1258 50 f. Poland 45 30
1259 50 f. Australia 45 30
1260 50 f. Japan 45 30
1261 50 f. Hungary 45 30
1262 50 f. Netherlands 45 30
1263 50 f. Denmark 45 30
1264 50 f. New Zealand 45 30
1265 50 f. Czechoslovakia 45 30
1266 50 f. Bahrain 45 30
1267 50 f. Honduras 45 30
1268 50 f. Turkey 45 30
1269 50 f. Greece 45 30
1270 50 f. Oman 45 30
1271 50 f. Qatar 45 30
1272 50 f. Belgium 45 30
1273 50 f. Sierra Leone 45 30
1274 50 f. Argentina 45 30
1275 50 f. Norway 45 30
1276 50 f. Canada 45 30
1277 50 f. Germany 45 30
1278 50 f. South Korea 45 30
1279 50 f. Bangladesh 45 30
1280 50 f. Bulgaria 45 30
1281 50 f. Senegal 45 30
1282 50 f. Spain 45 30
1283 50 f. Niger 45 30
1284 50 f. Pakistan 45 30

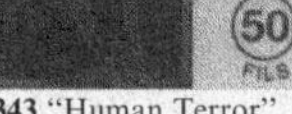

343 "Human Terror" **344** Emblem

1991. 1st Anniv of Iraqi Invasion. Multicoloured.
1286 50 f. Type **343** 80 50
1287 100 f. "Invasion of Kuwait" 1·60 1·00
1288 150 f. "Environmental Terrorism" (horiz) 2·40 1·60

1991. 30th Anniv (1990) of Organization of Petroleum Exporting Countries.
1290 **344** 25 f. multicoloured 45 30
1291 50 f. multicoloured 80 50
1292 150 f. multicoloured 2·40 1·60

345 National Flag, Arabic Script and Broken Chains

1991. Campaign to Free Kuwaiti Prisoners of War. Each black and yellow.
1293 50 f. Type **345** 70 45
1294 150 f. Prison bars, "Don't Forget Our P.O.W.'s" and broken chains 2·00 1·25

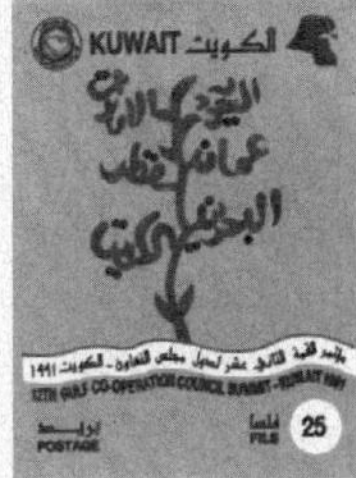

346 Names of Member Countries forming Tree

1991. 12th Gulf Co-operation Council Summit Conference, Kuwait. Multicoloured.
1296 25 f. Type **346** 35 25
1297 150 f. National flags as leaves of plant 2·00 1·25

347 I.L.Y. Emblem

1992. International Literacy Year (1990).
1299 **347** 50 f. blue and brown 70 45
1300 100 f. blue and yellow 1·40 90
1301 150 f. blue and mauve 2·00 1·25

348 Doves and National Flag

1992. 31st National Day (1302) and 1st Anniv of Liberation (1303).
1302 **348** 50 f. black, green and red 40 25
1303 – 150 f. multicoloured 1·25 80
DESIGN: 150 f. Assisting nations' flags.

349 Dromedaries

1992.
1305 **349** 25 f. multicoloured 15 10
1306 50 f. multicoloured 30 20
1307 150 f. multicoloured 95 60
1308 200 f. multicoloured 1·25 80
1309 350 f. multicoloured 2·10 1·25

350 Paddle, La Giralda Tower and Kuwaiti Pavilion

1992. "Expo '92" World's Fair, Seville. Multicoloured.
1310 50 f. Type **350** 30 20
1311 50 f. Dhows 30 20
1312 50 f. Dhow 30 20
1313 50 f. Kuwaiti Pavilion and dhow 30 20
1314 150 f. Kuwaiti Pavilion on Spanish flag 90 60
1315 150 f. Paddle and La Giralda Tower on hoist of Kuwaiti flag 90 60
1316 150 f. Paddle, La Giralda Tower and dhow on Spanish flag 90 60
1317 150 f. Kuwaiti Pavilion and dhow on fly of Kuwaiti flag 90 60

351 Snake around Top of Palm Tree

1992. 2nd U.N. Conference on Environment and Development, Rio de Janeiro, Brazil. Mult.
1319 150 f. Type **351** 1·25 80
1320 150 f. Snakes, Kuwait colours on map and palm tree 1·25 80
1321 150 f. Skull, snake around tree trunk and dead fish 1·25 80
1322 150 f. Snake around camel's neck and bird 1·25 80
Nos. 1319/22 were issued together, se-tenant, forming a composite design of the painting "Environmental Terrorism".

352 Palace of Justice

1992.
1324 **352** 25 f. multicoloured 20 10
1325 50 f. multicoloured 40 25
1326 100 f. multicoloured 80 50
1327 150 f. multicoloured 1·25 80
1328 250 f. multicoloured 2·00 1·25

353 Running and Handball

1992. Olympic Games, Barcelona. Multicoloured.
1329 50 f. Swimming and football 65 40
1330 100 f. Type **353** 1·25 80
1331 150 f. Judo and show jumping 1·90 1·25
Each value also portrays the Olympic flag and Prince Fahed al-Ahmad al-Sabah, President of several sports organizations, who was killed in the Iraqi invasion.

354 Tanks, Demonstrators with Placards and Executed Civilians

1992. 2nd Anniv of Iraqi Invasion. Children's Drawings. Multicoloured.
1332 50 f. Type **354** 30 20
1333 50 f. Soldiers rounding up civilians 30 20
1334 50 f. Military vehicles and Kuwait Towers 30 20
1335 50 f. Battle scene 30 20
1336 150 f. Tanks, bleeding eye and soldiers 95 60
1337 150 f. Battle scene around fortifications 95 60
1338 150 f. Liberation 95 60
1339 150 f. Soldiers and military vehicles 95 60

355 Burning Well

1992. 1st Anniv of Extinguishing of Oil Well Fires. Multicoloured.
1341 25 f. Type **355** 15 10
1342 50 f. Spraying dampener on fire 30 20
1343 150 f. Close-up of spraying 95 60
1344 250 f. Extinguished well (horiz) 1·60 1·00

356 Kuwait Towers **357** Laying Bricks to form "32"

1993.
1345 **356** 25 f. multicoloured 15 10
1346 100 f. multicoloured 70 45
1347 150 f. multicoloured 95 60

1993. 32nd National Day.
1348 **357** 25 f. multicoloured 15 10
1349 50 f. multicoloured 30 20
1350 150 f. multicoloured 95 60

358 Symbols of Oppression and Freedom **359** Hands Signing

1993. 2nd Anniv of Liberation.
1351 **358** 25 f. multicoloured 15 10
1352 50 f. multicoloured 30 20
1353 150 f. multicoloured 95 60

1993. Deaf Child Week.
1354 **359** 25 f. multicoloured 15 10
1355 50 f. multicoloured 30 20
1356 150 f. multicoloured 95 60
1357 350 f. multicoloured 2·10 1·40

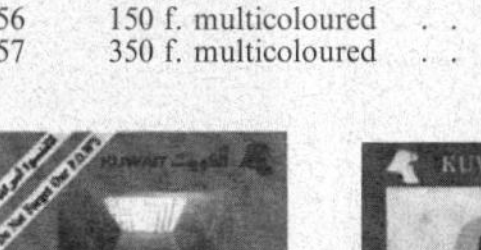

360 Chained Prisoner **361** Hand scratching Map

1993. Campaign to Free Kuwaiti Prisoners of War. Multicoloured.
1358 50 f. Type **360** 35 20
1359 150 f. Chained hand, hoopoe and barred window (horiz) 1·10 70
1360 200 f. Screaming face on wall of empty cell 1·50 1·00

1993. 3rd Anniv of Iraqi Invasion.
1361 **361** 50 f. multicoloured 30 20
1362 150 f. multicoloured 85 55

362 Emblem

1993. 40th Anniv of Kuwait Air Force.
1363 **362** 50 f. multicoloured 40 25
1364 150 f. multicoloured 1·10 70

363 Flower and Dove **364** Anniversary Emblem

1994. 33rd National Day.
1365 **363** 25 f. multicoloured 15 10
1366 50 f. multicoloured 30 20
1367 150 f. multicoloured 90 60

1994. 3rd Anniv of Liberation.
1368 **364** 25 f. multicoloured 15 10
1369 50 f. multicoloured 30 20
1370 150 f. multicoloured 90 60

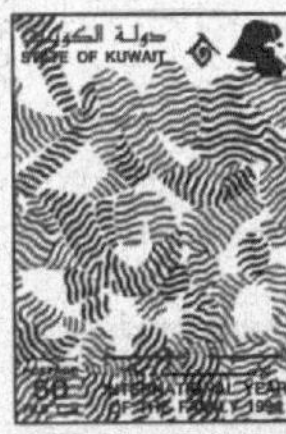

365 Anniversary Emblem **366** Stylized Emblems

1994. 25th Anniv of Central Bank of Kuwait.
1371 **365** 25 f. multicoloured 15 10
1372 50 f. multicoloured 30 20
1373 150 f. multicoloured 90 60

1994. Int Year of the Family. Mult.
1374 50 f. Type **366** 30 20
1375 150 f. Three I.Y.F. emblems 90 60
1376 200 f. Globe, emblem and spheres (horiz) 1·00 65

367 Emblem on Sky **368** Fingerprint in Water

1994. 20th Anniv of Industrial Bank of Kuwait.
1377 **367** 50 f. multicoloured 25 10
1378 100 f. gold, blue and black 55 35
1379 150 f. multicoloured 80 50

1994. Martyrs' Day. Multicoloured.
1380 50 f. Type **368** 30 10
1381 100 f. Fingerprint in sand 60 40
1382 150 f. Fingerprint in national colours 90 60
1383 250 f. Fingerprint in clouds over Kuwait Towers 1·50 1·00

369 Anniversary Emblem

370 Free and Imprisoned Doves

1994. 75th Anniv of I.L.O.

No.	Type	Description	Mint	Used
1385	369	50 f. multicoloured	25	10
1386		150 f. multicoloured	80	50
1387		350 f. gold, blue and black	1·75	1·10

1994. 4th Anniv of Iraqi Invasion.

No.	Type	Description	Mint	Used
1388	370	50 f. multicoloured	25	10
1389		150 f. multicoloured	80	50
1390		350 f. multicoloured	1·75	1·10

371 Emblem

372 Anniversary Emblem

1994. Kuwait Ports Authority.

No.	Type	Description	Mint	Used
1391	371	50 f. multicoloured	25	10
1392		150 f. multicoloured	80	50
1393		350 f. multicoloured	1·75	1·10

1994. 20th Anniv of Kuwait Science Club.

No.	Type	Description	Mint	Used
1394	372	50 f. multicoloured	25	10
1395		100 f. multicoloured	55	35
1396		150 f. multicoloured	75	50

373 Map and Building

374 I.C.A.O. and Kuwait International Airport Emblems

1994. Inauguration of Arab Towns Organization Permanent Headquarters. Multicoloured.

No.	Type	Description	Mint	Used
1397		50 f. Type **373**	25	10
1398		100 f. Close-up of arched facade	55	35
1399		150 f. Door	75	50

1994. 50th Anniv of I.C.A.O. Mult.

No.	Type	Description	Mint	Used
1400		100 f. Type **374**	55	35
1401		150 f. Emblems and control tower	85	55
1402		350 f. Airplane and "50 years"	1·90	1·25

375 Anniversary Emblem

376 Family

1994. 40th Anniv of Kuwait Airways.

No.	Type	Description	Mint	Used
1403	375	50 f. multicoloured	20	10
1404		100 f. multicoloured	50	35
1405		150 f. multicoloured	75	50

1995. Population Census.

No.	Type	Description	Mint	Used
1406	376	50 f. multicoloured	25	10
1407		100 f. multicoloured	45	30
1408		150 f. multicoloured	70	45

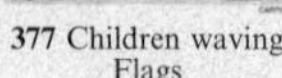

377 Children waving Flags

378 Falcon dragging Kuwaiti Flag from Snake's Grip

1995. 34th National Day.

No.	Type	Description	Mint	Used
1409	377	25 f. multicoloured	10	10
1410		50 f. multicoloured	25	10
1411		150 f. multicoloured	70	45

1995. 4th Anniv of Liberation.

No.	Type	Description	Mint	Used
1412	378	25 f. multicoloured	10	10
1413		50 f. multicoloured	25	10
1414		150 f. multicoloured	70	45

379 Conference Venue

1995. International Medical Conference. Mult.

No.	Type	Description	Mint	Used
1415		50 f. Type **379**	25	10
1416		100 f. Lecture	45	30
1417		150 f. Emblem on map of Kuwait in national colours	70	45

380 Anniversary Emblem and Flags

381 Emblem

1995. 50th Anniv of Arab League. Multicoloured.

No.	Type	Description	Mint	Used
1418		50 f. Type **380**	25	10
1419		100 f. Kuwaiti and League flags and League emblem (horiz)	45	30
1420		150 f. Handshake and League emblem	70	45

1995. World Health Day. "A World without Polio".

No.	Type	Description	Mint	Used
1421	381	50 f. multicoloured	25	10
1422		150 f. multicoloured	70	45
1423		200 f. multicoloured	90	60

382 "100"

383 Olive Branch falling from Wounded Dove's Beak

1995. Centenary of Volleyball.

No.	Type	Description	Mint	Used
1424	382	50 f. multicoloured	25	10
1425		100 f. multicoloured	45	30
1426		150 f. multicoloured	70	45

1995. 5th Anniv of Iraqi Invasion.

No.	Type	Description	Mint	Used
1427	383	50 f. multicoloured	20	10
1428		100 f. multicoloured	40	25
1429		150 f. multicoloured	60	40

384 Doves and Anniversary Emblem

385 Farmer with Animals

1995. 50th Anniv of U.N.O.

No.	Type	Description	Mint	Used
1430	384	25 f. multicoloured	10	10
1431		50 f. multicoloured	20	10
1432		150 f. multicoloured	60	40

1995. 50th Anniv of F.A.O. Multicoloured.

No.	Type	Description	Mint	Used
1433		50 f. Type **385**	20	10
1434		100 f. Fish market	40	25
1435		150 f. Agriculture	60	40

386 Emblems within Ruler

387 "Onobrychis ptolemaica"

1995. World Standards Day. Multicoloured.

No.	Type	Description	Mint	Used
1437		50 f. Type **386**	20	10
1438		100 f. Emblems and aspects of industry (48 × 27 mm)	40	25
1439		150 f. As No. 1438	60	40

1995. Flowers. Multicoloured.

No.	Type	Description	Mint	Used
1440		5 f. Type **387**	10	10
1441		15 f. "Convolvulus oxyphyllus"	10	10
1442		25 f. Corn poppy	10	10
1443		50 f. "Moltkiopsis ciliata"	20	10
1444		150 f. "Senecio desfontainei"	60	40

388 Coins forming Map of Kuwait

389 Boy Scout in Watchtower

1996. Money Show.

No.	Type	Description	Mint	Used
1445	388	25 f. multicoloured	10	10
1446		100 f. multicoloured	40	25
1447		150 f. multicoloured	60	40

1996. 60th Anniv of Scout Movement in Kuwait. Multicoloured.

No.	Type	Description	Mint	Used
1448		50 f. Type **389**	20	10
1449		100 f. Scout drawing water from well	40	25
1450		150 f. Scouts planting sapling	60	40

390 Hands supporting Ear of Wheat

391 Dove trailing National Colours, Falcon and City

1996.

No.	Type	Description	Mint	Used
1451	390	50 f. multicoloured	20	10
1452		100 f. multicoloured	40	25
1453		150 f. multicoloured	60	40

1996. 35th National Day.

No.	Type	Description	Mint	Used
1454	391	25 f. multicoloured	10	10
1455		50 f. multicoloured	20	10
1456		150 f. multicoloured	60	40

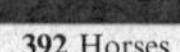

392 Horses

393 View through Gateway

1996. 5th Anniv of Liberation.

No.	Type	Description	Mint	Used
1457	392	25 f. multicoloured	10	10
1458		50 f. multicoloured	20	10
1459		150 f. multicoloured	60	40

1996. Arab City Day.

No.	Type	Description	Mint	Used
1460	393	50 f. multicoloured	20	10
1461		100 f. multicoloured	40	25
1462		150 f. multicoloured	60	40

394 Emblem

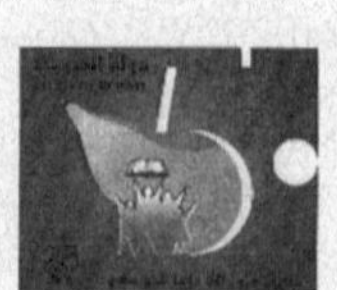

395 Figures holding Open Book within Bird

1996. 7th Kuwait Dental Association Conference.

No.	Type	Description	Mint	Used
1463	394	25 f. multicoloured	10	10
1464		50 f. multicoloured	20	10
1465		150 f. multicoloured	60	40

1996. 50th Anniv of U.N.E.S.C.O.

No.	Type	Description	Mint	Used
1466	395	25 f. multicoloured	10	10
1467		100 f. multicoloured	40	25
1468		150 f. multicoloured	60	40

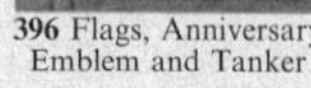

396 Flags, Anniversary Emblem and Tanker

397 Shaikh Mubarak al-Sabah

1996. 50th Anniv of First Oil Shipment from Kuwait.

No.	Type	Description	Mint	Used
1469	396	25 f. multicoloured	10	10
1470		100 f. multicoloured	40	25
1471		150 f. multicoloured	60	40

1996. Centenary of Accession as Emir of Shaikh Mubarak al-Sabah. Multicoloured.

No.	Type	Description	Mint	Used
1472		25 f. Type **397**	10	10
1473		50 f. Shaikh Mubarak al-Sabah and ribbons	20	10
1474		150 f. Type **397**	60	40

398 Rifle Shooting

1996. Olympic Games, Atlanta. Multicoloured.

No.	Type	Description	Mint	Used
1475		25 f. Type **398**	10	10
1476		50 f. Running	20	10
1477		100 f. Weightlifting	40	25
1478		150 f. Fencing	60	40

POSTAGE DUE STAMPS

D 34 D 51

1963.

No.	Type	Description	Mint	Used
D199	D 34	1 f. brown and black	10	20
D200		2 f. lilac and black	15	25
D201		5 f. blue and black	25	20
D202		8 f. green and black	50	35
D203		10 f. yellow and black	70	65
D204		25 f. red and black	1·60	2·00

The above stamps were not sold to the public unused until 1st July, 1964.

1965.

No.	Type	Description	Mint	Used
D276	D 51	4 f. pink and yellow	15	20
D277		15 f. red and blue	50	35
D278		40 f. blue and green	1·00	75
D279		50 f. green and mauve	1·40	1·00
D280		100 f. blue and yellow	2·50	2·00

KYRGYZSTAN Pt. 10

Formerly Kirghizia, a constituent republic of the Soviet Union, Kyrgyzstan became independent in 1991. Its capital Frunze reverted to its previous name of Bishkek.

1992. 100 kopeks = 1 rouble.
1993. 100 tyin = 1 som.

1 Sary-Chelek Nature Reserve — **2** Golden Eagle

1992.

1	**1**	15 k. multicoloured	50	50

1992.

2	**2**	50 k. multicoloured	20	20

3 "Cattle at Issyk-kule" (G. A. Aitiev)

1992.

3	**3**	1 r. multicoloured	50	50

4 Carpet and Samovar

1992.

4	**4**	1 r. 50 multicoloured	70	70

5 Cave Paintings

1993. National Monuments. Multicoloured.

5	10 k. Type **5**	10	10
6	50 k. 11th-century tower, Burana (vert)	10	10
7	1 r. + 25 k. Tomb, Talas (vert)	10	10
8	2 r. + 50 k. Mausoleum, Uzgen	15	15
9	3 r. Yurt	25	25
10	5 r. + 50 k. Statue of Manas, Bishkek	45	45
11	9 r. Cultural complex, Bishkek	85	85

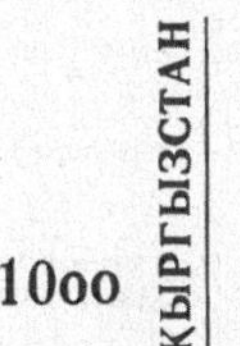

(6)

20 т. КЫРГЫЗСТАН

(7)

1993. Nos. 5940, 6073 and 4671 of Russia surch as T **6**.

13	10 k. on 1 k. brown	60	60
14	20 k. on 2 k. brown	1·25	1·25
15	30 k. on 3 k. red	1·75	1·75

1993. Nos. 4672/3 of Russia surch as T **7**.

16	20 t. on 4 k. red	40	40
17	30 t. on 6 k. blue	60	60

8 Map

1993. 2nd Anniv of Independence (18) and 1st Anniv of Admission to United Nations (19). Multicoloured.

18	50 t. Type **8**	1·00	1·00
19	60 t. U.N. emblem, national flag and Government Palace, Bishkek (vert)	1·40	1·40

9 Komuz

1993. Music.

20	**9**	30 t. multicoloured	25	25

10 Dog — **12** Mauve Flowers

11 Adult and Cub

1994. New Year. Year of the Dog.

22	**10**	60 t. multicoloured	55	55

1994. The Snow Leopard. Multicoloured.

23	10 t. Type **11**	10	10
24	20 t. Lying curled-up	10	10
25	30 t. Sitting	10	10
26	40 t. Head	10	10

1994. Flowers. Multicoloured.

27	1 t. Type **12**	10	10
28	3 t. Daisies (horiz)	10	10
29	10 t. Tulip	10	10
30	16 t. Narcissi	10	10
31	20 t. Deep pink flower	15	15
32	30 t. White flower	20	20
33	40 t. Yellow flower	25	25

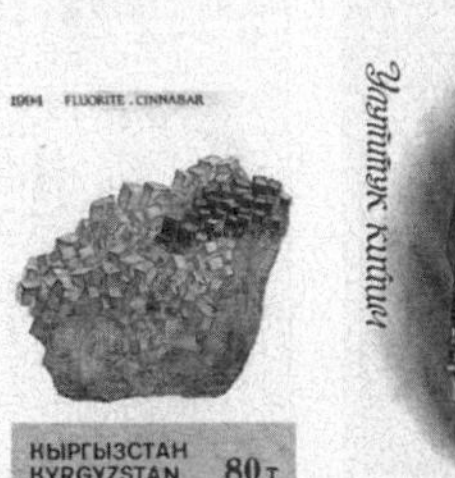

13 Fluorite — **15** Woman with Rug

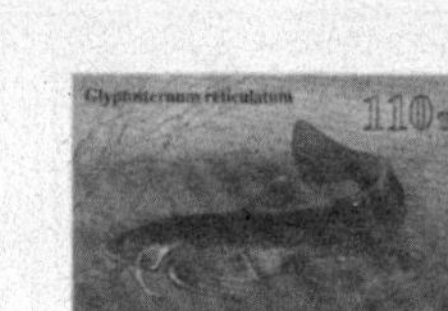

14 Turkestan Catfish

1994. Minerals. Multicoloured.

36	80 t. Type **13**	10	10
37	90 t. Calcite	10	10
38	100 t. Getchellite	15	15
39	110 t. Barite	20	20
40	120 t. Auripigment	25	25
41	140 t. Antimonite	30	30

1994. Fishes. Multicoloured.

43	110 t. Type **14**	10	10
44	120 t. Schmidt's dace	25	25
45	130 t. Scaleless osman	25	25
46	140 t. Spotted stone loach	30	30

1995. Traditional Costumes. Multicoloured.

48	50 t. Type **15**	10	10
49	50 t. Musician	10	10
50	100 t. Falconer	15	15
51	100 t. Woman with long plaits	15	15

16 Butterfly, Traffic Lights and Emblem — **17** Bear

1995. Road Safety Week.

52	**16**	200 t. multicoloured	30	30

1995. Animals. Multicoloured.

53	110 t. Type **17**	10	10
54	120 t. Snow leopard (horiz)	15	15
55	130 t. Eagle	20	20
56	140 t. Rodent (horiz)	25	25
57	150 t. Eagle (different) (horiz)	25	25
58	160 t. Vulture	30	30
59	190 t. Fox (horiz)	35	35

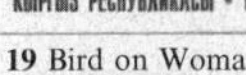

19 Bird on Woman's Hand — **20** Osprey

1995. Millenary of "Manas" (epic poem). Each blue and gold.

62	10 t. + 5 t. Type **19**	10	10
63	20 t. + 10 t. Hoopoe on youth's wrist	10	10
64	30 t. + 10 t. Women around baby	10	10
65	30 t. + 10 t. Woman carrying spear and leading horse	10	10
66	40 t. + 15 t. Warrior astride dead dragon	15	15
67	50 t. + 15 t. Mounted warrior with battle-axe	20	20
68	50 t. + 15 t. Man wearing tall hat on horseback	20	20
69	50 t. + 15 t. Mounted warrior with sword	20	20

1995. Birds. Multicoloured.

71	10 t. Type **20**	10	10
72	50 t. Tawny eagle	10	10
73	100 t. Himalayan griffon	10	10
74	140 t. Saker falcon	15	15
75	150 t. Short-toed eagle	15	15
76	200 t. Lammergeier	20	20
77	300 t. Golden eagle	30	30

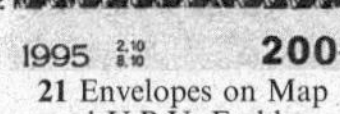

21 Envelopes on Map and U.P.U. Emblem — **22** State Arms

1995. Postage Stamp Week.

79	**21**	200 t. multicoloured	45	45

1995.

80	**22**	20 t. violet	10	10
81		50 t. blue	10	10
82		100 t. brown	25	25
86		500 t. green	1·10	1·10

23 Mare and Foal Galloping

1995. Horses. Multicoloured.

89	10 t. Type **23**	20	20
90	50 t. Palamino mare and foal (vert)	20	20
91	100 t. Brown mare and foal (vert)	20	20
92	140 t. Chestnut mare and foal (vert)	30	30
93	150 t. Chestnut mare and foal	30	30
94	200 t. Grey mare and foal	40	40
95	300 t. Pair of foals	60	60

25 River Nile, Egypt

1995. Natural Wonders of the World. Multicoloured.

98	10 t. Type **25**	10	10
99	50 t. Mt. Kilimanjaro, Tanzania	15	15
100	100 t. Sahara Desert, Algeria	20	20
101	140 t. Amazon River, Brazil (vert)	35	35
102	150 t. Grand Canyon, U.S.A. (vert)	40	40
103	200 t. Victoria Falls, Zimbabwe (vert)	45	45
104	350 t. Mt. Everest, Nepal	90	90
105	400 t. Niagara Falls, Canada	2·00	1·00

No. 98 is wrongly inscribed "Egipt".

26 Steppe Ribbon Snake

1996. Reptiles. Multicoloured.

107	20 t. Type **26**	10	10
108	50 t. Fat-tailed panther gecko	15	15
109	50 t. Tessellated water snake	15	15
110	100 t. Central Asian viper	20	20
111	150 t. Arguta	40	40
112	200 t. Dione snake	45	45
113	250 t. "Asyblepharus sp." (wrongly inscr "Asymblepharus")	50	50

LA AGUERA — Pt. 9

An administrative district of Spanish Sahara whose stamps it later used.

1920. Rio de Oro stamps optd **LA AGUERA.**

1	15	1 c. green	1·60	1·60
2		2 c. brown	1·60	1·60
3		5 c. green	1·60	1·60
4		10 c. red	1·60	1·60
5		15 c. yellow	1·60	1·60
6		20 c. violet	1·60	1·60
7		25 c. blue	1·60	1·60
8		30 c. brown	1·60	1·60
9		40 c. pink	1·60	1·60
10		50 c. blue	5·25	5·25
11		1 p. red	9·50	9·50
12		4 p. purple	30·00	30·00
13		10 p. orange	60·00	60·00

2

1923.

14	2	1 c. blue	70	70
15		2 c. green	70	70
16		5 c. green	70	70
17		10 c. red	70	70
18		15 c. brown	70	70
19		20 c. yellow	70	70
20		25 c. blue	70	70
21		30 c. brown	70	70
22		40 c. red	90	90
23		50 c. purple	3·25	3·25
24		1 p. mauve	6·25	6·25
25		4 p. violet	16·00	16·00
26		10 p. orange	25·00	25·00

LAOS — Pt. 21

Previously part of French Indo-China, the Kingdom of Laos was proclaimed in 1947. In 1949 it became an Associated State within the French Union and in 1953 it became fully independent within the Union.

Laos left the French Union in 1956. In 1976 it became a Republic.

1951. 100 cents = 1 piastre.
1955. 100 cents = 1 kip.

1 River Mekong 2 King Sisavang Vong

1951.

1	1	10 c. green and turquoise	20	20
2		20 c. red and purple	20	30
3		30 c. blue and indigo	1·00	85
4	–	50 c. brown and deep brown	50	35
5	–	60 c. orange and red	45	50
6	–	70 c. turquoise and blue	45	50
7	–	1 p. violet and deep violet	45	50
8	2	1 p. 50 purple and brown	85	65
9	–	2 p. green and turquoise	16·00	4·00
10	–	3 p. red and purple	90	75
11	–	5 p. blue and indigo	1.25	80
12	–	10 p. purple and brown	2·75	1·25

DESIGNS—As Type **1**: 50 c. to 70 c. Luang Prabang; 1 p. and 2 p. to 10 p. Vientiane.

3 Laotian Woman

4 Laotian Woman Weaving

1952.

13	3	30 c. violet and blue (post)	40	35
14		80 c. turquoise and green	40	35
15		1 p. 10 red and crimson	90	35
16		1 p. 90 blue and indigo	1·40	80
17		3 p. deep brown and brown	1·40	80
18	–	3 p. 30 violet and deep violet (air)	85	60
19	4	10 p. green and blue	1·90	1·25
20		20 p. red and crimson	3·25	2·00
21		30 p. brown and black	4·75	3·50

DESIGN—As Type **4**: 3 p. 30, Vat Pra Keo shrine.

5 King Sisavang Vong and U.P.U. Monument

1952. 1st Anniv of Admission to U.P.U.

22	5	80 c. violet, bl & ind (postage)	75	85
23		1 p. brown, red and lake	75	75
24		1 p. 20 blue and violet	75	85
25		1 p. 50 brown, emerald & grn	75	85
26		1 p. 90 turquoise and sepia	1·10	1·25
27		25 p. indigo and blue (air)	4·25	4·75
28		50 p. sepia, purple and brown	5·00	5·50

6 Girl carrying her Brother 7 Court of Love

1953. Red Cross Fund. Cross in red.

29	6	1 p. 50 + 1 p. purple & blue	2·75	2·75
30		3 p. + 1 p. 50 red and green	2·50	2·75
31		3 p. 90 + 2 p. 50 pur & brn	2·50	2·75

1953.

32	7	4 p. 50 turquoise and blue	1·00	85
33		6 p. brown and slate	1·10	85

8 Buddha

1953. Air. Statues of Buddha.

34	–	4 p. green	95	85
35	–	6 p. 50 green	1·40	1·10
36	–	9 p. green	2·00	1·50
37	8	11 p. 50 orange, brown & red	2·75	2·50
38	–	40 p. purple	6·50	2·50
39	–	100 p. green	13·50	10·50

DESIGNS—HORIZ: 4 p. Reclining. VERT: 6 p. 50, Seated; 9 p. Standing (full-face); 40 p. Standing (facing right); 100 p. Buddha and temple dancer.

9 Vientiane

1954. Golden Jubilee of King Sisavang Vong.

40	9	2 p. violet and blue (postage)	50·00	35·00
41		3 p. red and brown	45·00	38·00
42		50 p. turquoise & blue (air)	£140	£160

10 Ravana

1955. Air. "Ramayana" (dramatic poem).

43	10	2 k. blue, emerald and green	1·00	90
44	–	4 k. red and brown	1·25	1·25
45	–	5 k. green, brown and red	2·50	1·75
46	–	10 k. black, orange & brown	4·50	3·00
47	–	20 k. olive, green and violet	5·50	4·25
48	–	30 k. black, brown and blue	7·50	5·50

DESIGNS—HORIZ: 4 k. Hanuman, the white monkey; 5 k. Ninh Laphath, the black monkey. VERT: 10 k. Sita and Rama; 20 k. Luci and Ravana's friend; 30 k. Rama.

11 Buddha and Worshippers

1956. 2500th Anniv of Buddhist Era.

49	11	2 k. brown (postage)	3·50	2·25
50		3 k. black	3·50	2·25
51		5 k. sepia	5·50	3·50
52		20 k. carmine and red (air)	35·00	30·00
53		30 k. green and bistre	35·00	32·00

Nos. 49/53 were wrongly inscribed as commemorating the birth anniversary of Buddha.

12 U.N. Emblem 13

1956. 1st Anniv of Admission to U.N.

54	12	1 k. black (postage)	50	45
55		2 k. blue	65	50
56		4 k. red	90	70
57		6 k. violet	1·10	90
58	13	15 k. blue (air)	4·00	4·00
59		30 k. lake	5·50	5·50

14 Flute Player

1957. Native Musicians.

60	14	2 k. multicoloured (postage)	1·25	80
61	–	4 k. multicoloured	1·25	80
62	–	8 k. blue, brown and orange	2·10	95
63	–	12 k. multicoloured (air)	1·90	1·90
64	–	14 k. multicoloured	2·25	2·25
65	–	20 k. multicoloured	2·50	2·50

DESIGNS—VERT: 4 k. Piper; 14 k. Violinist; 20 k. Drummer. HORIZ: 8 k. Xylophonist; 12 k. Bells player.

15 Harvesting Rice

1957. Rice Cultivation.

66	15	3 k. multicoloured	70	40
67	–	5 k. brown, red and green	70	50
68	–	16 k. violet, olive and blue	1·50	90
69	–	26 k. chocolate, brown & grn	1·90	1·50

DESIGNS—VERT: 5 k. Drying rice; 16 k. Winnowing rice. HORIZ: 26 k. Polishing rice.

16 "The Offertory" 18 Mother and Child

17 Carrier Elephants

1957. Air. Buddhism.

70	16	10 k. multicoloured	60	60
71	–	15 k. brown, yellow & choc	90	90
72	–	18 k. yellow and green	1·25	1·25
73	–	24 k. red, black and yellow	2·40	2·40

DESIGNS—As T **16**: HORIZ: 15 k. "Meditation" (children on river craft). 48 × 36½ mm: 24 k. "The Great Renunciation" (dancers with horse). VERT: 18 k. "Serenity" (head of Buddhist).

1958. Laotian Elephants. Multicoloured.

74		10 c. Type **17**	45	20
75		20 c. Elephant's head with head-dress	45	20
76		30 c. Elephant with howdah (vert)	45	20
77		2 k. Elephant hauling log	65	35
78		5 k. Elephant walking with calf (vert)	1·90	75
79		10 k. Caparisoned elephant (vert)	2·25	90
80		13 k. Elephant bearing throne (vert)	3·75	1·50

1958. Air. 3rd Anniv of Laotian Red Cross. Cross in red.

81	18	8 k. black and grey	90	90
82		12 k. olive and brown	90	90
83		15 k. turquoise and green	1·10	1·10
84		20 k. violet and bistre	1·25	1·25

19

1958. Inauguration of U.N.E.S.C.O. Headquarters Building, Paris.

85	19	50 c. blue, orange and red	25	20
86	–	60 c. violet, brown and green	25	20
87	–	70 c. blue, brown and red	25	20
88	–	1 k. red, blue and bistre	45	25

DESIGNS—VERT: 60 c. Woman, children and part of exterior of U.N.E.S.C.O. building; 70 c. Woman and children hailing U.N.E.S.C.O. building superimposed on globe. HORIZ: 1 k. General view of U.N.E.S.C.O. building and Eiffel Tower.

20 King Sisavang Vong

1959.

89	20	4 k. lake	30	30
90		6 k. 50 red	30	30
91		9 k. mauve	30	30
92		13 k. green	30	30

21 Stage Performance 22 Portal of Vat Phou Temple, Pakse

1959. Education and Fine Arts.

93	21	1 k. multicoloured	20	15
94	–	2 k. lake, violet and black	25	15
95	–	3 k. black, green and purple	30	20
96	–	5 k. green, yellow and violet	45	35

DESIGNS—VERT: 2 k. Student and "Lamp of Learning"; 5 k. Stage performers and Buddhist temple. HORIZ: 3 k. Teacher and children with "Key to Education".

1959. Laotian Monuments. Multicoloured.

97		50 c. Type **22**	15	15
98		1 k. 50 That Ing Hang, Savannakhet	15	15
99		2 k. 50 Vat Phou Temple, Pakse	20	20
100		7 k. That Luang, Vientiane	30	30
101		11 k. As 7 k., but different view	30	30
102		12 k. 50 Phou-Si Temple, Luang Prabang	45	45

The 1 k. 50, 2 k. 50 and 11 k. are horiz and the rest vert.

1960. World Refugee Year. Nos. 89 and 79 surch

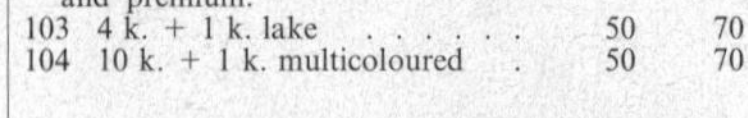

ANNEE MONDIALE DU REFUGIE 1959–1960 and premium.

103		4 k. + 1 k. lake	50	70
104		10 k. + 1 k. multicoloured	50	70

24 Plain of Jars, Xieng Khouang 25 Funeral Urn

1960. Air. Tourism.
105 **24** 9 k. 50 red, bistre and blue . . 25 25
106 – 12 k. brown violet and green . . 35 30
107 – 15 k. red, green and brown . . 50 45
108 – 19 k. brown, orange and green . . 60 50
DESIGNS—HORIZ: 12 k. Phapheng Falls, Champassak; 15 k. Pair of bullocks with cart. VERT: 19 k. Buddhist monk and village.

1961. Funeral of King Sisavang Vong.
109 **25** 4 k. bistre, black and red . . 30 30
110 – 6 k. 50 brown and black . . 30 30
111 – 9 k. brown and black . . . 30 30
112 – 25 k. black 70 70
DESIGNS: 6 k. 50, Urn under canopy; 9 k. Catafalque on dragon carriage; 25 k. King Sisavang Vong.

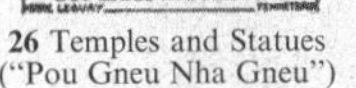

26 Temples and Statues ("Pou Gneu Nha Gneu") **27** King Savang Vatthana

1962. Air. Festival of Makha Bousa.
113 **26** 11 k. brown, red and green . . 30 30
114 – 14 k. blue and orange . . . 30 30
115 – 20 k. green, yellow and mauve . 50 50
116 – 25 k. red, blue and green . . 60 60
DESIGNS—As T **26**: 14 k. Bird ("Garuda"); 20 k. Flying deities ("Hanuman"). 36×48 mm: 25 k. Warriors ("Nang Teng One").

1962.
117 **27** 1 k. brown, red and blue . . 10 10
118 2 k. brown, red and mauve . . 15 15
119 5 k. brown, red and blue . . 25 15
120 10 k. brown, red and bistre . . 40 25

28 Laotian Boy **29** Royal Courier

1962. Malaria Eradication.
121 **28** 4 k. olive, black & green . . 20 10
122 – 9 k. brown, black & turq . . 20 20
123 – 10 k. red, yellow & olive . . 40 25
DESIGNS: 9 k. Laotian girl; 10 k. Campaign emblem.

1962. Philatelic Exhibition, Vientiane, and Stamp Day.
124 – 50 c. multicoloured 60 80
125 – 70 c. multicoloured 20 20
126 – 1 k. black, green and red . . 35 35
127 **29** 1 k. 50 multicoloured . . . 35 35
DESIGNS—HORIZ: 50 c. Modern mail transport; 70 c. Dancer and globe. VERT: 1 k. Royal courtier on elephant.

30 Fisherman

1963. Freedom from Hunger.
128 **30** 1 k. bistre, violet and green . . 20 15
129 – 4 k. blue, brown and green . . 20 20
130 – 5 k. blue, bistre and green . . 25 25
131 – 9 k. blue, green and brown . . 40 40
DESIGNS—VERT: 4 k. Threshing rice; 9 k. Harvesting rice. HORIZ: 5 k. Ploughing paddy field.

31 Queen of Laos **32** Laotian supporting U.N. Emblem

1963. Red Cross Centenary.
132 **31** 4 k. red, blue and brown . . 20 20
133 6 k. multicoloured 25 25
134 10 k. red, blue and brown . . 30 30

1963. 15th Anniv of Declaration of Human Rights.
135 **32** 4 k. purple, blue and red . . 50 30

33 Temple, Map and Rameses II

1964. Nubian Monuments Preservation.
136 **33** 4 k. multicoloured 20 20
137 6 k. multicoloured 30 30
138 10 k. multicoloured . . . 35 35

34 Offertory Vase and Horn

1964. "Constitutional Monarchy". Multicoloured.
139 10 k. Type **34** 20 15
140 15 k. Seated Buddha of Vat Pra Keo 30 20
141 20 k. Laotians walking across map 35 30
142 40 k. Royal Palace, Luang Prabang 70 55

35 Phra Vet and Wife **36** Meo Warrior

1964. Folklore. Phra Vet Legend. Multicoloured.
143 10 k. Type **35** 25 25
144 32 k. "Benediction" 35 35
145 45 k. Phame and wife 40 40
146 55 k. Arrest of Phame 70 70

1964. "People of Laos".
147 – 25 k. black, brown and green (postage) 60 60
148 **36** 5 k. multicoloured (air) . . 25 15
149 – 10 k. flesh, slate and purple . 35 20
150 – 50 k. brown, drab and lilac . 1·40 85
DESIGNS: 10 k. Kha hunter; 25 k. Girls of three races; 50 k. Thai woman.

37 Red Lacewing

1965. Butterflies and Moths.
151 **37** 10 k. chestnut, brown and green (postage) 75 40
152 – 25 k. blue, black & yellow . 1·10 60
153 – 40 k. yellow, brown & grn . 1·90 90
154 – 20 k. red and yellow (air) . 1·10 60
BUTTERFLIES—As Type **37**: 25 k. Yellow pansy. 48×27 mm: 20 k. Atlas moth; 40 k. "Dysphania militaris" (moth).

38 Wattay Airport ("French Aid")

1965. Foreign Aid.
155 **38** 25 k. mauve, brown & turq . . 30 20
156 – 45 k. brown and green . . . 35 30
157 – 55 k. brown and blue . . . 50 40
158 – 75 k. multicoloured 60 50
DESIGNS—VERT: 45 k. Mother bathing child (water resources: "Japanese Aid"); 75 k. School and plants (education and cultivation: "American Aid"). HORIZ: 55 k. Studio of radio station ("British Aid").

39 Hophabang

1965.
159 **39** 10 k. multicoloured 20 15

40 Teleprinter-operator, Globe and Map

1965. I.T.U. Centenary.
160 **40** 5 k. brown, violet & purple . 20 15
161 – 30 k. brown, blue & green . 30 30
162 – 50 k. multicoloured 50 35
DESIGNS: 30 k. Globe, map, telephonist and radio operator; 50 k. Globe, radio receiver and mast.

1965. Surch.
163 **20** 1 k. on 4 k. lake 20 15
164 5 k. on 6 k. 50 brown . . . 25 20

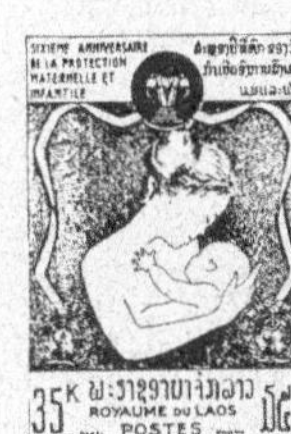

42 Mother and Baby **43** Leopard Cat

1965. 6th Anniv of U.N. "Protection of Mother and Child".
165 **42** 35 k. blue and red 70 30

1965. Air. Laotian Fauna.
166 **43** 22 k. yellow, brown & grn . 30 25
167 – 55 k. brown, sepia & blue . 40 30
168 – 75 k. brown and green . . . 65 40
169 – 100 k. brown, black & yell . 90 60
170 – 200 k. black and red . . . 1·90 1·40
DESIGNS: 55 k. Phayre's flying squirrel; 75 k. Javan mongoose; 100 k. Chinese porcupine; 200 k. Binturong.

44 U.N. Emblem on Map **45** Bulls in Combat

1965. 20th Anniv of U.N.
171 **44** 5 k. blue, grey and green . . 20 15
172 25 k. blue, grey and mauve . 25 20
173 40 k. blue, grey and turquoise 35 35

1965. Laotian Pastimes.
174 **45** 10 k. brown, black and orange 25 20
175 – 20 k. blue, red and green . 30 25
176 – 25 k. red, blue and green . 45 30
177 – 50 k. multicoloured 50 40
DESIGNS: 20 k. Tikhy (form of hockey); 25 k. Pirogue race; 50 k. Rocket festival.

46 Slaty-headed Parakeet

1966. Birds.
178 **46** 5 k. green, brown and red . 70 20
179 – 15 k. brown, black & turq . 80 40
180 – 20 k. sepia, ochre and blue . 1·10 60
181 – 45 k. blue, sepia and violet . 3·50 2·10
BIRDS: 15 k. White-crested laughing thrush; 20 k. Osprey; 45 k. Indian roller (or "blue jay").

47 W.H.O. Building

1966. Inaug of W.H.O. Headquarters, Geneva.
182 **47** 10 k. blue and turquoise . . 20 20
183 25 k. green and red 25 20
184 50 k. black and blue . . . 45 45

48 Ordination of Priests

1966. Laotian Ceremonies. Multicoloured.
186 10 k. Type **48** 25 15
187 25 k. Sand-hills ceremony . . 25 20
188 30 k. "Wax pagoda" procession (vert) 35 30
189 40 k. "Sou-Khouan" ceremony (vert) 40 35

49 U.N.E.S.C.O. Emblem

1966. 20th Anniv of U.N.E.S.C.O.
190 **49** 20 k. orange and black . . 15 15
191 30 k. blue and black . . . 25 20
192 40 k. green and black . . . 30 25
193 60 k. red and black 45 40

50 Letter, Carrier Pigeon and Emblem

1966. International Correspondence Week.
195 **50** 5 k. blue, brown and red . . 20 15
196 20 k. purple, black & green . 30 20
197 40 k. brown, red and blue . 40 25
198 45 k. black, green & purple . 45 30

51 Flooded Village **52** Carving, Siprapouthbat Pagoda

1967. Mekong Delta Flood Relief. Multicoloured.
200 20 k. + 5 k. Type **51** 25 25
201 40 k. + 10 k. Flooded market-place 40 40
202 60 k. + 15 k. Flooded airport . 1·10 1·10

1967. Buddhist Art.
204 **52** 5 k. green and brown . . . 15 15
205 – 20 k. blue and sepia . . . 25 20
206 – 50 k. purple and sepia . . . 35 35
207 – 70 k. grey and brown . . . 45 35
DESIGNS (carvings in temple pagodas, Luang Prabang): 30 k. Visoun; 50 k. Xiengthong; 70 k. Visoun (different).

53 General Post Office

1967. Opening of New G.P.O. Building, Vientiane.
208 **53** 25 k. brown, green and pur . 20 20
209 50 k. blue, green and slate . 30 25
210 70 k. red, green and brown . 50 35

54 "Ophicephalus micropeltes" 55 "Cassia fistula"

1967. Fishes.

211 **54** 20 k. black, bistre and blue . . 25 25
212 – 35 k. slate, bistre and blue . . 30 25
213 – 45 k. sepia, ochre and green . . 50 30
214 – 60 k. black, bistre and green . . 65 40

DESIGNS: 35 k. "Pangasianodon gigas"; 45 k. "Mastocembelus armatus"; 60 k. "Notopterus".

1967. Flowers.

215 **55** 30 k. yellow, green and mauve . . 25 25
216 – 55 k. red, green and orange . . 35 30
217 – 75 k. red, green and blue . . 50 40
218 – 80 k. yellow, mauve and green . . 60 45

DESIGNS: 55 k. "Cucuma singulario"; 75 k. "Poinciana regia"; 80 k. "Plumeria acutifolia".

56 Harvesting

1967. 10th Anniv of Laotian Red Cross.

219 **56** 20 k. + 5 k. multicoloured . . 25 25
220 50 k. + 10 k. multicoloured . . 85 35
221 60 k. + 15 k. multicoloured . . 55 55

57 Banded Krait

1967. Reptiles.

223 **57** 5 k. blue, yellow and green . . 20 15
224 – 40 k. brown, bistre and green . . 25 20
225 – 100 k. chocolate, brown and green . . 75 50
226 – 200 k. black, brown and green . 1·60 1·25

DESIGNS: 40 k. Marsh crocodile; 100 k. Pit viper; 200 k. Water monitor.

58 Human Rights Emblem

1968. Human Rights Year. Emblem in red and green.

227 **58** 20 k. green . . 20 20
228 30 k. brown . . 25 20
229 50 k. blue . . 50 35

59 Military Parade **60** W.H.O. Emblem

1968. Army Day. Multicoloured.

231 15 k. Type **59** (postage) . . 20 15
232 20 k. Soldiers and tank in battle . . 30 15
233 60 k. Soldiers and Laotian flag . . 50 25
234 200 k. Parade of colours before National Assembly building (air) . . 75 55
235 300 k. As 200 k. . . 1·25 70

1968. 20th Anniv of W.H.O.

237 **60** 15 k. brown, red & purple . . 25 20
238 30 k. brown, green & blue . . 30 20
239 70 k. brown, purple & red . . 50 30
240 110 k. light brown, purple and brown . . 70 45
241 250 k. brown, blue & green . 1·75 1·00

61 "Chrysochroa mnizechi" **62** "Mangifera indica"

1968. Beetles.

243 **61** 30 k. blue, yellow and green (postage) . . 40 25
244 – 50 k. black, orange & pur . . 55 35
245 – 90 k. blue, orange & ochre . 1·10 55
246 – 120 k. black & orange (air) . 1·10 55
247 – 160 k. multicoloured . . 1·40 75

INSECTS—VERT: 50 k. "Aristobia approximator"; 90 k. "Eutaenia corbetti". HORIZ: 120 k. "Dorysthenes walkeri"; 160 k. "Megaloxantha bicolor".

1968. Laotian Fruits.

248 **62** 20 k. green, blue & black . . 15 15
249 – 50 k. green, red and blue . . 30 25
250 – 180 k. green, brown & orge . . 80 70
251 – 250 k. green, brown & yell . 1·25 90

DESIGNS—VERT: 50 k. "Tamarindus indica". HORIZ: 180 k. "Artocarpus intregrifolia"; 250 k. "Citrullus vulgaris".

63 Hurdling

1968. Olympic Games, Mexico.

252 **63** 15 k. green, blue & brown . . 20 15
253 – 80 k. brown, turq & blue . . 40 30
254 – 100 k. blue, brown & green . . 55 30
255 – 110 k. brown, red and blue . . 65 40

DESIGNS: 80 k. Tennis; 100 k. Football; 110 k. High jumping.

64 Oriental Door, Wat Ongtu (detail)

1969. Wat Ongtu Temple.

256 **64** 150 k. gold, black and red . 1·10 60
257 – 200 k. gold, black and red . 1·75 90

DESIGN: 200 k. Central door, Wat Ongtu.

65 "Pharak praying to the Gods"

1969. Laotian "Ballet Royal". Designs showing dance characters. Multicoloured.

258 10 k. Type **65** (postage) . . 25 15
259 15 k. "Soukhib ordered to attack" . . 35 20
260 20 k. "Thotsakan reviewing troops" . . 40 30
261 30 k. "Nang Sida awaiting punishment" . . 60 35
262 40 k. "Pharam inspecting his troops" . . 75 35
263 60 k. "Hanuman about to rescue Nang Sida" . . 1·25 50
264 110 k. "Soudagnou battling with Thotsakan" (air) . . 1·75 1·25
265 300 k. "Pharam dancing with Thotsakkan" . . 3·75 2·25

66 Handicrafts Workshop, Vientiane

1969. 10th Anniv of I.L.O.

267 **66** 30 k. violet & purple (postage) . 25 20
268 60 k. brown and green . . 60 30
269 – 300 k. black & brown (air) . 2·25 1·40

DESIGN: 300 k. Elephants moving logs.

67 Chinese Pangolin

1969. "Wild Animals" (1st series). Multicoloured.

270 15 k. Type **67** (postage) . . 30 20
271 30 k. Type **67** . . 30 25
272 70 k. Sun bear (air) . . 35 30
273 120 k. Common gibbon (vert) . . 75 50
274 150 k. Tiger . . 80 60

See also Nos. 300/3 and 331/5.

68 Royal Mausoleum, Luang Prabang

1969. 10th Death Anniv of King Sisavang Vong.

275 **68** 50 k. ochre, blue and green . . 60 40
276 – 70 k. ochre and lake . . 70 40

DESIGN: 70 k. King Sisavang Vong (medallion).

69 "Lao Woman being Groomed" (Leguay)

1969. Air. Paintings by Marc Leguay (1st series). Multicoloured.

277 10 k. Type **69** . . 1·25 70
278 150 k. "Village Market" (horiz) . 1·75 90

See also Nos. 285, 307/9 and 357/61.

70 Carved Capital, Wat Xiengthong

1970. Laotian Pagodas. Multicoloured.

279 70 k. Type **70** (postage) . . 60 50
280 100 k. Library, Wat Sisaket (air) . 90 40
281 120 k. Wat Xiengthong (horiz) . 1·50 70

71 "Noon" Drum

1970. Laotian Drums.

282 **71** 30 k. mult (postage) . . 65 50
283 – 55 k. black, green & brown . 1·00 65
284 – 125 k. brown, yellow and flesh (air) . . 1·75 1·00

DESIGNS—HORIZ: 55 k. Bronze drum. VERT: 125 k. Wooden drum.

1970. Air. Paintings by Marc Leguay (2nd series). As T **69**. Multicoloured.

285 150 k. "Banks of the Mekong" (horiz) . . 1·75 90

72 Franklin D. Roosevelt

1970. Air. 25th Death Anniv of Franklin D. Roosevelt (American statesman).

286 **72** 120 k. slate and green . . 1·00 70

73 "Lenin explaining Electrification Plan" (L. Shmatko)

1970. Birth Centenary of Lenin.

287 **73** 30 k. multicoloured . . 35 25
288 70 k. multicoloured . . 45 40

1970. "Support for War Victims". Nos. 258/65 ("Ballet Royal") surch **Soutien aux Victimes de la Guerre** and premium.

289 10 k. + 5 k. mult (postage) . 40 40
290 15 k. + 5 k. multicoloured . 40 40
291 20 k. + 5 k. multicoloured . 40 40
292 30 k. + 5 k. multicoloured . 40 40
293 40 k. + 5 k. multicoloured . 70 70
294 60 k. + 5 k. multicoloured . 90 90
295 110 k. + 5 k. mult (air) . . 1·75 1·75
296 300 k. + 5 k. multicoloured . 2·75 2·75

75 Weaving Silk

1970. "EXPO 70" World Fair, Osaka, Japan. Laotian Silk Industry.

297 **75** 30 k. bl, brn & red (postage) . 40 25
298 – 70 k. multicoloured . . 70 45
299 – 125 k. multicoloured (air) . 85 70

DESIGNS: 70 k. Silk-spinning; 125 k. Winding skeins.

76 Wild Boar **77** Buddha, U.N. Emblem and New York H.Q.

1970. Wild Animals (2nd series).

300 **76** 20 k. brown & grn (postage) . 45 25
301 – 60 k. brown and olive . . 75 40

302 – 210 k. brown, red and yellow (air) . . . . 2·00 1·25
303 – 500 k. green, brown & orge 4·00 2·40
ANIMALS: 210 k. Leopard. 500 k. Gaur.

1970. 25th Anniv of U.N.O.
304 **77** 30 k. brown, mauve and blue (postage) 40 30
305 70 k. brown, blue and green 60 50
306 – 125 k. multicoloured (air) . 1·25 85
DESIGN—26 × 36 mm: 125 k. Nang Thorani ("Goddess of the Earth") and New York Headquarters.

1970. Air. Paintings by Marc Leguay (3rd series). As T **69**. Multicoloured.
307 100 k. "Village Track" 50 40
308 120 k. "Paddy-field in the Rainy Season" (horiz) 70 50
309 150 k. "Village Elder" 80 60

78 "Nakhanet"

1971. Laotian Mythology (1st series). Frescoes from Triumphal Arch, Vientiane. Multicoloured.
310 **78** 70 k. orange, brown and red (postage) 50 35
311 – 85 k. green, yellow & blue 60 45
312 – 125 k. multicoloured (air) 1·25 65
DESIGNS: As T **78**: 85 k. "Rahu". 49 × 36 mm: 125 k. "Underwater duel between Nang Matsa and Hanuman".
See also Nos. 352/4 and 385/7.

79 Silversmiths

1971. Laotian Traditional Crafts. Multicoloured.
313 30 k. Type **79** 20 20
314 50 k. Potters 40 20
315 70 k. Pirogue-builder (49 × 36 mm) 50 30

80 Laotian and African Children

1971. Racial Equality Year.
316 **80** 30 k. blue, red and green . 25 15
317 – 60 k. violet, red and yellow 45 30
DESIGN: 60 k. Laotian dancers and musicians.

81 Buddhist Monk at That Luang

1971. 50th Anniv of Vientiane Rotary Club.
318 **81** 30 k. violet, brown & blue 35 20
319 – 70 k. grey, red and blue . . 50 35
DESIGN—VERT: 70 k. Laotian girl on "Dragon" staircase.

82 "Dendrobium agregatum"

83 Dancers from France and Laos

1971. Laotian Orchids. Multicoloured.
320 30 k. Type **82** (postage) . . . 45 25
321 40 k. "Rynchostylis giganterum" 65 40
322 50 k. "Ascocentrum miniatur" (horiz) 70 40
323 60 k. "Paphiopedilum exul" . 90 50
324 70 k. "Trichoglottis fasciata" (horiz) 95 65
325 80 k. Cattleya (horiz) . . . . 1·10 65
326 125 k. Brazilian cattleya (horiz) (air) . . . . 1·75 80
327 150 k. "Vanda teres" (horiz) 1·90 1·10
Nos. 321, 323 and 325 are smaller, 22 × 36 or 36 × 22 mm. Nos. 326/7 are larger, 48 × 27 mm.

1971. Air. "Twin Cities" of St. Astier (France) and Keng-Kok (Laos).
328 **83** 30 k. brown and light brown 20 15
329 70 k. purple and plum . . 30 20
330 100 k. green & deep green 55 35

84 Common Palm Civet

1971. Wild Animals (3rd series).
331 **84** 25 k. black, violet and blue (postage) 20 20
332 40 k. black, green and olive 30 30
333 – 50 k. orange and green . . 45 40
334 – 85 k. brown, green & emerald 70 60
335 – 300 k. brown and green (air) 1·40 1·00
DESIGNS: 50 k. Lesser Malay chevrotain; 85 k. Sambar; 300 k. Javan rhinoceros.

85 Laotian Woman (design from 1952 issue)

1971. 20th Anniv of Laotian Stamps.
336 **85** 30 k. chocolate, brown and violet (postage) 20 20
337 – 40 k. multicoloured . . . 20 20
338 – 50 k. black, flesh and blue 35 25
339 – 125 k. violet, brn & grn (air) 70 50
DESIGNS—36 × 48 mm: 40 k. Violinist (As No. 64); 50 k. Rama (As No. 48); 125 k. "The Offertory" (As Type **16**).

86 "Sunset on the Mekong"

1971. Air. Paintings by Chamnane Prisayane. Mult.
341 125 k. Type **86** 55 45
342 150 k. "Quiet Morning at Ban Tane Pieo" 75 65

87 Children reading Book

1972. International Book Year.
343 **87** 30 k. green (postage) . . . 20 15
344 – 70 k. brown 30 25
345 – 125 k. violet (air) 70 45
DESIGNS—36 × 22 mm: 70 k. Laotian illustrating manuscript. 48 × 27 mm: 125 k. Father showing manuscripts to children.

88 Nam Ngum Dam and Obelisk

1972. 25th Anniv of U.N. Economic Commission for Asia and the Far East (E.C.A.F.E.). Multicoloured.
346 40 k. Type **88** (postage) 20 20
347 80 k. Type **88** 30 25
348 145 k. Lake and spill-way, Nam Ngum Dam (air) 80 50

89 "The Water-carrier"

1972. 25th Anniv of U.N.I.C.E.F. Drawings by Lao Schoolchildren. Multicoloured.
349 50 k. Type **89** (postage) 25 20
350 80 k. "Teaching Bamboo-weaving" 30 25
351 120 k. "Riding a Water-buffalo" (air) 70 45

90 "Nakharath"

1972. Air. Laotian Mythology (2nd series).
352 **90** 100 k. turquoise 40 30
353 – 120 k. lilac 70 45
354 – 150 k. brown 80 55
DESIGNS: 120 k. "Nang Kinnali"; 150 k. "Norasing".

91 Festival Offerings

1972. Air. That Luang Religious Festival.
355 **91** 110 k. brown 45 35
356 – 125 k. purple 65 50
DESIGN: 125 k. Festival procession.

1972. Air. Paintings by Marc Leguay (4th series). As T **69**. Multicoloured.
357 50 k. "In the Paddy Field" (detail) 25 20
358 50 k. "In the Paddy Field" (different detail) 25 20
359 70 k. "Village in the Rainy Season" (detail) 35 25
360 70 k. "Village in the Rainy Season" (different detail) . . 35 25
361 120 k. "Laotian Mother" . . . 70 45
Nos. 357/8 and 359/60 when placed together form the complete painting in each case.

92 Attopeu Religious Costume

93 "Lion" Guardian, That Luang

1973. Regional Costumes.
362 **92** 40 k. yellow, mauve & brown (postage) 40 20
363 – 90 k. black, lake & brown 70 30
364 – 120 k. brown, sepia and mauve (air) 70 35
365 – 150 k. ochre, lake & brown 90 45
DESIGNS: 90 k. Phongsaly festival costume; 120 k. Luang Prabang wedding costume; 150 k. Vientiane evening dress.

1973. 55th Anniv of Lions International.
366 **93** 40 k. red, purple and blue . 35 20
367 80 k. red, yellow and blue . 55 35
368 – 150 k. multicoloured (air) . 1·00 70
DESIGN—48 × 27 mm: 150 k. Lions emblems and statue of King Saysetthathirath, Vientiane.

94 Satellite passing Rahu

1973. Traditional and Modern Aspects of Space. Multicoloured.
369 80 k. Type **94** 35 20
370 150 k. Landing module and Laotian festival rocket. . . 80 40

95 Dr. Gerhard Hansen and Map of Laos

1973. Centenary of Identification of Leprosy Bacillus by Hansen.
371 **95** 40 k. purple, dp pur & orge 45 30
372 80 k. purple, brown & yellow 70 40

96 "Benediction"

97 "Nang Mekhala". (Goddess of the Sea)

1973. 25th Anniv of Laotian Boy Scouts Association.
373 **96** 70 k. yellow & brn (postage) 55 35
374 – 110 k. violet & orange (air) 55 20
375 – 150 k. blue, drab & brown 75 35
DESIGNS—48 × 27 mm: 110 k. Campfire entertainment; 150 k. Scouts helping flood victims, Vientiane, 1966.

1973. Air. Centenary of World Meteorological Organization.
376 **97** 90 k. lilac, red and brown . 55 30
377 – 150 k. brown, red & lt brn 1·00 50
DESIGN—HORIZ: 150 k. "Chariot of the Sun".

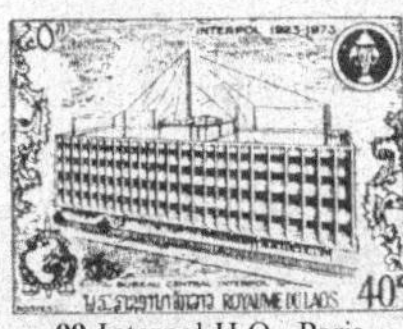
99 Interpol H.Q., Paris

1973. 50th Anniv of Int Criminal Police Organization (Interpol).
382 **99** 40 k. blue (postage) . . . 30 20
383 80 k. brown and light brown 35 20
384 – 150 k. violet, red and green (air) 80 35
DESIGN—48 × 27 mm: 150 k. Woman in opium-poppy field.

100 "Phra Sratsvady"

1974. Air. Laotian Mythology (3rd series).
385 **100** 100 k. red, brown & lilac . 70 30
386 – 110 k. brown, lilac & red . 85 40
387 – 150 k. violet, brown and light brown . . . . 1·25 60
DESIGNS: 110 k. "Phra Indra"; 150 k. "Phra Phrom".

101 Boy and Postbox

102 "Eranthemum nervosum"

1974. Centenary of U.P.U.

388 **101** 70 k. brown, green and blue (postage) 40 25
389 80 k. brown, blue & green 50 30
390 – 200 k. brown & red (air) 1·75 1·00
DESIGN—48×36 mm: 200 k. Laotian girls with letters, and U.P.U. Monument, Berne (Type **105**).

1974. Laotian Flora.

391 **102** 30 k. violet & grn (postage) 35 25
392 – 50 k. multicoloured . . . 50 30
393 – 80 k. red, green & brown . 80 40
394 – 500 k. green & brown (air) 3·50 1·90
DESIGNS—As T **102**: HORIZ: 50 k. Water lily; 80 k. Red silk-cotton. 36×36 mm: 500 k. Pitcher plant.

103 Mekong Ferry carrying Bus

1974. Laotian Transport.

395 **103** 25 k. brown & orge (postage) 45 20
396 – 90 k. brown and bistre . . 1·10 70
397 – 250 k. brown & green (air) 2·00 1·25
DESIGNS—VERT: 90 k. Bicycle rickshaw. HORIZ: 250 k. Mekong house boat.

104 Marconi, and Laotians with Transistor Radio

1974. Birth Centenary of Guglielmo Marconi (radio pioneer).

398 **104** 60 k. grey, green & brown (postage) 30 20
399 90 k. grey, brown & green 45 30
400 – 200 k. blue & brown (air) 1·50 60
DESIGN: 200 k. Communications methods.

105 U.P.U. Monument and Laotian Girls

1974. Air. Centenary of U.P.U.

401 **105** 500 k. lilac and red . . . 2·25 1·75

106 "Diastocera wallichi"

1974. Beetles.

403 **106** 50 k. brown, black & green (postage) 55 45
404 – 90 k. black, turq & grn . . 1·10 60
405 – 100 k. black, orange & brn 1·25 85
406 – 110 k. violet, red & grn (air) 1·25 55
DESIGNS: 90 k. "Macrochenus isabellunus"; 100 k. "Purpuricenus malaccensis"; 110 k. "Sternocera multipunctata".

107 Pagoda and Sapphire

1974. "Mineral Riches".

407 **107** 100 k. brown, green & blue 40 30
408 – 110 k. brown, blue & yellow 50 30
DESIGN: 110 k. Gold-panning and necklace.

108 King Savang Vatthana, Prince Souvanna Phouma and Prince Souvanouvong

1975. 1st Anniv (1974) of Laotian Peace Treaty.

409 **108** 80 k. brown, ochre & grn 30 25
410 300 k. brown, ochre & pur 70 50
411 420 k. brown, ochre and turquoise 80 60

109 Fortune-teller's Chart

1975. Chinese New Year ("Year of the Rabbit").

413 **109** 40 k. brown and green . 35 20
414 – 200 k. black, brown and green . . . . 1·10 50
415 – 350 k. brown, green and blue 2·00 90
DESIGNS—HORIZ: 200 k. Fortune-teller. VERT: 350 k. Woman riding hare.

110 U.N. Emblem and Frieze

112

1975. International Women's Year.

416 **110** 100 k. blue and turquoise 40 25
417 – 200 k. orange and green . 70 35
DESIGN: 200 k. I.W.Y. Emblem.

1975. "Pravet Sandone" Religious Festival.

420 **112** 80 k. multicoloured . . . 35 20
421 – 110 k. multicoloured . . 45 25
422 – 120 k. multicoloured . . 55 45
423 – 130 k. multicoloured . . 90 50
DESIGNS: 110 k. to 130 k. various legends.

113 Buddha and Stupas

1975. U.N.E.S.C.O. Campaign for Preservation of Borobudur Temple (in Indonesia).

424 **113** 100 k. green, blue & brn . 30 25
425 – 200 k. ochre, green & brn 55 30
DESIGN: 200 k. Temple sculptures.

114 Laotian Arms

115 Thathiang, Vien-Tran

1976. Multicoloured, background colour given.

427 **114** 1 k. blue 10 10
428 2 k. mauve 10 10
429 5 k. green 15 10
430 10 k. violet 20 20
431 200 k. orange . . . . . 1·00 1·00

1976. Pagodas. Multicoloured.

433 1 k. Type **115** 10 10
434 2 k. Phonsi, Luang Prabang . 10 10
435 30 k. Type **115** 10 10
436 80 k. As 2 k. 40 30
437 100 k. As 2 k. 50 45
438 300 k. Type **115** . . . . . . 1·50 90

116 Silversmith

1977. Laotian Crafts. Multicoloured.

440 1 k. Type **116** 10 10
441 2 k. Weaver 10 10
442 20 k. Potter 25 25
443 50 k. Basket-weaver (vert) . . 30 25

117 Gubarev, Grechko and "Salyut" Space Station

1977. 60th Anniv of Russian Revolution. Multicoloured.

445 5 k. Type **117** 10 10
446 20 k. Lenin 10 10
447 50 k. As 20 k. 20 20
448 60 k. Type **117** 35 25
449 100 k. Government Palace, Vientiane, and Kremlin, Moscow (horiz) 70 50
450 250 k. As 100 k. . . . . . . 1·60 1·25

118 Laotian Arms

119 Soldiers with Flag

1978.

452 **118** 5 k. yellow and black . . . 10 10
453 10 k. sepia and black . . . 10 10
454 50 k. purple and black . . 15 10
455 100 k. green and black . . 50 25
456 250 k. violet and black . . 1·25 70

1978. Army Day. Multicoloured.

457 20 k. Type **119** 10 10
458 40 k. Soldiers attacking village (horiz) 15 15
459 300 k. Anti-aircraft guns . . . 1·60 75

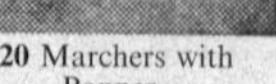

120 Marchers with Banner

121 Printed Circuit and Map of Laos

1978. National Day. Multicoloured.

460 20 k. Type **120** 10 10
461 50 k. Women with flag 25 15
462 400 k. Dancer . . . . 1·75 75

1979. World Telecommunications Day.

464 **121** 30 k. orange, brown & sil 10 10
465 – 250 k. multicoloured . . . 70 50
DESIGN: 250 k. Printed circuit, map of Laos and transmitter tower.

122 Woman posting Letter

1979. 15th Anniv of Asian-Oceanic Postal Union. Multicoloured.

466 5 k. Type **122** 10 10
467 10 k. Post Office counter . . 10 10
468 80 k. As 10 k. 40 25
469 100 k. Type **122** 50 30

123 Children playing Ball

1979. International Year of the Child (1st issue). Multicoloured. Without gum.

470 20 k. Type **123** 10 10
471 50 k. Children at school (horiz) 25 15
472 200 k. Mother feeding child . 1·50 45
473 500 k. Nurse immunising child 4·25 1·10

124 Elephant, Buffalo and Pirogues

1979. Transport. Multicoloured.

475 5 k. Type **124** 15 10
476 10 k. Buffalo carts 15 10
477 70 k. As No. 476 . . . . . . 50 15
478 500 k. Type **124** . . . . . . 2·25 1·25

125 Dancing Child

1979. International Year of the Child (2nd issue). Multicoloured. Without gum.

479 100 k. Children playing musical instruments (horiz) 40 25
480 200 k. Child releasing dove . 65 40
481 600 k. Type **125** . . . . . . 2·25 1·25

126 Forest and Paddy Field

1980. 5th Anniv of Republic (1st issue) and 25th Anniv of People's Front. Mult. Without gum.

483 30 c. Type **126** 15 10
484 50 c. Classroom and doctor examining baby (horiz) . . 20 10
485 1 k. Three women 50 20
486 2 k. Dam and electricity pylons (horiz) . . . . 1·10 65

127 Lenin Reading

1980. 110th Birth Anniv of Lenin. Multicoloured.

488 1 k. Type **127** 15 10
489 2 k. Lenin writing 35 15
490 3 k. Lenin and Red Flag (vert) 55 20
491 4 k. Lenin making speech (vert) 90 30

MINIMUM PRICE

The minimum price quoted is 10p which represents a handling charge rather than a basis for valuing common stamps. For further notes about prices, see introductory pages.

128 Workers in Field

1980. 5th Anniv of Republic (2nd issue). Multicoloured. Without gum.

493	50 c. Type **128**	10	10
494	1 k. 60 Loading logs on lorry and elephant hauling logs	30	15
495	4 k. 60 Veterinary workers tending animals	70	35
496	5 k. 40 Workers in paddy field	1·00	45

129 Emblems of Industry, Technology, Transport, Sport and Art

1981. 26th P.C.U.S. (Communist Party) Congress. Multicoloured.

498	60 c. Type **129**	15	10
499	4 k. 60 Communist star breaking manacles and globe	80	30
500	5 k. Laurel branch and broken bomb	1·00	35

131 Player heading Ball

132 Disabled Person on Telephone

1981. World Cup Football Championship, Spain (1982) (1st issue). Multicoloured.

503	1 k. Type **131**	20	10
504	2 k. Receiving ball	35	10
505	3 k. Passing ball	55	20
506	4 k. Goalkeeper diving for ball (horiz)	80	25
507	5 k. Dribbling	1·10	40
508	6 k. Kicking ball	1·50	50

See also Nos. 545/50.

1981. International Year of Disabled Persons. Multicoloured.

509	3 k. Type **132**	50	20
510	5 k. Disabled teacher	1·10	40
511	12 k. Person in wheelchair mending net	3·00	60

133 Wild Cat

1981. Wild Cats. Multicoloured.

512	10 c. Type **133**	10	10
513	20 c. Fishing cat	10	10
514	30 c. Caracal	10	10
515	40 c. Clouded leopard	15	10
516	50 c. Flat-headed cat	15	10
517	9 k. Jungle cat	3·00	70

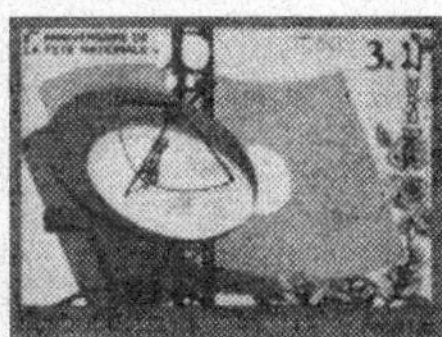
134 Dish Aerial and Flag

1981. 6th National Day Festival. Multicoloured.

518	3 k. Type **134**	50	30
519	4 k. Soldier and flag	65	40
520	5 k. Girls presenting flowers to soldier, flag and map of Laos	95	50

135 Indian Elephant

1982. Indian Elephant. Multicoloured.

521	1 k. Type **135**	20	10
522	2 k. Elephant carrying log	45	15
523	3 k. Elephant with passengers	70	25
524	4 k. Elephant in trap	90	35
525	5 k. Elephant and young	1·25	35
526	5 k. 50 Herd of elephants	1·60	50

136 Laotian Wrestling

1982. Wrestling.

527	**136**	50 c. multicoloured	10	10
528	–	1 k. 20 multicoloured	20	10
529	–	2 k. multicoloured	35	20
530	–	2 k. 50 multicoloured	55	30
531	–	4 k. multicoloured	80	35
532	–	5 k. multicoloured	1·40	45

DESIGNS: 1 k. 20 to 5 k. Various wrestling scenes.

137 "Nymphaea zanzibariensis"

1982. Water Lilies. Multicoloured.

533	30 c. Type **137**	10	10
534	40 c. "Nelumbo nucifera" "Gaertn Rose"	10	10
535	60 c. "Nymphaea rosea"	10	10
536	3 k. "Nymphaea nouchali"	60	35
537	4 k. "Nymphaea" White	95	40
538	7 k. "Nelumbo nucifera" "Gaertn White"	1·90	50

138 Barn Swallow

1982. Birds. Multicoloured.

539	50 c. Type **138**	30	15
540	1 k. Hoopoe	60	40
541	2 k. Common kingfisher	1·25	60
542	3 k. Black-naped blue monarch	1·90	80
543	4 k. Grey wagtail (horiz)	2·10	1·25
544	10 k. Long-tailed tailor bird (horiz)	7·25	2·40

139 Football

1982. World Cup Football Championship, Spain (2nd issue).

545	**139**	1 k. multicoloured	20	10
546	–	2 k. multicoloured	40	10
547	–	3 k. multicoloured	55	20
548	–	4 k. multicoloured	70	25
549	**139**	5 k. multicoloured	1·10	40
550	–	6 k. multicoloured	1·40	45

DESIGNS: 2 k. to 6 k. Various football scenes.

140 "Herona marathus"

1982. Butterflies. Multicoloured.

552	1 k. Type **140**	20	10
553	2 k. "Neptis paraka"	40	20
554	3 k. "Euripus halitherses"	70	30
555	4 k. "Lebadea martha"	1·10	40
556	5 k. "Iton semamora" (42 × 26 mm)	1·75	75
557	6 k. Common Palm Fly (59 × 41 mm)	2·00	1·00

142 Raft

1982. River Craft. Multicoloured.

559	50 c. Type **142**	10	10
560	60 c. Sampan	15	10
561	1 k. House boat	25	10
562	2 k. Passenger steamer	50	25
563	3 k. Ferry	70	30
564	8 k. Self-propelled barge	1·90	70

143 Vat Chanh

1982. Pagodas. Multicoloured.

565	50 c. Type **143**	10	10
566	60 c. Vat Inpeng	15	10
567	1 k. Vat Dong Mieng	25	10
568	2 k. Ho Tay	50	20
569	3 k. Vat Ho Pha Keo	70	25
570	8 k. Vat Sisaket	1·90	60

1982. Various stamps optd **1982**.

571	**114**	1 k. multicoloured
572	**116**	1 k. multicoloured
573	–	2 k. multicoloured (441)
574	**117**	5 k. multicoloured
575	**118**	5 k. yellow and black
576	**122**	5 k. multicoloured
577	**124**	5 k. multicoloured
578	–	10 k. multicoloured (467)
579	–	10 k. multicoloured (476)
580	–	20 k. multicoloured (446)
581	**119**	20 k. multicoloured
582	**121**	30 k. orange, brown and silver
583	–	40 k. multicoloured (458)
584	–	50 k. multicoloured (443)
585	–	70 k. multicoloured (477)
586	–	80 k. multicoloured (468)
587	**122**	100 k. multicoloured
588	**114**	200 k. multicoloured
589	**121**	250 k. multicoloured

145 Poodle

1982. Dogs. Multicoloured.

591	50 c. Type **145**	10	10
592	60 c. Samoyed	10	10
593	1 k. Boston terrier	25	10
594	2 k. Cairn terrier	65	20
595	3 k. Chihuahua	90	25
596	8 k. Bulldog	2·50	60

146 Woman watering Crops

1982. World Food Day. Multicoloured.

597	7 k. Type **146**	1·40	45
598	8 k. Woman transplanting rice	1·75	55

147 Fiat, 1925

1982. Cars. Multicoloured.

599	50 c. Type **147**	10	10
600	60 c. Peugeot, 1925	10	10
601	1 k. Berliet, 1925	25	10
602	2 k. Ballot, 1925	65	20
603	3 k. Renault, 1926	90	25
604	8 k. Ford, 1925	2·50	60

148 President Souphanouvong

1982. 7th Anniv of Republic. Multicoloured.

605	50 c. Type **148**	10	10
606	1 k. Tractors (horiz)	25	10
607	2 k. Cow (horiz)	35	20
608	3 k. Lorry passing dish aerial (horiz)	50	35
609	4 k. Nurse examining child	75	35
610	5 k. Classroom (horiz)	95	45
611	6 k. Dancer	1·40	50

149 Dimitrov, Flag and Arms of Bulgaria

1982. Birth Centenary of Georgi Dimitrov (Bulgarian statesman).

612	**149**	10 k. multicoloured	1·90	1·25

150 Kremlin and Arms of U.S.S.R.

151 Hurdling

1982. 60th Anniv of U.S.S.R. Multicoloured.

613	3 k. Type **150**	60	40
614	4 k. Doves and maps of U.S.S.R. and Laos	90	70

1983. Olympic Games, Los Angeles (1984) (1st issue). Multicoloured.

616	50 c. Type **151**	10	10
617	1 k. Javelin	20	10
618	2 k. Basketball	40	15
619	3 k. Diving	60	25
620	4 k. Gymnastics	80	40
621	10 k. Weightlifting	2·25	60

See also Nos. 708/14.

152 Bucking Horse

1983. Horses. Multicoloured.

623	50 c. Type **152**	10	10
624	1 k. Rearing black horse	20	10
625	2 k. Trotting brown horse	40	15
626	3 k. Dappled grey horse	65	25
627	4 k. Wild horse crossing snow	90	40
628	10 k. Horse in paddock	2·50	60

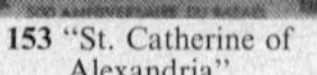

153 "St. Catherine of Alexandria"   **154** A. Gubarev (Soviet) and V. Remek (Czechoslovak)

1983. 500th Birth Anniv of Raphael (artist). Multicoloured.

629 50 c. Type **153** 10 10
630 1 k. "Adoration of the Kings" 20 10
631 2 k. "Madonna of the Grand Duke" 40 15
632 3 k. "St. George and the Dragon" 65 25
633 4 k. "The Vision of Ezekiel" 90 35
634 10 k. "Adoration of the Kings" (different) 2·50 60

1983. Cosmonauts. Multicoloured.

636 50 c. Type **154** 10 10
637 50 c. P. Klimuk (Soviet) and Miroslaw Hermaszewski (Polish) 10 10
638 1 k. V. Bykovsky (Soviet) and Sigmund Jahn (East German) 20 10
639 1 k. Nikolai Rukavishnikov (Soviet) and Georgi Ivanov (Bulgarian) 20 10
640 2 k. V. Kubasov (Soviet) and Bertalan Farkas (Hungarian) 40 15
641 3 k. V. Dzhanibekov (Soviet) and Gurragchaa (Mongolian) 65 25
642 4 k. L. Popov (Soviet) and D. Prunariu (Rumanian) 80 35
643 6 k. Soviet cosmonaut and Arnaldo Tamayo (Cuban) 1·25 40
644 10 k. Soviet and French cosmonauts 2·40 60

155 Jacques Charles's Hydrogen Balloon, 1783

1983. Bicentenary of Manned Flight. Mult.

646 50 c. Type **155** 10 10
647 1 k. Blanchard and Jeffries' balloon, 1785 20 10
648 2 k. Vincenzo Lunardi's balloon (London–Ware flight), 1784 40 15
649 3 k. Modern hot-air balloon over city 75 25
650 4 k. Massed balloon ascent, 1890 80 30
651 10 k. Auguste Piccard's stratosphere balloon "F.N.R.S.", 1931 2·50 60

157 "Dendrobium sp."

1983. Flowers. Multicoloured.

654 1 k. Type **157** 20 10
655 2 k. "Aerides odoratum" 40 15
656 3 k. "Dendrobium aggregatum" 70 25
657 4 k. "Dendrobium" 80 30
658 5 k. "Moschatum" 1·00 40
659 6 k. "Dendrobium sp." (different) 1·25 45

158 Downhill Skiing

1983. Winter Olympic Games, Sarajevo (1984) (1st issue). Multicoloured.

660 50 c. Type **158** 10 10
661 1 k. Slalom 25 10
662 2 k. Ice hockey 50 15
663 3 k. Speed skating 75 25
664 4 k. Ski jumping 1·00 30
665 10 k. Luge 2·40 80

See also Nos. 696/702.

160 "Notopterеus chitala"

1983. Fishes of Mekong River. Multicoloured.

668 1 k. Type **160** 20 10
669 2 k. "Cyprinus carpio" 40 15
670 3 k. "Pangasius sp." 65 25
671 4 k. "Catlocarpio siamensis" 75 30
672 5 k. "Morulius sp." 1·00 40
673 6 k. "Tilapia nilotica" 1·25 45

161 Magellan and "Vitoria"

1983. Explorers and their Ships. Multicoloured.

674 1 k. Type **161** 35 20
675 2 k. Jacques Cartier and "Grande Hermine" 75 30
676 3 k. Columbus and "Santa Maria" 1·25 50
677 4 k. Pedro Alvares Cabral and "El Ray" 1·40 60
678 5 k. Cook and H.M.S. "Resolution" 1·90 80
679 6 k. Charcot and "Pourquoi-pas?" 2·25 90

No. 679 is wrongly inscribed "Cabot".

162 Tabby Cat

1983. Domestic Cats. Multicoloured.

680 1 k. Type **162** 20 10
681 2 k. Long-haired Persian 40 15
682 3 k. Siamese 65 25
683 4 k. Burmese 75 30
684 5 k. Persian 1·00 40
685 6 k. Tortoiseshell 1·25 45

1983. Nos. 430 and 466 optd **1983.**

685a **122** 5 k. multicoloured
685b **114** 10 k. multicoloured

163 Marx, Book, Sun and Signature

1983. Death Centenary of Karl Marx. Mult.

686 1 k. Marx, dove, globe and flags 30 10
687 4 k. Type **163** 90 35
688 6 k. Marx and flags 1·60 65

164 Elephant dragging Log

1983. 8th Anniv of Republic. Multicoloured.

689 1 k. Type **164** 30 10
690 4 k. Cattle and pig (horiz) 90 35
691 6 k. Crops 1·60 65

165 Carrier Pigeon and Telex Machine

1983. World Communications Year. Multicoloured.

692 50 c. Type **165** 10 10
693 1 k. Early telephone, handset and receiver 25 10
694 4 k. Television tube and aerial 80 35
695 6 k. Satellite and dish aerial 1·50 55

166 Ice Skating   **167** Tiger

1984. Winter Olympic Games, Sarajevo (2nd issue). Multicoloured.

696 50 c. Type **166** 10 10
697 1 k. Speed skating 30 10
698 2 k. Biathlon 40 15
699 3 k. Luge (horiz) 80 30
700 4 k. Downhill skiing (horiz) 95 35
701 5 k. Ski jumping 1·40 45
702 6 k. Slalom 1·60 55

1984. Endangered Animals. The Tiger. Mult.

704 25 c. Type **167** 10 10
705 25 c. Tigers (horiz) 10 10
706 3 k. Tiger and cubs (horiz) 90 30
707 4 k. Tiger cubs 1·10 40

168 Diving

1984. Olympic Games, Los Angeles (2nd issue). Multicoloured.

708 50 c. Type **168** 10 10
709 1 k. Volleyball 25 10
710 2 k. Running 40 15
711 4 k. Basketball 85 25
712 5 k. Judo 1·10 35
713 6 k. Football 1·50 40
714 7 k. Gymnastics 1·75 50

169 Tuned Drums

1984. Musical Instruments. Multicoloured.

716 1 k. Type **169** 20 10
717 2 k. Xylophone 35 15
718 3 k. Pair of drums 70 25
719 4 k. Hand drum 90 25
720 5 k. Barrel drum 1·10 35
721 6 k. Pipes and string instrument 1·75 55

170 National Flag   **171** Chess Game

1984. National Day. Multicoloured.

722 60 c. Type **170** 15 10
723 1 k. National arms 35 10
724 2 k. As No. 723 50 20

1984. 60th Anniv of World Chess Federation. Multicoloured.

725 50 c. Type **171** 10 10
726 1 k. Renaissance game from "The Three Ages of Man" (miniature attr. to Estienne Porchier) 25 10
727 2 k. Woman teaching girls 40 15
728 2 k. Margrave Otto IV of Brandenburg playing chess with his wife 40 15
729 3 k. Four men at chessboard 75 30
730 4 k. Two women playing 1·00 35
731 8 k. Two men playing 2·25 55

Nos. 725, 727 and 729/31 show illustrations from King Alfonso X's "Book of Chess, Dice and Tablings".

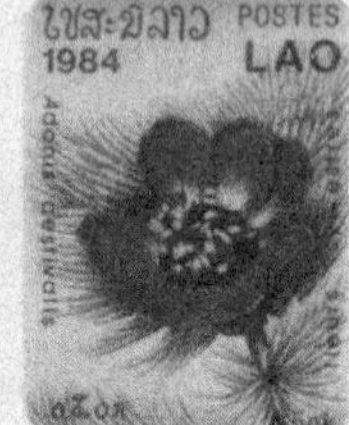

172 "Cardinal Nino de Guevara" (El Greco)   **173** "Adonis aestivalis"

1984. "Espana 84" International Stamp Exhibition, Madrid. Multicoloured.

733 50 c. Type **172** 10 10
734 1 k. "Gaspar de Guzman, Duke of Olivares, on Horseback" (Velazquez) 25 10
735 2 k. "The Annunciation" (Murillo) 40 15
736 2 k. "Portrait of a Lady" (Zurbaran) 40 15
737 3 k. "The Family of Charles IV" (Goya) 75 30
738 4 k. "Two Harlequins" (Picasso) 1·00 35
739 8 k. "Abstract" (Miro) 2·25 55

1984. Woodland Flowers. Multicoloured.

741 50 c. Type **173** 10 10
742 1 k. "Alpinia speciosa" 25 10
743 2 k. "Cassia lechenaultiana" 40 15
744 2 k. "Aeschynanthus speciosus" 40 15
745 3 k. "Datura meteloides" 75 30
746 4 k. "Quamoclit pennata" 95 35
747 8 k. "Commelina benghalensis" 2·25 55

174 Nazzaro

1984. 19th Universal Postal Union Congress Philatelic Salon, Hamburg. Cars. Multicoloured.

748 50 c. Type **174** 10 10
749 1 k. Daimler 25 10
750 2 k. Delage 40 15
751 2 k. Fiat "S 57/14B" 40 15
752 3 k. Bugatti 75 30
753 4 k. Itala 1·10 35
754 8 k. Blitzen Benz 2·25 55

175 "Madonna and Child"

1984. 450th Death Anniv of Correggio (artist). Multicoloured.

756 50 c. Type **175** 10 10
757 1 k. Detail showing horsemen resting 25 10
758 2 k. "Madonna and Child" (different) 40 15
759 2 k. "Mystical Marriage of St. Catherine" 40 15
760 3 k. "Four Saints" 75 30
761 4 k. "Noli me Tangere" 95 35
762 8 k. "Christ bids Farewell to the Virgin May" 1·90 55

176 "Luna 1"

1984. Space Exploration. Multicoloured.

764 50 c. Type **176** 10 10
765 1 k. "Luna 2" 25 10
766 2 k. "Luna 3" 40 15
767 2 k. Kepler and "Sputnik 2" 40 15
768 3 k. Newton & Lunokhod 2 . 75 30
769 4 k. Jules Verne and "Luna 13" 1·00 35
770 8 k. Copernicus and space station 2·10 60

177 Malaclemys Terrapin

1984. Reptiles. Multicoloured.

771 50 c. Type **177** 10 10
772 1 k. Banded krait 25 10
773 2 k. Indian python (vert) . . . 40 15
774 2 k. Reticulated python . . . 40 15
775 3 k. Tokay gecko 80 30
776 4 k. "Natrix subminiata" (snake) 1·10 40
777 8 k. Dappled ground gecko . . 2·40 65

178 Greater Glider

1984. "Ausipex 84" International Stamp Exhibition, Melbourne. Marsupials. Multicoloured.

778 50 c. Type **178** 10 10
779 1 k. Platypus 25 10
780 2 k. Southern hairy-nosed wombat ("Lasiorhinus latifrons") 40 15
781 2 k. Tasmanian devil ("Sarcophilus harrisii") . . 40 15
782 3 k. Thylacine 75 30
783 4 k. Tiger cat . . . . 1·00 35
784 8 k. Wallaby . . . . 2·10 60

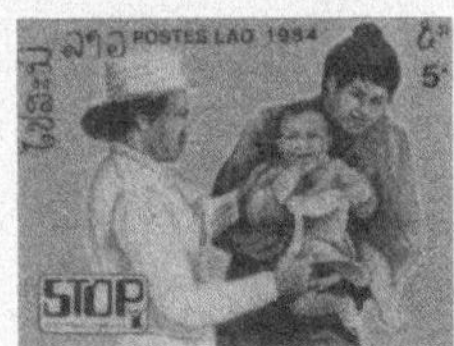

179 Nurse with Mother and Child

1984. Anti-poliomyelitis Campaign. Multicoloured.

786 5 k. Type **179** . . . . 1·10 50
787 6 k. Doctor inoculating child 1·40 55

180 Dragon Stair-rail

1984. Laotian Art. Multicoloured.

788 50 c. Type **180** 10 10
789 1 k. Capital of column 25 10
790 2 k. Decorative panel depicting god 40 15
791 2 k. Decorative panel depicting leaves 40 15
792 3 k. Stylized leaves (horiz) . . 70 30
793 4 k. Triangular flower decoration (horiz) . . . . 1·00 35
794 8 k. Circular lotus flower decoration . . . . 1·90 60

181 River House Boats

1984. 9th Anniv of Republic. Multicoloured.

795 1 k. Type **181** 45 15
796 2 k. Passengers boarding Fokker Friendship airliner 50 20
797 4 k. Building a bridge . . . . 1·10 45
798 10 k. Building a road . . . . 2·50 1·00

182 Players with Ball

1985. World Cup Football Championship, Mexico (1986) (1st issue). Multicoloured.

799 50 c. Type **182** 10 10
800 1 k. Heading the ball 25 10
801 2 k. Defending the ball . . . 45 15
802 3 k. Running with ball . . . 70 20
803 4 k. Taking possession of ball 1·10 35
804 5 k. Heading the ball (different) 1·40 45
805 6 k. Saving a goal . . . . . 1·75 55

See also Nos. 868/74.

183 Motor Cycle

1985. Centenary of Motor Cycle. Multicoloured.

807 50 c. Type **183** 10 10
808 1 k. Gnome Rhone, 1920 . . 25 10
809 2 k. F.N. "M67C", 1928 . . 45 15
810 3 k. Indian "Chief", 1930 . . 70 20
811 4 k. Rudge Multi, 1914 . . . 1·10 35
812 5 k. Honda "Benly J", 1953 . 1·40 45
813 6 k. CZ, 1938 . . . . 1·75 55

1985. Various stamps optd **1985**.

813a – 40 k. multicoloured (458)
813b – 50 k. multicoloured (443)
813c – 50 k. multicoloured (447)
813d – 70 k. multicoloured (477)
813e – 80 k. multicoloured (468)
813f – 100 k. multicoloured (449)
813g **122** 100 k. multicoloured .
813h **114** 200 k. multicoloured .
813i – 250 k. multicoloured (450)
813j **118** 250 k. violet and black
813k **121** 250 k. multicoloured
813m – 300 k. multicoloured (459)

184 Fly Agaric

1985. Fungi. Multicoloured.

814 50 c. Type **184** 15 10
815 1 k. Cep 30 10
816 2 k. Shaggy ink cap ("Coprinus comatus") 70 20
817 2 k. The blusher ("Amanita rubescens") 70 20
818 3 k. Downy boletus . . . . . 1·25 30
819 4 k. Parasol mushroom . . . 2·10 45
820 8 k. Brown roll-rim . . . . . 3·25 90

184a Battle Plan, Kursk, and Tanks

1985. 40th Anniv of End of Second World War. Multicoloured.

820a 1 k. Type **184a** 30 15
820b 2 k. Monument and military parade, Red Square, Moscow 60 25
820c 4 k. Street battle and battle plan, Stalingrad . . . . . 1·25 40
820d 5 k. Battle plan and Reichstag, Berlin . . . . 1·50 50
820e 6 k. Soviet Memorial, Berlin-Treptow, and military parade at Brandenburg Gate . . 1·75 60

185 Lenin reading "Pravda"

1985. 115th Birth Anniv of Lenin. Multicoloured.

821 1 k. Type **185** 25 10
822 2 k. Lenin (vert) 45 30
823 10 k. Lenin addressing meeting (vert) . . . . 2·40 1·50

186 "Cattleya percivaliana"

1985. "Argentina '85" International Stamp Exhibition, Buenos Aires. Orchids. Multicoloured.

824 50 c. Type **186** 10 10
825 1 k. "Odontoglossum luteo-purpureum" 25 10
826 2 k. "Cattleya lueddemanniana" 45 15
827 2 k. "Maxillaria sanderiana" 45 15
828 3 k. "Miltonia vexillaria" . . . 70 25
829 4 k. "Oncidium varicosum" . . 1·10 35
830 8 k. "Cattleya dowiana" . . . 2·50 70

187 Rhesus Macaque

188 "Saturn" Rocket on Launch Pad

1985. Mammals. Multicoloured.

832 2 k. Type **187** 45 15
833 3 k. Kouprey 70 25
834 4 k. Porcupine (horiz) . . . . 1·10 35
835 5 k. Asiatic black bear (horiz) 1·40 45
836 10 k. Chinese pangolin . . . . 2·75 90

1985. 10th Anniv of "Soyuz"–"Apollo" Space Link. Multicoloured.

837 50 c. Type **188** 10 10
838 1 k. Soviet rocket on launch pad 25 10
839 2 k. "Apollo" approaching "Soyuz 19" (horiz) 50 15
840 2 k. "Soyuz 19" approaching "Apollo" (horiz) 50 15
841 3 k. "Apollo" and crew T. Stafford, V. Brand and and D. Stayton (horiz) 80 25
842 4 k. "Soyuz 19" and crew A. Leonov and V. Kubasov (horiz) . . . . 1·10 35
843 8 k. "Apollo" and "Soyuz 19" docked (horiz) . . . . 2·25 70

189 Fiat Biplane

1985. "Italia '85" International Stamp Exhibition, Rome. Multicoloured. (a) Aircraft. As T **189**.

844 50 c. Type **189** 15 10
845 1 k. Cant Z.501 Gabbiano flying boat 30 10
846 2 k. Marina Fiat MF.5 flying boat 60 15
847 3 k. Macchi Castoldi MC-100 flying boat 90 25
848 4 k. Anzani biplane . . . . . 1·25 35
849 5 k. Ambrosini biplane . . . . 1·50 45
850 6 k. Piaggio P-148 . . . . . . 1·90 55

(b) Columbus and his Ships. Size 40 × 29 mm.

852 1 k. "Pinta" 30 10
853 2 k. "Nina" 60 10
854 3 k. "Santa Maria" 90 25
855 4 k. Christopher Columbus . . 1·25 35
856 5 k. Map of Columbus's first voyage . . . . 1·50 45

190 U.N. and National Flags on Globe

191 Woman feeding Child

1985. 40th Anniv of U.N.O. Multicoloured.

857 2 k. Type **190** 65 40
858 3 k. U.N. emblem and Laotian arms on globe 95 55
859 10 k. Map on globe . . . . . 3·25 1·75

1985. Lao Health Services. Multicoloured.

860 1 k. Type **191** 25 15
861 3 k. Red Cross nurse injecting child (horiz) 90 40
862 4 k. Red Cross nurse tending patient (horiz) . . . . . . 1·10 70
863 10 k. Mother breast-feeding baby 2·50 1·50

192 Soldier, Workers and Symbols of Industry and Agriculture

1985. 10th Anniv of Republic. Multicoloured.

864 3 k. Type **192** 80 50
865 10 k. Soldier, workers and symbols of transport and communications . . . . . 2·75 1·75

193 Soldier with Flag and Workers

1985. 30th Anniv of Lao People's Revolutionary Party. Multicoloured.

866 2 k. Type **193** 70 40
867 8 k. Soldier with flag and workers (different) . . . . 2·40 1·40

194 Footballers

194a Cosmonaut, "Mir" Space Complex and Earth

1986. World Cup Football Championship, Mexico (2nd issue).

868 **194** 50 c. multicoloured . . . 10 10
869 – 1 k. multicoloured 25 10
870 – 2 k. multicoloured 50 15
871 – 3 k. multicoloured 75 25
872 – 4 k. multicoloured 90 30
873 – 5 k. multicoloured . . . . 1·10 40
874 – 6 k. multicoloured . . . . 1·40 55

DESIGNS: 1 k. to 6 k. Various football scenes.

1986. 17th Soviet Communist Party Congress. Multicoloured.

875a 4 k. Type **194a** 90 35
875b 20 k. Lenin and Red Flag . . 4·50 95

195 "Pelargonium grandiflorum"

196 "Aporia hippia"

1986. Flowers. Multicoloured.

876 50 c. Type **195** 10 10
877 1 k. Columbine 25 10
878 2 k. "Fuchsia globosa" . . . 50 15
879 3 k. "Crocus aureus" 75 25
880 4 k. Hollyhock 90 30
881 5 k. "Gladiolus purpureo" . . . 1·10 45
882 6 k. "Hyacinthus orientalis" 1·75 65

1986. Butterflies. Multicoloured.

883 50 c. Type **196** 10 10
884 1 k. "Euthalia irrubescens" . . 25 10
885 2 k. "Japonica lutea" 50 15
886 3 k. "Pratapa ctesia" 75 25
887 4 k. Leaf butterfly 90 30
888 5 k. yellow orange-tip . . . . 1·10 45
889 6 k. Chestnut tiger . . . . . 1·75 65

197 Rocket launch at Baikanur Space Centre **198** Giraffe

1986. 25th Anniv of First Man in Space. Multicoloured.

890 50 c. Type **197** 10 10
891 1 k. "Molniya" communications satellite 20 10
892 2 k. "Salyut" space station (horiz) 50 20
893 3 k. Yuri Gargarin, "Sputnik 1" and rocket debris (horiz) 70 30
894 4 k. "Luna 3" and moon 95 40
895 5 k. Vladimir Komarov on first space walk 1·40 50
896 6 k. "Luna 16" lifting off from moon 1·60 90

1986. Animals. Multicoloured.

898 50 c. Type **198** 10 10
899 1 k. Lion 20 10
900 2 k. African elephant 40 20
901 3 k. Red kangaroo 60 30
902 4 k. Koala 80 40
903 5 k. Greater flamingo 1·25 50
904 6 k. Giant panda 1·75 90

199 Boeing 747-100

1986. Air. Aircraft. Multicoloured.

906 20 k. Type **199** 2·50 1·90
907 50 k. Ilyushin Il-86 7·00 5·25

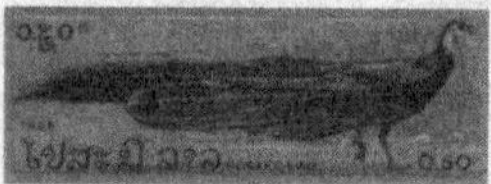

200 Great Argus Pheasant ($\frac{1}{2}$-size illustration)

1986. Pheasants. Multicoloured.

908 50 c. Type **200** 10 10
909 1 k. Silver pheasant 25 10
910 2 k. Ring-necked pheasant 50 20
911 3 k. Lady Amherst's pheasant 75 30
912 4 k. Reeves's pheasant 90 40
913 5 k. Golden pheasant 1·10 50
914 6 k. Copper pheasant 1·75 90

201 Scarlet King Snake

1986. Snakes. Multicoloured.

915 50 c. Corn snake 10 10
916 1 k. Type **201** 25 10
917 1 k. Richard's blind snake (vert) 25 10
918 2 k. Western ring-necked snake 50 25
919 4 k. Mangrove snake 90 40
920 5 k. Indian python 1·10 50
921 6 k. Common cobra (vert) 1·75 90

202 Bayeux Tapestry (detail) and Comet Head

1986. Appearance of Halley's Comet. Multicoloured.

922 50 c. Comet over Athens (65 × 21 mm) 10 10
923 1 k. Type **202** 30 10
924 2 k. Edmond Halley (astronomer) and comet tail (20 × 21 mm) 60 20
925 3 k. "Vega" space probe and comet head 90 30
926 4 k. Galileo and comet tail (20 × 21 mm) 1·10 40
927 5 k. Comet head (20 × 21 mm) 1·40 50
928 6 k. "Giotto" space probe and comet tail 1·75 90

Nos. 923/4, 925/6 and 927/8 resepctively were issued together, se-tenant, each pair forming a composite design.

203 Keeshond **204** "Mammillaria matudae"

1986. "Stockholmia 86" International Stamp Exhibition. Dogs. Multicoloured.

930 50 c. Type **203** 10 10
931 1 k. Elkhound (horiz) 20 10
932 2 k. Bernese (horiz) 45 25
933 3 k. Pointing griffon (horiz) 70 35
934 4 k. Collie (horiz) 90 45
935 5 k. Irish water spaniel (horiz) 1·10 55
936 6 k. Briard (horiz) 1·60 80

1986. Cacti. Multicoloured.

938 50 c. Type **204** 10 10
939 1 k. "Mammillaria theresae" 25 10
940 2 k. "Ariocarpus trigonus" 45 20
941 3 k. "Notocactus crassigibbus" 65 30
942 4 k. "Astrophytum asterias" hybrid 80 40
943 5 k. "Melocactus manzanus" 1·00 50
944 6 k. "Astrophytum ornatum" hybrid 1·25 60

205 Arms and Dove on Globe **206** Vat Phu Champasak

1986. International Peace Year.

945 **205** 3 k. multicoloured 85 40
946 – 5 k. black, blue and red 1·25 60
947 – 10 k. multicoloured 2·50 1·25

DESIGNS: 5 k. Dove on smashed bomb; 10 k. People supporting I.P.Y. emblem.

1984. 40th Anniv of U.N.E.S.C.O. Multicoloured.

948 3 k. Type **206** 75 30
949 4 k. Dish aerial and map of Laos on globe 1·00 40
950 9 k. People reading books (horiz) 2·00 80

207 Speed Skating

1987. Winter Olympic Games, Calgary (1988). (1st issue). Multicoloured.

951 50 c. Type **207** 10 10
952 1 k. Biathlon 25 10
953 2 k. Figure skating (pairs) 50 25
954 3 k. Luge (horiz) 70 35
955 4 k. Four-man bobsleigh (horiz) 90 45
956 5 k. Ice hockey (horiz) 1·10 55
957 6 k. Ski jumping (horiz) 1·40 70

See also Nos. 1046/51.

208 Gymnast and Urn

1987. Olympic Games, Seoul (1988) (1st issue). Sports and Greek Pottery. Multicoloured.

959 50 c. Type **208** 10 10
960 1 k. Throwing the discus and vase (horiz) 25 10
961 2 k. Running and urn 50 25
962 3 k. Show jumping and bowl (horiz) 70 35
963 4 k. Throwing the javelin and plate 90 45
964 5 k. High jumping and bowl with handles (horiz) 1·10 55
965 6 k. Wrestling and urn 1·40 70

See also Nos. 1053/9.

209 Great Dane

1987. Dogs. Multicoloured.

967 50 c. Type **209** 10 10
968 1 k. Black labrador 25 10
969 2 k. St. Bernard 50 15
970 3 k. Tervuren shepherd dog 70 25
971 4 k. German shepherd 90 30
972 5 k. Beagle 1·10 45
973 6 k. Golden retriever 1·50 50

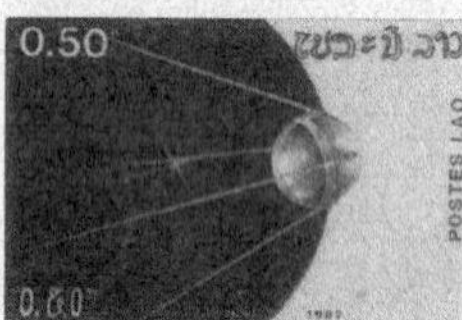

210 "Sputnik 1"

1987. 30th Anniv of Launch of First Artificial Satellite. Multicoloured.

974 50 c. Type **210** 10 10
975 1 k. "Sputnik 2" 20 10
976 2 k. "Cosmos 97" 40 20
977 3 k. "Cosmos" 60 30
978 4 k. "Mars" 75 35
979 5 k. "Luna 1" 95 45
980 9 k. "Luna 3" (vert) 1·50 75

211 "MONTREAL" Handstamp on Letter to Quebec and "Tern" (schooner)

1987. "Capex 87" International Stamp Exhibition, Toronto. Ships and Covers. Multicoloured.

981 50 c. Type **211** 10 10
982 1 k. "PAID MONTREAL" on letter and "Malahet" (schooner) 20 10
983 2 k. Letter from Montreal to London and "William D. Lawrence" (full-rigged ship) 40 20
984 3 k. 1840 letter to Williamsburgh and "Neptune" (early screw-steamer) 60 30
985 4 k. 1844 letter to London and "Athabasca" (early screw-steamer) 80 40
986 5 k. 1848 letter and "Chicora" (paddle-steamer) 1·00 50
987 6 k. 1861 letter and "Passport" (paddle-steamer) 1·25 60

212 Horse

1987. Horses. Multicoloured.

989 50 c. Type **212** 10 10
990 1 k. Chestnut (vert) 25 15
991 2 k. Black horse with sheepskin noseband (vert) 50 30
992 3 k. Dark chestnut (vert) 75 45
993 4 k. Black horse (vert) 1·00 60
994 5 k. Chestnut with plaited mane (vert) 1·40 85
995 6 k. Grey (vert) 1·75 1·00

213 Volvo "480"

1987. Motor Cars. Multicoloured.

996 50 c. Type **213** 10 10
997 1 k. Alfa Romeo "33" 20 10
998 2 k. Ford "Fiesta" 40 20
999 3 k. Ford "Fiesta" (different) 65 30
1000 4 k. Ford "Granada" 80 40
1001 5 k. Citroen "AX" 1·25 60
1002 6 k. Renault "21" 1·40 70

214 "Vanda teres"

1987. Orchids. Multicoloured.

1004 3 k. Type **214** 10 10
1005 7 k. "Laeliocattleya" sp. 15 10
1006 10 k. "Paphiopedilum" hybrid 25 10
1007 39 k. "Sobralia" sp. 85 40
1008 44 k. "Paphiopedilum" hybrid (different) 95 45
1009 47 k. "Paphiopedilum" hybrid (different) 1·10 50
1010 50 k. "Cattleya trianaei" 1·25 60

215 Elephants

1987. "Hafnia 87" International Stamp Exhibition, Copenhagen. Elephants. Multicoloured.

1012 50 c. Type **215** 10 10
1013 1 k. Three elephants 20 10
1014 2 k. Elephant feeding 40 20
1015 3 k. Elephant grazing on grass 60 30
1016 4 k. Adult with calf 80 40
1017 5 k. Elephant walking 1·10 60
1018 6 k. Elephant (vert) 1·40 70

216 Building Bamboo House

1987. International Year of Shelter for the Homeless. Multicoloured.

1020 1 k. Type **216** 10 10
1021 27 k. Building wooden house 60 30
1022 46 k. House on stilts 1·25 60
1023 70 k. Street of houses on stilts 1·75 90

217 Clown Loach

1987. Fishes. Multicoloured.

1024 3 k. Type **217** 10 10
1025 7 k. Harlequin file fish 15 10
1026 10 k. "Adioryx caudimaculatus" 25 10
1027 39 k. "Synchiropus splendidus" 85 40
1028 44 k. "Cephalopolis miniatus" 95 45
1029 47 k. Dwarf lion fish 1·10 50
1030 50 k. Semicircle angel fish 1·25 60

218 Watering Seedlings

1987. World Food Day. Multicoloured.
1031 1 k. Type **218** 10 10
1032 3 k. Harvesting maize (vert) 10 10
1033 5 k. Harvesting rice 15 10
1034 63 k. Children with fish (vert) 1·50 70
1035 142 k. Tending pigs and poultry 3·50 1·50

219 Wounded Soldiers on Battlefield

1987. 70th Anniv of Russian Revolution. Multicoloured.
1036 1 k. Type **219** 20 10
1037 2 k. Mother and baby . . . 40 20
1038 4 k. Storming the Winter Palace 80 40
1039 8 k. Lenin amongst soldiers and sailors . . . . 1·50 70
1040 10 k. Lenin labouring in Red Square . . . . 1·90 90

220 Hoeing

1987. Rice Culture in Mountain Regions. Mult.
1041 64 k. Type **220** . . . . 1·40 70
1042 100 k. Working in paddy fields 2·25 1·10

221 Laotheung Costume

1987. Ethnic Costumes. Multicoloured.
1043 7 k. Type **221** 25 10
1044 38 k. Laoloum costume . . . 90 40
1045 144 k. Laosoun costume . . 3·00 1·40

222 Two-man Bobsleigh

1988. Winter Olympic Games, Calgary (2nd issue). Multicoloured.
1046 1 k. Type **222** 10 10
1047 4 k. Biathlon (shooting) . . . 15 10
1048 20 k. Cross-country skiing . . 50 25
1049 42 k. Ice hockey . . . . . . 1·00 50
1050 63 k. Speed skating . . . . . 1·50 75
1051 70 k. Slalom . . . . 1·75 90

223 Throwing the Javelin

1988. Olympic Games, Seoul (2nd issue). Mult.
1053 2 k. Type **223** 10 10
1054 5 k. Triple jumping 15 10
1055 10 k. Men's gymnastics . . . 25 15
1056 12 k. Pirogue racing 30 15
1057 38 k. Women's gymnastics . . 90 45
1058 46 k. Fencing . . . . 1·10 50
1059 100 k. Wrestling . . . . . . 2·50 1·25

224 Tyrannosaurus

1988. "Juvalux 88" Youth Philately Exhibition, Luxembourg. Prehistoric Animals. Multicoloured.
1061 3 k. Type **224** (wrongly inscr "Trachodon") 10 10
1062 7 k. "Ceratosaurus nasicornis" (vert) 15 10
1063 39 k. "Iguanodon bernissartensis" (vert) . . 80 35
1064 44 k. Scolosaurus (vert) . . 1·25 60
1065 47 k. "Phororhacus" sp. (vert) 1·25 60
1066 50 k. Anatosaurus (wrongly inscr "Tyrannosaurus") . 1·40 65

225 Adults in Hygiene Class

1988. 40th Anniv of W.H.O. Multicoloured.
1068 5 k. Type **225** 10 10
1069 27 k. Fumigating houses . . 55 25
1070 164 k. Woman pumping fresh water (vert) . . . . 3·50 1·40

226 "Sans Pareil", 1829 **227** Red Frangipani

1988. "Essen 88" International Stamp Fair. Early Railway Locomotives. Multicoloured.
1071 6 k. Type **226** 10 10
1072 15 k. Stephenson's "Rocket", 1829 . . . . 30 15
1073 20 k. "Royal George", 1827 (horiz) 40 20
1074 25 k. Trevithick's locomotive, 1804 (horiz) 50 25
1075 30 k. "Novelty", 1829 (horiz) 65 30
1076 100 k. "Tom Thumb", 1829 (horiz) . . . . 2·25 1·10

1988. "Finlandia 88" International Stamp Exhibition, Helsinki. Flowers. Multicoloured.
1078 8 k. Type **227** 20 10
1079 9 k. Hollyhock 25 10
1080 15 k. Flame-of-the-forest . . 35 15
1081 33 k. Golden shower 75 35
1082 64 k. "Dahlia coccinea" (red) 1·50 70
1083 69 k. "Dahlia coccinea" (yellow) . . . . 1·75 90

228 Sash Pattern

1988. Decorative Stencil Patterns.
1085 **228** 1 k. multicoloured . . . 10 10
1086 – 2 k. yellow, red and black 10 10
1087 – 3 k. multicoloured . . . 10 10
1088 – 25 k. multicoloured . . 50 25
1089 – 163 k. multicoloured . . 3·50 1·25
DESIGNS (stencils for)—VERT: 2 k. Pagoda doors; 3 k. Pagoda walls. HORIZ: 25 k. Pagoda pillars; 163 k. Skirts.

229 Dove and Figures **230** Stork-billed Kingfisher

1988. 125th Anniv of Red Cross Movement. Multicoloured.
1090 4 k. Type **229** 10 10
1091 52 k. Red Cross workers with handicapped people . . . 1·00 50
1092 144 k. Red Cross worker vaccinating baby (horiz) . . 3·50 1·10

1988. Birds. Multicoloured.
1093 6 k. Type **230** 20 10
1094 10 k. Japanese quail 25 10
1095 13 k. Blossom-headed parakeet 35 15
1096 44 k. Orange-breasted green pigeon 80 40
1097 63 k. Black-crested bulbul . . 1·40 70
1098 64 k. Mountain imperial pigeon 1·60 80

231 Red Cross Workers loading Supplies into Pirogue

1988. Completion of 1st Five Year Plan. Multicoloured.
1099 20 k. Type **231** 50 10
1100 40 k. Library 90 45
1101 50 k. Irrigating fields . . . . 1·25 60
1102 100 k. Improvement in communications . . . . . 2·50 1·40

232 Ruy Lopez Segura

1988. Chess Masters. Multicoloured.
1103 1 k. Type **232** 10 10
1104 2 k Karl Anderssen 10 10
1105 3 k. Paul Morphy (wrongly inscr "Murphy") 15 10
1106 6 k. Wilhelm Steinitz 25 10
1107 7 k. Emanuel Lasker 30 15
1108 12 k. Jose Raul Capablanca 50 20
1109 172 k. Aleksandr Alekhine . . 4·25 1·75

233 Tortoiseshell and White

1989. "India 89" International Stamp Exhibition, New Delhi. Cats. Multicoloured.
1110 5 k. Type **233** 10 10
1111 6 k. Brown tabby 15 10
1112 10 k. Black and white 25 10
1113 20 k. Red tabby 50 15
1114 50 k. Black . . . . 1·00 35
1115 172 k. Silver tabby and white 3·50 1·25

234 Gunboat, Tank, Soldiers and Flags

1989. 40th Anniv of People's Army. Multicoloured.
1117 1 k. Type **234** 10 10
1118 2 k. Soldier teaching mathematics (vert) 10 10
1119 3 k. Army medics vaccinating civilians 15 10
1120 250 k. Peasant, revolutionary, worker and soldiers . . . . 5·50 1·00

235 Footballers

1989. World Cup Football Championship, Italy (1990) (1st issue). Multicoloured.
1121 10 k. Type **235** 15 10
1122 15 k. Footballer looking to pass ball 25 10
1123 20 k. Ball hitting player on chest 40 15
1124 25 k. Tackle 55 20
1125 45 k. Dribbling ball 90 35
1126 105 k. Kicking ball . . . . . 2·25 90
See also Nos. 1168/73.

236 Couple planting Sapling

1989. Preserve Forests Campaign. Multicoloured
1128 4 k. Type **236** 10 10
1129 10 k. Burning and fallen trees 20 10
1130 12 k. Man felling tree (vert) 25 15
1131 200 k. Trees on map (vert) 4·00 2·50

237 Camilo Cienfuegos, Fidel Castro and Flag **238** Skaters

1989. 30th Anniv of Cuban Revolution. Multicoloured.
1132 45 k. Type **237** . . . . . . 1·25 35
1133 50 d. Cuban and Laotian flags 1·25 35

1989. Winter Olympic Games, Albertville (1992) (1st issue). Figure Skating. Multicoloured.
1134 9 k. Type **238** 20 10
1135 10 k. Pair (horiz) 20 10
1136 15 k. Ice dancing 35 15
1137 24 k. Female skater 50 25
1138 29 k. Pair 55 25
1139 114 k. Male skater . . . . . 2·50 1·00
See also Nos. 1196/1201, 1237/41 and 1276/80.

239 High Jumping **241** Sapodillas

240 "Poor on Seashore"

1989. Olympic Games, Barcelona (1992) (1st issue). Multicoloured.
1141 5 k. Type **239** 15 10
1142 15 k. Gymnastics 45 25
1143 20 k. Cycling (horiz) 60 30
1144 25 k. Boxing (horiz) 75 40
1145 70 k. Archery . . . . 1·90 1·00
1146 120 k. Swimming . . . . . . 3·75 2·10
See also Nos. 1179/84, 1231/5 and 1282/6.

1989. "Philexfrance '89" International Stamp Exhibition, Paris. Paintings by Picasso. Mult.
1148 5 k. Type **240** 10 10
1149 7 k. "Motherhood" 15 10
1150 8 k. "Portrait of Jaime S. le Bock" 20 15
1151 9 k. "Harlequins" 25 15
1152 105 k. "Boy with Dog" . . . 2·25 1·00
1153 114 k. "Girl on Ball" . . . . 2·25 1·00

1989. Fruits. Multicoloured.
1155 5 k. Type **241** 10 10
1156 20 k. Sugar-apples 45 20
1157 20 k. Guavas 45 20
1158 30 k. Durians 70 30
1159 50 k. Pomegranates . . . . . 1·10 50
1160 172 k. "Moridica charautia" 3·75 1·75

242 Sikhotabong Temple, Khammouane

243 Nehru and Woman

1989. Temples. Multicoloured.

1161	5 k. Type **242**	10	10
1162	15 k. Dam Temple, Vientiane	35	20
1163	61 k. Ing Hang Temple, Savannakhet	1·10	65
1164	161 k. Ho Vay Phra Luang Temple, Vientiane	3·75	2·10

1989. Birth Centenary of Jawaharlal Nehru (Indian statesman). Multicoloured.

1165	1 k. Type **243**	10	10
1166	60 k. Nehru and group of children (horiz)	1·25	35
1167	200 k. Boy garlanding Nehru	4·25	1·25

244 Footballer

1990. World Cup Football Championship, Italy (2nd issue).

1168	**244**	10 k. multicoloured	25	10
1169	–	15 k. multicoloured	35	15
1170	–	20 k. multicoloured	50	25
1171	–	25 k. multicoloured	60	30
1172	–	45 k. multicoloured	1·10	55
1173	–	105 k. multicoloured	2·75	1·25

DESIGNS: 15 to 105 k. Different footballing scenes.

245 Teacher and Adult Class

1990. International Literacy Year. Multicoloured.

1175	10 k. Type **245**	25	10
1176	50 k. Woman teaching child (vert)	1·40	70
1177	60 k. Monk teaching adults	1·50	75
1178	150 k. Group reading and writing under tree	3·75	1·75

246 Basketball

1990. Olympic Games, Barcelona (1992) (2nd issue). Multicoloured.

1179	10 k. Type **246**	20	10
1180	30 k. Hurdling	60	25
1181	45 k. High jumping	95	40
1182	50 k. Cycling	1·10	45
1183	60 k. Throwing the javelin	1·25	50
1184	90 k. Tennis	2·00	80

247 Great Britain 1840 Penny Black and Mail Coach

1990. "Stamp World London 90" International Stamp Exhibition. Multicoloured.

1186	15 k. Type **247**	35	15
1187	20 k. U.S. 1847 5 c. stamp and early steam locomotive	45	20
1188	40 k. France 1849 20 c. stamp and mail balloons, Paris, 1870	90	35
1189	50 k. Sardinia 1851 5 c. stamp and post rider	1·10	45
1190	60 k. Indo-China 1892 1 c. stamp and elephant	1·40	50
1191	100 k. Spain 1850 6 c. stamp and galleon	2·25	90

248 Ho Chi Minh addressing Crowd

1990. Birth Centenary of Ho Chi Minh. Mult.

1193	40 k. Type **248**	85	35
1194	60 k. Ho Chi Minh and Laotian President	1·25	50
1195	160 k. Ho Chi Minh and Vietnamese flag (vert)	3·50	1·40

249 Speed Skating

1990. Winter Olympic Games, Albertville (1992) (2nd issue). Multicoloured.

1196	10 k. Type **249**	20	10
1197	25 k. Cross-country skiing (vert)	55	20
1198	30 k. Downhill skiing	65	25
1199	35 k. Tobogganing	75	30
1200	80 k. Figure skating (pairs) (vert)	1·75	70
1201	90 k. Biathlon	2·00	80

250 That Luang, 1990

1990. 430th Anniv of That Luang. Multicoloured.

1203	60 k. That Luang, 1867 (horiz)	1·40	55
1204	70 k. That Luang, 1930 (horiz)	1·50	60
1205	130 k. Type **250**	2·75	1·10

251 Tui

1990. "New Zealand 1990" International Stamp Exhibition, Auckland. Multicoloured.

1206	10 k. Type **251**	20	10
1207	15 k. Sky lark	30	10
1208	20 k. New Zealand sooty oystercatcher	40	15
1209	50 k. Common cormorant	1·00	40
1210	60 k. Eastern reef heron	1·25	50
1211	100 k. Brown kiwi	2·50	1·00

252 Brown-antlered Deer

1990. Mammals. Multicoloured.

1213	10 k. Type **252**	25	10
1214	20 k. Gaur	50	20
1215	40 k. Wild water buffalo	1·00	40
1216	45 k. Kouprey	1·00	40
1217	120 k. Javan rhinoceros	3·00	1·25

253 Surgeons Operating

1990. 40th Anniv of United Nations Development Programme. Multicoloured.

1218	30 k. Type **253**	60	25
1219	45 k. Fishermen inspecting catch	1·00	40
1220	80 k. Air-traffic controller (vert)	1·60	65
1221	90 k. Electricity plant workers	1·75	70

254 Rice Ceremony

1990. New Year. Multicoloured.

1222	5 k. Type **254**	10	10
1223	10 k. Elephant in carnival parade	25	10
1224	50 k. Making offerings at temple	1·25	50
1225	150 k. Family ceremony	3·75	1·50

255 Memorial, Wreath and Eternal Flame

1990. 15th National Day Festival. Multicoloured.

1226	15 k. Type **255**	40	15
1227	20 k. Celebration parade	50	20
1228	80 k. Hospital visit	2·00	80
1229	120 k. Girls parading with banner	2·75	1·10

257 Two-man Kayak

1991. Olympic Games, Barcelona (1992) (3rd issue). Multicoloured.

1231	22 k. Type **257**	10	10
1232	32 k. Canoeing	10	10
1233	285 k. Diving (vert)	95	40
1234	330 k. Yachting (vert)	1·10	45
1235	1000 k. Swimming	3·25	1·25

258 Bobsleighing

1991. Winter Olympic Games, Albertville (1992) (3rd issue). Multicoloured.

1237	32 k. Type **258**	10	10
1238	135 k. Cross-country skiing (horiz)	45	20
1239	250 k. Ski jumping (horiz)	85	35
1240	275 k. Biathlon (horiz)	95	40
1241	900 k. Speed skating (horiz)	3·00	1·25

259 Pha Pheng Falls, Champassak

1991. Tourism. Multicoloured.

1243	155 k. Type **259**	45	15
1244	220 k. Pha Tang mountains, Vangvieng	65	25
1245	235 k. Tat Set waterfall, Saravane (vert)	75	30
1246	1000 k. Plain of Jars, Xieng Khouang (vert)	2·75	1·10

260 Match Scene

1991. World Cup Football Championship, U.S.A. (1994) (1st issue). Multicoloured.

1247	32 k. Type **260**	10	10
1248	330 k. Goalkeeper catching ball	1·10	45
1249	340 k. Player controlling ball (vert)	1·25	50
1250	400 k. Player dribbling ball	1·50	60
1251	500 k. Tackle	1·90	75

See also Nos. 1292/6, 1370/4 and 1386/90.

261 Planting Saplings

1991. National Tree Planting Day. Multicoloured.

1253	350 k. Type **261**	70	25
1254	700 k. Planting saplings (different)	2·00	80
1255	800 k. Removing saplings from store	2·40	95

262 Mallard

1991. "Espamer '91" Spain-Latin America Stamp Exhibition, Buenos Aires. Railway Locomotives. Multicoloured.

1256	25 k. Type **262**	10	10
1257	32 k. Pacific "231" steam locomotive	15	10
1258	285 k. American locomotive	1·10	45
1259	650 k. Canadian Pacific steam locomotive	2·40	95
1260	750 k. Beyer-Garratt (wrongly inscr "Garrant")	3·00	1·25

263 Spindle Festival

1991. Traditional Music. Multicoloured.

1262	20 k. Type **263**	10	10
1263	220 k. Mong player (vert)	60	25
1264	275 k. Siphandone singer (vert)	70	25
1265	545 k. Khap ngum singer	1·60	60
1266	690 k. Phouthaydam dance	2·00	80

264 Great Purple

1991. "Phila Nippon '91" International Stamp Exhibition, Tokyo. Butterflies. Multicoloured.

1267	55 k. Type **264**	20	10
1268	90 k. "Luehdorfia puziloi" (wrongly inscr "Luendorfia")	30	10
1269	255 k. "Papilio bianor"	75	30
1270	285 k. Swallowtail	85	35
1271	900 k. Mikado swallowtail	2·75	1·10

265 Emblem and Pattern

266 Bobsleighing

1991. International Decade for Cultural Development (1988–97). Multicoloured.

1273	285 k. Type **265**	45	20
1274	330 k. Emblem and drum	55	20
1275	1000 k. Emblem and pipes	1·60	65

1992. Winter Olympic Games, Albertville (4th issue). Multicoloured.

1276	200 k. Type **266**	60	25
1277	220 k. Slalom skiing	65	25
1278	250 k. Downhill skiing (horiz)	75	30
1279	500 k. One-man luge	1·50	60
1280	600 k. Figure skating	1·75	70

267 Running

269 Argentinian and Italian Players and Flags

268 Pest Control

1992. Olympic Games, Barcelona (4th issue). Multicoloured.

1282	32 k. Type **267**	10	10
1283	245 k. Baseball	75	30
1284	275 k. Tennis	80	30
1285	285 k. Basketball	85	35
1286	900 k. Boxing (horiz)	2·75	1·10

1992. World Health Day. Multicoloured.

1288	200 k. Type **268**	60	25
1289	255 k. Anti-smoking campaign	75	30
1290	330 k. Donating blood	1·00	40
1291	1000 k. Vaccinating child (vert)	3·25	1·25

1992. World Cup Football Championship, U.S.A. (1994) (2nd issue). Multicoloured.

1292	260 k. Type **269**	60	25
1293	305 k. German and English players and flags	85	35
1294	310 k. United States flag, ball and trophy	90	35
1295	350 k. Italian and English players and flags	1·10	45
1296	800 k. German and Argentinian players and flags	2·50	1·00

270 Common Cobra

1992. Snakes. Multicoloured.

1298	280 k. Type **270**	75	30
1299	295 k. Common cobra	80	30
1300	420 k. Wagler's pit viper	1·10	45
1301	700 k. King cobra (vert)	2·25	90

271 Doorway and Ruins

1992. Restoration of Wat Phou. Multicoloured.

1302	185 k. Type **271**	50	20
1303	220 k. Doorway (different)	60	25
1304	1200 k. Doorway with collapsed porch (horiz)	3·50	1·40

272 "Pinta" and Juan Martinez's Map

1992. "Genova '92" International Thematic Stamp Exhibition. Multicoloured.

1305	100 k. Type **272**	30	10
1306	300 k. Piri Reis's letter and caravelle (vert)	90	35
1307	350 k. Magellan's ship and Paolo del Pozo Toscanelli's world map	1·10	45
1308	400 k. Gabriel de Vallesca's map and Vasco da Gama's flagship "Sao Gabriel"	1·25	50
1309	455 k. Juan Martinez's map and Portuguese four-masted caravel	1·40	55

273 Woman in Traditional Costume

274 Boy Drumming

1992. Traditional Costumes of Laotian Mountain Villages.

1311	**273**	25 k. multicoloured	10	10
1312	–	55 k. multicoloured	15	10
1313	–	400 k. multicoloured	1·10	45
1314	–	1200 k. multicoloured	3·75	1·25

DESIGNS: 55 to 1200 k. Different costumes.

1992. International Children's Day. Children at Play. Multicoloured.

1315	220 k. Type **274**	75	30
1316	285 k. Girls skipping (horiz)	1·00	40
1317	330 k. Boys racing on stilts	1·10	45
1318	400 k. Girls playing "escape" game (horiz)	1·40	55

275 Praying before Buddha

276 Crested Gibbon

1992. National Customs. Multicoloured.

1319	100 k. Type **275**	30	10
1320	140 k. Wedding (horiz)	40	15
1321	160 k. Religious procession (horiz)	50	20
1322	1500 k. Monks receiving alms (horiz)	4·75	1·90

1992. Climbing Mammals. Multicoloured.

1323	10 k. Type **276**	10	10
1324	100 k. Variegated langur	30	10
1325	250 k. Pileated gibbon	70	30
1326	430 k. Francois's monkey	1·25	50
1327	800 k. Lesser slow loris	2·25	90

277 New York

1993. 130th Anniv of Underground Railway Systems. Multicoloured.

1328	15 k. Type **277**	10	10
1329	50 k. Berlin	20	10
1330	100 k. Paris	40	15
1331	200 k. London	80	30
1332	900 k. Moscow	3·50	1·40

278 Malayan Bullfrog

1993. Amphibians. Multicoloured.

1334	55 k. Type **278**	20	10
1335	90 k. Muller's clawed frog	30	10
1336	100 k. Glass frog (vert)	35	15
1337	185 k. Giant toad	70	30
1338	1200 k. Common tree frog (vert)	4·25	1·75

279 Common Tree-shrew

280 Noble Scallop

1993. Mammals. Multicoloured.

1339	45 k. Type **279**	15	10
1340	60 k. Philippine flying lemur	20	10
1341	120 k. Loris	35	15
1342	500 k. Eastern tarsier	1·50	60
1343	600 k. Giant gibbon	1·75	70

1993. Molluscs. Multicoloured.

1344	20 k. Type **280**	10	10
1345	30 k. Precious wentletrap	10	10
1346	70 k. Spider conch	25	10
1347	500 k. Aulicus cone	1·75	70
1348	1000 k. Milleped spider conch	3·50	1·40

281 Drugs and Skull smoking

1993. Anti-drugs Campaign. Multicoloured.

1349	200 k. Type **281**	70	30
1350	430 k. Burning seized drugs	1·50	60
1351	900 k. Instructing on dangers of drugs	3·00	1·25

282 House

283 Greater Spotted Eagle

1993. Traditional Houses. Multicoloured.

1352	32 k. Type **282**	10	10
1353	200 k. Thatched house with gable end (horiz)	70	30
1354	650 k. Thatched house (horiz)	2·25	90
1355	750 k. House with tiled roof (horiz)	2·50	1·00

1993. Birds of Prey. Multicoloured.

1356	10 k. Type **283**	10	10
1357	100 k. Spotted little owl	35	15
1358	330 k. Pied harrier (horiz)	1·10	45
1359	1000 k. Short-toed eagle	3·50	1·40

284 Fighting Forest Fire

1993. Environmental Protection. Multicoloured.

1360	32 k. Type **284**	10	10
1361	40 k. Wildlife on banks of River Mekong	15	10
1362	260 k. Paddy fields	85	35
1363	1100 k. Oxen in river	1·40	55

285 "Narathura atosia"

1993. "Bangkok 1993" International Stamp Exhibition. Butterflies. Multicoloured.

1364	35 k. Type **285**	10	10
1365	80 k. "Parides philoxenus"	25	10
1366	150 k. "Euploea harrisi"	50	20
1367	220 k. Yellow orange-tip	75	30
1368	500 k. Female common palm fly	1·75	70

286 Footballer

287 Hesperornis

1993. World Cup Football Championship, U.S.A. (3rd issue). Multicoloured.

1370	10 k. Type **286**	10	10
1371	20 k. Brazil player	10	10
1372	285 k. Uruguay player	90	35
1373	400 k. Germany player	1·25	50
1374	800 k. Forward challenging goalkeeper	2·50	1·00

1994. Prehistoric Birds. Multicoloured.

1376	10 k. Type **287**	10	10
1377	20 k. Mauritius dodo	10	10
1378	150 k. Archaeopteryx	50	20
1379	600 k. Phororhachos	2·00	80
1380	700 k. Giant moa	2·25	90

288 Olympic Flag and Flame

289 Bridge and National Flags

1994. Centenary of International Olympic Committee. Multicoloured.

1382	100 k. Type **288**	35	10
1383	250 k. Ancient Greek athletes (horiz)	90	30
1384	1000 k. Pierre de Coubertin (founder) and modern athlete	3·50	1·10

1994. Opening of Friendship Bridge between Laos and Thailand.

1385	**289**	500 k. multicoloured	70	25

290 World Map and Players

1994. World Cup Football Championship, U.S.A. (4th issue).

1386	**290**	40 k. multicoloured	10	10
1387	–	50 k. multicoloured	10	10
1388	–	60 k. multicoloured	10	10
1389	–	320 k. multicoloured	45	15
1390	–	900 k. multicoloured	1·25	45

DESIGNS: 50 to 900 k. Different players on world map.

291 Pagoda

1994. Pagodas.

1392	**291**	30 k. multicoloured	10	10
1393	–	150 k. multicoloured	20	10
1394	–	380 k. multicoloured	55	20
1395	–	1100 k. multicoloured	1·60	55

DESIGNS: 150 to 1100 k. Different gabled roofs.

292 Bear eating

1994. The Malay Bear. Multicoloured.

1396	50 k. Type **292**	10	10
1397	90 k. Bear's head	15	10
1398	200 k. Adult and cub	30	10
1399	220 k. Bear	30	10

293 Grass Snake

1994. Amphibians and Reptiles. Multicoloured.

1400	70 k. Type **293**	10	10
1401	80 k. Tessellated snake	10	10
1402	90 k. Fire salamander	15	10
1403	600 k. Alpine newt	85	30
1404	800 k. Green lizard (vert)	1·10	40

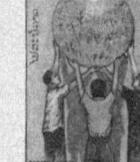

294 Phra Xayavoraman 7 — 295 Family supporting Healthy Globe

1994. Buddhas. Multicoloured.

1406	15 k. Type **294**	10	10
1407	280 k. Phra Thong Souk	40	15
1408	390 k. Phra Manolom	55	20
1409	800 k. Phra Ongtu	1·10	40

1994. International Year of the Family. Multicoloured.

1410	200 k. Type **295**	30	10
1411	500 k. Mother taking child to school (horiz)	70	25
1412	700 k. Mother and children	1·00	35

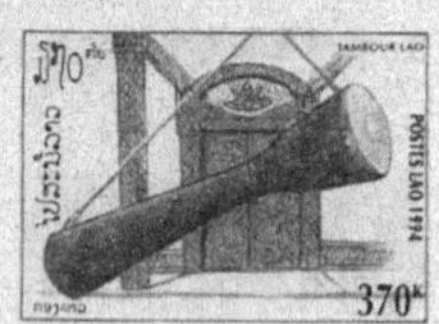

296 Kong Hang

1994. Traditional Laotian Drums. Multicoloured.

1414	370 k. Type **296**	50	20
1415	440 k. Kong Leng (portable drum)	60	20
1416	450 k. Kong Toum (drum on stand)	65	25
1417	600 k. Kong Phene (hanging drum)	85	30

297 Elephant in Procession

1994. Ceremonial Elephants. Multicoloured.

1418	140 k. Type **297**	20	10
1419	400 k. Elephant in pavilion	55	20
1420	890 k. Elephant in street procession (vert)	1·25	45

298 Theropodes

1994. Prehistoric Animals. Multicoloured.

1421	50 k. Type **298**	10	10
1422	380 k. Iguanodontides	55	20
1423	420 k. Sauropodes	60	20

299 Playing Musical Instruments

1995. 20th Anniv of World Tourism Organization. Multicoloured.

1424	60 k. Type **299**	10	10
1425	250 k. Women dancing	35	15
1426	400 k. Giving alms to monks	55	20
1427	650 k. Waterfall (vert)	90	30

300 Trachodon

1995. Prehistoric Animals. Multicoloured.

1429	50 k. Type **300**	10	10
1430	70 k. Protoceratops	10	10
1431	300 k. Brontosaurus	40	15
1432	400 k. Stegosaurus	55	20
1433	600 k. Tyrannosaurus	85	30

301 Indian Jungle Mynah

1995. Birds. Multicoloured.

1434	50 k. Type **301**	10	10
1435	150 k. Jerdon's starling	20	10
1436	300 k. Common mynah	40	15
1437	700 k. Southern grackle	1·00	35

303 Pole Vaulting — 304 Chalice

1995. Olympic Games, Atlanta. Multicoloured.

1441	60 k. Type **303**	10	10
1442	80 k. Throwing the javelin	10	10
1443	200 k. Throwing the hammer	25	10
1444	350 k. Long jumping	45	15
1445	700 k. High jumping	95	35

1995. Antique Vessels. Multicoloured.

1447	70 k. Type **304**	10	10
1448	200 k. Resin and silver bowl (horiz)	25	10
1449	450 k. Geometrically-decorated bowl (horiz)	60	20
1450	600 k. Religious chalice (horiz)	80	30

305 Procession

1995. Rocket Festival. Multicoloured.

1451	80 k. Launching rocket (vert)	10	10
1452	160 k. Type **305**	20	10
1453	500 k. Musicians in procession	70	25
1454	700 k. Crowds and rockets	95	35

306 Red Tabby Longhair

1995. Cats. Multicoloured.

1455	40 k. Type **306**	10	10
1456	50 k. Siamese sealpoint	10	10
1457	250 k. Red tabby longhair (different)	35	15
1458	400 k. Tortoiseshell shorthair	55	20
1459	650 k. Head of tortoiseshell shorthair (vert)	90	30

307 "Nepenthes villosa"

1995. Insectivorous Plants. Multicoloured.

1461	90 k. Type **307**	10	10
1462	100 k. "Dionaea muscipula"	15	10
1463	350 k. "Sarracenia flava"	45	15
1464	450 k. "Sarracenia purpurea"	60	20
1465	500 k. "Nepenthes ampullaria"	70	25

308 Stag Beetle

1995. Insects. Multicoloured.

1467	40 k. Type **308**	10	10
1468	50 k. May beetle	10	10
1469	500 k. Blue carpenter beetle	70	25
1470	800 k. Great green grasshopper	1·10	40

309 Cattle grazing

1995. 50th Anniv of F.A.O. Multicoloured.

1471	80 k. Type **309**	10	10
1472	300 k. Working paddy field	40	15
1473	1000 k. Agriculture	1·40	50

310 At Meeting

1995. 50th Anniv of U.N.O. Peoples of Different Races. Multicoloured.

1474	290 k. Type **310**	40	15
1475	310 k. Playing draughts	40	15
1476	440 k. Children playing	60	20

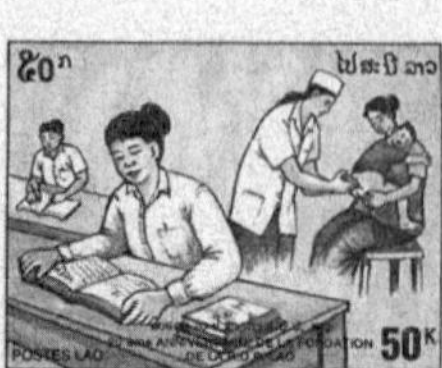

311 Students and Nurse vaccinating Child

1995. 20th Anniv of Republic. Multicoloured.

1477	50 k. Type **311**	10	10
1478	280 k. Agricultural land	40	15
1479	600 k. Bridge	80	30

POSTAGE DUE STAMPS

D 5 Vat Sisaket Shrine — D 6 Sampans — D 98 Serpent

1952.

D22	D 5	10 c. brown	20	35
D23		20 c. violet	20	35
D24		50 c. red	20	30
D25		1 p. green	25	35
D26		2 p. blue	25	35
D27		5 p. purple	70	80
D28	D 6	10 p. blue	1·10	1·25

1973.

D378	D 98	10 k. black, brn & yell	10	10
D379		15 k. black, yell & grn	10	10
D380		20 k. black, green & bl	15	15
D381		50 k. black, blue & red	30	30

APPENDIX

The following stamps have either been issued in excess of postal needs or have not been available to the public in reasonable quantities at face value. Such stamps may later be given full listing if there is evidence of regular postal use.

1975.

Centenary of U.P.U. Postage 10, 15, 30, 40 k; Air 1000, 1500 k. On gold foil 2500, 3000 k.

"Apollo-Soyuz" Space Link. Postage 125, 150, 200, 300 k.; Air 450, 700 k.

Bicentenary of American Revolution. Postage 10, 15, 40, 50, 100, 125, 150, 200 k.; Air 1000, 1500 k.

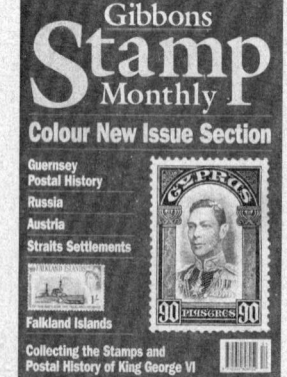

LATAKIA Pt. 19

The former state of the Alaouites which changed its name to Latakia in 1930.
Latakia was merged with Syria in 1936.

100 centimes = 1 piastre.

1931. As 1930 stamps of Syria (T **26/7**) optd **LATTAQUIE** in French and Arabic.

65 0 p. 10 mauve 90 60
66 0 p. 20 blue . . . . 40 1·40
67 0 p. 20 red . . . . 85 1·25
68 0 p. 25 green . . . . 40 1·40
69 0 p. 25 violet . . . . 1·50 1·75
70 0 p. 50 violet . . . . 90 1·60
71 0 p. 75 red . . . . 1·75 1·75
72 1 p. green 90 95
73 1 p. 50 brown . . . . 2·25 2·25
74 1 p. 50 green . . . . 2·25 2·25
75 2 p. violet . . . . 2·25 1·40
76 3 p. green . . . . 3·25 3·00
77 4 p. orange . . . . 3·00 2·25
78 4 p. 50 red . . . . 3·00 3·25
79 6 p. green . . . . 2·75 3·25
80 7 p. 50 blue . . . . 3·00 3·25
81 10 p. brown . . . . 4·75 5·00
82 15 p. green . . . . 6·25 7·00
83 25 p. purple . . . . 14·50 14·50
84 50 p. brown . . . . 12·00 12·50
85 100 p. red . . . . 35·00 38·00

1931. Air. As 1931 air stamps of Syria optd **LATTAQUIE** in French and Arabic.

86 0 p. 50 yellow . . . . 1·40 1·40
87 0 p. 50 brown . . . . 1·10 1·60
88 1 p. brown . . . . 1·75 1·90
89 2 p. blue . . . . 2·25 2·25
90 3 p. green . . . . 2·50 2·50
91 5 p. purple . . . . 5·25 5·50
92 10 p. blue . . . . 6·75 6·75
93 15 p. red . . . . 9·00 9·00
94 25 p. orange . . . . 17·00 17·00
95 50 p. black . . . . 24·00 25·00
96 100 p. mauve . . . . 25·00 24·00

POSTAGE DUE STAMPS

1931. Nos. D197/8 of Syria optd **LATTAQUIE** in French and Arabic.

D86 8 p. black on blue . . . . . 15·00 16·00
D87 15 p. black on pink . . . . . 11·00 12·50

LATVIA Pt. 10

A country on the Baltic Sea. Previously part of the Russian Empire, Latvia was independent from 1918 to 1940 when it became part of the U.S.S.R. Following the dissolution of the U.S.S.R. in 1991, Latvia once again became an independent republic.

1918. 100 kapeikas = 1 rublis.
1923. 100 santimu = 1 lats.
1991. 100 kopeks = 1 (Russian) rouble.
1992. 100 kopeks = 1 Latvian rouble.
1993. 100 santimu = 1 lats.

1 4 5 Rising Sun

1918. Printed on back of German war maps. Imperf or perf.

15 **1** 3 k. lilac 10 10
16 5 k. red 10 10
17 10 k. blue 10 10
18 15 k. green 10 10
41 20 k. orange 10 10
20 25 k. grey 50 35
21 35 k. brown 20 20
42 40 k. purple 30 10
22 50 k. violet 20 20
44 75 k. green 25 15
29 3 r. red and blue . . . . . . 1·25 75
30 5 r. red and brown . . . . . 1·00 85

1919. Liberation of Riga. Imperf.

24 **4** 5 k. red 20 15
25 15 k. green 20 15
26 35 k. brown 35 10

For stamps of Type **1** and **4** optd with a cross, with or without Russian letters "Z A". see under North-West Russia Nos. 21/42.

1919. Imperf or perf.

27 **5** 10 k. blue 45 35

6 7

1919. 1st Anniv of Independence. (a) Size 33 × 45 mm.

32 **6** 10 k. red and brown . . . . 1·00 1·60

(b) Size 28 × 38 mm.

33 **6** 10 k. red and brown 20 20
34 35 k. green and blue 20 20
35 1 r. red and green 50 50

1919. Liberation of Courland.

36 **7** 10 k. red and brown 10 10
37 25 k. green and blue 20 20
38 35 k. blue and black 30 30
39 1 r. brown and green 85 85

8

1920. Red Cross stamps. (a) On backs of blue Bolshevist notes. Perf.

46 **8** 20-30 k. red and brown . . . 1·00 1·40
47 40-55 k. red and blue . . . . 1·00 1·40
48 50-70 k. red and green . . . 85 2·00
49 1 r.-1 r. 30 red and grey . . . 1·10 2·00

(b) On backs of green Western Army notes. Perf.

50 **8** 20-30 k. red and brown . . . 1·00 1·25
51 40-55 k. red and blue . . . . 1·00 1·25
52 50-70 k. red and green . . . 85 1·60
53 1 r.-1 r. 30 red and grey . . . 1·50 3·25

(c) On backs of red, green and brown Bolshevist notes. Imperf.

54 **8** 20-30 k. red and brown . . . 1·50 3·00
55 40-55 k. red and blue . . . . 1·50 3·00
56 50-70 k. red and green . . . 1·50 3·00
57 1 r.-1 r. 30 red and grey . . . 3·75 4·75

CHARITY PREMIUMS. In the above and later issues where two values are expressed, the lower value represents the franking value and the higher the price charged, the difference being the charity premium.

9 10

1920. Liberation of Latgale.

58 **9** 50 k. pink and green 65 20
59 1 r. brown and green 65 30

1920. 1st Constituent Assembly.

60 **10** 50 k. red 50 20
61 1 r. blue 50 15
62 3 r. green and brown . . . 65 70
63 5 r. purple and grey . . . . 1·60 80

1920. Surch in white figures on black oval.

64 **6** 10 r. on 1 r. red and green . 2·00 2·00
65 20 r. on 1 r. red and green . 4·00 4·00
66 30 r. on 1 r. red and green . 5·00 5·00

1920. Surch **2 DIWI RUBLI**. Perf.

67 **1** 2 r. on 10 k. blue . . . . . 4·00 5·00
68 **4** 2 r. on 35 k. brown . . . . 50 3·00

1920. (a) Surch **WEENS** or **DIVI**, value and **RUBLI**.

69 **7** 1 (WEENS) r. on 35 k. blue and black 30 30
70 2 (DIVI) r. on 10 k. red and brown 85 85
71 2 (DIVI) r. on 25 k. green and blue 70 30

(b) Surch **DIWI RUBLI 2.**

72 **6** 2 r. on 35 k. green and blue . . 50 40

(c) Surch **DIVI 2 RUB. 2.**

73 **10** 2 r. on 50 k. red 85 85

(d) Surch **Desmit rubli.**

74 **6** 10 r. on 10 r. on 1 r. red and green (No. 64) . . . . . 2·00 65

1921. Red Cross. Nos. 51/3 surch **RUB 2 RUB.**

75 **8** 2 r. on 20-30 k. red & brown . 3·00 5·00
76 2 r. on 40-55 k. red and blue . 3·00 5·00
77 2 r. on 50-70 k. red & green . 3·00 5·00
78 2 r. on 1 r.-1 r. 30 k. red and grey 3·00 5·00

1921. Surch in figures and words over thick bar of crossed lines.

79 **9** 10 r. on 50 k. pink and green . 1·60 70
80 20 r. on 50 k. pink and green . 5·00 4·00
81 30 r. on 50 k. pink and green . 4·00 3·75
82 50 r. on 50 k. pink and green . 10·00 6·75
83 100 r. on 50 k. pink and green . 20·00 17·00

19

1921. Air. Value in "RUBLU". Imperf or perf.

84 **19** 10 r. green . . . . 5·00 5·00
85 20 r. blue . . . . 5·00 1·60

See also Nos. 155/7.

21 Latvian Coat of Arms

22 Great Seal of Latvia

1921. Value in "Kopeks" or "Roubles".

86 **21** 50 k. violet 25 10
87 1 r. yellow 25 25
88 2 r. green 20 10
89 3 r. green 30 25
90 5 r. red 80 10
91 6 r. red . . . . 1·25 1·00
92 9 r. orange 90 50
93 10 r. blue 85 10
94 15 r. blue . . . . 2·50 60
95 20 r. lilac . . . . 13·50 1·40
96 **22** 50 r. brown . . . . 17·00 4·25
97 100 r. blue . . . . 18·00 3·75

1923. Value in "Santimi" or "Lats".

127 **21** 1 s. mauve 15 10
129 2 s. yellow 15 10
130 3 s. red 15 10
100 4 s. green 45 10
132 5 s. green . . . . 1·60 10
133 6 s. green on yellow . . . 10 10
134 7 s. green 30 15
103 10 s. red 85 10
136 10 s. green on yellow . . . 10·00 10
104 12 s. mauve 25 20
105a 15 s. purple on red . . . . 3·75 10
107 20 s. blue . . . . 2·00 10
139 20 s. pink . . . . 5·75 10
108 25 s. blue 50 10
109 30 s. pink . . . . 4·75 15
140 30 s. blue . . . . 1·60 10
141 35 s. blue . . . . 1·75 10
110 40 s. purple . . . . 1·90 15
143 50 s. grey . . . . 3·00 15
144 **22** 1 l. brown and bistre . . . 5·75 15
116 2 l. blue and light blue . . 18·00 1·60
117 5 l. green and light green . 55·00 4·75
118 10 l. red and light red . . . 5·00 6·00

1923. Charity. War Invalids. Surch **KARA INVALIDIEM S.10S.** and cross.

112 **21** 1 s. + 10 s. mauve . . . . 50 1·00
113 2 s. + 10 s. yellow . . . . 50 1·00
114 4 s. + 10 s. green . . . . . 50 1·40

24 Town Hall

28 Pres. J. Cakste

1925. 300th Anniv of City of Libau.

119 – 6-12 s. blue and red . . . . 4·00 6·75
120 **24** 15-25 s. brown and blue . . 2·75 4·00
121 – 25-35 s. green and violet . 4·00 4·00
122 – 30-40 s. lake and blue . . . 6·75 13·00
123 – 50-60 s. violet and green . . 9·50 17·00

DESIGNS—HORIZ: 6-12 s. Harbour and lighthouse; 25-35 s. Spa health pavilion. VERT: 30-40 s. St. Anna's Church; 50-60 s. Arms of Libau.

1927. Surch.

124 **1** 15 s. on 40 k. purple . . . 50 40
125 15 s. on 50 k. violet . . . . 2·00 1·60
126 **10** 1 l. on 3 r. green & brown . 17·00 6·75

1928. Death of President Cakste and Memorial Fund.

150 **28** 2-12 s. orange . . . . . . 4·00 4·00
151 6-16 s. green . . . . 4·00 4·00
152 15-25 s. lake . . . . 4·00 4·00
153 25-35 s. blue . . . . 4·00 4·00
154 30-40 s. red . . . . 4·00 4·00

1928. Air. Value in "SANTIMU" or "SANTIMI".

155 **19** 10 s. green . . . . 2·75 1·50
156 15 s. red . . . . 2·75 1·50
157 25 s. blue . . . . 5·00 2·00

29 Ruins at Rezekne

30 Venta

1928. 10th Anniv of Independence. Views.

158 **29** 6 s. purple and green . . . 1·00 15
159 – 15 s. green and brown . . . 1·00 15
160 – 20 s. green and red . . . . 1·40 50
161 – 30 s. brown and blue . . . 1·60 20
162 – 50 s. pink and grey . . . . 2·00 2·00
163 – 1 l. sepia and brown . . . . 4·00 1·75

DESIGNS: 15 s. Jelgava (Mitau); 20 s. Cesis (Wenden); 30 s. Liepaja (Libau); 50 s. Riga; 1 l. National Theatre, Riga.

1928. Liberty Memorial Fund. Imperf or perf.

164 **30** 6-16 s. green . . . . 3·25 3·25
165 – 10-20 s. red . . . . 3·25 3·25
166 – 15-25 s. brown . . . . . . 3·25 3·25
167 – 30-40 s. blue . . . . 3·25 3·25
168 – 50-60 s. black . . . . . . 3·25 3·25
169 – 1 l.-1 l. 10 s. purple . . . . 3·25 3·25

DESIGNS: 10-20 s. "Latvia" (Woman); 15-25 s. Mitau; 30-40 s. National Theatre, Riga; 50-60 s. Wenden; 1 l.-1 l. 10 s. Trenches, Riga Bridge.

32 Z. A. Meierovics

33 J. Rainis

1929. 3rd Death Anniv of Meierovics (Foreign Minister). Imperf or perf.

170 **32** 2-4 s. yellow . . . . 5·00 5·00
171 6-12 s. green . . . . 5·00 5·00
172 15-25 s. purple . . . . . . 5·00 5·00
173 25-35 s. blue . . . . 5·00 5·00
174 30-40 s. blue . . . . 5·00 5·00

1930. Memorial Fund for J. Rainis (writer and politician). Imperf or perf.

175 **33** 1-2 s. purple . . . . 1·00 2·75
176 2-4 s. orange . . . . 1·00 2·75
177 4-8 s. green . . . . 1·00 2·75
178 6-12 s. brown and green . . 1·00 2·75
179 10-20 s. red . . . . 27·00 40·00
180 15-30 s. green and brown . 27·00 40·00

34 Durbe Castle

1930. Air. J. Rainis Memorial Fund. Imperf or perf.

181 **34** 10-20 s. green and red . . 10·00 17·00
182 15-30 s. red and green . . 10·00 17·00

35 36

1930. Anti-T.B. Fund.

183 – 1-2 s. red and purple . . . 50 50
184 – 2-4 s. red and orange . . . 50 50
185 **35** 4-8 s. red and green . . . 1·00 80
186 – 5-10 s. brown and green . . 1·40 1·10
187 – 6-12 s. yellow and green . . 1·40 1·10
188 – 10-20 s. black and red . . 2·00 1·60
189 – 15-30 s. green and brown . 1·75 1·50
190 – 20-40 s. blue and red . . . 2·00 2·00
191 – 25-50 s. lilac, blue and red . 3·00 2·50
192 **36** 30-60 s. lilac, green & blue . 3·50 4·25

DESIGNS—VERT: As Type **35**: 1-2 s., 2-4 s. The Crusaders' Cross; 5-10 s. G. Zemgalis; 6-12 s. Tower; 10-20 s. J. Cakste; 15-30 s. Floral design; 20-40 s. A. Kviesis. HORIZ: As Type **36**: 25-50 s. Sanatorium.

1931. Nos. 183/92 surch.

196 9 on 6-12 s. yellow and green . 65 1·60
197 16 on 1-2 s. red and purple . . 13·50 20·00
198 17 s. 2-4 s. red and orange . . 1·25 1·60
199 19 on 4-8 s. red and green . . 4·75 7·50
200 20 on 5-10 s. brown and green . 2·50 7·50
201 23 on 15-30 s. green & brown . 1·00 1·00
202 25 on 10-20 s. black and red . 2·75 4·25
203 35 on 20-40 s blue and red . . 4·00 6·00
204 45 on 25-50 s. lilac, blue and red 11·50 18·00
205 55 on 30-60 s. lilac, green & bl . 13·50 28·00

1931. Air. Charity. Nos. 155/7 surch **LATVIJAS AIZSARGI** and value. Imperf or perf.

206 **19** 50 on 10 s. green . . . . . 13·50 18·00
207 1 l. on 15 s. red . . . . . 13·50 18·00
208 1 l. 50 on 2 s. blue . . . . 13·50 18·00

38 Foreign Invasion

1932. Militia Maintenance Fund. Imperf or perf.

209 – 1-11 s. blue and purple . . 3·25 3·75
210 **38** 2-17 s. orange and olive . . 3·25 3·75
211 – 3-23 s. red and brown . . . 3·25 3·75
212 – 4-34 s. green . . . . . . 3·25 3·75
213 – 5-45 s. green . . . . . . 3·25 3·75

DESIGNS: 1-11 s. The Holy Oak and Kriva telling stories; 3-23 s. Lacplesis, the deliverer; 4-34 s. The Black Knight (enemy) slaughtered; 5-45 s. Laimdota, the spirit of Latvia, freed.

39 Infantry Manoeuvres

1932. Militia Maintenance Fund. Imperf or perf.
214 – 6-25 s. purple and brown . . 5·75 6·75
215 **39** 7-35 s. blue and green . . . 5·75 6·75
216 – 10-45 s. sepia and green . . 5·75 6·75
217 – 12-55 s. green and red . . . 5·75 6·75
218 – 15-75 s. violet and red . . . 5·75 6·75
DESIGNS—HORIZ: 6-25 s. Troops on march. VERT: 10-45 s. First aid to soldier; 12-55 s. Army kitchen; 15-75 s. Gen. J. Balodis.

41

1932. Air. Charity. Imperf or perf.
219 **41** 10-20 s. black and green . . 17·00 23·00
220 15-30 s. red and grey . . . 17·00 23·00
221 25-50 s. blue and grey . . . 17·00 23·00

1932. Riga Exn of Lettish Products. Optd **Latvijas razojumu izstade Riga. 1932.g.10.-18.IX.**
222 **21** 3 s. red 50 40
223 10 s. green on yellow . . . 1·50 80
224 20 s. pink . . . . 2·00 70
225 35 s. blue . . . . 3·25 85

43 Leonardo da Vinci 44 "Mourning Mother" Memorial, Riga

1932. Air. Charity. Pioneers of Aviation. Imperf or perf.
226 – 5-25 s. green and brown . . 17·00 17·00
227 **43** 10-50 s. green and brown 17·00 17·00
228 – 15-75 s. green and red . . . 17·00 17·00
229 – 20-100 s. mauve and green 17·00 17·00
230 – 25-125 s. blue and brown 17·00 17·00
DESIGNS—VERT: 5 s. Icarus; 15 s. Charles's hydrogen balloon. HORIZ: 20 s. Wright Type A; 25 s. Bleriot XI.

1933. Air. Wounded Latvian Airmen Fund. Imperf or perf.
231 – 2-52 s. brown and black . . 13·50 17·00
232 **44** 3-53 s. red and black . . . 13·50 17·00
233 – 10-60 s. green and black . . 13·50 17·00
234 – 20-70 s. red and black . . . 13·50 17·00
DESIGNS: 2 s. Fall of Icarus; 10 s., 20 s. Proposed tombs for airmen.

1933. Air. Charity. Riga–Bathurst Flight. Nos. 155/7 optd **LATVIJA-AFRIKA 1933** or surch also.
235 10 s. green . . . . 50·00 70·00
236 15 s. red . . . . 50·00 70·00
237 25 s. blue . . . . 50·00 70·00
238 50 s. on 15 s. red £225 £425
239 100 s. on 25 s. blue £225 £425
In the event the aircraft crashed at Neustettin, Germany, and the mail was forwarded by ordinary post.

46 Biplane under Fire at Riga

1933. Air. Charity. Wounded Latvian Airmen Fund. Imperf or perf.
240 – 3-53 s. blue and orange . . 30·00 32·00
241 **46** 7-57 s. brown and blue . . 30·00 32·00
242 – 35-135 s. black and blue . . 30·00 32·00
DESIGNS: 3 s. Monoplane taking off; 35 s. Map and aircraft.

47 Glanville Brothers' Gee-Bee Super Sportster

1933. Air. Charity. Wounded Latvian Airmen Fund. Imperf or perf.
243 **47** 8-68 s. grey and brown . . 40·00 60·00
244 – 12-112 s. green and purple 40·00 60·00
245 – 30-130 s. grey and blue . . 48·00 60·00
246 – 40-190 s. blue and purple 40·00 60·00
DESIGNS: 12 s. Supermarine S6B seaplane; 30 s. Airship "Graf Zeppelin" over Riga; 40 s. Dornier Do-X flying boat.

48 President's Palace 50 A. Kronvalds 51

1934. 15th Anniv of New Constitution.
247 **48** 3 s. red 10 15
248 – 5 s. green 15 10
249 – 10 s. green . . . . 2·00 10
250 – 20 s. red . . . . 2·00 10
251 – 35 s. blue 10 15
252 **48** 40 s. brown 10 15
DESIGNS: 5, 10 s. Arms and shield; 20 s. Allegory of Latvia; 35 s. Government Building.

1936. Lettish Intellectuals.
253 **50** 3 s. red . . . . 1·60 4·25
254 – 10 s. green . . . . 1·60 4·25
255 – 20 s. mauve . . . . 1·60 5·00
256 – 35 s. blue . . . . 1·60 5·00
PORTRAITS: 10 s. A. Pumpurs; 20 s. J. Maters; 35 s. Auseklis.

1936. White Cross Fund. Designs incorporating Cross and Stars device as in T **51**.
257 **51** 3 s. red . . . . 1·75 3·25
258 – 10 s. green . . . . 1·75 3·25
259 – 20 s. mauve . . . . 1·75 4·00
260 – 35 s. blue . . . . 1·75 4·00
DESIGNS: 10 s. Oak leaves; 20 s. Doctors and patient; 35 s. Woman holding shield.

53 Independence Monument, Rauna (Ronneburg) 54 President Ulmanis

1937. Monuments.
261 **53** 3 s. red . . . . 35 1·40
262 – 5 s. green 35 60
263 – 10 s. green 35 35
264 – 20 s. red . . . . 85 1·00
265 – 30 s. blue . . . . 1·40 1·25
266 – 35 s. blue . . . . 1·40 1·50
267 – 40 s. brown . . . . 2·25 2·50
DESIGNS—VERT: 10 s. Independence Monument, Jelgava (Mitau); 20 s. War Memorial, Valka (Walk); 30 s. Independence Monument, Iecava (Eckau); 35 s. Independence Monument, Riga; 40 s. Col. Kalpak's Grave, Visagalas Cemetery. HORIZ: 5 s. Cemetery Gate, Riga.

1937. President Ulmanis's 60th Birthday.
268 **54** 3 s. red and orange . . . 15 10
269 5 s. light green and green 15 15
270 10 s. deep green and green 25 35
271 20 s. purple and red . . . 55 35
272 25 s. grey and blue . . . 1·10 65
273 30 s. deep blue and blue . 1·10 60
274 35 s. indigo and blue . . . 1·00 50
275 40 s. lt brown and brown 85 75
276 50 s. green and black . . . 90 80

56 Gaizinkalns, Livonia 57 General J. Balodis

1938. 20th Anniv of Independence.
278 **56** 3 s. red 10 10
279 – 5 s. green 10 10
280 **57** 10 s. green 20 10
281 – 20 s. mauve 20 10
282 – 30 s. blue 60 20
283 – 35 s. slate 65 10
284 – 40 s. mauve 80 15
DESIGNS: As Type **56**: 5 s. Latgale landscape; 30 s; City of Riga; 35 s. Rumba waterfall, Courland; 40 s. Zemgale landscape. As Type **57**: 20 s. President Ulmanis.

58 Elementary School, Riga

1939. 5th Anniv of Authoritarian Government.
285 **58** 3 s. brown 50 85
286 – 5 s. green 50 85
287 – 10 s. green . . . . 2·00 1·00
288 – 20 s. red . . . . 2·75 1·40
289 – 30 s. blue . . . . 2·00 1·00
290 – 35 s. blue . . . . 2·50 1·50
291 – 40 s. purple . . . . 3·50 1·00
292 – 50 s. black . . . . 5·00 1·00
DESIGNS: 5 s. Jelgava Castle; 10 s. Riga Castle; 2 s. Independence Memorial; 30 s. Eagle and National Flag; 35 s. Town Hall, Daugavpils; 40 s. War Museum and Powder-magazine, Riga; 50 s. Pres. Ulmanis.

59 Reaping 60 Arms of Courland, Livonia and Latgale 61 Arms of Latvian Soviet Socialist Republic

1939. Harvest Festival. Dated "8 X 1939".
294 **59** 10 s. green . . . . 65 1·00
295 – 20 s. red (Apples) . . . . 1·00 65

1940.
296 **60** 1 s. violet 15 20
297 2 s. yellow 15 20
298 3 s. red 10 15
299 5 s. brown 10 10
300 7 s. green 10 40
301 10 s. green . . . . 1·00 10
302 20 s. red . . . . 1·00 10
303 30 s. brown . . . . 1·40 25
304 35 s. blue 10 70
305 50 s. green . . . . 2·00 2·00
306 1 l. olive . . . . 4·00 2·75

1940. Incorporation of Latvia in U.S.S.R.
307 **61** 1 s. violet 15 20
308 2 s. yellow 15 15
309 3 s. red 10 10
310 5 s. olive 10 10
311 7 s. green . . . . 10 1·00
312 10 s. green . . . . 1·40 10
313 20 s. red 65 10
314 30 s. blue . . . . 2·40 1·00
315 35 s. blue 10 55
316 40 s. brown . . . . 1·40 1·40
317 50 s. grey . . . . 2·00 1·40
318 1 l. brown . . . . 2·75 2·00
319 5 l. green . . . . 20·00 13·50

63 Latvian Arms 64

1991.
320 **63** 5 k. silver, brown & lt brn 15 15
321 10 k. silver, brown & drab 15 15
322 15 k. silver, sepia & brown 15 15
323 20 k. silver, blue & lt blue 60 60
324 40 k. silver, green and light green . . . . 1·25 1·25
325 50 k. silver, brown and lilac 1·40 1·40
326 **64** 100 k. multicoloured . . . 2·75 2·75
327 200 k. multicoloured . . . 5·00 5·00

1991. Nos. 4672, 6073 and 6077 of Russia surch **LATVIJA** and new value.
328 100 k. on 7 k. blue 20 20
329 300 k. on 2 k. brown 65 65
330 500 k. on 2 k. brown . . . . 1·10 1·10
331 1000 k. on 2 k. brown . . . 2·25 2·25
358 25 r. on 4 k. red . . . . . . 2·40 2·40

67 Main Statue, Liberty Monument, Riga 68 Olympic Committee Symbol

1991.
336 **67** 10 k. multicoloured 10 10
337 15 k. multicoloured 10 10
338 20 k. multicoloured 10 10
339 30 k. multicoloured 10 10
340 50 k. multicoloured 55 55
341 100 k. multicoloured . . . 1·10 1·10

1992. Recognition of Latvian Olympic Committee.
342 **68** 50 k. + 25 k. red, silver and drab 65 65
343 – 50 k. + 25 k. red, silver and grey 65 65
344 **68** 100 k. + 50 k. red, gold and bistre . . . . 1·40 1·40
DESIGN: No. 343. As T **68** but symbols smaller and inscribed "BERLIN 18.09.91." at left.

69 Vaidelotis 72 Children in Fancy Dress around Christmas Tree

1992. Statues from the base of the Liberty Monument, Riga.
345 – 10 k. black and brown . . 10 10
346 **69** 20 k. brown and grey . . . 10 10
347 – 30 k. deep lilac and lilac . 10 10
348 **69** 30 k. deep brown & brown 10 10
349 – 40 k. blue and grey 35 35
350 **69** 50 k. green and grey . . . 40 40
351 – 50 k. black and grey . . . 40 40
352 – 100 k. purple and mauve . 85 85
353 – 200 k. deep blue and blue 1·60 1·60
DESIGNS: Nos. 345, 347 and 353, Kurzeme (warrior with shield): Nos. 349 and 351/2, Lachplesis (two figures).

1992. Birds of the Baltic. As Nos. 506/9 of Lithuania.
359 5 r. black and red 15 15
360 5 r. brown, black and red . . 15 15
361 5 r. sepia, brown and red . . 15 15
362 5 r. brown, black and red . . 15 15
DESIGNS: Nos 359, Osprey ("Pandion haliaetus"); 360, Black-tailed godwit ("Limosa limosa"); 361, Goosander ("Mergus merganser"); 362, Common shelducks ("Tadorna tadorna").

1992. Christmas. Multicoloured.
363 2 r. Type **72** 20 20
364 3 r. Angel choir 50 50
365 10 r. Type **72** . . . . 1·75 1·75
366 15 r. Adoration of the Kings 2·50 2·50

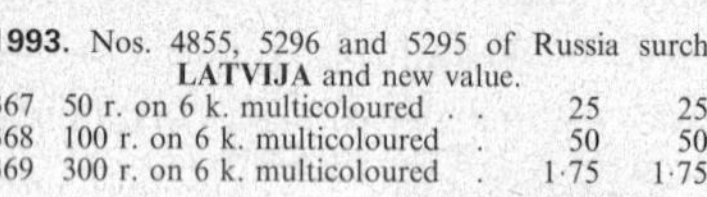

1993. Nos. 4855, 5296 and 5295 of Russia surch **LATVIJA** and new value.
367 50 r. on 6 k. multicoloured . . 25 25
368 100 r. on 6 k. multicoloured . 50 50
369 300 r. on 6 k. multicoloured . 1·75 1·75

74 Kuldiga Couple 75 Emblem

1993. Costumes (1st series). Multicoloured.
370 5 s. Type **74** 10 10
371 10 s. Alsunga 25 25
372 20 s. Lielvarde 45 45
373 50 s. Rucava . . . . 1·25 1·25
374 100 s. Zemgale . . . . 2·40 2·40
375 500 s. Ziemellatgale . . . . 12·00 12·00
See also Nos. 428 and 442.

1993. National Song Festival.
377 **75** 3 s. black, gold and brown 10 10
378 5 s. black, gold and lilac . 10 10
379 – 15 s. multicoloured 35 35
DESIGN: 15 s. Abstract.

76 Pope John Paul II 77 Flags

1993. Papal Visit.
380 **76** 15 s. multicoloured 35 35

1993. 75th Anniv of First Republic.
381 **77** 5 s. multicoloured 10 10
382 15 s. multicoloured 35 35

78 Valters 79 Biathlon

1994. 1000th Birthday of Evalds Valters (actor).
383 **78** 15 s. brown, light brown and gold 35 35

1994. Winter Olympic Games, Lillehammer, Norway. Multicoloured.
384 5 s. Type **79** 10 10
385 10 s. Two-man bobsleigh . . . 20 20
386 15 s. One-man luge 35 35
387 100 s. Figure skating . . . . . 2·25 2·25

80 Reed Hut

1994. 70th Anniv of Latvian Ethnological Open-air Museum, Bergi.
389 **80** 5 s. multicoloured 10 10

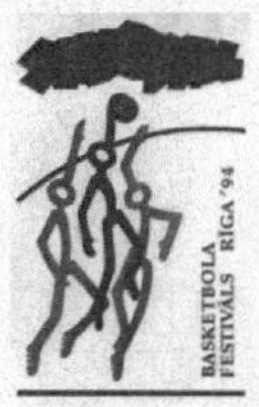
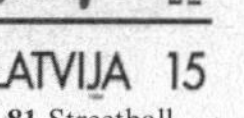

81 Streetball **82** Kurzeme

1994. Basketball Festival, Riga.
390 **81** 15 s. black, grey and orange 35 35

1994. Arms. (a) Size 18 × 21 mm.
391 **82** 1 s. red, black and silver . 10 10
391a – 2 s. multicoloured 10 10
392 – 3 s. silver, black and blue . 10 10
393 – 5 s. silver, black and red . 10 10
393a – 8 s. silver, black and blue . 20 20
394 – 10 s. silver, black and blue 20 20
394a – 13 s. black, gold and silver 30 30
395 – 16 s. multicoloured . . . 40 40
396 – 20 s. silver, black and grey 50 50
397 – 24 s. green, black and silver 60 60
397a – 28 s. multicoloured . . . 65 65
398 – 30 s. multicoloured . . . 75 75
398a – 36 s. silver, black and red 80 80
399 – 50 s. multicoloured . . . 1·25 1·25

(b) Size 29 × 23½ mm.
400 – 100 s. multicoloured . . . 2·40 2·40
401 – 200 s. multicoloured . . . 4·75 4·75
DESIGNS: 2 s. Auce; 3 s. Zemgale; 5 s. Vidzeme; 8 s. Livani; 10 s. Latgale; 13 s. Preili; 16 s. Ainazi; 20 s. Grobina; 24 s. Tukums; 28 s. Madona; 30, 100 s. Riga; 36 s. Priekule; 50, 200 s. State arms.

83 Emblem **84** Coins in Scales

1994. 75th Anniv of Latvia University.
405 **83** 5 s. gold, blue and green . 10 10

1994. Europa. Multicoloured.
406 10 s. Type **84** 20 20
407 50 s. Money chest and notes in scales . . . . 1·10 1·10

85 Eating Cherries **86** Angel

1994. The Fat Dormouse. Multicoloured.
408 5 s. Type **85** 10 10
409 10 s. Eating strawberries . . . 20 20
410 10 s. On leafy branch 20 20
411 15 s. On branch of apple tree . 35 35

1994. Christmas. Multicoloured.
412 3 s. Type **86** 10 10
413 8 s. Angels playing violin and flute 20 20
414 13 s. Angels singing 30 30
415 100 s. Wreath of candles . . . 2·25 2·25

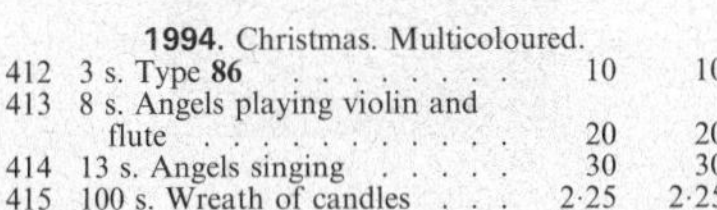

87 Gnome with Candle **88** Emblem

1994. 80th Birthday of Margarita Staraste (children's writer and illustrator). Multicoloured.
416 5 s. Type **87** 10 10
417 10 s. Bear 25 25
418 10 s. Child on sledge 25 25

1994. Roa Safety Year.
419 **88** 10 s. multicoloured . . . 25 25

89 Emblem **90** Bauska Castle (Latvia)

1995. 50th Anniv of U.N.O.
420 **89** 15 s. blue, red and silver . 35 35

1995. Via Baltica Motorway Project. Multicoloured.
421 **90** 8 s. multicoloured 20 20

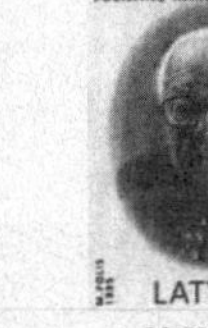

91 White-backe Woodpecker **92** Vaivods

1995. European Nature Conservation Year. Birds. Multicoloured.
423 8 s. Type **91** 20 20
424 20 s. Corncrake 50 50
425 24 s. White-winged black tern 60 60

1995. Birth Centenary of Cardinal Julijans Vaivods.
426 **92** 8 s. multicoloured 20 20

93 Sun and Open Book

1995. 60th Anniv of Karlis Ulmaris Schools Appeal.
427 **93** 8 s. multicoloured 20 20

1995. Costumes (2nd series). As T **74**. Multicoloured.
428 8 s. Nica 20 20

94 National Opera House **95** Lacplesis, the Bear Slayer

1995. 800th Anniv of Riga (1st issue). Multicoloured.
430 8 s. Type **94** 20 20
431 16 s. National Theatre . . . 40 40
432 24 s. Art School (44 x 26 mm) 60 60
433 36 s. Art Museum (44 x 26 mm) 85 85
See also Nos. 456/9

1995. Europan Peace and Freedom. Multicoloured.
434 16 s. Type **95** 40 40
435 50 s. Spidola . . . . 1·25 1·25

96 Christmas Tree at Night **97** Stradins

1995. Christmas. Multicoloured.
436 6 s. Type **96** 15 15
437 6 s. Elf flying with candle . . 15 15
438 15 s. Cottage at night 35 35
439 24 s. Elf with dog and cat . . 60 60

1996. Birth Centenary of Pauls Stradins (surgeon).
440 **97** 8 s. multicoloured 20 20

98 Zenta Maurina (writer) **100** Cycling

1996. Europa. Famous Women.
441 **98** 36 s. multicoloured 80 80

1996. Costumes (3rd series). As T **74**. Multicoloured.
442 8 s. Barta 20 20

1996. Olympic Games, Atlanta. Multicoloured.
445 8 s. Type **100** 20 20
446 16 s. Basketball 35 35
447 24 s. Walking 55 55
448 36 s. Canoeing (horiz) 80 80

101 Swallowtail

1996. Butterflies. Multicoloured.
450 8 s. Type **101** 20 20
451 24 s. Clifden's nonpareil . . . 55 55
452 80 s. Large tiger moth . . . . 1·75 1·75

102 1912 Russo-Balt Fire Engine **103** Apartment Block (E. Laube)

1996. Latvian Car Production. Multicoloured.
453 8 s. Type **102** 20 20
454 24 s. 1899 Leutner-Russia carriage 55 55
455 36 s. 1939 Ford-Vairogs motor car 80 80

1996. 800th Anniv of Riga (2nd issue). Multicoloured.
456 8 s. Type **103** 20 20
457 16 s. Stained glass window (F. Sefels) (30 × 26 mm) . . 35 35
458 24 s. Turreted buildings (E. Laube) (38 × 26 mm) . 55 55
459 30 s. Couple welcoming charioteer (mural, J. Rozentals) (38 × 26 mm) 70 70

104 Elves and Presents

1996. Christmas. Multicoloured.
460 6 s. Type **104** 15 15
461 14 s. Children with dog and Father Christmas on skis . . 30 30
462 20 s. Child at tree and Father Christmas in armchair . . . 45 45

LEBANON Pt. 19

A territory north of the Holy Land, formerly part of the Turkish Empire, Greater Lebanon was given a separate status under French Mandate in 1920. Until September 1923, the French occupation stamps of Syria were used and these were followed by the joint issue of 1923, Nos. 97 etc., of Syria. Independence was proclaimed in 1941, but the country was not evacuated by French troops until 1946.

100 centimes = 1 piastre;
100 piastres = 1 Lebanese pound

1924. Stamps of France surch **GRAND LIBAN** and value. (a) Definitive stamps.
1 **11** 10 c. on 2 c. purple . . . . 50 1·00
2 **18** 25 c. on 5 c. orange 55 85
3 50 c. on 10 c. green . . . . 70 1·10
4 **15** 75 c. on 15 c. green . . . . 90 1·75
5 **18** 1 p. on 20 c. brown . . . . 1·25 1·00
6 1,25 p. on 25 c. blue . . . . 2·50 2·25
7 1,50 p. on 30 c. orange . . 1·50 1·75
8 1,50 p. on 30 c. red . . . . 95 1·75
9 **15** 2,50 p. on 50 c. blue . . . . 1·00 1·25
10 **13** 2 p. on 40 c. red and blue . 1·25 2·25
11 3 p. on 60 c. violet and blue 5·00 4·25
12 5 p. on 1 f. red and yellow . 5·50 5·75
13 10 p. on 2 f. orange and green 9·00 6·75
14 25 p. on 5 f. blue and buff . 12·50 15·00

(b) Pasteur issue.
15 **30** 50 c. on 10 c. green . . . . 95 1·40
16 1,50 p. on 30 c. red . . . . 1·40 2·00
17 2,50 p. on 50 c. blue . . . . 1·00 1·60

(c) Olympic Games issue.
18 **31** 50 c. on 10 c. green and light green . . . . 20·00 35·00
19 – 1,25 p. on 25 c. deep red and red . . . . 18·00 35·00
20 – 1,50 p. on 30 c. red & black 20·00 35·00
21 – 2,50 p. on 50 c. blue . . . . 18·00 35·00

1924. Air. Stamps of France surch **Poste par Avion GRAND LIBAN** and value.
22 **13** 2 p. on 40 c. red and blue . 8·25 8·50
23 3 p. on 60 c. violet and blue 8·25 8·50
24 5 p. on 1 f. red and yellow . 7·25 8·00
25 10 p. on 2 f. orange and green 8·25 8·25

1924. Stamps of France surch **Grand Liban** (T **13**) or **Gd Liban** (others) and value in French and Arabic. (a) Definitive stamps.
26 **11** 0 p. 10 on 2 c. purple . . . 60 90
27 **18** 0 p. 25 on 5 c. orange . . . 60 85
28 0 p. 50 on 10 c. green . . . 1·25 1·10
29 **15** 0 p. 75 on 15 c. green . . . 1·00 1·50
30 **18** 1 p. on 20 c. brown 50 50
31 1 p. 25 on 25 c. blue . . . . 1·50 1·75
32 1 p. 50 on 30 c. red . . . . 1·25 1·50
33 1 p. 50 on 30 c. orange . . 40·00 42·00
34 2 p. on 35 c. violet . . . . 1·40 1·90
35 **13** 2 p. on 40 c. red and blue . 1·10 85
36 2 p. on 45 c. green and blue 12·00 14·00
37 3 p. on 60 c. violet and blue 1·50 1·40
38 **15** 3 p. on 60 c. violet . . . . 1·60 2·00
39 4 p. on 85 c. red . . . . . 65 1·75
40 **13** 5 p. on 1 f. red and yellow . 2·00 2·25
41 10 p. on 2 f. orange & green 4·25 6·75
42 25 p. on 5 f. blue and buff . 5·25 9·00

(b) Pasteur issue.
43 **30** 0 p. 50 on 10 c. green . . . 60 30
44 0 p. 75 on 15 c. green . . . 1·25 1·75
45 1 p. 50 on 30 c. red . . . . 1·25 1·10
46 2 p. on 45 c. red . . . . . 2·00 2·25
47 2 p. 50 on 50 c. blue 70 60
48 4 p. on 75 c. blue . . . . . 1·25 2·25

(c) Olympic Games issue.
49 **31** 0 p. 50 on 10 c. green and light green . . . . 20·00 40·00
50 – 1 p. 25 on 25 c. deep red and red . . . . 18·00 40·00
51 – 1 p. 50 on 30 c. red & black 18·00 40·00
52 – 2 p. 50 on 50 c. ultramarine and blue . . . . 19·00 40·00

(d) Ronsard issue.
53 **35** 4 p. on 75 c. blue on bluish 95 2·25

1924. Air. Stamps of France surch **Gd Liban Avion** and value in French and Arabic.
54 **13** 2 p. on 40 c. red and blue . 6·75 8·75
55 3 p. on 60 c. violet and blue 5·00 8·75
56 5 p. on 1 f. red and yellow . 4·75 8·75
57 10 p. on 2 f. orange and green 4·75 8·75

5 Cedar of Lebanon **7** Tripoli

6 Beirut

1925. Views.
58 **5** 0 p. 10 violet 25 40
59 **6** 0 p. 25 black 35 85
60 – 0 p. 50 green (Tripoli) . . . 30 95
61 – 0 p. 75 red (Beit ed-Din) . . 75 1·10
62 – 1 p. purple (Baalbek ruins) . 1·10 55
63 – 1 p. 25 green (Mouktara) . . 1·60 1·75

64 – 1 p. 50 pink (Tyre) 45 50
65 – 2 p. brown (Zahle) 95 35
66 – 2 p. 50 blue (Baalbek) 50 45
67 – 3 p. brown (Deir el-Kamar) 1·25 50
68 – 5 p. violet (Sidon) 8·25 6.00
69 **7** 10 p. purple 8·00 7·25
70 – 25 p. blue (Beirut) 16·00 18·00

1925. Air. Nos. 65 and 67/9 optd **AVION** in French and Arabic.
71 – 2 p. brown 4·00 3·25
72 – 3 p. brown 4·00 3·25
73 – 5 p. violet 4·00 3·25
74 **7** 10 p. purple 4·00 3·25

1926. Air. Nos. 65 and 67/9 optd with Bleriot XI airplane.
75 – 2 p. brown 2·25 3·25
76 – 3 p. brown 2·25 3·25
77 – 5 p. violet 2·25 3·25
78 **7** 10 p. purple 2·25 3·25

1926. War Refugee Charity. Various stamps surch **Secours aux Refugies Afft** and premium in French and Arabic. (a) Postage. Stamps of 1925.
79 **6** 0 p. 25 + 0 p. 25 black 1·75 3·00
80 – 0 p. 50 + 0 p. 25 green 2·50 3·25
81 – 0 p. 75 + 0 p. 25 red 2·00 3·25
82 – 1 p. + 0 p. 50 purple 2·25 3·25
83 – 1 p. 25 + 0 p. 50 green 2·75 4·00
84 – 1 p. 50 + 0 p. 50 pink 2·75 4·00
85 – 2 p. + 0 p. 75 brown 2·75 3·50
86 – 2 p. 50 + 0 p. 75 blue 2·75 4·75
87 – 3 p. + 1 p. brown 2·75 4·50
88 – 5 p. + 1 p. violet 3·75 4·75
89 **7** 10 p. + 2 p. purple 6·25 6·75
90 – 25 p. + 5 p. blue 6·00 8·25

(b) Air. Nos. 75/78 surch.
91 – 2 p. + 1 p. brown 5·50 8·75
92 – 3 p. + 2 p. brown 5·50 8·50
93 – 5 p. + 3 p. violet 5·50 8·75
94 **7** 10 p. + 5 p. purple 5·50 8·50

1926. Stamps of 1925 surch in English and Arabic.
95 – 3 p. 50 on 0 p. 75 red 1·50 1·50
96 **6** 4 p. on 0 p. 25 black 2·00 2·00
98 – 4 p. 50 on 0 p. 75 red 2·10 2·10
99 – 6 p. on 2 p. 50 blue 2·00 2·00
100 – 7 p. 50 on 2 p. 50 blue 2·00 2·00
101 – 12 p. on 1 p. 25 green 1·90 2·00
102 – 15 p. on 25 p. blue 3·00 3·00
103 – 20 p. on 1 p. 25 green 4·75 4·50

1927. Stamps of 1925 and provisional stamps of Lebanon optd **Republique Libanaise.**
104 **5** 0 p. 10 violet 60 70
105 – 0 p. 50 green 20 90
106 – 1 p. purple 50 15
107 – 1 p. 50 pink 70 75
108 – 2 p. brown 1·00 90
109 – 3 p. brown 85 75
110 **6** 4 p. on 0 p. 25 black (No. 96) 65 85
111 – 4 p. 50 on 0 p. 75 red (No. 98) 70 40
112 – 5 p. violet 3·00 3·00
113 – 7 p. 50 on 2 p. 50 blue (No. 100) 1·25 1·00
114 **7** 10 p. purple 4·00 4·00
115 – 15 p. on 25 p. blue (No. 102) 12·50 11·00
117 – 25 p. blue 14·00 15·00

1927. Air. Nos. 75/78 optd **Republique Libanaise.**
118 – 2 p. brown 3·00 3·25
119 – 3 p. brown 3·00 3·25
120 – 5 p. violet 3·00 3·25
121 **7** 10 p. purple 3·00 3·25

الجمهورية اللبنانية
(10)

1928. Nos. 104/117 optd with T **10** or surch also.
145 **5** 05 on 0 p. 10 violet 15 70
124 0 p. 10 violet 80 30
125 – 0 p. 50 green 2·50 2·50
146 – 0 p. 50 on 0 p. 75 red 45 45
126 – 1 p. purple 95 90
127 – 1 p. 50 pink 2·50 2·50
128 – 2 p. brown 2·75 2·75
147 – 2 p. on 1 p. 25 green 1·40 50
129 – 3 p. brown 2·00 1·75
148 **6** 4 p. on 0 p. 25 black 90 30
131 – 4 p. 50 on 0 p. 75 red 2·50 2·50
132a – 5 p. violet 1·75 2·25
149 – 7 p. 50 on 2 p. 50 blue 1·00 45
134 **7** 10 p. purple 7·00 6·00
123 – 15 p. on 25 p. blue 10·00 8·75
136 – 25 p. blue 12·00 12·00

1928. Air. Optd or surch with airplane, **Republique Libanaise** and line of Arabic as T **10**.
151 – 0 p. 50 green 40 1·25
152 – 0 p. 50 on 0 p. 75 red (No. 146) 55 1·25
153 – 1 p. purple 85 1·25
141 – 2 p. brown 2·25 2·75
154 – 2 p. on 1 p. 25 grn (No. 147) 1·10 1·00
142 – 3 p. brown 1·75 2·00
143 – 5 p. violet 2·50 2·75
144 **7** 10 p. purple 2·75 2·50
155 – 15 p. on 25 p. blue (No. 123) £225 £250
156 – 25 p. blue £170 £150

14 Silkworm Larva, Cocoon and Moth

1930. Silk Congress.
157 **14** 4 p. sepia 11·00 12·00
158 4½ p. red 11·00 13·00
159 7½ p. blue 11·00 10·00
160 10 p. violet 11·00 13·00
161 15 p. green 12·00 10·00
162 25 p. purple 11·00 11·00

15 Cedars of Lebanon

16a Baalbek

1930. Views.
163b – 0 p. 10 orange (Beirut) 40 35
164 **15** 0 p. 20 brown 35 60
165 – 0 p. 25 blue (Baalbek) 30 50
166 – 0 p. 50 brown (Bickfaya) 95 60
166b – 0 p. 75 brown (Baalbek) 2·00 2·25
167 – 1 p. green (Saida) 3·25 2·75
167a – 1 p. purple (Saida) 3·25 90
168 – 1 p. 50 purple (Beit ed-Din) 5·00 5·50
168a – 1 p. 50 green (Beit ed-Din) 5·25 90
169 – 2 p. blue (Tripoli) 6·00 5·50
170 – 3 p. sepia (Baalbek) 6·50 5·50
171 – 4 p. brown (Nahr-el-Kalb) 7·00 2·50
172 – 4 p. 50 red (Beaufort) 7·00 4·50
173 – 5 p. green (Beit ed-Din) 2·50 1·50
251 – 5 p. blue (Nahr el-Kalb) 95 20
174 – 6 p. purple (Tyre) 8·00 2·50
175 **16a** 7 p. 50 blue 6·00 1·25
176 – 10 p. green (Hasbaya) 12·00 3·25
177 – 15 p. purple (Afka Falls) 17·00 5·00
178 – 25 p. green (Beirut) 20·00 7·25
179 – 50 p. grn (Deir el-Kamar) 70·00 25·00
180 – 100 p. black (Baalbek) 70·00 28·00

17 Jebeil (Byblos)

1930. Air. Potez 29-4 biplane and views as T **17**.
181 0 p. 50 purple (Rachaya) 35 85
182 1 p. green (Broumana) 30 35
183 2 p. orange (Baalbek) 1·25 90
184 3 p. red (Hasroun) 1·10 95
185 5 p. green (Byblos) 90 70
186 10 p. red (Kadisha) 2·25 1·60
187 15 p. brown (Beirut) 2·50 1·10
188 25 p. violet (Tripoli) 1·75 1·00
189 50 p. lake (Kabelais) 5·50 4·25
190 100 p. brown (Zahle) 9·00 8·25

18 Skiing

1936. Air. Tourist Propaganda.
191 **18** 0 p. 50 green 1·60 2·25
192 – 1 p. orange 2·25 2·50
193 **18** 2 p. violet 1·60 2·75
194 – 3 p. green 1·90 2·50
195 **18** 5 p. red 2·25 2·50
196 – 10 p. brown 2·25 2·50
197 – 15 p. red 48·00 45·00
198 **18** 25 p. green £120 £180
DESIGN: 1, 3, 10, 15 p. Jounieh Bay.

20 Cedar of Lebanon

21 President Edde

22 Lebanese Landscape

1937.
199 **20** 0 p. 10 red 15 20
200 0 p. 20 blue 40 70
201 0 p. 25 lilac 25 1·00
202 0 p. 50 mauve 20 20
203 0 p. 75 brown 60 30
207 **21** 3 p. violet 1·40 60
208 4 p. brown 25 25
209 4 p. 50 red 1·10 30
211 **22** 10 p. red 1·10 35
212 12½ p. blue 95 20
213 15 p. green 1·10 50
214 20 p. brown 1·60 25
215 25 p. red 3·50 75
216 50 p. violet 5·00 2·50
217 100 p. sepia 7·50 2·75

23 Exhibition Pavilion, Paris

1937. Air. Paris International Exhibition.
218 **23** 0 p. 50 black 85 90
219 1 p. green 75 1·60
220 2 p. brown 80 1·60
221 3 p. green 80 1·60
222 5 p. green 1·10 2·00
223 10 p. red 6·25 7·50
224 15 p. purple 6·00 7·50
225 25 p. brown 11·00 12·50

25 Ruins of Baalbek

1937. Air.
226 – 0 p. 50 blue 10 20
227 – 1 p. red 75 60
228 – 2 p. sepia 90 70
229 – 3 p. red 1·60 1·10
230 – 5 p. green 1·10 40
231 **25** 10 p. violet 40 35
232 – 15 p. blue 1·50 1·60
233 – 25 p. violet 3·75 3·00
234 – 50 p. green 8·00 4·00
235 – 100 p. brown 3·50 2·75
DESIGN: 0 p. 50 to 5 p. Beit ed-Din.

1938. Surch in English and Arabic figures.
236 **21** 2 p. on 3 p. violet 50 40
237 2½ p. on 4 p. brown 50 45

27 Medical College, Beirut

1938. Air. Medical Congress.
238 **27** 2 p. green 1·75 2·25
239 3 p. orange 1·75 2·50
240 5 p. violet 2·75 4·00
241 10 p. red 7·25 9·75

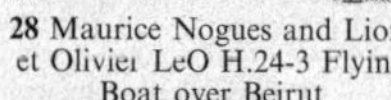
28 Maurice Nogues and Liore et Olivier LeO H.24-3 Flying Boat over Beirut
32 Emir Bechir Chehab

1938. Air. 10th Anniv of 1st Air Service between France and Lebanon.
242 **28** 10 p. purple 2·40 3·25

1938. Surch.
243 **16a** 6 p. on 7 p. 50 blue 1·40 1·00
244 – 7 p. 50 on 50 p. grn (No. 179) 1·40 1·25
245 – 7 p. 50 on 100 p. blk (No. 180) 1·25 1·40
246 **22** 12 p. 50 on 7 p. 50 blue 2·50 2·50
247 12½ on 7 p. 50 blue 45 40

1939. As T **16a**, but with differing figures and Arabic inscriptions in side panels, and imprint at foot "IMP. CATHOLIQUE-BEYROUTH-LIBAN" instead of "HELIO VAUGIRARD".
248 1 p. green 1·10 35
249 1 p. 50 purple 90 60
250 7 p. 50 red 1·60 65
DESIGN: 1 p. to 7 p. 50, Beit ed-Din.

1942. 1st Anniv of Proclamation of Independence.
252 **32** 0 p. 50 green (postage) 2·00 2·00
253 1 p. 50 purple 2·00 2·00
254 6 p. red 2·00 2·00
255 15 p. blue 2·00 2·00

256 – 10 p. purple (air) 3·75 3·75
257 – 50 p. green 3·75 3·75
DESIGN: 10, 50 p. Airplane over mountains.

1943. Surch in English and Arabic and with old values cancelled with ornaments.
258 **21** 2 p. on 4 p. brown 4·25 3·75
261 – 2 p. on 5 p. blue (251) 55 40
262 – 3 p. on 5 p. blue (251) 55 40
259 – 6 p. on 7 p. 50 red (No. 250) 85 55
263 **22** 6 p. on 12½ p. blue 75 55
264 7½ p. on 12½ p. blue 1·25 1·25
260 10 p. on 12½ p. blue 95 65

37 Parliament House

38 Bechamoun

1944. 2nd Anniv of Proclamation of Independence.
265 **37** 25 p. red (postage) 7·50 7·50
266 – 50 p. blue 7·50 7·50
267 **37** 150 p. blue 7·50 7·50
268 – 200 p. purple 7·50 7·50
DESIGN: 50 p., 200 p. Government House.

269 **38** 25 p. green (air) 2·25 2·00
270 50 p. orange 3·25 2·50
271 – 100 p. brown 3·50 2·25
272 – 200 p. violet 4·75 3·75
273 – 300 p. green 15·00 12·00
274 – 500 p. brown 35·00 25·00
DESIGNS: 100 p., 200 p. Rachaya Citadel; 300 p., 500 p. Beirut.

38a Beirut Isolation Hospital

(39)

1944. 6th Medical Congress. Optd with T **39**.
275 **38a** 10 p. red (postage) 5·00 5·00
276 20 p. blue 5·00 5·00

277 – 20 p. orange (air) 2·25 2·25
278 – 50 p. blue 2·25 2·25
279 – 100 p. purple 3·75 3·75
DESIGN: Nos. 277/9, Bhannes Sanatorium.

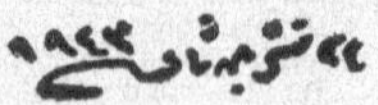
(**40** Trans "Nov. 23, 1943")

1944. 1st Anniv of President's Return to Office. Nos. 265/74 optd with T **40**.
280 **37** 25 p. red (postage) 10·00 10·00
281 – 50 p. blue 10·00 10·00
282 **37** 150 p. blue 10·00 10·00
283 – 200 p. purple 10·00 10·00

284 **38** 25 p. green (air) 3·75 3·75
285 – 50 p. orange 6·75 6·75
286 – 100 p. brown 8·75 8·75
287 – 200 p. violet 16·00 16·00
288 – 300 p. green 21·00 21·00
289 – 500 p. brown 40·00 40·00

41 Crusader Castle, Byblos
42 Falls of R. Litani

1945.
397 **41** 7 p. 50 red (postage) 2·40 20
398 10 p. purple 3·75 25
399 12 p. 50 blue 8·75 30
290 15 p. brown 2·50 2·25
291 20 p. green 2·50 2·25
292 – 25 p. blue 2·50 2·25
400 **41** 25 p. violet 16·00 65
293 – 50 p. red 4·75 2·50
401 **41** 50 p. green 38·00 4·25

294 **42** 25 p. brown (air) 1·90 1·25
295 50 p. purple 2·50 1·90
296 – 200 p. violet 8·75 3·25
297 – 300 p. black 18·00 6·25
DESIGNS—HORIZ: Nos. 292, 293, Crusader Castle, Tripoli; Nos. 296/7, Cedar of Lebanon and skier.

43 V(ictory) and National Flag

44 V(ictory) and Lebanese Soldiers at Bir-Hakeim

1946. Victory. "V" in design. (a) Postage.
298 **43** 7 p. 50 brown, red & pink 70 10
299 10 p. purple, pink and red 1·00 10
300 12 p. 50 purple, blue and red 1·25 15
301 15 p. green, emerald & red 1·25 25
302 20 p. myrtle, green and red 2·00 25
303 25 p. blue, lt blue and red 3·00 45
304 50 p. blue, violet and red 5·75 1·50
305 100 p. black, blue and red 9·50 3·50

(b) Air.
306 **44** 15 p. blue, yellow and red 50 20
307 20 p. red and blue 50 35
308 25 p. blue, yellow and red 60 35
309 50 p. black, violet and red 1·00 40
310 100 p. violet and red 3·25 90
311 150 p. brown and red 4·00 1·75

1946. As T **43** but without "V" sign.
312 7 p. 50 lake, red and mauve 70 10
313 10 p. violet, mauve and red 1·00 10
314 12 p. 50 brown, green and red 1·25 20
315 15 p. brown, pink and red 2·25 25
316 20 p. blue, orange and red 1·90 25
317 25 p. myrtle, green and red 3·25 40
318 50 p. blue, lt blue and red 7·00 1·50
319 100 p. black, blue and red 11·50 3·50

45 Grey Herons

1946.
320 **45** 12 p. 50 red (postage) 14·00 50
321 10 p. orange (air) 3·50 65
322 25 p. blue 5·00 30
323 50 p. green 12·00 95
324 100 p. purple 21·00 4·50

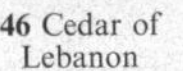
46 Cedar of Lebanon **47**

1946.
325 **46** 0 p. 50 c. brown 25 20
326 1 p. purple 35 20
327 2 p. 50 violet 1·25 20
328 5 p. red 1·90 20
329 6 p. grey 2·50 20

1946. Air. Arab Postal Congress.
330 **47** 25 p. blue 75 50
331 50 p. green 1·10 75
332 75 p. red 1·90 1·25
333 150 p. violet 4·50 2·25

48 Cedar of Lebanon **49** President, Bridge and Tablet

1947.
333a **48** 0 p. 50 brown 1·00 10
333b 2 p. 50 green 1·50 10
333c 5 p. red 2·50 20

1947. Air. Evacuation of Foreign Troops from Lebanon.
334 **49** 25 p. blue 75 65
335 50 p. red 1·10 95
336 75 p. black 2·50 1·25
337 150 p. green 4·50 2·50

50 Crusader Castle, Tripoli

51 Jounieh Bay

1947.
338 **50** 12 p. 50 red (postage) 6·25 30
339 25 p. blue 7·75 40
340 50 p. green 25·00 75
341 100 p. violet 32·00 5·50

342 **51** 5 p. green (air) 30 10
343 10 p. mauve 40 10
344 15 p. red 60 10
403 15 p. green 7·50 1·00
345 20 p. orange 95 10
345a 20 p. red 1·25 20
346 25 p. blue 1·25 10
347 50 p. red 3·00 25
348 **51** 100 p. purple 6·25 25
349 – 150 p. purple 12·50 1·10
350 – 200 p. slate 19·00 5·00
351 – 300 p. black 30·00 11·50
DESIGN: 150 p. to 300 p. Grand Serail Palace.

54 Phoenician Galley

1947. Air. 12th Congress of U.P.U., Paris.
352 – 10 p. blue 75 35
353 – 15 p. red 1·10 50
354 – 25 p. blue 1·50 85
355 **54** 50 p. green 3·50 1·00
356 – 75 p. violet 4·50 1·40
357 – 100 p. brown 6·25 3·00
DESIGN—VERT: 10 p. to 25 p. Posthorn.

55 Faraya Bridge and Statue

1947. Air. Red Cross Fund. Cross in red.
358 **55** 12 p. 50 + 25 p. green 6·25 5·00
359 25 p. + 50 p. blue 7·00 5·75
360 – 50 p. + 100 p. brown 9·50 7·00
361 – 75 p. + 150 p. violet 20·00 14·00
362 – 100 p. + 200 p. grey 35·00 25·00
DESIGN: 50 p. to 100 p. Djounie Bay and statue.

56 Cedar of Lebanon **58** Lebanese Landscape

1948.
363 **56** 0 p. 50 blue (postage) 15 10
364 1 p. brown 65 10
395 1 p. orange 30 10
365 2 p. 50 mauve 60 10
366 3 p. green 1·40 10
367 5 p. red 2·00 10
368 – 7 p. 50 red 5·00 20
369 – 10 p. purple 3·25 20
370 – 12 p. 50 blue 8·25 25
371 – 25 p. blue 11·00 65
372 – 50 p. green 25·00 5·00

373 **58** 5 p. red (air) 50 10
374 10 p. mauve 1·10 10
375 15 p. brown 2·75 10
376 20 p. slate 4·50 20
377 25 p. blue 8·25 90
378 50 p. black 14·50 1·75
DESIGN—As T **58**: Nos. 368/72, Zebaide Aqueduct.

59 Europa on Bull **61** Apollo on Sun Chariot

1948. 3rd Meeting of U.N.E.S.C.O., Beirut.
379 **59** 10 p. orange and red (postage) 1·90 1·25
380 12 p. 50 mauve and violet 2·50 1·90
381 25 p. green and light green 3·00 1·90
382 – 30 p. buff and brown 3·75 2·25
383 – 40 p. green and turquoise 5·75 2·25
DESIGN—VERT: 30, 40 p. Avicenna (philosopher and scientist).

384 **61** 7 p. 50 blue and light blue (air) 1·60 1·25
385 15 p. black and grey 1·90 1·25
386 20 p. brown and pink 3·25 1·90
387 – 35 p. red 5·25 2·50
388 – 75 p. green 10·50 5·50
DESIGN—HORIZ: 35, 75 p. Symbolical figure.

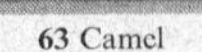
63 Camel

64 Sikorsky S-51 Helicopter

1949. 75th Anniv of U.P.U.
389 **63** 5 p. violet (postage) 1·00 75
390 7 p. 50 red 1·50 1·25
391 12 p. 50 blue 2·25 1·60

392 **64** 25 p. blue (air) 5·00 2·50
393 50 p. green 7·50 3·75

65 Cedar of Lebanon **66** Nahr el-Kalb Bridge

1950.
407 **65** 0 p. 50 red 25 10
408 1 p. red 65 10
409 2 p. 50 violet 1·00 10
410 5 p. purple 1·90 10
411 **66** 7 p. 50 red 2·25 10
412 10 p. lilac 2·75 10
413 12 p. 50 blue 4·50 20
414 25 p. blue 8·75 95
415 50 p. green 25·00 5·00

67 Congressional Flags

1950. Lebanese Emigrants' Congress. Inscr "MOIS DES EMIGRES-ETE 1950".
416 **67** 7 p. 50 green (postage) 65 20
417 12 p. mauve 65 20

418 – 5 p. blue (air) 2·00 50
419 – 15 p. violet 2·50 75
420 – 25 p. brown 1·25 75
421 – 35 p. green 2·50 1·25
DESIGNS: 5, 15 p. House Martins; 25, 35 p. Pres. Bishara al-Khoury and building.

70 Crusader Castle, Sidon

1950. Air.
422 **70** 10 p. brown 50 20
423 15 p. green 1·00 15
424 20 p. red 2·25 30
425 25 p. blue 5·00 1·25
426 50 p. grey 7·50 2·50

1950. Surch with figures and bars.
427 **56** 1 p. on 3 p. green 50 20
428 **46** 2 p. 50 on 6 p. grey 75 20

73 Cedar of Lebanon

74 Nahr el-Kalb Bridge

75 Crusader Castle, Sidon

1951.
429 **73** 0 p. 50 red (postage) 25 10
430 1 p. brown 50 10
431 2 p. 50 grey 2·50 10
432 5 p. purple 2·75 10
433 **74** 7 p. 50 red 3·00 30
434 10 p. purple 3·75 20
435 12 p. 50 turquoise 7·50 35
436 25 p. blue 11·50 1·25
437 50 p. green 25·00 6·75

438 **75** 10 p. turquoise (air) 80 10
439 15 p. brown 1·75 10
440 20 p. red 1·75 20
441 25 p. blue 2·00 20
442 35 p. mauve 5·00 2·50
443 50 p. blue 9·00 2·00
Type **74** is similar to Type **66** but left value tablets differ.
For design as Type **74** but inscr "LIBAN", see Nos. 561/3.

76 Cedar of Lebanon

77 Baalbek

1952.
444 **76** 0 p. 50 green (postage) 60 10
445 1 p. brown 60 10
446 2 p. 50 blue 90 20
447 5 p. red 1·60 25
448 **77** 7 p. 50 red 1·90 45
449 10 p. violet 4·50 50
450 12 p. 50 blue 4·50 50
451 25 p. blue 5·75 1·25
452 – 50 p. green 17·00 2·25
453 – 100 p. brown 35·00 7·00

454 – 5 p. red (air) 30 10
455 – 10 p. grey 45 10
456 – 15 p. mauve 80 10
457 – 20 p. orange 1·25 30
458 – 25 p. blue 1·25 40
459 – 35 p. blue 2·10 45
460 – 50 p. green 7·00 50
461 – 100 p. blue 48·00 2·10
462 – 200 p. green 28·00 4·00
463 – 300 p. sepia 38·00 8·75
DESIGNS—As Type **77**: Nos. 452/3, Beaufort Castle; 454/9, Beirut Airport; 460/3, Amphitheatre, Byblos.

78 Cedar of Lebanon

79 General Post Office

80 Douglas DC-4

1953.
559 **78** 0 p. 50 blue (postage) 20 10
465 1 p. red 70 10
466 2 p. 50 violet 90 20
560 2 p. 50 purple 60 10
467 5 p. green 1·60 25
468 **79** 7 p. 50 red 2·50 35
469 10 p. green 3·00 50
470 12 p. 50 turquoise 4·25 55
471 25 p. blue 6·25 1·10
472 50 p. brown 11·50 2·50

473 **80** 5 p. green (air) 30 10
474 10 p. red 55 10
475 15 p. red 80 10
476 20 p. turquoise 1·25 10
477 25 p. blue 3·25 10
478 35 p. brown 4·50 20
479 50 p. blue 6·50 45
480 100 p. sepia 12·00 4·25
For 20 p. green as Type **79** see No. 636.

81 Cedar of Lebanon

82 Beit ed-Din Palace

83 Baalbek

1954.
481 **81** 0 p. 50 blue (postage) 20 10
482 1 p. orange 35 10
483 2 p. 50 violet 60 20
484 5 p. green 1·10 20
485 **82** 7 p. 50 red 1·90 45
486 10 p. green 2·75 45
487 12 p. 50 blue 4·50 60
488 25 p. deep blue 6·25 2·25
489 50 p. turquoise 11·00 3·75
490 100 p. sepia 25·00 7·50

491 **83** 5 p. green (air) 40 10
492 10 p. lilac 70 10
493 15 p. red 80 10
494 20 p. brown 1·10 10
495 25 p. blue 1·25 20
496 35 p. sepia 1·75 25
497 – 50 p. green 5·50 40
498 – 100 p. red 9·00 60
499 – 200 p. sepia 20·00 1·90
500 – 300 p. blue 32·00 3·75
DESIGN—As T **83**: 50 p. to 300 p. Litani Irrigation Canal.
For other values as Nos. 497/500, see Nos. 564/7.

MINIMUM PRICE

The minimum price quoted is 10p which represents a handling charge rather than a basis for valuing common stamps. For further notes about prices, see introductory pages.

84 Khalde Airport, Beirut

1954. Air. Opening of Beirut International Airport.
501 **84** 10 p. red and pink 45 25
502 25 p. blue and ultramarine 1·25 40
503 35 p. brown and sepia . . . 1·75 65
504 65 p. green and turquoise . 4·25 2·50

1955. Arab Postal Union. As T **96a** of Syria but smaller, 27 × 37 mm. Inscr "LIBAN" at top.
505 12 p. 50 green (postage) . . . 50 35
506 25 p. violet 75 35
507 2 p. 50 brown (air) 40 30

85 Rotary Emblem 86 Cedar of Lebanon

87 Jeita Grotto 88 Skiers

1955. Air. 50th Anniv of Rotary International.
508 **85** 35 p. green 90 65
509 65 p. blue . . . . 1·60 95

1955.
510 **86** 0 p. 50 blue (postage) . . 20 10
511 1 p. red 25 10
512 2 p. 50 violet 45 10
552 2 p. 50 blue . . . . 6·25 25
513 5 p. green 70 10
514 **87** 7 p. 50 orange 95 10
515 10 p. green . . . . 1·60 10
516 12 p. 50 blue . . . . . . 1·60 10
517 25 p. blue . . . . 4·00 25
518 50 p. green . . . . 5·75 75
519 **88** 5 p. turquoise (air) 50 35
520 15 p. red 85 20
521 20 p. violet . . . . 1·50 20
522 25 p. blue . . . . 2·75 30
523 35 p. brown . . . . . . 4·50 50
524 50 p. brown . . . . . . 7·50 70
525 65 p. blue . . . . 14·00 2·25

The face value on No. 510 reads "0.50 PIASTRE"; on No. 512 the "2" and "50" are different sizes and the 1 and 5 p. have no dash under "P".

For other colours and new values as Type **88** see Nos. 568/70 and for redrawn Type **86** see Nos. 582/5, 686 and 695/7.

89 Visitor from Abroad 90 Cedar of Lebanon 91 Globe and Columns

92 Oranges

1955. Air. Tourist Propaganda.
526 **89** 2 p. 50 slate and purple . . 10 10
527 12 p. 50 blue & ultramarine 30 20
528 25 p. blue and indigo . . . 80 35
529 35 p. blue and green . . . 1·25 50

1955.
530 **90** 0.50 p. blue (postage) . . . 20 10
531 1 p. orange 20 10
532 2 p. 50 violet 25 10
533 5 p. green 50 10
534 **91** 7 p. 50 red and orange . . 65 10
535 10 p. green and brown . . 75 10
536 12 p. 50 blue and green . . 95 10
537 25 p. blue and mauve . . 1·90 20
538 50 p. green and blue . . 2·75 35
539 100 p. brown and orange . 4·50 1·10
540 **92** 5 p. yellow and green (air) 25 10
541 10 p. orange and green . . 60 10
542 15 p. orange and green . . 60 10
543 20 p. orange and brown . 1·00 10
544 – 25 p. violet and blue . . . 1·25 10
545 – 35 p. purple and green . . 2·50 25
546 – 50 p. yellow and black . . 2·50 25
547 – 65 p. yellow and green . . 5·00 35
548 – 100 p. orange and green . 8·25 1·00
549 – 200 p. red and green . . . 15·00 4·50

DESIGNS—VERT: 25 p. to 50 p. Grapes. HORIZ: 4 p. to 200 p. Quinces.

93 U.N. Emblem 94 Masks, Columns and Gargoyle

1956. Air. 10th Anniv of U.N.
550 **93** 35 p. blue . . . . 4·00 3·25
551 65 p. green . . . . 5·25 3·75

1956. Air. Baalbek International Drama Festival. Inscr "FESTIVAL INTERNATIONAL DE BAALBECK".
553 **94** 2 p. 50 sepia 30 15
554 10 p. green 45 25
555 – 12 p. 50 blue 45 35
556 – 25 p. violet . . . . 1·00 45
557 – 35 p. purple . . . . 1·90 65
558 – 65 p. slate . . . . 3·00 1·90

DESIGNS—HORIZ: 12 p. 50, 25 p. Temple ruins at Baalbek. VERT: 35 p., 65 p. Double bass, masks and columns.

1957. As earlier designs but redrawn. (a) Postage. As T **74** but inscr "LIBAN".
561 7 p. 50 red . . . . 1·10 10
562 10 p. brown . . . . 1·60 10
563 12 p. 50 blue . . . . 1·90 10

(b) Air. Arabic inscription changed. New values and colours.
564 – 10 p. violet 25 10
565 – 15 p. orange 40 10
566 – 20 p. green 50 10
567 – 25 p. blue 60 10
568 **88** 35 p. green . . . . 2·10 20
569 65 p. purple . . . . . . 3·75 55
570 100 p. brown . . . . . . 6·25 1·25

DESIGN: 10 p. to 25 p. As Nos. 497/500.

95 Pres. Chamoun and King Faisal II of Iraq

1957. Air. Arab Leaders' Conference, Beirut.
571 **95** 15 p. orange 65 40
572 – 15 p. blue 65 40
573 – 15 p. maroon 65 40
574 – 15 p. purple 65 40
575 – 15 p. green 65 40
576 – 25 p. turquoise 65 40
577 – 100 p. brown . . . . . . 4·50 2·25

DESIGNS—As T **95**: 15 p. values show Pres. Chamoun and; King Hussein of Jordan (No. 572), Abdallah Khalil of Sudan (No. 573), Pres. Shukri Bey al-Quwatli of Syria (No. 574) and King Saud of Saudi Arabia (No. 575); 25 p. Map and Pres. Chamoun. 44 × 44 mm (Diamond shape); 100 p. The six Arab Leaders.

97 Runners 98 Miners

1957. 2nd Pan-Arabian Games, Beirut.
578 **97** 2 p. 50 sepia (postage) . . 65 40
579 – 12 p. 50 blue 95 50
580 – 35 p. purple (air) . . . . 2·50 1·00
581 – 50 p. green . . . . 3·00 1·50

DESIGNS—VERT: 12 p. 50, Footballers. HORIZ: 35 p. Fencers; 50 p. Stadium.

1957.
582 **86** 0 p. 50 blue (16½ × 20½ mm) (postage) 15 10
582a 0 p. 50 violet (17 × 21½ mm) 25 10
583 1 p. brown (16½ × 20½ mm) 20 10
583a 1 p. purple (17 × 21½ mm) 25 10
584 2 p. 50 violet (16½ × 20½ mm) 35 10
584a 2 p. 50 blue (17 × 21½ mm) 40 10
585 5 p. green (16½ × 20½ mm) 50 10
586 **98** 7½ p. pink 75 10
587 10 p. brown . . . . 1·00 10
588 12½ p. blue . . . . 1·40 10
589 – 25 p. blue . . . . 1·40 10
590 – 50 p. green . . . . 2·50 30
591 – 100 p. brown . . . . . . 4·50 90
592 – 5 p. green (air) 20 10
593 – 10 p. orange 25 10
594 – 15 p. brown 25 10
595 – 20 p. purple 40 10
596 – 25 p. blue 50 15
597 – 35 p. purple 80 30
598 – 50 p. green . . . . 1·50 45
599 – 65 p. brown . . . . 2·50 45
600 – 100 p. grey . . . . 3·25 1·25

DESIGNS: POSTAGE—As Type **86**: 50 c. inscr "0 P.50", 2 p. 50, Figures in uniform size; 1 p., 5 p. Short dash under "P". As Type **98**: VERT: 25 p. to 100 p. Potter. AIR—As Type **98**: HORIZ: 5 p. to 25 p. Cedar of Lebanon with signs of the Zodiac, bird and ship. 35 to 100 p. Chamoun Electric Power Station.

99 Cedar of Lebanon 100 Soldier and Flag

101 Douglas DC-6B at Khalde Airport

1959.
601 **99** 0 p. 50 blue (postage) . . 15 10
602 1 p. orange 25 10
603 2 p. 50 violet 35 10
604 5 p. green 50 10
605 **100** 12 p. 50 blue . . . . . . 1·00 10
606 25 p. blue . . . . 1·10 10
607 50 p. brown . . . . . . 1·90 25
608 100 p. sepia . . . . . . 3·50 45
609 **101** 5 p. green (air) 55 10
610 10 p. purple 55 10
611 15 p. violet 80 10
612 20 p. red . . . . 1·10 15
613 25 p. violet . . . . . . 1·50 25
614 – 35 p. myrtle . . . . . . 1·10 25
615 – 50 p. turquoise . . . . . 1·40 25
616 – 65 p. sepia . . . . 2·75 45
617 – 100 p. blue . . . . 3·25 75

DESIGN—HORIZ: Nos. 614/17, Factory, cogwheel and telegraph pylons.

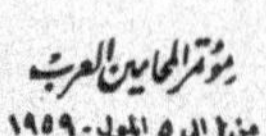
(102)

1959. Lawyers' Conference. Nos. 538 and 546 surch as T **102**.
618 30 p. on 50 p. myrtle and blue (postage) . . . . 1·10 65
619 40 p. on 50 p. yellow and black (air) . . . . 1·00 65

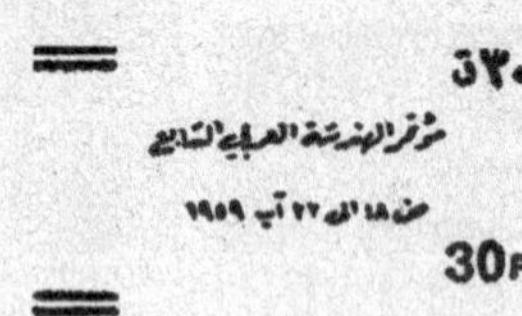
(103)

1959. Air. Engineers' Conference. Nos. 614 and 616 surch as T **103**.
620 30 p. on 35 p. myrtle 65 50
621 40 p. on 65 p. sepia . . . . 1·25 75

(104) 105 Discus Thrower

1959. Emigrants' Conference. No. 590 surch as T **104**.
622 30 p. on 50 p. green 75 30
623 40 p. on 50 p. green . . . . 1·10 60

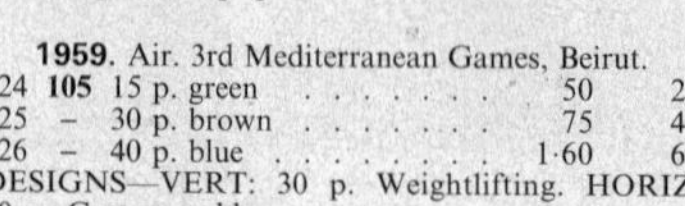

1959. Air. 3rd Mediterranean Games, Beirut.
624 **105** 15 p. green 50 25
625 – 30 p. brown 75 40
626 – 40 p. blue . . . . 1·60 65

DESIGNS—VERT: 30 p. Weightlifting. HORIZ: 40 p. Games emblem.

106 Soldiers with Standard 108 Planting Tree

1959. Air. 16th Anniv of Independence.
627 **106** 40 p. red and black . . . 95 65
628 60 p. red and green . . . 1·25 90

1959. Surch.
629 **100** 7 p. 50 on 12 p. 50 blue . 50 10
630 10 p. on 12 p. 50 blue . . 65 10
631 15 p. on 25 p. blue . . . 75 10
632 – 40 p. on 50 p. green (No. 590) . . . . 1·25 90
633 **88** 40 p. on 65 p. purple (No. 569) (air) . . . . 2·50 60

1960. Air. 25th Anniv of Friends of the Tree Society.
634 **108** 20 p. purple and green . . 75 50
635 40 p. sepia and green . . 1·10 75

1960. Air. As T **79** but colours of name and value tablets reversed.
636 20 p. green 70 45

109 Pres. Chehab

1960. Air.
637 **109** 5 p. green 10 10
638 10 p. blue 10 10
639 15 p. brown 10 10
640 20 p. sepia 15 10
641 30 p. olive 20 10
642 40 p. red 45 15
643 50 p. blue 60 20
644 70 p. purple . . . . . . 1·10 25
645 100 p. green . . . . . . 2·25 65

110 Arab League Centre 111 "Uprooted Tree"

1960. Inaug of Arab League Centre, Cairo.
646 **110** 15 p. turquoise 50 40

1960. Air. World Refugee Year. (a) Size 20½ × 36½ mm.
647 **111** 25 p. brown 75 50
648 40 p. green . . . . 1·10 75

(b) Size 19¾ × 35¼ mm.
648b **111** 25 p. brown . . . . . . 1·00 1·00
648c 40 p. green . . . . 1·25 1·25

112 Martyrs' Monument

1960. Air. Martyrs' Commemoration.
649 **112** 20 p. purple and green . . 50 30
650 40 p. blue and green . . 75 50
651 – 70 p. olive and black . . 1·60 75

DESIGN—VERT: 70 p. Detail of statues on monument.

113 Pres. Chehab and King Mohammed V 114 Pres. Chehab

1960. Air. Visit of King Mohammed V of Morocco.
652 **113** 30 p. chocolate and brown 75 50
653 70 p. brown and black . . 1·50 75

1960.

654 **114** 50 c. green 10 10
655 2 p. 50 olive 10 10
656 5 p. green 15 10
657 7 p. 50 red 30 10
658 15 p. blue 50 25
659 50 p. purple . . . . 1·25 30
660 100 p. brown . . . . . . 2·50 50

115 Child 116 Dove, Map and Flags

1960. Air. Mother and Child Days.

661 **115** 20 p. red and yellow . . . 50 25
662 20 p. + 10 p. red & yellow 75 40
663 – 60 p. blue & light blue . . 1·25 85
664 – 60 p. + 15 p. blue & lt bl 1·90 1·00
DESIGN: Nos. 663/4, Mother and child.

1960. Air. World Lebanese Union Meeting. Beirut. Multicoloured.

665 20 p. Type **116** 25 20
666 40 p. Cedar of Lebanon and homing pigeons 75 40
667 70 p. Globes and Cedar of Lebanon (horiz) 90 50

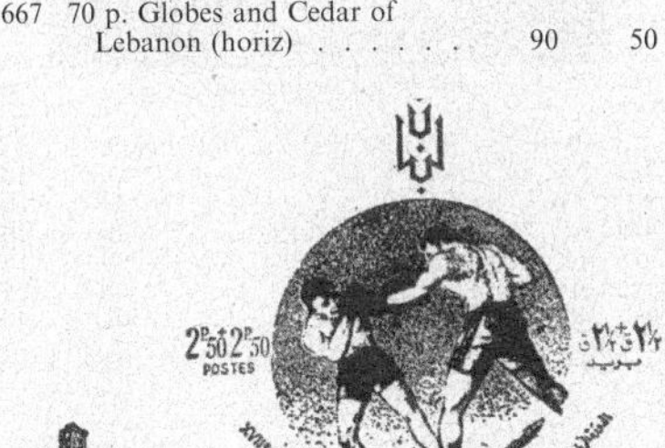

(117) 119 Boxing

1960. Arabian Oil Congress, Beirut. Optd with T **117**.

668 **86** 5 p. green (No. 585) . . . 30 10
669 **110** 15 p. turquoise 65 40

1960. Air. World Refugee Year. Nos. 648b/c surch in English and Arabic.

669a **111** 20 p. + 10 p. on 40 p. grn 7·00 7·00
669b 30 p. + 15 p. on 25 p. brn 10·00 10·00

1961. Olympic Games.

670 **119** 2 p. 50 + 2 p. 50 brown and blue (postage) 20 20
671 – 5 p. + 5 p. brown and orge 30 25
672 – 7 p. 50 + 7 p. 50 brn & vio 50 40
673 – 15 p. + 15 p. brown & red (air) . . . . 2·50 2·25
674 – 25 p. + 25 p. brown & grn 2·50 2·25
675 – 35 p. + 35 p. brown & bl 2·50 2·25
DESIGNS: 5 p. Wrestling; 7 p. 50, Putting the shot; 15 p. Fencing; 25 p. Cycling; 35 p. Swimming.

120 Pres. Chehab 121 Pres. Chehab and Map of Lebanon 122 U.N. Emblem and Map

1961.

676 **120** 2 p. 50 ultramarine and blue (postage) 20 10
677 7 p. 50 violet and mauve . 25 10
678 10 p. brown and yellow . 50 10
679 **121** 5 p. green & lt green (air) 15 10
680 10 p. brown and ochre . . 45 10
681 70 p. violet and mauve . . 1·90 60
682 – 200 p. blue and bistre . . 4·25 2·50
DESIGN—HORIZ: 200 p. Casino, Maameltein.

1961. Air. 15th Anniv of U.N.O.

683 **122** 20 p. purple and blue . . 50 25
684 – 30 p. green and brown . . 75 40
685 – 50 p. blue and ultramarine 1·25 60
DESIGNS—VERT: 30 p. U.N. emblem and Baalbek ruins. HORIZ: 50 p. View of U.N. Headquarters and Manhattan.

123 Cedar of Lebanon 124 Bay of Maameltein

1961. Redrawn version of T **86** (different arrangement at foot). Shaded background.

686 **123** 2 p. 50 myrtle 50 10
See also Nos. 695/7.

1961. Air.

687 **124** 15 p. lake 40 20
688 30 p. blue 65 30
689 40 p. sepia 90 45

125 Weaving

1961. Air. Labour Day.

690 – 30 p. red . . . . 1·25 60
691 **125** 70 p. blue . . . . 2·50 1·25
DESIGN: 30 p. Pottery.

126 Water-skiers

1961. Air. Tourist Month.

692 – 15 p. violet and blue . . 60 35
693 **126** 40 p. blue and flesh . . . 1·25 50
694 – 70 p. olive and flesh . . . 1·90 1·00
DESIGNS—VERT: 15 p. Firework display. HORIZ: 70 p. Tourists in punt.

1961. As T **123** but plain background.

695 2 p. 50 yellow 30 10
696 5 p. lake 40 15
697 10 p. black 65 25

127 G.P.O., Beirut

1961.

698 **127** 2 p. 50 mauve (postage) . 30 10
699 5 p. green 50 20
700 15 p. blue . . . . 1·00 35
701 – 35 p. green (air) 60 45
702 – 50 p. brown 90 55
703 – 100 p. black . . . . . . 1·25 90
DESIGN: 35 p. to 100 p. Motor highway, Dora.

128 Cedars of Lebanon 129 Tyre Waterfront

1961.

704 **128** 0 p. 50 green (postage) . 10 10
705 1 p. brown 10 10
706 2 p. 50 blue 10 10
707 5 p. red 25 10
708 7 p. 50 violet 35 10
709 – 10 p. purple 80 10
710 – 15 p. blue . . . . 1·10 20
711 – 50 p. green . . . . . . 1·25 75
712 – 100 p. black . . . . . . 3·00 1·10
713 **129** 5 p. red (air) 20 10
714 10 p. violet 25 10
715 15 p. blue 45 10
716 20 p. orange 45 10
717 30 p. green 50 15
718 – 40 p. purple 75 25
719 – 50 p. blue 90 40
720 – 70 p. green . . . . . . 1·25 60
721 – 100 p. sepia . . . . . . 2·25 95
DESIGNS—HORIZ: Nos. 709/12, Zahle. VERT: Nos. 718/21, Afka Falls.
See also Nos. 729/34.

130 U.N.E.S.C.O. Building, Beirut

1961. Air. 15th Anniv of U.N.E.S.C.O. Mult.

722 20 p. Type **130** 35 25
723 30 p. U.N.E.S.C.O. emblem and cedar (vert) 65 40
724 50 p. U.N.E.S.C.O. Building, Paris . . . . 1·00 60

131 Tomb of Unknown Soldier 132 Scout Bugler

1961. Independence and Evacuation of Foreign Troops Commem. Multicoloured.

725 10 p. Type **131** (postage) . . . 35 10
726 15 p. Soldier and flag 50 10
727 25 p. Cedar emblem (air) . . . 45 25
728 50 p. Emirs Bashir and Fakhreddine 65 50
The 25 p. and 50 p. are horiz.

1962. As Nos. 704/21 but with larger figures of value.

729 **128** 50 c. green (postage) . . . 20 10
730 1 p. brown 20 10
731 2 p. 50 blue 25 10
732 – 15 p. blue . . . . 3·00 25
733 **129** 5 p. red (air) 35 10
734 – 40 p. purple . . . . . . 5·50 75

1962. Lebanese Scout Movement Commemorative.

735 $\frac{1}{2}$ p. black, yell & grn (postage) 10 10
736 1 p. multicoloured 10 10
737 $2\frac{1}{2}$ p. green, black and red . . 10 10
738 6 p. multicoloured 35 10
739 10 p. yellow, black and blue . 65 10
740 15 p. multicoloured (air) . . . 65 25
741 20 p. yellow, black and violet 75 35
742 25 p. multicoloured . . . . . 1·25 65
DESIGNS—VERT: $\frac{1}{2}$ p. Type **132**; 6 p. Lord Baden-Powell; 20 p. Saluting hand. HORIZ: 1 p. Scout with flag, cedar and badge; $2\frac{1}{2}$ p. Stretcher party, badge and laurel; 10 p. Scouts at campfire; 15 p. Cedar and Guide badge; 25 p. Cedar and Scout badge.

133 Arab League Centre, Cairo, and Emblem 134 Blacksmith

1962. Air. Arab League Week.

743 **133** 20 p. ultramarine and blue 40 25
744 30 p. lake and pink . . . 45 40
745 50 p. geeen and turquoise 75 65
See also Nos. 792/5.

1962. Air. Labour Day.

746 **134** 5 p. green and blue 20 10
747 10 p. blue and pink . . . 30 10
748 – 25 p. violet and pink . . . 50 20
749 – 35 p. mauve and blue . . . 65 40
DESIGN—HORIZ: 25 p., 35 p. Tractor.

1962. European Shooting Championships Nos. 670/5 optd **CHAMPIONNAT D'EUROPE DE TIR 2 JUIN 1962** in French and Arabic.

750 **119** 2 p. 50 + 2 p. 50 (postage) 40 25
751 – 5 p. + 5 p. 65 50
752 – 7 p. 50 + 7 p. 50 . . . . 95 60
753 – 15 p. + 15 p. (air) 95 95
754 – 25 p. + 25 p. . . . . . . 2·25 2·25
755 – 35 p. + 35 p. . . . . . . 2·50 2·50

136 Hand grasping Emblem 137 Rock Temples of Abu Simbel

1962. Air. Malaria Eradication.

756 **136** 30 p. brown & lt brown . 75 50
757 – 70 p. violet and lilac . . 1·25 75
DESIGN: 70 p. Campaign emblem.

1962. Nubian Monuments.

758 **137** 5 p. bl & ultram (postage) 50 20
759 15 p. lake and brown . . . 75 25
760 – 30 p. yellow and grn (air) 1·25 60
761 – 50 p. olive and grey . . . 2·50 1·25
DESIGNS: 30 p., 50 p. Bas-relief.

138 Playing-card Symbols 139 Schoolboy

1962. Air. European Bridge Championships.

762 **138** 25 p. multicoloured . . . 3·00 1·90
763 40 p. multicoloured . . . 3·25 1·90

1962. Schoolchildren's Day.

764 **139** 30 p. mult (postage) . . . 50 25
765 – 45 p. multicoloured (air) . 75 40
DESIGN: 45 p. Teacher.

140 141 Cherries

1962. Air. 19th Anniv of Independence.

766 **140** 25 p. green, red & turq . 75 35
767 25 p. violet, red & turq . 75 35
768 25 p. blue, red & turquoise 75 35

1962. Fruits. Multicoloured.

769 0 p. 50 Type **141** (postage) . . 25 10
770 1 p. Figs 25 10
771 2 p. 50 Type **141** 40 10
772 5 p. Figs 50 10
773 7 p. 50 Type **141** 25 10
774 10 p. Grapes 35 10
775 17 p. 50 Grapes 75 10
776 30 p. Grapes . . . . 1·25 25
777 50 p. Oranges . . . . 2·25 65
778 100 p. Pomegranates . . . . 5·00 140
779 5 p. Apricots (air) 20 10
780 10 p. Plums 25 10
781 20 p. Apples 55 10
782 30 p. Plums 75 25
783 40 p. Apples 90 25
784 50 p. Pears . . . . 1·10 40
785 70 p. Medlars . . . . 1·90 50
786 100 p. Lemons . . . . . . 3·25 1·10

142 Reaping 143 Nurse tending Baby

1963. Air. Freedom from Hunger.

787 **142** 2 p. 50 yellow and blue . 15 10
788 5 p. yellow and green . . 15 10
789 7 p. 50 yellow & purple . 20 10
790 – 15 p. green and red . . . 50 25
791 – 20 p. green and red . . . 65 40
DESIGN—HORIZ: 15 p., 20 p. Three ears of wheat within hand.

1963. Air. Arab League Week. As T **133** but inscr "1963".

792 5 p. violet and blue 10 10
793 10 p. green and blue 20 20
794 15 p. brown and blue 30 25
795 20 p. grey and blue 65 45

1963. Air. Red Cross Centenary.

796 – 5 p. green and red 10 10
797 – 20 p. blue and red 30 10
798 **143** 35 p. red and black . . . 55 25
799 40 p. violet and red . . . 90 45
DESIGN—HORIZ: 5, 20 p. Blood transfusion.

144 Allegory of Music 145 Flag and rising Sun

1963. Air. Baalbek Festival.

800 **144** 35 p. orange and blue . . 95 50

1963. Air. 20th Anniv of Independence. Flag and sun in red and yellow.

801 **145** 5 p. turquoise 15 10
802 10 p. green 25 25
803 25 p. blue 50 40
804 40 p. drab 75 65

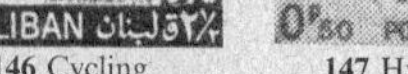
146 Cycling 147 Hyacinth

1964. 4th Mediterranean Games, Naples (1963).

805	146	2 p. 50 brown and purple (postage)	20	10
806	–	5 p. orange and blue	25	10
807	–	10 p. brown and violet	40	10
808	–	15 p. orange & green (air)	40	25
809	–	17 p. 50 brown & blue	50	30
810	–	30 p. brown & turq	75	50

DESIGNS—VERT: 5 p. Basketball; 10 p. Running; 15 p. Tennis. HORIZ: 17 p. 50 Swimming; 30 p. Skiing.

1964. Flowers. Multicoloured.

811	0 p. 50 Type **147** (postage)	10	10
812	1 p. Type **147**	10	10
813	2 p. 50 Type **147**	10	10
814	5 p. Cyclamen	10	10
815	7 p. 50 Cyclamen	15	10
816	10 p. Poinsettia	25	10
817	17 p. 50 Anemone	50	10
818	30 p. Iris	1·10	40
819	50 p. Poppy	2·50	65
820	5 p. Lily (air)	25	20
821	10 p. Ranunculus	45	20
822	20 p. Anemone	60	20
823	40 p. Tuberose	1·00	40
824	45 p. Rhododendron	1·10	40
825	50 p. Jasmine	1·25	40
826	70 p. Yellow broom	1·90	65

Nos. 816/26 are vert, size 26½ × 37 mm.

148 Cedar of Lebanon 149

1964.

827	148	0 p. 50 green	25	10
828	149	0 p. 50 green	15	10
829		2 p. 50 blue	15	10
830		5 p. mauve	20	10
831		7 p. 50 orange	40	10
832		17 p. 50 purple	70	10

150 Child on Rocking-horse

152 "Flame of Freedom"

151 League Session

1964. Air. Children's Day.

833	–	5 p. red, orange and green	15	10
834	–	10 p. red, orange and brown	25	15
835	150	20 p. orange, blue and ultramarine	50	35
836		40 p. yellow, blue and purple	90	65

DESIGN—HORIZ: 5 p., 10 p. Girls skipping.

1964. Air. Arab League Meeting.

837	151	5 p. buff, brown and black	25	20
838		10 p. black	35	25
839		15 p. turquoise	65	40
840		20 p. mauve, brn & sepia	1·00	45

1964. Air. 15th Anniv of Declaration of Human Rights.

841	152	20 p. red, pink and brown	25	25
842	–	40 p. orange, blue and light blue	50	35

DESIGN: 40 p. Flame on pedestal bearing U.N. emblem.

153 Sick Child

154 Clasped Wrists

1964. Air. "Bal des Petits Lits Blancs" (Ball for children's charity).

843	153	2 p. 50 multicoloured	15	10
844		5 p. multicoloured	15	10
845		15 p. multicoloured	25	10
846	–	17 p. 50 multicoloured	40	25
847	–	20 p. multicoloured	50	25
848	–	40 p. multicoloured	80	40

DESIGN—55 × 25½ mm: 17 p. 50 to 40 p. Children in front of palace (venue of ball).

1964. Air. World Lebanese Union Congress, Beirut.

849	154	20 p. black, yellow & grn	50	25
850		40 p. black, yellow & pur	90	50

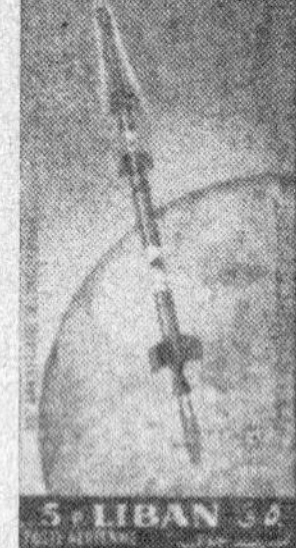
155 Rocket in Flight

156 Temple Columns

1964. Air. 21st Anniv of Independence.

851	155	5 p. multicoloured	25	20
852		10 p. multicoloured	25	20
853	–	40 p. blue and black	95	45
854	–	70 p. purple and black	1·40	1·10

DESIGNS—HORIZ: 40 p. to 70 p. "Struggle for Independence" (battle scene).

1965. Baalbek Festival.

855	156	2 p. 50 black and orange (postage)	25	20
856	–	7 p.50 black and blue	50	35
857	–	10 p. multicoloured (air)	10	10
858	–	15 p. multicoloured	25	10
859	–	25 p. multicoloured	50	40
860	–	40 p. multicoloured	1·00	50

DESIGNS—28 × 55 mm: 10 p., 15 p. Man in costume; 25 p., 40 p. Woman in costume.

157 Swimming

1965. Olympic Games, Tokyo.

861	157	2 p. 50 black, blue and mauve (postage)	20	10
862	–	7 p. 50 purple, green & brn	75	50
863	–	10 p. grey, brown & green	95	60
864	–	15 p. black and green (air)	25	10
865	–	25 p. green and purple	50	25
866	–	40 p. brown and blue	80	40

DESIGNS—HORIZ: 7 p. 50 Fencing; 15 p. Horse-jumping; 40 p. Gymnastics. VERT: 10 p. Basketball; 25 p. Rifle-shooting.

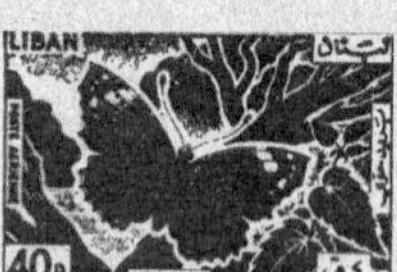
158 Red Admiral

1965. (a) Postage. Birds.

867	–	5 p. multicoloured	40	10
868	–	10 p. multicoloured	55	10
869	–	15 p. chocolate, orge & brn	1·00	10
870	–	17 p. 50 purple, red & blue	1·40	10
871	–	20 p. black, yellow & green	1·60	10
872	–	32 p. 50 yellow, brn & grn	4·00	65

(b) Air. Butterflies.

873	–	30 p. yellow, brown & red	75	10
874	–	35 p. blue, red & bistre	1·10	20
875	158	40 p. brown, red & green	1·40	20
876	–	45 p. brown, yellow & blue	1·75	40
877	–	70 p. multicoloured	2·75	50
878	–	85 p. black, orange & green	3·00	65
879	–	100 p. blue and plum	4·50	75
880	–	200 p. brown, blue & pur	8·00	90
881	–	300 p. sepia, yellow & green	12·00	2·50
882	–	500 p. brown, blue and light blue	20·00	5·00

DESIGNS—As T**158**. BIRDS: 5 p. Bullfinch; 10 p. Goldfinch; 15 p. Hoopoe; 17 p. 50, Red-legged partridge; 20 p. Golden oriole; 32 p. 50, European bee eater. BUTTERFLIES: 30 p. Large tiger moth; 35 p. Small postman; 45 p. Common grayling; 70 p. Swallowtail; 85 p. Orange-tip; 100 p. Blue morpho; 200 p. "Erasmia sanguiflua"; 300 p. "Papilio crassus". 35½ × 25 mm: 500 p. Amelia's charakes.

159 Pope Paul and Pres. Helou

1965. Air. Pope Paul's Visit to Lebanon.

883	159	45 p. violet and gold	3·25	1·90

160 Sheep

1965.

884	–	50 c. multicoloured	50	10
885	–	1 p. grey, black and mauve	65	10
886	160	2 p. 50 yellow, sepia & grn	75	10

DESIGNS: 50 c. Cow and calf; 1 p. Rabbit.

161 "Cedars of Friendship" 162 "Silk Manufacture"

1965. Air.

887	161	40 p. multicoloured	1·25	25

1965. Air. World Silk Congress, Beirut. Multicoloured.

888	2 p. 50 Type **162**	20	10
889	5 p. Type **162**	20	10
890	7 p. 50 Type **162**	25	10
891	15 p. Weaver and loom	25	10
892	30 p. As 15 p.	65	25
893	40 p. As 15 p.	1·00	40
894	50 p. As 15 p.	1·25	50

163 Parliament Building

1965. Air. Centenary of Lebanese Parliament.

895	163	35 p. brown, ochre & red	40	25
896		40 p. brown, ochre & green	65	40

164 U.N. Emblem and Headquarters 165 Playing-card "King"

1965. Air. 20th Anniv of U.N.O.

897	164	2 p. 50 blue	10	10
898		10 p. red	10	10
899		17 p. 50 violet	10	10
900		30 p. green	40	25
901		40 p. brown	50	40

1965. Air. World Bridge Chamipionships, Beirut.

902	165	2 p. 50 multicoloured	20	10
903		15 p. multicoloured	45	10
904		17 p. 50 multicoloured	65	25
905		40 p. multicoloured	1·25	50

166 Dagger on Deir Yassin, Palestine 167 I.T.U. Emblem and Symbols

1965. Air. Deir Yassin Massacre.

906	166	50 p. multicoloured	2·25	50

1966. Air. Centenary (1965) of I.T.U.

907	167	2 p. 50 multicoloured	20	10
908		15 p. multicoloured	20	10
909		17 p. 50 multicoloured	45	15
910		25 p. multicoloured	75	30
911		40 p. multicoloured	1·00	40

168 Stage Performance

1966. Air. Baalbek Festival. Multicoloured.

912	2 p. 50 Type **168**	20	10
913	5 p. Type **168**	20	10
914	7 p. 50 Ballet performance	20	10
915	15 p. Ballet performance	30	10
916	30 p. Concert	65	25
917	40 p. Concert	1·00	40

The 7 p. 50 and 15 p. are vert.

169 Tabarja

170 W.H.O. Building

1966. Tourism. Multicoloured.

918	50 c. Hippodrome, Beirut (postage)	10	10
919	1 p. Pigeon Grotto, Beirut	10	10
920	2 p. 50 Type **169**	10	10
921	5 p. Ruins, Beit-Mery	10	10
922	7 p. 50 Ruins, Anjar	10	10
923	10 p. Djezzine Falls (air)	10	10
924	15 p. Sidon Castle	15	10
925	20 p. Amphitheatre, Byblos	25	10
926	30 p. Sun Temple, Baalbek	40	10
927	50 p. Palace, Beit ed-Din	65	10
928	60 p. Nahr-el Kalb	1·00	25
929	70 p. Tripoli	1·25	40

1966. Air. Inauguration of W.H.O. Headquarters, Geneva.

930	170	7 p. 50 green	25	10
931		17 p. 50 red	35	25
932		25 p. blue	65	35

171 Skiing

1966. Air. International Cedars Festival.

933	171	2 p. 50 brown, red & green	25	10
934	–	5 p. multicoloured	25	10
935	–	17 p. 50 multicoloured	35	20
936	–	25 p. red, brown & green	1·00	40

DESIGNS: 5 p. Toboganning; 17 p. 50, Cedar in snow; 25 p. Ski-lift.

172 Inscribed Sarcophagus

1966. Air. Phoenician Invention of the Alphabet.

937	172	10 p. brown, black & grn	10	10
938	–	15 p. brown, ochre & mve	25	10
939	–	20 p. sepia, blue & ochre	40	25
940	–	30 p. brown, orange & yell	65	40

DESIGNS: 15 p. Phoenician sailing ship; 20 p. Mediterranean route map showing spread of Phoenician alphabet; 30 p. Kadmus with alphabet tablet.

173 Child in Bath — 174 Decade Emblem

1966. Air. Int Children's Day. Multicoloured.

941	2 p. Type **173**	10	10
942	5 p. Boy and doll in rowing boat	15	10
943	7 p. 50 Girl skiing	25	10
944	15 p. Girl giving food to bird	40	25
945	20 p. Boy doing homework	65	40

1966. Air. International Hydrological Decade.

947	**174** 5 p. ultramarine, bl & orge	20	10
948	10 p. red, blue and orange	20	10
949	– 15 p. sepia, green & orange	25	15
950	– 20 p. blue, green & orange	40	25

DESIGN: 15 p., 20 p. Similar "wave" pattern.

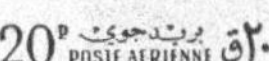

175 Rev. Daniel Bliss (founder) — 176 I.T.Y. Emblem

177 Beit ed-Din Palace

1966. Air. Centenary of American University, Beirut.

951	**175** 20 p. brown, yellow & grn	35	15
952	– 30 p. green, brown & blue	45	30

DESIGN: 30 p. University Chapel.

1967. International Tourist Year (1st issue).

(a) Postage.

954	**176** 50 c. multicoloured	10	10
955	1 p. multicoloured	10	10
956	2 p. 50 multicoloured	10	10
957	5 p. multicoloured	15	10
958	7 p. 50 multicoloured	25	10

(b) Air. Multicoloured.

959	10 p. Tabarja	20	10
960	15 p. Pigeon Rock, Beirut	25	10
961	17 p. 50 Type **177**	30	10
962	20 p. Sidon	30	10
963	25 p. Tripoli	35	10
964	30 p. Byblos	45	10
965	35 p. Ruins, Tyre	55	10
966	40 p. Temple, Baalbek	75	10

See also Nos. 977/80.

178 Signing Pact, and Flags

1967. Air. 22nd Anniv of Arab League Pact.

967	**178** 5 p. multicoloured	10	10
968	10 p. multicoloured	15	10
969	15 p. multicoloured	25	20
970	20 p. multicoloured	35	30

179 Veterans War Memorial Building, San Francisco

1967. Air. San Francisco Pact of 1945. Mult.

971	2 p. 50 Type **179**	60	20
972	5 p. Type **179**	60	20
973	7 p. 50 Type **179**	60	20
974	10 p. Scroll and flags of U.N. and Lebanon	20	20
975	20 p. As 10 p.	25	20
976	30 p. As 10 p.	50	20

180 Temple Ruins, Baalbek

1967. Air. International Tourist Year (2nd issue). Multicoloured.

977	5 p. Type **180**	10	10
978	10 p. Ruins, Anjar	15	10
979	15 p. Ancient bridge, Nahr-Ibrahim	25	10
980	20 p. Grotto, Jeita	40	15

181

1967. Air. India Day.

981	**181** 2 p. 50 red	10	10
982	5 p. purple	10	10
983	7 p. 50 brown	10	10
984	10 p. blue	20	10
985	15 p. green	45	15

182

1967. Air. 22nd Anniv of Lebanon's Admission to U.N.O.

986	**182** 2 p. 50 red	10	10
987	5 p. blue	10	10
988	7 p. 50 green	10	10
989	– 10 p. red	10	10
990	– 20 p. blue	25	10
991	– 30 p. green	45	25

DESIGN: 10, 20, 30 p. U.N. Emblem.

183 Goat and Kid

1967. Animals and Fishes. Multicoloured.

992	50 c. Type **183** (postage)	20	10
993	1 p. Cattle	20	10
994	2 p. 50 Sheep	20	10
995	5 p. Dromedaries	20	10
996	10 p. Donkey	25	10
997	15 p. Horses	55	10
998	20 p. Shark (air)	60	10
999	30 p. Needle-fish	60	10
1000	40 p. Pollack	85	10
1001	50 p. Wrasse	95	20
1002	70 p. Red mullet	2·50	25
1003	100 p. Salmon	3·75	25

184 Ski Jumping

1968. Air. International Ski Congress. Beirut.

1004	**184** 2 p. 50 multicoloured	10	10
1005	– 5 p. multicoloured	20	10
1006	– 7 p. 50 multicoloured	20	10
1007	– 10 p. multicoloured	25	20
1008	– 25 p. multicoloured	50	25

DESIGNS: 5 p. to 10 p. Skiing (all different); 25 p. Congress emblem of Cedar and skis.

185 Princess Khaskiah

1968. Air. Emir Fakhreddine II Commem. Mult.

1009	2 p. 50 Type **185**	10	10
1010	5 p. Emir Fakhreddine II	10	10
1011	10 p. Sidon Citadel	10	10
1012	15 p. Chekif Citadel	25	10
1013	17 p. 50 Beirut Citadel	40	15

The 10 p., 15 p. and 17 p. 50 are horiz designs.

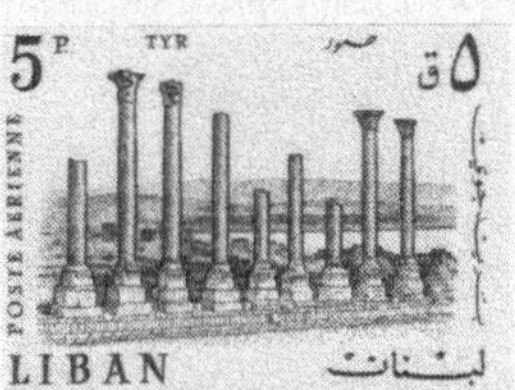

186 Colonnade

1968. Air. Tyre Antiquities.

1014	– 2 p. 50 brn, cream & pink	20	10
1015	**186** 5 p. brown, blue & yellow	20	10
1016	– 7 p. 50 brown, buff & grn	25	20
1017	– 10 p. brown, blue & orange	25	20

DESIGNS—VERT: 2 p. 50, Roman bust; 10 p. Bas-relief. HORIZ: 7 p. 50, Arch.

187 Justinian and Mediterranean Map

1968. Air. 1st Anniv of Faculty of Law, Beirut.

1019	5 p. Justinian (vert)	10	10
1020	10 p. Justinian (vert)	10	10
1021	15 p. Type **187**	20	10
1022	20 p. Type **187**	25	15

188 Arab League Emblem — 190 Jupiter's Temple Ruins, Baalbek

189 Cedar on Globe

1968. Air. Arab Appeal Week.

1023	**188** 5 p. multicoloured	10	10
1024	10 p. multicoloured	10	10
1025	15 p. multicoloured	25	15
1026	20 p. multicoloured	40	15

1968. Air. 3rd World Lebanese Union Congress, Beirut.

1027	**189** 2 p. 50 multicoloured	10	10
1028	5 p. multicoloured	10	10
1029	7 p. 50 multicoloured	20	10
1030	10 p. multicoloured	20	15

1968. Air. Baalbek Festival. Multicoloured.

1031	5 p. Type **190**	10	10
1032	10 p. Bacchus's Temple	10	10
1033	15 p. Corniche, Jupiter's Temple	25	15
1034	20 p. Portal, Bacchus's Temple	40	20
1035	25 p. Columns, Bacchus's Temple	50	30

191 Long Jumping and Atlantes

1968. Air. Olympic Games, Mexico.

1036	**191** 5 p. black, yellow & blue	10	10
1037	– 10 p. black, blue & purple	10	10
1038	– 15 p. multicoloured	25	10
1039	– 20 p. multicoloured	40	20
1040	– 25 p. brown	65	40

DESIGNS (each incorporating Aztec relic): 10 p. High jumping; 15 p. Fencing; 20 p. Weightlifting; 25 p. "Sailing boat" with oars.

192 Lebanese driving Tractor ("Work protection") — 193 Minshiya Stairs

1968. Air. Human Rights Year. Multicoloured.

1041	10 p. Type **192**	10	10
1042	15 p. Citizens ("Social Security")	20	10
1043	25 p. Young men of three races ("Unity")	25	20

1968. Air. Centenary of 1st Municipal Council (Deir el-Kamar). Multicoloured.

1044	10 p. Type **193**	10	10
1045	15 p. Serai kiosk	20	10
1046	25 p. Ancient highway	25	20

194 Nurse and Child

1969. Air. U.N.I.C.E.F. Multicoloured.

1047	**194** 5 p. black, brown & blue	10	10
1048	– 10 p. black, green & yell	10	10
1049	– 15 p. black, red & purple	10	10
1050	– 20 p. black, blue & yellow	25	20
1051	– 25 p. black, ochre & mve	40	20

DESIGNS: 10 p. Produce; 15 p. Mother and child; 20 p. Child with book; 25 p. Children with flowers.

195 Ancient Coin

1969. Air. 20th Anniv of International Museums Council (I.C.O.M.). Exhibits in National Museum, Beirut. Multicoloured.

1052	2 p. 50 Type **195**	10	·10
1053	5 p. Gold dagger, Byblos	20	10
1054	7 p. 50 Detail of Ahiram's Sarcophagus	20	10
1055	30 p. Jewelled pectoral	40	25
1056	40 p. Khalde "bird" vase	50	40

196 Water-skiing

1969. Air. Water Sports. Multicoloured.

1057	2 p. 50 Type **196**	10	10
1058	5 p. Water-skiing (group)	10	10
1059	7 p. 50 Paraskiing (vert)	35	10
1060	30 p. Sailing (vert)	50	35
1061	40 p. Yacht-racing	75	60

197 Frontier Guard

1969. Air. 25th Anniv of Independence. The Lebanese Army.

1062 2 p. Type **197** 10 10
1063 5 p. Unknown Soldier's Tomb 10 10
1064 7 p. 50 Army Foresters . . . 20 10
1065 15 p. Road-making 20 15
1066 30 p. Military ambulance and Sud Aviation Alouette III helicopter 40 35
1067 40 p. Skiing patrol 60 50

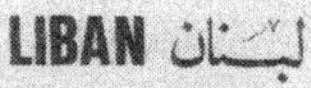

198 Concentric Red Crosses

1971. Air. 25th Anniv of Lebanese Red Cross.

1068 **198** 15 p. red and black . . . 40 25
1069 – 85 p. red and black . . . 1·50 1·00

DESIGN: 85 p. Red Cross in shape of cedar of Lebanon.

199 Foil and Flags of Arab States

1971. Air. 10th International Fencing Championships. Multicoloured.

1070 10 p. Type **199** 10 10
1071 15 p. Foil and flags of foreign nations 10 10
1072 35 p. Contest with foils . . . 50 40
1073 40 p. Epee contest 65 40
1074 50 p. Contest with sabres . . 80 50

200 "Farmers at Work" (12th-century Arab painting)

1971. Air. 50th Anniv (1969) of I.L.O.

1075 **200** 10 p. multicoloured . . . 20 10
1076 40 p. multicoloured . . . 65 40

201 U.P.U. Monument and New H.Q. Building, Berne

1971. Air. New U.P.U. Headquarters Building, Berne.

1077 **201** 15 p. red, black & yellow 20 10
1078 35 p. yell, black and orange 65 40

202 "Ravens setting fire to Owls" (14th-century painting)

1971. Air. Children's Day. Multicoloured.

1079 15 p. Type **202** 35 20
1080 85 p. "The Lion and the Jackal" (13th-century painting), (39 × 29 mm) . . . . 1·60 75

203 Arab League Flag and Map

1971. Air. 25th Anniv of Arab League.

1081 **203** 30 p. multicoloured . . 40 15
1082 70 p. multicoloured . . 75 50

204 Jamhour Electricity Sub-station

1971. Air. Multicoloured.

1083 5 p. Type **204** 10 10
1084 10 p. Maameltein Bridge . . 10 10
1085 15 p. Hoteliers' School . . . 10 10
1086 20 p. Litani Dam 20 10
1087 25 p. Interior of T.V. set . . 25 10
1088 35 p. Bziza Temple 40 10
1089 40 p. Jounieh Harbour . . . 40 15
1090 45 p. Radar scanner, Beirut Airport 55 20
1091 50 p. Hibiscus 75 20
1092 70 p. School of Sciences Building . . . . 1·00 25
1093 85 p. Oranges . . . . 1·25 40
1094 100 p. Satellite Communications Station, Arbanieh . 1·50 65

205 Insignia of Imam al Ouzai (theologian)

1971. Air. Lebanese Celebrities.

1095 **205** 25 p. brown, gold & grn 35 20
1096 – 25 p. brown, gold & yell 35 20
1097 – 25 p. brown, gold & yell 35 20
1098 – 25 p. brown, gold & grn 35 20

PORTRAITS: No. 1096, Bechara el Khoury (poet and writer); 1097, Hassan Kamel el Sabbah (scientist); 1098, Gibran Khalil Gibran (writer).

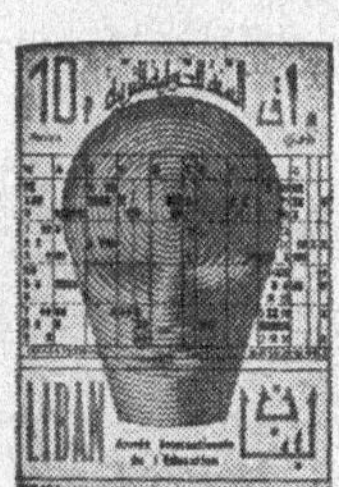

206 I.E.Y. Emblem and Computer Card

1971. Air. International Education Year.

1099 **206** 10 p. black, blue and violet 10 10
1100 40 p. black, yellow and red 40 25

207 Dahr-el-Basheq Sanatorium

208 "Solar Wheel" Emblem

1971. Air. Tuberculosis Relief Campaign.

1101 **207** 50 p. multicoloured . . 75 40
1102 – 100 p. multicoloured . . 1·10 65

DESIGN: 100 p. Different view of Sanatorium.

1971. Air. 16th Baalbek Festival.

1103 **208** 15 p. orange and blue . 20 10
1104 – 85 p. black, blue & orge 80 55

DESIGN: 85 p. Corinthian capital.

209 Field-gun

1971. Air. Army Day. Multicoloured.

1105 15 p. Type **209** 25 20
1106 25 p. Dassault Mirage IIICJ jet fighters 80 30
1107 40 p. Army Command H.Q. 75 50
1108 70 p. "Tarablous" (naval patrol boat) . . . . 1·25 90

210 Interior Decoration

212 U.N. Emblem

211 Lenin

1971. Air. 2nd Anniv of Burning of Al-Aqsa Mosque, Jerusalem.

1109 **210** 15 p. brown and deep brown 50 20
1110 35 p. brown and deep brown . . . . 1·00 65

1971. Air. Birth Centenary of Lenin. Mult.

1111 30 p. Type **211** 50 25
1112 70 p. Lenin in profile . . . . 1·10 65

1971. Air. 25th Anniv of United Nations.

1113 **212** 15 p. multicoloured . . . 20 10
1114 85 p. multicoloured . . . 95 50

213 "Europa" Mosaic, Byblos

1971. Air. World Lebanese Union.

1115 **213** 10 p. multicoloured . . . 25 10
1116 40 p. multicoloured . . . 1·00 40

1972. Various stamps surch.

1117 5 p. on 7 p. 50 (No. 922) (postage) 10 10
1118 5 p. on 7 p. 50 (No. 958) . . 10 10
1119 25 p. on 32 p. 50 (No. 872) 90 10
1120 5 p. on 7 p. 50 (No. 1016) (air) 10 10
1121 100 p. on 300 p. (No. 881) . . 3·25 90
1122 100 p. on 500 p. (No. 882) . . 3·25 90
1123 200 p. on 300 p. (No. 881) . . 4·50 1·75

217 Morning Glory

218 Ornate Arches

1973. Air. Multicoloured.

1124 2 p. 50 Type **217** 10 10
1125 5 p. Roses 20 10
1126 15 p. Tulips 25 10
1127 25 p. Lilies 40 10
1128 40 p. Carnations 50 20
1129 50 p. Iris 75 10
1130 70 p. Apples . . . . 1·25 20
1131 75 p. Grapes . . . . 1·25 20
1132 100 p. Peaches . . . . . . 2·00 60
1133 200 p. Pears . . . . 3·25 45
1134 300 p. Cherries . . . . . . 4·50 85
1135 500 p. Oranges . . . . . . 6·25 1·50

1973. Air. Lebanese Domestic Architecture.

1136 – 35 p. multicoloured . . . 50 25
1137 **218** 50 p. multicoloured . . . 75 35
1138 – 85 p. multicoloured . . . 1·25 45
1139 – 100 p. multicoloured . . . 1·40 60

DESIGNS: Nos. 1136 and 1138/39, Various Lebanese dwellings.

219 Girl with Lute

1973. Air. Ancient Costumes. Multicoloured.

1140 5 p. Woman with rose . . . 15 10
1141 10 p. Shepherd 25 10
1142 20 p. Horseman 25 20
1143 25 p. Type **219** 40 20

220 Swimming

1973. Air. 5th Pan-Arab Schools' Games, Beirut. Multicoloured.

1144 5 p. Type **220** 10 10
1145 10 p. Running 15 10
1146 15 p. Gymnastics 25 10
1147 20 p. Volleyball 40 10
1148 25 p. Basketball 40 20
1149 50 p. Table-tennis 75 35
1150 75 p. Handball . . . . 1·00 45
1151 100 p. Football . . . . . . 2·00 1·10

221 Brasilia

1973. Air. 150th Anniv of Brazil's Independence. Multicoloured.

1153 5 p. Type **221** 10 10
1154 20 p. Salvador (Bahia) in 1823 25 10
1155 25 p. Map and Phoenician galley 40 20
1156 50 p. Emperor Pedro I and Emir Fakhreddine II 85 40

222 Marquetry

223 Cedar of Lebanon

1973. Air. Lebanese Handicrafts. Multicoloured.

1157 10 p. Type **222** 15 10
1158 20 p. Weaving 25 10
1159 35 p. Glass-blowing 40 15
1160 40 p. Pottery 65 20
1161 50 p. Metal-working 75 20
1162 70 p. Cutlery-making . . . . 1·00 25
1163 85 p. Lace-making . . . . . 1·40 40
1164 100 p. Handicrafts Museum 1·75 50

1974.

1165 **223** 50 c. green, brn & orge 20 10

224 Camp Site and Emblems

1974. Air. 11th Arab Scout Jamboree, Smar-Jubeil, Lebanon. Multicoloured.

1166 2 p. 50 Type **224** 10 10
1167 5 p. Scout badge and map . . 10 10
1168 7 p. 50 Map of Arab countries 20 10
1169 10 p. Lord Baden-Powell and Baalbek 20 10
1170 15 p. Guide and camp . . . 20 10
1171 20 p. Lebanese Guide and Scout badge 30 10
1172 25 p. Scouts around campfire 45 10
1173 30 p. Globe and Scout badge 50 20
1174 35 p. Flags of participating countries 70 20
1175 50 p. Scout chopping wood for old man . . . . 1·00 35

225 Mail Train

1974. Centenary of U.P.U. Multicoloured.

1176 5 p 50 Type **225** 60 35
1177 20 p. Container ship 45 10
1178 25 p. Congress building, Lausanne, and U.P.U. H.Q., Berne 45 10
1179 50 p. Mail plane 75 45

226 Congress Building, Sofar
227 "Mountain Road" (O. Onsi)

1974. Air. 25th Anniv of Arab Postal Union. Multicoloured.

1180 5 p. Type **226** 10 10
1181 20 p. View of Sofar 20 10
1182 25 p. A.P.U. H.Q., Cairo . . 25 10
1183 50 p. Ministry of Posts, Beirut 1·00 55

1974. Air. Lebanese Paintings. Multicoloured.

1184 50 p. Type **227** 65 30
1185 50 p. "Clouds" (M. Farroukh) 65 30
1186 50 p. "Woman" (G. K. Gebran) 65 30
1187 50 p. "Embrace" (C. Gemayel) 65 30
1188 50 p. "Self-portrait" (H. Serour) 65 30
1189 50 p. "Portrait" (D. Corm) 65 30

228 Hunter killing Lion

1974. Air. Hermel Excavations. Multicoloured.

1190 5 p. Type **228** 10 10
1191 10 p. Astarte 15 10
1192 25 p. Dogs hunting boar . . 40 20
1193 35 p. Greco-Roman tomb . . 65 40

229 Book Year Emblem

1974. Air. International Book Year (1972).

1194 **229** 5 p. multicoloured . . . 10 10
1195 10 p. multicoloured . . . 15 10
1196 25 p. multicoloured . . . 40 15
1197 35 p. multicoloured . . . 50 60

230 Magnifying Glass
231 Georgina Rizk in Lebanese Costume

1974. Air. Stamp Day. Multicoloured.

1198 5 p. Type **230** 10 10
1199 10 p. Linked posthorns . . . 10 10
1200 15 p. Stamp-printing 20 10
1201 20 p. "Stamp" in mount . . 35 20

1974. Air. Miss Universe 1971 (Georgina Rizk). Multicoloured.

1202 5 p. Type **231** 10 10
1203 20 p. Head-and-shoulders portrait 15 10
1204 25 p. Type **231** 25 15
1205 50 p. As 20 p. 65 40

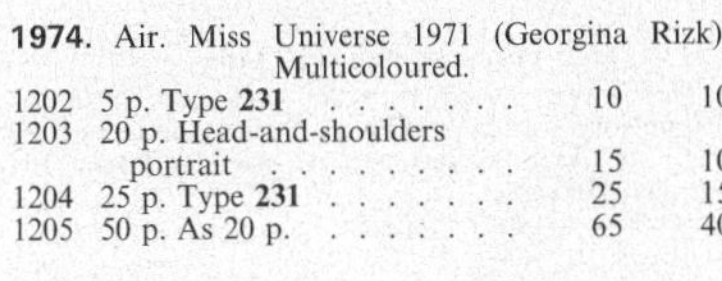

232 Winds
234 Discus-throwing

233 U.N.I.C.E.F. Emblem and Sikorsky S-55 Helicopter

1974. Air. U.N. Conference on Human Environment, Stockholm, 1972. Multicoloured.

1207 5 p. Type **232** 10 10
1208 25 p. Mountains and plain . 40 10
1209 30 p. Trees and flowers . . 40 20
1210 10 p. Sea 50 40

1974. Air. 25th Anniv of U.N.I.C.E.F. Multicoloured.

1212 20 p. Type **233** 45 10
1213 25 p. Emblem and child welfare clinic 25 10
1214 35 p. Emblem and kindergarten class 45 20
1215 70 p. Emblem and schoolgirls in laboratory 85 25

1974. Air. Olympic Games, Munich (1972). Mult.

1217 5 p. Type **234** 10 10
1218 10 p. Putting the shot . . . 10 10
1219 15 p. Weight-lifting 15 10
1220 35 p. Running 50 25
1221 50 p. Wrestling 65 25
1222 85 p. Javelin-throwing . . . 1·25 40

235 Symbols of Archaeology

1975. Air. Beirut — "University City". Multicoloured.

1224 20 p. Type **235** 25 10
1225 25 p. Science and medicine . 25 10
1226 35 p. Justice and commerce 45 35
1227 70 p. Industry and commerce 90 50

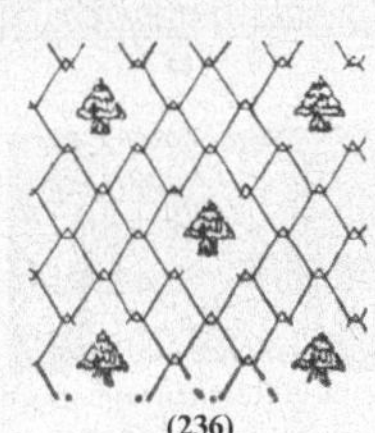

(236)

1978. Air. Various stamps optd with different patterns as T **236**. (a) Tourist Views. Nos. 1090, 1092/3.

1228 45 p. Radar scanner, Beirut Airport 45 20
1229 70 p. School of Sciences Building 90 25
1230 85 p. Oranges . . . . 1·00 35

(b) Flowers and Fruits. Nos. 1124/35.

1231 2 p. 50 Type **217** 10 10
1232 5 p. Roses 10 10
1233 15 p. Tulips 25 10
1234 25 p. Lilies 45 10
1235 40 p. Carnations 45 15
1236 50 p. Iris 65 15
1237 70 p. Apples 90 25
1238 75 p. Grapes . . . . 1·25 25
1239 100 p. Peaches . . . . 1·25 40
1240 200 p. Pears . . . . 2·50 1·40
1241 300 p. Cherries . . . . . . 3·75 2·50
1242 500 p. Oranges . . . . . . 6·25 3·75

(c) Lebanese Domestic Architecture. Nos. 1136/9.

1243 – 35 p. multicoloured . . 55 10
1244 **218** 50 p. multicoloured . . 65 15
1245 – 85 p. multicoloured . . 1·00 35
1246 – 100 p. multicoloured . . 1·25 40

(d) Ancient Costumes. Nos. 1140/3.

1247 5 p. Woman with rose . . . 10 10
1248 10 p. Shepherd 15 10
1249 20 p. Horseman 30 10
1250 25 p. Type **219** 45 10

(e) Lebanese Handicrafts. Nos. 1157/8, 1160/4.

1251 10 p. Type **222** 15 10
1252 20 p. Weaving 30 10
1253 40 p. Pottery 45 15
1254 50 p. Metal-working 75 15
1255 70 p. Cutlery-making . . . 90 25
1256 85 p. Lace-making . . . . . 1·00 35
1257 100 p. Handicraft Museum . 1·25 40

237 Mikhail Naimy (poet) and View of al-Chakroub Baskinta

1978. Air. Mikhail Naimy Festival Week. Mult.

1258 25 p. Mikhail Naimy and Sannine mountains 25 10
1259 50 p. Type **237** 50 25
1260 75 p. Mikhail Naimy (vert) . 80 40

238 Heart and Arrow
239 Army Badge

1978. Air. World Health Day. "Down with Blood Pressure".

1261 **238** 50 p. blue, red and black 75 40

1980. Army Day. Multicoloured.

1262 25 p. Type **239** (postage) . . 40 20
1263 50 p. Statue of Emir Fakhr el Dine on horseback (air) . . 65 25
1264 75 p. Soldiers with flag (horiz) 95 25

240 13th-century European King

1980. Air. 50th Anniv (1974) of International Chess Federation. Multicoloured.

1265 50 p. Rook, knight and Jubilee emblem (horiz) 75 25
1266 75 p. Type **240** . . . . 1·25 40
1267 100 p. Rook and Lebanon Chess Federation emblem . 1·90 65
1268 150 p. 18th-century French rook, king and knight . . . 2·50 1·00
1269 200 p. Painted faience rook, queen and bishop . . . . . 3·25 1·50

241 Congress, U.P.U. and Lebanon Post Emblems

1981. Air. 18th U.P.U. Congress, Rio de Janeiro (1979).

1270 **241** 25 p. blue, brown and black 40 15
1271 50 p. pink, brown & black 65 25
1272 75 p. green, brown & black 1·00 40

242 Children on Raft
243 President Sarkis

1981. Air. International Year of the Child (1979).

1273 **242** 100 p. multicoloured . . 1·25 65

1981. 5th Anniv of Election of President Sarkis.

1274 **243** 125 p. multicoloured . . 95 50
1275 300 p. multicoloured . . 2·75 1·10
1276 500 p. multicoloured . . 4·50 1·60

244 Society Emblem and Children

1981. Air. Centenary (1978) of Al-Makassed Islamic Welfare Society. Multicoloured.

1277 50 p. Type **244** 50 15
1278 75 p. Institute building . . . 75 20
1279 100 p. Al-Makassed (founder) 95 35

245 Stork carrying Food

1982. World Food Day (1981). Multicoloured.

1280 50 p. Type **245** 50 25
1281 75 p. Ear of wheat and globe 75 40
1282 100 p. Fruit, fish and grain 1·10 65

246 W.C.Y. Emblem
247 Phoenician Galley flying Scout Flag

1983. World Communications Year.

1283 **246** 300 p. multicoloured . . 2·50 1·25

1983. 75th Anniv of Boy Scout Movement. Multicoloured.

1284 200 p. Type **247** . . . . . . 1·90 95
1285 300 p. Scouts lowering flag and signalling by semaphore . 2·50 1·25
1286 500 p. Camp . . . . 4·50 1·90

248 "The Soul is Back"

1983. Birth Centenary of Gibran (poet and painter). Multicoloured.

1287 200 p. Type **248** . . . . . . 1·90 95
1288 300 p. "The Family" . . . . 2·50 1·25
1288 500 p. "Gibran" . . . . . . 4·50 1·90
1289 1000 p. "The Prophet" . . . 8·75 4·75

249 Cedar of Lebanon
250 Iris

1984.

1292 **249** 5 p. multicoloured . . . 20 10

1984. Flowers. Multicoloured.

1293 10 p. Type **250** 25 10
1294 25 p. Periwinkle 40 25
1295 50 p. Barberry 95 40

251 Dove with Laurel over Buildings

1984. Lebanese Army. Multicoloured.

1296 75 p. Type **251** 70 40
1297 150 p. Cedar and soldier holding rifle . . . . 1·50 90
1298 300 p. Broken chain, hand holding laurel wreath and cedar . . . . 3·25 1·90

252 Temple Ruins, Fakra

1984. Multicoloured.

1299		100 p. Type **252**	95	40
1300		200 p. Temple ruins, Bziza	1·90	90
1301		500 p. Roman arches and relief, Tyre	4·75	1·90

253 President taking Oath

1988. Installation of President Amin Gemayel.

1302	**253**	L£25 multicoloured	60	40

254 Map of South America and Cedar of Lebanon

1989. 1st World Festival of Lebanese Youth in Uruguay.

1303	**254**	L£5 multicoloured	20	10

255 Satellite, Flags and Earth

256 Children

1988. "Arabsat" Telecommunications Satellite.

1304	**255**	L£10 multicoloured	40	25

1988. U.N.I.C.E.F. Child Survival Campaign.

1305	**256**	L£15 multicoloured	65	40

257 Arabic "75" and Scout Emblems

258 President, Map and Dove

1988. 75th Anniv (1987) of Arab Scouts Movement.

1306	**257**	L£20 multicoloured	65	40

1988. International Peace Year (1986).

1307	**258**	L£50 multicoloured	1·25	65

259 Red Cross and Figures

260 Cedar of Lebanon

1988. Red Cross.

1308	**259**	L£10 + L£1 red, silver and black	40	25
1309	–	L£20 + L£2 multicoloured	65	40
1310	–	L£30 + L£3 silver, green and red	1·00	60

DESIGNS: L£20, Helmeted heads; L£30, Globe, flame, and dove holding map of Lebanon.

1989.

1311	**260**	L£50 green and mauve	25	15
1312		L£70 green and brown	40	20
1313		L£100 green and yellow	65	30
1314		L£200 green and blue	1·25	65
1315		L£500 dp green and green	3·25	1·60

261 Dining in the Open at Zahle, 1883

1993. 50th Anniv of Independence. Multicoloured.

1316	L£200 Type **261**	40	25
1317	L£300 Castle ruins, Saida (vert)	55	40
1318	L£500 Presidential Palace, Baabda	95	65
1319	L£1000 Sword ceremony (vert)	1·90	1·25
1320	L£3000 Model for the rebuilding of central Beirut	5·50	3·00
1321	L£5000 President Elias Hrawi and state flag (vert)	10·00	6·75

262 Protection of Plants

263 Martyrs' Monument, Beirut

1994. Environmental Protection. Multicoloured.

1323	L£100 Type **262**	15	10
1324	L£200 Protection against forest fires	30	20
1325	L£500 Reforesting with cedars	75	50
1326	L£1000 Creation of urban green zones	1·50	1·00
1327	L£2000 Trees	2·50	1·60
1328	L£5000 Green tree in town	8·00	5·25

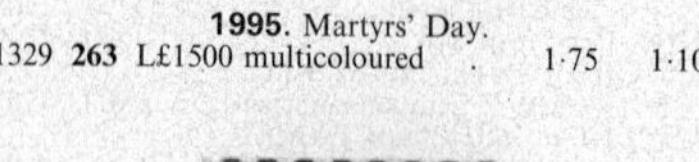

1995. Martyrs' Day.

1329	**263**	L£1500 multicoloured	1·75	1·10

264 Arabic Script under Magnifying Glass and Headquarters

1996. Anniversaries and Events. Multicoloured.

1330	L£100 Type **264** (inauguration of Postal Museum, Arab League Head-quarters, Cairo)	10	10
1331	L£500 Anniversary emblem (50th anniv of U.N.I.C.E.F.) (horiz)	40	25
1332	L£500 Ears of wheat and anniversary emblem (50th anniv (1995) of F.A.O.)	40	25
1333	L£1000 U.N. Building (New York) and anniversary emblem (50th anniv (1995) of U.N.O.)	80	55
1334	L£1000 Emblem (International Year of the Family (1994)) (horiz)	80	55
1335	L£2000 Anniversary emblem (75th anniv (1994) of I.L.O.) (horiz)	1·60	1·10
1336	L£2000 Emblem (50th anniv of Arab League)	1·60	1·10
1337	L£3000 Emblem (75th anniv (1994) of Lebanese Law Society)	2·40	1·60
1338	L£3000 Rene Moawad (former President, 70th birth anniv (1995))	2·40	1·60

POSTAGE DUE STAMPS

1924. Postage Due stamps of France surch **GRAND LIBAN** and value in "CENTIEMES" or "PIASTRES".

D26	**D 11**	50 c. on 10 c. brown	1·90	3·00
D27		1 p. on 20 c. green	2·75	3·75
D28		2 p. on 30 c. red	1·90	3·75
D29		3 p. on 50 c. purple	1·90	3·75
D30		5 p. on 1 f. purple on yellow	1·90	3·50

1924. Postage Due stamps of France surch **Gd Liban** and value in French and Arabic.

D58	**D 11**	0 p. 50 on 10 c. brown	1·00	3·75
D59		1 p. on 20 c. green	1·40	3·75
D60		2 p. on 30 c. red	1·40	2·75
D61		3 p. on 50 c. purple	1·40	3·50
D62		5 p. on 1 f. purple on yell	90	3·75

D 7 Nahr el-Kalb

1925.

D75	**D 7**	0 p. 50 brown on yellow	35	50
D76	–	1 p. red on pink	40	1·10
D77	–	2 p. black on blue	55	1·75
D78	–	3 p. brown on orange	1·40	2·50
D79	–	5 p. black on green	1·75	3·25

DESIGNS—HORIZ: 1 p. Pine Forest, Beirut; 2 p. Pigeon Grotto, Beirut; 3 p. Beaufort Castle; 5 p. Baalbeck.

1927. Optd **Republique Libanaise**.

D122	**D 7**	0 p. 50 brown on yellow	40	1·25
D123	–	1 p. red on pink	70	1·75
D124	–	2 p. black on blue	1·50	2·00
D125	–	3 p. brown on orange	2·50	3·00
D126	–	5 p. black on green	3·75	4·25

1928. Nos. D 122/6 optd with T **10**.

D145	**D 7**	0 p. 50 brown on yellow	1·00	1·90
D146	–	1 p. red on pink	1·10	2·00
D147	–	2 p. black on blue	2·00	2·50
D148	–	3 p. brown on orange	3·00	4·25
D149	–	5 p. black on green	3·25	4·50

D 18

D 19 Bas-relief from Sarcophagus of King Ahiram at Byblos

D 32

1931.

D191	**D 18**	0 p. 50 black on pink	55	55
D192	–	1 p. black on blue	80	75
D193	–	2 p. black on yellow	90	1·75
D194	–	3 p. black on green	1·75	1·60
D195	**D 32**	5 p. black on orange	5·25	6·25
D196	**D 19**	8 p. black on pink	3·75	3·50
D252	**D 32**	10 p. green	5·00	4·50
D197	–	15 p. black	2·50	3·00

DESIGNS: 1 p. Bas-relief of Phoenician galley; 2 p. Arabesque; 3 p. Garland; 15 p. Statuettes.

D 43 National Museum

1945.

D298	**D 43**	2 p. black on lemon	2·75	2·75
D299		5 p. blue on pink	3·25	3·25
D300		25 p. blue on green	4·75	4·75
D301		50 p. purple on blue	5·00	5·00

D 53

1947.

D352	**D 53**	5 p. black on green	3·75	1·25
D353		25 p. black on yellow	38·00	3·25
D354		50 p. black on blue	22·00	8·25

D 59 Monument at Hermel

1948.

D379	**D 59**	2 p. black on yellow	2·50	65
D380		3 p. black on pink	5·75	2·50
D381		10 p. black on blue	14·00	5·00

D 67

1950.

D416	**D 67**	1 p. red	95	20
D417		5 p. blue	2·75	75
D418		10 p. green	5·00	1·60

D 78

1952.

D464	**D 78**	1 p. mauve	20	10
D465		2 p. violet	30	20
D466		3 p. green	45	20
D467		5 p. blue	65	25
D468		10 p. brown	1·25	50
D469		25 p. black	9·75	1·25

D 81

D 93

1953.

D481	**D 81**	1 p. red	15	10
D482		2 p. green	15	10
D483		3 p. orange	15	10
D484		5 p. purple	25	20
D485		10 p. brown	65	20
D486		15 p. blue	1·25	65

1955.

D550	**D 93**	1 p. brown	10	10
D551		2 p. green	10	10
D552		3 p. turquoise	10	10
D553		5 p. purple	10	10
D554		10 p. green	30	20
D555		15 p. blue	30	20
D556		25 p. purple	75	50

D 178

D 184 Emir Fakhreddine II

1967.

D967	**D 178**	1 p. green	10	10
D968		5 p. mauve	10	10
D969		15 p. blue	30	30

1968.

D1004	**D 184**	1 p. slate and grey	10	10
D1005		2 p. turquoise & green	10	10
D1006		3 p. orange & yellow	10	10
D1007		5 p. purple and red	10	10
D1008		10 p. olive & yellow	10	10
D1009		15 p. blue and violet	35	35
D1010		25 p. blue & lt blue	60	60

POSTAL TAX STAMPS

These were issued between 1945 and 1962 for compulsory use on inland mail (and sometimes on mail to Arab countries) to provide funds for various purposes.

T 41

(T 42)

1945. Lebanese Army. Fiscal stamp as Type **T 41** surch with Type **T 42**.

T289	**T 41**	5 p. on 30 c. brown	£425	1·75

ضريبة فلسطين (T 50) طابع فلسطين (T 51)

ضريبة فلسطين (T 52) طابع فلسطين (T 56 "Palestine stamp").

1947. Aid to War in Palestine. Surch as Type **T 42** but
(a) With top line Type **T 50**.
T338 **T 41** 5 p. on 25 c. green 13·00 1·40
T339 5 p. on 30 c. brown 18·00 2·75
T340 5 p. on 60 c. blue 27·00 2·00
T341 5 p. on 3 p. pink 13·50 2·50
T342 5 p. on 15 p. blue 13·50 1·00

(b) With top line Type **T 51**.
T343 **T 41** 5 p. on 10 p. red 60·00 3·00

(c) With top line Type **T 52**.
T344 **T 41** 5 p. on 3 p. pink 13·50 1·75

(d) As No. T344 but with figure "5" at left instead of "0" and without inscr between figures.
T345 **T 41** 5 p. on 3 p. pink £300 22·00

1948. Palestine Aid. No. T289 optd with Type **T 56**.
T363 **T 41** 5 p. on 30 c. brown 18·00 2·40

T 95 Family and Ruined House

1956. Earthquake Victims.
T559 **T 95** 2 p. 50 brown 2·00 20

T 99 Rebuilding

T 100 Rebuilding

1957. Earthquake Victims.
T601 **T 99** 2 p. 50 brown 2·00 20
T602 2 p. 50 green 1·25 20
T603 **T 100** 2 p. 50 brown 1·25 10

T 132 Rebuilding

T 133 Rebuilding

1961. Earthquake Victims.
T729 **T 132** 2 p. 50 brown 1·25 10
T730 **T 133** 2 p. 50 blue 1·00 10

LIBERIA Pt. 13

A republic on the W. coast of Africa, founded as a home for freed slaves.

100 cents = 1 dollar.

1

2

1860.
7 **1** 6 c. red 23·00 32·00
2 12 c. blue 22·00 27·00
3 24 c. green 22·00 27·00

1880.
13 **1** 1 c. blue 3·25 4·75
14 2 c. red 2·25 3·25
15 6 c. mauve 4·25 5·50
16 12 c. yellow 4·25 6·00
17 24 c. red 5·00 6·75

1881.
18 **2** 3 c. black 4·25 3·25

3

4

5 "Alligator" (first settlers' ship)

1882.
47 **3** 8 c. blue 2·50 2·50
20 16 c. red 3·75 3·00

1886.
49 **3** 1 c. red 60 65
50 2 c. green 60 75
23 3 c. mauve 70 75
52 4 c. brown 80 75
27 6 c. grey 1·75 1·75
54 **4** 8 c. grey 2·75 2·75
55 16 c. yellow 3·75 3·75
29 **5** 32 c. blue 12·00 12·00

7 Liberian Star

8 African Elephant

9 Oil Palm

10 Pres. H. R. W. Johnson

11 Vai Woman

12 Seal

13 Star

15 Hippopotamus

17 President Johnson

1892.
75 **7** 1 c. red 30 30
76 2 c. blue 30 30
77 **8** 4 c. black and green 2·10 1·60
78 **9** 6 c. green 85 75
79 **10** 8 c. black and brown 60 75
80 **11** 12 c. red 60 85
81 **12** 16 c. lilac 2·10 1·60
82 **13** 24 c. green on yellow 1·50 1·25
83 **12** 32 c. blue 3·00 3·25
84 **15** $1 black and blue 8·75 7·75
85 **13** $2 brown on buff 4·25 3·75
86 **17** $5 black and red 5·50 5·50

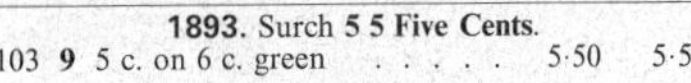
1893. Surch **5 5 Five Cents.**
103 **9** 5 c. on 6 c. green 5·50 5·50

24

1894. Imperf or roul.
117 **24** 5 c. black and red 3·25 3·25

35

36

1897.
144 **9** 1 c. purple 45 35
145 1 c. green 85 50
146 **15** 2 c. black and bistre 1·50 1·10
147 2 c. black and red 1·60 1·40
148 **8** 5 c. black and lake 1·60 1·10
149 5 c. black and blue 3·00 2·00
150 **10** 10 c. blue and yellow 1·00 50
151 **11** 15 c. black 85 65
152 **12** 20 c. red 1·90 1·60
153 **13** 25 c. green 1·50 1·50
154 **12** 30 c. blue 4·25 4·00
155 **35** 50 c. black and brown 2·75 2·75

The prices in the "used" column of sets marked with a dagger (†) against the date of issue are for stamps "cancelled to order" from remainder stocks. Postally used specimens are worth appreciably more.

†1897.
156 **36** 3 c. red and green 25 10

1901. Official stamps of 1892–98 optd **ORDINARY.**
175 **9** 1 c. purple (No. O157) 50·00 35·00
176 1 c. green (O158) 18·00 18·00
177 **7** 2 c. blue (O120) 50·00 50·00
178 **15** 2 c. black and brn (O159) £100 45·00
179 2 c. black & red (O160) 25·00 30·00
180 **24** 5 c. green and lilac (O130) £130 £130
181 **8** 5 c. black and red (O161) £100 £100
182 5 c. black and bl (O162) 20·00 25·00
183 **10** 8 c. black and brn (O122) 75·00
184 10 c. blue and yell (O163) 25·00 30·00
169 **11** 12 c. red (O92) £100 £100
185 15 c. black (O164) 18·00 25·00
170 **12** 16 c. lilac (O93)
186 16 c. lilac (O124) £140 £140
187 20 c. red (O165) 22·00 28·00
171 **13** 24 c. green and yell (O94) £225 £250
188 24 c. green on yell (O125) 25·00 30·00
189 25 c. green (O166) 28·00 38·00
190 **12** 30 c. blue (O167) 20·00 27·00
191 **13** 32 c. blue (O126) £150 £150
192 **35** 50 c. black & brn (O168) 25·00 30·00
172 **15** $1 black and bl (O96) £1000 £1000
193 $1 black and bl (O127) £170 £250
194 **13** $2 brown on buff (O128) £1300 £1300
174 **17** $5 black and red (O98) £2500 £2500
196 $5 black and red (O129) £1400 £1400

1902. Surch **75 c.** and bar.
206 **15** 75 c. on $1 black & blue 7·50 10·00

40 Liberty

1903.
209 **40** 3 c. black 25 15

1903. Surch in words.
216 **12** 10 c. on 16 c. lilac 2·50 4·50
217 **13** 15 c. on 24 c. green on yell 2·50 5·00
218 **12** 20 c. on 32 c. blue 3·75 4·75

1904. Surch
219 **9** 1 c. on 5 c. on 6 c. green (No. 103) 60 80
220 **8** 2 c. on 4 c. black and green (No. O89) 3·75 4·50
221 **12** 2 c. on 30 c. blue (No. 154) 5·25 7·75

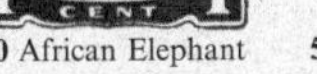
50 African Elephant

51 Head of Mercury

52 Mandingo Tribesmen

53 Pres. Barclay and Executive Mansion

†1906.
224 **50** 1 c. black and green 1·00 50
225 **51** 2 c. black and red 15 15
226 – 5 c. black and blue 2·00 75
227 – 10 c. black and red 8·00 90
228 – 15 c. green and violet 7·00 2·75
229 – 20 c. black and orange 10·00 2·10
230 – 25 c. grey and blue 75 20
231 – 30 c. violet 70 15
232 – 50 c. black and green 75 20
233 – 75 c. black and brown 7·00 2·10
234 – $1 black and pink 1·90 25
235 **52** $2 black and green 3·00 35
236 **53** $5 grey and red 5·75 50

DESIGNS—As Type **50**: 5 c. Chimpanzee; 15 c. Agama lizard; 75 c. Pygmy hippopotamus. As Type **51**: 10 c. Great blue turaco; 20 c. Great egret; 25 c. Head of Liberty on coin; 30 c. Figures "30"; 50 c. Liberian flag. As Type **53**: $1 Head of Liberty.

55 Coffee Plantation

56 Gunboat "Lark"

57 Commerce

†1909. The 10 c. is perf or roul.
250 **55** 1 c. black and green 25 15
251 – 2 c. black and red 25 15
252 **56** 5 c. black and blue 1·75 35
254 **57** 10 c. black and purple 25 20
255 – 15 c. black and blue 1·25 35
256 – 20 c. green and red 2·50 50
257 – 25 c. black and brown 1·75 35
258 – 30 c. brown 1·75 35
259 – 50 c. black and green 2·75 60
260 – 75 c. black and brown 2·25 45

DESIGNS—As Type **55**: 2 c. Pres. Barclay; 15 c. Vai woman spinning cotton; 20 c. Pepper plant; 25 c. Village hut; 30 c. Pres. Barclay (in picture frame). As Type **56**: 50 c. Canoeing; 75 c. Village (design shaped like a book).

1909. No. 227 surch **Inland 3 Cents.**
261 – 3 c. on 10 c. black & red 3·50 5·00

†1910. Surcharged **3 CENTS INLAND POSTAGE.** Perf or rouletted.
274 **57** 3 c. on 10 c. black & purple 35 25

1913. Various types surch with new value and bars or ornaments.
322 – 1 c. on 2 c. black and red (No. 251) 2·25 3·00
290 **57** + 2 c. on 3 c. on 10 c. blk and purple 60 1·25
323 **56** 2 c. on 5 c. black & blue 2·25 3·50
292 – 2 c. on 15 c. black and blue (No. 255) 1·25 1·25
279 – 2 c. on 25 c. grey & blue (A) (No. 230) 7·50 5·00
281 – 2 c. on 25 c. black and brown (A) (No. 257) 7·50 5·00
295 – 2 c. on 25 c. black and brown (B) (No. 257) 4·50 4·50
296 – 5 c. on 20 c. green & red (No. 256) 85 3·25
280 – 5 c. on 30 c. violet (C) (No. 231) 7·50 5·00
282 – 5 c. on 30 c. brown (C) (No. 258) 7·50 5·00
297 – 5 c. on 30 c. brown (D) (No. 258) 3·75 3·75
278 **36** 8 c. on 3 c. red and green 60 30
283 – 10 c. on 50 c. black and green (E) (No. 259) 9·25 9·25
301 – 10 c. on 50 c. black and green (F) (No. 259) 8·25 8·25
303 – 20 c. on 75 c. black and brown (No. 260) 3·25 6·25
304 **53** 25 c. on $1 black & pink 23·00 23·00
305 – 50 c. on $2 black and green (No. 235) 7·50 7·50
308 – $1 on $5 grey and red (No. 236) 28·00 28·00

Descriptions of surcharges. (A) **1914 2 CENTS.** (B) **2** over ornaments. (C) **1914 5 CENTS.** (D) **5** over ornaments. (E) **1914 10 CENTS.** (F) **10** and ornaments.

64 House on Providence Is

65 Monrovia Harbour, Providence Is

†1915.
288 **64** 2 c. red 20 10
289 **65** 3 c. violet 20 10

1916. Liberian Frontier Force. Surch **LFF 1 C.**
332 **9** 1 c. on 1 c. green . . . . . 75·00 75·00
333 **50** 1 c. on 1 c. black and grn . £275 £275
334 **55** 1 c. on 1 c. black and grn . 1·75 3·75
335 – 1 c. on 2 c. black and red (No. 251) . . . . 1·75 3·75

1916. Surch **1916** over new value.
339 **1** 3 c. on 6 c. mauve . . . . . 23·00 23·00
340 5 c. on 12 c. yellow . . . . 4·00 5·00
341 10 c. on 24 c. red . . . . . 4·00 4·50

1917. Surch **1917** and value in words.
342 **13** 4 c. on 25 c. green . . . . 6·00 7·50
343 **52** 5 c. on 30 c. violet (No. 231) 30·00 38·00

1918. Surch **3 CENTS.**
345 **57** 3 c. on 10 c. black & purple 2·40 5·00

91 Bongo 93

92 African Palm Civet

94 Traveller's Tree

†1918.
349 **91** 1 c. black and green . . . 65 25
350 **92** 2 c. black and red 65 25
351 – 5 c. black and blue 15 10
352 **93** 10 c. green 20 10
353 – 15 c. green and black . . . 2·50 20
354 – 20 c. black and red 50 15
355 **94** 25 c. green . . . . 3·25 25
356 – 30 c. black and mauve . . . 13·00 70
357 – 50 c. black and blue . . . 11·50 1·10
358 – 75 c. black and olive . . . 1·00 25
359 – $1 blue and brown . . . . 4·00 25
360 – $2 black and violet . . . . 6·00 30
361 – $5 brown . . . . 6·00 40
DESIGNS—As Type **91**: 5 c. Coat of Arms; 15 c. Oil palm; 20 c. Statue of Mercury; 75 c. Heads of Mandingos; $5 "Liberia" seated. As Type **92**: 50 c. Lungfish (or Mudskipper); $1 Coast view; $2 Liberia College. As Type **93**: 30 c. Palm-nut Vulture.

1918. Geneva Red Cross Fund. Surch **TWO CENTS** and red cross.
375 **91** 1 c. + 2 c. black and green 75 75
376 **92** 2 c. + 2 c. black and red 75 75
377 – 5 c. + 2 c. black and blue 25 1·00
378 **93** 10 c. + 2 c. green . . . . 50 1·00
379 – 15 c. + 2 c. green & black 2·40 1·75
380 – 20 c. + 2 c. black and red 1·50 3·00
381 **94** 25 c. + 2 c. green . . . . 3·25 3·25
382 – 30 c. + 2 c. black & mve 8·75 4·75
383 – 50 c. + 2 c. black & blue 7·00 5·75
384 – 75 c. + 2 c. black & olive 2·10 5·25
385 – $1 + 2 c. blue and brown 4·25 7·00
386 – $2 + 2 c. black and violet 5·75 11·50
387 – $5 + 2 c. brown . . . . . 14·00 23·00

1920. Surch **1920** and value and two bars.
393 **91** 3 c. on 1 c. black & grn 1·50 2·75
394 **92** 4 c. on 2 c. black & red 1·50 3·00
395 R **42** 5 c. on 10 c. black & bl 3·75 4·25
396 5 c. on 10 c. black & red 3·75 4·25
397 5 c. on 10 c. black & grn 3·75 4·25
398 5 c. on 10 c. black & vio 3·75 4·25
399 5 c. on 10 c. black & red 3·75 4·25

100 Cape Mesurado 101 Pres. D. E. Howard

†1921.
402 **100** 1 c. green 20 10
403 **101** 5 c. black and blue . . . 25 10
404 – 10 c. blue and red 80 10
405 – 15 c. green and purple . . 3·00 50
406 – 20 c. green and red . . . 1·50 25
407 – 25 c. black and yellow . . 2·75 50
408 – 30 c. purple and green . . 1·00 15
409 – 50 c. blue and yellow . . 1·00 25
410 – 75 c. sepia and red . . . 1·00 40
411 – $1 black and red . . . . 17·00 1·00
412 – $2 violet and yellow . . . 30·00 1·75
413 – $5 red and purple . . . . 22·00 1·50
DESIGNS—VERT: 10 c. Arms. HORIZ: 15 c. Crocodile; 20 c. Pepper plant; 25 c. Leopard; 30 c. Village; 50 c. "Kru" boatman; 75 c. St. Paul's River; $1 Bongo (antelope); $2 Great Indian hornbill; $5 African elephant.

†1921. Optd **1921**.
414 **100** 1 c. green . . . . 2·75 50
415 **64** 2 c. red . . . . 2·75 50
416 **65** 3 c. violet . . . . 3·50 50
417 **101** 5 c. black and blue . . . 2·25 50
418 – 10 c. blue and red . . . . 5·25 50
419 – 15 c. green and purple . . 7·00 1·00
420 – 20 c. green and red . . . 3·25 60
421 – 25 c. black and yellow . . 7·00 1·00
422 – 30 c. purple and green . . 3·75 50
423 – 50 c. blue and yellow . . 3·00 70
424 – 75 c. sepia and red . . . 3·00 50
425 – $1 black and red . . . . 18·00 1·50
426 – $2 violet and yellow . . . 32·00 2·50
427 – $5 red and purple . . . . 23·00 3·25

107 Arrival of First Settlers in "Alligator"

†1923. Centennial issue.
466 **107** 1 c. black and blue . . . 16·00 70
467 2 c. brown and red . . . 16·00 70
468 5 c. blue and olive . . . 12·50 70
469 10 c. mauve and green . . 4·75 70
470 $1 brown and red . . . . 7·00 70

108 J. J. Roberts Memorial 109 House of Representatives, Monrovia

110 Rubber Plantation

†1923.
471 **108** 1 c. green . . . . 3·25 10
472 **109** 2 c. brown and red . . . 3·25 10
473 – 3 c. black and lilac . . . 25 10
474 – 5 c. black and blue . . . 28·00 15
475 – 10 c. brown and grey . . . 25 10
476 – 15 c. blue and bistre . . . 17·00 50
477 – 20 c. mauve and green . . 2·00 50
478 – 25 c. brown and red . . . 38·00 50
479 – 30 c. mauve and brown . . 50 20
480 – 50 c. orange and purple . 1·00 40
481 – 75 c. blue and grey . . . 1·50 65
482 **110** $1 violet and red . . . . 3·25 1·00
483 – $2 blue and orange . . . 3·75 65
484 – $5 brown and green . . . 10·00 65
DESIGNS—As Type **108**: 3 c. Star; 5, 10 c. Pres. King; 50 c. Pineapple. As Type **109**: 15 c. Hippopotamus; 20 c. Kob (antelope); 25 c. African buffalo; 30 c. Natives making palm oil; 75 c. Carrying elephant tusk. As Type **110**: $2 Stockton lagoon; $5 Styles of huts.

1926. Surch **Two Cents** and thick bar or wavy lines or ornamental scroll.
504 **91** 2 c. on 1 c. black & green 2·75 4·25

116 Palm Trees

117 Map of Africa 118 President King

1928.
511 **116** 1 c. green 15 15
512 2 c. violet 20 20
513 3 c. brown 35 20
514 **117** 5 c. blue 55 35
515 **118** 10 c. grey 70 35
516 **117** 15 c. purple . . . . . . 3·25 1·40
517 $1 brown . . . . 28·00 13·50

1936. Nos. O518 and 512/13 surch **AIR MAIL SIX CENTS.**
525 **116** 6 c. on 1 c. green . . . . £140 85·00
526 6 c. on 2 c. violet . . . . £140 85·00
527 6 c. on 3 c. brown . . . . £140 85·00

122 Ford "Tin Goose"

1936. Air. 1st Air Mail Service of 28th February.
530 **122** 1 c. black and green . . . 25 10
531 2 c. black and red 25 10
532 3 c. black and violet . . . 40 10
533 4 c. black and orange . . . 40 15
534 5 c. black and blue 45 15
535 6 c. black and green . . . 45 20

1936. Nos. 350/61 surch **1936** and new values in figures.
536 1 c. on 2 c. black and red . . . 30 50
537 3 c. on 5 c. black and blue . . 30 45
538 4 c. on 10 c. green 25 40
539 6 c. on 15 c. green and black . 30 55
540 8 c. on 20 c. black and red . . 20 60
541 12 c. on 30 c. black and mauve 2·75 2·25
542 14 c. on 50 c. black and blue . 1·50 1·75
543 16 c. on 75 c. black and olive . 50 1·00
544 18 c. on $1 blue and brown . . 60 1·40
545 22 c. on $2 black and violet . . 60 1·50
546 24 c. on $5 brown . . . . . . 75 1·60

1936. Nos. O363/74 optd with Star and **1936** or surch also in figures and words.
547 1 c. on 2 c. black and red . . . 30 50
548 3 c. on 5 c. black and blue . . 25 50
549 4 c. on 10 c. green 20 45
550 6 c. on 15 c. green & brown . . 25 60
551 8 c. on 20 c. black and lilac . . 30 60
552 12 c. on 30 c. black & violet . 2·50 2·00
553 14 c. on 50 c. black & brown . 1·00 1·50
554 16 c. on 75 c. black & brown . 45 90
555 18 c. on $1 blue and olive . . 50 1·00
556 22 c. on $2 black and olive . . 60 1·25
557 24 c. on $5 green . . . . . . 75 1·50
558 25 c. green and brown . . . . 1·00 2·00

126 Hippopotamus

1937.
559 – 1 c. black and green . . . 1·25 35
560 – 2 c. black and red. . . . 1·00 30
561 – 3 c. black and purple . . . 1·00 35
562 **126** 4 c. black and orange . . . 1·50 60
563 – 5 c. black and blue . . . 2·75 50
564 – 6 c. black and green . . . 45 20
DESIGNS: 1 c. Black and white casqued hornbill; 2 c. Bushbuck; 3 c. African buffalo; 5 c. Western reef heron; 6 c. Pres. Barclay.

127 Tawny Eagle in Flight 128 Three-engine Flying Boat

129 Little Egrets

1938. Air.
565 **127** 1 c. green 50 10
566 **128** 2 c. red 15 10
567 – 3 c. olive 40 10
568 **129** 4 c. orange 50 10
569 – 5 c. green 60 10
570 **128** 10 c. violet 25 10
571 – 20 c. mauve 30 15
572 – 30 c. grey . . . . 1·40 15
573 **127** 50 c. brown . . . . 3·00 25
574 – $1 blue . . . . 1·40 25
DESIGNS—VERT: 20 c., $1 Sikorsky S-43 amphibian. HORIZ: 3, 30 c. Lesser black-backed gull in flight.

130 Immigrant Ships nearing Liberian Coast

1940. Centenary of Founding of Liberian Commonwealth.
575 **130** 3 c. blue 50 15
576 – 5 c. brown 20 10
577 – 10 c. green 25 15
DESIGNS: 5 c. Seal of Liberia and Flags of original Settlements; 10 c. Thos. Buchanan's house and portrait.

1941. Centenary of First Postage Stamps. Nos. 575/7 optd **POSTAGE STAMP CENTENNIAL 1840-1940** and portrait of Rowland Hill.
578 **130** 3 c. blue (postage) . . . . 1·75 1·75
579 – 5 c. brown . . . . 1·75 1·75
580 – 10 c. green . . . . 1·75 1·75
581 **130** 3 c. blue (air) . . . . . . 1·40 1·40
582 – 5 c. brown . . . . 1·40 1·40
583 – 10 c. green . . . . 1·40 1·40
Nos. 581/3 are additionally optd with airplane and **AIR MAIL.**

1941. Red Cross Fund. Nos. 575/7 surch **RED CROSS** plus Red Cross and **TWO CENTS.**
584 **130** + 2 c. on 3 c. blue (post) 1·40 1·40
585 – + 2 c. on 5 c. brown . . 1·40 1·40
586 – + 2 c. on 10 c. green . . 1·40 1·40
587 **130** + 2 c. on 3 c. blue (air) 1·40 1·40
588 – + 2 c. on 5 c. brown . . 1·40 1·40
589 – + 2 c. on 10 c. green . . 1·40 1·40
Nos. 587/9 are additionally optd with airplane and **AIR MAIL.**

1941. Air. 1st Flight to U.S.A. Nos. 565/74 surch **First Flight LIBERIA-U.S. 1941, 50 c.** and bar.
594 **127** 50 c. on 1 c. £2000 £250
595 **128** 50 c. on 2 c. . . . . . . £150 75·00
596 – 50 c. on 3 c. . . . . . . £225 75·00
597 **129** 50 c. on 4 c. . . . . . . 70·00 35·00
598 50 c. on 5 c. . . . . . . 70·00 35·00
599 **128** 50 c. on 10 c. . . . . . 48·00 38·00
600 – 50 c. on 20 c. £1500 £150
601 – 50 c. on 30 c. . . . . . 80·00 30·00
602 **127** 50 c. brown . . . . . . 80·00 35·00
603 – $1 blue . . . . 48·00 30·00
The first flight was cancelled and covers were sent by ordinary mail. The flight took place in 1942 and the stamps were reissued but with the date obliterated.

1942. As Nos. 594/601 but with date "1941" obliterated by two bars.
604 **127** 50 c. on 1 c. green . . . . 8·50 8·50
605 **128** 50 c. on 2 c. red . . . . . 6·00 6·75
606 – 50 c. on 3 c. green . . . . 7·50 7·50
607 **129** 50 c. on 4 c. orange . . . 7·00 7·00
608 50 c. on 5 c. green . . . . 7·00 7·00
609 **128** 50 c. on 10 c. violet . . . 5·25 6·25
610 – 50 c. on 20 c. mauve . . . 5·25 6·25
611 – 50 c. on 30 c. grey . . . . 7·50 7·50
612 **127** 50 c. brown . . . . 7·50 7·50
613 – $1 blue . . . . 6·25 7·50

138 Miami–Monrovia Air Route

1942. Air.
614 **138** 10 c. red 20 10
615 – 12 c. blue 30 10
616 – 24 c. green 35 10
617 **138** 30 c. green 35 10
618 35 c. lilac 40 15
619 50 c. purple 50 15
620 70 c. olive 55 30
621 $1.40 red 75 50
DESIGN: 12, 24 c. Boeing 247 airliner over Liberian Agricultural and Industrial Fair.

139 Bushbuck

1942.

622 – 1 c. brown and violet . . 80 20
623 – 2 c. brown and blue . . . 80 20
624 – 3 c. brown and green . . 1·25 45
625 **139** 4 c. red and black . . . . 2·00 70
626 – 5 c. brown and olive . . . 1·75 70
627 – 10 c. black and red . . . 3·75 1·10
DESIGNS—HORIZ: 1 c. Royal antelope; 2 c. Water chevrotain; 3 c. Jentink's duiker; 5 c. Banded duiker. VERT: 10 c. Diana monkey.

1944. Stamps of 1928 and 1937 surch.

628 **116** 1 c. on 2 c. violet . . . . 7·50 7·50
634 **126** 1 c. on 4 c. black & orge 48·00 40·00
629 **118** 1 c. on 10 c. grey . . . . 9·25 5·50
635 – 2 c. on 3 c. black and purple (No. 561) . . . . . . 48·00 40·00
630 **117** 2 c. on 5 c. blue . . . . . 3·25 3·25
632 **116** 3 c. on 2 c. violet . . . . 27·00 30·00
636 – 4 c. on 5 c. black and blue (No. 563) . . . . . . 28·00 28·00
633 **118** 4 c. on 10 c. grey . . . . 3·25 3·25
637 – 5 c. on 1 c. black and green (No. 559) . . . . . . 85·00 55·00
638 – 6 c. on 2 c. black and red (No. 560) . . . . . . 12·50 16·00
639 – 10 c. on 6 c. black and green (No. 564) . . . . . . 14·00 16·00

1944. Air stamps of 1936 and 1938 surch.

643 **128** 10 c. on 2 c. red . . . . . 27·00 30·00
644 **129** 10 c. on 5 c. green . . . . 11·50 11·50
640 **122** 30 c. on 1 c. black & grn 70·00 50·00
645 30 c. on 3 c. olive (No. 567) £100 85·00
646 **129** 30 c. on 4 c. orange . . . . 11·50 11·50
641 **122** 50 c. on 3 c. black & vio 20·00 23·00
642 70 c. on 2 c. black & red 50·00 50·00
647 – $1 on 3 c. olive (No. 567) 42·00 42·00
648 **127** $1 on 50 c. brown . . . . 27·00 22·00

150 Pres. Roosevelt reviewing Troops

1945. Pres. Roosevelt Memorial.

650 **150** 3 c. black & pur (postage) 15 15
651 5 c. black and blue . . . 30 25
652 70 c. black & brown (air) 1·00 1·00

151 Opening Monrovia Harbour Project

1946. Opening of Monrovia Harbour Project by Pres. Tubman.

653 **151** 5 c. blue (postage) 25 15
654 24 c. green (air) . . . . . 2·40 2·75

1947. As T **151**, but without inscr at top.

655 5 c. violet (postage) 15 15
656 25 c. red (air) . . . . 1·00 1·75

152 1st Postage Stamps of United States and Liberia

1947. U.S. Postage Stamps Centenary and 87th Anniv of Liberian Postal Issues.

657 **152** 5 c. red (postage) 20 15
658 12 c. green (air) 30 15
659 22 c. violet 40 20
660 50 c. blue 50 25

153 Matilda Newport Firing Canon

1947. 125th Anniv of Defence of Monrovia.

662 **153** 1 c. black & green (post) 15 10
663 3 c. black and violet . . 20 10
664 5 c. black and blue . . . 20 15
665 10 c. black and yellow . . 1·25 45
666 25 c. black and red (air) 95 35

154 Liberty

156 Douglas DC-3

1947. Centenary of National Independence.

667 – 1 c. green (postage) . . . 20 10
668 **154** 2 c. purple 20 10
669 – 3 c. purple 30 15
670 – 5 c. blue 40 15
671 – 12 c. orange (air) 60 20
672 – 25 c. red 75 35
673 – 50 c. brown 90 70
DESIGNS—VERT: 1 c. Liberian star; 3 c. Arms of Liberia; 4 c. Map of Liberia; 12 c. J. J. Roberts Monument; 25 c. Liberian Flag; 50 c. ($26\frac{1}{2} \times 33$ mm) Centenary Monument.

1948. Air. First Liberian International Airways Flight (Monrovia-Dakar).

674 **156** 25 c. red . . . . 1·50 1·00
675 50 c. blue . . . . 2·40 1·50

157 Joseph J. Roberts

1949. Liberian Presidents. Portrait and name in black. (a) Postage.

676 – 1 c. green (Roberts) . . . 1·60 3·25
677 **157** 1 c. green 15 10
678 – 1 c. pink (Roberts) . . . 25 15
679 – 2 c. pink (Benson) . . . 35 35
680 – 2 c. yellow (Benson) . . . 35 15
681 – 3 c. mauve (Warner) . . . 35 35
682 – 4 c. olive (Payne) 35 55
683 – 5 c. blue (Mansion) . . . 45 55
684 – 6 c. orange (Roye) . . . 55 95
685 – 7 c. green (Gardner and Russell) . . . . 70 1·25
686 – 8 c. red (Johnson) . . . . 70 1·40
687 – 9 c. purple (Cheeseman) . 1·10 1·10
688 – 10 c. yellow (Coleman) . . 75 35
689 – 10 c. grey (Coleman) . . 40 20
690 – 15 c. orange (Gibson) . . 85 40
691 – 15 c. blue (Gibson) . . . 25 15
692 – 20 c. grey (A. Barclay) . 1·25 70
693 – 20 c. red (A. Barclay) . . 50 45
694 – 25 c. red (Howard) . . . 1·60 1·10
695 – 25 c. blue (Howard) . . . 50 45
696 – 50 c. turquoise (King) . . 3·25 95
697 – 50 c. purple (King) . . . 70 60
698 – $1 mauve (E. Barclay) . . 5·75 70
699 – $1 brown (E. Barclay) . . 4·00 55

(b) Air.

700 – 25 c. blue (Tubman) . . . 1·00 55
701 – 25 c. green (Tubman) . . . 75 35
Nos. 676 and 678 have a different portrait of Roberts wearing a moustache.

158 Colonists and Map

159 Hand holding Book

1949. Multicoloured.

702 1 c. Settlers approaching village (postage) 50 75
703 2 c. Rubber tapping and planting 50 75
704 3 c. Landing of first colonists in 1822 . . . . 1·00 1·50
705 5 c. Jehudi Ashmun and Matilda Newport defending stockade 50 75
706 25 c. Type **158** (air) . . . . . 1·25 1·50
707 50 c. Africans and coat of arms 2·75 3·25

1950. National Literacy Campaign.

708 **159** 5 c. blue (postage) . . . 20 15
709 – 25 c. red (air) 70 70
DESIGN—VERT: 25 c. Open book and rising sun.

160 U.P.U. Monument, Berne

1950. 75th Anniv of U.P.U.

711 **160** 5 c. black and grn (post) 20 15
712 – 10 c. black and mauve . . 30 30
713 – 25 c. purple & orge (air) 3·25 3·25
DESIGNS—HORIZ: 10 c. Standehaus, Berne. VERT: 25 c. U.P.U. Monument, Berne.

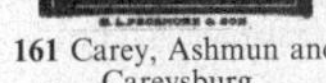

161 Carey, Ashmun and Careysburg

162 U.N. Headquarters

163 Flags and U.N. Emblem

1952. Designs all show portrait of Ashmun.

715 – 1 c. green (postage) . . . 10 10
716 **161** 2 c. blue and red 10 10
717 – 3 c. green and purple . . . 10 10
718 – 4 c. green and brown . . . 15 10
719 – 5 c. red and blue 20 15
720 – 10 c. blue and red 25 20
721 – 25 c. black & pur (air) . . 35 35
722 – 50 c. red and blue . . . . 1·00 45
DESIGNS—VERT: 1 c. Seal of Liberia; 3 c. Harper and Harper City; 5 c. Buchanan and Upper Buchanan. HORIZ: 4 c. Marshall and Marshall City; 10 c. Roberts and Robertsport; 25 c. Monroe and Monrovia; 50 c. Tubman and map.

1952. U.N. Commem.

724 **162** 1 c. blue (postage) 10 10
725 – 4 c. blue and pink 15 10
726 – 10 c. brown and yellow . . 25 20
727 **163** 25 c. red and blue (air) . . 55 45
DESIGNS—HORIZ: 4 c. Liberian and U.N. flags and scroll; 10 c. Liberian and U.N. emblems.

164 Modern Road-building

1953. Air. Transport.

729 **164** 12 c. brown 15 15
730 – 25 c. purple 75 30
731 – 35 c. violet . . . . 1·00 35
732 – 50 c. orange 65 25
733 – 70 c. green . . . . 1·25 40
734 – $1 blue . . . . 1·40 55
DESIGNS: 25 c. "African Glen" (freighter) in Monrovia Harbour; 35 c. Diesel locomotive; 50 c. Free Port of Monrovia; 70 c. Roberts Field Airport; $1 Tubman Bridge.

165 Common Bulbul

166 Blue-throated Roller

1953. Imperf or perf.

735 **165** 1 c. red and blue . . . . . 1·00 20
736 **166** 3 c. blue and salmon . . . 1·00 20
737 – 4 c. brown and yellow . . 1·50 25
738 – 5 c. turquoise & mauve . . 1·75 30
739 – 10 c. mauve and green . . 1·75 30
740 – 12 c. orange and brown . . 2·90 40
BIRDS: As Type **165**: 4 c. Yellow-casqued hornbill; 5 c. Giant kingfisher. As Type **166**: 10 c. African jacana; 12 c. Broad-tailed paradise whydah.

167 Hospital

1954. Liberian Govt. Hospital Fund.

741 – 5 c. + 5 c. black and purple (postage) 20 15
742 – 10 c. + 5 c. black and red (air) 15 20
743 **167** 20 c. + 5 c. black & grn 25 25
744 – 25 c. + 5 c. black, red and blue 30 20
DESIGNS—As Type **167**: 5 c. Medical research workers; 10 c. Nurses. 46 × 35 mm: 25 c. Doctor examining patient.

168 Children of the World

1954. Air. U.N.I.C.E.F.

745 **168** $5 ultramarine, red & blue 27·00 23·00

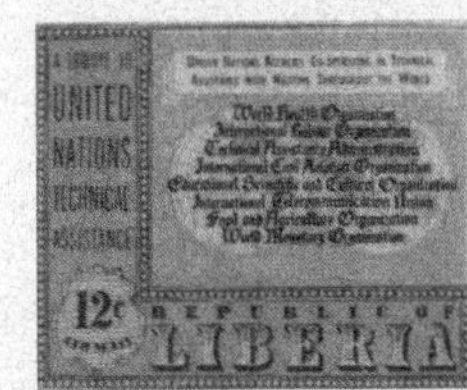

169 U.N. Organizations

1954. Air. U.N. Technical Assistance.

746 **169** 12 c. black and blue . . . 25 15
746 – 15 c. brown and yellow . . 25 15
747 – 20 c. black and green . . 30 20
749 – 25 c. blue and red 35 25
DESIGNS: 15 c. Printers; 20 c. Mechanic; 25 c. Teacher and students.

1954. Air. Visit of President Tubman to U.S.A. As Nos. 729/34 but colours changed and inscr "COMMEMORATING PRESIDENTIAL VISIT TO U.S.A."

750 12 c. orange 20 20
751 25 c. blue 80 25
752 35 c. red . . . . 3·25 1·40
753 50 c. mauve 80 30
754 70 c. brown . . . . 1·10 50
755 $1 green . . . . 1·60 3·25

170 Football

171 "Callichilia stenosepala"

1955. Sports.

756 – 3 c. red & grn (post) . . . 15 10
757 **170** 5 c. black and orange . . 15 10
758 – 25 c. violet and yellow . . 25 20
759 – 10 c. blue & mve (air) . . 20 15
760 – 12 c. brown and blue . . 15 15
761 – 25 c. red and green . . . 20 20
DESIGNS—VERT: 3 c. Tennis; 25 c. Boxing (No. 758). HORIZ: 10 c. Baseball; 12 c. Swimming; 25 c. Running (No. 761).

1955. Flowers.

763 **171** 6 c. yellow, salmon & green (postage) 15 10
764 – 7 c. red, yellow & green . 15 10
765 – 8 c. buff, blue and green 20 10
766 – 9 c. green and orange . . 25 15
767 – 20 c. yellow, green and violet (air) 15 15
768 – 25 c. yellow, green & red 20 20
FLOWERS—VERT: 7 c. "Gomphia subcordata"; 8 c. "Listrostachys chudata"; 9 c. "Mussaenda isertiana". HORIZ: 20 s. "Costus"; 25 c. "Barteria nigritiana".

172 U.N. General Assembly

173 Tapping Rubber and Rotary Emblem

1955. Air. 10th Anniv of U.N.

769 – 10 c. blue and red 20 10
770 **172** 15 c. black and violet . . 25 15
771 – 25 c. brown and green . . 35 15
772 – 50 c. green and red . . . 1·00 20

DESIGNS—VERT: 10 c. U.N. emblem; 25 c. Liberian Secretary of State signing U.N. Charter. HORIZ: 50 c. Page from U.N. Charter.

1955. 50th Anniv of Rotary International.

773 **173** 5 c. green & yell (postage) 25 15
774 – 10 c. blue and red (air) . . 15 50
775 – 15 c. brown, yellow & red 20 65

DESIGNS: 10 c. Rotary International H.Q., Evanston; 15 c. View of Monrovia.

174 Coliseum, New York

1956. 5th International Philatelic Exhibition, New York.

777 – 3 c. brown and green (postage) 15 10
778 **174** 4 c. brown and green . . 10 25
779 – 6 c. purple and black . . 20 10
780 **174** 10 c. blue and red (air) . . 25 15
781 – 12 c. violet and orange . . 20 15
782 – 15 c. purple & turquoise 25 20

DESIGNS—VERT: 3 c., 15 c. Statue of Liberty. HORIZ: 6 c., 12 c. The Globe.

175 Chariot Race

1956. Olympic Games.

784 – 4 c. brown & olive (post) 15 15
785 – 6 c. black and green . . . 15 10
786 – 8 c. brown and blue . . . 20 10
787 **175** 10 c. black and red . . . 25 10
788 – 12 c. purple and grn (air) 20 15
789 – 20 c. multicoloured . . . 30 20

DESIGNS—HORIZ: 4 c. Olympic rings, eastern grey kangaroo and emu; 8 c. Goddess of Victory; 12 c., 20 c. Olympic torch superimposed on map of Austrialia. VERT: 6 c. Discus thrower.

176 Douglas DC-6B "John Alden" at Idelwild Airport

1957. 1st Anniv of Inauguration of Liberia–U.S. Direct Air Service.

791 **176** 3 c. blue & orge (postage) 15 15
792 – 5 c. black and mauve . . 20 20
793 **176** 12 c. blue & green (air) . . 30 25
794 – 15 c. black and brown . . 30 25
795 **176** 25 c. blue and red . . . 45 25
796 – 50 c. black and blue . . . 85 30

DESIGN: 5, 15, 50 c. President Tubman and "John Alden" at Roberts Field, Liberia.

177 Children's Playground

1957. Inaug of Antoinette Tubman Child Welfare Foundation. Inscr as in T **177**.

797 **177** 4 c. green & red (postage) 10 10
798 – 5 c. brown & turquoise . 15 10
799 – 6 c. violet and bistre . . 15 10
800 – 10 c. blue and red 20 15
801 – 15 c. brown & blue (air) 20 15
802 – 35 c. purple and grey . . 35 25

DESIGNS: 5 c. Teacher with pupil; 6 c. National anthem with choristers; 10 c. Children viewing welfare home; 15 c. Nurse inoculating youth; 35 c. Kamara triplets.

178 German Flag and Brandenburg Gate

1958. Pres. Tubman's European Tour. Flags in national colours.

804 **178** 5 c. blue (postage) . . . 15 10
805 – 5 c. brown 15 10
806 – 5 c. red 15 10
807 – 10 c. black (air) 25 15
808 – 15 c. green 25 20
809 – 15 c. blue 25 20
810 – 15 c. violet 25 20

DESIGNS: Flags of: Netherlands and windmill (No. 805); Sweden and Royal Palace, Stockholm (No. 806); Italy and Colosseum (No. 807); France and Arc de Triomphe (No. 808); Switzerland and Alpine chalet (No. 809); Vatican City and St. Peter's Basilica (No. 810).

179 Map of the World

180 Africans and Map

1958. 10th Anniv of Declaration of Human Rights.

811 **179** 3 c. blue and black . . . 25 15
812 – 5 c. brown and blue . . . 20 20
813 – 10 c. orange and black . 30 75
814 – 12 c. black and red . . . 40 35

DESIGNS: 5 c. U.N. Emblem and H.Q. building; 10 c. U.N. Emblem; 12 c. U.N. Emblem and initials of U.N. agencies.

1959. Africa Freedom Day.

816 **180** 20 c. orge & brn (postage) 30 30
817 – 25 c. brown & blue (air) 35 20

DESIGN: 25 c. Two Africans looking at Pres. Tubman's declaration of Africa Freedom Day.

181

182 Abraham Lincoln

1959. Inaug of U.N.E.S.C.O. Building, Paris.

818 **181** 25 c. pur & grn (postage) 35 40
819 – 25 c. red and blue (air) . 35 30

DESIGN—HORIZ: No. 819 U.N.E.S.C.O. Headquarters, Paris.

1959. 150th Birth Anniv of Abraham Lincoln.

821 **182** 10 c. blk & blue (postage) 25 30
822 15 c. black and orange . 30 30
823 25 c. black & grn (air) . . 55 50

183 Presidents Toure, Tubman and Nkrumah at Conference Table

184 "Care of Refugees"

1960. "Big Three" Conf, Saniquellie, Liberia.

825 **183** 25 c. black & red (postage) 35 25
826 – 25 c. black, bl & buff (air) 35 25

DESIGN: No. 826, Medallion portraits of Presidents Toure (Guinea), Tubman (Liberia) and Nkrumah (Ghana).

1960. World Refugee Year.

827 **184** 25 c. green & blk (postage) 35 30
828 25 c. blue & black (air) . 55 40

185

186 Weightlifting

1960. 10th Anniv of African Technical Co-operation (C.C.T.A.).

830 **185** 25 c. green & blk (postage) 35 50
831 – 25 c. brown and blue (air) 45 35

DESIGN: No. 831, Map of Africa with symbols showing fields of assistance.

1960. Olympic Games, Rome.

832 **186** 5 c. brn and grn (postage) 20 15
833 – 10 c. brown and purple . . 40 75
834 – 15 c. brown and orange . . 35 30
835 – 25 c. brown & blue (air) 70 80

DESIGNS—HORIZ: 10 c. Rowing; 25 c. Javelin-throwing. VERT: 15 c. Walking.

187 Stamps of 1860 and Map

188 "Guardians of Peace"

1960. Liberian Stamp Centenary. Stamps, etc., in green, red and blue. Colours of map and inscriptions given.

837 **187** 5 c. black (postage) . . . 25 15
838 20 c. brown 40 40
839 25 c. blue (air) 50 40

1961. Membership of U.N. Security Council.

841 **188** 25 c. blue & red (postage) 45 35
842 – 25 c. blue and red (air) . . 45 25

DESIGN—HORIZ: No. 842, Dove of Peace, Globe and U.N. Emblem.

189 Anatomy Class, University of Liberia

190 President Roberts

1961. 15th Anniv of U.N.E.S.C.O.

845 **189** 25 c. brn & grn (postage) 35 35
846 – 25 c. brown & violet (air) 35 25

DESIGN: No. 846, Science class, University of Liberia.

1961. 150th Birth Anniv of Joseph J. Roberts (first President of Liberia).

848 **190** 5 c. sepia & orge (postage) 20 15
849 – 10 c. sepia and blue . . . 35 15
850 – 25 c. sepia & green (air) . 45 35

DESIGNS—HORIZ: 10 c. Pres. Roberts and old and new presidential mansions; 25 c. Pres. Roberts and Providence Is.

191 Scout and Sports

1961. Liberian Boy Scout Movement.

852 **191** 5 c. sepia & vio (postage) 25 20
853 – 10 c. ochre and blue . . . 30 20
854 – 25 c. sepia & green (air) . 40 30

DESIGNS—HORIZ: 10 c. Scout badge and scouts in camp. VERT: 25 c. Scout and badge.

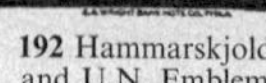

192 Hammarskjold and U.N. Emblem

193 Campaign Emblem

1962. Dag Hammarskjold Commem.

856 **192** 20 c. blk & blue (postage) 30 20
857 25 c. black & pur (air) . . 35 25

1962. Malaria Eradication.

859 **193** 25 c. green & red (postage) 35 25
860 – 25 c. orange & violet (air) 35 25

DESIGN—HORIZ: No. 860, Campaign emblem and slogan.

194 Pres. Tubman and New York Skyline

1962. Air. President's Visit to U.S.A.

862 **194** 12 c. multicoloured . . . 25 15
863 25 c. multicoloured . . . 35 30
864 50 c. multicoloured . . . 70 55

195 U.N. Emblem

1962. U.N. Day.

865 **195** 20 c. bistre & grn (postage) 35 30
866 – 25 c. blue & dp blue (air) 45 30

DESIGN: 25 c. U.N. emblem and flags.

196 Treasury Building

197 F.A.O. Emblem, Bowl and Spoon

1962. Liberian Government Buildings.

868 – 1 c. orge & blue (postage) 10 15
869 **196** 5 c. violet and blue . . . 15 10
870 – 10 c. brown and buff . . 20 15
871 – 15 c. blue and salmon . . 25 20
872 – 80 c. yellow and brown . 1·60 1·00
873 – 12 c. lake & green (air) . 25 15
874 – 50 c. blue and orange . . 1·00 90
875 – 70 c. blue and mauve . . 1·40 1·00
876 **196** $1 black and orange . . . 2·00 1·10

BUILDINGS: 1 c., 80 c. Executive; 10 c., 50 c. Information; 12 c., 15 c., 70 c. Capitol.

1963. Freedom from Hunger.

877 **197** 5 c. pur & turq (postage) 15 10
878 – 25 c. yellow & green (air) 35 20

DESIGN: 25 c. F.A.O. emblem and Globe.

198 Rocket

1963. Space Exploration.

880 **198** 10 c. yell & blue (postage) 20 15
881 – 15 c. brown and blue . . 35 40
882 – 25 c. green & orge (air) . 45 30

DESIGNS—HORIZ: 15 c. Space capsule. VERT: 25 c. "Telstar" TV satellite.

199 Red Cross

200 "Unity" Scroll

1963. Red Cross Centenary.

884 **199** 5 c. green & red (postage) 15 15
885 – 10 c. grey and red 20 20
886 – 25 c. violet & red (air) . . 35 30
887 – 50 c. blue and red . . . 1·00 85

DESIGNS—VERT: 10 c. Emblem and torch. HORIZ: 25 c. Red Cross and Globe; 50 c. Emblem and Globe.

1963. Conference of African Heads of State, Addis Ababa.

No.	Type	Description	Unused	Used
888	200	20 c. brn & grn (postage)	40	35
889	–	25 c. red and green (air)	45	30

DESIGN: 25 c. Map of Africa (inscr "AFRICAN SUMMIT CONFERENCE").

201 Ski-jumping **202** President Kennedy

1963. Winter Olympic Games, Innsbruck. (1964).

No.	Type	Description	Unused	Used
890	201	5 c. blue and red (postage)	20	20
891	–	10 c. red and blue (air)	25	25
892	–	25 c. orange and green	35	35

DESIGNS—VERT: 10 c. Olympic flame. HORIZ: 25 c. Olympic rings. All have mountain scenery as backgrounds.

1964. President Kennedy Memorial Issue.

No.	Type	Description	Unused	Used
894	202	20 c. blk & blue (postage)	35	20
895	–	25 c. black & pur (air)	45	25

DESIGN—VERT: 25 c. Pres. Kennedy, full face portrait.

203 "Relay I" Satellite **204** Mt. Fuji

1964. Space Communications.

No.	Type	Description	Unused	Used
897	–	10 c. orange and green	20	15
898	203	15 c. blue and mauve	25	20
899	–	25 c. yellow, black & blue	45	25

SATELLITES—HORIZ: 10 c. "Syncom"; 25 c. "Mariner II".

1964. Olympic Games, Tokyo.

No.	Type	Description	Unused	Used
901	204	10 c. green and yellow	15	10
902	–	15 c. purple and red	20	15
903	–	25 c. red and buff	45	20

DESIGNS: 15 c. Japanese arch and Olympic Flame; 25 c. Cherry blossom and stadium.

205 Scout Bugle **206** "The Great Emancipator" (statue)

1965. Liberian Boy Scouts.

No.	Type	Description	Unused	Used
905	–	5 c. brown and blue (postage)	25	15
906	205	10 c. ochre and green	40	25
907	–	25 c. blue and red (air)	50	35

DESIGNS—VERT: 5 c. Scout badge and saluting hand; 25 c. Liberian flag within scout badge.

1965. Death Centenary of Abraham Lincoln.

No.	Type	Description	Unused	Used
909	206	5 c. brown and sepia	20	25
910	–	20 c. green & lt brown	35	30
911	–	25 c. blue and purple	40	40

DESIGNS—HORIZ: 20 c. Bust of Lincoln, and Pres. Kennedy. VERT: 25 c. Lincoln statue, Chicago (after St. Gaudens).

207 I.C.Y. Emblem

1965. International Co-operation Year.

No.	Type	Description	Unused	Used
913	207	12 c. brown and orange	70	25
914		25 c. brown and blue	40	25
915		50 c. brown and green	80	70

208 I.T.U. Emblem and Symbols

1965. Centenary of I.T.U.

No.	Type	Description	Unused	Used
917	208	25 c. brn & grn (post)	40	50
918		35 c. mauve and black	60	50
919		50 blue and red (air)	80	45

209 Pres. Tubman and Flag **210** Sir Winston Churchill

1965. Pres. Tubman's 70th Birthday. Multicoloured.

No.	Type	Description	Unused	Used
921		25 c. Type **209** (postage)	35	30
922		25 c. President and Liberian arms (air)	35	25

1966. Churchill Commemoration.

No.	Type	Description	Unused	Used
924	210	15 c. black & orge (postage)	30	30
925	–	20 c. black and green	35	25
926	–	25 c. black and blue (air)	40	30

DESIGNS—HORIZ: 20 c. Churchill in uniform of Trinity House Elder Brother; 25 c. Churchill and Houses of Parliament.

211 Pres. Roberts **212** Footballers and Hemispheres

1966. Liberian Presidents.

No.	Type	Description	Unused	Used
928	211	1 c. black & pink (postage)	10	10
929	–	2 c. black and yellow	10	10
930	–	3 c. black and violet	10	10
931	–	4 c. black and yellow	75	50
932	–	5 c. black and orange	10	10
933	–	10 c. black and green	15	10
934	–	25 c. black and blue	35	20
935	–	50 c. black and mauve	70	65
936	–	80 c. black and red	1·25	95
937	–	$1 black and brown	1·40	15
938	–	$2 black and purple	3·25	2·75
939	–	25 c. black and green (air)	35	25

PRESIDENTS: 2 c. Benson; 3 c. Warner; 4 c. Payne; 5 c. Roye; 10 c. Coleman; 25 c. (postage) Howard; 25 c. (air) Tubman; 50 c. King; 80 c. Johnson; $1 Barclay; $2 Cheesman.

1966. World Cup Football Championships.

No.	Type	Description	Unused	Used
940	212	10 c. brown & turquoise	15	15
941	–	25 c. brown and mauve	35	30
942	–	35 c. brown and orange	50	45

DESIGNS—VERT: 25 c. Presentation cup, football and boots; 35 c. Footballer.

213 Pres. Kennedy taking Oath

1966. 3rd Death Anniv (Nov. 22nd) of Pres. Kennedy.

No.	Type	Description	Unused	Used
944	213	15 c. black & red (postage)	25	15
945	–	20 c. purple and blue	35	20
946	–	25 c. blue, black and ochre (air)	45	30
947	–	35 c. blue and pink	85	45

DESIGNS: 20 c. Kennedy stamps of 1964; 25 c. U.N. General Assembly and Pres. Kennedy; 35 c. Pres. Kennedy and rocket on launching pad.

214 Children on See-saw

1966. 20th Anniv of U.N.I.C.E.F.

No.	Type	Description	Unused	Used
949	214	5 c. blue and red	20	20
950	–	80 c. brown and green	1·50	1·50

DESIGN: 80 c. Child playing "Doctors".

215 Giraffe **216** Scout Emblem and Various Sports

1966. Wild Animals. Multicoloured.

No.	Type	Description	Unused	Used
951		2 c. Type **215**	10	10
952		3 c. Lion	20	15
953		5 c. Crocodile (horiz)	15	10
954		10 c. Chimpanzees	40	20
955		15 c. Leopard (horiz)	50	25
956		20 c. Black rhinoceros (horiz)	60	40
957		25 c. African elephant	70	50

1967. World Scout Jamboree, Idaho.

No.	Type	Description	Unused	Used
958	–	10 c. purple and green	20	15
959	216	25 c. red and blue	35	50
960	–	40 c. brown and green	85	60

DESIGNS—VERT: 10 c. Jamboree emblem. HORIZ: 40 c. Scout by campfire, and Moon landing.

217 Pre-Hispanic Sculpture **218** W.H.O. Building, Brazzaville

1967. Publicity for Olympic Games, Mexico (1968).

No.	Type	Description	Unused	Used
962	217	10 c. violet and orange	75	85
963	–	25 c. orange, black & blue	35	40
964	–	40 c. red and green	60	65

DESIGNS—VERT: 25 c. Aztec calendar. HORIZ: 40 c. Mexican sombrero, guitar and ceramics.

1967. Inauguration of W.H.O.'s Regional Office, Brazzaville.

No.	Type	Description	Unused	Used
966	218	5 c. yellow and blue	20	20
967	–	80 c. green and yellow	1·25	1·25

DESIGN—VERT: 80 c. As Type **218** but in vertical format.

219 Boy with Rattle **220** Ice-hockey

1967. Musicians and Instruments. Multicoloured.

No.	Type	Description	Unused	Used
968		2 c. Type **219**	15	15
969		3 c. Tomtom and soko violin	20	20
970		5 c. Mang harp	25	25
971		10 c. Alimilim	30	30
972		15 c. Xylophone drums	35	35
973		25 c. Tomtoms	50	40
974		35 c. Oral harp	75	60

The 3 c. and 5 c. are horiz designs.

1967. Publicity for Winter Olympic Games, Grenoble (1968).

No.	Type	Description	Unused	Used
975	220	10 c. blue and green	15	20
976	–	25 c. violet and blue	35	30
977	–	40 c. brown and orange	85	50

DESIGNS: 25 c. Ski-jumping; 40 c. Tobogganing.

221 Pres. Tubman **222** Human Rights Emblem

1967. Re-election of Pres. Tubman for 6th Term.

No.	Type	Description	Unused	Used
979	221	25 c. brown and blue	35	25

1968. Human Rights Year.

No.	Type	Description	Unused	Used
981	222	3 c. blue and red	10	10
982		80 c. green and brown	1·60	1·60

223 Dr. King and Hearse **224** Throwing the Javelin and Statue of Diana

1968. Martin Luther King Commem.

No.	Type	Description	Unused	Used
984	223	15 c. brown and blue	25	20
985	–	25 c. brown and blue	40	30
986	–	35 c. black and olive	60	65

DESIGNS—VERT: 25 c. Dr. Martin Luther King. HORIZ: Dr. King and Lincoln Monument.

1968. Olympic Games, Mexico.

No.	Type	Description	Unused	Used
988	224	15 c. violet and brown	25	15
989	–	25 c. blue and red	35	15
990	–	35 c. brown and green	50	30

DESIGNS: 25 c. Throwing the discus and Quetzalcoatl sculpture; 35 c. High-diving and Xochilcalco bas-relief.

225 President Tubman **226** I.L.O. Symbol

1968. 25th Anniv of Pres. Tubman's Administration.

No.	Type	Description	Unused	Used
992	225	25 c. black, brown & silver	45	50

1969. 50th Anniv of I.L.O.

No.	Type	Description	Unused	Used
994	226	25 c. blue & gold (postage)	35	35
995	–	80 c. green & gold (air)	1·50	1·40

DESIGN: 80 c. As Type **226** but vertical.

227 "Prince Balthasar Carlos" (Velasquez) **228** Bank Emblem on "Tree"

1969. Paintings (1st series). Multicoloured.

No.	Type	Description	Unused	Used
996		3 c. Type **227**	10	10
997		5 c. "Red Roofs" (Pissarro)	20	10
998		10 c. "David and Goliath" (Caravaggio)	30	15
999		12 c. "Still Life" (Chardin)	30	15
1000		15 c. "The Last Supper" (Leonardo da Vinci)	35	15
1001		20 c. "Regatta at Argenteuil" (Monet)	50	20
1002		25 c. "Judgement of Solomon" (Giorgione)	45	25
1003		35 c. "The Sistine Madonna" (Raphael)	60	30

Nos. 997/1001 are horiz.
See also Nos. 1010/1017.

1969. 5th Anniv of African Development Bank.

No.	Type	Description	Unused	Used
1004	228	25 c. brown and blue	45	40
1005		80 c. red and green	1·50	1·10

229 Memorial Plaque

1969. 1st Man on the Moon.

No.	Type	Description	Unused	Used
1006	229	15 c. blue and ochre	25	15
1007	–	25 c. blue and orange	35	20
1008	–	35 c. red and slate	50	25

DESIGNS—VERT: 25 c. Moon landing and Liberian; 35 c. "Kennedy" stamp of 1966; 35 c. Module lifting off from Moon.

1969. Paintings (2nd series). As T **227**. Multicoloured.

No.	Type	Description	Unused	Used
1010		3 c. "The Gleaners" (Millet)	15	10
1011		5 c. "View of Toledo" (El Greco)	20	15
1012		10 c. "Heads of Negroes" (Rubens)	30	15
1013		12 c. "The Last Supper" (El Greco)	30	20
1014		15 c. "Peasants Dancing" (Brueghel)	35	20
1015		20 c. "Hunters in the Snow" (Brueghel)	40	25
1016		25 c. "Descent from the Cross" (detail, Weyden)	45	30
1017		35 c. "The Conception" (Murillo)	60	40

Nos. 1010, 1012/15 are horiz.

230 Peace Dove and Emblems

1970. 25th Anniv of United Nations.
1018 **230** 5 c. grn & silver (postage) . . 15 25
1019 – $1 blue and silver (air) . . 1·25 1·00
DESIGN: $1, U.N. emblem and olive branch.

231 World Cup "Football" Emblem

1970. World Cup Football Championships, Mexico.
1020 **231** 5 c. brown and blue . . . 20 15
1021 – 10 c. brown and green . . 25 20
1022 – 25 c. gold and purple . . 45 30
1023 – 35 c. red and blue . . . 60 45
DESIGN—VERT: 10 c. Tialoc, Mexican Rain God; 25 c. Jules Rimet Cup. HORIZ: 35 c. Football in sombrero.

232 Japanese Singer and Festival Plaza

1970. Expo 70. Multicoloured.
1025 2 c. Type **232** 10 10
1026 3 c. Japanese singer and Expo hall 15 10
1027 5 c. Aerial view of "EXPO 70" 15 10
1028 7 c. "Tanabata" Festival . . 30 10
1029 8 c. "Awa" Dance Festival . 30 15
1030 25 c. "Sado-Okesa" Dance Festival 45 25

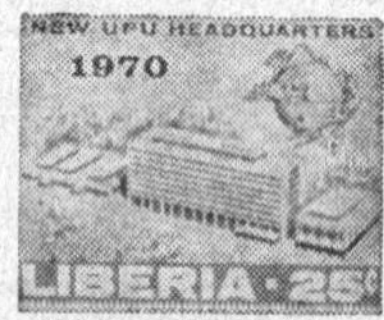

233 New H.Q. Building

1970. Inauguration of New U.P.U. Headquarters Building, Berne.
1032 **233** 25 c. brown and blue . . 35 35
1033 – 80 c. brown & chestnut 1·50 1·50
DESIGN—VERT: 80 c. Similar to Type **233** but with larger U.P.U. monument.

234 "The First Consul" (Vien)

1970. Birth Bicentenary of Napoleon Bonaparte. Multicoloured.
1034 3 c. Type **234** 20 10
1035 5 c. "Napoleon visiting school" (unknown artist) 30 15
1036 10 c. "Napoleon Bonaparte" (detail, Isabey) 35 15
1037 12 c. "The French Campaign" (Meissonier) 40 20
1038 20 c. "The Abdication" (Bouchot) 50 30
1039 25 c. "Meeting of Napoleon and Pope Pius VII" (Demarne) 60 35
Design of 10 c. is incorrectly attributed to Gerard on the stamp.

235 Pres. Tubman

1970. Pres. Tubman's 75th Birthday.
1041 **235** 25 c. multicoloured . . 35 25

236 "Adoration of the Magi" (Van der Weyden)

1970. Christmas. "The Adoration of the Magi" by artists as below. Multicoloured.
1043 3 c. Type **236** 10 10
1044 5 c. H. Memling 15 10
1045 10 c. S. Lochner 25 15
1046 12 c. A. Altdorfer (vert) . . 30 15
1047 20 c. H. van der Goes . . . 35 15
1048 25 c. H. Bosch (vert) 40 30

237 Bapende Mask

239 Pres. Tubman and Women at Ballot Box

238 Astronauts on Moon

1971. African Ceremonial Masks. Masks from different tribes. Multicoloured.
1050 2 c. Type **237** 10 10
1051 3 c. Dogon 15 10
1052 5 c. Baoule 15 15
1053 6 c. Dedougou 20 15
1054 9 c. Dan 25 15
1055 15 c. Bamileke 30 20
1056 20 c. Bapende (different) . . 40 30
1057 25 c. Bamileke costume . . 60 30

1971. "Apollo 14". Moon Mission. Multicoloured.
1058 3 c. Type **238** 15 10
1059 5 c. Astronaut and Moon vehicle 15 10
1060 10 c. Erecting U.S. flag on Moon 20 10
1061 12 c. Splashdown 40 15
1062 20 c. Astronauts leaving capsule 45 15
1063 25 c. "Apollo 14" crew . . . 60 20

1971. 25th Anniv of Liberian Women's Suffrage.
1065 **239** 3 c. blue and brown . . 15 30
1066 – 80 c. brown and green . 1·50 1·50
DESIGN—HORIZ: 80 c. Pres. Tubman, women and map.

240 Hall of Honour, Munich

1971. Olympic Games, Munich (1972) (1st issue). Views of Munich. Multicoloured.
1067 3 c. Type **240** 15 10
1068 5 c. View of central Munich 15 10
1069 10 c. National Museum . . . 20 10
1070 12 c. Max Joseph's Square . . 25 10
1071 20 c. Propylaen, King's Square 40 15
1072 25 c. Liesel-Karistadt Fountain 60 20

241 American Scout

242 Pres. William Tubman

1971. World Scout Jamboree, Asagiri, Japan. Scouts in national uniforms. Multicoloured.
1074 3 c. Type **241** 15 10
1075 5 c. West Germany 15 10
1076 10 c. Australia 20 15
1077 12 c. Great Britain 25 15
1078 20 c. Japan 40 20
1079 25 c. Liberia 60 30

1971. Pres. Tubman Memorial Issue.
1081 **242** 3 c. brown, blue & black 10 10
1082 25 c. brown, pur & blk 35 35

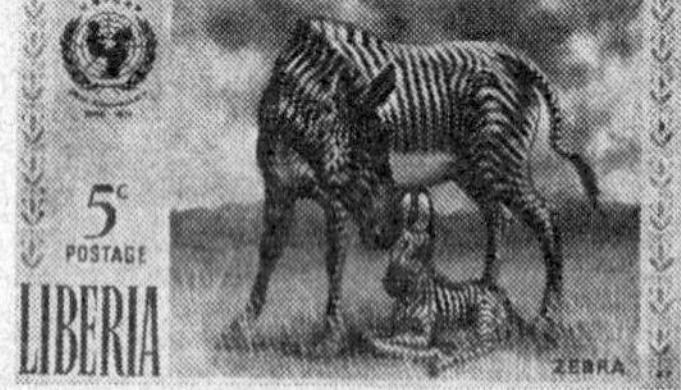

243 Common Zebra and Foal

1971. 25th Anniv of U.N.I.C.E.F. Animals with young. Multicoloured.
1083 5 c. Type **243** 20 10
1084 7 c. Koalas 30 15
1085 8 c. Guanaco 35 15
1086 10 c. Red fox and cubs . . . 45 15
1087 20 c. Savanna monkeys . . . 65 25
1088 25 c. Brown bears 90 35

244 Cross-country Skiing and Sika Deer

1971. Winter Olympic Games, Sapporo, Japan. Sports and Hokkaido Animals. Multicoloured.
1090 2 c. Type **244** 10 10
1091 3 c. Tobogganing and black woodpecker 70 15
1092 5 c. Ski-jumping and Brown bear 15 10
1093 10 c. Bob-sleighing and common guillemots . . . . 1·00 15
1094 15 c. Figure-skating and Northern pika 30 20
1095 25 c. Slalom-skiing and Manchurian cranes . . . . 2·00 45

245 A.P.U. Emblem, Dove and Letter

1971. 10th Anniv of African Postal Union.
1097 **245** 25 c. orange and blue . . 35 50
1098 80 c. brown and grey . . 1·60 1·50

246 "Elizabeth" (emigrant ship) at Providence Island

1972. 150th Anniv of Liberia.
1099 **246** 3 c. green and blue . . . 50 50
1100 – 20 c. blue and orange . . 35 20
1101 **246** 25 c. purple & orange . . 1·50 55
1102 – 35 c. purple and green . . 60 40
DESIGNS—VERT: 20 c., 35 c. Arms and Founding Fathers Monument, Monrovia.

247 Pres. Tolbert and Map

1972. Inaug of Pres. Wm. R. Tolbert Jnr.
1104 **247** 25 c. brown and green . 35 25
1105 – 80 c. brown and blue . . 1·60 80
DESIGN—VERT: 80 c. Pres. Tolbert standing by desk.

248 Football

1972. Olympic Games, Munich (2nd issue). Multicoloured.
1106 3 c. Type **248** 10 10
1107 5 c. Swimming 15 10
1108 10 c. Show-jumping 25 10
1109 12 c. Cycling 30 15
1110 20 c. Long-jumping 45 20
1111 25 c. Running 60 25

249 Globe and Emblem

251 Emperor Haile Selassie

250 Astronaut and Moon Rover

1972. 50th Anniv of Int Y's Men's Clubs.
1113 **249** 15 c. violet and gold . . 40 15
1114 – 90 c. green and blue . . 1·75 1·75
DESIGN: 90 c. Club emblem on World Map.

1972. Moon Mission of "Apollo 16". Mult.
1115 3 c. Type **250** 10 10
1116 5 c. Reflection on visor . . . 10 10
1117 10 c. Astronauts with cameras 15 10
1118 12 c. Setting up equipment . 20 15
1119 20 c. "Apollo 16" emblem . 40 20
1120 25 c. Astronauts in Moon Rover 50 50

1972. Emperor Haile Selassie of Ethiopia's 80th Birthday.
1122 **251** 20 c. green and yellow . 40 30
1123 25 c. purple & yellow . 45 40
1124 35 c. brown & yellow . . 60 60

252 H.M.S. "Ajax" (ship of the line), 1809

1972. Famous Ships of the British Royal Navy. Multicoloured.
1125 3 c. Type **252** 35 25
1126 5 c. H.M.S. "Hogue" (screw ship of the line), 1848 . . 65 25
1127 7 c. H.M.S. "Ariadne" (frigate), 1816 . . . . 85 30
1128 15 c. H.M.S. "Royal Adelaide" (ship of the line), 1828 . . 1·00 55
1129 20 c. H.M.S. "Rinaldo" (screw sloop), 1860 . . . . . 1·40 70
1130 25 c. H.M.S. "Nymphe" (screw sloop), 1888 . . . . . . 1·90 1·00

253 Pres. Tolbert taking Oath

1972. First Year President Tolbert Presidency.

1132 **253** 15 c. multicoloured . . . 35 15
1133 25 c. multicoloured . . . 70 70

254 Klaus Dibiasi and Italian Flag

1973. Olympic Games, Munich. Gold-medal Winners. Multicoloured.

1135 5 c. Type **254** 10 10
1136 8 c. Borzov and Soviet flag 15 10
1137 10 c. Yanagida and Japanese flag 15 10
1138 12 c. Spitz and U.S. flag . . 20 15
1139 15 c. Keino and Kenyan flag 25 15
1140 25 c. Meade and Union Jack 35 25

255 Astronaut on Moon

1973. Moon Flight of "Apollo 17". Multicoloured.

1142 2 c. Type **255** 10 10
1143 3 c. Testing lunar rover at Cape Kennedy 10 10
1144 10 c. Collecting Moon rocks 15 10
1145 15 c. Lunar rover on Moon 20 15
1146 20 c. "Apollo 17" crew at Cape Kennedy 30 20
1147 25 c. Astronauts on Moon . 35 25

256 British G.W.R. Locomotive

1973. Historical Railways. Steam locomotives of 1895-1905. Multicoloured.

1149 2 c. Type **256** 20 10
1150 3 c. Holland 30 10
1151 10 c. France 55 15
1152 15 c. U.S.A. 75 20
1153 20 c. Japan . . . . 1·60 25
1154 25 c. Germany . . . . . . 2·50 30

257 O.A.U. Emblem

1973. 10th Anniv of Organization of African Unity.

1156 **257** 3 c. multicoloured . . . 10 10
1157 5 c. multicoloured . . . 10 10
1158 10 c. multicoloured . . . 15 10
1159 15 c. multicoloured . . . 20 15
1160 25 c. multicoloured . . . 35 25
1161 50 c. multicoloured . . . 70 70

258 Edward Jenner and Roses

1973. 25th Anniv of W.H.O. Multicoloured.

1162 1 c. Type **258** 15 10
1163 4 c. Sigmund Freud and violets 15 10
1164 10 c. Jonas Salk and chrysanthemums 25 10
1165 15 c. Louis Pasteur and scabious 40 15
1166 20 c. Emil von Behring and mallow 45 20
1167 25 c. Sir Alexander Fleming and rhododendrons 85 25

259 Stanley Steamer, 1910

1973. Vintage Cars. Multicoloured.

1169 2 c. Type **259** 10 10
1170 3 c. Cadillac Model A, 1903 10 10
1171 10 c. Clement-Baynard, 1904 15 10
1172 15 c. Rolls-Royce Silver Ghost tourer, 1907 . . . . 25 15
1173 20 c. Maxwell gentleman's speedster, 1905 . . . . . 35 20
1174 25 c. Chadwick, 1907 . . . 50 25

260 Copernicus, Armillary Sphere and Satellite Communications System

1973. 500th Birth Anniv of Copernicus. Mult.

1176 1 c. Type **260** 10 10
1177 4 c. Eudoxus solar system . 10 10
1178 10 c. Aristotle, Ptolemy and Copernicus 15 10
1179 15 c. "Saturn" and "Apollo" spacecraft 25 15
1180 20 c. Astronomical observatory satellite 35 20
1181 25 c. Satellite tracking-station 50 25

261 Radio Mast and Map of Africa

1974. 20th Anniv of "Eternal Love Winning Africa". Radio Station. Multicoloured.

1183 13 c. Type **261** 25 25
1184 15 c. Radio Mast and map of Liberia 35 25
1185 17 c. Type **261** 35 50
1186 25 c. As 15 c. 50 40

262 "Thomas Coutts" (full-rigged sailing ship) and "Aureol" (liner)

1974. Cent of U.P.U. Multicoloured.

1187 2 c. Type **262** 20 10
1188 3 c. Boeing 707 airliner and liner, satellite and Monrovia Post Office 30 10
1189 10 c. U.S. and Soviet Telecommunications satellites 15 10
1190 15 c. Postal runner and Boeing 707 airliner 25 20
1191 20 c. British Rail High-speed Train and Liberian mail-van 55 25
1192 25 c. American Pony Express rider 50 35

263 Fox Terrier

1974. Dogs. Multicoloured.

1194 5 c. Type **263** 15 10
1195 10 c. Boxer 20 10
1196 16 c. Chihuahua 30 15
1197 19 c. Beagle 35 20
1198 25 c. Golden retriever 40 25
1199 50 c. Collie 75 50

264 West Germany v. Chile Match

1974. World Cup Football Championships, West Germany. Scenes from semi-final matches. Multicoloured.

1201 1 c. Type **264** 10 10
1202 2 c. Australia v. East Germany 10 10
1203 5 c. Brazil v. Yugoslavia . . . 15 10
1204 10 c. Zaire v. Scotland . . . 20 10
1205 12 c. Netherlands v. Uruguay 25 15
1206 15 c. Sweden v. Bulgaria . . . 30 15
1207 20 c. Italy v. Haiti 40 20
1208 25 c. Poland v. Argentina . . 60 25

265 "Chrysiridia madagascariensis"

1974. Tropical Butterflies. Multicoloured.

1210 1 c. Type **265** 10 10
1211 2 c. "Catagramma sorana" . 10 10
1212 5 c. "Erasmia pulchella" . . . 20 10
1213 17 c. "Morpho cypris" . . . 50 25
1214 25 c. "Agrias amydon" . . . 70 35
1215 40 c. "Vanessa cardui" . . . 1·40 45

266 Pres. Tolbert and Gold Medallion

1974. "Family of Man" Award to President Tolbert. Multicoloured.

1217 3 c. Type **266** 10 25
1218 $1 Pres. Tolbert, medallion and flag . . . . 1·40 1·40

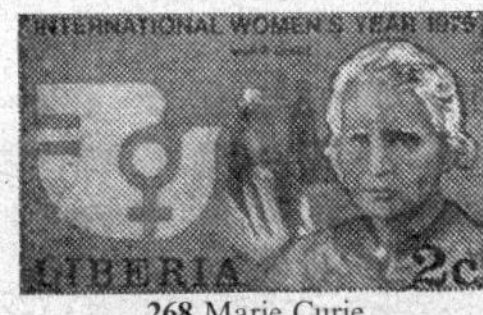

267 Churchill with Troops

1974. Birth Centenary of Sir Winston Churchill. Multicoloured.

1219 3 c. Type **267** 10 10
1220 10 c. Churchill and aerial combat 30 10
1221 15 c. Churchill aboard "Liberty" ship in Channel 55 15
1222 17 c. Churchill reviewing troops in desert 30 15
1223 20 c. Churchill crossing Rhine 40 20
1224 25 c. Churchill with Roosevelt 50 25

268 Marie Curie

1978. International Women's Year. Multicoloured.

1226 2 c. Type **268** 10 10
1227 3 c. Mahalia Jackson 10 10
1228 5 c. Joan of Arc 10 10
1229 10 c. Eleanor Roosevelt . . . 15 10
1230 25 c. Matilda Newport . . . 50 25
1231 50 c. Valentina Tereshkova 70 55

269 Old State House, Boston, and U.S. 2 c. "Liberty Bell" Stamp of 1926

1975. Bicentenary of American Independence.

1233 5 c. Type **269** 15 10
1234 10 c. George Washington and 1928 "Valley Forge" stamp 30 10
1235 15 c. Philadelphia and 1937 "Constitution" stamp . . 45 15
1236 20 c. Benjamin Franklin and 1938 "Ratification" stamp 50 15
1237 25 c. Paul Revere's Ride and 1925 "Lexington-Concord" stamp 70 20
1238 50 c. "Santa Maria" and 1893 "Columbus' Landing" stamp 2·00 55

270 Dr. Schweitzer, Yellow Baboon and Lambarene Hospital

1975. Birth Centenary of Dr Albert Schweitzer. Multicoloured.

1240 1 c. Type **270** 10 10
1241 3 c. Schweitzer, African elephant and canoe 15 10
1242 5 c. Schweitzer, African buffalo and canoe . . . . 1·25 20
1243 6 c. Schweitzer, kob and dancer 30 10
1244 25 c. Schweitzer, lioness and village woman 75 25
1245 50 c. Schweitzer, common zebras and clinic scene . . 1·40 65

271 "Apollo" Spacecraft

1975. "Apollo-Soyuz" Space Link. Multicoloured.

1247 5 c. Type **271** 10 10
1248 10 c. "Soyuz" spacecraft . . 15 10
1249 15 c. American-Russian hand-clasp 20 15
1250 20 c. Flags and maps of America and Russia . . . 25 15
1251 25 c. Leonov and Kubasov 35 20
1252 50 c. Slayton, Brand and Stafford 95 50

272 Presidents Tolbert and Stevens, and Signing Ceremony

1975. Liberia–Sierra Leone Mano River Union Agreement.

1254 **272** 2 c. multicoloured . . . 10 10
1255 3 c. multicoloured . . . 10 10
1256 5 c. multicoloured . . . 10 10
1257 10 c. multicoloured . . . 15 10
1258 25 c. multicoloured . . . 35 25
1259 50 c. multicoloured . . . 70 70

273 Figure Skating

1976. Winter Olympic Games, Innsbruck. Multicoloured.

1260 1 c. Type **273** 10 10
1261 4 c. Ski jumping 20 20
1262 10 c. Skiing (slalom) 30 20
1263 25 c. Ice hockey 60 30
1264 35 c. Speed skating 90 40
1265 50 c. Two-man bobsledding 1·25 65

274 Pres. Tolbert taking Oath

1976. Inauguration of President William R. Tolbert, Jr. Multicoloured.
1267 3 c. Type **274** 10 10
1268 25 c. Pres. Tolbert in Presidential Chair (vert) 35 25
1269 $1 Liberian crest, flat and commemorative gold coin 1·90 1·40

275 Weightlifting

1976. Olympic Games, Montreal. Multicoloured.
1270 2 c. Type **275** 10 10
1271 3 c. Pole-vaulting 10 10
1272 10 c. Hammer and shot-put 30 15
1273 25 c. Sailing 65 35
1274 35 c. Gymnastics 90 60
1275 50 c. Hurdling . . . . 1·25 65

276 Bell's Telephone and Receiver

1976. Telephone Centenary. Multicoloured.
1277 1 c. Type **276** 10 10
1278 4 c. Mail-coach 10 10
1279 5 c. "Intelsat 4" satellite . . 15 10
1280 25 c. Cable-ship "Dominia", 1926 . . . . 1·00 30
1281 40 c. Futuristic train . . . . 1·00 50
1282 50 c. Wright Flyer I, airship "Graf Zeppelin" and Concorde . . . . 1·75 60

277 Gold Nugget Pendant

1976. Liberian Products (1st series). Multicoloured.
1284 1 c. Mano River Bridge . . 10 10
1285 3 c. Type **277** 10 10
1286 5 c. "V" ring 10 10
1286a 7 c. As No. 1286 . . . . . 15 25
1287 10 c. Rubber tree and tyre 15 10
1287a 15 c. Combine harvester . . 20 10
1287b 17 c. As No. 1289 . . . . . 35 10
1287c 20 c. Hydro-electric plant . 30 15
1288 25 c. Mesurado shrimp . . . 35 25
1288a 27 c. Dress and woman tie-dying cloth 40 25
1289 55 c. Barracuda . . . . 1·10 35
1289a $1 Train carrying iron ore 1·10 25

For designs as Type **277** but in a smaller size, see Nos. 1505/8.

278 Black Rhinoceros

1976. Animals. Multicoloured.
1290 2 c. Type **278** 10 10
1291 3 c. Bongo 10 10
1292 5 c. Chimpanzee (vert) . . . 15 10
1293 15 c. Pygmy hippopotamus 40 15
1294 25 c. Leopard 80 40
1295 $1 Gorilla . . . . 3·00 90

279 Statue of Liberty and Unification Monument on Maps of U.S.A. and Liberia

1976. Bicentenary of American Revolution. Multicoloured.
1297 25 c. Type **279** 35 25
1298 $1 Presidents Washington and Ford (U.S.A.), Roberts and Tolbert (Liberia) . . . . . 1·40 1·25

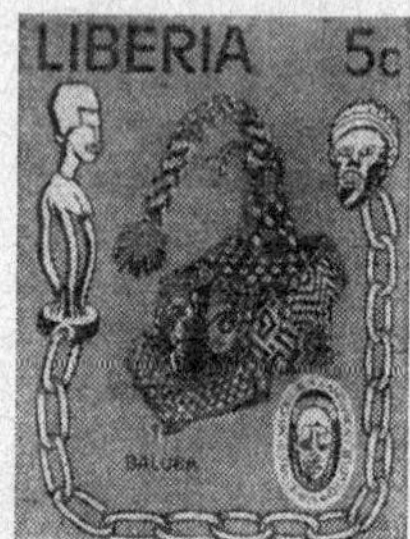

280 Baluba Masks

1977. Second World Black and African Festival of Arts and Culture, Lagos (Nigeria). Tribal Masks. Multicoloured.
1300 5 c. Type **280** 10 10
1301 10 c. Bateke 15 10
1302 15 c. Basshilele 20 15
1303 20 c. Igungun 30 15
1304 25 c. Maisi 35 20
1305 50 c. Kifwebe 70 45

281 Latham's Francolin

1977. Liberian Wild Birds. Multicoloured.
1307 5 c. Type **281** 65 10
1308 10 c. Narina trogon 95 15
1309 15 c. Rufous-crowned roller 95 20
1310 20 c. Brown-cheeked hornbill 1·00 25
1311 25 c. Common bulbul . . . 1·25 30
1312 50 c. African fish eagle . . . 2·40 80

282 Alwin Schockemohle (individual jumping)

1977. Olympic Games, Montreal. Equestrian Gold-medal Winners. Multicoloured.
1314 5 c. Edmund Coffin (military dressage) (postage) 15 10
1315 15 c. Type **282** 40 20
1316 20 c. Christine Stuckelberger (dressage) 50 30
1317 25 c. "Nations Prize" (French team) 70 35
1318 55 c. Military dressage (U.S.A. team) (air) . . . . 1·25 70

283 Queen Elizabeth II

1977. Silver Jubilee of Queen Elizabeth II. Multicoloured.
1320 15 c. Type **283** 35 15
1321 25 c. Queen Elizabeth and Prince Philip with President and Mrs. Tubman of Liberia 55 25
1322 80 c. Queen Elizabeth, Prince Philip and Royal Arms . . 2·40 70

284 "Blessing the Children"

1977. Christmas. Multicoloured.
1324 20 c. Type **284** 50 25
1325 25 c. "The Good Shepherd" 70 35
1326 $1 "Jesus and the Woman of Samaria at the Well" . . . 2·00 1·00

285 Dornier Do-X Flying Boat

1978. "Progress in Aviation". Multicoloured.
1327 2 c. Type **285** 10 10
1328 3 c. Space shuttle "Enterprise" on Boeing 747 . . . . . 10 10
1329 5 c. Edward Rickenbacker and Douglas DC-3 . . . . . 10 10
1330 25 c. Charles Lindbergh and "Spirit of St. Louis" . . . 45 20
1331 35 c. Louis Bleriot and Bleriot XI monoplane 65 35
1332 50 c. Wright Brothers and Flyer I 90 55

286 Santos-Dumont's Airship "Ballon No. 9 La Badaleuse", 1903

1978. 75th Anniv of First Zeppelin Flight. Multicoloured.
1334 2 c. Type **286** 10 10
1335 3 c. Thomas Baldwin's airship "U.S. Military No. 1", 1908 10 10
1336 5 c. Tissandier brothers' airship, 1883 . . . . 10 10
1337 25 c. Parseval airship PL-VII, 1912 . . . . 40 20
1338 40 c. Airship "Nulli Secundus II", 1908 . . . . 75 35
1339 50 c. Beardmore airship R-34, 1919 . . . . 85 55

287 Tackling **288** Coronation Chair

1978. World Cup Football Championship, Argentina.
1341 **287** 2 c. multicoloured 10 10
1342 – 3 c. mult (horiz) 10 10
1343 – 10 c. mult (horiz) 15 10
1344 – 25 c. mult (horiz) 35 20
1345 – 35 c. multicoloured . . . 50 25
1346 – 50 c. mult (horiz) . . . . 1·00 50

DESIGNS: Nos. 1342/6 Different match scenes.

1978. 25th Anniv of Coronation. Multicoloured.
1348 5 c. Type **288** 10 25
1349 25 c. Imperial State Crown . 35 25
1350 $1 Buckingham Palace (horiz) 1·40 1·00

289 Mohammed Ali Jinnah and Flags

1978. Birth Centenary of Mohammed Ali Jinnah (first Governor-General of Pakistan).
1352 **289** 30 c. multicoloured . . . 1·50 1·50

290 Carter and Tolbert Families

1978. Visit of President Carter of U.S.A. Mult.
1353 5 c. Type **290** 10 10
1354 25 c. Presidents Carter and Tolbert with Mrs. Carter at microphones 25 20
1355 $1 Presidents Carter and Tolbert in open car . . . . 1·40 1·40

291 Italy v. France **292** Timber Truck

1978. Argentina's Victory in World Cup Football Championship. Multicoloured.
1356 1 c. Brazil v. Spain (horiz) . 10 10
1357 2 c. Type **291** 10 10
1358 10 c. Poland v. West Germany (horiz) 15 10
1359 27 c. Peru v. Scotland . . . 40 25
1360 35 c. Austria v. West Germany 50 25
1361 50 c. Argentinian players with Cup . . . . 1·00 50

1978. 8th World Forestry Congress, Djakarta. Multicoloured.
1363 5 c. Chopping up log (horiz) 10 10
1364 10 c. Type **292** 15 10
1365 25 c. Felling trees (horiz) . . 25 20
1366 50 c. Loggers (horiz) 70 70

293 Presidents Gardner and Tolbert with Monrovia Post Office

1979. Centenary of U.P.U. Membership. Mult.
1367 5 c. Type **293** 10 10
1368 35 c. Presidents Gardner and Tolbert with U.P.U. emblem 50 65

294 "25" and Radio Waves

1979. 25th Anniv of Radio ELWA. Multicoloured.
1369 35 c. Type **294** 50 25
1370 $1 Radio tower . . . . . . 1·40 1·40

295 I.Y.C., Decade of the African Child and S.O.S. Villages Emblems

1979. International Year of the Child. Multicoloured.

1371 5 c. Type **295** 10 10
1372 25 c. As Type **295** but with UNICEF instead of S.O.S. Villages emblem 25 20
1373 35 c. Type **295** 50 25
1374 $1 As No. 1372 . . . . . . 1·40 1·40

296 Clasped Arms and Torches

1979. Organization for African Unity Summit Conference, Monrovia. Multicoloured.

1375 5 c. Type **296** 10 10
1376 27 c. Masks 40 25
1377 35 c. African animals 50 50
1378 50 c. Thatched huts and common bulbuls . . . . . 1·75 70

297 Sir Rowland Hill and Liberian 15 c. Stamp, 1974

1979. Death Centenary of Sir Rowland Hill. Multicoloured.

1379 3 c. Type **297** 10 10
1380 10 c. Pony Express rider . . . 15 10
1381 15 c. British mail coach . . . 20 35
1382 25 c. "John Penn" (paddle-steamer) 75 55
1383 27 c. Stanier Pacific locomotive 75 60
1384 50 c. Concorde . . . . 1·50 90

298 President Tolbert giving Blood

1979. National Red Cross Blood Donation Campaign. Multicoloured.

1386 30 c. Type **298** 45 25
1387 50 c. President Tolbert and Red Cross 70 70

299 "World Peace" (tanker)

1979. 2nd World Maritime Day and 30th Anniv of Liberia Maritime Programme. Multicoloured.

1388 5 c. Type **299** 30 15
1389 $1 "World Peace" (different) 2·25 2·00

300 "A Good Turn"

1979. Scout Paintings by Norman Rockwell. Multicoloured.

1390 5 c. Scout giving first aid to pup ("A Good Scout") 20 15
1391 5 c. Type **300** 20 15
1392 5 c. "Good Friends" 20 15
1393 5 c. "Spirit of America" . . . 20 15
1394 5 c. "Scout Memories" . . . 20 15
1395 5 c. "The Adventure Trail" 20 15
1396 5 c. "On My Honour" . . . 20 15
1397 5 c. "A Scout is Reverent" . 20 15
1398 5 c. "The Right Way" . . . 20 15
1399 5 c. "The Scoutmaster" . . . 20 15
1400 10 c. "A Scout is Loyal" . . 35 20
1401 10 c. "An Army of Friendship" 35 20
1402 10 c. "Carry on" 35 20
1403 10 c. "A Good Scout" . . . 35 20
1404 10 c. "The Campfire Story" 35 20
1405 10 c. "High Adventure" . . 35 20
1406 10 c. "Mighty Proud" . . . 35 20
1407 10 c. "Tomorrow's Leader" 35 20
1408 10 c. "Ever Onward" . . . 35 20
1409 10 c. "Homecoming" . . . 35 20
1410 15 c. "Scouts of Many Trails" 40 25
1411 15 c. "America builds for Tomorrow" 40 25
1412 15 c. "The Scouting Trail" . 40 25
1413 15 c. "A Scout is Reverent" 40 25
1414 15 c. "A Scout is Helpful" . 40 25
1415 15 c. "Pointing the Way" . . 40 25
1416 15 c. "A Good Sign All Over the World" 40 25
1417 15 c. "To Keep Myself Physically Strong" 40 25
1418 15 c. "A Great Moment" . . 40 25
1419 15 c. "Growth of a Leader" 40 25
1420 25 c. "A Scout is Loyal" . . 60 35
1421 25 c. "A Scout is Friendly" 60 35
1422 25 c. "We Too, Have a Job to Do" 60 35
1423 25 c. "I Will do my Best" . 60 35
1424 25 c. "A Guiding Hand" . . 60 35
1425 25 c. "Breakthrough for Freedom" 60 35
1426 25 c. "Scouting is Outing" . 60 35
1427 25 c. "Beyond the Easel" . . 60 35
1428 25 c. "Come and Get It" . . 60 35
1429 25 c. "America's Manpower begins with Boypower" . . 60 35
1430 35 c. "All Together" 80 45
1431 35 c. "Men of Tomorrow" . 80 45
1432 35 c. "Friend in Need" . . . 80 45
1433 35 c. "Our Heritage" 80 45
1434 35 c. "Forward America" . 80 45
1435 35 c. "Can't Wait" 80 45
1436 35 c. "From Concord to Tranquility" 80 45
1437 35 c. "We Thank Thee" . . 80 45
1438 35 c. "So Much Concern" . . 80 45
1439 35 c. "Spirit of '76" 80 45

301 Mrs. Tolbert and Children

1979. S.O.S. Children's Village, Monrovia. Multicoloured.

1440 25 c. Mrs. Tolbert and children (different) (horiz) 35 50
1441 40 c. Type **301** 60 50

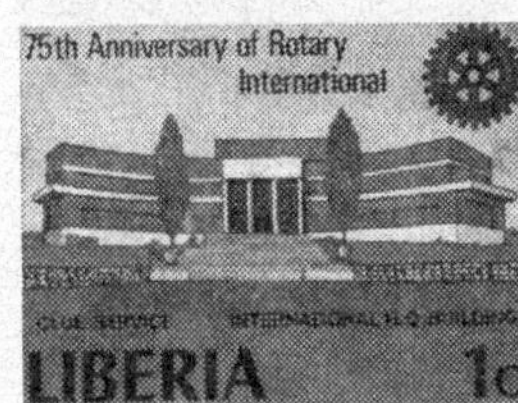

302 International Headquarters, Evanston, Illinois

1979. 75th Anniv of Rotary International. Multicoloured.

1442 1 c. Type **302** 10 10
1443 5 c. Vocational services . . . 10 10
1444 17 c. Wheelchair patient and nurse (community service) (vert) 20 35
1445 27 c. Flags (international service) 40 50
1446 35 c. Different races holding hands around globe (health, hunger and humanity) . . 50 50
1447 50 c. President Tolbert and map of Africa (17th anniv of Monrovia Rotary Club) (vert) 1·00 1·00

303 Ski Jumping

1980. Winter Olympic Games, Lake Placid. Multicoloured.

1449 1 c. Type **303** 10 10
1450 5 c. Pairs figure skating . . 10 10
1451 17 c. Bobsleigh 20 35
1452 27 c. Cross-country skiing . 50 50
1453 35 c. Speed skating 50 50
1454 50 c. Ice hockey . . . . . . 1·00 1·00

304 Presidents Tolbert of Liberia and Stevens of Sierra Leone and View of Mano River

1980. 5th Anniv of Mano River Union and 1st Anniv (1979) of Postal Union.

1456 **304** 8 c. multicoloured 10 10
1457 27 c. multicoloured . . . 40 50
1458 35 c. multicoloured . . . 50 50
1459 80 c. multicoloured . . . 1·50 1·50

305 Redemption Horn

1981. People's Redemption Council (1st series). Multicoloured.

1460 1 c. Type **305** 10 10
1461 10 c. M/Sgt. Doe and allegory of redemption (horiz) . . . 10 10
1462 14 c. Map, soldier and citizens (horiz) 15 15
1463 $2 M/Sgt. Samuel Doe (chairman of Council) . . . 3·75 3·75

See also Nos. 1475/8.

306 Players and Flags of Argentine, Uruguay, Italy and Czechoslovakia

1981. World Cup Football Championships, Spain (1982). Multicoloured.

1464 3 c. Type **306** 10 10
1465 5 c. Players and flags of Hungary, Italy, Germany, Brazil and Sweden 10 10
1466 20 c. Players and flags of Italy, Germany, Brazil and Sweden 20 20
1467 27 c. Players and flags of Czechoslovakia, Brazil, Great Britain and Germany . . . 25 25
1468 40 c. Players and flags of Italy, Brazil, Germany and Netherlands 60 60
1469 55 c. Players and flags of Netherlands and Uruguay 80 80

307 M/Sgt. Doe and Crowd

1981. 1st Anniv of People's Redemption Council. Multicoloured.

1471 22 c. Type **307** 20 20
1472 27 c. M/Sgt. Doe and national flag 25 25
1473 30 c. Hands clasping arms, sunrise and map 45 45
1474 $1 M/Sgt. Doe, "Justice" and soldiers . . . . 1·40 1·40

1981. People's Redemption Council (2nd series).

1475 6 c. Type **305** 10 10
1476 23 c. As No. 1461 . . . . . 20 20
1477 31 c. As No. 1462 . . . . . 45 45
1478 41 c. As No. 1463 . . . . . 60 60

MINIMUM PRICE

The minimum price quoted is 10p which represents a handling charge rather than a basis for valuing common stamps. For further notes about prices, see introductory pages.

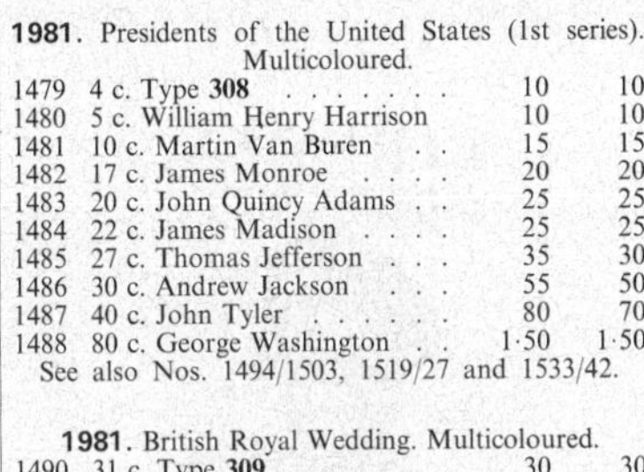

308 John Adams **309** Prince Charles and Lady Diana Spencer

1981. Presidents of the United States (1st series). Multicoloured.

1479 4 c. Type **308** 10 10
1480 5 c. William Henry Harrison 10 10
1481 10 c. Martin Van Buren . . 15 15
1482 17 c. James Monroe 20 20
1483 20 c. John Quincy Adams . . 25 25
1484 22 c. James Madison 25 25
1485 27 c. Thomas Jefferson . . . 35 30
1486 30 c. Andrew Jackson . . . 55 50
1487 40 c. John Tyler 80 70
1488 80 c. George Washington . . 1·50 1·50

See also Nos. 1494/1503, 1519/27 and 1533/42.

1981. British Royal Wedding. Multicoloured.

1490 31 c. Type **309** 30 30
1491 41 c. Intertwined initials . . 40 40
1492 62 c. St. Paul's Cathedral . . 60 60

1981. Presidents of the United States (2nd series). As T **308**. Multicoloured.

1494 6 c. Rutherford B. Hayes . . 10 10
1495 12 c. Ulysses S. Grant . . . 15 15
1496 14 c. Millard Fillmore . . . 20 15
1497 15 c. Zachary Taylor 20 15
1498 20 c. Abraham Lincoln . . . 25 20
1499 27 c. Andrew Johnson . . . 30 25
1500 31 c. James Buchanan . . . 50 45
1501 41 c. James A. Garfield . . . 70 60
1502 50 c. James K. Polk 80 70
1503 55 c. Franklin Pierce . . . . 1·00 85

1981. Liberian Products (2nd series). As T **277**, but smaller, 33 × 20 mm. Multicoloured.

1504a 1 c. Mano River Bridge . . 10 10
1505 3 c. Type **277** 10 10
1506 6 c. Rubber tree and tyre . . 10 10
1506a 15 c. Combine harvester . . 20 15
1507 25 c. Mesurado shrimp . . 35 35
1508 31 c. Hydro-electric plant . 45 45
1509 41 c. Dress and woman tie-dying cloth 60 55
1509a 80 c. Barracuda . . . . . . 1·90 1·50
1510 $1 Diesel train carrying iron ore . . . . 2·50 1·50

310 Disabled Children **312** Lady Diana Spencer

311 Examination Room

1982. International Year of Disabled People (1981). Multicoloured.

1515 23 c. Type **310** 35 35
1516 62 c. Child leading blind woman 1·25 95

1982. 30th Anniv of West African Examination Council.

1517 **311** 6 c. multicoloured . . . 10 10
1518 31 c. multicoloured . . . 45 45

1982. Presidents of the United States (3rd series). As T **308**. Multicoloured.

1519 4 c. William Taft 10 25
1520 5 c. Calvin Coolidge 10 10
1521 6 c. Benjamin Harrison . . 15 15
1522 10 c. Warren Harding . . . 20 25
1523 22 c. Grover Cleveland . . . 45 45
1524 27 c. Chester Arthur 50 70
1525 31 c. Woodrow Wilson . . . 60 60
1526 41 c. William McKinley . . 70 80
1527 80 c. Theodore Roosevelt . . 1·50 1·60

1982. Princess of Wales. 21st Birthday. Mult.

1529 31 c. Type **312** 45 45
1530 41 c. Lady Diana Spencer (different) 60 60
1531 62 c. Lady Diana accepting flower . . . . 1·25 1·25

1982. Presidents of the United States (4th series). As T **308**. Multicoloured.

No.	Description		
1533	4 c. Jimmy Carter	10	10
1534	6 c. Gerald Ford	15	15
1535	14 c. Harry Truman	25	25
1536	17 c. Franklin D. Roosevelt	30	30
1537	23 c. Lyndon B. Johnson	40	40
1538	27 c. Richard Nixon	45	50
1539	31 c. John F. Kennedy	50	60
1540	35 c. Ronald Reagan	60	80
1541	50 c. Herbert Hoover	80	90
1542	55 c. Dwight D. Eisenhower	1·00	1·00

1982. Birth of Prince William of Wales. Nos. 1529/31 optd **ROYAL BABY 21-6-82 PRINCE WILLIAM.**

No.	Description		
1544	31 c. Type **312**	45	45
1545	41 c. Lady Diana Spencer (different)	60	60
1546	62 c. Lady Diana accepting flower	95	95

314 Lt. Col. Fallah nGaida Varney

1983. 3rd Anniv of National Redemption Day. Multicoloured.

No.	Description		
1548	3 c. Type **314**	10	10
1549	6 c. Commander-in-Chief Samuel Doe	10	10
1550	10 c. Major-General Jlatoh Nicholas Podier	15	15
1551	15 c. Brigadier-General Jeffery Sei Gbatu	20	15
1552	31 c. Brigadier-General Thomas Gunkama Quiwonkpa	50	45
1553	41 c. Colonel Abraham Doward Kollie	60	80

315 National Archives Centre

1983. Opening of National Archives Centre. Multicoloured.

No.	Description		
1555	6 c. Type **315**	10	10
1556	31 c. National Archives Centre	50	45

316 "Circumcision of Christ"

1983. Christmas. 500th Birth Anniv of Raphael. Multicoloured.

No.	Description		
1557	6 c. Type **316**	10	10
1558	15 c. "Adoration of the Magi" (detail)	20	15
1559	25 c. "The Annunciation" (detail)	40	35
1560	31 c. "Madonna of the Baldachino"	50	45
1561	41 c. "Holy Family" (detail)	60	55
1562	62 c. "Madonna and Child with Five Saints" (detail)	90	85

317 Graduates of M.U.R. Training Programmes

1984. 10th Anniv (1983) of Mano River Union. Multicoloured.

No.	Description		
1564	6 c. Type **317**	10	10
1565	25 c. Map of Africa	40	35
1566	31 c. Presidents and map of member states	50	45
1567	41 c. President of Guinea signing Accession Agreement	70	85

318 Redemption Day Hospital, New Kru Town

1984. 4th Anniv of National Redemption Day. Multicoloured.

No.	Description		
1569	3 c. Type **318**	10	10
1570	10 c. Ganta-Harpa Highway project	15	15
1571	20 c. Opening of Constitution Assembly	35	30
1572	31 c. Commander-in-Chief Doe launching Ganta-Harper Highway project	50	45
1573	41 c. Presentation of Draft Constitution	70	85

319 "Adoration of the Magi"

1984. Rubens Paintings (1st series). Multicoloured.

No.	Description		
1574	6 c. Type **319**	10	10
1575	15 c. "Coronation of Catherine"	25	20
1576	25 c. "Adoration of the Magi"	70	70
1577	31 c. "Madonna and Child with Halo"	85	85
1578	41 c. "Adoration of the Shepherds"	1·10	1·10
1579	62 c. "Madonna and Child with Saints"	1·75	1·75

See also Nos. 1612/17.

320 Jesse Owens

1984. Olympic Games, Los Angeles. Multicoloured.

No.	Description		
1581	3 c. Type **320**	10	10
1582	4 c. Rafer Johnson	10	10
1583	25 c. Miruts Yifter	65	65
1584	41 c. Kipchoge Keino	1·10	1·10
1585	62 c. Muhammad Ali	1·75	1·75

321 Liberian Ducks and Water Birds

1984. Louisiana World Exposition. Multicoloured.

No.	Description		
1587	6 c. Type **321**	1·25	30
1588	31 c. Bulk carrier loading ore at Buchanan Harbour	1·25	75
1589	41 c. Liberian fishes	1·10	1·10
1590	62 c. Diesel train carrying iron ore	1·75	1·75

322 Mother and Calf

1984. Pygmy Hippopotami. Multicoloured.

No.	Description		
1591	6 c. Type **322**	20	10
1592	10 c. Pair of hippopotami	30	15
1593	20 c. Close-up of hippopotamus	70	35
1594	31 c. Hippopotamus and map	1·00	50

323 Mrs. Doe and Children

1984. Indigent Children's Home, Bensonville. Multicoloured.

No.	Description		
1595	6 c. Type **323**	10	10
1596	31 c. Mrs. Doe and children (different)	85	85

324 New Soldiers' Barracks

1985. 5th Anniv of National Redemption Day. Multicoloured.

No.	Description		
1597	6 c. Type **324**	10	10
1598	31 c. Pan-African Plaza	85	85

325 Bohemian Waxwing

1985. Birth Bicentenary of John J. Audubon (ornithologist). Multicoloured.

No.	Description		
1599	1 c. Type **325**	15	10
1600	3 c. Bay-breasted warbler	30	10
1601	6 c. White-winged crossbill	35	15
1602	31 c. Grey phalarope	1·90	85
1603	41 c. Eastern bluebird	2·50	1·25
1604	62 c. Common cardinal	3·50	2·00

326 Germany v. Morocco, 1970

1985. World Cup Football Championship, Mexico (1986). Multicoloured.

No.	Description		
1605	6 c. Type **326**	10	10
1606	15 c. Zaire v. Brazil, 1974	20	15
1607	25 c. Tunisia v. Germany, 1978	60	60
1608	31 c. Cameroun v. Peru, 1982 (vert)	75	75
1609	41 c. Algeria v. Germany, 1982	95	95
1610	62 c. Senegal team	1·40	1·40

327 "Mirror of Venus" (detail)

328 Women transplanting Rice

1985. Rubens Paintings (2nd series). Mult.

No.	Description		
1612	6 c. Type **327**	10	10
1613	15 c. "Adam and Eve in Paradise" (detail)	20	15
1614	25 c. "Andromeda" (detail)	60	60
1615	31 c. "The Three Graces" (detail)	75	75
1616	41 c. "Venus and Adonis" (detail)	95	95
1617	62 c. "The Daughters of Leucippus" (detail)	1·40	1·40

1985. World Food Day.

No.	Description		
1619	**328** 25 c. multicoloured	1·25	85
1620	31 c. multicoloured	1·50	1·10

329 Queen Mother in Garter Robes

330 Alamo, San Antonio, Texas

1985. 85th Birthday of Queen Elizabeth the Queen Mother. Multicoloured.

No.	Description		
1621	31 c. Type **329**	35	30
1622	41 c. At the races	55	50
1623	62 c. Waving to the crowds	80	70

1986. "Ameripex '86" International Stamp Exhibition, Chicago. Multicoloured.

No.	Description		
1625	25 c. Type **330**	60	60
1626	31 c. Liberty Bell, Philadelphia	75	75
1627	80 c. Magnifying glass, emblem and Liberian stamps	1·90	1·90

331 Unveiling Ceremony, 1886 (after E. Moran)

333 Royal Theatre. Gendarmenmarkt

332 Max Julen (Men's Giant Slalom)

1986. Centenary of Statue of Liberty. Multicoloured.

No.	Description		
1628	20 c. Type **331**	30	50
1629	31 c. Frederic-Auguste Bartholdi (sculptor) and statue	75	75
1630	$1 Head of statue	2·40	2·40

1987. Winter Olympic Games, Calgary (1988). 1984 Games Gold Medallists. Multicoloured.

No.	Description		
1631	3 c. Type **332**	10	10
1632	6 c. Debbi Armstrong (women's giant slalom)	10	10
1633	31 c. Peter Angerer (biathlon)	35	55
1634	60 c. Bill Johnson (men's downhill)	1·10	1·10
1635	80 c. East German team (four-man bobsleigh)	1·40	1·40

1987. Liberian–German Friendship. 750th Anniv of Berlin. Multicoloured.

No.	Description		
1637	6 c. Type **333**	10	10
1638	31 c. Kaiser Friedrich Museum, River Spree	35	55
1639	60 c. Charlottenburg Palace	1·10	1·10
1640	80 c. Kaiser Wilhelm Memorial Church	1·40	1·40

334 Othello and Desdemona ("Othello")

1987. William Shakespeare. Multicoloured.

No.	Description		
1642	3 c. Type **334**	10	10
1643	6 c. Romeo and Juliet ("Romeo and Juliet")	10	10
1644	10 c. Falstaff ("The Merry Wives of Windsor")	15	10
1645	15 c. Falstaff, Doll Tearsheet and Prince Hal ("Henry IV", Part 2)	20	15
1646	31 c. Hamlet holding Yorick's skull ("Hamlet")	35	50
1647	60 c. Macbeth and the three witches ("Macbeth")	1·00	1·00
1648	80 c. Lear and companions in the storm ("King Lear")	1·40	1·40
1649	$2 William Shakespeare and Globe Theatre, Southwark	3·25	3·25

335 Emblem

1987. Amateur Radio Week. 25th Anniv of Liberia Radio Amateur Association. Multicoloured.

1650 10 c. Type **335** 15 10
1651 10 c. Amateur radio enthusiasts 15 10
1652 35 c. Certificate awarded to participants in anniversary "On the Air" activity 40 30
1653 35 c. Globe, flags and banner 40 30

336 Illuminated Torch Flame

1987. Centenary of Statue of Liberty. Multicoloured.

1654 6 c. Type **336** 10 10
1655 6 c. Scaffolding around statue's head 10 10
1656 6 c. Men working on head 10 10
1657 6 c. Men working on crown 10 10
1658 6 c. Statue's toes 10 10
1659 15 c. Statue behind "Sir Winston Churchill" (cadet schooner) 35 20
1660 15 c. "Bay Queen" (harbour ferry) 35 20
1661 15 c. Posters on buildings and crowd 20 15
1662 15 c. Tug and schooner in bay 35 20
1663 15 c. Decorated statues around building 20 15
1664 31 c. Fireworks display around statue 35 25
1665 31 c. Statue floodlit 35 25
1666 31 c. Statue's head 35 25
1667 31 c. Fireworks display around statue (different) 35 25
1668 31 c. Statue (half-length) 35 25
1669 60 c. Wall poster on building (vert) 70 85
1670 60 c. Yachts and cabin cruisers on river (vert) 1·25 75
1671 60 c. Measuring statue's nose (vert) 70 85
1672 60 c. Plastering nose (vert) 70 85
1673 60 c. Finishing off repaired nose (vert) 70 85

337 Dr. Doe (President), Dr. Moniba (Vice-President), Flags and Hands

1988. 2nd Anniv of Second Republic.

1674 **337** 10 c. multicoloured 15 10
1675 35 c. multicoloured 40 30

338 Breast-feeding

1988. U.N.I.C.E.F. Child Survival and Development Campaign. Multicoloured.

1676 3 c. Type **338** 10 10
1677 6 c. Oral rehydration therapy (vert) 10 10
1678 31 c. Immunization 35 25
1679 $1 Growth monitoring (vert) 1·50 1·50

339 Chief Justice Emmanuel N. Gbalazeh swearing-in Dr. Samuel Kanyon Doe

1988. Inauguration of Second Republic.

1680 **339** 6 c. multicoloured 10 10

340 Footballer and Stadium

1988. 2nd Anniv of Opening of Samuel Kanyon Doe Sports Complex.

1681 **340** 31 c. multicoloured 35 25

341 Child and Volunteer reading

1988. 25th Anniv of U.S. Peace Corps in Liberia.

1682 **341** 10 c. multicoloured 10 10
1683 35 c. multicoloured 40 30

342 Pres. Doe, Farm Workers and Produce

1988. Green Revolution.

1684 **342** 10 c. multicoloured 25 10
1685 35 c. multicoloured 85 35

344 Emblem

345 "GP 10" Locomotive, Nimba

1988. 25th Anniv of Organization of African Unity.

1687 **344** 10 c. multicoloured 10 10
1688 35 c. multicoloured 40 60
1689 $1 multicoloured 1·60 1·60

1988. Locomotives. Multicoloured.

1690 10 c. Type **345** 10 10
1691 35 c. Triple engined iron ore train 80 80

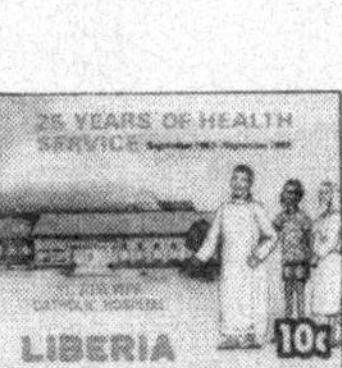

346 Helping Boy to Walk

347 Baseball

1988. 25th Anniv of St. Joseph's Catholic Hospital. Multicoloured.

1693 10 c. Type **346** 10 10
1694 10 c. Medical staff and hospital 10 10
1695 35 c. Monk, child, candle and hospital 65 65
1696 $1 Map behind doctor with nurse holding baby 1·90 1·90

1988. Olympic Games, Seoul. Multicoloured.

1697 10 c. Type **347** 10 10
1698 35 c. Hurdling 65 65
1699 45 c. Fencing 80 80
1700 80 c. Synchronised swimming 1·40 1·40
1701 $1 Yachting 1·75 1·75

348 Monkey Bridge

349 Tending Crops

1988.

1703 10 c. Type **348** 10 10
1704 35 c Sasa players (horiz) 40 60
1705 45 c. Snake dancers 75 75

1988. 10th Anniv of International Fund for Agricultural Development. Multicoloured.

1706 10 c. Type **349** 10 10
1707 35 c. Farmers tending livestock and spraying crops 40 60

350 Destruction of Royal Exchange, 1838

1988. 300th Anniv of Lloyd's of London. Multicoloured.

1708 10 c. Type **350** 10 10
1709 35 c. Britten Norman Islander airplane (horiz) 60 60
1710 45 c. "Chevron Antwerp" (tanker) (horiz) 70 75
1711 $1 "Lakonia" (liner) ablaze, 1963 1·75 1·75

351 Honouring Head of Operational Smile Team

1989. 3rd Anniv of Second Republic.

1712 **351** 10 c. black and blue 10 10
1713 35 c. black and red 40 60
1714 – 50 c. black and mauve 85 85

DESIGN: 50 c. Pres. Samuel Doe at John F. Kennedy Memorial Hospital.

1989. Presidents of United States (5th series). As T **308**. Multicoloured.

1715 $1 George Bush 1·60 1·60

352 "Harmony"

353 Union Glass Factory, Gardersville, Monrovia

1989. Liberia–Japan Friendship. 50th Anniv of Rissho Kosei-Kai (lay Buddhist association). Multicoloured.

1716 10 c. Type **352** 10 10
1717 10 c. Nikkyo Niwano (founder and president of association) 10 10
1718 10 c. Rissho Kosei-Kai headquarters, Tokyo 10 10
1719 50 c. Eternal Buddha, Great Sacred Hall 85 85

1989. 15th Anniv of Mano River Union. Mult.

1721 10 c. Type **353** 15 10
1722 35 c. Presidents of Guinea, Sierra Leone and Liberia 40 30
1723 45 c. Monrovia–Freetown highway 55 45
1724 50 c. Flags, map and mail van 85 85
1725 $1 Presidents at 1988 Summit 1·60 1·60

354 Symbols of International Co-operation

357 Recovery Ship U.S.S. "Okinawa"

1989. World Telecommunications Day.

1726 **354** 50 c. multicoloured 85 85

1989. 20th Anniv of First Manned Landing on Moon. Multicoloured.

1728 10 c. Type **357** 30 10
1729 35 c. Edwin Aldrin, Neil Armstrong and Michael Collins (crew) (28 × 28 mm) 40 60
1730 45 c. "Apollo 11" flight emblem (28 × 28 mm) 1·00 80
1731 $1 Aldrin descending to Moon's surface 1·75 1·75

358 Renovation of Statue of Liberty

360 Nehru and Flag

1989. "Philexfrance '89" International Stamp Exhibition, Paris, and "World Stamp Expo '89" International Stamp Exhibition, Washington D.C. Multicoloured.

1733 25 c. Type **358** 30 20
1734 25 c. French contingent at statue centenary celebrations 30 20
1735 25 c. Statue, officials and commemorative plaque 30 20

1989. Birth Centenary of Jawaharlal Nehru (Indian statesman). Multicoloured.

1737 45 c. Type **360** 55 70
1738 50 c. Nehru 60 80

361 Close View of Station

1990. New Standard A Earth Satellite Station. Multicoloured.

1739 10 c. Type **361** 15 10
1740 35 c. Distant view of station 40 55

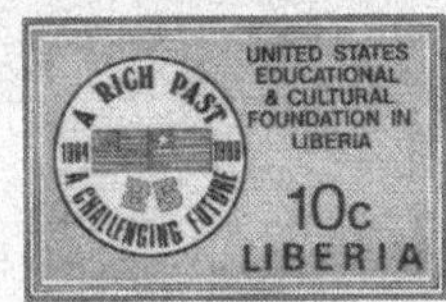

362 Emblem

1990. 25th Anniv of United States Educational and Cultural Foundation in Liberia. Multicoloured.

1741 10 c. Type **362** 15 10
1742 45 c. Similar to Type **362** but differently arranged 55 70

363 Flags, Arms, Map and Union Emblem

364 Bomi County

1990. 10th Anniv of Pan-African Postal Union.

1743 **363** 35 c. multicoloured 40 55

1990. County Flags. Multicoloured.

1744 10 c. Type **364** 10 10
1745 10 c. Bong 10 10
1746 10 c. Grand Bassa 10 10
1747 10 c. Grand Cape Mount 10 10
1748 10 c. Grand Gedeh 10 10
1749 10 c. Grand Kru 10 10
1750 10 c. Lofa 10 10
1751 10 c. Margibi 10 10
1752 10 c. Maryland 10 10
1753 10 c. Montserrado 10 10
1754 10 c. Nimba 10 10
1755 10 c. Rivercress 10 10
1756 10 c. Sinoe 10 10
1757 35 c. Type **364** 40 55
1758 35 c. Bong 40 55
1759 35 c. Grand Bassa 40 55
1760 35 c. Grand Cape Mount 40 55
1761 35 c. Grand Gedeh 40 55
1762 35 c. Grand Kru 40 55
1763 35 c. Lofa 40 55
1764 35 c. Margibi 40 55
1765 35 c. Maryland 40 55
1766 35 c. Montserrado 40 55
1767 35 c. Nimba 40 55
1768 35 c. Rivercress 40 55
1769 35 c. Sinoe 40 55
1770 45 c. Type **364** 50 70
1771 45 c. Bong 50 70

1772 45 c. Grand Bassa 50 70
1773 45 c. Grand Cape Mount . . 50 70
1774 45 c. Grand Gedeh 50 70
1775 45 c. Grand Kru 50 70
1776 45 c. Lofa 50 70
1777 45 c. Margibi 50 70
1778 45 c. Maryland 50 70
1779 45 c. Montserrado 50 70
1780 45 c. Nimba 50 70
1781 45 c. Rivercress 50 70
1782 45 c. Sinoe 50 70
1783 50 c. Type **364** 80 80
1784 50 c. Bong 80 80
1785 50 c. Grand Bassa 80 80
1786 50 c. Grand Cape Mount . . 80 80
1787 50 c. Grand Gedeh 80 80
1788 50 c. Grand Kru 80 80
1789 50 c. Lofa 80 80
1790 50 c. Margibi 80 80
1791 50 c. Maryland 80 80
1792 50 c. Montserrado 80 80
1793 50 c. Nimba 80 80
1794 50 c. Rivercress 80 80
1795 50 c. Sinoe 80 80
1796 $1 Type **364** . . . . 1·60 1·60
1797 $1 Bong . . . . 1·60 1·60
1798 $1 Grand Bassa . . . . . . 1·60 1·60
1799 $1 Grand Cape Mount . . . 1·60 1·60
1800 $1 Grand Gedeh . . . . . . 1·60 1·60
1801 $1 Grand Kru . . . . 1·60 1·60
1802 $1 Lofa . . . . 1·60 1·60
1803 $1 Margibi . . . . 1·60 1·60
1804 $1 Maryland . . . . 1·60 1·60
1805 $1 Montserrado . . . . . . 1·60 1·60
1806 $1 Nimba . . . . 1·60 1·60
1807 $1 Rivercress . . . . 1·60 1·60
1808 $1 Sinoe . . . . 1·60 1·60

365 Lady Elizabeth Bowes-Lyon as Girl

368 Boxing

367 Clasped Hands and Map

1991. 90th Birthday (1990) of Queen Elizabeth the Queen Mother. Multicoloured.
1809 10 c. Type **365** 15 10
1810 $2 As Duchess of York (29 × 36½ mm) . . . . 3·25 3·25

1991. National Unity. Multicoloured.
1812 35 c. Type **367** 40 50
1813 45 c. National flag and map of Africa (ECOMOG (West African States Economic Community peace-keeping forces)) 50 65
1814 50 c. Brewer, Konneh and Michael Francis (co-chairmen) and national flag (All-Liberia Conference) . 60 75

1992. Olympic Games, Barcelona. Multicoloured.
1815 45 c. Type **368** 60 65
1816 50 c. Football 70 75
1817 $1 Weightlifting . . . . . . 1·40 1·50
1818 $2 Water polo . . . . 3·00 3·00

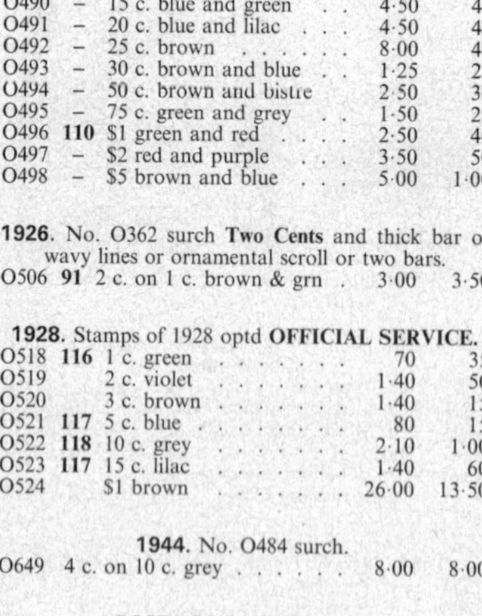

369 "Disarm Today"

1993. Peace and Redevelopment. Multicoloured.
1820 50 c. Type **369** 70 45
1821 $1 "Join your Parents and build Liberia" . . . . 1·40 85
1822 $2 "Peace must prevail in Liberia" . . . . 2·75 1·75

OFFICIAL STAMPS

1892. 1892 stamps optd **OFFICIAL.**
O 87 **7** 1 c. red 30 40
O 88 2 c. blue 30 50
O 89 **8** 4 c. black and green . . 2·50 4·00
O104 **9** 5 c. on 6 c. green (No. 89) 1·00 1·75
O 90 6 c. green 60 90
O 91 **10** 8 c. black and brown . . 1·00 1·25
O 92 **11** 12 c. red . . . . 1·50 1·75
O 93 **12** 16 c. lilac . . . . . . 2·00 2·50
O 94 **13** 24 c. green on yellow . . 1·40 1·75
O 95 **12** 32 c. blue . . . . 3·00 4·50
O 96 **15** $1 black and blue . . . 15·00 18·00
O 97 **13** $2 brown on buff . . . 10·00 12·00
O 98 **17** $5 black and red . . . 12·00 15·00

1894. 1892 stamps optd **O S.**
O119 **7** 1 c. red 30 60
O120 2 c. blue 35 70
O121 **8** 4 c. black and green . . 2·75 3·00
O122 **10** 8 c. black and brown . . 1·50 2·00
O123 **11** 12 c. red . . . . 1·75 2·50
O124 **12** 16 c. lilac . . . . . . 2·50 3·00
O125 **13** 24 c. green on yellow . . 2·00 2·50
O126 **12** 32 c. blue . . . . 3·50 4·00
O127 $1 black and blue . . . 20·00 22·00
O128 $2 brown on buff . . . 12·50 16·00
O129 $5 black and red . . . . 70·00 70·00

1894. 1894 stamp in different colours optd **O S.** Imperf or roul.
O130 **24** 5 c. green and lilac . . . 1·75 2·00

1898. 1897 stamps optd **O S.**
O157 **9** 1 c. purple 35 35
O158 1 c. green 35 35
O159 **15** 2 c. black and bistre . . 1·50 2·00
O160 2 c. black and red . . . 2·00 2·50
O161 **8** 5 c. black and lake . . . 2·25 1·75
O162 5 c. black and blue . . . 2·50 2·50
O163 **10** 10 c. blue and yellow . . 1·00 1·25
O164 **11** 15 c. black . . . . . . 1·00 1·50
O165 **12** 20 c. red . . . . 1·25 2·00
O166 **13** 25 c. green . . . . . . 1·50 2·00
O167 **12** 30 c. blue . . . . 2·00 2·75
O168 **35** 50 c. black and brown . 1·75 2·50

†1903. Stamp of 1903, but different colour, optd **O S.**
O210 **40** 3 c. green 20 15

1904. Nos. O104 and 167 surch **ONE O.S.** and bars or **OS 2** and bars.
O222 **9** 1 c. on 5 c. on 6 c. green 1·10 1·10
O223 **12** 2 c. on 30 c. blue . . . . 6·75 6·75

†1906. Stamps of 1906, but different colours, optd **OS.**
O237 **50** 1 c. black and green . . 50 50
O238 **51** 2 c. black and red . . . 15 8
O239 – 5 c. black and blue . . . 2·00 35
O240 – 10 c. black and violet . . 6·00 60
O241 – 15 c. black and brown . . 4·00 75
O242 – 20 c. black and green . . 6·00 75
O243 – 25 c. grey and purple . . 60 15
O244 – 30 c. brown 50 15
O245 – 50 c. green and brown . . 90 20
O246 – 75 c. black and blue . . 3·00 75
O247 – $1 black and green . . . 1·00 25
O248 **52** $2 black and purple . . 1·50 25
O249 **53** $5 black and orange . . 3·50 30

†1909. Stamps of 1909, but different colours, optd **OS.** 10 c. perf or roul.
O262 **55** 1 c. black and green . . 15 10
O263 – 2 c. brown and red . . . 15 10
O264 **56** 5 c. black and blue . . . 1·00 15
O266 **57** 10 c. blue and black . . 50 25
O267 – 15 c. black and purple . . 50 25
O268 – 20 c. green and bistre . . 1·25 45
O269 – 25 c. green and blue . . 70 50
O270 – 30 c. blue . . . . 1·00 40
O271 – 50 c. green and brown . 2·25 40
O272 – 75 c. black and violet . . 1·50 40

1910. No. O266 surch **3 CENTS INLAND POSTAGE.** Perf or roul.
O276 **57** 3 c. on 10 c. blue & black 90 45

1914. Official stamps surch: (A) **1914 2 CENTS.** (B) + **2 c.** (C) **5.** (D) **CENTS 20 OFFICIAL.**
O291 **57** + 2 c. on 3 c. on 10 c. blue and black (B) (No. O275) 60 1·25
O284 – 2 c. on 25 c. grey and pur (A) (No. O243) . . . 15·00 7·50
O285 – 5 c. on 30 c. blue (C) (No. O270) . . . . 11·00 4·50
O286 – 20 c. on 75 c. black and violet (D) (No. O272) 11·00 4·50

1914. No. 233 surch **CENTS 20 OFFICIAL.**
O287 20 c. on 75 c. black and brown 11·00 4·50

1915. Official stamps of 1906 and 1909 surch in different ways.
O325 – 1 c. on 2 c. brown and red (No. O263) . . . . . 2·25 2·50
O326 **56** 2 c. on 5 c. black and blue (No. O264) . . . . . 2·50 3·00
O310 – 2 c. on 15 c. black and purple (No. O267) . . 95 1·25
O311 – 2 c. on 25 c. green and blue (No. O269) . . . . 5·50 5·50
O312 – 5 c. on 20 c. green and bistre (No. O268) . . . . 1·25 1·50
O313 – 5 c. on 30 c. green and brown (No. O270) . . 5·50 5·50
O314 – 10 c. on 50 c. green and brown (No. O271) . . 6·50 7·50
O316 – 20 c. on 75 c. black and violet (No. O272) . . 2·75 3·50
O317 – 25 c. on $1 black and green (No. O247) . . . . 11·00 12·00
O318 **52** 50 c. on $2 black and purple (No. O248) . . . . 13·00 15·00
O320 **53** $1 on $5 black and orange (No. O249) . . . . . 15·00 18·00

1915. No. O168 surch **10 10** and ornaments and bars.
O321 **35** 10 c. on 50 c. black & brn 9·75 9·75

1915. Military Field Post. Official stamps surch **L E F 1 c.**
O336 **50** 1 c. on 1 c. black and green (No. O237) £325 £325
O337 **55** 1 c. on 1 c. black and green (No. O262) . . . . . 2·50 3·50
O338 – 1 c. on 2 c. brown and red (No. O263) . . . . . . 2·00 3·00

1917. No. O244 surch **FIVE CENTS 1917** and bars.
O344 – 5 c. on 30 c. brown . . . . 13·50 13·50

1918. No. O266 surch **3 CENTS.**
O348 **57** 3 c. on 10 c. blue & black 1·40 1·50

†1918. Stamps of 1918, but in different colours, optd **O S.**
O362 **91** 1 c. brown and green . . 50 15
O363 **92** 2 c. black and red 50 15
O364 – 5 c. black and blue . . . 75 10
O365 **93** 10 c. blue 35 10
O366 – 15 c. green and brown . . 1·75 40
O367 – 20 c. black and lilac . . . 55 10
O368 **94** 25 c. green and brown . . 3·25 45
O369 – 30 c. black and violet . . 4·00 50
O370 – 50 c. black and brown . . 5·00 50
O371 – 75 c. black and brown . . 2·00 15
O372 – $1 blue and olive . . . . 3·75 30
O373 – $2 black and olive . . . . 6·25 20
O374 – $5 green . . . . 8·25 20

1920. Nos. O362/3 surch **1920** and value and two bars.
O400 **91** 3 c. on 1 c. brown & grn 1·50 2·00
O401 **92** 4 c. on 2 c. black and red 2·00 2·50

†1921. Stamps of 1915 and 1921, in different colours, optd **O S** or **OFFICIAL.**
O428 **100** 1 c. green 70 10
O429 **64** 2 c. red . . . . 3·75 10
O430 **65** 3 c. brown 70 10
O431 **101** 5 c. brown and blue . . 70 10
O432 – 10 c. black and purple . . 35 15
O433 – 15 c. green and black . . 2·10 50
O434 – 20 c. blue and brown . . 1·10 25
O435 – 25 c. green and orange . . 3·00 50
O436 – 30 c. red and brown . . 75 15
O437 – 50 c. green and black . . 75 25
O438 – 75 c. purple and blue . . 1·50 25
O439 – $1 black and blue . . . 12·00 1·50
O440 – $2 green and orange . . 22·00 1·50
O441 – $5 blue and green . . . 17·00 1·75

†1921. Nos. O400/41 optd **1921.**
O442 **100** 1 c. green . . . . 3·25 20
O443 **64** 2 c. red . . . . 3·25 20
O444 **65** 3 c. brown . . . . 3·25 25
O445 **101** 5 c. brown and blue . . 1·90 25
O446 – 10 c. black and purple . . 3·25 25
O447 – 15 c. green and black . . 3·75 15
O448 – 20 c. blue and brown . . 3·75 35
O449 – 25 c. green and orange . . 4·25 40
O450 – 30 c. red and brown . . 3·25 30
O451 – 50 c. green and black . . 4·00 15
O452 – 75 c. purple and blue . . 2·40 15
O453 – $1 black and blue . . . 10·00 1·50
O454 – $2 green and orange . . 21·00 2·50
O455 – $5 blue and green . . . 16·00 3·00

†1923. Stamps of 1923, but different colours, optd **O S.**
O485 **108** 1 c. black and green . . 50 10
O486 **109** 2 c. brown and red . . . 50 10
O487 – 3 c. black and blue . . . 50 10
O488 – 5 c. green and orange . . 1·25 10
O489 – 10 c. purple and olive . . 80 10
O490 – 15 c. blue and green . . 4·50 40
O491 – 20 c. blue and lilac . . . 4·50 40
O492 – 25 c. brown . . . . . . 8·00 40
O493 – 30 c. brown and blue . . 1·25 20
O494 – 50 c. brown and bistre . 2·50 30
O495 – 75 c. green and grey . . 1·50 25
O496 **110** $1 green and red . . . 2·50 40
O497 – $2 red and purple . . . 3·50 50
O498 – $5 brown and blue . . . 5·00 1·00

1926. No. O362 surch **Two Cents** and thick bar or wavy lines or ornamental scroll or two bars.
O506 **91** 2 c. on 1 c. brown & grn . 3·00 3·50

1928. Stamps of 1928 optd **OFFICIAL SERVICE.**
O518 **116** 1 c. green 70 35
O519 2 c. violet . . . . 1·40 50
O520 3 c. brown . . . . 1·40 15
O521 **117** 5 c. blue 80 15
O522 **118** 10 c. grey . . . . 2·10 1·00
O523 **117** 15 c. lilac . . . . 1·40 60
O524 $1 brown . . . . 26·00 13·50

1944. No. O484 surch.
O649 4 c. on 10 c. grey . . . . . . 8·00 8·00

POSTAGE DUE STAMPS

1892. Stamps of 1886 surch **POSTAGE DUE** and value in frame.
D 99 **4** 3 c. on 3 c. mauve . . . . 2·00 3·00
D100 6 c. on 6 c. grey . . . . . 4·75 4·75

D 23

1894.
D110 **D 23** 2 c. black and orange on yellow . . . . . . 95 1·00
D111 4 c. blk & red on rose 95 1·00
D112 6 c. blk & brn on buff 95 1·00
D113 8 c. black & blue on bl 1·00 1·50
D114 10 c. black and green on mauve . . . . . . 1·25 2·00
D115 20 c. black and violet on grey . . . . . . 1·25 2·00
D116 40 c. black and brown on green . . . . 2·10 2·50

REGISTRATION STAMPS

R 22

1893.
R105 **R 22** (10 c.) black (Buchanan) £275 £350
R106 (10 c.) black ("Grenville") . . . £1000 £1250
R107 (10 c.) black (Harper) £1000 £1250
R108 (10 c.) black (Monrovia) 40·00 £175
R109 (10 c.) blk (Robertsport) £500 £575

1894. Surch **10 CENTS 10** twice.
R140 **R 22** 10 c. blue on pink (Buchanan) . . . . 3·75 3·75
R141 10 c. green on buff (Harper) . . . . . 3·75 3·75
R142 10 c. red on yellow (Monrovia) . . . . 3·75 3·75
R143 10 c. red on blue (Robertsport) . . . 3·75 3·75

R 42 Pres. Gibson

†1904.
R211 **R 42** 10 c. black and blue (Buchanan) . . . . 1·50 25
R212 10 c. black and red ("Grenville") . . . 1·50 25
R213 10 c. black and green (Harper) . . . . 1·50 25
R214 10 c. black and violet (Monrovia) . . . . 1·50 25
R215 10 c. black and purple (Robertsport) . . . 1·50 25

R 96 Patrol Boat "Quail"

1919. Roul or perf.
R388 **R 96** 10 c. blue and black (Buchanan) . . . . 90 5·75
R389 10 c. black and brown ("Grenville") . . . 90 7·50
R390 10 c. black and green (Harper) . . . . . 90 5·25
R391 10 c. blue and violet (Monrovia) . . . . 90 5·75
R392 10 c. black and red (Robertsport) . . . 90 7·50

R 106 Gabon Viper

†1921.
R456 **R 106** 10 c. black and red (Buchanan) . . . . 23·00 2·50
R457 10 c. black and red (Greenville) . . . . 14·00 2·50
R458 10 c. black and blue (Harper) . . . . 18·00 2·50
R459 10 c. black and orange (Monrovia) . . . . 14·00 2·50
R460 10 c. black and green (Robertsport) . . . 14·00 2·50

†1921. Optd **1921.**
R461 **R 106** 10 c. black and lake 17·00 4·25
R462 10 c. black and red 17·00 4·25
R463 10 c. black and blue 17·00 4·25
R464 10 c. black and orange 17·00 4·25
R465 10 c. black and green 17·00 4·25

R **111** Sailing Skiff (Buchanan)

†**1923**. Various sea views.

R499	R **111**	10 c. red and black	8·50	55
R500	–	10 c. green and black	8·50	55
R501	–	10 c. orange and black	8·50	55
R502	–	10 c. blue and black	8·50	55
R503	–	10 c. violet and black	8·50	55

DESIGNS: No. R500, Lighter (Greenville); R501, Full-rigged sailing ship (Harper); R502, "George Washington" (liner) (Monrovia); R503, Canoe (Robertsport).

1941. No. 576 surch **REGISTERED 10 CENTS 10.**

R592	10 c. on 5 c. brown (postage)	1·40	1·40
R593	10 c. on 5 c. brown (air) . .	1·40	1·40

No. R593 is additionally optd with airplane and **AIR MAIL**.

SPECIAL DELIVERY STAMPS

1941. No. 576 surch with postman and **SPECIAL DELIVERY 10 CENTS 10.**

S590	10 c. on 5 c. brown (postage)	1·40	1·40
S591	10 c. on 5 c. brown (air) . .	1·40	1·40

No. S591 is additionally optd with airplane and **AIR MAIL**.

LIBYA Pt. 8; Pt. 13

A former Italian colony in N. Africa, comprising the governorates of Cyrenaica and Tripolitania. From the end of 1951 an independent kingdom including the Fezzan also. Following a revolution in 1969 the country became the Libyan Arab Republic.

1912. 100 centesimi = 1 lira.
1952. 1000 milliemes = 1 Libyan pound.
1972. 1000 dirhams = 1 dinar.

A. ITALIAN COLONY.

1912. Stamps of Italy optd **LIBIA** (No. 5) or **Libia** (others).

No.	Type	Description	Unused	Used
1	30	1 c. brown	20	60
2	31	2 c. brown	20	35
3	37	5 c. green	20	30
4		10 c. red	20	20
5	41	15 c. grey	18·00	1·50
6	37	15 c. grey	2·00	3·50
7	33	20 c. orange	30	35
8	41	20 c. orange	1·25	3·00
9	39	25 c. blue	50	50
10		40 c. brown	80	1·25
11	33	45 c. green	7·50	11·00
12	39	50 c. violet	2·25	1·00
13		60 c. red	4·25	12·00
14	34	1 l. brown and green	24·00	2·00
15		5 l. blue and red	£120	£170
16		10 l. green and pink	9·50	40·00

1915. Red Cross stamps of Italy optd **LIBIA.**

No.	Type	Description	Unused	Used
17	53	10 c. + 5 c. red	1·25	3·50
18	54	15 c. + 5 c. grey	5·00	8·00
19		20 c. on 15 c. + 5 c. grey	5·00	8·00
20		20 c. + 5 c. orange	2·00	4·75

1916. No. 100 of Italy optd **LIBIA.**

No.	Type	Description	Unused	Used
21	41	20 c. on 15 c. grey	18·00	5·00

4 Roman Legionary 5 Goddess of Plenty

6 Roman Galley leaving Tripoli 7 Victory

1921.

No.	Type	Description	Unused	Used
22	4	1 c. brown and black	20	90
23		2 c. brown and black	20	90
24		5 c. green and black	40	55
50		7½ c. brown and black	30	1·25
51	5	10 c. pink and black	10	10
52		15 c. orange and brown	1·90	60
27		25 c. blue and deep blue	30	15
54	6	30 c. brown and black	10	35
55		50 c. green and black	10	10
30		55 c. violet and black	1·90	5·00
57	7	75 c. red and purple	10	10
58a		1 l. brown	1·25	10
59	6	1 l. 25 blue and indigo	10	10
32	7	5 l. blue and black	9·00	7·00
33		10 l. green and blue	40·00	55·00

1922. Victory stamps of Italy optd **LIBIA.**

No.	Type	Description	Unused	Used
34	62	5 c. green	50	2·00
35		10 c. red	50	2·00
36		15 c. grey	50	3·25
37		25 c. blue	50	3·00

1922. Nos. 9 and 12 of Libya surch.

No.	Type	Description	Unused	Used
38	39	40 c. on 50 c. mauve	1·10	1·40
39		80 c. on 25 c. blue	1·60	5·00

9 "Libyan Sibyl" by Michelangelo 10 Bedouin Woman

1924.

No.	Type	Description	Unused	Used
41	9	20 c. green	30	10
42		40 c. brown	1·10	40
43		60 c. blue	30	10
44		1 l. 75 orange	10	10
45		2 l. red	1·60	80
46		2 l. 55 violet	1·60	2·75

1928. Air. Air stamps of Italy optd **Libia.**

No.	Type	Description	Unused	Used
63	88	50 c. pink	3·00	4·50
64		80 c. brown and purple	6·00	19·00

1928. Types of Italy optd **LIBIA** (No. 67) or **Libia** (others).

No.	Type	Description	Unused	Used
65	92	7½ c. brown	6·00	15·00
66	34	1 l. 25 blue	24·00	11·00
67	91	1 l. 75 brown	28·00	1·25

1936. 10th Tripoli Trade Fair.

No.	Type	Description	Unused	Used
68	10	50 c. violet	70	1·40
69		1 l. 25 blue	90	4·25

1936. Air. Nos. 96 and 99 of Cyrenaica optd **LIBIA.**

No.	Type	Description	Unused	Used
70	–	50 c. violet	80	10
71	17	1 l. black	2·75	19·00

1937. Air. Stamps of Tripolitania optd **LIBIA.**

No.	Type	Description	Unused	Used
72	18	50 c. red	30	10
73		60 c. red	40	
74		75 c. blue	40	12·00
75		80 c. purple	40	12·00
76	19	1 l. blue	1·00	60
77		1 l. 20 brown	40	15·00
78		1 l. 50 orange	40	
79		5 l. green	40	

11 Triumphal Arch 12 Roman Theatre, Sabrata

1937. Inauguration of Coastal Highway.

No.	Type	Description	Unused	Used
80	11	50 c. red (postage)	1·50	3·00
81		1 l. 25 blue	1·50	7·00
82	12	50 c. purple (air)	1·50	4·00
83		1 l. black	1·50	6·50

1937. 11th Tripoli Trade Fair. Optd **XI FIERA DI TRIPOLI.**

No.	Type	Description	Unused	Used
84	11	50 c. red (postage)	5·00	12·00
85		1 l. 25 blue	5·00	12·00
86	12	50 c. purple (air)	5·00	12·00
87		1 l. black	5·00	12·00

14 Benghazi Waterfront

1938. 12th Tripoli Trade Fair.

No.	Type	Description	Unused	Used
88	14	5 c. brown (postage)	30	50
89	–	10 c. brown	30	50
90	14	25 c. green	50	50
91	–	50 c. violet	50	40
92	14	75 c. red	60	2·00
93	–	1 l. 25 blue	60	2·00

DESIGN: 10 c., 50 c., 1 l. 25, Fair Buildings.

No.	Type	Description	Unused	Used
94		50 c. brown (air)	1·00	1·00
95		1 l. blue	1·00	3·00

DESIGN—VERT: View of Tripoli.

16 Statue of Augustus 17 Eagle and Serpent

1938. Birth Bimillenary of Augustus the Great.

No.	Type	Description	Unused	Used
96	16	5 c. green (postage)	30	85
97	–	10 c. red	30	85
98	16	25 c. green	50	65
99	–	50 c. mauve	50	35
100	16	75 c. red	75	1·40
101	–	1 l. 25 blue	75	1·40
102	17	50 c. brown (air)	50	1·10
103		1 l. mauve	75	2·50

DESIGN: 10, 50 c., 1 l. 25, Statue of Goddess of Plenty.

18 Agricultural Landscape

1939. 13th Tripoli Trade Fair. Inscr "XIII FIERA CAMPIONARIA DE TRIPOLI" etc.

No.	Type	Description	Unused	Used
104	18	5 c. green (postage)	20	55
105	–	20 c. red	40	55
106	18	50 c. mauve	50	30
107	–	75 c. red	60	90
108	18	1 l. 25 blue	60	90

DESIGN: 20, 75 c. View of Ghadames.

No.	Type	Description	Unused	Used
109	–	25 c. green (air)	40	1·10
110	–	50 c. green	50	90
111	–	1 l. mauve	50	1·10

DESIGNS—Fiat G18V airplane over: 25 c., 1 l. Arab and camel in desert; 50 c. Fair entrance.

19 Buildings

1940. Naples Exhibition.

No.	Type	Description	Unused	Used
112	19	5 c. brown (postage)	20	35
113	–	10 c. orange	20	35
114	–	25 c. green	60	85
115	19	50 c. violet	60	85
116	–	75 c. red	60	1·25
117	–	1 l. 25 blue	60	1·40
118	–	2 l. + 75 c. red	60	2·00

DESIGNS—HORIZ: 10, 75 c., 2 l. Oxen and plough. VERT: 25 c., 1 l. 25, Mosque.

No.	Type	Description	Unused	Used
119	–	50 c. black (air)	40	1·40
120	–	1 l. brown	40	1·40
121	–	2 l. + 75 c. blue	65	2·25
122	–	5 l. + 2 l. 50 brown	65	2·25

DESIGNS—HORIZ: 50 c., 2 l. Savoia Marchetti S.M.75 airplane over city; 1, 5 l. Savoia Marchetti S-73 airplane over oasis.

19a Hitler and Mussolini

1941. Rome-Berlin Axis Commemoration.

No.	Type	Description	Unused	Used
123	19a	5 c. orange (postage)	20	3·00
124		10 c. brown	20	3·00
125		20 c. purple	50	3·00
126		25 c. green	50	3·00
127		50 c. violet	50	3·00
128		75 c. red	50	5·00
129		1 l. 25 blue	50	5·00
130		50 c. green (air)	60	10·00

B. INDEPENDENT.

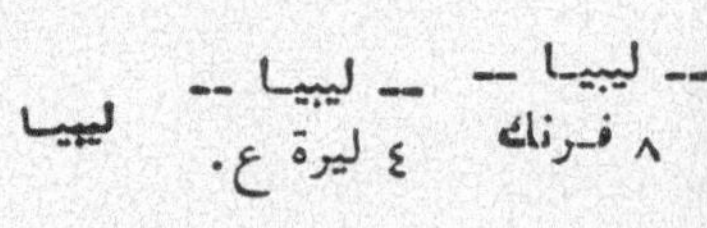

(20) (21) (22)

1951. Stamps of Cyrenaica optd. (a) For use in Cyrenaica, optd as T **20.**

No.	Type	Description	Unused	Used
131	24	1 m. brown	15	15
132		2 m. red	20	20
133		3 m. yellow	25	25
134		4 m. green	28·00	19·00
135		5 m. brown	35	35
136		8 m. orange	40	40
137		10 m. violet	60	60
138		12 m. red	1·10	1·10
139		20 m. blue	1·50	1·50
140	25	50 m. blue and brown	8·75	8·75
141		100 m. red and black	14·50	14·50
142		200 m. violet and blue	45·00	40·00
143		500 m. yellow and green	£150	£130

(b) For use in Tripolitania. Surch as T **21** in Military Authority lire.

No.	Type	Description	Unused	Used
151	24	1 mal. on 2 m. red	25	25
152		2 mal. on 4 m. green	25	25
153		4 mal. on 8 m. orange	25	25
154		5 mal. on 10 m. violet	35	35
155		6 mal. on 12 m. red	35	35
156		10 mal. on 20 m. blue	65	65
157	25	24 mal. on 50 m. blue and brown	3·00	3·00
158		48 mal. on 100 m. red	11·00	11·00
159		96 mal. on 200 m. violet and blue	27·00	27·00
160		240 mal. on 500 m. yellow and green	70·00	70·00

(c) For use in the Fezzan. Surch as T **22.**

No.	Type	Description	Unused	Used
166	24	2 f. on 2 m. red	20	20
167		4 f. on 4 m. green	30	30
168		8 f. on 8 m. orange	35	40
169		10 f. on 10 m. violet	50	50
170		12 f. on 12 m. red	75	75
171		20 f. on 20 m. blue	2·00	2·00
172	25	48 f. on 50 m. blue & brn	38·00	35·00
173		96 f. on 100 m. red and black	40·00	35·00
174		192 f. on 200 m. violet and blue	£110	80·00
175		480 f. on 500 m. yellow and green	£190	£190

23 King Idris (28) 30

1952.

No.	Type	Description	Unused	Used
176	23	2 m. brown	10	10
177		4 m. grey	10	10
178		5 m. green	12·50	35
179		8 m. red	40	25
180	23	10 m. violet	12·50	15
181		12 m. red	75	15
182		20 m. blue	13·50	45
183		25 m. brown	13·50	45
184	–	50 m. blue and brown	1·75	65
185	–	100 m. red and black	3·75	1·90
186	–	200 m. violet and blue	6·00	3·50
187	–	500 m. orange and green	25·00	17·00

Nos. 184/7 are larger.

1955. Arab Postal Union. As T **96a** of Syria but inscr "LIBYE" at top.

No.	Type	Description	Unused	Used
200		5 m. brown	1·25	60
201		10 m. green	1·90	90
202		30 m. violet	4·25	2·00

1955. 2nd Arab Postal Congress, Cairo. Nos. 200/2 optd with T **28.**

No.	Type	Description	Unused	Used
203		5 m. brown	40	30
204		10 m. green	95	50
205		30 m. violet	2·25	1·25

1955. No. 177 surch.

No.	Type	Description	Unused	Used
206	23	5 m. on 4 m. grey	1·25	45

1955.

No.	Type	Description	Unused	Used
207	30	1 m. black on yellow	10	10
208		2 m. bistre	1·40	50
209		2 m. brown	10	10
210		3 m. blue	10	10
211		4 m. black	1·50	50
212		4 m. lake	20	15
213		5 m. green	40	20
214		10 m. lilac	65	25
215		18 m. red	15	10
216		20 m. orange	25	15
217		30 m. blue	50	20
218		35 m. brown	65	25
219		40 m. lake	1·10	40
220		50 m. olive	85	25
221	–	100 m. purple and slate	1·75	50
222	–	200 m. lake and blue	9·25	1·40
223	–	500 m. orange and green	15·00	7·25
224	–	£L1 green, brown on yellow	21·00	11·50

Nos. 221/4 are larger 27 x 32 mm.
See also Nos. 242/57.

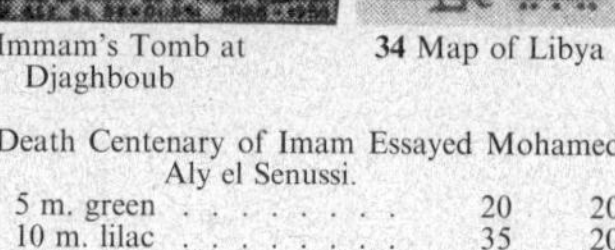

33 Immam's Tomb at Djaghboub 34 Map of Libya

1956. Death Centenary of Imam Essayed Mohamed Aly el Senussi.

No.	Type	Description	Unused	Used
225	33	5 m. green	20	20
226		10 m. lilac	35	20
227		15 m. red	95	75
228		30 m. blue	1·60	1·25

1956. 1st Anniv of Admission to U.N.

No.	Type	Description	Unused	Used
229	34	15 m. buff and blue	30	15
230		35 m. buff, purple & blue	1·00	30

35 36

1957. Arab Postal Congress, Tripoli.

No.	Type	Description	Unused	Used
231	35	15 m. blue	1·75	90
232		500 m. brown	12·50	6·50

1958. 10th Anniv of Declaration of Human Rights.

No.	Type	Description	Unused	Used
233	36	10 m. violet	20	15
234		15 m. green	25	20
235		30 m. blue	95	50

37 F.A.O. Emblem and Date Palms 39

1959. 1st Int Dates Conf, Tripoli.

No.	Type	Description	Unused	Used
236	37	10 m. black and violet	20	15
237		15 m. black and green	50	20
238		45 m. black and blue	1·00	50

1960. Inauguration of Arab League Centre, Cairo. As T **154a** of Syria. but with Arms of Libya and inscr "LIBYA".
239 10 m. black and green 50 20

1960. World Refugee Year.
240 **39** 10 m. black and violet . . 25 15
241 45 m. black and blue . . . 1·25 75

1960. As Nos. 207 etc. On coloured paper.
242 **30** 1 m. black on grey 10 10
243 2 m. brown on buff 10 10
244 3 m. indigo on blue 10 10
245 4 m. lake on red 10 10
246 5 m. green on green 10 10
247 10 m. lilac on violet 10 10
248 15 m. sepia on buff 10 10
249 20 m. orange on orange . . 20 10
250 30 m. red on pink 20 15
251 40 m. lake on red 30 20
252 45 m. blue on blue 35 20
253 50 m. olive on bistre . . . 35 20
254 – 100 m. purple & slate on blue 1·25 35
255 – 200 m. lake & blue on blue 3·25 1·40
256 – 500 m. orange & green on green . . . . 23·00 5·50
257 – £L1 green & brown on brn 23·00 11·00

40 Palm Tree and Radio Mast 41 Military Watchtower (medallion)

1960. 3rd Arab Telecommunications Conf, Tripoli.
258 **40** 10 m. violet 15 10
259 15 m. turquoise 20 10
260 45 m. lake . . . . 1·40 65

1961. Army Day.
261 **41** 5 m. brown and green . . . 20 10
262 15 m. brown and blue . . . 60 15

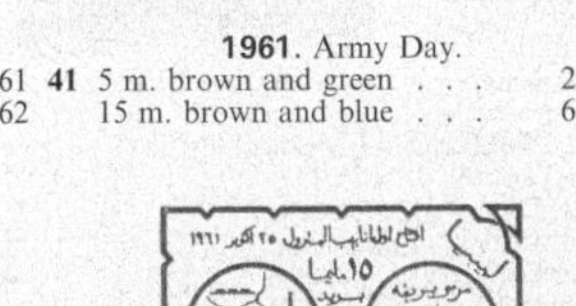

42 Zelten Field and Marsa Brega Port

1961. Inaug of First Libyan Petrol Pipeline.
263 **42** 15 m. green and buff . . . 25 10
264 50 m. brown and lavender 75 40
265 100 m. blue and light blue 2·25 90

43 Broken Chain and Agricultural Scenes

1961. 10th Anniv of Independence.
266 **43** 15 m. sepia, turquoise and green 15 10
267 – 50 m. sepia, brown & buff 45 25
268 – 100 m. sepia, blue & salmon 2·10 80
DESIGNS—(embodying broken chain): 50 m. Modern highway and buildings; 100 m. Industrial machinery.

44 Tuareg Camel Riders

1962. International Fair, Tripoli.
269 **44** 10 m. chestnut and brown 60 10
270 – 15 m. green and purple . . 75 25
271 – 50 m. blue and green . . . 2·00 1·60
DESIGNS: 15 m. Well; 50 m. Oil derrick.

45 Campaign Emblem 46 Ahmed Rafik

1962. Malaria Eradication.
273 **45** 15 m. multicoloured . . . 25 20
274 50 m. multicoloured . . . 1·10 90

1962. 1st Death Anniv of Ahmed Rafik el Mehdawi (poet).
276 **46** 15 m. green 15 10
277 20 m. brown 55 20

47 Scout Badge and Handclasp 48 City within Oildrop

1962. 3rd Boy Scouts' Meeting, Tripoli.
278 **47** 5 m. sepia, red and yellow 10 10
279 – 10 m. sepia, yellow & blue 20 10
280 – 15 m. sepia, yellow & grey 25 20
DESIGNS: 10 m. Scouts and badge; 15 m. Badge and camp.

1962. Inauguration of Essider Terminal, Sidrah Oil Pipeline.
282 **48** 15 m. purple and green . . 45 15
283 50 m. olive and brown . . 1·10 45

49 Red Crescent encircling Globe

1963. International Red Cross Centenary.
284 **49** 10 m. multicoloured . . . 20 15
285 15 m. multicoloured . . . 25 20
286 20 m. multicoloured . . . 90 60

50 Rainbow over Map of Tripoli

1963. International Trade Fair, Tripoli.
287 **50** 15 m. multicoloured . . . 25 20
288 30 m. multicoloured . . . 70 20
289 50 m. multicoloured . . . 1·40 60

51 Palm and Well 52 "Emancipation"

1963. Freedom from Hunger.
290 **51** 10 m. green, brown & blue 20 10
291 – 15 m. ochre, purple & grn 25 20
292 – 45 m. sepia, blue & salmon 1·10 75
DESIGNS: 15 m. Camel and sheep; 45 m. Farmer sowing and tractor.

1963. 15th Anniv of Declaration of Human Rights.
293 **52** 5 m. brown and blue . . . 10 10
294 15 m. purple and blue . . 20 10
295 50 m. green and blue . . . 45 30

54 Map and Fair Entrance 55 Child playing in Sun

1964. International Fair, Tripoli.
300 **54** 10 m. green, brown and red 75 15
301 15 m. green, brown & purple 1·00 50
302 30 m. green, brown & blue 1·40 75

1964. Children's Day. Sun gold.
303 **55** 5 m. violet, red and pink . . 10 10
304 – 15 m. brown, bistre & buff 20 15
305 **55** 45 m. violet, blue & lt blue 1·25 65
DESIGN: 15 m. Child in bird's nest.

56 Lungs and Stethoscope

1964. Anti-Tuberculosis Campaign.
307 **56** 20 m. violet 90 25

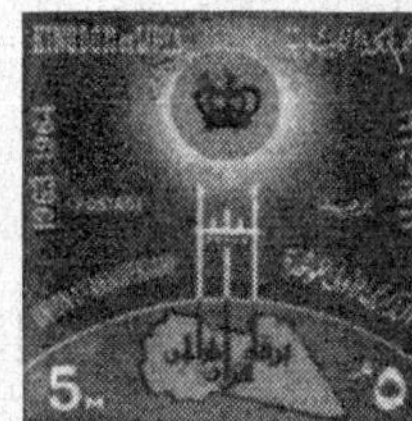

57 Crown and Map 58 Libyan Woman, Silk Moth and Cocoon

1964. 1st Anniv of Libyan Union.
308 **57** 5 m. orange and green . . . 15 10
309 50 m. yellow and blue . . . 1·00 50

1964. Emancipation of Libyan Women.
310 **58** 10 m. blue and green . . . 15 10
311 20 m. blue and yellow . . . 55 35
312 35 m. blue and pink 85 80

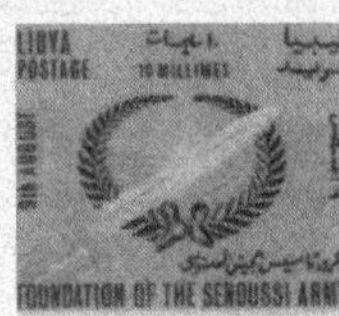

59 Flags and Scout Salute 60 Bayonet

1964. Libyan Scouts. Multicoloured.
314 10 m. Type **59** 65 20
315 20 m. Scout badge and saluting hands . . . . 1·25 60

1964. Foundation of the Senussi Army.
317 **60** 10 m. brown and green . . 15 10
318 20 m. black and orange . . 65 40

61 Ahmed Bahloul (poet) 62 Football

1964. Ahmed Bahloul El-Sharef Commem.
319 **61** 15 m. purple 20 10
320 20 m. blue 65 20

1964. Olympic Games, Tokyo. Rings in Gold.
321 5 m. black and blue (Type **62**) 25 20
322 10 m. black & purple (Cycling) 25 20
323 20 m. black and red (Boxing) 50 20
324 30 m. black and buff (Runner) 65 50
325 35 m. black and olive (High-diving) 65 50
326 50 m. black & grn (Hurdling) 65 50
Nos. 321/6 were arranged together se-tenant in the sheets, each block of six being superimposed with the Olympic "rings" symbol.

63 A.P.U. Emblem 64 I.C.Y. Emblem

1964. 10th Anniv of Arab Postal Union.
328 **63** 10 m. blue and yellow . . 10 10
329 15 m. brown and lilac . . 20 10
330 30 m. brown and green . . 95 65

1965. International Co-operation Year.
331 **64** 5 m. gold & blue (postage) 25 10
332 15 m. gold and red 90 25
333 50 m. gold and violet (air) 1·50 35

65 European Bee Eater

1965. Birds. Multicoloured.
335 5 m. Long-legged buzzard . . 95 20
336 10 m. Type **65** . . . . 1·25 20
337 15 m. Black-bellied sandgrouse 1·75 20
338 20 m. Houbara bustard . . . 2·10 30
339 30 m. Spotted sandgrouse . . 2·75 55
340 40 m. Barbary partridge . . . 3·25 80
The 5 m. and 40 m. are vert.

66 Fair Emblem

1965. International Trade Fair, Tripoli.
341 **66** 50 m. multicoloured . . . 75 50

67 Compass, Rocket and Balloons

1965. World Meteorological Day.
342 **67** 10 m. multicoloured . . . 10 10
343 15 m. multicoloured . . . 20 15
344 50 m. multicoloured . . . 1·00 70

68 I.T.U. Emblem and Symbols

1965. Centenary of I.T.U.
345 **68** 10 m. brown 10 10
346 20 m. purple 15 10
347 50 m. mauve 90 65

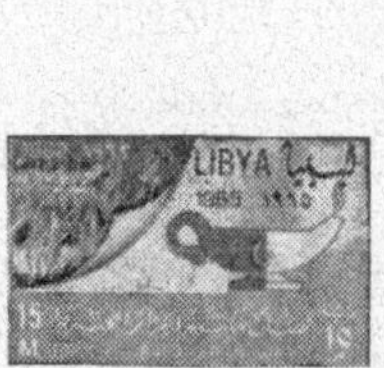

69 Lamp and Burning Library 70 Rose

1965. Reconstitution of Burnt Algiers Library.
348 **69** 15 m. multicoloured . . . 20 10
349 50 m. multicoloured . . . 90 25

1965. Flowers. Multicoloured.
351 1 m. Type **70** 10 10
352 2 m. Iris 10 10
353 3 m. Cactus flower 10 10
354 4 m. Sunflower 50 10

71 Sud Aviation Super Caravelle over Globe 72 Forum, Cyrene

1965. Inaug of Kingdom of Libya Airlines.
355 **71** 5 m. multicoloured 10 10
356 10 m. multicoloured . . . 20 10
357 15 m. multicoloured . . . 70 10

1965.
358 **72** 50 m. olive and blue . . . 70 25
359 – 100 m. brown and blue . . 1·25 45
360 – 200 m. blue and purple . . 3·00 95
361 – 500 m. green and red . . . 6·50 2·75
362 – £L1 brown and green . . . 14·00 6·50
DESIGNS—VERT: 100 m. Trajan's Arch, Leptis Magna; 200 m. Apollo's Temple, Cyrene. HORIZ: 500 m. Antonine Temple, Sabratha; £L1 Theatre, Sabratha.

73 "Helping Hands"

1966. Air. Nubian Monuments Preservation.
363 **73** 10 m. brown and bistre . . 20 10
364 15 m. brown and green . . 25 10
365 40 m. brown and chestnut 1·10 50

74 Germa Mausoleum

1966.
367 **74** 70 m. violet and brown . . 1·40 75
See also No. E368.

75 Globe and Satellites

1966. International Trade Fair, Tripoli.
369 **75** 15 m. black, gold & green 20 10
370 45 m. black, gold and blue 70 20
371 55 m. black, gold & purple 95 60

76 League Centre, Cairo, and Emblem

77 W.H.O. Building

1966. Arab League Week.
372 **76** 20 m. red, green and black 10 10
373 55 m. blue, red and black 65 50

1966. Air. Inauguration of W.H.O. Headquarters, Geneva.
374 **77** 20 m. black, yellow & blue 20 10
375 50 m. black, green and red 65 25
376 65 m. black, salmon & lake 95 70

78 Tuareg with Camel

80 Leaping Deer

1966. Tuaregs.
378 **78** 10 m. red 95 65
379 – 20 m. blue . . . . . . 2·25 1·25
380 – 50 m. multicoloured . . . 4·50 3·25
DESIGNS—VERT: 20 m. As Type **78** but positions of Tuareg and camel reversed. 62 x 39 mm: 50 m. Tuareg with camel (different).

1966. 1st Arab Girl Scouts Camp (5 m.) and 7th Arab Boy Scouts Camp (25 and 65 m.). Multicoloured.
382 5 m. Type **80** 10 10
383 25 m. Boy scouts 20 10
384 65 m. Camp emblem (vert) . . 1·00 50

81 Airline Emblem

1966. Air. 1st Anniv of Kingdom of Libya Airlines.
385 **81** 25 m. multicoloured . . . 20 15
386 60 m. multicoloured . . . 1·00 75
387 85 m. multicoloured . . . 1·40 1·00

82 U.N.E.S.C.O. Emblem

83 Castle of Columns, Tolemaide

1967. 20th Anniv of U.N.E.S.C.O.
388 **82** 15 m. multicoloured . . . 20 10
389 25 m. multicoloured . . . 90 20

1967. Tourism.
390 **83** 25 m. black, brown & violet 20 10
391 – 55 m. brown, violet & black 90 50
DESIGN—HORIZ: 55 m. Sebba Fort.

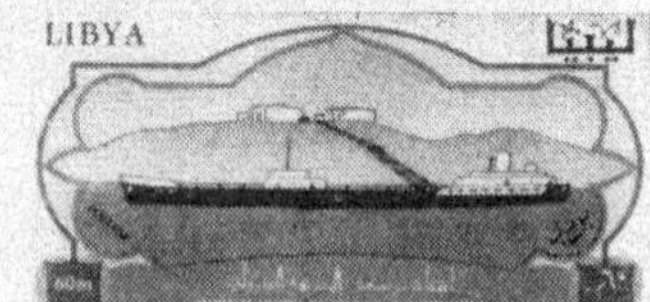

84 "British Confidence" (tanker) at Oil Terminal

1967. Inaug of Marsa al Hariga Oil Terminal.
392 **84** 60 m. multicoloured . . . 1·75 65

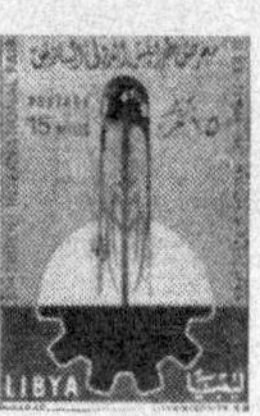

85 Fair Emblem

86 I.T.Y. Emblem

1967. International Fair, Tripoli.
393 **85** 15 m. multicoloured . . . 50 10
394 55 m. multicoloured . . . 75 50

1967. International Tourist Year.
395 **86** 5 m. black and blue . . . 10 10
396 10 m. blue and black . . . 10 10
397 45 m. black, blue and pink 60 15

87 Running

88 Open Book and Arab League Emblem

1967. Mediterranean Games, Tunisia. Designs showing action "close-ups".
398 **87** 5 m. black, orange and blue 10 10
399 – 10 m. black, brown & blue 10 10
400 – 15 m. black, violet and blue 10 10
401 – 45 m. black, red and blue 30 25
402 – 75 m. black, green and blue 75 30
DESIGNS: 10 m. Throwing the javelin; 15 m. Cycling; 45 m. Football; 75 m. Boxing.

1967. Literacy Campaign.
403 **88** 5 m. orange and violet . . 10 10
404 10 m. green and violet . . 10 10
405 15 m. purple and violet . . 15 10
406 25 m. blue and violet . . . 20 15

89 Human Rights Emblem

90 Cameleers, Fokker Friendship, Oil Rig and Map

1968. Human Rights Year.
407 **89** 15 m. red and green 15 10
408 60 m. blue and orange . . . 65 25

1968. International Fair, Tripoli.
409 **90** 55 m. multicoloured 95 30

91 Arab League Emblem

1968. Arab League Week.
410 **91** 10 m. red and blue 10 10
411 45 m. green and orange . . 65 50

92 Children "Wrestling" (statue)

93 W.H.O. Emblem and Reaching Hands

1968. Children's Day. Multicoloured.
412 25 m. Type **92** 45 15
413 55 m. Libyan mother and children 80 55

1968. 20th Anniv of W.H.O.
414 **93** 25 m. blue and purple . . . 25 15
415 55 m. brown and blue . . . 40 25

94 Oil Pipeline Map

1968. Inauguration of Zueitina Oil Terminal.
416 **94** 10 m. multicoloured 20 10
417 60 m. multicoloured . . . . 1·10 65

95 "Teaching the People"

1968. "Eliminate Illiteracy".
418 **95** 5 m. mauve 10 10
419 10 m. orange 10 10
420 15 m. blue 10 10
421 20 m. green 20 20

96 Conference Emblem

1968. 4th Session of Arab Labour Ministries Conference, Tripoli.
422 **96** 10 m. multicoloured . . . 10 10
423 15 m. multicoloured . . . 20 10

97 Treble Clef, Eye and T.V. Screen

1968. Inauguration of Libyan Television Service.
424 **97** 10 m. multicoloured . . . 10 10
425 30 m. multicoloured . . . 65 20

98 Bridge, Callipers and Road Sign

1968. Opening of Wadi El Kuf Bridge.
426 **98** 25 m. multicoloured . . . 15 15
427 60 m. multicoloured . . . 70 25

99 Melons

100 Fair Emblem

1969. Fruits. Multicoloured.
428 5 m. Type **99** 10 10
429 10 m. Dates 10 10
430 15 m. Lemons 10 10
431 20 m. Oranges 15 10
432 25 m. Peaches 50 15
433 35 m. Pears 90 50

1969. 8th International Trade Fair, Tripoli.
434 **100** 25 m. multicoloured . . . 15 10
435 35 m. multicoloured . . . 25 15
436 40 m. multicoloured . . . 60 20

101 Hoisting Weather Balloon

1969. World Meteorological Day.
437 **101** 60 m. multicoloured . . . 1 10 65

102 Family on Staircase within Cogwheel

103 I.L.O. Emblem

1969. 10th Anniv of Libyan Social Insurance.
438 **102** 15 m. multicoloured . . . 15 10
439 55 m. multicoloured . . . 30 25

1969. 50th Anniv of I.L.O.
440 **103** 10 m. green, black & turq 10 10
441 60 m. green, black and red 70 50

104 Emblem and Desert Scene

1969. African Tourist Year.
442 **104** 15 m. multicoloured . . . 15 10
443 30 m. multicoloured . . . 65 50

105 Members of the Armed Forces and Olive Branch
106 Dish Aerial and Flags

1969. Revolution of 1st September.

444 **105** 5 m. multicoloured . . . 25 10
445 10 m. multicoloured . . . 35 20
446 15 m. multicoloured . . . 55 25
447 25 m. multicoloured . . . 85 40
448 45 m. multicoloured . . . 1·00 60
449 60 m. multicoloured . . . 2·10 1·00

On Nos. 444/9 the value is in white and the designer's name appears at the foot of design.

1970. 5th Anniv of Arab Satellite Communications Co-operation Agreement.

450 **106** 15 m. multicoloured . . . 50 15
451 20 m. multicoloured . . . 75 20
452 25 m. multicoloured . . . 1·00 25
453 40 m. multicoloured . . . 1·50 75

107 Arab League Flag, Arms and Map

1970. Silver Jubilee of Arab League.

454 **107** 10 m. sepia, green & blue 10 10
455 15 m. brown, green & orge 15 15
456 20 m. purple, grn & olive 50 25

1970. Revolution of 1st September. Designs as T **105**, but without imprint "M. A. Siala" at foot, and figures of value differently inscr

457 **87** 5 m. multicoloured 25 10
458 10 m. multicoloured . . . 35 20
459 15 m. multicoloured . . . 55 25
460 25 m. multicoloured . . . 85 40
461 45 m. multicoloured . . . 1·00 60
462 60 m. multicoloured . . . 2·10 1·00

108 New Headquarters Building
109 Arms and Soldiers

1970. New U.P.U. Headquarters Building, Berne.

463 **108** 10 m. multicoloured . . . 15 10
464 25 m. multicoloured . . . 20 20
465 60 m. multicoloured . . . 95 60

1970. Nos. 358 and 360/2 with "KINGDOM OF LIBYA" inscriptions obliterated.

465a **72** 50 m. olive and blue . . .
466 – 200 m. blue and purple . .
467 – 500 m. green and pink . .
468 – £L1 brown and green . .

These stamps were sold only for use on parcel post items. Other values may exist so overprinted, but were unauthorised.

See also Nos. 518/23.

1970. Evacuation of Foreign Military Bases in Libya.

469 **109** 15 m. black and red . . . 15 15
470 25 m. yellow, blue & red 45 20
471 45 m. yellow, red & green 1·25 30

110 Soldiers and Libyan Flag
111 U.N. Emblem, Dove and Scales

1970. 1st Anniv of Libyan Arab Republic.

472 **110** 20 m. multicoloured . . . 55 15
473 25 m. multicoloured . . . 70 15
474 30 m. multicoloured . . . 1·25 75

1970. 25th Anniv of United Nations.

475 **111** 5 m. brown, red & green 25 10
476 10 m. green, red & emerald 65 15
477 60 m. green, red and blue 1·75 75

112 Map and Flags
113 Dove, U.N. Emblem and Globe

1970. Signing of Tripoli Charter of Co-operation.

478 **112** 15 m. green, black & red 5·00 1·50

1971. 10th Anniv of U.N. De-colonisation Declaration.

479 **113** 15 m. multicoloured . . . 50 15
480 20 m. multicoloured . . . 75 20
481 60 m. multicoloured . . . 1·90 75

114 Education Year Emblem
115 Palestinian Guerrilla

1971. International Education Year.

482 **114** 5 m. brown, red & black 15 10
483 10 m. green, red & black 50 10
484 20 m. blue, red & black 1·10 15

1971. "Al-Fatah" Movement for the Liberation of Palestine.

485 **115** 5 m. multicoloured . . . 15 10
486 10 m. multicoloured . . . 50 15
487 100 m. multicoloured . . 1·75 1·00

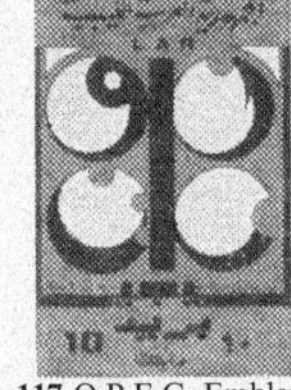

116 Fair Emblem
117 O.P.E.C. Emblem

1971. 9th International Trade Fair, Tripoli.

488 **116** 15 m. multicoloured . . . 15 10
489 30 m. multicoloured . . . 65 20

1971. Organization of Petroleum Exporting Countries (O.P.E.C.).

490 **117** 10 m. brown and yellow 15 10
491 70 m. violet and pink . . 1·25 65

118 Global Symbol

1971. World Telecommunications Day (Nos. 494/5) and Pan-African Telecommunications Network.

492 – 5 m. multicoloured . . . 10 10
493 – 15 m. multicoloured . . . 10 10
494 **118** 25 m. multicoloured . . . 20 15
495 35 m. multicoloured . . . 50 25

DESIGN: 5 m., 15 m. Telecommunications map of Africa.

119 Soldier, Torch and Flag
120 Ramadan Suehli

1971. 1st Anniv of Evacuation of Foreign Troops.

496 **119** 5 m. multicoloured . . . 10 10
497 10 m. multicoloured . . . 15 10
498 15 m. multicoloured . . . 20 15

1971. Ramadan Suehli (patriot). Commem.

499 **120** 15 m. multicoloured . . . 15 10
500 55 m. multicoloured . . . 75 35

For similar portraits see Nos. 503/4, 507/8, 526/7 and 553/4.

121 Palm and Dates
122 Pres. Gamal Nasser

1971. 2nd Anniv of 1st September Revolution.

501 **121** 5 m. multicoloured 20 10
502 15 m. multicoloured . . . 1·00 15

1971. 40th Death Anniv of Omar el Mukhtar (patriot). As T **120.**

503 5 m. multicoloured 10 10
504 100 m. multicoloured . . . . . 1·75 90

1971. 1st Death Anniv of Pres. Nasser of Egypt.

505 **122** 5 m. black, green & pur 10 10
506 15 m. black, purple & grn 95 10

1971. 21st Death Anniv of Ibrahim Usta Omar (poet). As T **120.**

507 25 m. multicoloured 25 15
508 30 m. multicoloured 80 20

123 Racial Equality Year Emblem
124 A.P.U. Emblem

1971. Racial Equality Year.

509 **123** 25 m. multicoloured . . . 25 15
510 35 m. multicoloured . . . 70 15

1971. 25th Anniv of Founding of Arab Postal Union at Sofar Conference.

511 **124** 5 m. multicoloured 10 10
512 10 m. multicoloured . . . 20 10
513 15 m. multicoloured . . . 15 10

125 Arab Postal Union. Emblem and Envelopes
126 Book Year Emblem

1971. 10th Anniv of African Postal Union. Mult.

514 10 m. Type **125** 10 10
515 15 m. Type **125** 15 10
516 25 m. A.P.U. Emblem and dove with letter 25 15
517 55 m. As 25 m. 95 35

1971. Nos. 423/33 with "KINGDOM OF LIBYA" inscriptions obliterated.

518 5 m. Type **99** . . . .
519 10 m. Dates . . . .
520 15 m. Lemons . . . .
521 20 m. Oranges . . . .
522 25 m. Peaches . . . .
523 35 m. Pears . . . .

1972. International Book Year.

524 **126** 15 m. multicoloured . . . 15 10
525 20 m. multicoloured . . . 25 20

1972. Ahmed Gnaba (poet). Commem. As T **120.**

526 20 m. multicoloured 25 10
527 35 m. multicoloured 65 20

127 Libyan Arms
128 Tombs, Ghirza

1972. Values in Milliemes.

528 **127** 5 m. multicoloured 10 10
529 10 m. multicoloured . . . 10 10
530 25 m. multicoloured . . . 15 10
531 30 m. multicoloured . . . 20 10
532 35 m. multicoloured . . . 25 10
533 40 m. multicoloured . . . 50 15
534 45 m. multicoloured . . . 60 15
535 55 m. multicoloured . . . 85 20
536 60 m. multicoloured . . . 1·00 35
537 90 m. multicoloured . . . 1·60 90

1972. Libyan Antiquities. Multicoloured.

538 5 m. Type **128** 10 10
539 10 m. Cufic inscription, Ajdabiya 10 10
540 15 m. Marcus Aurelius' Arch, Tripoli (horiz) 15 10
541 25 m. Exchanging Weapons (cave painting, Wadi Zigza) 65 15

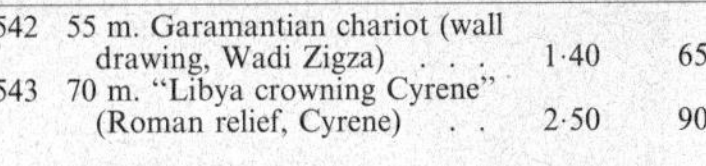

542 55 m. Garamantian chariot (wall drawing, Wadi Zigza) . . . 1·40 65
543 70 m. "Libya crowning Cyrene" (Roman relief, Cyrene) . . 2·50 90

129 Fair Emblem
130 Heart and Skeletal Arm

1972. 10th Int Trade Fair, Tripoli.

544 **129** 25 m. multicoloured . . . 20 15
545 35 m. multicoloured . . . 25 20
546 50 m. multicoloured . . . 95 25
547 70 m. multicoloured . . . 1·40 35

1972. World Health Day.

548 **130** 15 m. multicoloured . . . 1·10 25
549 25 m. multicoloured . . . 2·25 75

131 "Unity" Symbol on Map
132

1972. 1st Anniv of Libyan-Egyptian Federation Agreement.

550 **131** 15 m. yellow, blue & black 10 10
551 20 m. yellow, green & emer 20 10
552 25 m. yellow, red & black 80 20

1972. Birth Centenary (1970) of Suleiman el Baruni (writer). As T **120.**

553 10 m. multicoloured 95 15
554 70 m. multicoloured . . . . . 1·25 75

1972. New Currency (Dirhams and Dinars). As Type **127.** (a) Size 19 x 24 mm.

555 **127** 15 dh. multicoloured . . 10 10
556 65 dh. multicoloured . . 75 50
557 70 dh. multicoloured . . 90 65
558 80 dh. multicoloured . . 1·25 65

(b) Size 27 x 32 mm.

559 **127** 100 dh. multicoloured . . 1·75 2·00
560 200 dh. multicoloured . . 3·25 1·60
561 500 dh. multicoloured . . 7·50 5·00
562 1 D. multicoloured . . . 13·50 10·00

1972.

563 **132** 5 m. multicoloured . . . 1·90 50
564 20 m. multicoloured . . . 7·50 1·40
565 50 m. multicoloured . . . 18·00 3·75

Nos. 563/5 were also issued with the Arabic face values expressed in the new currency.

See also Nos. 657/9.

133 Environmental Emblem
134 Olympic Emblems

1972. U.N. Environmental Conservation Conference, Stockholm.

566 **133** 15 dh. multicoloured . . 50 10
567 55 dh. multicoloured . . 1·10 35

1972. Olympic Games, Munich.

568 **134** 25 dh. multicoloured . . 1·50 35
569 35 dh. multicoloured . . 2·25 90

135 Symbolic Tree and "Fruit"
136 Dome of the Rock

1972. 3rd Anniv of 1st September Revolution.

570 **135** 15 dh. multicoloured . . 15 10
571 25 dh. multicoloured . . 70 15

1973. Dome of the Rock, Jerusalem.

572 **136** 10 dh. multicoloured . . 10 10
573 25 dh. multicoloured . . 50 15

137 Nicolas Copernicus

138 Libyan Eagle and Fair

1973. 500th Birth Anniv of Copernicus. Mult.
574 15 dh. Type **137** 15 10
575 25 dh. "Copernicus in his Observatory" (horiz) 50 15

1973. 11th International Trade Fair, Tripoli.
576 **138** 5 dh. multicoloured . . . 15 10
577 10 dh. multicoloured . . . 50 10
578 15 dh. multicoloured . . . 90 15

139 Blind Persons and Occupations

140 Map and Laurel

1973. Role of the Blind in Society.
579 **139** 20 dh. multicoloured . . . 5·50 1·25
580 25 dh. multicoloured . . . 10·00 2·50

1973. 10th Anniv of Organization of African Unity.
584 **140** 15 dh. multicoloured . . . 20 10
585 25 dh. multicoloured . . . 65 45

141 Interpol H.Q., Paris

1973. 50th Anniv of International Criminal Police Organization (Interpol).
586 **141** 10 dh. multicoloured . . . 10 10
587 15 dh. multicoloured . . . 15 10
588 25 dh. multicoloured . . . 60 20

142 Map and Emblems

143 W.M.O. Emblem

1973. Census.
589 **142** 10 dh. blue, black & red 3·00 65
590 25 dh. green, black & blue 4·25 1·25
591 35 dh. orange, black & grn 8·00 2·50

1973. W.M.O. Centenary.
592 **143** 5 dh. blue, black and red 10 10
593 10 dh. blue, black & green 15 10

144 Footballers

1973. 2nd Palestine Cup Football Championship.
594 **144** 5 dh. brown and green . . 45 20
595 25 dh. brown and red . . 80 15

145 Revolutionary Torch

146 "Writing Ability"

1973. 4th Anniv of September 1st Revolution.
596 **145** 15 dh. multicoloured . . . 20 10
597 25 dh. multicoloured . . . 85 10

1973. Literacy Campaign.
598 **146** 25 dh. multicoloured . . 50 15

147 Doorway of Old City Hall

148 Militiamen and Flag

1973. Cent of Tripoli Municipality. Mult.
599 10 dh. Type **147** 20 10
600 25 dh. Khondok fountain . . 50 10
601 35 dh. Clock tower 75 40

1973. Libyan Militia.
602 **148** 15 dh. multicoloured . . 15 10
603 25 dh. multicoloured . . 55 10

149 Arabic Quotation from Speech of 15 April 1973

1973. Declaration of Cultural Revolution by Col. Gaddafi. Multicoloured.
604 25 dh. Type **149** 20 10
605 70 dh. As Type **149** but text in English 60 30

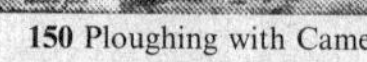
150 Ploughing with Camel

151 Human Rights Emblem

1973. 10th Anniv of World Food Programme.
606 **150** 10 dh. multicoloured . . 10 10
607 25 dh. multicoloured . . 20 10
608 35 dh. multicoloured . . 55 15

1973. 25th Anniv of Declaration of Human Rights.
609 **151** 25 dh. red, purple & blue 20 10
610 70 dh. red, green and blue 1·10 30

152 Mullet

154 Emblem formed with National Flags

153 Lookout Post and Scout Salute

1973. Fishes. Multicoloured.
611 5 dh. Type **152** 10 10
612 10 dh. Seabream 45 10
613 15 dh. Perch 60 10
614 20 dh. Seaperch 90 15
615 25 dh. Tunny . . . . 1·60 20

1974. 20th Anniv of Scouting in Libya.
616 **153** 5 dh. multicoloured . . . 95 10
617 20 dh. multicoloured . . 2·50 50
618 25 dh. multicoloured . . 4·00 1·25

1974. 12th International Trade Fair, Tripoli.
619 **154** 10 dh. multicoloured . . 50 10
620 25 dh. multicoloured . . 75 15
621 35 dh. multicoloured . . 1·25 35

155 Family within Protective Hands

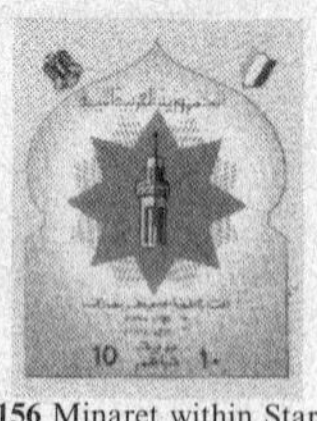
156 Minaret within Star

1974. World Health Day.
622 **155** 5 dh. multicoloured . . . 15 10
623 25 dh. multicoloured . . . 50 20

1974. Inauguration of Benghazi University.
624 **156** 10 dh. multicoloured . . . 20 10
625 25 dh. multicoloured . . . 75 15
626 35 dh. multicoloured . . . 1·10 25

157 U.P.U. Emblem within Star

158 Traffic Lights and Signs

1974. Centenary of U.P.U.
627 **157** 25 dh. multicoloured . . . 5·50 75
628 70 dh. multicoloured . . . 10·00 1·50

1974. Motoring and Touring Club of Libya.
629 **158** 5 dh. multicoloured . . . 10 10
630 10 dh. multicoloured . . . 15 10
631 25 dh. multicoloured . . . 15 10

159 Tank, Refinery and Pipeline

160 W.P.Y. Emblem and People

1974. 5th Anniv of 1st September Revolution.
632 **159** 5 dh. multicoloured . . . 10 10
633 20 dh. multicoloured . . . 15 10
634 25 dh. multicoloured . . . 15 10
635 35 dh. multicoloured . . . 20 15

1974. World Population Year.
637 **160** 25 dh. multicoloured . . . 20 10
638 35 dh. multicoloured . . . 50 20

161

162 Congress Emblem

1975. 13th International Trade Fair, Tripoli. Libyan Costumes.
639 **161** 5 dh. multicoloured . . . 10 10
640 – 10 dh. multicoloured . . . 10 10
641 – 15 dh. multicoloured . . . 10 10
642 – 20 dh. multicoloured . . . 20 10
643 – 25 dh. multicoloured . . . 75 10
644 – 50 dh. multicoloured . . . 1·10 20
DESIGNS: 10 dh. to 50 dh. Various costumes.

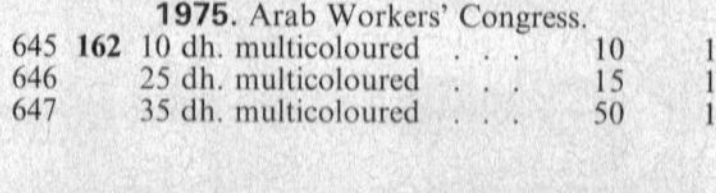

1975. Arab Workers' Congress.
645 **162** 10 dh. multicoloured . . . 10 10
646 25 dh. multicoloured . . . 15 15
647 35 dh. multicoloured . . . 50 15

163 Teacher at Blackboard

164 Human Figures, Text and Globe

1975. Teachers' Day.
648 **163** 10 dh. multicoloured . . 10 10
649 25 dh. multicoloured . . 20 10

1975. World Health Day.
650 **164** 20 dh. multicoloured . . 15 10
651 25 dh. multicoloured . . 20 10

165 Readers and Bookshelves

166 Festival Emblem

1975. Arab Book Exhibition.
652 **165** 10 dh. multicoloured . . 10 10
653 20 dh. multicoloured . . 20 10
654 25 dh. multicoloured . . 50 15

1975. 2nd Arab Youth Festival.
655 **166** 20 dh. multicoloured . . 15 10
656 25 dh. multicoloured . . 20 15

1975. As Nos. 563/5 but without "L.A.R.".
657 **132** 5 dh. black, orange & blue 35 10
658 20 dh. black, yellow & bl 75 10
659 50 dh. black, green & blue 1·40 15

167 Games Emblem

168 Dove of Peace

1975. 7th Mediterranean Games, Algiers.
660 **167** 10 dh. multicoloured . . 10 10
661 25 dh. multicoloured . . 45 10
662 50 dh. multicoloured . . 85 20

1975. 6th Anniv of September 1st Revolution. Multicoloured.
663 25 dh. Type **168** 20 10
664 70 dh. Peace dove with different background 95 25

169 Khalil Basha Mosque

170 Arms and Crowds

1975. Mosques. Multicoloured.
666 5 dh. Type **169** 10 10
667 10 dh. Sidi Abdulla El Shaab 10 10
668 15 dh. Sidi Ali El Fergani . . 10 10
669 20 dh. Al Kharruba (vert) . . 15 10
670 25 dh. Katiktha (vert) 20 10
671 30 dh. Murad Agha (vert) . . 45 15
672 35 dh. Maulai Mohamed (vert) 55 15

1976. National People's Congress.
673 **170** 35 dh. multicoloured . . 20 10
674 40 dh. multicoloured . . 25 10

171 Dialogue Emblem

172 Woman blowing Bugle

1976. Islamic-Christian Dialogue Seminar.
675 **171** 40 dh. multicoloured . . 50 15
676 115 dh. multicoloured . . 1·40 60

1976. International Trade Fair, Tripoli. Mult.
677 10 dh. Type **172** 10 10
678 20 dh. Lancer 15 10
679 30 dh. Drummer 65 10
680 40 dh. Bagpiper 75 20
681 100 dh. Woman with jug on head 1·90 35

173 Early and Modern Telephones

1976. Telephone Centenary. Multicoloured.
682 40 dh. Type **173** . . . . 1·60 15
683 70 dh. Alexander Graham Bell 2·75 50

174 Mother and Child

175 Hands supporting Eye

1976. International Children's Day.
685 **174** 85 dh. multicoloured . . . 75 30
686 110 dh. multicoloured . . 1·10 40

1976. World Health Day.
687 **175** 30 dh. multicoloured . . . 20 10
688 35 dh. multicoloured . . . 20 10
689 40 dh. multicoloured . . . 50 15

176 Little Bittern

1976. Libyan Birds. Multicoloured.
690 5 dh. Type **176** 75 25
691 10 dh. Great grey shrike . . . 1·40 40
692 15 dh. Fulvous babbler . . . 2·00 50
693 20 dh. European bee eater (vert) 2·75 70
694 25 dh. Hoopoe . . . . 3·00 95

177 Barabekh Plant

178 Cycling

1976. Natural History Museum. Multicoloured.
695 10 dh. Type **177** 10 10
696 15 dh. Fin whale (horiz) . . . 15 10
697 30 dh. Lizard (horiz) 20 10
698 40 dh. Elephant's skull (horiz) 70 15
699 70 dh. Bonnelli's eagle . . . . 3·00 70
700 115 dh. Barbary sheep . . . . 2·00 40

1976. Olympic Games, Montreal. Multicoloured.
701 15 dh. Type **178** 10 10
702 25 dh. Boxing 20 10
703 70 dh. Football 95 20

179 Global "Tree"

180 Agricultural and Industrial Symbols

1976. Non-Aligned Countries' Colombo Conference.
705 **179** 115 dh. multicoloured . . 95 35

1976. 7th Anniv of Revolution.
706 **180** 30 dh. multicoloured . . . 15 10
707 40 dh. multicoloured . . . 45 15
708 100 dh. multicoloured . . 90 55

181 Various Sports

182 Chessboard and Pieces

1976. 5th Arab Games, Damascus.
710 **181** 15 dh. multicoloured . . 10 10
711 30 dh. multicoloured . . 15 10
712 100 dh. multicoloured . . 1·00 55

1976. Arab Chess Olympiad, Tripoli.
714 **182** 15 dh. multicoloured . . 95 15
715 30 dh. multicoloured . . 1·60 60
716 100 dh. multicoloured . . 5·00 95

183 Ratima

186 Kaaba, Mecca

184 Emblem and Text

1976. Libyan Flora. Multicoloured.
717 15 dh. Type **183** 15 10
718 20 dh. "Sword of Crow" . . . 15 10
719 35 dh. "Lasef" 50 10
720 40 dh. "Yadid" 80 15
721 70 dh. Esparto grass . . . . 1·90 25

1976. International Archives Council.
722 **184** 15 dh. multicoloured . . 10 10
723 35 dh. multicoloured . . 15 10
724 70 dh. multicoloured . . 55 20

1976. Pilgrimage to Mecca.
729 **186** 15 dh. multicoloured . . 10 10
730 30 dh. multicoloured . . 15 10
731 70 dh. multicoloured . . 30 20
732 100 dh. multicoloured . . 75 30

187

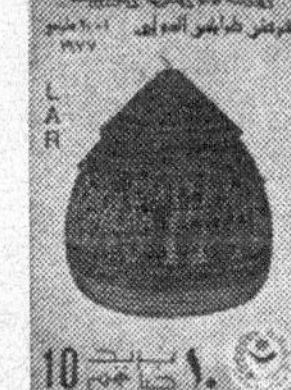
188 Basket

1977. Coil Stamps.
733 **187** 5 dh. multicoloured . . . 10 10
734 20 dh. multicoloured . . 10 10
735 50 dh. multicoloured . . 55 40

1977. 15th International Trade Fair, Tripoli. Mult.
736 10 dh. Type **188** 10 10
737 20 dh. Leather bag 10 10
738 30 dh. Vase 15 10
739 40 dh. Slippers 45 15
740 50 dh. Saddle 60 15

189 Girl with Flowers

1977. Children's Day. Multicoloured.
742 10 dh. Type **189** 10 10
743 30 dh. Clothes shop 15 10
744 40 dh. Orchard 20 15

190 Fighters and Machine-gun

191 Protected Child

1977. 9th Anniv of Battle of Al-Karamah.
745 **190** 15 dh. multicoloured . . . 10 10
746 25 dh. multicoloured . . . 15 10
747 70 dh. multicoloured . . . 80 25

1977. World Health Day.
748 **191** 15 dh. multicoloured . . . 10 10
749 30 dh. multicoloured . . . 15 10

192 A.P.U. Emblem

1977. 25th Anniv of Arab Postal Union.
750 **192** 15 dh. multicoloured . . . 10 10
751 20 dh. multicoloured . . . 15 10
752 40 dh. multicoloured . . . 20 15

193 Maps of Libya and Africa

194 Heart on Map of Libya

1977. Organization of African Unity Conference, Tripoli.
753 **193** 40 dh. multicoloured . . . 1·00 20
754 70 dh. multicoloured . . . 1·50 30

1977. Red Crescent Commemoration.
755 **194** 5 dh. multicoloured . . . 10 10
756 10 dh. multicoloured . . . 15 10
757 30 dh. multicoloured . . . 65 15

195 Messenger and Jet Fighter

1977. Communications Progress. Multicoloured.
758 20 dh. Type **195** 15 10
759 25 dh. Arab rider and Concorde 30 15
760 60 dh. Satellite and aerial . . . 55 20
761 115 dh. Television relay via satellite . . . . 1·10 65
762 150 dh. Camel rider and Boeing 727 airliner loading . . . . 1·75 90
763 200 dh. "Apollo-Soyuz" link 2·25 1·10

196 Mosque

197 Archbishop Capucci

1977. Libyan Mosques.
765 **196** 40 dh. multicoloured . . . 20 15
766 – 50 dh. multicoloured . . . 50 15
767 – 70 dh. multicoloured . . . 70 20
768 – 90 dh. multicoloured . . . 85 30
769 – 100 dh. multicoloured . . 1·00 35
770 – 115 dh. multicoloured . . 1·25 75
DESIGNS: 50 dh. to 115 dh. Various mosques. The 50 dh. and 100 dh. are vertical.

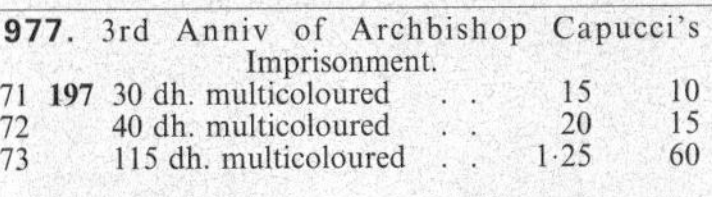
1977. 3rd Anniv of Archbishop Capucci's Imprisonment.
771 **197** 30 dh. multicoloured . . 15 10
772 40 dh. multicoloured . . 20 15
773 115 dh. multicoloured . . 1·25 60

198 Clasped Hands and Emblems

199 Swimming

1977. 8th Anniv of Revolution.
774 **198** 15 dh. multicoloured . . 10 10
775 30 dh. multicoloured . . 15 10
776 85 dh. multicoloured . . 80 25

1977. Arab School Sports. Multicoloured.
778 5 dh. Type **199** 10 10
779 10 dh. Handball (horiz) . . . 10 10
780 15 dh. Football 15 10
781 25 dh. Table tennis (horiz) . . 50 20
782 40 dh. Basketball . . . . . . 1·10 65

200 Championship Emblem

201 Dome of the Rock

1977. 1st International Turf Championships, Tripoli. Multicoloured.
783 5 dh. Horse jumping (facing left) 10 10
784 10 dh. Arab horseman 10 10
785 15 dh. Type **200** 15 10
786 45 dh. Horse jumping fence (facing right) 55 15
787 115 dh. Arab horseman racing 1·40 80

1977. Palestine Welfare.
789 **201** 5 dh. multicoloured . . . 10 10
790 10 dh. multicoloured . . 10 10

202 Fort, and Hands writing Arabic Script in Book

203 Emblem

1977. "The Green Book". Multicoloured.
791 35 dh. Type **202** 15 10
792 40 dh. Type **202** (text in English) 20 15
793 115 dh. Dove with "Green Book" and map . . . . . 1·25 70

1977. World Standards Day.
794 **203** 5 dh. multicoloured . . . 10 10
795 15 dh. multicoloured . . 10 10
796 30 dh. multicoloured . . 15 10

204 Giraffe

1978. Rock Drawings from Wadi Mathendous. Multicoloured.
797 10 dh. Crocodiles (horiz) . . . 10 10
798 15 dh. Elephant hunt (horiz) 10 10
799 20 dh. Type **204** 15 10
800 30 dh. Antelope (horiz) . . . 45 15
801 40 dh. Elephant (horiz) . . . 65 20

205 Silver Pendant

206 Compass and Lightning Flash

1978. 16th Tripoli International Fair.
802 **205** 5 dh. silver, black and red . . 10 10
803 – 10 dh. silver, black & violet . . 10 10
804 – 20 dh. silver, black & green . . 10 10
805 – 25 dh. silver, black & blue . . 15 10
806 – 115 dh. silver, black & blue . . 1·10 70
DESIGNS: 10 dh. Silver ornamental plate; 20 dh. Necklace with three pendants; 25 dh. Crescent-shaped silver brooch; 115 dh. Silver armband.

1978. Arab Cultural Education Organisation.
807 **206** 30 dh. multicoloured . . . 20 15
808 115 dh. multicoloured . . 1·40 65

207 Dancing a Round

1978. Children's Day. Children's Paintings. Multicoloured.
809 40 dh. Type **207** 20 15
810 40 dh. Children with placards . . 20 15
811 40 dh. Shopping street 20 15
812 40 dh. Playground 20 15
813 40 dh. Wedding ceremony . . 20 15

208 Brickwork Clenched Fist

1978. The Arabs.
814 **208** 30 dh. multicoloured . . . 20 15
815 115 dh. multicoloured . . 1·10 35

209 Blood Pressure Meter

211 Games Emblem

210 Microwave Antenna

1978. World Hypertension Month.
816 **209** 30 dh. multicoloured . . . 15 15
817 115 dh. multicoloured . . 1·25 35

1978. World Telecommunications Day.
818 **210** 30 dh. multicoloured . . . 15 15
819 115 dh. multicoloured . . 1·00 35

1978. 3rd African Games, Algiers.
820 **211** 15 dh. copper, violet & blk . . 10 10
821 30 dh. silver, lilac & black . . 15 10
822 115 dh. gold, purple & blk . . 1·10 35

212 Aerial View of Airport

1978. Inauguration of Tripoli International Airport. Multicoloured.
823 40 dh. Type **212** 30 10
824 115 dh. Terminal building . . 1·25 65

213 Ankara

1978. Turkish-Libyan Friendship.
825 **213** 30 dh. multicoloured . . 15 10
826 35 dh. multicoloured . . 15 10
827 115 dh. multicoloured . . 1·10 35

214 "Armed Forces"

215 Crater

1978. 9th Anniv of 1st September Revolution. Multicoloured.
828 30 dh. Type **214** 40 15
829 35 dh. Tower, Green Book and symbols of progress 15 10
830 115 dh. "Industry" 95 70

1978. 2nd Symposium on Geology of Libya. Multicoloured.
832 30 dh. Type **215** 15 10
833 40 dh. Oasis 20 15
834 115 dh. Crater (different) . . 1·10 60

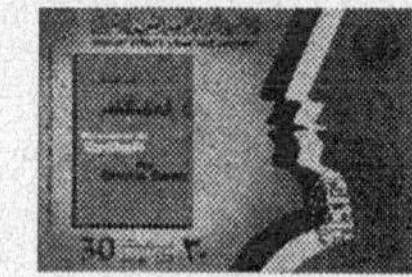
216 "Green Book" and Different Races

1978. International Anti-Apartheid Year.
835 **216** 30 dh. multicoloured . . 15 10
836 40 dh. multicoloured . . 20 15
837 115 dh. multicoloured . . 85 35

217 Pilgrims, Minarets and Kaaba

218 Clasped Hands and Globe

1978. Pilgrimage to Mecca.
838 **217** 5 dh. multicoloured . . . 10 10
839 10 dh. multicoloured . . . 10 10
840 15 dh. multicoloured . . . 10 10
841 20 dh. multicoloured . . . 15 10

1978. U.N. Conference for Technical Co-operation between Developing Countries.
842 **218** 30 dh. multicoloured . . 15 10
843 40 dh. multicoloured . . 20 15
844 115 dh. multicoloured . . 85 35

219 Workers, Rifles, Torch and Flag

220 Human Figure and Scales

1978. Arab Countries Summit Conference. Multicoloured.
845 30 dh. Type **219** 15 10
846 40 dh. Map of Middle East, eagle and crowd (horiz) 20 15
847 115 dh. As 40 dh. 85 35
848 145 dh. Type **219** . . . . . . 1·00 45

1978. 30th Anniv of Declaration of Human Rights.
849 **220** 15 dh. multicoloured . . . 10 10
850 30 dh. multicoloured . . . 20 15
851 115 dh. multicoloured . . 50 35

221 Horse Racing and Fort

222 Lilienthal's Biplane Glider

1978. Libyan Study Centre.
852 **221** 20 dh. multicoloured . . . 15 10
853 40 dh. multicoloured . . . 20 15
854 115 dh. multicoloured . . 95 60

1978. 75th Anniv of First Powered Flight. Mult.
855 20 dh. Type **222** 10 10
856 25 dh. Lindbergh's "Spirit of St. Louis" 10 10
857 30 dh. Admiral Richard Byrd's Trimotor "Floyd Bennett" . 1·25 25
858 50 dh. Bleriot 5190 Santos Dumont flying boat and airship "Graf Zeppelin" . . . . . . 1·50 35
859 115 dh. Wright brothers and Wright Type A . . . . . . 1·10 75

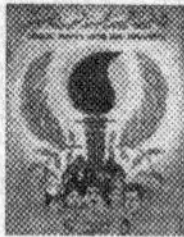
223 Libyans, Torch and Laurel Wreath

224 Mounted Dorcas Gazelle Head

1979.
861 **223** 5 dh. multicoloured . . . 10 10
862 10 dh. multicoloured . . 10 10
863 15 dh. multicoloured . . 10 10
864 30 dh. multicoloured . . 20 10
865 50 dh. multicoloured . . 20 10
866 60 dh. multicoloured . . 25 15
867 70 dh. multicoloured . . 30 15
868 100 dh. multicoloured . . 75 25
869 115 dh. multicoloured . . 85 30
870 200 dh. multicoloured . . 1·10 45
871 250 dh. multicoloured . . 1·90 65
871 500 dh. multicoloured . . 3·50 65
872 1000 dh. multicoloured 6·75 3·50
872a 1500 dh. multicoloured 12·50 4·25
872b 2500 dh. multicoloured 23·00 7·50
Nos. 861/9 measure 18 x 23 mm and Nos. 870/2b 26 x 32 mm.

1979. Coil Stamps.
873 **224** 5 dh. multicoloured . . . 15 10
874 20 dh. multicoloured . . . 25 10
875 50 dh. multicoloured . . . 80 25

225 Tortoise

1979. Libyan Animals. Multicoloured.
876 5 dh. Type **225** 10 10
877 10 dh. Addax (vert) 10 10
878 15 dh. Algerian hedgehog . . . 20 10
879 20 dh. North African crested porcupine 20 10
880 30 dh. Dromedaries 30 15
881 35 dh. Wild cat (vert) 40 15
882 45 dh. Dorcas gazelle (vert) . . 95 25
883 115 dh. Cheetah . . . . 1·90 75

226 Carpet

1979. 17th Tripoli International Trade Fair.
884 **226** 10 dh. multicoloured . . . 10 10
885 – 15 dh. multicoloured . . . 10 10
886 – 30 dh. multicoloured . . 15 10
887 – 45 dh. multicoloured . . 15 10
888 – 115 dh. multicoloured . . 85 35
DESIGNS: 15 dh. to 115 dh. Different carpets

227 Aircraft and People

1979. International Year of the Child. Children's Paintings (1st series). Multicoloured.
889 20 dh. Type **227** 10 10
890 20 dh. Shepherd with flock . . 10 10
891 20 dh. Open air cafe 10 10
892 20 dh. Boat in storm 10 10
893 20 dh. Policeman on traffic duty 10 10
See also Nos. 975/9.

228 World Map, Koran and Symbols of Arab Achievements

229 Radar Tower and Map

1979. The Arabs.
894 **228** 45 dh. multicoloured . . 20 15
895 70 dh. multicoloured . . 55 20

1979. World Meteorological Day.
896 **229** 15 dh. multicoloured . . 10 10
897 30 dh. multicoloured . . 15 10
898 50 dh. multicoloured . . 20 15

230 Medical Care

1979. World Health Day.
899 **230** 40 dh. multicoloured . . 20 15

231 "Carpobrotus acinaciformis"

232 Farmer and Sheep

1979. Libyan Flowers. Multicoloured.
900 10 dh. Type **231** 10 10
901 15 dh. "Caralluma europaea" 10 10
902 20 dh. "Arum cirenaicum" . . 10 10
903 35 dh. "Lavatera arborea" . . 50 15
904 40 dh. "Capparis spinosa" . . 50 15
905 50 dh. "Ranunculus asiaticus" 60 15

1979. 10th Anniv of Revolution. Mult.
906 15 dh. Type **232** 10 10
907 15 dh. Crowd with Green Book 10 10
908 15 dh. Oil field 10 10
909 15 dh. Refinery 10 10
910 30 dh. Dish aerial 15 10
911 30 dh. Hospital 15 10
912 30 dh. Doctor examining patient 15 10
913 30 dh. Surgeon 15 10
914 40 dh. Street, Tripoli . . . 20 15
915 40 dh. Steel mill 20 15
916 40 dh. Tanks 20 15
917 40 dh. Tuareg horsemen . . . 20 15
918 70 dh. Revolutionaries and Green Book 70 20
919 70 dh. Crowd within map of Libya 70 20
920 70 dh. Mullah 70 20
921 70 dh. Student 70 20

233 Volleyball

234 Emblem

1979. "Universiada '79" World University Games, Mexico City. Multicoloured.

923	45 dh. Type **233**	20	15
924	115 dh. Football	1·10	30

1979. 3rd World Telecommunications Exhibition, Geneva.

925 **234**	45 dh. multicoloured	20	15
926	115 dh. multicoloured	1·25	30

235 Seminar Emblem and Crowd

1979. International Seminar on the "Green Book". Multicoloured.

927	10 dh. Type **235**	10	10
928	35 dh. Seminar in progress	45	15
929	100 dh. Colonel Gaddafi with "Green Book"	1·00	30

No. 928 is horizontal, 70 x 43 mm.

236 Horsemen in Town

1979. Evacuation of Foreign Forces. Multicoloured.

931	30 dh. Type **236**	15	10
932	40 dh. Tuareg horsemen	20	15

237 Football Match

1979. Mediterranean Games, Split.

934 **237**	15 dh. multicoloured	10	10
935	30 dh. multicoloured	50	10
936	70 dh. multicoloured	1·25	20

238 Cyclist and Emblem

1979. Junior Cycling Championships, Tripoli. Multicoloured.

937	15 dh. Type **238**	10	10
938	30 dh. Cyclists and emblem	15	10

239 Horse-jumping

1979. Pre-Olympics. Multicoloured.

939	45 dh. Type **239**	20	15
940	60 dh. Javelin	55	15
941	115 dh. Hurdles	1·10	55
942	160 dh. Football	1·40	65

Nos. 939/42 exist from sheets on which an overall Moscow Olympics emblem in silver was superimposed on the stamps.

240 Figure clothed in Palestinian Flag

241 Ploughing

1979. Solidarity with Palestinian People.

944 **240**	30 dh. multicoloured	15	10
945	115 dh. multicoloured	1·10	30

1980. World Olive Oil Year.

946 **241**	15 dh. multicoloured	10	10
947	30 dh. multicoloured	15	10
948	45 dh. multicoloured	20	15

242 Hockey (left)

243 Pipes

1980. National Sports. Multicoloured.

949	10 dh. Type **242**	10	10
950	10 dh. Hockey (right)	10	10
951	10 dh. Leap-frog (left)	10	10
952	10 dh. Leap-frog (right)	10	10
953	15 dh. Long jump (left)	10	10
954	15 dh. Long jump (right)	10	10
955	15 dh. Ball catching (left)	10	10
956	15 dh. Ball catching (right)	10	10
957	20 dh. Wrestling (left)	10	10
958	20 dh. Wrestling (right)	10	10
959	20 dh. Stone throwing (left)	10	10
960	20 dh. Stone throwing (right)	10	10
961	30 dh. Tug-of-war (left)	15	10
962	30 dh. Tug-of-war (right)	15	10
963	30 dh. Jumping (left)	15	10
964	30 dh. Jumping (right)	15	10
965	45 dh. Horsemen (left)	45	15
966	45 dh. Horsemen (right)	45	15
967	45 dh. Horsemen with whips (left)	45	15
968	45 dh. Horsemen with whips (right)	45	15

Nos. 949/68 were issued together, divided into se-tenant blocks of four within the sheet, each horizontal pair forming a composite design.

1980. 18th Tripoli International Fair. Multicoloured.

969	5 dh. Drum (horiz)	10	10
970	10 dh. Drum (different) (horiz)	10	10
971	15 dh. Type **243**	10	10
972	20 dh. Bagpipes (horiz)	10	10
973	25 dh. Stringed instrument and bow (horiz)	15	10

1980. International Year of the Child (1979) (2nd issue). As T **227**. Multicoloured.

975	20 dh. "Horse Riding"	10	10
976	20 dh. "Beach scene"	10	10
977	20 dh. "Fish"	10	10
978	20 dh. "Birthday party"	10	10
979	20 dh. "Sheep Festival"	10	10

244 Mosque and Kaaba

1980. 400th Anniv of Hejira.

980 **244**	50 dh. multicoloured	25	15
981	115 dh. multicoloured	1·10	55

245 Surgical Operation and Hospital

1980. World Health Day.

982 **245**	20 dh. multicoloured	10	10
983	50 dh. multicoloured	50	15

246 Battle of Shoghab "Shahat", 1913

1980. Battles (1st series). Multicoloured.

984	20 dh. Gardabia, 1915	20	15
986	20 dh. Type **246**	10	10
988	20 dh. Fundugh al-Shibani "Garian"	10	10
990	20 dh. Yefren	10	10
992	20 dh. Ghira "Brak"	20	15
994	20 dh. El Hani (Shiat)	35	15
996	20 dh. Sebah	20	15
998	20 dh. Sirt	10	10
985	35 dh. Gardabia	10	10
987	35 dh. Shoghab "Shahat"	20	15
989	35 dh. Fundagh al-Shibani "Garian"	20	15
991	35 dh. Yefren	20	15
993	35 dh. Ghira "Brak"	20	15
995	35 dh. El Hani (Shiat)	60	25
997	35 dh. Sebah	20	15
999	35 dh. Sirt	10	10

The two values commemorating each battle were issued in se-tenant pairs, each pair forming a composite design.

See also Nos. 1027/50, 1132/51 and 1232/39.

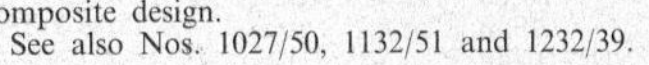

247 Flame

248 Ghadames

1980. Sheikh Zarruq Festival.

1000 **247**	40 dh. multicoloured	20	15
1001	115 dh. multicoloured	1·00	65

1980. Arabian Towns Organization. Mult.

1003	15 dh. Type **248**	10	10
1004	30 dh. Derna	15	10
1005	50 dh. Ahmad Pasha Mosque, Tripoli	50	15

249 Guides on Hike

1980. 14th Pan-Arab Scout Jamboree. Multicoloured.

1006	15 dh. Type **249**	10	10
1007	30 dh. Guides cooking	15	10
1008	50 dh. Cub Scouts cooking	25	15
1009	115 dh. Scouts map-reading	1·10	60

250 Oil Refinery

1980. 11th Anniv of Revolution. Multicoloured.

1011	5 dh. Type **250**	10	10
1012	10 dh. Recreation and youth	10	10
1013	15 dh. Agriculture	10	10
1014	25 dh. Boeing 727-200 airplane and liner	50	15
1015	40 dh. Education	20	15
1016	115 dh. Housing	95	30

251 Camels, Map of Libya and Conference Emblem

1980. World Tourism Conference, Manila. Mult.

1018	45 dh. Type **251**	20	15
1019	115 dh. Emblem, map and camel riders	95	30

252 Figures supporting O.P.E.C. Emblem

253a Map of Libya and Science Symbols

253 Death of Omar el Mukhtar

1980. 20th Anniv of Organization of Petroleum Exporting Countries. Multicoloured.

1020	45 dh. O.P.E.C. emblem and globe	20	15
1021	115 dh. Type **252**	95	30

1980. 49th Death Anniv of Omar el Mukhtar (patriot).

1022 **253**	20 dh. multicoloured	10	10
1023	35 dh. multicoloured	20	15

1980. Birth Millenary of Avicenna (philosopher) and School Scientific Exhibition. Multicoloured.

1025	45 dh. Type **253a**	20	15
1026	115 d. Avicenna and Exhibition Emblem	1·10	30

1981. Battles (2nd series). As T **246**. Mult.

1027	20 dh. Zuara	10	10
1029	20 dh. Tawargha	10	10
1031	20 dh. Dernah	10	10
1033	20 dh. Bir Tagreft	10	10
1035	20 dh. Funduk El Jamel "Misurata"	10	10
1037	20 dh. Sidi El Khemri "Gusbat"	10	10
1039	20 dh. El Khoms	10	10
1041	20 dh. Roghdalin "Menshia"	10	10
1043	20 dh. Ain Zara "Tripoli"	10	10
1045	20 dh. Rughbat el Naga "Benina"	10	10
1047	20 dh. Tobruk	10	10
1049	20 dh. Ikshadia "Werfella"	10	10
1028	35 dh. Zuara	15	15
1030	35 dh. Tawargha	15	15
1032	35 dh. Dernah	15	15
1034	35 dh. Bir Tagreft	15	15
1036	35 dh. Funduk El Jamel "Misurata"	15	15
1038	35 dh. Sidi El Khemri "Gusbat"	15	15
1040	35 dh. El khoms	15	15
1042	35 dh. Roghdalin "Menshia"	15	15
1044	35 dh. Ain Zara "Tripoli"	15	15
1046	35 dh. Rughbat el Naga "Benina"	15	15
1048	35 dh. Tobruk	15	15
1050	35 dh. Ikshadia "Werfella"	15	15

The two values commemorating each battle were issued in se-tenant pairs, each pair forming a composite design.

254 Tent, Trees and Sun

1981. Children's Day. Children's Paintings. Multicoloured.

1051	20 dh. Type **254**	10	10
1052	20 dh. Women	10	10
1053	20 dh. Picnic	10	10
1054	20 dh. Aeroplane and playing children	10	10
1055	20 dh. Mosque and man with camel	10	10

255 Central Bank

257 Crowd and "Green Book" Stamp of 1977

256 Pots

1981. 25th Anniv of Central Bank of Libya.

1056	**255**	45 dh. multicoloured . .	15	15
1057		115 dh. multicoloured . .	95	35

1981. Tripoli International Fair. Multicoloured.

1059	5 dh. Type **256**	10	10
1060	10 dh. Silver coffee pot (vert)	10	10
1061	15 dh. Long-necked vase (vert)	10	10
1062	45 dh. Round-bellied vase . .	45	15
1063	115 dh. Jug	1·10	35

1981. People's Authority Declaration.

1064	**257**	50 dh. multicoloured . .	15	15
1065		115 dh. multicoloured . .	95	35

258 Tajoura Hospital, Medical Complex, Patients receiving Treatment and W.H.O. Emblem

1981. World Health Day.

1066	**258**	45 dh. multicoloured . .	15	15
1067		115 dh. multicoloured . .	95	35

259 Eye and Man on Crutches

1981. International Year of Disabled People.

1068	**259**	20 dh. green, blue & blk .	10	10
1069	–	45 dh. green, black & bl .	15	15
1070	–	115 dh. blue and green .	1·00	35

DESIGNS: 45 dh. Globe and I.Y.D.P. emblem; 115 dh. Hands holding shield with I.Y.D.P. emblem, eye and man on crutch.

260 Horse

1981. Libyan Mosaics. Multicoloured.

1071	10 dh. Type **260**	10	10
1072	20 dh. Ship	10	10
1073	30 dh. Birds, fish and flowers	10	10
1074	40 dh. Leopard	40	15
1075	50 dh. Man playing musical instrument	50	15
1076	115 dh. Fishes	1·10	35

INDEX

Countries can be quickly located by referring to the index at the end of this volume.

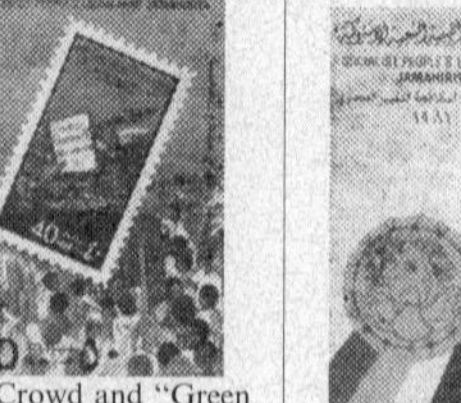

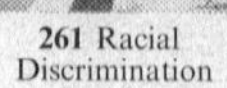

261 Racial Discrimination Emblem

262 Jet Fighters and Sud Aviation Alouette III Helicopter (left-hand stamp)

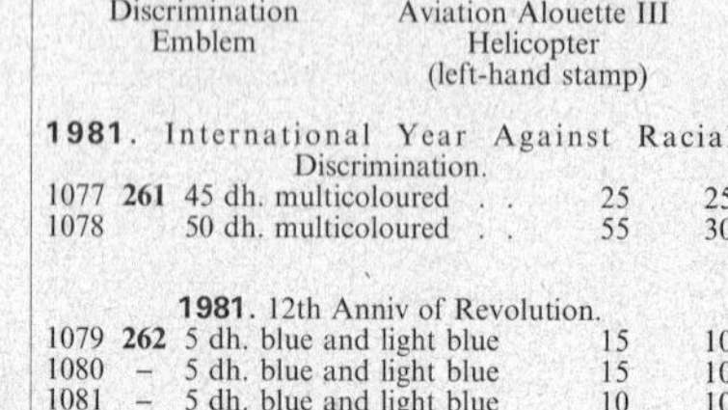

1981. International Year Against Racial Discrimination.

1077	**261**	45 dh. multicoloured . .	25	25
1078		50 dh. multicoloured . .	55	30

1981. 12th Anniv of Revolution.

1079	**262**	5 dh. blue and light blue	15	10
1080	–	5 dh. blue and light blue	15	10
1081	–	5 dh. blue and light blue	10	10
1082	–	5 dh. blue and light blue	10	10
1083	–	10 dh. black and blue .	10	10
1084	–	10 dh. black and blue .	10	10
1085	–	10 dh. black and blue .	10	10
1086	–	10 dh. black and blue .	10	10
1087	–	15 dh. brown & lt brown	10	10
1088	–	15 dh. brown & lt brown	10	10
1089	–	15 dh. brown & lt brown	10	10
1090	–	15 dh. brown & lt brown	10	10
1091	–	20 dh. blue and green .	15	15
1092	–	20 dh. blue and green .	15	15
1093	–	20 dh. blue and green .	15	15
1094	–	20 dh. blue and green .	15	15
1095	–	25 dh. brown and yellow	15	15
1096	–	25 dh. brown and yellow	15	15
1097	–	25 dh. brown and yellow	15	15
1098	–	25 dh. brown and yellow	15	15

DESIGNS—VERT: No. 1080, Jet fighter (right-hand stamp); Nos. 1081/2, Parachutists; Nos. 1083/4, Tank parade; Nos. 1085/6, Marching frogmen; Nos. 1087/8, Anti-aircraft rocket trucks; Nos. 1089/90, Missile trucks. HORIZ: Nos. 1091/2, Marching sailors; Nos. 1093/4, Jeeps and anti-aircraft rocket trucks; Nos. 1095/6, Armoured vehicles and landrovers; Nos. 1097/8, Tank parade.

Each pair forms a horizontal composite design, the first number being the left-hand stamp in each instance.

263 Wheat and Plough

1981. World Food Day.

1100	**263**	45 dh. multicoloured . .	25	25
1101		200 dh. multicoloured .	1·75	95

264 "Pseudotergumia fidia"

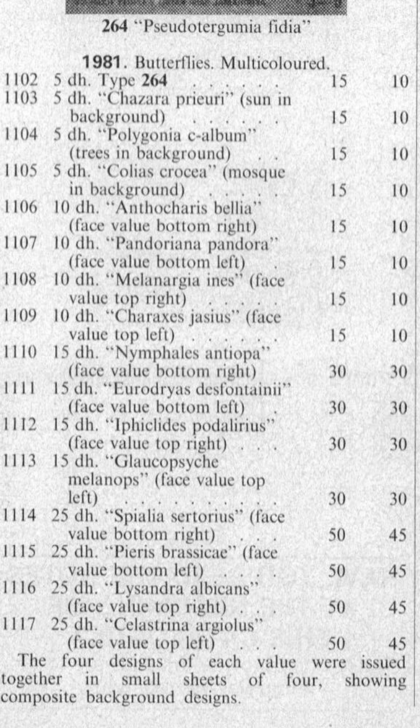

1981. Butterflies. Multicoloured.

1102	5 dh. Type **264**	15	10
1103	5 dh. "Chazara prieuri" (sun in background)	15	10
1104	5 dh. "Polygonia c-album" (trees in background) . .	15	10
1105	5 dh. "Colias crocea" (mosque in background)	15	10
1106	10 dh. "Anthocharis bellia" (face value bottom right)	15	10
1107	10 dh. "Pandoriana pandora" (face value bottom left) .	15	10
1108	10 dh. "Melanargia ines" (face value top right)	15	10
1109	10 dh. "Charaxes jasius" (face value top left)	15	10
1110	15 dh. "Nymphales antiopa" (face value bottom right)	30	30
1111	15 dh. "Eurodryas desfontainii" (face value bottom left) .	30	30
1112	15 dh. "Iphiclides podalirius" (face value top right) . . .	30	30
1113	15 dh. "Glaucopsyche melanops" (face value top left)	30	30
1114	25 dh. "Spialia sertorius" (face value bottom right) . . .	50	45
1115	25 dh. "Pieris brassicae" (face value bottom left)	50	45
1116	25 dh. "Lysandra albicans" (face value top right) . . .	50	45
1117	25 dh. "Celastrina argiolus" (face value top left) . . .	50	45

The four designs of each value were issued together in small sheets of four, showing composite background designs.

265 Grapes

266 I.Y.D.P. Emblem and Globe

1981. Fruit. Multicoloured.

1119	5 dh. Type **265**	10	10
1120	10 dh. Dates	10	10
1121	15 dh. Lemons	10	10
1122	20 dh. Oranges	15	15
1123	35 dh. Barbary figs	20	20
1124	55 dh. Pomegranate	65	30

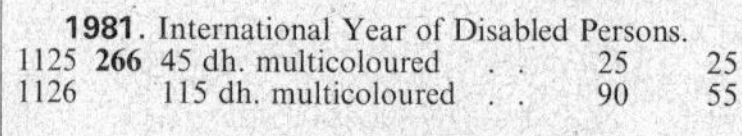

1981. International Year of Disabled Persons.

1125	**266**	45 dh. multicoloured . .	25	25
1126		115 dh. multicoloured . .	90	55

267 Animals (looking right)

1982. Libyan Mosaics. Multicoloured.

1127	45 dh. Type **267**	50	25
1128	45 dh. Orpheus	50	25
1129	45 dh. Animals (looking left)	50	25
1130	45 dh. Fishes	50	25
1131	45 dh. Fishermen	50	25
1132	45 dh. Fishes and ducks . . .	50	25
1133	45 dh. Farm	50	25
1134	45 dh. Birds and fruit	50	25
1135	45 dh. Milking	50	25

268 Koran Texts leading to Ka'aba

269 Grinding Flour

1982. Third Koran Reading Contest. Multicoloured.

1136	10 dh. Type **268**	10	10
1137	35 dh. Koran and formation of the World	20	20
1138	115 dh. Reading the Koran	95	55

1982. Battles (3rd series). As T **246**. Multicoloured.

1140	20 dh. Hun "Gioffra"	15	15
1142	20 dh. Gedabia	15	15
1144	20 dh. El Asaba "Gianduba"	15	15
1146	20 dh. El Habela	15	15
1148	20 dh. Suk El Ahad "Tarhuna"	15	15
1150	20 dh. El Tangi	15	15
1152	20 dh. Sokna	15	15
1154	20 dh. Wadi Smalus "Jabel El Akdar"	15	15
1156	20 dh. Sidi Abuagela "Agelat"	15	15
1158	20 dh. Sidi Surur "Zeliten"	15	15
1160	20 dh. Kuefia	15	15
1162	20 dh. Abunjeim	15	15
1141	35 dh. Hun "Gioffra"	20	20
1143	35 dh. Gedabia	20	20
1145	35 dh. El Asaba "Gianduba"	20	20
1147	35 dh. El Habela	20	20
1149	35 dh. Suk El Ahad "Tarhuna"	20	20
1151	35 dh. El Tangi	20	20
1153	35 dh. Sokna	20	20
1155	35 dh. Wadi Smalus "Jabel El Akdar"	20	20
1157	35 dh. Sidi Abuagela "Agelat"	20	20
1159	35 dh. Sidi Surur "Zeliten"	20	20
1161	35 dh. Kuefia	20	20
1163	35 dh. Abunjeim	20	20

The two values commemorating each battle were issued in se-tenant pairs, each pair forming a composite design.

1982. Tripoli International Fair. Multicoloured.

1164	5 dh. Type **269**	10	10
1165	10 dh. Ploughing	10	10
1166	25 dh. Stacking hay	15	15
1167	35 dh. Weaving	20	20
1168	45 dh. Cooking	50	25
1169	100 dh. Harvesting	95	50

270 "ALFATAH" forming Farm Vehicle

1982. People's Authority Declaration. Multicoloured.

1170	100 dh. Type **270**	75	50
1171	200 dh. Colonel Gaddafi, old man, "Green Book" and guns	1·75	95
1172	300 dh. Rejoicing crowd . .	2·50	1·40

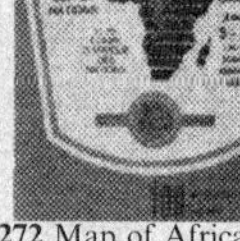

271 Scout flying Model Airship

272 Map of Africa and A.F.C. Emblem

1982. 75th Anniv of Boy Scout Movement. Mult.

1173	100 dh. Type **271**	75	50
1174	200 dh. Scouts helping injured dog	1·75	95
1175	300 dh. Scout reading to old man	1·75	1·40
1176	400 dh. Scout with model rocket	3·75	2·25

1982. African Football Cup Competition.

1178	**272**	100 dh. multicoloured .	95	50
1179		200 dh. multicoloured .	1·90	95

273 Footballer

1982. World Cup Football Championship, Spain. Multicoloured.

1180	45 dh. Type **273**	25	25
1181	100 dh. Footballer (different)	75	50
1182	200 dh. As No. 1173	1·60	95
1183	300 dh. Footballer and goalkeeper	2·25	1·40

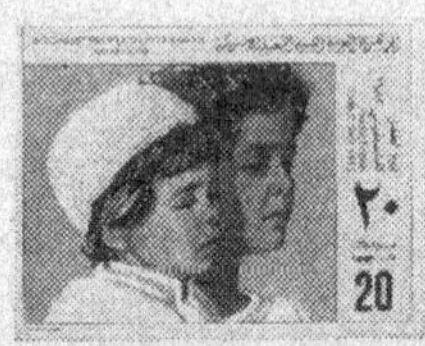

274 Palestinian Children

1982. Palestinian Children's Day. Multicoloured.

1185	20 dh. Type **274**	15	15
1186	20 dh. Girl with dish	15	15
1187	20 dh. Child with turban . .	15	15
1188	20 dh. Young child	15	15
1189	20 dh. Young boy	15	15

275 Lanner Falcon

277 Map of Libya and A.P.U. Emblem

276 Nurses' Class, Operating Theatre and Doctor examining Child

1982. Birds. Multicoloured.

No.	Description	Unused	Used
1190	15 dh. Type **275**	55	35
1191	15 dh. Common swift	55	35
1192	15 dh. Peregrine falcon	55	35
1193	15 dh. Greater flamingo	55	35
1194	25 dh. Whitethroat	90	50
1195	25 dh. Turtle dove	90	50
1196	25 dh. Black-bellied sandgrouse	90	50
1197	25 dh. Egyptian vulture	90	50
1198	45 dh. Golden oriole	1·50	85
1199	45 dh. European bee eater	1·50	85
1200	45 dh. Common kingfisher	1·50	85
1201	45 dh. Common roller	1·50	85
1202	95 dh. Barbary partridge	3·00	1·60
1203	95 dh. Barn owl	3·00	1·60
1204	95 dh. Cream-coloured courser	3·00	1·60
1205	95 dh. Hoopoe	3·00	1·60

The four designs of each value were printed together in se-tenant blocks of four, forming a composite design.

1982. Teaching Hospitals.

No.	Description	Unused	Used
1207	**276** 95 dh. multicoloured	85	50
1208	100 dh. multicoloured	85	50
1209	205 dh. multicoloured	2·00	1·10

1982. 30th Anniv of Arab Postal Union.

No.	Description	Unused	Used
1210	**277** 100 dh. multicoloured	95	50
1211	200 dh. multicoloured	1·90	95

278 19th-century Chinese King and Diagram of Fischer v Spassky, 1972

1982. World Chess Championship, Moscow. Mult.

No.	Description	Unused	Used
1212	100 dh. Type **278**	1·25	50
1213	100 dh. African king and diagram of Karpov v Korchnoi, 1978	1·25	50
1214	100 dh. Modern bishop and diagram of Smyslov v Karpov, 1971	1·25	50
1215	100 dh. 19th-century European rook and diagram of Tal v Vadasz, 1977	1·25	50

Nos. 1212/15 were printed together, se-tenant, forming a composite design.

279 Hexagonal Pattern

1982. World Telecommunications Day.

No.	Description	Unused	Used
1217	**279** 100 dh. multicoloured	75	50
1218	200 dh. multicoloured	1·50	95

280 Map of Libya and "Green Book"

1982. 51st Anniv of International Philatelic Federation (F.I.P.).

No.	Description	Unused	Used
1219	**280** 200 dh. multicoloured	1·75	95

281 Family & Flag **283** Palm Tree and Red Crescent

282 Pres. Gaddafi and Jet Aircraft

1982. Organization of African Unity Summit. Multicoloured.

No.	Description	Unused	Used
1221	50 dh. Type **281**	30	30
1222	100 dh. Map, dove and symbols of industry and agriculture	75	50
1223	200 dh. Pres. Gaddafi and crowd with "Green Book" (65 x 36 mm.)	1·90	95

1982. 13th Anniv of Revolution. Multicoloured.

No.	Description	Unused	Used
1225	15 dh. Type **282**	15	10
1226	20 dh. Gaddafi, soldiers and rockets	15	10
1227	30 dh. Gaddafi, sailors and naval vessels	50	25
1228	45 dh. Gaddafi, soldiers and tanks	25	25
1229	70 dh. Gaddafi, and armed forces	60	35
1230	100 dh. Gaddafi and women soldiers	90	50

1982. 25th Anniv of Libyan Red Crescent. Multicoloured.

No.	Description	Unused	Used
1232	100 dh. Type **283**	95	50
1233	200 dh. "25" within crescents	1·90	95

284 Globe, Dove and Rifle **286** Philadelphus

285 Gaddafi, Crowd, "Green Book" and Emblems

1982. Solidarity with Palestinian People.

No.	Description	Unused	Used
1234	**284** 100 dh. black, mauve and green	95	40
1235	200 dh. black, blue and green	1·90	80

1982. Al Fateh University Symposium on the "Green Book". Multicoloured.

No.	Description	Unused	Used
1236	100 dh. Type **285**	95	45
1237	200 dh. Gaddafi, "Green Book", map and emblems	1·90	95

1983. Flowers. Multicoloured.

No.	Description	Unused	Used
1238	25 dh. Type **286**	15	10
1239	25 dh. Hypericum	15	10
1240	25 dh. Antirrhinum	15	10
1241	25 dh. Lily	15	10
1242	25 dh. Capparis	15	10
1243	25 dh. Tropaeolum	15	10
1244	25 dh. Roses	15	10
1245	25 dh. Chrysanthemum	15	10
1246	25 dh. "Nigella damascena"	15	10
1247	25 dh. "Guilladia lanceolata"	15	10
1248	25 dh. Dahlia	15	10
1249	25 dh. "Dianthus caryophyllus"	15	10
1250	25 dh. "Notobasis syriaca"	15	10
1251	25 dh. "Nerium oleander"	15	10
1252	25 dh. "Iris histroides"	15	10
1253	25 dh. "Scolymus hispanicus"	15	10

287 Customs Council Building, Brussels, and Warrior on Horseback **288** Camel

1983. 30th Anniv of Customs Co-operation Council. Multicoloured.

No.	Description	Unused	Used
1254	25 dh. Type **287**	15	10
1255	50 dh. Customs building	25	20
1256	100 dh. Customs building and warrior with sword	50	45

1983. Battles (4th series). As T **246**. (a) Battle of Ghaser Ahmed.

No.	Description	Unused	Used
1257	50 dh. multicoloured	25	20
1258	50 dh. multicoloured	25	20
	(b) Battle of Sidi Abuarghub.		
1259	50 dh. multicoloured	25	20
1260	50 dh. multicoloured	25	20
	(c) Battle of Ghar Yunes.		
1261	50 dh. multicoloured	25	20
1262	50 dh. multicoloured	25	20
	(d) Battle of Bir Otman.		
1263	50 dh. multicoloured	25	20
1264	50 dh. multicoloured	25	20
	(e) Battle of Sidi Sajeh.		
1265	50 dh. multicoloured	25	20
1266	50 dh. multicoloured	25	20
	(f) Battle of Ras el-Hamam.		
1267	50 dh. multicoloured	25	20
1268	50 dh. multicoloured	25	20
	(g) Battle of Zawiet Ishghefa.		
1269	50 dh. multicoloured	25	20
1270	50 dh. multicoloured	25	20
	(h) Battle of Wadi Essania.		
1271	50 dh. multicoloured	25	20
1272	50 dh. multicoloured	25	20
	(i) Battle of El-Meshiashta.		
1273	50 dh. multicoloured	25	20
1274	50 dh. multicoloured	25	20
	(j) Battle of Gharara.		
1275	50 dh. multicoloured	25	20
1276	50 dh. multicoloured	25	20
	(k) Battle of Abughelan.		
1277	50 dh. multicoloured	20	20
1278	50 dh. multicoloured	20	20
	(l) Battle of Mahruka.		
1279	50 dh. multicoloured	20	20
1280	50 dh. multicoloured	20	20

The two values for each battle were printed together in se-tenant pairs, forming composite designs.

1983. Farm Animals. Multicoloured.

No.	Description	Unused	Used
1281	25 dh. Type **288**	15	10
1282	25 dh. Cow	15	10
1283	25 dh. Horse	15	10
1284	25 dh. Bull	15	10
1285	25 dh. Goat	15	10
1286	25 dh. Sheep dog	15	10
1287	25 dh. Ewe	15	10
1288	25 dh. Ram	15	10
1289	25 dh. Greylag goose	15	10
1290	25 dh. Helmet guineafowl	15	10
1291	25 dh. Rabbit	15	10
1292	25 dh. Wood pigeon	15	10
1293	25 dh. Common turkey	15	10
1294	25 dh. Cockerel	15	10
1295	25 dh. Hen	15	10
1296	25 dh. Goose	15	10

289 Musician with Twin-horned Pipe

1983. Tripoli International Fair. Multicoloured.

No.	Description	Unused	Used
1297	40 dh. Type **289**	20	15
1298	45 dh. Bagpipes (horiz)	25	20
1299	50 dh. Horn	25	20
1300	55 dh. Flute (horiz)	30	25
1301	75 dh. Pipe	65	35
1302	100 dh. Man and woman at well	90	45

290 Phoenician Galley

1983. 25th Anniv of International Maritime Organization. Multicoloured.

No.	Description	Unused	Used
1303	100 dh. Type **290**	1·25	55
1304	100 dh. Ancient Greek galley	1·25	55
1305	100 dh. Ancient Egyptian ship	1·25	55
1306	100 dh. Roman sailing ship	1·25	55
1307	100 dh. Viking longship	1·25	55
1308	100 dh. Libyan xebec	1·25	55

291 Motorist

1983. Children's Day. Multicoloured.

No.	Description	Unused	Used
1309	20 dh. Type **291**	10	10
1310	20 dh. Tractor and trailer	10	10
1311	20 dh. Child with dove and globe	10	10
1312	20 dh. Scout camp	10	10
1313	20 dh. Dinosaur	10	10

292 Pres. Gaddafi with Children

1983. World Health Day. Multicoloured.

No.	Description	Unused	Used
1314	25 dh. Type **292**	15	10
1315	50 dh. Gaddafi and old man in wheelchair	25	20
1316	100 dh. Gaddafi visiting sick girl (horiz)	80	45

293 Gaddafi, Map and "Green Book" **294** Economic Emblems on Map of Africa

1983. 1st World "Green Book" Symposium. Multicoloured.

No.	Description	Unused	Used
1317	50 dh. Type **293**	25	20
1318	70 dh. Syposium in session and emblem (56 x 37 mm)	60	30
1319	80 dh. Gaddafi, "Green Book", emblem and "Jamahiriya"	65	35

1983. 25th Anniv of African Economic Committee.

No.	Description	Unused	Used
1321	**294** 50 dh. multicoloured	25	20
1322	100 dh. multicoloured	90	45
1323	250 dh. multicoloured	1·90	1·10

296 "Labrus bimaculatus"

1983. Fishes. Multicoloured.

No.	Description	Unused	Used
1325	25 dh. Type **296**	15	10
1326	25 dh. "Trigoporus lastoviza"	15	10
1327	25 dh. "Thalassoma pavo"	15	10
1328	25 dh. "Apogon imberbis"	15	10
1329	25 dh. "Scomber scombrus"	15	10
1330	25 dh. "Spondyliosoma cantharus"	15	10
1331	25 dh. "Trachinus draco"	15	10
1332	25 dh. "Blennius pavo"	15	10
1333	25 dh. "Scorpaena notata"	15	10
1334	25 dh. "Serranus scriba"	15	10
1335	25 dh. "Lophius piscatorius"	15	10
1336	25 dh. "Uranoscopus scaber"	15	10
1337	25 dh. "Auxis thazard"	15	10
1338	25 dh. "Zeus faber"	15	10
1339	25 dh. "Dactylopterus volitans"	15	10
1340	25 dh. "Umbrina cirrosa"	15	10

297 "Still-life" (Gauguin)

1983. Paintings. Multicoloured.

No.	Description	Unused	Used
1341	50 dh. Type **297**	25	20
1342	50 dh. Abstract	25	20
1343	50 dh. "The Conquest of Tunis by Charles V" (Rubens)	25	20
1344	50 dh. "Arab Band in Horse-drawn Carriage"	25	20
1345	50 dh. "Apotheosis of Gaddafi" (vert)	25	20
1346	50 dh. Horses (detail of Raphael's "The Triumph of David over the Assyrians") (vert)	25	20
1347	50 dh. "Workers" (vert)	25	20
1348	50 dh. "Sunflowers" (Van Gogh) (vert)	25	20

298 Basketball

1983. Olympic Games, Los Angeles. Mult.

No.	Description	Unused	Used
1349	10 dh. Type **298**	10	10
1350	15 dh. High jumping	10	10
1351	25 dh. Running	15	10
1352	50 dh. Gymnastics	25	20
1353	100 dh. Windsurfing	80	45
1354	200 dh. Shot-putting	1·50	95

299 I.T.U. Building, Antenna and W.C.Y. Emblem

1983. World Communications Year.

No.	Description	Unused	Used
1356 **299**	10 dh. multicoloured	10	10
1357	50 dh. multicoloured	25	20
1358	100 dh. multicoloured	75	45

300 "The House is to be served by its Residents"

1983. Extracts from the Green Book. Mult.

No.	Description	Unused	Used
1359	10 dh. Type **300**	10	10
1360	15 dh. "Power, wealth and arms are in the hands of the people"	10	10
1361	20 dh. "Masters in their own castles" (vert)	10	10
1362	35 dh. "No democracy without popular congresses"	20	15
1363	100 dh. "The authority of the people" (vert)	50	45
1364	140 dh. "The Green Book is the guide of humanity for final release"	1·10	70

301 Handball

1983. 2nd African Youth Festival. Multicoloured.

No.	Description	Unused	Used
1366	100 dh. Type **301**	85	45
1367	100 dh. Basketball	85	45
1368	100 dh. High jumping	85	45
1369	100 dh. Running	85	45
1370	100 dh. Football	85	45

302 Marching Soldiers

1983. 14th Anniv of September Revolution. Mult.

No.	Description	Unused	Used
1371	65 dh. Type **302**	35	30
1372	75 dh. Weapons and communications training	40	35
1373	90 dh. Women with machine-guns and bazookas	70	40
1374	100 dh. Machine-gun training	75	45
1375	150 dh. Bazooka training	1·10	70
1376	250 dh. Rifle training	2·00	1·10

303 Saluting Scouts

1983. Scout Jamborees. Multicoloured.

No.	Description	Unused	Used
1378	50 dh. Type **303**	25	20
1379	100 dh. Scouts around camp fire	90	45

EVENTS. 50 dh. Second Islamic Scout Jamboree; 100 dh. 15th Pan Arab Scout Jamboree.

304 Traffic Cadets

305 Saadun

1983. Traffic Day. Multicoloured.

No.	Description	Unused	Used
1381	30 dh. Type **304**	40	15
1382	70 dh. Traffic policeman	70	30
1383	200 dh. Police motorcyclists	1·90	1·25

1983. 90th Birth Anniv of Saadun (patriot soldier).

No.	Description	Unused	Used
1384 **305**	100 dh. multicoloured	90	45

306 Walter Wellman's airship "America", 1910

1983. Bicentenary of Manned Flight. Mult.

No.	Description	Unused	Used
1385	100 dh. Type **306**	1·00	55
1386	100 dh. Airship "Nulli Secundus", 1907	1·00	55
1387	100 dh. Jean-Baptiste Meusnier's balloon design, 1784	1·00	55
1388	100 dh. Blanchard and Jeffries' Channel crossing, 1785 (vert)	1·00	55
1389	100 dh. Pilatre de Rozier's hydrogen/hot-air balloon flight, 1784 (vert)	1·00	55
1390	100 dh. First Montgolfier balloon, 1783 (vert)	1·00	55

307 Globe and Dove

1983. Solidarity with Palestinian People.

No.	Description	Unused	Used
1393 **307**	200 dh. green, blue & blk	1·60	95

308 Gladiators fighting

1983. Mosaics. Multicoloured.

No.	Description	Unused	Used
1394	50 dh. Type **308**	50	20
1395	50 dh. Gladiators fighting (different)	50	20
1396	50 dh. Gladiators and slave	50	20
1397	50 dh. Two musicians	50	20
1398	50 dh. Three musicians	50	20
1399	50 dh. Two gladiators	50	20
1400	50 dh. Two Romans and bound victim	50	20
1401	50 dh. Leopard and man hunting deer	50	20
1402	50 dh. Deer and man with boar	50	20

309 Traditional Architecture

1983. Achievements of the Revolution. Mult.

No.	Description	Unused	Used
1403	10 dh. Type **309**	10	10
1404	15 dh. Camels drinking and mechanization of farming	10	10
1405	20 dh. Computer operator and industrial scene	10	10
1406	35 dh. Modern architecture	15	10
1407	100 dh. Surgeons and nurses treating patients and hospital	90	40
1408	140 dh. Airport and airplane	1·25	75

310 Flooding a River Bed

311 Mahmud Burkis

1983. Colonel Gaddafi–River Builder. Multicoloured.

No.	Description	Unused	Used
1410	50 dh. Type **310**	20	15
1411	50 dh. Irrigation pipe and agricultural produce	20	15
1412	100 dh. Colonel Gaddafi, irrigation pipe and farmland (62 x 44 mm)	1·00	40
1413	100 dh. Colonel Gaddafi and map (68 x 32 mm)	1·00	40
1414	150 dh. Colonel Gaddafi explaining irrigation project (35 x 32 mm)	1·40	65

Nos. 1410/12 were printed together in se-tenant strips of three forming a composite design.

1984. Personalities. Multicoloured.

No.	Description	Unused	Used
1416	100 dh. Type **311**	1·00	40
1417	100 dh. Ahmed el-Bakbak	1·00	40
1418	100 dh. Mohamed el-Misurati	1·00	40
1419	100 dh. Mahmud Ben Musa	1·00	40
1420	100 dh. Abdulhamid el-Sherif	1·00	40
1421	100 dh. Mehdi el-Sherif	1·00	40
1422	100 dh. Mahmud Mustafa Dreza	1·00	40
1423	100 dh. Hosni Fauzi el-Amir	1·00	40
1424	100 dh. Ali Haidar el-Saati	1·00	40
1425	200 dh. Ahmed el-Feghi Hasan	1·50	80
1426	200 dh. Bashir el-Jawab	1·50	80
1427	200 dh. Ali el-Gariani	1·50	80
1428	200 dh. Muktar Shakshuki	1·50	80
1429	200 dh. Abdurrahman el-Busayri	1·50	80
1430	200 dh. Ibbrahim Bakir	1·50	80
1431	200 dh. Mahmud el-Janzuri	1·50	80

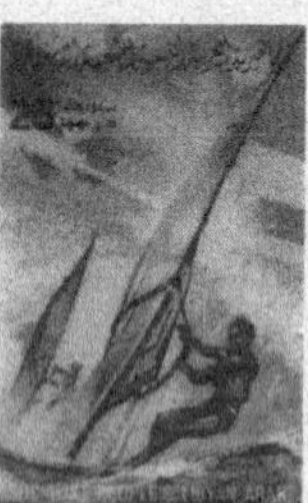

312 Windsurfing

313 Col. Gaddafi with Schoolchildren

1984. Water Sports. Multicoloured.

No.	Description	Unused	Used
1432	25 dh. Type **312**	20	10
1433	25 dh. Dinghy sailing (orange and red sails)	20	10
1434	25 dh. Dinghy sailing (mauve sails)	20	10
1435	25 dh. Hang-gliding on water skis	20	10
1436	25 dh. Water-skiing	20	10
1437	25 dh. Angling from boat	20	10
1438	25 dh. Men in speed boat	20	10
1439	25 dh. Water-skiing (different)	20	10
1440	25 dh. Fishing	20	10
1441	25 dh. Canoeing	20	10
1442	25 dh. Surfing	20	10
1443	25 dh. Water-skiing (different)	20	10
1444	25 dh. Scuba diving	20	10
1445	25 dh. Diving	20	10
1446	25 dh. Swimming in snorkel and flippers	20	10
1447	25 dh. Scuba diving for fish	20	10

1984. African Children's Day. Multicoloured.

No.	Description	Unused	Used
1448	50 dh. Type **313**	50	15
1449	50 dh. Colonel Gaddafi and children in national dress	50	15
1450	100 dh. Colonel Gaddafi on map and children at various activities (62 x 43 mm)	1·10	40

314 Women in National, Casual and Military Dress

1984. Libyan Women's Emancipation. Multicoloured.

No.	Description	Unused	Used
1451	55 dh. Type **314**	50	20
1452	70 dh. Women in traditional, casual and military dress (vert)	75	25
1453	100 dh. Colonel Gaddafi and women in military dress	95	40

315 Theatre, Sabratha

1984. Roman Ruins of Cyrenaica. Multicoloured.

No.	Description	Unused	Used
1454	50 dh. Type **315**	20	15
1455	60 dh. Temple, Cyrene	50	20
1456	70 dh. Monument, Sabratha (vert)	60	25
1457	100 dh. Amphitheatre, Leptis Magna	90	40
1458	150 dh. Temple, Cyrene (different)	1·40	65
1459	200 dh. Basilica, Leptis Magna	1·90	80

316 Silver Dirham, 115 h.

318 Muktar Shiaker Murabet

317 Men at Tea Ceremony

1984. Arabic Islamic Coins (1st series).

No.	Description	Unused	Used
1460 **316**	200 dh. silver, yellow and black	1·90	85
1461 –	200 dh. silver, mauve and black	1·90	85
1462 –	200 dh. silver, green and black	1·90	85
1463 –	200 dh. silver, orange and black	1·90	85
1464 –	200 dh. silver, blue and black	1·90	85

DESIGNS: No. 1461, Silver dirham, 93 h; 1462, Silver dirham, 121 h; 1463, Silver dirham, 49 h; 1464, Silver dirham, 135 h.

See also Nos. 1643/5.

1984. International Trade Fair, Tripoli. Mult.

No.	Description	Unused	Used
1465	25 dh. Type **317**	15	10
1466	35 dh. Woman making tea	15	15
1467	45 dh. Men taking tea	20	15
1468	55 dh. Family taking tea	50	20
1469	75 dh. Veiled women pouring tea	70	30
1470	100 dh. Robed men taking tea	1·00	40

1984. Musicians. Multicoloured.

No.	Description	Unused	Used
1471	100 dh. Type **318**	1·25	65
1472	100 dh. El-Aref el-Jamal	1·25	65
1473	100 dh. Ali Shiaalia	1·25	65
1474	100 dh. Bashir Fehmi	1·25	65

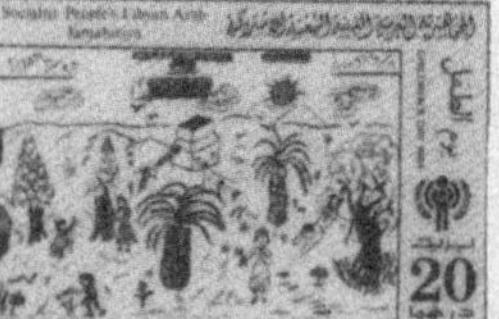

319 Playing among Trees

1984. Children's Day. Designs showing children's paintings. Multicoloured.

1475 20 dh. Type **319** 10 10
1476 20 dh. A rainy day 10 10
1477 20 dh. Weapons of war . . . 10 10
1478 20 dh. Playing on the swing 10 10
1479 20 dh. Playing in the park . . 10 10

320 Crest and "39"

1984. 39th Anniv of Arab League.

1480 **320** 30 dh. multicoloured . . 15 15
1481 40 dh. multicoloured . . 20 15
1482 50 dh. multicoloured . . 55 20

321 Red Four-seater Car

1984. Motor Cars and Locomotives. Mult.

1483 100 dh. Type **321** . . . . . . 1·25 65
1484 100 dh. Red three-seater car 1·25 65
1485 100 dh. Yellow two-seater car with three lamps . . . . . 1·25 65
1486 100 dh. Covered red four-seater car . . . . 1·25 65
1487 100 dh. Yellow two-seater car with two lamps . . . . . . 1·25 65
1488 100 dh. Cream car with spare wheel at side . . . . 1·25 65
1489 100 dh. Green car with spare wheel at side . . . . 1·25 65
1490 100 dh. Cream four-seater car with spare wheel at back . 1·25 65
1491 100 dh. Locomotive pulling wagon and coach . . . . . 1·25 65
1492 100 dh. Purple and blue locomotive . . . . 1·25 65
1493 100 dh. Cream locomotive . . 1·25 65
1494 100 dh. Lavender and brown locomotive . . . . 1·25 65
1495 100 dh. Lavender and black locomotive with red wheels 1·25 65
1496 100 dh. Cream and red locomotive . . . . 1·25 65
1497 100 dh. Purple and black locomotive with red wheels 1·25 65
1498 100 dh. Green and orange locomotive . . . . 1·25 65

322 Stylised People and Campaign Emblem

1984. World Health Day. Anti-Polio Campaign. Multicoloured.

1499 20 dh. Type **322** 10 10
1500 30 dh. Stylised people and 1981 20 dh. stamp 15 15
1501 40 dh. Stylised people and Arabic emblem 50 15

323 Man making Slippers

1984. Handicrafts. Multicoloured.

1502 150 dh. Type **323** . . . . . . 1·60 65
1503 150 dh. Man making decorative harness . . . . 1·60 65
1504 150 dh. Women forming cotton into skeins . . . . 1·60 65
1505 150 dh. Woman spinning by hand . . . . 1·60 65
1506 150 dh. Man weaving . . . . 1·60 65
1507 150 dh. Women weaving . . 1·60 65

324 Telephones, Dial and Mail

1984. Postal and Telecommunications Union Congress. Multicoloured.

1508 50 dh. Type **324** 50 20
1509 50 dh. Woman working at computer console, dial and man working on computer 50 20
1510 100 dh. Satellite, map, laurel branches and telephone handset . . . . 1·00 40

325 Armed Soldiers and Civilians **326** Children behind Barbed Wire

1984. Abrogation of 17th May Treaty. Multicoloured.

1511 50 dh. Type **325** 65 20
1512 50 dh. Map, dove and burning banner 65 20
1513 50 dh. Soldiers shaking hands and crowd with banners (30 x 40 mm) 65 20
1514 100 dh. Hands tearing treaty, Gaddafi and crowd (62 x 40 mm) . . . . 1·25 40
1515 100 dh. Gaddafi addressing crowd . . . . 1·25 40

Nos. 1512/14 were printed together in se-tenant strips of three, forming a composite design.

1984. Child Victims of Invasion Day. Multicoloured.

1516 70 dh. Torn flags on barbed wire 70 25
1517 100 dh. Type **326** . . . . . 1·00 40

327 "The Party System Aborts Democracy" **328** Man in Brown Robes

1984. Quotations from "The Green Book". Multicoloured.

1518 100 dh. Type **327** 95 40
1519 100 dh. Colonel Gaddafi . . 95 40
1520 100 dh. "Partners not wage-workers" 95 40
1521 100 dh. "No representation in lieu of the people. Representation is falsification" 95 40
1522 100 dh. The Green Book . . 95 40
1523 100 dh. "Committees everywhere" 95 40
1524 100 dh. "Forming parties splits societies" 95 40
1525 100 dh. Skyscraper and earthmover 95 40
1526 100 dh. "No democracy without popular congresses" . . . 95 40

1984. Costumes. Multicoloured.

1527 100 dh. Type **328** . . . . . 1·25 65
1528 100 dh. Woman in green dress and red shawl . . . . . . 1·25 65
1529 100 dh. Man in ornate costume and turban . . . . 1·25 65
1530 100 dh. Man in short trousers and plain shirt . . . . . 1·25 65
1531 100 dh. Woman in shift and trousers with white shawl 1·25 65
1532 100 dh. Man in long white robe and red shawl . . . . . . 1·25 65

329 Footballer tackling

1984. World Cup Football Championship. Multicoloured.

1533 70 dh. Type **329** 70 25
1534 70 dh. Footballers in magenta and green shirts 70 25
1535 70 dh. Footballers in orange and lemon shirts 70 25
1536 70 dh. Goalkeeper failing to save ball 70 25
1537 70 dh. Footballers in yellow and brown shirts 70 25
1538 70 dh. Top of Trophy and footballer in green striped shirt 70 25
1539 70 dh. Top of Trophy and footballers in blue and pink shirts 70 25
1540 70 dh. Footballers in black and white striped and green and red striped shirts 70 25
1541 70 dh. Footballers in green and red striped shirts 70 25
1542 70 dh. Foot of trophy and footballers in orange striped and blue shirts 70 25
1543 70 dh. Foot of trophy and goalkeeper 70 25
1544 70 dh. Goalkeeper saving headed ball 70 25
1545 70 dh. Referee and footballers 70 25
1546 70 dh. Footballers in white with red striped sleeves and orange shirts 70 25
1547 70 dh. Footballers in white and green striped and orange shirts 70 25
1548 70 dh. Footballer in pink shirt 70 25

Nos. 1533/48 were printed in sheetlets of 16 stamps, the backgrounds to the stamps forming an overall design of a stadium.

330 Football **331** Palm Trees

1984. Olympic Games, Los Angeles. Mult.

1549 100 dh. Type **330** . . . . . . 1·25 65
1550 100 dh. Swimming . . . . . 1·25 65
1551 100 dh. Throwing the discus 1·25 65
1552 100 dh. Windsurfing . . . . 1·25 65
1553 100 dh. Basketball . . . . . 1·25 65
1554 100 dh. Running . . . . . . 1·25 65

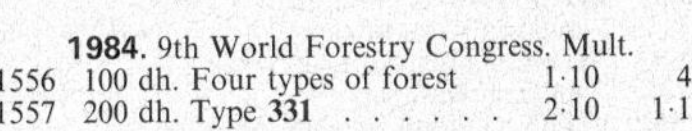

1984. 9th World Forestry Congress. Mult.

1556 100 dh. Four types of forest 1·10 40
1557 200 dh. Type **331** . . . . . . 2·10 1·10

332 Modern Building

1984. 15th Anniv of Revolution. Multicoloured.

1558 25 dh. Type **332** 15 10
1559 25 dh. Front of building . . . 15 10
1560 25 dh. Building by pool . . . 15 10
1561 25 dh. Col. Gaddafi (three-quarter portrait) 15 10
1562 25 dh. High-rise block 15 10
1563 25 dh. Crane and mosque . . 15 10
1564 25 dh. Motorway interchange 15 10
1565 25 dh. House and garden . . 15 10
1566 25 dh. Shepherd and flock . . 15 10
1567 25 dh. Combine harvester . . 15 10
1568 25 dh. Tractors 15 10
1569 25 dh. Scientific equipment 15 10
1570 25 dh. Col Gaddafi (full face) 15 10
1571 25 dh. Water pipeline 15 10
1572 25 dh. Lighthouse 15 10
1573 25 dh. Liner at quay 30 10

333 Armed Man

334 Soldier flogging Civilian

1984. Evacuation of Foreign Forces. Mult. (a) As T **333.**

1574 50 dh. Type **333** 50 20
1575 50 dh. Armed man (different) 50 20
1576 100 dh. Men on horseback charging (62 x 40 mm) . . 1·00 40

(b) As T **334.**

1577 100 dh. Type **334** . . . . . 1·00 40
1578 100 dh. Girl on horse charging soldiers . . . . 1·00 40
1579 100 dh. Mounted soldiers and wounded being tended by women . . . . 1·00 40

335 Woman riding Skewbald Showjumper

1984. Equestrian Events. Multicoloured.

1580 25 dh. Type **335** 15 10
1581 25 dh. Man riding black showjumper (stands in background) 15 10
1582 25 dh. Jockey riding chestnut horse (stands in background) 15 10
1583 25 dh. Man on chestnut horse jumping in cross-country event 15 10
1584 25 dh. Man riding bay horse in showjumping competition 15 10
1585 25 dh. Woman on black horse in dressage competition . . . 15 10
1586 25 dh. Man on black horse in dressage competition . . . 15 10
1587 25 dh. Woman riding chestnut horse in cross-country event 15 10
1588 25 dh. Jockey riding bay horse 15 10
1589 25 dh. Woman on bay horse in dressage competition . . . 15 10
1590 25 dh. Man on grey horse in dressage competition . . . 15 10
1591 25 dh. Jockey riding grey steeplechaser 15 10
1592 25 dh. Woman riding grey showjumper 15 10
1593 25 dh. Woman riding through water in cross-country competition 15 10
1594 25 dh. Woman on chestnut horse in cross-country competition 15 10
1595 25 dh. Man riding dun showjumper 15 10

Nos. 1580/95 were printed together in sheetlets of 16 stamps, the backgrounds of the stamps forming an overall design of an equestrian ring.

336 Man cleaning Corn **337** Map and Pharmaceutical Equipment

1984. Traditional Agriculture. Multicoloured.

1596 100 dh. Type **336** . . . . . 1·25 65
1597 100 dh. Man using oxen to draw water from well . . . . . 1·25 65
1598 100 dh. Man making straw goods . . . . 1·25 65
1599 100 dh. Shepherd with sheep 1·25 65
1600 100 dh. Man treating animal skin . . . . 1·25 65
1601 100 dh. Man climbing coconut tree . . . . 1·25 65

1984. 9th Conference of Arab Pharmacists Union.

1602 **337** 100 dh. multicoloured . 1·25 40
1603 200 dh. multicoloured . 2·50 1·10

338 Crowd with Banner showing Map of North Africa

1984. Arab-African Unity. Multicoloured.
1604 100 dh. Type **338** . . . . . . 1·25 65
1605 100 dh. Crowd and men holding flags . . . . 1·25 65

339 1982 and 1983 Solidarity Stamps and Map of Palestine

1984. Solidarity with Palestinian People.
1606 **339** 100 dh. multicoloured . . 1·25 40
1607 150 dh. multicoloured . . 1·90 1·00

340 Boeing 747SP, 1975

1984. 40th Anniv of International Civil Aviation Organization. Multicoloured.
1608 70 dh. Type **340** 95 30
1609 70 dh. Concorde, 1969 . . . 95 30
1610 70 dh. Lockheed TriStar 500, 1978 . . . . 95 30
1611 70 dh. Airbus Industrie A310, 1982 . . . . 95 30
1612 70 dh. Tupolev Tu-134A, 1962 95 30
1613 70 dh. Shorts 360, 1981 . . . 95 30
1614 70 dh. Boeing 727-100, 1963 . 95 30
1615 70 dh. Sud Aviation Caravelle 10R, 1965 . . . . 95 30
1616 70 dh. Fokker Friendship, 1955 95 30
1617 70 dh. Lockheed Constellation, 1946 . . . . 95 30
1618 70 dh. Martin M-130 flying boat, 1955 . . . . 95 30
1619 70 dh. Douglas DC-3, 1936 95 50
1620 70 dh. Junkers Ju-52/3m, 1932 95 30
1621 70 dh. Lindbergh's "Spirit of St. Louis", 1927 . . . . 95 30
1622 70 dh. De Havilland Moth, 1925 95 30
1623 70 dh. Wright Flyer I, 1903 . . 95 30
Nos. 1608/23 were printed together in sheetlets of 16 stamps, the backgrounds of the stamps forming an overall design of a runway.

341 Coin

342 Mother and Son

1984. 20th Anniv of African Development Bank. Multicoloured.
1624 50 dh. Type **341** 55 20
1625 70 dh. Map of Africa and "20" 1·00 25
1626 100 dh. "20" and symbols of industry and agriculture . . 1·25 65

1985. U.N.I.C.E.F. Child Survival Campaign. Multicoloured.
1627 70 dh. Type **342** . . . . . . 1·00 50
1628 70 dh. Couple and children 1·00 50
1629 70 dh. Col. Gaddafi and children . . . . 1·00 50
1630 70 dh. Boys in uniform . . . 1·00 50

343 Mohamed Hamdi

344 Pipeline, River, Plants and Map

1985. Musicians and Instruments. Multicoloured.
1631 100 dh. Kamel el-Ghadi . . 1·25 65
1632 100 dh. Fiddle rebab . . . . 1·25 65
1633 100 dh. Ahmed el-Khogia . 1·25 65
1634 100 dh. Violin . . . . 1·25 65
1635 100 dh. Mustafa el-Fallah . 1·25 65
1636 100 dh. Zither . . . . 1·25 65
1637 100 dh. Type **343** . . . . . 1·25 65
1638 100 dh. Mask . . . . 1·25 65

1985. Col. Gaddafi–River Builder. Multicoloured.
1639 100 dh. Type **344** . . . . . 1·25 65
1640 100 dh. Water droplet, river and flowers . . . . 1·25 65
1641 100 dh. Dead tree with branch thriving in water droplet . 1·25 65

345 Gold Dinar, 105 h.

1985. Arabic Islamic Coins (2nd series). Mult.
1643 200 dh. Type **345** . . . . . 2·50 1·25
1644 200 dh. Gold dinar, 91 h. . . 2·50 1·25
1645 200 dh. Gold dinar, 77 h. . . 2·50 1·25

346 Fish

347 Gaddafi in Robes and Hat

1985. Fossils. Multicoloured.
1647 150 dh. Type **346** . . . . . 1·90 55
1648 150 dh. Frog . . . . 1·90 55
1649 150 dh. Mammal . . . . . 1·90 55

1985. People's Authority Declaration. Mult.
1650 100 dh. Type **347** . . . . . 1·25 65
1651 100 dh. Gaddafi in black robe holding book . . . . . . 1·25 65
1652 100 dh. Gaddafi in dress uniform without cap . . . 1·25 65
1653 100 dh. Gaddafi in black dress uniform with cap . . . . 1·25 65
1654 100 dh. Gaddafi in white dress uniform . . . . 1·25 65

348 Cymbal Player

1985. International Trade Fair, Tripoli. Mult.
1655 100 dh. Type **348** . . . . . 1·25 65
1656 100 dh. Piper and drummer . 1·25 65
1657 100 dh. Drummer and bagpipes player . . . . 1·25 65
1658 100 dh. Drummer . . . . . 1·25 65
1659 100 dh. Tambour player . . 1·25 65

349 Goalkeeper catching Ball

350 Emblem, Radio Transmitter and Satellite

1985. Children's Day. Multicoloured.
1660 20 dh. Type **349** 10 10
1661 20 dh. Child on touchline with ball 10 10
1662 20 dh. Letters of alphabet as players 10 10
1663 20 dh. Goalkeeper saving ball 10 10
1664 20 dh. Player heading ball . 10 10

1985. International Communications Development Programme.
1665 **350** 30 dh. multicoloured . . 15 10
1666 70 dh. multicoloured . . 75 25
1667 100 dh. multicoloured . . 1·10 65

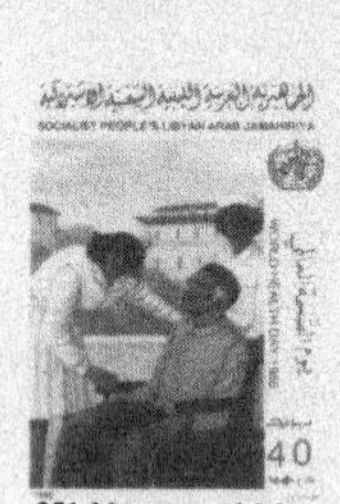

351 Nurses and Man in Wheelchair

352 "Mytilidae"

1985. World Health Day. Multicoloured.
1668 40 dh. Type **351** 50 10
1669 60 dh. Nurses and doctors . . 75 15
1670 100 dh. Nurse and child . . . 1·25 65

1985. Sea Shells. Multicoloured.
1671 25 dh. Type **352** 40 15
1672 25 dh. Purple dye murex ("Muricidae") 40 15
1673 25 dh. Tuberculate cockle ("Cardiidae") 40 15
1674 25 dh. "Corallophilidae" . . 40 15
1675 25 dh. Trunculus murex ("Muricidae") 40 15
1676 25 dh. "Muricacea" 40 15
1677 25 dh. "Turridae" 40 15
1678 25 dh. Nodose paper nautilus ("Argonautidae") 40 15
1679 25 dh. Giant tun ("Tonnidae") 40 15
1680 25 dh. Common pelican's-foot ("Aporrhaidae") 40 15
1681 25 dh. "Trochidae" 40 15
1682 25 dh. "Cancellariidae" . . . 40 15
1683 25 dh. "Epitoniidae" 40 15
1684 25 dh. "Turbinidae" 40 15
1685 25 dh. Zoned mitre ("Mitridae") 40 15
1686 25 dh. Cat's-paw scallop ("Pectinidae") 40 15
Nos. 1671/86 were printed se-tenant, the backgrounds forming an overall design of the sea bed.

353 Books and Emblem

354 Girls Skipping

1985. International Book Fair, Tripoli.
1687 **353** 100 dh. multicoloured . . 1·25 60
1688 200 dh. multicoloured . . 2·25 1·25

1985. International Youth Year. Multicoloured.
1689 20 dh. Type **354** 10 10
1690 20 dh. Boys playing with stones 10 10
1691 20 dh. Girls playing hopscotch 10 10
1692 20 dh. Boys playing with sticks 10 10
1693 20 dh. Boys playing with spinning top 10 10

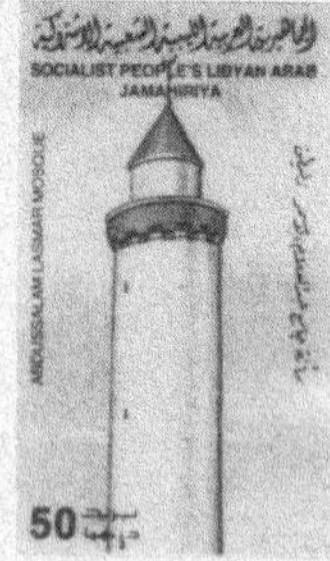

355 Abdussalam Lasmar Mosque

356 Jamila Zemerli

1985. Minarets. Multicoloured.
1695 50 dh. Type **355** 50 15
1696 50 dh. Zaoviat Kadria Mosque 50 15
1697 50 dh. Zaoviat Amura Mosque 50 15
1698 50 dh. Gurgi Mosque 50 15
1699 50 dh. Mizran Mosque . . . 50 15
1700 50 dh. Salem Mosque 50 15
1701 50 dh. Ghat Mosque 50 15
1702 50 dh. Ahmed Karamanli Mosque 50 15
1703 50 dh. Atya Mosque 50 15
1704 50 dh. El Kettani Mosque . . 50 15
1705 50 dh. Benghazi Mosque . . 50 15
1706 50 dh. Derna Mosque 50 15
1707 50 dh. El Derug Mosque . . 50 15
1708 50 dh. Ben Moussa Mosque . 50 15
1709 50 dh. Ghadames Mosque . . 50 15
1710 50 dh. Abdulwahab Mosque . 50 15

1985. Teachers' Day. Multicoloured.
1711 100 dh. Type **356** . . . . . 1·25 65
1712 100 dh. Hamida El-Anezi . . 1·25 65

357 "Philadelphia" exploding

358 Gaddafi and Followers

1985. Battle of the "Philadelphia". Multicoloured.
1713 50 dh. Type **357** 60 20
1714 50 dh. Men with swords . . 60 20
1715 100 dh. Men fighting and ship's rigging (59 x 45 mm) . . . 1·25 45
Nos. 1713/15 were printed together, se-tenant, forming a composite design.

1986. Colonel Gaddafi's Islamic Pilgrimage. Multicoloured.
1716 200 dh. Gaddafi writing . . 2·50 1·25
1717 200 dh. Gaddafi praying . . 2·50 1·25
1718 200 dh. Gaddafi, crowds and Kaaba . . . . 2·50 1·25
1719 200 dh. Gaddafi and mirror 2·50 1·25
1720 200 dh. Type **358** . . . . . 2·50 1·25

359 "Leucopaxillus lepistoides"

1985. Mushrooms. Multicoloured.
1722 50 dh. Type **359** . . . . . . 1·10 25
1723 50 dh. "Amanita caesarea" . 1·10 25
1724 50 dh. "Coriolus hirsutus" . 1·10 25
1725 50 dh. "Cortinarius subfulgens" 1·10 25
1726 50 dh. "Dermocybe pratensis" 1·10 25
1727 50 dh. "Macrolepiota excoriata" . . . . 1·10 25
1728 50 dh. "Amanita curtipes" . 1·10 25
1729 50 dh. "Trametes ljubarskyi" . 1·10 25
1730 50 dh. "Pholiota aurivella" . 1·10 25
1731 50 dh. "Boletus edulis" . . . 1·10 25
1732 50 dh. "Geastrum sessile" . . 1·10 25
1733 50 dh. "Russula sanguinea" . 1·10 25
1734 50 dh. "Cortinarius herculeus" 1·10 25
1735 50 dh. "Pholiota lenta" . . . 1·10 25
1736 50 dh. "Amanita rubescens" . 1·10 25
1737 50 dh. "Seleroderma polyrhizum" . . . . 1·10 25
Nos. 1722/37 were printed together, se-tenant, the backgrounds of the stamps forming an overall design of map of Mediterranean.

360 Woman in Purple Striped Dress

361 "In Need Freedom is Latent"

1985. Traditional Women's Costumes. Multicoloured.
1738 100 dh. Type **360** . . . . . 1·25 65
1739 100 dh. Woman in robes covering her face . . . . . 1·25 65
1740 100 dh. Woman in colourful robes with heavy jewellery 1·25 65
1741 100 dh. Woman in long blue striped dress . . . . 1·25 65
1742 100 dh. Woman in red dress and trousers . . . . 1·25 65

1985. Quotations from "The Green Book".
1743 **361** 100 dh. lt grn, grn & blk 45 35
1744 – 100 dh. multicoloured . 45 35
1745 – 100 dh. lt grn, grn & blk 45 35
1746 – 100 dh. lt grn, grn & blk 45 35
1747 – 100 dh. multicoloured . 45 35
1748 – 100 dh. lt grn, grn & blk 45 35
1749 – 100 dh. lt grn, grn & blk 45 35
1750 – 100 dh. multicoloured . 45 35
1751 – 100 dh. lt grn, grn & blk 45 35
DESIGNS: No. 1744, Gaddafi in uniform reading; 1745, "To make a party you split society"; 1746, "Public sport is for all the masses"; 1747, "Green Books" and doves; 1748, "Wage-workers are a type of slave, however improved their wages may be"; 1749, "People are only harmonious with their own arts and heritages"; 1750, Gaddafi addressing crowd; 1751, "Democracy means popular rule not popular expression".

362 Tree and Citrus Fruits

1985. 16th Anniv of Revolution. Multicoloured.
1752 100 dh. Type **362** 1·25 65
1753 100 dh. Oil pipeline and tanks 1·25 65
1754 100 dh. Capital and olive branch 1·25 65
1755 100 dh. Mosque and modern buildings 1·25 65
1756 100 dh. Flag and mountains 1·25 65
1757 100 dh. Telecommunications 1·25 65

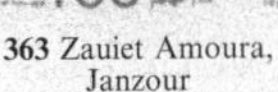

363 Zauiet Amoura, Janzour
364 Players in Red No. 5 and Green Shirts

1985. Mosque Gateways. Multicoloured.
1759 100 dh. Type **363** 1·25 65
1760 100 dh. Shiaieb El-Ain, Tripoli 1·25 65
1761 100 dh. Zauiet Abdussalam El-Asmar, Zliten 1·25 65
1762 100 dh. Karamanli, Tripoli 1·25 65
1763 100 dh. Gurgi, Tripoli 1·25 65

1985. Basketball. Multicoloured.
1764 25 dh. Type **364** 15 10
1765 25 dh. Players in green number 7 and red shirts 15 10
1766 25 dh. Players in green number 8 and red shirts 15 10
1767 25 dh. Players in red number 6 and green shirts 15 10
1768 25 dh. Players in red number 4 and green number 7 shirts 15 10
1769 25 dh. Players in green numbers 6 and 5 and red number 9 shirts 15 10
1770 25 dh. Basket and one player in red and two in green shirts 15 10
1771 25 dh. Players in red number 8 and green number 7 shirts 15 10
1772 25 dh. Two players in green shirts and two in red shirts, one number 4 15 10
1773 25 dh. Players in red numbers 4 and 7 and green shirts 15 10
1774 25 dh. Players in red numbers 4 and 9 and green numbers 7 and 4 shirts 15 10
1775 25 dh. Players in red number 6 and green shirts 15 10
1776 25 dh. Players in red number 9 and green number 8 shirts 15 10
1777 25 dh. Players in red number 8 and green number 5 shirts 15 10
1778 25 dh. Players in red number 4 and green shirts 15 10
1779 25 dh. Players in red number 5 and green number 10 shirts 15 10

Nos. 1764/79 were printed together se-tenant, the backgrounds of the stamps forming an overall design of baseball court and basket.

365 People in Light Ray

1985. Evacuation of Foreign Forces. Multicoloured.
1780 100 dh. Man on crutches in web and light shining on tree 1·25 65
1781 100 dh. Hands pulling web away from man 1·25 65
1782 100 dh. Type **365** 1·25 65

MINIMUM PRICE

The minimum price quoted is 10p which represents a handling charge rather than a basis for valuing common stamps. For further notes about prices, see introductory pages.

366 Stockbook, Magnifying Glass and Stamps
367 Players

1985. Stamp Day. "Italia '85" International Stamp Exhibition, Rome. Multicoloured.
1783 50 dh. Man and desk on flying stamp above globe 65 15
1784 50 dh. Type **366** 65 15
1785 50 dh. Stamps escaping from wallet 65 15

1986. World Cup Football Championship, Mexico (1st issue). Multicoloured.
1786 100 dh. Type **367** 1·25 65
1787 100 dh. Players in red and white number 10 and yellow shirts 1·25 65
1788 100 dh. Goalkeeper and player defending goal against attack 1·25 65
1789 100 dh. Goalkeeper diving to make save 1·25 65
1790 100 dh. Goalkeeper jumping to make save 1·25 65
1791 100 dh. Player in red and white shirt tackling player in lime shirt 1·25 65

See also Nos. 1824/9.

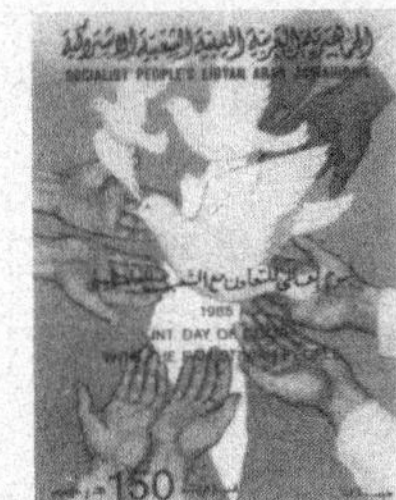
368 Hands releasing Dove

1985. Solidarity with Palestinian People.
1793 **368** 100 dh. multicoloured 95 35
1794 150 dh. multicoloured 1·60 75

370 Headquarters and Dish Aerial
371 Paper and Quill in Hand

1986. 1st Anniv of General Posts and Telecommunications Corporation.
1807 **370** 100 dh. multicoloured 1·00 30
1808 150 dh. multicoloured 1·50 75

1986. Peoples' Authority Declaration. Multicoloured.
1809 50 dh. Type **371** 65 40
1810 50 dh. Paper and globe in hand 65 40
1811 100 dh. "Green Books" and dove (53 x 37 mm) 1·25 65

372 Flute

1986. International Trade Fair, Tripoli. Mult.
1812 100 dh. Type **372** 1·25 65
1813 100 dh. Drums 1·25 65
1814 100 dh. Double pipes 1·25 65
1815 100 dh. Tambourines 1·25 65
1816 100 dh. Drum hung from shoulder 1·25 65

373 Boy Scout with Fish on Hook

1986. Children's Day. Multicoloured.
1817 50 dh. Type **373** 65 15
1818 50 dh. Boy on camel 65 15
1819 50 dh. Boy catching butterflies 65 15
1820 50 dh. Boy playing drum 65 15
1821 50 dh. Boy and giant goalkeeper on football pitch 65 15

374 Emblem, Man and Skull in Blood Droplet

1986. World Health Day. Multicoloured, background colours given.
1822 **374** 250 dh. silver 2·50 1·25
1823 250 dh. gold 2·50 1·25

375 Footballers

1986. World Cup Football Championship, Mexico (2nd issue). Multicoloured.
1824 50 dh. Type **375** 65 15
1825 50 dh. Player jumping over player on ground 65 15
1826 50 dh. Referee and players 65 15
1827 50 dh. Goalkeeper trying to save ball 65 15
1828 50 dh. Player about to tackle 65 15
1829 50 dh. Player jumping over ball 65 15

376 Peas
377 Health Programmes

1986. Vegetables. Multicoloured.
1831 50 dh. Type **376** 45 15
1832 50 dh. Marrow 45 15
1833 50 dh. Beans 45 15
1834 50 dh. Aubergine 45 15
1835 50 dh. Corn on the cob 45 15
1836 50 dh. Tomato 45 15
1837 50 dh. Red pepper 45 15
1838 50 dh. Zucchini 45 15
1839 50 dh. Garlic 45 15
1840 50 dh. Cabbage 45 15
1841 50 dh. Cauliflower 45 15
1842 50 dh. Celery 45 15
1843 50 dh. Onions 45 15
1844 50 dh. Carrots 45 15
1845 50 dh. Potato 45 15
1846 50 dh. Radishes 45 15

Nos. 1831/46 were printed together in sheetlets of 16 stamps, the backgrounds of the stamps forming an overall design of a garden.

1986. Jamahiriya Thought. Multicoloured.
1847 50 dh. Type **377** 50 15
1848 50 dh. Education programmes 50 15
1849 100 dh. "Green Book", agricultural scenes and produce (agriculture programmes) (62 x 41 mm) 1·00 30

378 Gaddafi studying Plane

1986. Colonel Gaddafi, "Great man-made River Builder". Multicoloured.
1850 100 dh. Type **378** 95 30
1851 100 dh. Gaddafi showing planned route on map 95 30
1852 100 dh. Gaddafi and old well 95 30
1853 100 dh. Gaddafi in desert 95 30
1854 100 dh. Gaddafi and pipe 95 30
1855 100 dh. Gaddafi at pumping station 95 30
1856 100 dh. Gaddafi and storage tank 95 30
1857 100 dh. Workers' hut 95 30
1858 100 dh. Water in cupped hands and irrigation equipment 95 30
1859 100 dh. Gaddafi turning wheel at opening ceremony 95 30
1860 100 dh. Laying pipes 95 30
1861 100 dh. Pipe sections on lorries 95 30
1862 100 dh. Gaddafi in robes holding "Green Book" 95 30
1863 100 dh. Boy giving Gaddafi bowl of fruit 95 30
1864 100 dh. Boy drinking from tap 95 30
1865 100 dh. Gaddafi praying 95 30

379 Gaddafi with Children

1986. Colonel Gaddafi, "Man of Peace". Multicoloured.
1866 100 dh. Type **379** 1·10 30
1867 100 dh. Reading book in tent 1·10 30
1868 100 dh. With his mother 1·10 30
1869 100 dh. Praying in tent with his sons 1·10 30
1870 100 dh. Talking to hospital patient 1·10 30
1871 100 dh. Driving tractor 1·10 30

380 General Dynamics F-111 Exploding above Man with injured Child

381 Gaddafi, Ruined buildings and Stretcher-bearers

1986. Battle of the U.S.S. "Philadelphia" and American Attack on Libya. Multicoloured.

(a) As T **380**.
1872 50 dh. Type **380** 40 25
1873 50 dh. American aircraft carrier and escaping family 40 25
1874 100 dh. "Philadelphia" exploding (59 x 38 mm) 1·00 50

(b) As T **381**.
1875 70 dh. Type **381** 80 20
1876 70 dh. Burning wreckage of car and man and boy in rubble 80 20
1877 70 dh. Woman and child by burning ruin 80 20
1878 70 dh. Men running from bomb strike 80 20
1879 70 dh. Covered body and rescue workers searching ruins 80 20
1880 70 dh. Libyans and General Dynamics F-111 airplane tail and wing 80 25
1881 70 dh. Libyans waving fists 80 20
1882 70 dh. Rescue workers lifting child from rubble 80 20
1883 70 dh. Weeping women and soldier carrying baby 80 20
1884 70 dh. Libyans and glare of explosion 80 20
1885 70 dh. Libyans and General Dynamics F-111 airplane wing and nose 80 25
1886 70 dh. Man carrying girl 80 20
1887 70 dh. Coffins held aloft by crowd 80 20
1888 70 dh. Crowd carrying pictures of Gaddafi 80 20
1889 70 dh. Wounded being tended 80 20
1890 70 dh. Hands tending wounded baby 80 20

(c) Size 89 x 32 mm.
1891 100 dh. General Dynamics F-111 bombers, Gaddafi and anti-aircraft rockets 1·25 35

Nos. 1872/4 were printed together in se-tenant strips of three within the sheet, each strip forming a composite design.

382 "The House must be served by its own Tenant"

1986. Quotations from the "Green Book".

1892 **382** 100 dh. lt grn, grn & blk . . 1·00 30
1893 – 100 dh. multicoloured . . 1·00 30
1894 – 100 dh. lt grn, grn & blk 1·00 30
1895 – 100 dh. lt grn, grn & blk 1·00 30
1896 – 100 dh. multicoloured . . 1·00 30
1897 – 100 dh. lt grn, grn & blk 1·00 30
1898 – 100 dh. lt grn, grn & blk 1·00 30
1899 – 100 dh. multicoloured . . 1·00 30
1900 – 100 dh. lt grn, grn & blk 1·00 30

DESIGNS: No. 1893, Gaddafi; 1894, "The Child is raised by his mother"; 1895, "Democracy is the Supervision of the People by the People"; 1896, "Green Books"; 1897, "Representation is a Falsification of Democracy"; 1898, "The Recognition of Profit is an Acknowledgement of Exploitation"; 1899, Vase of roses, iris, lilies and jasmine; 1900, "Knowledge is a Natural Right of every Human Being which Nobody has the Right to deprive him of under any Pretext".

383 Map, Chrysanthemum and Health Services

1986. 17th Anniv of Revolution. Multicoloured.

1901 200 dh. Type **383** . . . . . . 2·50 95
1902 200 dh. Map, sunflower and agriculture programme . . 2·50 95
1903 200 dh. "Sunflowers" (Van Gogh) . . . . 2·50 95
1904 200 dh. Map, rose and defence programme . . . . . . 2·50 95
1905 200 dh. Map, campanula and oil exploration programme . . 2·50 95

384 Moroccan and Libyan Women

1986. Arab-African Union. Multicoloured.

1906 250 dh. Type **384** . . . . . . 2·50 80
1907 250 dh. Libyan and Moroccan horsemen . . . . 2·50 80

385 Libyan Horseman

1986. Evacuation of Foreign Forces. Multicoloured.

1908 50 dh. Type **385** 50 15
1909 100 dh. Libyan horsemen trampling Italian soldiers 1·10 30
1910 150 dh. Italian soldiers charging 1·50 50

386 Globe and Rose

1986. International Peace Year. Multicoloured, background colours given.

1911 **386** 200 dh. green . . . . . . 1·90 70
1912 200 dh. blue . . . . . . 1·90 70

387 Brick "Fists" and Maps within Laurel Wreath

1986. Solidarity with Palestinian People. Multicoloured, background colours given.

1913 **387** 250 dh. blue . . . . . . 2·50 80
1914 250 dh. red . . . . . . 2·50 80

388 Drummer

1986. Folk Music. Multicoloured.

1915 70 dh. Type **388** 95 20
1916 70 dh. Masked stick dancer 95 20
1917 70 dh. Woman dancer with pot headdress 95 20
1918 70 dh. Bagpipe player . . . 95 20
1919 70 dh. Tambour player . . . 95 20

389 Gazelles

1987. Endangered Animals. Sand Gazelle. Multicoloured.

1920 100 dh. Type **389** . . . . . 1·25 30
1921 100 dh. Mother and calf . . 1·25 30
1922 100 dh. Gazelle drinking . . 1·25 30
1923 100 dh. Gazelle lying down 1·25 30

390 Oil Derricks and Crowd

391 Sheep and Shepherd

1987. People's Authority Declaration. Multicoloured.

1924 500 dh. Type **390** . . . . . 4·00 1·75
1925 500 dh. Buildings and crowd 4·00 1·75
1926 1000 dh. Gaddafi addressing crowd and globe (40 x 38 mm) 8·00 3·25

1987. 18th Anniv of Revolution. Multicoloured.

1927 150 dh. Type **391** . . . . . 1·50 50
1928 150 dh. Col. Gaddafi in robes 1·50 50
1929 150 dh. Mosque . . . . . . 1·50 50
1930 150 dh. Water flowing from irrigation pipe . . . . . . 1·50 50
1931 150 dh. Combine harvester . 1·50 50
1932 150 dh. Col. Gaddafi in army uniform with microphone 1·50 50
1933 150 dh. Harvesting crop . . 1·50 50
1934 150 dh. Irrigation . . . . . 1·50 50
1935 150 dh. Soldier with rifle . . 1·50 50
1936 150 dh. Buildings behind Libyan with rifle . . . . 1·50 50
1937 150 dh. Fountain . . . . . 1·50 50
1938 150 dh. Buildings and beach 1·50 50
1939 150 dh. Fort and girls . . . 1·50 50
1940 150 dh. Children and hand on rifle butt . . . . 1·50 50
1941 150 dh. Theatre . . . . . . 1·50 50
1942 150 dh. Couple . . . . . . 1·50 50

392 Omar Abed Anabi al Mansusri

1988. Personalities. Multicoloured.

1943 100 dh. Type **392** 75 30
1944 200 dh. Ahmed Ali al Emrayd 1·50 70
1945 300 dh. Khalifa Said Ben Asker 2·50 1·00
1946 400 dh. Mohamed Ben Farhat Azawi . . . . 3·00 1·10
1947 500 dh. Mohamed Souf al Lafi al Marmori . . . . 3·75 1·50

393 Gaddafi and Crowd with Raised Fists around Earthmover Bucket

1988. Freedom Festival Day.

1948 **393** 100 dh. multicoloured . . 95 30
1949 150 dh. multicoloured . . 1·60 75
1950 250 dh. multicoloured . . 2·50 1·25

394 Woman and Children running

1988. 2nd Anniv of American Attack on Libya. Multicoloured.

1951 150 dh. Type **394** . . . . . . 1·40 50
1952 150 dh. Gaddafi playing chess with boy . . . . 1·40 50
1953 150 dh. Gaddafi and children 1·40 50
1954 150 dh. Gaddafi in robes . . 1·40 50
1955 150 dh. Gaddafi and boys praying . . . . 1·40 50
1956 150 dh. Gaddafi and injured girl 1·40 50
1957 150 dh. Gaddafi in robes with children (horiz) . . . . . 1·40 50
1958 150 dh. Gaddafi making speech (horiz) . . . . 1·40 50
1959 150 dh. Gaddafi and family (horiz) . . . . 1·40 50

395 Roses

1988. 19th Anniv of Revolution.

1961 **395** 100 dh. multicoloured . . 75 30
1962 250 dh. multicoloured . . 2·00 80
1963 300 dh. multicoloured . . 2·25 1·00
1964 500 dh. multicoloured . . 4·25 1·50

396 Relay

397 Dates

1988. Olympic Games, Seoul. Multicoloured.

1965 150 dh. Type **396** . . . . . . 1·25 50
1966 150 dh. Cycling . . . . . . 1·25 50
1967 150 dh. Football . . . . . . 1·25 50
1968 150 dh. Tennis . . . . . . 1·25 50
1969 150 dh. Running . . . . . . 1·25 50
1970 150 dh. Showjumping . . . . 1·25 50

1988. The Palm Tree. Multicoloured.

1972 500 dh. Type **397** . . . . . . 4·25 1·50
1973 1000 dh. Tree . . . . 8·00 3·75

398 Petrol Bomb, Sling and Map

399 Globe, Declaration and Dove

1988. Palestinian "Intifada" Movement. Mult.

1974 100 dh. Type **398** 95 30
1975 200 dh. Boy holding stones (45 x 38 mm) . . . . . . 1·60 70
1976 300 dh. Map and flag . . . 2·50 1·00

1989. People's Authority Declaration.

1977 **399** 260 dh. multicoloured . 1·10 65
1978 500 dh. multicoloured . 2·00 1·25

400 Crowd and Green Books (½-size illustration)

1989. 20th Anniv of Revolution. Multicoloured.

1979 150 dh. Type **400** . . . . . 1·25 40
1980 150 dh. Soldiers, Colonel Gaddafi and water pipeline 1·25 40
1981 150 dh. Military hardware, Gaddafi in uniform, education, communications and medicine . . . . . . 1·25 40
1982 150 dh. Armed horsemen . . 1·25 40
1983 150 dh. U.S.S. "Philadelphia" exploding . . . . 1·25 55

401 Execution Victims, Soldiers and Colonel Gaddafi

1989. 78th Anniv of Deportation of Libyans to Italy. Multicoloured.

1985 100 dh. Type **401** 40 25
1986 100 dh. Colonel Gaddafi and Libyans 40 25
1987 100 dh. Soliders, deportees and Gaddafi 40 25
1988 100 dh. Deportees on jetty and in boats 55 25
1989 100 dh. Gaddafi and corpses 40 25

402 Demoliton of Wall

403 Emblem of Committee for supporting "Intifida"

1989. "Demolition of Borders".

1991 **402** 150 dh. multicoloured . 1·60 1·60
1992 200 dh. multicoloured . 2·10 2·10

1989. Palestinian "Intifida" Movement. Mult.

1993 100 dh. Type **403** . . . . . 1·10 1·10
1994 300 dh. Crowd of youths . . 3·00 3·00
1995 500 dh. Emblem (1st anniv of declaration of State of Palestine) . . . . 4·75 4·75

404 Circulation Diagram and Annafis

1989. Ibn Annafis (physician) Commemorative.

1996 **404** 100 dh. multicoloured . 1·25 1·25
1997 150 dh. multicoloured . 1·90 1·90

405 Green Books and Fort

406 Libyan People and Soldier

1990. People's Authority Declaration.

1998 **405** 300 dh. multicoloured . 2·75 2·75
1999 500 dh. multicoloured . 5·00 5·00

1990. 20th Anniv of American Forces Evacuation.

2000 **406** 100 dh. multicoloured . 1·00 1·00
2001 400 dh. multicoloured . 4·00 4·00

407 Eagle

408 Anniversary Emblem

1990. 21st Anniv of Revolution.
2002 **407** 100 dh. multicoloured . . 1·00 1·00
2003 400 dh. multicoloured . . 4·00 4·00
2004 1000 dh. multicoloured 10·50 10·50

1990. 30th Anniv of Organization of Petroleum Exporting Countries.
2006 **408** 100 dh. multicoloured . . 1·00 1·00
2007 400 dh. multicoloured . . 4·00 4·00

409 I.L.Y. Emblem and Figures

410 Player, Globe and Ball

1990. International Literacy Year.
2008 **409** 100 dh. multicoloured . . 1·10 1·10
2009 300 dh. multicoloured . . 3·00 3·00

1990. World Cup Football Championship, Italy.
2010 **410** 100 dh. multicoloured . . 1·00 1·00
2011 400 dh. multicoloured . . 4·00 4·00
2012 500 dh. multicoloured . . 5·00 5·00

411 Hand holding Ears of Wheat

412 Members' Flags

1990. World Food Day. Multicoloured.
2014 500 dh. Type **411** . . . . . . 5·00 5·00
2015 2000 dh. Ploughing . . . . . 20·00 20·00

1991. 2nd Anniv of Union of Arab Maghreb.
2016 **412** 100 dh. multicoloured . . 1·10 1·10
2017 300 dh. multicoloured . . 3·00 3·00

413 Flame, Scroll and Koran

1991. People's Authority Declaration.
2018 **413** 300 dh. multicoloured . . 2·75 2·75
2019 400 dh. multicoloured . . 3·75 3·75

414 Girl and International Year of the Child Emblem

415 World Health Organization Emblem

1991. Children's Day. Multicoloured.
2020 100 dh. Type **414** 95 95
2021 400 dh. Boy and Day of the African Child emblem . . 3·75 3·75

1991. World Health Day. Multicoloured.
2022 100 dh. Type **415** 95 95
2023 200 dh. As Type **415** but with emblem additionally inscr "W.H.O. O.M.S." . . . . 1·90 1·90

416 Wadi el Hayat

417 Digging Riverbed and laying Pipes

1991. Scenes from Libya. Multicoloured.
2024 100 dh. Type **416** 95 95
2025 250 dh. Mourzuk (horiz) . . 2·50 2·50
2026 500 dh. Ghadames (horiz) . 5·00 5·00

1991. Great Man-made River. Multicoloured.
2027 50 dh. Type **417** 25 15
2028 50 dh. Col. Gaddafi, agricultural projects and livestock (59 x 37 mm) . . 25 15
2029 50 dh. Produce 25 15
Nos. 2027/9 were printed together, se-tenant, forming a composite design.

418 "22", Roses and Broken Chain

1991. 22nd Anniv of Revolution. Multicoloured.
2030 300 dh. Type **418** . . . . . 2·75 2·75
2031 400 dh. "22" within wheat/cogwheel wreath and broken chain . . . . 3·75 3·75

419 Emblem and Globe

1991. "Telecom 91" International Telecommunications Exhibition, Geneva. Multicoloured.
2033 100 dh. Type **419** 95 95
2034 500 dh. Buldings and dish aerial (horiz) . . . . 4·50 4·50

420 Monument and Soldier

1991. 80th Anniv of Deportation of Libyans to Italy. Multicoloured.
2035 100 dh. Type **420** 95 95
2036 400 dh. Naval transport, Libyans and soldiers . . . 3·75 3·75

421 Map

1991. Arab Unity.
2038 **421** 50 dh. multicoloured . . 20 10
2039 100 dh. multicoloured . 40 20

422 Lorry

424 State Arms

423 Gaddafi and Camels

1991. Paris–Dakar Trans-Sahara Rally. Mult.
2040 50 dh. Type **422** 20 10
2041 50 dh. Blue lorry 20 10
2042 50 dh. African Product lorry . 20 10
2043 50 dh. Tomel lorry 20 10
2044 50 dh. All-terrain vehicle No. 173 . . . . 20 10
2045 50 dh. Mitsusuki all-terrain vehicle 20 10
2046 50 dh. Michedop all-terrain vehicle 20 10
2047 50 dh. All-terrain vehicle No. 401 . . . . 20 10
2048 50 dh. Motor cycle No. 100 20 10
2049 50 dh. Rider pushing red motor cycle 20 10
2050 50 dh. Rider pushing white motor cycle 20 10
2051 50 dh. Motor cycle No. 98 . . 20 10
2052 50 dh. Motor cycle No. 101 20 10
2053 50 dh. Motor cycle No. 80 . . 20 10
2054 50 dh. Motor cycle No. 12 . . 20 10
2055 50 dh. Motor cycle No. 45 . . 20 10

1992. "Gaddafi, Man of Peace 1992". Multicoloured, colour of frame given.
2056 **423** 100 dh. green 40 20
2057 100 dh. grey 40 20
2058 100 dh. red 40 20
2059 100 dh. ochre 40 20

1992.
2061 **424** 100 dh. green, brn & yell 40 20
2062 150 dh. green, brn & grey 60 30
2063 200 dh. green, brown & bl 85 45
2064 250 dh. green, brn & orge 1·10 55
2065 300 dh. green, brn & vio 1·25 65
2066 400 dh. green, brn & mve 1·75 90
2067 450 dh. emerald, brn & grn 1·90 95

425 1991 100 dh. Stamp, Tweezers, Magnifying Glass and Stamps

1992. 3rd Anniv of Union of Arab Maghreb.
2068 **425** 75 dh. multicoloured . . 30 15
2069 80 dh. multicoloured . . 35 20

426 Horse-drawn Carriage

1992. International Trade Fair, Tripoli. Mult.
2070 50 dh. Type **426** 20 10
2071 100 dh. Horse-drawn cart . . 40 20

427 Emblem

429 Fish with Spines

428 Emblem and Camel Rider

1992. People's Authority Declaration.
2072 **427** 100 dh. multicoloured . . 40 20
2073 150 dh. multicoloured . . 60 30

1992. African Tourism Year.
2074 **428** 50 dh. multicoloured . . 20 10
2075 100 dh. multicoloured . . 40 20

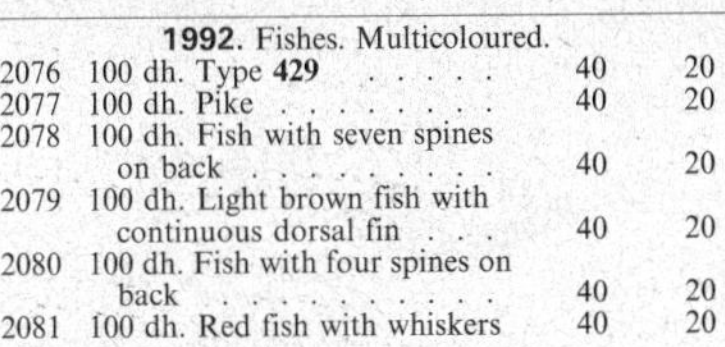

1992. Fishes. Multicoloured.
2076 100 dh. Type **429** 40 20
2077 100 dh. Pike 40 20
2078 100 dh. Fish with seven spines on back 40 20
2079 100 dh. Light brown fish with continuous dorsal fin . . . 40 20
2080 100 dh. Fish with four spines on back 40 20
2081 100 dh. Red fish with whiskers 40 20

430 Horsewoman with Rifle

431 Long Jumping

1992. Horse Riders. Multicoloured.
2082 100 dh. Type **430** 40 20
2083 100 dh. Man on rearing white horse 40 20
2084 100 dh. Man on brown horse with ornate bridle 40 20
2085 100 dh. Roman soldier on brown horse 40 20
2086 100 dh. Man in blue coat on brown horse 40 20
2087 100 dh. Arab on white horse 40 20

1992. Olympic Games, Barcelona. Multicoloured.
2089 50 dh. Type **431** 20 10
2090 50 dh. Throwing the discus 20 10
2091 50 dh. Tennis 20 10

432 Palm Trees

1992. Achievements of the Revolution. Mult.
2093 100 dh. Type **432** 40 20
2094 150 dh. Ingots and foundry 60 30
2095 250 dh. Container ship . . . 1·10 55
2096 300 dh. Airplane . . . . . . 1·25 65
2097 400 dh. Assembly hall . . . 1·75 90
2098 500 dh. Water pipes and Gaddafi . . . . 2·10 1·10

433 Gaddafi

434 Laurel Wreath, Torch and "23"

1992. Multicoloured, background colours given.
2099 **433** 500 dh. green . . . . . 2·50 1·10
2100 1000 dh. pink . . . . . 5·00 2·50
2101 2000 dh. blue . . . . . 10·00 5·00
2102 5000 dh. violet . . . . 25·00 12·50
2103 6000 dh. orange . . . . 32·00 16·00

1992. 23rd Anniv of Revolution. Multicoloured.
2104 50 dh. Type **434** 20 10
2105 100 dh. Laurel wreath, flag, sun and "23" 40 20

435 Antelope drinking

436 Horse and Broken Chain

1992. Oases. Multicoloured.
2107 100 dh. Type **435** 40 20
2108 200 dh. Sun setting behind camel train (vert) 85 45
2109 300 dh. Camel rider . . . . 1·25 65

1992. Evacuation of Foreign Forces. Multicoloured.
2110 75 dh. Type **436** 30 15
2111 80 dh. Flag and broken chain 35 20

437 Monument and Dates

1992. 81st Anniv of Deportation of Libyans to Italy.
2112 **437** 100 dh. multicoloured . . 40 20
2113 250 dh. multicoloured . . 1·10 55

438 Dome of the Rock and Palestinian

1992. Palestinian "Intifida" Movement. Mult.
2114 100 dh. Type **438** 40 20
2115 300 dh. Map, Dome of the Rock, flag and fist (vert) . 1·25 65

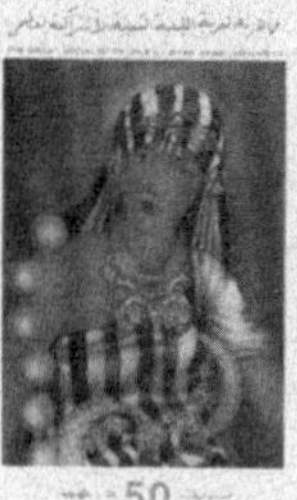

439 Red and White Striped Costume — **440** Mohamed Ali Imsek

1992. Women's Costumes. Multicoloured.
2116 50 dh. Type **439** 20 10
2117 50 dh. Large red hat with silver decorations, white tunic and red wrap 20 10
2118 50 dh. Brown and orange striped costume with small gold necklace and horseshoe brooch 20 10
2119 50 dh. Purple and white costume 20 10
2120 50 dh. Orange striped costume 20 10

1993. Physicians
2121 **440** 40 dh. black, yellow and silver 15 10
2122 – 60 dh. black, green and gold 20 15
DESIGN: 60 dh. Aref Adhani Arif.

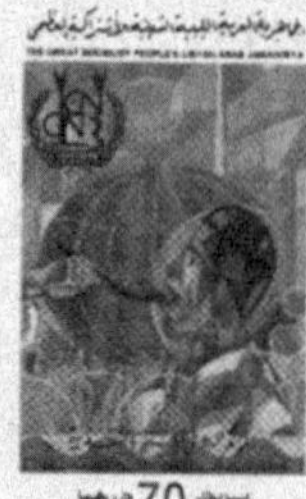
441 Globe, Crops and Spoon-feeding Man

1993. International Nutrition Conference, Rome.
2123 **441** 70 dh. multicoloured . . 35 25
2124 80 dh. multicoloured . . 40 30

442 Gaddafi, Eagle and Oil Refinery

1993. People's Authority Declaration.
2125 **442** 60 dh. multicoloured . . 20 15
2126 65 dh. multicoloured . . 25 15
2127 75 dh. multicoloured . . 25 15

MINIMUM PRICE

The minimum price quoted is 10p which represents a handling charge rather than a basis for valuing common stamps. For further notes about prices, see introductory pages.

443 Crowd with Tambours — **445** Girl

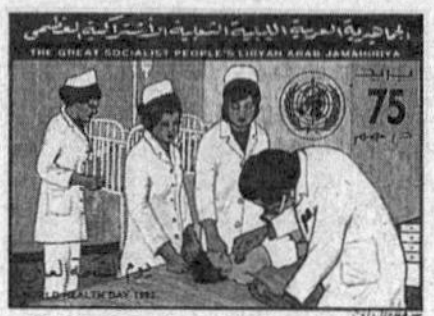
444 Examining Baby

1993. International Trade Fair, Tripoli. Mult.
2128 60 dh. Type **443** 20 15
2129 60 dh. Crowd with camel . 20 15
2130 60 dh. Dance of veiled men (horiz) 20 15
2131 60 dh. Women preparing food (horiz) 20 15

1993. World Health Day. Multicoloured.
2133 75 dh. Type **444** 25 15
2134 85 dh. Medical staff attending patient 30 20

1993. Children's Day. Multicoloured.
2135 75 dh. Type **445** 25 15
2136 75 dh Girl wearing blue and white veil and gold cuff . 25 15
2137 75 dh. Girl with white fluted collar and silver veil . . . 25 15
2138 75 dh. Girl with hands clasped 25 15
2139 75 dh. Girl wearing blue scallop-edged veil 25 15

446 Phoenician Ship

1993. Ships. Multicoloured
2140 50 dh. Type **446** 20 15
2141 50 dh. Arab galley 20 15
2142 50 dh. Pharaonic ship . . . 20 15
2143 50 dh. Roman bireme . . . 20 15
2144 50 dh. Carvel 20 15
2145 50 dh. Yacht (globe showing Italy) 20 15
2146 50 dh. Yacht (globe showing Greece) 20 15
2147 50 dh. Galleass 20 15
2148 50 dh. Nau 20 15
2149 50 dh. Yacht (globe showing left half of Libya) 20 15
2150 50 dh. Yacht (globe showing right half of Libya) . . . 20 15
2151 50 dh. "Santa Maria" . . . 20 15
2152 50 dh. "France" (liner) . . . 20 15
2153 50 dh. Schooner 20 15
2154 50 dh. Sail/steam warship . 20 15
2155 50 dh. Modern liner 20 15
Nos. 2140/55 were issued together, se-tenant, the centre four stamps forming a composite design.

447 Combine Harvesters — **448** Woman tending Youth

1993. 24th Anniv of Revolution. Multicoloured.
2156 50 dh. Type **447** 20 15
2157 50 dh. Col. Gaddafi 20 15
2158 50 dh. Cattle behind men filling sack with grain 20 15
2159 50 dh. Chickens behind shepherd with flock 20 15
2160 50 dh. Oil rig 20 15
2161 50 dh. Eagle and camel . . . 20 15
2162 50 dh. Industrial plant . . . 20 15
2163 50 dh. Water pipeline . . . 20 15
2164 50 dh. Man harvesting dates 20 15
2165 50 dh. Man in field and boxes of produce 20 15
2166 50 dh. Pile of produce . . . 20 15
2167 50 dh. Man picking courgettes 20 15
2168 50 dh. Children reading . . 20 15
2169 50 dh. Typist and laboratory worker 20 15
2170 50 dh. Hand-picking crop and ploughing with tractor . . . 20 15
2171 50 dh. Tractor towing circular harrow 20 15
Nos. 2156/71 were issued together, se-tenant, forming several composite designs.

1993. 82nd Anniv of Deportation of Libyans to Italy. Multicoloured.
2172 50 dh. Type **448** 20 15
2173 50 dh. Soldiers and Libyan family 20 15
2174 50 dh. Col. Gaddafi (in turban) 20 15
2175 50 dh. Libyans in food queue 20 15
2176 50 dh. Man being flogged . . 20 15
2177 50 dh. Horseman charging between soldiers and Libyans 20 15
2178 50 dh. Soldier with manacled Libyan before court 20 15
2179 50 dh. Libyans gazing at hanged man 20 15
2180 50 dh. Crowd of Libyans and two soldiers 20 15
2181 50 dh. Soldiers guarding procession of Libyans . . . 20 15
2182 50 dh. Soldiers and manacled Libyans on quayside . . . 20 15
2183 50 dh. Deportees in boat . . 20 15
2184 50 dh. Col. Gaddafi (bare-headed) 20 15
2185 50 dh. Two Libyan families and branch of palm tree 20 15
2186 50 dh. Soldiers in disarray (ruins in background) 20 15
2187 50 dh. Libyan horsemen . . . 20 15
Nos. 2172/87 were issued together, se-tenant, forming several composite designs.

449 Brooch — **451** Player and Trophy

450 Gaddafi, Soldiers and Jet Fighters

1994. Silver Jewellery. Multicoloured.
2188 55 dh. Type **449** 20 15
2189 55 dh. Armlet 20 15
2190 55 dh. Pendant 20 15
2191 55 dh. Pendants hanging from oblong 20 15
2192 55 dh. Necklace 20 15
2193 55 dh. Slippers 20 15

1994. 25th Anniv of Revolution. Multicoloured.
2194 100 dh. Type **450** 35 25
2195 100 dh. Libyan tribesmen and Gaddafi in uniform (59 × 38 mm) 35 25
2196 100 dh. Peaceful pursuits and elderly couple 35 25
Nos. 2194/6 were issued together, se-tenant, forming a composite design.

1994. World Cup Football Championship, U.S.A. Multicoloured.
2198 100 dh. Type **451**
2199 100 dh. Kicking ball with inside of foot 35 25
2200 100 dh. Kicking ball in air . . 35 25
2201 100 dh. Goalkeeper 35 25
2202 100 dh. Running with ball . . 35 25
2203 100 dh. Player taking ball on chest 35 25

452 Gaddafi

1994. 83rd Anniv of Deportation of Libyans to Italy. Multicoloured.
2205 95 dh. Type **452** 35 25
2206 95 dh. Light plane over rifleman 35 25
2207 95 dh. Couple running from biplane 35 25
2208 95 dh. Biplane flying over men and boy 35 25
2209 95 dh. Man trapped beneath fallen horse 35 25
2210 95 dh. Soldiers and Libyans fighting (camel's head and neck in foreground) . . . 35 25
2211 95 dh. Soldiers surrounding fallen Libyan 35 25
2212 95 dh. Man carrying boy . . 35 25
2213 95 dh. Soldier with whip raised 35 25
2214 95 dh. Robed man shouting . 35 25
2215 95 dh. Tank and battle scene 35 25
2216 95 dh. Women fleeing mounted soliers 35 25
2217 95 dh. Man being flogged and woman cradling head of fallen Libyan 35 25
2218 95 dh. Soldiers and Libyans fighting (camels in background) 35 25
2219 95 dh. Women and soldiers on quayside 35 25
2220 95 dh. Deportees in two boats 35 25
Nos. 2205/20 were issued together, se-tenant, forming several composite designs.

453 Darghut — **454** Armed Forces

1994. Mosques. Multicoloured.
2221 70 dh. Type **453** 25 15
2222 70 dh. Benghazi 25 15
2223 70 dh. Kabao 25 15
2224 70 dh. Gouzgu 25 15
2225 70 dh. Siala 25 15
2226 70 dh. El Kettani 25 15

1994. People's Authority Declaration. Multicoloured.
2227 80 dh. Type **454** 30 20
2228 80 dh. Truck, hand holding Green Book and ears of wheat 30 20
2229 80 dh. Pipes on trailers, water pipeline and family 30 20
2230 80 dh. Crowd with Green Books 30 20
2231 80 dh. Col. Gaddafi 30 20
2232 80 dh. Youths and produce . 30 20
Nos. 2227/32 were issued together, se-tenant, forming a composite design.

455 Sun over Cemetery, National Flag, Dove and Footprints — **457** Declaration and Flowers

456 Men with Weapons and Troops in Background

1994. Evacuation of Foreign Forces.
2233 **455** 65 dh. multicoloured . . 25 15
2234 95 dh. multicoloured . . 35 20

1994. Gaddafi Prize for Human Rights. Multicoloured.
2235 95 dh. Type **456** 35 20
2236 95 dh. Men with weapons . . 35 20
2237 95 dh. President Nelson Mandela of South Africa . 35 20
2238 95 dh. President Gaddafi . . 35 20
2239 95 dh. Amerindian meditating 35 20
2240 95 dh. Warriors on horseback 35 20
2241 95 dh. Amerindian chief . . 35 20
2242 95 dh. Amerindian 35 20
2243 95 dh. Riflemen and aircraft 35 20
2244 95 dh. Bomber, women, fire and left page of book 35 20
2245 95 dh. Right page of book and surgeon operating 35 20
2246 95 dh. Surgeons operating . . 35 20
2247 95 dh. Masked revolutionaries with flag 35 20

2248 95 dh. Revolutionaries raising arms with flag 35 20
2249 95 dh. Young boys with stones 35 20
2250 95 dh. Revolutionaries, fire and troops 35 20
Nos. 2235/50 were issued together, se-tenant, forming a composite design.

1995. People's Authority Declaration. Multicoloured, colour of background given.
2251 **457** 100 dh. yellow 35 20
2252 100 dh. blue 35 20
2253 100 dh. green 35 20

458 Emblem, Members' Flags and Map showing Member Countries

1995. 50th Anniv of Arab League. Multicoloured, frame colour given.
2254 **458** 200 f. blue 70 45
2255 200 f. green 70 45

459 Messaud Zentuti

1995. 60th Anniv of National Football Team. Designs showing players. Multicoloured.
2257 100 dh. Type **459** 35 20
2258 100 dh. Salem Shermit . . . 35 20
2259 100 dh. Ottoman Marfua . . 35 20
2260 100 dh. Ghaleb Siala 35 20
2261 100 dh. Team, 1935 . . . . . 35 20
2262 100 dh. Senussi Mresila . . . 35 20
Nos. 2257/62 were issued together, se-tenant, forming a composite design.

460 Dromedary **461** Grapefruit

1995. Libyan Zoo. Multicoloured.
2263 100 dh. Type **460** 35 20
2264 100 dh. Secretary bird . . . 35 20
2265 100 dh. African wild dog . . 35 20
2266 100 dh. Oryx 35 20
2267 100 dh. Baboon 35 20
2268 100 dh. Golden jackal . . . 35 20
2269 100 dh. Crowned eagle . . . 35 20
2270 100 dh. Eagle owl 35 20
2271 100 dh. Desert hedgehog . . 35 20
2272 100 dh. Sand gerbil 35 20
2273 100 dh. Addax 35 20
2274 100 dh. Fennec fox 35 20
2275 100 dh. Lanner falcon . . . 35 20
2276 100 dh. Desert wheatear . . 35 20
2277 100 dh. Pin-tailed sandgrouse 35 20
2278 100 dh. Jerboa 35 20
Nos. 2263/78 were issued together, se-tenant, the backgrounds forming a composite design.

1995. Fruit. Multicoloured.
2279 100 dh. Type **461** 35 20
2280 100 dh. Wild cherry 35 20
2281 100 dh. Mulberry 35 20
2282 100 dh. Strawberry 35 20
2283 100 dh. Plum 35 20
2284 100 dh. Pear 35 20
2285 100 dh. Apricot 35 20
2286 100 dh. Almond 35 20
2287 100 dh. Prickly pear 35 20
2288 100 dh. Lemon 35 20
2289 100 dh. Peach 35 20
2290 100 dh. Dates 35 20
2291 100 dh. Olive 35 20
2292 100 dh. Orange 35 20
2293 100 dh. Fig 35 20
2294 100 dh. Grape 35 20
Nos. 2279/94 were issued together, se-tenant, the backgrounds forming a composite design.

462 Students

1995. 26th Anniv of Revolution. Multicoloured.
2295 100 dh. Type **462** 35 20
2296 100 dh. Mosque, teacher and students 35 20
2297 100 dh. President Gaddafi . 35 20
2298 100 dh. Laboratory workers 35 20
2299 100 dh. Hospital patient, doctor examining child and nurse 35 20
2300 100 dh. Surgeons operating . 35 20
2301 100 dh. Cobblers and keyboard operator 35 20
2302 100 dh. Sound engineers and musician 35 20
2303 100 dh. Crane and apartment block 35 20
2304 100 dh. Silos 35 20
2305 100 dh. Oil rig platform . . 35 20
2306 100 dh. Airplane and ships . 35 20
2307 100 dh. Animals grazing and farmer 35 20
2308 100 dh. Pipeline 35 20
2309 100 dh. Camels at trough and crops 35 20
2310 100 dh. Crops and farm vehicle 35 20
Nos. 2295/2310 were issued together, se-tenant, forming a composite design.

463 Scout Badge and Wildlife

1995. Scouting. Multicoloured.
2311 250 dh. Type **463** 85 55
2312 250 dh. Badge, butterflies and scouts with animals (59 x 39 mm) 85 55
2313 250 dh. Badge and scouts . . 85 55
Nos. 2311/13 were issued together, se-tenant, forming a composite design.

464 Warships and Rocket

1995. 9th Anniv of American Attack on Libya. Multicoloured.
2314 100 dh. Type **464** 35 20
2315 100 dh. Bombers, helicopters, warships and Libyans (59 x 49 mm) 35 20
2316 100 dh. Bomber and woman holding baby 35 20
Nos. 2314/16 were issued together, se-tenant, forming a composite design.

465 Gaddafi on Horseback **466** Dromedary and Woman with Water Jars

1995. International Trade Fair, Tripoli. Multicoloured.
2317 100 dh. Type **465** 35 20
2318 100 dh. Horseman 35 20
2319 100 dh. Horseman (horse galloping to right) 35 20
2320 100 dh. Horsemen with whips (horiz) 35 20
2321 100 dh. Horseman holding rifle (horiz) 35 20
2322 100 dh. Horsewoman brandishing rifle in air (horiz) 35 20

1995. City of Ghadames. Multicoloured.
2324 100 dh. Type **466** 35 20
2325 100 dh. Making cheeses . . . 35 20
2326 100 dh. Woman holding jar . 35 20
2327 100 dh. Feeding chickens . . 35 20
2328 100 dh. Spinning wool . . . 35 20
2329 100 dh. Woman in traditional costume 35 20
2330 100 dh. Drying grain 35 20
2331 100 dh. Milking goat 35 20
2332 100 dh. Making shoes 35 20
2333 100 dh. Weaving 35 20
2334 100 dh. Engraving brass tabletops 35 20
2335 100 dh. Harvesting dates . . 35 20
2336 100 dh. Reading scriptures . . 35 20
2337 100 dh. Potter 35 20
2338 100 dh. Washing clothes in well 35 20
2339 100 dh. Picking fruit 35 20

467 Family with Torch and National Flag

1995. Evacuation of Foreign Forces.
2340 **467** 50 dh. multicoloured . . 20 10
2341 100 dh. multicoloured . 35 20
2342 200 dh. multicoloured . 70 45

468 Honeycomb and Bees on Flowers

1995. Arab Beekeepers' Association. Multicoloured, colour of border given.
2343 **468** 100 dh. mauve 35 20
2344 100 dh. lilac 35 20
2345 100 dh. green 35 20

469 Stubbing out Cigarette and holding Rose **470** Dr. Mohamed Feituri

1995. World Health Day. Multicoloured, colour of central band given.
2346 **469** 100 dh. yellow 35 20
2347 100 dh. orange 35 20

1995.
2348 **470** 200 dh. multicoloured . 70 45

471 Gaddafi and Horsemen

1995. 84th Anniv of Deportation of Libyans to Italy. Multicoloured.
2349 100 dh. Type **471** 35 20
2350 100 dh. Horsemen 35 20
2351 100 dh. Battle scene 35 20
2352 100 dh. Bomber over battle scene 35 20
2353 100 dh. Libyans with rifles . . 35 20
2354 100 dh. Soldiers fighting with Libyans 35 20
2355 100 dh. Soldiers with weapons and man on ground 35 20
2356 100 dh. Soldiers with rifles and building in background . . 35 20
2357 100 dh. Libyans 35 20
2358 100 dh. Soldiers charging men on ground 35 20
2359 100 dh. Soldiers shooting at horseman 35 20
2360 100 dh. Soldiers pushing Libyan to ground 35 20
2361 100 dh. Horsemen charging . 35 20
2362 100 dh. Horses falling to ground 35 20
2363 100 dh. Children 35 20
2364 100 dh. Deportees in boats . 35 20
Nos. 2349/64 were issued together, se-tenant, forming a composite design.

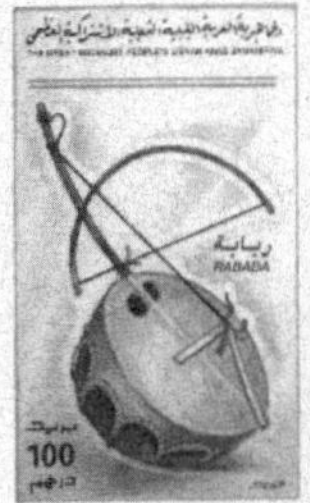

472 Rababa **473** Blue Door

1995. Musical Instruments. Multicoloured.
2365 100 dh. Type **472** 35 20
2366 100 dh. Nouba 35 20
2367 100 dh. Clarinet 35 20
2368 100 dh. Drums 35 20
2369 100 dh. Magruna 35 20
2370 100 dh. Zukra 35 20
2371 100 dh. Zil 35 20
2372 100 dh. Kaman 35 20
2373 100 dh. Guitar 35 20
2374 100 dh. Trumpet 35 20
2375 100 dh. Tapla 35 20
2376 100 dh. Gonga 35 20
2377 100 dh. Saxophone 35 20
2378 100 dh. Piano 35 20
2379 100 dh. Ganoon 35 20
2380 100 dh. Ood 35 20

1995. Doors from Mizda. Multicoloured.
2381 100 dh. Type **473** 35 20
2382 100 dh. Door with arch detail 35 20
2383 100 dh. Door made of logs . 35 20
2384 100 dh. Arched door 35 20
2385 100 dh. Wide door with bolts 35 20

474 Sports within Olympic Rings

1995. Centenary of International Olympic Committee. Multicoloured, colour of face value given.
2386 **474** 100 dh. black 35 20
2387 100 dh. red 35 20

475 Baryonyx

1995. Prehistoric Animals. Multicoloured.
2388 100 dh. Type **475** 35 20
2389 100 dh. Oviraptor 35 20
2390 100 dh. Stenonychosaurus . 35 20
2391 100 dh. Tenontosaurus . . . 35 20
2392 100 dh. Yangchuanosaurus . 35 20
2393 100 dh. Stegotetrabelodon (facing right) 35 20
2394 100 dh. Stegotetrabelodon (facing left) 35 20
2395 100 dh. Psittacosaurus . . . 35 20
2396 100 dh. Heterodontosaurus . 35 20
2397 100 dh. "Loxodonta atlantica" 35 20
2398 100 dh. "Mammuthus africanavus" 35 20
2399 100 dh. Erlikosaurus 35 20
2400 100 dh. Cynognathus 35 20
2401 100 dh. Plateosaurus 35 20
2402 100 dh. Staurikosaurus . . . 35 20
2403 100 dh. Lystrosaurus 35 20
Nos. 2388/2403 were issued together, se-tenant, the backgrounds forming a composite design.

476 Child and Dinosaur walking with Stick

1995. Children's Day. Multicoloured.
2405 100 dh. Type **476** 35 20
2406 100 dh. Child on mammoth's back 35 20
2407 100 dh. Child on way to school and tortoise under mushroom 35 20
2408 100 dh. Dinosaur playing football 35 20
2409 100 dh. Child pointing rifle at pteranodon 35 20

477 Helicopter, Soldier and Stone-thrower

1995. Palestinian "Intifida" Movement. Multicoloured.
2410 100 dh. Type **477** 35 20
2411 100 dh. Dome of the Rock and Palestinian with flag 35 20
2412 100 dh. Women with flag 35 20
Nos. 2410/12 were issued together, se-tenant, forming a composite design.

478 Airplane, Control Tower and Tailfin

1995. 50th Anniv of I.C.A.O. Multicoloured, colour of face value given.
2413 **478** 100 dh. blue 35 20
2414 100 dh. black 35 20

479 Headquarters, New York
480 "Iris germanica"

1995. 50th Anniv of U.N.O. Multicoloured, colour of background given.
2415 **479** 100 dh. pink 35 20
2416 100 dh. lilac 35 20

1995. Flowers. Multicoloured.
2417 200 dh. Type **480** 35 20
2418 200 dh. "Canna edulis" 35 20
2419 200 dh. "Nerium oleander" 35 20
2420 200 dh. Corn poppy ("Papaver rhoeas") 35 20
2421 200 dh. Bird of Paradise flower ("Strelitzia reginae") 35 20
2422 200 dh. "Amygdalus communis" 35 20

CONCESSIONAL LETTER POST

1929. No. CL227 of Italy optd **LIBIA**.
CL68 CL **93** 10 c. blue 11·00 12·00

1941. No. CL267 of Italy optd **LIBIA**.
CL123 CL **109** 10 c. brown 5·00 5·00

EXPRESS LETTER STAMPS

A. ITALIAN ISSUES.

1915. Express Letter stamps of Italy optd **Libia**.
E17 E **35** 25 c. pink 9·00 8·00
E18 E **41** 30 c. blue and pink 6·00 16·00

E 8

1921.
E34 E **8** 30 c. red and blue 1·10 2·75
E35 50 c. brown and red 1·60 4·25
E42 60 c. brown and red 2·50 7·00
E43 2 l. red and blue 5·00 15·00
Nos. E34 and E43 are inscribed "EXPRES".

1922. Nos. E17/18 surch.
E40 E **35** 60 c. on 25 c. pink 3·75 7·00
E41 E **41** 1 l. 60 on 30 c. blue and pink 5·00 17·00

1926. Nos. E42/3 surch.
E62 E **8** 70 on 60 c. brown and red 3·25 7·00
E64 1 l. 25 on 60 c. brown and red 2·75 1·00
E63 2.50 on 2 l. red and blue 3·75 14·00

B. INDEPENDENT ISSUE

1966. Design similar to T **74** inscr "EXPRES".
E368 90 m. red and green 2·25 1·25
DESIGN—HORIZ: 90 m. Saracen Castle, Zuela.

OFFICIAL STAMPS

1952. Optd **Official** in English and Arabic.
O192 **23** 2 m. brown 40 35
O193 4 m. grey 65 50
O194 5 m. green 4·50 1·60
O195 8 m. red 2·50 75
O196 10 m. violet 3·75 1·25
O197 12 m. red 6·75 2·50
O198 20 m. blue 13·50 5·25
O199 25 m. brown 17·00 6·75

PARCEL POST STAMPS

Unused prices are for complete pairs, used prices for a half.

1915. Parcel Post stamps of Italy optd **LIBIA** on each half of the stamp.
P17 P **53** 5 c. brown 80 30
P18 10 c. blue 80 30
P19 20 c. black 1·00 30
P20 25 c. red 2·00 30
P21 50 c. orange 2·00 30
P22 1 l. violet 1·75 30
P23 2 l. green 2·40 30
P24 3 l. yellow 3·00 30
P25 4 l. grey 3·00 30
P26 10 l. purple 35·00 7·00
P27 12 l. brown 65·00 7·00
P28 15 l. green 65·00 10·00
P29 20 l. purple 65·00 12·00

1927. Parcel Post stamps of Italy optd **LIBIA** on each half of the stamp.
P62 P **92** 5 c. brown £8000
P63 10 c. blue 1·60 35
P64 25 c. red 1·60 35
P65 30 c. blue 50 35
P66 50 c. orange 70·00 10·00
P67 60 c. red 50 35
P68 1 l. violet 24·00 3·50
P69 2 l. green 30·00 3·50
P70 3 l. bistre 1·00 40
P71 4 l. black 1·00 40
P72 10 l. mauve £160 15·00
P73 20 l. purple £160 15·00

POSTAGE DUE STAMPS

A. ITALIAN ISSUES.

1915. Postage Due stamps of Italy optd **Libia.**
D17 D **12** 5 c. mauve and orange 60 1·90
D18 10 c. mauve and orange 1·00 2·00
D19 20 c. mauve and orange 1·40 3·50
D20 30 c. mauve and orange 2·00 3·50
D21 40 c. mauve and orange 2·25 3·50
D22 50 c. mauve and orange 2·00 3·50
D23 60 c. mauve and orange 3·00 5·00
D24 60 c. brown and orange 45·00 80·00
D25 1 l. mauve and blue 2·00 2·00
D26 2 l. mauve and blue 30·00 35·00
D27 5 l. mauve and blue 35·00 50·00

1934. Postage Due stamps of Italy optd **LIBIA.**
D68 D **141** 5 c. brown 15 70
D69 10 c. blue 15 70
D70 20 c. red 80 55
D71 25 c. green 80 55
D72 30 c. red 80 1·10
D73 40 c. brown 80 1·75
D74 50 c. violet 1·10 20
D75 60 c. blue 1·60 2·75
D76 D **142** 1 l. orange 1·40 20
D77 2 l. green 24·00 4·50
D78 5 l. violet 48·00 15·00
D79 10 l. blue 7·00 15·00
D80 20 l. red 7·00 17·00

B. INDEPENDENT ISSUES

1951. Postage Due stamps of Cyrenaica optd. (a) For use in Cyrenaica. Optd as T **20.**
D144 D **26** 2 m. brown 5·00 5·00
D145 4 m. green 5·00 5·00
D146 8 m. red 6·75 6·25
D147 10 m. orange 7·50 6·25
D148 20 m. yellow 11·00 10·00
D149 40 m. blue 30·00 20·00
D150 100 m. black 40·00 23·00

(b) For use in Tripolitania. Surch as T **21.**
D161 D **26** 1 mal. on 2 m. brown 5·50 5·00
D162 2 mal. on 4 m. green 7·50 5·50
D163 4 mal. on 8 m. red 12·50 10·00
D164 10 mal. on 20 m. yellow 27·00 20·00
D165 20 mal. on 40 m. blue 45·00 35·00

D 25
D 53 Government Building, Tripoli

1952.
D188 D **25** 2 m. brown 65 25
D189 5 m. green 95 50
D190 10 m. red 2·25 95
D191 50 m. blue 7·50 2·25

1964.
D296 D **53** 2 m. brown 10 10
D297 6 m. green 20 10
D298 10 m. red 70 45
D299 50 m. blue 1·25 85

D **185** Men in Boat

1976. Ancient Mosaics. Multicoloured.
D725 5 dh. Type D **185** 10 10
D726 10 dh. Head of Medusa 10 10
D727 20 dh. Peacock 10 10
D728 50 dh. Fish 50 15

LIECHTENSTEIN Pt. 8

A small independent principality lying between Austria and Switzerland.

1912. 100 heller = 1 krone.
1921. 100 rappen = 1 franc (Swiss).

1 Prince John II

1912.
4 **1** 5 h. green 8·00 11·00
2 10 h. red 50·00 8·00
3 25 h. blue 50·00 30·00

2

3

1917.
7 **2** 3 h. violet 1·00 1·10
8 5 h. green 1·00 1·10
9 **3** 10 h. purple 1·00 1·10
10 15 h. brown 1·00 1·10
11 20 h. green 1·00 1·10
12 25 h. blue 1·00 1·10

1918. 60th Anniv of Prince John's Accession. As T **3** but dated "1858–1918" in upper corners.
13 **3** 20 h. green 50 1·50

1920. Optd with a scroll pattern.
14 **2** 5 h. green 2·00 5·50
15 **3** 10 h. purple 2·00 5·50
16 25 h. blue 2·00 5·50

1920. Surch.
17 **2** 40 h. on 3 h. violet 2·00 5·50
18 **3** 1 k. on 15 h. brown 2·00 5·50
19 2½ k. on 20 h. green 2·00 5·50

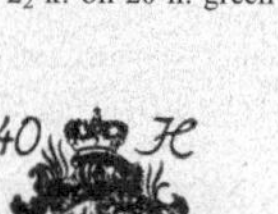

7

8 Castle of Vaduz

1920. Imperf.
20 **7** 5 h. bistre 15 3·50
21 10 h. orange 15 3·50
22 15 h. blue 15 3·50
23 20 h. brown 15 3·50
24 25 h. green 15 3·50
25 30 h. grey 15 3·50
26 40 h. red 15 3·50
27 **8** 1 k. blue 15 3·50

9 Prince John I

10 Arms

1920. Perf.
28 **7** 5 h. bistre 15 40
29 10 h. orange 15 40
30 15 h. blue 15 40
31 20 h. brown 15 40
32 – 25 h. green 15 40
33 **7** 30 h. grey 15 40
34 – 40 h. purple 15 40
35 – 50 h. green 15 40
36 – 60 h. brown 15 40
37 – 80 h. pink 15 40
38 **8** 1 k. lilac 15 40
39 – 2 k. blue 25 70
40 **9** 5 k. black 50 1·25
41 – 7½ k. grey 65 1·50
42 **10** 10 k. brown 75 2·00
DESIGNS: As Type **8**: 25 h. St. Mamertus Chapel; 40 h. Gutenberg Castle; 50 h. Courtyard, Vaduz Castle; 60 h. Red House, Vaduz; 80 h. Church Tower, Schaan; 2 k. Bendern. As Type **9**: 7½ k. Prince John II.

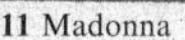

11 Madonna

14 Arms

15 St. Mamertus Chaple

16 Vaduz

1920. Prince John's 80th Birthday. Imperf or perf.

43 **11** 50 h. green . . . . 30 1·10
44 80 h. red . . . . 30 1·10
45 2 k. blue . . . . 30 1·10

1921. Surch **2 Rp.** and bars.

47 **7** 2 r. on 10 h. orge (No. 21) . 35 16·00

1921.

47a **14** 2 r. yellow . . . . 55 8·00
48 $2\frac{1}{2}$ r. brown . . . . 55 8·00
49 3 r. orange . . . . 55 8·00
50 5 r. green . . . . 7·50 1·25
51 $7\frac{1}{2}$ r. blue . . . . 3·75 25·00
65 10 r. green . . . . 15·00 1·50
53 13 r. brown . . . . 7·50 60·00
54 15 r. violet . . . . 14·00 12·00
55 **15** 20 r. black and violet . . . 55·00 1·00
56 – 25 r. black and red . . . . 2·00 1·75
57 – 30 r. black and green . . . 55·00 8·00
66 – 30 r. black and blue . . . 12·00 1·50
58 – 35 r. black and brown . . . 3·25 9·50
59 – 40 r. black and blue . . . 5·00 2·75
60 – 50 r. black and green . . . 7·00 4·00
61 – 80 r. black and grey . . . 20·00 55·00
62 **16** 1 f. black and red . . . . . 40·00 32·00

DESIGNS—As Type **15**: 25 r. Vaduz Castle; 30 r. Bendern; 35 r. Prince John II; 40 r. Church Tower at Schaan; 50 r. Gutenberg Castle; 80 r. Red House, Vaduz.

1924. Surch.

63 **14** 5 on $7\frac{1}{2}$ r. blue . . . . 1·00 2·00
64 10 on 13 r. brown . . . . . 60 1·50

19 Vine-dresser

21 Government Bldg. and Church, Vaduz

1924.

67 **19** $2\frac{1}{2}$ r. mauve and green . . . 1·00 5·00
68 5 r. blue and brown . . . . 2·00 70
69 $7\frac{1}{2}$ r. brown and green . . . 1·40 5·00
70 – 10 r. green . . . . 8·00 55
71 **19** 15 r. green and purple . . . 6·50 25·00
72 – 20 r. red . . . . 30·00 70
73 **21** $1\frac{1}{2}$ f. blue . . . . 60·00 75·00

DESIGN—As Type **19**: 10, 20 r. Castle of Vaduz.

22 Prince John II

23

1925. 85th Birthday of Prince John.

74 **22** 10 + 5 r. green . . . . . . 35·00 15·00
75 20 + 5 r. red . . . . 18·00 15·00
76 30 + 5 r. blue . . . . 5·50 5·00

1927. 87th Birthday of Prince. Arms multicoloured.

77 **23** 10 + 5 r. green . . . . . . 6·50 17·00
78 20 + 5 r. purple . . . . . . 6·50 17·00
79 30 + 5 r. blue . . . . 6·50 14·00

24 Salvage Work by Austrian soldiers

1928. Flood Relief.

80 – 5 r. + 5 r. brown and purple 16·00 18·00
81 – 10 r. + 10 r. brown & green 14·00 22·00
82 **24** 20 r. + 10 r. brown and red 17·00 22·00
83 – 30 r. + 10 r. brown & blue 14·00 22·00

DESIGNS: 5 r. Railway bridge between Buchs and Schaan; 10 r. Village of Ruggell; 30 r. Salvage work by Swiss soldiers.

26 Prince John II, 1858-1928

1928. 70th Anniv of Accession of Prince John II.

84 – 10 r. green and brown . . . 3·00 4·00
85 – 20 r. green and red . . . . 5·00 6·50
86 – 30 r. green and blue . . . . 20·00 16·00
87 – 60 r. green and mauve . . . 45·00 70·00
88 **26** 1 f. 20 blue . . . . 40·00 80·00
89 1 f. 50 brown . . . . 70·00 £160
90 2 f. red . . . . 70·00 £160
91 5 f. green . . . . 70·00 £180

DESIGN—VERT: 10 r. to 60 r. Prince John II.

28 Prince Francis I

31 Girl Vintager

32 Prince Francis I and Princess Elsa

34 Monoplane over Vaduz Castle and Rhine Valley

1929. Accession of Prince Francis I.

92 – 10 r. green . . . . 50 2·75
93 **28** 20 r. red . . . . 60 4·00
94 – 30 r. blue . . . . 1·00 16·00
95 – 70 r. brown . . . . 16·00 90·00

PORTRAITS: 10 r. Prince Francis I as a boy; 30 r. Princess Elsa; 70 r. Prince Francis and Princess Elsa.

1930.

96 **31** 3 r. red . . . . 55 1·00
97 – 5 r. green . . . . 1·50 1·00
98 – 10 r. lilac . . . . 1·40 1·00
99 – 20 r. red . . . . 22·00 1·10
100 – 25 r. green . . . . 5·00 32·00
101 – 30 r. blue . . . . 4·00 1·75
102 – 35 r. green . . . . 6·00 14·00
103 – 40 r. brown . . . . 6·50 3·00
104 – 50 r. black . . . . 70·00 13·00
105 – 60 r. green . . . . 55·00 18·00
106 – 90 r. purple . . . . 60·00 £100
107 – 1 f. 20 brown . . . . . . 80·00 £180
108 – 1 f. 50 blue . . . . 35·00 40·00
109 **32** 2 f. brown and green . . . 45·00 80·00

DESIGNS—VERT: 5 r. Mt. Three Sisters-Edelweiss; 10 r. Alpine cattle–alpine roses; 20 r. Courtyard of Vaduz Castle; 25 r. Mt. Naafkopf; 30 r. Valley of Samina; 35 r. Rofenberg Chapel; 40 r. St. Mamertus' Chapel; 50 r. Kurhaus at Malbun; 60 r. Gutenberg Castle; 90 r. Schellenberg Monastery; 1 f. 20, Vaduz Castle; 1 f. 50, Pfaelzer club hut.

1930. Air.

110 – 15 r. brown . . . . 5·00 10·00
111 – 20 r. green . . . . 12·00 15·00
112 – 25 r. brown . . . . 6·00 25·00
113 – 35 r. blue . . . . 12·00 25·00
114 **34** 45 r. green . . . . 25·00 60·00
115 1 f. purple . . . . 38·00 40·00

DESIGNS—VERT: 15, 20 r. Biplane over snowy mountain peak. HORIZ: 25, 35 r. Biplane over Vaduz Castle.

35 Airship "Graf Zeppelin" over Alps

1931. Air.

116 **35** 1 f. green . . . . 40·00 80·00
117 – 2 f. blue . . . . 90·00 £225

DESIGN: 2 f. Airship "Graf Zeppelin" (different).

37 Princess Elsa

38 Mt. Naafkopf

39 Prince Francis I

1932. Youth Charities.

118 – 10 r. + 5 r. green . . . . 16·00 25·00
119 **37** 20 r. + 5 r. red . . . . . 16·00 25·00
120 – 30 r. + 10 r. blue . . . . 16·00 32·00

DESIGNS—22 × 29 mm: 10 r. Arms of Liechtenstein. As Type **37**: 30 r. Prince Francis.

1933.

121 **38** 25 r. orange . . . . £160 50·00
122 – 90 r. green . . . . 7·50 65·00
123 – 1 f. 20 brown . . . . . . 80·00 £200

DESIGNS: 90 r. Gutenberg Castle; 1 f. 20, Vaduz Castle.

1933. Prince Francis's 80th Birthday.

124 **39** 10 r. violet . . . . 18·00 30·00
125 20 r. red . . . . 18·00 30·00
126 30 r. blue . . . . 18·00 30·00

40

41 "Three Sisters"

42 Vaduz Castle

44 Prince Francis I

45 Arms of Liechtenstein

46 Golden Eagle

1933.

127 **40** 3 r. red 15 45
128 **41** 5 r. green . . . . 3·00 75
129 – 10 r. violet 75 50
130 – 15 r. orange 20 85
131 – 20 r. red 50 45
132 – 25 r. brown . . . . 18·00 42·00
133 – 30 r. blue . . . . 3·25 90
134 – 35 r. green . . . . 70 5·50
135 – 40 r. brown . . . . 90 3·50
136 **42** 50 r. brown . . . . 18·00 13·00
137 – 60 r. purple . . . . 1·25 4·75
138 – 90 r. green . . . . 6·00 16·00
139 – 1 f. 20 blue . . . . 1·75 18·00
140 – 1 f. 50 brown . . . . . . 2·00 21·00
141 – 2 f. brown . . . . 50·00 £150
142 **44** 3 f. blue . . . . 70·00 £150
143 **45** 5 f. purple £275 £750

DESIGNS—As Type **41**: 10 r. Schaan Church; 15 r. Bendern am Rhein; 20 r. Town Hall, Vaduz; 25 r. Saminatal. As Type **44**: 2 f. Princess Elsa. As Type **42**: 30 r. Saminatal (different); 35 r. Schellenberg ruins; 40 r. Government Building, Vaduz; 60 r. Vaduz Castle (different); 90 r. Gutenberg Castle; 1 f. 20, Pfalzer Hut, Bettlerjoch; 1 f. 50, Valuna.

See also Nos. 174, 225/6 and 258.

1934. Air.

145 **46** 10 r. violet . . . . 8·00 24·00
146 – 15 r. orange . . . . 18·00 35·00
147 – 20 r. red . . . . 18·00 35·00
148 – 30 r. blue . . . . 18·00 35·00
149 – 50 r. green . . . . 14·00 28·00

DESIGNS: 10 r. to 20 r. Golden eagles in flight; 30 r. Ospreys in nest; 50 r. Golden eagle on rock.

1935. Air. No. 115 surch 60 Rp.

150 **34** 60 r. on 1 f. purple . . . . 24·00 40·00

49 "Hindenburg" and Schaan Church

1936. Air.

151 **49** 1 f. red . . . . 26·00 65·00
152 – 2 f. violet . . . . 22·00 65·00

DESIGN: 2 f. "Graf Zeppelin" over Schaan Airport.

51 Masescha am Triesenberg

52 Schellenberg Castle

1937.

154 – 3 r. brown 15 50
155 **51** 5 r. green and buff 15 20
156 – 10 r. violet and buff 15 15
157 – 15 r. black and buff . . . 20 60
158 – 20 r. red and buff 20 30
159 – 25 r. brown and buff . . . 55 2·00
160 – 30 r. blue and buff . . . . 3·00 60
161 **52** 40 r. green and buff . . . 2·25 1·50
162 – 50 c. brown and buff . . . 85 2·00
163 – 60 r. purple and buff . . . 2·25 2·00
164 – 90 r. violet and buff . . . 9·00 13·00
165 – 1 f. purple and buff . . . 2·00 10·00
166 – 1 f. 20 brown and buff . . 8·00 20·00
167 – 1 f. 50 grey and buff . . . 2·50 20·00

DESIGNS—As Type **51**: 3 r. Schalun ruins; 10 r. Knight and Vaduz Castle; 15 r. Upper Saminatal; 20 r. Church and Bridge at Bendern; 25 r. Steg Chapel and girl. As Type **52**: 30 r. Farmer and orchard, Triesenberg; 50 r. Knight and Gutenberg Castle; 60 r. Baron von Brandis and Vaduz Castle; 90 r. "Three Sisters" mountain; 1 f. Boundary-stone on Luziensteig; 1 f. 20, Minstrel and Gutenberg Castle; 1 f. 50, Lawena (Schwarzhorn).

53 Roadmakers at Triesenberg

1937. Workers' Issue.

168 – 10 r. mauve 80 70
169 **53** 20 r. red . . . . 1·10 1·25
170 – 30 r. blue . . . . 1·50 1·50
171 – 50 r. brown . . . . 1·00 2·50

DESIGNS: 10 r. Bridge at Malbun; 30 r. Binnen Canal Junction; 50 r. Francis Bridge, near Planken.

1938. Death of Prince Francis I.

174 **44** 3 f. black on yellow . . . 8·50 65·00

54 Josef Rheinberger

55 Black-headed Gulls

1939. Birth Centenary of Rheinberger (composer).

175 **54** 50 r. grey . . . . 65 3·50

1939. Air.

176 – 10 r. violet (Barn swallows) 40 40
177 **55** 15 r. orange . . . . 65 1·50
178 – 20 r. red (Herring gull) . . 1·75 45
179 – 30 r. blue (Common buzzard) 1·60 1·25
180 – 50 r. green (Northern goshawk) . . . . . 5·00 2·00
181 – 1 f. red (Lammergeier) . . 4·25 13·00
182 – 2 f. violet Lammergeier . . 4·00 13·00

56 Offering Homage to First Prince

1939. Homage to Francis Joseph II.

183 **56** 20 r. red . . . . 60 1·60
184 30 r. blue . . . . 60 1·60
185 50 r. green . . . . 60 1·60

57 Francis Joseph II

1939.

186 – 2 f. green on cream . . . . 6·00 32·00
187 – 3 f. violet on cream . . . 4·50 32·00
188 **57** 5 f. brown on cream . . . 11·00 20·00

DESIGNS: 2 f. Cantonal Arms; 3 f. Arms of Principality.

58 Prince John when a Child

1940. Birth Centenary of Prince John II.

189 **58** 20 r. red . . . . 40 1·75
190 – 30 r. blue . . . . 55 2·75
191 – 50 r. green . . . . 1·00 9·00

192 – 1 f. violet . . . . 6·00 60·00
193 – 1 f. 50 black . . . . 5·00 50·00
194 – 3 f. brown . . . . 3·50 20·00
DESIGNS–As Type **58**: Portraits of Prince John in early manhood (30 r.), in middle age (50 r.) and in later life (1 f.), and Memorial tablet (1 f. 50). As Type **44**: 3 f. Framed portrait of Prince John II.

60 Wine Press

1941. Agricultural Propaganda.
195 – 10 r. brown 35 80
196 **60** 20 r. purple . . . . 60 1·25
197 – 30 r. blue . . . . 60 2·00
198 – 50 r. green . . . . 1·60 13·00
199 – 90 r. violet . . . . 1·60 15·00
DESIGNS: 10 r. Harvesting maize; 30 r. Sharpening scythe; 50 r. Milkmaid and cow; 90 r. Girl wearing traditional headdress.

61 Madonna and Child **62** Prince Hans Adam

1941.
200 **61** 10 f. purple on stone . . . 45·00 95·00

1941. Princes (1st issue).
201 **62** 20 r. red . . . . 30 1·25
202 – 30 r. blue (Wenzel) . . . . 35 2·00
203 – 1 f. grey (Anton Florian) . 1·40 14·00
204 – 1 f. 50 green (Joseph) . . . 1·50 14·00
See also Nos. 210/13 and 217/20.

63 St. Lucius preaching

1942. 600th Anniv of Separation from Estate of Montfort.
205 **63** 20 r. red on pink 90 80
206 – 30 r. blue on pink . . . . . 90 2·00
207 – 50 r. green on pink . . . . 1·75 6·00
208 – 1 f. brown on pink . . . . 2·25 12·00
209 – 2 f. violet on pink . . . . 2·25 12·00
DESIGNS: 30 r. Count of Montfort replanning Vaduz; 50 r. Counts of Montfort-Werdenberg and Sargans signing treaty; 1 f. Battle of Gutenberg; 2 f. Homage to Prince of Liechtenstein.

64 Prince John Charles **65** Princess Georgina

1942. Princes (2nd issue).
210 **64** 20 r. pink 30 80
211 – 30 r. blue (Francis Joseph I) 45 1·50
212 – 1 f. purple (Alois I) . . . . 1·40 13·00
213 – 1 f. 50 brown (John I) . . . 1·40 13·00

1943. Marriage of Prince Francis Joseph II and Countess Georgina von Wildczek.
214 – 10 r. purple 45 80
215 **65** 20 r. red 45 80
216 – 30 r. blue 45 80
PORTRAITS—VERT: 10 r. Prince Francis Joseph II. HORIZ (44×25 mm): 30 r. Prince and Princess.

66 Alois II **67** Marsh Land

1943. Princes (3rd issue).
217 **66** 20 r. brown 30 65
218 – 30 r. blue . . . . 60 1·25
219 – 1 f. brown . . . . 90 6·50
220 – 1 f. 50 green . . . . 90 6·50
PORTRAITS: 30 r. John II; 1 f. Francis I; 1 f. 50, Francis Joseph II.

1943. Completion of Irrigation Canal.
221 **67** 10 r. violet 20 40
222 – 30 r. blue . . . . 40 1·90
223 – 50 r. green . . . . 75 7·00
224 – 2 f. brown . . . . 2·00 11·00
DESIGNS: 30 r. Draining the canal; 50 r. Ploughing reclaimed land; 2 f. Harvesting crops.

1943. Castles. As T **41**.
225 10 r. grey (Vaduz) 40 35
226 20 r. brown (Gutenberg) . . 55 80

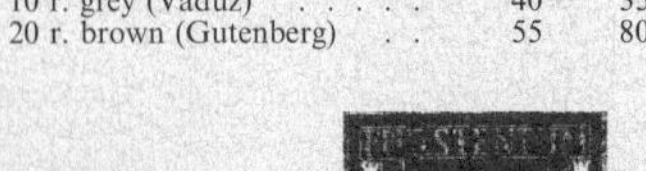

69 Planken **70** Prince Francis Joseph II

1944. Various designs. Buff backgrounds.
227 **69** 3 r. brown 15 20
228 – 5 r. green (Bendern) . . . 15 10
228a – 5 r. brown (Bendern) . . 28·00 60
229 – 10 r. grey (Triesen) . . . 20 10
230 – 15 r. grey (Ruggell) . . . 30 85
231 – 20 r. red (Vaduz) 30 20
232 – 25 r. brown (Triesenberg) 30 1·00
233 – 30 r. blue (Schaan) . . . 30 25
234 – 40 r. brown (Balzers) . . 60 1·10
235 – 50 r. blue (Mauren) . . . 70 1·50
236 – 60 r. green (Schellenberg) 3·75 4·25
237 – 90 r. green (Eschen) . . . 3·75 4·50
238 – 1 f. purple (Vaduz Castle) 2·25 3·75
239 – 1 f. 20 brown (Valunatal) 2·50 5·00
240 – 1 f. 50 blue (Lawena) . . 2·50 5·00

1944.
241 **70** 2 f. brown and buff . . . 4·75 14·00
242 – 3 f. green and buff . . . . 3·00 11·00
DESIGN: 3 f. Princess Georgina.
See also Nos. 302/3.

72 **73**

1945. Birth of Crown Prince Johann Adam Pius (known as Prince Hans Adam).
243 **72** 20 r. red, yellow and gold 1·00 40
244 30 r. blue, yellow and gold 1·00 1·40
245 100 r. grey, yellow and gold 2·25 5·00

1945.
246 **73** 5 f. blue on buff . . . . . 19·00 28·00
247 5 f. brown on buff . . . . 24·00 38·00

74 First Aid **75** St. Lucius

1945. Red Cross. Cross in red.
248 – 10 r. + 10 r. purple and buff 1·00 1·50
249 **74** 20 r. + 20 r. purple and buff 1·00 2·25
250 – 1 f. + 1 f. 40 blue and buff 6·00 22·00
DESIGNS: 10 r. Mother and children; 1 f. Nurse and invalid.

1946.
251 **75** 10 f. grey on buff . . . . 35·00 28·00

76 Red Deer Stag **79** Wilbur Wright

1946. Wild Life.
252 **76** 20 r. red . . . . 1·75 2·25
255 – 20 r. red (Chamois) . . . 3·50 4·00
283 – 20 r. red (Roebuck) . . . 9·00 3·75
253 – 30 r. blue (Arctic hare) . . 2·40 3·00
256 – 30 r. blue (Alpine marmot) 5·50 4·25
284 – 30 r. green (Black grouse) 22·00 6·00
285 – 80 r. brown (Eurasian badger) 38·00 38·00
254 – 1 f. 50 green (Capercaillie) 9·50 11·00
257 – 1 f. 50 brown (Golden eagle) 9·50 14·00

1947. Death of Princess Elsa. As No. 141.
258 – 2 f. black on yellow . . . . 3·50 14·00

1948. Air. Pioneers of Flight.
259 – 10 r. green 65 20
260 – 15 r. violet . . . . 65 1·10
261 – 20 r. brown 80 20
262 – 25 r. red . . . . 1·25 1·90
263 – 40 r. blue . . . . 1·75 1·00
264 – 50 r. blue . . . . 1·75 1·75
265 – 1 f. purple . . . . 2·50 3·00
266 – 2 f. purple . . . . 4·50 4·75
267 **79** 5 f. green . . . . 5·50 6·50
268 – 10 f. black . . . . 32·00 16·00
PORTRAITS: 10 r. Leonardo da Vinci; 15 r. Joseph Montgolfier; 20 r. Jakob Degen; 25 r. Wilhelm Kress; 40 r. Etienne Robertson; 50 r. William Henson; 1 f. Otto Lilienthal; 2 f. Salomon Andree; 10 f. Icarus.

80 "Ginevra de Benci" (Da Vinci)

1949. Paintings.
269 **80** 10 r. green 45 30
270 – 20 r. red . . . . 1·25 60
271 – 30 r. brown . . . . 3·00 1·25
272 – 40 r. blue . . . . 6·00 65
273 – 50 r. violet . . . . 5·00 6·50
274 – 60 r. grey . . . . 11·00 5·50
275 – 80 r. brown . . . . 2·50 4·00
276 – 90 r. green . . . . 11·00 5·00
277 – 120 r. mauve . . . . . . 2·50 4·75
DESIGNS: 20 r. "Portrait of a Young Girl" (Rubens); 30 r. Self-portrait of Rembrandt in plumed hat; 40 r. "Stephan Gardiner, Bishop of Winchester" (Quentin Massys); 50 r. "Madonna and Child" (Hans Memling); 60 r. "Franz Meister in 1456" (Jehan Fouquet); 80 r. "Lute Player" (Orazio Gentileschi); 90 r. "Portrait of a Man" (Bernhardin Strigel); 120 r. "Portrait of a Man (Duke of Urbino)" (Raphael).

1949. No. 227 surch **5 Rp**. and bars.
278 **69** 5 r. on 3 r. brown and buff 60 40

82 Posthorn and Map of World

1949. 75th Anniv of U.P.U.
279 **82** 40 r. blue . . . . 3·00 3·75

83 Rossauer Castle **86** Boy cutting Loaf

1949. 250th Anniv of Acquisition of Domain of Schellenberg.
280 **83** 20 r. purple . . . . 2·00 2·00
281 – 40 r. blue . . . . 7·00 6·50
282 – 1 f. 50 red . . . . 9·50 8·50
DESIGN—HORIZ: 40 r. Bendern Church. VERT: 1 f. 50, Prince Johann Adam I.

1950. Surch **100 100**.
286 **82** 100 r. on 40 r. blue . . . . 18·00 42·00

1951. Agricultural scenes.
287 **86** 5 r. mauve 20 10
288 – 10 r. green 45 10
289 – 15 r. brown . . . . 4·50 5·00
290 – 20 r. brown . . . . 1·00 20
291 – 25 r. purple . . . . 4·50 4·50
292 – 30 r. green . . . . 3·25 55
293 – 40 r. blue . . . . 8·50 7·00
294 – 50 r. purple . . . . 7·50 3·00
295 – 60 r. brown . . . . 7·00 3·00
296 – 80 r. brown . . . . 9·00 8·00
297 – 90 r. green . . . . 18·00 4·75
298 – 1 f. blue . . . . 55·00 6·00
DESIGNS: 10 r. Man whetting scythe; 15 r. Mowing; 20 r. Girl and sweet corn; 25 r. Haywain; 30 r. Gathering grapes; 40 r. Man with scythe; 50 r. Herdsman with cows; 60 r. Ploughing; 80 r. Girl carrying basket of fruit; 90 r. Woman gleaning; 1 f. Tractor hauling corn.

87 "Lock on the Canal" (Aelbert Cuyp) **88** "Willem von Heythuysen, Burgomaster of Haarlem" (Frans Hals)

1951. Paintings.
299 **87** 10 r. + 10 r. green . . . . 8·00 6·00
300 **88** 20 r. + 10 r. brown . . . . 8·00 12·00
301 – 40 r. + 10 r. blue . . . . 8·00 8·00
DESIGN—As Type **87**: 40 r. "Landscape" (Jacob van Ruysdael).

90 Vaduz Castle **96** Lord Baden-Powell

1951.
302 **70** 2 f. blue . . . . 13·00 30·00
303 – 3 f. brown . . . . £150 90·00
304 **90** 5 f. green £170 £150
DESIGN: 3 f. Princess Georgina.

1952. No. 281 surch **1.20**
308 1 f. 20 on 40 r. blue . . . . 18·00 48·00

1952. Paintings from Prince's Collection. (a) As T **80** but size 25×30 mm.
309 10 r. green 80 80
305 20 r. purple . . . . 32·00 3·00
307 40 r. blue . . . . 12·00 5·00
312 40 r. blue . . . . 27·00 42·00
PAINTINGS: No. 309, "Portrait of a Young Man" (A. G.); 305, "Portrait" (Giovanni Salvoldo); 307, "St. John" (Andrea del Sarto); 312, "Leonhard, Count of Hag" (Hans von Kulmbach).

(b) As T **88** ($22\frac{1}{2}\times24$ mm).
310 20 r. brown . . . . 12·00 2·25
306 30 r. green . . . . 22·00 7·50
311 30 r. brown . . . . 25·00 6·50
PAINTINGS: No. 310, "St. Nicholas" (Bartholomaus Zeitblom); 306, "Madonna and Child" (Sandro Botticelli); 311, "St. Christopher" (Lucas Cranach the elder).

1953. 14th International Scout Conf.
313 **96** 10 r. green . . . . 1·25 1·00
314 20 r. brown . . . . 12·00 2·25
315 25 r. red . . . . 10·00 16·00
316 40 r. blue . . . . 8·00 6·00

97 Alemannic Ornamental Disc, (c. A. D. 600) **98** Prehistoric Walled Settlement, Borscht

1953. Opening of National Museum, Vaduz.
317 **97** 10 r. brown . . . . 8·00 12·00
318 **98** 20 r. green . . . . 8·00 10·00
319 – 1 f. 20 blue . . . . . . 42·00 26·00
DESIGN—VERT: 1 f. 20, Rossen jug (3000 B.C.).

99 Footballers **100** Madonna and Child

1954. Football.
320 **99** 10 r. brown and red . . . 2·00 1·00
321 – 20 r. deep green and green 8·00 1·50
322 – 25 r. deep brown & brown 20·00 30·00
323 – 40 r. violet and grey . . . 16·00 9·00
DESIGNS: 20 r. Footballer kicking ball; 25 r. Goal-keeper; 40 r. Two footballers.
For stamps in similar designs see Nos. 332/5, 340/3, 351/4 and 363/6.

1954. Nos. 299/301 surch in figures.
324 **87** 35 r. on 10 r. + 10 r. green 3·00 2·00
325 **88** 60 r. on 20 r. + 10 r. brown 15·00 9·00
326 – 65 r. on 40 r. + 10 r. blue 5·00 7·00

1954. Termination of Marian Year.
327 **100** 20 r. brown . . . . 2·00 2·00
328 40 r. black . . . . 15·00 17·00
329 1 f. brown . . . . 16·00 16·00

101 Princess Georgina **102** Crown Prince John Adam Pius

1955.
330 – 2 f. brown . . . . 65·00 35·00
331 **101** 3 f. green . . . . 65·00 35·00
PORTRAIT: 2 f. Prince Francis Joseph II.

1955. Mountain Sports. As T **99.**
332 10 r. purple and blue . . . . 1·00 70
333 20 r. green and bistre . . . . 6·00 70
334 25 r. brown and blue . . . . 16·00 14·00
335 40 r. green and red . . . . . 16·00 6·00
DESIGNS: 10 r. Slalom racer; 20 r. Mountaineer hammering in piton; 25 r. Skier; 40 r. Mountaineer resting on summit.

1955. 10th Anniv of Liechtenstein Red Cross. Cross in red.
336 **102** 10 r. violet . . . . 1·25 60
337 – 20 r. green . . . . 4·50 1·75
338 – 40 r. brown . . . . 6·50 7·00
339 – 60 r. red . . . . 6·50 3·50
PORTRAITS: 20 r. Prince Philip; 40 r. Prince Nicholas; 60 r. Princess Nora.
See also No. 350.

1956. Athletics. As T **99.**
340 10 r. green and brown 80 60
341 20 r. purple and green . . . . 3·00 70
342 40 r. brown and blue . . . . 4·50 4·50
343 1 f. brown and red . . . . . 10·00 12·00
DESIGNS: 10 r. Throwing the javelin; 20 r. Hurdling; 40 r. Pole vaulting; 1 f. Running.

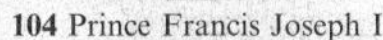
103 **104** Prince Francis Joseph II

1956. 150th Anniv of Sovereignty of Liechtenstein.
344 **103** 10 r. purple and gold . . 2·00 75
345 1 f. 20 blue and gold . . . 9·00 3·50

1956. 50th Birthday of Prince Francis Joseph II.
346 **104** 10 r. green . . . . 1·40 40
347 15 r. blue . . . . 3·00 2·50
348 25 r. purple . . . . 3·25 2·50
349 60 r. brown . . . . 7·00 2·50

1956. 6th Philatelic Exhibition, Vaduz. As T **102** but inscr "6. BRIEFMARKEN-AUSSTELLUNG".
350 20 r. green . . . . 2·50 40

1956. Gymnastics. As T **99.**
351 10 r. green and pink . . . . . 1·25 75
352 15 r. purple and green . . . . 4·50 6·00
353 25 r. green and drab . . . . . 6·00 7·00
354 1 f. 50 brown and yellow . . . 16·00 14·00
DESIGNS: 10 r. Somersaulting; 15 r. Vaulting; 25 r. Exercising with rings; 1 f. 50, Somersaulting on parallel bars.

105 Norway Spruce **106** Lord Baden-Powell

1957. Liechtenstein Trees and Bushes.
355 **105** 10 r. purple . . . . 3·50 1·75
356 – 20 r. red . . . . 3·50 70
357 – 1 f. green . . . . 5·50 5·50
DESIGNS: 20 r. Wild rose bush; 1 f. Silver birch.
See also Nos. 369/71, 375/7 and 401/3.

1957. 50th Anniv of Boy Scout Movement and Birth Centenary of Lord Baden-Powell (founder).
358 – 10 r. blue . . . . 1·00 1·25
359 **106** 20 r. brown . . . . 1·00 1·25
DESIGN: 10 r. Torchlight procession.

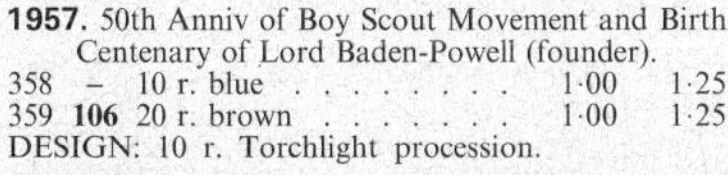

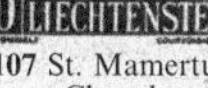

107 St. Mamertus Chapel **108** Relief Map of Liechtenstein

1957. Christmas.
360 **107** 10 r. brown 70 20
361 – 40 r. blue . . . . 2·75 6·00
362 – 1 f. 50 purple . . . . . . 8·00 9·50
DESIGNS—(from St. Mamertus Chapel): 40 r. Altar shrine; 1 f. 50, "Pieta" (sculpture).
See also Nos. 372/4 and 392/4.

1958. Sports. As T **99.**
363 15 r. violet and blue . . . . 1·00 1·25
364 30 r. green and purple . . . . 5·00 6·00
365 40 r. green and orange . . . . 8·50 7·50
366 90 r. brown and green . . . . 2·50 3·50
DESIGNS: 15 r. Swimmer; 30 r. Fencers; 40 r. Tennis player; 90 r. Racing cyclists.

1958. Brussels International Exhibition.
367 **108** 25 r. violet, stone and red 50 55
368 40 r. purple, blue and red 60 55

1958. Liechtenstein Trees and Bushes. As T **105.**
369 20 r. brown (Sycamore) . . . 3·00 60
370 50 r. green (Holly) . . . . . 12·00 3·50
371 90 r. violet (Yew) . . . . . . 3·00 2·75

1958. Christmas. As T **107.**
372 20 r. green . . . . 2·50 2·25
373 35 r. violet . . . . 2·50 2·25
374 80 r. brown . . . . 2·75 2·25
DESIGNS: 20 r. "St. Maurice and St. Agatha"; 35 r. "St. Peter"; 80 r. St. Peter's Chapel, Mals-Balzers.

1959. Liechtenstein Trees and Bushes. As T **105.**
375 20 r. lilac (Red-berried larch) 4·50 2·25
376 50 r. red (Red-berried elder) . 4·00 2·25
377 90 r. green (Linden) . . . . . 3·50 3·00

109 **111** Harvester

110 Flags of Vaduz Castle and Rhine Valley

1959. Pope Pius XII Mourning.
378 **109** 30 r. purple and gold . . 65 75

1959. Views.
379 – 5 r. brown 10 10
380 **110** 10 r. purple 10 10
381 – 20 r. mauve 25 10
382 – 30 r. red 30 15
383 – 40 r. green 75 35
384 – 50 r. blue 45 30
385 – 60 r. blue 65 40
386 **111** 75 r. brown . . . . . . 1·00 1·25
387 – 80 r. green 75 55
388 – 90 r. purple 90 65
389 – 1 f. brown 90 50
390 – 1 f. 20 red . . . . . . 1·25 1·00
390a – 1 f. 30 green . . . . . . 1·00 90
391 – 1 f. 50 blue . . . . . . 1·50 1·00
DESIGNS—HORIZ: 5 r. Bendern Church; 20 r. Rhine Dam; 30 r. Gutenberg Castle; 40 r. View from Schellenberg; 50 r. Vaduz Castle; 60 r. Naafkopf-Falknis Mountains (view from the Bettlerjoch); 1 f. 20, Harvesting apples; 1 f. 30, Farmer and wife; 1 f. 50, Saying grace at table. VERT: 80 r. Alpine haymaker; 90 r. Girl in vineyard; 1 f. Mother in kitchen.

1959. Christmas. As T **107.**
392 5 r. green 50 15
393 60 r. brown . . . . 5·00 4·50
394 1 f. purple . . . . 4·50 2·50
DESIGNS: 5 r. Bendern Church belfry; 60 r. Relief on bell of St. Theodul's Church; 1 f. Sculpture on tower of St. Lucius's Church.

112 Bell 47J Ranger Helicopter

1960. Air. 30th Anniv of 1st Liechtenstein Air Stamps.
395 **112** 30 r. red . . . . 2·00 2·25
396 – 40 r. blue . . . . 3·50 2·25
397 – 50 r. purple . . . . . . 8·50 4·00
398 – 75 r. green . . . . . . 1·50 2·50
DESIGNS: 40 r. Boeing 707 jetliner; 50 r. Convair Coronado jetliner; 75 r. Douglas DC-8 jetliner.

1960. World Refugee Year. Nos. 367/8 surch **WELTFLUCHTLINGSJAHR 1960,** uprooted tree and new value.
399 **108** 30 + 10 r. on 40 r. purple, blue and red 60 85
400 50 + 10 r. on 25 r. violet, stone and red . . . . . 80 1·40

1960. Liechtenstein Trees and Bushes. As T **105.**
401 20 r. brown (Beech) . . . . . 6·00 3·50
402 30 r. purple (Juniper) . . . . 6·00 7·00
403 50 r. turquoise (Mountain pines) 19·00 9·00

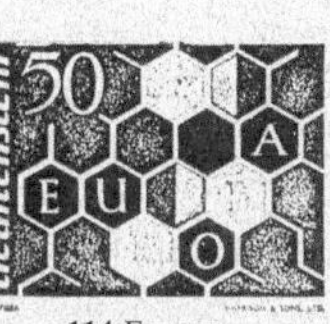

114 Europa "Honeycomb" **115** Princess Gina

1960. Europa.
404 **114** 50 r. multicoloured . . . . 75·00 45·00

1960.
404a – 1 f. 70 violet . . . . . . 1·00 85
405 **115** 2 f. blue . . . . 1·75 1·40
406 – 3 f. brown . . . . 1·90 1·50
PORTRAITS: 1 f. 70, Crown Prince Hans Adam; 3 f. Prince Francis Joseph II.

116 Heinrich von Frauenberg **117** "Power Transmission"

1961. Minnesingers (1st issue). Multicoloured. Reproduction from the Manessian Manuscript of Songs.
407 15 r. Type **116** 30 35
408 25 r. Ulrich von Liechtenstein 50 50
409 35 r. Ulrich von Gutenberg . . 60 70
410 1 f. Konrad von Altstatten . . 1·40 1·50
411 1 f. 50 Walther von der Vogelweide . . . . 7·25 12·00
See also Nos. 415/18 and 428/31.

1961. Europa.
412 **117** 50 r. multicoloured 20 25

118 Clasped Hands **119** Campaign Emblem

1962. Europa.
413 **118** 50 r. red and blue 40 40

1962. Malaria Eradication.
414 **119** 50 r. blue 35 35

1962. Minnesingers (2nd issue). As T **116.** Mult.
415 20 r. King Konradin 20 20
416 30 r. Kraft von Toggenburg . . 60 60
417 40 r. Heinrich von Veldig . . . 60 60
418 2 f. Tannhauser . . . . 1·50 1·50

120 Pieta **121** Prince Francis Joseph II

1962. Christmas.
419 **120** 30 r. mauve 40 40
420 – 50 r. red 55 55
421 – 1 f. 20 blue 95 95
DESIGNS: 50 r. Fresco with angel; 1 f. 20, View of Mauren.
See also Nos. 438/40.

1963. 25th Anniv of Reign of Prince Francis Joseph II.
422 **121** 5 f. green . . . . 3·50 2·75

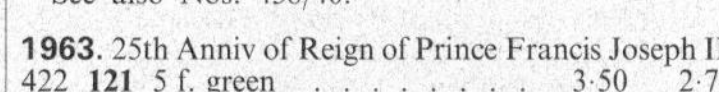

122 Milk and Bread

1963. Freedom from Hunger.
423 **122** 50 r. brown, purple & red . 35 35

123 "Angel of Annunciation" **124** "Europa"

1963. Red Cross Cent. Cross in red; background grey.
424 **123** 20 r. yellow and green . . 25 25
425 – 80 r. violet and mauve . . 60 60
426 – 1 f. blue and ultramarine . 80 80
DESIGNS: 80 r. "The Epiphany"; 1 f. "Family".

1963. Europa.
427 **124** 50 r. multicoloured 75 65

1963. Minnesingers (3rd issue). As T **116.** Mult.
428 25 r. Heinrich von Sax 25 25
429 30 r. Kristan von Hamle . . . 40 40
430 75 r. Werner von Teufen . . . 75 75
431 1 f. 70 Hartmann von Aue . . 1·50 1·50

125 Olympic Rings and Flags **126** Arms of Counts of Werdenberg, Vaduz

1964. Olympic Games, Tokyo.
432 **125** 50 r. red, black and blue 30 30

1964. Arms (1st issue). Multicoloured.
433 20 f. Type **126** 20 15
434 30 f. Barons of Brandis . . . 30 20
435 80 f. Counts of Sulz 75 65
436 1 f. 50 Counts of Hohenems 1·10 90
See also Nos. 443/6.

127 Roman Castle, Schaan **128** P. Kaiser

1964. Europa.
437 **127** 50 f. multicoloured . . . 1·10 70

1964. Christmas. As T **120.**
438 10 r. purple 10 10
439 40 r. blue 25 25
440 1 f. 30 purple 80 80
DESIGNS: 10 r. Masescha Chapel; 40 r. "Mary Magdalene" (altar painting); 1 f. 30, "St. Sebastian, Madonna and Child, and St. Rochus" (altar painting).

1964. Death Centenary of Peter Kaiser (historian).
441 **128** 1 f. green on cream . . . 30 45

129 "Madonna" (wood sculpture, c. 1700) **130** Europa "Links" (ancient belt-buckle)

1965.
442 **129** 10 f. red . . . . 5·50 3·50

1965. Arms (2nd issue). As T **126.** Multicoloured.
443 20 r. Von Schellenberg . . . 20 15
444 30 r. Von Gutenberg 25 20
445 80 r. Von Frauenberg 75 70
446 1 f. Von Ramschwag 75 70

1965. Europa.
447 **130** 50 r. brown, grey and blue 30 40

131 "Jesus in the Temple"

1965. Birth Centenary of Ferdinand Nigg (painter).
448 – 10 r. deep green and green 10 10
449 – 30 r. brown and orange . . 15 15
450 **131** 1 f. 20 green and blue . . 40 40
DESIGNS—VERT: 10 r. "The Annunciation"; 30 r. "The Magi".

132 Princess Gina and Prince Franz (after painting by Pedro Leitao) **133** Telecommunications Symbols

1965. Special Issue.
451 **132** 75 r. multicoloured . . . 30 40
See also No. 457.

1965. Centenary of I.T.U.
452 **133** 25 r. multicoloured . . . 20 20

134 Tree ("Wholesome Earth")

1966. Nature Protection.

453 **134** 10 r. green and yellow . . 10 10
454 – 20 r. blue and light blue . 15 15
455 – 30 r. blue and green . . . 15 15
456 – 1 f. 50 red and yellow . . 45 45
DESIGNS: 20 r. Bird ("Pure Air"); 30 r. Fish ("Clean Water"); 1 f. 50, Sun ("Protection of Nature").

1966. Prince Franz Joseph II's 60th Birthday. As T **132**, but with portrait of Prince Franz and inscr "1906–1966".

457 – 1 f. multicoloured 30 45

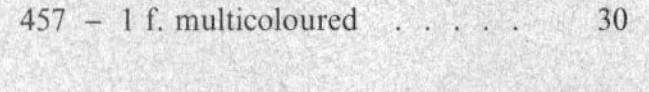

135 Arms of Herren von Richenstein **136** Europa "Ship"

1966. Arms of Triesen Families. Multicoloured.

458 20 r. Type **135** 15 15
459 30 r. Jinker Vaistli 20 20
460 60 r. Edle von Trisun 25 25
461 1 f. 20 Die von Schiel 50 50

1966. Europa.

462 **136** 50 r. multicoloured . . . 30 30

137 Vaduz Parish Church **138** Cogwheels

1966. Restoration of Vaduz Parish Church.

463 **137** 5 r. green and red 10 10
464 – 20 r. purple and bistre . . 15 10
465 – 30 r. blue and red 20 20
466 – 1 f. 70 brown and green . 60 90
DESIGNS: 20 r. St. Florin; 30 r. Madonna; 1 f. 70, God the Father.

1967. Europa.

467 **138** 50 r. multicoloured . . . 30 30

139 "The Man from Malanser" **141** "Alpha and Omega"

1967. Liechtenstein Sagas (1st series). Multicoloured.

468 20 r. Type **139** 20 10
469 30 r. "The Treasure of Gutenberg" 25 15
470 1 f. 20 "The Giant of Guflina" 65 40
See also Nos. 492/4 and 516/18.

1967. Christian Symbols. Multicoloured.

472 20 r. Type **141** 10 10
473 30 r. "Tropaion" (Cross as victory symbol) 10 10
474 70 r. Christ's monogram . . . 30 30

142 Father J. B. Buchel (educator, historian and poet) **143** "E.F.T.A."

1967. Buchel Commemoration.

475 **142** 1 f. red and green 35 35

1967. European Free Trade Association.

476 **143** 50 r. multicoloured . . . 30 25

144 "Peter and Paul", Mauren **145** Campaign Emblem

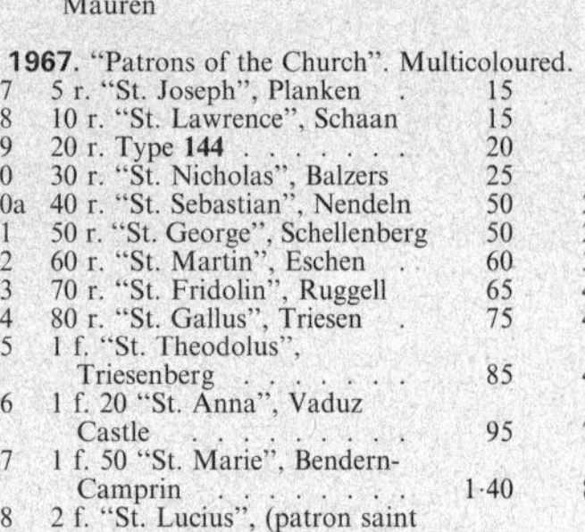

1967. "Patrons of the Church". Multicoloured.

477 5 r. "St. Joseph", Planken . 15 10
478 10 r. "St. Lawrence", Schaan 15 10
479 20 r. Type **144** 20 10
480 30 r. "St. Nicholas", Balzers 25 10
480a 40 r. "St. Sebastian", Nendeln 50 25
481 50 r. "St. George", Schellenberg 50 20
482 60 r. "St. Martin", Eschen . 60 30
483 70 r. "St. Fridolin", Ruggell 65 40
484 80 r. "St. Gallus", Triesen . 75 45
485 1 f. "St. Theodolus", Triesenberg 85 40
486 1 f. 20 "St. Anna", Vaduz Castle 95 70
487 1 f. 50 "St. Marie", Bendern-Camprin . . . . 1·40 80
488 2 f. "St. Lucius", (patron saint of Liechtenstein) . . . . . 2·00 1·10

1967. "Technical Assistance".

489 **145** 50 r. + 20 r. multicoloured 30 30

146 Europa "Key"

1968. Europa.

490 **146** 50 r. multicoloured . . . 30 25

147 Arms of Liechtenstein and Wilczek **148** Sir Rowland Hill

1968. Silver Wedding Anniv of Prince Francis Joseph II and Princess Gina.

491 **147** 75 r. multicoloured . . . 45 40

1968. Liechtenstein Sagas (2nd series). As T **139**. Multicoloured.

492 30 r. "The Treasure of St. Mamerten" 20 15
493 50 r. "The Hobgoblin in the Bergerwald" 25 25
494 80 r. "The Three Sisters" . . 40 40

1968. "Pioneers of Philately" (1st series).

495 **148** 20 r. green 15 10
496 – 30 r. brown 20 15
497 – 1 f. black 50 40
PORTRAITS: 30 r. Philippe de Ferrary; 1 f. Maurice Burrus.
See also Nos. 504/5 and 554/6.

150 Arms of Liechtenstein **151** Colonnade

1969.

498 **150** 3 f. 50 brown . . . . . . 2·00 1·25

1969. Europa.

499 **151** 50 r. multicoloured . . . 35 30

152 "Biology"

1969. 250th Anniv of Liechtenstein. Multicoloured.

500 10 r. Type **152** 10 10
501 30 r. "Physics" 20 15
502 50 r. "Astronomy" 40 30
503 80 r. "Art" 60 60

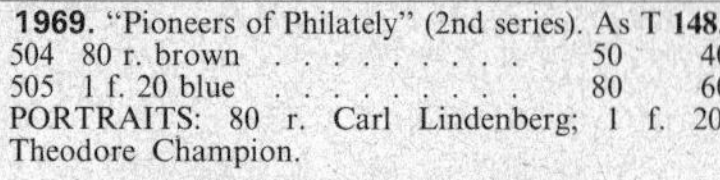

1969. "Pioneers of Philately" (2nd series). As T **148**.

504 80 r. brown 50 40
505 1 f. 20 blue 80 60
PORTRAITS: 80 r. Carl Lindenberg; 1 f. 20, Theodore Champion.

153 Arms of St. Luzi Monastery **154** Symbolic "T"

1969. Arms of Church Patrons. Multicoloured.

506 20 r. St. Johann's Abbey . . . 20 10
507 30 r. Type **153** 25 20
508 30 r. Ladies' Priory, Schanis 25 20
509 30 r. Knights Hospitallers, Feldkirch 25 20
510 50 r. Pfafers Abbey 35 30
511 50 r. Weingarten Abbey . . . 35 30
512 75 r. St. Gallen Abbey . . . 70 50
513 1 f. 20 Ottobeuren Abbey . . . 1·10 80
514 1 f. 50 Chur Episcopate . . . 1·40 90

1969. Centenary of Liechtenstein Telegraph System.

515 **154** 30 r. multicoloured 15 15

1969. Liechtenstein Sagas (3rd series). As T **139**. Multicoloured.

516 20 r. "The Cheated Devil" . . 20 15
517 50 r. "The Fiery Red Goat" 45 25
518 60 r. "The Grafenberg Treasure" 65 35

155 Orange Lily **156** "Flaming Sun"

1970. Nature Conservation Year. Multicoloured.

519 20 r. Type **155** 25 15
520 30 r. Wild orchid 45 20
521 50 r. Ranunculus 60 40
522 1 f. 20 Bog bean . . . . . . 1·25 1·00
See also Nos. 532/5 and 548/51.

1970. Europa.

523 **156** 50 r. yellow, blue & green 35 30

157 Prince Wenzel **158** Prince Francis Joseph II

1970. 25th Anniv of Liechtenstein Red Cross.

524 **157** 1 f. multicoloured 55 45

1970.

526 – 1 f. 70 green 80 80
526a – 2 f. 50 blue . . . . 1·25 1·25
527 **158** 3 f. black . . . . 1·40 1·40
DESIGNS: 1 f. 70, Prince Hans Adam; 2 f. 50, Princess Gina.

159 "Mother and Child" (R. Schadler) **160** Bronze Boar (La Tene period)

1970. Christmas.

528 **159** 30 r. multicoloured 20 15

1971. National Museum Inauguration

529 **160** 25 r. black, blue & ultram 20 15
530 – 30 r. green and brown . . 30 15
531 – 75 r. multicoloured 60 40
DESIGNS: 30 r. Ornamental peacock (Roman, 2nd-century); 75 r. Engraved bowl (13th-century).

1971. Liechtenstein Flowers (2nd series). As T **155**. Multicoloured.

532 10 r. Cyclamen 20 10
533 20 r. Moonwort 20 15
534 50 r. Superb pink 45 35
535 1 f. 50 Alpine columbine . . . 1·40 1·00

161 Europa Chain

1971. Europa.

536 **161** 50 r. yellow, blue & black 30 30

162 Part of Text **163** Cross-country Skiing

1971. 50th Anniv of 1921 Constitution. Mult.

537 70 r. Type **162** 60 50
538 80 r. Princely crown 65 55

1971. Winter Olympic Games, Sapporo, Japan (1972). Multicoloured.

539 15 r. Type **163** 20 10
540 40 r. Ice hockey 35 25
541 65 r. Downhill skiing 55 40
542 1 f. 50 Figure skating . . . . 1·10 95

164 "Madonna and Child" (sculpture, Andrea della Robbia) **165** Gymnastics

1971. Christmas.

543 **164** 30 r. multicoloured . . . 20 15

1972. Olympic Games, Munich. Multicoloured.

544 10 r. Type **165** 15 10
545 20 r. High jumping 20 15
546 40 r. Running 40 25
547 60 r. Throwing the discus . . 50 35

1972. Liechtenstein Flowers (3rd series). As T **155**. Multicoloured.

548 20 r. Sulphur anemone . . . 20 15
549 30 r. Turk's-cap lily 30 20
550 60 r. Alpine centaury 60 40
551 1 f. 20 Reed-mace . . . . . . 1·00 75

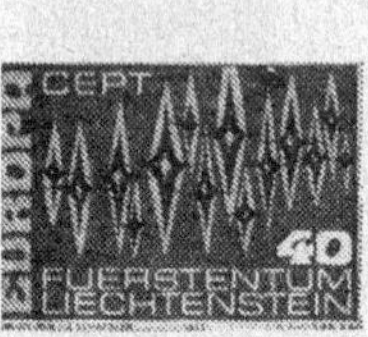

166 "Communications" **168** "Faun"

1972. Europa.

552 **166** 40 r. multicoloured . . . 30 25

1972. "Pioneers of Philately" (3rd series). As T **148**.

554 30 r. green 25 25
555 40 r. purple 30 30
556 1 f. 30 blue . . . . 1·10 85
PORTRAITS: 30 r. Emilio Diena; 40 r. Andre de Cock; 1 f. 30, Theodore E. Steinway.

1972. "Natural Art". Motifs fashioned from roots and branches. Multicoloured.

557 20 r. Type **168** 15 15
558 30 r. "Dancer" 20 20
559 1 f. 10 "Owl" 65 65

169 "Madonna with Angels" (F. Nigg) **170** Lawena Springs

1972. Christmas.

560 **169** 30 r. multicoloured . . . 25 20

1972. Landscapes.

561 – 5 r. purple and yellow . . 10 10
562 **170** 10 r. green and light green 10 10
563 – 15 r. brown and green . . 10 10
564 – 25 r. purple and blue . . 25 20

565 – 30 r. purple and brown 30 10
566 – 40 r. purple and brown 40 20
567 – 50 r. blue and lilac 30 20
568 – 60 r. green and yellow 30 30
569 – 70 r. blue and cobalt 35 35
570 – 80 r. green and light green 40 40
571 – 1 f. brown and green 70 45
572 – 1 f. 30 blue and green 75 75
573 – 1 f. 50 brown and blue 75 75
574 – 1 f. 80 brown & lt brown 1·25 1·10
575 – 2 f. brown and blue 1·60 1·00

DESIGNS: 5 r. Silum; 15 r. Ruggeller Reed; 25 r. Steg Kirchlispitz; 30 r. Feld Schellenberg; 40 r. Rennhof Mauren; 50 r. Tidrufe; 60 r. Eschner Riet; 70 r. Mittagspitz; 80 r. Schaan Forest; 1 f. St. Peter's Chapel, Mals; 1 f. 30, Frommenhaus; 1 f. 50, Ochsenkopf; 1 f. 80, Hehlawangspitz; 2 f. Saminaschlucht.

171 Europa "Posthorn"

1973. Europa.
576 **171** 30 r. multicoloured 25 20
577 40 r. multicoloured 35 30

172 Chambered Nautilus Goblet — 173 Arms of Liechtenstein

1973. Treasures from Prince's Collection (1st issue). Drinking Vessels. Multicoloured.
578 30 r. Type **172** 25 20
579 70 r. Ivory tankard 60 45
580 1 f. 10 Silver cup 80 70
See also Nos. 589/92.

1973.
581 **173** 5 f. multicoloured 3·00 2·40

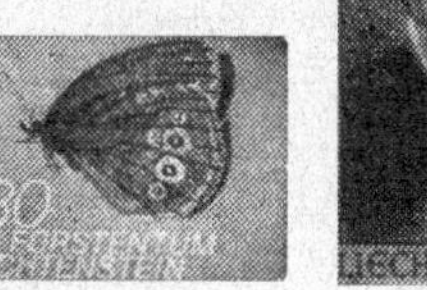

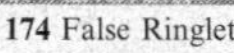

174 False Ringlet — 175 "Madonna" (Bartolomeo di Tommaso da Foligno)

1973. Small Fauna of Liechtenstein (1st series). Multicoloured.
582 30 r. Type **174** 35 20
583 40 r. Curlew 1·25 30
584 60 r. Edible frog 60 40
585 80 r. Grass snake 80 55
See also Nos. 596/9.

1973. Christmas.
586 **175** 30 r. multicoloured 25 20

176 "Shouting Horseman" (sculpture, Andrea Riccio) — 177 Footballers

1974. Europa. Multicoloured.
587 30 r. Type **176** 25 20
588 40 r. "Squatting Aphrodite" (sculpture, Antonio Susini) 35 30

1974. Treasures from Prince's Collection (2nd issue). Porcelain. As T **172**. Multicoloured.
589 30 r. Vase, 19th century 25 20
590 50 r. Vase, 1740 40 30
591 60 r. Vase, 1830 50 40
592 1 f. Vase, c. 1700 80 75

1974. World Cup Football Championship, West Germany.
593 **177** 80 f. multicoloured 80 55

178 Posthorn and U.P.U. Emblem — 179 Bishop Marxer

1974. Centenary of Universal Postal Union.
594 **178** 40 r. black, green & gold 30 25
595 60 r. black, red and gold 40 40

1974. Small Fauna of Liechtenstein (2nd series). As T **174**. Multicoloured.
596 15 r. Mountain newt 20 10
597 25 r. Adder 25 15
598 70 r. Cynthia's fritillary (butterfly) 1·75 60
599 1 f. 10 Three-toed woodpecker 2·75 85

1974. Death Centenary of Bishop Franz Marxer.
600 **179** 1 f. multicoloured 40 50

180 Prince Francis Joseph II and Princess Gina

1974.
601 **180** 10 f. brown and gold 5·50 4·50

181 "St. Florian" — 182 Prince Constantin

1974. Christmas. Glass Paintings. Multicoloured.
602 30 r. Type **181** 20 15
603 50 r. "St. Wendelin" 35 30
604 60 r. "St. Mary, Anna and Joachim" 45 40
605 70 r. "Jesus in Manger" 55 50

1975. Liechtenstein Princes.
606 **182** 70 r. green and gold 55 50
607 – 80 r. purple and gold 70 60
608 – 1 f. 20 blue and gold 95 85
PORTRAITS: 80 r. Prince Maximilian; 1 f. 20, Prince Alois.

183 "Cold Sun" (M. Frommelt) — 184 Imperial Cross

1975. Europa. Paintings. Multicoloured.
609 30 r. Type **183** 25 20
610 60 r. "Village" (L. Jager) 55 45

1975. Imperial Insignia (1st series). Multicoloured.
611 30 r. Type **184** 25 20
612 60 r. Imperial sword 40 35
613 1 f. Imperial orb 80 70
614 1 f. 30 Imperial robe (50 × 32 mm) 10·00 8·50
615 2 f. Imperial crown 2·00 1·75
See also Nos. 670/3.

185 "Red Cross Activities" — 186 St. Mamerten, Triesen

1975. 30th Anniv of Liechtenstein Red Cross.
616 **185** 60 r. multicoloured 45 35

1975. European Architectural Heritage Year. Multicoloured.
617 40 r. Type **186** 25 25
618 50 r. Red House, Vaduz 30 30
619 70 r. Prebendary buildings, Eschen 50 60
620 1 f. Gutenberg Castle, Balzers 75 85

187 Speed Skating — 188 "Daniel in the Lions' Den"

1975. Winter Olympic Games, Innsbruck (1976). Multicoloured.
621 20 r. Type **187** 20 10
622 25 r. Ice hockey 25 15
623 70 r. Downhill skiing 70 50
624 1 f. 20 Slalom 1·10 85

1975. Christmas and Holy Year. Capitals in Chur Cathedral.
625 **188** 30 r. violet and gold 25 20
626 – 60 r. green and gold 50 40
627 – 90 r. red and gold 75 65
DESIGNS: 60 r. "Madonna"; 90 r. "St. Peter".

189 Mouflon — 190 Crayfish

1976. Europa. Ceramics by Prince Hans von Liechtenstein. Multicoloured.
628 40 r. Type **189** 50 25
629 80 r. "Ring-necked Pheasant and Brood" 80 60

1976. World Wildlife Fund. Multicoloured.
630 25 r. Type **190** 25 20
631 40 r. Turtle 50 30
632 70 r. European otter 75 65
633 80 r. Lapwing 3·00 90

191 Roman Fibula — 193 Judo

1976. 75th Anniv of National Historical Society.
634 **191** 90 r. multicoloured 75 60

1970. Olympic Games, Montreal. Multicoloured.
636 35 r. Type **193** 25 20
637 50 r. Volleyball 35 35
638 80 r. Relay 50 50
639 1 f. 10 Long jumping 70 75

194 "Singing Angels" — 195 "Pisces"

1976. 400th Birth Anniv (1977) of Peter Paul Rubens (painter). Multicoloured.
640 50 r. Type **194** 50 60
641 70 r. "Sons of the Artist" 75 85
642 1 f. "Daughters of Cecrops" (49 × 39 mm) 3·50 4·25

1976. Signs of the Zodiac (1st series). Multicoloured.
643 20 r. Type **195** 15 15
644 40 r. "Aries" 30 25
645 80 r. "Taurus" 50 55
646 90 r. "Gemini" 70 75
See also Nos. 666/9 and 710/13.

196 "Child Jesus of Prague" — 197 Sarcophagus Statue, Chur Cathedral

1976. Christmas. Monastic Wax Sculptures. Mult.
647 20 r. Type **196** 15 10
648 50 r. "The Flight into Egypt" (vert) 40 35
649 80 r. "Holy Trinity" (vert) 60 55
650 1 f. 50 "Holy Family" 1·10 1·00

1976. Bishop Ortlieb von Brandis of Chur Commemoration.
651 **197** 1 f. 10 brown and gold 70 65

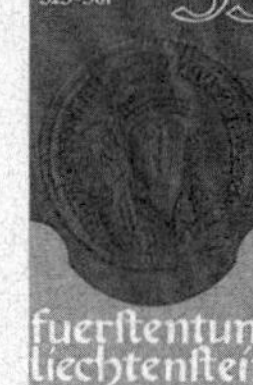

199 Map of Liechtenstein, 1721 (J. Heber) — 200 Coin of Emperor Constantine II

1977. Europa. Multicoloured.
664 40 r. Type **199** 20 20
665 80 r. "View of Vaduz, 1815" (F. Bachmann) 45 45

1977. Signs of the Zodiac (2nd series). As T **195**. Multicoloured.
666 40 r. "Cancer" 25 20
667 70 r. "Leo" 45 45
668 80 r. "Virgo" 55 55
669 1 f. 10 "Libra" 65 70

1977. Imperial Insignia (2nd series). As T **184**. Multicoloured.
670 40 r. Holy Lance and Reliquary with Particle of the Cross 30 25
671 50 r. "St. Matthew" (Imperial Book of Gospels) 35 30
672 80 r. St. Stephen's Purse 55 55
673 90 r. Tabard of Imperial Herald 75 75

1977. Coins (1st series). Multicoloured.
674 35 r. Type **200** 30 25
675 70 r. Lindau Brakteat 50 50
676 80 r. Coin of Ortlieb von Brandis 60 60
See also Nos. 707/9.

201 Frauenthal Castle, Styria — 202 Children in Costume

1977. Castles.
677 **201** 20 r. green and gold 15 15
678 – 50 r. red and gold 30 30
679 – 80 r. lilac and gold 45 50
680 – 90 r. blue and gold 50 60
DESIGNS: 50 r. Gross-Ullersdorf, Moravia; 80 r. Liechtenstein Castle, near Modling, Austria; 90 r. Palais Liechtenstein, Alserbachstrasse, Vienna.

1977. National Costumes. Multicoloured.
681 40 r. Type **202** 25 25
682 70 r. Two girls in traditional costume 40 45
683 1 f. Woman in festive costume 60 65

203 Princess Tatjana

1977. Princess Tatjana.
684 **203** 1 f. 10 lt brn, brn & gold 1·00 80

204 "Angel" **205** Palais Liechtenstein, Bankgasse, Vienna

1977. Christmas. Sculptures by Erasmus Kern. Multicoloured.
685 20 r. Type **204** 15 15
686 50 r. "St. Rochus" 30 30
687 80 r. "Madonna" 45 55
688 1 f. 50 "God the Father" . . . 85 1·00

1978. Europa.
689 **205** 40 r. blue and gold . . . 30 25
690 – 80 r. red and gold 70 55
DESIGN: 80 r. Feldsberg Castle.

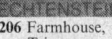

206 Farmhouse, Triesen **207** Vaduz Castle

1978. Buildings. Multicoloured.
691 10 r. Type **206** 10 10
692 20 r. Upper village of Triesen 15 10
693 35 r. Barns at Balzers 30 20
694 40 r. Monastery building, Bendern 30 10
695 50 r. Rectory tower, Balzers-Mals 40 25
696 70 r. Rectory, Mauren 50 30
697 80 r. Farmhouse, Schellenberg 70 45
698 90 r. Rectory, Balzers 75 70
699 1 f. Rheinberger House, Vaduz 80 55
700 1 f. 10 Vaduz Mitteldorf . . . 90 70
701 1 f. 50 Town Hall, Triesenberg 1·25 95
702 2 f. National Museum and Administrator's residence, Vaduz . . . . 1·50 1·10

1978. 40th Anniv of Prince Francis Joseph II's Accession. Royal Residence. Multicoloured.
703 40 r. Type **207** 40 40
704 50 r. Courtyard 40 40
705 70 r. Hall 65 65
706 80 r. High Altar, Castle Chapel 75 75

208 Coin of Prince Charles **209** "Portrait of a Piebald" (J. G. von Hamilton and A. Faistenberger)

1978. Coins (2nd series). Multicoloured.
707 40 r. Type **208** 30 30
708 50 r. Coin of Prince John Adam 40 40
709 80 r. Coin of Prince Joseph Wenzel 65 65

1978. Signs of the Zodiac (3rd series). As T **195.** Multicoloured.
710 40 r. "Scorpio" 30 25
711 50 r. "Sagittarius" 40 35
712 80 r. "Capricorn" 65 60
713 1 f. 50 "Aquarius" . . . . . 1·25 1·10

1978. Paintings. Multicoloured.
714 70 r. Type **209** 50 50
715 80 r. "Portrait of a Blackish-brown Stallion" (J. G. von Hamilton) 65 65
716 1 f. 10 "Golden Carriage of Prince Joseph Wenzel" (Martin von Meytens) (48½ × 38 mm) 85 85

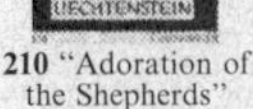

210 "Adoration of the Shepherds" **211** Comte AC-8 Mail Plane "St. Gallen" over Schaan

1978. Christmas. Church Windows, Triesenberg. Multicoloured.
717 20 r. Type **210** 15 15
718 50 r. "Enthroned Madonna with St. Joseph" 40 30
719 80 r. "Adoration of the Magi" 70 65

1979. Europa. Multicoloured.
720 40 r. Type **211** 50 45
721 80 r. Airship "Graf Zeppelin" over Vaduz Castle 80 70

212 Child Drinking **213** Ordered Wave-field

1979. International Year of the Child. Multicoloured.
722 80 r. Type **212** 40 50
723 90 r. Child eating 50 60
724 1 f. 10 Child reading 55 70

1979. 50th Anniv of International Radio Consultative Committee (CCIR).
725 **213** 50 r. blue and black . . . 40 30

214 Abstract Composition **215** Sun rising over Continents

1979. Liechtenstein's Entry into Council of Europe.
726 **214** 80 r. multicoloured . . . 70 55

1979. Development Aid.
727 **215** 1 f. multicoloured 80 70

216 Arms of Carl Ludwig von Sulz **217** Sts. Lucius and Florian (fresco, Waltensberg-Vuorz Church)

1979. Heraldic Windows in the Liechtenstein National Museum. Multicoloured.
728 40 r. Type **216** 30 25
729 70 r. Arms of Barbara von Sulz 65 55
730 1 f. 10 Arms of Ulrich von Ramschwag and Barbara von Hallwil 90 80

1979. Patron Saints.
731 **217** 20 f. multicoloured . . . 9·00 8·50

218 Base of Ski Slope, Valuna

1979. Winter Olympic Games, Lake Placid (1980). Multicoloured.
732 40 r. Type **218** 35 25
733 70 r. Malbun and Ochsenkopf 65 55
734 1 f. 50 Ski-lift, Sareis . . . . 1·25 1·00

219 "The Annunciation"

1979. Christmas. Embroideries by Ferdinand Nigg. Multicoloured.
735 20 r. Type **219** 15 10
736 50 r. "Christmas" 40 30
737 80 r. "Blessed are the Peacemakers" 60 50

220 Maria Leopoldine von Esterhazy (bust by Canova) **221** Arms of Andreas Buchel, 1690

1980. Europa.
738 **220** 40 r. green, turq & gold . 35 35
739 – 80 r. brown, red and gold 50 50
DESIGN: 80 r. Maria Theresia von Liechtenstein (after Martin von Meytens).

1980. Arms of Bailiffs (1st series). Multicoloured.
740 40 r. Type **221** 30 25
741 70 r. Georg Marxer, 1745 . . . 60 55
742 80 r. Luzius Frick, 1503 . . . 70 60
743 1 f. 10 Adam Oehri, 1634 . . . 85 80
See also Nos. 763/6, and 788/91.

222 3 r. Stamp of 1930 **223** Milking Pail

1980. 50th Anniv of Postal Museum.
744 **222** 80 r. red, green and grey . 75 60

1980. Alpine Dairy Farming Implements. Mult.
745 20 r. Type **223** 15 15
746 50 r. Wooden heart dairy herd descent marker 40 30
747 80 r. Butter churn 65 55

224 Crossbow

1980. Hunting Weapons.
748 **224** 80 r. brown and lilac . . . 70 60
749 – 90 r. black and green . . . 80 70
750 – 1 f. 10 black and stone . . 90 80
DESIGNS: 90 r. Spear and knife; 1 f. 10, Rifle and powder-horn.

225 Triesenberg Costumes

1980. Costumes. Multicoloured.
751 40 r. Type **225** 30 25
752 70 r. Dancers, Schellenberg . . 65 55
753 80 r. Brass band, Mauren . . . 70 65

226 Beech Trees, Matrula (spring) **227** Angel bringing Shepherds Good Tidings

1980. The Forest in the Four Seasons. Multicoloured.
754 40 r. Type **226** 30 30
755 50 r. Firs in the Valorsch (summer) 45 40
756 80 r. Beech tree, Schaan (autumn) 70 60
757 1 f. 50 Edge of forest at Oberplanken (winter) . . . . 1·25 1·25

1980. Christmas. Multicoloured.
758 20 r. Type **227** 15 15
759 50 r. Crib 40 30
760 80 r. Epiphany 65 60

228 National Day Procession **230** Scout Emblems

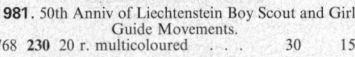

1981. Europa. Multicoloured.
761 40 r. Fireworks at Vaduz Castle 35 25
762 80 r. Type **228** 75 65

1981. Arms of Bailiffs (2nd series). As T **221.** Multicoloured.
763 40 r. Anton Meier, 1748 . . . 30 25
764 70 r. Kaspar Kindle, 1534 . . 60 50
765 80 r. Hans Adam Negele, 1600 70 60
766 1 f. 10 Peter Matt, 1693 . . . 90 80

1981. 50th Anniv of Liechtenstein Boy Scout and Girl Guide Movements.
768 **230** 20 r. multicoloured . . . 30 15

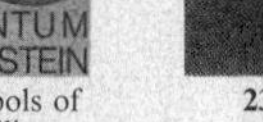

231 Symbols of Disability **232** St. Theodul (sculpture)

1981. International Year of Disabled Persons.
769 **231** 40 r. multicoloured . . . 30 25

1981. 1600th Birth Anniv of St. Theodul.
770 **232** 80 r. multicoloured . . . 65 55

233 "Xanthoria parietina"

1981. Mosses and Lichens. Multicoloured.
771 40 r. Type **233** 30 25
772 50 r. "Parmelia physodes" . . 50 40
773 70 r. "Sphagnum palustre" . . 65 55
774 80 r. "Amblystegium serpens" 80 65

234 Gutenberg Castle

1981. Gutenberg Castle. Multicoloured.
775 20 r. Type **234** 20 15
776 40 r. Courtyard 30 25
777 50 r. Parlour 40 35
778 1 f. 10 Great Hall 95 85

235 Cardinal Karl Borromaus von Mailand **236** St. Nicholas blessing Children

1981. Famous Visitors to Liechtenstein (1st series). Multicoloured.
779 40 r. Type **235** 30 30
780 70 r. Johann Wolfgang von Goethe (writer) 65 60
781 89 r. Alexander Dumas the younger (writer) 75 65
782 1 f. Hermann Hesse (writer) . 85 80
See also Nos. 804/7 and 832/5.

1981. Christmas. Multicoloured.
783 20 r. Type **236** 15 15
784 50 r. Adoration of the Kings . 40 30
785 80 r. Holy Family 70 55

237 Peasant Revolt, 1525

1982. Europa. Multicoloured.
786 40 r. Type **237** 40 30
787 80 r. King Wenceslaus with Counts (Imperial direct rule, 1396) 85 65

1982. Arms of Bailiffs (3rd series). As T **221**. Multicoloured.
788 40 r. Johann Kaiser, 1664 40 30
789 70 r. Joseph Anton Kaufmann, 1748 70 60
790 80 r. Christoph Walser, 1690 80 75
791 1 f. 10 Stephan Banzer, 1658 1·10 1·00

238 Triesenberg Sports Ground
239 Crown Prince Hans Adam

1982. World Cup Football Championship, Spain. Multicoloured.
792 15 r. Type **238** 20 15
793 25 r. Eschen/Mauren playing fields 25 25
794 1 f. 80 Rheinau playing fields, Balzers 1·75 1·60

1982. "Liba 82" Stamp Exhibition. Multicoloured.
795 1 f. Type **239** 90 85
796 1 f. Princess Marie Aglae 90 85

240 Tractor (agriculture)

1982. Rural Industries. Multicoloured.
797 30 r. Type **240** 30 25
798 50 r. Cutting flowers (horticulture) 50 40
799 70 r. Workers with logs (forestry) 70 65
800 150 r. Worker and milk (dairy farming) 1·50 1·40

241 "Neu Schellenberg"

1982. 150th Birth Anniv of Mortiz Menzinger (artist). Multicoloured.
801 40 r. Type **241** 30 25
802 50 r. "Vaduz" 55 40
803 100 r. "Bendern" 90 80

242 Angelika Kauffmann (artist, self-portrait)
243 Angel playing Lute

1982. Famous Visitors to Liechtenstein (2nd series). Multicoloured.
804 40 r. Emperor Maximilian I (after Benhard Strigel) 30 25
805 70 f. Georg Jenatsch (liberator of Grisons) 65 50
806 80 r. Type **242** 75 60
807 1 f. St. Fidelis of Sigmaringen 1·00 90

1982. Christmas. Details from High Altar by Jakob Russ, Chur Cathedral. Multicoloured.
808 20 r. Type **243** 15 15
809 50 r. Madonna and child 45 35
810 80 r. Angel playing organ 70 60

244 Notker Balbulus of St. Gall
245 Shrove Thursday

1983. Europa. Multicoloured.
811 40 r. Type **244** 30 25
812 80 r. Hildegard of Bingen 70 55

1983. Shrovetide and Lent Customs. Mult.
813 40 r. Type **245** 30 25
814 70 r. Shrovetide carnival 55 50
815 1 f. 80 Lent Sunday bonfire 1·40 1·40

246 River Bank
247 "Schaan"

1983. Anniversaries and Events. Multicoloured.
816 20 r. Type **246** 30 20
817 40 r. Montgolfier Brothers' balloon 35 30
818 50 r. Airmail envelope 50 35
819 80 r. Plant and hands holding spade 70 65

EVENTS: 20 r. Council of Europe river and coasts protection campaign; 40 r. Bicentenary of manned flight; 50 r. World Communications Year; 80 r. Overseas aid.

1983. Landscape Paintings by Anton Ender. Mult.
820 40 r. Type **247** 35 25
821 50 r. "Gutenberg Castle" 55 45
822 200 r. "Steg Reservoir" 2·00 2·00

248 Princess Gina
249 Pope John Paul II

1983. Multicoloured.
823 2 f. 50 Type **248** 2·25 1·75
824 3 f. Prince Francis Joseph II 2·75 2·00

1983. Holy Year.
825 **249** 80 r. multicoloured 75 60

250 Snowflakes and Stripes
251 Seeking Shelter

1983. Winter Olympic Games, Sarajevo. Mult.
826 40 r. Type **250** 35 25
827 80 r. Snowflake 75 65
828 1 f. 80 Snowflake and rays 1·75 1·75

1983. Christmas. Multicoloured.
829 20 r. Type **251** 15 15
830 50 r. Infant Jesus 50 35
831 80 r. Three Kings 75 65

252 Aleksandr Vassilievich Suvorov (Russian general)
253 Bridge

1984. Famous Visitors to Liechtenstein (3rd series). Multicoloured.
832 40 r. Type **252** 40 30
833 70 r. Karl Rudolf von Buol-Schauenstein, Bishop of Chur 65 60
834 80 r. Carl Zuckmayer (dramatist) 75 65
835 1 f. Curt Goetz (actor) 95 90

1984. Europa. 25th Anniv of E.P.T. Conf.
836 **253** 50 r. blue and deep blue 50 40
837 80 r. pink and brown 75 70

254 The Warning Messenger
255 Pole Vaulting

1984. Liechtenstein Legends. The Destruction of Trisona. Each brown, grey and blue.
838 35 r. Type **254** 30 25
839 50 r. The buried town 55 40
840 80 r. The spared family 80 70

1984. Olympic Games, Los Angeles. Mult.
841 70 r. Type **255** 60 55
842 80 r. Throwing the discus 70 65
843 1 f. Putting the shot 85 80

256 Currency (trade and banking)

1984. Occupations. Multicoloured.
844 5 r. Type **256** 10 10
845 10 r. Plumber adjusting pipe (building trade) 15 10
846 20 r. Operating machinery (industry–production) 20 15
847 35 r. Draughtswoman (building trade–planning) 35 20
848 45 r. Office worker and world map (industry–sales) 50 35
849 50 r. Cook (tourism) 55 30
850 60 r. Carpenter (building trade–interior decoration) 70 45
851 70 r. Doctor injecting patient (medical services) 75 60
852 80 r. Scientist (industrial research) 80 55
853 100 r. Bricklayer (building trade) 90 65
854 120 r. Flow chart (industry–administration) 1·25 1·10
855 150 r. Handstamping covers (post and communications) 1·60 1·00

257 Princess Marie
258 Annunciation

1984. Multicoloured.
856 1 f. 70 Type **257** 1·50 1·25
857 2 f. Crown Prince Hans Adam 2·00 1·50

1984. Christmas. Multicoloured.
858 35 r. Type **258** 30 25
859 50 r. Holy Family 50 40
860 80 r. The Three Kings 80 70

259 Apollo and the Muses playing Music (detail from 18th-century harpsichord lid)

1985. Europa. Music Year. Multicoloured.
861 50 r. Type **259** 60 50
862 80 r. Apollo and the Muses playing music (different) 80 75

260 St. Elisabeth Convent, Schaan

1985. Monasteries. Multicoloured.
863 50 r. Type **260** 50 40
864 1 f. Schellenberg Convent 1·00 1·00
865 1 f. 70 Gutenberg Mission, Balzers 1·75 1·75

261 Princess Gina and handing out of Rations

1985. 40th Anniv of Liechtenstein Red Cross. Multicoloured.
866 20 r. Type **261** 30 30
867 50 r. Princess Gina and Red Cross ambulance 75 75
868 120 r. Princess Gina with refugee children 1·50 1·50

262 Justice
264 "Portrait of a Canon" (Quentin Massys)

1985. Cardinal Virtues. Multicoloured.
869 35 r. Type **262** 30 30
870 50 r. Temperance 50 50
871 70 r. Prudence 70 70
872 1 f. Fortitude 1·10 1·10

1985. Paintings in Metropolitan Museum, New York. Multicoloured.
874 50 r. Type **264** 60 60
875 1 f. "Clara Serena Rubens" (Rubens) 1·50 1·50
876 1 f. 20 "Duke of Urbino" (Raphael) 1·25 1·25

265 Halberd used by Charles I's Bodyguard

1985. Guards' Weapons and Armour. Mult.
877 35 r. Type **265** 35 30
878 50 r. Morion used by Charles I's bodyguard 70 70
879 80 r. Halberd used by Carl Eusebius's bodyguard 90 90

266 Frankincense
267 Puppets performing Tragedy

1985. Christmas. Multicoloured.
880 35 r. Type **266** 35 25
881 50 r. Gold 60 50
882 80 r. Myrrh 90 90

1985. Theatre. Multicoloured.
883 50 r. Type **267** 70 70
884 80 r. Puppets performing comedy 90 90
885 1 f. 50 Opera 1·75 1·75

268 Courtyard
269 Barn Swallows

1986. Vaduz Castle. Multicoloured.
886 20 r. Type **268** 20 15
887 25 r. Keep 40 30
888 50 r. Castle 60 45
889 90 r. Inner gate 75 60
890 1 f. 10 Castle from gardens 1·40 1·25
891 1 f. 40 Courtyard (different) 1·75 1·40

1986. Europa. Birds. Multicoloured.
892 50 r. Type **269** 1·25 1·25
893 90 r. European robin 1·75 1·75

270 "Offerings"
271 Palm Sunday

1986. Lenten Fast.
894 270 1 f. 40 multicoloured . . . 1·50 1·50

1986. Religious Festivals. Multicoloured.
895 35 r. Type **271** 40 30
896 50 r. Wedding 70 60
897 70 r. Rogation Day procession 90 80

272 Karl Freiherr Haus von Hausen

273 Francis Joseph II

1986. 125th Anniv of Liechtenstein Land Bank.
898 272 50 r. brown, ochre & buff 55 55

1986. 80th Birthday of Prince Francis Joseph II.
899 273 3 f. 50 multicoloured . . . 3·00 2·75

274 Roebuck in Ruggeller Riet

275 Cabbage and Beetroot

1986. Hunting. Multicoloured.
900 35 r. Type **274** 45 45
901 50 r. Chamois at Rappenstein 80 80
902 1 f. 70 Stag in Lawena . . . . 2·25 2·25

1986. Field Crops. Multicoloured.
903 50 r. Type **275** 70 70
904 80 r. Red cabbages . . . . . 1·00 1·00
905 90 r. Potatoes, onions and garlic 1·25 1·25

276 Archangel Michael

277 Silver Fir

1986. Christmas. Multicoloured.
906 35 r. Type **276** 35 30
907 50 r. Archangel Gabriel . . . 70 70
908 90 r. Archangel Raphael . . . 1·40 1·40

1986. Tree Bark. Multicoloured.
909 35 r. Type **277** 30 30
910 90 r. Norway spruce . . . . . 1·40 1·40
911 1 f. 40 Pedunculate oak . . . 1·90 1·90

278 Gamprin Primary School

280 Niklaus von Flue

1987. Europa. Multicoloured.
912 50 r. Type **278** 60 60
913 90 r. Schellenberg parish church 1·40 1·40

1986. 500th Death Anniv of Niklaus von Flue (martyr).
914 280 1 f. 10 multicoloured . . . 1·25 1·25

281 Miller's Thumb

282 Princes Alois (frame as in first stamps)

1987. Fishes (1st series). Multicoloured.
915 50 r. Type **281** 70 70
916 90 r. Brook trout . . . . . . 1·25 1·25
917 1 f. 10 European grayling . . 1·75 1·75
See also Nos. 959/61.

1987. 75th Anniv of First Liechtenstein Stamps.
918 282 2 f. multicoloured . . . . 2·40 2·40

283 Staircase

284 Arms

1987. Liechtenstein City Palace, Vienna. Multicoloured.
919 35 r. Type **283** 35 30
920 50 r. Minoritenplatz doorway 70 70
921 90 r. Staircase (different) . . 1·25 1·25

1987. 275th Anniv of Transfer of County of Vaduz to House of Liechtenstein.
922 284 1 f. 40 multicoloured . . 1·50 1·50

285 Constitution Charter, 1862

286 St. Matthew

1987. 125th Anniv of Liechtenstein Parliament.
923 285 1 f. 70 multicoloured . . 1·75 1·75

1987. Christmas. Illuminations from Golden Book of Pfafers Abbey. Multicoloured.
924 35 r. Type **286** 35 30
925 50 r. St. Mark 75 75
926 60 r. St. Luke 85 85
927 90 r. St. John . . . . 1·40 1·40

287 "The Toil of the Cross-Country Skier"

288 Dish Aerial

1987. Winter Olympic Games, Calgary (1988). Multicoloured.
928 25 r. Type **287** 30 30
929 90 r. "The Courageous Pioneers of Skiing" . . . . 1·40 1·40
930 1 f. 10 "As our Grandfathers used to ride on a Bobsled" 1·60 1·60

1988. Europa. Transport and Communications. Mult.
931 50 r. Type **288** 50 50
932 90 r. Maglev monorail . . . 1·25 1·25

289 Agriculture

1988. European Campaign for Rural Areas. Multicoloured.
933 80 r. Type **289** . . . . . . 1·00 1·00
934 90 r. Village centre . . . . . 1·40 1·40
935 1 f. 70 Road . . . . 1·75 1·75

290 Headphones on Books (Radio Broadcasts)

292 St. Barbara's Shrine, Balzers

1988. Costa Rica–Liechtenstein Cultural Co-operation.
936 290 50 r. multicoloured . . . 65 65
937 – 1 f. 40 red, brown and green 2·00 2·00
DESIGN: 1 f. 40, Man with pen and radio (Adult education).

1988. Wayside Shrines. Multicoloured.
939 25 r. Type **292** 40 40
940 35 r. Shrine containing statues of Christ, St. Peter and St. Paul at Oberdorf, Vaduz 50 50
941 50 r. St. Anthony of Egypt's shrine, Fallagass, Ruggel . . 85 85

293 Cycling

294 Joseph and Mary

1988. Olympic Games, Seoul. Multicoloured.
942 50 r. Type **293** 70 70
943 80 r. Gymnastics . . . . . . 1·25 1·25
944 90 r. Running . . . . 1·50 1·50
945 1 f. 40 Equestrian event . . . 2·10 2·10

1988. Christmas. Multicoloured.
946 35 r. Type **294** 35 30
947 50 r. Baby Jesus 70 70
948 90 r. Wise Men presenting gifts to Jesus . . . . 1·40 1·40

295 Letter beside Footstool (detail)

296 "Cat and Mouse"

1988. "The Letter" (portrait of Marie-Theresa, Princesse de Lamballe by Anton Hickel). Multicoloured.
949 50 r. Type **295** 65 65
950 90 r. Desk and writing materials (detail) . . . . 1·10 1·10
951 2 f. "The Letter" (complete painting) . . . . 2·00 2·00

1989. Europa. Children's Games. Multicoloured.
952 50 r. Type **296** 90 90
953 90 r. "Hide and Seek" . . . . 1·50 1·50

298 Rheinberger and Score

299 Little Ringed Plover

1989. 150th Birth Anniv of Josef Gabriel Rheinberger (composer).
954 298 2 f. 90 black, blue & pur 3·50 3·00

1989. Endangered Animals. Multicoloured.
955 25 r. Type **299** 85 40
956 35 r. Green tree frog 60 50
957 50 r. "Libelloides coccajus" (lace-wing) 80 75
958 90 r. Polecat . . . . 1·60 1·50

300 Northern Pike

1989. Fishes (2nd series). Multicoloured.
959 50 r. Type **300** 60 60
960 1 f. 10 Lake trout . . . . . . 1·40 1·40
961 1 f. 40 Stone loach . . . . . 1·90 1·90

301 Return of Cattle from Alpine Pastures

302 Falknis

1989. Autumn Customs. Multicoloured.
962 35 r. Type **301** 40 40
963 50 r. Peeling corn cobs 65 65
964 80 r. Cattle market . . . . . . 1·10 1·10

1989. Mountains. Watercolours by Josef Schadler.
965 – 5 r. multicoloured 10 10
966 – 10 r. multicoloured . . . 10 10
967 – 35 r. multicoloured . . . 30 25
968 – 40 r. multicoloured . . . 35 25
969 – 45 r. multicoloured . . . 40 30
970 302 50 r. multicoloured . . . 45 35
971 – 60 r. multicoloured . . . 55 40
972 – 70 r. multicoloured . . . 65 50
973 – 75 r. multicoloured . . . 70 55
974 – 80 r. violet, brown & black 75 60
975 – 1 f. multicoloured 90 70
976 – 1 f. 20 multicoloured . . 1·10 85
977 – 1 f. 50 multicoloured . . 1·40 1·00
978 – 1 f. 60 multicoloured . . 1·50 1·10
979 – 2 f. multicoloured . . . . 2·00 1·50
DESIGNS: 5 r. Augstenberg; 10 r. Hahnenspiel; 35 r. Nospitz; 40 r. Ochsenkopf; 45 r. Three Sisters; 60 r. Kuhgrat; 70 r. Galinakopf; 75 r. Plassteikopf; 80 pf. Naafkopf; 1 f. Schonberg; 1 f. 20, Bleikaturm; 1 f. 50, Garselliturm; 1 f. 60, Schwarzhorn; 2 f. Scheienkopf.

303 "Melchior and Balthasar"

304 Mace Quartz

1989. Christmas. Details of triptych by Hugo van der Goes. Multicoloured.
981 35 r. Type **303** 50 50
982 50 r. "Kaspar and Holy Family" (27 × 34 mm) 75 70
983 90 r. "St. Stephen" . . . . . 1·25 1·25

1989. Minerals. Multicoloured.
984 50 r. Type **304** 80 80
985 1 f.10 Globe pyrite . . . . . 1·50 1·50
986 1 f. 50 Calcite . . . . 2·10 2·10

305 Nendeln Forwarding Agency, 1864

306 Penny Black

1990. Europa. Post Office Buildings. Mult.
987 50 r. Type **305** 70 70
988 90 r. Vaduz post office, 1976 1·10 1·10

1990. 150th Anniv of the Penny Black.
989 306 1 f. 50 multicoloured . . 2·00 1·90

307 Footballers

308 Tureen, Oranges and Grapes

1990. World Cup Football Championship, Italy.
990 307 2 f. multicoloured . . . . 2·50 2·40

1990. 9th Death Anniv of Benjamin Steck (painter). Multicoloured.
991 50 r. Type **308** 70 70
992 80 r. Apples and pewter bowl 1·00 1·00
993 1 f. 50 Basket, apples, cherries and pewter jug . . . . . . 1·90 1·90

309 Princess Gina

310 Ring-necked Pheasant

1990. Prince Francis Joseph II and Princess Gina Commemoration. Multicoloured.
994 2 f. Type **309** . . . . 2·40 2·40
995 3 f. Prince Francis Joseph II 3·50 3·50

1990. Game Birds. Multicoloured.
996 25 r. Type **310** 40 40
997 50 r. Black grouse 70 70
998 2 f. Mallard . . . . 2·75 2·75

311 Annunciation 312 St. Nicholas

1990. Christmas. Paintings. Multicoloured.
999 35 r. Type **311** 50 45
1000 50 r. Nativity 65 60
1001 90 r. Adoration of the Magi 1·10 1·00

1990. Winter Customs. Multicoloured.
1002 35 r. Type **312** 45 45
1003 50 r. Awakening on New Year's Eve 60 60
1004 1 f. 50 Giving New Year greetings 1·60 1·60

313 Mounted Courier 314 "Olympus 1" Satellite

1990. 500th Anniv of Regular European Postal Services.
1005 **313** 90 r. multicoloured 1·10 1·00

1991. Europa. Europe in Space. Multicoloured.
1006 50 r. Type **314** 55 55
1007 90 r. "Meteosat" satellite 1·00 95

315 St. Ignatius de Loyola (founder of Society of Jesus) 316 U.N. Emblem and Dove

1991. Anniversaries. Multicoloured.
1008 80 r. Type **315** (500th birth anniv) 85 85
1009 90 r. Wolfgang Amadeus Mozart (composer, death bicentenary) 95 95

1991. Admission to U.N. Membership (1990).
1010 **316** 2 f. 50 multicoloured 2·75 2·75

317 Non-Commissioned Officer and Private 318 "Near Maloja" (Giovanni Giacometti)

1991. 125th Anniv of Last Mobilization of Liechtenstein's Military Contingent (to the Tyrol). Multicoloured.
1011 50 r. Type **317** 55 55
1012 70 r. Tunic, chest and portrait 75 55
1013 1 f. Officer and private 1·10 1·10

1991. 700th Anniv of Swiss Confederation. Paintings by Swiss artists. Multicoloured.
1014 50 r. Type **318** 55 55
1015 80 r. "Rhine Valley" (Ferdinand Gehr) 85 85
1016 90 r. "Bergell" (Augusto Giacometti) 95 95
1017 1 f. 10 "Hoher Kasten" (Hedwig Scherrer) 1·25 1·25

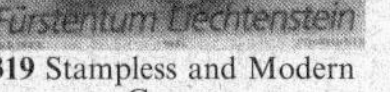

319 Stampless and Modern Covers 320 Princess Marie

1991. "Liba 92" National Stamp Exhibition, Vaduz.
1018 **319** 90 r. multicoloured 90 90

1991. Multicoloured.
1019 3 f. Type **320** 3·00 3·00
1020 3 f. 40 Prince Hans Adam II 3·50 3·50

321 Virgin of the Annunciation (exterior of left wing) 322 Cross-country Skiers and Testing for Drug Abuse

1991. Christmas. Details of the altar from St. Mamertus Chapel, Triesen. Multicoloured.
1021 50 r. Type **321** 50 50
1022 80 r. Madonna and Child (wood-carving attr. Jorg Syrlin, inner shrine) 80 80
1023 90 r. Angel Gabriel (exterior of right wing) 90 90

1991. Winter Olympic Games, Albertville. Mult.
1024 70 r. Type **322** 80 70
1025 80 r. Ice hockey player tackling opponent and helping him after fall 90 80
1026 1 f. 60 Downhill skier and fallen skier caught in safety net 1·75 1·60

323 Relay Race, Drugs and Shattered Medal 324 Aztecs

1992. Olympic Games, Barcelona. Multicoloured.
1027 50 r. Type **323** 50 45
1028 70 r. Cycling road race 1·00 65
1029 2 f. 50 Judo 3·00 2·25

1992. Europa. 500th Anniv of Discovery of America by Columbus. Multicoloured.
1030 80 r. Type **324** 75 75
1031 90 r. Statue of Liberty and New York skyline 85 85

325 Clown in Envelope ("Good Luck") 327 "Blechnum spicant"

1992. Greetings Stamps. Multicoloured.
1032 50 r. Type **325** 50 45
1033 50 r. Wedding rings in envelope and harlequin violinist 50 45
1034 50 r. Postman blowing horn (31×21 mm) 50 45
1035 50 r. Flying postman carrying letter sealed with heart (31×21 mm) 50 45

1992. Ferns. Multicoloured.
1037 40 r. Type **327** 40 35
1038 50 r. Maidenhair spleenwort 50 45
1039 70 r. Hart's-tongue 70 65
1040 2 f. 50 "Asplenium ruta-muraria" 2·40 2·25

328 Reading Edict 329 Chapel of St. Mamertus, Triesen

1992. 650th Anniv of County of Vaduz.
1041 **328** 1 f. 60 multicoloured 1·75 1·50

1992. Christmas. Multicoloured.
1042 50 r. Type **329** 50 45
1043 90 r. Crib, St. Gallus's Church, Triesen 90 85
1044 1 f. 60 St. Mary's Chapel, Triesen 1·75 1·50

330 Crown Prince Alois 331 "Nafkopf and Huts, Steg"

1992.
1045 **330** 2 f. 50 multicoloured 2·50 2·25

1993. 1400th Birth Anniv of Hans Gantner (painter). Multicoloured.
1046 50 r. Type **331** 50 45
1047 60 r. "Hunting Lodge, Sass" 55 50
1048 1 f. 80 "Red House, Vaduz" 1·75 1·60

332 "910805" (Bruno Kaufmann) 333 "Tale of the Ferryman" (painting)

1993. Europa. Contemporary Art. Multicoloured.
1049 80 r. Type **332** 85 80
1050 1 f. "The Little Blue" (Evi Kliemand) 95 90

1993. Tibetan Collection in the National Museum. Multicoloured.
1051 60 r. Type **333** 70 65
1052 80 r. Religious dance mask 85 80
1053 1 f. "Tale of the Fish" (painting) 1·00 95

334 "Tree of Life" 335 "The Black Hatter"

1993. Missionary Work.
1054 **334** 1 f. 80 multicoloured 1·90 1·75

1993. Homage to Liechtenstein.
1055 **335** 2 f. 80 multicoloured 2·75 2·50

337 Origanum 338 Eurasian Badger

1993. Flowers. Illustrations from "Hortus Botanicus Liechtensteinsis". Multicoloured.
1057 50 r. Type **337** 60 55
1058 60 r. Meadow sage 70 65
1059 1 f. "Seseli annuum" 1·10 1·00
1060 2 f. 50 Large self-heal 2·40 2·25

1993. Animals. Multicoloured.
1061 60 r. Type **338** 70 65
1062 80 r. Beech marten 95 90
1063 1 f. Red fox 1·25 1·10

339 "Now that the Quiet Days are Coming..." (Rainer Maria Rilke) 340 Ski Jump

1993. Christmas. Multicoloured.
1064 60 r. Type **339** 60 55
1065 80 r. "Can You See the Light..." (Th. Friedrich) 85 80
1066 1 f. "Christmas, Christmas..." (R. A. Schroder) 95 90

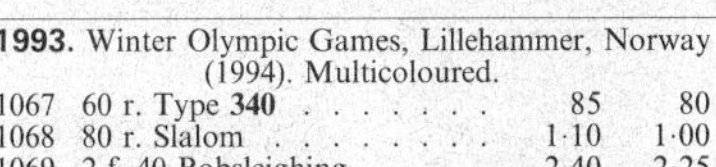
1993. Winter Olympic Games, Lillehammer, Norway (1994). Multicoloured.
1067 60 r. Type **340** 85 80
1068 80 r. Slalom 1·10 1·00
1069 2 f. 40 Bobsleighing 2·40 2·25

341 Seal and Title Page 342 Andean Condor

1994. Anniversaries. Multicoloured.
1070 60 r. Type **341** (275th anniv of Principality) 70 70
1071 1 f. 80 State, Prince's and Olympic flags (centenary of International Olympic Committee) 1·75 1·75

1994. Europa. Discoveries of Alexander von Humboldt. Multicoloured.
1072 80 r. Type **342** 80 80
1073 1 f. "Rhexia cardinalis" (plant) 90 90

343 Football Pitch and Hopi Indians playing Kickball 344 Elephant with Letter

1994. World Cup Football Championship, U.S.A.
1074 **343** 2 f. 80 multicoloured 2·75 2·75

1994. Greetings Stamps. Multicoloured.
1075 60 r. Type **344** 70 70
1076 60 r. Cherub with flower and hearts 70 70
1077 60 r. Pig with four-leaf clover 70 70
1078 60 r. Dog holding bunch of tulips 70 70

345 "Eulogy of Madness" (mobile, Jean Tinguely)

1994. Homage to Liechtenstein.
1079 **345** 4 f. black, pink and violet 4·50 4·50

346 Spring

1994. Seasons of the Vine. Multicoloured.
1080 60 r. Type **346** 70 70
1081 60 r. Vine leaves (Summer) 70 70
1082 60 r. Trunk in snowy landscape (Winter) 70 70
1083 60 r. Grapes (Autumn) 70 70

Nos. 1080/3 were issued together, se-tenant, forming a composite design.

347 Strontium

1994. Minerals. Multicoloured.
1084 60 r. Type **347** 70 70
1085 80 r. Quartz 90 90
1086 3 f. 50 Iron dolomite 3·50 3·50

HAVE YOU READ THE NOTES AT THE BEGINNING OF THIS CATALOGUE?

These often provide the answers to the enquiries we receive.

348 "The True Light"

349 Earth

1994. Christmas. Multicoloured.

No.	Description	Unused	Used
1087	60 r. Type **348**	70	70
1088	80 r. "Peace on Earth"	90	90
1089	1 f. "Behold, the House of God"	1·10	1·10

1994. The Four Elements. Multicoloured.

No.	Description	Unused	Used
1090	60 r. Type **349**	70	70
1091	80 r. Water	90	90
1092	1 f. Fire	1·10	1·10
1093	2 f. 50 Air	2·75	2·75

350 "The Theme of all our Affairs must be Peace"
351 U.N. Flag and Bouquet of Flowers

1995. Europa. Peace and Freedom. Quotations of Franz Josef II. Multicoloured.

No.	Description	Unused	Used
1094	80 r. Type **350**	85	85
1095	1 f. "Through Unity comes Strength and the Bearing of Sorrows"	1·10	1·10

1995. Anniversaries and Event. Multicoloured.

No.	Description	Unused	Used
1096	60 r. Princess Marie with children (50th anniv of Liechtenstein Red Cross) (horiz)	65	65
1097	1 f. 80 Type **351** (50th anniv of U.N.O.)	1·75	1·75
1098	3 f. 50 Alps (European Nature Conservation Year)	3·75	3·75

352 "Falknis Mountains"
353 "One Heart and One Soul"

1995. Birth Centenary of Anton Frommelt (painter). Multicoloured.

No.	Description	Unused	Used
1099	60 r. Type **352**	65	65
1100	80 r. "Three Oaks"	85	85
1101	4 f. 10 "The Rhine"	4·00	4·00

1995. Greetings Stamps. Multicoloured.

No.	Description	Unused	Used
1102	60 r. Type **353**	65	65
1103	60 r. Bandage round sunflower ("Get Well")	65	65
1104	60 r. Baby arriving over rainbow ("Hurrah! Here I am")	65	65
1105	60 r. Delivering letter by hot-air balloon ("Write again")	65	65

354 Coloured Ribbons woven through River
355 Arnica

1995. Liechtenstein–Switzerland Co-operation.

No.	Description	Unused	Used
1106	60 r. multicoloured Type **354**	65	65

No. 1106 was valid for use in both Liechtenstein and Switzerland (see No. 1308 of Switzerland).

1995. Medicinal Plants. Multicoloured.

No.	Description	Unused	Used
1107	60 r. Type **355**	65	65
1108	80 r. Giant nettle	85	85
1109	1 f. 80 Common valerian	1·75	1·75
1110	3 f. 50 Fig-wort	3·25	3·25

356 Angel (detail of painting)

357 "Lady with Lap-dog" (Paul Wunderlich)

1995. Christmas. Painting by Lorenzo Monaco. Multicoloured.

No.	Description	Unused	Used
1111	60 r. Type **356**	50	50
1112	80 r. "Virgin Mary with Infant and Two Angels"	70	70
1113	1 f. Angel facing left (detail of painting)	85	85

1995. Homage to Liechtenstein.

No.	Type	Description	Unused	Used
1114	**357**	4 f. multicoloured	3·50	3·50

358 Eschen

359 Crucible

1996. Scenes. Multicoloured.

No.	Description	Unused	Used
1115	10 r. Type **358**	20	40
1116	5 f. Vaduz Castle	4·25	4·25

1996. Brozne Age in Europe.

No.	Type	Description	Unused	Used
1117	**359**	90 r. multicoloured	75	75

360 Kinsky and Diary Extract, 7 March 1917

1996. Europa. Famous Women. Nora, Countess Kinsky (mother of Princess Gina of Liechtenstein)

No.	Type	Description	Unused	Used
1118	**360**	90 r. grey, purple and blue	75	75
1119	–	1 f. 10 grey, blue and purple	95	95

DESIGN: 1 f.10, Kinsky and diary extract for 28 February 1917.

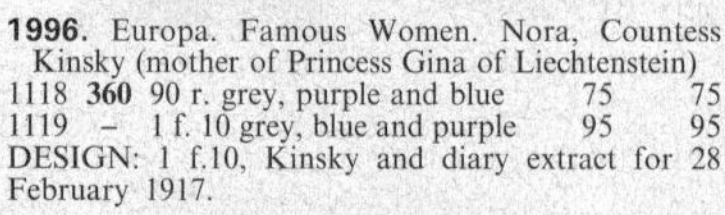
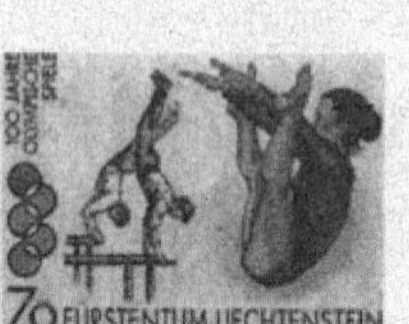
361 Gymnastics

1996. Centenary of Modern Olympic Games. Multicoloured.

No.	Description	Unused	Used
1120	70 r. Type **361**	60	60
1121	90 r. Hurdling	75	75
1122	1 f. 10 Cycling	95	95

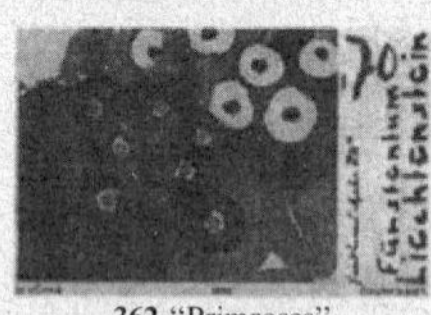
362 "Primroses"

1996. Birth Centenary of Ferdinand Gehr (painter). Multicoloured.

No.	Description	Unused	Used
1123	70 r. Type **362**	60	60
1124	90 r. "Daisies"	75	75
1125	1 f. 10 "Poppy"	95	95
1126	1 f. 80 "Buttercups" (33 × 23 mm)	1·50	1·50

363 State Arms

1996.

No.	Type	Description	Unused	Used
1127	**363**	10 f. multicoloured	8·50	8·50

364 Veldkirch, 1550

1996. Millenary of Austria.

No.	Type	Description	Unused	Used
1128	**364**	90 r. multicoloured	75	75

OFFICIAL STAMPS

1932. Stamps of 1930 optd **REGIERUNGS DIENSTSACHE** under crown.

No.	Description	Unused	Used
O118	5 r. green (No. 97)	8·00	8·00
O119	10 r. lilac	50·00	8·00
O120	20 r. red	55·00	8·00
O121	30 r. blue	12·00	8·00
O122	35 r. green	7·00	18·00
O123	50 r. black	45·00	13·00
O124	60 r. green	9·50	28·00
O125	1 f. 20 brown	£100	£250

1933. Nos. 121 and 123 optd **REGIERUNGS DIENSTSACHE** in circle round crown.

No.	Type	Description	Unused	Used
O126	**38**	25 r. orange	28·00	32·00
O127	–	1 f. 20 brown	60·00	£225

1934. Nos. 128 etc. optd **REGIERUNGS DIENSTSACHE** in circle round crown.

No.	Type	Description	Unused	Used
O150	**41**	5 r. green	80	1·50
O151	–	10 r. violet	1·10	1·25
O152	–	15 r. orange	35	1·40
O153	–	20 r. red	40	1·40
O155	–	25 r. brown	1·50	11·00
O156	–	30 r. blue	3·00	5·50
O157	**42**	50 r. brown	1·00	2·00
O158	–	90 r. green	5·50	32·00
O159	–	1 f. 50 brown	26·00	£140

1937. Stamps of 1937 optd **REGIERUNGS DIENSTSACHE** in circle round crown.

No.	Type	Description	Unused	Used
O174	**51**	5 r. green and buff	20	50
O175	–	10 r. violet and buff	40	90
O176	–	20 r. red and buff	75	1·25
O177	–	25 r. brown and buff	30	1·25
O178	–	30 r. blue and buff	1·00	70
O179	–	50 r. brown and buff	75	90
O180	–	1 f. purple and buff	75	5·50
O181	–	1 f. 50 grey and buff	2·10	9·00

1947. Stamps of 1944 optd **DIENSTMARKE** and crown.

No.	Description	Unused	Used
O255	5 r. green	1·25	60
O256	10 r. violet	1·25	85
O257	20 r. red	1·50	85
O258	30 r. blue	2·00	1·40
O259	50 r. grey	2·00	3·00
O260	1 f. red	9·00	10·00
O261	1 f. 50 blue	9·00	10·00

O 86

O 198 Government Building, Vaduz

1950. Buff paper.

No.	Type	Description	Unused	Used
O287	**O 86**	5 r. purple and grey	10	10
O288		10 r. green and mauve	10	10
O289		20 r. brown and blue	15	15
O290		30 r. purple and red	30	25
O291		40 r. blue and brown	30	30
O292		55 r. green and red	1·00	1·00
O293		60 r. grey and mauve	1·00	1·00
O294		80 r. orange and grey	75	75
O295		90 r. brown and blue	80	1·00
O296		1 f. 20 turquoise and orange	1·50	1·50

1968. White paper.

No.	Type	Description	Unused	Used
O495	**O 86**	5 r. brown and orange	10	10
O496		10 r. violet and red	10	10
O497		20 r. red and green	15	15
O498		30 r. green and red	25	25
O499		50 r. blue and red	40	40
O500		60 r. orange and blue	50	50
O501		70 r. purple and green	60	60
O502		80 r. green and red	70	70
O503		95 r. green and red	1·00	1·00
O504		1 f. purple & turquoise	90	90
O505		1 f. 20 brown & turq	1·40	1·40
O506		2 f. brown and orange	1·60	1·60

1976.

No.	Type	Description	Unused	Used
O652	**O 198**	10 r. brown and violet	10	10
O653		20 r. red and blue	15	15
O654		35 r. blue and red	20	20
O655		40 r. violet and green	25	25
O656		50 r. green and mauve	30	30
O657		70 r. purple and green	40	40
O658		80 r. green and purple	50	50
O659		90 r. violet and blue	60	60
O660		1 f. grey and purple	65	65
O661		1 f. 10 brown and blue	70	70
O662		1 f. 50 green and red	90	90
O663		2 f. orange and blue	1·40	1·40
O664		5 f. purple and orange	3·75	3·50

POSTAGE DUE STAMPS

D 11 D 25 D 58

1920.

No.	Type	Description	Unused	Used
D43	**D 11**	5 h. red	10	25
D44		10 h. red	10	25
D45		15 h. red	10	25
D46		20 h. red	10	25
D47		25 h. red	15	30
D48		30 h. red	15	30
D49		40 h. red	15	30
D50		50 h. red	15	30
D51		80 h. red	15	30
D52		1 k. blue	20	50
D53		2 k. blue	20	50
D54		5 k. blue	20	50

1928.

No.	Type	Description	Unused	Used
D84	**D 25**	5 r. red and violet	1·00	2·50
D85		10 r. red and violet	1·25	2·50
D86		15 r. red and violet	2·50	10·00
D87		20 r. red and violet	2·50	2·50
D88		25 r. red and violet	2·50	7·50
D89		30 r. red and violet	7·00	11·00
D90		40 r. red and violet	8·00	12·00
D91		50 r. red and violet	8·50	15·00

1940.

No.	Type	Description	Unused	Used
D189	**D 58**	5 r. red and blue	1·25	4·25
D190		10 r. red and blue	50	75
D191		15 r. red and blue	75	4·50
D192		20 r. red and blue	80	1·25
D193		25 r. red and blue	1·40	3·25
D194		30 r. red and blue	3·00	5·00
D195		40 r. red and blue	3·00	4·50
D196		50 r. red and blue	3·00	5·50

LITHUANIA Pt. 10

A country on the Baltic Sea, under Russian rule until occupied by the Germans in the first World War (see German Eastern Command). It was an independent republic from 1918 to 1940, when it was incorporated into the U.S.S.R.

Lithuania declared its independence in 1990, and the U.S.S.R. formally recognised the republic in 1991.

1918. 100 skatiku = 1 auksinas.
1922. 100 centu = 1 litas.
1990. 100 kopeks = 1 rouble.
1992. Talons.
1993. 100 centu = 1 litas.

Lietuvos 30 skatikų pašta — 1
Lietuvos 10 skatikų paštas — 2

1918.
3 **1** 10 s. black on buff . . . . . . 50·00 25·00
4 15 s. black on buff . . . . . . 50·00 25·00
5 20 s. black on buff . . . . . . 6·75 3·50
6 30 s. black on buff . . . . . . 6·75 3·50
7 40 s. black on buff . . . . . . 6·75 3·50
8 50 s. black on buff . . . . . . 10·00 8·75

1919.
9 **2** 10 s. black on buff . . . . . 6·75 3·50
10 15 s. black on buff . . . . . 6·75 3·50
11 20 s. black on buff . . . . . 6·75 3·50
12 30 s. black on buff . . . . . 6·75 3·50

Lietuvos paštas 10 sk. — 3
Lietuvos paštas sk. 10 sk. — 4

1919.
13 **3** 10 s. black on buff . . . . . 3·25 2·00
14 15 s. black on buff . . . . . 3·25 2·00
15 20 s. black on buff . . . . . 3·25 2·00
16 30 s. black on buff . . . . . 3·25 2·00
17 40 s. black on buff . . . . . 3·25 2·75
18 50 s. black on buff . . . . . 3·25 2·75
19 60 s. black on buff . . . . . 3·25 3·25

1919.
20 **4** 10 s. black on buff . . . . . 2·00 1·50
21 15 s. black on buff . . . . . 2·00 1·50
22 20 s. black on buff . . . . . 2·00 1·50
23 30 s. black on buff . . . . . 2·00 1·50
24 40 s. black on buff . . . . . 2·00 1·50
25 50 s. black on buff . . . . . 2·00 1·50
26 60 s. black on buff . . . . . 2·00 1·50

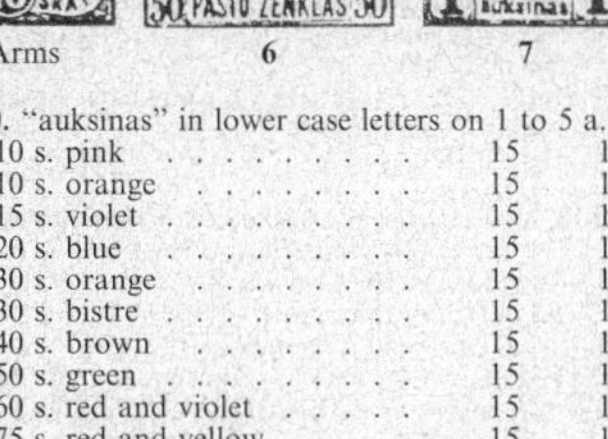

5 Arms **6** **7**

1919. "auksinas" in lower case letters on 1 to 5 a.
40 **5** 10 s. pink 15 15
50 10 s. orange 15 10
51 15 s. violet 15 10
52 20 s. blue 15 10
43 30 s. orange 15 15
53 30 s. bistre 15 10
54 40 s. brown 15 10
55 **6** 50 s. green 15 10
56 60 s. red and violet 15 10
57 75 s. red and yellow 15 10
37 **7** 1 a. red and grey 35 20
38 3 a. red and brown 35 20
39 5 a. red and green 40 30

1921. As T **4**, but "AUKSINAS" or "AUKSINAI" in capital letters.
58 **7** 1 a. red and grey 15 10
59 3 a. red and brown 25 15
60 5 a. red and green 40 25

11 Lithuania receiving Independence **12** Lithuania arises

1920. 2nd Anniv of Independence.
65 **11** 10 s. lake . . . . 2·00 2·00
66 15 s. lilac . . . . 2·00 2·00
67 20 s. blue . . . . 2·00 2·00
68 **12** 30 s. brown . . . . 2·00 2·00
69 – 40 s. green and brown . . . 2·00 2·00
70 **12** 50 s. red . . . . 2·00 2·00
71 60 s. lilac . . . . 2·00 2·00
72 – 80 s. red and violet . . . . 2·00 2·00
73 – 1 a. red and green . . . . 2·00 2·00
74 – 3 a. red and brown . . . . 2·00 2·00
75 – 5 a. red and green . . . . 2·00 2·00
DESIGNS—VERT: 40 s., 80 s., 1 a. Lithuania with chains broken; 3, 5 a. (25×25 mm) Arms.

16 Arms **17** Vytautas

1920. National Assembly.
76 **16** 10 s. red 30 25
77 15 s. violet 45 35
78 **17** 20 s. green 45 35
79 **16** 30 s. brown 45 45
80 – 40 s. violet and green . . . 45 45
81 **17** 50 s. brown and orange . . . 45 45
82 60 s. red and orange . . . 55 45
83 – 80 s. red, grey and black . . 55 55
84 – 1 a. yellow and black . . . 55 55
85 – 3 a. green and black . . . 65 65
86 – 5 a. violet and black . . . 2·75 2·00
DESIGNS—As Type **17**: 40 s., 80 s. Gediminas. As Type **16**: 1 a. to 5 a. Sacred Oak and Altar.

20 Sower **21** Kestutis **22** Reaper

23 **28** Allegory of Flight

24 Flying Posthorn **25** Junkers F-13 over R. Niemen

1921.
87 **20** 10 s. red . . . . 15 1·40
88 15 s. mauve . . . . 15 1·60
89 20 s. blue 10 10
90 **22** 30 s. brown . . . . 40 4·00
91 **21** 40 s. red 15 10
92 **22** 50 s. olive 10 10
93 60 s. mauve and green . . . 30 5·00
94 **21** 80 s. red and orange . . . 20 15
95 1 a. green and brown . . . 15 10
96 2 a. red and blue 15 10
97 **23** 3 a. blue and brown . . . 40 85
124 **20** 4 a. blue and yellow . . . 30 20
98 **23** 5 a. red and grey . . . . 50 2·00
125 **20** 8 a black and green . . . 65 20
99 **23** 10 a. mauve and red . . . 1·00 35
100 25 a. green and brown . . . 1·10 65
101 100 a. grey and red . . . 4·00 10·00

1921. Air. Inauguration of Kaunas–Konigsberg Air Service.
102 **24** 20 s. blue . . . . 1·00 85
103 40 s. orange . . . . 1·00 85
104 60 s. green . . . . 1·00 65
105 80 s. red . . . . 1·10 1·00
106 **25** 1 a. green and red . . . . 2·00 1·25
107 – 2 a. brown and blue . . . 2·00 1·50
108 – 5 a. grey and yellow . . . 2·75 2·75
DESIGNS—As Type **25**: 2 a. Three Junkers F-13 monoplanes; 5 a. Junkers F-13 over Gediminas Castle.

1921. Air. Inauguration of Air Mail Service.
109 **28** 20 s. lilac and orange . . . 1·10 2·00
110 40 s. red and blue . . . . 1·10 2·00
111 60 s. olive and blue . . . 1·10 2·00
112 80 s. green and yellow . . . 1·10 2·00
113 1 a. blue and green . . . 1·10 2·00
114 2 a. red and grey . . . . 1·10 2·00
115 5 a. green and purple . . . 1·10 2·00

1922. Surch **4 AUKSINAI** with or without frame.
116 **6** 4 a. on 75 s. red and yellow 40 1·00

30 Junkers F-13

1922. Air.
118 **30** 1 a. red and brown . . . . 1·60 2·75
119 3 a. green and violet . . . 1·60 2·75
120 5 a. yellow and blue . . . 1·60 2·75

31 Gediminas Castle **33** Pte. Luksis

1922. Air.
121 **31** 2 a. red and blue . . . . . 1·00 2·00
122 4 a. red and brown . . . . 1·00 2·00
123 10 a. blue and black . . . . 2·40 1·90

1922. "De jure" Recognition of Lithuania by League of Nations. Inscr "LIETUVA DE JURE".
126 **33** 20 s. red and black 65 65
127 – 40 s. violet and green . . . 65 65
128 – 50 s. blue and purple . . . 65 65
129 – 60 s. orange and violet . . . 65 65
130 – 1 a. blue and red 65 65
131 – 2 a. brown and blue 65 65
132 – 3 a. blue and brown 65 65
133 – 4 a. purple and green . . . 65 65
134 – 5 a. red and brown 65 65
135 – 6 a. blue 65 65
136 – 8 a. yellow and blue . . . 65 65
137 – 10 a. green and violet . . . 65 65
DESIGNS—VERT: 40 s. Lt. Juozapavicius; 50 s. Dr. Basanavicius; 60 s. Mrs. Petkevicaite; 1 a. Prof. Voldemaras; 2 a. Dovidaitis; 3 a. Dr. Slezevicius; 4 a. Dr. Galvanauskas; 5 a. Dr. Grinius; 6 a. Dr. Stulginskis; 8 a. Pres. Smetona. HORIZ: (39×27 mm): 10 a. Stauguitis, Pres. Smetona and Silingas.

1922. Surch.
138 **5** 1 c. on 10 s. orange (postage) 25 5·00
139 1 c. on 15 s. violet . . . . 25 5·00
143 1 c. on 20 s. blue . . . . . 25 5·00
144 1 c. on 30 s. orange . . . . 35·00 60·00
145 1 c. on 30 s. bistre 15 40
146 1 c. on 40 s. brown . . . . 50 4·00
148 **22** 1 c. on 50 s. olive 10 10
149 **6** 2 c. on 50 s. green . . . . 65 4·00
150 2 c. on 60 s. red and violet 10 10
151 2 c. on 75 s. red and yellow 75 5·00
152 **20** 3 c. on 10 s. red . . . . . 3·25 6·00
153 3 c. on 15 s. mauve 15 15
154 3 c. on 20 s. blue . . . . . 20 3·25
155 **22** 3 c. on 30 s. brown . . . . 5·00 8·50
156 **21** 3 c. on 40 s. red 15 60
157 **7** 3 c. on 1 a. (No. 37) . . . 85·00 £130
158 3 c. on 1 a. (No. 58) . . . 15 1·25
159 3 c. on 3 a. (No. 38) . . . 70·00 £120
160 3 c. on 3 a. (No. 59) . . . 10 65
161 3 c. on 5 a. (No. 39) . . . 40·00 50·00
162 3 c. on 5 a. (No. 60) . . . 10 80
163 **22** 5 c. on 50 s. olive 10 10
164 5 c. on 60 s. mauve & green 6·75 15·00
165 **21** 5 c. on 80 s. red & orange 10 40
166 **6** 5 c. on 4 a. on 75 s. red and yellow . . . . 30 12·50
168 **21** 10 c. on 1 a. green & brown 25 10
169 10 c. on 2 a. red and blue 10 10
170 **20** 15 c. on 4 a. blue & yellow 10 10
171 **23** 25 c. on 3 a. blue and green 10·00 25·00
172 25 c. on 5 a. red and grey 3·50 6·75
173 25 c. on 10 a. mauve & red 1·00 1·60
174 **20** 30 c. on 8 a. black & green 65 35
175 **23** 50 c. on 25 a. green & brown 1·50 3·00
176 1 l. on 100 a grey and red 2·75 3·25
177 **24** 10 c. on 20 s. blue (air) . . 1·40 3·75
178 10 c. on 40 s. orange . . . 1·40 5·75
179 10 c. on 60 s. green . . . 1·10 5·75
180 10 c. on 80 s. red . . . . 1·40 5·75
181 **25** 20 c. on 1 a. green and red 4·75 12·50
182 – 20 c. on 2 a. (No. 107) . . 11·00 18·00
183 **31** 25 c. on 2 a. red and blue 1·00 85
184 30 c. on 4 a. red and brown 1·00 80
185 – 50 c. on 5 a. (No. 108) . . 1·40 1·25
186 **31** 50 c. on 10 a. blue & black 65 1·25
187 **30** 1 l. on 5 a. yellow & blue 12·50 27·00

38 Wayside Cross **39** Ruins of Kaunas Castle **40** Seminary Church

1923.
201 **38** 2 c. brown 60 30
202 3 c. bistre 85 25
203 5 c. green 85 10
204 10 c. violet . . . . 2·00 10
189 15 c. red . . . . 1·40 10
190 20 c. green . . . . 1·40 15
191 25 c. blue . . . . 1·40 10
206 36 c. brown . . . . 7·50 65
192 **39** 50 c. green . . . . 1·40 15
193 60 c. red . . . . 1·40 10
194 **40** 1 l. orange and green . . . 6·75 10
195 3 l. red and grey . . . . 5·25 55
196 5 l. brown and blue . . . 10·00 90

43 Arms of Memel **44** Ruins of Trakai

1923. Union of Memel with Lithuania.
210 **43** 1 c. red and green . . . . 1·10 1·25
211 – 2 c. mauve . . . . 1·10 1·25
212 – 3 c. yellow . . . . 1·25 1·25
213 **43** 5 c. buff and blue . . . . 1·40 1·25
214 – 10 c. red . . . . 1·50 1·50
215 – 15 c. green . . . . 1·50 1·50
216 **44** 25 c. violet . . . . 2·40 2·40
217 – 30 c. red . . . . 2·75 3·25
218 – 60 c. green . . . . 2·75 3·25
219 – 1 l. green . . . . 2·75 3·25
220 – 2 l. red . . . . 6·75 10·00
221 **44** 3 l. blue . . . . 7·50 10·00
222 – 5 l. blue . . . . 10·00 11·50
DESIGNS—As Type **43**: 3 c., 2 l. Chapel of Biruta; 10 c., 15 c. War Memorial Kaunas; As Type **44**: 2, 30 c. Arms of Lithuania; 60 c., 5 l. Memel Lighthouse; 1 l. Memel Harbour.

45

46

1924. Air.
223 **45** 20 c. yellow . . . . 1·40 85
224 40 c. green . . . . 1·40 85
225 60 c. red . . . . 1·60 65
226 **46** 1 l. brown . . . . 3·25 55

1924. Charity. War Orphans Fund. Surch **KARO NASLAICIAMS** and premium.
227 **38** 2 c. + 2 c. bistre (postage) 2·00 2·00
228 3 c. + 3 c. bistre . . . . 2·00 2·00
229 5 c. + 5 c. green . . . . 2·00 2·00
231 10 c. + 10 c. violet . . . 2·75 3·00
232 15 c. + 15 c. red . . . . 3·00 3·00
233 20 c. + 20 c. olive . . . 4·00 4·00
235 25 c. + 25 c. blue . . . . 9·50 9·50
236 36 c. + 34 c. brown . . . 10·00 10·00
237 **39** 50 c. + 50 c. green . . . 10·00 10·00
238 60 c. + 60 c. red . . . . 13·50 13·50
239 **40** 1 l. + 1 l. orange and green 13·50 13·50
240 3 l. + 2 l. red and grey . . 23·00 23·00
241 5 l. + 3 l. brown and blue 32·00 32·00
242 **45** 20 c. + 20 c. yellow (air) 13·50 13·50
243 40 c. + 40 c. green . . . 13·50 13·50
244 60 c. + 60 c. red . . . . 13·50 13·50
245 **46** 1 l. + 1 l. brown . . . . 17·00 17·00

49 Swallow carrying Letter **56** **57**

1926. Air.
246 **49** 20 c. red 70 30
247 40 c. orange and mauve . . 70 30
248 60 c. black and blue . . . 2·10 40

1926. Charity. War Invalids. Nos. 227/39 surch with new values and small ornaments.
249 **38** 1 c. + 1 c. on 2 c. + 2 c. 1·40 1·40
250 2 c. + 2 c. on 3 c. + 3 c. 1·40 1·40
251 2 c. + 2 c. on 5 c. + 5 c. 1·40 1·40
253 5 c. + 5 c. on 10 c. + 10 c. 2·75 2·75
254 5 c. + 5 c. on 15 c. + 15 c. 2·75 2·75
255 10 c. + 10 c. on 20 c. + 20 c. 2·75 2·75
257 10 c. + 10 c. on 25 c. + 25 c. 6·75 6·75
258 14 c. + 14 c. on 36 c. + 34 c. 8·00 8·00
259 **39** 20 c. + 20 c. on 50 c. + 50 c. 6·75 6·75
260 25 c. + 25 c. on 60 c. + 60 c. 10·00 10·00
261 **40** 30 c. + 30 c. on 1 l. + 1 l. 17·00 17·00

1926. Charity. War Orphans. Nos. 227/39 surch **V.P.** and new values in circular ornament.
262 **38** 1 c. + 1 c. on 2 c. + 2 c. 1·40 1·40
263 2 c. + 2 c. on 3 c. + 3 c. 1·40 1·40
264 2 c. + 2 c. on 5 c. + 5 c. 1·40 1·40
266 5 c. + 5 c. on 10 c. + 10 c. 2·75 2·75
267 10 c. + 10 c. on 15 c. + 15 c. 2·75 2·75
268 15 c. + 15 c. on 20 c. + 20 c. 2·75 2·75
270 15 c. + 15 c. on 25 c. + 25 c. 6·75 6·75
271 19 c. + 19 c. on 36 c. + 34 c. 6·75 6·75
272 **39** 25 c. + 25 c. on 50 c. + 50 c. 8·00 8·00
273 30 c. + 30 c. on 60 c. + 60 c. 13·50 13·50
274 **40** 50 c. + 50 c. on 1 l. + 1 l. 20·00 20·00

1927.

275 **56** 2 c. orange 55 10
276 3 c. brown 55 10
277 5 c. green . . . . 1·10 10
278 10 c. violet . . . . 2·00 10
279 15 c. red . . . . 1·60 10
280 25 c. blue . . . . 1·60 10
283 30 c. blue . . . . 5·50 10

1927. Dr. Basanavicius Mourning issue.

285 **57** 15 c. red . . . . 1·40 1·00
286 25 c. blue . . . . 1·40 1·00
287 50 c. green . . . . 1·40 1·00
288 60 c. violet . . . . 2·75 2·75

58 "Vytis" of the Lithuanian Arms

1927.

289 **58** 1 l. green and grey . . . . 1·25 65
290 3 l. violet and green . . . . 3·25 50
291 5 l. brown and grey . . . . 6·50 1·25

59 President Antanas Smetona **60** Lithuania liberated

1928. 10th Anniv of Independence.

292 **59** 5 c. green and brown . . . 15 10
293 10 c. black and violet . . . 15 10
294 15 c. brown and orange . . 15 10
295 25 c. slate and blue 50 10
296 **60** 50 c. purple and blue . . . 90 20
297 60 c. black and red . . . . 1·10 35
298 – 1 l. brown . . . . 1·75 1·00

DESIGN—HORIZ: 1 l. Lithuania's resurrection (angel and soldiers). Dated 1918-1928.

62 **63**

64 J. Tubelis **66** Railway Station, Kaunas

1930. 500th Death Anniv of Grand Duke Vytautas. (a) Postage.

299 **62** 2 c. brown 25 10
300 3 c. violet and brown . . . 25 10
301 5 c. red and green 25 10
302 10 c. green and violet . . . 25 10
303 15 c. violet and red . . . 25 10
304 30 c. purple and blue . . . 50 10
305 36 c. olive and purple . . . 35 15
306 50 c. blue and green . . . 35 20
307 60 c. red and blue 60 35
308 **63** 1 l. purple, grey and green . 2·00 65
309 3 l. violet, pink and mauve . 2·75 1·25
310 5 l. red, grey and brown . . 5·00 1·75
311 10 l. black and blue . . . . 18·00 18·00
312 25 l. green and brown . . . 50·00 60·00

(b) Air.

313 **64** 5 c. brown, yellow & black 35 35
314 10 c. black, drab and blue 40 40
315 15 c. blue, grey and purple 40 40
316 – 20 c. red, orange & brown 1·00 55
317 – 40 c. violet, lt blue and blue 1·40 80
318 – 60 c. black, lilac and green 1·60 1·40
319 – 1 l. black, lilac and red . . 3·00 1·50

DESIGNS—HORIZ: 20 c., 40 c. Vytautas and Kaunas; 60 c., 1 l. Vytautas and Smetona.

1932. Orphans' Fund. Imperf or perf.

320 **66** 5 c. blue and brown 30 30
321 10 c. purple and brown . . 30 30
322 – 15 c. brown and green . . 30 30
323 – 25 c. blue and green . . . 75 75
324 – 50 c. grey and olive . . . 1·40 2·00
325 – 60 c. grey and mauve . . . 1·75 6·00
326 – 1 l. blue and grey . . . . 2·75 3·25
327 – 3 l. purple and green . . . 3·75 6·00

DESIGNS—As Type **66**: 15, 25 c. "The Two Pines" (painting); 50 c. G.P.O. VERT: 60 c., 1, 3 l. Vilnius Cathedral.

68 Map of Lithuania, Memel and Vilna

1932. Air. Orphans' Fund. Imperf or perf.

328 **68** 5 c. red and green 25 25
329 10 c. purple and brown . . 25 25
330 – 15 c. blue and buff . . . 40 40
331 – 20 c. black and brown . . 2·40 2·00
332 – 40 c. purple and yellow . . 3·25 3·25
333 – 60 c. blue and buff . . . 4·00 6·00
334 – 1 l. purple and green . . . 5·00 6·00
335 – 2 l. blue and green . . . . 5·00 6·75

DESIGNS: 15, 20 c. Airplane over R. Niemen; 40, 60 c. Town Hall, Kaunas; 1, 2 l. Vytautas Church, Kaunas.

69 Vytautas escapes from Prison

71 Coronation of Mindaugas

1932. 15th Anniv of Independence. Imperf or perf.

336 **69** 5 c. purple and red (postage) 50 50
337 10 c. brown and grey . . . 50 50
338 – 15 c. green and red 50 50
339 – 25 c. brown and purple . . 1·00 1·60
340 – 50 c. brown and green . . 1·40 2·40
341 – 60 c. red and green . . . . 1·90 5·00
342 – 1 l. black and blue . . . . 2·00 3·50
343 – 3 l. green and purple . . . 2·75 6·75

344 – 5 c. lilac and green (air) . 15 20
345 – 10 c. red and green 15 25
346 **71** 15 c. brown and violet . . 20 30
347 – 20 c. black and red 45 45
348 – 40 c. black and purple . . 2·00 2·75
349 – 60 c. black and orange . . 2·75 8·25
350 – 1 l. green and violet . . . 3·50 4·00
351 – 2 l. brown and blue . . . . 5·00 8·25

DESIGNS—POSTAGE. As Type **69**: 15, 25 c. Vytautas and Jagello preaching the gospel; 50, 60 c. Battle of Grunewald; 1, 3 l. Proclamation of Independence. AIR. As Type **71**: 5, 10 c. Battle of Saules; 40 c. Gediminas in Council; 60 c. Founding of Vilnius; 1 l. Russians surrendering to Gediminas; 2 l. Algirdas before Moscow.

72 A. Visteliauskas

1933. 50th Anniv of Publication of "Ausra".

352 **72** 5 c. red and green 20 25
353 10 c. red and blue 20 25
354 – 15 c. red and orange . . . 20 25
355 – 25 c. brown and blue . . . 85 1·00
356 – 50 c. blue and green . . . 1·25 1·60
357 – 60 c. deep brown & lt brn 3·00 5·00
358 – 1 l. purple and red . . . . 3·25 4·25
359 – 3 l. purple and blue . . . 5·75 6·75

PORTRAITS: 15, 25 c. P. Vileisis; 50, 60 c. J. Sliupas; 1, 3 l. J. Basanavicius.

73 Trakai Castle

1933. Air. 550th Death Anniv of Grand Duke Kestutis.

360 **73** 5 c. blue and green 20 35
361 10 c. brown and violet . . 20 35
362 – 15 c. violet and blue . . . 20 35
363 – 20 c. purple and brown . . 55 80
364 – 40 c. purple and blue . . . 3·25 1·90
365 – 60 c. blue and red . . . . 5·00 7·75
366 – 1 l. blue and green . . . . 5·00 6·75
367 – 2 l. green and violet . . . 6·00 10·00

DESIGNS: 15, 20 c. Kestutis encounters Birute; 40, 60 c. Birute; 1, 2 l. Kestutis and Algirdas.

74 Mother and Child

75 J. Tumas Vaizgantas

1933. Child Welfare. (a) Postage.

373 **74** 5 c. brown and green . . . 15 20
374 10 c. blue and red 15 20
375 – 15 c. purple and green . . . 20 25
376 – 25 c. black and orange . . 65 1·00
377 – 50 c. red and green . . . . 1·00 1·60
378 – 60 c. orange and black . . 2·40 5·00
379 – 1 l. blue and brown . . . . 2·75 5·00
380 – 3 l. green and purple . . . 4·75 8·25

DESIGNS—VERT: 15, 25 c. Boy reading a book; 50, 60 c. Boy with building bricks; 1, 3 l. Mother and child weaving.

(b) Air. Various medallion portraits in triangular frames.

381 – 5 c. blue and red 15 15
382 – 10 c. green and violet . . . 15 15
383 **75** 15 c. brown and green . . . 15 15
384 20 c. blue and red 25 35
385 – 40 c. green and lake . . . . 1·40 1·60
386 – 60 c. brown and blue . . . . 1·75 3·75
387 – 1 l. blue and yellow . . . . 2·40 3·75
388 – 2 l. lake and green . . . . 3·75 6·00

DESIGNS: 5, 10 c. Maironis; 40, 60 c. Vincas Kudirka; 1, 2 l. Zemaite.

76 Captains S. Darius and S. Girenas

78 "Flight" mourning over Wreckage **81** President A. Smetona

1934. Air. Death of Darius and Girenas (trans-Atlantic airmen).

389 **76** 20 c. red and black 10 10
390 – 40 c. blue and red 10 10
391 **76** 60 c. violet and black . . . 10 10
392 **78** 1 l. black and red 35 15
393 – 3 l. orange and green . . . 1·00 2·00
394 – 5 l. blue and brown . . . . 4·00 4·25

DESIGNS—HORIZ: 40 c. Bellanca monoplane "Lituanica" over Atlantic. VERT: 3 l. "Lituanica" and globe; 5 l. "Lituanica" and Vytis.

1934. President's 60th Birthday.

395 **81** 15 c. red . . . . 3·25 10
396 30 c. green . . . . 6·75 15
397 60 c. blue . . . . 13·50 70

82 **83** **84** Gleaner

85

1934.

398 **82** 2 c. red and orange 25 10
399 5 c. green 30 10
400 **83** 10 c. brown . . . . 1·00 10
401 **84** 25 c. brown and green . . . 2·40 10
402 **83** 35 c. red . . . . 2·40 10
403 **84** 50 c. blue . . . . 4·00 10
404 **85** 1 l. purple and red . . . . 32·00 10
405 3 l. green 20 10
406 – 5 l. purple and blue 20 20
407 – 10 l. brown and yellow . . 1·60 1·25

DESIGNS—HORIZ: as Type **85**: 5 l., 10 l. Knight. For design as Type **82** but smaller, see Nos. 411/12.

1935. Air. Honouring Atlantic Flyer Vaitkus. No. 390 optd **F. VAITKUS nugalejo Atlanta 21-22-IX-1935**.

407a – 40 c. blue and red £300 £350

87 Vaitkus and Air Route **88** President Smetona

1936. Air. Vaitkus' New York–Ireland Flight.

408 **87** 15 c. purple . . . . 1·25 45
409 30 c. green . . . . 1·60 1·10
410 60 c. blue . . . . 2·75 1·10

1936. As T **82** but smaller (18 × 23 mm).

411 **82** 2 c. orange 10 10
412 5 c. green 10 10

1936.

413 **88** 15 c. red . . . . 4·00 10
414 30 c. green . . . . 11·50 10
415 60 c. blue . . . . 6·75 10

89 **90** Archer

1937.

416 **89** 10 c. green . . . . 1·10 10
417 25 c. mauve 10 10
418 35 c. red 60 10
419 50 c. brown 30 10
419a 1 l. blue 15 30

1938. 1st National Olympiad Fund.

420 **90** 5 c. + 5 c. green . . . . . 8·25 10·00
421 – 15 c. + 5 c. red . . . . . 9·25 10·00
422 – 30 c. + 10 c. blue . . . . 13·50 13·50
423 – 60 c. + 15 c. brown . . . 20·00 20·00

DESIGNS: 15 c. Throwing the javelin; 30 c. Diving; 60 c. Relay runner breasting tape.

1938. Scouts' and Guides' National Camp Fund. Nos. 420/3 optd **TAUTINE SKAUCIU** (or **SKAUTU**) **STOVYKLA** and badge.

424 **90** 5 c. + 5 c. green . . . . . 10·00 10·00
425 – 15 c. + 5 c. red . . . . . 10·00 10·00
426 – 30 c. + 10 c. blue . . . . 10·00 13·50
427 – 60 c. + 15 c. brown . . . 20·00 22·00

92 President Smetona **93** Scoring a Goal

1939. 20th Anniv of Independence.

428 – 15 c. red 30 10
429 **92** 30 c. green 85 45
430 – 35 c. mauve . . . . 1·00 55
431 **92** 60 c. blue . . . . 1·40 85

DESIGN: 15, 35 c. Dr. Basanvicius proclaiming Lithuanian independence.

1939. 3rd European Basketball Championship and Physical Culture Fund.

432 – 15 c. + 10 c. brown . . . 6·75 6·75
433 **93** 30 c. + 15 c. green . . . . 6·75 6·75
434 – 60 c. + 40 c. violet . . . . 17·00 20·00

DESIGNS—VERT: 15 c. Scoring a goal. HORIZ: ($40\frac{1}{2} \times 36$ mm); 60 c. International flags and ball.

1939. Recovery of Vilnius. Nos. 428/31 optd **VILNIUS 1939-X-10** and trident.

435 – 15 c. red 55 30
436 **92** 30 c. green . . . . 1·00 40
437 – 35 c. mauve . . . . 1·10 55
438 **92** 60 c. blue . . . . 1·50 85

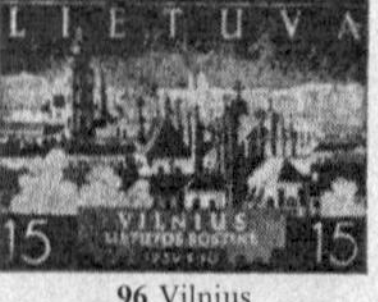

95 Vytis **96** Vilnius

1940. "Liberty" Issue.

439 **95** 5 c. brown 10 10
440 – 10 c. green 65 30
441 – 15 c. orange 10 10
442 – 25 c. brown 10 30
443 – 30 c. green 10 10
444 – 35 c. orange 10 45

DESIGNS: 10 c. Angel; 15 c. Woman releasing a dove; 25 c. Mother and children; 30 c. "Liberty Bell"; 35 c. Mythical animal.

1940. Recovery of Vilnius.
445 **96** 15 c. brown 30 15
446 – 30 c. green 85 25
447 – 60 c. blue . . . . 1·60 90
DESIGNS—VERT: 30 c. Portrait of Gediminas. HORIZ: 60 c. Ruins of Trakai Castle.

1940. Incorporation of Lithuania in U.S.S.R. Optd **LTSR 1940 VII 21.**
448 **82** 2 c. red and orange 15 40
449 **95** 5 c. brown 15 40
450 – 10 c. green (No. 440) . . . 5·00 5·00
451 – 15 c. orange (No. 441) . . 15 50
452 – 25 c. brown (No. 442) . . . 20 75
453 – 30 c. green (No. 443) . . . 25 80
454 – 35 c. orange (No. 444) . . 60 1·50
455 **89** 50 c. brown . . . . 50 1·40

From 1940 to 1990 Lithuania used stamps of Russia.

99 Angel and Map

1990. No gum. Imperf.
456 **99** 5 k. green 10 10
457 10 k. lilac 20 20
458 20 k. blue 40 40
459 50 k. red . . . . 1·50 1·50

1990. No gum. Imperf (simulated perfs).
460 **99** 5 k. green and brown . . . 10 10
461 10 k. purple and brown . . 20 20
462 20 k. blue and brown . . . 40 40
463 50 k. red and brown . . . 1·00 1·00

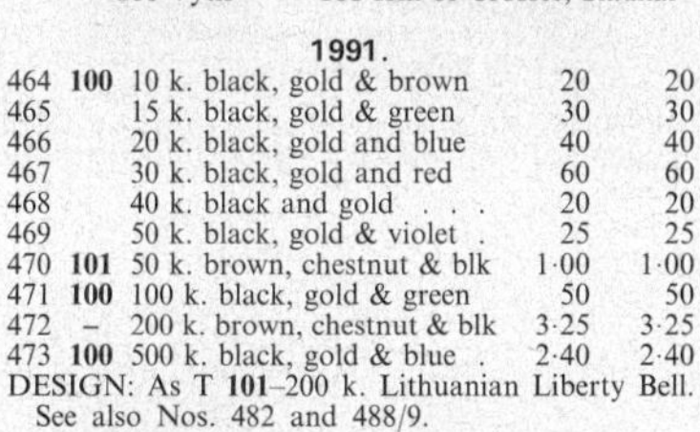

100 Vytis **101** Hill of Crosses, Siauliai

1991.
464 **100** 10 k. black, gold & brown 20 20
465 15 k. black, gold & green 30 30
466 20 k. black, gold and blue 40 40
467 30 k. black, gold and red 60 60
468 40 k. black and gold . . . 20 20
469 50 k. black, gold & violet . 25 25
470 **101** 50 k. brown, chestnut & blk 1·00 1·00
471 **100** 100 k. black, gold & green 50 50
472 – 200 k. brown, chestnut & blk 3·25 3·25
473 **100** 500 k. black, gold & blue . 2·40 2·40
DESIGN: As T **101**–200 k. Lithuanian Liberty Bell.
See also Nos. 482 and 488/9.

102 Liberty Statue, Kaunas **103** Angel with Trumpet

1991. National Day.
480 **102** 20 k. mauve, silver & blk 40 40

1991. 1st Anniv of Declaration of Independence from U.S.S.R.
481 **103** 20 k. dp green & green . . 40 40

1991. No gum. Imperf (simulated perfs).
482 **100** 15 k. green 30 30

104 Wayside Crosses

1991.
483 **104** 40 k. green and silver . . 55 55
484 – 70 k. brown, buff & gold . 95 95
485 – 100 k. brown, yell & silver 1·40 1·40
DESIGNS: 70 k. "Madonna" (icon from Pointed Gate Chapel, Vilnius); 100 k. Towers of St. Anne's Church, Vilnius.

105 Candle

1991. 50th Anniv of Resistance to Soviet and German Occupations.
486 **105** 20 k. yellow, black & bis 40 40
487 – 50 k. rose, black and red 1·00 1·00
488 – 70 k. multicoloured . . . 1·10 1·10
DESIGNS: 50 k. Shield pierced by swords; 70 k. Sword and wreath.

1991. No gum. Imperf.
489 **100** 25 k. black and brown . 50 50
490 30 k. black and purple . 60 60

106 World Map and Games Emblem **107** Lithuanian Flag on Ice-axe and Mt. Everest

1991. 4th International Lithuanians' Games.
491 **106** 20 k. green, black & yell 40 40
492 – 50 k. green, black & yell 1·40 1·40
DESIGN: 50 k. Symbolic female athlete.

1991. Lithuanian Expedition to Mt. Everest.
493 **107** 20 k. multicoloured . . . 40 40
494 70 k. multicoloured . . . 1·75 1·75

108 Trakai Castle **109** Black Storks

1991. 650th Death Anniv of Grand Duke Gediminas. Each brown, ochre and green.
495 30 k. Type **108** 60 60
496 50 k. Gediminas 75 75
497 70 k. Vilnius in 14th century 1·10 1·10

1991. Birds in the Red Book. Multicoloured.
498 30 k. + 15 k. Type **109** . . . 1·00 1·00
499 50 k. Common cranes . . . . 1·25 1·25

110 U.N. and National Emblems and National Flag **111** National Team Emblem and Colours

1992. Admission to U.N.O.
500 **110** 100 k. multicoloured . . 50 50

1992. Winter Olympic Games, Albertville, and Summer Games, Barcelona. Multicoloured.
501 50 k. + 25 k. Type **111** . . . 35 35
502 130 k. Winter Games emblem 60 60
503 280 k. Summer Games emblem 1·10 1·10

112 Slipper Orchid **113** Goosander ("Mergus merganser")

1992. Plants in the Red Book. Multicoloured.
504 200 k. Type **112** 65 65
505 300 k. Sea holly . . . . . . 1·00 1·00

1992. Birds of the Baltic. No value expressed.
506 **113** B (15 t.) black and green 20 20
507 – B (15 t.) brown, blk & grn 20 20
508 – B (15 t.) sepia, brn & grn 20 20
509 – B (15 t.) brown, blk & grn 20 20
DESIGNS: No. 506, Osprey ("Pandion haliaetus"); 507, Black-tailed godwit ("Limosa limosa"); 509, Common shelduck ("Tadorna tadorna").

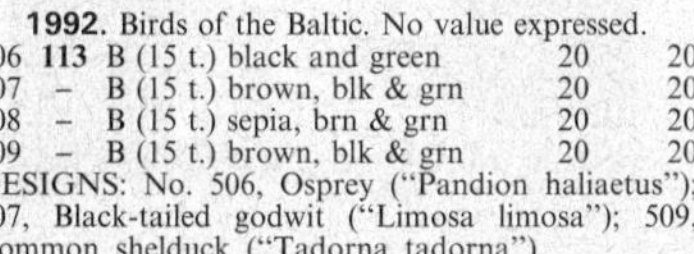

114 Kedainiai **115** Couple

1992. Arms. Multicoloured.
510 2 t. Type **114** 15 15
511 3 t. Vilnius 20 20
512 10 t. State arms 65 65
See also Nos. 531/3, 569/71, 594/5 and 628/30.

1992. Costumes of Suvalkija.
513 **115** 2 t. multicoloured 15 15
514 – 5 t. multicoloured 30 30
515 – 7 t. multicoloured 45 45
DESIGNS: 5, 7 t. Different costumes.

116 Zapyskis Church

1993. Churches.
516 **116** 3 t. black and stone . . . 15 15
517 – 10 t. black and blue . . . 55 55
518 – 15 t. black and grey . . . 85 85
DESIGNS: 10 t. Church of St. Peter and St. Paul, Vilnius; 15 t. Church of the Resurrection, Kaunas.

1993. Nos. 467, 490 and 468 surch.
519 **100** 1 t. on 30 k. blk, gold & red 10 10
520 1 t. on 30 k. black & pur 10 10
521 3 t. on 40 k. black & gold 35 35

118 Jonas Basanavicius (statesman)

1993. National Day. No value expressed.
522 **118** A (3 t.) red, cinnamon and brown 15 15
523 – B (15 t.) green, stone and brown 85 85
DESIGN: No. 523, Jonas Vileisis (politician).

119 Vytautas **120** Simonas Daukantas (historian)

1993. 600th Anniv (1987) of Accession of Grand Duke Vytautas.
524 – 5 t. gold, red and black . . 25 25
525 **119** 10 t. green, black and red 55 55
526 – 15 t. black, yellow & red 80 80
DESIGNS: 5 t. Seal; 15 t. "Battle of Grunwald" (Jan Matejka).

1993. Birth Anniversaries. Each brown and yellow.
528 1000 t. Type **120** (bicent) . . . 50 50
529 2000 t. Vydunas (125th anniv) 1·25 1·25
530 4500 t. Vincas Mykolaitis-Putinas (philosopher, centenary) . . . . 2·75 2·75

1993. Town Arms. As T **114**. Multicoloured.
531 5 c. Skuodas 10 10
532 30 c. Telsiai 10 10
533 50 c. Klaipeda 20 20

121 "Watchtower" (M. K. Ciurlionis) **122** State Arms

1993. World Unity Day (5 c.) and Transatlantic Flight (80 c.). Multicoloured.
534 5 c. Type **121** 10 10
535 80 c. Steponas Dariaus and Stasys Gireno 30 30

1993. No value expressed.
536 **122** A, green, brown and red 10 10
537 B, red, green and bistre 30 30

123 Pope John Paul II and View of Siluva **124** Couple

1993. Papal Visit. Multicoloured.
538 60 c. Type **123** 20 20
539 60 c. Pope and Hill of Crosses 20 20
540 80 c. Pope and Kaunas . . . 30 30
541 80 c. Pope and Ausra Gates, Vilnius 30 30

1993. Costumes of Dzukai.
542 **124** 60 c. multicoloured . . . 20 20
543 – 80 c. multicoloured . . . 30 30
544 – 1 l. multicoloured 35 35
DESIGNS: 80 c. to 1 l. Different costumes.

125 Klaipeda Post Office

1993. 75th Anniv of First Lithuanian Postage Stamps.
545 **125** 60 c. multicoloured . . . 20 20
546 – 60 c. multicoloured . . . 20 20
547 – 80 c. multicoloured . . . 25 25
548 – 1 l. black, brown and green 30 30
DESIGNS: No. 546, Kaunas post office; 547, Ministry for Post and Information, Vilnius; 548, First Lithuanian stamp.

126 "The Ladle Carver" (A. Gudaitis) **127** European Pond Turtle

1993. Europa. Contemporary Art.
549 **126** 80 c. multicoloured . . . 25 25

1993. Pond Life. Multicoloured.
550 80 c. Type **127** 25 25
551 1 l. Running toad 30 30

128 Games Emblem and Team Colours **130** Kristijonas Donelaitis

129 Antanas Smetona (President 1919–22 and 1926–40)

1994. Winter Olympic Games, Lillehammer, Norway.
552 **128** 1 l. 10 multicoloured . . 35 35

1994. National Day.
553 **129** 1 l. red and black 30 30
554 – 1 l. brown and black . . . 30 30
DESIGN: No. 554, Aleksandras Stulginskis (President 1922–26).

1994. Writers. Each cream, brown and orange.
555 60 c. Type **130** 20 20
556 80 c. Vincas Kudirka 25 25
557 1 l. Jonas Maciulis Maironis . 30 30

131 State Arms **132** Rockets by Kazimieras Simonavicius (illus from "Artis Magnae Artilleriae")

1994.

558 **131** 5 c. brown 10 10
559 10 c. lilac 10 10
560 20 c. green 10 10
609 40 c. purple 10 10

1994. Europa. Inventions and Discoveries.
561 **132** 80 c. multicoloured . . . 25 25

133 Couple **134** Music Note, Globe and Flag

1994. 19th-century Costumes of Zemaiciai (Lowlands).
563 **133** 5 c. multicoloured 10 10
564 – 80 c. multicoloured . . . 25 25
565 – 1 l. multicoloured 30 30
DESIGNS: 80 c., 1 l., Different costumes from Zemaiciai.

1994. Lithuanians of the World Song Festival.
566 **134** 10 c. multicoloured . . . 10 10

135 State Arms **136** Common Bat

1994.
567 **135** 2 l. multicoloured 65 65
568 3 l. multicoloured 95 95

1994. Town Arms. As T **114** but size 25 × 32 mm. Multicoloured.
569 10 c. Punia 10 10
570 60 c. Alytus 20 20
571 80 c. Perloja 25 25

1994. Mammals. Multicoloured.
572 20 c. Type **136** 10 10
573 20 c. Fat dormouse 10 10

137 Kaunas Town Hall

1994. Town Halls.
574 **137** 10 c. black and mauve . . 10 10
575 – 60 c. black and blue . . . 20 20
576 – 80 c. black and green . . 25 25
DESIGNS: 60 c. Kedainiai; 80 c. Vilnius.

138 Madonna and Child

1994. Christmas.
577 **138** 20 c. multicoloured . . . 10 10

139 Steponas Kairys

1995. National Day. Signatories to 1918 Declaration of Independence.
578 **139** 20 c. lilac, grey and black 10 10
579 – 20 c. blue, grey and black 10 10
DESIGN: No. 579, Pranas Dovydaitis (Head of Government, Mar–Apr 1919).

140 Kaunas (Lithuania) **141** "Lithuanian School, 1864–1904" (P. Rimsa)

1995. Via Baltica Motorway Project.
581 **140** 20 c. multicoloured . . . 10 10

1995. Europa. Peace and Freedom.
583 **141** 1 l. multicoloured 30 30

142 Couple **143** Motiejus Valancius (120th death)

1995. Costumes of the Highlands.
584 – 20 c. multicoloured . . . 10 10
585 – 70 c. multicoloured . . . 20 20
586 **142** 1 l. multicoloured 30 30
DESIGNS: 70 c. to 1 l. Different 19th-century costumes.

1995. Anniversaries.
587 **143** 30 c. cream, purple and yellow 10 10
588 – 40 c. cream, green and orange 15 15
589 – 70 c. cream, deep blue and pink 25 25
DESIGNS: 40 c. Zemaite (150th birth); 70 c. Kipras Petrauskas (110th birth).

144 Pieta **145** Torch-bearer

1995. Day of Mourning and Hope.
590 **144** 20 c. multicoloured . . . 10 10

1995. 5th World Lithuanians Games.
591 **145** 30 c. multicoloured . . . 10 10

146 "Baptria tibiale" **147** "Valerija Mesalina"

1995. Butterflies and Moths in "The Red Book". Multicoloured.
592 30 c. Type **146** 10 10
593 30 c. Cream-spot tiger moth ("Arctia villica") 10 10

1995. Town Arms. As T **114**. Multicoloured.
594 40 c. Virbalis 15 15
595 1 l. Kudirkos Naumiestis (horiz) 30 30

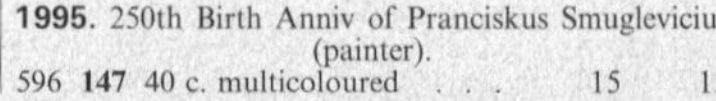

1995. 250th Birth Anniv of Pranciskus Smuglevicius (painter).
596 **147** 40 c. multicoloured . . . 15 15

148 Trakai Island Castle

1995. Castles.
597 – 40 c. multicoloured 15 15
598 **148** 70 c. blue, deep blue and black 25 25
599 – 1 l. multicoloured 30 30
DESIGNS: 40 c. Vilnius Upper Castle; 1 l. Birzai Castle.

149 Star over Winter Scene **150** Bison

1995. Christmas. Multicoloured.
600 40 c. Type **149** 15 15
601 1 l. Churchgoers with lanterns 30 30

1996. The European Bison. Multicoloured.
602 30 c. Type **150** 1 10
603 40 c. Pair of bison 15 15
604 70 c. Adult and calf 25 25
605 1 l. Parents and calf 30 30

151 Kazys Grinius (130th)

1996. Birth Anniversaries.
606 **151** 40 c. cream, brown and blue 15 15
607 – 1 l. cream, bistre and yellow 30 30
608 – 1 l. cream, blue and red . 30 30
DESIGNS: No. 607, Antanas Zmuidzinavicius (120th); 608, Balys Sruoga (centenary).

152 Vladas Mironas

1996. National Day. Signatories to 1918 Declaration of Independence.
615 **152** 40 c. cream, grey and black 10 10
616 – 40 c. bistre, brown and black 10 10
DESIGN: No. 616, Jurgis Saulys.

153 Barbora Radvilaite **154** Couple

1996. Europa. Famous Women
617 **153** 1 l. multicoloured 30 30

1996. Costumes of Klaipeda. 19th-century costumes. Multicoloured.
618 40 c. Type **154** 10 10
619 1 l. Woman in red skirt and man in frock-coat 30 30
620 1 l. Woman in black skirt and man in blue waistcoat . . . 30 30

155 Angel **156** "The Discus Thrower"

1996. Day of Mourning and Hope.
621 **155** 40 c. blue, red and black . 10 10
622 – 40 c. green, red and black 10 10
DESIGN: No. 622, Head of crucifix.

1996. Olympic Games, Atlanta. Multicoloured.
623 1 l. Type **156** 30 30
624 1 l. Basketball 30 30

157 "Sacrifice" **159** Angels heralding

1996. 85th Death Anniv of Mikolajus Ciurlionis (artist). Multicoloured.
625 40 c. Type **157** 10 10
626 40 c. "Cemetery" 10 10

1996. Town Arms. As T **114** but size 25 × 32 mm.
628 50 c. multicoloured 15 15
629 90 c. red, black and yellow . . 30 30
630 1 l. 20 multicoloured 35 35
DESIGN: 50 c. Seduva; 90 c. Panevezys; 1 l. 20, Zarasai.

1996. Christmas. Multicoloured.
632 50 c. Type **159** 15 15
633 1 l. 20 Elf riding on "Pegasus" 35 35

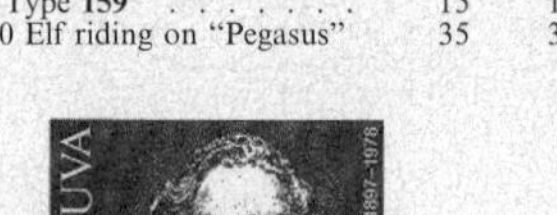

160 Ieva Simonaityte (writer, birth centenary)

1997. Anniversaries.
634 **160** 50 c. stone, brown and green 15 15
635 – 90 c. stone, grey and yellow 30 30
636 – 1 l. 20 stone, green and orange 35 35
DESIGNS: 90 c. Jonas Sliupas (physician, 53rd death); 1 l. 20, Vladas Jurgutis (financier, 31st death).

LOMBARDY AND VENETIA Pt. 2

Formerly known as Austrian Italy. Although these provinces used a different currency the following issues were valid throughout Austria. Lombardy was annexed by Sardinia in 1859 and Venetia by Italy in 1866.

1850. 100 centesimi = 1 lira.
1858. 100 soldi = 1 florin.
100 kreuzer = 1 gulden.

1 Arms of Austria

1850. Imperf.

No.	Type	Description	Unused	Used
1c	1	5 c. orange	£950	55·00
2c		10 c. black	£1000	42·00
7		15 c. red	£325	75
4		30 c. brown	£1300	3·50
5e		45 c. blue	£4250	8·50

1859. As T **4** and **5** of Austria (Emperor Francis Joseph I) but value in soldi. Perf.

No.	Type	Description	Unused	Used
16	5	2 s. yellow	£275	50·00
17	4	3 s. black	£900	£150
18		3 s. green	£225	50·00
19	5	5 s. red	£120	2·25
20		10 s. brown	£180	23·00
21		15 s. blue	£1100	40·00

3 Emperor Francis Joseph I

4 Arms of Austria

1861.

No.	Type	Description	Unused	Used
25	3	5 s. red	£900	1·40
26		10 s. brown	£900	13·00

1863.

No.	Type	Description	Unused	Used
27	4	2 s. yellow	55·00	£110
33		3 s. green	12·00	9·00
34		5 s. red	1·75	1·00
35		10 s. blue	11·00	3·00
36		15 s. brown	55·00	38·00

JOURNAL STAMPS

J 5

1858. Imperf.

No.	Type	Description	Unused	Used
J22	J 5	1 k. black	£1100	£3000
J23		2 k. red	£130	40·00
J24		4 k. red	£25000	£3000

LOURENCO MARQUES Pt. 9

A Portuguese colony in E. Africa, now part of Mozambique, whose stamps it uses.

1895. 1000 reis = 1 milreis.
1913. 100 centavos = 1 escudo.

1895. "Figures" key-type inscr "LOURENCO MARQUES".

No.	Type	Description	Unused	Used
1	R	5 r. yellow	20	15
2		10 r. mauve	25	15
3		15 r. brown	40	35
4		20 r. lilac	40	35
10		25 r. green	30	15
12		50 r. blue	35	15
18		75 r. pink	80	40
14		80 r. green	1·10	75
7		100 r. brown on yellow	85	50
16		150 r. red on pink	90	75
8		200 r. blue on blue	1·50	90
9		300 r. blue on brown	1·50	90

1895. 700th Death Anniv of St. Anthony. Optd **L. MARQUES CENTENARIO DE S. ANTONIO MDCCCXCV** on (a) "Embossed" key-type inscr "PROVINCIA DE MOCAMBIQUE".

No.	Type	Description	Unused	Used
19	Q	5 r. black	4·50	4·00
20		10 r. green	7·00	4·50
21		20 r. red	8·00	5·50
22		25 r. purple	10·00	7·25
23		40 r. brown	8·00	6·75
27a		50 r. blue	5·50	4·50
25		100 r. brown	15·00	11·00
26		200 r. violet	12·00	11·00
27		300 r. orange	18·00	16·00

(b) "Figures" key-type inscr "MOCAMBIQUE".

No.	Type	Description	Unused	Used
28	R	5 r. orange	5·25	3·75
29		10 r. mauve	8·50	7·50
30		50 r. blue	13·00	7·50
35		75 r. pink	14·00	9·50
32		80 r. green	23·00	17·00
33		100 r. brown on yellow	25·00	23·00
35a		150 r. red on pink	16·00	13·00

1897. No. 9 surch **50 reis**.

No.	Type	Description	Unused	Used
36	R	50 r. on 300 r. blue on brown	70·00	50·00

1898. "King Carlos" key-type inscr "LOURENCO MARQUES". Name and value in black.

No.	Type	Description	Unused	Used
37	S	2½ r. grey	15	15
38		5 r. orange	15	15
39		10 r. green	15	15
40		15 r. brown	50	45
83		15 r. green	20	15
41		20 r. lilac	30	15
42		25 r. green	35	15
84		25 r. red	20	15
43		50 r. blue	50	25
85		50 r. brown	45	35
86		65 r. blue	2·25	2·00
44		75 r. pink	1·00	80
87		75 r. purple	65	60
45		80 r. mauve	95	65
46		100 r. blue on blue	50	25
88		115 r. brown on pink	2·50	2·00
89		130 r. brown on yellow	2·50	2·00
47		150 r. brown on yellow	85	75
48		200 r. purple on pink	1·50	75
49		300 r. blue on pink	1·00	80
90		400 r. blue on yellow	2·50	2·00
50		500 r. black on blue	2·10	1·25
51		700 r. mauve on yellow	3·75	2·75

1899. Green and brown fiscal stamps of Mozambique, as T **9** of Macao, bisected and each half surch **Correio de Lourenco Marques** and value. Imperf.

No.	Type	Description	Unused	Used
55	–	5 r. on half of 10 r.	60	30
56	–	25 r. on half of 10 r.	60	30
57	–	50 r. on half of 30 r.	60	30
58	–	50 r. on half of 800 r.	90	50

1899. No. 44 surch **50 Reis**.

No.	Type	Description	Unused	Used
59	S	50 r. on 75 r. pink	1·50	1·10

1902. "Figures" and "Newspaper" key-types surch.

No.	Type	Description	Unused	Used
60	V	65 r. on 2½ r. brown	1·25	1·10
62	R	65 r. on 5 r. yellow	1·25	1·10
63		65 r. on 15 r. brown	1·25	1·10
64		65 r. on 20 r. lilac	1·25	1·10
66		115 r. on 10 r. mauve	1·25	1·10
67		115 r. on 200 r. blue on bl	1·25	1·10
68		115 r. on 300 r. bl on brn	1·25	1·10
70		130 r. on 25 r. green	1·25	1·10
72		130 r. on 80 r. green	1·25	1·10
73		130 r. on 150 r. red on pink	1·25	1·10
74		400 r. on 50 r. blue	4·25	1·90
76		400 r. on 75 r. pink	3·25	2·10
78		400 r. on 100 r. brown on yellow	2·10	1·40

1902. "King Carlos" key-type inscr "LOURENCO MARQUES" optd **PROVISORIO**.

No.	Type	Description	Unused	Used
79	S	15 r. brown	75	50
80		25 r. green	65	40
81		50 r. blue	80	60
82		75 r. pink	1·25	75

1905. No. 86 surch **50 Reis**.

No.	Type	Description	Unused	Used
91	S	50 r. on 65 r. blue	1·00	95

1911. "King Carlos" key-type inscr "LOURENCO MARQUES" optd **REPUBLICA**.

No.	Type	Description	Unused	Used
92	S	2½ r. grey	10	10
93		5 r. orange	10	10
94		10 r. green	15	15
95		15 r. green	15	15
96		20 r. lilac	30	20
97		25 r. red	20	15
98		50 r. brown	35	25
99		75 r. purple	35	25
100		100 r. blue on blue	35	25
178		115 r. brown on pink	35	35
102		130 r. brown on yellow	30	25
103		200 r. purple on pink	30	25
104		400 r. blue on yellow	50	35
105		500 r. black on blue	60	50
106		700 r. mauve on yellow	80	50

1913. Surch **REPUBLICA LOURENCO MARQUES** and value on "Vasco da Gama" issues of (a) Portuguese Colonies.

No.	Description	Unused	Used
107	¼ c. on 2½ r. green	50	45
108	½ c. on 5 r. red	50	45
109	1 c. on 10 r. purple	50	45
110	2½ c. on 25 r. green	50	45
111	5 c. on 50 r. blue	50	45
112	7½ c. on 75 r. brown	1·25	85
113	10 c. on 100 r. brown	65	45
114	15 c. on 150 r. brown	65	45

(b) Macao.

No.	Description	Unused	Used
115	¼ c. on ½ a. green	60	45
116	½ c. on 1 a. red	60	45
117	1 c. on 2 a. purple	60	45
118	2½ c. on 4 a. green	60	45
119	5 c. on 8 a. blue	60	45
120	7½ c. on 12 a. brown	1·00	85
121	10 c. on 16 a. brown	75	45
122	15 c. on 24 a. brown	75	45

(c) Timor.

No.	Description	Unused	Used
123	¼ c. on ½ a. green	60	45
124	½ c. on 1 a. red	60	45
125	1 c. on 2 a. purple	60	45
126	2½ c. on 4 a. green	60	45
127	5 c. on 8 a. blue	60	45
128	7½ c. on 12 a. brown	1·00	90
129	10 c. on 16 a. brown	80	45
130	15 c. on 24 a. brown	80	45

1914. "Ceres" key-type inscr "LOURENCO MARQUES".

No.	Type	Description	Unused	Used
147	U	¼ c. green	10	10
148		½ c. black	10	10
149		1 c. green	10	10
150		1½ c. brown	15	15
151		2 c. red	15	15
152		2½ c. violet	15	15
153		5 c. blue	15	15
154		7½ c. brown	15	15
155	U	8 c. grey	15	15
140		10 c. red	80	40
157		15 c. purple	35	35
142		20 c. green	45	35
143		30 c. brown on green	70	50
144		40 c. brown on pink	2·50	2·00
145		50 c. orange on orange	1·00	90
146		1 e. green on blue	1·10	90

1914. Provisionals of 1902 overprinted **REPUBLICA**.

No.	Type	Description	Unused	Used
166	R	115 r. on 10 r. mauve	30	30
167		115 r. on 200 r. blue on bl	35	30
168		115 r. on 300 r. blue on brown	30	30
161		130 r. on 25 r. green	50	40
164		130 r. on 80 r. green	50	40
169		130 r. on 150 r. red on pink	30	30
184		400 r. on 50 r. blue	80	45
185		400 r. on 75 r. pink	80	25

1915. Nos. 93 and 148 perf diagonally and each half surch ¼.

No.	Type	Description	Unused	Used
170	S	¼ on half of 5 r. orange	1·40	1·10
171	U	¼ on half of ½ c. black	1·40	1·10

Prices of Nos. 170/1 are for whole stamps.

1915. Surch **Dois centavos**.

No.	Type	Description	Unused	Used
172	S	2 c. on 15 r. (No. 83)	45	35
173		2 c. on 15 c. (No. 95)	45	35

1918. Red Cross Fund. "Ceres" key-type inscr "LOURENCO MARQUES", optd **9-3-18** and Red Cross or surch with value in figures and bars also.

No.	Type	Description	Unused	Used
188	U	¼ c. green	85	85
189		½ c. black	85	85
190		1 c. green	85	85
191		2½ c. violet	85	85
192a		5 c. blue	85	85
193		10 c. red	1·75	85
194		20 c. on 1½ c. brown	1·75	85
195		30 c. brown on green	1·75	1·50
196		40 c. on 2 c. red	1·75	1·50
197		50 c. on 7½ c. brown	1·75	1·50
198		70 c. on 8 c. grey	1·75	1·50
199		1 e. on 15 c. purple	1·75	1·50

1920. No. 166 surch **Um quarto de centavo**.

No.	Type	Description	Unused	Used
200	R	¼ c. on 115 r. on 10 r. mauve	30	20

1920. No. 152 surch in figures or words.

No.	Type	Description	Unused	Used
201	U	1 c. on 2½ c. violet	20	15
202		1½ c. on 2½ c. violet	20	15
203		4 c. on 2½ c. violet	20	15

For other surcharges on "Ceres" key-type of Lourenco Marques, see Mozambique Nos. 309/10 and Nos. D44 and 46.

NEWSPAPER STAMPS

1893. "Newspaper" key-type inscr "LOURENCO MARQUES".

No.	Type	Description	Unused	Used
N1	V	2½ r. brown	15	15

1895. 700th Death Anniv of St. Anthony. "Newspaper" key-type inscr "MOCAMBIQUE" optd **L. MARQUES CENTENARIO DE S. ANTONIO MDCCCXCV**.

No.	Type	Description	Unused	Used
N36	V	2½ r. brown	2·25	1·90

LUBECK Pt. 7

Formerly one of the free cities of the Hanseatic League. In 1868 joined the North German Confederation.

16 schilling = 1 mark

1

3

1859. Imperf.

No.	Type	Description	Unused	Used
9	1	½ s. lilac	12·00	£1400
10		1 s. orange	27·00	£1400
3		2 s. brown	14·00	£225
4		2½ s. red	38·00	£650
6		4 s. green	13·00	£350

1863. Rouletted.

No.	Type	Description	Unused	Used
11	3	½ s. green	35·00	80·00
13		1 s. orange	£120	£140
14		2 s. red	18·00	55·00
16		2½ s. blue	45·00	£325
17		4 s. bistre	32·00	£110

4

5

1864. Imperf.

No.	Type	Description	Unused	Used
19	4	1¼ s. brown	22·00	60·00

1865. Roul.

No.	Type	Description	Unused	Used
21	5	1½ s. mauve	20·00	80·00

LUXEMBOURG Pt. 4

An independent Grand Duchy lying between Belgium and the Saar District. Under German Occupation from 1940 to 1944.

1852. 12½ centimes = 1 silver groschen.
100 centimes = 1 franc.
1940. 100 pfennig = 1 reichsmark.
1944. 100 centimes = 1 franc (Belgian).

1 Grand Duke William III

3

4

1852. Imperf.

No.	Type	Description	Unused	Used
2	1	10 c. black	£1900	40·00
3a		1 s. red	£1300	70·00

1859. Imperf or roul.

No.	Type	Description	Unused	Used
23	3	1 c. brown	35·00	4·50
21		1 c. orange	30·00	6·00
17		2 c. black	15·00	13·00
8		4 c. yellow	£180	£170
20		4 c. green	35·00	20·00
10	4	10 c. blue	£190	17·00
24		10 c. purple	£110	2·00
25		10 c. lilac	£120	2·00
28		12½ c. red	£170	5·00
30		20 c. brown	£120	6·00
12		25 c. brown	£375	£250
32		25 c. blue	£800	14·00
13		30 c. purple	£300	£200
14		37½ c. green	£300	£170
35		37½ c. bistre	£500	£250
39		40 c. orange	38·00	80·00

1872. Surch **UN FRANC**. Roul.

No.	Type	Description	Unused	Used
37	4	1 f. on 37½ c. bistre	£900	70·00

1874. Perf.

No.	Type	Description	Unused	Used
64	3	1 c. brown	7·50	4·00
65		2 c. black	7·00	75
42		4 c. green	1·00	8·00
43		5 c. yellow	£170	24·00
67	4	10 c. lilac	£160	70
61		12½ c. red	£190	£180
69		20 c. brown	42·00	15·00
70		25 c. blue	£250	4·00
71		30 c. red	3·50	18·00
55		40 c. orange	50	8·00

1879. Surch **Un Franc**. Perf.

No.	Type	Description	Unused	Used
56	4	1 f. on 37½ c. bistre	7·00	24·00

7 Agriculture and Trade

8 Grand Duke Adolf

9

1882.

No.	Type	Description	Unused	Used
116	7	1 c. grey	15	25
117		2 c. brown	10	20
118		4 c. bistre	35	1·00
119		5 c. green	50	20
120		10 c. red	5·00	20
98		12½ c. blue	1·00	25·00
122		20 c. orange	2·00	2·00
123		25 c. blue	£150	1·60
101		30 c. green	15·00	12·00
124		50 c. brown	65	9·00
103		1 f. lilac	70	25·00
104		5 f. orange	30·00	£160

1891.

No.	Type	Description	Unused	Used
127	8	10 c. red	15	25
145		12½ c. green	50	50
146		20 c. orange	10·00	50
147		25 c. blue	40	30
148		30 c. green	1·00	1·00
149		37½ c. green	2·00	2·00
150		50 c. brown	6·00	2·00
151		1 f. purple	12·00	5·00
135		2½ f. black	1·25	20·00
136		5 f. lake	30·00	65·00

1895.

No.	Type	Description	Unused	Used
152	9	1 c. grey	1·50	30
153		2 c. brown	10	20
154		4 c. bistre	15	1·00
155		5 c. green	1·50	20
156		10 c. red	6·00	20

10

11 Grand Duke William IV

13 Grand Duchess Adelaide

1906.

No.	Type	Description	Unused	Used
157	10	1 c. grey	10	20
158		2 c. brown	10	20
159		4 c. bistre	15	25
160		5 c. green	25	20
231		5 c. mauve	15	20
161		6 c. lilac	10	30
161a		7½ c. orange	10	3·00

162 **11** 10 c. red 80 20
163 12½ slate 1·00 40
164 15 c. brown 1·00 60
165 20 c. orange 1·50 50
166 25 c. blue 50·00 30
166a 30 c. olive 55 50
167 37½ c. green 55 50
168 50 c. brown 3·00 60
169 87½ c. blue 1·00 9·00
170 1 f. purple 4·00 1·50
171 2½ f. red 40·00 80·00
172 5 f. purple 8·00 50·00

1912. Surch **62½ cts.**
173 **11** 62½ c. on 87½ c. blue 1·00 2·00
173a 62½ c. on 2½ f. red 1·50 4·00
173b 62½ c. on 5 f. purple 40 3·00

1914.
174 **13** 10 c. purple 10 20
175 12½ c. green 10 20
176 15 c. brown 10 20
176a 17½ c. brown 10 40
177 25 c. blue 10 20
178 30 c. brown 10 40
179 35 c. blue 10 40
180 37½ c. brown 10 40
181 40 c. red 20 40
182 50 c. grey 20 40
183 62½ c. green 30 3·00
183a 87½ c. orange 30 3·00
184 1 f. brown 2·00 60
185 2½ f. red 40 3·00
186 5 f. violet 8·00 45·00

1916. Surch in figures and bars.
187 **10** 2½ on 5 c. green 10 20
188 3 on 2 c. brown 10 20
212 5 on 1 c. grey 10 20
213 5 on 4 c. bistre 10 40
214 5 on 7½ c. orange 10 20
215 6 on 2 c. brown 20 25
189 **13** 7½ on 10 c. red 10 20
190 17½ on 30 c. brown 10 40
191 20 on 17½ c. brown 10 20
216 25 on 37½ c. sepia 10 20
217 75 on 62½ c. green 10 20
218 80 on 87½ c. orange 10 20
192 87½ on 1 f. brown 50 6·00

17 Grand Duchess Charlotte
18 Vianden Castle

1921. Perf.
194 **17** 2 c. brown 10 20
195 3 c. green 10 20
196 6 c. purple 10 20
197 10 c. green 10 20
193a 15 c. red* 10 20
198 15 c. green 10 20
234 15 c. orange 10 20
199 20 c. orange 10 30
235 20 c. green 10 20
200 25 c. green 10 20
201 30 c. red 10 20
202 40 c. orange 10 20
203 50 c. blue 10 40
236 50 c. red 10 20
204 75 c. red 10 1·10
237 75 c. blue 10 20
205 80 c. black 10 85
206a **18** 1 f. red 10 30
238 1 f. blue 10 50
207 – 2 f. blue 50 50
239 – 2 f. brown 2·00 2·00
208 – 5 f. violet 8·00 8·00
DESIGNS—As Type **18**: 2 f. Factories at Esch; 5 f. Bridge over Alzette.
*No. 193a was originally issued on the occasion of the birth of Crown Prince Jean.
See also Nos. 219/20.

21 Monastery at Clervaux

1921. War Monument Fund.
209 **21** 10 c. + 5 c. green 15 3·50
210 – 15 c. + 10 c. orange 15 6·00
211 – 25 c. + 10 c. green 15 3·50
DESIGNS—HORIZ: 15 c. Pfaffenthal; 25 c. as Type **26**.

1922. Philatelic Exhibition. Imperf.
219 **17** 25 c. green 1·60 5·50
220 30 c. red 1·60 5·50

26 Luxembourg
28 Echternach

1923.
222a **26** 10 f. black 4·00 12·00

1923. Unveiling of War Memorial by Prince Leopold of Belgium. Nos. 209/11 surch **27 mai 1923** and additional values.
223 **21** 10 + 5 + 25 c. green 1·00 15·00
224 – 15 + 10 + 25 c. orange 1·00 20·00
225 – 25 + 10 + 25 c. green 1·00 15·00

1923.
226a **28** 3 f. blue 60 50

1924. Charity. Death of Grand Duchess Marie Adelaide. Surch **CARITAS** and new value.
227 **13** 12½ c. + 7½ c. green 10 3·00
228 35 c. + 10 c. blue 10 3·00
229 2½ f. + 1 f. red 80 30·00
230 5 f. + 2 f. violet 50 20·00

1925. Surch **5**.
240 **17** 5 on 10 c. green 10 20

31
32 Grand Duchess Charlotte

1925. Anti-T.B. Fund.
241 **31** 5 c. + 5 c. violet 10 60
242 30 c. + 5 c. orange 10 3·00
243 50 c. + 5 c. brown 10 6·00
244 1 f. + 10 c. blue 25 15·00

1926.
245 **32** 5 c. mauve 10 20
246 10 c. olive 10 10
246a 15 c. black 10 20
247 20 c. orange 10 30
248 25 c. green 10 30
248a 25 c. brown 10 30
248b 30 c. green 10 30
248c 30 c. violet 30 20
248d 35 c. violet 1·50 30
248e 35 c. green 10 20
249 40 c. brown 10 20
250 50 c. brown 10 20
250a 60 c. green 1·50 20
251 65 c. brown 15 1·40
251a 70 c. violet 10 10
252 75 c. red 10 50
252a 75 c. brown 10 20
253 80 c. brown 15 1·50
253a 90 c. red 50 1·40
254 1 f. black 40 30
254a 1 f. red 40 25
255 1¼ f. blue 10 50
255a 1¼ f. yellow 5·00 1·25
255b 1¼ f. green 30 20
255c 1¼ f. red 10·00 2·00
255d 1½ f. blue 1·00 1·50
255e 1¾ f. blue 70 25

33 Prince Jean
34 Grand Duchess and Prince Felix

1926. Child Welfare.
256 **33** 5 c. + 5 c. black and mauve 10 50
257 40 c. + 10 c. black & green 10 1·00
258 50 c. + 15 c. black & yellow 10 1·00
259 75 c. + 20 c. black & red 20 12·00
260 1 f. 50 c. + 30 c. blk and bl 20 13·00

1927. International Philatelic Exhibition.
261 **34** 25 c. purple 1·00 11·00
262 50 c. green 1·50 17·00
263 75 c. red 1·00 11·00
264 1 f. black 1·00 11·00
265 1½ f. blue 1·00 11·00

35 Princess Elisabeth
37 Clervaux

1927. Child Welfare.
266 **35** 10 c. + 5 c. black and blue 10 50
267 50 c. + 10 black & brown 10 1·00
268 75 c. + 20 c. black & orge 10 1·50
269 1 f. + 30 c. black and red 20 12·00
270 1½ f. + 50 c. black & blue 20 12·00

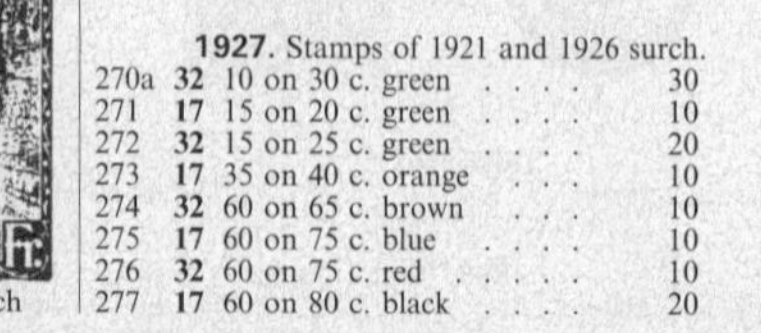

1927. Stamps of 1921 and 1926 surch.
270a **32** 10 on 30 c. green 30 40
271 **17** 15 on 20 c. green 10 20
272 **32** 15 on 25 c. green 20 60
273 **17** 35 on 40 c. orange 10 20
274 **32** 60 on 65 c. brown 10 40
275 **17** 60 on 75 c. blue 10 20
276 **32** 60 on 75 c. red 10 40
277 **17** 60 on 80 c. black 20 40

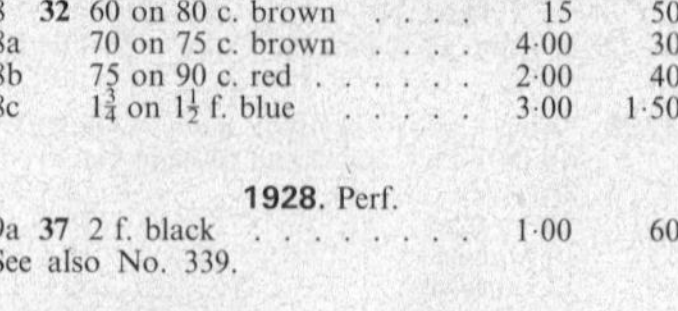

278 **32** 60 on 80 c. brown 15 50
278a 70 on 75 c. brown 4·00 30
278b 75 on 90 c. red 2·00 40
278c 1¾ on 1½ f. blue 3·00 1·50

1928. Perf.
279a **37** 2 f. black 1·00 60
See also No. 339.

38 Princess Marie Adelaide
39 Princess Marie Gabrielle

1928. Child Welfare.
280 **38** 10 c. + 5 c. purple & green 20 1·00
281 60 c. + 10 c. olive & brown 30 3·00
282 75 c. + 15 c. green and red 50 8·00
283 1 f. + 25 c. brown & green 1·50 24·00
284 1½ f. + 50 c. blue & yellow 1·50 24·00

1928. Child Welfare.
285 **39** 10 c. + 10 c. green & brn 20 1·00
286 35 c. + 15 c. brown & grn 1·00 7·00
287 75 c. + 30 c. black and red 1·00 10·00
288 1¼ f. + 50 c. green and red 2·00 24·00
289 1¾ f. + 75 c. black & blue 3·00 30·00

40 Prince Charles
41 Arms of Luxembourg

1930. Child Welfare.
290 **40** 10 c. + 5 c. brown & green 20 1·00
291 75 c. + 10 c. green & brn 1·25 5·00
292 1 f. + 25 c. violet and red 2·50 20·00
293 1¼ f. + 75 c. black & yell 4·00 25·00
294 1¾ f. + 1 f. 50 brown & bl 4·50 25·00

1930.
295 **41** 5 c. red 50 30
296 10 c. green 60 20

42 Biplane over the Alzette
43 Luxembourg, Lower Town

1931. Air.
296a **42** 50 c. green 55 1·00
297 75 c. brown 50 1·00
298 1 f. red 50 1·25
299 1¼ f. purple 50 1·50
300 1¾ f. blue 50 1·50
300a 3 f. black 1·00 6·00

1931.
301 **43** 20 f. green 3·00 18·00

44 Princess Alix
45 Countess Ermesinde
46 Emperor Henry VII

1931. Child Welfare.
302 **44** 10 c. + 5 c. grey & brown 20 1·00
303 75 c. + 10 c. green and red 4·00 15·00
304 1 f. + 25 c. grey and green 7·00 30·00
305 1¼ f. + 75 c. green & violet 7·00 30·00
306 1¾ f. + 1 f. 50 grey & blue 12·00 55·00

1932. Child Welfare.
307 **45** 10 c. + 5 c. brown 30 80
308 75 c. + 10 c. violet 2·00 15·00
309 1 f. + 25 c. red 10·00 35·00
310 1¼ f. + 75 c. lake 10·00 40·00
311 1¾ f. + 1 f. 50 blue 10·00 40·00

1933. Child Welfare.
312 **46** 10 c. + 5 c. brown 30 80
313 75 c. + 10 c. purple 5·00 15·00
314 1 f. + 25 c. red 12·00 40·00
315 1¼ f. + 75 c. brown 15·00 50·00
316 1¾ f. + 1 f. 50 blue 15·00 55·00

47 Gateway of the Three Towers
48 Arms of John the Blind

1934.
317 **47** 5 f. green 1·00 7·50

1934. Child Welfare.
318 **48** 10 c. + 5 c. violet 10 1·00
319 35 c. + 10 c. green 2·50 10·00
320 75 c. + 15 c. red 2·50 10·00
321 1 f. + 25 c. red 15·00 50·00
322 1¼ f. + 75 c. orange 15·00 50·00
323 1¾ f. + 1½ f. blue 15·00 50·00

50 Surgeon

1935. International Relief Fund for Intellectuals.
324 – 5 c. violet 15 1·40
325 – 10 c. red 30 1·40
326 – 15 c. olive 30 2·00
327 – 20 c. orange 45 2·50
328 – 35 c. green 80 3·50
329 – 50 c. black 90 5·00
330 – 70 c. green 1·50 6·00
331 **50** 1 f. red 1·00 7·00
332 – 1 f. 25 turquoise 8·00 55·00
333 – 1 f. 75 blue 10·00 55·00
334 – 2 f. brown 30·00 £120
335 – 3 f. brown 40·00 £160
336 – 5 f. blue 70·00 £300
337 – 10 f. purple £180 £500
338 **50** 20 f. green £200 £600
DESIGNS — HORIZ: 5 c., 10 f. Schoolteacher; 15 c., 3 f. Journalist; 20 c. 1 f. 75, Engineer; 35 c., 1 f. 25, Chemist. VERT: 10 c., 2 f. "The Arts"; 50 c., 5 f. Barrister; 70 c. University.
This set was sold at the P.O. at double face value.

1935. Esch Philatelic Exhibition. Imperf.
339 **37** 2 f. (+ 50 c.) black 5·00 16·00

52 Vianden

1935.
340 **52** 10 f. green 1·40 12·00

53 Charles I
54 Town Hall

1935. Child Welfare.
341 **53** 10 c. + 5 c. violet 10 40
342 35 c. + 10 c. green 30 60
343 70 c. + 20 c. brown 1·00 1·50
344 1 f. + 25 c. red 14·00 40·00
345 1 f. 25 + 75 c. brown 14·00 40·00
346 1 f. 75 + 1 f. 50 blue 14·00 50·00

1936. 11th Int Philatelic Federation Congress.
347 **54** 10 c. brown 20 50
348 35 c. green 30 1·00
349 70 c. orange 35 1·50
350 1 f. red 1·00 9·00
351 1 f. 25 violet 2·00 12·00
352 1 f. 75 blue 1·00 10·00

55 Wenceslas I
56 Wenceslas II

1936. Child Welfare.
353 55 10 c. + 5 c. brown 10 30
354 35 c. + 10 c. green 20 60
355 70 c. + 20 c. slate 40 80
356 1 f. + 25 c. red . . . . 2·50 15·00
357 1 f. 25 + 75 c. violet . . . 5·00 30·00
358 1 f. 75 + 1 f. 50 blue . . . 5·00 20·00

1937. Child Welfare.
360 56 10 c. + 5 c. black and red . 10 40
361 35 c. + 10 c. green & pur 20 50
362 70 c. + 20 c. red and blue . 20 50
363 1 f. + 25 c. red and green . 1·00 17·00
364 1 f. 25 + 75 c. purple and brown . . . . 1·50 17·00
365 1 f. 75 + 1 f. 50 blue and black . . . . 2·00 20·00

57 St. Willibrord

61 Sigismond of Luxembourg

1938. Echternach Abbey Restoration Fund (1st issue). 1200th Death Anniv of St. Willibrord.
366 57 35 c. + 10 c. green 25 50
367 – 70 c. + 10 c. black 70 60
368 – 1 f. 25 + 25 c. red . . . . 90 2·50
369 – 1 f. 75 + 50 c. blue . . . . 2·00 3·00
370 – 3 f. + 2 f. red . . . . . 6·00 9·00
371 – 5 f. + 5 f. violet . . . . 6·00 8·00
DESIGNS—As Type **57**: 70 c. Town Hall, Echternach; 1 f. 25, Pavilion, Echternach Municipal Park; 31 × 51 mm. 1 f 75, St. Willibrord (from miniature); 42 × 38 mm: 3 f. Echternach Basilica; 5 f. Whitsuntide dancing procession.
See also Nos. 492/7 and 569/70.

1938. Child Welfare.
372 61 10 c. + 5 c. black & mauve 10 40
373 35 c. + 10 c. black & green 20 50
374 70 c. + 20 c. black & brn 30 50
375 1 f. + 25 c. black and red 2·00 16·00
376 1 f. 25 + 75 c. black & grey 2·00 16·00
377 1 f. 75 + 1 f. 50 black and blue . . . . 3·00 24·00

62 Arms of Luxembourg

63 William I

1939. Centenary of Independence.
378 62 35 c. green 15 20
379 63 50 c. orange 25 20
380 – 70 c. green 10 20
381 – 75 c. olive . . . . 50 1·00
382 – 1 f. red . . . . 1·25 2·00
383 – 1 f. 25 violet 15 20
384 – 1 f. 75 blue 15 20
385 – 3 f. brown 30 50
386 – 5 f. black . . . . 30 8·00
387 – 10 f. red . . . . 1·00 11·00
PORTRAITS—As Type **63**: 70 c. William II; 75 c. William III; 1 f. Prince Henry; 1 f. 25 Grand Duke Adolphe; 1 f. 75 William IV; 3 f. Marie-Anne, wife of William IV; 5 f. Grand Duchess Marie Adelaide; 10 f. Grand Duchess Charlotte.

1939. Surch in figures.
388 32 30 c. on 60 c. green . . . . 10 1·50

65 Allegory of Medicinal Spring

66 Prince Jean

1939. Mondorf-les-Bains Propaganda.
389 65 2 f. red . . . . 30 3·00

MINIMUM PRICE

The minimum price quoted is 10p which represents a handling charge rather than a basis for valuing common stamps. For further notes about prices, see introductory pages.

1939. 20th Anniv of Reign and of Royal Wedding.
390 66 10 c. + 5 c. brn on cream 10 30
391 – 35 c. + 10 c. green on cream 20 1·00
392 – 70 c. + 20 c. black on cream 55 1·50
393 66 1 f. + 25 c. red on cream 4·00 35·00
394 – 1 f. 25 + 75 c. violet on cream 5·00 55·00
395 – 1 f. 75 + 1 f. 50 blue on cream 6·00 70·00
PORTRAITS: 35 c., 1 f. 25, Prince Felix; 70 c., 1 f. 75, Grand Duchess Charlotte.

1940. Anti-T.B. Fund. Surch with Cross of Lorraine and premium.
396 65 2 f. + 50 c. grey . . . . . 1·00 15·00

1940-44. GERMAN OCCUPATION.

1940. T **94** of Germany optd **Luxemburg**.
397 94 3 pf. brown 15 50
398 4 pf. blue 15 60
399 5 pf. green 15 50
400 6 pf. green 15 50
401 8 pf. red 15 50
402 10 pf. brown 15 50
403 12 pf. red 15 20
404 15 pf. purple 50 65
405 20 pf. blue . . . . 50 1·10
406 25 pf. blue . . . . 80 1·00
407 30 pf. green 80 60
408 40 pf. mauve . . . . 80 1·00
409 50 pf. black and green . . 60 1·50
410 60 pf. black and purple . . 2·00 4·00
411 80 pf. black and blue . . . 7·00 20·00
412 100 pf. black and yellow . 2·50 4·00

1940. Types of Luxembourg surch.
413 32 3 Rpf. on 15 c. black . . . 10 50
414 4 Rpf. on 20 c. orange . . 10 50
415 5 Rpf. on 35 c. green . . . 10 50
416 6 Rpf. on 10 c. green . . . 10 50
417 8 Rpf. on 25 c. brown . . 10 50
418 10 Rpf. on 40 c. brown . . 10 50
419 12 Rpf. on 60 c. green . . 10 50
420 15 Rpf. on 1 f. red . . . . 40 4·00
421 20 Rpf. on 50 c. brown . . 10 1·00
422 25 Rpf. on 5 c. mauve . . 80 4·00
423 30 Rpf. on 70 c. violet . . 15 1·00
424 40 Rpf. on 75 c. brown . . 15 1·00
425 50 Rpf. on 1¼ f. greeen . . 15 1·00
426 65 60 Rpf. on 2 f. red . . . 3·50 24·00
427 47 80 Rpf. on 5 f. green . . . 50 3·25
428 52 100 Rpf. on 10 f. green . . . 50 3·25

1941. Nos. 739/47 of Germany optd **Luxemburg**.
429 3 pf. + 2 pf. brown 50 75
430 4 pf. + 3 pf. blue 50 75
431 5 pf. + 3 pf. green 50 75
432 6 pf. + 4 pf. green 50 75
433 8 pf. + 4 pf. orange 50 75
434 12 pf. + 6 pf. red 50 75
435 15 pf. + 10 pf. purple . . . 3·50 9·00
436 25 pf. + 15 pf. blue . . . 3·50 9·00
437 40 pf. + 35 pf. purple . . . 3·50 9·00

1944. INDEPENDENCE REGAINED.

70 Grand Duchess Charlotte

71 "Britannia"

1944.
438 70 5 c. brown 10 10
439 10 c. slate 10 10
440 20 c. orange 20 10
441 25 c. brown 10 10
442 30 c. red 30 30
443 35 c. green 15 30
444 40 c. blue 30 30
445 50 c. violet 10 10
445a 60 c. orange . . . . 1·50 15
446 70 c. red 15 20
447 70 c. green . . . . 50 1·00
448 75 c. brown 30 20
449 1 f. olive 10 10
450 1¼ f. orange 20 20
451 1½ f. orange 30 15
452 1¾ f. blue 30 30
453 2 f. red . . . . 3·50 15
454 2½ f. mauve . . . . 5·00 5·00
455 3 f. green 50 50
456 3½ f. blue 60 85
457 5 f. green 20 20
458 10 f. red . . . . 30 1·40
459 20 f. blue . . . . 50 20·00

1945. Liberation.
460 – 60 c. + 1 f. 40 green . . . 10 20
461 – 1 f. 20 + 1 f. 80 red . . . 10 20
462 71 2 f. 50 + 3 f. 50 blue . . . 10 20
463 – 4 f. 20 + 4 f. 80 violet . . 10 20
DESIGNS: 60 c. Ship symbol of Paris between Cross of Lorraine and Arms of Luxembourg; 1 f. 20, Man killing snake between Arms of Russia and Luxembourg; 4 f. 20, Eagle between Arms of U.S.A. and Luxembourg.

72 Statue of the Madonna in Procession

74 Lion of Luxembourg

73 Altar and Shrine of the Madonna

1945. Our Lady of Luxembourg.
464 72 60 c. + 40 c. green 20 80
465 – 1 f. 20 + 80 c. red 20 80
466 – 2 f. 50 + 2 f. 50 blue . . . 30 5·00
467 – 5 f. 50 + 6 f. 50 violet . . 1·25 70·00
468 73 20 f. + 20 f. brown . . . . 1·25 70·00
DESIGNS: As Type **72**: 1 f. 20, The Madonna; 2 f. 50, The Madonna and Luxembourg; 5 f. 50, Portal of Notre Dame Cathedral.

1945.
469 74 20 c. black 20 20
470 30 c. green 20 20
470a 60 c. violet 30 20
471 75 c. brown 30 20
472 1 f. 20 red 20 20
473 1 f. 50 violet 20 20
474 2 f. 50 blue 30 30

75 Members of the Maquis

76

1945. National War Victims Fund.
475 75 20 c. + 30 c. green & buff 20 1·00
476 – 1 f. 50 + 1 f. red and buff 20 1·00
477 – 3 f. 50 + 3 f. 50 blue & buff 40 10·00
478 – 5 f. + 10 f. brown & buff 30 10·00
DESIGNS: 1 f. 50, Mother and children; 3 f. 50, Political prisoner; 5 f. Executed civilian.

1946. Air.
479 – 1 f. green and blue 20 20
480 76 2 f. brown and yellow . . . 20 20
481 – 3 f. brown and yellow . . . 20 20
482 – 4 f. violet and grey 30 30
483 76 5 f. purple and yellow . . . 25 25
484 – 6 f. purple and blue 30 30
485 – 10 f. brown and yellow . . 1·50 30
486 76 20 f. blue and grey . . . . 1·75 1·00
487 – 50 f. green and light green . 3·50 1·50
DESIGNS: 1, 4, 10 f. Airplane wheel; 3, 6, 50 f. Airplane engine and castle.

77 John the Blind, King of Bohemia

78 Exterior Ruins of St. Willibrord Basilica

79 St. Willibrord

1946. 600th Death Anniv of John the Blind.
488 77 60 c. + 40 c. green & grey 15 1·50
489 1 f. 50 + 50 c. red & buff 25 2·00
490 3 f. 50 + 3 f. 50 blue & grey 2·00 26·00
491 5 f. + 10 f. brown & grey 1·00 22·00

1947. Echternach Abbey Restoration (2nd issue). Inscr "ECHTERNACH".
492 78 20 c. + 10 c. black 30 30
493 – 60 c. + 10 c. green 60 50
494 – 75 c. + 25 c. red . . . . 1·00 80
495 – 1 f. 50 c. + 50 c. brown . . 1·25 80
496 – 3 f. 50 c. + 2 f. 50 blue . . 6·00 5·00
497 79 25 f. + 25 f. purple . . . 32·00 25·00
DESIGNS—As Type **78**: 60 c. Statue of Abbot Bertels; 75 c. Echternach Abbey emblem; 1 f. 50, Ruined interior of Basilica; 3 f. 50, St. Irmine and Pepin II carrying model of Abbey.

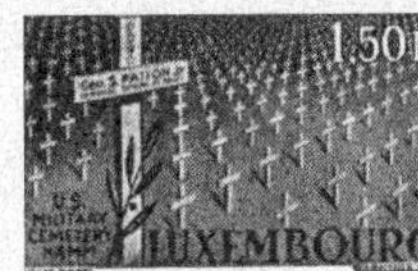

80 U.S. Military Cemetery, Hamm

82 Michel Lentz (national poet)

1947. Honouring Gen. George S. Patton.
498 80 1 f. 50 red and buff 50 20
499 – 3 f. 50 blue and buff . . . 2·50 3·00
500 80 5 f. green and grey . . . . 2·50 2·00
501 – 10 f. purple and grey . . . 11·00 40·00
PORTRAIT: 3 f. 50, 10 f. Gen. G. S. Patton.

1947. National Welfare Fund.
502 82 60 c. + 40 c. brown & buff 55 60
503 1 f. 50 + 50 c. pur & buff 80 60
504 3 f. 50 + 3 f. 50 blue & grey 6·50 20·00
505 10 f. + 5 f. green and grey 6·00 20·00

83 L'Oesling

85 "Dicks" (Edmund de la Fontaine)

1948. Tourist Propaganda.
505a – 2 f. 50 brown & chocolate 1·50 40
505b – 3 f. violet . . . . 6·00 1·25
505c – 4 f. blue . . . . 4·00 1·25
506 83 7 f. brown . . . . 20·00 80
507 – 10 f. green . . . . 2·50 20
508 – 15 f. red . . . . 2·50 40
509 – 20 f. blue . . . . 2·50 40
DESIGNS—HORIZ: 2 f. 50, Television transmitter, Dudelange; 3 f. Radio Luxembourg; 4 f. Victor Hugo's house, Vianden; 10 f. River Moselle; 15 f. Mining district. VERT: 20 f. Luxembourg.

1948. National Welfare Fund.
510 85 60 c. + 40 c. brown & bis 45 50
511 1 f. 50 + 50 c. red & pink 60 70
512 3 f. 50 + 3 f. 50 blue & grey 9·50 18·00
513 10 f. + 5 f. green and grey 8·50 18·00

86 Grand Duchess Charlotte

87 Date-stamp and Map

1948.
513a 86 5 c. orange 10 10
513b 10 c. blue 10 10
514 15 c. olive 15 10
514a 20 c. purple 20 10
515 25 c. grey 20 10
515a 30 c. olive 20 10
515b 40 c. red 30 30
515c 50 c. orange 40 15
516 60 c. bistre 30 20
517 80 c. green 30 20
518 1 f. red . . . . 1·00 10
518a 1 f. 20 black . . . . 1·00 30
518b 1 f. 25 brown . . . . 1·00 40
519 1 f. 50 turquoise . . . . . 1·00 10
520 1 f. 60 grey . . . . 1·00 1·00
521 2 f. purple . . . . 1·00 10
521a 2 f. 50 red . . . . 1·50 10
521b 3 f. blue . . . . 12·00 40
521c 3 f. 50 red . . . . 3·50 40
522 4 f. blue . . . . 3·50 40
522a 5 f. violet . . . . 9·50 40
523 6 f. purple . . . . 7·00 40
524 8 f. green . . . . 5·00 80

1949. 75th Anniv of U.P.U.
525 87 80 c. green, lt green & black 50 60
526 2 f. 50 red, pink and black 2·50 1·50
527 4 f. ultramarine, blue & black 5·00 6·00
528 8 f. brown, buff and black 17·00 32·00

88 Michel Rodange

89 Young Girl

1949. National Welfare Fund.
529 88 60 c. + 40 c. green & grey 50 50
530 2 f. + 1 f. purple & claret 5·00 6·00
531 4 f. + 2 f. blue and grey 9·00 12·00
532 10 f. + 5 f. brown & buff 9·00 14·00

1950. War Orphans Relief Fund.

533	–	60 c. + 15 c. turquoise	2·00	50
534	**89**	1 f. + 20 c. red	5·00	1·25
535	–	2 f. + 30 c. brown	3·00	1·25
536	**89**	4 f. + 75 c. blue	12·00	15·00
537	–	8 f. + 3 f. black	32·00	40·00
538	**89**	10 f. + 5 f. purple	32·00	40·00

DESIGN: 60 c., 2 f., 8 f. Mother and boy.

90 J. A. Zinnen (composer)

91 Ploughman and Factories

1950. National Welfare Week.

539	**90**	60 c. + 10 c. violet & grey	55	30
540		2 f. + 15 c. red and buff	1·00	40
541		4 f. + 15 c. blue and grey	7·00	7·00
542		8 f. + 5 f. brown and buff	20·00	28·00

1951. To Promote United Europe.

543	**91**	80 c. green and light green	10·00	10·00
544	–	1 f. violet and light violet	5·00	50
545	–	2 f. brown and grey	25·00	50
546	**91**	2 f. 50 red and orange	25·00	20·00
547	–	3 f. brown and yellow	40·00	30·00
548	–	4 f. blue and light blue	60·00	40·00

DESIGNS: 1, 3 f. Map, people and "Rights of Man" Charter; 2, 4 f. Scales balancing "United Europe" and "Peace".

92 L. Menager (composer)

1951. National Welfare Fund.

549	**92**	60 c. + 10 c. black & grey	40	40
550		2 f. + 15 c. green and grey	40	40
551		4 f. + 15 c. blue and grey	5·00	4·00
552		8 f. + 5 f. purple and grey	25·00	32·00

92a T **1** and **86**

92b T **1**

1952. National Philatelic Exhibition ("CENTILUX") and Stamp Centenary.

552a	**92a**	80 c. black, purple and green (air)	50	50
552b		2 f. 50 black, pur & red	80	1·50
552c		4 f. black, purple & blue	1·75	3·00
552d		8 f. black, purple & red	35·00	55·00
552e		10 f. black, purple & brn	24·00	45·00
552f	**92b**	2 f. black and green (postage)	30·00	35·00
552g		4 f. red and green	30·00	35·00

93 Hurdling

1952. 15th Olympic Games, Helsinki.

553	**93**	1 f. black and green	60	30
554	–	2 f. black and light brown (Football)	3·00	30
555	–	2 f. 50 black and pink (Boxing)	4·00	1·60
556	–	3 f. blk & drab (Water polo)	5·00	1·60
557	–	4 f. black & blue (Cycling)	25·00	7·00
558	–	8 f. black & lilac (Fencing)	16·00	4·50

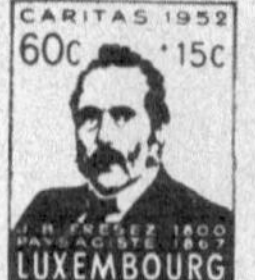

94 J. B. Fresez (painter)

95 Prince Jean and Princess Josephine Charlotte

1952. National Welfare Fund.

559	**94**	60 c. + 15 c. green & blue	40	40
560		2 f. + 25 c. brown & orange	40	40
561		4 f. + 25 c. violet and grey	4·00	4·00
562		8 f. + 4 f. 75 purple & lt pur	30·00	32·00

1953. Royal Wedding.

563	**95**	80 c. violet & deep mauve	45	35
564		1 f. 20 deep brown & brown	45	35
565		2 f. deep green and green	1·50	35
566		3 f. deep purple and purple	1·50	50
567		4 f. deep blue and blue	7·00	1·00
568		9 f. brown and red	7·00	1·00

96 Echternach Basilica

97 Pierre D'Aspelt

1953. Echternach Abbey Restoration (3rd issue).

569	**96**	2 f. red	4·00	35
570	–	2 f. 50 olive	6·00	6·00

DESIGN: 2 f. 50, Interior of Basilica.

1953. 7th Birth Centenary of Pierre D'Aspelt.

571	**97**	4 f. black	8·00	5·00

98 "Candlemas Singing"

99 Foils, Mask and Gauntlet

1953. National Welfare Fund.

572	**98**	25 c. + 15 c. carmine and red	30	40
573	–	80 c. + 20 c. blue & brown	30	40
574	–	1 f. 20 + 30 c. green & turq	70	80
575	**98**	2 f. + 25 c. brown and red	60	40
576	–	4 f. + 50 c. blue & turquoise	6·00	7·00
577	–	7 f. + 3 f. 35 lilac & violet	19·00	22·00

DESIGNS: 80 c., 4 f. "The Rattles"; 1 f. 20, 7 f. "The Easter-eggs".

1954. World Fencing Championships.

578	**99**	2 f. deep brown and brown on cream	4·00	80

100 Fair Emblem

101 Earthenware Whistle

1954. Luxembourg International Fair.

579	**100**	4 f. multicoloured	10·00	4·00

1954. National Welfare Fund.

580	**101**	25 c. + 5 c. red & orange	40	50
581	–	80 c. + 20 c. grey & black	40	50
582	–	1 f. 20 + 30 c. green and cream	1·50	1·50
583	**101**	2 f. + 25 c. brown & buff	60	60
584	–	4 f. + 50 c. dp blue & blue	7·00	7·00
585	–	7 f. + 3 f. 45 violet & mve	23·00	27·00

DESIGNS: 80 c., 4 f. Sheep and drum; 1 f. 20, 7 f. Merry-go-round horses.

102 Tulips

103

1955. Mondorf-les-Bains Flower Show.

586	**102**	80 c. red, green & brown	30	30
587	–	2 f. yellow, green and red	40	30
588	–	3 f. purple, green & emer	3·50	3·50
589	–	4 f. orange, green & blue	5·50	5·50

FLOWERS: 2 f. Daffodils; 3 f. Hyacinths; 4 f. Parrot tulips.

1955. 1st National Crafts Exhibition.

590	**103**	2 f. black and grey	1·50	25

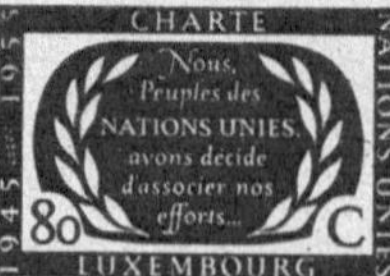

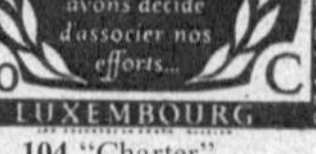

104 "Charter"

105 "Christmas Day"

1955. 10th Anniv of U.N.

591	**104**	80 c. blue and black	45	50
592	–	2 f. brown and red	5·00	15
593	–	4 f. red and blue	4·00	4·00
594	–	9 f. green and brown	2·00	1·00

SYMBOLIC DESIGNS: 2 f. "Security"; 4 f. "Justice"; 9 f. "Assistance".

1955. National Welfare Fund.

595	–	25 c. + 5 c. red and pink	30	30
596	**105**	80 c. + 20 c. black & grey	30	30
597	–	1 f. 20 + 30 c. deep green and green	60	80
598	–	2 f. + 25 c. deep brown and brown	60	30
599	**105**	4 f. + 50 c. blue & lt blue	6·00	11·00
600	–	7 f. + 3 f. 45 pur & mve	14·00	16·00

ALLEGORICAL DESIGNS: 25 c., 2 f. "St. Nicholas's Day"; 1 f. 20, 7 f. "Twelfth Night".

1956. Mondorf-les-Bains Flower Show. As T **102** but inscription at top in one line. Multicoloured.

601	2 f. Anemones	65	30
602	3 f. Crocuses	2·50	2·50

1956. Roses. As T **102** but inscr at top "LUXEMBOURG-VILLE DES ROSES". Multicoloured.

603	2 f. 50 Yellow roses	5·50	5·00
604	4 f. Red roses	2·50	2·50

108 Steel Plant and Girder

109 Blast Furnaces and Map

1956. 50th Anniv of Esch-sur-Alzette.

605	**108**	2 f. red, black and turq	2·50	40

1956. European Coal and Steel Community. Inscr as in T **109**.

606	**109**	2 f. red	30·00	40
607	–	3 f. blue	30·00	24·00
608	–	4 f. green	6·00	5·00

DESIGNS—VERT: 3 f. Girder supporting City of Luxembourg. HORIZ: 4 f. Chain and miner's lamp.

110

111 Luxembourg Central Station

1956. Europa.

609	**110**	2 f. black and brown	£225	25
610		3 f. red and orange	40·00	40·00
611		4 f. deep blue and blue	3·00	3·00

1956. Electrification of Luxembourg Railways.

612	**111**	2 f. sepia and black	3·00	50

112 I. de la Fontaine

113 Arms of Echternach

1956. Council of State Centenary. Inscr as in T **112**.

613	**112**	2 f. sepia	1·50	30
614	–	7 f. purple	3·00	80

DESIGN: 7 f. Grand Duchess Charlotte.

1956. National Welfare Fund. Inscr "CARITAS 1956". Arms. Multicoloured.

615	25 c. + 5 c. Type **113**	25	30
616	80 c. + 20 c. Esch-sur-Alzette	25	30
617	1 f. 20 + 30 c. Grevenmacher	30	80
618	2 f. + 25 c. Type **113**	25	30
619	4 f. + 50 c. Esch-sur-Alzette	4·00	5·00
620	7 f. + 3 f. 45 Grevenmacher	8·00	13·00

114 Lord Baden-Powell and Scout Emblems

115 Prince Henri

1957. Birth Centenary of Lord Baden-Powell, and 50th Anniv of Scouting Movement.

621	**114**	2 f. brown and green	1·00	30
622	–	2 f. 50 red and violet	2·50	3·75

DESIGN: 2 f. 50, as Type **114** but showing Girl Guide emblems.

1957. "Prince Jean and Princess Josephine-Charlotte Foundation" Child Welfare Clinic.

623	**115**	2 f. dp brown and brown	1·00	20
624	–	3 f. dp green and green	4·00	4·00
625	–	4 f. deep blue and blue	2·00	3·00

DESIGNS—HORIZ: 3 f. Children's Clinic Project. VERT: 4 f. Princess Marie-Astrid.

116 "Peace"

117 Fair Entrance and Flags

1957. Europa.

626	**116**	2 f. brown	2·00	15
627		3 f. red	35·00	18·00
628		4 f. purple	30·00	16·00

1957. National Welfare Fund. Arms as T **113** inscr "CARITAS 1957". Multicoloured.

629	25 c. + 5 c. Luxembourg	30	40
630	80 c. + 20 c. Mersch	30	40
631	1 f. 20 + 30 c. Vianden	40	50
632	2 f. + 25 c. Luxembourg	30	30
633	4 f. + 50 c. Mersch	4·50	5·50
634	7 f. + 3 f. 45 Vianden	5·50	8·00

1958. 10th Anniv of Luxembourg Int Fair.

635	**117**	2 f. multicoloured	15	15

118 Luxembourg Pavilion

119 St. Willibrord holding Child (after Puseel)

1958. Brussels Exhibition.

636	**118**	2 f. 50 blue and red	15	15

1958. 1300th Birth Anniv of St. Willibrord.

637	–	1 f. red	20	30
638	**119**	2 f. 50 sepia	25	15
639	–	5 f. blue	1·00	90

DESIGNS: 1 f. St. Willibrord and St. Irmina holding inscribed plaque; 5 f. St. Willibrord and Suppliant. (Miracle of the wine-cask).

119a Europa

120 Open-air Theatre at Wiltz

1958. Europa.

640	**119a**	2 f. 50 blue and red	15	15
641		3 f. 50 brown and green	20	25
642		5 f. red and blue	80	75

1958. Wiltz Open-air Theatre Commemoration.

643	**120**	2 f. 50 sepia and grey	60	15

121 Vineyard

122 Grand Duchess Charlotte

1958. Bimillenary of Moselle Wine Industry.
644 **121** 2 f. 50 brown and green . . . 60 15

1958. National Welfare Fund. Arms as T **113** inscr "CARITAS 1958". Multicoloured.
645 30 c. + 10 c. Capellen 30 30
646 1 f. + 25 c. Diekirch 30 30
647 1 f. 50 + 25 c. Redange . . . 50 50
648 2 f. 50 + 50 c. Capellen . . . 30 30
649 5 f. + 50 c. Diekirch . . . . 4·50 5·00
650 8 f. 50 + 4 f. 60 Redange . . 5·00 8·00

1959. 40th Anniv of Accession of Grand Duchess Charlotte.
651 **122** 1 f. 50 dp green and green 80 25
652 2 f. 50 brown and lt brown 80 20
653 5 f. lt blue & ultramarine 1·60 1·25

123 N.A.T.O. Emblem

123a Europa

1959. 10th Anniv of N.A.T.O.
654 **123** 2 f. 50 blue and olive . . 15 10
655 8 f. 50 blue and brown . . 40 40

1959. Mondorf-les-Bains Flower Show. As T **102** but inscr "1959".
656 1 f. violet, yellow and turquoise 25 30
657 2 f. 50 red, green and blue . . 30 20
658 3 f. blue, green and purple . . 50 70
FLOWERS: 1 f. Iris; 2 f. 50, Peony; 3 f. Hortensia.

1959. Europa.
659 **123a** 2 f. 50 green 40 15
660 5 f. blue 90 75

124 Early Locomotive and First Bars of Hymn "De Feierwon"

1959. Railways Centenary.
661 **124** 2 f. 50 blue and red . . . 2·00 40

1959. National Welfare Fund. Arms as T **113** inscr "CARITAS 1959". Multicoloured.
662 30 c. + 10 c. Clervaux 30 30
663 1 f. + 25 c. Remich 30 30
664 1 f. 50 + 25 c. Wiltz 50 50
665 2 f. 50 + 50 c. Clervaux . . . 30 30
666 5 f. + 50 c. Remich . . . . . 1·50 2·00
667 8 f. 50 + 4 f. 60 Wiltz . . . . 7·00 12·00

125 Refugees seeking Shelter

126 Steel Worker

1960. World Refugee Year.
668 **125** 2 f. 50 blue and salmon . . 15 15
669 – 5 f. blue and violet 20 35
DESIGN—HORIZ: 5 f. "The Flight into Egypt" (Biblical scene).

1960. 10th Anniv of Schuman Plan.
670 **126** 2 f. 50 lake 20 15

127 European School, Luxembourg

128 Grand Duchess Charlotte

1960. European School Commemoration.
671 **127** 5 f. black and blue . . . 1·00 1·00

1960.
672 **128** 10 c. red 10 20
673 20 c. red 10 20
673a 25 c. orange 20 20
674 30 c. drab 10 20
675 50 c. green 50 20
676 1 f. violet 50 10
677 1 f. 50 mauve 50 15
678 2 f. turquoise 60 10
679 2 f. 50 purple . . . . . 1·00 15
680 3 f. dull purple . . . . 2·50 10
680a 3 f. 50 turquoise . . . 3·00 2·50
681 5 f. brown . . . . . . 1·50 20
681a 6 f. turquoise . . . . . 2·50 20

129 Heraldic Lion, and Tools

1960. 2nd National Crafts Exhibition.
682 **129** 2 f. 50 multicoloured . . 1·60 20

129a Conference Emblem

130 Princess Marie-Astrid

1960. Europa.
683 **129a** 2 f. 50 green and black . . 20 15
684 5 f. black and red . . . 60 25

1960. National Welfare Fund. Inscr "CARITAS 1960". Centres and inscr in sepia.
685 **130** 30 c. + 10 c. blue . . . 20 20
686 – 1 f. + 25 c. pink 20 20
687 – 1 f. 50 + 25 c. turquoise 40 50
688 **130** 2 f. 50 + 50 c. yellow . . 35 25
689 – 5 f. + 50 c. lilac . . . . 1·00 2·50
690 – 8 f. 50 + 4 f. 60 sage . . 10·00 13·00
DESIGNS: Princess Marie-Astrid standing (1, 5 f.), sitting with book on lap (1 f. 50, 8 f. 50).

131 Great Spotted Woodpecker

132 Patton Monument, Ettelbruck

1961. Animal Protection Campaign. Inscr "PROTECTION DES ANIMAUX".
691 **131** 1 f. multicoloured 50 15
692 – 1 f. 50 buff, blue and black 25 25
693 – 3 f. brown, buff and violet 40 40
694 – 8 f. 50 multicoloured . . 70 50
DESIGNS—VERT: 8 f. 50, Dachshund. HORIZ: 1 f. 50, Cat; 3 f. Horse.

1961. Tourist Publicity.
695 **132** 2 f. 50 blue and black . . 60 20
696 – 2 f. 50 green 60 20
DESIGN—VERT: No. 696, Clervaux.

133 Doves

134 Prince Henri

1961. Europa.
697 **133** 2 f. 50 red 10 10
698 5 f. blue 20 20

1961. National Welfare Fund. Inscr "CARITAS 1961". Centres and inscr in sepia.
699 **134** 30 c. + 10 c. mauve . . 20 20
700 – 1 f. + 25 c. lavender . . 20 20
701 – 1 f. 50 + 25 c. salmon . . 35 45
702 **134** 2 f. 50 + 50 c. green . . 35 30
703 – 5 f. + 50 c. yellow . . . 2·50 3·00
704 – 8 f. 50 + 4 f. 60 grey . . 4·50 7·00
DESIGNS: Prince Henri when young boy (1, 5 f.); youth in formal dress (1 f. 50, 8 f. 50).

MINIMUM PRICE
The minimum price quoted is 10p which represents a handling charge rather than a basis for valuing common stamps. For further notes about prices, see introductory pages.

135 Cyclist carrying Cycle

136 Europa "Tree"

1962. World Cross-country Cycling Championships, Esch-sur-Alzette.
705 **135** 2 f. 50 multicoloured . . . 30 15
706 – 5 f. multicoloured (Emblem) 30 40

1962. Europa.
707 **136** 2 f. 50 multicoloured . . . 15 10
708 5 f. brown, green & purple 15 20

137 St. Laurent's Church, Diekirch

138 Prince Jean and Princess Margaretha as Babies

1962.
709 **137** 2 f. 50 black and brown . . 30 15

1962. National Welfare Fund. inscr "CARITAS 1962". Centres and inscr in sepia.
710 **138** 30 c. + 10 c. buff 20 20
711 – 1 f. + 25 c. blue 20 20
712 – 1 f. 50 + 25 c. olive . . . 30 40
713 – 2 f. 50 + 50 c. pink . . . 30 25
714 – 5 f. + 50 c. green . . . . 1·60 2·50
715 – 8 f. 50 + 4 f. 60 violet . . 3·50 5·50
PORTRAITS—VERT: 1 f., 2 f. 50, Prince Jean and: 2 f. 50, 5 f. Princess Margaretha, at various stages of childhood. HORIZ: 8 f. 50, The Royal Children.

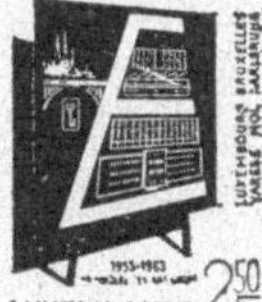

139 Blackboard

140 Benedictine Abbey, Munster

1963. 10th Anniv of European Schools.
716 **139** 2 f. 50 green, red and grey 10 10

1963. Millenary of City of Luxembourg and International Philatelic Exhibition. (a) Horiz views.
717 – 1 f. blue 15 30
718 **140** 1 f. 50 red 15 30
719 – 2 f. 50 green 15 30
720 – 3 f. brown 40 30
721 – 5 f. violet 15 30
722 – 11 f. blue . . . . 1·50 1·75
VIEWS: 1 f. Bock Rock; 2 f. 50, Rham Towers; 3 f. Grand Ducal Palace; 5 f. Castle Bridge; 11 f. Millenary Buildings.

(b) Vert multicoloured designs.
723 1 f. "Three Towers" Gate . . 10 10
724 1 f. 50 Great Seal 15 15
725 2 f. 50 "The Black Virgin" (statue), St. John's Church 15 15
726 3 f. Citadel 15 15
727 5 f. Town Hall 35 70

141 Colpach Castle

142 "Human Rights"

1963. Red Cross Centenary.
728 **141** 2 f. 50 red and slate . . . 15 10

1963. 10th Anniv of European "Human Rights" Convention.
729 **142** 2 f. 50 blue on gold . . . 20 10

143 "Co-operation"

144 Trout snapping Bait

1963. Europa.
730 **143** 3 f. green, orange & turq 20 10
731 6 f. orange, red & brown 20 25

1963. World Fishing Championships, Wormeldange.
732 **144** 3 f. slate 15 15

145 Telephone Dial

146 St. Roch (patron saint of bakers)

1963. Inauguration of Automatic Telephone System.
733 **145** 3 f. green, black and blue 15 15

1963. National Welfare Fund. Patron Saints of Crafts and Guilds. Inscr "CARITAS 1963". Multicoloured.
734 50 c. + 10 c. Type **146** . . . 15 15
735 1 f. + 25 c. St. Anne (tailors) 15 15
736 2 f. + 25 c. St. Eloi (smiths) 15 40
737 3 f. + 50 c. St. Michel (haberdashers) 15 15
738 6 f. + 50 c. St. Barthelemy (butchers) . . . . 1·25 2·00
739 10 f. + 5 f. 90 St. Thibaut (seven crafts) . . . . 2·00 3·00

147 Power House

148 Barge entering Canal

1964. Inauguration of Vianden Reservoir.
740 **147** 2 f. blue, brown and red 20 15
741 – 3 f. light blue, turq & red 20 15
742 – 6 f. brown, blue and green 30 15
DESIGNS—HORIZ: 3 f. Upper reservoir. VERT: 6 f. Lohmuhle Dam.

1964. Inauguration of Moselle Canal.
743 **148** 3 f. indigo and blue . . . 30 15

149 Europa "Flower"

150 Students thronging "New Athenaeum"

1964. Europa.
744 **149** 3 f. blue, brown & cream 15 10
745 6 f. sepia, green & yellow 15 20

1964. Opening of "New Athenaeum" (education centre).
746 **150** 3 f. black and green . . . 10 10

150a King Baudouin, Queen Juliana and Grand Duchess Charlotte

1964. 20th Anniversary of "BENELUX".
747 **150a** 3 f. brown, yellow & blue 10 10

151 Grand Duke Jean and Princess Josephine-Charlotte **152** Three Towers

1964. Accession of Grand Duke Jean.
748 **151** 3 f. deep blue & lt blue . . 30 10
749 6 f. sepia and light brown 30 20

1964. National Welfare Fund. Inscr "CARITAS 1964". Multicoloured.
750 50 c. + 10 c. Type **152** . . . 15 15
751 1 f. + 25 c. Grand Duke Adolphe Bridge 15 15
752 2 f. + 25 c. Lower Town . . 15 15
753 3 f. + 50 c. Type **152** 15 15
754 6 f. + 50 c. Grand Duke Adolphe Bridge . . . . . . 1·00 2·00
755 10 f. + 5 f. 90 Lower Town 1·50 4·50

153 Rotary Emblem and Cogwheels **154** Grand Duke Jean

1965. 60th Anniv of Rotary International.
756 **153** 3 f. multicoloured 15 10

1965.
757 **154** 25 c. brown 10 10
758 50 c. red 10 10
759 1 f. blue 10 10
760 1 f. 50 purple 10 10
761a 2 f. red 10 10
762 2 f. 50 orange 10 10
763a 3 f. green 20 10
763b 3 f. 50 brown 20 20
764a 4 f. purple 20 10
764ba 5 f. green 50 10
765a 6 f. lilac 30 10
765b 7 f. orange 30 10
765c 8 f. blue 50 10
766 9 f. green 40 20
766a 10 f. black 60 10
767 12 f. red . . . . . 1·00 10
767a 14 f. blue 50 40
767b 16 f. green 70 25
767c 18 f. green 80 30
767d 20 f. blue 80 20
767e 22 f. brown 80 60

155 I.T.U. Emblem and Symbols

1965. Centenary of I.T.U.
768 **155** 3 f. blue, lake and violet 10 10

156 Europa "Sprig" **157** "The Roman Lady of the Titelberg"

1965. Europa.
769 **156** 3 f. turquoise, red and black 15 10
770 6 f. brown, blue and green 15 20

1965. National Welfare Fund. Fairy Tales. Inscr "CARITAS 1965". Multicoloured.
771 50 c. + 10 c. Type **157** . . . 15 20
772 1 f. + 25 c. "Schappchen, the Huntsman" 15 20
773 2 f. + 25 c. "The Witch of Koerich" 15 20
774 3 f. + 50 c. "The Goblins of Schoendels" 15 20
775 6 f. + 50 c. "Tollchen, Watchman of Hesperange" 30 1·50
776 10 f. + 5 f. 90 "The Old Spinster of Heispelt" . . . . 1·25 3·00

158 "Flag" and Torch **159** W.H.O. Building

1966. 50th Anniv of Luxembourg Workers' Union.
777 **158** 3 f. red and grey 10 10

1966. Inaug of W.H.O. Headquarters, Geneva.
778 **159** 3 f. green 10 10

160 Golden Key **161** Europa "Ship"

1966. Tercentenary of Solemn Promise to Our Lady of Luxembourg.
779 **160** 1 f. 50 green 10 20
780 – 2 f. red 10 20
781 – 3 f. blue 10 20
782 – 6 f. brown 20 30
DESIGNS: 2 f. Interior of Luxembourg Cathedral (after painting by J. Martin); 3 f. Our Lady of Luxembourg (after engraving by R. Collin); 6 f. Gallery pillar, Luxembourg Cathedral (after sculpture by D. Muller).

1966. Europa.
783 **161** 3 f. blue and grey 10 10
784 6 f. green and brown . . 20 20

162 Diesel Locomotive

1966. Luxembourg Railwaymen's Philatelic Exhibition. Multicoloured.
785 1 f. 50 Type **162** 30 25
786 3 f. Electric locomotive . . . 30 20

163 Grand Duchess Charlotte Bridge **164** Kirchberg Building and Grand Duke Adolphe Railway Bridge

1966. Tourism.
787 **163** 3 f. lake 10 10
See also Nos. 807/8, 828 and 844/5.

1966. "Luxembourg-European Centre".
788 **164** 1 f. 50 green 20 20
789 – 13 f. blue (Robert Schuman monument) 60 15

165 "Mary, Veiled Matron of Wormeldange" **166** City of Luxembourg, 1850 (after engraving by N. Liez)

1966. National Welfare Fund. Luxembourg Fairy Tales. Multicoloured.
790 50 c. + 10 c. Type **165** . . . 10 20
791 1 f. 50 + 25 c. "Jekel Warden of the Wark" 10 20
792 2 f. + 25 c. "The Black Gentleman of Vianden" . . 10 20
793 3 f. + 50 c. "The Gracious Fairy of Rosport" 15 20
794 6 f. + 1 f. "The Friendly Shepherd of Donkolz" . . 35 1·00
795 13 f. + 6 f. 90 "The Little Sisters of Trois-Vierges" . . . . . 70 2·50

1967. Centenary of Treaty of London.
796 **166** 3 f. brown, blue and green 25 10
797 – 6 f. red, brown and blue 20 30
DESIGN—VERT: 6 f. Plan of Luxembourg fortress c. 1850 (after T. de Cederstolpe).

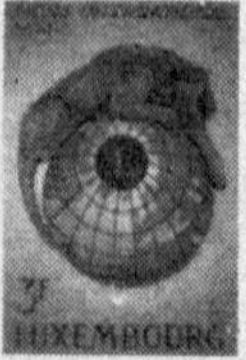

167 Cogwheels **168** Lion on Globe

1967. Europa.
798 **167** 3 f. purple, grey and buff 15 10
799 6 f. sepia, purple and blue 15 20

1967. 50th Anniv of Lions International.
800 **168** 3 f. yellow, purple & black 10 10

169 European Institutions Building, Luxembourg **170** Hikers and Hostel

1967. N.A.T.O. Council Meeting, Luxembourg.
801 **169** 3 f. turquoise and green . 10 10
802 6 f. red and pink 25 35

1967. Luxembourg Youth Hostels.
803 **170** 1 f. 50 multicoloured . . . 10 15

171 Shaving-dish (after Degrotte) **172** "Gardener"

1967. "200 Years of Luxembourg Pottery".
804 **171** 1 f. 50 multicoloured . . . 10 15
805 – 3 f. multicoloured 20 15
DESIGN—VERT: 3 f. Vase, circa 1820.

1967. "Family Gardens" Congress, Luxembourg.
806 **172** 1 f. 50 orange and green 10 15

1967. Tourism. As T **163**.
807 3 f. indigo and blue 20 15
808 3 f. purple, green and blue . . 50 15
DESIGNS—HORIZ: No. 807, Moselle River and quayside, Mertert. VERT: No. 808, Moselle, Church and vines, Wormeldange.

173 Prince Guillaume **174** Football

1967. National Welfare Fund. Royal Children and Residence.
809 **173** 50 c. + 10 c. brown & buff 15 20
810 – 1 f. 50 + 25 c. brown & bl 15 20
811 – 2 f. + 25 c. brown & red 15 20
812 – 3 f. + 50 c. brown & yell 80 20
813 – 6 f. + 1 f. brown & lav 40 1·00
814 – 13 f. + 6 f. 90 brn, grn & bl 70 3·00
DESIGNS: 1 f. 50, Princess Margaretha; 2 f. Prince Jean; 3 f. Prince Henri; 6 f. Princess Marie-Astrid; 13 f. Berg Castle.

1968. Olympic Games, Mexico.
815 – 50 c. light blue and blue . 10 15
816 **174** 1 f. 50 green & emerald . . 10 15
817 – 2 f. yellow and green . . . 10 15
818 – 3 f. lt orange and orange . 10 10
819 – 6 f. green and blue 15 20
820 – 13 f. red and crimson . . . 30 30
DESIGNS: 50 c. Diving; 2 f. Cycling; 3 f. Running; 6 f. Walking; 13 f. Fencing.

175 Europa "Key"

1968. Europa.
821 **175** 3 f. brown, black & green 10 10
822 6 f. green, black & orange 20 30

176 Thermal Bath Pavilion, Mondorf-les-Bains

1968. Mondorf-les-Bains Thermal Baths.
823 **176** 3 f. multicoloured 15 10

177 Fair Emblem

1968. 20th Anniv of Luxembourg Int Fair.
824 **177** 3 f. multicoloured 15 10

178 Village Project **179** "Blood Transfusion"

1968. Luxembourg SOS Children's Village.
825 **178** 3 f. purple and green . . . 10 10
826 – 6 f. black, blue and purple 20 30
DESIGN—VERT: 6 f. Orphan with foster-mother.

1968. Blood Donors of Luxembourg Red Cross.
827 **179** 3 f. red and blue 20 10

180 Fokker Friendship over Luxembourg **181** Cap Institute

1968. Tourism.
828 **180** 50 f. dp blue, brown & bl 3·00 40

1968. National Welfare Fund. Luxembourg Handicapped Children.
829 **181** 50 c. + 10 c. brown and blue 15 20
830 – 1 f. 50 + 25 c. brn and grn 15 20
831 – 2 f. + 25 c. brown & yell 20 30
832 – 3 f. + 50 c. brown & blue 25 20
833 – 6 f. + 1 f. brown & buff 40 1·00
834 – 13 f. + 6 f. 90 brown and pink . . . . 1·50 3·50
DESIGNS: 1 f. 50, Deaf and dumb child; 2 f. Blind child; 3 f. Nurse supporting handicapped child; 6 f. and 13 f. Mentally handicapped children (different).

183 Colonnade

1969. Europa.
836 **183** 3 f. multicoloured 15 10
837 6 f. multicoloured 30 30

184 "The Wooden Horse" (Kutter)

1969. 75th Birth Anniv of Joseph Kutter (painter). Multicoloured.
838 3 f. Type **184** 50 15
839 6 f. "Luxembourg" (Kutter) 50 30

185 ILO Emblem **186** National Colours

1969. 50th Anniv of Int Labour Organization.
840 **185** 3 f. gold, violet and green 10 10

1969. 25th Anniv of "BENELUX" Customs Union.
841 **186** 3 f. multicoloured 20 10

187 N.A.T.O. Emblem

188 Ear of Wheat and Agrocentre, Mersch

1969. 20th Anniv of N.A.T.O.
842 **187** 3 f. orange and brown . . 20 10

1969. "Modern Agriculture".
843 **188** 3 f. grey and green 10 10

189 Echternach

190 Vianden Castle

1969. Tourism.
844 **189** 3 f. indigo and blue . . . 20 10
845 – 3 f. blue and green 20 10
DESIGN: No. 845, Wiltz.

1969. National Welfare Fund. Castles (1st series). Multicoloured.
846 50 c. + 10 c. Type **190** . . . 15 20
847 1 f. 50 + 25 c. Lucilinburhuc 15 20
848 2 f. + 25 c. Bourglinster . . . 15 20
849 3 f. + 50 c. Hollenfels 15 20
850 6 f. + 1 f. Ansembourg . . . 45 1·50
851 13 f. + 6 f. 90 Beaufort . . . 1·00 3·50
See also Nos. 862/7.

191 Pasque Flower

192 Firecrest

1970. Nature Conservation Year. Multicoloured.
852 3 f. Type **191** 20 10
853 6 f. West European hedgehogs 60 40

1970. 50 Years of Bird Protection.
854 **192** 1 f. 50 green, black & orge 20 15

193 "Flaming Sun"

1970. Europa.
855 **193** 3 f. multicoloured 10 10
856 6 f. multicoloured 20 30

194 Road Safety Assoc. Emblem and Traffic

1970. Road Safety.
857 **194** 3 f. black, red and lake . . 30 15

195 "Empress Kunegonde and Emperor Henry II" (stained-glass windows, Luxembourg Cathedral)

1970. Centenary of Luxembourg Diocese.
858 **195** 3 f. multicoloured 15 20

196 Population Pictograph

1970. Population Census.
859 **196** 3 f. red, blue and green 15 10

197 Facade of Town Hall, Luxembourg

1970. 50th Anniv of Union of Four Suburbs with Luxembourg City.
860 **197** 3 f. brown, ochre & blue 15 10

198 U.N. Emblem

199 Monks in the Scriptorium

1970. 25th Anniv of United Nations.
861 **198** 1 f. 50 violet and blue . . 10 10

1970. National Welfare Fund. Castles (2nd series). Designs as T **190**.
862 50 c. + 10 c. Clervaux . . . 15 20
863 1 f. 50 + 25 c. Septfontaines 15 20
864 2 f. + 25 c. Bourschied . . . 15 20
865 3 f. + 50 c. Esch-sur-Sure . . 15 20
866 6 f. + 1 f. Larochette . . . . 60 1·50
867 13 f. + 6 f. 90 Brandenbourg 1·10 3·50

1971. Medieval Miniatures produced at Echternach. Multicoloured.
868 1 f. 50 Type **199** 10 15
869 3 f. Vine-growers going to work 15 10
870 6 f. Vine-growers at work and returning home 25 20
871 13 f. Workers with spades and hoe 45 55

200 Europa Chain

1971.
872 **200** 3 f. black, brown and red 20 15
873 6 f. black, brown & green 35 50

201 Olympic Rings and Arms of Luxembourg

202 "50" and Emblem

1971. Int Olympic Committee Meeting, Luxembourg.
874 **201** 3 f. red, gold and blue . . 10 10

1971. 50th Anniv of Luxembourg's Christian Workers' Union (L.C.G.B.).
875 **202** 3 f. purple, orange & yell 10 10

203 Artificial Lake, Upper Sure Valley

204 Child with Coin

1971. Man-made Landscapes.
876 **203** 3 f. blue, grey and brown 40 20
877 – 3 f. brown, green and blue 40 25
878 – 15 f. black, blue & brown 60 20
DESIGNS: No. 877, Water-processing plant, Esch-sur-Sure; No. 878, ARBED (United Steelworks) Headquarters Building, Luxembourg.

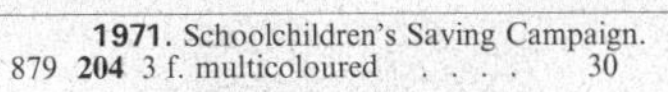
1971. Schoolchildren's Saving Campaign.
879 **204** 3 f. multicoloured 30 10

205 "Bethlehem Children"

206 Coins of Belgium and Luxembourg

1971. National Welfare Fund. "The Nativity"– wood-carvings in Beaufort Church. Multicoloured.
880 1 f. + 25 c. Type **205** 30 20
881 1 f. 50 + 25 c. "Shepherds" 30 20
882 3 f. + 50 c. "Virgin, Child Jesus and St. Joseph" 30 20
883 8 f. + 1 f. "Herdsmen" . . . 1·00 2·50
884 18 f. + 6 f. 50 "One of the Magi" 2·00 5·50

1972. 50th Anniv of Belgium-Luxembourg Economic Union.
885 **206** 1 f. 50 silver, black & grn 15 15

207 Bronze Mask (1st cent.)

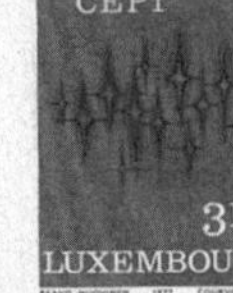
208 "Communications"

1972. Gallo-Roman Exhibits from Luxembourg State Museum. Multicoloured.
886 1 f. Samian bowl (2nd cent) (horiz) 15 15
887 3 f. Type **207** 30 15
888 8 f. Limestone head (2nd/3rd century) 60 80
889 15 f. Glass "head" flagon (4th century) 50 60

1972. Europa.
890 **208** 3 f. multicoloured 40 10
891 8 f. multicoloured 85 85

209 Archer

210 R. Schuman (after bronze by R. Zilli)

1972. 3rd European Archery Championships, Luxembourg.
892 **209** 3 f. multicoloured 30 10

1972. 20th Anniv of Establishment of European Coal and Steel Community in Luxembourg.
893 **210** 3 f. green and grey 40 15

211 National Monument

212 "Renert"

1972. Monuments and Buildings.
894 **211** 3 f. brown, green & violet 50 15
895 – 3 f. brown, green and blue 50 15
DESIGN: No. 895, European Communities' Court of Justice.

1972. Cent of Publication of Michel Rodange's "Renert" (satirical poem).
896 **212** 3 f. multicoloured 30 10

213 "Angel"

214 "Epona on Horseback"

1972. National Welfare Fund. Stained Glass Windows in Luxembourg Cathedral. Multicoloured.
897 1 f. + 25 c. Type **213** 15 20
898 1 f. 50 + 25 c. "St. Joseph" 15 20
899 3 f. + 50 c. "Holy Virgin with Child Jesus" 15 20
900 8 f. + 1 f. "People of Bethlehem" 1·00 2·50
901 18 f. + 6 f. 50 "Angel" (facing left) . . . . 3·00 7·00

1973. Archaeological Relics. Multicoloured.
902 1 f. Type **214** 15 20
903 4 f. "Panther attacking swan" (horiz) 30 10
904 8 f. Celtic gold coin . . . . . 1·10 1·10
905 15 f. Bronze boar (horiz) . . 90 65

215 Europa "Posthorn"

216 Bee on Honeycomb

1973. Europa.
906 **215** 4 f. orange, blue & violet 35 10
907 8 f. green, yellow & purple 90 1·00

1973. Bee-keeping.
908 **216** 4 f. multicoloured 30 10

217 Nurse and Child

218 Capital, Vianden Castle

1973. Day Nurseries in Luxembourg.
909 **217** 4 f. multicoloured 30 10

1973. Romanesque Architecture in Luxembourg.
910 **218** 4 f. purple and green . . 20 10
911 – 8 f. blue and brown . . . 80 75
DESIGN: 8 f. Detail of altar, St. Irmina's Chapel, Rosport.

219 Labour Emblem

220 J. de Busleyden

1973. 50th Anniv of Luxembourg Board of Labour.
912 **219** 3 f. multicoloured 20 10

1973. 500th Anniv of Great Council of Malines.
913 **220** 4 f. purple and brown . . 20 10

221 Monument, Wiltz

222 Joachim and St. Anne

1973. National Strike Monument.
914 **221** 4 f. green, brown and grey 20 10

1973. National Welfare Fund. "The Nativity". Details from 16th-century reredos, Hachiville Hermitage. Multicoloured.
915 1 f. + 25 c. Type **222** 15 20
916 3 f. + 25 c. "Mary meets Elizabeth" 15 20
917 4 f. + 50 c. "Magus presenting gift" 20 20
918 8 f. + 1 f. "Shepherds at the manger" . . . . 1·00 2·50
919 15 f. + 7 f. "St. Joseph with Candle" . . . . 3·00 7·00

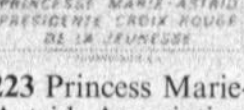

223 Princess Marie-Astrid, Association President

224 Flame Emblem

1974. Luxembourg Red Cross Youth Association.
920 **223** 4 f. multicoloured . . . . 1·60 15

1974. 50th Anniv of Luxembourg Mutual Insurance Federation.
921 **224** 4 f. multicoloured 50 10

225 Seal of Henry VII, King of the Romans

226 "Hind" (A. Tremont)

1974. Seals in Luxembourg State Archives.
922 **225** 1 f. brown, yellow & pur . 10 10
923 – 3 f. brown, yellow & grn . 20 25
924 – 4 f. dark brown, yell & brn 30 10
925 – 19 f. brown, yellow & bl . 1·00 90
DESIGNS: 3 f. Equestrian seal of John the Blind, King of Bohemia; 4 f. Municipal seal of Diekirch; 19 f. Seal of Marienthal Convent.

1974. Europa. Sculptures. Multicoloured.
926 4 f. Type **226** 80 10
927 8 f. "Abstract" (L. Wercollier) 2·00 1·25

227 Churchill Memorial, Luxembourg

228 Diagram of Fair

1974. Birth Centenary of Sir Winston Churchill.
928 **227** 4 f. multicoloured 30 10

1974. New International Fair, Luxembourg-Kirchberg.
929 **228** 4 f. multicoloured 20 10

229 "Theis the Blind" (artist unknown)

230 "Crowning of St. Cecily and St. Valerien" (Hollenfels Church)

1974. 150th Death Anniv of "Theis the Blind" (Mathias Schou, folk singer).
930 **229** 3 f. multicoloured 20 30

1974. Gothic Architecture.
931 **230** 4 f. brown, green & violet 30 30
932 – 4 f. black, brown & blue 30 20
DESIGN: No. 932, Interior of Septfontaines Church.

231 U.P.U. Emblem on "100"

1974. Centenary of Universal Postal Union.
933 **231** 4 f. multicoloured 20 10
934 8 f. multicoloured 80 70

232 "Benelux"

1974. 30th Anniv of Benelux (Customs Union).
935 **232** 4 f. turquoise, green & bl 1·00 15

233 Differdange

1974. Tourism.
936 **233** 4 f. purple . . . . 1·00 15

234 "Annunciation"

236 The Fish Market, Luxembourg

1974. National Welfare Fund. Illustrations from "Codex Aureus Epternacensis". Multicoloured.
937 1 f. + 25 c. Type **234** 15 20
938 3 f. + 25 c. "Visitation" . . 15 20
939 4 f. + 50 c. "Nativity" . . . 20 20
940 8 f. + 1 f. "Adoration of the Magi" . . . . 1·25 3·00
941 15 f. + 7 f. "Presentation at the Temple" . . . . 2·40 6·00

1975. European Architectural Heritage Year.
943 **236** 1 f. green 70 20
944 – 3 f. brown . . . . 1·25 30
945 – 4 f. lilac . . . . 1·40 15
946 – 19 f. red . . . . 1·50 1·00
DESIGNS—HORIZ: 3 f. Bourglinster Castle; 4 f. Market Square, Echternach. VERT: 19 f. St. Michael's Square, Mersch.

237 "Joseph Kutter" (self-portrait)

238 Dr. Albert Schweitzer

1975. Luxembourg Culture, and Europa. Paintings. Multicoloured.
947 1 f. Type **237** 15 15
948 4 f. "Remich Bridge" (N. Klopp) (horiz) . . . . 1·00 20
949 8 f. "Still Life" (J. Kutter) (horiz) 2·00 1·90
950 20 f. "The Dam" (D. Lang) . 1·50 45

1975. Birth Centenary of Dr. Albert Schweitzer (medical missionary).
951 **238** 4 f. blue . . . . 1·00 15

239 Robert Schuman, G. Martino and P.-H. Spaak

240 Civil Defence Emblem

1975. 25th Anniv of Robert Schuman Declaration for European Unity.
952 **239** 4 f. black, gold and green 60 15

1975. 15th Anniv of Civil Defence Reorganization.
953 **240** 4 f. multicoloured 60 10

241 Ice Skating

242 Fly Orchid

1975. Sports. Multicoloured.
954 **241** 3 f. purple, blue and green 45 25
955 – 4 f. brown, grn & dp brn 65 15
956 – 15 f. blue, brown & green 1·40 65
DESIGNS — HORIZ: 4 f. Water-skiing. VERT: 15 f. Rock-climbing.

1975. National Welfare Fund. Protected Plants (1st series). Multicoloured.
957 1 f. + 25 c. Type **242** 20 20
958 3 f. + 25 c. Pyramid orchid . 40 35
959 4 f. + 50 c. Marsh helleborine 50 15
960 8 f. + 1 f. Pasque flower . . . 1·50 2·00
961 15 f. + 7 f. Bee orchid . . . . 3·50 6·00
See also Nos. 976/80 and 997/1001.

243 Grand Duchess Charlotte (80th)

244 7th-century Disc-shaped Brooch

1976. Royal Birthdays. Multicoloured.
962 6 f. Type **243** . . . . 1·50 20
963 6 f. Prince Henri (21st) . . . . 1·50 20

1976. Luxembourg Culture. Ancient Treasures from Merovingian Tombs. Multicoloured.
964 2 f. Type **244** 15 20
965 5 f. 5th-6th cent. glass beaker (horiz) 30 30
966 6 f. Ancient pot (horiz) . . . 30 15
967 12 f. 7th cent. gold coin . . . 1·00 1·00

245 Soup Tureen

1976. Europa. 19th century Pottery. Multicoloured.
968 6 f. Type **245** 50 15
969 12 f. Bowl . . . . 1·50 1·25

246 Independence Hall, Philadelphia

247 Symbol representing "Strength and Impetus"

1976. Bicentenary of American Revolution.
970 **246** 6 f. multicoloured 30 10

1976. Olympic Games, Montreal.
971 **247** 6 f. gold, magenta and mauve 20 10

248 Association Emblem and "Sound Vibrations"

249 "Virgin and Child"

1976. 30th Anniv of "Jeunesses Musicales" (Youth Music Association).
972 **248** 6 f. multicoloured 30 10

1976. Renaissance Art. Multicoloured.
973 6 f. Type **249** 30 10
974 12 f. Bernard de Velbruck, Lord of Beaufort (funeral monument) . . . . 1·00 80

250 Alexander Graham Bell

1976. Telephone Centenary.
975 **250** 6 f. green 30 10

1976. National Welfare Fund. Protected Plants (2nd series). As T **242**. Multicoloured.
976 2 f. + 25 c. Gentian 20 20
977 5 f. + 25 c. Wild daffodil . . 20 20
978 6 f. + 50 c. Red helleborine (orchid) 40 25
979 12 f. + 1 f. Late spider orchid 1·00 2·00
980 20 f. + 8 f. Twin leaved squill 3·00 6·00

251 Johann von Goethe (poet)

252 Fish Market, Luxembourg

1977. Luxembourg Culture. Famous Visitors to Luxembourg.
981 **251** 2 f. purple 15 10
982 – 5 f. violet 25 20
983 – 6 f. black 60 15
984 – 12 f. violet 70 75
DESIGNS: 5 f. Joseph Mallard William Turner (painter); 6 f. Victor Hugo (writer); 12 f. Franz Liszt (musician).

1977. Europa. Multicoloured.
985 6 f. Type **252** 35 10
986 12 f. Grand Duke Adolphe railway bridge and European Investment Bank . . . . . 1·25 1·00

253 Esch-sur-Sure

254 Marguerite de Busbach (founder)

1977. Tourism.
987 **253** 5 f. blue 50 20
988 – 6 f. brown 40 10
DESIGNS 6 f. Ehnen.

1977. Anniversaries. Multicoloured.
989 6 f. Type **254** 40 15
990 6 f. Louis Braille (after Filippi) 40 15
ANNIVERSARIES: No. 989, 350th anniv of foundation of Notre Dame Congregation; No. 990, 125th death anniv.

256 St. Gregory the Great

257 Head of Medusa

1977. Baroque Art. Sculpture from Feulen Parish Church pulpit attributed to J.-G. Scholtus.
992 **256** 6 f. purple 40 15
993 – 12 f. grey 80 80
DESIGN: 12 f. St. Augustine.

1977. Roman Mosaic at Diekirch.
994 **257** 6 f. multicoloured 60 20

258 Scene from "Orpheus and Eurydice" (Gluck)

1977. 25th Wiltz International Festival.
995 **258** 6 f. multicoloured 60 15

259 Map of E.E.C. and "Europa" (R. Zilli)

1977. 20th Anniv of Rome Treaties.
996 **259** 6 f. multicoloured 40 15

1977. National Welfare Fund. Protected Plants (3rd series). As T **242**. Multicoloured.
997 2 f. + 25 c. Lily of the valley 15 15
998 5 f. + 25 c. Columbine . . . 30 25
999 6 f. + 50 c. Mezereon . . . 50 25
1000 12 f. + 1 f. Early spider orchid 1·75 1·50
1001 20 f. + 8 f. Spotted orchid 3·00 5·00

262 Charles IV

263 Head of Our Lady of Luxembourg

1978. Europa.
1004 **262** 6 f. lilac 40 10
1005 – 12 f. red . . . . 1·25 1·00
DESIGN: 12 f. Pierre d'Aspelt (funeral monument, Mainz Cathedral).

1978. Anniversaries. Multicoloured.
1006 6 f. Type **263** (300th anniv of election as patron saint) . . 40 15
1007 6 f. Trumpeters (135th anniv of Grand Ducal Military Band) 40 15

264 Emile Mayrisch (after T. van Rysselberghe)

265 Child with Ear of Millet

1978. 50th Death Anniv of Emile Mayrisch (iron and steel magnate).
1008 **264** 6 f. multicoloured . . . . 1·00 15

1978. "Solidarity 1978". Multicoloured.
1009 2 f. Type **265** (Terre des Hommes) 10 20
1010 5 f. Flower and lungs (70th anniv of Luxembourg Anti-Tuberculosis League) . . . 30 20
1011 6 f. Open cell (Amnesty International and 30th anniv of Declaration of Human Rights) 35 15

266 Perfect Ashlar

267 "St. Matthew"

1978. 175th Anniv of Luxembourg Grand Lodge.
1012 **266** 6 f. blue 60 15

1978. National Welfare Fund. Glass Paintings (1st series). Multicoloured.
1013 2 f. + 25 c. Type **267** . . . 15 20
1014 5 f. + 25 c. "St. Mark" . . . 30 30
1015 6 f. + 50 c. "Nativity" . . . 40 30
1016 12 f. + 1 f. "St. Luke" . . . 1·50 1·00
1017 20 f. + 8 f. "St. John" . . . 2·00 4·50
See also Nos. 1035/9 and 1055/8.

268 Denarius of Gaius Julius Caesar

269 Mondorf-les-Bains

1979. Luxembourg Culture. Roman Coins in the State Museum. Multicoloured.
1018 5 f. Type **268** 30 15
1019 6 f. Sestertius of Faustina I 50 15
1020 9 f. Follis of Helena 80 50
1021 26 f. Solidus of Valens . . . 1·75 1·40
See also Nos. 1040/3 and 1060/3.

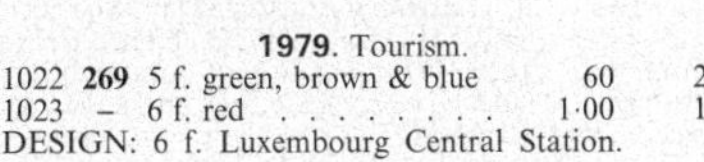

1979. Tourism.
1022 **269** 5 f. green, brown & blue 60 20
1023 – 6 f. red . . . . 1·00 10
DESIGN: 6 f. Luxembourg Central Station.

270 Stage Coach

271 Antoine Meyer (poet)

1979. Europa. Multicoloured.
1024 6 f. Type **270** . . . . . . 2·00 15
1025 12 f. Old wall telephone (vert) 2·00 1·50

1979. Anniversaries.
1026 – 2 f. purple 35 20
1027 **271** 5 f. red 35 20
1028 – 6 f. turquoise 35 20
1029 – 9 f. grey-black 40 25
DESIGNS—36 × 36 mm: 2 f. Michel Pintz on trial (after L. Piedboeuf) and monument to rebels (180th anniv of peasant uprising against French). 22 × 36 mm: 5 f. Type **271** (150th anniv of first publication in Luxembourg dialect); 6 f. S. G. Thomas (cent of purchase of Thomas patent for steel production); 9 f. "Abundance crowning Work and Saving" (ceiling painting by August Vinet) (50th anniv of Stock Exchange).

272 "European Assembly"

273 Blindfolded Cherub with Chalice

1979. First Direct Elections to European Assembly.
1030 **272** 6 f. multicoloured . . . 1·25 60

1979. Rococo Art. Details from altar of St. Michael's Church by Barthelemy Namur. Multicoloured.
1031 6 f. Type **273** 40 15
1032 12 f. Cherub with anchor . . 70 70

274 Child with Traffic Symbol Balloons jumping over Traffic

1979. International Year of the Child.
1033 **274** 2 f. blue, brown and red 15 15

275 Radio Waves, "RTL" and Dates

1979. 50th Anniv of Broadcasting in Luxembourg.
1034 **275** 6 f. blue and red 50 15

1979. National Welfare Fund. Glass Paintings (2nd series). As T **267**. Multicoloured.
1035 2 f. + 25 c. "Spring" . . . 15 15
1036 5 f. + 25 c. "Summer" . . . 30 30
1037 6 f. + 50 c. "Charity" . . . 40 30
1038 12 f. + 1 f. "Autumn" . . . 80 1·50
1039 20 f. + 8 f. "Winter" . . . 1·50 4·50

1980. Luxembourg Culture. Medieval Coins in the State Museum. As T **268**. Multicoloured.
1040 2 f. Grosso of Emperor Henry VII 20 20
1041 5 f. Grosso of John the Blind of Bohemia 20 20
1042 6 f. "Mouton d'or" of Wenceslas I and Jeanne, Duke and Duchess of Brabant 80 15
1043 20 f. Grosso of Wenceslas II, Duke of Luxembourg . . 2·00 80

276 State Archives Building

277 Jean Monnet (statesman)

1980. Tourism.
1044 **276** 6 f. purple, ultram & bl 50 15
1045 – 6 f. red and brown . . . 60 15
DESIGN—VERT: No. 1045, Ettelbruck Town Hall.

1980. Europa.
1046 **277** 6 f. black 50 15
1047 – 12 f. olive . . . . 1·00 85
DESIGN: 12 f. St. Benedict of Nursia (founder of Benedictine Order) (statue in Echternach Abbey).

278 Sports Equipment

279 Gloved Hand protecting Worker from Machinery

1980. "Sports for All".
1048 **278** 6 f. black, orange & grn 1·40 30

1980. 9th World Congress on the Prevention of Accidents at Work and Occupational Diseases, Amsterdam.
1049 – 2 f. multicoloured 20 15
1050 **279** 6 f. brown, grey and red 40 15
DESIGN—VERT: 2 f. Worker pouring molten iron.

280 "Mercury" (Jean Mich)

281 Postcoded Letter

1980. Art Nouveau Sculpture. Statues beside entrance to State Savings Bank.
1051 **280** 8 f. lilac 45 15
1052 – 12 f. blue 55 60
DESIGN: 12 f. "Ceres" (Jean Mich).

1980. Postcode Publicity.
1053 **281** 4 f. brown, ochre and red 60 15

282 Policemen and Patrol Car

1980. 50th Anniv of National Police Force.
1054 **282** 8 f. multicoloured 80 20

1980. National Welfare Fund. Glass Paintings (3rd series). As T **267**. Multicoloured.
1055 4 f. + 50 c. "St. Martin" . . 30 20
1056 6 f. + 50 c. "St. Nicholas" 30 25
1057 8 f. + 1 f. "Virgin and child" 40 1·00
1058 30 f. + 10 f. "St. George" . . 2·25 5·00

1981. Luxembourg Culture. Coins in the State Museum. As T **268**.
1060 4 f. Patagon of Philip IV of Spain, 1635 . . . . 25 20
1061 6 f. 12 sols coin of Maria Theresa, 1775 . . . . . . 30 20
1062 8 f. 12 sols coin of Emperor Joseph II, 1789 . . . . . 30 15
1063 30 f. Siege crown of Emperor Francis II, 1795 . . . . . 1·40 80

MINIMUM PRICE

The minimum price quoted is 10p which represents a handling charge rather than a basis for valuing common stamps. For further notes about prices, see introductory pages.

284 European Parliament Building, Luxembourg

285 Cock-shaped Whistle sold at Easter Monday Market

1981. Tourism.
1064 **284** 8 f. brown and blue . . 30 15
1065 – 8 f. red and blue 30 15
DESIGN: No. 1065, National Library.

1981. Europa. Multicoloured.
1066 8 f. Procession of beribboned sheep and town band to local fair 40 15
1067 12 f. Type **285** 60 50

286 Staunton Knight on Chessboard

287 Prince Henri and Princess Maria Teresa

1981. Anniversaries.
1068 **286** 4 f. multicoloured . . . 40 15
1069 – 8 f. ochre, brown & silver 40 15
1070 – 8 f. multicoloured . . . 40 15
DESIGNS—VERT: 4 f. Type **286** (50th anniv of Luxembourg Chess Federation); 8 f. (1070), Passbook and State Savings Bank (125th anniv of State Savings Bank). HORIZ: 8 f. (1069), First Luxembourg banknote (125th anniv of International Bank of Luxembourg's issuing rights).

1981. Royal Wedding.
1071 **287** 8 f. multicoloured . . . 50 40

288 Gliders over Useldange

289 Flame

1981. Aviation. Multicoloured.
1072 8 f. Type **288** 30 15
1073 16 f. Cessna 172F Skyhawk and 182H Skylane sports planes 80 60
1074 35 f. Boeing 747-200F 182H over Luxembourg-Findel airport terminal . . . . . 1·60 85

1981. Energy Conservation.
1075 **289** 8 f. multicoloured . . . 30 15

290 Arms of Petange

291 "Apple Trees in Blossom" (Frantz Seimetz)

1981. National Welfare Fund. Arms of Local Authorities (1st series). Multicoloured.
1076 4 f. + 50 c. Type **290** . . . 15 15
1077 6 f. + 50 c. Larochette . . . 25 25
1078 8 f. + 1 f. "Adoration of the Magi" (School of Rubens) 40 30
1079 16 f. + 2 f. Stadtbredimus 80 2·00
1080 35 f. + 12 f. Weiswampach 2·50 5·00
See also Nos. 1097/1101 and 1119/23.

1982. Luxembourg Culture. Landscapes through the Four Seasons. Multicoloured.
1081 4 f. Type **291** 20 15
1082 6 f. "Landscape" (Pierre Blanc) 30 30
1083 8 f. "The Larger Hallerbach" (Guido Oppenheim) . . . 45 15
1084 16 f. "Winter Evening" (Eugene Mousset) . . . . 1·00 70

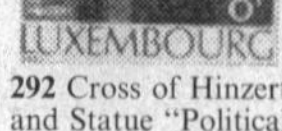

292 Cross of Hinzert and Statue "Political Prisoner" (Lucien Wercollier)
293 Treaty of London, 1867, and Luxembourg Fortress

1982. National Monument of the Resistance and Deportation, Notre-Dame Cemetery.
1085 **292** 8 f. multicoloured 40 15

1982. Europa. Multicoloured.
1086 8 f. Type **293** 50 15
1087 16 f. Treaty of Paris, 1951, and European Coal and Steel Community Building, Luxembourg 90 75

294 St. Theresa of Avila (wood statue, Carmel Monastery)
295 State Museum

1982. Anniversaries. Multicoloured.
1088 4 f. Type **294** (400th death anniv) 30 15
1089 8 f. Raoul Follereau (social worker for lepers, 5th death anniv) 50 15

1982. Tourism.
1090 **295** 8 f. brown, blue & black 50 15
1091 – 8 f. buff, black and blue . 40 15
DESIGN: No. 1091, Luxembourg Synagogue.

296 Bourscheid Castle
297 Key in Lock

1982. Classified Monuments (1st series).
1092 **296** 6 f. blue 30 15
1093 – 8 f. red 50 15
DESIGN—HORIZ: 8 f. Vianden Castle.
See also Nos. 1142/3, and 1165/6.

1982. Anniversaries. Multicoloured.
1094 4 f. Type **297** (50th anniv of International Youth Hostel Federation) 50 15
1095 8 f. Scouts holding hands around globe (75th anniv of Scouting Movement) (vert) 60 15

298 Monument to Civilian and Military Deportation

1982. Civilian and Military Deportation Monument, Hollerich Station.
1096 **298** 8 f. multicoloured 40 15

1982. National Welfare Fund. Arms of Local Authorities (2nd series) and Stained Glass Window (8 f.). As T **290**. Multicoloured.
1097 4 f. + 50 c. Bettembourg . . 25 20
1098 6 f. + 50 c. Frisange 30 25
1099 8 f. + 1 f. "Adoration of the Shepherds" (Gustav Zanter, Hoscheid parish church) . 45 30
1100 16 f. + 2 f. Mamer . . . . 90 2·00
1101 35 f. + 12 f. Heinerscheid . . 4·00 7·00

299 Modern Fire Engine
300 "Mercury" (Auguste Tremont)

1983. Centenary of National Federation of Fire Brigades. Multicoloured.
1102 8 f. Type **299** 65 15
1103 16 f. Hand fire-pump (18th century) 80 65

1983. Anniversaries and Events.
1104 **300** 4 f. multicoloured . . . 20 20
1105 – 6 f. multicoloured . . . 50 30
1106 – 8 f. brown, black and blue 50 15
1107 – 8 f. deep blue and blue 50 15
DESIGNS: No. 1104, Type **300** (25th Congress of International Association of Foreign Exchange Dealers); 1105, N.A.T.O. emblem surrounded by flags of member countries (25th anniv of N.A.T.O.); 1106, Echternach Cross of Justice (30th Congress of International Union of Barristers); 1107, Globe and customs emblem (30th anniv of Customs Co-operation Council).

301 Robbers attacking Traveller

1983. Europa. Miniatures from "Codex Aureus Escorialensis", illustrating Parable of the Good Samaritan. Multicoloured.
1108 8 f. Type **301** . . . . 1·00 20
1109 16 f. Good Samaritan helping traveller . . . . 2·50 80

302 Initial "H" from "Book of Baruch"
303 Despatch Rider and Postcode

1983. Luxembourg Culture. Echternach Abbey Giant Bible. Multicoloured.
1110 8 f. Type **302** 45 20
1111 35 f. Initial "B" from letter of St. Jerome to Pope Damasius I . . . . 1·50 1·00

1983. World Communications Year. Mult.
1112 8 f. Type **303** 80 20
1113 8 f. Europan Communications Satellite (horiz) . . . . . 2·00 30

304 St. Lawrence's Church, Diekirch
305 Basketball

1983. Tourism.
1114 **304** 7 f. orange, brown and blue 30 15
1115 – 10 f. orange, brown & bl 40 20
DESIGN—HORIZ: 10 f. Dudelange Town Hall.

1983. Anniversaries and Events. Multicoloured.
1116 7 f. Type **305** (50th anniv of Luxembourg basketball Federation) 55 20
1117 10 f. Sheepdog (European Working Dog Championships) 80 20
1118 10 f. City of Luxembourg ("The Green Heart of Europe") 1·25 20

1983. National Welfare Fund. Arms of Local Authorities (3rd series) and Painting. As T **290**. Multicoloured.
1119 4 f. + 1 f. Winseler 30 20
1120 7 f. + 1 f. Beckerich 40 30
1121 10 f. + 1 f. "Adoration of the Shepherds" (Lucas Bosch) 50 35
1122 16 f. + 2 f. Feulen . . . . 1·10 2·00
1123 40 f. + 13 f. Mertert . . . . 2·50 5·00

306 Lion and First Luxembourg Stamp
307 Pedestrian Precinct

1984. Anniversaries. Each black, red and blue.
1124 10 f. Type **306** 70 30
1125 10 f. Lion and ministry buildings 70 30
1126 10 f. Lion and postman's bag 70 30
1127 10 f. Lion and locomotive . . 70 30
ANNIVERSARIES: No. 1124, 50th anniv of Federation of Luxembourg Philatelic Societies; 1125, 75th anniv of Civil Service Trade Union Movement; 1126, 75th anniv of Luxembourg Postmen's Trade Union; 1127, 125th anniv of Luxembourg Railways.

1984. Environmental Protection. Multicoloured.
1128 7 f. Type **307** 30 30
1129 10 f. City of Luxembourg sewage treatment plant . . 40 20

308 Hands supporting European Parliament Emblem
309 Bridge

1984. 2nd Direct Elections to European Parliament.
1130 **308** 10 f. multicoloured . . . 60 20

1984. Europa. 25th Anniv of European Post and Telecommunications Conference.
1131 **309** 10 f. green, dp grn & blk 1·50 20
1132 16 f. orange, brown & blk 3·00 75

310 "The Smoker" (David Teniers the Younger)
311 "The Race" (Jean Jacoby)

1984. Paintings. Multicoloured.
1133 4 f. Type **310** 50 30
1134 7 f. "Young Turk caressing his Horse" (Eugene Delacroix) (horiz) 70 30
1135 10 f. "Ephiphany" (Jan Steen) (horiz) . . . . 1·00 20
1136 50 f. "The Lacemaker" (Pieter van Slingelandt) . . . . . 4·00 2·00

1984. Olympic Games, Los Angeles.
1137 **311** 10 f. orange, black & bl 65 20

312 "Pecten sp."
313 "American Soldier" (statue by Michel Heitz at Clervaux)

1984. Luxembourg Culture. Fossils in the Natural History Museum. Multicoloured.
1138 4 f. Type **312** 45 20
1139 7 f. Devil's toe-nail 85 35
1140 10 f. "Coeloceras raquinianum" (ammonite) . . . . 1·60 15
1141 16 f. "Dapedius sp." (fish) . . 1·50 95

1984. Classified Monuments (2nd series). As T **296**.
1142 7 f. turquoise 35 30
1143 10 f. brown 45 15
DESIGNS: 7 f. Hollenfels Castle; 10 f. Larochette Castle.

1984. 40th Anniv of Liberation.
1144 **313** 10 f. black, red and blue 1·50 20

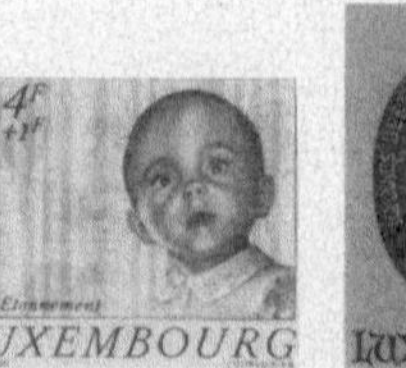

314 Infant astounded by Surroundings
315 Jean Bertels (abbot of Echternach Abbey)

1984. National Welfare Fund. The Child. Mult.
1145 4 f. + 1 f. Type **314** 40 40
1146 7 f. + 1 f. Child dreaming . 60 60
1147 10 f. + 1 f. "Nativity (crib, Steinsel church) . . . . . 1·00 50
1148 16 f. + 2 f. Child sulking . . 2·50 3·00
1149 40 f. + 13 f. Girl admiring flower . . . . 7·00 8·00

1985. Luxembourg Culture. Portrait Medals in State Museum (1st series). Multicoloured.
1150 4 f. Type **315** (steatite medal, 1595) 20 20
1151 7 f. Emperor Charles V (bronze medal, 1537) 30 30
1152 10 f. King Philip II of Spain (silver medal, 1555) 40 20
1153 30 f. Maurice of Orange-Nassau (silver medal, 1615) . . . . 1·60 90
See also Nos. 1173/6.

316 Fencing
317 Papal Arms

1985. Anniversaries. Multicoloured.
1154 10 f. Type **316** (50th anniv of Luxembourg Fencing Federation) 60 20
1155 10 f. Benz "Velo" (centenary of automobile) 60 20
1156 10 f. Telephone within concentric circles (centenary of Luxembourg telephone service) 60 20

1985. Visit of Pope John Paul II.
1157 **317** 10 f. multicoloured . . . 60 20

318 Treble Clef within Map of National Anthem
320 Little Owl

1965. Europa. Music Year. Multicoloured.
1158 10 f. Type **318** (Grand Duke Adolphe Union of choral, instrumental and folklore societies) . . . . 1·50 30
1159 16 f. Neck of violin, music school and score of Beethoven's Violin Concerto opus 61 . . . . 3·00 95

1985. Endangered Animals. Multicoloured.
1161 4 f. Type **320** . . . . 1·00 40
1162 7 f. European wildcat (horiz) 2·00 30
1163 10 f. Red admiral (horiz) . . 3·00 30
1164 50 f. European tree frog . . 6·00 2·00

1985. Classified Monuments (3rd series). As T **296**.
1165 7 f. red 50 20
1166 10 f. green 50 15
DESIGNS—HORIZ: 7 f. Echternach orangery. VERT: 10 f. Mohr de Waldt house.

321 Mansfeld Arms (book binding)
322 Application

1985. Luxembourg Culture.
1167 **321** 10 f. multicoloured . . . 50 30

1985. National Welfare Fund. Multicoloured.
1168 4 f. + 1 f. Type **322** 40 30
1169 7 f. + 1 f. Friendship . . . 60 50
1170 10 f. + 1 f. "Adoration of the Magi" (16th century alabaster sculpture) . . . . 1·00 50
1171 16 f. + 2 f. Child identifying with his favourite characters 2·50 3·00
1172 40 f. + 13 f. Shame . . . . 7·50 10·00

1986. Luxembourg Culture. Portrait Medals in State Museum (2nd series). As T **315**.
1173 10 f. multicoloured 50 30
1174 12 f. multicoloured 60 20
1175 18 f. black, grey and blue . . 80 50
1176 20 f. multicoloured . . . . . 1·25 80
DESIGNS: 10 f. Count of Monterey (silver medal, 1675); 12 f. Louis XIV of France (silver medal, 1684); 18 f. Pierre de Weyms (president of Provincial Council) (pewter medal, 1700); 20 f. Duke of Marlborough (silver medal, 1706).

323 Bee on Flower **324** Forest and City

1986. Anniversaries. Multicoloured.

1177 12 f. Type **323** (centenary of Federation of Luxembourg Beekeeper's Association) . . 80 20
1178 12 f. Table tennis player (50th anniv of Luxembourg Table Tennis Federation) 80 20
1179 11 f. Mosaic of woman with water jar (centenary of Mondorf State Spa) . . . 80 20

1986. Europa. Multicoloured.

1180 12 f. Type **324** . . . . 1·00 15
1181 20 f. Mankind, industry and countryside . . . . 1·75 75

325 Fort Thungen **326** Schuman

1986. Luxembourg Town Fortifications. Mult.

1182 15 f. Type **325** . . . . 1·00 50
1183 18 f. Invalids' Gate (vert) . . 1·25 50
1184 50 f. Malakoff Tower (vert) 3·00 1·50

1986. Birth Centenary of Robert Schuman (politician).

1185 **326** 2 f. black and red 10 10
1186 10 f. black and blue . . . 40 30

327 Road through Red Triangle on Map **328** Ascent to Chapel of the Cross, Grevenmacher

1986. European Road Safety Year.

1187 **327** 10 f. multicoloured . . . 75 20

1986. Tourism.

1188 **328** 12 f. multicoloured . . . 70 30
1189 – 12 f. brown, stone & red 70 30
DESIGN: No. 1189, Relief from Town Hall facade, Esch-sur-Alzette.

329 Presentation of Letter of Freedom to Echternach (after P. H. Witkamp) **330** Annunciation

1986. 800th Birth Anniv of Countess Ermesinde of Luxembourg.

1190 **329** 12 f. brown and stone . . 50 30
1191 – 30 f. buff, black and grey 1·50 80
DESIGN: 30 f. Seal, 1238.

1986. National Welfare Fund. Illustrations from 15th-century "Book of Hours". Multicoloured.

1192 6 f. + 1 f. Type **330** . . . . 1·00 30
1193 10 f. + 1 f. Angel appearing to shepherds 50 40
1194 12 f. + 2 f. Nativity . . . . 1·00 50
1195 18 f. + 2 f. Adoration of the Magi . . . . 3·00 3·50
1196 20 f. + 8 f. Flight into Egypt 5·00 6·50

331 Garden Dormouse **332** Network Emblem

1987. Endangered Animals. Multicoloured.

1197 6 f. Type **331** 50 30
1198 10 f. Banded agrion (vert) . 1·00 55
1199 12 f. Dipper (vert) . . . . . 1·50 65
1200 25 f. Salamander . . . . . 2·50 80

1987. 50th Anniversaries. Multicoloured.

1201 12 f. Type **332** (Amateur Short Wave Network) 55 30
1202 12 f. Anniversary Emblem (International Fair) . . . 55 30

333 "St. Bernard of Siena and St. John the Baptist" **334** National Swimming Centre (Roger Taillibert)

1987. Paintings by Giovanni Ambrogio Bevilacqua in State Museum. Multicoloured.

1203 10 f. Type **333** 50 40
1204 18 f. "St. Jerome and St. Francis of Assisi" 90 60

1987. Europa. Architecture. Multicoloured.

1205 12 f. Type **334** . . . . 1·00 30
1206 20 f. European Communities' Court of Justice . . . . . 2·00 80

335 "Consecration" (stained glass window by Gustav Zanter) **336** Charles Metz (first President) (after Jean-Baptiste Fresez)

1987. Millenary of St. Michael's Church. Multicoloured.

1207 12 f. Type **335** 50 30
1208 20 f. Baroque organ-chest . 1·10 70

1987. Chamber of Deputies.

1209 **336** 6 f. brown 30 20
1210 – 12 f. blue 50 40
DESIGN: 12 f. Chamber of Deputies building.

337 Hennesbau, Niederfeulen **338** Annunciation

1987. Rural Architecture. Each ochre, brown and blue.

1211 10 f. Type **337** 60 30
1212 12 f. 18th-century dwelling house converted to health centre, Mersch 60 30
1213 100 f. 18th-century house converted to Post Office, Bertrange . . . . 4·00 1·00

1987. National Welfare Fund. Illustrations from 15th-century Paris "Book of Hours". Multicoloured.

1214 6 f. + 1 f. Type **338** 70 50
1215 10 f. + 1 f. Visitation . . . 1·25 1·00
1216 12 f. + 2 f. Adoration of the Magi . . . . 1·50 1·00
1217 18 f. + 2 f. Presentation in the Temple . . . . 3·00 3·00
1218 20 f. + 8 f. Flight into Egypt 6·00 6·00

339 Lilies and Water-lily **340** Rail, Road and Water Transport

1988. Luxembourg Culture. Flower Illustrations by Pierre-Joseph Redouté. Multicoloured.

1219 6 f. Type **339** 75 30
1220 10 f. Primulas and double narcissus 75 40
1221 12 f. Tulips and chrysanthemums . . . . . 2·00 50
1222 50 f. Irises and gorterias . . 4·00 2·00

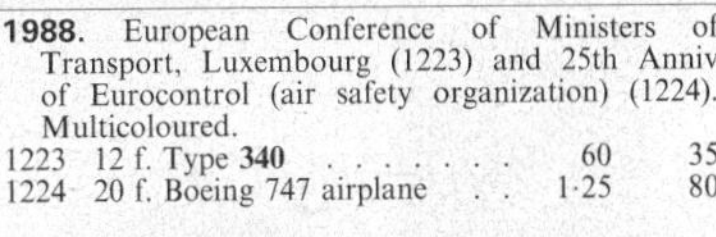

1988. European Conference of Ministers of Transport, Luxembourg (1223) and 25th Anniv of Eurocontrol (air safety organization) (1224). Multicoloured.

1223 12 f. Type **340** 60 35
1224 20 f. Boeing 747 airplane . . 1·25 80

342 Wiltz Town Hall and Cross of Justice

1988. Tourism. Multicoloured.

1226 10 f. Type **342** 70 30
1227 12 f. Differdange Castle (vert) 70 30
See also Nos. 1254/5 and 1275/6.

343 Athletes

1988. 50th Anniv of League of Luxembourg Student Sports Associations.

1228 **343** 12 f. multicoloured . . . 60 15

344 Automated Mail Sorting

1988. Europa. Transport and Communications. Multicoloured.

1229 12 f. Type **344** . . . . 2·00 20
1230 20 f. Electronic communications . . . . 2·50 1·25

345 Jean Monnet (statesman, birth centenary) **346** Emblem and Flame

1988. European Anniversaries.

1231 **345** 12 f. pink, brown and light brown 75 20
1232 – 12 f. brown and green . . 1·00 20
DESIGN: No. 1232, European Investment Bank headquarters, Kirchberg (30th anniv).

1988. Olympic Games, Seoul.

1233 **346** 12 f. multicoloured . . . 60 15

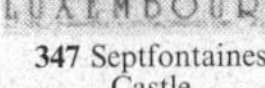

347 Septfontaines Castle **348** Annunciation to Shepherds

1988. Doorways.

1234 **347** 12 f. black and brown . . 70 15
1235 – 25 f. black and green . . 1·50 80
1236 – 50 f. black and brown . . 2·50 1·50
DESIGNS: 25 f. National Library; 50 f. Holy Trinity Church.

1988. National Welfare Fund. Illustrations from 16th-century "Book of Hours". Multicoloured.

1237 9 f. + 1 f. Type **348** 60 40
1238 12 f. + 2 f. Adoration of the Magi 70 40
1239 18 f. + 2 f. Madonna and Child 2·50 2·50
1240 20 f. + 8 f. Pentecost . . . . 3·00 3·00

349 C. M. Spoo (promoter of Luxembourgish) **350** Grand Ducal Family Vault Bronze (Auguste Tremont)

1989. Anniversaries.

1241 **349** 12 f. black, red & brown 60 25
1242 – 18 f. multicoloured . . . 90 50
1243 – 20 f. red, black and grey 1·25 75
DESIGNS: 12 f. Type **349** (75th death anniv); 18 f. Stylized inking pad (125th anniv of Book Workers' Federation); 20 f. Henri Dunant (founder of International Red Cross) (75th anniv of Luxembourg Red Cross).

1989. 150th Anniv of Independence.

1244 **350** 12 f. multicoloured . . . 60 30

351 "Astra" Satellite and Map on T.V. Screens **352** Cyclist

1989. Launch of 16-channel T.V. Satellite.

1245 **351** 12 f. multicoloured . . . 60 30

1989. Start in Luxembourg of Tour de France Cycling Race.

1246 **352** 9 f. multicoloured . . . 70 30

353 Assembly and Flag **354** Emblem

1989. 40th Anniv of Council of Europe.

1247 **353** 12 f. multicoloured . . . 70 30

1989. Centenary of Interparliamentary Union.

1248 **354** 12 f. yellow, blue & ind 70 30

355 Hands **356** "Three Children in a Park" (anon)

1989. 3rd Direct Elections to European Parliament.

1249 **355** 12 f. multicoloured . . . 70 30

1989. Europa. Children's Games and Toys. Multicoloured.

1250 12 f. Type **356** 75 30
1251 20 f. "Child with Drum" (anon) 1·50 95

357 Grand Duke Jean **358** Charles IV

1989. 25th Anniv of Accession of Grand Duke Jean.

1252 **357** 3 f. black and orange . . 60 60
1253 9 f. black and green . . 80 80

1989. Tourism. As T **342**. Multicoloured.

1254 12 f. Clervaux Castle 50 30
1255 18 f. 1st-century bronze wild boar, Titelberg 90 65

1989. Luxembourg History. Stained Glass Windows by Joseph Oterberger, Luxembourg Cathedral. Multicoloured.
1256 12 f. Type **358** 75 30
1257 20 f. John the Blind . . . . 1·00 85
1258 25 f. Wenceslas II . . . . . 1·00 85

359 St. Lambert and St. Blase, Fennange **360** Funfair (650th anniv of Schueberfouer)

1989. National Welfare Fund. Restored Chapels (1st series). Multicoloured.
1259 9 f. + 1 f. Type **359** 50 30
1260 12 f. + 2 f. St. Quirinus, Luxembourg (horiz) . . . 60 50
1261 18 f. + 3 f. St. Anthony the Hermit, Reisdorf (horiz) . 2·00 2·00
1262 25 f. + 8 f. The Hermitage, Hachiville . . . . 3·00 3·00
See also Nos. 1280/3 and 1304/7.

1990. Anniversaries.
1263 **360** 9 f. multicoloured 80 30
1264 – 12 f. brown, pink & black 55 30
1265 – 18 f. multicoloured . . . 90 50
DESIGNS: 12 f. Batty Weber (writer, 50th death anniv); 18 f. Dish aerial (125th anniv of International Telecommunications Union).

361 Troops at Fortress

1990. Luxembourg Culture. Etchings of the Fortress by Christoph Wilhelm Selig. Multicoloured.
1266 9 f. Type **361** 60 30
1267 12 f. Soldiers by weir 70 40
1268 20 f. Distant view of fortress 1·50 1·00
1269 25 f. Walls . . . . 2·00 90

362 Paul Eyschen (75th anniv)

363 "Psallus pseudoplatini" (male and female) on Maple

1990. Statesmen's Death Anniversaries.
1270 **362** 9 f. brown and blue . . . 50 30
1271 – 12 f. blue and brown . . . 60 40
DESIGN: 12 f. Emmanuel Servais (centenary).

1990. Centenary of Luxembourg Naturalists' Society.
1272 **363** 12 f. multicoloured . . . 70 40

364 General Post Office, Luxembourg City

365 Hammelsmarsch Fountain (Will Lofy)

1990. Europa. Post Office Buildings.
1273 **364** 12 f. black and brown . . 1·00 30
1274 – 20 f. black and blue . . . 1·50 70
DESIGN—VERT: 20 f. Esch-sur-Alzette Post Office.

1990. Tourism. As T **342**. Multicoloured.
1275 12 f. Mondercange administrative offices . . . 65 30
1276 12 f. Schifflange town hall and church 65 30

1990. Fountains. Multicoloured.
1277 12 f. Type **365** 60 30
1278 25 f. Doves Fountain . . . . 1·25 80
1279 50 f. Maus Ketty Fountain, Mondorf-les-Bains (Will Lofy) . . . . 2·25 1·50

366 Congregation of the Blessed Virgin Mary, Vianden

368 "Geastrum varians"

1990. National Welfare Fund. Restored Chapels (2nd series). Multicoloured.
1280 9 f. + 1 f. Type **366** 60 40
1281 12 f. + 2 f. Notre Dame, Echternach (horiz) 70 50
1282 18 f. + 3 f. Consoler of the Afflicted, Grentzingen (horiz) 1·75 1·75
1283 25 f. + 8 f. St. Pirmin, Kaundorf . . . . 3·00 3·00

1991. Fungi. Illustrations by Pierre-Joseph Redoute. Multicoloured.
1285 14 f. Type **368** . . . . 1·00 40
1286 14 f. "Agaricus (Gymnopus) thiebautii" . . . . 1·00 40
1287 18 f. "Agaricus (Lepiota) lepidocephalus" . . . . . 1·50 75
1288 25 f. "Morchella favosa" . . 2·00 1·25

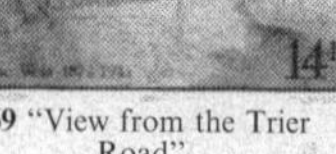

369 "View from the Trier Road"

370 Dicks (after Jean Goedert)

1991. Luxembourg Culture. 50th Death Anniv of Sosthene Weis (painter). Multicoloured.
1289 14 f. Type **369** 80 40
1290 18 f. "Vauban Street and the Viaduct" . . . . 1·00 60
1291 25 f. "St. Ulric Street" (vert) 1·50 1·00

1991. Death Centenary of Edmond de la Fontaine (pen-name Dicks) (poet).
1292 **370** 14 f. multicoloured . . . 70 40

371 Claw grasping Piece of Metal (after Emile Kirscht)

372 National Miners' Monument, Kayl

1991. 75th Anniv of Trade Union Movement in Luxembourg.
1293 **371** 14 f. multicoloured . . . 70 40

1991. Tourism. Multicoloured.
1294 14 f. Type **372** 75 40
1295 14 f. Magistrates' Court, Redange-sur-Attert (horiz) 75 40

373 Earth and Orbit of "Astra 1A" and "1B" Satellites

374 Telephone

1991. Europa. Europe in Space. Multicoloured.
1296 14 f. Type **373** 90 40
1297 18 f. Betzdorf Earth Station 1·50 85

1991. Posts and Telecommunications.
1298 **374** 4 f. brown . . . . 1·00 1·00
1299 – 14 f. blue 60 50
DESIGN: 14 f. Postbox.

375 1936 International Philatelic Federation Congress Stamp

376 Girl's Head

1991. 50th Stamp Day.
1300 **375** 14 f. multicoloured . . . 60 40
The stamp illustrated on No. 1300 incorrectly shows a face value of 10 f.

1991. Mascarons (stone faces on buildings) (1st series).
1301 **376** 14 f. black, buff & brown 60 40
1302 – 25 f. black, buff and pink 1·00 80
1303 – 50 f. black, buff and blue 2·00 1·60
DESIGNS: 25 f. Woman's head; 50 f. Man's head.
See also Nos. 1320/22.

377 Chapel of St. Donatus, Arsdorf

378 Jean-Pierre Pescatore Foundation

1991. National Welfare Fund. Restored Chapels (3rd series). Multicoloured.
1304 14 f. + 2 f. Type **377** 80 60
1305 14 f. + 2 f. Chapel of Our Lady of Sorrows, Brandenbourg (horiz) 80 60
1306 18 f. + 3 f. Chapel of Our Lady, Luxembourg (horiz) . . . . 1·60 1·60
1307 22 f. + 7 f. Chapel of the Hermitage, Wolwelange . . 3·00 3·00

1992. Buildings. Multicoloured.
1308 14 f. Type **378** 80 35
1309 14 f. Higher Technology Institute, Kirchberg 80 35
1310 14 f. New Fairs and Congress Centre, Kirchberg 80 35

379 Inner Courtyard, Bettembourg Castle

1992. Tourism. Multicoloured.
1311 18 f. Type **379** 75 45
1312 25 f. Walferdange Railway Station . . . . 1·25 60

380 Athlete (detail of mural, Armand Strainchamps)

1992. Olympic Games, Barcelona.
1313 **380** 14 f. multicoloured . . . 1·50 35

381 Luxembourg Pavilion

382 Lions Emblem

1992. "Expo '92" World's Fair, Seville.
1314 **381** 14 f. multicoloured . . . 55 35

1992. 75th Anniv of Lions International.
1315 **382** 14 f. multicoloured . . . 55 35

383 Memorial Tablet (Lucien Wercollier) **384** Nicholas Gonner (editor)

1992. 50th anniv of General Strike.
1316 **383** 18 f. brown, grey and red 75 70

1992. Europa. 500th anniv of Discovery of America by Columbus. Luxembourg Emigrants to America.
1317 **384** 14 f. brown, black and grn 1·00 35
1318 – 22 f. blue, black & orange 1·50 1·00
DESIGN: 22 f. Nicolas Becker (writer).

385 Star and European Community Emblem

386 Posthorn and Letters

1992. Single European Market.
1319 **385** 14 f. multicoloured . . . 55 35

1992. Mascarons (2nd series). As T **376**.
1320 14 f. black, buff and green . . 55 35
1321 22 f. black, buff and blue . . 90 1·00
1322 50 f. black, buff and purple . 2·00 1·60
DESIGNS: 14 f. Ram's head; 22 f. Lion's head; 50 f. Goat's head.

1992. 150th Anniv of Post and Telecommunications Office. Designs showing stained glass windows by Auguste Tremont. Multicoloured.
1323 14 f. Type **386** 55 35
1324 22 f. Post rider . . . . 90 1·00
1325 50 f. Telecommunications . . 2·00 1·60

387 Hazel Grouse

388 Grand Duke Jean

1992. National Welfare Fund. Birds (1st series). Multicoloured.
1326 14 f. + 2 f. Type **387** 65 50
1327 14 f. + 2 f. Golden oriole (vert) 65 50
1328 18 f. + 3 f. Black stork . . . 1·60 1·60
1329 22 f. + 7 f. Red kite (vert) . . 3·00 3·00
See also Nos. 1364/7 and 1383/6.

1993.
1330 **388** 1 f. black and yellow . . 10 10
1331 2 f. black and green . . 10 10
1332 5 f. black and yellow . . 20 10
1334 7 f. black and brown . . 30 20
1335 10 f. black and blue . . 45 30
1337 14 f. black and purple . 55 35
1338 15 f. black and green . . 55 35
1339 16 f. black and orange . 70 45
1340 18 f. black and yellow . 75 45
1341 20 f. black and red . . . 75 45
1343 22 f. black and green . . 90 55
1345 25 f. black and blue . . 1·00 60
1349 100 f. black and brown . 3·00 2·50

389 Old Ironworks Cultural Centre, Steinfort

1993. Tourism. Multicoloured.
1350 14 f. Type **389** 55 35
1351 14 f. "Children with Grapes" Fountain, Schwebsingen . 55 35

390 Collage by Maurice Esteve

1993. New Surgical Techniques.
1352 **390** 14 f. multicoloured . . . 55 35

391 Hotel de Bourgogne (Prime Minister's offices)

1993. Historic Houses. Multicoloured.
1353 14 f. Type **391** 55 35
1354 20 f. Simons House (now Ministry of Agriculture) . 85 50
1355 50 f. Cassal House . . . . . 2·50 1·60

392 "Rezlop" (Fernand Roda)

1993. Europa. Contemporary Art. Multicoloured.
1356 14 f. Type **392** 55 35
1357 22 f. "So Close" (Sonja Roef) 90 1·00

393 Monument (detail D. Donzelli), Tetange Cemetery

394 Emblem

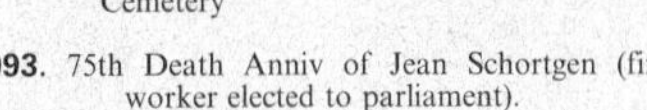

1993. 75th Death Anniv of Jean Schortgen (first worker elected to parliament).
1358 **393** 14 f. multicoloured . . . 55 35

1993. Centenary of Artistic Circle of Luxembourg.
1359 **394** 14 f. mauve and violet . 55 35

395 European Community Ecological Label

396 Tram Motor Unit No. 1 (Transport Museum, Luxembourg)

1993. Protection of Environment.
1360 **395** 14 f. blue, grn & emer . . 55 35

1993. Museum Exhibits (1st series). Multicoloured.
1361 14 f. Type **396** 55 35
1362 22 f. Iron ore tipper wagon (National Mining Museum, Rumelange) . . . . 85 1·00
1363 60 f. Horse-drawn carriage (Arts and Ancient Crafts Museum, Wiltz) . . . . . 2·25 2·00
See also Nos. 1404/6.

1993. National Welfare Fund. Birds (2nd series). As T **387**. Multicoloured.
1364 14 f. + 2 f. Common snipe ("Becassine") 65 50
1365 14 f. + 2 f. Common kingfisher ("Martin-Pecheur") (vert) . 65 50
1366 18 f. + 3 f. Little ringed plover ("Petit Gravelot") . . . . 1·60 1·50
1367 22 f. + 7 f. Sand martin ("Hirondelle de Rivage") (vert) . . . . 2·50 2·50

397 "Snow-covered Landscape" (Joseph Kutter)

1994. Artists' Birth Centenaries. Multicoloured.
1368 14 f. Type **397** 60 40
1369 14 f. "The Moselle" (Nico Klopp) 60 40

398 Members' Flags

399 17th-Century Herald's Tabard

1994. 4th Direct Elections to European Parliament.
1370 **398** 14 f. multicoloured . . . 60 40

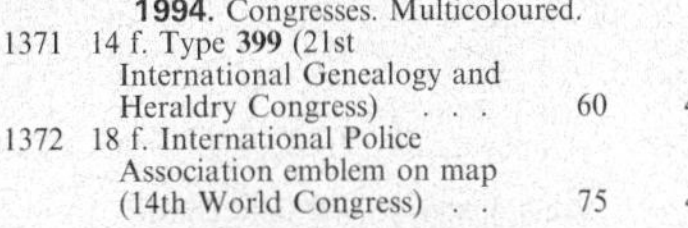

1994. Congresses. Multicoloured.
1371 14 f. Type **399** (21st International Genealogy and Heraldry Congress) . . . 60 40
1372 18 f. International Police Association emblem on map (14th World Congress) . . 75 45

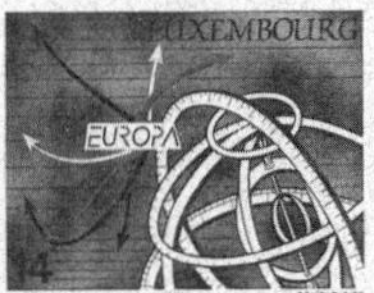

400 Arrows and Terrestrial Globe

1994. Europa. Discoveries. Multicoloured.
1373 14 f. Type **400** 60 40
1374 22 f. Chart, compass rose and sails . . . . 90 1·00

401 "Family" (Laura Lammar)

1994. International Year of the Family.
1375 **401** 25 f. multicoloured . . . 1·00 60

402 Crowds cheering American Soldiers

1994. 50th Anniv of Liberation.
1376 **402** 14 f. multicoloured . . . 60 40

403 Western European Union Emblem (40th anniv)

1994. Anniversaries and Campaigns.
1377 **403** 14 f. blue, lilac and ultramarine 60 40
1378 – 14 f. multicoloured . . . 60 40
1379 – 14 f. multicoloured . . . 60 40
DESIGNS—No. 1378, Emblem (25th anniv in Luxembourg of European Communities' Office for Official Publications); 1379, 10th-century B.C. ceramic bowl from cremation tomb, Bigelbach (European Bronze Age Campaign).

404 Munster Abbey (General Finance Inspectorate)

1994. Former Refuges now housing Government Offices. Multicoloured.
1380 15 f. Type **404** 65 40
1381 25 f. Holy Spirit Convent (Ministry of Finance) . . 1·00 1·00
1382 60 f. St. Maximine Abbey of Trier (Ministry of Foreign Affairs) . . . . 2·50 2·00

1994. National Welfare Fund. Birds (3rd series). As T **387**. Multicoloured.
1383 14 f. + 2 f. Stonechat ("Traquet Patre") (vert) 65 50
1384 14 f. + 2 f. Grey partridge ("Perdix Grise") 65 60
1385 18 f. + 3 f. Yellow wagtail ("Bergeronnette Printaniere") 1·50 1·40
1386 22 f. + 7 f. Great grey shrike ("Pie-Grieche Grise") (vert) 2·00 2·00

405 "King of the Antipodes"

406/409 Panoramic View of City (½-size illustration)

1995. Luxembourg, European City of Culture.
1387 **405** 16 f. multicoloured . . . 70 45
1388 – 16 f. multicoloured . . . 70 45
1389 – 16 f. multicoloured . . . 70 45
1390 **406** 16 f. multicoloured . . . 70 45
1391 **407** 16 f. multicoloured . . . 70 45
1392 **408** 16 f. multicoloured . . . 70 45
1393 **409** 16 f. multicoloured . . . 70 45
1394 – 16 f. multicoloured . . . 70 45
DESIGNS—As T **405**: No. 1388, "House with Arcades and Yellow Tower"; 1389, "Small Path" (maze). 35 × 26 mm: No. 1394, Emblem.
Nos. 1390/3 were issued together, se-tenant, forming the composite design illustrated.

410 Landscape and Slogan

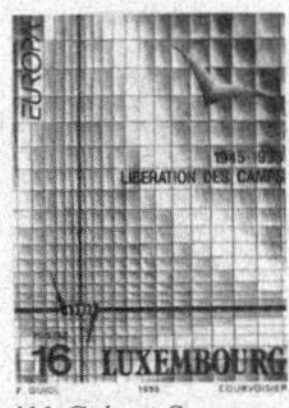

411 Colour Spectrum and Barbed Wire

1995. European Nature Conservation Year.
1395 **410** 16 f. multicoloured . . . 70 45

1995. Europa. Peace and Freedom. 50th Anniv of Liberation of Concentration Camps. Mult.
1396 16 f. Type **411** 70 45
1397 25 f. Wire barbs breaking through symbolic sky and earth . . . . 1·10 70

412 Emblem

1995. Anniversaries and Event. Multicoloured.
1398 16 f. Type **412** (6th Small European States Games, Luxembourg) 70 45
1399 32 f. Diagram of section through Earth (27th anniv of underground Geodynamics Laboratory, Walferdange) (33 × 34 mm) . . . . . . 1·40 85
1400 80 f. Anniversary emblem (50th anniv of U.N.O.) . . . . . 3·25 2·50

413 Boeing 757

1995. 40th Anniv of Luxembourg–Iceland Air Link.
1401 **413** 16 f. multicoloured . . . 70 45

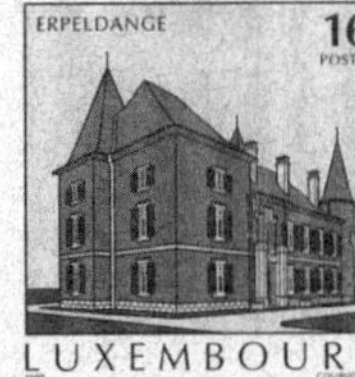

414 Erpeldange Castle

415 Stained Glass Window from Alzingen Church

1995. Tourism. Multicoloured.
1402 16 f. Type **414** 70 45
1403 16 f. Schengen Castle 70 45

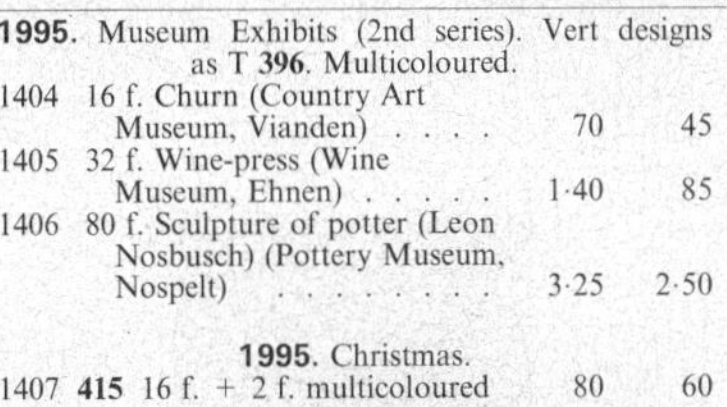

1995. Museum Exhibits (2nd series). Vert designs as T **396**. Multicoloured.
1404 16 f. Churn (Country Art Museum, Vianden) 70 45
1405 32 f. Wine-press (Wine Museum, Ehnen) . . . . . 1·40 85
1406 80 f. Sculpture of potter (Leon Nosbusch) (Pottery Museum, Nospelt) . . . . 3·25 2·50

1995. Christmas.
1407 **415** 16 f. + 2 f. multicoloured 80 60

416 Broad-leaved Linden ("Tilia platyphyllos")

417 Mayrisch (after Theo van Rysselberghe)

1995. National Welfare Fund. Trees (1st series). Multicoloured.
1408 16 f. + 2 f. Type **416** 80 60
1409 16 f. + 2 f. Horse chestnut ("Aesculus hippocastanum") (horiz) 80 60
1410 20 f. + 3 f. Pedunculate oak (horiz) . . . . 1·00 1·00
1411 32 f. + 7 f. Silver birch . . . 1·75 1·75
See also Nos. 1432/5.

1996. 68th Death Anniv of Emile Mayrisch (engineer).
1412 **417** A (16 f.) multicoloured . 65 40

418 Mounument, Place Clairefontaine (Jean Cardot)

420 "Marie Munchen"

419 Two-car Electric Train

1996. Birth Centenary of Grand Duchess Charlotte.
1413 **418** 16 f. multicoloured . . . 65 40

1996. 50th Anniv of Luxembourg National Railway Company. Multicoloured.
1414 16 f. Type **419** 65 40
1415 16 f. Linked cars 65 40
1416 16 f. Train (right-hand detail) 65 40
Nos. 1414/16 were issued together, se-tenant, forming a composite design of the train.

1996. 96th Death Anniv of Mihaly Munkacsy (painter). Multicoloured.
1417 16 f. Type **420** 65 40
1418 16 f. Munkacsy (after Edouard Charlemont) (horiz) . . . 65 40

421 Workers and Emblem

422 Marie de Bourgogne

1996. Anniversaries.
1419 **421** 16 f. green, orange and black 65 40
1420 – 20 f. multicoloured . . . 80 50
1421 – 25 f. multicoloured . . . 1·00 60
1422 – 32 f. multicoloured . . . 1·25 75
DESIGNS—HORIZ: 16 f. Type **421** (75th anniv of Luxembourg Confederation of Christian Trade Unions); 32 f. Film negative (centenary of motion pictures). VERT: 20 f. Transmitter and radiowaves (centenary of Guglielmo Marconi's patented wireless telegraph); 25 f. Olympic flame and rings (centenary of modern Olympic Games).

1996. Europa. Famous Women. Duchesses of Luxembourg. Multicoloured.
1423 16 f. Type **422** 65 40
1424 25 f. Maria-Theresa of Austria 1·00 60

423 Handstamp

1996. Bicentenary (1995) of Registration and Property Administration.
1425 **423** 16 f. multicoloured . . . 65 40

424 Children of different Cultures (Michele Dockendorf)

1996. "Let us Live Together". Multicoloured.
1426 16 f. Type **424** 65 40
1427 16 f. "L'Abbraccio" (statue, Marie-Josee Kerschen) (vert) 65 40

425 Eurasian Badger

1996. Mammals. Multicoloured.
1428 16 f. Type **425** 65 40
1429 20 f. Polecat 80 50
1430 80 f. European otter . . . . 3·25 2·00

426 "The Birth of Christ" (icon, Eva Mathes) 427 John the Blind

1996. Christmas.
1431 **426** 16 f. + 2 f. multicoloured 70 55

1996. National Welfare Fund. Trees (2nd series). As T **416**. Multicoloured.
1432 16 f. + 2 f. Willow ("Salix sp.") (horiz) 70 55
1433 16 f. + 2 f. Ash ("Fraxinus excelsior") 70 55
1434 20 f. + 3 f. Mountain ash (horiz) 90 90
1435 32 f. + 7 f. Common beech . . 1·50 1·50

1996. 700th Birth Anniv of John the Blind (King of Bohemia and Count of Luxembourg).
1436 **427** 32 f. multicoloured . . . 1·25 75

OFFICIAL STAMPS

1875. Stamps of 1859–72 optd **OFFICIEL**. Roul.
O79 **3** 1 c. brown . . . . 30·00 40·00
O80 2 c. black . . . . 30·00 40·00
O81 **4** 10 c. lilac £2250 £2500
O82 12½ c. red £500 £600
O83 20 c. brown . . . . 40·00 60·00
O84 25 c. blue £275 £150
O85 30 c. purple . . . . 35·00 80·00
O88 40 c. orange £180 £250
O87 1 f. on 37½ c. bistre (No. 37) £160 25·00

1875. Stamps of 1874–79 optd **OFFICIEL**. Perf.
O 89 **3** 1 c. brown . . . . 10·00 30·00
O 90 2 c. black . . . . 12·00 35·00
O 91 4 c. green £100 £160
O 92 5 c. yellow . . . . 70·00 80·00
O 93a **4** 10 c. lilac £100 £110
O111 12½ c. red . . . . 90·00 £110
O 98 20 c. brown . . . .
O 99a 25 c. blue . . . . 2·00 2·50
O 96 1 f. on 37½ c. bistre (No. 56) 35·00 60·00

1881. Stamp of 1859 optd **S. P.** Roul.
O116 **3** 40 c. orange . . . . . . 40·00 70·00

1881. Stamps of 1874–79 optd **S. P.** Perf.
O128 **3** 1 c. brown . . . . 8·00 10·00
O129 2 c. black . . . . 10·00 10·00
O118 4 c. green £180 £200
O123 5 c. yellow £150 £200
O124 **4** 10 c. lilac £150 £200
O131 12½ c. red £180 £225
O132 20 c. brown . . . . 70·00 £100
O133 25 c. blue . . . . 70·00 £100
O134 30 c. red . . . . 80·00 £120
O120 1 f. on 37½ c. bistre (No. 56) 35·00 50·00

1882. Stamps of 1882 optd **S. P.**
O141 **7** 1 c. grey 25 40
O142 2 c. brown 25 40
O143 4 c. olive 25 50
O144 5 c. green 30 60
O181 10 c. red . . . . 12·00 16·00
O158 12½ c. blue . . . . 1·50 5·00
O159 20 c. orange . . . . 1·50 4·00
O183 25 c. blue . . . . 20·00 25·00
O149 30 c. olive . . . . 4·00 9·00
O150 50 c. brown . . . . 1·00 3·00
O151 1 f. lilac . . . . 1·00 3·00
O152 5 f. orange . . . . 12·00 40·00

1891. Stamps of 1891 optd **S. P.**
O188 **8** 10 c. red 25 50
O191 12½ c. green . . . . 7·00 7·00
O192 20 c. orange . . . . 12·00 9·00
O193 25 c. blue 30 55
O194 30 c. green . . . . 7·00 9·00
O195 37½ c. green . . . . 7·00 9·00
O196 50 c. brown . . . . 6·00 10·00
O197 1 f. purple . . . . 6·00 12·00
O198 2½ f. black . . . . 40·00 75·00
O199 5 f. lake . . . . 35·00 55·00

1898. Stamps of 1895 optd **S. P.**
O213 **9** 1 c. grey . . . . 2·00 2·00
O214 2 c. brown . . . . 1·00 1·50
O215 4 c. bistre . . . . 1·00 1·50
O216 5 c. green . . . . 4·00 5·00
O217 10 c. red . . . . 25·00 35·00

1908. Stamps of 1906 optd **Officiel.**
O218 **10** 1 c. grey 10 30
O219 2 c. brown 10 30
O220 4 c. bistre 10 30
O221 5 c. green 10 30
O271 5 c. mauve 10 30
O222 6 c. lilac 10 30
O223 7½ c. yellow 10 30
O224 10 c. red 20 40
O225 12½ c. slate 20 50
O226 15 c. brown 30 50
O227 20 c. orange 30 60
O228 25 c. blue 30 60
O229 30 c. olive . . . . 4·00 7·00
O230 37½ c. green 50 60
O231 50 c. brown . . . . 80 1·25
O232 87½ c. blue . . . . 2·00 3·50
O233 1 f. purple . . . . 3·00 4·00
O234 2½ f. red . . . . 70·00 60·00
O235 5 f. purple . . . . 60·00 45·00

1915. Stamps of 1914 optd **Officiel.**
O236 **13** 10 c. purple 20 70
O237 12½ c. green 20 70
O238 15 c. brown 20 70
O239 17½ c. brown 20 70
O240 25 c. blue 20 70
O241 30 c. brown . . . . 1·50 5·00
O242 35 c. blue . . . . 20 1·25
O243 37½ c. brown . . . . 20 1·50
O244 40 c. red . . . . 30 1·25
O245 50 c. grey . . . . 30 1·00
O246 62½ c. green . . . . 30 1·50
O247 87½ c. orange . . . . . . 30 2·00
O248 1 f. brown . . . . 30 1·50
O249 2½ f. red . . . . 30 3·00
O250 5 f. violet . . . . 30 3·50

1922. Stamps of 1921 optd **Officiel.**
O251 **17** 2 c. brown 10 20
O252 3 c. green 10 20
O253 6 c. purple 10 40
O272 10 c. green 10 30
O273 15 c. green 10 30
O274 15 c. orange 10 30
O256 20 c. orange 10 40
O275 20 c. green 10 30
O257 25 c. green 10 40
O258 30 c. red 10 40
O259 40 c. orange 10 40
O260 50 c. blue 20 60
O276 50 c. red 20 50
O261 75 c. red 20 60
O277 75 c. blue 20 50
O266 80 c. black 20 50
O263 **18** 1 f. red . . . . 30 2·00
O278 1 f. blue . . . . 30 1·00
O267 – 2 f. blue . . . . 40 2·00
O279 – 2 f. brown . . . . 1·50 5·00
O269 – 5 f. violet . . . . 3·00 10·00

1922. Stamps of 1923 optd **Officiel.**
O268b **28** 3 f. blue . . . . 40 1·50
O270 **26** 10 f. black . . . . 9·00 24·00

1926. Stamps of 1926 optd **Officiel.**
O280 **32** 5 c. mauve 10 20
O281 10 c. green 10 20
O298 15 c. black 30 80
O282 20 c. orange 10 20
O283 25 c. green 10 20
O300 25 c. brown 20 60
O301 30 c. green . . . . 30 1·40
O302 30 c. violet 30 80
O303 35 c. violet 30 80
O304 35 c. green 30 80
O286 40 c. brown 10 20
O287 50 c. brown 10 20
O307 60 c. green 30 60
O288 65 c. brown 10 40
O308 70 c. violet . . . . 3·00 6·00
O289 75 c. red 10 40
O309 75 c. brown 30 60
O291 80 c. brown 10 40
O292 90 c. red 20 60
O293 1 f. black 20 50
O312 1 f. red . . . . 40 2·00
O294 1¼ f. blue 10 50
O313 1¼ f. yellow . . . . 2·00 6·00
O314 1¾ f. green . . . . 1·90 4·00
O315 1½ f. blue . . . . 30 1·40
O316 1¾ f. blue . . . . 40 1·50

1928. Stamp of 1928 optd **Officiel.**
O317 **37** 2 f. black . . . . 40 1·50

1931. Stamp of 1931 optd **Officiel.**
O318 **43** 20 f. green . . . . 2·00 8·50

1934. Stamp of 1934 optd **Officiel.**
O319 **47** 5 f. green . . . . 1·40 6·00

1935. No. 340 optd **Officiel.**
O341 **52** 10 f. green . . . . 1·50 7·00

POSTAGE DUE STAMPS

D 12 Arms of Luxembourg D 77

1907.
D173 **D 12** 5 c. black and green 10 20
D174 10 c. black and green 1·10 20
D175 12½ c. black and green 30 80
D176 20 c. black and green 60 80
D177 25 c. black and green 13·00 1·25
D178 50 c. black and green 50 3·00
D179 1 f. black and green . . 30 3·00

1920. Surch.
D193 **D 12** 15 on 12½ c. blk & grn 1·50 8·00
D194 30 on 25 c. blk & grn 1·50 9·00

1922.
D221 **D 12** 5 c. red and green . . 20 40
D222 10 c. red and green . . 20 30
D223 20 c. red and green . . 20 30
D224 25 c. red and green . . 20 30
D225 30 c. red and green . . 40 30
D226 35 c. red and green . . 40 20
D227 50 c. red and green . . 40 30
D228 60 c. red and green . . 30 30
D229 70 c. red and green . . 40 30
D230 75 c. red and green . . 40 20
D231 1 f. red and green . . 20 50
D232 2 f. red and green . . 40 7·00
D233 3 f. red and green . . 1·25 13·00

1946.
D488 **D 77** 5 c. green 30 30
D489 10 c. green 30 30
D490 20 c. green 30 30
D491 30 c. green 30 30
D492 50 c. green 30 30
D493 70 c. green 40 55
D494 75 c. green . . . . . . 1·50 30
D495 1 f. red 30 30
D496 1 f. 50 red 30 30
D497 2 f. red 30 30
D498 3 f. red 80 30
D499 5 f. red . . . . 1·25 30
D500 10 f. red . . . . 2·00 3·00
D501 20 f. red . . . . 4·00 20·00

MACAO Pt. 9

A Portuguese territory in China at the mouth of the Canton River.

1884. 1000 reis = 1 milreis.
1894. 78 avos = 1 rupee.
1913. 100 avos = 1 pataca.

1884. "Crown" key-type inscr "MACAU".
10 **P** 5 r. black . . . . 5·75 4·25
2 10 r. orange . . . . 8·50 8·00
21 10 r. green . . . . 8·50 7·00
12 20 r. bistre . . . . 14·00 10·50
27 20 r. red . . . . 14·00 12·00
13 25 r. red . . . . 5·00 4·25
22 25 r. lilac . . . . 8·50 7·00
14 40 r. blue . . . . 22·00 22·00
23 40 r. buff . . . . 13·00 10·50
15 50 r. green . . . . 24·00 22·50
24 50 r. blue . . . . 8·50 8·50
31 80 r. grey . . . . 24·00 21·00
16 100 r. lilac . . . . 14·00 12·50
17 200 r. orange . . . . . . 14·00 12·50
9 300 r. brown . . . . . . 13·50 13·50

1885. "Crown" key type of Macao surch **80 reis** in circle. No gum.
19a **P** 80 r. on 100 r. lilac . . . . 21·00 20·00

1885. "Crown" key type of Macao surch in Reis. With gum, (43, 44, 45), no gum (others).
32 **P** 5 r. on 25 r. pink . . . . 7·00 6·00
43 5 r. on 80 r. grey . . . . 6·00 5·25
46 5 r. on 100 r. lilac . . . . 28·00 24·00
33 10 r. on 25 r. pink . . . . 10·50 8·50
38 10 r. on 50 r. green . . . . 50·00 42·00
44 10 r. on 80 r. grey . . . . 13·50 11·00
47 10 r. on 200 r. orange . . . 28·00 24·00
35 20 r. on 50 r. green . . . . 9·25 6·25
45 20 r. on 80 r. grey . . . . 18·00 15·00
40 40 r. on 50 r. green . . . . 42·00 32·00

1885. "Crown" key-type of Macao surch with figure of value only and bar. No gum.
41 **P** 5 on 25 r. red . . . . . . 11·00 8·50
42a 10 on 50 r. green . . . . . 8·50 7·00

9

1887. Fiscal stamps as T **9** surch **CORREIO** and new value. No gum.
50 5 r. on 10 r. green and brown 55·00 55·00
51 5 r. on 20 r. green and brown 55·00 55·00
52 5 r. on 60 r. green and brown 55·00 55·00
53 10 r. on 10 r. green and brown 65·00 60·00
54 10 r. on 60 r. green and brown 65·00 60·00
55 40 r. on 20 r. green and brown £110 90·00

1888. "Embossed" key-type inscr "PROVINCIA DE MACAU".
56 **Q** 5 r. black . . . . 6·00 5·00
57 10 r. green . . . . 6·00 5·00
58 20 r. red . . . . 10·50 5·00
59 25 r. mauve . . . . 10·50 5·00
60 40 r. brown . . . . 10·50 5·00
61 50 r. blue . . . . 10·50 5·00
62 80 r. grey . . . . 13·00 8·50
63 100 r. brown . . . . 14·00 8·50
71 200 r. lilac . . . . 18·00 8·50
72 300 r. orange . . . . . . 16·00 8·50

1892. No. 71 surch **30 30.**
73 **Q** 30 on 200 r. lilac . . . . . 14·50 11·00

1894. "Embossed" key-type of Macao surch **PROVISORIO**, value and Chinese characters. No gum.
75b **Q** 1 a. on 5 r. black . . . . 3·25 1·90
76 3 a. on 20 r. red . . . . . 5·25 2·50
77 4 a. on 25 r. violet . . . . 7·00 3·25
89 5 a. on 30 on 200 r. lilac (No. 73) . . . . 45·00 42·00
78 6 a. on 40 r. brown . . . . 5·75 5·25
79 8 a. on 50 r. blue . . . . 14·00 8·50
80 13 a. on 80 r. grey . . . . 7·00 5·75
81 16 a. on 100 r. brown . . . 11·00 6·00
82 31 a. on 200 r. lilac . . . 21·00 20·00
83 47 a. on 300 r. orange . . . 21·00 12·50

1894. "Figures" key-type inscr "MACAU".
91 **R** 5 r. yellow . . . . 2·75 1·90
92 10 r. mauve . . . . 2·75 1·90
93 15 r. brown . . . . 4·50 3·00
94 20 r. lilac . . . . 5·00 3·00
95 25 r. green . . . . 11·00 7·00
96 50 r. blue . . . . 13·50 7·00
97 75 r. pink . . . . 21·00 17·00
98 80 r. green . . . . 14·00 13·50
99 100 r. brown on buff . . . 14·50 10·50
100 150 r. red on pink . . . . 15·00 10·50
101 200 r. blue on blue . . . 20·00 14·00
102 300 r. blue on brown . . . 25·00 14·00

1898. As Vasco da Gama types of Portugal but inscr "MACAU".
104 ½ a. green . . . . 2·75 1·90
105 1 a. red . . . . 2·75 1·90
106 2 a. purple . . . . 2·75 1·90
107 4 a. green . . . . 3·00 1·90
108 8 a. blue . . . . 5·25 2·75

109 12 a. brown . . . . 5·75 3·25
110 16 a. brown . . . . 5·75 2·75
111 24 a. brown . . . . 7·00 5·00

1898. "King Carlos" key-type inscr "MACAU". Name and value in black.

112 S ½ a. grey . . . . 1·10 45
113 1 a. yellow . . . . 1·10 45
114 2 a. green . . . . 1·10 45
115 2½ a. brown . . . . 1·90 1·10
116 3 a. lilac . . . . 1·90 1·10
174 3 a. grey . . . . 1·75 1·25
117 4 a. green . . . . 2·75 2·00
175 4 a. red . . . . 1·75 1·25
176 5 a. brown . . . . 2·40 1·90
177 6 a. brown . . . . 2·75 2·00
119 8 a. blue . . . . 2·75 2·00
178 8 a. brown . . . . 2·75 2·00
120 10 a. blue . . . . 2·75 2·00
121 12 a. pink . . . . 5·00 4·00
179 12 a. purple . . . . 12·50 8·75
122 13 a. mauve . . . . 5·00 4·00
180 13 a. lilac . . . . 5·25 4·25
123 15 a. green . . . . 13·00 8·75
124 16 a. blue on blue . . . . 5·75 4·00
181 18 a. brown on pink . . . 10·50 8·75
125 20 a. brown on cream . . 6·00 4·00
126 24 a. brown on yellow . . 7·00 5·00
127 31 a. purple . . . . 8·50 5·00
182 31 a. purple on pink . . . 10·50 9·75
128 47 a. blue on pink . . . . 12·50 7·25
183 47 a. blue on yellow . . . 14·50 11·00
129 78 a. black on blue . . . . 14·00 8·75

1900. "King Carlos" key-type of Macao surch **PROVISORIO** and new value.

132 S 5 on 13 a. mauve . . . . . 3·50 2·50
133 10 on 16 a. blue on blue . . 4·50 3·00
134 15 on 24 a. brown on yell . 5·25 3·00
135 20 on 31 a. purple . . . . 5·25 3·00

1902. Various types of Macao surch.

138 Q 6 a. on 5 r. black . . . . . 2·75 1·90
142 R 6 a. on 5 r. yellow . . . . 2·75 2·00
136 P 6 a. on 10 r. yellow . . . . 6·00 5·00
137 6 a. on 10 r. green . . . . 4·00 4·00
139 Q 6 a. on 10 r. green . . . . 2·75 1·90
143 R 6 a. on 10 r. mauve . . . 4·25 3·50
144 6 a. on 15 r. brown . . . 4·25 3·50
145 6 a. on 25 r. green . . . . 2·75 2·00
140 Q 6 a. on 40 r. brown . . . 2·75 1·90
146 R 6 a. on 80 r. green . . . . 2·75 2·00
148 6 a. on 100 r. brn on buff 5·25 2·75
149 6 a. on 200 r. blue on blue 2·75 2·00
151 V 18 a. on 2½ r. brown . . . 3·50 3·00
153 Q 18 a. on 20 r. red . . . . 5·00 3·25
162 R 18 a. on 20 r. lilac . . . 6·25 3·50
154 Q 18 a. on 25 r. mauve . . . 29·00 20·00
163 R 18 a. on 50 r. blue . . . . 6·25 3·50
165 18 a. on 75 r. pink . . . . 6·25 3·50
155 Q 18 a. on 80 r. grey . . . 40·00 32·00
156 18 a. on 100 r. brown . . 7·00 6·00
166 R 18 a. on 150 r. red on pink 6·25 3·50
158 Q 18 a. on 200 r. lilac . . . 30·00 30·00
160 18 a. on 300 r. orange . . 8·50 5·25
167 R 18 a. on 300 r. blue on brn 6·25 3·50

1902. "King Carlos" type of Macao optd **PROVISORIO**.

168 S 2 a. green . . . . 6·00 3·50
169 4 a. green . . . . 6·00 3·50
170 8 a. blue . . . . 6·00 3·50
171 10 a. blue . . . . 6·25 4·25
172 12 a. pink . . . . 10·50 6·00

1905. No. 179 surch **10 AVOS** and bar.

184 S 10 a. on 12 a. purple . . . 9·25 7·50

1910. "Due" key-type of Macao, but with words "PORTEADO" and "RECEBER" cancelled.

185 W ½ a. green . . . . 5·25 4·00
186 1 a. green . . . . 5·25 4·00
187 2 a. grey . . . . 5·25 4·00

1911. "King Carlos" key-type of Macao optd **REPUBLICA**.

188 S ½ a. grey 55 50
189 1 a. orange 55 50
190 2 a. green 55 50
191 3 a. grey 55 50
192 4 a. red . . . . 1·90 1·90
193 5 a. brown . . . . 1·90 1·40
194 6 a. brown . . . . 1·90 1·40
195 8 a. brown . . . . 1·90 1·40
196 10 a. blue . . . . 1·90 1·40
197 13 a. lilac . . . . 2·75 1·50
198 16 a. blue on blue . . . . 2·75 1·60
199 18 a. brown on pink . . . 4·75 3·25
200 20 a. brown on cream . . 4·75 3·25
201 31 a. purple on pink . . . 4·75 3·25
202 47 a. blue on yellow . . . 7·00 5·25
203 78 a. black on blue . . . . 10·00 10·50

30 32

1911. Fiscal stamp surch **POSTAL 1 AVO** and bar.

204 30 1 a. on 5 r. brown, yellow and black . . . . 3·50 2·75

1911. Stamps bisected and surch.

205 S 2 a. on half of 4 a. red (No. 175) . . . . 12·50 8·50
206 5 a. on half of 10 a. blue (No. 120) . . . . 38·00 38·00
207 5 a. on half of 10 a. blue (No. 171) . . . . 38·00 38·00

1911.

208 32 1 a. black £250 £250
209 2 a. black £275 £275

1913. Provisionals of 1902 surch in addition with new value and bars over old value and optd **REPUBLICA**.

212 R 2 a. on 18 a. on 20 r. lilac (No. 162) . . . . 2·75 2·00
213 2 a. on 18 a. on 50 r. blue (No. 163) . . . . 2·75 2·00
215 2 a. on 18 a. on 75 r. pink (No. 165) . . . . 2·75 2·00
216 2 a. on 18 a. on 150 r. red on pink (No. 166) . . . . 2·75 2·00

1913. Provisionals of 1902 and 1905 optd **REPUBLICA**.

218 Q 6 a. on 5 r. (No. 138) . . 3·25 2·75
284 R 6 a. on 5 r. (No. 142) . . 1·90 1·60
217 P 6 a. on 10 r. (No. 137) . . 8·50 7·00
285 Q 6 a. on 10 r. (No. 139) . . 1·75 1·25
286 R 6 a. on 10 r. (No. 143) . . 1·90 1·60
287 6 a. on 15 r. (No. 144) . . 1·40 1·25
288 6 a. on 25 r. (No. 145) . . 1·40 1·25
220 Q 6 a. on 40 r. (No. 140) . . 3·50 2·40
289 R 6 a. on 80 r. (No. 146) . . 1·40 1·25
291 6 a. on 100 r. (No. 148) . 2·50 1·90
292 6 a. on 200 r. (No. 149) . 1·40 1·25
281 S 8 a. (No. 170) . . . . . 1·60 1·25
282 10 a. (No. 171) . . . . . 1·60 1·25
283 S 10 a. on 12 a. (No. 184) . 1·60 1·25
293 V 18 a. on 2½ r. (No. 151) . 1·40 1·25
229 Q 18 a. on 20 r. (No. 153) . 5·25 5·25
295 R 18 a. on 20 r. (No. 162) . 3·25 2·25
296 18 a. on 50 r. (No. 163) . 3·50 2·75
298 18 a. on 75 r. (No. 165) . 3·50 2·75
230 Q 18 a. on 100 r. (No. 156) . 20·00 20·00
299 R 18 a. on 150 r. (No. 166) . 3·50 2·75
233 Q 18 a. on 300 r. (No. 160) . 9·50 7·25
300 R 18 a. on 300 r. (No. 167) . 7·25 4·00

1913. Stamps of 1911 issue surch.

252 S ½ a. on 5 a. brown . . . . 2·75 1·90
255 1 a. on 13 a. lilac . . . . 3·00 2·25
253 4 a. on 8 a. brown . . . . 3·50 2·75

1913. Vasco da Gama stamps of Macao optd **REPUBLICA**, and the 12 a. surch **10 A**.

256 ½ a. green . . . . 1·90 1·10
257 1 a. red . . . . 2·10 1·10
258 2 a. purple . . . . 2·10 1·10
259 4 a. green . . . . 1·90 1·10
260 8 a. blue . . . . 2·10 1·50
261 10 a. on 12 a. brown . . . 5·00 1·00
262 16 a. brown . . . . 3·00 1·90
263 24 a. brown . . . . 4·25 2·40

1913. "Ceres" key-type inscr "MACAU".

264 U ½ a. green . . . . 1·00 55
310 1 a. black . . . . 1·00 55
311 1½ a. green 85 45
280 2 a. green . . . . 1·00 55
313 3 a. orange . . . . 2·40 1·75
267 4 a. red . . . . 1·90 1·10
315 4 a. yellow . . . . 2·00 1·75
268 5 a. brown . . . . 2·25 1·40
269 6 a. violet . . . . 2·25 1·40
270 8 a. brown . . . . 2·25 1·40
271 10 a. blue . . . . 2·25 1·40
272 12 a. brown . . . . 2·25 1·40
320 14 a. mauve . . . . 5·75 5·75
321 16 a. grey . . . . 4·00 3·25
274 20 a. red . . . . 5·50 3·75
322 24 a. green . . . . 5·75 5·00
323 32 a. brown . . . . 8·75 7·00
275 40 a. purple . . . . 5·75 4·00
324 56 a. pink . . . . 11·50 10·50
276 58 a. brown on green . . . 10·50 8·00
325 72 a. brown . . . . 15·00 8·25
277 76 a. brown on pink . . . 11·00 8·75
278 1 p. orange on orange . . 13·50 11·00
326 1 p. orange . . . . 22·00 16·00
279 3 p. green on blue . . . . 40·00 35·00
327 3 p. turquoise . . . . . . 60·00 55·00
328 5 p. red . . . . 85·00 85·00

1919. Surch.

301 U ½ a. on 5 a. brn (No. 268) 17·00 14·00
330 1 a. on 24 a. grn (No. 322) 2·00 1·60
302 R 2 on 6 a. on 25 r. green (No. 288) . . . . 25·00 21·00
303 2 on 6 a. on 80 r. green (No. 289) . . . . 12·50 10·50
304 S 2 a. on 6 a. (No. 177) . . 20·00 18·00
331 U 2 a. on 32 a. (No. 323) . . 2·00 1·60
332 4 a. on 12 a. (No. 272) . . 2·00 1·60
329 5 a. on 6 a. vio (No. 269) . 2·75 2·50
334 7 a. on 8 a. brn (No. 270) . 2·75 2·25
335 12 a. on 14 a. (No. 320) . 2·75 2·25
336 15 a. on 16 a. (No. 321) . 2·75 2·25
337 20 a. on 56 a. pink (No. 324) 21·00 19·00

50 "Portugal" and Galleasse

1934.

338 50 ½ a. brown 30 30
339 1 a. brown 30 30
340 2 a. green 45 40
341 3 a. mauve 45 40
342 4 a. black 55 50
343 5 a. grey 55 50
344 6 a. brown 55 50
345 7 a. red 75 60
346 8 a. blue 75 60
347 10 a. red . . . . 1·10 1·00
348 12 a. blue . . . . 1·10 1·00
349 14 a. green . . . . 1·10 1·00
350 15 a. purple . . . . 1·10 1·00
351 20 a. orange . . . . 1·10 1·00
352 30 a. green . . . . 2·75 1·90
353 40 a. violet . . . . 2·75 1·90
354 50 a. brown . . . . 5·25 3·50
355 1 p. blue . . . . 13·00 7·75
356 2 p. brown . . . . 19·00 11·50
357 3 p. green . . . . 29·00 17·00
358 5 p. mauve . . . . 42·00 22·00

1936. Air. Stamps of 1934 optd **Aviso** and with Greek characters or surch also.

359 40 2 a. green . . . . 2·50 1·50
360 3 a. mauve . . . . 2·50 1·50
361 5 a. on 6 a. brown . . . . 2·50 1·50
362 7 a. red . . . . 2·50 1·50
363 8 a. blue . . . . 4·25 3·00
364 15 a. purple . . . . 13·00 7·50

54 Vasco da Gama 56 Airplane over Globe

1938. Name and value in black.

365 54 1 a. green (postage) 45 45
366 2 a. brown 45 45
367 3 a. violet 45 45
368 4 a. green 45 45
369 – 5 a. red 45 45
370 – 6 a. grey 80 75
371 – 8 a. purple 80 75
372 – 10 a. mauve 95 80
373 – 12 a. red 95 80
374 – 15 a. orange 95 80
375 – 20 a. blue . . . . 1·25 1·25
376 – 40 a. black . . . . 2·50 1·25
377 – 50 a. brown . . . . 2·50 1·25
378 – 1 p. red . . . . 9·75 5·25
379 – 2 p. green . . . . 18·00 8·00
380 – 3 p. blue . . . . 23·00 12·50
381 – 5 p. brown . . . . 38·00 16·00
382 56 1 a. red (air) 35 35
383 2 a. violet 45 35
384 3 a. orange 45 35
385 5 a. blue . . . . 1·00 60
386 10 a. red . . . . 1·75 95
387 20 a. green . . . . 2·75 1·50
388 50 a. brown . . . . 4·75 2·25
389 70 a. red . . . . 9·25 4·00
390 1 p. mauve . . . . 17·00 5·50

DESIGNS: Nos. 369/71, Mousinho de Albuquerque; Nos. 372/4, Henry the Navigator; Nos. 375/7, Dam; Nos. 378/81, Afonso de Albuquerque.

1940. Surch.

391 50 1 a. on 6 a. brn (No. 344) 3·75 2·75
394 2 a. on 6 a. brn (No. 344) 1·60 1·60
395 3 a. on 6 a. brn (No. 344) 1·60 1·60
401 – 3 a. on 6 a. grey (No. 370) 28·00 20·00
396 50 5 a. on 7 a. red (No. 345) 1·60 1·60
397 5 a. on 8 a. blue (No. 346) 1·60 1·60
398 8 a. on 30 a. (No. 352) . . 4·00 3·25
399 8 a. on 40 a. (No. 353) . . 4·00 3·25
400 8 a. on 50 a. (No. 354) . . 4·00 3·25

61 Mountain Fort 62 Our Lady of Fatima

1948.

410 – 1 a. brown and orange . . 1·25 40
427 – 1 a. violet and pink . . . 40 25
411 61 2 a. purple 85 40
428 2 a. brown and yellow . . . 40 25
412 – 3 a. purple . . . . 1·60 85
429 – 3 a. orange 85 40
413 – 8 a. red . . . . 2·10 1·25
430 – 8 a. grey . . . . 2·00 65
414 – 10 a. purple . . . . 2·50 1·25
431 – 10 a. brown and orange . 2·50 85
415 – 20 a. blue . . . . 5·00 1·25
416 – 30 a. grey . . . . 5·00 1·25
432 – 30 a. blue . . . . 6·75 1·75
417 – 50 a. brown and buff . . 8·50 1·60
433 – 50 a. olive and green . . . 12·50 2·50
418 – 1 p. green . . . . 30·00 11·00
419 – 1 p. blue . . . . 42·00
434 – 1 p. brown . . . . 25·00 4·25
420 – 2 p. red . . . . 38·00 9·75
421 – 3 p. green . . . . 45·00 10·50
422 – 5 p. violet . . . . 60·00 16·00

DESIGNS—HORIZ: 1 a. Macao house; 3 a. Port of Macao; 8 a. Praia Grande Bay; 10 a. Leal Senado Sq; 20 a. Sao Jerome Hill; 30 a. Street scene, Macao; 50 a. Relief of goddess of Ma (allegory); 5 p. Forest road. VERT: 1 p. Cerco Gateway; 2 p. Barra Pagoda, Ma-Cok-Miu; 3 p. Post Office.

1948. Honouring the Statue of Our Lady of Fatima.

423 62 8 a. red . . . . 10·00 4·00

64 Globe and Letter 65 Bells and Dove

1949. 75th Anniv of U.P.U.

424 64 32 a. purple . . . . 29·00 8·50

1950. Holy Year.

425 65 32 a. black . . . . 6·75 3·25
426 – 50 a. red . . . . 10·00 5·00

DESIGN: 50 a. Angel holding candelabra.

66 Arms and Dragon

1950.

435 66 1 a. yellow on cream . . . 85 40
436 2 a. green on green 85 40
437 10 a. purple on green . . . 2·50 85
438 10 a. mauve on green . . . 2·50 85

67 F. Mendes Pinto 68 Junk

1951.

439 67 1 a. indigo and blue . . . 40 20
440 – 2 a. brown and green . . . 85 20
441 – 3 a. green & light green . 1·25 25
442 – 6 a. violet and blue . . . 2·10 40
443 – 10 a. brown and orange . . 3·25 85
444 67 20 a. purple & lt purple . . 6·75 1·40
445 – 30 a. brown and green . . 11·00 2·10
446 – 50 a. red and orange . . . 16·00 3·25

DESIGNS: 2, 10 a. St. Francis Xavier; 3, 50 a. J. Alvaras; 6, 30 a. L. da Camoens.

1951.

447 – 1 p. ultramarine & blue . . 8·50 1·75
448 – 3 p. black and blue . . . 38·00 12·50
449 68 5 p. brown and orange . . 60·00 12·50

DESIGNS—HORIZ: 1 p. Sampan. VERT: 3 p. Junk.

69 Our Lady of Fatima

71 St. Raphael Hospital

1951. Termination of Holy Year.

450 69 60 a. mauve and pink . . . 21·00 5·00

1952. 1st Tropical Medicine Congress, Lisbon.

451 71 6 a. lilac and black . . . . 4·00 85

72 St. Francis Xavier Statue

73 The Virgin

1952. 400th Death Anniv of St. Francis Xavier.

452 72 3 a. black on cream . . . 1·25 40
453 – 16 a. brown on buff . . . 4·00 1·60
454 – 40 a. black on blue . . . . 8·50 2·50

DESIGNS: 16 a. Miraculous Arm of St. Francis; 40 a. Tomb of St. Francis.

1953. Missionary Art Exhibition.

455 73 8 a. brown and drab . . . 1·25 40
456 10 a. blue and brown . . . 3·25 1·25
457 50 a. green and drab . . . 8·50 2·50

74 Honeysuckle

75 Portuguese Stamp of 1853 and Arms of Portuguese Overseas Provinces

1953. Indigenous Flowers.

458 74 1 a. yellow, green and red . 25 10
459 – 3 a. purple, green & yellow 25 10
460 – 5 a. red, green and brown . 25 10
461 – 10 a. multicoloured 25 15
462 – 16 a. yellow, green & brown 50 15

463 – 30 a. pink, brown & green . . 1·10 35
464 – 39 a. multicoloured . . . . 1·25 35
465 – 1 p. yellow, green & purple . 3·00 65
466 – 3 p. red, brown and grey . . 9·25 1·60
467 – 5 p. yellow, green and red . 15·00 3·25

FLOWERS: 3 a. Myosotis; 5 a. Dragon claw; 10 a. Nunflower; 16 a. Narcissus; 30 a. Peach blossom; 39 a. Lotus blossom; 1 p. Chrysanthemum; 3 p. Plum blossom; 5 p. Tangerine blossom.

1954. Portuguese Stamp Centenary.
468 **75** 10 a. multicoloured . . . . 5·00 85

76 Father M. de Nobrega and View of Sao Paulo

77 Map of Macao

1954. 4th Centenary of Sao Paulo.
469 **76** 39 a. multicoloured . . . . 6·75 1·60

1956. Map multicoloured. Values in red, inscr in brown. Colours given are of the backgrounds.
470 **77** 1 a. drab 15 10
471 3 a. slate 30 10
472 5 a. brown 85 10
473 10 a. buff . . . . 1·25 30
474 30 a. blue . . . . 2·50 50
475 40 a. green . . . . 3·25 1·00
476 90 a. grey . . . . 7·50 1·25
477 1 p. 50 pink . . . . 13·50 2·10

78 Exhibition Emblem and Atomic Emblems

79 "Cinnamomum camphora"

1958. Brussels International Exhibition.
478 **78** 70 a. multicoloured . . . . 3·25 1·25

1958. 6th International Congress of Tropical Medicine.
479 **79** 20 a. multicoloured . . . . 4·50 1·25

80 Globe girdled by Signs of the Zodiac

81 Boeing 707 over Ermida da Penha

1960. 500th Death Anniv of Prince Henry the Navigator.
480 **80** 2 p. multicoloured . . . . 5·75 1·60

1960. Air. Multicoloured.
481 50 a. Praia Grande Bay . . . . 1·60 40
482 76 a. Type **81** . . . . 2·10 85
483 3 p. Macao . . . . 4·00 85
484 5 p. Mong Ha . . . . 10·00 85
485 10 p. Shore of Praia Grande Bay 12·50 1·25

82 Hockey

83 "Anopheles hycranus sinensis"

1962. Sports. Multicoloured.
486 10 a. Type **82** 10 10
487 16 a. Wrestling 40 10
488 20 a. Table tennis 50 25
489 50 a. Motor cycle racing . . . 80 25
490 1 p. 20 Relay racing . . . . . 8·50 1·60
491 2 p. 50 Badminton . . . . . . 17·00 4·25

1962. Malaria Eradication.
492 **83** 40 a. multicoloured . . . . 4·25 1·25

84 Bank Building

85 I.T.U. Emblem and St. Gabriel

1964. Centenary of National Overseas Bank.
493 **84** 20 a. multicoloured . . . 5·00 1·25

1965. Centenary of I.T.U.
494 **85** 10 a. multicoloured . . . 2·75 50

86 Infante Dom Henrique Academy and Visconde de Sao Januario Hospital

87 Drummer, 1548

1966. 40th Anniv of Portuguese National Revolution.
495 **86** 10 a. multicoloured . . . 4·25 40

1966. Portuguese Military Uniforms. Multicoloured.
496 10 a. Type **87** 80 25
497 15 a. Soldier, 1548 . . . . . 1·25 25
498 20 a. Arquebusier, 1649 . . . 1·25 25
499 40 a. Infantry officer, 1783 . . 2·10 50
500 50 a. Infantryman, 1783 . . . 2·75 60
501 60 a. Infantryman, 1902 . . . 3·75 1·25
502 1 p. Infantryman, 1903 . . . 5·50 1·60
503 3 p. Infantryman, 1904 . . . 12·50 5·00

88 O. E. Carmo and Patrol Boat "Vega"

89 Arms of Pope Paul VI, and "Golden Rose"

1967. Centenary of Military Naval Assn. Mult.
504 10 a. Type **88** 85 55
505 20 a. Silva Junior and sail frigate "Don Fernando" . . . . . 2·75 1·00

1967. 50th Anniv of Fatima Apparitions.
506 **89** 50 a. multicoloured . . . 4·00 80

90 Cabral Monument, Lisbon

91 Adm. Gago Coutinho with Sextant

1968. 500th Birth Anniv of Pedro Cabral (explorer). Multicoloured.
507 20 a. Type **90** . . . . 2·75 40
508 70 a. Cabral's statue, Belmonte 4·50 80

1969. Birth Centenary of Admiral Gago Coutinho.
509 **91** 20 a. multicoloured . . . 2·75 50

92 Church and Convent of Our Lady of the Reliquary, Vidigueira

93 L. A. Rebello da Silva

1969. 500th Birth Anniv of Vasco da Gama (explorer).
510 **92** 1 p. multicoloured . . . . 10·00 1·25

1969. Centenary of Overseas Administrative Reforms.
511 **93** 90 a. multicoloured . . . 2·50 40

94 Bishop D. Belchoir Carneiro

95 Facade of Mother Church, Golega

1969. 400th Anniv of Misericordia Monastery, Macao.
512 **94** 50 a. multicoloured . . . . 2·50 35

1969. 500th Birth Anniv of King Manoel I.
513 **95** 30 a. multicoloured . . . . 4·25 85

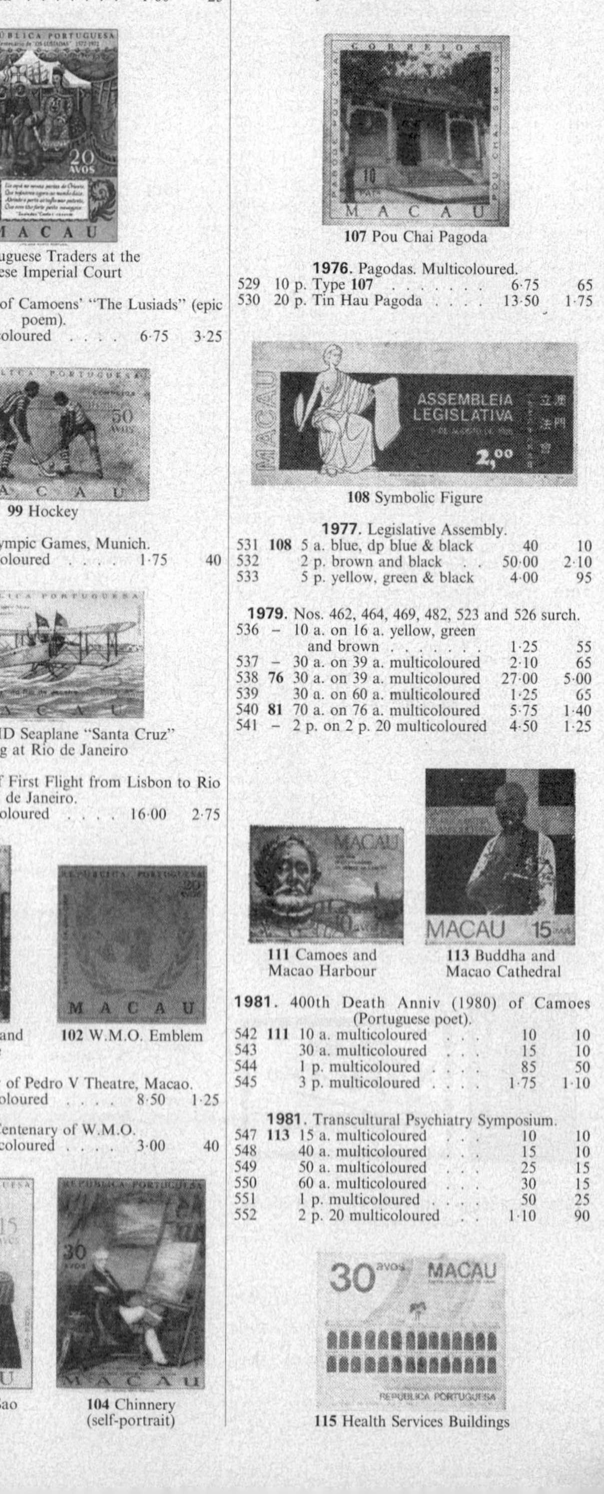

96 Marshal Carmona

97 Dragon Mask

1970. Birth Centenary of Marshal Carmona.
514 **96** 5 a. multicoloured. 40 15

1971. Chinese Carnival Masks. Multicoloured.
515 5 a. Type **97** 85 15
516 10 a. Lion mask . . . . 1·60 25

98 Portuguese Traders at the Chinese Imperial Court

1972. 400th Anniv of Camoens' "The Lusiads" (epic poem).
517 **98** 20 a. multicoloured . . . . 6·75 3·25

99 Hockey

1972. Olympic Games, Munich.
518 **99** 50 a. multicoloured . . . . 1·75 40

100 Fairey IIID Seaplane "Santa Cruz" arriving at Rio de Janeiro

1972. 50th Anniv of First Flight from Lisbon to Rio de Janeiro.
519 **100** 5 p. multicoloured . . . . 16·00 2·75

101 Lyre Emblem and Theatre Facade

102 W.M.O. Emblem

1972. Centenary of Pedro V Theatre, Macao.
520 **101** 2 p. multicoloured . . . . 8·50 1·25

1973. Centenary of W.M.O.
521 **102** 20 a. multicoloured . . . . 3·00 40

103 Visconde de Sao Januario

104 Chinnery (self-portrait)

1974. Centenary of Visconde de Sao Januario Hospital. Multicoloured.
522 15 a. Type **103** 40 10
523 60 a. Hospital buildings of 1874 and 1974 . . . . 1·60 40

1974. Birth Bicent of George Chinnery (painter).
524 **104** 30 a. multicoloured . . . 1·60 40

105 Macao–Taipa Bridge

1975. Inauguration of Macao–Taipa Bridge. Multicoloured.
525 20 a. Type **105** 85 30
526 2 p. 20 View of Bridge from below . . . . 5·75 1·10

106 Man waving Banner

1975. 1st Anniv of Portuguese Revolution.
527 **106** 10 a. multicoloured . . . 80 10
528 1 p. multicoloured . . . . 7·50 80

107 Pou Chai Pagoda

1976. Pagodas. Multicoloured.
529 10 p. Type **107** . . . . 6·75 65
530 20 p. Tin Hau Pagoda . . . . 13·50 1·75

108 Symbolic Figure

1977. Legislative Assembly.
531 **108** 5 a. blue, dp blue & black 40 10
532 2 p. brown and black . . . 50·00 2·10
533 5 p. yellow, green & black 4·00 95

1979. Nos. 462, 464, 469, 482, 523 and 526 surch.
536 – 10 a. on 16 a. yellow, green and brown . . . . 1·25 55
537 – 30 a. on 39 a. multicoloured 2·10 65
538 **76** 30 a. on 39 a. multicoloured 27·00 5·00
539 30 a. on 60 a. multicoloured 1·25 65
540 **81** 70 a. on 76 a. multicoloured 5·75 1·40
541 – 2 p. on 2 p. 20 multicoloured 4·50 1·25

111 Camoes and Macao Harbour

113 Buddha and Macao Cathedral

1981. 400th Death Anniv (1980) of Camoes (Portuguese poet).
542 **111** 10 a. multicoloured . . . 10 10
543 30 a. multicoloured . . . 15 10
544 1 p. multicoloured 85 50
545 3 p. multicoloured . . . . 1·75 1·10

1981. Transcultural Psychiatry Symposium.
547 **113** 15 a. multicoloured . . . 10 10
548 40 a. multicoloured . . . 15 10
549 50 a. multicoloured . . . 25 15
550 60 a. multicoloured . . . 30 15
551 1 p. multicoloured 50 25
552 2 p. 20 multicoloured . . . 1·10 90

115 Health Services Buildings

1982. Buildings.

554 – 10 a. grey, blue & yellow . . 10 10
555 – 20 a. black, green & lt grn . 10 10
556 115 30 a. green, grey & stone . 15 10
557 – 40 a. yellow, lt grn & grn . 15 10
558 – 60 a. orange, chocolate and brown 15 15
559 – 80 a. pink, green & brown 25 10
560 – 90 a. purple, blue and red 15 15
561 – 1 p. multicoloured 30 15
562 – 1 p. 50 yellow, brn & grey 30 15
563 – 2 p. purple, ultramarine and blue 65 30
564 – 2 p. 50 ultramarine, pink and blue 50 30
565 – 3 p. yellow, green and olive 40 30
566 – 7 p. 50 lilac, blue and red 1·25 1·00
567 – 10 p. grey, lilac & mauve . 3·25 1·75
568 – 15 p. yellow, brown & red 1·60 1·00

DESIGNS: 10 a. Social Welfare Institute; 20 a. Holy House of Mercy; 40 a. Guia lighthouse; 60 a. St. Lawrence's Church; 80 a. St. Joseph's Seminary; 90 a. Pedro V Theatre; 1 p. Cerco city gate; 1 p. 50, St. Domenico's Church; 2 p. Luis de Camoes Museum; 2 p. 50, Ruins of St. Paul's Church; 3 p. Palace of St. Sancha (Governor's residence); 7 p. 50, Senate House; 10 p. Schools Welfare Service building; 15 p. Barracks of the Moors (headquarters of Port Captaincy and Maritime Police).

116 Heng Ho (Moon goddess)

1982. Autumn Festival. Multicoloured.

569 40 a. Type 116 . . . . 40 40
560 1 p. Decorated gourds . . . . 1·25 40
561 2 p. Paper lantern . . . . . . 1·60 65
562 5 p. Warrior riding lion . . . 3·25 80

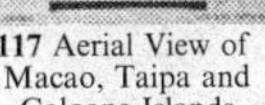

117 Aerial View of Macao, Taipa and Coloane Islands

118 "Switchboard Operators" (Lou Sok Man)

1982. Macao's Geographical Situation. Multicoloured.

573 50 a. Type 117 . . . . 25 15
574 3 p. Map of South China . . 3·00 1·50

1983. World Communications Year. Children's Drawings. Multicoloured.

575 60 a. Type 118 . . . . 15 10
576 3 p. Postman and pillar box (Lai Sok Pek) 65 30
577 6 p. Globe with methods of communication (Loi Chak Keong) . . . . 1·60 85

119 "Asclepias curassavica"

120 Galleon and Map of Macao (left)

1983. Medicinal Plants. Multicoloured.

578 20 a. Type 119 . . . . 15 10
579 40 a. "Acanthus ilicifolius" . . 30 15
580 60 a. "Melastoma sanguineum" 50 15
581 70 a. Indian lotus ("Nelumbo nucifera") 55 25
582 1 p. 50 "Bombax malabaricum" 1·25 65
583 2 p. 50 "Hibiscus mutabilis" 2·10 1·25

1983. 16th Century Portuguese Discoveries. Multicoloured.

585 4 p. Type 120 . . . . 1·40 1·25
586 4 p. Galleon, astrolabe and map of Macao (right) . . . . . 1·40 1·25

Nos. 585/6 were printed together, se-tenant, forming a composite design.

MINIMUM PRICE

The minimum price quoted is 10p which represents a handling charge rather than a basis for valuing common stamps. For further notes about prices, see introductory pages.

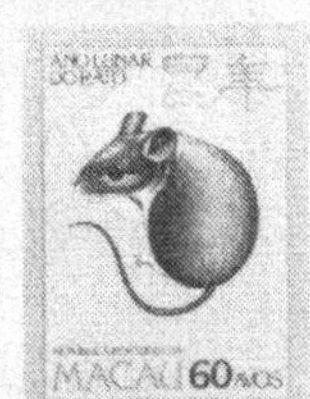

121 Rat

122 Detail of First Macao Stamp, 1884

1984. New Year. "Year of the Rat".

587 121 60 a. multicoloured . . . 2·50 1·25

1984. Centenary of Macao Stamps.

588 122 40 a. black and red . . . 15 15
589 3 p. black and red . . . 1·25 65
590 5 p. black and brown . . 1·75 1·00

123 Jay

1984. "Ausipex 84" International Stamp Exhibition, Melbourne. Birds. Multicoloured.

592 30 a. White-breasted kingfisher 35 20
593 40 a. Type 123 . . . . 45 20
594 50 a. Japanese white eye . . . 50 30
595 70 a. Hoopoe 70 30
596 2 p. 50 Pekin robin . . . . . 2·10 85
597 6 p. Mallard . . . . 4·25 2·10

124 Hok Lou T'eng

1984. "Philakorea 84" International Stamp Exhibition, Seoul. Fishing Boats. Multicoloured.

598 20 a. Type 124 . . . . 20 20
599 60 a. Tai Tong 55 30
600 2 p. Tai Mei Chai . . . . . 1·00 70
601 5 p. Ch'at Pong T'o . . . . 2·50 1·75

125 Ox and Moon

126 Open Hand with Stylized Doves

1985. New Year. Year of the Ox.

602 125 1 p. multicoloured . . . 85 55

1985. International Youth Year. Multicoloured.

603 2 p. 50 Type 126 . . . . . . 60 35
604 3 p. Open hands and plants . 70 50

127 Pres. Eanes

1985. Visit of President Ramalho Eanes of Portugal.

605 127 1 p. 50 multicoloured . . 85 30

128 Riverside Scene

129 "Euploea midamus"

1985. 25th Anniv of Luis de Camoes Museum. Paintings by Cheng Chi Yun. Multicoloured.

606 2 p. 50 Type 128 . . . . . . 1·25 1·00
607 2 p. 50 Man on seat and boy filling jar from river . . . . 1·25 1·00
608 2 p. 50 Playing harp in summerhouse . . . . 1·25 1·00
609 2 p. 50 Three men by river . . 1·25 1·00

1985. World Tourism Day. Butterflies. Mult.

610 30 a. Type 129 . . . . 15 10
611 50 a. Great orange-tip 15 15
612 70 a. "Lethe confusa" 30 15
613 2 p. Purple sapphire 70 45
614 4 p. "Euthalia phemius seitzi" 1·25 85
615 7 p. 50 Common birdwing . . 2·50 1·60

130 Tou (sailing barge)

131 Tiger and Moon

1985. "Italia '85" International Stamp Exhibition, Rome. Cargo Boats. Multicoloured.

617 50 a. Type 130 . . . . 25 25
618 70 a. "Veng Seng Lei" (motor junk) 35 25
619 1 p. "Tong Heng Long No. 2" (motor junk) 55 25
620 6 p. "Fong Vong San" (container ship) . . . . 3·25 2·00

1986. New Year. Year of the Tiger.

621 131 1 p. 50 multicoloured . . . 1·25 50

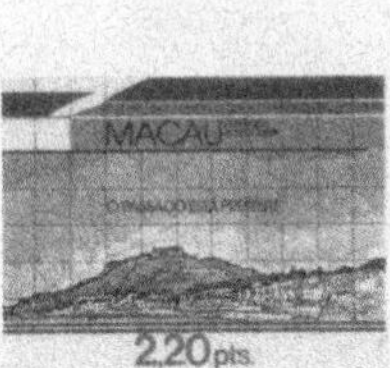

132 View of Macao

133 Suo-na

1986. Macao, "the Past is still Present".

622 132 2 p. 20 multicoloured . . . 1·25 50

1986. "Ameripex '86" International Stamp Exn, Chicago. Musical Instruments. Multicoloured.

623 20 a. Type 133 . . . . 10 10
624 50 a. Sheng (pipes) 15 15
625 60 a. Er-hu (bowed instrument) 25 25
626 70 a. Ruan (string instrument) 40 25
627 5 p. Cheng (harp) . . . . . . 2·50 1·60
628 8 p. Pi-pa (lute) . . . . 4·00 2·50

134 Hydrofoil

1986. "Stockholmia 86" International Stamp Exhibition. Passenger Ferries. Multicoloured.

630 10 a. Type 134 . . . . 25 20
631 40 a. "Tejo" (hovercraft) . . . 30 25
632 3 p. "Tercera" (jetfoil) . . . . 1·25 80
633 7 p. 50 High speed ferry . . . 3·50 3·00

135 Taipa Fortress

136 Sun Yat-sen

1986. 10th Anniv of Security Forces. Fortresses. Multicoloured.

634 2 p. Type 135 . . . . 2·50 1·60
635 2 p. St. Paul on the Mount . . 2·50 1·60
636 2 p. St. Francis . . . . 2·50 1·60
637 2 p. Guia . . . . 2·50 1·60

Nos. 634/7 were printed together, se-tenant, forming a composite design.

1986. 120th Birth Anniv of Dr. Sun Yat-sen.

638 136 70 a. multicoloured 65 20

137 Hare and Moon

138 Wa To (physician)

1987. New Year. Year of the Hare.

640 137 1 p. 50 multicoloured . . . 2·10 55

1987. Shek Wan Ceramics. Multicoloured.

641 2 p. 20 Type 138 . . . . . . 1·60 1·60
642 2 p. 20 Choi San, God of Fortune 1·60 1·60
643 2 p. 20 Yi, Sun God . . . . . 1·60 1·60
644 2 p. 20 Cung Kuei, Keeper of Demons . . . . 1·60 1·60

139 Boats

1987. Dragon Boat Festival. Multicoloured.

645 50 a. Type 139 . . . . 40 10
646 5 p. Dragon boat prow . . . 1·60 80

140 Circular Fan

141 Fantan

1987. Fans. Multicoloured.

647 30 a. Type 140 . . . . 15 15
648 70 a. Folding fan with tree design 25 25
649 1 p. Square-shaped fan with peacock design . . . . . . 1·60 1·25
650 6 p. Heart-shaped fan with painting of woman and tree 4·50 3·25

1987. Casino Games. Multicoloured.

652 20 a. Type 141 . . . . 15 15
653 40 a. Cussec 25 25
654 4 p. Baccarat . . . . 1·60 85
655 7 p. Roulette . . . . 6·25 2·10

142 Goods Hand-cart

143 Dragon and Moon

1987. Traditional Vehicles. Multicoloured.

656 10 a. Type 142 . . . . 15 10
657 70 a. Open sedan chair . . . 25 10
658 90 a. Rickshaw 85 65
659 10 p. Cycle rickshaw . . . . 3·25 1·60

1988. New Year. Year of the Dragon.

661 143 2 p. 50 multicoloured . . 2·50 1·00

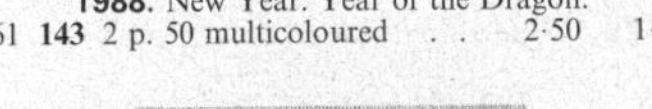

144 West European Hedgehog

1988. Protected Mammals. Multicoloured.

662 3 p. Type 144 . . . . 1·25 1·00
663 3 p. Eurasian badger . . . . 1·25 1·00
664 3 p. European otter . . . . 1·25 1·00
665 3 p. Chinese pangolin . . . . 1·25 1·00

145 Breastfeeding

1988. 40th Anniv of W.H.O. Multicoloured.

666 60 a. Type 145 . . . . 15 10
667 80 a. Vaccinating child . . . 30 25
668 2 p. 40 Donating blood . . . 1·10 65

146 Bicycles

1988. Transport. Multicoloured.
669 20 a. Type **146** 10 10
670 50 a. Lambretta and Vespa . . 15 10
671 3 p. 30 Open-sided motor car 1·00 80
672 5 p. Renault delivery truck, 1912 2·10 1·50

147 Hurdling **148** Intelpost (electronic mail)

1988. Olympic Games, Seoul. Multicoloured.
674 40 a. Type **147** 15 10
675 60 a. Basketball 25 15
676 1 p. Football 80 65
677 8 p. Table tennis . . . . . . 2·50 1·60

1988. New Postal Services. Multicoloured.
679 13 p. 40 Type **148** . . . . . . 1·60 85
680 40 p. Express Mail Service (EMS) 4·00 2·75

149 B.M.W. Saloon Car **150** Snake and Moon

1988. 35th Macao Grand Prix. Multicoloured.
681 80 a. Type **149** 15 15
682 2 p. 80 Motor cycle 85 65
683 7 p. Formula 3 car . . . . . 2·50 1·60

1989. New Year. Year of the Snake.
685 **150** 3 p. multicoloured . . . . 1·75 45

151 Water Carrier **152** White Building

1989. Traditional Occupations (1st series). Multicoloured.
686 50 a. Type **151** 15 10
687 1 p. Tan-kya (boat) woman . . 25 15
688 4 p. Tin-tin man (pedlar) . . . 1·00 85
689 5 p. Tao-fu-fa (soya bean cheese) vendor . . . . 1·50 1·00
See also Nos. 714/17 and 743/6.

1989. Paintings by George Vitalievich Smirnoff in Luis Camoes Museum Multicoloured.
690 2 p. Type **152** 40 40
691 2 p. Building with railings . . 40 40
692 2 p. Street scene 40 40
693 2 p. White thatched cottage . . 40 40

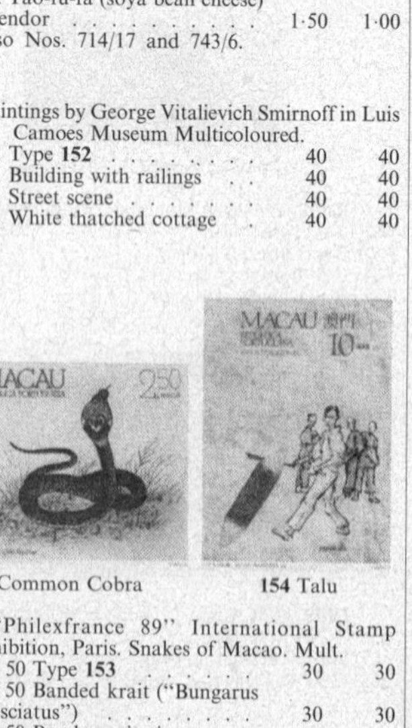

153 Common Cobra **154** Talu

1989. "Philexfrance 89" International Stamp Exhibition, Paris. Snakes of Macao. Mult.
694 2 p. 50 Type **153** 30 30
695 2 p. 50 Banded krait ("Bungarus fasciatus") 30 30
696 2 p. 50 Bamboo pit viper ("Trimeresurus albolabris") 30 30
697 2 p. 50 Rat snake ("Elaphe radiata") 30 30

1989. Traditional Games. Multicoloured.
698 10 a. Type **154** 10 10
699 60 a. Triol (marbles) 25 10
700 3 p. 30 Chiquia (shuttlecock) 85 30
701 5 p. Chinese chequers . . . . 1·25 1·10

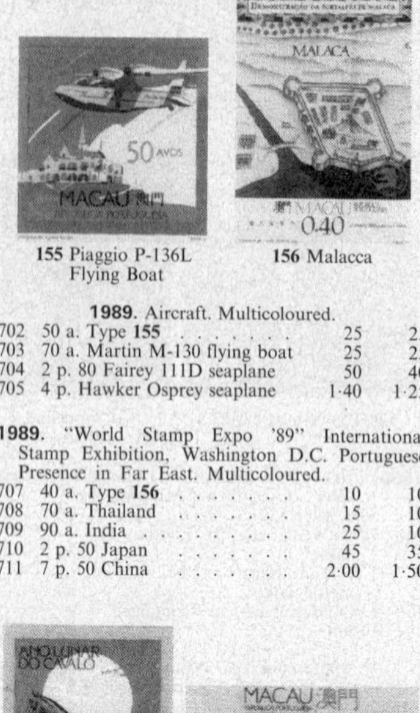

155 Piaggio P-136L Flying Boat **156** Malacca

1989. Aircraft. Multicoloured.
702 50 a. Type **155** 25 25
703 70 a. Martin M-130 flying boat 25 25
704 2 p. 80 Fairey 111D seaplane 50 40
705 4 p. Hawker Osprey seaplane 1·40 1·25

1989. "World Stamp Expo '89" International Stamp Exhibition, Washington D.C. Portuguese Presence in Far East. Multicoloured.
707 40 a. Type **156** 10 10
708 70 a. Thailand 15 10
709 90 a. India 25 10
710 2 p. 50 Japan 45 35
711 7 p. 50 China . . . . 2·00 1·50

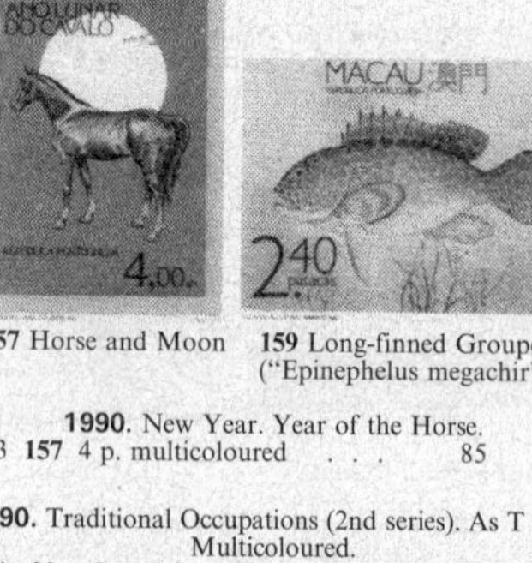

157 Horse and Moon **159** Long-finned Grouper ("Epinephelus megachir")

1990. New Year. Year of the Horse.
713 **157** 4 p. multicoloured . . . 85 45

1990. Traditional Occupations (2nd series). As T **151**. Multicoloured.
714 30 a. Long-chau singer . . . 10 10
715 70 a. Cobbler 15 10
716 1 p. 50 Travelling penman . . 40 35
717 7 p. 50 Fisherman with wide nets 1·75 1·10

1990. Fishes. Multicoloured.
719 2 p. 40 Type **159** 30 30
720 2 p. 40 Malabar snapper ("Lutianus malabaricus") . 30 30
721 2 p. 40 Snakehead ("Ophiocepalus maculatus") 30 30
722 2 p. 40 Common paradise fish ("Macropodus opercularis") 30 30

160 Porcelain

1990. "New Zealand 1990" International Stamp Exhibition, Auckland. Industrial Diversification. Multicoloured.
723 3 p. Type **160** 30 30
724 3 p. Furniture 30 30
725 3 p. Toys 30 30
726 3 p. Artificial flowers 30 30

161 Cycling **162** Rose by Lazaro Luis

1990. 11th Asian Games, Peking. Multicoloured.
728 80 a. Type **161** 10 10
729 1 p. Swimming 15 10
730 3 p. Judo 55 30
731 4 p. 20 Shooting . . . . . . 1·25 1·00

1990. Compass Roses. Designs showing roses from ancient charts by cartographer named. Mult.
733 50 a. Type **162** 10 10
734 1 p. Diogo Homem 20 10
735 3 p. 50 Diogo Homem (different) 70 35
736 6 p. 50 Fernao Vaz Dourado . . 1·50 1·00

HAVE YOU READ THE NOTES AT THE BEGINNING OF THIS CATALOGUE?
These often provide the answers to the enquiries we receive.

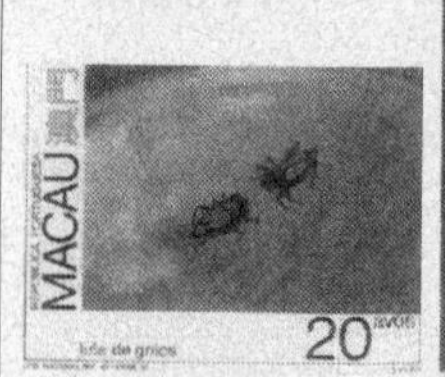

163 Cricket Fight **164** Goat and Moon

1990. Betting on Animals. Multicoloured.
738 20 a. Type **163** 15 10
739 80 a. Hwamei fight 35 15
740 1 p. Greyhound racing 40 25
741 10 p. Horse racing . . . . . . 1·60 1·10

1991. New Year. Year of the Goat.
742 **164** 4 p. 50 multicoloured . . . 85 40

1991. Traditional Occupations (3rd series). As T **151**. Multicoloured.
743 80 a. Knife-grinder 15 10
744 1 p. 70 Flour-puppets vendor 35 25
745 3 p. 50 Street barber 65 50
746 4 p. 20 Fortune-teller . . . . . 1·00 85

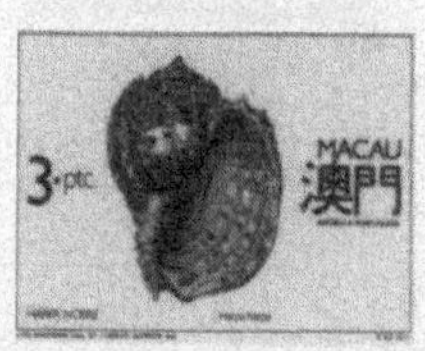

165 True Harp ("Harpa harpa")

1991. Sea Shells. Multicoloured.
747 3 p. Type **165** 60 40
748 3 p. Oil-lamp tun ("Tonna zonata") 60 40
749 3 p. Bramble murex ("Murex pecten") 60 40
750 3 p. Rose-branch murex ("Chicoreus rosarius") . . . 60 40
The Latin names on Nos. 749/50 are incorrect.

166 Character and Backcloth

1991. Chinese Opera. Multicoloured.
751 **166** 60 a. multicoloured 40 35
752 – 80 a. multicoloured 40 35
753 – 1 p. multicoloured 85 65
754 – 10 p. multicoloured . . . 3·75 2·10
DESIGNS: Nos. 752/4, Different backcloths and costumes.

167 "Delonix regia" and Lou Lim Ioc Garden

1991. Flowers and Gardens (1st series). Mult.
755 1 p. 70 Type **167** 35 25
756 3 p. "Ipomoea cairica" and Sao Francisco Garden 60 50
757 3 p. 50 "Jasminum mesyi" and Sun Yat Sen Park 75 60
758 4 p. 20 "Bauhinia variegata" and Seac Pai Van Park 85 65
See also Nos. 815/18.

168 Portuguese Traders unloading Boats **169** Firework Display

1991. Cultural Exchange. Nambam Paintings attr. Kano Domi. Multicoloured.
760 4 p. 20 Type **168** 85 55
761 4 p. 20 Portuguese traders displaying goods to buyers 70 40

1991. Christmas. Multicoloured.
763 1 p. 70 Type **169** 30 20
764 3 p. Father Christmas 50 40
765 3 p. 50 Man dancing 60 45
766 4 p. 20 January 1st celebrations 70 55

170 Concertina Door

1992. Doors and Windows. Multicoloured.
767 1 p. 70 Type **170** 30 20
768 3 p. Window with four shutters 50 40
769 3 p. 50 Window with two shutters 60 45
770 4 p. 20 Louvred door 70 55

171 Monkey and Moon **172** T'it Kuai Lei

1992. New Year. Year of the Monkey.
771 **171** 4 p. 50 multicoloured . . 75 60

1992. Gods of Chinese Mythology (1st series). Multicoloured.
772 3 p. 50 (1) Type **172** . . . . . 1·25 1·00
773 3 p. 50 (2) Chong Lei Kun . . 1·25 1·00
774 3 p. 50 (3) Cheong Kuo Lou on donkey . . . . 1·25 1·00
775 3 p. 50 (4) Loi Tong Pan . . 1·25 1·00
See also Nos. 796/9.

173 Lion Dance **174** High Jumping

1992. "World Columbian Stamp Expo '92", Chicago. Chinese Dances. Multicoloured.
776 1 p. 70 Type **173** 15 10
777 2 p. 70 Lion dance (different) 60 35
778 6 p. Dragon dance . . . . . 1·40 85

1992. Olympic Games, Barcelona. Multicoloured
779 80 a. Type **174** 15 10
780 4 p. 20 Badminton 70 55
781 4 p. 70 Roller hockey 80 60
782 5 p. Yachting 85 65

175 Na Cha Temple

1992. Temples (1st series). Multicoloured.
784 1 p. Type **175** 15 10
785 1 p. 50 Kun Iam 35 25
786 1 p. 70 Hong Kon 40 30
787 6 p. 50 A Ma . . . . 1·40 1·10
See also Nos. 792/5 and 894/8.

176 Tung Sin Tong Services **177** Rooster and Dragon

1992. Centenary of Tung Sin Tong (medical and educational charity).
788 **176** 1 p. multicoloured 25 20

1992. Portuguese–Chinese Friendship.
789 **177** 10 p. multicoloured . . . 1·60 1·25

178 Red Junglefowl

179 Children carrying Banners

1992. New Year. Year of the Cock.

791 **178** 5 p. multicoloured 85 65

1993. Temples (2nd series). As T **175**. Mult.

792 50 a. T'am Kong 10 10
793 2 p. T'in Hau 35 25
794 3 p. 50 Lin Fong 60 45
795 8 p. Pau Kong . . . . 1·40 1·10

1993. Gods of Chinese Mythology (2nd series). As T **172**. Multicoloured.

796 3 p. 50 (1) Lam Ch'oi Wo flying on crane 60 45
797 3 p. 50 (2) Ho Sin Ku (goddess) on peach blossom 60 45
798 3 p. 50 (3) Hon Seong Chi crossing sea on basket of flowers 60 45
799 3 p. 50 (4) Ch'ou Kuok K'ao crossing river on plank . . . 60 45

1993. Chinese Wedding. Multicoloured.

800 3 p. Type **179** 50 40
801 3 p. Bride 50 40
802 3 p. Bridegroom 50 40
803 3 p. Wedding guests 50 40

Nos. 800/3 were issued together, se-tenant, forming a composite design.

180 Bird perched on Hand

181 Scops Owl

1993. Environmental Protection.

805 **180** 1 p. multicoloured 25 20

1993. Birds of Prey. Multicoloured.

806 3 p. Type **181** 50 40
807 3 p. Barn owl ("Tyto alba") . . . 50 40
808 3 p. Peregrine falcon ("Falco peregrinus") 50 40
809 3 p. Golden eagle ("Aquila obrysaetos") 50 40

182 Town Hall

1993. Union of Portuguese-speaking Capital Cities.

811 **182** 1 p. 50 green, blue & red 25 20

183 Portuguese Missionaries

1993. 450th Anniv of First Portuguese Visit to Japan. Multicoloured.

812 50 a. Japanese man with musket 15 10
813 3 p. Type **183** 50 40
814 3 p. 50 Traders carrying goods 60 45

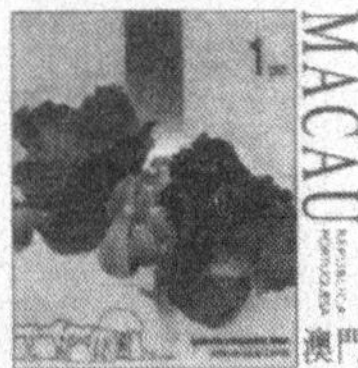

184 "Spathodea campanulata" and Luis de Camoes Garden

1993. Flowers and Gardens (2nd series). Multicoloured.

815 1 p. Type **184** 15 10
816 2 p. "Tithonia diversifolia" and Montanha Russa Garden . . 35 25
817 3 p. "Rhodomyrtus tomentosa" and Cais Garden 50 40
818 8 p. "Passiflora foetida" and Flora Garden . . . . . . 1·40 1·10

185 Caravel

1993. 16th-century Sailing Ships. Multicoloured.

820 1 p. Type **185** 15 10
821 2 p. Caravel (different) . . . 35 25
822 3 p. 50 Nau 60 45
823 4 p. 50 Galleon 75 60

186 Saloon Car

1993. 40th Anniv of Macao Grand Prix. Multicoloured.

825 1 p. 50 Type **186** 25 20
826 2 p. Motor cycle 35 25
827 4 p. 50 Racing car 75 60

187 Chow-chow and Moon

1994. New Year. Year of the Dog.

828 **187** 5 p. multicoloured . . . 85 65

188 Map and Prince Henry (½-size illustration)

1994. 600th Birth Anniv of Prince Henry the Navigator.

829 **188** 3 p. multicoloured . . . 50 40

189 Lakeside Hut

1994. Birth Bicentenary of George Chinnery (artist). Multicoloured.

830 3 p. 50 Type **189** 60 45
831 3 p. 50 Fisherman on sea wall 60 45
832 3 p. 50 Harbour 60 45
833 3 p. 50 Sao Tiago Fortress . 60 45

190 Lai Sis Exchange

1994. Spring Festival of Lunar New Year. Multicoloured.

835 1 p. Type **190** 15 10
836 2 p. Flower and tangerine tree decorations 35 25
837 3 p. 50 Preparing family meal 60 45
838 4 p. 50 Paper decorations bearing good wishes 75 60

191 "Longevity"

192 Footballer

1994. Legends and Myths (1st series). Chinese Gods. Multicoloured.

839 3 p. Type **191** 50 40
840 3 p. "Prosperity" 50 40
841 3 p. "Happiness" 50 40

See also Nos. 884/7 and 930/2.

1994. World Cup Football Championship, U.S.A.

843 2 p. Type **192** 35 25
844 3 p. Tackling 50 40
845 3 p. 50 Heading ball 60 45
846 4 p. 50 Goalkeeper saving goal 75 60

193 Rice Shop

194 Astrolabe

1994. Traditional Chinese Shops. Multicoloured.

848 1 p. Type **193** 15 10
849 1 p. 50 Medicinal tea shop . . 25 20
850 2 p. Salt-fish shop 35 25
851 3 p. 50 Pharmacy 60 45

1994. Nautical Instruments. Multicoloured.

852 3 p. Type **194** 50 40
853 3 p. 50 Quadrant 60 45
854 4 p. 50 Sextant 75 65

195 Fencing

1994. 12th Asian Games, Hiroshima, Japan. Multicoloured.

855 1 p. Type **195** 15 10
856 2 p. Gymnastics 35 25
857 3 p. Water-polo 50 40
858 3 p. 50 Pole vaulting 60 45

196 Nobre de Carvalho Bridge

1994. Bridges. Multicoloured.

859 1 p. Type **196** 15 10
860 8 p. Friendship Bridge . . . . 1·40 1·10

197 Carp

199 Pig and Moon

198 Angel's Head (stained glass window, Macao Cathedral)

1994. Good Luck Signs. Multicoloured.

861 3 p. Type **197** 50 40
862 3 p. 50 Peaches 60 45
863 4 p. 50 Water lily 75 60

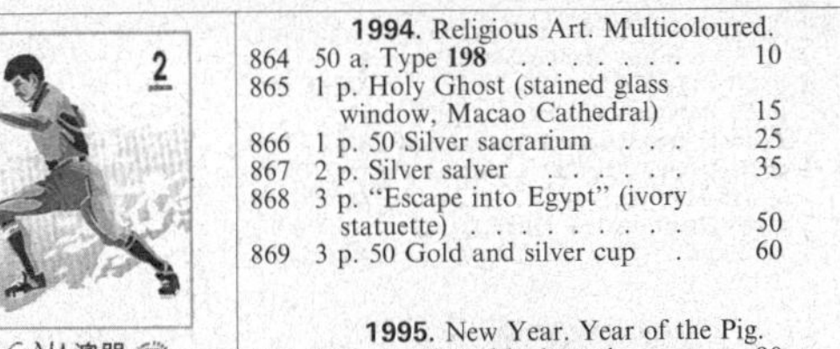

1994. Religious Art. Multicoloured.

864 50 a. Type **198** 10 10
865 1 p. Holy Ghost (stained glass window, Macao Cathedral) 15 10
866 1 p. 50 Silver sacrarium . . . 25 20
867 2 p. Silver salver 35 25
868 3 p. "Escape into Egypt" (ivory statuette) 50 40
869 3 p. 50 Gold and silver cup . 60 45

1995. New Year. Year of the Pig.

870 **199** 5 p. 50 multicoloured . . 90 70

200 "Lou Lim Iok Garden"

1995. Paintings of Macao by Lio Man Cheong. Multicoloured.

871 50 a. Type **200** 10 10
872 1 p. "Guia Fortress and Lighthouse" 15 10
873 1 p. 50 "Barra Temple" 25 20
874 2 p. "Avenida da Praia, Taipa" 35 25
875 2 p. 50 "Kun Iam Temple" . . 40 30
876 3 p. "St. Paul's Seminary" . . 50 40
877 3 p. 50 "Penha Hill" 60 45
878 4 p. "Gates of Understanding Monument" 65 50

201 Magnifying Glass over Goods

1995. World Consumer Day.

879 **201** 1 p. multicoloured 15 10

202 Pangolin

203 Kun Sai Iam

1995. Protection of Chinese ("Asian") Pangolin. Multicoloured.

880 1 p. 50 In fork of tree 25 20
881 1 p. 50 Hanging from tree by tail 25 20
882 1 p. 50 On leafy branch . . . 25 20
883 1 p. 50 Type **202** 25 20

1995. Legends and Myths (2nd series). Kun Sai Iam (Buddhist god). Multicoloured.

884 3 p. Type **203** 50 40
885 3 p. Holding baby 50 40
886 3 p. Sitting behind water lily . 50 40
887 3 p. With water lily and dragon-fish 50 40

204/7 Senado Square (½-size illustration)

1995. Senado Square.

889 **204** 2 p. multicoloured 35 25
890 **205** 2 p. multicoloured 35 25
891 **206** 2 p. multicoloured 35 25
892 **207** 2 p. multicoloured 35 25

Nos. 889/92 were issued together, se-tenant, forming the composite design illustrated.

1995. Temples (3rd series). As T **175**. Multicoloured.

894 50 a. Kuan Tai 10 10
895 1 p. Pak Tai 15 10
896 1 p. 50 Lin K'ai 25 20
897 3 p. Se Kam Tong 50 40
898 3 p. 50 Fok Tak 60 45

208 Pekin Robin ("Leiothrix lutea")

1995. "Singapore'95" International Stamp Exhibition. Birds. Multicoloured.

899 2 p. 50 Type **208** 40 30
900 2 p. 50 Japanese white eye ("Zosterops japonica") . . . 40 30
901 2 p. 50 Canary ("Serinus canarius canarius") 40 30
902 2 p. 50 Nightingale ("Gurrulax canonus") 40 30

209 Pipa

1995. International Music Festival. Musical Instruments. Multicoloured.

904 1 p. Type **209** 15 10
905 1 p. Erhu (string instrument) . 15 10
906 1 p. Gong (hand-held drum) . 15 10
907 1 p. Sheng (string instrument) 15 10
908 1 p. Xiao (flute) 15 10
909 1 p. Tambor (drum) 15 10

210 Anniversary Emblem, World Map and U.N. Headquarters, New York

1995. 50th Anniv of United Nations Organization.

911 **210** 4 p. 50 multicoloured . . . 75 60

211 Terminal Building

1995. Inauguration of Macao International Airport. Multicoloured.

912 1 p. Type **211** 15 10
913 1 p. 50 Terminal (different) . . 25 20
914 2 p. Loading airplane and cargo building 35 20
915 3 p. Control tower 50 40

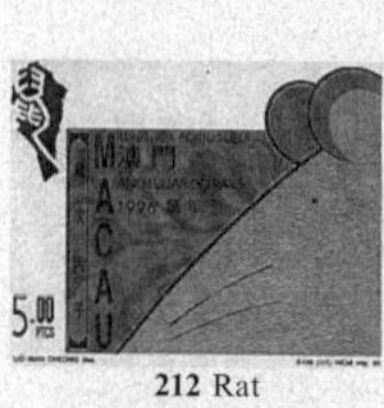

212 Rat

213 Cage

1996. New Year. Year of the Rat.

918 **212** 5 p. multicoloured 85 65

1996. Traditional Chinese Cages.

920 **213** 1 p. multicoloured 15 10
921 – 1 p. 50 multicoloured . . 25 20
922 – 3 p. multicoloured . . . 50 40
923 – 4 p. 50 multicoloured . . 75 60

DESIGNS: 1 p. 50 to 4 p. 50, Different cages.

214 Street

215 Tou Tei (God of Earth)

1996. Paintings of Macao by Herculano Estominho. Multicoloured.

925 50 a. Fishing boats (horiz) . . 10 10
926 1 p. 50 Town square 25 20
927 3 p. Type **214** 50 40
928 5 p. Townscape (horiz) 85 65

1996. Legends and Myths (3rd series). Multicoloured.

930 3 p. 50 Type **215** 60 45
931 3 p. 50 Choi San (God of Fortune) 60 45
932 3 p. 50 Chou Kuan (God of the Kitchen) 60 45

216 Customers

1996. Traditional Chinese Tea Houses. Multicoloured.

934 2 p. Type **216** 35 25
935 2 p. Waiter with tray of steamed stuffed bread 35 25
936 2 p. Newspaper vendor 35 25
937 2 p. Waiter pouring tea at table 35 25

Nos. 934/7 were issued together, se-tenant, forming a composite design.

217 Get Well Soon

1996. Greetings stamps. Multicoloured.

939 50 a. Type **217** 10 10
940 1 p. 50 Congratulations on new baby 25 20
941 3 p. Happy birthday 50 40
942 4 p. Wedding congratulations 65 50

218 Swimming

1996. Olympic Games, Atlanta, U.S.A. Multicoloured.

943 2 p. Type **218** 30 20
944 3 p. Football 45 35
945 3 p. 50 Gymnastics 55 40
946 4 p. 50 Yachting 70 55

219 Crane (civil, 1st rank)

1996. Civil and Military Insignia of the Mandarins. Multicoloured.

948 2 p. 50 Type **219** 40 30
949 2 p. 50 Lion (military, 2nd rank) 40 30
950 2 p. 50 Golden pheasant (civil, 2nd rank) 40 30
951 2 p. 50 Leopard (military, 3rd rank) 40 30

220 Trawler with Multiple Nets

1996. Nautical Sciences: Fishing Nets. Multicoloured.

952 3 p. Type **220** 45 35
953 3 p. Modern trawler with net from stern 45 35
954 3 p. Two sailing junks with common net 45 35
955 3 p. Junk with two square nets at sides 45 35

Nos. 952/5 were issued together, se-tenant, forming a composite design.

221 National Flag and Statue

1996. 20th Anniv of Legislative Assembly.

956 **221** 2 p. 80 multicoloured . . 45 35

222 Dragonfly

1996. Paper Kites. Multicoloured.

958 3 p. 50 Type **222** 55 40
959 3 p. 50 Butterfly 55 40
960 3 p. 50 Owl 55 40
961 3 p. 50 Swallow 55 40

223 Doll

1996. Traditional Chinese Toys. Multicoloured.

963 50 a. Type **223** 10 10
964 1 p. Fish 15 10
965 3 p. Painted doll 45 35
966 4 p. 50 Dragon 70 55

CHARITY TAX STAMPS

The notes under this heading in Portugal also apply here.

43

C 48 Our Lady of Charity (altarpiece, Macao Cathedral)

1919. Fiscal stamp optd **TAXA DE GUERRA**.

C305 **43** 2 a. green . . . . 3·75 2·75
C306 11 a. green . . . . 5·75 5·25

The above was for use in Timor as well as Macao.

1925. As Marquis de Pombal issue of Portugal but inscr "MACAU".

C329 **C 73** 2 a. red . . . . 1·25 1·00
C330 – 2 a. red . . . . 1·40 1·25
C331 **C 75** 2 a. red . . . . 1·40 1·40

1930. No gum.

C332 **C 48** 5 a. brown and buff 25·00 20·00

1945. As Type C **48** but values in Arabic and Chinese numerals left and right, at bottom of design. No gum.

C486 1 a. olive and green 40 25
C487 2 a. purple and grey 40 25
C415 5 a. brown and yellow . . . 17·00 25·00
C416 5 a. blue and light blue . . . 25·00 21·00
C417 10 a. green and light green . 16·00 12·50
C488 10 a. blue and green 80 25
C418 15 a. orange & lt orange . . 16·00 12·50
C419 20 a. red and orange . . . . 29·00 21·00
C489 20 a. brown and yellow . . . 1·25 40
C420 50 a. lilac and buff . . . . 29·00 21·00
C472 50 a. red and pink . . . . . 12·50 8·50

1981. No. C487 and similar higher (fiscal) values surch **20 avos** and Chinese characters.

C546 20 a. on 2 a. purple on grey . 1·60 1·60
C534 20 a. on 1 p. green & lt grn . 2·10 1·25
C535 20 a. on 3 p. black and pink . 2·10 1·25
C536 20 a. on 5 p. brown & yellow

1981. No. C418 surch **10 avos** and Chinese characters.

C553 10 a. on 15 a. orange and light orange . . . . 1·60 1·60

NEWSPAPER STAMPS

1892. "Embossed" key-type of Macao surch **JORNAES** and value. No gum.

N73 Q $2\frac{1}{2}$ r. on 10 r. green . . . . 3·25 1·90
N74 $2\frac{1}{2}$ r. on 40 r. brown . . . . 3·25 1·90
N75 $2\frac{1}{2}$ r. on 80 r. grey . . . . 3·25 1·90

1893. "Newspaper" key-type inscr "Macau".

N80 V $2\frac{1}{2}$ r. brown . . . . 2·50 1·75

1894. "Newspaper" key-type of Macao surch $\frac{1}{2}$ **avo PROVISORIO** and Chinese characters.

N82 V $\frac{1}{2}$ a. on $2\frac{1}{2}$ r. brown . . . . 2·75 2·00

POSTAGE DUE STAMPS

1904. "Due" key-type inscr "MACAU". No gum (12 a. to 1p.), with or without gum (others).

D184 W $\frac{1}{2}$ a. green 90 80
D185 1 a. green 90 80
D186 2 a. grey 95 80
D187 4 a. brown 95 80
D188 5 a. orange . . . . . . 1·50 1·10
D189 8 a. brown . . . . . . 1·50 1·10
D190 12 a. brown . . . . . . 2·25 1·60
D191 20 a. blue . . . . 5·25 3·75
D192 40 a. red . . . . 5·75 4·50
D193 50 a. orange . . . . . 10·50 9·25
D194 1 p. lilac . . . . 22·00 17·00

1911. "Due" key-types of Macao optd **REPUBLICA**.

D204 W $\frac{1}{2}$ a. green 75 75
D205 1 a. green 75 75
D206 2 a. grey 75 75
D207 4 a. brown 75 75
D208 5 a. orange 75 75
D209 8 a. brown 75 75
D287 12 a. brown . . . . . . 1·50 1·00
D211 20 a. blue . . . . 2·10 1·60
D212 40 a. red . . . . 4·25 2·75
D290 50 a. orange . . . . . 7·25 5·25
D291 1 p. lilac . . . . 5·00 8·50

1925. Marquis de Pombal issue, as Nos. C329/31 optd **MULTA**.

D329 C 73 4 a. red . . . . 1·10 1·10
D330 – 4 a. red . . . . 1·10 1·10
D331 C 75 4 a. red . . . . 1·10 1·10

1947. As Type D **1** of Portuguese Colonies, but inscr "MACAU".

D410 **D 1** 1 a. black and purple . 45 20
D411 2 a. black and violet . 45 20
D412 4 a. black and blue . . 80 45
D413 5 a. black and brown . 80 45
D414 8 a. black and purple . 1·25 80
D415 12 a. black and brown . 2·10 1·60
D416 20 a. black and green . 4·00 2·50
D417 40 a. black and red . . 6·75 3·25
D418 50 a. black and yellow . 9·25 3·25
D419 1 p. black and blue . . 18·00 3·25

1949. Postage stamps of 1934 surch **PORTEADO** and new value.

D424 **50** 1 a. on 4 a. black . . . . 1·60 85
D425 2 a. on 6 a. brown . . . 1·60 85
D426 4 a. on 8 a. blue . . . . 1·60 85
D427 5 a. on 10 a. red . . . . 1·60 85
D428 8 a. on 12 a. blue . . . . 2·50 1·25
D429 12 a. on 30 a. green . . 4·00 3·00
D430 20 a. on 40 a. violet . . 7·50 5·75

1951. Optd **PORTEADO** or surch also.

D439 **66** 1 a. yellow on cream . . 1·25 40
D440 2 a. green on green . . 1·25 85
D441 7 a. on 10 a. mauve on green 1·25 85

D 70

1952. Numerals in red. Name in black.

D451 **D 70** 1 a. blue and green . . 40 15
D452 3 a. brown and salmon 40 15
D453 5 a. slate and blue . . 40 15
D454 10 a. red and blue . . 85 85
D455 30 a. blue and brown . 1·60 1·25
D456 1 p. brown & grey . . 3·25 1·60

MACEDONIA Pt. 3

Part of Austro-Hungarian Empire until 1918 when it became part of Yugoslavia. Separate stamps were issued during German Occupation in the Second World War.

In 1991 Macedonia became an independent republic.

A. GERMAN OCCUPATION

100 stotinki = 1 lev

Македония
8. IX. 1944
1 лв.
(1)

1944. Stamps of Bulgaria, 1940-44. (a) Surch as T **1**.
G1 1 l. on 10 st. orange . . . . . 3·75 9·25
G2 3 l. on 15 st. blue . . . . . . 3·75 9·25

(b) Surch similar to T **1** but larger.
G3 6 l. on 10 st. blue . . . . . . 6·25 14·00
G4 9 l. on 15 st. green . . . . . . 6·25 14·00
G5 9 l. on 15 st. green . . . . . . 7·75 19·00
G6 15 l. on 4 l. black . . . . . . 15·00 40·00
G7 20 l. on 7 l. blue . . . . 15·00 40·00
G8 30 l. on 14 l. brown . . . . . 30·00 75·00

B. INDEPENDENT REPUBLIC

1991. 100 paras = 1 dinar
1992. 100 deni (de.) = 1 denar (d.)

1 Trumpeters

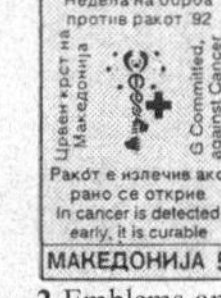

2 Emblems and Inscriptions

1991. Obligatory Tax. Independence.
1 **1** 2 d. 50 black and orange . . . 50 50

1992. Obligatory Tax. Anti-cancer Week. (a) T **2** showing Red Cross symbol at bottom left.
2 **2** 5 d. mauve, black and blue . 75 75
3 – 5 d. multicoloured 75 75
4 – 5 d. multicoloured 75 75
5 – 5 d. multicoloured 75 75
DESIGNS: No. 3, Flowers, columns and scanner; 4, Scanner and couch; 5, Computer cabinet.

(b) As T **2** but with right-hand inscr reading down instead of up and without Red Cross symbol.
6 5 d. mauve, black & blue (as No. 2) 75 75
7 5 d. multicoloured (as No. 3) . . 75 75
8 5 d. multicoloured (as No. 4) . . 75 75
9 5 d. multicoloured (as No. 5) . . 75 75

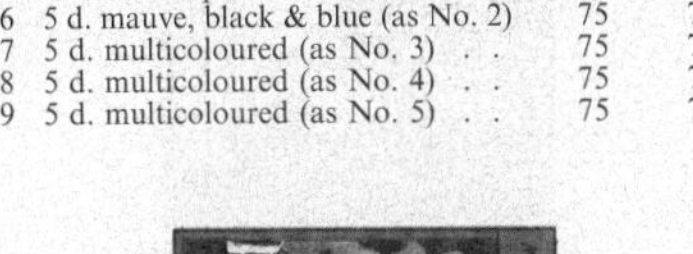

3 Red Cross Aircraft dropping Supplies

1992. Obligatory Tax. Red Cross Week. Multicoloured.
10 10 d. Red Cross slogans 40 40
11 10 d. Type **3** 40 40
12 10 d. Treating road accident victim 40 40
13 10 d. Evacuating casualties from ruined building 40 40
The three pictorial designs are taken from children's paintings.

4 "Skopje Earthquake"

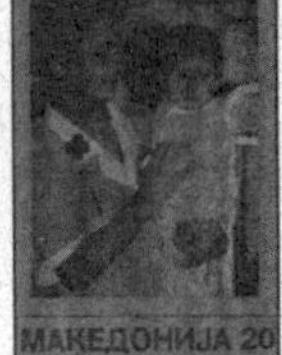

6 Nurse with Baby

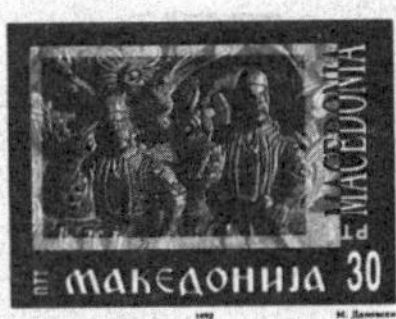

5 "Wood-carvers Petar and Makarie" (icon), St. Joven Bigorsk Monastery, Debar

1992. Obligatory Tax. Solidarity Week.
14 **4** 20 d. black and mauve . . 50 50
15 – 20 d. multicoloured 50 50
16 – 20 d. multicoloured 50 50
17 – 20 d. multicoloured 50 50
DESIGNS: No. 15, Red Cross nurse with child; 16, Mothers carrying toddlers at airport; 17, Family at airport.

1992. 1st Anniv of Independence.
18 **5** 30 d. multicoloured 50 50
For 40 d. in same design see No. 33.

1992. Obligatory Tax. Anti-tuberculosis Week. Multicoloured.
19 20 d. Anti-tuberculosis slogans 40 40
20 20 d. Type **6** 40 40
21 20 d. Nurse giving oxygen . . 40 40
22 20 d. Baby in cot 40 40

7 "The Nativity" (fresco, Slepce Monastery)

9 Radiography Equipment

8 Mixed Bouquet

1992. Christmas. Multicoloured.
23 100 d. Type **7** 10 10
24 500 d. "Madonna and Child" (fresco), Zrze Monastery . . 50 50

1993. Obligatory Tax. Red Cross Fund. Multicoloured.
25 20 d. Red Cross slogans . . . 40 40
26 20 d. Marguerites 40 40
27 20 d. Carnations 40 40
28 20 d. Type **8** 40 40

1993. Obligatory Tax. Anti-cancer Week. Multicoloured.
29 20 d. Anti-cancer slogans . . . 25 25
30 20 d. Type **9** 25 25
31 20 d. Overhead treatment unit 25 25
32 20 d. Scanner 25 25

1993. As No. 18 but changed value.
33 **5** 40 d. multicoloured 30 30

10 Macedonian Flag

1993.
34 **10** 10 d. multicoloured 15 15
35 40 d. multicoloured 50 50
36 50 d. multicoloured 60 60

11 Roach

1993. Fishes from Lake Ohrid. Multicoloured.
37 50 d. Type **11** 10 10
38 100 d. Ohrid trout 20 20
39 1000 d. Type **11** . . . . . . 1·00 1·00
40 2000 d. As No. 38 . . . . . . 2·25 2·25

12 Crucifix, St. George's Monastery

1993. Easter.
41 **12** 300 d. multicoloured . . . 1·25 1·25

13 Diagram of Telecommunications Cable and Map

1993. Opening of Trans-Balkan Telecommunications Line.
42 **13** 500 d. multicoloured 75 75

14 Red Cross Worker with Baby

1993. Obligatory Tax. Red Cross Week. Multicoloured.
43 50 d. Red Cross inscriptions . . 20 20
44 50 d. Type **14** 20 20
45 50 d. Physiotherapist and child in wheelchair 20 20
46 50 d. Stretcher party 20 20
See also No. 73.

15 Unloading U.N.I.C.E.F. Supplies from Lorry

1993. Obligatory Tax. Solidarity Week.
47 – 50 de. black, mauve and silver 20 20
48 **15** 50 de. multicoloured 20 20
49 – 50 de. multicoloured 20 20
50 – 50 de. multicoloured 20 20
DESIGNS: No. 47, "Skopje Earthquake"; 49, Labelling parcels in warehouse; 50, Consignment of parcels on fork-lift truck.
See also No. 72.

16 U.N. Emblem and Rainbow

1993. Admission to United Nations Organization.
51 **16** 10 d. multicoloured . . . . 1·50 1·50

17 "Insurrection" (detail) (B. Lazeski)

19 Tapestry

18 Children in Meadow

1993. 90th Anniv of Macedonian Insurrection.
52 **17** 10 d. multicoloured . . . . 1·50 1·50

1993. Obligatory Tax. Anti-tuberculosis Week. Multicoloured.
54 50 de. Anti-tuberculosis slogans 25 25
55 50 de. Type **18** 25 25
56 50 de. Bee on flower 25 25
57 50 de. Goat behind boulder . . 25 25
See also No. 71.

1993. Centenary of Founding of Inner Macedonia Revolutionary Organization.
58 **19** 4 d. multicoloured 25 25

20 "The Nativity" (fresco from St. George's Monastery, Rajcica)

1993. Christmas. Multicoloured.
60 2 d. Type **20** 10 10
61 20 d. "The Three Kings" (fresco from Slepce Monastery) . . 1·25 1·25

21 Lily

1994. Obligatory Tax. Anti-cancer Week. Multicoloured.
62 1 d. Red Cross and anti-cancer emblems 20 20
63 1 d. Type **21** 20 20
64 1 d. Mushroom 20 20
65 1 d. Mute swans on lake . . . 20 20

1994. Nos. 1, 18 and 34 surch.
66 **5** 2 d. on 30 d. multicoloured . 35 35
67 **1** 8 d. on 2 d. 50 black and orange 1·60 1·60
68 **6** 15 d. on 10 d. multicoloured 2·75 2·75

23 Decorated Eggs

24 Kosta Ratsin (writer)

1994. Easter.
69 **23** 2 d. multicoloured 10 10

1994. Obligatory Tax. Red Cross Week. As previous designs but values, and date (70), changed. Multicoloured.
70 1 d. Red Cross inscriptions (dated "8-15 Maj 1994") 10 10
71 1 d. Type **18** 10 10
72 1 d. As No. 50 . . . . 10 10
73 1 d. Type **14** 10 10

1994. Revolutionaries. Portraits by Dimitar Kondovski. Multicoloured.
74 8 d. Type **24** 25 25
75 15 d. Grigor Prlichev (writer) . 50 50
76 20 d. Nikola Vaptsarov (Bulgarian poet) 70 70
77 50 d. Gotse Delchev (founder of Internal Macedonian–Odrin Revolutionary Organization) 1·75 1·75

25 "Skopje Earthquake"

26 Tree and Family

1994. Obligatory Tax. Solidarity Week.
78 **25** 1 d. black, red and silver . . 10 10

1994. Census.
79 **26** 2 d. multicoloured 10 10

27 St. Prokhor Pchinski Monastery (venue)

28 Swimmer

1994. 50th Anniv of Macedonian National Liberation Council.
80 **27** 5 d. multicoloured 15 15

1994. Swimming Marathon, Ohrid.
82 **28** 8 d. multicoloured 25 25

29 Turkish Cancellation and 1992 30 d. Stamp on Cover

1994. 150th Anniv (1993) of Postal Service in Macedonia.
83 29 2 d. multicoloured 10 10

30 Mastheads

1994. 50th Anniversaries of "Nova Makedonija", "Mlad Borets" and "Makedonka" (newspapers).
84 30 2 d. multicoloured 10 10

31 Open Book

1994. 50th Anniv of St. Clement of Ohrid Library. Multicoloured.
85 2 d. Type 31 . . . . 10 10
86 10 d. Page of manuscript (vert) 35 35

32 Globe

33 Wireless and Gramophone Record

1994. Obligatory Tax. Anti-AIDS Week.
87 – 2 d. red and black 10 10
88 32 2 d. black, red and blue . . 10 10
89 – 2 d. black, yellow and red . 10 10
90 – 2 d. black and red 10 10
DESIGNS: No. 87, Inscriptions in Cyrillic (dated "01-08.12.1994"); 89, Exclamation mark in warning triangle; 90, Safe sex campaign emblem.

1994. 50th Anniv of Macedonian Radio.
91 33 2 d. multicoloured 10 10

34 Macedonian Pine

1994. Flora and Fauna. Multicoloured.
92 5 d. Type 34 . . . . 15 15
93 10 d. Lynx 35 35

35 Emblems and Inscriptions

38 Voluntary Workers

37 Fresco

1995. Obligatory Tax. Anti-Cancer Week. Multicoloured.
94 1 d. + 50 de. Type 35 . . . . 10 10
95 1 d. + 50 de. White lilies . . . 10 10
96 1 d. + 50 de. Red lilies . . . 10 10
97 1 d. + 50 de. Red roses . . . 10 10

1995. Nos. 35 and 33 surch.
98 10 2 d. on 40 d. multicoloured 10 10
100 5 5 d. on 40 d. multicoloured 15 15

1995. Easter.
101 37 4 d. multicoloured 15 15

1995. Obligatory Tax. Red Cross.
102 1 d. black, pink and blue . 10 10
103 38 1 d. multicoloured 10 10
104 – 1 d. multicoloured 10 10
105 – 1 d. multicoloured 10 10
DESIGNS: No. 102, Cross and inscriptions in Cyrillic (dated "8–15 MAJ 1995"); 104, Volunteers in t-shirts; 105, Globe, red cross and red crescent.

39 Troops on Battlefield

1995. 50th Anniv of End of Second World War.
106 39 2 d. multicoloured 10 10

40 Anniversary Emblem

1995. 50th Anniv of Macedonian Red Cross.
107 40 2 d. multicoloured 10 10

41 Rontgen and X-Ray Lamp

1995. Centenary of Discovery of X-Rays by Wilhelm Rontgen.
108 41 2 d. multicoloured 10 10

42 "Skopje Earthquake"

1995. Obligatory Tax. Solidarity Week.
109 42 1 d. black, red and gold . 10 10

43 Cernodrinski (dramatist)

1995. 50th Anniv of Vojdan Cernodrinski Theatre Festival.
110 43 10 d. multicoloured . . . 35 35

44 Kraljevic (fresco, Markov Monastery, Skopje)

1995. 600th Death Anniv of Marko Kraljevic (Serbian Prince).
111 44 20 d. multicoloured 70 70

45 Pulęski

1995. Death Centenary of Gorgi Puleski (linguist and revolutionary).
112 45 2 d. multicoloured 10 10

46 Manuscript, Bridge and Emblem

1995. Writers' Festival, Struga.
113 46 2 d. multicoloured 10 10

47 Robert Koch (discoverer of tubercule bacillus)

1995. Obligatory Tax. Anti-tuberculosis Week.
114 47 1 d. brown, black and red . 10 10

49 Maleshevija

50 Interior of Mosque

1995. Buildings. Multicoloured.
116 2 d. Type 49 . . . . 10 10
117 20 d. Krakornitsa . . . . . . 1·25 1·25

1995. Tetovo Mosque.
118 50 15 d. multicoloured 95 95

51 Lumiere Brothers (inventors of cine-camera)

1995. Centenary of Motion Pictures. Multicoloured.
119 10 d. Type 51 . . . . 65 65
120 10 d. Manaki brothers (Macedonian cinematographers) 65 65
Nos. 119/20 were issued together, se-tenant, forming a composite design.

52 Globe in Nest within Frame

1995. 50th Anniv of U.N.O. Multicoloured.
121 20 d. Type 52 . . . . 1·25 1·25
122 50 d. Sun within frame . . . . 3·00 3·00

53 Male and Female Symbols

1995. Obligatory Tax. Anti-AIDS Week.
123 53 1 d. multicoloured 10 10

54 Madonna and Child

1995. Christmas.
124 54 15 d. multicoloured . . . 95 95

55 Dalmatian Pelican

1995. Birds. Multicoloured.
125 15 d. Type 55 . . . . 95 95
126 40 d. Lammergeier . . . . . 2·50 2·50

56 Letters of Alphabet and Jigsaw Pieces

1995. Alphabet Reform.
127 56 5 d. multicoloured 15 15

57 St. Kliment of Ohrid (detail of fresco)

1995. 700th Anniv of Fresco, St. Bogorodica's Church, Ohrid.
128 57 8 d. multicoloured 20 20

58 Postal Headquarters, Skopje

59 Zip joining Flags

1995. 2nd Anniv of Membership of U.P.U.
130 58 10 d. multicoloured . . . 65 65

1995. Entry to Council of Europe and Organization for Security and Co-operation in Europe.
131 59 20 d. multicoloured . . . 1·25 1·25

60 Hand holding out Apple

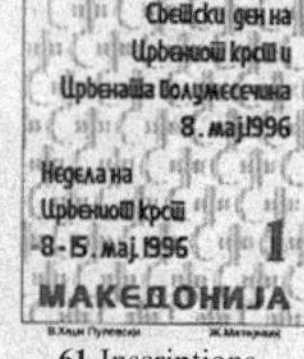

61 Inscriptions

1996. Obligatory Tax. Anti-cancer Week.
132 60 1 d. multicoloured 10 10

1996. Obligatory Tax. Red Cross Week. Each red, black and yellow.

133		1 d. Type **61**	10	10
134		1 d. Red Cross principles in Macedonian	10	10
135		1 d. Red Cross principles in English	10	10
136		1 d. Red Cross principles in French	10	10
137		1 d. Red Cross principles in Spanish	10	10

62 Canoeing **63** "Skopje Earthquake"

1996. Olympic Games, Atlanta. Designs showing statue of discus thrower and sport. Multicoloured.

138		2 d. Type **62**	10	10
139		8 d. Basketball (vert)	20	20
140		15 d. Swimming	45	45
141		20 d. Wrestling	60	60
142		40 d. Boxing (vert)	1·25	1·25
143		50 d. Running (vert)	1·40	1·40

1996. Obligatory Tax. Solidarity Week.

144	**63**	1 d. gold, red and black	10	10

MADAGASCAR AND DEPENDENCIES Pt. 6

A large island in the Indian Ocean off the east coast of Africa. French Post Offices operated there from 1885.

In 1896 the island was declared a French colony, absorbing Diego-Suarez and Ste. Marie de Madagascar in 1898 and Nossi-Be in 1901.

Madagascar became autonomous as the Malagasy Republic in 1958.

100 centimes = 1 franc.

A. FRENCH POST OFFICES

1889. Stamps of French Colonies "Commerce" type surch with value in figures.

1	J	05 on 10 c. black on lilac	£475	£150
2		05 on 25 c. black on red	£475	£140
4		05 on 40 c. red on yellow	£110	70·00
5		5 on 10 c. black on lilac	£160	90·00
6		5 on 25 c. black on red	£160	95·00
7		15 on 25 c. black on red	£110	70·00
3		25 on 40 c. red on yellow	£425	£120

5

1891. No gum. Imperf.

9	**5**	5 c. black on green	£100	17·00
10		10 c. black on blue	70·00	22·00
11		15 c. blue on blue	75·00	24·00
12		25 c. brown on buff	14·00	8·50
13		1 f. black on yellow	£800	£200
14		5 f. black and lilac on lilac	£1500	£900

1895. Stamps of France optd **POSTE FRANCAISE Madagascar**.

15	**10**	5 c. green	4·75	3·75
16		10 c. black on lilac	30·00	19·00
17		15 c. blue	40·00	7·00
18		25 c. black on red	55·00	6·00
19		40 c. red on yellow	45·00	12·00
20		50 c. red	65·00	12·00
21		75 c. brown on orange	60·00	27·00
22		1 f. olive	85·00	18·00
23		5 f. mauve on lilac	£110	50·00

1896. Stamps of France surch with value in figures in oval.

29	**10**	5 c. on 1 c. black on blue	£4000	£1500
30		15 c. on 2 c. brown on yell	£1500	£750
31		25 c. on 3 c. grey	£1700	£750
32		25 c. on 4 c. red on grey	£4250	£1400
33		25 c. on 40 c. red on yellow	£900	£550

B. FRENCH COLONY

1896. "Tablet" key-type inscr "MADAGASCAR ET DEPENDANCES".

1	D	1 c. black & red on blue	50	50
2		2 c. brown & blue on buff	60	60
2a		2 c. brown & blk on buff	2·75	2·75
3		4 c. brown & bl on grey	85	40
17		5 c. green and red	75	30
6		10 c. black & blue on lilac	4·75	60
18		10 c. red and blue	1·00	25
7		15 c. blue and red	6·00	55
19		15 c. grey and red	1·10	30
8		20 c. red & blue on green	3·50	85
9		25 c. black & red on pink	4·75	40
20		25 c. blue and red	12·50	14·00
10		30 c. brown & bl on drab	4·75	1·50
21		35 c. black & red on yell	28·00	3·50
11		40 c. red & blue on yellow	5·25	1·00
12		50 c. red & blue on pink	6·75	85
22		50 c. brown & red on blue	20·00	16·00
13		75 c. violet & red on orge	2·25	1·50
14		1 f. green and red	7·00	1·90
15		1 f. green and blue	12·50	8·00
16		5 f. mauve & blue on lilac	25·00	16·00

1902. "Tablet" key-type stamps as above surch.

27	D	0,01 on 2 c. brown and blue on buff	4·50	3·00
27a		0,01 on 2 c. brown and black on buff	2·50	4·00
29		0,05 on 30 c. brown and blue on drab	3·50	3·50
23		05 on 50 c. red and blue on pink	2·00	1·50
31		0,10 on 50 c. red and blue on pink	3·00	3·50
24		10 on 5 f. mauve and blue on lilac	14·00	12·00
32		0,15 on 75 c. violet and red on orange	1·75	1·75
33		0,15 on 1 f. green & red	1·75	2·50
25		15 on 1 f. green and red	3·50	1·75

1902. Nos. 59 and 61 of Diego-Suarez surch.

35	D	0,05 on 30 c. brown and blue on drab	85·00	£100
36		0,10 on 50 c. red and blue on pink	£3250	£3000

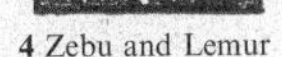

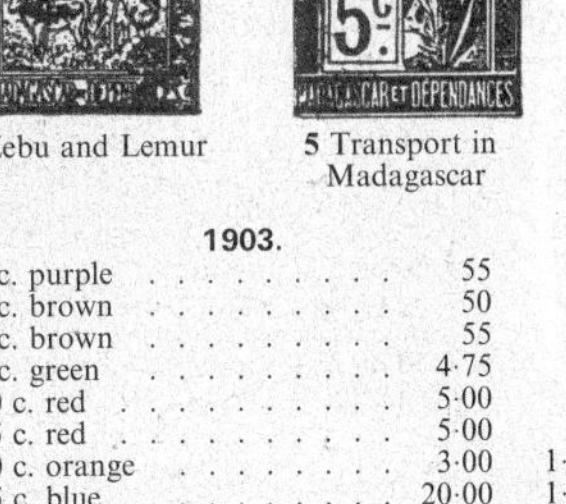

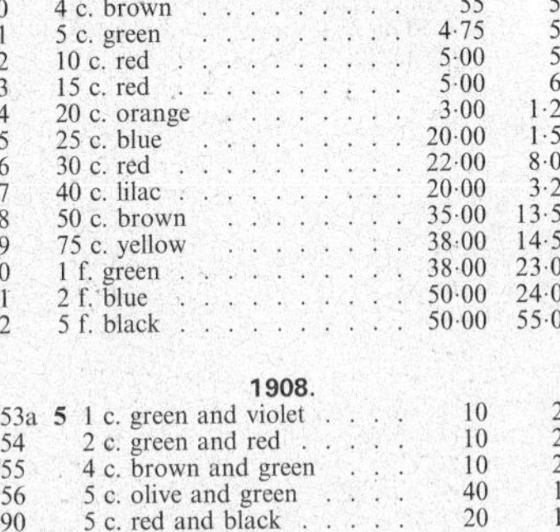

4 Zebu and Lemur **5** Transport in Madagascar

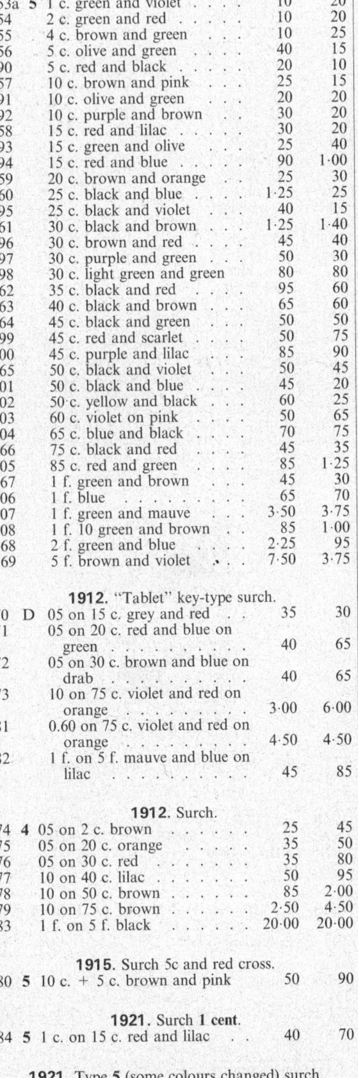

1903.

38	**4**	1 c. purple	55	30
39		2 c. brown	50	50
40		4 c. brown	55	55
41		5 c. green	4·75	55
42		10 c. red	5·00	50
43		15 c. red	5·00	65
44		20 c. orange	3·00	1·25
45		25 c. blue	20·00	1·50
46		30 c. red	22·00	8·00
47		40 c. lilac	20·00	3·25
48		50 c. brown	35·00	13·50
49		75 c. yellow	38·00	14·50
50		1 f. green	38·00	23·00
51		2 f. blue	50·00	24·00
52		5 f. black	50·00	55·00

1908.

53a	**5**	1 c. green and violet	10	20
54		2 c. green and red	10	20
55		4 c. brown and green	10	25
56		5 c. olive and green	40	15
90		5 c. red and black	20	10
57		10 c. brown and pink	25	15
91		10 c. olive and green	20	20
92		10 c. purple and brown	30	20
58		15 c. red and lilac	30	20
93		15 c. green and olive	25	40
94		15 c. red and blue	90	1·00
59		20 c. brown and orange	25	30
60		25 c. black and blue	1·25	25
95		25 c. black and violet	40	15
61		30 c. black and brown	1·25	1·40
96		30 c. brown and red	45	40
97		30 c. purple and green	50	30
98		30 c. light green and green	80	80
62		35 c. black and red	95	60
63		40 c. black and brown	65	60
64		45 c. black and green	50	50
99		45 c. red and scarlet	50	75
100		45 c. purple and lilac	85	90
65		50 c. black and violet	50	45
101		50 c. black and blue	45	20
102		50 c. yellow and black	60	25
103		60 c. violet on pink	50	65
104		65 c. blue and black	70	75
66		75 c. black and red	45	35
105		85 c. red and green	85	1·25
67		1 f. green and brown	45	30
106		1 f. blue	65	70
107		1 f. green and mauve	3·50	3·75
108		1 f. 10 green and brown	85	1·00
68		2 f. green and blue	2·25	95
69		5 f. brown and violet	7·50	3·75

1912. "Tablet" key-type surch.

70	D	05 on 15 c. grey and red	35	30
71		05 on 20 c. red and blue on green	40	65
72		05 on 30 c. brown and blue on drab	40	65
73		10 on 75 c. violet and red on orange	3·00	6·00
81		0.60 on 75 c. violet and red on orange	4·50	4·50
82		1 f. on 5 f. mauve and blue on lilac	45	85

1912. Surch.

74	**4**	05 on 2 c. brown	25	45
75		05 on 20 c. orange	35	50
76		05 on 30 c. red	35	80
77		10 on 40 c. lilac	50	95
78		10 on 50 c. brown	85	2·00
79		10 on 75 c. brown	2·50	4·50
83		1 f. on 5 f. black	20·00	20·00

1915. Surch 5c and red cross.

80	**5**	10 c. + 5 c. brown and pink	50	90

1921. Surch **1 cent.**

84	**5**	1 c. on 15 c. red and lilac	40	70

1921. Type **5** (some colours changed) surch.

109	**5**	25 c. on 15 c. red and lilac	40	45
85		0,25 on 35 c. black and red	3·00	3·00
86		0,25 on 40 c. black & brown	2·50	2·75
87		0,25 on 45 c. black & green	2·00	2·25
110		25 c. on 2 f. green and blue	30	40
112		25 c. on 5 f. brown & violet	50	60
88		0,30 on 40 c. black & brown	1·10	1·10
113		50 c. on 1 f. green & brown	80	20
89		0,60 on 75 c. black and red	1·90	2·00
114		60 on 75 c. violet on pink	40	40
115		65 c. on 75 c. black and red	90	1·50
116		85 c. on 45 c. black & green	90	1·50
117		90 c. on 75 c. pink and red	45	55
118		1 f. 25 on 1 f. blue	30	40
119		1 f. 50 on 1 f. lt blue & blue	50	20
120		3 f. on 5 f. violet and green	1·50	1·00
121		10 f. on 5 f. mauve and red	4·50	3·25
122		20 f. on 5 f. blue and mauve	6·25	5·50

HAVE YOU READ THE NOTES AT THE BEGINNING OF THIS CATALOGUE?

These often provide the answers to the enquiries we receive.

14 Sakalava Chief **15** Zebus

17 Betsileo Woman **18** General Gallieni

1930.

123	**18**	1 c. blue	20	40
124	**15**	1 c. green and blue	20	25
125	**14**	2 c. brown and red	10	10
177	**18**	3 c. blue	15	25
126	**14**	4 c. mauve and brown	15	35
127	**15**	5 c. red and green	15	15
128	–	10 c. green and red	10	10
129	**17**	15 c. red	10	10
130	**15**	20 c. blue and brown	20	20
131	–	25 c. brown and lilac	20	10
132	**17**	30 c. green	40	30
133	**14**	40 c. red and green	30	35
134	**17**	45 c. lilac	55	50
178	**18**	45 c. green	35	40
179		50 c. brown	20	10
180		60 c. mauve	15	30
136	**15**	65 c. mauve and brown	55	25
181	**18**	70 c. red	35	35
137	**17**	75 c. brown	50	25
138	**15**	90 c. red	85	80
182	**18**	90 c. brown	30	15
139	–	1 f. blue and brown	1·00	90
140	–	1 f. red and scarlet	45	45
140a	–	1 f. 25 brown and blue	95	75
183	**18**	1 f. 40 orange	50	35
141	**14**	1 f. 50 ultramarine & blue	4·50	1·25
142		1 f. 50 red and brown	50	55
278		1 f. 50 brown and red	20	50
184	**18**	1 f. 60 violet	50	40
143	**14**	1 f. 75 red and brown	2·50	1·00
185	**18**	2 f. red	35	20
186a		3 f. green	55	60
146	**14**	5 f. brown and mauve	70	40
147	**18**	10 f. orange	2·75	1·90
148	**14**	20 f. blue and brown	1·40	1·40

DESIGN—VERT. 10 c., 25 c., 1 f., 1 f. 25, Hova girl.

1931. "Colonial Exhibition" key-types inscr "MADAGASCAR".

149	E	40 c. black and green	55	55
150	F	50 c. black and mauve	1·25	70
151	G	90 c. black and red	85	90
152	H	1 f. 50 black and blue	1·40	1·00

19 Bloch 120 over Madagascar **20** J. Laborde and Tananarivo Palace

1935. Air.

153	**19**	50 c. red and green	50	55
154		90 c. red and green	35	40
155		1 f. 25 red and lake	35	40
156		1 f. 50 red and blue	40	45
157		1 f. 60 red and blue	20	25
158		1 f. 75 red and orange	5·25	3·25
159		2 f. red and blue	50	30
160		3 f. red and orange	35	30
161		3 f. 65 red and black	35	40
162		3 f. 90 red and green	30	30
163		4 f. red and carmine	35·00	1·90
164		4 f. 50 red and black	18·00	80
165		5 f. 50 red and green	45	40
166		6 f. red and mauve	40	40
167		6 f. 90 red and purple	40	40
168		8 f. red and mauve	70	90
169		8 f. 50 red and green	80	95
170		9 f. red and green	45	50
171		12 f. red and brown	55	65
172		12 f. 50 red and violet	1·25	95
173		15 f. red and orange	60	60
174		16 f. red and green	1·25	1·25
175		20 f. red and brown	1·90	1·40
176		50 f. red and blue	3·25	3·00

1937. International Exhibition, Paris. As Nos. 168/73 of St.-Pierre et Miquelon.

187		20 c. violet	60	75
188		30 c. green	75	85
189		40 c. red	50	50
190		50 c. brown and agate	45	60
191		90 c. red	45	60
192		1 f. 50 blue	45	90

1938. 60th Death Anniv of Jean Laborde (explorer).
193 **20** 35 c. green 35 45
194 55 c. violet 40 45
195 65 c. red 35 50
196 80 c. purple 45 40
197 1 f. red 35 30
198 1 f. 25 red 45 40
199 1 f. 75 blue 90 35
200 2 f. 15 brown . . . . . . 1·75 1·25
201 2 f. 25 blue 75 75
202 2 f. 50 brown 40 45
203 10 f. green 60 60

1938. Int Anti-Cancer Fund. As T **22** of Mauritania.
204 1 f. 75 + 50 c. blue . . . . . 3·75 6·00

1939. New York World's Fair. As T **28** of Mauritania.
205 1 f. 25 red 75 80
206 2 f. 25 blue 80 85

1939. 150th Anniv of French Revolution. As T **29** of Mauritania.
207 45 c. + 25 c. green and black (postage) . . . . 4·75 5·75
208 70 c. + 30 c. brown and black 5·25 5·75
209 90 c. + 35 c. orange and black 4·75 5·75
210 1 f. 25 + 1 f. red and black . 4·75 5·75
211 2 f. 25 + 2 f. blue and black 5·00 5·75
212 4 f. 50 + 4 f. black and orange (air) . . . . 9·00 10·00

1942. Surch **50** and bars.
213 **15** 50 on 65 c. mauve & brown 95 35

1942. Free French Administration. Optd **FRANCE LIBRE** or surch also.
214 **14** 2 c. brown and red (postage) 65 65
215 **18** 3 c. blue . . . . 85·00 90·00
216 **15** 0,05 on 1 c. green and blue 50 60
217 **20** 0,10 on 55 c. violet 75 90
218 **17** 15 c. red . . . . 6·25 6·25
219 **20** 0,30 on 65 c. red 50 60
220 **15** 0 f. 50 on 0,05 on 1 c. green and blue 50 65
221 50 on 65 c. mauve & brown 55 25
222 **18** 50 on 90 c. brown 40 20
223 **15** 65 c. mauve and brown . . 65 65
224 **18** 70 c. red 55 60
225 **20** 80 c. purple . . . . 1·40 1·40
226 – 1,00 on 1 f. 25 brown and blue (No. 140a) . . . . 1·40 1·40
227 **20** 1,00 on 1 f. 25 red . . . . 5·00 5·00
228 **18** 1 f. 40 orange 60 60
229 **5** 1 f. 50 on 1 f. blue . . . 90 85
230 **14** 1 f. 50 ultramarine & blue 90 90
231 1 f. 50 red and brown . . . 90 90
232 **18** 1,50 on 1 f. 60 violet . . . 55 55
233 **14** 1,50 on 1 f. 75 red & brown 55 50
234 **20** 1,50 on 1 f. 75 blue . . . 55 55
235 **18** 1 f. 60 violet 50 60
236 **20** 2,00 on 2 f. 15 brown . . . 50 50
237 2 f. 25 blue 55 55
238 – 2 f. 25 blue (No. 206) . . . 55 55
239 **20** 2 f. 50 brown . . . . . . 2·00 2·25
240 **5** 10 f. on 5 f. mauve & red . 5·50 5·25
241 **20** 10 f. green . . . . 2·75 3·00
242 **5** 20 f. on 5 f. blue & mauve 7·75 8·00
243 **14** 20 f. blue and brown . . . £550 £650
244 **19** 1,00 on 1 f. 25 red and lake (air) . . . . 3·00 3·25
245 1 f. 50 red and blue . . . 3·75 3·75
246 1 f. 75 red and orange . . 55·00 60·00
247 3,00 on 3 f. 65 red & black 65 25
248 8 f. red and purple 80 75
249 8,00 on 8 f. 50 red & green 60 30
250 12 f. red and brown . . . . 1·75 1·60
251 12 f. 50 red and violet . . . 90 85
252 16 f. red and green . . . . 3·25 3·25
253 50 f. red and blue . . . . 2·75 2·75

24 Traveller's Tree

29 Gen. Gallieni

1943. Free French Issue.
254 **24** 5 c. brown 10 25
255 10 c. mauve 10 10
256 25 c. green 10 20
257 30 c. orange 10 10
258 40 c. blue 20 20
259 80 c. purple 10 10
260 1 f. blue 15 15
261 1 f. 50 c. red 20 15
262 2 f. yellow 15 10
263 2 f. 50 c. blue 20 25
264 4 f. blue and red 20 10
265 5 f. green and black 45 15
266 10 f. red and blue 60 20
267 20 f. violet and brown . . . 40 40

1943. Free French Administration. Air. As T **30** of New Caledonia, but inscr "MADAGASCAR".
268 1 f. orange 40 40
269 1 f. 50 c. red 40 40
270 5 f. purple 40 40
271 10 f. black 40 45
272 25 f. blue 85 45
273 50 f. green . . . . 1·40 70
274 100 f. red 50 80

1944. Mutual Aid and Red Cross Funds. As T **31** of New Caledonia.
275 5 f. + 20 f. green 50 80

1944. Surch **1 f. 50**.
276 **24** 1 f. 50 on 5 c. brown . . . 35 55
277 1 f. 50 on 10 c. mauve . . 50 80

1945. Eboue. As T **32** of New Caledonia.
279 2 f. black 20 35
280 25 f. green 50 85

1946. Air. Victory. As T **34** of New Caledonia.
281 8 f. red 40 40

1945. Surch with new value.
282 **24** 50 c. on 5 c. brown . . . 35 35
283 60 c. on 5 c. brown . . . 40 45
284 70 c. on 5 c. brown . . . 35 40
285 1 f. 20 on 5 c. brown . . . 35 35
286 2 f. 40 on 25 c. green . . . 35 45
287 3 f. on 25 c. green 30 30
288 4 f. 50 on 25 c. green . . . 45 50
289 15 f. on 2 f. 50 blue . . . 35 45

1946. Air. From Chad to the Rhine. As Nos. 300/305 of New Caledonia.
290 5 f. blue 75 85
291 10 f. red 80 90
292 15 f. green 80 90
293 20 f. brown . . . . 1·00 1·10
294 25 f. violet . . . . 1·25 1·40
295 50 f. red . . . . 1·10 1·40

1946.
296 – 10 c. green (postage) . . . 10 25
297 – 30 c. orange 10 25
298 – 40 c. olive 10 25
299 – 50 c. purple 10 10
300 – 60 c. blue 10 25
301 – 80 c. green 10 25
302 – 1 f. sepia 10 10
303 – 1 f. 20 green 20 20
304 **29** 1 f. 50 red 10 10
305 – 2 f. black 10 10
306 – 3 f. purple 10 10
307 – 3 f. 60 red 60 60
308 – 4 f. blue 25 20
309 – 5 f. orange 35 15
310 – 6 f. blue 20 10
311 – 10 f. lake 25 25
312 – 15 f. brown 35 20
313 – 20 f. blue 45 35
314 – 25 f. brown 80 45
315 – 50 f. blue and red (air) . . 90 45
316 – 100 f. brown and red . . . 1·75 85
317 – 200 f. brown and green . . 3·50 2·00
DESIGNS—As T **29**. VERT: 10 to 50 c. Native with spear; 6, 10 f. Gen. Duchesne; 15, 20, 25 f. Lt.-Col. Joffre. HORIZ: 60, 80 c. Zebus; 1 f., 1 f. 20, Sakalava man and woman; 3 f. 60, 4, 5 f. Betsimisaraka mother and child. 49×28 mm: 50 f. Aerial view of Port of Tamatave. 28×51 mm: 100 f. Allegory of flight. 51×28 mm: Douglas DC-2 airplane and map of Madagascar.

36 Gen. Gallieni and View

1946. 50th Anniv of French Protectorate.
318 **36** 10 f. + 5 f. purple 35 45

1948. Air. Discovery of Adelie Land, Antarctic. No. 316 optd **TERRE ADELIE DUMONT D'URVILLE 1840.**
319 – 100 f. brown and red . . . 35·00 50·00

1949. Air. 75th Anniv of U.P.U. As T **38** of New Caledonia.
320 25 f. multicoloured . . . . . 2·75 1·90

1950. Colonial Welfare Fund. As T **39** of New Caledonia.
321 10 f. + 2 f. purple and green 3·50 4·00

38 Cacti and Succulents

39 Long-tailed Ground Roller

40 Woman and Forest Road

1952.
322 **38** 7 f. 50 green & blue (postage) 70 35
323 **39** 8 f. lake . . . . 1·75 35
324 15 f. blue and green . . . . 3·00 30
325 – 50 f. green and blue (air) . 2·25 40
326 – 100 f. black, brown & blue 12·00 1·50
327 – 200 f. brown and green . . 12·50 4·50
328 **40** 500 f. brown, sepia & green 21·00 5·00
DESIGNS—As Type **40**: 50 f. Palm trees; 100 f. Antsirabe Viaduct; 200 f. Ring-tailed lemurs.

1952. Military Medal Centenary As T **40** of New Caledonia.
329 15 f. turquoise, yellow & green 1·50 1·90

1954. Air. 10th Anniv of Liberation. As T **42** of New Caledonia.
330 15 f. purple and violet . . . . 2·00 1·50

41 Marshal Lyautey

1954. Birth Centenary of Marshal Lyautey.
331 **41** 10 f. indigo, blue & ultram 65 10
332 40 f. lake, grey and black 1·00 10

42 Gallieni School

43 Cassava

1956. Economic and Social Development Fund.
333 – 3 f. brown and grey . . . 20 10
334 **42** 5 f. brown and chestnut . . 15 10
335 – 10 f. blue and grey 30 15
336 – 15 f. green and turquoise . 40 15
DESIGNS: 3 f. Tamatave and tractor; 10 f. Dredging canal; 15 f. Irrigation.

1956. Coffee. As T **44** of New Caledonia.
337 20 f. sepia and brown 40 15

1957. Plants.
338 **43** 2 f. green, brown and blue 25 10
339 – 4 f. red, brown and green 25 15
340 – 12 f. green, brown & violet 45 15
DESIGNS: 4 f. Cloves; 12 f. Vanilla.

PARCEL POST STAMPS

1919. Receipt stamp of France surch **MADAGASCAR ET DEPENDANCES 0fr.10 COLIS POSTAUX.**
P81 0 f. 10 on 10 c. grey . . . . . 2·75 2·75

1919. Fiscal stamp of Madagascar surch **COLIS POSTAUX 0f.10.**
P82 0 f. 10 on 1 f. pink . . . . . 70·00 42·00

1919. Fiscal stamps surch **Madagascar et Dependances** (in capitals on No. P83) **COLIS POSTAUX 0f.10.**
P83 0 f. 10 pink . . . . 6·25 4·75
P84 0 f. 10 red and green . . . . 1·50 1·25
P85 0 f. 10 black and green . . . . 1·75 1·25

POSTAGE DUE STAMPS

1896. Postage Due stamps of Fr. Colonies optd **Madagascar et DEPENDANCES.**
D17 U 5 c. blue . . . . 5·00 4·75
D18 10 c. brown . . . . 5·00 4·25
D19 20 c. yellow . . . . 4·50 5·00
D20 30 c. red . . . . 5·50 5·00
D21 40 c. mauve . . . . 50·00 30·00
D22 50 c. violet . . . . 6·00 5·00
D23 1 f. green . . . . 55·00 35·00

D **6** Governor's Palace, Tananarive

D **37**

1908.
D70 D **6** 2 c. red 10 10
D71 4 c. violet 10 15
D72 5 c. green 10 20
D73 10 c. red 10 20
D74 20 c. olive 10 30
D75 40 c. brown on cream . . 15 30
D76 50 c. brown on blue . . . 15 25
D77 60 c. red 20 45
D78 1 f. blue 25 55

1924. Surch in figures.
D123 D **6** 60 c. on 1 f. red . . . . 1·00 1·40
D124 2 f. on 1 f. purple . . . 45 60
D125 3 f. on 1 f. blue 45 60

1942. Free French Administration. Optd **FRANCE LIBRE** or surch also.
D254 D **6** 10 c. red 55 65
D255 20 c. green 55 65
D256 D **6** 0,30 on 5 c. green . . . 55 65
D257 40 c. brown on cream . . 55 65
D258 50 c. brown and blue . . 55 65
D259 60 c. red 55 65
D260 1 f. blue 55 65
D261 1 f. on 2 c. purple . . . 3·00 3·50
D262 2 f. on 4 c. violet . . . 1·25 1·50
D263 2 f. on 1 f. mauve . . . 55 65
D264 3 f. on 1 f. blue 55 65

1947.
D319 D **37** 10 c. mauve 10 25
D320 30 c. brown 10 25
D321 50 c. green 10 25
D322 1 f. brown 10 25
D323 2 f. red 20 30
D324 3 f. brown 15 30
D325 4 f. blue 15 40
D326 5 f. red 25 45
D327 10 f. green 35 55
D328 20 f. blue . . . . 40 1·00

For later issues see **MALAGASY REPUBLIC**.

MADEIRA Pt. 9

A Portuguese island in the Atlantic Ocean off the N.W. coast of Africa. From 1868 to 1929 and from 1980 separate issues were made.

1868. 1000 reis = 1 milreis.
1912. 100 centavos = 1 escudo.

Nos. 1/78b are stamps of Portugal optd **MADEIRA**.

1868. With curved value label. Imperf.
1 **14** 20 r. bistre £180 £140
2 50 r. green £180 £140
3 80 r. orange £190 £140
4 100 r. lilac £100 £140

1868. With curved value label. Perf.
10 **14** 5 r. black . . . . 50·00 35·00
13 10 r. yellow . . . . 85·00 75·00
14 20 r. bistre £130 £100
15 25 r. red . . . . 50·00 11·00
16 50 r. green £160 £140
17 80 r. orange £160 £140
19 100 r. mauve £160 £140
20 120 r. blue . . . . £100 80·00
21 240 r. mauve £450 £400

1871. With straight value label.
30 **15** 5 r. black . . . . 8·25 5·75
47 10 r. yellow . . . . 26·00 20·00
72a 10 r. green . . . . 60·00 50·00
48 15 r. brown . . . . 18·00 11·00
49 20 r. bistre . . . . 29·00 20·00
34 25 r. pink . . . . 10·50 4·00
51 50 r. green . . . . 60·00 27·00
71 50 r. blue . . . . £110 55·00
36 80 r. orange . . . . £100 75·00
53 100 r. mauve . . . . 80·00 48·00
38 120 r. blue . . . . £100 80·00
55 150 r. blue £160 £130
74 150 r. yellow £250 £225
39 240 r. lilac £650 £500
67 300 r. lilac . . . . 70·00 65·00

1880. Stamps of 1880.
79 **16** 5 r. black . . . . 24·00 20·00
78 25 r. grey . . . . 26·00 20·00
78b 25 r. brown . . . . 26·00 20·00
77 **17** 25 r. grey . . . . 26·00 20·00

1898. Vasco da Gama. As Nos. 378/85 of Portugal.
134 2½ r. green . . . . 2·25 1·25
135 5 r. red . . . . 2·25 1·25
136 10 r. purple . . . . 3·00 1·50
137 25 r. green . . . . 2·50 1·25
138 50 r. blue . . . . 8·25 3·25
139 75 r. brown . . . . 10·00 6·75
140 100 r. brown . . . . 10·00 6·75
141 150 r. brown . . . . 13·50 11·00
For Nos. 134/41 with **REPUBLICA** overprint, see Nos. 455/62 of Portugal.

6 Ceres

7 20 r. Stamp, 1868

1929. Funchal Museum Fund. Value in black.
148 **6** 3 c. violet 60 60
149 4 c. yellow 60 60
150 5 c. blue 60 60
151 6 c. brown 75 75
152 10 c. red 75 75
153 15 c. green 75 75
154 16 c. brown 75 75
155 25 c. purple 80 80
156 32 c. green 80 80
157 40 c. brown 80 80
158 50 c. grey 80 80
159 64 c. blue 80 80
160 80 c. brown 80 80
161 96 c. red . . . . 3·25 3·25
162 1 e. black 70 70
163 1 e. 20 pink 70 70
164 1 e. 60 blue 70 70
165 2 e. 40 yellow . . . . . . 1·00 1·00
166 3 e. 36 green . . . . 1·25 1·25
167 4 e. 50 red . . . . 1·25 1·25
168 7 e. blue . . . . 2·50 2·50

1980. 112th Anniv of First Overprinted Madeira Stamps.

169 **7** 6 e. 50 black, bistre & green . . . 20 10
170 – 19 e. 50 black, purple & red . . . 75 50

DESIGN: 19 e. 50, 100 r. stamp, 1868.

8 Ox Sledge

1980. World Tourism Conference, Manila, Philippines. Multicoloured.

172 50 c. Type **8** . . . 10 10
173 1 e. Wine and grapes . . . 10 10
174 5 e. Map of Madeira . . . 40 10
175 6 e. 50 Basketwork . . . 40 10
176 8 e. Orchid . . . 65 25
177 30 e. Fishing boat . . . 1·60 50

9 O Bailinho (folk dance)

1981. Europa.

178 **9** 22 e. multicoloured . . . 1·10 60

10 Portuguese Caravel approaching Madeira

11 "Dactylorhiza foliosa"

1981. 560th Anniv (1980) of Discovery of Madeira. Multicoloured.

180 8 e. Type **10** . . . 35 10
181 33 e. 50 Prince Henry the Navigator and map of Atlantic Ocean . . . 1·60 50

1981. Regional Flowers. Multicoloured.

182 7 e. Type **11** . . . 25 10
183 8 e. 50 "Geranium maderense" . . . 35 10
184 9 e. "Goodyera macrophylla" . . . 35 10
185 10 e. "Armeria maderensis" . . . 35 10
186 12 e. 50 "Matthiola maderensis" . . . 15 10
187 20 e. "Isoplexis sceptrum" . . . 50 35
188 27 e. "Viola paradoxa" . . . 1·00 45
189 30 e. "Erica maderensis" . . . 60 25
190 33 e. 50 "Scilla maderensis" . . . 1·10 70
191 37 e. 50 "Cirsium latifolium" . . . 75 45
192 50 e. "Echium candicans" . . . 1·25 65
193 100 e. "Clethra arborea" . . . 2·10 80

12 First Sugar Mill

13 Dancer holding Dolls on Staff

1982. Europa.

199 **12** 33 e. 50 multicoloured . . . 1·75 70

1982. O Brinco Dancing Dolls. Multicoloured.

201 27 e. Type **13** . . . 1·00 55
202 33 e. 50 Dancers . . . 1·50 75

14 Los Levadas Irrigation Channels

1983. Europa.

203 **14** 37 e. 50 multicoloured . . . 1·25 55

15 Flag of Madeira

16 Rally Car

1983. Flag.

205 **15** 12 e. 50 multicoloured . . . 65 10

1984. Europa. As T **398** of Portugal but additionally inscr "MADEIRA".

206 51 e. multicoloured . . . 1·60 95

1984. 25th Anniv of Madeira Rally. Multicoloured.

208 16 e. Type **16** . . . 40 10
209 51 e. Rally car (different) . . . 1·50 55

17 Basket Sledge

18 Braguinha Player

1984. Transport (1st series). Multicoloured.

210 16 e. Type **17** . . . 25 10
211 35 e. Hammock . . . 90 50
212 40 e. Borracheiros (wine carriers) . . . 1·10 50
213 51 e. Carreira local sailing boat . . . 1·40 50

See also Nos. 218/21.

1985. Europa.

214 **18** 60 e. multicoloured . . . 1·75 75

19 Black Scabbard Fish

1985. Fishes (1st series). Multicoloured.

216 40 e. Type **19** . . . 1·10 40
217 60 e. Moon fish . . . 1·50 60

See also Nos. 222/3 and 250/3.

1985. Transport (2nd series). As T **17**. Multicoloured.

218 20 e. Ox sledge . . . 30 10
219 40 e. Mountain railway . . . 95 40
220 46 e. Fishing boat and basket used by pesquitos (itinerant fish sellers) . . . 1·10 65
221 60 e. Coastal ferry . . . 1·25 90

1986. Fishes (2nd series). As T **19**. Multicoloured.

222 20 e. Big eye tuna . . . 55 10
223 75 e. Red bream . . . 2·10 65

20 Cory's Shearwater and Tanker

1986. Europa.

224 **20** 68 e. 50 multicoloured . . . 1·75 80

21 Sao Lourenco Fort, Funchal

1986. Fortresses. Multicoloured.

226 22 e. 50 Type **21** . . . 50 10
227 52 e. 50 Sao Joao do Pico Fort, Funchal . . . 1·25 60
228 68 e. 50 Sao Tiago Fort, Funchal . . . 1·75 70
229 100 e. Nossa Senhora do Amparo Fort, Machico . . . 2·50 85

22 Firecrest

24 Funchal Cathedral

23 Social Services Centre, Funchal (Raul Chorao Ramalho)

1987. Birds (1st series). Multicoloured.

230 25 e. Type **22** . . . 50 15
231 57 e. Trocaz pigeon . . . 1·25 65
232 74 e. 50 Barn owl . . . 1·75 90
233 125 e. Soft-plumaged petrel . . . 2·50 1·25

See also Nos. 240/3.

1987. Europa. Architecture.

234 **23** 74 e. 50 multicoloured . . . 1·60 85

1987. Historic Buildings. Multicoloured.

236 51 e. Type **24** . . . 1·10 60
237 74 e. 50 Old Town Hall, Santa Cruz . . . 1·50 65

25 "Maria Cristina" (mail boat)

1988. Europa. Transport and Communications.

238 **25** 80 e. multicoloured . . . 1·60 65

1988. Birds (2nd series). As T **22** but horiz. Multicoloured.

240 27 e. European robin . . . 40 15
241 60 e. Rock sparrow . . . 1·10 60
242 80 e. Chaffinch . . . 1·50 70
243 100 e. European sparrow hawk . . . 2·00 80

26 Columbus and Funchal House

27 Child flying Kite

1988. Christopher Columbus's Houses in Madeira. Multicoloured.

244 55 e. Type **26** . . . 1·10 60
245 80 e. Columbus and Porto Santo house (horiz) . . . 1·50 60

1989. Europa. Children's Games and Toys.

246 **27** 80 e. multicoloured . . . 1·40 70

28 Church of St. John the Evangelist

29 Silver Hatchetfish

1989. "Brasiliana 89" Stamp Exhibition, Rio de Janeiro. Madeiran Churches. Multicoloured.

248 29 e. Type **28** . . . 45 10
249 87 e. St. Clara's Church and Convent . . . 1·40 85

1989. Fishes (3rd series). Multicoloured.

250 29 e. Type **29** . . . 30 15
251 60 e. "Pseudolepidaplois scrofa" . . . 95 50
252 87 e. Rainbow wrasse . . . 1·50 75
253 100 e. Scorpion fish . . . 1·75 1·10

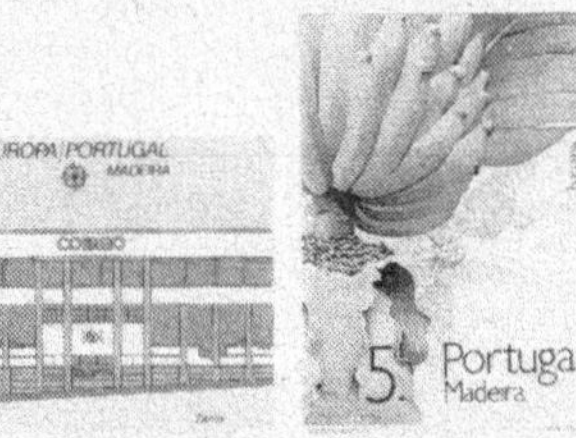

30 Zarco Post Office

31 Bananas

1990. Europa. Post Office Buildings.

254 **30** 80 e. multicoloured . . . 1·10 60

1990. Sub-tropical Fruits. Multicoloured.

256 5 e. Type **31** . . . 10 10
257 10 e. Thorn apple . . . 10 10
258 32 e. Avocado . . . 40 15
259 35 e. Mangoes . . . 35 10

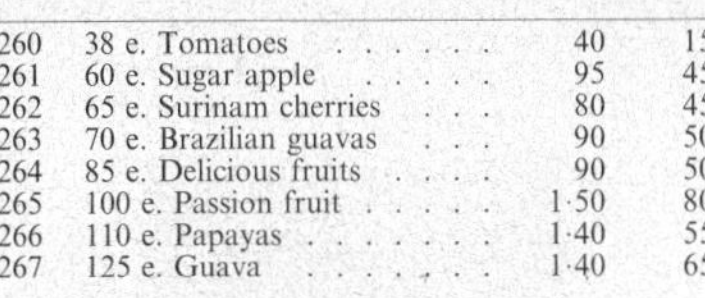

260 38 e. Tomatoes . . . 40 15
261 60 e. Sugar apple . . . 95 45
262 65 e. Surinam cherries . . . 80 45
263 70 e. Brazilian guavas . . . 90 50
264 85 e. Delicious fruits . . . 90 50
265 100 e. Passion fruit . . . 1·50 80
266 110 e. Papayas . . . 1·40 55
267 125 e. Guava . . . 1·40 65

32 Tunny Boat

1990. Boats. Multicoloured.

270 32 e. Type **32** . . . 35 15
271 50 e. Desert Islands boat . . . 85 45
272 70 e. Maneiro . . . 1·00 50
275 95 e. Chavelha . . . 1·50 85

33 Trocaz Pigeon

1991. The Trocaz Pigeon. Multicoloured.

274 35 e. Type **33** . . . 55 25
275 35 e. Two pigeons . . . 55 25
276 35 e. Pigeon on nest . . . 55 25
277 35 e. Pigeon alighting on twig . . . 55 25

Nos. 264/7 were issued together, se-tenant, forming a composite design.

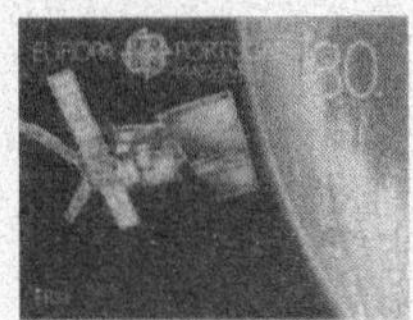

34 European Remote Sensing ("ERS1") Satellite

1991. Europa. Europe in Space.

278 **34** 80 e. multicoloured . . . 1·00 60

35 Columbus and Funchal House

1992. Europa. 500th Anniv of Discovery of America by Columbus.

280 **35** 85 e. multicoloured . . . 80 50

36 "Gaviao" (ferry)

1992. Inter-island Ships. Multicoloured.

281 38 e. Type **36** . . . 35 15
282 65 e. "Independencia" (catamaran ferry) . . . 60 35
283 85 e. "Madeirense" (car ferry) . . . 80 45
284 120 e. "Funchalense" (freighter) . . . 1·25 60

37 "Shadow thrown by Christa Maar" (Lourdes Castro)

39 Window of St. Francis's Convent, Funchal

38 Seals Swimming

1993. Europa. Contemporary Art.
285 **37** 90 e. multicoloured . . . . 1·00 50

1993. Mediterranean Monk Seal. Multicoloured.
287 42 e. Type **38** 45 20
288 42 e. Seal basking 45 20
289 42 e. Two seals on rocks . . . 45 20
290 42 e. Mother suckling young 45 20
Nos. 287/90 were issued together, se-tenant, forming a composite design.

1993. Regional Architecture. Multicoloured.
291 42 e. Type **39** 40 20
292 130 e. Window of Mercy, Old Hospital, Funchal . . . . . 1·25 60

40 Native of Cape of Good Hope and Explorer with Model Caravel

1994. Europa. Discoveries.
293 **40** 100 e. multicoloured . . . 90 50

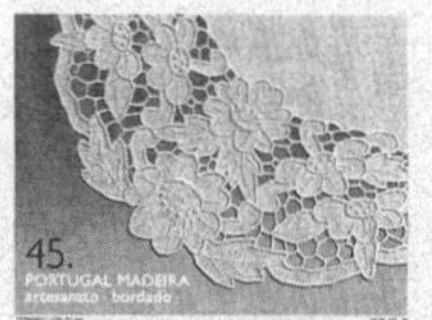

41 Embroidery

1994. Traditional Crafts (1st series). Multicoloured.
295 45 e. Type **41** 35 20
296 75 e. Tapestry 65 35
297 100 e. Boots 90 45
298 140 e. Wicker chair back . . . 1·25 60
See also Nos. 301/4.

42 Funchal

43 Bread Dough Figures

1994. District Arms. Multicoloured.
299 45 e. Type **42** 35 20
300 140 e. Porto Santo . . . . . 1·10 55

1995. Traditional Crafts (2nd series). Multicoloured.
301 45 e. Type **43** 35 20
302 80 e. Inlaid wooden box . . . 65 35
303 95 e. Bamboo cage 75 40
304 135 e. Woollen bonnet . . . . 1·10 55

44 Guiomar Vilhena (entrepreneur)

1996. Europa. Famous Women.
305 **44** 98 e. multicoloured 80 40

45 "Adoration of the Magi"

1996. Religious Paintings by Flemish Artists. Multicoloured.
307 47 e. Type **45** 40 20
308 78 e. "St. Mary Magdalene" . 65 35
309 98 . "The Annunciation" (horiz) 80 40
310 140 e. "Saints Peter, Paul and Andrew" (horiz) . . . . . 1·10 55

CHARITY TAX STAMPS

The note under this heading in Portugal also applies here.

1925. As Marquis de Pombal stamps of Portugal but inscr "MADEIRA".
C142 C **73** 15 c. grey . . . . . . 1·25 1·25
C143 – 15 c. grey . . . . . . 1·25 1·25
C144 C **75** 15 c. grey . . . . . . 1·25 1·25

NEWSPAPER STAMP

1876. Newspaper stamp of Portugal optd **MADEIRA**.
N69 N **17** $2\frac{1}{2}$ r. green . . . . . . 8·00 3·25

POSTAGE DUE STAMPS

1925. Marquis de Pombal stamps as Nos. C1/3 optd **MULTA**.
D145 C **73** 30 c. grey . . . . . . 1·25 1·25
D146 – 30 c. grey . . . . . . 1·25 1·25
D147 C **75** 30 c. grey . . . . . . 1·25 1·25

MALAGASY REPUBLIC Pt. 6; Pt. 13

The former areas covered by Madagascar and Dependencies were renamed the Malagasy Republic within the French Community on 14 Oct., 1958.

1958. 100 centimes = 1 franc.
1976. 5 francs = 1 ariary.

1958. 10th Anniv of Declaration of Human Rights. As T **48** of New Caledonia.
1 10 f. brown and blue 65 45

1959. Tropical Flora. As T **47** of New Caledonia.
2 6 f. green, brown and yellow . . 15 10
3 25 f. multicoloured 40 15
DESIGNS—HORIZ: 6 f. "Datura"; 25 f. Poinsettia.

1 Malagasy Flag and Assembly Hall

1959. Proclamation of Malagasy Republic and "French Community" Commemorative (60 f.).
4 **1** 20 f. red, green and purple . . 30 20
5 – 25 f. red, green and grey . . . 40 25
6 – 60 f. multicoloured 75 45
DESIGNS—VERT: 25 f. Malagasy flag on map of Madagascar; 60 f. Natives holding French and Malagasy flags.

2 "Chionaema pauliani" (butterfly)

3 Reafforestation

1960.
7 – 30 c. multicoloured (postage) 15 10
8 – 40 c. brown, choc & green . . 15 10
9 – 50 c. turquoise and purple . . 15 10
10 **2** 1 f. red, purple and black . . 20 15
11 – 3 f. black, red and olive . . . 35 20
12 – 5 f. green, brown and red . . 10 10
13 – 6 f. yellow and green 10 10
14 – 8 f. black, green and red . . . 15 10
15 – 10 f. green, brown & turq . . 20 10
16 – 15 f. green and brown 25 15
17 – 30 f. multicoloured (air) . . . 75 25
18 – 40 f. brown and turquoise . . . 85 30
19 – 50 f. multicoloured . . . . . 2·50 50
20 – 100 f. multicoloured . . . . . 4·00 85
21 – 200 f. yellow and violet . . . 7·50 1·50
22 – 500 f. brown, blue and green 7·50 2·00
BUTTERFLIES—As Type **2**: 30 c. Purple-tip; 40 c. "Acraea hova"; 50 c. Clouded mother-of-pearl; 3 f. "Hypolimnas dexithea". 48 × 27 mm: 50 f. "Charaxes antamboulou"; 100 f. Sunset moth. 27 × 48 mm: 200 f. Tailed comet moth.
OTHER DESIGNS—As Type **2**: HORIZ: 5 f. Sisal; 8 f. Pepper; 15 f. Cotton. VERT: 6 f. Ylang ylang (flower); 10 f. Rice. $48\frac{1}{2} \times 27$ mm: 30 f. Sugar-cane trucks; 40 f. Tobacco plantation; 500 f. Mandrare Bridge.

1960. Trees Festival.
23 **3** 20 f. brown, green and ochre 35 25

4

5 Pres. Philibert Tsiranana

1960. 10th Anniv of African Technical Co-operation Commission.
24 **4** 25 f. lake and green 45 35

1960.
25 **5** 20 f. brown and green 30 15

6 Young Athletes

7 Pres. Tsiranana

1960. 1st Youth Games, Tananarive.
26 **6** 25 f. brown, chestnut & blue 50 30

1960.
27 **7** 20 f. black, red and green . . 25 10

1960. Independence. Surch + **10 F FETES DE L'INDEPENDANCE**.
28 **7** 20 f. + 10 f. black, red & grn 55 35

9 Ruffed Lemur

1961. Lemurs.
29 – 2 f. purple & turq (postage) 15 15
30 **9** 4 f. black, brown and myrtle 20 15
31 – 12 f. brown and green . . . 50 30
32 – 65 f. brown, sepia and myrtle (air) . . . . 1·75 65
33 – 85 f. black, sepia and green 2·25 1·00
34 – 250 f. purple, black and turq 6·50 2·75
LEMURS—VERT: As Type **9**: 2 f. Grey gentle lemur; 12 f. Mongoose-lemur. 48 × 27 mm: 65 f. Diadem sifaka; 85 f. Indris; 250 f. Verreaux's sifaka.

10 Diesel Train

11 U.N. and Malagasy Flags, and Govt. Building, Tananarive

1962.
35 **10** 20 f. myrtle 90 20
36 – 25 f. blue 35 15
DESIGN: 25 f. President Tsiranana Bridge.

1962. Admission into U.N.O.
37 **11** 25 f. multicoloured 35 20
38 85 f. multicoloured 95 55

1962. Malaria Eradication. As T **43** of Mauritania.
39 25 f. + 5 f. green 50 50

12 Ranomafana

1962. Tourist Publicity.
40 **12** 10 f. purple, myrtle and blue (postage) 20 15
41 – 30 f. purple, blue and myrtle 40 15
42 – 50 f. blue, myrtle and purple 60 25
43 – 60 f. myrtle, purple and blue 80 35
44 – 100 f. brown, myrtle and blue (air) . . . . 1·75 95
DESIGNS—As Type **12**: 30 f. Tritriva Lake; 50 f. Foulpointe; 60 f. Fort Dauphin. $27 \times 47\frac{1}{2}$ mm: 100 f. Boeing 707 airliner over Nossi-Be.

13 G.P.O., Tamatave

1962. Stamp Day.
45 **13** 25 f. + 5 f. brown, myrtle and blue 35 40

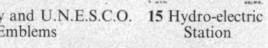

14 Malagasy and U.N.E.S.C.O. Emblems

15 Hydro-electric Station

1962. U.N.E.S.C.O. Conference on Higher Education in Africa, Tananarive.
46 **14** 20 f. black, green and red . . 35 25

1962. 1st Anniv of Union of African and Malagasy States. As T **45** of Mauritania.
47 30 f. green 45 35

1962. Malagasy Industrialisation.
48 **15** 5 f. multicoloured 10 10
49 – 8 f. multicoloured 15 10
50 – 10 f. multicoloured 20 10
51 – 15 f. brown, black and blue . . 35 15
52 – 20 f. multicoloured 35 20
DESIGNS—HORIZ: 8 f. Atomic plant; 15 f. "Esso Gasikara" (tanker); 20 f. Hertzian aerials at Tananarive-Fianarantsoa. VERT: 10 f. Oilwell.

16 Globe and Factory

1963. International Fair, Tamatave.
53 **16** 25 f. orange and black . . . 30 20

1963. Freedom from Hunger. As T **51** of Mauritania.
54 25 f. + 5 f. lake, brown & red 60 60

17 Douglas DC-8 Airliner

1963. Air. Malagasy Commercial Aviation.
55 **17** 500 f. blue, red and green . 8·50 3·25

18 Central Post Office, Tananarive
19 Madagascar Blue Pigeon

1963. Stamp Day.
56 **18** 20 f. + 5 f. brown & turq 30 35

1963. Malagasy Birds and Orchids (8 f. to 12 f.). Multicoloured. (a) Postage as T **19**.
57 1 f. Type **19** 75 30
58 2 f. Blue Madagascar coucal . . 75 30
59 3 f. Madagascar red fody . . . 75 30
60 6 f. Madagascar pygmy kingfisher 90 30
61 8 f. "Gastrorchis humblotii" . . 20 15
62 10 f. "Eulophiella roempleriana" 30 25
63 12 f. "Angraceum sesquipedale" 30 25

(b) Air. Horiz: 49½ × 28 mm.
64 40 f. Helmet bird . . . . 3·25 45
65 100 f. Pitta-like Ground roller 8·00 1·25
66 200 f. Crested wood ibis . . . 17·00 3·50

20 Centenary Emblem and Map
21 U.P.U. Monument, Berne, and Map of Malagasy

1963. Red Cross Centenary.
67 **20** 30 f. multicoloured 80 60

1963. Air. African and Malagasy Posts and Telecommunications Union. As T **56** of Mauritania.
68 85 f. multicoloured . . . . . . 1·00 90

1963. Air. 2nd Anniv of Malagasy's admission to U.P.U.
69 **21** 45 f. blue, red and turquoise 50 25
70 85 f. blue, red and violet . . 90 50

22 Arms of Fianarantsoa
23 Flame, Globe and Hands

1963. Town Arms (1st series). Multicoloured.
71 1 f. 50 Antsirabe 10 10
72 5 f. Antalaha 15 10
73 10 f. Tulear 20 10
74 15 f. Majunga 30 15
75 20 f. Type **22** 40 15
75a 20 f. Manajary 25 10
76 25 f. Tananarive 45 15
76a 30 f. Nossi Be 35 15
77 50 f. Diego-Suarez 85 50
77a 90 f. Antsohihy . . . . 1·40 55
See also Nos. 174/7 and 208/9.

1963. 15th Anniv of Declaration of Human Rights.
78 **23** 60 f. ochre, bronze & mauve 55 45

24 Met Station, Tananarive

1964. Air. World Meteorological Day.
79 **24** 90 f. brown, blue and grey 1·50 1·25

25 Postal Cheques and Savings Bank Building, Tananarive
26 Scouts beside Campfire

1964. Stamp Day.
80 **25** 25 f. + 5 f. brown, bl & grn 50 60

1964. 40th Anniv of Malagasy Scout Movement.
81 **26** 20 f. multicoloured 55 25

27 Symbolic Bird and Globe within "Egg"
28 Statuette of Woman

1964. "Europafrique".
82 **27** 45 f. brown and green . . . 45 35

1964. Malagasy Art.
83 **28** 6 f. brown, blue and indigo (postage) 25 15
84 – 30 f. brown, bistre & green 45 20
85 – 100 f. brown, red & vio (air) 1·50 95
DESIGNS: 30 f. Statuette of squatting vendor. 27 × 48½ mm: 100 f. Statuary of peasant family, ox and calf.

1964. French, African and Malagasy Co-operation. As T **68** of Mauritania.
86 25 f. brown, chestnut and black 40 25

29 Tree on Globe
30 Cithern

1964. University of Malagasy Republic.
87 **29** 65 f. black, red and green 50 25

1965. Malagasy Musical Instruments.
88 – 3 f. brown, blue and mauve (postage) 20 10
89 **30** 6 f. sepia, purple and green 25 10
90 – 8 f. brown, black and green 35 10
91 – 25 f. multicoloured 90 50
92 – 200 f. brown, orange and green (air) . . . . 4·00 2·25
DESIGNS—As Type **30**: 3 f. Kabosa (lute); 8 f. Hazolahy (sacred drum). LARGER—VERT: 35½ × 48 mm: 25 f. "Valiha Player" (after E. Ralambo). 27 × 48 mm: 200 f. Bara violin.

31 Foulpointe Post Office

1965. Stamp Day.
93 **31** 20 f. brown, green & orange 20 15

32 I.T.U. Emblem
33 J.-J. Rabearivelo (poet)

1965. I.T.U. Centenary.
94 **32** 50 f. green, blue and red . . 1·00 45

1965. Rabearivelo Commemorative.
95 **33** 40 f. brown and orange . . . 40 25

34 Nurse weighing Baby

1965. Air. International Co-operation Year.
96 **34** 50 f. black, bistre and blue 60 35
97 – 100 f. purple, brown & blue 1·25 60
DESIGN: 100 f. Boy and girl.

35 Pres. Tsiranana
36 Bearer

1965. Pres. Tsiranana's 55th Birthday.
98 **35** 20 f. multicoloured 25 15
99 25 f. multicoloured 30 20

1965. Postal Transport.
102 – 3 f. violet, blue and brown 30 15
103 – 4 f. blue, brown and green 25 15
104 **36** 10 f. multicoloured 25 15
105 – 12 f. multicoloured 30 20
106 – 20 f. multicoloured 50 20
107 – 25 f. multicoloured 50 20
108 – 30 f. red, brown and blue 1·25 60
109 – 65 f. brown, blue & violet 1·50 50
DESIGNS—HORIZ: 3 f. Early car; 4 f. Filanzane (litter); 12 f. Pirogue; 20 f. Horse-drawn mail-cart; 25 f. Bullock cart; 30 f. Early railway postal carriage; 65 f. Hydrofoil, "Porthos", Betsiboka.

37 Diseased Hands

1966. World Leprosy Day.
110 **37** 20 f. purple, red and green 35 20

38 Planting Trees

1966. Reafforestation Campaign.
111 **38** 20 f. violet, brown & turq 35 20

39 "Cicindelidac chaetodera andriana"

1966. Malagasy Insects. Multicoloured.
112 1 f. Type **39** 10 10
113 6 f. "Mantodea tisma freiji" . 20 10
114 12 f. "Cerambycini mastododera nodicollis" 45 20
115 45 f. "Trachelophoru giraffa" 85 30

40 Madagascar 1 c. Stamp of 1903
41 Betsileo Dance

1966. Stamp Day.
116 **40** 25 f. bistre and red 35 25

1966. Folk Dances. Multicoloured.
117 2 f. Bilo Sakalava dance (vert) (postage) 15 10
118 5 f. Type **41** 25 15
119 30 f. Antandroy dance (vert) 55 20
120 200 f. Southern Malagasy dancer (air) . . . . 3·50 1·50
121 250 f. Sakalava Net Dance . . 4·00 2·25
Nos. 120/1 are size 27 × 48 mm.

43 "Tree" of Emblems

1966. O.C.A.M. Conference, Tananarive.
122 **43** 25 f. multicoloured 30 15
The above was issued with "Janvier 1966" obliterated by bars, and optd "**JUIN 1966**".

44 Singing Anthem
45 U.N.E.S.C.O. Emblem

1966. National Anthem.
123 **44** 20 f. brn, mauve and green 25 10

1966. 20th Anniv of U.N.E.S.C.O.
124 **45** 30 f. blue, bistre and red . 35 20

46 Lions Emblem
47 Harvesting Rice

1967. 50th Anniv of Lions Int.
125 **46** 30 f. multicoloured 40 20

1967. International Rice Year.
126 **47** 20 f. multicoloured 30 15

48 Adventist Temple, Tanambao-Tamatave

1967. Religious Buildings (1st series).
127 **48** 3 f. ochre, blue and green 10 10
128 – 5 f. lilac, purple and green 10 10
129 – 10 f. purple, blue and green 25 10
BUILDINGS—VERT: 5 f. Catholic Cathedral, Tananarive. HORIZ: 10 f. Mosque, Tamatave.
See also Nos. 148/50.

49 Raharisoa at Piano

1967. 4th Death Anniv of Norbert Raharisoa (composer).
130 **49** 40 f. multicoloured 55 20

50 Jean Raoult's Bleriot XI, 1911

1967. "History of Malagasy Aviation".
131 **50** 5 f. brown, blue and green (postage) 35 15
132 – 45 f. black, blue & brown 90 35
133 – 500 f. black, blue and ochre (air) . . . . 8·75 3·75
DESIGNS: 45 f. Bernard Bougault and flying boat, 1926. 48 × 27 mm: 500 f. Jean Dagnaux and Breguet 19A2 biplane, 1927.

51 Ministry of Communications, Tananarive
52 Church, Torch and Map

1967. Stamp Day.
134 **51** 20 f. green, blue & orange 25 15

1967. Air. 5th Anniv of U.A.M.P.T. As T **101** of Mauritania.
135 100 f. mauve, bistre and red 1·25 60

1967. Centenary of Malagasy Lutheran Church.
136 **52** 20 f. multicoloured 30 15

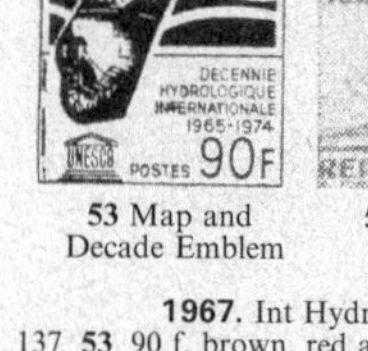

53 Map and Decade Emblem
54 Woman's Face and Scales of Justice

1967. Int Hydrological Decade.
137 **53** 90 f. brown, red and blue 85 45

1967. Women's Rights Commission.
138 **54** 50 f. blue, ochre and green 50 25

55 Human Rights Emblem

56 Congress and W.H.O. Emblems

1968. Human Rights Year.
139 **55** 50 f. red, green and black 40 25

1968. Air. 20th Anniv of W.H.O. and Int Medical Sciences Congress, Tananarive.
140 **56** 200 f. red, blue and ochre 2·00 1·25

57 International Airport, Tananarive-Ivato

1968. Air. Stamp Day.
141 **57** 500 f. blue, green & brown 4·25 3·00

1968. Nos. 33 and 38 surch.
142 **11** 20 f. on 85 f. (postage) . . 40 30
143 – 20 f. on 85 f. (No. 33) (air) 50 30

59 "Industry and Construction"
61 Isotry Protestant Church, Fitiavana, Tananarive

60 Church and Open Bible

1968. Five-Year Plan (1st issue).
144 **59** 10 f. plum, red and green 15 10
145 – 20 f. black, red and green 20 15
146 – 40 f. blue, brown & ultram 85 35
DESIGNS—VERT: 20 f. "Agriculture". HORIZ: 40 f. "Transport".
See also Nos. 156/7.

1968. 150th Anniv of Christianity in Madagascar.
147 **60** 20 f. multicoloured 25 10

1968. Religious Buildings (2nd series).
148 **61** 4 f. brown, green and red 10 10
149 – 12 f. brown, blue and violet 20 10
150 – 50 f. indigo, blue and green 45 25
DESIGNS: 12 f. Catholic Cathedral, Fianarantsoa; 50 f. Aga Khan Mosque, Tananarive.

62 President Tsiranana and Wife
63 Cornucopia, Coins and Map

1968. 10th Anniv of Republic.
151 **62** 20 f. brown, red and yellow 20 10
152 30 f. brown, red and blue 25 15

1968. 50th Anniv of Malagasy Savings Bank.
154 **63** 20 f. multicoloured 25 10

64 "Dance of the Whirlwind"

1968. Air.
155 **64** 100 f. multicoloured . . . 1·10 65

65 Malagasy Family

1968. Five Year Plan (2nd issue).
156 **65** 15 f. red, yellow and blue 15 10
157 – 45 f. multicoloured 40 25
DESIGN—VERT: 45 f. Allegory of "Achievement".

1968. Air. "Philexafrique" Stamp Exn., Abidjan (1969) (1st issue). As T **113a** of Mauritania.
158 100 f. multicoloured . . . . 1·75 80
DESIGN: 100 f. "Young Woman sealing a Letter". (J. B. Santerre).

1969. Air. "Philexafrique" Stamp Exn., Abidjan, Ivory Coast (2nd issue). As T **114a** of Mauritania.
159 50 f. red, green and drab . . 1·00 90
DESIGN: 50 f. Malagasy Arms, map and Madagascar stamp of 1946.

68 "Queen Adelaide receiving Malagasy Mission, London" (1836-37)

1969.
160 **68** 250 f. multicoloured . . . . 3·00 2·50

69 Hand with Spanner, Cogwheels and I.L.O. Emblem

1969. 50th Anniv of I.L.O.
161 **69** 20 f. multicoloured 25 15

70 Post and Telecommunications Building, Tananarive

1969. Stamp Day.
162 **70** 30 f. multicoloured 35 20

71 Map, Steering Wheel and Vehicles
72 President Tsiranana making Speech

1969. 20th Anniv of Malagasy Motor Club.
163 **71** 65 f. multicoloured 60 35

1969. 10th Anniv of President Tsiranana's Assumption of Office.
164 **72** 20 f. multicoloured 20 10

73 Bananas
74 Start of Race and Olympic Flame

1969. Fruits.
165 **73** 5 f. green, brown and blue 15 10
166 – 15 f. red, myrtle and green 30 10
DESIGN: 15 f. Lychees.

1969. Olympic Games, Mexico (1968).
167 **74** 15 f. brown, red and green 25 20

75 "Malagasy Seashore, East Coast" (A. Razafinjohany)

1969. Air. Paintings by Malagasy Artists. Multicoloured.
168 100 f. Type **75** . . . . 1·25 80
169 150 f. "Sunset on the High Plateaux" (H. Ratovo) . . . 2·50 1·40

76 Imerino House, High Plateaux

77 Ambalavao Arms

1969. Malagasy Traditional Dwellings (1st series).
170 – 20 f. red, blue and green . . 20 10
171 – 20 f. brown, red and blue 20 10
172 **76** 40 f. red, blue and indigo 40 20
173 – 60 f. purple, green & blue 60 25
HOUSES—HORIZ: 20 f. (No. 170), Tsimihety hut, East Coast; 60 f. Betsimisaraka dwellings, East Coast. VERT: 20 f. (No. 171), Betsileo house, High Plateaux.
See also Nos. 205/6.

1970. Town Arms (2nd series). Multicoloured.
174 10 f. Type **77** 20 10
175 25 f. Morondava 35 15
176 25 f. Ambatondrazaka 35 15
177 80 f. Tamatave 90 35
See also Nos. 208/9.

78 Agate
80 U.N. Emblem and Symbols

1970. Semi-precious Stones. Multicoloured.
178 5 f. Type **78** 55 20
179 20 f. Ammonite . . . . 2·75 80

1970. New U.P.U. Headquarters Building, Berne. As T **81** of New Caledonia.
180 20 f. blue, brown and mauve 30 20

1970. 25th Anniv of United Nations.
181 **80** 50 f. black, blue & orange 40 25

81 Astronaut and Module on Moon

1970. Air. 1st Anniv of "Apollo 11" Moon-landing.
182 **81** 75 f. green, slate and blue 85 40

82 Malagasy Fruits

1970.
183 **82** 20 f. multicoloured 30 15

83 Delessert's Lyria

1970. Sea Shells (1st series). Multicoloured.
184 5 f. Type **83** 50 15
185 10 f. Bramble murex 65 25
186 20 f. Thorny oyster . . . . . 1·40 50

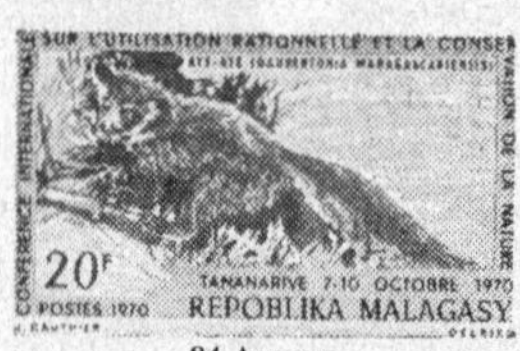

84 Aye-aye

1970. Int Nature Conservation Conference, Tananarive.
187 **84** 20 f. multicoloured 40 30

85 Boeing 737 in Flight

1970. Air.
188 **85** 200 f. red, green and blue 2·40 1·25

86 Pres. Tsiranana **87** Calcite

1970. Pres. Tsiranana's 60th Birthday.
189 **86** 30 f. brown and green . . . 30 15

1971. Minerals Multicoloured.
190 12 f. Type **87** 75 20
191 15 f. Quartz . . . . 1·10 35

88 Soap Works, Tananarive

1971. Malagasy Industries.
192 **88** 5 f. multicoloured 15 10
193 – 15 f. black, brown and blue 25 10
194 – 50 f. multicoloured 55 15
DESIGNS: 15 f. Chrome works, Comina-Andriamena; 50 f. Textile complex, Sotema-Majunga.

89 Globe and Emblems

1971. Council Meeting of Common Market Countries with African and Malagasy Associated States, Tananarive.
195 **89** 5 f. multicoloured 15 15

90 Rural Mobile Post Office **91** Gen. De Gaulle

1971. Stamp Day.
196 **90** 25 f. multicoloured 35 15

1971. Death (1970) of Gen. Charles de Gaulle.
197 **91** 30 f. black, red and blue . 70 35

92 Palm Beach Hotel, Nossi-Be **93** Forestry Emblem

1971. Malagasy Hotels.
198 **92** 25 f. multicoloured 30 20
199 – 65 f. brown, blue & green 60 30
DESIGN: 65 f. Hilton Hotel, Tananarive.

1971. Forest Preservation Campaign.
200 **93** 3 f. multicoloured 15 10

MINIMUM PRICE

The minimum price quoted is 10p which represents a handling charge rather than a basis for valuing common stamps. For further notes about prices, see introductory pages.

94 Jean Ralaimongo **96** Vezo Dwellings, South-east Coast

1971. Air. Malagasy Celebrities.
201 **94** 25 f. brown, red & orange 30 15
202 – 65 f. brown, myrtle & green 40 25
203 – 100 f. brown, ultram & bl 90 40
CELEBRITIES: 65 f. Albert Sylla; 100 f. Joseph Ravoahangy Andrianavalona.

1971. Air. 10th Anniv of African and Malagasy Posts and Telecommunications Union. As T **139a** of Mauritania.
204 100 f. U.A.M.P.T. H.Q. Brazzaville, and painting "Mpisikidy" (G. Rakotovao) 1·00 60

1971. Malagasy Traditional Dwellings (2nd series). Multicoloured.
205 5 f. Type **96** 15 10
206 10 f. Antandroy hut, South coast 20 10

97 "Children and Cattle in Meadow" (G. Rasoaharijaona)

1971. 25th Anniv of U.N.I.C.E.F.
207 **97** 50 f. multicoloured 65 30

1972. Town Arms (3rd series). As T **77**. Mult.
208 1 f. Maintirano Arms 10 10
209 25 f. Fenerive-Est 35 20

99 Cable-laying train

1972. Co-axial Cable Link, Tananarive-Tamatave.
210 **99** 45 f. brown, green and red 1·40 80

100 Telecommunications Station

1972. Inauguration of Philibert Tsiranana Satellite Communications Station.
211 **100** 85 f. multicoloured . . . 75 45

101 Pres. Tsiranana and Voters **102** "Moped" Postman

1972. Presidential Elections.
212 **101** 25 f. multicoloured . . . 40 35

1972. Stamp Day.
213 **102** 10 f. multicoloured . . . 40 20

1972. De Gaulle Memorial. No. 197 surch **MEMORIAL +20F**.
214 **91** 30 f. + 20 f. blk, red & bl 60 60

104 Exhibition. Emblem and Stamps **105** Road and Monument

1972. 2nd National Stamp Exn, Antanarive.
215 **104** 25 f. multicoloured 35 30
216 40 f. multicoloured 60 35
217 100 f. multicoloured . . . 1·25 75

1972. Opening of Andapa-Sambava Highway.
219 **105** 50 f. multicoloured 35 25

106 Petroleum Refinery, Tamatave **107** R. Rakotobe

1972. Malagasy Economic Development.
220 **106** 2 f. blue, green and yellow 20 10
221 – 100 f. multicoloured . . . 2·40 40
DESIGN: 100 f. "3600 CV" railway locomotive.

1972. Air. 1st Death Anniv of Rene Rakotobe (poet).
222 **107** 40 f. brown, purple & orge 40 20

108 College Buildings

1972. 150th Anniv of Razafindrahety College, Tananarive.
223 **108** 10 f. purple, brown & blue 15 10

109 Volleyball

1972. African Volleyball Championships.
224 **109** 12 f. black, orange & brn 40 15

110 Runners breasting Tape

1972. Air. Olympic Games, Munich. Multicoloured.
225 100 f. Type **110** . . . . 1·00 60
226 200 f. Judo . . . . 1·75 90

111 Hospital Complex

1972. Inauguration of Ravoahangy Andrianavalona Hospital.
227 **111** 6 f. multicoloured 20 15

112 Mohair Goat

1972. Air. Malagasy Wool Production.
228 **112** 250 f. multicoloured . . . 3·50 2·25

113 Ploughing with Oxen

1972. Agricultural Expansion.
229 **113** 25 f. multicoloured . . . 25 15

114 "Virgin and Child" (15th-cent. Florentine School)

1972. Air. Christmas. Religious Paintings. Mult.
230 85 f. Type **114** 85 55
231 150 f. "Adoration of the Magi" (A. Mantegna) (horiz) . . . 2·00 85

115 Betsimisarka Women

1972. Traditional Costumes. Multicoloured.
232 10 f. Type **115** 20 10
233 15 f. Merina mother and child 30 20

116 Astronauts on Moon **117** "Natural Produce"

1973. Air. Moon Flight of "Apollo 17".
234 **116** 300 f. purple, brown & grey 3·00 1·75

1973. 10th Anniv of Malagasy Freedom from Hunger Campaign Committee.
235 **117** 25 f. multicoloured . . . 30 15

118 "The Entombment" (Grunewald)

1973. Air. Easter. Multicoloured.
236 100 f. Type **118** . . . . 1·00 55
237 200 f. "The Resurrection" (Grunewald) (vert) . . . . 2·00 1·10

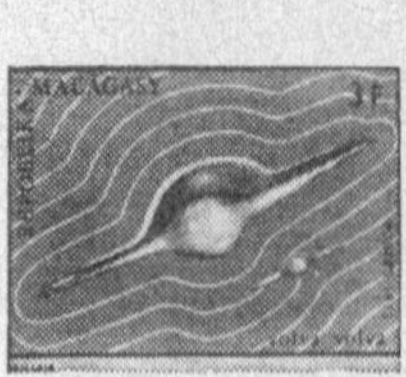

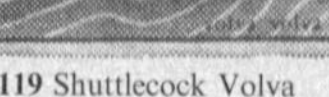

119 Shuttlecock Volva **120** Postal Courier, Tsimandoa

1973. Sea Shells (2nd series). Multicoloured.
238 3 f. Type **119** 15 10
239 10 f. Arthritic spider conch . . 25 20
240 15 f. Common harp 50 30
241 25 f. Type **119** 70 45
242 40 f. As 15 f. . . . . 1·10 50
243 50 f. As 10 f. . . . . 2·25 60

1973. Stamp Day.
244 **120** 50 f. blue, green & brown 45 20

121 "Africa" within Scaffolding **122** "Cameleon campani"

1973. 10th Anniv of Organization of African Unity.
245 **121** 25 f. multicoloured . . . 30 15

1973. Malagasy Chameleons. Multicoloured.
246 1 f. Type **122** 10 10
247 5 f. "Cameleon nasutus" (male) 10 10
248 10 f. "Cameleon nasutus" (female) 15 10
249 40 f. As 5 f. 55 25
250 60 f. Type **122** 85 35
251 85 f. As 10 f. . . . . 1·25 65

123 Excursion Carriage

1973. Air. Early Malagasy Railways. Multicoloured.
252 100 f. Type **123** . . . . . . 1·75 80
253 150 f. Steam locomotive . . . 2·50 1·25

124 "Cypripedium"

1973. Orchids. Multicoloured.
254 10 f. Type **124** 30 15
255 25 f. "Nepenthes pervillei" . . 50 20
256 40 f. As 25 f. . . . . 1·00 35
257 100 f. Type **124** . . . . 2·25 85

1973. Pan African Drought Relief. No. 235 surch **SECHERESSE SOLIDARITE AFRICAINE** and value.
258 **117** 100 f. on 25 f. multicoloured 1·10 60

126 Dish Aerial and Met. Station **128** Greater Dwarf Lemur

1973. Air. W.M.O. Centenary.
259 **126** 100 f. orange, blue & blk 1·25 65

1973. 12th Anniv of African and Malagasy Posts and Telecommunications. As T **155a** of Mauritania.
260 100 f. red, violet and green . . 90 45

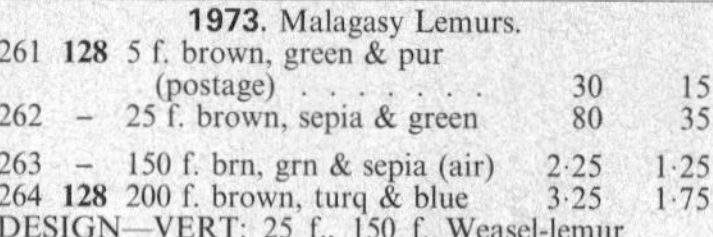

1973. Malagasy Lemurs.
261 **128** 5 f. brown, green & pur (postage) 30 15
262 – 25 f. brown, sepia & green 80 35
263 – 150 f. brn, grn & sepia (air) 2·25 1·25
264 **128** 200 f. brown, turq & blue 3·25 1·75
DESIGN—VERT: 25 f., 150 f. Weasel-lemur.

129 Pres. Kennedy

1973. Air. 10th Death Anniv of Pres. John Kennedy.
265 **129** 300 f. multicoloured . . . 2·25 1·75

130 Footballers

1973. Air. World Cup Football Championships. West Germany.
266 **130** 500 f. mauve, brown and light brown . . . . . 5·50 2·50

CURRENCY. Issues from No. 267 to No. 389 have face values shown as "Fmg". This abbreviation denotes the Malagasy Franc which was introduced in 1966.

131 Copernicus, Satellite and Diagram

1974. Air. 500th Birth Anniv of Copernicus.
267 **131** 250 f. blue, brown & green 2·75 1·50

1974. No. 76a surch.
268 25 f. on 30 f. multicoloured . 25 15

133 Agricultural Training **135** Family and House

134 Male Player, and Hummingbird on Hibiscus

1974. 25th World Scouting Conference, Nairobi, Kenya.
269 **133** 4 f. grey, blue and green (postage) 10 10
270 – 15 f. purple, green & blue 20 15
271 – 100 f. ochre, red & blue (air) 80 45
272 – 300 f. brown, blue & black 2·75 1·50
DESIGNS—VERT: 15 f. Building construction. HORIZ: 100 f. First Aid training; 300 f. Fishing.

1974. Air. Asia, Africa and Latin America Table-Tennis Championships, Peking.
273 **134** 50 f. red, blue and brown 80 30
274 – 100 f. red, blue and violet 1·60 70
DESIGN: 100 f. Female player, and stylised bird.

1974. World Population Year.
275 **135** 25 f. red, orange and blue 25 10

INDEX

Countries can be quickly located by referring to the index at the end of this volume.

136 Micheline Rail Car

1974. Air. Malagasy Railway Locomotives.
276 **136** 50 f. green, red & brown 65 40
277 – 85 f. red, blue and green 1·10 50
278 – 200 f. blue, lt blue & brn 2·75 1·25
DESIGNS: 85 f. Track-inspection trolley; 200 f. Garratt steam locomotive.

137 U.P.U. Emblem and Letters

1974. Air. Centenary of U.P.U.
279 **137** 250 f. red, blue and violet 1·75 1·40

138 Rainibetsimisaraka

1974. Rainibetsimisaraka Commemoration.
280 **138** 25 f. multicoloured 35 20

1974. Air. West Germany's Victory in World Cup Football Championships. No. 266 optd **R.F.A. 2 HOLLANDE 1**.
281 **130** 500 f. mauve, brown & light brown . . . . 4·75 2·50

140 "Apollo" and "Soyuz" spacecraft

1974. Air. Soviet–U.S. Space Co-operation.
282 **140** 150 f. orange, green & blue 1·10 60
283 – 250 f. green, blue & brn 2·00 1·00
DESIGN: No. 283, As Type **140** but different view.

141 Marble Slabs **143** Faces and Maps

1974. Marble Industry. Multicoloured.
284 4 f. Type **141** 25 15
285 25 f. Quarrying 75 25

1974. Air. Universal Postal Union. Centenary (2nd issue). No. 279 optd **100 ANS COLLABORATION INTERNATIONALE**.
286 **137** 250 f. red, blue and violet 1·40 1·00

1974. Europafrique.
287 **143** 150 f. brown, red & orange 1·40 70

144 "Food in Hand"

1974. "Freedom from Hunger".
288 **144** 80 f. blue, brown & grey 65 35

145 "Coton" **146** Malagasy People

1974. Malagasy Dogs. Multicoloured.
289 50 f. Type **145** . . . . . . 1·40 45
290 100 f. Hunting dog . . . . . 2·00 1·10

1974. Founding of "Fokonolona" Commune.
291 **146** 5 f. multicoloured 15 10
292 10 f. multicoloured . . . 15 10
293 20 f. multicoloured . . . 20 10
294 60 f. multicoloured . . . 60 30

147 "Discovering Talent"

1974. National Development Council.
295 **147** 25 f. multicoloured . . . 20 10
296 35 f. multicoloured . . . 30 15

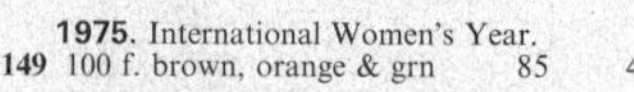

148 "Adoration of the Magi" (David) **149** Malagasy Girl and Rose

1974. Air. Christmas. Multicoloured.
297 200 f. Type **148** . . . . . . 1·75 95
298 300 f. "Virgin of the Cherries and Child" (Metzys) . . . . . . 3·00 1·25

1975. International Women's Year.
299 **149** 100 f. brown, orange & grn 85 40

150 Colonel Richard Ratsimandrava (Head of Government)

1975.
300 **150** 15 f. brown, black & yell 15 10
301 25 f. brown, black & blue 20 15
302 100 f. brown, black & grn 80 35

151 Sofia Bridge

1975.
303 **151** 45 f. multicoloured . . . 50 20

152 U.N. Emblem and Part of Globe

1975. Air. 30th Anniv of U.N. Charter.
304 **152** 300 f. multicoloured . . . 2·25 1·25

153 De Grasse (after Mauzaisse) and "Randolph"

1975. Bicentenary of American Revolution (1st issue). Multicoloured.

305 40 f. Type **153** (postage) 55 25
306 50 f. Lafayette, "Lexington" and H.M.S. "Edward" 65 30
307 100 f. D'Estaing and "Languedoc" (air) . . . . . 1·25 50
308 200 f. Paul Jones, "Bonhomme Richard" and H.M.S. "Serapis" . . . . 2·25 1·10
309 300 f. Benjamin Franklin, "Millern" and "Montgomery" 3·25 1·60

154 "Euphorbia viguieri"

1975. Malagasy Flora. Multicoloured.

311 15 f. Type **154** (postage) . . . 25 15
312 25 f. "Hibiscus rosesinensis" . . 40 20
313 30 f. "Plumeria rubra acutitolia" 55 20
314 40 f. "Pachypodium rosulatum" 1·00 30
315 85 f. "Turraea sericea" (air) . 1·75 1·00

1975. Air. "Apollo" - "Soyuz" Space Link Nos. 282/3 optd **JONCTION 17 JUILLET 1975**.

316 **140** 150 f. orange, grn & blue 1·00 60
317 – 250 f. green, blue & brown 2·00 1·00

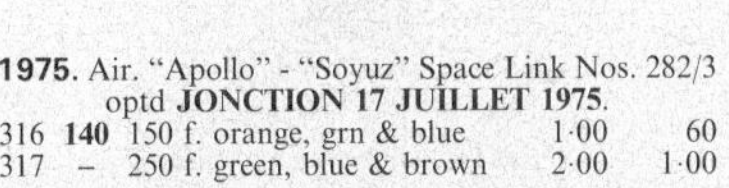

156 Temple Frieze

1975. Air. "Save Borobudur Temple" (in Indonesia) Campaign.

318 **156** 50 f. red, orange and blue 1·00 50

157 "Racial Unity" **159** Lily Waterfall

158 Pryer's Woodpecker

1975. Namibia Day.

319 **157** 50 f. multicoloured . . . 45 20

1975. International Exposition, Okinawa. Fauna. Multicoloured.

320 25 f. Type **158** (postage) . . . 3·00 45
321 40 f. Ryukyu rabbit 50 20
322 50 f. Toad 70 30
323 75 f. Tortoise . . . . 1·10 40
324 125 f. Sika deer (air) . . . . . 1·50 55

1975. Lily Waterfall. Multicoloured.

326 25 f. Type **159** 40 15
327 40 f. Lily Waterfall (distant view) 60 15

160 Hurdling

1975. Air. "Pre-Olympic Year". Olympic Games, Montreal (1976). Multicoloured.

328 75 f. Type **160** 60 35
329 200 f. Weightlifting (vert) . . 1·50 75

161 Bobsleigh "Fours"

1975. Winter Olympic Games, Innsbruck. Multicoloured.

330 75 f. Type **161** (postage) . . . 50 25
331 100 f. Ski-jumping 80 35
332 140 f. Speed-skating . . . . 1·25 50
333 200 f. Cross-country skiing (air) 1·75 75
334 245 f. Downhill skiing . . . . 2·00 90

162 Pirogue

1975. Malagasy Sailing-vessels. Multicoloured.

336 8 f. Type **162** 15 15
337 45 f. Malagasy schooner . . . 60 25

163 Canoeing

1976. Olympic Games, Montreal. Multicoloured.

338 40 f. Type **163** (postage) . . . 25 15
339 50 f. Sprinting and hurdling . 35 20
340 100 f. Putting the shot, and long-jumping (air) 65 35
341 200 f. Gymnastics-horse and parallel bars . . . . 1·40 75
342 300 f. Trampoline-jumping and high-diving . . . . 2·00 1·00

164 "Apollo 14" Lunar Module and Flight Badge

1976. Air. 5th Anniv of "Apollo 14" Mission.

344 **164** 150 f. blue, red and green 1·25 65

1976. Air. 5th Anniv of "Apollo 14" Mission. No. 344 optd **5e Anniversaire de la mission APOLLO XIV**.

345 **164** 150 f. blue, red and green 1·25 75

166 "Graf Zeppelin" over Fujiyama

1976. 75th Anniv of Zeppelin. Multicoloured.

346 40 f. Type **166** (postage) . . . 35 15
347 50 f. "Graf Zeppelin" over Rio de Janeiro 40 15
348 75 f. "Graf Zeppelin" over New York 80 25
349 100 f. "Graf Zeppelin" over Sphinx and pyramids 95 35
350 200 f. "Graf Zeppelin" over Berlin (air) . . . . 2·00 75
351 300 f. "Graf Zeppelin" over London . . . . 3·00 1·00

167 "Prevention of Blindness"

1976. World Health Day.

353 **167** 100 f. multicoloured . . . 1·25 55

168 Aragonite

1976. Minerals and Fossils. Multicoloured.

354 25 f. Type **168** 50 15
355 50 f. Fossilised wood 85 30
356 150 f. Celestyte . . . . 2·75 1·10

169 Alexander Graham Bell and Early Telephone

1976. Telephone Centenary. Multicoloured.

357 25 f. Type **169** 15 10
358 50 f. Cable maintenance, 1911 30 15
359 100 f. Telephone operator and switchboard, 1895 . . . . . 60 25
360 200 f. "Emile Baudot" cable ship 1·75 70
361 300 f. Man with radio-telephone 2·00 80

170 Children reading Book

1976. Children's Books Promotion. Multicoloured.

363 10 f. Type **170** 15 10
364 25 f. Children reading book (vert) 35 15

1976. Medal winners, Winter Olympic Games, Innsbruck. Nos. 330/4 optd **VAINQUEUR** and medal winner.

365 75 f. Type **161** (postage) . . . 50 25
366 100 f. Ski-jumping 80 40
367 140 f. Skating . . . . 1·25 50
368 200 f. Cross-country skiing (air) 1·40 75
369 245 f. Downhill skiing . . . . . 1·90 1·00

OPTS: 75 f. **ALLEMAGNE FEDERALE**; 100 f. **KARL SCHNABL, AUTRICHE**; 140 f. **SHEILA YOUNG, ETATS-UNIS**; 200 f. **IVAR FORMO, NORVEGE**; 245 f. **ROSI MITTERMAIER, ALLEMAGNE DE L'OUEST**.

The subject depicted on No. 367 is speed-skating, an event in which the gold medal was won by J. E. Storholt, Norway.

1976. Bicentenary of American Revolution (2nd issue). Nos. 305/9 optd **"4 JUILLET 1776-1976"**.

371 **153** 40 f. multicoloured (postage) 35 25
372 – 50 f. multicoloured 40 30
373 – 100 f. multicoloured (air) 75 50
374 – 200 f. multicoloured . . . 1·50 85
375 – 300 f. multicoloured . . . 2·25 1·25

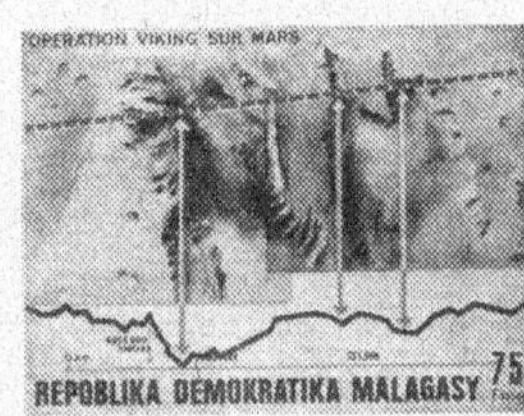

173 Descent Trajectory

1976. "Viking" Landing on Mars. Multicoloured.

377 75 f. Type **173** 40 20
378 100 f. "Viking" landing module separation 60 25
379 200 f. "Viking" on Martian surface . . . . 1·25 55
380 300 f. "Viking" orbiting Mars 2·00 80

174 Rainandriam-ampandry **175** Doves over Globe

1976. 30th Anniv of Treaties signed by Rainandriamampandry (Foreign Minister).

382 **174** 25 f. multicoloured . . . 30 20

1976. Indian Ocean – "Zone of Peace". Multicoloured.

383 60 f. Type **175** 35 20
384 160 f. Doves flying across Indian Ocean (horiz) . . . . 1·10 55

1976. Olympic Games Medal – winners. Nos. 338/342 optd with names of two winners on each stamp.

385 **163** 40 f. multicoloured (postage) 25 15
386 – 50 f. multicoloured . . . 35 25
387 – 100 f. multicoloured (air) 70 40
388 – 200 f. multicoloured . . . 1·40 65
389 – 300 f. multicoloured . . . 2·00 1·00

OVERPRINTS: 40 f. **V. DIBA, A. ROGOV**; 50 f. **H. CRAWFORD, J. SCHALLER**; 100 f. **U. BEYER, A. ROBINSON**; 200 f. **N. COMANECI, N. ANDRIANOV**; 300 f. **K. DIBIASI, E. VAYTSEKHOVSKAIA**.

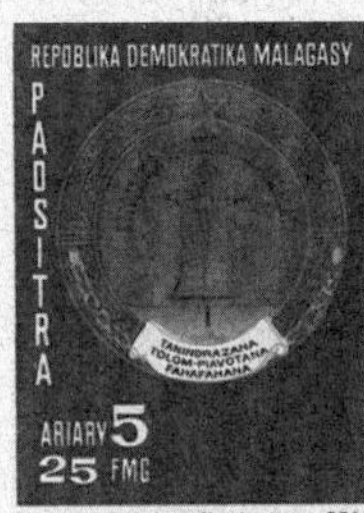

177 Malagasy Arms

1976. 1st Anniv of Malagasy Democratic Republic.

391 **177** 25 f. multicoloured . . . 20 10

178 Rabezavana (Independence Movement leader)

1977. National Heroes. Multicoloured.

392 25 f. Type **178** 20 10
393 25 f. Lt. Albert Randriamaromanana . . . 20 10
394 25 f. Ny Avana Ramanantoanina (politician) 20 10
395 100 f. Fasam-Pirenena National Mausoleum, Tananarive (horiz) 75 40

179 Family

1977. World Health Day.

396 **179** 5 f. multicoloured 15 10

180 Medical School, Antananarivo

1977. 80th Anniv of Medical School Antananarivo.
397 **180** 250 f. multicoloured . . . 1·75 95

181 Rural Post Van

1977. Rural Mail.
398 **181** 35 f. multicoloured . . . 30 15

182 Morse Key and Man with Headphones

1977. 90th Anniv of Antananarivo–Tamatave Telegraph.
399 **182** 15 f. multicoloured . . . 15 10

183 Academy Emblem

1977. 75th Anniv of Malagasy Academy.
400 **183** 10 f. multicoloured . . . 15 10

184 Lenin and Russian Flag

1977. 60th Anniv of Russian Revolution.
401 **184** 25 f. multicoloured . . . 15 10

185 Raoul Follereau

1978. 25th Anniv of World Leprosy Day.
402 **185** 5 f. multicoloured 20 10

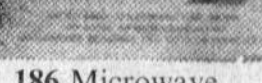

186 Microwave Antenna **187** "Co-operation"

1978. World Telecommunications Day.
403 **186** 20 f. multicoloured . . . 15 10

1978. Anti-Apartheid Year.
404 **187** 60 f. red, black & yellow 40 25

188 Children with Instruments of Revolution **189** Tractor, Factory and Labourers

1978. "Youth–Pillar of the Revolution".
405 **188** 25 f. multicoloured . . . 75 45

1978. Socialist Co-operatives.
406 **189** 25 f. multicoloured . . . 15 10

190 Women at Work **191** Children with Books, Instruments and Fruit

1979. "Women, Pillar of the Revolution".
407 **190** 40 f. multicoloured . . . 25 15

1979. International Year of the Child.
408 **191** 10 f. multicoloured . . . 20 10

192 Ring-tailed Lemur **193** J. V. S. Razakandraina

1979. Animals. Multicoloured.
409 25 f. Type **192** (postage) . . . 25 15
410 125 f. Black lemur . . . . 1·10 30
411 1000 f. Malagasy civet . . . 8·00 2·25
412 20 f. Tortoise (air) 20 20
413 95 f. Black lemur (different) . 1·00 40

1979. J. V. S. Razakandraina (poet) Commem.
414 **193** 25 f. multicoloured . . . 15 10

194 "Centella asiatica"

1979. Medicinal Plant.
415 **194** 25 f. multicoloured . . . 15 10

195 Map of Malagasy and Ste. Marie Telecommunications Station

1979. Telecommunications.
416 **195** 25 f. multicoloured . . . 20 10

196 Post Office, Antsirabe

1979. Stamp Day.
417 **196** 500 f. multicoloured . . . 2·75 1·10

197 Palestinians with Flag

1979. Air. Palestinian Solidarity.
418 **197** 60 f. multicoloured 50 20

198 Concorde and Map of Africa

1979. 20th Anniv of ASECNA (African Air Safety Organization).
419 **198** 50 f. multicoloured 60 20

199 Lenin addressing Meeting

1980. 110th Birth Anniv of Lenin.
420 **199** 25 f. multicoloured 20 10

200 Taxi-Bus **201** Map illuminated by Sun

1980. 5th Anniv of Socialist Revolution.
421 **200** 30 f. multicoloured 20 10

1980. 20th Anniv of Independence.
422 **201** 75 f. multicoloured 50 30

202 Military Parade

1980. 20th Anniv of Army.
423 **202** 50 f. multicoloured 35 15

203 Joseph Raseta

1980. Dr. Joseph Raseta Commemoration.
424 **203** 30 f. multicoloured 20 10

204 Anatirova Temple

1980. Anatirova Temple Centenary.
425 **204** 30 f. multicoloured . . . 20 10

205 Boxing

1980. Olympic Games, Moscow. Multicoloured.
426 30 f. Hurdling 20 10
427 75 f. Type **205** 45 25
428 250 f. Judo . . . . 1·50 75
429 500 f. Swimming . . . . . . 2·75 1·50

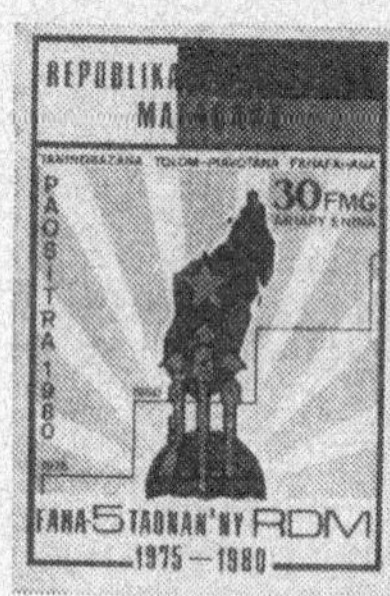

206 Emblem, Map and Sun

1980. 5th Anniv of Malagasy Democratic Republic.
430 **206** 30 f. multicoloured . . . 20 10

207 Skier

1981. Winter Olympic Games, Lake Placid (1980).
431 **207** 175 f. multicoloured . . . 1·10 55

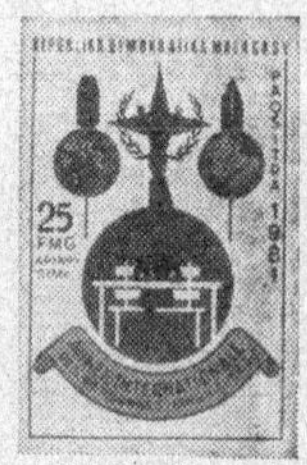

208 "Angraecum leonis" **209** Handicapped Student

1981. Flowers. Multicoloured.
432 5 f. Type **208** 10 10
433 80 f. "Angraecum famosum" 60 25
434 170 f. "Angraecum sesquipedale" 1·25 55

1981. International Year of Disabled People. Multicoloured.
435 25 f. Type **209** 20 10
436 80 f. Disabled carpenter . . . 55 25

210 Ribbons forming Caduceus, I.T.U. and W.H.O. Emblems

1981. World Telecommunications Day.
437 **210** 15 f. blue, black & yellow 15 10
438 45 f. multicoloured . . . 35 15

211 Valentina Tereshkova (first woman in space)

1981. Space Achievements. Multicoloured.

439	30 f. Type **211**	15	10
440	80 f. Astronaut on Moon	55	25
441	90 f. Yuri Gagarin (first man in space)	65	30

212 Raphael-Louis Rafiringa

1981. Raphael-Louis Rafiringa Commemoration.

442	**212**	30 f. multicoloured	20	10

213 Child writing Alphabet

1981. World Literary Day.

443	**213**	30 f. multicoloured	20	10

214 Ploughing and Sowing

1981. World Food Day.

444	**214**	200 f. multicoloured	1·25	60

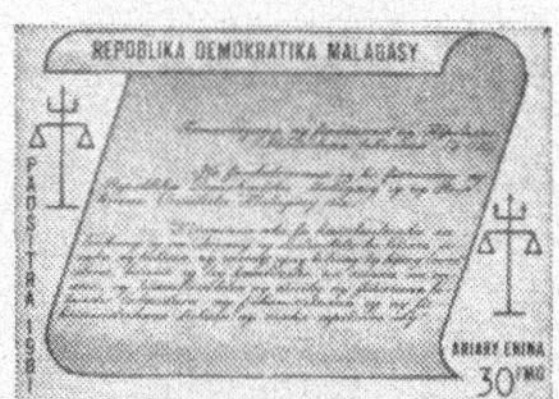

215 Magistrates' Oath

1981. Renewal of Magistrates' Oath.

445	**215**	30 f. mauve and black	20	10

216 "Dove"

1981. Birth Centenary of Pablo Picasso.

446	**216**	80 f. multicoloured	60	25

217 U.P.U. Emblem and Malagasy Stamps

1981. 20th Anniv of Admission to U.P.U.

447	**217**	5 f. multicoloured	10	10
448		30 f. multicoloured	20	10

218 Stamps forming Map of Malagasy

1981. Stamp Day.

449	**218**	90 f. multicoloured	65	30

219 Hook-billed Vanga

1982. Birds. Multicoloured.

450	25 f. Type **219**	1·40	55
451	30 f. Courol	1·40	55
452	200 f. Madagascar fish eagle (vert)	8·25	3·25

220 Vaccination

221 Jeannettee Mpihira

1982. Centenary of Discovery of Tubercule Bacillus.

453	**220**	30 f. multicoloured	30	15

1982. Jeannette Mpihira Commemoration.

454	**221**	30 f. multicoloured	20	10

222 Woman's Head formed from Map of Africa

223 Pierre Louis Boiteau

1982. Air. 20th Anniv of Panafrican Women's Organization.

455	**222**	80 f. multicoloured	60	30

1982. Pierre Louis Boiteau Commemoration.

456	**223**	30 f. multicoloured	20	15

224 Andekaleka Dam

1982. Air. Andekaleka Hydro-electric Complex.

457	**224**	80 f. multicoloured	60	30

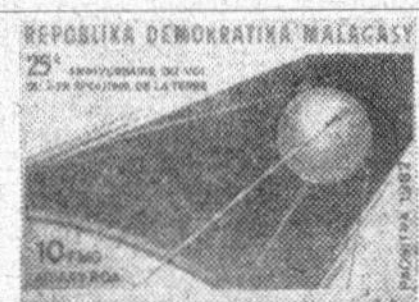

225 "Sputnik I"

1982. 25th Anniv of First Artificial Satellite. Multicoloured.

458	10 f. Type **225**	10	10
459	80 f. Yuri Gagarin	60	30
460	100 f. "Soyuz-Salyut" space station	75	35

226 Heading Ball

1982. World Cup Football Championship, Spain. Multicoloured.

461	30 f. Type **226**	20	10
462	40 f. Running with ball	30	15
463	80 f. Tackle	60	30

227 Ploughing, Sowing and F.A.O. Emblem

1982. World Food Day.

465	**227**	80 f. multicoloured	50	30

228 Bar Scene

1982. 150th Anniv of Edouard Manet (artist). Multicoloured.

466	5 f. Type **228**	15	15
467	30 f. Woman in white	25	10
468	170 f. Man with pipe	1·40	65

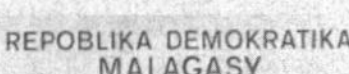

229 "Lutianus sebae"

1982. Fishes. Multicoloured.

470	5 f. Type **229**	15	15
471	20 f. "Istiophorus platypterus"	20	15
472	30 f. "Pterois volitans"	25	15
473	50 f. "Thunnus albacares"	40	15
474	200 f. "Epinephelus fasciatus"	1·75	65

230 Fort Mahavelona

1982. Landscapes. Multicoloured.

476	10 f. Type **230** (postage)	10	10
477	30 f. Ramena coast	20	10
478	400 f. Jacarandas in flower (air)	2·75	1·50

231 Flags of Russia and Malagasy, Clasped Hands and Tractors

1982. 60th Anniv of U.S.S.R. Multicoloured.

479	10 f. Type **231**	10	10
480	15 f. Flags, clasped hands and radio antenna	10	10
481	30 f. Map of Russia, Kremlin and Lenin	15	10
482	150 f. Flags, clasped hands, statue and arms of Malagasy	1·00	45

232 Television, Drums, Envelope and Telephone

1983. World Communications Year. Multicoloured.

483	30 f. Type **232**	15	10
484	80 f. Stylized figures holding cogwheel	55	25

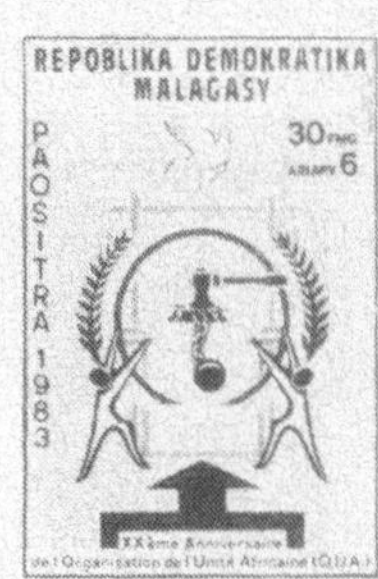

233 Axe breaking Chain on Map of Africa

234 Henri Douzon

1983. 20th Anniv of Organization of African Unity.

485	**233**	30 f. multicoloured	20	10

1983. Henri Douzon (lawyer) Commemorative.

486	**234**	30 f. multicoloured	20	10

237 Ruffed Lemur

1984. Lemurs. Multicoloured.

489	30 f. Type **237**	35	20
490	30 f. Verreaux's sifaka	35	20
491	30 f. Lesser mouse-lemur (horiz)	35	20
492	30 f. Aye-aye (horiz)	35	20
493	200 f. Indri (horiz)	2·00	1·10

238 Ski Jumping

1984. Winter Olympic Games, Sarajevo. Mult.

495	20 f. Type **238**	15	10
496	30 f. Ice hockey	20	10
497	30 f. Downhill skiing	20	10
498	30 f. Speed skating	20	10
499	200 f. Ice dancing	1·40	70

239 Renault, 1907

1984. Early Motor Cars. Multicoloured.
501 15 f. Type **239** 20 10
502 30 f. Benz, 1896 . . . . 30 15
503 30 f. Baker, 1901 . . . . . . 30 15
504 30 f. Blake, 1901 . . . . . . 30 15
505 200 f. F.I.A.L., 1908 . . . . . 2·00 75

240 Pastor Ravelojaona **241** "Noli me Tangere"

1984. Pastor Ravelojaona (encylopedist) Commemoration.
507 **240** 30 f. multicoloured . . . 20 15

1984. 450th Death Anniv of Correggio. Paintings by Artist.
508 **241** 5 f. multicoloured . . . 10 10
509 – 20 f. multicoloured . . . 15 10
510 – 30 f. multicoloured . . . 25 15
511 – 80 f. multicoloured . . . 45 25
512 – 200 f. multicoloured . . . 1·40 65

242 Paris Landmarks and Emblem **243** Football

1984. 60th Anniv of International Chess Federation. Multicoloured.
514 5 f. Type **242** 15 15
515 20 f. Wilhelm Steinitz and stylized king 20 15
516 30 f. Vera Menchik and stylized queen 35 15
517 30 f. Anatoly Karpov and trophy 35 15
518 215 f. Nona Gaprindashvili and trophy . . . . 2·75 90

1984. Olympic Games, Los Angeles.
520 **243** 100 f. multicoloured . . . 45 30

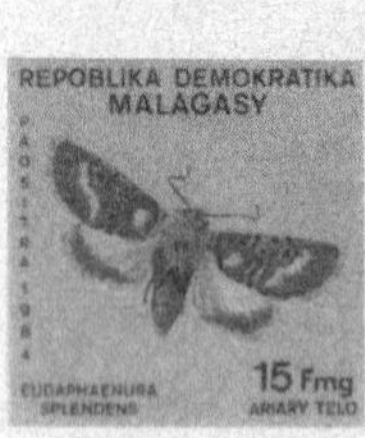

244 "Eudaphaenura splendens" **245** Ralaimongo

1984. Butterflies. Multicoloured.
521 15 f. Type **244** 20 15
522 50 f. "Acraea hova" 60 20
523 50 f. "Othreis boesae" 60 20
524 50 f. "Pharmocophagus antenor" 60 20
525 200 f. "Epicausis smithii" . . . 2·25 1·00

1984. Birth Centenary of Jean Ralaimongo (politician).
527 **245** 50 f. multicoloured . . . 30 15

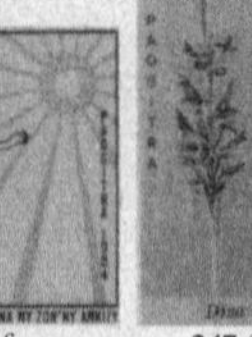

246 Children in Brief-case **247** "Disa incarnata"

1984. 25th Anniv of Children's Rights Legislation.
528 **246** 50 f. multicoloured . . . 40 15

1984. Orchids. Multicoloured.
529 20 f. Type **247** (postage) . . . 20 10
530 235 f. "Eulophiella roempleriana" . . . . . . 2·25 85
531 50 f. "Eulophiella roempleriana" (horiz) (air) 60 25
532 50 f. "Grammangis ellisii" (horiz) 60 25
533 50 f. "Grammangis spectabilis" 60 25

248 U.N. Emblem and Cotton Plant **249** "Sun Princess" (Sadio Diouf)

1984. 20th Anniv of United Nations Conference on Commerce and Development.
535 **248** 100 f. multicoloured . . . 60 30

1984. 40th Anniv of International Civil Aviation Organization.
536 **249** 100 f. multicoloured . . . 65 30

250 Bible, Map and Gothic Letters

1985. 150th Anniv of First Bible in Malagasy Language.
537 **250** 50 f. brown, pink and black 30 15

251 Farming Scenes, Census-taker and Farmer **252** Lap-dog

1985. Agricultural Census.
538 **251** 50 f. grey, black and mauve 30 15

1985. Cats and Dogs. Multicoloured.
539 20 f. Type **252** 20 15
540 20 f. Siamese cat 20 15
541 50 f. Abyssinian cat (vert) . . 60 20
542 100 f. Cocker spaniel (vert) . . 1·25 35
543 235 f. Poodle . . . . 2·50 90

253 Russian Soldiers in Berlin

1985. 40th Anniv of Victory in Second World War.
545 20 f. Type **253** 15 10
546 50 f. Arms of French squadron and fighter planes 40 15
547 100 f. Victory parade, Red Square, Moscow 75 30
548 100 f. French troops entering Paris (vert) 75 30

254 Parade in Stadium

1985. 10th Anniv of Malagasy Democratic Republic.
549 **254** 50 f. multicoloured 40 15

255 Medal and Independence Obelisk **256** Peace Dove and Stylised People

1985. 25th Anniv of Independence.
550 **255** 50 f. multicoloured 40 15

1985. 12th World Youth and Students' Festival, Moscow.
551 **256** 50 f. multicoloured 40 15

257 I.Y.Y. Emblem and Map of Madagascar **258** Red Cross Centres and First Aid Post

1985. International Youth Year.
552 **257** 100 f. multicoloured . . . 60 25

1985. 70th Anniv of Malagasy Red Cross.
553 **258** 50 f. multicoloured 60 25

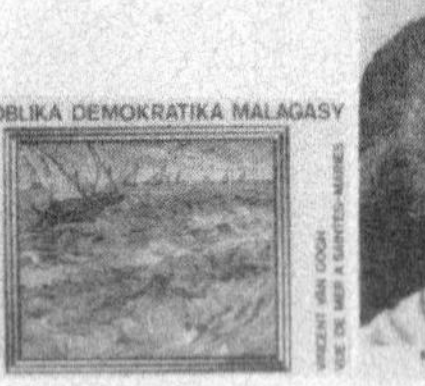

259 "View of Sea at Saintes-Maries" (Vincent van Gogh) **260** Indira Gandhi

1985. Impressionist Paintings. Multicoloured.
554 20 f. Type **259** 20 10
555 20 f. "Rouen Cathedral in the Evening" (Claude Monet) (vert) 15 10
556 45 f. "Young Girls in Black" (Pierre-Auguste Renoir) (vert) 30 20
557 50 f. "Red Vineyard at Arles" (van Gogh) 30 20
558 100 f. "Boulevard des Capucines, Paris" (Monet) 85 40

1985. Indira Gandhi (Indian Prime Minister) Commemoration.
560 **260** 100 f. multicoloured . . . 80 30

261 Figures and Dove on Globe and Flag **262** "Aeranthes grandiflora"

1985. 40th Anniv of U.N.O.
561 **261** 100 f. multicoloured . . . 65 25

1985. Orchids. Multicoloured.
562 20 f. Type **262** 20 10
563 45 f. "Angraecum magdalenae" and "Nephele oenopion" (insect) (horiz) 35 15
564 50 f. "Aerangis stylosa" . . . 35 15
565 100 f. "Angraecum eburneum longicalcar" and "Hippotion batschi" (insect) 80 35
566 100 f. "Angraecum sesquipedale" and "Xanthopan morganipredicta" (insect) . . 80 35

263 Russian and Czechoslovakian Cosmonauts

1985. Russian "Interkosmos" Space Programme. Multicoloured.
568 20 f. Type **263** 15 10
569 20 f. Russian and American flags and "Apollo"–"Soyuz" link 15 10
570 50 f. Russian and Indian cosmonauts 30 15
571 100 f. Russian and Cuban cosmonauts 50 25
572 200 f. Russian and French cosmonauts . . . . 1·25 60

264 Emblem in "10" **265** Headquarters

1985. 10th Anniv of Malagasy Democratic Republic.
574 **264** 50 f. multicoloured . . . 30 15

1986. 10th Anniv of ARO (State insurance system).
575 **265** 50 f. yellow and brown . 30 15

266 "David and Uriah" (Rembrandt) **268** Sombrero, Football and Player

267 Comet

1986. Foreign Paintings in Hermitage Museum, Leningrad. Multicoloured.
576 20 f. Type **266** 20 10
577 50 f. "Portrait of Old Man in Red" (Rembrandt) . . . 50 30
578 50 f. "Danae" (Rembrandt) (horiz) 50 30
579 50 f. "Marriage of Earth and Water" (Rubens) 50 30
580 50 f. "Portrait of Infanta Isabella's Maid" (Rubens) 50 30

1968. Air. Appearance of Halley's Comet.
582 **267** 150 f. multicoloured . . . 1·00 50

1986. Russian Paintings in the Tretyakov Gallery, Moscow. As T **266**. Multicoloured.
583 20 f. "Fruit and Flowers" (I. Khroutsky) (horiz) . . . 15 10
584 50 f. "The Rooks have Returned" (A. Savrasov) . . 30 20
585 50 f. "Unknown Woman" (I. Kramskoi) (horiz) 30 20
586 50 f. "Aleksandr Pushkin" (O. Kiprenski) 30 20
587 100 f. "March, 1895" (I. Levitan) (horiz) 60 40

1986. World Cup Football Championship, Mexico.
589 **268** 150 f. multicoloured . . . 1·10 30

269 Child Care **270** Jungle Cat

1986. U.N.I.C.E.F. Child Survival Campaign.
590 **269** 60 f. multicoloured . . . 40 15

1986. Wild Cats. Multicoloured.

591 10 f. Type **270** 20 10
592 10 f. Wild cat 20 10
593 60 f. Caracal 45 20
594 60 f. Leopard cat 45 20
595 60 f. Serval 45 20

271 Dove above Hands holding Globe

1986. International Peace Year. Multicoloured.

597 60 f. Type **271** 40 15
598 150 f. Doves above emblem and map . . . . 1·00 45

272 U.P.U. Emblem on Dove

273 U.P.U. Emblem on Globe

1986. World Post Day.

599 **272** 60 f. multicoloured (postage) 40 15
600 150 f. blue, black and red (air) . . . . 1·10 50

1986. Air. 25th Anniv of Admission to U.P.U.

601 **273** 150 f. multicoloured . . . 1·10 50

274 Giant Madagascar Coucal

1986. Birds. Multicoloured.

602 60 f. Type **274** . . . . 1·60 60
603 60 f. Crested Madagascar coucal 1·60 60
604 60 f. Rufous vangas (vert) . . 1·60 60
605 60 f. Red-tailed vangas (vert) 1·60 60
606 60 f. Sicklebill . . . . 1·60 60

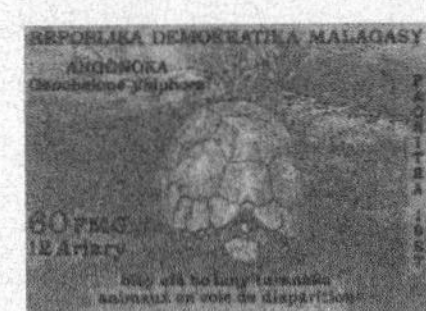

275 Tortoise

1987. Endangered Animals. Multicoloured.

608 60 f. Type **275** 50 20
609 60 f. Crocodile 50 20
610 60 f. Crested wood ibis (vert) 50 20
611 60 f. Vasa parrot 50 20

276 Crowd in "40"

1987. 40th Anniv of Anti-Colonial Uprising.

613 **276** 60 f. brown, red & yellow 35 15
614 – 60 f. multicoloured . . . 35 15

DESIGN: No. 614, Hands in broken manacles, map, rifleman and spearman.

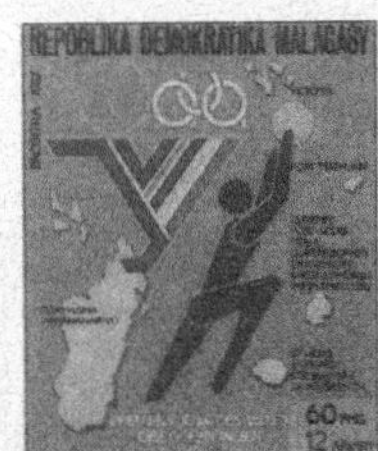

277 Emblems, Map and Pictogram

1987. 1st Indian Ocean Towns Games.

615 **277** 60 f. multicoloured . . . 35 15
616 150 f. multicoloured . . . 1·10 35

278 "Sarimanok"

1987. The "Sarimanok" (replica of early dhow). Multicoloured.

617 60 f. Type **278** 40 15
618 150 f. "Sarimanok" (different) 1·10 35

279 Coffee Plant

280 Rifle Shooting and Satellite

1987. 25th Anniv of African and Malagasy Coffee Producers Organization. Multicoloured.

619 60 f. Type **279** 35 15
620 150 f. Map showing member countries . . . . 1·10 35

1987. Winter Olympic Games, Calgary (1988). Multicoloured.

621 60 f. Type **280** 25 10
622 150 f. Slalom 60 20
623 250 f. Luge . . . . 1·25 40
624 350 f. Speed skating . . . . 1·40 50
625 400 f. Ice hockey . . . . . . 1·60 60
626 450 f. Ice skating (pairs) . . . 2·00 70

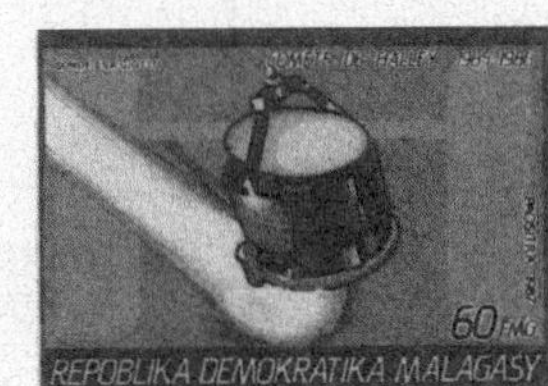

281 "Giotto" Space Probe

1987. Appearance of Halley's Comet (1986). Space Probes. Multicoloured.

628 60 f. Type **281** 25 10
629 150 f. "Vega 1" 60 20
630 250 f. "Vega 2" . . . . . . 1·25 40
631 350 f. "Planet A 1" . . . . . 1·40 50
632 400 f. "Planet B 1" . . . . . 1·60 60
633 450 f. "I.C.E." . . . . 2·00 70

282 Piper Aztec

283 Rabearivelo

1987. Air. 25th Anniv of Air Madagascar. Multicoloured.

635 60 f. Type **282** 40 20
636 60 f. De Havilland Twin Otter 40 20
637 150 f. Boeing 747-200 . . . 1·00 40

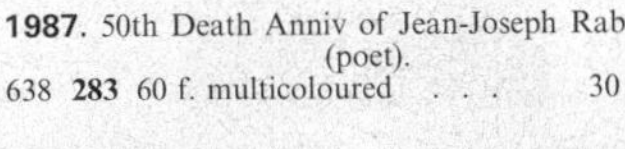

1987. 50th Death Anniv of Jean-Joseph Rabearivelo (poet).

638 **283** 60 f. multicoloured . . . 30 15

284 Communications Equipment Robot and Print-out Paper

285 Emblem

1987. National Telecommunications Research Laboratory.

639 **284** 60 f. green, black and red 30 15

1987. 150th Anniv of Execution of Rafaravavy Rasalama (Christian martyr).

640 **285** 60 f. black, deep blue and blue 30 15

286 Hand using Key and Telegraphist

1987. Centenary of Antananarivo–Tamatave Telegraph.

641 **286** 60 f. multicoloured 30 15

287 Bartholomeu Dias and Departure from Palos, 1492

1987. 500th Anniv (1992) of Discovery of America by Columbus. Multicoloured.

642 60 f. Type **287** 20 10
643 150 f. Route around Samana Cay and Henry the Navigator . . 45 20
644 250 f. Columbus and crew disembarking, 1492, and A. de Marchena 75 30
645 350 f. Building Fort Navidad and Paolo del Pozzo Toscanelli 1·10 40
646 400 f. Columbus in Barcelona, 1493, and Queen Isabella of Spain . . . . 1·25 50
647 450 f. Columbus and "Nina" 1·50 50

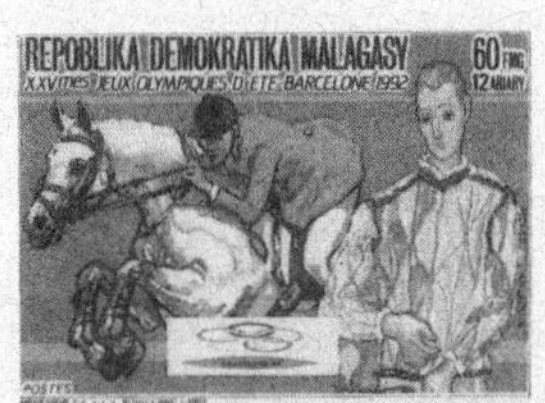

288 Showjumping and "Harlequin" (Picasso)

1987. Olympic Games, Barcelona (1992). Multicoloured.

649 60 f. Type **288** (postage) . . . 15 10
650 150 f. Weightlifting and Barcelona Cathedral 40 20
651 250 f. Hurdling and Canaletas Fountain 70 30
652 350 f. High jumping and Parc d'Attractions . . . . 1·00 40
653 400 f. Gymnast on bar and church (air) . . . . 1·40 50
654 450 f. Gymnast with ribbon and Triumphal Arch . . . . . . 1·50 50

289 Anniversary Emblem, T.V. Tower and Interhotel "Berlin"

290 Musician and Dancers

1987. 750th Anniv of Berlin.

656 **289** 150 f. multicoloured . . . 25 15

1987. Schools Festival.

657 **290** 60 f. multicoloured 15 10

291 Madagascar Pasteur Institute and Pasteur

1987. Centenary of Pasteur Institute, Paris.

658 **291** 250 f. multicoloured . . . 60 25

292 "After the Shipwreck" (Eugene Delacroix)

1987. Paintings in Pushkin Museum of Fine Arts, Moscow. Multicoloured.

659 10 f. Type **292** 15 10
660 60 f. "Jupiter and Callisto" (Francois Boucher) (vert) . 15 10
661 60 f. "Still Life with Swan" (Frans Snyders) 15 10
662 60 f. "Chalet in the Mountains" (Gustave Courbet) 15 10
663 150 f. "At the Market" (Joachim Bueckelaer) 40 15

293 Emblem

294 Family and House on Globe

1987. 10th Anniv of Pan-African Telecommunications Union.

665 **293** 250 f. multicoloured . . . 40 20

1988. International Year of Shelter for the Homeless (1987). Multicoloured.

666 80 f. Type **294** 15 10
667 250 f. Hands forming house protecting family from rain 35 20

295 Lenin addressing Crowd

1988. 70th Anniv of Russian Revolution. Mult.

668 60 f. Type **295** 15 10
669 60 f. Revolutionaries 15 10
670 150 f. Lenin in crowd 25 15

296 Broad-nosed Gentle Lemur

1988. Endangered Species. Multicoloured.

671 60 f. Type **296** 15 10
672 150 f. Diadem sifaka 20 15
673 250 f. Indri 35 15
674 350 f. Ruffed lemur 60 25
675 550 f. Purple herons (horiz) . 1·25 70
676 1500 f. Nossi-be chameleon (horiz) . . . . 2·40 1·25

297 Ice Skating

1988. Winter Olympic Games, Calgary. Mult.

678 20 f. Type **297** 10 10
679 60 f. Speed-skating 10 10
680 60 f. Slalom 10 10
681 100 f. Cross-country skiing . . 20 10
682 250 f. Ice hockey 45 20

298 Dove, Axe breaking Chain and Map

1988. 25th Anniv of Organization of African Unity.
684 **298** 80 f. multicoloured . . . 15 10

299 Institute Building

1988. 20th Anniv of National Posts and Telecommunications Institute.
685 **299** 80 f. multicoloured . . . 15 10

300 College

1988. Centenary of St. Michael's College.
686 **300** 250 f. multicoloured . . . 30 20

301 Pierre and Marie Curie in Laboratory **302** Emblem

1988. 90th Anniv of Discovery of Radium.
687 **301** 150 f. brown and mauve 40 15

1988. 10th Anniv of Alma-Ata Declaration (on health and social care).
688 **302** 60 f. multicoloured . . . 15 10

303 Emblem **304** Ring-tailed Lemurs on Island

1988. 40th Anniv of W.H.O.
689 **303** 150 f. brown, blue and black 20 15

1988. 50th Anniv of Tsimbazaza Botanical and Zoological Park. Multicoloured.
690 20 f. Type **304** 15 10
691 80 f. Ring-tailed lemur with young (25 × 37 mm) 20 10
692 250 f. Palm tree and ring-tailed lemur within "Zoo" (47 × 32 mm) 40 20

305 Hoopoe and Blue Madagascar Coucal **306** Cattle grazing

1988. Scouts, Birds and Butterflies. Multicoloured.
694 80 f. Type **305** 60 30
695 250 f. "Chrysiridia croesus" (butterfly) 40 20
696 270 f. Nelicourvi weaver and red forest fody . . . . 1·25 50
697 350 f. "Papilio dardanus" (butterflies) 60 40
698 550 f. Crested Madagascar coucal . . . . 2·25 1·00
699 1500 f. "Argema mittrei" (butterfly) . . . . 2·50 2·00

1988. 10th Anniv of International Fund for Agricultural Development.
701 **306** 250 f. multicoloured . . . 30 20

307 Karl Bach and Clavier **308** Books

1988. Musicians' Anniversaries. Multicoloured.
702 80 f. Type **307** (death bicentenary) 15 10
703 250 f. Franz Schubert and piano (160th death) 40 15
704 270 f. Georges Bizet and scene from "Carmen" (150th birth) 40 20
705 350 f. Claude Debussy and scene from "Pelleas et Melisande" (70th death) 50 25
706 550 f. George Gershwin at piano writing score of "Rhapsody in Blue" (90th birth) 75 45
707 1500 f. Elvis Presley (10th death (1987)) . . . . 2·50 1·25

1988. "Ecole en Fete" Schools Festival.
709 **308** 80 f. multicoloured . . . 15 10

309 "Black Sea Fleet at Feodosiya" (Ivan Aivazovski) **310** "Tragocephala crassicornis"

1988. Paintings of Sailing Ships. Multicoloured.
710 20 f. Type **309** 25 15
711 80 f. "Lesnoie" (N. Semenov) 25 15
712 80 f. "Seascape with Sailing Ships" (Simon de Vlieger) . 25 15
713 100 f. "Orel" (N. Golitsine) (horiz) 30 15
714 250 f. "Naval Battle Exercises" (Adam Silo) 75 25

1988. Endangered Beetles. Multicoloured.
716 20 f. Type **310** 15 10
717 80 f. "Polybothris symptuosa-gema" 55 25
718 250 f. "Euchroea auripigmenta" 1·25 60
719 350 f. "Stellognata maculata" 1·60 80

311 Stretcher Bearers and Anniversary Emblem **312** Symbols of Human Rights

1988. 125th Anniv of International Red Cross. Multicoloured.
720 80 f. Type **311** 15 10
721 250 f. Red Cross services, emblem and Henri Dunant (founder) 35 20

1988. 40th Anniv of Declaration of Human Rights. Multicoloured.
722 80 f. Type **312** 15 10
723 250 f. Hands with broken manacles holding "40" 35 15

313 Mercedes-Benz "Blitzen-Benz", 1909

1989. Cars and Trains. Multicoloured.
724 80 f. Type **313** 15 10
725 250 f. Micheline "ZM 517 Tsikirity" Antananarivo-Moramanga line 35 15
726 270 f. Bugatti coupe binder, "41" 40 20
727 350 f. German class "1020" electric locomotive 60 25
728 1500 f. Souleze "710" diesel train, Malagasy . . . . . . 2·25 1·25
729 2500 f. Opel racing car, 1913 3·50 2·00

314 Tyrannosaurus

1989. Prehistoric Animals. Multicoloured.
731 20 f. Type **314** 15 10
732 80 f. Stegosaurus 20 10
733 250 f. Arsinoitherium 40 15
734 450 f. Triceratops 80 30

315 "Tahitian Girls"

1989. Woman in Art. Multicoloured.
736 20 f. Type **315** 10 10
737 80 f. "Portrait of a Girl" (Jean-Baptiste Greuze) 15 10
738 80 f. "Portrait of a Young Woman" (Titian) 15 10
739 100 f. "Woman in Black" (Auguste Renoir) 20 10
740 250 f. "The Lace-maker" (Vasily Tropinine) 35 15

316 "Sobennikoffia robusta" **317** Nehru

1989. Orchids. Multicoloured.
742 5 f. Type **316** 15 10
743 10 f. "Grammangis fallax" (horiz) 15 10
744 80 f. "Angraecum sororium" 20 10
745 80 f. "Cymbidiella humblotii" 20 10
746 250 f. "Oenia oncidiiflora" . . 60 20

1989. Birth Centenary of Jawaharlal Nehru (Indian statesman).
748 **317** 250 f. multicoloured . . . 45 15

318 Mahamasina Sports Complex, Lake Anosy and Ampefiloha Quarter

1989. Antananarivo. Multicoloured.
749 5 f. Type **318** 10 10
750 20 f. Andravoahangy and Anjanahary Quarters 10 10
751 80 f. Zoma market and Faravohitra Quarter 15 10
752 80 f. Andohan' Analekely Quarter and 29 March Column 15 10
753 250 f. Avenue de l'Independance and Jean Ralaimongo Column 35 15
754 550 f. Lake Anosy, Queen's Palace and Andohalo School 70 35

319 Rose Quartz

1989. Ornamental Minerals. Multicoloured.
755 80 f. Type **319** 20 10
756 250 f. Fossilized wood 60 20

320 Pope and Rasoamanarivo **321** Map and Runner with Torch

1989. Visit of Pope John Paul II and Beatification of Victoire Rasoamanarivo. Multicoloured.
757 80 f. Type **320** 20 10
758 250 f. Map and Pope 55 20

1989. Town Games.
759 **321** 80 f. + 20 f. multicoloured 15 15

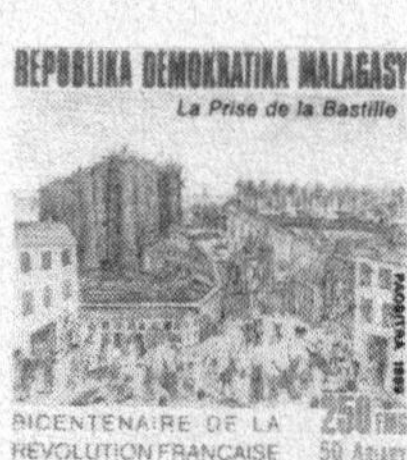

322 "Storming the Bastille"

1989. Bicentenary of French Revolution (1st issue).
760 **322** 250 f. multicoloured . . . 35 15
See also Nos. 773/5.

323 Mirabeau and Gabriel Riqueti at Meeting of States General

1989. "Philexfrance 89" International Stamp Exhibition, Paris. Multicoloured.
761 250 f. Type **323** 30 15
762 350 f. Camille Desmoulins' call to arms 45 20
763 1000 f. Lafayette and crowd demanding bread . . . . . 1·25 60
764 1500 f. Trial of King Louis XVI 2·00 80
765 2500 f. Assassination of Marat 3·25 1·25

324 "Mars 1"

1989. Space Probes. Multicoloured.
767 20 f. Type **324** 10 10
768 80 f. "Mars 3" 15 10
769 80 f. "Zond 2" 15 10
770 250 f. "Mariner 9" 35 15
771 270 f. "Viking 2" 40 20

325 "Liberty guiding the People" (Eugene Delacroix)

1989. Bicentenary of French Revolution (2nd issue). Multicoloured.

773 5 f. Type **325** (postage) 10 10
774 80 f. "La Marseillaise" (Francois Rude) 15 10
775 250 f. "Oath of the Tennis Court" (Jacques Louis David) (air) 35 15

326 Rene Cassin (founder)
327 Mother and Young on Bamboo

1989. 25th Anniv of International Human Rights Institute for French Speaking Countries.

776 **326** 250 f. multicoloured . . . 30 15

1989. Golden Gentle Lemur.

777 **327** 250 f. multicoloured . . . 40 20

328 Footballer and Cavour Monument, Turin
330 Long Jumping

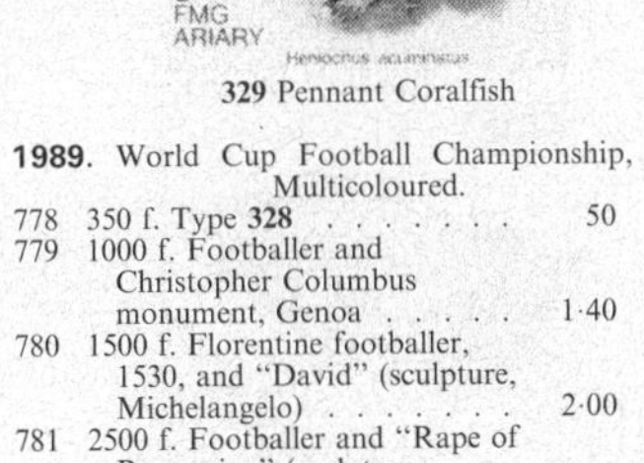

329 Pennant Coralfish

1989. World Cup Football Championship, Italy. Multicoloured.

778 350 f. Type **328** 50 20
779 1000 f. Footballer and Christopher Columbus monument, Genoa . . . . . 1·40 50
780 1500 f. Florentine footballer, 1530, and "David" (sculpture, Michelangelo) . . . . 2·00 75
781 2500 f. Footballer and "Rape of Proserpina" (sculpture, Bernini), Rome . . . . . . 3·25 1·40

1990. Fishes. Multicoloured.

783 5 f. Type **329** 10 10
784 20 f. Snub-nosed parasitic eel (vert) 10 10
785 80 f. Southern guitar-fish (vert) 15 10
786 250 f. Red-banded grouper . . 40 15
787 320 f. Common hammerhead shark 55 20

1990. Olympic Games, Barcelona (1992). Mult.

789 80 f. Type **330** 10 10
790 250 f. Pole vaulting 35 15
791 550 f. Hurdling 65 25
792 1500 f. Cycling . . . . 2·00 60
793 2000 f. Baseball . . . . 2·50 80
794 2500 f. Tennis . . . . 3·25 1·25

331 "Queen of the Isalo" (rock)

1990. Natural Features. Multicoloured.

796 70 f. Type **331** 15 10
797 150 f. Lonjy Island (as T **332**) 25 15

332 Pipe

1990. Sakalava Craft. Multicoloured.

798 70 f. Type **332** 15 10
799 150 f. Combs (as T **331**) . . . 25 15

333 Emblem and Projects

1990. 25th Anniv of African Development Bank.

800 **333** 80 f. multicoloured . . . 15 10

334 "Voyager II" and Neptune

1990. 20th Anniv of First Manned Landing on Moon. Multicoloured.

801 80 f. Type **334** 15 10
802 250 f. Hughes Hercules flying boat, Boeing 747 airliner and flying boat "of the future" 40 15
803 550 f. "Noah" satellite tracking elephants 70 25
804 1500 f. Venus and "Magellan" space probe . . . . 1·25 55
805 2000 f. Halley's Comet and Concorde . . . . 2·25 90
806 2500 f. "Apollo 11" landing capsule and crew . . . . . 3·00 1·00

335 Liner on Globe
336 Maps showing Development between 1975 and 1990

1990. 30th Anniv of International Maritime Organization.

808 **335** 250 f. ultramarine, bl & blk 45 15

1990. Air. 15th Anniv of Malagasy Socialist Revolution.

809 **336** 100 f. multicoloured . . . 15 10
810 – 350 f. black and grey . . 45 25

DESIGN: 350 f. Presidential Palaces, 1975 and 1990.

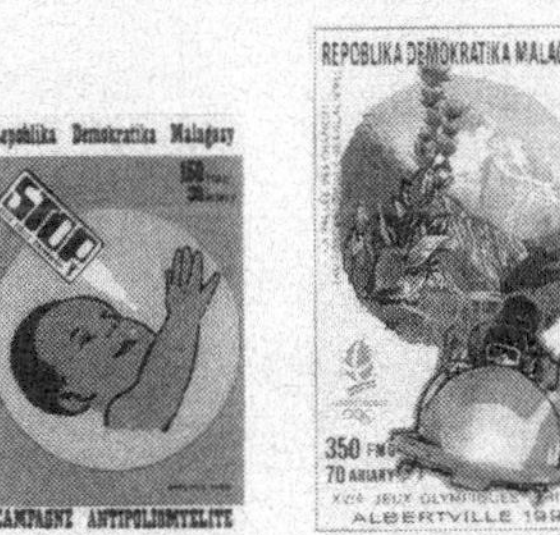

337 Oral Vaccination
338 Four-man Bobsleigh

1990. Anti-Polio Campaign.

811 **337** 150 f. multicoloured . . . 30 15

1990. Winter Olympic Games, Albertville (1992) (1st issue). Multicoloured.

812 350 f. Type **338** 40 20
813 1000 f. Speed skating . . . . 1·25 40
814 1500 f. Cross-country skiing . 2·00 65
815 2500 f. Downhill skiing . . . 3·00 1·10

See also Nos. 862/8.

339 Society Emblem

340 Mascot

1990. Air. 25th Anniv of Malagasy Bible Society.

817 **339** 25 f. multicoloured 10 10
818 – 100 f. blue, black & green 15 10

DESIGN—VERT: 100 f. Society emblem.

1990. 3rd Indian Ocean Island Games, Malagasy (1st issue).

819 **340** 100 f. + 20 f. on 80 f. + 20 f. multicoloured . . . 15 15
820 350 f. + 20 f. on 250 f. + 20 f. multicoloured . . . 45 40

The games were originally to be held in 1989 and the stamps were printed for release then. The issued stamps are handstamped with the correct date and new value.

See also Nos. 822/3.

341 Symbols of Agriculture and Industry
342 Torch

1990. 30th Anniv of Independence.

821 **341** 100 f. multicoloured . . . 15 10

1990. 3rd Indian Ocean Island Games, Malagasy (2nd issue).

822 **342** 100 f. multicoloured . . . 15 10
823 350 f. multicoloured . . . 45 20

343 Envelopes forming Map and Mail Transportation

1990. Air. World Post Day.

824 **343** 350 f. multicoloured . . . 75 30

344 Ho Chi Minh
345 "Avahi laniger"

1990. Birth Centenary of Ho Chi Minh (President of North Vietnam, 1945–69).

825 **344** 350 f. multicoloured . . . 40 20

1990. Lemurs. Multicoloured.

826 10 f. Type **345** 10 10
827 20 f. "Lemur fulvus albifrons" 10 10
828 20 f. "Lemur fulvus sanfordi" 10 10
829 100 f. "Lemur fulvus collaris" 25 15
830 100 f. "Lepulemur ruficaudatus" 25 15

346 Fluted Giant Clam
347 Letters in Book

1990. Shells. Multicoloured.

832 40 f. Type **346** 25 15
833 50 f. Dimidiate and subulate augers 35 15

1990. International Literacy Year. Multicoloured.

834 20 f. Type **347** 10 10
835 100 f. Open book and hand holding pen (horiz) 20 15

348 Cep
349 De Gaulle, Leclerc and Parod under Arc de Triomphe, 1944

1991. Fungi. Multicoloured.

836 25 f. Type **348** 10 10
837 100 f. Butter mushroom . . . 35 10
838 350 f. Fly agaric 55 20
839 450 f. Scarlet-stemmed boletus 75 25
840 680 f. Flaky-stemmed witches' mushroom . . . . 1·10 40
841 800 f. Brown birch bolete . . 1·25 45
842 900 f. Orange birch bolete . . 1·40 55

1991. Multicoloured.

844 100 f. Type **349** 10 10
845 350 f. "Galileo" space probe near Jupiter 25 10
846 800 f. Crew of "Apollo 11" on moon 55 25
847 900 f. De Gaulle and Free French emblem, 1942 . . . . . . 65 30
848 1250 f. Concorde aircraft and German "ICE" high speed train . . . . 1·40 55
849 2500 f. Gen. Charles de Gaulle (French statesman) . . . . 1·90 95

350 Industrial and Agricultural Symbols and Arms

351 Baobab Tree

1991. 15th Anniv (1990) of Republic.

851 **350** 100 f. multicoloured . . . 10 10

1991. Trees. Multicoloured.

852 140 f. Type **351** 10 10
853 500 f. "Dideria madagascariensis" 35 15

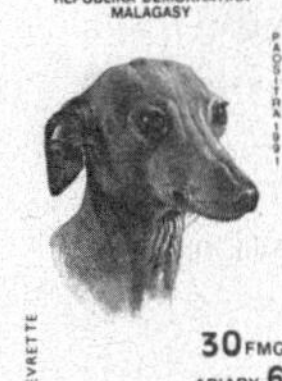

352 Whippet

353 Cross-country Skiing

1991. Dogs. Multicoloured.

854 30 f. Type **352** 10 10
855 50 f. Japanese spaniel 10 10
856 140 f. Toy terrier 10 10
857 350 f. Chow-chow 25 10
858 500 f. Chihuahua 35 15
859 800 f. Afghan hound 55 25
860 1140 f. Papillon 85 40

1991. Winter Olympic Games, Albertville (2nd issue). Multicoloured.

862 5 f. Type **353** 10 10
863 15 f. Biathlon 10 10
864 60 f. Ice hockey 10 10
865 140 f. Skiing 10 10
866 640 f. Ice skating 45 30
867 1000 f. Ski jumping 70 50
868 1140 f. Speed skating 80 60

354 "Helictopleurus splendidicollis"

1992. Scouts, Insects and Fungi. Multicoloured.
870 140 f. Type **354** 10 10
871 500 f. "Russula radicans" (mushroom) 50 25
872 640 f. "Cocles contemplator" (insect) 45 30
873 1025 f. "Russula singeri" (mushroom) 90 50
874 1140 f. "Euchroea oberthurii" (beetle) 80 60
875 3500 f. "Lactariopsis pandani" (mushroom) . . . . 3·00 2·00

355 Former and Present Buildings

1992. 90th Anniv (1991) of Paul Minault College.
877 **355** 140 f. multicoloured . . . 10 10

356 Repairing Space Telescope

1992. Space. Multicoloured.
878 140 f. Type **356** 10 10
879 500 f. "Soho" sun probe . . . 35 25
880 640 f. "Topex-Poseidon" oceanic survey satellite 45 30
881 1025 f. "Hipparcos" planetary survey satellite 70 50
882 1140 f. "Voyager 2" Neptune probe 80 60
883 5000 f. "ETS-VI" Japanese test communications satellite . . . 3·50 2·50

357 Ryuichi Sakamoto

1992. Entertainers. Multicoloured.
885 100 f. Type **357** 10 10
886 350 f. John Lennon 25 15
887 800 f. Bruce Lee 55 40
888 900 f. Sammy Davis jun . . . 65 45
889 1250 f. John Wayne 85 60
890 2500 f. James Dean . . . . . 1·75 1·25

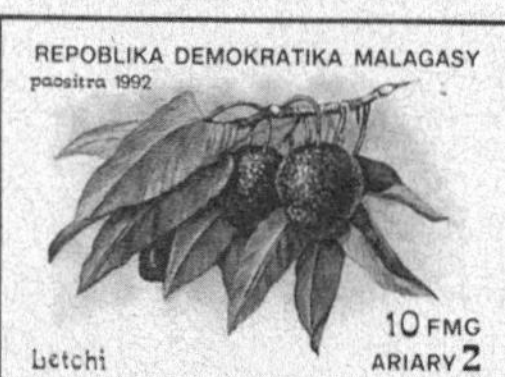

358 Lychees

1992. Fruits. Multicoloured.
892 10 f. Type **358** 10 10
893 50 f. Oranges 10 10
894 60 f. Apples 10 10
895 140 f. Peaches 10 10
896 555 f. Bananas (vert) 40 30
897 800 f. Avocados (vert) 55 40
898 1400 f. Mangoes (vert) . . . . 1·00 75

359 9th-century Galley

360 Couple in Heart

1992. Sailing Ships. Multicoloured.
900 15 f. Type **359** 10 10
901 65 f. Full-rigged sailing ship, 1878 . . . . 10 10
902 140 f. "Golden Hind" (Drake's flagship) 10 10
903 500 f. 18th-century dhow . . 35 25
904 640 f. "Ostrust" (galleon), 1721 (vert) 45 30
905 800 f. Dutch caravelle, 1599 (vert) 55 40
906 1025 f. "Santa Maria" (Columbus's flagship), 1492 70 50

1992. Anti-AIDS Campaign.
908 **360** 140 f. black and mauve . . 10 10

361 Tending Trees

362 Children with Mascot

1992. Reforestation.
909 **361** 140 f. dp green, blk & grn 10 10

1992. School Sports Festival (1990).
910 **362** 140 f. multicoloured . . . 10 10

363 Environmental Projects

364 Post Box and Globe

1992. Air. World Environment Day.
911 **363** 140 f. multicoloured . . . 10 10

1992. Air. World Post Day.
912 **364** 500 f. multicoloured . . . 35 25

365 Basenji

1992. Domestic Animals. Multicoloured.
913 140 f. Type **365** 10 10
914 500 f. Anglo Arab horse . . 35 25
915 640 f. Tortoiseshell cat and kitten 45 30
916 1025 f. Siamese and colour-point (cats) 70 50
917 1140 f. Holstein horse 80 60
918 5000 f. German shepherd dogs 3·50 2·50

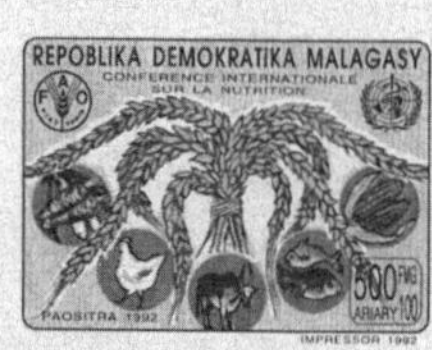

366 Foodstuffs

1992. International Nutrition Conference, Rome.
920 **366** 500 f. multicoloured . . . 35 25

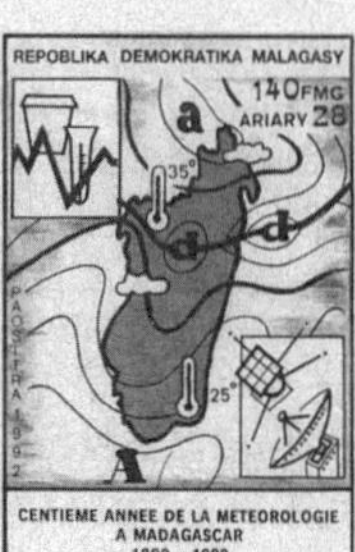

367 Weather Map

1992. Centenary of Meteorological Service.
921 **367** 140 f. multicoloured . . . 10 10

368 "Eusemia bisma"

1992. Butterflies and Moths. Multicoloured.
922 15 f. Type **368** 10 10
923 35 f. Tailed comet moth (vert) 10 10
924 65 f. "Alcides aurora" 10 10
925 140 f. "Agarista agricola" . . 10 10
926 600 f. "Trogonoptera croesus" 40 30
927 850 f. "Trogonodtera priamus" 60 45
928 1300 f. "Pereute leucodrosime" 90 70

369 Barn Swallow

1992. Birds. Multicoloured.
930 40 f. Type **369** 10 10
931 55 f. Pied harrier (vert) 10 10
932 60 f. European cuckoo (vert) . 10 10
933 140 f. Sacred ibis 10 10
934 210 f. Purple swamphen . . . 15 10
935 500 f. Common roller 35 25
936 2000 f. Golden oriole . . . . . 1·40 1·10

370 Gymnastics

1992. Olympic Games, Barcelona. Multicoloured.
938 65 f. Type **370** 10 10
939 70 f. High jumping 10 10
940 120 f. Archery 10 10
941 140 f. Cycling 10 10
942 675 f. Weightlifting 45 30
943 720 f. Boxing 50 35
944 1200 f. Two-man kayak . . . 85 60

371 Pusher-tug, Pangalanes Canal

1993.
946 **371** 140 f. multicoloured . . . 10 10

372 BMW

373 Hyacinth Macaw

1993. Motor Cars. Multicoloured.
947 20 f. Type **372** 10 10
948 40 f. Toyota "Carina" 10 10
949 60 f. Cadillac 10 10
950 65 f. Volvo 10 10
951 140 f. Mercedes-Benz 10 10
952 640 f. Ford "Sierra" 45 30
953 3000 f. Honda "Concerto" . . 2·10 1·50

1993. Parrot Family. Multicoloured.
955 50 f. Type **373** 10 10
956 60 f. Cockatiel 10 10
957 140 f. Budgerigar 10 10
958 500 f. Jandaya conure 35 25
959 675 f. Budgerigar (different) . 50 35
960 800 f. Red-fronted parakeet . . 60 45
961 1750 f. Kea . . . . 1·25 90

MINIMUM PRICE

The minimum price quoted is 10p which represents a handling charge rather than a basis for valuing common stamps. For further notes about prices, see introductory pages.

375 Albert Einstein (physics, 1921) and Niels Bohr (physics, 1922)

1993. Nobel Prize Winners. Multicoloured.
964 500 f. Type **375** 35 25
965 500 f. Wolfgang Pauli (physics, 1945) and Max Born (physics, 1954) 35 25
966 500 f. Joseph Thomson (physics, 1906) and Johannes Stark (physics, 1919) 35 25
967 500 f. Otto Hahn (physics, 1944) and Hideki Yukawa (physics, 1949) 35 25
968 500 f. Owen Richardson (physics, 1928) and William Shockley (physics, 1956) 35 25
969 500 f. Albert Michelson (physics, 1907) and Charles Townes (physics, 1964) 35 25
970 500 f. Wilhelm Wien (physics, 1911) and Lev Landau (physics, 1962) 35 25
971 500 f. Carl Braun (physics, 1909) and Sir Edward Appleton (physics, 1947) 35 25
972 500 f. Percy Bridgman (physics, 1946) and Nikolai Semyonov (physics, 1956) 35 25
973 500 f. Sir William Ramsay (chemistry, 1904) and Glenn Seaborg (chemistry, 1951) . 35 25
974 500 f. Otto Wallach (chemistry, 1910) and Hermann Staudinger (chemistry, 1953) 35 25
975 500 f. Richard Synge (chemistry, 1952) and Axel Theorell (chemistry, 1955) 35 25
976 500 f. Thomas Morgan (medicine, 1933) and Hermann Muller (medicine, 1946) . . 35 25
977 500 f. Allvar Gullstrand (medicine, 1911) and Willem Einthoven (Medicine, 1924) 35 25
978 500 f. Sir Charles Sherrington (medicine, 1932) and Otto Loewi (medicine, 1936) . . 35 25
979 500 f. Jules Bordet (medicine, 1936) and Sir Alexander Fleming (medicine, 1945) . 35 25

376 1956 Bugatti

1993. Racing Cars and Railway Locomotives. Multicoloured.
980 20 f. Type **376** 10 10
981 20 f. 1968 Ferrari 10 10
982 20 f. 1948 Class "C-62" steam locomotive 10 10
983 20 f. 1975 SZD electric locomotive 10 10
984 140 f. 1962 Lotus Mk 25 . . . 10 10
985 140 f. 1970 Matra 10 10
986 140 f. 1954 MU locomotive . 10 10
987 140 f. 1982 Series 26 locomotive 10 10
988 1250 f. 1963 Porsche 90 65
989 1250 f. 1980 Ligier JS 11 . . . 90 65
990 1250 f. 1967 PRR Metroliner . 90 65
991 1250 f. 1982 V.I.A. locomotive 90 65
992 3000 f. 1967 Honda . . . . . 2·10 1·50
993 3000 f. 1992 Benetton B-192 . 2·10 1·50
994 3000 f. 1969 Union Pacific locomotive . . . . 2·10 1·50
995 3000 f. 1990 TGV Atlantique . 2·10 1·50

377 Pharaonic Ship

1993. Ships. Multicoloured.
996 5 f. Type **377** 10 10
997 5 f. Mediterranean carrack . 10 10
998 5 f. "Great Western" (sail paddle-steamer), 1837 . . 10 10
999 5 f. "Mississippi" (paddle-steamer), 1850 . . . . . 10 10
1000 15 f. Phoenician bireme . . . 10 10
1001 15 f. Viking ship 10 10
1002 15 f. "Clermont" (first commercial paddle-steamer), 1806 . . . . 10 10
1003 15 f. "Pourquoi Pas?" (Charcot's ship), 1936 . . 10 10
1004 140 f. "Santa Maria" (Columbus's ship), 1492 . 10 10

1005 140 f. H.M.S. "Victory" (ship of the line), 1765 . . . . . . 10 10
1006 140 f. Motor yacht 10 10
1007 140 f. "Bremen" (liner), 1950 10 10
1008 10000 f. "Sovereign of the Seas" (galleon), 1637 . . . . . . 7·25 5·25
1009 10000 f. "Cutty Sark" (clipper) 7·25 5·25
1010 10000 f. "Savannah" (nuclear-powered freighter) . . . . 7·25 5·25
1011 10000 f. "Condor" (hydrofoil) 7·25 5·25
No. 999 is wrongly inscribed "Mississipi".

378 Johannes Gutenberg and Printing Press

1993. Inventors. Multicoloured.
1012 500 f. Type **378** 35 25
1013 500 f. Sir Isaac Newton and telescope 35 25
1014 500 f. John Dalton and atomic theory 35 25
1015 500 f. Louis Jacques Daguerre and camera 35 25
1016 500 f. Michael Faraday and electric motor 35 25
1017 500 f. Wright brothers and "Flyer" 35 25
1018 500 f. Alexander Bell and telephone 35 25
1019 500 f. Thomas Edison and telegraph 35 25
1020 500 f. Karl Benz and motor vehicle 35 25
1021 500 f. Sir Charles Parsons and steam turbine 35 25
1022 500 f. Rudolph Diesel and diesel locomotive 35 25
1023 500 f. Guglielmo Marconi and early radio 35 25
1024 500 f. Lumiere brothers and cine-camera 35 25
1025 500 f. Herman Oberth and space rocket 35 25
1026 500 f. John Mauchly, J. Prosper Eckert and computer . . . 35 25
1027 500 f. Arthur Shawlow, compact disc and laser . . 35 25

379 Leonardo da Vinci and "Virgin of the Rocks"

1993. Painters. Multicoloured.
1028 50 f. Type **379** 10 10
1029 50 f. Titian and "Sacred and Profane Love" 10 10
1030 50 f. Rembrandt and "Jeremiah crying" 10 10
1031 50 f. J. M. W. Turner and "Ulysses" 10 10
1032 640 f. Michelangelo and the Doni Tondo 45 30
1033 640 f. Peter Paul Rubens and "Self-portrait" 45 30
1034 640 f. Francisco Goya and "Don Manuel Osorio de Zuniga" 45 30
1035 640 f. Eugene Delacroix and "Christ on Lake Gennesaret" 45 30
1036 1000 f. Claude Monet and "Poppyfield" 70 50
1037 1000 f. Paul Gauguin and "Two Tahitians" 70 50
1038 1000 f. Henri Marie de Toulouse-Lautrec and "Woman with a Black Boa" 70 50
1039 1000 f. Salvador Dali and "St. James of Compostela" . . 70 50
1040 2500 f. Pierre Auguste Renoir and "Child carrying Flowers" 1·75 1·25
1041 2500 f. Vincent Van Gogh and "Dr. Paul Gachet" . . . . 1·75 1·25
1042 2500 f. Pablo Picasso and "Crying Woman" . . . . 1·75 1·25
1043 2500 f. Andy Warhol and "Portrait of Elvis" . . . . 1·75 1·25

380 Sunset Moth ("Chrysiridia madagascariensis")

1993. Butterflies, Moths and Birds. Multicoloured.
1044 45 f. Type **380** 10 10
1045 45 f. African monarch ("Hypolimnas misippus") . 10 10
1046 45 f. Southern crested Madagascar coucal ("Coua verreauxi") 10 10
1047 45 f. African marsh owl ("Asio helvola") 10 10
1048 60 f. "Charaxes antamboulou" 10 10
1049 60 f. "Papilio antenor" . . . 10 10
1050 60 f. Crested Madagascar coucal ("Coua cristata") . 10 10
1051 60 f. Helmet bird ("Euryceros prevostii") 10 10
1052 140 f. "Hypolimnas dexithea" 10 10
1053 140 f. "Charaxes andronodorus" 10 10
1054 140 f. Giant Madagascar coucal ("Couca gigas") 10 10
1055 140 f. Madagascar red fody ("Foudia madagascarensis") 10 10
1056 3000 f. "Euxanthe madagascarensis" . . . . 2·10 1·50
1057 3000 f. "Papilio grosesmithi" 2·10 1·50
1058 3000 f. Sicklebill ("Falculea palliata") . . . . 2·10 1·50
1059 3000 f. Madagascar serpent eagle ("Eutriorchis astur") 2·10 1·50
Nos. 1044/59 were issued together, se-tenant, the butterfly and bird designs respectively forming composite designs.

381 Henri Dunant and Volunteers unloading Red Cross Lorry

1993. Anniversaries and Events. Multicoloured.
1060 500 f. Type **381** (award of first Nobel Peace Prize, 1901) . 35 25
1061 640 f. Charles de Gaulle and battlefield (50th anniv of Battle of Bir-Hakeim (1992)) 45 30
1062 1025 f. Crowd at Brandenburg Gate (bicentenary (1991) and fourth anniv of breach of Berlin Wall) 75 55
1063 1500 f. Doctors giving health instruction to women (Rotary International and Lions International) . . . . . . 1·10 80
1064 3000 f. Konrad Adenauer (German chancellor 1949–63, 24th death anniv (1991)) . 2·10 1·50
1065 3500 f. "LZ-4" (airship), 1908, and Count Ferdinand von Zeppelin (75th death anniv (1992)) . . . . 2·50 1·75

382 Guides and Anniversary Emblem

383 Player, Trophy and Ficklin Home, Macon

1993. Air. 50th Anniv of Madagascar Girl Guides.
1067 **382** 140 f. multicoloured . . 10 10

1993. World Cup Football Championship, United States (1992). Multicoloured.
1068 140 f. Type **383** 10 10
1069 640 f. Player, trophy and Herndon Home, Atlanta . 45 35
1070 1025 f. Player, trophy and Cultural Centre, Augusta . 75 55
1071 5000 f. Player, trophy and Old Governor's Mansion, Milledgeville . . . . . . 3·50 1·75

1993. Various stamps optd with emblem and inscription. (a) Germany, World Cup Football Champion, 1990. Nos. 778/81 optd **VAINQUEUR:ALLEMAGNE.**
1073 **328** 350 f. multicoloured . . 25 15
1074 – 1000 f. multicoloured . 70 50
1075 – 1500 f. multicoloured . 1·10 80
1076 – 2500 f. multicoloured . 1·75 1·25

(b) Gold Medallists at Winter Olympic Games, Albertville (1992). Nos. 812/15 optd with olympic rings, "**MEDAILLE D'OR** " and further inscr as below.
1077 350 f. **BOB A QUATRE (AUT) INGO APPELT HARALD WINKLER GERHARD HAIDACHER THOMAS SCROLL** 25 15
1078 1000 f. **1000 M. - OLAF ZINKE (GER)** 70 50
1079 1500 f. **50 KM LIBRE BJOERN DAEHLIE (NOR)** 1·10 80
1080 2500 f. **SUPER G MESSIEURS KJETIL-ANDRE AAMODT (NOR)** . . . . 1·75 1·25

(c) Anniversaries. Nos. 1060, 675 and 707 optd as listed below.
1082 500 f. Red Cross and **130e ANNIVERSAIRE DE LA CREATION DE LA CROIX-ROUGE 1863-1993** 35 25
1083 550 f. Lions emblem and **75eme ANNIVERSAIRE LIONS** . 40 30
1084 1500 f. Guitar and **THE ELVIS'S GUITAR 15TH ANNIVERSARY OF HIS DEATH 1977-1992** . . . . 1·10 80
1085 1500 f. Guitar and **GUITARE ELVIS 15eme ANNIVERSAIRE DE SA MORT 1977-1992** . . . . . 1·10 80

(d) 50th Death Anniv of Robert Baden-Powell (founder of Boy Scouts). Optd **50eme ANNIVERSAIRE DE LA MORT DE BADEN POWEL** and emblem. (i) On Nos. 870/5 with scout badge in wreath.
1086 **354** 140 f. multicoloured . . 10 10
1087 – 500 f. multicoloured . . 35 25
1088 – 640 f. multicoloured . . 45 30
1089 – 1025 f. multicoloured . . 75 55
1090 – 1140 f. multicoloured . . 80 60
1091 – 3500 f. multicoloured . . 2·50 1·75

(ii) On No. 676 with profile of Baden-Powell.
1093 1500 f. multicoloured . . . . 1·10 80

(e) Bicentenary of French Republic. Nos. 761/5 optd **Republique Francaise** and emblem within oval and **BICENTENAIRE DE L'AN I DE LA REPUBLIQUE FRANCAISE**.
1094 250 f. multicoloured 20 15
1095 350 f. multicoloured 25 15
1096 1000 f. multicoloured 70 50
1097 1500 f. multicoloured . . . . 1·10 80
1098 2500 f. multicoloured . . . . 1·75 1·25

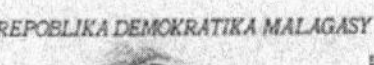

385 Great Green Turban

1993. Molluscs. Multicoloured.
1100 40 f. Type **385** 10 10
1101 60 f. Episcopal mitre 10 10
1102 65 f. Common paper nautilis . 10 10
1103 140 f. Textile cone 10 10
1104 500 f. European sea hare . . 35 25
1105 675 f. "Harpa amouretta" . . 50 35
1106 2500 f. Tiger cowrie . . . . . 1·75 1·25

386 Tiger Leopard Shark

1993. Sharks. Multicoloured.
1108 10 f. Type **386** 10 10
1109 45 f. Japanese saw shark . . . 10 10
1110 140 f. Whale basking shark . 10 10
1111 270 f. Common hammerhead shark 20 15
1112 600 f. Oceanic white-tip shark 45 30
1113 1200 f. "Stegostoma tigrinum" 85 60
1114 1500 f. Goblin shark . . . . 1·10 80

387 Map of Africa and Industry

1993. Air. African Industrialization Day.
1116 **387** 500 f. red, yellow and blue 35 25

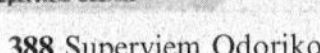

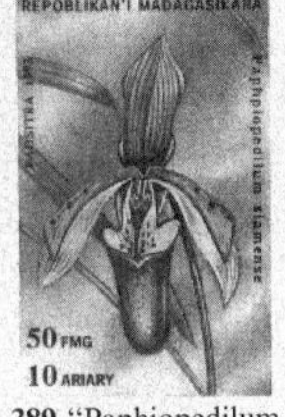

388 Superviem Odoriko

389 "Paphiopedilum siamense"

1993. Electric Locomotives. Multicoloured.
1117 5 f. Type **388** 10 10
1118 15 f. Morrison Knudsen Corporation 10 10
1119 140 f. ER-200 . . . . 10 10
1120 265 f. General Motors 20 15
1121 300 f. New Jersey Transit . . 20 15
1122 575 f. Inter City Express Siemens 40 30
1123 2500 f. Sweden's fast train . . 1·75 1·25
No. 1123 is wrongly inscribed "Fas".

1993. Orchids. Multicoloured.
1125 50 f. Type **389** (wrongly inscr "Paphiopedilum") . . . 10 10
1126 65 f. "Cypripedium calceolus" 10 10
1127 70 f. "Ophrys oestrifera" . . 10 10
1128 140 f. "Cephalanthera rubra" 10 10
1129 300 f. "Cypripedium macranthon" 20 15
1130 640 f. "Calanthe vestita" . . 45 30
1131 2500 f. "Cypripedium guttatum" . . . . 1·75 1·25

POSTAGE DUE STAMPS

D 13 Independence Obelisk

1962.
D45 **D 13** 1 f. green 10 10
D46 2 f. brown 10 10
D47 3 f. violet 10 10
D48 4 f. slate 10 10
D49 5 f. red 10 10
D50 10 f. green 15 15
D51 20 f. purple 20 20
D52 40 f. blue 50 45
D53 50 f. red 75 70
D54 100 f. black . . . . . 1·40 1·25

APPENDIX

The following stamps have either been issued in excess of postal needs or have not been available to the public in reasonable quantities at face value.

1987.
Winter Olympic Games, Calgary (1988). 1500 f. (on gold foil).

1989.
Scout and Butterfly. 5000 f. (on gold foil).
"Philexfrance 89" Int. Stamp Exhibition, Paris. 5000 f. (on gold foil).
World Cup Football Championship, Italy. 5000 f. (on gold foil).

1990.
Winter Olympic Games, Albertville (1992). 5000 f. (on gold foil).

1991.
Birth Centenary of De Gaulle. 5000 f. (on gold foil).

1992.
Olympic Games, Barcelona. 500 f. (on gold foil).

1993.
Bicentenary of French Republic. 1989 "Philexfrance 89" issue optd. 5000 f.

MALI Pt. 6; Pt. 13

Federation of French Sudan and Senegal, formed in 1959 as an autonomous republic within the French Community. In August 1960 the Federation was split up and the French Sudan part became the independent Mali Republic.

100 centimes = 1 franc

A. FEDERATION.

1 Map, Flag, Mali and Torch

1959. Establishment of Mali Federation.
1 **1** 25 f. multicoloured 50 50

2

1959. Air. 300th Anniv of St. Louis, Senegal.
2 **2** 85 f. multicoloured . . . . . 1·50 1·25

3 Parrot Fish

4 Violet Starling

1960. (a) Postage. Fish as T **3**.
3 **3** 5 f. orange, blue and bronze . . 30 15
4 – 10 f. black, brown & turquoise . . 30 25
5 – 15 f. brown, slate and blue . . 40 25
6 – 20 f. black, bistre and green . . 50 35
7 – 25 f. yellow, sepia and green . . 60 40
8 – 30 f. red, purple and blue . . . 80 50
9 – 85 f. red, blue and green . . . 1·75 1·50

(b) Air. Birds as T **4**.
10 **4** 100 f. multicoloured . . . . 6·75 1·75
11 – 200 f. multicoloured . . . . 15·00 5·50
12 – 500 f. multicoloured . . . . 40·00 15·00
DESIGNS—HORIZ: 10 f. Trigger fish; 15 f. Batfish; 20 f. Threadfish; 25 f. Butterfly fish; 30 f. Surgeon; 85 f. Sea bream; 200 f. Bateleur. VERT: 500 f. Common gonolek.

1960. 10th Anniv of African Technical Co-operation Commission. As T **4** of Malagasy Republic.
13 25 f. purple and violet . . . . . 1·00 75

B. REPUBLIC.

1960. Nos. 6, 7, 9 and 10/12 optd **REPUBLIQUE DU MALI** and bar or bars or surch also.
14 20 f. black, bistre and green (postage) . . . . 1·25 60
15 25 f. red, purple and blue . . . 1·75 60
16 85 f. red, blue and green . . . 3·00 1·50
17 100 f. multicoloured (air) . . . 5·50 1·50
18 200 f. multicoloured . . . . . 8·50 3·50
19 300 f. on 500 f. multicoloured . . 14·00 6·00
20 500 f. multicoloured . . . . . 28·00 17·00

7 Pres. Mamadou Konate

1961.
21 **7** 20 f. sepia & green (postage) . . 25 15
22 – 25 f. black and purple 35 15
23 **7** 200 f. sepia and red (air) . . . 3·00 1·00
24 – 300 f. black and green . . . . 4·25 1·25
DESIGN: 25, 300 f. President Keita. Nos. 23/4 are larger 27 × 38 mm.

8 U.N. Emblem, Flag and Map

1961. Air. Proclamation of Independence and Admission into U.N.
25 **8** 100 f. multicoloured . . . . 1·25 90

9 Sankore Mosque, Timbuktu

1961. Air.
26 **9** 100 f. brown, blue and sepia . . 1·75 55
27 – 200 f. brown, red and green . . 4·00 1·50
28 – 500 f. green, brown and blue . . 11·00 3·25
DESIGN: 200 f. View of Timbuktu; 500 f. Arms and view of Bamako.

10 Africans learning Vowels

1961. 1st Anniv of Independence.
29 **10** 25 f. multicoloured 45 30

11 Sheep at Pool

12 African Map and King Mohammed V of Morocco

1961.
30 **11** 50 c. sepia, myrtle and red . . 15 15
31 A 1 f. bistre, green and blue . . 15 15
32 B 2 f. red, green and blue . . . 15 15
33 C 3 f. brown, green and blue . . 15 15
34 D 4 f. blue, green and bistre . . 15 15
35 **11** 5 f. purple, green and blue . . 20 15
36 A 10 f. brown, myrtle & blue . . 20 15
37 B 15 f. brown, green & blue . . 20 15
38 C 20 f. red, green and blue . . . 30 25
39 D 25 f. brown and blue 40 20
40 **11** 30 f. brown, green & violet . . 55 30
41 A 40 f. brown, green & blue . . 1·25 30
42 B 50 f. lake, green and blue . . 50 30
43 C 60 f. brown, green and blue . . 15 15
44 D 85 f. brown, bistre & blue . . 1·75 35
DESIGNS: A, Oxen at pool; B, House of Arts, Mali; C, Land tillage; D, Combine-harvester in rice field.

1962. 1st Anniv of African Conf, Casablanca.
45 **12** 25 f. multicoloured 25 15
46 50 f. multicoloured 50 20

13 Patrice Lumumba

1962. 1st Death Anniv of Patrice Lumumba (Congo leader).
47 **13** 25 f. brown and bistre 20 20
48 100 f. brown and green . . . 75 50

1962. Malaria Eradication. As T **43** of Mauritania.
49 25 f. + 5 f. blue 50 60

14 Pegasus and U.P.U. Emblem

1962. 1st Anniv of Admission into U.P.U.
50 **14** 85 f. multicoloured . . . . . 1·00 65

14a Posthorn on Map of Africa

15 Sansanding Dam

1962. African Postal Union Commem.
51 **14a** 25 f. green and brown . . . 25 20
52 85 f. orange and green . . . 75 50

1962.
53 **15** 25 f. black, green and blue . . 30 20
54 – 45 f. multicoloured . . . . . 1·10 50
DESIGN—HORIZ: 45 f. Cotton plant.

16 "Telstar" Satellite, Globe and Television Receiver

1962. 1st Trans-Atlantic Telecommunications Satellite Link.
55 **16** 45 f. brown, violet and lake . . 70 40
56 55 f. violet, olive and green . . 80 60

17 Soldier and Family

18 Bull's Head, Laboratory Equipment and Chicks

1962. Mali–Algerian Solidarity.
57 **17** 25 f. + 5 f. multicoloured . . 30 30

1963. Zoological Research Centre, Sobuta.
58 **18** 25 f. turq & brn (postage) . . 35 25
59 – 200 f. turquoise, purple and bistre (air) . . . . 3·00 1·25
DESIGN: 200 f. As Type **18** but horiz 47 × 27 mm.

19 Tractor and Campaign Emblem

1963. Freedom from Hunger.
60 **19** 25 f. purple, black and blue . . 35 20
61 45 f. brown, green & turq . . 65 35

20 Balloon and W.M.O. Emblem

1963. Atmospheric Research.
62 **20** 25 f. multicoloured 30 20
63 45 f. multicoloured 60 35
64 60 f. multicoloured 80 50

21 Race Winners

22 Centenary Emblem and Globe

1963. Youth Week. Multicoloured.
65 5 f. Type **21** 15 10
66 10 f. Type **21** 20 15
67 20 f. Acrobatic dance 35 20
68 85 f. Football . . . . 1·40 55
Nos. 67/8 are horiz.

1963. Red Cross Centenary. Inscr in black.
69 **22** 5 f. multicoloured 20 15
70 10 f. red, yellow and grey . . 30 20
71 85 f. red, yellow and grey . . 1·10 60

23 Stretcher case entering Aero 145 Ambulance Airplane

1963. Air.
72 **23** 25 f. brown, blue and green . . 35 20
73 – 55 f. blue, ochre and brown . . 1·00 40
74 – 100 f. blue, brown and green . 1·60 75
DESIGNS: 55 f. Douglas DC-3 airliner on tarmac; 100 f. Illyushin Il-18 airliner taking off.

24 South African Crowned Crane standing on Giant Tortoise

26 "Kaempferia aethiopica"

25 U.N. Emblem, Doves and Banner

1963. Air. Fauna Protection.
75 **24** 25 f. brown, red and orange . . 2·00 50
76 200 f. multicoloured . . . . 6·00 2·25

1963. Air. 15th Anniv of Declaration of Human Rights.
77 **25** 50 f. yellow, red and green . . 75 40

1963. Tropical Flora. Multicoloured.
78 30 f. Type **26** 45 25
79 70 f. "Bombax costatum" . . . 1·40 50
80 100 f. "Adenium honghel" . . . 2·75 65

27 Pharaoh and Cleopatra, Philae

28 Locust on Map of Africa

1964. Air. Nubian Monuments Preservation.
81 **27** 25 f. brown and purple . . . 60 25
82 55 f. olive and purple . . . 1·40 50

1964. Anti-Locust Campaign.
83 **28** 5 f. brown, green and purple . . 20 15
84 – 10 f. brown, green and olive . . 30 20
85 – 20 f. brown, green and bistre . . 50 25
DESIGNS—VERT: 10 f. Locust and map. HORIZ: 20 f. Air-spraying, locust and village.

29 Football

1964. Olympic Games, Tokyo.
86 29 5 f. purple, green and red . . 15 10
87 – 10 f. brown, blue and sepia 20 20
88 – 15 f. red and violet 25 20
89 – 85 f. green, brown & violet 1·00 70
DESIGNS—VERT: 10 f. Boxing; 15 f. Running and Olympic Flame. HORIZ: 85 f. Hurdling. Each design has a stadium in the background.

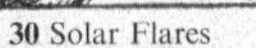

30 Solar Flares — 32 Map of Vietnam

31 President Kennedy

1964. Int Quiet Sun Years.
90 30 45 f. olive, red and blue . . 60 35

1964. Air. 1st Death Anniv of Pres. Kennedy.
91 31 100 f. multicoloured . . . . 1·40 1·25

1964. Mali–South Vietnam Workers' Solidarity Campaign.
92 32 30 f. multicoloured 30 20

33 Knysna Turacos

1965. Air. Birds.
93 33 100 f. green, blue and red . 5·50 1·75
94 – 200 f. black, red and blue . 13·50 3·75
95 – 300 f. black, ochre and green 19·00 5·00
96 – 500 f. red, brown and green 29·00 9·50
BIRDS—VERT: 200 f. Abyssinian ground hornbills; 300 f. Egyptian vultures. HORIZ: 500 f. Goliath herons.

34 I.C.Y. Emblem and U.N. Headquarters — 36 Abraham Lincoln

35 African Buffalo

1965. Air. International Co-operation Year.
97 34 55 f. ochre, purple and blue 75 40

1965. Animals.
98 – 1 f. brown, blue and green 10 10
99 35 5 f. brown, orange & green 15 10
100 – 10 f. brown, mauve & green 40 25
101 – 30 f. brown, green and red 75 30
102 – 90 f. brown, grey and green 2·25 95
ANIMALS—VERT: 1 f. Waterbuck; 10 f. Scimitar oryx; 90 f. Giraffe. HORIZ: 30 f. Leopard.

1965. Death Centenary of Abraham Lincoln.
103 36 45 f. multicoloured 60 40
104 55 f. multicoloured 65 50

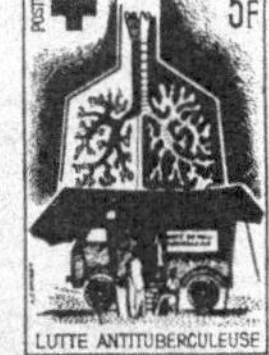

37 Hughes' Telegraph — 38 "Lungs" and Mobile X-Ray Unit (Anti-T.B.)

1965. Centenary of I.T.U.
105 – 20 f. black, blue & orange 30 25
106 37 30 f. green, brn & orange 45 25
107 – 50 f. green, brown & orge 75 45
DESIGNS—VERT: 20 f. Denis's Pneumatic tube; 50 f. Lescurre's heliograph.

1965. Mali Health Service.
108 38 5 f. violet, red and crimson 15 15
109 – 10 f. green, bistre and red 25 15
110 – 25 f. green and brown . . 40 20
111 – 45 f. green and brown . . 75 40
DESIGNS: 10 f. Mother and children (Maternal and Child Care); 25 f. Examining patient (Marchoux Institute); 45 f. Nurse (Biological Laboratory).

39 Diving

1965. 1st African Games, Brazzaville, Congo.
112 39 5 f. red, brown and blue . 15 10
113 – 15 f. turquoise, brown and red (Judo) 60 30

40 Pope John XXIII — 41 Sir Winston Churchill

1965. Air. Pope John Commemoration.
114 40 100 f. multicoloured . . . 1·90 75

1965. Air. Churchill Commemoration.
115 41 100 f. blue and brown . . 1·75 75

42 Dr. Schweitzer and Young African

1965. Air. Dr. Albert Schweitzer Commemoration.
116 42 100 f. multicoloured . . . 2·00 75

43 Leonov

1966. International Astronautic Conference, Athens (1965). Multicoloured.
117 100 f. Type 43 . . . . 1·60 60
118 100 f. White . . . . 1·60 60
119 300 f. Cooper, Conrad, Leonov and Beliaiev (vert) . . . . 4·25 2·00

44 Vase, Quill and Cornet

1966. World Festival of Negro Arts, Dakar, Cameroun.
120 44 30 f. black, red and ochre 30 20
121 – 55 f. red, black and green 60 35
122 – 90 f. brown, orange & blue 1·10 60
DESIGNS: 55 f. Mask, brushes and palette, microphones; 90 f. Dancers, Mask, patterned cloth.

45 W.H.O. Building

1966. Inaug of W.H.O. Headquarters, Geneva.
123 45 30 f. green, blue and yellow 40 20
124 45 f. red, blue and yellow 60 35

46 Fisherman with Net

1966. River Fishing.
125 46 3 f. brown and blue 15 15
126 – 4 f. purple, blue and brown 20 15
127 – 20 f. purple, green and blue 35 15
128 46 25 f. purple, blue and green 50 20
129 – 60 f. purple, lake and green 85 35
130 – 85 f. plum, green and blue 1·25 50
DESIGNS: 4 f., 60 f. Collective shore fishing; 20 f., 85 f. Fishing pirogue.

47 Papal Arms, U.N. and Peace Emblems

1966. Air. Pope Paul's Visit to U.N.
131 47 200 f. blue, green & turq . . 2·50 1·10

48 Initiation Ceremony — 49 People and U.N.E.S.C.O. Emblem

1966. Mali Pioneers. Multicoloured.
132 5 f. Type 48 . . . . 15 15
133 25 f. Pioneers dancing 50 20

1966. Air. 20th Anniv of U.N.E.S.C.O.
134 49 100 f. red, green and blue 1·75 70

50 Footballers, Globe, Cup and Football

1966. Air. World Cup Football Championships, England.
135 50 100 f. multicoloured . . . . 1·75 70

51 Cancer ("The Crab") — 52 U.N.I.C.E.F. Emblem and Children

1966. Air. 9th International Cancer Congress, Tokyo.
136 51 100 f. multicoloured . . . 1·60 55

1966. 20th Anniv of U.N.I.C.E.F.
137 52 45 f. blue, purple & brown 60 25

53 Inoculating Cattle

1967. Campaign for Preventing Cattle Plague.
138 53 10 f. multicoloured 25 10
139 30 f. multicoloured 50 20

54 Desert Vehicles in Pass

1967. Air. Crossing of the Hoggar (1924).
140 54 200 f. green, brown & vio 4·50 2·25

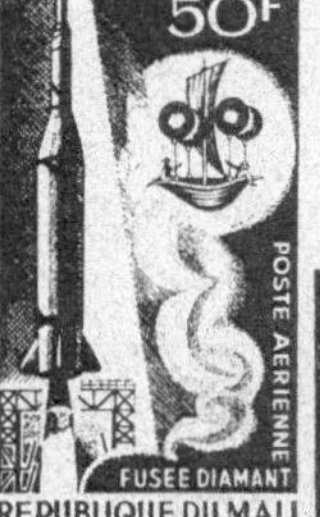

55 "Diamant" Rocket and Francesco de Lana-Terzis's "Aerial Ship" — 56 Ancient City

1967. Air. French Space Rockets and Satellites.
141 55 50 f. blue, turquoise & pur 70 30
142 – 100 f. lake, purple & turq 1·40 50
143 – 200 f. purple, olive and blue 2·40 1·00
DESIGNS: 100 f. Satellite "A 1" and Jules Verne's "rocket"; 200 f. Satellite "D 1" and Da Vinci's "bird-powered" flying machine.

1967. International Tourist Year.
144 56 25 f. orange, blue and violet 30 20

57 Amelia Earhart and Mail Route-map

1967. Air. 30th Anniv of Amelia Earhart's Flight, via Gao.
145 57 500 f. multicoloured . . . 7·00 3·25

58 "The Bird Cage" — 59 Scout Emblems and Rope Knots

1967. Air. Picasso Commemoration. Designs showing paintings. Multicoloured.
146 50 f. Type 58 . . . . 1·00 30
147 100 f. "Paul as Harlequin" . . 1·75 70
148 250 f. "The Pipes of Pan" . . 3·50 1·50
See also Nos. 158/9 and 164/7.

1967. Air. World Scout Jamboree, Idaho.
149 59 70 f. red and green . . . . 1·00 30
150 – 100 f. black, lake and green 1·25 45
DESIGN: 100 f. Scout with "walkie-talkie" radio.

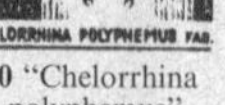

60 "Chelorrhina polyphemus" 61 School Class

1967. Insects.
151 **60** 5 f. green, brown and blue . . . 30 20
152 – 15 f. purple, brown & green . . 50 25
153 – 50 f. red, brown and green . . 1·10 55
INSECTS—HORIZ: 15 f. "Ugada grandicollis"; 50 f. "Phymateus cinctus".

1967. International Literacy Day.
154 **61** 50 f. black, red and green . . . 60 20

62 "Europafrique" 63 Lions Emblem and Crocodile

1967. Europafrique.
155 **62** 45 f. multicoloured 70 25

1967. 50th Anniv of Lions International.
156 **63** 90 f. multicoloured 95 55

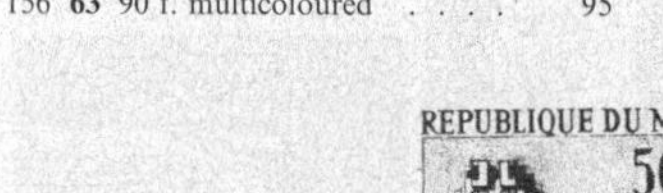

64 "Water Resources" 65 Block of Flats, Grenoble

1967. International Hydrological Decade.
157 **64** 25 f. black, blue and bistre . . 30 20

1967. Air. Toulouse-Lautrec Commemoration. Paintings as T **58**. Multicoloured.
158 100 f. "Gazelle" (horse's head) (horiz) . . . . 2·00 1·10
159 300 f. "Gig drawn by Cob" (vert) 4·75 2·25

1968. Air. Winter Olympic Games, Grenoble.
160 **65** 50 f. brown, green and blue . 70 35
161 – 150 f. brown, blue and ultramarine . . . . . . 1·60 65
DESIGN: 150 f. Bob-sleigh course, Huez mountain.

66 W.H.O. Emblem

1968. 20th Anniv of W.H.O.
162 **66** 90 f. blue, lake and green . . 70 30

67 Human Figures and Entwined Hearts

1968. World "Twin Towns" Day.
163 **67** 50 f. red, violet and green . . 40 15

1968. Air. Flower Paintings. As T **58**. Mult.
164 50 f. "Roses and Anemones" (Van Gogh) 50 25
165 150 f. "Vase of Flowers" (Manet) 1·50 55
166 300 f. "Bouquet of Flowers" (Delacroix) . . . . 3·00 1·10
167 500 f. "Marguerites" (Millet) 4·50 2·00
SIZES: 50 f., 300 f. 40×41½ mm; 150 f. 36×47½ mm; 500 f. 50×36 mm.

68 Dr. Martin Luther King 69 "Draisienne" Bicycle, 1809

1968. Air. Martin Luther King Commemoration.
168 **68** 100 f. black, pink & purple . 85 35

1968. Veteran Bicycles and Motor Cars.
169 **69** 2 f. brown, mauve and green (postage) 20 15
170 – 5 f. red, blue and bistre . . 30 20
171 – 10 f. blue, brown and green . 50 25
172 – 45 f. black, green & brown . 80 40
173 – 50 f. red, green & brn (air) . 1·00 25
174 – 100 f. blue, mauve & bistre . 2·00 60
DESIGNS—HORIZ: 5 f. De Dion-Bouton, 1894; 45 f. Panhard-Levassor, 1914; 100 f. Mercedes-Benz, 1927. VERT: 10 f. Michaux Bicycle, 1861; 50 f. "Bicyclette, 1918".

70 Books, Graph and A.D.B.A. Emblem

1968. 10th Anniv of International African Libraries and Archives Development Association.
175 **70** 100 f. red, black and brown . 65 30

71 Football

1968. Air. Olympic Games, Mexico. Multicoloured.
176 100 f. Type **71** 75 40
177 150 f. Long-jumping (vert) . . 1·25 60

1968. Air. "Philexafrique" Stamp Exhibition, Abidjan, Ivory Coast, 1969 (1st issue). As T **113a** of Mauritania. Multicoloured.
178 200 f. "The Editors" (F. M. Granet) . . . . 2·00 1·50

1969. Air. "Philexafrique" Stamp Exn., Abidjan, Ivory Coast (2nd issue). As T **114a** of Mauritania.
179 100 f. purple, red and violet . 1·25 1·25
DESIGN: 100 f. Carved animal and French Sudan stamp of 1931.

1969. Air. Birth Bicentenary of Napoleon Bonaparte. Multicoloured. As T **114b** of Mauritania.
180 150 f. "Napoleon Bonaparte, First Consul" (Gros) . . . 2·25 1·25
181 200 f. "The Bivouac–Battle of Austerlitz" (Lejeune) (horiz) 4·00 1·75

73 Montgolfier Balloon

1969. Air. Aviation History. Multicoloured.
182 50 f. Type **73** 50 20
183 150 f. Ferdinand Ferber's Glider No. 5 . . . . 1·50 40
184 300 f. Concorde . . . . . . 3·00 1·40

74 African Tourist Emblem

1969. African Tourist Year.
185 **74** 50 f. red, green and blue . . 25 20

75 "O.I.T." and I.L.O. Emblem

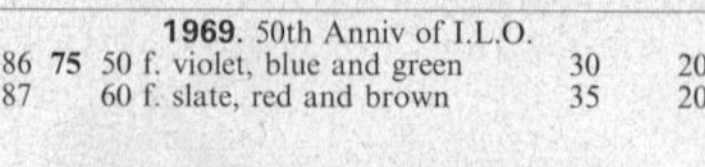

1969. 50th Anniv of I.L.O.
186 **75** 50 f. violet, blue and green . 30 20
187 60 f. slate, red and brown . . 35 20

76 Panhard of 1897 and Model "24-CT"

1969. French Motor Industry.
188 **76** 25 f. lake, black and bistre (postage) 50 20
189 – 30 f. green and black . . . 60 20
190 – 55 f. red, black and purple (air) . . . . 1·00 35
191 – 90 f. blue, black and red . . 1·40 45
DESIGNS: 30 f. Citroen of 1923 and Model "DS-21"; 55 f. Renault of 1898 and Model "16"; 90 f. Peugeot of 1893 and Model "404".

77 Clarke (Australia), 10,000 metres (1965)

1969. Air. World Athletics Records.
192 **77** 60 f. brown and blue . . . 30 25
193 – 90 f. brown and red 45 25
194 – 120 f. brown and green . . 55 35
195 – 140 f. brown and slate . . . 70 35
196 – 150 f. black and red 85 50
DESIGNS: 90 f. Lusis (Russia), Javelin (1968); 120 f. Miyake (Japan), Weightlifting (1967); 140 f. Matson (U.S.A.), Shot-putting (1968); 150 f. Keino (Kenya), 3,000 metres (1965).

78 Hollow Blocks

1969. International Toy Fair, Nuremberg.
197 **78** 5 f. red, yellow and grey . . 15 10
198 – 10 f. multicoloured 15 10
199 – 15 f. green, red and pink . . 20 10
200 – 20 f. orange, blue and red . 25 15
DESIGNS: 10 f. Toy donkey on wheels; 15 f. "Ducks"; 20 f. Model car and race-track.

79 "Apollo 8", Earth and Moon

1969. Air. Moon Flight of "Apollo 8".
201 **79** 2,000 f. gold . . . . 14·00 14·00
This stamp is embossed on gold foil.

1969. Air. 1st Man on the Moon. Nos. 182/4 optd **L'HOMME SUR LA LUNE JUILLET 1969** and Apollo 11.
202 50 f. multicoloured 95 65
203 150 f. multicoloured . . . . . 2·00 1·25
204 300 f. multicoloured . . . . . 3·25 2·50

81 Sheep

1969. Domestic Animals.
205 **81** 1 f. olive, brown and green . 10 10
206 – 2 f. brown, grey and red . . 10 10
207 – 10 f. olive, brown and blue . 20 10
208 – 35 f. slate and red 60 30
209 – 90 f. brown and blue . . . 1·25 55
ANIMALS: 2 f. Goat; 10 f. Donkey; 35 f. Horse; 90 f. Dromedary.

1969. 5th Anniv of African Development Bank. As T **122a** of Mauritania.
210 50 f. brown, green and purple 25 20
211 90 f. orange, green and brown 45 20

83 "Mona Lisa" (Leonardo da Vinci)

1969. Air. 450th Death Anniv of Leonardo da Vinci.
212 **83** 500 f. multicoloured . . . 4·00 3·25

84 Vaccination 85 Mahatma Gandhi

1969. Campaign against Smallpox and Measles.
213 **84** 50 f. slate, brown & green . . 40 15

1969. Air. Birth Centenary of Mahatma Gandhi.
214 **85** 150 f. brown and green . . 1·60 55

1969. 10th Anniv of Aerial Navigation Security Agency for Africa and Madagascar (A.S.E.C.N.A.). As T **94a** of Niger.
215 100 f. green 60 25

87 West African Map and Posthorns

1970. Air. 11th Anniv of West African Postal Union (C.A.P.T.E.A.O.).
216 **87** 100 f. multicoloured . . . 60 35

1970. Air. Religious Paintings. As T **83**. Mult.
217 100 f. "Virgin and Child" (Van der Weydan School) 70 40
218 150 f. "The Nativity" (The Master of Flamalle) . . . . 1·10 65
219 250 f. "Virgin, Child and St. John the Baptist" (Low Countries School) . . . . 2·40 1·40

89 Franklin D. Roosevelt 91 Lenin

90 Women of Mali and Japan

1970. Air. 25th Death Anniv of Franklin D. Roosevelt.
220 **89** 500 f. black, red and blue . 3·50 2·00

1970. "EXPO 70" World Fair, Osaka, Japan.
221 **90** 100 f. orange, brown & blue . 60 20
222 – 150 f. red, green & yellow . 80 30
DESIGN: 150 f. Flags and maps of Mali and Japan.

1970. Air. Birth Centenary of Lenin.
223 **91** 300 f. black, green & flesh . 2·25 1·00

92 Verne and Moon Rockets

1970. Air. Jules Verne "Prophet of Space Travel". Multicoloured.
224 50 f. Type **92** 60 25
225 150 f. Moon orbit . . . . . . 1·50 50
226 300 f. Splashdown . . . . . . 2·25 1·10

93 I.T.U. Emblem and Map

1970. World Telecommunications Day.
227 **93** 90 f. red, brown and sepia 60 25

1970. New U.P.U. Headquarters Building, Berne. As Type **81** of New Caledonia.
228 50 f. brown, green and red . . 30 20
229 60 f. brown, blue and mauve 40 20

1970. Air. Space Flight of "Apollo 13". Nos. 224/6 optd **APOLLO XIII EPOPEE SPATIALE 11-17 AVRIL 1970** in three lines.
230 50 f. multicoloured 40 25
231 150 f. multicoloured . . . . . 1·10 45
232 300 f. multicoloured . . . . . 2·00 1·25

96 "Intelstat 3" Satellite

1970. Air. Space Telecommunications.
233 **96** 100 f. indigo, blue & orange 60 35
234 – 200 f. purple, grey and blue 1·25 50
235 – 300 f. brown, orge & slate 2·25 1·10
236 – 500 f. brown, blue & indigo 3·50 1·60
DESIGNS: 200 f. "Molnya I" satellite; 300 f. Dish aerial, Type PB **2**; 500 f. "Symphony Project" satellite.

97 Auguste and Louis Lumiere, Jean Harlow and Marilyn Monroe

1970. Air. Lumiere Brothers (inventors of the cine camera). Commemoration.
237 **97** 250 f. multicoloured . . . 2·50 1·25

98 Footballers

1970. Air. World Cup Football Championships, Mexico.
238 **98** 80 f. green, brown and red 50 25
239 200 f. red, brown and blue 1·25 55

99 Rotary Emblem, Map and Antelope
100 "Supporting United Nations"

1970. Air. Rotary International.
240 **99** 200 f. multicoloured . . . 1·75 60

1970. Air. 25th Anniv of U.N.O.
241 **100** 100 f. blue, brown & violet 70 35

101 Page from 11th century Baghdad Koran

1970. Air. Ancient Muslim Art. Multicoloured.
242 50 f. Type **101** 50 25
243 200 f. "Tree and wild Animals" (Jordanian mosaic, c.730) . 1·25 55
244 250 f. "The Scribe" (Baghdad miniature, 1287) . . . . . 2·00 90

1970. Air. Moon Landing of "Luna 16". Nos. 234/5 surch **LUNA 16 PREMIERS PRELEVEMENTS AUTOMATIQUES SUR LA LUNE SEPTEMBRE 1970** and new values.
245 150 f. on 200 f. purple, grey and blue . . . . 1·00 40
246 250 f. on 300 f. brown, orange and grey . . . . 1·50 60

103 G.P.O., Bamako

1970. Public Buildings.
247 **103** 30 f. olive, green & brown 20 20
248 – 40 f. purple, brown & grn 30 20
249 – 60 f. grey, green and red 40 20
250 – 80 f. brown, green and grey 50 25
BUILDINGS: 40 f. Chamber of Commerce, Bamako; 60 f. Ministry of Public Works, Bamako; 80 f. Town Hall, Segou.

104 Pres. Nasser
106 Gallet "0-30-T" Locomotive

105 "The Nativity" (Antwerp School 1530)

1970. Air. Pres. Gamal Nasser of Egypt. Commemoration.
251 **104** 1000 f. gold . . . . . . 7·50 7·50

1970. Air. Christmas. Paintings. Multicoloured.
252 100 f. Type **105** 70 40
253 250 f. "Adoration of the Shepherds" (Memling) . . 1·60 95
254 300 f. "Adoration of the Magi" (17th century Flemish school) 2·25 1·25

1970. Mali Railway Locomotives from the Steam Era (1st series).
255 **106** 20 f. black, red and green 1·40 1·25
256 – 40 f. black, green & brown 1·75 1·60
257 – 50 f. black, green & brown 2·10 1·90
258 – 80 f. black, red and green 3·00 2·75
259 – 100 f. black, green & brn 3·50 3·25
LOCOMOTIVES: 40 f. Felou "0-3-0T"; 50 f. Bechevel "2-3-0T"; 80 f. "231"; 100 f. Type "**411**".
See also Nos. 367/70.

107 Scouts crossing Log-bridge
108 Bambara de San Mask

1970. Scouting in Mali. Multicoloured.
260 5 f. Type **107** 20 15
261 30 f. Bugler and scout camp (vert) 35 15
262 100 f. Scouts canoeing 90 35

1971. Mali Masks and Ideograms. Multicoloured.
263 29 f. Type **108** 15 10
264 25 f. Dogon de Bandiagara mask 20 10
265 59 f. Kanaga ideogram 45 15
266 89 f. Bambara ideogram . . . 60 25

109 General De Gaulle

1971. Air. Charles De Gaulle Commem. Die-stamped on gold foil.
267 **109** 2000 f. gold, red and blue 30·00 30·00

110 Alfred Nobel
111 Tennis Player (Davis Cup)

1971. Air. 75th Death Anniv of Alfred Nobel (philanthropist).
268 **110** 300 f. red, brown & green 2·25 1·25

1971. Air. World Sporting Events.
269 **111** 100 f. slate, purple & blue 75 25
270 – 150 f. olive, brown & grn 1·40 40
271 – 200 f. brown, olive & blue 2·00 60
DESIGNS—HORIZ: 150 f. Steeplechase (inscr "Derby at Epsom" but probably represents the Grand National). VERT: 200 f. Yacht (America Cup).

112 Youth, Sun and Microscope

1971. 50th Anniv of 1st B.C.G. Vaccine Innoculation.
272 **112** 100 f. brown, green & red 85 40

113 "The Thousand and One Nights"

1971. Air. "Tales of the Arabian Nights". Mult.
273 120 f. Type **113** 70 30
274 180 f. "Ali Baba and the Forty Thieves" . . . . 1·00 40
275 200 f. "Aladdin's Lamp" . . . 1·40 50

114 Scouts, Japanese Horseman and Mt. Fuji

1971. 13th World Scout Jamboree, Asagiri, Japan.
276 **114** 80 f. plum, green and blue 60 20

115 Rose between Hands
116 Rural Costume

1971. 25th Anniv of U.N.I.C.E.F.
277 **115** 50 f. brown, red and orge 30 20
278 – 60 f. blue, green & brown 40 20
DESIGN—VERT: 60 f. Nurses and children.

1971. National Costumes. Multicoloured.
279 5 f. Type **116** 15 10
280 10 f. Rural costume (female) 20 15
281 15 f. Tuareg 20 15
282 60 f. Embroidered "boubou" 45 20
283 80 f. Women's ceremonial costume 60 25

117 Olympic Rings and Events

1971. Air. Olympic Games Publicity.
284 **117** 80 f. blue, purple & green 40 20

118 Telecommunications Map

1971. Pan-African Telecommunications Network Year.
285 **118** 50 f. multicoloured . . . 25 20

119 "Mariner 4" and Mars

1971. Air. Exploration of Outer Space.
286 **119** 200 f. green, blue & brown 1·25 50
287 – 300 f. blue, plum & purple 1·75 60
DESIGN: 300 f. "Venera 5" and Venus.

120 "Santa Maria" (1492)

1971. Air. Famous Ships.
288 **120** 100 f. brown, violet & blue 70 35
289 – 150 f. violet, brown & grn 1·25 45
290 – 200 f. green, blue and red 1·60 75
291 – 250 f. red, blue and black 2·25 90
DESIGNS: 150 f. "Mayflower" (1620); 200 f. Battleship "Potemkin" (1905); 250 f. Liner "Normandie" (1935).

121 "Hibiscus rose-sinensis"

1971. Flowers. Multicoloured.

292 20 f. Type **121** 20 10
293 50 f. "Euphorbia pulcherrima" 45 15
294 60 f. "Adenium obesum" . . . 70 20
295 80 f. "Allamanda cathartica" 1·00 25
296 100 f. "Satanocrater berhautii" 1·25 35

122 Allegory of Justice

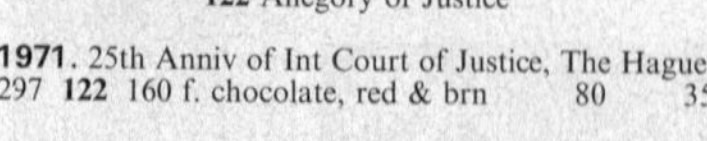

1971. 25th Anniv of Int Court of Justice, The Hague.

297 **122** 160 f. chocolate, red & brn 80 35

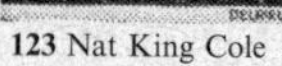

123 Nat King Cole

124 Statue of Olympic Zeus (by Phidias)

1971. Air. Famous Negro Musicians. Multicoloured.

298 130 f. Type **123** . . . . 1·25 25
299 150 f. Erroll Garner . . . . 1·25 30
300 270 f. Louis Armstrong . . . 1·75 45

1971. Air. "The Seven Wonders of the Ancient World".

301 **124** 70 f. blue, brown & purple 35 20
302 – 80 f. black, brown & blue 40 20
303 – 100 f. blue, red and violet 50 25
304 – 130 f. black, purple & blue 75 30
305 – 150 f. brown, green & bl 1·10 35
306 – 270 f. blue, brown & pur 1·60 75
307 – 280 f. blue, purple & brn 2·00 85

DESIGNS—VERT: 80 f. Pyramid of Cheops, Egypt; 130 f. Pharos of Alexandria; 270 f. Mausoleum of Halicarnassos; 280 f. Colossus of Rhodes. HORIZ: 100 f. Temple of Artemis, Ephesus; 150 f. Hanging Gardens of Babylon.

125 "Family Life" (carving)

1971. 15th Anniv of Social Security Service.

308 **125** 70 f. brown, green and red 40 20

126 Slalom-skiing and Japanese Girl

128 Hands clasping Flagpole

127 "Santa Maria della Salute" (Caffi)

1972. Air. Winter Olympic Games, Sapporo, Japan.

309 **126** 150 f. brown, green & orge 1·00 35
310 – 200 f. green, brown & red 1·50 55

DESIGN: 200 f. Ice-hockey and Japanese actor.

1972. Air. U.N.E.S.C.O. "Save Venice" Campaign. Multicoloured.

312 130 f. Type **127** 70 35
313 270 f. "Rialto Bridge" . . . . 1·40 60
314 280 f. "St. Mark's Square" (vert) 1·60 70

1972. Air. Int Scout Seminar, Cotonou, Dahomey.

315 **128** 200 f. green, orange & brn 1·40 55

129 Heart and Red Cross Emblems

1972. Air. World Heart Month.

316 **129** 150 f. red and blue . . . 1·00 40

130 Football

1972. Air. Olympic Games, Munich (1st issue). Sports and Munich Buildings.

317 **130** 50 f. blue, brown & green 25 20
318 – 150 f. blue, brown & green 70 30
319 – 200 f. blue, brown & green 80 50
320 – 300 f. blue, brown & green 1·25 70

DESIGNS—VERT: 150 f. Judo; 200 f. Hurdling. HORIZ: 300 f. Running.

See also Nos. 357/62.

131 "Apollo 15" and Lunar Rover

1972. Air. History of Transport Development.

322 **131** 150 f. red, green and lake 80 40
323 – 250 f. red, blue and green 2·00 1·00

DESIGN: 250 f. Montgolfier's balloon and Cugnot's steam car.

132 "UIT" on T.V. Screen

1972. World Telecommunications Day.

324 **132** 70 f. black, blue and red 40 20

133 Clay Funerary Statue

134 Samuel Morse and Early Telegraph

1972. Mali Archaeology. Multicoloured.

325 30 f. Type **133** 20 15
326 40 f. Female Figure (wood-carving) 30 20
327 50 f. "Warrior" (stone-painting) 40 20
328 100 f. Wrought-iron ritual figures 1·00 35

1972. Death Centenary of Samuel Morse (inventor of telegraph).

329 **134** 80 f. purple, green and red 45 20

135 "Cinderella"

136 Weather Balloon

1972. Air. Charles Perrault's Fairy Tales.

330 **135** 70 f. green, red and brown 45 20
331 – 80 f. brown, red and green 50 25
332 – 150 f. violet, purple & blue 1·10 35

DESIGNS: 80 f. "Puss in Boots"; 150 f. "The Sleeping Beauty".

1972. World Meteorological Day.

333 **136** 130 f. multicoloured . . . 60 30

137 Astronauts and Lunar Rover

1972. Air. Moon Flight of "Apollo 16".

334 **137** 500 f. brown, violet & grn 3·00 1·25

138 Book Year Emblem

1972. Air. International Book Year.

335 **138** 80 f. gold, green and blue 40 25

139 Sarakole Dance, Kayes

140 Learning the Alphabet

1972. Traditional Dances. Multicoloured.

336 10 f. Type **139** 25 15
337 20 f. Malinke dance, Bamako 30 15
338 50 f. Hunter's dance, Bougouni 45 20
339 70 f. Bambara dance, Segou . 60 20
340 80 f. Dogon dance, Sanga . 70 30
341 120 f. Targuie dance, Timbukto 1·25 45

1972. International Literacy Day.

342 **140** 80 f. black and green . . . 40 15

141 Statue and Musical Instruments

142 Club Banner

1972. 1st Anthology of Malinenne Music.

343 **141** 100 f. multicoloured . . . 70 30

1972. Air. 10th Anniv of Bamako Rotary Club.

344 **142** 170 f. purple, blue and red 1·00 40

143 Aries the Ram

1972. Signs of the Zodiac.

345 **143** 15 f. brown and purple 25 20
346 – 15 f. black and brown . . 25 20
347 – 35 f. blue and red 40 25
348 – 35 f. red and green 40 25
349 – 40 f. brown and blue . . . 50 30
350 – 40 f. brown and purple . . 50 30
351 – 45 f. red and blue 60 35
352 – 45 f. green and red 60 35
353 – 65 f. blue and violet . . . 90 35
354 – 65 f. brown and violet . . 90 35
355 – 90 f. blue and mauve . . 1·40 65
356 – 90 f. green and mauve . . 1·40 65

DESIGNS: No. 346, Taurus the Bull; No. 347, Gemini the Twins; No. 348, Cancer the Crab; No. 349, Leo the Lion; No. 350, Virgo the Virgin; No. 351, Libra the Scales; No. 352, Scorpio the Scorpion; No. 353, Sagittarius the Archer; No. 354, Capricornus the Goat; No. 355, Aquarius the Water-carrier; No. 356, Pisces the Fish.

1972. Air. Olympic Games, Munich (2nd issue). Sports and Locations of Games since 1952. As Type **130**.

357 70 f. blue, brown and red . . . 25 15
358 90 f. green, red and blue . . . 35 20
359 140 f. olive, green and brown 60 20
360 150 f. brown, green and red . 65 25
361 170 f. blue, brown and purple 75 30
362 210 f. blue, red and green . . 90 40

DESIGNS—VERT: 70 f. Boxing, Helsinki Games (1952); 150 f. Weightlifting, Tokyo Games (1964). HORIZ: 90 f. Hurdling, Melbourne Games (1956); 140 f. 200 metres, Rome Games (1960); 170 f. Swimming, Mexico Games (1968); 210 f. Throwing the javelin, Munich Games (1972).

1972. Medal Winners, Munich Olympic Games. Nos. 318/20 and 362 optd with events and names, etc.

363 150 f. blue, brown and green 70 30
364 200 f. blue, brown and green 90 40
365 210 f. blue, red and green . . 90 40
366 300 f. blue, brown and green 1·25 70

OVERPRINTS: 150 f. **JUDO RUSKA 2 MEDAILLES D'OR**; 200 f. **STEEPLE KEINO MEDAILLE D'OR**; 210 f. **MEDAILLE D'OR 90 m. 48**; 300 f. **100 m.-200m BORZOV 2 MEDAILLES D'OR**

1972. Mali Locomotives (2nd series). As T **106**.

367 10 f. blue, green and red . . . 1·25 1·00
368 30 f. blue, green and brown 2·50 2·25
369 60 f. blue, brown and green 3·00 2·75
370 120 f. purple, green and black 5·00 4·50

LOCOMOTIVES: 10 f. First Locomotive to arrive at Bamako, 1906; 30 f. Locomotive from the Thies–Bamako line, 1920; 60 f. Type "141" locomotive, Thies–Bamako line, 1927;. 120 f. Alsthom "BB" coupled diesels, Dakar–Bamako line, 1947.

146 Emperor Haile Selassie

1972. Air. 80th Birth Anniv of Emperor Haile Selassie.

371 **146** 70 f. multicoloured . . . 30 20

147 Balloon, Breguet 14T Biplane and Map

1972. Air. First Mali Airmail Flight by Balloon, Bamako to Timbuktu. Multicoloured.

372 200 f. Type **147** . . . . 1·00 45
373 300 f. Balloon, Concorde and map . . . . 1·40 60

148 High Jumping

1973. 2nd African Games, Lagos, Nigeria. Mult.

374 70 f. Type **148** 30 20
375 270 f. Throwing the discus . . 1·25 60
376 280 f. Football . . . . 1·40 65

149 14th-century German Bishop

150 Interpol Headquarters, Paris

1973. Air. World Chess Championship, Reykjavik, Iceland.

377 **149** 100 f. lt blue, blue & brn 1·25 35
378 – 200 f. red, lt red & black 2·50 75

DESIGN: 200 f. 18th-century Indian knight (elephant).

1973. 50th Anniv of International Criminal Police Organization (Interpol).

379 **150** 80 f. multicoloured . . . 65 20

151 Emblem and Dove with letter

152 "Fauna Protection" Stamp of 1963

1973. 10th Anniv (1971) of African Postal Union.
380 **151** 70 f. multicoloured . . . 35 20

1973. Air. Stamp Day.
381 **152** 70 f. orange, red & brown 1·25 30

153 Astronauts on Moon

155 Handicapped Africans

154 Copernicus

1973. Moon Mission of "Apollo" 17.
382 **153** 250 f. brown and blue . . 1·60 65

1973. 500th Birth Anniv of Copernicus.
384 **154** 300 f. purple and blue . . 2·00 1·10

1973. "Help the Handicapped".
385 **155** 70 f. orange, black and red 35 20

156 Dr. G. A. Hansen

1973. Centenary of Hansen's Identification of the Leprosy Bacillus.
386 **156** 200 f. green, black and red 1·60 60

157 Bentley and Alfa Romeo, 1930

1973. 50th Anniv of Le Mans 24 hour Endurance Race.
387 **157** 50 f. green, orange & blue 35 15
388 – 100 f. green, blue and red 75 25
389 – 200 f. blue, green and red 1·75 50
DESIGNS: 100 f. Jaguar and Talbot, 1953; 200 f. Matra and Porsche, 1952.

158 Scouts around Campfire

1973. International Scouting Congress, Addis Ababa and Nairobi.
390 **158** 50 f. brown, red and blue 30 15
391 – 70 f. brown, red and blue 40 20
392 – 80 f. red, brown and green 50 20
393 – 130 f. green, blue & brown 70 30
394 – 270 f. red, violet and grey 1·40 60
DESIGNS—VERT: 70 f. Scouts saluting flag; 130 f. Lord Baden-Powell. HORIZ: 80 f. Standard-bearers; 270 f. Map of Africa and Scouts and Guides in ring.

159 Swimming and National Flags

1973. 1st Afro-American Sports Meeting, Bamako.
395 **159** 70 f. green, red and blue 30 20
396 – 80 f. green, red and blue 35 25
397 – 330 f. blue and red . . . 1·50 70
DESIGNS—VERT: 80 f. Throwing the discus and javelin. HORIZ: 330 f. Running.

1973. Pan-African Drought Relief. No. 296 surch **SECHERESSE SOLIDARITE AFRICAINE** and value.
398 200 f. on 100 f. multicoloured 1·10 65

1973. Air. African Fortnight, Brussels. As T **168a** of Niger.
399 70 f. violet, blue and brown 30 20

162 "Perseus" (Cellini)

164 "Apollo 11" First Landing

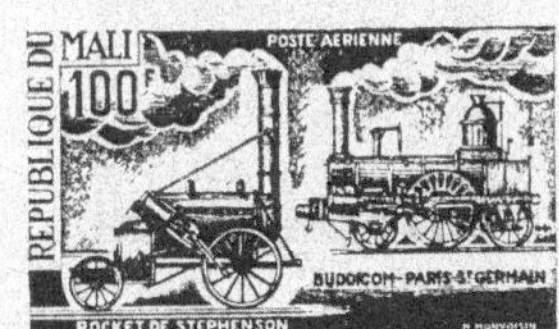

163 Stephenson's "Rocket" and French "Buddicom" Locomotive

1973. Air. Famous Sculptures.
400 **162** 100 f. green and red . . . 55 25
401 – 150 f. purple and red . . 85 35
402 – 250 f. green and red . . . 1·50 65
DESIGNS: 150 f. "Pieta" (Michelangelo); 250 f. "Victory of Samothrace".

1973. Air. Famous Locomotives.
403 **163** 100 f. black, blue & brown 1·25 60
404 – 150 f. multicoloured . . . 1·60 65
405 – 200 f. blue, slate and brown 2·50 1·00
DESIGNS: 150 f. Union Pacific and Santa Fe Railroad locomotives; 200 f. "Mistral" and "Tokaido" trains.

1973. Conquest of the Moon.
406 **164** 50 f. purple, red & brown 25 20
407 – 75 f. grey, blue and red . 30 20
408 – 100 f. slate, brown and blue 55 30
409 – 280 f. blue, green and red 1·25 65
410 – 300 f. blue, red and green 1·50 80
DESIGNS: 75 f. "Apollo 13" Recovery capsule; 100 f. "Apollo 14" Lunar trolley; 280 f. "Apollo 15" Lunar rover; 300 f. "Apollo 17" lift off from Moon.

165 Picasso

166 Pres. John Kennedy

1973. Air. Pablo Picasso (artist). Commem.
411 **165** 500 f. multicoloured . . . 2·75 1·25

1973. Air. 10th Death Anniv of Pres. Kennedy.
412 **166** 500 f. black, purple & gold 2·50 1·25

1973. Air. Christmas. As T **105** but dated "1973". Multicoloured.
413 100 f. "The Annunciation" (V. Carpaccio) (horiz) 50 25
414 200 f. "Virgin of St. Simon" (F. Baroccio) . . . . 1·25 50
415 250 f. "Flight into Egypt" (A. Solario) . . . . 1·60 70

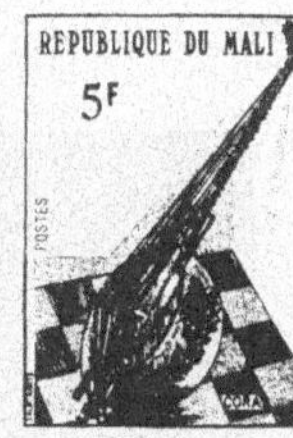

167 Player and Football

168 Cora

1973. Air. World Football Cup Championships, West Germany.
416 **167** 150 f. red, brown & green 75 35
417 – 250 f. green, brown & violet 1·50 60
DESIGN: 250 f. Goalkeeper and ball.

1973. Musical Instruments.
419 **168** 5 f. brown, red and green 20 10
420 – 10 f. brown and blue . . . 20 10
421 – 15 f. brown, red & yellow 25 15
422 – 20 f. brown and red . . . 30 15
423 – 25 f. brown, red & yellow 35 15
424 – 30 f. black and blue . . . 50 20
425 – 35 f. sepia, brown and red 60 20
426 – 40 f. brown and red . . . 65 30
DESIGNS—HORIZ: 10 f. Balafon. VERT: 15 f. Djembe; 20 f. Guitar; 25 f. N'Djarka; 30 f. M'Bolon; 35 f. Dozo N'Goni; 40 f. N'Tamani.

169 "Musicians" (mosaic)

1974. Roman Frescoes and Mosaics from Pompeii.
427 **169** 150 f. red, brown and grey 75 35
428 – 250 f. brown, red & orange 1·25 60
429 – 350 f. brown, orange and olive . . . . 1·75 75
DESIGNS—VERT: 250 f. "Alexander the Great" (mosaic); 350 f. "Bacchante" (fresco).

170 Corncob, Worker and "Kibaru" Newspaper

171 Sir Winston Churchill

1974. 2nd Anniv of Rural Press.
430 **170** 70 f. brown and green . . 35 20

1974. Air. Birth Cent of Sir Winston Churchill.
431 **171** 500 f. black . . . . 2·50 1·50

172 Chess-pieces on Board

1974. Air. 21st Chess Olympiad, Nice.
432 **172** 250 f. indigo, red and blue 2·50 75

173 "The Crucifixion" (Alsace School c. 1380)

1974. Air. Easter. Multicoloured.
433 400 f. Type **173** . . . . . . 1·60 1·00
434 500 f. "The Entombment" (Titian) (horiz) . . . . . . 2·25 1·25

174 Lenin

1974. Air. 50th Death Anniv of Lenin.
435 **174** 150 f. purple and violet . 70 30

175 Goalkeeper and Globe

177 Full-rigged Sailing Ship and Modern Liner

176 Horse-jumping Scenes

1974. World Cup Football Championships, West Germany.
436 **175** 270 f. red, green and lilac 1·25 80
437 – 280 f. blue, brown and red 1·60 80
DESIGN: 280 f. World Cup emblem on football.

1974. Air. World Equestrian Championships, La Baule.
438 **176** 130 f. brown, lilac and blue 1·50 60

1974. Centenary of Universal Postal Union.
439 **177** 80 f. purple, lilac & brown 55 25
440 – 90 f. orange, grey and& blue 40 30
441 – 270 f. purple, olive & grn 2·00 90
DESIGNS: 90 f. Breguet 14T biplane and Douglas DC-8; 270 f. Early steam and modern electric trains.
See also Nos. 463/4.

178 "Skylab" over Africa

1974. Air. Survey of Africa by "Skylab" Space Station.
442 **178** 200 f. indigo, blue & orge 1·00 40
443 – 250 f. blue, purple & orge 1·25 60
DESIGN: 250 f. Astronaut servicing cameras.

1974. Air. 11th Arab Scout Jamboree, Lebanon. Nos. 391/2 surch **130 f. 11e JAMBOREE ARABE AOUT 1974 LIBAN** or **170 f. CONGRES PAN-ARABE LIBAN AOUT 1974**.
444 130 f. on 70 f. brown, red & bl 70 40
445 170 f. on 80 f. blue, grn & red 75 50

1974. Air. 5th Anniv of First landing on Moon. Nos. 408/9 surch **130 f. 1er DEBARQUEMENT SUR LA LUNE 20-VII-69** or **300 f. 1er PAS SUR LA LUNE 21-VII-69**.
446 130 f. on 100 f. slate, brown and blue 70 45
447 300 f. on 280 f. blue, grn & red 1·40 70

1974. West Germany's Victory in World Cup Football Championships. Nos. 436/7 surch **R.F.A. 2 HOLLANDE 1** and value.
448 **175** 300 f. on 270 f. red, green and lilac . . . . 1·40 80
449 – 330 f. on 280 f. blue, brown and red . . . . 1·60 80

182 Weaver

183 River Niger near Gao

1974. Crafts and Craftsmen. Multicoloured.
450 50 f. Type **182** 25 15
451 60 f. Potter 30 15
452 70 f. Smith 40 20
453 80 f. Wood-carver 55 20

1974. Mali Views. Multicoloured.
454 10 f. Type **183** 15 10
455 20 f. "The Hand of Fatma" (rock formation, Hombori) (vert) 15 10
456 40 f. Waterfall, Gouina . . . 35 15
457 70 f. Hill-dwellings, Dogon (vert) 60 20

184 "C3-PLM" (1906) and "150-P" (1939) Locomotives

1974. Air. Steam Locomotives.
458 **184** 90 f. indigo, red and blue 75 40
459 – 120 f. brown, orange & bl 85 50
460 – 210 f. brown, orange & bl 1·60 70
461 – 330 f. black, green & blue 2·40 1·40
DESIGNS: 120 f. Baldwin "2-2-0" (1870) and Pacific (1920) locomotives; 210 f. "241-A1" (1925) and Buddicom (1847) locomotives; 330 f. Hudson (1938) and "La Gironde" (1839) locomotives.

185 Skiing

1974. Air. 50th Anniv of Winter Olympics.
462 **185** 300 f. red, blue and green 1·40 80

1974. Berne Postal Convention. Cent. Nos. 439 and 441 surch **9 OCTOBRE 1974** and value.
463 **177** 250 f. on 80 f. purple, lilac and brown . . . . . . 1·40 80
464 – 300 f. on 270 f. purple, olive and green . . . . . . 1·90 80

187 Mao Tse-tung and Great Wall of China
188 "The Nativity" (Memling)

1974. 25th Anniv of Chinese People's Republic.
465 **187** 100 f. blue, red and green 50 30

1974. Air. Christmas. Multicoloured.
466 290 f. Type **188** . . . . 1·25 70
467 310 f. "Virgin and Child" (Bourgogne School) . . . . 1·50 75
468 400 f. "Adoration of the Magi" (Schongauer) . . . . 1·90 1·10

189 Raoul Follereau (missionary)
191 Dr. Schweitzer

190 Electric Train and Boeing 707

1974. Air. Raoul Follereau, "Apostle of the Lepers".
469 **189** 200 f. blue . . . . 1·25 55
469a 200 f. brown . . . . . . 1·75 1·10

1974. Air. Europafrique.
470 **190** 100 f. green, brown & bl 1·75 65
471 110 f. blue, violet & brn 1·75 65

1975. Birth Centenary of Dr Albert Schweitzer.
472 **191** 150 f. turquoise, grn & blue 90 40

192 Patients making Handicrafts and Lions International Emblem

1975. 5th Anniv of Samanko (Leprosy rehabilitation village). Multicoloured.
473 90 f. Type **192** 50 20
474 100 f. View of Samanko . . . 60 25

193 "The Pilgrims at Emmaus" (Champaigne)

1975. Air. Easter. Multicoloured.
475 200 f. Type **193** 90 45
476 300 f. "The Pilgrims at Emmaus" (Veronese) . . . . 1·25 60
477 500 f. "Christ in Majesty" (Limoges enamel) (vert) . . 2·25 1·25

194 "Journey to the Centre of the Earth"

1975. Air. 70th Death Anniv of Jules Verne.
478 **194** 100 f. green, blue & brn 45 25
479 – 170 f. brown, bl & lt brn 75 35
480 – 190 f. blue, turquoise & brn 1·25 55
481 – 220 f. brown, purple & bl 1·50 60
DESIGNS: 170 f. Jules Verne and "From the Earth to the Moon"; 190 f. Giant octopus–"Twenty Thousand Leagues Under the Sea"; 220 f. "A Floating City".

195 Head of "Dawn" (Tomb of the Medici)
197 Astronaut

196 "Tetrodon fahaka"

1975. Air. 500th Birth Anniv of Michelangelo (artist). Multicoloured.
482 400 f. Type **195** . . . . 1·75 1·10
483 500 f. "Moses" (marble statue, Rome) . . . . 2·25 1·25

1975. Fishes (1st series).
484 **196** 60 f. brown, yellow & grn 50 20
485 – 70 f. black, brown & grey 55 25
486 – 80 f. multicoloured . . . 70 25
487 – 90 f. blue, grey and green 1·00 35
488 – 110 f. black and blue . . 1·25 45
DESIGNS: 70 f. "Malopterurus electricus"; 80 f. "Citharinus latus"; 90 f. "Hydrocyon forskali"; 110 f. "Lates niloticus".
See also Nos. 544/8.

1975. Air. Soviet–U.S. Space Co-operation.
489 **197** 290 f. red, blue and black 1·10 50
490 – 300 f. red, blue and black 1·10 60
491 – 370 f. green, purple & blk 1·40 80
DESIGNS: 300 f. "America and Russia"; 370 f. New York and Moscow landmarks.

198 Einstein and Equation
199 Woman with Bouquet

1975. Air. 20th Death Anniv of Albert Einstein.
492 **198** 90 f. blue, purple & brown 55 30
See also Nos. 504, 507 and 519.

1975. International Women's Year.
493 **199** 150 f. red and green . . . 70 35

200 Morris "Oxford", 1913

1975. Early Motor-cars.
494 **200** 90 f. violet, brown & blue 50 20
495 – 130 f. red, grey and blue 80 25
496 – 190 f. deep blue, green and blue . . . . 1·25 40
497 – 230 f. brown, blue and red 1·50 45
DESIGNS—MOTOR-CARS: 130 f. Franklin "E", 1907; 190 f. Daimler, 1900; 230 f. Panhard & Levassor, 1895.

201

1975. Air. "Nordjamb 75" World Scout Jamboree, Norway.
498 **201** 100 f. blue, brown & lake 55 25
499 – 150 f. green, brown & bl 75 30
500 – 290 f. lake, brown & blue 1·40 75
DESIGNS: 150 f., 290 f. Scouts and emblem (different).

202 Lafayette and Battle Scene

1975. Air. Bicentenary of American Revolution. Mult.
501 290 f. Type **202** . . . . 1·50 65
502 300 f. Washington and battle scene . . . . 1·50 65
503 370 f. De Grasse and Battle of the Chesapeake, 1781 . . . 1·90 95

1975. 20th Death Anniv of Sir Alexander Fleming (scientist). As T **198**.
504 150 f. brown, purple and blue 80 35

204 Olympic Rings

1975. Air. "Pre-Olympic Year".
505 **204** 350 f. violet and blue . . . 1·00 65
506 – 400 f. blue . . . . 1·10 80
DESIGNS: 400 f. Emblem of Montreal Olympics (1976).

1975. Birth Bicentenary of Andre-Marie Ampere. As T **198**.
507 90 f. brown, red and violet . . 45 20

205 Tristater of Carthage

1975. Ancient Coins.
508 **205** 130 f. black, blue & purple 50 25
509 – 170 f. black, green & brn 70 35
510 – 190 f. black, green & red 1·00 65
511 – 260 f. black, blue & orange 1·75 1·25
COINS: 170 f. Decadrachm of Syracuse; 190 f. Tetradrachm of Acanthe; 260 f. Didrachm of Eretrie.

1975. Air. "Apollo–Soyuz" Space Link. Nos. 489/91 optd **ARRIMAGE 17 Juil. 1975.**
512 **197** 290 f. red, blue and black 1·25 65
513 – 300 f. red, blue and black 1·25 65
514 – 370 f. green, purple & blk 1·50 95

207 U.N. Emblem and Names of Agencies forming "ONU"

1975. 30th Anniv of United Nations Charter.
515 **207** 200 f. blue and green . . 70 45

208 "The Visitation" (Ghirlandaio)

1975. Air. Christmas. Religious Paintings.
516 290 f. Type **208** . . . . 1·40 55
517 300 f. "Nativity" (Fra Filippo Lippi School) . . . . . . 1·40 65
518 370 f. "Adoration of the Magi" (Velasquez) . . . . 1·60 1·10

1975. Air. 50th Death Anniv of Clement Ader (aviation pioneer). As T **198**.
519 100 f. purple, red and blue . . 55 20

209 Concorde in Flight

1976. Air. Concorde's First Commercial Flight.
520 **209** 500 f. multicoloured . . . 3·50 1·50

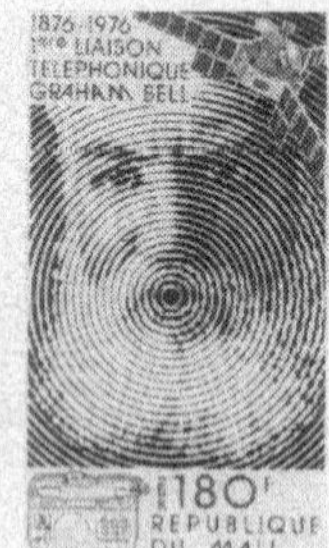

210 Figure-Skating
211 Alexander Graham Bell

1976. Air. Winter Olympic Games, Innsbruck. Multicoloured.
521 120 f. Type **210** 50 25
522 420 f. Ski-jumping . . . . . 1·50 65
523 430 f. Skiing (slalom) . . . . 1·50 75

1976. Telephone Centenary.
524 **211** 180 f. blue, brown and light brown 65 35

212 Chameleon

1976. Reptiles. Multicoloured.
525 20 f. Type **212** 20 15
526 30 f. Lizard 25 15
527 40 f. Tortoise 30 20
528 90 f. Python 65 25
529 120 f. Crocodile . . . . . . 1·10 50

213 Nurse and Patient

215 Constructing Orbital Space Station

214 Dr. Adenauer and Cologne Cathedral

1976. Air. World Health Day.
530 **213** 130 f. multicoloured . . . 55 25

1976. Birth Centenary Dr. Konrad Adenauer.
531 **214** 180 f. purple and brown 90 40

1976. Air. "The Future in Space".
532 **215** 300 f. deep blue, blue and orange . . . . 1·25 60
533 – 400 f. blue, red and purple 1·90 90
DESIGN: 400 f. Sun and space-ship with solar batteries.

216 American Bald Eagle and Liberty Bell

1976. Air. American Revolution Bicentenary and "Interphil '76" Int Stamp Exn, Philadelphia.
534 **216** 100 f. blue, purple & black 1·00 20
535 – 400 f. brown, blue & blk 3·50 85
536 – 440 f. violet, green & blk 2·75 85
DESIGNS—HORIZ: 400 f. Warships and American bald eagle. VERT: 440 f. Red Indians and American bald eagle.

217 Running

218 Scouts marching

1976. Air. Olympic Games, Montreal.
537 **217** 200 f. black, brown & red 70 40
538 – 250 f. brown, green & bl 80 50
539 – 300 f. black, blue & green 1·25 60
540 – 400 f. black, blue & green 1·60 90
DESIGNS: 250 f. Swimming; 300 f. Handball; 440 f. Football.

1976. Air. 1st All-African Scout Jamboree, Nigeria.
541 **218** 140 f. brown, blue & green 70 35
542 – 180 f. brown, green & grey 1·00 40
543 – 200 f. violet and brown . 1·10 50
DESIGNS—HORIZ: 180 f. Scouts tending calf. VERT: 200 f. Scout surveying camp at dusk.

1976. Fishes (2nd series). As T **196**.
544 100 f. black and blue 50 20
545 120 f. yellow, brown & green 55 25
546 130 f. turquoise, brown & blk 65 25
547 150 f. yellow, drab and green 75 30
548 220 f. black, green and brown 1·25 50
DESIGNS: 100 f. "Heterotis niloticus"; 120 f. "Synodontis budgetti"; 130 f. "Heterobranchus bidorsalis"; 150 f. "Tilapia mondodi"; 220 f. "Alestes malerolepidotus".

220 Scenes from Children's Book

221 "Roi de L'Air"

1976. Literature for Children.
549 **220** 130 f. grey, green and red 45 25

1976. 1st Issue of "L'Essor" Newspaper.
550 **221** 120 f. multicoloured . . . 1·00 30

222 Fall from Scaffolding

1976. 20th Anniv of National Social Insurance.
551 **222** 120 f. multicoloured . . . 35 25

223 Moenjodaro

1976. Air. U.N.E.S.C.O. "Save Moenjodaro" (Pakistan) Campaign.
552 **223** 400 f. purple, blue & black 1·75 80
553 – 500 f. red, yellow and blue 2·00 1·25
DESIGN: 500 f. Effigy, animals and remains.

224 Freighter, Vickers Viscount 800 and Map

1976. Air. Europafrique.
554 **224** 200 f. purple and blue . . 1·10 45

225 Cascade of Letters

1976. 25th Anniv of U.N. Postal Administration.
555 **225** 120 f. orange, green & lilac 45 25

226 Moto Guzzi "254" (Italy)

1976. Motorcycling.
556 **226** 90 f. red, grey and brown 45 20
557 – 120 f. violet, blue & black 55 25
558 – 130 f. red, grey and green 70 25
559 – 140 f. blue, green and grey 90 30
DESIGNS: 120 f. B.M.W. "900" (Germany); 130 f. Honda "Egli" (Japan); 140 f. Motobecane "LT3" (France).

227 "The Nativity" (Taddeo Gaddi)

1976. Air. Christmas. Religious Paintings. Mult.
560 280 f. Type **227** . . . . 1·25 50
561 300 f. "Adoration of the Magi" (Hans Memling) . . . . . . 1·40 60
562 320 f. "The Nativity" (Carlo Crivelli) . . . . 1·50 75

228 Muscat Fishing Boat

1976. Ships.
563 **228** 160 f. purple, green & blue 65 30
564 – 180 f. green, red and blue 65 35
565 – 190 f. purple, blue & green 70 40
566 – 200 f. green, red and blue 75 40
DESIGNS: 180 f. Cochin Chinese junk; 190 f. Dunkirk lightship "Ruytingen"; 200 f. Nile felucca.

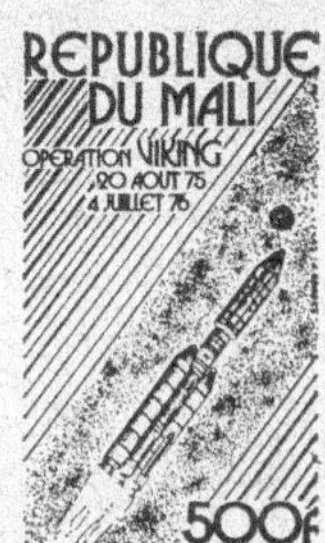

229 Rocket in Flight

1976. Air. Operation "Viking".
567 **229** 500 f. blue, red and lake 1·75 1·25
568 – 1000 f. lake, blue and deep blue . . . . 3·00 1·90
DESIGN: 1000 f. Spacecraft on Mars.

230 Pres. Giscard d'Estaing and Sankore Mosque, Timbuktu

1977. Air. Visit of Pres. Giscard d'Estaing of France.
570 **230** 430 f. multicoloured . . . 2·00 80

231 Rocket on Launch-pad, Newton and Apple

1977. Air. 250th Death Anniv of Isaac Newton.
571 **231** 400 f. purple, red & green 2·00 75

232 Prince Philip and Queen Elizabeth II

1977. Air. "Personalities of Decolonisation". Mult.
572 180 f. Type **232** 65 35
573 200 f. General De Gaulle (vert) 1·10 50
574 250 f. Queen Wilhelmina of the Netherlands (vert) 75 55
575 300 f. King Baudouin and Queen Fabiola of Belgium . . . . 1·10 70
576 480 f. Crowning of Queen Elizabeth II (vert) . . . . . 2·00 1·25

233 Lindbergh and "Spirit of St. Louis"

1977. Air. 50th Anniv of Lindbergh's Transatlantic Flight.
577 **233** 420 f. orange and violet . 1·90 85
578 – 430 f. blue, orange & green 1·90 85
DESIGN: 430 f. "Spirit of St. Louis" crossing the Atlantic.

234 Village Indigobird

236 Printed Circuit

235 Louis Braille and Hands reading Book

1977. Mali Birds. Multicoloured.
579 15 f. Type **234** 50 15
580 25 f. Yellow-breasted barbet 80 15
581 30 f. Vitelline masked weaver 80 55
582 40 f. Carmine bee eater . . . 1·00 60
583 50 f. Senegal parrot . . . . . 1·10 60

1977. 125th Death Anniv of Louis Braille (inventor of "Braille" system of reading and writing for the blind".
584 **235** 200 f. blue, red and green 1·10 45

1977. World Telecommunications Day.
585 **236** 120 f. red and brown . . 35 20

236a Chateau Sassenage, Grenoble

1977. Air. 10th Anniv of International French Language Council.
586 **236a** 300 f. multicoloured . . 1·00 50

237 Airship LZ-1 over Lake Constance

1977. Air. History of the Zeppelin.
587 **237** 120 f. green, brown & blue 55 25
588 – 130 f. deep blue, brown and blue 55 25
589 – 350 f. red, blue and deep blue 1·60 75
590 – 500 f. deep blue, green and blue . . . . 2·25 95
DESIGNS: 130 f. "Graf Zeppelin" over Atlantic; 350 f. Burning of "Hindenburg" at Lakehurst; 500 f. Count Ferdinand von Zeppelin and "Graf Zeppelin" at mooring mast.

238 "Anaz imperator"

1977. Insects. Multicoloured.
591 5 f. Type **238** 20 15
592 10 f. "Sphadromantis viridis" 25 15
593 20 f. "Vespa tropica" 25 15
594 35 f. "Melolontha melolantha" 30 15
595 60 f. Stag beetle 55 20

239 Knight and Rook 240 Henri Dunant

1977. Chess Pieces.
596 **239** 120 f. black, green & brn 1·00 30
597 – 130 f. green, red and black 1·10 30
598 – 300 f. green, red and blue 2·50 75
DESIGNS—VERT: 130 f. Pawn and Bishop. HORIZ: 300 f. King and Queen.

1977. Air. Nobel Peace Prize Winners. Multicoloured.
599 600 f. Type **240** (founder of Red Cross) 2·00 1·00
600 700 f. Martin Luther King 2·25 1·10

241 Ship 242 "Head of Horse"

1977. Europafrique.
601 **241** 400 f. multicoloured 1·25 75

1977. 525th Birth Anniv of Leonardo da Vinci.
602 **242** 200 f. brown and black 75 50
603 – 300 f. brown 1·10 60
604 – 500 f. red 2·00 85
DESIGNS: 300 f. "Head of Young Girl"; 500 f. Self-portrait.

243 Footballers 245 Dome of the Rock

244 Friendship Hotel

1977. Air. Football Cup Elimination Rounds.
605 – 180 f. brown, green & orge 50 30
606 **243** 200 f. brown, green & orge 60 35
607 – 420 f. grey, green and lilac 1·25 70
DESIGNS—HORIZ: 180 f. Two footballers; 420 f. Tackling.

1977. Inauguration of Friendship Hotel, Bamako.
608 **244** 120 f. multicoloured 35 25

1977. Palestinian Welfare.
609 **245** 120 f. multicoloured 55 20
610 180 f. multicoloured 70 30

246 Mao Tse-tung and "Comatex" Hall, Bamako

1977. Air. Mao Tse-tung Memorial.
611 **246** 300 f. red 1·25 50

1977. Air. First Commercial Paris–New York Flight by Concorde. Optd **PARIS-NEW YORK 22.11.77.**
612 **209** 500 f. multicoloured 7·00 4·50

248 "Adoration of the Magi" (Rubens)

1977. Air. Christmas. Details from "Adoration of the Magi" by Rubens.
613 **248** 400 f. multicoloured 1·25 75
614 – 500 f. multicoloured 1·60 95
615 – 600 f. multicoloured 2·00 1·10
The 600 f. is a horizontal design.

249 "Hercules and the Nemean Lion"

1978. 400th Birth Anniv of Peter Paul Rubens. Multicoloured.
616 200 f. "Battle of the Amazons" (horiz) 70 35
617 300 f. "Return from Labour in the Fields" (horiz) 1·00 55
618 500 f. Type **249** 1·75 95

250 Schubert and Mute Swans

1978. Air. 150th Death Anniv of Franz Schubert (composer). Multicoloured.
619 300 f. Schubert and bars of music (vert) 1·50 60
620 420 f. Type **250** 4·00 70

251 Cook and Shipboard Scene

1978. Air. 250th Birth Anniv of Captain James Cook.
621 **251** 200 f. blue, red and violet 1·25 40
622 – 300 f. brown, blue & green 1·75 70
DESIGN: 300 f. Capt. Cook meeting natives.

252 African and Chained Building

1978. World Anti-Apartheid Year.
623 **252** 120 f. violet, brown & blue 40 20
624 – 130 f. violet, blue & orge 40 20
625 – 180 f. brown, pur & orge 60 30
DESIGNS: 130 f. Statue of Liberty and Africans walking to open door; 180 f. African children and mule in fenced enclosure.

253 Players and Ball 254 "Head of Christ"

1978. Air. World Cup Football Championship, Argentina.
626 **253** 150 f. red, green & brown 60 30
627 – 250 f. red, brown & green 1·25 45
628 – 300 f. red, brown and blue 1·50 50
DESIGNS—VERT: 250 f. HORIZ: 300 f. Different football scenes.

1978. Air. Easter. Works by Durer.
630 **254** 420 f. green and brown 1·60 75
631 – 430 f. blue and brown 1·60 75
DESIGN: 430 f. "The Resurrection".

255 Red-cheeked Cordon-bleu

1978. Birds. Multicoloured.
632 20 f. Type **255** 20 15
633 30 f. Black-faced fire finch 50 20
634 50 f. Red-billed fire finch 60 40
635 70 f. African collared dove 1·10 40
636 80 f. White-billed buffalo weaver 1·50 50

256 C-3 "Trefle"

1978. Air. Birth Centenary of Andre Citroen (automobile pioneer).
637 **256** 120 f. brown, lake & green 60 20
638 – 130 f. grey, orange & blue 70 25
639 – 180 f. blue, green and red 1·10 30
640 – 200 f. black, red and lake 1·25 40
DESIGNS: 130 f. B-2 "Croisiere Noir" track-laying vehicle, 1924; 180 f. B-14 G Saloon, 1927; 200 f. Model-11 front-wheel drive car, 1934.

1978. 20th Anniv of Bamako Lions Club. Nos. 473/4 surch **XXe ANNIVERSAIRE DU LIONS CLUB DE BAMAKO 1958-1978** and value.
641 120 f. on 90 f. Type **192** 45 20
642 130 f. on 100 f. View of Samanko 55 30

258 Names of 1978 U.P.U. members forming Map of the World

1978. Centenary of U.P.U. Foundation Congress, Paris.
643 **258** 120 f. green, orange & mve 45 20
644 – 130 f. yellow, red & green 45 20
DESIGN: 130 f. Names of 1878 member states across globe.

259 Desert Scene

1978. Campaign against Desertification.
645 **259** 200 f. multicoloured 70 35

260 Mahatma Gandhi 262 Dominoes

261 "Dermestes bromius"

1978. 30th Anniv of Gandhi's Assassination.
646 **260** 140 f. brown, red & black 85 30

1978. Insects. Multicoloured.
647 15 f. Type **261** 20 15
648 25 f. "Calosoma sp." 25 15
649 90 f. "Lopocerus variegatus" 45 20
650 120 f. "Coccinella septempunctata" 55 25
651 140 f. "Goliathus giganteus" 70 30

1978. Social Games.
652 **262** 100 f. black, green and red 40 20
653 – 130 f. red, black and blue 85 25
DESIGN: 130 f. Bridge hand.

263 Ostrich on Nest (Syrian Manuscript)

1978. Air. Europafrique. Multicoloured.
654 100 f. Type **263** 1·25 20
655 110 f. Common zebra (Mansur miniature) 50 30

1978. Air. World Cup Football Championship Finalists. Nos. 626/8 optd with results.
656 **253** 150 f. red, green & brown 60 25
657 – 250 f. red, brown & green 1·00 45
658 – 300 f. red, brown & blue 1·25 60
OPTS: 150 f. **CHAMPION 1978 ARGENTINE**; 250 f. **2e HOLLANDE**; 300 f. **3e BRESIL 4e ITALIE.**

265 Coronation Coach

1978. Air. 25th Anniv of Coronation of Queen Elizabeth II. Multicoloured.
660 500 f. Type **265** 1·50 70
661 1000 f. Queen Elizabeth II 2·75 1·40

266 Aristotle and African Animals 267 Douglas DC-3 and U.S.A. 1918 24 c. stamp

1978. 2300th Death Anniv of Aristotle (Greek philosopher).
662 **266** 200 f. brow red and grn 90 35

1978. Air. History of Aviation.

No.	Type	Description	Unused	Used
663	**267**	80 f. deep blue, red & blue	35	15
664	–	100 f. multicoloured	40	20
665	–	120 f. black, blue and red	50	25
666	–	130 f. green, red & black	55	30
667	–	320 f. violet, blue & red	1·25	65

DESIGNS: 100 f. Stampe and Renard SV-4 and Belgium Balloon stamp of 1932; 120 f. Clement Ader's Avion III and France Concorde stamp of 1976; 130 f. Junkers Ju–52/3m and Germany Biplane stamp of 1919; 320 f. Mitsubishi A6M Zero-Sen and Japan Pagoda stamp of 1951.

268 "The Annunciation"

1978. Air. Christmas. Works by Durer.

No.	Type	Description	Unused	Used
668	**268**	420 f. brown and black	1·25	60
669	–	430 f. brown and green	1·25	60
670	–	500 f. black and brown	1·60	75

DESIGNS: 430 f. "Virgin and Child"; 500 f. "Adoration of the Magi".

269 Launch of "Apollo 8" and Moon

1978. Air. 10th Anniv of First Manned Flight around the Moon.

No.	Type	Description	Unused	Used
671	**269**	200 f. red, green and violet	60	30
672	–	300 f. violet, green and red	1·10	50

DESIGN: 300 f. "Apollo 8" in orbit around the Moon.

270 U.N. and Human Rights Emblems

1978. 30th Anniv of Declaration of Human Rights.

No.	Type	Description	Unused	Used
673	**270**	180 f. red, blue and brown	60	35

271 Concorde and Clement Ader's "Eole"

1979. Air. 3rd Anniv of First Commercial Concorde Flight. Multicoloured.

No.	Type	Description	Unused	Used
674		120 f. Type **271**	60	25
675		130 f. Concorde and Wright Flyer 1	70	30
676		200 f. Concorde and "Spirit of St. Louis"	1·25	45

1979. Air. "Philexafrique" Stamp Exhibition, Libreville, Gabon (1st issue) and International Stamp Fair, Essen, West Germany. As T **262** of Niger. Multicoloured.

No.	Type	Description	Unused	Used
677		200 f. Ruff (bird) and Lubeck 1859 ½ s. stamp	1·10	75
678		200 f. Dromedary and Mali 1965 200 f. stamp	1·90	1·25

See also Nos. 704/5.

1979. Air. Birth Centenary of Albert Einstein (physicist). No. 492 surch **"1879–1979" 130F.**

No.	Type	Description	Unused	Used
679	**198**	130 f. on 90 f. blue, purple and brown	55	30

273 "Christ carrying the Cross"

1979. Air. Easter. Works by Durer.

No.	Type	Description	Unused	Used
680	**273**	400 f. black and turquoise	1·40	60
681	–	430 f. black and red	1·40	60
682	–	480 f. black and blue	1·60	1·00

DESIGNS: 430 f. "Christ on the Cross"; 480 f. "The Great Lamentation".

274 Basketball and St. Basil's Cathedral, Moscow

275 African Manatee

1979. Air. Pre-Olympic Year. Multicoloured.

No.	Type	Description	Unused	Used
683		420 f. Type **274**	1·50	75
684		430 f. Footballer and Kremlin	1·50	75

1979. Endangered Animals. Multicoloured.

No.	Type	Description	Unused	Used
685		100 f. Type **275**	45	20
686		120 f. Chimpanzee	55	30
687		130 f. Topi	65	35
688		180 f. Gemsbok	80	40
689		200 f. Giant eland	90	55

276 Child and I.Y.C. Emblem

1979. International Year of the Child.

No.	Type	Description	Unused	Used
690	**276**	120 f. green, red & brown	40	20
691	–	200 f. purple and green	70	35
692	–	300 f. brown, mauve and deep brown	1·00	50

DESIGNS: 200 f. Girl and scout with birds; 300 f. Children with calf.

277 Judo

1979. World Judo Championships, Paris.

No.	Type	Description	Unused	Used
693	**277**	200 f. sepia, red and ochre	80	40

278 Wave Pattern and Human Figures

279 Goat's Head and Lizard Fetishes

1979. World Telecommunications Day.

No.	Type	Description	Unused	Used
694	**278**	120 f. multicoloured	35	20

1979. World Museums Day. Multicoloured.

No.	Type	Description	Unused	Used
695		90 f. Type **279**	30	15
696		120 f. Seated figures (wood carving)	40	20
697		130 f. Two animal heads and figurine (wood carving)	50	25

280 Rowland Hill and Mali 1961 25 f. stamp

281 Cora Players

1979. Death Centenary of Sir Rowland Hill.

No.	Type	Description	Unused	Used
698	**280**	120 f. multicoloured	40	20
699	–	130 f. red, blue and green	40	20
700	–	180 f. black, green & blue	60	30
701	–	200 f. black, red & purple	70	35
702	–	300 f. blue, deep blue and red	1·25	50

DESIGNS: 130 f. Airship "Graf Zeppelin" and Saxony stamp of 1850; 180 f. Concorde and France stamp of 1849; 200 f. Stage coach and U.S.A. stamp of 1849; 300 f. U.P.U. emblem and Penny Black.

1979.

No.	Type	Description	Unused	Used
703	**281**	200 f. multicoloured	1·00	40

282 Sankore Mosque and "Adenium obesum"

1979. "Philexafrique" Exhibition, Libreville, Gabon (2nd issue).

No.	Type	Description	Unused	Used
704	**282**	120 f. multicoloured	90	55
705	–	300 f. red, blue and orange	1·90	1·25

DESIGN: 300 f. Horseman and satellite.

283 Map of Mali showing Conquest of Desert

1979. Operation "Sahel Vert". Multicoloured.

No.	Type	Description	Unused	Used
706		200 f. Type **283**	70	30
707		300 f. Planting a tree	1·10	50

284 Lemons

285 Sigmund Freud

1979. Fruit (1st series). Multicoloured.

No.	Type	Description	Unused	Used
708		10 f. Type **284**	15	10
709		60 f. Pineapple	30	15
710		100 f. Papaw	50	15
711		120 f. Sweet-sops	55	20
712		130 f. Mangoes	65	25

See also Nos. 777/81.

1979. 40th Death Anniv of Sigmund Freud (psychologist).

No.	Type	Description	Unused	Used
713	**285**	300 f. sepia and violet	1·25	60

286 Caillie and Camel approaching Fort

1979. 180th Birth Anniv of Rene Caillie (explorer).

No.	Type	Description	Unused	Used
714	**286**	120 f. sepia, brown & blue	50	20
715	–	130 f. blue, green & brown	60	25

DESIGN: 130 f. Rene Caillie and map of route across Sahara.

287 "Eurema brigitta"

1979. Butterflies and Moths (1st series). Mult.

No.	Type	Description	Unused	Used
716		100 f. Type **287**	60	20
717		120 f. "Papilio pylades"	65	20
718		130 f. "Melanitis leda satyridae"	80	40
719		180 f. "Gonimbrasis belina occidentalis"	1·25	45
720		200 f. "Bunaea alcinoe"	1·50	50

See also Nos. 800/4.

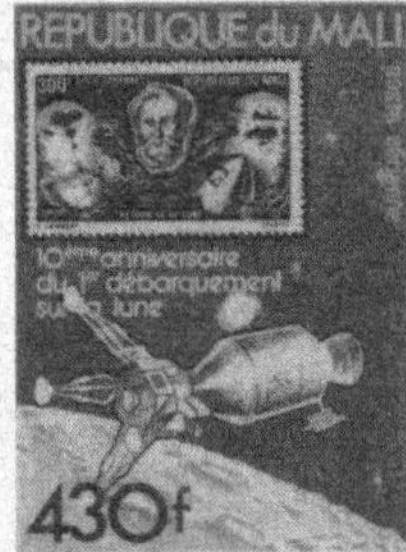

288 Mali 1970 300 f. Stamp and Modules orbiting Moon

1979. Air. 10th Anniv of First Moon Landing.

No.	Type	Description	Unused	Used
721		430 f. Type **288**	1·40	60
722		500 f. 1973 250 f. stamp and rocket launch	1·60	95

289 Capt. Cook and H.M.S. "Resolution" off Kerguelen Islands

1979. Air. Death Bicent of Captain James Cook.

No.	Type	Description	Unused	Used
723		300 f. Type **289**	1·50	80
724		400 f. Capt. Cook and H.M.S. "Resolution" off Hawaii	2·25	1·10

290 Menaka Greyhound

1979. Dogs. Multicoloured.

No.	Type	Description	Unused	Used
725		20 f. Type **290**	20	15
726		50 f. Water spaniel	35	15
727		70 f. Beagle	45	15
728		80 f. Newfoundland	55	20
729		90 f. Sheepdog	70	20

291 David Janowski

1979. Air. Chess Grand-masters.

No.	Type	Description	Unused	Used
730	**291**	100 f. red and brown	70	30
731	–	140 f. red, brown and blue	1·00	30
732	–	200 f. blue, violet & green	1·60	50
733	–	300 f. brown, ochre & red	2·00	70

DESIGNS: 140 f. Alexander Alekhine; 200 f. Willi Schlage; 300 f. Efim Bogoljubow.

292 "The Adoration of the Magi" 1511 (detail, Durer)

1979. Air. Christmas. Works by Durer.

No.	Type	Description	Unused	Used
734	**292**	300 f. brown and orange	1·00	50
735	–	400 f. brown and blue	1·25	75
736	–	500 f. brown and green	1·60	95

DESIGNS: 400 f. "Adoration of the Magi" (1503); 500 f. "Adoration of the Magi" (1511, different).

1979. Air. 20th Anniv of ASECNA (African Air Safety Organization). As T **198** of Malagasy but 36 × 27 mm.

No.	Type	Description	Unused	Used
737		120 f. multicoloured	40	20

293 Globe, Rotary Emblem and Diesel Train

294 African Ass

1980. Air. 75th Anniv of Rotary International. Multicoloured.

738 220 f. Type **293** . . . . 1·25 50
739 250 f. Globe, Rotary emblem and Douglas DC-10 airliner . . 1·00 45
740 430 f. Bamako Rotary Club and emblem . . . . 1·40 75

1980. Protected Animals. Multicoloured.

741 90 f. Type **294** 50 20
742 120 f. Addax 60 20
743 130 f. Cheetahs 65 35
744 140 f. Barbary sheep 70 45
745 180 f. African buffalo 90 50

295 Speed Skating

1980. Air. Winter Olympics Game, Lake Placid. Multicoloured.

746 200 f. Type **295** 70 30
747 300 f. Ski jump . . . . 1·10 60

296 Stephenson's "Rocket" and Mali 30 f. Stamp, 1972

1980. Air. 150th Anniv of Liverpool and Manchester Railway.

749 **296** 200 f. blue, brown & green 90 45
750 – 300 f. black, brown & turq 1·60 80

DESIGN: 300 f. "Rocket" and Mali 50 f. railway stamp, 1970.

297 Horse Jumping

1980. Air. Olympic Games, Moscow.

751 **297** 200 f. green, brown & blue 70 30
752 – 300 f. blue, brown & green 1·00 50
753 – 400 f. red, green & lt green 1·50 75

DESIGN: 300 f. Sailing. 400 f. Football.

298 Solar Pumping Station, Koni

1980. Solar Energy. Multicoloured.

755 90 f. Type **298** 30 15
756 100 f. Solar capture tables, Dire 35 15
757 120 f. Solar energy cooker . . 50 20
758 130 f. Solar generating station, Dire 55 25

299 Nioro Horse

1980. Horses. Multicoloured.

759 100 f. Mopti 50 15
760 120 f. Type **299** 55 15
761 130 f. Koro 65 20
762 180 f. Lake zone horse . . . 80 35
763 200 f. Banamba 95 40

300 "Head of Christ" (Maurice Denis)

1980. Air. Easter.

764 **300** 480 f. red and brown . . 1·60 95
765 – 500 f. brown and red . . 1·60 95

DESIGN: 500 f. "Christ before Pilate" (Durer).

301 Kepler and Diagram of Earth's Orbit

1980. Air. 350th Death Anniv of J. Kepler (astronomer).

766 **301** 200 f. lt blue, blue & red 80 35
767 – 300 f. mauve, violet & grn 1·25 55

DESIGN: 300 f. Kepler, Copernicus and diagram of solar system.

302 Pluto and Diagram of Orbit

1980. Air. 50th Anniv of Discovery of Planet Pluto.

768 **302** 402 f. blue, grey & mauve 1·90 85

303 "Lunokhod 1" (10th Anniv)

1980. Air. Space Events.

769 **303** 480 f. black, red and blue 1·50 85
770 – 500 f. grey, blue and red 1·50 85

DESIGN: 500 f. "Apollo" - "Soyuz" link-up.

304 Fleming and Laboratory

1980. Sir Alexander Fleming (discoverer of penicillin). Commemoration.

771 **304** 200 f. green, sepia & brn 80 35

305 Avicenna, Medical Instruments and Herbs

306 Pilgrim at Mecca

1980. Birth Millenary of Avicenna (Arab physician and philosopher).

772 **305** 120 f. blue, red and brown 40 20
773 – 180 f. dp brn, turq & brn 60 25

DESIGN: 180 f. Avicenna as teacher.

1980. 1400th Anniv of Hegira. Multicoloured.

774 120 f. Type **306** 40 15
775 130 f. Praying hands 40 20
776 180 f. Pilgrims (horiz) 60 30

1980. Fruit (2nd series). As T **284**. Multicoloured.

777 90 f. Guavas 45 20
778 120 f. Cashews 50 20
779 130 f. Oranges 65 25
780 140 f. Bananas 75 25
781 180 f. Grapefruit 90 35

307 Rochambeau and French Fleet at Rhode Island, 1780

1980. Air. French Support for American Independence.

782 **307** 420 f. brown, turq & red 1·50 75
783 – 430 f. black, blue and red 1·50 80

DESIGN: 430 f. Rochambeau, Washington and Eagle.

308 Dove and U.N. Emblem

1980. 60th Anniv of League of Nations.

784 **308** 200 f. blue, red and violet 60 35

309 Scene from "Around the World in 80 Days"

1980. Air. 75th Death Anniv of Jules Verne (writer).

785 **309** 100 f. red, green & brown 1·50 75
786 – 100 f. brown, chestnut and turquoise . . . . 1·50 30
787 – 150 f. green, brn & dp brn 1·00 40
788 – 150 f. blue, violet & dp bl 1·00 40

DESIGNS: No. 786, Concorde; No. 787, "From the Earth to the Moon"; No. 788, Astronaut on Moon.

310 Xylophone, Mask and Emblem

1980. 6th Arts and Cultural Festival, Bamako.

789 **310** 120 f. multicoloured . . . 40 20

311 Map of Africa and Asia

313 Conference Emblem

1980. 25th Anniv of Afro-Asian Bandung Conference.

790 **311** 300 f. green, red and blue 90 55

1980. Air. Olympic Medal Winners. Nos. 751/3 optd

791 200 f. green, brown and blue 70 35
792 300 f. blue, brown and green 1·00 55
793 400 f. red, green & light green 1·40 75

OVERPRINTS: 200 f. **CONCOURS COMPLET INDIVIDUEL ROMAN (It.) BLINOV (Urss) SALNIKOV (Urss)**; 300 f. **FINN RECHARDT (Fin.) MAYRHOFER (Autr.) BALACHOV (Urss)**; 400 f. **TCHECOSLOVAQUIE ALLEMAGNE DE L'EST URSS.**

1980. World Tourism Conference, Manila. Mult.

795 120 f. Type **313** 35 15
796 180 f. Encampment outside fort and Conference emblem . . 50 30

314 Dam and Rural Scene

1980. 20th Anniv of Independence. Multicoloured.

797 100 f. Type **314** 40 15
798 120 f. National Assembly Building 40 20
799 130 f. Independence Monument (vert) 45 25

1980. Butterflies. (2nd series). As T **287** but dated "1980". Multicoloured.

800 50 f. "Uterheisa pulchella" (postage) 30 20
801 60 f. "Mylothis chloris pieridae" 40 20
802 70 f. "Hypolimnas mishippus" 50 20
803 80 f. "Papilio demodocus" . . 65 20
804 420 f. "Denaus chrysippus" (48 × 36 mm) (air) . . . . . 2·25 1·25

315 Pistol firing Cigarette and Target over Lungs

1980. Anti-Smoking Campaign.

805 **315** 200 f. multicoloured . . . 75 35

316 Train, Boeing 737 and Globe

1980. Europafrique.

806 **316** 300 f. multicoloured . . . 1·25 60

317 Map of West Africa and Agricultural Symbols

318 Gen. de Gaulle and Map of France

1980. 5th Anniv of West African Economic Council. Multicoloured.

807 100 f. Type **317** 35 15
808 120 f. "Transport" . . . . . . 1·40 45
809 130 f. "Industry" 45 25
810 140 f. "Energy" 50 25

1980. Air. 10th Death Anniv of Gen. Charles de Gaulle. Multicoloured.

811 420 f. Type **318** . . . . 1·75 75
812 430 f. De Gaulle and Cross of Lorraine . . . . 1·75 75

319 "Tokaido" (Japan) and Mali 1972 10 f. Stamp

1980. Air. Locomotives.
813 **319** 120 f. blue, green and red 65 20
814 – 130 f. green, blue and red 75 25
815 – 200 f. orange, black & grn 1·00 40
816 – 480 f. black, red and green 2·50 95
DESIGNS—HORIZ: 130 f. "RTG" train of Amtrack, U.S.A. and 20 f. locomotive stamp of 1970; 200 f. "Rembrandt" train, Germany and 100 f. locomotive stamp of 1970. VERT: 480 f. "TGV 001" express train, France and 80 f. locomotive stamp of 1970.

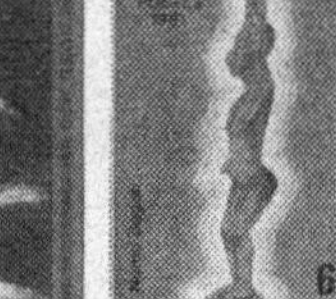

320 "Flight into Egypt" (Rembrandt) **321** Nomo Dogon

1980. Air. Christmas. Multicoloured.
817 300 f. "St. Joseph showing the infant Jesus to St. Catherine" (Lorenzo Lotto) (horiz) . . 1·00 55
818 400 f. Type **320** . . . . 1·40 80
819 500 f. "Christmas Night" (Gauguin) (horiz) . . . . . 1·60 90

1980. 5th Anniv of African Posts and Telecommunications Union. As T **292** of Niger.
820 130 f. multicoloured 40 20

1981. Statuettes. Multicoloured.
821 60 f. Type **321** 20 15
822 70 f. Senoufo fertility symbol 25 15
823 90 f. Bamanan fertility statuette 35 15
824 100 f. Senoufo captives snuff-box 40 15
825 120 f. Dogon fertility statuette 50 20

322 "Self-portrait" (Blue period) **323** Mambie Sidibe

1981. Birth Bicentenary of Pablo Picasso (artist).
826 **322** 1000 f. multicoloured . . 3·25 1·75

1981. Mali Thinkers and Savants.
827 **323** 120 f. brown, buff and red 40 20
828 – 130 f. brown, buff & black 40 25
DESIGN: 130 f. Amadou Hampate Ba.

324 Mosque and Ka'aba **325** Tackle

1981. 1400th Anniv of Hejira.
829 **324** 120 f. multicoloured . . . 40 20
830 180 f. multicoloured . . . 60 30

1981. Air. World Cup Football Championship Eliminators. Multicoloured.
831 100 f. Type **325** 40 20
832 200 f. Heading the ball . . . 85 35
833 300 f. Running for ball . . . 1·40 50

326 Kaarta Zeba **327** Crinum de Moore "Crinum moorei"

1981. Cattle. Multicoloured.
835 20 f. Type **326** 15 15
836 30 f. Peul du Macina sebu . . 15 15
837 40 f. Maure zebu 25 15
838 80 f. Touareg zebu 50 15
839 100 f. N'Dama cow 60 20

1981. Flowers. Multicoloured.
840 50 f. Type **327** 30 15
841 100 f. Double rose hibiscus "Hibiscus rosa-sinensis" . . 70 15
842 120 f. Pervenche "Catharanthus roseus" 80 20
843 130 f. Frangipani "Plumeria rubra" 80 25
844 180 f. Orgueil de Chine "Caesalpinia pulcherrima" 1·25 40

328 Mozart and Musical Instruments

1981. Air. 225th Birth Anniv of Mozart. Mult.
845 420 f. Type **328** . . . . 1·75 85
846 430 f. Mozart and musical instruments (different) . . . 1·75 85

329 "The Fall on the Way to Calvary" (Raphael) **330** Yury Gagarin

1981. Air. Easter.
847 500 f. Type **329** . . . . 1·50 85
848 600 f. "Ecce Homo" (Rembrandt) . . . . 2·00 1·25

1981. Air. Space Anniversaries and Events.
849 **330** 200 f. blue, black and red 75 30
850 – 200 f. blue, black & lt blue 75 30
851 – 380 f. multicoloured . . . 1·25 55
852 – 430 f. violet, black & blue 1·50 70
DESIGNS—VERT: No. 849, Type **330**: first man in space (20th anniv); No. 850, Alan Shepard, first American in space (20th anniv); No. 851, Saturn and moons (exploration of Saturn). HORIZ: No. 852, Sir William Herschel, and diagram of Uranus, (Discovery bicentenary)

331 Blind and Sighted Faces **332** Caduceus (Telecommunications and Health)

1981. International Year of Disabled People.
853 **331** 100 f. light brown, brown and green 35 15
854 – 120 f. violet, blue and purple 45 20
DESIGN: 120 f. Mechanical hand and human hand with spanner.

1981. World Telecommunications Day.
855 **332** 130 f. multicoloured . . . 40 25

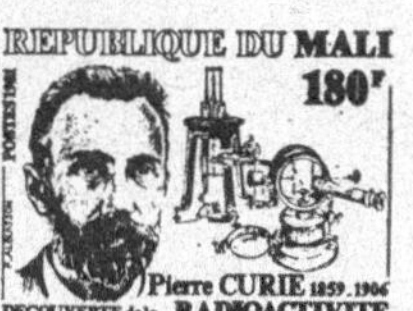

333 Pierre Curie and Instruments

1981. 75th Death Anniv of Pierre Curie (discoverer of radioactivity).
856 **333** 180 f. blue, black & orange 90 30

334 Scouts at Well and Dorcas Gazelle

1981. 4th African Scouting Conference, Abidjan. Multicoloured.
857 110 f. Type **334** 55 30
858 160 f. Scouts signalling and patas monkey . . . . 1·00 60
859 300 f. Scouts saluting and cheetah (vert) . . . . 1·50 85

1981. Air. World Railway Speed Record. No. 816 optd **28 fevrier 1981/Record du monde de vitesse–380 km/h**.
861 480 f. black, red and blue . . . 2·25 90

336 Columbus, Fleet and U.S. Columbus Stamp of 1892

1981. Air. 475th Death Anniv of Christopher Columbus.
862 **336** 180 f. brown, black & bl 80 40
863 – 200 f. green, blue & brown 1·00 40
864 – 260 f. black, violet and red 1·50 60
865 – 300 f. lilac, red and green 1·60 70
DESIGNS—VERT: 200 f. "Nina" and 1 c. Columbus stamp of Spain; 260 f. "Pinta" and 5 c. Columbus stamp of Spain. HORIZ: 300 f. "Santa Maria" and U.S. 3 c. Columbus stamp.

1981. 23rd World Scouting Conference, Dakar. Nos. 857/9 optd **"DAKAR 8 AOUT 1981/28e CONFERENCE MOUNDIALE DU SCOUTISME"**.
866 **334** 110 f. multicoloured . . . 40 20
867 – 160 f. multicoloured . . . 50 30
868 – 300 f. multicoloured . . . 1·25 55

338 Space Shuttle after Launching

1981. Air. Space Shuttle. Multicoloured.
870 200 f. Type **338** 75 30
871 500 f. Space Shuttle in orbit . 2·00 75
872 600 f. Space Shuttle landing . . 2·25 1·25

339 "Harlequin on a Horse"

1981. Air. Birth Centenary of Pablo Picasso. Mult.
874 600 f. Type **339** . . . . 2·50 1·25
875 750 f. "Child with Pigeon" . . . 3·00 1·40

340 Prince Charles, Lady Diana Spencer and St. Paul's Cathedral

1981. Air. British Royal Wedding. Multicoloured.
876 500 f. Type **340** . . . . 1·25 75
877 700 f. Prince Charles, Lady Diana Spencer and coach . 1·75 1·10

342 Maure Sheep **343** Heinrich von Stephan (founder of U.P.U.), Latecoere 28 and Concorde

1981. Sheep. Multicoloured.
886 10 f. Type **342** 15 10
887 25 f. Peul sheep 20 10
888 140 f. Sahael sheep 50 25
889 180 f. Touareg sheep 75 35
890 200 f. Djallonke ram 85 35

1981. Universal Postal Union Day.
891 **343** 400 f. red and green . . . 1·60 70

344 Woman drinking from Bowl

1981. World Food Day.
892 **344** 200 f. brown, orge & mve 65 30

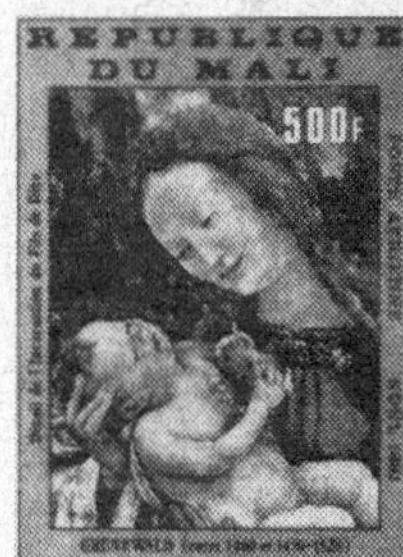

345 "The Incarnation of the Son of God" (detail, Grunewald)

1981. Air. Christmas. Multicoloured.
893 500 f. Type **345** . . . . 1·75 75
894 700 f. "The Campori Madonna" (Correggio) . . . . 2·25 1·25

347 Transport and Hands holding Map of Europe and Africa

1981. Europafrique.
896 **347** 700 f. blue, brown & orge 3·00 1·60

348 Guerin, Calmette, Syringe and Bacillus

1981. 60th Anniv of First B.C.G. Innoculation.
897 **348** 200 f. brown, violet & blk 85 40

1982. Air. World Chess Championship, Merano. Nos. 731 and 733 optd.
898 140 f. red, brown and blue . . 1·10 50
899 300 f. brown, ochre and red . . 2·00 75
OPTS: 140 f. **ANATOLI KARPOV VICTOR KORTCHNOI MERANO (ITALIE) (Octobre-Novembre 1981**; 300 f. **Octobre-Novembre 1981 ANATOLI KARPOV Champion du Monde 1981**.

350 "Nymphaea lotus"

1982. Flowers. Multicoloured.
900 170 f. Type **350** 75 35
901 180 f. "Bombax costatum" . . 80 35
902 200 f. "Parkia biglobosa" . . 85 40
903 220 f. "Gloriosa simplex" . . 1·10 45
904 270 f. "Satanocrater berhautii" 1·25 50

351 Lewis Carroll and Characters from "Alice" Books

1982. Air. 150th Birth Anniv of Lewis Carroll (Revd. Charles Dodgson).
905 110 f. Type **351** 55 25
906 130 f. Characters from "Alice" books 60 30
907 140 f. Characters from "Alice" books (different) 75 30

352 "George Washington" (Gilbert Stuart)

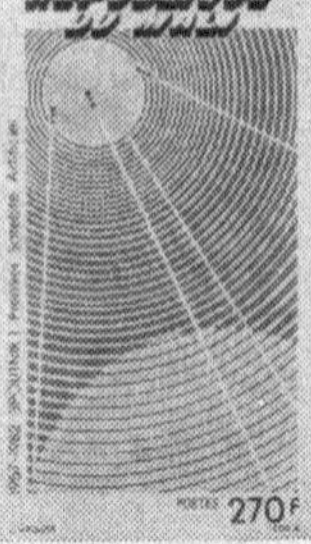
353 Ciwara Bamanan

1982. Air. 250th Birth Anniv of George Washington.
908 **352** 700 f. multicoloured . . . 2·00 1·25

1982. Masks. Multicoloured.
909 5 f. Type **353** 10 10
910 35 f. Kanga Dogon 15 10
911 180 f. N Domo Bamanan . . 1·00 40
912 200 f. Cimier (Sogoninkum Bamanan . . . . 1·00 40
913 250 f. Kpelie Senoufo . . . . 1·10 45

354 Football

355 "Sputnik 1"

1982. Air. World Cup Football Championship, Spain.
914 **354** 220 f. multicoloured . . . 80 45
915 – 420 f. multicoloured . . . 1·50 90
916 – 500 f. multicoloured . . . 1·75 90
DESIGNS: 420 f., 500 f. Football scenes.

1982. 25th Anniv of First Artificial Satellite.
918 **355** 270 f. violet, blue and red 1·25 50

356 Lord Baden-Powell, Tent and Scout Badge

1982. Air. 125th Birth Anniv of Lord Baden-Powell.
919 300 f. Type **356** . . . . 1·50 50
920 500 f. Saluting scout . . . . 2·25 90

357 "The Transfiguration" (Fra Angelico)

1982. Air. Easter. Multicoloured.
921 680 f. Type **357** . . . . 2·00 1·25
922 1000 f. "Pieta" (Giovanni Bellini) 3·00 1·90

358 Doctor giving Child Oral Vaccine

360 "En Bon Ami" (N'Teri)

359 Lions Emblem and Blind Person

1982. Anti-Polio Campaign.
923 **358** 180 f. multicoloured . . . 80 35

1982. Lions Club Blind Day.
924 **359** 260 f. orange, blue and red 1·25 50

1982. Hairstyles. Multicoloured.
925 140 f. Type **360** 35 30
926 150 f. Tucked-in pony tail . . 60 35
927 160 f. "Pour l'Art" 70 45
928 180 f. "Bozo Kun" 75 50
929 270 f. "Fulaw Kun" . . . . 1·25 60

361 Arms Stamp of Mali and France

1982. Air. "Philexfrance 82" International Stamp Exhibition, Paris. Multicoloured.
930 180 f. Type **361** 60 35
931 200 f. Dromedary caravan and 1979 "Philexafrique II" stamp 1·00 70

362 Fire-engine, 1850

1982. Fire-engines. Multicoloured.
932 180 f. Type **362** 85 35
933 200 f. Fire-engine, 1921 . . . 1·25 40
934 270 f. Fire-engine, 1982 . . . 1·50 50

363 Gobra

1982. Zebu. Cattle. Multicoloured.
935 10 f. Type **363** 10 10
936 60 f. Azaouak 25 15
937 110 f. Maure 35 25
938 180 f. Toronke 65 35
939 200 f. Peul Sambourou 75 40

1982. Air. World Cup Football Championship Winners. Nos. 914/16 optd.
940 **354** 220 f. multicoloured . . . 75 45
941 – 420 f. multicoloured . . . 1·50 90
942 – 500 f. multicoloured . . . 1·75 90
OPTS: 220 f. **1 ITALIE 2 RFA 3 POLOGNE**; 420 f. **POLOGNE FRANCE 3-2**; 500 f. **ITALIE RFA 3-1**.

365 "Urchin with Cherries"

1982. Air. 150th Birth Anniv of Edouard Manet (painter).
944 **365** 680 f. multicoloured . . . 2·50 1·25

366 "Virgin and Child" (detail) (Titian)

367 Wind-surfing

1982. Air. Christmas. Multicoloured.
945 500 f. Type **366** . . . . 1·50 90
946 1000 f. "Virgin and Child" (Giovanni Bellini) . . . . 2·75 1·90

1982. Introduction of Wind-surfing as Olympic Event. Multicoloured.
947 200 f. Type **367** 80 45
948 270 f. Wind-surfer . . . . . . 1·25 55
949 300 f. Wind-surfer (different) 1·40 55

368 Goethe

1982. Air. 150th Death Anniv of Goethe (poet).
950 **368** 500 f. brown, light brown and black . . . . 1·75 90

369 Valentina Tereshkova

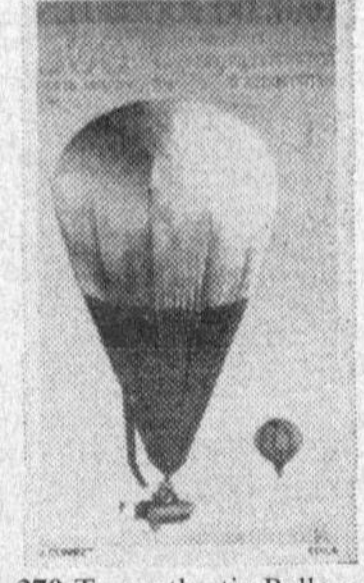
370 Transatlantic Balloon "Double Eagle II"

1983. Air. 20th Anniv of Launching of Vostok VI.
951 **369** 400 f. multicoloured . . . 1·25 75

1983. Air. Bicentenary of Manned Flight. Mult.
952 500 f. Type **370** . . . . 2·00 90
953 700 f. Montgolfier balloon . . 2·50 1·25

371 Football

1983. Air. Olympic Games, Los Angeles. Mult.
954 180 f. Type **371** 50 30
955 270 f. Hurdles 75 40
956 300 f. Windsurfing . . . . . 1·10 55

372 "The Transfiguration" (detail)

373 Martin Luther King

1983. Air. Easter. Multicoloured.
957 400 f. Type **372** . . . . 1·25 75
958 600 f. "The Entombment" (detail from Baglioni Retable) . . 2·00 1·10

1983. Celebrities.
959 **373** 800 f. brown, blue & pur 2·50 1·40
960 – 800 f. brown, red & dp red 2·50 1·40
DESIGN: No. 960, President Kennedy.

374 Oua Hairstyle

375 "Family of Acrobats with Monkey"

1983. Hairstyles. Multicoloured.
961 180 f. Type **374** 60 30
962 200 f. Nation (Diamani) . . . 70 30
963 270 f. Rond Point 90 40
964 300 f. Naamu-Naamu . . . . 1·00 45
965 500 f. Bamba-Bamba . . . . 2·50 1·40

1983. Air. 10th Death Anniv of Picasso.
966 **375** 680 f. multicoloured . . . 2·00 1·25

376 Lions Club Emblem and Lions

1983. Air. Lions and Rotary Clubs. Mult.
967 700 f. Type **376** . . . . 2·25 2·00
968 700 f. Rotary Club emblem, container ship, diesel railcar and Boeing 737 airliner . . 4·50 2·50

377 Satellite, Antenna and Telephone

1983. World Communications Year.
969 **377** 180 f. multicoloured . . . 55 30

378 Lavoisier and Apparatus

379 Banzoumana Sissoko

1983. Bicent of Lavoisier's Analysis of Water.
970 **378** 300 f. green, brown & blue . . 1·10 50

1983. Mali Musicians. Multicoloured.
971 200 f. Type **379** 75 30
972 300 f. Batourou Sekou Kouyate 1·25 45

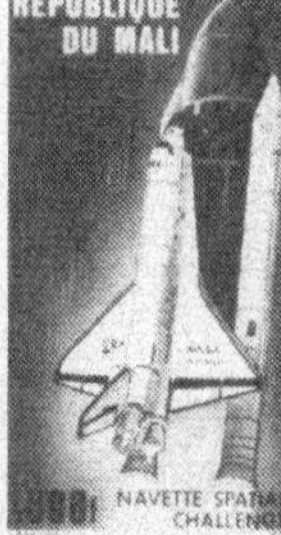

380 Nicephore Niepce and Camera

381 Space Shuttle "Challenger"

1983. 150th Death Anniv of Nicephore Niepce (pioneer of photography).
973 **380** 400 f. blue, green & dp grn 1·40 65

1983. Air. Space Shuttle.
974 **381** 1000 f. multicoloured . . 3·00 1·75

382 Young People and Map of Africa

1983. 2nd Panafrican Youth Festival. Mult.
975 240 f. Type **382** 75 40
976 270 f. Hands reaching for map of Africa 75 40

383 Mercedes, 1914

1983. Air. Paris–Dakar Rally. Multicoloured.
977 240 f. Type **383** . . . . 1·25 40
978 270 f. Mercedes SSK, 1929 . . 1·25 50
979 500 f. Mercedes W 196, 1954 2·25 80

384 Liner and U.P.U. Emblem

385 Pawn and Bishop

1983. U.P.U. Day.
981 **384** 240 f. red, black and blue 1·25 50

1983. Air. Chess Pieces.
982 **385** 300 f. grey, violet and green 1·60 60
983 – 420 f. green, pink and grey 2·00 85
984 – 500 f. blue, dp blue & green 2·75 1·00
DESIGNS: 420 f. Rook and knight; 500 f. King and queen.

386 "Canigiani Madonna"

1983. Air. Christmas. 500th Birth Anniv of Raphael. Multicoloured.
986 700 f. Type **386** . . . . 2·00 1·00
987 800 f. "Madonna of the Lamb" 2·25 1·25

387 Sahara Goat

1984. Goats. Multicoloured.
988 20 f. Type **387** 15 10
989 30 f. Billy goat 20 10
990 50 f. Billy goat (different) . . 25 15
991 240 f. Kaarta goat . . . . . 1·00 40
992 350 f. Southern goat . . . . 1·40 75

388 "Leopold Zborowski" (Modigliani)

389 Henri Dunant (founder of Red Cross)

1984. Air. Birth Centenary of Modigliani (painter).
993 **388** 700 f. multicoloured . . . 2·50 1·25

1984. Air. Celebrities.
994 **389** 400 f. dp blue, red & blue 1·50 65
995 – 540 f. dp blue, red & blue 1·60 85
DESIGN: 540 f. Abraham Lincoln.

390 Sidney Bechet

1984. Air. Jazz Musicians. Multicoloured.
996 470 f. Type **390** . . . . 2·25 75
997 500 f. Duke Ellington . . . . 2·25 80

391 Microlight Aircraft

1984. Air. Microlight Aircraft. Multicoloured.
998 270 f. Type **391** . . . . 1·00 40
999 350 f. Lazor Gemini motorized hang-glider . . . . 1·25 55

392 Weightlifting

1984. Air. Olympic Games, Los Angeles. Multicoloured.
1000 265 f. Type **392** 75 40
1001 440 f. Show jumping 90 70
1002 500 f. Hurdles . . . . 1·10 80

393 "Crucifixion" (Rubens)

1984. Air. Easter.
1004 **393** 940 f. brown & dp brown 3·00 1·50
1005 – 970 f. brown and red . . 3·00 1·50
DESIGN—HORIZ: 970 f. "The Resurrection" (Mantegna).

1984. Currency revaluation. Various stamps surch. (i) U.P.U. Day (No. 981).
1006 **384** 120 f. on 240 f. red, black and blue (postage) . . 1·10 50

(ii) Goats (Nos. 988/92)
1007 **387** 10 f. on 20 f. mult 10 10
1008 – 15 f. on 30 f. mult 15 10
1009 – 25 f. on 50 f. mult 20 15
1010 – 125 f. on 240 f. mult . . 95 40
1011 – 175 f. on 350 f. mult . . 1·75 65

(iii) Paris–Dakar Rally (No. 977)
1012 **383** 120 f. on 240 f. mult (air) 1·10 40

395 Mercedes "Simplex"

1984. Air. 150th Birth Anniv of Gottlieb Daimler (motor car designer).
1035 **395** 350 f. olive, blue and mauve 2·25 1·10
1036 – 470 f. green, violet and plum . . . . 3·00 1·50
1037 – 485 f. blue, violet and plum 3·25 1·75
DESIGNS: 470 f. Mercedes-Benz Type "370 S"; 485 f. Mercedes-Benz "500 S EC".

396 Farm Workers

1984. Progress in Countryside and Protected Essences. Multicoloured.
1038 5 f. Type **396** 10 10
1039 90 f. Carpentry 60 30
1040 100 f. Tapestry making . . . 70 35
1041 135 f. Metal work 80 40
1042 515 f. "Borassus flabelifer" 3·25 1·90
1043 1225 f. "Vitelaria paradoxa" 7·50 3·75

397 Emblem and Child

1984. United Nations Children's Fund.
1044 **397** 120 f. red, brown and green 80 40
1045 – 135 f. red, blue and brown 90 50
DESIGN: 135 f. Emblem and two children.

398 U.P.U. Emblem, Anchor and Hamburg

1984. Universal Postal Union Congress, Hamburg.
1046 **398** 135 f. mauve, green and blue 80 40

1984. Air. Olympic Winners, Los Angeles. No. 1000/1002 optd.
1047 135 f. on 265 f. Optd **HALTERES 56 KGS / 1. WU (CHINE). 2. LAI (CHINE). 3. KOTAKA (JAPON)** . . 80 40
1048 220 f. on 440 f. Optd **DRESSAGE / PAR EQUIPES / 1. RFA 2. SUISSE / 3. SUEDE** . . . 1·10 75
1049 250 f. on 500 f. Optd **ATHLETISME 3000 METRES STEEPLE / 1. KORIR (KENYA). / 2. MAHMOUD (FRANCE). / 3. DIEMER (E-U).** . . . . 1·40 1·00

400 Emblem

1984. 10th Anniv of Economic Community of West Africa.
1051 **400** 350 f. multicoloured . . 1·75 1·10

401 Dimetrodon

1984. Prehistoric Animals. Multicoloured.
1052 10 f. Type **401** 15 15
1053 25 f. Iguanodon (vert) . . . 25 15
1054 30 f. Archaeopteryx (vert) . . 70 45
1055 120 f. Type **401** . . . . . . 1·50 45
1056 175 f. As No. 1053 . . . . . 1·75 70
1057 350 f. As No. 1054 . . . . . 4·50 2·75
1058 470 f. Triceratops . . . . . 5·00 2·50

402 "Virgin and Child between St. Joseph and St. Jerome" (detail, Lorenzo Lotto)

1984. Air. Christmas.
1059 **402** 500 f. multicoloured . . 3·00 1·60

1984. Drought Aid. No. 758 surch.
1060 **298** 470 f. on 130 f. mult . . 2·75 1·75

404 Horse Galloping

405 "Clitocybe nebularis"

1985. Horses. Multicoloured.
1061 90 f. Type **404** 70 35
1062 135 f. Beledougou horse . . 1·25 40
1063 190 f. Nara horse . . . . . 1·50 70
1064 530 f. Trait horse . . . . . 4·50 2·00

1985. Fungi. Multicoloured.
1065 120 f. Type **405** . . . . . . 1·75 65
1066 200 f. "Lepiota cortinarius" 2·40 1·00
1067 485 f. "Agaricus semotus" . 6·00 2·40
1068 525 f. "Lepiota procera" . . 6·50 2·75

406 Emile Marchoux and Marchoux Institute

1985. Health. Multicoloured.
1069 120 f. Type **406** (World Lepers' Day and 40th anniv of Marchoux Institute) (postage) 80 30
1070 135 f. Lions' emblem and Samanto Village (15th anniv) 85 35
1071 470 f. Laboratory technicians and polio victim (anti-polio campaign) (air) 3·50 1·50

407 Profiles and Emblem

1985. 15th Anniv of Technical and Cultural Co-operation Agency.
1072 **407** 540 f. green and brown 3·50 1·90

408 Common Kingfisher

1985. Air. Birth Bicentenary of John J. Audubon (ornithologist). Multicoloured.
1073 180 f. Type **408** 1·75 90
1074 300 f. Great bustard (vert) 2·75 1·40
1075 470 f. Ostrich (vert) 4·25 2·40
1076 540 f. Ruppell's griffon 4·50 3·00

409 National Pioneers Movement Emblem

1985. International Youth Year. Multicoloured.
1077 120 f. Type **409** 80 40
1078 190 f. Boy leading oxen 1·40 70
1079 500 f. Sports motifs and I.Y.Y. emblem 3·50 1·75

410 Sud Aviation Caravelle, Boeing 727-200 and Agency Emblem

1985. Air. 25th Anniv of Aerial Navigation Security Agency for Africa and Madagascar (ASECNA).
1080 **410** 700 f. multicoloured 4·50 2·50

411 Lion, and Scouts collecting Wood

1985. Air. "Philexafrique" Stamp Exhibition, Lome. Multicoloured.
1081 200 f. Type **411** 1·50 1·25
1082 200 f. Satellite, dish aerial and globe 1·50 1·25

412 U.P.U. Emblem, Computer and Reservoir (Development)

1985. "Philexafrique" Stamp Exhibition, Lome, Togo (2nd issue). Multicoloured.
1083 250 f. Type **412** 1·75 1·25
1084 250 f. Satellite, girls writing and children learning from television (Youth) 1·75 1·25

413 Grey Cat

1986. Cats. Multicoloured.
1085 150 f. Type **413** 1·50 60
1086 200 f. White cat 2·25 80
1087 300 f. Tabby cat 2·50 1·10

414 Hands releasing Doves and Globe

1986. Anti-apartheid Campaign. Multicoloured.
1088 100 f. Type **414** 65 40
1089 120 f. People breaking chain around world 85 50

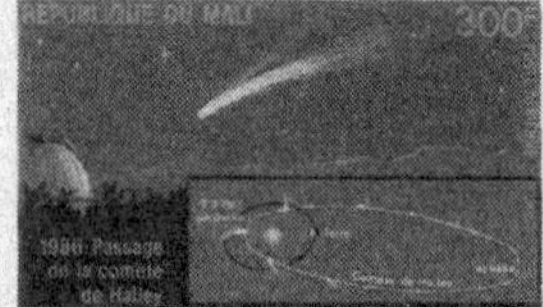

415 Comet and Diagram of Orbit

1986. Air. Appearance of Halley's Comet.
1090 **415** 300 f. multicoloured 2·25 1·25

416 Internal Combustion Engine

1986. Air. Centenaries of First Motor Car with Internal Combustion Engine and Statue of Liberty. Multicoloured.
1091 400 f. Type **416** 3·00 1·50
1092 600 f. Head of statue, and French and American flags 4·00 2·25

417 Robeson

1986. Air. 10th Death Anniv of Paul Robeson (singer).
1093 **417** 500 f. multicoloured 4·00 2·00

418 Women tending Crop

1986. World Communications Day.
1094 **418** 200 f. multicoloured 1·50 80

419 Players

1986. World Cup Football Championship, Mexico. Multicoloured.
1095 160 f. Type **419** 1·40 65
1096 225 f. Player capturing ball 1·90 90

420 Watt

1986. 250th Birth Anniv of James Watt (inventor).
1098 **420** 110 f. multicoloured 85 45

421 Eberth and Microscope **422** Chess Pieces on Board

1986. Air. 60th Death Anniv of Karl Eberth (discoverer of typhoid bacillus).
1099 **421** 550 f. multicoloured 4·00 1·90

1986. Air. World Chess Championship, London and Leningrad. Multicoloured.
1100 400 f. Type **422** 3·50 1·75
1101 500 f. Knight and board 4·50 2·25

1986. World Cup Winners. Nos. 1095/6 optd **ARGENTINE 3 R.F.A. 2.**
1102 160 f. multicoloured 1·25 85
1103 225 f. multicoloured 1·60 1·00

424 Head

1986. Endangered Animals. Giant Eland. Mult.
1105 5 f. Type **424** 10 10
1106 20 f. Standing by dead tree 25 10
1107 25 f. Stepping over fallen branch 25 10
1108 200 f. Mother and calf 1·90 95

425 Mermoz and "Croix du Sud"

1986. Air. 50th Anniv of Disappearance of Jean Mermoz (aviator). Multicoloured.
1109 150 f. Type **425** 1·25 60
1110 600 f. CAMS 53 flying boat and monoplane 4·25 2·25
1111 625 f. Map and seaplane "Comte de la Vaulx" 4·50 2·50

1986. 10th Anniv of Concorde's First Commercial Flight. Nos. 674/6 surch **1986–10e Anniversaire du 1er Vol Commercial Supersonique.**
1112 175 f. on 120 f. Type **271** 1·40 80
1113 225 f. on 130 f. Concorde and Wright Flyer I 1·75 1·00
1114 300 f. on 200 f. Concorde and Lindbergh's "Spirit of St. Louis" 2·75 1·50

427 Hansen and Follereau

1987. Air. 75th Death Anniv of Gerhard Hansen (discoverer of bacillus) and 10th Death Anniv of Raoul Follereau (leprosy pioneer).
1115 **427** 500 f. multicoloured 3·50 1·90

428 Model "A", 1903

1987. 40th Death Anniv of Henry Ford (motor car manufacturer). Multicoloured.
1116 150 f. Type **428** 1·25 55
1117 200 f. Model "T", 1923 1·75 75
1118 225 f. "Thunderbird", 1968 1·75 95
1119 300 f. "Continental", 1963 2·00 1·25

429 Konrad Adenauer **431** Scenes from "The Jazz Singer"

430 Runners and Buddha's Head

1987. Air. 20th Death Anniv of Konrad Adenauer (German statesman).
1120 **429** 625 f. stone, brown and red 4·00 2·25

1987. Air. Olympic Games, Seoul (1988) (1st issue).
1121 **430** 400 f. black and brown 2·00 1·40
1122 – 500 f. dp green, grn & red 2·75 1·75
DESIGN: 500 f. Footballers.
See also Nos. 1133/4.

1987. Air. 60th Anniv of First Talking Picture.
1123 **431** 550 f. red, brn & dp brn 4·00 2·25

432 "Apis florea"

1987. Bees. Multicoloured.
1124 100 f. Type **432** 80 50
1125 150 f. "Apis dorsata" 1·40 70
1126 175 f. "Apis adonsonii" 1·60 80
1127 200 f. "Apis mellifera" 1·75 1·00

433 Map, Dove and Luthuli

1987. Air. 20th Death Anniv of Albert John Luthuli (Nobel Peace Prize winner).
1128 **433** 400 f. mauve, blue & brn 2·50 1·50

434 Profiles and Lions Emblem

1987. Air. Lions International and Rotary International. Multicoloured.
1129 500 f. Type **434** 3·00 1·75
1130 500 f. Clasped hands and Rotary emblem 3·00 1·75

435 Anniversary Emblem and Symbols of Activities

1988. 30th Anniv of Lions International in Mali.
1131 **435** 200 f. multicoloured . . 1·25 75

436 Emblem and Doctor examining Boy

1988. 40th Anniv of W.H.O.
1132 **436** 150 f. multicoloured . . 1·10 60

437 Coubertin and Ancient and Modern Athletes

1988. Air. Olympic Games, Seoul (2nd issue). 125th Birth Anniv of Pierre de Coubertin (founder of modern games). Multicoloured.
1133 240 f. Type **437** . . . . . . 1·10 90
1134 400 f. Stadium, Olympic rings and sports pictograms . . 1·90 1·40

438 "Harlequin"

1988. Air. 15th Death Anniv of Pablo Picasso (painter).
1135 **438** 600 f. multicoloured . . 4·00 2·25

439 Concorde and Globe

1988. Air. 15th Anniv of First North Atlantic Crossing by Concorde.
1136 **439** 500 f. multicoloured . . 3·75 2·00

440 Pres. Kennedy 442 Map

1988. 25th Death Anniv of John Fitzgerald Kennedy (American President).
1137 **440** 640 f. multicoloured . . 4·00 2·40

1988. Mali Mission Hospital, Mopti. No. 1132 surch **MISSION MALI HOPITAL de MOPTI 300F** and **MEDECINS DU MONDE** emblem.
1138 **436** 300 f. on 150 f. mult . . 2·40 1·75

1988. 25th Anniv of Organization of African Unity.
1139 **442** 400 f. multicoloured . . 2·50 1·25

443 Map, Leaf and Stove

1989. Air. "Improved Stoves: For a Green Mali". Multicoloured.
1140 5 f. Type **443** 10 10
1141 10 f. Tree and stove 10 10
1142 25 f. Type **443** 15 10
1143 100 f. As No. 1141 . . . . . 60 35

444 Astronauts on Moon

1989. Air. 20th Anniv of First Manned Moon Landing.
1144 **444** 300 f. blue, purple & grn 2·00 1·25
1145 – 500 f. purple, blue & brn 3·25 1·75
DESIGN: 500 f. Astronauts on moon (diff).

445 Emblem and Crossed Syringes

1989. Vaccination Programme. Multicoloured.
1146 20 f. Type **445** 15 10
1147 30 f. Doctor vaccinating woman 20 10
1148 50 f. Emblem and syringes . 40 15
1149 175 f. Doctor vaccinating child 1·40 65

446 Emblem

1989. 25th Anniv of International Law Institute of French-speaking Countries.
1150 **446** 150 f. multicoloured . . 1·10 55
1151 200 f. multicoloured . . 1·40 70

447 Crowd 448 U.P.U. Emblem and Hands holding Envelopes

1989. Air. Bicentenary of French Revolution and "Philexfrance 89" International Stamp Exn, Paris.
1152 **447** 400 f. red, blue & purple 2·50 1·25
1153 – 600 f. violet, pur & mve 3·50 2·00
DESIGN: 600 f. Marianne and Storming of Bastille.

1989. World Post Day.
1154 **448** 625 f. multicoloured . . 3·50 2·25

449 Pope and Cathedral

1990. Visit of Pope John Paul II.
1155 **449** 200 f. multicoloured . . 1·60 80

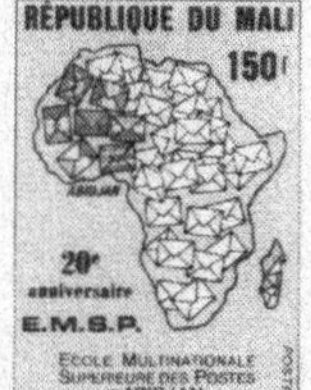
450 Envelopes on Map

1990. 20th Anniv of Multinational Postal Training School, Abidjan.
1156 **450** 150 f. multicoloured . . . 1·25 55

451 Footballers

1990. Air. World Cup Football Championship, Italy. Multicoloured.
1157 200 f. Type **451** . . . . 1·50 75
1158 225 f. Footballers (different) 1·75 85

1990. World Cup Result. Nos. 1157/8 optd. Mult.
1160 200 f. **ITALIE : 2 / ANGLETERRE : 1** . . . . 1·50 85
1161 225 f. **R.F.A. : 1 / ARGENTINE : 0** . . . . 1·75 85

453 Pres. Moussa Traore and Bamako Bridge

1990. 30th Anniv of Independence.
1163 **453** 400 f. multicoloured . . . 2·50 1·50

454 Man writing and Adults learning to Read 455 Woman carrying Water and Cattle at Well

1990. International Literacy Year.
1164 **454** 150 f. multicoloured . . . 1·25 55
1165 200 f. multicoloured . . . 1·50 75

1991. Lions Club (1166) and Rotary International (1167) Projects. Multicoloured.
1166 200 f. Type **455** (6th anniv of wells project) . . . . 1·40 75
1167 200 f. Bamako branch emblem and hand (30th anniv of anti-polio campaign) . . . . . 1·40 75

456 Sonrai Dance, Takamba 457 Bank Emblem and Map of France

1991. Dances. Multicoloured.
1168 50 f. Type **456** 30 15
1169 100 f. Malinke dance, Mandiani 60 30
1170 150 f. Bamanan dance, Kono 90 50
1171 200 f. Dogon dance, Songho 1·10 75

1991. 50th Anniv of Central Economic Co-operation Bank.
1172 **457** 200 f. multicoloured . . . 1·25 75

458 Women with Torch and Banner

1992. National Women's Movement for the Safeguarding of Peace and National Unity.
1173 **458** 150 f. multicoloured . . 75 40

1992. Various stamps surch.
1174 – 25 f. on 470 f. mult (No. 1058) (postage) 15 10
1175 **420** 30 f. on 110 f. mult . . . 15 10
1176 – 50 f. on 300 f. mult (No. 1087) 25 15
1177 – 50 f. on 1225 f. mult (No. 1043) 25 15
1178 – 150 f. on 135 f. mult (No. 1070) 75 40
1179 – 150 f. on 190 f. mult (No. 1063) 75 40
1180 – 150 f. on 190 f. mult (No. 1078) 75 40
1181 **400** 150 f. on 350 f. mult . . 75 40
1182 – 150 f. on 485 f. mult (No. 1067) . . . . 1·25 50
1183 – 150 f. on 525 f. mult (No. 1068) . . . . 1·25 50
1184 – 150 f. on 530 f. mult (No. 1064) 75 40
1185 **440** 200 f. on 640 f. mult . . 1·00 50
1186 – 240 f. on 350 f. mult (No. 1057) . . . . 1·25 65
1187 **448** 240 f. on 625 f. mult . . 1·25 65
1188 **410** 20 f. on 700 f. mult (air) 10 10
1189 **415** 20 f. on 300 f. mult . . . 10 10
1190 – 25 f. on 470 f. mult (No. 1071) 15 10
1191 **408** 30 f. on 180 f. mult . . . 15 10
1192 – 30 f. on 500 f. purple, blue and brown (No. 1145) 15 10
1193 – 100 f. on 540 f. mult (No. 1076) 50 25
1194 **438** 100 f. on 600 f. mult . . 50 25
1195 **444** 150 f. on 300 f. blue, purple and green 75 40
1196 **447** 150 f. on 400 f. red, blue and purple 75 40
1197 – 200 f. on 300 f. mult (No. 1074) . . . . 1·00 50
1198 – 240 f. on 600 f. violet, purple & mve (No. 1153) 1·25 65

1992. (a) Postage. No. 1095 surch **150 f "Euro 92"**.
1199 **419** 150 f. on 160 f. mult . . 75 40

(b) Air. No. 1134 surch **150F "Barcelone 92"**.
1200 150 f. on 400 f. multicoloured 75 40

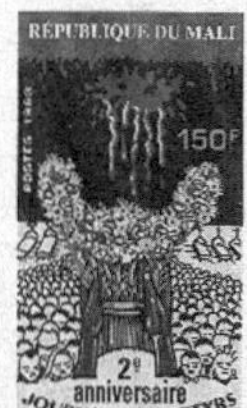
462 Blood, Memorial and Martyrs

1993. 2nd Anniv of Martyrs' Day.
1203 **462** 150 f. multicoloured . . 70 35
1204 160 f. multicoloured . . 75 40

464 Lecture on Problem Issues

1993. 35th Anniv of Lions International in Mali.
1207 **464** 200 f. multicoloured . . 90 45
1208 225 f. multicoloured . . 1·00 50

466 Figure Skating 467 Juan Schiaffino (Uruguay)

1994. Winter Olympic Games, Lillehammer. Multicoloured.

1219 150 f. Type **466** 35 20
1220 200 f. Giant slalom 50 25
1221 225 f. Ski jumping 55 30
1222 750 f. Speed skating 1·75 90

1994. World Cup Football Championship, U.S.A. Players from Different Teams. Multicoloured.

1224 200 f. Type **467** 50 25
1225 240 f. Diego Maradona (Argentine Republic) 60 30
1226 260 f. Paolo Rossi (Italy) 65 35
1227 1000 f. Franz Beckenbauer (Germany) 2·40 1·25

468 Scaphonyx

1994. Prehistoric Animals. Multicoloured.

1229 5 f. Type **468** 10 10
1230 10 f. Cynognathus 10 10
1231 15 f. Lesothosaurus 10 10
1232 20 f. Scutellosaurus 10 10
1233 25 f. Ceratosaurus 10 10
1234 30 f. Dilophosaurus 10 10
1235 40 f. Dryosaurus 10 10
1236 50 f. Heterodontosaurus 10 10
1237 60 f. Anatosaurus 15 10
1238 70 f. Saurornithoides 15 10
1239 80 f. Avimimus 20 10
1240 90 f. Saltasaurus 20 10
1241 300 f. Dromaeosaurus 75 40
1242 400 f. Tsintaosaurus 95 50
1243 600 f. Velociraptor 1·50 75
1244 700 f. Ouranosaurus 1·75 90

Nos. 1229/44 were issued together, se-tenant, forming a composite design.

469 "Sternuera castanea"

1994. Insects. Multicoloured.

1246 40 f. Type **469** 10 10
1247 50 f. "Eudicella gralli" (horiz) 10 10
1248 100 f. "Homoderus mellyi" 25 15
1249 200 f. "Kraussaria angulifera" (horiz) 50 25

470 Vaccinating Child

1994. Vaccination Campaign.

1250 **470** 150 f. green and black 35 20
1251 200 f. blue and black 50 25

471 Rock Doves

1994. Birds. Multicoloured.

1252 25 f. Type **471** 10 10
1253 30 f. Helmet guineafowl 10 10
1254 150 f. Crowned cranes (vert) 35 20
1255 200 f. Red junglefowl (vert) 50 25

MORE DETAILED LISTS

are given in the Stanley Gibbons Catalogues referred to in the country headings. For lists of current volumes see introduction

472 Family   473 Kirk Douglas in "Spartacus"

1994. International Year of the Family.

1256 **472** 200 f. multicoloured 50 25

1994. Film Stars. Multicoloured.

1257 100 f. Type **473** (postage) 25 15
1258 150 f. Elizabeth Taylor in "Cleopatra" 35 20
1259 225 f. Marilyn Monroe in "The River of No Return" 55 30
1260 500 f. Arnold Swarzenegger in "Conan the Barbarian" 1·25 65
1261 1000 f. Elvis Presley in "Loving You" 2·40 1·25
1263 200 f. Clint Eastwood in "A Mule for Sister Sara" (inscr "SIERRA TORRIDE") (air) 50 25

474 Ella Fitzgerald

1994. Jazz Singers. Multicoloured.

1264 200 f. Type **474** 50 25
1265 225 f. Lionel Hampton 55 30
1266 240 f. Sarah Vaughan 60 30
1267 300 f. Count Basie 75 40
1268 400 f. Duke Ellington 95 50
1269 600 f. Miles Davis 1·50 75

475 Soldiers caught in Explosion

1994. 50th Anniv of Second World War D-Day Landings. Multicoloured. (a) Villers-Bocage.

1271 200 f. Type **475** 50 25
1272 200 f. Tank (29 × 47 mm) 50 25
1273 200 f. Troops beside tank 50 25

(b) Beaumont-sur-Sarthe.

1274 300 f. Bombers and troops under fire 75 40
1275 300 f. Bombers and tanks (29 × 47 mm) 75 40
1276 300 f. Tank and soldier with machine gun 75 40

(c) Utah Beach (wrongly inscr "Utha").

1277 300 f. Wounded troops and bow of boat 75 40
1278 300 f. Troops in boat (29 × 47 mm) 75 40
1279 300 f. Troops in boats 75 40

(d) Air Battle.

1280 400 f. Bombers 95 50
1281 400 f. Aircraft (29 × 47 mm) 95 50
1282 400 f. Airplane on fire 95 50

(e) Sainte-Mere-Eglise.

1283 400 f. Troops firing at paratrooper 95 50
1284 400 f. Church and soldier (29 × 47 mm) 95 50
1285 400 f. Paratroopers and German troops 95 50

Nos. 1271/3, 1274/6, 1277/9, 1280/2 and 1283/5 respectively were issued together, se-tenant, forming composite designs.

476 Olympic Rings on National Flag

1994. Centenary of International Olympic Committee (1st issue).

1286 **476** 150 f. multicoloured 35 20
1287 200 f. multicoloured 50 25

See also Nos. 1342/5.

477 Couple holding Condoms

1994. Anti-AIDS Campaign. Multicoloured.

1288 150 f. Type **477** 35 20
1289 225 f. Nurse treating patient and laboratory worker 55 30

478 "Venus of Brassempoury"

1994. Ancient Art. Multicoloured.

1290 15 f. Type **478** 10 10
1291 25 f. Cave paintings, Tanum 10 10
1292 45 f. Prehistoric men painting mural 10 10
1293 50 f. Cave paintings, Lascaux (horiz) 10 10
1294 55 f. Painting from tomb of Amonherkhopeshef 15 10
1295 65 f. God Anubis laying out Pharoah (horiz) 15 10
1296 75 f. Sphinx and pyramid, Mycerinus (horiz) 20 10
1297 85 f. Bust of Nefertiti 20 10
1298 95 f. Statue of Shibum 25 15
1299 100 f. Cavalry of Ur (horiz) 25 15
1300 130 f. Head of Mesopotamian harp 30 15
1301 135 f. Mesopotamian tablet (horiz) 35 20
1302 140 f. Assyrian dignitary 35 20
1303 180 f. Enamel relief from Babylon (horiz) 45 25
1304 190 f. Assyrians hunting 45 25
1305 200 f. "Mona Lisa of Nimrod" 50 25
1306 225 f. Phoenician coins (horiz) 55 30
1307 250 f. Phoenician sphinx 60 30
1308 275 f. Persian archer 65 35
1309 280 f. Glass paste mask 70 35

479 "Polyptychus roseus"

1994. Multicoloured. (a) Butterflies and Moths.

1310 20 f. Type **479** 10 10
1311 30 f. "Elymniopsis bammakoo" 10 10
1312 40 f. Silver-striped hawk moth 10 10
1313 150 f. Crimson-speckled moth 35 20
1314 180 f. Foxy charaxes 45 25
1315 200 f. Common dotted border 50 25

(b) Plants.

1316 25 f. "Disa kewensis" 10 10
1317 50 f. "Angraecum eburneum" 10 10
1318 100 f. "Ansellia africana" 25 15
1319 140 f. Sorghum 35 20
1320 150 f. Onion 35 20
1321 190 f. Maize 45 25
1322 200 f. Clouded agaric 50 25
1323 225 f. Parasol mushroom 55 30
1324 500 f. "Lepiota aspera" 1·25 65

(c) Insects.

1325 225 f. Goliath beetle 55 30
1326 240 f. Cricket 60 30
1327 350 f. Praying mantis 85 45

1994. Winter Olympic Games Medal Winners, Lillehammer. Nos. 1219/22 optd.

1328 150 f. **O GRISHSHUK Y. PLATOV RUSSIE** 35 20
1329 150 f. **Y. GORDEYEVA S. GRINKOV RUSSIE** 35 20
1330 200 f. **M. WASMEIER ALLEMAGNE** 50 25
1331 200 f. **D. COMPAGNONI ITALIE** 50 25
1332 225 f. **T. WEISSFLOG ALLEMAGNE** 55 30
1333 225 f. **E. BREDESEN NORVEGE** 55 30
1334 750 f. **J.O. KOSS NORVEGE** 1·75 90
1335 750 f. **B. BLAIR U.S.A.** 1·75 90

A sheetlet also exists containing Nos. 1219/22 each optd with both of the inscriptions for that value.

1994. Results of World Cup Football Championship. Nos. 1224/27 optd **1. BRESIL 2. ITALIE 3. SUEDE**.

1337 200 f. multicoloured 50 25
1338 240 f. multicoloured 60 30
1339 260 f. multicoloured 65 35
1340 1000 f. multicoloured 2·40 1·25

482 Pierre de Coubertin (founder) and Torchbearer   483 Statue and Village

1994. Centenary of International Olympic Committee (2nd issue). Multicoloured.

1342 225 f. Type **482** 55 30
1343 240 f. Coubertin designing Olympic rings 60 30
1344 300 f. Athlete bearing torch and Coubertin (horiz) 75 40
1345 500 f. Olympic rings and Coubertin at desk (horiz) 1·25 65

1994. 20th International Tourism Day. Multicoloured.

1347 150 f. Type **483** 35 20
1348 200 f. Sphinx, pyramids and Abu Simbel temple (horiz) 50 25

OFFICIAL STAMPS

O 9 Dogon Mask   O 30 Mail Flag and Emblems

1961.

O26 **O 9** 1 f. violet 10 10
O27 2 f. red 10 10
O28 3 f. slate 10 10
O29 5 f. turquoise 15 15
O30 10 f. brown 20 15
O31 25 f. blue 35 15
O32 30 f. red 40 20
O33 50 f. myrtle 70 25
O34 85 f. purple 1·10 65
O35 100 f. green 1·40 65
O36 200 f. purple 2·75 1·40

1964. Centre and flag multicoloured; frame colour given.

O 90 **O 30** 1 f. green 10 10
O 91 2 f. lavender 10 10
O 92 3 f. slate 10 10
O 93 5 f. purple 10 10
O 94 10 f. blue 15 10
O 95 25 f. ochre 20 15
O 96 30 f. green 25 15
O 97 50 f. orange 35 15
O 98 85 f. brown 50 20
O 99 100 f. red 65 30
O100 200 f. blue 1·50 60

O 341 Arms of Gao

1981. Town Arms. Multicoloured.

O878 5 f. Type **O 341** 10 10
O879 15 f. Tombouctou 10 10
O880 50 f. Mopti 20 10
O881 180 f. Segou 60 30
O882 200 f. Sikasso 80 30
O883 680 f. Koulikoro 2·50 95
O884 700 f. Kayes 2·75 1·25
O885 1000 f. Bamako 4·00 1·50

1984. Nos. O878/85 surch.

O1013 15 f. on 5 f. Type **O 341** 15 10
O1014 50 f. on 15 f. Tombouctou 30 15
O1015 120 f. on 50 f. Mopti 70 25
O1016 295 f. on 180 f. Segou 2·00 90
O1017 470 f. on 200 f. Sikasso 3·00 1·50
O1018 515 f. on 680 f. Koulikoro 3·50 1·90
O1019 845 f. on 700 f. Kayes 6·00 2·50
O1020 1225 f. on 1000 f. Bamako 7·50 3·75

POSTAGE DUE STAMPS

D 9 Bambara Mask

1961.

D26	**D 9**	1 f. black	10	10
D27		2 f. blue	10	10
D28		5 f. mauve	20	10
D29		10 f. orange	25	15
D30		20 f. turquoise	50	25
D31		25 f. purple	65	30

D **28** "Polyptychus roseus"

1964. Butterflies and Moths. Multicoloured.

D83	1 f. Type D **28**	10	10
D84	1 f. "Deilephila nerii"	10	10
D85	2 f. "Bunaea alcinoe"	15	15
D86	2 f. "Gynanisa maja"	15	15
D87	3 f. "Teracolus eris"	35	30
D88	3 f. "Colotis antevippe"	35	30
D89	5 f. "Manatha microcera"	35	30
D90	5 f. "Charaxes epijasius"	35	30
D91	10 f. "Hypokopelates otraeda"	45	35
D92	10 f. "Lipaphnaeus leonina"	45	35
D93	20 f. "Lobobunaea christyi"	75	70
D94	20 f. "Gonimbrasia hecate"	75	70
D95	25 f. "Hypolimnas misippus"	1·10	90
D96	25 f. "Castopsilia florella"	1·10	90

1984. Nos. D83/96 surch.

D1021	5 f. on 1 f. Type D **28**	10	10
D1022	5 f. on 1 f. "Deilephila nerii"	10	10
D1023	10 f. on 2 f. "Bunaea alcinoe"	10	10
D1024	10 f. on 2 f. "Gynanisa maja"	10	10
D1025	15 f. on 3 f. "Teracolus eris"	15	10
D1026	15 f. on 3 f. "Colotis antevippe"	15	10
D1027	25 f. on 5 f. "Manatha microcera"	15	15
D1028	25 f. on 5 f. "Charaxes epijasius"	15	15
D1029	50 f. on 10 f. "Hypokopelates otraeda"	30	30
D1030	50 f. on 10 f. "Lipaphnaeus leonina"	30	30
D1031	100 f. on 20 f. "Lobobunaea christyi"	60	60
D1032	100 f. on 20 f. "Gonimbrasia hecate"	60	60
D1033	125 f. on 25 f. "Hypolimnas misippus"	75	75
D1034	125 f. on 25 f. "Catopsilia florella"	75	75

APPENDIX

The following stamps have either been issued in excess of postal needs or have not been available to the public in reasonable quantities at face value. Such stamps may later be given full listing if there is evidence of regular postal use.

All on gold foil.

1994.

World Cup Football Championship, U.S.A. Air. 3000 f.

Film Stars. Air. 3000 f.

MANAMA Pt. 19

A dependency of Ajman.

100 dirhams = 1 riyal

1966. Nos. 10, 12, 14 and 18 of Ajman surch **Manama** in English and Arabic and new value.

1	40 d. on 40 n.p. multicoloured	25	15
2	70 d. on 70 n.p. multicoloured	50	15
3	1 r. 50 on 1 r. 50 multicoloured	1·40	45
4	10 r. on 10 r. multicoloured	6·50	6·00

1967. Nos. 140/8 of Ajman optd **MANAMA** in English and Arabic. (a) Postage.

5	15 d. blue and brown	10	10
6	30 d. brown and black	15	15
7	50 d. black and brown	35	35
8	70 d. violet and black	60	50
	(b) Air.		
9	1 r. green and brown	40	25
10	2 r. mauve and black	70	50
11	3 r. black and brown	1·10	1·75
12	5 r. brown and black	3·50	3·50
13	10 r. blue and brown	6·50	6·50

APPENDIX

The following stamps have either been issued in excess of postal needs or have not been available to the public in reasonable quantities at face value. Such stamps may later be given full listing if there is evidence of regular postal use.

1966.

New Currency Surcharges. Stamps of Ajman surch **Manama** in English and Arabic and new value.

(a) Nos. 19/20 and 22/4 (Kennedy). 10 d. on 10 n.p., 15 d. on 15 n.p., 1 r. on 1 r., 2 r. on 2 r., 3 r. on 3 r.

(b) Nos. 27, 30 and 35/6 (Olympics). 5 d. on 5 n.p., 25 d. on 25 n.p., 3 r. on 3 r., 5 r. on 5 r.

(c) Nos. 80/2 and 85 (Churchill). 50 d. on 50 n.p., 75 d. on 75 n.p., 1 r. on 1 r., 5 r. on 5 r.

(d) Nos. 95/8 (Space). Air 50 d. on 50 n.p., 1 r. on 1 r., 3 r. on 3 r., 5 r. on 5 r.

1967.

World Scout Jamboree, Idaho. Postage 30, 70 d., 1 r.; Air 2, 3, 4 r.

Olympic Games, Mexico (1968). Postage 35, 65, 75 d., 1 r.; Air 1 r. 25, 2, 3, 4 r.

Winter Olympic Games, Grenoble (1968). Postage 5, 35, 60, 75 d.; Air 1, 1 r. 25, 2, 3 r.

Paintings by Renoir and Terbrugghen. Air 35, 65 d., 1, 2 r. × 3.

1968.

Paintings by Velazquez. Air 1 r. × 2, 2 r. × 2.

Costumes. Air 30 d. × 2, 70 d. × 2, 1 r. × 2, 2 r. × 2.

Olympic Games, Mexico. Postage 1 r. × 4; Air 2 r. x 4.

Satellites and Spacecraft. Air 30 d. × 2, 70 d. × 2, 1 r. × 2, 2 r. × 2, 3 r. × 2.

Human Rights Year. Kennedy Brothers and Martin Luther King. Air 1 r. × 3, 2 r. × 3.

Sports Champions, Famous Footballers. Postage 15, 20, 50, 75 d., 1 r.; Air 10 r.

Heroes of Humanity. Circular designs on gold or silver foil. 60 d. × 12.

Olympic Games, Mexico. Circular designs on gold or silver foil. Air 3 r. × 8.

Mothers' Day. Paintings. Postage 1 r. × 6.

Kennedy Brothers Commem. Postage 2 r.; Air 5 r.

Cats (1st series). Postage 1, 2, 3 d.; Air 2, 3 r.

5th Death Anniv of Pres. Kennedy. Air 10 r.

Space Exploration. Postage 5, 10, 15, 20, 25 d.; Air 15 r.

Olympic Games, Mexico. Gold Medals. Postage 2 r. × 4; Air 5 r. × 4.

Christmas. Air 5 r.

1969.

Sports Champions. Cyclists. Postage 1, 2, 5, 10, 15, 20 d.; Air 12 r.

Sports Champions. German Footballers. Postage 5, 10, 15, 20, 25 d.; Air 10 r.

Sports Champions. Motor-racing Drivers. Postage 1, 5, 10, 15, 25 d.; Air 10 r.

Motor-racing Cars. Postage 1, 5, 10, 15, 25 d.; Air 10 r.

Sports Champions. Boxers. Postage 5, 10, 15, 20 d.; Air 10 r.

Sports Champions. Baseball Players. Postage 1, 2, 5, 10, 15 d.; Air 10 r.

Birds. Air 1 r. × 11.

Roses. Postage 1 r. × 6.

Animals. Air 1 r. × 6.

Paintings by Italian Artists. 5, 10, 15, 20 d., 10 r.

Great Composers. Air 5, 10, 25 d., 10 r.

Paintings by French Artists. 1 r. × 4.

Nude Paintings. Air 2 r. × 4.

Kennedy Brothers. Air 2, 3, 10 r.

Olympic Games, Mexico. Gold Medal Winners. Postage 1, 2 d., 10 r.; Air 10 d., 5, 10 r.

Paintings of the Madonna. Postage 10 d.; Air 10 r.

Space Flight of "Apollo 9". Optd on 1968 Space Exploration issue. Air 15 r.

Space Flight of "Apollo 10". Optd on 1968 Space Exploration issue. Air 15 r.

1st Death Anniv of Gagarin. Optd on 1968 Space Exploration issue. 5 d.

2nd Death Anniv of Edward White (astronaut). Optd on 1968 Space Exploration issue. 10 d.

1st Death Anniv of Robert Kennedy. Optd on 1969 Kennedy Brothers issue. Air 2 r.

Olympic Games, Munich (1972). Optd on 1969 Mexico Gold Medal Winners issue. Air 10 d., 5, 10 r.

Moon Mission of "Apollo 11". Air 1, 2, 3 r.

Christmas. Paintings by Brueghel. Postage 1, 2, 4, 5, 10 d.; Air 6 r.

1970.

"Soyuz" and "Apollo" Space Programmes. Postage 1, 2, 4, 5, 10 d.; Air 3, 5 r.

Kennedy and Eisenhower Commem. Embossed on gold foil. Air 20 r.

Lord Baden-Powell Commem. Embossed on gold foil. Air 20 r.

World Cup Football Championship, Mexico. Postage 20, 40, 60, 80 d., 1 r.; Air 3 r.

Brazil's Victory in World Cup Football Championship. Optd on 1970 World Cup issue. Postage 20, 40, 60, 80 d., 1 r.; Air 3 r.

Paintings by Michelangelo. Postage 1, 2, 4, 5, 10 d.; Air 6 r.

World Fair "Expo 70", Osaka, Japan. Air 25, 50, 75 d., 1, 2, 3, 12 r.

Paintings by Renoir. Postage 1, 2, 5, 6, 10 d.; Air 5, 12 r.

Olympic Games, Rome, Tokyo, Mexico and Munich. Postage 15, 30, 50, 70 d.; Air 2, 5 r.

Winter Olympic Games, Sapporo (1972) (1st issue). Postage 2, 3, 4, 10 d.; Air 2, 5 r.

Christmas. Flower Paintings by Brueghel. Postage 5, 20, 25, 30, 50 d.; Air 60 d., 1, 2 r.

1971.

Winter Olympic Games, Sapporo (2nd issue). Postage 1, 2, 3, 4, 5, 6, 8, 10, 12, 15, 20, 25, 30, 35, 40, 50 d.; Air 75 d, 1, 2, 2 r. 50.

Roses. Postage 5, 20, 25, 30, 50 d.; Air 60 d., 1, 2 r.

Birds. Postage 5, 20, 25, 30, 50 d.; Air 60 d., 1, 2 r.

Paintings by Modigliani. Air 25, 50, 60, 75 d., 1 r. 50, 3 r.

Paintings by Rubens. Postage 1, 2, 3, 4, 5, 10 d.; Air 2, 3 r.

"Philatokyo '71" Stamp Exhibition, Paintings by Hokusai and Hiroshige. Postage 10, 15, 20, 25, 50, 75 d.; Air 1, 2 r.

25th Anniv of United Nations. Optd on 1970 Christmas issue. Postage 5, 20, 25, 30, 50 d.; Air 60 d., 1, 2 r.

British Military Uniforms. Postage 5, 20, 25, 30, 50 d.; Air 60 d., 1, 2 r.

Space Flight of "Apollo 14". Postage 15, 25, 50, 60, 70 d.; Air 5 r.

Space Flight of "Apollo 15". Postage 25, 40, 50, 60 d.; Air 1, 6 r.

13th World Scout Jamboree, Asagiri, Japan (1st issue). Postage 1, 2, 3, 5, 7, 10, 12, 15, 20, 25, 30, 35, 40, 50, 65, 80 d.; Air 1, 1 r. 25, 1 r. 50, 2 r.

World Wild Life Conservation. Postage 1, 2, 3, 5, 7, 10, 12, 15, 20, 25, 30, 35, 40, 50, 65, 80 d.; Air 1 r., 1 r. 25, 1 r. 50, 2 r.

13th World Scout Jamboree, Asagiri, Japan (2nd issue). Stamps. Postage 10, 15, 20, 25, 50, 75 d.; Air 1, 2 r.

Winter Olympic Games, Sapporo (3rd issue). Postage 1, 2, 3, 4, 5, 10 d.; Air 2, 3 r.

Cats (2nd series). Postage 15, 25, 40, 60 d.; Air 3, 10 r.

Lions International Clubs. Optd on 1971 Uniforms issue. Postage 5, 20, 25, 30, 50 d.; Air 60 d., 1, 2 r.

Paintings of Ships. Postage 15, 20, 25, 30, 50 d.; Air 60 d., 1, 2 r.

Great Olympic Champions. Postage 25, 50, 75 d., 1 r.; Air 5 r.

Prehistoric Animals. Postage 15, 20, 25, 30, 50, 60 d.; Air 1, 2 r.

Footballers. Postage 5, 10, 15, 20, 40 d.; Air 5 r.

Royal Visit of Queen Elizabeth II to Japan. Postage 10, 20, 30, 40, 50 d.; Air 2, 3 r.

Fairy Tales. Stories by Hans Andersen. Postage 1, 2, 4, 5, 10 d.; Air 3 r.

World Fair, Philadelphia (1976). American Paintings. Postage 20, 25, 50, 60, 75 d.; Air 3 r.

Fairy Tales. Well-known stories. Postage 1, 2, 4, 5, 10 d.; Air 3 r.

Space Flight of "Apollo 16". Postage 20, 30, 40, 50, 60 d.; Air 3, 4 r.

Tropical Fishes. Postage 1, 2, 3, 4, 5, 10 d.; Air 2, 3 r.

European Tour of Emperor Hirohito of Japan. Postage 1, 2, 4, 5, 10 d.; Air 6 r.

Meeting of Pres. Nixon and Emperor Hirohito of Japan in Alaska. Optd on 1971 Emperor's Tour issue. Air 6 r.

2500th Anniv of Persian Empire. Postage 10, 20, 30, 40, 50 d.; Air 3 r.

Space Flight of "Apollo 15" and Future Developments in Space. Postage 10, 15, 20, 25, 50 d.; Air 1, 2 r.

1972.

150th Death Anniv (1971) of Napoleon. Postage 10, 20, 30, 40 d.; Air 1, 2, 3, 4 r.

1st Death Anniv of Gen. de Gaulle. Postage 10, 20, 30, 40 d.; Air 1, 2, 3, 4 r.

Paintings from the "Alte Pinakothek", Munich. Postage 5, 10, 15, 20, 25 d.; Air 5 r.

"Tour de France" Cycle Race. Postage 5, 10, 15, 20, 25, 30, 35, 40, 45, 50, 55, 60 d.; Air 65, 70, 75, 80, 85, 90, 95 d., 1 r.

Cats and Dogs. Postage 10, 20, 30, 40, 50 d.; Air 1 r.

25th Anniv of U.N.I.C.E.F. Optd on 1971 World Scout Jamboree, Asagiri (2nd issue). Postage 10, 15, 20, 25, 50, 75 d.; Air 1, 2 r.

Past and Present Motorcars. Postage 10, 20, 30, 40, 50 d.; Air 1 r.

Military Uniforms. 1 r. × 11.

The United Arab Emirates Ministry of Communications took over the Manama postal service on 1 August 1972. Further stamps inscribed "Manama" issued after that date were released without authority and had no validity.

MANCHUKUO Pt. 17

Issues for the Japanese puppet Government set up in 1932 under President (later Emperor) Pu Yi.

100 fen = 1 yuan

1 White Pagoda, Liaoyang

2 Pu Yi, later Emperor Kang-teh

1932. (a) With five characters in top panel as T **1** and **2**.

1	**1**	½ f. brown	75	25
2		1 f. lake	75	10
25		1½ f. mauve	1·50	75
4		2 f. slate	2·25	20
27		3 f. brown	2·50	10
6		4 f. olive	50	10
7		5 f. green	75	15
8		6 f. red	2·75	40
9		7 f. grey	1·25	20
10		8 f. brown	9·00	6·00
11		10 f. orange	1·50	15
12	**2**	13 f. brown	3·50	4·25
13		15 f. red	15·00	75
14		16 f. blue	12·00	2·25
15		20 f. brown	2·75	40
16		30 f. orange	3·25	1·25
17		50 f. green	3·75	70
31		1 y. violet	17·00	6·50
		(b) With six characters in top panel.		
40	**1**	½ f. sepia	25	10
41		1 f. lake	25	10
42		1½ f. mauve	60	40
43		3 f. brown	40	10
44		5 f. blue	8·50	60
45		5 f. slate	3·50	40
46		6 f. red	1·00	15
47		7 f. grey	1·25	40
48		9 f. orange	1·25	20
55		10 f. blue	4·25	10
56	**2**	13 f. brown	3·75	4·25
49		15 f. red	2·00	25
50		18 f. green	12·00	3·50
51		20 f. sepia	2·25	20
52		30 f. brown	3·35	35
53		50 f. olive	3·75	30
54		1 y. violet	10·00	3·50

3 Map and Flags

6 Emperor's Palace

1933. 1st Anniv of Republic.

19	**3**	1 f. orange	1·00	1·00
20	–	2 f. green	7·50	7·50
21	**3**	4 f. red	1·00	50
22	–	10 f. blue	11·00	11·00

DESIGN: 2, 10 f. Council Hall, Hsinking.

1934. Enthronement of Emperor.

32	**6**	1½ f. brown	1·00	40
33	–	3 f. red	1·00	20
34	**6**	6 f. green	4·25	3·75
35	–	10 f. blue	5·75	3·75

DESIGN: 3 f., 10 f. Phoenixes.

1934. Stamps of 1932 surch with four Japanese characters.

36	**1**	1 f. on 4 f. olive (No. 6)	3·50	2·25
38		3 f. on 4 f. olive (No. 6)	22·00	18·50
39	**2**	3 f. on 16 f. blue (No. 14)	6·50	6·50

In No. 38 the left hand upper character of the surcharge consists of three horizontal lines.

12 Orchid Crest of Manchukuo

13 Changpai Mountain and Sacred Lake

1935. China Mail.

64	12	2 f. green	45	15
65		2½ f. violet	35	15
66	13	4 f. green	1·00	30
67		5 f. blue	25	10
68	12	8 f. yellow	1·75	30
60	13	12 f. red	4·50	2·25
70		13 f. brown	50	15

15 Mt. Fuji

16 Phoenixes

1935. Visit of Emperor Kang-teh to Japan.

71	15	1½ f. green	1·00	80
72	16	3 f. orange	1·00	25
73	15	6 f. red	3·25	3·25
74	16	10 f. blue	3·25	2·50

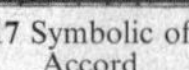

17 Symbolic of Accord

19 State Council Building, Hsinking

20 Chengte Palace, Jehol

1936. Japan–Manchukuo Postal Agreement.

75	17	1½ f. sepia	1·75	1·50
76	–	3 f. mauve	1·50	25
77	17	6 f. red	6·50	6·50
78	–	10 f. blue	5·50	3·50

DESIGN—HORIZ: 3 f., 10 f. Department of Communications.

1936.

79	19	½ f. brown	25	15
80		1 f. red	25	10
81		1½ f. violet	2·50	2·00
82	A	2 f. green	20	10
83	19	3 f. brown	25	15
84	B	4 f. green	20	10
149	19	5 f. grey	10	1·00
86	A	6 f. red	75	10
87	B	7 f. black	1·00	10
88		9 f. red	75	20
89	20	10 f. blue	40	10
90	B	12 f. orange	25	10
91		13 f. brown	10·00	20·00
92		15 f. red	1·25	30
93	C	18 f. green	7·50	7·50
94		19 f. green	3·50	1·50
95	A	20 f. brown	1·50	35
96	20	30 f. brown	1·75	30
97	D	38 f. blue	6·50	6·00
98		39 f. blue	1·00	1·00
99	A	50 f. green	2·25	30
154	20	1 y. violet	45	2·75

DESIGNS: A, Carting soya-beans; B. Peiling Mausoleum; C, Airplane and grazing sheep (domestic and China air mail); D, Fokker F.VII b/3m airplane over R. Sungari bridge (air mail to Japan).

21 Sun rising over Fields

22 Shadowgraph of old and new Hsinking

1937. 5th Anniv of Founding of State.

101	21	1½ f. red	5·00	6·00
102	22	3 f. green	1·50	1·75

1937. China Mail. Surch in Chinese characters.

108	12	2½ f. on 2 f. green	2·75	2·00
110	13	5 f. on 4 f. green	2·75	2·50
111		13 f. on 12 f. brown	9·50	7·00

27 Pouter Pigeon and Hsinking

1937. Completion of Five Year Reconstruction Plan for Hsinking.

112	27	2 f. mauve	2·00	1·00
113	–	4 f. red	2·00	25
114	27	10 f. green	6·50	4·00
115	–	20 f. blue	7·50	5·00

DESIGN: 4, 20 f. Flag over Imperial Palace.

29 Manchukuo

30 Japanese Residents Assn. Building

1937. Japan's Relinquishment of Extra-territorial Rights.

116	29	2 f. red	1·00	25
117	30	4 f. green	2·75	75
118		8 f. orange	3·25	2·00
119	–	10 f. blue	2·75	50
120	–	12 f. violet	3·50	3·00
121	–	20 f. brown	4·75	2·75

DESIGNS—As Type **30**: 10, 20 f. Dept. of Communications Bldg. HORIZ: 12 f. Ministry of Justice.

32 "Twofold Happiness"

33 Red Cross on Map and Globe

1937. New Year's Greetings.

122	32	2 f. red and blue	2·00	30

1938. Inaug of Manchukuo Red Cross Society.

123	33	2 f. red	1·00	1·25
124		4 f. green	1·00	25

34 Map of Railway Lines

35 "Asia" Express

1939. Completion of 10,000 Kilometres of Manchurian Railways.

125	34	2 f. blue and orange	1·50	1·75
126	35	4 f. deep blue and blue	1·50	1·75

36 Manchurian Cranes over Shipmast

37 Census Official and Manchukuo

38 Census Slogans in Chinese and Mongolian

1940. 2nd Visit of Emperor Kang-teh to Japan.

127	36	2 f. purple	1·00	1·50
128		4 f. green	1·00	1·50

1940. National Census.

129	37	2 f. brown and yellow	55	1·50
130	38	4 f. deep green and green	55	1·50

39 Message of Congratulation

40 Dragon Dance

1940. 2600th Anniv of Founding of Japanese Empire.

131	39	2 f. red	15	1·50
132	40	4 f. blue	15	1·50

41 Recruit

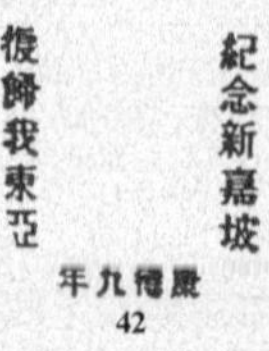

42

1941. Enactment of Conscription Law.

133	41	2 f. red	40	1·50
134		4 f. blue	55	1·50

1942. Fall of Singapore. Stamps of 1936 optd with T **42**.

135	A	2 f. green	85	2·00
136	B	4 f. olive	85	2·00

43 Kenkoku Shrine

44 Achievement of Fine Crops

45 Women of Five Races Dancing

46 Map of Manchukuo

1942. 10th Anniv of Founding of State.

137	43	2 f. red	15	75
138	44	3 f. orange	1·75	2·25
139	43	4 f. lilac	25	75
140	45	6 f. green	1·75	2·50
141	46	10 f. red on yellow	60	1·50
142	–	20 f. blue on yellow	65	1·50

DESIGN—HORIZ: 20 f. Flag of Manchukuo.

1942. 1st Anniv of "Greater East Asia War". Stamps of 1936 optd with native characters above date **8.12.8.**

143	19	3 f. brown	75	1·75
144	A	6 f. red	75	1·75

1943. Labour Service Law Proclamation. Stamps of 1936 optd with native characters above heads of pick and shovel.

145	19	3 f. brown	75	1·75
146	A	6 f. red	75	1·75

49 Nurse and Stretcher

50 Furnace at Anshan Plant

1943. 5th Anniv of Manchukuo Red Cross Society.

147	49	6 f. green	50	2·50

1943. 2nd Anniv of "Greater East Asia War".

148	50	6 f. red	50	2·50

51 Chinese characters

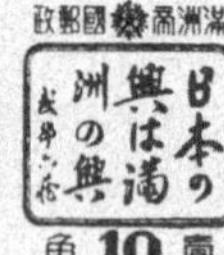

52 Japanese characters

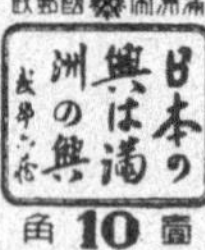

53 "One Heart One Soul"

1944. Friendship with Japan. (a) Chinese characters

155	51	10 f. red	25	75
156		40 f. green	75	1·00

(b) Japanese characters.

157	52	10 f. red	25	75
158		40 f. green	75	1·00

1945. 10th Anniv of Emperor's Edict.

159	53	10 f. red	1·25	4·50

MARIANA ISLANDS Pt. 7

A group of Spanish Islands in the Pacific Ocean of which Guam was ceded to the U.S.A. and the others to Germany. The latter are now under U.S. Trusteeship.

100 pfennig = 1 mark

1899. German stamps optd **Marianen**.

7	8	3 pf. brown	12·00	32·00
8		5 pf. green	14·00	32·00
9	9	10 pf. red	18·00	38·00
10		20 pf. blue	22·00	£110
11		25 pf. orange	60·00	£160
12		50 pf. brown	60·00	£190

1901. "Yacht" key-type inscr "MARIANEN".

13	N	3 pf. brown	70	90
14		5 pf. green	70	90
15		10 pf. red	70	2·75
16		20 pf. blue	1·00	6·00
17		25 pf. black & red on yell	1·25	13·00
18		30 pf. black & orge on buff	1·25	13·00
19		40 pf. black and red	1·25	13·00
20		50 pf. black & pur on buff	1·40	15·00
21		80 pf. black & red on rose	2·00	24·00
22	O	1 m. red	2·75	70·00
23		2 m. blue	4·50	90·00
24		3 m. black	6·50	£130
25		5 m. red and black	£130	£500

MARIENWERDER Pt. 7

A district of E. Prussia where a plebiscite was held in 1920. As a result the district remained part of Germany. After the War of 1939-45 it was returned to Poland and reverted to its original name of Kwidzyn.

100 pfennig = 1 mark

1

1920.

1	1	5 pf. green	35	35
2		10 pf. red	25	20
3		15 pf. grey	35	35
4		20 pf. brown	30	20
5		25 pf. blue	50	45
6		30 pf. orange	85	65
7		40 pf. brown	50	45
8		50 pf. violet	50	40
9		60 pf. brown	3·50	2·50
10		75 pf. brown	70	75
11		1 m. brown and green	60	55
12		2 m. purple	4·75	2·40
13		3 m. red	4·50	3·25
14		5 m. blue and red	10·00	17·00

1920. Stamps of Germany inscr "DEUTSCHES REICH" optd or surch **Commission Interalliee Marienwerder**.

15	10	5 pf. green	12·00	25·00
16		20 pf. blue	5·00	16·00
17		50 pf. black & pur on buff	£350	£650
18		75 pf. black and green	3·50	6·00
19		80 pf. black and red on rose	70·00	£110
25	12	1 m. red	2·40	4·50
21	24	1 m. on 2 pf. grey	20·00	35·00
26	12	1 m. 25 green	3·00	5·00
27		1 m. 50 brown	4·00	7·00
22	24	2 m. on 2½ pf. grey	8·00	12·00
28	13	2 m. 50 purple	2·40	4·50
23	10	3 m. on 3 pf. brown	12·00	14·00
24	24	5 m. on 7½ pf. orange	8·50	14·00

1920. As T **1**, with inscription at top changed to "PLEBISCITE".

29		5 pf. green	2·75	2·50
30		10 pf. red	2·75	2·50
31		15 pf. grey	12·00	12·00
32		20 pf. brown	1·50	1·60
33		25 pf. blue	14·00	13·00
34		30 pf. orange	1·40	1·00
35		40 pf. brown	1·00	70
36		50 pf. violet	1·75	1·25
37		60 pf. brown	5·25	4·00
38		75 pf. brown	6·50	5·50
39		1 m. brown and green	1·00	1·00
40		2 m. purple	1·40	1·10
41		3 m. red	1·75	1·25
42		5 m. blue and red	2·75	1·40

MARSHALL ISLANDS Pts. 7, 22

A group of islands in the Pacific Ocean, a German protectorate from 1885. From 1920 to 1947 it was a Japanese mandated territory and from 1947 part of the United States Trust Territory of the Pacific Islands, using United States stamps. In 1984 it assumed control of its postal services.

A. GERMAN PROTECTORATE

100 pfennig = 1 mark

1897. Stamps of Germany (a) optd **Marschall-Inseln**.

G1	8	3 pf. brown	£120	£450
G2		5 pf. green	£100	£400
G3	9	10 pf. red	30·00	£110
G4		20 pf. blue	30·00	£110

(b) optd **Marshall-Inseln**.

G 5	8	3 pf. brown	3·00	5·00
G 6		5 pf. green	7·50	5·50
G 7	9	10 pf. red	10·00	14·00
G 8		20 pf. blue	13·00	23·00
G 9		25 pf. orange	17·00	40·00
G10		50 pf. brown	27·00	48·00

1901. "Yacht" key-type inscr "MARSHALL INSELN".

G11	N	3 pf. brown	60	1·00
G12		5 pf. green	60	1·10
G13		10 pf. red	60	4·00
G14		20 pf. blue	75	9·00
G15		25 pf. black & red on yell	80	15·00
G16		30 pf. blk & orge on buff	80	15·00
G17		40 pf. black and red	80	15·00
G18		50 pf. blk & pur on buff	1·10	20·00
G19		80 pf. blk & red on rose	2·00	32·00
G20	O	1 m. red	3·25	75·00
G21		2 m. blue	4·50	£120
G22		3 m. black	7·00	£200
G23		5 m. red and black	£110	£500

B. REPUBLIC

100 cents = 1 dollar

1 Canoe

1984. Inauguration of Postal Independence. Multicoloured.

1 20 c. Type **1** 55 30
2 20 c. Fishes and net 55 30
3 20 c. Navigational stick-chart . . 55 30
4 20 c. Islet with coconut palms . 55 30

2 Mili Atoll

3 German Marshall Islands 1900 3 pf. Optd Stamp

1984. Maps. Multicoloured.

5 1 c. Type **2** 10 10
6 3 c. Likiep Atoll 10 10
7 5 c. Ebon Atoll 15 10
8 10 c. Jaluit Atoll 15 10
9 13 c. Ailinginae Atoll 25 15
10 14 c. Wotho Atoll 25 15
11 20 c. Kwajalein and Ebeye Atolls 40 20
12 22 c. Enewetak Atoll 40 20
13 28 c. Ailinglaplap Atoll 65 35
14 30 c. Majuro Atoll 65 25
15 33 c. Namu Atoll 70 40
16 37 c. Rongelap Atoll 75 45
16a 39 c. Taka and Utirik Atolls 75 45
16b 44 c. Ujelang Atoll 85 50
16c 50 c. Aur and Maloclap Atolls 1·00 65
17 $1 Arno Atoll . . . . 2·25 75
18 $2 Wotje and Erikub Atolls . 4·00 2·50
19 $5 Bikini Atoll . . . . 10·00 8·00
20 $10 Mashallese stick chart (31 × 31 mm) . . . . . . 16·00 13·00

1984. 19th Universal Postal Union Congress Philatelic Salon, Hamburg.

21 **3** 40 c. brown, black & yellow 75 50
22 – 40 c. brown, black & yellow 75 50
23 – 40 c. blue, black and yellow 75 50
24 – 40 c. multicoloured 75 50

DESIGNS: No. 22, German Marshall Islands 1901 3 pf. "Yacht" stamp; 23, German Marshall Islands 1897 20 pf. stamp; 24, German Marshall Islands 1901 5 m. "Yacht" stamp.

4 Common Dolphin

1984. "Ausipex 84" International Stamp Exhibition, Melbourne. Dolphins. Multicoloured.

25 20 c. Type **4** 55 35
26 20 c. Risso's dolphin 55 35
27 20 c. Spotter dolphins 55 35
28 20 c. Bottle-nosed dolphin . . . 55 35

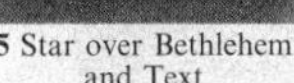

5 Star over Bethlehem and Text

6 Traditional Chief and German and Marshallese Flags

1984. Christmas. Multicoloured.

29 20 c. Type **5** 50 30
30 20 c. Desert landscape 50 30
31 20 c. Two kings on camels . . 50 30
32 20 c. Third king on camel . . . 50 30

1984. 5th Anniv of Constitution. Multicoloured.

33 20 c. Type **6** 45 30
34 20 c. Pres. Amata Kabua and American and Marshallese flags 45 30
35 20 c. Admiral Chester W. Nimitz and Japanese and Marshallese flags 45 30
36 20 c. Trygve H. Lie (first Secretary-General of United Nations) and U.N. and Marshallese flags 45 30

7 Leach's Storm Petrel

1985. Birth Bicentenary of John J. Audubon (ornithologist). Multicoloured.

37 22 c. Type **7** (inscr "Fork-tailed Petrel") (postage) 65 30
38 22 c. Pectoral sandpiper . . . 65 30
39 44 c. Brown booby (inscr "Booby Gannet") (air) . . . . 1·25 80
40 44 c. Whimbrel (inscr "Great Esquimaux Curlew") . . . . 1·25 80

8 Black-spotted Triton

1985. Sea Shells (1st series). Multicoloured.

41 22 c. Type **8** 65 35
42 22 c. Monodon murex 65 35
43 22 c. Diana conch 65 35
44 22 c. Great green turban . . . 65 35
45 22 c. Rose-branch murex . . . 65 35

See also Nos. 85/9, 131/5 and 220/4.

9 Woman as Encourager and Drum

1985. International Decade for Women. Mult.

46 22 c. Type **9** 50 30
47 22 c. Woman as Peacemaker and palm branches 50 30
48 22 c. Woman as Nurturer and pounding stone 50 30
49 22 c. Woman as Benefactress and lesser frigate bird 50 30

Nos. 46/9 were printed together in se-tenant blocks of four within the sheet, each block forming a composite design.

10 White-barred Surgeon Fish

1985. Lagoon Fishes. Multicoloured.

50 22 c. Type **10** 60 40
51 22 c. White-blotched squirrel fish 60 40
52 22 c. White-spotted boxfish . . 60 40
53 22 c. Saddleback butterfly fish 60 40

11 Basketball

1985. International Youth Year. Multicoloured.

54 22 c. Type **11** 45 30
55 22 c. Elderly woman recording for oral history project 45 30
56 22 c. Islander explaining navigational stick charts . . 45 30
57 22 c. Dancers at inter-atoll music and dance competition . . . 45 30

12 American Board of Commissions for Foreign Missions Stock Certificate

1985. Christmas. "Morning Star I" (first Christian missionary ship to visit Marshall Islands). Multicoloured.

58 14 c. Type **12** 30 15
59 22 c. Launching of "Morning Star I", 1856 . . . . 45 30
60 33 c. Departure from Honolulu, 1857 . . . . 70 50
61 44 c. Entering Ebon Lagoon, 1857 80 60

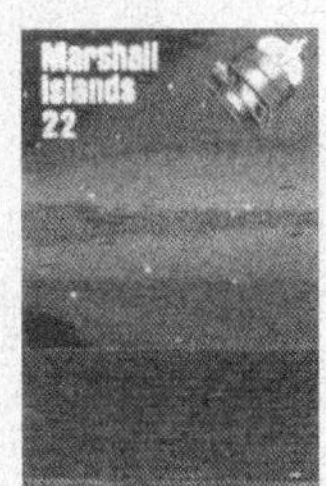

13 "Giotto" and Section of Comet Tail

1985. Appearance of Halley's Comet. Designs showing comet over Roi-Namur Island. Multicoloured.

62 22 c. Space shuttle and comet 1·00 55
63 22 c. "Planet A" space probe and dish aerial . . . . 1·00 55
64 22 c. Type **13** . . . . 1·00 55
65 22 c. "Vega" satellite and buildings on island . . . . . 1·00 55
66 22 c. Sir Edmund Halley, satellite communications ship and airplane . . . . 1·00 55

Nos. 62/6 were printed together, se-tenant, forming a composite design.

14 Mallow

1985. Medicinal Plants. Multicoloured.

67 22 c. Type **14** 50 35
68 22 c. Half-flower 50 35
69 22 c. "Guettarda speciosa" . . 50 35
70 22 c. Love-vine 50 35

15 Trumpet Triton

1986. World Wildlife Fund. Marine Life. Mult.

71 14 c. Type **15** 45 30
72 14 c. Giant clam 45 30
73 14 c. Small giant clam 45 30
74 14 c. Coconut crab 45 30

16 Consolidated PBY-5A Catalina Amphibian

1986. Air. "Ameripex 86" International Stamp Exhibition, Chicago. Mail Planes. Multicoloured.

75 44 c. Type **16** 85 65
76 44 c. Grumman SA-16 Albatross 85 65
77 44 c. Douglas DC-6B 85 65
78 44 c. Boeing 727-100 . . . . . 85 65

17 Islanders in Outrigger Canoe

1986. 40th Anniv of Operation Crossroads (atomic bomb tests on Bikini Atoll). Multicoloured.

80 22 c. Type **17** 55 35
81 22 c. Advance landing of amphibious DUKW from U.S.S. "Sumner" 55 35
82 22 c. Loading "LST 1108" (tank landing ship) for islanders' departure 55 35
83 22 c. Man planting coconuts as part of reclamation programme 55 35

1986. Sea Shells (2nd series). As T **8**. Multicoloured.

85 22 c. Ramose ("Rose") murex . 55 35
86 22 c. Orange spider conch . . . 55 35
87 22 c. Red-mouth frog shell . . . 55 35
88 22 c. Laciniate conch 55 35
89 22 c. Giant frog shell 55 35

18 Blue Marlin

1986. Game Fishes. Multicoloured.

90 22 c. Type **18** 50 40
91 22 c. Wahoo 50 40
92 22 c. Dolphin fish 50 40
93 22 c. Yellowfin tuna 50 40

19 Flowers (top left)

1986. International Peace Year. Multicoloured.

94 22 c. Type **19** (Christmas) (postage) 50 35
95 22 c. Flowers (top right) . . . 50 35
96 22 c. Flowers (bottom left) . . 50 35
97 22 c. Flowers (bottom right) . 50 35
98 44 c. Head of Statue crowned with flowers (24 × 39 mm) (cent of Statue of Liberty) (air) . . 1·00 70

Nos. 94/7 were issued together, se-tenant, in blocks of four within the sheet, each block forming a composite design of mixed flower arrangement.

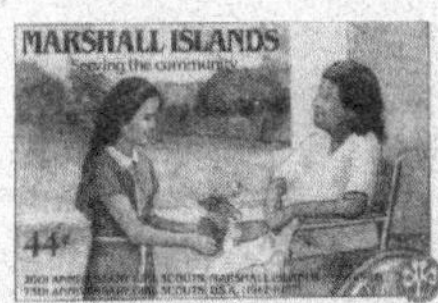

20 Girl Scout giving Plant to Patient

1986. Air. 20th Anniv of Marshall Island Girl Scouts and 75th Anniv (1987) of United States Girl Scout Movement. Multicoloured.

99 44 c. Type **20** 90 70
100 44 c. Giving salute 90 70
101 44 c. Girl scouts holding hands in circle 90 70
102 44 c. Weaving pandana and palm branch mats 90 70

21 Wedge-tailed Shearwater

1987. Air. Sea Birds. Multicoloured.

103 44 c. Type **21** 90 70
104 44 c. Red-footed booby . . . 90 70
105 44 c. Red-tailed tropic bird . . 90 70
106 44 c. Lesser frigate bird . . . 90 70

22 "James T. Arnold", 1854

1987. Whaling Ships. Multicoloured.

107 22 c. Type **22** 60 45
108 22 c. "General Scott", 1859 . 60 45
109 22 c. "Charles W. Morgan", 1865 60 45
110 22 c. "Lucretia", 1884 . . . . 60 45

23 "Spirit of St. Louis" and Congressional Medal of Honour, 1927

1987. Aviators. Multicoloured.

111 33 c. Type **23** 70 45
112 33 c. Charles Lindbergh and Chance Vought F4U Corsair, Marshall Islands, 1944 . . . 70 45
113 39 c. William Bridgeman and Consolidated B-24 Liberator bomber, Kwajalein, 1944 . 80 60

114 39 c. Bridgeman and Douglas Skyrocket, 1951 . . . 80 60
115 44 c. John Glenn and Chance Vought F4U Corsair fighters, Marshall Islands, 1944 . . . 1·00 75
116 44 c. Glenn and "Friendship 7" space capsule . . . 1·00 75

24 Lockheed Electra taking off from Lae, New Guinea

1987. Air. "Capex '87" International Stamp Exhibition, Toronto. 50th Anniv of Amelia Earhart's Round the World Flight Attempt. Multicoloured.
117 44 c. Type **24** . . . 90 65
118 44 c. U.S. Coastguard cutter "Itasca" waiting off Howland Island for Electra . . . 90 65
119 44 c. Islanders and crashed Electra on Mili Atoll . . . 90 65
120 44 c. Japanese patrol boat "Koshu" recovering Electra . . . 90 65

25 "We, the people of the Marshall Islands ..."

1987. Bicentenary of United States of America Constitution. Multicoloured.
122 14 c. Type **25** . . . 30 25
123 14 c. Marshall Is. and U.S.A. emblems . . . 30 25
124 14 c. "We the people of the United States..." . . . 30 25
125 22 c. "All we have and are today as a people..." . . . 45 25
126 22 c. Marshall Is. and U.S.A. flags . . . 45 25
127 22 c. "... to establish Justice..." . . . 45 25
128 44 c. "With this Constitution..." . . . 85 75
129 44 c. Marshall Is. stick chart and U.S. Liberty Bell . . . 85 75
130 44 c. "... to promote the general Welfare..." . . . 85 75

The three designs of each value were printed together, se-tenant, the left hand stamp of each strip bearing quotations from the preamble to the Marshall Islands Constitution and the right hand stamp, quotations from the United States Constitution preamble.

1987. Sea Shells (3rd series). As T **8**. Multicoloured.
131 22 c. Magnificent cone . . . 60 35
132 22 c. Pacific partridge tun . . . 60 35
133 22 c. Scorpion conch . . . 60 35
134 22 c. Common hairy triton . . . 60 35
135 22 c. Arthritic ("Chiragra") spider conch . . . 60 35

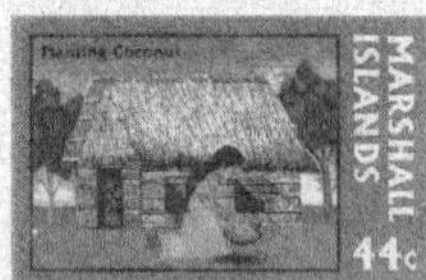

26 Planting Coconut

1987. Copra Industry. Multicoloured.
136 44 c. Type **26** . . . 80 65
137 44 c. Making copra . . . 80 65
138 44 c. Bottling extracted coconut oil . . . 80 65

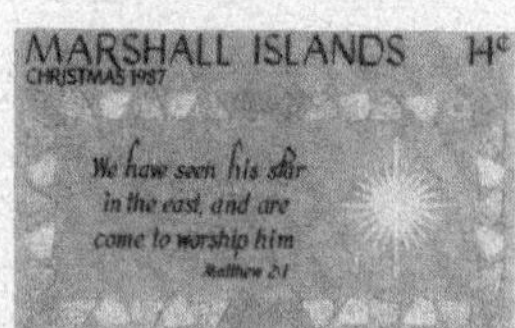

27 "We have seen his star in the east..."

1987. Christmas. Multicoloured.
139 14 c. Type **27** . . . 35 25
140 22 c. "Glory to God in the highest;..." . . . 50 30
141 33 c. "Sing unto the Lord a new song..." . . . 70 40
142 44 c. "Praise him in the cymbals and dances;..." . . . 95 65

28 Eastern Reef Heron

1988. Shore and Water Birds. Multicoloured.
143 44 c. Type **28** . . . 75 50
144 44 c. Bar-tailed godwit . . . 75 50
145 44 c. Blue-faced booby . . . 75 50
146 44 c. Common shoveler . . . 75 50

29 Damselfish **30** Javelin Thrower

1988. Fishes. Multicoloured.
147 1 c. Type **29** . . . 10 10
148 3 c. Blackface butterfly fish . . . 10 10
149 14 c. Hawkfish . . . 20 10
150 15 c. Balloonfish . . . 20 10
151 17 c. Trunk fish . . . 25 15
152 22 c. Lyretail wrasse . . . 30 20
153 25 c. Parrotfish . . . 30 20
154 33 c. White-spotted boxfish . . . 40 25
155 36 c. Spotted boxfish . . . 45 30
156 39 c. Surgeonfish . . . 50 40
157 44 c. Long-snouted butterfly fish . . . 55 45
158 45 c. Trumpetfish . . . 55 45
159 56 c. Sharp nosed puffer . . . 70 50
160 $1 Seahorse . . . 1·25 70
161 $2 Ghost pipefish . . . 2·50 1·50
162 $5 Big spotted triggerfish . . . 6·00 4·50
163 $10 Blue jacks (50 × 28 mm) . . . 12·00 9·00

1988. Olympic Games, Seoul. Multicoloured.
166 15 c. Type **30** . . . 25 15
167 15 c. Drawing javelin back and star . . . 25 15
168 15 c. Javelin drawn back fully (value at left) . . . 25 15
169 15 c. Commencing throw (value at right) . . . 25 15
170 15 c. Releasing javelin . . . 25 15
171 25 c. Runner and star (left half) . . . 35 25
172 25 c. Runner and star (right half) . . . 35 25
173 25 c. Runner (value at left) . . . 35 25
174 25 c. Runner (value at right) . . . 35 25
175 25 c. Finish of race . . . 35 25

Nos. 166/70 were printed together, se-tenant, forming a composite design of a javelin throw with background of the Marshallese flag. Nos. 171/5 were similarly arranged forming a composite design of a runner and flag.

31 "Casco" sailing through Golden Gate of San Francisco

1988. Centenary of Robert Louis Stevenson's Pacific Voyages. Multicoloured.
176 25 c. Type **31** . . . 50 35
177 25 c. "Casco" at the Needles of Ua-Pu, Marquesas . . . 50 35
178 25 c. "Equator" leaving Honolulu . . . 50 35
179 25 c. Chieftain's canoe, Majuro Lagoon . . . 50 35
180 25 c. Bronze medallion depicting Stevenson by Augustus St. Gaudens, 1887 . . . 50 35
181 25 c. "Janet Nicoll" (inter-island steamer), Majuro Lagoon . . . 50 35
182 25 c. Stevenson's visit to maniap of King Tembinoka of Gilbert Islands . . . 50 35
183 25 c. Stevenson in Samoan canoe, Apia Harbour . . . 50 35
184 25 c. Stevenson on horse Jack at Valima (Samoan home) . . . 50 35

32 Spanish Ragged Cross Ensign (1516-1785) and Magellan's Ship "Vitoria"

1988. Exploration Ships and Flags. Multicoloured.
185 25 c. Type **32** . . . 50 35
186 25 c. British red ensign (1707–1800), "Charlotte" and "Scarborough" . . . 50 35
187 25 c. American flag and ensign (1837–45), U.S.S. "Flying Fish" and U.S.S. "Peacock" . . . 50 35
188 25 c. German flag and ensign (1867–1919) and "Planet" . . . 50 35

33 Father Christmas in Sleigh **34** Nuclear Test on Bikini Atoll

1988. Christmas. Multicoloured.
189 25 c. Type **33** . . . 35 25
190 25 c. Reindeer over island with palm huts and trees . . . 35 25
191 25 c. Reindeer over island with palm trees . . . 35 25
192 25 c. Reindeer and flying fish . . . 35 25
193 25 c. Reindeer over island with outrigger canoe . . . 35 25

1988. 25th Anniv of Assassination of John F. Kennedy (American President). Multicoloured.
194 25 c. Type **34** . . . 40 25
195 25 c. Kennedy signing Test Ban Treaty . . . 40 25
196 25 c. Kennedy . . . 40 25
197 25 c. Kennedy using hot-line between Washington and Moscow . . . 40 25
198 25 c. Peace Corps volunteers . . . 40 25

35 "SV-5D PRIME" Vehicle Launch from Vandenberg Air Force Base

1988. Kwajalein Space Shuttle Tracking Station. Multicoloured.
199 25 c. Type **35** (postage) . . . 45 30
200 25 c. Re-entry of "SV-5D" . . . 45 30
201 25 c. Recovery of "SV-5D" off Kwajalein . . . 45 30
202 25 c. Space shuttle "Discovery" over Kwajalein . . . 45 30
203 45 c. Shuttle and astronaut over Rongelap (air) . . . 75 55

Nos. 199/202 were printed together, se-tenant, forming a composite design.

36 1918 Typhoon Monument, Majuro

1989. Links with Japan. Multicoloured.
204 45 c. Type **36** . . . 80 55
205 45 c. Japanese seaplane base and railway, Djarret Islet, 1940s . . . 80 55
206 45 c. Japanese fishing boats . . . 80 55
207 45 c. Japanese skin-divers . . . 80 55

37 "Island Woman"

1989. Links with Alaska. Oil Paintings by Claire Fejes. Multicoloured.
208 45 c. Type **37** . . . 75 55
209 45 c. "Kotzebue, Alaska" . . . 75 55
210 45 c. "Marshallese Madonna" . . . 75 55

38 Dornier Do-228

1989. Air. Airplanes. Multicoloured.
212 12 c. Type **38** . . . 30 20
214 36 c. Boeing 737 . . . 55 40
215 39 c. Hawker Siddeley H.S.748 . . . 65 45
216 45 c. Boeing 727 . . . 75 55

1989. Sea Shells (4th series). As T **8**. Mult.
220 25 c. Pontifical mitre . . . 55 35
221 25 c. Tapestry turban . . . 55 35
222 25 c. Flame mouthed ("Bull-mouth") helmet . . . 55 35
223 25 c. Prickly Pacific drupe . . . 55 35
224 25 c. Blood-mouth conch . . . 55 35

40 Wandering Tattler

1989. Birds. Multicoloured.
226 45 c. Type **40** . . . 85 60
227 45 c. Turnstone . . . 85 60
228 45 c. Pacific golden plover . . . 85 60
229 45 c. Sanderling . . . 85 60

41 "Bussard" (German cruiser) and 1897 Ship's Post Cancellation

1989. "Philexfrance 89" International Stamp Exhibition, Paris. Marshall Islands Postal History. Multicoloured.
230 25 c. Type **41** . . . 80 50
231 25 c. First Day Cover bearing first Marshall Islands stamps and U.S. 10 c. stamp . . . 80 50
232 25 c. Consolidated PBY-5 Catalina flying boats, floating Fleet Post Office ("L.S.T. 119"), Majuro, and 1944 U.S. Navy cancellation . . . 80 50
233 25 c. Nakajima A6M2 "Rufe" seaplane, mailboat off Mili Island and Japanese cancellation . . . 80 50
234 25 c. Majuro Post Office . . . 80 50
235 25 c. Consolidated PBY-5A Catalina amphibian, outrigger canoe and 1951 U.S. civilian mail cancellation . . . 80 50
236 45 c. "Morning Star V" (missionary ship) and 1905 Jaluit cancellation . . . 85 55
237 45 c. 1906 registered cover with Jaluit cancellation . . . 85 55
238 45 c. "Prinz Eitel Freiderich" (auxiliary cruiser) and 1914 German ship's post cancellation . . . 85 55
239 45 c. "Scharnhorst" (cruiser) leading German Asiatic Squadron and 1914 ship's post cancellation . . . 85 55

Nos. 230/5 were printed together, se-tenant, Nos. 231 and 234 forming a composite design to commemorate the 5th anniversary of Marshall Islands Independent Postal Service.

42 Launch of "Apollo 11"

1989. 20th Anniv of First Manned Moon Landing. Multicoloured.
241 25 c. Type **42** . . . 75 75
242 25 c. Neil Armstrong . . . 75 75
243 25 c. Descent of lunar module to moon's surface . . . 75 75
244 25 c. Michael Collins . . . 75 75
245 25 c. Planting flag on Moon . . . 75 75
246 25 c. Edwin "Buzz" Aldrin . . . 75 75

43 Polish Cavalry and German Tanks

1989. History of Second World War. Multicoloured. (a) 1st issue. Invasion of Poland, 1939.
248 25 c. Type **43** . . . 45 35

(b) 2nd issue. Sinking of H.M.S. "Royal Oak", 1939.
249 49 c. U-boat and burning battleship . . . 75 55

(c) 3rd issue. Invasion of Finland, 1939.
250 45 c. Troops on skis and tanks . . . 70 55

(d) 4th issue. Battle of the River Plate, 1939.

251 45 c. H.M.S. "Exeter" (cruiser) 70 55
252 45 c. H.M.S. "Ajax" (cruiser) 70 55
253 45 c. "Admiral Graf Spee" (German pocket battleship) 70 55
254 45 c. H.M.N.Z.S. "Achilles" (cruiser) 70 55

See also Nos. 320/44, 359/84, 409/40, 458/77, 523/48 and 575/95.

44 Angel with Horn

45 Dr. Robert Goddard

1989. Christmas. Multicoloured.

255 25 c. Type **44** 55 35
256 25 c. Angel singing 55 35
257 25 c. Angel with lute 55 35
258 25 c. Angel with lyre 55 35

1989. Milestones in Space Exploration. Multicoloured.

259 45 c. Type **45** (first liquid fuel rocket launch, 1926) 85 55
260 45 c. "Sputnik 1" (first man-made satellite, 1957) 85 55
261 45 c. Rocket lifting off (first American satellite, 1958) 85 55
262 45 c. Yury Gagarin (first man in space, 1961) 85 55
263 45 c. John Glenn (first American in Earth orbit, 1962) 85 55
264 45 c. Valentina Tereshkova (first woman in space, 1963) 85 55
265 45 c. Aleksei Leonov (first space walk, 1965) 85 55
266 45 c. Edward White (first American space walk, 1965) 85 55
267 45 c. "Gemini 6" and "7" (first rendezvous in space, 1965) 85 55
268 45 c. "Luna 9" (first soft landing on the Moon, 1966) 85 55
269 45 c. "Gemini 8" (first docking in space, 1966) 85 55
270 45 c. "Venera 4" (first successful Venus probe, 1967) 85 55
271 45 c. Moon seen from "Apollo 8" (first manned orbit of Moon, 1968) 85 55
272 45 c. Neil Armstrong and U.S. flag (first man on Moon, 1969) 85 55
273 45 c. "Soyuz 11" and "Salyut 1" space station (first space station crew, 1971) 85 55
274 45 c. Lunar rover of "Apollo 15" (first manned lunar vehicle, 1971) 85 55
275 45 c. "Skylab 1" (first American space station, 1973) 85 55
276 45 c. "Pioneer 10" and Jupiter (first flight past Jupiter, 1973) 85 55
277 45 c. "Apollo" and "Soyuz" craft approaching each other (first international joint space flight, 1975) 85 55
278 45 c. "Viking 1" on Mars (first landing on Mars, 1976) 85 55
279 45 c. "Voyager 1" and Saturn's rings (first flight past Saturn, 1979) 85 55
280 45 c. "Columbia" (first space shuttle flight, 1981) 85 55
281 45 c. Satellite in outer space (first probe beyond the solar system, 1983) 85 55
282 45 c. Astronaut (first untethered space walk, 1984) 85 55
283 45 c. Launch of space shuttle "Discovery", 1988 85 55

46 White-capped Noddy

1990. Birds. Multicoloured.

284 1 c. Red-tailed tropic bird 10 10
285 5 c. Type **46** 10 10
286 9 c. Whimbrel 10 10
287 10 c. Sanderling 15 15
288 12 c. Black-naped tern 15 15
289 15 c. Wandering tattler 20 20
290 20 c. Bristle-thighed curlew 25 25
291 22 c. Greater scaup 30 30
292 23 c. Common (inscr "Northern") shoveler 30 30
293 25 c. Common (inscr "Brown") noddy 35 35
294 27 c. Sooty tern 35 35
295 28 c. Sharp-tailed sandpiper 35 35
296 29 c. Wedge-tailed shearwater 40 40
297 30 c. American (inscr "Pacific") golden plover 40 40
298 35 c. Brown booby 45 45
299 36 c. Red-footed booby 50 50
300 40 c. White tern 55 55
301 45 c. Green-winged (inscr "Common") teal 60 60
302 50 c. Great frigate bird 65 65
303 52 c. Crested tern (inscr "Great Crested Tern") 70 70
304 65 c. Mongolian (inscr "Lesser Sand") plover 85 85
305 75 c. Little tern 1·00 1·00
306 $1 Eastern (inscr "Pacific") reef heron 1·40 1·40
307 $2 Blue-faced (inscr "Masked") booby 2·50 2·50

47 Lodidean (coconut-palm leaf windmill)

1990. Children's Games. Multicoloured.

309 25 c. Type **47** 30 25
310 25 c. Lejonjon (juggling green coconuts) 30 25
311 25 c. Etobobo (coconut leaf musical instrument) 30 25
312 25 c. Didmakol (pandanus leaf flying-toy) 30 25

48 Penny Black

1990. 150th Anniv of the Penny Black. Multicoloured.

313 25 c. Type **48** 65 65
314 25 c. Essay of James Chalmers's cancellation 65 65
315 25 c. Stamp essay by Robert Sievier 65 65
316 25 c. Stamp essay by Charles Whiting 65 65
317 25 c. Stamp essay by George Dickinson 65 65
318 25 c. "City" medal by William Wyon (struck to commemorate Queen Victoria's first visit to City of London) 65 65

1990. History of Second World War. As T **43**. Multicoloured. (a) 5th issue. Invasions of Denmark and Norway, 1940.

320 25 c. German soldier and "Stuka" dive bombers in Copenhagen 30 25
321 25 c. Norwegian soldiers, burning building and German column 30 25

(b) 6th issue. Katyn Forest Massacre of Polish Prisoners, 1940.

322 25 c. Bound hands and grave (vert) 30 25

(c) 7th issue. Appointment of Winston Churchill as Prime Minister of Great Britain, 1940.

323 45 c. Union Jack, Churchill and war scenes 55 40

(d) 8th issue. Invasion of Low Countries, 1940.

324 25 c. Bombing of Rotterdam 30 25
325 25 c. Invasion of Belgium 30 25

(e) 9th issue. Evacuation at Dunkirk, 1940.

326 45 c. British bren-gunner on beach 55 40
327 45 c. Soldiers queueing for boats 55 40

Nos. 326/7 were issued together, se-tenant, forming a composite design.

(f) 10th issue. German Occupation of Paris, 1940.

328 45 c. German soldiers marching through Arc de Triomphe (vert) 55 40

(g) 11th issue. Battle of Mers-el-Kebir, 1940.

329 25 c. Vice-Admiral Sir James Somerville, Vice-Admiral Marcel Gensoul and British and French battleships 30 25

(h) 12th issue. The Burma Road, 1940.

330 25 c. Allied and Japanese forces (vert) 30 25

(i) 13th issue. British Bases and American Destroyers Lend-lease Agreement, 1940.

331 45 c. H.M.S. "Georgetown" (formerly U.S.S. "Maddox") 55 40
332 45 c. H.M.S. "Banff" (formerly U.S.C.G.C. "Saranac") 55 40
333 45 c. H.M.S. "Buxton" (formerly U.S.S. "Edwards") 55 40
334 45 c. H.M.S. "Rockingham" (formerly U.S.S. "Swasey") 55 40

(j) 14th issue. Battle of Britain, 1940.

335 45 c. Supermarine Spitfire Mk 1A fighters 55 40
336 45 c. Hawker Hurricane Mk 1 and Spitfire fighters 55 40
337 45 c. Messerschmitt Bf 109E fighters 55 40
338 45 c. Junkers Ju 87B-2 "Stuka" dive bomber 55 40

Nos. 335/8 were issued together, se-tenant, forming a composite design.

(k) 15th issue. Tripartite Pact, 1940.

339 45 c. Officers' caps of Germany, Italy and Japan (vert) 55 40

(l) 16th issue. Election of Franklin D. Roosevelt for Third United States Presidential Term, 1940.

340 25 c. Roosevelt (vert) 30 25

(m) 17th issue. Battle of Taranto, 1940.

341 25 c. H.M.S. "Illustrious" (aircraft carrier) 30 25
342 25 c. Fairey Swordfish bomber 30 25
343 25 c. "Andrea Doria" (Italian battleship) 30 25
344 25 c. "Conte di Cavour" (Italian battleship) 30 25

Nos. 341/4 were issued together, se-tenant, forming a composite design.

49 Pacific Green Turtles

1990. Endangered Turtles. Multicoloured.

345 25 c. Type **49** 45 35
346 25 c. Pacific green turtle swimming 45 35
347 25 c. Hawksbill turtle hatching 45 35
348 25 c. Hawksbill turtle swimming 45 35

50 Stick Chart, Outrigger Canoe and Flag

1990. 4th Anniv of Ratification of Compact of Free Association with United States.

349 **50** 25 c. multicoloured 35 25

51 Brandenburg Gate, Berlin

1990. Re-unification of Germany.

350 **51** 45 c. multicoloured 80 60

52 Outrigger Canoe and Stick Chart

1990. Christmas. Multicoloured.

351 25 c. Type **52** 45 35
352 25 c. Missionary preaching and "Morning Star" (missionary ship) 45 35
353 25 c. British sailors dancing 45 35
354 25 c. Electric guitar and couple dancing 45 35

53 Harvesting Breadfruit

1990. Breadfruit. Multicoloured.

355 25 c. Type **53** 45 35
356 25 c. Peeling breadfruit 45 35
357 25 c. Soaking breadfruit 45 35
358 25 c. Kneading dough 45 35

1991. History of Second World War. As T **43**. Multicoloured. (a) 18th issue. Four Freedoms Speech to U.S. Congress by President Franklin Roosevelt, 1941.

359 30 c. Freedom of Speech 35 25
360 30 c. Freedom from Want 35 25
361 30 c. Freedom of Worship 35 25
362 30 c. Freedom from Fear 35 25

(b) 19th issue. Battle of Beda Fomm, 1941.

363 30 c. Tank battle 35 25

(c) 20th issue. German Invasion of Balkans, 1941.

364 29 c. German Dornier DO-17Z bombers over Acropolis, Athens (Greece) (vert) 35 25
365 29 c. German tank and Yugoslavian Parliament building (vert) 35 25

(d) 21st issue. Sinking of the "Bismarck" (German battleship), 1941.

366 50 c. H.M.S. "Prince of Wales" (battleship) 60 45
367 50 c. H.M.S. "Hood" (battle cruiser) 60 45
368 50 c. "Bismarck" 60 45
369 50 c. Fairey Swordfish torpedo bombers 60 45

(e) 22nd issue. German Invasion of Russia, 1941.

370 30 c. German tanks 35 25

(f) 23rd issue. Declaration of Atlantic Charter by United States and Great Britain, 1941.

371 29 c. U.S.S. "Augusta" (cruiser) and Pres. Roosevelt of United States (vert) 35 25
372 29 c. H.M.S. "Prince of Wales" (battleship) and Winston Churchill (vert) 35 25

Nos. 371/2 were issued together, se-tenant, forming a composite design.

(g) 24th issue. Siege of Moscow, 1941.

373 29 c. German tanks crossing snow-covered plain 35 25

(h) 25th issue. Sinking of U.S.S. "Reuben James", 1941.

374 30 c. U.S.S. "Reuben James" (destroyer) 35 25
375 30 c. German U-boat 562 (submarine) 35 25

Nos. 374/5 were issued together, se-tenant, forming a composite design.

(i) 26th issue. Japanese Attack on Pearl Harbor, 1941.

376 50 c. American airplanes (inscr "Peal Harbor") (vert) 60 45
376b As No. 376 but inscr "Pearl Harbor" 60 45
377 50 c. Japanese dive bombers (vert) 60 45
378 50 c. U.S.S. "Arizona" (battleship) (vert) 60 45
379 50 c. "Akagi" (Japanese aircraft carrier) (vert) 60 45

Nos. 376/9 were issued together, se-tenant, forming a composite design.

(j) 27th issue. Japanese Capture of Guam, 1941.

380 29 c. Japanese troops (vert) 35 25

(k) 28th issue. Fall of Singapore to Japan, 1941.

381 29 c. Japanese soldiers with Japanese flag, Union Jack and white flag 35 25

(l) 29th issue. Formation of "Flying Tigers" (American volunteer group), 1941.

382 50 c. American Curtiss Tomahawk fighters 60 45
383 50 c. Japanese Mitsubishi Ki-21 "Sally" bombers 60 45

Nos. 382/3 were issued together, se-tenant, forming a composite design.

(m) 30th issue. Fall of Wake Island to Japan, 1941.

384 29 c. American Grumman Wildcat fighters and Japanese Mitsubishi G3M "Nell" bombers over Wake Island 35 25

54 Boeing 747 carrying "Columbia" to Launch Site

1991. Ten Years of Space Shuttle Flights. Multicoloured.

385 50 c. Type **54** 75 55
386 50 c. Orbital release of Long Duration Exposure Facility from "Challenger", 1984 75 55
387 50 c. Shuttle launch at Cape Canaveral 75 55
388 50 c. Shuttle landing at Edwards Air Force Base 75 55

Nos. 385/8 were issued together, se-tenant, the backgrounds forming a composite design.

55 "Ixora carolinensis"

1991. Native Flowers. Multicoloured.

389 52 c. Type **55** 65 50
390 52 c. Glory-bower ("Clerodendum inerme") 65 50
391 52 c. "Messerschmidia argentea" 65 50
392 52 c. "Vigna marina" 65 50

56 American Bald Eagle and Marshall Islands and U.S. Flags

1991. United States Participation in Operation Desert Storm (campaign to liberate Kuwait).
394 56 29 c. multicoloured 35 25

57 Red-footed Booby

1991. Birds. Multicoloured.
395 29 c. Type 57 . . . . 35 25
396 29 c. Great frigate bird (facing right) 35 25
397 29 c. Brown booby 35 25
398 29 c. White tern 35 25
399 29 c. Great frigate bird (facing left) 35 25
400 29 c. White-capped ("Black") noddy 35 25

58 Dornier Do-228

1991. Passenger Aircraft. Multicoloured.
402 12 c. Type 58 . . . . 15 10
403 29 c. Douglas DC-8 jetliner . . 35 25
404 50 c. Hawker Siddeley H.S.748 airliner 60 45
405 50 c. Saab 2000 . . . . 60 45

59 U.N. and State Emblems and Outrigger Canoe

1991. Admission of Marshall Islands to the United Nations.
406 59 29 c. multicoloured 40 30

60 Dove and Glory-bower Flowers

1991. Christmas.
407 60 30 c. multicoloured 45 35

61 State Flag and Dove

1991. 25th Anniv of Peace Corps in Marshall Islands.
408 61 29 c. multicoloured 35 25

1992. History of Second World War. As T 43. Multicoloured. (a) 31st issue. Arcadia Conference, Washington D.C., 1942.
409 29 c. Pres. Franklin Roosevelt of U.S.A., Winston Churchill of Great Britain, White House and United Nations emblem 35 25

(b) 32nd issue. Fall of Manila to Japan, 1942.
410 50 c. Japanese tank moving through Manila 60 45

(c) 33rd issue. Capture of Rabaul by Japan, 1942.
411 29 c. Japanese flag, Admiral Yamamoto, General Douglas MacArthur and U.S. flag . . 35 25

(d) 34th issue. Battle of the Java Sea, 1942.
412 29 c. Sinking of the "De Ruyter" (Dutch cruiser) 35 25

(e) 35th issue. Capture of Rangoon by Japan, 1942.
413 50 c. Japanese tank and soldiers in Rangoon (vert) 60 45

(f) 36th issue. Japanese Landing on New Guinea, 1942.
414 29 c. Japanese soldiers coming ashore 35 25

(g) 37th issue. Evacuation of General Douglas MacArthur from Corregidor, 1942.
415 29 c. MacArthur 35 25

(h) 38th issue. British Raid on Saint Nazaire, 1942.
416 29 c. H.M.S. "Campbeltown" and motor torpedo boat . . 35 25

(i) 39th issue. Surrender of Bataan, 1942.
417 29 c. Prisoners on "death" march (vert) 35 25

(j) 40th issue. Doolittle Raid on Tokyo, 1942.
418 50 c. North American B-25 Mitchell bomber taking off from U.S.S. "Hornet" (aircraft carrier) (vert) 60 45

(k) 41st issue. Fall of Corregidor to Japan, 1942.
419 29 c. Lt.-Gen. Jonathan Wainwright 35 25

(l) 42nd issue. Battle of the Coral Sea, 1942.
420 50 c. U.S.S. "Lexington" (aircraft carrier) and Grumman F4F-3 Wildcat fighter (inscr "U.S.S. Lexington") 60 45
420b As No. 420 but additionally inscr with aircraft name . 60 45
421 50 c. Japanese Aichi D3A 1 "Val" and Nakajima B5N2 "Kate" dive bombers (wrongly inscr 'Mitsubishi A6M2 "Zero" ') 60 45
422 50 c. American Douglas TBD-1 Devastator torpedo bombers (wrongly inscr "U.S. Douglas SBD Dauntless") 60 45
422a As No. 422 but with inscr corrected 60 45
423 50 c. "Shoho" (Japanese aircraft carrier) and Mitsubishi A6M2 Zero-Sen fighters (inscr "Japanese carrier Shoho") . 60 45
423a As No. 423 but additionally inscr with aircraft name . 60 45

The four designs were issued together, se-tenant, each pair forming a composite design.

(m) 43rd issue. Battle of Midway, 1942.
424 50 c. "Akagi" (Japanese aircraft carrier) 60 45
425 50 c. U.S.S. "Yorktown" (aircraft carrier) 60 45
426 50 c. American Douglas SBD Dauntless dive bombers . . 60 45
427 50 c. Japanese Nakajima B5N2 "Kate" dive bombers . . 60 45

Nos. 424/7 were issued together, se-tenant, forming a composite design.

(n) 44th issue. Destruction of Lidice (Czechoslovakian village), 1942.
428 29 c. Cross and memorial at Lidice 35 25

(o) 45th issue. German Capture of Sevastopol, 1942.
429 29 c. German siege gun "Dora" (vert) 35 25

(p) 46th issue. Destruction of Convoy PQ-17, 1942.
430 29 c. British merchant ship . 35 25
431 29 c. German U-boat 35 25

(q) 47th issue. Marine Landing on Guadalcanal, 1942.
432 29 c. American marines landing on beach 35 25

(r) 48th issue. Battle of Savo Island, 1942.
433 29 c. Admiral Mikawa of Japan (vert) 35 25

(s) 49th issue. Dieppe Raid, 1942.
434 29 c. Soldiers landing at Dieppe 35 25

(t) 50th issue. Battle of Stalingrad, 1942.
435 50 c. Heroes monument and burning buildings (vert) . . 60 45

(u) 51st issue. Battle of Eastern Solomon Islands, 1942.
436 29 c. Aircraft over U.S.S. "Enterprise" (aircraft carrier) 35 25

(v) 52nd issue. Battle of Cape Esperance, 1942.
437 50 c. American cruiser firing guns at night 60 45

(w) 53rd issue. Battle of El Alamein, 1942.
438 29 c. Gen. Bernard Montgomery of Great Britain and Gen. Erwin Rommel of Germany 35 25

(x) 54th issue. Battle of Barents Sea, 1942.
439 29 c. H.M.S. "Sheffield" (cruiser) 35 25
440 29 c. "Admiral Hipper" (German cruiser) 35 25

62 "Emlain" (bulk carrier) 63 Northern Pintail

1992. Ships flying the Marshall Islands Flag. Multicoloured.
441 29 c. Type 62 . . . . 30 25
442 29 c. "CSK Valiant" (tanker) 30 25
443 29 c. "Ionmeto" (fisheries protection vessel) 30 25
444 29 c. "Micro Pilot" (inter-island freighter) 30 25

1992. Nature Protection.
445 63 29 c. multicoloured . . . 60 45

64 Tipnol (outrigger canoe) 65 Basket Making

1992. Legends of Discovery. Multicoloured.
446 50 c. Type 64 . . . . 60 60
447 50 c. "Santa Maria" (reconstruction of Columbus's flagship) 60 60
448 50 c. Constellation Argo Navis 60 60
449 50 c. Sailor and tipnol 60 60
450 50 c. Christopher Columbus and "Santa Maria" 60 60
451 50 c. Astronaut and Argo Navis constellation 60 60

1992. Handicrafts. Multicoloured.
453 29 c. Type 65 . . . . 35 25
454 29 c. Boy holding model outrigger canoe 35 25
455 29 c. Man carving boat 35 25
456 29 c. Fan making 35 25

66 Christmas Offering

1992. Christmas.
457 66 29 c. multicoloured 35 25

1993. History of Second World War. As T 43. Multicoloured. (a) 55th issue. Casablanca Conference, 1943.
458 29 c. Pres. Franklin Roosevelt and Winston Churchill . . . 35 25

(b) 56th issue. Liberation of Kharkov, 1943.
459 29 c. Russian tank in Kharkov 35 25

(c) 57th issue. Battle of the Bismarck Sea, 1943.
460 50 c. Japanese Mitsubishi A6M Zero-Sen fighters and "Arashio" (Japanese destroyer) 60 45
461 50 c. American Lockheed P-38 Lightnings and Australian Bristol Beaufighter fighters . 60 45
462 50 c. "Shirayuki" (Japanese destroyer) 60 45
463 50 c. American A-20 Havoc and North American B-52 Mitchell bombers 60 45

Nos 460/63 were issued together, se-tenant, forming a composite design.

(d) 58th issue. Interception of Yamamoto, 1943.
464 50 c. Admiral Yamamoto 60 45

(e) 59th issue. Battle of Kursk, 1943.
465 29 c. German "Tiger 1" tank . 35 25
466 29 c. Soviet "T-34" tank . . . 35 25

Nos. 465/6 were issued together, se-tenant, forming a composite design.

(f) 60th issue. Allied Invasion of Sicily, 1943.
467 52 c. Gen. George Patton, Jr . 65 50
468 52 c. Gen. Bernard Montgomery 65 50
469 52 c. Americans landing at Licata 65 50
470 52 c. British landing south of Syracuse 65 50

(g) 61st issue. Raids on Schweinfurt, 1943.
471 50 c. American Boeing B-17F Flying Fortress bombers and German Messerschmitt Bf 109 fighter 60 45

(h) 62nd issue. Liberation of Smolensk, 1943.
472 29 c. Russian soldier and burning buildings (vert) 35 25

(i) 63rd issue. Landing at Bougainville, 1943.
473 29 c. American Marines on beach at Empress Augusta Bay . . 35 25

(j) 64th issue. U.S. Invasion of Tarawa, 1943.
474 50 c. American Marines . . . 50 45

(k) 65th issue. Teheran Allied Conference, 1943.
475 52 c. Winston Churchill of Great Britain, Pres. Franklin Roosevelt of U.S.A. and Iosif Stalin of Russia (vert) . . . 65 50

(l) 66th issue. Battle of North Cape, 1943.
476 29 c. H.M.S. "Duke of York" (British battleship) 35 25
477 29 c. "Scharnhorst" (German battleship) 35 25

67 Butterfly Fish

1993. Reef Life. Multicoloured.
478 50 c. Type 67 . . . . 60 45
479 50 c. Soldierfish 60 45
480 50 c. Damselfish 60 45
481 50 c. Filefish 60 45
482 50 c. Hawkfish 60 45
483 50 c. Surgeonfish 60 45

68 "Britannia" (full-rigged ship)

1993. Ships. Multicoloured. (a) Size 35 x 20 mm.
485 10 c. "San Jeronimo" (Spanish galleon) 10 10
486 14 c. U.S.C.G. "Cape Corwin" (fisheries patrol vessel) . . . 15 10
487 15 c. Type 68 . . . . 20 15
488 19 c. "Micro Palm" (inter-island ship) 20 15
489 20 c. "Eendracht" (Dirk Hartog's ship) 25 15
490 23 c. H.M.S. "Cornwallis" (sail frigate) 30 20
491 24 c. U.S.S. "Dolphin" (schooner) 30 20
492 29 c. "Morning Star I" (missionary brigantine) . . 35 25
493 30 c. "Rurik" (Otto von Kotzebue's brig) (inscr "Rurick") 35 25
494 32 c. "Santa Maria de la Vittoria" (Spanish galleon) . 40 25
495 35 c. "Nautilus" (German cruiser) 45 30
496 40 c. "Nautilus" (brig) 50 30
497 45 c. "Nagara" and "Isuzu" (Japanese cruisers) 55 35
498 46 c. "Equator" (schooner) . . 55 35
499 50 c. U.S.S. "Lexington" (aircraft carrier) 60 40
500 52 c. H.M.S. "Serpent" (brig) . 65 45
501 55 c. "Potomac" (whaling ship) 70 45
502 60 c. U.S.C.G. "Assateague" (cutter) 75 50
503 75 c. "Scarborough" (transport) 95 60
504 78 c. "Charles W. Morgan" (whaling ship) 95 60
505 95 c. "Tanager" (inter-island steamer) . . . . 1·25 80
506 $1 "Tole Mour" (hospital schooner) . . . . 1·25 80
507 $2.90 Fishing vessels . . . . 3·50 2·25
508 $3.00 "Victoria" (whaling ship) 3·75 2·40

(b) Size 46 x 26 mm.
509 $1 Enewetak outrigger canoe . 1·25 80
510 $2 Jaluit outrigger canoe . . . 3·50 2·25
511 $5 Ailuk outrigger canoe . . . 6·25 4·00
512 $10 Racing outrigger canoes . 12·50 8·00

See also Nos. 669/92.

69 Capitol Complex

1993. Inauguration of New Capitol Complex, Majuro. Multicoloured.
513 29 c. Type 69 . . . . 35 25
514 29 c. Parliament building . . 35 25
515 29 c. National seal (vert) . . . 35 25
516 29 c. National flag (vert) . . . 35 25

71 Woman with Breadfruit

1993. Marshallese Life in the 1800s. Designs adapted from sketches by Louis Choris. Multicoloured.
518 29 c. Type 71 . . . . 35 25
519 29 c. Canoes and warrior . . . 35 25
520 29 c. Chief and islanders . . . 35 25
521 29 c. Drummer and dancers . 35 25

72 Singing Silent Night

1993. Christmas.
522 72 29 c. multicoloured . . . 35 25

1994. History of Second World War. As T 43. Multicoloured.
(a) 67th issue. Appointment of Gen. Dwight D. Eisenhower as Commander of Supreme Headquarters, Allied Expeditionary Force, 1944.
523 29 c. Eisenhower 35 25

(b) 68th issue. Invasion of Anzio, 1944.
524 50 c. Troops landing 60 45

(c) 69th issue. Lifting of Siege of Leningrad, 1944.
525 52 c. St. Isaac's Cathedral and soldier with Soviet flag . . 65 50

(d) 70th issue. U.S. Liberation of Marshall Islands, 1944.
526 29 c. Douglas SBD Dauntless dive bombers 35 25

(e) 71st issue. Japanese Defeat at Truk, 1944.
527 29 c. Admirals Spruance and Marc Mitscher (vert) 35 25

(f) 72nd issue. U.S. Bombing of Germany, 1944.
528 52 c. Boeing B-17 Flying Fortress bombers 65 50

(g) 73rd issue. Allied Liberation of Rome, 1944.
529 50 c. Lt.-Gen. Mark Clark and flowers in gun barrel (vert) . 60 45

(h) 74th issue. Allied Landings in Normandy, 1944.
530 75 c. Airspeed A.S.51 Horsa gliders (inscr "Horsa Gliders") 95 70
530b As No. 530 but inscr "Horsa Gliders, Parachute Troops" 95 70
531 75 c. Hawker Typhoon 1B and North American P-51B Mustang fighters (wrongly inscr "U.S. P51B Mustangs, British Hurricanes") . . . 95 70
531a As No. 531 but inscr corrected 95 70
532 75 c. German gun defenses (inscr "German Gun Defenses") 95 70
532a As No. 523 but inscr "German Gun Defences, Pointe du Hoc" 95 70
533 75 c. Allied amphibious landing 95 70

The four designs were issued together, se-tenant, forming a composite design.

(i) 75th issue. V-1 Bombardment of England, 1944.
534 50 c. V-1 flying bomb over River Thames 60 45

(j) 76th issue. U.S. Marines Land on Saipan, 1944.
535 29 c. U.S. and Japanese troops 35 25

(k) 77th issue. First Battle of the Philippine Sea, 1944.
536 50 c. Grumman F6F-3 Hellcat fighter 60 45

(l) 78th issue. U.S. Liberation of Guam, 1944.
537 29 c. Naval bombardment . . 35 25

(m) 79th issue. Warsaw Uprising, 1944.
538 50 c. Polish Home Army fighter 60 45

(n) 80th issue. Liberation of Paris, 1944.
539 50 c. Allied troops marching along Champs Elysee . . . 60 45

(o) 81st issue. U.S. Marines Land on Peleliu, 1944.
540 29 c. Amphibious armoured tracked vehicle 35 25

(p) 82nd issue. General Douglas MacArthur's Return to Philippines, 1944.
541 52 c. McArthur and soldiers . . 65 50

(q) 83rd issue. Battle of Leyte Gulf, 1944.
542 52 c. American motor torpedo boat and Japanese warships 65 50

(r) 84th issue. Sinking of the "Tirpitz" (German battleship), 1944.
543 50 c. Avro Lancaster bombers 60 45
544 50 c. Tirpitz burning 60 45

(s) 85th issue. Battle of the Bulge, 1944.
545 50 c. Infantrymen 60 45
546 50 c. Tank driver and tanks . 60 45
547 50 c. Pilot and aircraft 60 45
548 50 c. Lt.-Col. Creighton Abrams and Brig.-Gen. Anthony McAuliffe shaking hands . . 60 45

75 Footballers

76 Neil Armstrong stepping onto Moon

1994. World Cup Football Championship, U.S.A. Multicoloured.
552 50 c. Type **75** 60 45
553 50 c. Footballers (different) . . 60 45

Nos. 552/53 were issued together, se-tenant, forming a composite design.

1994. 25th Anniv of First Manned Moon Landing. Multicoloured.
554 75 c. Type **76** 95 70
555 75 c. Planting U.S. flag on moon 95 70
556 75 c. Astronauts saluting . . . 95 70
557 75 c. Pres. John F. Kennedy and Armstrong 95 70

77 Solar System

1994. The Solar System. Multicoloured.
559 50 c. Type **77** 60 45
560 50 c. Sun 60 45
561 50 c. Moon 60 45
562 50 c. Mercury 60 45
563 50 c. Venus 60 45
564 50 c. Earth 40 45
565 50 c. Mars 60 45
566 50 c. Jupiter 60 45
567 50 c. Saturn 60 45
568 50 c. Uranus 60 45
569 50 c. Neptune 60 45
570 50 c. Pluto 60 45

79 Church and Christmas Tree (Ringo Baso)

1994. Christmas.
573 **79** 29 c. multicoloured . . . 35 25

1995. History of Second World War. As T **43**. Multicoloured.

(a) 86th issue. Yalta Conference, 1945.
575 32 c. Iosif Stalin of U.S.S.R., Winston Churchill of Great Britain and Franklin Roosevelt of U.S.A. (vert) 40 30

(b) 87th issue. Allied Bombing of Dresden, 1945.
576 55 c. "Europe" Meissen porcelain statuette, flames and bombers (vert) 70 55

(c) 88th issue. U.S. Marine Invasion of Iwo Jima, 1945.
577 $1 Marines planting flag on Mt. Suribachi (vert) . . . . . . 1·25 95

(d) 89th issue. U.S. Capture of Remagen Bridge, Germany, 1945.
578 32 c. Troops and tanks crossing bridge (vert) 40 30

(e) 90th issue. U.S. Invasion of Okinawa, 1945.
579 55 c. Soldiers throwing grenades (vert) 70 55

(f) 91st issue. Death of Franklin D. Roosevelt, 1945.
580 50 c. Funeral cortege 60 45

(g) 92nd issue. U.S. and U.S.S.R. Troops meet at Elbe, 1945.
581 32 c. American and Soviet troops 40 30

(h) 93rd issue. Capture of Berlin by Soviet Troops, 1945.
582 60 c. Soviet Marshal Georgi Zhukov and Berlin landmarks 75 55

(i) 94th issue. Allied Liberation of Concentration Camps, 1945.
583 55 c. Inmates and soldier cutting barbed-wire fence 70 55

(j) 95th issue. V-E (Victory in Europe) Day, 1945.
584 75 c. Signing of German surrender, Rheims 95 70
585 75 c. Soldier kissing girl, Times Square, New York 95 70
586 75 c. Victory Parade, Red Square, Moscow 95 70
587 75 c. Royal Family and Churchill on balcony of Buckingham Palace, London 95 70

(k) 96th issue. Signing of United Nations Charter, 1945.
588 32 c. U.S. President Harry S. Truman and Veterans' Memorial Hall, San Francisco 40 30

(l) 97th issue. Potsdam Conference, 1945.
589 55 c. Pres. Harry S. Truman of U.S.A., Winston Churchill and Clement Attlee of Great Britain and Iosif Stalin of U.S.S.R. 70 55

(m) 98th issue. Resignation of Winston Churchill, 1945.
590 60 c. Churchill leaving 10 Downing Street (vert) . . . 75 55

(n) 99th issue. Dropping of Atomic Bomb on Hiroshima, 1945.
591 $1 Boeing B-29 Superfortress bomber "Enola Gay" and mushroom cloud . . . . . . 1·25 95

(o) 100th issue. V-J (Victory in Japan) Day, 1945.
592 75 c. Mount Fuji and warships in Tokyo Bay 95 70
593 75 c. U.S.S. "Missouri" (battleship) 95 70
594 75 c. Admiral Chester Nimitz signing Japanese surrender watched by Gen. Douglas MacArthur and Admirals William Halsey and Forest Sherman 95 70
595 75 c. Japanese Foreign Minister Shigemitsu, General Umezu and delegation 95 70

Nos. 592/5 were issued together, se-tenant, each pair forming a composite design.

81 Scuba Diver, Meyer's Butterfly Fish and Achilles Tang

1995. Undersea World. Multicoloured.
596 55 c. Type **81** 70 55
597 55 c. Moorish idols and scuba diver 70 55
598 55 c. Pacific green turtle and fairy basslets 70 55
599 55 c. Fairy basslets, emperor angelfish and orange-fin anemone fish 70 55

Nos. 596/9 were issued together, se-tenant, forming a composite design.

82 U.S.S. "PT 109" (motor torpedo boat)

83 Marilyn Monroe

1995. 35th Anniv of Election of John F. Kennedy as U.S. President. Multicoloured.
600 55 c. Type **82** (Second World War command) 70 55
601 55 c. Presidential inauguration 70 55
602 55 c. Peace corps on agricultural project in Marshall Islands . 70 55
603 55 c. U.S. airplane and warships superintending removal of Soviet missiles from Cuba . 70 55
604 55 c. Kennedy signing Nuclear Test Ban Treaty, 1963 . . . 70 55
605 55 c. Eternal flame on Kennedy's grave, Arlington National Cemetery, Washington D.C. 70 55

1995. 69th Birth Anniv of Marilyn Monroe (actress). Multicoloured.
606 75 c. Type **83** 95 70
607 75 c. Monroe (face value top right) 95 70
608 75 c. Monroe (face value bottom left) 95 70
609 75 c. Monroe (face value bottom right) 95 70

85 "Mir" (Soviet space station)

86 Siamese and Exotic Shorthair

1995. Docking of Atlantis with "Mir" Space Station (611/12) and 20th Anniv of "Apollo"–"Soyuz" Space Link (613/14). Multicoloured.
611 75 c. Type **85** 95 70
612 75 c. "Atlantis" (U.S. space shuttle) 95 70
613 75 c. "Apollo" (U.S. spacecraft) 95 70
614 75 c. "Soyuz" (Soviet spacecraft) 95 70

Nos. 611/14 were issued together, se-tenant, forming a composite design.

1995. Cats. Multicoloured.
615 32 c. Type **86** 40 30
616 32 c. American shorthair tabby and red Persian 40 30
617 32 c. Maine coon and Burmese 40 30
618 32 c. Himalayan and Abyssinian 40 30

87 Pacific Sailfish

1995. Pacific Game Fish. Multicoloured.
619 60 c. Type **87** 75 55
620 60 c. Albacores 75 55
621 60 c. Wahoo 75 55
622 60 c. Pacific blue marlin . . . 75 55
623 60 c. Yellowfin tunas 75 55
624 60 c. Giant trevally 75 55
625 60 c. Dolphin fish 75 55
626 60 c. Mako sharks 75 55

Nos. 619/26 were issued together, se-tenant, forming a composite design.

88 Inedel's Magic Kite

91 Shepherds gazing at Sky

1995. Folk Legends (1st series). Multicoloured.
627 32 c. Type **88** 40 30
628 32 c. Lijebake rescues her granddaughter 40 30
629 32 c. Jebro's mother invents the sail 40 30
630 32 c. Limajnon escapes to the moon 40 30

See also Nos. 727/30.

1995. Christmas.
633 **91** 32 c. multicoloured . . . 40 30

92 Messerschmit Me 262-1a Schwalbe

93 Rabin

1995. Jet Fighters. Multicoloured.
634 32 c. Type **92** 40 30
635 32 c. Gloster Meteor F Mk 8 40 30
636 32 c. Lockheed F-80 Shooting Star 40 30
637 32 c. North American F-86 Sabre 40 30
638 32 c. F9F-2 Panther 40 30
639 32 c. Mikoyan Gurevich MiG-15 40 30
640 32 c. North American F-100 Super Sabre 40 30
641 32 c. Convair TF-102A Delta Dagger 40 30
642 32 c. Lockheed F-104 Starfighter 40 30
643 32 c. Mikoyan Gurevich MiG-21 MT 40 30
644 32 c. F8U Crusader 40 30
645 32 c. Republic F-105 Thunderchief 40 30
646 32 c. Saab J35 Draken 40 30
647 32 c. Fiat G-91Y 40 30
648 32 c. McDonnell Douglas F-4 Phantom II 40 30
649 32 c. Saab JA 37 Viggen . . . 40 30
650 32 c. Dassault Mirage F1C . . 40 30
651 32 c. Grumman F-14 Tomcat . 40 30
652 32 c. F-15 Eagle 40 30
653 32 c. General Dynamics F-16 Fighting Falcon 40 30
654 32 c. Panavia Tornado F Mk 3 40 30
655 32 c. Sukhoi Su-27UB 40 30
656 32 c. Dassault Mirage 2000C . 40 30
657 32 c. Hawker Siddeley Sea Harrier FRS.MK1 . . . . 40 30
658 32 c. F-117 Nighthawk . . . 40 30

1995. Yitzhak Rabin (Israeli Prime Minister) Commemoration.
659 **93** 32 c. multicoloured . . . 40 30

95 Blue-grey Noddy

1996. Birds. Multicoloured.
661 32 c. Type **95** 40 30
662 32 c. Spectacled ("Gray-backed") tern 40 30
663 32 c. Blue-faced ("Masked") booby 40 30
664 32 c. Black-footed albatross . 40 30

96 Cheetah

1996. Big Cats. Multicoloured.
665 55 c. Type **96** 70 55
666 55 c. Tiger 75 55
667 55 c. Lion 70 55
668 55 c. Jaguar 70 55

1996. Ships. As Nos. 485/508 but face values changed, and new design (No. 681). Multicoloured.
669 32 c. Type **68** 40 30
670 32 c. U.S.S. "Dolphin" (schooner) 40 30
671 32 c. "Morning Star I" (missionary brigantine) . . 40 30
672 32 c. U.S.S. "Lexington" (aircraft carrier) 40 30
673 32 c. "Micro Palm" (inter-island ship) 40 30
674 32 c. H.M.S. "Cornwallis" (sail frigate) 40 30
675 32 c. H.M.S. "Serpent" (brig) 40 30
676 32 c. "Scarborough" (transport) 40 30
677 32 c. "San Jeronimo" (Spanish galleon) 40 30

678 32 c. "Rurik" (Otto van Kotzebue's brig) (inscr "Rurick") 40 30
679 32 c. "Nautilus" (German cruiser) 40 30
680 32 c. Fishing vessels 40 30
681 32 c. Malmel outrigger canoe . 40 30
682 32 c. "Eendracht" (Dirk Hartog's ship) 40 30
683 32 c. "Nautilus" (brig) 40 30
684 32 c. "Nagara" and "Isuzu" (Japanese cruisers) 40 30
685 32 c. "Potomac" (whaling ship) 40 30
686 32 c. "Santa Maria de la Vittoria" (Spanish galleon) (dated "1996") 40 30
687 32 c. U.S.C.G. "Assateague" (cutter) 40 30
688 32 c. "Charles W. Morgan" (whaling ship) 40 30
689 32 c. "Victoria" (whaling ship) 40 30
690 32 c. U.S.C.G. "Cape Corwin" (fisheries patrol vessel) . . . 40 30
691 32 c. "Equator" (schooner) . . 40 30
692 32 c. "Tanager" (inter-island steamer) 40 30

97 5 l. Stamp

1996. Centenary of Modern Olympic Games. Designs reproducing 1896 Greek Olympic stamps. Multicoloured.
694 60 c. Type **97** 75 55
695 60 c. 60 l. stamp 75 55
696 60 c. 40 l. stamp 75 55
697 60 c. 1 d. stamp 75 55

98 Undersea Eruptions form Islands

99 Presley

1996. History of Marshall Islands. Multicoloured.
698 55 c. Type **98** 70 55
699 55 c. Coral reefs grow around islands 70 55
700 55 c. Storm-driven birds carry seeds to atolls 70 55
701 55 c. First human inhabitants arrive, 1500 B.C. 70 55
702 55 c. Spanish explorers discover islands, 1527 . . . . 70 55
703 55 c. John Marshall charts islands, 1788 . . . . 70 55
704 55 c. German Protectorate, 1885 70 55
705 55 c. Japanese soldier on beach, 1914 . . . . 70 55
706 55 c. American soldiers liberate islands, 1944 . . . . 70 55
707 55 c. Evacuation of Bikini Atoll for nuclear testing, 1946 . . 70 55
708 55 c. Marshall Islands becomes United Nations Trust Territory, 1947 . . . . . . 70 55
709 55 c. People and national flag (independence, 1986) 70 55

1996. 40th Anniv of Elvis Presley's First Number One Hit Record "Heartbreak Hotel".
710 **99** 32 c. multicoloured 40 30

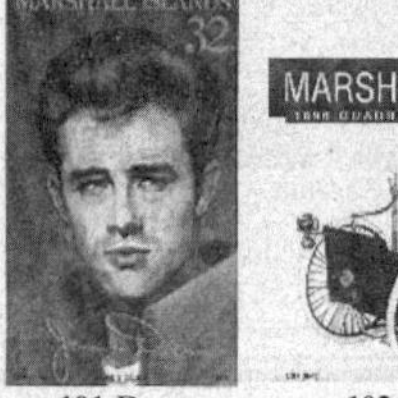

101 Dean

102 1896 Quadricycle

1996. 65th Birth Anniv of James Dean (actor).
712 **101** 32 c. multicoloured . . . 40 30

1996. Centenary of Ford Motor Vehicle Production. Multicoloured.
713 60 c. Type **102** 75 55
714 60 c. 1903 Model A Roadster . 75 55
715 60 c. 1909 Model T touring car 75 55
716 60 c. 1929 Model A station wagon 75 55
717 60 c. 1955 "Thunderbird" . . 75 55
718 60 c. 1964 "Mustang" convertible 75 55
719 60 c. 1995 "Explorer" 75 55
720 60 c. 1996 "Taurus" 75 55

103 Evacuees boarding "L.S.T. 1108" (tank landing ship)

1996. 50th Anniv of Operation Crossroads (nuclear testing) at Bikini Atoll. Multicoloured.
721 32 c. + 8 c. Type **103** 50 50
722 32 c. + 8 c. U.S. Navy preparation of site 50 50
723 32 c. + 8 c. Explosion of "Able" (first test) 50 50
724 32 c. + 8 c. Explosion of "Baker" (first underwater test) 50 50
725 32 c. + 8 c. Ghost fleet (targets) 50 50
726 32 c. + 8 c. Bikinian family . 50 50

1996. Folk Legends (2nd series). As T **88**. Multicoloured.
727 32 c. Letao gives gift of fire . 40 30
728 32 c. Mennin Jobwodda flying on giant bird 40 30
729 32 c. Koko chasing Letao in canoe 40 30
730 32 c. Mother and girl catching Kouj (octopus) to cook . . 40 30

104 Pennsylvania Railroad Class "K4"

1996. Steam Railway Locomotives. Multicoloured.
731 55 c. Type **104** 75 55
732 55 c. "Big Boy" 75 55
733 55 c. "Mallard" 75 55
734 55 c. Renfe Class "242" . . . 75 55
735 55 c. DB Class "01" 75 55
736 55 c. FS Group "691" 75 55
737 55 c. "Royal Hudson" . . . 75 55
738 55 c. "Evening Star" 75 55
739 55 c. SAR "520" Class . . . 75 55
740 55 c. SNCF "232.U1" 75 55
741 55 c. QJ "Advance Forward" 75 55
742 55 c. C62 "Swallow" 75 55

105 Stick Chart, Outrigger Canoe and Flag

1996. 10th Anniv of Ratification of Compact of Free Association with U.S.A.
744 **105** $3 multicoloured . . . . 3·75 2·75

106 "Madonna and Child with Four Saints" (detail, Rosso Fiorentino)

1996. Christmas.
745 **106** 32 c. multicoloured . . . 40 30

107 Curtiss JN-4 "Jenny"

1996. Biplanes. Multicoloured.
746 32 c. Type **107** 40 30
747 32 c. SPAD XIII 40 30
748 32 c. Albatros 40 30
749 32 c. De Havilland D.H.4 Liberty 40 30
750 32 c. Fokker Dr-1 . . . . . 40 30
751 32 c. Sopwith Camel 40 30
752 32 c. Martin MB-2 . . . . . 40 30
753 32 c. Martin MB-3A Tommy 40 30
754 32 c. Curtiss TS-1 . . . . . 40 30
755 32 c. P-1 Hawk 40 30
756 32 c. Boeing PW-9 . . . . . 40 30
757 32 c. Douglas O-2-H 40 30
758 32 c. LB-5 Pirate 40 30
759 32 c. O2U-1 Corsair 40 30
760 32 c. Curtiss F8C Helldiver . 40 30
761 32 c. Boeing F4B-4 . . . . . 40 30
762 32 c. J6B Gerfalcon 40 30
763 32 c. Martin BM 40 30
764 32 c. FF-1 Fifi 40 30
765 32 c. C.R.32 Cricket 40 30
766 32 c. Polikarpov I-15 Gull . . 40 30
767 32 c. Fairey Swordfish 40 30
768 32 c. Aichi D1A2 . . . . . . 40 30
769 32 c. Grumman F3F 40 30
770 32 c. SOC-3 Seagull 40 30

108 Fan-making

1996. Traditional Crafts. Multicoloured.
771 32 c. Type **108** 45 30
772 32 c. Boys sailing model outrigger canoes 45 30
773 32 c. Carving canoes 45 30
774 32 c. Weaving baskets 45 30

MARTINIQUE Pt. 6

An island in the West Indies, now an overseas department using the stamps of France.

100 centimes = 1 franc

1886. Stamp of French Colonies, "Commerce" type.
(a) Surch **MARTINIQUE** and new value.
3 J 01 on 20 c. red on green . . 8·75 9·00
1 5 on 20 c. red on green . . . 30·00 26·00
4 05 on 20 c. red on green . . 7·00 4·50
2 5 c. on 20 c. red on green . . £10000 £10000
6 015 on 20 c. red on green . . 35·00 35·00
5 15 on 20 c. red on green . . £130 £110

(b) Surch **MQE 15 c**.
7 J 15 c. on 20 c. red on green . 60·00 55·00

1888. Stamps of French Colonies, "Commerce" type, surch **MARTINIQUE** and value, thus **01 c**.
10 01 c. on 4 c. brn on grey . . 7·00 1·75
11 05 c. on 4 c. brn on grey . . £800 £675
12 05 c. on 10 c. black & lilac . 60·00 30·00
13 05 c. on 20 c. red on green . 12·50 9·25
14 05 c. on 30 c. brn on drab . 16·00 14·50
15a 05 c. on 35 c. blk on yell . . 10·00 7·75
16 05 c. on 40 c. red on yell . . 32·00 25·00
17 15 c. on 4 c. brn on grey . . £7000 £6000
18 15 c. on 20 c. red on green . 70·00 50·00
19 15 c. on 25 c. blk on pink . . 9·25 8·00
20 15 c. on 75 c. red on pink . . £110 90·00

1891. Postage Due stamps of French Colonies surch **TIMBRE-POSTE MARTINIQUE** and value in figures.
21 U 05 c. on 5 c. black . . . . 7·75 7·00
25 05 c. on 10 c. black . . . . 4·25 5·00
22 05 c. on 15 c. black . . . . 5·50 4·00
23 15 c. on 20 c. black . . . . 8·00 5·50
24 15 c. on 30 c. black . . . . 8·00 6·50

1891. Stamp of French Colonies, "Commerce" type, surch **TIMBRE-POSTE 01c. MARTINIQUE**.

1892. Stamp of French Colonies, "Commerce" type, surch **1892 MARTINIQUE** and new value.
31 15 c. on 25 c. black on pink 15·00 15·00

1892. "Tablet" key-type inscr "MARTINIQUE", in red (1, 5, 15, 25, 75 c., 1 f.) or blue (others).
33 D 1 c. black on blue 80 80
34 2 c. brown on buff 90 85
35 4 c. brown on grey 90 85
36 5 c. green on green . . . . 1·25 45
37 10 c. black on lilac . . . . 5·50 70
47 10 c. red . . . . 1·75 50
38 15 c. blue . . . . 21·00 3·50
48 15 c. grey . . . . 6·25 70
39 20 c. red on green . . . . 10·00 4·00
40 25 c. black on pink . . . . 11·50 1·00
49 25 c. blue . . . . 8·50 7·50
41 30 c. brown on drab . . . 21·00 7·75
50 35 c. black on yellow . . . 9·50 4·75
42 40 c. red on yellow . . . . 21·00 7·50
43 50 c. red on pink . . . . . 20·00 9·75
51 50 c. brown on blue . . . . 21·00 15·00
44 75 c. brown on orange . . 20·00 10·00
45 1 f. green . . . . 16·00 8·25
52 2 f. violet on pink . . . . 65·00 50·00
53 5 f. mauve on lilac . . . . 75·00 60·00

1903. Postage Due stamp of French Colonies surch **TIMBRE POSTE 5 F. MARTINIQUE COLIS POSTAUX**.
53a U 5 f. on 60 c. brown on buff £400 £425

Despite the surcharge Nos. 53a was for use on letters as well as parcels.

1904. Surch **10 c**.
55 10 c. on 5 f. mve on lilac . . 6·25 6·25

1904. Surch **1904 0f10**.
57 0 f. 10 on 40 c. red on yell . . 10·50 10·50
58 0 f. 10 on 50 c. red on pink . 10·50 10·50
59 0 f. 10 on 75 c. brown on orange 9·75 9·75
60 0 f. 10 on 1 f. green . . . . . 10·50 10·50
61 0 f. 10 on 5 f. mve on lilac . . £140 £140

13 Martinique Woman

15 Woman and Sugar Cane

14 Fort-de-France

1908.
62 **13** 1 c. chocolate and brown 15 20
63 2 c. brown and green . . . 15 25
64 4 c. brown and purple . . 15 25
65 5 c. brown and green . . . 25 15
87 5 c. brown and orange . . 15 15
66 10 c. brown and red . . . 45 25
88 10 c. olive and green . . . 20 30
89 10 c. red and purple . . . 20 25
67 15 c. red and purple . . . 15 30
90 15 c. olive and green . . . 20 30

91 13 15 c. red and blue 50 70
68 20 c. brown and lilac 50 55
69 14 25 c. brown and blue 75 20
92 25 c. brown and orange 25 15
93 30 c. brown and red 35 35
94 30 c. red and carmine 20 35
95 30 c. brown and lt brown 20 25
96 30 c. green and blue 70 75
71 35 c. brown and lilac 30 45
72 40 c. brown and green 30 40
73 45 c. chocolate and brown 35 45
74 50 c. brown and red 75 45
97 50 c. brown and blue 70 75
98 50 c. green and red 30 20
99 60 c. pink and blue 20 30
100 65 c. brown and violet 90 95
75 75 c. brown and black 70 60
101 75 c. blue and deep blue 20 30
102 75 c. blue and brown 1·40 1·50
103 90 c. carmine and red 3·25 3·25
76 15 1 f. brown and red 40 40
104 1 f. blue 30 40
105 1 f. green and red 95 1·25
106 1 f. 10 brown and violet 2·00 2·00
107 1 f. 50 light blue and blue 3·50 3·50
77 2 f. brown and grey 1·90 1·00
108 3 f. mauve on pink 5·25 5·25
78 5 f. brown and red 6·25 6·00

1912. Stamps of 1892 surch.
79 05 on 15 c. grey 50 45
80 05 on 25 c. black on pink 75 85
81 10 on 40 c. red on yellow 90 1·00
82 10 on 5 f. mauve on lilac 1·25 1·40

1915. Surch **5c** and red cross.
83 13 10 c. + 5 c. brown and red 1·00 1·00

1920. Surch in figures.
115 13 0,01 on 2 c. brown and grn 1·10 1·40
109 0,01 on 15 c. red and purple 25 35
110 0,02 on 15 c. red and purple 15 35
84 05 on 1 c. chocolate & brn 1·00 1·00
111 0,05 on 15 c. red and pur 25 35
116 0,05 on 20 c. brown & lilac 1·25 1·40
85 10 on 2 c. brown and green 85 90
117 14 0,15 on 30 c. brown & red 6·50 7·00
86 13 25 on 15 c. red and purple 65 70
121 25 c. on 15 c. red & purple 25 35
119 14 0,25 on 50 c. brown and red £170 £170
120 0,25 on 50 c. brown & blue 2·75 3·00
122 15 25 c. on 2 f. brown & grey 20 35
123 25 c. on 5 f. brown and red 95 60
112 14 60 on 75 c. pink and blue 20 35
113 65 on 45 c. brown & lt brn 60 70
114 85 on 75 c. brown & black 65 80
124 90 c. on 75 c. carmine and red 1·90 2·00
125 15 1 f. 25 on 1 f. blue 20 30
126 1 f. 50 on 1 f. ultramarine and blue 70 80
127 3 f. on 5 f. green and red 1·25 1·40
128 10 f. on 5 f. red and green 6·00 6·25
129 20 f. on 5 f. violet & brown 9·25 9·00

1931. "Colonial Exhibition" key-types inscr "MARTINIQUE".
130 E 40 c. black and green 2·25 2·25
131 F 50 c. black and mauve 2·00 2·00
132 G 90 c. black and red 2·25 2·25
133 H 1 f. 50 black and blue 2·25 2·25

26 Basse Pointe Village

27 Government House, Fort-de-France

28 Martinique Woman

1933.
134 26 1 c. red on pink 15 25
135 27 2 c. blue 15 30
136 3 c. purple 20 30
137 26 4 c. green 15 30
138 27 5 c. purple 15 25
139 26 10 c. black on pink 15 25
140 27 15 c. black on red 15 25
141 28 20 c. brown 15 25
142 26 25 c. purple 20 35
143 27 30 c. green 25 25
144 30 c. blue 25 30
145 28 35 c. green 25 35
146 40 c. brown 25 35
147 27 45 c. brown 1·00 1·10
148 45 c. green 30 45
149 50 c. red 20 15
150 26 55 c. red 45 55
151 60 c. blue 25 35
152 28 65 c. red on blue 35 30
153 70 c. purple 35 30
154 26 75 c. brown 50 50
155 27 80 c. violet 35 35
156 26 90 c. red 1·10 95
157 90 c. purple 35 40
158 27 1 f. black on green 1·10 30
159 1 f. red 40 40
160 28 1 f. 25 violet 45 45
161 1 f. 25 red 45 40
162 28 1 f. 40 blue 40 40
163 27 1 f. 50 blue 35 35
164 1 f. 60 brown 45 45
165 28 1 f. 75 green 5·50 2·50
166 1 f. 75 blue 40 35
167 26 2 f. blue on green 40 30
168 28 2 f. 25 blue 50 45
169 26 2 f. 50 purple 55 60
170 28 3 f. purple 25 25
171 5 f. red on pink 70 40
172 26 10 f. blue on blue 45 30
173 27 20 f. red on yellow 85 65

30 Belain d'Esnambuc, 1635

31 Schoelcher and Abolition of Slavery, 1848

1935. West Indies Tercentenary.
174 30 40 c. brown 1·10 1·00
175 50 c. red 1·10 1·00
176 1 f. 50 blue 8·00 8·00
177 31 1 f. 75 red 7·25 7·50
178 5 f. brown 7·25 7·50
179 10 f. green 5·25 5·50

1937. International Exhibition, Paris. As Nos. 168/73 of St.-Pierre et Miquelon.
180 20 c. violet 85 95
181 30 c. green 85 95
182 40 c. red 85 95
183 50 c. brown and agate 80 1·10
184 90 c. red 90 1·10
185 1 f. 50 blue 1·00 1·10

1938. Int Anti-Cancer Fund. As T **22** of Mauritania.
186 1 f. 75 + 50 c. blue 6·50 6·50

1939. New York World's Fair. As T **28** of Mauritania.
187 1 f. 25 red 70 70
188 2 f. 25 blue 70 70

1939. 150th Anniv of French Revolution. As T **29** of Mauritania.
189 45 c. + 25 c. green and black 4·50 4·50
190 70 c. + 30 c. brown and black 4·50 4·50
191 90 c. + 35 c. orange and black 4·50 4·50
192 1 f. 25 + 1 f. red and black 4·50 4·50
193 2 f. 25 + 2 f. blue and black 4·50 4·50

1944. Mutual Aid and Red Cross Funds. As T **31** of New Caledonia.
194 5 f. + 20 f. violet 65 80

1945. Eboue. As T **32** of New Caledonia.
195 2 f. black 20 35
196 25 f. green 55 65

1945. Surch.
197 27 1 f. on 2 c. blue 40 40
198 26 2 f. on 4 c. olive 40 40
199 27 3 f. on 2 c. blue 40 40
200 28 5 f. on 65 c. red on blue 60 60
201 10 f. (DIX f.) on 65 c. red on blue 60 60
202 27 20 f. (VINGT f.) on 3 c. purple 75 75

33 Victor Schoelcher

1945.
203 33 10 c. blue and violet 15 30
204 30 c. brown and red 20 30
205 40 c. blue and light blue 25 35
206 50 c. red and purple 30 30
207 60 c. orange and yellow 30 40
208 70 c. purple and brown 30 40
209 80 c. green and light green 30 40
210 1 f. blue and light blue 30 40
211 1 f. 20 violet and purple 30 40
212 1 f. 50 red and orange 30 40
213 2 f. black and grey 30 40
214 2 f. 40 red and pink 75 90
215 3 f. pink and light pink 30 20
216 4 f. ultramarine and blue 35 40
217 4 f. 50 turquoise and green 50 35
218 5 f. light brown and brown 40 50
219 10 f. purple and mauve 50 30
220 15 f. red and pink 60 45
221 20 f. olive and green 80 75

1945. Air. As T **30** of New Caledonia.
222 50 f. green 50 35
223 100 f. red 55 45

1946. Air. Victory. As T **34** of New Caledonia.
224 8 f. blue 50 75

1946. Air. From Chad to the Rhine. As Nos. 300/305 of New Caledonia.
225 5 f. orange 40 50
226 10 f. green 40 50
227 15 f. red 40 50
228 20 f. brown 50 60
229 25 f. blue 60 70
230 50 f. grey 80 90

34 Martinique Woman

39 Mountains and Palms

35 Local Fishing Boats and Rocks

40 West Indians and Flying Boat

1947.
231 34 10 c. lake (postage) 20 30
232 30 c. blue 15 25
233 50 c. brown 15 30
234 35 60 c. green 25 35
235 1 f. lake 25 35
236 1 f. 50 violet 25 35
237 – 2 f. green 60 45
238 – 2 f. 50 brown 60 50
239 – 3 f. blue 45 45
240 – 4 f. brown 45 45
241 – 5 f. green 40 45
242 – 6 f. mauve 45 45
243 – 10 f. blue 75 65
244 – 15 f. lake 90 85
245 – 20 f. brown 1·25 1·00
246 39 25 f. violet 1·40 1·25
247 40 f. green 1·50 1·40

248 40 50 f. purple (air) 2·50 2·00
249 – 100 f. green 3·75 2·50
250 – 200 f. violet 48·00 17·00

DESIGNS—HORIZ: As Type **35**: 2 f. to 3 f. Gathering sugar cane; 4 f. to 6 f. Mount Pele; 10 f. to 20 f. Fruit products. As Type **40**—VERT: 100 f. Aeroplane over landscape. HORIZ: 200 f. Wandering albatross in flight.

POSTAGE DUE STAMPS

1927. Postage Due stamps of France optd **MARTINIQUE**.
D130 D 11 5 c. blue 50 85
D131 10 c. brown 80 1·00
D132 20 c. olive 90 1·00
D133 25 c. red 1·25 1·50
D134 30 c. red 1·60 1·75
D135 45 c. green 1·75 1·75
D136 50 c. purple 3·50 3·75
D137 60 c. green 4·25 4·25
D138 1 f. red on yellow 5·25 5·25
D139 2 f. mauve 7·25 7·25
D140 3 f. red 8·25 8·25

D 29 Fruit

D 43 Map of Martinique

1933.
D174 D 29 5 c. blue on green 15 40
D175 10 c. brown 20 40
D176 20 c. blue 60 65
D177 25 c. red on pink 60 65
D178 30 c. purple 40 45
D179 45 c. red on yellow 30 35
D180 50 c. brown 45 75
D181 60 c. green 45 75
D182 1 f. black on red 65 90
D183 2 f. purple 55 75
D184 3 f. blue on blue 70 85

1947.
D251 D 43 10 c. blue 15 20
D252 30 c. green 15 30
D253 50 c. blue 15 30
D254 1 f. orange 20 35
D255 2 f. purple 45 60
D256 3 f. purple 45 60
D257 4 f. brown 55 70
D258 5 f. red 60 70
D259 10 f. black 90 1·25
D260 20 f. green 90 1·25

MAURITANIA Pt. 6; Pt. 13

A French colony extending inland to the Sahara, incorporated in French West Africa from 1945 to 1959. In 1960 Mauritania became an independent Islamic republic.

1906. 100 centimes = 1 franc.
1973. 100 cents = 1 ouguiya (um).

1906. "Faidherbe", "Palms" and "Balay" key-types inscr "MAURITANIE" in blue (10, 40 c., 5 f.) or red (others).
1 I 1 c. grey 25 25
2 2 c. brown 50 40
3 4 c. brown on blue 75 50
4 5 c. green 45 50
5 10 c. pink 4·50 3·00
6 J 20 c. black on blue 11·00 8·50
7 25 c. blue 4·50 3·25
8 30 c. brown on pink 70·00 40·00
9 35 c. black on yellow 4·25 3·00
10 40 c. red on blue 4·50 3·50
11 45 c. brown on green 4·25 3·50
12 50 c. violet 4·50 3·50
13 75 c. green on orange 4·00 3·50
14 K 1 f. black on blue 9·50 8·00
15 2 f. blue on pink 35·00 30·00
16 5 f. red on yellow £100 85·00

6 Merchants crossing Desert

1913.
18 6 1 c. brown and lilac 10 20
19 2 c. blue and black 10 20
20 4 c. black and violet 15 25
21 5 c. green and light green 25 40
37 5 c. red and purple 10 25
22 10 c. orange and pink 55 75
38 10 c. green and light green 10 25
39 10 c. pink on blue 15 30
23 15 c. black and brown 30 40
24 20 c. orange and brown 20 45
25 25 c. ultramarine and blue 80 85
40 25 c. red and green 40 65
26 30 c. pink and green 50 80
41 30 c. orange and red 50 70
42 30 c. yellow and black 15 35
43 30 c. light green and green 70 95
27 35 c. violet and brown 25 45
44 35 c. light green and green 25 50
28 40 c. green and brown 70 1·10
29 45 c. brown and orange 35 55
30 50 c. pink and lilac 35 50
45 50 c. ultramarine and blue 40 50
46 50 c. blue and green 40 60
47 60 c. violet on pink 15 35
48 65 c. blue and brown 50 70
31 75 c. brown and blue 40 70
49 85 c. brown and green 40 60
50 90 c. pink and red 85 90
32 1 f. black and red 40 65
51 1 f. 10 red and mauve 6·50 6·75
52 1 f. 25 brown and blue 1·10 1·25
53 1 f. 50 blue and light blue 70 75
54 1 f. 75 red and green 70 75
55 1 f. 75 ultramarine and blue 75 70
33 2 f. violet and orange 1·00 1·40
56 3 f. mauve on pink 1·00 1·40
34 5 f. blue and violet 1·40 1·50

1915. Surch **5c** and red cross.
35 6 10 c. + 5 c. orange and pink 40 70
36 15 c. + 5 c. black and brown 40 75

1922. Surch in figures and bars (some colours changed).
60 6 25 c. on 2 f. violet and orange 60 60
57 60 on 75 c. violet on pink 50 70
58 65 on 15 c. black and brown 1·00 1·40
59 85 on 75 c. brown and blue 75 1·10
61 90 c. on 75 c. pink and red 1·40 1·40
62 1 f. 25 on 1 f. ultram and blue 55 75
63 1 f. 50 on 1 f. blue and lt blue 65 80
64 3 f. on 5 f. mauve and brown 5·00 5·00
65 10 f. on 5 f. green and mauve 4·25 4·50
66 20 f. on 5 f. orange and blue 4·25 4·50

1931. "Colonial Exhibition" key-types inscr "MAURITANIE".
67 E 40 c. green and black 5·00 5·25
68 F 50 c. purple and black 2·50 2·50
69 G 90 c. red and black 2·50 2·50
70 H 1 f. 50 blue and black 2·50 2·50

1937. International Exhibition, Paris. As Nos. 168/73 of St.-Pierre et Miquelon.
71 20 c. violet 60 75
72 30 c. green 60 80
73 40 c. red 50 75
74 50 c. brown 50 70
75 90 c. red 50 80
76 1 f. 50 blue 55 80

22 Pierre and Marie Curie

1938. International Anti-Cancer Fund.
76b 22 1 f. 75 + 50 c. blue 3·50 5·00

23 Man on Camel

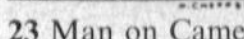

24 Warriors

25 Encampment 26 Mauritanians

1938.

No.	Type	Description	Unused	Used
77	23	2 c. purple	15	30
78		3 c. blue	10	30
79		4 c. lilac	10	30
80		5 c. red	10	30
81		10 c. red	20	35
82		15 c. violet	15	30
83	24	20 c. red	10	30
84		25 c. blue	30	55
85		30 c. purple	20	30
86		35 c. green	35	55
87		40 c. red	35	50
88		45 c. green	35	45
89		50 c. violet	35	55
90	25	55 c. lilac	55	70
91		60 c. violet	40	50
92		65 c. green	40	55
93		70 c. red	50	60
94		80 c. blue	95	1·00
95		90 c. lilac	40	55
96		1 f. red	90	1·10
97		1 f. green	25	45
98		1 f. 25 red	50	90
99		1 f. 40 blue	50	65
100		1 f. 50 violet	45	70
101		1 f. 60 brown	90	1·00
102	26	1 f. 75 blue	75	70
103		2 f. lilac	60	75
104		2 f. 25 blue	45	65
105		2 f. 50 brown	65	80
106		3 f. green	50	70
107		5 f. red	60	90
108		10 f. purple	90	1·40
109		20 f. red	95	1·40

27 Rene Caillie (explorer)

1939. Caillie.

No.	Type	Description	Unused	Used
110	27	90 c. orange	50	80
111		2 f. violet	50	80
112		2 f. 25 blue	50	80

28

1939. New York World's Fair.

No.	Type	Description	Unused	Used
113	28	1 f. 25 red	45	65
114		2 f. 25 blue	45	65

29 Storming the Bastille

1939. 150th Anniv of French Revolution.

No.	Type	Description	Unused	Used
115	29	45 c. + 25 c. green & black	4·75	5·00
116		70 c. + 30 c. brown & black	4·75	5·00
117		90 c. + 35 c. orange & black	4·75	5·00
118		1 f. 25 + 1 f. red and black	4·75	5·00
119		2 f. 25 + 2 f. blue & black	4·75	5·00

30 Twin-engine Airliner over Jungle

1940. Air.

No.	Type	Description	Unused	Used
120	30	1 f. 90 blue	45	60
121		2 f. 90 red	45	60
122		4 f. 50 green	45	60
123		4 f. 90 olive	60	75
124		6 f. 90 orange	65	85

1941. National Defence Fund. Surch **SECOURS NATIONAL** and value.

No.	Description	Unused	Used
124a	+ 1 f. on 50 c. (No. 89)	2·00	2·00
124b	+ 2 f. on 80 c. (No. 94)	4·00	4·00
124c	+ 2 f. on 1 f. 50 (No. 100)	4·00	4·00
124d	+ 3 f. on 2 f. (No. 103)	4·00	4·00

31a Ox Caravan

1942. Marshal Petain issue.

No.	Type	Description	Unused	Used
124e	31a	1 f. green	20	1·25
124f		2 f. 50 blue	15	1·25

1942. Air. Colonial Child Welfare Fund. As Nos. 98g/i of Niger.

No.	Description	Unused	Used
124g	1 f. 50 + 3 f. 50 green		15
124h	2 f. + 6 f. brown		15
124i	3 f. + 9 f. red		15

1942. Air. Imperial Fortnight. As No. 98j of Niger.

No.	Description	Unused	Used
124j	1 f. 20 + 1 f. 80 blue and red		15

32 Twin-engine Airliner over Camel Caravan

1942. Air. T **32** inscr "MAURITANIE" at foot.

No.	Type	Description	Unused	Used
124k	32	50 f. orange and yellow	75	1·10

1944. Surch

No.	Type	Description	Unused	Used
125	25	3 f. 50 on 65 c. green	25	20
126		4 f. on 65 c. green	30	35
127		5 f. on 65 c. green	40	60
128		10 f. on 65 c. green	40	50
129	27	15 f. on 90 c. orange	65	70

ISLAMIC REPUBLIC.

35 Flag of Republic

37 Well

38 Slender-billed Gull

1960. Inauguration of Islamic Republic.

No.	Type	Description	Unused	Used
130	35	25 f. bistre, green and brown on rose	40	35

1960. 10th Anniv of African Technical Co-operation Commission. As T **4** of Malagasy Republic.

No.	Description	Unused	Used
131	25 f. blue and turquoise	40	35

1960.

No.	Type	Description	Unused	Used
132	37	50 c. purple & brn (postage)	10	10
133	–	1 f. bistre, brown and green	10	10
134	–	2 f. brown, green and blue	15	10
135	–	3 f. red, sepia and turquoise	20	20
136	–	4 f. buff and green	20	20
137	–	5 f. chocolate, brown & red	15	10
138	–	10 f. blue, black & brown	20	15
139	–	15 f. multicoloured	40	15
140	–	20 f. brown and green	30	15
141	–	25 f. blue and green	30	15
142	–	30 f. blue, violet & bistre	50	15
143	–	50 f. brown and green	80	40
144	–	60 f. purple, red and green	1·25	40
145	–	85 f. brown, sepia & blue	3·50	1·50
146	–	100 f. brown, chocolate and blue (air)	8·00	3·00
147	–	200 f. myrtle, brn and sepia	17·00	6·25
148	38	500 f. sepia, blue & brn	35·00	13·00

DESIGNS—VERT: (As Type **37**) 2 f. Harvesting dates; 5 f. Harvesting millet; 25, 30 f. Seated dance; 50 f. "Telmidi" (symbolic figure); 60 f. Metalsmith; 85 f. Scimitar oryx; 100 f. Greater flamingo; 200 f. African spoonbill. HORIZ: 3 f. Barbary sheep; 4 f. Fennec foxes; 10 f. Cordwainer; 15 f. Fishing-boat; 20 f. Nomad school.

39 Flag and Map

43 Campaign Emblem

42 European, African and Boeing 707 Airliners

1960. Proclamation of Independence.

No.	Type	Description	Unused	Used
149	39	25 f. green, brown and chest	50	50

1962. Air. Air Afrique Airline.

No.	Type	Description	Unused	Used
150	42	100 f. green, brown & bistre	1·75	1·10

1962. Malaria Eradication.

No.	Type	Description	Unused	Used
151	43	25 f. + 5 f. olive	50	50

44 U.N. Headquarters and View of Nouakchott

1962. Admission to U.N.O.

No.	Type	Description	Unused	Used
152	44	15 f. brown, black and blue	20	20
153		25 f. brown, myrtle and blue	35	35
154		85 f. brown, purple and blue	1·00	1·00

45 Union Flag

1962. 1st Anniv of Union of African and Malagasy States.

No.	Type	Description	Unused	Used
155	45	30 f. blue	45	45

46 Eagle and Crescent over Nouakchott

1962. 8th Endemic Diseases Eradication Conference, Nouakchott.

No.	Type	Description	Unused	Used
156	46	30 f. green, brown and blue	45	35

47 Diesel Mineral Train

1962.

No.	Type	Description	Unused	Used
157	47	50 f. multicoloured	2·25	85

1962. Air. 1st Anniv of Admission to U.N.O. As T **44** but views from different angles and inscr "1 er ANNIVERSAIRE 27 OCTOBRE 1962".

No.	Description	Unused	Used
158	100 f. blue, brown & turquoise	1·10	90

49 Map and Agriculture

1962. 2nd Anniv of Independence.

No.	Type	Description	Unused	Used
159	49	30 f. green and purple	45	30

50 Congress Representatives

1962. 1st Anniv of Unity Congress.

No.	Type	Description	Unused	Used
160	50	25 f. brown, myrtle & blue	45	40

51 Globe and Emblem

1962. Freedom from Hunger.

No.	Type	Description	Unused	Used
161	51	25 f. + 5 f. blue, brown & pur	55	55

52 Douglas DC-3 Airliner over Nouakchott Airport

1963. Air. Creation of National Airline.

No.	Type	Description	Unused	Used
162	52	500 f. myrtle, brown & blue	12·00	4·50

53 Open-cast Mining, Zouerate

1963. Air. Mining Development. Multicoloured.

No.	Description	Unused	Used
163	100 f. Type **53**	2·50	60
164	200 f. Port-Etienne	4·50	1·75

54 Striped Hyena

56 "Posts and Telecommunications"

1963. Animals.

No.	Type	Description	Unused	Used
165	54	50 c. black, brown & myrtle	10	10
166	–	1 f. black, blue and buff	10	10
167	–	1 f. 50 brown, olive & pur	20	15
168	–	2 f. purple, green and red	15	15
169	–	5 f. bistre, blue and ochre	25	20
170	–	10 f. black and ochre	40	20
171	–	15 f. purple and blue	40	20
172	–	20 f. bistre, purple and blue	50	20
173	–	25 f. ochre, brown & turq	70	25
174	–	30 f. bistre, brown and blue	1·25	30
175	–	50 f. bistre, brown & green	1·75	60
176	–	60 f. bistre, brown & turq	2·25	90

ANIMALS—HORIZ: 1 f. Spotted hyena; 2 f. Guinea baboons; 10 f. Leopard; 15 f. Bongos; 20 f. Aardvark; 30 f. North African crested porcupine; 60 f. Chameleon. VERT: 1 f. 50, Cheetah; 5 f. Dromedaries; 25 f. Patas monkeys; 50 f. Dorcas gazelle.

1963. Air. African and Malagasy Posts and Telecommunications Union.

No.	Type	Description	Unused	Used
177	56	85 f. multicoloured	1·00	65

57 "Telstar" Satellite

1963. Air. Space Telecommunications.

No.	Type	Description	Unused	Used
178	57	50 f. brown, purple & green	65	45
179	–	100 f. blue, brown and red	1·25	80
180	–	150 f. turquoise and brown	2·25	1·50

DESIGNS: 100 f. "Syncom" satellite; 150 f. "Relay" satellite.

58 "Tiros" Satellite

60 U.N. Emblem, Sun and Birds

59 Airline Emblem

1963. Air. World Meteorological Day.
181 **58** 200 f. brown, blue & green . . 3·50 1·75

1963. Air. 1st Anniv of "Air Afrique" and DC-8 Service Inauguration.
182 **59** 25 f. multicoloured 50 25

1963. Air. 15th Anniv of Declaration of Human Rights.
183 **60** 100 f. blue, violet & purple 1·25 85

61 Cogwheels and Wheat 62 Lichtenstein's Sandgrouse

1964. Air. European–African Economic Convention.
184 **61** 50 f. multicoloured . . . . 1·10 70

1964. Air. Birds.
185 **62** 100 f. ochre, brown & green 10·00 2·00
186 – 200 f. black, brown & blue 16·00 4·50
187 – 500 f. slate, red and green 35·00 12·50
DESIGNS: 200 f. Reed cormorant; 500 f. Dark chanting goshawk.

63 Temple, Philae

1964. Air. Nubian Monuments Preservation.
188 **63** 10 f. brown, black and blue 45 30
189 25 f. slate, brown and blue 70 60
190 60 f. chocolate, brown & bl 1·50 1·10

64 W.M.O. Emblem. Sun and Lightning 65 Radar Antennae and Sun Emblem

1964. World Meteorological Day.
191 **64** 85 f. blue, orange & brown 1·25 80

1964. International Quiet Sun Years.
192 **65** 25 f. red, green and blue . 35 25

66 Bowl depicting Horse-racing

1964. Air. Olympic Games, Tokyo.
193 **66** 15 f. brown and bistre . . 30 25
194 – 50 f. brown and blue . . . 60 50
195 – 85 f. brown and red . . . 1·10 1·00
196 – 100 f. brown and green . . 1·50 1·25
DESIGNS—VERT: 50 f. Running (vase); 85 f. Wrestling (vase). HORIZ: 100 f. Chariot-racing (bowl).

67 Grey Mullet 68 "Co-operation"

1964. Marine Fauna.
197 **67** 1 f. green, blue and brown 15 15
198 – 5 f. purple, green & brown 20 15
199 – 10 f. green, ochre and blue 35 20
200 – 60 f. slate, green and brown 2·00 85
DESIGNS—VERT: 5 f. Lobster ("Panulirus mauritanicus"); 10 f. Lobster ("Panulirus regius"). HORIZ: 60 f. Meagre.

1964. French, African and Malagasy Co-operation.
201 **68** 25 f. brown, green & mauve 40 30

69 Pres. Kennedy 70 "Nymphaea lotus"

1964. Air. 1st Death Anniv of Pres. Kennedy.
202 **69** 100 f. multicoloured . . . 1·40 1·00

1965. Mauritanian Flowers.
203 **70** 5 f. green, red and blue . . 15 15
204 – 10 f. green, ochre & purple 25 15
205 – 20 f. brown, red and sepia 45 20
206 – 45 f. turquoise, purple & grn 1·10 60
FLOWERS—VERT: 10 f. "Acacia gommier"; 45 f. "Caralluma retrospiciens". HORIZ: 20 f. "Adenium obesum".

71 "Hardine" 72 Abraham Lincoln

1965. Musical Instruments and Musicians.
207 **71** 2 f. brown, bistre and blue 15 15
208 – 8 f. brown, bistre and red 30 15
209 – 25 f. brown, black & green 60 20
210 – 40 f. black, blue and violet 80 35
DESIGNS: 8 f. "Tobol" (drums); 25 f. "Tidinit" ("Violins"); 40 f. Native band.

1965. Death Centenary of Abraham Lincoln.
211 **72** 50 f. multicoloured 70 35

73 Early Telegraph and Relay Satellite

1965. Air. Centenary of I.T.U.
212 **73** 250 f. green, mauve & blue 4·25 3·25

74 Palms in the Adrar

1965. "Tourism and Archaeology" (1st series).
213 **74** 1 f. green, brown and blue 10 10
214 – 4 f. brown, red and blue . 15 10
215 – 15 f. multicoloured 30 20
216 – 60 f. sepia, brown and green 90 45
DESIGNS—VERT: 4 f. Chinguetti Mosque. HORIZ: 15 f. Clay-pits; 60 f. Carved doorway, Qualata.
See also Nos. 255/8.

75 "Attack on Cancer" (the Crab) 76 Wooden Tea Service

1965. Air. Campaign against Cancer.
217 **75** 100 f. red, blue and ochre 1·50 60

1965. Native Handicrafts.
218 **76** 3 f. brown, ochre and slate 15 15
219 – 7 f. purple, orange and blue 20 20
220 – 25 f. brown, black and red 35 20
221 – 50 f. red, green and orange 75 35
DESIGNS—VERT: 7 f. Snuff-box and pipe; 25 f. Damasquine dagger. HORIZ: 50 f. Mederdra chest.

77 Nouakchott Wharf 78 Sir Winston Churchill

1965. Mauritanian Development.
222 – 5 f. green and brown . . . 90 60
223 **77** 10 f. red, turquoise and blue 15 10
224 – 30 f. red, brown and purple 1·75 60
225 – 85 f. violet, lake and blue 1·25 55
DESIGNS—VERT: 5 f., 30 f. Choum Tunnel. HORIZ: 85 f. Nouakchott Hospital.

1965. Air. Churchill Commem.
226 **78** 200 f. multicoloured . . . . 2·50 1·25

79 Rocket "Diamant"

1966. Air. French Satellites.
227 **79** 30 f. green, red and blue . . 50 25
228 – 60 f. purple, blue & turquoise 1·00 45
229 – 90 f. lake, violet and blue 1·50 75
DESIGNS—HORIZ: 60 f. Satellite "A 1" and Globe; 90 f. Rocket "Scout" and satellite "FR 1".

80 Dr. Schweitzer and Hospital Scene

1966. Air. Schweitzer Commem.
230 **80** 50 f. multicoloured . . . . 1·10 50

81 Stafford, Schirra and "Gemini 6"

1966. Air. Space Flights. Multicoloured.
231 50 f. Type **81** 60 25
232 100 f. Borman, Lovell and "Gemini 7" . . . . 1·25 60
233 200 f. Beliaiev, Leonov and "Voskhod 2" . . . . 2·50 1·25

82 African Woman and Carved Head

1966. World Festival of Negro Arts, Dakar.
234 **82** 10 f. black, brown & grn 20 10
235 – 30 f. purple, black and blue 35 20
236 – 60 f. purple, red and orange 75 45
DESIGNS: 30 f. Dancers and hands playing cornet; 60 f. Cine-camera and village huts.

83 "Dove" over Map of Africa 84 Satellite "D 1"

1966. Air. Organization of African Unity (O.A.U.).
237 **83** 100 f. multicoloured . . . 1·00 50

1966. Air. Launching of Satellite "D 1".
238 **84** 100 f. plum, brown & blue 1·10 75

85 Breguet 14T2 Salon

1966. Air. Early Aircraft.
239 **85** 50 f. indigo, blue and bistre 80 25
240 – 100 f. green, purple & blue 1·75 50
241 – 150 f. turquoise, brn & blue 2·50 75
242 – 200 f. indigo, blue & purple 3·50 1·25
AIRCRAFT: 100 f. Farman Goliath; 150 f. Couzinet "Arc en Ciel"; 200 f. Latecoere 28-3 seaplane "Comte de la Vaulx".

86 "Acacia ehrenbergiana"

1966. Mauritanian Flowers. Multicoloured.
243 10 f. Type **86** 25 15
244 15 f. "Schouwia purpurea" . . 35 15
245 20 f. "Ipomaea asarifolia" . . 45 20
246 25 f. "Grewia bicolor" 55 25
247 30 f. "Pancratium trianthum" 90 25
248 60 f. "Blepharis linariifolia" . 1·40 55

87 DC-8F and "Air Afrique" Emblem

1966. Air. Inauguration of Douglas DC-8F Air Services.
249 **87** 30 f. grey, black and red . 40 15

88 "Raft of the Medusa" (after Gericault)

1966. Air. 150th Anniv of Shipwreck of the "Medusa".
250 **88** 500 f. multicoloured . . . 9·00 6·50

89 "Myrina silenus" **90** "Hunting" (petroglyph from Tenses, Adrar)

1966. Butterflies. Multicoloured.
251 5 f. Type **89** 30 20
252 30 f. "Colotis danae" . . . . 1·00 40
253 45 f. "Hypolimnas misippus" 1·75 60
254 60 f. "Danaus chrysippus" . . 2·50 85

1966. Tourism and Archaeology (2nd series).
255 **90** 2 f. chestnut and brown . . 15 15
256 – 3 f. brown and blue 20 20
257 – 30 f. green and red 55 25
258 – 50 f. brown, green & pur . 1·25 80
DESIGNS: 3 f. "Fighting" (petroglyph from Tenses, Adrar); 30 f. Copper jug (from Le Mreyer, Adrar); 50 f. Camel and caravan.

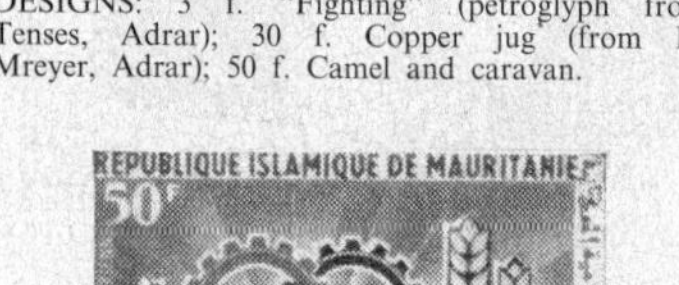

91 Cogwheels and Ears of Wheat

1966. Air. Europafrique.
259 **91** 50 f. multicoloured 70 40

92 U.N.E.S.C.O. Emblem

1966. 20th Anniv of U.N.E.S.C.O.
260 **92** 30 f. multicoloured 45 20

93 Olympic Village, Grenoble

1967. Publicity for Olympic Games (1968).
261 – 20 f. brown, blue and green 30 20
262 **93** 30 f. brown, green and blue 40 30
263 – 40 f. brown, purple & blue 60 40
264 – 100 f. brown, green & blk 1·10 70
DESIGNS—VERT: 20 f. Old and new buildings, Mexico City; 40 f. Ice rink, Grenoble and Olympic torch. HORIZ: 100 f. Olympic stadium, Mexico City.

94 South African Crowned Crane **95** Globe, Rockets and Eye

1967. Air. Birds. Multicoloured.
265 100 f. Type **94** . . . . 4·50 1·60
266 200 f. Great egret . . . . . . 9·00 2·25
267 500 f. Ostrich . . . . 20·00 7·25

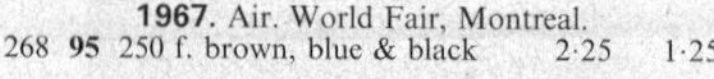

1967. Air. World Fair, Montreal.
268 **95** 250 f. brown, blue & black 2·25 1·25

96 Prosopis **97** Jamboree Emblem and Scout Kit

1967. Trees.
269 **96** 10 f. green, blue and brown 20 10
270 – 15 f. green, blue and purple 25 15
271 – 20 f. green, purple and blue 30 15
272 – 25 f. brown and green . . 40 20
273 – 30 f. brown, green and red 55 25
TREES: 15 f. Jujube; 20 f. Date palm; 25 f. Peltophorum; 30 f. Baobab.

1967. World Scout Jamboree, Idaho.
274 **97** 60 f. blue, green and brown 70 35
275 – 90 f. blue, green and red . 1·10 50
DESIGN—HORIZ: 90 f. Jamboree emblem and scouts.

98 Weaving **99** Atomic Symbol

1967. Advancement of Mauritanian Women.
276 **98** 5 f. red, black and violet . 15 10
277 – 10 f. black, violet and green 20 10
278 – 20 f. black, purple and blue 35 15
279 – 30 f. blue, black and brown 45 25
280 – 50 f. black, violet & indigo 70 30
DESIGNS—VERT: 10 f. Needlework; 30 f. Laundering. HORIZ: 20 f. Nursing; 50 f. Sewing (with machines).

1967. Air. International Atomic Energy Agency.
281 **99** 200 f. blue, green and red . 2·25 1·10

100 Cattle

1967. Campaign for Prevention of Cattle Plague.
282 **100** 30 f. red, blue and green . 35 25

101 Map of Africa, Letters and Pylons

1967. Air. 5th Anniv of U.A.M.P.T.
283 **101** 100 f. green, brown & pur 1·00 60

102 "Francois of Rimini" (Ingres) **103** Currency Tokens

1967. Air. Death Centenary of Jean Ingres (painter). Multicoloured.
284 90 f. Type **102** . . . . 1·10 60
285 200 f. "Ingres in his Studio" (Alaux) . . . . 2·10 1·25
See also Nos. 306/8.

1967. 5th Anniv of West African Monetary Union.
286 **103** 30 f. grey and orange . . 35 15

104 "Hyphaene thebaica" **105** Human Rights Emblem

1967. Mauritanian Fruits.
287 **104** 1 f. brown, green & purple 15 10
288 – 2 f. yellow, green & brown 15 10
289 – 3 f. olive, green and violet 15 10
290 – 4 f. red, green and brown 15 10
291 – 5 f. orange, brown & green 20 10
FRUITS—HORIZ: 2 f. "Balanites aegypticaca"; 4 f. "Ziziphus lotus". VERT: 3 f. "Adansonia digitata"; 5 f. "Phoenix dactylifera".

1968. Human Rights Year.
292 **105** 30 f. yellow, green & black 30 20
293 50 f. yellow, brown & black 55 35

106 Chancellor Adenauer **108** Mosque, Nouakchott

107 Skiing

1968. Air. Adenauer Commemoration.
294 **106** 100 f. sepia, brown & blue 1·25 60

1968. Air. Olympic Games, Grenoble and Mexico.
296 **107** 20 f. purple, indigo & blue 30 10
297 – 30 f. brown, green & plum 35 15
298 – 50 f. green, blue and ochre 55 25
299 – 100 f. green, red & brown 1·00 50
DESIGNS—VERT: 30 f. Horse-vaulting; 50 f. Ski-jumping. HORIZ: 100 f. Hurdling.

1968. Tourism. Multicoloured.
300 30 f. Type **108** 25 20
301 45 f. Amogjar Pass 35 20
302 90 f. Cavaliers' Tower, Boutilimit 65 35

109 Man and W.H.O. Emblem

1968. Air. 20th Anniv of W.H.O.
303 **109** 150 f. blue, purple & brn . 1·50 75

110 U.N.E.S.C.O. Emblem and "Movement of Water"

1968. International Hydrological Decade.
304 **110** 90 f. green and lake . . . 70 40

111 U.P.U. Building, Berne

1968. Admission of Mauritania to U.P.U.
305 **111** 30 f. brown and red . . . 35 20

1968. Air. Paintings by Ingres. As T **102**. Mult.
306 100 f. "Man's Torso" . . . . 1·10 65
307 150 f. "The Iliad" . . . . 1·75 95
308 250 f. "The Odyssey" . . . . 2·75 1·60

112 Land-yachts crossing Desert **113** Dr. Martin Luther King

1968. Land-yacht Racing.
309 **112** 30 f. blue, yellow & orange 45 25
310 – 40 f. purple, blue & orange 55 30
311 – 60 f. green, yellow & orge 85 50
DESIGNS—HORIZ: 40 f. Racing on shore. VERT: 60 f. Crew making repairs.

1968. Air. "Apostles of Peace".
312 **113** 50 f. brown, blue and olive 1·00 40
313 – 50 f. brown and blue . . 60 25
DESIGN: No. 313, Mahatma Gandhi.

113a "Surprise Letter" (C. A. Coypel) **114** Donkey and Foal

1968. Air. "Philexafrique" Stamp Exn Abidjan, Ivory Coast, (1969) (1st issue).
315 **113a** 100 f. multicoloured . . 1·75 1·75

1968. Domestic Animals. Multicoloured.
316 5 f. Type **114** 15 10
317 10 f. Ewe and lamb 20 15
318 15 f. Dromedary and calf . . 25 15
319 30 f. Mare and foal 45 25
320 50 f. Cow and calf 70 35
321 90 f. Goat and kid . . . . . 1·40 50

114a Forest Scene and Stamp of 1938

1969. Air. "Philexafrique" Stamp Exhibition, Abidjan, Ivory Coast (2nd issue).
322 **114a** 50 f. purple, green & brown 1·10 1·10

114b "Napoleon at Council of Five Hundred" (Bouchot) **115** Map and I.L.O. Emblem

1969. Air. Birth Bicentenary of Napoleon Bonaparte. Multicoloured.
323 50 f. **114b** . . . . 1·50 90
324 90 f. "Napoleon's Installation by the Council of State" (Conder) 2·00 1·25
325 250 f. "The Farewell of Fontainebleau" (Vernet) . . 5·00 3·25

1969. 50th Anniv of I.L.O.
326 **115** 50 f. multicoloured . . . 50 25

116 Monitor Lizard **117** Date Palm, "Parlatoria blanchardi" and "Pharoscymus anchorage"

1969. Reptiles. Multicoloured.

327 5 f. Type **116** 25 20
328 10 f. Horned viper 45 30
329 30 f. Black-collared cobra . . 1·10 35
330 60 f. Rock python . . . . . . 1·75 1·10
331 85 f. Nile crocodile . . . . . 2·75 1·40

1969. Date-palms. Protection Campaign.

332 **117** 30 f. blue, red and green . 30 15

118 Camel and Emblem

1969. Air. African Tourist Year.

333 **118** 50 f. purple, blue & orange 70 35

119 Dancers and Baalbek Columns

1969. Baalbek Festival, Lebanon.

334 **119** 100 f. brown, red and blue 1·25 55

120 "Apollo 8" and Moon

1969. Air. Moon Flight of "Apollo 8". Embossed on gold foil.

335 **120** 1,000 f. gold . . . . 14·00 14·00

121 Wolde (marathon) **122a** Bank Emblem

122 London–Istanbul Route-Map

1969. Air. Gold Medal Winners, Mexico Olympic Games.

336 **121** 30 f. red, brown and blue 25 15
337 – 70 f. red, brown and green 50 30
338 – 150 f. green, bistre and red 1·25 70

DESIGNS: 70 f. Beamon (athletics); 150 f. Vera Caslavska (gymnastics).

1969. Air. London–Sydney Motor Ralley.

339 **122** 10 f. brown, blue & purple 15 10
340 – 20 f. brown, blue & purple 30 15
341 – 50 f. brown, blue & purple 60 25
342 – 70 f. brown, blue & purple 85 30

ROUTE-MAPS: 20 f. Ankara-Teheran; 50 f. Kandahar–Bombay; 70 f. Perth-Sydney.

1969. 5th Anniv of African Development Bank. Multicoloured.

344 **122a** 30 f. brown, green & blue 30 15

123 Pendant **124** Sea-water Desalination Plant, Nouakchott

1969. Native Handicrafts.

345 **123** 10 f. brown and purple . 20 15
346 – 20 f. red, black and blue . 40 20

DESIGN—HORIZ: 20 f. Rahla headdress.

1969. Economic Development.

347 **124** 10 f. blue, purple and red 20 15
348 – 15 f. black, lake and blue 25 15
349 – 30 f. black, purple & blue 30 20

DESIGNS: 15 f. Fishing quay, Nouadhibou; 30 f. Meat-processing plant, Kaedi.

125 Lenin **126** "Sternocera interrupta"

1970. Birth Centenary of Lenin.

350 **125** 30 f. black, red and blue . 30 20

1970. Insects.

351 **126** 5 f. black, buff and brown 25 15
352 – 10 f. brown, yellow & lake 35 15
353 – 20 f. olive, purple & brown 50 25
354 – 30 f. violet, green & brn 80 45
355 – 40 f. brown, blue and lake 1·50 70

INSECTS: 10 f. "Anoplocnemis curvipes"; 20 f. "Julodis aequinoctialis"; 30 f. "Thermophilum sexmaculatum marginatum"; 40 f. "Plocaederus denticornis".

127 Footballers and Hemispheres **128** Japanese Musician, Emblem and Map on Palette

1970. World Cup Football Championships, Mexico.

356 **127** 25 f. multicoloured . . . 30 20
357 – 30 f. multicoloured . . . 35 20
358 – 70 f. multicoloured . . . 70 30
359 – 150 f. multicoloured . . . 1·60 75

DESIGNS: 30, 70, 150 f. As Type **127**, but with different players.

1970. New U.P.U. Headquarters Building. As T **81** of New Caledonia.

360 30 f. red, brown and green . 35 20

1970. Air. "EXPO 70" World Fair, Osaka, Japan. Multicoloured.

361 50 f. Type **128** 50 20
362 75 f. Japanese fan 75 35
363 150 f. Stylised bird, map and boat . . . . 1·40 80

129 U.N. Emblem and Examples of Progress

1970. Air. 25th Anniv of U.N.O.

364 **129** 100 f. green, brown & blue 1·00 60

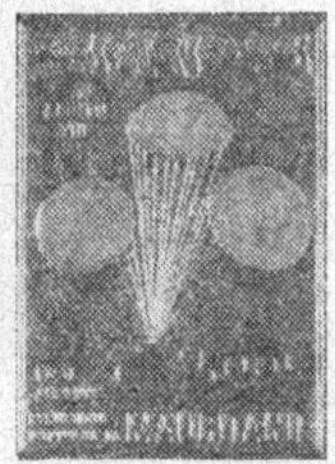

130 Vladimir Komarov **131** Descent of "Apollo 13"

1970. Air. "Lost Heroes of Space" (1st series).

365 **130** 150 f. brown, orge & slate 1·50 70
366 – 150 f. brown, blue and slate 1·50 70
367 – 150 f. brown, orge & slate 1·50 70

HEROES: No. 366, Elliott See; 367, Yuri Gagarin. See also Nos. 376/8.

1970. Air. Space Flight of "Apollo 13".

369 **131** 500 f. red, blue and gold . 5·00 5·00

132 Woman in Traditional Costume **133** Arms and State House

1970. Traditional Costumes. As T **132**.

370 **132** 10 f. orange and brown . . 20 15
371 – 30 f. blue, red and brown 40 20
372 – 40 f. brown, purple & red 50 30
373 – 50 f. blue and brown . . . 70 35
374 – 70 f. brown, choc & bl . . 90 45

1970. Air. 10th Anniv of Independence.

375 **133** 100 f. multicoloured . . . 1·00 45

1970. Air. "Lost Heroes of Space" (2nd series). As T **130**.

376 150 f. brown, blue & turquoise 1·50 70
377 150 f. brown, blue & turquoise 1·50 70
378 150 f. brown, blue and orange 1·50 70

HEROES: No. 376, Roger Chaffee; No. 377, Virgil Grissom; No. 378, Edward White.

134 Greek Wrestling

1971. Air. "Pre-Olympics Year".

380 **134** 100 f. brown, purple & bl 1·10 75

135 People of Different Races

1971. Racial Equality Year.

381 **135** 30 f. plum, blue & brown 30 15
382 – 40 f. black, red and blue 35 20

DESIGN—VERT: 40 f. European and African hands.

136 Pres. Nasser

1971. Air. Pres. Gamal Nasser of Egypt Commemoration.

383 **136** 100 f. multicoloured . . . 85 40

137 Gen. De Gaulle in Uniform **138** Scout Badge, Scout and Map

1971. De Gaulle Commem. Multicoloured.

384 40 f. Type **137** . . . . 1·25 60
385 100 f. De Gaulle as President of France . . . . 2·75 1·40

1971. Air. 13th World Scout Jamboree, Asagiri, Japan.

387 **138** 35 f. multicoloured . . . 40 20
388 40 f. multicoloured . . . 50 20
389 100 f. multicoloured . . . 1·25 45

139 Diesel Locomotive

1971. Miferma Iron-ore Mines. Multicoloured.

390 35 f. Iron ore train . . . . . 1·10 60
391 100 f. Type **139** . . . . 2·40 1·40

Nos. 390/1 were issued together, se-tenant, forming a composite design.

139a Headquarters, Brazzaville, and Ardin Musicians

1971. Air. 10th Anniv of African and Malagasy Posts and Telecommunications Union.

392 **139a** 100 f. multicoloured . . 1·10 60

140 A.P.U. Emblem and Airmail Envelope

1971. Air. 10th Anniv of African Postal Union.

393 **140** 35 f. multicoloured . . . 40 25

141 U.N.I.C.E.F. Emblem and Child

1971. 25th Anniv of U.N.I.C.E.F.

394 **141** 35 f. black, brown & blue 35 20

142 "Moslem King" (c. 1218)

1972. Air. Moslem Miniatures. Multicoloured.

395 35 f. Type **142** 45 20
396 40 f. "Enthroned Prince" (Egypt, c. 1334) 60 25
397 100 f. "Pilgrims' Caravan" (Maquamat, Baghdad 1237) 1·50 70

1972. Air. U.N.E.S.C.O. "Save Venice" Campaign. As T **127** of Mali. Multicoloured.

398 45 f. "Quay and Ducal Palace" (Carlevaris) (vert) 60 25

399 100 f. "Grand Canal" (Canaletto) . . . . 1·40 60
400 250 f. "Santa Maria della Salute" (Canaletto) . . . . 3·00 1·50

143 Hurdling

1972. Air. Olympic Games, Munich.
401 **143** 75 f. purple, orange & grn 55 30
402 100 f. purple, blue & brn 75 40
403 200 f. purple, lake & green 1·60 70

144 Nurse tending Baby
145 Samuel Morse and Morse Key

1972. Mauritanian Red Crescent Fund.
405 **144** 35 f. + 5 f. multicoloured 60 60

1972. World Telecommunications Day. Mult.
406 35 f. Type **145** 35 20
407 40 f. "Relay" satellite and hemispheres 45 20
408 75 f. Alexander Graham Bell and early telephone 70 35

146 Spirifer Shell

1972. Fossil Shells. Multicoloured.
409 25 f. Type **146** . . . . 1·00 35
410 75 f. Trilobite . . . . 2·75 1·10

147 "Luna 16" and Moon Probe

151 Mediterranean Monk Seal with Young

149 Africans and 500 f. Coin

1972. Air. Russian Exploration of the Moon.
411 **147** 75 f. brown, blue & green 60 30
412 – 100 f. brown, grey & violet 90 50
DESIGN—HORIZ: 100 f. "Lunokhod 1".

1972. Air. Gold Medal-Winners, Munich. Nos. 401/3 optd as listed below.
413 **143** 75 f. purple, orange & grn 60 30
414 100 f. purple, blue & brn 80 50
415 200 f. purple, lake & green 1·60 1·00
OVERPRINTS: 75 f. **110m. HAIES MILBURN MEDAILLE D'OR**; 100 f. **400m. HAIES AKII-BUA MEDAILLE D'OR**; 200 f. **3,000m. STEEPLE KEINO MEDAILLE D'OR**.

1972. 10th Anniv of West African Monetary Union.
416 **149** 35 f. grey, brown & green 30 20

1973. Air. Moon Flight of "Apollo 17". No. 267 surch **Apollo XVII Decembre 1972** and value.
417 250 f. on 500 f. multicoloured 4·00 2·00

1973. Seals. Multicoloured.
418 40 f. Type **151** (postage) . . . 1·25 50
419 135 f. Head of Mediterranean monk seal (air) . . . . . . 3·75 2·00

152 "Lion and Crocodile" (Delacroix)

1973. Air. Paintings by Delacroix. Mult.
420 100 f. Type **152** . . . . 1·50 75
421 250 f. "Lion attacking Forest Hog" . . . . 3·25 2·00

153 "Horns of Plenty"

1973. 10th Anniv of World Food Programme.
422 **153** 35 f. multicoloured . . . 30 20

154 U.P.U. Monument, Berne, and Globe

1973. World U.P.U. Day.
423 **154** 100 f. blue, orange & grn 1·00 65

155 Nomad Encampment and Eclipse

1973. Total Eclipse of the Sun.
424 **155** 35 f. purple and green . . 35 20
425 – 40 f. purple, red and blue 45 20
426 – 140 f. purple and red . . 1·60 75
DESIGNS—VERT: 40 f. Rocket and Concorde. HORIZ: 140 f. Observation team.

1973. "Drought Relief". African Solidarity. No. 320 surch **SECHERESSE SOLIDARITE AFRICAINE** and value.
428 20 um. on 50 f. multicoloured 65 45

155a Crane with Letter and Union Emblem

1973. 12th Anniv of African and Malagasy Posts and Telecommunications Union.
429 **155a** 20 um. brown, lt brn & orge 70 45

157 Detective making Arrest and Fingerprint

1973. 50th Anniv of International Criminal Police Organization (Interpol).
430 **157** 15 um. violet, red & brown 1·10 45

1974. Various stamps surch with values in new currency. (a) Postage.

(i) Nos. 345/6.
431 **123** 27 um. on 10 f. brown and purple . . . . 1·50 70
432 – 28 um. on 20 f. red, black and blue . . . . 1·75 90

(ii) Nos. 351/5.
433 **126** 5 um. on 5 f. black, buff and brown 70 50
434 – 7 um. on 10 f. brown, yellow and lake 60 30
435 – 8 um. on 20 f. olive, purple and brown 70 35
436 – 10 um. on 30 f. violet, purple and brown . . . . 1·00 45
437 – 20 um. on 4 f. brown, blue and lake . . . . 2·00 1·10

(iii) Nos. 409/10.
438 **146** 5 um. on 25 f. mult . . . 60 40
439 – 15 um. on 75 f. mult . . . 1·75 1·00

(iv) No. 418.
440 **151** 8 um. on 40 f. multicoloured 90 45

(b) Air.
(i) Nos. 395/7.
441 **142** 7 um. on 35 f. mult . . . 40 20
442 – 8 um. on 40 f. mult . . . 40 20
443 – 20 um. on 100 f. mult . . 1·50 70

(ii) No. 419.
444 – 27 um. on 135 f. multicoloured . . . . . . 2·25 85

(iii) Nos. 420/1.
445 **152** 20 um. on 100 f. mult . . 1·60 70
446 – 50 um. on 250 f. mult . . 3·75 2·00

(iv) Nos. 424/6.
447 **155** 7 um. on 35 f. purple and green 45 20
448 – 8 um. on 40 f. purple, red and blue 45 20
449 – 28 um. on 140 f. purple and red . . . . 1·90 70

159 Footballers

161 Sir Winston Churchill

160 Jules Verne and Scenes from Books

1974. Air. World Cup Football Championships, West Germany.
450 **159** 7 um. multicoloured . . . 40 20
451 8 um. multicoloured . . . 40 20
452 20 um. multicoloured . . . 1·10 50

1974. Air. Jules Verne "Prophet of Space Travel" and "Skylab" Flights Commemoration.
454 **160** 70 um. silver . . . . 4·50 4·50
455 – 70 um. silver . . . . 4·50 4·50
456 **160** 250 um. gold . . . . . 12·00 12·00
457 – 250 um. gold . . . . . 12·00 12·00
DESIGNS: Nos. 455, 457, "Skylab" in Space.

1974. Air. Birth Centenary of Sir Winston Churchill.
458 **161** 40 um. red and purple . . 1·75 95

162 U.P.U. Monument and Globes

1974. Centenary of U.P.U.
459 **162** 30 um. red, green and deep green . . . . 1·25 75
460 50 um. red, light blue and blue . . . . 2·00 1·25

163 5 Ouguiya Coin and Banknote

1974. 1st Anniv of Introduction of Ouguiya Currency.
461 **163** 7 um. black, green and blue 35 20
462 – 8 um. black, mauve and green 40 20
463 – 20 um. black, blue and red . . . . 1·00 50
DESIGNS: 8 u. 10 ouguiya coin and banknote; 20 um. 20 ouguiya coin and banknote.

164 Lenin

166 Two Hunters

1974. Air. 50th Death Anniv of Lenin.
464 **164** 40 um. green and red . . 2·00 95

1974. Treaty of Berne Centenary. Nos. 459/60 optd **9 OCTOBRE 100 ANS D'UNION POSTALE INTERNATIONALE.**
465 **162** 30 um. red, green and deep green . . . . 1·60 80
466 50 um. red, light blue and blue . . . . 2·00 1·25

1975. Nos. 287/91 surch in new currency.
467 – 1 um. on 5 f. orange, brown and green 10 10
468 – 2 um. on 4 f. red, green and brown 15 15
469 – 3 um. on 2 f. yellow, green and brown 20 15
470 **104** 10 um. on 1 f. brown, green and purple 60 20
471 – 12 um. on 3 f. olive, green and violet 75 30

1975. Rock-carvings, Zemmour.
472 **166** 4 um. red and brown . . 40 15
473 – 5 um. purple 45 25
474 – 10 um. blue and light blue 80 35
DESIGNS—VERT: 5 um. Ostrich. HORIZ: 10 um. Elephant.

167 Mauritanian Women

1975. Air. International Women's Year.
475 **167** 12 um. purple, brown & bl 50 25
476 – 40 um. purple, brown & bl 1·75 85
DESIGNS: 40 um. Head of Mauritanian woman.

168 Combined European and African Heads

169 Dr. Schweitzer

1975. Europafrique.
477 **168** 40 um. brown, red & bistre 1·60 95

1975. Birth Centenary of Dr. Albert Schweitzer.
478 **169** 60 um. olive, brown & green 2·50 1·50

1975. Pan-African Drought Relief. Nos. 301/2 surch **SECHERESSE SOLIDARITE AFRICAINE** and value.
479 15 um. on 45 f. multicoloured 1·00 50
480 25 um. on 90 f. multicoloured 1·40 75

171 Akoujt Plant and Man with Camel

172 Fair Emblem

1975. Mining Industry.
481 **171** 10 um. brown, blue & orge 1·00 30
482 – 12 um. blue, red and brown 1·25 40
DESIGN: 12 um. Mining operations.

1975. Nouakchott National Fair.
483 **172** 10 um. multicoloured . . 40 25

173 Throwing the Javelin

1975. Air. "Pre-Olympic Year". Olympic Games, Montreal (1976).
484 **173** 50 um. red, green & brown 1·60 1·40
485 – 52 um. blue, brown and red 1·75 1·40
DESIGN: 52 um. Running.

174 Commemorative Medal

1975. 15th Anniv of Independence. Multicoloured.
486 10 um. Type **174** 50 30
487 12 um. Map of Mauritania . . 60 35

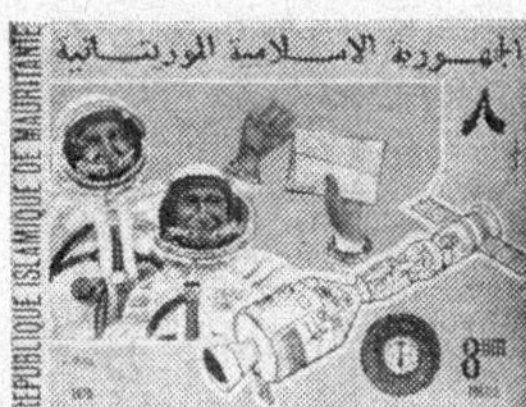

175 "Soyuz" Cosmonauts Leonov and Kubasov

1975. "Apollo-Soyz" Space Link. Multicoloured.
488 8 um. Type **175** (postage) . . 45 20
489 10 um. "Soyuz" on launch-pad 55 25
490 20 um. "Apollo" on launch-pad (air) 70 45
491 50 um. Cosmonauts meeting astronauts . . . . 2·00 1·00
492 60 um. Parachute splashdown 2·25 1·25

176 Foot-soldier of Lauzun's Legion

1976. Bicentenary of American Independence. Multicoloured.
494 8 um. Type **176** (postage) . . 60 20
495 10 um. "Green Mountain" infantryman 70 20
496 20 um. Lauzun Hussar's officer (air) 90 40
497 50 um. Artillery officer of 3rd Continental Regiment . . . 2·40 1·00
498 60 um. Grenadier of Gatinais' Regiment . . . . 3·00 1·25

1976. 10th Anniv of Arab Labour Charter. No. 408 surch **10e ANNIVERSAIRE DE LA CHARTE ARABE DU TRAVAIL** in French and Arabic.
500 12 um. on 75 f. blue, blk & grn 55 30

178 Commemorative Text on Map

1976. Reunification of Mauritania.
501 **178** 10 um. green, lilac and deep green 45 30

181 Running

1976. Air. Olympic Games, Montreal.
514 **181** 10 um. brown, green and violet 40 25
515 – 12 um. brown, green and violet 50 35
516 – 52 um. brown, green and violet . . . . 1·75 1·25
DESIGNS: 12 um. Vaulting (gymnastics); 52 um. Fencing.

182 LZ-4 at Friedrichshafen

1976. 75th Anniv of Zeppelin Airship. Mult.
517 5 um. Type **182** (postage) . . 25 15
518 10 um. "Schwaben" over German Landscape 40 20
519 12 um. "Hansa" over Heligoland 50 25
520 20 um. "Bodensee" and Doctor H. Durr . . . . 2·50 75
521 50 um. "Graf Zeppelin" over Capitol, Washington (air) . 2·25 90
522 60 um. "Graf Zeppelin II" crossing Swiss Alps . . . . 3·00 1·25

183 Temple and Bas-relief

1976. U.N.E.S.C.O. "Save Moenjodaro" (Pakistan) Campaign.
524 **183** 15 um. multicoloured . . 80 40

184 Sacred Ibis and Yellow-billed Stork

185 Alexander Graham Bell, Early Telephone and Satellite

1976. Air. Mauritanian Birds. Multicoloured.
525 50 um. Type **184** . . . . . . 5·00 1·90
526 100 um. Marabou storks (horiz) 8·50 4·25
527 200 um. Long-crested and Martial eagles . . . . . . 18·00 7·25

1976. Telephone Centenary.
528 **185** 10 um. blue, lake and red 50 25

186 Mohammed Ali Jinnah

1976. Birth Centenary of Mohammed Ali Jinnah (first Governor-General of Pakistan).
529 **186** 10 um. multicoloured . . 35 20

187 Capsule Assembly

1977. "Viking" Space Mission. Multicoloured.
530 10 um. Misson Control (horiz) 50 15
531 12 um. Type **187** 55 20
532 20 um. "Viking" in flight (horiz) (air) 80 25
533 50 um. "Viking" over Mars (horiz) . . . . 2·00 60
534 60 um. Parachute descent . . . 2·25 65

188 Bush Hare

1977. Mauritanian Animals. Multicoloured.
536 5 um. Type **188** 30 15
537 10 um. Golden jackals 55 30
538 12 um. Warthogs 75 40
539 14 um. Lion and lioness . . . 85 50
540 15 um. African elephants . . . 1·75 80

189 Frederic and Irene Joliot-Curie (Chemistry, 1935)

1977. Nobel Prize-winners. Multicoloured.
541 12 um. Type **189** (postage) . . 75 15
542 15 um. Emil von Behring and nurse inoculating patient (1901) 75 20
543 14 um. George Bernard Shaw and scene from "Androcles and the Lion" (1925) (air) . 75 30
544 55 um. Thomas Mann and scene from "Joseph and his Brethren" (1929) . . . . . . 1·90 60
545 60 um. International Red Cross and scene on Western Front (Peace Prize) (1917) . . . . 2·25 70

190 A.P.U. Emblem

1977. 25th Anniv of Arab Postal Union.
547 **190** 12 um. multicoloured . . . 45 30

191 Oil Lamp

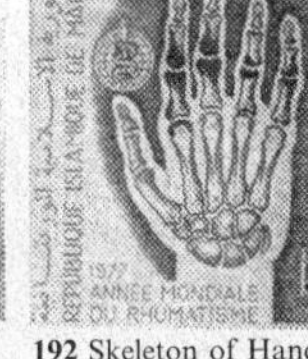

192 Skeleton of Hand

1977. Pottery from Tegdaoust.
548 **191** 1 um. olive, brown and blue 10 10
549 – 2 um. mauve, brown & blue 15 10
550 – 5 um. orange, brown & blue 25 10
551 – 12 um. brown, green and red 55 20
DESIGNS: 2 um. Four-handled tureen; 5 um. Large jar; 12 um. Narrow-necked jug.

1977. World Rheumatism Year.
552 **192** 40 um. orange, brown & grn 2·00 1·25

193 Holy Kaaba, Mecca

1977. Air. Pilgrimage to Mecca.
553 **193** 12 um. multicoloured . . 60 40

194 Charles Lindbergh and "Spirit of St. Louis"

1977. History of Aviation. Multicoloured.
554 12 um. Type **194** 50 15
555 14 um. Clement Ader and "Eole" 60 25
556 15 um. Louis Bleriot and Bleriot XI 70 25
557 55 um. General Italo Balbo and Savoia Marchetti S-55X flying boats . . . . 2·25 70
558 60 um. Concorde . . . . . . 2·50 85

195 Dome of the Rock

197 "Helene Fourment and Her Children" (Rubens)

196 Two Players

1977. Palestinian Welfare.
560 **195** 12 um. multicoloured . . 70 30
561 14 um. multicoloured . . 80 35

1977. World Cup Football Championships–Elimination Rounds. Multicoloured.
562 12 um. Type **196** (postage) . . 40 15
563 14 um. Sir Alf Ramsey and Wembley Stadium 50 20
564 15 um. A "throw-in" 60 20
565 50 um. Football and emblems (air) . . . . 2·00 60
566 60 um. Eusebio Ferreira . . . 2·40 1·00

1977. 400th Birth Anniv of Rubens. Paintings. Multicoloured.
568 12 um. Type **197** 50 15
569 14 um. "The Marquis of Spinola" 60 20
570 67 um. "The Four Philosophers" 2·25 75
571 69 um. "Steen Castle and Park" (horiz) . . . . 2·50 85

198 Addra Gazelles

1978. Endangered Animals. Multicoloured.
573 5 um. Scimitar oryx (horiz) . . 35 15
574 12 um. Type **198** 65 25
575 14 um. African manatee (horiz) 80 35
576 55 um. Barbary sheep . . . . 3·00 1·00
577 60 um. African elephant (horiz) 3·25 1·25
578 100 um. Ostrich . . . . 4·50 1·75

199 Clasped Hands and President Giscard d'Estaing of France

1978. Air. Franco-African Co-operation. Embossed on foil.
579 **199** 250 um. silver . . . . . . 7·00 7·00
580 500 um. gold . . . . . . 14·00 14·00

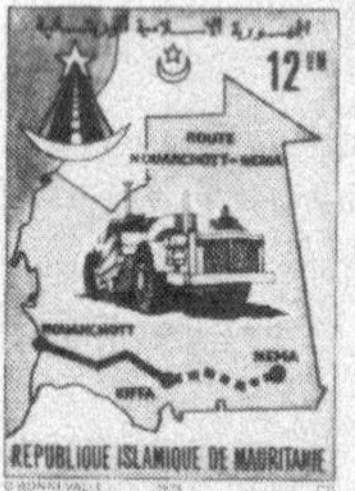

199a Earth-mover and Route Map   200 Footballers

1978. Nouakchott–Nema Highway. Mult.
580a 12 um. Type **199a** . . . . . 2·00 1·50
580b 14 um. Bulldozer and route map 2·25 1·75

1978. World Cup Football Championship, Argentina. Multicoloured.
581 12 um. Type **200** 40 20
582 14 um. World Cup 50 25
583 20 um. F.I.F.A. flag and football 85 35

201 Raoul Follereau and St. George fighting Dragon

1978. 25th Anniv of Raoul Follereau Foundation.
585 **201** 12 um. brown and green . 70 40

202 Emblem and People holding Hands   203 Charles de Gaulle

1978. International Anti-Apartheid Year.
586 – 25 um. brown, blue and red 90 60
587 **202** 30 um. brown, blue & green 1·10 70
DESIGN—HORIZ: 25 um. Emblem and people behind fence.

1978. Personalities. Multicoloured.
588 12 um. Type **203** 90 30
589 14 um. King Baudouin of Belgium 90 30
590 55 um. Queen Elizabeth II (25th anniv of Coronation) . . . 2·00 90

1978. Air. "Philexafrique" Stamp Exhibition, Libreville (Gabon) (1st issue), and 2nd International Stamp Fair, Essen (West Germany). As T **262** of Niger. Multicoloured.
591 20 um. Water rail and Hamburg 1859 ½ s. stamp . . . . . . 1·00 65
592 20 um. Spotted hyena and Mauritania 1967 100 f. South African crowned crane stamp 1·00 65
See also Nos. 619/20.

1978. Argentina's Victory in World Cup Football Championship. Nos. 562/6 optd **ARGENTINE–PAYS BAS 3-1** in English and Arabic.
593 **196** 12 um. mult (postage) . . 50 25
594 – 14 um. multicoloured . . 55 30
595 – 15 um. multicoloured . . 65 30
596 – 50 um. multicoloured (air) 1·75 1·10
597 – 60 um. multicoloured . . 2·25 1·40

205 View of Nouakchott

1978. 20th Anniv of Nouakchott.
599 **205** 12 um. multicoloured . . 45 30

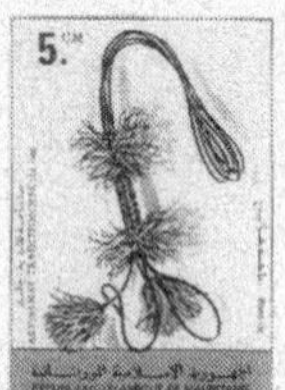

206 Human Rights Emblem   208 Key Chain

207 Wright Flyer I and Clement Ader's Avion III

1978. 30th Anniv of Declaration of Human Rights.
600 **206** 55 um. red and blue . . . 1·60 1·25

1979. Air. 75th Anniv of First Powered Flight.
601 **207** 15 um. grey, red and blue 75 35
602 – 40 um. violet, blue & brn 1·75 1·10
DESIGN: 40 um. Concorde and Wright Flyer I.

1979. Handicrafts. Multicoloured.
603 5 um. Type **208** 25 15
604 7 um. Tooth-brush case . . . 30 20
605 10 um. Knife sheath 45 25

209 "Market Peasant and Wife"   210 Seated Buddha, Temple of Borobudur

1979. 450th Birth Anniv of Albrecht Durer (artist).
606 **209** 12 um. black and red . . 70 30
607 – 14 um. black and red . . 60 25
608 – 55 um. black and red . . 1·60 75
609 – 60 um. black and red . . 1·90 1·00
DESIGNS: 14 um. "Young Peasant and his Wife"; 55 um. "Mercenary with Banner"; 60 um. "St. George and the Dragon".

1979. U.N.E.S.C.O. Campaign for Preservation of Historic Monuments. Multicoloured.
611 12 um. Type **210** 50 30
612 14 um. Carthaginian warrior and hunting dog 60 30
613 55 um. Erechtheum Caryatid, Acropolis. . . . . 1·75 1·25

211 Rowland Hill and Paddle-steamer "Sirius"

1979. Death Centenary of Sir Rowland Hill. Multicoloured.
614 12 um. Type **211** 50 25
615 14 um. Hill and "Great Republic" (paddle-steamer) . 65 25
616 55 um. Hill and "Mauretania I" (liner) . . . . 2·00 60
617 60 um. Hill and "Stirling Castle" (liner) . . . . 2·50 85

212 Satellite over Earth

1979. "Philexafrique" Exhibition, Libreville (2nd issue).
619 – 12 um. multicoloured . . . 60 50
620 **212** 30 um. red, blue and lilac . 1·40 1·25
DESIGN—HORIZ: 12 um. Embossed leather cushion cover.

213 Mother and Children   215 Sprinter on Starting-blocks

1979. International Year of the Child. Multicoloured.
621 12 um. Type **213** 45 25
622 14 um. Mother with sleeping baby 55 35
623 40 um. Children playing with ball 1·50 90

1979. 10th Anniv of "Apollo 11" Moon Landing. Nos. 530/4 optd **ALUNISSAGE APOLLO XI JUILLET 1969**, with Lunar module, or surch also.
624 10 um. Mission Control (horiz) (postage) 40 25
625 12 um. Type **187** 45 30
626 14 um. on 20 u. "Viking" in flight (horiz) (air) 60 25
627 50 um. "Viking" over Mars (horiz) . . . . 1·60 1·00
628 60 um. Parachute descent . . . 1·90 1·10

1979. Pre-Olympic Year. Multicoloured.
630 12 um. Type **215** 35 15
631 14 um. Female runner 40 15
632 55 um. Male runner leaving start 1·50 60
633 60 um. Hurdling . . . . 1·60 60

215a "Scomberesox saurus"

1979. Fishes. Multicoloured.
634a 1 um. Type **215a** 10 10
634b 2 um. Swordfish 10 10
634c 3 um. "Trigla lucerna" . . . 15 15

216 Ice Hockey

1979. Winter Olympic Games, Lake Placid (1980). Ice Hockey. Multicoloured.
635 10 um. Type **216** 40 20
636 12 um. Saving a goal 45 25
637 14 um. Goalkeeper and player 55 25
638 55 um. Two players . . . . . 2·00 60
639 60 um. Goalkeeper . . . . . 2·25 65
640 100 um. Tackle . . . . 3·50 1·25

217 Woman pouring out Tea

1980. Taking Tea.
641 **217** 1 um. multicoloured . . . 10 10
642 5 um. multicoloured . . . 20 10
643 12 um. multicoloured . . 45 20

218 Koran, World Map and Symbols of Arab Achievements

1980. The Arabs.
644 **218** 12 um. multicoloured . . 40 25
645 15 um. multicoloured . . 50 30

1980. Winter Olympics Medal Winners. Nos. 635/40 optd.
646 10 um. **Medaille de bronze SUEDE** 35 20
647 12 um. **MEDAILLE DE BRONZE SUEDE** 40 20
648 14 um. **Medaille d'argent U.R.S.S.** 45 25
649 55 um. **MEDAILLE D'ARGENT U.R.S.S.** . . . . 1·50 80
650 60 um. **MEDAILLE D'OR ETATS-UNIS** . . . . 1·75 90
651 100 um. **Medaille d'or ETATS-UNIS** . . . . 3·00 1·50

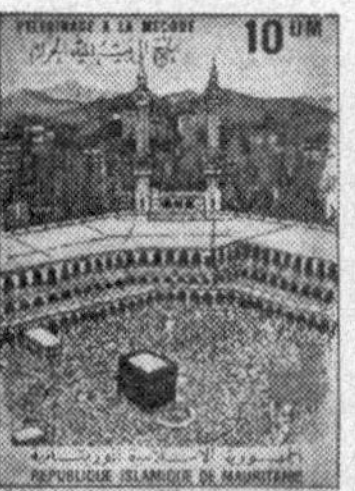

220 Holy Kaaba, Mecca   221 Mother and Child

1980. Pilgrimage to Mecca. Multicoloured.
652 10 um. Type **220** 40 20
653 50 um. Pilgrims outside Mosque 1·60 1·10

1980. World Red Cross Societies Day.
654 **221** 20 um. multicoloured . . 70 40

222 Crowd greeting Armed Forces

1980. Armed Forces Festival.
655 **222** 12 um. multicoloured . . 35 20
656 14 um. multicoloured . . 40 25

223 Horse jumping Bar   224 Trees on Map of Mauritania

1980. Olympic Games, Moscow. Multicoloured.
657 10 um. Type **223** 30 20
658 20 um. Water polo 55 30
659 50 um. Horse jumping brick wall (horiz) . . . . 1·40 55
660 70 um. Horse jumping stone wall 1·90 75

1980. Tree Day.

662	224	12 um. multicoloured . .	35	20

225 "Rembrandt's Mother"

1980. Paintings by Rembrandt. Multicoloured.

663	10 um. "Self-portrait"	30	20
664	20 um. Type **225**	55	30
665	50 um. "Portrait of a Man in Oriental Costume"	1·40	55
666	70 um. "Titus Lisant"	1·90	75

226 Footballers

1980. Air. World Cup Football Championship, Spain (1982). Multicoloured.

668	10 um. Type **226**	30	20
669	12 um. Goalkeeper and players	35	20
670	14 um. Goalkeeper catching ball	40	25
671	20 um. Fighting for possession	55	30
672	67 um. Tackle	1·90	75

1980. Olympic Medal Winners. Nos. 657/60 optd.

674	10 um. **VAINQUEUR KOWALLZYK (POL)** . . .	30	20
675	20 um. **VAINQUEUR THEURER (AUTR)**	55	30
676	50 um. **VAINQUEUR URSS** .	1·40	55
677	70 um. **VAINQUEUR ROMAN (IT)**	1·90	75

228 Giovi "Mastodont"

1980. Locomotives. Multicoloured.

679	10 um. Type **228**	40	15
680	12 um. SNIM-SEM diesel ore train	45	15
681	14 um. Steam locomotive of Chicago, Milwaukee and St. Paul Railway	55	20
682	20 um. Bury steam locomotive 1837	75	25
683	67 um. Steam locomotive of French Reseau du Nord line	2·50	55
684	100 um. Steam locomotive of Berlin–Potsdam line	3·75	95

229 Palm Tree, Crescent and Star, Maize and Map

1980. 20th Anniv of Independence.

685	229	12 um. multicoloured . .	40	20
686		15 um. multicoloured . .	50	30

230 El Haram Mosque

1981. 15th Century of Hegira. Multicoloured.

687	2 um. Type **230**	10	10
688	12 um. Medine Mosque . . .	40	20
689	14 um. Chinguetti Mosque . .	50	30

231 Space Shuttle in Orbit

1981. Air. Space Shuttle. Multicoloured.

690	12 um. Type **231**	40	20
691	20 um. Shuttle and space station	70	30
692	50 um. Shuttle performing experiment	1·60	75
693	70 um. Shuttle landing . . .	2·25	1·00

232 "The Harlequin"

1981. Air. Birth Centenary of Pablo Picasso. Multicoloured.

695	12 um. Type **232**	50	20
696	20 um. "Vase of Flowers" . .	75	30
697	50 um. "Three Women at a Fountain" (horiz)	1·40	75
698	70 um. "Dinard Landscape" (horiz)	2·25	1·00
699	100 um. "Le Dejeuner sur l'Herbe" (horiz)	3·00	1·50

233 I.Y.D.P. Emblem

1981. International Year of Disabled People.

700	233	12 um. violet, gold & blue	45	30

234 Open Landau

1981. British Royal Wedding. Multicoloured.

701	14 um. Type **234**	40	20
702	18 um. Light carriage	45	20
703	77 um. Closed coupe	1·40	1·10

235 George Washington

1981. Bicentenary of Battles of Yorktown and Chesapeake Bay. Multicoloured.

705	14 um. Type **235**	45	25
706	18 um. Admiral de Grasse . .	55	25
707	63 um. Surrender of Cornwallis at Yorktown (horiz) . . .	1·75	95
708	81 um. Battle of Chesapeake Bay (horiz)	2·25	1·50

236 Columbus and "Pinta"

1981. 450th Death Anniv of Christopher Columbus. Multicoloured.

709	19 um. Type **236**	1·00	40
710	55 um. Columbus and "Santa Maria"	2·75	1·10

237 Wheat and F.A.O. Emblem

238 Kemal Ataturk

1981. World Food Day.

711	237	19 um. multicoloured . . .	60	40

1981. Birth Centenary of Kemal Ataturk (Turkish statesman).

712	238	63 um. multicoloured . . .	2·00	1·25

239 Eastern White Pelicans

1981. Birds of the Arguin. Multicoloured.

713	2 um. Type **239**	40	15
714	18 um. Greater flamingoes . .	1·60	70

240 Hand holding Torn Flag

1981. Battle of Karameh Commemoration.

715	240	14 um. multicoloured . . .	45	30

241 "Dermochelys coiacer"

1981. Turtles. Multicoloured.

716	1 um. Type **241**	20	15
717	3 um. "Chelonia mydas" . . .	30	15
718	4 um. "Eretmochelys imbricata"	35	15

242 Sea Scouts

1982. 75th Anniv of Boy Scout Movement. Multicoloured.

719	14 um. Type **242**	55	25
720	19 um. Scouts boarding rowing boat	90	35
721	22 um. Scouts in rowing boat .	1·00	40
722	92 um. Scouts in yacht	3·00	1·25

243 Deusenberg, 1921

1982. 75th Anniv of French Grand Prix Motor Race. Multicoloured.

724	7 um. Type **243**	40	20
725	12 um. Alfa Romeo, 1932 . .	50	20
726	14 um. Juan Fangio	60	35
727	18 um. Renault, 1979	75	40
728	19 um. Niki Lauda	75	45

244 A.P.U. Emblem

245 Hexagonal Pattern

1982. 30th Anniv of Arab Postal Union.

730	244	14 um. orange and brown	45	30

1982. World Telecommunications Day.

731	245	21 um. multicoloured . .	65	45

246 Environmental Emblem on Map

1982. 10th Anniv of U.N. Environmental Programme.

732	246	14 um. blue and light blue	45	30

247 Princess of Wales

1982. 21st Birthday of Princess of Wales. Mult.

733	21 um. Type **247**	75	35
734	77 um. Princess of Wales (different)	2·40	1·10

248 Straw Hut

1982. Traditional Houses. Multicoloured.

736	14 um. Type **248**	45	30
737	18 um. Thatched hut	55	45
738	19 um. Tent	60	45

1982. Birth of Prince William of Wales. Nos. 701/3 surch **NAISSANCE ROYALE 1982**.

739	14 um. Type **234**	45	35
740	18 um. Light carriage	55	40
741	77 um. Closed coupe	2·40	1·25

1982. Air. World Cup Football Championship Results. Nos. 668/72 optd **ITALIE 3 ALLEMAGNE (R.F.A.) 1**.

743	10 um. Type **226**	40	25
744	12 um. Goalkeeper punching ball	40	30
745	14 um. Goalkeeper catching ball	45	30
746	20 um. Three players	70	40
747	67 um. Tackle	2·25	1·40

251 Cattle at Collinaire Dam, Hodh El Gharbi

1992. Agricultural Development.

749	14 um. Type **251**	1·25	1·10
750	18 um. Irrigation canal, Gorgol	1·75	1·25

252 Desert Rose

1982. Desert Rose.
751 **252** 21 um. multicoloured . . 1·50 1·00

253 Montgolfier Balloon, 1783

1983. Bicent of Manned Flight. Multicoloured.
752 14 um. Type **253** 65 20
753 18 um. Charles's hydrogen balloon ascent, 1783 (horiz) 65 30
754 19 um. Goodyear Aerospace airship 65 30
755 55 um. Nieuport 11 "Bebe" biplane (horiz) . . . . . . 1·75 70
756 63 um. Concorde (horiz) . . . 3·00 1·00
757 77 um. "Apollo 11" on Moon 2·50 1·00
No. 754 is wrongly inscribed "Zeppelin".

254 Ouadane

1983. Protection of Ancient Sites. Multicoloured.
758 14 um. Type **254** 40 25
759 18 um. Chinguetti 50 30
760 24 um. Oualata 70 45
761 30 um. Tichitt . . . . 1·00 55

255 Manuscript **256** I.M.O. Emblem

1983. Ancient Manuscripts. Multicoloured.
762 2 um. Type **255** 10 10
763 5 um. Decorated manuscript . 15 15
764 7 um. Shield-shaped patterned manuscript 25 20

1983. 25th Anniv of I.M.O.
765 **256** 18 um. multicoloured . . 50 30

257 W.C.Y. Emblem

1983. World Communications Year.
766 **257** 14 um. multicoloured . . 55 30

258 Customs Emblems

1983. 30th Anniv of Customs Co-operation Council.
767 **258** 14 um. multicoloured . . 45 30

259 Pilatre de Rozier and Montgolfier Balloon **260** Grinding Stone

1983. Bicentenary of Manned Flight. Mult.
768 10 um. Type **259** (postage) . . 40 20
769 14 um. John Wise and balloon "Atlantic" 50 30
770 25 um. Charles Renard and Renard and Krebs' airship "La France" (horiz) 85 35
771 100 um. Henri Juillot and Lebaudy-Juillot airship "Patrie" (air) (horiz) . . . 3·75 1·25

1983. Prehistoric Grindstones. Multicoloured.
773 10 um. Type **260** 50 30
774 14 um. Pestle and mortar . . 75 40
775 18 um. Grinding dish . . . . 1·00 60

261 Basketball

1983. Pre-Olympic Year. Multicoloured.
776 1 um. Type **261** (postage) . . 10 10
777 20 um. Wrestling 60 25
778 50 um. Show-jumping . . . . 1·50 80
779 77 um. Running (air) . . . . 2·25 1·25

262 Lord Baden-Powell (founder of Scout Movement)

1984. Celebrities. Multicoloured.
781 5 um. Type **262** (postage) . . 15 10
782 14 um. Goethe (poet) 45 20
783 25 um. Rubens and detail of painting "The Virgin and Child" 75 45
784 100 um. P. Harris (founder of Rotary International) (air) . 3·00 1·40

263 Tunny

1984. Fishing Resources. Multicoloured.
786 1 um. Type **263** 10 10
787 2 um. Mackerel 10 10
788 5 um. Hake 25 15
789 14 um. Chinchard 70 45
790 18 um. Building a fishing boat 85 55

264 Durer and "Madonna and Child"

1984. Multicoloured.
791 10 um. Type **264** (postage) . . 35 20
792 12 um. "Apollo 11" and astronaut (15th anniv of first manned Moon landing) . . 40 25
793 50 um. Chess pieces and globe 2·00 80
794 77 um. Prince and Princess of Wales (air) . . . . 2·25 1·40

265 Start of Race

1984. Olympic Games, Los Angeles. Multicoloured.
796 14 um. Type **265** 40 25
797 18 um. Throwing the discus (vert) 55 25
798 19 um. Hurdling (vert) 55 25
799 44 um. Throwing the javelin (vert) . . . . 1·25 65
800 77 um. High jumping . . . . 2·00 1·25

266 Feeding Dehydrated Child from Glass **267** Aerial View of Complex

1984. Infant Survival Campaign. Multicoloured.
802 1 um. Type **266** 10 10
803 4 um. Breast-feeding baby . . 15 10
804 10 um. Vaccinating baby . . . 30 20
805 14 um. Weighing baby 45 30

1984. Nouakchott Olympic Complex.
806 **267** 14 um. multicoloured . . . 50 40

268 Tents and Mosque Courtyard

1984. Pilgrimage to Mecca. Multicoloured.
807 14 um. Type **268** 50 30
808 18 um. Tents and courtyard (different) 75 40

269 Emblem

1984. 10th Anniv of West African Economic Community.
809 **269** 14 um. multicoloured . . . 45 30

270 S. van den Berg (windsurfing)

1984. Air. Olympic Games Yachting Gold Medallists. Multicoloured.
810 14 um. Type **270** 55 25
811 18 um. R. Coutts ("Finn" class) 75 25
812 19 um. Spain ("470" class) . . 1·00 25
813 44 um. U.S.A. ("Soling" class) 1·90 60

1984. Drought Relief. No. 537 surch **Aide au Sahel 84.**
815 18 um. on 10 um. multicoloured 70 50

272 Profiles and Emblem

1985. 15th Anniv of Technical and Cultural Co-operation Agency.
816 **272** 18 um. blue, deep blue and red 60 45

273 Animal drinking in Water Droplet and Skeletons **274** Replanting Trees

1985. Campaign against Drought. Multicoloured.
817 14 um. Type **273** . . . . . . 1·10 50
818 18 um. Lush trees by river in water droplet and dead trees 1·10 50

1985. Anti-desertification Campaign. Multicoloured.
819 10 um. Type **274** 35 25
820 14 um. Animals fleeing from forest fire 55 30
821 18 um. Planting grass to hold sand dunes 65 50

275 Emblem

1985. 30th Anniv (1984) of Arab League.
822 **275** 14 um. green and black . 45 30

276 Map, I.Y.Y. Emblem and Youths

1985. Air. "Philexafrique" Stamp Exhibition, Lome. Multicoloured.
823 40 um. Type **276** (International Youth Year) . . . . 1·50 1·25
824 40 um. Nouadhibou oil refinery 1·50 1·25

277 Bonaparte's Gulls

1985. Air. Birth Bicentenary of John J. Audubon (ornithologist). Multicoloured.
825 14 um. Wester tanager and scarlet tanager . . . . . . 1·10 45
826 18 um. Type **277** . . . . . . 1·40 50
827 19 um. Blue jays . . . . . . 1·50 75
828 44 um. Black skimmer . . . . 4·25 2·50

278 "Der Adler", 1835

1985. Anniversaries. Multicoloured.
830 12 um. Type **278** (German railways. 150th anniv) . . . 60 25
831 18 um. Class 10 locomotive, 1956 (German railways. 150th anniv) 90 25
832 44 um. Johann Sebastian Bach (composer, 300th birth anniv European Music Year) . . 1·60 70

833 77 um. Georg Frederick Handel (composer, 300th birth anniv European Music Year) . . . 2·75 1·25
834 90 um. Statue of Liberty (centenary) (vert) . . . . . 2·75 1·40

279 Globe and Emblem

1985. World Food Day.
836 **279** 18 um. multicoloured . . 55 35

280 Tending Sheep and reading Book

1985. Air. "Philexafrique" Stamp Exhibition, Lome, Togo (2nd issue). Multicoloured.
837 50 um. Type **280** . . . . . . 2·00 1·50
838 50 um. Dock, iron ore mine and train . . . . 2·00 1·50

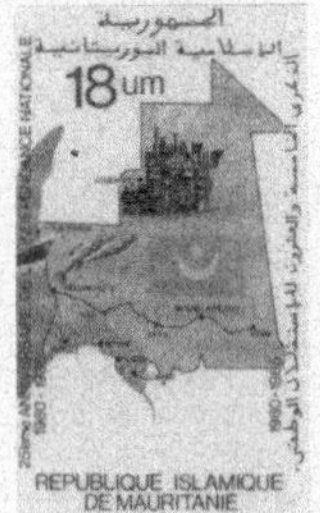

281 Map showing Industries

1985. 25th Anniv of Independence.
839 **281** 18 um. multicoloured . . 60 40

282 Development

1986. International Youth Year. Multicoloured.
840 18 um. Type **282** 60 30
841 22 um. Re-afforestation (voluntary work) 70 40
842 25 um. Hands reaching from globe to dove (peace) (vert) . 75 50

283 Latecoere Seaplane "Comte de la Vaulx" and Map

1986. Air. 55th Anniv (1985) of First Commercial South Atlantic Flight. Multicoloured.
843 18 um. Type **283** 60 35
844 50 um. Piper Twin Commanche airplanes crossing between maps of Africa and South America . . . . 1·75 1·25

284 Toujounine Earth Receiving Station

1986.
845 **284** 25 um. multicoloured . . 90 50

285 Heads of Mother and Pup

1986. World Wildlife Fund. Mediterranean Monk Seal. Multicoloured.
846 2 um. Type **285** 20 15
847 5 um. Mother and pup on land 25 15
848 10 um. Mother and pup swimming 40 15
849 18 um. Seal family 80 25

286 Player and 1970 25 f. Stamp

1986. Air. World Cup Football Championship, Mexico. Multicoloured.
851 8 um. Type **286** 25 10
852 18 um. Player and 1970 30 f. stamp 60 20
853 22 um. Player and 1970 70 f. stamp 70 30
854 25 um. Player and 1970 150 f. stamp 85 35
855 40 um. Player and World Cup trophy on "stamp" . . . . 1·25 60

287 Weaving

1986.
857 **287** 18 um. multicoloured . . 60 35

288 Emblem, Boeing 737, Douglas DC-10 and Map

1986. Air. 25th Anniv of Air Afrique.
858 **288** 26 um. multicoloured . . 1·00 40

289 Indian, "Santa Maria" and Route Map

1987. 500th Anniv (1992) of Discovery of America by Christopher Columbus. Multicoloured.
859 2 um. Type **289** (postage) . . 10 10
860 22 um. Indian, "Nina" and map 65 30
861 35 um. Indian, "Pinta" and map 1·10 50
862 150 um. Indian, map and Christopher Columbus (air) 4·50 1·60

290 J. H. Dort, Comet Picture and Space Probe "Giotto"

1986. Appearance of Halley's Comet. Multicoloured.
864 5 um. Type **290** (postage) . . . 15 10
865 18 um. William Huggins (astronomer) and "Ariane" space rocket 60 20
866 26 um. E. J. Opik and space probes "Giotto" and "Vega" 80 30
867 80 um. F. L. Whipple and "Planet A" space probe (air) 2·75 1·25

291 Astronauts

1986. "Challenger" Astronauts Commemoration. Multicoloured.
869 7 um. Type **291** (postage) . . . 20 10
870 22 um. Judith Resnik and astronaut 60 30
871 32 um. Ellison Onizuka and Ronald McNair . . . . . . 1·00 45
872 43 um. Christa Corrigan McAuliffe (air) . . . . . . 1·50 60

292 Sea Bream

1986. Fishes and Birds. Multicoloured.
874 4 um. Type **292** 20 15
875 22 um. White spoonbills . . . 2·25 80
876 32 um. Bridled terns . . . . . 2·50 1·10
877 98 um. Sea trout . . . . 3·25 2·25
See also Nos. 896/900.

293 Arrow through Victim 294 Fisherman

1986. 4th Anniv of Massacre of Palestinian Refugees in Sabra and Shatila Camps, Lebanon.
878 **293** 22 um. black, gold & red . 80 40

1986. World Food Day.
879 **294** 22 um. multicoloured . . . 80 40

295 Dome of the Rock

1987. "Arab Jerusalem".
880 **295** 22 um. multicoloured . . . 80 40

REPUBLIQUE ISLAMIQUE DE MAURITANIE

296 Boxing

1987. Air. Olympic Games, Seoul (1988) (1st issue). Multicoloured.
881 30 um. Type **296** 80 40
882 40 um. Judo . . . . 1·00 55
883 50 um. Fencing . . . . 1·25 70
884 75 um. Wrestling . . . . . . 2·00 1·10
See also Nos. 902/5.

297 Cordoue Mosque

1987. 1200th Anniv of Cordoue Mosque.
886 **297** 30 um. multicoloured . . 1·00 50

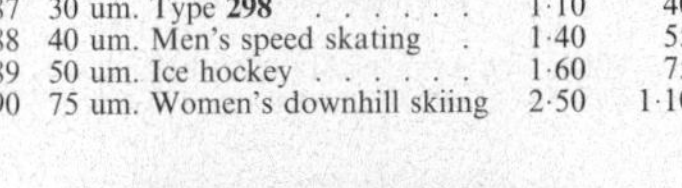

298 Women's Slalom

1987. Air. Winter Olympic Games, Calgary (1988). Multicoloured.
887 30 um. Type **298** . . . . . . 1·10 40
888 40 um. Men's speed skating . 1·40 55
889 50 um. Ice hockey . . . . . . 1·60 75
890 75 um. Women's downhill skiing 2·50 1·10

299 Adults at Desk

1987. Literacy Campaign. Multicoloured.
892 18 um. Type **299** 60 40
893 20 um. Adults and children reading 80 50

300 People queueing for Treatment

1987. World Health Day.
894 **300** 18 um. multicoloured . . 70 40

301 Map within Circle

1988. National Population and Housing Census.
895 **301** 20 um. multicoloured . . 60 35

1988. Fishes and Birds. Horiz designs as T **292**. Multicoloured.
896 1 um. White wrasse 10 10
897 7 um. Trigger fish 30 15
898 15 um. Striped bonitos . . . 50 30
899 18 um. Common cormorants . 70 40
900 80 um. Royal terns . . . . . 3·00 2·00

302 People with Candles 303 Hammer Throwing

1988. 40th Anniv of W.H.O.
901 **302** 30 um. multicoloured . . 1·00 40

1988. Air. Olympic Games, Seoul (2nd issue). Multicoloured.

902 20 um. Type **303** 50 25
903 24 um. Discus 60 30
904 30 um. Putting the shot . . . 80 40
905 150 um. Javelin throwing . . . 4·00 2·10

1988. Winter Olympic Games Gold Medal Winners. Nos. 887/90 optd.

907 30 um. Optd **Medaille d'or/Vreni Schneider (Suisse)** . . . . . 1·00 50
908 40 um. Optd **Medaille d'or/1500 m./Andre Hoffman (R.D.A.)** 1·10 75
909 50 um. Optd **Medaille d'or/ U.R.S.S.** . . . . 1·50 1·00
910 75 um. Optd **Medaille d'or/ Marina Kiehl (R.F.A.)** . . . 2·25 1·50

305 Flags and Globe

1988. 75th Anniv of Arab Scout Movement.

912 **305** 35 um. multicoloured . . 1·25 55

306 Men at Ballot Box

1988. 1st Municipal Elections. Multicoloured.

913 20 um. Type **306** 60 30
914 24 um. Woman at ballot box . 80 40

307 Emblem **308** Ploughing with Oxen

1988. 25th Anniv of Organization of African Unity.

915 **307** 40 um. multicoloured . . 1·25 60

1988. 10th Anniv of International Agricultural Development Fund.

916 **308** 35 um. multicoloured . . 1·10 70

309 Port Activities

1989. 1st Anniv of Nouakchott Free Port.

917 **309** 24 um. multicoloured . . 1·25 65

310 "Heliothis armigera"

311 "Nomadacris septemfasciata"

1989. Plant Pests. Multicoloured.

918 2 um. Type **310** 15 15
919 6 um. "Aphis gossypii" . . . 20 15
920 10 um. "Agrotis ypsilon" . . 35 15
921 20 um. "Chilo sp." 75 30
922 24 um. "Plitella xylostella" . . 85 40
923 30 um. "Henosepilachna elaterii" 1·25 55
924 42 um. "Trichoplusia ni" . . . 1·50 70

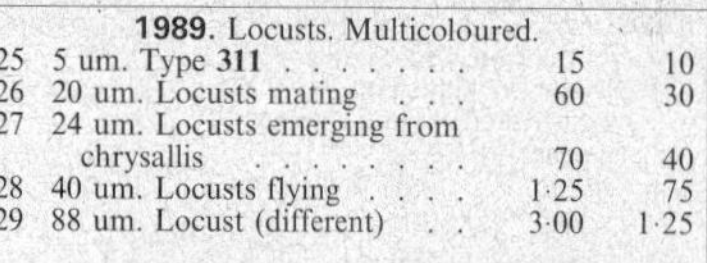

1989. Locusts. Multicoloured.

925 5 um. Type **311** 15 10
926 20 um. Locusts mating . . . 60 30
927 24 um. Locusts emerging from chrysallis 70 40
928 40 um. Locusts flying . . . . 1·25 75
929 88 um. Locust (different) . . 3·00 1·25

312 Men of Different Races embracing

313 Footballers

1989. "Philexfrance '89" Int Stamp Exn, Paris, and Bicent of French Revolution.

930 **312** 35 um. multicoloured . . 1·10 60

1989. World Cup Football Championship, Italy (1990) (1st issue).

931 **313** 20 um. multicoloured . . 70 40
See also Nos. 937/41.

314 Attan'eem Migat, Mecca

1989. Pilgrimage to Mecca.

932 **314** 20 um. multicoloured . . 75 30

315 Emblem

317 Youths

316 Carpet

1989. 25th Anniv of African Development Bank.

933 **315** 37 um. black and mauve . 1·00 50

1989.

934 **316** 50 um. multicoloured . . 1·50 80

1989. 2nd Anniv of Palestinian "Intifida" Movement.

935 **317** 35 um. multicoloured . . 1·25 50

318 Member Countries' Leaders (½-size illustration)

1990. 1st Anniv of Arab Maghreb Union.

936 **318** 50 um. multicoloured . . 1·50 70

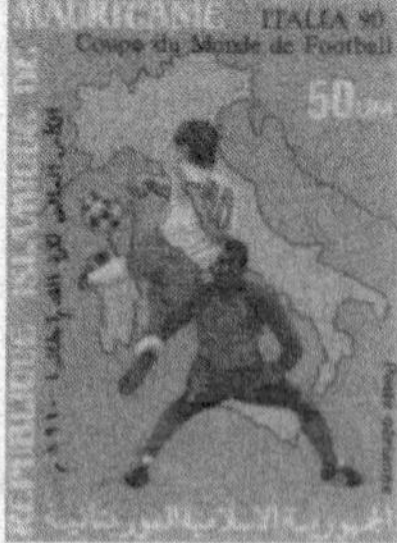

319 Players

320 Envelopes on Map

1990. Air. World Cup Football Championship, Italy (2nd issue).

937 **319** 50 um. multicoloured . . 1·50 50
938 – 60 um. multicoloured . . . 1·90 60
939 – 70 um. multicoloured . . . 2·00 75
940 – 90 um. multicoloured . . . 2·75 75
941 – 150 um. multicoloured . . 4·50 1·25
DESIGNS: 60 to 150 um. Show footballers.

1990. 20th Anniv of Multinational Postal Training School, Abidjan.

942 **320** 50 um. multicoloured . . . 1·10 50

321 Books and Desk

1990. International Literacy Year.

943 **321** 60 um. multicoloured . . . 1·75 1·00

322 Maps and Earth-moving Vehicles

1990. Mineral Resources.

944 **322** 60 um. multicoloured . . . 2·25 1·25

323 Dressage

324 Emblem

1990. Olympic Games, Barcelona (1992). Mult.

945 5 um. Type **323** (postage) . . . 20 15
946 50 um. Archery . . . . 1·40 40
947 60 um. Throwing the hammer . 1·50 50
948 75 um. Football . . . . 2·00 50
949 90 um. Basketball . . . . . . 2·75 65
950 220 um. Table tennis (air) . . . 6·00 1·40

1990. 2nd Anniv of Declaration of State of Palestine.

952 **324** 85 um. multicoloured . . . 1·75 1·10

325 Camp

1990. Integration of Repatriates from Senegal. Multicoloured.

953 50 um. Type **325** 90 60
954 75 um. Women's sewing group 1·25 1·00
955 85 um. Water collection . . . 1·40 1·00

326 Map, Dove and Mandela

1990. Release from South African Prison of Nelson Mandela.

956 **326** 85 um. multicoloured . . 1·60 1·10

327 Downhill skiing

1990. Winter Olympic Games, Albertville (1992). Multicoloured.

957 60 um. Type **327** (postage) . . 1·00 60
958 75 um. Cross-country skiing . 1·50 75
959 90 um. Ice hockey . . . . . . 1·75 95
960 220 um. Figure skating (pairs) (air) . . . . 3·75 2·25

328 Blue Leg

1991. Scouts, Fungi and Butterflies. Multicoloured.

962 5 um. Type **328** (postage) . . 30 20
963 50 um. "Agaricus bitorquis edulis" . . . . 2·25 80
964 60 um. "Bunea alcinoe" (butterfly) . . . . 2·00 75
965 90 um. "Salamis cytora" (butterfly) . . . . 2·50 1·10
966 220 um. "Bronze boletus" . . 6·00 3·00
967 75 um. "Cyrestis camillus" (butterfly) (air) . . . . . 2·00 85

329 Dish Aerials and Transmitting Tower **330** Woman carrying Bucket of Water

1991. 30th Anniv of Independence. Multicoloured.

968 50 um. Type **329** . . . . . 1·00 65
969 60 um. Container ship in dock 2·00 85
970 100 um. Workers in field . . 1·75 1·00

1991. World Meteorological Day.

972 **330** 100 um. multicoloured . . 1·75 1·10

331 Health Centre

1991. 20th Anniv of Medecins sans Frontieres (international medical relief organization).

973 **331** 60 um. multicoloured . . 70 45

332 Cats

1991. Domestic Animals. Multicoloured.

974 50 um. Type **332** 55 35
975 60 um. Basenji dog 70 45

333 Globe and Stylized Figures

1991. World Population Day.

976 **333** 90 um. multicoloured . . 1·00 60

334 Blind Woman with Sight restored

1991. Anti-blindness Campaign.

977 **334** 50 um. multicoloured . . 55 35

335 Nouakchott Electricity Station

1991. 2nd Anniv of Nouakchott Electricity Station.

978 **335** 50 um. multicoloured . . 55 35

336 Quarrying

1993. Mineral Exploitation, Haoudat. Multicoloured.

979 50 um. Type **336** 55 35
980 60 um. Dry land 65 40

337 Camel Train **338** Palestinians

1993.

981 **337** 50 um. multicoloured . . 55 35
982 60 um. multicoloured . . 65 40

1993. Palestinian "Intifida" Movement. Multicoloured.

983 50 um. Type **338** 55 35
984 60 um. Palestinian children by fire (horiz) 65 40

339 Four-man Bobsleighing **340** Soldier Field, Chicago

1993. Winter Olympic Games, Lillehammer. Multicoloured.

985 10 um. Type **339** 10 10
986 50 um. Luge 55 35
987 60 um. Figure skating 65 40
988 80 um. Skiing 85 55
989 220 um. Cross-country skiing . . 2·40 1·50

1994. World Cup Football Championship, U.S.A. Players and Stadiums. Multicoloured.

991 10 um. Type **340** 10 10
992 50 um. Foxboro Stadium, Boston 50 30
993 60 um. Robert F. Kennedy Stadium, Washington D.C. . 65 40
994 90 um. Stanford Stadium, San Francisco 95 60
995 220 um. Giant Stadium, New York . . . . 2·25 1·40

341 Anniversary Emblem and 1962 15 f. Stamp

1995. 50th Anniv of U.N.O.

997 **341** 60 um. multicoloured . . 60 40

342 Stabilising Desert

1995. 50th Anniv of F.A.O. Multicoloured.

998 50 um. Type **342** 50 30
999 60 um. Fishermen launching boat 60 40
1000 90 um. Planting crops . . . 85 55

OFFICIAL STAMPS

O **41** Cross of Trarza

O **179**

1961.

O150 O **41** 1 f. purple and blue . . 10 10
O151 3 f. myrtle and red . . 10 10
O152 5 f. brown and green 10 10
O153 10 f. blue and turquoise 20 10
O154 15 f. orange and blue 30 15
O155 20 f. green and myrtle 35 20
O156 25 f. red and orange . 40 30
O157 30 f. green and purple 45 30
O158 50 f. sepia and red . . 1·00 45
O159 100 f. blue and orange 1·60 75
O160 200 f. red and green . 3·00 1·60

1976.

O502 O **179** 1 u. multicoloured . 10 10
O503 2 u. multicoloured . 15 10
O504 5 u. multicoloured . 20 15
O505 10 u. multicoloured 40 20
O506 12 u. multicoloured 55 30
O507 40 u. multicoloured 1·75 1·00
O508 50 u. multicoloured 2·25 1·25

POSTAGE DUE STAMPS

1906. Stamps of 1906 optd **T** in a triangle.

D18 I 5 c. green and red . . . . — 27·00
D19 10 c. pink and blue . . . — 27·00
D20 J 20 c. black & red on blue — 40·00
D21 25 c. blue and red . . . . — 40·00
D22 30 c. brown & red on pink — £110
D23 50 c. violet and red . . . — £110
D24 K 1 f. black & red on blue . — £160

1906. "Natives" key-type inscr "MAURITANIE" in blue (10, 30 c.) or red (others).

D25 L 5 c. green . . . . 1·25 1·25
D26 10 c. purple . . . . . . 1·75 1·75
D27 15 c. blue on blue . . . . 4·00 3·25
D28 20 c. black on yellow . . 6·00 6·00
D29 30 c. red on cream . . . 6·00 6·75
D30 50 c. violet . . . . . . 9·25 9·25
D31 60 c. black on buff . . 6·50 6·75
D32 1 f. black on pink . . . . 11·50 9·25

1914. "Figure" key-type inscr "MAURITANIE".

D35 M 5 c. green 10 25
D36 10 c. red 15 25
D37 15 c. grey 15 30
D38 20 brown 15 30
D39 30 c. blue 25 40
D40 50 c. black 50 95
D41 60 c. orange 40 50
D42 1 f. violet 60 80

1927. Surch in figures.

D67 M 2 f. on 1 f. purple . . . 1·25 1·75
D68 3 f. on 1 f. brown . . . 1·25 2·00

D **40** Qualata Motif D **55** Ruppell's Griffon

1961.

D150 D **40** 1 f. yellow and purple 10 10
D151 2 f. grey and red . . 10 10
D152 5 f. pink and red . . 20 15
D153 10 f. green and myrtle 25 15
D154 15 f. brown and drab 30 15
D155 20 f. blue and red . . 35 20
D156 25 f. red and green . 55 35

1963. Birds. Multicoloured.

D177 50 c. Type D **55** 60 20
D178 50 c. Common crane 60 20
D179 1 f. Eastern white pelican . . 70 25
D180 1 f. Garganey 70 25
D181 2 f. Golden oriole 85 30
D182 2 f. Variable sunbird 85 30
D183 5 f. Great snipe 95 60
D184 5 f. Common shoveler . . . 95 60
D185 10 f. Vulturine guineafowl . 1·75 1·10
D186 10 f. Black stork . . . . . . 1·75 1·10
D187 15 f. Grey heron . . . . . . 2·00 1·50
D188 15 f. White stork . . . . . . 2·00 1·50
D189 20 f. Paradise whydah . . . 2·40 1·75
D190 20 f. Red-legged partridge . 2·40 1·75
D191 25 f. Little stint . . . . . . 3·00 2·10
D192 25 f. Arabian bustard . . . 3·00 2·10

D **180**

1976.

D509 D **180** 1 u. multicoloured . . 10 10
D510 3 u. multicoloured . . 15 15
D511 10 u. multicoloured 35 35
D512 12 u. multicoloured 40 40
D513 20 u. multicoloured 70 70

APPENDIX

The following stamps have either been issued in excess of postal needs or have not been available to the public in a reasonable quantities at face value. Such stamps may later be given full listing if there is evidence of regular postal use.

1962.

World Refugee Year (1960). Optd on 1960–61 Definitive issue, 30, 50, 60 f.

Olympic Games in Rome (1960) and Tokyo (1964). Surch on 1960–61 Definitive issue 75 f. on 15 f., 75 f. on 20 f.

European Steel and Coal Community and Exploration of Iron-ore in Mauritania. Optd on 1960–61 Definitive issue. Air 500 f.

Malaria Eradication. Optd on 1960–61 Definitive issue. Air. 100, 200 f.

MAYOTTE Pt. 6

One of the Comoro Islands adjacent to Madagascar.

In 1974 (when the other islands became an independent state) Mayotte was made an Overseas Department of France, using French stamps from 1997 it again had its own issues.

100 centimes = 1 franc

1892. "Tablet" key-type inscr "MAYOTTE".

1	D	1 c. black and red on blue	40	40
2		2 c. brown & blue on buff	50	50
3		4 c. brown & blue on grey	70	60
4		5 c. green & red on green	1·50	1·00
5		10 c. black & blue on lilac	2·00	2·00
15		10 c. red and blue	26·00	20·00
6		15 c. blue and red	6·00	4·00
16		15 c. grey and red	60·00	45·00
7		20 c. red & blue on green	5·25	4·50
8		25 c. black & red on pink	3·75	2·50
17		25 c. blue and red	4·00	3·50
9		30 c. brown & bl on drab	8·25	5·75
18		35 c. black & red on yellow	2·50	2·50
10		40 c. red & blue on yellow	6·75	5·75
19		45 c. black on green	7·50	6·00
11		50 c. red and blue on pink	12·50	8·00
20		50 c. brown & red on blue	6·25	8·25
12		75 c. brown & red on orge	14·00	9·00
13		1 f. green and red	10·50	8·00
14		5 f. mauve & blue on lilac	70·00	60·00

1912. Surch in figures.

21	D	05 on 20 c. brown and blue on buff	90	90
22		05 on 4 c. brown and blue on grey	35	30
23		05 on 15 c. blue and red	50	50
24		05 on 20 c. red and blue on green	50	60
25		05 on 25 c. black and red on pink	50	60
26		05 on 30 c. brown and blue on drab	60	65
27		10 on 40 c. red and blue on yellow	50	70
28		10 on 45 c. black and red on green	55	55
29		10 on 50 c. red and blue on pink	1·50	1·75
30		10 on 75 c. brown and red on orange	85	1·00
31		10 on 1 f. green and red	1·00	1·10

MECKLENBURG-SCHWERIN Pt. 7

In northern Germany. Formerly a Grand Duchy, Mecklenburg-Schwerin joined the North German Confederation in 1868.

48 schilling = 1 thaler

1

2

1856. Imperf.

1a	1	¼ s. red	10·00	10·00
1		¼ s. red	£130	£110
3	2	3 s. yellow	75·00	50·00
4		5 s. blue	£200	£275

See note below No. 7.

1864. Roul.

5a	1	¼ s. red	£120	£140
6a		¼ s. red	6·00	6·00
5		¼ s. red	£2250	£1800
6		¼ s. red	48·00	48·00
11	2	2 s. purple	£200	£225
9		3 s. yellow	£150	95·00
7		5 s. bistre	£130	£225

Nos. 1, 1a, 5, 5a have a dotted background, Nos 6 and 6a a plain background. Prices for Nos. 1a, 5a and 6a are for quarter stamps; prices for Nos. 1, 5 and 6 are for the complete stamp (four quarters) as illustrated in Type **1**.

MECKLENBURG-STRELITZ Pt. 7

In northern Germany. Formerly a Grand Duchy, Mecklenburg-Strelitz joined the North German Confederation in 1868.

30 silbergroschen = 1 thaler

1

2

1864. Roul. Various frames.

2	1	¼ sgr. orange	£150	£2250
3		⅓ sgr. green	50·00	£1200
6		1 sch. mauve	£275	£3500
7	2	1 sgr. red	£130	£190
9		2 sgr. blue	28·00	£750
11		3 sgr. bistre	28·00	£1200

MEMEL Pt. 7

A seaport and district on the Baltic Sea, formerly part of Germany. Under Allied control after the 1914–18 war, it was captured and absorbed by Lithuania in 1923 and returned to Germany in 1939. From 1945 the area has been part of Lithuania.

1920. 100 pfennig = 1 mark.
16.4.23. 100 centu = 1 litas.

1920. Stamps of France surch **MEMEL** and **pfennig** or **mark** with figure of value.

1	18	5 pf. on 5 c. green	10	30
2		10 pf. on 10 c. red	10	20
3		20 pf. on 25 c. blue	10	20
4		30 pf. on 30 c. orange	10	20
5		40 pf. on 20 c. brown	10	20
6		50 pf. on 35 c. violet	10	35
7	13	60 pf. on 40 c. red & blue	20	55
8		80 pf. on 45 c. green & blue	15	35
9		1 m. on 50 c. brown & lilac	10	20
10		1 m. 25 on 60 c. violet & bl	70	1·75
11		2 m. on 1 f. red and green	15	25
12		3 m. on 2 f. orange & green	10·00	22·00
13		3 m. on 5 f. blue and buff	11·00	22·00
14		4 m. on 2 f. orange & green	15	35
15		10 m. on 5 f. blue & buff	1·50	5·00
16		20 m. on 5 f. blue & buff	30·00	65·00

1920. Stamps of Germany inscr "DEUTSCHES REICH" optd **Memel- gebiet** or **Memelgebiet**.

17	10	5 pf. green	25	40
18		10 pf. red	2·40	7·00
19		10 pf. orange	15	35
20	24	15 pf. brown	2·25	6·50
21	10	20 pf. blue	15	15
22		30 pf. black & orge on buff	1·25	2·00
23		30 pf. blue	15	35
24		40 pf. black and red	10	15
25		50 pf. black & pur on buff	10	15
26		60 pf. green	45	2·25
27		75 pf. black and green	2·00	5·00
28		80 pf. blue	90	2·75
29	12	1 m. red	20	45
30		1 m. 25 green	11·00	26·00
31		2 m. 50 brown	3·50	7·00
32	13	2 m. blue	1·50	3·25
33		2 m. 50 purple	9·50	22·00

1921. Nos. 2/3, 5/6, 9, 11 and 41 further surch in large figures.

34	18	15 on 10 pf. on 10 c. red	20	35
35		15 on 20 pf. on 25 c. blue	20	55
36		15 on 50 pf. on 35 c. violet	15	45
37		60 on 40 pf. on 20 c. brown	15	15
38	13	75 on 60 pf. on 40 c. red and blue (41)	40	1·00
39		1,25 on 1 m. on 50 c. brown and lilac	15	40
40		5,00 on 2 m. on 1 f. red and green	45	1·25

1921. Surch **MEMEL** and **Pfennig** or **Mark** with figure of value.

54	18	5 pf. on 5 c. orange	10	20
55		10 pf. on 10 c. red	40	1·10
56		10 pf. on 10 c. green	10	20
57		15 pf. on 10 c. green	10	30
58		20 pf. on 20 c. brown	2·75	8·50
59		20 pf. on 25 c. blue	2·75	8·50
60		25 pf. on 5 c. orange	10	15
61		30 pf. on 30 c. red	40	1·75
86		35 pf. on 35 c. violet	10	20
64	13	40 pf. on 40 c. red and blue	10	15
62	15	50 pf. on 50 c. blue	10	15
41	13	60 pf. on 40 c. red and blue	3·00	7·00
87	15	75 pf. on 15 c. green	10	15
63	18	75 pf. on 35 c. violet	10	15
65	13	80 pf. on 45 c. green & blue	10	15
88	18	1 m. on 25 c. blue	10	10
66	13	1 m. on 40 c. red and blue	10	15
89	18	1¼ m. on 30 c. red	10	20
67	13	1 m. 25 on 60 c. violet & bl	10	20
68		1 m. 50 on 45 c. green & bl	10	25
90		2 m. on 45 c. green & blue	10	15
69		2 m. on 1 f. red and green	10	20
91		2¼ m. on 40 c. red and blue	10	20
92		2½ m. on 60 c. violet & blue	20	45
113	18	3 m. on 5 c. orange	10	1·10
70	13	3 m. on 60 c. violet & blue	45	85
93		4 m. on 45 c. green & blue	10	15
71		5 m. on 1 f. red and green	15	45
114	15	6 m. on 15 c. green	15	80
94	13	6 m. on 60 c. violet & blue	10	15
72		6 m. on 2 f. orange & green	15	45
115	18	8 m. on 30 c. red	35	2·25
95	13	9 m. on 1 f. red and green	15	30
73		9 m. on 5 f. blue and buff	20	60
116		10 m. on 45 c. green & blue	35	1·00
43		10 m. on 5 f. blue and buff	65	1·50
96		12 m. on 40 c. red and blue	15	30
117		20 m. on 40 c. red and blue	35	1·60
44		20 m. on 45 c. green & blue	3·75	10·00
97		20 m. on 2 f. orange & grn	15	40
118		30 m. on 60 c. violet & blue	35	1·50
98		30 m. on 5 f. blue and buff	2·25	6·50
119		40 m. on 1 f. red and green	35	1·75
99		50 m. on 2 f. orange & grn	7·00	18·00
120		80 m. on 2 f. orange & grn	35	1·75
121		100 m. on 5 f. blue & buff	45	3·00

1921. Air. Nos. 7/9, 11, 14, 41 and 70 optd **FLUGPOST** in double-lined letters.

47	13	60 pf. on 40 c. red and blue	25·00	70·00
48		60 pf. on 40 c. red and blue (No. 41)	2·00	7·00
49		80 pf. on 45 c. green & blue	2·00	6·00
50		1 m. on 50 c. brown & lilac	1·40	4·50
51		2 m. on 1 f. red and green	2·00	4·50
52		3 m. on 60 c. violet and blue (No. 70)	2·00	6·50
53		4 m. on 2 f. orange & green	2·25	10·00

1922. Air. Optd **Flugpost** in script letters.

74	13	40 pf. on 40 c. red and blue (No. 64)	25	1·00
75		80 pf. on 45 c. green and blue (No. 65)	25	1·00
76		1 m. on 40 c. red and blue (No. 66)	25	1·00
77		1 m. 25 on 60 c. violet and blue (No. 67)	40	1·75
78		1 m. 50 on 45 c. green and blue (No. 68)	40	1·75
79		2 m. on 1 f. red and green (No. 69)	40	1·75
80		3 m. on 60 c. violet and blue (No. 70)	40	1·75
82		4 m. on 2 f. orange and green (No. 14)	40	1·75
83		5 m. on 1 f. red and green (No. 71)	45	2·00
84		6 m. on 2 f. orange and green (No. 72)	45	2·00
85		9 m. on 5 f. blue and buff (No. 73)	55	2·00

1922. Air. Surch as in 1921 and optd **FLUGPOST** in ordinary capitals.

100	13	40 pf. on 40 c. red and blue	1·00	6·00
101		1 m. on 40 c. red & blue	1·00	6·00
102		1 m. 25 on 60 c. violet and blue	1·00	6·00
103		1 m. 50 on 45 c. green and blue	1·00	6·00
104		2 m. on 1 f. red & green	1·00	6·00
105		3 m. on 60 c. violet & blue	1·00	6·00
106		4 m. on 2 f. orange & green	1·00	6·00
107		5 m. on 1 f. red & green	1·00	6·00
108		6 m. on 2 f. orange & green	1·00	6·00
109		9 m. on 5 f. blue & buff	1·00	6·00

1922. Surch as in 1921 but with additional surch **Mark** obliterating **Pfennig**.

110	18	10 m. on 10 pf. on 10 c. green (No. 56)	50	2·50
111		20 m. on 20 pf. on 20 c. brown (No. 58)	40	85
112	15	50 m. on 50 pf. on 50 c. blue (No. 62)	1·25	5·50

1923. Nos. 64 and 67 with additional surch.

122	13	"Mark" on 40 pf. on 40 c. red and blue	50	1·50
123		"80—" on 1 m. 25 on 60 c. violet and blue	50	2·00

1923. Nos. 90 and 88 surch with large figures.

124	13	"10" on 2 m. on 45 c. green and blue	1·00	3·50
125	18	"25" on 1 m. on 25 c. blue	1·00	3·50

LITHUANIAN OCCUPATION

The port and district of Memel was captured by Lithuanian forces in 1923 and incorporated in Lithuania.

1

5

1923. (a) Surch **KLAIPEDA (MEMEL)** and value over curved line and **MARKIU**.

1	1	10 m. on 5 c. blue	35	75
2		25 m. on 5 c. blue	35	75
3		50 m. on 25 c. red	35	75
4		100 m. on 25 c. red	50	1·40
5		400 m. on 1 l. brown	1·25	2·50

(b) **Klaipeda (Memel)** and value over two straight lines and **Markiu**.

6	1	10 m. on 5 c. blue	65	1·75
7		25 m. on 5 c. blue	65	1·75
8		50 m. on 25 c. red	65	1·75
9		100 m. on 25 c. red	65	1·75
10		400 m. on 1 l. brown	70	2·25
11		500 m. on 1 l. brown	70	2·25

(c) **KLAIPEDA (Memel)** and value over four stars and **MARKIU**.

12	1	10 m. on 5 c. blue	55	1·75
13		20 m. on 5 c. blue	55	1·75
14		25 m. on 25 c. red	55	1·75
15		50 m. on 25 c. red	65	2·25
16		100 m. on 1 l. brown	80	2·75
17		200 m. on 1 l. brown	80	2·75

1923.

18	5	10 m. brown	20	45
19		20 m. yellow	20	45
20		25 m. orange	20	45
21		40 m. violet	20	45
22		50 m. green	75	85
23		100 m. red	40	40
24		300 m. green	2·50	45·00
25		400 m. brown	45	65
26		500 m. purple	2·50	45·00
27		1,000 m. blue	65	80

7 Liner, Memel Port

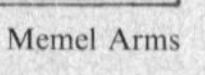

8 Memel Arms

9 Memel Lighthouse

1923. Uniting of Memel with Lithuania and Amalgamation of Memel Harbours.

28	7	40 m. green	2·50	12·00
29		50 m. brown	2·50	12·00
30		80 m. green	2·50	12·00
31		100 m. red	2·50	12·00
32	8	200 m. blue	2·50	12·00
33		300 m. brown	2·50	12·00
34		400 m. purple	2·50	12·00
35		500 m. orange	2·50	12·00
36		600 m. green	2·50	12·00
37	9	800 m. blue	2·50	12·00
38		1000 m. purple	2·50	12·00
39		2000 m. red	2·50	12·00
40		3000 m. green	2·50	12·00

1923. No. 123 of Memel surch **Klaipeda**, value and large **M** between bars, sideways.

41		100 m. on 80 on 1 m. 25 on 60 c.	4·00	12·00
42		400 m. on 80 on 1 m. 25 on 60 c.	4·00	12·00
43		500 m. on 80 on 1 m. 25 on 60 c.	4·00	12·00

1923. Surch (thin or thick figures) in **CENT.** or **LITAS**.

60	5	2 c. on 10 m. brown	1·25	5·50
44		2 c. on 20 m. yellow	2·25	3·25
45		2 c. on 50 m. green	2·25	3·25
63		3 c. on 10 m. brown	2·00	5·50
46		3 c. on 40 m. violet	2·50	3·50
47		3 c. on 300 m. green	2·50	3·50
48		5 c. on 100 m. red	2·50	3·50
49		5 c. on 300 m. green	3·00	4·25
50		10 c. on 400 m. brown	5·00	7·00
67		15 c. on 25 m. orange	70·00	£350
51		30 c. on 500 m. purple	3·00	3·50
68		50 c. on 1000 m. blue	1·50	4·75
69		1 l. on 1000 m. blue	3·25	9·00

1923. Surch in **CENTU**.

53	5	2 c. on 300 m. green	3·75	6·25
54		3 c. on 300 m. green	3·75	6·25
55		10 c. on 25 m. orange	3·75	6·25
56		15 c. on 25 m. orange	3·75	6·25
57		20 c. on 500 m. purple	4·50	7·75
58		30 c. on 500 m. purple	3·75	6·25
59		50 c. on 500 m. purple	10·00	17·00

1923. Surch in **CENT.** or **LITAS**.

70	7	15 c. on 40 m. green	3·25	12·00
71		30 c. on 50 m. brown	2·50	6·50
72		30 c. on 80 m. green	3·25	10·00
73		30 c. on 100 m. red	2·50	6·50
74	8	50 c. on 200 m. blue	3·25	10·00
75		50 c. on 300 m. brown	2·50	6·50
76		50 c. on 400 m. purple	3·25	11·00
77		50 c. on 500 m. orange	2·50	6·50
78		1 l. on 600 m. green	3·25	11·00
79	9	1 l. on 800 m. blue	3·25	11·00
80		1 l. on 1000 m. purple	3·25	11·00
81		1 l. on 2000 m. red	3·25	11·00
82		1 l. on 3000 m. green	3·25	11·00

1923. Surch in large figures and **Centu** and bars reading upwards.

83	1	10 c. on 25 m. on 5 c. blue (No. 2)	17·00	40·00
84		15 c. on 100 m. on 25 c. red (No. 4)	20·00	£110
85		30 c. on 400 m. on 1 l. brown (No. 5)	4·00	16·00
86		60 c. on 50 m. on 25 c. red (No. 8)	20·00	£130

1923. Surch in large figures and **CENT.** and bars.

87	7	15 c. on 50 m. brown	£225	£1400
88		25 c. on 100 m. red	£110	£900
89	8	30 c. on 300 m. brown	£180	£1000
90		60 c. on 500 m. orange	£110	£900

1923. Surch in **Centu** or **Centai** (25 c.) between bars.

91	5	15 c. on 10 m. brown	5·00	20·00
92		15 c. on 20 m. yellow	2·25	10·00
93		15 c. on 25 m. orange	2·75	12·00
94		15 c. on 40 m. violet	2·25	10·00
95		15 c. on 50 m. green	1·50	8·00
96		15 c. on 100 m. red	1·50	8·00
97		15 c. on 400 m. brown	1·25	6·00
98		15 c. on 1000 m. blue	45·00	£250
99		25 c. on 10 m. brown	3·25	16·00
100		25 c. on 20 m. yellow	2·25	9·50
101		25 c. on 25 m. orange	2·75	12·00
102		25 c. on 40 m. violet	2·25	10·00
103		25 c. on 50 m. green	1·40	7·50
104		25 c. on 100 m. red	1·40	7·50
105		25 c. on 400 m. brown	1·25	6·00
106		25 c. on 1000 m. blue	50·00	£275
107		30 c. on 10 m. brown	4·50	19·00
108		30 c. on 20 m. yellow	2·50	10·00
109		30 c. on 25 m. orange	3·25	12·00
110		30 c. on 40 m. violet	2·50	10·00
111		30 c. on 50 m. green	1·40	6·50
112		30 c. on 100 m. red	1·40	7·00
113		30 c. on 400 m. brown	1·25	6·00
114		30 c. on 1000 m. blue	45·00	£250

MEXICO Pt. 15

A republic of Central America. From 1864–67 an Empire under Maximilian of Austria.

8 reales = 100 centavos = 1 peso

1 Miguel Hidalgo y Costilla 2

1856. With or without optd district name. Imperf.

1c 1 ½ r. blue . . . . 12·50 14·00
8c ½ r. black on buff . . . . 12·50 17·00
6 1 r. orange . . . . 11·00 1·60
9b 1 r. black on green . . . . 2·50 2·75
7b 2 r. green . . . . 10·50 1·60
10c 2 r. black on red . . . . 1·40 3·25
4b 4 r. red . . . . 55·00 75·00
11b 4 r. black on yellow . . . . 22·00 35·00
12a 4 r. red on yellow . . . . 50·00 60·00
5c 8 r. lilac . . . . 75·00 95·00
13a 8 r. black on brown . . . . 48·00 95·00
14a 8 r. green on brown . . . . 60·00 80·00

1864. Perf.

15a 2 1 r. red 10
16a 2 r. blue 15
17a 4 r. brown 25
18a 1 p. black 95

3 Arms of Mexico 4 Emperor Maximilian

1864. Imperf.

30 3 3 c. brown £600 £1200
19a ½ r. brown . . . . 85·00 £225
31 ½ r. purple . . . . 35·00 28·00
31c ½ r. grey . . . . 40·00 40·00
32b 1 r. blue . . . . 8·25 5·00
33 2 r. orange . . . . 2·50 1·60
34 4 r. green . . . . 55·00 32·00
35b 8 r. red . . . . 80·00 48·00

1864. Imperf.

40 4 7 c. purple £225 £2500
36c 7 c. grey . . . . 32·00 60·00
41 13 c. blue . . . . 3·75 5·50
42 25 c. orange . . . . 3·25 5·00
39c 50 c. green . . . . 11·50 11·50

7 Hidalgo 8 Hidalgo 9 Hidalgo

10 Hidalgo 15 Benito Juarez 16

1868. Imperf or perf.

67 7 6 c. black on brown . . . . 4·50 2·50
68 12 c. black on green . . . . 1·90 60
69 25 c. blue on pink . . . . 3·50 45
70b 50 c. black on yellow . . . . 60·00 7·50
71 100 c. black on brown . . . . 60·00 22·00
76 100 c. brown on brown . . . . 95·00 28·00

1872. Imperf or perf.

87 8 6 c. green . . . . 6·25 6·25
88 12 c. blue 80 65
94 25 c. red . . . . 3·50 75
90 50 c. yellow . . . . 70·00 16·00
91 100 c. lilac . . . . 48·00 25·00

1874. Various frames. Perf.

102a 9 4 c. orange . . . . 3·50 6·25
97 10 5 c. brown . . . . 2·10 1·40
98 9 10 c. black 85 50
105 10 c. orange 85 50
99 10 25 c. blue 35 30
107 9 50 c. green . . . . 7·00 6·25
108 100 c. red . . . . 9·50 8·25

1879.

115 15 1 c. brown . . . . 1·90 1·75
116 2 c. violet . . . . 1·75 1·50
117 5 c. orange . . . . 1·25 60
118 10 c. blue . . . . 1·60 1·25
127a 10 c. brown on green . . . . 1·25
128 12 c. brown . . . . 3·25 3·25
129 18 c. brown . . . . 3·75 3·25
130 24 c. mauve . . . . 3·75 3·25
119 25 c. red . . . . 4·00 4·75
132 25 c. brown . . . . 2·10
120 50 c. green . . . . 6·25 6·00
134 15 50 c. yellow . . . . 35·00 38·00
121 85 c. violet . . . . 11·00 9·50
122 100 c. black . . . . 12·50 11·00
137 100 c. orange . . . . 40·00 48·00

1882.

138 16 2 c. green . . . . 3·25 2·50
139 3 c. red . . . . 3·25 2·50
140 6 c. blue . . . . 2·50 1·90

17 Hidalgo 18

1884.

141 17 1 c. green . . . . 1·25 15
142 2 c. green . . . . 1·90 25
157 2 c. red . . . . 6·25 1·40
143 3 c. green . . . . 3·75 80
158 3 c. brown . . . . 8·75 2·50
144 4 c. green . . . . 5·00 80
159 4 c. red . . . . 12·50 7·50
145 5 c. green . . . . 5·00 60
160 5 c. blue . . . . 8·75 1·60
146 6 c. green . . . . 4·50 45
161 6 c. brown . . . . 10·00 2·50
147 10 c. green . . . . 4·75 15
162 10 c. orange . . . . 7·50 45
148 12 c. green . . . . 8·75 1·25
163 12 c. brown . . . . 16·00 3·75
149 20 c. green . . . . 25·00 95
150 25 c. green . . . . 45·00 1·90
164 25 c. blue . . . . 55·00 8·75
151 50 c. green . . . . 40 1·25
152 1 p. blue . . . . 40 4·75
153 2 p. blue . . . . 40 8·75
154 5 p. blue . . . . £120 80·00
155 10 p. blue . . . . £170 95·00

1886.

196 18 1 c. green 30 10
209 2 c. red 35 10
167 3 c. lilac . . . . 2·50 1·25
189 3 c. red 30 10
198 3 c. orange 95 35
168 4 c. lilac . . . . 4·50 95
211 4 c. red 75 50
199 4 c. orange . . . . 1·10 50
191 5 c. blue 20 10
170 6 c. lilac . . . . 5·00 60
213 6 c. red 95 60
200 6 c. orange . . . . 1·40 35
171 10 c. lilac . . . . 5·00 15
193 10 c. red 10 10
185a 10 c. brown . . . . 8·75 1·90
201 10 c. orange . . . . 7·50 35
172 12 c. lilac . . . . 5·00 3·25
215 12 c. red . . . . 3·25 3·75
173 20 c. lilac . . . . 40·00 22·00
194 20 c. red 50 20
202 20 c. orange . . . . 12·50 1·60
174 25 c. lilac . . . . 16·00 3·75
217 25 c. red 95 25
203 25 c. orange . . . . 4·00 1·10
206 5 p. red £350 £225
207 10 p. red £550 £350

19 Foot Postman 20 Mounted Postman and Pack Mules 21 Statue of Cuauhtemoc

22 Mailcoach 23 Steam Train

1895.

253 19 1 c. green 20 10
219 2 c. red 30 10
220 3 c. brown 30 10
221 20 4 c. orange . . . . 1·50 25
257 21 5 c. blue 35 10
223 22 10 c. purple 50 10
224 20 12 c. olive . . . . 8·25 3·75
225 22 15 c. blue . . . . 4·00 80
226 20 c. red . . . . 4·00 40
227 50 c. mauve . . . . 12·00 4·75
228 23 1 p. brown . . . . 23·00 11·50
229 5 p. red . . . . 80·00 48·00
230 10 p. blue . . . . £130 85·00

27 28 Juanacatlan Falls

29 Popocatepetl 30 Cathedral, Mexico

1899. Various frames for T **27**.

266 27 1 c. green 80 10
276 1 c. purple 60 10
267 2 c. red . . . . 2·40 10
277 2 c. green 80 10
268 3 c. brown . . . . 1·60 10
278 4 c. red . . . . 2·50 20
269 5 c. blue . . . . 2·50 10
279 5 c. orange 45 10
270 10 c. brown and purple . . . . 3·25 15
280 10 c. orange and blue . . . . 2·50 10
271 15 c. purple and lavender . . . . 4·25 10
272 20 c. blue and red . . . . 4·75 15
273a 28 50 c. black and purple . . . . 19·00 1·25
281 50 c. black and red . . . . 40·00 3·50
274 29 1 p. black and blue . . . . 42·00 1·90
275 30 5 p. black and red . . . . £130 6·25

32 Josefa Ortiz 40 Hidalgo at Dolores

1910. Centenary of First Independence Movement.

282 32 1 c. purple 10 10
283 – 2 c. green 10 10
284 – 3 c. brown 25 10
285 – 4 c. red . . . . 1·25 20
286 – 5 c. orange 10 10
287 – 10 c. orange and blue 80 10
288 – 15 c. lake and slate . . . . 4·50 20
289 – 20 c. blue and lake . . . . 2·50 10
290 40 50 c. black and brown . . . . 6·25 95
291 – 1 p. black and blue . . . . 7·50 1·10
292 – 5 p. black and red . . . . 28·00 2·75

DESIGNS: As Type **32**: 2 c. L. Vicario; 3 c. L. Rayon; 4 c. J. Aldama; 5 c. M. Hidalgo; 10 c. I. Allende; 15 c. E. Gonzalez; 20 c. M. Abasolo. As Type **40**: 1 p. Mass on Mt. of Crosses; 5 p. Capture of Granaditas.

REVOLUTIONARY PROVISIONALS

For full list of the provisional issues made during the Civil War from 1913 onwards, see the Stanley Gibbons Part 15 (Central America) Catalogue.

CONSTITUTIONALIST GENERAL ISSUES.

CT 1

1914. "Transitorio".

CT1 CT 1 1 c. blue 20 15
CT2 2 c. green 30 15
CT3 4 c. blue . . . . 7·00 1·60
CT4 5 c. green . . . . 7·00 1·90
CT9 5 c. green 10 10
CT5 10 c. red 15 15
CT6 20 c. brown 25 25
CT7 50 c. red . . . . 1·60 2·10
CT8 1 p. violet . . . . 8·75 10·00

The words of value on No. CT4, are 2 × 14 mm and on No. CT9 are 2½ × 16 mm.

1914. Victory of Torreon. Nos. CT1/7 optd **Victoria de TORREON ABRIL 2 - 1914.**

CT10 CT 1 1 c. blue . . . . 95·00 80·00
CT11 2 c. green . . . . £110 95·00
CT12 4 c. blue £130 £160
CT13 5 c. green . . . . 11·50 12·50
CT14 10 c. red . . . . 60·00 60·00
CT15 20 c. brown £1100 £1100
CT16 50 c. red £1200 £1200

CT 3 CT 4

1914. Handstamped with Type CT 3.

(a) Nos. D282/6.

CT17 D 32 1 c. blue . . . . 8·75 10·00
CT18 2 c. blue . . . . 8·75 10·00
CT19 4 c. blue . . . . 8·75 10·00
CT20 5 c. blue . . . . 8·75 10·00
CT21 10 c. blue . . . . 8·75 10·00

(b) Nos. 282/92.

CT22 32 1 c. purple 35 30
CT23 – 2 c. green 95 80
CT24 – 3 c. brown 95 80
CT25 – 4 c. red . . . . 1·60 1·25
CT26 – 5 c. orange 20 10
CT27 – 10 c. orange and blue . . . . 1·90 1·25
CT28 – 15 c. lake and slate . . . . 3·25 1·90
CT29 – 20 c. blue and lake . . . . 6·25 3·75
CT30 40 50 c. black and brown . . . . 7·50 5·00
CT31 – 1 p. black and blue . . . . 16·00 6·25
CT32 – 5 p. black and red . . . . £100 95·00

1914.

CT33 CT 4 1 c. pink . . . . 80 12·50
CT34 2 c. green . . . . 80 11·50
CT35 3 c. orange . . . . 80 12·50
CT36 5 c. red . . . . 60 5·00
CT37 10 c. green . . . . 60 22·00
CT38 25 c. blue . . . . 10·00

CT 5

1914. "Denver" issue.

CT39 CT 5 1 c. blue 15 20
CT40 2 c. green 15 15
CT41 3 c. orange 25 15
CT42 5 c. red 25 15
CT43 10 c. red 35 40
CT44 15 c. mauve . . . . 60 1·10
CT45 50 c. yellow . . . . 1·25 1·60
CT46 1 p. violet . . . . 5·25 7·50

1914. Optd **GOBIERNO CONSTITUCIONALISTA.**

(a) Nos. 279 and 271/2.

CT50 – 5 c. orange . . . . 48·00 35·00
CT51 – 15 c. purple and lavender . . . . 95·00 95·00
CT52 – 20 c. blue and red £300 £250

(b) Nos. D282/6.

CT53 D 32 1 c. blue . . . . 1·10 1·10
CT54 2 c. blue . . . . 1·25 1·25
CT55 4 c. blue . . . . 9·50 9·50
CT56 5 c. blue . . . . 9·50 9·50
CT57 10 c. blue . . . . 1·60 1·60

(c) Nos. 282/92.

CT58 32 1 c. purple 10 10
CT59 – 2 c. green 10 10
CT60 – 3 c. brown 20 20
CT61 – 4 c. red 25 25
CT62 – 5 c. orange 10 10
CT63 – 10 c. orange and blue 10 10
CT64 – 15 c. lake and slate 35 30
CT65 – 20 c. blue and lake 35 35
CT66 40 50 c. black and brown . . . . 1·10 75
CT67 – 1 p. black and blue . . . . 4·75 3·25
CT68 – 5 p. black and red . . . . 25·00 19·00

CONVENTIONIST ISSUES

(CV 1) Villa-Zapata Monogram

1914. Optd with Type CV 1. (a) Nos. 266/75.

CV 1 27 1 c. green . . . . 60·00
CV 2 2 c. red . . . . 60·00
CV 3 3 c. brown . . . . 32·00
CV 4 5 c. blue . . . . 60·00
CV 5 10 c. brown and purple . . . . 60·00
CV 6 15 c. purple and lavender . . . . 60·00
CV 7 20 c. blue and red . . . . 60·00
CV 8 28 50 c. black and red £160
CV 9 29 1 p. black and blue £160
CV10 30 5 p. black and red £300

(b) Nos. 276/80.

CV11 27 1 c. purple . . . . 60·00
CV12 2 c. green . . . . 60·00
CV13 4 c. red . . . . 60·00
CV14 5 c. orange . . . . 7·75
CV15 10 c. orange and blue . . . . 48·00

(c) Nos. D282/6.

CV16 D 32 1 c. blue . . . . 6·00 6·25
CV17 2 c. blue . . . . 6·00 6·25
CV18 4 c. blue . . . . 6·00 6·25
CV19 5 c. blue . . . . 6·00 6·25
CV20 10 c. blue . . . . 60·00 6·25

(d) Nos. 282/92.

CV21 32 1 c. purple 40 40
CV22 – 2 c. green 45 20
CV23 – 3 c. brown 30 30
CV24 – 4 c. red . . . . 1·25 1·25
CV25 – 5 c. orange 10 10
CV26 – 10 c. orange and blue 95 95
CV27 – 15 c. lake and slate 95 95
CV28 – 20 c. blue and lake 95 95
CV29 40 50 c. black and brown . . . . 6·25 6·25
CV30 – 1 p. black and blue . . . . 9·50 9·50
CV31 – 5 p. black and red . . . . 95·00 95·00

CONSTITUTIONALIST PROVISIONAL ISSUES

CT 10 CT 11 Carranza Monogram

1914. Nos. 282/92 handstamped with Type CT **10**.

CT69 32 1 c. purple . . . . 6·00 5·50
CT70 – 2 c. green . . . . 6·00 5·50
CT71 – 3 c. brown . . . . 6·00 5·50

CT72 – 4 c. red 7·50 7·00
CT73 – 5 c. orange 90 90
CT74 – 10 c. orange and blue 7·00 6·25
CT75 – 15 c. lake and slate 7·00 6·25
CT76 – 20 c. blue and lake 8·75 5·75
CT77 **40** 50 c. black and brown 19·00 19·00
CT78 – 1 p. black and blue 28·00
CT79 – 5 p. black and red £100

1915. Optd with Type CT **11**. (a) No. 271.
CT80 – 15 c. purple and lavender 50·00 50·00

(b) No. 279.
CT81 – 5 c. orange 12·50 12·50

(c) Nos. D282/6.
CT82 D **32** 1 c. blue 7·00
CT83 2 c. blue 7·00
CT84 4 c. blue 7·00
CT85 5 c. blue 7·00
CT86 10 c. blue 7·00

(d) Nos. 282/92.
CT87 **32** 1 c. purple 35 35
CT88 – 2 c. green 35 30
CT89 – 3 c. brown 35 35
CT90 – 4 c. red 1·25 1·25
CT91 – 5 c. orange 10 10
CT92 – 10 c. orange and blue 75 75
CT93 – 15 c. lake and slate 75 75
CT94 – 20 c. blue and lake 75 75
CT95 **40** 50 c. black and brown 6·25 6·25
CT96 – 1 p. black and blue 9·50 9·50
CT97 – 5 p. black and red 95·00 95·00

GENERAL ISSUES.

43 Coat of Arms
44 Statue of Cuauhtemoc 
45 Ignacio Zaragoza 

1915. Portraits as T **45**. Roul or perf.
293 **43** 1 c. violet 10 10
294 **44** 2 c. green 20 15
304 **45** 3 c. brown 20 15
305 4 c. red (Morelos) 20 20
306 5 c. orange (Madero) 25 15
307 10 c. blue (Juarez) 15 10

46 Map of Mexico
47 Lighthouse, Veracruz 
48 Post Office, Mexico City 

1915.
299 **46** 40 c. grey 30 30
433 40 c. mauve 1·25 25
300 **47** 1 p. grey and brown 35 60
411 1 p. grey and blue 22·00 60
301 **48** 5 p. blue and lake 5·00 5·50
412 5 p. grey and green 50 60

(49)
50 V. Carranza 

1916. Silver Currency. Optd with T **49**. (a) No. 271.
309 – 15 c. purple and lavender £250 £250

(b) No. 279.
309a – 5 c. orange 55·00 55·00

(c) Nos. 282/92.
310 **32** 1 c. purple 2·10 3·25
311 – 2 c. green 25 15
312 – 3 c. brown 25 15
313 – 4 c. red 3·75 5·00
314 – 5 c. orange 10 10
315 – 10 c. orange and blue 60 95
316 – 15 c. lake and slate 1·10 1·90
317 – 20 c. blue and lake 1·10 1·90
318 **40** 50 c. black and brown 5·25 3·25
319 – 1 p. black and blue 9·50 4·00
320 – 5 p. black and red 95·00 80·00

(d) Nos. CT1/3 and CT5/8.
320b CT **1** 1 c. blue 15·00
320c 2 c. green 7·50
320d 4 c. blue £160
320e 10 c. red 1·40
320f 20 c. brown 1·90
320g 50 c. red 9·50
320h 1 p. violet 15·00

(e) Nos. CT39/46.
321 CT **5** 1 c. blue 2·40 12·00
322 2 c. green 2·40 7·00
323 3 c. orange 45 7·00
324 5 c. red 45 7·00
325 10 c. red 45 3·25
326 15 c. mauve 45 7·00
327 50 c. yellow 70 8·00
328 1 p. violet 6·00 15·00

(f) Nos. CT58/68.
329 **32** 1 c. purple 1·60 2·50
330 – 2 c. green 35 30
331 – 3 c. brown 30 30
332 – 4 c. red 30 30
333 – 5 c. orange 50 15
334 – 10 c. orange and blue 35 30
335 – 15 c. lake and slate 40 40
336 – 20 c. blue and lake 40 40
337 **40** 50 c. black and brown 4·75 3·75
338 – 1 p. black and blue 10·00 10·00
339 – 5 p. black and red 95·00 85·00

(g) Nos. CV22/9.
340 **32** 1 c. purple 7·00 9·50
341 – 2 c. green 75 45
342 – 3 c. brown 2·00 2·75
343 – 4 c. red 8·25 9·50
344 – 5 c. orange 2·75 3·75
345 – 10 c. orange and blue 7·50 8·75
346 – 15 c. lake and slate 7·50 8·75
347 – 20 c. blue and lake 7·50 8·75

(h) Nos. CT87/97.
348 **32** 1 c. purple 1·60 2·10
349 – 2 c. green 30 30
350 – 3 c. brown 25 20
351 – 4 c. red 3·25 3·75
352 – 5 c. orange 40 10
353 – 10 c. orange and blue 75 1·25
354 – 15 c. lake and slate 60 30
355 – 20 c. blue and lake 60 55
356 **40** 50 c. black and brown 4·75 5·50
357 – 1 p. black and blue 7·00 7·50

1916. Carranza's Triumphal Entry into Mexico City.
358 **50** 10 c. brown 7·50 8·25
359 10 c. blue 60 30

(51)

1916. Optd with T **51**. (a) Nos. D282/6.
360 D **32** 5 c. on 1 c. blue 1·60 1·60
361 10 c. on 2 c. blue 1·60 1·60
362 20 c. on 4 c. blue 1·60 1·60
363 25 c. on 5 c. blue 1·60 1·60
364 60 c. on 10 c. blue 75 75
365 1 p. on 1 c. blue 75 75
366 1 p. on 2 c. blue 75 75
367 1 p. on 4 c. blue 40 40
368 1 p. on 5 c. blue 1·60 1·60
369 1 p. on 10 c. blue 1·60 1·60

(b) Nos. 282, 286 and 283.
370 **32** 5 c. on 1 c. purple 10 10
371 10 c. on 1 c. purple 10 10
372 – 20 c. on 5 c. orange 10 10
373 – 25 c. on 5 c. orange 15 15
374 – 60 c. on 2 c. green 10·50 12·50

(c) Nos. CT39/40.
375 CT **5** 60 c. on 1 c. blue 1·90 3·75
376 60 c. on 2 c. green 1·90 3·75

(d) Nos. CT58, CT62 and CT59.
377 **32** 5 c. on 1 c. purple 10 10
378 – 10 c. on 1 c. purple 60 60
379 – 25 c. on 5 c. purple 15 15
380 – 60 c. on 2 c. green £130 £170

(e) No. CV25.
381 – 25 c. on 5 c. orange 15 10

(f) Nos. CT87, CT91 and CT88.
382 **32** 5 c. on 1 c. purple 9·50 12·50
383 – 10 c. on 1 c. purple 3·25 4·75
385 – 25 c. on 5 c. orange 50 95
386 – 60 c. on 2 c. green £140

1916. Nos. D282/6 surch **GPM** and value.
387 D **32** $2.50 on 1 c. blue 60 60
388 $2.50 on 2 c. blue 6·25 6·25
389 $2.50 on 4 c. blue 6·25 6·25
390 $2.50 on 5 c. blue 6·25 6·25
391 $2.50 on 10 c. blue 6·25 6·25

52a Arms
53 Zaragoza 

1916.
392 **52a** 1 c. purple 15 15

1917. Portraits. Roul or perf.
393 **53** 1 c. violet 25 10
393a 1 c. grey 70 20
394 – 2 c. green (Vazquez) 35 10
395 – 3 c. brown (Suarez) 35 10
396 – 4 c. red (Carranza) 60 20
397 – 5 c. blue (Herrera) 85 10
398 – 10 c. blue (Madero) 1·40 10
399 – 20 c. lake (Dominguez) 14·00 35
400 – 30 c. purple (Serdan) 38·00 60
401 – 30 c. black (Serdan) 45·00 60

1919. Red Cross Fund. Surch with cross and premium.
413 5 c. + 3 c. blue (No. 397) 9·00 9·50
414 10 c. + 5 c. blue (No. 398) 11·00 9·50

56 Meeting of Iturbide and Guerrero

1921. Centenary of Declaration of Independence.
415 **56** 10 c. brown and blue 9·50 1·90
416 – 10 p. black and brown 9·50 22·00
DESIGN: 10 p. Entry into Mexico City.

58 Golden Eagle

1922. Air.
454 **58** 25 c. sepia and lake 90 20
455 25 c. sepia and green 95 25
456 50 c. red and blue 1·25 35

59 Morelos Monument
60 Fountain and Aqueduct 
61 Pyramid of the Sun, Teotihuacan 
62 Castle of Chapultepec 
63 Columbus Monument 
74 Benito Juarez 
64 Juarez Colonnade 
65 Monument to Dona Josefa Ortiz de Dominguez 
66 Cuauhtemoc Monument 
68 Ministry of Communications 
69 National Theatre and Palace of Fine Arts 

1923. Roul or perf.
436 **59** 1 c. brown 25 10
437 **60** 2 c. red 15 10
438 **61** 3 c. brown 10 10
429 **62** 4 c. green 60 10
440 **63** 4 c. green 15 10
441 5 c. orange 10 10
453 **74** 8 c. orange 15 10
423 **64** 10 c. brown 4·75 10
442 **66** 10 c. lake 15 10
443 **65** 20 c. blue 35 10
426 **66** 30 c. green 35·00 2·50
432 **64** 30 c. green 45 10
434 **68** 50 c. brown 30 10
435 **69** 1 p. blue and lake 50 25

70
72 Sr. Francisco Garcia y Santos 
73 Post Office, Mexico City 

1926. 2nd Pan-American Postal Congress. Inscr as in T **70/3**.
445 **70** 2 c. red 1·25 35
446 – 4 c. green 1·25 40
447 **70** 5 c. orange 1·25 25
448 – 10 c. red 1·90 25
449 **72** 20 c. blue 1·90 50
450 30 c. green 3·25 1·90
451 40 c. mauve 6·25 1·60
452 **73** 1 p. blue and brown 12·50 3·75
DESIGN—As Type **70**: 4 c., 10 c. Map of North and South America.

1929. Child Welfare. Optd **Protection a la Infancia**.
457 **59** 1 c. brown 25 15

77
79 Capt. Emilio Carranza 

1929. Obligatory Tax. Child Welfare.
459 **77** 1 c. violet 10 10
461 2 c. green 20 10
462 5 c. brown 15 10

1929. Air. 1st Death Anniv of Carranza (airman).
463 **79** 5 c. sepia and green 55 30
464 10 c. red and sepia 65 35
465 15 c. green and violet 1·90 60
466 20 c. black and sepia 60 35
467 50 c. black and red 3·75 1·25
468 1 p. sepia and black 7·75 1·75

80

1929. Air. Perf or roul (10, 15, 20, 50 c.), roul (5, 25 c.), perf (others).
476a **80** 5 c. blue 10 10
477 10 c. violet 10 10
478 15 c. red 15 10
479 20 c. brown 75 10
480 25 c. purple 45 40
472 30 c. black 10 10
473 35 c. blue 15 10
481 50 c. red 45 35
474 1 p. blue and black 60 30
475 5 p. blue and red 2·50 2·10
476 10 p. brown and violet 3·75 4·50

81
87 

1929. Air. Aviation Week.
482 **81** 20 c. violet 60 50
483 40 c. green 55·00 48·00

1930. 2nd Pan-American Postal Congress issue optd **HABILITADO 1930**.
484 **70** 2 c. red 2·10 1·40
485 – 4 c. green 2·10 1·25
486 **70** 5 c. orange 2·10 1·10
487 – 10 c. red 3·75 1·25
488 **72** 20 c. blue 5·00 1·90
489 30 c. green 4·50 2·10
490 40 c. mauve 6·25 4·50
491 **73** 1 p. blue and brown 5·50 3·75

1930. Air. National Tourist Congress. Optd **Primer Congreso Nacional de Turismo. Mexico. Abril 20-27 de 1930.**
492 **80** 10 c. violet (No. 477) 1·25 60

1930. Obligatory Tax. Child Welfare. Surch **HABILITADO $0.01**.
494 **77** 1 c. on 2 c. green 30 15
495 1 c. on 5 c. brown 60 15

1930. Air. Optd **HABILITADO 1930**.
496 **79** 5 c. sepia and green . . . . 3·50 2·75
497 15 c. green and violet . . . . 5·50 4·75

1930. Air. Optd **HABILITADO Aereo 1930-1931**.
498 **79** 5 c. sepia and green . . . . 3·75 4·00
499 10 c. red and sepia . . . . 2·10 2·50
500 15 c. green and violet . . . 4·00 4·50
501 20 c. black and sepia . . . 4·50 3·50
502 50 c. black and red . . . . 8·75 6·25
503 1 p. sepia and black . . . . 2·50 1·75

1931. Obligatory Tax. Child Welfare. No. CT58 optd **PRO INFANCIA**.
504 **32** 1 c. purple 20 15

1931. Fourth Centenary of Puebla.
505 **87** 10 c. brown and blue . . . 1·60 25

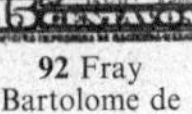

88 92 Fray Bartolome de las Casas

1931. Air. Aeronautic Exhibition.
506 **88** 25 c. lake . . . . 2·00 1·60

1931. Nos. 446/52 optd **HABILITADO 1931**.
508 – 4 c. green . . . . 35·00
509 **70** 5 c. orange . . . . 6·25
510 – 10 c. red . . . . 6·25
511 **72** 20 c. blue . . . . 6·25
512 30 c. green . . . . 11·00
513 40 c. mauve . . . . 16·00
514 **73** 1 p. blue and brown . . . . 14·00

1931. Air. Surch **HABILITADO Quince centavos**. Perf or rouletted.
516 **80** 15 c. on 20 c. sepia 20 10

1932. Air. Surch in words and figures. Perf. or roul.
517 **88** 20 c. on 25 c. lake 30 15
521 **80** 30 c. on 20 c. sepia 15 10
519 **58** 40 c. on 25 c. sepia & lake 90 65
520 40 c. on 25 c. sepia & green 25·00 25·00
522 **80** 80 c. on 25 c. (No. 480) . . 90 60

1932. Air. 4th Death Anniv of Emilio Carranza. Optd **HABILITADO AEREO–1932**.
523 **79** 5 c. sepia and green . . . . 3·75 3·25
524 10 c. red and sepia . . . . 3·25 1·90
525 15 c. green and violet . . . 3·75 2·50
526 20 c. black and sepia . . . 3·25 1·75
527 50 c. black and red . . . . 22·00 22·00

1933. Roul.
528 **92** 15 c. blue 15 10

93 Mexican Geographical and Statistical Society's Arms
94 National Theatre and Palace of Fine Arts

1933. 21st Int Statistical Congress and Centenary of Mexican Geographical and Statistical Society.
529 **93** 2 c. green (postage) 75 20
530 5 c. brown . . . . 1·10 25
531 10 c. blue 35 10
532 1 p. violet . . . . 32·00 38·00
533 **94** 20 c. violet and red (air) . . 2·10 85
534 30 c. violet and brown . . 4·25 3·75
535 1 p. violet and green . . . 42·00 45·00

95 Mother and Child
98 Nevada de Toluca

1934. National University. Inscr "PRO-UNIVERSIDAD".
543 **95** 1 c. orange (postage) . . . 10 10
544 – 5 c. green . . . . 1·00 15
545 – 10 c. lake . . . . 1·25 30
546 – 20 c. blue . . . . 5·00 3·25
547 – 30 c. black . . . . 8·75 7·50
548 – 40 c. brown . . . . 15·00 10·00
549 – 50 c. blue . . . . 28·00 32·00
550 – 1 p. black and red . . . . 32·00 30·00
551 – 5 p. brown and black . . . £120 £160
552 – 10 p. violet and brown . . . £500 £650
DESIGNS: 5 c. Archer; 10 c. Festive headdress; 20 c. Woman decorating pot; 30 c. Indian and Inca Lily; 40 c. Potter; 50 c. Sculptor; 1 p. Gold craftsman; 5 p. Girl offering fruit; 10 p. Youth burning incense.

553 **98** 20 c. orange (air) . . . . 1·75 1·75
554 – 30 c. purple and mauve . . 3·50 4·25
555 – 50 c. brown and green . . 4·00 6·25
556 – 75 c. green and black . . . 4·75 8·75
557 – 1 p. blue and green . . . . 5·00 6·25
558 – 5 p. blue and brown . . . 26·00 60·00
559 – 10 p. red and blue . . . . 80·00 £130
560 – 20 p. red and brown . . . £475 £750
DESIGNS—Airplane over: 30 c. Pyramids of the Sun and Moon, Teotihuacan; 50 c. Mt. Ajusco; 75 c. Mts. Ixtaccihuatl and Popocatepetl; 1 p. Bridge over R. Papagallo; 5 p. Chapultepec Castle entrance; 10 p. Orizaba Peak, Mt. Citlaltepetl; 20 p. Girl and Aztec calendar stone.

101 Zapoteca Indian Woman
110 Coat of Arms

1934. Pres. Cardenas' Assumption of Office. Designs as Type **101** and **110**. Imprint "OFICINA IMPRESORA DE HACIENDA-MEXICO" at foot of stamp. (a) Postage.
561 – 1 c. orange 30 10
562 **101** 2 c. green 30 10
563 – 4 c. red 45 15
564 – 5 c. brown 30 10
565 – 10 c. blue 40 10
565a – 10 c. violet 80 10
566 – 15 c. blue . . . . 2·50 15
567 – 20 c. green . . . . 1·25 10
567a – 20 c. blue 85 10
568 – 30 c. red 35 10
653 – 30 c. blue 40 10
569 – 40 c. brown 40 10
570 – 50 c. black 45 10
571 **110** 1 p. red and brown . . . 1·60 10
572 – 5 p. violet and orange . . 4·75 55
DESIGNS: 1 c. Yalalteca Indian; 4 c. Revolution Monument; 5 c. Los Remedios Tower; 10 c. Cross of Palenque; 15 c. Independence Monument, Mexico City; 20 c. Independence Monument, Puebla; 30 c. "Heroic Children" Monument, Mexico City; 40 c. Sacrificial Stone; 50 c. Ruins of Mitla, Oaxaca; 5 p. Mexican "Charro" (Horseman).

112 Mictlantecuhtli
120 "Peasant admiration"

(b) Air.
573 **112** 5 c. black 20 10
574 – 10 c. brown 45 10
575 – 15 c. green 90 10
576 – 20 c. red . . . . 1·90 10
577 – 30 c. olive 35 10
577a – 40 c. blue 60 10
578 – 50 c. green . . . . 1·60 10
579 – 1 p. red and green . . . 2·50 10
580 **120** 5 p. black and red . . . 4·50 25
DESIGNS—HORIZ: 10 c. Temple at Quetzalcoatl; 15 c. Aeroplane over Citlaltepetl; 20 c. Popocatepetl; 30 c. Pegasus; 50 c. Uruapan pottery; 1 p. "Warrior Eagle". VERT: 40 c. Aztec idol.

121 Tractor
122 Arms of Chiapas

1935. Industrial Census.
581 **121** 10 c. violet . . . . 2·50 25

1935. Air. Amelia Earhart Flight to Mexico. No. 576 optd **AMELIA EARHART VUELO DE BUENA VOLUNTAD MEXICO 1935**.
581a 20 c. red £1900 £2500

1935. Annexation of Chiapas Centenary.
582 **122** 10 c. blue 35 15

123 E. Zapata
124 Francisco Madero

1935. 25th Anniv of Revolutionary Plans of Ayala and San Luis Potosi.
583 **123** 10 c. violet (postage) . . 35 10
584 **124** 20 c. red (air) 20 10

129 Nuevo Laredo Road
131 Rio Corona Bridge

1936. Opening of Nuevo Laredo Highway (Mexico City-U.S.A.).
591 – 5 c. red & green (postage) 15 10
592 – 10 c. grey 25 10
593 **129** 20 c. green and brown . . 75 50
DESIGNS: As Type **129**: 5 c. Symbolical Map of Mexico–U.S.A. road; 10 c. Matalote Bridge.
594 – 10 c. blue (air) 30 10
595 **131** 20 c. orange and violet . . 30 10
596 – 40 c. green and blue . . . 40 30
DESIGNS: As Type **131**: 10 c. Tasquillo Bridge over Rio Tula; 40 c. Guayalejo Bridge.

1936. 1st Congress of Industrial Medicine and Hygiene. Optd **PRIMER CONGRESO NAL DE HIGIENE V. MED. DEL TRABAJO**.
597 – 10 c. violet (No. 565a) . . . 30 20

1937. As Nos. 561/4, 565a and 576, but smaller. Imprint at foot changed to "TALLERES DE IMP.(RESION) DE EST.(AMPILLAS) Y VALORES-MEXICO".
708 1 c. orange (postage) 25 10
709 2 c. green 25 10
600 4 c. red 40 10
601 5 c. brown 35 10
602 10 c. violet 25 10
603 20 c. red (air) 80 10

134 Blacksmith

1938. Carranza's "Plan of Guadelupe". 25th Anniv Inscr "CONMEMORATIVO PLAN DE GUADALUPE", etc.
604 **134** 5 c. brown & blk (postage) 30 10
605 – 10 c. brown 10 10
606 – 20 c. orange and brown . . 3·25 50
607 – 20 c. blue and red (air) . . 20 10
608 – 40 c. red and blue 45 15
609 – 1 p. blue and yellow . . . 3·00 1·40
DESIGNS—VERT: 10 c. Peasant revolutionary; 20 c. Preaching revolt. HORIZ: 20 c. Horseman; 40 c. Biplane; 1 p. Mounted horseman.

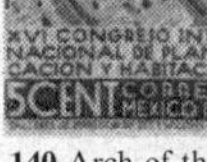

140 Arch of the Revolution
141 Cathedral and Constitution Square

1938. 16th Int Town Planning and Housing Congress, Mexico City. Inscr as in T **140/1**.
610 **140** 5 c. brown (postage) . . . 80 30
611 – 5 c. olive . . . . 1·60 1·40
612 – 10 c. orange . . . . 8·75 7·00
613 – 10 c. brown 30 10
614 – 20 c. black . . . . 2·10 2·50
615 – 20 c. lake . . . . 11·50 9·50
DESIGNS: As Type **140**: 10 c. National Theatre; 20 c. Independence Column.
616 **141** 20 c. red (air) 15 10
617 – 20 c. violet . . . . 8·75 6·25
619 – 40 c. green . . . . 4·50 3·25
620 – 1 p. slate . . . . 4·50 3·25
621 – 1 p. light blue . . . . . . 4·50 3·25
DESIGNS: As Type **141**: 40 c. Chichen Itza Ruins (Yucatan); 1 p. Acapulco Beach.

142 Mosquito and Malaria Victim

1939. Obligatory Tax. Anti-Malaria Campaign.
622 **142** 1 c. blue 95 10

INDEX

Countries can be quickly located by referring to the index at the end of this volume.

143 Statue of an Indian
144 Statue of Woman Pioneer and Child

1939. Tulsa Philatelic Convention, Oklahoma.
623 **143** 10 c. red (postage) 20 10
624 **144** 20 c. brown (air) 50 20
625 40 c. green . . . . 1·25 60
626 1 p. violet 80 45

145 Mexican Pavilion, World's Fair
146 Morelos Statue on Mexican Pavilion

1939. Air. F. Sarabia non-stop Flight to New York. Optd **SARABIA Vuela MEXICO-NUEVA YORK**.
626a **146** 20 c. blue and red . . . £160 £300

1939. New York World's Fair.
627 **145** 10 c. green & bl (postage) 30 10
628 **146** 20 c. green (air) 60 25
629 40 c. purple . . . . . . 1·60 60
630 1 p. brown and red . . . 1·00 50

147 J. de Zumarraga
152 "Building"

154 "Transport"

1939. 400th Anniv of Printing in Mexico.
631 **147** 2 c. black (postage) . . . 35 10
632 – 5 c. green 35 10
633 – 10 c. red 10 10
634 – 20 c. blue (air) 10 10
635 – 40 c. green 30 10
636 – 1 p. red and brown . . . 55 35
DESIGNS: 5 c. First printing works in Mexico; 10 c. Antonio D. Mendoza; 20 c. Book frontispiece; 40 c. Title page of first law book printed in America; 1 p. Oldest Mexican Colophon.

1939. National Census. Inscr "CENSOS 1939 1940".
637 **152** 2 c. red (postage) 60 10
638 – 5 c. green 10 10
639 – 10 c. brown 10 10
640 **154** 20 c. blue (air) 70 25
641 – 40 c. orange 35 10
642 – 1 p. violet and blue . . . 1·75 35
DESIGNS: As Type **152**: 5 c. "Agriculture"; 10 c. "Commerce". As Type **154**: 40 c. "Industry"; 1 p. "Seven Censuses".

155 "Penny Black"
156 Roadside Monument

1940. Centenary of First Adhesive Postage Stamps.
643 **155** 5 c. yellow & black (postage) 45 25
644 10 c. purple 10 10
645 20 c. red and blue 15 10
646 1 p. red and grey 4·50 2·50
647 5 p. blue and black 23·00 19·00
648 5 c. green and black (air) 45 30
649 10 c. blue and brown 35 10
650 20 c. violet and red 25 10
651 1 p. brown and red 2·10 3·25
652 5 p. brown and green 25·00 35·00

1940. Opening of Highway from Mexico City to Guadalajara.
654 **156** 6 c. green 35 10

159 Original College at Patzcuaro

1940. 4th Centenary of National College of St. Nicholas de Hidalgo.
655 – 2 c. violet (postage) 65 25
656 – 5 c. red 40 10
657 – 10 c. olive 40 10
658 **159** 20 c. green (air) 20 10
659 – 40 c. orange 25 10
660 – 1 p. violet, brown & orange 60 45
DESIGNS—VERT: 2 c. V. de Quiroga; 5 c. M. Ocampo; 10 c. St. Nicholas College Arms; 40 c. Former College at Morelia. HORIZ: 1 p. Present College at Morelia.

163 Pirate Galleon

1940. 400th Anniv of Campeche. Inscr as in T **163**.
661 – 10 c. red & brown (postage) 1·90 60
662 **163** 20 c. brown and red (air) 70 35
663 – 40 c. green and black 75 25
664 – 1 p. black and blue 3·25 1·90
DESIGNS: 10 c. Campeche City Arms; 40 c. St. Miguel Castel; 1 p. Temple of San Francisco.

165 Helmsman
166 Miguel Hidalgo y Costilla

1940. Inauguration of Pres. Camacho.
665 **165** 2 c. orange & black (postage) 1·00 30
666 5 c. blue and brown 3·75 2·10
667 10 c. olive and brown 1·40 40
668 20 c. grey & orange (air) 1·25 60
669 40 c. brown and green 1·25 95
670 1 p. purple and red 2·10 1·25

1940. Compulsory Tax. Dolores Hidalgo Memorial Fund.
671 **166** 1 c. red 30 10

168 Javelin throwing
169 Dark Nebula in Orion

1941. National Athletic Meeting.
675 **168** 10 c. green 2·10 25

1942. Inauguration of Astro-physical Observatory at Tonanzintla, Puebla.
676 **169** 2 c. blue & violet (postage) 80 50
677 – 5 c. blue 5·50 1·25
678 – 10 c. blue and orange 5·50 25
679 – 20 c. blue and green (air) 7·75 1·90
680 – 40 c. blue and red 7·00 2·50
681 – 1 p. black and orange 7·00 2·75
DESIGNS: 5 c. Solar Eclipse; 10 c. Spiral Galaxy of the "Hunting Dog"; 20 c. Extra-Galactic Nebula in Virgo; 40 c. Ring Nebula in Lyra; 1 p. Russell Diagram.

171 Ruins of Chichen-Itza
172 Merida Nunnery

1942. 400th Anniv of Merida. Inscr as in T **171/2**.
682 **171** 2 c. brown (postage) 70 30
683 – 5 c. red 1·40 30
684 – 10 c. violet 80 10
685 **172** 20 c. blue (air) 95 25
686 – 40 c. green 1·40 1·25
687 – 1 p. red 1·60 1·25
DESIGNS—VERT: 5 c. Mayan sculpture; 10 c. Arms of Merida; 40 c. Montejo University Gateway. HORIZ: 1 p. Campanile of Merida Cathedral.

173 "Mother Earth"
175 Hidalgo Monument

1942. 2nd Inter-American Agricultural Conference.
688 **173** 2 c. brown (postage) 40 20
689 – 5 c. blue 1·90 55
690 – 10 c. orange 60 25
691 – 20 c. green (air) 1·25 25
692 – 40 c. brown 75 25
693 – 1 p. violet 1·60 1·25
DESIGNS: 5 c. Sowing wheat; 10 c. Western Hemisphere carrying torch; 20 c. Corn; 40 c. Coffee; 1 p. Bananas.

1942. 400th Anniv of Guadalajara.
694 **175** 2 c. brown & bl (postage) 15 15
695 – 5 c. red and black 60 25
696 – 10 c. blue and red 60 20
697 – 20 c. black and green (air) 80 35
698 – 40 c. green and olive 1·10 50
699 – 1 p. violet and brown 80 60
DESIGNS—VERT: 5 c. Government Palace; 10 c. Guadalajara. HORIZ: 20 c. St. Paul's Church, Zapopan; 40 c. Sanctuary of Our Lady of Guadalupe; 1 p. Arms of Guadalajara.

186 Saltillo Athenaeum, Coahuila

1942. 75th Anniv of Saltillo Athenaeum.
700 **186** 10 c. black 90 20

189 Birthplace of Allende

1943. 400th Anniv of San Miguel de Allende.
701 – 2 c. blue (postage) 50 15
702 – 5 c. brown 55 15
703 – 10 c. black 2·10 50
704 – 20 c. green (air) 45 30
705 **189** 40 c. purple 60 30
706 – 1 p. red 1·75 1·60
DESIGNS—VERT: 2 c. Cupola de las Monjas; 5 c. Gothic Church; 10 c. Gen. de Allende. HORIZ: 20 c. San Miguel de Allende; 1 p. Church seen through cloisters.

190 "Liberty"
192 Dr. de Castorena
194 "Flight"

1944.
707 **190** 12 c. brown 20 10

1944. 3rd National Book Fair.
732 **192** 12 c. brown (postage) 40 10
733 – 25 c. green (air) 45 10
DESIGN: 25 c. Microphone, book and camera.

1944. Air.
734 **194** 25 c. brown 30 10

195 Hands clasping Globe

1945. Inter-American Conference.
735 **195** 12 c. red (postage) 25 10
736 1 p. green 45 10
737 5 p. brown 3·50 2·75
738 10 p. black 6·25 5·00
739 25 c. orange (air) 10 10
740 1 p. green 15 10
741 5 p. blue 1·25 1·10
742 10 p. red 3·50 2·75
743 20 p. blue 7·25 7·00

196 La Paz Theatre, San Luis Potosi

1945. Reconstruction of La Paz Theatre, San Luis Potosi.
744 **196** 12 c. pur & blk (postage) 20 10
745 1 p. blue and black 30 10
746 5 p. red and black 3·50 3·25
747 10 p. green and black 7·75 7·50
748 30 c. green (air) 10 10
749 1 p. purple and green 15 10
750 5 p. black and green 1·40 1·25
751 10 p. blue and green 2·75 2·10
752 20 p. green and black 6·00 5·25

197 Fountain of Diana the Huntress
198 Removing Bandage

1945.
753 **197** 3 c. violet 40 10

1945. Literacy Campaign.
754 **198** 2 c. blue (postage) 15 10
755 6 c. orange 20 10
756 12 c. blue 20 10
757 1 p. olive 25 10
758 5 p. red and black 2·10 1·90
759 10 p. green and blue 12·50 12·50
760 30 c. green (air) 10 10
761 1 p. red 15 10
762 5 p. blue 1·60 1·40
763 10 p. red 2·75 2·75
764 20 p. brown and green 13·00 12·50

199 Founder of National Post Office
200 O.N.U., Olive Branch and Globe

201 O.N.U. and Flags of United Nations

1946. Foundation of Posts in Mexico in 1580.
765 **199** 8 c. black 60 10

1946. United Nations.
766 **200** 2 c. olive (postage) 15 10
767 6 c. brown 15 10
768 12 c. blue 10 10
769 1 p. green 30 10
770 5 p. red 3·25 3·25
771 10 p. blue 14·00 12·50
772 **201** 3 c. brown (air) 10 10
773 1 p. grey 10 10
774 5 p. green and brown 70 50
775 10 p. brown and sepia 2·75 2·00
776 20 p. red and slate 6·00 4·75

202 Zacatecas City Arms
205 Don Genaro Codina and Zacatecas

1946. 400th Anniv of Zacatecas.
777 **202** 2 c. olive (postage) 25 10
778 – 12 c. blue 15 10
779 – 1 p. mauve 30 10
780 – 5 p. red 3·50 1·90
781 – 10 p. black and blue 19·00 6·25
DESIGNS: 1 p. Statue of Gen. Ortega; 5 p. R. L. Velarde (poet); 10 p. F. G. Salinas.
782 – 30 c. grey (air) 10 10
783 **205** 1 p. green and brown 15 10
784 – 5 p. green and red 1·60 1·60
785 – 10 p. brown and green 5·50 2·75
PORTRAITS: 30 c. Fr. Margil de Jesus; 5 p. Gen. Enrique Estrada; 10 p. D. Fernando Villalpando.

207 Learning Vowels
208 Postman

1946. Education Plan.
786 **207** 1 c. sepia 20 10

1947.
787 **208** 15 c. blue 15 10

209 Roosevelt and First Mexican Stamp
210 10 c. U.S.A. 1847 and Mexican Eagle

1947. U.S.A. Postage Stamp Centenary.
788 **209** 10 c. brown (postage) 80 60
789 – 15 c. green 10 10
790 – 25 c. blue (air) 35 20
791 **210** 30 c. black 25 10
792 – 1 p. blue and red 50 15
DESIGNS: 15 c. as Type **209** but vert, 25 c., 1 p. as Type **210** but horiz.

213 Justo Sierra
214 Ministry of Communications

212 Douglas DC-4

1947.
795 **213** 10 p. green and brown (postage) 55·00 9·50
796 **214** 20 p. mauve and green 80 1·25
793 – 10 p. red and brown (air) 75 80
794 **212** 20 p. red and blue 1·50 1·25
DESIGN—HORIZ: 10 p. E. Carranza.

215 Manuel Rincon 217 Vicente Suarez

1947. Battle Centenaries. Portraits of "Child Heroes" etc. Inscr "1er CENTENARIO CHAPULTEPEC ("CHURUBUSCO" or "MOLINO DEL REY") 1847 1947".

797 – 2 c. black (postage) . . . 30 10
798 – 5 c. red 15 10
799 – 10 c. brown 15 10
800 – 15 c. green 15 10
801 **215** 30 c. olive 20 10
802 – 1 p. blue 30 15
803 – 5 p. red and blue . . . . 1·25 1·25

DESIGNS—VERT: 2 c. Francisco Marquez; 5 c. Fernando Montes de Oca; 10 c. Juan Escutin; 15 c. Agustin Melgar; 1 p. Lucas Balderas; 5 p. Flag of San Blas Battalion.

804 **217** 25 c. violet (air) 15 10
805 – 30 c. blue 15 10
806 – 50 c. green 25 10
807 – 1 p. violet 30 10
808 – 5 p. brown and blue . . . 80 80

DESIGNS—HORIZ: 30 c. Juan de la Barrera; 50 c. Military Academy; 1 p. Pedro Maria Anaya; 5 p. Antonio de Leon.

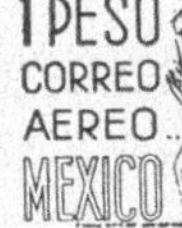

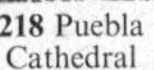

218 Puebla Cathedral 221 Dance of the Half Moons, Puebla

1950. (a) Postage. As T **218**.

835 – 3 c. blue 15 10
874 – 5 c. brown 25 10
875 – 10 c. green . . . . . . 1·50 10
876 – 15 c. green 20 10
877e **218** 20 c. blue 30 10
840 – 30 c. red 25 10
879 – 30 c. brown 35 10
880b – 40 c. orange 95 10
1346b – 50 c. blue 10 10
1327b – 80 c. green 35 10
843 – 1 p. brown . . . . . . 2·75 10
1346f – 1 p. green 10 10
1011ab – 1 p. grey 30 10
1327d – 3 p. red 55 10
1012a – 5 p. blue and green . . 1·10 60
1013ab – 10 p. black and blue . . 2·50 1·25
846 – 20 p. violet and green . . 6·25 6·25
1014a – 20 p. violet and black . . 5·00 2·50
1327e – 50 p. orange and green . 6·25 4·75

DESIGNS: 3 c, 3 p. La Purisima Church, Monterrey; 5 c. Modern building, Mexico City; 10 c. Convent of the Nativity, Tepoztlan; 15 c, 50 p. Benito Juarez; 30 c., 80 c. Indian dancer, Michoacan; 40 c. Sculpture, Tabasco; 50 c. Carved head, Veracruz; 1 p. Actopan Convent and carved head; 5 p. Galleon, Campeche; 10 p. Francisco Madero; 20 p. Modern building, Mexico City.

(b) Air. As T **221**.

897 – 5 c. blue 15 10
898 – 10 c. brown 85 15
899a – 20 c. red 35 10
850 – 25 c. brown 60 10
851 – 30 c. olive 15 10
852 – 35 c. violet . . . . . . 1·25 10
1327f – 40 c. blue 10 10
904c – 50 c. green 35 10
1056 – 80 c. red 60 70
906a **221** 1 p. grey 45 10
1327h – 1 p. 60 red 60 10
1327i – 1 p. 90 red 35 10
907a – 2 p. brown . . . . . . 6·25 25
908 – 2 p. 25 purple 60 45
1327j – 4 p. 30 blue 45 10
1017a – 5 p. orange and brown . . 2·75 35
1327k – 5 p. 20 lilac 70 25
1327l – 5 p. 60 green . . . . . 1·40 30
895 – 10 p. blue and black . . 3·00 60
1019a – 20 p. blue and red . . . 4·50 4·75

DESIGNS: 5 c., 1 p. 90 Bay of Acapulco; 10 c., 4 p. 30, Dance of the Plumes, Oaxaca; 20 c. Mayan frescoes, Chiapas; 25 c., 2 p. 25, 5 p. 60, Masks, Michoacan; 30 c. Cuauhtemoc; 35 c., 2 p., 5 p. 20, Taxco, Guerrero; 40 c. Sculpture, San Luis Potosi; 50 c., 1 p. 60, Ancient carvings, Chiapas; 80 c. University City, Mexico City; 5 p. Architecture, Queretaro; 10 p. Hidalgo; 20 p. National Music Conservatoire, Mexico City.

222 Arterial Road 224 Train and Map

1950. Opening of Mexican Section of Pan-American Highway. Inscr "CARRETERA INTER-NACIONAL 1950".

860 – 15 c. violet (postage) . . 30 10
861 **222** 20 c. blue 20 10
862 – 25 c. pink (air) . . . . . 1·60 20
863 – 35 c. green 10 10

DESIGNS—HORIZ: 15 c. Bridge; 25 c. Pres. M. Aleman, bridge and map; 35 c. B. Juarez and map.

1950. Inauguration of Mexico–Yucatan Rly.

864 – 15 c. purple (postage) . . 80 10
865 **224** 20 c. red 25 10
866 – 25 c. green (air) 25 10
867 – 35 c. blue 40 30

DESIGNS—VERT: 15 c. Rail-laying. HORIZ: 25 c. Diesel trains; 35 c. M. Aleman and suspension bridge.

227 Hands and Globe

1950. 75th Anniv of U.P.U.

868 – 50 c. violet (postage) . . 25 10
869 – 25 c. red (air) 35 10
870 **227** 80 c. blue 30 20

DESIGNS—HORIZ: 25 c. Aztec runner. VERT: 50 c. Letters "U.P.U.".

228 Miguel Hidalgo 229

1953. Birth Bicentenary of Hidalgo.

871 **228** 20 c. sepia & blue (postage) 1·10 10
872 – 25 c. lake and blue (air) . 35 10
873 **229** 35 c. green 35 10

DESIGN: As Type **229**: 25 c. Full face portrait.

231 Aztec Athlete 232 View and Mayan Bas-relief

1954. 7th Central American and Caribbean Games.

918 **231** 20 c. blue & pink (postage) 55 10
919 **232** 25 c. brown and green (air) 35 15
920 – 35 c. turquoise and purple 30 10

DESIGN: 35 c. Stadium.

233 234

1954. Mexican National Anthem Centenary.

921 **233** 5 c. lilac & blue (postage) 45 15
922 20 c. brown and purple . 55 10
923 1 p. green and red . . . 30 20
924 **234** 25 c. blue and lake (air) . 45 15
925 35 c. purple and blue . . 20 10
926 80 c. green and blue . . . 25 15

235 Torchbearer and Stadium 236 Aztec God and Map

1955. 2nd Pan-American Games, Mexico City. Inscr "II JUEGOS DEPORTIVOS PANAMER-ICANOS".

927 **235** 20 c. green & brn (postage) 40 10
928 **236** 25 c. blue and brown (air) 30 10
929 – 35 c. brown and red . . . 30 10

DESIGN: As Type **236**: 35 c. Stadium and map.

237 Olin Design

238 Feathered Serpent and Mask

1956. Mexican Stamp Centenary.

930 **237** 5 c. green & brn (postage) 30 10
931 – 10 c. blue and grey 30 10
932 – 30 c. purple and red . . . 20 10
933 – 50 c. brown and blue . . . 25 10
934 – 1 p. black and green . . . 35 10
935 – 5 p. sepia and bistre . . . 1·25 1·40

DESIGNS: As Type **237**: 10 c. Tohtli bird; 30 c. Zochitl flower; 50 c. Centli corn; 1 p. Mazatl deer; 5 p. Teheutli man's head.

937 **238** 5 c. black (air) 15 10
938 – 10 c. blue 15 10
939 – 50 c. purple 10 10
940 – 1 p. violet 15 10
941 – 1 p. 20 mauve 15 10
942 – 5 p. turquoise 50 50

DESIGNS: As Type **238**: 10 c. Bell tower, coach and Viceroy Enriquez de Almanza; 50 c. Morelos and cannon; 1 p. Mother, child and mounted horseman; 1 p. 20, Sombrero and spurs; 5 p. Emblems of food and education and pointing hand.

239 Stamp of 1856

1956. Centenary Int Philatelic Exn, Mexico City.

944 **239** 30 c. blue and brown . . . 45 15

240 F. Zarco 241 V. Gomez Farias and M. Ocampo

1956. Inscr "CONSTITUYENTE(S) DE 1857".

945 – 25 c. brown (postage) . . 35 10
946 – 45 c. blue 15 10
947 – 60 c. purple 15 10
1346d **240** 70 c. blue 20 10
1327c – 2 p. 30 blue 55 10
949 **241** 15 c. blue (air) 20 10
1327g – 60 c. green 15 15
950 – 1 p. 20 violet and green 35 15
951 **241** 2 p. 75 purple 50 30

PORTRAITS: As T **240** (postage): 25, 45 c., 2 p. 30, G. Prieto; 60 c. P. Arriagan. As T **41** (air): 60 c., 1 p. 20, L. Guzman and I. Ramirez.

242 Paricutin Volcano

1956. Air. 20th International Geological Congress.

952 **242** 50 c. violet 30 10

243 Map of Central America and the Caribbean

1956. Air. 4th Inter-American Congress of Caribbean Tourism.

953 **243** 25 c. blue and grey 20 10

244 Assembly of 1857 245 Mexican Eagle and Scales

1957. Centenary of 1857 Constitution.

958 – 30 c. gold & lake (postage) 35 10
959 **244** 1 p. green and sepia . . . 25 10
960 **245** 50 c. brown & green (air) 20 10
961 – 1 p. lilac and blue 30 15

DESIGNS—VERT: 30 c. Emblem of Constitution. HORIZ: 1 p. (Air), "Mexico" drafting the Constitution.

246 Globe, Weights and Dials

1957. Air. Centenary of Adoption of Metric System in Mexico.

962 **246** 50 c. black and silver . . 30 10

247 Train Disaster 248 Oil Derrick

1957. Air. 50th Anniv of Heroic Death of J. Garcia (engine driver) at Nacozari.

963 **247** 50 c. purple and red . . . 20 25

1958. 20th Anniv of Nationalization of Oil Industry.

964 **248** 30 c. black & bl (postage) 25 10
965 – 5 p. red and blue . . . . 2·50 2·50
966 – 50 c. green and black (air) 10 10
967 – 1 p. black and red 20 10

DESIGNS—HORIZ: 50 c. Oil storage tank and "AL SERVICIO DE LA PATRIA" ("At the service of the Fatherland"); 1 p. Oil refinery at night. VERT: 5 p. Map of Mexico and silhouette of oil refinery.

249 Angel, Independence Monument, Mexico City 250 U.N.E.S.C.O. Headquarters, Paris

1958. Air. 10th Anniv of Declaration of Human Rights.

968 **249** 50 c. blue 20 10

1959. Inauguration of U.N.E.S.C.O. Headquarters Building, Paris.

969 **250** 30 c. black and purple . . 30 10

251 U.N. Headquarters, New York 252 President Carranza

1959. U.N. Economic and Social Council Meeting, Mexico City.

970 **251** 30 c. blue and yellow . . 30 10

1960. "President Carranza Year" (1959) and his Birth Centenary.

971 **252** 30 c. pur & grn (postage) 20 10
972 – 50 c. violet & salmon (air) 20 10

DESIGN—HORIZ: 50 c. Inscription "Plan de Guadalupe Constitucion de 1917" and portrait as Type **252**.

253 Alexander von Humboldt (statue) 254 Alberto Braniff's Voisin "Boxkite" and Bristol Britannia

1960. Death Centenary of Alexander von Humboldt (naturalist).
973 **253** 40 c. green and brown . . 20 10

1960. Air. 50th Anniv of Mexican Aviation.
974 **254** 50 c. brown and violet . . 40 10
975 1 p. brown and green . . 40 15

255 Francisco I. Madero **257** Dolores Bell **259** Children at Desk, University and School Buildings

1960. Visit to Mexico of Members of Elmhurst Philatelic Society (American Society of Mexican Specialists). Inscr "HOMENAJE AL COLECCIONISTA".
976 **255** 10 p. sepia, green and purple (postage) . . . . 22·00 26·00
977 – 20 p. sepia, green and purple (air) . . . . 26·00 50·00
DESIGN: As No. 1019a 20 p. National Music Conservatoire inscr "MEX. D.F.".

1960. 150th Anniv of Independence.
978 **257** 30 c. red & grn (postage) 60 10
979 – 1 p. sepia and green . . . 25 10
980 – 5 p. blue and purple . . . 3·25 3·25
981 – 50 c. red and green (air) 15 10
982 – 1 p. 20 sepia and blue . . 20 10
983 – 5 p. sepia and green . . . 2·75 1·10
DESIGNS—VERT: No. 979, Independence Column; No. 980, Hidalgo, Dolores Bell and Mexican Eagle. HORIZ: No. 981, Mexican Flag; No. 982, Eagle breaking chain and bell tolling; No. 983, Dolores Church.

1960. 50th Anniv of Mexican Revolution.
984 – 10 c. multicoloured (postage) 30 10
985 – 15 c. brown and green . . 1·75 10
986 – 20 c. blue and brown . . 50 10
987 – 30 c. violet and sepia . . . 20 10
988 **259** 1 p. slate and purple . . . 25 10
989 – 5 p. grey and purple . . . 2·10 2·10
990 – 50 c. black and blue (air) 20 10
991 – 1 p. green and red 20 10
992 – 1 p. 20 sepia and green . . 20 10
993 – 5 p. lt blue, blue & mauve 1·25 45
DESIGNS: No. 984, Pastoral scene (35½ × 45½ mm). As Type **259** VERT: No. 985, Worker and hospital buildings; No. 986, Peasant, soldier and marine; No. 987, Power lines and pylons; No. 989, Coins, banknotes and bank entrance. HORIZ: No. 990, Douglas DC-8 airliner; No. 991, Riggers on oil derrick; No. 992, Main highway and map; No. 993, Barrage.

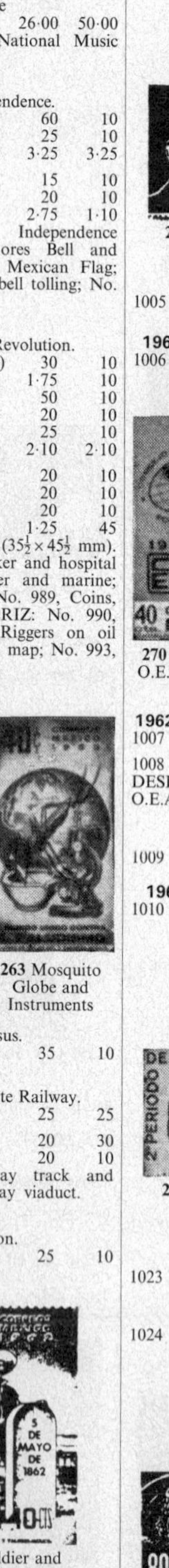

261 Count S. de Revillagigedo **262** Railway Tunnel **263** Mosquito Globe and Instruments

1960. Air. National Census.
994 **261** 60 c. black and lake . . . 35 10

1961. Opening of Chihuahua State Railway.
995 **262** 40 c. black & grn (postage) 25 25
996 – 60 c. blue and black (air) 20 30
997 – 70 c. black and blue . . . 20 10
DESIGNS—HORIZ: 60 c. Railway track and outline map of Mexico; 70 c. Railway viaduct.

1962. Malaria Eradication.
998 **263** 40 c. brown and blue . . 25 10

264 Pres. Goulart of Brazil **265** Soldier and Memorial Stone

1962. Visit of President of Brazil.
999 **264** 40 c. bistre 65 10

1962. Centenary of Battle of Puebla.
1000 **265** 40 c. sepia and green (postage) 25 10
1001 – 1 p. olive and green (air) 35 10
DESIGN—HORIZ: 1 p. Statue of Gen. Zaragoza.

266 Draughtsman and Surveyor **267** Plumb-line

1962. 25th Anniv of National Polytechnic Institute.
1002 **266** 40 c. turquoise and blue (postage) 65 10
1003 – 1 p. olive and blue (air) 35 10
DESIGN—HORIZ: 1 p. Scientist and laboratory assistant.

1962. Mental Health.
1004 **267** 20 c. blue and black . . 90 15

268 Pres. J. F. Kennedy **269** Tower and Cogwheels

1962. Air. Visit of U.S. President.
1005 **268** 80 c. blue and red . . . 75 15

1962. "Century 21" Exn ("World's Fair"), Seattle.
1006 **269** 40 c. black and green . . 35 10

270 Globe and O.E.A. Emblem **271** Pres. Alessandri of Chile **272** Balloon over Mexico City

1962. Inter-American Economic and Social Council.
1007 **270** 40 c. sepia & grey (post) 25 10
1008 – 1 p. 20 sepia & violet (air) 35 15
DESIGN—HORIZ: 1 p. 20, Globe, Scroll and O.E.A. emblem.

1962. Visit of President of Chile.
1009 **271** 20 c. brown 45 10

1962. Air. 1st Mexican Balloon Flight Centenary
1010 **272** 80 c. black and blue . . 90 25

273 "ALALC" Emblem **274** Pres. Betancourt of Venezuela

1963. Air. 2nd "ALALC" Session.
1023 **273** 80 c. purple and orange 65 20

1963. Visit of President of Venezuela.
1024 **274** 20 c. blue 35 10

275 Petroleum Refinery **276** Congress Emblem

1963. Air. 25th Anniv of Nationalization of Mexican Petroleum Industry.
1025 **275** 80 c. slate and orange . . 35 10

1963. 19th International Chamber of Commerce Congress, Mexico City.
1026 **276** 40 c. brown and black (postage) 45 10
1027 – 80 c. black and blue (air) 55 20
DESIGN—HORIZ: 80 c. World map and "C.I.C." emblem.

277 Campaign Emblem **278** Arms and Mountain **279** B. Dominguez

1963. Freedom from Hunger.
1028 **277** 40 c. red and blue 45 15

1963. 4th Centenary of Durango.
1029 **278** 20 c. brown and blue . . 45 15

1963. Birth Centenary of B. Dominguez (revolutionary).
1030 **279** 20 c. olive and green . . 45 15

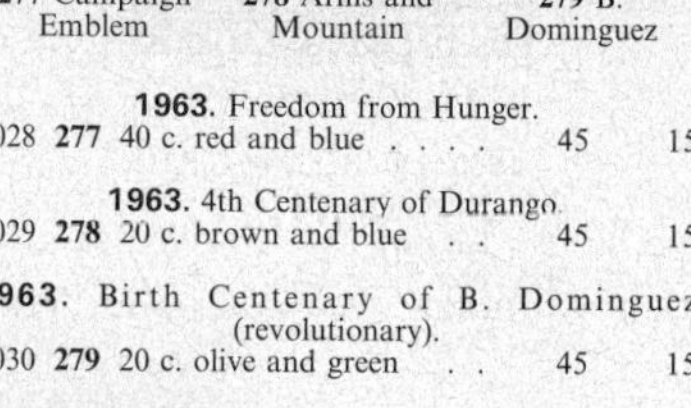

280 Exhibition Stamp of 1956 **281** Pres. Tito

1963. 77th American Philatelic Society Convention, Mexico City.
1031 **280** 1 p. brown & bl (postage) 60 45
1032 – 5 p. red (air) . . . . . . 1·40 75
DESIGN—HORIZ: 5 p. EXMEX "stamp" and "postmark".

1963. Air. Visit of President of Yugoslavia.
1033 **281** 2 p. green and violet . . 1·10 30

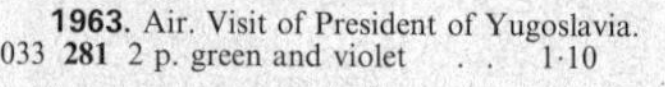

283 Part of U.I.A. Building **284** Red Cross on Tree **285** Pres. Estenssoro

1963. Air. International Architects' Day.
1034 **283** 80 c. grey and blue . . . 45 15

1963. Red Cross Centenary.
1035 **284** 20 c. red & grn (postage) 30 15
1036 – 80 c. red and green (air) . 70 25
DESIGN—HORIZ: 80 c. Red Cross on dove.

1963. Visit of President of Bolivia.
1037 **285** 40 c. purple and brown 45 15

286 Jose Morelos **287** Don Quixote as Skeleton

1963. 150th Anniv of First Anahuac Congress.
1038 **286** 40 c. bronze and green 40 15

1963. Air. 50th Death Anniv of Jose Posada (satirical artist).
1039 **287** 1 p. 20 black 75 20

288 University Arms **289** Diesel Train

1963. 90th Anniv of Sinaloa University.
1040 **288** 40 c. bistre and green . . 45 15

1963. 11th Pan-American Railways Congress, Mexico City.
1041 **289** 20 c. brn & blk (postage) 55 30
1042 – 1 p. 20 blue and violet (air) 50 20
DESIGN: 1 p. 20, Steam and diesel locomotives and horse-drawn tramcar.

290 "F.S.T.S.E." Emblem **291** Mrs. Roosevelt, Flame and U.N. Emblem

1964. 25th Anniv of Workers' Statute.
1075 **290** 20 c. sepia and orange . 30 10

1964. Air. 15th Anniv of Declaration of Human Rights.
1076 **291** 80 c. blue and orange . . 50 10

292 Pres. De Gaulle

1964. Air. Visit of President of France.
1077 **292** 2 p. blue and brown . . 1·25 35

293 Pres. Kennedy and Pres. A. Lopez Mateos

1964. Air. Ratification of Chamizal Treaty (1963).
1078 **293** 80 c. black and blue . . 55 15

294 Queen Juliana and Arms **295** Academy Emblem

1964. Air. Visit of Queen Juliana of the Netherlands.
1079 **294** 20 c. bistre and blue . . 70 15

1964. Centenary of National Academy of Medicine.
1080 **295** 20 c. gold and black . . 30 10

296 Lieut. Jose Azueto and Cadet Virgillo Uribe

1964. Air. 50th Anniv of Heroic Defence of Veracruz.
1081 **296** 40 c. green and brown . 30 10

297 Arms and World Map

1964. Air. International Bar Assn Conf, Mexico City.
1082 **297** 40 c. blue and brown . . 45 10

298 Colonel G. Mendez 299 Dr. Jose Rizal 300 Zacatecas

1964. Centenary of Battle of the Jahuactal Tabasco.
1083 **298** 40 c. olive and brown . . 35 10

1964. 400 Years of Mexican–Philippine Friendship. Inscr "1564 AMISTAD MEXICANO–FILIPINA 1964".
1084 **299** 20 c. blue & grn (postage) 35 10
1085 – 40 c. blue and violet . . 40 10
1086 – 80 c. blue & lt blue (air) 1·40 25
1087 – 2 p. 75 black and yellow 1·75 70
DESIGNS—As Type **299**: VERT: 40 c. Legaspi. HORIZ: 80 c. Galleon. LARGER (44×36 mm): 2 p. 75, Ancient map of Pacific Ocean.

1964. 50th Anniv of Conquest of Zacatecas.
1088 **300** 40 c. green and red . . . 40 10

301 Morelos Theatre, Aguascalientes 302 Andres Manuel del Rio

1965. 50th Anniv of Aguascalientes Convention.
1089 **301** 20 c. purple and grey . . 30 10

1965. Andres M. del Rio Commemoration.
1090 **302** 30 c. black 35 10

303 Netzahualcoyotl Dam 304 J. Morelos (statue)

1965. Air. Inauguration of Netzahualcoyotl Dam.
1091 **303** 80 c. slate and purple . . 30 10

1965. 150th Anniv (1964) of First Constitution.
1092 **304** 40 c. brown and green . 40 10

305 Microwave Tower 306 Fir Trees

1965. Air. Centenary of I.T.U.
1093 **305** 80 c. blue and indigo . . 40 20
1094 – 1 p. 20 green and black 45 20
DESIGN: 1 p. 20, Radio-electric station.

1965. Forest Conservation.
1095 **306** 20 c. green and blue . . 30 10
The inscription "!CUIDALOS!" means "CARE FOR THEM!".

307 I.C.Y. Emblem

1965. International Co-operation Year.
1096 **307** 40 c. brown and green . 25 10

308 Camp Fire and Tent

1965. Air. World Scout Conference, Mexico City.
1097 **308** 30 c. ultramarine & blue 40 20

309 King Baudouin and Queen Fabiola

1965. Air. Visit of Belgian King and Queen.
1098 **309** 2 p. blue and green . . 75 20

310 Mexican Antiquities and Unisphere 311 Dante (after R. Sanzio)

1965. Air. New York World's Fair.
1099 **310** 80 c. green and yellow . 30 15

1965. Air. Dante's 700th Birth Anniv.
1100 **311** 2 p. red . . . . 1·00 55

312 Sling-thrower 313 Jose M. Morelos y Pavon (leader of independence movement)

1965. Olympic Games (1968) Propaganda (1st series). Museum pieces.
1101 **312** 20 c. blue & olive (postage) 45 10
1102 – 40 c. sepia and red . . . 15 10
1103 – 80 c. slate and red (air) 35 10
1104 – 1 p. 20 indigo and blue 45 15
1105 – 2 p. brown and blue . . 35 10
DESIGNS—As Type **312**: VERT: 40 c. Batsman. HORIZ: 2 p. Ball game. HORIZ (36×20 mm): 80 c. Fieldsman. 1 p. 20, Scoreboard.

1965. 150th Anniv of Morelos's Execution.
1108 **313** 20 c. black and blue . . 30 10

314 Agricultural Produce 315 Ruben Dario

1966. Centenary of Agrarian Reform Law.
1109 **314** 20 c. red 30 10
1110 – 40 c. black 40 10
DESIGN: 40 c. Emilio Zapata, pioneer of agrarian reform.

1966. Air. 50th Death Anniv of Ruben Dario (Nicaraguan poet).
1111 **315** 1 p. 20 sepia 55 20

316 Father Andres de Urdaneta and Compass Rose 317 Flag and Postal Emblem

1966. Air. 400th Anniv of Father Andres de Urdaneta's Return from the Philippines.
1112 **316** 2 p. 75 black 85 45

1966. 9th Postal Union of Americas and Spain Congress (U.P.A.E.), Mexico City.
1113 **317** 40 c. blk & grn (postage) 35 10
1114 – 80 c. black & mauve (air) 30 15
1115 – 1 p. 20 black and blue . . 35 15
DESIGNS—VERT: 80 c. Flag and posthorn. HORIZ: 1 p. 20, U.P.A.E. emblem and flag.

318 Friar B. de Las Casas 319 E.S.I.M.E. Emblem and Diagram

1966. 400th Death Anniv of Friar Bartolome de Las Casas ("Apostle of the Indies").
1116 **318** 20 c. black on buff . . . 35 10

1966. 50th Anniv of Higher School of Mechanical and Electrical Engineering.
1117 **319** 20 c. green and grey . . . 30 10

320 U Thant and U.N. Emblem 321 "1966 Friendship Year"

1966. Air. U.N. Secretary-General U Thant's Visit to Mexico.
1118 **320** 80 c. black and blue . . . 30 15

1966. Air. "Year of Friendship" with Central American States.
1119 **321** 80 c. green and red . . . 25 10

322 F.A.O. Emblem 323 Running and Jumping

1966. International Rice Year.
1120 **322** 40 c. green 30 10

1966. Olympic Games (1968) Propaganda (2nd series).
1121 **323** 20 c. black & bl (postage) 55 10
1122 – 40 c. black and lake . . . 25 10
1124 – 80 c. black & brown (air) 35 10
1125 – 2 p. 25 black and green 55 25
1126 – 2 p. 75 black and violet 60 35
DESIGNS: 40 c. Wrestling. LARGER (57×20 mm): 80 c. Obstacle race; 2 p. 25, American football; 2 p. 75, Lighting Olympic flame.

324 U.N.E.S.C.O. Emblem

1966. Air. 20th Anniv of U.N.E.S.C.O.
1128 **324** 80 c. multicoloured . . . 30 10

325 Constitution of 1917 326 Earth and Satellite 327 Oil Refinery

1967. 50th Anniv of Mexican Constitution.
1129 **325** 40 c. black (postage) . . 45 10
1130 – 80 c. brown & ochre (air) 35 10
DESIGN: 80 c. President V. Carranza.

1967. Air. World Meteorological Day.
1131 **326** 80 c. blue and black . . . 30 20

1967. 7th World Petroleum Congress, Mexico City.
1132 **327** 40 c. black and blue . . 30 10

328 Nayarit Indian 329 Degollado Theatre

1967. 50th Anniv of Nayarit State.
1133 **328** 20 c. black and green . . 30 10

1967. Cent. of Degollado Theatre, Guadalajara.
1134 **329** 40 c. brown and mauve 10 10

330 Mexican Eagle and Crown 331 School Emblem

1967. Centenary of Triumph over the Empire.
1135 **330** 20 c. black and ochre . . 30 10

1967. Air. 50th Anniv of Military Medical School.
1136 **331** 80 c. green and yellow . 35 15

332 Capt. H. Ruiz Gavino 333 Marco Polo

1967. Air. 50th Anniv of 1st Mexican Airmail Flight. Pachuca–Mexico City.
1137 **332** 80 c. brown and black . 30 10
1138 – 2 p. brown and black . 70 20
DESIGN—HORIZ: 2 p. De Havilland D.H.6A biplane.

1967. Air. International Tourist Year.
1139 **333** 80 c. red and black . . . 20 10

334 Canoeing 335 A. del Valle-Arizpe (writer)

1967. Olympic Games (1968) Propaganda (3rd series).
1140 **334** 20 c. black & bl (postage) 20 10
1141 – 40 c. black and red . . 15 10
1142 – 50 c. black and green . . 15 10
1143 – 80 c. black and violet . . 25 10
1144 – 2 p. black and orange . 40 15
1146 – 80 c. black & mauve (air) 15 10
1147 – 1 p. 20 black and green 15 10
1148 – 2 p. black and lemon . . 60 20
1149 – 5 p. black and yellow . . 1·00 35
DESIGNS: 40 c. Basketball; 50 c. Hockey; 80 c. (No. 1143), Cycling; 80 c. (No. 1146), Diving; 1 p. 20, Running; 2 p. (No. 1144), Fencing; 2 p. (No. 1148), Weightlifting; 5 p. Football.

1967. Centenary of Fuente Athenaeum, Saltillo.
1151 **335** 20 c. slate and brown . . 30 10

336 Hertz and Clark Maxwell 337 P. Moreno

1967. Air. International Telecommunications Plan Conference, Mexico City.
1152 **336** 80 c. green and black . . 30 10

1967. 150th Death Anniv of Pedro Moreno (revolutionary).
1153 **337** 40 c. black and blue . . 30 15

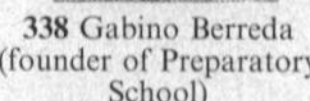

338 Gabino Berreda (founder of Preparatory School)
339 Exhibition Emblem

1968. Centenary of National Preparatory and Engineering Schools.
1154 **338** 40 c. red and blue . . . 35 10
1155 – 40 c. blue and black . . . 35 10
DESIGN: No. 1155, Staircase, Palace of Mining.

1968. Air. "Efimex '68" International Stamp Exn, Mexico City.
1156 **339** 80 c. green and black . . 25 30
1157 2 p. red and black . . . 25 30
The emblem reproduces the "Hidalgo" Official stamp design of 1884.

1968. Olympic Games (1968) Propaganda (4th series). Designs as T **334**, but inscr "1968".
1158 20 c. black & olive (postage) 25 10
1159 40 c. black and purple . . . 25 10
1160 50 c. black and green . . . 25 10
1161 80 c. black and mauve . . . 25 10
1162 1 p. black and brown . . . 1·50 25
1163 2 p. black and grey . . . . 1·75 95
1165 80 c. black and blue (air) . . 30 10
1166 1 p. black and turquoise . . 35 15
1167 2 p. black and yellow . . . 35 20
1168 5 p. black and brown . . . 80 70
DESIGNS: 20 c. Wrestling; 40 c. Various sports; 50 c. Water-polo; 80 c. (No. 1161), Gymnastics; 80 c. (No. 1165), Yachting; 1 p. (No. 1162), Boxing; 1 p. (No. 1166), Rowing; 2 p. (No. 1163), Pistol-shooting; 2 p. (No. 1167), Volleyball; 5 p. Horse-racing.

340 Dr. Martin Luther King

1968. Air. Martin Luther King Commemorative.
1170 **340** 80 c. black and grey . . 35 15

341 Olympic Flame **342** Emblems of Games

1968. Olympic Games, Mexico. (i) Inaug Issue.
1171 **341** 10 p. multicoloured . . . 2·00 1·25

(ii) Games Issue. Multicoloured designs as T **341**. (20, 40, 50 c. postage and 80 c., 1, 2 p. air) or as T **342** (others).
1172 20 c. Dove of Peace on map (postage) 25 10
1173 40 c. Stadium 30 10
1174 50 c. Telecommunications Tower, Mexico City . . . 30 10
1175 2 p. Palace of Sport, Mexico City 55 25
1176 5 p. Cultural symbols of Games 1·50 80
1178 80 c. Dove and Olympic rings (air) 15 10
1179 1 p. "The Discus-thrower" . 15 10
1180 2 p. Olympic medals 45 25
1181 5 p. Type **342** . . . . . . 1·75 85
1182 10 p. Line-pattern based on "Mexico 68" & rings . . . 1·50 95

343 Arms of Vera Cruz
344 "Father Palou" (M. Guerrero)

1969. 450th Anniv of Vera Cruz.
1185 **343** 40 c. multicoloured . . 30 10

1969. Air. 220th Anniv of Arrival in Mexico of Father Serra (coloniser of California).
1186 **344** 80 c. multicoloured . . 35 10
It was intended to depict Father Serra in this design, but the wrong detail of the painting by Guerrero, which showed both priests, was used.

345 Football and Spectators

1969. Air. World Cup Football Championship (1st issue). Multicoloured.
1187 80 c. Type **345** 25 10
1188 2 p. Foot kicking ball . . . 35 10
See also Nos. 1209/10.

346 Underground Train

1969. Inauguration of Mexico City Underground Railway System.
1189 **346** 40 c. multicoloured . . 20 10

347 Mahatma Gandhi **348** Footprint on Moon

1969. Air. Birth Centenary of Mahatma Gandhi.
1190 **347** 80 c. multicoloured . . 30 10

1969. Air. 1st Man on the Moon.
1191 **348** 2 p. black 30 25

349 Bee and Honeycomb
350 "Flying" Dancers and Los Nichos Pyramid, El Tajin

1969. 50th Anniv of I.L.O.
1192 **349** 40 c. brown, blue & yell 20 10

1969. Tourism (1st series). Multicoloured.
1193 40 c. Type **350** 25 10
1193a 40 c. Puerto Vallarta, Jalisco (vert) 25 10
1194 80 c. Acapulco (air) 60 15
1195 80 c. Pyramid, Teotihuacan 60 15
1196 80 c. "El Caracol" (Maya ruin), Yucatan 60 15
See also Nos. 1200/2 and 1274/7.

351 Red Crosses and Sun
352 "General Allende" (D. Rivera)

1969. Air. 50th Anniv of League of Red Cross Societies.
1197 **351** 80 c. multicoloured . . . 30 10

1969. Birth Bicent of General Ignacio Allende ("Father of Mexican Independence").
1198 **352** 40 c. multicoloured . . . 20 10

353 Dish Aerial **354** Question Marks

1969. Air. Inauguration of Satellite Communications Station, Tulancingo.
1199 **353** 80 c. multicoloured . . . 35 10

1969. Tourism (2nd series). As T **350** but dated "1970". Multicoloured.
1200 40 c. Puebla Cathedral . . . 40 10
1201 40 c. Anthropological Museum, Mexico City 40 10
1202 40 c. Belaunzaran Street, Guanajuato 40 10

1970. 9th National and 5th Agricultural Census. Multicoloured.
1204 20 c. Type **354** 30 10
1205 40 c. Horse's head and agricultural symbols 25 10

355 Diagram of Human Eye

1970. 21st International Opthalmological Congress, Mexico City.
1206 **355** 40 c. multicoloured . . . 25 10

356 Cadet Ceremonial Helmet and Kepi **357** Jose Pino Suarez

1970. 50th Anniv of Military College Reorganization.
1207 **356** 40 c. multicoloured . . . 20 10

1970. Birth Centenary (1969) of Jose Maria Pino Suarez (statesman).
1208 **357** 40 c. multicoloured . . . 20 10

358 Football and Masks **360** Composition by Beethoven

1970. Air. World Cup Football Championship (2nd issue). Multicoloured.
1209 80 c. Type **358** 30 15
1210 2 p. Football and Mexican idols 25 25

1970. Air. Birth Bicentenary of Beethoven.
1212 **360** 2 p. multicoloured . . . 50 25

361 Arms of Celaya **362** "General Assembly"

1970. 400th Anniv of Celaya.
1213 **361** 40 c. multicoloured . . . 20 10

1970. Air. 25th Anniv of U.N.O.
1214 **362** 80 c. multicoloured . . . 30 10

363 "Eclipse de Sol" **364** "Galileo" (Susterman)

1970. Total Eclipse of the Sun (7.3.70).
1215 **363** 40 c. black 20 10

1971. Air. Conquest of Space. Early Astronomers. Multicoloured.
1216 2 p. Type **364** 25 10
1217 2 p. "Kepler" (unknown artist) 25 10
1218 2 p. "Sir Isaac Newton" (Kneller) 25 10

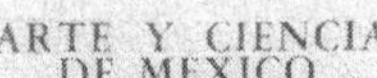

365 "Sister Juana" (M. Cabrera)

1971. Air. Mexican Arts and Sciences (1st series). Paintings. Multicoloured.
1219 80 c. Type **365** 40 15
1220 80 c. "El Paricutin" (volcano) (G. Murillo) 40 15
1221 80 c. "Men of Flames" (J. C. Orozco) 40 15
1222 80 c. "Self-portrait" (J. M. Velasco) 40 15
1223 80 c. "Mayan Warriors" ("Dresden Codex") 40 15
See also Nos. 1243/7, 1284/8, 1323/7, 1351/5, 1390/4, 1417/21, 1523/7, 1540/4, 1650/4, 1688/92, 1834 and 1845.

366 Stamps from Venezuela, Mexico and Colombia

1971. Air. "Philately for Peace". Latin-American Stamp Exhibitions 1968–70.
1224 **366** 80 c. multicoloured . . . 35 15

367 Lottery Balls

1971. Bicentenary of National Lottery.
1225 **367** 40 c. black and green . . 25 10

368 "Francisco Clavijero" (P. Carlin)

1971. Air. Return of the Remains of Francisco Javier Clavijero (historian) to Mexico (1970).
1226 **368** 2 p. brown and green . . 50 25

369 Vasco de Quiroga and "Utopia" (O'Gorman)
370 "Amado Nervo" (artist unknown)

1971. 500th Birth Anniv of Vasco de Quiroga, Archbishop of Michoacan.
1227 **369** 40 c. multicoloured . . . 20 10

1971. Birth Centenary of Amado Nervo (writer).
1228 **370** 80 c. multicoloured . . . 20 10

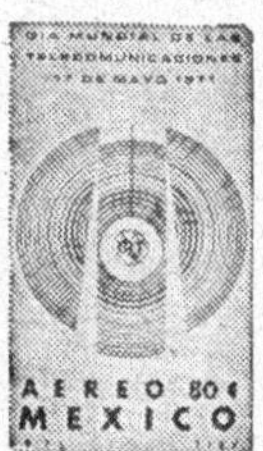
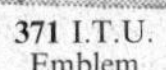

371 I.T.U. Emblem

372 "Mariano Matamoros" (D. Rivera)

1971. Air. World Telecommunications Day.
1229 **371** 80 c. multicoloured . . . 25 10

1971. Air. Birth Bicentenary of Mariano Matamoros (patriot).
1230 **372** 2 p. multicoloured . . . 45 25

373 "General Guerrero" (O'Gorman)

374 Loudspeaker and Sound Waves

1971. Air. 150th Anniv of Independence from Spain.
1231 **373** 2 p. multicoloured . . . 45 25

1971. 50th Anniv of Radio Broadcasting in Mexico.
1232 **374** 40 c. black, blue & green 25 10

375 Pres. Cardenas and Banners

376 Stamps of Venezuela, Mexico, Colombia and Peru

1971. 1st Death Anniv of General Lazaro Cardenas.
1233 **375** 40 c. black and lilac . . . 25 10

1971. Air. "EXFILIMA 71" Stamp Exhibition Lima, Peru.
1234 **376** 80 c. multicoloured . . . 45 15

377 Abstract of Circles

378 Piano Keyboard

1971. Air. 25th Anniv of U.N.E.S.C.O.
1235 **377** 80 c. multicoloured . . . 30 15

1971. 1st Death Anniv of Agustin Lara (composer).
1236 **378** 40 c. black, blue & yellow 30 10

379 "Mental Patients"

380 City Arms of Monterrey

1971. Air. 5th World Psychiatric Congress, Mexico City.
1237 **379** 2 p. multicoloured . . . 25 20

1971. 375th Anniv of Monterrey.
1238 **380** 40 c. multicoloured . . . 10 10

381 Durer's Bookplate

1971. Air. 500th Anniv of Albrecht Durer (artist).
1239 **381** 2 p. black and brown . 40 25

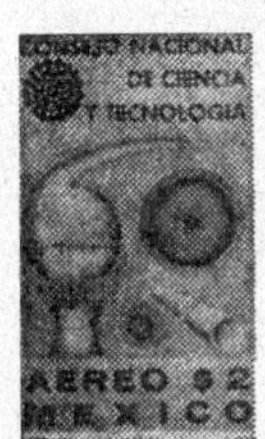

382 Scientific Symbols

383 Emblem of Mexican Cardiological Institute

1972. Air. 1st Anniv of National Council of Science and Technology.
1240 **382** 2 p. multicoloured . . . 20 10

1972. World Health Month. Multicoloured.
1241 40 c. Type **383** (postage) . . 10 10
1242 80 c. Heart specialists (air) 10 10

1972. Air. Mexican Arts and Sciences (2nd series). Portraits. As T **365**.
1243 80 c. brown and black . . . 75 15
1244 80 c. green and black . . . 75 15
1245 80 c. brown and black . . . 75 15
1246 80 c. blue and black 75 15
1247 80 c. red and black 75 15
PORTRAITS: Nos. 1243, King Netzahualcoyotl of Texcoco (patron of the arts); No. 1244, J. R. de Alarcon (lawyer); No. 1245, J. J. Fernandez de Lizardi (writer); No. 1246, E. G. Martinez (poet); No. 1247, R. L. Velardo (author).

384 Rotary Emblems

385 Indian Laurel and Fruit

1972. Air. 50th Anniv of Rotary Movement in Mexico.
1248 **384** 80 c. multicoloured . . 10 10

1972. Centenary of Chilpancingo as Capital of Guerrero State.
1249 **385** 40 c. black, gold & green 10 10

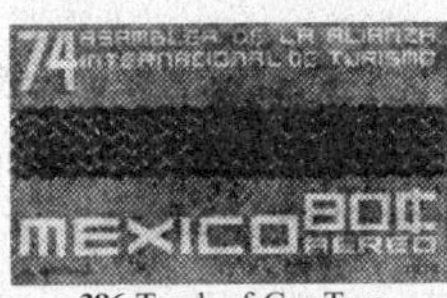

386 Track of Car Tyre

1972. Air. 74th Assembly of International Tourist Alliance, Mexico City.
1250 **386** 80 c. black and grey . . 10 10

387 First issue of "Gaceta De Mexico"

388 Emblem of Lions Organization

1972. 250th Anniv of Publication of "Gaceta De Mexico" (1st newspaper to be published in Latin America).
1251 **387** 40 c. multicoloured . . . 10 10

1972. Lions' Clubs Convention, Mexico City.
1252 **388** 40 c. multicoloured . . . 10 10

389 "Zaragoza" (cadet sail corvette)

390 "Margarita Maza de Juarez" (artist unknown)

1972. 75th Anniv of Naval Academy, Veracruz.
1253 **389** 40 c. multicoloured . . . 30 10

1972. Death Centenary of Pres. Benito Juarez.
1254 **390** 20 c. mult (postage) . . . 35 10
1255 – 40 c. multicoloured . . . 35 10
1256 – 80 c. black and blue (air) 10 10
1257 – 1 p. 20 multicoloured . . 15 10
1258 – 2 p. multicoloured . . . 20 10
DESIGNS: 40 c. "Benito Juarez" (D. Rivera); 80 c. Page of Civil Register with Juarez signature; 1 p. 20, "Benito Juarez" (P. Clave); 2 p. "Benito Juarez" (J. C. Orozco).

391 "Emperor Justinian I" (mosaic)

392 Atomic Emblem

1972. 50th Anniv of Mexican Bar Association.
1259 **391** 40 c. multicoloured . . . 55 10

1972. Air. 16th General Conference of Int Atomic Energy Organization, Mexico City.
1260 **392** 2 p. black, blue and grey 15 10

393 Caravel on "Stamp"

394 "Sobre las Olas" (sheet-music cover by O'Brandstetter)

1972. Stamp Day of the Americas.
1261 **393** 80 c. violet and brown . . 15 10

1972. Air. 28th International Authors' and Composers' Society Congress, Mexico City.
1262 **394** 80 c. brown 15 10

395 "Mother and Child" (G. Galvin)

1972. Air. 25th Anniv of U.N.I.C.E.F.
1263 **395** 80 c. multicoloured . . . 50 10

396 "Father Pedro de Gante" (Rodriguez y Arangorti)

397 Olympic Emblems

1972. Air. 400th Death Anniv of Father Pedro de Gante (founder of first school in Mexico).
1264 **396** 2 p. multicoloured . . . 25 10

1972. Olympic Games, Munich.
1265 **397** 40 c. multicoloured (postage) 10 10
1266 – 80 c. multicoloured (air) 15 10
1267 – 2 p. black, green and blue 25 10
DESIGNS—HORIZ: 80 c. "Football". VERT: 2 p. Similar to Type **397**.

398 Books on Shelves

400 "Footprints on the Americas"

399 Fish ("Pure Water")

1972. Int Book Year.
1268 **398** 40 c. multicoloured . . . 10 10

1972. Anti-Pollution Campaign.
1269 **399** 40 c. black & bl (postage) 10 10
1270 – 80 c. black and blue (air) 15 10
DESIGN–VERT: 80 c. Pigeon on cornice ("Pure Air").

1972. Air. Tourist Year of the Americas.
1271 **400** 80 c. multicoloured . . . 15 10

401 Stamps of Mexico, Colombia, Venezuela, Peru and Brazil

1973. Air. "EXFILBRA 72" Stamp Exhibition, Rio de Janeiro, Brazil.
1272 **401** 80 c. multicoloured . . . 15 10

402 "Metlac Viaduct" (J. M. Velasco)

1973. Centenary of Mexican Railways.
1273 **402** 40 c. multicoloured . . . 90 10

403 Ocotlan Abbey

1973. Tourism (3rd series). Multicoloured.
1274 40 c. Type **403** (postage) . . 20 10
1275 40 c. Indian hunting dance, Sonora (vert) 20 10
1276 80 c. Girl in local costume (vert) (air) 35 15
1277 80 c. Sport fishing, Lower California 35 10

404 "God of the Winds"

1973. Air. Centenary of W.M.O.
1278 **404** 80 c. black, blue & mauve 35 10

405 Copernicus

406 Cadet

1973. Air. 500th Birth Anniv of Copernicus (astronomer).
1279 **405** 80 c. green 15 10

1973. 150th Anniv of Military College.
1280 **406** 40 c. multicoloured 10 10

407 "Francisco Madero" (D. Rivera)

408 Antonio Narro (founder)

1973. Birth Centenary of Pres. Francisco Madero.
1281 **407** 40 c. multicoloured 10 10

1973. 50th Anniv of "Antonio Narro" Agricultural School, Saltillo.
1282 **408** 40 c. grey 10 10

409 San Martin Statue

410 Caryon Molecules

1973. Air. Argentina's Gift of San Martin Statue to Mexico City.
1283 **409** 80 c. multicoloured 15 10

1973. Air. "Mexican Arts and Sciences" (3rd series). Astronomers. As T **365** but dated "1973".
1284 80 c. green and red 10 10
1285 80 c. multicoloured 10 10
1286 80 c. multicoloured 10 10
1287 80 c. multicoloured 10 10
1288 80 c. multicoloured 10 10
DESIGNS: No. 1284, Aztec "Sun" stone; No. 1285, Carlos de Siguenza y Gongora; No. 1286, Francisco Diaz Covarrubias; No. 1287, Joaquin Gallo; No. 1288, Luis Enrique Erro.

1973. 25th Anniv of Chemical Engineering School.
1289 **410** 40 c. black, yellow & red 10 10

411 Fist with Pointing Finger

412 "EXMEX 73" Emblem

1974. Promotion of Exports.
1294 **411** 40 c. black and green 10 10

1974. "EXMEX 73" National Stamp Exhibition, Cuernavaca.
1295 **412** 40 c. black (postage) 10 10
1296 – 80 c. multicoloured (air) 15 10
DESIGN: 80 c. Cortes' Palace, Cuernavaca.

413 Manuel Ponce

1974. 25th Death Anniv (1973) of Manuel M. Ponce (composer).
1297 **413** 40 c. multicoloured 10 10

414 Gold Brooch, Mochica Culture

1974. Air. Exhibition of Peruvian Gold Treasures, Mexico City.
1298 **414** 80 c. multicoloured 15 10

415 C.E.P.A.L. Emblem and Flags

416 Baggage

1974. Air. 25th Anniv of U.N. Economic Commission for Latin America (C.E.P.A.L.).
1299 **415** 80 c. multicoloured 15 10

1974. Air. 16th Confederation of Latin American Tourist Organizations (C.O.T.A.L.) Convention, Acapulco.
1300 **416** 80 c. multicoloured 15 10

417 Silver Statuette

419 "Dancing Dogs" (Indian statuette)

418 "The Enamelled Saucepan" (Picasso)

1974. 1st International Silver Fair, Mexico City.
1301 **417** 40 c. multicoloured 10 10

1974. Air. 1st Death Anniv of Pablo Picasso (artist).
1302 **418** 80 c. multicoloured 15 10

1974. 6th Season of Dog Shows.
1303 **419** 40 c. multicoloured 10 10

420 Mariano Azuela

1974. Birth Cent (1973) of Mariano Azuela (writer).
1304 **420** 40 c. multicoloured 10 10

421 Tepotzotlan Viaduct

1974. National Engineers' Day.
1305 **421** 40 c. black and blue 55 15

422 R. Robles (surgeon)

1974. 25th Anniv of W.H.O.
1306 **422** 40 c. brown and green 10 10

423 U.P.U. Emblem

1974. "Exfilmex 74" Inter-American Stamp Exhibition, Mexico City.
1307 **423** 40 c. black and green on yellow (postage) 10 10
1308 80 c. black and brown on yellow (air) 15 10

424 Demosthenes

426 Map and Indian Head

425 Lincoln Standard Biplane

1974. 2nd Spanish-American Reading and Writing Studies Congress, Mexico City.
1309 **424** 20 c. green and brown 35 10

1974. Air. 50th Anniv of "Mexicana" (Mexican Airlines). Multicoloured.
1310 80 c. Type **425** 15 10
1311 2 p. Boeing 727-200 jetliner 40 10

1974. 150th Anniv of Union with Chiapas.
1312 **426** 20 c. green and brown 10 10

427 "Sonar Waves"

1974. Air. 1st International Electrical and Electronic Communications Congress, Mexico City.
1313 **427** 2 p. multicoloured 15 10

428 S. Lerdo de Tejada

429 Manuscript of Constitution

1974. Centenary of Restoration of Senate.
1314 **428** 40 c. black and blue 10 10

1974. 150th Anniv of Federal Republic.
1315 **429** 40 c. black and green 10 10

430 Ball in Play

1974. Air. 8th World Volleyball Championships, Mexico City.
1316 **430** 2 p. black, brown & orge 15 10

432 F. C. Puerto

433 Mask, Bat and Catcher's Glove

1974. Air. Birth Centenary of Felipe Carrillo Puerto (politician and journalist).
1318 **432** 80 c. brown and green 10 10

1974. Air. 50th Anniv of Mexican Baseball League.
1319 **433** 80 c. brown and green 10 10

434 U.P.U. Monument

1974. Centenary of U.P.U.
1320 **434** 40 c. brown and blue (postage) 10 10
1321 – 80 c. multicoloured (air) 10 10
1322 – 2 p. brown and green 20 10
DESIGNS: 80 c. Man's face as letter-box, Colonial period; 2 p. Heinrich von Stephan, founder of U.P.U.

1974. Air. Mexican Arts and Sciences (4th series). Music and Musicians. As T **365** but dated "1974". Multicoloured.
1323 80 c. "Musicians" – Mayan painting, Bonampak 15 10
1324 80 c. First Mexican-printed score, 1556 15 10
1325 80 c. Angela Peralta (soprano and composer) 15 10
1326 80 c. "Miguel Lerdo de Tejada" (composer) 15 10
1327 80 c. "Silvestre Revueltas" (composer) (bronze by Carlos Bracho) 15 10

435 I.W.Y. Emblem

436 Economic Charter

1975. Air. International Women's Year.
1328 **435** 1 p. 60 black and red . . 15 10

1975. Air. U.N. Declaration of Nations' Economic Rights and Duties.
1329 **436** 1 p. 60 multicoloured . . 15 10

437 Jose Maria Mora

439 Dr. M. Jimenez

438 Balsa Raft "Acali"

1975. 150th Anniv of Federal Republic.
1330 **437** 20 c. multicoloured . . . 10 10

1975. Air. Trans-Atlantic Voyage of "Acali". Canary Islands to Yucatan (1973).
1331 **438** 80 c. multicoloured . . . 30 10

1975. Air. 5th World Gastroenterological Congress.
1332 **439** 2 p. multicoloured 15 10

440 Aztec Merchants with Goods ("Codex Florentino")

1975. Centenary (1974) of Mexican Chamber of Commerce.
1333 **440** 80 c. multicoloured . . . 10 10

441 Miguel de Cervantes Saavedra (Spanish author)

443 Salvador Novo

442 4-reales Coin of 1675

1975. Air. 3rd International Cervantes Festival, Guanajuato.
1334 **441** 1 p. 60 red and black . . 15 10

1975. Air. International Numismatics Convention "Mexico 74".
1335 **442** 1 p. 60 bronze and blue 15 10

1975. Air. 1st Death Anniv of Salvador Novo (poet and writer).
1336 **443** 1 p. 60 multicoloured . . 15 10

444 "Self-portrait" (Siqueiros)

1975. Air. 1st Death Anniv of David Alfaro Siqueiros (painter).
1337 **444** 1 p. 60 multicoloured . 15 10

445 General Juan Aldama (detail from mural by Diego Rivera)

1975. Birth Bicentenary (1974) of General Aldama.
1338 **445** 80 c. multicoloured . . 10 10

446 U.N. and I.W.Y. Emblems

1975. Air. International Women's Year and World Conference.
1339 **446** 1 p. 60 blue and pink . 15 10

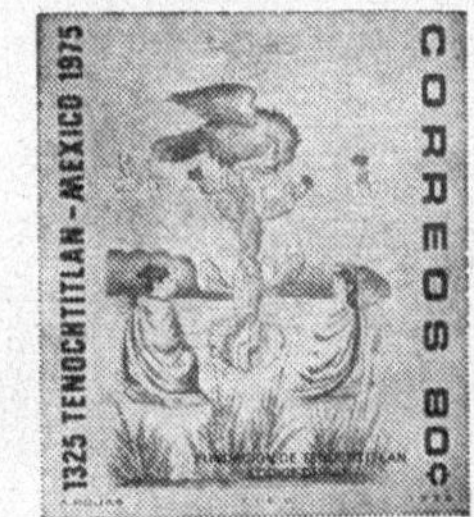

447 Eagle and Snake ("Codex Duran")

1975. 650th Anniv of Tenochtitlan (now Mexico City). Multicoloured.
1340 80 c. Type **447** (postage) . . 10 10
1341 1 p. 60 Arms of Mexico City (air) 15 10

448 Domingo F. Sarmiento (educator and statesman)

449 Teachers' Monument, Mexico City

1975. Air. 1st International Congress of "Third World" Educators, Acapulco.
1342 **448** 1 p. 60 green and brown 15 10

1975. Air. Mexican–Lebanese Friendship.
1343 **449** 4 p. 30 green and brown 25 10

450 Games' Emblem

1975. Air. 7th Pan-American Games, Mexico City.
1344 **450** 1 p. 60 multicoloured . 15 10

INDEX

Countries can be quickly located by referring to the index at the end of this volume.

451 Julian Carrillo (composer)

452 Academy Emblem

1975. Birth Centenary of J. Carrillo.
1345 **451** 80 c. brown and green . . 10 10

1975. Cent of Mexican Languages Academy.
1346 **452** 80 c. yellow and brown 10 10

453 University Building

1975. 50th Anniv of Guadalajara University.
1347 **453** 80 c. black, brown & pink 10 10

454 Dr. Atl

455 Road Builders

1975. Air. Atl (Gerardo Murillo-painter and writer). Birth Centenary.
1348 **454** 4 p. 30 multicoloured . . 25 10

1975. "50 Years of Road Construction" and 15th World Road Congress, Mexico City.
1349 **455** 80 c. black & green (post) 10 10
1350 – 1 p. 60 black & blue (air) 15 10
DESIGN: 1 p. 60, Congress emblem.

1975. Air. Mexican Arts and Sciences (5th series). As T **365**, but dated "1975". Multicoloured.
1351 1 p. 60 Title page, F. Hernandez' "History of New Spain" 15 10
1352 1 p. 60 A. L. Herrera (naturalist) 15 10
1353 1 p. 60 Page from "Badiano Codex" (Aztec herbal) . . . 15 10
1354 1 p. 60 A. Rosenblueth Stearns (neurophysiologist) 15 10
1355 1 p. 60 A. A. Duges (botanist and zoologist) 15 10

456 Car Engine Parts

457 Aguascalientes Cathedral

1975. Mexican Exports. Multicoloured.
1356 – 5 c. blue (postage) . . . 35 10
1471 – 20 c. black 35 10
1356b – 40 c. brown 30 10
1356c **456** 50 c. blue 35 10
1472 50 c. black 10 10
1473 – 80 c. red 10 10
1474 – 1 p. violet and yellow 10 10
1358a – 1 p. black and orange 10 10
1475 – 2 p. blue and turquoise 55 10
1476 – 3 p. brown 25 10
1359b – 4 p. red and brown . . 25 10
1359e – 5 p. brown 10 10
1359ed – 6 p. red 10 10
1359ee – 6 p. grey 10 10
1359f – 7 p. blue 10 10
1359g – 8 p. brown 10 10
1359h – 9 p. blue 10 10
1479 – 10 p. lt green and green 95 45
1360ac – 10 p. red 10 10
1360ad – 15 p. orange and brown 15 10
1360b – 20 p. black 15 10
1360bc – 20 p. black and red . . 10 10
1360be – 25 p. brown 25 10
1360bh – 35 p. yellow and mauve 25 10
1360bk – 40 p. yellow and brown 25 10
1360bl – 40 p. gold and green . 25 10
1360bm – 40 p. black 10 10
1360c – 50 p. multicoloured . . 1·25 35
1360d – 50 p. yellow and blue 35 20
1360da – 50 p. red and green . . 35 20
1360db – 60 p. brown 30 15
1360dc – 70 p. brown 35 20
1360de – 80 p. gold and mauve 20 50
1360df – 80 p. blue 80 50
1360dg – 90 p. blue and green . 1·25 55
1360e – 100 p. red, green and grey 70 35
1360ea – 100 p. brown 10 10
1360f – 200 p. yellow, green and grey . . . . 1·90 30
1360fb – 200 p. yellow and green 10 10
1360g – 300 p. blue, red and grey 60 60
1360gb – 300 p. blue and red . . 15 10
1360h – 400 p. bistre, brown and grey 95 35
1360hb – 450 p. brown & mauve 20 10
1360i – 500 p. green, orange and grey . . . . 1·90 30
1360ib – 500 p. grey and blue . 20 10
1360j – 600 p. multicoloured . 30 10
1360k – 700 p. black, red and green 35 10
1360kb – 750 p. black, red and green 30 10
1360l – 800 p. brown & dp brown 40 10
1360m **456** 900 p. black 50 10
1360n – 950 p. blue 40 20
1481a – 1000 p. black, red and grey 50 20
1360pa – 1000 p. red and black 40 8
1360q – 1100 p. grey 60 30
1360r – 1300 p. red, green and grey 60 30
1360rb – 1300 p. red and green 50 25
1360rg – 1400 p. black 50 20
1360s – 1500 p. brown 55 45
1360t – 1600 p. orange 65 30
1360u – 1700 p. green and deep green 70 30
1360w – 1900 p. blue and green 2·25 75
1481b – 2000 p. black and grey 1·25 50
1360xa – 2000 p. black 80 55
1360y – 2100 p. black, orange and grey 80 55
1360ya – 2100 p. black and red 80 55
1360yb – 2200 p. red 90 60
1360z – 2500 p. blue and grey 95 65
1360za – 2500 p. blue 95 65
1630zc – 2800 p. black . . . . 1·10 75
1481c – 3000 p. green, grey and orange . . . . . . 1·75 75
1360zf **456** 3600 p. black and grey 1·50 1·00
1360zg – 3900 p. grey and blue 1·60 1·10
1481d – 4000 p. yellow, grey and red . . . . 2·40 1·25
1360zj – 4800 p. red, green and grey . . . . 1·90 1·25
1481e – 5000 p. grey, green and orange . . . . . . 3·00 1·50
1360zn – 6000 p. green, yellow and grey . . . . 2·40 1·60
1360zq – 7200 p. multicoloured 3·00 2·00
1361 – 30 c. bronze (air) . . . 30 10
1482 – 50 c. green and brown 10 10
1361a – 80 c. blue 10 10
1483 – 1 p. 60 black & orange 10 10
1484 – 1 p. 90 red and green 15 10
1361d – 2 p. gold and blue . . 25 10
1485 – 2 p. 50 red and green 10 10
1361e – 4 p. yellow and brown 25 10
1361f – 4 p. 30 mauve & green 10 20
1361g – 5 p. blue and yellow . 95 20
1361h – 5 p. 20 black and red 25 25
1361i – 5 p. 60 green & yellow 10 30
1488 – 10 p. green and light green 55 40
1361j – 20 p. black, red and green 2·75 85
1361k – 50 p. multicoloured . . 1·60 95

DESIGNS—POSTAGE. 5 c., 6, 1600 p. Steel tubes; 20 c., 40 (1360bm), 1400, 2800 p. Laboratory flasks; 40 c., 100 p. (1360ea) Cup of coffee; 80 c., 10 (1360ac), 2200 p. Steer marked with beef cuts; 1, 3000 p. Electric cable; 2, 90, 1900 p. Abalone shell; 3, 60 p. Men's shoes; 4 p. Ceramic tiles; 5, 1100 p. Chemical formulae; 7, 8, 9, 80 (1360df), 2500 p. Textiles; 10 (1479), 1700 p. Tequila; 15 p. Honeycomb; 20 (1360b), 2000 p. Wrought iron; 20 (1360bc), 2100 p. Bicycles; 25, 70, 1500 p. Hammered copper vase; 35, 40 (1360bk/bl), 50 (1360d), 80 p. (1360de) Books; 50 (1360c), 600 p. Jewellery; 50 (1360da), 4800 p. Tomato; 100 (1360e), 1300 p. Strawberries; 200, 6000 p. Citrus fruit; 300 p. Motor vehicles; 400, 450 p. Printed circuit; 500 (1360i), 5000 p. Cotton boll; 500 (1360ib), 3900 p. Valves (petroleum) industry; 700, 750, 7200 p. Film; 800 p. Construction materials; 1000 p. Farm machinery; 4000 p. Bee and honeycomb. AIR. 30 c. Hammered copper vase; 50 c. Electronic components; 80 c. Textiles; 1 p. 60, Bicycles; 1 p. 90, Valves (petroleum) industry; 2 p. Books; 2 p. 50, Tomato; 4 p. Bee and honeycomb; 4 p. 30, Strawberry; 5 p. Motor vehicles; 5 p. 20, Farm machinery; 5 p. 60, Cotton boll; 10 p. Citrus fruit; 20 p. Film; 50 p. Cotton.

1975. 400th Anniv of Aguascalientes.
1362 **457** 50 c. black and green . . 35 10

458 J. T. Bodet

460 "Death of Cuautemoc" (Chavez Morado)

459 "Fresco" (J. C. Orozco)

1975. 1st Death Anniv of Jaime T. Bodet (author and late Director-General of U.N.E.S.C.O.).
1363 **458** 80 c. brown and blue . . 10 10

1975. 150th Anniv of Mexican Supreme Court of Justice.
1364 **459** 80 c. multicoloured 10 10

1975. 450th Death Anniv of Emperor Cuautemoc.
1365 **460** 80 c. multicoloured . . . 10 10

461 Allegory of Irrigation

1976. 50th Anniv of Nat Irrigation Commission.
1366 **461** 80 c. deep blue and blue 10 10

462 City Gateway

1976. 400th Anniv of Leon de los Aldamas, Guanajuato.
1367 **462** 80 c. yellow and purple 10 10

463 Early Telephone **464** Gold Coin

1976. Air. Telephone Centenary.
1368 **463** 1 p. 60 black and grey . 10 10

1976. Air. 4th Int Numismatics Convention.
1369 **464** 1 p. 60 gold, brown & blk 10 10

465 Tlaloc (Aztec god of rain) and Calles Dam

1976. Air. 12th Int Great Dams Congress.
1370 **465** 1 p. 60 purple and green 20 10

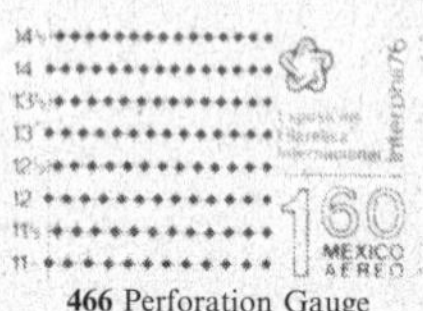

466 Perforation Gauge

1976. Air. "Interphil '76" International Stamp Exhibition, Philadelphia.
1371 **466** 1 p. 60 black, red & blue 20 10

467 Rainbow over Industrial Skyline **470** Liberty Bell

1976. Air. U.N. Conf on Human Settlements.
1372 **467** 1 p. 60 multicoloured . . 20 10

1976. Air. Bicentenary of American War of Independence.
1378 **470** 1 p. 60 blue and mauve 20 10

471 Forest Fire

1976. Fire Prevention Campaign.
1379 **471** 80 c. multicoloured 10 10

472 Peace Texts **473** Children on TV Screen

1976. Air. 30th International Asian and North American Science and Humanities Congress, Mexico City.
1380 **472** 1 p. 60 multicoloured . 15 10

1976. Air. 1st Latin-American Forum on Children's Television.
1381 **473** 1 p. 60 multicoloured . 20 10

474 Scout's Hat **475** Exhibition Emblem

1976. 50th Anniv of Mexican Boy Scout Movement.
1382 **474** 80 c. olive and brown . 10 10

1976. "Mexico Today and Tomorrow" Exhibition.
1383 **475** 80 c. black, red & turq . 10 10

476 New Buildings **477** Dr. R. Vertiz

1976. Inaug of New Military College Buildings.
1384 **476** 50 c. brown and ochre . 10 10

1976. Centenary of Opthalmological Hospital of Our Lady of the Light.
1385 **477** 80 c. brown and black . 10 10

478 Guadalupe Basilica

1976. Inauguration of Guadalupe Basilica.
1386 **478** 50 c. bistre and black . 10 10

479 "40" and Emblem

1976. 40th Anniv of National Polytechnic Institute.
1387 **479** 80 c. black, red and green 10 10

480 Blast Furnace

1976. Inauguration of Lazaro Cardenas Steel Mill, Las Truchas.
1388 **480** 50 c. multicoloured . . 10 10

481 Natural Elements

1976. Air. World Urbanisation Day.
1389 **481** 1 p. 60 multicoloured . . 10 10

1976. Air. Mexican Arts and Sciences (6th series). As T **365** but dated "1976". Multicoloured.
1390 1 p. 60 black and red 10 10
1391 1 p. 60 multicoloured 10 10
1392 1 p. 60 black and yellow . . . 10 10
1393 1 p. 60 multicoloured 10 10
1394 1 p. 60 brown and black . . . 10 10
DESIGNS: No. 1390, "The Signal" (Angela Gurria); No. 1391, "The God of Today" (L. Ortiz Monasterio); No. 1392, "The God Coatlicue" (traditional Mexican sculpture); No. 1393, "Tiahuicole" (Manuel Vilar); No. 1394, "The Horseman" (Manuel Tolsa).

482 Score of "El Pesebre"

1977. Air. Birth Centenary of Pablo Casals (cellist).
1395 **482** 4 p. 30 blue and brown 15 10

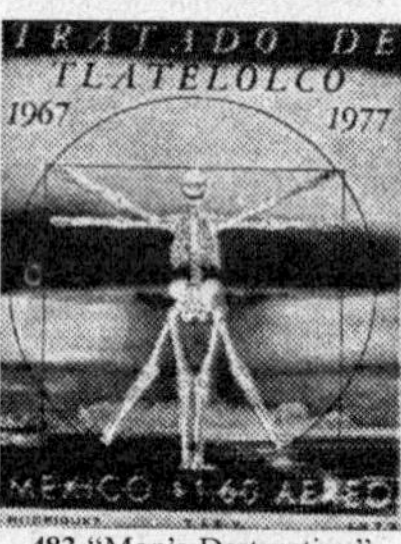

483 "Man's Destruction"

1977. Air. 10th Anniv of Treaty of Tlatelolco.
1396 **483** 1 p. 60 multicoloured . . 10 10

484 Saltillo Cathedral **485** Light Switch, Pylon and Engineers

1977. 400th Anniv of Founding of Saltillo.
1397 **484** 80 c. brown and yellow 10 10

1977. 40 years of Development in Mexico. Federal Electricity Commission.
1398 **485** 80 c. multicoloured . . . 10 10

486 Footballers

1977. Air. 50th Anniv of Mexican Football Federation.
1399 **486** 1 p. 60 multicoloured . . 10 10
1400 – 4 p. 30 yellow, blue & blk 15 10
DESIGN: 4 p. 30, Football emblem.

487 Hands and Scales

1977. Air. 50th Anniv of Federal Council of Reconciliation and Arbitration.
1401 **487** 1 p. 60 orange, brn & blk 10 10

MORE DETAILED LISTS
are given in the Stanley Gibbons Catalogues referred to in the country headings. For lists of current volumes see introduction

488 Flags of Spain and Mexico **489** Tlaloc (weather god)

1977. Resumption of Diplomatic Relations with Spain.
1402 **488** 50 c. multicoloured (postage) 10 10
1403 80 c. multicoloured . . . 10 10
1404 – 1 p. 60 black & grey (air) 10 10
1405 – 1 p. 90 red, grn & lt grn 10 10
1406 – 4 p. 30 grey, brown & grn 15 10
DESIGNS: 1 p. 60, Arms of Mexico and Spain; 1 p. 90, Maps of Mexico and Spain; 4 p. 30, President Jose Lopez Portillo and King Juan Carlos.

1977. Air. Centenary of Central Meterological Observatory.
1407 **489** 1 p. 60 multicoloured . . 10 10

490 Ludwig van Beethoven **491** A. Serdan

1977. Air. 150th Death Anniv of Beethoven.
1408 **490** 1 p. 60 green and brown 10 10
1409 4 p. 30 red and blue . . 15 10

1977. Birth Centenary of Aquiles Serdan (revolutionary martyr).
1410 **491** 80 c. black, turq & grn 10 10

492 Mexico City–Guernavaca Highway

1977. Air. 25th Anniv of First National Highway.
1411 **492** 1 p. 60 multicoloured . 10 10

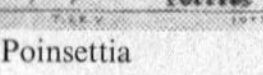

493 Poinsettia **494** Arms of Campeche

1977. Christmas.
1412 **493** 50 c. multicoloured . . . 10 10

1977. Air. Bicentenary of Naming of Campeche.
1413 **494** 1 p. 60 multicoloured . . 10 10

495 Tractor and Dam

1977. Air. U.N. Desertification Conference, Mexico City.
1414 **495** 1 p. 60 multicoloured . . 10 10

496 Congress Emblem

1977. Air. 20th World Education, Hygiene and Recreation Congress.
1415 **496** 1 p. 60 multicoloured . . 10 10

497 Freighter "Rio Yaqui" 498 Mayan Dancer

1977. Air. 60th Anniv of National Merchant Marine.
1416 **497** 1 p. 60 multicoloured . . 40 10

1977. Air. Mexican Arts and Sciences (7th series). Pre-colonial statuettes.
1417 **498** 1 p. 60 red, black & pink 10 10
1418 – 1 p. 60 blue, black and lt blue 10 10
1419 – 1 p. 60 grey, black and yellow 10 10
1420 – 1 p. 60 green, black and turquoise 10 10
1421 – 1 p. 60 red, black and grey 10 10
DESIGNS: No. 1418, Aztec god of dance; No. 1419, Snake dance; No. 1420, Dancer, Monte Alban; No. 1421, Dancer, Totonaca.

499 Hospital Scene

1978. Air. 35th Anniv of Mexican Social Insurance Institute. Multicoloured.
1422 1 p. 60 Type **499** 10 10
1423 4 p. 30 Workers drawing benefits 15 10

500 Moorish Fountain

1978. Air. 450th Anniv of Chiapa de Corzo, Chiapas.
1424 **500** 1 p. 60 multicoloured . . 10 10

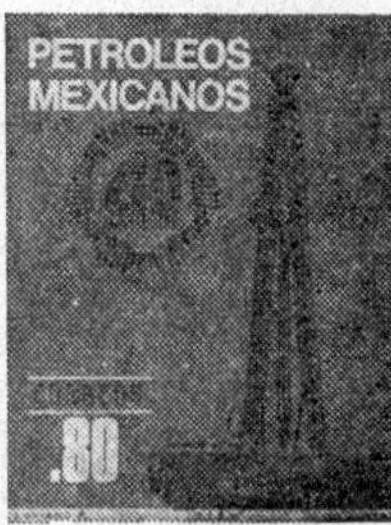

501 Telephones, 1878 and 1978 502 Oilwell

1978. Centenary of Mexican Telephone.
1425 **501** 80 c. red and salmon . . 10 10

1978. 40th Anniv of Nationalization of Oil Resources.
1426 **502** 80 c. red and salmon (postage) 10 10
1427 – 1 p. 60 blue and red (air) 10 10
1428 – 4 p. 30 black, light blue and blue 35 10
DESIGNS: 1 p. 60, General I. Cardenas (President, 1938); 4 p. 30, Oil rig, Gulf of Mexico.

INDEX

Countries can be quickly located by referring to the index at the end of this volume.

503 Arms of San Cristobal de las Casas

1978. Air. 450th Anniv of San Cristobal de las Casas, Chiapas.
1429 **503** 1 p. 60 purple, pink and black 10 10

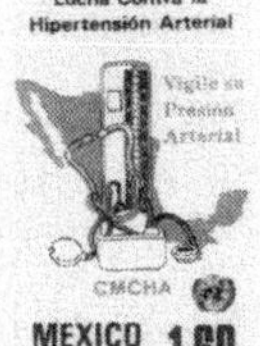

504 Fairchild FC-71 Mail Plane 506 Blood Pressure Gauge and Map of Mexico

505 Globe and Cogwheel

1978. Air. 50th Anniv of First Mexican Airmail Route.
1430 **504** 1 p. 60 multicoloured . 20 10
1431 4 p. 30 multicoloured . 30 10

1978. Air. World Conference on Technical Co-operation between Underdeveloped Countries. Multicoloured.
1432 1 p. 60 Type **505** 10 10
1433 4 p. 30 Globe and cogwheel joined by flags 15 10

1978. Air. World Hypertension Month and World Health Day.
1434 **506** 1 p. 60 blue and red . . 10 10
1435 – 4 p. 30 salmon and blue 15 10
DESIGN: 4 p. 30, Hand with stethoscope.

507 Kicking Ball 508 Francisco (Pancho) Villa

1978. Air. World Cup Football Championship, Argentina.
1436 **507** 1 p. 60 bl, lt orge & orge 10 10
1437 – 1 p. 90 blue, brn & orge 10 10
1438 – 4 p. 30 blue, grn & orge 15 10
DESIGNS: 1 p. 90, Saving a goal; 4 p. 30, Footballer.

1978. Air. Birth Centenary of Francisco Villa (revolutionary leader).
1439 **508** 1 p. 60 multicoloured . 10 10

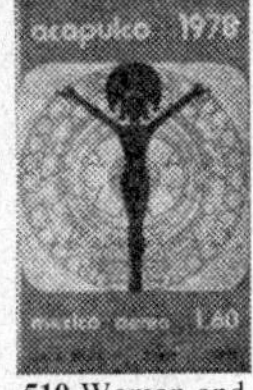

509 Emilio Carranza Stamp of 1929 510 Woman and Calendar Stone

1978. Air. 50th Anniv of Mexico–Washington Flight by Emilio Carranza.
1440 **509** 1 p. 60 red and brown . 10 10

1978. Air. Miss Universe Contest, Acapulco.
1441 **510** 1 p. 60 black, brn & red 10 10
1442 1 p. 90 black, brn & grn 10 10
1443 4 p. 30 black, brn & red 15 10

511 Alvaro Obregon (J. Romero)

1978. Air. 50th Death Anniv of Alvaro Obregon (statesman).
1444 **511** 1 p. 60 multicoloured . . 10 10

512 Institute Emblem

1978. 50th Anniv of Pan-American Institute for Geography and History.
1445 **512** 80 c. blue and black (postage) 10 10
1446 – 1 p. 60 green & blk (air) 10 10
1447 – 4 p. 30 brown and black 15 10
DESIGNS: 1 p. 60, 4 p. 30, Designs as Type **512**, showing emblem.

513 Sun rising over Ciudad Obregon 514 Mayan Statue, Rook and Pawn

1978. Air. 50th Anniv of Ciudad Obregon.
1448 **513** 1 p. 60 multicoloured . . 10 10

1978. Air. World Youth Team Chess Championship, Mexico City.
1449 **514** 1 p. 60 multicoloured . . 10 10
1450 4 p. 30 multicoloured . . 20 10

515 Aristotle 516 Mule Deer

1978. Air. 2300th Death Anniv of Aristotle.
1451 **515** 1 p. 60 grey, blue and yellow 10 10
1452 – 4 p. 30 grey, red and yellow 20 10
DESIGN: 4 p. 30, Statue of Aristotle.

1978. Air. World Youth Team Chess Championship, Mexico City.
1453 1 p. 60 Type **516** 20 10
1454 1 p. 60 Ocelot 20 10
See also Nos. 1548/9, 1591/2, 1638/9 and 1683/4.

517 Man's Head and Dove 518 "Dahlia coccinea". ("Dalia" on stamp)

1978. Air. International Anti-Apartheid Year.
1455 **517** 1 p. 60 grey, red and black 10 10
1456 – 4 p. 30 grey, lilac and black 15 10
DESIGN: 4 p. 30, Woman's head and dove.

1978. Mexican Flowers (1st series). Multicoloured.
1457 50 c. Type **518** 10 10
1458 80 c. "Plumeria rubra" . . . 10 10
See also Nos. 1550/1, 1593/4, 1645/6, 1681/2, 1791/2 and 1913/14.

519 Emblem 520 Dr. Rafael Lucio

1978. Air. 12th World Architects' Congress.
1459 **519** 1 p. 60 red, black and orange 10 10

1978. Air. 11th International Leprosy Congress.
1460 **520** 1 p. 60 green 10 10

521 Franz Schubert and "Death and the Maiden" 522 Decorations and Candles

1978. Air. 150th Death Anniv of Franz Schubert (composer).
1461 **521** 4 p. 30 brown, black and green 15 10

1978. Christmas. Multicoloured.
1462 50 c. Type **522** (postage) . . 10 10
1463 1 p. 60 Children and decoration (air) 10 10

523 Antonio Vivaldi 524 Wright Flyer III

1978. Air. 300th Birth Anniv of Antonio Vivaldi (composer).
1464 **523** 4 p. 30 red, stone and brown 15 10

1978. Air. 75th Anniv of First Powered Flight.
1465 **524** 1 p. 60 orge, yell & mve 15 10
1466 – 4 p. 30 yellow, red & flesh 30 10
DESIGN: 4 p. 30, Side view of Wright Flyer I.

525 Albert Einstein and Equation

1979. Air. Birth Centenary of Albert Einstein (physicist).
1467 **525** 1 p. 60 multicoloured . . 10 10

526 Arms of Hermosillo 527 Sir Rowland Hill

1979. Centenary of Hermosillo, Sonora.
1468 **526** 80 c. multicoloured . . . 10 10

1979. Air. Death Centenary of Sir Rowland Hill.
1469 **527** 1 p. 60 multicoloured . . 10 10

528 "Children" (Adriana Blas Casas)

1979. Air. International Year of the Child.
1470 **528** 1 p. 60 multicoloured . . 10 10

529 Registered Letter from Mexico to Rome, 1880

1979. Air. "Mepsipex 79", Third International Exhibition of Elmhurst Philatelic Society, Mexico City.
1499 **529** 1 p. 60 multicoloured . . 10 10

530 Football **531** Josefa Ortiz de Dominguez

1979. "Universiada 79", 10th World University Games, Mexico City (1st issue).
1500 **530** 50 c. grey, black and blue (postage) 10 10
1501 – 80 c. multicoloured . . . 10 10
1502 – 1 p. multicoloured . . . 10 10
1504 – 1 p. 60 multicoloured (air) 10 10
1505 – 4 p. 30 multicoloured . . 15 10
DESIGNS—VERT: 80 c. Aztec ball player; 1 p. Wall painting of athletes; 1 p. 60, Games emblem; 4 p. 30, Flame and doves.
See also Nos. 1514/19.

1979. 150th Death Anniv of Josefa Ortiz de Dominguez (Mayor of Queretaro).
1507 **531** 80 c. pink, black and bright pink 10 10

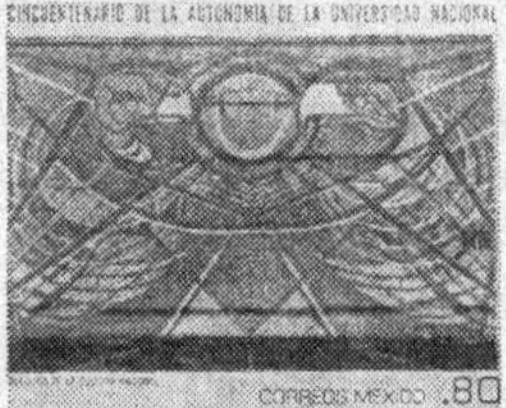

532 "Allegory of National Culture" (Alfaro Siqueiros)

1979. 50th Anniv of National University's Autonomy. Multicoloured.
1508 80 c. Type **532** (postage) . . 10 10
1509 3 p. "The Conquest of Energy" (Chavez Morado) 20 10
1510 1 p. 60 "The Return of Quetzalcoatl" (Chavez Morado) (air) 10 10
1511 4 p. 30 "Students reaching for Culture" (Alfaro Siqueiros) 15 10

533 Messenger and U.P.U. Emblem **534** Emiliano Zapata (after Diego Rivera)

1979. Air. Centenary of Mexico's Admission to U.P.U.
1512 **533** 1 p. 60 yellow, black and brown 10 10

1979. Birth Centenary of Emiliano Zapata (revolutionary).
1513 **534** 80 c. multicoloured . . . 10 10

535 Football **536** Tepoztlan, Morelos

1979. "Universiada '79", 10th World University Games, Mexico City (2nd issue). Multicoloured.
1514 50 c. Type **535** (postage) . . 10 10
1515 80 c. Volleyball 10 10
1516 1 p. Basketball 10 10
1518 1 p. 60 Tennis (air) 10 10
1519 5 p. 50 Swimming 30 20

1979. Tourism (1st series). Multicoloured.
1526 80 c. Type **536** (postage) . . 10 10
1527 80 c. Mexacaltitan, Nayarit 10 10
1528 1 p. 60 Agua Azul waterfall, Chipas (air) 10 10
1529 1 p. 60 King Coliman statue, Colima 10 10
See also Nos. 1631/4 and 1675/8.

537 Congress Emblem **538** Edison Lamp

1979. Air. 11th Congress and Assembly of International Industrial Design Council.
1530 **537** 1 p. 60 black, mauve and turquoise 10 10

1979. Air. Centenary of Electric Light.
1531 **538** 1 p. 60 multicoloured . 10 10

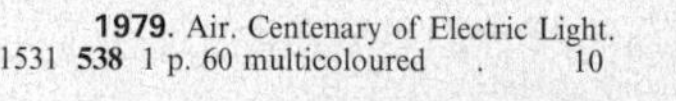

539 Martin de Olivares (postmaster) **540** Assembly Emblem

1979. 400th Anniv of Royal Proclamation of Mail Services in the New World. Multicoloured.
1532 80 c. Type **539** (postage) . . 10 10
1533 1 p. 60 Martin Enriquez de Almanza (viceroy of New Spain) (air) 10 10
1534 5 p. 50 King Philip II of Spain 35 20

1979. Air. 8th General Assembly of Latin American Universities Union.
1536 **540** 1 p. 60 multicoloured . 10 10

541 Shepherd **542** Moon Symbol from Mexican Codex

1979. Christmas. Multicoloured.
1537 50 c. Type **541** (postage) . . 10 10
1538 1 p. 60 Girl and Christmas tree (air) 10 10

1979. Air. 10th Anniv of First Man on Moon.
1539 **542** 2 p. 50 multicoloured . 15 10

543 Church, Yanhuitlan

1980. Air. Mexican Arts and Sciences (8th series). Multicoloured.
1540 1 p. 60 Type **543** 10 10
1541 1 p. 60 Monastery, Yuriria . 10 10
1542 1 p. 60 Church, Tlayacapan 10 10
1543 1 p. 60 Church, Actopan . 10 10
1544 1 p. 60 Church, Acolman . . 10 10

544 Steps and Snake's Head

1980. National Pre-Hispanic Monuments (1st series). Multicoloured.
1545 80 c. Type **544** (postage) . . . 10 10
1546 1 p. 60 Doble Tlaloc (rain god) (air) 10 10
1547 5 p. 50 Coyolzauhqui (moon goddess) 35 20
See also Nos. 1565/7 and 1605/7.

1980. Mexican Fauna (2nd series). As T **516**. Multicoloured.
1548 80 c. Common turkey (postage) 50 10
1549 1 p. 60 Greater flamingo (air) 1·00 25

1980. Mexican Flowers (2nd series). As T **518**. Multicoloured.
1550 80 c. "Tajetes erecta" (postage) 15 10
1551 1 p. 60 "Vanilla planifolia" (air) 25 10

545 Jules Verne

1980. Air. 75th Death Anniv of Jules Verne (author).
1552 **545** 5 p. 50 brown and black 35 20

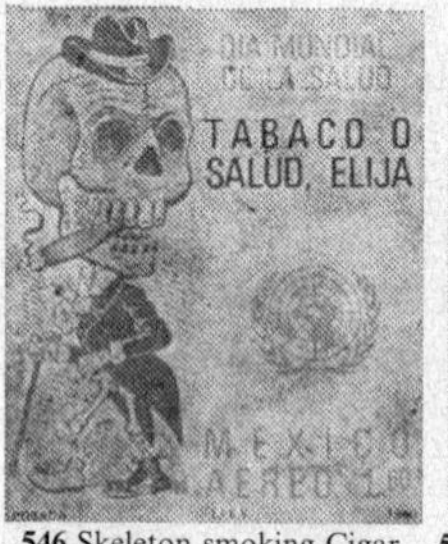

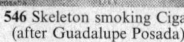

546 Skeleton smoking Cigar (after Guadalupe Posada) **547** China Poblana, Puebla

1980. Air. World Health Day. Anti-Smoking Campaign.
1553 **546** 1 p. 60 purple, blue & red 10 10

1980. National Costumes (1st series). Multicoloured.
1554 50 c. Type **547** (postage) . . . 10 10
1555 80 c. Jarocha, Veracruz . . . 10 10
1556 1 p. 60 Chiapaneca, Chiapas (air) 10 10
See also Nos. 1588/90.

548 Family **549** Cuauhtemoc (last Aztec Emperor)

1980. 10th Population and Housing Census.
1557 **548** 3 p. black and silver . . . 20 10

1980. Pre-Hispanic Personages (1st series). Multicoloured.
1558 80 c. Type **549** 10 10
1559 1 p. 60 Nezahualcoyotl (governor of Tetzcoco) . . 10 10
1560 5 p. 50 Eight Deer Tiger's Claw (11th Mixtec king) 35 20
See also Nos. 1642/4 and 1846/8.

550 Xipe (Aztec god of medicine) **551** Bronze Medal

1980. 22nd World Biennial Congress of International College of Surgeons, Mexico City.
1561 **550** 1 p. 60 multicoloured . . 10 10

1980. Olympic Games, Moscow.
1562 **551** 1 p. 60 bronze, black and turquoise 10 10
1563 – 3 p. silver, black and blue 20 10
1564 – 5 p. 50 gold, black & red 35 20
DESIGNS: 3 p. Silver medal; 5 p. 50, Gold medal.

1980. National Pre-Hispanic Monuments (2nd series). As T **554**. Multicoloured.
1565 80 c. Sacred glass 10 10
1566 1 p. 60 Stone snail 10 10
1567 5 p. 50 Chac Mool (god) . . 35 20

552 Sacromonte Sanctuary, Amecameca

1980. Colonial Architecture (1st series).
1568 **552** 2 p. 50 grey and black . 20 10
1569 – 2 p. 50 grey and black . 20 10
1570 – 3 p. grey and black . . . 25 10
1571 – 3 p. grey and black . . . 25 10
DESIGNS—HORIZ: No. 1552, St. Catherine's Convent, Patzcuaro; No. 1554, Hermitage, Cuernavaca. VERT: No. 1553, Basilica, Culiapan.
See also Nos. 1617/20, 1660/3, 1695/8 and 1784/7.

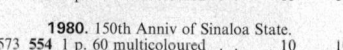

553 Quetzalcoatl (god) **554** Arms of Sinaloa

1980. World Tourism Conference, Manila, Philippines.
1572 **553** 2 p. 50 multicoloured . . 15 10

1980. 150th Anniv of Sinaloa State.
1573 **554** 1 p. 60 multicoloured . . 10 10

555 Straw Angel **556** Congress Emblem

1980. Christmas. Multicoloured.
1574 50 c. Type **555** 10 10
1575 1 p. 60 Poinsettia in a jug . . 10 10

1980. 4th International Civil Justice Congress.
1576 **556** 1 p. 60 multicoloured . . 10 10

557 Glass Demijohn and Animals **558** "Simon Bolivar" (after Paulin Guerin)

1980. Mexican Crafts (1st series). Multicoloured.
1577 50 c. Type **557** 10 10
1578 1 p. Poncho 10 10
1579 3 p. Wooden mask 20 15
See also Nos. 1624/6.

1980. 150th Death Anniv of Simon Bolivar.
1580 **558** 4 p. multicoloured . . . 30 20

559 Vicente Guerrero

560 Valentin Gomez Farias

1981. 150th Death Anniv of Vicente Guerrero (liberator).
1581 **559** 80 c. multicoloured . . . 10 10

1981. Birth Bicentenary of Valentin Gomez Farias.
1582 **560** 80 c. black and green . . 10 10

561 Table Tennis Balls in Flight

1981. 1st Latin-American Table Tennis Cup.
1583 **561** 4 p. multicoloured . . . 30 20

562 Jesus Gonzalez Ortega

563 Gabino Barreda

1981. Death Centenary of Jesus Gonzalez Ortega.
1584 **562** 80 c. lt brown & brown 10 10

1981. Death Centenary of Gabino Barreda (politician).
1585 **563** 80 c. pink, black & green 10 10

564 Benito Juarez

565 Foundation Monument

1981. 175th Birth Anniv of Benito Juarez (patriot).
1586 **564** 1 p. 60 grn, brn & lt brn 15 10

1981. 450th Anniv of Puebla City.
1587 **565** 80 c. multicoloured . . . 10 10

1981. National Costumes (2nd series). Vert designs as T **547**. Multicoloured.
1588 50 c. Purepecha, Michoacan 10 10
1589 80 c. Charra, Jalisco 10 10
1590 1 p. 60 Mestiza, Yucatan . . 15 10

1981. Mexican Fauna (3rd series). Vert designs as T **516**. Multicoloured.
1591 80 c. Northern Mockingbird 65 15
1592 1 p. 60 Mountain Trogon . . 1·10 35

1981. Mexican Flowers (3rd series). Vert designs as T **518**. Multicoloured.
1593 80 c. Avocado 10 10
1594 1 p. 60 Cacao 15 10

566 "Martyrs of Cananea" (David A. Siqueiros)

1981. 75th Anniv of Martyrs of Cananea.
1595 **566** 1 p. 60 multicoloured . 15 10

567 Toy Drummer with One Arm

568 Arms of Queretaro

1981. International Year of Disabled People.
1596 **567** 4 p. multicoloured . . . 30 20

1981. 450th Anniv of Queretaro City.
1597 **568** 80 c. multicoloured . . 10 10

569 Mexican Stamp of 1856 and Postal Service Emblem

1981. 125th Anniv of First Mexican Stamp.
1598 **569** 4 p. multicoloured . . . 30 20

570 Sir Alexander Fleming

572 St. Francisco Xavier Claver

571 Union Congress Building and Emblem

1981. Birth Centenary of Sir Alexander Fleming (discoverer of penicillin).
1599 **570** 5 p. blue and orange . . 35 10

1981. Opening of New Union Congress Building.
1600 **571** 1 p. 60 green and red . . 10 10

1981. 250th Birth Anniv of St. Francis Xavier Claver.
1601 **572** 80 c. multicoloured . . 10 10

573 "Desislava" (detail of Bulgarian Fresco)

1981. 1300th Anniv of Bulgarian State. Mult.
1602 1 p. 60 Type **573** 10 10
1603 4 p. Horse-headed cup from Thrace 25 20
1604 7 p. Madara Horseman (relief) 40 30

1981. Pre-Hispanic Monuments. As T **544**. Multicoloured.
1605 80 c. Seated God 10 10
1606 1 p. 60 Alabaster deer's head 15 10
1607 4 p. Jade Fish 30 20

574 Pablo Picasso

1981. Birth Centenary of Pablo Picasso (artist).
1608 **574** 5 p. deep green & green 35 20

575 Shepherd

576 Wheatsheaf

1981. Christmas. Multicoloured.
1609 50 c. Type **575** 10 10
1610 1 p. 60 Praying girl 15 10

1981. World Food Day.
1611 **576** 4 p. multicoloured . . . 25 15

577 Thomas Edison, Lightbulb and Gramophone

1981. 50th Death Anniv of Thomas Edison (inventor).
1612 **577** 4 p. stone, brown & green 25 15

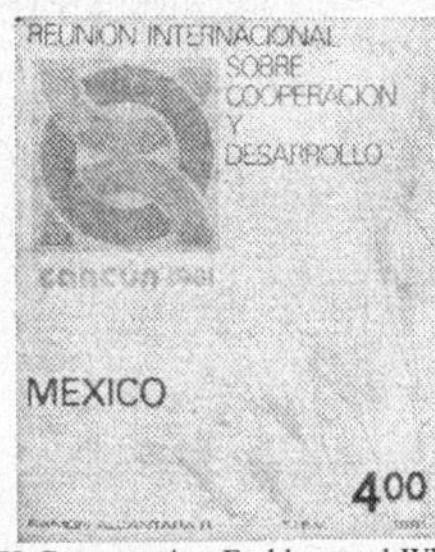

578 Co-operation Emblem and Wheat

1981. International Meeting on Co-operation and Development, Cancun.
1613 **578** 4 p. blue, grey and black 25 20

579 Globe and Diesel Locomotive

1981. 15th Pan-American Railway Congress.
1614 **579** 1 p. 60 multicoloured . . 35 10

580 Film Frame

1981. 50th Anniv of Mexican Sound Movies.
1615 **580** 4 p. grey, black and green 25 20

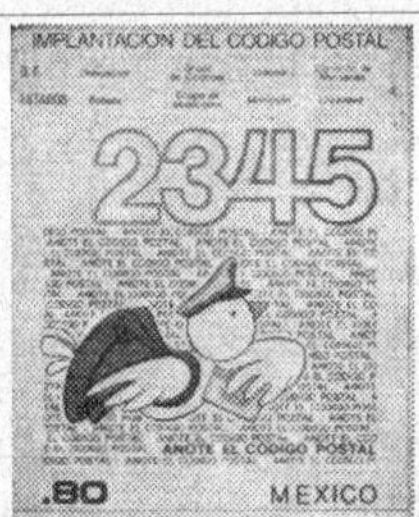

581 Postcode and Bird delivering Letter

1981. Inauguration of Postcodes.
1616 **581** 80 c. multicoloured . . . 10 10

1981. Colonial Architecture (2nd series). As T **522**. Multicoloured.
1617 4 p. Mascarones House . . . 25 15
1618 4 p. La Merced Convent . . 25 15
1619 5 p. Chapel of the Third Order, Texcoco 30 20
1620 5 p. Father Tembleque Aqueduct, Otumba 30 20

582 "Martyrs of Rio Blanco" (Orozco)

1982. 75th Anniv of Martyrs of Rio Blanco.
1621 **582** 80 c. multicoloured . . . 10 10

583 Ignacio Lopez Rayon

1982. 150th Death Anniv of Ignacio Lopez Rayon.
1622 **583** 1 p. 60 green, red & black 10 10

584 Postal Headquarters

1982. 75th Anniv of Postal Headquarters.
1623 **584** 4 p. pink and green . . . 25 20

1982. Mexican Crafts (2nd series). As T **557**. Multicoloured.
1624 50 c. "God's Eye" (Huichol art) 10 10
1625 1 p. Ceramic snail 10 10
1626 3 p. Tiger mask 20 15

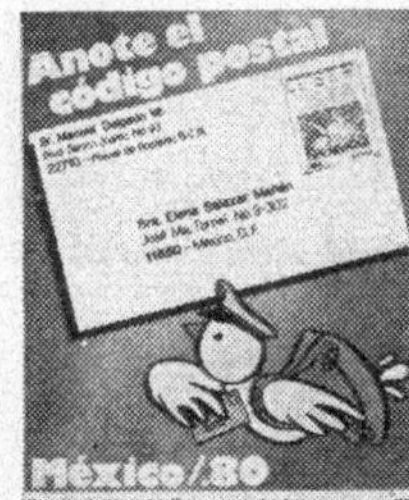

585 Postcoded Letter and Bird

1982. Postcode Publicity.
1627 **585** 80 c. multicoloured . . . 10 10

586 Dr. Robert Koch and Cross of Lorraine

1982. Centenary of Discovery of Tubercle Bacillus.
1628 **586** 4 p. multicoloured . . . 15 10

587 Military Academy 588 Arms of Oaxaca

1982. 50th Anniv of Military Academy.
1629 **587** 80 c. yellow, black & gold 10 10

1982. 450th Anniv of Oaxaca City.
1630 **588** 1 p. 60 multicoloured . . 10 10

1982. Tourism (2nd series). As T **563**. Multicoloured.
1631 80 c. Basaseachic Falls, Chihuahua 10 10
1632 80 c. Natural rock formation, Pueblo Nuevo, Durango . 10 10
1633 1 p. 60 Mayan City of Edzna, Campeche 10 10
1634 1 p. 60 La Venta (Olmeca sculpture, Tabasco) 10 10

589 Footballers

1982. World Cup Football Championship, Spain. Multicoloured.
1635 1 p. 60 Type **589** 10 10
1636 4 p. Dribbling 15 10
1637 7 p. Tackling 25 15

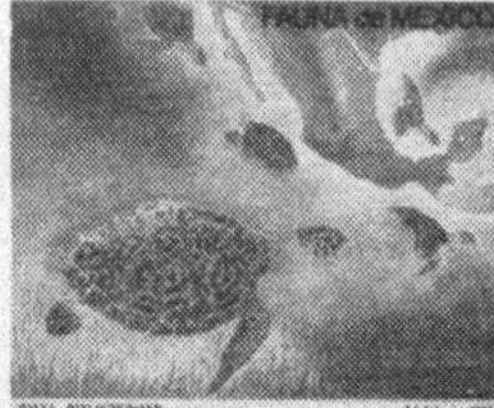
590 Hawksbill Turtles

1982. Mexican Fauna. Multicoloured.
1638 1 p. 60 Type **590** 10 10
1639 4 p. Grey Whales 15 30

591 Vicente Guerrero

1982. Birth Bicentenary of Vicente Guerrero (independence fighter).
1640 **591** 80 c. multicoloured . . . 10 10

592 Symbols of Peace and Communication

1982. Second U.N. Conference on the Exploration and Peaceful Uses of Outer Space, Vienna.
1641 **592** 4 p. multicoloured . . . 10 10

1982. Pre-Hispanic Personalities (2nd series). As T **549**. Multicoloured.
1642 80 c. Tariacuri 10 10
1643 1 p. 60 Acamapichtli 10 10
1644 4 p. Ten Deer Tiger's breastplate 10 10

593 Pawpaw ("Carica papaya")

1982. Mexican Flora. Multicoloured.
1645 80 c. Type **593** 10 10
1646 1 p. 60 Maize ("Zea mays") 10 10

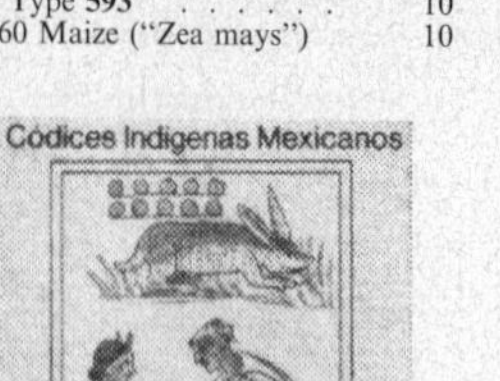

594 Astrologer

1982. Native Mexican Codices. Florentine Codex. Multicoloured.
1647 80 c. Type **594** 10 10
1648 1 p. 60 Arriving at School . 10 10
1649 4 p. Musicians 10 10

595 Manuel Gamio (anthropologist)

1982. Mexican Arts and Scientists. Multicoloured.
1650 1 p. 60 Type **595** 10 10
1651 1 p. 60 Isaac Ochoterena (biologist) 10 10
1652 1 p. 60 Angel Maria Garibay (philologist) 10 10
1653 1 p. 60 Manuel Sandoval Vallarta (nuclear physicist) 10 10
1654 1 p. 60 Guillermo Gonzalez Camarena (electronics engineer) 10 10

596 State Archives Building

1982. Inaug of State Archives Building.
1655 **596** 1 p. 60 black and green 10 10

597 Dove and Peace Text

1982. Christmas. Multicoloured.
1656 50 c. Type **597** 10 10
1657 1 p. 60 Dove and Peace text (different) 10 10

598 Hands holding Food

1982. Mexican Food System.
1658 **598** 1 p. 60 multicoloured . 10 10

MINIMUM PRICE

The minimum price quoted is 10p which represents a handling charge rather than a basis for valuing common stamps. For further notes about prices, see introductory pages.

599 "Revolutionary Mexico" Stamp, 1956

1982. Inauguration of Revolution Museum, Chihuahua.
1659 **599** 1 p. 60 grey and green . . 10 10

1982. Colonial Architecture (3rd series). As T **552**. Multicoloured.
1660 1 p. 60 College of Sts. Peter and Paul, Mexico City 10 10
1661 8 p. Convent of Jesus Maria, Mexico City 15 10
1662 10 p. Open Chapel, Tlalmanalco 20 15
1663 14 p. Convent, Actopan . . . 25 20

600 Alfonso Garcia Robles and Laurel 601 Jose Vasconcelos

1982. Alfonso Garcia Robles (Nobel Peace Prize Winner) Commemoration.
1664 **600** 1 p. 60 grey, black & gold 10 10
1665 – 14 p. pink, black & gold 25 20
DESIGN: 14 p. Robles and medal.

1982. Birth Centenary of Jose Vasconcelos (philosopher).
1666 **601** 1 p. 60 black and blue . . 10 10

602 W.C.Y. Emblem and Methods of Communication

1983. World Communications Year.
1667 **602** 16 p. multicoloured . . . 20 15

603 Sonora State Civil War Stamp, 1913

1983. "Herfilex 83" Mexican Revolution Stamp Exhibition.
1668 **603** 6 p. brown, black & green 10 10

604 "Nauticas Mexico" (container ship), World Map and I.M.O. Emblem

1983. 25th Anniv of International Maritime Organization.
1669 **604** 16 p. multicoloured . . . 80 20

605 Doctor treating Patient

1983. Constitutional Right to Health Protection.
1670 **605** 6 p. green and red . . . 10 10

606 Valentin Gomez Farias (founder) and Arms of Society

1983. 150th Anniv of Mexican Geographical and Statistical Society.
1671 **606** 6 p. multicoloured . . . 10 10

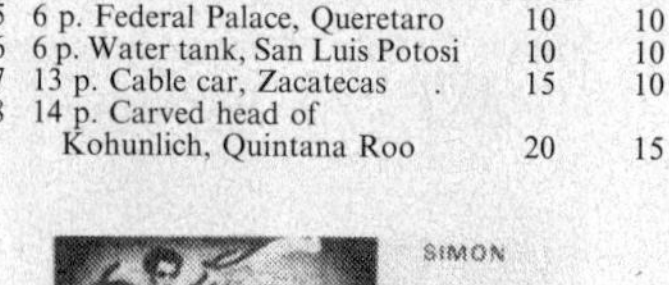

607 Football

1983. Second World Youth Football Championship, Mexico.
1672 **607** 6 p. black and green . . 10 10
1673 13 p. black and red . . . 15 10
1674 14 p. black and blue . . 20 15

1983. Tourism. As T **536**. Multicoloured.
1675 6 p. Federal Palace, Queretaro 10 10
1676 6 p. Water tank, San Luis Potosi 10 10
1677 13 p. Cable car, Zacatecas . 15 10
1678 14 p. Carved head of Kohunlich, Quintana Roo 20 15

608 Bolivar on Horseback

1983. Birth Bicentenary of Simon Bolivar.
1679 **608** 21 p. multicoloured . . . 25 15

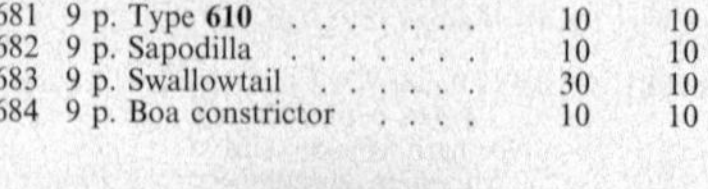

609 Angela Peralta 610 Agave

1983. Death Centenary of Angela Peralta (opera singer).
1680 **609** 9 p. light brown & brown 10 10

1983. Mexican Flora and Fauna (5th series). Multicoloured.
1681 9 p. Type **610** 10 10
1682 9 p. Sapodilla 10 10
1683 9 p. Swallowtail 30 10
1684 9 p. Boa constrictor 10 10

611 Two Candles

1983. Christmas. Multicoloured.
1685 9 p. Type **611** 10 10
1686 20 p. Three candles 25 15

612 S.C.T. Emblem

1983. Integral Communications and Transport System.
1687 **612** 13 p. blue and black . . 15 10

613 Carlos Chavez (musician)

1983. Mexican Arts and Sciences (10th series). Contemporary Artists. Multicoloured.
1688 **613** 9 p. brown, light brown and deep brown 10 10
1689 – 9 p. brown, light brown and deep brown 10 10
1690 – 9 p. deep brown, light brown and brown . . 10 10
1691 – 9 p. light brown, deep brown and brown . . 10 10
1692 – 9 p. deep brown, stone and brown 10 10
DESIGNS: No. 1689, Francisco Goitia (painter); No. 1690, S. Diaz Miron (poet); No. 1691, Carlos Bracho (sculptor); No. 1692, Fanny Anitua (singer).

614 Orozco (self-portrait)

1983. Birth Centenary of Jose Clemente Orozco (artist).
1693 **614** 9 p. multicoloured . . . 10 10

615 Human Rights Emblem

1983. 35th Anniv of Human Rights Declaration.
1694 **615** 20 p. deep blue, yellow and blue 25 15

1983. Colonial Architecture (4th series). As T **552**. Each grey and black.
1695 9 p. Convent, Malinalco . . 10 10
1696 20 p. Cathedral, Cuernavaca 25 15
1697 21 p. Convent, Tepeji del Rio 25 15
1698 24 p. Convent, Atlatlahucan 30 20

616 Antonio Caso and Books

1983. Birth Centenary of Antonio Caso (philospher).
1699 **616** 9 p. blue, lilac and red . 10 10

617 Joaquin Velazquez

1983. Bicentenary of Royal Legislation on Mining.
1700 **617** 9 p. multicoloured . . . 10 10

618 Book and Envelopes

1984. Centenary of First Postal Laws.
1701 **618** 12 p. multicoloured . . 15 10

619 Children dancing around Drops of Anti-Polio Serum

1984. World Anti-Polio Campaign.
1702 **619** 12 p. multicoloured . . 15 10

620 Muscovy Duck

1984. Mexican Fauna (6th series). Multicoloured.
1703 12 p. Type **620** 65 20
1704 20 p. Red-billed whistling duck 1·10 30

621 Xoloitzcuintle Dog

1984. World Dog Show.
1705 **621** 12 p. multicoloured . . 15 10

623 Hands holding Trees 624 Throwing the Discus

1984. Protection of Forest Resources.
1707 **623** 20 p. multicoloured . . . 20 15

1984. Olympic Games, Los Angeles. Multicoloured.
1708 14 p. Type **624** 15 15
1709 20 p. Show jumping 20 15
1710 23 p. Gymnastics (floor exercise) 25 20
1711 24 p. Diving 25 20
1712 25 p. Boxing 25 20
1713 26 p. Fencing 25 20

625 Mexican and Russian Flags

1984. 60th Anniv of Diplomatic Relations with U.S.S.R.
1715 **625** 23 p. multicoloured . . . 25 20

626 Hand holding U.N. emblem

1984. International Population Conference.
1716 **626** 20 p. multicoloured . . . 20 15

627 Gen. Mugica

1984. Birth Centenary of General Francisco Mugica (politician).
1717 **627** 14 p. brown and black . . 15 15

628 Emblem and Dates 629 Airline Emblem

1984. 50th Anniv of Economic Culture Fund.
1718 **628** 14 p. brown, black and red 15 15

1984. 50th Anniv of Aeromexico (state airline).
1719 – 14 p. multicoloured . . . 15 15
1720 **629** 20 p. black and red . . . 20 15
DESIGN—36 × 44 mm: 14 p. "Red Cactus" (sculpture, Sebastian).

630 Palace of Fine Arts

1984. 50th Anniv of Palace of Fine Arts.
1721 **630** 14 p. blue, black and brown 15 15

631 Metropolitan Cathedral (detail of facade) 633 Dove and Hand holding Flame

632 Coatzacoalcos Bridge

1984. 275th Anniv of Chihuahua City.
1722 **631** 14 p. brown and black . 15 15

1984. Inaug of Coatzacoalcos Bridge.
1723 **632** 14 p. multicoloured . . . 15 15

1984. World Disarmament Week.
1724 **633** 20 p. multicoloured . . . 20 15

634 Christmas Tree and Toy Train

1984. Christmas. Multicoloured.
1725 14 p. Type **634** 45 15
1726 20 p. Breaking the pinata (balloon filled with gifts) (vert) 20 15

635 Ignacio Manuel Altamirano

1984. 150th Birth Anniv of Ignacio Manuel Altamirano (politician and journalist).
1727 **635** 14 p. red and black . . . 15 15

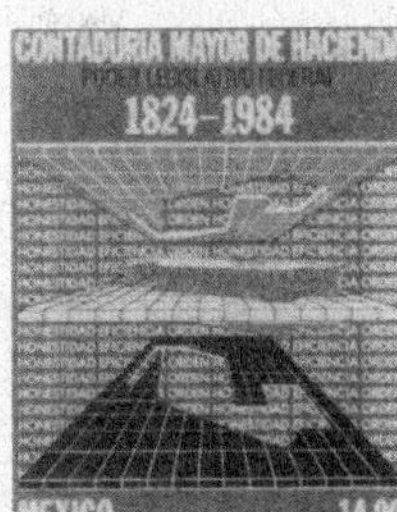

636 Maps, Graph and Text

1984. 160th Anniv of State Audit Office.
1728 **636** 14 p. multicoloured . . . 15 15

622 Bank Headquarters

1984. Centenary of National Bank.
1706 **622** 12 p. multicoloured . . 15 10

637 Half a Football and Mexican Colours

1984. Mexico, Site of 1986 World Cup Football Championship. Multicoloured.
1729 20 p. Type **637** 20 15
1730 24 p. Football and Mexican colours 25 20

638 Romulo Gallegos **639** State Arms and Open Register

1984. Birth Centenary of Romul Gallegos.
1731 **638** 20 p. black and blue . . 20 15

1984. 125th Anniv of Mexican Civil Register.
1732 **639** 24 p. blue 25 20

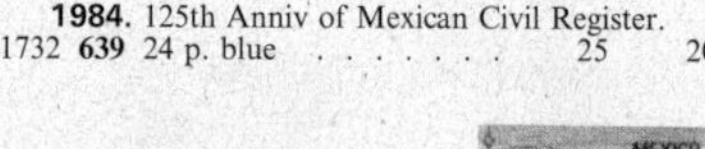

640 Mexican Flag **641** Johann Sebastian Bach

1985. 50th Anniv of National Flag.
1733 **640** 22 p. multicoloured . . . 25 20

1985. 300th Birth Anniv of Johann Sebastian Bach (composer).
1734 **641** 35 p. red and black . . . 15 30

642 I.Y.Y. Emblem **643** Children and Fruit within Book

1985. International Youth Year.
1735 **642** 35 p. purple, gold and black 15 30

1985. Child Survival Campaign.
1736 **643** 36 p. multicoloured . . . 15 10

644 Commemorative Medallion

1985. 450th Anniv of State Mint.
1737 **644** 35 p. gold, mauve & blue 15 10

645 Victor Hugo, Text and Gateway

1985. Death Centenary of Victor Hugo (novelist).
1738 **645** 35 p. grey 15 10

646 Hidalgo 8 r. Stamp, 1856

1985. "Mexifil 85" Stamp Exhibition.
1739 **646** 22 p. grey, black and purple 10 10
1740 – 35 p. grey, black and blue 15 10
1741 – 36 p. multicoloured . . 15 10
DESIGNS: 35 p. Carranza 10 c. stamp, 1916; 36 p. Juarez 50 p. stamp, 1975.

647 Rockets, Satellite, Nurse and Computer Operator

1985. Launching of First Morelos Satellite. Multicoloured.
1743 22 p. Type **647** 10 10
1744 36 p. Camera, dish aerial, satellite and computers . . 15 10
1745 90 p. Camera, dish aerial, satellite, television and couple telephoning 25 20
Nos. 1743/5 were printed together, se-tenant, forming a composite design.

648 Conifer

1985. 9th World Forestry Congress, Mexico.
1747 **648** 22 p. brown, black and green 10 10
1748 – 35 p. brown, black and green 15 10
1749 – 36 p. brown, black and green 15 10
DESIGNS: 35 p. Silk-cotton trees; 36 p. Mahogany tree.

649 Martin Luis Guzman

1985. Mexican Arts and Sciences (11th series). Contemporary Writers.
1750 **649** 22 p. grey and blue . . 10 10
1751 – 22 p. grey and blue . . 10 10
1752 – 22 p. grey and blue . . 10 10
1753 – 22 p. grey and blue . . 10 10
1754 – 22 p. grey and blue . . 10 10
DESIGNS: No. 1751, Augustin Yanez; 1752, Alfonso Reyes; 1753, Jose Ruben Romero; 1754, Artemio de Valle-Arizpe.

650 Miguel Hidalgo

1985. 175th Anniv of Independence Movement. Each green, black and red.
1755 22 p. Type **650** 10 10
1756 35 p. Jose Ma. Morelos . . . 10 10
1757 35 p. Ignacio Allende 10 10
1758 36 p. Leona Vigario 10 10
1759 110 p. Vicente Guerrero . . . 20 15

651 San Ildefonso

1985. 75th Anniv of National University. Mult.
1761 26 p. Type **651** 10 10
1762 26 p. Emblem 10 10
1763 40 p. Modern building . . . 10 10
1764 45 p. 1910 crest and Justo Sierra (founder) 10 10
1765 90 p. University crest 15 10

652 Rural and Industrial Landscapes

1985. 25th Anniv of Inter-American Development Bank.
1766 **652** 26 p. multicoloured . . . 10 10

653 Guns and Doves **654** Hands and Dove

1985. United Nations Disarmament Week.
1767 **653** 36 p. multicoloured . . . 10 10

1985. 40th Anniv of U.N.O.
1768 **654** 26 p. multicoloured . . . 10 10

655 "Girls Skipping" (Mishinoya K. Maki)

1985. Christmas. Children's Paintings. Mult.
1769 26 p. Disabled and able-bodied children playing (Margarita Salazar) 10 10
1770 35 p. Type **655** 10 10

656 Soldadera

1985. 75th Anniv of 1910 Revolution. Each red, black and green.
1771 26 p. Type **656** 10 10
1772 35 p. Pancho Villa 10 10
1773 40 p. Emiliano Zapata . . . 10 10
1774 45 p. Venustiano Carranza . . 10 10
1775 110 p. Francisco I. Madero . 20 15

657 "Vigilante" (Federico Silva)

1985. 2nd "Morelos" Telecommunications Satellite Launch.
1777 – 26 p. black and blue . . 10 10
1778 **657** 35 p. grey, pink and black 10 10
1779 – 45 p. multicoloured . . . 10 10
DESIGNS—VERT: 26 p. "Cosmonaut" (sculpture by Sebastian). HORIZ: 45 p. "Mexican Astronaut" (painting by Cauduro).

658 "Mexico" holding Book

1985. 25th Anniv of Free Textbooks National Commission.
1781 **658** 26 p. multicoloured . . . 10 10

659 Olympic Stadium, University City

1985. World Cup Football Championship, Mexico. Each grey and black.
1782 26 p. Type **659** 10 10
1783 45 p. Azteca Stadium 10 10

1985. Colonial Architecture (5th series). Vert designs as T **552**. Each brown and black.
1784 26 p. Vizcayan College, Mexico City 10 10
1785 35 p. Counts of Heras y Soto Palace, Mexico City . . . 10 10
1786 40 p. Counts of Calimaya Palace, Mexico City . . . 10 10
1787 45 p. St. Carlos Academy, Mexico City 10 10

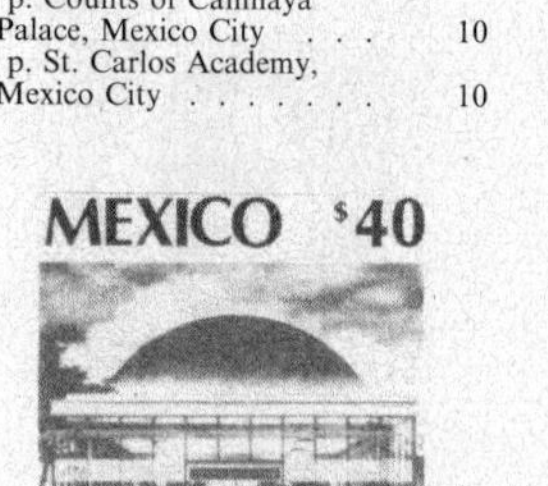

661 Luis Enrique Erro Planetarium

1986. 50th Anniv of National Polytechnic Institute. Multicoloured.
1788 40 p. Type **661** 10 10
1789 65 p. National School of Arts and Crafts 10 10
1790 75 p. Founders, emblem and "50" 10 10

1985. Mexican Flowers (6th series). As T **518**. Multicoloured.
1791 40 p. Calabash 10 10
1792 65 p. "Nopalea coccinellifera" (cactus) 10 10

663 Doll

1986. World Health Day.
1793 **663** 65 p. multicoloured . . . 10 10

664 Halley and Comet

1986. Appearance of Halley's Comet.
1794 **664** 90 p. multicoloured . . . 15 10

665 Emblem

1986. Centenary of Geological Institute.
1795 **665** 40 p. multicoloured . . . 10 10

666 "Three Footballers with Berets"

1986. World Cup Football Championship, Mexico (2nd issue). Paintings by Angel Zarraga. Multicoloured.
1796 30 p. Type **666** 10 10
1797 40 p. "Portrait of Ramon Novaro" 10 10
1798 65 p. "Sunday" 10 10
1799 70 p. "Portrait of Ernest Charles Gimpel" 10 10
1800 90 p. "Three Footballers" . . 15 10

667 Ignacio Allende

1986. 175th Death Annivs of Independence Heroes. Multicoloured.
1802 40 p. Type **667** 10 10
1803 40 p. Miguel Hidalgo (after J. C. Orozco) 10 10
1804 65 p. Juan Aldama 10 10
1805 75 p. Mariano Jimenez . . . 10 10

668 Mexican Arms over "FTF"

669 Nicolas Bravo

1986. 50th Anniv of Fiscal Tribunal.
1806 **668** 40 p. black, blue & grey 10 10

1986. Birth Bicentenary of Nicolas Bravo (independence fighter).
1807 **669** 40 p. multicoloured . . . 10 10

670 "Zapata Landscape"

1986. Paintings by Diego Rivera. Multicoloured.
1808 50 p. Type **670** 10 10
1809 80 p. "Nude with Arum Lilies" 10 10
1810 110 p. "Vision of a Sunday Afternoon Walk on Central Avenue" (horiz) 20 15

671 Guadalupe Victoria

1986. Birth Bicentenary of Guadalupe Victoria (first President).
1811 **671** 50 p. multicoloured . . 10 10

672 People depositing Produce

1986. 50th Anniv of National Depositories.
1812 **672** 40 p. multicoloured . . 10 10

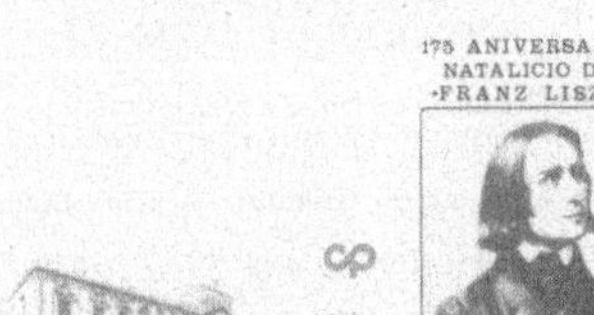

673 Pigeon above Hands holding Posthorn

674 Emblem

1986. World Post Day.
1813 **673** 120 p. multicoloured . . 20 15

1986. Foundation of National Commission to Mark 500th Anniv (1992) of Discovery of America.
1814 **674** 50 p. black and red . . 10 10

675 Ministry of Mines

676 Liszt

1986. 15th Pan-American Roads Congress.
1815 **675** 80 p. grey and black . . 10 10

1986. 175th Birth Anniv of Franz Liszt (composer).
1816 **676** 100 p. brown and black 15 10

677 U.N. and "Pax Cultura" Emblems

1986. International Peace Year.
1817 **677** 80 p. blue, red and black 10 10

678 Jose Maria Pino Suarez (1st Vice-President of Revolutionary Govt.)

1986. Famous Mexicans buried in The Rotunda of Illustrious Men (1st series).
1818 **678** 50 p. multicoloured . . . 10 10
See also Nos. 1823/4, 1838 and 1899.

679 King

680 "Self-portrait"

1986. Christmas. Multicoloured.
1819 50 p. Type **679** 10 10
1820 80 p. Angel 10 10

1986. Birth Centenary of Diego Rivera (artist).
1821 **680** 80 p. multicoloured . . . 10 10

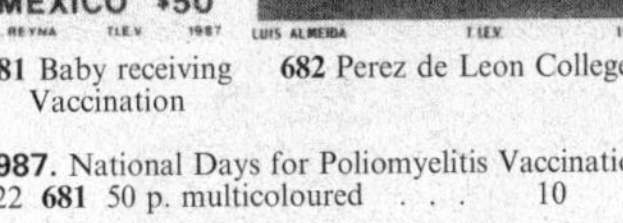

681 Baby receiving Vaccination

682 Perez de Leon College

1987. National Days for Poliomyelitis Vaccination.
1822 **681** 50 p. multicoloured . . . 10 10

1987. Famous Mexicans buried in The Rotunda of Illustrious Men (2nd series). As T **678**. Mult.
1823 100 p. Jose Maria Iglesias . . 10 10
1824 100 p. Pedro Sainz de Baranda 10 10

1987. Centenary of Higher Education.
1825 **682** 100 p. multicoloured . . 10 10

683 Kino and Map

1987. 300th Anniv of Father Eusebio Francisco Kino's Mission to Pimeria Alta.
1826 **683** 100 p. multicoloured . . 10 10

684 Baby's Head

1987. Child Immunization Campaign.
1827 **684** 100 p. deep blue & blue 10 10

685 Staircase

686 "5th of May, 1862, and the Siege of Puebla" Exhibition Poster, 1887

1987. 50th Anniv of Puebla Independent University.
1828 **685** 200 p. grey, pink and black 10 10

1987. 125th Anniv of Battle of Puebla.
1829 **686** 100 p. multicoloured . . 10 10

687 Stylized City

1987. "Metropolis 87" World Association of Large Cities Congress.
1830 **687** 310 p. red, black and green 45 30

688 Lacquerware Tray, Uruapan, Michoacan

689 Genaro Estrada (author and pioneer of democracy)

1987. Handicrafts. Multicoloured.
1831 100 p. Type **688** 10 10
1832 200 p. Woven blanket, Santa Ana Chiautempan, Tlaxcala 10 10
1833 230 p. Ceramic jar with lid, Puebla, Puebla 15 10

1987. Mexican Arts and Sciences (12th series).
1834 **689** 100 p. brown, black and pink 10 10
See also Nos. 1845, 1880 and 1904/5.

BANCO NACIONAL DE COMERCIO EXTERIOR

MERCADO INTERIOR INDIGENA 1961 P. O'HIGGINS

50 ANIVERSARIO

MEXICO $100

690 "Native Traders" (mural, P. O'Higgins)

1987. 50th Anniv of National Foreign Trade Bank.
1835 **690** 100 p. multicoloured . . 10 10

691 Diagram of Longitudinal Section through Ship's Hull

1987. 400th Anniv of Publication of First Shipbuilding Manual in America, Diego Garcia de Palacio's "Instrucion Nautica".
1836 **691** 100 p. green, blue & brn 10 10

692 Man carrying Sack of Maize Flour

1987. 50th Anniv of National Food Programme.
1837 **692** 100 p. multicoloured . . 10 10

1987. Mexicans in Rotunda of Illustrious Men (3rd series). As T **678**. Multicoloured.
1838 100 p. Leandro Valle 10 10

693 "Self-portrait with Skull"

1987. Paintings by Saturnino Herran.
1839 **693** 100 p. brown and black 15 10
1840 – 100 p. multicoloured . . 15 10
1841 – 400 p. multicoloured . . 60 50
DESIGNS: No. 1840, "The Offering"; 1841, "Creole with Shawl".

694 Flags of Competing Countries

1987. 10th Pan-American Games, Indianapolis.
1842 **694** 100 p. multicoloured . . 10 10
1843 – 200 p. black, red and green 10 10
DESIGN: 200 p. Running.

695 Electricity Pylon

1987. 50th Anniv of Federal Electricity Commission.
1844 **695** 200 p. multicoloured . . 10 10

1987. Mexican Arts and Sciences (13th series). As T **689**. Multicoloured.
1845 100 p. J. E. Hernandez y Davalos (author) 10 10

1987. Pre-Hispanic Personages (3rd series). As T **549**. Multicoloured.
1846 100 p. Xolotl (Chichimeca commander) 10 10
1847 200 p. Nezahualpilli (leader of Tezcoco tribe) 10 10
1848 400 p. Motecuhzoma Ilhuicamina (leader of Tenochtitlan tribe) 45 10

696 Stylized Racing Car

1987. Mexico Formula One Grand Prix.
1849 **696** 100 p. multicoloured . . 10 10

697 Mexican Cultural Centre, Mexico City
698 "Santa Maria" and 1922 Mexican Festival Emblem

1987. Mexican Tourism.
1850 **697** 100 p. multicoloured . . 10 10

1987. 500th Anniv of "Meeting of Two Worlds" (discovery of America by Columbus) (1st issue).
1851 **698** 150 p. multicoloured . . 30 15
See also Nos. 1902, 1941, 1979, 2038 and 2062/6.

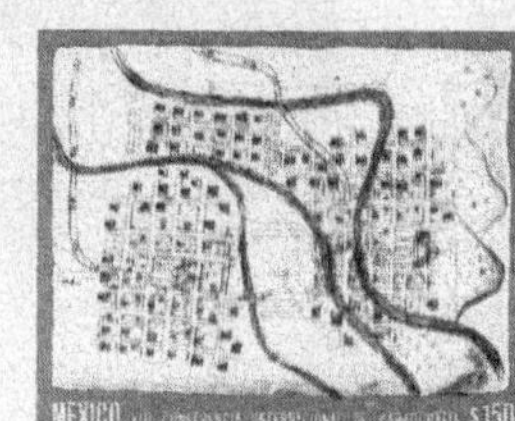

699 16th-century Spanish Map of Mexico City

1987. 13th International Cartography Conference.
1852 **699** 150 p. multicoloured . . 10 10

1987. Mexican Tourism. As T **697**. Multicoloured.
1853 150 p. Michoacan 15 10
1854 150 p. Garcia Caves, Nuevo Leon 10 10
1855 150 p. View of Mazatlan, Sinaloa 10 10

700 Pre-Hispanic Wedding Ceremony

1987. Native Codices. Mendocino Codex. Mult.
1856 150 p. Type **700** 10 10
1857 150 p. Moctezuma's council chamber 10 10
1858 150 p. Foundation of Tenochtitlan 10 10

701 Dove with Olive Twig

1987. Christmas.
1859 **701** 150 p. mauve 10 10
1860 – 150 p. blue 10 10
DESIGN: No. 1860, As T **701** but dove facing left.

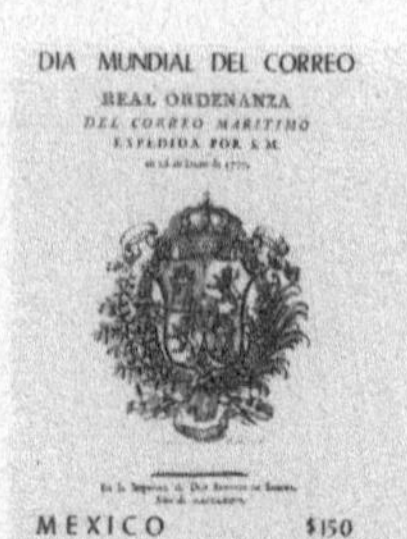

702 "Royal Ordinance for the Carriage of Maritime Mail" Title Page

1987. World Post Day.
1861 **702** 150 p. green and grey . . 10 10

703 Circle of Flags

1987. 1st Meeting of Eight Latin-American Presidents, Acapulco. Multicoloured.
1863 250 p. Type **703** 10 10
1864 500 p. Flags and doves . . . 25 10

704 "Dualidad 1964"

1987. Rufino Tamayo (painter). "70 Years of Creativity".
1865 **704** 150 p. multicoloured . . 10 10

705 Train on Metlac Railway Bridge

1987. 50th Anniv of Railway Nationalization.
1866 **705** 150 p. multicoloured . . 35 10

706 Stradivarius at Work (detail, 19th-century engraving)

1987. 250th Death Anniv of Antonio Stradivarius (violin-maker).
1867 **706** 150 p. light violet and violet 10 10

707 Statue of Manuel Crescensio Rejon (promulgator of Yucatan State Constitution)

1988. Constitutional Tribunal, Supreme Court of Justice.
1868 **707** 300 p. multicoloured . . 15 10

708 American Manatee

1988. Animals. Multicoloured.
1869 300 p. Type **708** 15 10
1870 300 p. Mexican mole salamander 15 10

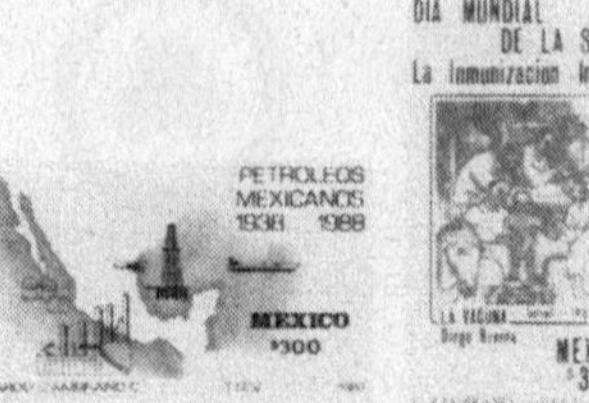

709 Map and Oil Industry Symbols
710 "The Vaccination"

1988. 50th Anniv of Pemex (Nationalized Petroleum Industry).
1871 **709** 300 p. blue and black . . 20 10
1872 – 300 p. multicoloured . . 15 10
1873 – 500 p. multicoloured . . 25 10
DESIGNS:—36 × 43 mm: No. 1872, PEMEX emblem. 43 × 36 mm: No. 1873, "50" and oil exploration platform.

1988. World Health Day (1874) and 40th Anniv of W.H.O. (1875). Paintings by Diego Rivera.
1874 **710** 300 p. brown and green 15 10
1875 – 300 p. multicoloured . . 15 10
DESIGN:—43 × 36 mm: No. 1875, "The People demand Health".

711 "Death Portrait" (Victor Delfin)

1988. 50th Death Anniv of Cesar Vallejo (painter and poet). Multicoloured.
1876 300 p. Type **711** 15 10
1877 300 p. Portrait by Arnold Belkin and "Hoy me palpo..." . . 15 10
1878 300 p. Portrait as in T **711** but larger (30 × 35 mm) . . . 15 10
1879 300 p. Portrait as in No. 1877 but larger (23 × 35 mm) . . 15 10

1988. Mexican Arts and Sciences (14th series). As T **689**.
1880 300 p. brown, black and violet 15 10
DESIGN: 300 p. Carlos Pellicer (poet).

712 Girl and Boy holding Stamp in Tweezers

1988. "Mepsirrey '88" Stamp Exhibition, Monterrey. Multicoloured.
1881 300 p. Type **712** 15 10
1882 300 p. Envelope with "Monterrey" hand-stamp 15 10
1883 500 p. Exhibition emblem . . 25 10

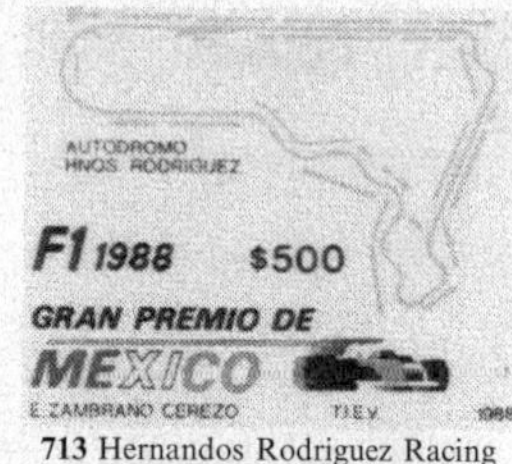

713 Hernandos Rodriguez Racing Circuit, Mexico City

1988. Mexico Formula One Grand Prix.
1884 **713** 500 p. multicoloured . . 25 10

714 Lopez Verlarde and Rose
715 Emblem

1988. Birth Centenary of Ramon Lopez Verlarde (poet). Multicoloured.
1885 300 p. Type **714** 15 10
1886 300 p. Abstract 15 10

1988. 50th Anniv of Military Sports.
1887 **715** 300 p. multicoloured . . 15 10

MORE DETAILED LISTS
are given in the Stanley Gibbons Catalogues referred to in the country headings. For lists of current volumes see introduction

716 Chrysanthemum, Container Ship and Flags

1988. Centenary of Mexico–Japan Friendship, Trade and Navigation Treaty.
1888 **716** 500 p. multicoloured . . 35 10

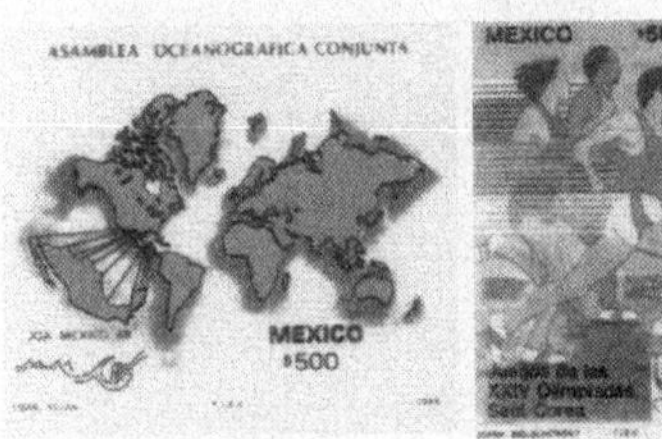

717 Map   718 Runners

1988. Oceanographical Assembly.
1889 **717** 500 p. multicoloured . . 25 10

1988. Olympic Games Seoul.
1890 **718** 500 p. multicoloured . . 25 10

719 Boxer and Flags

1988. 25th Anniv of World Boxing Council.
1892 **719** 500 p. multicoloured . . 25 10

720 Hospital and Emblem

1988. 125th Anniv of Red Cross.
1893 **720** 300 p. grey, red and black 15 10

721 Posada

1988. 75th Death Anniv of Jose Guadalupe Posada (painter).
1894 **721** 300 p. black and silver . 15 10

722 "Danaus plexippus"

1988. Endangered Insects. The Monarch Butterfly. Multicoloured.
1895 300 p. Type **722** 30 10
1896 300 p. Butterflies on wall . . 30 10
1897 300 p. Butterflies on leaves . . 30 10
1898 300 p. Caterpillar, butterfly and chrysalis 30 10

1988. Mexicans in Rotunda of Illustrious Persons (4th series). As T **678**. Multicoloured.
1899 300 p. Manuel Sandoval Vallarta 15 10

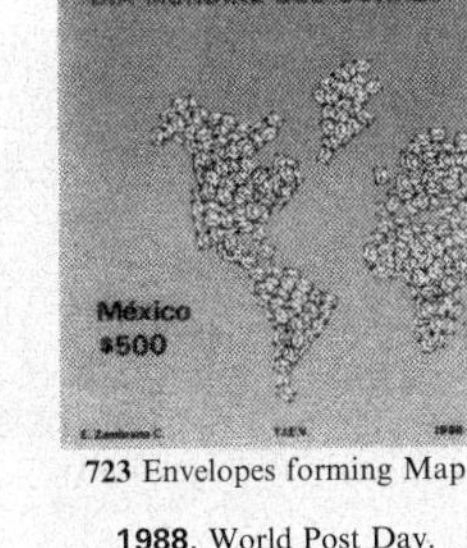

723 Envelopes forming Map

1988. World Post Day.
1900 **723** 500 p. black and blue . 20 10

724 Indian and Monk writing

1988. 500th Anniv of "Meeting of Two Worlds" (2nd issue). Yanhuitian Codex.
1902 **724** 500 p. multicoloured . . 20 10

725 Man watering Plant

1988. World Food Day. "Rural Youth".
1903 **725** 500 p. multicoloured . . 20 10

1988. Mexican Arts and Sciences (15th series). As T **689**.
1904 300 p. black and grey . . . 15 10
1905 300 p. brown, black & yellow 15 10
DESIGNS: No. 1904, Alfonso Caso; 1905, Vito Alessio Robles.

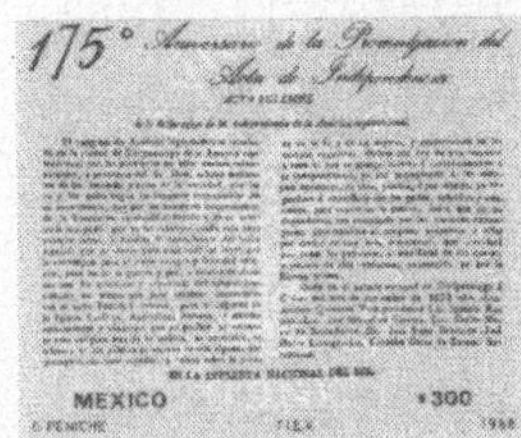

726 Act

1988. 175th Anniv of Promulgation of Act of Independence.
1906 **726** 300 p. flesh and brown 15 10

727 "Self-portrait 1925"   728 Children and Kites

1988. 25th Death Anniv of Antonio Ruiz (painter). Multicoloured.
1907 300 p. Type **727** 15 10
1908 300 p. "La Malinche" . . . 15 10
1909 300 p. "March Past" 15 10

1988. Christmas. Multicoloured.
1910 300 p. Type **728** 15 10
1911 300 p. Food (horiz) 15 10

729 Emblem

1988. 50th Anniv of Municipal Workers Trade Union.
1912 **729** 300 p. black and brown 15 10

1988. Mexican Flowers (7th series). As T **518**. Multicoloured.
1913 300 p. "Mimosa tenuiflora" 15 10
1914 300 p. "Ustilago maydis" . . 30 10

731 "50" and Emblem

1989. 50th Anniv of State Printing Works.
1915 **731** 450 p. brown, grey & red 20 10

732 Arms and Score of National Anthem

1989. 145th Anniv of Dominican Independence.
1916 **732** 450 p. multicoloured . . 20 10

733 Emblem

1989. Centenary of International Boundary and Water Commission.
1917 **733** 1100 p. multicoloured . . 50 50

734 Emblem

1989. 10th International Book Fair, Mineria.
1918 **734** 450 p. multicoloured . . 20 10

735 Composer at Work

1989. 25th Anniv of Society of Authors and Composers.
1919 **735** 450 p. multicoloured . . 20 10

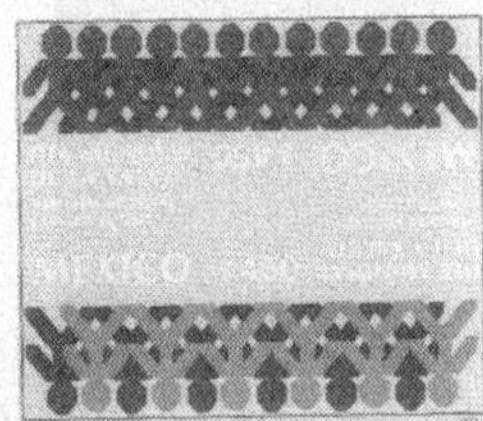

736 People

1989. Anti-Aids Campaign.
1920 **736** 450 p. multicoloured . . 20 10

737 Vicario   738 Statue of Reyes

1989. Birth Bicentenary of Leona Vicario (Independence fighter).
1921 **737** 450 p. brown, deep brown and black 20 10

1989. Birth Centenary of Alfonso Reyes (writer).
1922 **738** 450 p. multicoloured . . 20 10

739 Speeding Cars

1989. Mexico Formula One Grand Prix.
1923 **739** 450 p. multicoloured . . 20 10

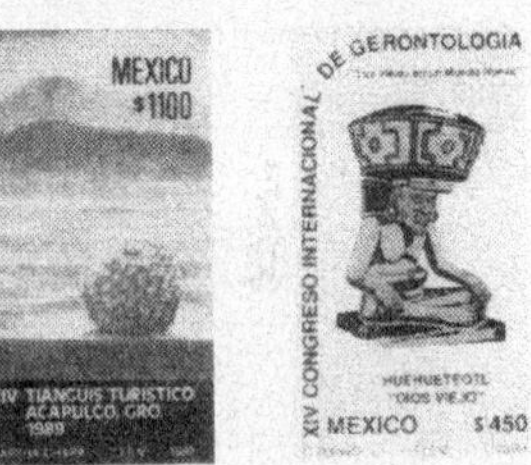

740 Sea and Mountains   741 Huehuetcotl (god)

1989. 14th Travel Agents' Meeting, Acapulco.
1924 **740** 1100 p. multicoloured . . 50 50

1989. 14th International Congress on Ageing.
1925 **741** 450 p. pink, black and stone 20 10

742 Revolutionary and Battle Site

1989. 75th Anniv of Battle of Zacatecas.
1926 **742** 450 p. black 20 10

743 Catchers

1989. Baseball Professionals' Hall of Fame. Multicoloured.
1927 550 p. Type **743** 20 10
1928 550 p. Striker 20 10
Nos. 1927/8 were printed together, se-tenant, forming a composite design.

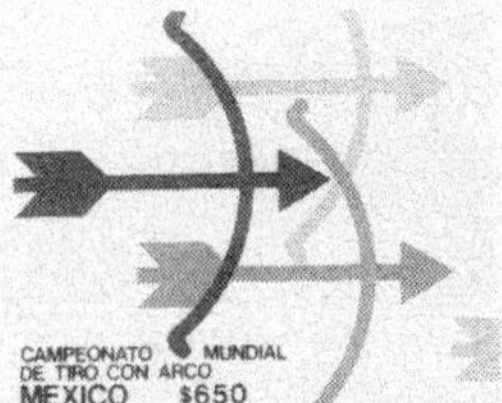

744 Bows and Arrows

1989. World Archery Championships, Switzerland. Multicoloured.
1929 650 p. Type **744** 25 10
1920 650 p. Arrows and target . . 25 10
Nos. 1929/30 were printed together, se-tenant, forming a composite design.

745 Arms

1989. Centenary of Tijuana.
1931 **745** 1100 p. multicoloured . . 50 20

746 Storming the Bastille

1989. Bicentenary of French Revolution.
1932 **746** 1300 p. multicoloured . . 60 50

747 Mina

1989. Birth Bicentenary of Francisco Xavier Mina (independence fighter).
1933 **747** 450 p. multicoloured . . 20 10

748 Cave Paintings

1989. 25th Anniv of National Anthropological Museum, Chapultepec.
1934 **748** 450 p. multicoloured . . 20 10

749 Runners

1989. 7th Mexico City Marathon.
1935 **749** 450 p. multicoloured . . 20 10

750 Printed Page

1989. 450th Anniv of First American and Mexican Printed Work.
1936 **750** 450 p. multicoloured . . 20 10

751 Posthorn and Cancellations

1989. World Post Day.
1937 **751** 1100 p. multicoloured . 50 20

752 "Aguascalientes in History" (Osvaldo Barra)

1989. 75th Anniv of Aguascalientes Revolutionary Convention.
1936 **752** 450 p. multicoloured . . 20 10

753 Patterns

1989. America. Pre-Columbian Culture.
1939 450 p. Type **753** 20 10
1940 450 p. Traditional writing . 20 10

754 Old and New World Symbols

755 Cross of Lorraine

1989. 500th Anniv of "Meeting of Two Worlds" (3rd issue).
1941 **754** 1300 p. multicoloured . 60 25

1989. 50th Anniv of Anti-tuberculosis National Committee.
1942 **755** 450 p. multicoloured . . 20 10

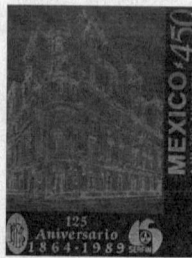
756 Mask of God Murcielago

1989.
1943 **756** 450 p. green, black & mve 20 10

757 Bank

1989. 125th Anniv of Serfin Commercial Bank.
1944 **757** 450 p. blue, gold & black 20 10

758 Cortines

759 Man with Sparkler

1989. Birth Centenary of Adolfo Ruiz Cortines (President, 1952–58).
1945 **758** 450 p. multicoloured . . 20 10

1989. Christmas. Multicoloured.
1946 450 p. Type **759** 20 10
1947 450 p. People holding candles (horiz) 20 10

760 Emblem

1989. 50th Anniv of National Institute of Anthropology and History.
1948 **760** 450 p. gold, red & black 20 10

761 Steam Locomotive, Modern Train and Felipe Pescador

1989. 80th Anniv of Nationalization of Railways.
1949 **761** 450 p. multicoloured . . 20 10

762 Bridge

1990. Opening of Tampico Bridge.
1950 **762** 600 p. black, gold & red 20 10

763 Smiling Children

1990. Child Vaccination Campaign.
1951 **763** 700 p. multicoloured . . 25 10

764 People in Houses

1990. 11th General Population and Housing Census.
1952 **764** 700 p. green, yell & lt grn 25 10

765 Stamp under Magnifying Glass

1990. 10th Anniv of Mexican Philatelic Association.
1953 **765** 700 p. multicoloured . . 25 10

766 Archive

1990. Bicentenary of National Archive.
1954 **766** 700 p. blue 25 10

767 Emblem and "90"

1990. 1st International Poster Biennale.
1955 **767** 700 p. multicoloured . . 25 10

768 Messenger, 1790

1990. "Stamp World London 90" International Stamp Exhibition.
1956 **768** 700 p. yellow, red & black 25 10

769 Penny Black

1990. 150th Anniv of the Penny Black.
1957 **769** 700 p. black, red & gold 25 10

770 National Colours and Pope John Paul II

1990. Papal Visit.
1958 **770** 700 p. multicoloured . . 25 10

771 Church 772 Mother and Child

1990. 15th Travel Agents' Congress.
1959 **771** 700 p. multicoloured . . 25 10

1990. Mother and Child Health Campaign.
1960 **772** 700 p. multicoloured . . 25 10

773 Smoke Rings forming Birds 774 Globe as Tree

1990. World Anti-Smoking Day.
1961 **773** 700 p. multicoloured . . 25 10

1990. World Environment Day.
1962 **774** 700 p. multicoloured . . 25 10

775 Racing Car and Chequered Flag

1990. Mexico Formula One Grand Prix.
1963 **775** 700 p. black, red & green 25 10

776 Aircraft Tailfin

1990. 25th Anniv of Airports and Auxiliary Services.
1964 **776** 700 p. multicoloured . . 25 10

777 Family

1990. United Nations Anti-drugs Decade.
1965 **777** 700 p. multicoloured . . 25 10

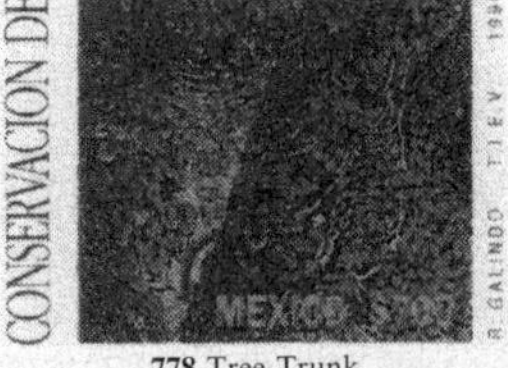

778 Tree Trunk

1990. Forest Conservation.
1966 **778** 700 p. multicoloured . . 25 10

779 Emblem

1990. "Solidarity".
1967 **779** 700 p. multicoloured . . 25 10
See also No. 2047.

780 Columns and Native Decoration

1990. World Heritage Site. Oaxaca.
1968 **780** 700 p. multicoloured . . 25 10

781 Elegant Tern

1990. Conservation of Rasa Island, Gulf of California.
1969 **781** 700 p. grey, black & red 1·25 30

782 Institute Activities

1990. 25th Anniv of Mexican Petroleum Institute.
1970 **782** 700 p. blue and black . 25 10

783 National Colours, City Monuments and Runners

1990. 18th International Mexico City Marathon.
1971 **783** 700 p. black, red & green 25 10

784 Facade

1990. 50th Anniv of Colima University.
1972 **784** 700 p. multicoloured . . 25 10

785 Abstract

1990. Mexico City Consultative Council.
1973 **785** 700 p. multicoloured . . 25 10

786 Electricity Worker

1990. 30th Anniv of Nationalization of Electricity Industry.
1974 **786** 700 p. multicoloured . . 25 10

787 Violin and Bow

1990. 50th Death Anniv of Silvestre Revueltas (violinist).
1975 **787** 700 p. multicoloured . . 25 10

788 Building

1990. 450th Anniv of Campeche.
1976 **788** 700 p. multicoloured . . 25 15

789 Crossed Rifle and Pen 790 Emblem

1990. 80th Anniv of San Luis Plan.
1977 **789** 700 p. multicoloured . . 25 15

1990. 14th World Supreme Councils Conference.
1978 **790** 1500 p. multicoloured . . 55 35

791 Spanish Tower and Mexican Pyramid

1990. 500th Anniv of "Meeting of Two Worlds" (4th issue).
1979 **791** 700 p. multicoloured . . 25 15

792 Glass of Beer, Ear of Barley and Hop 793 Carving

1990. Centenary of Brewing Industry.
1980 **792** 700 p. multicoloured . . 25 15

1990. Bicentenary of Archaeology in Mexico.
1981 **793** 1500 p. multicoloured . . 55 35

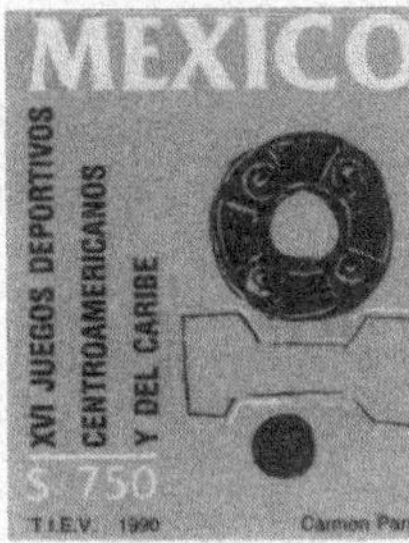

794 Ball-game Field 795 Globe and Poinsettia

1990. 16th Central American and Caribbean Games. Multicoloured.
1982 750 p. Type **794** 30 20
1983 750 p. Amerindian ball-game player 30 20
1984 750 p. Amerindian ball-game player (different) (horiz) . 30 20
1985 750 p. Yutsil and Balam (mascots) (horiz) 30 20

1990. Christmas. Multicoloured.
1986 700 p. Type **795** 25 15
1987 700 p. Fireworks and candles 25 15

796 Dog (statuette)

1990. 50th Anniv of Mexican Canine Federation.
1988 **796** 700 p. multicoloured . . 25 15

797 Microscope, Dolphin and Hand holding Map

1991. 50th Anniv of Naval Secretariat.
1989 **797** 1000 p. gold, black & bl 40 25

798 Means of Transport

1991. Accident Prevention.
1990 **798** 700 p. multicoloured . . 40 15

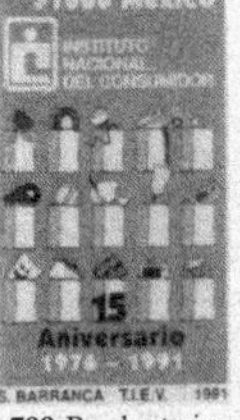

799 Products in Bags 800 "In order to Decide, Register"

1991. 15th Anniv of National Consumer Institute.
1991 **799** 1000 p. multicoloured . . 40 25

1991. Electoral Register.
1992 **800** 1000 p. orange, grn & blk 40 25

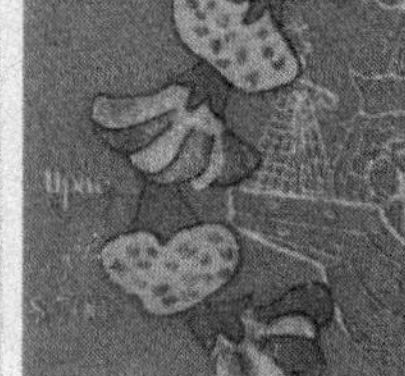

801 Basketball Player **802** Flowers and Caravel

1991. Olympic Games, Barcelona (1992) (1st issue).
1993 **801** 1000 p. black and yellow . . 40 25
See also Nos. 2050, 2057 and 2080/9.

1991. America (1990). Natural World. Mult.
1994 700 p. Type **802** 40 15
1995 700 p. Right half of caravel, blue and yellow macaw and flowers 40 15
Nos. 1994/5 were issued together, se-tenant, forming a composite design.

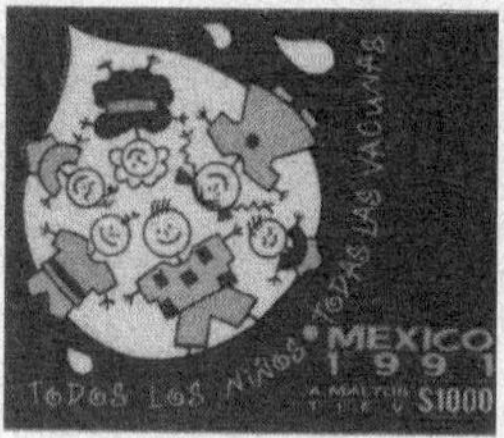

803 Children in Droplet

1991. Children's Month. Vaccination Campaign.
1996 **803** 1000 p. multicoloured . . 40 25

804 Map **805** Dove and Children

1991. World Post Day (1990).
1997 **804** 1500 p. multicoloured . . 55 35

1991. Children's Days for Peace and Development.
1998 **805** 1000 p. multicoloured . . 40 25

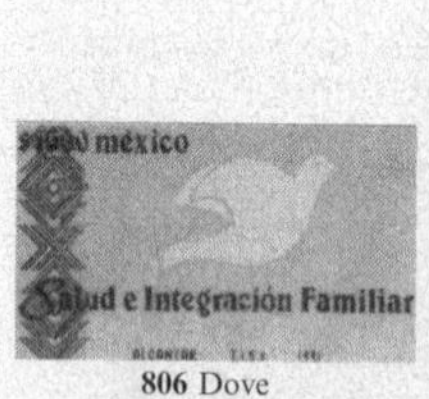

806 Dove **807** Mining

1991. Family Health and Unity.
1999 **806** 1000 p. multicoloured . . 40 25

1991. 500th Anniv of Mining.
2000 **807** 1000 p. multicoloured . . 40 25

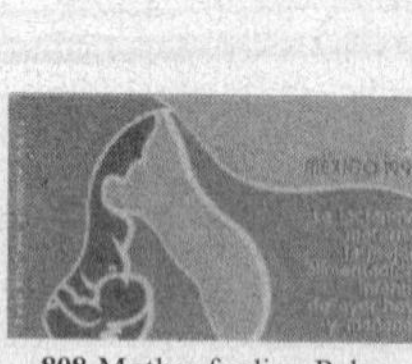

808 Mother feeding Baby **809** Emblem

1991. Breastfeeding Campaign.
2001 **808** 1000 p. buff, blue & brn 40 25

1991. 16th Tourism Fair, Acapulco.
2002 **809** 1000 p. green & dp green 40 25

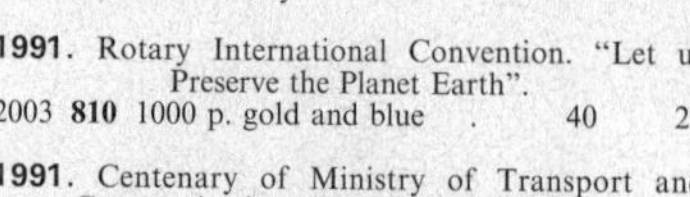

810 Rotary Emblem and Independence Monument, Mexico City **811** "Communication"

1991. Rotary International Convention. "Let us Preserve the Planet Earth".
2003 **810** 1000 p. gold and blue . 40 25

1991. Centenary of Ministry of Transport and Communications (S.C.T.). Multicoloured.
2004 1000 p. Type **811** 40 35
2005 1000 p. Boeing 737 landing . 40 25
2006 1000 p. Facsimile machine . 40 25
2007 1000 p. Van 40 25
2008 1000 p. Satellites and Earth 40 25
2009 1000 p. Railway freight cars on bridge 40 25
2010 1000 p. Telephone users . . 40 25
2011 1000 p. Road bridge over road 40 25
2012 1000 p. Road bridge and cliffs 40 25
2013 1000 p. Stern of container ship and dockyard 40 25
2014 1000 p. Television camera and presenter 40 25
2015 1000 p. Front of truck at toll gate 40 25
2016 1000 p. Roadbuilding ("Solidarity") 40 25
2017 1500 p. Boeing 737 and control tower 55 35
2018 1500 p. Part of fax machine, transmitters and dish aerials on S.C.T. building 55 35
2019 1500 p. Satellite (horiz) . . . 55 35
2020 1500 p. Railway locomotives 55 35
2021 1500 p. S.C.T. building . . . 55 35
2022 1500 p. Road bridge over ravine 55 35
2023 1500 p. Bow of container ship and dockyard 55 35
2024 1500 p. Bus at toll gate . . . 55 35
2025 1500 p. Rear of truck and trailer at toll gate 55 35
Nos. 2005/25 were issued together, se-tenant, each block containing several composite designs.

812 Jaguar

1991. Lacandona Jungle Conservation.
2026 **812** 1000 p. black, orge & red 40 25

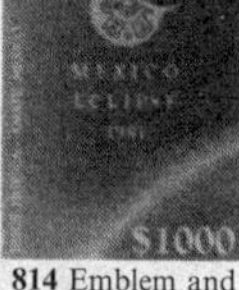

813 Driver and Car **814** Emblem and Left-hand Sections of Sun and Earth

1991. Mexico Formula 1 Grand Prix.
2027 **813** 1000 p. multicoloured . . 40 25

1991. Total Eclipse of the Sun. Multicoloured.
2028 1000 p. Type **814** 40 25
2029 1000 p. Emblem and right-hand sections of sun and Earth 40 25
2030 1500 p. Emblem and centre of sun and Earth showing north and central America . . . 55 35
Nos. 2028/30 were issued together, se-tenant, forming a composite design.

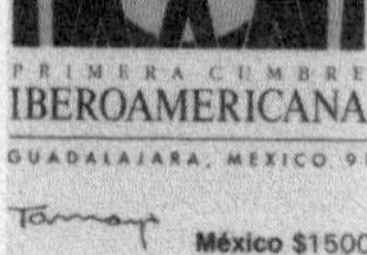

815 "Solidarity" (Rufino Tamayo) **816** Bridge

1991. 1st Latin American Presidential Summit, Guadalajara.
2031 **815** 1500 p. black, orge & yell 55 35

1991. Solidarity between Nuevo Leon and Texas.
2032 **816** 2000 p. multicoloured . . 1·10 75

817 Runners **819** Emblem

818 Cogwheel

1991. 9th Mexico City Marathon.
2033 **817** 1000 p. multicoloured . . 40 25

1991. 50th Anniv (1990) of National Chambers of Industry and Commerce.
2034 **818** 1500 p. multicoloured . . 55 35

1991. 55th Anniv of Federation Fiscal Tribunal.
2035 **819** 1000 p. silver and blue . . 40 25

820 National Colours forming Emblem

1991. "Solidarity–Let us Unite in order to Progress".
2036 **820** 1000 p. multicoloured . . 40 25

821 Dove with Letter **822** World Map

1991. World Post Day.
2037 **821** 1500 p. multicoloured . . 40 25

1991. 500th Anniv of "Meeting of Two Worlds" (5th issue).
2038 **822** 1000 p. multicoloured . . 40 25

823 Caravel, Sun and Trees

1991. America. Voyages of Discovery. Mult.
2039 1000 p. Type **823** 40 25
2040 1000 p. Storm cloud, caravel and broken snake 40 25

824 Flowers and Pots

1991. Christmas. Multicoloured.
2041 1000 p. Type **824** 40 25
2042 1000 p. Children with decoration 40 25

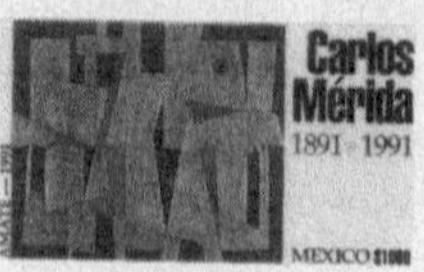

825 Abstract

1991. Carlos Merida (artist) Commemoration.
2043 **825** 1000 p. multicoloured . . 40 25

826 Score and Portrait

1991. Death Bicentenary of Wolfgang Amadeus Mozart (composer).
2044 **826** 1000 p. multicoloured . . 40 25

827 Kidney Beans and Maize

1991. Self-sufficiency in Kidney Beans and Maize.
2045 **827** 1000 p. multicoloured . . 40 25

828 City Plan

1991. 450th Anniv of Morelia.
2046 **828** 1000 p. brown, stone and red 40 25

1991. "Solidarity". As No. 1967 but new value.
2047 **779** 1000 p. multicoloured . . 40 25

829 Merida

1992. 450th Anniv of Merida.
2048 **829** 1300 p. multicoloured . . 60 40

830 Colonnade

1992. Bicentenary of Engineering Training in Mexico.
2049 **830** 1300 p. blue and red . . 60 40

831 Horse Rider

1992. Olympic Games, Barcelona (2nd issue).
2050 **831** 2000 p. multicoloured . . 90 60

MINIMUM PRICE

The minimum price quoted is 10p which represents a handling charge rather than a basis for valuing common stamps. For further notes about prices, see introductory pages.

832 City Arms

1992. 450th Anniv of Guadalajara. Multicoloured.

2051 1300 p. Type **832** 60 40
2052 1300 p. "Guadalajara Town Hall" (Jorge Navarro) . . 60 40
2053 1300 p. "Guadalajara Cathedral" (Gabriel Flores) 60 40
2054 1900 p. "Founding of Guadalajara" (Rafael Zamarripa) 85 55
2055 1900 p. Anniversary emblem (Ignacio Vazquez) 85 55

833 Children and Height Gauge **834** Olympic Torch and Rings

1992. Child Health Campaign.

2056 **833** 2000 p. multicoloured . . 90 60

1992. Olympic Games, Barcelona (3rd issue).

2057 **834** 2000 p. multicoloured . . 90 60

835 Horse and Racing Car

1992. "500th Anniv of the Wheel and the Horse in America". Mexico Formula 1 Grand Prix.

2058 **835** 1300 p. multicoloured . . 60 40

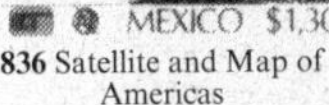

836 Satellite and Map of Americas **837** Human Figure and Cardiograph

1992. "Americas Telecom '92" Telecommunications Exhibition.

2059 **836** 1300 p. multicoloured . . 60 40

1992. World Health Day.

2060 **837** 1300 p. black, red & blue 60 40

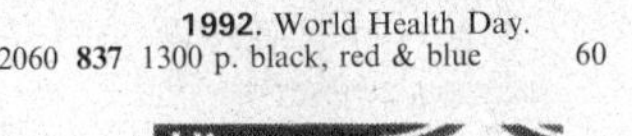

838 Emblem

1992. 60th Anniv of Military Academy.

2061 **838** 1300 p. red, yellow & blk 60 40

839 "Inspiration of Christopher Columbus" (Jose Maria Obregon) **840** Complex

1992. 500th Anniv of "Meeting of Two Worlds" (6th issue). "Granada 92" International Stamp Exhibition.

2062 1300 p. Type **839** 60 40
2063 1300 p. "Racial Encounter" (Jorge Gonazalez Camarena) 60 40
2064 2000 p. "Origin of the Sky" (Selden Codex) 90 60
2065 2000 p. "Quetzalcoatl and Tezcatlipoca" (Borhomico Codex) 90 60
2066 2000 p. "From Spaniard and Indian, mestizo" 90 60

1992. National Medical Centre.

2068 **840** 1300 p. multicoloured . 60 40

841 Children, Dove and Globe **842** New-born Baby

1992. Children's Rights.

2069 **841** 1300 p. multicoloured . 60 40

1992. Traditional Childbirth.

2070 **842** 1300 p. multicoloured . 60 40

1992. "World Columbian Stamp Expo '92", Chicago. Nos. 2062/6 optd **WORLD COLUMBIAN STAMP EXPO '92 MAY 22-31, 1992 - CHICAGO** and emblem.

2071 1300 p. mult (No. 2062) . . 50 35
2072 1300 p. mult (No. 2063) . . 50 35
2073 2000 p. mult (No. 2064) . . 80 55
2074 2000 p. mult (No. 2065) . . 80 55
2075 2000 p. mult (No. 2066) . . 80 55

845 Arms of Colleges

1992. Bicentenary of Mexico Notary College.

2078 **845** 1300 p. multicoloured . 50 35

846 Trees and Cacti

1992. Tree Day.

2079 **846** 1300 p. multicoloured . 50 35

847 Boxing **848** Athlete

1992. Olympic Games, Barcelona (4th issue). Mult.

2080 1300 p. Type **847** 50 35
2081 1300 p. High jumping . . . 50 35
2082 1300 p. Fencing 50 35
2083 1300 p. Shooting 50 35
2084 1300 p. Gymnastics 50 35
2085 1900 p. Rowing 75 50
2086 1900 p. Running 75 50
2087 1900 p. Football 75 50
2088 1900 p. Swimming 75 50
2089 2000 p. Equestrian 80 55

1992. 10th Mexico City Marathon.

2091 **848** 1300 p. multicoloured . 50 35

TERCERA SEMANA NACIONAL
Solidaridad
Unidos para progresar
MEXICO $1,300

849 Emblem

1992. "Solidarity".

2092 **849** 1300 p. multicoloured . 50 35

851 Television, Map and Radio

1992. 50th Anniv of National Chamber of Television and Radio Industry.

2094 **851** 1300 p. multicoloured . . 50 35

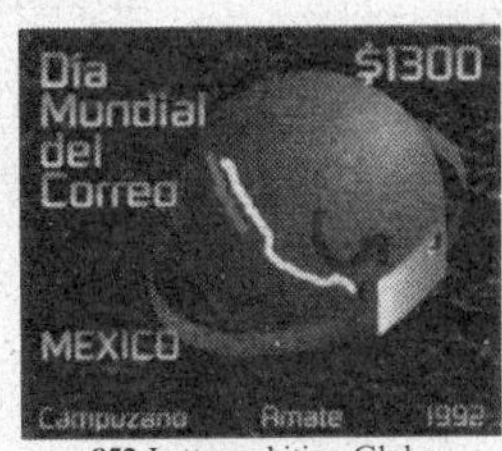

852 Letter orbiting Globe

1992. World Post Day.

2095 **852** 1300 p. multicoloured . . 50 35

853 Satellite above South and Central America and Flags

1992. American Cadena Communications System.

2096 **853** 2000 p. multicoloured . . 80 55

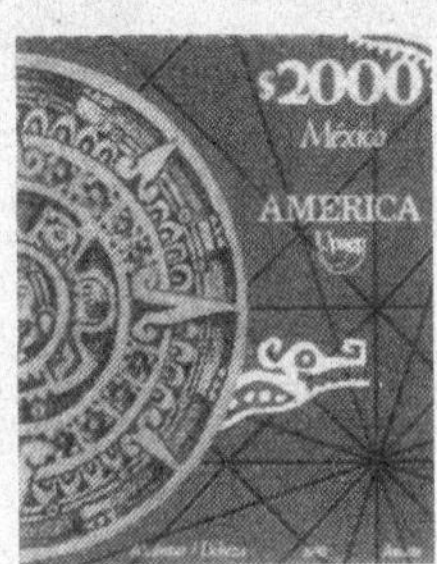

854 Gold Compass Rose

1992. America. 500th Anniv of Discovery of America by Columbus. Multicoloured.

2097 2000 p. Type **854** 80 55
2098 2000 p. Compass rose (different) and fish 80 55

Nos. 2097/8 were issued together, se-tenant, forming a composite design.

855 Scroll

1992. 400th Anniv of San Luis Potosi.

2099 **855** 1300 p. black and mauve 50 35

856 Berrendos Deer

1992. Conservation.

2100 **856** 1300 p. multicoloured . . 50 35

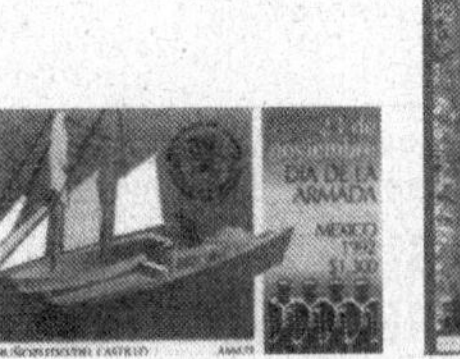

857 Schooner, Landing Ship, Emblem and Sailors **858** Christmas Tree, Children and Crib

1992. Navy Day.

2101 **857** 1300 p. multicoloured . . 50 35

1992. Christmas. Children's Drawings. Mult.

2102 1300 p. Type **858** 50 35
2103 2000 p. Street celebration (horiz) 80 55

Currency Reform. 1 (new) peso = 1000 (old) pesos.

Sociedad Mexicana de Oftalmologia
CENTENARIO
N$ 1.30
México
1993

859 Anniversary Emblem **860** Emblem

1993. 50th Anniv of Mexican Social Security Institute (1st issue).

2104 **859** 1 p. 50 green, gold & blk 60 40

See also Nos. 2110 and 2152/3.

1993. Centenary of Mexican Opthalmological Society.

2105 **860** 1 p. 30 multicoloured . . 50 35

861 Children **862** Society Arms and Founders

1993. Children's Month.

2106 **861** 1 p. 30 multicoloured . . 50 35

1993. 160th Anniv of Mexican Geographical and Statistical Society.

2107 **862** 1 p. 30 multicoloured . . 50 35

863 1824 Constitution **864** Gomez, Children and Hospital

1993. 150th Death Anniv of Miguel Ramos Arizpe, "Father of Federalism".

2108 **863** 1 p. 30 multicoloured . . 50 35

1993. 50th Anniv of Federico Gomez Children's Hospital.

2109 **864** 1 p. 30 multicoloured . . 50 35

865 Doctor with Child

1993. 50th Anniv of Mexican Social Security Institute (2nd issue). Medical Services.

2110 **865** 1 p. 30 multicoloured . . 50 35

866 Mother feeding Baby

1993. "Health begins at Home".

2111 **866** 1 p. 30 multicoloured . . 50 35

867 Seal and Map

1993. Upper Gulf of California Nature Reserve.

2112 **867** 1 p. 30 multicoloured . . 50 35

868 Cantinflas

1993. Mexican Film Stars. Mario Moreno (Cantinflas).
2113 **868** 1 p. 30 black and blue . . 50 35
See also Nos. 2156/60.

869 Campeche

1993. Tourism. Multicoloured.
2114 90 c. Type **869** 35 25
2115 1 p. Guanajuato 40 25
2116 1 p. 30 Colima 50 35
2117 1 p. 90 Michoacan (vert) . . 75 50
2118 2 p. Coahuila 80 55
2119 2 p. 20 Queretaro 90 60
2120 2 p. 50 Sonora . . . . . . 1·00 65
2121 2 p. 80 Zacatecas (vert) . . . 1·10 75
2122 3 p. 70 Sinaloa . . . . . 1·50 1·00
2123 4 p. 40 Yucatan . . . . . . 1·75 1·10
2124 4 p. 80 Chiapas . . . . . 1·90 1·25
2125 6 p. Mexico City . . . . . 2·40 1·60
See also Nos. 2263/90.

870 Dr. Maximiliano Ruiz Castaneda

1993. 50th Anniv of Health Service. Multicoloured.
2126 1 p. 30 Type **870** 50 35
2127 1 p. 30 Dr. Bernardo Sepulveda Gutierrez 50 35
2128 1 p. 30 Dr. Ignacio Chavez Sanchez 50 35
2129 1 p. 30 Dr. Mario Salazar Mallen 50 35
2130 1 p. 30 Dr. Gustavo Baz Prada 50 35

871 Brazil 30 r. "Bull's Eye" Stamp 872 Runners

1993. 150th Anniv of First Brazilian Stamps.
2131 **871** 2 p. multicoloured . . . 80 55

1993. 11th Mexico City Marathon.
2132 **872** 1 p. 30 multicoloured . . 50 35

873 Emblem 874 Open Book and Symbols

1993. "Solidarity".
2133 **873** 1 p. 30 multicoloured . . 50 35

1993. 50th Anniv of Monterrey Institute of Technology and Higher Education. Multicoloured.
2134 1 p. 30 Type **874** 50 35
2135 2 p. Buildings and mountains 80 55
Nos. 2134/5 were issued together, se-tenant, forming a composite design.

875 Cogwheels and Emblem 876 Torreon

1993. 75th Anniv of Concamin.
2136 **875** 1 p. 30 multicoloured . 50 35

1993. Centenary of Torreon.
2137 **876** 1 p. 30 multicoloured . 50 35

877 Emblem

1993. "Europalia 93 Mexico" Festival.
2138 **877** 2 p. multicoloured . . . 80 55

878 Globe in Envelope 879 Gen. Guadalupe Victoria

1993. World Post Day.
2139 **878** 2 p. multicoloured . . . 80 55

1993. 150th Death Anniv of General Manuel Guadalupe Victoria (first President, 1824–28).
2140 **879** 1 p. 30 multicoloured . 50 35

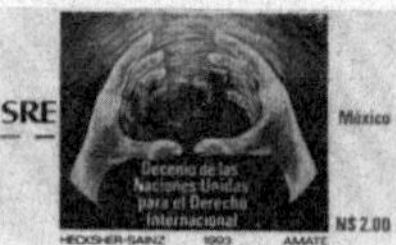
880 Emblem 881 Hands protecting Foetus

1993. National Civil Protection System and International Day for Reduction of Natural Disasters.
2141 **880** 1 p. 30 red, blk and yell 50 35

1993. United Nations Decade of International Law.
2142 **881** 2 p. multicoloured . . . 80 55

882 Torch Carrier

1993. 20th National Wheelchair Games.
2143 **882** 1 p. 30 multicoloured . 50 35

883 Peon y Contreras

1993. 150th Birth Anniv of Jose Peon y Contreras (poet, dramatist and founder of National Romantic Theatre).
2144 **883** 1 p. 30 violet and black 50 35

884 Horned Guan 885 Presents around Trees

1993. America. Endangered Birds. Multicoloured.
2145 2 p. Type **884** 80 55
2146 2 p. Resplendent quetzal on branch (horiz) 80 55

1993. Christmas. Multicoloured.
2147 1 p. 30 Type **885** 50 35
2148 1 p. 30 Three wise men (horiz) 50 35

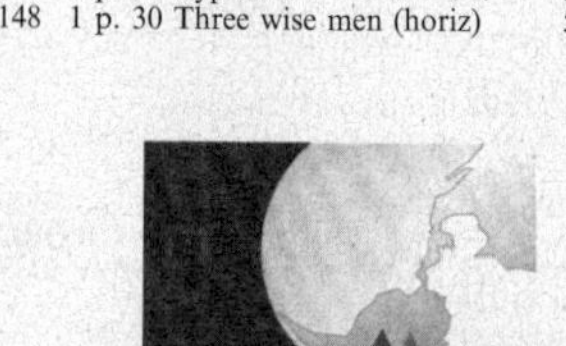

886 Satellites orbiting Earth

1993. "Solidarity".
2149 **886** 1 p. 30 multicoloured . . 50 35

887 School and Arms

1993. 125th Anniv of National Preparatory School.
2150 **887** 1 p. 30 multicoloured . . 50 35

888 Emblem on Map

1993. 55th Anniv of Municipal Workers Trade Union.
2151 **888** 1 p. 30 multicoloured . . 50 35

889 Hands

1993. 50th Anniv of Mexican Social Security Institute (3rd issue). Multicoloured.
2152 1 p. 30 Type **889** (social security) 50 35
2153 1 p. 30 Ball, building blocks, child's painting and dummy (day nurseries) 50 35

890 Mezcala Solidarity Bridge

1993. Tourism. Multicoloured.
2154 1 p. 30 Type **890** 50 35
2155 1 p. 30 Mexico City–Acapulco motorway 50 35

1993. Mexican Film Stars. As T **868**.
2156 1 p. 30 black and blue 50 35
2157 1 p. 30 black and orange . . 50 35
2158 1 p. 30 black and green . . 50 35
2159 1 p. 30 black and violet . . . 50 35
2160 1 p. 30 black and pink . . . 50 35
DESIGNS:—No, 2156, Pedro Armendariz in "Juan Charrasqueado"; 2157, Maria Felix in "The Lover"; 2158, Pedro Infante in "Necesito dinero"; 2159, Jorge Negrete in "It is not enough to be a Peasant"; 2160, Dolores del Rio in "Flor Silvestre".

891 Estefania Castaneda Nunez

1994. 72nd Anniv of Secretariat of Public Education. Educationists. Multicoloured.
2161 1 p. 30 Type **891** 50 35
2162 1 p. 30 Lauro Aguirre Espinosa 50 35
2163 1 p. 30 Rafael Ramirez Castaneda 50 35
2164 1 p. 30 Moises Saenz Garza . 50 35
2165 1 p. 30 Gregorio Torres Quintero 50 35
2166 1 p. 30 Jose Vasconcelos . . 50 35
2167 1 p. 30 Rosaura Zapato Cano 50 35

892 Zapata (after H. Velarde) 893 Emblem and Worker

1994. 75th Death Anniv of Emiliano Zapata (revolutionary).
2168 **892** 1 p. 30 multicoloured . . 50 35

1994. 75th Anniv of I.L.O.
2169 **893** 2 p. multicoloured . . . 80 50

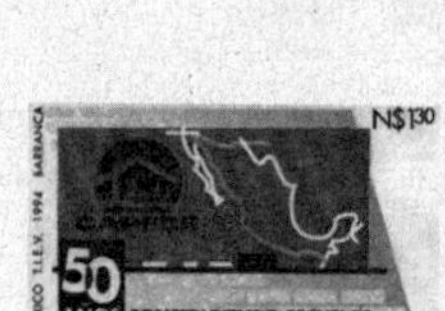

894 Map and Emblem 895 "Earth and Communication" (frieze, detail)

1994. 50th Anniv of National Schools Building Programme Committee.
2170 **894** 1 p. 30 multicoloured . . 50 35

1994. 3rd Death Anniv of Francisco Zuniga (sculptor).
2171 **895** 1 p. 30 multicoloured . . 50 35

896 Flower and Children

1994. Children's Organization for Peace and Development.
2172 **896** 1 p. 30 multicoloured . . 50 35

897 Greater Flamingo

1994. DUMAC Nature Protection Organization.
2173 **897** 1 p. 30 multicoloured . . 50 35

898 Children and Silhouette of Absentee

1994. Care and Control of Minors.
2174 **898** 1 p. 30 black and green . 50 35

899 Man and Letters

900 Route Map

1994. 34th World Advertising Congress, Cancun.
2175 **899** 2 p. multicoloured . . . 80 35

1994. 50th Anniv of National Association of Importers and Exporters.
2176 **900** 1 p. 30 multicoloured . . 50 35

901 Head and Emblem

1994. International Telecommunications Day.
2177 **901** 2 p. multicoloured . . . 80 55

902 Animals

1994. Yumka Wildlife Centre, Villahermosa.
2178 **902** 1 p. 30 multicoloured . . 50 35

903 Town Centre

904 Mother and Baby

1994. U.N.E.S.C.O. World Heritage Site, Zacatecas.
2179 **903** 1 p. 30 multicoloured . . 50 35

1994. Friendship Hospital. Mother and Child Health Month.
2180 **904** 1 p. 30 multicoloured . . 30 20

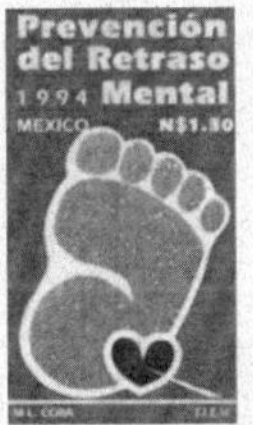

905 Foot and Heart

906 Song and Ornamental Birds

1994. Prevention of Mental Retardation.
2181 **905** 1 p. 30 multicoloured . . 30 20

1994. Nature Conservation. Multicoloured.

2182	1 p. 30 Type **906**	30	20
2183	1 p. 30 Game birds (silhouettes)	30	20
2184	1 p. 30 Threatened animals (silhouettes)	30	20
2185	1 p. 30 Animals in danger of extinction (silhouettes) . .	30	20
2186	1 p. 30 Orange-fronted conures	30	20
2187	1 p. 30 Yellow-tailed oriole .	30	20
2188	1 p. 30 Pyrrhuloxias	30	20
2189	1 p. 30 Loggerhead shrike . .	30	20
2190	1 p. 30 Northern mockingbird	30	20
2191	1 p. 30 Common turkey . . .	30	20
2192	1 p. 30 White-winged dove .	30	20
2193	1 p. 30 Red-billed whistling duck	30	20
2194	1 p. 30 Snow goose	30	20
2195	1 p. 30 Gambel's quail . . .	30	20
2196	1 p. 30 Peregrine falcon . . .	30	20
2197	1 p. 30 Jaguar	30	20
2198	1 p. 30 Jaguarundi	30	20
2199	1 p. 30 Mantled howler monkey	30	20
2200	1 p. 30 Californian sealions .	30	20
2201	1 p. 30 Pronghorn	30	20
2202	1 p. 30 Scarlet macaw	30	20
2203	1 p. 30 Mexican prairie dogs	30	20
2204	1 p. 30 Wolf	30	20
2205	1 p. 30 American manatee . .	30	20

907 Player

908 Fish

1994. World Cup Football Championship, U.S.A. Multicoloured.
2206 2 p. Type **907** 45 30
2207 2 p. Goalkeeper 45 30
Nos. 2206/7 were issued together, se-tenant, forming a composite design.

1994. International Fishing Festival, Veracruz.
2208 **908** 1 p. 30 multicoloured . 30 20

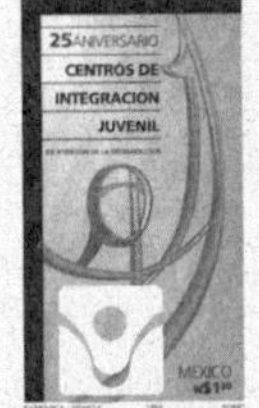

909 Stylized Figure and Emblem

910 "Butterflies" (Carmen Parra)

1994. 25th Anniv of Juvenile Integration Centres.
2209 **909** 1 p. 30 multicoloured . 30 20

1994. 50th Aniv of Diplomatic Relations with Canada.
2210 **910** 2 p. multicoloured . . . 45 30

911 Emblems

912 Emblem and Family

1994. 20th Anniv of National Population Council.
2211 **911** 1 p. 30 multicoloured . 30 20

1994. International Year of the Family.
2212 **912** 2 p. multicoloured . . . 45 30

913 Runner breasting Tape

914 Giant Panda

1994. 12th Mexico City International Marathon.
2213 **913** 1 p. 30 multicoloured . 30 20

1994. Chapultepec Zoo.
2214 **914** 1 p. 30 multicoloured . 30 20

915 Tree

916 Anniversary Emblem

1994. Tree Day.
2215 **915** 1 p. 30 brown and green 30 20

1994. 60th Anniv of Economic Culture Fund.
2216 **916** 1 p. 30 multicoloured . 30 20

917 Statue and Underground Train

918 Cathedral and Gardens

1994. 25th Anniv of Mexico City Transport System.
2217 **917** 1 p. 30 multicoloured . . 30 20

1994. 350th Anniv of Salvatierra City, Guanajuato.
2218 **918** 1 p. 30 purple, grey and black 30 20

919 State Flag and National Anthem

1994. National Symbols Week.
2219 **919** 1 p. 30 multicoloured . . 30 20

920 Building and Anniversary Emblem

921 Figures with Flags

1994. 40th Anniv of University City.
2220 **920** 1 p. 30 multicoloured . . 30 20

1994. 5th Solidarity Week.
2221 **921** 1 p. 30 black, red and green 30 20

922 Lopez Mateos

923 Palace Facade

1994. 25th Death Anniv of Adolfo Lopez Mateos (President, 1958–64).
2222 **922** 1 p. 30 multicoloured . . 30 20

1994. 60th Anniv of Palace of Fine Arts.
2223 **923** 1 p. 30 black and grey . . 30 20

924 Rings and "100"

1994. Centenary of International Olympic Committee.
2224 **924** 2 p. multicoloured . . . 45 30

925 Quarter Horse (Juan Rayas)

1994. Horses. Paintings by artists named. Multicoloured.
2225 1 p. 30 Aztec horse (Heladio Velarde) 30 20
2226 1 p. 30 Type **925** 30 20
2227 1 p. 30 Quarter horse (Rayas) (different) 30 20
2228 1 p. 30 Vaquero on horseback (Velarde) 30 20
2229 1 p. 30 Aztec horse (Velarde) 30 20
2230 1 p. 30 Rider with lance (Velarde) 30 20

926 Emblem

927 Saint-Exupery and The Little Prince (book character)

1994. Inauguration of 20th November National Medical Centre.
2231 **926** 1 p. 30 multicoloured . . 30 20

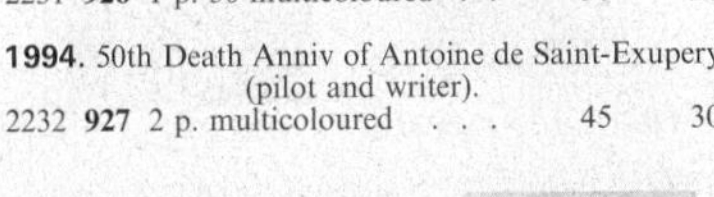

1994. 50th Death Anniv of Antoine de Saint-Exupery (pilot and writer).
2232 **927** 2 p. multicoloured . . . 45 30

928 Man writing Letters to Woman

929 Urban Postman on Bicycle

1994. World Post Day.
2233 **928** 2 p. multicoloured . . . 35 25

1994. America. Postal Transport. Multicoloured.
2234 2 p. Type **929** 35 25
2235 2 p. Rural postman with bicycle 35 25
Nos. 2234/5 were issued together, se-tenant, forming a composite design.

930 Couple (Sofia Bassi)

1994. Ancestors' Day.
2236 **930** 1 p. 30 multicoloured . . 20 15

931 Water Drop and Hand

932 Dr. Mora

1994. National Clean Water Programme.
2237 **931** 1 p. 30 multicoloured . . 20 15

1994. Birth Bicentenary of Dr. Jose Maria Luis Mora (journalist and politician).
2238 **932** 1 p. 30 multicoloured . . 20 15

933 Theatre and Soler (actor)

1994. 15th Anniv of Fernando Soler Theatre, Saltillo, Coahuila.
2239 **933** 1 p. 30 multicoloured . . 20 15

MINIMUM PRICE

The minimum price quoted is 10p which represents a handling charge rather than a basis for valuing common stamps. For further notes about prices, see introductory pages.

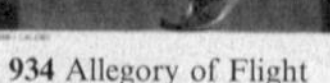

934 Allegory of Flight

935 Museum's Central Pillar

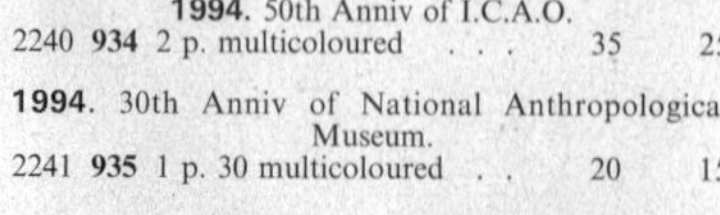

1994. 50th Anniv of I.C.A.O.
2240 **934** 2 p. multicoloured . . . 35 25

1994. 30th Anniv of National Anthropological Museum.
2241 **935** 1 p. 30 multicoloured . . 20 15

936 Theatrical Masks

937 Allende

1994. 60th Anniv of National Association of Actors.
2242 **936** 1 p. 30 multicoloured . . 20 15

1994. 225th Birth Anniv of Ignacio Allende (independence hero).
2243 **937** 1 p. 30 multicoloured . . 20 15

938 Chapultepec Castle

1994. 50th Anniv of National History Museum.
2244 **938** 1 p. 30 multicoloured . . 20 15

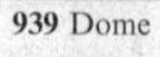

939 Dome

940 Anniversary Emblem

1994. Centenary of Coahuila School.
2245 **939** 1 p. 30 multicoloured . . 20 15

1994. 40th Anniv of Pumas University Football Club.
2246 **940** 1 p. 30 blue and gold . . 20 15

941 Decorated Tree

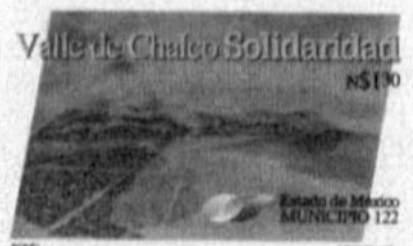

942 Valley

1994. Christmas. Multicoloured.
2247 2 p. Type **941** 35 25
2248 2 p. Couple watching shooting star (horiz) 35 25

1994. "Solidarity". Chalco Valley.
2249 **942** 1 p. 30 multicoloured . . 20 15

943 Ines de la Cruz (after Miguel de Cabrera)

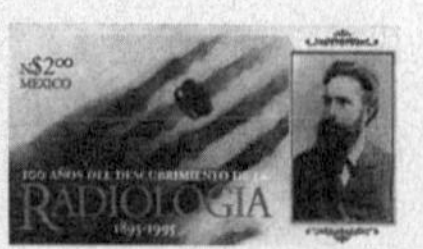

944 X-Ray of Hand and Rontgen

1995. 300th Birth Anniv of Juana Ines de la Cruz (mystic poet).
2250 **943** 1 p. 80 multicoloured . . 30 20

1995. Centenary of Discovery of X-Rays by Wilhelm Rontgen.
2251 **944** 2 p. multicoloured . . 35 25

945 Ignacio Altamirano

946 Emblem

1995. Teachers' Day.
2252 **945** 1 p. 80 black, grn & bl . . 30 20

1995. World Telecommunications Day. "Telecommunications and the Environment".
2253 **946** 2 p. 70 multicoloured . . 45 30

947 Anniversary Emblem

948 Marti

1995. 40th Anniv of National Institute of Public Administration.
2254 **947** 1 p. 80 grn, mve & lilac . . 30 20

1995. Death Centenary of Jose Marti (Cuban writer and revolutionary).
2255 **948** 2 p. 70 multicoloured . . 35 25

949 Carranza

950 Kite

1995. 75th Death Anniv of Venustiano Carranza (President 1914–20).
2256 **949** 1 p. 80 multicoloured . . 30 20

1995. 20th Anniv of National Tourist Organization.
2257 **950** 2 p. 70 multicoloured . . 40 25

951 Drugs, Skull and Unhappy Face

952 Cardenas del Rio

1995. International Day against Drug Abuse and Trafficking. Multicoloured.
2258 1 p. 80 Type **951** 30 20
2259 1 p. 80 Drug addict on swing . . 30 20
2260 1 p. 80 Faces behind bars . . . 30 20

1995. Birth Centenary of Gen. Lazaro Cardenas del Rio (President 1934–40).
2261 **952** 1 p. 80 black 30 20

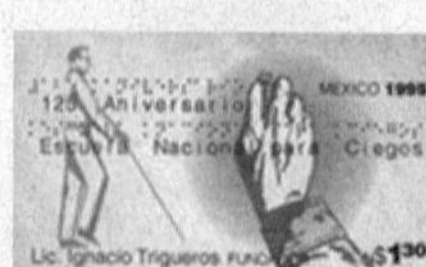

953 Man with White Stick and Hand reading Braille

1995. 125th Anniv of National Blind School.
2262 **953** 1 p. 30 brown and black . . 20 15

1995. As Type **869**.
2263 1 p. 10 Guanajuato 15 10
2264 1 p. 80 Chiapas 30 20
2265 1 p. 80 Coahuila 30 20
2266 1 p. 80 Colima 30 20
2269 2 p. As No. 2266 . . . . . 30 20
2271 2 p. 30 Sinaloa 35 25
2272 2 p. 40 Yucatan 40 25
2274 2 p. 70 Mexico City 40 25
2276 3 p. Type **869** 45 30
2278 3 p. 40 As No. 2271 . . . . 55 35
2280 3 p. 80 As No. 2272 . . . . . 60 40
2290 6 p. 50 Sonora . . . . 1·00 65

954 Pintails

1995. Animals. Multicoloured.
2295 2 p. 70 Type **954** 40 25
2296 2 p. 70 Belted kingfisher . . . 40 25
2297 2 p. 70 Orange tiger 40 25
2298 2 p. 70 Hoary bat 40 25

955 Runners

956 Envelopes

1995. 13th International Marathon, Mexico City.
2299 **955** 2 p. 70 multicoloured . . 40 25

1995. 16th Congress of Postal Union of the Americas, Spain and Portugal, Mexico City.
2300 **956** 2 p. 70 multicoloured . . 40 25

957 Pasteur

958 Hands holding Envelopes

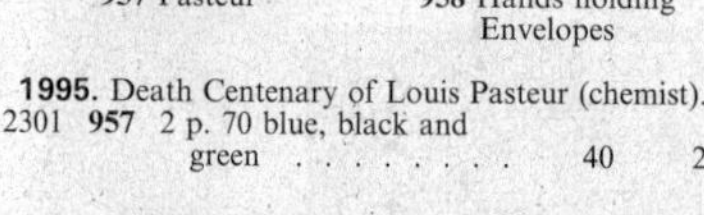

1995. Death Centenary of Louis Pasteur (chemist).
2301 **957** 2 p. 70 blue, black and green 40 25

1995. World Post Day.
2302 **958** 2 p. 70 multicoloured . . 40 25

959 Basket of Shopping

960 Anniversary Emblem

1995. World Food Day.
2303 **959** 1 p. 80 multicoloured . . 30 20

1995. 50th Anniv of F.A.O.
2304 **960** 2 p. 70 multicoloured . . 40 25

961 Elias Calles

962 Cuauhtemoc

1995. 50th Death Anniv of General Plutarco Elias Calles (President 1924–28).
2305 **961** 1 p. 80 multicoloured . . 30 20

1995. 500th Birth Anniv of Cuauhtemoc (Aztec Emperor of Tenochtitlan).
2306 **962** 1 p. 80 multicoloured . . 30 20

963 National Flag, National Anthem and Constitution

964 Flags as Tail of Dove

1995. National Constitution and Patriotic Symbols Day.
2307 **963** 1 p. 80 multicoloured . 30 20

1995. 50th Anniv of U.N.O.
2308 **964** 2 p. 70 multicoloured . 40 25

965 Airplane, Train and Motor Vehicle

1995. International Passenger Travel Year.
2309 **965** 2 p. 70 multicoloured . 40 25

966 "The Holy Family" (Andres de Concha)

1995. 30th Anniv of Museum of Mexican Art in the Vice-regency Period.
2310 **966** 1 p. 80 multicoloured . 30 20

967 Pedro Maria Anaya

1995. Generals in Mexican History. Each black, yellow and gold.
2311 1 p. 80 Type **967** 30 20
2312 1 p. 80 Felipe Berriozabal . . 30 20
2313 1 p. 80 Santos Degollado . . 30 20
2314 1 p. 80 Sostenes Rocha . . . 30 20
2315 1 p. 80 Leandro Valle . . . 30 20
2316 1 p. 80 Ignacio Zaragoza . . 30 20

968 Children playing in Garden (Pablo Osorio Gomez)

969 Emblem

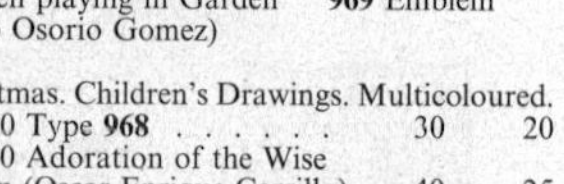

1995. Christmas. Children's Drawings. Multicoloured.
2317 1 p. 80 Type **968** 30 20
2318 2 p. 70 Adoration of the Wise Men (Oscar Enrique Carrillo) 40 25

1995. 10th Anniv of Mexican Health Foundation.
2319 **969** 1 p. 80 multicoloured . 30 20

970 Ocelot

971 Louis Lumiere and Cine-camera

1995. Nature Conservation.
2320 **970** 1 p. 80 multicoloured . . 30 20

1995. Centenary of Motion Pictures.
2321 **971** 1 p. 80 black, mauve and blue 30 20

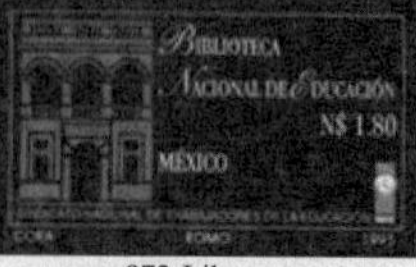

972 Library

1995. National Education Library, Mexico City.
2322 **972** 1 p. 80 green, blue and yellow 30 20

973 "Proportions of Man" (Leonardo da Vinci)

974 Pedro Vargas

1995. 50th Anniv of National Science and Arts Prize.
2323 **973** 1 p. 80 multicoloured . . 30 20

1995. Radio Personalities. Multicoloured.
2324 1 p. 80 Type **974** 30 20
2325 1 p. 80 Agustin Lara 30 20
2326 1 p. 80 Aguila Sisters 30 20
2327 1 p. 80 Tona "La Negra" . . 30 20
2328 1 p. 80 F. Gabilondo Soler "Cri-Cri" 30 20
2329 1 p. 80 Emilio Teuro 30 20
2330 1 p. 80 Gonzalo Curiel . . . 30 20
2331 1 p. 80 Lola Beltran 30 20

975 Robot Hand holding Optic Fibres

1995. 25th Anniv of Science and Technology Council.
2332 **975** 1 p. 80 multicoloured . 30 20

976 Airplane

1996. National Aviation Day. Multicoloured.
2333 1 p. 80 Type **976** 30 20
2334 1 p. 80 Squadron 201, 1945 . 30 20
2335 2 p. 70 Ley Airport 40 25
2336 2 p. 70 Modern jetliner and biplane 40 25

977 Child and Caso

1996. Birth Centenary of Dr. Alfonso Caso (anthropologist).
2337 **977** 1 p. 80 multicoloured . 30 20

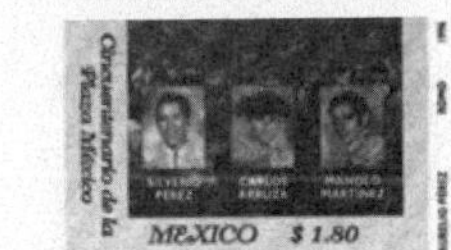

978 Silverio Perez, Carlos Arruza and Manolo Martinez

1996. 50th Anniv of Plaza Mexico (bullring). Matadors. Multicoloured.
2338 1 p. 80 Type **978** 30 20
2339 2 p. 70 Roldolfo Gaona, Fermin Espinosa and Lorenzo Garza 40 25
Nos. 2338/9 were issued together, se-tenant, forming a composite design of the bullring.

979 Bag of Groceries

1996. 20th Anniv of Federal Consumer Council.
2340 **979** 1 p. 80 multicoloured . 30 20

980 "Treatment of Fracture" (from Sahagun Codex)

1996. 50th Anniv of Mexican Society of Orthopaedics.
2341 **980** 1 p. 80 multicoloured . 30 20

981 Rulfo

1996. 10th Death Anniv of Juan Rulfo (writer).
2342 **981** 1 p. 80 multicoloured . 30 20

982 Anniversary Emblem and Map of Mexico

1996. 60th Anniv of National Polytechnic Institute.
2343 **982** 1 p. 80 grey, black and red 30 20

EXPRESS LETTER STAMPS

E 55 Express Service Messenger

1919.
E445 **E 55** 20 c. black and red . . 35 15

E 95

1934.
E536 **E 95** 10 c. blue and red . . . 15 30

E 121 Indian Archer

E 222

1934. New President's Assumption of Office. Imprint "OFICINA IMPRESORA DE HACIENDA–MEXICO".
E581 **E 121** 10 c. violet . . . . . . 1·00 20

1938. Imprint "TALLERES DE IMP. DE EST. Y VALORES-MEXICO".
E610 **E 121** 10 c. violet 55 20
E731 20 c. orange 25 30

1940. Optd **1940.**
E665 **E 55** 20 c. black and red . . 20 15

1950.
E860 **E 222** 25 c. orange 20 10
E910 – 60 c. green . . . . . . 1·10 35
DESIGN: 60 c. Hands and letter.

E 244

E 245

1956.
E 954 **E 244** 35 c. purple 25 10
E1065 50 c. green 45 10
E 956 **E 245** 80 c. red 50 80
E1066 1 p. 20 lilac . . . . 1·50 75
E1346p **E 244** 2 p. orange 20 15
E1346q **E 245** 5 p. blue 20 60

E 468 Watch Face

1979.
E1373 **E 468** 2 p. black & orange 10 60

INSURED LETTER STAMPS

IN 125 Safe

IN 222 P.O. Treasury Vault

1935. Inscr as in Type IN 125.
IN583 – 10 c. red . . . . . . 1·10 30
IN733 – 50 c. blue 75 25
IN734 **IN 125** 1 p. green 75 35
DESIGNS: 10 c. Bundle of insured letters; 50 c. Registered mailbag.

1950.
IN911 **IN 222** 20 c. blue 15 10
IN912 40 c. purple 15 10
IN913 1 p. green 20 10
IN914 5 p. green and blue 65 60
IN915 10 p. blue and red 3·00 1·50

IN 469 Padlock

1976.
IN1374 **IN 469** 40 c. black & turq 10 10
IN1522 1 p. black & turq 10 10
IN1376 2 p. black and blue 10 10
IN1380 5 p. black & turq 10 10
IN1524 10 p. black & turq 10 10
IN1525 20 p. black & turq 10 10
IN1383 50 p. black & turq 95 95
IN1384 100 p. black & turq 60 60
The 5, 10, 20 p. exist with the padlock either 31 or 32½ mm high.

OFFICIAL STAMPS

O 18 Hidalgo

1884. No value shown.
O156 **O 18** Red 30 20
O157 Brown 15 10
O158 Orange 80 15
O159 Green 30 15
O160 Blue 45 35

1894. Stamps of 1895 handstamped **OFICIAL**.
O231 **19** 1 c. green . . . . 3·75 1·25
O232 2 c. red . . . . 4·50 1·25
O233 3 c. brown . . . . . . 3·75 1·25
O234 **20** 4 c. orange . . . . . . 5·50 2·50
O235 **21** 5 c. blue . . . . 7·50 2·50
O236 **22** 10 c. purple . . . . . . 7·00 50
O237 **20** 12 c. olive . . . . . . 15·00 6·25
O238 **22** 15 c. blue . . . . 8·75 3·75
O239 20 c. red . . . . 8·75 3·75
O240 50 c. mauve . . . . . 19·00 9·50
O241 **23** 1 p. brown . . . . 48·00 19·00
O242 5 p. red . . . . £110 55·00
O243 10 p. blue £190 £100

1899. Stamps of 1899 handstamped **OFICIAL**.
O276 **27** 1 c. green . . . . 9·50 60
O286 1 c. purple . . . . . . 8·75 95
O277 2 c. red . . . . 12·50 95
O287 2 c. green . . . . . . 8·75 95
O278 3 c. brown . . . . . . 12·50 60
O288 4 c. red . . . . 16·00 45
O279 5 c. blue . . . . 12·50 1·10
O289 5 c. orange . . . . . . 16·00 3·25
O280 10 c. brown and purple 16·00 1·40
O290 10 c. orange and blue 19·00 95
O281 15 c. purple and lavender 16·00 1·40
O282 20 c. blue and red . . . 19·00 45
O283 **28** 50 c. black and purple . 38·00 6·25
O291 50 c. black and red . . 48·00 6·25
O284 **29** 1 p. black and blue . . . 80·00 6·25
O285 **30** 5 p. black and red . . . 50·00 19·00

1911. Independence stamps optd **OFICIAL**.
O301 **32** 1 c. purple . . . . 1·25 1·25
O302 – 2 c. green 75 45
O303 – 3 c. brown . . . . 1·25 45
O304 – 4 c. red . . . . 1·90 45
O305 – 5 c. orange . . . . . . 3·25 1·75
O306 – 10 c. orange and blue . 1·90 45
O307 – 15 c. lake and slate . . . 3·25 2·00
O308 – 20 c. blue and lake . . . 2·50 45
O309 **40** 50 c. black and brown . 8·75 3·75
O310 – 1 p. black and blue . . . 15·00 6·25
O311 – 5 p. black and red . . . 55·00 32·00

1915. Stamps of 1915 optd **OFICIAL**.
O321 **43** 1 c. violet 30 55
O322 **44** 2 c. green 30 55
O323 **45** 3 c. brown 30 55
O324 4 c. red 30 55
O325 5 c. orange 30 55
O326 10 c. blue 30 55

1915. Stamps of 1915 optd **OFICIAL**.
O318 **46** 40 c. grey . . . . 2·50 2·75
O455 40 c. mauve . . . . . . 3·75 1·90
O319 **47** 1 p. grey and brown . . 3·25 3·75
O456 1 p. grey and blue . . . 9·50 6·25
O320 **48** 5 p. blue and lake . . . 19·00 16·00
O457 5 p. grey and green . . 55·00 95·00

1916. Nos. O301/11 optd with T **49**.
O358 **32** 1 c. purple . . . . 1·90
O359 – 2 c. green 30
O360 – 3 c. brown 35
O361 – 4 c. red . . . . 2·00
O362 – 5 c. orange 35
O363 – 10 c. orange and blue . . 35
O364 – 15 c. lake and slate . . . 35
O365 – 20 c. blue and lake . . . 40

O366 40 50 c. black and brown . . 55·00
O367 – 1 p. black and blue . . . 3·25
O368 – 5 p. black and red . . . £1600

1918. Stamps of 1917 optd **OFICIAL**.
O424 53 1 c. violet . . . . 1·25 60
O446 1 c. grey 30 20
O447 – 2 c. green 20 20
O448 – 3 c. brown 25 20
O449 – 4 c. red . . . . 3·75 45
O450 – 5 c. blue 20 20
O451 – 10 c. blue 30 15
O452 – 20 c. lake . . . . 2·50 2·50
O454 – 30 c. black . . . . . . 3·75 1·40

1923. No. 416 optd **OFICIAL**.
O485 10 p. black and brown . . . 60·00 95·00

1923. Stamps of 1923 optd **OFICIAL**.
O471 59 1 c. brown 20 20
O473 60 2 c. red 25 25
O475 61 3 c. brown 55 40
O461 62 4 c. green . . . . 1·90 1·90
O476 63 4 c. green 40 40
O477 5 c. orange 70 65
O489 74 8 c. orange . . . . . . 3·75 2·50
O479 66 10 c. lake 55 55
O480 65 20 c. blue . . . . 3·25 2·50
O464 64 30 c. green 35 25
O467 68 50 c. brown 55 55
O469 69 1 p. blue and lake . . . . 4·75 4·75

1929. Air. Optd **OFICIAL**.
O501 80 5 c. blue (roul) 45 25
O502 81 20 c. violet 55 55
O492 58 25 c. sepia and lake . . . 3·50 2·75
O490 25 c. sepia and green . . 1·75 1·25

1929. Air. As 1926 Postal Congress stamp optd **HABILITADO Servicio Oficial Aereo.**
O493 70 2 c. black . . . . 26·00 26·00
O494 – 4 c. black . . . . 26·00 26·00
O495 70 5 c. black . . . . 26·00 26·00
O496 – 10 c. black . . . . . . 26·00 26·00
O497 72 20 c. black . . . . . . 26·00 26·00
O498 30 c. black . . . . 26·00 26·00
O499 40 c. black . . . . 26·00 26·00
O500 73 1 p. black £950 £950

O 85

1930. Air.
O503 O 85 20 c. grey . . . . . . 2·75 2·75
O504 35 c. violet 40 95
O505 40 c. blue and brown . . 50 90
O506 70 c. sepia and violet . . 50 95

1931. Air. Surch **HABILITADO Quince centavos.**
O515 O 85 15 c. on 20 c. grey . . 45 45

1932. Air. Optd **SERVICIO OFICIAL** in one line.
O532 80 10 c. violet (perf or roul) . . 30 30
O533 15 c. red (perf or roul) . . 85 85
O534 20 c. sepia (roul) 85 85
O531 58 50 c. red and blue 90 70

1932. Stamps of 1923 optd **SERVICIO OFICIAL** in two lines.
O535 59 1 c. brown 15 15
O536 60 2 c. red 10 10
O537 61 3 c. brown 95 95
O538 63 4 c. green . . . . 3·25 2·50
O539 5 c. red . . . . 3·75 2·50
O540 66 10 c. lake . . . . 1·10 75
O541 65 20 c. blue . . . . 4·75 3·25
O544 64 30 c. green . . . . . . 2·50 95
O545 46 40 c. mauve . . . . . . 4·75 1·90
O546 68 50 c. brown 80 95
O547 69 1 p. blue and lake 95 95

1933. Air. Optd **SERVICIO OFICIAL** in two lines.
O553 58 50 c. red and blue . . . . 1·00 70

1933. Air. Optd **SERVICIO OFICIAL** in two lines.
O548 80 5 c. blue (No. 476a) . . . 30 30
O549 10 c. violet (No. 477) . . . 30 30
O550 20 c. sepia (No. 479) . . . 30 60
O551 50 c. lake (No. 481) . . . 40 95

1934. Optd **OFICIAL**.
O565 92 15 c. blue 35 35

1938. Nos. 561/71 optd **OFICIAL**.
O622 1 c. orange . . . . 70 1·25
O623 2 c. green 45 45
O624 4 c. red 45 45
O625 10 c. violet 45 80
O626 20 c. blue 55 80
O627 30 c. red . . . . 70 1·25
O628 40 c. brown . . . . 70 1·25
O629 50 c. black . . . . 1·00 1·00
O630 1 p. red and brown . . . . 2·50 3·75

PARCEL POST STAMPS

P 167 Mail Train

1941.
P732 P 167 10 c. red . . . . . . 1·75 40
P733 20 c. violet . . . . . . 2·00 50

P 228 Mail Train

1951.
P916 P 228 10 c. pink . . . . . . 1·25 15
P917 20 c. violet . . . . . . 1·75 25

POSTAGE DUE STAMPS

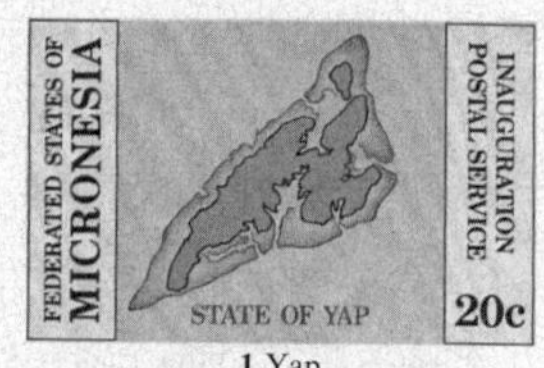

D 32

1908.
D282 D 32 1 c. blue . . . . 1·00 1·00
D283 2 c. blue . . . . 1·00 1·00
D284 4 c. blue . . . . 1·00 1·00
D285 5 c. blue . . . . 1·00 1·100
D286 10 c. blue . . . . . . 1·00 1·00

MICRONESIA Pt. 22

A group of islands in the Pacific, from 1899 to 1914 part of the German Caroline Islands. Occupied by the Japanese in 1914 the islands were from 1920 a Japanese mandated territory, and from 1947 part of the United States Trust Territory of the Pacific Islands, using United States stamps. Micronesia assumed control of its postal services in 1984.

100 cents = 1 dollar

1 Yap

1984. Inauguration of Postal Independence. Maps. Multicoloured.
1 20 c. Type **1** 60 45
2 20 c. Truk 60 45
3 20 c. Pohnpei 60 45
4 20 c. Kosrae 60 45

2 Fernandez de Quiros

3 Boeing 727-100

1984.
5 2 1 c. blue 10 10
6 – 2 c. brown 10 10
7 – 3 c. blue 10 10
8 – 4 c. green 10 10
9 – 5 c. brown and olive 10 10
10 – 10 c. purple 15 10
11 – 13 c. blue 20 10
11a – 15 c. red 20 10
12 – 17 c. brown 25 10
13 2 19 c. purple 30 10
14 – 20 c. green 30 10
14a – 22 c. green 30 15
14b – 25 c. orange 30 15
15 – 30 c. red 45 15
15a – 36 c. blue 50 20
16 – 37 c. violet 50 20
16a – 45 c. green 60 30
17 – 50 c. brown and sepia . . . 80 35
18 – $1 olive . . . . 1·50 85
19 – $2 blue . . . . 3·00 1·50
20 – $5 brown . . . . 8·00 4·50
20a – $10 blue . . . . 15·00 11·00
DESIGNS: 2, 20 c. Louis Duperrey; 3, 30 c. Fyodor Lutke; 4, 37 c. Jules Dumont d'Urville; 5 c. Men's house, Yap; 10, 45 c. Sleeping Lady (mountains), Kosrae; 13, 15 c. Liduduhriap waterfall, Pohnpei; 17, 25 c. Tonachau Peak, Truk; 22, 36 c. "Senyavin" (full-rigged sailing ship); 50 c. Devil mask, Truk; $1 Sokehs Rock, Pohnpei; $2 Outrigger canoes, Kosrae; $5 Stone money, Yap; $10 Official seal.

1984. Air. Multicoloured.
21 28 c. Type **3** 55 30
22 35 c. Grumman SA-16 Albatros flying boat 70 50
23 40 c. Consolidated PBY-5A Catalina amphibian 90 60

4 Truk Post Office

1984. "Ausipex 84" International Stamp Exhibition, Melbourne. Multicoloured.
24 20 c. Type **4** (postage) 50 20
25 28 c. German Caroline Islands 1919 3 pf. yacht stamp (air) . . 60 40
26 35 c. German 1900 20 pf. stamp optd for Caroline Islands . . 70 50
27 40 c. German Caroline Islands 1915 5 m. yacht stamp . . . 80 65

5 Baby in Basket

1984. Christmas. Multicoloured.
28 20 c. Type **5** (postage) 50 25
29 28 c. Open book showing Christmas scenes (air) 60 40
30 35 c. Palm tree decorated with lights 70 50
31 40 c. Women preparing food . . 80 65

6 U.S.S. "Jamestown" (warship)

1985. Ships.
32 6 22 c. black & brn (postage) . . 65 35
33 – 33 c. black and lilac (air) . . 85 50
34 – 39 c. black and green . . . . 1·00 70
35 – 44 c. black and red . . . . 1·40 85
DESIGNS: 33 c. "L'Astrolabe" (D'Urville's ship); 39 c. "La Coquille" (Duperrey's ship); 44 c. "Shenandoah" (Confederate warship).

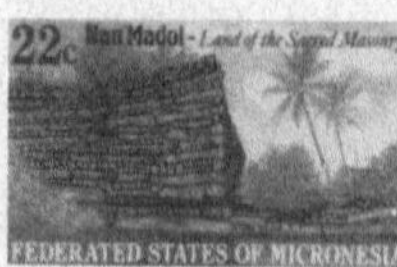

7 Lelu Protestant Church, Kosrae

1985. Christmas.
36 7 22 c black and orange (postage) 70 30
37 – 33 c. black and violet (air) . . 95 50
38 – 44 c. black and green . . . . 1·50 70
DESIGNS: 33 c. Dublon Protestant Church; 44 c. Pohnpei Catholic Church.

8 "Noddy Tern"

1985. Birth Bicentenary of John J. Audubon (ornithologist). Multicoloured.
39 22 c. Type **8** (postage) 70 50
40 22 c. "Turnstone" 70 50
41 22 c. "Golden Plover" 70 50
42 22 c. "Black-bellied Plover" . . 70 50
43 44 c. "Sooty Tern" (air) . . . . 1·25 80

9 Land of Sacred Masonry

1985. Nan Madol, Pohnpei. Multicoloured.
44 22 c. Type **9** (postage) 45 25
45 33 c. Nan Tauas inner courtyard (air) 60 45
46 39 c. Nan Tauas outer wall . . . 75 60
47 44 c. Nan Tauas burial vault . . 90 70

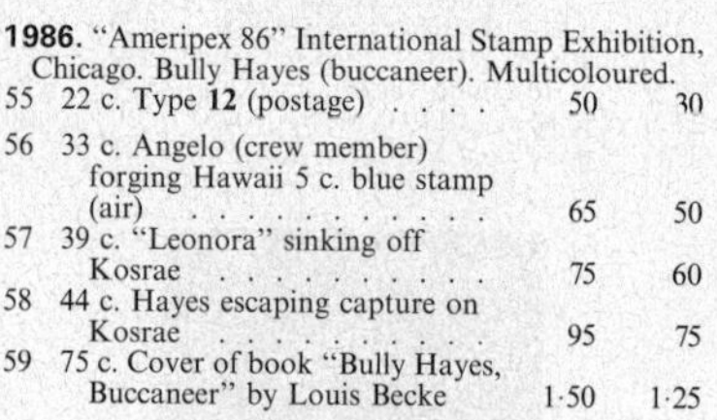

10 Doves, "LOVE" and Hands

12 Bully Hayes

1986. Anniversaries and Events. Multicoloured.
48 22 c. Type **10** (Interntional Peace Year) 60 35
49 44 c. Halley's comet . . . . . 1·40 80
50 44 c. "Trienza" (cargo liner) arriving at jetty (40th anniv of return of Nauruans from Truk) 1·40 80

1986. Nos. 1/4 surch.
51 22 c. on 20 c. Type **1** 55 45
52 22 c. on 20 c. Truk 55 45
53 22 c. on 20 c. Pohnpei 55 45
54 22 c. on 20 c. Kosrae 55 45

1986. "Ameripex 86" International Stamp Exhibition, Chicago. Bully Hayes (buccaneer). Multicoloured.
55 22 c. Type **12** (postage) 50 30
56 33 c. Angelo (crew member) forging Hawaii 5 c. blue stamp (air) 65 50
57 39 c. "Leonora" sinking off Kosrae 75 60
58 44 c. Hayes escaping capture on Kosrae 95 75
59 75 c. Cover of book "Bully Hayes, Buccaneer" by Louis Becke 1·50 1·25

13 "Madonna and Child"

1986. Christmas. "Madonna and Child" Paintings.
61 – 5 c. multicoloured (postage) 15 10
62 – 22 c. multicoloured 70 30
63 – 33 c. multicoloured (air) . . 95 65
64 13 44 c. multicoloured . . . . 1·25 1·00

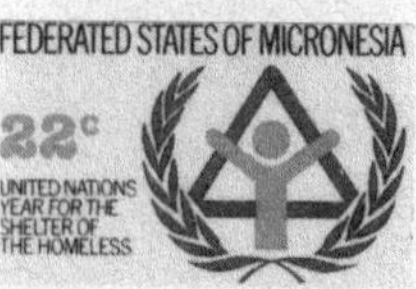

14 Passports on Globe

1986. 1st Micronesian Passport.
65 14 22 c. blue, black and yellow 60 35

15 Emblem (International Year of Shelter for the Homeless)

1987. Anniversaries and Events.
66 15 22 c. blue, red and black (postage) 35 30
67 – 33 c. green, red and black (air) 50 40
68 – 39 c. blue, black and red . . 60 50
69 – 44 c. blue, red and black . . 75 60
DESIGNS: 33 c. Dollar sign (bicentenary of dollar currency); 39 c. Space capsule (25th anniv of first American to orbit Earth); 44 c. "200 USA" (bicentenary of US constitution).

16 Archangel Gabriel appearing to Mary

1987. Christmas. Multicoloured.
71 22 c. Type **16** (postage) 40 30
72 33 c. Joseph praying and Mary with baby Jesus (air) 60 45
73 39 c. Shepherds with their sheep 75 60
74 44 c. Wise men 90 75

17 Spanish Missionary and Flag

1988. Micronesian History. Multicoloured.

75 22 c. Type **17** (postage) 50 35
76 22 c. Natives producing copra and German flag 50 35
77 22 c. School pupils and Japanese flag 50 35
78 22 c. General store and U.S. flag 50 35
79 44 c. Traditional boatbuilding and fishing skills (air) . . . . . . 1·00 75
80 44 c. Welcoming tourists from Douglas DC-10 airliner and divers investigating World War II wreckage . . . . 1·00 75

18 Ponape White Eye 19 Marathon

1988. Birds. Multicoloured.

81 3 c. Type **18** (postage) 10 10
82 14 c. Truk monarch 25 10
83 22 c. Ponape starling 35 20
84 33 c. Truk white eye (air) . . . 55 35
85 44 c. Blue-faced parrot finch . . 75 60
86 $1 Yap monarch . . . . 1·50 1·40

1988. Olympic Games, Seoul. Multicoloured.

87 25 c. Type **19** 45 25
88 25 c. Hurdling 45 25
89 45 c. Basketball 70 55
90 45 c. Volleyball 70 55

20 Girls decorating Tree

1988. Christmas. Multicoloured.

91 25 c. Type **20** 45 30
92 25 c. Dove with mistletoe in beak and children holding decorations 45 30
93 25 c. Boy in native clothing and girl in floral dress sitting at base of tree 45 30
94 25 c. Boy in T-shirt and shorts and girl in native clothing sitting at base of tree 45 30

Nos. 91/4 were printed together in blocks of four, se-tenant, forming a composite design.

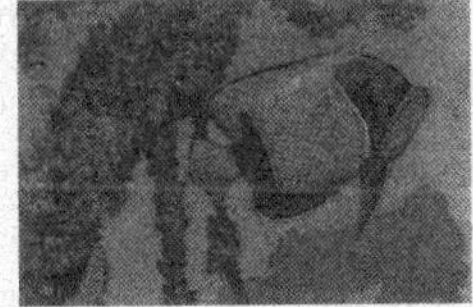

21 Sun and Stars Angelfish

1988. Truk Lagoon, "Micronesia's Living War Memorial". Multicoloured.

95 25 c. Type **21** 40 30
96 25 c. Jellyfish and shoal of small fishes 40 30
97 25 c. Snorkel divers 40 30
98 25 c. Two goldenjack (black-striped fishes facing left) . . 40 30
99 25 c. Blacktip reef shark . . . 40 30
100 25 c. Deck railings of wreck and fishes 40 30
101 25 c. Squirrelfish (red fish) . . 40 30
102 25 c. Batfish and aircraft cockpit 40 30
103 25 c. Three Moorish idols (fishes with long dorsal fins) . . . 40 30
104 25 c. Four barracuda and shoal 40 30
105 25 c. Two spot-banded butterfly fishes (facing alternate directions) 40 30
106 25 c. Three-spot damselfish and aircraft propeller 40 30
107 25 c. Foxface (fish) and shoal 40 30
108 25 c. Lionfish (fish with spines) 40 30
109 25 c. Scuba diver 40 30
110 25 c. Tubular corals 40 30
111 25 c. Ornate butterfly fish and brain coral 40 30
112 25 c. Clown fish, giant clam and sea plants 40 30

Nos. 95/112 were printed together, se-tenant, in sheetlets of 18 stamps, the backgrounds of the stamps forming an overall design of the remains of a Japanese ship and "Zero" fighter plane on the Lagoon bed colonized by marine life.

22 Flag of Pohnpei

1989. Air. State Flags. Multicoloured.

113 45 c. Type **22** 85 60
114 45 c. Truk 85 60
115 45 c. Kosrae 85 60
116 45 c. Yap 85 60

23 Plumeria and Headdress

1989. Mwarmwarms (floral decorations). Multicoloured.

117 45 c. Type **23** 85 60
118 45 c. Hibiscus and lei 85 60
119 45 c. Jasmine and Yap religious mwarmwarm 85 60
120 45 c. Bougainvillea and Truk dance mwarmwarm 85 60

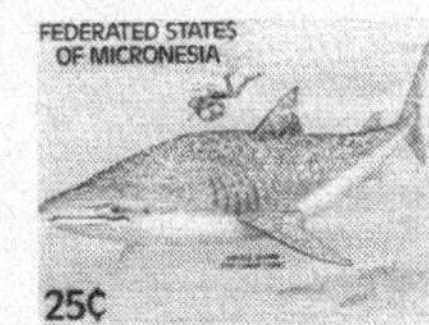

24 White Shark

1989. Sharks. Multicoloured.

121 25 c. Type **24** 65 40
122 25 c. Hammerhead shark . . 65 40
123 45 c. Tiger shark (vert) . . . 1·10 75
124 45 c. Great white shark (vert) 1·10 75

26 "Explorer 1" Satellite over North America

1989. 20th Anniv of First Manned Landing on the Moon. Multicoloured.

126 25 c. Bell XS-15 rocket plane 40 30
127 25 c. Type **26** 40 30
128 25 c. Ed White on space walk during "Gemini 4" mission 40 30
129 25 c. "Apollo 18" spacecraft 40 30
130 25 c. "Gemini 4" space capsule over South America 40 30
131 25 c. Space shuttle "Challenger" 40 30
132 25 c. Italian "San Marco 2" satellite 40 30
133 25 c. Russian "Soyuz 19" spacecraft 40 30
134 25 c. Neil Armstrong descending ladder to Moon's surface during "Apollo 11" mission 40 30
135 $2.40 Lunar module "Eagle" on Moon (34 × 46 mm) . . . . 3·50 2·75

Nos. 126/34 were printed together in se-tenant sheetlets of nine stamps, the backgrounds of the stamps forming an overall design of Earth as viewed from the Moon.

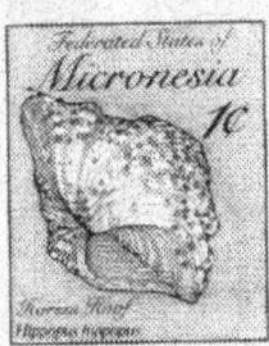

27 Horse's Hoof

1989. Sea Shells. Multicoloured.

136 1 c. Type **27** 10 10
137 3 c. Rare spotted cowrie . . . 10 10
138 15 c. Commercial trochus . . 20 10
139 20 c. General cone 25 10
140 25 c. Trumpet triton 30 20
141 30 c. Laciniate conch 35 25
142 36 c. Red-mouth olive 45 35
143 45 c. All-red map cowrie . . 55 45
144 50 c. Textile cone 60 50
145 $1 Orange spider conch . . . 1·25 1·00
146 $2 Golden cowrie . . . . . 2·50 2·00
147 $5 Episcopal mitre . . . . . 6·00 4·50

28 Oranges

1989. "World Stamp Expo '89" International Stamp Exhibition, Washington D.C. "Kosrae–The Garden State". Multicoloured.

155 25 c. Type **28** 45 30
156 25 c. Limes 45 30
157 25 c. Tangerines 45 30
158 25 c. Mangoes 45 30
159 25 c. Coconuts 45 30
160 25 c. Breadfruit 45 30
161 25 c. Sugar cane 45 30
162 25 c. Kosrae house 45 30
163 25 c. Bananas 45 30
164 25 c. Children with fruit and flowers 45 30
165 25 c. Pineapples 45 30
166 25 c. Taro 45 30
167 25 c. Hibiscus 45 30
168 25 c. Ylang ylang 45 30
169 25 c. White ginger 45 30
170 25 c. Plumeria 45 30
171 25 c. Royal poinciana 45 30
172 25 c. Yellow allamanda 45 30

29 Angel over Micronesian Village

1989. Christmas. Multicoloured.

173 25 c. Type **29** 50 25
174 45 c. Truk children dressed as Three Kings 75 60

30 Young Kingfisher and Sokehs Rock, Pohnpei

1990. World Wide Fund for Nature. Micronesian Kingfisher and Micronesian Pigeon.

175 10 c. Type **30** 15 10
176 15 c. Adult kingfisher and rain forest, Pohnpei 25 15
177 20 c. Pigeon flying over lake at Sleeping Lady, Kosrae . . . 35 25
178 25 c. Pigeon perched on leaf, Tol Island, Truk 45 40

31 Wooden Whale Stamp and "Lyra"

1990. "Stamp World London 90" International Stamp Exhibition. 19th-century British Whaling Ships. Multicoloured.

179 45 c. Type **31** 55 45
180 45 c. Harpoon heads and "Prudent" 55 45
181 45 c. Carved whale bone and "Rhone" 55 45
182 45 c. Carved whale tooth and "Sussex" 55 45

33 Beech 18 over Kosrae Airport 34 School Building

1990. Air. Airplanes. Multicoloured.

185 22 c. Type **33** 30 15
186 36 c. Boeing 727 landing at Truk 50 30
187 39 c. Britten Norman Islander over Pohnpei 50 30
188 45 c. Beech Queen Air over Yap 60 35

1990. 25th Anniv of Pohnpei Agriculture and Trade School. Multicoloured.

190 25 c. Type **34** 25 15
191 25 c. Fr. Costigan (founder) and students 25 15
192 25 c. Fr. Hugh Costigan . . . 25 15
193 25 c. Ispahu Samuel Hadley (Metelanim chief) and Fr. Costigan 25 15
194 25 c. Statue of Liberty, New York City Police Department badge and Empire State Building 25 15

36 Loading Mail Plane at Pohnpei Airport

1990. Pacific Postal Transport. Multicoloured.

196 25 c. Type **36** 35 20
197 45 c. Launch meeting "Nantaku" (inter-island freighter) in Truk Lagoon to exchange mail, 1940 65 40

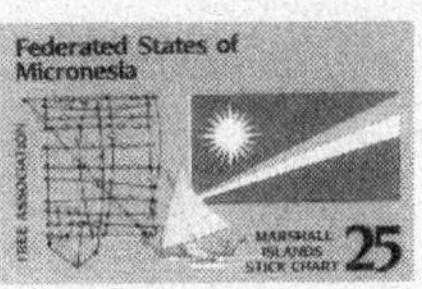

37 Marshallese Stick Chart, Outrigger Canoe and Flag

1990. 4th Anniv of Ratification of Micronesia and Marshall Islands Compacts of Free Association. Multicoloured.

198 25 c. Type **37** 35 20
199 25 c. Great frigate bird, U.S.S. "Constitution" (frigate), U.S. flag and American bald eagle 35 20
200 25 c. Micronesian outrigger canoe and flag 35 20

38 "Caloptilia sp." and New Moon

1990. Moths. Multicoloured.

201 45 c. Type **38** 60 50
202 45 c. "Anticrates sp." (inscr "Yponomeatidae") and waxing moon 60 50
203 45 c. "Cosmopterigidae" family and full moon 60 50
204 45 c. "Cosmopteridigae" family and waning moon 60 50

39 Cherub above Roof 41 Hawksbill Turtle returning to Sea

1990. Christmas. "Micronesian Holy Night". Multicoloured.

205 25 c. Type **39** 30 20
206 25 c. Two cherubs and Star of Bethlehem 30 20
207 25 c. Cherub blowing horn . . 30 20
208 25 c. Lambs, goat, pig and chickens 30 20
209 25 c. Native wise men offering gifts to Child 30 20
210 25 c. Children and dog beside lake 30 20
211 25 c. Man blowing trumpet triton 30 20
212 25 c. Adults and children on path 30 20
213 25 c. Man and children carrying gifts 30 20

Nos. 205/13 were printed together, se-tenant, forming a composite design.

1991. Sea Turtles. Multicoloured.

215 29 c. Type **41** 45 25
216 29 c. Green turtles swimming underwater 45 25
217 50 c. Hawksbill turtle swimming underwater 45 25
218 50 c. Leatherback turtle swimming underwater . . . 45 25

42 Boeing E-3 Sentry

1991. Operations Desert Shield and Desert Storm (liberation of Kuwait). Multicoloured.

219 29 c. Type **42** 40 25
220 29 c. Grumman F-14 Tomcat 40 25
221 29 c. U.S.S. "Missouri" (battleship) 40 25
222 29 c. Multiple Launch Rocket System 40 25
223 $2.90 Great frigate bird with yellow ribbon and flag of Micronesia (50 × 37 mm) . . 3·75 2·75

43 "Evening Flowers, Toloas, Truk"

1991. "Phila Nippon '91" International Stamp Exhibition, Tokyo. 90th Birth Anniv (1992) of Paul Jacoulet (artist). Micronesian Ukiyo-e Prints by Jacoulet. Multicoloured.

225	29 c. Type **43**	40	25
226	29 c. "The Chief's Daughter, Mogomog"	40	25
227	29 c. "Yagourouh and Mio, Yap"	40	25
228	50 c. "Yap Beauty and Orchids"	70	45
229	50 c. "The Yellow-Eyed Boys, Ohlol"	70	45
230	50 c. "Violet Flowers, Tomil, Yap"	70	45

44 Sheep and Holy Family

1991. Christmas. Shell Cribs. Multicoloured.

232	29 c. Type **44**	40	25
233	40 c. Three Kings arriving at Bethlehem	55	35
234	50 c. Sheep around manger	65	45

45 Pohnpei Fruit Bat

1991. Pohnpei Rain Forest. Multicoloured.

235	29 c. Type **45**	40	25
236	29 c. Purple-capped fruit dove	40	25
237	29 c. Micronesian kingfisher	40	25
238	29 c. Birdnest fern	40	25
239	29 c. Carolines ("Island") swiftlets	40	25
240	29 c. Ponape ("Long-billed") white eye	40	25
241	29 c. Common ("Brown") noddy	40	25
242	29 c. Ponape lory	40	25
243	29 c. Ponape myiagra flycatcher	40	25
244	29 c. Truk Island ("Caroline") ground dove	40	25
245	29 c. White-tailed tropic bird	40	25
246	29 c. Cardinal ("Micronesian") honeyeater	40	25
247	29 c. Ixora	40	25
248	29 c. Rufous ("Pohnpei") fantail	40	25
249	29 c. Grey-brown ("Gray") white eye	40	25
250	29 c. Blue-faced parrot finch	40	25
251	29 c. Slender-billed grey bird ("Cicadabird")	40	25
252	29 c. Green skink	40	25

Nos. 235/52 were issued together, se-tenant, forming a composite design.

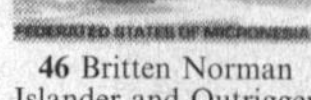

46 Britten Norman Islander and Outrigger Canoe

47 Volunteers learning Crop Planting

1992. Air. Multicoloured.

253	40 c. Type **46**	55	35
254	50 c. Boeing 727-200 airliner and outrigger canoe (different)	65	45

INDEX

Countries can be quickly located by referring to the index at the end of this volume.

1992. 25th Anniv of Presence of United States Peace Corps in Micronesia. Multicoloured.

255	29 c. Type **47**	40	25
256	29 c. Education	40	25
257	29 c. Pres. John Kennedy announcing formation of Peace Corps	40	25
258	29 c. Public health nurses	40	25
259	29 c. Recreation	40	25

48 Queen Isabella of Spain

1992. 500th Anniv of Discovery of America by Christopher Columbus. Multicoloured.

260	29 c. Type **48**	40	25
261	29 c. "Santa Maria"	40	25
262	29 c. Christopher Columbus	40	25

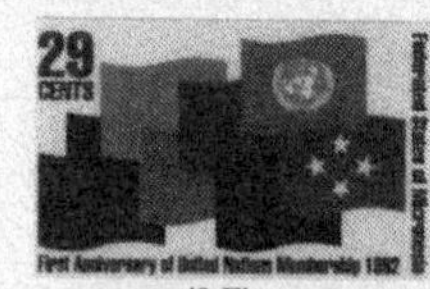

49 Flags

1992. 1st Anniv of U.N. Membership.

264	**49** 29 c. multicoloured	40	25
265	50 c. multicoloured	65	45

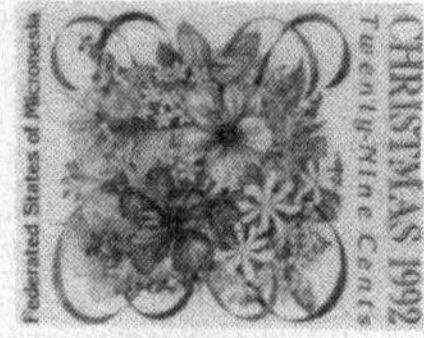

50 Bouquet

1992. Christmas.

266	**50** 29 c. multicoloured	40	25

51 Edward Rickenbacker (fighter pilot)

1993. Pioneers of Flight (1st series). Pioneers and aircraft. Multicoloured.

267	29 c. Type **51**	40	25
268	29 c. Manfred von Richthofen (fighter pilot)	40	25
269	29 c. Andrei Tupolev (aeronautical engineer)	40	25
270	29 c. John Macready (first non-stop crossing of U.S.A.)	40	25
271	29 c. Sir Charles Kingsford-Smith (first trans-Pacific flight)	40	25
272	29 c. Igor Sikorsky (aeronautical engineer)	40	25
273	29 c. Lord Trenchard ("Father of the Royal Air Force")	40	25
274	29 c. Glenn Curtiss (builder of U.S. Navy's first aircraft)	40	25

See also Nos. 322/9, 364/71, 395/402, 418/25, 441/8, 453/60 and 514/21.

52 Bigscale Soldierfish

1993. Fishes. Multicoloured.

275	10 c. Type **52**	15	10
276	19 c. Bennett's butterflyfish	25	15
277	20 c. Peacock grouper	25	15
278	22 c. Great barracuda	30	20
278a	23 c. Yellow-finned tuna	30	20
279	25 c. Coral grouper	30	20
280	29 c. Regal angelfish	40	25
281	30 c. Bleeker's parrotfish	40	25
282	32 c. Saddled butterflyfish (dated "1995")	40	25
283	35 c. Picassofish	45	30
284	40 c. Mandarinfish	50	35
285	45 c. Blue-banded surgeonfish	60	40
285a	46 c. Achilles tang	60	40
286	50 c. Orange-striped triggerfish	65	45
287	52 c. Palette surgeonfish	70	45
288	55 c. Moorish idol	70	45
288a	60 c. Skipjack tuna	80	55
289	75 c. Oriental sweetlips	95	65
290	78 c. Square-spot fairy basslet	1·00	65
290a	95 c. Blue-lined snapper	1·25	85
291	$1 Zebra moray	1·25	85
292	$2 Foxface rabbitfish	2·50	1·60
293	$2.90 Orange-spine unicornfish	3·75	2·50
294	$3 Flame angelfish	3·75	2·50
295	$5 Cave grouper	6·50	4·25

See also Nos. 465/89 and 522/5.

53 "Great Republic"

54 Jefferson

1993. Sailing Ships. Multicoloured.

301	29 c. Type **53**	40	25
302	29 c. "Benjamin F. Packard"	40	25
303	29 c. "Stag Hound"	40	25
304	29 c. "Herald of the Morning"	40	25
305	29 c. "Rainbow and junk"	40	25
306	29 c. "Flying Cloud"	40	25
307	29 c. "Lightning"	40	25
308	29 c. "Sea Witch"	40	25
309	29 c. "Columbia"	40	25
310	29 c. "New World"	40	25
311	29 c. "Young America"	40	25
312	29 c. "Courier"	40	25

1993. 250th Birth Anniv of Thomas Jefferson (U.S. President, 1801–09).

313	**54** 29 c. multicoloured	40	25

55 Yap Outrigger Canoe

1993. Traditional Canoes. Multicoloured.

314	29 c. Type **55**	40	25
315	29 c. Kosrae outrigger canoe	40	25
316	29 c. Pohnpei lagoon outrigger canoe	40	25
317	29 c. Chuuk war canoe	40	25

56 Ambilos Iehsi

57 Kepirohi Falls

1993. Local Leaders (1st series). Multicoloured.

318	29 c. Type **56** (Pohnpei)	40	25
319	29 c. Andrew Roboman (Yap)	40	25
320	29 c. Joab Sigrah (Kosrae)	40	25
321	29 c. Petrus Mailo (Chuuk)	40	25

See also Nos. 409/12.

1993. Pioneers of Flight (2nd series). As T **51**. Multicoloured.

322	50 c. Lawrence Sperry (inventor of the gyro)	65	45
323	50 c. Alberto Santos-Dumont (first powered flight in Europe)	65	45
324	50 c. Hugh Dryden (developer of first guided missile)	65	45
325	50 c. Theodore von Karman (space pioneer)	65	45
326	50 c. Orville Wright (first powered flight)	65	45
327	50 c. Wilbur Wright (second powered flight)	65	45
328	50 c. Otto Lilienthal (first heavier-than-air flight)	65	45
329	50 c. Sir Thomas Sopwith (aircraft designer)	65	45

1993. Pohnpei Tourist Sites. Multicoloured.

330	29 c. Type **57**	40	25
331	50 c. Spanish Wall	65	45

See also Nos. 357/9.

58 Female Common ("Great") Eggfly

59 "We Three Kings"

1993. Butterflies. Multicoloured.

333	29 c. Type **58**	40	25
334	29 c. Female common ("great") eggfly (variant)	40	25
335	50 c. Male monarch	65	45
336	50 c. Male common ("great") eggfly	65	45

See also Nos. 360/3.

1993. Christmas. Carols. Multicoloured.

337	29 c. Type **59**	40	25
338	50 c. "Silent Night, Holy Night"	65	45

60 Baby Basket

1993. Yap. Multicoloured.

339	29 c. Type **60**	40	25
340	29 c. Bamboo raft	40	25
341	29 c. Basketry	40	25
342	29 c. Fruit bat	40	25
343	29 c. Forest	40	25
344	29 c. Outrigger canoes	40	25
345	29 c. Dioscorea yams	40	25
346	29 c. Mangroves	40	25
347	29 c. Manta ray	40	25
348	29 c. "Cyrtosperma taro"	40	25
349	29 c. Fish weir	40	25
350	29 c. Seagrass and fishes	40	25
351	29 c. Taro bowl	40	25
352	29 c. Thatched house	40	25
353	29 c. Coral reef	40	25
354	29 c. Lavalava	40	25
355	29 c. Dancers	40	25
356	29 c. Stone money	40	25

1994. Kosrae Tourist Sites. As T **57** but horiz. Multicoloured.

357	29 c. Sleeping Lady (mountains)	40	25
358	40 c. Walung	50	35
359	50 c. Lelu Ruins	65	45

1994. "Hong Kong '94" International Stamp Exhibition. Designs as Nos. 333/6 but with inscriptions in brown and additionally inscribed "Hong Kong '94 Stamp Exhibition" in English (361/2) or Chinese (others).

360	29 c. As No. 333	40	25
361	29 c. As No. 334	40	25
362	50 c. As No. 335	65	45
363	50 c. As No. 336	65	45

1994. Pioneers of Flight (3rd series). As T **51**. Multicoloured.

364	29 c. Octave Chanute (early glider designer)	40	25
365	29 c. T. Claude Ryan (founder of first commercial airline)	40	25
366	29 c. Edwin (Buzz) Aldrin ("Apollo 11" crew member and second man to step onto moon)	40	25
367	29 c. Neil Armstrong (commander of "Apollo 11" and first man on moon)	40	25
368	29 c. Frank Whittle (developer of jet engine)	40	25
369	29 c. Waldo Waterman (aircraft designer)	40	25
370	29 c. Michael Collins ("Apollo 11" crew member)	40	25
371	29 c. Wernher von Braun (rocket designer)	40	25

61 Spearfishing

1994. 3rd Micronesian Games. Multicoloured.

372	29 c. Type **61**	40	25
373	29 c. Basketball	40	25
374	29 c. Coconut husking	40	25
375	29 c. Tree climbing	40	25

62 Pohnpei

64 "Fagraea berteriana" (Kosrae)

63 People

1994. Traditional Costumes. Multicoloured.

376 29 c. Type **62** 40 25
377 29 c. Kosrae 40 25
378 29 c. Chuuk 40 25
379 29 c. Yap 40 25

1994. 15th Anniv of Constitution.

380 **63** 29 c. multicoloured 40 25

1994. Native Flowers. Multicoloured.

381 29 c. Type **64** 40 25
382 29 c. "Pangium edule" (Yap) . . 40 25
383 29 c. "Pittosporum ferrugineum" (Chuuk) 40 25
384 29 c. "Sonneratia caseolaris" (Pohnpei) 40 25

Nos. 381/4 were issued together, se-tenant, forming a composite design.

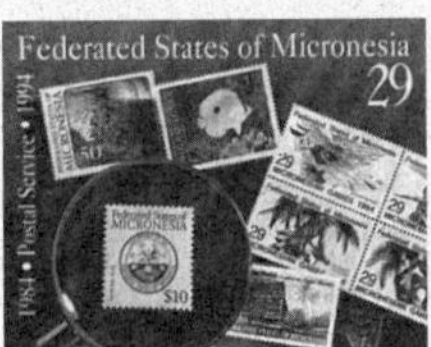

65 1985 $10 Definitive under Magnifying Glass

1994. 10th Anniv of Postal Independence. Multicoloured.

385 29 c. Type **65** 40 25
386 29 c. 1993 traditional canoes block 40 25
387 29 c. 1984 postal independence block 40 25
388 29 c. 1994 native costumes block 40 25

Nos. 385/8 were issued together, se-tenant, forming a composite design of various Micronesian stamps. Nos. 386/8 are identified by the block in the centre of the design.

66 Players

68 Iguanodons

69 Oriental Cuckoo

1994. World Cup Football Championship, U.S.A. Multicoloured.

389 50 c. Type **66** 65 45
390 50 c. Ball and players 65 45

Nos. 389/90 were issued together, se-tenant, forming a composite design.

1994. "Philakorea 1994" International Stamp Exhibition, Seoul. Prehistoric Animals. Multicoloured.

392 29 c. Type **68** 40 25
393 52 c. Iguanodons and coelurosaurs 70 45
394 $1 Camarasaurus . . . . . . 1·25 85

Nos. 392/4 were issued together, se-tenant, forming a composite design.

1994. Pioneers of Flight (4th series). As T **51**. Multicoloured.

395 50 c. Yury Gagarin (first man in space) 65 45
396 50 c. Alan Shepard Jr. (first American in space) 65 45
397 50 c. William Bishop (fighter pilot) 65 45
398 50 c. "Atlas" (first U.S. intercontinental ballistic missile) and Karel Bossart (aerospace engineer) 65 45
399 50 c. John Towers (world endurance record, 1912) . . 65 45
400 50 c. Hermann Oberth (space flight pioneer) 65 45
401 50 c. Marcel Dassault (aircraft producer) 65 45
402 50 c. Geoffrey de Havilland (aircraft designer) 65 45

1994. Migratory Birds. Multicoloured.

403 29 c. Type **69** 40 25
404 29 c. Long-tailed koel ("Cuckoo") 40 25
405 29 c. Short-eared owl 40 25
406 29 c. Eastern broad-billed roller ("Dollarbird") 40 25

70 Doves

1994. Christmas. Multicoloured.

407 29 c. Type **70** 40 25
408 50 c. Angels 65 45

1994. Local Leaders (2nd series). As T **56**. Multicoloured.

409 32 c. Anron Ring Buas . . . 40 25
410 32 c. Belarmino Hatheylul . . 40 25
411 32 c. Johnny Moses 40 25
412 32 c. Paliknoa Sigrah (King John) 40 25

72 Diver and Coral

1995. Chuuk Lagoon. Multicoloured.

414 32 c. Type **72** 40 25
415 32 c. Butterfly fish and lionfish 40 25
416 32 c. Diver and butterfly fish 40 25
417 32 c. Two fish amongst anemone tentacles 40 25

Nos. 414/17 were issued together, se-tenant, forming a composite design.

1995. Pioneers of Flight (5th series). As T **51**. Multicoloured.

418 32 c. Robert Goddard (first liquid-fuelled rocket) . . . 40 25
419 32 c. Leroy Grumman (first fighter with retractable landing gear) 40 25
420 32 c. Louis-Charles Breguet (aeronautics engineer) . . . 40 25
421 32 c. Juan de la Cierva (inventor of autogyro) 40 25
422 32 c. Hugo Junkers (aircraft engineer) 40 25
423 32 c. James Lovell Jr. (astronaut) 40 25
424 32 c. Donald Douglas (aircraft designer) 40 25
425 32 c. Reginald Mitchell (designer of Spitfire fighter) 40 25

73 West Highland White Terrier

1995. Dogs. Multicoloured.

426 32 c. Type **73** 40 25
427 32 c. Welsh springer spaniel . 40 25
428 32 c. Irish setter 40 25
429 32 c. Old English sheepdog . 40 25

74 "Hibiscus tiliaceus"

1995. Hibiscus. Multicoloured.

430 32 c. Type **74** 40 25
431 32 c. "Hibiscus huegelii" . . 40 25
432 32 c. "Hibiscus trionum" . . 40 25
433 32 c. "Hibiscus splendens" . 40 25

Nos. 430/3 were issued together, se-tenant, forming a composite design.

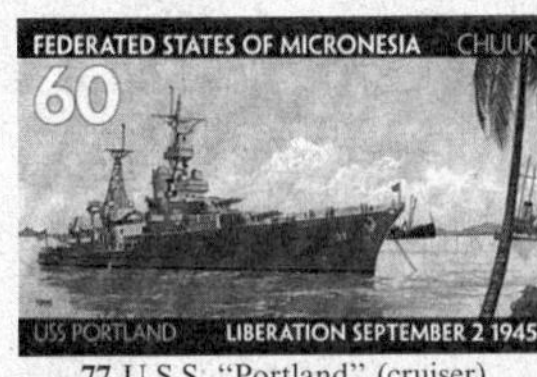

77 U.S.S. "Portland" (cruiser)

1995. 50th Anniv of End of Second World War. Liberation of Micronesia. Multicoloured.

436 60 c. Type **77** (liberation of Chuuk) 80 55
437 60 c. U.S.S. "Tillman" (destroyer) (Yap) 80 55
438 60 c. U.S.S. "Soley" (destroyer) (Kosrae) 80 55
439 60 c. U.S.S. "Hyman" (destroyer) (Pohnpei) 80 55

1995. Pioneers of Flight (6th series). As T **51**. Multicoloured.

441 60 c. Frederick Rohr (devoloper of mass-production techniques) 80 55
442 60 c. Juan Trippe (founder of Pan-American Airways) . . 80 55
443 60 c. Konstantin Tsiolkovsky (rocket pioneer) 80 55
444 60 c. Count Ferdinand von Zeppelin (airship inventor) . 80 55
445 60 c. Air Chief Marshal Hugh Dowding (commander of R.A.F. Fighter Command, 1940) 80 55
446 60 c. William Mitchell (pioneer of aerial bombing) 80 55
447 60 c. John Northrop (aircraft designer) 80 55
448 60 c. Frederick Handley Page (producer of first twin-engine bomber) 80 55

79 Poinsettia **80** Rabin

1995. Christmas.

449 **79** 32 c. multicoloured 40 25
450 60 c. multicoloured 80 55

1995. Yitzhak Rabin (Israeli Prime Minister) Commemoration.

451 **80** 32 c. multicoloured 40 25

1995. Pioneers of Flight (7th series). As T **51**. Multicoloured.

453 32 c. James Doolittle (leader of America's Second World War bomb raid on Japan) 40 25
454 32 c. Claude Dornier (aircraft designer) 40 25
455 32 c. Ira Eaker (leader of air effort against occupied Europe during Second World War) . 40 25
456 32 c. Jacob Ellehammer (first European manned flight) . . 40 25
457 32 c. Henry Arnold (Commander of U.S. air operations during Second World War) 40 25
458 32 c. Louis Bleriot (first flight across the English Channel) . 40 25
459 32 c. William Boeing (founder of Boeing Corporation) 40 25
460 32 c. Sydney Camm (aircraft designer) 40 25

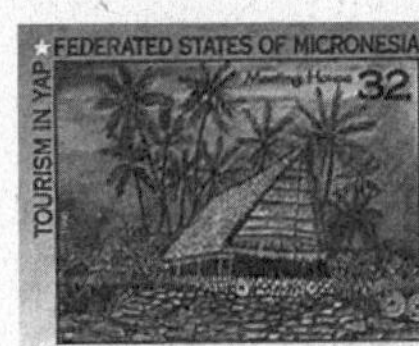

82 Meeting House

1995. Tourism in Yap. Multicoloured.

461 32 c. Type **82** 40 25
462 32 c. Stone money 40 25
463 32 c. Churu dancing 40 25
464 32 c. Traditional canoe 40 25

1995. Fishes. As Nos. 275/95 but face values changed. Multicoloured.

465 32 c. Bennett's butterflyfish . . 40 25
466 32 c. Regal angelfish 40 25
467 32 c. Orange-striped triggerfish 40 25
468 32 c. Zebra moray 40 25
469 32 c. Great barracuda 40 25
470 32 c. Bleeker's parrotfish . . . 40 25
471 32 c. Mandarinfish 40 25
472 32 c. Blue-banded surgeonfish . 40 25
473 32 c. Bigscale soldierfish . . . 40 25
474 32 c. Peacock grouper 40 25
475 32 c. Picassofish 40 25
476 32 c. Orange-spine unicornfish 40 25
477 32 c. Achilles tang 40 25
478 32 c. Coral grouper 40 25
479 32 c. Palette surgeonfish . . . 40 25
480 32 c. Oriental sweetlips 40 25
481 32 c. Foxface rabbitfish . . . 40 25
482 32 c. Saddled butterflyfish (dated "1996") 40 25
483 32 c. Moorish idol 40 25
484 32 c. Square-spot fairy basslet . 40 25
485 32 c. Flame angelfish 40 25
486 32 c. Yellow-fin tuna 40 25
487 32 c. Skipjack tuna 40 25
488 32 c. Bluelined snapper 40 25
489 32 c. Cave grouper 40 25

See also Nos. 522/5.

83 Necklace Sea Star

1996. Starfishes. Multicoloured.

490 55 c. Type **83** 70 45
491 55 c. Rhinoceros sea star . . 70 45
492 55 c. Blue sea star 70 45
493 55 c. Thick-skinned sea star . 70 45

Nos. 490/3 were issued together, se-tenant, forming a composite design.

84 10 l. Stamp

1996. Centenary of Modern Olympic Games. Designs reproducing 1896 Greek Olympic Issue. Multicoloured.

494 60 c. Type **84** 75 50
495 60 c. 25 l. stamp 75 50
496 60 c. 20 l. stamp 75 50
497 60 c. 10 d. stamp 75 50

85 "Palikir"

1996. Patrol Boats. Multicoloured.

498 32 c. Type **85** 40 25
499 32 c. "Micronesia" 40 25

Nos. 498/9 were issued together, se-tenant, forming a composite design.

87 1896 Quadricycle

1996. Centenary of Ford Motor Vehicle Production. Multicoloured.

501 55 c. Type **87** 70 45
502 55 c. 1917 Model T Truck . . 70 45
503 55 c. 1928 Model A Tudor Sedan 70 45
504 55 c. 1932 V-8 Sport Roadster 70 45
505 55 c. 1941 Lincoln Continental 70 45
506 55 c. 1953 F-100 Truck . . . 70 45
507 55 c. 1958 Thunderbird convertible 70 45
508 55 c. 1996 Mercury Sable . . 70 45

88 Reza **89** Oranges

1996. Reza (National Police Drug Enforcement Unit's dog).

509 **88** 32 c. multicoloured 40 25

1996. Citrus Fruits. Multicoloured.

510 50 c. Type **89** 60 40
511 50 c. Limes 60 40
512 50 c. Lemons 60 40
513 50 c. Tangerines 60 40

Nos. 510/13 were issued together, se-tenant, forming a composite design.

1996. Pioneers of Flight (8th series). As T **51**. Multicoloured.

514 60 c. Curtis LeMay (commander of Strategic Air Command) . . 75 50
515 60 c. Grover Loening (first American graduate in aeronautical engineering) . 75 50
516 60 c. Gianni Caproni (aircraft producer) 75 50

517 60 c. Henri Farman (founder of Farman Airlines) 75 50
518 60 c. Glenn Martin (aircraft producer) 75 50
519 60 c. Alliot Verdon Roe (aircraft designer) 75 50
520 60 c. Sergei Korolyov (rocket scientist) 75 50
521 60 c. Isaac Laddon (aircraft designer) 75 50

1996. 10th Asian International Stamp Exhibition, Taipeh. Fishes. As previous designs but additionally inscr for the exhibition in English (522, 525) or Chinese (523/4).
522 32 c. As No. 465 . . . . . . 40 25
523 32 c. As No. 468 . . . . . . 40 25
524 32 c. As No. 475 . . . . . . 40 25
525 32 c. As No. 483 . . . . . . 40 25

90 Wise Men following Star

1996. Christmas.
526 **90** 32 c. multicoloured 40 25
527 60 c. multicoloured 75 50

91 Outrigger Canoe and State Flag

1996. 10th Anniv of Ratification of Compact of Free Association with U.S.A.
528 **91** $3 multicoloured . . . . . 3·75 2·50

MIDDLE CONGO Pt. 6

One of three colonies into which Fr. Congo was divided in 1906. Became part of Fr. Equatorial Africa in 1937. Became part of the Congo Republic within the French Community on 28th November, 1958.

100 centimes = 1 franc

1 Leopard in Ambush

2 Bakalois Woman

3 Coconut Palms, Libreville

1907.
1 **1** 1 c. olive and brown 10 10
2 2 c. violet and brown 10 10
3 4 c. blue and brown 10 10
4 5 c. green and blue 10 10
21 5 c. yellow and blue 35 45
5 10 c. red and blue 15 10
22 10 c. green and light green . . 1·25 1·25
6 15 c. purple and pink 85 55
7 20 c. brown and blue . . . . 1·25 1·00
8 **2** 25 c. blue and green 45 35
23 25 c. green and grey 35 45
9 30 c. pink and green 55 45
24 30 c. red 75 75
10 35 c. brown and blue 55 55
11 40 c. green and brown 55 55
12 45 c. violet and orange . . . 2·10 1·90
13 50 c. green and orange . . . 75 70
25 50 c. blue and green 85 85
14 75 c. brown and blue . . . . 3·50 2·50
15 **3** 1 f. green and violet . . . . 6·00 4·50
16 2 f. violet and green . . . . 5·00 3·25
17 5 f. blue and pink . . . . . 18·00 16·00

1916. Surch **5c** and red cross.
20 **1** 10 c. + 5 c. red and blue . . 45 55

1924. Surch **AFRIQUE EQUATORIALE FRANCAISE** and new value.
26 **3** 25 c. on 2 f. green and violet 35 35
27 25 c. on 5 f. pink and blue . 35 35
28 65 on 1 f. brown and orange 45 55
29 85 on 1 f. brown and orange 55 55
30 **2** 90 on 75 c. scarlet and red . 65 55
31 1 f. 25 on 1 f. ultramarine & bl 25 25
32 1 f. 50 on 1 f. blue & ultram 85 65
33 3 f. on 5 f. pink and brown 1·10 85
34 10 f. on 5 f. green and red . 5·50 4·00
35 20 f. on 5 f. purple and brown 8·00 5·50

1924. Optd **AFRIQUE EQUATORIALE FRANCAISE.**
36 **1** 1 c. olive and brown 15 20
37 2 c. violet and brown 20 20
38 4 c. blue and brown 20 20
39 5 c. yellow and blue 20 20
40 10 c. green and light green . 20 20
41 10 c. red and grey 20 20
42 15 c. purple and pink 25 25
43 20 c. brown and blue 25 25
44 20 c. green and light green . 25 25
45 20 c. brown and mauve 45 25
46 **2** 25 c. green and grey 25 25
47 30 c. red 45 25
48 30 c. grey and mauve 20 10
49 30 c. deep green and green . 25 25
50 35 c. brown and blue 25 25
51 40 c. green and brown 40 25
52 45 c. violet and orange . . . 75 45
53 50 c. blue and green 50 25
54 50 c. yellow and black 25 15
55 65 c. brown and blue . . . . 1·10 90
56 75 c. brown and blue 35 25
57 90 c. red and pink . . . . . 2·25 1·60
58 **3** 1 f. green and violet 75 55
59 1 f. 10 mauve and brown . . 1·75 1·10
60 1 f. 50 ultramarine and blue 3·25 2·40
61 2 f. violet and green 85 65
62 3 f. mauve on pink . . . . . 3·50 3·00
63 5 f. blue and pink . . . . . 2·50 1·25

1931. "Colonial Exhibition" key-types inscr "MOYEN CONGO".
65 E 40 c. green and black . . . 2·00 1·90
66 F 50 c. mauve and black . . . 1·10 1·00
67 G 90 c. red and black . . . . 1·40 1·10
68 H 1 f. 50 blue and black . . . 2·00 1·10

15 Mindouli Viaduct

1933.
69 **15** 1 c. brown 10 50
70 2 c. blue 10 50
71 4 c. olive 10 50
72 5 c. red 20 30
73 10 c. green 40 50
74 15 c. purple . . . . 75 1·25
75 20 c. red on rose . . . . . 4·50 3·00
76 25 c. orange 75 75
77 30 c. green . . . . 1·75 1·25
78 – 40 c. brown 85 55
79 – 45 c. black on green 90 65
80 – 50 c. purple 55 35
81 – 65 c. red on green 55 45
82 – 75 c. black on red . . . . . 5·50 3·50
83 – 90 c. red 55 55
84 – 1 f. red 55 45
85 – 1 f. 25 green 90 60
86 – 1 f. 50 blue . . . . 3·25 1·50
87 – 1 f. 75 violet . . . . 1·00 75
88 – 2 f. olive 85 65
89 – 3 f. black on red . . . . . 1·75 1·60
90 – 5 f. grey . . . . 8·00 6·50
91 – 10 f. black . . . . 35·00 18·00
92 – 20 f. brown . . . . 22·00 14·00
DESIGNS: 40 c. to 1 f. 50 Pasteur Institute, Brazzaville; 1 f. 75 to 20 f. Government Building, Brazzaville.

POSTAGE DUE STAMPS

1928. Postage Due type of France optd **MOYEN-CONGO A. E. F.**
D64 **D 11** 5 c. blue 25 25
D65 10 c. brown 25 25
D66 20 c. olive 55 55
D67 25 c. red 55 55
D68 30 c. red 55 55
D69 45 c. green 55 55
D70 50 c. purple 65 75
D71 60 c. brown on cream . . . 95 95
D72 1 f. red on cream . . . . 1·00 1·00
D73 2 f. red . . . . 1·75 1·90
D74 3 f. violet . . . . 3·25 3·25

D 13 Village

1930.
D75 **D 13** 5 c. olive and blue . . . 35 45
D76 10 c. brown and red . . 55 55
D77 20 c. brown and green 1·50 1·50
D78 25 c. brown and blue 2·00 2·25
D79 30 c. green and brown 3·00 3·25
D80 45 c. olive and green . . 3·00 3·25
D81 50 c. brown and mauve 3·00 3·25
D82 60 c. black and violet 3·50 3·50
D83 – 1 f. black and brown . . 6·00 6·00
D84 – 2 f. brown and mauve 6·50 6·50
D85 – 3 f. brown and red . . . 6·50 6·50
DESIGN: 1 to 3 f. "William Guinet" (steamer) on the River Congo.

D 17 "Le Djoue"

1933.
D 93 **D 17** 5 c. green 40 45
D 94 10 c. blue on blue . . . 45 45
D 95 20 c. red on yellow . . 55 55
D 96 25 c. red 55 55
D 97 30 c. red 65 75
D 98 45 c. purple 65 75
D 99 50 c. black . . . . . 1·25 1·25
D100 60 c. black on red . . . 1·75 1·75
D101 1 f. red . . . . 2·50 2·50
D102 2 f. orange . . . . . 3·75 3·75
D103 3 f. blue . . . . . . 6·25 6·25

For later issues see **FRENCH EQUATORIAL AFRICA.**

MODENA Pt. 8

A state in Upper Italy, formerly a duchy and now part of Italy. Used stamps of Sardinia after the cessation of its own issues in 1860. Now uses Italian stamps.

100 centesimi = 1 lira

1 Arms of Este

5 Cross of Savoy

1852. Imperf.
9 **1** 5 c. black on green . . . . . 10·00 23·00
3 10 c. black on pink . . . . . £200 55·00
4 15 c. black on yellow . . . . 15·00 12·00
5 25 c. black on buff . . . . . 18·00 12·00
12 40 c. black on blue . . . . . 19·00 85·00
13 1 l. black on white . . . . . 35·00 £1600

1859. Imperf.
18 **5** 5 c. green £500 £475
19 15 c. brown £800 £2250
20 15 c. grey £100
21 20 c. black . . . . £800 75·00
22 20 c. lilac . . . . 26·00 £400
23 40 c. red . . . . 80·00 £700
24 80 c. brown . . . . 85·00 £12000

NEWSPAPER STAMPS

1853. As T **1** but in the value tablet inscr "B.G. CEN" and value. Imperf.
N15 **1** 9 c. black on mauve . . . £140 40·00
N16 10 c. black on lilac . . . . 20·00 £160

N 4

1859. Imperf.
N17 **N 4** 10 c. black £400 £1800

MOHELI Pt. 6

An island in the Comoro Archipelago adjacent to Madagascar. A separate French dependency until 1914 when the whole archipelago was placed under Madagascar whose stamps were used until 1950. Now part of the Comoro Islands.

100 centimes = 1 franc

1906. "Tablet" key-type inscr "MOHELI" in blue (2, 4, 10, 20, 30, 40 c., 5 f.) or red (others).
1 D 1 c. black on blue 85 80
2 2 c. brown on buff 85 60
3 4 c. brown on grey . . . . 90 1·10
4 5 c. green . . . . 1·25 1·00
5 10 c. red . . . . 1·60 1·00
6 20 c. red on green . . . . 6·00 4·00
7 25 c. blue . . . . 6·25 3·00
8 30 c. brown on drab . . . 9·50 7·00
9 35 c. black on yellow . . . 4·75 2·25
10 40 c. red on yellow . . . . 7·00 4·25
11 45 c. black on green . . . 45·00 30·00
12 50 c. brown on blue . . . . 13·00 8·00
13 75 c. brown on orange . . . 13·00 11·50
14 1 f. green . . . . 8·50 8·25
15 2 f. violet on pink . . . . 21·00 19·00
16 5 f. mauve on lilac . . . . 90·00 75·00

1912. Surch in figures.
17 D 05 on 4 c. brown and blue on grey 55 70
18 05 on 20 c. red and blue on green . . . . 90 2·00
19 05 on 30 c. brown and blue on drab . . . . 80 1·00
20 10 on 40 c. red and blue on yellow . . . . 80 1·00
21 10 on 45 c. black and red on green 60 80
22 10 on 50 c. brown and red on blue . . . . 90 1·25

MOLDOVA Pt. 10

Formerly Moldavia, a constituent republic of the Soviet Union. Moldova declared its sovereignty within the Union in 1990 and became independent in 1991.

1991. 100 kopeks = 1 rouble.
1993. Kupon (temporary currency).
1993. 100 bani = 1 leu.

1 Arms

2 Codrii Nature Reserve

1991. 1st Anniv of Declaration of Sovereignty. Multicoloured. Imperf.
1 7 k. Type **1** 10 10
2 13 k. Type **1** 20 20
3 30 k. Flag (35 × 23 mm) 45 45

1992.
4 **2** 25 k. multicoloured 45 45

3 Arms

4 Tupolev Tu-144

1992.
5 **3** 35 k. green 10 10
6 50 k. red 20 20
7 65 k. brown 30 30
8 1 r. purple 45 45
9 1 r. 50 blue 75 75

1992. Air.
15 4 1 r. 75 red . . . 30 30
16 2 r. 50 mauve . . . 45 45
17 7 r. 75 violet . . . 1·50 1·50
18 8 r. 50 green . . . 1·90 1·90
See also Nos. 70/3.

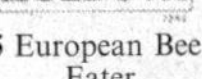

5 European Bee Eater 6 St. Panteleimon Church

1992. Birds. Multicoloured.
19 50 k. Type **5** . . . 20 20
20 65 k. Golden oriole . . . 25 25
21 2 r. 50 Green woodpecker . . . 65 65
22 6 r. Common roller . . . 1·10 1·10
23 7 r. 50 Hoopoe . . . 1·25 1·25
24 15 r. European cuckoo . . . 2·50 2·50
See also Nos. 63/9.

1992. Centenary (1991) of St. Panteleimon Church, Chisinau.
25 **6** 1 r. 50 multicoloured . . . 35 35

7 Wolf suckling Romulus and Remus 9 High Jumping

1992. Trajan Memorial, Chisinau.
26 **7** 5 r. multicoloured . . . 95 95

1992. Various stamps of Russia surch **MOLDOVA** and value.
27 2 r. 50 on 4 k. red (No. 4672) 25 25
28 6 r. on 3 k. red (No. 4671) . . 65 65
29 8 r. 50 on 4 k. red (No. 4672) 95 95
30 10 r. on 3 k. turq (No. 5941) . 1·25 1·25

1992. Olympic Games, Barcelona. Multicoloured.
31 35 k. Type **9** . . . 10 10
32 65 k. Wrestling . . . 45 45
33 1 r. Archery . . . 65 65
34 2 r. 50 Swimming . . . 1·00 1·00
35 10 r. Show jumping . . . 1·50 1·50

1992. Moldovan Olympic Games Medal Winners. Nos. 33/4 optd.
37 1 r. Archery (optd **NATALIA VALEEV / bronz** and emblem) 50 50
38 2 r. 50 Swimming (optd **IURIE BASCATOV / argint** and emblem) . . . 1·40 1·40

12 Moldovan Flag, Statue of Liberty and U.N. Emblem and Building

1992. Admission of Moldova to U.N.O. Mult.
40 1 r. 30 Type **12** . . . 15 15
41 12 r. As Type **12** but with motifs differently arranged . . . 1·25 1·25

13 Moldovan Flag and Prague Castle

1992. Admission of Moldova to European Security and Co-operation Conf Multicoloured.
42 2 r. 50 Type **13** . . . 20 20
43 25 r. Helsinki Cathedral and Moldovan flag . . . 1·60 1·60

1992. Nos. 4533, 4670/1 of Russia surch **MOLDOVA**, new value and bunch of grapes.
44 – 45 k. on 2 k. mauve . . . 15 15
45 – 46 k. on 2 k. mauve . . . 15 15
46 **1753** 63 k. on 1 k. green . . . 25 25
47 – 63 k. on 3 k. red . . . 25 25
48 **1753** 70 k. on 1 k. green . . . 15 15
49 4 r. on 1 k. green . . . 80 80

15 Carpet and Pottery 16 Galleon

1992. Folk Art.
50 **15** 7 r. 50 multicoloured . . . 2·50 2·50

1992. 500th Anniv of Discovery of America by Columbus. Multicoloured.
51 1 r. Type **16** . . . 15 15
52 6 r. Carrack . . . 1·10 1·10
53 6 r. Caravel . . . 1·10 1·10

17 Letter Sorter, Train, State Flag and U.P.U. Emblem

1992. Admission to U.P.U. Multicoloured.
55 5 r. Type **17** . . . 95 95
56 10 r. Douglas DC-10 airplane, computerized letter sorting equipment, state flag and U.P.U. emblem . . . 1·75 1·75

18 Aesculapius Snake

1993. Protected Animals. Snakes. Multicoloured.
57 3 r. Type **18** . . . 35 35
58 3 r. Aesculapius in tree . . . 35 35
59 3 r. Aesculapius on path . . . 35 35
60 3 r. Aesculapius on rock . . . 35 35
61 15 r. Grass snake . . . 1·10 1·10
62 25 r. Adder . . . 3·00 3·00
Nos. 57/60 were issued together, se-tenant, forming a composite design.

1993. Birds. As Nos. 19/24 but with values changed and additional design. Multicoloured.
63 2 r. Type **5** . . . 10 10
64 3 r. As No. 20 . . . 10 10
65 5 r. As No. 21 . . . 15 15
66 10 r. As No. 22 . . . 30 30
67 15 r. As No. 23 . . . 65 65
68 50 r. As No. 24 . . . 1·50 1·50
69 100 r. Barn swallow . . . 2·75 2·75

1993. Air.
70 **4** 25 r. red . . . 55 55
71 45 r. brown . . . 1·10 1·10
72 50 r. green . . . 1·40 1·40
73 90 r. blue . . . 2·40 2·40

19 Arms 20

1993.
74 **19** 2 k. blue . . . 10 10
75 3 k. purple . . . 10 10
76 6 k. green . . . 10 10
77 – 10 k. violet and green . . . 10 10
78 – 15 k. violet and green . . . 10 10
79 – 20 k. violet and grey . . . 15 15
80 – 30 k. violet and yellow . . . 20 20
81 – 50 k. violet and red . . . 50 50
82 **20** 100 k. multicoloured . . . 1·00 1·00
83 250 k. multicoloured . . . 2·75 2·75
DESIGN: 10 to 50 k. Similar to Type **19** but with inscription and value at foot differently arranged.

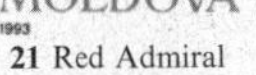

21 Red Admiral 22 "Tulipa bibersteiniana"

1993. Butterflies and Moths. Multicoloured.
94 6 b. Type **21** . . . 10 10
95 10 b. Swallowtail . . . 15 15
96 50 b. Peacock . . . 75 75
97 250 b. Emperor moth . . . 3·75 3·75

1993. Flowers. Multicoloured.
98 6 b. Type **22** . . . 20 20
99 15 b. Lily of the valley . . . 45 45
100 25 b. Snowdrop . . . 70 70
101 30 b. Peony . . . 90 90
102 50 b. Snowdrop . . . 1·50 1·50
103 90 b. Pasque flower . . . 2·75 2·75

23 Dragos Voda (1352–53) 24 "Story of One Life" (M. Grecu)

1993. 14th-century Princes of Moldavia. Multicoloured.
105 6 b. Type **23** . . . 15 15
106 25 b. Bogdan Voda I (1359–65) 25 25
107 50 b. Latcu Voda (1365–75) . . 50 50
108 100 b. Petru I Musat (1375–91) 1·00 1·00
109 150 b. Roman Voda Musat (1391–94) . . . 1·50 1·50
110 200 b. Stefan I (1394–99) . . . 2·10 2·10

1993. Europa. Contemporary Art. Multicoloured.
111 3 b. Type **24** . . . 10 10
112 150 b. "Coming of Spring" (I. Vieru) . . . 2·10 1·10

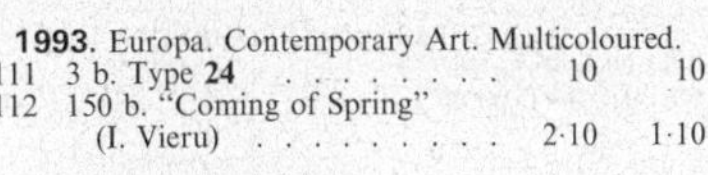

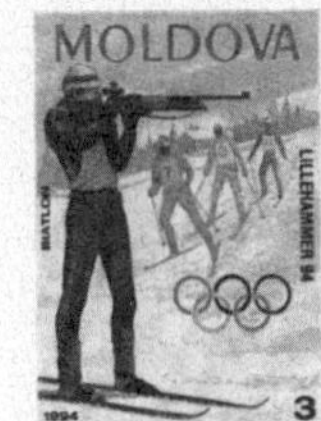

25 Biathletes 27 State Arms

1994. Winter Olympic Games, Lillehammer, Norway. Multicoloured.
113 3 b. Type **25** . . . 10 10
114 150 b. Close-up of biathlete shooting . . . 2·10 2·10

1994. No. 4533 of Russia surch **MOLDOVA**, grapes and value.
115 **1753** 3 b. on 1 k. green . . . 10 10
116 25 b. on 1 k. green . . . 40 40
117 50 b. on 1 k. green . . . 90 90

1994.
118 **27** 1 b. multicoloured . . . 10 10
120 10 b. multicoloured . . . 10 10
121 30 b. multicoloured . . . 10 10
122 38 b. multicoloured . . . 10 10
123 45 b. multicoloured . . . 15 15
125 75 b. multicoloured . . . 30 15
127 1 l. 50 multicoloured . . . 55 55
128 1 l. 80 multicoloured . . . 60 60
129 2 l. 50 mult (24×29 mm) . . 75 75
130 4 l. 50 multicoloured . . . 1·25 1·25
131 5 l. 40 multicoloured . . . 1·40 1·40
132 6 l. 90 multicoloured . . . 1·50 1·50
133 7 l. 20 mult (24×29 mm) . . 1·75 1·75
134 13 l. mult (24×29 mm) . . 3·50 3·30
135 24 l. mult (24×29 mm) . . 7·00 7·00

28 Launch of "Titan II" Rocket 29 Maria Cibotari (singer)

1994. Europa. Inventions and Discoveries. 25th Anniv of First Manned Moon Landing. Multicoloured.
136 1 b. Type **28** . . . 10 10
137 45 b. Ed White (astronaut) on space walk ("Gemini 4" flight, 1965) . . . 10 10
138 2 l. 50 Lunar module landing, 1969 . . . 1·10 1·10

1994. Entertainers' Death Anniversaries. Mult.
139 3 b. Type **29** (45th) . . . 10 10
140 90 b. Dumitru Caraciobanu (actor, 14th) . . . 25 25
141 150 b. Eugeniu Coca (composer, 40th) . . . 45 45
142 250 b. Igor Vieru (actor, 11th) 1·25 1·25

30 Preparing Stamp Design

1994. Stamp Day.
143 **30** 10 b. black, blue and mauve 10 10
144 – 45 b. black, mauve and yellow 25 25
145 – 2 l. multicoloured . . . 1·10 1·10
DESIGNS: 45 b. Printing stamps; 2 l. Checking finished sheets.

31 Pierre de Coubertin (founder) 32 Map

1994. Centenary of International Olympic Committee. Multicoloured.
146 60 b. Type **31** . . . 20 20
147 1 l. 50 Rings and "Paris 1994" centenary congress emblem 65 65

1994. Partnership for Peace Programme (co-operation of N.A.T.O. and Warsaw Pact members).
148 – 60 b. black, ultramarine and blue . . . 15 15
149 **32** 2 l. 50 multicoloured . . . 70 70
DESIGN: 60 b. Manfred Worner (Secretary-General of N.A.T.O.) and President Mircea Snegur of Moldova.

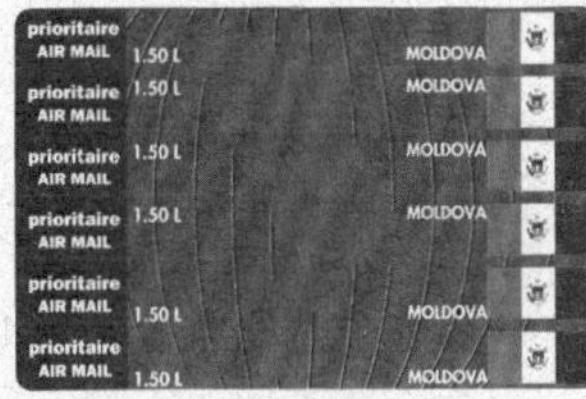

34 Map
(½-size illustration)

1994. Air. Self-adhesive. Roul.
152 **34** 1 l. 50 multicoloured . . . 45 45
153 4 l. 50 multicoloured . . . 1·25 1·25
The individual stamps are peeled directly from the card backing. Each card contains six different designs with the same face value forming the composite design illustrated. Each stamp is a horizontal strip with a label indicating the main class of mail covered by the rate at the left, separated by a vertical line of rouletting. The outer edges of the cards are imperforate.

35 Family 36 Handshake

1994. International Year of the Family. Multicoloured.
154 30 b. Type **35** . . . 10 10
155 60 b. Mother breastfeeding baby 15 15
156 1 l. 50 Child drawing . . . 45 45

1994. Preliminary Rounds of European Cup Football Championship, England (1996). Multicoloured.
157 10 b. Type **36** . . . 10 10
158 40 b. Players competing for ball . . . 10 20
159 2 l. 40 Goalkeeper making save 70 70

37 "Birth of Jesus Christ" (anon)

38 Cracked Green Russula

1994. Christmas. Multicoloured.

161	20 b. Type **37**	10	10
162	3 l. 60 "Birth of Jesus Christ" (Gherasim)	1·00	1·00

1995. Fungi. Multicoloured.

163	4 b. Type **38**	10	10
164	10 b. Oak mushroom	10	10
165	20 b. Chanterelle	10	10
166	90 b. "Leccinum aurantiacum"	25	25
167	1 l. 80 "Leccinum duriusculum"	50	50

39 Booted Eagle

1995. European Nature Conservation Year. Multicoloured.

168	4 b. Type **39**	10	10
169	45 b. Roe deer	15	15
170	90 b. Wild boar	25	25

40 Earthenware Urns and Necklace

1995. National Museum Exhibits. Multicoloured.

171	4 b. Type **40**	10	10
172	10 b. + 2 b. Representation and skeleton of "Dinotherium gigantissimum"	10	10
173	1 l. 80 + 30 b. Silver coins	60	60

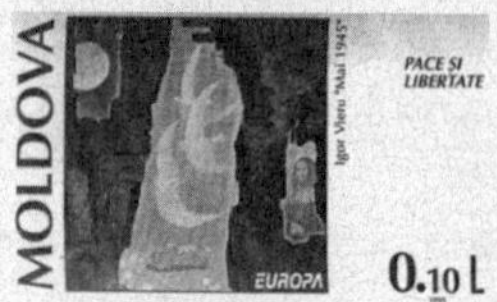

41 "May 1945" (Igor Vieru)

1995. Europa. Peace and Freedom. Paintings. Multicoloured.

174	10 b. Type **41**	10	10
175	40 b. "Peace" (Sergiu Cuciuc)	10	10
176	2 l. 20 "Spring 1944" (Cuciuc)	70	70

42 Constantin Stere (writer, 130th birth)

43 Alexandru cel Bun (1400–32)

1995. Anniversaries.

177	**42**	9 b. brown and grey	10	10
178	–	10 b. purple and grey	10	10
179	–	40 b. lilac and grey	10	10
180	–	1 l. 80 green and grey	50	50

DESIGNS: 10 b. Tamara Ceban (singer, 5th death); 40 b. Alexandru Plamadeala (sculptor, 55th death); 1 l. 80, Lucian Blaga (philosopher, birth centenary).

1995. 15th–16th Century Princes of Moldavia. Multicoloured.

181	10 b. Type **43**	10	10
182	10 b. Petru Aron (1451–52 and 1454–57)	10	10
183	10 b. Stefan cel Mare (1457–1504)	10	10
184	45 b. Petru Rares (1527–38 and 1541–46)	15	15
185	90 b. Alexandru Lapusneanu (1552–61 and 1564–68)	25	25
186	1 l. 80 Ioan Voda cel Cumplit (1572–74)	50	50

44 Soroca Castle

1995. Castles. Multicoloured.

188	10 b. Type **44**	10	10
189	20 b. Tighina Castle	10	10
190	60 b. Alba Castle	15	15
191	1 l. 30 Hotin Castle	35	35

45 Seal in Eye

46 "50" and Emblem

1995. 50th Anniv of U.N.O. Multicoloured. (a) Ordinary gum. Perf.

192	10 b. Type **45**	10	10
193	10 b. Airplane in eye	10	10
194	1 l. 50 Child's face and barbed wire in eye	40	40

(b). Self-adhesive. Rouletted.

195	90 b. Type **46**	25	25
196	1 l. 50 Type **46**	40	40

47 "Last Moon of Autumn"

48 Fly Agaric

1995. Centenary of Motion Pictures.

197	**47**	10 b. red and black	10	10
198	–	40 b. green and black	10	10
199	–	2 l. 40 blue and black	65	65

DESIGNS: 40 b. "Lautarii"; 2 l. 40, "Dimitrie Cantemir".

1996. Fungi. Multicoloured.

200	10 b. Type **48**	10	10
201	10 b. Satan's mushroom	10	10
202	65 b. Death cap	20	20
203	1 l. 30 "Hypholoma fasciculare"	35	35
204	2 l. 40 Destroying angel	65	65

49 Weightlifting

50 Rudi Monastery

1996. Olympic Games, Atlanta, U.S.A. Multicoloured.

205	10 b. Type **49**	10	10
206	20 b. + 5 b. Judo	10	10
207	45 b. + 10 b. Running	15	15
208	2 l. 40 + 30 b. Kayaking	75	75

1996. Monasteries. Multicoloured.

210	10 b. Type **50**	10	10
211	90 b. Japca	25	25
212	1 l. 30 Curchi	35	35
213	2 l. 80 Saharna	95	95
214	4 l. 40 Capriana	1·25	1·25

51 Moorhens

52 Elena Alistar (president of Women's League)

1996. Birds. Multicoloured.

215	9 b. Type **51**	10	10
216	10 b. Greylag geese	10	10
217	2 l. 20 Turtle doves	60	60
218	4 l. 40 Mallard	1·25	1·25

1996. Europa. Famous Women. Multicoloured.

220	10 b. Type **52**	10	10
221	3 l. 70 Marie Sklodowska-Curie (physicist)	1·00	1·00

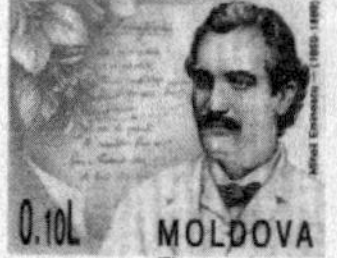

53 Mihail Eminescu (poet) (146th birth anniv)

54 Town Hall

1996. Birth Anniversaries.

223	**53**	10 b. brown and deep brown	10	10
224	–	10 b. sepia and brown	10	10
225	–	2 l. 20 green and brown	60	60
226	–	3 l. 30 green and deep brown	90	90
227	–	5 l. 40 brown and deep brown	1·50	1·50

DESIGNS: 10 b. Gavriil Banulescu-Bodoni (Metropolitan of Chisinau, 250th); 2 l. 20, Ion Creanga (writer, 159th); 3 l. 30, Vasile Alecsandri (writer, 172nd); 5 l. 40, Petru Movila and printing press (400th).

1996. 560th Anniv of Chisinau. Multicoloured.

229	10 b. Type **54**	10	10
230	1 l. 30 Cultural Palace	35	35
231	2 l. 40 Mazarache Church	65	65

POSTAGE DUE STAMPS

D 33 Postal Emblems

1994.

D150	D **33**	30 b. brown and green	15	15
D151		40 b. green and lilac	20	20

One stamp in the pair was put on insufficiently franked mail, the other stamp on associated documents.

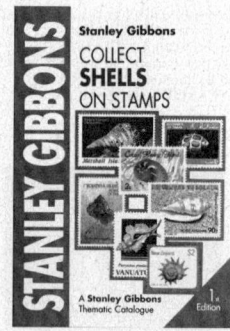

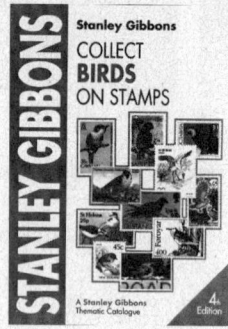

MONACO Pt. 6

A principality on the S. coast of France including the town of Monte Carlo.

100 centimes = 1 French franc

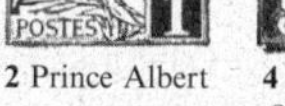

1 Prince Charles III 2 Prince Albert 4 War Widow and Monaco

1885.

1 1 1 c. olive 19·00 16·00
2 2 c. lilac 55·00 27·00
3 5 c. blue 75·00 35·00
4 10 c. brown on yellow 85·00 35·00
5 15 c. red £375 16·00
6 25 c. green £750 65·00
7 40 c. blue on red 85·00 42·00
8 75 c. black on red £275 £110
9 1 f. black on yellow £1900 £500
10 5 f. red on green £3250 £2000

1891.

11 2 1 c. green 75 75
12 2 c. purple 85 85
13 5 c. blue 60·00 5·50
22 5 c. green 45 25
14 10 c. brown on yellow £140 14·00
23 10 c. red 4·50 60
15 15 c. pink £225 6·75
24 15 c. brown on yellow 2·50 60
25 15 c. green 1·75 2·50
16 25 c. green £375 32·00
26 25 c. blue 14·00 4·25
17 40 c. black on pink 4·50 2·50
18 50 c. brown on orange 8·75 4·25
19 75 c. brown on buff 15·00 21·00
20 1 f. black on yellow 25·00 8·75
21 5 f. red on green £130 80·00
28 5 f. mauve £250 £250
29 5 f. green 20·00 26·00

1914. Surcharged **+5c.**

30 2 10 c. + 5 c. red 7·50 6·25

1919. War Orphans Fund.

31 4 2 c. + 3 c. mauve 28·00 30·00
32 5 c. + 5 c. green 15·00 18·00
33 15 c. + 10 c. red 15·00 18·00
34 25 c. + 15 c. blue 40·00 45·00
35 50 c. + 50 c. brown on orge £180 £160
36 1 f. + 1 f. black on yellow £300 £375
37 5 f. + 5 f. red £1000 £1100

1920. Princess Charlotte's Marriage. Nos. 33/7 optd **20 mars 1920** or surch also.

38 4 2 c. + 3 c. on 15 c. + 10 c. 40·00 40·00
39 2 c. + 3 c. on 25 c. + 15 c. 40·00 40·00
40 2 c. + 3 c. on 50 c. + 50 c. 40·00 40·00
41 5 c. + 5 c. on 1 f. + 1 f. 40·00 40·00
42 5 c. + 5 c. on 5 f. + 5 f. 40·00 40·00
43 15 c. + 10 c. red 28·00 28·00
44 25 c. + 15 c. blue 12·50 12·50
45 50 c. + 50 c. brown on orge 55·00 55·00
46 1 f. + 1 f. black on yellow 75·00 75·00
47 5 f. + 5 f. red £6500 £6500

1921. Princess Antoinette's Baptism. Optd **28 DECEMBRE 1920** or surch also.

48 2 5 c. green 45 50
49 75 c. brown on buff 4·50 6·25
50 2 f. on 5 f. mauve 38·00 55·00

1922. Surch.

51 2 20 c. on 15 c. green 1·25 1·50
52 25 c. on 10 c. red 75 1·00
53 50 c. on 1 f. black on yellow 5·50 6·25

8 Prince Albert I

9 St. Devote Viaduct

1922.

54 8 25 c. brown 3·00 4·25
55 – 30 c. green 65 1·10
56 – 30 c. red 40 45
57 9 40 c. brown 50 50
58 – 50 c. blue 3·25 4·00
59 – 60 c. grey 20 25
60 – 1 f. black on yellow 20 20
61a – 2 f. red 40 35
62 – 5 f. brown 32·00 32·00
63 – 5 f. green on blue 7·50 38·00
64 – 10 f. red 12·50 9·25

DESIGNS: As Type **9**: 30 c., 50 c. Oceanographic Museum; 60 c., 1 f., 2 f. The Rock; 5 f., 10 f. Prince's Palace, Monaco.

12 Prince Louis

13 Prince Louis and Palace

1923.

65 12 10 c. green 35 35
66 15 c. red 50 75
67 20 c. brown 30 30
68 25 c. purple 25 30
69 13 50 c. blue 25 30

1924. Surch with new value and bars.

70 2 45 c. on 50 c. brown on orge 50 75
71 75 c. on 1 f. black on yellow 30 30
72 85 c. on 5 f. green 30 30

14 15 16

17 St. Devote Viaduct

1924.

73 14 1 c. grey 10 10
74 2 c. brown 10 10
75 3 c. mauve 2·75 1·90
76 5 c. orange 20 20
77 10 c. blue 10 10
78 15 15 c. green 10 10
79 15 c. violet 2·50 1·50
80 20 c. mauve 15 10
81 20 c. pink 20 10
82 25 c. pink 10 10
83 25 c. red on yellow 15 15
84 30 c. orange 10 10
85 40 c. brown 15 10
86 40 c. blue on blue 15 10
87 45 c. black 70 40
88 16 50 c. green 15 15
89 15 50 c. brown on yellow 10 10
90 16 60 c. brown 10 10
91 15 60 c. green on green 10 10
92 75 c. green on green 20 15
93 75 c. red on yellow 15 10
94 75 c. black 40 50
95 80 c. red on yellow 25 20
96 90 c. red on yellow 2·00 1·25
97 17 1 f. black on yellow 20 15
98 1 f. 05 mauve 20 35
99 1 f. 10 green 8·00 6·25
100 15 1 f. 25 blue on blue 15 15
101 1 f. 50 blue on blue 3·75 1·50
102 – 2 f. brown and mauve 95 60
103 – 3 f. lilac and red on yellow 17·00 10·00
104 – 5 f. red and green 7·00 5·00
105 – 10 f. blue and brown 18·00 17·00

DESIGN—As Type **17**: 2 f. to 10 f. Monaco.

1926. Surch.

106 15 30 c. on 25 c. pink 20 10
107 50 c. on 60 c. green on grn 1·25 15
108 17 50 c. on 1 f. 05 mauve 90 60
109 50 c. on 1 f. 10 green 8·75 6·25
110 15 50 c. on 1 f. 25 blue on blue 1·40 30
111 1 f. 25 on 1 f. blue on blue 65 20
112 – 1 f. 50 on 2 f. brown and mauve (No. 102) 5·00 4·75

20 Prince Charles III, Louis II and Albert I

1928. International Philatelic Exn, Monte Carlo.

113 20 50 c. red 2·10 3·75
114 1 f. 50 blue 2·10 3·75
115 3 f. violet 2·10 3·75

20a

21 Palace Entrance

22 St. Devote's Church

23 Prince Louis II

1933.

116 20a 1 c. plum 10 10
117 2 c. green 10 10
118 3 c. purple 10 10
119 5 c. red 10 10
120 10 c. blue 10 10
121 15 c. violet 75 70
122 21 15 c. red 85 10
123 20 c. brown 85 10
124 A 25 c. sepia 1·25 30
125 22 30 c. green 1·50 30
126 23 40 c. sepia 3·75 1·60
127 B 45 c. brown 3·25 1·25
128 23 50 c. violet 3·00 85
129 C 65 c. green 3·25 65
130 D 75 c. blue 4·25 2·50
131 23 90 c. red 2·75 2·50
132 22 1 f. brown 27·00 6·75
133 D 1 f. 25 red 6·25 3·75
134 23 1 f. 50 blue 32·00 8·75
135 A 1 f. 75 red 32·00 8·75
136 1 f. 75 red 20·00 12·50
137 B 2 f. blue 11·00 4·25
138 21 3 f. violet 18·00 7·50
139 A 3 f. 50 orange 45·00 30·00
140 22 5 f. purple 25·00 17·00
141 A 10 f. blue £120 65·00
142 C 20 f. black £160 £130

DESIGNS—As Type **21**—HORIZ: A, The Prince's Residence; B, The Rock of Monaco; C, Palace Gardens; D, Fortifications and Harbour.

For other stamps in Type **20a** see Nos. 249, etc.

1933. Air. Surch with Bleriot XI airplane and **1f50.**

143 – 1 f. 50 on 5 f. red and green (No. 104) 22·00 23·00

28 Palace Gardens

1937. Charity.

144 28 50 c. + 50 c. green 2·50 2·50
145 – 90 c. + 90 c. red 2·50 2·50
146 – 1 f. 50 + 1 f. 50 blue 5·00 5·00
147 – 2 f. + 2 f. violet 11·00 11·00
148 – 5 f. + 5 f. red 85·00 85·00

DESIGNS—HORIZ: 90 c. Exotic gardens; 1 f. 50, The Bay of Monaco. VERT: 2, 5 f. Prince Louis II.

1937. Postage Due stamps optd **POSTES** or surch also.

149 D 18 5 on 10 c. violet 70 70
150 10 c. violet 70 70
151 15 on 30 c. bistre 70 70
152 20 on 30 c. bistre 70 70
153 25 on 60 c. red 1·25 1·25
154 30 c. bistre 2·25 2·00
155 40 on 60 c. red 2·00 1·90
156 50 on 60 c. red 2·25 2·50
157 65 on 1 f. blue 2·25 2·25
158 85 on 1 f. blue 5·25 4·75
159 1 f. blue 6·50 6·50
160 2 f. 15 on 2 f. red 7·25 7·25
161 2 f. 25 on 2 f. red 17·00 17·00
162 2 f. 50 on 2 f. red 27·00 25·00

31 Prince Louis II

33 Monaco Hospital

1938.

164 31 55 c. brown 3·25 1·50
165 65 c. violet 26·00 12·50
166 70 c. brown 15 15
167 90 c. violet 15 15
168 1 f. red 10·50 6·25
169 1 f. 25 red 20 15
170 1 f. 75 blue 15·00 8·00
171 2 f. 25 blue 20 15

1938. Anti-Cancer Fund. 40th Anniv of Discovery of Radium.

172 – 65 c. + 25 c. green 8·75 8·75
173 33 1 f. 75 + 50 c. blue 11·00 11·00

DESIGN—VERT: 65 c. Pierre and Marie Curie.

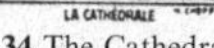
34 The Cathedral

38 Monaco Harbour

1939.

174 34 20 c. mauve 15 15
175 – 25 c. brown 30 20
176 – 30 c. green 20 20
177 – 40 c. red 20 20
178 – 45 c. purple 20 20
179 – 50 c. green 25 15
180 – 60 c. red 20 20
181 – 60 c. green 20 50
182 38 70 c. lilac 35 20
183 75 c. green 35 20
184 – 1 f. black 20 20
185 – 1 f. 30 brown 20 20
186 – 2 f. purple 20 20
187 – 2 f. 50 red 22·00 13·00
188 – 2 f. 50 blue 1·25 1·25
189 38 3 f. red 40 20
190 34 5 f. blue 4·25 2·50
191 – 10 f. green 1·10 1·25
192 – 20 f. blue 1·25 1·25

DESIGNS—VERT: 25, 40 c., 2 f. Place St. Nicholas; 30, 60 c., 20 f. Palace Gateway; 50 c., 1 f., 1 f. 30, Palace of Monaco. HORIZ: 45 c., 2 f. 50, 10 f. Aerial view of Monaco.

40 Louis II Stadium 41 Lucien

1939. Inauguration of Louis II Stadium, Monaco.

198 40 10 f. green £110 £110

1939. National Relief. XVI–XVIII-century portrait designs and view.

199 41 5 c. + 5 c. black 1·75 1·25
200 – 10 c. + 10 c. purple 1·75 1·25
201 – 45 c. + 15 c. green 5·00 4·25
202 – 70 c. + 30 c. mauve 8·75 8·00
203 – 90 c. + 35 c. violet 9·25 9·25
204 – 1 f. + 1 f. blue 23·00 22·00
205 – 2 f. + 2 f. red 22·00 23·00
206 – 2 f. 25 + 1 f. 25 blue 30·00 25·00
207 – 3 f. + 3 f. red 40·00 42·00
208 – 5 f. + 5 f. red 75·00 85·00

DESIGNS—VERT: 10 c. Honore II; 45 c. Louis I; 70 c. Charlotte de Gramont; 90 c. Antoine I; 1 f. Marie de Lorraine; 2 f. Jacques I; 2 f. 25, Louise-Hippolyte; 3 f. Honore III. HORIZ: 5 f. The Rock of Monaco.

1939. 8th International University Games. As T **40** but inscr "VIIIeme JEUX UNIVERSITAIRES INTERNATIONAUX 1939".

209 40 c. green 1·25 1·25
210 70 c. brown 1·75 1·75
211 90 c. violet 2·00 2·00
212 1 f. 25 red 3·00 3·00
213 2 f. 25 blue 4·25 4·25

1940. Red Cross Ambulance Fund. As Nos. 174/92 in new colours surch with Red Cross and premium.

214 34 20 c. + 1 f. violet 3·25 3·25
215 – 25 c. + 1 f. green 3·25 3·25
216 – 30 c. + 1 f. red 3·25 3·25
217 – 40 c. + 1 f. blue 3·25 3·25
218 – 45 c. + 1 f. red 3·50 3·50
219 – 50 c. + 1 f. brown 3·50 3·50
220 – 60 c. + 1 f. green 3·50 3·50
221 38 75 c. + 1 f. black 3·50 3·50
222 – 1 f. + 1 f. red 4·25 4·25
223 – 2 f. + 1 f. slate 4·25 4·25
224 – 2 f. 50 + 1 f. green 10·00 10·00
225 38 3 f. + 1 f. blue 11·00 11·00
226 34 5 f. + 1 f. black 13·50 13·50
227 – 10 f. + 5 f. blue 22·00 22·00
228 – 20 f. + 5 f. purple 25·00 25·00

44 Prince Louis II

1941.

229 44 40 c. red 20 50
230 80 c. green 20 50
231 1 f. violet 10 10
232 1 f. 20 green 10 10
233 1 f. 50 red 10 10
234 1 f. 50 violet 10 10
235 2 f. green 10 10
236 2 f. 40 red 10 10
237 2 f. 50 blue 60 1·25
238 4 f. blue 10 10

45

46

1941. National Relief Fund.

239 45 25 c. + 25 c. purple 1·40 1·40
240 46 50 c. + 25 c. brown 1·40 1·40
241 75 c. + 50 c. purple 2·10 2·10
242 45 1 f. + 1 f. blue 2·10 2·10
243 46 1 f. 50 + 1 f. 50 red 3·00 3·00
244 45 2 f. + 2 f. green 3·00 3·00
245 46 2 f. 50 + 2 f. blue 3·75 3·75
246 45 3 f. + 3 f. brown 3·75 3·75
247 46 5 f. + 5 f. green 6·25 6·25
248 45 10 f. + 8 f. sepia 10·50 10·50

1941. New values and colours.

249	**20a**	10 c. black	10	10
250	–	30 c. red (as No. 176)	20	15
251	**20a**	30 c. green	10	10
252		40 c. red	10	10
253		50 c. violet	10	10
362	**34**	50 c. brown	10	10
254	**20a**	60 c. blue	10	10
363	–	60 c. pink (as No. 175)	10	15
255	**20a**	70 c. brown	10	10
256	**34**	80 c. green	10	10
257	–	1 f. brown (as Nos. 178)	10	10
258	**38**	1 f. 20 blue	15	15
259	–	1 f. 50 blue (as Nos. 175)	15	15
260	**38**	2 f. blue	10	10
261	–	2 f. green (as No. 179)	10	10
262	–	3 f. black (as No. 175)	10	10
364	–	3 f. purple (as No. 176)	20	20
391	–	3 f. green (as No. 175)	40	20
263	**34**	4 f. mauve	10	50
365	–	4 f. green (as No. 175)	20	20
264	–	4 f. 50 violet (as No. 179)	10	10
265	–	5 f. green (as No. 176)	10	10
392	–	5 f. green (as No. 178)	20	10
393	–	5 f. red (as No. 176)	35	35
266	–	6 f. violet (as No. 179)	60	30
368	–	8 f. brown (as No. 179)	1·75	1·90
267	**34**	10 f. blue	10	10
370	–	10 f. brown (as No. 179)	1·75	1·25
394	**38**	10 f. yellow	60	20
268		15 f. red	20	15
269	–	20 f. brown (as No. 178)	20	15
373	–	20 f. red (as No. 178)	75	80
270	**38**	25 f. green	1·25	85
374		25 f. black	15·00	14·00
397	–	25 f. blue (as No. 176)	23·00	14·00
398	–	25 f. red (as No. 179)	1·75	55
399	–	30 f. blue (as No. 176)	5·25	4·00
400	–	35 f. blue (as No. 179)	3·75	2·00
401	**34**	40 f. red	3·00	3·75
402		50 f. violet	2·50	65
403	–	65 f. violet (as No. 178)	6·25	6·25
404	**34**	70 f. yellow	6·25	7·50
405	–	75 f. green (as No. 175)	13·50	8·00
406	–	85 f. red (as No. 175)	8·75	8·00
407	–	100 f. turquoise (as No. 178)	8·75	8·00

47 Caudron Rafale over Monaco **48** Propeller and Palace

49 Arms, Airplane and Globe **50** Charles II

1942. Air.

271	**47**	5 f. green	20	20
272		10 f. blue	20	30
273	**48**	15 f. brown	55	35
274	–	20 f. brown	55	45
275	–	50 f. purple	3·00	1·75
276	**49**	100 f. red and purple	3·00	1·75

DESIGNS—VERT: 20 f. Pegasus. HORIZ: 50 f. Common gull over Bay of Monaco.

1942. National Relief Fund. Royal Personnages.

277	–	2 c. + 3 c. blue	10	50
278	**50**	5 c. + 5 c. red	10	50
279	–	10 c. + 5 c. black	10	50
280	–	20 c. + 10 c. green	10	50
281	–	30 c. + 30 c. purple	10	50
282	–	40 c. + 40 c. red	10	50
283	–	50 c. + 50 c. violet	10	50
284	–	75 c. + 75 c. purple	10	50
285	–	1 f. + 1 f. green	10	50
286	–	1 f. 50 + 1 f. red	10	50
287	–	2 f. 50 + 2 f. 50 violet	3·00	5·00
288	–	3 f. + 3 f. blue	3·00	5·00
289	–	5 f. + 5 f. sepia	3·75	6·25
290	–	10 f. + 5 f. purple	3·75	6·75
291	–	20 f. + 5 f. blue	3·75	6·75

PORTRAITS: 2 c. Rainier Grimaldi; 10 c. Jeanne Grimaldi; 20 c. Charles Auguste, Goyon de Matignon; 30 c. Jacques I; 40 c. Louise-Hippolyte; 50 c. Charlotte Grimaldi; 75 c. Marie Charles Grimaldi; 1 f. Honore III; 1 f. 50, Honore IV; 2 f. 50, Honore V; 3 f. Florestan I; 5 f. Charles III; 10 f. Albert I; 20 f. Princess Marie-Victoire.

52 Prince Louis II

1943.

292	**52**	50 f. violet	85	85

53 St. Devote **54** Blessing the Sea

55 Arrival of St. Devote at Monaco

1944. Charity. Festival of St. Devote.

293	**53**	50 c. + 50 c. brown	15	15
294	–	70 c. + 80 c. blue	15	15
295	–	80 c. + 70 c. green	15	15
296	–	1 f. + 1 f. purple	15	15
297	–	1 f. 50 + 1 f. 50 red	15	50
298	**54**	2 f. + 2 f. purple	20	75
299	–	5 f. + 2 f. violet	35	75
300	–	10 f. + 40 f. blue	35	75
301	**55**	20 f. + 60 f. blue	3·00	5·50

DESIGNS—VERT: 70 c., 1 f. Various processional scenes; 1 f. 50, Burning the boat; 10 f. Trial scene. HORIZ: 80 c. Procession; 5 f. St. Devote's Church.

1945. Air. For War Dead and Deported Workers. As Nos. 272/6 (colours changed) surch.

302	1 f. + 4 f. on 10 f. red	35	35
303	1 f. + 4 f. on 15 f. brown	35	35
304	1 f. + 4 f. on 20 f. brown	35	35
305	1 f. + 4 f. on 50 f. blue	35	35
306	1 f. + 4 f. on 100 f. purple	35	35

57 Prince Louis II **58**

1946.

361	**57**	30 c. black	10	10
389		50 c. olive	10	10
390		1 f. violet	10	10
307		2 f. 50 green	15	10
308		3 f. mauve	15	10
366		5 f. brown	20	15
309		6 f. red	15	10
367		6 f. purple	1·00	1·75
310		10 f. blue	15	10
369		10 f. orange	10	10
371		12 f. red	3·00	2·50
395		12 f. slate	4·25	5·50
396		15 f. lake	4·25	3·75
372		18 f. blue	5·00	6·25
311	**58**	50 f. grey	1·50	1·75
312		100 f. red	2·10	2·25

59 Child Praying **60** Nurse and Baby

1946. Child Welfare Fund.

313	**59**	1 f. + 3 f. green	20	20
314		2 f. + 4 f. red	20	20
315		4 f. + 6 f. blue	20	20
316		5 f. + 40 f. mauve	55	55
317		10 f. + 60 f. red	55	55
318		15 f. + 100 f. blue	90	90

1946. Anti-tuberculosis Fund.

319	**60**	2 f. + 8 f. blue	35	35

1946. Air. Optd **POSTE AERIENNE** over Sud Ouest Cassiopees airplane.

320	**58**	50 f. grey	3·00	2·75
321		100 f. red	5·00	4·25

INDEX

Countries can be quickly located by referring to the index at the end of this volume.

62 Steamship and Chart

1946. Stamp Day.

322	**62**	3 f. + 2 f. blue	20	20

63

1946. Air.

323	**63**	40 f. red	60	85
324		50 f. brown	70	90
325		100 f. green	1·40	1·60
326		200 f. violet	1·50	2·50
326a		300 f. blue & ultramarine	35·00	60·00
326b		500 f. green & deep green	25·00	35·00
326c		1000 f. violet and brown	35·00	60·00

64 Pres. Roosevelt and Palace of Monaco

66 Pres. Roosevelt

1946. President Roosevelt,Commemorative.

327	**66**	10 c. mauve (postage)	10	10
328	–	30 c. blue	15	15
329	**64**	60 c. green	15	15
330	–	1 f. sepia	30	75
331	–	2 f. + 3 f. green	55	1·10
332	–	3 f. violet	1·00	1·40
333	–	5 f. red (air)	30	60
334	–	10 f. black	60	40
335	**66**	15 f. + 10 f. orange	1·90	1·40

DESIGNS—HORIZ: 30 c., 5 f. Rock of Monaco; 2 f. Viaduct and St. Devote. VERT: 1 f., 3 f., 10 f. Map of Monaco.

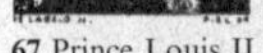

67 Prince Louis II **68** Pres. Roosevelt as a Philatelist

69 Statue of Liberty and New York Harbour **70** Prince Charles III

1947. Participation in the Centenary International Philatelic Exhibition, New York. (a) Postage.

336	**67**	10 f. blue	2·00	3·75

(b) Air. Dated "1847 1947"

337	**68**	50 c. violet	40	1·00
338	–	1 f. 50 mauve	30	25
339	–	3 f. orange	30	50
340	–	10 f. blue	2·00	3·75
341	**69**	15 f. red	3·00	5·00

DESIGNS—HORIZ: As Type **68**: 1 f. 50, G.P.O., New York; 3 f. Oceanographic Museum, Monte Carlo. As Type **69**: 10 f. Bay of Monaco.

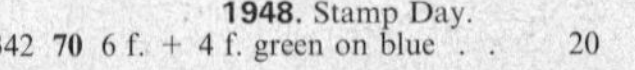

1948. Stamp Day.

342	**70**	6 f. + 4 f. green on blue	20	50

71 Diving **72** Tennis

1948. Olympic Games, Wembley. Inscr "JEUX OLYMPIQUES 1948".

343	–	50 c. green (postage)	15	15
344	–	1 f. red	15	15
345	–	2 f. blue	85	85
346	–	2 f. 50 red	1·75	1·75
347	**71**	4 f. slate	2·50	2·50
348	–	5 f. + 5 f. brown (air)	6·25	10·50
349	–	6 f. + 9 f. violet	9·25	16·00
350	**72**	10 f. + 15 f. red	13·50	22·00
351	–	15 f. + 25 f. blue	20·00	32·00

DESIGNS—HORIZ: 50 c. Hurdling; 15 f. Yachting. VERT: 1 f. Running; 2 f. Throwing the discus; 2 f. 50, Basketball; 5 f. Rowing; 6 f. Skiing.

75 The Salmacis Nymph **77** F. J. Bosio (wrongly inscr. "J. F.")

1948. Death Centenary of Francois Joseph Bosio (sculptor).

352	**75**	50 c. green (postage)	10	10
353	–	1 f. red	20	20
354	–	2 f. blue	60	75
355	–	2 f. 50 violet	1·10	1·50
356	**77**	4 f. mauve	1·40	2·10
357	–	5 f. + 5 f. blue (air)	7·50	13·50
358	–	6 f. + 9 f. green	8·00	14·50
359	–	10 f. + 15 f. red	10·50	17·00
360	–	15 f. + 25 f. brown	15·00	23·00

DESIGNS—VERT: 1, 5 f. Hercules struggling with Achelous; 2, 6 f. Aristaeus (Garden God); 15 f. The Salmacis Nymph (36 × 48 mm). HORIZ: 2 f. 50, 10 f. Hyacinthus awaiting his turn to throw a quoit.

79 Exotic Gardens **80** "Princess Alice II"

1949. Birth Centenary of Prince Albert I.

375	–	2 f. blue (postage)	25	20
376	**79**	3 f. green	10	10
377	–	4 f. brown and blue	20	20
378	**80**	5 f. red	1·25	1·25
379	–	6 f. violet	45	45
380	–	10 f. sepia	80	1·50
381	–	12 f. pink	1·25	2·00
382	–	18 f. orange and brown	2·50	3·50
383	–	20 f. brown (air)	30	55
384	–	25 f. blue	30	55
385	–	40 f. green	1·00	1·90
386	–	50 f. green, brown & black	1·40	2·50
387	–	100 f. red	14·50	8·50
388	–	200 f. orange	8·00	13·50

DESIGNS—HORIZ: 2 f. Yacht "Hirondelle I" (1870); 4 f. Oceanographic Museum, Monaco; 10 f. "Hirondelle II" (1914); 12 f. Albert harpooning whale; 18 f. Buffalo (Palaeolithic mural); 20 f. Constitution Day, 1911; 25 f. Paris Institute of Palaeontology; 200 f. Coin with effigy of Albert. VERT: 6 f. Statue of Albert at tiller; 40 f. Anthropological Museum; 50 f. Prince Albert I; 100 f. Oceanographic Institute, Paris.

83 Palace of Monaco and Globe

1949. 75th Anniv of U.P.U.

410	**83**	5 f. green (postage)	10	10
411		10 f. orange	5·75	5·75
412		15 f. red	20	25
413		25 f. blue (air)	55	45
414		40 f. sepia and brown	1·25	2·00
415		50 f. blue and green	1·60	2·75
416		100 f. blue and red	2·75	4·50

84 Prince Rainier III and Monaco Palace

85 Prince Rainier III

1950. Accession of Prince Rainier III.

No.	Type	Description	Unused	Used
417	84	10 c. purple & red (postage)	10	10
418		50 c. brown, light brown and orange	10	10
419		1 f. violet	10	10
420		5 f. deep green and green	1·10	1·90
421		15 f. carmine and red	2·25	3·75
422		25 f. blue, green and ultramarine	3·75	6·25
423		50 f. brown and black (air)	3·00	5·50
424		100 f. blue, deep brown and brown	5·50	10·00

1950.

No.	Type	Description	Unused	Used
425	85	50 c. violet	10	10
426		1 f. brown	10	10
434		5 f. green	8·75	5·00
427		6 f. green	65	85
428		8 f. green	2·25	2·00
429		8 f. orange	90	35
435		10 f. orange	11·00	7·50
430		12 f. blue	1·25	25
431		15 f. red	1·75	35
432		15 f. blue	1·10	50
433		18 f. red	3·00	1·50

86 Prince Albert I

87 Edmond and Jules de Goncourt

1951. Unveiling of Prince Albert Statue.

No.	Type	Description	Unused	Used
436	86	15 f. blue	10·50	8·00

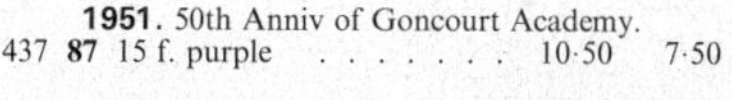

1951. 50th Anniv of Goncourt Academy.

No.	Type	Description	Unused	Used
437	87	15 f. purple	10·50	7·50

88 St. Vincent de Paul

90 St. Peter's Keys and Papal Bull

89 Judgement of St. Devote

1951. Holy Year.

No.	Type	Description	Unused	Used
438	88	10 c. blue, ultram & red	15	15
439	–	50 c. violet and red	15	15
440	89	1 f. green and brown	20	20
441	90	2 f. red and purple	30	30
442	–	5 f. green	30	30
443	–	12 f. violet	40	40
444	–	15 f. red	5·25	3·00
445	–	20 f. brown	7·50	4·25
446	–	25 f. blue	10·00	6·25
447	–	40 f. violet and mauve	11·00	6·75
448	–	50 f. brown and olive	15·00	9·25
449	–	100 f. brown	30·00	19·00

DESIGNS—TRIANGULAR: 50 c. Pope Pius XII. As Type 90—HORIZ: 5 f. Mosaic. VERT: 12 f. Prince Rainier III in St. Peter's; 15 f. St. Nicholas of Patara; 20 f. St. Romain; 25 f. St. Charles Borromeo; 40 f. Coliseum; 50 f. Chapel of St. Devote. As Type 89: VERT: 100 f. Rainier of Westphalia.

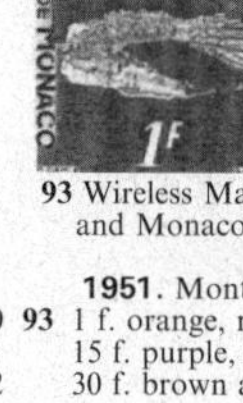

93 Wireless Mast and Monaco

94 Seal of Prince Rainier III

1951. Monte Carlo Radio Station.

No.	Type	Description	Unused	Used
450	93	1 f. orange, red and blue	55	20
451		15 f. purple, red and violet	3·00	1·25
452		30 f. brown and blue	11·00	6·25

1951.

No.	Type	Description	Unused	Used
453	94	1 f. violet	1·00	65
454		5 f. black	6·75	2·50
512		5 f. violet	3·75	1·25
513		6 f. red	3·00	1·75
455		8 f. red	6·75	4·25
514		8 f. brown	5·50	3·75
456		15 f. green	11·00	8·00
515		15 f. blue	21·00	5·00
457		30 f. blue	20·00	12·50
516		30 f. green	20·00	16·00

95 Gallery of Hercules

1952. Monaco Postal Museum.

No.	Type	Description	Unused	Used
460	95	5 f. chestnut and brown	30	30
461		15 f. violet and purple	55	30
462		30 f. indigo and blue	2·25	1·00

96 Football

1953. 15th Olympic Games, Helsinki. Inscr "HELSINKI 1952".

No.	Type	Description	Unused	Used
463	–	1 f. mauve & violet (postage)	20	15
464	96	2 f. blue and green	20	20
465	–	3 f. pale and deep blue	25	20
466	–	5 f. green and brown	70	30
467	–	8 f. red and lake	2·25	1·10
468	–	15 f. brown, green and blue	1·50	1·10
469	–	40 f. black (air)	11·00	9·25
470	–	50 f. violet	12·50	9·25
471	–	100 f. green	18·00	15·00
472	–	200 f. red	23·00	11·00

DESIGNS: 1 f. Basketball; 3 f. Yachting; 5 f. Cycling; 8 f. Gymnastics; 15 f. Louis II Stadium, Monaco; 40 f. Running; 50 f. Fencing; 100 f. Rifle target and Arms of Monaco; 200 f. Olympic torch.

97 "Journal Inedit"

1953. Centenary of Publication of Journal by E. and J. de Goncourt.

No.	Type	Description	Unused	Used
473	97	5 f. green	75	50
474		15 f. brown	3·00	75

98 Physalia, Yacht "Princess Alice", Prince Albert, Richet and Portier

1953. 50th Anniv of Discovery of Anaphylaxis.

No.	Type	Description	Unused	Used
475	98	2 f. violet, green and brown	10	10
476		5 f. red, lake and green	1·00	25
477		15 f. lilac, blue and green	3·00	1·60

99 F. Ozanam

100 St. Jean-Baptiste de la Salle

1954. Death Centenary of Ozanam (founder of St. Vincent de Paul Conferences).

No.	Type	Description	Unused	Used
478	99	1 f. red	10	10
479	–	5 f. blue	25	60
480	99	15 f. black	2·10	2·00

DESIGN: 5 f. Outline drawing of Sister of Charity.

1954. St. J.-B. de la Salle (educationist).

No.	Type	Description	Unused	Used
481	100	1 f. red	10	10
482	–	5 f. sepia	25	60
483	100	15 f. blue	2·10	2·00

DESIGN: 5 f. Outline drawing of De la Salle and two children.

101 102 103

1954. Arms.

No.	Type	Description	Unused	Used
484	–	50 c. red, black and mauve	10	10
485	–	70 c. red, black and blue	10	10
486	101	80 c. red, black and green	10	10
487	–	1 f. red, black and blue	10	10
488	102	2 f. red, black and orange	10	10
489	–	3 f. red, black and green	10	10
490	103	5 f. multicoloured	10	10

DESIGNS—HORIZ: 50 c. as Type **101**. VERT: 70 c., 1, 3 f. as Type **102**.

104 Seal of Prince Rainier III

1954. Precancelled.

No.	Type	Description	Unused	Used
491	104	4 f. red	65	20
492		5 f. blue	20	10
493		8 f. green	65	90
494		8 f. purple	55	20
495		10 f. green	20	10
496		12 f. violet	5·00	1·90
497		15 f. orange	1·25	1·00
498		20 f. green	1·60	1·50
499		24 f. brown	9·25	5·25
500		30 f. blue	1·75	1·00
501		40 f. brown	3·00	1·25
502		45 f. red	2·75	1·40
503		55 f. blue	5·75	3·00

See also Nos. 680/3.

105 Lambarene

106 Dr. Albert Schweitzer

1955. 80th Birthday of Dr. Schweitzer (humanitarian).

No.	Type	Description	Unused	Used
504	105	2 f. green, turquoise and blue (postage)	10	10
505	106	5 f. blue and green	1·40	1·40
506	–	15 f. purple, black and green	3·25	3·25
507	–	200 f. slate, green and blue (air)	40·00	32·00

DESIGNS—As Type **106**: 15 f. Lambarene Hospital. HORIZ—(48×27 mm): 200 f. Schweitzer and jungle scene.

107 Common Cormorants

1955. Air.

No.	Type	Description	Unused	Used
508a	–	100 f. indigo and blue	15·00	12·00
509	–	200 f. black and blue	18·00	9·50
510	–	500 f. grey and green	30·00	16·00
511a	107	1,000 f. black, turquoise and green	75·00	45·00

DESIGNS—As Type **107**: 100 f. Roseate tern; 200 f. Herring gull; 500 f. Wandering albatrosses.

108 Eight Starting Points

109 Prince Rainier III

1955. 25th Monte Carlo Car Rally.

No.	Type	Description	Unused	Used
517	108	100 f. red and brown	75·00	50·00

1955.

No.	Type	Description	Unused	Used
518	109	6 f. purple and green	10	10
519		8 f. violet and red	10	10
520		12 f. green and red	20	10
521		15 f. blue and purple	75	15
522		18 f. blue and orange	2·50	20
523		20 f. turquoise	1·50	30
524		25 f. black and orange	1·25	60
525		30 f. sepia and blue	16·00	7·50
526		30 f. violet	4·25	2·25
527		35 f. brown	4·25	2·25
528		50 f. lake and green	3·75	2·50

See also Nos. 627/41.

110 "La Maison a Vapeur"

111 "The 500 Millions of the Begum"

113 U.S.S. "Nautilus"

112 "Round the World in Eighty Days"

1955. 50th Death Anniv of Jules Verne (author). Designs illustrating his works.

No.	Type	Description	Unused	Used
529	–	1 f. blue & brown (postage)	10	10
530	–	2 f. sepia, indigo and blue	10	10
531	110	3 f. blue, black and brown	10	10
532	–	5 f. sepia and red	10	10
533	111	6 f. grey and sepia	25	25
534	–	8 f. turquoise and olive	35	35
535	–	10 f. sepia, turquoise & ind	1·25	1·10
536	112	15 f. red and brown	1·10	85
537	–	25 f. black and green	2·50	1·90
538	113	30 f. black, purple & turq	6·25	5·25

539 – 200 f. indigo & blue (air) 24·00 22·00
DESIGNS—As Type **111**—VERT: 1 f. "Five Weeks in a Balloon". HORIZ: 5 f. "Michael Strogoff"; 8 f. "Le Superbe Orenoque". As Type **110**: HORIZ: 2 f. "A Floating Island"; 10 f. "Journey to the Centre of the Earth"; 25 f. "20,000 Leagues under the Sea"; 200 f. "From Earth to Moon".

114 "The Immaculate Virgin" (F. Brea)

1955. Marian Year.
540 **114** 5 f. green, grey and brown 20 20
541 – 10 f. green, grey & brown 30 30
542 – 15 f. brown and sepia 40 40
DESIGNS—As Type **114**: 10 f. "Madonna" (L. Brea). As Type **113**: 15 f. Bienheureux Rainier.

115 Rotary Emblem

1955. 50th Anniv of Rotary International.
543 **115** 30 f. blue and yellow 1·10 1·10

116 George Washington

118 President Eisenhower

117 Abraham Lincoln

1956. 5th International Stamp Exhibition, New York.
544 **116** 1 f. violet and lilac 10 10
545 – 2 f. lilac and purple 10 10
546 **117** 3 f. blue and violet 10 10
547 **118** 5 f. red 20 20
548 – 15 f. brown and chocolate 45 45
549 – 30 f. black, indigo & blue 3·50 2·25
550 – 40 f. brown 4·25 1·90
551 – 50 f. red 4·25 2·50
552 – 100 f. green 5·00 3·00
DESIGNS—As Type **117**: 2 f. F. D. Roosevelt. As Type **116**—HORIZ: 15 f. Monaco Palace in the 18th century; 30 f. Landing of Columbus. LARGER (48 × 36 mm): 50 f. Aerial view of Monaco Palace in the 18th century; 100 f. Louisiana landscape in 18th century. As Type **118**: 40 f. Prince Rainier III.

120

1956. 7th Winter Olympic Games, Cortina d'Ampezzo and 16th Olympic Games, Melbourne.
553 – 15 f. brown, green & pur 1·25 55
554 **120** 30 f. red 2·50 1·75
DESIGN: 15 f. "Italia" ski-jump.

1956. Nos. D482/95 with "TIMBRE TAXE" barred out and some surch also. (a) Postage.
555 2 f. on 4 f. slate and brown 30 30
556 2 f. on 4 f. brown and slate 30 30
557 3 f. lake and green 35 35
558 3 f. green and lake 35 35
559 5 f. on 4 f. slate and brown 75 30
560 5 f. on 4 f. brown and slate 75 30
561 10 f. on 4 f. slate and brown 1·10 55
562 10 f. on 4 f. brown and slate 1·10 55
563 15 f. on 5 f. violet and blue 2·00 1·00
564 15 f. on 5 f. blue and violet 2·00 1·00
565 20 f. violet and blue 3·00 1·75
566 20 f. blue and violet 3·00 1·75
567 25 f. on 20 f. violet and blue 5·25 3·00
568 25 f. on 20 f. blue and violet 5·25 3·00
569 30 f. on 10 f. indigo and blue 7·25 4·50
570 30 f. on 10 f. blue and indigo 7·25 4·50
571 40 f. on 50 f. brown and red 10·00 6·75
572 40 f. on 50 f. red and brown 10·00 6·75
573 50 f. on 100 f. green and purple 13·50 9·25
574 50 f. on 100 f. purple and green 13·50 9·25

(b) Air. Optd **POSTE AERIENNE** also.
575 100 f. on 20 f. violet and blue 10·50 10·50
576 100 f. on 20 f. blue and violet 10·50 10·50

121 Route Map from Glasgow

1956. 26th Monte Carlo Car Rally.
577 **121** 100 f. brown and red 25·00 16·00

122 Princess Grace and Prince Rainier III

1956. Royal Wedding.
578 **122** 1 f. black & grn (postage) 10 10
579 2 f. black and red 10 10
580 3 f. black and blue 20 15
581 5 f. black and green 55 25
582 15 f. black and brown 80 40
583 100 f. brown & purple (air) 1·10 60
584 200 f. brown and red 1·75 1·00
585 500 f. brown and grey 4·00 2·50

123 Princess Grace

124 Princess Grace with Princess Caroline

1957. Birth of Princess Caroline.
586 **123** 1 f. grey 10 10
587 2 f. olive 10 10
588 3 f. brown 10 10
589 5 f. red 10 10
590 15 f. pink 10 10
591 25 f. blue 1·10 10
592 30 f. violet 1·10 10
593 50 f. red 2·10 75
594 75 f. orange 3·00 2·10

1958. Birth of Prince Albert.
595 **124** 100 f. black 8·00 6·25

125 Order of St. Charles

126 Route Map from Munich

1958. Centenary of Creation of National Order of St. Charles.
596 **125** 100 f. multicoloured 2·50 2·25

1958. 27th Monte Carlo Rally.
597 **126** 100 f. multicoloured 9·25 7·50

127 Statue of the Holy Virgin and Popes Pius IX and Pius XII

1958. Centenary of Apparition of Virgin Mary at Lourdes.
598 **127** 1 f. grey & brown (postage) 10 10
599 – 2 f. violet and blue 10 10
600 – 3 f. sepia and green 10 10
601 – 5 f. blue and sepia 10 10
602 – 8 f. multicoloured 15 15
603 – 10 f. multicoloured 15 10
604 – 12 f. multicoloured 20 15
605 – 20 f. myrtle and purple 30 20
606 – 35 f. myrtle, bistre and brown 40 30
607 – 50 f. blue, green and lake 65 55
608 – 65 f. turquoise and blue 90 70
609 – 100 f. grey, myrtle and blue (air) 1·75 1·50
610 – 200 f. brown and chestnut 2·50 2·50
DESIGNS—VERT: ($26\frac{1}{2} \times 36$ mm): 2 f. St. Bernadette; 3 f. St. Bernadette at Bartres; 5 f. The Miracle of Bourriette; 20 f. St. Bernadette at prayer; 35 f. St. Bernadette's canonization. (22 × 36 mm): 8 f. Stained-glass window. As Type **127**: 50 f. St. Bernadette, Pope Pius XI, Mgr. Laurence and Abbe Peyramale. HORIZ: (48 × 36 mm): 10 f. Lourdes grotto; 12 f. Interior of Lourdes grotto. ($36 \times 26\frac{1}{2}$ mm): 65 f. Shrine of St. Bernadette; (48 × 27 mm): 100 f. Lourdes Basilica; 200 f. Pope Pius X and subterranean interior of Basilica.

128 Princess Grace and Clinic

1959. Opening of new hospital block in "Princess Grace" Clinic, Monaco.
611 **128** 100 f. grey, brown & green 3·00 1·75

129 U.N.E.S.C.O. Headquarters, Paris, and Cultural Emblems

1959. Inaug of U.N.E.S.C.O. Headquarters Building.
612 **129** 25 f. multicoloured 15 10
613 – 50 f. turquoise, black & ol 35 30
DESIGN: 50 f. As Type **129** but with heads of children and letters of various alphabets in place of the emblems.

130 Route Map from Athens

131 Prince Rainier and Princess Grace

1959. 28th Monte Carlo Rally.
614 **130** 100 f. blue, red & grn on blue 6·25 3·75

1959. Air.
615 **131** 300 f. violet 12·50 10·50
616 500 f. blue 21·00 17·00
See also Nos. 642/3.

132 "Princess Caroline" Carnation

1959. Flowers.
617 **132** 5 f. mve, grn and brn 10 10
618 – 10 f. on 3 f. pink, green and brown 10 10
619 – 15 f. on 1 f. yellow & green 15 10
620 – 20 f. purple and green 1·00 60
621 – 25 f. on 6 f. red, yellow and green 1·25 85
622 – 35 f. pink and green 2·50 2·00
623 – 50 f. green and sepia 3·00 2·00
624 – 85 f. on 65 f. lavender, bronze and green 4·00 3·25
625 – 100 f. red and green 5·25 5·00
FLOWERS—As Type **132**: 10 f. "Princess Grace" carnation; 100 f. "Grace of Monaco" rose. VERT: (22 × 36 mm): 15 f. Mimosa; 25 f. Geranium. HORIZ: (36 × 22 mm): 20 f. Bougainvillea; 35 f. "Laurier" rose; 50 f. Jasmine; 85 f. Lavender.

(New currency. 100 (old) francs = 1 (new franc.)

133 "Uprooted Tree"

134 Oceanographic Museum

1960. World Refugee Year.
626 **133** 25 c. green, blue and black 15 15

1960. Prince Rainier types with values in new currency.
627 **109** 25 c. blk & orge (postage) 50 10
628 30 c. violet 20 10
629 40 c. red and brown 85 10
630 45 c. brown and grey 30 10
631 50 c. red and green 40 20
632 50 c. red and brown 40 10
633 60 c. brown and green 1·60 50
634 60 c. brown and purple 1·60 50
635 65 c. blue and brown 11·00 5·00
636 70 c. blue and plum 80 40
637 85 c. green and violet 1·60 1·25
638 95 c. blue 1·50 1·25
639 1 f. 10 blue and brown 3·00 1·75
640 1 f. 30 brown and red 2·75 2·25
641 2 f. 30 purple and orange 3·00 1·00
642 **131** 3 f. violet (air) 48·00 23·00
643 5 f. blue 48·00 32·00

1960.
644 – 5 c. green, black and blue 10 10
645 **134** 10 c. brown and blue 80 10
646 – 10 c. blue, violet and green 10 10
647 – 40 c. purple, grn & dp grn 85 10
648 – 45 c. brown, green & blue 5·00 75
649 – 70 c. brown, red and green 75 20
650 – 80 c. red, green and blue 1·60 1·25
651 – 85 c. black, brown & grey 8·00 2·25
652 – 90 c. red, blue and black 1·00 40
653 – 1 f. multicoloured 1·25 25
654 – 1 f. 15 black, red and blue 2·25 1·75
655 – 1 f. 30 brown, green & bl 2·50 2·25
656 – 1 f. 40 orange, green & vio 8·25 2·75
DESIGNS—HORIZ: 5 c. Palace of Monaco; 10 c. (No. 646), Aquatic Stadium; 40, 45, 80 c., 1 f. 40, Aerial view of Palace; 70, 85, 90 c., 1 f. 15, 1 f. 30, Court of Honour, Monaco Palace; 1 f. Palace floodlit.

134a St. Devote

1960. Air.
668 **134a** 2 f. violet, blue and green 1·40 75
669 3 f. brown, green and blue 2·25 1·10
670 5 f. red 5·00 2·25
671 10 f. brown, grey and green 8·75 2·25

135 Sea Horse

136 Route Map from Lisbon

1960. Marine Life and Plants. (a) Marine Life.
672 – 1 c. red and turquoise .. 10 10
673 – 12 c. brown and blue .. 55 10
674 **135** 15 c. green and red .. 65 10
675 – 20 c. multicoloured .. 60 10
DESIGNS—HORIZ: 1 c. "Macrocheira kampferi" (crab); 20 c. "Pterois volitans". VERT: 12 c. Trapezium horse conch.

(b) Plants.
676 – 2 c. multicoloured .. 10 10
677 – 15 c. orange, brown & olive 65 10
678 – 18 c. multicoloured .. 55 10
679 – 20 c. red, olive and brown 55 10
PLANTS—VERT: 2 c. "Selenicereus sp."; 15 c. "Cereus sp."; 18 c. "Aloe ciliaris"; 20 c. "Nopalea dejecta".

1960. Prince Rainier Seal type with values in new currency. Precancelled.
680 **104** 8 c. purple .. 1·40 60
681 20 c. green .. 2·75 60
682 40 c. brown .. 4·50 1·25
683 55 c. blue .. 6·75 1·90

1960. 29th Monte Carlo Rally.
684 **136** 25 c. black, red and blue on blue .. 1·90 1·90

137 Stamps of Monaco 1885, France and Sardinia, 1860

1960. 75th Anniv of 1st Stamp.
685 **137** 25 c. bistre, blue and violet 70 70

138 Aquarium

1960. 50th Anniv of Oceanographic Museum, Monaco.
686 – 5 c. black, blue and purple 20 15
687 **138** 10 c. grey, brown and grn 35 35
688 – 15 c. black, bistre and blue 20 15
689 – 20 c. black, blue & mauve 85 50
690 – 25 c. turquoise .. 2·00 1·25
691 – 50 c. brown and blue .. 2·50 1·90
DESIGNS—VERT: 5 c. Oceanographic Museum (similar to Type **134**). HORIZ: 15 c. Conference Hall; 20 c. Hauling-in catch; 25 c. Museum, aquarium and under-water research equipment; 50 c. Prince Albert, "Hirondelle I" (schooner) and "Princess Alice" (steam yacht).

139 Horse-jumping

1960. Olympic Games.
692 **139** 5 c. brown, red and green 10 10
693 – 10 c. brown, blue & green 20 20
694 – 15 c. red, brown & purple 20 20
695 – 20 c. black, blue and green 3·00 3·00
696 – 25 c. purple, turq & grn 1·00 1·00
697 – 50 c. purple, blue & turq 1·25 1·25
DESIGNS: 10 c. Swimming; 15 c. Long jumping; 20 c. Throwing the javelin; 25 c. Free-skating; 50 c. Skiing.

MORE DETAILED LISTS
are given in the Stanley Gibbons Catalogues referred to in the country headings. For lists of current volumes see introduction

140 Rally Badge, Old and Modern Cars

1961. 50th Anniv of Monte Carlo Rally.
698 **140** 1 f. violet, red and brown 1·90 1·90

141 Route Map from Stockholm

142 Marine-life

1961. 30th Monte Carlo Rally.
699 **141** 1 f. multicoloured .. 1·10 1·10

1961. World Aquariological Congress. Orange network background.
700 **142** 25 c. red, sepia and violet 15 15

143 Leper in Town of Middle Ages

145 Insect within Protective Hand

144 Semi-submerged Sphinx of Ouadi-es-Saboua

1961. Sovereign Order of Malta.
701 **143** 25 c. black, red and brown 15 15

1961. U.N.E.S.C.O. Campaign for Preservation of Nubian Monuments.
702 **144** 50 purple, blue and brown 1·00 1·00

1962. Nature Preservation.
703 **145** 25 c. mauve and purple . 15 15

146 Chevrolet, 1912

1961. Veteran Motor Cars.
704 1 c. brown, green and chestnut 10 10
705 2 c. blue, purple and red .. 10 10
706 3 c. purple, black and mauve 10 10
707 4 c. blue, brown and violet 10 10
708 5 c. green, red and olive .. 10 10
709 10 c. brown, red and blue .. 10 10
710 15 c. green and turquoise .. 15 15
711 20 c. brown, red and violet 20 20
712 25 c. violet, red and brown 35 35
713 30 c. lilac and green .. 1·10 1·10
714 45 c. green, purple and brown 2·25 2·25
715 50 c. blue, red and brown .. 2·50 2·50
716 65 c. brown, red and grey .. 3·00 3·00
717 1 f. blue, red and violet .. 4·00 4·00
MOTOR CARS: 1 c. Type **146**: 2 c. Peugeot, 1898; 3 c. Fiat, 1901; 4 c. Mercedes, 1901; 5 c. Rolls Royce, 1903;. 10 c. Panhard-Lavassor, 1899; 15 c. Renault, 1898; 20 c. Ford "N", 1906 (wrongly inscr "FORD-S-1908"); 25 c. Rochet-Schneider, 1894; 30 c. FN-Herstal, 1901; 45 c. De Dion Bouton, 1900; 50 c. Buick, 1910; 65 c. Delahaye, 1901; 1 f. Cadillac, 1906.

147 Racing Car and Race Route

1962. 20th Monaco Motor Grand Prix.
718 **147** 1 f. purple .. 1·75 1·75

148 Route Map from Oslo

1962. 31st Monte Carlo Rally.
719 **148** 1 f. multicoloured .. 1·10 1·25

149 Louis XII and Lucien Grimaldi

1962. 450th Anniv of Recognition of Monegasque Sovereignty by Louis XII.
720 **149** 25 c. black, red and blue 20 20
721 – 50 c. brown, lake and blue 20 20
722 – 1 f. red, green and brown 55 55
DESIGNS: 50 c. Parchment bearing declaration of sovereignty; 1 f. Seals of two Sovereigns.

150 Mosquito and Swamp

1962. Malaria Eradication.
723 **150** 1 f. green and olive .. 50 60

151 Sun, Bouquet and "Hope Chest"

1962. National Multiple Sclerosis Society, New York.
724 **151** 20 c. multicoloured .. 15 10

152 Harvest Scene

1962. Europa.
725 **152** 25 c. brown, green and blue (postage) .. 15 15
726 50 c. olive and turquoise 25 25
727 1 f. olive and purple .. 55 55
728 – 2 f. slate, brown and green (air) .. 1·25 1·25
DESIGN: 2 f. Mercury in flight over Europe.

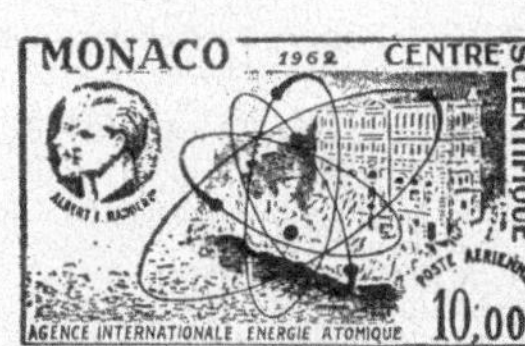

153 Atomic Symbol and Scientific Centre, Monaco

1962. Air. Scientific Centre, Monaco.
729 **153** 10 f. violet, brown & blue 5·50 5·50

154 Yellow Wagtails

155 Galeazzi's Diving Turret

1962. Protection of Birds useful to Agriculture.
730 **154** 5 c. yellow, brown & green 10 10
731 – 10 c. red, bistre and purple 10 10
732 – 15 c. multicoloured .. 15 10
733 – 20 c. sepia, green & mauve 50 10
734 – 25 c. multicoloured .. 60 50
735 – 30 c. brown, blue & myrtle 70 40
736 – 45 c. brown and violet .. 1·40 1·00
737 – 50 c. black, olive & turq 2·00 1·25
738 – 85 c. multicoloured .. 2·25 1·90
739 – 1 f. sepia, red and green 3·00 2·25
BIRDS: 10 c. European robins; 15 c. Goldfinches; 20 c. Blackcaps; 25 c. Greater spotted woodpeckers; 30 c. Nightingale; 45 c. Barn owls; 50 c. Common starlings; 85 c. Red crossbills; 1 f. White storks.

1962. Underwater Exploration.
740 – 5 c. black, violet and blue 10 10
741 **155** 10 c. blue, violet & brown 10 10
742 – 25 c. bistre, green and blue 10 10
743 – 45 c. black, blue and green 35 25
744 – 50 c. green, bistre and blue 75 75
745 – 85 c. blue and turquoise 1·25 1·25
746 – 1 f. brown, green and blue 1·90 1·90
DESIGNS—HORIZ: 5 c. Divers; 25 c. Williamson's photosphere (1914) and bathyscape "Trieste"; 45 c. Klingert's diving-suit (1797) and modern diving-suit; 50 c. Diving saucer; 85 c. Fulton's "Nautilus" (1800) and modern submarine; 1 f. Alexander the Great's diving bell and Beebe's bathysphere.

156 Donor's Arm and Globe

158 Feeding Chicks in Nest

157 "Ring-a-ring o' Roses"

1962. 3rd Int Blood Donors' Congress' Monaco.
747 **156** 1 f. red, sepia and orange 40 40

1963. U.N. Children's Charter.
748 **157** 5 c. red, blue and ochre . 10 10
749 **158** 10 c. green, sepia and blue 10 10
750 – 15 c. blue, red and green 10 10
751 – 20 c. multicoloured .. 10 10
752 – 25 c. blue, purple & brown 20 20
753 – 50 c. multicoloured .. 75 30
754 – 95 c. multicoloured .. 1·40 75
755 – 1 f. purple, red & turq .. 2·00 1·50
DESIGNS—As Type **157**: 1 f. Prince Albert and Princess Caroline; Children's paintings as Type **158**: HORIZ: 15 c. Children on scales; 50 c. House and child. VERT: 20 c. Sun's rays and children of three races; 25 c. Mother and child; 95 c. Negress and child.

159 Ship's Figurehead

160 Racing Cars

1963. International Red Cross Centenary.
756 **159** 50 c. red, brown & turquoise 50 50
757 – 1 f. multicoloured .. 80 80
DESIGN—HORIZ: 1 f. Moynier, Dunant and Dufour.

1963. European Motor Grand Prix.
758 **160** 50 c. multicoloured .. 75 35

161 Emblem and Charter

1963. Founding of Lions Club of Monaco.
759 **161** 50 c. blue, bistre and violet 40 40

162 Hotel des Postes and U.P.U. Monument, Berne

1963. Paris Postal Conference Centenary.
760 **162** 50 c. lake, green & yellow 60 60

163 "Telstar" Satellite and Globe

1963. 1st Link Trans-Atlantic T.V. Satellite.
761 **163** 50 c. brown, green & pur . 40 40

164 Route Map from Warsaw

1963. 32nd Monte Carlo Rally.
762 **164** 1 f. multicoloured . . . . 1·40 1·40

165 Feeding Chicks

1963. Freedom from Hunger.
763 **165** 1 f. multicoloured 75 75

166 Allegory

1963. 2nd Ecumenical Council, Vatican City.
764 **166** 1 f. turquoise, green and red 40 40

167 Henry Ford and Ford "A" Car of 1903

1963. Birth Centenary of Henry Ford (motor pioneer).
765 **167** 20 c. green and purple . . 20 20

168 H. Garin (winner of 1903 race) cycling through Village

1963. 50th "Tour de France" Cycle Race.
766 **168** 25 c. green, brown & blue 20 20
767 – 50 c. sepia, green & blue 25 25
DESIGN: 50 c. Cyclist passing Desgrange Monument, Col du Galibier, 1963.

169 P. de Coubertin and Discus-thrower

1963. Birth Centenary of Pierre de Coubertin (reviver of Olympic Games).
768 **169** 1 f. brown, red and lake . 75 75

170 Roland Garros and Morane Saulnier Type I

1963. Air. 50th Anniv of 1st Aerial Crossing of Mediterranean Sea.
769 **170** 2 f. sepia and blue . . . 1·10 1·25

171 Route Map from Paris

173 "Europa"

172 Children with Stamp Album

1963. 33rd Monte Carlo Rally.
770 **171** 1 f. red, turquoise and blue 1·25 1·25

1963. "Scolatex" International Stamp Exn, Monaco.
771 **172** 50 c. blue, violet and red 20 20

1963. Europa.
772 **173** 25 c. brown, red and green 20 20
773 50 c. sepia, red and& blue 60 30

174 Wembley Stadium

1963. Cent of (English) Football Association.
774 **174** 1 c. violet, green and red 10 10
775 – 2 c. red, black and green 10 10
776 – 3 c. orange, olive and red 10 10
777 – 4 c. multicoloured 10 10
Multicoloured horiz designs depicting (a) "Football through the Centuries".
778 10 c. "Calcio", Florence (16th cent) 10 10
779 15 c. "Soule", Brittany (19th cent) 10 10
780 20 c. English military college (after Cruickshank, 1827) 10 10
781 25 c. English game (after Overend, 1890) 10 10
(b) "Modern Football".
782 30 c. Tackling 50 50
783 50 c. Saving goal 55 55
784 95 c. Heading ball . . . . . . 1·10 1·10
785 1 f. Corner kick . . . . 1·40 1·40
DESIGNS—As Type **174**: 4 c. Louis II Stadium, Monaco. This stamp is optd in commemoration of the Association Sportive de Monaco football teams in the French Championships and in the Coupe de France, 1962–63. HORIZ: (36×22 mm): 2 c. Footballer making return kick; 3 c. Goalkeeper saving ball.
Nos. 778/81 and 782/5 were respectively issued together in sheets and arranged in blocks of 4 with a football in the centre of each block.

175 Communications in Ancient Egypt, and Rocket

1964. "PHILATEC 1964" Int Stamp Exn, Paris.
786 **175** 1 f. brown, indigo & blue . 75 75

176 Reproduction of Rally Postcard Design

1964. 50th Anniv of 1st Aerial Rally, Monte Carlo.
787 1 c. olive, blue & grn (postage) 10 10
788 2 c. bistre, brown and blue . . 10 10
789 3 c. brown, blue and green . . 10 10
790 4 c. red, turquoise and blue . . 10 10
791 5 c. brown, red and violet . . 10 10
792 10 c. violet, brown and blue . 10 10
793 15 c. orange, brown and blue . 10 10
794 20 c. sepia, green and blue . 20 10
795 25 c. brown, blue and red . . 30 35
796 30 c. myrtle, purple and blue . 40 50
797 45 c. sepia, turquoise & brn . . 85 60
798 50 c. ochre, olive and violet . 1·00 85
799 65 c. red, slate and turquoise 1·40 1·10
800 95 c. turquoise, red and bistre 1·90 1·50
801 1 f. brown, blue and turquoise 2·50 1·90
802 5 f. sepia, blue & brown (air) 3·75 3·75
DESIGNS: 1 c. Type **176**. 48×27 mm—Rally planes: 2 c. Renaux's Farman M.F.7 floatplane; 3 c. Espanet's Nieuport 4 seaplane; 4 c. Moineau's Breguet HU-3 seaplane; 5 c. Roland Garros' Morane Saulnier Type I seaplane; 10 c. Hirth's WDD Albatros seaplane; 15 c. Prevost's Deperdussin Monocoque Racer. Famous planes and flights: 20 c. Vickers–Vimy (Ross Smith: London–Port Darwin, 1919); 25 c. Douglas World Cruiser seaplane (U.S. World Flight, 1924); 30 c. Savoia Marchetti S-55M flying boat "Santa Maria" (De Pinedo's World Flight, 1925); 45 c. Fokker F. VIIa/3m "Josephine Ford" (Flight over North Pole, Byrd and Bennett, 1925); 50 c. Ryan NYP Special "Spirit of St. Louis" (1st solo crossing of N. Atlantic, Lindbergh, 1927); 65 c. Breguet 19 "Point d'Interrogation" (Paris–New York, Coste and Bellonte, 1930); 95 c. Latecoere 28-3 seaplane "Comte de la Vaulx" (Dakar–Natal, first S. Atlantic airmail flight, Mermoz, 1930); 1 f. Dornier Do-X flying boat (Germany–Rio de Janeiro, Christiansen, 1930); 5 f. Convair B-58 Hustler (New York–Paris in 3 hours, 19"41" Major Payne, U.S.A.F., 1961).

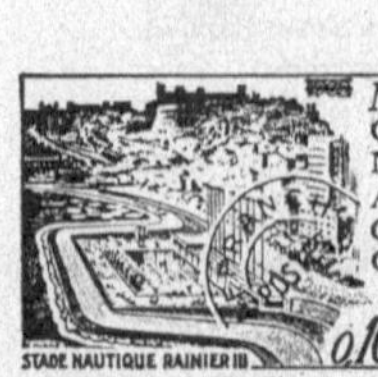
177 Aquatic Stadium 178 Europa "Flower"

1964. Precancelled.
803 **177** 10 c. multicoloured . . . 2·00 20
803a 15 c. multicoloured . . . 75 20
804 25 c. turquoise, blue & blk 75 20
805 50 c. violet, turq & blk . 2·00 1·10
The "1962" date has been obliterated with two bars.
See also Nos. 949/51a and 1227/1230.

1964. Europa.
806 **178** 25 c. red, green and blue . 20 20
807 50 c. brown, bistre and bl 40 40

179 Weightlifting

1964. Olympic Games, Tokyo and Innsbruck.
808 **179** 1 c. red, brown and blue (postage) 10 10
809 – 2 c. red, green and olive . 10 10
810 – 3 c. blue, brown and red . 10 10
811 – 4 c. green, olive and red . 10 10
812 – 5 f. red, brown and blue (air) 3·00 3·00
DESIGNS: 2 c. Judo; 3 c. Pole vaulting; 4 c. Archery; 5 f. Bobsleighing.

180 Pres. Kennedy and Space Capsule

1964. Pres. Kennedy Commemoration.
813 **180** 50 c. indigo and blue . . 75 75

181 Monaco and Television Set

1964. 5th Int Television Festival, Monte Carlo.
814 **181** 50 c. brown, blue and red 30 30

182 F. Mistral and Statue

1964. 50th Death Anniv of Frederic Mistral (poet).
815 **182** 1 f. brown and olive . . . 60 60

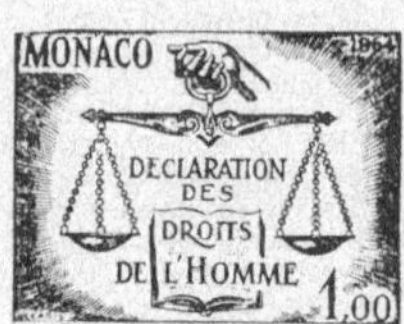
183 Scales of Justice

1964. 15th Anniv of Declaration of Human Rights.
816 **183** 1 f. green and brown . . 40 40

184 Route Map from Minsk

1964. 34th Monte Carlo Rally.
817 **184** 1 f. brown, turq & ochre 85 85

185 FIFA Emblem

1964. 60th Anniv of Federation Internationale de Football Association (FIFA).
818 **185** 1 f. bistre, blue and red . 60 60

186 "Syncom 2" and Globe

1965. Cent of I.T.U.
819 **186** 5 c. green & ultra (postage) 10 10
820 – 10 c. chestnut, brown & bl 10 10
821 – 12 c. purple, red and grey 10 10
822 – 18 c. blue, red and purple 10 10
823 – 25 c. violet, bistre & purple 10 10
824 – 30 c. bistre, brown & sepia 20 20
825 – 50 c. blue and green . . . 25 25
826 – 60 c. blue and brown . . 75 75
827 – 70 c. sepia, orange & blue 1·00 1·00
828 – 95 c. black, indigo & blue 1·10 1·10
829 – 1 f. brown and blue . . . 1·60 1·60
830 – 10 f. green, blue and brown (air) . . . . 5·00 5·00
DESIGNS—As Type **186**: HORIZ: 10 c. "Echo 2"; 18 c. "Lunik 3"; 30 c. A. G. Bell and telephone; 50 c. S. Morse and telegraph; 60 c. E. Belin and "belinograph". VERT: 12 c. "Relay"; 10 f. Monte Carlo television transmitter. LARGER (48½ × 27 mm): 25 c. "Telstar" and Pleumeur-Bodou Station; 70 c. Roman beacon and Chappe's telegraph; 95 c. Cable-laying ships "Great Eastern" and "Alsace"; 1 f. E. Branly, G. Marconi and English Channel.

187 Europa "Sprig"

1965. Europa.
831 **187** 30 c. brown and green . . 50 15
832 60 c. violet and red . . . 75 30

188 Monaco Palace (18th cent)

1966. 750th Anniv of Monaco Palace.
833 **188** 10 c. violet, green and blue 10 10
834 – 12 c. bistre, blue and black 10 10
835 – 18 c. green, black & blue 15 15
836 – 30 c. brown, black & blue 20 20
837 – 60 c. green, blue & bistre 75 75
838 – 1 f. 30 brown and green 1·40 1·40
DESIGNS: (Different views of Palace): 12 c. 17th century; 18 c. 18th century; 30 c. 19th century; 60 c. 19th century; 1 f. 30, 20th century.

189 Dante

1966. 700th Anniv of Dante's Birth.
839 **189** 30 c. green, deep green and red 20 20
840 – 60 c. blue, turquoise & grn 75 75
841 – 70 c. black, green and red 55 55
842 – 95 c. blue, violet & purple 80 80
843 – 1 f. turquoise, blue & dp bl 80 80
DESIGNS: (Scenes from Dante's works): 60 c. Dante harassed by the panther (envy); 70 c. Crossing the 5th circle; 95 c. Punishment of the arrogant; 1 f. Invocation of St. Bernard.

190 "The Nativity"

1966. World Association of Children's Friends (A.M.A.D.E.).
844 **190** 30 c. brown 20 20

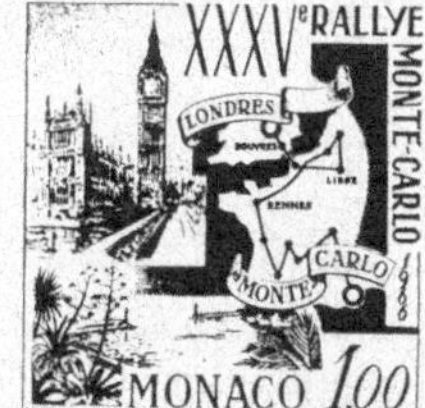

191 Route Map from London

1966. 35th Monte Carlo Rally.
845 **191** 1 f. blue, purple and red . 1·00 1·00

192 Princess Grace with Children

1966. Air. Princess Stephanie's 1st Birthday.
846 **192** 3 f. brown, blue and violet 3·00 2·50

193 Casino in 19th Century **194** Europa "Ship"

1966. Centenary of Monte Carlo.
847 – 12 c. black, red and blue (postage) 10 10
848 **193** 25 c. multicoloured . . . 10 10
849 – 30 c. multicoloured . . . 10 10
850 – 40 c. multicoloured . . . 20 20
851 – 60 c. multicoloured . . . 30 30
852 – 70 c. blue and lake . . . 30 30
853 – 95 c. black and purple . . 65 65
854 – 1 f. 30 purple, brown and chestnut . . . . 1·25 1·25
855 – 5 f. lake, ochre and blue (air) 2·25 2·25
DESIGNS—VERT: 12 c. Prince Charles III. HORIZ: 40 c. Charles III Monument; 95 c. Massenet and Saint-Saens; 1 f. 30, Faure and Ravel. LARGER (48 × 27 mm): 30 c. F. Blanc, originator of Monte Carlo, and view of 1860; 60 c. Prince Rainier III and projected esplanade; 70 c. Rene Blum and Diaghilev, ballet character from "Petrouchka". (36 × 36 mm): 5 f. Interior of Opera House, 1879.

1966. Europa.
856 **194** 30 c. orange 15 15
857 60 c. green 50 50

195 Prince Rainier and Princess Grace **197** "Learning to Write"

196 Prince Albert I and Yachts "Hirondelle I" and "Princess Alice"

1966. Air.
858 **195** 2 f. slate and red . . . 1·25 40
859 3 f. slate and green . . . 2·50 1·00
860 5 f. slate and blue . . . 3·00 1·40
861 10 f. slate and bistre . . 6·25 4·00
862 20 f. brown and orange . 55·00 42·00

1966. 1st International Oceanographic History Congress, Monaco.
861 **196** 1 f. lilac and blue . . . . 1·40 1·00

1966. 20th Anniv of U.N.E.S.C.O.
862 **197** 30 c. purple and mauve . . 10 10
863 60 c. brown and blue . . . 25 25

198 T.V. Screen, Cross and Monaco Harbour **200** W.H.O. Building

199 "Precontinent III"

1966. 10th Meeting of International Catholic Television Association (U.N.D.A.), Monaco.
864 **198** 60 c. red, purple & crimson 20 15

1966. 1st Anniv of Underwater Research Craft "Precontinent III".
865 **199** 1 f. yellow, brown & blue . 35 30

1966. Inaug of W.H.O. Headquarters, Geneva.
866 **200** 30 c. brown, grn and blue 10 10
867 60 c. brown, red and green 20 20

201 Bugatti, 1931 **202** Dog (Egyptian bronze)

1967. 25th Motor Grand Prix, Monaco. Multicoloured. (a) Postage.
868 1 c. Type **201** 10 10
869 2 c. Alfa-Romeo, 1932 . . . . 10 10
870 5 c. Mercedes, 1936 . . . . . 10 10
871 10 c. Maserati, 1948 . . . . . 10 10
872 18 c. Ferrari, 1955 . . . . . 50 10
873 20 c. Alfa-Romeo, 1950 . . . 10 10
874 25 c. Maserati, 1957 . . . . 15 15
875 30 c. Cooper-Climax, 1958 . . 50 15
876 40 c. Lotus-Climax, 1960 . . 60 50
877 50 c. Lotus-Climax, 1961 . . . 85 50
878 60 c. Cooper-Climax, 1962 . . 1·10 60
879 70 c. B.R.M., 1963-6 . . . . 1·50 1·10
880 1 f. Walter Christie, 1907 . . 1·75 1·25
881 2 f. 30 Peugeot, 1910 . . . . 3·00 2·50
(b) Air. Diamond. 50 × 50 mm.
882 3 f. black and blue . . . . . . 2·50 2·50
DESIGN: 3 f. Panhard-Phenix, 1895.

1967. Int Cynological Federation Congress, Monaco.
883 **202** 30 c. black, purple & green 25 25

203 View of Monte Carlo

1967. International Tourist Year.
884 **203** 30 c. brown, green & blue 15 10

204 Pieces on Chessboard

1967. Int Chess Grand Prix, Monaco.
885 **204** 60 c. black, plum and blue 65 50

205 Melvin Jones (founder), Lions Emblem and Monte Carlo

1967. 50th Anniv of Lions International.
886 **205** 60 c. blue, ultramarine and brown 30 20

206 Rotary Emblem and Monte Carlo

1967. Rotary International Convention.
887 **206** 1 f. bistre, blue and green 75 30

207 Fair Buildings

1967. World Fair, Montreal.
888 **207** 1 f. red, slate and blue . . 30 30

208 Squiggle on Map of Europe **209** Cogwheels

1967. European Migration Committee (C.I.M.E.).
889 **208** 1 f. brown, bistre and blue 30 25

1967. Europa.
890 **209** 30 c. violet, purple and red 20 20
891 60 c. green, turq & emerald 30 30

210 Dredger and Coastal Chart

1967. 9th Int Hydrographic Congress, Monaco.
892 **210** 1 f. brown, blue and green 60 30

211 Marie Curie and Scientific Equipment

1967. Birth Centenary of Marie Curie.
893 **211** 1 f. blue, olive & brown . 1·00 60

212 Skiing

1967. Winter Olympic Games, Grenoble.
894 **212** 2 f. 30 brown, blue & slate 1·40 1·25

213 "Prince Rainier I" (E. Charpentier)

1967. Paintings. "Princes and Princesses of Monaco". Multicoloured.

895		1 f. Type **213**	85	85
896		1 f. "Lucien Grimaldi" (A. di Predis)	85	85

See also Nos. 932/3, 958/9, 1005/6, 1023/4, 1070/1, 1108/9, 1213/14, 1271/2, 1325, 1380/1, 1405/6, 1460/1 and 1531/2.

214 Putting the Shot

1968. Olympic Games, Mexico.

897	**214**	20 c. blue, brown and green (postage)	10	10
898	–	30 c. brown, blue & plum	10	10
899	–	60 c. blue, purple and red	20	20
900	–	70 c. red, blue and ochre	25	25
901	–	1 f. blue, brown and orange	50	50
902	–	2 f. 30 olive, blue and lake	1·10	1·10
903	–	3 f. blue, violet & grn (air)	1·90	1·90

DESIGNS: 30 c. High-jumping; 60 c. Gymnastics; 70 c. Water-polo; 1 f. Greco-Roman wrestling; 2 f. 30, Gymnastics (different); 3 f. Hockey.

215 "St. Martin"

1968. 20th Anniv of Monaco Red Cross.

904	**215**	2 f. 30 blue and brown	1·40	1·25

216 "Anemones" (after Raoul Dufy)

217 Insignia of Prince Charles III and Pope Pius IX

1968. Monte Carlo Floral Exhibitions.

905	**216**	1 f. multicoloured	55	55

1968. Centenary of "Nullius Diocesis" Abbey.

906	**217**	10 c. brown and red	10	10
907	–	20 c. red, green and brown	10	10
908	–	30 c. brown and blue	20	20
909	–	60 c. brown, blue & green	25	25
910	–	1 f. indigo, bistre and blue	40	40

DESIGNS—VERT: 20 c. "St. Nicholas" (after Louis Brea); 30 c. "St. Benedict" (after Simone Martini); 60 c. Subiaco Abbey. HORIZ: 1 f. Old St. Nicholas' Church (on site of present cathedral).

218 Europa "Key"

1968. Europa.

911	**218**	30 c. red and orange	20	20
912		60 c. blue and red	75	30
913		1 f. brown and green	1·75	1·10

219 Type 0-3-0 Steam Locomotive (1868)

1968. Centenary of Nice–Monaco Railway.

914	**219**	20 c. black, blue & purple	30	25
915	–	30 c. black, blue and olive	75	60
916	–	60 c. black, blue and ochre	90	1·10
917	–	70 c. black, violet & brown	2·00	1·60
918	–	1 f. black, blue and red	3·00	2·75
919	–	2 f. 30 blue, black and red	5·00	4·00

DESIGNS: 30 c. Type "C-220" steam locomotive (1898); 60 c. Type "230-C" steam locomotive (1910); 70 c. Type "231-F" steam locomotive (1925); 1 f. Type "241-A" steam locomotive (1952); 2 f. 30, Type "BB" electric locomotive (1968).

220 Chateaubriand and Combourg Castle

1968. Birth Centenary of Chateaubriand (novelist).

920	**220**	10 c. plum, green & myrtle	10	10
921	–	20 c. violet, purple & blue	10	10
922	–	25 c. brown, violet & blue	10	10
923	–	30 c. violet, choc & brn	15	15
924	–	60 c. brown, grn & red	25	25
925	–	2 f. 30 brown, mve & blue	1·25	1·25

Scenes from Chateaubriand's novels: 20 c. "Le Genie du Christianisme"; 25 c. "Rene"; 30 c. "Le Dernier Abencerage"; 60 c. "Les Martyrs"; 2 f. 30, "Atala".

221 Law Courts, Paris, and statues–"La France et la Fidelite"

1968. Birth Centenary of J. F. Bosio (Monegasque sculptor).

926	**221**	20 c. brown and purple	10	10
927	–	25 c. brown and red	10	10
928	–	30 c. blue and green	10	10
929	–	60 c. green and myrtle	60	20
930	–	2 f. 30 black and slate	1·10	1·00

DESIGNS—VERT: (26×36 mm): 25 c. "Henry IV as a Child"; 30 c. "J. F. Bosio" (lithograph); 60 c. "Louis XIV". HORIZ: As Type **221**: 2 f. 30, "Napoleon I, Louis XVIII and Charles X".

222 W.H.O. Emblem

1968. 20th Anniv of W.H.O.

931	**222**	60 c. multicoloured	25	20

1968. Paintings. "Princes and Princesses of Monaco". As T **213**. Multicoloured.

932		1 f. "Prince Charles II" (Mimault)	30	30
933		2 f. 30 "Princess Jeanne Grimaldi" (Mimault)	1·25	1·25

223 The Hungarian March

1969. Death Centenary of Hector Berlioz (composer).

934	**223**	10 c. brown, violet and green (postage)	10	10
935	–	20 c. brown, olive & mauve	10	10
936	–	25 c. brown, blue & mauve	10	10
937	–	30 c. black, green & black	10	10
938	–	40 c. red, black and slate	10	10
939	–	50 c. brown, slate & purple	15	15
940	–	70 c. brown, slate & green	25	20
941	–	1 f. black, mauve & brown	35	50
942	–	1 f. 15 black, blue & turq	75	75
943	–	2 f. black, blue & grn (air)	1·40	1·25

DESIGNS—HORIZ: 20 c. Mephistopheles appears to Faust; 25 c. Auerbach's tavern; 30 c. Sylphs' ballet; 40 c. Minuet of the goblins; 50 c. Marguerite's bedroom; 70 c. "Forests and caverns"; 1 f. The journey to Hell; 1 f. 15, Heaven; All scenes from Berlioz's "The Damnation of Faust". VERT: 2 f. Bust of Berlioz.

224 "St. Elisabeth of Hungary"

1969. Monaco Red Cross.

944	**224**	3 f. blue, brown and red	1·90	1·50

225 "Napoleon I" (P. Delaroche)

1969. Birth Bicentenary of Napoleon Bonaparte.

945	**225**	3 f. multicoloured	1·90	1·60

226 Colonnade

227 "Head of Woman" (Da Vinci)

1969. Europa.

946	**226**	40 c. red and purple	30	10
947		70 c. blue, brown & black	1·40	1·00
948		1 f. ochre, brown and blue	1·90	1·25

1969. Precancelled. As T **177**. No date.

949		22 c. brown, blue and black	35	10
949a		26 c. violet, blue and black	40	15
949b		30 c. multicoloured	65	15
950		35 c. multicoloured	45	10
950a		45 c. multicoloured	1·00	35
951		70 c. black and blue	1·00	35
951a		90 c. green, blue and black	1·60	60

1969. 450th Death Anniv of Leonardo da Vinci.

952	**227**	30 c. brown	10	10
953	–	40 c. red and brown	15	10
954	–	70 c. green	25	20
955	–	80 c. sepia	35	25
956	–	1 f. 15 brown	85	45
957	–	3 f. brown	2·00	1·40

DRAWINGS: 40 c. Self-portrait; 70 c. "Head of an Old Man"; 80 c. "Head of St. Madeleine"; 1 f. 15, "Man's Head"; 3 f. "The Condottiere".

1969. Paintings. "Princes and Princesses of Monaco". As T **213**. Multicoloured.

958		1 f. "Prince Honore II" (Champaigne)	35	35
959		3 f. "Princess Louise-Hippolyte" (Champaigne)	1·50	1·50

228 Marine Fauna, King Alfonso XIII of Spain and Prince Albert I of Monaco

229 I.L.O. Emblem

1969. 50th Anniv of Int Commission for Scientific Exploration of the Mediterranean, Madrid.

960	**228**	40 c. blue and black	50	50

1969. 50th Anniv of I.L.O.

961	**229**	40 c. multicoloured	20	20

230 Aerial View of Monaco and T.V. Camera

1969. 10th International Television Festival.

962	**230**	40 c. purple, lake and blue	15	15

231 J.C.C. Emblem

1969. 25th Anniv of Junior Chamber of Commerce.

963	**231**	40 c. violet, bistre and blue	15	15

232 Alphonse Daudet and Scenes from "Lettres"

1969. Centenary of Daudet's "Lettres de Mon Moulin".

964	**232**	30 c. lake, violet and green	10	10
965	–	40 c. green, brown & blue	20	20
966	–	70 c. multicoloured	30	25
967	–	80 c. violet, brown & grn	60	30
968	–	1 f. 15 brown, orange & bl	75	75

DESIGNS: (Scenes from the book): 40 c. "Installation" (Daudet writing); 70 c. "Mule, Goat and Wolf"; 80 c. "Gaucher's Elixir" and "The Three Low Masses"; 1 f. 15, Daudet drinking, "The Old Man" and "The Country Sub-Prefect".

233 Conference Building, Albert I and Rainier III

1970. Interparliamentary Union's Spring Meeting, Monaco.

969	**233**	40 c. black, red and purple	15	10

234 Baby Common Seal

1970. Protection of Baby Seals.

970	**234**	40 c. drab, blue and purple	1·00	60

235 Japanese Print 236 Dobermann

1970. Expo 70.
971 **235** 20 c. brown, green and red 10 10
972 – 30 c. brown, buff & green 25 20
973 – 40 c. bistre and violet 15 15
974 – 70 c. grey and red 75 75
975 – 1 f. 15 red, green & purple 85 85
DESIGNS—VERT: 30 c. Manchurian Cranes (birds); 40 c. Shinto temple gateway. HORIZ: 70 c. Cherry blossom; 1 f. 15, Monaco Palace and Osaka Castle.

1970. International Dog Show, Monte Carlo.
976 **236** 40 c. black and brown 1·10 85

237 Apollo

1970. 20th Anniv of World Federation for Protection of Animals.
977 **237** 30 c. black, red and blue 40 20
978 – 40 c. brown, blue & green 40 20
979 – 50 c. brown, ochre & blue 85 40
980 – 80 c. brown, blue & green 10·00 1·00
981 – 1 f. brown, bistre and slate 2·50 2·25
982 – 1 f. 15 brown, green & blue 3·00 2·50
DESIGNS—HORIZ: 40 c. Basque ponies; 50 c. Common seal. VERT: 80 c. Chamois; 1 f. White-tailed sea eagles; 1 f. 15, European otter.

238 "St. Louis" (King of France)

1970. Monaco Red Cross.
983 **238** 3 f. green, brown and slate 1·90 1·90
See also Nos. 1022, 1041, 1114, 1189 and 1270.

239 "Roses and Anemones" (Van Gogh)

1970. Monte Carlo Flower Show.
984 **239** 3 f. multicoloured 2·75 2·50
See also Nos. 1042 and 1073.

240 Moon Plaque, Presidents Kennedy and Nixon

1970. 1st Man on the Moon (1969). Multicoloured.
985 40 c. Type **240** 60 35
986 80 c. Astronauts on Moon 1·10 75

241 New U.P.U. Building and Monument 242 "Flaming Sun"

1970. New U.P.U. Headquarters Building.
987 **241** 40 c. brown, black & green 15 10

1970. Europa.
988 **242** 40 c. purple 50 10
989 80 c. green 1·10 1·00
990 1 f. blue 1·90 1·50

243 Camargue Horse

1970. Horses.
991 **243** 10 c. slate, olive and blue (postage) 10 10
992 – 20 c. brown, olive and blue 20 10
993 – 30 c. brown, green & blue 50 15
994 – 40 c. grey, brown & slate 85 60
995 – 50 c. brown, olive & blue 1·25 85
996 – 70 c. brown, orange & grn 2·00 1·50
997 – 85 c. blue, green and olive 2·25 1·90
998 – 1 f. 15 black, green & blue 2·75 2·50

999 – 3 f. multicoloured (air) 2·25 2·25
HORSES—HORIZ: 20 c. Anglo-Arab; 30 c. French saddle-horse; 40 c. Lippizaner; 50 c. Trotter; 70 c. English thoroughbred; 85 c. Arab; 1 f. 15, Barbary. DIAMOND (50×50 mm): 3 f. Rock-drawings of horses in Lascaux grotto.

244 Dumas, D'Artagnan and the Three Musketeers

1970. Birth Centenary of Alexandre Dumas (pere) (author).
1000 **244** 30 c. slate, brown & blue 10 10

245 Henri Rougier and Voisin "Boxkite"

1970. 60th Anniv of First Mediterranean Flight.
1001 **245** 40 c. brown, blue & slate 20 10

246 De Lamartine and scene from "Meditations Poetiques"

1970. 150th Birth Anniv of A. de Lamartine (writer).
1002 **246** 80 c. brown, blue & turq 30 15

247 Beethoven

1970. Birth Bicentenary of Beethoven.
1003 **247** 1 f. 30 brown and red 2·10 1·25

1970. 50th Death Anniv of Modigliani. Vert Painting as T **213**. Multicoloured.
1004 3 f. "Portrait of Dedie" 3·00 2·25

1970. Paintings. "Princes and Princesses of Monaco". As T **213**.
1005 1 f. red and black 30 30
1006 3 f. multicoloured 1·50 1·40
PORTRAITS: 1 f. "Prince Louis I" (F. de Troy); 3 f. "Princess Charlotte de Gramont" (S. Bourdon).

248 Cocker Spaniel 249 Razorbill

1971. International Dog Show, Monte Carlo.
1007 **248** 50 c. multicoloured 2·50 1·90
See also Nos. 1036, 1082, 1119, 1218 and 1239.

1971. Campaign Against Pollution of the Sea.
1008 **249** 50 c. indigo and blue 65 35

250 Hand holding Emblem

1971. 7th Int Blood-Donors Federation Congress.
1009 **250** 80 c. red, violet and grey 75 30

251 Sextant, Scroll and Underwater Scene

1971. 50th Anniv of Int Hydrographic Bureau.
1010 **251** 80 c. brown, grn & slate 40 30

252 Detail of Michelangelo Painting ("The Arts")

1971. 25th Anniv of U.N.E.S.C.O.
1011 **252** 30 c. brown, blue & vio 10 10
1012 – 50 c. blue and brown 20 10
1013 – 80 c. brown and green 30 35
1014 – 1 f. 30 green 75 40
DESIGNS—VERT: 50 c. Alchemist and dish aerial ("Sciences"); 1 f. 30, Prince Pierre of Monaco (National U.N.E.S.C.O. Commission). HORIZ: 80 c. Ancient scribe, book and T.V. screen ("Culture").

253 Europa Chain

1971. Europa.
1015 **253** 50 c. red 85 50
1016 80 c. blue 1·50 1·10
1017 1 f. 30 green 2·75 2·10

254 Old Bridge, Sospel

1971. Protection of Historic Monuments.
1018 **254** 50 c. brown, blue & green 15 10
1019 – 80 c. brown, green & grey 50 15
1020 – 1 f. 30 red, green & brn 55 40
1021 – 3 f. slate, blue and olive 1·75 1·25
DESIGNS—HORIZ: 80 c. Roquebrune Chateau; 1 f. 30, Grimaldi Chateau, Cagnes-sur-Mer. VERT: 3 f. Roman "Trophy of the Alps", La Turbie.

1971. Monaco Red Cross. As T **238**.
1022 3 f. brown, olive and green 1·90 1·60
DESIGN: 3 f. St. Vincent de Paul.

1972. Paintings. "Princes and Princesses of Monaco". As T **213**. Multicoloured.
1023 1 f. "Prince Antoine I" (Rigaud) 40 50
1024 3 f. "Princess Marie de Lorraine" (18th-century French School) 1·75 1·60

255 La Fontaine and Animal Fables (350th)

1972. Birth Anniversaries (1971).
1025 **255** 50 c. brown, emer & grn 30 20
1026 – 1 f. 30 purple, blk & red 1·10 85
DESIGNS: 1 f. 30, Baudelaire, nudes and cats (150th).

256 Saint-Saens and scene from Opera, "Samson and Delilah"

1972. 50th Death Anniv (1971) of Camile Saint-Saens.
1027 **256** 90 c. brown and sepia 40 50

257 Battle Scene

1972. 400th Anniv (1971) of Battle of Lepanto.
1028 **257** 1 f. blue, brown and red 60 40

258 "Christ before Pilate" (engraving by Durer)

1972. 500th Birth Anniv (1971) of Albrecht Durer.
1029 **258** 2 f. black and brown 1·60 1·25

259 "The Cradle" (B. Morisot)

1972. 25th Anniv (1971) of U.N.I.C.E.F.
1030 **259** 2 f. multicoloured 1·60 1·10

INDEX

Countries can be quickly located by referring to the index at the end of this volume.

260 "Gilles" (Watteau)

1972. 250th Death Anniv (1971) of Watteau.
1031 **260** 3 f. multicoloured . . . . 2·50 1·90

261 Santa Claus

1972. Christmas (1971).
1032 **261** 30 c. red, blue and brown 10 10
1033 50 c. red, green & orange 25 10
1034 90 c. red, blue and brown 40 20

262 Steam Locomotive and Modern Turbo Express

1972. 50th Anniv of International Railway Union.
1035 **262** 50 c. purple, lilac and red 1·00 75

1972. Int Dog Show, Monte Carlo. As T **248**.
1036 60 c. multicoloured . . . . . 2·50 1·90
DESIGN: 60 c. Great Dane.

263 "Pollution Kills"

1972. Anti-Pollution Campaign.
1037 **263** 90 c. brown, green & blk 50 30

264 Ski-jumping

1972. Winter Olympic Games, Sapporo, Japan.
1038 **264** 90 c. black, red and green 40 30

265 "Communications" **266** "SS. Giovanni e Paolo" (detail, Canaletto)

1972. Europa.
1039 **265** 50 c. blue and orange . 1·10 75
1040 90 c. blue and green . . 2·00 1·75

1972. Monaco Red Cross. As T **238**.
1041 3 f. brown and purple . . . 2·00 1·60
DESIGN: 3 f. St. Francis of Assisi.

1972. Monte Carlo Flower Show. As T **239**.
1042 3 f. multicoloured . . . . . 3·50 3·00
DESIGN: 3 f. "Vase of Flowers" (Cezanne).

1972. U.N.E.S.C.O. "Save Venice" Campaign.
1043 **266** 30 c. red 25 20
1044 – 60 c. violet 35 20
1045 – 2 f. blue . . . . 2·00 1·60
DESIGNS—27×48 mm: 60 c. "S. Pietro di Castello" (F. Guradi). As Type **266**: 2 f. "Piazzetta S. Marco" (B. Bellotto).

267 Dressage

1972. Olympic Games, Munich. Equestrian Events.
1046 **267** 60 c. brown, blue & lake 40 40
1047 – 90 c. lake, brown & blue 1·25 1·25
1048 – 1 f. 10 blue, lake & brown 1·90 1·90
1049 – 1 f. 40 brown, lake & blue 3·00 3·00
DESIGNS: 90 c. Cross country; 1 f. 10, Show jumping (wall); 1 f. 40, Show jumping (parallel bars).

268 Escoffier and Birthplace

1972. 125th Birth Anniv of Auguste Escoffier (master chef).
1050 **268** 45 c. black and brown . 25 15

269 Drug Addiction **270** Globe, Birds and Animals

1972. Campaign Against Drugs.
1051 **269** 50 c. red, brown & orange 50 20
1052 90 c. green, brown & blue 60 30
See also Nos. 1088/91 and 1280/1.

1972. 17th Int Congress of Zoology, Monaco.
1053 **270** 30 c. green, brown & red 15 10
1054 – 50 c. brown, purple and red 30 10
1055 – 90 c. blue, brown & red 40 20
DESIGNS—HORIZ: 50 c. VERT: 90 c. Similar symbolic design.

271 Bouquet **272** "The Nativity" and Child's face

1972. Monte Carlo Flower Show, 1973 (1st issue). Multicoloured.
1056 30 c. Lilies in vase 60 35
1057 50 c. Type **271** . . . . . 1·00 60
1058 90 c. Flowers in Vase . . . . 1·90 1·25
See also Nos. 1073, 1105/7, 1143/4, 1225/6, 1244, 1282/3 and 1316/17.

1972. Christmas.
1059 **272** 30 c. grey, blue & purple 10 10
1060 50 c. red, purple & brown 20 10
1061 90 c. violet, plum & pur 40 20

273 Louis Bleriot and Bleriot XI

1972. Birth Anniversaries.
1062 **273** 30 c. blue and brown . . 15 10
1063 – 50 c. blue, turquoise and new blue . . . . . . 1·10 75
1064 – 90 c. brown and buff . . 2·50 1·90
DESIGNS AND ANNIVERSARIES: 30 c. (birth centenary); 50 c. Amundsen and polar scene (birth centenary); 90 c. Pasteur and laboratory scene (150th birth anniv).

274 "Gethsemane"

1972. Protection of Historical Monuments. Frescoes by J. Canavesio. Chapel of Notre-Dame des Fontaines, La Brigue.
1065 **274** 30 c. red 10 10
1066 – 50 c. grey 20 15
1067 – 90 c. green 40 50
1068 – 1 f. 40 red 55 75
1069 – 2 f. purple . . . . . . 1·10 1·10
DESIGNS: 50 c. "Christ Outraged"; 90 c. "Ascent to Calvary"; 1 f. 40, "The Resurrection"; 2 f. "The Crucifixion".

1972. Paintings. "Princes and Princesses of Monaco". As T **213**. Multicoloured.
1070 1 f. "Prince Jacques 1" (N. Largillière) 40 50
1071 3 f. "Princess Louise-Hippolyte" (J. B. Vanloo) . 1·90 1·75

1973. Monte Carlo Flower Show (2nd issue). As T **239**.
1073 3 f. 50 multicoloured . . . . 5·50 4·25
DESIGN: 3 f. 50, "Bouquet of Flowers".

276 Europa "Posthorn"

1973. Europa.
1074 **276** 50 c. orange . . . . . . 2·50 1·25
1075 90 c. green . . . . 3·75 2·50

277 Moliere and Characters from "Le Malade Imaginaire" **278** Colette, Cat and Books

1973. 300th Death Anniv of Moliere.
1076 **277** 20 c. red, brown and blue 30 20

1973. Birth Anniversaries.
1077 **278** 30 c. black, blue and red 1·00 50
1078 – 45 c. multicoloured . . . 2·25 1·40
1079 – 50 c. lilac, purple & blue 30 20
1080 – 90 c. multicoloured . . . 75 60
DESIGNS AND ANNIVERSARIES—HORIZ: 30 c., Type **278** (nature writer, birth cent); 45 c. J.-H. Fabre and insects (entomologist, 150th birth anniv); 90 c. Sir George Cayley and his "convertiplane" (aviation pioneer, birth bicent). VERT: 50 c. Blaise Pascal (philosopher and writer, 350th birth anniv).

HAVE YOU READ THE NOTES AT THE BEGINNING OF THIS CATALOGUE?
These often provide the answers to the enquiries we receive.

279 E. Ducretet, "Les Invalides" and Eiffel Tower

1973. 75th Anniv of Eugene Ducretet's First Hertzian Radio Link.
1081 **279** 30 c. purple and brown . 20 15

1973. International Dog Show, Monte Carlo. As T **248**. Inscr "1973". Multicoloured.
1082 45 c. Alsatian . . . . 6·25 4·25

280 C. Peguy and Chartres Cathedral

1973. Birth Bicentenary of Charles Peguy (writer).
1083 **280** 50 c. brown, mauve & grey 30 25

281 Telecommunications Equipment **282** Stage Characters

1973. 5th World Telecommunications Day.
1084 **281** 60 c. violet, blue & brown 30 20

1973. 5th World Amateur Theatre Festival.
1085 **282** 60 c. lilac, blue and red . 60 50

283 Ellis and Rugby Tackle

1973. 150th Anniv of Founding of Rugby Football by William Web Ellis.
1086 **283** 90 c. red, lake and brown 85 60

284 St. Theresa

1973. Birth Centenary of St. Theresa of Lisieux.
1087 **284** 1 f. 40 multicoloured . . 65 75

285 Drug Addiction

1973. Campaign Against Drugs.
1088 **285** 50 c. red, green and blue 20 15
1089 – 50 c. multicoloured . . . 20 15
1090 **285** 90 c. violet, green and red 75 30
1091 – 90 c. multicoloured . . . 60 40
DESIGN: Nos. 1089, 1091, Children, syringes and addicts.

286 "Institution of the Creche" (Giotto)

1973. 750th Anniv of St. Francis of Assisi Creche.
1092 **286** 30 c. purple (postage) . . 30 20
1093 – 45 c. red . . . . 1·00 75
1094 – 50 c. brown 80 85
1095 – 1 f. green . . . . 2·10 1·50
1096 – 2 f. brown . . . . 4·00 3·25
1097 – 3 f. blue (air) . . . . . . 3·75 3·00
DESIGN—HORIZ: 45 c. "The Nativity" (School of F. Lippi); 50 c. "The Birth of Jesus Christ" (Giotto). VERT: 1 f. "The Nativity" (15th century miniature); 2 f. "The Birth of Jesus" (Fra Angelico); 3 f. "The Nativity" (Flemish school).

287 Country Picnic

1973. 50th Anniv of National Committee for Monegasque Traditions.
1098 **287** 10 c. blue, green & brown 10 10
1099 – 20 c. violet, blue & green 10 10
1100 – 30 c. sepia, brown & grn 15 15
1101 – 45 c. red, violet & purple 50 50
1102 – 50 c. black, red & brown 60 60
1103 – 60 c. red, violet and blue 75 75
1104 – 1 f. violet, blue & brown 1·25 1·25
DESIGNS—VERT: 20 c. Maypole dance. HORIZ: 30 c. "U Bradi" (local dance); 45 c. St. Jean fire-dance; 50 c. Blessing the Christmas loaf; 60 c. Blessing the sea Festival of St. Devote; 1 f. Corpus Christi procession.

1973. Monte Carlo Flower Show, 1974. As T **271**. Multicoloured.
1105 45 c. Roses and Strelitzia . . 1·25 75
1106 60 c. Mimosa and myosotis . 1·75 1·10
1107 1 f. "Vase of Flowers" (Odilon Redon) . . . . 3·25 1·90

1973. Paintings. "Princes and Princesses of Monaco". As T **213**. Multicoloured.
1108 2 f. "Charlotte Grimaldi" (in day dress, P. Gobert) . . . 2·10 1·90
1109 2 f. "Charlotte Grimaldi" (in evening dress, P. Gobert) . 2·10 1·90

289 U.P.U. Emblem and Symbolic Heads
290 Farman, Farman F.60 Goliath and Farman H.F.III

1974. Centenary of Universal Postal Union.
1111 **289** 50 c. purple and brown . 25 10
1112 – 70 c. multicoloured . . . 35 20
1113 – 1 f. 10 multicoloured . . 80 55
DESIGNS: 70 c. Hands holding letters; 1 f. 10, "Countries of the World" (famous buildings).

1974. Monaco Red Cross. As T **238**.
1114 3 f. blue, green and purple . 1·90 1·75
DESIGN: 3 f. St. Bernard of Menthon.

1974. Birth Centenary of Henry Farman (aviation pioneer).
1115 **290** 30 c. brown, purple & bl 10 10

291 Marconi, Circuit Plan and Destroyers

1974. Birth Centenary of Guglielmo Marconi (radio pioneer).
1116 **291** 40 c. red, dp blue & blue 20 10

292 Duchesne and "Penicillium glaucum"

1974. Birth Centenary of Ernest Duchesne (microbiologist).
1117 **292** 45 c. black, blue & purple 30 10

293 Forest and Engine

1974. 60th Death Anniv of Fernand Forest (motor engineer and inventor).
1118 **293** 50 c. purple, red & black 20 10

1974. International Dog Show, Monte Carlo. As T **248**, inscr "1974".
1119 60 c. multicoloured . . . . 3·75 3·00
DESIGN: 60 c. Schnauzer.

294 Ronsard and Characters from "Sonnet to Helene"

1974. 450th Birth Anniv of Pierre de Ronsard (poet).
1120 **294** 70 c. brown and red . . 40 35

295 Sir Winston Churchill (after bust by O. Nemon)

297 "The King of Rome" (Bosio)

296 Interpol Emblem, and Views of Monaco and Vienna

1974. Birth Centenary of Sir Winston Churchill.
1121 **295** 1 f. brown and grey . . 50 30

1974. 60th Anniv of 1st International Police Judiciary Congress and 50th Anniv of International Criminal Police Organization (Interpol).
1122 **296** 2 f. blue, brown & green 1·25 80

1974. Europa. Sculptures by J. F. Bosio.
1123 **297** 45 c. green and brown . 1·10 1·10
1124 – 1 f. 10 bistre and brown 2·00 1·75
DESIGN: 1 f. 10, "Madame Elizabeth".

298 "The Box" (A. Renoir)

1974. "The Impressionists". Multicoloured.
1126 1 f. Type **298** . . . . . . 2·00 2·00
1127 1 f. "The Dance Class" (E. Degas) . . . . 2·00 2·00
1128 2 f. "Impression-Sunrise" (C. Monet) (horiz) . . . . 4·00 3·25
1129 2 f. "Entrance to Voisins Village" (C. Pissarro) (horiz) 4·00 3·25
1130 2 f. "The Hanged Man's House" (P. Cezanne) (horiz) 4·00 3·25
1131 2 f. "Floods at Port Marly" (A. Sisley) (horiz) . . . . 4·00 3·25

299 Tigers and Trainer

1974. 1st International Circus Festival, Monaco.
1132 **299** 2 c. brown, green & blue 10 10
1133 – 3 c. brown and purple 10 10
1134 – 5 c. blue, brown and red 10 10
1135 – 45 c. brown, black & red 40 20
1136 – 70 c. multicoloured . . 90 75
1137 – 1 f. 10 brown, grn & red 1·60 1·25
1138 – 5 f. green, blue & brown 5·75 4·75
DESIGNS—VERT: 3 c. Performing horse; 45 c. Equestrian act; 1 f. 10, Acrobats; 5 f. Trapeze act. HORIZ: 5 c. Performing elephants; 70 c. Clowns.

300 Honore II on Medal

1974. 350th Anniv of Monegasque Numismatic Art.
1139 **300** 60 c. green and red . . . 50 35

301 Marine Flora and Fauna

1974. 24th Congress of the International Commission for the Scientific Exploration of the Mediterranean. Multicoloured.
1140 45 c. Type **301** . . . . 1·25 85
1141 70 c. Sea-bed flora and fauna 1·60 1·25
1142 1 f. 10 Sea-bed flora and fauna (different) . . . . 2·75 2·25
Nos. 1141/2 are larger, size 52 × 31 mm.

1974. Monte Carlo Flower Show. As T **271**. Multicoloured.
1143 70 c. Honeysuckle and violets 1·10 85
1144 1 f. 10 Iris and chrysanthemums 1·60 1·40

302 Prince Rainier III (F. Messina)

303

1974.
1145 **302** 60 c. green (postage) . . 60 15
1146 80 c. red 75 25
1147 80 c. green 40 10
1148 1 f. brown . . . . . . 1·40 60
1149 1 f. red 75 10
1149a 1 f. green 40 10
1149b 1 f. 10 green 40 10
1150 1 f. 20 violet . . . . . 4·75 2·50
1150a 1 f. 20 red 65 10
1150b 1 f. 20 green . . . . . 1·00 10
1151 1 f. 25 blue . . . . . 1·50 1·10
1151a 1 f. 30 red 65 15
1152 1 f. 40 red . . . . . . 1·10 10
1152a 1 f. 50 black . . . . . 1·00 40
1153 1 f. 60 grey . . . . . 1·10 50
1153a 1 f. 70 blue 90 75
1153b 1 f. 80 blue . . . . . 1·75 1·50
1154 2 f. mauve . . . . . 2·50 1·60
1154a 2 f. 10 brown . . . . . 1·60 1·25
1155 2 f. 30 violet . . . . . 2·25 1·50
1156 2 f. 50 black . . . . . 2·25 1·90
1157 9 f. violet . . . . . . 6·25 4·00
1158 **303** 10 f. violet (air) . . . . 7·50 3·00
1159 15 f. red . . . . 10·50 7·50
1160 20 f. blue . . . . 16·00 10·00

304 Coastline, Monte Carlo
305 "Haagocereus chosicensis"

1974.
1161 **304** 25 c. blue, green & brown 1·50 60
1162 – 25 c. brown, green & blue 20 20
1163 – 50 c. brown and blue . . 85 60
1164 **304** 65 c. blue, brown & green 30 20
1165 – 70 c. multicoloured . . . 75 60
1166 **304** 1 f. 10 brown, green & bl 2·25 1·25
1167 – 1 f. 10 black, brown & bl 85 60
1168 – 1 f. 30 brown, green & bl 65 30
1169 – 1 f. 40 green, grey & brn 2·25 1·25
1170 – 1 f. 50 green, blue & blk 1·50 1·25
1171 – 1 f. 70 brown, green & bl 3·75 2·50
1172 – 1 f. 80 brown, green & bl 1·50 1·10
1173 – 2 f. 30 brown, grey & bl 2·50 1·90
1174 – 3 f. brown, grey & green 4·75 1·90
1175 – 5 f. 50 brown, green & blue 9·25 4·25
1176 – 6 f. 50 brown, blue & grn 4·25 3·25
DESIGNS—VERT: 50 c. Palace clock tower; 70 c. Botanical gardens; 1 f. 30, Monaco Cathedral; 1 f. 40, 1 f. 50, Prince Albert I statue and Museum; 3 f. Fort Antoine. HORIZ: 25 c. (1162), 1 f. 70, "All Saints" Tower; 1 f. 10, (1167), Palais de Justice; 1 f. 80, 5 f. 50, La Condamine; 2 f. 30, North Galleries of Palace; 6 f. 50, Aerial view of hotels and harbour.

1975. Plants. Multicoloured.
1180 10 c. Type **305** 10 10
1181 20 c. "Matucana madisoniarum" 35 10
1182 30 c. "Parodia scopaioides" . 65 35
1183 85 c. "Mediolobivia arachnacantha" . . . . . 2·50 1·25
1184 1 f. 90 "Matucana yanganucensis" . . . . . 4·25 2·75
1185 4 f. "Echinocereus marksianus" 6·75 5·00

306 "Portrait of a Sailor" (P. Florence)
308 "Prologue"

307 "St. Bernardin de Sienne"

1975. Europa.
1186 **306** 80 c. purple . . . . . . 1·10 1·00
1187 – 1 f. 20 blue . . . . . . 1·90 1·50
DESIGN: 1 f. 20, "St. Devote" (Ludovic Brea).

1975. Monaco Red Cross.
1189 **307** 4 f. blue and purple . . 3·00 2·50

1975. Centenary of "Carmen" (opera by Georges Bizet).
1190 **308** 30 c. violet, brown & blk 10 10
1191 – 60 c. grey, green and red 20 10
1192 – 80 c. green, brown & blk 75 50
1193 – 1 f. 40 purple, brown and ochre . . . . 1·25 1·00
DESIGNS—HORIZ: 60 c. Lilla Pastia's tavern; 80 c. "The Smuggler's Den"; 1 f. 40, "Confrontation at Seville".

309 Saint-Simon

310 Dr. Albert Schweitzer

1975. 300th Birth Anniv of Louis de Saint-Simon (writer).
1194 **309** 40 c. blue 25 15

1975. Birth Centenary of Dr. Schweitzer (Nobel Peace Prize Winner).
1195 **310** 60 c. red and brown . . 75 20

311 "Stamp" and Calligraphy

1975. "Arphila 75" International Stamp Exhibition, Paris.
1196 **311** 80 c. brown and orange . 50 35

312 Seagull and Sunrise

1975. International Exposition, Okinawa.
1197 **312** 85 c. blue, green & orange 1·00 75

313 Pike smashing Crab

1975. Anti-Cancer Campaign.

1198	313	1 f. multicoloured	65	60

314 Christ with Crown of Thorns

1975. Holy Year.

1199	314	1 f. 15 black, brn & pur	1·00	75

315 Villa Sauber, Monte Carlo

1975. European Architectural Heritage Year.

1200	315	1 f. 20 green, brown & bl	90	85

316 Woman's Head and Globe

1975. International Women's Year.

1201	316	1 f. 20 multicoloured . .	90	85

317 Rolls-Royce "Silver Ghost" (1907)

1975. Evolution of the Motor Car.

1202	317	5 c. blue, green & brown	10	10
1203	–	10 c. indigo and blue . .	10	10
1204	–	20 c. blue, ultram & blk .	20	10
1205	–	30 c. purple and mauve .	40	20
1206	–	50 c. blue, purple & mve	80	75
1207	–	60 c. red and green . . .	1·10	65
1208	–	80 c. indigo and blue . .	2·00	1·50
1209	–	85 c. brown, orge & grn .	2·50	2·25
1210	–	1 f. 20 blue, red and green	3·75	3·00
1211	–	1 f. 40 green and blue . .	5·00	3·25
1212	–	5 f. 50 blue, emerald and green	15·00	10·50

MOTOR CARS: 10 c. Hispano-Suiza "H.6B" (1926); 20 c. Isotta Fraschini "8A" (1928); 30 c. Cord "L.29"; 50 c. Voisin "V12" (1930); 60 c. Duesenberg "SJ" (1933); 80 c. Bugatti "57 C" (1938); 85 c. Delahaye "135 M" (1940); 1 f. 20, Cisitalia "Pininfarina" (1945); 1 f. 40, Mercedes-Benz "300 SL" (1955); 5 f. 50, Lamborghini "Countach" (1974).

1975. Paintings. "Princes and Princesses of Monaco". As T **213**. Multicoloured.

1213	2 f. "Prince Honore III" . . .	1·90	1·25
1214	4 f. "Princess Catherine de Brignole"	3·75	3·00

318 Dog behind Bars 319 Maurice Ravel

1975. 125th Birth Anniv of Gen. J. P. Delmas de Grammont (author of Animal Protection Code).

1215	318	60 c. black and brown .	1·10	75
1216	–	80 c. black and brown .	1·60	1·10
1217	–	1 f. 20 green and purple	2·25	1·90

DESIGNS—VERT: 80 c. Cat chased up tree. HORIZ: 1 f. 20, Horse being ill-treated.

1975. International Dog Show, Monte Carlo. As T **248**, but inscr "1975". Multicoloured.

1218	60 c. black and purple . . .	3·75	3·00

DESIGN: 60 c. French poodle.

1975. Birth Centenaries of Musicians.

1219	319	60 c. brown and purple .	1·10	60
1220	–	1 f. 20 black and purple	2·25	1·60

DESIGN: 1 f. 20, Johann Strauss (the younger).

320 Circus Clown 322 Andre Ampere with Electrical Meter

321 Monaco Florin Coin, 1640

1975. 2nd International Circus Festival.

1221	320	80 c. multicoloured . .	1·25	40

1975. Monaco Numismatics.

1222	321	80 c. brown and blue . .	75	30

See also Nos. 1275, 1320 and 1448.

1975. Birth Centenary of Andre Ampere (physicist).

1223	322	85 c. indigo and blue . .	60	60

323 "Lamentations for the Dead Christ"

1975. 500th Birth Anniv of Michelangelo.

1224	323	1 f. 40 olive and black .	1·10	60

1975. Monte Carlo Flower Show (1976). As T **271**. Multicoloured.

1225	60 c. Bouquet of wild flowers	90	60
1226	80 c. Ikebana flower arrangement	1·60	1·00

1975. Precancelled. Surch.

1227	42 c. on 26 c. violet, blue and black (No. 949a)	2·50	1·25
1228	48 c. on 30 c. red, blue, lilac & black (No. 949b)	3·00	1·90
1229	70 c. on 45 c. blue, violet, turq & black (No. 950a)	5·00	2·50
1230	1 f. 35 on 90 c. green, blue and black (No. 951a)	6·25	3·00

325 Prince Pierre de Monaco

1976. 25th Anniv of Literary Council of Monaco.

1231	325	10 c. black	10	10
1232	–	20 c. blue and red . . .	20	10
1233	–	25 c. blue and red . . .	20	10
1234	–	30 c. brown	20	15
1235	–	50 c. blue, red and purple	30	20
1236	–	60 c. brown, grn & lt brn	40	50
1237	–	80 c. purple and blue . .	1·00	75
1238	–	1 f. 20 violet, blue & mve	1·60	1·40

COUNCIL MEMBERS—HORIZ: 20 c. A. Maurois and Colette; 25 c. Jean and Jerome Tharaud; 30 c. E. Henriot, M. Pagnol and G. Duhamel; 50 c. Ph. Heriat, J. Supervielle and L. Pierard; 60 c. R. Dorgeles, M. Achard and G. Bauer; 80 c. F. Hellens, A. Billy and Mgr. Grente; 1 f. 20, J. Giono, L. Pasteur Vallery-Radot and M. Garcon.

326 Dachshunds

1976. International Dog Show, Monte Carlo.

1239	326	60 c. multicoloured . . .	5·00	3·75

327 Bridge Table and Monte Carlo Coast

1976. 5th Bridge Olympiad, Monte Carlo.

1240	327	60 c. brown, green & red	55	30

328 Alexander Graham Bell and Early Telephone

1976. Telephone Centenary.

1241	328	80 c. brown, light brown and grey	50	30

329 Federation Emblem on Globe

1976. 50th Anniv of International Philatelic Federation.

1242	329	1 f. 20 red, blue & green .	80	60

330 U.S.A. 2 c. Stamp, 1926

1976. Bicent of American Revolution.

1243	330	1 f. 70 black and purple .	1·10	1·10

331 "The Fritillaries" (Van Gogh)

1976. Monte Carlo Flower Show.

1244	331	3 f. multicoloured	7·50	6·25

332 Diving 333 Decorative Plate

1976. Olympic Games, Montreal.

1245	332	60 c. brown and blue . .	25	20
1246	–	80 c. blue, brown & green	40	30
1247	–	85 c. blue, green & brown	50	40
1248	–	1 f. 20 brown, green & bl	80	60
1249	–	1 f. 70 brown, blue & grn	1·40	1·25

DESIGNS—VERT: 80 c. Gymnastics; 85 c. Hammer-throwing. HORIZ: 1 f. 20, Rowing; 1 f. 70, Boxing.

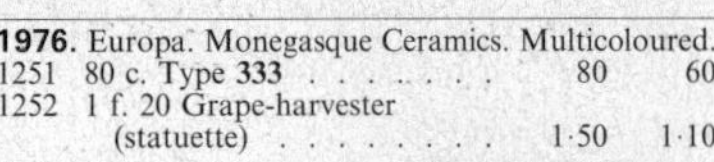

1976. Europa. Monegasque Ceramics. Multicoloured.

1251	80 c. Type **333**	80	60
1252	1 f. 20 Grape-harvester (statuette)	1·50	1·10

334 Palace Clock Tower 335 "St. Louise de Marillac" (altar painting)

1976. Precancelled.

1254	334	50 c. red	60	30
1255		52 c. orange	30	15
1256		54 c. green	40	20
1257		60 c. green	60	40
1258		62 c. mauve	40	50
1259		68 c. yellow	60	30
1260		90 c. violet	90	65
1261		95 c. red	1·00	60
1262		1 f. 05 brown	85	60
1263		1 f. 60 blue	1·50	90
1264		1 f. 70 turquoise	1·50	1·10
1265		1 f. 85 brown	1·75	1·10

1976. Monaco Red Cross.

1270	335	4 f. black, purple & green	2·75	2·50

1976. Paintings. "Princes and Princesses of Monaco". As T **213**.

1271	2 f. purple	2·50	1·90
1272	4 f. multicoloured	4·25	3·00

DESIGNS: 2 f. "Prince Honore IV"; 4 f. "Princess Louise d'Aumont-Mazarin".

336 St. Vincent-de-Paul 337 Marie de Rabutin Chantal

1976. Centenary of St. Vincent-de-Paul Conference, Monaco.

1273	336	60 c. black, brown & blue	30	20

1976. 350th Birth Anniv of Marquise de Sevigne (writer).

1274	337	80 c. black, violet and red	40	25

338 Monaco 2 g. "Honore II" Coin, 1640

1976. Monaco Numismatics.

1275	338	80 c. blue and green . .	55	30

339 Richard Byrd, "Josephine Ford", Airship "Norge" and Roald Amundsen

1976. 50th Anniv of First Flights over North Pole.

1276	339	85 c. black, blue & green	1·90	1·25

340 Gulliver and Lilliputians 341 Girl's Head and Christmas Decorations

1976. 250th Anniv of Jonathan Swift's "Gulliver's Travels".
1277 **340** 1 f. 20 multicoloured . . 60 45

1976. Christmas.
1278 **341** 60 c. multicoloured . . . 40 20
1279 1 f. 20 green, orge & pur 65 40

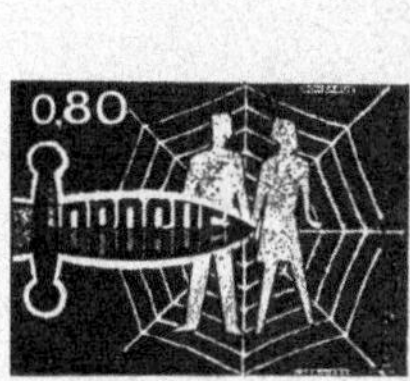

342 "Drug" Dagger piercing Man and Woman
343 Circus Clown

1976. Campaign against Drug Abuse.
1280 **342** 80 c. blue, orge & bronze 50 30
1281 1 f. 20 lilac, purple & brn 1·00 40

1976. Monte Carlo Flower Show (1977). As T **271**. Multicoloured.
1282 80 c. Flower arrangement . . 1·50 1·00
1283 1 f. Bouquet of flowers . . . 2·25 1·75

1976. 3rd International Circus Festival, Monte Carlo.
1284 **343** 1 f. multicoloured . . . . 1·90 1·10

344 Schooner "Hirondelle"

1977. 75th Anniv of Publication of "Career of a Navigator" by Prince Albert I (1st issue). Illustrations by L. Tinayre.
1285 **344** 10 c. brown, blue & turq 10 10
1286 – 20 c. black, brown & lake 10 10
1287 – 30 c. green, blue & orge 15 15
1288 – 80 c. black, blue and red 35 50
1289 – 1 f. black and brown . . 55 60
1290 – 1 f. 25 olive, green & vio 1·25 1·00
1291 – 1 f. 40 brown, olive & grn 1·90 1·50
1292 – 1 f. 90 blue, lt blue & red 3·00 2·50
1293 – 2 f. 50 brown, blue and turquoise . . . . . . 4·25 3·25
DESIGNS—VERT: 20 c. Prince Albert I; 1 f. Helmsman; 1 f. 90, Bringing in the trawl. HORIZ: 30 c. Crew-members; 80 c. "Hirondelle" in a gale; 1 f. 25, Securing the lifeboat; 1 f. 40, Shrimp fishing; 2 f. 50, Capture of a moon-fish.
See also Nos. 1305/13.

345 Pyrenean Sheep and Mountain Dogs

1977. International Dog Show, Monte Carlo.
1294 **345** 80 c. multicoloured . . . 5·00 3·75

346 "Maternity" (M. Cassatt)

1977. World Association of the "Friends of Children".
1295 **346** 80 c. deep brown, brown and black . . . . . . 1·10 75

347 Archers

1977. 10th International Archery Championships.
1296 **347** 1 f. 10 black, brown & bl 60 40

INDEX

Countries can be quickly located by referring to the index at the end of this volume.

348 Charles Lindbergh and "Spirit of St. Louis"

1977. 50th Anniv of Lindbergh's Transatlantic Flight.
1297 **348** 1 f. 90 light blue, blue and brown . . . . 2·00 1·40

349 "Harbour, Deauville"

1977. Birth Centenary of Raoul Dufy (painter).
1298 **349** 2 f. multicoloured . . . 4·25 3·00

350 "Portrait of a Young Girl"
351 "L'Oreillon" Tower

1977. 400th Birth Anniv of Peter Paul Rubens (painter).
1299 **350** 80 c. orange, brn & blk . 85 60
1300 – 1 f. red . . . . 1·25 75
1301 – 1 f. 40 orange and red . 2·25 1·50
DESIGNS: 1 f. "Duke of Buckingham"; 1 f. 40, "Portrait of a Child".

1977. Europa. Monaco Views.
1302 **351** 1 f. brown and blue . . 90 60
1303 – 1 f. 40 blue, brown and bistre . . . . 1·40 1·40
DESIGN: 1 f. 40, St. Michael's Church, Menton.

1977. 75th Anniv of Publication of "Career of a Navigator" by Prince Albert I (2nd issue). Illustrations by L. Tinayre. As T **344**.
1305 10 c. black and blue 10 10
1306 20 c. blue 10 10
1307 30 c. blue, light blue and green 20 20
1308 80 c. brown, black and green 60 30
1309 1 f. grey and green 75 60
1310 1 f. 25 black, brown and lilac 1·10 85
1311 1 f. 40 purple, blue & brown 1·90 1·50
1312 1 f. 90 black, blue and light blue 3·00 2·50
1313 3 f. blue, brown and green . 4·25 3·50
DESIGNS—HORIZ: 10 c. "Princess Alice" (steam yacht) at Kiel; 20 c. Ship's laboratory; 30 c. "Princess Alice" in ice floes; 1 f. Polar scene; 1 f. 25, Bridge of "Princess Alice" during snowstorm; 1 f. 40, Arctic camp; 1 f. 90, Ship's steam launch in floating ice; 3 f. "Princess Alice" passing iceberg. VERT: 80 c. Crewmen in Arctic dress.

352 Santa Claus & Sledge
353 Face, Poppy and Syringe

1977. Christmas.
1314 **352** 80 c. red, green and blue 35 25
1315 1 f. 40 multicoloured . . 65 35

1977. Monte Carlo Flower Show. As T **271**. Mult.
1316 80 c. Snapdragons and campanula 80 75
1317 1 f. Ikebana . . . . 1·50 1·25

1977. Campaign Against Drug Abuse.
1318 **353** 1 f. black, red and violet 55 30

354 Clown and Flags

1977. 4th International Festival of Circus, Monaco.
1319 **354** 1 f. multicoloured . . . . 1·90 1·10

355 Gold Coin of Honore II

1977. Monaco Numismatics.
1320 **355** 80 c. brown and red . . . 50 35

356 Mediterranean divided by Industry

1977. Protection of the Mediterranean Environment.
1321 **356** 1 f. black, green and blue 60 35

357 Dr. Guglielminetti and Road Tarrers

1977. 75th Anniv of First Experiments at Road Tarring in Monaco.
1322 **357** 1 f. 10 black, bistre and brown 75 60

358 F.M.L.T. Badge and Monte Carlo

1977. 50th Anniv of Monaco Lawn Tennis Federation.
1323 **358** 1 f. blue, red and brown 1·25 60

359 Wimbledon and First Championships

1977. Centenary of Wimbledon Lawn Tennis Championships.
1324 **359** 1 f. 40 grey, green & brown 1·75 1·00

1977. Paintings. "Princes and Princesses of Monaco". As T **213**. Multicoloured.
1325 6 f. "Prince Honore V" . . . 5·00 3·75

360 St. Jean Bosco

1977. Monaco Red Cross. Monegasque Art.
1326 **360** 4 f. green, brown & blue 2·50 2·25

1978. Precancelled. Surch.
1327 **334** 58 c. on 54 c. green . . . 60 30
1328 73 c. on 68 c. yellow . . 1·00 40
1329 1 f. 15 on 1 f. 05 brown 1·50 1·00
1330 2 f. on 1 f. 85 brown . . 2·50 1·60

362 Aerial Shipwreck from "L'Ile Mysterieuse"

1978. 150th Birth Anniv of Jules Verne.
1331 **362** 5 c. brown, red and olive 10 10
1332 – 25 c. turquoise, blue & red 10 10
1333 – 30 c. blue, brown & lt blue 15 10
1334 – 80 c. black, green & orge 35 50
1335 – 1 f. brown, lake and blue 85 60
1336 – 1 f. 40 bistre, brown and green . . . . 1·10 65
1337 – 1 f. 70 brown, lt blue and blue . . . . 1·60 1·50
1338 – 5 f. 50 violet and blue . 4·00 3·50
DESIGNS: 25 c. The abandoned ship from "L'Ile Mysterieuse"; 30 c. The secret of the island from "L'Ile Mysterieuse"; 80 c. "Robur the Conqueror"; 1 f. "Master Zacharius"; 1 f. 40, "The Castle in the Carpathians"; 1 f. 70, "The Children of Captain Grant"; 5 f. 50, Jules Verne and allegories.

363 Aerial View of Congress Centre

1978. Inauguration of Monaco Congress Centre.
1339 **363** 1 f. brown, blue and green 40 30
1340 – 1 f. 40 blue, brown & grn 65 40
DESIGN: 1 f. 40, View of Congress Centre from sea.

364 Footballers and Globe

1978. World Cup Football Championship, Argentina.
1341 **364** 1 f. blue, slate and green 65 55

365 Antonio Vivaldi
366 "Ramoge" (research vessel) and Grimaldi Palace

1978. 300th Birth Anniv of Antonio Vivaldi (composer).
1342 **365** 1 f. brown and red . . . 1·00 85

1978. Environment Protection. "RAMOGE" Agreement.
1343 **366** 80 c. multicoloured . . . 40 50
1344 – 1 f. red, blue and green 65 40
DESIGN—HORIZ: (48 × 27 mm): 1 f. Map of coastline between St. Raphael and Genes.

367 Monaco Cathedral
368 Monaco Congress Centre

1978. Europa. Monaco Views.
1345 **367** 1 f. green, brown & blue 80 45
1346 – 1 f. 40 brown, green & bl 1·25 1·10
DESIGN: 1 f. 40, View of Monaco from the east.

1978. Precancelled.
1348 **368** 61 c. orange 30 10
1349 64 c. green 30 10
1350 68 c. blue 30 10
1351 78 c. purple 40 20
1352 83 c. violet 40 20
1353 88 c. orange 40 20
1354 1 f. 25 brown . . . . . 1·00 60
1355 1 f. 30 red 65 40
1356 1 f. 40 green . . . . . 1·00 40
1357 2 f. 10 blue . . . . . . 1·50 1·00
1358 2 f. 25 orange . . . . . 1·40 80
1359 2 f. 35 mauve . . . . . 1·60 80

369 "Cinderella"

1978. 350th Birth Anniv of Charles Perrault (writer).
1360 **369** 5 c. red, olive and violet 10 10
1361 – 25 c. black, brown & mve 10 10
1362 – 30 c. green, lake & brown 15 10
1363 – 80 c. multicoloured . . . 60 50
1364 – 1 f. red, brown and olive 75 60
1365 – 1 f. 40 mauve, ultram & blue . . . . 1·00 65
1366 – 1 f. 70 green, blue & grey 1·40 1·10
1367 – 1 f. 90 multicoloured . . 1·90 1·40
1368 – 2 f. 50 blue, orange & grn 2·50 1·90
DESIGNS: 25 c. "Puss in Boots"; 30 c. "The Sleeping Beauty"; 80 c. "Donkey's Skin"; 1 f. "Little Red Riding Hood"; 1 f. 40, "Bluebeard"; 1 f. 70, "Tom Thumb"; 1 f. 90, "Riquet with a Tuft"; 2 f. 50, "The Fairies".

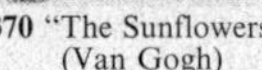

370 "The Sunflowers" (Van Gogh) **371** Afghan Hound

1978. Monte Carlo Flower Show (1979) and 125th Birth Anniv of Vincent Van Gogh. Multicoloured.
1369 1 f. Type **370** . . . . 2·50 1·90
1370 1 f. 70 "The Iris" (Van Gogh) 3·75 2·50

1978. International Dog Show, Monte Carlo. Multicoloured.
1371 1 f. Type **371** . . . . 3·00 2·50
1372 1 f. 20 Borzoi . . . . 4·25 3·00

372 Girl with Letter **374** Juggling Seals

373 Catherine and William Booth

1978. Christmas.
1373 **372** 1 f. brown, blue and red 55 40

1978. Centenary of Salvation Army.
1374 **373** 1 f. 70 multicoloured . . 1·40 1·25

1978. 5th International Circus Festival, Monaco.
1375 **374** 80 c. orange, black & blue 40 50
1376 – 1 f. multicoloured 65 75
1377 – 1 f. 40 brown, mauve and bistre . . . . 1·40 1·10
1378 – 1 f. 90 blue, lilac and mauve 2·10 2·00
1379 – 2 f. 40 multicoloured . . 3·00 2·50
DESIGNS—HORIZ: 1 f. 40, Horseback acrobatics; 1 f. 90, Musical monkeys; 2 f. 40, Trapeze. VERT: 1 f. Lion tamer.

1978. Paintings. "Princes and Princesses of Monaco". As T **213**. Multicoloured.
1380 2 f. "Prince Florestan I" (G. Dauphin) . . . . . . 2·50 1·90
1381 4 f. "Princess Caroline Gilbert de la Metz" (Marie Verroust) 4·25 3·75

377 "Jongleur de Notre-Dame" (Massenet)

1979. Centenary of "Salle Garnier" (Opera House) (1st issue).
1384 **377** 1 f. blue, orange & mauve 40 20
1385 – 1 f. 20 violet, blk & turq 65 30
1386 – 1 f. 50 maroon, grn & turq 80 65
1387 – 1 f. 70 multicoloured . . 1·75 1·40
1388 – 2 f. 10 turquoise & violet 2·25 2·00
1389 – 3 f. multicoloured . . . . 3·00 2·50
DESIGNS—HORIZ: 1 f. 20, "Hans the Flute Player" (L. Ganne); 1 f. 50, "Don Quixote" (J. Massenet); 2 f. 10, "The Child and the Sorcerer" (M. Ravel); 3 f. Charles Garnier (architect) and south facade of Opera House. VERT: 1 f. 70, "L'Aiglon" (A. Honegger and J. Ibert).
See also Nos. 1399/1404.

378 Flower, Bird and Butterfly

1979. International Year of the Child. Children's Paintings.
1390 **378** 50 c. pink, green & black 20 15
1391 – 1 f. slate, green & orange 45 50
1392 – 1 f. 20 slate, orange & mve 65 75
1393 – 1 f. 50 yellow, brown & bl 1·25 1·10
1394 – 1 f. 70 multicoloured . . 1·75 1·60
DESIGNS: 1 f. Horse and Child; 1 f. 20, "The Gift of Love"; 1 f. 50, "Peace in the World"; 1 f. 70, "Down with Pollution".

379 Armed Foot Messenger

1979. Europa.
1395 **379** 1 f. 20 brown, green & bl 65 30
1396 – 1 f. 50 brown, turq & bl 80 40
1397 – 1 f. 70 brown, green & bl 95 70
DESIGNS: 1 f. 50, 18th cent felucca; 1 f. 70, Arrival of 1st train at Monaco.

380 "Instrumental Music" (G. Boulanger) (detail of Opera House interior)

1979. Centenary of "Salle Garnier" (Opera House) (2nd issue).
1399 – 1 f. brown, orange & turq 55 20
1400 – 1 f. 20 multicoloured . . 65 40
1401 – 1 f. 50 multicoloured . . 1·25 1·00
1402 – 1 f. 70 blue, brown & red 1·75 1·40
1403 – 2 f. 10 red, violet & black 2·25 2·00
1404 **380** 3 f. green, brown and light green . . . . 3·00 2·50
DESIGNS: As Type **377**. HORIZ: 1 f. "Les Biches" (F. Poulenc); 1 f. 20, "The Sailors" (G. Auric); 1 f. 70, "Gaiete Parisienne" (J. Offenbach). VERT: 1 f. 50, "La Spectre de la Rose" (C. M. Weber) (after poster by Jean Cocteau); 2 f. 10, "Salome" (R. Strauss).

1979. Paintings. "Princes and Princesses of Monaco". As T **213**. Multicoloured.
1405 3 f. "Prince Charles III" (B. Biard) . . . . 2·50 1·90
1406 4 f. "Antoinette de Merode" 3·75 2·50

381 St. Pierre Claver **382** "Princess Grace" Orchid

1979. Monaco Red Cross.
1407 **381** 5 f. multicoloured . . . 3·00 2·75

1979. Monte Carlo Flora 1980.
1408 **382** 1 f. multicoloured . . . 2·50 1·90

383 "Princess Grace" Rose **384** Clown balancing on Ball

1979. Monte Carlo Flower Show.
1409 **383** 1 f. 20 multicoloured . . 2·50 1·90

1979. 6th International Circus Festival.
1410 **384** 1 f. 20 multicoloured . . 2·10 1·40

385 Sir Rowland Hill and Penny Black **386** Albert Einstein

1979. Death Centenary of Sir Rowland Hill.
1411 **385** 1 f. 70 brown, blue & blk 65 45

1979. Birth Centenary of Albert Einstein (physicist).
1412 **386** 1 f. 70 brown, grey & red 1·00 75

387 St. Patrick's Cathedral **388** Nativity Scene

1979. Centenary of St. Patrick's Cathedral, New York.
1413 **387** 2 f. 10 black, blue & brn . 1·00 60

1979. Christmas.
1414 **388** 1 f. 20 blue, orange & mve 85 60

389 Early Racing Cars

1979. 50th Anniv of Grand Prix Motor Racing.
1415 **389** 1 f. multicoloured . . . . 1·10 75

390 Arms of Charles V and Monaco

1979. 450th Anniv of Visit of Emperor Charles V.
1416 **390** 1 f. 50 brown, blue & blk 60 40

391 Setter and Pointer

1979. International Dog Show, Monte Carlo.
1417 **391** 1 f. 20 multicoloured . . 3·75 3·00

392 Spring

1980. Precancels. The Seasons.
1418 **392** 76 c. brown and green . . 35 20
1419 88 c. olive, emerald & grn 35 20
1420 – 99 c. green and brown . . 75 60
1421 – 1 f. 14 green, emer & brn 75 60
1422 – 1 f. 60 brown, grey & deep brown . . . . 1·25 65
1423 – 1 f. 84 lake, grey & brown 1·25 85
1424 – 2 f. 65 brown, lt blue & bl 1·90 1·25
1425 – 3 f. 05, brown, bl & slate 1·90 1·50
DESIGNS: 99 c., 1 f. 14, Summer; 1 f. 60, 1 f. 84, Autumn; 2 f. 65, 3 f. 05, Winter.

394 Paul P. Harris (founder) and View of Chicago

1980. 75th Anniv of Rotary International.
1434 **394** 1 f. 80 olive, blue & turq 90 65

395 Gymnastics

1980. Olympic Games, Moscow and Lake Placid.
1435 **395** 1 f. 10 blue, brn & grey 30 20
1436 – 1 f. 30 red, brown & blue 40 30
1437 – 1 f. 60 red, blue & brown 55 40
1438 – 1 f. 80 brown, bis & grn 65 40
1439 – 2 f. 30 grey, violet & mve 1·00 65
1440 – 4 f. green, blue & brown 1·40 1·25
DESIGNS: 1 f. 30, Handball; 1 f. 60, Pistol shooting; 1 f. 80, Volleyball; 2 f. 30, Ice hockey; 4 f. Skiing.

396 Colette (novelist) **397** "La Source"

1980. Europa. Each black, green and red.
1441 1 f. 30 Type **396** 35 25
1442 1 f. 80 Marcel Pagnol (writer) 45 30

1980. Birth Bicentenary of Jean Ingres (artist).
1444 **397** 4 f. multicoloured . . . 6·25 5·00

398 Montaigne **399** Guillaume Apollinaire (after G. Pieret)

1980. 400th Anniv of Publication of Montaigne's "Essays".
1445 **398** 1 f. 30 black, red and blue 75 60

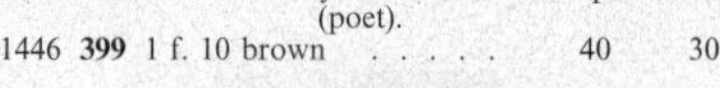
1980. Birth Centenary of Guillaume Apollinaire (poet).
1446 **399** 1 f. 10 brown 40 30

400 Congress Centre

1980. Kiwanis International European Convention.
1447 **400** 1 f. 30 black, blue and red 75 50

401 Honore II Silver Ecu, 1649

1980. Numismatics.
1448 **401** 1 f. 50 black and blue . 65 40

MINIMUM PRICE

The minimum price quoted is 10p which represents a handling charge rather than a basis for valuing common stamps. For further notes about prices, see introductory pages.

402 Lhassa Apso and Shih Tzu

1980. International Dog Show, Monte Carlo.
1449 **402** 1 f. 30 multicoloured . . 4·00 3·00

403 "The Princess and the Pea"

1980. 175th Birth Anniv of Hans Christian Andersen.
1450 **403** 70 c. sepia, red & brown 25 20
1451 – 1 f. 30 blue, turq & red 75 60
1452 – 1 f. 50 black, blue & turq 1·00 1·00
1453 – 1 f. 60 red, black & brn 1·40 1·00
1454 – 1 f. 80 yellow, brn & turq 1·50 1·25
1455 – 2 f. 30 brown, pur & vio 1·90 1·50
DESIGNS: 1 f. 30, "The Little Mermaid"; 1 f. 50, "The Chimneysweep and Shepherdess"; 1 f. 60, "The Brave Little Lead Soldier"; 1 f. 80, "The Little Match Girl"; 2 f. 30, "The Nightingale".

404 "The Road" (M. Vlaminck)

1980. 75th Anniv of 1905 Autumn Art Exhibition. Multicoloured.
1456 2 f. Type **404** . . . . 2·50 1·90
1457 3 f. "Woman at Balustrade" (Van Dongen) . . . . . . 3·75 2·50
1458 4 f. "The Reader" (Henri Matisse) . . . . 5·00 4·25
1459 5 f. "Three Figures in a Meadow" (A. Derain) . . 6·25 5·00

1980. Paintings. "Princes and Princesses of Monaco". As T **213**. Multicoloured.
1460 4 f. "Prince Albert I" (L. Bonnat) . . . . 3·00 2·50
1461 4 f. "Princess Marie Alice Heine" (. Maeterlinck) . . 3·00 2·50

405 "Sunbirds"

1980. Monaco Red Cross.
1462 **405** 6 f. red, bistre and brown 3·75 3·00

406 "MONACO" balanced on Tightrope

1980. Seventh International Circus Festival, Monaco.
1463 **406** 1 f. 30 red, turquoise & blue 1·90 1·25

407 Children and Nativity

1980. Christmas.
1464 **407** 1 f. 10 blue, carmine and red 35 25
1465 2 f. 30 violet, orange and pink . . . . 1·10 55

1980. Monte Carlo Flower Show, 1981. As T **383**. Multicoloured.
1466 1 f. 30 "Princess Stephanie" Rose . . . . 1·25 85
1467 1 f. 80 Ikebana . . . . 2·10 1·25

408 "Alcyonium" **409** Fish with Hand for Tail

1980. Marine Fauna. Multicoloured.
1468 5 c. "Spirographis spallanzanli" 10 10
1469 10 c. "Anemonia sulcata" . 10 10
1470 15 c. "Leptopsammia pruvoit" 10 10
1471 20 c. "Pteroides" 10 10
1472 30 c. "Paramuricea clavata" (horiz) 30 10
1473 40 c. Type **408** 30 10
1474 50 c. "Corallium rubrum" . 40 20
1475 60 c. Trunculus murex ("Calliactis parasitica") (horiz) . . . . 1·00 75
1476 70 c. "Cerianthus membranaceus" (horiz) . . 1·25 85
1477 1 f. "Actinia equina" (horiz) 1·40 85
1478 2 f. "Protula" (horiz) . . . 2·75 1·10

1981. "Respect the Sea".
1479 **409** 1 f. 20 multicoloured . . 85 40

410 Prince Rainier and Princess Grace

1981. Royal Silver Wedding.
1480 **410** 1 f. 20 black and green . 1·50 1·00
1481 1 f. 40 black and red . . 2·00 1·50
1482 1 f. 70 black and green . 2·50 1·90
1483 1 f. 80 black and brown 2·75 2·25
1484 2 f. black and blue . . . 3·75 2·75

411 Mozart (after Lorenz Vogel) **412** Palm Cross

1981. 225th Birth Anniv of Wolfgang Amadeus Mozart (composer).
1485 **411** 2 f. brown, dp brn & bl 1·40 1·00
1486 – 2 f. 50 blue, brn & dp brn 2·10 1·75
1487 – 3 f. 50 dp brown, bl & brn 2·75 2·25
DESIGNS—HORIZ: 2 f. 50, "Mozart at 7 with his Father and Sister" (engraving by Delafoose after drawing by Carmontelle); 3 f. 50 ,"Mozart directing Requiem two Days before his Death" (painting by Baude).

1981. Europa. Multicoloured.
1488 **412** 1 f. 40 green, brown & red 35 25
1489 – 2 f. multicoloured . . . 60 40
DESIGN: 2 f. Children carrying palm crosses.

413 Paris Football Stadium, Cup and Footballer

1981. 25th Anniv of European Football Cup.
1491 **413** 2 f. black and blue . . . 1·25 85

414 I.Y.D.P. Emblem and Girl in Wheelchair

1981. International Year of Disabled Persons.
1492 **414** 1 f. 40 blue and green . . 1·00 40

415 Palace flying Old Flag, National Flag and Monte Carlo

1981. Centenary of National Flag.
1493 **415** 2 f. red, blue and brown . 1·50 1·00

416 Oceanographic Institute, Paris and Oceanographic Museum, Monaco

1981. 75th Anniv of Oceanographic Institute.
1494 **416** 1 f. 20 blue, black & brn 1·00 75

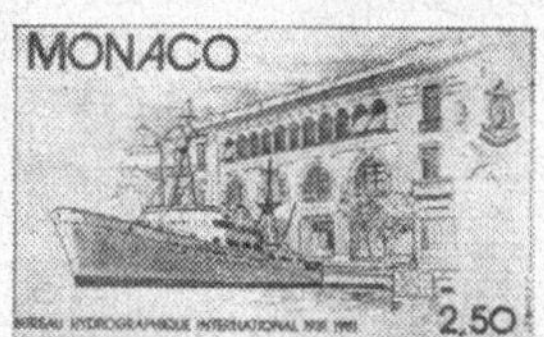

417 Bureau Building and "Faddey Bellingshausen" (hydrographic research ship)

1981. 50th Anniv of Int Hydrographic Bureau.
1495 **417** 2 f. 50 sepia, brown & light brown . . . . 1·90 1·50

418 Rough Collies and Shetland Sheepdogs

1981. International Dog Show, Monte Carlo.
1496 **418** 1 f. 40 multicoloured . . 4·25 3·00

419 Rainier III and Prince Albert **421** Arctic Scene and Map

1981. (a) 23 × 28 mm.
1497 **419** 1 f. 40 green (postage) . . 1·00 10
1498 1 f. 60 red . . . . 1·50 10
1499 1 f. 60 green 85 10
1500 1 f. 70 green . . . . . . 1·10 10
1501 1 f. 80 red . . . . 1·00 10
1502 1 f. 80 green . . . . . . 1·00 10
1503 1 f. 90 green . . . . . . 2·25 40
1504 2 f. red . . . . 1·00 10
1505 2 f. green . . . . 1·25 10
1506 2 f. 10 red . . . . 1·25 10
1507 2 f. 20 red . . . . 1·00 10
1508 2 f. 30 blue . . . . . . 3·50 3·00
1509 2 f. 50 brown . . . . . . 1·75 85
1510 2 f. 60 blue . . . . . . 2·75 2·50
1511 2 f. 80 blue . . . . . . 2·75 2·00
1512 3 f. blue . . . . 3·25 2·50
1513 3 f. 20 blue . . . . . . 3·00 2·50
1514 3 f. 40 blue . . . . . . 4·00 2·50
1515 3 f. 60 blue . . . . . . 2·75 1·60
1516 4 f. brown . . . . 1·60 85
1517 5 f. 50 black . . . . . . 2·25 1·75
1518 10 f. purple . . . . . . 3·75 1·10
1519 15 f. green . . . . . . 10·00 2·50
1520 20 f. blue . . . . 10·00 3·00

(b) 36 × 27 mm.
1521 – 5 f. violet (air) . . . . . 1·75 60
1522 – 10 f. red . . . . 6·25 1·25
1523 – 15 f. green . . . . 6·75 1·75
1524 – 20 f. blue . . . . 8·00 2·50
1525 – 30 f. brown . . . . 12·50 5·00
DESIGN: Nos. 1521/5, Double portrait and monograms.

1981. 1st International Congress on Discovery and History of Northern Polar Regions, Rome.
1530 **421** 1 f. 50 multicoloured . . 1·75 1·25

1981. Paintings. "Princes and Princesses of Monaco". Vert designs as T **213**. Multicoloured.
1531 3 f. "Prince Louis II" (P.-A. de Laszlo) . . . . . 2·50 1·25
1532 5 f. "Princess Charlotte" (P.-A. de Laszlo) . . . . . 3·75 2·50

422 Hercules fighting the Nemean Lion

1981. Monaco Red Cross. The Twelve Labours of Hercules (1st series).
1533 **422** 2 f. 50 + 50 c. green, brown and red . . . . 1·50 1·50
1534 – 3 f. 50 + 50 c. blue, green and red . . . . 1·90 1·90
DESIGN: 3 f. 50, Slaying the Hydra of Lerna.
See also Nos. 1584/5, 1631/2, 1699/1700, 1761/2 and 1794/5.

423 Ettore Bugatti (racing car designer) (Cent) **424** Eglantines and Morning Glory

1981. Birth Anniversaries.
1535 **423** 1 f. indigo, blue and red 1·25 85
1536 – 2 f. black, blue & brown 1·10 85
1537 – 2 f. 50 brown, black and red 1·40 1·10
1538 – 4 f. multicoloured . . . 3·75 3·25
1539 – 4 f. multicoloured . . . 3·75 3·25
DESIGNS: No. 1536, George Bernard Shaw (dramatist, 125th anniv); 1537, Fernand Leger (painter, centenary). LARGER: 37 × 48 mm: 1538, Pablo Picasso (self-portrait) (centenary); 1539, Rembrandt (self-portrait) (375th anniv).

1981. Monte Carlo Flower Show (1982). Mult.
1540 1 f. 40 Type **424** . . . . . . 1·50 1·00
1541 2 f. "Ikebana" (painting by Ikenobo) . . . . 2·25 1·75

425 "Catherine Deneuve" **426** Tiger, Clown, Acrobat and Elephants

1981. 1st International Rose Show, Monte Carlo.
1542 **425** 1 f. 80 multicoloured . . 3·75 2·50

1981. 8th International Circus Festival, Monaco.
1543 **426** 1 f. 40 violet, mve & blk 2·50 1·50

427 Praying Children and Nativity

1981. Christmas.
1544 **427** 1 f. 20 blue, mauve & brn 85 60

428 "Lancia-Stratos" Rally Car

1981. 50th Monte Carlo Rally (1982).
1545 **428** 1 f. blue, red & turquoise 1·40 1·00

430 "Hoya bella" 431 Spring

1981. Plants in Exotic Garden. Multicoloured.
1547 1 f. 40 Type **430** . . . . . . 3·75 1·50
1548 1 f. 60 "Bolivicereus samaipatanus" . . . . . . 2·25 1·25
1549 1 f. 80 "Trichocereus grandiflorus" (horiz) . . . 2·75 1·25
1550 2 f. "Argyroderma roseum" . 1·90 60
1551 2 f. 30 "Euphorbia milii" . . 2·25 2·00
1552 2 f. 60 "Echinocereus fitchii" (horiz) . . . . 2·25 2·00
1553 2 f. 90 "Rebutia heliosa" (horiz) 2·50 2·25
1554 4 f. 10 "Echinopsis multiplex cristata" (horiz) . . . . . 4·50 3·50

1982. Precancels. The Seasons of the Peach Tree.
1555 **431** 97 c. mauve and green . 40 25
1556 – 1 f. 25 green, orge & mve 75 60
1557 – 2 f. 03 brown . . . . . 1·25 65
1558 – 3 f. 36 brown and blue . 1·90 1·50
DESIGNS: 1 f. 25, Summer; 2 f. 03, Autumn; 3 f. 36, Winter.

432 Nutcracker 433 Capture of Monaco Fortress, 1297

1982. Birds from Mercantour National Park.
1559 **432** 60 c. black, brown & grn 1·00 85
1560 – 70 c. black and mauve . 1·25 1·00
1561 – 80 c. red, black & orange 1·25 1·10
1562 – 90 c. black, red and blue 1·90 1·60
1563 – 1 f. 40 brown, blk & red 2·75 2·25
1564 – 1 f. 60 brown, black & blue 3·75 2·50
DESIGNS—VERT: 70 c. Black grouse; 80 c. Rock partridge; 1 f. 60, Golden eagle. HORIZ: 90 c. Wallcreeper; 1 f. 40, Rock ptarmigan.

1982. Europa.
1565 **433** 1 f. 60 blue, brown and red 50 30
1566 – 2 f. 30 blue, brown and red 75 45
DESIGN: 2 f. 30, Signing the Treaty of Peronne, 1641.

434 Old Quarter

1982. Fontvieille.
1568 **434** 1 f. 40 blue, brown & grn 1·00 50
1569 – 1 f. 60 light brown, brown and red . . . . 1·10 60
1570 – 2 f. 30 purple . . . . . . 1·60 1·10
DESIGNS: 1 f. 60, Land reclamation; 2 f. 30, Urban development.

435 Stadium

1982. Fontvieille Sports Stadium (1st series).
1571 **435** 2 f. 30 green, brown & blue 1·50 1·25
See also No. 1616.

436 Arms of Paris

1982. "Philexfrance" International Stamp Exhibition, Paris.
1572 **436** 1 f. 40 red, grey and deep red . . . . 1·00 75

437 Old English Sheepdog

1982. International Dog Show, Monte Carlo. Multicoloured.
1573 60 c. Type **437** . . . . . . 2·50 1·90
1574 1 f. Briard . . . . 3·00 1·90

438 Monaco Cathedral and Arms

1982. Creation of Archbishopric of Monaco (1981).
1575 **438** 1 f. 60 black, blue and red 90 75

439 St. Francis of Assisi 440 Dr. Robert Koch

1982. 800th Birth Anniv of St. Francis of Assisi.
1576 **439** 1 f. 40 grey and light grey 85 75

1982. Centenary of Discovery of Tubercle Bacillus.
1577 **440** 1 f. 40 purple and lilac . 1·25 1·00

441 Lord Baden-Powell 443 St. Hubert (18th-century medallion)

1982. 125th Birth Anniv of Lord Baden-Powell (founder of Boy Scout Movement).
1578 **441** 1 f. 60 brown and black 1·50 1·25

1982. 29th Meeting of International Hunting Council, Monte Carlo.
1580 **443** 1 f. 60 multicoloured . . 1·40 1·10

444 Books, Reader and Globe

1982. International Bibliophile Association General Assembly, Monte Carlo.
1581 **444** 1 f. 60 blue, purple & red 90 75

445 "Casino, 1870"

1982. Monaco in the "Belle Epoque" (1st series). Paintings by Hubert Clerissi. Multicoloured.
1582 3 f. Type **445** . . . . . . 1·90 1·40
1583 5 f. "Porte d'Honneur, Royal Palace, 1893" . . . . . 3·75 2·00
See also Nos. 1629/30, 1701/2, 1763/4, 1801/2, 1851/2, 1889/90 and 1965/6.

1982. Monaco Red Cross. The Twelve Labours of Hercules (2nd series). As T **422**.
1584 2 f. 50 + 50 c. green, red and bright red . . . . 1·50 1·50
1585 3 f. 50 + 50 c. brown, blue and red . . . . 1·90 1·90
DESIGNS: 2 f. 50, Capturing the Erymanthine Boar. 3 f. 50, Shooting the Stymphalian Birds.

446 Nicolo Paganini (violinist and composer, bicent) 447 Vase of Flowers

1982. Birth Anniversaries.
1586 **446** 1 f. 60 brown and purple 1·25 1·00
1587 – 1 f. 80 red, mauve & brn 1·75 1·25
1588 – 2 f. 60 green and red . . 2·00 1·50
1589 – 4 f. multicoloured . . . . 3·75 3·00
1590 – 4 f. multicoloured . . . . 3·75 3·00
DESIGNS—VERT: No. 1587, Anna Pavlova (ballerina, centenary); 1588, Igor Stravinsky (composer, centenary). HORIZ: (47 × 36 mm): 1589, "In a Boat" (Édouard Manet, 150th anniv); 1590, "The Black Fish" (Georges Braque, centenary).

1982. Monte Carlo Flower Show (1983). Mult.
1591 1 f. 60 Type **447** . . . . . . 1·90 1·40
1592 2 f. 60 Ikebana arrangement . 2·50 1·90

448 Bowl of Flowers 449 The Three Kings

1982.
1593 **448** 1 f. 60 multicoloured . . 1·90 1·40

1982. Christmas.
1594 **449** 1 f. 60 green, blue & orge 55 30
1595 – 1 f. 80 green, blue & orge 65 30
1596 – 2 f. 60 green, blue & orge 1·00 55
DESIGNS: 1 f. 80, The Holy Family; 2 f. 60, Shepherds and angels.

450 Prince Albert I and Polar Scene

1982. Centenary of First International Polar Year.
1598 **450** 1 f. 60 brown, green & bl 2·00 1·75

451 Viking Longships off Greenland

1982. Millenary of Discovery of Greenland by Erik the Red.
1599 **451** 1 f. 60 blue, brown & blk 2·00 1·75

452 Julius Caesar in the Port of Monaco ("Aeneid", Book VI)

1982. 2000th Death Anniv of Virgil (poet).
1600 **452** 1 f. 80 deep blue, blue and brown . . . . 2·00 1·75

453 Spring 454 Tourism

1983. Precancels. The Seasons of the Apple Tree.
1601 **453** 1 f. 05 purple, green and yellow 75 30
1602 – 1 f. 35 lt green, dp grn & turquoise 85 40
1603 – 2 f. 19 red, brown & grey 1·50 1·00
1604 – 3 f. 63 yellow and brn . 2·10 1·60
DESIGNS: 1 f. 35, Summer; 2 f. 19, Autumn; 3 f. 63, Winter.

1983. 50th Anniv of Exotic Garden. Mult.
1605 1 f. 80 Type **454** . . . . . . 1·50 1·10
1606 2 f. Cactus plants (botanical collections) . . . . 1·75 1·25
1607 2 f. 30 Cactus plants (international flower shows) 2·00 1·75
1608 2 f. 60 Observatory grotto (horiz) . . . . 2·50 1·90
1609 3 f. 30 Museum of Prehistoric Anthropology (horiz) . . . 3·50 2·75

455 Alaskan Malamute 457 St. Charles Borromee and Church

1983. International Dog Show, Monte Carlo.
1610 **455** 1 f. 80 multicoloured . . 5·00 3·75

1983. Centenary of St. Charles Church, Monte Carlo.
1612 **457** 2 f. 60 deep blue, blue and green . . . . 1·25 1·00

458 Montgolfier Balloon, 1783 459 Franciscan College

1983. Europa.
1613 **458** 1 f. 80 blue, brown & grey 55 30
1614 – 2 f. 60 grey, blue & brown 1·00 40
DESIGN: 2 f. 60, Space shuttle.

1983. Centenary of Franciscan College, Monte Carlo.
1616 **459** 2 f. grey, brown and red 90 75

460 Stadium

1983. Fontvieille Sports Stadium (2nd series).
1617 **460** 2 f. green, blue & brown 1·00 40

461 Early and Modern Cars

1983. Centenary of Petrol-driven Motor Car.
1618 **461** 2 f. 90 blue, brown & green 3·00 1·90

462 Blue Whale

1983. International Commission for the Protection of Whales.
1619 **462** 3 f. 30 blue, light blue and grey . . . . 3·75 3·00

463 Dish Aerial, Pigeon, W.C.Y. Emblem and Satellite

1983. World Communications Year.
1620 **463** 4 f. lilac and mauve . . . 1·90 1·40

464 Smoking Moor

1983. Nineteenth Century Automata from the Galea Collection. Multicoloured.
1621 50 c. Type **464** 15 10
1622 60 c. Clown with diabolo . . . 20 10
1623 70 c. Smoking monkey . . . 20 15
1624 80 c. Peasant with pig 60 60
1625 90 c. Buffalo Bill smoking . . 75 60
1626 1 f. Snake charmer 75 60
1627 1 f. 50 Pianist . . . . 1·10 85
1628 2 f. Young girl powdering herself . . . . 1·75 1·25

1983. Monaco in the "Belle Epoque" (2nd series). As T **445**. Multicoloured.
1629 3 f. "The Beach, 1902" . . . 3·00 2·50
1630 5 f. "Cafe de Paris, 1905" . . 4·25 3·75

1983. Monaco Red Cross. The Twelve Labours of Hercules (3rd series). As T **422**.
1631 2 f. 50 + 50 c. brn, bl & red 1·75 1·75
1632 3 f. 50 + 50 c. vio, mauve & red 1·90 1·90
DESIGNS: 2 f. 50, Capturing the Hind of Ceryneia; 3 f. 50, Cleaning the Augean stables.

465 Johannes Brahms (composer)

1983. Birth Anniversaries.
1633 **465** 3 f. deep brown, brown and green . . . . 1·50 1·25
1634 – 3 f. black, brown and red 1·60 1·25
1635 – 4 f. multicoloured . . . . 3·00 2·50
1635 – 4 f. multicoloured . . . . 3·00 2·50
DESIGNS—HORIZ: No. 1633, Type **465** (150th anniv); 1634, Giacomo Puccini (composer) and scene from "Madame Butterfly" (125th anniv). VERT: (37×48 mm): 1635, "Portrait of a Young Man" (Raphael (artist), 500th anniv); 1636, "Cottin Passage" (Utrillo (artist), centenary).

466 Circus Performers

467 Bouquet

1983. 9th International Circus Festival, Monaco.
1637 **466** 2 f. blue, red and green . 1·90 1·50

1983. Monte Carlo Flower Show (1984). Mult.
1638 1 f. 60 Type **467** . . . . . . 1·50 1·00
1639 2 f. 60 Arrangement of poppies 2·25 1·50

468 Provencale Creche

1983. Christmas.
1640 **468** 2 f. multicoloured . . . . 1·90 1·25

469 Nobel Literature Prize Medal

1983. 150th Birth Anniv of Alfred Nobel (inventor of dynamite and founder of Nobel Prizes).
1641 **469** 2 f. black, grey and red . 1·40 1·10

470 O. F. Ozanam (founder) and Paris Headquarters
471 "Tazerka" (oil rig)

1983. 150th Anniv of Society of St. Vincent de Paul.
1642 **470** 1 f. 80 violet and purple 1·00 40

1983. Oil Industry.
1643 **471** 5 f. blue, brown & turq . 2·10 1·40

474 Skater and Stadium

1984. Winter Olympic Games, Sarajevo.
1646 **474** 2 f. blue, green and turquoise 65 55
1647 – 4 f. blue, violet & purple 1·40 1·25
DESIGN: 4 f. Skater and snowflake.

475 Bridge
476 Balkan Fritillary

1984. Europa. 25th Anniv of European Post and Telecommunications Conference.
1648 **475** 2 f. blue . . . . 1·00 30
1649 3 f. green . . . . 1·25 1·00

1984. Butterflies and Moths in Mercantour National Park. Multicoloured.
1651 1 f. 60 Type **476** . . . . . . 1·50 1·10
1652 2 f. "Zygaena vesubiana" . . 1·90 1·25
1653 2 f. 80 False mnestra ringlet 2·00 1·75
1654 3 f. Small apollo (horiz) . . 2·75 2·10
1655 3 f. 60 Southern swallowtail (horiz) . . . . 3·75 2·50

477 Auvergne Pointer

478 Sanctuary and Statue of Virgin

1984. International Dog Show, Monte Carlo.
1656 **477** 1 f. 60 multicoloured . . 2·50 1·90

1984. Our Lady of Laghet Sanctuary.
1657 **478** 2 f. blue, brown and green 90 40

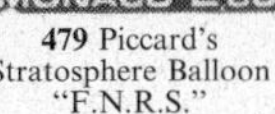
479 Piccard's Stratosphere Balloon "F.N.R.S."

480 Concert

1984. Birth Centenary of Auguste Piccard (physicist).
1658 **479** 2 f. 80 black, green & bl 90 55
1659 – 4 f. blue, green & turq 1·40 1·00
DESIGN: 4 f. Bathyscaphe.

1984. 25th Anniv of Palace Concerts.
1660 **480** 3 f. 60 blue and deep blue 1·40 1·00

481 Place de la Visitation
482 Spring

1984. Bygone Monaco (1st series). Paintings by Hubert Clerissi.
1661 **481** 5 c. brown 10 15
1662 – 10 c. red 10 10
1663 – 15 c. violet 10 10
1664 – 20 c. blue 10 10
1665 – 30 c. blue 15 10
1666 – 40 c. green 75 10
1667 – 50 c. red 20 10
1668 – 60 c. blue 10 10
1669 – 70 c. orange . . . . . . 1·25 35
1670 – 80 c. green 20 10
1671 – 90 c. mauve 25 20
1672 – 1 f. blue 30 15
1673 – 2 f. black 85 50
1674 – 3 f. red . . . . 2·50 1·00
1675 – 4 f. blue . . . . 1·75 80
1676 – 5 f. green . . . . 1·10 65
1677 – 6 f. green . . . . 1·50 1·25
DESIGNS: 10 c. Town Hall; 15 c. Rue Basse; 20 c. Place Saint-Nicolas; 30 c. Quai du Commerce; 40 c. Rue des Iris; 50 c. Ships in harbour; 60 c. St. Charles's Church; 70 c. Religious procession; 80 c. Olive tree overlooking harbour; 90 c. Quayside; 1 f. Palace Square; 2 f. Fishing boats in harbour; 3 f. Bandstand; 4 f. Railway station; 5 f. Mail coach; 6 f. Monte Carlo Opera House.
See also Nos. 2015/27.

1984. Precancels. The Seasons of the Quince.
1678 **482** 1 f. 14 red and green . . 75 30
1679 – 1 f. 47 dp green & green 85 40
1680 – 2 f. 38 olive, turquoise & green . . . . 1·50 1·00
1681 – 3 f. 95 green . . . . . . 2·10 1·60
DESIGNS: 1 f. 47, Summer; 2 f. 38, Autumn; 3 f. 95, Winter.

483 Shepherd
485 Bowl of Mixed Flowers

484 Gargantua and Cattle

1984. Christmas. Crib Figures from Provence. Multicoloured.
1682 70 c. Type **483** 25 15
1683 1 f. Blind man 35 50
1684 1 f. 70 Happy man . . . . . 1·10 1·00
1685 2 f. Spinner . . . . 1·25 1·10
1686 2 f. 10 Angel playing trumpet 1·40 1·25
1687 2 f. 40 Garlic seller . . . . . 1·60 1·50
1688 3 f. Drummer . . . . 1·90 1·60
1689 3 f. 70 Knife grinder . . . . 2·25 2·00
1690 4 f. Elderly couple . . . . . 2·75 2·50

1984. 450th Anniv of First Edition of "Gargantua" by Francois Rabelais.
1691 **484** 2 f. black, red and brown 1·00 40
1692 – 2 f. black, red and blue 1·10 40
1693 – 4 f. green . . . . 2·25 1·25
DESIGNS:—As T **484**: No. 1692, Panurge's sheep. 36×48 mm: 1693, Francois Rabelais.

1984. Monte Carlo Flower Show (1985). Mult.
1694 2 f. 10 Type **485** . . . . . . 1·50 1·00
1695 3 f. Ikebana arrangement . . 2·25 1·50

486 Television Lights and Emblem

1984. 25th International Television Festival, Monte Carlo.
1696 **486** 2 f. 10 blue, grey and mauve 1·00 40
1697 – 3 f. grey, blue and red . . 1·25 65
DESIGN: 3 f. "Golden Nymph" (Grand Prix).

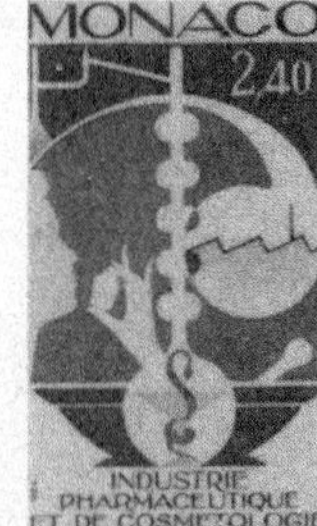
487 Chemical Equipment

1984. Pharmaceutical and Cosmetics Industry.
1698 **487** 2 f. 40 blue, deep blue and green 75 35

1984. Monaco Red Cross. The Twelve Labours of Hercules (4th series). As T **422**.
1699 3 f. + 50 c. brown, light brown and red . . . . 1·40 1·40
1700 4 f. + 50 c. green, brown and red . . . . 1·75 1·75
DESIGNS: 3 f. Killing the Cretan bull; 4 f. Capturing the Mares of Diomedes.

1984. Monaco in the "Belle Epoque" (3rd series). Paintings by Hubert Clerissi. As T **445**. Mult.
1701 4 f. "Grimaldi Street, 1908" (vert) . . . . 3·25 2·50
1702 5 f. "Railway Station, 1910" (vert) . . . . 5·25 3·75

489 "Woman with Chinese Vase"

1984. 150th Birth Anniv of Edgar Degas (artist).
1704 **489** 6 f. multicoloured . . . 5·00 3·00

490 Spring

1985. Precancels. Seasons of the Cherry.
1705 **490** 1 f. 22 olive, green and blue 75 30
1706 – 1 f. 57 red, green and yellow 85 40
1707 – 2 f. 55 orange and brown 1·50 1·00
1708 – 4 f. 23 purple, green and blue . . . . 2·25 1·90
DESIGNS: 1 f. 57, Summer; 2 f. 55, Autumn; 4 f. 23, Winter.

491 First Stamp

1985. Centenary of First Monaco Stamps.
1709 **491** 1 f. 70 green 65 30
1710 2 f. 10 red 80 10
1711 3 f. blue . . . . 1·40 85

493 "Berardia subacaulis"

495 Nadia Boulanger (composer)

1985. Flowers in Mercantour National Park. Mult.
1724 1 f. 70 Type **493** 65 75
1725 2 f. 10 "Saxifraga florulenta" (vert) . . . . 1·00 85
1726 2 f. 40 "Fritillaria moggridgei" (vert) . . . . 1·25 1·00
1727 3 f. "Sempervivum allionii" (vert) . . . . 1·60 1·25
1728 3 f. 60 "Silene cordifolia" (vert) 2·50 1·60
1729 4 f. "Primula allionii" . . . . 2·75 2·00

1985. 25th Anniv of First Musical Composition Competition.
1731 **495** 1 f. 70 brown . . . . . 1·00 60
1732 – 2 f. 10 blue . . . . . . 1·25 85
DESIGN: 2 f. 10, Georges Auric (composer).

496 Stadium and Runners

1985. Inauguration of Louis II Stadium, Fontvieille, and Athletics and Swimming Championships.
1733 **496** 1 f. 70 brown, red and violet 55 40
1734 – 2 f. 10 blue, brown and green . . . . 1·00 40
DESIGN: 2 f. 10, Stadium and swimmers.

497 Prince Antoine I

1985. Europa.
1735 **497** 2 f. 10 blue 65 30
1736 – 3 f. red . . . . 1·25 85
DESIGN: 3 f. John-Baptiste Lully (composer).

498 Museum, "Hirondelle" (schooner) and "Denise" (midget submarine)

1985. 75th Anniv of Oceanographic Museum.
1738 **498** 2 f. 10 black, green and blue 1·10 75

499 Boxer

1985. International Dog Show, Monte Carlo.
1739 **499** 2 f. 10 multicoloured . . 2·50 1·90

500 Scientific Motifs

1985. 25th Anniv of Scientific Centre.
1740 **500** 3 f. blue, black and violet 1·00 55

501 Children and Hands holding Seedling and Emblem

502 Regal Angelfish

1985. International Youth Year.
1741 **501** 3 f. brown, green and light brown . . . . 1·25 55

1985. Fishes in Oceanographic Museum Aquarium (1st series). Multicoloured.
1742 1 f. 80 Type **502** . . . . . . 1·50 1·25
1743 1 f. 90 Type **502** . . . . . . 2·25 1·00
1744 2 f. 20 Powder blue tang surgeonfish . . . . . . 1·50 1·00
1745 3 f. 20 "Chaetodon collare" 2·00 1·90
1746 3 f. 40 As No. 1745 . . . . 4·00 2·50
1747 3 f. 90 Spotted triggerfish . . 2·50 2·10
1748 7 f. Fishes in aquarium (36 × 48 mm) . . . . 5·00 3·75
See also Nos. 1857/62.

504 Rome Buildings and Emblem

1985. "Italia '85" International Stamp Exhibition, Rome.
1750 **504** 4 f. black, green and red 1·75 1·10

505 Clown

506 Decorations

1985. 11th International Circus Festival, Monaco.
1751 **505** 1 f. 80 multicoloured . . 1·50 1·10

1985. Christmas.
1752 **506** 2 f. 20 multicoloured . . 1·25 40

507 Ship and Marine Life

508 Arrangement of Roses, Tulips and Jonquil

1985. Fish Processing Industry.
1753 **507** 2 f. 20 blue, turquoise and brown . . . . 1·00 40

1985. Monte Carlo Flower Show (1986). Mult.
1754 2 f. 20 Type **508** . . . . . . 1·50 1·25
1755 3 f. 20 Arrangement of chrysanthemums and heather 2·25 1·90

509 Globe and Satellite

1985. European Telecommunications Satellite Organization.
1756 **509** 3 f. black, blue and violet 1·50 1·00

510 Sacha Guitry (actor, centenary)

1985. Birth Anniversaries.
1757 **510** 3 f. orange and brown 1·40 1·00
1758 – 4 f. blue, brown and mauve 1·75 1·25
1759 – 5 f. turquoise, blue and grey 2·25 1·75
1760 – 6 f. blue, brown and black 2·75 2·25
DESIGNS: 4 f. Wilhelm and Jacob Grimm (folklorists, bicentenaries); 5 f. Frederic Chopin and Robert Schumann (composers, 175th annivs); 6 f. Johann Sebastian Bach and Georg Friedrich Handel (composers, 300th annivs).

1985. Monaco Red Cross. The Twelve Labours of Hercules (5th series). As T **422**.
1761 3 f. + 70 c. green, deep red and red . . . . 1·40 1·40
1762 4 f. + 80 c. brown, bl & red 1·75 1·75
DESIGNS: 3 f. The Cattle of Geryon; 4 f. The Girdle of Hippolyte.

1985. Monaco in the "Belle Epoque" (4th series). As T **445**, showing paintings by Hubert Clerissi. Multicoloured.
1763 4 f. "Port of Monaco, 1912" . 3·00 1·90
1764 6 f. "Avenue de la Gare 1920" 3·75 3·00

512 Spring

1986. Precancels. Seasons of the Hazel Tree.
1766 **512** 1 f. 28 brown, green & bl 75 30
1767 – 1 f. 65 green, brn & yell 85 40
1768 – 2 f. 67 grey, brown and deep brown . . . . 1·50 1·00
1769 – 4 f. 44 green and brown 2·25 1·90
DESIGNS: 1 f. 65, Summer; 2 f. 67, Autumn; 4 f. 44, Winter.

513 Ancient Monaco

1986. 10th Anniv of "Annales Monegasques" (historical review).
1770 **513** 2 f. 20 grey, blue and brown 1·10 35

514 Scotch Terriers

1986. International Dog Show, Monte Carlo.
1771 **514** 1 f. 80 multicoloured . . 4·25 3·00

515 Mouflon **516** Research Vessel "Ramoge"

1986. Mammals in Mercantour National Park. Multicoloured.
1772 2 f. 20 Type **515** . . . . . . 1·10 60
1773 2 f. 50 Ibex . . . . 1·40 1·00
1774 3 f. 20 Chamois . . . . 1·90 1·60
1775 3 f. 90 Alpine marmot (vert) . 2·75 2·00
1776 5 f. Arctic hare (vert) . . . . 3·50 2·75
1777 7 f. 20 Stoat (vert) . . . . . 4·25 3·25

1986. Europa. Each green, blue and red.
1778 2 f. 20 Type **516** 80 40
1779 3 f. 20 Underwater nature reserve, Larvotto beach . . 1·25 90

517 Prince Albert I and National Council Building

1986. Anniversaries and Events.
1781 **517** 2 f. 50 brown and green . . 1·25 85
1782 – 3 f. 20 brown, red and black 2·50 2·25
1783 – 3 f. 90 purple and red . . . 3·00 2·50
1784 – 5 f. green, red and blue . . 1·75 1·25
DESIGNS—HORIZ: 2 f. 50, Type **517** (75th anniv of First Constitution); 3 f. 20, Serge Diaghilev and dancers (creation of new Monte Carlo ballet company); 3 f. 90, Henri Rougier and Turcat-Mery car (75th Anniv of first Monte Carlo Rally). VERT: 5 f. Flags and Statue of Liberty (centenary).

518 Chicago and Flags

1986. "Ameripex '86" International Stamp Exhibition, Chicago.
1785 **518** 5 f. black, red and blue 1·75 1·00

520 Comet, Telescopes and 1532 Chart by Apian

1986. Appearance of Halley's Comet.
1787 **520** 10 f. blue, brown & green 4·25 3·00

521 Monte Carlo and Congress Centre

1986. 30th International Insurance Congress.
1788 **521** 3 f. 20 blue, brown & grn 1·75 1·10

522 Christmas Tree Branch and Holly

523 Clown's Face and Elephant on Ball

1986. Christmas. Multicoloured.
1789 1 f. 80 Type **522** 65 25
1790 2 f. 50 Christmas tree branch and poinsettia 90 35

1986. 12th International Circus Festival, Monaco.
1791 **523** 2 f. 20 multicoloured . . 1·75 1·00

524 Posy of Roses and Acidanthera

525 Making Plastic Mouldings for Car Bodies

1986. Monte Carlo Flower Show (1987). Mult.
1792 2 f. 20 Type **524** . . . . . . 1·50 75
1793 3 f. 90 Lilies and beech in vase 2·50 1·75

1986. Monaco Red Cross. The Twelve Labours of Hercules (6th series). As T **422**.
1794 3 f. + 70 c. green, yell & red 1·50 1·50
1795 4 f. + 80 c. blue, brn & red . 1·90 1·90
DESIGNS: 3 f. The Golden Apples of the Hesperides; 4 f. Capturing Cerberus.

1986. Plastics Industry.
1796 **525** 3 f. 90 turquoise, red and grey . . . . 1·40 55

526 Scenes from "Le Cid" (Pierre Corneille)

1986. Anniversaries.
1797 **526** 4 f. dp brown and brown 1·40 90
1798 – 5 f. brown and blue . . 1·75 1·40
DESIGNS: 4 f. Type **526** (350th anniv of first performance); 5 f. Franz Liszt (composer) and bible (175th birth anniv).

527 Horace de Saussure, Mont Blanc and Climbers

1986. Bicentenary of First Ascent of Mont Blanc by Dr. Paccard and Jacques Balmat.
1799 **527** 5 f. 80 blue, red & black . . . 2·25 1·75

528 "The Olympic Diver" (Emma de Sigaldi)

1986. 25th Anniv of Unveiling of "The Olympic Diver" (statue).
1800 **528** 6 f. multicoloured . . . . 2·25 1·40

1986. Monaco in the "Belle Epoque" (5th series). Paintings by Hubert Clerissi. As T **445**. Mult.
1801 6 f. "Bandstand and Casino, 1920" (vert) . . . . 3·75 2·50
1802 7 f. "Avenue du Beau Rivage, 1925" (vert) . . . . 5·50 35

530 Spring

1987. Precancels. Seasons of the Chestnut.
1804 **530** 1 f. 31 green, yell & brn . . 75 30
1805 – 1 f. 69 green and brown . . 1·00 75
1806 – 2 f. 74 brown, yell & bl . . 1·60 1·25
1807 – 4 f. 56 brown, grn & grey . 2·25 1·90
DESIGNS: 1 f. 69, Summer; 2 f. 74, Autumn; 4 f. 56, Winter.

531 Golden Hunter

1987. Insects in Mercantour National Park. Multicoloured.
1808 1 f. Type **531** 40 50
1809 1 f. 90 Golden wasp (vert) . . 1·00 75
1810 2 f. Green tiger beetle . . . . 1·25 1·00
1811 2 f. 20 Brown aeshna (vert) . . 1·60 8·50
1812 3 f. Leaf beetle . . . . 2·50 1·60
1813 3 f. 40 Grasshopper (vert) . . 3·00 2·10

532 St. Devote Church 533 Dogs

1987. Centenary of St. Devote Parish Church.
1814 **532** 1 f. 90 brown 85 25

1987. International Dog Show, Monte Carlo.
1815 **533** 1 f. 90 grey, black & brn . . 1·90 1·25
1816 – 2 f. 70 black and green . . 3·00 1·90
DESIGN: 2 f. 70, Poodle.

534 Stamp Album

1987. Stamp Day.
1817 **534** 2 f. 20 red, purple and mauve . . . . 1·00 50

535 Louis II Stadium, Fontvieille 536 Cathedral

1987. Europa. Each blue, green and red.
1818 2 f. 20 Type **535** . . . . . . 1·00 30
1819 3 f. 40 Crown Prince Albert Olympic swimming pool . 1·50 85

1987. Centenary of Monaco Diocese.
1821 **536** 2 f. 50 green 80 30

538 Lawn Tennis

1987. 2nd European Small States Games, Monaco.
1823 **538** 3 f. black, red and purple . 2·25 1·75
1824 – 5 f. blue and black . . . 2·75 2·00
DESIGN: 5 f. Sailing dinghies and windsurfer.

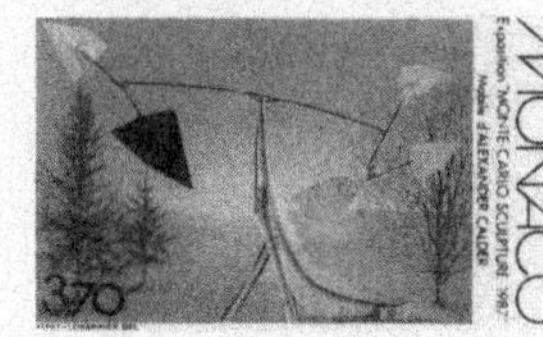

539 "Red Curly Tail" (Alexander Calder)

1987. "Monte Carlo Sculpture 1987" Exhibition.
1825 **539** 3 f. 70 multicoloured . . 2·00 1·25

540 Prince Rainier III 541 Swallowtail on Stamp

1987. 50th Anniv of Monaco Stamp Issuing Office.
1826 **540** 4 f. blue . . . . 1·40 1·40
1827 – 4 f. red . . . . 1·40 1·40
1828 – 8 f. black . . . . 3·25 3·25
DESIGNS: No. 1827, Prince Louis II. (47 × 37 mm): 1829, Villa Miraflores.

1987. International Stamp Exhibition.
1829 **541** 1 f. 90 deep green and green 55 25
1830 2 f. 20 purple and red . 65 45
1831 2 f. 50 purple and mauve . 90 60
1832 3 f. 40 deep blue and blue 1·60 90

542 Festival Poster (J. Ramel) 543 Christmas Scenes

1987. 13th International Circus Festival, Monaco (1988).
1833 **542** 2 f. 20 multicoloured . . 2·00 1·00

1987. Christmas.
1834 **543** 2 f. 20 red 85 20

544 Strawberry Plants and Campanulas in Bowl 545 Obverse and Reverse of Honore V 5 f. Silver Coin

1987. Monte Carlo Flower Show (1988). Mult.
1835 2 f. 20 Type **544** . . . . . . 1·25 60
1836 3 f. 40 Ikebana arrangement of water lilies and dog roses (horiz) . . . . 1·90 1·25

1987. 150th Anniv of Revival of Monaco Coinage.
1837 **545** 2 f. 50 black and red . . . 1·10 40

546 Graph, Factory, Electron Microscope and Printed Circuit

1987. Electro-Mechanical Industry.
1838 **546** 2 f. 50 blue, green and red 1·00 40

547 St. Devote

1987. Monaco Red Cross. St. Devote, Patron Saint of Monaco (1st series). Multicoloured.
1839 4 f. Type **547** . . . . 1·40 65
1840 5 f. St. Devote and her nurse 1·75 1·25
See also Nos. 1898/9, 1956/7, 1980/1, 2062/3 and 2101/2.

548 Oceanographic Museum and I.A.E.A. Headquarters, Vienna

1987. 25th Anniv of International Marine Radioactivity Laboratory, Monaco.
1842 **548** 5 f. black, brown and blue 2·10 1·40

549 Jouvet

1987. Birth Centenary of Louis Jouvet (actor).
1843 **549** 3 f. black . . . . 1·10 65

550 River Crossing

1987. Bicentenary of First Edition of "Paul and Virginia" by Bernardin de Saint-Pierre.
1844 **550** 3 f. green, orange and blue 1·25 65

551 Marc Chagall (painter)

1987. Anniversaries.
1845 **551** 4 f. black and red . . . . 1·75 1·00
1846 – 4 f. purple, red and brown 1·75 1·00
1847 – 4 f. red, blue and brown . 1·75 1·00
1848 – 4 f. green, brown & pur . 1·75 1·00
1849 – 5 f. blue, brown and green 2·25 1·25
1850 – 5 f. brown, green and blue 2·25 1·25
DESIGNS: No. 1845, Type **551** (birth centenary); 1846, Chapel of Ronchamp and Charles Edouard Jeanneret (Le Corbusier) (architect, birth centenary); 1847, Sir Isaac Newton (mathematician) and diagram (300th anniv of publication of "Principia Mathematica"); 1848, Key and Samuel Morse (inventor, 150th Anniv of Morse telegraph); 1849, Wolfgang Amadeus Mozart and scene from "Don Juan" (opera, bicentenary of composition); 1850, Hector Berlioz (composer) and scene from "Mass for the Dead" (150th anniv of composition).

1987. Monaco in the "Belle Epoque" (6th series). As T **445** showing paintings by Hubert Clerissi. Multicoloured.
1851 6 f. "Main Ramp to Palace Square, 1925" (vert) . . . 3·75 2·50
1852 7 f. "Monte Carlo Railway Station, 1925" (vert) . . . 5·00 3·75

552 Coat of Arms 553 Spanish Hogfish

1987.
1853 **552** 2 f. multicoloured . . 85 30
1854 2 f. 20 multicoloured . . 65 60

1988. Fishes in Oceanographic Museum Aquarium (2nd series). Multicoloured.
1857 2 f. Type **553** . . . . 1·25 75
1858 2 f. 20 Longnose butterfly fish ("Chelmon rostratus") . . 1·75 30
1859 2 f. 50 Harlequin filefish ("Oxymonacanthus longirostrus") . . . . . 2·00 1·10
1860 3 f. Blue trunkfish . . . . . 1·40 75
1861 3 f. 70 Lionfish . . . . . . 2·75 2·10
1862 7 f. Moon wrasse (horiz) . . 3·25 2·25

554 Spring 556 Dachshunds

1988. Precancels. Seasons of the Pear Tree. Multicoloured.
1863 1 f. 36 Type **554** 75 30
1864 1 f. 75 Summer . . . . . . 1·00 75
1865 2 f. 83 Autumn . . . . . . 1·60 1·25
1866 4 f. 72 Winter . . . . 2·25 1·90
See also Nos. 1952/5.

1988. European Dachshunds Show, Monte Carlo.
1868 **556** 3 f. multicoloured . . . 2·50 1·90

557 Children of different Races around Globe 558 Satellite Camera above Man with World as Brain

1988. 25th Anniv of World Association of Friends of Children.
1869 **557** 5 f. green, brown & blue 2·50 1·90

1988. Europa. Transport and Communications. Each black, brown and red.
1870 2 f. 20 Type **558** . . . . . . 1·25 75
1871 3 f. 60 High-speed mail train and aircraft propeller . . . 2·25 1·75

559 Coxless Four

1988. Centenary of Monaco Nautical Society (formerly Regatta Society).
1873 **559** 2 f. blue, green and red . 1·00 60

560 Jean Monnet (statesman) 561 "Leccinum rotundifoliae"

1988. Birth Centenaries.
1874 **560** 2 f. black, brown & blue 2·50 1·60
1875 – 2 f. black and blue . . 2·50 1·60
DESIGN: No. 1875, Maurice Chevalier (entertainer).

1988. Fungi in Mercantour National Park. Multicoloured.
1876 2 f. Type **561** 70 30
1877 2 f. 20 Crimson wax cap . . 80 30
1878 2 f. 50 "Pholiota flammans" . 95 55
1879 2 f. 70 "Lactarius lignyotus" . 1·10 75
1880 3 f. Goaty smell (vert) . . . 1·25 75
1881 7 f. "Russula olivacea" (vert) 3·00 1·75

562 Nansen

563 Church and "Miraculous Virgin"

1988. Centenary of First Crossing of Greenland by Fridtjof Nansen (Norwegian explorer).
1882 **562** 4 f. violet . . . . 2·50 1·90

1988. Restoration of Sanctuary of Our Lady of Laghet.
1883 **563** 5 f. multicoloured . . . . 2·10 1·50

564 Anniversary Emblem

1988. 40th Anniv of W.H.O.
1884 **564** 6 f. red and blue . . . . 2·50 1·50

565 Anniversary Emblem

1988. 125th Anniv of Red Cross.
1885 **565** 6 f. red, grey and black . 2·50 1·50

566 Congress Centre

1988. 10th Anniv of Monte Carlo Congress Centre.
1886 **566** 2 f. green . . . . 1·00 1·00
1887 – 3 f. red . . . . 1·25 1·25
DESIGN: 3 f. Auditorium.

1988. Monaco in the "Belle Epoque" (7th series). Paintings by Hubert Clerissi. As T **445**. Mult.
1889 6 f. "Steam packet in Monte Carlo Harbour, 1910" . . 3·75 2·50
1890 7 f. "Place de la Gare, 1910" 4·25 3·00

568 Festival Poster (J. Ramel)

NOËL 88
MONACO 2,00
569 Star Decoration

1988. 14th International Circus Festival, Monaco (1989).
1891 **568** 2 f. multicoloured . . . . 1·50 85

1988. Christmas.
1892 **569** 2 f. multicoloured . . . . 1·10 60

570 Arrangement of Fuchsias, Irises, Roses and Petunias

571 Models

1988. Monte Carlo Flower Show (1989).
1893 **570** 3 f. multicoloured . . . 2·00 1·25

1988. Ready-to-Wear Clothing Industry.
1894 **571** 3 f. green, orange & black 1·25 85

572 Lord Byron (bicentenary)

574 "Le Nain and his Brothers" (Antoine Le Nain)

1988. Writers' Birth Anniversaries.
1895 **572** 3 f. black, brown and blue 1·50 85
1896 – 3 f. purple and blue . . 1·50 90
DESIGN: No. 1896, Pierre de Marivaux (300th anniv).

1988. Monaco Red Cross. St. Devote, Patron Saint of Monaco (2nd series). As T **547**. Multicoloured.
1898 4 f. Roman governor Barbarus arriving at Corsica . . . . 1·90 1·00
1899 5 f. St. Devote at the Roman senator Eutychius's house 2·50 1·50

1988. Artists' Birth Anniversaries.
1900 **574** 5 f. brown olive and red 2·75 1·90
1901 – 5 f. black, green and blue 2·75 1·90
DESIGNS: No. 1912, Type **574** (400th anniv): 1913, "The Great Archaeologists" (bronze statue, Giorgio de Chirico) (centenary).

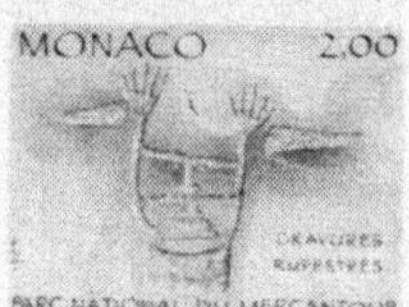

575 Sorcerer

1989. Rock Carvings in Mercantour National Park. Multicoloured.
1902 2 f. Type **575** 85 75
1903 2 f. 20 Oxen in yoke . . . . 1·00 75
1904 3 f. Hunting implements . . 1·40 1·25
1905 3 f. 60 Tribal chief . . . . 2·10 1·60
1906 4 f. Puppet (vert) . . . . 2·50 1·75
1907 5 f. Jesus Christ (vert) . . . 2·75 2·00

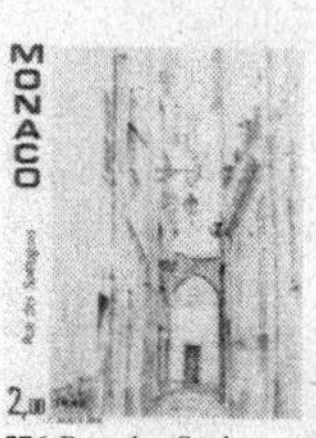

576 Rue des Spelugues

577 Prince Rainier

1989. Old Monaco (1st series). Multicoloured.
1908 2 f. Type **576** 90 40
1909 2 f. 20 Place Saint Nicolas . 1·00 45
See also Nos. 1969/70 and 2090/1.

1989.
1910 **577** 2 f. blue and azure . . . 1·10 10
1911 2 f. 10 blue and azure . 1·25 10
1912 2 f. 20 brown and pink . 1·40 10
1913 2 f. 20 blue and azure . 1·00 10
1914 2 f. 30 brown and pink . 1·25 10
1915 2 f. 40 blue and azure . 85 10
1916 2 f. 50 brown and pink . 1·00 10
1917 2 f. 70 blue 65 40
1918 2 f. 80 brown and pink . 1·00 10
1919 3 f. brown and pink . . 75 45
1920 3 f. 20 blue and cobalt . 1·50 1·00
1922 3 f. 40 blue and cobalt . 2·00 1·10
1923 3 f. 60 blue and cobalt . 2·50 1·25
1924 3 f. 70 blue and cobalt . 1·25 85
1925 3 f. 80 purple and lilac . 2·00 60
1926 3 f. 80 blue and cobalt . 90 55
1927 4 f. purple and lilac . 1·00 50
1930 5 f. brown and pink . . 1·10 40
1932 10 f. dp green and green 2·50 1·00

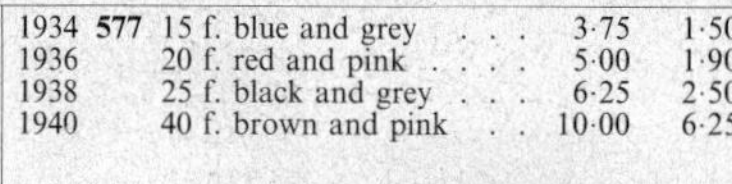
1934 **577** 15 f. blue and grey . . . 3·75 1·50
1936 20 f. red and pink . . . . 5·00 1·90
1938 25 f. black and grey . . . 6·25 2·50
1940 40 f. brown and pink . . 10·00 6·25

578 Yorkshire Terrier

1989. International Dog Show, Monte Carlo.
1941 **578** 2 f. 20 multicoloured . . 1·25 55

579 Magician, Dove and Cards

1989. 5th Grand Prix of Magic, Monte Carlo.
1942 **579** 2 f. 20 black, blue & red . 1·50 75

580 Nuns and Monks around "Our Lady of Misericorde"

1989. 350th Anniv of Archiconfrerie de la Misericorde.
1943 **580** 3 f. brown, black and red 1·10 75

581 Charlie Chaplin (actor) and Film Scenes

1989. Birth Centenaries.
1944 – 3 f. green, blue & mauve 1·50 1·10
1945 **581** 4 f. purple, green and red 2·25 1·75
DESIGN: 3 f. Jean Cocteau (writer and painter), scene from "The Double-headed Eagle" and frescoes in Villefrance-sur-Mer chapel.

583 Boys playing Marbles

586 "Artist's Mother" (Philibert Florence)

1989. Europa. Children's Games. Each mauve, brown and grey.
1947 2 f. 20 Type **583** . . . . . 1·00 60
1948 3 f. 60 Girls skipping . . . . 1·50 1·10

1989. Precancels. As Nos. 1863/6 but values changed. Multicoloured.
1952 1 f. 39 Type **554** 75 50
1953 1 f. 79 Summer . . . . . . 1·00 75
1954 2 f. 90 Autumn . . . . . . 1·60 1·25
1955 4 f. 84 Winter . . . . . . 2·25 1·90

1989. Monaco Red Cross. St. Devote, Patron Saint of Monaco (3rd series). As T **547**. Multicoloured.
1956 4 f. St. Devote beside the dying Eutychius . . . . 1·90 1·25
1957 5 f. Barbarus condemns St. Devote to torture for refusing to make a sacrifice to the gods 2·50 1·50

1989. Artists' 150th Birth Anniversaries.
1958 **586** 4 f. brown . . . . 2·25 1·60
1959 – 6 f. multicoloured . . . 3·25 2·10
1960 – 8 f. multicoloured . . . 4·25 3·00
DESIGNS—HORIZ: 6 f. "Molesey Regatta" (Alfred Sisley). VERT: 8 f. "Farmyard at Auvers" (Paul Cezanne).

587 Poinsettia, Christmas Roses and Holly

1989. Christmas.
1961 **587** 2 f. multicoloured . . . 2·50 75

588 Map and Emblem

1989. Centenary of Interparliamentary Union.
1962 **588** 4 f. black, green and red 1·90 1·00

590 Monaco Palace, White House, Washington, and Emblem

1989. 20th U.P.U. Congress, Washington D.C.
1964 **590** 6 f. blue, brown and black 2·50 1·75

1989. Monaco in the "Belle Epoque" (8th series). Paintings by Hubert Clerissi. As T **445**. Mult.
1965 7 f. "Barque in Monte Carlo Harbour, 1915" (vert) . . 3·75 2·50
1966 8 f. "Gaming Tables, Casino, 1915" (vert) . . . . . . 4·25 3·00

591 World Map

592 Clown and Horses

1989. 10th Anniv of Monaco Aide et Presence (welfare organization).
1967 **591** 2 f. 20 brown and red . 1·75 85

1989. 15th International Circus Festival, Monte Carlo.
1968 **592** 2 f. 20 multicoloured . . 2·50 1·00

1990. Old Monaco (2nd series). Paintings by Claude Rosticher. As T **576**. Multicoloured.
1969 2 f. 10 La Rampe Major . . 75 40
1970 2 f. 30 Town Hall Courtyard 90 45

593 Phalaenopsis "Princess Grace"

594 Bearded Collie

1990. International Garden and Greenery Exposition, Osaka, Japan. Multicoloured.
1971 2 f. Type **593** 55 60
1972 3 f. Iris "Grace Patricia" . . 1·25 85
1973 3 f. "Paphiopedilum" "Prince Rainier III" . . . . . . 1·25 75
1974 4 f. "Cattleya" "Principessa Grace" . . . . 1·50 1·00
1975 5 f. Rose "Caroline of Monaco" 2·75 1·75

1990. International Dog Show, Monte Carlo.
1976 **594** 2 f. 30 multicoloured . . 1·60 1·10

595 Noghes and Racing Car

1990. Birth Centenary of Antony Noghes (founder of Monaco Grand Prix and Monte Carlo Rally).
1977 **595** 3 f. red, lilac and black . 1·50 1·00

596 Cyclist and Lancia Rally Car

1990. Centenary of Automobile Club of Monaco (founded as Cycling Racing Club).
1978 **596** 4 f. blue, brown & purple 2·25 1·75

597 Telephone, Satellite and Dish Aerial

1990. 125th Anniv of I.T.U.
1979 **597** 4 f. lilac, mauve and blue 1·90 1·25

1990. Monaco Red Cross. St. Devote, Patron Saint of Monaco (4th series). As T **547**. Multicoloured.
1980 4 f. St. Devote being flogged 1·90 1·25
1981 5 f. Placing body of St. Devote in fishing boat . . . . . . 2·50 1·75

598 Sir Rowland Hill and Penny Black

1990. 150th Anniv of Penny Black.
1982 **598** 5 f. blue and black . . . 3·00 2·00

599 "Post Office, Place de la Mairie"

601 Anatase

1990. Europa. Post Office Buildings. Paintings by Hubert Clerissi. Multicoloured.
1983 2 f. 30 Type **599** . . . . . . 1·00 30
1984 3 f. 70 "Post Office, Avenue d'Ostende" . . . . 1·50 85

1990. Minerals in Mercantour National Park. Mult.
1987 2 f. 10 Type **601** 85 50
1988 2 f. 30 Albite . . . . 1·00 50
1989 3 f. 20 Rutile . . . . 1·40 1·10
1990 3 f. 80 Chlorite . . . . 2·00 1·25
1991 4 f. Brookite (vert) . . . . . 2·50 1·90
1992 6 f. Quartz (vert) . . . . . . 3·50 2·75

602 Powerboat

603 Pierrot writing (mechanical toy)

1990. World Offshore Powerboat Racing Championship.
1993 **602** 2 f. 30 brown, red & blue 1·25 75

1990. Philatelic Round Table.
1994 **603** 3 f. blue . . . . 1·60 75

604 Christian Samuel Hahnemann (founding of homeopathy)

1990. Bicentenaries.
1995 **604** 3 f. purple, green & black 1·40 85
1996 – 5 f. chestnut, brown & bl 2·00 1·40
DESIGN: 5 f. Jean-Francois Champollion (Egyptologist) and hieroglyphics (birth bicentenary).

605 Monaco Heliport, Fontvieille

606 Petanque Player

1990. 30th International Civil Airports Association Congress, Monte Carlo.
1997 **605** 3 f. black, red and brown 1·25 60
1998 – 5 f. black, blue & brown 2·10 1·25
DESIGN: 5 f. Aerospatiale Ecureuil helicopters over Monte Carlo Congress Centre.

1990. 26th World Petanque Championship.
1999 **606** 6 f. blue, brown & orange 2·75 1·60

607 Spring

608 Miller on Donkey

1990. Precancels. Seasons of the Plum Tree. Multicoloured.
2000 1 f. 46 Type **607** 75 50
2001 1 f. 89 Summer . . . . . . 1·00 75
2002 3 f. 06 Autumn . . . . . . 1·60 1·25
2003 5 f. 10 Winter . . . . 2·25 1·90

1990. Christmas. Crib figures from Provence. Multicoloured.
2004 2 f. 30 Type **608** . . . . . . 1·10 50
2005 3 f. 20 Woman carrying faggots 1·40 75
2006 3 f. 80 Baker . . . . 1·90 1·00
See also Nos. 2052/4, 2097/9, 2146/8 and 2191/3.

610 Pyotr Ilich Tchaikovsky (composer)

611 Clown playing Concertina

1990. 150th Birth Anniversaries.
2008 **610** 5 f. blue and green . . . 2·00 1·25
2009 – 5 f. bistre and blue . . . 2·00 1·25
2010 – 7 f. multicoloured . . . 5·25 3·75
DESIGNS:—As T **610**: No. 2009, "Cathedral" (Auguste Rodin, sculptor). 48 × 37 mm: "The Magpie" (Claude Monet, painter).

1991. 16th International Circus Festival, Monte Carlo.
2011 **611** 2 f. 30 multicoloured . . 1·40 75
See also No. 2069.

1991. Bygone Monaco (2nd series). Paintings by Hubert Clerissi. As T **481**.
2015 20 c. purple 10 10
2017 40 c. green 10 10
2018 50 c. red 10 10
2019 60 c. blue 15 10
2020 70 c. green 15 10
2021 80 c. blue 20 15
2022 90 c. lilac 30 15
2023 1 f. blue 30 15
2024 2 f. red 75 30
2025 3 f. black 75 35
2027 7 f. grey and black . . . . . 1·75 1·10
DESIGNS: 20 c. Rock of Monaco and Fontvieille; 40 c. Place du Casino; 50 c. Place de la Cremaillere and railway station; 60 c. National Council building; 70 c. Palace and Rampe Major; 80 c. Avenue du Beau Rivage; 90 c. Fishing boats, Fontvieille; 1 f. Place d'Armes; 2 f. Marche de la Condamine; 3 f. Yacht; 7 f. Oceanographic Museum.

612 Abdim's Stork

613 Phytoplankton

1991. International Symposium on Bird Migration. Multicoloured.
2029 2 f. Type **612** . . . . 1·00 40
2030 3 f. Broad-tailed humming birds 1·25 1·00
2031 4 f. Garganeys . . . . 2·00 1·40
2032 5 f. Eastern broad-billed roller 2·50 2·00
2033 6 f. European bee eaters . . . 3·25 2·50

1991. Oceanographic Museum (1st series).
2034 **613** 2 f. 10 multicoloured . . 1·40 75
See also Nos. 2095/6.

614 Schnauzer

615 Cyclamen, Lily-of-the-Valley and Pine Twig in Fir-cone

1991. International Dog Show, Monte Carlo.
2035 **614** 2 f. 50 multicoloured . . 1·40 1·00

1991. Monte Carlo Flower Show.
2036 **615** 3 f. multicoloured . . . . 1·50 85

616 Corals

617 Control Room, "Eutelsat" Satellite and Globe

1991. "Joys of the Sea" Exhibition. Multicoloured.
2037 2 f. 20 Type **616** . . . . . . 1·25 75
2038 2 f. 40 Coral necklace . . . . 1·25 85

1991. Europa. Europe in Space. Each blue, black and green.
2039 2 f. 30 Type **617** . . . . . . 1·10 30
2040 3 f. 20 Computer terminal, "Inmarsat" satellite, research ship transmitting signal and man with receiving equipment 1·40 60

618 Cross-country Skiers and Statue of Skiers by Emma de Sigaldi

1991. 1992 Olympic Games. (a) Winter Olympics, Albertville.
2042 **618** 3 f. green, blue and olive . 1·50 1·25
2043 – 4 f. green, blue and olive . 2·00 1·60

(b) Olympic Games, Barcelona.
2044 – 3 f. green, lt brown & brown 1·50 1·25
2045 – 5 f. black, brown and green 2·50 2·10
DESIGNS: No. 2043, Right-hand part of statue and cross-country skiers; 2044, Track, relay runners and left part of statue of relay runners by Emma de Sigaldi; 2045, Right part of statue, view of Barcelona and track.

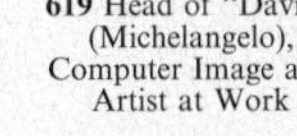
619 Head of "David" (Michelangelo), Computer Image and Artist at Work

620 Prince Pierre, Open Book and Lyre

1991. 25th International Contemporary Art Prize.
2046 **619** 4 f. green, dp green & lilac 1·60 1·10

1991. 25th Anniv of Prince Pierre Foundation.
2047 **620** 5 f. black, blue & brown 2·00 1·50

621 Tortoises

1991. Hermann's Tortoise. Multicoloured.
2048 1 f. 25 Type **621** . . . . . . 1·25 75
2049 1 f. 25 Head of tortoise . . . 1·25 75
2050 1 f. 25 Tortoise in grass . . . 1·25 75
2051 1 f. 25 Tortoise emerging from among plants . . . . . . 1·25 75

1991. Christmas. As T **608** showing crib figures from Provence. Multicoloured.
2052 2 f. 50 Consul . . . . 1·25 50
2053 3 f. 50 Arlesian woman . . . 1·75 1·10
2054 4 f. Mayor . . . . 2·00 1·50

622 Norway Spruce

1991. Conifers in Mercantour National Park. Multicoloured.
2055 2 f. 50 Type **622** . . . . . . 1·00 20
2056 3 f. 50 Silver fir . . . . . . 1·25 75
2057 4 f. "Pinus uncinata" . . . . 1·50 1·00
2058 5 f. Scots pine (vert) . . . . 2·00 1·25
2059 6 f. Arolla pine . . . . . . 2·50 1·60
2060 7 f. European larch (vert) . . 3·00 1·90

1991. Monaco Red Cross. St. Devote, Patron Saint of Monaco (5th series). As T **547**. Multicoloured.
2062 4 f. 50 Fishing boat carrying body caught in storm . . . 1·90 90
2063 5 f. 50 Dove guiding boat-man to port of Monaco . . . . 2·50 1·50

624 "Portrait of Claude Monet"

1991. 150th Birth Anniv of Auguste Renoir (painter).
2064 **624** 5 f. multicoloured . . . 2·50 1·90

625 Prince Honore II of Monaco

1991. 350th Anniv of Treaty of Peronne (giving French recognition of sovereignty of Monaco). Paintings by Philippe de Champaigne. Mult.
2065 6 f. Type **625** . . . . 3·00 2·50
2066 7 f. King Louis XIII of France 3·75 2·50

626 Princess Grace (after R. Samini)

1991. 10th Anniv of Princess Grace Theatre.
2067 **626** 8 f. multicoloured . . . . 4·25 3·75

1992. 16th International Circus Festival, Monte Carlo. As No. 2011 but value and dates changed.
2069 **611** 2 f. 50 multicoloured . . 1·25 85
The 1991 Festival was cancelled.

628 Two-man Bobsleighs

1992. Winter Olympic Games, Albertville (7 f.), and Summer Games, Barcelona (8 f.).
2070 **628** 7 f. blue, turquoise & blk 2·75 1·60
2071 – 8 f. purple, blue and green 3·25 2·10
DESIGN: 8 f. Football.

630 Spring

1992. Precancels. Seasons of the Walnut Tree. Mult.
2073 1 f. 60 Type **630** 85 50
2074 2 f. 08 Summer . . . . 1·00 75
2075 2 f. 98 Autumn . . . . 1·50 1·25
2076 5 f. 28 Winter . . . . 2·25 1·90

631 Golden Labrador

1992. International Dog Show, Monte Carlo.
2077 **631** 2 f. 20 multicoloured . . 1·25 75

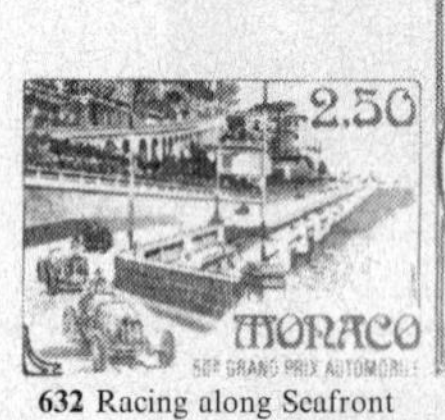

632 Racing along Seafront **633** Mixed Bouquet

1992. 50th Monaco Grand Prix.
2078 **632** 2 f. 50 black, purple & bl 1·10 75

1992. 25th Monte Carlo Flower Show.
2079 **633** 3 f. 40 multicoloured . . 1·50 1·25

634 Ford Sierra Rally Car

1992. 60th Monte Carlo Car Rally.
2080 **634** 4 f. black, green and red 1·90 1·25

636 "Pinta" off Palos

1992. Europa. 500th Anniv of Discovery of America by Columbus. Multicoloured.
2082 2 f. 50 Type **636** . . . . . 1·10 40
2083 3 f. 40 "Santa Maria" in the Antilles . . . . 1·60 1·00
2084 4 f. "Nina" off Lisbon . . . 2·00 1·50

637 Produce

1992. "Ameriflora" Horticultural Show, Columbus, Ohio. Multicoloured.
2086 4 f. Type **637** . . . . 1·90 1·25
2087 5 f. Vase of mixed flowers . 2·50 1·90

638 Prince Rainier I and Fleet (detail of fresco by E. Charpentier, Spinola Palace, Genoa)

1992. Columbus Exhibition, Genoa (6 f.), and "Expo '92" World's Fair, Seville (7 f.).
2088 **638** 6 f. brown, red and blue 2·50 1·60
2089 – 7 f. brown, red and blue 2·75 2·00
DESIGN: 7 f. Monaco pavilion.

1992. Old Monaco (3rd series). Paintings by Claude Rosticher. As T **576**. Multicoloured.
2090 2 f. 20 La Porte Neuve (horiz) 1·00 30
2091 2 f. 50 La Placette Bosio (horiz) 1·00 35

639 "Christopher Columbus"

1992. "Genova '92" International Thematic Stamp Exhibition. Roses. Multicoloured.
2092 3 f. Type **639** . . . . . . 1·40 1·00
2093 4 f. "Prince of Monaco" . . 1·75 1·25

640 Lammergeier

1992.
2094 **640** 2 f. 20 orange, blk & grn 1·00 75

1992. Oceanographic Museum (2nd series). As T **613**. Multicoloured.
2095 2 f. 20 "Ceratium ranipes" . 1·10 75
2096 2 f. 50 "Ceratium hexacanthum" . . . . . . 1·40 35

1992. Christmas. As T **608** showing crib figures from Provence. Multicoloured.
2097 2 f. 50 Basket-maker . . . . 1·25 35
2098 3 f. 40 Fishwife . . . . . . 1·50 45
2099 5 f. Rural constable . . . . 2·25 1·50

641 "Seabus" (tourist submarine)

1992.
2100 **641** 4 f. blue, red and brown 1·50 1·25

642 Burning Boat Ceremony, St. Devote's Eve

1992. Monaco Red Cross. St. Devote, Patron Saint of Monaco (6th series).
2101 **642** 6 f. red, blue and brown . 2·50 1·90
2102 – 8 f. purple, orange & red 3·00 2·50
DESIGN: 8 f. Procession of reliquary, St. Devote's Day.

643 Athletes, Sorbonne University and Coubertin

1992. Centenary of Pierre de Coubertin's Proposal for Revival of Olympic Games.
2103 **643** 10 f. blue . . . . 3·75 2·50

644 Baux de Provence and St. Catherine's Chapel

1992. Titles of Princes of Monaco. Marquis of Baux de Provence.
2104 **644** 15 f. multicoloured . . . 5·50 3·75

646 Clown and Tiger **647** Short-toed Eagles

1993. 17th Int Circus Festival, Monte Carlo.
2106 **646** 2 f. 50 multicoloured . . 1·10 35

1993. Birds of Prey in Mercantour National Park.
2107 **647** 2 f. chestnut, brown and orange 75 30
2108 – 3 f. indigo, orange & blue 1·25 75
2109 – 4 f. brown, ochre & blue 1·60 1·10
2110 – 5 f. brown, chestnut and green . . . . 2·00 1·40
2111 – 6 f. brown, mauve & grn 2·50 2·00
DESIGNS—HORIZ: 3 f. Peregrine falcon. VERT: 4 f. Eagle owl; 5 f. Honey buzzard; 6 f. Tengmalm's owl.

650 Mixed Bouquet **652** Fire Fighting and Rescue

651 Pennants, Auditorium and Masks

1993. Monte Carlo Flower Show.
2114 **650** 3 f. 40 multicoloured . . . 1·40 85

1993. 10th International Amateur Theatre Festival.
2115 **651** 4 f. 20 multicoloured . . . 1·60 60

1993. World Civil Protection Day.
2116 **652** 6 f. black, red and green . 3·00 1·90

653 Newfoundland **654** Golfer

1993. International Dog Show, Monte Carlo.
2117 **653** 2 f. 20 multicoloured . . 1·00 75

1993. 10th Monte Carlo Open Golf Tournament.
2118 **654** 2 f. 20 multicoloured . . 1·00 75

655 Princess Grace **656** Mirror and Candelabra

1993. 10th Death Anniv (1992) of Princess Grace.
2119 **655** 5 f. blue . . . . 1·10 1·25

1993. 10th Antiques Biennale.
2120 **656** 7 f. multicoloured . . . 2·75 1·75

657 "Echinopsis multiplex" **658** Monte Carlo Ballets

1993. Cacti.
2121 **657** 2 f. 50 green, pur & yell 60 35
2122 – 2 f. 50 green and purple 60 35
2123 – 2 f. 50 green, pur & yell 60 35
2124 – 2 f. 50 green and yellow 60 35
DESIGNS: No. 2122, "Zygocactus truncatus"; 2123, "Echinocereus procumbens"; 2124, "Euphorbia virosa".
See also Nos. 2154/66.

1993. Europa. Contemporary Art.
2125 **658** 2 f. 50 black, brn & pink 1·00 35
2126 – 4 f. 20 grey and brown 1·60 1·00
DESIGN: 4 f. 20, "Evolution" (sculpture, Emma de Sigaldi).

660 State Arms and Olympic Rings

1993. 110th International Olympic Committee Session, Monaco.
2129 **660** 2 f. 80 red, brown & blue 65 75
2130 – 2 f. 80 blue, lt blue & red 60 75
2131 – 2 f. 80 brown, blue & red 65 75
2132 – 2 f. 80 blue, lt blue & red 65 75
2133 – 2 f. 80 brown, blue & red 65 75
2134 – 2 f. 80 blue, lt blue & red 65 75
2135 – 2 f. 80 brown, blue & red 65 75
2136 – 2 f. 80 blue, lt blue & red 65 75
2137 – 4 f. 50 multicoloured . . 1·00 1·10
2138 – 4 f. 50 black, yellow & bl 1·00 1·10
2139 – 4 f. 50 red, yellow & blue 1·00 1·10
2140 – 4 f. 50 black, yellow & bl 1·00 1·10
2141 – 4 f. 50 red, yellow & blue 1·00 1·10
2142 – 4 f. 50 black, yellow & bl 1·00 1·10
2143 – 4 f. 50 red, yellow & blue 1·00 1·10
2144 – 4 f. 50 red, yellow & blue 1·00 1·10
DESIGNS: Nos. 2129, 2137, Type **660** 2130, Bobsleighing; 2131, Skiing; 2132, Yachting; 2133, Rowing; 2134, Swimming; 2135, Cycling; 2136, 2144, Commemorative inscription; 2138, Gymnastics (rings exercise); 2139, Judo; 2140, Fencing; 2141, Hurdling; 2142, Archery; 2143, Weightlifting.

661 Examining 1891 1 c. Stamp

1993. Centenary of Monaco Philatelic Union.
2145 **661** 2 f. 40 multicoloured . . 85 35

1993. Christmas. Crib figures from Provence. As T **608**. Multicoloured.

2146 2 f. 80 Donkey 65 40
2147 3 f. 70 Shepherd holding lamb 1·25 85
2148 4 f. 40 Ox lying down in barn 1·60 1·25

662 Grieg, Music and Trolls

1993. 150th Birth Anniv of Edvard Grieg (composer).

2149 **662** 4 f. blue 2·00 1·25

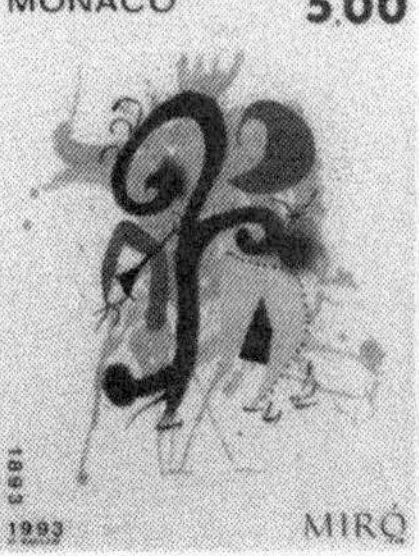

663 Abstract Lithograph **664** Monaco Red Cross Emblem

1993. Birth Centenary of Joan Miro (painter and sculptor).

2150 **663** 5 f. multicoloured 2·00 1·75

1993. Monaco Red Cross.

2151 **664** 5 f. red, yellow and black 1·90 1·25
2152 – 6 f. red and black 2·50 1·90

DESIGN: 6 f. Crosses inscribed with fundamental principles of the International Red Cross.

665 "St. Joseph the Carpenter"

1993. 400th Birth Anniv of Georges de la Tour (painter).

2153 **665** 6 f. multicoloured 2·50 1·75

1994. Cacti. As Nos. 2121/4 but values changed and additional designs.

2153a 10 c. green, orange and red 10 10
2154 20 c. green, purple & yell 10 10
2155 30 c. green and purple 10 10
2156 40 c. green and yellow 10 10
2157 50 c. green, red and olive 15 10
2158 60 c. green, red and yellow 15 10
2159 70 c. green, red and blue 15 10
2160 80 c. green, orange and red 20 15
2162 1 f. green, brown and yellow 25 15
2164 2 f. green, red and yellow 50 35
2166 4 f. green, purple and yellow 95 85
2167 5 f. green, black and brown 1·25 75

DESIGNS: 10 c. "Bromelia brevifolia"; 20 c. Type **657**; 30 c. "Zygocactus truncatus"; 40 c. "Euphorbia virosa"; 50 c. "Selenicereus grandiflorus"; 60 c. "Opuntia basilaris"; 70 c. "Aloe plicatilis"; 80 c. "Opuntia hybride"; 1 f. "Stapelia flavirostris"; 2 f. "Aporocactus flagelliformis"; 4 f. "Echinocereus procumbens"; 5 f. "Cereus peruvianus".

666 Festival Poster **667** Artist/Poet

1994. 18th Int Circus Festival, Monte Carlo.

2168 **666** 2 f. 80 multicoloured 1·10 40

1994. Mechanical Toys.

2169 **667** 2 f. 80 blue 65 40
2170 – 2 f. 80 red 65 40
2171 – 2 f. 80 purple 65 40
2172 – 2 f. 80 green 65 40

DESIGNS: No. 2170, Bust of Japanese woman; 2171, Shepherdess with sheep; 2172, Young Parisienne.

669 King Charles Spaniels

1994. International Dog Show, Monte Carlo.

2175 **669** 2 f. 40 multicoloured 1·00 40

670 Couple, Leaves and Pollution **671** Iris

1994. Monaco Committee of Anti-tuberculosis and Respiratory Diseases Campaign.

2176 **670** 2 f. 40 + 60 c. mult 1·10 85

1994. Monte Carlo Flower Show.

2177 **671** 4 f. 40 multicoloured 1·60 1·00

672 Levitation Trick

1994. 10th Monte Carlo Magic Grand Prix.

2178 **672** 5 f. blue, black and red 1·90 1·25

673 Ingredients and Dining Table overlooking Harbour

1994. 35th Anniv of Brotherhood of Cordon d'Or French Chefs.

2179 **673** 6 f. multicoloured 2·25 1·50

674 Isfjord, Prince Albert I, Map of Spitzbergen and "Princess Alice II"

1994. Europa. Discoveries made by Prince Albert I. Each black, blue and red.

2180 2 f. 80 Type **674** 1·00 45
2181 4 f. 50 Oceanographic Museum, mirrorbelly and "Eryoneicus alberti" (crustacean) 1·50 1·00

675 Olympic Flag and Sorbonne University **676** Dolphins through Porthole

1994. Centenary of International Olympic Committee.

2183 **675** 3 f. multicoloured 1·10 75

1994. Economic Institute of the Rights of the Sea Conference, Monaco.

2184 **676** 6 f. multicoloured 2·50 1·90

677 Family around Tree of Hearts **678** Footballer's Legs and Ball

1994. International Year of the Family.

2185 **677** 7 f. green, orange and blue 2·50 1·75

1994. World Cup Football Championship, U.S.A.

2186 **678** 8 f. red and black 3·00 2·10

679 Athletes and Villa Miraflores

1994. Inauguration of New Seat of International Amateur Athletics Federation.

2187 **679** 8 f. blue, purple and bistre 3·00 2·10

680 De Dion Bouton, 1903

1994. Vintage Car Collection of Prince Rainier III.

2188 **680** 2 f. 80 black, brown and mauve 1·10 45

681 Emblem and Monte Carlo **682** Emblem and Korean Scene

1994. 1st Association of Postage Stamp Catalogue Editors and Philatelic Publications Grand Prix.

2189 **681** 3 f. multicoloured 1·10 45

1994. 21st Universal Postal Union Congress, Seoul.

2190 **682** 4 f. 40 black, blue and red 1·60 1·10

1994. Christmas. As T **608** showing crib figures from Provence. Multicoloured.

2191 2 f. 80 Virgin Mary 1·00 45
2192 4 f. 50 Baby Jesus 1·50 70
2193 6 f. Joseph 1·90 90

683 Prince Albert I **684** Three Ages of Voltaire (writer, 300th anniv)

1994. Inaug of Stamp and Coin Museum (1st issue). Coins.

2194 **683** 3 f. stone, brown and red 1·25 85
2195 – 4 f. grey, brown and red 1·60 1·40
2196 – 7 f. stone, brown and red 2·75 2·10

DESIGNS: 4 f. Arms of House of Grimaldi; 7 f. Prince Rainier III.

See also Nos. 2265/7 and 2283/5.

1994. Birth Anniversaries.

2198 **684** 5 f. green 1·90 1·50
2199 – 6 f. brown and purple 2·25 1·75

DESIGN—HORIZ: 6 f. Sarah Bernhardt (actress, 150th anniv).

685 Heliport and Helicopter

1994. 50th Anniv of International Civil Aviation Organization.

2200 **685** 5 f. green, black and blue 1·90 1·25
2201 – 7 f. brown, black and red 2·50 1·90

DESIGN: 7 f. Harbour and helicopter.

687 Blood Vessels on Woman (anti-cancer)

1994. Monaco Red Cross. Health Campaigns.

2203 **687** 6 f. blue, black and red 2·25 1·75
2204 – 8 f. green, black and red 3·00 2·25

DESIGN: 8 f. Tree and woman (anti-AIDS).

688 Robinson Crusoe and Friday

1994. Anniversaries. Multicoloured.

2205 7 f. Type **688** (275th anniv of publication of "Robinson Crusoe" by Daniel Defoe) 2·50 1·90
2206 9 f. "The Snake Charmer" (150th birth anniv of Henri Rousseau, painter) 3·00 2·10

689 Clown playing Trombone **690** Crown Prince Albert

1995. 19th Int Circus Festival, Monte Carlo.

2207 **689** 2 f. 80 multicoloured 1·00 45

1995. 35th Television Festival, Monte Carlo.

2208 **690** 8 f. brown 3·00 1·90

691 Fontvieille

1995. European Nature Conservation Year.

2209 **691** 2 f. 40 multicoloured 85 40

692 American Cocker Spaniel

1995. International Dog Show, Monte Carlo.

2210 **692** 4 f. multicoloured 1·50 1·00

693 Parrot Tulips

1995. Monte Carlo Flower Show.
2211 **693** 5 f. multicoloured . . . . 1·90 1·10

694 "Acer palmatum"

1995. European Bonsai Congress.
2212 **694** 6 f. multicoloured . . . . 2·25 1·50

695 Alfred Nobel (founder of Nobel Prizes) and Dove

1995. Europa. Peace and Freedom. Multicoloured.
2213 2 f. 80 Type **695** . . . . . . 1·00 45
2214 5 f. Roses, broken chain and watchtower . . . . 1·90 1·25

696 Emblem of Monagasque Disabled Children Association

1995. International Special Olympics, New Haven, U.S.A.
2215 **696** 3 f. multicoloured . . . . 1·10 75

697 Emblem

1995. Rotary International Convention, Nice.
2216 **697** 4 f. blue . . . . 1·50 1·00

699 Jean Giono

701 Princess Caroline (President)

700 Saint Hubert (patron saint of hunting)

1995. Writers' Birth Centenaries.
2218 **699** 5 f. lilac, brown and green 1·90 1·10
2219 – 6 f. brown, violet and green . . . . 2·25 1·50
DESIGN: 6 f. Marcel Pagnol.

1995. General Assembly of International Council for Hunting and Conservation of Game.
2220 **700** 6 f. blue . . . . 2·25 1·25

1995. World Association of Friends of Children General Assembly, Monaco.
2221 **701** 7 f. blue . . . . 2·50 1·90

702 Athletes and Medal

1995. International Amateur Athletics Federation Grand Prix, Monaco.
2222 **702** 7 f. mauve, purple and grey 2·50 1·50

703 "Trophee des Alpes" (Hubert Clerissi)

1995. 2000th Anniv of Emperor Augustus Monument, La Turbie.
2223 **703** 8 f. multicoloured . . . 3·00 1·90

704 Prince Pierre (after Philip Laszlo de Lombos)

706 St. Antony (wooden statue)

1995. Birth Centenary of Prince Pierre of Monaco.
2224 **704** 10 f. purple . . . . . . 3·75 2·50

1995. 800th Birth Anniv of St. Antony of Padua.
2226 **706** 2 f. 80 multicoloured . . 1·00 45

707 United Nations Charter and Peacekeeping Soldiers

1995. 50th Anniv of U.N.O.
2227 **707** 2 f. 50 multicoloured . . 90 40
2228 – 2 f. 50 multicoloured . . 90 40
2229 – 2 f. 50 multicoloured . . 90 40
2230 – 2 f. 50 blue, black and brown 90 40
2231 – 3 f. black, brown and blue 1·10 75
2232 – 3 f. multicoloured . . . 1·10 75
2233 – 3 f. multicoloured . . . 1·10 75
2234 – 3 f. multicoloured . . . 1·10 75
DESIGNS: No. 2228, Wheat ears, boy and arid ground; 2229, Children from different nationalities; 2230, Head of Colossus, Abu Simbel Temple; 2231, United Nations meeting; 2232, Growing crops and hand holding seeds; 2233, Figures and alphabetic characters; 2234, Lute and U.N.E.S.C.O. headquarters, Paris.
Nos. 2228 and 2232 commemorate the F.A.O., Nos. 2229 and 2233 International Year of Tolerance, Nos. 2230 and 2234 U.N.E.S.C.O.

708 Rose "Grace de Monaco"

709 Balthazar

1995. Flowers. Multicoloured.
2236 3 f. Type **708** 80 50
2237 3 f. Fuchsia "Lakeland Princess" 80 50
2238 3 f. Carnation "Centenaire de Monte-Carlo" 80 50
2239 3 f. Fuchsia "Grace" 80 50
2240 3 f. Rose "Princesse de Monaco" 80 50
2241 3 f. Alstroemeria "Gracia" . . 80 50
2242 3 f. Lily "Princess Gracia" . . 80 50
2243 3 f. Carnation "Princesse Caroline" 80 50
2244 3 f. Rose "Stephanie de Monaco" 80 50
2245 3 f. Carnation "Prince Albert" 80 50
2246 3 f. Sweet pea "Grace de Monaco" 80 50
2247 3 f. Gerbera "Gracia" 80 50

1995. Christmas. Crib Figures from Provence of the Three Wise Men. Multicoloured.
2248 3 f. Type **709** 80 50
2249 5 f. Gaspard . . . . 1·25 75
2250 6 f. Melchior . . . . 1·60 1·00

710 Tree, Bird, Seahorse and Association Emblem

1995. 20th Anniv of Monaco Association for Nature Protection.
2251 **710** 4 f. green, black and red . 1·50 60

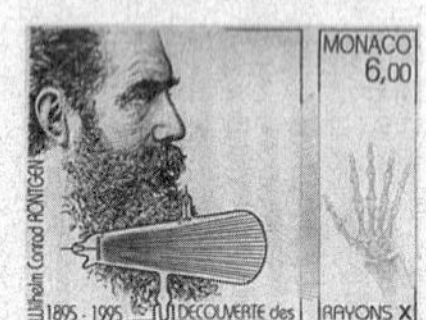

711 Rontgen and X-Ray of Hand

1995. Centenary of Discovery of X-Rays by Wilhelm Rontgen.
2252 **711** 6 f. black, yellow and green . . . . 2·25 1·25

712 First Screening to Paying Public, Paris, December 1895

1995. Centenary of Motion Pictures.
2253 **712** 7 f. blue . . . . 2·50 1·90

713 Allegory of Anti-Leprosy Campaign

1995. Monaco Red Cross. Multicoloured.
2254 7 f. Type **713** . . . . 2·25 1·50
2255 8 f. Doctors Prakash and Mandakini Amte (anti-leprosy campaign in India) . 2·75 1·90

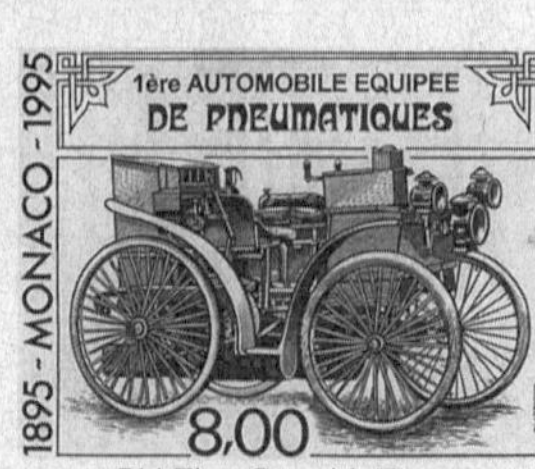

714 First Car with Tyres

1995. Centenary of Invention of Inflatable Tyres.
2256 **714** 8 f. purple and claret . . 2·75 1·90

715 "Spring"

1995. 550th Birth Anniv of Sandro Botticelli (artist).
2257 **715** 15 f. blue . . . . 5·25 3·75

716 Poster

718 Rhododendron

717 Illusion

1996. 20th International Circus Festival, Monte Carlo.
2258 **716** 2 f. 40 multicoloured . 60 40

1996. Magic Festival, Monte Carlo.
2259 **717** 2 f. 80 black 70 45

1996. Monte Carlo Flower Show.
2260 **718** 3 f. multicoloured . . . 75 45

719 Wire-haired Fox Terrier

1996. International Dog Show, Monte Carlo.
2261 **719** 4 f. multicoloured . . . 95 60

720 "Chapel" (Hubert Clerissi)

1996. 300th Anniv of Chapel of Our Lady of Mercy.
2262 **720** 6 f. multicoloured . . . 1·50 90

721 Prince Albert I of Monaco (½-size illustration)

1996. Centenary of Oceanographic Expeditions. Multicoloured.
2263 3 f. Type **721** 75 45
2264 4 f. 50 King Carlos I of Portugal . . . . 1·10 70

722 Prince Rainier III (after F. Messina) 723 Princess Grace

1996. Inauguration of Stamp and Coin Museum (2nd issue). 1974 Prince Rainier design.

2265	722	10 f. violet	2·40	1·50
2266		15 f. brown	3·75	2·25
2267		20 f. blue	4·75	3·00

1996. Europa. Famous Women.

2268	723	3 f. brown and red	75	45

724 Fishes, Sea and Coastline

1996. 20th Anniv of Ramoge Agreement on Environmental Protection of Mediterranean.

2269	724	3 f. multicoloured	75	45

727 Code and Monaco 728 Throwing the Javelin

1996. Introduction of International Dialling Code "377".

2272	727	3 f. blue	75	45
2273		3 f. 80 red	90	55

1996. Olympic Games, Atlanta. Multicoloured.

2274	3 f. Type **728**	75	45
2275	3 f. Baseball	75	45
2276	4 f. 50 Running	1·10	70
2277	4 f. 50 Cycling	1·10	70

729 Children of Different Races with Balloon 730 Angel and Star

1996. 50th Anniv of U.N.I.C.E.F.

2278	729	3 f. brown, blue and lilac	75	45

1996. Christmas. Multicoloured.

2279	3 f. Type **730**	75	45
2280	6 f. Angels heralding	1·50	90

731 Planet and Neptune, God of the Sea (after Roman mosaic, Sousse)

1996. Anniversaries.

2281	731	4 f. red, blue and black	95	60
2282	–	5 f. blue and red	1·25	75

DESIGNS—4 f. Type **731** (150th anniv of discovery of planet Neptune by Johann Galle); 5 f. Rene Descartes (after Franz Hals) (philosopher and scientist, 400th birth anniv).

732 Coins and Press

1996. Inauguration of Stamp and Coin Museum (3rd issue).

2283	732	5 f. brown and blue	1·25	75
2284	–	5 f. brown and purple	1·25	75
2285	–	10 f. blue and brown	2·40	1·50

DESIGNS—As T **733**: 5 f. Stamp press and engraver. 48 × 37 mm: 10 f. Museum entrance.

733 Camille Corot (bicentenary)

1996. Artists' Birth Anniversaries. Self-portraits. Multicoloured.

2287	6 f. Type **733**	1·50	90
2288	7 f. Francisco Goya (250th anniv)	1·75	1·10

734 Allegory

1996. Monaco Red Cross. Anti-Tuberculosis Campaign. Multicoloured.

2289	7 f. Type **734**	1·75	1·10
2290	8 f. Camille Guerin and Albert Calmette (developers of vaccine)	1·90	1·25

POSTAGE DUE STAMPS

D 3 D 4 D 18

1906.

D 29a	D 3	1 c. green	50	60
D 30		5 c. green	35	45
D 31a		10 c. red	25	60
D 32		10 c. brown	£325	£120
D 33		15 c. purple on cream	2·50	1·25
D113		20 c. bistre on buff	50	15
D 34		30 c. blue	30	35
D114		40 c. mauve	15	15
D 35		50 c. brown on buff	6·25	3·75
D115		50 c. green	15	15
D116		60 c. black	40	40
D117		60 c. mauve	15·00	25·00
D118		1 f. purple on cream	50	10
D119		2 f. red	1·10	1·90
D120		3 f. red	1·10	1·60
D121		5 f. blue	60	85

1910.

D36	D 4	1 c. olive	20	50
D37		10 c. lilac	30	60
D38		30 c. bistre	£180	£160

1919. Surch.

D39	D 4	20 c. on 10 c. lilac	6·75	6·75
D40		40 c. on 30 c. bistre	6·75	6·75

1925.

D106	D 18	1 c. olive	60	50
D107		10 c. violet	60	60
D108		30 c. bistre	50	75
D109		60 c. red	60	85
D110		1 f. blue	60·00	60·00
D111		2 f. red	£160	85·00

1925. Surch **1 franc a percevoir**.

D112	D 3	1 f. on 50 c. brown on buff	65	65

D 64 D 65

1946.

D327	D 64	10 c. black	10	10
D328		30 c. violet	10	10
D329		50 c. blue	10	10
D330		1 f. green	15	15
D331		2 f. brown	15	15
D332		3 f. mauve	20	20
D333		4 f. red	30	35
D334	D 65	5 f. brown	20	20
D335		10 f. blue	30	60
D336		20 f. turquoise	40	45
D337		50 f. red and mauve	32·00	60·00
D338		100 f. red and green	7·50	12·50

D 99 Early Steam Locomotive

1953.

D478	–	1 f. red and green	10	10
D479	–	1 f. green and red	10	10
D480	–	2 f. turquoise and blue	10	10
D481	–	2 f. blue and turquoise	10	10
D482	D 99	3 f. lake and green	20	20
D483	–	3 f. green and lake	20	20
D484	–	4 f. slate and brown	15	15
D485	–	4 f. brown and slate	15	15
D486	–	5 f. violet and blue	40	40
D487	–	5 f. blue and violet	40	40
D488	–	10 f. indigo and blue	5·50	9·25
D489	–	10 f. blue and indigo	5·50	9·25
D490	–	20 f. violet and blue	3·00	5·00
D491	–	20 f. blue and violet	3·00	5·00
D492	–	50 f. brown and red	6·75	11·00
D493	–	50 f. red and brown	6·75	11·00
D494	–	100 f. green and purple	12·50	20·00
D495	–	100 f. purple and green	12·50	20·00

TRIANGULAR DESIGNS: Nos. D478, Pigeons released from mobile loft; D479, Sikorsky S-51 helicopter; D480, Brig; D481, "United States" (liner); D483, Streamlined steam locomotive; D484, Santos-Dumont's monoplane No. 20 Demoiselle; D485, De Havilland Comet 1 airliner; D486, Old motor car; D487, "Sabre" racing-car; D488, Leonardo da Vinci's flying machine; D489, Postal rocket; D490, Mail balloon, Paris, 1870; D491, Airship "Graf Zeppelin"; D492, Postilion; D493, Motor cycle messenger; D494, Mail coach; D495, Railway mail van.

D 140 18th-Century Felucca

1960.

D698	D 140	1 c. brown, grn & bl	10	10
D699	–	2 c. sepia, bl & grn	15	15
D700	–	5 c. purple, blk & turq	15	25
D701	–	10 c. black, grn & bl	10	10
D702	–	20 c. purple, grn & bl	1·50	1·50
D703	–	30 c. brown, bl & grn	90	90
D704	–	50 c. blue, brn & myrtle	2·10	2·10
D705	–	1 f. brown, myrtle & bl	2·75	2·75

DESIGNS: 2 c. Paddle-steamer "La Palmaria"; 5 c. Arrival of first railway train at Monaco; 10 c. 15th-16th-century armed messenger; 20 c. 18th-century postman; 30 c. "Charles III" (paddle-steamer); 50 c. 17th-century courier; 1 f. Mail coach (19th-century).

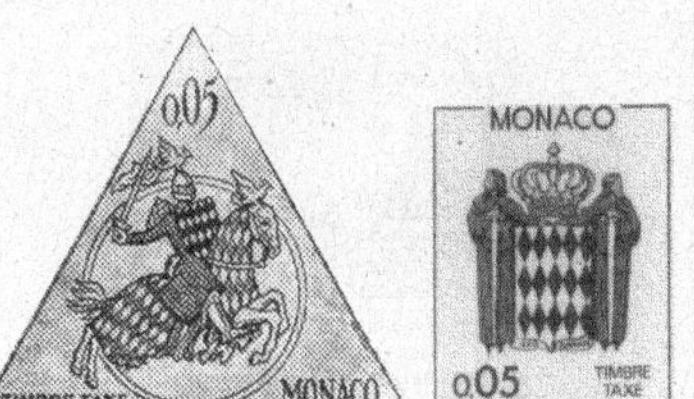

D 393 Prince's Seal D 492 Coat of Arms

1980.

D1426	D 393	5 c. red and brown	10	10
D1427		10 c. orange and red	10	10
D1428		15 c. violet and red	10	10
D1429		20 c. green and red	10	10
D1430		30 c. blue and red	15	15
D1431		40 c. bistre and red	20	20
D1432		50 c. violet and red	50	50
D1433		1 f. grey and blue	1·00	1·00
D1434		2 f. brown & black	1·25	1·25
D1435		3 f. red and green	1·90	1·90
D1436		4 f. green and red	2·50	2·50
D1437		5 f. brown & mauve	3·00	3·00

1985.

D1712	D 492	5 c. multicoloured	10	10
D1713		10 c. multicoloured	10	10
D1714		15 c. multicoloured	10	10
D1715		20 c. multicoloured	10	10
D1716		30 c. multicoloured	10	10
D1717		40 c. multicoloured	10	10
D1718		50 c. multicoloured	10	10
D1719		1 f. multicoloured	30	30
D1720		2 f. multicoloured	65	65
D1721		3 f. multicoloured	1·50	1·50
D1722		4 f. multicoloured	1·90	1·90
D1723		5 f. multicoloured	2·50	2·50

MONGOLIA Pt. 10

A republic in Central Asia between China and Russia, independent since 1921.

1924. 100 cents = 1 dollar (Chinese).
1926. 100 mung = 1 tugrik.

1 Eldev-Otchir Symbol
2 Soyombo Symbol

1924. Inscr in black.
1 1 1 c. brown, pink and grey on bistre . . . . 3·25 3·25
2 2 c. brown, blue and red on brown . . . . 3·25 2·75
3 5 c. grey, red and yellow . . . . 20·00 14·00
4 10 c. blue and brown on blue . 7·50 5·50
5 20 c. grey, blue and white on blue 12·00 8·50
6 50 c. red and orange on pink . 20·00 14·00
7 $1 bistre, red and white on yellow 32·00 22·00
Stamps vary in size according to the face value.

1926. Fiscal stamps as T 2 optd **POSTAGE** in frame in English and Mongolian.
8 2 1 c. blue . . . . 6·50 6·50
9 2 c. buff . . . . 7·50 7·50
10 5 c. purple . . . . 8·50 8·50
11 10 c. green . . . . 10·00 10·00
12 20 c. brown . . . . 13·00 13·00
13 50 c. brown and yellow . . . £120 £120
14 $1 brown and pink £325 £375
15 $5 red and olive £350
Stamps vary in size according to the face value.

4 State Emblem: Soyombo Symbol 5

1926. New Currency.
16 4 5 m. black and lilac . . . . 4·00 4·00
17 20 m. black and blue . . . . 3·50 3·50

1926.
18 5 1 m. black and yellow . . . . 1·00 80
19 2 m. black and brown . . . . 1·10 90
20 5 m. black and lilac (A) . . . . 2·00 1·40
28 5 m. black and lilac (B) . . . . 13·00 8·50
21 10 m. black and blue . . . . 1·40 1·10
30 20 m. black and blue . . . . 14·00 8·00
22 25 m. black and green . . . . 3·00 1·75
23 40 m. black and yellow . . . . 4·50 2·00
24 50 m. black and brown . . . . 6·00 3·25
25 1 t. black, green and brown . 14·00 6·50
26 3 t. black, yellow and red . . 30·00 25·00
27 5 t. black, red and purple . . 45·00 40·00
In (A) the Mongolian numerals are in the upper and in (B) in the lower value tablets.
These stamps vary in size according to the face value.

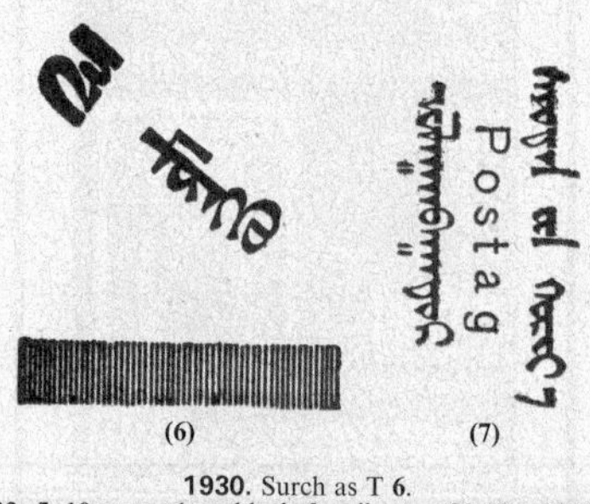

(6) (7)

1930. Surch as T 6.
32 5 10 m. on 1 m. black & yellow 20·00 30·00
33 20 m. on 2 m. black & brown 30·00 30·00
34 25 m. on 40 m. black & yell . 35·00 35·00

1931. Optd with T 7.
35 2 1 c. blue . . . . 17·00 8·00
36 2 c. buff . . . . 12·00 6·00
37 5 c. purple . . . . 18·00 6·00
38 10 c. green . . . . 18·00 6·00
39 20 c. brown . . . . 27·00 8·50
40 50 c. brown and yellow . . . 70·00 70·00
41 $1 brown and pink . . . .

1931. Surch **Postage** and value in "Menge".
43 2 5 m. on 5 c. purple . . . . 18·00 6·00
44 10 m. on 10 c. green . . . . 30·00 15·00
45 20 m. on 20 c. brown . . . . 40·00 20·00

9 Govt Building, Ulan Bator
11 Sukhe Bator

12 Lake and Mountain Scenery

1932.
46 – 1 m. brown . . . . 1·40 1·00
47 – 2 m. red . . . . 1·40 1·00
48 – 5 m. blue 35 30
49 9 10 m. green 35 30
50 – 15 m. brown 35 30
51 – 20 m. red 35 30
52 – 25 m. violet 45 30
53 11 40 m. black 45 40
54 – 50 m. blue 35 30
55 12 1 t. green 60 50
56 – 3 t. violet . . . . 1·75 1·25
57 – 5 t. brown . . . . 10·00 7·50
58 – 10 t. blue . . . . 17·00 13·00
DESIGNS—As Type **9**: 1 m. Weavers; 5 m. Machinist. As Type **11**: 2 m. Telegraphist; 15 m. Revolutionary soldier carrying flag; 20 m. Mongols learning Latin alphabet; 25 m. Soldier; 50 m. Sukhe Bator's monument. As Type **12**: 3 t. Sheep-shearing; 5 t. Camel caravan; 10 t. Lassoing wild horses (after painting by Sampilon).

13 Mongol Man
14 Camel Caravan

1943. Network background in similar colour to stamps.
59 13 5 m. green . . . . 3·50 3·50
60 – 10 m. blue . . . . 6·00 3·75
61 – 15 m. red . . . . 7·00 5·00
62 14 20 m. brown . . . . 11·00 9·00
63 – 25 m. brown . . . . 11·00 11·00
64 – 30 m. red . . . . 12·00 12·00
65 – 45 m. purple . . . . 17·00 17·00
66 – 60 m. green . . . . 28·00 28·00
DESIGNS—VERT: 10 m. Mongol woman; 15 m. Soldier; 30 m. Arms of the Republic; 45 m. Portrait of Sukhe Bator, dated 1894–1923. HORIZ: 25 m. Secondary school; 60 m. Pastoral scene.

15 Marshal Kharloin Choibalsan
17 Victory Medal

16 Choibalsan and Sukhe Bator

1945. 50th Birthday of Choibalsan.
67 15 1 t. black . . . . 7·50 7·50

1946. 25th Anniv of Independence. As T **16/17**.
68 – 30 m. bistre . . . . 4·50 3·50
69 16 50 m. purple . . . . 5·50 4·00
70 – 60 m. brown . . . . 5·50 5·50
71 – 60 m. black . . . . 8·00 5·50
72 17 80 m. brown . . . . 7·50 7·50
73 – 1 t. blue . . . . 11·00 12·00
74 – 2 t. brown . . . . 14·00 16·00
DESIGNS—VERT: (21½×32 mm): 30 m. Choibalsan, aged four. As Type **17**: 60 m. (No. 71), Choibalsan when young man; 1 t. 25th Anniversary Medal; 2 t. Sukhe Bator. HORIZ: As Type **16**: 60 m. (No. 70), Choibalsan University.

17a Flags of Communist Bloc

1951. Struggle for Peace.
75 17a 1 t. multicoloured . . . . 7·50 7·50

17b Lenin (after P. Vasilev)
19 Sukhe Bator

18 State Shop

1951. Honouring Lenin.
76 17b 3 t. multicoloured . . . . 16·00 16·00

1951. 30th Anniv of Independence.
77 – 15 m. green on azure . . . . 3·25 3·25
78 18 20 m. orange . . . . 3·25 3·25
79 – 20 m. multicoloured . . . . 3·75 3·75
80 – 25 m. blue on azure . . . . 3·75 3·75
81 – 30 m. multicoloured . . . . 4·25 4·25
82 – 40 m. violet on pink . . . . 4·50 4·50
83 – 50 m. brown on azure . . . . 9·00 9·00
84 – 60 m. black on pink . . . . 8·00 8·00
85 19 2 t. brown . . . . 15·00 15·00
DESIGNS—HORIZ: (As Type **18**): 15 m. Altai Hotel; 40 m. State Theatre, Ulan Bator; 50 m. Pedagogical Institute. 55½×26 mm: 25 m. Choibalsan University. VERT: (As Type **19**): 20 m. (No. 79); 30 m. Arms and flag; 60 m. Sukhe Bator Monument.

20 School-children

1952. Culture.
86 – 5 m. brown on pink . . . . 2·00 1·75
87 20 10 m. blue on pink . . . . 2·50 2·50
DESIGN: 5 m. New houses.

21 Choibalsan in National Costume
22 Choibalsan and Farm Worker

1953. 1st Death Anniv of Marshal Choibalsan. As T **21/22**.
88 21 15 m. blue . . . . 2·50 2·75
89 22 15 m. green . . . . 2·50 2·75
90 21 20 m. green . . . . 5·00 6·00
91 22 20 m. sepia . . . . 2·50 2·50
92 – 20 m. blue . . . . 2·50 2·50
93 – 30 m. sepia . . . . 3·25 3·25
94 – 50 m. brown . . . . 3·25 3·25
95 – 1 t. red . . . . 4·00 4·00
96 – 1 t. purple . . . . 4·00 4·00
97 – 2 t. red . . . . 4·00 4·00
98 – 3 t. purple . . . . 5·00 5·00
99 – 5 t. red . . . . 19·00 19·00
DESIGNS: As Type **21**: 1 t. (96); 2 t. Choibalsan in uniform. 33×48 mm: 3, 5 t. Busts of Choibalsan and Sukhe Bator. 33×46 mm: 50 m., 1 t. (95), Choibalsan and young pioneer. 48×33 mm: 20 m. (92); 30 m. Choibalsan and factory hand.

23 Arms of the Republic
23a Lenin

1954.
100 23 10 m. red . . . . 6·50 4·00
101 20 m. red . . . . 11·00 5·00
102 30 m. red . . . . 6·00 4·50
103 40 m. red . . . . 7·00 4·50
104 60 m. red . . . . 6·50 4·50

1955. 85th Birth Anniv of Lenin.
105 23a 2 t. blue . . . . 3·75 2·00

23b Flags of the Communist Bloc
24 Sukhe Bator and Choibalsan

1955. Struggle for Peace.
106 23b 60 m. multicoloured . . . 1·00 55

1955.
107 24 30 m. green 30 20
108 – 30 m. blue 50 20
109 – 30 m. red 40 40
110 – 40 m. purple . . . . 1·00 40
111 – 50 m. brown . . . . 1·00 45
112 – 1 t. multicoloured . . . . 2·75 1·25
DESIGNS—HORIZ: 30 m. blue, Lake Khobsogol; 50 m. Choibalsan University. VERT: 30 m. red, Lenin Statue, Ulan Bator; 40 m. Sukhe Bator and dog; 1 t. Arms and flag of the Republic.

24a Train linking Ulan Bator and Moscow
25 Arms of the Republic

1956. Mongol–Soviet Friendship. Multicoloured.
113 1 t. Type **24a** . . . . 22·00 10·00
114 2 t. Flags of Mongolia and Russia . . . . 3·50 2·00

1956.
115 25 20 m. brown 50 30
116 30 m. brown 65 35
117 40 m. blue 80 45
118 60 m. green . . . . 1·00 65
119 1 t. red . . . . 1·60 80

26 Hunter and Golden Eagle
27 Arms

27a Wrestlers

1956. 35th Anniv of Independence.
120 26 30 m. brown . . . . 38·00 16·00
121 27 30 m. blue . . . . 5·00 4·00
122 27a 60 m. green . . . . 15·00 15·00
123 – 60 m. orange . . . . 15·00 15·00
DESIGN: As Type **26**: 60 m. (No. 123), Children. Also inscr "xxxv".

28
29

1958. With or without gum.
124 28 20 m. red . . . . 1·50 1·00

1958. 13th Mongol People's Revolutionary Party Congress. With or without gum.
125 **29** 30 m. red and salmon . . . 3·00 3·25

1958. As T **27a** but without "xxxv". With or without gum.
126 50 m. brown on pink . . . . 5·00 3·75

30 Dove and Globe

1958. 4th Congress of International Women's Federation, Vienna. With or without gum.
127 **30** 60 m. blue . . . . 3·25 2·00

31 Ibex

32 Yak

1958. Mongolian Animals. As T **31/2**.
128 – 30 m. pale blue . . . . . . 15·00 2·50
129 – 30 m. turquoise . . . . . . 15·00 2·50
130 **31** 30 m. green . . . . 3·00 1·50
131 30 m. turquoise . . . . . . 3·00 1·00
132 **32** 60 m. bistre . . . . 3·50 2·00
133 60 m. orange . . . . 3·50 1·25
134 – 1 t. blue . . . . 5·00 2·50
135 – 1 t. light blue . . . . 4·00 1·75
136 – 1 t. red . . . . 5·00 3·25
137 – 1 t. red . . . . 4·00 2·00
DESIGNS—VERT: 30 m. (Nos. 128/9), Dalmatian pelicans. HORIZ: 1 t. (Nos. 134/5), Yak, facing right; 1 t. (Nos. 136/7), Bactrian camels.

33 Goat

34 "Tulaga"

1958. Mongolian Animals.
138 **33** 5 m. sepia and yellow . . . 15 10
139 – 10 m. sepia and green . . . 20 10
140 – 15 m. sepia and lilac . . . 35 10
141 – 20 m. sepia and blue . . . 35 10
142 – 25 m. sepia and red 40 10
143 – 30 m. purple and mauve . . 50 10
144 **33** 40 m. green 50 10
145 – 50 m. brown and salmon . 60 20
146 – 60 m. blue 80 20
147 – 1 t. bistre and yellow . . . 1·75 50
ANIMALS: 10, 30 m. Ram; 15, 60 m. Stallion; 20, 50 m. Bull; 25 m., 1 t. Bactrian camel.

1959.
148 **34** 1 t. multicoloured . . . . . 3·25 1·10

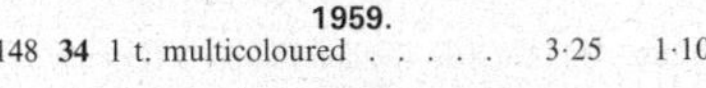

35 Taming a Wild Horse

1959. Mongolian Sports. Centres and inscriptions multicoloured: frame colours given below.
149 **35** 5 m. yellow and orange . . 20 10
150 – 10 m. purple 20 10
151 – 15 m. yellow and green . . 20 10
152 – 20 m. lake and red 25 10
153 – 25 m. blue 40 15
154 – 30 m. yellow, green & turq 55 15
155 – 70 m. red and yellow . . . 70 30
156 – 80 m. purple . . . . . . 1·10 60
DESIGNS: 10 m. Wrestlers; 15 m. Introducing young rider; 20 m. Archer; 25 m. Galloping horseman; 30 m. Archery contest; 70 m. Hunting a wild horse; 80 m. Proclaiming a champion.

36 Child Musician

1959. Mongolian Youth Festival (1st issue).
157 **36** 5 m. purple and blue . . . 20 10
158 – 10 m. brown and green . . 25 10
159 – 20 m. green and purple . . 25 10
160 – 25 m. blue and green . . . 50 25
161 – 40 m. violet and myrtle . . 95 40
DESIGNS—VERT: 10 m. Young wrestlers; 20 m. Youth on horse; 25 m. Artists in national costume. HORIZ: 40 m. Festival parade.

37 Festival Badge

38 Kalmuck Script

1959. Mongolian Youth Festival (2nd issue).
162 **37** 30 m. purple and blue . . 30 20

1959. Mongolists' Congress. Designs as T **38** incorporating "MONGOL" in various scripts.
163 – 30 m. multicoloured . . . 5·00 5·00
164 – 40 m. red, blue and yellow 5·00 5·00
165 **38** 50 m. multicoloured . . . 7·00 7·00
166 – 60 m. red, blue and yellow 11·00 11·00
167 – 1 t. yellow, turquoise & orge 14·00 14·00
SCRIPTS (29½ × 42½ mm): 30 m. Stylized Ulghur; 40 m. Soyombo; 60 m. Square (Pagspa). (21½ × 31 mm): 1 t. Cyrillic.

39 Military Monument

40 Herdswoman and Lamb

1959. 20th Anniv of Battle of Khalka River.
168 – 40 m. red, brown & yellow 55 15
169 **39** 50 m. multicoloured . . . 55 15
DESIGN: 40 m. Mounted horseman with flag (emblem), inscr "AUGUST 1959 HALHIN GOL".

1959. 2nd Meeting of Rural Economy Co-operatives.
170 **40** 30 m. green . . . . 3·50 3·50

41 Sable

1959. Mongolian Fauna.
171 **41** 5 m. purple, yellow & blue 15 10
172 – 10 m. multicoloured . . . 90 10
173 – 15 m. black, green and red 45 10
174 – 20 m. purple, blue and red 45 15
175 – 30 m. myrtle, purple & grn 50 15
176 – 50 m. black, blue and green 1·10 30
177 – 1 t. black, green and red 1·75 40
ANIMALS—HORIZ: (58 × 21 mm): 10 m. Ring-necked pheasants; 20 m. European otter; 50 m. Saiga; 1 t. Siberian musk deer. As Type **41**: 15 m. Muskrat; 30 m. Argali.

42 "Lunik 3" in Flight

44 "Flower" Emblem

43 Motherhood Badge

1959. Launching of "Lunik 3" Rocket.
178 **42** 30 m. yellow and violet . . 65 25
179 – 50 m. red, green and blue . 80 35
DESIGN—HORIZ: 50 m. Trajectory of "Lunik 3" around the Moon.

1960. International Women's Day.
180 **43** 40 m. bistre and blue . . . 50 15
181 **44** 50 m. yellow, green & blue . 75 30

45 Lenin

46 Larkspur

1960. 90th Birth Anniv of Lenin.
182 **45** 40 m. red 60 15
183 50 m. violet 40 30

1960. Flowers.
184 **46** 5 m. blue, green and bistre . 15 10
185 – 10 m. red, green and orange 20 10
186 – 15 m. violet, green & bistre 25 10
187 – 20 m. yellow, green & olive 30 10
188 – 30 m. violet, green & emer . 35 15
189 – 40 m. orange, green & violet 65 15
190 – 50 m. violet, green and blue 85 35
191 – 1 t. mauve, green & lt green 1·60 80
FLOWERS: 10 m. Tulip; 15 m. Jacob's ladder; 20 m. Asiatic globe flower; 30 m. Clustered bellflower; 40 m. Grass of Parnassus; 50 m. Meadow cranes-bill; 1 t. "Begonia vansiana".

47 Horse-jumping

1960. Olympic Games. Inscr "ROMA 1960" or "ROMA MCMLX". Centres in greenish grey.
192 **47** 5 m. red, black & turquoise 10 10
193 – 10 m. violet and yellow . . 15 10
194 – 15 m. turquoise, black & red 20 20
195 – 20 m. red and blue 20 10
196 – 30 m. ochre, black & green 35 10
197 – 50 m. blue and turquoise . 50 10
198 – 70 m. green, black & violet 60 30
199 – 1 t. mauve and green . . . 90 50
DESIGNS—DIAMOND SHAPED: 10 m. Running; 20 m. Wrestling; 50 m. Gymnastics; 1 t. Throwing the discus. As Type **47**: 15 m. Diving; 30 m. Hurdling; 70 m. High jumping.

48

1960. Red Cross.
200 **48** 20 m. red, yellow and blue . 70 25

49 Newspapers

1960. 40th Anniv of Mongolian Newspaper "Unen" ("Truth").
201 **49** 20 m. buff, green and red . 20 10
202 30 m. red, yellow and green 30 15

50 Hoopoe

1961. Mongolian Song-birds.
203 – 5 m. mauve, black and grn 75 25
204 **50** 10 m. red, black and green 85 25
205 – 15 m. yellow, black & green 1·00 35
206 – 20 m. green, black & bistre 1·25 35
207 – 50 m. blue, black and red . 1·75 35
208 – 70 m. yellow, black & mve 1·90 65
209 – 1 t. mauve, orange & black 2·40 90
BIRDS: As Type **50**: 15 m. Golden oriole; 20 m. Siberian capercaillie. Inverted triangulars: 5 m. Rose-coloured starling; 50 m. Eastern broad-billed roller; 70 m. Tibetan sandgrouse; 1 t. Mandarin.

51 Foundry Worker

52 Patrice Lumumba

1961. 15th Anniv of World Federation of Trade Unions.
210 **51** 30 m. red and black . . . 30 10
211 – 50 m. red and violet . . . 35 20
DESIGN—HORIZ: 50 m. Hemispheres.

1961. Patrice Lumumba (Congolese politician) Commemoration.
212 **52** 30 m. brown . . . . 1·50 1·00
213 50 m. purple . . . . 2·00 1·25

53 Bridge

54 Gagarin with Capsule

1961. 40th Anniv of Independence (1st issue). Mongolian Modernization.
214 **53** 5 m. green 10 10
215 – 10 m. blue 10 10
216 – 15 m. red 15 10
217 – 20 m. brown 15 10
218 – 30 m. blue 20 15
219 – 50 m. green 30 20
220 – 1 t. violet 50 25
DESIGNS: 10 m. Shoe-maker; 15 m. Store at Ulan Bator; 30 m. Government Building, Ulan Bator; 50 m. Machinist; 1 t. Ancient and modern houses. (59 × 20½ mm): 20 m. Choibalsan University.
See also Nos. 225/32, 233/41, 242/8 and 249/56.

1961. World's First Manned Space Flight. Mult.
221 20 m. Type **54** 50 15
222 30 m. Gagarin and globe (horiz) 60 30
223 50 m. Gagarin in capsule making parachute descent 90 60
224 1 t. Globe and Gagarin (horiz) 1·40 90

55 Postman with Reindeer

1961. 40th Anniv of Independence (2nd issue). Mongolian Postal Service.
225 **55** 5 m. red, brown and blue (postage) 15 10
226 – 15 m. violet, brown & bistre 30 10
227 – 20 m. blue, black and green 20 10
228 – 25 m. violet, bistre & green 30 15
229 – 30 m. green, black & lav 3·50 80
230 – 10 m. orange, black and green (air) 35 10
231 – 50 m. black, pink and green 1·00 25
232 – 1 t. multicoloured . . . . 1·10 35
DESIGNS: Postman with: 10 m. Horses; 15 m. Camels; 20 m. Yaks; 25 m. Postman on quayside; 30 m. Diesel mail train; 50 m. Ilyushin Il-14M mail plane over map; 1 t. Postal emblem.

56 Rams

1961. 40th Anniv of Independence (3rd issue). Animal Husbandry.

233 **56** 5 m. black, red and blue . . 10 10
234 – 10 m. black, green & purple 15 10
235 – 15 m. black, red and green 20 10
236 – 20 m. sepia, blue & brown . 25 10
237 – 25 m. black, yellow & green 30 15
238 – 30 m. black, red and violet 35 15
239 – 40 m. black, green and red 40 15
240 – 50 m. black, brown & blue 65 25
241 – 1 t. black, violet and olive . 90 50

DESIGNS: 10 m. Oxen; 15 m. Camels; 20 m. Pigs and poultry; 25 m. Angora goats; 30 m. Mongolian horses; 40 m. Ewes; 50 m. Cows; 1 t. Combine-harvester.

57 Children Wrestling

1961. 40th Anniv of Independence (5th issue). Mongolian Sports.

242 **57** 5 m. multicoloured 15 10
243 – 10 m. sepia, red and green 20 10
244 – 15 m. purple blue & yellow 25 10
245 – 20 m. red, black and green 55 25
246 – 30 m. purple, green & lav 80 30
247 – 50 m. indigo, orange & blue 1·00 35
248 – 1 t. purple, blue and grey 1·60 70

DESIGNS: 10 m. Horse-riding; 15 m. Children on camel and pony; 20 m. Falconry; 30 m. Skiing; 50 m. Archery; 1 t. Dancing.

58 Young Mongol

1961. 40th Anniv of Independence (6th issue). Mongolian Culture.

249 **58** 5 m. purple and green . . . 10 10
250 – 10 m. blue and red 10 10
251 – 15 m. brown and blue . . . 15 10
252 – 20 m. green and violet . . 25 10
253 – 30 m. red and blue 35 15
254 – 50 m. violet and bistre . . 80 20
255 – 70 m. green and mauve . . 90 25
256 – 1 t. red and blue . . . . . 1·25 70

DESIGNS—HORIZ. 10 m. Mongol chief; 70 m. Orchestra; 1 t. Gymnast. VERT: 15 m. Sukhe Bator Monument; 20 m. Young singer; 30 m. Young dancer; 50 m. Dombra-player.

59 Mongol Arms 60 Congress Emblem

1961. Arms multicoloured; inscr in blue; background colours given.

257 **59** 5 m. salmon 15 10
258 10 m. lilac 20 10
259 15 m. brown 25 10
260 20 m. turquoise 35 10
261 30 m. ochre 45 15
262 50 m. mauve 50 20
263 70 m. olive 60 25
264 1 t. orange . . . . 1·00 35

1961. 5th World Federation of Trade Unions Congress, Moscow.

265 **60** 30 m. red, yellow and blue 30 15
266 50 m. red, yellow and sepia 35 20

61 Dove, Map and Globe

1962. Admission of Mongolia to U.N.O.

267 **61** 10 m. multicoloured . . . 20 10
268 – 30 m. multicoloured . . . 30 15
269 – 50 m. multicoloured . . . 40 15
270 – 60 m. multicoloured . . . 60 25
271 – 70 m. multicoloured . . . 70 35

DESIGNS: 30 m. U.N. Emblem and Mongol Arms; 50 m. U.N. and Mongol flags; 60 m. U.N. Headquarters and Mongolian Parliament building; 70 m. U.N. and Mongol flags, and Assembly.

62 Football, Globe and Flags

1962. World Cup Football Championship, Chile. Multicoloured.

272 10 m. Type **62** 10 10
273 30 m. Footballers, globe and ball 25 10
274 50 m. Footballers playing in stadium 40 15
275 60 m. Goalkeeper saving goal 50 25
276 70 m. Stadium . . . . 1·10 35

63 D. Natsagdorj 64 Torch and Handclasp

1962. 3rd Congress of Mongolian Writers.

277 **63** 30 m. brown 20 15
278 50 m. green 30 15

1962. Afro-Asian People's Solidarity.

279 **64** 20 m. multicoloured . . . 15 10
280 30 m. multicoloured . . . 25 20

65 Flags of Mongolia and U.S.S.R 67 Victory Banner

1962. Mongol-Soviet Friendship.

281 **65** 30 m. multicoloured . . . 25 10
282 50 m. multicoloured . . . 35 20

1962. Malaria Eradication. Nos. 1849/91 optd with Campaign emblem and **LUTTE CONTRE LE PALUDISME**.

283 **46** 5 m. 20 20
284 – 10 m. 20 20
285 – 15 m. 20 20
286 – 20 m. 20 20
287 – 30 m. 40 30
288 – 40 m. 40 30
289 – 50 m. 55 50
290 – 1 t. . . . . 1·10 80

1962. 800th Birth Anniv of Genghis Khan.

291 **67** 20 m. multicoloured . . . 5·50 5·50
292 – 30 m. multicoloured . . . 5·50 5·50
293 – 50 m. black, brown and red 12·00 12·00
294 – 60 m. buff, blue and brown 12·00 12·00

DESIGNS: 30 m. Engraved lacquer tablets; 50 m. Obelisk; 60 m. Genghis Khan.

68 Perch

1962. Fish. Multicoloured.

295 5 m. Type **68** 15 10
296 10 m. Burbot 15 10
297 15 m. Arctic grayling 20 10
298 20 m. Bullhead 30 15
299 30 m. Pike-perch 45 20
300 50 m. Sturgeon 70 30
301 70 m. Dace 95 45
302 1 t. 50 Sculpin . . . . 1·50 70

69 Sukhe Bator

1963. 70th Birth Anniv of Sukhe Bator.

303 **69** 30 m. blue 15 10
304 60 m. lake 30 20

70 Dog "Laika" and "Sputnik 2"

1963. Space Flights. Multicoloured.

305 5 m. Type **70** 20 10
306 15 m. Rocket blasting off . . . 35 10
307 25 m. "Lunik 2" (1959) . . . 35 15
308 70 m. Nikolaev and Popovich 65 35
309 1 t. Rocket "Mars" (1962) . . 90 55

SIZES: As Type **70**: 70 m., 1 t. VERT: (21 × 70 mm): 15 m., 25 m.

71 Children packing Red Cross Parcels

1963. Red Cross Centenary Multicoloured.

310 20 m. Type **71** 35 10
311 30 m. Blood transfusion . . . 45 15
312 50 m. Doctor treating child . . 60 20
313 60 m. Ambulance at street accident 75 20
314 1 t. 30 Centenary emblem . . 90 40

72 Karl Marx 73 Woman

1963. 145th Birth Anniv of Karl Marx.

315 **72** 30 m. blue 20 10
316 60 m. lake 25 20

1963. 5th World Congress of Democratic Women, Moscow.

317 **73** 30 m. multicoloured 25 20

74 "Inachis io"

1963. Mongolian Butterflies. Multicoloured.

318 5 m. Type **74** 30 10
319 10 m. "Gonepteryx rhamni L." 35 10
320 15 m. "Aglais urticae L." . . 85 15
321 20 m. "Parnassius apollo L." . 55 20
322 30 m. "Papilio machaon L." . 85 25
323 60 m. "Agrodiaetus damon Schiff" . . . . 1·25 45
324 1 t. "Limenitis populi L." . . 1·75 60

75 Globe and Scales of Justice

1963. 15th Anniv of Declaration of Human Rights.

325 **75** 30 m. red, blue and brown 20 15
326 60 m. black, blue & yellow 30 20

76 "Coprinus comatus"

1964. Mushrooms. Multicoloured.

327 5 m. Type **76** 30 10
328 10 m. "Lactarius torminosus" 40 15
329 15 m. "Psalliota campestris" . 55 15
330 20 m. "Russula delica" . . . 60 15
331 30 m. "Ixocomus granulatus" . 90 20
332 50 m. "Lactarius scobiculatus" 1·25 45
333 70 m. "Lactarius deliciosus" . 1·60 60
334 1 t. "Ixocomus variegatus" . . 2·25 80

77 Lenin when a Young Man

1964. 60th Anniv of London Bolshevik (Communist) Party.

335 **77** 30 m. red and brown . . . 30 30
336 50 m. ultramarine and blue 35 30

78 Gymnastics

1964. Olympic Games, Tokyo. Multicoloured.

337 5 m. Type **78** 10 10
338 10 m. Throwing the javelin . . 10 10
339 15 m. Wrestling 15 10
340 20 m. Running 20 10
341 30 m. Horse-jumping 30 15
342 50 m. High-diving 40 20
343 60 m. Cycling 65 30
344 1 t. Emblem of Tokyo Games 90 50

79 Congress Emblem

1964. 4th Mongolian Women's Congress.

345 **79** 30 m. multicoloured . . . 35 20

80 "Lunik 1"

1964. Space Research. Multicoloured.

346 5 m. Type **80** 15 10
347 10 m. "Vostoks 1 and 2" . . . 15 10
348 15 m. "Tiros" (vert) 20 10
349 20 m. "Cosmos" (vert) 20 10
350 30 m. "Mars Probe" (vert) . . 30 10
351 60 m. "Luna 4" (vert) 45 15
352 80 m. "Echo 2" 60 25
353 1 t. Radio telescope 65 45

81 Horseman and Flag

1964. 40th Anniv of Mongolian Constitution.

354 **81** 25 m. multicoloured . . . 30 10
355 50 m. multicoloured . . . 35 20

82 Marine Exploration

1965. International Quiet Sun Year. Multicoloured.

356 5 m. Type **82** (postage) 30 10
357 10 m. Weather balloon 15 10
358 60 m. Northern Lights 60 20
359 80 m. Geomagnetic emblems . . 70 25
360 1 t. Globe and I.Q.S.Y. emblem 1·10 50

361 15 m. Weather satellite (air) . 40 10
362 20 m. Antarctic exploration . 3·00 55
363 30 m. Space exploration . . . 55 15

83 Horses Grazing

1965. Mongolian Horses. Multicoloured.

364 5 m. Type **83** 30 10
365 10 m. Hunting with golden eagles 1·25 15
366 15 m. Breaking-in wild horse . 45 15
367 20 m. Horses racing 45 15
368 30 m. Horses jumping 55 15
369 60 m. Hunting wolves 70 25
370 80 m. Milking a mare 85 40
371 1 t. Mare and colt . . . . . . 1·40 60

84 Farm Girl with Lambs

1965. 40th Anniv of Mongolian Youth Movement.

372 **84** 5 m. orange, bistre & green 10 10
373 – 10 m. bistre, blue and red 15 10
374 – 20 m. ochre, red and violet 20 15
375 – 30 m. lilac, brown & green 45 20
376 – 50 m. orange, buff and blue 75 45

DESIGNS: 10 m. Young drummers; 20 m. Children around campfire; 30 m. Young wrestlers; 50 m. Emblem.

85 Chinese Perch

1965. Mongolian Fishes. Multicoloured.

377 5 m. Type **85** 20 10
378 10 m. "Brachymistrax lenok" 20 10
379 15 m. Siberian sturgeon . . . 25 15
380 20 m. Taimen 35 15
381 30 m. Banded catfish 55 20
382 60 m. Amur catfish 85 20
383 80 m. Pike 90 40
384 1 t. River perch . . . . . . 1·25 60

86 Marx and Lenin

87 I.T.U. Emblem and Symbols

1965. Organization of Socialist Countries' Postal Administrations Conference, Peking.

385 **86** 10 m. black and red . . . 25 15

1965. Air. I.T.U. Centenary.

386 **87** 30 m. blue and bistre . . . 40 15
387 50 m. red, bistre and blue 60 20

88 Sable

1966. Mongolian Fur Industry.

388 **88** 5 m. purple, black & yellow 15 10
389 – 10 m. brown, black & grey 15 10
390 – 15 m. brown, black & blue 25 10
391 – 20 m. multicoloured . . . 25 10
392 – 30 m. brown, black & mve 35 10
393 – 60 m. brown, black & green 55 25
394 – 80 m. multicoloured . . . 85 40
395 – 1 t. blue, black and olive . 1·90 50

DESIGNS (Fur animals): HORIZ: 10 m. Red fox; 30 m. Pallas's cat; 60 m. Beech marten. VERT: 15 m. European otter; 20 m. Cheetah; 80 m. Stoat; 1 t. Woman in fur coat.

89 W.H.O. Building

1966. Inauguration of W.H.O. Headquarters, Geneva.

396 **89** 30 m. blue, gold and green 35 15
397 50 m. blue, gold and red . 50 20

HAVE YOU READ THE NOTES AT THE BEGINNING OF THIS CATALOGUE?

These often provide the answers to the enquiries we receive.

90 Footballers

1966. World Cup Football Championships. Multicoloured.

398 10 m. Type **90** 15 10
399 30 m. Footballers (different) . 25 10
400 60 m. Goalkeeper saving goal . 40 25
401 80 m. Footballers (different) . 65 30
402 1 t. World Cup flag . . . . . 1·10 35

92 Sukhe Bator and Parliament Buildings, Ulan Bator

1966. 15th Mongolian Communist Party Congress.

404 **92** 30 m. multicoloured 15 10

93 Wrestling

95 State Emblem

1966. World Wrestling Championships Toledo (Spain). Similar wrestling designs.

405 **93** 10 m. black, mauve & pur . 10 10
406 – 30 m. black, mauve & grey . 20 15
407 – 60 m. black, mauve & brn . 30 15
408 – 80 m. black, mauve & lilac . 40 20
409 – 1 t. black, mauve and turq . 55 20

1966. 45th Anniv of Independence. Mult.

411 30 m. Type **95** 75 20
412 50 m. Sukhe Bator, emblems of agriculture and industry (horiz) . . . . 1·75 30

96 "Physochlaena physaloides"

1966. Flowers. Multicoloured.

413 5 m. Type **96** 20 10
414 10 m. Onion 20 10
415 15 m. Red lily 25 10
416 20 m. "Thermopsis lanceolata" 35 10
417 30 m. "Amygdalus mongolica" 50 20
418 60 m. Bluebeard 60 30
419 80 m. "Piptanthus mongolicus" 75 40
420 1 t. "Iris bungei" 95 55

1966. 60th Birth Anniv of D. Natsagdorj. Nos. 277/8 optd **1906 1966.**

420a **63** 30 m. brown . . . . 6·50 6·50
420b 50 m. green . . . . 6·50 6·50

97 Child with Dove

1966. Children's Day. Multicoloured.

421 10 m. Type **97** 20 10
422 15 m. Children with reindeer . 20 10
423 20 m. Boys wrestling 25 10
424 30 m. Boy riding horse . . . 50 15
425 60 m. Children on camel . . . 60 20
426 80 m. Shepherd boy with sheep 75 25
427 1 t. Boy archer . . . . 1·40 55

The 15 m., 30 m. and 80 m. are horiz.

98 "Proton 1"

1966. Space Satellites. Multicoloured.

428 5 m. "Vostok 2" (vert) . . . 10 10
429 10 m. Type **98** 10 10
430 15 m. "Telstar 1" (vert) . . . 15 10
431 20 m. "Molniya 1" (vert) . . 15 10
432 30 m. "Syncom 3" (vert) . . . 20 15
433 60 m. "Luna 9" (vert) 40 15
434 80 m. "Luna 12" (vert) . . . 60 30
435 1 t. Mars and photographs taken by "Mariner 4" 85 40

99 Tarbosaurus

1966. Prehistoric Animals. Multicoloured.

436 5 m. Type **99** 40 10
437 10 m. Talararus 40 10
438 15 m. Protoceratops 55 15
439 20 m. Indricotherium 55 15
440 30 m. Saurolophus 90 20
441 60 m. Mastodon . . . . . . 1·40 30
442 80 m. Mongolotherium . . . 1·60 45
443 1 t. Mammuthus . . . . . . 1·75 70

100 Congress Emblem

101 Sukhe Bator and Mongolian and Soviet Soldiers

1967. 9th International Students' Union Congress.

444 **100** 30 m. ultramarine and blue 25 15
445 50 m. blue and pink . . . 35 20

1967. 50th Anniv of October Revolution.

446 **101** 40 m. multicoloured . . . 35 20
447 – 60 m. multicoloured . . . 40 25

DESIGN: 60 m. Lenin, and soldiers with sword.

102 Vietnamese Mother and Child

1967. Help for Vietnam.

448 **102** 30 m. + 20 m. brown, red and blue 30 25
449 50 m. + 30 m. brown, blue and red 50 40

103 Figure Skating

1967. Winter Olympic Games, Grenoble. Mult.

450 5 m. Type **103** 10 10
451 10 m. Speed skating 10 10
452 15 m. Ice hockey 30 10
453 20 m. Skijumping 40 10
454 30 m. Bob sleighing 45 20
455 60 m. Figure skating (pairs) . 60 30
456 80 m. Downhill skiing 80 40

104 Bactrian Camel and Calf

1968. Young Animals. Multicoloured.

458 5 m. Type **104** 15 10
459 10 m. Yak 15 10
460 15 m. Lamb 20 10
461 20 m. Foal 30 10
462 30 m. Calf 30 10
463 60 m. Bison 40 15
464 80 m. Roe deer 55 30
465 1 t. Reindeer 80 40

105 Prickly Rose

ДЭХБ
20 ЖИЛ
WHO
(**106**)

1968. Mongolian Berries.

466 **105** 5 m. ultramarine on blue . 15 10
467 – 10 m. brown on buff . . . 15 10
468 – 15 m. emerald on green . 20 10
469 – 20 m. red on cream . . . 20 10
470 – 30 m. red on pink 25 10
471 – 60 m. brown on orange . 45 20
472 – 80 m. turquoise on blue . 60 25
473 – 1 t. red on cream 80 40

DESIGNS: 10 m. Blackcurrant; 15 m. Gooseberry; 20 m. Crabapple; 30 m. Strawberry; 60 m. Redcurrant; 80 m. Cowberry; 1 t. Sea buckthorn.

1968. 20th Anniv of World Health Organization. Nos. 396/7 optd with T **106**.

474 **89** 30 m. blue, gold and green 2·50 2·50
475 50 m. blue, gold and red . 2·50 2·50

107 Human Rights Emblem

109 "Portrait of Artist Sharab" (A. Sangatzohyo)

108 "Das Kapital"

1968. Human Rights Year.

476 **107** 30 m. green and blue . . . 30 10

1968. 150th Birth Anniv of Karl Marx. Mult.

477 30 m. Type **108** 20 10
478 50 m. Karl Marx 35 20

1968. Mongolian Paintings. Multicoloured.

479 5 m. Type **109** 15 10
480 10 m. "On Remote Roads" (A. Sangatzohyo) 20 10
481 15 m. "Camel Calf" (B. Avarzad) 25 10
482 20 m. "The Milk" (B. Avarzad) 30 15
483 30 m. "The Bowman" (B. Gombosuren) 50 30
484 80 m. "Girl Sitting on a Yak" (A. Sangatzohyo) 70 40
485 1 t. 40 "Cagan Dara Ekke" (Janaivajara) . . . . . . 1·25 75

110 Volleyball

1968. Olympic Games, Mexico. Multicoloured.

487 5 m. Type **110** 10 10
488 10 m. Wrestling 10 10
489 15 m. Cycling 15 10
490 20 m. Throwing the javelin . 15 10
491 30 m. Football 15 15
492 60 m. Running 35 25
493 80 m. Gymnastics 55 25
494 1 t. Weightlifting 90 40

111 Hammer and Spade

1968. 7th Anniv of Darkhan Town.

496 **111** 50 m. orange and blue . . 20 10

112 Gorky

113 "Madonna and Child" (Boltraffio)

1968. Birth Centenary of Maksim Gorky (writer).

497 **112** 60 m. ochre and blue . . 20 10

1968. 20th Anniv (1966) of U.N.E.S.C.O. Paintings by European Masters in National Gallery, Budapest. Multicoloured.

498 5 m. Type **113** 15 10
499 10 m. "St. Roch healed by an angel" (Moretto of Brescia) 20 10
500 15 m. "Madonna and Child with St. Anne" (Macchietti) . . 25 10
501 20 m. "St. John on Patmos" (Cano) 35 15
502 30 m. "Young lady with viola da gamba" (Kupetzky) 35 15
503 80 m. "Study of a head" (Amerling) 60 50
504 1 t. 40 "The death of Adonis" (Furini) . . . . 1·25 75

114 Paavo Nurmi (running)

1969. Olympic Games' Gold-medal Winners. Multicoloured.

506 5 m. Type **114** 10 10
507 10 m. Jesse Owens (running) . 10 10
508 15 m. F. Blankers-Koen (hurdling) 15 10
509 20 m. Laszlo Papp (boxing) . 15 10
510 30 m. Wilma Rudolph (running) 25 15
511 60 m. Boris Sahlin (gymnastics) 35 20
512 80 m. D. Schollander (swimming) 40 25
513 1 t. A. Nakayama (ring exercises) 80 45

115 Bayit Costume (woman)

1969. Mongolian Costumes. Multicoloured.

515 5 m. Type **115** 20 10
516 10 m. Torgut (man) 20 10
517 15 m. Sakhchin (woman) . . . 25 10
518 20 m. Khalka (woman) 35 10
519 30 m. Daringanga (woman) . . 40 15
520 60 m. Mingat (woman) 55 20
521 80 m. Khalka (man) 75 25
522 1 t. Barga (woman) . . . . . 1·25 40

116 Emblem and Helicopter Rescue

1969. 30th Anniv of Mongolian Red Cross.

523 **116** 30 m. red and blue 60 20
524 – 50 m. red and violet . . . 50 25

DESIGN: 50 m. Shepherd and ambulance.

117 Yellow Lion's-foot

1969. Landscapes and Flowers. Multicoloured.

525 5 m. Type **117** 15 10
526 10 m. Variegated pink 15 10
527 15 m. Superb pink 25 10
528 20 m. Meadow cranesbill . . . 25 10
529 30 m. Mongolian pink 40 15
530 60 m. Asiatic globe flower . . 50 15
531 80 m. Long-lipped larkspur . . 70 30
532 1 t. Saxaul 85 40

118 "Bullfight" (O. Tsewegdjaw)

1969. 10th Anniv of Co-operative Movement. Paintings in National Gallery, Ulan Bator. Mult.

533 5 m. Type **118** 10 10
534 10 m. "Colts Fighting" (O. Tsewegdjaw) 10 10
535 15 m. "Horse-herd" (A. Sengetsohyo) 20 10
536 20 m. "Camel Caravan" (D. Damdinsuren) 20 10
537 30 m. "On the Steppe" (N. Tsultem) 35 15
538 60 m. "Milking Mares" (O. Tsewegdjaw) 40 15
539 80 m. "Off to School" (B. Avarzad) 50 30
540 1 t. "After Work" (G. Odon) . 80 40

120 Army Crest

БНМАУ-ыг
тунхагласны
45
жилийн ой
1969—XI—26
(**121**)

1969. 30th Anniv of Battle of Khalka River.

543 **120** 50 m. multicoloured . . . 30 10

1969. 45th Anniv of Mongolian People's Republic. Nos. 411/12 optd with T **121**.

544 **95** 30 m. multicoloured . . . 1·50 1·40
545 – 50 m. multicoloured . . . 3·00 2·10

122 "Sputnik 3"

1969. Exploration of Space. Multicoloured.

546 5 m. Type **122** 15 10
547 10 m. "Vostok 1" 15 10
548 15 m. "Mercury 7" 20 10
549 20 m. Space-walk from "Voskhod 2" 30 10
550 30 m. "Apollo 8" in Moon orbit 40 15
551 60 m. Space-walk from "Soyuz 5" 45 25
552 80 m. "Apollo 12" and Moon landing 55 30

123 Wolf

1970. Wild Animals. Multicoloured.

554 5 m. Type **123** 25 10
555 10 m. Brown bear 30 10
556 15 m. Lynx 55 10
557 20 m. Wild Boar 55 10
558 30 m. Elk 60 20
559 60 m. Bobak marmot 70 20
560 80 m. Argali 80 35
561 1 t. "Hun Hunter and Hound" (tapestry) 90 50

124 "Lenin Centenary" (silk panel, Cerenhuu)

1970. Birth Centenary of Lenin. Multicoloured.

562 20 m. Type **124** 15 10
563 50 m. "Mongolians meeting Lenin" (Sangatzohyo) (horiz) 30 15
564 1 t. "Lenin" (Mazhig) 45 20

125 "Fairy Tale" Pavilion

1970. "EXPO 70" World Fair, Osaka, Japan.

565 **125** 1 t. 50 multicoloured . . 65 55

126 Footballers

1970. World Cup Football Championships, Mexico.

567 **126** 10 m. multicoloured . . . 15 10
568 – 20 m. multicoloured . . . 15 10
569 – 30 m. multicoloured . . . 20 10
570 – 50 m. multicoloured . . . 25 10
571 – 60 m. multicoloured . . . 45 15
572 – 1 t. multicoloured 55 15
573 – 1 t. 30 multicoloured . . 70 40

DESIGNS: Nos. 568/73, Different football scenes.

127 Common Buzzard

1970. Birds of Prey. Multicoloured.

575 10 m. Type **127** 70 10
576 20 m. Tawny owls 90 10
577 30 m. Northern goshawk . . . 1·10 15
578 50 m. White-tailed sea eagle . 1·25 20
579 60 m. Peregrine falcon . . . . 1·75 40
580 1 t. Common kestrels . . . . 2·00 45
581 1 t. 30 Black kite . . . . . . 2·40 55

128 Soviet Memorial, Treptow, Berlin
129 Mongol Archery

1970. 25th Anniv of Victory in Second World War.

582 **128** 60 m. multicoloured . . . 35 15

1970. Mongolian Traditional Life. Multicoloured.

583 10 m. Type **129** 30 15
584 20 m. Bodg-gegeen's Palace, Ulan Bator 30 15
585 30 m. Mongol horsemen . . . 30 20
586 40 m. "The White Goddess-Mother" 30 25
587 50 m. Girl in National costume 65 45
588 60 m. "Lion's Head" (statue) . 75 45
589 70 m. Dancer's mask 85 65
590 80 m. Gateway, Bogd-gegeen's Palace . . . . 1·00 1·00

131 I.E.Y. and U.N. Emblems with Flag

1970. International Education Year.

592 **131** 60 m. multicoloured . . . 25 15

132 Horseman, "50" and Sunrise

1970. 50th Anniv of National Press.

593 **132** 30 m. multicoloured . . . 35 20

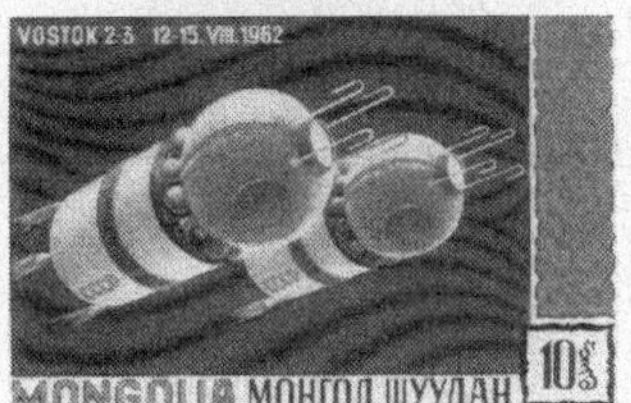

133 "Vostok 3" and "4"

1971. Space Research. Multicoloured.

594 10 m. Type **133** 15 10
595 20 m. Space-walk from "Voskhod 2" 15 15
596 30 m. "Gemini 6" and "7" . . 15 15
597 50 m. Docking of "Soyuz 4" and "5" 25 20
598 60 m. "Soyuz 6", "7" and "8" 35 20
599 80 m. "Apollo 11" and lunar module 50 35
600 1 t. "Apollo 13" damaged . . 60 30
601 1 t. 30 "Luna 16" 75 30

No. 594 is incorrectly inscribed "Vostok 2–3". The date refers to flight of "Vostoks 3" and "4".

134 Sukhe Bator addressing Meeting

1971. 50th Anniv of Revolutionary Party. Mult.

603 30 m. Type **134** 15 10
604 60 m. Horseman with flag . . 25 10
605 90 m. Sukhe Bator with Lenin 30 15
606 1 t. 20 Mongolians with banner 40 25

136 Tsam Mask

1971. Mongol Tsam Masks.

608 **136** 10 m. multicoloured . . . 15 10
609 – 20 m. multicoloured . . . 25 10
610 – 30 m. multicoloured . . . 30 10
611 – 50 m. multicoloured . . . 35 10
612 – 60 m. multicoloured . . . 45 20
613 – 1 t. multicoloured 80 30
614 – 1 t. 30 multicoloured . . 1·00 50

DESIGNS: Nos. 609/14, Different dance masks.

137 Banner and Party Emblems

1971. 16th Revolutionary Party Congress.

615 **137** 60 m. multicoloured . . . 20 10

138 Steam Locomotive

1971. "50 Years of Transport Development". Multicoloured.

616 20 m. Type **138** 60 15
617 30 m. Diesel locomotive . . . 65 15
618 40 m. Russian "Urals" truck 65 15
619 50 m. Russian "Moskovich 412" car 75 15
620 60 m. Polikarpov Po-2 biplane 90 25
621 80 m. Antonov AN-24B airliner 1·10 40
622 1 t. Lake steamer "Sukhe Bator" 2·00 70

139 Soldier
140 Emblem and Red Flag

1971. 50th Anniv of People's Army and Police. Multicoloured.

623 60 m. Type **139** 40 10
624 1 t. 50 Policeman and child . 85 20

1971. 50th Anniv of Revolutionary Youth Organization.

625 **140** 60 m. multicoloured . . . 30 20

141 Mongolian Flag and Year Emblem

1971. Racial Equality Year.

626 **141** 60 m. multicoloured . . . 30 15

142 "The Old Man and the Tiger"

1971. Mongolian Folk Tales. Multicoloured.

627 10 m. Type **142** 20 10
628 20 m. "The Boy Giant-killer" . 20 10
629 30 m. Cat and mice 20 10
630 50 m. Mongolians riding on eagle 25 10
631 60 m. Girl on horseback ("The Wise Bride") 40 15
632 80 m. King and courtiers with donkey 55 20
633 1 t. Couple kneeling before empty throne ("Story of the Throne") 80 25
634 1 t. 30 "The Wise Bird" . . . 95 40

143 Yaks

1971. Livestock Breeding. Multicoloured.

635 20 m. Type **143** 20 10
636 30 m. Bactrian camels 20 10
637 40 m. Sheep 25 10
638 50 m. Goats 40 10
639 60 m. Cattle 50 20
640 80 m. Horses 60 25
641 1 t. Pony 95 45

144 Cross-country Skiing

1972. Winter Olympic Games, Sapporo, Japan. Multicoloured.

642 10 m. Type **144** 25 10
643 20 m. Bobsleighing 30 10
644 30 m. Figure skating 30 10
645 50 m. Slalom skiing 35 10
646 60 m. Speed skating 40 15
647 80 m. Downhill skiing 50 20
648 1 t. Ice hockey 70 25
649 1 t. 30 Pairs figure skating . . 85 40

145 "Horse-breaking" (A. Sengatzohyo)

1972. Paintings by Contemporary Artists from the National Gallery, Ulan Bator. Multicoloured.

651 10 m. Type **145** 15 10
652 20 m. "Black Camel" (A. Sengatzohyo) 20 10
653 30 m. "Jousting" (A. Sengatzohyo) 25 10
654 50 m. "Wrestling Match" (A. Sengatzohyo) 30 10
655 60 m. "Waterfall" (A. Sengatzohyo) 40 10
656 80 m. "Old Musician" (U. Yadamsuren) 50 20
657 1 t. "Young Musician" (U. Yadamsuren) 60 25
658 1 t. 30 "Ancient Prophet" (B. Avarzad) 85 40

147 "Calosoma fischeri"

1972. Insects. Multicoloured.

660 10 m. Type **147** 20 10
661 20 m. "Mylabris mongolica" . 25 10
662 30 m. "Sternoplax zichyi" . . 30 10
663 50 m. "Rhaebus komarovi" . 40 15
664 60 m. "Meloe centripubens" . 55 15
665 80 m. "Eodorcadion mongolicum" 75 25
666 1 t. "Platyope maongolica" . 90 30
667 1 t. 30 "Lixus nigrolineatus" . 1·40 50

149 Satellite and Dish Aerial ("Telecommunications")

1972. Air. National Achievements. Multicoloured.

669 20 m. Type **149** 20 10
670 30 m. Horse-herd ("Livestock Breeding") 30 10
671 40 m. Diesel train and Tupolev Tu-144 aircraft ("Transport") 90 15
672 50 m. Corncob and farm ("Agriculture") 35 15
673 60 m. Ambulance and hospital ("Public Health") 70 20
674 80 m. Actors ("Culture") . . 70 25
675 1 t. Factory ("Industry") . . 75 40

150 Globe, Flag and Dish Aerial

1972. Air. World Telecommunications Day.

676 **150** 60 m. multicoloured . . . 40 15

151 Running

1972. Olympic Games, Munich. Multicoloured.

677 10 m. Type **151** 15 10
678 15 m. Boxing 15 10
679 20 m. Judo 20 10
680 25 m. High jumping 20 10
681 30 m. Rifle-shooting 30 15
682 60 m. Wrestling 45 20
683 80 m. Weightlifting 55 25
684 1 t. Mongolian flag and Olympic emblems 80 45

152 E.C.A.F.E. Emblem

1972. 25th Anniv of E.C.A.F.E.
686 **152** 60 m. blue, gold and red . 20 10

153 Mongolian Racerunner

1972. Reptiles. Multicoloured.
687 10 m. Type **153** 20 10
688 15 m. Radde's toad 25 10
689 20 m. Halys viper 85 10
690 25 m. Toad-headed agama . . 40 15
691 30 m. Asiatic grass frog . . . 55 15
692 60 m. Plate-tailed geckol . . . 70 25
693 80 m. Steppe ribbon snake . . 85 35
694 1 t. Mongolian agama . . . . 1·25 55

154 "Technical Knowledge"

1972. 30th Anniv of Mongolian State University. Multicoloured.
695 50 m. Type **154** 35 10
696 60 m. University building . . 45 15

155 "Madonna and Child with St. John the Baptist and a Holy Woman" (Bellini)

1972. Air. U.N.E.S.C.O. "Save Venice" Campaign. Paintings. Multicoloured.
697 10 m. Type **155** 15 10
698 20 m. "The Transfiguration" (Bellini) (vert) 20 10
699 30 m. "Blessed Virgin with the Child" (Bellini) (vert) . . . 25 10
700 50 m. "Presentation of the Christ in the Temple" (Bellini) . . 40 15
701 60 m. "St. George" (Bellini) (vert) 50 20
702 80 m. "Departure of Ursula" (detail, Carpaccio) (vert) . . 65 35
703 1 t. "Departure of Ursula" (different detail, Carpaccio) . 85 45

156 Manlay-Bator Damdinsuren

157 Spassky Tower, Moscow Kremlin

1972. National Heroes. Multicoloured.
705 10 m. Type **156** 15 10
706 20 m. Ard Ayus in chains (horiz) 25 10
707 50 m. Hatan-Bator Magsarzhav 40 15
708 60 m. Has-Bator on the march (horiz) 55 20
709 1 t. Sukhe Bator 85 30

1972. 50th Anniv of U.S.S.R.
710 **157** 60 m. multicoloured . . . 50 15

158 Snake and "Mars 1"

1972. Air. Animal Signs of the Mongolian Calendar and Progress in Space Exploration. Multicoloured.
711 60 m. Type **158** 70 25
712 60 m. Horse and "Apollo 8" (square) 70 25
713 60 m. Sheep and "Electron 2" (square) 70 25
714 60 m. Monkey and "Explorer 6" 70 25
715 60 m. Dragon and "Mariner 2" 70 25
716 60 m. Pig and "Cosmos 110" (square) 70 25
717 60 m. Dog and "Ariel 2" (square) 70 25
718 60 m. Cockerel and "Venus 1" 70 25
719 60 m. Hare and "Soyuz 5" . 70 25
720 60 m. Tiger and "Gemini 7" (square) 70 25
721 60 m. Ox and "Venus 4" (square) 70 25
722 60 m. Rat and "Apollo 15" lunar rover 70 25
The square designs are size 40×40 mm.

159 Swimming Gold Medal (Mark Spitz, U.S.A.)

1972. Gold Medal Winners, Munich Olympic Games. Multicoloured.
723 5 m. Type **159** 15 10
724 10 m. High jumping (Ulrike Meyfarth, West Germany) . 25 10
725 20 m. Gymnastics (Savao Kato, Japan) 25 10
726 30 m. Show jumping (Andras Balczo, Hungary) 35 10
727 60 m. Running (Lasse Viren, Finland) 50 20
728 80 m. Swimming (Shane Gould, Australia) 70 25
729 1 t. Putting the shot (Anatoli Bondarchuk, U.S.S.R.) . . 85 35

160 Monkey on Cycle

1973. Mongolian Circus (1st series). Mult.
731 5 m. Type **160** 20 10
732 10 m. Seal with ball 20 10
733 15 m. Bear on mono-wheel . . 30 10
734 20 m. Acrobat on camel . . . 30 10
735 30 m. Acrobat on horse . . . 50 10
736 50 m. Clown playing flute . . 60 15
737 60 m. Contortionist 70 30
738 1 t. New Circus Hall, Ulan Bator 1·00 45
See also Nos. 824/30.

161 Mounted Postman

162 Sukhe Bator receiving Traditional Gifts

1973.
739 **161** 50 m. brown (postage) . . 60 10
740 – 60 m. green . . . . 1·75 15
741 – 1 t. purple . . . . 1·00 20
742 – 1 t. 50 blue (air) . . . . . 1·75 25
DESIGNS: 60 m. Diesel train; 1 t. Mail truck; 1 t. 50, Antonov An-24 airliner.

1973. 80th Birth Anniv of Sukhe Bator. Mult.
743 10 m. Type **162** 15 10
744 20 m. Holding reception . . . 25 10
745 50 m. Leading army 35 10
746 60 m. Addressing council . . . 45 10
747 1 t. Giving audience (horiz) . . 65 20

163 W.M.O. Emblem and Meteorological Symbols

1973. Air. Centenary of World Meteorological Organization.
748 **163** 60 m. multicoloured . . . 45 15

164 "Copernicus" (anon)

167 Marx and Lenin

Нэгдлийн Холбооны IV Их
Хурал 1973-6-11
(166)

1973. 500th Birth Anniv of Nicholas Copernicus (astronomer). Multicoloured.
749 50 m. Type **164** 40 15
750 60 m. "Copernicus in his Observatory" (J. Matejko) (55×35 mm) 50 15
751 1 t. "Copernicus" (Jan Matejko) 70 30

1973. 4th Agricultural Co-operative Congress, Ulan Bator. No. 538 optd with T **166**.
754 60 m. multicoloured . . . . .

1973. 9th Organization of Socialist States Postal Ministers Congress, Ulan Bator.
755 **167** 60 m. multicoloured . . . 30 15

168 Russian Stamp and Emblems

1973. Air. Council for Mutual Economic Aid Posts and Telecommunications Conference, Ulan Bator. Multicoloured.
756 30 m. Type **168** 30 15
757 30 m. Mongolia 45 20
758 30 m. Bulgaria 45 20
759 30 m. Hungary 45 20
760 30 m. Czechoslovakia 45 20
761 30 m. German Democratic Republic 45 20
762 30 m. Cuba 45 20
763 30 m. Rumania 45 20
764 30 m. Poland 70 20

169 Common Shelduck

1973. Aquatic Birds. Multicoloured.
765 5 m. Type **169** 45 10
766 10 m. Black-throated diver . . 65 10
767 15 m. Bar-headed geese . . . 1·00 15
768 30 m. Great crested grebe . . 1·25 20
769 50 m. Mallard . . . . 1·90 40
770 60 m. Mute swan . . . . . . 2·25 40
771 1 t. Greater scaups . . . . . 2·50 60

170 Siberian Weasel

1973. Small Fur Animals. Multicoloured.
772 5 m. Type **170** 20 10
773 10 m. Siberian chipmunk . . 20 10
774 15 m. Siberian flying squirrel . 20 10
775 20 m. Eurasian badger 25 15
776 30 m. Eurasian red squirrel . 35 15
777 60 m. Wolverine 70 30
778 80 m. American mink 85 45
779 1 t. Arctic hare . . . . . . 1·25 60

171 Launching "Soyuz" Spacecraft

1973. Air. "Apollo" and "Soyuz" Space Programmes. Multicoloured.
780 5 m. Type **171** 15 10
781 10 m. "Apollo 8" 15 10
782 15 m. "Soyuz 4" and "5" linked 20 15
783 20 m. "Apollo 11" module on Moon 20 15
784 30 m. "Apollo 14" after splash-down 30 15
785 50 m. Triple flight by "Soyuz 6", "7" and "8" 35 20
786 60 m. "Apollo 16" lunar rover 45 25
787 1 t "Lunokhod 1" 65 30

172 Global Emblem

1973. 15th Anniv of Review "Problems of Peace and Socialism".
789 **172** 60 m. red, gold and blue . 35 15

173 Alpine Aster

1973. Mongolian Flowers. Multicoloured.
790 5 m. Type **173** 15 10
791 10 m. Mongolian catchfly . . 25 10
792 15 m. "Rosa davurica" . . . 30 10
793 20 m. Mongolian dandelion . 40 15
794 30 m. "Rhododendron dahuricum" 55 20
795 50 m. "Clematis tangutica" . 70 40
796 60 m. Siberian primrose . . . 85 40
797 1 t. Pasque flower . . . . . . 1·25 60

174 "Limenitis populi"

1974. Butterflies and Moths. Multicoloured.

798 5 m. Type **174** 30 10
799 10 m. "Arctia hebe" 35 10
800 15 m. "Rhyparia purpurata" . 40 10
801 20 m. "Catocala pacta" . . . 55 10
802 30 m. "Isoceras kaszabi" . . . 70 15
803 50 m. "Celerio costata" . . . 1·00 30
804 60 m. "Arctia caja" . . . . . 1·10 40
805 1 t. "Diacrisia sannio" . . . . 1·50 50

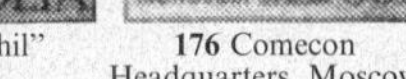

175 "Hebe Namshil" (L. Merdorsh)

176 Comecon Headquarters, Moscow

1974. Mongolian Opera and Drama. Multicoloured.

806 15 m. Type **175** 25 10
807 20 m. "Sive Hiagt" (D. Luvsansharav) (horiz) . 25 10
808 25 m. "Edre" (D. Namdag) . 30 10
809 30 m. "The Three Khans of Sara-gol" (horiz) 40 15
810 60 m. "Amarsana" (B. Damdinsuren) 65 20
811 80 m. "Edre" (different scene) 80 25
812 1 t. "Edre" (different scene) . 1·25 55

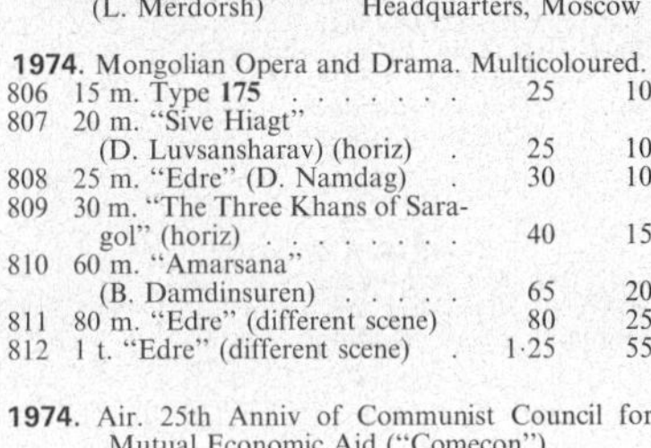

1974. Air. 25th Anniv of Communist Council for Mutual Economic Aid ("Comecon").

813 **176** 60 m. multicoloured . . . 30 20

177 Government Building and Sukhe Bator Monument, Ulan Bator

1974. 50th Anniv of Renaming of Capital as Ulan Bator.

814 **177** 60 m. multicoloured . . . 30 20

179 Mounted Courier

1974. Air. Centenary of U.P.U. Multicoloured.

816 50 m. Type **179** . . . . 1·50 40
817 50 m. Reindeer mail sledge . . 1·50 40
818 50 m. Mail coach . . . . . . 1·50 40
819 50 m. Balloon post . . . . . . 2·00 40
820 50 m. Lake steamer "Sukhe Bator" and Polikarpov Po-2 biplane . . . . 2·25 40
821 50 m. Mail train and P.O. truck 1·75 40
822 50 m. Rocket in orbit . . . . 1·50 40

MINIMUM PRICE

The minimum price quoted is 10p which represents a handling charge rather than a basis for valuing common stamps. For further notes about prices, see introductory pages.

180 Performing Horses

1974. Mongolian Circus (2nd series). Multicoloured.

824 10 m. Type **180** (postage) . . 20 10
825 20 m. Juggler (vert) 30 10
826 30 m. Elephant on ball (vert) 40 15
827 40 m. Performing yak 60 20
828 60 m. Acrobats (vert) 75 25
829 80 m. Trick cyclist (vert) . . . 1·10 45
830 1 t. Contortionist (vert) (air) . 1·10 45

181 "Training a Young Horse"

1974. Int Children's Day. Drawings by Lhamsurem. Multicoloured.

831 10 m. Type **181** 20 10
832 20 m. "Boy with Calf" . . . 30 10
833 30 m. "Riding untamed Horse" 35 10
834 40 m. "Boy with Foal" . . . 45 20
835 60 m. "Girl dancing with Doves" 60 20
836 80 m. "Wrestling" 65 30
837 1 t. "Hobby-horse Dance" . . 1·10 45

182 Archer on Foot

1974. "Nadam" Sports Festival. Multicoloured.

838 10 m. Type **182** 20 10
839 20 m. "Kazlodanie" (Kazakh mounted game) 30 10
840 30 m. Mounted archer . . . 40 10
841 40 m. Horse-racing 50 20
842 60 m. Bucking horse-riding . 60 20
843 80 m. Capturing wild horse . 70 30
844 1 t. Wrestling 80 45

183 Giant Panda

1974. Bears. Multicoloured.

845 10 m. Brown bear 15 10
846 20 m. Type **183** 25 10
847 30 m. Giant Panda 45 15
848 40 m. Brown bear 45 20
849 60 m. Sloth bear 70 30
850 80 m. Asiatic black bear . . . 80 50
851 1 t. Brown bear . . . . . . 1·40 65

184 Red Deer

1974. Games Reserves. Fauna. Multicoloured.

852 10 m. Type **184** 15 10
853 20 m. Eurasian beaver 30 10
854 30 m. Leopard 40 15
855 40 m. Herring gull . . . . . . 1·25 30
856 60 m. Roe deer 80 30
857 80 m. Argali 85 35
858 1 t. Siberian musk deer . . . . 1·40 65

185 Detail of Buddhist Temple, Palace of Bogdo Gegen

1974. Mongolian Architecture. Multicoloured.

859 10 m. Type **185** 20 10
860 15 m. Buddhist temple (now museum) 20 10
861 30 m. "Charity" Temple, Ulan Bator 40 15
862 50 m. Yurt (tent) 55 20
863 80 m. Arbour in court-yard . . 75 40

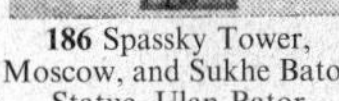

186 Spassky Tower, Moscow, and Sukhe Bator Statue, Ulan Bator

187 Proclamation of the Republic

1974. Brezhnev's Visit to Mongolia.

864 **186** 60 m. multicoloured . . . 30 20

1974. 50th Anniv of Mongolian People's Republic. Multicoloured.

865 60 m. Type **187** 35 20
866 60 m. "First Constitution" (embroidery) 35 20
867 60 m. Mongolian flag 35 20

188 Gold Decanter

1974. Goldsmiths' Treasures of the 19th Century. Multicoloured.

868 10 m. Type **188** 20 10
869 20 m. Silver jug 30 10
870 30 m. Night lamp 35 10
871 40 m. Tea jug 45 20
872 60 m. Candelabra 55 20
873 80 m. Teapot 75 30
874 1 t. Silver bowl on stand . . . 1·00 40

189 Lapwing

1974. Protection of Water and Nature Conservation. Multicoloured.

875 10 m. Type **189** (postage) . . . 80 15
876 20 m. Sturgeon 45 10
877 30 m. Marsh marigolds 50 15
878 40 m. Dalmatian pelican . . . 1·40 20
879 60 m. Perch 75 25
880 80 m. Sable 90 40
881 1 t. Hydrologist with jar of water (air) . . . . 1·00 40

190 U.S. Mail Coach

1974. Centenary of U.P.U. Multicoloured.

883 10 m. Type **190** 15 10
884 20 m. French postal cart . . . 20 10
885 30 m. Changing horses, Russian mail and passenger carriage 35 15
886 40 m. Swedish postal coach with caterpillar tracks 45 20
887 50 m. First Hungarian mail van 50 25
888 60 m. German Daimler-Benz mail van and trailer 65 40
889 1 t. Mongolian postal courier 95 55

191 Red Flag

193 Mongolian Woman

192 "Zygophyllum xanthoxylon" (½-size illustration)

1975. 30th Anniv of Victory.

891 **191** 60 m. multicoloured . . . 35 20

1975. 12th International Botanical Conference. Rare Medicinal Plants. Multicoloured.

892 10 m. Type **192** 25 10
893 20 m. "Incarvillea potaninii" . 35 10
894 30 m. "Lancea tibetica" . . . 55 15
895 40 m. "Jurinea mongolica" . . 55 20
896 50 m. "Saussurea involucrata" 70 20
897 60 m. "Allium mongolicum" . 80 30
898 1 t. "Adonis mongolica" . . . 1·40 40

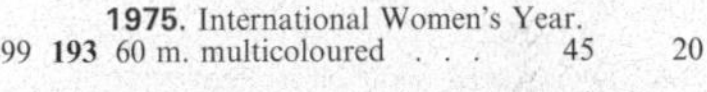

1975. International Women's Year.

899 **193** 60 m. multicoloured . . . 45 20

194 "Soyuz" on Launch-pad

1975. Air. Joint Soviet–American Space Project. Multicoloured.

900 10 m. Type **194** 10 10
901 20 m. Launch of "Apollo" . . 15 10
902 30 m. "Apollo" and "Soyuz" spacecraft 30 10
903 40 m. Docking manoeuvre . . 35 20
904 50 m. Spacecraft docked together 45 20
905 60 m. "Soyuz" in orbit . . . 50 30
906 1 t. "Apollo" and "Soyuz" spacecraft and communications satellite . . 80 40

195 Child and Lamb

1975. International Children's Day. Multicoloured.

908 10 m. Type **195** 20 10
909 20 m. Child riding horse . . . 40 10
910 30 m. Child with calf 40 10
911 40 m. Child and "orphan camel" 40 15
912 50 m. "The Obedient Yak" . . 50 25
913 60 m. Child riding on swan . 60 30
914 1 t. Two children singing . . 95 45

See also Nos. 979/85.

196 Pioneers tending Tree

Тээвэр—50
1975—7—15.

(197)

1975. 50th Anniv of Mongolian Pioneer Organization. Multicoloured.

915 50 m. Type **196** 30 15
916 60 m. Children's study circle . 50 20
917 1 t. New emblem of Mongolian pioneers 65 30

1975. 50th Anniv of Public Transport. Nos. 616/22 optd with T **197**.

918 **138** 20 m. multicoloured . . . 2·50 2·50
919 – 30 m. multicoloured . . . 2·50 2·50
920 – 40 m. multicoloured . . . 1·90 1·90
921 – 50 m. multicoloured . . . 1·90 1·90
922 – 60 m. multicoloured . . . 2·50 2·50
923 – 80 m. multicoloured . . . 3·00 3·00
924 – 1 t. multicoloured . . . . 3·75 3·75

198 Argali

1975. Air. South Asia Tourist Year.

925 **198** 1 t. 50 multicoloured . . . 90 40

199 Golden Eagle attacking Red Fox

1975. Hunting Scenes. Multicoloured.

926 10 m. Type **199** 90 15
927 20 m. Lynx-hunting (vert) . . 45 10
928 30 m. Hunter stalking bobak marmots 50 15
929 40 m. Hunter riding on reindeer (vert) 60 20
930 50 m. Shooting wild boar . . 60 25
931 60 m. Wolf in trap (vert) . . . 75 35
932 1 t. Hunters with brown bear . 1·00 50

200 "Mesocottus haitej"

1975. Fishes. Multicoloured.

933 10 m. Type **200** 20 10
934 20 m. "Pseudaspius lepto cephalus" 30 10
935 30 m. "Oreoleuciscus potanini" 35 15
936 40 m. "Tinca tinca" 45 20
937 50 m. "Coregonus lavaretus" . 65 25
938 60 m. "Erythroculter mongolicus" 75 30
939 1 t. "Carassius auratus" . . . 1·25 55

201 "Morin Hur" (musical instrument)

202 Revolutionary with Banner

1975. Mongolian Handicrafts. Multicoloured.

940 10 m. Type **201** 15 10
941 20 m. Saddle 25 10
942 30 m. Headdress 30 10
943 40 m. Boots 40 15
944 50 m. Cap 50 20
945 60 m. Pipe and tobacco pouch 60 25
946 1 t. Fur hat 90 40

1975. 70th Anniv of 1905 Russian Revolution.

947 **202** 60 m. multicoloured . . . 35 20

203 "Taming a Wild Horse"

1975. Mongolian Paintings. Multicoloured.

948 10 m. Type **203** 10 10
949 20 m. "Camel Caravan" (horiz) 25 10
950 30 m. "Man playing Lute" . 35 10
951 40 m. "Woman adjusting Headdress" (horiz) 40 15
952 50 m. "Woman in ceremonial Costume" 40 25
953 60 m. "Woman fetching Water" 50 30
954 1 t. "Woman playing Yaga" (musical instrument) . . . 75 40

204 Ski Jumping

205 "House of Young Technicians"

1975. Winter Olympic Games, Innsbruck. Multicoloured.

956 10 m. Type **204** 10 10
957 20 m. Ice hockey 30 10
958 30 m. Slalom skiing 35 10
959 40 m. Bobsleighing 45 15
960 50 m. Rifle shooting (biathlon) 55 25
961 60 m. Speed skating 60 25
962 1 t. Figure skating 90 45

1975. Public Buildings.

964 **205** 50 m. blue 40 10
965 – 60 m. green 50 15
966 – 1 t. brown 70 25

DESIGNS: 60 m. Hotel, Ulan Bator; 1 t. "Museum of the Revolution".

206 "Molniya" Satellite

1976. Air. 40th Anniv of Mongolian Meteorological Office.

967 **206** 60 m. blue and yellow . . 55 20

209 "National Economy" Star

1976. 17th Mongolian People's Revolutionary Party Congress, Ulan Bator.

970 **209** 60 m. multicoloured . . . 35 20

210 Archery

1976. Olympic Games, Montreal. Multicoloured.

971 10 m. Type **210** 15 10
972 20 m. Judo 20 10
973 30 m. Boxing 35 10
974 40 m. Gymnastics 35 15
975 60 m. Weightlifting 45 20
976 80 m. High jumping 55 25
977 1 t. Rifle shooting 80 35

1976. Int Children's Day. As T **195**. Mult.

979 10 m. Gobi Desert landscape . 20 10
980 20 m. Horse-taming 30 10
981 30 m. Horse-riding 35 10
982 40 m. Pioneers' camp 45 20
983 60 m. Young musician 60 20
984 80 m. Children's party 80 30
985 1 t. Mongolian wrestling . . . 1·00 45

211 Cavalry Charge

1976. 55th Anniv of Revolution. Multicoloured.

986 60 m. Type **211** (postage) . . . 65 20
987 60 m. Man and emblem (vert) . 65 20
988 60 m. "Industry and Agriculture" (air) 65 20

213 Osprey

1976. Protected Birds. Multicoloured.

990 10 m. Type **213** 75 15
991 20 m. Griffon vulture . . . . 1·00 15
992 30 m. Lammergeier . . . . . 1·40 20
993 40 m. Marsh harrier . . . . . 1·75 20
994 60 m. European black vulture . 2·00 30
995 80 m. Golden eagle . . . . . 2·50 35
996 1 t. Tawny eagle . . . . . . 2·75 40

214 "Rider on Wild Horse"

1976. Paintings by O. Tsewegdjaw. Multicoloured.

997 10 m. Type **214** 15 10
998 20 m. "The First Nadam" (game on horse-back) (horiz) 20 10
999 30 m. "Harbour on Khobsogol Lake" (horiz) 55 15
1000 40 m. "Awakening the Steppe" (horiz) 45 20
1001 80 m. "Wrestling" (horiz) . . 60 25
1002 1 t. "The Descent" (yak hauling timber) . . . . 1·00 50

215 "Industrial Development"

1976. Mongolian–Soviet Friendship.

1003 **215** 60 m. multicoloured . . 90 20

216 John Naber of U.S.A. (Swimming)

217 Tablet on Tortoise

1976. Olympic Games, Montreal. Gold Medal Winners. Multicoloured.

1004 10 m. Type **216** 10 10
1005 20 m. Nadia Comaneci of Rumania (gymnastics) . . 15 10
1006 30 m. Kornelia Ender of East Germany (swimming) . . . 30 10
1007 40 m. Mitsuo Tsukahara of Japan (gymnastics) 40 15
1008 60 m. Gregor Braun of West Germany (cycling) 50 25
1009 80 m. Lasse Viren of Finland (running) 60 30
1010 1 t. Nikolai Andrianov of U.S.S.R. (gymnastics) . . 70 35

1976. Archaeology.

1012 **217** 50 m. brown and blue . 40 15
1013 – 60 m. black and green . 40 15

DESIGN: 60 m. 6th-century stele.

218 R-1 Biplane

1976. Aircraft. Multicoloured.

1014 10 m. Type **218** 20 10
1015 20 m. Polikarpov R-5 biplane 30 10
1016 30 m. Kalinin K-5 . . . . . 40 10
1017 40 m. Polikarpov Po-2 biplane 45 15
1018 60 m. Polikarpov I-16 jet fighter 60 20
1019 80 m. Yakovlev Ya-6 Air 6 . . 75 35
1020 1 t. Junkers F-13 . . . . . . 95 40

219 Dancers in Folk Costume

1977. Mongolian Folk Dances. Multicoloured.

1021 10 m. Type **219** 25 10
1022 20 m. Dancing girls in 13th-century costume 35 10
1023 30 m. West Mongolian dance 45 10
1024 40 m. "Ekachi" dance . . . 50 15
1025 60 m. "Bielge" ("Trunk") dance 80 20
1026 80 m. "Hodak" dance . . . 95 30
1027 1 t. "Dojarka" dance . . . . 1·10 45

220 Gravitational Effects on "Pioneer"

1977. 250th Death Anniv of Sir Isaac Newton (mathematician). Multicoloured.

1028 60 m. Type **220** (postage) . . 45 15
1029 60 m. Apple tree (25 × 32 mm) 45 15
1030 60 m. Planetary motion and sextant 45 15
1031 60 m. Sir Isaac Newton (25 × 32 mm) 45 15
1032 60 m. Spectrum of light . . . 45 15
1033 60 m. Attraction of Earth . . 45 15
1034 60 m. Laws of motion of celestial bodies (25 × 32 mm) 45 15
1035 60 m. Space-walking (air) . . 45 15
1036 60 m. "Pioneer 10" and Jupiter 45 15

221 Natsagdorj, Mongolian Scenes and Extract from poem "Mother"

1977. Natsagdorj (poet) Commem. Mult.

1037 60 m. Type **221** 40 25
1038 60 m. Border stone, landscape and extract from poem "My Homeland" 40 25

222 Horse Race

1977. Horses. Multicoloured.

1039 10 m. Type **222** 20 10
1040 20 m. Girl on white horse . . 25 10
1041 30 m. Rangeman on brown horse 30 10
1042 40 m. Tethered horses . . . 40 20
1043 60 m. White mare with foal . 55 20
1044 80 m. Brown horse with shepherd 70 30
1045 1 t. White horse 85 45

223 "Mongolemys elegans"

1977. Prehistoric Animals. Multicoloured.

1046 10 m. Type **223** 30 10
1047 20 m. "Embolotherium ergiliense" 45 10
1048 30 m. "Psittacosaurus mongoliensis" 55 15
1049 40 m. Enthelodon 70 20
1050 60 m. "Spirocerus kiakhtensis" 1·00 25
1051 80 m. Hipparion . . . . . . 1·40 40
1052 1 t. "Bos primigenius" . . . 1·60 55

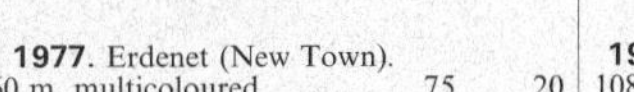

225 Child feeding Lambs **226** Industrial Plant and Transport

1977. Children's Day and 1st Balloon Flight in Mongolia. Multicoloured.

1054 10 m. + 5 m. Type **225** . . . 30 15
1055 20 m. + 5 m. Boy playing flute and girl dancing 45 15
1056 30 m. + 5 m. Girl chasing butterflies 55 20
1057 40 m. + 5 m. Girl with ribbon 60 25
1058 60 m. + 5 m. Girl with flowers 70 40
1059 80 m. + 5 m. Girl with bucket 80 50
1060 1 t. + 5 m. Boy going to school 1·00 60

1977. Erdenet (New Town).

1062 **226** 60 m. multicoloured . . 75 20

227 Trade Unions Emblem

1977. Air. 11th Mongolian Trade Unions Congress.

1063 **227** 60 m. multicoloured . . 50 15

228 Mounting Bell-shaped Gear on Rocket (⅔-size illustration)

1977. Air. 11th Anniv of "Intercosmos" Co-operation. Multicoloured.

1064 10 m. Type **228** 10 10
1065 20 m. Launch of "Intercosmos 3" 20 10
1066 30 m. Tracking ship "Kosmonaut Yury Gargarin" 60 15
1067 40 m. Observation of lunar eclipse 50 20
1068 60 m. Earth station's multiple antennae 70 25
1069 80 m. Magnetosphere examination, Van Allen Zone 90 35
1070 1 t. Meteorological satellites 1·25 65

229 Fire-fighters' Bucket Chain

1977. Mongolian Fire-fighting Services. Multicoloured.

1072 10 m. Type **229** 20 10
1073 20 m. Horse-drawn hand pump 30 10
1074 30 m. Horse-drawn steam pump 40 15
1075 40 m. Fighting forest fire . . 50 20
1076 60 m. Mobile foam extinguisher 70 25
1077 80 m. Modern fire engine . . 85 30
1078 1 t. Mil Mi-8 helicopter spraying fire . . . . 1·25 45

230 "Molniya" Satellite and Dish Aerial on TV Screen

1977. 40th Anniv of Technical Institute.

1079 **230** 60 m. blue, black & grey 45 20

231 "Aporia crataegi"

1977. Butterflies and Moths. Multicoloured.

1080 10 m. Type **231** 20 10
1081 20 m. "Gastropacha quercifolia" 35 15
1082 30 m. "Colias chrysoteme" . . 50 15
1083 40 m. "Dasychira fascelina" 70 20
1084 60 m. "Malocosoma neustria" 1·00 25
1085 80 m. "Diacrisia sannio" . . 1·40 35
1086 1 t. "Heodes virgaureae" . . 1·60 50

232 Lenin Museum

1977. Inauguration of Lenin Museum, Ulan Bator.

1087 **232** 60 m. multicoloured . . 40 20

233 Cruiser "Aurora" and Soviet Flag

1977. 60th Anniv of Russian Revolution. Mult.

1088 50 m. Type **233** 60 15
1089 60 m. Dove and globe (horiz) 50 15
1090 1 t. 50 Freedom banner around the globe (horiz) 75 35

234 Giant Pandas

1977. Giant Pandas. Multicoloured.

1091 10 m. Eating bamboo shoot (vert) 20 10
1092 20 m. Type **234** 35 10
1093 30 m. Female and cub in washtub (vert) 45 15
1094 40 m. Male and cub with bamboo shoot 60 20
1095 60 m. Female and cub (vert) 80 30
1096 80 m. Family (horiz) . . . . 1·40 50
1097 1 t. Male on hind legs (vert) 1·60 65

236 Montgolfier Balloon

1977. Air. Airships and Balloons. Multicoloured.

1099 20 m. Type **236** 25 10
1100 30 m. Airship "Graf Zeppelin" over North Pole 30 10
1101 40 m. Airship "Osoaviachim" over the Arctic 40 15
1102 50 m. Airship "North" 55 20
1103 60 m. Aereon 340 design . . 65 20
1104 80 m. Nestrenko's planned airship 70 35
1105 1 t. 20 "Flying Crane" airship 1·00 60

237 Ferrari "312-T2"

1978. Racing Cars. Multicoloured.

1107 20 m. Type **237** 25 10
1108 30 m. Ford McLaren "M-23" 30 10
1109 40 m. Soviet experimental car 40 20
1110 50 m. Japanese Mazda . . . 50 20
1111 60 m. Porsche "936-Turbo" . 60 25
1112 80 m. Model of Soviet car . . 65 25
1113 1 t. 20 American rocket car "Blue Flame" 95 40

238 "Boletus variegatus". (½-size illustration)

1978. Mushrooms. Multicoloured.

1114 20 m. Type **238** 50 15
1115 30 m. "Russula cyanoxantha" 75 20
1116 40 m. "Boletus aurantiacus" . 80 25
1117 50 m. "Boletus scaber" . . . 1·00 30
1118 60 m. "Russula flava" . . . . 1·25 35
1119 80 m. "Lactarius resimus" . . 1·50 50
1120 1 t. 20 "Flammula spumosa" 2·00 75

239 A. F. Mozhaiski and Monoplane

1978. Air. History of Aviation. Multicoloured.

1121 20 m. Type **239** 20 10
1122 30 m. Henri Farman and Farman H.F.III biplane . 25 10
1123 40 m. Geoffrey de Havilland and De Havilland FE.1 biplane 30 15
1124 50 m. Charles Lindbergh and "Spirit of St. Louis" . . . 45 20
1125 60 m. Shagdarsuren, Dembral, biplane and glider 55 20
1126 80 m. Chalkov, Baidukov, Beliadov and Tupolev ANT-25 . . . . 65 35
1127 1 t. 20 A. N. Tupolev and Tu-154 . . . . 90 55

240 Footballers and View of Rio de Janeiro

1978. World Cup Football Championship, Argentina. Multicoloured.

1129 20 m. Type **240** 20 10
1130 30 m. Footballers and Old Town Tower, Berne . . . 25 10
1131 40 m. Footballers and Stockholm Town Hall . . 30 15
1132 50 m. Footballers and University of Chile 40 20
1133 60 m. Footballers, Houses of Parliament and Tower of London 55 25
1134 80 m. Footballers and Theatre Degolladeo of Guadalajara, Mexico 60 25
1135 1 t. 20 Footballers and Munich Town Hall 85 40

241 Mongolian Youth and Girl

1978. Mongolian Youth Congress, Ulan Bator.

1137 **241** 60 m. multicoloured . . 35 15

242 Eurasian Beaver and 1954 Canadian Beaver Stamp

1978. "CAPEX '78". International Stamp Exhibition, Toronto. Multicoloured.

1138 20 m. Type **242** 20 10
1139 30 m. Tibetan sandgrouse and Canada S.G. 620 . . . . . 40 10
1140 40 m. Black-throated diver and Canada S.G. 495 . . . . . 50 10
1141 50 m. Argali and Canada S.G. 449 . . . . 70 35
1142 60 m. Brown bear and Canada S.G. 447 . . . . 80 40
1143 80 m. Elk and Canada S.G. 448 90 45
1144 1 t. 20 Herring gull and Canada S.G. 474 . . . . 1·50 25

243 Marx, Engels and Lenin

1978. 20th Anniv of Review "Problems of Peace and Socialism".

1146 **243** 60 m. red, gold and black 40 15

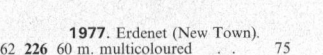

244 Map of Cuba, Liner, Tupolev Tu-134 and Emblem

1978. Air. 11th World Youth Festival, Havana.
1147 **244** 1 t. multicoloured 90 20

245 "Open-air Repose"

1978. 20th Anniv of Philatelic Co-operation between Mongolia and Hungary. Paintings by P. Angalan. Multicoloured.
1148 1 t. 50 Type **245** 90 90
1149 1 t. 50 "Winter Night" 90 90
1150 1 t. 50 "Saddling" 90 90

247 Butterfly Dog

1978. Dogs. Multicoloured.
1152 10 m. Type **247** 20 10
1153 20 m. Black Mongolian sheepdog 25 10
1154 30 m. Puli (Hungarian sheepdog) 35 15
1155 40 m. St. Bernard 40 20
1156 50 m. German shepherd dog 55 25
1157 60 m. Mongolian watchdog 65 25
1158 70 m. Semoyedic Spitz 75 35
1159 80 m. Laika (space dog) 90 35
1160 1 t. 20 Black and white poodles and cocker spaniel 1·10 55

248 Open Book showing Scenes from Mongolian Literary Works

1978. 50th Anniv of Mongolian Writers' Association.
1161 **248** 60 m. blue and red 35 15

249 "Dressed Maja" (Goya, 150th death anniv)

1978. Painters' Anniversaries. Multicoloured.
1162 1 t. 50 Type **249** 90 90
1163 1 t. 50 "Ta Matete" (Gaugin - 75th death anniv) 90 90
1164 1 t. 50 "Bridge at Arles" (Van Gogh - 125th birth anniv) 90 90

250 Young Bactrian Camel

1978. Bactrian Camels. Multicoloured.
1166 20 m. Camel with Foal 25 15
1167 30 m. Type **250** 30 15
1168 40 m. Two camels 45 20
1169 50 m. Woman leading loaded camel 55 25
1170 60 m. Camel in winter coat 70 30
1171 80 m. Camel-drawn water waggon 90 45
1172 1 t. 20 Camel racing 1·25 60

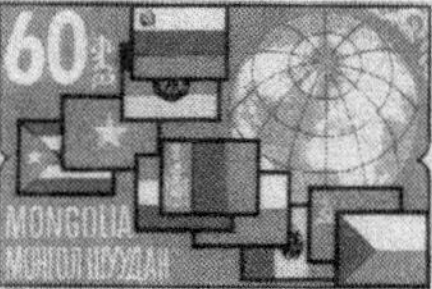
251 Flags of COMECON Countries

1979. 30th Anniv of Council of Mutual Economic Assistance.
1173 **251** 60 m. multicoloured 35 25

252 Children riding Camel

1979. International Year of the Child. Multicoloured.
1174 10 m. + 5 m. Type **252** 15 15
1175 30 m. + 5 m. Children feeding chickens 25 15
1176 50 m. + 5 m. Children with deer 35 15
1177 60 m. + 5 m. Children picking flowers 45 20
1178 70 m. + 5 m. Children watering tree 50 25
1179 80 m. + 5 m. Young scientists 60 35
1180 1 t. + 5 m. Making music and dancing 80 50

253 Silver Tabby

1978. Domestic Cats. Multicoloured.
1182 10 m. Type **253** 20 10
1183 30 m. White Persian 35 15
1184 50 m. Red Persian 55 15
1185 60 m. Blue-cream Persian 70 20
1186 70 m. Siamese 80 30
1187 80 m. Smoke Persian 90 35
1188 1 t. Birman 1·25 50

254 "Potaninia mongolica"

1979. Flowers. Multicoloured.
1189 10 m. Type **254** 20 10
1190 30 m. "Sophora alopecuroides" 30 10
1191 50 m. "Halimodendron halodendron" 35 15
1192 60 m. "Myosotis asiatica" 50 20
1193 70 m. "Scabiosa comosa" 50 30
1194 80 m. "Leucanthemum sibiricum" 60 30
1195 1 t. "Leontopodium ochroleucum" 80 45

255 Finland v. Czechoslovakia

1979. World Ice Hockey Championships, Moscow. Multicoloured.
1196 10 m. Type **255** 15 10
1197 30 m. West Germany v. Sweden 30 10
1198 50 m. U.S.A. v. Canada 50 20
1199 60 m. Russia v. Sweden 60 20
1200 70 m. Canada v. Russia 65 25
1201 80 m. Swedish goalkeeper 75 25
1202 1 t. Czechoslovakia v. Russia 1·00 35

256 Lambs (Sanzhid)

1979. Agriculture Paintings. Multicoloured.
1203 10 m. Type **256** 10 10
1204 30 m. "Milking camels" (Budbazar) 20 10
1205 50 m. "Aircraft bringing help" (Radnabazar) 40 15
1206 60 m. "Herdsmen" (Budbazar) 40 15
1207 70 m. "Milkmaids" "Nanzadsguren) (vert) 50 30
1208 80 m. "Summer Evening" (Sanzhid) 70 40
1209 1 t. "Country Landscape" (Tserendondog) 80 50

257 First Mongolian and Bulgarian Stamps

1979. Death Centenary of Sir Rowland Hill, and "Philaserdica 79" International Stamp Exn, Sofia. Each black, grey and brown.
1211 1 t. Type **257** 1·50 1·00
1212 1 t. American mail coach 1·50 1·00
1213 1 t. Travelling post office, London-Birmingham railway 1·50 1·00
1214 1 t. Paddle-steamer "Hindoostan" 1·75 1·00

258 Stephenson's "Rocket"

1979. Development of Railways. Multicoloured.
1215 10 m. Type **258** 25 10
1216 20 m. German "Der Adler" locomotive, 1835 30 10
1217 30 m. American locomotive, 1860 40 10
1218 40 m. Mongolian locomotive, 1931 50 15
1219 50 m. Mongolian locomotive, 1936 55 20
1220 60 m. Mongolian locomotive, 1970 65 25
1221 70 m. Japanese high-speed electric train, 1963 80 30
1222 80 m. French "Orleans" aerotrain 90 40
1223 1 t. 20 Russian experimental jet train "Rapidity" 1·00 50

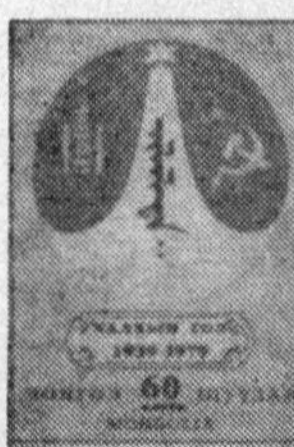
259 Flags of Mongolia and Russia

262 East German Flag, Berlin Buildings and "Soyuz 31"

260 Pallas's Cat

1979. 40th Anniv of Battle of Khalka River.
1224 **259** 60 m. gold, red and yellow 40 35
1225 – 60 m. red, yellow & blue 40 35
DESIGN: No. 1225, Ribbons, badge and military scene.

1979. Wild Cats. Multicoloured.
1226 10 m. Type **260** 15 10
1227 30 m. Lynx 30 15
1228 50 m. Tiger 55 25
1229 60 m. Snow leopard 65 25
1230 70 m. Leopard 75 35
1231 80 m. Cheetah 80 35
1232 1 t. Lion 1·25 50

1979. 30th Anniv of German Democratic Republic (East Germany).
1234 **262** 60 m. multicoloured 60 30

263 Demoiselle Crane

1979. Air. Protected Birds. Multicoloured.
1235 10 m. Type **263** 35 10
1236 30 m. Barred warbler 55 10
1237 50 m. Ruddy shelduck 65 15
1238 60 m. Azure-winged magpie 75 15
1239 70 m. Goldfinch 75 20
1240 80 m. Great tit 85 25
1241 1 t. Golden oriole 1·10 30

264 "Venus 5" and "6"

1979. Air. Space Research. Multicoloured.
1242 10 m. Type **264** 10 10
1243 30 m. "Mariner 5" 20 10
1244 50 m. "Mars 3" 35 20
1245 60 m. "Viking 1" and "2" 40 20
1246 70 m. "Luna 1", "2" and "3" 45 25
1247 80 m. "Lunokhod 2" 50 25
1248 1 t. "Apollo 15" Moon-rover 65 40

265 Cross-country Skiing

1980. Winter Olympic Games, Lake Placid. Multicoloured.
1250 20 m. Type **265** 20 10
1251 30 m. Biathlon 25 15
1252 40 m. Ice hockey 30 20
1253 50 m. Ski jumping 40 25
1254 60 m. Slalom 50 30
1255 80 m. Speed skating 60 30
1256 1 t. 20 Four-man bobsleigh 85 45

266 "Andrena scita"

1980. Air. Wasps and Bees. Multicoloured.

1258	20 m. Type **266**	25	15
1259	30 m. "Paravespula germanica"	30	20
1260	40 m. "Perilampus ruficornis"	40	25
1261	50 m. "Bombus terrestris"	60	30
1262	60 m. "Apis mellifera"	70	35
1263	80 m. "Stilbum cyanurum"	80	45
1264	1 t. 20 "Parnopes grandior"	1·25	60

267 Weightlifting

1980. Olympic Games, Moscow. Multicoloured.

1266	20 m. Type **267**	15	10
1267	30 m. Archery	20	15
1268	40 m. Gymnastics	25	15
1269	50 m. Running	35	20
1270	60 m. Boxing	40	25
1271	80 m. Judo	50	25
1272	1 t. 20 Cycling	75	40

268 Zlin Akrobat Specials

1980. Air. World Acrobatic Championship, Oshkosh, Wisconsin. Multicoloured.

1274	20 m. Type **268**	25	10
1275	30 m. Socata Sportsman	30	10
1276	40 m. Grumman Yankee	40	15
1277	50 m. MJ-2 Tempete	55	20
1278	60 m. Pitts S-2A biplane	65	25
1279	80 m. Hirth Acrostar	75	35
1280	1 t. 20 Yakovlev Yak-50	1·00	60

269 Swimming

1980. Olympic Medal Winners. Multicoloured.

1282	20 m. Type **269**	15	10
1283	30 m. Fencing	20	10
1284	50 m. Judo	30	15
1285	60 m. Athletics	40	20
1286	80 m. Boxing	50	25
1287	1 t. Weightlifting	55	30
1288	1 t. 20 Kayak-canoe	75	35

270 Sukhe Bator

271 Gubarev

1980. Mongolian Politicians.

1290	**270**	60 m. brown	40	20
1291	–	60 m. blue	40	20
1292	–	60 m. turquoise	40	20
1293	–	60 m. bronze-green	40	20
1294	–	60 m. deep green	40	20
1295	–	60 m. red	40	20
1296	–	60 m. brown	40	20

DESIGNS—VERT: No. 1291, Marshal Choibalsan; No. 1292, Yu. Tsedenbal aged 13; No. 1293, Tsedenbal as soldier, 1941; No. 1294, Pres. Tsedenbal in 1979; No. 1295, Tsedenbal with children. HORIZ: No. 1296, Tsedenbal and President Brezhnev of Russia.

1980. "Intercosmos" Space Programme. Multicoloured.

1297	40 m. Type **271**	30	20
1298	40 m. Czechoslovak stamp showing Gubarev and Remek	30	20
1299	40 m. P. Klimuk	30	20
1300	40 m. Polish stamp showing M. Hermaszewski	30	20
1301	40 m. V. Bykovsky	30	20
1302	40 m. East German stamp showing S. Jahn	30	20
1303	40 m. N. Rukavishnikov	30	20
1304	40 m. Bulgarian stamp showing G. Ivanov	30	20
1305	40 m. V. Kubasov	30	20
1306	40 m. Hungarian stamp showing Kubasov and B. Farkas	30	20

272 Benz, 1885

1980. Classic Cars. Multicoloured.

1307	20 m. Type **272**	25	10
1308	30 m. "President" Czechoslovakia, 1897	30	10
1309	40 m. Armstrong Siddeley, 1904	35	25
1310	50 m. Russo-Balt, 1909	45	20
1311	60 m. Packard, 1909	50	20
1312	80 m. Lancia, 1911	70	30
1313	1 t. 60 "Marne" taxi, 1914	1·40	60

273 Adelie Penguin

276 "The Shepherd speaking the Truth"

1980. Antarctic Exploration. Multicoloured.

1315	20 m. Type **273**	75	15
1316	30 m. Blue whales	70	20
1317	40 m. Wandering albatross and Jacques Cousteau's bathysphere	95	30
1318	50 m. Weddell seals and mobile research station	90	30
1319	60 m. Emperor penguins	1·50	35
1320	70 m. Great skuas	1·75	40
1321	80 m. Killer whales	1·60	55
1322	1 t. 20 Adelie penguins, research station, Ilyushin Il-18B airplane and tracked vehicle	2·75	75

1980. Nursery Tales. Multicoloured.

1326	20 m. Type **276**	25	10
1327	30 m. Children under umbrella and rainbow ("Above them the Sky is always clear")	30	10
1328	40 m. Children on sledge and skis ("Winter's Joys")	35	15
1329	50 m. Girl watching boy playing flute ("Little Musicians")	40	15
1330	60 m. Boys giving girl leaves ("Happy Birthday")	55	20
1331	80 m. Children with flowers and briefcase ("First Schoolday")	65	30
1332	1 t. 20 Girls dancing ("May Day")	90	40

277 Soldier

1981. 60th Anniv of Mongolian People's Army.

1334	**277**	60 m. multicoloured	60	30

MINIMUM PRICE

The minimum price quoted is 10p which represents a handling charge rather than a basis for valuing common stamps. For further notes about prices, see introductory pages.

278 Economy Emblems within Party Initials

1981. 60th Anniv of Mongolian Revolutionary People's Party.

1335	**278**	60 m. gold, red and black	45	25

279 Motocross

1981. Motor Cycle Sports. Multicoloured.

1336	10 m. Type **279**	15	10
1337	20 m. Tour racing	25	10
1338	30 m. Ice racing	30	15
1339	40 m. Road racing	40	20
1340	50 m. Motocross (different)	50	25
1341	60 m. Road racing (different)	55	25
1342	70 m. Speedway	60	30
1343	80 m. Sidecar racing	70	35
1344	1 t. 20 Road racing (different)	95	45

280 Cosmonauts entering Space Capsule

1981. Soviet–Mongolian Space Flight. Mult.

1345	20 m. Type **280**	30	10
1346	30 m. Rocket and designer S. P. Korolev	35	10
1347	40 m. "Vostok 1" and Yuri Gagarin	40	15
1348	50 m. "Soyuz"–"Sallyut" space station	50	20
1349	60 m. Spectral photography	60	25
1350	80 m. Crystal and space station	70	30
1351	1 t. 20 Space complex, Moscow Kremlin and Sukhe Bator statue, Ulan Bator	90	45

281 Ulan Bator Buildings and 1961 Mongolian Stamp

1981. Stamp Exhibitions.

1353	**281**	1 t. multicoloured	1·75	80
1354	–	1 t. multicoloured	1·75	80
1355	–	1 t. black, blue and magenta	1·75	80
1356	–	1 t. multicoloured	1·75	80

DESIGNS: No. 1353, Type **281** (Mongolian stamp exhibition); No. 1354, Wurttemberg stamps of 1947 and 1949 and view of Old Stuttgart ("Naposta '81" exhibition); No. 1355, Parliament building and sculpture, Vienna, and Austrian stamp of 1933 ("WIPA 1981" exhibition); No. 1356, Japanese stamp of 1964, cherry blossom and girls in Japanese costume ("Japex '81" exhibition, Tokyo).

282 Star and Industrial and Agricultural Scenes

1981. 18th Mongolian Revolutionary People's Party Congress.

1357	**282**	60 m. multicoloured	45	25

284 Sheep Farming

1981. "Results of the People's Economy". Multicoloured.

1359	20 m. Type **284**	30	10
1360	30 m. Transport	70	15
1361	40 m. Telecommunications	90	15
1362	50 m. Public health service	50	20
1363	60 m. Agriculture	60	25
1364	80 m. Electrical industry	70	30
1365	1 t. 20 Housing	1·00	45

286 Pharaonic Ship (15th century B.C.)

1981. Sailing Ships. Multicoloured.

1367	10 m. Type **286**	30	10
1368	20 m. Mediterranean sailing ship (9th century)	40	15
1369	40 m. Hanse kogge (12th century) (vert)	60	20
1370	50 m. Venetian felucca (13th century) (vert)	75	30
1371	60 m. Columbus's "Santa Maria" (vert)	90	35
1372	80 m. Cook's H.M.S. "Endeavour" (vert)	1·00	50
1373	1 t. "Poltava" (18th-century Russian ship of the line) (vert)	1·40	60
1374	1 t. 20 American schooner (19th century) (vert)	1·60	75

287 Arms of Mongolia and Russia

1981. Soviet–Mongolian Friendship Pact.

1375	**287**	60 m. red, blue and gold	45	25

288 "Hendrickje in Bed"

290 White-tailed Sea Eagle and German 1 m. "Zeppelin" Stamp

289 Billy Goat (pawn)

1981. 375th Birth Anniv of Rembrandt (artist). Multicoloured.

1376	20 m. "Flora"	20	10
1377	30 m. Type **288**	25	15
1378	40 m. "Young Woman with Earrings"	40	20
1379	50 m. "Young girl in the Window"	45	25
1380	60 m. "Hendrickje like Flora"	55	30
1381	80 m. "Saskia with Red Flower"	70	35
1382	1 t. 20 "The Holy Family with Drape" (detail)	85	45

1981. Mongolian Chess Pieces. Multicoloured.

1384 20 m. Type **289** 50 15
1385 40 m. Horse-drawn cart (rook) 75 25
1386 50 m. Camel (bishop) 90 35
1387 60 m. Horse (knight) . . . . 1·25 40
1388 80 m. Lion (queen) . . . . . 1·60 60
1389 1 t. 20 Man with dog (king) . 2·00 85

1981. Air. 50th Anniv of "Graf Zeppelin" Polar Flight. Multicoloured.

1391 20 m. Type **290** 40 15
1392 30 m. Arctic Fox and German 2 m. "Zeppelin" stamp . . 40 20
1393 40 m. Walrus and German 4 m. "Zeppelin" stamp 50 25
1394 50 m. Polar Bear and Russian 30 k. "Zeppelin" stamp . . 60 30
1395 60 m. Snowy Owl and Russian 35 k. "Zeppelin" stamp . . 1·00 20
1396 80 m. Atlantic Puffin and Russian 1 r. "Zeppelin" stamp . . . . 1·25 20
1397 1 t. 20 Northern sealion and Russian 2 r. "Zeppelin" stamp . . . . 1·50 65

291 Circus Camel and Circus Building, Ulan Bator

1981. Mongolian Sport and Art. Multicoloured.

1399 10 m. Type **291** 10 10
1400 20 m. Horsemen and stadium (National holiday cavalcade) 20 15
1401 40 m. Wrestling and Ulan Bator stadium 40 25
1402 50 m. Archers and stadium . 55 30
1403 60 m. Folk singer-dancer and House of Culture 65 35
1404 80 m. Girl playing jatga (folk instrument) and Ulan Bator Drama Theatre 80 40
1405 1 t. Ballet dancers and Opera House . . . . 1·25 50
1406 1 t. 20 Exhibition Hall and statue of man on bucking horse . . . . 1·40 70

292 Mozart and scene from "The Magic Flute"

1981. Composers. Multicoloured.

1407 20 m. Type **292** 40 15
1408 30 m. Beethoven and scene from "Fidelio" 50 20
1409 40 m. Bartok and scene from "The Miraculous Mandarin" 60 25
1410 50 m. Verdi and scene from "Aida" 80 35
1411 60 m. Tchaikovsky and scene from "The Sleeping Beauty" 90 40
1412 80 m. Dvorak and score of "New World" symphony . 1·25 50
1413 1 t. 20 Chopin, piano, score and quill pens . . . . 1·60 75

293 "Mongolian Women in Everyday Life" (detail, Davaakhuu)

294 Gorbatko

1981. International Decade for Women. Mult.

1414 20 m. Type **293** 25 10
1415 30 m. "Mongolian Women in Everyday Life" (different detail) 35 15
1416 40 m. "National Day" (detail, Khishigbaiar) 40 20
1417 50 m. "National Day" (detail) (different) 50 25
1418 60 m. "National Day" (detail) (different) 60 35
1419 80 m. "Ribbon Weaver" (Ts. Baidi) 85 40
1420 1 t. 20 "Expectant Mother" (Senghesokhio) . . . . . . 1·25 65

1981. "Intercosmos" Space Programme. Mult.

1422 50 m. Type **294** 50 30
1423 50 m. Vietnam stamp showing Gorbatko and Pham Tuan 50 30
1424 50 m. Romanenko 50 30
1425 50 m. Cuban stamp showing Tamayo 50 30
1426 50 m. Dzhanibekov 50 30
1427 50 m. Mongolian stamp showing Dzhanibekov and Gurrugchaa 50 30
1428 50 m. Popov 50 30
1429 50 m. Rumanian stamp showing "Salyut" space station and "Soyuz" space ship . . . 50 30

295 Karl von Drais Bicycle, 1816

1982. History of the Bicycle. Multicoloured.

1430 10 m. Type **295** 20 10
1431 20 m. Macmillan bicycle, 1838 30 10
1432 40 m. First American pedal bicycle by Pierre Lallament, 1866 . . . . 50 20
1433 50 m. First European pedal bicycle by Ernest Michaux 55 25
1434 60 m. "Kangaroo" bicycle, 1877 60 30
1435 80 m. Coventry Rotary Tandem, 1870s 75 45
1436 1 t. Chain-driven bicycle, 1878 95 60
1437 1 t. 20 Modern bicycle . . . 4·50 2·40

296 Footballers (Brazil, 1950)

1982. World Cup Football Championship, Spain. Multicoloured.

1439 10 m. Type **296** 15 10
1440 20 m. Switzerland, 1954 . . 25 10
1441 40 m. Sweden, 1958 . . . . 40 20
1442 50 m. Chile, 1962 . . . . . 55 25
1443 60 m. England, 1966 . . . . 60 30
1444 80 m. Mexico, 1970 . . . . 75 40
1445 1 t. West Germany, 1974 . . 95 50
1446 1 t. 20 Argentina, 1978 . . . 1·25 55

297 Trade Union Emblem and Economic Symbols

299 Dimitrov

1982. 12th Mongolian Trade Unions Congress.

1448 **297** 60 m. multicoloured . . 50 30

1982. Birth Centenary of Georgi Dimitrov (Bulgarian statesman).

1450 **299** 60 m. black, grey & gold 55 30

300 Chicks

1982. Young Animals. Multicoloured.

1451 10 m. Type **300** 20 10
1452 20 m. Colt 30 15
1453 30 m. Lamb 40 20
1454 40 m. Roe deer fawn . . . 50 25
1455 50 m. Bactrian camel 65 30
1456 60 m. Kid 70 35
1457 70 m. Calf 80 40
1458 1 t. 20 Wild piglet . . . . . 1·10 60

301 Coal-fired Industry

1982. Coal Mining.

1459 **301** 60 m. multicoloured . . . 70 30

302 Emblem

304 Revsomol Emblem within "Flower"

303 Siberian Pine

1982. 18th Revsomol Youth Congress.

1460 **302** 60 m. multicoloured . . . 55 30

1982. Trees. Multicoloured.

1461 20 m. Type **303** 25 15
1462 30 m. Siberian fir 35 20
1463 40 m. Poplar 45 25
1464 50 m. Siberian larch 55 30
1465 60 m. Scots pine 65 35
1466 80 m. Birch 75 45
1467 1 t. 20 Spruce . . . . . . 1·10 60

1982. 60th Anniv of Revsomol Youth Organization.

1449 **304** 60 m. multicoloured . . . 55 30

305 World Map and Satellite

1982. Air. I.T.U. Delegates' Conference, Nairobi.

1469 **305** 60 m. multicoloured . . . 70 30

306 Japanese "Iseki-6500" Tractor

1982. Tractors. Multicoloured.

1470 10 m. Type **306** 15 10
1471 20 m. West German "Deutz-DX230" 25 10
1472 40 m. British "Bonser" . . . 40 20
1473 50 m. American "International-884" 55 25
1474 60 m. French Renault "TX 145-14" 60 30
1475 80 m. Russian "Belarus-611" . 75 40
1476 1 t. Russian "K-7100" . . . 95 50
1477 1 t. 20 Russian "DT-75" . . . 1·10 55

307 Fish and Lake Hevsgel

1982. Landscapes and Animals. Multicoloured.

1478 20 m. Type **307** 35 15
1479 30 m. Zavkhan Highlands and sheep 40 20
1480 40 m. Lake Hovd and Eurasian beaver 50 25
1481 50 m. Lake Uvs and horses . 65 30
1482 60 m. Bajankhongor Steppe and goitred gazelle 80 35
1483 80 m. Bajan-Elgii Highlands and rider with golden eagle 2·25 35
1484 1 t. 20 Gobi Desert and bactrian camels . . . . 1·40 65

308 "Sputnik 1"

1982. Air. Second U.N. Conference on the Exploration and Peaceful Uses of Outer Space. Multicoloured.

1485 60 m. Type **308** 60 30
1486 60 m. "Sputnik 2" and Laika (first dog in space) 60 30
1487 60 m. "Vostok 1" and Yuri Gagarin (first man in space) 60 30
1488 60 m. "Venera 8" 60 30
1489 60 m. "Vostok 6" and V. Tereshkova (first woman in space) 60 30
1490 60 m. Aleksei Leonov and space walker 60 30
1491 60 m. Neil Armstrong and astronaut on Moon's surface 60 30
1492 60 m. V. Dzhanibekov, Jean-Loup Chretien and "Soyuz T-6" 60 30

309 Montgolfier Brothers' Balloon, 1783

1982. Air. Bicentenary of Manned Flight. Mult.

1494 20 m. Type **309** 30 10
1495 30 m. Blanchard and Jefferies crossing the channel, 1785 40 20
1496 40 m. Green's flight to Germany in "Royal Vauxhall", 1836 55 25
1497 50 m. Andree's North Pole flight in "Oernen", 1897 . 60 30
1498 60 m. First Gordon Bennett balloon race, Paris, 1906 . 70 35
1499 80 m. First stratosphere flight in "F.N.R.S.", Switzerland, 1931 . . . . 90 45
1500 1 t. 20 USSR VR-62 flight, 1933 1·25 65

310 Sorcerer tells Mickey Mouse to clean up Quarters

1983. Drawings from "The Sorcerer's Apprentice" (section of Walt Disney's film "Fantasia"). Mult.

1502 25 m. Type **310** 20 10
1503 35 m. Mickey notices Sorcerer has left his cap behind . . 30 15
1504 45 m. Mickey puts cap on and commands broom to fetch water 35 20
1505 55 m. Broom carrying water 40 25
1506 65 m. Mickey sleeps while broom continues to fetch water, flooding the room . 50 30
1507 75 m. Mickey uses axe on broom to try to stop it . . 55 35
1508 85 m. Each splinter becomes a broom which continues to fetch water 65 40

1509 1 t. 40 Mickey, clinging to Sorcerer's Book of Spells, caught in whirlpool . . . . 1·00 55
1510 2 t. Mickey handing cap back to Sorcerer . . . . 1·40 75

311 Foal with Mother

1983. "The Foal and the Hare" (folk tale). Mult.
1512 10 m. Type **311** 10 10
1513 20 m. Foal wanders off alone 15 10
1514 30 m. Foal finds sack 25 15
1515 40 m. Foal unties sack . . . 30 15
1516 50 m. Wolf jumps out of sack 40 20
1517 60 m. Hare appears as wolf is about to eat foal 45 25
1518 70 m. Hare tricks wolf into re-entering sack 50 30
1519 80 m. Hare ties up sack with wolf inside 60 35
1520 1 t. 20 Hare and foal look for foal's mother 90 50

312 Antonov An-24B Aircraft

1983. Tourism. Multicoloured.
1524 20 m. Type **312** 35 10
1525 30 m. Skin tent 35 15
1526 40 m. Roe deer 40 20
1527 50 m. Argali 55 25
1528 60 m. Imperial eagle . . . . 2·00 30
1529 80 m. Khan Museum, Ulan Bator 90 40
1530 1 t. 20 Sukhe Bator statue, Ulan Bator . . . . 1·00 60

313 Rose

1983. Flowers. Multicoloured.
1531 20 m. Type **313** 30 10
1532 30 m. Dahlia 40 15
1533 40 m. Marigold 50 20
1534 50 m. Narcissus 60 25
1535 60 m. Viola 70 30
1536 80 m. Tulip 85 40
1537 1 t. 20 Sunflower . . . . . . 1·25 60

314 Border Guard

1983. 50th Anniv of Border Guards.
1538 **314** 60 m. multicoloured . . 1·00 40

316 Karl Marx

1983. Death Centenary of Karl Marx.
1540 **316** 60 m. red, gold and blue 70 40

317 Agriculture

1983. 18th Communist Party Congress Five Year Plan. Multicoloured.
1541 10 m. Type **317** 15 10
1542 20 m. Power industry . . . 25 10
1543 30 m. Textile industry . . . 30 15
1544 40 m. Science in industry and agriculture 45 25
1545 60 m. Improvement of living standards 60 35
1546 80 m. Communications . . . 1·40 50
1547 1 t. Children (education) . . 1·00 60

318 Young Inventors

1983. Children's Year. Multicoloured.
1548 10 m. Type **318** 15 10
1549 20 m. In school 25 10
1550 30 m. Archery 40 15
1551 40 m. Shepherdess playing flute 50 20
1552 50 m. Girl with deer 65 30
1553 70 m. Collecting rocks and mushrooms . . . . 2·25 60
1554 1 t. 20 Girl playing lute and boy singing . . . . 1·25 60

319 Skating

1983. 10th Anniv of Children's Fund. Multicoloured.
1555 20 m. Type **319** 15 15
1556 30 m. Shepherds 25 15
1557 40 m. Tree-planting 50 25
1558 50 m. Playing by the sea . . 65 35
1559 60 m. Carrying water . . . 80 40
1560 80 m. Folk dancing . . . . 1·00 65
1561 1 t. 20 Ballet . . . . 1·75 85

320 Pallas's Pika

1983. Small Mammals. Multicoloured.
1563 20 m. Type **320** 35 20
1564 30 m. Long-eared jerboa . . 45 25
1565 40 m. Eurasian red squirrel . 55 30
1566 50 m. Daurian hedgehog . . 65 40
1567 60 m. Harvest mouse . . . 80 45
1568 80 m. Eurasian water shrew 1·25 70
1569 1 t. 20 Siberian chipmunk . 1·75 95

322 Bobsleighing

1984. Winter Olympic Games, Sarajevo. Mult.
1571 20 m. Type **322** 30 15
1572 30 m. Cross-country skiing . 40 20
1573 40 m. Ice hockey 55 30
1574 50 m. Speed skating 65 35
1575 60 m. Ski jumping 75 40
1576 80 m. Ice dancing . . . . . 1·25 70
1577 1 t. 20 Biathlon (horiz) . . . 1·60 90

323 Mail Van

1984. World Communications Year. Multicoloured.
1579 10 m. Type **323** 15 10
1580 20 m. Earth receiving station . 30 20
1581 40 m. Airliner 75 30
1582 50 m. Central Post Office, Ulan Bator 70 35
1583 1 t. Transmitter . . . . . . 1·10 70
1584 1 t. 20 Diesel train . . . . . 2·50 1·00

325 Cycling

326 Flag, Rocket and Coastal Scene

1984. Olympic Games, Los Angeles. Multicoloured.
1587 20 m. Gymnastics (horiz) . . 25 15
1588 30 m. Type **325** 35 20
1589 40 m. Weightlifting 45 25
1590 50 m. Judo 55 30
1591 60 m. Archery 65 35
1592 80 m. Boxing 90 60
1593 1 t. 20 High jumping (horiz) . 1·25 75

1984. 25th Anniv of Cuban Revolution.
1595 **326** 60 m. multicoloured . . . 80 40

328 Douglas DC-10

329 Speaker, Radio and Transmitter

1984. Air. Civil Aviation. Multicoloured.
1597 20 m. Type **328** 35 15
1598 30 m. Airbus Industrie A300B2 55 20
1599 40 m. Concorde 70 30
1600 50 m. Boeing 747-200 . . . 85 35
1601 60 m. Ilyushin Il-62M . . . . 1·00 40
1602 80 m. Tupolev Tu-154 . . . . 1·40 70
1603 1 t. 20 Ilyushin Il-86 . . . . 1·75 85

1984. 50th Anniv of Mongolian Broadcasting.
1605 **329** 60 m. multicoloured . . . 75 40

330 Silver and Gold Coins

331 Golden Harp

1984. 60th Anniv of State Bank.
1606 **330** 60 m. multicoloured . . 75 40

1984. Scenes from Walt Disney's "Mickey and the Beanstalk" (cartoon film). Multicoloured.
1607 25 m. Type **331** 20 10
1608 35 m. Mickey holding box of magic beans 30 15
1609 45 m. Mickey about to eat bean 40 20
1610 55 m. Mickey looking for magic bean 50 25
1611 65 m. Goofy, Mickey and Donald at top of beanstalk 55 30
1612 75 m. Giant holding Mickey 60 35
1613 85 m. Giant threatening Mickey 80 40
1614 140 m. Goofy, Mickey and Donald cutting down beanstalk . . . . 1·40 65
1615 2 t. Goofy and Donald rescuing golden harp . . . . 1·60 75

1984. 60th Anniv of Ulan Bator City.
1617 **332** 60 m. multicoloured . . 75 40

333 Arms, Flag and Landscape

334 Rider carrying Flag

1984. 60th Anniv of Mongolian People's Republic.
1618 **333** 60 m. multicoloured . . . 75 40

1984. 60th Anniv of Mongolian People's Revolutionary Party.
1619 **334** 60 m. multicoloured . . 75 40

335 Gaetan Boucher (speed skating)

1984. Winter Olympic Gold Medal Winners. Multicoloured.
1620 20 m. Type **335** 30 10
1621 30 m. Eirik Kvalfoss (biathlon) 40 20
1622 40 m. Marja-Liisa Hamalainen (cross-country skiing) . . . 55 25
1623 50 m. Max Julen (slalom) . . 70 35
1624 60 m. Jens Weissflog (ski jumping) (vert) 85 40
1625 80 m. W. Hoppe and D. Schauerhammer (two-man bobsleigh) (vert) . . . . . 1·25 60
1626 1 t. 20 J. Valova and O. Vassiliev (pairs figure skating) (vert) . . . . 1·75 85

336 Donshy Mask

1984. Traditional Masks. Multicoloured.
1628 20 m. Type **336** 10 10
1629 30 m. Zamandi 10 10
1630 40 m. Ulaan-Yadam 15 10
1631 50 m. Lkham 20 10
1632 60 m. Damdinchoizhoo . . . 25 10
1633 80 m. Ochirvaan 30 15
1634 1 t. 20 Namsrai 50 25

337 Collie

1984. Dogs. Multicoloured.

1636 20 m. Type **337** 10 10
1637 30 m. German shepherd 10 10
1638 40 m. Papillon 15 10
1639 50 m. Cocker spaniel 20 10
1640 60 m. Terrier puppy (diamond-shaped) 25 10
1641 80 m. Dalmatians (diamond-shaped) 30 15
1642 1 t. 20 Mongolian shepherd 50 25

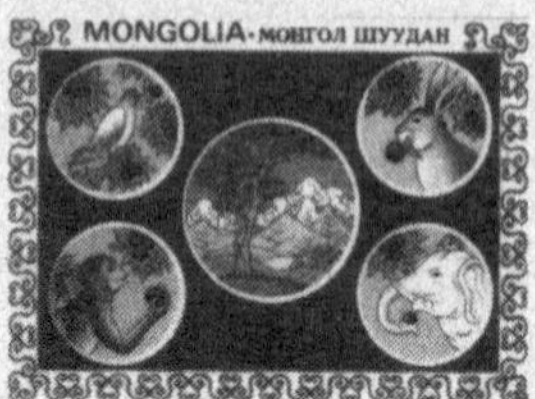

338 Four Animals and Tree

1984. "The Four Friendly Animals" (fairy tale). Multicoloured.

1643 10 m. Type **338** 10 10
1644 20 m. Animals discussing who was the oldest 10 10
1645 30 m. Monkey and elephant beside tree 10 10
1646 40 m. Elephant as calf and young tree 15 10
1647 50 m. Monkey and young tree 20 10
1648 60 m. Hare and young tree 25 10
1649 70 m. Dove and sapling 30 15
1650 80 m. Animals around mature tree 30 15
1651 1 t. 20 Animals supporting each other so that dove could reach fruit 50 25

339 Fawn

1984. Red Deer. Multicoloured.

1653 50 m. Type **339** 20 10
1654 50 m. Stag 20 10
1655 50 m. Adults and fawn by river 20 10
1656 50 m. Doe in woodland 20 10

340 Flag and Pioneers **342** Black Stork

341 Shar Tarlan

1985. 60th Anniv of Mongolian Pioneer Organization.

1657 **340** 60 m. multicoloured 25 10

1985. Cattle. Multicoloured.

1658 20 m. Type **341** 10 10
1659 30 m. Bor khalium 10 10
1660 40 m. Sarlag 15 10
1661 50 m. Dornod talin bukh 20 10
1662 60 m. Char tarlan 25 15
1663 80 m. Nutgiin uulderiin unee 30 15
1664 1 t. 20 Tsagaan tolgoit 50 25

1985. Birds. Multicoloured.

1666 20 m. Type **342** 10 10
1667 30 m. White-tailed sea eagle 10 10
1668 40 m. Great white crane 15 10
1669 50 m. Heude's parrotbill 20 10
1670 60 m. Hooded crane 25 15
1671 80 m. Japanese white-necked crane 30 15
1672 1 t. 20 Rough-legged buzzard 50 25

343 Footballers **344** Monument

1985. World Junior Football Championship, U.S.S.R.

1674 **343** 20 m. multicoloured 10 10
1675 – 30 m. multicoloured 10 10
1676 – 40 m. multicoloured 15 10
1677 – 50 m. multicoloured 20 10
1678 – 60 m. multicoloured 25 10
1679 – 80 m. multicoloured 30 15
1680 – 1 t. 20 multicoloured 50 25

DESIGNS: 30 m. to 1 t. 20 Different footballing scenes.

1985. 40th Anniv of Victory in Europe.

1682 **344** 60 m. multicoloured 25 15

345 Snow Leopards

1985. The Snow Leopard. Multicoloured.

1683 50 m. Type **345** 20 10
1684 50 m. Leopard 20 10
1685 50 m. Leopard on cliff ledge 20 10
1686 50 m. Mother and cubs 20 10

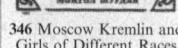

346 Moscow Kremlin and Girls of Different Races **347** Monument

1985. 12th World Youth and Students' Festival, Moscow.

1687 **346** 60 m. multicoloured 25 10

1985. 40th Anniv of Victory in Asia.

1688 **347** 60 m. multicoloured 25 10

348 "Rosa dahurica"

1985. Plants. Multicoloured.

1689 20 m. Type **348** 10 10
1690 30 m. False chamomile 10 10
1691 40 m. Dandelion 15 10
1692 50 m. "Saxzitraga nirculus" 20 10
1693 60 m. Cowberry 25 10
1694 80 m. "Sanguisorba officinalis" 30 15
1695 1 t. 20 "Plantago major" 50 25

See also Nos. 1719/25.

349 Camel

1985. The Bactrian Camel. Multicoloured.

1697 50 m. Type **349** 20 10
1698 50 m. Adults and calf 20 10
1699 50 m. Calf 20 10
1700 50 m. Adult 20 10

350 "Soyuz" Spacecraft

1985. Space. Multicoloured.

1701 20 m. Type **350** 10 10
1702 30 m. "Kosmos" satellite 10 10
1703 40 m. "Venera-9" satellite 15 10
1704 50 m. "Salyut" space station 20 10
1705 60 m. "Luna-9" landing vehicle 25 10
1706 80 m. "Soyuz" rocket on transporter 30 15
1707 1 t. 20 Dish aerial receiving transmission from "Soyuz" 50 25

352 U.N. and Mongolian Flags and U.N. Headquarters, New York **354** Congress Emblem

353 "Tricholoma mongolica"

1985. 40th Anniv of U.N.O.

1710 **352** 60 m. multicoloured 25 10

1985. Fungi. Multicoloured.

1711 20 m. Type **353** 20 10
1712 30 m. Chanterelle 30 15
1713 40 m. Boot-lace fungus 40 20
1714 50 m. Caesar's mushroom 55 25
1715 70 m. Chestnut mushroom 75 35
1716 80 m. Red-staining mushroom 85 40
1717 1 t. 20 Cep 1·40 55

1986. 19th Mongolian Revolutionary People's Party Congress.

1718 **354** 60 m. multicoloured 25 10

1986. Plants. As T **348**. Multicoloured.

1719 20 m. "Valeriana officinalis" 10 10
1720 30 m. "Hyoscymus niger" 10 10
1721 40 m. "Ephedra sinica" 15 10
1722 50 m. "Thymus gobica" 20 10
1723 60 m. "Paeonia anomalia" 25 10
1724 80 m. "Achilea millefolium" 30 15
1725 1 t. 20 "Rhododendron adamsii" 50 25

355 Scene from Play

1986. 80th Birth Anniv of D. Natsagdorj (writer).

1726 **355** 60 m. multicoloured 25 10

356 Thalmann **357** Man wearing Patterned Robe

1986. Birth Centenary of Ernst Thalmann (German politician).

1727 **356** 60 m. multicoloured 25 10

1986. Costumes. Multicoloured.

1728 60 m. Type **357** 25 10
1729 60 m. Man in blue robe and fur-lined hat with ear flaps 25 10
1730 60 m. Woman in black and yellow dress and bolero 25 10
1731 60 m. Woman in pink dress patterned with stars 25 10
1732 60 m. Man in cream robe with fur cuffs 25 10
1733 60 m. Man in brown robe and mauve and yellow tunic 25 10
1734 60 m. Woman in blue dress with black, yellow and red overtunic 25 10

358 Footballers

1986. World Cup Football Championship, Mexico.

1735 **358** 20 m. multicoloured 10 10
1736 – 30 m. multicoloured 10 10
1737 – 40 m. multicoloured 15 10
1738 – 50 m. multicoloured 20 10
1739 – 60 m. multicoloured 25 10
1740 – 80 m. multicoloured 30 15
1741 – 1 t. 20 multicoloured 50 25

DESIGNS: 30 m. to 1 t. 20. Different footballing scenes.

359 Mink

1986. Mink. Multicoloured.

1743 60 m. Type **359** 25 10
1744 60 m. Mink on rock 25 10
1745 60 m. Mink on snow covered branch 25 10
1746 60 m. Two mink 25 10

See also Nos. 1771/4, 1800/3, 1804/7, 1840/3 and 1844/7.

360 "Neptis coenobita" **361** Sukhe Bator Statue

1986. Butterflies and Moths. Multicoloured.

1747 20 m. Type **360** 10 10
1748 30 m. "Colias tycha" 10 10
1749 40 m. "Leptidea amurensis" 15 10
1750 50 m. "Oeneis tarpenledevi" 20 10
1751 60 m. "Mesoacidalia charlotta" 25 10
1752 80 m. Eyed hawk moth 30 15
1753 1 t. 20 Large tiger moth 50 25

1986. 65th Anniv of Independence.

1754	**361**	60 m. multicoloured	25	10

362 Yak and Goats Act

1986. Circus. Multicoloured.

1755	20 m. Type **362**	10	10
1756	30 m. Acrobat	10	10
1757	40 m. Yak act	15	10
1758	50 m. Acrobats (vert)	20	10
1759	60 m. High wire act (vert)	25	10
1760	80 m. Fire juggler on camel (vert)	30	15
1761	1 t. 20 Acrobats on camel-drawn cart (vert)	50	25

363 Morin Khuur **364** Flag and Emblem

1986. Musical Instruments. Multicoloured.

1762	20 m. Type **363**	10	10
1763	30 m. Bishguur (wind instrument)	10	10
1764	40 m. Ever buree (wind)	15	10
1765	50 m. Shudarga (string)	20	10
1766	60 m. Khiil (string)	25	10
1767	80 m. Janchir (string) (horiz)	30	15
1768	1 t. 20 Jatga (string) (horiz)	50	25

1986. International Peace Year.

1770	**364**	10 m. multicoloured	10	10

1986. Przewalski's Horse. As T **359**. Mult.

1771	50 m. Horses grazing on sparsely grassed plain	20	10
1772	50 m. Horses grazing on grassy plain	20	10
1773	50 m. Adults with foal	20	10
1774	50 m. Horses in snow	20	10

365 Temple

1986. Ancient Buildings. Multicoloured.

1775	60 m. Type **365**	25	10
1776	60 m. Temple with light green roof and white doors	25	10
1777	60 m. Temple with porch	25	10
1778	60 m. White building with three porches	25	10

366 Redhead ("Aythya americana")

1986. Birds. Multicoloured.

1779	60 m. Type **366**	25	10
1780	60 m. Ruffed grouse ("Bonasa umbellus")	25	10
1781	60 m. Whistling swan ("Olor columbianus")	25	10
1782	60 m. Rock pipit ("Anthus spinoletta")	60	20

367 Alfa Romeo "RL Sport", 1922

1986. Cars. Multicoloured.

1783	20 m. Type **367**	10	10
1784	30 m. Stutz "Bearcat", 1912	10	10
1785	40 m. Mercedes "Simplex", 1902	15	10
1786	50 m. Tatra "11", 1923	20	10
1787	60 m. Ford Model "T", 1908	25	10
1788	80 m. Vauxhall, 1905	30	15
1789	1 t. 20 Russo-Balt "K", 1913	50	25

368 Wilhelm Steinitz and Bardeleben Game, 1895

1986. World Chess Champions. Multicoloured.

1791	20 m. Type **368**	10	10
1792	30 m. Emanuel Lasker and Pilsberi game, 1895	10	10
1793	40 m. Alexander Alekhine and Retti game, 1925	15	10
1794	50 m. Mikhail Botvinnik and Capablanca game, 1938	20	10
1795	60 m. Anatoly Karpov and Untsiker game, 1975	25	10
1796	80 m. Nona Gaprindashvili and Lasarevich game, 1961	30	15
1797	1 t. 20 M. Chirburdanidze and Levitina game, 1984	50	25

1986. Saiga Antelope ("Saiga tatarica"). As T **359**. Multicoloured.

1800	60 m. Male	25	10
1801	60 m. Female with calf	25	10
1802	60 m. Male and female	25	10
1803	60 m. Male and female in snow	25	10

1986. Pelicans. As T **359**. Multicoloured.

1804	60 m. Dalmatian pelican ("Pelecanus crispus")	25	10
1805	60 m. Dalmatian pelican preening	25	10
1806	60 m. Eastern white pelican ("Pelecanus onocrotalus")	25	10
1807	60 m. Eastern white pelicans in flight	25	10

370 Siamese Fighting Fish

1987. Aquarium Fishes. Multicoloured.

1808	20 m. Type **370**	10	10
1809	30 m. Goldfish	10	10
1810	40 m. "Rasbora hengeli"	15	10
1811	50 m. "Aequidens sp."	20	10
1812	60 m. Moonfish	25	10
1813	80 m. Green swordtail	30	15
1814	1 t. 20 Angel fish (vert)	50	25

371 Lassooing Horse

1987. Traditional Equestrian Sports. Mult.

1816	20 m. Type **371**	10	10
1817	30 m. Breaking horse	10	10
1818	40 m. Mounted archer	15	10
1819	50 m. Race	20	10
1820	60 m. Horseman snatching flag from ground	25	10
1821	80 m. Tug of war	30	15
1822	1 t. 20 Racing wolf	50	25

372 Grey-headed Green Woodpecker **373** Butterfly Hunting

1987. Woodpeckers. Multicoloured.

1823	20 m. Type **372**	10	10
1824	30 m. Wryneck	10	10
1825	40 m. Great spotted woodpecker	15	10
1826	50 m. White-backed woodpecker	20	10
1827	60 m. Lesser spotted woodpecker	25	10
1828	80 m. Black woodpecker	30	15
1829	1 t. 20 Three-toed woodpecker	50	25

1987. Children's Activities. Multicoloured.

1831	20 m. Type **373**	10	10
1832	30 m. Feeding calves	10	10
1833	40 m. Drawing on ground in chalk	15	10
1834	50 m. Football	20	10
1835	60 m. Go-carting	25	10
1836	80 m. Growing vegetables	30	15
1837	1 t. 20 Playing string instrument	50	25

374 Industry and Agriculture

1987. 13th Congress and 60th Anniv of Mongolian Trade Union.

1838	**374**	60 m. multicoloured	25	10

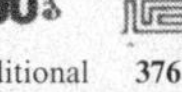
375 Women in Traditional Costume **376** Flags of Member Countries

1987. 40th Anniv of Mongol–Soviet Friendship.

1839	**375**	60 m. multicoloured	25	10

1987. Argali ("Ovis ammon"). As T **359**. Mult.

1840	60 m. On grassy rock (full face)	25	10
1841	60 m. On rock (three-quarter face)	25	10
1842	60 m. Family	25	10
1843	60 m. Close-up of head and upper body	25	10

1987. Swans. As T **359**. Multicoloured.

1844	60 m. Mute Swan ("Cygnus olor") in water	25	10
1845	60 m. Mute swan on land	25	10
1846	60 m. Whistling swan ("Cygnus bewickii")	25	10
1847	60 m. Whistling swan, "Cygnus gunus" and mute swan	25	10

1987. 25th Anniv of Membership of Council for Mutual Economic Aid.

1848	**376**	60 m. multicoloured	25	10

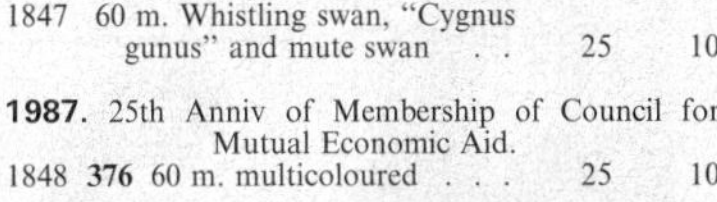

377 Sea Buckthorn **378** Couple in Traditional Costume

1987. Fruits. Multicoloured.

1849	20 m. Type **377**	10	10
1850	30 m. Blackcurrants	10	10
1851	40 m. Redcurrants	15	10
1852	50 m. Redcurrants	20	10
1853	60 m. Raspberries	25	10
1854	80 m. "Padus asiatica"	30	15
1855	1 t. 20 Strawberries	50	25

1987. Folk Art. Multicoloured.

1857	20 m. Type **378**	10	10
1858	30 m. Gold-inlaid baton and pouch	10	10
1859	40 m. Gold and jewelled ornaments	15	10
1860	50 m. Bag and dish	20	10
1861	60 m. Earrings	25	10
1862	80 m. Pipe, pouch and bottle	30	15
1863	1 t. 20 Decorative headdress	50	25

379 Dancer

1987. Dances.

1864	**379**	20 m. multicoloured	10	10
1865	–	30 m. multicoloured	10	10
1866	–	40 m. multicoloured	15	10
1867	–	50 m. multicoloured	20	10
1868	–	60 m. multicoloured	25	10
1869	–	80 m. multicoloured	30	15
1870	–	1 t. 20 multicoloured	50	25

DESIGNS: 30 m. to 1 t. 20, Different dances.

381 Scottish Fold

1987. Cats. Multicoloured.

1872	20 m. Type **381**	10	10
1873	30 m. Grey	10	10
1874	40 m. Oriental	15	10
1875	50 m. Abyssinian (horiz)	20	10
1876	60 m. Manx (horiz)	25	10
1877	80 m. Black shorthair (horiz)	30	15
1878	1 t. 20 Spotted (horiz)	50	25

382 Mil Mi-V12

1987. Helicopters. Multicoloured.

1880	20 m. Type **382**	10	10
1881	30 m. Westland WG-30	15	10
1882	40 m. Bell LongRanger II	20	10
1883	50 m. Kawasaki-Hughes 369HS	25	10
1884	60 m. Kamov Ka-32	30	10
1885	80 m. Mil Mi-17	35	15
1886	1 t. 20 Mil Mi-10K	60	25

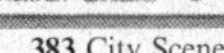

383 City Scene **384** Kremlin, Lenin and Revolutionaries

1987. 19th Mongolian People's Revolutionary Party Congress. Multicoloured.

1887	60 m. Type **383**	25	10
1888	60 m. Clothing and mining industries	25	10
1889	60 m. Agriculture	25	10
1890	60 m. Family	25	10
1891	60 m. Workers, factories and fields	25	10
1892	60 m. Building construction	25	10
1893	60 m. Scientist	25	10

1987. 70th Anniv of Russian October Revolution.

1894	**384**	60 m. multicoloured	25	10

385 Seven with One Blow

1987. Walt Disney Cartoons. Mult (a) "The Brave Little Tailor" (Grimm Brothers).
1895 25 m. Type **385** 10 10
1896 35 m. Brought before the King 15 10
1897 45 m. Rewards for bravery . 20 10
1898 55 m. Fight between Mickey and the giant 25 10
1899 2 t. Happy ending 80 40
(b) "The Celebrated Jumping Frog of Calaveras County" (Mark Twain).
1901 65 m. "He'd bet on anything" 25 10
1902 75 m. "He never done nothing but...learn that frog to jump" 30 15
1903 85 m. "What might it be that you've got in that box?" . 35 15
1904 1 t. "40 He got the frog out and filled him full of quail shot" 60 30

386 Head

1987. The Red Fox. Multicoloured.
1906 60 m. Type **386** 25 10
1907 60 m. Vixen and cubs . . . 25 10
1908 60 m. Stalking 25 10
1909 60 m. In the snow 25 10

388 Bobsleighing 389 Sukhe Bator

1988. Air. Winter Olympic Games, Calgary. Mult.
1911 20 m. Type **388** 10 10
1912 30 m. Ski jumping 10 10
1913 40 m. Skiing 15 10
1914 50 m. Biathlon 20 10
1915 60 m. Speed skating 25 10
1916 80 m. Figure skating 30 15
1917 1 t. 20 Ice hockey 50 25

1988. 95th Birth Anniv of Sukhe Bator.
1919 **389** 60 m. multicoloured . . 25 10

390 "Invitation"

1988. Roses. Multicoloured.
1920 20 m. Type **390** 10 10
1921 30 m. "Meilland" 10 10
1922 40 m. "Pascali" 15 10
1923 50 m. "Tropicana" 20 10
1924 60 m. "Wendy Cussons" . . 25 10
1925 80 m. "Rosa sp" (wrongly inscr "Blue Moon") 30 15
1926 1 t. 20 "Diorama" 50 25

391 "Ukhaant Ekhner"

1988. Puppets. Multicoloured.
1928 20 m. Type **391** 10 10
1929 30 m. "Altan Everte Mungun Turuut" 10 10
1930 40 m. "Aduuchyn Khuu" . . 15 10
1931 50 m. "Suulenkhuu" 20 10
1932 60 m. "Khonchyn Khuu" . . 25 10
1933 80 m. "Argat Byatskhan Baatar" 30 15
1934 1 t. 20 "Botgochyn Khuu" . 50 25

393 Judo 394 Marx

1988. Olympic Games, Seoul. Multicoloured.
1936 20 m. Type **393** 10 10
1937 30 m. Archery 10 10
1938 40 m. Weightlifting 15 10
1939 50 m. Gymnastics 20 10
1940 60 m. Cycling 25 10
1941 80 m. Running 30 15
1942 1 t. 20 Wrestling 50 25

1988. 170th Birth Anniv of Karl Marx.
1944 **394** 60 m. multicoloured . . 25 10

395 Couple and Congress Banner 396 "Kosmos"

1988. 19th Revsomol Youth Congress.
1945 **395** 60 m. multicoloured . . 25 10

1988. Spacecraft and Satellites. Multicoloured.
1946 20 m. Type **396** 10 10
1947 30 m. "Meteor" 10 10
1948 40 m. "Salyut"–"Soyuz" space complex 15 10
1949 50 m. "Prognoz-6" 20 10
1950 60 m. "Molniya-1" 25 10
1951 80 m. "Soyuz" 30 15
1952 1 t. 20 "Vostok" 50 25

397 Buddha 398 Emblem

1988. Religious Sculptures.
1954 **397** 20 m. multicoloured . . 10 10
1955 – 30 m. multicoloured . . 10 10
1956 – 40 m. multicoloured . . 15 10
1957 – 50 m. multicoloured . . 20 10
1958 – 60 m. multicoloured . . 25 10
1959 – 80 m. multicoloured . . 30 15
1960 – 1 t. 20 multicoloured . . 50 25
DESIGNS: 30 m. to 1 t. 20, Different buddhas.

1988. 30th Anniv of Problems of "Peace and Socialism" (magazine).
1962 **398** 60 m. multicoloured . . 25 10

399 Eagle

1988. White-tailed Sea Eagle. Multicoloured.
1963 60 m. Type **399** 25 10
1964 60 m. Eagle on fallen branch and eagle landing 25 10
1965 60 m. Eagle on rock 25 10
1966 60 m. Eagle (horiz) 25 10

400 Ass

1988. Asiatic Wild Ass. Multicoloured.
1967 60 m. Type **400** 25 10
1968 60 m. Head of ass 25 10
1969 60 m. Two adults 25 10
1970 60 m. Mare and foal 25 10

401 Athlete 403 U.S.S.R. (ice hockey)

1988. Traditional Sports. Multicoloured.
1971 10 m. Type **401** 10 10
1972 20 m. Horseman 10 10
1973 30 m. Archery 10 10
1974 40 m. Wrestling 15 10
1975 50 m. Archery (different) . . 20 10
1976 70 m. Horsemen (national holiday cavalcade) 30 15
1977 1 t. 20 Horsemen, wrestlers and archers 50 25

1988. Winter Olympic Games Gold Medal Winners. Multicoloured.
1979 1 t. 50 Type **403** 60 30
1980 1 t. 50 Bonnie Blair (speed skating) 60 30
1981 1 t. 50 Alberto Tomba (slalom) 60 30
1982 1 t. 50 Matti Nykanen (ski jumping) (horiz) 60 30

404 Brown Goat

1988. Goats. Multicoloured.
1984 20 m. Type **404** 10 10
1985 30 m. Black goat 10 10
1986 40 m. White long-haired goats 15 10
1987 50 m. Black long-haired goat 20 10
1988 60 m. White goat 25 10
1989 80 m. Black short-haired goat 30 15
1990 1 t. 20 Nanny and kid 50 25

405 Emblem

1989. 60th Anniv of Mongolian Writers' Association.
1992 **405** 60 m. multicoloured . . . 25 10

406 Beaver gnawing Trees

1989. Eurasian Beaver. Multicoloured.
1993 60 m. Type **406** 25 10
1994 60 m. Beaver with young . . 25 10
1995 60 m. Beavers beside tree stump and in water 25 10
1996 60 m. Beaver rolling log . . . 25 10

407 Dancers

1989. Ballet.
1997 **407** 20 m. multicoloured . . 10 10
1998 – 30 m. multicoloured . . 10 10
1999 – 40 m. multicoloured (vert) 15 10
2000 – 50 m. multicoloured . . 20 10
2001 – 60 m. multicoloured . . 25 10
2002 – 80 m. multicoloured (vert) 30 15
2003 – 1 t. 20 multicoloured (vert) 50 25
DESIGNS: 30 m. to 1 t. 20, Different dancing scenes.

408 "Ursus pruinosis"

1989. Bears. Multicoloured.
2004 20 m. Type **408** 10 10
2005 30 m. Brown bear 10 10
2006 40 m. Asiatic black bear . . 15 10
2007 50 m. Polar bear 20 10
2008 60 m. Brown bear 25 10
2009 80 m. Giant panda 30 15
2010 1 t. 20 Brown bear 50 25

409 "Soyuz" Spacecraft

1989. Space. Multicoloured.
2012 20 m. Type **409** 10 10
2013 30 m. "Apollo"–"Soyuz" link 10 10
2014 40 m. "Columbia" space shuttle (vert) 15 10
2015 50 m. "Hermes" spacecraft . 20 10
2016 60 m. "Nippon" spacecraft (vert) 25 10
2017 80 m. "Energy" rocket (vert) 30 15
2018 1 t. 20 "Buran" space shuttle (vert) 50 25

411 Nehru 412 "Opuntia microdasys"

1989. Birth Centenary of Jawaharial Nehru (Indian statesman).
2021 **411** 10 m. multicoloured . . 10 10

1989. Cacti. Multicoloured.
2022 20 m. Type **412** 10 10
2023 30 m. "Echinopsis multipiex" 10 10
2024 40 m. "Rebutia tephracanthus" 15 10
2025 50 m. "Brasilicactus haselbergii" 20 10
2026 60 m. "Gymnocalycium mihanovichii" 25 10
2027 80 m. "C. strausii" 30 15
2028 1 t. 20 "Horridocactus tuberisvicatus" 50 25

1989. 800th Anniv of Coronation of Genghis Khan. Nos. 291/4 optd **CHINGGIS KHAN CROWNATION 1189.**
2030 **67** 20 m. multicoloured . . . 10 10
2031 – 30 m. multicoloured . . . 10 10
2032 – 50 m. black, brown & red 20 10
2033 – 60 m. buff, blue & brown 25 10

415 Citroen "BX"

1989. Motor Cars. Multicoloured.
2035 20 m. Type **415** 10 10
2036 30 m. Volvo "760 GLF" . . 10 10
2037 40 m. Honda "Civic" 15 10
2038 50 m. Volga 20 10
2039 60 m. Ford "Granada" . . . 25 10
2040 80 m. Baz "21099" 30 15
2041 1 t. 20 Mercedes "190" . . . 50 25

416 Monument **417** Florence Griffith-Joyner (running)

1989. 50th Anniv of Battle of Khalka River.
2043 **416** 60 m. multicoloured . . 30 10

1989. Olympic Games Medal Winners. Mult.
2044 60 m. Type **417** 25 10
2045 60 m. Stefano Cerioni (fencing) 25 10
2046 60 m. Gintautas Umaras (cycling) 25 10
2047 60 m. Kristin Otto (swimming) 25 10

418 "Malchin Zaluus" (N. Sandagsuren)

1989. 30th Anniv of Co-operative Movement. Paintings. Multicoloured.
2049 20 m. Type **418** 10 10
2050 30 m. "Tsaatny Tukhai Dursamkh" (N. Sandagsuren) (vert) 10 10
2051 40 m. "Uul Shig Tushigtei" (D. Amgalan) 15 10
2052 50 m. "Goviin Egshig" (D. Amgalan) 20 10
2053 60 m. "Tsagaan Sar" (Ts. Dagvanyam) 25 10
2054 80 m. "Tumen Aduuny Bayar" (M. Butemkh) (vert) . . . 30 15
2055 1 t. 20 "Bilcheer Deer" (N. Tsultem) 50 25

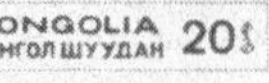

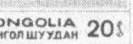

419 Four-man Bobsleighing **420** Victory Medal

1989. Ice Sports. Multicoloured.
2057 20 m. Type **419** 10 10
2058 30 m. Luge 10 10
2059 40 m. Figure skating 15 10
2060 50 m. Two-man bobsleighing 20 10
2061 60 m. Ice dancing 25 10
2062 80 m. Speed skating 30 15
2063 1 t. 20 Ice speedway 50 25

1989. Orders. Designs showing different badges and medals. Multicoloured, background colour given.
2065 **420** 60 m. blue 25 10
2066 – 60 m. orange 25 10
2067 – 60 m. mauve 25 10
2068 – 60 m. violet 25 10
2069 – 60 m. green 25 10
2070 – 60 m. blue 25 10
2071 – 60 m. red 25 10

422 Chu Lha **423** Sukhe Bator Statue

1989. Buddhas. Multicoloured.
2073 20 m. Damdin Sandub . . . 10 10
2074 30 m. Pagwa Lama 10 10
2075 40 m. Type **422** 15 10
2076 50 m. Agwanglobsan 20 10
2077 60 m. Dorje Dags Dan . . . 25 10
2078 80 m. Wangchikdorje . . . 30 15
2079 1 t. 20 Buddha 50 25

1990. New Year.
2081 **423** 10 m. multicoloured . . 75 35

424 Newspapers and City **425** Emblem

1990. 70th Anniv of "Khuvisgalt Khevlel" (newspaper).
2082 **424** 60 m. multicoloured . . 65 30

1990. 20th Mongolian People's Revolutionary Party Congress.
2083 **425** 60 m. multicoloured . . 50 25

426 Male Character

1990. "Mandukhai the Wise" (film).
2084 **426** 20 m. multicoloured . . 20 10
2085 – 30 m. multicoloured . . 30 15
2086 – 40 m. multicoloured . . 45 20
2087 – 50 m. multicoloured . . 55 30
2088 – 60 m. multicoloured . . 75 35
2089 – 80 m. multicoloured . . 90 45
2090 – 1 t. 20 multicoloured . . 1·25 65
DESIGNS: 30 m. to 1 t. 20, Different characters from the film.

427 Trophy and Players

1990. World Cup Football Championship, Italy.
2092 **427** 20 m. multicoloured . . 20 10
2093 – 30 m. multicoloured . . 30 15
2094 – 40 m. multicoloured . . 40 20
2095 – 50 m. multicoloured . . 60 30
2096 – 60 m. multicoloured . . 70 35
2097 – 80 m. multicoloured . . 95 40
2098 – 1 t. 20 multicoloured . . 1·25 65
DESIGNS: 30 m. to 1 t. 20, Trophy and different players.

428 Lenin

1990. 120th Birth Anniv of Lenin.
2100 **428** 60 m. black, red and gold 65 30

429 Mother with Fawn

1990. Siberian Musk Deer. Multicoloured.
2101 60 m. Type **429** 65 30
2102 60 m. Deer in wood 65 30
2103 60 m. Deer on river bank . . 65 30
2104 60 m. Deer in winter landscape 65 30

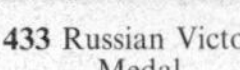

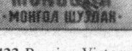

433 Russian Victory Medal **434** Crane

1990. 45th Anniv of End of Second World War.
2108 **433** 60 m. multicoloured . . . 65 30

1990. The Japanese White-necked Crane. Multicoloured.
2109 60 m. Type **434** 45 25
2110 60 m. Crane feeding (horiz) . 45 25
2111 60 m. Cranes flying (horiz) . 45 25
2112 60 m. Crane on river bank . . 45 25

435 Fin Whale

1990. Marine Mammals. Multicoloured.
2113 20 m. Type **435** 15 10
2114 30 m. Humpback whale . . . 25 10
2115 40 m. Narwhal 35 15
2116 50 m. Risso's dolphin 45 20
2117 60 m. Bottle-nosed dolphin . 50 25
2118 80 m. Atlantic white-sided dolphin 70 35
2119 1 t. 20 Bowhead whale 90 45

436 Weapons and Black Standard **437** Panda

1990. 750th Anniv of "Secret History of the Mongols" (book). Multicoloured.
2121 10 m. Type **436** 10 10
2122 10 m. Weapons and white standard 10 10
2123 40 m. Brazier ($17\frac{1}{2}\times22$ mm) . 30 15
2124 60 m. Genghis Khan ($17\frac{1}{2}\times22$ mm) 55 25
2125 60 m. Horses galloping . . . 55 25
2126 60 m. Tartar camp 55 25
2127 80 m. Men kneeling to ruler . 60 30
2128 80 m. Court 60 30

1990. The Giant Panda. Multicoloured.
2129 10 m. Type **437** 10 10
2130 20 m. Panda eating bamboo 15 10
2131 30 m. Adult eating bamboo, and cub 25 10
2132 40 m. Panda on tree branch (horiz) 35 15
2133 50 m. Adult and cub resting (horiz) 40 20
2134 60 m. Panda and mountains (horiz) 55 25
2135 80 m. Adult and cub playing (horiz) 60 30
2136 1 t. 20 Panda on snow-covered river bank (horiz) . . . . 1·25 60

438 Chasmosaurus

1990. Prehistoric Animals. Multicoloured.
2138 20 m. Type **438** 15 10
2139 30 m. Stegosaurus 25 10
2140 40 m. Probactrosaurus . . . 35 15
2141 50 m. Opisthocoelicaudia . . 45 20
2142 60 m. Iguanodon (vert) . . . 50 25
2143 80 m. Tarbosaurus 70 35
2144 1 t. 20 Mamenchisaurus (after Mark Hallett) (60×22 mm) 90 45

439 Lighthouse, Alexandria, Egypt **440** Kea

1990. Seven Wonders of the World. Mult.
2146 20 m. Type **439** 15 10
2147 30 m. Pyramids of Egypt (horiz) 25 10
2148 40 m. Statue of Zeus, Olympia 35 15
2149 50 m. Colossus of Rhodes . 45 25
2150 60 m. Mausoleum, Halicarnassus 50 25
2151 80 m. Temple of Artemis, Ephesus (horiz) 70 35
2152 1 t. 20 Hanging Gardens of Babylon 90 45

1990. Parrots. Multicoloured.
2154 20 m. Type **440** 15 10
2155 30 m. Hyacinth macaw 25 10
2156 40 m. Australian king parrot . 35 15
2157 50 m. Grey parrot 45 20
2158 60 m. Kakapo 55 25
2159 80 m. Alexandrine parakeet . 75 35
2160 1 t. 20 Scarlet macaw 90 45

441 Purple Bear Moth

1990. Moths and Butterflies. Multicoloured.
2162 20 m. Type **441** 15 10
2163 30 m. Great night peacock butterfly 25 10
2164 40 m. Moth 35 15
2165 50 m. Magpie moth 45 20
2166 60 m. Chequered moth . . . 50 25
2167 80 m. Swallowtail 70 35
2168 1 t. 20 Butterfly 90 45

442 Jetsons in Flying Saucer

1991. The Jetsons (cartoon characters). Mult.

2170 20 m. Type **442** 10 10
2171 25 m. Family walking on planet and dragon (horiz) 10 10
2172 30 m. Jane, George, Elroy and dog Astro 10 10
2173 40 m. George, Judy, Elroy and Astro crossing river 15 10
2174 50 m. Flying in saucer (horiz) 35 15
2175 60 m. Jetsons and Cosmo Spacely (horiz) 45 20
2176 70 m. George and Elroy flying with jetpacks
2177 80 m. Elroy (horiz) 55 25
2178 1 t. 20 Judy and Astro watching Elroy doing acrobatics on tree 95 45

443 Dino and Bam-Bam meeting Mongolian Boy with Camel

1991. The Flintstones (cartoon characters). Mult.

2180 25 m. Type **443** 10 10
2181 35 m. Bam-Bam and Dino posing with boy (vert) 15 10
2182 45 m. Mongolian mother greeting Betty Rubble, Wilma Flintstone and children 20 10
2183 55 m. Barney Rubble and Fred riding dinosaurs 25 10
2184 65 m. Flintstones and Rubbles by river 30 15
2185 75 m. Bam-Bam and Dino racing boy on camel 40 20
2186 85 m. Fred, Barney and Bam-Bam with Mongolian boy 55 25
2187 1 t. 40 Flintstones and Rubbles in car 90 45
2188 2 t. Fred and Barney taking refreshments with Mongolian 1·40 70

444 Party Emblem

445 Black-capped Chickadee

1991. 70th Anniv of Mongolian People's Revolutionary Party.

2190 **444** 60 m. multicoloured 50 25

1991. "Stamp World London 90" International Stamp Exhibition. Multicoloured.

2191 25 m. Type **445** 10 10
2192 35 m. Common cardinal 15 10
2193 45 m. Crested shelduck 20 10
2194 55 m. Mountain bluebird 25 10
2195 65 m. Northern oriole 30 10
2196 75 m. Bluethroat (horiz) 35 10
2197 85 m. Eastern bluebird 45 15
2198 1 t. 40 Great red warbler 85 40
2199 2 t. Golden eagle 1·10 55

446 Black Grouse

1991. Birds. Multicoloured.

2201 20 m. Type **446** 15 10
2202 30 m. Common shelduck 25 10
2203 40 m. Ring-necked pheasant 35 15
2204 50 m. Long-tailed duck 50 25
2205 60 m. Hazel grouse 60 30
2206 80 m. Red-breasted merganser 80 40
2207 1 t. 20 Goldeneye 1·10 55

447 Emblem **448** Superb Pink

1991. 70th Anniv of Mongolian People's Army.

2209 **447** 60 m. multicoloured 50 25

1991. Flowers. Multicoloured.

2210 20 m. Type **448** 15 10
2211 30 m. "Gentiana pneumonanthe" (wrongly inscr "puenmonanthe") 25 10
2212 40 m. Dandelion 35 15
2213 50 m. Siberian iris 50 25
2214 60 m. Turk's-cap lily 60 30
2215 80 m. "Aster amellus" 80 40
2216 1 t. 20 "Ciszium rivulare" 1·10 55

449 Stag Beetle

1991. Beetles. Multicoloured.

2218 20 m. Type **449** 15 10
2219 30 m. "Chelorrhina polyphemus" 25 15
2220 40 m. "Coptolabrus coelestis" 35 15
2221 50 m. "Epepeotes togatus" 50 25
2222 60 m. Tiger beetle 60 30
2223 80 m. "Macrodontia cervicornis" 80 40
2224 1 t. 20 Hercules beetle 1·10 55

450 Defend

1991. Buddhas. Multicoloured.

2226 20 m. Type **450** 15 10
2227 30 m. Badmasanhava 25 10
2228 40 m. Avalokitecvara 35 15
2229 50 m. Buddha 50 25
2230 60 m. Mintugwa 60 30
2231 80 m. Shyamatara 70 35
2232 1 t. 20 Samvara 1·10 55

451 Zebras

1991. African Wildlife. Multicoloured.

2234 20 m. Type **451** 15 10
2235 30 m. Cheetah (wrongly inscr "Cheetan") 25 10
2236 40 m. Black rhinoceros 35 15
2237 50 m. Giraffe (vert) 50 25
2238 60 m. Gorilla 60 30
2239 80 m. Elephants 80 40
2240 1 t. 20 Lion (vert) 1·10 55

452 Communications

1991. Meiso Mizuhara Stamp Exhibition, Ulan Bator.

2242 **452** 1 t. 20 multicoloured 55 25

453 Scotch Bonnet

1991. Fungi. Multicoloured.

2243 20 m. Type **453** 15 10
2244 30 m. Oak mushroom 20 10
2245 40 m. "Hygrophorus marzuelus" 30 15
2246 50 m. Chanterelle 40 20
2247 60 m. Field mushroom 55 25
2248 80 m. Bronze boletus 70 30
2249 1 t. 20 Caesar's mushroom 1·25 50
2250 2 t. "Tricholoma terreum" 2·10 95

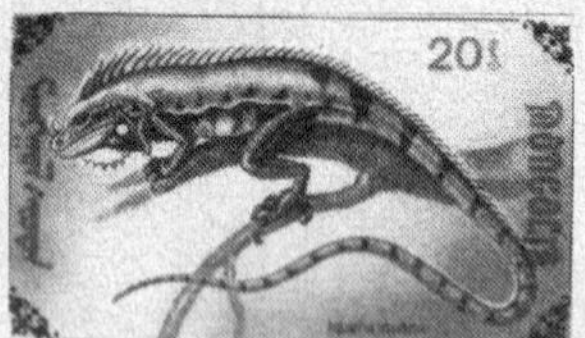

455 Green Iguana

1991. Reptiles. Multicoloured.

2253 20 m. Type **455** 15 10
2254 30 m. Flying gecko 30 15
2255 40 m. Frilled lizard 40 20
2256 50 m. Common cape lizard 50 25
2257 60 m. Common basilisk 60 30
2258 80 m. Common tegu 80 40
2259 1 t. 20 Marine iguana 1·25 65

456 Warrior

1991. Masked Costumes. Multicoloured.

2261 35 m. Type **456** 15 10
2262 45 m. Mask with fangs 25 10
2263 55 m. Bull mask 40 20
2264 65 m. Dragon mask 50 25
2265 85 m. Mask with beak 60 30
2266 1 t. 40 Old man 1·10 55
2267 2 t. Gold mask with earrings 1·25 60

457 German Shepherd

1991. Dogs. Multicoloured.

2269 20 m. Type **457** 15 10
2270 30 m. Dachshund (vert) 30 15
2271 40 m. Yorkshire terrier (vert) 40 20
2272 50 m. Standard poodle 50 25
2273 60 m. Springer spaniel 60 30
2274 80 m. Norfolk terrier 80 40
2275 1 t. 20 Keeshund 1·25 60

458 Siamese

1991. Cats. Multicoloured.

2277 20 m. Type **458** 15 10
2278 30 m. Black and white longhaired (vert) 30 15
2279 40 m. Ginger red 40 20
2280 50 m. Tabby (vert) 50 25
2281 60 m. Red and white (vert) 60 30
2282 80 m. Maine coon (vert) 80 40
2283 1 t. 20 Blue-eyed white persian (vert) 1·25 60

459 Pagoda **460** Butterfly

1991. "Phila Nippon '91" International Stamp Exhibition, Tokyo. Multicoloured.

2285 1 t. Type **459** 25 10
2286 2 t. Japanese woman 50 25
2287 3 t. Mongolian woman 80 40
2288 4 t. Temple 1·25 60

1991. Butterflies and Flowers. Multicoloured.

2289 20 m. Type **460** 10 10
2290 25 m. Yellow roses 15 10
2291 30 m. Butterfly 20 10
2292 40 m. Butterfly 25 10
2293 50 m. Butterfly 30 15
2294 60 m. Butterfly 35 15
2295 70 m. Red rose 40 20
2296 80 m. Marguerites 50 25
2297 1 t. 20 Lily 75 35

1991. "Expo '90" International Garden and Greenery Exhibition, Osaka. Nos. 2289/97 optd **EXPO '90** and symbol.

2298 20 m. multicoloured 10 10
2299 25 m. multicoloured 15 10
2300 30 m. multicoloured 20 10
2301 40 m. multicoloured 25 10
2302 50 m. multicoloured 30 15
2303 60 m. multicoloured 35 15
2304 70 m. multicoloured 40 20
2305 80 m. multicoloured 50 25
2306 1 t. 20 multicoloured 75 35

462 Poster for 1985 Digital Stereo Re-issue

1991. 50th Anniv (1990) of Original Release of Walt Disney's "Fantasia" (cartoon film). Multicoloured.

2308 1 t. 70 Type **462** 10 10
2309 2 t. 1940 poster for original release 15 10
2310 2 t. 30 Poster for 1982 digital re-issue 20 10
2311 2 t. 60 Poster for 1981 stereo re-issue 25 10
2312 4 t. 20 Poster for 1969 "Psychedelic Sixties" release 45 20
2313 10 t. 1941 poster for original release 1·50 75
2314 15 t. Mlle. Upanova (sketch by Campbell Grant) 1·75 85
2315 16 t. Mickey as the Sorcerer's Apprentice (original sketch) 2·10 1·00

463 Speed Skating **465** Elk

1992. Winter Olympic Games, Albertville. Multicoloured.
2317 60 m. Type **463** 15 10
2318 80 m. Ski jumping 35 15
2319 1 t. Ice hockey 65 30
2320 1 t. 20 Ice skating 70 35
2321 1 t. 50 Biathlon (horiz) . . . 90 45
2322 2 t. Skiing (horiz) . . . . . . 1·25 60
2323 2 t. 40 Two-man bobsleigh (horiz) . . . . 1·50 75

1992. The Elk. Multicoloured.
2326 3 t. Type **465** 85 40
2327 3 t. Female with young (horiz) 85 40
2328 3 t. Adult male (horiz) . . . 85 40
2329 3 t. Female 85 40

466 Tank Locomotive, Darjeeling–Himalaya Railway, India

1992. Multicoloured. (a) Railways of the World.
2330 3 t. Type **466** 45 20
2331 3 t. "The Royal Scot", Great Britain 45 20
2332 6 t. Train on bridge, Burma–Siam Railway . . . . . . 1·00 50
2333 6 t. Baltic tank engine, Burma 1·00 50
2334 8 t. Baldwin locomotive, Thailand . . . . 1·25 60
2335 8 t. Western Railway locomotive, Pakistan . . . 1·25 60
2336 16 t. Class "P.36" locomotive, U.S.S.R. . . . . 2·60 1·25
2337 16 t. Shanghai–Peking express, China . . . . 2·60 1·25

(b) "Orient Express".
2339 3 t. 1931 advertising poster . 45 20
2340 3 t. 1928 advertising poster . 45 20
2341 6 t. Dawn departure . . . . 1·00 50
2342 6 t. "The Golden Arrow" leaving Victoria Station, London . . . . 1·00 50
2343 8 t. Standing in station, Yugoslavia . . . . 1·25 60
2344 8 t. Train passing through mountainous landcape, early 1900s . . . . 1·25 60
2345 16 t. "Fleche d'Or" approaching Etaples . . . . 2·60 1·25
2346 16 t. Arrival in Istanbul . . . 2·60 1·25

468 Magpie

1992. Multicoloured. (a) Birds.
2349 3 t. Type **468** 40 20
2350 3 t. Eagle owl 40 20
2351 6 t. Black-headed gull (horiz) 80 40
2352 6 t. Redstart (horiz) 80 40
2353 8 t. Demoiselle crane . . . . 1·10 55
2354 8 t. Black stork (horiz) . . . 1·10 55
2355 16 t. Rough-legged buzzard . . 2·25 1·10
2356 16 t. Golden eagle (horiz) . . 2·25 1·10

(b) Butterflies and Moths.
2358 3 t. Scarce swallowtail (horiz) 40 20
2359 3 t. Small tortoiseshell . . . 40 20
2360 6 t. "Thyria jacobaeae" (value at right) (horiz) 80 40
2361 6 t. Peacock (value at left) (horiz) 80 40
2362 8 t. Camberwell beauty (value at left) (horiz) . . . . . . 1·10 55
2363 8 t. Red admiral (value at right) (horiz) . . . . 1·10 55
2364 16 t. "Hyporhaia audica" (horiz) . . . . 2·25 1·10
2365 16 t. Large tortoiseshell (flying over river) (horiz) . . . . 2·25 1·10

472 Fleet

1992. 500th Anniv of Discovery of America by Columbus (2nd issue). Multicoloured.
2370 3 t. Type **472** 20 10
2371 7 t. Amerindians' canoe approaching "Santa Maria" 40 20
2372 10 t. "Pinta" 55 25
2373 16 t. "Santa Maria" in open sea (vert) 80 40
2374 30 t. "Santa Maria" passing coastline . . . . 1·75 85
2375 40 t. Dolphins and "Santa Maria" . . . . 2·25 1·10
2376 50 t. "Nina" . . . . 2·75 1·60

474 Long Jumping

1992. Olympic Games, Barcelona. Multicoloured.
2379 3 t. Type **474** 10 10
2380 6 t. Gymnastics (pommel exercise) 15 10
2381 8 t. Boxing 25 10
2382 16 t. Wrestling 50 25
2383 20 t. Archery (vert) 55 25
2384 30 t. Cycling 75 35
2385 40 t. Show jumping . . . . 1·10 55
2386 50 t. High jumping . . . . 1·25 60
2387 60 t. Weightlifting . . . . . 1·50 75

476 Black Grouse

1993. Birds. Multicoloured.
2390 3 t. Type **476** 10 10
2391 8 t. Moorhen 35 15
2392 10 t. Golden-crowned kinglet 45 20
2393 16 t. Common kingfisher . . 70 35
2394 30 t. Red-throated diver . . 1·25 60
2395 40 t. Grey heron . . . . . . 1·75 85
2396 50 t. Hoopoe . . . . 2·25 1·10
2397 60 t. Blue-throated niltava . 2·50 1·25

477 Orange-tip

1993. Butterflies and Moths. Multicoloured.
2399 3 t. Type **477** 10 10
2400 8 t. Peacock 35 15
2401 10 t. High brown fritillary . . 45 20
2402 16 t. "Limenitis reducta" . . 70 35
2403 30 t. Common burnet . . . 1·25 60
2404 40 t. Common blue . . . . 1·75 80
2405 50 t. Apollo . . . . 2·25 1·10
2406 60 t. Great peacock . . . . 2·50 1·25

1993. No. 1221 surch.
2408 15 t. on 70 m. multicoloured 25 10

479 Nicolas Copernicus (astronomer)

1993. "Polska'93" International Stamp Exhibition, Poznan. Multicoloured.
2409 30 t. Type **479** (520th birth anniv) . . . . 1·25 60
2410 30 t. Frederic Chopin (composer) . . . . 1·25 60
2411 30 t. Pope John Paul II . . 1·25 60

1993. No. 263 surch.
2413 8 t. on 70 m. multicoloured . 50 25

482 Hologram of Airship

1993. Airship Flight over Ulan Bator.
2415 **482** 80 t. multicoloured . . 2·10 1·00

483 Buddha

1993. "Bangkok 1993" International Stamp Exhibition. Multicoloured.
2416 50 t. Buddha on throne . . . 1·10 55
2417 100 t. Buddha (different) . . 2·25 1·10
2418 150 t. Type **483** . . . . . . 3·25 1·60
2419 200 t. Multi-armed Buddha . 4·50 2·25

484 Clouds, Mountains and Dog

1994. New Year. Year of the Dog. Multicoloured.
2421 60 t. Type **484** 90 45
2422 60 t. Dog reclining between mountains and waves (horiz) 90 45

485 Uruguay (1930, 1950)

1994. World Cup Football Championship, U.S.A. Previous Winners. Multicoloured.
2423 150 t. Type **485** 45 20
2424 150 t. Italy (1934) 45 20
2425 150 t. German Federal Republic (1954) 45 20
2426 150 t. Brazil (1958) 45 20
2427 150 t. Argentina (1978, 1986) 45 20
2428 200 t. Italy (1938) 50 25
2429 200 t. Brazil (1962) 50 25
2430 200 t. German Federal Republic (1974) 50 25
2431 250 t. Brazil (1970) 65 30
2432 250 t. Italy (1982) 65 30
2433 250 t. German Federal Republic (1990) 65 30

488 Biathlon

1994. Winter Olympic Games, Lillehammer, Norway. Multicoloured.
2437 50 t. Type **488** 30 15
2438 60 t. Two-man bobsleigh . . 40 20
2439 80 t. Skiing 50 25
2440 100 t. Ski jumping 70 35
2441 120 t. Ice skating 75 35
2442 200 t. Speed skating . . . . . 1·40 70

490 Eagle

1994. Wildlife. Multicoloured.
2445 60 t. Type **490** 45 20
2446 60 t. Woodpecker on tree trunk 45 20
2447 60 t. Cranes 45 20
2448 60 t. Osprey 45 20
2449 60 t. Golden oriole on branch 45 20
2450 60 t. Swallows 45 20
2451 60 t. Eagle perched on rock . 45 20
2452 60 t. White birds in flight . . 45 20
2453 60 t. Squirrel on branch . . 45 20
2454 60 t. Dragonfly 45 20
2455 60 t. Black stork 45 20
2456 60 t. Duck 45 20
2457 60 t. Brown bird standing on rock 45 20
2458 60 t. Marmot 45 20
2459 60 t. Ladybird on flower . . 45 20
2460 60 t. Clutch of eggs in ground nest 45 20
2461 60 t. Grasshopper 45 20
2462 60 t. Butterfly 45 20
Nos. 2445/62 were issued together, se-tenant, forming a composite design.

491 Command Module **492** Flowers

1994. 25th Anniv of First Manned Moon Landing. Multicoloured.
2463 200 t. Type **491** 95 45
2464 200 t. Earth, astronaut in chair and shuttle wing 95 45
2465 200 t. Shuttle approaching Earth 95 45
2466 200 t. Astronaut on Moon . . 95 45

1994.
2468 **492** 10 t. green and black . 10 10
2469 – 18 t. purple and black . 10 10
2470 – 22 t. blue and black . . 15 10
2471 – 44 t. purple and black . 20 10
DESIGNS: 18, 44 t. Argali; 22 t. Airplane.

493 Korean Empire 1884 5 m. Stamp

1994. "Philakorea 1994" International Stamp Exhibition, Seoul. Multicoloured.
2472 600 t. Type **493** 65 30
2473 600 t. Mongolia 1924 1 c. stamp 65 30
2474 600 t. Mongolia 1966 Children's Day 15 m. stamp (47 × 34 mm) 65 30
2475 600 t. South Korea 1993 New Year 110 w. stamp (47 × 34 mm) 65 30

494 Butterfly

1994. "Singpex '94" National Stamp Exhibition, Singapore. Year of the Dog.
2477 **494** 300 t. multicoloured . . 1·00 50

496 Mammoth

1994. Prehistoric Animals. Multicoloured.
2480 60 t. Type **496** 35 15
2481 80 t. Stegosaurus 50 25
2482 100 t. Talararus (horiz) . . . 75 35
2483 120 t. Gorythosaurus (horiz) 90 45
2484 200 t. Tyrannosaurus (horiz) 1·50 75

497 National Flags

1994. Mongolia–Japan Friendship and Co-operation.

2486	**497**	20 t. multicoloured	40	25

498 Boar and Mountains

1995. New Year. Year of the Pig. Multicoloured.

2487	200 t. Type **498**	65	30
2488	200 t. Boar reclining amongst clouds (vert)	65	30

499 Dancer

1995. Tsam Religious Mask Dance.

2489	**499**	20 t. multicoloured	10	10
2490	–	50 t. multicoloured	20	10
2491	–	60 t. multicoloured	30	15
2492	–	100 t. multicoloured	50	25
2493	–	120 t. multicoloured	60	30
2494	–	150 t. multicoloured	65	30
2495	–	200 t. multicoloured	85	40

DESIGNS: 50 t. to 200 t. Different masked characters.

500 Saiga

1995. The Saiga. Multicoloured.

2497	40 t. Type **500**	15	10
2498	50 t. Male and female	20	10
2499	70 t. Male running	35	15
2500	200 t. Head and neck of male	85	40

502 Yellow Oranda

1995. Goldfish. Multicoloured.

2502	20 t. Type **502**	20	10
2503	50 t. Red and white wen-yu	30	15
2504	60 t. Brown oranda with red head	40	20
2505	100 t. Calico pearl-scale with phoenix tail	65	30
2506	120 t. Red lion-head	85	45
2507	150 t. Brown oranda	1·10	55
2508	200 t. Red and white oranda with narial	1·40	70

503 Bishop

1995. X-Men (comic strip). Designs showing characters. Multicoloured.

2511	30 t. Type **503**	10	10
2512	50 t. Beast	15	10
2513	60 t. Rogue	20	10
2514	70 t. Gambit	25	10
2515	80 t. Cyclops	30	15
2516	100 t. Storm	45	20
2517	200 t. Professor X	85	40
2518	250 t. Wolverine	1·00	50

505 Presley

1995. 60th Birth Anniv of Elvis Presley (entertainer). Multicoloured.

2521	60 t. Type **505**	30	15
2522	80 t. Wearing cap	35	15
2523	100 t. Holding microphone	45	20
2524	120 t. Wearing blue and white striped T-shirt	60	30
2525	150 t. With guitar and microphone	70	35
2526	200 t. On motor bike with girl	85	40
2527	250 t. On surfboard	1·00	50
2528	300 t. Pointing with left hand	1·40	70
2529	350 t. Playing guitar and girl clapping	1·75	85

Nos. 2521/9 were issued together, se-tenant, forming a composite design.

506 Monroe smiling

1995. 70th Birth Anniv (1996) of Marilyn Monroe (actress). Multicoloured.

2531	60 t. Type **506**	30	15
2532	80 t. Wearing white dress	35	15
2533	100 t. Pouting	45	20
2534	120 t. With naval officer and cello player	60	30
2535	150 t. Wearing off-the-shoulder blouse	70	35
2536	200 t. Using telephone and wearing magenta dress	85	40
2537	250 t. Man kissing Monroe's shoulder	1·00	50
2538	300 t. With white fur collar	1·40	70
2539	350 t. With Clark Gable	1·75	85

Nos. 2531/9 were issued together, se-tenant, forming a composite design.

507 Rat sitting between Mountains

1996. New Year. Year of the Rat. Multicoloured.

2541	150 t. Type **507**	70	35
2542	200 t. Rat crouching between mountains and waves (horiz)	85	40

MONG-TSEU (MENGTSZ) Pt. 17

An Indo-Chinese P.O. in Yunnan province, China, closed in 1922.

1903. 100 centimes = 1 franc.
1919. 100 cents = 1 piastre.

Stamps of Indo-China surcharged.

1903. "Tablet" key-type surch **MONGTZE** and value in Chinese.

1	D	1 c. black and red on buff	3·50	3·50
2		2 c. brown & blue on buff	2·25	2·25
3		4 c. brown & blue on grey	3·50	3·50
4		5 c. green and red	2·75	3·00
5		10 c. red and blue	4·00	4·00
6		15 c. grey and red	5·00	4·50
7		20 c. red and blue on green	5·25	5·25
8		25 c. blue and red	5·75	5·50
9		25 c. black and red on pink	£400	£400
10		30 c. brown & bl on drab	4·75	5·00
11		40 c. red & blue on yellow	38·00	38·00
12		50 c. red and blue on pink	£190	£190
13		50 c. brown & red on blue	60·00	60·00
14		75 c. brown & red on orge	60·00	60·00
15		1 f. green and red	60·00	60·00
16		5 f. mauve & blue on lilac	60·00	60·00

1906. Surch **Mong-Tseu** and value in Chinese.

17	**8**	1 c. green	90	85
18		2 c. purple on yellow	90	85
19		4 c. mauve on blue	90	85
20		5 c. green	90	85
21		10 c. pink	1·10	1·10
22		15 c. brown on blue	1·10	1·10
23		20 c. red on green	2·00	2·00
24		25 c. blue	2·25	2·25
25		30 c. brown on cream	3·50	3·50
26		35 c. black on yellow	2·50	2·50
27		40 c. black on grey	3·25	3·25
28		50 c. brown	9·50	9·50
29	D	75 c. brown & red on orange	23·00	23·00
30	**8**	1 f. green	11·00	11·00
31		2 f. brown on yellow	27·00	27·00
32	D	5 f. mauve and blue on lilac	60	60
34	**8**	10 f. red on green	80·00	80·00

1908. Surch **MONGTSEU** and value in Chinese.

35	**10**	1 c. black and brown	35	40
36		2 c. black and brown	40	45
37		4 c. black and blue	50	55
38		5 c. black and green	60	60
39		10 c. black and red	85	90
40		15 c. black and violet	95	95
41	**11**	20 c. black and violet	2·50	2·25
42		25 c. black and blue	3·25	3·25
43		30 c. black and brown	2·25	2·00
44		35 c. black and green	2·25	2·00
45		40 c. black and brown	2·25	2·25
46		50 c. black and red	2·25	2·25
47	**12**	75 c. black and orange	5·50	5·50
48	–	1 f. black and red	6·00	6·25
49	–	2 f. black and green	8·00	8·25
50	–	5 f. black and blue	55·00	60·00
51	–	10 f. black and violet	65·00	70·00

1919. Nos. 35/51 further surch in figures and words.

52	**10**	$\frac{2}{5}$ c. on 1 c. black & brown	45	45
53		$\frac{4}{5}$ c. on 2 c. black & brown	45	40
54		$1\frac{3}{5}$ c. on 4 c. black & blue	90	90
55		2 c. on 5 c. black and green	55	55
56		4 c. on 10 c. black and red	1·10	1·00
57		6 c. on 15 c. black and violet	1·10	1·00
58	**11**	8 c. on 20 c. black and violet	2·00	2·00
59		10 c. on 25 c. black and blue	1·60	1·60
60		12 c. on 30 c. black & brown	1·60	1·60
61		14 c. on 35 c. black & green	1·60	1·50
62		16 c. on 40 c. black & brown	2·00	2·00
63		20 c. on 50 c. black and red	2·25	2·00
64	**12**	30 c. on 75 c. black & orge	2·00	2·00
65	–	40 c. on 1 f. black and red	4·25	4·25
66	–	80 c. on 2 f. black and green	2·75	2·75
67	–	2 p. on 5 f. black and blue	70·00	75·00
68	–	4 p. on 10 f. black and violet	13·00	13·00

MONTENEGRO Pt. 3

Formerly a monarchy on the Adriatic Sea and part of Yugoslavia. In Italian and German occupation during 1939-45 war.

1874. 100 novcic = 1 florin.
1902. 100 heller = 1 krone.
1907. 100 para = 1 krone (1910 = 1 perper).

1 Prince Nicholas

Прослава
1493 1893
Штампарије
(2)

1874.

45	**1**	1 n. pale blue	10	15
38		2 n. yellow	2·50	1·90
51		2 n. green	10	15
39		3 n. green	40	50
52		3 n. red	10	15
40		5 n. red	40	40
53		5 n. orange	25	15
19		7 n. mauve	29·00	19·00
41		7 n. pink	40	40
54		7 n. grey	15	20
42		10 n. blue	40	40
55		10 n. purple	15	10
56		15 n. brown	15	15
46		20 n. brown	10	15
7		25 n. purple	£225	£200
44		25 n. brown	40	1·50
57		25 n. blue	10	25
47	**1**	30 n. brown	10	15
48		50 n. blue	10	20
49		1 f. green	25	1·40
50		2 f. red	80	2·25

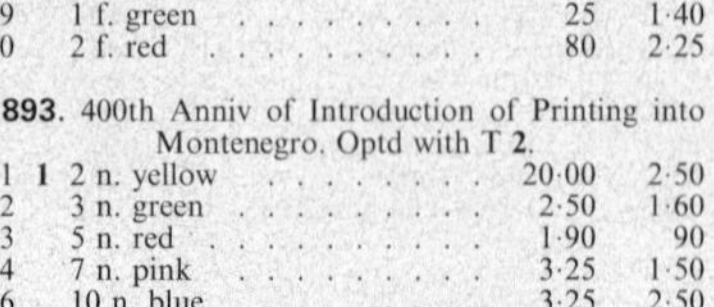

1893. 400th Anniv of Introduction of Printing into Montenegro. Optd with T **2**.

81	**1**	2 n. yellow	20·00	2·50
82		3 n. green	2·50	1·60
83		5 n. red	1·90	90
84		7 n. pink	3·25	1·50
86		10 n. blue	3·25	2·50
87		15 n. bistre	3·50	3·25
89		25 n. brown	3·25	1·50

3 Monastery near Cetinje, Royal Mausoleum

1896. Bicentenary of Petrovich Niegush Dynasty.

90	**3**	1 n. brown and blue	10	80
91		2 n. yellow and purple	10	80
92		3 n. green and brown	10	80
93		5 n. brown and green	10	80
94		10 n. blue and yellow	10	80
95		15 n. green and blue	10	80
96		20 n. blue and green	10	80
97		25 n. yellow and blue	10	80
98		30 n. brown and purple	10	80
99		50 n. slate and red	10	70
100		1 f. slate and pink	15	1·25
101		2 f. grey and brown	15	1·25

4

УСТАВ
Constitution
Никољдан
1905
(5)

7

1902.

102	**4**	1 h. blue	15	15
103		2 h. purple	20	15
104		5 h. green	15	10
105		10 h. red	20	10
106a		25 h. blue	15	15
107		50 h. green	35	30
108		1 k. brown	30	30
109		2 k. brown	35	35
110		5 k. orange	50	90

1905. Granting of Constitution. Optd with T **5**.

111	**4**	1 h. blue	15	15
112		2 h. mauve	15	15
113		5 h. green	15	15
114		10 h. red	15	15
124		25 h. blue	15	15
125		50 h. green	15	15
126		1 k. brown	15	15
127		2 k. brown	15	15
119		5 k. orange	50	1·50

1907.

129	**7**	1 p. yellow	10	20
130		2 p. black	10	20
131		5 p. green	65	10
132		10 p. red	1·60	10
133		15 p. blue	10	15
134		20 p. orange	10	20
135		25 p. blue	10	15
136		35 p. brown	15	15
137		50 p. lilac	30	35
138		1 k. red	30	30
139		2 k. green	35	30
140		5 k. red	75	60

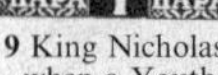
9 King Nicholas when a Youth

10 King Nicholas and Queen Milena

11 Prince Nicholas

12 Nicholas I

1910. Fiftieth Year of King's Reign.

141	**9**	1 p. black	15	10
142	**10**	2 p. purple	15	10
143	–	5 p. green	10	10
144	–	10 p. red	10	10
145	–	15 p. blue	10	10
146	**10**	20 p. olive	20	15
147	–	25 p. blue	15	10
148	–	35 p. brown	50	40
149	–	50 p. violet	20	20
150	–	1 per. lake	30	30
151	–	2 per. green	70	45
152	**11**	5 per. blue	75	75

DESIGNS: As Type 9: 5 p., 10 p., 25 p., 35 p. Nicholas I in 1910; 15 p. Nicholas I in 1878; 50 p., 1 per., 2 per. Nicholas I in 1890.

1913.
153 12 1 p. orange 10 10
154 2 p. purple 10 10
155 5 p. green 10 10
156 10 p. red 10 10
157 15 p. blue 15 15
158 20 p. brown 15 15
159 25 p. blue 15 15
160 35 p. red 40 40
161 50 p. blue 20 20
162 1 per. brown 20 20
163 2 per. lilac 40 40
164 5 per. green 40 40

ITALIAN OCCUPATION

Montenegro
Црна Гора
17-IV-41-XIX (1) **ЦРНА ГОРА** (2)

1941. Stamps of Yugoslavia optd with T 1.

(a) Postage. On Nos. 414, etc.
1 99 25 p. black 10 45
2 1 d. green 10 45
3 1 d. 50 red 10 45
4 2 d. mauve 10 45
5 3 d. brown 10 45
6 4 d. blue 10 45
7 5 d. blue . . . . 1·25 2·25
8 5 d. 50 violet . . . . 1·25 2·25
9 6 d. blue . . . . 1·25 2·25
10 8 d. brown . . . . 1·40 2·25
11 12 d. violet . . . . 1·25 2·25
12 16 d. purple . . . . 1·25 2·25
13 20 d. blue . . . . 50·00 95·00
14 30 d. pink . . . . 25·00 45·00

(b) Air. On Nos. 360/7.
15 80 50 p. brown . . . . 2·50 5·00
16 – 1 d. green . . . . 1·75 3·25
17 – 2 d. blue . . . . 1·75 3·25
18 – 2 d. 50 red . . . . 2·50 5·00
19 80 5 d. violet . . . . 22·00 38·00
20 – 10 d. red . . . . 16·00 32·00
21 – 20 d. green . . . . 22·00 45·00
22 – 30 d. blue . . . . 16·00 32·00

1941. Stamps of Italy optd with T 2. (a) On Postage stamps of 1929.
28 98 5 c. brown 10 35
29 – 10 c. brown 10 35
30 – 15 c. green 10 35
31 99 20 c. red 10 35
32 – 25 c. green 10 35
33 103 30 c. brown 10 35
34 50 c. violet 10 35
35 – 75 c. red 10 35
36 – 1 l. 25 blue 10 35

(b) On Air stamp of 1930.
37 110 50 c. brown 10 35

1942. Nos. 416 etc of Yugoslavia optd **Governatorato del Montenegro Valore LIRE**.
43 99 1 d. green 25 40
44 1 d. 50 red . . . . 11·00 22·00
45 3 d. brown 25 40
46 4 d. blue 30 40
47 5 d. 50 violet 30 40
48 6 d. blue 30 40
49 8 d. brown 30 40
50 12 d. violet 30 40
51 16 d. purple 30 40

1942. Air. Nos. 360/7 of Yugoslavia optd **Governatorato del Montenegro Valore in Lire**.
52 80 0.50 l. brown . . . . 1·40 3·00
53 – 1 l. green . . . . 1·40 3·00
54 – 2 l. blue . . . . 1·40 3·00
55 – 2.50 l. red . . . . 1·40 3·00
56 80 5 l. violet . . . . 1·40 3·00
57 – 10 l. brown . . . . 1·40 3·00
58 – 20 l. green . . . . 55·00 £120
59 – 30 l. blue . . . . 12·50 27·00

4 Prince Bishop Peter Njegos and View

1943. National Poem Commemoratives. Each stamp has fragment of poetry inscr at back.
60 4 5 c. violet 10 60
61 – 10 c. green 10 60
62 – 15 c. brown 10 60
63 – 20 c. orange 10 60
64 – 25 c. green 15 60
65 – 50 c. mauve 15 60
66 – 1 l. 25 blue 15 85
67 – 2 l. green . . . . 30 1·25
68 – 5 l. red on buff . . . . 1·75 4·75
69 – 20 l. purple on grey . . . . 3·75 11·00
DESIGNS—HORIZ: 10 c. Meadow; 15 c. Country chapel; 20 c. Chiefs Meeting; 25, 50 c. Folk-dancing; 1 l. 25, Taking the Oath; 2 l. Procession; 5 l. Watch over wounded standard-bearer. VERT: 20 l. Portrait of Prince Bishop Peter Njegos.

INDEX

Countries can be quickly located by referring to the index at the end of this volume.

5 Cetinje

1943. Air.
70 5 50 c. brown 10 70
71 – 1 l. blue 15 70
72 – 2 l. mauve . . . . 20 1·00
73 – 5 l. green . . . . 45 1·90
74 – 10 l. purple on buff . . . . 3·00 8·00
75 – 20 l. blue on pink . . . . 5·00 13·00
DESIGNS—HORIZ: 1 l. Coastline; 2 l. Budva; 5 l. Mt. Lovcen; 10 l. Lake of Scutari. VERT: 20 l. Mt. Durmitor.

GERMAN OCCUPATION

1943. Nos. 419/20 of Yugoslavia surch **Deutsche Militaer-Verwaltung Montenegro** and new value in lire.
76 99 50 c. on 3 d. brown . . . . 3·00 18·00
77 1 l. on 3 d. brown . . . . 3·00 18·00
78 1 l. 50 on 3 d. brown . . . . 3·00 18·00
79 2 l. on 3 d. brown . . . . 6·25 38·00
80 4 l. on 3 d. brown . . . . 6·25 38·00
81 5 l. on 4 d. blue . . . . 6·25 38·00
82 8 l. on 4 d. blue . . . . 7·75 75·00
83 10 l. on 4 d. blue . . . . 14·00 £120
84 20 l. on 4 d. blue . . . . 25·00 £250

1943. Appointment of National Administrative Committee. Optd **Nationaler Verwaltungsausschuss 10.XI.1943**. (a) Postage. On Nos. 64/8.
85 25 c. green . . . . 9·25 £140
86 50 c. mauve . . . . 9·25 £140
87 1 l. 25 blue . . . . 9·25 £140
88 2 l. green . . . . 9·25 £140
89 5 l. red on buff £250 £1900

(b) Air. On Nos. 70/4.
90 5 50 c. brown . . . . 17·00 £160
91 1 l. blue . . . . 17·00 £160
92 2 l. mauve . . . . 17·00 £160
93 5 l. green . . . . 17·00 £160
94 10 l. purple on buff £3250 £12000

1944. Refugees Fund. Surch **Fluchtlingshilfe Montenegro** and new value in German currency. (a) On Nos. 419/20 of Yugoslavia.
95 99 0.15 + 0.85 Rm. on 3 d. . . 9·25 £140
96 0.15 + 0.85 Rm. on 4 d. . . 9·25 £140

(b) On Nos. 46/9.
97 – 0.15 + 0.85 Rm. on 25 c. . . 9·25 £140
98 – 0.15 + 1.35 Rm. on 50 c. . . 9·25 £140
99 – 0.25 + 1.75 Rm. on 1 l. 25 . . 9·25 £140
100 – 0.25 + 1.75 Rm. on 2 l. . . 9·25 £140

(c) Air. On Nos. A52/4.
101 5 0.15 + 0.85 Rm. on 50 c. . . 9·25 £140
102 – 0.25 + 1.25 Rm. on 1 l. . . 9·25 £140
103 – 0.50 + 1.50 Rm. on 2 l. . . 9·25 £140

1944. Red Cross. Surch + **Crveni Krst Montenegro** and new value in German currency.
(a) On Nos. 419/20 of Yugoslavia.
104 99 0.50 + 2.50 Rm. on 3 d. . . 9·25 £110
105 0.50 + 2.50 Rm. on 4 d. . . 9·25 £110

(b) On Nos. 64/5.
106 – 0.15 + 0.85 Rm. on 25 c. . . 9·25 £110
107 – 0.15 + 1.35 Rm. on 50 c. . . 9·25 £110

(c) Air. On Nos. 70/2.
108 5 0.25 + 1.75 Rm. on 50 c. . . 10·50 £110
109 – 0.25 + 2.75 Rm. on 1 l. . . 10·50 £110
110 – 0.50 + 2 Rm. on 2 l. . . . 10·50 £110

ACKNOWLEDGEMENT OF RECEIPT STAMPS

A 3

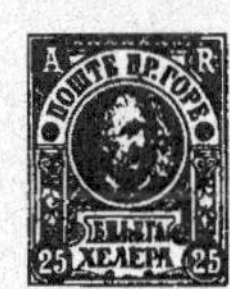
A 4

1895.
A90 A 3 10 n. blue and red . . . 10 30

1902.
A111 A 4 25 h. orange and red . 40 40

1905. Optd with T 5.
A130 A 4 25 h. orange and red . 10 15

1907. As T 7, but letters "A" and "R" in top corners.
A141 7 25 p. olive 20 35

1913. As T 12, but letters "A" and "R" in top corners.
A169 12 25 p. olive 20 35

POSTAGE DUE STAMPS

D 3

D 4

D 8

1894.
D90 D 3 1 n. red . . . . 1·90 1·25
D91 2 n. green 15 15
D92 3 n. orange 15 15
D93 5 n. green 15 15
D94 D 3 10 n. purple 15 15
D95 20 n. blue 15 20
D96 30 n. green 15 20
D97 50 n. pale green 15 20

1902.
D111 D 4 5 h. orange 10 10
D112 10 h. olive 15 10
D113 25 h. purple 15 10
D114 50 h. green 15 10
D115 1 k. pale green 20 20

1905. Optd with T 5.
D120 D 4 5 h. orange 25 25
D121 10 h. olive 15 20
D122 25 h. purple 25 25
D123 50 h. green 25 25
D124 1 k. pale green 40 40

1907.
D141 D 8 5 p. brown 15 15
D142 10 p. violet 15 15
D143 25 p. red 15 15
D144 50 p. green 15 15

1913. As T 12 but inscr "HOPTOMAPKA" at top.
D165 5 p. grey 50 50
D166 10 p. violet 25 25
D167 25 p. blue 25 25
D168 50 p. red 40 35

ITALIAN OCCUPATION

1941. Postage Due stamps of Yugoslavia optd **Montenegro Upha 17-IV-41-XIX**.
D23 D 56 50 p. violet 20 65
D24 1 d. mauve 20 65
D25 2 d. blue 20 65
D26 5 d. orange . . . . 9·25 18·00
D27 10 d. brown . . . . 1·60 3·25

1942. Postage Due stamps of Italy optd **UPHATOPA**.
D38 D 141 10 c. blue 10 80
D39 20 d. red 10 80
D40 30 c. orange 10 80
D41 50 c. violet 10 80
D42 1 l. orange 20 80

MOROCCO Pt. 13

An independent kingdom, established in 1956, comprising the former French and Spanish International Zones.

A. NORTHERN ZONE.

100 centimes = 1 peseta

1 Sultan of Morocco

2 Polytechnic

1956.
1 1 10 c. brown 10 10
2 – 15 c. brown 10 10
3 2 25 c. violet 10 10
4 – 50 c. green 25 25
5 1 80 c. green 90 90
6 – 2 p. lilac . . . . 7·50 7·50
7 2 3 p. blue . . . . 15·00 15·00
8 – 10 p. green . . . . 31·00 31·00
DESIGNS—HORIZ: 15 c., 2 p. Villa Sanjurjo harbour. VERT: 50 c., 10 p. Cultural Delegation building, Tetuan.

3 Lockheed Super Constellation over Lau Dam

1956. Air.
9 3 25 c. purple 20 15
10 – 1 p. 40 mauve 90 60
11 3 3 p. 40 red . . . . 1·90 1·50
12 – 4 p. 80 purple . . . . 3·50 2·50
DESIGN: 1 p. 40, 4 p. 80, Lockheed Super Constellation over Rio Nekor Bridge.

1957. 1st Anniv of Independence. As T 7 but with Spanish inscriptions and currency.
13 80 c. green 65 50
14 1 p. 50 olive . . . . 1·90 1·40
15 3 p. red . . . . 4·25 3·25

1957. As T 5 but with Spanish inscriptions and currency.
16 30 c. indigo and blue 10 10
17 70 c. purple and brown 20 10
18 80 c. purple . . . . 1·60 40
19 1 p. 50 lake and green 50 15
20 3 p. green 75 50
21 7 p. red . . . . 5·25 1·50

1957. Investiture of Prince Moulay el Hassan. As T 9 but with Spanish inscriptions and currency.
22 80 c. blue 65 25
23 1 p. 50 green . . . . 1·60 80
24 3 p. red . . . . 4·75 2·50

1957. Nos. 17 and 19 surch.
25 15 c. on 70 c. purple and brown . 75 75
26 1 p. 20 on 1 p. 50 lake and green . 1·40 1·40

1957. 30th Anniv of Coronation of Sultan Sidi Mohammed ben Yusuf. As T 10 but with Spanish inscription and currency.
27 1 p. 20 green and black 65 50
28 1 p. 80 red and black 90 75
29 3 p. violet and black . . . . 1·60 1·50

B. SOUTHERN ZONE

100 centimes = 1 franc

5 Sultan of Morocco

6 Classroom

7 Sultan of Morocco

1956.
30 5 5 f. indigo and blue 20 10
31 10 f. sepia and brown 15 10
32 15 f. lake and green 25 10
33 25 f. purple . . . . 1·10 10
34 30 f. green . . . . 1·90 10
35 50 f. red . . . . 3·00 15
36 70 f. brown and sepia . . . . 4·25 60

1956. Education Campaign.
37 – 10 f. violet and purple . . . 1·90 1·25
38 – 15 f. lake and red . . . . 2·40 1·50
39 6 20 f. green and turquoise . . 2·50 2·50
40 – 30 f. red and lake . . . . 4·50 2·75
41 – 50 f. blue and indigo . . . 7·50 5·00
DESIGNS: 10 f. Peasants reading book; 15 f. Two girls reading; 30 f. Child reading to old man; 50 f. Child teaching parents the alphabet.

1957. 1st Anniv of Independence.
42 7 15 f. green . . . . 1·60 1·25
43 25 f. olive . . . . 2·25 1·25
44 30 f. red . . . . 4·00 1·90

8 Emblem over Casablanca

9 Crown Prince Moulay el Hassan

1957. Air. International Fair, Casablanca.
45 8 15 f. green and red . . . . 1·25 1·00
46 25 f. turquoise . . . . 2·25 1·40
47 30 f. brown . . . . 2·75 1·75

1957. Investiture of Crown Prince Moulay el Hassan.
48 9 15 f. blue . . . . 1·50 95
49 25 f. green . . . . 1·75 1·25
50 30 f. red . . . . 2·75 1·60

10 King Mohammed V

11 Moroccan Pavilion

1957. 30th Anniv of Coronation of King Mohammed V.
51 10 15 f. green and black . . . 95 50
52 25 f. red and black . . . . 1·50 1·00
53 30 f. violet and black . . . 1·60 1·10

C. ISSUES FOR THE WHOLE OF MOROCCO.

1958. 100 centimes = 1 franc.
1962. 100 francs = 1 dirham.

1958. Brussels International Exhibition.
54 11 15 f. turquoise 25 20
55 25 f. red 25 25
56 30 f. blue 35 30

12 King Mohammed V and U.N.E.S.C.O. Headquarters, Paris

1958. Inauguration of U.N.E.S.C.O. Headquarters Building, Paris.

57 **12** 15 f. green 25 20
58 25 f. lake 25 25
59 30 f. blue 35 30

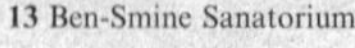

13 Ben-Smine Sanatorium

14 King Mohammed V on Horseback

1959. "National Aid".

60 **13** 50 f. bistre, green and red . 70 35

1959. King Mohammed V's 50th Birthday.

61 **14** 15 f. lake 65 30
62 25 f. blue 95 35
63 45 f. green . . . . 1·10 45

15 Princess Lalla Amina

16

1959. Children's Week.

64 **15** 15 f. blue 25 20
65 25 f. green 30 25
66 45 f. purple 60 30

1960. Meeting of U.N. African Economic Commission, Tangier.

67 **16** 45 f. green, brown & violet 1·10 50

+10 f

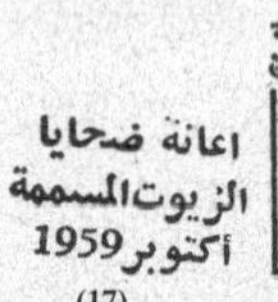

(17)

18 Arab Refugees

1960. Adulterated Cooking Oil Victims Relief Fund. Surch as T **17**.

68 **5** 5 f. + 10 f. indigo and blue 35 30
69 10 f. + 10 f. sepia and brown 70 45
70 15 f. + 10 f. lake and green 1·25 95
71 25 f. + 15 f. purple . . . . 1·40 1·10
72 30 f. + 20 f. green . . . . . 2·25 2·00

1960. World Refugee Year.

73 **18** 15 f. black, green and ochre 25 20
74 – 45 f. green and black 65 35

DESIGNS: 45 f. "Uprooted tree" and Arab refugees.

19 Marrakesh

20 Lantern

1960. 900th Anniv of Marrakesh.

75 **19** 100 f. green, brown and blue 1·40 95

1960. 1100th Anniv of Karaouiyne University.

76 **20** 15 f. purple 60 50
77 – 25 f. blue (Fountain) 65 55
78 – 30 f. brown (Minaret) . . . 1·25 60
79 – 35 f. black (Frescoes) . . . 1·60 80
80 – 45 f. green (Courtyard) . . . 2·25 1·40

21 Arab League Centre and King Mohammed V

(22)

1960. Inauguration of Arab League Centre, Cairo.

81 **21** 15 f. black and green . . . 20 20

1960. Solidarity Fund. Nos. 458/9 (Mahakma, Casablanca) of French Morocco surch as T **22**.

82 **106** 15 f. + 3 f. on 18 f. myrtle 55 55
83 + 5 f. on 20 f. lake . . . 80 80

23 Wrestling

24 Runner

1960. Olympic Games.

84 **23** 5 f. purple, green and violet 10 10
85 – 10 f. chocolate, blue & brn 15 10
86 – 15 f. brown, blue and green 20 15
87 – 20 f. purple, blue and bistre 25 20
88 – 30 f. brown, violet and red . 30 25
89 – 40 f. brown, blue and violet 60 25
90 – 45 f. blue, green and purple 75 35
91 – 70 f. black, blue and brown 1·40 45

DESIGNS: 10 f. Gymnastics; 15 f. Cycling; 20 f. Weightlifting; 30 f. Running; 40 f. Boxing; 45 f. Sailing; 70 f. Fencing.

1961. 3rd Pan-Arab Games, Casablanca.

92 **24** 20 f. green 20 15
93 30 f. lake 65 20
94 50 f. blue 75 60

25 Post Office and Letters

26 King Mohammed V and African Map

27 Lumumba and Congo Map

1961. African Postal and Telecommunications Conference, Tangier.

95 **25** 20 f. purple and mauve . . 35 30
96 – 30 f. turquoise and green . 45 35
97 – 90 f. ultramarine and blue . 85 60

DESIGNS—VERT: 30 f. Telephone operator. HORIZ: 90 f. Sud Aviation Caravelle mail plane over Tangier.

1962. 1st Anniv of African Charter of Casablanca.

98 **26** 20 f. purple and buff . . . 20 20
99 30 f. indigo and blue . . . 25 25

1962. Patrice Lumumba Commemorative.

100 **27** 20 f. black and bistre . . . 20 20
101 30 f. black and brown . . 30 25

28 King Hassan II

29 "Pupils of the Nation"

1962. Air.

102 **28** 90 f. black 75 15
103 1 d. red 90 15
104 2 d. blue . . . . 1·10 45
105 3 d. green . . . . . . 2·25 1·10
106 5 d. violet . . . . . . 4·50 1·60

1962. Children's Education.

107 **29** 20 f. blue, red and green . 35 25
108 30 f. sepia, brown and green 40 35
109 90 f. blue, purple and green 90 50

1962. Arab League Week. As T **76** of Libya.

110 20 f. brown 20 15

30 King Hassan II

31 Scout with Banner

1962.

111 **30** 1 f. olive 10 10
112 2 f. violet 10 10
113 5 f. sepia 10 10
114 10 f. brown 10 10
115 15 f. turquoise 15 10
116 20 f. purple (18 × 22 mm) 20 10
116a 20 f. purple ($17\frac{1}{2} \times 23\frac{1}{2}$ mm) 30 10
116b 25 f. red 20 10
117 30 f. green 25 10
117a 35 f. slate 65 10
117b 40 f. blue 65 10
118 50 f. purple 80 10
118a 60 f. purple . . . . . . 1·10 10
119 70 f. blue . . . . 1·25 10
120 80 f. lake . . . . 2·10 15

1962. 5th Arab Scout Jamboree, Rabat.

121 **31** 20 f. purple and blue . . . 20 15

32 Campaign Emblem and Swamp

33 Aquarium and Fish

1962. Malaria Eradication Campaign.

122 **32** 20 f. blue and green 20 15
123 – 50 f. lake and green 35 25

DESIGN—VERT: 50 f. Sword piercing mosquito.

1962. Casablanca Aquarium. Multicoloured.

124 20 f. Type **33** 65 25
125 30 f. Aquarium and eel 65 25

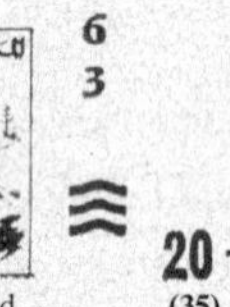

34 Mounted Postman and 1912 Sherifian Stamp

(35)

1962. First National Philatelic Exhibition, Rabat, and Stamp Day.

126 **34** 20 f. green and brown . . . 75 35
127 – 30 f. black and red 90 40
128 – 50 f. bistre and blue . . . 1·25 50

DESIGNS: 30 f. Postman and circular postmark; 50 f. Sultan Hassan I and octagonal postmark. (Both stamps commemorate 70th anniv of Sherifian post.)

1963. Flood Relief Fund. Surch as T **35**.

129 **5** 20 + 5 f. on 5 f. indigo and blue 90 85
130 30 + 10 f. on 50 f. red . . . 1·00 85

36 King Moulay Ismail

37 Ibn Batota (voyager)

1963. 300th Anniv of Meknes.

131 **36** 20 f. sepia 25 20

1963. "Famous Men of Maghreb".

132 **37** 20 f. purple 45 20
133 – 20 f. black 45 20
134 – 20 f. myrtle 25 25
134a **37** 40 f. blue 30 10

PORTRAITS: No. 133, Ibn Khaldoun (historian); 134, Al Idrissi (geographer).

38 Sugar Beet and Refinery

39 Isis (bas relief)

1963. Freedom from Hunger.

135 **38** 20 f. black, brown & green 25 20
136 – 50 f. black, brown & blue . 65 35

DESIGN—VERT: 50 f. Fisherman and tunny.

1963. Nubian Monuments Preservation.

137 – 20 f. black and grey . . . 20 15
138 **39** 30 f. violet 25 25
139 – 50 f. purple 60 35

DESIGNS—HORIZ: 20 f. Heads of Colossi, Abu Simbel; 50 f. Philae Temple.

40 Agadir before Earthquake

1963. Reconstruction of Agadir.

140 **40** 20 f. red and blue 35 35
141 30 f. red and blue 45 35
142 – 50 f. red and blue 80 40

DESIGNS: 30 f. is optd with large red cross and date of earthquake, 29th February, 1960; 50 f. Reconstructed Agadir.

41 Plan of new Agadir Hospital

42 Emblems of Morocco and Rabat

1963. Centenary of International Red Cross.

143 **41** 30 f. multicoloured 50 20

1963. Opening of Parliament.

144 **42** 20 f. multicoloured 45 20

43 Hands breaking Chain

44 National Flag

1963. 15th Anniv of Declaration of Human Rights.

145 **43** 20 f. brown, sepia & green 45 20

1963. Evacuation of Foreign Troops from Morocco.

146 **44** 20 f. red, green and black . 25 25

45 "Moulay Abdurrahman" (after Delacroix)

1964. 3rd Anniv of King Hassan's Coronation.

147 **45** 1 d. multicoloured . . . . 2·75 1·90

46 Map, Chart and W.M.O. Emblem

1964. World Meteorological Day. Multicoloured.
148 20 f. African weather map (postage) (vert) 25 20
149 30 f. Type **46** 40 35
150 90 f. Globe and weather vane (air) (vert) 90 45

47 Fair Entrance

1964. Air. 20th Anniv of Casablanca Int Fair.
151 **47** 1 d. red, drab and blue 95 60

48 Moroccan Pavilion at Fair

1964. Air. New York World's Fair.
152 **48** 1 d. multicoloured 1·25 65

49 Children Playing in the Sun

50 Olympic Torch

1964. Postal Employees' Holiday Settlements.
153 **49** 20 f. multicoloured 25 20
154 – 30 f. multicoloured 35 25
DESIGN: 30 f. Boy, girl and holiday settlement.

1964. Olympic Games, Tokyo.
155 **50** 20 f. green, violet and red 25 25
156 30 f. purple, blue and grn 35 30
157 50 f. red, blue and green 75 35

51 Lighthouse and Sultan Mohamed ben Abdurrahman (founder)

52 Tangier Iris

1964. Centenary of Cape Spartel Lighthouse.
158 **51** 25 f. multicoloured 55 45

1965. Flowers. Multicoloured.
159 25 f. Type **52** 1·00 45
160 40 f. Gladiolus (vert) 1·25 55
161 60 f. Caper (horiz) 1·90 1·40

53 Return of King Mohammed

54 Early Telegraph Receiver

1965. 10th Anniv of Return of King Mohammed V from Exile.
162 **53** 25 f. green 50 20

1965. Centenary of I.T.U. Multicoloured.
163 25 f. Type **54** 20 20
164 40 f. "TIROS" weather satellite 35 30

55 I.C.Y. Emblem

59 Corn

1965. International Co-operation Year.
165 **55** 25 f. black and green 25 20
166 60 f. lake 40 35

1965. Sea Shells. As T **52**. Multicoloured, background colours given.
167 25 f. violet 55 25
168 25 f. blue 55 25
169 25 f. yellow 55 25
SEASHELLS: No. 167, Knobbed triton ("Charonia nodifera"); 168, Smooth callista ("Pitaria chione"); 169, "Cymbium tritonis".

1965. Shellfish. As T **52**. Multicoloured.
170 25 f. Helmet Crab 70 50
171 40 f. Mantis shrimp 1·60 95
172 1 d. Royal prawn (horiz) 2·25 1·40

1965. Orchids. As T **52**. Multicoloured.
173 25 f. "Ophrys speculum" (vert) 60 45
174 40 f. "Ophrys fusca" (vert) 95 50
175 60 f. "Ophrys tenthredinifera" (horiz) 1·75 1·25

1966. Agricultural Products (1st issue).
176 **59** 25 f. black and ochre 20 15
See also Nos. 188/9 and 211.

60 Flag, Map and Dove

1966. 10th Anniv of Independence.
177 **60** 25 f. red and green 20 15

61 King Hassan II and Crown

1966. 5th Anniv of King Hassan's Coronation.
178 **61** 25 f. blue, green and red 20 15

62 Cross-country Runner

1966. 53rd "Cross des Nations" (Cross-country Race).
179 **62** 25 f. green 20 15

63 W.H.O. Building

1966. Inaug of W.H.O. Headquarters, Geneva.
180 **63** 25 f. black and purple 20 15
181 – 40 f. black and blue 25 20
DESIGN: 40 f. W.H.O. Building (different view).

64 King Hassan and Parachutist

65 Brooch

1966. 10th Anniv of Royal Armed Forces.
182 **64** 25 f. black and gold 60 25
183 – 40 f. black and gold 60 25
DESIGN: 40 f. Crown Prince Hassan kissing hand of King Mohammed.

1966. Palestine Week. As No. 110 but inscr "SEMAINE DE LA PALESTINE" at foot and dated "1966".
184 25 f. blue 20 15

1966. Red Cross Seminar. Moroccan Jewellery. Multicoloured.
185 25 f. + 5 f. Type **65** 90 45
186 40 f. + 10 f. Pendant 1·25 55
See also Nos. 203/4, 246/7, 274/5, 287/8, 303/4, 324/5, 370/1, 397/8, 414/15, 450/1 and 493.

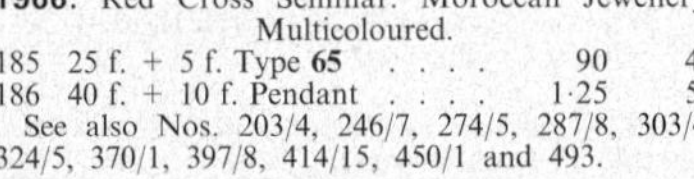

66 Rameses II, Abu Simbel

67 Diesel Train

1966. Air. 20th Anniv of U.N.E.S.C.O.
187 **66** 1 d. red and yellow 1·25 75

1966. Agricultural Products (2nd and 3rd issue). As T **59**.
188 40 f. multicoloured 25 10
189 60 f. multicoloured 35 20
DESIGNS—VERT: 40 f. Citrus fruits. HORIZ: 60 f. Olives.

1966. Moroccan Transport. Multicoloured.
190 25 f. Type **67** (postage) 75 35
191 40 f. Liner "Maroc" 80 40
192 1 d. Tourist coach 95 60
193 3 d. Sud Aviation Caravelle of Royal Air Maroc (48 × 27½ mm) (air) 4·50 1·90

68 Shad

1967. Fishes. Multicoloured.
194 25 f. Type **68** 75 20
195 40 f. Pale bonito 90 25
196 1 d. Bluefish 1·90 1·25

69 Hilton Hotel, Ancient Ruin and Map

1967. Opening of Hilton Hotel, Rabat.
197 **69** 25 f. black and blue 20 15
198 1 d. purple and blue 50 20

70 Ait Aadel Dam

1967. Inauguration of Ait Aadel Dam.
199 **70** 25 f. grey, blue and green 25 15
200 40 f. bistre and blue 65 20

71 Moroccan Scene and Lions Emblem

1967. 50th Anniv of Lions Int.
201 **71** 40 f. blue and gold 50 20
202 1 d. green and gold 1·00 25

1967. Moroccan Red Cross. As T **65**. Mult.
203 60 f. + 5 f. Necklace 95 95
204 1 d. + 10 f. Two bracelets 1·90 1·90

72 Three Hands and Pickaxe

73 I.T.Y. Emblem

1967. Communal Development Campaign.
205 **72** 25 f. green 20 15

1967. International Tourist Year.
206 **73** 1 d. blue and cobalt 80 35

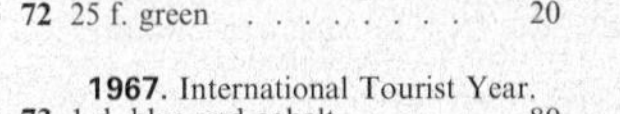

74 Arrow and Map

75 Horse-jumping

1967. Mediterranean Games, Tunis.
207 **74** 25 f. multicoloured 25 20
208 40 f. multicoloured 30 20

1967. International Horse Show.
209 **75** 40 f. multicoloured 30 20
210 1 d. multicoloured 75 35

1967. Agricultural Products (4th issue). As T **59**.
211 40 f. mult (Cotton plant) 65 15

76 Human Rights Emblem

77 Msouffa Woman

1968. Human Rights Year.
212 **76** 25 f. slate 20 20
213 1 d. lake 35 25

1968. Moroccan Costumes. Multicoloured.
214 10 f. Ait Moussa or Ali 65 25
215 15 f. Ait Mouhad 90 30
216 25 f. Barquemaster of Rabat-Sale 1·00 35
217 25 f. Townsman 1·90 75
218 40 f. Townswoman 1·10 45
219 60 f. Royal Mokhazni 1·50 60
220 1 d. Type **77** 1·50 95
221 1 d. Riff 1·50 95
222 1 d. Zemmour woman 1·90 1·25
223 1 d. Meknassa 1·90 60

78 King Hassan

79 Red Crescent Nurse and Child

1968.
224 **78** 1 f. multicoloured 10 10
225 2 f. multicoloured 10 10
226 5 f. multicoloured 10 10
227 10 f. multicoloured 10 10
228 15 f. multicoloured 10 10
229 20 f. multicoloured 10 10
230 25 f. multicoloured 15 10
231 30 f. multicoloured 15 10
232 35 f. multicoloured 45 10
233 40 f. multicoloured 45 10
234 50 f. multicoloured 50 10
235 60 f. multicoloured 50 10
236 70 f. multicoloured 4·00 90
237 75 f. multicoloured 1·00 15
238 80 f. multicoloured 70 20
239 – 90 f. multicoloured 1·40 20
240 – 1 d. multicoloured 2·00 20
241 – 2 d. multicoloured 2·50 35
242 – 3 d. multicoloured 5·00 80
243 – 5 d. multicoloured 8·75 2·50
Nos. 239/43 bear a similar portrait of King Hassan, but are larger, 26½ × 40½ mm.

1968. 20th Anniv of W.H.O.
244 **79** 25 f. brown, red & blue 20 10
245 40 f. brown, red & slate 25 15

1968. Red Crescent. Moroccan Jewellery. As T **65**. Multicoloured.
246 25 f. Pendant brooch 80 40
247 40 f. Bracelet 1·25 50

80 Rotary Emblem, Conference Building and Map

1968. Rotary Int District Conf, Casablanca.
248 **80** 40 f. gold, blue and green 65 20
249 1 d. gold, ultramarine & blue 75 30

81 Belt Pattern

82 Princess Lalla Meryem

1968. "The Belts of Fez". Designs showing ornamental patterns.

250 **81** 25 f. multicoloured . . . . 1·90 70
251 – 40 f. multicoloured . . . . 2·25 1·25
252 – 60 f. multicoloured . . . . 3·50 1·75
253 – 1 d. multicoloured . . . . 6·00 3·25

1968. World Children's Day. Multicoloured.

254 25 f. Type **82** 25 20
255 40 f. Princess Lalla Asmaa . . 65 25
256 1 d. Crown Prince Sidi Mohammed . . . . 1·10 55

83 Wrestling

1968. Olympic Games, Mexico. Multicoloured.

257 15 f. Type **83** 15 15
258 20 f. Basketball 15 15
259 25 f. Cycling 50 15
260 40 f. Boxing 60 15
261 60 f. Running 75 15
262 1 d. Football . . . . 1·25 45

84 Silver Crown

85 Costumes of Zagora, South Morocco

1968. Ancient Moroccan Coins.

263 **84** 20 f. silver & purple 55 20
264 – 25 f. gold and purple . . . 80 25
265 – 40 f. silver and green . . . 1·40 65
266 – 60 f. gold and red . . . . 1·60 65

COINS: 25 f. Gold dinar; 40 f. Silver dirham; 60 f. Gold piece.

See also Nos. 270/1.

1969. Traditional Women's Costumes. Mult.

267 15 f. Type **85** (postage) . . . . 1·25 75
268 25 f. Ait Adidou costumes . . 1·90 1·10
269 1 d. Ait Ouaouzguit costumes (air) . . . . 2·50 1·25

1969. 8th Anniv of Coronation of Hassan II. As T **84** (silver coins).

270 1 d. silver and blue . . . . . 4·25 1·60
271 5 d. silver and violet . . . . . 10·00 6·00

COINS: 1 d. One dirham coin of King Mohammed V; 5 d. One dirham coin of King Hassan II.

86 Hands "reading" Braille on Map

1969. Protection of the Blind Week.

272 **86** 25 f. + 10 f. multicoloured 45 15

87 "Actor"

89 King Hassan II

1969. World Theatre Day.

273 **87** 1 d. multicoloured 45 25

1969. 50th Anniv of League of Red Cross Societies. Moroccan Jewellery as T **65**. Multicoloured.

274 25 f. + 5 f. Bracelets 90 45
275 40 f. + 10 f. Pendant . . . . 1·25 55

1969. King Hassan's 40th Birthday.

276 **89** 1 d. multicoloured . . . . 1·25 35

(90)

91 Mahatma Gandhi

1969. Islamic Summit Conf, Rabat (1st issue). No. 240 optd with T **90**.

278 1 d. multicoloured . . . . . 5·00 4·00

1969. Birth Centenary of Mahatma Gandhi.

279 **91** 40 f. brown and lavender . 60 15

92 I.L.O. Emblem

1969. 50th Anniv of I.L.O.

280 **92** 50 f. multicoloured 50 20

93 King Hassan on Horseback

1969. Islamic Summit Conference, Rabat (2nd issue).

281 **93** 1 d. multicoloured . . . . 1·10 35

94 "Spahi Horseman" (Haram al Glaoui)

1970. Moroccan Art.

282 **94** 1 d. multicoloured . . . . 1·10 30

1970. Flood Victims Relief Fund. Nos. 227/8 surch.

283 **78** 10 f. + 25 f. multicoloured 3·50 3·50
284 15 f. + 25 f. multicoloured 3·50 3·50

96 Drainage System, Fez

97 "Dance of the Guedra" (P. Beaubrun)

1970. 50th Congress of Public and Municipal Health Officials, Rabat.

285 **96** 60 f. multicoloured 35 20

1970. Folklore Festival, Marrakesh.

286 **97** 40 f. multicoloured 75 20

1970. Red Crescent. Moroccan Jewellery as T **65**. Multicoloured.

287 25 f. + 5 f. Necklace . . . . 1·00 65
288 50 f. + 10 f. Pendant . . . . 1·50 1·40

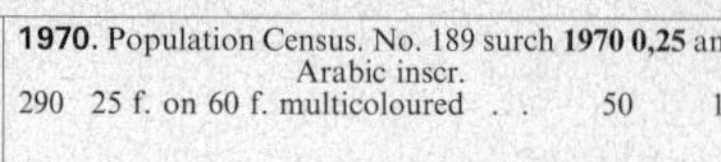

1970. Population Census. No. 189 surch **1970 0,25** and Arabic inscr.

290 25 f. on 60 f. multicoloured . . 50 10

99 Dish Aerial, Souk el Arba des Sehoul Communications Station

100 Ruddy Shelduck

1970. 17th Anniv of Revolution.

291 **99** 1 d. multicoloured 80 35

1970. Nature Protection, Wild Birds. Multicoloured.

292 25 f. Type **100** . . . . 1·50 35
293 40 f. Houbara bustard . . . . 2·50 45

101 I.E.Y. Emblem and Moroccan with Book

1970. International Education Year.

294 **101** 60 f. multicoloured 65 20

102 Symbols of U.N

1970. 25th Anniv of U.N.O.

295 **102** 50 f. multicoloured 55 15

103 League Emblem, Map and Laurel

1970. 25th Anniv of Arab League.

296 **103** 50 f. multicoloured 50 15

104 Olive Grove and Extraction Plant

1970. World Olive-oil Production Year.

297 **104** 50 f. black, brown & green 55 15

105 Es Sounna Mosque

1971. Restoration of Es Sounna Mosque, Rabat.

298 **105** 60 f. multicoloured 60 15

106 "Heart" within Horse

107 King Hassan II and Dam

1971. European and North African Heart Week.

299 **106** 50 f. multicoloured 50 20

1971. 10th Anniv of King Hassan's Accession.

300 **107** 25 f. multicoloured 45 10

108 Palestine on Globe

1971. Palestine Week.

302 **108** 25 f. + 10 f. multicoloured 25 20

1971. Red Crescent, Moroccan Jewellery. As T **65**. Multicoloured.

303 25 f. + 5 f. "Arrow-head" brooch 75 50
304 40 f. + 10 f. Square pendant . 1·10 90

109 Hands holding Peace Dove

1971. Racial Equality Year.

305 **109** 50 f. multicoloured . . . 50 15

110 Musical Instrument

1971. Protection of the Blind Week.

306 **110** 40 f. + 10 f. multicoloured 60 20

111 Children at Play

112 Shah Mohammed Reza Pahlavi of Iran

1971. International Children's Day.

307 **111** 40 f. multicoloured . . . 45 15

1971. 2,500th Anniv of Persian Empire.

308 **112** 1 d. multicoloured 70 30

113 Aerial View of Mausoleum

1971. Mausoleum of Mohammed V. Multicoloured.

309 25 f. Type **113** 15 15
310 50 f. Tomb of Mohammed V . . 20 20
311 1 d. Interior of Mausoleum (vert) 80 50

114 Football and Emblem

116 Sun and Landscape

115 A.P.U. Emblem

1971. Mediterranean Games, Izmir, Turkey. Multicoloured.
312 40 f. Type **114** 55 15
313 60 f. Athlete and emblem . . 70 20

1971. 25th Anniv of Founding of Arab Postal Union at Sofar Conference.
314 **115** 25 f. red, blue & light blue 15 10

1971. 50th Anniv of Sherifian Phosphates Office.
315 **116** 70 f. multicoloured . . . 55 20

117 Torch and Book Year Emblem
118 Lottery Symbol

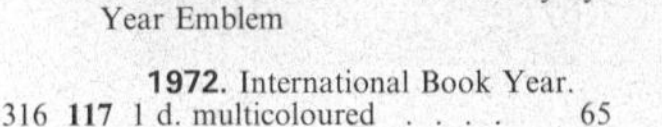

1972. International Book Year.
316 **117** 1 d. multicoloured 65 25

1972. Creation of National Lottery.
317 **118** 25 f. gold, black & brown 15 10

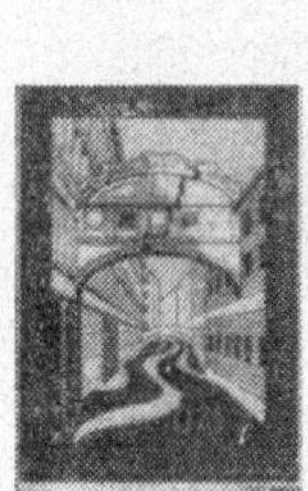

119 Bridge of Sighs
120 Mizmar (double-horned flute)

1972. U.N.E.S.C.O. "Save Venice" Campaign. Multicoloured.
318 25 f. Type **119** 15 15
319 50 f. St. Mark's Basilica (horiz) 20 15
320 1 d. Lion of St. Marks (horiz) 65 20

1972. Protection of the Blind Week.
321 **120** 25 f. + 10 f. multicoloured 60 20

121 Bridge and Motorway

1972. 2nd African Highways Conference, Rabat.
322 **121** 75 f. multicoloured . . . 75 20

122 Moroccan Stamp of 1969, and Postmark

1972. Stamp Day.,
323 **122** 1 d. multicoloured 65 20

1972. Red Crescent. Moroccan Jewellery. As T **65**. Multicoloured.
324 25 f. + 5 f. Jewelled bangles . 75 75
325 70 f. + 10 f. Filigree pendant 1·10 1·10

123 "Betrothal of Imilchil" (Tayeb Lahlou)
124 Dove on African Map

1972. Folklore Festival, Marrakesh.
326 **123** 60 f. multicoloured . . . 90 35

1972. 9th Organisation of African Unity Summit Conference, Rabat.
327 **124** 25 f. multicoloured . . . 15 15

125 Polluted Beach

1972. U.N. Environmental Conservation Conference, Stockholm.
328 **125** 50 f. multicoloured . . . 50 20

126 Running
127 "Sonchus pinnatifidus"

1972. Olympic Games, Munich.
329 **126** 25 f. red, pink & black . 15 15
330 – 50 f. violet, lilac & black 20 15
331 – 75 f. green, yell and blk . 60 20
332 – 1 d. blue, light bl & blk . 75 25
DESIGNS: 50 f. Wrestling; 75 f. Football; 1 d. Cycling.

1972. Moroccan Flowers (1st series). Multicoloured.
333 25 f. Type **127** 45 15
334 40 f. "Amberboa crupinoides" 55 15
See also Nos. 375/6.

128 Sand Gazelle
129 Rabat Carpet

1972. Nature Protection. Fauna. Multicoloured.
335 25 f. Type **128** 75 25
336 40 f. Barbary sheep . . . . . 1·00 60

1972. Moroccan Carpets (1st series). Multicoloured.
337 50 f. Type **129** . . . . 1·00 35
338 75 f. Rabat carpet with "star-shaped" centre . . . . . . 1·50 50
See also Nos. 380/1, 406/7, 433/4, 485/7 and 513.

130 Mother and Child with U.N. Emblem
132 Global Weather Map

131 "Postman" and "Stamp"

1972. International Children's Day.
339 **130** 75 f. blue, yellow & green 35 30

1973. Stamp Day.
340 **131** 25 f. multicoloured . . . 15 10

1973. Centenary of W.M.O.
341 **132** 70 f. multicoloured . . . 70 20

133 King Hassan and Arms

1973.
342 **133** 1 f. multicoloured 10 10
343 2 f. multicoloured 10 10
344 5 f. multicoloured 10 10
345 10 f. multicoloured . . . 10 10
346 15 f. multicoloured . . . 10 10
347 20 f. multicoloured . . . 10 10
348 25 f. multicoloured . . . 10 10
349 30 f. multicoloured . . . 15 10
350 35 f. multicoloured . . . 15 10
351 40 f. multicoloured . . . 5·00 70
352 50 f. multicoloured . . . 50 10
353 60 f. multicoloured . . . 60 15
354 70 f. multicoloured . . . 25 15
355 75 f. multicoloured . . . 30 15
356 80 f. multicoloured . . . 60 20
357 90 f. multicoloured . . . 75 15
358 1 d. multicoloured . . . 2·00 20
359 2 d. multicoloured . . . 4·25 55
360 3 d. multicoloured . . . 6·25 1·25
361 5 d. mult (brown background) . . . . . 4·25 1·25
361a 5 d. mult (pink background) 4·00 90

مناظرة
السياحة
1973
(134)

1973. Nat Tourist Conf. Nos. 324/5 surch with T **134**.
362 **65** 25 f. on 5 f. multicoloured . 2·50 2·50
363 70 f. on 10 f. multicoloured 2·50 2·50
On No. 363 the Arabic text is arranged in one line.

135 Tambours

1973. Protection of the Blind Week.
364 **135** 70 f. + 10 f. multicoloured 75 55

136 Kaaba, Mecca, and Mosque, Rabat

1973. Prophet Mohammed's Birthday.
365 **136** 25 f. multicoloured 15 10

137 Roses and M'Gouna

1973. M'Gouna Rose Festival.
366 **137** 25 f. multicoloured 45 10

138 Handclasp and Torch
139 Folk-dancers

1973. 10th Anniv of Organization of African Unity.
367 **138** 70 f. multicoloured 30 15

1973. Folklore Festival, Marrakesh. Multicoloured.
368 50 f. Type **139** 50 15
369 1 d. Folk-musicians 75 25

1973. Red Crescent. Moroccan Jewellery. As T **65**. Multicoloured.
370 25 f. + 5 f. Locket . . . . . 1·00 50
371 70 f. + 10 f. Bracelet inlaid with pearls . . . . 1·10 60

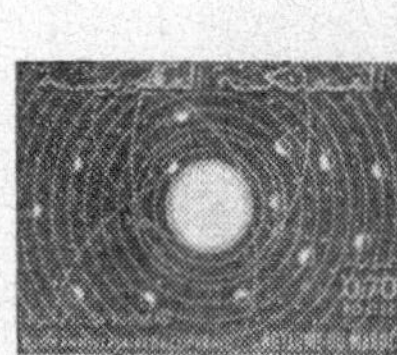

140 Solar System
141 Microscope

1973. 500th Birth Anniv of Nicholas Copernicus.
372 **140** 70 f. multicoloured . . . 60 20

1973. 25th Anniv of W.H.O.
373 **141** 70 f. multicoloured . . . 55 20

142 Interpol Emblem and Fingerprint

1973. 50th Anniv of International Criminal Police Organization (Interpol).
374 **142** 70 f. multicoloured . . . 30 25

1973. Moroccan Flowers (2nd series). As T **127**. Multicoloured.
375 25 f. "Chrysanthemum carinatum" (horiz) 75 35
376 1 d. "Amberboa muricata" . 1·25 55

143 Striped Hyena

1973. Nature Protection. Multicoloured.
377 25 f. Type **143** 95 40
378 50 f. Eleonora's Falcon (vert) 3·25 55

144 Map and Arrows

1973. Meeting of Maghreb Committee for Co-ordination of Posts and Telecommunications, Tunis.
379 **144** 25 f. multicoloured . . . 15 10

1973. Moroccan Carpets (2nd series). As T **129**. Multicoloured.
380 25 f. Carpet from the High Atlas 1·00 25
381 70 f. Tazenakht carpet . . . . 1·50 50

المؤتمر الاسلامي - لاهور
1394

145 Golf Club and Ball
(146)

1974. International "Hassan II Trophy" Golf Grand Prix, Rabat.
382 **145** 70 f. multicoloured . . . 1·25 60

1974. Islamic Summit Conference, Lahore, Pakistan. No. 281 optd with T **146**.
383 1 d. multicoloured . . . . . 2·75 1·60

147 Human Rights Emblem
148 Vanadinite

1974. 25th Anniv (1973) of Declaration of Human Rights.
384 **147** 70 f. multicoloured . . . 50 20

1974. Moroccan Mineral Sources. Multicoloured.
385 25 f. Type **148** 95 50
386 70 f. Erythrine . . . . 1·90 1·00

149 Marrakesh Minaret

150 U.P.U. Emblem and Congress Dates

1974. 173rd District of Rotary International Annual Conference, Marrakesh.
387 **149** 70 f. multicoloured 70 20

1974. Centenary of U.P.U.
388 **150** 25 f. black, red and green 15 10
389 – 1 d. multicoloured 70 25
DESIGN—HORIZ: 1 d. Commemorative scroll.

151 Drummers and Dancers

1974. 15th Folklore Festival, Marrakesh. Multicoloured.
390 25 f. Type **151** 35 15
391 70 f. Juggler with woman . . . 1·25 30

152 Environmental Emblem and Scenes

154 Flintlock Pistol

1974. World Environmental Day.
392 **152** 25 f. multicoloured 20 15

1974. Red Crescent. Moroccan Firearms. Multicoloured.
397 25 f. + 5 f. Type **154** 75 75
398 70 f. + 10 f. Gunpowder box 1·10 1·10

155 Stamps, Postmark and Magnifying Glass

الاحصاء الفلاحي
.1،00
(156)

1974. Stamp Day.
399 **155** 70 f. multicoloured 60 20

1974. No. D393 surch with T **156**.
400 1 d. on 5 f. orange, grn & blk 1·90 1·25

157 World Cup Trophy

158 Erbab (two-string fiddle)

1974. World Cup Football Championship, West Germany.
401 **157** 1 d. multicoloured 85 65

1974. Blind Week.
402 **158** 70 f. + 10 f. multicoloured 1·00 50
See also No. 423.

160 Double-spurred Francolin

162 Jasmine

1974. Moroccan Animals. Multicoloured.
404 25 f. Type **160** . . . . 1·60 50
405 70 f. Leopard (horiz) 95 40

1974. Moroccan Carpets (3rd series). As T **129**. Multicoloured.
406 25 f. Zemmour carpet 65 10
407 1 d. Beni M'Guild carpet . . 1·25 50

1975. Flowers (1st series). Multicoloured.
408 25 f. Type **162** 50 10
409 35 f. Orange lilies 60 10
410 70 f. Poppies 85 35
411 90 f. Carnations . . . . . . 1·10 50
See also Nos. 417/20.

163 Aragonite

165 "The Water-carrier" (Feu Taieb-Lalou)

1975. Minerals. Multicoloured.
412 50 f. Type **163** 75 40
413 1 d. Agate . . . . 1·50 75
See also Nos. 543 and 563/4.

1975. Red Crescent. Moroccan Jewellery. As T **65**. Multicoloured.
414 25 f. + 5 f. Pendant 75 75
415 70 f. + 10 f. Earring . . . . 1·10 1·00

1975. "Moroccan Painters".
416 **165** 1 d. multicoloured . . . . 1·10 30

1975. Flowers (2nd series). As T **162**. Multicoloured.
417 10 f. Daisies 10 10
418 50 f. Pelargoniums 60 10
419 60 f. Orange blossom 75 30
420 1 d. Pansies . . . . 1·10 60

166 Collector with Stamp Album

167 Dancer with Rifle

1975. Stamp Day.
421 **166** 40 f. multicoloured 20 10

1975. 16th Nat Folklore Festival, Marrakesh.
422 **167** 1 d. multicoloured 65 30

1975. Blind Week. As T **158**. Multicoloured.
423 1 d. Mandolin 85 25

168 "Animals in Forest" (child's drawing)

1975. Children's Week.
424 **168** 25 f. multicoloured 15 10

169 Games Emblem and Athletes

1975. 7th Mediterranean Games, Algiers.
425 **169** 40 f. multicoloured 45 10

170 Waldrapp

1975. Fauna. Multicoloured.
426 40 f. Type **170** . . . . 3·00 70
427 1 d. Caracal (vert) . . . . . . 1·50 75
See also Nos. 470/71.

1975. "Green March" (1st issue). Nos. 370/1 optd **1975** and Arabic inscr.
428 25 f. (+ 5 f.) multicoloured . . 2·50 2·50
429 70 f. (+ 10 f.) multicoloured . 2·50 2·50
The premiums on the stamps are obliterated.

172 King Mohammed V greeting Crowd

1975. 20th Anniv of Independence. Mult.
430 40 f. Type **172** 15 10
431 1 d. King Hassan (vert) . . . 75 45
432 1 d. King Hassan V wearing fez (vert) 75 45

1975. Moroccan Carpets (4th series). As T **129**. Multicoloured.
433 25 f. Ouled Besseba carpet . . 60 35
434 1 d. Ait Ouaouzguid carpet . . 90 45
See Nos. 485/7 and 513.

173 Marchers crossing Desert

174 Fez Coin of 1883/4

1975. "Green March" (2nd issue).
435 **173** 40 f. multicoloured 15 10

1976. Moroccan Coins (1st series). Multicoloured.
436 5 f. Type **174** 10 10
437 15 f. Rabat silver coin 1774/5 . 10 10
438 35 f. Sabta coin, 13/14th centuries 75 35
439 40 f. Type **174** 50 10
440 50 f. As No. 437 . . . . 75 35
441 65 f. As No. 438 . . . . 75 50
442 1 d. Sabta coin, 12/13th centuries 1·10 60
See also Nos. 458/67a.
For Nos. 439/40 in smaller size, see Nos. 520/b.

175 Interior of Mosque

1976. Millennium of Ibn Zaidoun Mosque. Multicoloured.
443 40 f. Type **175** 15 10
444 65 f. Interior archways (vert) . 50 15

176 Moroccan Family

1976. Family Planning.
445 **176** 40 f. multicoloured 15 10

177 Bou Anania College, Fez

1976. Moroccan Architecture.
446 **177** 1 d. multicoloured 70 20

178 Temple Sculpture

1976. Borobudur Temple Preservation Campaign. Multicoloured.
447 40 f. Type **178** 15 15
448 1 d. View of Temple 60 20

179 Dome of the Rock, Jerusalem

1976. 6th Anniv of Islamic Conference.
449 **179** 1 d. multicoloured 70 20

1976. Red Crescent. Moroccan Jewellery. As T **65**. Multicoloured.
450 40 f. Jewelled purse 15 10
451 1 d. Jewelled pectoral 65 25

180 George Washington, King Hassan I, Statue of Liberty and Mausoleum of Mohammed V

181 Wrestling

1976. Bicentenary of American Revolution. Multicoloured.
452 40 f. Flags of USA and Morocco (horiz) 45 15
453 1 d. Type **180** 65 25

1976. Olympic Games, Montreal. Multicoloured.
454 35 f. Type **181** 10 10
455 40 f. Cycling 15 10
456 50 f. Boxing 50 15
457 1 d. Running 70 25

1976. Moroccan Coins (2nd series). As T **174**. Multicoloured.
458 5 f. Medieval silver mohur . 10 10
459 10 f. Gold mohur 10 10
460 15 f. Gold coin 10 10
461 20 f. Gold coin (different) . . 10 10
461a 25 f. As No. 437 . . . . . 1·25 50
462 30 f. As No. 459 . . . . . . 35 10
463 35 f. Silver dinar 45 10
464 60 f. As No. 458 . . . . . . 50 15
465 70 f. Copper coin 80 15
466 75 f. As No. 463 . . . . . . 50 15
466a 80 f. As No. 460 . . . . . . 2·50 75
467 75 f. As No. 465 . . . . . . 60 35
467a 3 d. As No. 461 . . . . . . 3·75 1·25

182 Early and Modern Telephones with Dish Aerial

1976. Telephone Centenary.
468 **182** 1 d. multicoloured 70 25

183 Gold Medallion

1976. Blind Week.
469 **183** 50 f. multicoloured . . . 50 10

1976. Birds. As T **170**. Multicoloured.
470 40 f. Dark chanting goshawk . 1·75 40
471 1 d. Purple swamphen . . . . 2·50 85
Nos. 470/1 are vert designs.

185 King Hassan, Emblems and Map (186)

1976. 1st Anniv of "Green March".
472 **185** 40 f. multicoloured . . . 45 10

1976. Fifth African Tuberculosis Conference. Nos. 414/15 optd with T **186**.
473 25 f. multicoloured . . . . . 1·90 1·90
474 70 f. multicoloured . . . . . 2·25 2·25

187 Globe and Peace Dove 188 African Nations Cup

1976. Conference of Non-Aligned Countries, Colombo.
475 **187** 1 d. red, black and blue . 30 20

1976. African Nations Football Championship.
476 **188** 1 d. multicoloured 65 20

189 Letters encircling Globe

1977. Stamp Day.
477 **189** 40 f. multicoloured . . . 40 10

190 "Aeonium arboreum"

1977. Flowers. Multicoloured.
478 40 f. Type **190** 30 10
479 50 f. "Malope trifida" (24 × 38 mm) 95 30
480 1 d. "Hesperolaburnum platyclarpum" . . . . 1·10 30

191 Ornamental Candle Lamps (192)

1977. Procession of the Candles, Sale.
481 **191** 40 f. multicoloured . . . 45 10

1977. Cherry Festival. No. D394 surch with T **192**.
482 40 f. on 10 f. Cherries 75 30

193 Map and Emblem

1977. 5th Congress, Organization of Arab Towns.
483 **193** 50 f. multicoloured . . . 15 10

194 A.P.U. Emblem

1977. 25th Anniv of Arab Postal Union.
484 **194** 1 d. multicoloured . . . 60 20

1977. Carpets (5th series). As T **129**. Multicoloured.
485 35 f. Marmoucha carpet . . . 25 15
486 40 f. Ait Haddou carpet . . . 40 20
487 1 d. Henbel rug, Sale 95 30

195 Zither 196 Mohammed Ali Jinnah

1977. Blind Week.
488 **195** 1 d. multicoloured . . . 85 25

1977. Birth Centenary of Mohammed Ali Jinnah.
489 **196** 70 f. multicoloured . . . 50 20

197 Marcher with Flag

1977. 2nd Anniv of "Green March".
490 **197** 1 d. multicoloured . . . 60 20

198 Assembly Hall

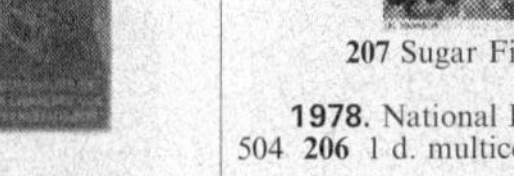

1977. Opening of House of Representatives.
491 **198** 1 d. multicoloured . . . 65 20

199 Silver Brooch 200 Bowl with Funnel

1977. Red Crescent.
493 **199** 1 d. multicoloured . . . . 1·25 60

1978. Moroccan Copperware. Multicoloured.
494 40 f. Type **200** 35 10
495 1 d. Bowl with cover 70 20

201 Development Emblem 202 Decorative Pot with Lid

1978. Sahara Development. Multicoloured.
496 40 f. Type **201** 35 10
497 1 d. Fishes in net and camels at oasis (horiz) 60 20

1978. Blind Week. Multicoloured.
498 1 d. Type **202** 90 30
499 1 d. Decorative jar 90 30

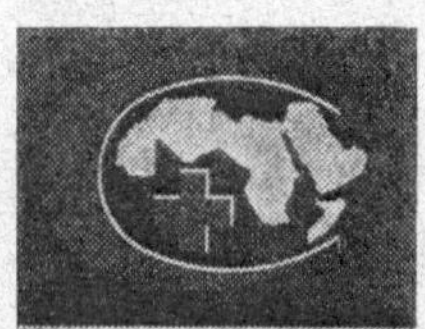

203 Map and Red Cross within Red Crescent

1978. 10th Conference of Arab Red Crescent and Red Cross Societies.
500 **203** 1 d. red and black 65 20

204 View of Fez 205 Dome of the Rock

1978. Rotary International Meeting, Fez.
501 **204** 1 d. multicoloured 65 20

1978. Palestine Welfare.
502 **205** 5 f. multicoloured 10 10
503 10 f. multicoloured 10 10

206 Flautist and Folk Dancers 208 Yacht

207 Sugar Field and Crushing Plant

1978. National Folklore Festival, Marrakesh.
504 **206** 1 d. multicoloured 55 20

1978. Sugar Industry.
505 **207** 40 f. multicoloured 15 10

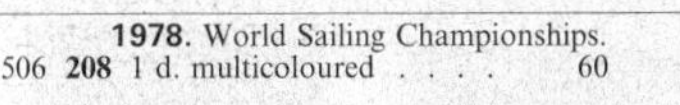

1978. World Sailing Championships.
506 **208** 1 d. multicoloured 60 20

209 Tree, Tent and Scout Emblem 211 Human Rights Emblem

210 Moulay Idriss

1978. Pan-Arab Scout Festival, Rabat.
507 **209** 40 f. multicoloured . . . 15 10

1978. Moulay Idriss Great Festival.
508 **210** 40 f. multicoloured . . . 15 10

1978. 30th Anniv of Declaration of Human Rights.
509 **211** 1 d. multicoloured 65 20

212 Houses in Agadir 214 Decorated Pot

213 Player, Football and Cup

1979. Southern Moroccan Architecture (1st series). Multicoloured.
510 40 f. Type **212** 15 10
511 1 d. Old fort at Marrakesh . . 60 15
See also Nos. 536 and 562.

1979. Mohammed V Football Cup.
512 **213** 40 f. multicoloured . . . 15 10

1979. Moroccan Carpets (6th series). As T **129**.
513 40 f. Marmoucha carpet . . . 40 15

1979. Blind Week.
514 **214** 1 d. multicoloured 65 20

215 "Procession from a Mosque" 216 Coffee Pot and Heater

1979. Paintings by Mohamed Ben Ali Rbati. Mult.
515 40 f. Type **215** 15 10
516 1 d. "Religious Ceremony in a Mosque" (horiz) 55 20

1979. Red Crescent. Brassware. Multicoloured.
517 40 f. Engraved Circular Boxes 25 15
518 1 d. Type **216** 85 30

217 Costumed Girls

218 Curved Dagger in Jewelled Sheath

1979. National Folklore Festival, Marrakesh.
519 **217** 40 f. multicoloured . . . 15 10

1979. Moroccan Coins. As T **174**, but smaller, $17\frac{1}{2} \times 22\frac{1}{2}$ mm.
520 40 f. multicoloured 10 10
520b 50 f. multicoloured 10 10

1979. Ancient Weapons.
521 **218** 1 d. black and yellow . . 75 20

219 King Hassan II

221 King Hassan II

220 Festival Emblem

1979. King Hassan's 50th Birthday.
522 **219** 1 d. multicoloured 70 20

1979. 4th Arab Youth Festival, Rabat.
523 **220** 1 d. multicoloured 70 20

1979. "25th Anniv of Revolution of King and People".
524 **221** 1 d. multicoloured 30 20

222 World Map superimposed on Open Book

1979. 50th Anniv of International Bureau of Education.
525 **222** 1 d. brown and yellow . . 60 20

223 Pilgrims in Wuquf, Arafat

1979. Pilgrimage to Mecca.
526 **223** 1 d. multicoloured 70 20

استرجاع اقليم وادى الذهب
1979-8-14
(224)

1979. Recovery of Oued Eddahab Province. Design as No. 497, with face value amended (40 f.), optd with T **224**.
527 40 f. multicoloured 15 10
528 1 d. multicoloured 65 20

225 Centaurium

226 Children around Globe

1979. Flowers. Multicoloured.
529 40 f. Type **225** 15 10
530 1 d. "Leucanthemum catananc" 55 20

1979. International Year of the Child.
531 **226** 40 f. multicoloured . . . 60 25

227 European Otter

228 Traffic Signs

1979. Wildlife. Multicoloured.
532 40 f. Type **227** 50 15
533 1 d. Moussier's redstart . . . 1·50 55

1980. Road Safety. Multicoloured.
534 40 f. Type **228** 15 10
535 1 d. Children at crossing . . 30 20

229 Fortress

1980. South Moroccan Architecture (2nd series).
536 **229** 1 d. multicoloured . . . 55 20

230 Copper Bowl with Lid

231 Pot

1980. Red Crescent. Multicoloured.
537 50 f. Type **230** 50 15
538 70 f. Copper kettle and brazier 60 20

1980. Blind Week.
539 **231** 40 f. multicoloured . . . 15 10

232 Mechanised Sorting Office, Rabat

1980. Stamp Day.
540 **232** 40 f. multicoloured . . . 15 10

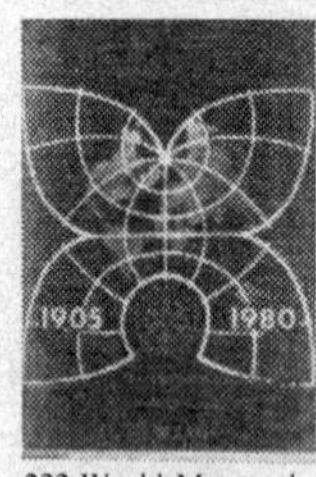
233 World Map and Rotary Emblem

234 Leather Bag and Cloth

1980. 75th Anniv of Rotary International.
541 **233** 1 d. multicoloured . . . 55 20

1980. 4th Textile and Leather Exhibition, Casablanca.
542 **234** 1 d. multicoloured . . . 55 20

1980. Minerals (2nd series). As T **163**. Multicoloured.
543 40 f. Gypsum 85 10

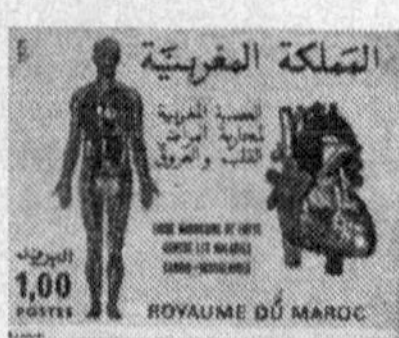
235 Peregrine Falcon

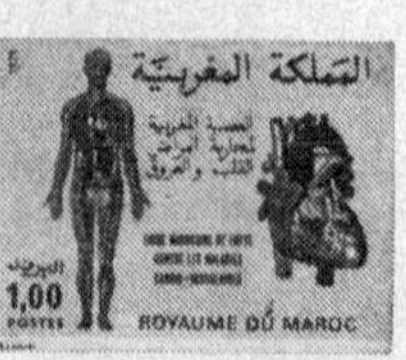
236 Diagram of Blood Circulation and Heart

1980. Hunting with Falcon.
544 **235** 40 f. multicoloured . . . . 1·50 45

1980. Campaign against Cardio-vascular Diseases.
545 **236** 1 d. multicoloured 65 20

237 Decade Emblem and Human Figures

238 Harnessed Horse

1980. Decade for Women.
546 **237** 40 f. mauve and blue . . . 15 10
547 – 1 d. multicoloured 55 20
DESIGN: 1 d. Decade and United Nations emblems.

1980. Ornamental Harnesses. Multicoloured.
548 40 f. Harnessed horse (different) 15 10
549 1 d. Type **238** 75 20

239 Satellite orbiting Earth and Dish Aerial

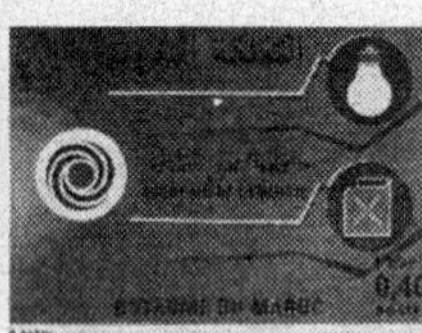
240 Light Bulb and Fuel Can

1980. World Meteorological Day.
550 **239** 40 f. multicoloured 15 10

1980. Energy Conservation. Multicoloured.
551 40 f. Type **240** 15 10
552 1 d. Hand holding petrol pump 55 20

241 Conference Emblem

1980. World Tourism Conference, Manila.
553 **241** 40 f. multicoloured 15 10

242 Tree bridging Straits of Gibraltar

1980. European–African Liaison over the Straits of Gibraltar.
554 **242** 1 d. multicoloured 60 20

243 Flame and Marchers

1980. 5th Anniv of "The Green March".
555 **243** 1 d. multicoloured 60 20

244 Holy Kaaba, Mecca

245 "Senecio antheuphorbium"

1980. 1400th Anniv of Hegira. Multicoloured.
556 40 f. Type **244** 15 10
557 1 d. Mosque, Mecca 60 20

1980. Flowers. Multicoloured.
558 40 f. Type **245** 60 10
559 1 d. "Periploca laevigata" . . 1·25 50

246 Painting by Aherdan

247 Nejjarine Fountain, Fez

1980. Paintings.
560 – 40 f. bistre and brown . . 15 10
561 **246** 1 d. multicoloured 60 20
DESIGN: 40 f. Composition of bird and feathers.

1981. Moroccan Architecture (3rd series).
562 **247** 40 f. multicoloured 10 10

1981. Minerals (3rd series). Vert designs as T **163**. Multicoloured.
563 40 f. Onyx 95 35
564 1 d. Malachite-azurite . . . . 1·60 75

248 King Hassan II

249 King Hassan II

1981. 25th Anniv of Independence. Mult.
565 60 f. Type **248** 35 10
566 60 f. Map, flags, broken chains and "25" 35 10
567 60 f. King V. Mohammed . . . 35 10

1981. 20th Anniv of King Hassan's Coronation.
568 **249** 1 d. 30 multicoloured . . 50 25

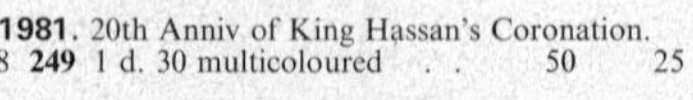

250 "Source" (Jillali Gharbaoul)

1981. Moroccan Painting.
569 **250** 1 d. 30 multicoloured . . 75 25

251 "Anagalis monelli"

252 King Hassan as Major General

1981. Flowers. Multicoloured.
570 40 f. Type **251** 20 10
571 70 f. "Bubonium intricatum" . 40 15

1981. 25th Anniv of Moroccan Armed Forces.
572 **252** 60 f. lilac, gold and green 35 10
573 – 60 f. multicoloured . . . 35 10
574 – 60 f. lilac, gold and green 35 10
DESIGNS: No. 573, Army badge; No. 574, King Mohammed V (founder).

253 Caduceus (Telecommunications and Health)

254 Plate with Pattern

1981. World Telecommunications Day.
575 **253** 1 d. 30 multicoloured . . 70 20

1981. Blind Week. Multicoloured.
576 50 f. Type **254** 10 10
577 1 d. 30 Plate with ship pattern 60 20

255 Musicians and Dancers
256 "Seboula" Dagger

1981. 22nd National Folklore Festival, Marrakesh.
578 **255** 1 d. 30 multicoloured . . 85 25

1981. Ancient Weapons.
579 **256** 1 d. 30 multicoloured . . 75 20

257 Pestle and Mortar
258 Hands holding I.Y.D.P. Emblem

1981. Red Crescent. Moroccan Copperware. Mult.
580 60 f. Type **257** 25 15
581 1 d. 30 Tripod brazier 80 25

1981. International Year of Disabled People.
582 **258** 60 f. multicoloured . . . 35 10

259 "Iphiclides feisthamelii Lotteri"
260 King Hassan and Marchers

1981. Butterflies (1st series). Multicoloured.
583 60 f. Type **259** 50 25
584 1 d. 30 "Zerynthina rumina africana" . . . . 1·25 60
See also Nos. 609/10.

1981. 6th Anniv of "Green March".
585 **260** 1 d. 30 multicoloured . . 70 20

261 Town Buildings and Congress Emblem

1981. 10th International Twinned Towns Congress, Casablanca.
586 **261** 1 d. 30 multicoloured . . 20 20

262 Dome of the Rock
264 Terminal Building and Runway

1981. Palestinian Solidarity Day.
587 **262** 60 f. multicoloured . . . 35 10

1981. 12th Arab Summit Conference, Fez. Nos. 502/3 surch **1981 0,40**.
588 **205** 40 f. on 5 f. multicoloured 4·00 4·00
588a 40 f. on 10 f. multicoloured 2·75 2·75

1981. 1st Anniv of Mohammed V Airport.
589 **264** 1 d. 30 multicoloured . . 70 20

265 Al Massira Dam
266 King Hassan II

1981. Al Massira Dam.
590 **265** 60 f. multicoloured . . . 35 10

1981.
591 **266** 5 f. red, blue and gold . 10 10
592 10 f. red, yellow and gold 10 10
593 15 f. red, green and gold 10 10
594 20 f. red, pink and gold 10 10
595 25 f. red, lilac and gold . 10 10
596 30 f. blue, lt bl & gold . 10 10
597 35 f. blue, yellow & gold 10 10
598 40 f. blue, green and gold 10 10
599 50 f. blue, pink and gold 10 10
600 60 f. blue, lilac and gold 10 10
601 65 f. blue, lilac and gold 10 10
602 70 f. violet, yellow and gold 10 10
603 75 f. violet, green and gold 15 15
604 80 f. violet, pink and gold 15 15
605 90 f. violet, lilac and gold 15 15
605a 1 d. 25 red, mauve & gold 20 15
605b 4 d. brown, yellow and gold 1·10 55
See also Nos. 624/9, 718/22, 759/61, 866 and 895/6.

267 Horse Jumping
268 Ait Quaquzguit

1981. Equestrian Sports.
606 **267** 1 d. 30 multicoloured . . 1·25 25

1982. Carpets (1st series). Multicoloured.
607 50 f. Type **268** 10 10
608 1 d. 30 Ouled Besseba 60 30
See also Nos. 653/4.

1982. Butterflies and Moths (2nd series). As T **259**. Multicoloured.
609 60 f. "Celerio oken lineata" . 70 25
610 1 d. 30 "Mesoacidalia aglaja lyauteyi" . . . . 1·50 55

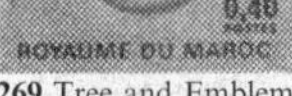

269 Tree and Emblem
270 Jug

1982. World Forestry Day.
611 **269** 40 f. multicoloured . . . 10 10

1982. Blind Week.
612 **270** 1 d. multicoloured . . . 50 25

271 Dancers
272 Candlestick

1982. Popular Art.
613 **271** 1 d. 40 multicoloured . . 60 35

1982. Red Crescent.
614 **272** 1 d. 40 multicoloured . . 60 35

273 Painting by M. Mezian
274 Buildings and People on Graph

1982. Moroccan Painting.
615 **273** 1 d. 40 multicoloured . . . 60 35

1982. Population and Housing Census.
616 **274** 60 f. multicoloured 15 15

275 Dr. Koch, Lungs and Apparatus
276 I.T.U. Emblem

1982. Centenary of Discovery of Tubercle Bacillus.
617 **275** 1 d. 40 multicoloured . . . 75 35

1982. I.T.U. Delegates' Conference, Nairobi.
618 **276** 1 d. 40 multicoloured . . . 60 35

277 Wheat, Globe, Sea and F.A.O. Emblem
278 Diesel Train and Route Map

1982. World Food Day.
619 **277** 60 f. multicoloured 15 15

1982. Unity Railway.
620 **278** 1 d. 40 multicoloured . . . 95 50

279 A.P.U. Emblem

1982. 30th Anniv of Arab Postal Union.
621 **279** 1 d. 40 multicoloured . . . 40 15

280 Dome of the Rock and Map of Palestine
281 Red Coral

1982. Palestinian Solidarity.
622 **280** 1 d. 40 multicoloured . . . 40 15

1982. Red Coral of Al Hoceima.
623 **281** 1 d. 40 multicoloured . . . 70 25

1983. As T **266** but inscribed "1982".
624 1 d. maroon, blue and gold . . 25 10
625 1 d. 40 brown, lt brn and gold 35 10
626 2 d. maroon, green and gold . 45 15
627 3 d. brown, yellow and gold . 65 25
628 5 d. brown, green and gold . . 1·40 50
629 10 d. brown, orange and gold . 2·75 90

282 Moroccan Stamps
283 King Hassan II

1983. Stamp Day.
630 **282** 1 d. 40 multicoloured . . . 60 20

1983.
631 **283** 1 d. 40 multicoloured . . . 25 20
632 2 d. multicoloured . . . 35 30
633 3 d. multicoloured . . . 80 50
634 5 d. multicoloured . . . 1·40 45
635 10 d. multicoloured . . . 2·75 1·10

284 Decorated Pot
286 Ornamental Stand

285 Musicians

1983. Blind Week.
636 **284** 1 d. 40 multicoloured . . . 60 20

1983. Popular Arts.
637 **285** 1 d. 40 multicoloured . . 75 20

1983. Red Crescent.
638 **286** 1 d. 40 multicoloured . . 75 20

287 Commission Emblem

1983. 25th Anniv of Economic Commission for Africa.
639 **287** 1 d. 40 multicoloured . . 55 20

288 "Tecoma sp."
290 Games Emblem and Stylized Sports

289 King Hassan II, Map and Sultan of Morocco

1983. Flowers. Multicoloured.
640 60 c. Type **288** 10 10
641 1 d. 40 "Strelitzia sp." 75 20

1983. 30th Anniv of Revolution.
642 **289** 80 c. multicoloured . . . 20 20

1983. 9th Mediterranean Games, Casablanca.
644 **290** 80 c. blue, silver and gold 20 20
645 – 1 d. multicoloured 20 20
646 – 2 d. multicoloured 60 30
DESIGNS—VERT: 1 d. Games emblem. HORIZ: 2 d. Stylized runner.

291 Ploughing

1983. Touiza.
648 **291** 80 c. multicoloured . . . 20 20

292 Symbol of "Green March"
293 Palestinian formed from Map and Globe

1983. 8th Anniv of "Green March".
649 **292** 80 f. multicoloured . . . 20 15

1983. Palestinian Welfare.
650 **293** 80 f. multicoloured . . . 20 15

294 Ouzoud Waterfall **295** Children's Emblem

1983. Ouzoud Waterfall.
651 **294** 80 f. multicoloured . . . 20 15

1983. Children's Day. Multicoloured.
652 **295** 2 d. multicoloured 70 30

1983. Carpets (2nd series). As T **268**. Mult.
653 60 f. Zemmouri 10 10
654 1 d. 40 Zemmouri (different) . 55 20

296 Transport and W.C.Y. Emblem

1983. World Communications Year.
655 **296** 2 d. multicoloured . . . . 1·25 50

297 Views of Jerusalem and Fez

1984. Twinned Towns.
656 **297** 2 d. multicoloured 95 20

298 Fennec Fox

1984. Animals. Multicoloured.
657 80 f. Type **298** 30 25
658 2 d. Lesser Egyptian jerboa . . 60 35

299 Map of League Members and Emblem

المهرجان 25 (**300**)

1984. 39th Anniv of League of Arab States.
659 **299** 2 d. multicoloured 70 20

1984. 25th National Folklore Festival, Marrakesh. No. 578 optd with T **300**.
660 **255** 1 d. 30 multicoloured . . 75 15

301 "Metha viridis" **302** Decorated Bowl

1984. Flowers. Multicoloured.
661 80 f. Type **301** 20 15
662 2 d. Aloe 75 30

1984. Blind Week.
663 **302** 80 f. multicoloured . . . 20 15

303 Lidded Container **304** Sports Pictograms

1984. Red Crescent.
664 **303** 2 d. multicoloured . . . 75 30

1984. Olympic Games, Los Angeles.
665 **304** 2 d. multicoloured . . . 75 30

305 Dove carrying Children **306** U.P.U. Emblem and Ribbons

1984. International Child Victims' Day.
666 **305** 2 d. multicoloured . . . 70 30

1984. Universal Postal Union Day.
667 **306** 2 d. multicoloured . . . 40 30

307 Hands holding Ears of Wheat **308** Stylized Bird, Airplane and Emblem

1984. World Food Day.
668 **307** 80 f. multicoloured . . . 20 15

1984. 40th Anniv of I.C.A.O.
669 **308** 2 d. multicoloured . . . 40 30

309 Inscribed Scroll

1984. 9th Anniv of "Green March".
670 **309** 80 f. multicoloured . . . 20 15

311 Flag and Dome of the Rock **312** Emblem and People

1984. Palestinian Welfare.
672 **311** 2 d. multicoloured . . . 60 25

1984. 36th Anniv of Human Rights Declaration.
673 **312** 2 d. multicoloured . . . 60 25

313 Aidi **314** Weighing Baby

1984. Dogs. Multicoloured.
674 80 f. Type **313** 50 10
675 2 d. Sloughi . . . . 1·10 25

1985. Infant Survival Campaign.
676 **314** 80 f. multicoloured 15 10

315 Children playing in Garden **316** Sherifian Mail Postal Cancellation, 1892

1985. 1st Moroccan S.O.S. Children's Village.
677 **315** 2 d. multicoloured 60 25

1985. Stamp Day.
678 **316** 2 d. grey, pink and black . 60 25
See also Nos. 698/9, 715/16, 757/8, 778/9, 796/7, 818/19, 841/2 and 877/8.

317 Emblem, Birds, Landscape and Fish **318** Musicians

1985. World Environment Day.
680 **317** 80 f. multicoloured 15 10

1985. National Folklore Festival, Marrakesh.
681 **318** 2 d. multicoloured 75 25

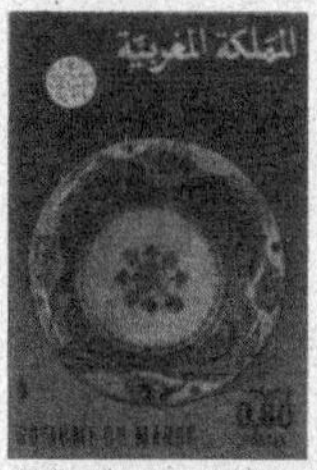

319 Decorated Plate **320** Bougainvillea

1985. Blind Week.
682 **319** 80 f. multicoloured 15 10

1985. Flowers. Multicoloured.
683 80 f. Type **320** 60 10
684 2 d. "Hibiscus rosasinensis" . . 1·25 50

321 Woman in Headdress **323** Map and Emblem

322 Musicians and Dancers

1985. Red Crescent.
685 **321** 2 d. multicoloured . . . . 1·25 50

1985. National Folklore Festival, Marrakesh.
686 **322** 2 d. multicoloured 95 25

1985. 6th Pan-Arab Games.
687 **323** 2 d. multicoloured 95 25

HAVE YOU READ THE NOTES AT THE BEGINNING OF THIS CATALOGUE?
These often provide the answers to the enquiries we receive.

324 Emblem on Globe **325** Emblem

1985. 40th Anniv of U.N.O.
688 **324** 2 d. multicoloured 60 25

1986. International Youth Year.
689 **325** 2 d. multicoloured 60 25

326 Medal **327** Clasped Hands around Flag

1985. 10th Anniv of "Green March".
690 **326** 2 d. multicoloured 60 25

1985. Palestinian Welfare.
691 **327** 2 d. multicoloured 60 25

328 "Euphydryas desfontainii" **329** Arms

1985. Butterflies (1st series). Multicoloured.
692 80 f. Type **328** 45 30
693 2 d. "Colotis evagore" . . . . 1·40 90
See also Nos. 713/14.

1986. 25th Anniv of King Hassan's Coronation. Multicoloured.
694 80 f. Type **329** 15 10
695 2 d. King Hassan II (horiz) . 60 25

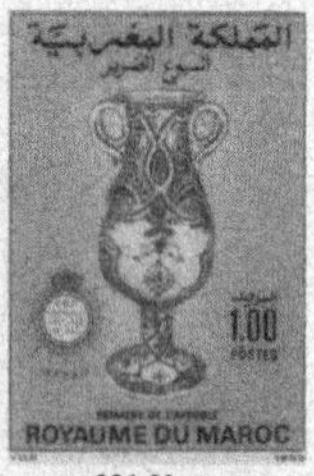

330 Emblem **331** Vase

1986. 26th International Military Medicine Congress.
697 **330** 2 d. multicoloured 60 25

1986. Stamp Day. As T **316**.
698 80 f. orange and black 15 10
699 2 d. green and black 60 25
DESIGNS: 80 f. Sherifian postal seal of Maghzen-Safi; 2 d. Sherifian postal seal of Maghzen-Safi (different).

1986. Blind Week.
700 **331** 1 d. multicoloured 15 10

332 Footballer and Emblem

1986. World Cup Football Championship, Mexico. Multicoloured.
701 1 d. Type **332** 50 10
702 2 d. Cup, pictogram of footballer and emblem . . . . 1·00 25

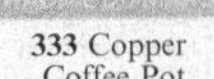

333 Copper Coffee Pot

334 "Warionia saharae"

1986. Red Crescent.
703 **333** 2 d. multicoloured . . . . 1·25 50

1986. Flowers. Multicoloured.
704 1 d. Type **334** 60 10
705 2 d. "Mandragora autumnalis" 1·25 50

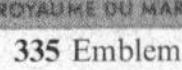

335 Emblem

336 Dove and Olive Branch

1986. 18th Parachute Championships.
706 **335** 2 d. multicoloured 90 25

1986. International Peace Year.
707 **336** 2 d. multicoloured 60 25

337 Horsemen

338 Book

1986. Horse Week.
708 **337** 1 d. light brown, pink and brown 60 10

1986. 11th Anniv of "Green March".
709 **338** 1 d. multicoloured 15 10

339 Stylized People and Wheat

340 Marrakesh

1986. Fight against Hunger.
710 **339** 2 d. multicoloured 60 25

1986. Aga Khan Architecture Prize.
711 **340** 2 d. multicoloured 60 25

341 Hands holding Wheat

الملتقى العالمي الاول
لخطباء الجمعة

(342)

1986. "1,000,000 Hectares of Grain".
712 **341** 1 d. multicoloured 15 10

1986. Butterflies (2nd series). As T **328**. Multicoloured.
713 1 d. "Elphinstonia charlonia" . 65 35
714 2 d. "Anthocharis belia" . . . 90 85

1987. Stamp Day. As T **316**.
715 1 d. blue and black 15 10
716 2 d. red and black 60 25
DESIGNS: 1 d. Circular postal cancellation of Tetouan; 2 d. Octagonal postal cancellation of Tetouan.

1987. Air. 1st World Reunion of Friday Preachers. Optd with T **342**.
717 **283** 2 d. multicoloured 90 60

1987. Size 25×32 mm. Inscribed "1986".
718 **266** 1 d. 60 red, brown and gold 25 20
719 2 d. 50 red, grey and gold 60 25
720 6 d. 50 red, brown and gold 1·50 35
721 7 d. red, brown and gold 1·75 45
722 8 d. 50 red, lilac and gold 2·00 50

343 Sidi Muhammad ben Yusuf addressing Crowd

1987. 40th Anniv of Tangier Conference. Each blue, silver and black.
723 1 d. Type **343** 15 10
724 1 d. King Hassan II making speech 15 10

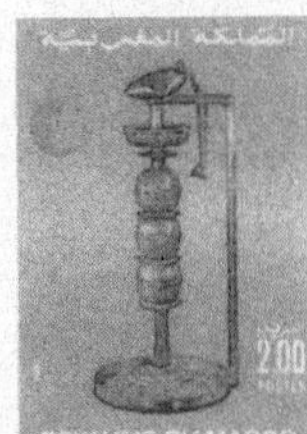

344 Copper Lamp

345 Woman with Baby and Packet of Salt being emptied into Beaker

1987. Red Crescent.
726 **344** 2 d. multicoloured . . . 60 25

1987. U.N.I.C.E.F. Child Survival Campaign.
727 **345** 1 d. multicoloured . . . 15 10

346 Decorated Pottery Jug

347 "Zygophyllum fontanesii"

1987. Blind Week.
728 **346** 1 d. multicoloured . . . 15 10

1987. Flowers. Multicoloured.
729 1 d. Type **347** 15 10
730 2 d. "Otanthus maritimus" . 60 25

348 Arabesque from Door, Dar Batha Palace, Fez

349 Map and King Hassan giving Blood

1987. Bicentenary of Diplomatic Relations with United States of America.
731 **348** 1 d. blue, red & black . . 15 10

1987. Blood Transfusion Service.
732 **349** 2 d. multicoloured . . . 95 25

350 Woman from Melhfa

351 Emblem and Irrigated Field

1987. Sahara Costumes. Multicoloured.
733 1 d. Type **350** 15 10
734 2 d. Man from Derraa . . . 60 25

1987. 13th International Irrigation and Drainage Congress.
735 **351** 1 d. multicoloured . . . 15 10

352 Baby on Hand and Syringe

353 Azurite

1987. United Nations Children's Fund Child Survival Campaign.
736 **352** 1 d. multicoloured 15 10

1987. Mineral Industries Congress, Marrakesh. Multicoloured.
737 1 d. Type **353** 50 10
738 2 d. Wulfenite . . . . 1·00 50

354 "12" on Scroll

1987. 12th Anniv of "Green March".
739 **354** 1 d. multicoloured 15 10

355 Activities

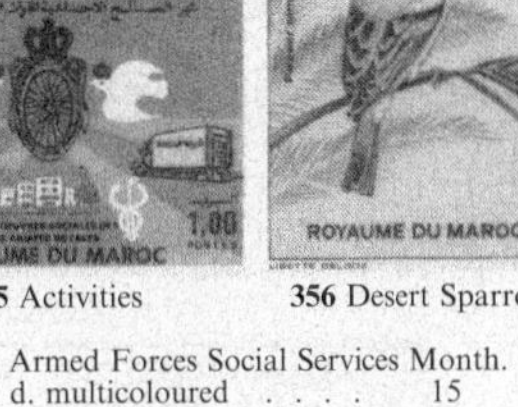

356 Desert Sparrow

1987. Armed Forces Social Services Month.
740 **355** 1 d. multicoloured 15 10

1987. Birds. Multicoloured.
741 1 d. Type **356** 90 30
742 2 d. Barbary partridge . . . . 1·60 70

357 1912 25 m. Stamp and Postmark

1987. 75th Anniv of Moroccan Stamps.
743 **357** 3 d. mauve, black and green 80 40

358 "Cetiosaurus mogrebiensis"

1988. Dinosaur of Tilougguite.
744 **358** 2 d. multicoloured . . . . 1·40 50

359 King Mohammed V

360 Map and Player in Arabesque Frame

1988. International Conference on King Mohammed V, Rabat.
745 **359** 2 d. multicoloured 60 25

1988. 16th African Nations Cup Football Competition.
746 **360** 3 d. multicoloured 75 40

361 Boy with Horse

1988. Horse Week.
747 **361** 3 d. multicoloured . . . . 1·50 60

362 Pottery Flask

363 Anniversary Emblem

1988. Blind Week.
748 **362** 3 d. multicoloured 75 35

1988. 125th Anniv of Red Cross.
749 **363** 3 d. black, red and pink . 75 35

364 "Citrullus colocynthis"

365 Breastfeeding Baby

1988. Flowers. Multicoloured.
750 3 d. 60 Type **364** 90 45
751 3 d. 60 "Calotropis procera" . 90 45

1988. U.N.I.C.E.F. Child Survival Campaign.
752 **365** 3 d. multicoloured 95 35

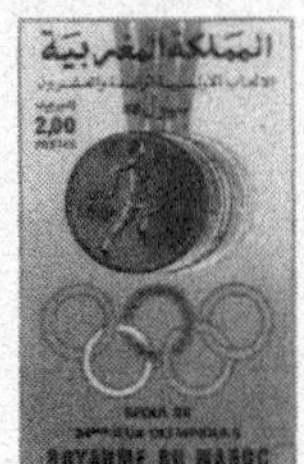

366 Olympic Medals and Rings

367 Greater Bustard

1988. Olympic Games, Seoul.
753 **366** 2 d. multicoloured 30 25

1988. Birds. Multicoloured.
754 3 d. 60 Type **367** . . . . . . 1·60 55
755 3 d. 60 Greater flamingo . . . 1·60 55

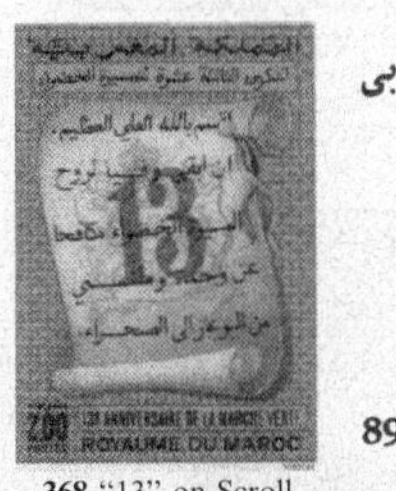

368 "13" on Scroll

اتحاد المغرب العربى

مراكش–فبراير 89

(370)

369 Housing of the Ksours and Csbaha

1988. 13th Anniv of "Green March".
756 **368** 2 d. multicoloured 60 25

1988. Stamp Day. As T **316**.
757 3 d. brown and black 95 35
758 3 d. violet and black 95 35
DESIGNS: No. 757, Octagonal postal cancellation of Maghzen el Jadida; 758, Circular postal cancellation of Maghzen el Jadida.

1988. Inscribed "1988".
759 **266** 1 d. 20 blue, lilac & gold . 15 10
760 3 d. 60 red and gold . . . 75 20
761 5 d. 20 brown, bis & gold 1·25 30

1989. Architecture.
762 **369** 2 d. multicoloured 60 25

1989. Union of Arab Maghreb. No. 631 optd with T **370**.
763 **283** 1 d. 40 multicoloured . . 50 15

371 King and Bishop with Chess Symbols

1989. 25th Anniv of Royal Moroccan Chess Federation.
764 **371** 2 d. multicoloured 85 25

372 Copper Vase **373** Ceramic Vase

1989. Red Crescent.
765 **372** 2 d. multicoloured 60 25

1989. Blind Week.
766 **373** 2 d. multicoloured 60 25

374 King Hassan **375** "Cerinthe major"

1989. 60th Birthday of King Hassan II. Mult.
767 2 d. Type **374** 75 25
768 2 d. King Hassan in robes . . 75 25

1989. Flowers. Multicoloured.
770 2 d. Type **375** 75 25
771 2 d. "Narcissus papyraceus" . 75 25

376 Telephone Handset linking Landmarks

1989. World Telecommunications Day.
772 **376** 2 d. multicoloured 60 25

377 Gender Symbols forming Globe, Woman and Eggs

1989. 1st World Fertility and Sterility Congress.
773 **377** 2 d. multicoloured 75 25

378 Desert Wheatear

1989. Birds. Multicoloured.
774 2 d. Type **378** 90 50
775 3 d. Shore lark . . . . 2·10 75

379 House of Representatives

1989. Centenary of Interparliamentary Union.
776 **379** 2 d. multicoloured . . . 60 25

380 Scroll

1989. 14th Anniv of "Green March".
777 **380** 3 d. multicoloured . . . 70 35

1990. Stamp Day. As T **316**.
778 2 d. orange and black 60 20
779 3 d. green and black 70 35
DESIGNS: 2 d. Round postal cancellation of Casablanca; 3 d. Octagonal postal cancellation of Casablanca.

381 Flags forming Map

1990. 1st Anniv of Union of Arab Maghreb.
780 **381** 2 d. multicoloured . . . 65 20

382 Oil Press

1990. 3rd World Olive Year. Multicoloured.
782 2 d. Type **382** 60 15
783 3 d. King Hassan and olives . 85 25

383 Decorated Pot

1990. Blind Week.
784 **383** 2 d. multicoloured . . . 55 15

384 Silver Teapot

1990. Red Crescent.
785 **384** 2 d. multicoloured . . . 60 15

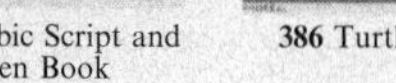

385 Arabic Script and Open Book **386** Turtle Dove

1990. International Literacy Year.
786 **385** 3 d. green, yellow & blk . 80 25

1990. Birds. Multicoloured.
787 2 d. Type **386** 85 40
788 3 d. Hoopoe (horiz) . . . . . 1·40 70

387 "15" on Scroll **388** "35", Sun's Rays and Flag

1990. 15th Anniv of "Green March".
789 **387** 3 d. multicoloured 80 25

1990. 35th Anniv of Independence.
790 **388** 3 d. multicoloured 80 25

389 Dam

1990.
791 **389** 3 d. multicoloured 80 25

390 Emblem **392** Projects and Emblem

391 Morse Code Apparatus

1990. 10th Anniv of Royal Academy of Morocco.
792 **390** 3 d. multicoloured 85 25

1990. 20th Anniv of National Postal Museum. Multicoloured.
793 2 d. Type **391** 60 15
794 3 d. Horse-drawn mail wagon, 1913 . . . . 85 25

1991. Stamp Day. As T **316**.
796 2 d. red and black 60 15
797 3 d. blue and black 85 25
DESIGNS: 2 d. Round postal cancellation of Rabat; 3 d. Octagonal postal cancellation of Rabat.

1991. 40th Anniv of United Nations Development Programme.
798 **392** 3 d. turquoise, yell & blk . 85 25

393 King Hassan **394** Mining

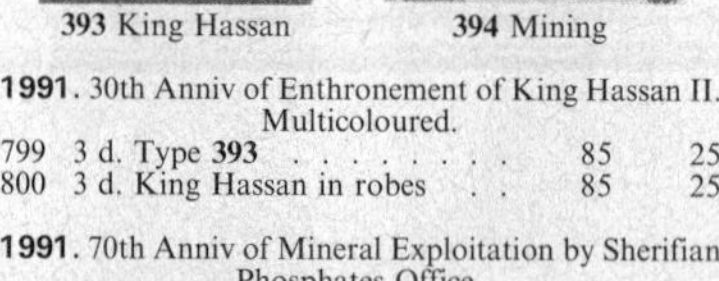

1991. 30th Anniv of Enthronement of King Hassan II. Multicoloured.
799 3 d. Type **393** 85 25
800 3 d. King Hassan in robes . . 85 25

1991. 70th Anniv of Mineral Exploitation by Sherifian Phosphates Office.
802 **394** 3 d. multicoloured 85 25

395 Kettle on Stand **396** Lantern

1991. Blind Week.
803 **395** 3 d. multicoloured 85 25

1991. Red Crescent.
804 **396** 3 d. multicoloured 85 25

397 "Cynara humilis" **398** Man

1991. Flowers. Multicoloured.
805 3 d. Type **397** 85 25
806 3 d. "Pyrus mamorensis" . . 85 25

1991. Ouarzazate Costumes. Multicoloured.
807 3 d. Type **398** 85 20
808 3 d. Woman 85 20

1991. Inscribed "1991".
809 **266** 1 d. 35 red, green & gold 20 10

399 Road **400** Members' Flags and Map

1991. 19th World Roads Congress, Marrakesh.
810 **399** 3 d. multicoloured 85 20

1991. 4th Ordinary Session of Arab Maghreb Union Presidential Council, Casablanca.
811 **400** 3 d. multicoloured 85 20

401 "16" on Scroll **402** White Stork

1991. 16th Anniv of "Green March".
812 **401** 3 d. multicoloured 85 20

1991. Birds. Multicoloured.
813 3 d. Type **402** 45 20
814 3 d. European bee eater . . . 45 20

403 Figures and Blood Splash **405** Zebra and Map of Africa

404 Emblem

1991. World AIDS Day.
815 **403** 3 d. multicoloured 85 20

1991. 20th Anniv of Islamic Conference Organization.
816 **404** 3 d. multicoloured 85 20

1991. African Tourism Year.
817 **405** 3 d. multicoloured 85 20

1992. Stamp Day. As T **316**.
818 3 d. green and black 85 20
819 3 d. violet and black 85 20
DESIGNS: No. 818, Circular postal cancellation of Essaouira; No. 819, Octagonal postal cancellation of Essaouira.

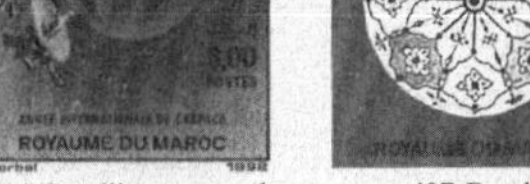

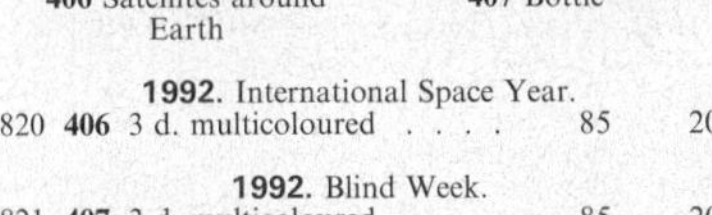

406 Satellites around Earth
407 Bottle

1992. International Space Year.
820 **406** 3 d. multicoloured 85 20

1992. Blind Week.
821 **407** 3 d. multicoloured 85 20

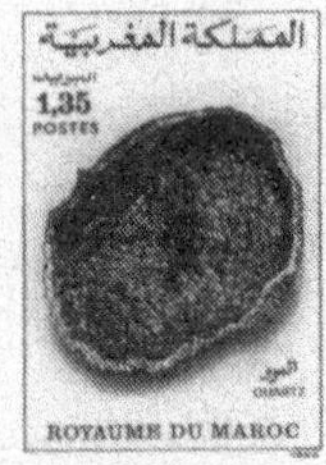

408 Brass Jug
409 Quartz

1992. Red Crescent.
822 **408** 3 d. multicoloured 85 50

1992. Minerals. Multicoloured.
823 1 d. 35 Type **409** 45 10
824 3 d. 40 Calcite . . . . 1·10 60

410 Woman
411 "Campanula afra"

1992. Tata Costumes. Multicoloured.
825 1 d. 35 Type **410** 20 10
826 3 d. 40 Man . . . . 1·10 60

1992. Flowers. Multicoloured.
827 1 d. 35 Type **411** 20 10
828 3 d. 40 "Thymus broussonetii" 1·10 60

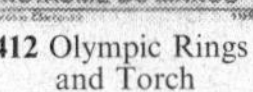

412 Olympic Rings and Torch
414 La Koutoubia, La Giralda (cathedral bell-tower) and Exhibition Emblem

413 Map of Africa and Methods of Transport and Communication

1992. Olympic Games, Barcelona.
829 **412** 3 d. 40 multicoloured . . 1·10 20

1992. Decade of Transport and Communications in Africa.
830 **413** 3 d. 40 multicoloured . . 1·10 50

1992. "Expo '92" World's Fair, Seville.
831 **414** 3 d. 40 multicoloured . . 1·10 50

415 Columbus's Fleet and Route Map

1992. 500th Anniv of Discovery of America by Columbus.
832 **415** 3 d. 40 multicoloured . . 1·25 50

416 Pin-tailed Sandgrouse

1992. Birds. Multicoloured.
833 3 d. Type **416** 40 20
834 3 d. Griffon vulture ("Gyps fulvus") (vert) 40 20

417 "17" on Scroll

1992. 17th Anniv of "Green March".
835 **417** 3 d. 40 multicoloured . . 1·10 20

418 Postal Messenger, Route Map and Cancellations

1992. Centenary of Sherifian Post. Multicoloured.
836 1 d. 35 Type **418** 20 10
837 3 d. 40 Postal cancellation, "100" on scroll and Sultan Mulay al-Hassan . . . . 1·10 50

419 Conference Emblem

1992. International Nutrition Conference, Rome.
839 **419** 3 d. 40 multicoloured . . 1·10 50

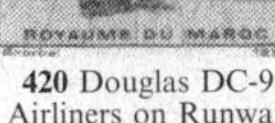

420 Douglas DC-9 Airliners on Runway
422 Satellite orbiting Earth

421 Dishes

1992. Al Massira Airport, Agadir.
840 **420** 3 d. 40 multicoloured . . 1·10 20

1993. Stamp Day. As T **316**.
841 1 d. 70 green and black 25 10
842 3 d. 80 orange and black . . . 1·10 50
DESIGNS: 1 d. 70, Round postal cancellation of Tangier; 3 d. 80, Octagonal postal cancellation of Tangier.

1993. Blind Week.
843 **421** 4 d. 40 multicoloured . . . 1·25 25

1993. World Meteorological Day.
844 **422** 4 d. 40 multicoloured . . . 1·25 25

423 Kettle on Stand
424 Emblem

1993. Red Crescent.
845 **423** 4 d. 40 multicoloured . . . 1·25 25

1993. World Telecommunications Day.
846 **424** 4 d. 40 multicoloured . . . 60 25

425 Woman extracting Argan Oil
426 Prince Sidi Mohammed

1993. Argan Oil. Multicoloured.
847 1 d. 70 Type **425** 25 10
848 4 d. 80 Branch and fruit of argan tree 70 30

1993. 30th Birthday of Prince Sidi Mohammed.
849 **426** 4 d. 80 multicoloured . . . 70 30

427 King Hassan and Mosque
428 Canopy, Sceptres, Flag and "40" on Sun

1993. Inauguration of King Hassan II Mosque.
850 **427** 4 d. 80 multicoloured . . . 70 30

1993. 40th Anniv of Revolution.
851 **428** 4 d. 80 multicoloured . . . 70 30

429 Post Box and Globe
430 Emblem

1993. World Post Day.
852 **429** 4 d. 80 multicoloured . . . 70 30

1993. Islamic Summer University.
853 **430** 4 d. 80 multicoloured . . . 70 30

431 "18" on Scroll
433 Flags, Scroll and "50"

432 Marbled Teal

1993. 18th Anniv of "Green March".
854 **431** 4 d. 80 multicoloured . . 70 30

1993. Waterfowl. Multicoloured.
855 1 d. 70 Type **432** 25 10
856 4 d. 80 Red-knobbed coot . . 70 30

1994. 50th Anniv of Istaqlal (Independence) Party.
857 **433** 4 d. 80 multicoloured . . 70 30

434 House
435 Decorated Vase

1994. Signing of Uruguay Round Final Act of General Agreement on Tariffs and Trade, Marrakesh.
858 **434** 1 d. 70 multicoloured . . 25 10
859 – 4 d. 80 multicoloured . . 70 30
DESIGN: 4 d. 80, Mosque.

1994. Blind Week.
861 **435** 4 d. 80 multicoloured . . 70 30

436 Copper Vessel
437 Couple

1994. Red Crescent.
862 **436** 4 d. 80 multicoloured . . 70 30

1994. National Congress on Children's Rights. Children's Drawings. Multicoloured.
863 1 d. 70 Type **437** 25 10
864 4 d. 80 Couple under sun . . 70 30

438 Ball, Moroccan and U.S.A. Flags, Pictogram and Trophy

1994. World Cup Football Championship, U.S.A.
865 **438** 4 d. 80 multicoloured . . 70 30

1994. Size 25 × 32 mm. Inscr "1994".
866 **266** 1 d. 70 red, blue and gold 25 10

439 King Hassan II and Arms

1994. 65th Birthday of King Hassan II. Multicoloured.
867 1 d. 70 Type **439** 25 10
868 4 d. 80 King Hassan II (vert) . 70 30

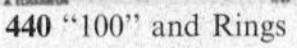

440 "100" and Rings
441 Saint-Exupery, Route Map and Biplane

1994. Centenary of International Olympic Committee.
869 **440** 4 d. 80 multicoloured . . 70 30

1994. 50th Death Anniv of Antoine de Saint-Exupery (writer and pilot).
870 **441** 4 d. 80 multicoloured . . 70 30

442 "Chamaeleon gummifer"

1994. Flowers. Multicoloured.
871 1 d. 70 Type **442** 25 10
872 4 d. 80 "Pancratium maritimum" (vert) 70 30

443 Curlew

1994. Birds. Multicoloured.
873 1 d. 70 Type **443** 25 10
874 4 d. 80 Audouin's gull 70 30

444 Scroll and March **445** Decorated Vase

1994. 19th Anniv of "Green March". Multicoloured.
875 1 d. 70 Type **444** 25 10
876 4 d. 80 Marchers and Moroccan coastline 70 30

1994. Stamp Day. As T **316.**
877 1 d. 70 blue and black 25 10
878 4 d. 80 red and black 70 30
DESIGNS: 1 d. 70, Round postal cancellation of Marrakesh; 4 d. 80, Octagonal postal cancellation of Marrakesh.

1995. Blind Week.
879 **445** 4 d. 80 multicoloured . . 70 30

446 Anniversary Emblem **447** Copper Vessel

1995. 50th Anniv of League of Arab States.
880 **446** 4 d. 80 multicoloured . . 70 30

1995. Red Crescent.
881 **447** 4 d. 80 multicoloured . . 70 30

448 "Malva hispanica" **449** Common Roller

1995. Flowers. Multicoloured.
882 2 d. Type **448** 30 10
883 4 d. 80 "Phlomis crinita" . . . 70 30

1995. Birds. Multicoloured.
884 1 d. 70 Type **449** 25 10
885 4 d. 80 Goldfinch 70 30

450 Anniversary Emblem, Building and Map

1995. 50th Anniv of F.A.O.
886 **450** 4 d. 80 multicoloured . . 70 30

451 "50" and Flags

1995. 50th Anniv of U.N.O. Multicoloured.
887 1 d. 70 Type **451** 25 10
888 4 d. 80 U.N. emblem, doves and map 70 30

452 "20" on Scroll **453** "40", National Flag and Crown

1995. 20th Anniv of "Green March". Multicoloured.
889 1 d. 70 Type **452** 25 10
890 4 d. 80 National flag, book and medal 70 30

1995. 40th Anniv of Independence.
891 **453** 4 d. 80 multicoloured . . 70 30

1995. Stamp Day. As T **316.**
893 1 d. 70 bistre and black . . . 25 10
894 4 d. 80 lilac and black 70 30
DESIGNS: 1 d. 70, Round postal cancellation of Meknes; 4 d. 80, Octagonal cancellation of Meknes.

1996. Size 25 × 32 mm. Dated "1996".
895 **266** 5 d. 50 brown, red and gold 80 35
896 20 d. brown, blue and gold . . . . 2·75 1·10

454 National Arms **455** Decorated Vase

1996. 35th Anniv of Enthronement of King Hassan II. Multicoloured.
897 2 d. Type **454** 30 15
898 5 d. 50 King Hassan II . . . 80 35

1996.
900 **455** 5 d. 50 multicoloured . . 80 35

456 Leather Flask **457** "Cleonia lusitanica"

1996.
901 **456** 5 d. 50 multicoloured . . 80 35

1996. Flowers. Multicoloured.
902 2 d. Type **457** 30 15
903 5 d. 50 "Tulipa sylvestris" . . 80 35

458 King Hassan II wearing Military Uniform

1996. 40th Anniv of Royal Armed Forces. Multicoloured.
904 2 d. Type **458** 30 15
905 5 d. 50 King Hassan II and globe 80 35

POSTAGE DUE STAMPS

D 53

1965.
D162 **D 53** 5 f. green . . . . . . 3·00 1·25
D163 10 f. brown 50 25
D164 20 f. red 50 25
D165 30 f. sepia . . . . . . 1·25 50

D **153** Peaches

1974.
D393 – 5 f. orge, grn & blk 10 10
D394 – 10 f. grn, red & blk 10 10
D395 – 20 f. green & black 50 10
D396 **D 153** 30 f. orge, grn & blk 60 35
D397 – 40 f. green and black 15 10
D398 – 60 f. orge, grn & blk 20 15
D399 – 80 f. orange, green and black 50 20
D399a – 1 d. multicoloured 20 15
D400 – 1 d. 20 multicoloured 50 15
D401 – 1 d. 60 multicoloured 60 20
D402 – 2 d. multicoloured 55 25
DESIGNS: 60 f., 1 d. 60, Peaches. VERT: 5 f. Oranges; 10 f., 1 d. 20, Cherries; 20 f. Raisins; 40 f. Grapes; 80 f. Oranges; 1 d. Apples; 2 d. Strawberries.

MOSUL Pt. 19

Stamps used by Indian forces in Mesopotamia (now Iraq) at the close of the 1914–18 war.

12 pies = 1 anna; 16 annas = 1 rupee

1919. Turkish Fiscal stamps surch **POSTAGE I.E.F. 'D'** and value in annas.
1 ½ a. on 1 pi. green and red . . . 1·40 1·40
2 1 a. on 20 pa. black on red . . 1·40 1·75
4 2½ a. on 1 pi. mauve & yellow . 1·50 1·50
5 3 a. on 20 pa. green . . . . . . 1·60 2·50
6 3 a. on 20 pa. green & orange . 25·00 45·00
7 4 a. on 1 pi. violet . . . . . . 3·00 3·50
8 8 a. on 10 pa. red . . . . 4·00 5·00

MOZAMBIQUE Pt. 9; Pt. 13

Former Overseas Province of Portugal in East Africa, granted independence in 1975.
Mozambique joined the Commonwealth on 12 November 1995.

1876. 1000 reis = 1 milreis.
1913. 100 centavos = 1 escudo.
1980. 100 centavos = 1 metical.

1876. "Crown" key-type inscr "MOCAMBIQUE".
1 P 5 r. black 50 40
11 10 r. yellow . . . . 1·60 1·40
19 10 r. green 40 30
3 20 r. bistre 50 30
20 20 r. red . . . . £100 75·00
4a 25 r. red 25 15
21 25 r. lilac . . . . 1·10 60
14 40 r. blue . . . . 4·00 2·50
22 40 r. buff 75 65
6 50 r. green . . . . 35·00 11·00
23 50 r. blue 40 30
7 100 r. lilac 40 25
8 200 r. orange . . . . 1·25 70
9 300 r. brown 95 65

1886. "Embossed" key-type inscr "PROVINCIA DE MOCAMBIQUE".
30 Q 5 r. black 50 35
32 10 r. green 45 35
34 20 r. red 50 35
48 25 r. lilac . . . . 3·25 1·75
37 40 r. brown 45 30
38 50 r. blue 70 35
40 100 r. brown 50 30
42 200 r. violet . . . . 1·10 75
43 300 r. orange . . . . 1·40 45

1893. No. 37 surch **PROVISORIO 5 5.**
53 Q 5 on 40 r. brown . . . . . 32·00 23·00

1894. "Figures" key-type inscr "MOCAMBIQUE".
56 R 5 r. orange 30 20
57 10 r. mauve 30 20
58 15 r. brown 35 25
59 20 r. lilac 35 20
65 25 r. green 30 15
60 50 r. blue . . . . 1·10 25
67 75 r. pink 65 45
61 80 r. green . . . . 1·10 65
62 100 r. brown on buff . . . 70 50
68 150 r. red on pink . . . . . 3·00 1·60
64 200 r. blue on blue . . . . 1·10 90
69 300 r. blue on brown . . . 1·60 1·25

1895. "Embossed" key-type of Mozambique optd **1195 CENTENARIO ANTONINO 1895.**
71 Q 5 r. black . . . . 2·25 1·60
72 10 r. green . . . . 2·25 1·75
73 20 r. red . . . . 2·40 2·00
74 25 r. purple . . . . 2·40 2·00
75 40 r. brown . . . . 2·40 2·25
76 50 r. blue . . . . 2·40 2·25
77 100 r. brown . . . . 2·40 2·25
78 200 r. lilac . . . . 7·50 5·50
79 300 r. orange . . . . 7·50 5·50

1897. No. 69 surch **50 reis.**
82 R 50 r. on 300 r. bl on brn . . 60·00 45·00

1898. Nos. 34 and 37 surch **MOCAMBIQUE** and value.
84 Q 2½ r. on 20 r. red . . . . . 7·00 5·50
85 5 r. on 40 r. brown . . . . 6·00 5·50

1898. "King Carlos" key type inscr "MOCAMBIQUE". Name and value in red (500 r.) or black (others).
86 S 2½ r. grey 15 15
87 5 r. red 15 15
88 10 r. green 15 15
89 15 r. brown . . . . 1·50 75
138 15 r. green 50 40
90 20 r. lilac 50 25
91 25 r. green 50 25
139 25 r. red 40 15
92 50 r. blue 55 30
140 50 r. brown . . . . 1·25 85
141 65 r. blue . . . . 3·00 3·00
93 75 r. pink . . . . 2·50 1·50
142 75 r. purple . . . . 1·00 85
94 80 r. mauve . . . . 2·50 1·50
95 100 r. blue on blue . . . . 1·25 65
143 115 r. brown on pink . . . 3·00 2·50
144 130 r. brown on yellow . . 3·00 2·50
96 150 r. brown on yellow . . 2·25 1·50
97 200 r. purple on pink . . . 1·00 70
98 300 r. blue on pink . . . . 2·00 1·25
145 400 r. blue on cream . . . 4·50 3·25
99 500 r. black on blue . . . 4·75 3·00
100 700 r. mauve on yellow . . 5·50 3·50

1902. Various types surch.
146 S 50 r. on 65 r. blue . . . . . 1·10 1·00
101 R 65 r. on 10 r. mauve 95 85
102 65 r. on 15 r. brown 95 85
105 Q 65 r. on 20 r. red . . . . . 1·40 1·00
106 R 65 r. on 20 r. lilac 95 85
108 Q 65 r. on 40 r. brown . . . . 1·25 1·25
110 65 r. on 200 r. violet . . . 1·50 1·00

111	V	115 r. on 2½ r. brown	95	90
113	Q	115 r. on 5 r. black	65	55
114	R	115 r. on 5 r. orange	90	75
115		115 r. on 25 r. green	95	85
117	Q	115 r. on 50 r. blue	60	50
120		130 r. on 25 r. mauve	70	45
121	R	130 r. on 75 r. red	95	90
122		130 r. on 100 r. brown on buff	2·25	2·25
123		130 r. on 150 r. red on pink	1·00	1·00
124		130 r. on 200 r. bl on bl	2·00	2·00
126	Q	130 r. on 300 r. orange	75	45
128		400 r. on 10 r. green	1·75	1·60
129	R	400 r. on 50 r. blue	60	50
130		400 r. on 80 r. green	60	50
132	Q	400 r. on 100 r. brown	12·50	8·50
133	R	400 r. on 300 r. blue on brown	60	50

1902. "King Carlos" key-type of Mozambique optd **PROVISORIO**.

134	S	15 r. brown	75	45
135		25 r. green	75	45
136		50 r. blue	1·25	95
137		75 r. pink	2·10	1·25

1911. "King Carlos" key-type of Mozambique optd **REPUBLICA**.

147	S	2½ r. grey	10	15
148		5 r. orange	15	15
149		10 r. green	40	25
150		15 r. green	15	10
151		20 r. lilac	40	20
152		25 r. red	15	10
153		50 r. brown	15	15
154		75 r. purple	30	25
155		100 r. blue on blue	30	25
156		115 r. brown on pink	40	30
157		130 r. brown on yellow	40	30
158		200 r. purple on pink	75	50
159		400 r. blue on yellow	70	45
160		500 r. black on blue	70	45
161		700 r. mauve on yellow	70	45

1912. "King Manoel" key-type inscr "MOCAMBIQUE" with opt **REPUBLICA**.

162	T	2½ r. lilac	15	10
163		5 r. black	15	10
164		10 r. green	15	10
165		20 r. red	35	25
166		25 r. brown	15	10
167		50 r. blue	20	15
168		75 r. brown	20	15
169		100 r. brown on green	20	15
170		200 r. green on orange	45	40
171		300 r. black on blue	45	40
172		500 r. brown and green	90	80

1913. Surch **REPUBLICA MOCAMBIQUE** and value on "Vasco da Gama" issues of (a) Portuguese Colonies.

173	¼ c. on 2½ r. green	45	30
174	½ c. on 5 r. red	40	30
175	1 c. on 10 r. purple	35	30
176	2½ c. on 25 r. green	35	30
177	5 c. on 50 r. blue	40	30
178	7½ c. on 75 r. brown	70	55
179	10 c. on 100 r. brown	50	45
180	15 c. on 150 r. brown	45	40

(b) Macao.

181	¼ c. on ½ a. green	60	50
182	½ c. on 1 a. red	55	50
183	1 c. on 2 a. purple	55	45
184	2½ c. on 4 a. green	55	45
185	5 c. on 8 a. blue	1·50	1·25
186	7½ c. on 12 a. brown	85	75
187	10 c. on 16 a. brown	60	50
188	15 c. on 24 a. brown	55	45

(c) Timor.

189	¼ c. on ½ a. green	60	50
190	½ c. on 1 a. red	60	50
191	1 c. on 2 a. purple	55	45
192	2½ c. on 4 a. green	55	45
193	5 c. on 8 a. blue	90	70
194	7½ c. on 12 a. brown	65	50
195	10 c. on 16 a. brown	50	45
196	15 c. on 24 a. brown	45	35

1914. "Ceres" key-type inscr "MOCAMBIQUE".

197	U	¼ c. green	10	10
198		½ c. black	10	10
199		1 c. green	10	10
200		1½ c. brown	10	10
201		2 c. red	10	10
270		2 c. grey	10	10
202		2½ c. violet	10	10
255		3 c. orange	10	10
256		4 c. pink	10	10
257		4½ c. grey	10	10
203		5 c. blue	10	10
275		6 c. mauve	10	10
259		7 c. blue	10	10
260		7½ c. brown	10	10
278		8 c. grey	10	10
279		10 c. red	10	10
280		12 c. brown	10	10
281		12 c. green	10	10
283		15 c. purple	10	10
284		20 c. green	15	15
285		24 c. blue	15	15
286		25 c. brown	20	20
209		30 c. brown on green	70	50
287		30 c. green	15	15
295		30 c. lilac on pink	70	55
210		40 c. brown on pink	75	60
288		40 c. turquoise	15	15
211		50 c. orange on orange	1·40	1·10
289		50 c. mauve	15	10
297		60 c. brown on pink	70	55
290		60 c. blue	45	25
291		60 c. pink	45	25
298		80 c. brown on blue	65	45
293		80 c. red	45	25
299		1 e. green on blue	1·10	65
264		1 e. pink	50	40
301		1 e. blue	70	45
300	U	2 e. mauve on pink	80	50
302		2 e. purple	40	30
303		5 e. brown	4·50	1·90
304		10 e. pink	6·75	2·50
305		20 e. green	18·00	8·25

1915. Provisional issues of 1902 optd **REPUBLICA**.

226	S	50 r. blue (136)	30	20
227		50 r. on 65 r. blue	30	25
213		75 r. pink (137)	70	40
228	V	115 r. on 2½ r. brown	30	25
216	Q	115 r. on 5 r. black	9·00	8·50
229	R	115 r. on 5 r. orange	30	25
230		115 r. on 25 r. green	30	25
231		130 r. on 75 r. red	30	25
220		130 r. on 100 r. brown on buff	55	45
232		130 r. on 150 r. red on pink	30	25
233		130 r. on 200 r. bl on bl	30	25
223		400 r. on 50 r. blue	65	60
224		400 r. on 80 r. green	65	60
225		400 r. on 300 r. bl on brn	65	60

1918. Charity Tax stamp surch **2½ CENTAVOS**. Roul or perf.

248	C 16	2½ c. on 5 c. red	40	25

1920. Charity Tax stamps surch. (a) **CORREIOS** and value in figures.

306	C 15	1 c. on 1 c. green	30	30
307	C 16	1½ c. on 5 c. red	30	25

(b) **SEIS CENTAVOS**.

308	C 16	6 c. on 5 c. red	40	30

1921. "Ceres" stamps of 1913 surch.

309	U	10 c. on ½ c. black	70	60
310		30 c. on 1½ c. brown	70	60
316		50 c. on 4 c. pink	55	35
311		60 c. on 2½ c. violet	90	70
328		70 c. on 2 e. purple	30	20
329		1 e. 40 on 2 e. purple	35	20

1922. "Ceres" key-type of Lourenco Marques surch.

312	U	10 c. on ½ c. black	50	45
314		30 c. on 1½ c. brown	50	45

1922. Charity Tax stamp surch **2$00**.

315	C 16	$2 on 5 c. red	60	35

1924. 4th Death Centenary of Vasco da Gama. "Ceres" key-type of Mozambique optd **Vasco da Gama 1924**.

317	U	80 c. pink	50	35

1925. Nos. 129 and 130 surch **Republica 40 C.**

318	R	40 c. on 400 r. on 50 r.	35	25
319		40 c. on 400 r. on 80 r.	35	30

1929. "Due" key-type inscr "MOCAMBIQUE" optd **CORREIOS**.

320	W	50 c. lilac	55	45

23 Mousinho de Albuquerque

25 "Portugal" and Camoens' "The Lusiads"

1930. Albuquerque's Victories Commemorative. Vignette in grey.

321	23	50 c. lake and red (Macontene)	2·75	2·50
322		50 c. orange and red (Mujenga)	2·75	2·50
323		50 c. mauve and brown (Coolela)	2·25	1·90
324		50 c. grey and green (Chaimite)	2·75	2·50
325		50 c. blue and indigo (Ibrahimo)	2·25	1·90
326		50 c. blue and black (Mucutomuno)	2·25	1·90
327		50 c. violet and lilac (Naguema)	2·25	1·90

The above were for compulsory use throughout Mozambique in place of ordinary postage stamps on certain days in 1930 and 1931. They are not listed among the Charity Tax stamps as the revenue was not applied to any charitable fund.

1938. Value in red (1, 15 c., 1 e. 40) or black (others).

330	25	1 c. brown	10	10
331		5 c. brown	10	10
332		10 c. purple	10	10
333		15 c. black	10	10
334		20 c. grey	10	10
335		30 c. green	10	10
336		35 c. green	2·50	1·40
337		40 c. red	10	10
338		45 c. blue	20	20
339		50 c. brown	15	10
340		60 c. green	20	15
341		70 c. brown	20	15
342		80 c. green	20	15
343		85 c. red	55	40
344		1 e. purple	25	15
345		1 e. 40 blue	3·75	1·25
346		1 e. 75 blue	2·40	1·10
347		2 e. lilac	65	25
348		5 e. green	1·25	30
349		10 e. brown	2·75	50
350		20 e. orange	12·50	80

1938. As 1938 issue of Macao. Name and value in black.

351	54	1 c. green (postage)	10	10
352		5 c. brown	10	10
353		10 c. red	10	10
354		15 c. purple	10	10
355		20 c. grey	10	10
356	–	30 c. purple	15	10
357	–	35 c. green	20	15
358	–	40 c. brown	20	15
359	–	50 c. mauve	20	10
360	–	60 c. black	20	10
361	–	70 c. violet	25	15
362	–	80 c. orange	25	15
363	–	1 e. red	30	15
364	–	1 e. 75 blue	90	30
365	–	2 e. red	90	30
366	–	5 e. green	2·25	30
367	–	10 e. blue	4·50	60
368	–	20 e. brown	11·00	1·00
369	56	10 c. red (air)	10	10
370		20 c. violet	10	10
371		50 c. orange	15	10
372		1 e. blue	20	10
373		2 e. red	40	15
374		3 e. green	60	20
375		5 e. brown	1·00	35
376		9 e. red	1·90	45
377		10 e. mauve	3·00	60

DESIGNS: 30 to 50 c. Mousinho de Albuquerque; 60 c. to 1 e. Dam; 1 e. 75, to 5 e. Henry the Navigator; 10, 20 e. Afonso de Albuquerque.

1938. No. 338 surch **40 centavos**.

378	25	40 c. on 45 c. blue	1·75	1·50

26a Route of President's Tour

27 New Cathedral, Lourenco Marques

1938. President Carmona's 2nd Colonial Tour.

379	26a	80 c. violet on mauve	1·50	75
380		1 e. 75 blue on blue	4·50	1·90
381		3 e. green on green	6·75	3·50
382		20 e. brown on cream	32·00	16·00

1944. 400th Anniv of Lourenco Marques.

383	27	50 c. brown	65	30
384	–	50 c. green	65	30
385	–	1 e. 75 blue	3·50	85
386a	–	20 e. black	2·75	30

DESIGNS—HORIZ: 1 e. 75, Lourenco Marques Central Railway Station; 20 e. Town Hall, Lourenco Marques.

See also No. 405.

1946. Nos. 354, 364 and 375 surch.

387	10 c. on 15 c. purple (postage)	40	30
388	60 c. on 1 e. 75 blue	60	35
389	3 e. on 5 e. brown (air)	4·00	1·75

1947. No. 386a surch.

390	2 e. on 20 e. black	1·25	1·10

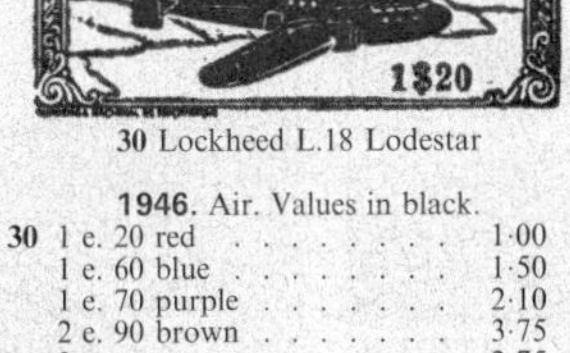

30 Lockheed L.18 Lodestar

1946. Air. Values in black.

391	30	1 e. 20 red	1·00	65
392		1 e. 60 blue	1·50	80
393		1 e. 70 purple	2·10	1·20
394		2 e. 90 brown	3·75	1·40
395		3 e. green	2·75	1·60

1947. Air. Optd **Taxe percue**. Values in red (50 c.) or black (others).

397	30	50 c. black	40	30
398		1 e. pink	50	30
399		3 e. green	80	40
400		4 e. 50 green	1·40	55
401		5 e. red	2·00	80
402		10 e. blue	5·50	1·90
403		20 e. violet	13·50	5·25
404		50 e. orange	30·00	12·00

1948. As T **27** but without commemorative inscr.

405	4 e. 50 red	1·25	40

31 Antonio Enes

33 Lourenco Marques

1948. Birth Centenary of Antonio Enes.

406	31	50 c. black and cream	1·00	20
407		5 e. purple and cream	4·25	80

1948.

408	–	5 c. brown	25	15
409	–	10 c. purple	25	15
410	–	20 c. brown	25	15
411	–	30 c. purple	25	15
412	–	40 c. green	25	15
413	33	50 c. grey	25	15
414	–	60 c. purple	30	15
415	33	80 c. violet	25	15
416	–	1 e. red	35	15
417	–	1 e. 20 grey	50	20
418	–	1 e. 50 violet	35	20
419	–	1 e. 75 blue	95	25
420	–	2 e. brown	60	15
421	–	2 e. 50 blue	2·10	20
422	–	3 e. green	90	20
423	–	3 e. 50 green	1·60	20
424	–	5 e. green	1·40	20
425	–	10 e. brown	3·25	35
426	–	15 e. red	8·00	1·50
427	–	20 e. orange	15·00	1·75

DESIGNS—VERT: 5, 30 c. Gogogo Peak; 20, 40 c. Zumbo River; 60 c., 3 e. 50, Nhanhangare Waterfall. HORIZ: 10 c., 1 e. 20, Bridge over Zambesi; 1, 5 e. Gathering coconuts; 1 e. 50, 2 e. River Pungue at Beira; 1 e. 75, 3 e. Polana beach, Lourenco Marques; 2 e. 50, 10 e. Bird's eye view of Lourenco Marques; 15, 20 e. Malema River.

1949. Honouring the Statue of Our Lady of Fatima. As T **62** of Macao.

428	50 c. blue	1·50	50
429	1 e. 20 mauve	3·00	1·00
430	4 e. 50 green	11·00	3·50
431	20 e. brown	21·00	5·25

35 Aircraft and Globe

36 "Balistoides conspicillum"

1949. Air.

432	35	50 c. brown	20	10
433		1 e. 20 violet	40	20
434		4 e. 50 blue	95	35
435		5 e. green	1·60	45
436		20 e. brown	4·75	1·00

1949. 75th Anniv of U.P.U. As T **64** of Macao.

437	4 e. 50 blue	1·50	60

1950. Holy Year. As Nos. 425/6 of Macao.

438	1 e. 50 orange	65	30
439	3 e. blue	90	45

1951. Fishes. Multicoloured.

440	5 c. Type **36**	15	10
441	10 c. "Chaetodon auriga"	10	10
442	15 c. "Chaetodon inula"	35	20
443	20 c. "Pterois volitans"	15	10
444	30 c. "Canthigaster margaritatus"	15	10
445	40 c. "Stephanolepis auratus"	10	10
446	50 c. "Teuthis nigrofuscus"	10	10
447	1 e. "Heniochus acuminatus" (vert)	15	10
448	1 e. 50 "Novaculichthys macrolepidotus"	15	10
449	2 e. "Gaterin schotaf"	15	10
450	2 e. 50 "Lutianus kasmira"	40	15
451	3 e. "Acauthurus triostegus"	40	15
452	3 e. 50 "Abalistes stellaris"	45	10
453	4 e. "Fistularia petimba"	70	20
454	4 e. 50 "Chaetodon vagabundus"	1·00	15
455	5 e. "Amblyapistus binotata"	1·00	10
456	6 e. "Platax pinnatus" (vert)	1·00	10
457	8 e. "Zanclus canescens" (vert)	1·75	25
458	9 e. "Tetrosomus concatenatus"	1·75	20
459	10 e. "Dactyloptena orientalis"	4·25	1·10
460	15 e. "Odonus niger"	28·00	7·50
461	20 e. "Rhinecanthus aculeatus"	14·50	3·25
462	30 e. "Lactoria cornutus"	17·00	4·50
463	50 e. "Lactoria fornasina"	26·00	10·00

1951. Termination of Holy Year. As T **69** of Macao.

464	5 e. red and orange	1·90	90

37 Victor Cordon (colonist)

39 Liner and Lockheed Constellation Airliner

1951. Birth Centenary of Cordon.

465	37	1 e. brown and light brown	1·25	30
466		5 e. black and blue	6·00	85

1952. 1st Tropical Medicine Congress. Lisbon. As T **71** of Macao.

467	3 e. orange and blue	90	45

DESIGN: Miguela Bombarda Hospital.

1952. 4th African Tourist Congress.

468	39	1 e. 50 multicoloured	65	30

40 Missionary   41 Citrus Butterfly

1953. Missionary Art Exhibition.
469 **40** 10 c. red and lilac 10 10
470 1 e. red and green 70 20
471 5 e. black and blue . . . . 1·40 40

1953. Butterflies and Moths. Multicoloured.
472 10 c. Type **41** 10 10
473 15 c. "Amphicallia thelwalli" . 10 10
474 20 c. Forest queen 10 10
475 30 c. Western scarlet 10 10
476 40 c. Black-barred red-tip . . 10 10
477 50 c. Mocker swallowtail . . . 10 10
478 80 c. "Nudaurelia hersilia dido" 15 15
479 1 e. African moon moth . . . 15 10
480 1 e. 50 Large striped swallowtail 15 10
481 2 e. "Athletes ethica" . . . . 4·50 30
482 2 e. 30 African monarch . . . 3·00 25
483 2 e. 50 Green swallowtail . . . 7·50 25
484 3 e. "Arniocera ericata" . . . 95 10
485 4 e. Apollo moth 50 10
486 4 e. 50 Peach moth 50 10
487 5 e. "Metarctica lateritia" . . 50 10
488 6 e. "Xanthospilopteryx mozambica" 55 15
489 7 e. 50 White bear . . . . . . 3·00 30
490 10 e. Flame-coloured charaxes 7·50 1·00
491 20 e. Fervid tiger moth . . . . 11·00 1·00

42 Stamps   43 Map of Mozambique

1953. Philatelic Exhibition, Lourenco Marques.
492 **42** 1 e. multicoloured 80 30
493 3 e. multicoloured . . . . 2·25 65

1953. Portuguese Postage Stamp Centenary. As T **75** of Macao.
494 50 c. multicoloured 50 35

1954. 4th Centenary of Sao Paulo. As T **76** of Macao.
495 3 e. 50 multicoloured 30 20

1954. Multicoloured map; Mozambique territory in colours given.
496 **43** 10 c. lilac 10 10
497 20 c. yellow 10 10
498 50 c. blue 10 10
499 1 e. yellow 10 10
500 2 e. 30 white 50 35
501 4 e. orange 50 25
502 10 e. green . . . . 1·40 20
503 20 e. brown . . . . 2·00 30

44 Arms of Beira   45 Mousinho de Albuquerque

1954. 1st Philatelic Exhibition, Manica and Sofala.
504 **44** 1 e. 50 multicoloured . . . 35 20
505 3 e. 50 multicoloured . . . 90 35

1955. Birth Centenary of M. de Albuquerque.
506 **45** 2 e. brown and grey 50 30
507 – 2 e. 50 multicoloured . . . 1·10 55
DESIGN: 2 e. 50, Equestrian statue of Albuquerque.

46 Arms and Inhabitants   47 Beira

1956. Visit of President to Mozambique. Multicoloured. Background in colours given.
508 **46** 1 e. cream 25 15
509 2 e. 50 blue 65 30

1957. 50th Anniv of Beira.
510 **47** 2 e. 50 multicoloured . . . 65 25

1958. 6th International Congress of Tropical Medicine. As T **79** of Macao.
511 1 e. 50 multicoloured . . . . 1·25 70
DESIGN: 1 e. 50, "Strophanthus grandiflorus" (plant).

1958. Brussels International Exn. As T **78** of Macao.
512 3 e. 50 multicoloured 25 15

48 Caravel   49 "Arts and Crafts"

1960. 500th Death Anniv of Prince Henry the Navigator.
513 **48** 5 e. multicoloured 45 20

1960. 10th Anniv of African Technical Co-operation Commission.
514 **49** 3 e. multicoloured 45 20

50 Arms of Lourenco Marques   51 Fokker F.27 Friendship and De Havilland D.H.89 Dragon Rapide over Route Map

1961. Arms. Multicoloured.
515 5 c. Type **50** 15 10
516 15 c. Chibuto 15 10
517 20 c. Nampula 15 10
518 30 c. Inhambane 15 10
519 50 c. Mozambique (city) . . . 15 10
520 1 e. Matola 30 15
521 1 e. 50 Quelimane 30 15
522 2 e. Mocuba 50 15
523 2 e. 50 Antonio Enes . . . . 1·10 15
524 3 e. Cabral 50 15
525 4 e. Manica 50 20
526 4 e. 50 Pery 50 15
527 5 e. St. Tiago de Tete . . . 60 20
528 7 e. 50 Porto Amelia 80 35
529 10 e. Chinde . . . . 1·40 35
530 20 e. Joao Belo . . . . . . 2·75 50
531 50 e. Beira . . . . 4·50 1·25

1962. Sports. As T **82** of Macao. Multicoloured.
532 50 c. Water-skiing 10 10
533 1 e. Wrestling 75 20
534 1 e. 50 Gymnastics 35 15
535 2 e. 50 Hockey 60 15
536 4 e. 50 Netball 90 40
537 15 e. Outboard speedboat racing 1·60 90

1962. Malaria Eradication. Mosquito design as T **83** of Macao. Multicoloured.
538 2 e. 50 "Anopheles funestus" . 50 30

1962. 25th Anniv of D.E.T.A. (Mozambique Airline).
539 **51** 3 e. multicoloured 45 20

52 Lourenco Marques in 1887 and 1962   53 Oil Refinery, Sonarep

1962. 75th Anniv of Lourenco Marques.
540 **52** 1 e. multicoloured 40 20

1962. Air. Multicoloured.
541 1 e. 50 Type **53** 50 10
542 2 e. Salazar Academy 30 10
543 3 e. 50 Aerial view of Lourenco Marques Port 40 15
544 4 e. 50 Salazar Barrage . . . 35 15
545 5 e. Trigo de Morais Bridge and Dam 40 15
546 20 e. Marcelo Caetano Bridge and Dam . . . . 1·10 50
Each design includes an airplane in flight.

54 Arms of Mozambique and Statue of Vasco da Gama   55 Nef, 1430

1963. Bicentenary of City of Mozambique.
547 **54** 3 e. multicoloured 35 20

1963. 10th Anniv of T.A.P. Airline. As T **52** of Portuguese Guinea.
548 2 e. 50 multicoloured 35 15

1963. Evolution of Sailing Ships. Multicoloured.
549 10 c. Type **55** 10 10
550 20 c. Caravel, 1436 (vert) . . . 10 10
551 30 c. Lateen-rigged caravel, 1460 (vert) 15 10
552 50 c. Vasco da Gama's ship "Sao Gabriel", 1497 (vert) 30 10
553 1 e. Don Manuel's nau, 1498 (vert) 55 10
554 1 e. 50 Galleon, 1530 (vert) . . 40 15
555 2 e. Nau "Flor de la Mer", 1511 (vert) 40 15
556 2 e. 50 Caravel "Redonda", 1519 45 15
557 3 e. 50 Nau, 1520 (vert) . . . 45 15
558 4 e. Portuguese Indies galley, 1521 . . . . 50 20
559 4 e. 50 Galleon "Santa Tereza", 1639 (vert) 50 20
560 5 e. Nau "N. Senhora da Conceicao", 1716 (vert) . . 10·00 30
561 6 e. Warship "N. Senhora do Bom Sucesso", 1764 . . . . 80 25
562 7 e. 50 Bomb launch, 1788 . . 90 35
563 8 e. Naval brigantine "Lebre", 1793 . . . . 90 35
564 10 e. Corvette "Andorinha", 1799 . . . . 95 35
565 12 e. 50 Naval schooner "Maria Teresa", 1820 . . . . . . 1·25 60
566 15 e. Warship "Vasco da Gama", 1841 . . . . 1·60 60
567 20 e. Sail frigate "Don Fernando II e Gloria", 1843 (vert) . . 2·00 75
568 30 e. Cadet barque "Sagres I", 1924 (vert) . . . . 3·50 1·25

1964. Centenary of National Overseas Bank. As T **84** of Macao but view of Bank building, Lourenco Marques.
569 1 e. 50 multicoloured 20 15

56 Pres. Tomas   57 State Barge of Joao V, 1728

1964. Presidential Visit.
570 **56** 2 e. 50 multicoloured . . . 15 10

1964. Portuguese Marine, 18th and 19th Centuries. Multicoloured.
571 15 c. Type **57** 10 10
572 35 c. State barge of Jose I, 1753 10 10
573 1 e. Barge of Alfandega, 1768 . 35 10
574 1 e. 50 Oarsman of 1780 (vert) 30 15
575 2 e. 50 State barge "Pinto da Fonseca", 1780 . . . . . . 20 10
576 5 e. State barge of Carlota Joaquina, 1790 . . . . . . 25 20
577 9 e. Don Miguel's state barge, 1831 . . . . 60 40

1965. I.T.U. Centenary. As T **85** of Macao.
578 1 e. multicoloured 30 20

1966. 40th Anniv of Portuguese National Revolution. As T **86** of Macao, but showing different building. Multicoloured.
579 1 e. Railway station, Beira and Antonio Enes Academy . . 40 30

58 Arquebusier, 1560   59 Luis de Camoens (poet)

1967. Portuguese Military Uniforms. Multicoloured.
580 20 c. Type **58** 10 10
581 30 c. Arquebusier, 1640 . . . 10 10
582 40 c. Infantryman, 1777 . . . 15 10
583 50 c. Infantry officer, 1777 . . 15 10
584 80 c. Drummer, 1777 . . . . . 35 20
585 1 e. Infantry sergeant, 1777 . . 30 10
586 2 e. Infantry major, 1784 . . . 30 15
587 2 e. 50 Colonial officer, 1788 . 40 15
588 3 e. Infantryman, 1789 . . . . 40 20
589 5 e. Colonial bugler, 1801 . . . 50 30
590 10 e. Colonial officer, 1807 . . 70 30
591 15 e. Infantryman, 1817 . . . 85 55

1967. Centenary of Military Naval Association. As T **88** of Macao. Multicoloured.
592 3 e. A. Coutinho and paddle-gunboat "Tete" 35 15
593 10 e. J. Roby and paddle-gunboat "Granada" 65 35

1967. 50th Anniv of Fatima Apparitions. As T **89** of Macao.
594 50 c. "Golden Crown" 15 10

1968. 500th Birth Anniv of Pedro Cabral (explorer). As T **90** of Macao.
595 1 e. Erecting the Cross at Porto Sequro (horiz) 10 10
596 1 e. 50 First mission service in Brazil (horiz) 20 10
597 3 e. Church of Grace, Santarem 40 15

1969. Birth Centenary of Admiral Gago Coutinho. As T **91** of Macao.
598 70 c. Admiral Gago Coutinho Airport, Lourenco Marques (horiz) 25 10

1969. 400th Anniv of Camoens' Visit to Mozambique. Multicoloured.
599 15 c. Type **59** 10 10
600 50 c. Nau of 1553 (horiz) . . 15 10
601 1 e. 50 Map of Mozambique, 1554 . . . . 20 15
602 2 e. 50 Chapel of Our Lady of Baluarte (horiz) 25 20
603 5 e. Part of the "Lusiad" (poem) 40 30

1969. 500th Birth Anniv of Vasco da Gama (explorer). As T **92** of Macao. Multicoloured.
604 1 e. Route map of Da Gama's Voyage to India (horiz) . . 15 10

1969. Centenary of Overseas Administrative Reforms. As T **93** of Macao.
605 1 e. 50 multicoloured 15 10

1969. 500th Birth Anniv of King Manoel I. As T **95** of Macao. Multicoloured.
606 80 c. Illuminated arms (horiz) 15 10

1970. Birth Centenary of Marshal Carmona. As T **96** of Macao. Multicoloured.
607 5 e. Portrait in ceremonial dress 25 15

60 Fossilized Fern

1971. Rocks, Minerals and Fossils. Mult.
608 15 c. Type **60** 15 10
609 50 c. "Lytodiscoides conduciensis" (fossilized snail) 20 10
610 1 e. Stibnite 20 10
611 1 e. 50 Pink beryl 20 10
612 2 e. Endothiodon and fossil skeleton 25 10
613 3 e. Tantalocolumbite 30 10
614 3 e. 50 Verdelite 40 15
615 4 e. Zircon 50 30
616 10 e. Petrified tree-stump . . 1·25 65

1972. 400th Anniv of Camoens' "The Lusiads" (epic poem). As T **98** of Macao. Multicoloured.
617 4 e. Mozambique Island in 16th century . . . . 1·25 30

1972. Olympic Games, Munich. As T **99** of Macao. Multicoloured.
618 3 e. Hurdling and swimming . 15 10

1972. 50th Anniv of 1st Flight, Lisbon–Rio de Janeiro. As T **100** of Macao. Multicoloured.
619 1 e. Fairey IIID seaplane "Santa Cruz" at Recife 15 10

61 Racing Yachts

1973. World Championships for "Vauriens" Class Yachts, Lourenco Marques.
620 **61** 1 e. multicoloured 15 10
621 – 1 e. 50 multicoloured . . . 15 10
622 – 3 e. multicoloured 30 20
DESIGNS: Nos. 621/2 similar to Type **61**.

1973. Centenary of I.M.O./W.M.O. As T **102** of Macao.
623 2 e. multicoloured 20 20

62 Dish Aerials

1974. Inauguration of Satellite Communications Station Network.
624 **62** 50 c. multicoloured 20 20

63 Bird with "Flag" Wings

1975. Implementation of Lusaka Agreement.

625 **63** 1 e. multicoloured 10 10
626 1 e. 50 multicoloured . . . 10 10
627 2 e. multicoloured 15 10
628 3 e. 50 multicoloured . . . 25 15
629 6 e. multicoloured 65 30

1975. Independence. Optd **INDEPENDENCIA 25 JUN 75**.

631 **43** 10 c. mult (postage) 25 25
632 – 40 c. mult (No. 476) . . . 10 10
633 **62** 50 c. multicoloured 20 15
634 **61** 1 e. multicoloured 30 25
635 – 1 e. 50 mult (No. 621) . . . 60 50
636 – 2 e. mult (No. 623) . . . . 1·75 1·75
637 – 2 e. 50 mult (No. 535) . . . 35 30
638 – 3 e. mult (No. 618) 40 35
639 – 3 e. mult (No. 622) 45 40
640 – 3 e. 50 mult (No. 614) . . . 1·75 1·75
641 – 4 e. 50 mult (No. 536) . . . 2·00 1·10
642 – 7 e. 50 mult (No. 489) . . . 55 30
643 – 10 e. mult (No. 616) . . . 1·00 35
644 – 15 e. mult (No. 537) . . . 1·25 1·10
645 **43** 20 e. multicoloured . . . . 1·25 1·10
646 – 3 e. 50 multicoloured (No. 543) (air) 35 25
647 – 4 e. 50 mult (No. 544) . . . 40 25
648 – 5 e. mult (No. 545) 90 50
649 – 20 e. mult (No. 546) . . . 1·50 90

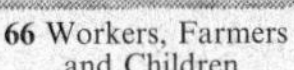
66 Workers, Farmers and Children

67 Farm Worker

1975. "Vigilance, Unity, Work". Multicoloured.

650 20 c. Type **66** 10 10
651 30 c. Type **66** 10 10
652 50 c. Type **66** 10 10
653 2 e. 50 Type **66** 15 10
654 4 e. 50 Armed family, workers and dancers 25 15
655 5 e. As No. 654 . . . . 35 15
656 10 e. As No. 654 . . . . 70 30
657 50 e. As No. 654 . . . . . . 3·00 1·50

1976. Women's Day.

659 **67** 1 e. black and green . . . 10 10
660 – 1 e. 50 black and brown . . 10 10
661 – 2 e. 50 black and blue . . . 15 10
662 – 10 e. black and red 65 40

DESIGNS: 1 e. 50, Teaching; 2 e. 50, Nurse; 10 e. Mother.

1976. Pres. Kaunda's First Visit to Mozambique. Optd **PRESIDENTE KENNETH KAUNDA PREMEIRA VISITA 20/4/1976**.

663 **63** 2 e. multicoloured 15 10
664 3 e. 50 multicoloured . . . 25 15
665 6 e. multicoloured 50 30

69 Arrival of President Machel

70 Mozambique Stamp of 1876 and Emblem

1976. 1st Anniv of Independence. Mult.

666 50 c. Type **69** 10 10
667 1 e. Proclamation ceremony . . 10 10
668 2 e. 50 Signing ceremony . . . 15 10
669 7 e. 50 Soldiers on parade . . . 40 20
670 20 e. Independence flame . . . 1·10 80

1976. Stamp Centenary.

671 **70** 1 e. 50 multicoloured . . . 10 10
672 6 e. multicoloured 30 20

1976. "FACIM" Industrial Fair. Optd **FACIM 1976**.

673 **66** 2 e. 50 multicoloured . . . 30 15

72 Weapons and Flag

73 Thick-tailed Bush baby

1976. Army Day.

674 **72** 3 e. multicoloured 20 10

1977. Animals. Multicoloured.

675 50 c. Type **73** 15 10
676 1 e. Ratel (horiz) 15 10
677 1 e. 50 Temminck's ground pangolin 20 10
678 2 e. Steenbok (horiz) 20 10
679 2 e. 50 Diademed monkey . . 25 10
680 3 e. Hunting dog (horiz) . . . 25 10
681 4 e. Cheetah (horiz) 35 10
682 5 e. Spotted hyena 50 15
683 7 e. 50 Warthog (horiz) . . . 75 25
684 8 e. Hippopotamus (horiz) . . 80 30
685 10 e. White rhinoceros (horiz) 80 30
686 15 e. Sable antelope . . . . . 1·25 65

74 Congress Emblem

75 "Women" (child's drawing)

1977. 3rd Frelimo Congress, Maputo. Mult.

687 3 e. Type **74** 15 10
688 3 e. 50 Macheje Monument (site of 2nd Congress) (34 × 24 mm) 20 10
689 20 e. Maputo Monument (23 × 34 mm) . . . . 1·10 50

1977. Mozambique Women's Day.

690 **75** 5 e. multicoloured 25 10
691 15 e. multicoloured . . . 65 25

76 Labourer and Farmer

77 Crowd with Arms and Crops

1977. Labour Day.

692 **76** 5 e. multicoloured 25 10

1977. 2nd Anniv of Independence.

693 **77** 50 c. multicoloured . . . 10 10
694 1 e. 50 multicoloured . . . 10 10
695 3 e. multicoloured 15 10
696 15 e. multicoloured . . . 60 25

78 "Encephalartos ferox"

79 "Chariesthes bella"

1978. Stamp Day. Nature Protection. Mult.

697 1 e. Type **78** 10 10
698 10 e. Nyala 50 20

1978. Beetles. Multicoloured.

699 50 c. Type **79** 10 10
700 1 e. "Tragocephalus variegata" 10 10
701 1 e. 50 "Monochamus leuconotus" 10 10
702 3 e. "Prosopocera lactator" . 25 10
703 5 e. "Dinocephalus ornatus" . 40 10
704 10 e. "Tragiscoschema nigroscriptus" 60 20

80 Violet-crested Turaco

81 Mother and Child

1978. Birds. Multicoloured.

705 50 c. Type **80** 30 10
706 1 e. Lilac-breasted roller . . . 40 10
707 1 e. 50 Red-headed weaver . . 40 10
708 2 e. 50 Violet starling . . . 45 15
709 3 e. Peters's twin-spot 70 20
710 15 e. European bee eater . . . 1·75 40

1978. Global Eradication of Smallpox.

711 **81** 15 e. multicoloured . . . 45 25

82 "Crinum delagoense"

83 First Stamps of Mozambique and Canada

1978. Flowers. Multicoloured.

712 50 c. Type **82** 10 10
713 1 e. "Gloriosa superba" . . . 10 10
714 1 e. 50 "Eulophia speciosa" . . 10 10
715 3 e. "Erithrina humeana" . . . 15 10
716 5 e. "Astripomoea malvacea" . 40 15
717 10 e. "Kigelia africana" . . . 50 30

1978. "CAPEX '78" International Stamp Exhibition, Toronto.

718 **83** 15 e. multicoloured 45 25

84 Mozambique Flag

85 Boy with Books

1978. 3rd Anniv of Independence. Multicoloured.

719 1 e. Type **84** 10 10
720 1 e. 50 Coat of Arms 10 10
721 7 e. 50 People and Constitution 25 15
722 10 e. Band and National Anthem 30 20

1978. 11th World Youth Festival, Havana. Multicoloured.

724 2 e. 50 Type **85** 10 10
725 3 e. Soldiers 15 10
726 7 e. 50 Harvesting wheat . . . 25 20

86 Czechoslovakian 50 h. Stamp, 1919

1978. "PRAGA '78" International Stamp Exhibition.

727 **86** 15 e. blue, ochre and red . . 45 30

87 Football

1978. Stamp Day. Sports. Multicoloured.

729 50 c. Type **87** 10 10
730 1 e. 50 Putting the shot 10 10
731 3 e. Hurdling 15 10
732 7 e. 50 Basketball 35 20
733 12 e. 50 Swimming 45 35
734 25 e. Roller-skate hockey . . . 95 60

88 U.P.U. Emblem and Dove

1979. Membership of U.P.U.

735 **88** 20 e. multicoloured 70 45

89 Eduardo Mondlane

1979. 10th Death Anniv of Eduardo Mondlane (founder of FRELIMO). Multicoloured.

736 1 e. Soldier handing gourd to woman 10 10
737 3 e. FRELIMO soldiers . . . 15 10
738 7 e. 50 Children learning to write 30 20
739 12 e. 50 Type **89** 40 30

90 Shaded Silver

91 I.Y.C. Emblem

1979. Domestic Cats. Multicoloured.

740 50 c. Type **90** 10 10
741 1 e. 50 Manx cat 10 10
742 2 e. 50 British blue 15 10
743 3 e. Turkish cat 20 10
744 12 e. 50 Long-haired tabby . . 50 30
745 20 e. African wild cat 85 55

1979. Obligatory Tax. International Year of the Child.

746 **91** 50 c. red 15 10

92 Wrestling

1979. Olympic Games, Moscow (1980). Mult.

747 1 e. Type **92** 10 10
748 2 e. Running 10 10
749 3 e. Horse jumping 15 10
750 5 e. Canoeing 15 10
751 10 e. High jump 30 20
752 15 e. Archery 50 40

93 Flowers

1979. International Year of the Child. Multicoloured.

754 50 c. Type **93** 10 10
755 1 e. 50 Dancers 10 10
756 3 e. In the city 15 10
757 5 e. Working in the country . 15 10
758 7 e. 50 Houses 25 15
759 12 e. 50 Transport 90 35

94 Flight from Colonialism

1979. 4th Anniv of Independence. Multicoloured.

760 50 c. Type **94** 10 10
761 2 e. Eduardo Mondlane (founder of FRELIMO) 10 10
762 3 e. Armed struggle, death of Mondlane 15 10
763 7 e. 50 Final fight for liberation 25 15
764 15 e. President Samora Machel proclaims victory 45 35

95 "Scorpaena mossambica"

1979. Tropical Fish. Multicoloured.

766 50 c. Type **95** 10 10
767 1 e. 50 "Caraux speciosus" . . 15 10
768 2 e. 50 "Gobius inhaca" . . . 15 10
769 3 e. "Acanthurus lineatus" . . 15 10
770 10 e. "Gobuchthys lemayi" . . 40 20
771 12 e. 50 "Variola louti" . . . 60 30

96 Quartz

1979. Minerals. Multicoloured.

No.	Description	Mint	Used
772	1 e. Type **96**	10	10
773	1 e. 50 Beryl	10	10
774	2 e. 50 Magnetite	15	10
775	5 e. Tourmaline	30	10
776	10 e. Euxenite	60	20
777	20 e. Fluorite	1·10	45

97 Soldier handing out Guns

1979. 15th Anniv of Fight for Independence.

No.	Description	Mint	Used
778	**97** 5 e. multicoloured	25	15

98 Locomotive

1979. Early Locomotives. Designs depicting various locomotives.

No.	Description	Mint	Used
779	**98** 50 c. multicoloured	10	10
780	– 1 e. 50 multicoloured	15	10
781	– 3 e. multicoloured	30	10
782	– 7 e. 50 multicoloured	50	15
783	– 12 e. 50 multicoloured	80	25
784	– 15 e. multicoloured	90	35

99 Dalmatian

1979. Dogs. Multicoloured.

No.	Description	Mint	Used
785	50 c. Basenji (vert)	10	10
786	1 e. 50 Type **99**	15	10
787	3 e. Boxer	15	10
788	7 e. 50 Blue gascon pointer	35	15
789	12 e. 50 English cocker spaniel	60	25
790	15 e. Pointer	85	30

100 "Papilio nireus"

1979. Stamp Day. Butterflies. Multicoloured.

No.	Description	Mint	Used
791	1 e. Type **100**	10	10
792	1 e. 50 "Amauris ochlea"	10	10
793	2 e. 50 "Pinacopterix eriphia"	15	10
794	5 e. "Junonia hierta"	35	10
795	10 e. "Nephronia argia"	60	20
796	20 e. "Catacroptera cloanthe"	1·25	55

101 "Dermacentor circumguttatus cunhasilvai" and African Elephant

1980. Ticks. Multicoloured.

No.	Description	Mint	Used
797	50 c. Type **101**	20	10
798	1 e. 50 "Dermacentor rhinocerinos" and black rhinoceros	30	10
799	2 e. 50 "Amblyomma hebraeum" and giraffe	40	15
800	3 e. "Amblyomma pomposum" and eland	50	15
801	5 e. "Amblyomma theilerae" and cow	60	15
802	7 e. 50 "Amblyomma eburneum" and African buffalo	85	30

102 Ford "Hercules" Bus, 1950

1980. Road Transport. Multicoloured.

No.	Description	Mint	Used
803	50 c. Type **102**	10	10
804	1 e. 50 Scania "Marco-polo" bus, 1978	10	10
805	3 e. Bussing Nag Bus, 1936	15	10
806	5 e. Ikarus articulated bus, 1978	20	10
807	7 e. 50 Ford Taxi, 1929	40	15
808	12 e. 50 Fiat "131" Taxi, 1978	65	20

103 Soldier and Map of Southern Africa

1980. Zimbabwe Independence.

No.	Description	Mint	Used
809	**103** 10 e. blue and brown	40	15

104 Marx, Engels and Lenin

1980. International Workers' Day.

No.	Description	Mint	Used
810	**104** 10 e. multicoloured	40	15

105 "Market" (Moises Simbine)

1980. "London 1980" International Stamp Exhibition. Multicoloured.

No.	Description	Mint	Used
811	50 c. "Heads" (Malangatana)	10	10
812	1 e. 50 Type **105**	10	10
813	3 e. "Heads with Helmets" (Malangatana)	15	10
814	5 e. "Women with Goods" (Machiana)	20	10
815	7 e. 50 "Crowd with Masks" (Malangatana)	25	15
816	12 e. 50 "Man and Woman with Spear" (Mankeu)	50	25

106 Telephone

1980. World Telecommunications Day.

No.	Description	Mint	Used
817	**106** 15 e. multicoloured	60	25

MINIMUM PRICE

The minimum price quoted is 10p which represents a handling charge rather than a basis for valuing common stamps. For further notes about prices, see introductory pages.

107 Mueda Massacre **108** Crowd waving Tools

1980. 20th Anniv of Mueda Massacre.

No.	Description	Mint	Used
818	**107** 15 e. green, brown and red	60	25

1980. 5th Anniv of Independence.

No.	Description	Mint	Used
819	– 1 e. black and red	10	10
820	**108** 2 e. multicoloured	10	10
821	– 3 e. multicoloured	15	10
822	– 4 e. multicoloured	20	10
823	– 5 e. black, yellow and red	20	10
824	– 10 e. multicoloured	40	15

DESIGNS—As T **108**: 1 e. Crowd, doctor tending patient, soldier and workers tilling land; 3 e. Crowd with flags and tools; 4 e. Stylised figures raising right hand; 5 e. Hand grasping flags, book and plants; 10 e. Figures carrying banners each with year date. 55 × 37 mm: 30 e. Soldiers.

109 Gymnastics

1980. Olympic Games, Moscow. Multicoloured.

No.	Description	Mint	Used
826	50 c. Type **109**	10	10
827	1 e. 50 Football	10	10
828	2 e. 50 Running	10	10
829	3 e. Volleyball	20	10
830	10 e. Cycling	40	15
831	12 e. 50 Boxing	45	20

110 Narina Trogon

1980. Birds. Multicoloured.

No.	Description	Mint	Used
832	1 m. Type **110**	30	10
833	1 m. 50 South African crowned crane	35	10
834	2 m. 50 Bare-throated francolin	40	10
835	5 m. Ostrich	75	20
836	7 m. 50 Spur-winged goose	85	20
837	12 m. 50 African fish eagle	1·00	30

111 Family and Census Officer

1980. First General Census.

No.	Description	Mint	Used
838	**111** 3 m. 50 multicoloured	25	10

112 Animals fleeing from Fire

1980. Campaign against Bush Fires.

No.	Description	Mint	Used
839	**112** 3 m. 50 multicoloured	25	10

113 Common Harp

1980. Stamp Day. Shells. Multicoloured.

No.	Description	Mint	Used
840	1 m. Type **113**	10	10
841	1 m. 50 Arthritic spider conch	15	10
842	2 m. 50 Venus comb murex	20	10
843	5 m. Clear sundial	40	15
844	7 m. 50 Ramose murex	50	20
845	12 m. 50 Diana conch	85	35

114 Pres. Machel, Electricity Pylons, Aircraft and Lorry

1981. "Decade for Victory over Underdevelopment".

No.	Description	Mint	Used
846	**114** 3 m. 50 blue and red	1·00	25
847	– 7 m. 50 brown and green	25	15
848	– 12 m. 50 mauve and blue	50	30

DESIGNS: 7 m. 50, Pres. Machel and armed forces on parade; 12 m. 50, Pres. Machel and classroom scenes.

115 Footballer and Athletic de Bilbao Stadium

1981. World Cup Football Championships, Spain (1982). Multicoloured.

No.	Description	Mint	Used
849	1 m. Type **115**	10	10
850	1 m. 50 Valencia, C.F.	10	10
851	2 m. 50 Oviedo C.F.	10	10
852	5 m. R. Betis Balompie	20	10
853	7 m. 50 Real Zaragoza	25	15
854	12 m. 50 R.C.D. Espanol	50	25

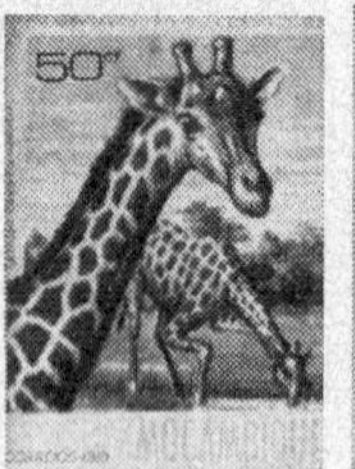

116 Giraffe **117** Chitende

1981. Protected Animals. Multicoloured.

No.	Description	Mint	Used
856	50 c. Type **116**	10	10
857	1 m. 50 Topi	10	10
858	2 m.50 Aardvark	10	10
859	3 m. African python	10	10
860	5 m. Loggerhead turtle	20	15
861	10 m. Marabou stork	70	30
862	12 m. 50 Saddle-bill stork	95	35
863	15 m. Kori bustard	1·25	45

1981. Musical Instruments. Multicoloured.

No.	Description	Mint	Used
864	50 c. Type **117**	10	10
865	2 m. Pankwe (horiz)	10	10
866	2 m. 50 Kanyembe	10	10
867	7 m. Nyanga (horiz)	30	20
868	10 m. Likuti and M'Petheni (horiz)	70	25

118 Disabled Persons making Baskets

1981. International Year of Disabled People.

No.	Description	Mint	Used
869	**118** 5 m. multicoloured	25	15

119 De Havilland Dragon Rapide

1981. Air. Mozambique Aviation History. Mult.

No.	Description	Mint	Used
870	50 c. Type **119**	10	10
871	1 m. 50 Junkers Ju 52/3m	10	10
872	3 m. Lockheed Super Electra	20	15
873	7 m. 50 De Havilland Dove	35	30
874	10 m. Douglas DC-3	50	35
875	12 m. 50 Fokker Friendship	75	50

120 Controlled Killing, Marromeu

1981. World Hunting Exhibition, Plovdiv. Mult.
876 2 m. Type **120** 30 15
877 5 m. Traditional hunting Cheringoma 20 15
878 6 m. Tourist hunting, Save . . 40 30
879 7 m. 60 Marksmanship Gorongosa 40 20
880 12 m. 50 African elephants, Gorongosa . . . . 1·25 60
881 20 m. Trap, Cabo Delgado . . 80 50

121 50 Centavos Coin **122** Sunflower

1981. 1st Anniv of New Currency. Mult.
883 50 c. Type **121** 10 10
884 1 m. One metical coin 10 10
885 2 m. 50 Two meticals 50 coin . 10 10
886 5 m. Five meticals coin . . . 20 15
887 10 m. Ten meticals coin . . . 50 25
888 20 m. Twenty meticals coin . . 1·10 55

1981. Agricultural Resources.
890 **122** 50 c. orange and red . . . 10 10
891 – 1 m. black and red 10 10
892 – 1 m. 50 blue and red . . . 10 10
893 – 2 m. 50 yellow and red . . 10 10
894 – 3 m. 50 green and red . . . 15 10
895 – 4 m. 50 grey and red . . . 15 10
896 – 10 m. blue and red 40 15
897 – 12 m. 50 brown and red . . 50 20
898 – 15 m. brown and red . . . 60 25
899 – 25 m. green and red . . . 1·10 40
900 – 40 m. orange and red . . . 1·60 60
901 – 60 m. brown and red . . . 2·25 1·00
DESIGNS: 1 m. Cotton; 1 m. 50, Sisal; 2 m. 50, Cashew; 3 m. 50, Tea; 4 m. 50, Sugar cane; 10 m. Castor oil; 12 m. 50, Coconut; 15 m. Tobacco; 25 m. Rice; 40 m. Maize; 60 m. Groundnut.

123 Archaeological Excavation, Manyikeni

1981. Archaeological Excavation. Mult.
902 1 m. Type **123** 10 10
903 1 m. 50 Hand-axe (Massingir Dam) 10 10
904 2 m. 50 Ninth century bowl (Chibuene) 10 10
905 7 m. 50 Ninth century pot (Chibuene) 30 20
906 12 m. 50 Gold beads (Manyikeni) 50 30
907 20 m. Gong (Manyikeni) . . . 80 50

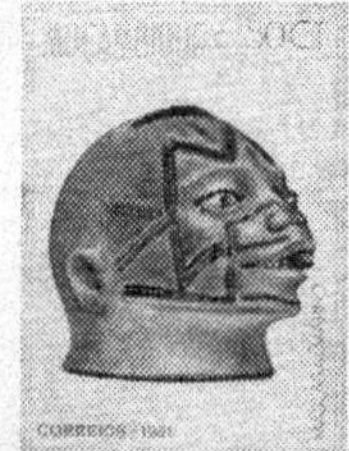
124 Mapiko Mask

1981. Sculptures. Multicoloured.
908 50 c. Type **124** 10 10
909 1 m. Woman who suffers . . . 10 10
910 2 m. 50 Woman with a child . 10 10
911 3 m. 50 The man who makes fire 15 10
912 5 m. Chietane 20 15
913 12 m. 50 Chietane (different) 70 30

125 Broken Loaf on Globe

1981. World Food Day.
914 **125** 10 m. multicoloured . . . 45 25

126 Tanker "Matchedje"

1981. Mozambique Ships. Multicoloured.
915 50 c. Type **126** 10 10
916 1 m. 50 Tug "Macuti" . . . 10 10
917 3 m. Trawler "Vega 7" . . . 20 10
918 5 m. Freighter "Linde" . . . 30 20
919 7 m. 50 Freighter "Pemba" . 50 30
920 12 m. 50 Dredger "Rovuma" . 95 55

127 "Portunus pelagicus"

1981. Crustaceans. Multicoloured.
921 50 c. Type **127** 10 10
922 1 m. 50 "Scylla serrata" . . . 10 10
923 3 m. "Penaeus indicus" . . . 15 10
924 7 m. 50 "Palinurus delagoae" . 35 20
925 12 m. 50 "Lysiosquilla maculata" 55 35
926 15 m. "Panulirus ornatus" . . 80 45

128 "Hypoxis multiceps" **129** Telex Tape, Telephone and Globe

1981. Flowers. Multicoloured.
927 1 m. Type **128** 10 10
928 1 m. 50 "Pelargonium luridun" 10 10
929 2 m. 50 "Caralluma melanathera" 10 10
930 7 m. 50 "Ansellia gigantea" . 35 20
931 12 m. 50 "Stapelia leendertsiae" 60 35
932 25 m. "Adenium multiflorum" 1·25 70

1982. 1st Anniv of Mozambique Post and Telecommunications. Multicoloured.
933 6 m. Type **129** 35 20
934 15 m. Winged envelope and envelope forming railway wagon 75 75

130 Diagram of Petrol Engine

1982. Fuel Saving. Multicoloured.
935 5 m. Type **130** 30 15
936 7 m. 50 Speeding car 45 25
937 10 m. Loaded truck 60 35

131 "Pelamis platurus"

1982. Reptiles. Multicoloured.
938 50 c. Type **131** 10 10
939 1 m. 50 "Naja mossambica mossambica" 10 10
940 3 m. "Thelotornis capensis mossambica" 20 15
941 6 m. "Dendroaspis polylepis polylepis" 35 25
942 15 m. "Dispholidus typus" . 80 50
943 20 m. "Bitis arietans arietans" 1·25 75

132 Dr. Robert Koch, Bacillus and X-Ray

1982. Centenary of Discovery of Tubercle Bacillus.
944 **132** 20 m. multicoloured . . . 1·40 75

133 Telephone Line **134** Player with Ball

1982. International Telecommunications Union. Plenipotentiary Conference.
945 **133** 20 m. multicoloured . . . 1·00 75

1982. World Cup Football Championship, Spain. Multicoloured.
946 1 m. 50 Type **134** 10 10
947 3 m. 50 Player heading ball . . 25 15
948 7 m. Two players fighting for ball 40 20
949 10 m. Player receiving ball . . 60 30
950 20 m. Goalkeeper . . . . . . 1·00 75

135 Political Rally **137** "Vangueria infausta"

1982. 25th Anniv of FRELIMO. Multicoloured.
953 4 m. Type **135** 25 15
954 8 m. Agriculture 45 25
955 12 m. Marching workers . . . 70 35

1982. Fruits. Multicoloured.
956 1 m. Type **137** 10 10
957 2 m. "Mimusops caffra" . . . 10 10
958 4 m. "Sclerocarya caffra" . . 25 15
959 8 m. "Strychnos spinosa" . . 45 25
960 12 m. "Salacia kraussi" . . . 70 40
961 32 m. "Trichilia emetica" . . . 1·50 85

138 "Sputnik I" **139** Vigilantes

1982. 25th Anniv of First Artificial Satellite. Multicoloured.
962 1 m. Type **138** 10 10
963 2 m. First manned space flight 10 10
964 4 m. First walk in space . . . 25 15
965 8 m. First manned flight to the moon 45 25
966 16 m. "Soyuz"–"Apollo" mission . . . . 1·00 70
967 20 m. "Intercosmos" rocket . . 1·25 70

1982. People's Surveillance Day.
968 **139** 4 m. multicoloured 25 15

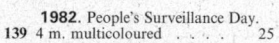

140 Caique **141** "Ophiomostix venosa"

1982. Traditional Boats. Multicoloured.
969 1 m. Type **140** 10 10
970 2 m. Machua 15 10
971 4 m. Calaua (horiz) 30 15
972 8 m. Chitatarro (horiz) 60 25
973 12 m. Cangaia (horiz) 80 35
974 16 m. Chata (horiz) . . . . . 1·40 60

1982. Starfishes and Sea Urchins. Multicoloured.
975 1 m. Type **141** 10 10
976 2 m. "Protoreaster lincki" . . . 10 10
977 4 m. "Tropiometra carinata" . 15 10
978 8 m. "Holothuria scabra" . . 35 20
979 12 m. "Prionocidaris baculosa" 60 35
980 16 m. "Colobocentrotus atnatus" 80 40

142 Soldiers defending Mozambique

1983. 4th Frelimo Party Congress. Multicoloured.
981 4 m. Type **142** 15 10
982 8 m. Crowd waving voting papers 30 20
983 16 m. Agriculture, industry and education 65 40

143 "Codium duthierae"

1983. Seaweeds. Multicoloured.
984 1 m. Type **143** 10 10
985 2 m. "Halimeda cunata" . . . 10 10
986 4 m. "Dictyota liturata" . . . 15 10
987 8 m. "Endorachne binghamiae" 40 20
988 12 m. "Laurencia flexuosa" . . 60 30
989 20 m. "Acrosorium sp." . . . 1·00 55

144 Diving and Swimming

1983. Olympic Games, Los Angeles (1st issue). Multicoloured.
990 1 m. Type **144** 10 10
991 2 m. Boxing 10 10
992 4 m. Basketball 20 10
993 8 m. Handball 35 20
994 12 m. Volleyball 55 30
995 16 m. Running 65 40
996 20 m. Yachting . . . . 1·00 65
See also Nos. 1029/34.

145 Mallet Type Locomotive

1983. Steam Locomotives. Multicoloured.
998 1 m. Type **145** 10 10
999 2 m. Baldwin Series "200" . . 15 10
1000 4 m. Henschel Series "1600" . 30 15
1001 8 m. Baldwin Series "05" . . 60 25
1002 16 m. Henschel Garratt type 1·10 50
1003 32 m. Henschel Series "50" . 2·25 1·00

146 O.A.U. Emblem

1983. 20th Anniv of Organization of African Unity.
1004 **146** 4 m. multicoloured . . . 20 15

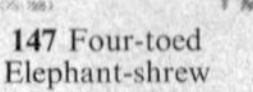

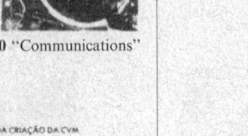

147 Four-toed Elephant-shrew
150 "Communications"

148 Aiding Flood Victims

1983. Mozambique Mammals. Multicoloured.

No.	Type	Description	Unused	Used
1005		1 m. Type **147**	10	10
1006		2 m. Four-striped grass mouse	15	10
1007		4 m. Vincent's bush squirrel	25	15
1008		8 m. Hottentot mole-rat	50	25
1009		12 m. Natal red hare	75	40
1010		16 m. Straw-coloured fruit bat	95	50

1983. 2nd Anniv of Mozambique Red Cross. Multicoloured.

No.	Type	Description	Unused	Used
1011		4 m. Type **148**	20	10
1012		8 m. Red Cross lorry	40	20
1013		16 m. First aid demonstration	75	40
1014		32 m. Agricultural worker performing first aid	1·50	75

1983. World Communications Year.

No.	Type	Description	Unused	Used
1016	**150**	8 m. multicoloured	60	25

151 Line Fishing

1983. Fishery Resources. Multicoloured.

No.	Type	Description	Unused	Used
1017		50 c. Type **151**	10	10
1018		2 m. Chifonho (basket trap)	10	10
1019		4 m. Spear fishing	20	15
1020		8 m. Gamboa (fence trap)	40	25
1021		16 m. Mono (basket trap)	1·00	40
1022		20 m. Lema (basket trap)	1·25	55

152 Kudu Horn
153 Swimming

1983. Stamp Day. Multicoloured.

No.	Type	Description	Unused	Used
1023		50 c. Type **152**	10	10
1024		1 m. Drum communication	10	10
1025		4 m. Postal runners	20	15
1026		8 m. Mail canoe	40	40
1027		16 m. Mail van	75	40
1028		20 m. Mail train	1·75	1·00

1984. Olympic Games, Los Angeles (2nd issue). Multicoloured.

No.	Type	Description	Unused	Used
1029		50 c. Type **153**	10	10
1030		4 m. Football	20	10
1031		8 m. Hurdling	35	20
1032		16 m. Basketball	90	50
1033		32 m. Handball	1·50	80
1034		60 m. Boxing	2·50	1·50

154 "Trichilia emetica"

1984. Indigenous Trees. Multicoloured.

No.	Type	Description	Unused	Used
1035		50 c. Type **154**	10	10
1036		2 m. "Brachystegia spiciformis"	10	10
1037		4 m. "Androstachys johnsonii"	20	10
1038		8 m. "Pterocarpus angolensis"	35	20
1039		16 m. "Milletia stuhlmannii"	80	40
1040		50 m. "Dalbergia melanoxylon"	2·25	1·40

155 Dove with Olive Sprig

1984. Nkomati South Africa–Mozambique Non-aggression Pact.

No.	Type	Description	Unused	Used
1041	**155**	4 m. multicoloured	25	10

156 State Arms

1984. Emblems of the Republic. Multicoloured.

No.	Type	Description	Unused	Used
1042		4 m. Type **156**	20	10
1043		8 m. State Flag	40	20

157 Makway Dance

1984. "Lubrapex '84" Portuguese–Brazilian Stamp Exhibition, Lisbon. Traditional Mozambican dances. Multicoloured.

No.	Type	Description	Unused	Used
1044		4 m. Type **157**	20	10
1045		8 m. Mapiko dance	40	20
1046		16 m. Wadjaba dance	1·10	50

158 Nampula Museum and Statuette of Woman with Water Jug

1984. Museums. Multicoloured.

No.	Type	Description	Unused	Used
1047		50 c. Type **158**	10	10
1048		4 m. Natural History Museum and secretary bird	45	10
1049		8 m. Revolution Museum and soldier carrying wounded comrade	35	20
1050		16 m. Colonial History Museum and cannon	65	40
1051		20 m. National Numismatic Museum and coins	1·00	65
1052		30 m. St. Paul's Palace and antique chair	1·25	95

159 "Alestes imberi"

1984. Fishes. Multicoloured.

No.	Type	Description	Unused	Used
1053		50 c. Type **159**	10	10
1054		4 m. "Labeo congoro"	20	10
1055		12 m. "Synodontis zambezensis"	60	35
1056		16 m. "Notobranchius rachovii"	75	50
1057		40 m. "Barbus paludinosus"	2·00	1·25
1058		60 m. "Barilius zambezensis"	2·75	1·75

160 Badge and Laurels
162 Knife and Club

161 Rural Landscape and Emblem

1984. International Fair, Maputo.

No.	Type	Description	Unused	Used
1059	**160**	16 m. multicoloured	70	50

1984. 20th Anniv of African Development Bank.

No.	Type	Description	Unused	Used
1060	**161**	4 m. multicoloured	30	10

1984. Traditional Weapons. Multicoloured.

No.	Type	Description	Unused	Used
1061		50 c. Type **162**	10	10
1062		4 m. Axes	20	10
1063		8 m. Spear and shield	35	15
1064		16 m. Bow and arrow	75	35
1065		32 m. Rifle	1·50	95
1066		50 m. Assegai and arrow	2·25	1·60

163 Workers and Emblem

1984. 1st Anniv of Organization of Mozambican Workers.

No.	Type	Description	Unused	Used
1067	**163**	4 m. multicoloured	20	10

164 Barue 1902 Postmark

1984. Stamp Day. Postmarks. Multicoloured.

No.	Type	Description	Unused	Used
1068		4 m. Type **164**	15	10
1069		8 m. Zumbo postmark and King Carlos 15 r. Mozambique "key type" stamp	35	20
1070		12 m. Mozambique Company postmark and 1935 airmail stamp	55	30
1071		16 m. Macequece postmark and 1937 2 e. Mozambique Company stamp	70	40

165 Keeper and Hive
166 Shot-putter and Emblem

1985. Bee-keeping. Multicoloured.

No.	Type	Description	Unused	Used
1072		4 m. Type **165**	15	10
1073		8 m. Worker bee	45	20
1074		16 m. Drone	1·00	40
1075		20 m. Queen bee	1·40	60

1985. "Olymphilex 85" Olympic Stamps Exhibition, Lausanne.

No.	Type	Description	Unused	Used
1076	**166**	16 m. blue, black & red	75	35

167 Forecasting Equipment and Desert

1985. World Meteorology Day.

No.	Type	Description	Unused	Used
1077	**167**	4 m. multicoloured	35	10

168 Map

1985. 5th Anniv of Southern African Development Co-ordination Conference. Multicoloured.

No.	Type	Description	Unused	Used
1078		4 m. Type **168**	15	10
1079		8 m. Map and pylon	45	20
1080		16 m. Industry and transport	1·00	50
1081		32 m. Member states' flags	1·60	95

169 Battle of Mujenga, 1896

1985. 10th Anniv of Independence. Mult.

No.	Type	Description	Unused	Used
1082		1 m. Type **169**	10	10
1083		4 m. Attack on Barue by Macombe, 1917	25	10
1084		8 m. Attack on Massangano, 1868	55	20
1085		16 m. Battle of Marracuene, 1895, and Gungunhana	1·25	50

170 U.N. Building, New York and Flag

1985. 40th Anniv of U.N.O.

No.	Type	Description	Unused	Used
1086	**170**	16 m. multicoloured	80	50

171 Mathacuzana

1985. Traditional Games and Sports. Multicoloured.

No.	Type	Description	Unused	Used
1087		50 c. Type **171**	10	10
1088		4 m. Mudzobo	20	10
1089		8 m. Muravarava (board game)	40	20
1090		16 m. N'tshuwa	90	50

172 "Rana angolensis"

1985. Frogs and Toads. Multicoloured.

No.	Type	Description	Unused	Used
1091		50 c. Type **172**	10	10
1092		1 m. "Hyperolius pictus"	10	10
1093		4 m. "Ptychadena porosissima"	15	10
1094		8 m. "Afrixalus formasinii"	50	20
1095		16 m. "Bufo regularis"	95	50
1096		32 m. "Hyperolius marmoratus"	2·00	95

HAVE YOU READ THE NOTES AT THE BEGINNING OF THIS CATALOGUE?

These often provide the answers to the enquiries we receive.

174 "Aloe ferox"   176 Comet and "Giotto" Space Probe

175 Mozambique Company, 1918 10 c. Stamp

1985. Medicinal Plants. Multicoloured.
1099 50 c. Type **174** 10 10
1100 1 m. "Boophone disticha" . . 10 10
1101 3 m. 50 "Gloriosa superba" . 15 10
1102 4 m. "Cotyledon orbiculata" 15 10
1103 8 m. "Homeria breyniana" . 55 20
1104 50 m. "Haemanthus coccineus" 3·00 1·50

1985. Stamp Day. Multicoloured.
1105 1 m. Type **175** 10 10
1106 4 m. Nyassa Co. 1911 25 r. stamp 15 10
1107 8 m. Mozambique Co. 1918 ½ c. stamp 50 20
1108 16 m. Nyassa Co. 1924 1 c. Postage Due stamp . . . . 1·10 50

1986. Appearance of Halley's Comet.
1109 **176** 4 m. blue & light blue . . 20 10
1110 – 8 m. violet & light violet 50 20
1111 – 16 m. multicoloured . . 95 50
1112 – 30 m. multicoloured . . 2·00 95
DESIGNS: 8 m. Comet orbits; 16 m. Small and large telescopes, comet and space probe; 30 m. Comet, stars and globe.

177 Vicente

1986. World Cup Football Championship, Mexico. Multicoloured.
1113 3 m. Type **177** 15 10
1114 4 m. Coluna 20 10
1115 8 m. Costa Pereira 40 20
1116 12 m. Hilario 65 35
1117 16 m. Matateu 95 50
1118 50 m. Eusebio . . . . 3·00 1·60

178 Dove and Emblem   179 "Amanita muscaria"

1986. International Peace Year.
1119 **178** 16 m. multicoloured . . 85 45

1986. Fungi. Multicoloured.
1120 4 m. Type **179** 50 20
1121 8 m. "Lactarius deliciosus" . 95 30
1122 16 m. "Amanita phaloides" . 2·00 65
1123 30 m. "Tricholoma nudum" . 4·25 1·25

181 Spiky Style

1986. Women's Hairstyles. Multicoloured.
1125 1 m. Type **181** 10 10
1126 4 m. Beaded plaits 25 10
1127 8 m. Plaited tightly to head . 50 20
1128 16 m. Plaited tightly to head with ponytail . . . . . . 1·25 55

182 Dugong

1986. Marine Mammals. Multicoloured.
1129 1 m. Type **182** 10 10
1130 8 m. Common dolphin . . . 35 20
1131 16 m. "Neobalena marginata" 1·25 50
1132 50 f. Fin whale . . . . . . 3·50 1·75

183 Children Studying

1986. 1st Anniv of Continuadores Youth Organization.
1133 **183** 4 m. multicoloured . . . 30 15

184 50 m. Notes

1986. Savings. Multicoloured.
1134 4 m. Type **184** 25 10
1135 8 m. 100 m. notes 50 20
1136 16 m. 500 m. notes . . . . 1·40 50
1137 30 m. 1000 m. notes . . . 2·50 1·25

185 Quelimane Post Office

1986. Stamp Day. Post Offices. Multicoloured.
1138 3 m. Type **185** 20 10
1139 4 m. Maputo 30 10
1140 8 m. Beira 65 20
1141 16 m. Nampula . . . . . . 1·40 50

186 Pyrite

1987. Minerals. Multicoloured.
1142 4 m. Type **186** 30 10
1143 8 m. Emerald 60 20
1144 12 m. Agate 85 40
1145 16 m. Malachite . . . . . . 1·40 50
1146 30 m. Garnet . . . . 2·25 1·25
1147 50 m. Amethyst . . . . . . 3·75 1·75

187 Crowd beneath Flag

1987. 10th Anniv of Mozambique Liberation Front.
1148 **187** 4 m. multicoloured . . . 30 15

188 Little Libombos Dam

1987.
1149 **188** 16 m. multicoloured . . . 1·40 60

189 Children being Vaccinated

1987. World Health Day. Vaccination Campaign.
1150 **189** 50 m. multicoloured . . . 1·60 1·50

190 Common Grenadier   191 Football

1987. Birds. Multicoloured.
1151 3 m. Type **190** 20 10
1152 4 m. Woodland kingfisher . . 25 15
1153 8 m. White-fronted bee eater . 50 30
1154 12 m. Lesser seedcracker . . 75 45
1155 16 m. Broad-billed roller . . 1·00 65
1156 30 m. Neergaard's sunbird . . 2·00 1·10

1987. Olympic Games, Seoul (1988) (1st issue). Multicoloured.
1157 12 m. 50, Type **191** 10 10
1158 25 m. Running 20 10
1159 50 m. Handball 40 20
1160 75 m. Chess . . . . 1·25 30
1161 100 m. Basketball . . . . . 1·25 35
1162 200 m. Swimming . . . . . 1·75 65
See also Nos. 1176/81.

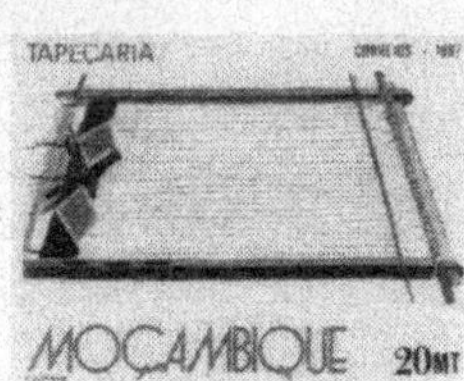

193 Work on Loom

1987. Weaving. Multicoloured.
1164 20 m. Type **193** 15 10
1165 40 m. Triangle and diamond design 40 10
1166 80 m. "Eye" design 70 20
1167 200 m. Red carpet . . . . . 1·75 60

194 Piper "Navajo"

1987. Air. History of Aviation in Mozambique. Multicoloured.
1168 20 m. Type **194** 15 10
1169 40 m. De Havilland Hornet moth 25 10
1170 80 m. Boeing 737 . . . . . 50 20
1171 120 m. Beechcraft King Air . 75 20
1172 160 m. Piper Aztec . . . . 1·00 35
1173 320 m. Douglas DC-10 . . . 2·00 75

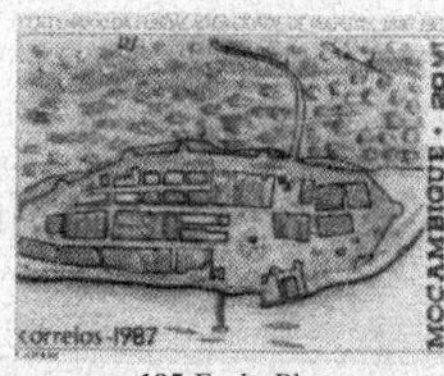

195 Early Plan

1987. Centenary of Maputo as City.
1174 **195** 20 m. multicoloured . . . 20 15

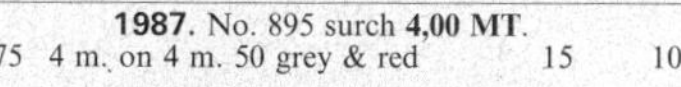

1987. No. 895 surch **4,00 MT**.
1175 4 m. on 4 m. 50 grey & red 15 10

197 Javelin throwing   198 "Boophane disticha"

1988. Olympic Games, Seoul (2nd issue). Mult.
1176 10 m. Type **197** 10 10
1177 20 m. Baseball 10 10
1178 40 m. Boxing 10 10
1179 80 m. Hockey 40 10
1180 100 m. Gymnastics 50 15
1181 400 m. Cycling . . . . 1·50 75

1988. Flowers. Multicoloured.
1182 10 m. "Heamanthus nelsonii" 10 10
1183 20 m. "Crinum polyphyllum" 15 10
1184 40 m. Type **198** 15 10
1185 80 m. "Cyrtanthus contractus" 35 10
1186 100 m. "Nerine angustifolia" 50 15
1187 400 m. "Cyrtanthus galpinnii" 1·75 75

199 Man refusing Cigarette

1988. 40th Anniv of W.H.O. Anti-smoking Campaign.
1188 **199** 20 m. multicoloured . . 20 10

201 Mat

1988. Basketry. Multicoloured.
1190 20 m. Type **201** 10 10
1191 25 m. Basket with lid 10 10
1192 80 m. Basket with handle . . 20 10
1193 100 m. Fan 30 10
1194 400 m. Dish . . . . 1·25 60
1195 500 m. Conical basket . . . 1·60 85

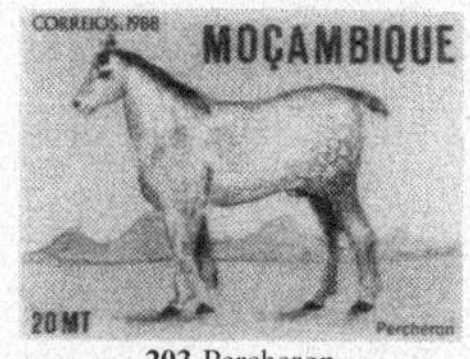

203 Percheron

1988. Horses. Multicoloured.
1197 20 m. Type **203** 15 10
1198 40 m. Arab 20 10
1199 80 m. Pure blood 40 10
1200 100 m. Pony 50 15

204 Machel

1988. 2nd Death Anniv of Samora Machel (President 1975–86).
1201 **204** 20 m. multicoloured . . 15 10

205 Inhambane

1988. Ports. Multicoloured.

1202 20 m. Type **205** 15 10
1203 50 m. Quelimane (vert) 10 10
1204 75 m. Pemba 15 10
1205 100 m. Beira 35 10
1206 250 m. Nacala (vert) 65 35
1207 500 m. Maputo 1·40 70

206 Mobile Post Office

1988. Stamp Day. Multicoloured.

1208 20 m. Type **206** 10 10
1209 40 m. Posting box (vert) 15 10

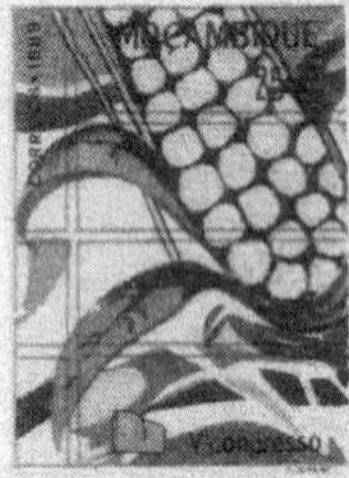

207 Maize **208** Mondlane

1989. 5th FRELIMO Congress. Multicoloured.

1210 25 m. Type **207** 10 10
1211 50 m. Hoe 10 10
1212 75 m. Abstract 10 10
1213 100 m. Cogwheels 20 10
1214 250 m. Right-half of cogwheel 50 25

Nos. 1210/14 were printed together, se-tenant, forming a composite design.

1989. 20th Anniv of Assassination of Pres. Mondlane.

1215 **208** 25 m. black, gold & red 15 10

209 "Storming the Bastille" (Thevenin)

1989. Bicentenary of French Revolution. Mult.

1216 100 m. Type **209** 25 10
1217 250 m. "Liberty guiding the People" (Delacroix) 60 35

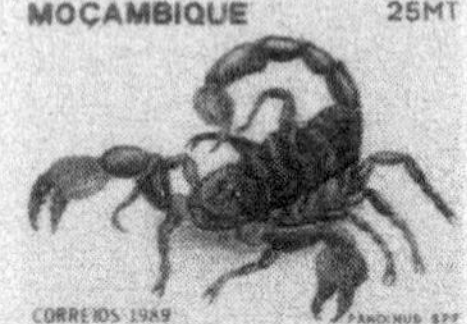
210 "Pandinus sp."

1989. Venomous Animals. Multicoloured.

1219 25 m. Type **210** 10 10
1220 50 m. Egyptian cobra 10 10
1221 75 m. "Bombus sp." (bee) 15 10
1222 100 m. "Paraphysa sp." (spider) 25 10
1223 250 m. Marble cone 90 40
1224 500 m. Devil firefish 1·40 70

211 "Acropora pulchra"

1989. Corals. Multicoloured.

1225 25 m. Type **211** 10 10
1226 50 m. "Eunicella papilosa" 15 10
1227 100 m. "Dendrophyla migrantus" 30 10
1228 250 m. "Favia fragum" 50 35

212 Footballers **213** Macuti Lighthouse

1989. World Cup Football Championship, Italy (1990). Designs showing various footballing scenes.

1229 **212** 30 m. multicoloured 10 10
1230 – 60 m. multicoloured 15 10
1231 – 125 m. multicoloured 30 10
1232 – 200 m. multicoloured 50 25
1233 – 250 m. multicoloured 65 35
1234 – 500 m. multicoloured 1·50 70

1989. Lighthouses. Multicoloured.

1235 30 m. Type **213** 15 10
1236 60 m. Pinda 15 10
1237 125 m. Cape Delgado 30 10
1238 200 m. Goa Island 60 25
1239 250 m. Caldeira Point 80 35
1240 500 m. Vilhena 1·50 70

214 Bracelet

1989. Silver Filigree Work.

1241 **214** 30 m. grey, red & black 10 10
1242 – 60 m. grey, blue & black 15 10
1243 – 125 m. grey, red & black 25 10
1244 – 200 m. grey, bl & black 40 25
1245 – 250 m. grey, pur & blk 55 35
1246 – 500 m. grey, grn & blk 1·25 70

DESIGNS: 60 m. Flower belt; 125 m. Necklace; 200 m. Casket; 250 m. Spoons; 500 m. Butterfly.

215 Flag and Soldiers **216** Rain Gauge

1989. 25th Anniv of Fight for Independence.

1247 **215** 30 m. multicoloured 15 10

1989. Meteorological Instruments. Multicoloured.

1248 30 m. Type **216** 10 10
1249 60 m. Radar graph 15 10
1250 125 m. Sheltered measuring instruments 30 10
1251 200 m. Computer terminal 55 25

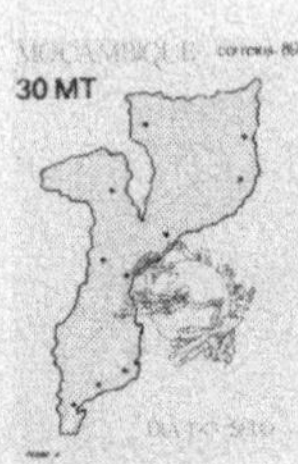
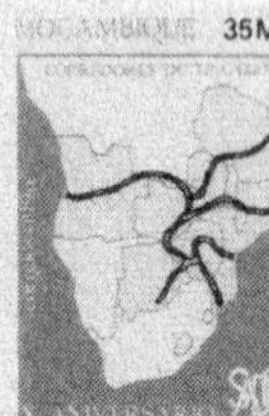
218 Map and U.P.U. Emblem **219** Railway Map

1989. Stamp Day.

1253 **218** 30 m. multicoloured 15 10
1254 – 60 m. black, green & red 15 10

DESIGN: 60 m. Map and Mozambique postal emblem.

1990. 10th Anniv of Southern Africa Development Co-ordination Conference.

1255 **219** 35 m. multicoloured 20 10

MINIMUM PRICE

The minimum price quoted is 10p which represents a handling charge rather than a basis for valuing common stamps. For further notes about prices, see introductory pages.

220 Cloth and Woman wearing Dress

1990. Traditional Dresses. Designs showing women wearing different dresses and details of cloth used.

1256 **220** 42 m. multicoloured 10 10
1257 – 90 m. multicoloured 15 10
1258 – 150 m. multicoloured 20 10
1259 – 200 m. multicoloured 25 15
1260 – 400 m. multicoloured 55 40
1261 – 500 m. multicoloured 65 50

221 Sena Fortress, Sofala

1990. Fortresses.

1262 **221** 45 m. blue and black 10 10
1263 – 90 m. blue and black 15 10
1264 – 150 m. multicoloured 20 10
1265 – 200 m. multicoloured 30 15
1266 – 400 m. red and black 55 40
1267 – 500 m. red and black 70 40

DESIGNS: 90 m. Sto. Antonio, Ibo Island; 150 m. S. Sebastiao, Mozambique Island; 200 m. S. Caetano, Sofala; 400 m. Our Lady of Conception, Maputo; 500 m. S. Luis, Tete.

223 Obverse and Reverse of 50 m. Coin

1990. 15th Anniv of Bank of Mozambique.

1269 **223** 100 m. multicoloured 20 15

224 Statue of Eduardo Mondlane (founder of FRELIMO)

1990. 15th Anniv of Independence. Mult.

1270 42 m. 50 Type **224** 10 10
1271 150 m. Statue of Samora Machel (President, 1975–86) 25 15

225 White Rhinoceros

1990. Endangered Animals. Multicoloured.

1272 42 m. 50 Type **225** 15 10
1273 100 m. Dugong 20 10
1274 150 m. African elephant 35 15
1275 200 m. Cheetah 40 15
1276 400 m. Spotted-necked otter 70 40
1277 500 m. Hawksbill turtle 85 50

226 "Dichrostachys cinerea" **227** Pillar Box waving to Kurika

1990. Environmental Protection. Plants. Mult.

1278 42 m. 50 Type **226** 10 10
1279 100 m. Forest fire 20 10
1280 150 m. Horsetail tree 25 10
1281 200 m. Mangrove 30 15
1282 400 m. "Estrato herbaceo" (grass) 65 40
1283 500 m. Pod mahogany 80 50

1990. Kurika (post mascot) at Work. Mult.

1284 42 m. 50 Type **227** 15 10
1285 42 m. 50 Hand cancelling envelopes 15 10
1286 42 m. 50 Leaping across hurdles 15 10
1287 42 m. 50 Delivering post to chicken 15 10

228 "10" and Posts Emblem **229** Bird-of-Paradise Flower

1991. 10th Anniv of National Posts and Telecommunications Enterprises, Mozambique.

1288 **228** 50 m. blue, red & blk 15 10
1289 – 50 m. brown, green & black 15 10

DESIGN: No. 1289, "10" and telecommunications emblem.

1991. Flowers. Multicoloured.

1290 50 m. Type **229** 15 10
1291 125 m. Flamingo lily 25 15
1292 250 m. Calla lily 50 30
1293 300 m. Canna lily 55 35

230 Two Hartebeest **231** Mpompine

1991. Lichtenstein's Hartebeest. Multicoloured.

1294 50 m. Type **230** 15 10
1295 100 m. Alert hartebeest 20 10
1296 250 m. Hartebeest grazing 50 30
1297 500 m. Mother feeding young 90 60

1991. Maputo Drinking Fountains. Mult.

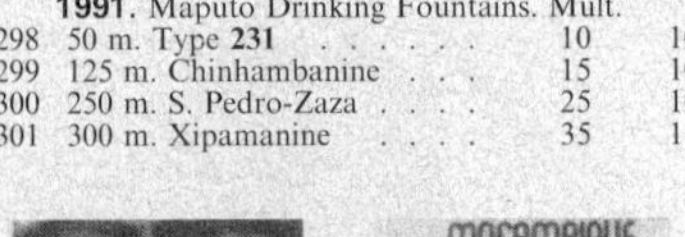

1298 50 m. Type **231** 10 10
1299 125 m. Chinhambanine 15 10
1300 250 m. S. Pedro-Zaza 25 10
1301 300 m. Xipamanine 35 15

232 Painting by Samate **233** Diving

1991. Paintings by Mozambican Artists. Mult.

1302 180 m. Type **232** 15 10
1303 250 m. Malangatana Ngwenya 20 15
1304 560 m. Malangatana Ngwenya (different) 40 30

1991. Olympic Games, Barcelona (1992). Mult.

1305 10 m. Type **233** 10 10
1306 50 m. Roller hockey 15 10
1307 100 m. Tennis 20 10
1308 200 m. Table tennis 30 10
1309 500 m. Running 50 20
1310 1000 m. Badminton 85 40

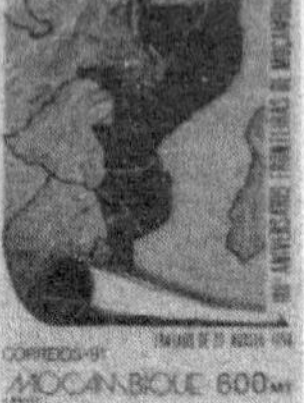

234 Proposed Boundaries in 1890 Treaty **236** Skipping

1991. Centenary of Settling of Mozambique Borders. Multicoloured.

1311 600 m. Type **234** 50 25
1312 800 m. Frontiers settled in English-Portuguese 1891 treaty 75 35

1991. Stamp Day. Children's Games. Multicoloured.

1314 40 m. Type **236** 10 10
1315 150 m. Spinning top 10 10
1316 400 m. Marbles 20 10
1317 900 m. Hopscotch 45 20

237 "Christ" **238** "Rhisophora mucronata"

1992. Stained Glass Windows. Multicoloured.

1318 40 m. Type **237** 10 10
1319 150 m. "Faith" 10 10
1320 400 m. "IC XC" 20 10
1321 900 m. Window in three sections 45 20

1992. Marine Flowers. Multicoloured.

1322 300 m. Type **238** 15 10
1323 600 m. "Cymodocea ciliata" . 30 15
1324 1000 m. "Sophora inhambanensis" 50 25

239 Spears **240** Amethyst Sunbird

1992. "Lubrapex 92" Brazilian–Portuguese Stamp Exhibition, Lisbon. Weapons. Multicoloured.

1325 100 m. Type **239** 10 10
1326 300 m. Tridents 15 10
1327 500 m. Axe 25 10
1328 1000 m. Dagger 50 25

1992. Birds. Multicoloured.

1329 150 m. Type **240** 10 10
1330 200 m. Mosque swallow . . . 10 10
1331 300 m. Red-capped robin chat 15 10
1332 400 m. Lesser blue-eared glossy starling 20 10
1333 500 m. Grey-headed bush shrike 25 10
1334 800 m. African golden oriole 40 20

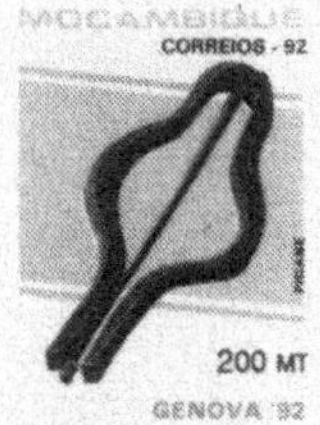

241 Emblem **242** Phiane

1992. 30th Anniv of Eduardo Mondlane University.

1335 **241** 150 m. green and brown . 10 10

1992. "Genova '92" International Thematic Stamp Exn. Musical Instruments. Multicoloured.

1336 200 m. Type **242** 10 10
1337 300 m. Xirupe (rattle) 15 10
1338 500 m. Ngulula (drum) . . . 25 10
1339 1500 m. Malimba (drum) . . 75 35

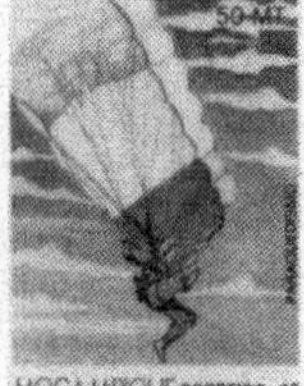

243 Children Eating **244** Parachutist

1992. International Nutrition Conference, Rome.

1341 **243** 450 m. multicoloured . . 20 10

1992. Parachuting. Multicoloured.

1342 50 m. Type **244** 10 10
1343 400 m. Parachutist and buildings 20 10
1344 500 m. Airplane dropping parachutists 25 10
1345 1500 m. Parachutist (different) 70 35

1992. No. 890 surch **50MT**.

1346 **122** 50 m. on 50 c. orange and red 10 10

246 Order of Peace and Friendship

1993. Mozambique Decorations. Multicoloured.

1347 400 m. Type **246** 20 10
1348 800 m. Bagamoyo Medal . . 40 20
1349 1000 m. Order of Eduardo Mondlane 50 25
1350 1500 m. Veteran of the Struggle for National Liberation Medal 70 35

247 Tree Stumps and Girl carrying Wood

1993. Pollution. Multicoloured.

1351 200 m. Type **247** 10 10
1352 750 m. Chimneys smoking . 35 15
1353 1000 m. Tanker sinking . . 50 25
1354 1500 m. Car exhaust fumes . 70 35

248 Lion (Gorongosa Park, Sofala)

1993. National Parks. Multicoloured.

1355 200 m. Type **248** 10 10
1356 800 m. Giraffes (Banhine Park, Gaza) 40 20
1357 1000 m. Dugongs (Bazoruto Park, Inhambane) 50 25
1358 1500 m. Ostriches (Zinave Park, Inhambane) 70 35

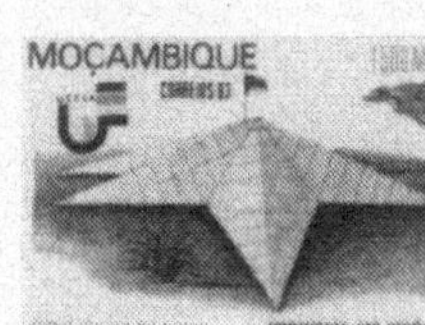

249 Heroes Monument, Maputo

1993. "Brasiliana 93" International Stamp Exhibition, Rio de Janeiro.

1359 **249** 1500 m. multicoloured . 55 25

250 Conference Emblem **251** "Cycas cercinalis"

1993. National Culture Conference, Maputo.

1360 **250** 200 m. multicoloured . . 10 10

1993. Forest Plants. Multicoloured.

1361 200 m. Type **251** 10 10
1362 250 m. "Cycas revoluta" . . 10 10
1363 900 m. "Encephalartos ferox" 25 10
1364 2000 m. "Equisetum ramosissimum" 50 25

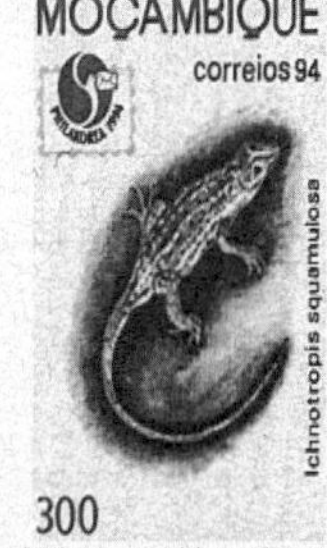

252 "Anacardium occidentale" **254** Mozambique Rough-scaled Sand Lizard

1994. Medicinal Plants. Multicoloured.

1365 200 m. Type **252** 10 10
1366 250 m. "Sclerocarya caffra" . 10 10
1367 900 m. "Annona senegalensis" 25 10
1368 2000 m. "Crinum delagoense" 50 25

1994. Various stamps surch.

1369 50 m. on 7 m. 50 multicoloured (No. 905) 10 10
1370 50 m. on 7 m. 50 multicoloured (No. 924) 10 10
1371 50 m. on 7 m. 50 multicoloured (No. 930) 10 10
1372 100 m. on 10 m. blue and red (No. 896) 10 10
1373 100 m. on 12 m. 50 mult (No. 931) 10 10
1374 200 m. on 12 m. 50 brown and red (No. 897) 10 10
1375 250 m. on 12 m. 50 mult (No. 925) 10 10

1994. "Philakorea 1994" International Stamp Exhibition, Seoul. Reptiles. Multicoloured.

1376 300 m. Type **254** 10 10
1377 500 m. Olive loggerhead turtle 10 10
1378 2000 m. Northern coppery snake 40 20
1379 3500 m. Marshall's chameleon 75 35

255 Crop-spraying

1994. 50th Anniv of I.C.A.O. Multicoloured.

1381 300 m. Type **255** 10 10
1382 500 m. Airport 10 10
1383 2000 m. Air transport . . . 40 20
1384 3500 m. Aircraft maintenance 75 35

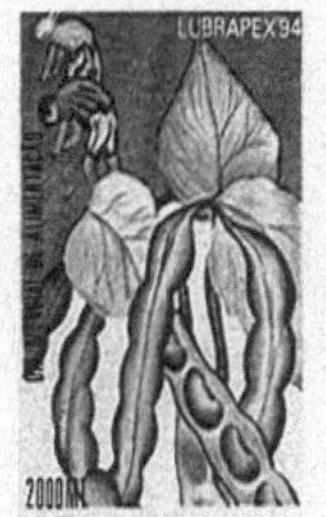

MOÇAMBIQUE correios94 900MT ELEIÇÕES MULTIPARTIDÁRIAS 27-28-OUTUBRO

256 Bean Plant **257** Queue of Voters

1994. "Lubrapex'94" Portuguese–Brazilian Stamp Exhibition. World Food Day.

1385 **256** 2000 m. multicoloured . . 40 20

1994. 1st Multiparty Elections.

1386 **257** 900 m. multicoloured . . 20 10

258 Document and Handshake **259** Couple using Drugs

1994. 20th Anniv of Lusaka Accord (establishing independence).

1387 **258** 1500 m. multicoloured . . 30 15

1994. Anti-drugs Campaign. Multicoloured.

1388 500 m. Type **259** 10 10
1389 1000 m. Couple, syringe, cigarette and skeleton . . 20 10
1390 2000 m. Addict 40 20
1391 5000 m. Sniffer dog capturing man with drugs . . . . . 1·00 50

260 Basket **261** Dress and Cloak

1995. Baskets and Bags. Multicoloured.

1392 250 m. Type **260** 10 10
1393 300 m. Bag with two handles 10 10
1394 1200 m. Circular bag with one handle 20 10
1395 5000 m. Bag with flap . . . 85 40

1995. Women's Costumes. Multicoloured.

1396 250 m. Type **261** 10 10
1397 300 m. Blouse and calf-length skirt 10 10
1398 1200 m. Blouse and ankle-length skirt 20 10
1399 5000 m. Strapless top and skirt 85 40

MOÇAMBIQUE CORREIOS-95 GALAGO 500MT

262 State Arms **263** Bushbaby

1995. Investiture (1994) of President Joaquim Chissano. Multicoloured.

1400 900 m. Type **262** 15 10
1401 2500 m. National flag . . . 45 20
1402 5000 m. Pres. Chissano . . 85 40

Nos. 1400/2 were issued together, se-tenant, the commemorative inscription at the foot extending across the strip.

1995. Mammals. Multicoloured.

1403 500 m. Type **263** 10 10
1404 2000 m. Greater kudu (horiz) 25 10
1405 3000 m. Bush pig (horiz) . . 40 20
1406 5000 m. Bushbuck 65 30

1995. Various stamps surch.

1407 250 m. on 12 m. 50 multicoloured (No. 931) . 10 10
1408 300 m. on 10 m. blue and red (No. 896) 10 10
1409 500 m. on 12 m. 50 multicoloured (No. 925) . 10 10
1410 900 m. on 12 e. 50 multicoloured (No. 771) . 10 10
1411 1000 m. on 12 m. 50 multicoloured (No. 837) . 15 10
1412 1500 m. on 16 m. multicoloured (No. 1064) 20 10
1413 2000 m. on 16 m. multicoloured (No. 995) 25 10
1414 2500 m. on 12 m. multicoloured (No. 880) 35 15

265 Family carrying Foodstuffs **266** Emblem

1995. 50th Anniv of F.A.O.

1415 **265** 5000 m. multicoloured . 65 30

1995. 50th Anniv of United Nations Organization.

1416 **266** 5000 m. blue and black . 65 30

Mozambique joined the Commonwealth on 12 November 1995. Later issues appear in volume 3.

CHARITY TAX STAMPS

The notes under this heading in Portugal also apply here.

C **15** Arms of Portugal and Mozambique and Allegorical Figures

C **16** Prow of Galley of Discoveries and Symbols of Declaration of War

1916. War Tax Fund. Imperf, roul or perf.

C234 **C 15** 1 c. green 35 25
C235 **C 16** 5 c. red 35 30

C 18 "Charity"

C 22 Society's Emblem

1920. 280th Anniv of Restoration of Portugal. Wounded Soldiers and Social Assistance Funds.
C309 C **18** ¼ c. green 70 70
C310 ½ c. black 75 70
C311 1 c. brown 75 70
C312 2 c. brown 75 75
C313 3 c. lilac 75 75
C314 4 c. green 75 75
C315 – 5 c. green 85 75
C316 – 6 c. blue 85 75
C317 – 7½ c. brown 85 75
C318 – 8 c. yellow 85 75
C319 – 10 c. lilac 85 85
C320 – 12 c. pink 85 85
C321 – 18 c. red 85 85
C322 – 24 c. brown . . . . . 1·10 85
C323 – 30 c. green . . . . . 1·10 85
C324 – 40 c. red . . . . . . 1·10 85
C325 – 50 c. yellow . . . . . 1·10 85
C326 – 1 e. blue . . . . . . 1·10 85
DESIGNS: 5 c. to 12 c. Wounded soldier and nurse; 18 c. to 1 e. Family scene.

1925. Marquis de Pombal stamps of Portugal, but inscr "MOCAMBIQUE".
C327 C **73** 15 c. brown 15 15
C328 – 15 c. brown 15 15
C329 C **75** 15 c. brown 15 15

1925. Red Cross. Surch **50 CENTAVOS**.
C330 C **22** 50 c. yellow and grey . 55 40

1926. Surch **CORREIOS** and value.
C337 C **22** 5 c. yellow and red . . 75 60
C338 10 c. yellow and green . 75 60
C339 20 c. yellow and grey . 75 60
C340 30 c. yellow and blue . 75 60
C331 40 c. yellow and grey . 80 75
C341 40 c. yellow and violet 75 60
C332 50 c. yellow and grey . 80 75
C342 50 c. yellow and red . 75 60
C333 60 c. yellow and grey . 80 75
C343 60 c. yellow and brown 75 60
C334 80 c. yellow and grey . 80 75
C344 80 c. yellow and blue . 75 60
C335 1 e. yellow and grey . . 90 75
C345 1 e. yellow and green . 75 60
C336 2 e. yellow and grey . . 90 75
C346 2 e. yellow and brown . 75 60

C 25

1928. Surch **CORREIOS** and value in black, as in Type C **25**.
C347 C **25** 5 c. yellow and green . 1·10 1·00
C348 10 c. yellow and blue . 1·10 1·00
C349 20 c. yellow and black . 1·10 1·00
C350 30 c. yellow and red . 1·10 1·00
C351 40 c. yellow and purple 1·10 1·00
C352 50 c. yellow and red . 1·10 1·00
C353 60 c. yellow and brown 1·10 1·00
C354 80 c. yellow and brown 1·10 1·00
C355 1 e. yellow and grey . . 1·10 1·00
C356 2 e. yellow and red . . 1·10 1·00

C 27

C 29 Pelican

C 28 "Charity"

1929. Value in black.
C357 C **27** 40 c. purple and blue . 85 85
C358 40 c. violet and red . . 85 85
C359 40 c. violet and green . 85 85
C360 40 c. red and brown . 85 85
C361 (No value) red & green 1·10 1·10
C362 40 c. blue and orange . 1·10 1·10
C363 40 c. blue and brown . 85 85
C364 40 c. purple and green . 1·10 1·00
C365 40 c. black and yellow . 1·10 1·10
C366 40 c. black and brown 1·10 1·10

1942.
C383 C **28** 50 c. pink and black . 2·00 90

1943. Inscr "Colonia de Mocambique". Value in black.
C390 C **29** 50 c. red . . . . . . 1·50 75
C389 50 c. blue . . . . . . 1·50 75
C386 50 c. violet . . . . . 1·50 75
C387 50 c. brown . . . . . 1·50 75
C393 50 c. green . . . . . 1·50 75

1952. Inscr "Provincia de Mocambique". Value in black.
C514 C **29** 30 c. yellow 45 35
C515 50 c. orange 45 35
C469 50 c. green 75 40
C470 50 c. brown 75 40

1957. No. C470 surch **$30**.
C511 C **29** 30 c. on 50 c. brown . 45 25

C 56 Women and Children

C 58 Telegraph Poles and Map

1963.
C569 C **56** 30 c. black, green & red 15 15
C570 50 c. black, bistre & red 20 15
C571 50 c. black, pink & red 20 15
C572 50 c. black, green & red 20 15
C573 50 c. black, blue & red 20 15
C574 50 c. black, buff & red 20 15
C575 50 c. black, grey & red 20 15
C576 50 c. black, yell & red 20 15
C577 1 e. grey, blk & red . 50 25
C578 1 e. black, buff & red 15 10
C578a 1 e. black, mve & red 15 10

1965. Mozambique Telecommunications Improvement.
C579 C **58** 30 c. black, pink & vio 10 10
C580 – 50 c. black, brown & bl 10 10
C581 – 1 e. black, orge & grn 20 20
DESIGN—19½ × 36 mm: 50 c., 1 e. Telegraph linesman.

A 2 e. 50 in Type C **58** was also issued for compulsory use on telegrams.

NEWSPAPER STAMPS

1893. "Embossed" key-type of Mozambique surch.
(a) **JORNAES 2½ 2½**.
N53 Q 2½ r. on 40 r. brown . . . 9·50 7·50
(b) **JORNAES 2½ REIS**.
N54 Q 2½ r. on 40 r. brown . . . 45·00 30·00
N57 5 r. on 40 r. brown . . . . 28·00 24·00

1893. "Newspaper" key-type inscribed "MOCAMBIQUE".
N58 V 2½ r. brown 25 20

POSTAGE DUE STAMPS

1904. "Due" key-type inscr "MOCAMBIQUE".
D146 W 5 r. green 15 15
D147 10 r. grey 15 15
D148 20 r. brown 15 15
D149 30 r. orange 30 20
D150 50 r. brown 30 20
D151 60 r. brown . . . . . 1·25 75
D152 100 r. mauve . . . . . 1·25 75
D153 130 r. blue 70 65
D154 200 r. red . . . . . . 1·25 65
D155 500 r. violet . . . . . 1·25 65

1911. "Due" key-type of Mozambique optd **REPUBLICA**.
D162 W 5 r. green 15 15
D163 10 r. grey 15 15
D164 20 r. brown 20 15
D165 30 r. orange 20 15
D166 50 r. brown 20 15
D167 60 r. brown 30 20
D168 100 r. mauve 30 20
D169 130 r. blue 50 40
D170 200 r. red 65 60
D171 500 r. lilac 65 60

1917. "Due" key-type of Mozambique, but currency changed.
D246 W ½ c. green 15 15
D247 1 c. grey 15 15
D248 2 c. brown 15 15
D249 3 c. orange 15 15
D250 5 c. brown 15 15
D251 6 c. brown 15 15
D252 10 c. mauve 15 15
D253 13 c. blue 30 25
D254 20 c. red 30 25
D255 50 c. lilac 30 25

1918. Charity Tax stamps optd **PORTEADO**.
D256 C **15** 1 c. green 50 40
D257 C **16** 5 c. red 50 40

1922. "Ceres" key-type of Lourenco Marques (½, 1½ c.) and of Mozambique (1, 2½, 4 c.) surch **PORTEADO** and value and bar.
D316 U 5 c. on ½ c. black . . . 55 40
D318 6 c. on 1 c. green . . . 60 40
D317 10 c. on 1½ c. brown . . 55 40
D319 20 c. on 2½ c. violet . . 60 40
D320 50 c. on 4 c. pink . . . 60 40

1924. "Ceres" key-type of Mozambique surch **Porteado** and value.
D321 U 20 c. on 30 c. green . . . 35 30
D323 50 c. on 60 c. blue . . . 55 40

1925. Marquis de Pombal charity tax designs as Nos. C327/9, optd **MULTA**.
D327 C **73** 30 c. brown 15 15
D328 – 30 c. brown 15 15
D329 C **75** 30 c. brown 15 15

1952. As Type D **70** of Macao, but inscr "MOCAMBIQUE".
D468 10 c. multicoloured 10 10
D469 30 c. multicoloured 10 10
D470 50 c. multicoloured 10 10
D471 1 e. multicoloured 20 20
D472 2 e. multicoloured 20 20
D473 5 e. multicoloured 25 25

MOZAMBIQUE COMPANY Pt. 9

The Mozambique Company was responsible from 1891 until 1942 for the administration of Manica and Sofala territory in Portuguese East Africa. Now part of Mozambique.

1899. 1000 reis = 1 milreis.
1913. 100 centavos = 1 escudo.

1892. "Embossed" key-type inscr "PROVINCA DE MOCAMBIQUE" optd **COMPA. DE MOCAMBIQUE**.
10 Q 5 r. black 25 20
2 10 r. green 35 15
3 20 r. red 45 15
4 25 r. mauve 30 20
5 40 r. brown 30 15
6 50 r. blue 35 20
7 100 r. brown 30 45
8 200 r. violet 60 45
9 300 r. orange 60 45

2

1895. Value in black or red (500, 1000 r.).
33 **2** 2½ r. yellow 10 10
114 2½ r. grey 50 25
17 5 r. orange 15 10
36 10 r. mauve 15 15
115 10 r. green 30 25
39 15 r. brown 15 15
116 15 r. green 30 25
20 20 r. lilac 15 15
45 25 r. green 15 15
117 25 r. red 45 20
46 50 r. blue 20 15
118 50 r. brown 45 30
109 65 r. blue 30 25
48 75 r. red 20 15
119 75 r. mauve 90 75
50 80 r. green 20 15
52 100 r. brown on buff . . . 25 15
120 100 r. blue on blue 90 75
110 115 r. pink on pink 80 70
121 115 r. brown on pink . . . 1·40 90
111 130 r. green on pink . . . 80 70
122 130 r. brown on yellow . . 1·40 90
54 150 r. orange on pink . . . 25 15
55 200 r. blue on blue 25 15
123 200 r. lilac on pink . . . 1·40 90
56 300 r. blue on brown . . . 25 15
112 400 r. black on blue . . . 80 70
124 400 r. blue on yellow . . . 1·75 1·40
58 500 r. black 35 25
125 500 r. black on blue . . . 1·75 40
126 700 r. mauve on buff . . . 1·90 1·60
59 1000 r. mauve 45 25

1895. Surch **PROVISORIO 25**.
77 **2** 25 on 80 r. green . . . . . . 6·50 4·50

1895. No. 6 optd **PROVISORIO**.
78 Q 50 r. blue . . . . 1·60 1·25

1898. Vasco da Gama. Optd **1498 Centenario da India 1898**.
80 **2** 2½ r. yellow 55 55
81 5 r. orange 65 60
82 10 r. mauve 65 55
84 15 r. brown 80 70
86 20 r. lilac 90 80
87 25 r. green . . . . 1·50 90
99 50 r. blue 85 80
89 75 r. red . . . . 1·50 1·25
91 80 r. green . . . . 1·50 1·10
101 100 r. brown on buff . . . 1·60 1·40
102 150 r. orange on pink . . . 1·60 1·50
94 200 r. blue on blue . . . . 2·00 1·75
104 300 r. blue on brown . . . 3·00 2·25

1899. Surch **25 PROVISORIO**.
105 **2** 25 on 75 r. red . . . . . . 1·25 1·10

1900. Surch **25 Reis** and bar.
106 **2** 25 r. on 5 r. orange . . . . 1·10 65

1900. Perforated through centre and surch **50 REIS**.
108 **2** 50 r. on half of 20 r. lilac . . 40 40

1911. Optd **REPUBLICA**.
145 **2** 2½ r. grey 15 10
147 5 r. orange 15 10
148 10 r. green 10 10
150 15 r. green 10 10
151 20 r. lilac 15 10
153 25 r. red 10 10
155 50 r. brown 10 10
156 75 r. mauve 15 10
157 100 r. blue on blue 20 10
159 115 r. brown on pink . . . 30 20
160 130 r. brown on yellow . . 30 20
161 200 r. lilac on pink 30 15
162 400 r. blue on yellow . . . 30 15
163 500 r. black on blue 30 15
164 700 r. mauve on yellow . . 35 30

1916. Surch **REPUBLICA** and value in figures.
166 **2** ¼ c. on 2½ r. grey 10 10
168 ½ c. on 5 r. orange 10 10
170 1 c. on 10 r. green 15 15
173 1½ c. on 15 r. green 15 15
175 2 c. on 20 r. lilac 15 15
178 2½ c. on 25 r. red 15 15
180 5 c. on 50 r. brown 15 15
181 7½ c. on 75 r. mauve 25 15
182 10 c. on 100 r. blue on blue 25 15
183 11½ c. on 115 r. brown on pink 50 30
184 13 c. on 130 r. brown on yell 50 25
185 20 c. on 200 r. lilac on pink 40 30
186 40 c. on 400 r. blue on yell . 40 30
187 50 c. on 500 r. black on blue 50 35
188 70 c. on 700 r. mauve on yell 50 35

1917. Red Cross Fund. Stamps of 1911 (optd **REPUBLICA**) optd with red cross and **31.7.17.**
189 **2** 2½ r. grey . . . . 1·50 1·25
190 10 r. green . . . . 2·00 1·75
191 20 r. lilac . . . . 2·00 1·75
192 50 r. brown . . . . 4·50 2·75
193 75 r. mauve . . . . 10·50 8·75
194 100 r. blue on blue . . . . 13·50 11·25
195 700 r. mauve on yellow . . 42·00 29·00

1918. Stamps of 1911 (optd **REPUBLICA**) surch with new value.
196 **2** ¼ c. on 700 r. mauve on yellow 80 70
197 2½ c. on 500 r. black on blue 80 70
198 5 c. on 400 r. blue on yellow 80 70

14 Native Village

15 Ivory

1918.
199 **14** ¼ c. green and brown . . . 15 15
233 ¼ c. black and green . . . 15 15
200 **15** ½ c. black 15 15
201 – 1 c. black and green . . . 15 15
202 – 1½ c. green and black . . 15 15
203 – 2 c. black and red 15 15
235 – 2 c. black and grey . . . 15 15
204 – 2½ c. black and lilac . . . 15 15
236 – 3 c. black and orange . . 15 15
205 – 4 c. brown and green . . 15 15
237 – 4 c. black and red 15 15
227 **14** 4½ c. black and grey . . . 20 15
206 – 5 c. black and blue . . . 15 15
207 – 6 c. blue and purple . . . 25 20
238 – 6 c. black and mauve . . . 15 15
228 – 7 c. black and blue 45 25
208 – 7½ c. green and orange . . 35 30
239 – 8 c. black and lilac 30 25
210 – 10 c. black and red 45 30
229 – 12 c. black and brown . . 65 45
241 – 12 c. black and green . . . 30 20
242 – 15 c. black and red 25 20
212 – 20 c. black and green . . 20 15
213 – 30 c. black and brown . . 40 30
244 – 30 c. black and green . . 40 30
214 – 40 c. black and green . . 30 20
246 – 40 c. black and blue . . . 45 30
215 – 50 c. black and orange . . 40 30
247 – 50 c. black and mauve . . 60 40
230 – 60 c. brown and red . . . 75 50
231 – 80 c. brown and blue . . 1·10 55
248 – 80 c. black and red . . . 75 50
216 – 1 e. black and green . . . 70 50
249 – 1 e. black and blue . . . 60 50
232 – 2 e. violet and red . . . 1·25 80
250 – 2 e. black and lilac . . . 1·00 50
DESIGNS—HORIZ: 1, 3 c. Maize field; 2 c. Sugar factory; 5 c., 2 e. Beira; 20 c. Law Court; 40 c. Mangrove swamp. VERT: 1½ c. India-rubber; 2½ c. River Buzi; 4 c. Tobacco bushes; 6 c. Coffee bushes; 7, 15 c. Steam train; 7½ c. Orange tree; 8, 12 c. Cotton plants; 10, 80 c. Sisal plantation; 30 c. Coconut palm; 50, 60 c. Cattle breeding; 1 e. Mozambique Co's Arms.

1920. Pictorial issue surch in words.
217 ½ c. on 30 c. (No. 213) . . . . 1·10 95
218 ½ c. on 1 e. (No. 216) . . . . 1·10 95
219 1½ c. on 2½ c. (No. 204) . . . 90 90
220 1½ c. on 5 c. (No. 206) . . . . 1·10 70
221 2 c. on 2½ c. (No. 204) 70 55
222 4 c. on 20 c. (No. 212) . . . . 1·10 75
223 4 c. on 40 c. (No. 214) . . . . 1·10 75
224 6 c. on 8 c. (No. 239) . . . . 1·10 75
225 6 c. on 50 c. (No. 215) . . . . 1·10 75

MINIMUM PRICE

The minimum price quoted is 10p which represents a handling charge rather than a basis for valuing common stamps. For further notes about prices, see introductory pages.

33

36 Tea

1925.
251 **33** 24 c. black and blue . . . 80 65
252 – 25 c. blue and brown . . . 80 65
253 **33** 85 c. black and red 60 50
254 – 1 e. 40 black and blue . . . 1·00 50
255 – 5 e. blue and brown 65 35
256 **36** 10 e. black and red 65 35
257 – 20 e. black and green . . . 80 35
DESIGNS—VERT: 25 c., 1 e. 40, Beira; 5 e. Tapping rubber. HORIZ: 20 e. River Zambesi.

38 Ivory

1931.
258 **38** 45 c. blue . . . . 1·50 80
259 – 70 c. brown . . . . 1·00 50
DESIGN—VERT: 70 c. Gold mining.

40 Zambesi Bridge

1935 Opening of Zambesi Bridge.
260 **40** 1 e. black and blue . . . . 1·75 1·10

41 Armstrong-Whitworth Atalanta Airliner over Beira

1935. Inauguration of Blantyre–Beira–Salisbury Air Route.
261 **41** 5 c. black and blue 40 25
262 10 c. black and red 40 25
263 15 c. black and red 40 25
264 20 c. black and green . . . 40 25
265 30 c. black and green . . . 40 25
266 40 c. black and blue . . . 50 35
267 45 c. black and blue . . . 50 35
268 50 c. black and purple . . 50 35
269 60 c. brown and red . . . 80 40
270 80 c. black and red 80 40

42 Armstrong-Whitworth Atalanta Airliner over Beira

1935. Air.
271 **42** 5 c. black and blue 10 10
272 10 c. black and red 10 10
273 15 c. black and red 10 10
274 20 c. black and green . . . 10 10
275 30 c. black and green . . . 10 10
276 40 c. black and green . . . 10 10
277 45 c. black and blue . . . 10 10
278 50 c. black and purple . . 10 10
279 60 c. brown and red . . . 10 10
280 80 c. black and red 10 10
281 1 e. black and blue 15 10
282 2 e. black and lilac 35 20
283 5 e. blue and brown 60 35
284 10 e. black and red 65 40
285 20 e. black and green . . . 1·40 85

43 Coastal Dhow

46 Palms at Beira

45 Crocodile

1937.
286 – 1 c. lilac and green 10 10
287 – 5 c. green and blue 10 10
288 **43** 10 c. blue and red 10 10
289 – 15 c. black and red 10 10
290 – 20 c. blue and green . . . 10 10
291 – 30 c. blue and green . . . 10 10
292 – 40 c. black and blue . . . 10 10
293 – 45 c. brown and blue . . . 10 10
294 **45** 50 c. green and violet . . 15 15
295 – 60 c. blue and red 15 15
296 – 70 c. green and brown . . 15 15
297 – 80 c. green and red 15 15
298 – 85 c. black and red 20 15
299 – 1 e. black and blue 15 15
300 **46** 1 e. 40 c. green and blue . 20 15
301 – 2 e. brown and lilac . . . 40 20
302 – 5 e. blue and brown . . . 60 25
303 – 10 e. black and red 55 35
304 – 20 e. purple and green . . 85 50
DESIGNS—VERT: 21 × 29 mm—1 c. Giraffe; 20 c. Common zebra; 70 c. Native woman. 23 × 31 mm—10 e. Old Portuguese gate, Sena; 20 e. Arms. HORIZ: 29 × 21 mm—5 c. Native huts. 15 c. S. Caetano fortress, Sofala; 60 c. Leopard; 80 c. Hippopotami. 37 × 22 mm—5 e. Railway bridge over River Zambesi. TRIANGULAR: 30 c. Python; 40 c. White rhinoceros; 45 c. Lion; 85 c. Vasco da Gama's flagship "Sao Gabriel"; 1 e. Native in dugout canoe; 2 e. Greater kudu.

1939. President Carmona's Colonial Tour. Optd **28-VII-1939 Visita Presidencial**.
305 – 30 c. (No. 291) 70 50
306 – 40 c. (No. 292) 70 50
307 – 45 c. (No. 293) 70 50
308 **45** 50 c. green and violet . . 70 50
309 – 85 c. (No. 298) 70 50
310 – 1 e. (No. 299) . . . . . . 1·10 90
311 – 2 e. (No. 301) . . . . . . 1·40 1·10

49 King Afonso Henriques

51 "Don John IV" after Alberto de Souza

1940. 800th Anniv of Portuguese Independence.
312 **49** 1 e. 75 light blue and blue 70 40

1940. Tercentenary of Restoration of Independence.
313 **51** 40 c. black and blue . . . 20 15
314 50 c. green and violet . . 20 15
315 60 c. blue and red 20 15
316 70 c. green and brown . . 20 15
317 80 c. green and red 20 15
318 1 e. black and blue 20 15

CHARITY TAX STAMPS

The notes under this heading in Portugal also apply here.

1932. No. 236 surch **Assistencia Publica 2 Ctvos. 2**.
C260 2 c. on 3 c. black & orge . 35 35

C 41 "Charity"

C 50

1934.
C261 C **41** 2 c. black and mauve . 45 1·10

1940.
C313 C **50** 2 c. blue and black . . 2·75 2·40

C 52

1941.
C319 C **52** 2 c. red and black . . 2·75 2·40

NEWSPAPER STAMP

1894. "Newspaper" key-type inscr "MOCAMBIQUE" optd **COMPA. DE MOCAMBIQUE**.
N15 V $2\frac{1}{2}$ r. brown 25 20

POSTAGE DUE STAMPS

D 9

D 32

1906.
D114 D **9** 5 r. green 20 20
D115 10 r. grey 20 20
D116 20 r. brown 20 20
D117 30 r. orange 35 25
D118 50 r. brown 35 25
D119 60 r. brown . . . . . . 1·75 1·60
D120 100 r. mauve 50 50
D121 130 r. blue . . . . . . 2·50 1·75
D122 200 r. red . . . . 1·10 70
D123 500 r. lilac . . . . . . 1·40 1·10

1911. Optd **REPUBLICA**.
D166 D **9** 5 r. green 15 15
D167 10 r. grey 15 15
D168 20 r. brown 15 15
D169 30 r. orange 15 15
D170 50 r. brown 15 15
D171 60 r. brown 30 20
D172 100 r. mauve 30 20
D173 130 r. blue 70 75
D174 200 r. red 80 70
D175 500 r. lilac 90 80

1916. Currency changed.
D189 D **9** $\frac{1}{2}$ c. green 15 15
D190 1 c. grey 15 15
D191 2 c. brown 15 15
D192 3 c. orange 15 15
D193 5 c. brown 15 15
D194 6 c. brown 15 15
D195 10 c. mauve 35 35
D196 13 c. blue 70 70
D197 20 c. red 70 70
D198 50 c. lilac 90 90

1919.
D217 D **32** $\frac{1}{2}$ c. green 10 10
D218 1 c. black 10 10
D219 2 c. brown 10 10
D220 3 c. orange 10 10
D221 5 c. brown 15 10
D222 6 c. brown 20 20
D223 10 c. red 20 20
D224 13 c. blue 25 25
D225 20 c. red 25 20
D226 50 c. grey 30 30

MUSCAT AND OMAN Pt. 19

Independent Sultanate in Eastern Arabia. The title of the Sultanate was changed in 1971 to Oman.

1966. 64 baizas = 1 rupee.
1970. 1000 baizas = 1 rial saidi.

12 Sultan's Crest

14 Nakhal Fort

1966.
94 **12** 3 b. purple 10 10
95 5 b. brown 10 10
96 10 b. brown 10 10
97 A 15 b. black and violet . . . 20 15
98 20 b. black and blue 30 20
99 25 b. black and orange . . 35 20
100 **14** 30 b. mauve and blue . . . 45 30
101 B 50 b. green and brown . . . 70 40
102 C 1 r. blue and orange . . . . 1·40 75
103 D 2 r. brown and green . . . 2·75 1·50
104 E 5 r. violet and red . . . . 6·75 4·50
105 F 10 r. red and violet . . . . 11·00 9·50
DESIGNS—VERT: $21\frac{1}{2} \times 25\frac{1}{2}$ mm: A, Crest and Muscat harbour. HORIZ (as Type **14**): B, Samail Fort; C, Sohar Fort; D, Nizwa Fort; E, Matrah Fort; F, Mirani Fort.

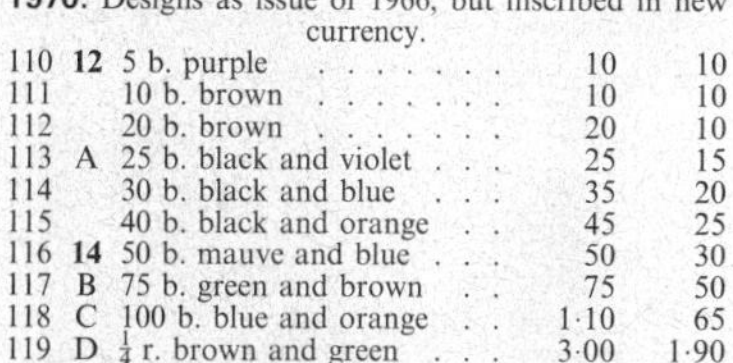

15 Mina el Fahal

1969. 1st Oil Shipment (July 1967). Multicoloured.
106 20 b. Type **15** 55 40
107 25 b. Storage tanks 70 50
108 40 b. Desert oil-rig . . . . . 1·10 85
109 1 r. Aerial view from "Gemini 4" 2·75 2·00

1970. Designs as issue of 1966, but inscribed in new currency.
110 **12** 5 b. purple 10 10
111 10 b. brown 10 10
112 20 b. brown 20 10
113 A 25 b. black and violet . . . 25 15
114 30 b. black and blue . . . 35 20
115 40 b. black and orange . . 45 25
116 **14** 50 b. mauve and blue . . . 50 30
117 B 75 b. green and brown . . 75 50
118 C 100 b. blue and orange . . 1·10 65
119 D $\frac{1}{4}$ r. brown and green . . . 3·00 1·90
120 E $\frac{1}{2}$ r. violet and red . . . . 6·00 3·75
121 F 1 r. red and violet . . . . 11·00 7·75

For later issues see **OMAN**.

MYANMAR Pt. 21

Formerly known as Burma.

100 pyas = 1 kyat

81 Fountain, National Assembly Park ($\frac{1}{2}$-size illustration)

1990. State Law and Order Restoration Council.
312 **81** 1 k. multicoloured . . . . 1·00 65

1990. As Nos. 258/61 of Burma but inscr "UNION OF MYANMAR".
313 15 p. deep green and green . . 20 15
314 20 p. black, brown and blue . 25 20
315 50 p. violet and brown . . . 45 25
316 1 k. violet, mauve and black . 90 65

82 Map and Emblem

83 Nawata Ruby

1990. 40th Anniv of United Nations Development Programme.
322 **82** 2 k. blue, yellow & black . 1·90 1·25

1991. Gem Emporium.
323 **83** 50 p. multicoloured 95 65

84 "Grandfather giving Sword to Grandson" (statuette, Nan Win)

85 Emblem

1992. 44th Anniv of Independence. Multicoloured.
324 50 p. Warrior defending personification of Myanmar and map (poster, Khin Thein) 50 40
325 2 k. Type **84** . . . . 2·00 1·50

1992. National Sports Festival.
326 **85** 50 p. multicoloured 55 40

86 Campaign Emblem

87 Fish, Water Droplet and Leaf

1992. Anti-AIDS Campaign.
327 **86** 50 p. red 40 30

1992. International Nutrition Conference, Rome.
328 **87** 50 p. multicoloured 30 20
329 1 k. multicoloured 55 40
330 3 k. multicoloured . . . . 1·60 1·10
331 5 k. multicoloured . . . . 2·75 1·90

88 Statue 89 Hintha (legendary bird)

1993. National Convention for Drafting of New Constitution.

332 **88** 50 p. multicoloured 25 20
333 3 k. multicoloured . . . . 1·50 1·00

1993. Statuettes. Multicoloured.

334 5 k. Type **89** . . . . 2·50 1·75
335 10 k. Lawkanat . . . . 5·00 3·50

90 Horseman aiming Spear at Target

1993. Festival of Traditional Equestrian Sports, Sittwe.

336 **90** 3 k. multicoloured . . . . 1·60 1·10

91 Tree, Globe and Figures

92 Association Emblem

1994. World Environment Day.

337 **91** 4 k. multicoloured . . . . 2·00 1·50

1994. 1st Anniv of Union Solidarity and Development Association.

338 **92** 3 k. multicoloured . . . . 1·75 1·25

93 City and Emblem

1995. 50th Anniv of Armed Forces Day.

339 **93** 50 p. multicoloured 10 10

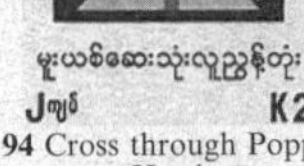

94 Cross through Poppy Head

95 Camera and Film

1995. International Day against Drug Abuse.

340 **94** 2 k. multicoloured 45 30

1995. 60th Anniv of Myanmar Film Industry.

341 **95** 50 p. multicoloured 10 10

96 Figures around Emblem

97 Convocation Hall

1995. 50th Anniv of United Nations Organization.

342 **96** 4 k. multicoloured 90 65

1995. 60th Anniv of Yangon University.

343 **97** 50 p. multicoloured . . . 10 10
344 2 k. multicoloured 45 30

98 Punt

1996. Visit Myanmar Year. Multicoloured.

345 50 p. Type **98** 10 10
346 4 k. Karaweik Hall 90 65
347 5 k. Mandalay Palace . . . . 1·10 75

99 Four-man Canoe

1996. International Letter Writing Week. "Unity equals Success". Multicoloured.

348 2 k. Type **99** 40 30
349 5 k. Human pyramid holding flag aloft (vert) . . . . 1·10 75

100 Breastfeeding

1996. 50th Anniv of U.N.I.C.E.F. Multicoloured.

350 1 k. Type **100** 20 15
351 2 k. Nurse inoculating child . 40 30
352 4 k. Children outside school . 85 60

NAKHICHEVAN Pt. 10

An autonomous province of Azerbaijan, separated from the remainder of the republic by Armenian territory. Nos. 1 and 2 were issued during a period when the administration of Nakhichevan was in dispute with the central government.

100 qopik = 1 manat

1 President Aliev

1993. 70th Birthday of President H. Aliev of Nakhichevan.

1 **1** 5 m. black and red . . . . . .
2 – 5 m. multicoloured . . . . . .

DESIGN: No. 2, Map of Nakhichevan.

NAPLES Pt. 8

A state on the S.W. coast of Central Italy, formerly part of the Kingdom of Sicily, but now part of Italy.

200 tornesi = 100 grano = 1 ducato

1 Arms under Bourbon Dynasty

4 Cross of Savoy

1858. The frames differ in each value. Imperf.

8 **1** $\frac{1}{2}$ t. blue £120000 £8000
1 $\frac{1}{2}$ g. red £650 £170
2 1 g. red . . . . £180 15·00
3 2 g. red . . . . £110 4·25
4 5 g. red . . . . £900 18·00
5 10 g. red . . . . £2000 65·00
6 20 g. red £1700 £275
7 50 g. red £4250 £2500

1860. Imperf.

9 **4** $\frac{1}{2}$ t. blue £16000 £3000

NEAPOLITAN PROVINCES Pt. 8

Temporary issues for Naples and other parts of S. Italy which adhered to the new Kingdom of Italy in 1860.

200 tornesi = 100 grano = 1 ducato

1

1861. Embossed. Imperf.

2 **1** $\frac{1}{2}$ t. green . . . . 3·25 55·00
5 $\frac{1}{2}$ g. brown . . . . £110 80·00
9 1 g. black . . . . £200 8·00
10 2 g. blue . . . . 45·00 3·75
15 5 g. red . . . . £130 40·00
18 10 g. orange . . . . £110 70·00
19 20 g. yellow £400 £700
23 50 g. slate . . . . 5·00 £6000

NEPAL Pt. 21

An independent Kingdom in the Himalayas N. of India.

1861. 16 annas = 1 rupee.
1907. 64 pice = 1 rupee.
1954. 100 paisa = 1 rupee.

1 (1 a.) Crown and Kukris

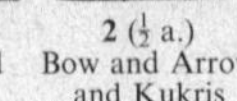

2 ($\frac{1}{2}$ a.) Bow and Arrow and Kukris

3 Siva Mahadeva (2 pice)

1881. Imperf or pin-perf.

34 **2** $\frac{1}{2}$ a. black . . . . 2·00 1·00
35 $\frac{1}{2}$ a. orange £300 £120
42 **1** 1 a. blue . . . . 4·00 1·60
14 1 a. green . . . . 26·00 26·00
16c 2 a. violet . . . . 12·00 12·00
40 2 a. brown . . . . 5·00 3·00
41 4 a. green . . . . 4·00 4·00

1907. Various sizes.

57 **3** 2 p. brown 20 20
58 4 p. green 60 40
59 8 p. red 40 30
60 16 p. purple . . . . 3·00 1·50
61 24 p. orange . . . . 3·00 1·00
62 32 p. blue . . . . 5·00 1·25
63 1 r. red . . . . 9·00 4·00
50 5 r. black and brown . . . . 14·00 8·00

5 Swayambhunath Temple, Katmandu

7 Guheswari Temple, Patan

8 Sri Pashupati (Siva Mahadeva)

1949.

64 **5** 2 p. brown 50 40
65 – 4 p. green 50 40
66 – 6 p. pink . . . . 1·00 40
67 – 8 p. red . . . . 1·00 60
68 – 16 p. purple . . . . 1·00 60
69 – 20 p. blue . . . . 2·00 1·00
70 **7** 24 p. red . . . . 1·60 60
71 – 32 p. blue . . . . 3·00 1·00
72 **8** 1 r. orange . . . . 12·00 6·00

DESIGNS—As Type **5**: 4 p. Pashupatinath Temple, Katmandu; 6 p. Tri-Chundra College; 8 p. Mahabuddha Temple. 26×30 mm: 16 p. Krishna Mandir Temple, Patan. As Type **7**: 20 p. View of Katmandu; 32 p. The twenty-two fountains, Balaju.

9 King Tribhuvana

10 Map of Nepal

1954. (a) Size 18×22 mm.

73 **9** 2 p. brown . . . . 1·00 20
74 4 p. green . . . . 2·00 60
75 6 p. red 80 20
76 8 p. lilac 60 20
77 12 p. orange . . . . 4·00 1·00

(b) Size $25\frac{1}{2} \times 29\frac{1}{2}$ mm.

78 **9** 16 p. brown 80 20
79 20 p. red . . . . 1·60 60
80 24 p. purple . . . . 1·40 60
81 32 p. blue . . . . 2·00 60
82 50 p. mauve . . . . 9·00 3·00
83 1 r. red . . . . 18·00 5·00
84 2 r. orange . . . . 9·00 4·00

(c) Size 30×18 mm.

85 **10** 2 p. brown 80 40
86 4 p. green . . . . 2·00 60
87 6 p. red . . . . 6·00 1·00
88 8 p. lilac 60 40
89 12 p. orange . . . . 6·00 1·00

(d) Size $38 \times 21\frac{1}{2}$ mm.

90 **10** 16 p. brown . . . . 1·00 40
91 20 p. red . . . . 1·60 40
92 24 p. purple . . . . 1·25 40
93 32 p. blue . . . . 3·00 80
94 50 p. mauve . . . . 11·00 3·00
95 1 r. red . . . . 20·00 4·00
96 2 r. orange . . . . 9·00 4·00

11 Mechanization of Agriculture

13 Hanuman Dhoka, Katmandu

1956. Coronation.

97 **11** 4 p. green . . . . 2·00 1·25
98 – 6 p. red and yellow . . . 1·25 60
99 – 8 p. violet 80 40
100 **13** 24 p. red . . . . 2·00 80
101 – 1 r. red . . . . 55·00 48·00

DESIGNS—As Type **11**: 8 p. Processional elephant. As Type **13**: 6 p. Throne; 1 r. King and Queen and mountains.

15 U.N. Emblem and Nepalese Landscape

16 Nepalese Crown

1956. 1st Anniv of Admission into U.N.O.

102 **15** 12 p. blue and brown . . . 2·75 1·60

1957. (a) Size 18 × 22 mm.

103 **16** 2 p. brown 40 25

104 4 p. green 60 40

105 6 p. red 40 40

106 8 p. violet 40 40

107 12 p. red . . . . 2·25 60

(b) Size $25\frac{1}{2} \times 29\frac{1}{2}$ mm.

108 **16** 16 p. brown . . . . 3·00 1·00

109 20 p. red . . . . 5·00 1·40

110 24 p. mauve . . . . 3·00 1·25

111 32 p. blue . . . . 4·00 1·40

112 50 p. pink . . . . 7·00 3·00

113 1 r. salmon . . . . 15·00 6·00

114 2 r. orange . . . . 7·00 4·00

17 Gaunthali carrying Letter

18 Temple of Lumbini

1958. Air. Inauguration of Nepalese Internal Airmail Service.

115 **17** 10 p. blue . . . . 1·10 1·10

1958. Human Rights Day.

116 **18** 6 p. yellow 80 80

19 Nepalese Map and Flag

1959. 1st Nepalese Elections.

117 **19** 6 p. red and green 30 25

20 Spinning Wheel

21 King Mahendra

1959. Cottage Industries.

118 **20** 2 p. brown 25 25

1959. Admission of Nepal to U.P.U.

119 **21** 12 p. blue 30 25

22 Vishnu

23 Nyatopol Temple, Bhaktapur

1959.

120 **22** 1 p. brown 10 10

121 – 2 p. violet 10 10

122 – 4 p. blue 30 20

123 – 6 p. pink 30 15

124 – 8 p. brown 20 10

125 – 12 p. grey 30 10

126 **23** 16 p. violet and brown . . 30 10

127 20 p. red and blue . . . . 1·00 40

128 24 p. red and green . . . . 1·00 40

129 32 p. blue and lilac 60 40

130 50 p. green and red . . . . 1·00 40

131 – 1 r. blue and brown . . . . 6·00 2·00

132 – 2 r. blue and purple . . . . 6·00 3·25

133 – 5 r. red and violet . . . . 45·00 38·00

DESIGNS—As Type **22**. HORIZ: 2 p. Krishna; 8 p. Siberian musk deer; 12 p. Indian rhinoceros. VERT: 4 p. Himalayas; 6 p. Gateway, Bhaktapur Palace. As Type **23**. VERT: 1 r., 2 r. Himalayan monal pheasant; 5 r. Satyr tragopan.

24 King Mahendra opening Parliament

25 Sri Pashupatinath

1959. Opening of 1st Nepalese Parliament.

134 **24** 6 p. red 60 60

1959. Renovation of Sri Pashupatinath Temple, Katmandu.

135 **25** 4 p. green (18 × 25 mm) . . 40 40

136 8 p. red ($21 \times 28\frac{1}{2}$ mm) . . 60 40

137 1 r. blue ($24\frac{1}{2} \times 33\frac{1}{2}$ mm) . . 5·00 3·25

26 Children, Pagoda and Mt. Everest

27 King Mahendra

1960. Children's Day.

137a **26** 6 p. blue . . . . 8·00 6·00

1960. King Mahendra's 41st Birthday.

138 **27** 1 r. purple 90 60

See also Nos. 163/4a.

28 Mt. Everest

29 King Tribhuvana

1960. Mountain Views.

139 – 5 p. brown and purple . . 20 10

140 **28** 10 p. purple and blue . . 30 15

141 – 40 p. brown and violet . . 70 45

DESIGNS: 5 p. Machha Puchhre; 40 p. Manaslu (wrongly inscr "MANSALU").

1961. 10th Democracy Day.

142 **29** 10 p. orange and brown . . 10 10

30 Prince Gyanendra cancelling Children's Day Stamps of 1960

31 King Mahendra

1961. Children's Day.

143 **30** 12 p. orange . . . . 20·00 20·00

1961. King Mahendra's 42nd Birthday.

144 **31** 6 p. green 20 20

145 12 p. blue 30 30

146 50 p. red 60 60

147 1 r. brown . . . . 1·00 1·00

32 Campaign Emblem and House

33 King Mahendra on Horseback

1962. Malaria Eradication.

148 **32** 12 p. blue 20 20

149 – 1 r. orange and red . . . 60 60

DESIGN: 1 r. Emblem and Nepalese flag.

1962. King Mahendra's 43rd Birthday.

150 **33** 10 p. blue 15 15

151 15 p. brown 20 20

152 45 p. brown 40 40

153 1 r. grey 60 60

34 Bhana Bhakta Acharya

1962. Nepalese Poets.

154 **34** 5 p. brown 20 20

155 – 10 p. turquoise 20 20

156 – 40 p. green 30 30

PORTRAITS: 10 p. Moti Ram Bhakta; 40 p. Sambhu Prasad.

35 King Mahendra

36

1962.

157 **35** 1 p. red 10 10

158 2 p. blue 10 10

158a 3 p. grey 30 20

159 5 p. brown 10 10

160 **36** 10 p. purple 10 10

161 40 p. brown 20 20

162 75 p. green . . . . 6·00 6·00

162a **35** 75 p. green 80 40

163 **27** 2 r. red 80 80

164 5 r. green . . . . 1·60 1·60

164a 10 r. violet . . . . 6·00 5·00

No. 162a is smaller, $17\frac{1}{2} \times 20$ mm.

37 Emblems of Learning

38 Hands holding Lamps

1963. U.N.E.S.C.O. "Education for All" Campaign.

165 **37** 10 p. black 20 10

166 15 p. brown 30 20

167 50 p. blue 50 40

1963. National Day.

168 **38** 5 p. blue 10 10

169 10 p. brown 10 10

170 50 p. purple 40 30

171 1 r. green 80 40

39 Campaign Symbols

40 Map of Nepal and Open Hand

1963. Freedom from Hunger.

172 **39** 10 p. orange 20 10

173 15 p. blue 30 20

174 50 p. green 60 40

175 1 r. brown 80 70

1963. Rastruya Panchayat.

176 **40** 10 p. green 10 10

177 15 p. purple 20 20

178 50 p. grey 50 30

179 1 r. blue 80 50

41 King Mahendra

42 King Mahendra and Highway Map

1963. King Mahendra's 44th Birthday.

180 **41** 5 p. violet 10 10

181 10 p. brown 20 10

182 15 p. green 30 20

1964. Inauguration of East–West Highway.

183 **42** 10 p. orange and blue . . 10 10

184 15 p. orange and blue . . 20 10

185 50 p. brown and green . . 30 20

43 King Mahendra at Microphone

44 Crown Prince Birendra

1964. King Mahendra's 45th Birthday.

186 **43** 1 p. brown 10 10

187 2 p. grey 10 10

188 2 r. brown 60 60

1964. Crown Prince's 19th Birthday.

189 **44** 10 p. green 50 40

190 15 p. brown 50 40

45 Flag, Kukris, Rings and Torch

46 Nepalese Family

1964. Olympic Games, Tokyo.

191 **45** 10 p. blue, red and pink . . 50 40

1965. Land Reform.

192 – 2 p. black and green . . . 20 20

193 – 5 p. brown and green . . . 20 20

194 – 10 p. purple and grey . . . 20 20

195 **46** 15 p. brown and yellow . . 30 30

DESIGNS: 2 p. Farmer ploughing; 5 p. Ears of wheat; 10 p. Grain elevator.

47 Globe and Letters

48 King Mahendra

1965. Introduction of International Insured and Parcel Service.

196 **47** 15 p. violet 20 20

1965. King Mahendra's 46th Birthday.

197 **48** 50 p. purple 50 40

49 Four Martyrs

50 I.T.U. Emblem

1965. "Nepalese Martyrs".

198 **49** 15 p. green 25 20

1965. I.T.U. Centenary.

199 **50** 15 p. black and purple . . 30 20

51 I.C.Y. Emblem

52 Devkota (poet)

1965. International Co-operation Year.

200 **51** 1 r. multicoloured 60 50

1965. Devkota Commemoration.
201 **52** 15 p. brown 20 20

54 Flag and King Mahendra

1966. Democracy Day.
202 **54** 15 p. red and blue 40 30

55 Siva Parvati and Pashuvati Temple
56 "Stamp" Emblem

1966. Maha Siva-Ratri Festival.
203 **55** 15 p. violet 25 20

1966. Nepalese Philatelic Exhibition, Katmandu.
204 **56** 15 p. orange and green . . 30 20

57 King Mahendra
58 Queen Mother

1966. King Mahendra's 47th Birthday.
205 **57** 15 p. brown and yellow . . 25 20

1966. Queen Mother's 60th Birthday.
206 **58** 15 p. brown 20 20

59 Queen Ratna
60 Flute-player and Dancer

1966. Children's Day.
207 **59** 15 p. brown and yellow . . 25 20

1966. Krishna Anniv.
208 **60** 15 p. violet and yellow . . 25 20

61 "To render service..."

1966. 1st Anniv of Nepalese Red Cross.
209 **61** 50 p. red and green . . . . 2·40 80

62 W.H.O. Building on Flag
63 Paudyal

1966. Inaug of W.H.O. Headquarters, Geneva.
210 **62** 1 r. violet . . . . 1·25 80

1966. Leknath Paudyal (poet) Commemoration.
211 **63** 15 p. blue 25 20

64 Rama and Sita
65 Buddha

1967. Rama Navami, 2024, birthday of Rama.
212 **64** 15 p. brown and yellow . 25 20

1967. Buddha Jayanti, birthday of Buddha.
213 **65** 75 p. purple and orange . 50 50

66 King Mahendra addressing Nepalese

1967. King Mahendra's 48th Birthday.
214 **66** 15 p. brown and blue . . 25 25

67 Queen Ratna and Children
68 Ama Dablam (mountain)

1967. Children's Day.
215 **67** 15 p. brown and cream . . 25 20

1967. International Tourist Year.
216 **68** 5 p. violet (postage) . . . 20 20
217 – 65 p. brown 40 40
218 – 1 r. 80 red and blue (air) . 1·00 80
DESIGNS—38 × 20 mm: 65 p. Bhaktapur Durbar Square. $35\frac{1}{2} \times 25\frac{1}{2}$ mm: 1 r. 80, Plane over Katmandu.

69 Open-air Class

1967. Constitution Day. "Go to the Village" Educational Campaign.
219 **69** 15 p. multicoloured . . . 25 20

70 Crown Prince Birendra, Campfire and Scout Emblem

1967. Diamond Jubilee of World Scouting.
220 **70** 15 p. blue 40 30

71 Prithvi Narayan Shah (founder of Kingdom)
72 Arms of Nepal

1968. Bicentenary of the Kingdom.
221 **71** 15 p. blue and red 40 30

1968. National Day.
222 **72** 15 p. blue and red 40 30

73 W.H.O. Emblem and Nepalese Flag

1968. 20th Anniv of W.H.O.
223 **73** 1 r. 20 blue, red & yellow . 1·75 1·25

74 Sita and Janaki Temple

1968. Sita Jayanti.
224 **74** 15 p. brown and violet . . 30 20

75 King Mahendra, Mountains and Himalayan Monal Pheasant

1968. King Mahendra's 49th Birthday.
225 **75** 15 p. multicoloured . . . . 1·00 30

76 Garuda and Airline Emblem

1968. Air. 10th Anniv of Royal Nepalese Airlines.
226 **76** 15 p. brown and blue . . . 20 20
227 – 65 p. blue 40 40
228 – 2 r. 50 blue and orange . . 1·50 1·25
DESIGNS—DIAMOND ($25\frac{1}{2} \times 25\frac{1}{2}$ mm): 65 p. Route-map. As Type **76**: 2 r. 50, Convair Metropolitan airliner over Mount Dhaulagiri.

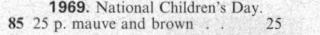

77 Flag, Queen Ratna and Children
78 Human Rights Emblem and Buddha

1968. Children's Day and Queen Ratna's 41st Birthday.
229 **77** 5 p. red, yellow and green . 20 15

1968. Human Rights Year.
230 **78** 1 r. red and green . . . . . 1·60 1·25

79 Crown Prince Birendra and Dancers

1968. Crown Prince Birendra's 24th Birthday, and National Youth Festival.
231 **79** 25 p. blue 40 30

80 King Mahendra, Flags and U.N. Building, New York
81 Amsu Varma (7th-century ruler)

1969. Nepal's Election to U.N. Security Council.
232 **80** 1 r. multicoloured 60 50

1969. Famous Nepalese.
233 **81** 15 p. violet and green . . . 30 30
234 – 25 p. turquoise 40 40
235 – 50 p. brown 50 50
236 – 1 r. purple and brown . . . 60 50
DESIGNS—VERT: 25 p. Ram Shah (17th-century King of Gurkha); 50 p. Bhimsen Thapa (19th-century Prime Minister). HORIZ: 1 r. Bal Bhadra Kunwar (19th-century warrior).

82 I.L.O. Emblem

1969. 50th Anniv of I.L.O.
237 **82** 1 r. brown and mauve . . . 3·00 2·00

83 King Mahendra
85 Queen Ratna, and Child with Toy

84 King Tribhuvana and Queens

1969. King Mahendra's 50th Birthday.
238 **83** 25 p. multicoloured 25 25

1969. 64th Birth Anniv of King Tribhuvana.
239 **84** 25 p. brown and yellow . . 25 25

1969. National Children's Day.
240 **85** 25 p. mauve and brown . . 25 25

86 Rhododendron
87 Durga, Goddess of Victory

1969. Flowers. Multicoloured.
241 25 p. Type **86** 35 30
242 25 p. Narcissus 35 30
243 25 p. Marigold 35 30
244 25 p. Poinsettia 35 30

1969. Durga Pooja Festival.
245 **87** 15 p. black and orange . . 20 20
246 50 p. violet and brown . . 45 40

88 Crown Prince Birendra and Princess Aishwarya

1970. Royal Wedding.
247 **88** 25 p. multicoloured 25 20

89 Produce, Cow and Landscape

1970. Agricultural Year.
248 **89** 25 p. multicoloured 25 20

90 King Mahendra, Mt. Everest and Nepalese Crown

1970. King Mahendra's 51st Birthday.
249 **90** 50 p. multicoloured 40 30

91 Lake Gosainkunda

1970. Nepalese Lakes. Multicoloured.
250 5 p. Type **91** 20 20
251 25 p. Lake Phewa Tal 30 30
252 1 r. Lake Rara Daha 50 50

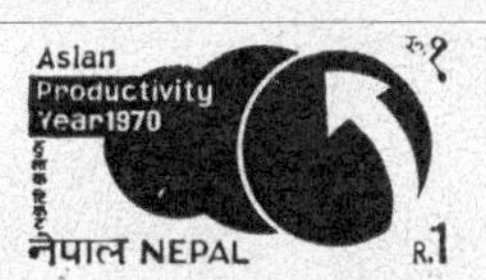

92 A.P.Y. Emblem

1970. Asian Productivity Year.
253 **92** 1 r. blue 50 40

93 Queen Ratna and Children's Palace, Taulihawa

1970. National Children's Day.
254 **93** 25 p. grey and brown . . . 25 20

94 New Headquarters Building

1970. New U.P.U. Headquarters, Berne.
255 **94** 2 r. 50 grey and brown . . 1·00 80

95 U.N. Flag

1970. 25th Anniv of United Nations.
256 **95** 25 p. blue and purple . . . 25 20

96 Durbar Square, Patan

1970. Tourism. Multicoloured.
257 15 p. Type **96** 20 10
258 25 p. Boudhanath Stupa (temple) (vert) 30 20
259 1 r. Mt. Gauri Shankar . . . 50 40

97 Statue of Harihar, Valmiki Ashram

98 Torch within Spiral

1971. Nepalese Religious Art.
260 **97** 25 p. black and brown . . 25 20

1971. Racial Equality Year.
261 **98** 1 r. red and blue 60 45

99 King Mahendra taking Salute

100 Sweta Bhairab

1971. King Mahendra's 52nd Birthday.
262 **99** 15 p. purple and blue . . . 25 20

1971. Bhairab Statues of Shiva.
263 **100** 15 p. brown and chestnut . 20 20
264 – 25 p. brown and green . . 20 20
265 – 50 p. brown and blue . . 40 40
DESIGNS: 25 p. Mahankal Bhairab; 50 p. Kal Bhairab.

101 Child presenting Queen Ratna with Garland

1971. National Children's Day.
266 **101** 25 p. multicoloured . . . 25 15

102 Iranian and Nepalese Flags on Map of Iran

1971. 2,500th Anniv of Persian Empire.
267 **102** 1 r. multicoloured 60 40

103 Mother and Child

1971. 25th Anniv of U.N.I.C.E.F.
268 **103** 1 r. blue 60 40

104 Mt. Everest

105 Royal Standard

1971. Tourism. Himalayan Peaks.
269 **104** 25 p deep brown, brown and blue 20 10
270 – 1 r. black, brown and blue 40 30
271 – 1 r. 80 green, brown and blue 70 50
DESIGNS: 1 r. Mt. Kanchenjunga; 1 r. 80, Mt. Annapurna I.

1972. National Day.
272 **105** 25 p. black and red . . . 25 15

106 Araniko and White Dagoba, Peking

107 Open Book

1972. Araniko (13th-century architect) Commem.
273 **106** 15 p. brown and blue . . 15 10

1972. International Book Year.
274 **107** 2 p. brown and buff . . . 10 10
275 5 p. black and brown . . . 10 10
276 1 r. black and blue . . . 50 40

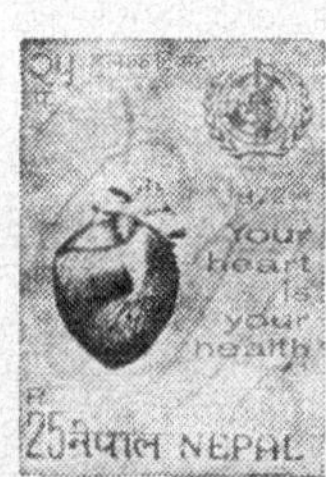

108 Human Heart

1972. World Heart Month.
277 **108** 25 p. red and green . . . 25 20

109 King Mahendra

110 King Birendra

1972. 1st Death Anniv of King Mahendra.
278 **109** 25 p. brown and black . . 25 15

1972. King Birendra's 28th Birthday.
279 **110** 50 p. purple and brown . . 30 25

111 Northern Border Costumes

112 Sri Baburam Acharya

1973. National Costumes. Multicoloured.
280 25 p. Type **111** 20 10
281 50 p. Hill-dwellers 25 20
282 75 p. Katmandu Valley 35 25
283 1 r. Inner Terai 50 35

1973. 85th Birth Anniv of Sri Baburam Acharya (historian).
284 **112** 25 p. grey and red 20 15

113 Nepalese Family

1973. 25th Anniv of W.H.O.
285 **113** 1 r. blue and orange . . . 50 40

114 Birthplace of Buddha, Lumbini

1973. Tourism. Multicoloured.
286 25 p. Type **114** 20 10
287 75 p. Mt. Makalu 30 20
288 1 r. Castle, Gurkha 40 40

115 Transplanting Rice

1973. 10th Anniv of World Food Programme.
289 **115** 10 p. brown & violet . . . 10 10

116 Interpol H.Q., Paris

1973. 50th Anniv of International Criminal Police Organization (Interpol).
290 **116** 25 p. blue and brown . . . 20 15

117 Shri Shom Nath Sigdyal

118 Cow

1973. 1st Death Anniv of Shri Shom Nath Sigdyal (scholar).
291 **117** 1 r. 25 violet 50 40

1973. Domestic Animals. Multicoloured.
292 2 p. Type **118** 10 10
293 3 r. 25 Yak 90 60

119 King Birendra

1974. King Birendra's 29th Birthday.
294 **119** 5 p. brown and black . . 10 10
295 15 p. brown and black . . 15 10
296 1 r. brown and black . . 40 30

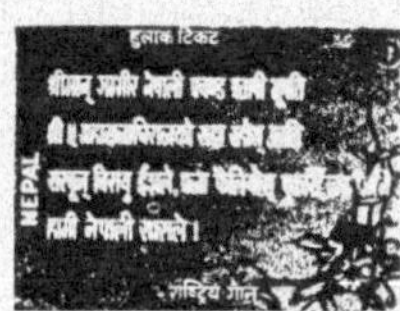

120 Text of National Anthem

121 King Janak seated on Throne

1974. National Day.
297 **120** 25 p. purple 20 10
298 – 1 r. green 30 25
DESIGN: 1 r. Anthem musical score.

1974. King Janak Commemoration.
299 **121** 2 r. 50 multicoloured . . 1·00 80

122 Emblem and Village

1974. 25th Anniv of SOS Children's Village International.
300 **122** 25 p. blue and red 15 15

123 Football

124 W.P.Y. Emblem

1974. Nepalese Games. Multicoloured.
301 2 p. Type **123** 10 10
302 2 r. 75 Baghchal (diagram) . . 60 50

1974. World Population Year.
303 **124** 5 p. blue and brown . . . 10 10

125 U.P.U. Monument, Berne

126 Red Lacewing

1974. Centenary of U.P.U.
304 **125** 1 r. black and green . . . 40 30

1974. Nepalese Butterflies. Multicoloured.
305 10 p. Type **126** 10 10
306 15 p. Leaf butterfly 40 15
307 1 r. 25 Leaf butterfly (underside) 1·00 70
308 1 r. 75 Red-breasted jezebel . 1·25 1·00

127 King Birendra

128 Muktinath

1974. King Birendra's 30th Birthday.
309 **127** 25 p. black and green . . 15 15

1974. "Visit Nepal" Tourism. Multicoloured.
310 25 p. Type **128** 20 10
311 1 r. Peacock window, Bhaktapur (horiz) 40 25

129 Guheswari Temple

1975. Coronation of King Birendra. Multicoloured.

312 25 p. Type **129** 20 10
313 50 p. Lake Rara (37 × 30 mm) 20 10
314 1 r. Throne and sceptre (46 × 26 mm) 30 20
315 1 r. 25 Royal Palace, Katmandu (46 × 26 mm) 60 30
316 1 r. 75 Pashupatinath Temple (25 × 31 mm) 40 40
317 2 r. 75 King Birendra and Queen Aishwarya (46 × 25 mm) . . 60 50

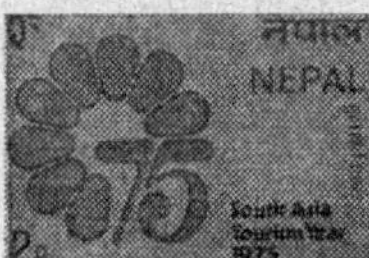

130 Tourism Year Emblem

1975. South Asia Tourism Year. Multicoloured.

319 2 p. Type **130** 10 10
320 25 p. Temple stupa (vert) . . . 20 20

131 Tiger

1975. Wildlife Conservation. Multicoloured.

321 2 p. Type **131** 20 20
322 5 p. Swamp deer (vert) 20 20
323 1 r. Lesser panda 40 40

132 Queen Aishwarya and I.W.Y. Emblem

1975. International Women's Year.

324 **132** 1 r. multicoloured 30 20

133 Rupse Falls 134 King Birendra

1975. Tourism. Multicoloured.

325 2 p. Mt. Ganesh Himal (horiz) 10 10
326 25 p. Type **133** 10 10
327 50 p. Kumari ("Living Goddess") 30 20

1975. King Birendra's 31st Birthday.

328 **134** 25 p. violet and mauve . . 15 10

136 Flag and Map 138 Flags of Nepal and Colombo Plan

137 Transplanting Rice

1976. Silver Jubilee of National Democracy Day.

330 **136** 2 r. 50 red and blue . . . 50 40

1976. Agriculture Year.

331 **137** 25 p. multicoloured . . . 15 10

1976. 25th Anniv of Colombo Plan.

332 **138** 1 r. multicoloured 30 25

139 Running 140 "Dove of Peace"

1976. Olympic Games, Montreal.

333 **139** 3 r. 25 black and blue . . 80 60

1976. 5th Non-aligned Countries' Summit Conference.

334 **140** 5 r. blue, yellow and black 1·10 70

141 Lakhe Dance

1976. Nepalese Dances. Multicoloured.

335 10 p. Type **141** 10 10
336 15 p. Maruni dance 10 10
337 30 p. Jhangad dance 20 10
338 1 r. Sebru dance 30 20

142 Nepalese Lily 143 King Birendra

1976. Flowers. Multicoloured.

339 30 p. Type **142** 30 10
340 30 p. "Meconopsis grandis" . . 30 10
341 30 p. "Cardiocrinum giganteum" (horiz) 30 10
342 30 p. "Megacodon stylophorus" (horiz) 30 10

1976. King Birendra's 32nd Birthday.

343 **143** 5 p. green 10 10
344 30 p. dp brown, brn & yell 15 10

144 Liberty Bell

1976. Bicentenary of American Revolution.

345 **144** 10 r. multicoloured . . . 1·50 1·40

145 Kaji Amarsingh Thapa

1977. Kaji Amarsingh Thapa (19th-century warrior) Commemoration

346 **145** 10 p. green and brown . 10 10

146 Terracotta Figurine and Kapilavastu

1977. Tourism.

347 **146** 30 p. violet 10 10
348 – 5 r. green and brown . . 80 60

DESIGN: 5 r. Ashokan pillar, Lumbini.

147 Great Indian Hornbill 148 Tukuche Himal and Police Flag

1977. Birds. Multicoloured.

349 5 p. Type **147** 45 10
350 15 p. Cheer pheasant (horiz) . 80 15
351 1 r. Green magpie (horiz) . . 1·25 45
352 2 r. 30 Spiny babbler . . . . . 2·25 95

1977. 1st Anniv of Ascent of Tukuche Himal by Police Team.

353 **148** 1 r. 25 multicoloured . . . 30 20

149 Map of Nepal and Scout Emblem 150 Dhanwantari, the Health-giver

1977. 25th Anniv of Scouting in Nepal.

354 **149** 3 r. 50 multicoloured . . . 60 40

1977. Health Day.

355 **150** 30 p. green 15 10

151 Map of Nepal and Flags 152 King Birendra

1977. 26th Consultative Committee Meeting of Colombo Plan, Katmandu.

356 **151** 1 r. multicoloured 20 15

1977. King Birendra's 33rd Birthday.

357 **152** 5 p. brown 10 10
358 1 r. brown 20 20

153 General Post Office, Katmandu, and Seal

1978. Centenary of Nepalese Post Office.

359 **153** 25 p. brown and agate . . 10 10
360 – 75 p. brown and agate . . 20 20

DESIGN: 75 p. General Post Office, Katmandu, and early postmark.

154 South-west Face of Mount Everest

1978. 25th Anniv of First Ascent of Mt. Everest.

361 **154** 2 r. 30 grey and brown . . 50 30
362 – 4 r. blue and green . . . 70 60

DESIGN: 4 r. South face of Mt. Everest.

155 Sun, Ankh and Landscape

1978. World Environment Day.

363 **155** 1 r. green and orange . . . 20 15

156 Queen Mother Ratna 157 Rapids, Tripsuli River

1978. Queen Mother's 50th Birthday.

364 **156** 2 r. 30 green 40 30

1978. Tourism. Multicoloured.

365 10 p. Type **157** 10 10
366 50 p. Window, Nara Devi, Katmandu 15 10
367 1 r. Mahakali dance (vert) . . 25 20

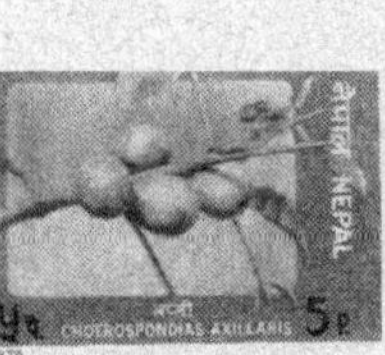

158 Lapsi ("Choerospondias axillaris") 159 Lamp and U.N. Emblem

1978. Fruits. Multicoloured.

368 5 p. Type **158** 15 10
369 1 r. Katus (vert) 25 20
370 1 r. 25 Rudrakshya 40 25

1978. 30th Anniv of Human Rights Declaration.

371 **159** 25 p. brown and red . . . 10 10
372 1 r. blue and red 20 15

160 Wright Flyer I and Boeing 727-100 161 King Birendra

1978. Air. 75th Anniv of First Powered Flight.

373 **160** 2 r. 30 blue and brown . 45 30

1978. King Birendra's 34th Birthday.

374 **161** 30 p. blue and brown . . 10 10
375 2 r. brown and violet . . 30 25

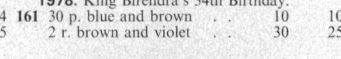

162 Red Machchhindranath and Kamroop and Patan Temples

1979. Red Machchhindranath (guardian deity) Festival.

376 **162** 75 p. brown and green . . 20 15

163 "Buddha's Birth" (carving, Maya Devi Temple) 164 Planting a Sapling

1979. Lumbini Year.

377 **163** 1 r. yellow and brown . . 20 15

1979. Tree Planting Festival.

378 **164** 2 r. 30 brown, grn & yell . 50 40

165 Chariot of Red Machchhindranath 166 Nepalese Scouts and Guides

1979. Bhoto Jatra (Vest Exhibition) Festival.
379 **165** 1 r. 25 multicoloured . . . 25 20

1979. International Year of the Child.
380 **166** 1 r. brown 25 20

167 Mount Pabil

168 Great Grey Shrike

1979. Tourism.
381 **167** 30 p. green 10 10
382 – 50 p. red and blue 10 10
383 – 1 r. 25 multicoloured . . . 25 25
DESIGNS: 50 p. Yajnashala, Swargadwari. 1 r. 25, Shiva-Parbati (wood carving, Gaddi Baithak Temple).

1979. International World Pheasant Association Symposium, Katmandu. Multicoloured.
384 10 p. Type **168** (postage) . . . 25 20
385 10 r. Fire-tailed sunbird . . . 7·25 3·50
386 3 r. 50 Himalayan monal pheasant (horiz) (air) . . . 2·50 1·90

169 Lichchhavi Coin (obverse)

170 King Birendra

1979. Coins.
387 **169** 5 p. orange and brown . . 10 10
388 – 5 p. orange and brown . . 10 10
389 – 15 p. blue and indigo . . 10 10
390 – 15 p. blue and indigo . . 10 10
391 – 1 r. blue and deep blue . . 20 20
392 – 1 r. blue and deep blue . . 20 20
DESIGNS: No. 388, Lichchhavi coin (reverse); No. 389, Malla coin (obverse); No. 390, Malla coin (reverse); No. 391, Prithvi Narayan Shah coin (obverse); No. 392, Prithvi Narayan Shah coin (reverse).

1979. King Birendra's 35th Birthday. Multicoloured.
393 25 p. Type **170** 10 10
394 2 r. 30 Reservoir 40 30

171 Samyak Pooja Festival

1980. Samyak Pooja Festival, Katmandu.
395 **171** 30 p. brown, grey & pur . 10 10

172 Sacred Basil

1980. Herbs. Multicoloured.
396 5 p. Type **172** 10 10
397 30 p. Valerian 10 10
398 1 r. Nepalese pepper 20 15
399 2 r. 30 Himalayan rhubarb . . 40 25

173 Gyandil Das

174 Everlasting Flame and Temple, Shirsasthan

1980. Nepalese Writers.
400 **173** 5 p. lilac and brown . . . 10 10
401 – 30 p. purple and brown . . 10 10
402 – 1 r. green and blue 15 15
403 – 2 r. 30 blue and green . . 55 25
DESIGNS: 30 p. Siddhidas Amatya; 1 r. Pahalman Singh Swanr; 2 r. 30, Jay Prithvi Bahadur Singh.

1980. Tourism. Multicoloured.
404 10 p. Type **174** 10 10
405 1 r. Godavari Pond 20 15
406 5 r. Mount Dhaulagiri . . . 70 50

175 Bhairab Dancer

176 King Birendra

1980. World Tourism Conference, Manila, Philippines.
407 **175** 25 r. multicoloured . . . 3·00 2·25

1980. King Birendra's 36th Birthday.
408 **176** 1 r. multicoloured 20 15

177 I.Y.D.P. Emblem and Nepalese Flag

1981. International Year of Disabled Persons.
409 **177** 5 r. multicoloured 80 60

178 Nepal Rastra Bank

179 One Anna Stamp of 1881

1981. 25th Anniv of Nepal Rastra Bank.
410 **178** 1 r. 75 multicoloured . . 25 20

1981. Nepalese Postage Stamp Centenary.
411 **179** 10 p. blue, brown and black 10 10
412 – 40 p. purple, brown and black 10 10
413 – 3 r. 40 green, brown and blk 50 40
DESIGNS: 40 p. 2 anna stamp of 1881; 3 r. 40, 4 a. stamp of 1881.

180 Nepalese Flag and Association Emblem

181 Hand holding Stamp

1981. 70th Council Meeting of International Hotel Association, Katmandu.
415 **180** 1 r. 75 multicoloured . . 25 20

1981. "Nepal 81" Stamp Exhibition, Katmandu.
416 **181** 40 p. multicoloured . . . 10 10

182 King Birendra

183 Image of Hrishikesh, Ridi

1981. King Birendra's 37th Birthday.
417 **182** 1 r. multicoloured 15 15

1981. Tourism. Multicoloured.
418 5 p. Type **183** 10 10
419 25 p. Tripura Sundari Temple, Baitadi 10 10
420 2 r. Mt. Langtang Lirung . . 25 15

184 Academy Building

185 Balakrishna Sama

1982. 25th Anniv of Royal Nepal Academy.
421 **184** 40 p. multicoloured . . . 10 10

1982. 1st Death Anniv of Balakrishna Sama (writer).
422 **185** 1 r. multicoloured 15 15

186 "Intelsat V" and Dish Aerial

187 Mount Nuptse

1982. Sagarmatha Satellite Earth Station, Balambu.
423 **186** 5 r. multicoloured 75 40

1982. 50th Anniv of Union of International Alpinist Associations. Multicoloured.
424 25 p. Type **187** 10 10
425 2 r. Mount Lhotse (31 × 31 mm) 30 20
426 3 r. Mount Everest (39 × 31 mm) 60 30
Nos. 424/6 were issued together, se-tenant, forming a composite design.

188 Games Emblem and Weights

189 Indra Sarobar Lake

1982. 9th Asian Games, New Delhi.
427 **188** 3 r. 40 multicoloured . . . 50 40

1982. Kulekhani Hydro-electric Project.
428 **189** 2 r. multicoloured 30 20

190 King Birendra

191 N.I.D.C. Emblem

1982. King Birendra's 38th Birthday.
429 **190** 5 p. multicoloured 10 10

1983. 25th Anniv (1984) of Nepal Industrial Development Corporation.
430 **191** 50 p. multicoloured . . . 10 10

192 Boeing 727 over Himalayas

1983. 25th Anniv of Royal Nepal Airlines.
431 **192** 1 r. multicoloured 40 15

193 W.C.Y. Emblem and Nepalese Flag

194 Sarangi

1983. World Communications Year.
432 **193** 10 p. multicoloured . . . 10 10

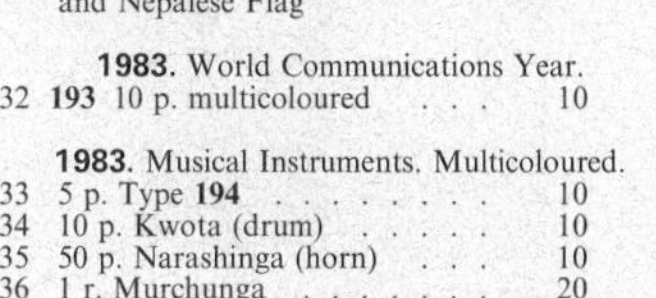

1983. Musical Instruments. Multicoloured.
433 5 p. Type **194** 10 10
434 10 p. Kwota (drum) 10 10
435 50 p. Narashinga (horn) . . . 10 10
436 1 r. Murchunga 20 20

195 Chakrapani Chalise

196 King Birendra and Doves

1983. Birth Centenary of Chakrapani Chalise (poet).
437 **195** 4 r. 50 multicoloured . . 60 45

1983. King Birendra's 39th Birthday.
438 **196** 5 r. multicoloured 70 40

197 Barahkshetra Temple and Image of Barah

1983. Tourism. Multicoloured.
439 1 r. Type **197** 15 10
440 2 r. 20 Temple, Triveni . . . 25 20
441 6 r. Mount Cho-oyu 70 50

198 Auditing Accounts

199 Antenna and Emblem

1984. 25th Anniv of Auditor General.
442 **198** 25 p. multicoloured . . . 10 10

1984. 20th Anniv of Asia-Pacific Broadcasting Union.
443 **199** 5 r. multicoloured 70 60

200 University Emblem

201 Boxing

1984. 25th Anniv of Tribhuvan University.
444 **200** 50 p. multicoloured . . . 15 10

1984. Olympic Games, Los Angeles.
445 **201** 10 r. multicoloured . . . 1·25 80

202 Family and Emblem

203 National Flag and Emblem

1984. 25th Anniv of Nepal Family Planning Association.
446 **202** 1 r. multicoloured 15 10

1984. Social Service Day.
447 **203** 5 p. multicoloured 10 10

204 Gharial

205 "Vishnu as Giant" (stone carving)

1984. Wildlife. Multicoloured.
448 10 p. Type **204** 10 10
449 25 p. Snow leopard 10 10
450 50 p. Blackbuck 20 20

1984. Tourism. Multicoloured.
451 10 p. Type **205** 10 10
452 1 r. Temple of Chhinna Masta Bhagavati and sculpture (horiz) 15 10
453 5 r. Mount Api 70 45

206 King Birendra

1984. King Birendra's 40th Birthday.
454 **206** 1 r. multicoloured 15 10

207 Animals and Mountains 208 Shiva

1985. Sagarmatha (Mt. Everest) National Park.
455 **207** 10 r. multicoloured . . . 2·50 70

1985. Traditional Paintings. Details of cover of "Shiva Dharma Purana". Multicoloured.
456 50 p. Type **208** 10 10
457 50 p. Multi-headed Shiva talking to woman 10 10
458 50 p. Brahma and Vishnu making offering (15 × 22 mm) 10 10
459 50 p. Shiva in single- and multi-headed forms 10 10
460 50 p. Shiva talking to woman . 10 10
Nos. 456/60 were printed together, se-tenant, forming a composite design.

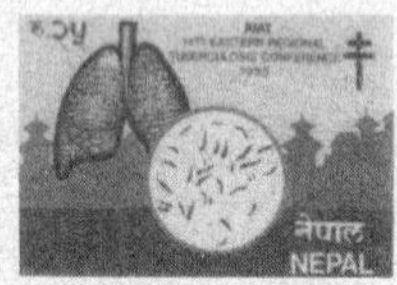

209 U.N. Flag 210 Lungs and Bacilli

1985. 40th Anniv of U.N.O.
461 **209** 5 r. multicoloured 60 40

1985. 14th Eastern Regional Tuberculosis Conference, Katmandu.
462 **210** 25 r. multicoloured . . . 2·75 2·00

211 Flags of Member Countries

1985. 1st South Asian Association for Regional Co-operation Summit.
463 **211** 5 r. multicoloured 60 40

212 Jaleshwar Temple 213 I.Y.Y. Emblem

1985. Tourism. Multicoloured.
464 10 p. Type **212** 10 10
465 1 r. Temple of Goddess Shaileshwari, Silgadi 10 10
466 2 r. Phoksundo Lake 25 15

1985. International Youth Year.
467 **213** 1 r. multicoloured 15 10

214 King Birendra 215 Devi Ghat Hydro-electric Project

1985. King Birendra's 41st Birthday.
468 **214** 50 p. multicoloured . . . 10 10

1985.
469 **215** 2 r. multicoloured 30 20

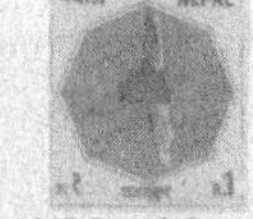

216 Emblem 217 Royal Crown

1986. 25th Anniv of Panchayat System (partyless government).
470 **216** 4 r. multicoloured 50 40

1986.
471 – 5 p. brown and deep brown 10 10
472 – 10 p. blue 10 10
474 – 50 p. blue 10 10
476 **217** 1 r. brown and ochre . . 15 10
DESIGNS: 5, 50 p. Pashupati Temple; 10 p. Mayadevi Temple of Lumbini (Buddha's birthplace).

218 Pharping Hydro-electric Station

1986. 75th Anniv of Pharping Hydro-electric Power Station.
480 **218** 15 p. multicoloured . . . 10 10

219 Emblem and Map

1986. 25th Anniv of Asian Productivity Organization.
481 **219** 1 r. multicoloured 15 10

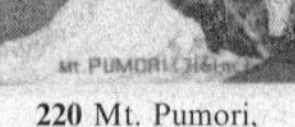

220 Mt. Pumori, Himalayas 221 King Birendra

1986. Tourism. Multicoloured.
482 60 p. "Budhanilkantha" (sculpture of reclining Vishnu), Katmandu Valley (38 × 22 mm) 10 10
483 8 r. Type **220** 80 60

1986. King Birendra's 42nd Birthday.
484 **221** 1 r. multicoloured 15 10

222 I.P.Y. Emblem 223 National Flag and Council Emblem

1986. International Peace Year.
485 **222** 10 r. multicoloured . . . 90 70

1987. 10th Anniv of National Social Service Co-ordination Council.
486 **223** 1 r. multicoloured 15 10

224 Emblem and Forest

1987. 1st Nepal Scout Jamboree, Katmandu.
487 **224** 1 r. brown, orange & bl . 20 10

225 Ashokan Pillar and Maya Devi

1987. Lumbini (Buddha's Birthplace) Development Project.
488 **225** 4 r. multicoloured 40 30

226 Emblem 227 Emblem

1987. 3rd South Asian Association for Regional Co-operation Summit, Katmandu.
489 **226** 60 p. gold and red 10 10

1987. 25th Anniv of Rastriya Samachar Samiti (news service).
490 **227** 4 r. purple, blue & red . . 40 30

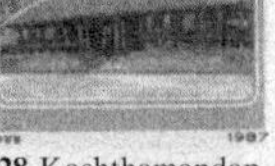

228 Kashthamandap, Katmandu 229 Gyawali

1987.
491 **228** 25 p. multicoloured . . . 10 10

1987. 89th Birth Anniv of Surya Bikram Gyawali.
492 **229** 60 p. multicoloured . . . 10 10

230 Emblem 231 King Birendra

1987. International Year of Shelter for the Homeless.
493 **230** 5 r. multicoloured 50 40

1987. King Birendra's 43rd Birthday.
494 **231** 25 p. multicoloured . . . 10 10

232 Mt. Kanjiroba

1987.
495 **232** 10 r. multicoloured 90 60

233 Crown Prince Dipendra

1988. Crown Prince Dipendra's 17th Birthday.
496 **233** 1 r. multicoloured 15 10

234 Baby in Incubator

1988. 25th Anniv of Kanti Children's Hospital, Katmandu.
497 **234** 60 p. multicoloured . . . 10 10

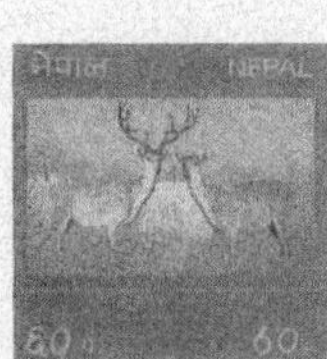

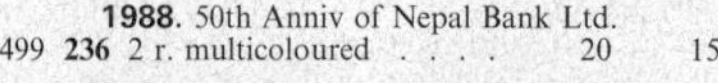

235 Swamp Deer 236 Laxmi, Goddess of Wealth

1988. 12th Anniv of Royal Shukla Phanta Wildlife Reserve.
498 **235** 60 p. multicoloured . . . 20 10

1988. 50th Anniv of Nepal Bank Ltd.
499 **236** 2 r. multicoloured 20 15

237 Queen Mother 238 Hands protecting Blood Droplet

1988. 60th Birthday of Queen Mother.
500 **237** 5 r. multicoloured 50 40

1988. 25th Anniv of Nepal Red Cross Society.
501 **238** 1 r. red and brown . . . 15 10

239 Temple and Statue

1988. Temple of Goddess Bindhyabasini, Pokhara.
502 **239** 15 p. multicoloured . . . 10 10

240 King Birendra 241 Temple

1988. King Birendra's 44th Birthday.
503 **240** 4 r. multicoloured 40 25

1989. Pashupati Area Development Trust.
504 **241** 1 r. multicoloured 15 10

242 Emblem 243 S.A.A.R.C. Emblem

1989. 10th Anniv of Asia-Pacific Telecommunity.
505 **242** 4 r. green, black & violet . 25 15

1989. South Asian Association for Regional Co-operation Year against Drug Abuse and Trafficking.
506 **243** 60 p. multicoloured . . . 10 10

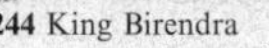

244 King Birendra 245 Child Survival Measures

1989. King Birendra's 45th Birthday.
507 **244** 2 r. multicoloured 20 10

1989. Child Survival Campaign.
508 **245** 1 r. multicoloured 10 10

246 Lake Rara **247** Mt. Amadablam

1989. Rara National Park.
509 **246** 4 r. multicoloured 25 15

1989.
510 **247** 5 r. multicoloured 40 20

248 Crown Prince Dipendra **249** Temple of Manakamana, Gorkha

1989. Crown Prince Dipendra's Coming-of-Age.
511 **248** 1 r. multicoloured 10 10

1990.
512 **249** 60 p. black and violet . . 10 10

250 Emblem and Children **251** Emblem

1990. 25th Anniv of Nepal Children's Organization.
513 **250** 1 r. multicoloured 10 10

1990. Centenary of Bir Hospital.
514 **251** 60 p. red, blue and yellow 10 10

252 Emblem **253** Goddess and Bageshwori Temple, Nepalgunj

1990. 20th Anniv of Asian–Pacific Postal Training Centre, Bangkok.
515 **252** 4 r. multicoloured 30 15

1990. Tourism. Multicoloured.
516 1 r. Type **253** 10 10
517 5 r. Mt. Saipal (36 × 27 mm) . 35 25

254 Leisure Activities

1990. South Asian Association for Regional Co-operation Girls' Year.
518 **254** 4 r. 60 multicoloured . . . 35 20

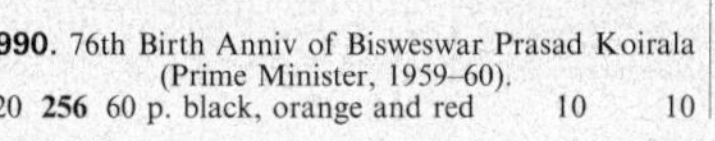

255 King Birendra **256** Koirala

1990. King Birendra's 46th Birthday.
519 **255** 2 r. multicoloured 15 10

1990. 76th Birth Anniv of Bisweswar Prasad Koirala (Prime Minister, 1959–60).
520 **256** 60 p. black, orange and red 10 10

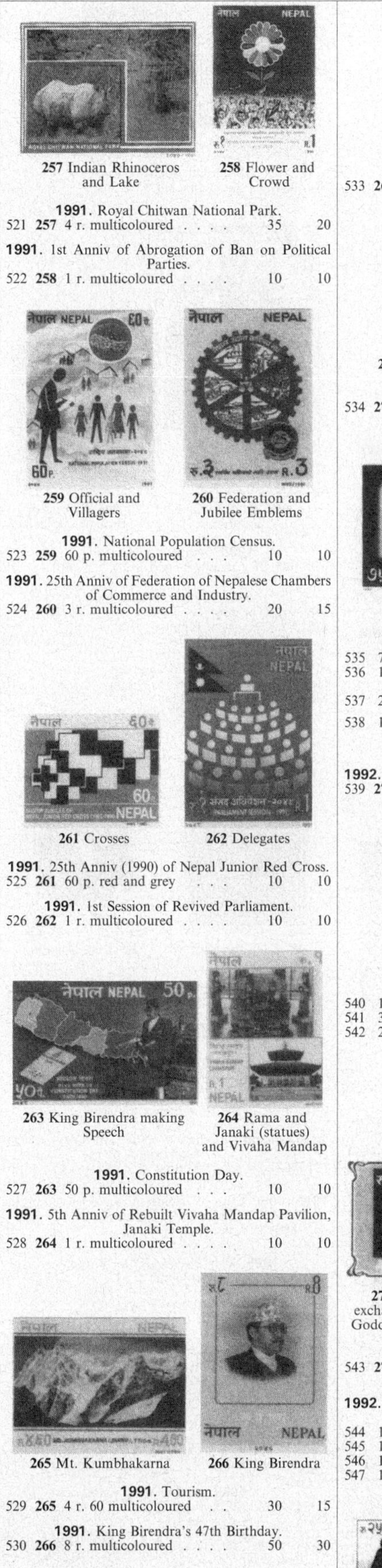

257 Indian Rhinoceros and Lake **258** Flower and Crowd

1991. Royal Chitwan National Park.
521 **257** 4 r. multicoloured 35 20

1991. 1st Anniv of Abrogation of Ban on Political Parties.
522 **258** 1 r. multicoloured 10 10

259 Official and Villagers **260** Federation and Jubilee Emblems

1991. National Population Census.
523 **259** 60 p. multicoloured . . . 10 10

1991. 25th Anniv of Federation of Nepalese Chambers of Commerce and Industry.
524 **260** 3 r. multicoloured 20 15

261 Crosses **262** Delegates

1991. 25th Anniv (1990) of Nepal Junior Red Cross.
525 **261** 60 p. red and grey . . . 10 10

1991. 1st Session of Revived Parliament.
526 **262** 1 r. multicoloured 10 10

263 King Birendra making Speech **264** Rama and Janaki (statues) and Vivaha Mandap

1991. Constitution Day.
527 **263** 50 p. multicoloured . . . 10 10

1991. 5th Anniv of Rebuilt Vivaha Mandap Pavilion, Janaki Temple.
528 **264** 1 r. multicoloured 10 10

265 Mt. Kumbhakarna **266** King Birendra

1991. Tourism.
529 **265** 4 r. 60 multicoloured . . 30 15

1991. King Birendra's 47th Birthday.
530 **266** 8 r. multicoloured 50 30

267 Houses **268** Glass magnifying Society Emblem

1991. South Asian Association for Regional Co-operation Year of Shelter.
531 **267** 9 r. multicoloured 50 35

1992. 25th Anniv (1991) of Nepal Philatelic Society.
532 **268** 4 r. multicoloured 25 15

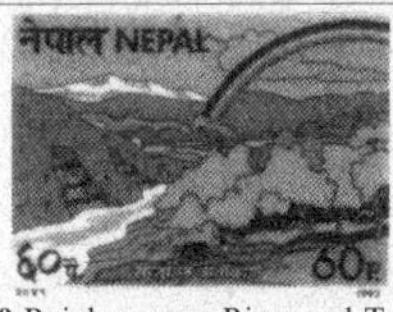

269 Rainbow over River and Trees

1992. Environmental Protection.
533 **269** 60 p. multicoloured . . . 10 10

270 Nutrition, Education and Health Care

1992. Rights of the Child.
534 **270** 1 r. multicoloured 10 10

271 Thakurdwara Temple, Bardiya **272** Bank Emblem

1992. Temples. Multicoloured.
535 75 p. Type **271** (postage) . . . 10 10
536 1 r. Namo Buddha Temple, Kavre 10 10
537 2 r. Narijhowa Temple, Mustang 10 10
538 11 r. Dantakali Temple, Bijayapur (air) 55 35

1992. 25th Anniv of Agricultural Development Bank.
539 **272** 40 p. brown and green . . 10 10

273 Pin-tailed Green Pigeon

1992. Birds. Multicoloured.
540 1 r. Type **273** 10 10
541 3 r. Bohemian waxwing . . . 15 10
542 25 r. Rufous-tailed desert (inscr "Finch") lark . . . . 1·25 80

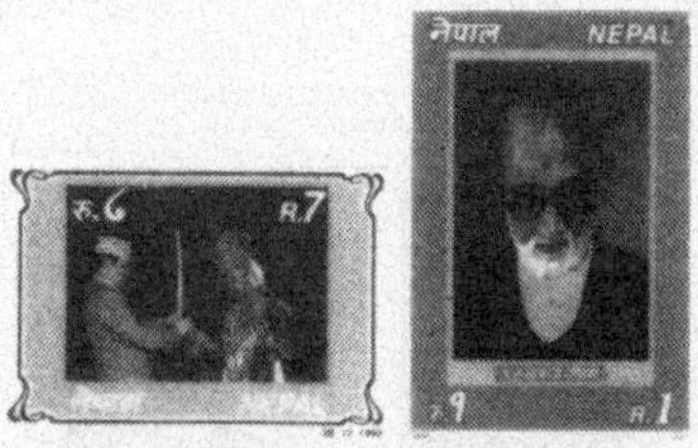

274 King Birendra exchanging Swords with Goddess Sree Bhadrakali **275** Pandit Kulchandra Gautam

1992. King Birendra's 48th Birthday.
543 **274** 7 r. multicoloured 35 25

1992. Poets. Multicoloured, frame colour given in brackets.
544 1 r. Type **275** 10 10
545 1 r. Chittadhar Hridaya (drab) 10 10
546 1 r. Vidyapati (stone) 10 10
547 1 r. Teongsi Sirijunga (grey) . 10 10

276 Shooting and Marathon **277** Barb

1992. Olympic Games, Barcelona.
548 **276** 25 r. multicoloured . . . . 1·25 80

1993. Fishes. Multicoloured.
549 25 p. Type **277** 10 10
550 1 r. Marinka 10 10
551 5 r. Indian eel 25 15
552 10 r. "Psilorhynchus pseudecheneis" 50 30

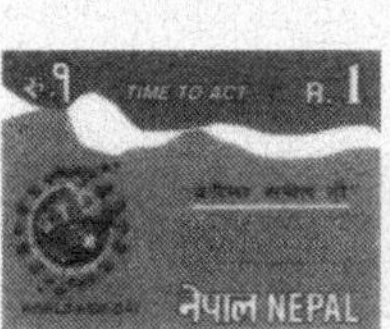

278 Antibodies attacking Globe **279** Tanka Prasad Acharya (Prime Minister, 1956–57)

1993. World AIDS Day.
554 **278** 1 r. multicoloured 10 10

1993. Death Anniversaries. Multicoloured.
555 25 p. Type **279** (1st anniv) . . 10 10
556 1 r. Sungdare Sherpa (mountaineer) (4th anniv) . 10 10
557 7 r. Siddhi Charan Shrestha (poet) (1st anniv) 30 20
558 15 r. Falgunanda (religious leader) (44th anniv) 60 40

280 Bagh Bairab Temple, Kirtipur

1993. Holy Places. Multicoloured.
559 1 r. 50 Halesi Mahadev cave (hiding place of Shiva), Khotang 10 10
560 5 r. Devghat (gods' bathing place), Tanahun 20 15
561 8 r. Type **280** 30 20

281 Tushahiti Fountain, Sundari Chowk, Patan **282** King Birendra

1993. Tourism. Multicoloured.
562 5 r. Type **281** 20 10
563 8 r. White-water rafting . . . 30 20

1993. King Birendra's 49th Birthday.
564 **282** 10 r. multicoloured . . . 40 25

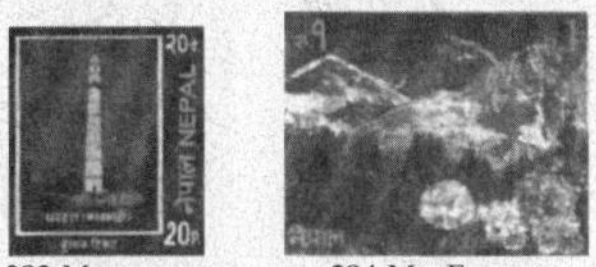

283 Monument **284** Mt. Everest

1994.
565 **283** 20 p. brown 10 10
566 – 25 p. red 10 10
567 – 30 p. green 10 10
568 **284** 1 r. multicoloured 10 10
569 – 5 r. multicoloured 20 10
DESIGNS—20 × 22 mm: 25 p. State arms. 22 × 20 mm: 30 p. Lumbini. 25 × 15 mm: 5 r. Map of Nepal, crown and state arms and flag.

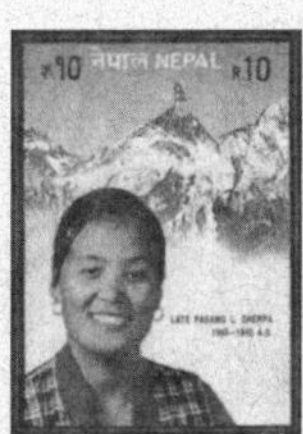

285 Pasang Sherpa

1994. 1st Death Anniv of Pasang Sherpa (mountaineer).
570 **285** 10 r. multicoloured . . . 30 20

286 Cigarette, Lungs and Crab's Claws **287** Postal Delivery

1994. Anti-smoking Campaign.
571 **286** 1 r. multicoloured 10 10

1994.
572 **287** 1 r. 50 multicoloured . . . 10 10

288 Khuda

1994. Weapons. Multicoloured.
573 5 r. Kukris (three swords and two scabbards) 15 10
574 5 r. Type **288** 15 10
575 5 r. Dhaal (swords and shield) 15 10
576 5 r. Katari (two daggers) . . . 15 10

289 Workers and Emblem

1994. 75th Anniv of I.L.O.
577 **289** 15 r. gold, blue & ultram . 40 25

290 Landscape

1994. World Food Day.
578 **290** 25 r. multicoloured . . . 65 40

291 "Dendrobium densiflorum"

292 Family

1994. Orchids. Multicoloured.
579 10 r. Type **291** 25 15
580 10 r. "Coelogyne flaccida" . . 25 15
581 10 r. "Cymbidium devonianum" 25 15
582 10 r. "Coelogyne corymbosa" 25 15

1994. International Year of the Family.
583 **292** 9 r. emerald, green and red 25 15

293 Emblem and Airplane

294 "Russula nepalensis"

1994. 50th Anniv of I.C.A.O.
584 **293** 11 r. blue, gold and deep blue 30 20

1994. Fungi. Multicoloured.
585 7 r. Type **294** 35 10
586 7 r. Morels ("Morchella conica") 35 10
587 7 r. Caesar's mushroom ("Amanita caesarea") . . . 35 10
588 7 r. "Cordyceps sinensis" . . . 35 10

295 Dharanidhar Koirala (poet)

1994. Celebrities. Multicoloured.
589 1 r. Type **295** 10 10
590 2 r. Narayan Gopal Guruwacharya (singer) . . 10 10
591 6 r. Bahadur Shah (vert) . . 15 10
592 7 r. Balaguru Shadananda . . 20 10

296 King Birendra, Flag, Map and Crown

1994. King Birendra's 50th Birthday (1st issue).
593 **296** 9 r. multicoloured 25 15
See also No. 621.

297 Lake Tilicho, Manang

298 Health Care

1994. Tourism. Multicoloured.
594 9 r. Type **297** 25 15
595 11 r. Taleju Temple, Katmandu (vert) 30 20

1994. Children's Activities. Multicoloured.
596 1 r. Type **298** 10 10
597 1 r. Classroom 10 10
598 1 r. Playground equipment . 10 10
599 1 r. Stamp collecting 10 10

299 Singhaduarbar

300 Crab on Lungs

1995.
600 **299** 10 p. green 10 10
601 – 50 p. blue 10 10
DESIGN—VERT: 50 p. Pashupati.

1995. Anti-cancer Campaign.
602 **300** 2 r. multicoloured . . . 10 10

301 Chandra Man Singh Maskey (artist)

302 Bhakti Thapa (soldier)

1995. Celebrities. Multicoloured.
603 3 r. Type **301** 10 10
604 3 r. Parijat (writer) 10 10
605 3 r. Bhim Nidhi Tiwari (writer) 10 10
606 3 r. Yuddha Prasad Mishra (writer) 10 10

1995. Celebrities. Multicoloured.
607 15 p. Type **302** 10 10
608 1 r. Madan Bhandari (politician) 10 10
609 4 r. Prakash Raj Kaphley (human rights activist) 10 10

303 Gaur ("Bos gaurus")

1995. "Singapore '95" International Stamp Exhibition. Mammals. Multicoloured.
610 10 r. Type **303** 20 10
611 10 r. Lynx ("Felis lynx") . . . 20 10
612 10 r. Assam macaque ("Macaca assamensis") 20 10
613 10 r. Striped hyena ("Hyaena hyaena") 20 10

304 Anniversary Emblem

1995. 50th Anniv of F.A.O.
614 **304** 7 r. multicoloured 15 10

305 Figures around Emblem

306 Bhimeswor Temple, Dolakha

1995. 50th Anniv of U.N.O.
615 **305** 50 r. multicoloured . . . 1·10 35

1995. Tourism. Multicoloured.
616 1 r. Type **306** 10 10
617 5 r. Ugra Tara Temple, Dadeldhura (horiz) 10 10
618 7 r. Mt. Nampa (horiz) 15 10
619 18 r. Nrity Aswora (traditional Pauba painting) (27 × 39 mm) 40 10
620 20 r. Lumbini (Buddha's birthplace) (28 × 28 mm) . . 45 15

307 King Birendra

309 King Birendra

308 Anniversary Emblem

1995. King Birendra's 50th Birthday (1994) (2nd issue).
621 **307** 1 r. multicoloured 10 10

1995. 10th Anniv of South Asian Association for Regional Co-operation.
622 **308** 10 r. multicoloured . . . 20 10

1995. King Birendra's 51st Birthday.
623 **309** 12 r. multicoloured . . . 25 10

OFFICIAL STAMPS

O 25 Nepalese Arms and Soldiers

काज सरकारी

(**O 28**)

1960. (a) Size 30 × 18 mm.
O135 **O 25** 2 p. brown 10 10
O136 4 p. green 10 10
O137 6 p. red 10 10
O138 8 p. violet 10 10
O139 12 p. orange 15 15

(b) Size 38 × 27 mm.
O140 **O 25** 16 p. brown 20 20
O141 24 p. red 35 25
O142 32 p. purple 35 35
O143 50 p. blue 65 55
O144 1 r. red . . . . 1·40 1·25
O145 2 r. orange . . . . . . 2·50 2·25

1960. Optd as Type O **28**.
O146 **27** 1 r. purple 50

1961. Optd with Type O **28**.
O148 **35** 1 p. red 10 10
O149 2 p. blue 10 10
O150 5 p. brown 10 10
O151 **36** 10 p. purple 10 10
O152 40 p. brown 10 10
O153 75 p. green 15 15
O154 **27** 2 r. red 30 30
O155 5 r. green 80 80

NETHERLANDS Pt. 4

A kingdom in the N.W. of Europe on the North Sea.

100 cents = 1 gulden (florin)

1 3 4
King William III

1852. Imperf.
1 **1** 5 c. blue . . . . £375 29·00
2 10 c. red . . . . £450 22·00
3b 15 c. orange £700 £100

1864. Perf.
8 **3** 5 c. blue . . . . £300 16·00
9 10 c. red . . . . £425 8·25
10 15 c. orange . . . . £1100 90·00

1867.
47 **4** 5 c. blue . . . . 75·00 2·00
30 10 c. red . . . . £130 2·75
46 15 c. brown . . . . £650 30·00
50 20 c. green . . . . £550 21·00
15 25 c. purple £2250 £100
16 50 c. gold £2500 £150

5 6

1869.
58 **5** $\frac{1}{2}$ c. brown . . . . 23·00 4·00
53 1 c. black . . . . £200 70·00
59 1 c. green . . . . 11·00 2·00
60 $1\frac{1}{2}$ c. red . . . . £130 75·00
61 2 c. yellow . . . . 50·00 14·50
62 $2\frac{1}{2}$ c. mauve . . . . £475 70·00

1872.
91 **6** 5 c. blue . . . . 9·00 15
92 $7\frac{1}{2}$ c. brown . . . . 38·00 18·00
112 10 c. red . . . . 55·00 1·25
113 $12\frac{1}{2}$ c. grey . . . . 65·00 1·25
95 15 c. brown . . . . £350 5·50
96 20 c. green . . . . £550 5·25
97 $22\frac{1}{2}$ c. green . . . . 80·00 45·00
98 25 c. lilac . . . . £550 4·00
100 50 c. bistre . . . . £700 11·00
101 1 g. violet . . . . £500 35·00
74 – 2 g. 50 blue and red £900 £110
No. 74 is similar to Type **6** but larger and with value and country scrolls transposed.

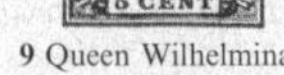

8 **9** Queen Wilhelmina

1876.
138d **8** $\frac{1}{2}$ c. red . . . . 3·00 10
140 1 c. green . . . . 2·25 10
143 2 c. yellow . . . . 32·00 2·75
145 $2\frac{1}{2}$ c. mauve . . . . 14·50 15

1891.
147a **9** 3 c. orange . . . . 9·25 2·10
148a 5 c. blue . . . . 4·00 10
149b $7\frac{1}{2}$ c. brown . . . . 17·00 5·50
150b 10 c. red . . . . 24·00 1·25
151b $12\frac{1}{2}$ c. grey . . . . 24·00 1·60
152a 15 c. brown . . . . 55·00 4·75
153b 20 c. green . . . . 60·00 3·00
154a $22\frac{1}{2}$ c. green . . . . . . 32·00 11·50
155 25 c. mauve . . . . £110 4·50
156a 50 c. bistre . . . . £500 16·00
159 – 50 c. brown and green . . 75·00 9·25
157 **9** 1 g. violet . . . . £550 75·00
160 – 1 g. green and brown . . . £180 18·00
161 – 2 g. 50 blue and red . . . £425 £130
165 – 5 g. red and green £750 £400
Nos. 159, 160, 161 and 165 are as Type **9** but larger and with value and country scrolls transposed.

11 12 13

1898. Nos. 174 and 176 also exist imperf.

No.	Type	Description	Unused	Used
167	12	½ c. lilac	90	15
168		1 c. red	2·75	10
226		1½ c. blue	8·00	25
170		2 c. brown	4·00	10
171		2½ c. green	9·00	10
172	13	3 c. orange	18·00	3·50
173		3 c. green	1·25	10
227		4 c. purple	1·50	70
228		4½ c. mauve	3·75	4·00
174		5 c. red	1·50	10
187a		5 c. red and blue	5·00	80
175		7½ c. brown	60	10
176		10 c. grey	6·75	10
177		12½ c. blue	3·50	15
178		15 c. brown	90·00	3·50
179		15 c. red and blue	6·50	10
180		17½ c. mauve	48·00	13·00
181		17½ c. brown and blue	16·00	85
182		20 c. green	£110	65
183		20 c. grey and green	11·00	30
184		22½ c. green and brown	10·50	40
185		25 c. blue and pink	10·00	10
230		30 c. purple and mauve	25·00	20
231		40 c. orange and green	38·00	75
186		50 c. red and green	£100	90
232		50 c. violet and grey	65·00	95
233		60 c. green and olive	38·00	90
202	11	1 g. green	50·00	30
203		2½ g. lilac	95·00	2·50
201		5 g. red	£225	5·25
198		10 g. red	£750	£650

14

1906. Society for the Prevention of Tuberculosis.

No.	Type	Description	Unused	Used
208	14	1 c. (+ 1 c.) red	14·50	9·00
209		3 c. (+ 3 c.) green	27·00	22·00
210		5 c. (+ 5 c.) violet	27·00	13·00

15 Admiral M. A. de Ruyter

16 William I

1907. Birth Tercentenary of Admiral de Ruyter.

No.	Type	Description	Unused	Used
211	15	½ c. blue	1·75	1·40
212		1 c. red	3·50	2·25
213		2½ c. red	7·50	2·25

1913. Independence Centenary.

No.	Type	Description	Unused	Used
214	16	2½ c. green on green	60	50
215	–	3 c. yellow on cream	90	90
216	–	5 c. red on buff	90	40
217	–	10 c. grey	3·50	2·00
218	16	12½ c. blue on blue	2·75	1·50
219	–	20 c. brown	13·00	11·00
220	–	25 c. blue	13·50	8·00
221	–	50 c. green	32·00	27·00
222	16	1 g. red	48·00	20·00
223	–	2½ g. lilac	£120	48·00
224	–	5 g. yellow on cream	£275	40·00
225	–	10 g. orange	£750	£750

DESIGNS: 3 c., 20 c., 2½ g. William II; 5 c., 25 c., 5 g. William III; 10 c., 50 c., 10 g. Queen Wilhelmina.

1919. Surch **Veertig Cent** (40 c.) or **Zestig Cent** (60 c.).

No.	Type	Description	Unused	Used
234	13	40 c. on 30 c. purple & mve	25·00	3·50
235		60 c. on 30 c. purple & mve	25·00	3·50

1920. Surch in figures.

No.	Type	Description	Unused	Used
238	13	4 c. on 4½ c. mauve	4·50	1·90
236	11	2.50 on 10 g. red	£150	£120
237	–	2.50 on 10 g. red (225)	£150	95·00

23

24

1921. Air.

No.	Type	Description	Unused	Used
239	23	10 c. red	1·75	1·25
240		15 c. green	6·50	2·00
241		60 c. blue	19·00	20

1921.

No.	Type	Description	Unused	Used
242	24	5 c. green	9·25	15
243		12½ c. red	18·00	2·10
244		20 c. blue	27·00	15

25 Lion in Dutch Garden and Orange Tree (emblematical of Netherlands)

26

27

1923.

No.	Type	Description	Unused	Used
248	25	1 c. violet	50	60
249		2 c. orange	5·50	10
250	26	2½ c. green	1·75	70
251	27	4 c. blue	1·25	45

1923. Surch.

No.	Type	Description	Unused	Used
252	12	2 c. on 1 c. red	45	20
253		2 c. on 1½ c. blue	45	20
254	13	10 c. on 3 c. green	4·50	15
255		10 c. on 5 c. red	8·50	55
256		10 c. on 12½ c. blue	7·50	55
257a		10 c. on 17½ c. brown & bl	3·00	3·50
258a		10 c. on 22½ c. olive & brn	3·00	3·50

30

31

1923. 25th Anniv of Queen's Accession.

No.	Type	Description	Unused	Used
259a	31	2 c. green	15	10
260a	30	5 c. green	25	10
261a	31	7½ c. red	40	10
262b		10 c. red	30	10
263		20 c. blue	3·75	55
264		25 c. yellow	5·50	90
265b		35 c. orange	5·50	2·50
266a		50 c. black	16·00	20
267	30	1 g. red	32·00	7·50
268		2½ g. black	£225	£200
269		5 g. blue	£200	£175

1923. Surch **DIENST ZEGEL PORTEN AAN TEEKEN RECHT** and value.

No.	Type	Description	Unused	Used
270	13	10 c. on 3 c. green	90	1·00
271		1 g. on 17½ c. brown & blue	70·00	17·00

33

1923. Culture Fund.

No.	Type	Description	Unused	Used
272	33	2 c. + 5 c. blue on pink	19·00	18·00
273	–	10 c. + 5 c. red on pink	19·00	18·00

DESIGN: 10 c. Two women.

35 Carrier Pigeon

36 Queen Wilhelmina

1924.

No.	Type	Description	Unused	Used
330	35	½ c. grey	40	25
423		1 c. red	10	10
332		1½ c. mauve	20	10
424a		1½ c. grey	10	10
425		2 c. orange	10	10
426a		2½ c. green	70	20
427		3 c. green	10	10
427a		4 c. blue	10	10
428	36	5 c. green	15	10
429		6 c. brown	15	10
279		7½ c. yellow	40	10
313		7½ c. violet	2·75	10
314		7½ c. red	20	10
279c		9 c. red and black	1·75	1·60
281		10 c. red	1·40	10
317		10 c. blue	2·50	10
282		12½ c. red	1·75	35
431		12½ c. blue	30	10
320		15 c. blue	7·25	15
432		15 c. yellow	1·60	10
433		20 c. blue	7·50	10
434		21 c. brown	26·00	90
323		22½ c. brown	7·50	3·00
434a		22½ c. orange	15·00	18·00
435		25 c. green	4·50	10
346		27½ c. grey	4·50	95
437		30 c. violet	10·00	10
286c		35 c. brown	35·00	6·75
437a		40 c. brown	10·00	15
329		50 c. green	5·50	10
289		60 c. violet	32·00	85
437c		60 c. black	29·00	90
301		1 g. blue (23 × 29 mm)	9·25	30
302		2½ g. red (23 × 29 mm)	95·00	4·50
303		5 g. black (23 × 29 mm)	£180	2·75

For further stamps in Type **35**, see Nos. 546/57.

1924. International Philatelic Exn, The Hague.

No.	Type	Description	Unused	Used
290	36	10 c. green	55·00	32·00
291		15 c. black	70·00	42·00
292		35 c. red	55·00	32·00

37

38

39

1924. Dutch Lifeboat Centenary.

No.	Type	Description	Unused	Used
293	37	2 c. brown	7·50	2·75
294	38	10 c. brown on yellow	13·00	13·00

1924. Child Welfare.

No.	Type	Description	Unused	Used
295	39	2 c. + 2 c. green	2·50	1·60
296		7½ c. + 3½ c. brown	11·50	5·75
297		10 c. + 2½ c. red	8·00	1·50

40 Arms of South Holland

46 Queen Wilhelmina

47 Red Cross Allegory

1925. Child Welfare. Arms as T **40**.

No.	Type	Description	Unused	Used
298	–	2 c. + 2 c. green & yell	1·40	80
299	–	7½ c. + 3½ c. violet & blue	7·75	4·75
300	40	10 c. + 2½ c. red & yellow	7·50	65

ARMS: 2 c. North Brabant; 7½ c. Gelderland. See also Nos. 350/3 and 359/62.

1926. Child Welfare. Arms as T **40**.

No.	Type	Description	Unused	Used
350		2 c. + 2 c. red and silver	1·25	40
351		5 c. + 3 c. green and blue	4·50	1·25
352		10 c. + 3 c. red and green	6·00	20
353		15 c. + 3 c. yellow & blue	13·50	6·00

ARMS: 2 c. Utrecht; 5 c. Zeeland; 10 c. North Holland; 15 c. Friesland.

1927. 60th Anniv of Dutch Red Cross Society.

No.	Type	Description	Unused	Used
354a	46	2 c. + 2 c. red	5·50	2·75
355	–	3 c. + 2 c. green	13·00	8·50
356	–	5 c. + 3 c. blue	1·90	1·10
357a	–	7½ c. + 3½ c. blue	11·00	1·60
358	47	15 c. + 5 c. red & blue	20·00	9·75

PORTRAITS: 2 c. King William III; 3 c. Queen Emma; 5 c. Henry, Prince Consort.

1927. Child Welfare. Arms as T **40**.

No.	Type	Description	Unused	Used
359		2 c. + 2 c. red and lilac	1·40	35
360		5 c. + 3 c. green & yellow	4·00	1·40
361		7½ c. + 3½ c. red and black	7·75	30
362		15 c. + 3 c. blue & brown	12·50	5·25

ARMS: 2 c. Drente; 5 c. Groningen; 7½ c. Limburg; 15 c. Overyssel.

48 Sculler

49 Footballer

1928. Olympic Games, Amsterdam.

No.	Type	Description	Unused	Used
363	48	1½ c. + 1 c. green	1·75	1·50
364	–	2 c. + 1 c. purple	2·50	1·75
365	49	3 c. + 1 c. green	2·50	2·10
366	–	5 c. + 1 c. blue	2·75	1·50
367	–	7½ c. + 2½ c. orange	2·75	1·60
368	–	10 c. + 2 c. red	7·50	5·75
369	–	15 c. + 2 c. blue	7·50	4·50
370	–	30 c. + 3 c. sepia	25·00	25·00

DESIGNS—HORIZ: 2 c. Fencer. VERT: 5 c. Yachting; 7½ c. Putting the weight; 10 c. Runner; 15 c. Horseman; 30 c. Boxer.

50 Lieut. Koppen

1928. Air.

No.	Type	Description	Unused	Used
371	50	40 c. red	45	45
372	–	75 c. green	45	45

DESIGN: 75 c. Van der Hoop.

52 J. P. Minckelers

53 Mercury

1928. Child Welfare.

No.	Type	Description	Unused	Used
373	52	1½ c. + 1½ c. violet	50	35
374	–	5 c. + 3 c. green	1·75	65
375a	–	7½ c. + 2½ c. red	3·25	25
376a	–	12½ c. + 3½ c. blue	10·00	7·50

PORTRAITS: 5 c. Boerhaave; 7½ c. H. A. Lorentz; 12½ c. G. Huygens.

1929. Air.

No.	Type	Description	Unused	Used
377	53	1½ g. black	2·50	1·60
378		4½ g. red	1·50	3·50
379		7½ g. green	27·00	4·50

1929. Surch **21**.

No.	Type	Description	Unused	Used
380	36	21 c. on 22½ c. brown	22·00	1·40

55 "Friendship and Security"

56 Rembrandt and "De Staalmeesters"

1929. Child Welfare.

No.	Type	Description	Unused	Used
381	55	1½ c. + 1½ c. grey	2·25	40
382		5 c. + 3 c. green	3·50	65
383		6 c. + 4 c. red	2·25	30
384		12½ c. + 3½ c. blue	14·00	13·00

1930. Rembrandt Society.

No.	Type	Description	Unused	Used
385	56	5 c. (+ 5 c.) green	7·50	7·50
386		6 c. (+ 5 c.) black	5·50	3·50
387		12½ c. (+ 5 c.) blue	9·25	9·25

57 Spring

58

59 Queen Wilhelmina

1930. Child Welfare.

No.	Type	Description	Unused	Used
388	57	1½ c. + 1½ c. red	1·50	35
389	–	5 c. + 3 c. green	2·25	65
390	–	6 c. + 4 c. purple	2·25	25
391	–	12½ c. + 3½ c. blue	17·00	10·00

DESIGNS (allegorical): 5 c. Summer; 6 c. Autumn; 12½ c. Winter.

1931. Gouda Church Restoration Fund.

No.	Type	Description	Unused	Used
392	58	1½ c. + 1½ c. green	18·00	18·00
393		6 c. + 4 c. red	22·00	20·00

1931.

No.	Type	Description	Unused	Used
395	–	70 c. blue and red (postage)	30·00	45
395b	–	80 c. green and red	£110	3·25
394	59	36 c. red and blue (air)	14·00	40

DESIGNS: 70 c. Portrait and factory; 80 c. Portrait and shipyard.

61 Mentally Deficient Child

62 Windmill and Dykes, Kinderdijk

63 Gorse (Spring)

1931. Child Welfare.

No.	Type	Description	Unused	Used
396	–	1½ c. + 1½ c. red and blue	1·40	50
397	61	5 c. + 3 c. green & purple	2·25	1·25
398	–	6 c. + 4 c. purple & green	1·75	40
399	–	12½ c. + 3½ c. blue & red	27·00	23·00

DESIGNS: 1½ c. Deaf mute; 6 c. Blind girl; 12½ c. Sick child.

1932. Tourist Propaganda.

No.	Type	Description	Unused	Used
400	62	2½ c. + 1½ c. green & black	7·50	5·50
401	–	6 c. + 4 c. grey & black	11·00	5·50
402	–	7½ c. + 3½ c. red & black	32·00	23·00
403	–	12½ c. + 2½ c. blue & black	35·00	20·00

DESIGNS: 6 c. Aerial view of Town Hall, Zierikzee; 7½ c. Bridges at Schipluiden and Moerdijk; 12½ c. Tulips.

1932. Child Welfare.

No.	Type	Description	Unused	Used
404	63	1½ c. + 1½ c. brown & yell	2·25	35
405	–	5 c. + 3 c. blue and red	3·00	65
406	–	6 c. + 4 c. green & orge	2·25	30
407	–	12½ c. + 3½ c. blue & orange	30·00	22·00

DESIGNS: Child and: 5 c. Cornflower (Summer); 6 c. Sunflower (Autumn); 12½ c. Christmas rose (Winter).

64 Arms of House of Orange

65 Portrait by Goltzius

1933. 4th Birth Centenary of William I of Orange. T **64** and portraits of William I inscr "1533", as T **65**.
408 **64** 1½ c. black 55 15
409 **65** 5 c. green . . . . 1·75 20
410 – 6 c. purple . . . . 2·75 10
411 – 12½ c. blue . . . . 17·00 3·75
DESIGNS: 6 c. Portrait by Key; 12½ c. Portrait attributed to Moro.

68 Dove of Peace

69 Projected Monument at Den Helder

70 "De Hoop" (hospital ship)

1933. Peace Propaganda.
412 **68** 12½ c. blue . . . . 9·25 25

1933. Seamen's Fund.
413 **69** 1½ c. + 1½ c. red . . . . . 3·50 1·90
414 **70** 5 c. + 3 c. green and red . 12·00 3·50
415 – 6 c. + 4 c. green . . . . . 17·00 2·75
416 – 12½ c. + 3½ c. blue . . . . 24·00 21·00
DESIGNS: 6 c. Lifeboat; 12½ c. Seaman and Seamen's Home.

73 Pander S.4 Postjager

1933. Air (Special Flights).
417 **73** 30 c. green 70 75

74 Child and Star of Epiphany **75** Princess Juliana

1933. Child Welfare.
418 **74** 1½ c. + 1½ c. orange & grey 1·50 45
419 5 c. + 3 c. yellow and brown 2·25 60
420 6 c. + 4 c. gold and green . 2·75 40
421 12½ c. + 3½ c. silver & blue 26·00 20·00

1934. Crisis stamps.
438 – 5 c. + 4 c. purple . . . . 13·00 3·50
439 **75** 6 c. + 5 c. blue . . . . . 11·00 4·50
DESIGN: 5 c. Queen Wilhelmina.

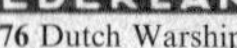

76 Dutch Warship

77 Dowager Queen Emma

1934. Tercentenary of Curacao.
440 – 6 c. black . . . . 4·00 10
441 **76** 12½ c. blue . . . . 26·00 2·75
DESIGN: 6 c. Willemstad Harbour.

1934. Anti-T.B. Fund.
442 **77** 6 c. + 2 c. blue . . . . . 13·00 1·60

78 Destitute child

79 H. D. Guyot

1934. Child Welfare.
443 **78** 1½ c. + 1½ c. brown . . . . 1·50 50
444 5 c. + 3 c. red . . . . . . 2·25 1·25
445 6 c. + 4 c. green . . . . . 2·25 25
446 12½ c. + 3½ c. blue . . . . 27·00 19·00

1935. Cultural and Social Relief Fund.
447 **79** 1½ c. + 1½ c. red . . . . . 1·90 1·90
448 – 5 c. + 3 c. brown . . . . 4·50 4·75
449 – 6 c. + 4 c. green . . . . 5·50 30
450 – 12½ c. + 3½ c. blue . . . 28·00 5·50
PORTRAITS: 5 c. A. J. M. Diepenbrock; 6 c. F. C. Donders; 12½ c. J. P. Sweelinck.
See also Nos. 456/9, 469/72, 478/82 and 492/6.

80 Aerial Map of Netherlands

81 Child picking Fruit

1935. Air Fund.
451 **80** 6 c. + 4 c. brown . . . . 29·00 11·00

1935. Child Welfare.
452 **81** 1½ c. + 1½ c. red 60 30
453 5 c. + 3 c. green . . . . 1·75 1·25
454 6 c. + 4 c. brown . . . . 1·50 30
455 12½ c. + 3½ c. blue . . . . 24·00 8·00

1936. Cultural and Social Relief Fund. As T **79**.
456 1½ c. + 1½ c. sepia . . . . . 85 1·00
457 5 c. + 3 c. green . . . . . 4·50 3·75
458 6 c. + 4 c. red . . . . . . 3·75 35
459 12½ c. + 3½ c. blue . . . . 15·00 3·25
PORTRAITS: 1½ c. H. Kamerlingh Onnes; 5 c. Dr. A. S. Talma; 6 c. Mgr. Dr. H. J. A. M. Schaepman; 12½ c. Desiderius Erasmus.

83 Pallas Athene

1936. Tercentenary of Utrecht University Foundation.
460 **83** 6 c. red . . . . 1·75 20
461 – 12½ c. blue . . . . 5·50 5·25
DESIGN: 12½ c. Gisbertus Voetius.

84 Child Herald

85 Scout Movement

1936. Child Welfare.
462 **84** 1½ c. + 1½ c. slate 50 25
463 5 c. + 3 c. green . . . . 2·50 75
464 6 c. + 4 c. brown . . . . 2·40 20
465 12½ c. + 3½ c. blue . . . . 16·00 5·00

1937. Scout Jamboree.
466 – 1½ c. black and green . . . 15 10
467 **85** 6 c. brown and black . . . 1·50 10
468 – 12½ c. black and blue . . . 3·75 1·60
DESIGNS: 1½ c. Scout Tenderfoot Badge; 12½ c. Hermes.

1937. Cultural and Social Relief Fund. Portraits as T **79**.
469 1½ c. + 1½ c. sepia 60 60
470 5 c. + 3 c. green . . . . . 5·00 3·75
471 6 c. + 4 c. purple . . . . . 1·10 25
472 12½ c. + 3½ c. blue . . . . 8·25 1·00
PORTRAITS: 1½ c. Jacob Maris; 5 c. F. de la B. Sylvius; 6 c. J. van den Vondel; 12½ c. A. van Leeuwenhoek.

86 "Laughing Child" by Frans Hals

87 Queen Wilhelmina

1937. Child Welfare.
473 **86** 1½ c. + 1½ c. black 15 15
474 3 c. + 2 c. green . . . . 1·75 1·25
475 4 c. + 2 c. red 60 50
476 5 c. + 3 c. green 50 15
477 12½ c. + 3½ c. blue . . . . 7·75 1·50

1938. Cultural and Social Relief Fund. As T **79**.
478 1½ c. + 1½ c. sepia 40 70
479 3 c. + 2 c. green 60 35
480 4 c. + 2 c. red . . . . . . 2·00 2·25
481 5 c. + 3 c. green . . . . . 2·50 30
482 12½ c. + 3½ c. blue . . . . 9·00 1·25
PORTRAITS: 1½ c. M. van St. Aldegonde; 3 c. O. G. Heldring; 4 c. Maria Tesselschade; 5 c. Rembrandt; 12½ c. H. Boerhaave.

1938. 40th Anniv of Coronation.
483 **87** 1½ c. black 20 10
484 5 c. red 25 10
485 12½ c. blue . . . . 3·75 1·40

88 Carrion Crow **89** Boy with Flute

1938. Air (Special Flights).
486 **88** 12½ c. blue and grey . . . 75 65
790a 25 c. blue and grey . . . 4·50 1·90

1938. Child Welfare.
487 **89** 1½ c. + 1½ c. black 15 20
488 3 c. + 2 c. brown 40 30
489 4 c. + 2 c. green 75 85
490 5 c. + 3 c. red 35 15
491 12½ c. + 3½ c. blue . . . . 9·00 2·00

1939. Cultural and Social Relief Fund. As T **79**.
492 1½ c. + 1½ c. brown 60 60
493 2½ c. + 2½ c. green . . . . 3·75 2·75
494 3 c. + 3 c. red . . . . . . 80 1·25
495 5 c. + 3 c. green . . . . . 2·75 30
496 12½ c. + 3½ c. blue . . . . 6·75 1·00
PORTRAITS: 1½ c. M. Maris; 2½ c. Anton Mauve; 3 c. Gerardus van Swieten; 5 c. Nicolas Beets; 12½ c. Pieter Stuyvesant.

91 St. Willibrord's landing in the Netherlands

92 Steam Locomotive "Der Arend"

93 Child and Cornucopia

1939. 12th Death Centenary of St. Willibrord.
497 **91** 5 c. green 75 10
498 – 12½ c. blue . . . . 5·50 3·00
DESIGN: 12½ c. St. Willibrord as Bishop of Utrecht.

1939. Centenary of Netherlands Railway.
499 **92** 5 c. green 75 15
500 – 12½ c. blue . . . . 9·50 3·50
DESIGN: 12½ c. Modern electric locomotive.

1939. Child Welfare.
501 **93** 1½ c. + 1½ c. black 15 20
502 2½ c. + 2½ c. green . . . . 5·00 3·00
503 3 c. + 3 c. red 60 25
504 5 c. + 3 c. green . . . . 1·00 10
505 12½ c. + 3½ c. blue . . . . 4·25 1·40

94 Queen Wilhelmina

95 Vincent Van Gogh

98 Girl with Dandelion

1940.
506 **94** 5 c. green 10 10
506a 6 c. brown 65 10
507 7½ c. red 10 10
508 10 c. purple 10 10
509 12½ c. blue 10 10
510 15 c. blue 15 10
510a 17½ c. blue . . . . 1·10 80
511 20 c. violet 20 10
512 22½ c. olive . . . . 1·10 95
513 25 c. red 20 10
514 30 c. ochre 45 30
515 40 c. green . . . . 1·40 85
515a 50 c. orange . . . . 7·75 60
515b 60 c. purple . . . . 7·50 2·50

1940. Cultural and Social Relief Fund.
516 **95** 1½ c. + 1½ c. brown . . . . 2·00 35
517 – 2½ c. + 2½ c. green . . . 6·50 1·25
518 – 3 c. + 3 c. red . . . . . 3·75 1·00
519 – 5 c. + 3 c. green . . . . 8·00 25
520 – 12½ c. + 3½ c. blue . . . 7·50 95
PORTRAITS: 1½ c. E. J. Potgieter; 3 c. Petrus Camper; 5 c. Jan Steen; 12½ c. Joseph Scaliger.
See also Nos. 558/62 and 656/60.

1940. As No. 519, colour changed. Surch.
521 7½ c. + 2½ c. on 5 c. + 3 c. red 35 25

1940. Surch with large figures and network.
522 **35** 2½ on 3 c. red . . . . . . 3·00 25
523 5 on 3 c. green 10 20
524 7½ on 3 c. red 10 10
525 10 on 3 c. green 10 15
526 12½ on 3 c. blue 15 30
527 17½ on 3 c. green 75 65
528 20 on 3 c. green 45 15
529 22½ on 3 c. green . . . . 90 1·10
530 25 on 3 c. green 55 30
531 30 on 3 c. green 75 50
532 40 on 3 c. green 90 70
533 50 on 3 c. green . . . . . 1·10 60
534 60 on 3 c. green . . . . . 1·90 1·25
535 70 on 3 c. green . . . . . 4·50 3·00
536 80 on 3 c. green . . . . . 6·25 5·50
537 100 on 3 c. green . . . . . 38·00 35·00
538 250 on 3 c. green . . . . . 42·00 42·00
539 500 on 3 c. green . . . . . 42·00 40·00

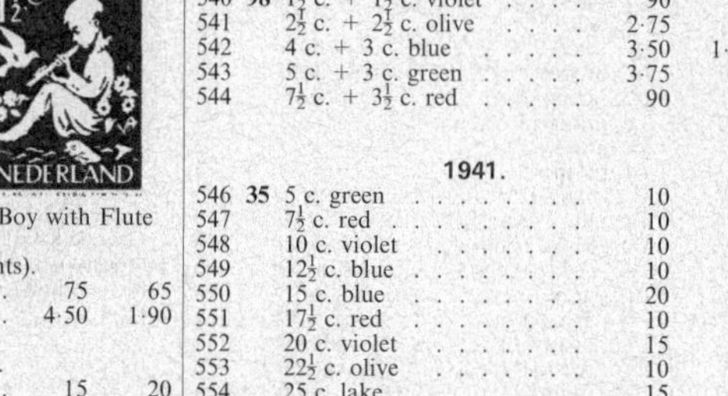

1940. Child Welfare.
540 **98** 1½ c. + 1½ c. violet 90 20
541 2½ c. + 2½ c. olive . . . . 2·75 90
542 4 c. + 3 c. blue . . . . . 3·50 1·10
543 5 c. + 3 c. green . . . . 3·75 15
544 7½ c. + 3½ c. red 90 15

1941.
546 **35** 5 c. green 10 10
547 7½ c. red 10 10
548 10 c. violet 10 10
549 12½ c. blue 10 30
550 15 c. blue 20 35
551 17½ c. red 10 15
552 20 c. violet 15 15
553 22½ c. olive 10 30
554 25 c. lake 15 25
555 30 c. brown . . . . 3·75 25
556 40 c. green 15 30
557 50 c. brown 10 15

1941. Cultural and Social Relief Fund. As T **95** but inscr "ZOMERZEGEL 31.12.46".
558 1½ c. + 1½ c. brown 90 30
559 2½ c. + 2½ c. green 90 30
560 4 c. + 3 c. red 90 30
561 5 c. + 3 c. green 90 30
562 7½ c. + 3½ c. purple 90 30
PORTRAITS: 1½ c. Dr. A. Mathijsen; 2½ c. J. Ingenhousz; 4 c. Aagje Deken; 5 c. Johan Bosboom; 7½ c. A. C. W. Staring.

100 "Titus Rembrandt"

101 Legionary

1941. Child Welfare.
563 **100** 1½ c. + 1½ c. black . . . 25 30
564 2½ c. + 2½ c. olive . . . 25 30
565 4 c. + 3 c. blue 25 30
566 5 c. + 3 c. green 25 30
567 7½ c. + 3½ c. red 25 30

1942. Netherlands Legion Fund.
568 **101** 7½ c. + 2½ c. red 90 75
569 – 12½ c. + 87½ c. blue . . . 6·75 7·00
DESIGN—HORIZ: 12½ c. Legionary with similar inscription.

1943. 1st European Postal Congress. As T **26** but larger (21 × 27½ mm) surch **EUROPEESCHE P T T VEREENIGING 19 OCTOBER 1942 10 CENT.**
570 **26** 10 c. on 2½ c. yellow . . . 10 15

103 Seahorse

104 Michiel A. de Ruyter

1943. Old Germanic Symbols.
571 **103** 1 c. black 10 10
572 – 1½ c. red 10 10
573 – 2 c. blue 10 10
574 – 2½ c. green 10 10
575 – 3 c. red 10 10
576 – 4 c. brown 10 10
577 – 5 c. olive 10 10
DESIGNS—VERT: 1½ c. Triple crowned tree; 2½ c. Birds in ornamental tree; 4 c. Horse and rider. HORIZ: 2 c. Swans; 3 c. Trees and serpentine roots; 5 c. Prancing horses.

1943. Dutch Naval Heroes.
578 **104** 7½ c. red 10 10
579 – 10 c. green 10 10
580 – 12½ c. blue 10 15
581 – 15 c. violet 15 15
582 – 17½ c. grey 10 10
583 – 20 c. brown 10 10
584 – 22½ c. red 10 20
585 – 25 c. purple 50 50
586 – 30 c. blue 10 10
587 – 40 c. grey 10 15
PORTRAITS: 10 c. Johan Evertsen; 12½ c. Maarten H. Tromp; 15 c. Piet Hein; 17½ c. Wilhelm Joseph van Gent; 20 c. Witte de With; 22½ c. Cornelis Evertsen; 25 c. Tjerk Hiddes de Fries; 30 c. Cornelis Tromp; 40 c. Cornelis Evertsen the younger.

105 Mail Cart

106 Child and Doll's House

1943. Stamp Day.
589 **105** 7½ c. + 7½ c. red 10 10

1944. Child Welfare and Winter Help Funds. Inscr "WINTERHULP" (1½ c. and 7½ c.) or "VOLKSDIENST" (others).
590 **106** 1½ c. + 3½ c. black 10 20
591 – 4 c. + 3½ c. brown 10 20
592 – 5 c. + 5 c. green 10 20
593 – 7½ c. + 7½ c. red 10 20
594 – 10 c. + 40 c. blue 10 20
DESIGNS: 4 c. Mother and child; 5 c., 10 c. Mother and children; 7½ c. Child and wheatsheaf.

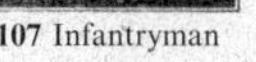
107 Infantryman

111 Queen Wilhelmina

1944.
595 **107** 1½ c. black 10 10
596 – 2½ c. green 10 10
597 – 3 c. brown 10 10
598 – 5 c. blue 10 10
599 **111** 7½ c. red 10 10
600 10 c. orange 10 10
601 12½ c. blue 10 10
602 15 c. red . . . . 1·10 1·10
603 17½ c. green . . . . 1·00 1·10
604 20 c. violet 25 20
605 22½ c. red 75 90
606 25 c. brown . . . . 1·50 1·50
607 30 c. green 20 15
608 40 c. purple . . . . 2·00 2·00
609 50 c. mauve . . . . 1·10 90
DESIGNS—HORIZ: 2½ c. "Nieuw Amsterdam" (liner); 3 c. Airman. VERT: 5 c. "De Ruyter" (cruiser).
The above set was originally for use on Netherlands warships serving with the Allied Fleet, and was used after liberation in the Netherlands.

112 Lion and Dragon
113

1945. Liberation.
610 **112** 7½ c. orange 10 10

1945. Child Welfare.
611 **113** 1½ c. + 2½ c. grey 30 25
612 2½ c. + 3½ c. green 30 25
613 5 c. + 5 c. brown 30 25
614 7½ c. + 4½ c. red 30 25
615 12½ c. + 5½ c. blue 30 25

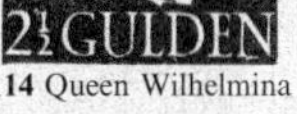
114 Queen Wilhelmina

115 Emblem of Abundance

1946.
616 **114** 1 g. blue 80 20
617 2½ g. red . . . . £140 9·00
618 5 g. green . . . . £140 30·00
619 10 g. violet . . . . £140 28·00

1946. War Victims' Relief Fund.
620 **115** 1½ c. + 3½ c. black 50 30
621 2½ c. + 5 c. green 60 60
622 5 c. + 10 c. violet 65 60
623 7½ c. + 15 c. red 45 20
624 12½ c. + 37½ c. blue 95 60

116 Princess Irene

117 Boy on Roundabout

1946. Child Welfare.
625 **116** 1½ c. + 1½ c. brown 50 50
626 – 2½ c. + 1½ c. green 50 60
627 **116** 4 c. + 2 c. red 65 65
628 – 5 c. + 2 c. brown 65 65
629 – 7½ c. + 2½ c. red 50 15
630 – 12½ c. + 7½ c. blue 50 65
PORTRAITS: 2½ c., 5 c. Princess Margriet; 7½ c., 12½ c. Princess Beatrix.

1946. Child Welfare.
631 **117** 2 c. + 2 c. violet 40 40
632 4 c. + 2 c. green 45 50
633 7½ c. + 2½ c. red 45 50
634 10 c. + 5 c. purple 60 15
635 20 c. + 5 c. blue 60 65

118 Numeral

119 Queen Wilhelmina
122 Children

1946.
636 **118** 1 c. red 10 10
637 2 c. blue 10 10
638 2½ c. orange . . . . 6·50 1·75
638a 3 c. brown 10 10
639 4 c. green 20 10
639a 5 c. orange 10 10
639c 6 c. grey 45 10
639d 7 c. red 20 10
639f 8 c. mauve 20 10

1947.
640 **119** 5 c. green . . . . 1·10 10
641 6 c. black 15 10
642 6 c. blue 40 10
643 7½ c. red 15 20
644 10 c. purple 40 10
645 12½ c. red 60 40
646 15 c. violet . . . . 6·25 10
647 20 c. blue . . . . 7·50 10
648 22½ c. green 70 70
649 25 c. blue . . . . 14·50 10
650 30 c. orange . . . . 14·50 20
651 35 c. blue . . . . 14·50 50
652 40 c. brown . . . . 18·00 50
653 – 45 c. blue . . . . 22·00 12·50
654 – 50 c. brown . . . . 14·50 25
655 – 60 c. red . . . . 18·00 2·25
Nos. 653/5 are as Type **119** but have the inscriptions in colour on white ground.

1947. Cultural and Social Relief Fund. As T **95** but inscr "ZOMERZEGEL...13.12.48".
656 2 c. + 2 c. red 70 50
657 4 c. + 2 c. green . . . . 1·50 75
658 7½ c. + 2½ c. violet . . . . 1·90 85
659 10 c. + 5 c. brown . . . . 1·75 15
660 20 c. + 5 c. blue . . . . 1·40 85
PORTRAITS: 2 c. H. van Deventer; 4 c. P. C. Hooft; 7½ c. Johan de Witt; 10 c. J. F. van Royen; 20 c. Hugo Grotius.

1947. Child Welfare.
661 **122** 2 c. + 2 c. brown 20 10
662 – 4 c. + 2 c. green . . . . 1·10 60
663 – 7½ c. + 2½ c. brown . . . . 1·50 90
664 – 10 c. + 5 c. lake . . . . 1·25 10
665 **122** 20 c. + 5 c. blue . . . . 1·50 90
DESIGN: 4 c. to 10 c. Baby.

124 Ridderzaal, The Hague

125 Queen Wilhelmina

1948. Cultural and Social Relief Fund.
666 **124** 2 c. + 2 c. brown . . . . 1·75 40
667 – 6 c. + 4 c. green . . . . 2·00 60
668 – 10 c. + 5 c. red . . . . 1·60 15
669 – 20 c. + 5 c. blue . . . . 2·00 90
BUILDINGS: 6 c. Palace on the Dam; 10 c. Kneuterdijk Palace; 20 c. Nieuwe Kerk, Amsterdam.

1948. Queen Wilhelmina's Golden Jubilee.
670 **125** 10 c. red 10 10
671 20 c. blue . . . . 2·25 2·10

126 Queen Juliana

127 Boy in Canoe

1948. Coronation.
672 **126** 10 c. brown . . . . 1·50 10
673 20 c. blue . . . . 2·00 50

1948. Child Welfare.
674 **127** 2 c. + 2 c. green 15 10
675 – 5 c. + 3 c. green . . . . 2·25 80
676 – 6 c. + 4 c. grey . . . . 1·40 15
677 – 10 c. + 5 c. red 45 10
678 – 20 c. + 8 c. blue . . . . 2·25 1·10
DESIGNS: 5 c. Girl swimming; 6 c. Boy on toboggan; 10 c. Girl on swing; 20 c. Boy skating.

128 Terrace near Beach

1949. Cultural and Social Relief Fund.
679 **128** 2 c. + 2 c. yell & blue . . . . 2·00 20
680 – 5 c. + 3 c. yell & blue . . . . 3·50 2·00
681 – 6 c. + 4 c. green . . . . 3·00 50
682 – 10 c. + 5 c. yell & blue . . . . 3·75 10
683 – 20 c. + 5 c. blue . . . . 3·50 2·25
DESIGNS: 5 c. Hikers in cornfield; 6 c. Campers by fire; 10 c. Gathering wheat; 20 c. Yachts.

129 Queen Juliana 130
131 Hands reaching for Sunflower

1949.
684 **129** 5 c. green 50 10
685 6 c. blue 40 10
686 10 c. orange 30 10
687 12 c. red . . . . 1·75 1·75
688 15 c. green . . . . 4·50 10
689 20 c. blue . . . . 3·75 10
690 25 c. brown . . . . 13·00 10
691 30 c. violet . . . . 9·25 10
692 35 c. blue . . . . 22·00 15
693 40 c. purple . . . . 40·00 20
694 45 c. orange . . . . 1·75 90
695 45 c. violet . . . . 50·00 30
696 50 c. green . . . . 10·50 15
697 60 c. brown . . . . 15·00 15
697a 75 c. red . . . . 75·00 1·25
698 **130** 1 g. red . . . . 3·75 10
699 2½ g. brown . . . . £190 2·40
700a 5 g. brown . . . . £450 4·00
701 10 g. violet . . . . £300 16·00

1949. Red Cross and Indonesian Relief Fund.
702 **131** 2 c. + 3 c. yellow & grey . . 90 30
703 6 c. + 4 c. yellow & red . . 65 40
704 10 c. + 5 c. yellow & bl . . 3·75 25
705 30 c. + 10 c. yellow & brn . . 9·50 3·00

132 Posthorns and Globe

133 "Autumn"

1949. 75th Anniv of U.P.U.
706 **132** 10 c. lake 55 10
707 20 c. blue . . . . 9·50 2·75

1949. Child Welfare Fund. Inscr "VOOR HET KIND".
708 **133** 2 c. + 3 c. brown 20 10
709 – 5 c. + 3 c. red . . . . 6·75 2·00
710 – 6 c. + 4 c. green . . . . 3·75 30
711 – 10 c. + 5 c. grey 20 10
712 – 20 c. + 7 c. blue . . . . 5·50 1·60
DESIGNS: 5 c. "Summer"; 6 c. "Spring"; 10 c. "Winter"; 20 c. "New Year".

134 Resistance Monument

135 Part of Moerdyk Bridge

1950. Cultural and Social Relief Fund. Inscr "ZOMERZEGEL 1950".
713 **134** 2 c. + 2 c. brown . . . . 2·00 1·25
714 – 4 c. + 2 c. green . . . . 11·50 11·00
715 – 5 c. + 3 c. grey . . . . 9·00 3·25
716 – 6 c. + 4 c. violet . . . . 4·50 75
717 **135** 10 c. + 5 c. slate . . . . 6·25 20
718 – 20 c. + 5 c. blue . . . . 17·00 14·50
DESIGNS—VERT: 4 c. Sealing dykes; 5 c. Rotterdam skyscraper. HORIZ: 6 c. Harvesting; 20 c. "Overijssel" (canal freighter).

1950. Surch with bold figure **6**.
719 **119** 6 c. on 7½ c. red . . . . 2·25 10

INDEX

Countries can be quickly located by referring to the index at the end of this volume.

137 Good Samaritan and Bombed Church
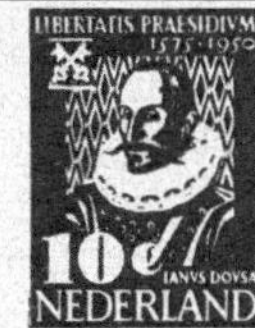
138 Janus Dousa

1950. Bombed Churches Rebuilding Fund.
720 **137** 2 c. + 2 c. olive . . . . 7·50 1·75
721 5 c. + 3 c. brown . . . . 11·00 11·00
722 6 c. + 4 c. green . . . . 7·50 3·00
723 10 c. + 5 c. red . . . . 18·00 35
724 20 c. + 5 c. blue . . . . 32·00 30·00

1950. 375th Anniv of Leyden University.
725 **138** 10 c. olive . . . . 5·00 10
726 – 20 c. blue . . . . 5·00 1·40
PORTRAIT: 20 c. Jan van Hout.

139 Baby and Bees

140 Bergh Castle

1950. Child Welfare. Inscr "VOOR HET KIND".
727 **139** 2 c. + 3 c. red 20 10
728 – 5 c. + 3 c. olive . . . . 10·50 4·50
729 – 6 c. + 4 c. green . . . . 3·75 60
730 – 10 c. + 5 c. purple 20 10
731 – 20 c. + 7 c. blue . . . . 11·00 10·50
DESIGNS: 5 c. Boy and fowl; 6 c. Girl and birds; 10 c. Boy and fish; 20 c. Girl, butterfly and frog.

1951. Cultural and Social Relief Fund. Castles.
732 – 2 c. + 2 c. violet . . . . 2·50 1·25
733 **140** 5 c. + 3 c. red . . . . 9·00 7·75
734 – 6 c. + 4 c. sepia . . . . 3·00 60
735 – 10 c. + 5 c. green . . . . 6·00 25
736 – 20 c. + 5 c. blue . . . . 8·50 8·50
DESIGNS—HORIZ: 2 c. Hillenraad; 6 c. Hernen. VERT: 10 c. Rechteren; 20 c. Moermond.

141 Girl and Windmill

142 Gull

143 Jan van Riebeeck

1951. Child Welfare.
737 **141** 2 c. + 3 c. green 30 10
738 – 5 c. + 3 c. blue . . . . 7·50 4·50
739 – 6 c. + 4 c. brown . . . . 5·50 60
740 – 10 c. + 5 c. lake 20 10
741 – 20 c. + 7 c. blue . . . . 7·50 7·50
DESIGNS: Each shows boy or girl: 5 c. Crane; 6 c. Fishing nets; 10 c. Factory chimneys; 20 c. Flats.

1951. Air.
742 **142** 15 g. brown £250 £125
743 25 g. black £275 £125

1952. Tercentenary of Landing in South Africa and Van Riebeeck Monument Fund.
744 **143** 2 c. + 3 c. violet . . . . 5·50 3·75
745 6 c. + 4 c. green . . . . 6·50 4·50
746 10 c. + 5 c. red . . . . 7·50 4·50
747 20 c. + 5 c. blue . . . . 5·50 3·75

144 Miner

145 Wild Rose

1952. 50th Anniv of State Mines, Limburg.
748 **144** 10 c. blue . . . . 2·50 10

1952. Cultural and Social Relief Fund. Floral designs inscr "ZOMERZEGEL 1952".
749 **145** 2 c. + 2 c. green & red . . 75 50
750 – 5 c. + 3 c. yellow & green . 2·50 2·50
751 – 6 c. + 4 c. green & red . . 2·25 1·10
752 – 10 c. + 5 c. green & orge . 2·00 15
753 – 20 c. + 5 c. green & blue . 13·00 12·00
FLOWERS: 5 c. Marsh Marigold; 6 c. Tulip; 10 c. Marguerite; 20 c. Cornflower.

146 Radio Masts

147 Boy feeding Goat

1952. Netherlands Stamp Centenary and Centenary of Telegraph Service.
754 – 2 c. violet 70 10
755 146 6 c. red 20 10
756 – 10 c. green 20 10
757 – 20 c. slate . . . . 7·75 2·25
DESIGNS: 2 c. Telegraph poles and train; 10 c. Postman delivering letters, 1852; 20 c. Postman delivering letters, 1952.

1952. International Postage Stamp Ex, Utrecht ("ITEP"). Nos. 754/7 but colours changed.
757a – 2 c. brown . . . . 17·00 13·00
757b 146 6 c. blue . . . . 17·00 13·00
757c – 10 c. lake . . . . 17·00 13·00
757d – 20 c. blue . . . . 17·00 13·00
Nos. 757a/d were sold only in sets at the Exhibition at face + 1 g. entrance fee.

1952. Child Welfare.
758 147 2 c. + 3 c. black & olive . 15 10
759 – 5 c. + 3 c. black & pink . 3·00 1·25
760 – 6 c. + 4 c. black & green 2·75 50
761 – 10 c. + 5 c. black & orge 20 10
762 – 20 c. + 7 c. black & blue 7·75 6·50
DESIGNS: 5 c. Girl riding donkey; 6 c. Girl playing with dog; 10 c. Boy and cat; 20 c. Boy and rabbit.

1953. Flood Relief Fund. Surch **19 53 10 c + 10 WATERSNOOD.**
763 129 10 c. + 10 c. orange . . . 65 10

149 Hyacinth

150 Red Cross

1953. Cultural and Social Relief Fund.
764 149 2 c. + 2 c. green & violet 60 35
765 – 5 c. + 3 c. green & orge . 2·10 2·00
766 – 6 c. + 4 c. yellow & green 2·00 55
767 – 10 c. + 5 c. green & red . 3·25 15
768 – 20 c. + 5 c. green & blue 13·50 13·50
FLOWERS: 5 c. African marigold; 6 c. Daffodil; 10 c. Anemone; 20 c. Dutch iris.

1953. Red Cross Fund. Inscr "RODE KRUIS".
769 150 2 c. + 3 c. red and sepia . 90 45
770 – 6 c. + 4 c. red and brown 3·75 3·50
771 – 7 c. + 5 c. red and olive . 1·00 50
772 – 10 c. + 5 c. red 60 10
773 – 25 c. + 8 c. red and blue . 8·00 5·50
DESIGNS: 6 c. Man with lamp; 7 c. Rescue worker in flooded area; 10 c. Nurse giving blood transfusion; 25 c. Red Cross flags.

151 Queen Juliana

152 Queen Juliana

1953.
775 151 10 c. brown 10 10
776 12 c. turquoise 10 10
777 15 c. red 10 10
777b 18 c. turquoise 20 10
778 20 c. purple 15 10
778b 24 c. olive 40 20
779 25 c. blue 20 10
780a 30 c. orange 40 15
781 35 c. brown 90 10
781a 37 c. turquoise 85 20
782 40 c. slate 35 10
783 45 c. red 40 10
784 50 c. green 35 10
785 60 c. brown 50 10
785a 62 c. red . . . . 3·25 2·75
785b 70 c. blue 60 10
786 75 c. purple 50 10
786a 80 c. violet 75 15
786b 85 c. green . . . . . . 1·40 20
786c 95 c. brown . . . . . . 2·25 25
787 152 1 g. red . . . . 1·75 10
788 2½ g. green . . . . . . 9·25 10
789 5 g. black . . . . 3·75 15
790 10 g. blue . . . . 18·00 1·25

153 Girl with Pigeon

154 M. Nijhoff (poet)

1953. Child Welfare. Inscr "VOOR HET KIND".
791 – 2 c. + 3 c. blue & yellow . 10 10
792 – 5 c. + 3 c. lake & green . 3·25 2·40
793 153 7 c. + 5 c. brown & blue . 3·25 80
794 – 10 c. + 5 c. lilac & bistre 10 10
795 – 25 c. + 8 c. turq & pink . 11·00 12·00
DESIGNS: 2 c. Girl, bucket and spade; 5 c. Boy and apple; 10 c. Boy and tjalk (sailing boat); 25 c. Girl and tulip.

1954. Cultural and Social Relief Fund.
796 154 2 c. + 3 c. blue . . . . . 1·75 1·75
797 – 5 c. + 3 c. brown . . . . 2·75 1·75
798 – 7 c. + 5 c. red . . . . . 3·75 1·40
799 – 10 c. + 5 c. green . . . 7·50 15
800 – 25 c. + 8 c. purple . . . 11·00 11·50
PORTRAITS: 5 c. W. Pijper (composer); 7 c. H. P. Berlage (architect); 10 c. J. Huizinga (historian); 25 c. Vincent van Gogh (painter).

155 St. Boniface

156 Boy and Model Glider

1954. 1200th Anniv of Martyrdom of St. Boniface.
801 155 10 c. blue . . . . 2·75 10

1954. National Aviation Fund.
802 156 2 c. + 2 c. green . . . . 1·40 90
803 – 10 c. + 4 c. blue . . . . 3·50 50
PORTRAIT: 10 c. Dr. A. Plesman (aeronautical pioneer).

157 Making Paperchains
158 Queen Juliana

1954. Child Welfare.
804 157 2 c. + 3 c. brown 10 10
805 – 5 c. + 3 c. olive . . . . 1·75 1·75
806 – 7 c. + 5 c. blue . . . . 1·50 50
807 – 10 c. + 5 c. red 10 10
808 – 25 c. + 8 c. blue . . . . 10·00 6·25
DESIGNS—VERT: 5 c. Girl brushing her teeth; 7 c. Boy and toy boat; 10 c. Nurse and child. HORIZ: 25 c. Invalid boy drawing in bed.

1954. Ratification of Statute for the Kingdom.
809 158 10 c. red 80 10

159 Factory, Rotterdam

160 "The Victory of Peace"

1955. Cultural and Social Relief Fund.
810 159 2 c. + 3 c. brown . . . . 1·25 1·25
811 – 5 c. + 3 c. green . . . . 1·50 1·10
812 – 7 c. + 5 c. red . . . . . 1·25 1·25
813 – 10 c. + 5 c. blue . . . . 2·10 15
814 – 25 c. + 8 c. brown . . . 12·00 11·00
DESIGNS—HORIZ: 5 c. Post Office, The Hague; 10 c. Town Hall, Hilversum; 25 c. Office Building, The Hague. VERT: 7 c. Stock Exchange, Amsterdam.

1955. 10th Anniv of Liberation.
815 160 10 c. red . . . . 1·60 10

161 Microscope and Emblem of Cancer

162 "Willem van Loon" (D. Dircks)

1955. Queen Wilhelmina Anti-Cancer Fund.
816 161 2 c. + 3 c. black & red . 60 50
817 5 c. + 3 c. green & red . 1·60 1·25
818 7 c. + 5 c. purple & red . 1·50 70
819 10 c. + 5 c. blue and red 85 10
820 25 c. + 8 c. olive & red . 7·50 6·50

1955. Child Welfare Fund.
821 162 2 c. + 3 c. green 10 10
822 – 5 c. + 3 c. red . . . . . 2·10 1·00
823 – 7 c. + 5 c. brown . . . . 4·00 80
824 – 10 c. + 5 c. blue 10 10
825 – 25 c. + 8 c. lilac . . . . 9·50 9·00
PORTRAITS: 5 c. "Portrait of a Boy" (J. A. Backer); 7 c. "Portrait of a Girl" (unknown); 10 c. "Philips Huygens" (A. Hanneman); 25 c. "Constantin Huygens" (A. Hanneman).

163 "Farmer"

1956. Cultural and Social Relief Fund and 350th Birth Anniv of Rembrandt. Details from Rembrandt's paintings.
826 163 2 c. + 3 c. slate . . . . . 2·75 2·75
827 – 5 c. + 3 c. olive . . . . 1·90 1·50
828 – 7 c. + 5 c. brown . . . . 4·50 4·50
829 – 10 c. + 5 c. green . . . . 12·50 25
830 – 25 c. + 8 c. brown . . . . 18·00 18·00
PAINTINGS: 5 c. "Young Tobias with Angel"; 7 c. "Persian wearing Fur Cap"; 10 c. "Old Blind Tobias"; 25 c. Self-portrait 1639.

164 Yacht

165 Amphora

167 "Portrait of a Boy" (Van Scorel)

1956. 16th Olympic Games, Melbourne.
831 164 2 c. + 3 c. black & blue . 75 75
832 – 5 c. + 3 c. black & yellow 1·10 1·10
833 165 7 c. + 5 c. black & brown 1·50 1·25
834 – 10 c. + 5 c. black & grey . 3·00 40
835 – 25 c. + 8 c. black & green 6·50 6·50
DESIGNS: As Type **164**: 5 c. Runner; 10 c. Hockey player; 25 c. Water polo player.

1956. Europa. As T **110** of Luxembourg.
836 10 c. black and lake . . . . . 1·75 10
837 25 c. black and blue . . . . . 45·00 1·75

1956. Child Welfare Fund. 16th century Dutch Paintings.
838 167 2 c. + 3 c. grey & cream . 10 10
839 – 5 c. + 3 c. olive & cream . 1·25 65
840 – 7 c. + 5 c. purple & cream 3·50 1·50
841 – 10 c. + 5 c. red & cream . 10 10
842 – 25 c. + 8 c. blue & cream 7·50 4·25
PAINTINGS: 5 c. "Portrait of a Boy"; 7 c. "Portrait of a Girl"; 10 c. "Portrait of a Girl"; 25 c. "Portrait of Eechie Pieters".

168 "Curacao" (trawler) and Fish Barrels

169 Admiral M. A. de Ruyter

1957. Cultural and Social Relief Fund. Ships.
843 – 4 c. + 3 c. blue . . . . . 1·25 90
844 – 6 c. + 4 c. lilac . . . . . 2·25 1·60
845 – 7 c. + 5 c. red . . . . . 1·90 1·50
846 168 10 c. + 8 c. green . . . . 4·00 15
847 – 30 c. + 8 c. brown . . . . 7·50 7·00
DESIGNS: 4 c. "Gaasterland" (freighter); 6 c. Coaster; 7 c. "Willem Barendsz" (whale factory ship) and whale; 30 c. "Nieuw Amsterdam" (liner).

1957. 350th Birth Anniv of M. A. de Ruyter.
848 169 10 c. orange 75 10
849 – 30 c. blue . . . . 5·00 1·75
DESIGN: 30 c. De Ruyter's flagship, "De Zeven Provincien".

170 Blood Donors' Emblem

171 "Europa" Star

1957. 90th Anniv of Netherlands Red Cross Society and Red Cross Fund.
850 170 4 c. + 3 c. blue & red . . 1·10 1·00
851 – 6 c. + 4 c. green & red . . 1·50 1·25
852 – 7 c. + 5 c. red & green . . 1·50 1·25
853 – 10 c. + 8 c. red & ochre . 1·25 10
854 – 30 c. + 8 c. red & blue . . 2·75 2·75
DESIGNS: 6 c. "J. Henry Dunant" (hospital ship); 7 c. Red Cross; 10 c. Red Cross emblem; 30 c. Red Cross on globe.

1957. Europa.
855 171 10 c. black and blue . . . 65 10
856 30 c. green and blue . . . 7·50 1·75

172 Portrait by B. J. Blommers

173 Walcheren Costume

1957. Child Fund Welfare. 19th/20th Century Paintings by Dutch Masters.
857 172 4 c. + 4 c. red 40 10
858 – 6 c. + 4 c. green . . . . 2·50 2·00
859 – 8 c. + 4 c. sepia . . . . 3·25 2·00
860 – 12 c. + 9 c. purple . . . 40 10
861 – 30 c. + 9 c. blue . . . . 8·50 7·50
PORTRAITS: Child paintings by: W. B. Tholen (6 c.); J. Sluyters (8 c.); M. Maris (12 c.); C. Kruseman (30 c.).

1958. Cultural and Social Relief Fund. Provincial Costumes.
862 173 4 c. + 4 c. blue 80 60
863 – 6 c. + 4 c. ochre . . . . 1·50 80
864 – 8 c. + 4 c. red . . . . . 5·00 1·75
865 – 12 c. + 9 c. brown . . . 2·00 15
866 – 30 c. + 9 c. lilac . . . . 7·75 7·50
COSTUMES: 6 c. Marken; 8 c. Scheveningen; 12 c. Friesland; 30 c. Volendam.

1958. Surch **12 C.**
867 151 12 c. on 10 c. brown . . . 1·10 10

1958. Europa. As T **119a** of Luxembourg.
868 12 c. blue and red 20 10
869 30 c. red and blue 90 70

176 Girl on Stilts and Boy on Tricycle

177 Cranes

1958. Child Welfare Fund. Children's Games.
870 176 4 c. + 4 c. blue 10 10
871 – 6 c. + 4 c. red . . . . . 2·50 1·75
872 – 8 c. + 4 c. green . . . . 1·75 1·25
873 – 12 c. + 9 c. red 10 10
874 – 30 c. + 9 c. blue . . . . 6·25 4·75
DESIGNS: 6 c. Boy and girl on scooter; 8 c. Boys playing leap-frog; 12 c. Boys on roller-skates; 30 c. Girl skipping and boy in toy car.

1959. 10th Anniv of N.A.T.O. As T **123** of Luxembourg (N.A.T.O. emblem).
875 12 c. blue and yellow 10 10
876 30 c. blue and red . . . . . . 1·00 60

1959. Cultural and Social Relief Fund. Prevention of Sea Encroachment.
877 – 4 c. + 4 c. blue on green 1·40 1·25
878 – 6 c. + 4 c. brown on grey 90 90
879 – 8 c. + 4 c. violet on blue 2·25 1·75
880 177 12 c. + 9 c. green on yell 4·00 15
881 – 30 c. + 9 c. black on red 6·75 6·75
DESIGNS: 4 c. Tugs and caisson; 6 c. Dredger; 8 c. Labourers making fascine mattresses; 30 c. Sand-spouter and scoop.

1959. Europa. As T **123a** of Luxembourg.
882 12 c. red 15 10
883 30 c. green . . . . 3·00 1·90

178 Silhouette of Douglas DC-8 Airliner and World Map

179 Child in Play-pen

1959. 40th Anniv of K.L.M. (Royal Dutch Airlines).
884 178 12 c. blue and red 20 10
885 – 30 c. blue and green . . . 2·00 1·25
DESIGN: 30 c. Silhouette of Douglas DC-8 airliner.

1959. Child Welfare Fund.
886 179 4 c. + 4 c. blue & brown 10 10
887 – 6 c. + 4 c. brown and green . . . . 1·75 1·40
888 – 8 c. + 4 c. blue and red . 3·00 1·90
889 – 12 c. + 9 c. red, black and blue 10 10
890 – 30 c. + 9 c. turquoise and yellow . . . . 4·00 4·00
DESIGNS: 6 c. Boy as "Red Indian" with bow and arrow; 8 c. Boy feeding geese; 12 c. Traffic warden escorting children; 30 c. Girl doing homework.

180 Refugee Woman **181** White Water-lily

1960. World Refugee Year.
891 **180** 12 c. + 8 c. purple . . . 25 15
892 30 c. + 10 c. green . . . 3·50 3·00

1960. Cultural and Social Relief Fund. Flowers.
893 – 4 c. + 4 c. red, green and grey 80 65
894 – 6 c. + 4 c. yellow, green and salmon . . . . 1·50 1·25
895 **181** 8 c. + 4 c. multicoloured . 3·25 2·50
896 – 12 c. + 8 c. red, green and buff . . . . 2·75 20
897 – 30 c. + 10 c. blue, green and yellow . . . . 6·25 6·00
FLOWERS—VERT: 4 c. "The Princess" tulip; 6 c. Gorse; 12 c. Poppy; 30 c. Blue sea-holly.

182 J. van der Kolk **183** Marken Costume **184** Herring Gull

1960. World Mental Health Year.
898 **182** 12 c. red 80 10
899 – 30 c. blue (J. Wier) . . . 6·75 2·75

1960. Europa. As T **113**a of Norway.
900 12 c. yellow and red 25 10
901 30 c. yellow and blue . . . . 3·00 2·25

1960. Child Welfare Fund. Costumes. Multicoloured portraits.
902 **183** 4 c. + 4 c. slate 30 10
903 – 6 c. + 4 c. ochre . . . . 2·50 1·25
904 – 8 c. + 4 c. turquoise . . . 5·25 2·25
905 – 12 c. + 9 c. violet 30 10
906 – 30 c. + 9 c. grey . . . . 7·50 6·75
DESIGNS: Costumes of: 6 c. Volendam; 8 c. Bunschoten; 12 c. Hindeloopen; 30 c. Huizen.

1961. Cultural and Social Relief Fund. Beach and Meadow Birds.
907 **184** 4 c. + 4 c. slate & yellow 1·50 1·50
908 – 6 c. + 4 c. sep. & brown . 1·50 1·50
909 – 8 c. + 4 c. brn & olive . . 1·40 1·25
910 – 12 c. + 8 c. blk & blue . 3·00 25
911 – 30 c. + 10 c. blk & green 5·50 4·00
BIRDS—HORIZ: 6 c. Oystercatcher; 12 c. Avocet. VERT: 8 c. Curlew; 30 c. Lapwing.

185 Doves **186** St. Nicholas

1961. Europa.
912 **185** 12 c. brown 10 10
913 30 c. turquoise 30 30

1961. Child Welfare.
914 **186** 4 c. + 4 c. red 10 10
915 – 6 c. + 4 c. blue . . . . 1·25 90
916 – 8 c. + 4 c. bistre . . . . 1·25 1·25
917 – 12 c. + 9 c. green 10 10
918 – 30 c. + 9 c. orange . . . 3·50 3·25
DESIGNS: 6 c. Epiphany; 8 c. Palm Sunday; 12 c. Whitsuntide; 30 c. Martinmas.

187 Queen Juliana and Prince Bernhard **188** Detail of "The Repast of the Officers of the St. Jorisdoelen" after Frans Hals

1962. Silver Wedding.
919 **187** 12 c. red 15 10
920 30 c. green . . . . 1·50 60

1962. Cultural, Health and Social Welfare Funds.
921 – 4 c. + 4 c. green . . . . 1·25 90
922 – 6 c. + 4 c. black 65 65
923 – 8 c. + 4 c. purple . . . . 1·50 1·50
924 – 12 c. + 8 c. bistre . . . . 1·50 25
925 **188** 30 c. + 10 c. blue . . . . 2·00 2·00
DESIGNS—HORIZ: 4 c. Roman cat (sculpture). VERT: 6 c. "Pleuroceras spinatus" (ammonite); 8 c. Pendulum clock (after principle of Huygens); 12 c. Ship's figurehead.

189 Telephone Dial **190** Europa "Tree"

1962. Completion of Netherlands Automatic Telephone System. Inscr "1962".
926 **189** 4 c. red and black 10 10
927 – 12 c. drab and black . . 55 10
928 – 30 c. ochre, blue & blk . 2·40 2·00
DESIGNS—VERT: 12 c. Diagram of telephone network. HORIZ: 30 c. Arch and telephone dial.

1962. Europa.
929 **190** 12 c. black, yellow & bis . 10 10
930 30 c. black, yellow & bl . 90 60

191 "Polder" Landscape (reclaimed area) **192** Children cooking Meal

1962.
935 – 4 c. deep blue and blue . 10 10
937 **191** 6 c. deep green & green . 40 10
938 – 10 c. dp purple & purple 10 10
DESIGNS: 4 c. Cooling towers, State mines, Limburg; 10 c. Delta excavation works.

1962. Child Welfare.
940 **192** 4 c. + 4 c. red 10 10
941 – 6 c. + 4 c. bistre 70 55
942 – 8 c. + 4 c. blue . . . . 1·75 1·50
943 – 12 c. + 9 c. green . . . 10 10
944 – 30 c. + 9 c. lake . . . . 2·75 2·75
DESIGNS—Children: 6 c. Cycling; 8 c. Watering flowers; 12 c. Feeding poultry; 30 c. Making music.

193 Ears of Wheat **194** "Gallery" Windmill

1963. Freedom from Hunger.
945 **193** 12 c. ochre and blue . . 10 10
946 30 c. ochre and red . . 1·00 75

1963. Cultural, Health and Social Welfare Funds. Windmill types.
947 **194** 4 c. + 4 c. blue . . . . . 1·00 1·00
948 – 6 c. + 4 c. violet . . . . 1·00 1·00
949 – 8 c. + 4 c. green . . . . 1·40 1·40
950 – 12 c. + 8 c. brown . . . 1·75 25
951 – 30 c. + 10 c. red . . . 2·40 2·40
WINDMILLS—VERT: 6 c. North Holland polder; 12 c. "Post"; 30 c. "Wip". HORIZ: 8 c. South Holland polder.

195 **196** Wayside First Aid Post

1963. Paris Postal Conference Centenary.
952 **195** 30 c. blue, green & blk . 1·25 1·00

1963. Red Cross Fund and Centenary (8 c.).
953 **196** 4 c. + 4 c. blue and red . 40 40
954 – 6 c. + 4 c. violet and red 25 30
955 – 8 c. + 4 c. red & black . 90 75
956 – 12 c. + 9 c. brown & red 35 15
957 – 30 c. + 9 c. green & red . 1·60 1·60
DESIGNS: 6 c. "Books" collection-box; 8 c. Crosses; 12 c. "International Aid" (Negro children at meal); 30 c. First aid party tending casualty.

197 "Co-operation" **198** "Auntie Luce sat on a goose ..."

1963. Europa.
958 **197** 12 c. orange and brown . . 10 10
959 30 c. orange and green . . 1·25 1·00

1963. Child Welfare.
960 **198** 4 c. + 4 c. ultra & bl . . . 10 10
961 – 6 c. + 4 c. green & red . . 70 65
962 – 8 c. + 4 c. brown & green 90 65
963 – 12 c. + 9 c. violet & yell . 10 10
964 – 30 c. + 8 c. blue & pink . 1·75 1·75
DESIGNS (Nursery rhymes): 6 c. "In the Hague there lives a count..."; 8 c. "One day I passed a puppet's fair..."; 12 c. "Storky, storky, Billy Spoon...."; 30 c. "Ride on a little pram...".

199 William, Prince of Orange, landing at Scheveningen **200** Knights' Hall, The Hague

1963. 150th Anniv of Kingdom of the Netherlands.
965 **199** 4 c. black, bistre & blue . 10 10
966 5 c. black, red and green . 10 10
967 – 12 c. bistre, blue & black . 10 10
968 – 30 c. red and black 50 50
DESIGNS: 12 c. Triumvirate: Van Hogendorp, Van Limburg, and Van der Duyn van Maasdam; 30 c. William I taking oath of allegiance.

1964. 500th Anniv of 1st States-General Meeting.
969 **200** 12 c. black and olive . . . 15 10

201 Guide Dog for the Blind

1964. Cultural, Health and Social Welfare Funds. Animals.
970 **201** 5 c. + 5 c. red, black and olive 60 50
971 – 8 c. + 5 c. brown, black and red 30 30
972 – 12 c. + 9 c. black, grey and bistre 55 15
973 – 30 c. + 9 c. multicoloured 85 70
DESIGNS: 8 c. Three red deer; 12 c. Three kittens; 30 c. European bison and calf.

202 University Arms **203** Station Signal

1964. 350th Anniv of Groningen University.
974 **202** 12 c. slate 10 10
975 – 30 c. brown 20 15
DESIGN: 30 c. "AG" monogram.

1964. 125th Anniv of Netherlands Railways.
976 **203** 15 c. black and green . . . 20 10
977 – 40 c. black and yellow . . 90 70
DESIGN: 40 c. Electric train at speed.

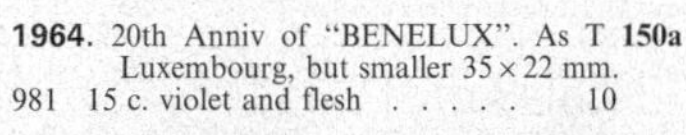

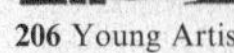
204 Bible and Dove **205** Europa "Flower"

1964. 150th Anniv of Netherlands Bible Society.
978 **204** 15 c. brown 10 10

1964. Europa.
979 **205** 15 c. green 15 10
980 20 c. brown 35 25

1964. 20th Anniv of "BENELUX". As T **150**a of Luxembourg, but smaller 35 × 22 mm.
981 15 c. violet and flesh 10 10

206 Young Artist **207** Queen Juliana

1964. Child Welfare.
982 **206** 7 c. + 3 c. blue & green . 40 50
983 – 10 c. + 5 c. red, pink and green 35 40
984 – 15 c. + 10 c. yellow, black and bistre 10 10
985 – 20 c. + 10 c. red, sepia and mauve 45 45
986 – 40 c. + 15 c. green & blue 1·00 70
DESIGNS: 10 c. Ballet-dancing; 15 c. Playing the recorder; 20 c. Masquerading; 40 c. Toy-making.

1964. 10th Anniv of Statute for the Kingdom.
987 **207** 15 c. green 10 10

208 "Killed in Action" (Waalwijk) and "Destroyed Town" (Rotterdam) (monuments) **209** Medal of Knight (Class IV)

1965. "Resistance" Commemoration.
988 **208** 7 c. black and red 10 10
989 – 15 c. black and olive . . . 10 10
990 – 40 c. black and red . . . 1·25 75
MONUMENTS: 15 c. "Docker" (Amsterdam) and "Killed in Action" (Waalwijk); 40 c. "Destroyed Town" (Rotterdam) and "Docker" (Amsterdam).

1965. 150th Anniv of Military William Order.
991 **209** 1 g. grey . . . . 2·00 80

210 I.T.U. Emblem and "Lines of Communication"

1965. Centenary of I.T.U.
992 **210** 20 c. blue and drab . . . 20 15
993 40 c. brown and blue . . 65 50

211 Veere

1965. Cultural, Health and Social Welfare Funds.
994 **211** 8 c. + 6 c. black & yellow 30 45
995 – 10 c. + 6 c. black & turq 45 40
996 – 18 c. + 12 c. blk & brn . 35 15
997 – 20 c. + 10 c. black & blue 45 40
998 – 40 c. + 10 c. black & grn 55 55
DESIGNS: (Dutch towns): 10 c. Thorn; 18 c. Dordrecht; 20 c. Staveren; 40 c. Medemblik.

212 Europa "Sprig"

1965. Europa.
999 **212** 18 c. black, red & brn . 20 10
1000 20 c. black, red & blue . 30 25

213 Girl's Head

1965. Child Welfare. Multicoloured.
1001 8 c. + 6 c. Type **213** 10 10
1002 10 c. + 6 c. Ship 50 50
1003 18 c. + 12 c. Boy (vert) . . 10 10
1004 20 c. + 10 c. Duck-pond . . 65 60
1005 40 c. + 10 c. Tractor . . . . 1·25 80

214 Marines of 1665 and 1965 **215** "Help them to a safe Haven" (Queen Juliana)

1965. Tercentenary of Marine Corps.
1007 **214** 18 c. blue and red . . . 10 10

1966. Intergovernmental Committee for European Migration (I.C.E.M.) Fund.

1008 **215** 10 c. + 7 c. yell & blk . 30 25
1009 40 c. + 20 c. red and blk 30 15

216 Writing Materials **217** Aircraft in Flight

1966. Cultural, Health and Social Welfare Funds. Gysbert Japicx Commem and 200th Anniv of Netherlands Literary Society. Multicoloured.

1011 10 c. + 5 c. Type **216** 30 35
1012 12 c. + 8 c. Part of MS, Japicx's poem "Wobbelke" 30 35
1013 20 c. + 10 c. Part of miniature, "Knight Walewein" 40 35
1014 25 c. + 10 c. Initial "D" and part of MS, novel, "Ferguut" 50 65
1015 40 c. + 20 c. 16th-cent printery (woodcut) 40 65

1966. Air (Special Flights).

1016 **217** 25 c. multicoloured . . . 30 40

218 Europa "Ship" **219** Infant

1966. Europa.

1017 **218** 20 c. green and yellow . 15 10
1018 40 c. deep blue & blue . 30 15

1966. Child Welfare.

1019 **219** 10 c. + 5 c. red & blue . 10 10
1020 – 12 c. + 8 c. green & red 10 10
1021 – 20 c. + 10 c. blue & red 10 10
1022 – 25 c. + 10 c. purple & bl 80 90
1023 – 40 c. + 20 c. red & green 95 80

DESIGNS: 12 c. Young girl; 20 c. Boy in water; 25 c. Girl with moped; 40 c. Young man with horse.

220 Assembly Hall **221** Common Northern Whelk Eggs

1967. 125th Anniv of Delft Technological University.

1025 **220** 20 c. sepia and yellow . . 10 10

1967. Cultural, Health and Social Welfare Funds. Marine Fauna.

1026 **221** 12 c. + 8 c. brown & grn 20 20
1027 – 15 c. + 10 c. blue, light blue and deep blue 20 20
1028 – 20 c. + 10 c. mult . . . 20 15
1029 – 25 c. + 10 c. purple, brown and bistre 45 50
1030 – 45 c. + 20 c. mult . . . 70 65

DESIGNS: 15 c. Common northern whelk; 20 c. Common blue mussel; 25 c. Jellyfish; 45 c. Crab.

222 Cogwheels **223** Netherlands 5 c. Stamp of 1852

1967. Europa.

1031 **222** 20 c. blue & light blue 40 10
1032 45 c. purple & lt purple . 1·00 70

1967. "Amphilex 67" Stamp Exn, Amsterdam.

1035 **223** 20 c. blue and black . . 2·40 2·25
1036 – 25 c. red and black . . . 2·40 2·25
1037 – 75 c. green and black . . 2·40 2·25

DESIGNS: 25 c. Netherlands 10 c. stamp of 1864; 75 c. Netherlands 20 c. stamp of 1867.

Nos. 1035/7 were sold at the Exhibition and at post offices at 3 g. 70, which included entrance fee to the Exhibition.

INDEX

Countries can be quickly located by referring to the index at the end of this volume.

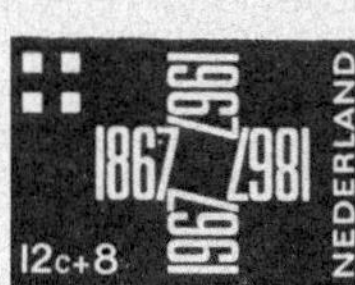

224 "1867-1967" **225** "Porcupine Lullaby"

1967. Centenary of Dutch Red Cross.

1038 12 c. + 8 c. blue and red . . 20 20
1039 15 c. + 10 c. red 35 35
1040 20 c. + 10 c. olive and red . 20 15
1041 25 c. + 10 c. green & red . 35 40
1042 45 c. + 20 c. grey and red . 60 70

DESIGNS: 12 c. Type **224**; 15 c. Red crosses; 20 c. "NRK" ("Nederlandsche Rood Kruis") in the form of a cross; 25 c. Maltese cross and "red" crosses; 45 c. "100" in the form of a cross.

1967. Child Welfare. Multicoloured.

1043 12 c. + 8 c. Type **225** . . . 10 10
1044 15 c. + 10 c. "The Whistling Kettle" 10 10
1045 20 c. + 10 c. "Dikkertje Dap" (giraffe) 10 10
1046 25 c. + 10 c. "The Flower-seller" 70 80
1047 45 c. + 20 c. "Pippeloentje" (bear) . . . . 1·10 95

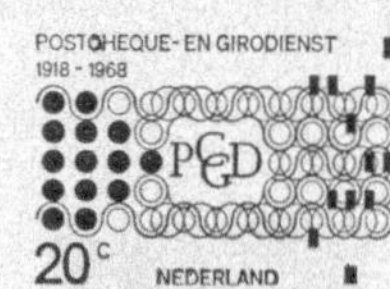

226 "Financial Automation"

1968. 50th Anniv of Netherlands Postal Cheque and Clearing Service.

1049 **226** 20 c. red, black & yell . 15 10

227 St. Servatius' Bridge, Maastricht

1968. Cultural, Health and Social Welfare Funds. Dutch Bridges.

1050 **227** 12 c. + 8 c. green . . . 40 50
1051 – 15 c. + 10 c. brown . . 60 70
1052 – 20 c. + 10 c. red . . . 1·50 25
1053 – 25 c. + 10 c. blue . . . 40 50
1054 – 45 c. + 20 c. blue . . . 85 80

BRIDGES: 15 c. Magere ("Narrow"), Amsterdam; 20 c. Railway, Culemborg; 25 c. Van Brienenoord, Rotterdam; 45 c. Oosterschelde, Zeeland.

228 Europa "Key"

1968. Europa.

1055 **228** 20 c. blue 20 10
1056 45 c. red 70 60

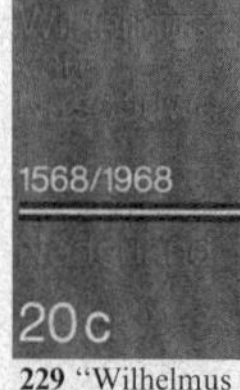

229 "Wilhelmus van Nassouwe" **230** Wright Type A and Cessna 150F

1968. 400th Anniv of Dutch National Anthem, "Wilhelmus".

1057 **229** 20 c. multicoloured . . 20 10

1968. Dutch Aviation Anniversaries.

1058 12 c. black, red & mauve . . 10 10
1059 20 c. black, emerald & grn . . 10 10
1060 45 c. black, blue & green . . 1·25 1·25

DESIGNS AND EVENTS: 12 c. T **230** (60th anniv (1967) of Royal Netherlands Aeronautical Assn); 20 c. Fokker F.II and Fellowship aircraft (50th anniv (1969) of Royal Netherlands Aircraft Factories "Fokker"); 45 c. De Havilland D.H.9B biplane and Douglas DC-9 airliner (50th anniv (1969) of Royal Dutch Airlines "KLM").

231 "Goblin"

1968. Child Welfare.

1061 **231** 12 c. + 8 c. pink, black and green 10 10
1062 – 15 c. + 10 c. pink, blue and black 10 10
1063 – 20 c. + 10 c. blue, green and black 10 10
1064 – 25 c. + 10 c. red, yellow and black . . . . . . 1·50 1·50
1065 – 45 c. + 20 c. yellow, orange and black . . . . . . 1·50 1·50

DESIGNS: 15 c. "Giant"; 20 c. "Witch"; 25 c. "Dragon"; 45 c. "Sorcerer".

232 "I A O" (Internationale Arbeidsorganisatie)

1969. 50th Anniv of I.L.O.

1067 **232** 25 c. red and black . . . 35 10
1068 45 c. blue and black . . . 1·00 95

233 Queen Juliana **234** Villa, Huis ter Heide (1915)

1969. (a) Type **233**.

1069 **233** 25 c. red . . . . 1·50 10
1069c 30 c. brown 15 10
1070a 35 c. blue 20 10
1071a 40 c. red 25 10
1072a 45 c. blue 30 10
1073a 50 c. purple 25 10
1073c 55 c. red 20 10
1074a 60 c. blue 20 10
1075 70 c. brown 40 10
1076 75 c. green 45 10
1077 80 c. red 45 10
1077a 90 c. grey 50 10

(b) Size 22 × 33 mm.

1078 – 1 g. green 80 10
1079 – 1 g. 25 lake 95 10
1080 – 1 g. 50 brown . . . . . . 1·10 10
1081 – 2 g. mauve . . . . 1·50 10
1082 – 2 g. 50 blue . . . . . . 1·90 10
1083 – 5 g. grey . . . . 3·75 10
1084 – 10 g. blue . . . . 7·50 1·10

DESIGNS: 1 g., 1 g. 25, 1 g. 50, 2 g., 2 g. 50, 5 g. and 10 g. similar to Type **233**.

1969. Cultural, Health and Social Welfare Funds. 20th-century Dutch Architecture.

1085 **234** 12 c. + 8 c. black & brn . 70 70
1086 – 15 c. + 10 c. black, red and blue 70 70
1087 – 20 c. + 10 c. black & vio 70 70
1088 – 25 c. + 10 c. brown & grn 70 30
1089 – 45 c. + 20 c. black, blue and yellow 70 70

DESIGNS: 15 c. Private House, Utrecht (1924); 20 c. Open-Air School, Amsterdam (1930); 25 c. Orphanage, Amsterdam (1960); 45 c. Congress Building, The Hague (1969).

235 Colonnade **236** Stylised "Crab" (of Cancer)

1969. Europa.

1090 **235** 25 c. blue 40 10
1901 45 c. red . . . . 1·50 1·40

1969. 20th Anniv of Queen Wilhelmina Cancer Fund.

1092 **236** 12 c. + 8 c. violet 75 75
1093 25 c. + 10 c. orange . . 1·00 30
1094 45 c. + 20 c. green . . 1·75 1·75

1969. 25th Anniv of "BENELUX" Customs Union. As T **186** of Luxembourg.

1095 25 c. multicoloured 30 10

238 Erasmus **239** Child with Violin

1969. 500th Birth Anniv of Desiderius Erasmus.

1096 **238** 25 c. purple on green . . 30 10

1969. Child Welfare.

1097 – 12 c. + 8 c. black, yellow and blue 10 10
1098 **239** 15 c. + 10 c. black and red 10 10
1099 – 20 c. + 10 c. black, yellow and red . . . . 1·90 2·00
1100 – 25 c. + 10 c. black, red and yellow 10 10
1101 – 45 c. + 20 c. black, red and green . . . . 1·90 2·00

DESIGNS—VERT: 12 c. Child with recorder; 20 c. Child with drum. HORIZ: 25 c. Three choristers; 45 c. Two dancers.

240 Queen Juliana and "Sunlit Road"

1969. 25th Anniv of Statute for the Kingdom.

1103 **240** 25 c. multicoloured . . . 30 10

241 Prof. E. M. Meijers (author of "Burgerlijk Wetboek")

1970. Introduction of New Netherlands Civil Code ("Burgerlijk Wetboek").

1104 **241** 25 c. ultramarine, green and blue 30 10

242 Netherlands Pavilion **243** "Circle to Square"

1970. Expo 70, World Fair, Osaka, Japan.

1105 **242** 25 c. grey, blue & red . . 30 10

1970. Cultural, Health and Social Welfare Funds.

1106 **243** 12 c. + 8 c. black on yell 1·10 1·25
1107 – 15 c. + 10 c. black on silver 1·10 1·25
1108 – 20 c. + 10 c. black . . . 1·10 1·25
1109 – 25 c. + 10 c. black on bl 1·10 70
1110 – 45 c. + 20 c. white on grey 1·10 1·25

DESIGNS: 15 c. Parallel planes in cube; 20 c. Overlapping scales; 25 c. Concentric circles in transition; 45 c. Spirals.

244 "V" Symbol **245** "Flaming Sun"

1970. 25th Anniv of Liberation.

1111 **244** 12 c. red, blue & brown . 40 10

1970. Europa.

1112 **245** 25 c. red 40 10
1113 45 c. blue . . . . 1·60 1·00

246 "Work and Co-operation" **247** Globe on Plinth

1970. Inter-Parliamentary Union Conference.

1114 **246** 25 c. green, blk & grey . 40 10

1970. 25th Anniv of United Nations.

1115 **247** 45 c. blk, violet and bl . 75 70

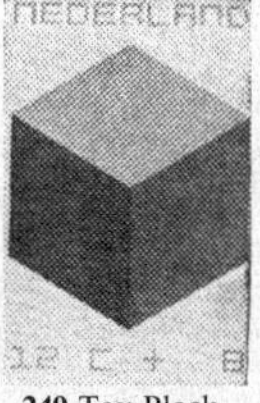

248 Human Heart **249** Toy Block

1970. Netherlands Heart Foundation.
1116 **248** 12 c. + 8 c. red, black and yellow 80 80
1117 25 c. + 10 c. red, black and mauve 80 65
1118 45 c. + 20 c. red, black and green 80 80

1970. Child Welfare. "The Child and the Cube".
1119 **249** 12 c. + 8 c. blue, violet and green 10 10
1120 – 15 c. + 10 c. green, blue and yellow . . . . . . 1·60 1·60
1121 **249** 20 c. + 10 c. mauve, red and violet . . . . . . 1·60 1·60
1122 – 25 c. + 10 c. red, yell and mauve 15 10
1123 **249** 45 c. + 20 c. grey, cream and black . . . . . . 2·00 2·00
DESIGN: 15 c., 25 c. As Type **249**, but showing underside of block.

250 "Fourteenth Census 1971"

1971. 14th Netherlands Census.
1125 **250** 15 c. purple 15 10

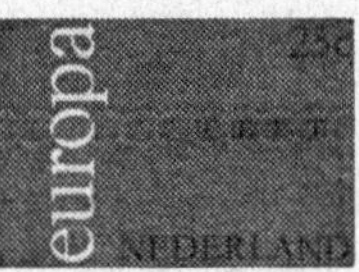

251 "50 years of Adult University Education" **252** Europa Chain

1971. Cultural, Health and Social Welfare Funds. Other designs show 15th-century wooden statues by unknown artists.
1126 **251** 15 c. + 10 c. black, red and yellow . . . . 1·50 1·50
1127 – 20 c. + 10 c. black and green on green . . . . 1·00 1·00
1128 – 25 c. + 10 c. black and orange on orge . . . . 1·25 60
1129 – 30 c. + 15 c. black and blue on blue . . . . 1·50 1·50
1130 – 45 c. + 20 c. black and red on pink . . . . 1·50 1·50
STATUES: 20 c. "Apostle Paul"; 25 c. "Joachim and Ann"; 30 c. "John the Baptist and Scribes"; 45 c. "Ann, Mary and Christ-Child" (detail).

1971. Europa.
1131 **252** 25 c. yellow, red & black 40 10
1132 45 c. yellow, blue & blk . 1·60 1·00

253 Carnation Symbol of Prince Bernhard Fund **254** "The Good Earth"

1971. Prince Bernhard's 60th Birthday.
1133 **253** 15 c. yellow, grey & blk . 15 10
1134 – 20 c. multicoloured . . . 25 15
1135 – 25 c. multicoloured . . . 25 10
1136 – 45 c. + 20 c. black, purple and yellow . . . . . . 2·75 2·75
DESIGNS—HORIZ: 20 c. Panda symbol of World Wildlife Fund. VERT: 25 c. Prince Bernhard; 45 c. Statue, Borobudur Temple, Indonesia.

1971. Child Welfare.
1137 **254** 15 c. + 10 c. red, purple and black 10 10
1138 – 20 c. + 10 c. mult . . . 30 15
1139 – 25 c. + 10 c. mult . . . 15 10
1140 – 30 c. + 15 c. blue, violet and black 85 70
1141 – 45 c. + 20 c. blue, green and black . . . . . . 1·75 2·00
DESIGNS—VERT: 20 c. Butterfly; 45 c. Reflecting water. HORIZ: 25 c. Sun waving; 30 c. Moon winking.

255 Delta Map **256** "Fruits"

1972. Delta Sea-Defences Plan.
1143 **255** 20 c. multicoloured . . 30 10

1972. Cultural, Health and Social Welfare Funds. "Floriade Flower Show" (20 c., 25 c.) and "Holland Arts Festival" (30 c., 45 c.). Mult.
1144 20 c. + 10 c. Type **256** . . . 1·25 1·00
1145 25 c. + 10 c. "Flower" . . 1·25 1·00
1146 30 c. + 15 c. "Sunlit Landscape" . . . . 1·25 70
1147 45 c. + 25 c. "Music" . . . 1·25 1·00

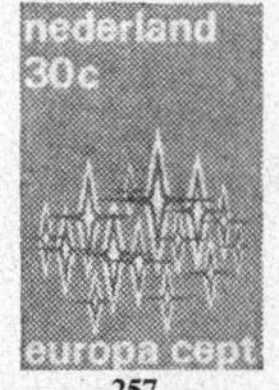

257 "Communications" **258** "There is more to be done in the world than ever before" (Thorbecke)

1972. Europa.
1148 **257** 30 c. brown and blue . . 85 10
1149 45 c. brown and orange 1·40 1·25

1972. Death Centenary of J. R. Thorbecke (statesman).
1150 **258** 30 c. black and blue . . 30 10

259 Netherlands Flag **260** Hurdling

1972. 400th Anniv of Netherlands Flag.
1151 **259** 20 c. multicoloured . . 60 15
1152 25 c. multicoloured . . 1·40 10

1972. Olympic Games, Munich. Multicoloured.
1153 20 c. Type **260** 15 10
1154 30 c. Diving 15 10
1155 45 c. Cycling . . . . 1·00 1·25

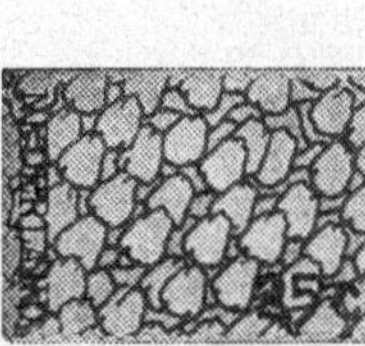

261 Red Cross **262** Prince Willem-Alexander

1972. Netherlands Red Cross.
1156 **261** 5 c. red 10 10
1157 – 20 c. + 10 c. red & pink 60 60
1158 – 25 c. + 10 c. red & orge 80 1·00
1159 – 30 c. + 15 c. red & black 75 35
1160 – 45 c. + 25 c. red & blue 85 95
DESIGNS: 20 c. Accident services; 25 c. Blood transfusion; 30 c. Refugee relief; 45 c. Child care.

1972. Child Welfare. Multicoloured.
1161 25 c. + 15 c. Type **262** . . . 15 15
1162 30 c. + 10 c. Prince Johan Friso 70 80
1163 35 c. + 15 c. Prince Constantin 70 10
1164 50 c. + 20 c. The Three Princes 2·40 2·50
Nos. 1162/4 are horiz.

263 Tulips in Bloom **264** "De Zeven Provincien" (De Ruyter's flagship)

1973. Tulip Exports.
1166 **263** 25 c. multicoloured . . 75 10

1973. Cultural, Health and Social Welfare Funds. Dutch Ships. Multicoloured.
1167 25 c. + 15 c. Type **264** . . . 1·25 1·50
1168 30 c. + 10 c. "W.A. Scholten" (steamship) (horiz) . . . . 1·25 1·50
1169 35 c. + 15 c. "Veendam" (liner) (horiz) . . . . 1·50 1·00
1170 50 c. + 20 c. Fishing boat (from etching by R. Nooms) . . . 1·50 1·50

265 Europa "Posthorn" **266** Hockey-players

1973. Europa.
1171 **265** 35 c. lt blue & blue . . . 45 40
1172 50 c. blue and violet . . . 80 75

1973. Events and Anniversaries. Multicoloured.
1173 25 c. Type **266** 25 10
1174 30 c. Gymnastics . . . . . . 2·25 55
1175 35 c. Dish aerial (vert) 35 10
1176 50 c. Rainbow 60 60
EVENTS—VERT: 25 c. 75th anniv of Royal Netherlands Hockey Association; 30 c. World Gymnastics Championships, Rotterdam. HORIZ: 35 c. Opening of Satellite Station, Burum; 50 c. Centenary of World Meteorological Organization.

267 Queen Juliana **268** "Co-operation"

1973. Silver Jubilee of Queen Juliana's Accession.
1177 **267** 40 c. multicoloured . . . 50 10

1973. International Development Co-operation.
1178 **268** 40 c. multicoloured . . . 1·00 10

269 "Chess" **270** Northern Goshawk

1973. Child Welfare.
1179 **269** 25 c. + 15 c. red, yellow and black 65 15
1180 – 30 c. + 10 c. green, mauve and black . . . . . . 1·00 70
1181 – 40 c. + 20 c. yellow, green and black 80 10
1182 – 50 c. + 20 c. blue, yellow and black . . . . . . 2·25 2·25
DESIGNS: 30 c. "Noughts and crosses"; 40 c. "Maze"; 50 c. "Dominoes".

1974. "Nature and Environment". Multicoloured.
1184 25 c. Type **270** . . . . 1·90 60
1185 25 c. Tree . . . . 1·25 60
1186 25 c. Fisherman and frog . . 1·25 60
Nos. 1184/6 were issued together se-tenant forming a composite design.

271 Bandsmen (World Band Contest, Kerkrade) **272** Football on Pitch

1974. Cultural, Health and Social Welfare Funds.
1187 **271** 25 c. + 15 c. multicoloured 90 90
1188 – 30 c. + 10 c. multicoloured 90 90
1189 – 40 c. + 20 c. brown, black and red 90 65
1190 – 50 c. + 20 c. purple, black and red 90 90
DESIGNS: 30 c. Dancers and traffic-lights ("Modern Ballet"); 40 c. Herman Heijermans; 50 c. "Kniertje" (character from Heijermans' play "Op hoop van zegan"). The 40 c. and 50 c. commemorate the 50th death anniv of the playwright.

1974. Sporting Events.
1191 **272** 25 c. multicoloured . . . 20 10
1192 – 40 c. yellow, red & mve . 30 10
DESIGNS AND EVENTS—HORIZ: 25 c. (World Cup Football Championships, West Germany). VERT: 40 c. Hand holding tennis ball (75th anniv of Royal Dutch Lawn Tennis Association).

273 Netherlands Cattle **274** "BENELUX" (30th Anniv of Benelux (Customs Union))

1974. Anniversaries. Multicoloured.
1193 25 c. Type **273** . . . . 9·25 2·25
1194 25 c. "Cancer" 15 15
1195 40 c. "Suzanna" (lifeboat) seen through binoculars 20 10
EVENTS AND ANNIVERSARIES: No. 1193, Cent of Netherlands Cattle Herdbook Society; No. 1194, 25th anniv of Queen Wilhelmina Cancer Research Fund; No. 1195, 150th anniv of Dutch Lifeboat Service.

1974. International Anniversaries.
1196 **274** 30 c. green, turq & bl . . 20 10
1197 – 45 c. deep blue, silver & bl 30 10
1198 – 45 c. yellow, blue & blk . 30 10
DESIGNS—VERT: No. 1197, NATO emblem (25th anniv); 1198, Council of Europe emblem (25th anniv).

275 Hands with Letters **276** Boy with Hoop

1974. Centenary of Universal Postal Union.
1199 **275** 60 c. multicoloured . . . 40 35

1974. 50th Anniv of Child Welfare Issues. Early Photographs.
1200 **276** 30 c. + 15 c. brown & blk 15 15
1201 – 35 c. + 20 c. brown . . 40 50
1202 – 45 c. + 20 c. black . . . 40 15
1203 – 60 c. + 20 c. black . . . 1·25 1·40
DESIGNS: 35 c. Child and baby; 45 c. Two young girls; 60 c. Girl sitting on balustrade.

277 Amsterdam **278** St. Hubertus Hunting Lodge, De Hoge Veluwe National Park

1975. Anniversaries. Multicoloured.
1205 30 c. Type **277** 20 10
1206 30 c. Synagogue and map . . 40 15
1207 35 c. Type **277** 35 10
1208 45 c. "Window" in human brain 40 15
ANNIVERSARIES: Nos. 1205, 1207, Amsterdam (700th anniv); No. 1206, Portuguese-Israelite Synagogue, Amsterdam (300th anniv); No. 1208, Leyden University and university education (400th anniv).

1975. Cultural, Health and Social Welfare Funds. National Monument Year. Preserved Monuments. Multicoloured.
1209 35 c. + 20 c. Type **278** . . . 50 50
1210 40 c. + 15 c. Bergijnhof (Beguinage), Amsterdam (vert) 50 50
1211 50 c. + 20 c. "Kuiperspoort" (Cooper's gate), Middelburg (vert) 65 50
1212 60 c. + 20 c. Orvelte village, Drenthe 75 90

279 Eye and Barbed Wire **280** Company Emblem and "Stad Middelburg" (schooner)

1975. 30th Anniv of Liberation.
1213 **279** 35 c. black and red . . . 30 10

1975. Centenary of Zeeland Shipping Company.
1214 **280** 35 c. multicoloured . . . 30 10

281 Dr. Albert Schweitzer crossing Lambarene River

1975. Birth Centenary of Dr. Schweitzer.
1215 **281** 50 c. multicoloured . . . 40 10

282 Man and Woman on "Playing-card" **283** Braille Reading

1975. International Events. Multicoloured.
1216 35 c. Type **282** (Int Women's Year) 20 10
1217 50 c. Metric scale (Metre Convention centenary) (horiz) 30 10

1975. 150th Anniv of Invention of Braille.
1218 **283** 35 c. multicoloured . . . 30 10

284 Dutch 25 c. Coins **285** "Four Orphans" (C. Simons), Torenstraat Orphanage, Medemblik

1975. Savings Campaign.
1219 **284** 50 c. grey, green & blue . 35 10

1975. Child Welfare. Historic Ornamental Stones. Multicoloured.
1220 35 c. + 15 c. Type **285** . . . 15 15
1221 40 c. + 15 c. "Milkmaid" Kooltuin Alkmaar 45 45
1222 50 c. + 25 c. "Four Sons of Aymon seated on Beyaert", Herengracht 30 10
1223 60 c. + 25 c. "Life at the Orphanage", Molenstraat Orphanage, Gorinchem . . 85 85

286 18th-century Lottery Ticket **287** Numeral

1976. 250th Anniv of National Lottery.
1225 **286** 35 c. multicoloured . . . 30 10

1976.
1226 **287** 5 c. grey 10 10
1227 10 c. blue 10 10
1228 25 c. violet 10 10
1229 40 c. brown 15 10
1230 45 c. blue 30 10
1231 50 c. mauve 30 10
1232 55 c. green 45 10
1233 60 c. yellow 45 10
1234 65 c. brown 45 10
1235 70 c. violet 45 10
1236 80 c. mauve 50 10

288 West European Hedgehog

1976. Cultural, Health and Social Welfare Funds. Nature Protection (40, 75 c.) and Anniversaries. Multicoloured.
1241 40 c. + 20 c. Type **288** . . . 60 60
1242 45 c. + 20 c. Open book (vert) 60 60
1243 55 c. + 20 c. People and organization initials . . . 70 25
1244 75 c. + 25 c. Frog and spawn (vert) 85 85
ANNIVERSARIES: No. 1242, 175th anniv of Primary education and centenary of Agricultural education; No. 1245, 75th anniv of Social Security Bank and legislation.

289 Admiral Michiel de Ruyter (statue)

1976. 300th Death Anniv of Admiral Michiel de Ruyter.
1245 **289** 55 c. multicoloured . . 35 10

290 Guillaume Groen van Prinsterer

1976. Death Centenary of Guillaume Groen van Prinsterer (statesman).
1246 **290** 55 c. multicoloured . . 35 10

291 Detail of 18th Century Calendar

1976. Bicentenary of American Revolution.
1247 **291** 75 c. multicoloured . . 50 35

292 Long-distance Marchers **293** The Art of Printing

1976. Sport and Recreation Anniversaries. Mult.
1248 40 c. Type **292** 20 15
1249 55 c. Runners "photo-finish" 60 15
ANNIVERSARIES: 40 c. 60th Nijmegen Long-Distance March; 55 c. Royal Dutch Athletics Society (75th anniv).

1976. Anniversaries.
1250 **293** 45 c. red and blue . . . 25 10
1251 – 55 c. + 25 c. multicoloured 45 45
DESIGNS AND EVENTS: 45 c. Type **293** (75th anniv of Netherlands Printers' organization); 55 c. Rheumatic patient "Within Care" (50th anniv of Dutch Anti-Rheumatism Association).

294 Dutch Tjalk and Reclaimed Land **295** Queen Wilhelmina 4½ c. Stamp, 1919

1976. Zuider Zee Project–Reclamation and Urbanization. Multicoloured.
1252 **294** 40 c. blue, olive and red 25 10
1253 – 75 c. yellow, red & blue 50 35
DESIGN: 75 c. Duck flying over reclaimed land.

1976. "Amphilex '77" International Stamp Exhibition, Amsterdam (1977) (1st series). Stamp Portraits of Queen Wilhelmina. Mult.
1254 – 55 c. + 55 c. blue, deep grey and grey 70 75
1255 **295** 55 c. + 55 c. purple, deep grey and grey 70 75
1256 – 55 c. + 55 c. brown, deep grey and grey 70 75
1257 – 75 c. + 75 c. turq, deep grey and grey 70 75
1258 – 75 c. + 75 c. blue, deep grey and grey 70 75
DESIGNS: No. 1254, 5 c. stamp, 1891; No. 1256, 25 c. stamp, 1924; No. 1257, 15 c. stamp, 1940; No. 1258, 25 c. stamp, 1947.
See also Nos. 1273/6.

296 "Football" (J. Raats)

1976. Child Welfare. Children's Paintings. Multicoloured.
1259 40 c. + 20 c. Type **296** . . . 25 25
1260 45 c. + 20 c. "Boat" (L Jacobs) 25 25
1261 55 c. + 20 c. "Elephant" (M. Lugtenburg) 30 10
1262 75 c. + 25 c. "Caravan" (A. Seeleman) 65 80

297 Ballot-paper and Pencil

1977. National Events. Multicoloured.
1264 40 c. "Energy" (vert) 30 10
1265 45 c. Type **297** 40 10
EVENTS: 40 c. "Be wise with energy" campaign; 45 c. Elections to Lower House of States General.
See also No. 1268.

298 Spinoza **299** Early Type Faces and "a" on Bible Script

1977. 300th Death Anniv of Barach (Benedictus) de Spinoza (philosopher).
1266 **298** 75 c. multicoloured . . . 60 30

1977. 500th Anniv of Printing of "Delft Bible".
1267 **299** 55 c. multicoloured . . . 40 30

1977. Elections to Lower House of States General. As T **297** but also inscribed "25 MEI '77".
1268 45 c. multicoloured 45 10

300 Altar of Goddess Nehalennia **301** "Kaleidoscope"

1977. Cultural, Health and Social Welfare Funds. Roman Archaeological Discoveries.
1269 – 40 c. + 20 c. mult . . . 30 30
1270 **300** 45 c. + 20 c. black, stone and green 30 25
1271 – 55 c. + 20 c. black, blue and red 30 20
1272 – 75 c. + 25 c. black, grey and yellow 40 45
DESIGNS: 40 c. Baths, Heerlen; 55 c. Remains of Zwammerdam ship; 75 c. Parade helmet.

1977. "Amphilex 1977" International Stamp Exhibition, Amsterdam (2nd series). As T **295**.
1273 55 c. + 45 c. grn, brn & grey 45 50
1274 55 c. + 45 c. bl, brn & grey . 45 50
1275 55 c. + 45 c. bl, brn & grey . 45 50
1276 55 c. + 45 c. red, brn & grey 45 50
DESIGNS: No. 1273, Queen Wilhelmina 1 g. stamp, 1898; No. 1274, Queen Wilhelmina 20 c. stamp, 1923; No. 1275, Queen Wilhelmina 12½ c. stamp, 1938; No. 1276, Queen Wilhelmina 10 c. stamp, 1948.

1977. Bicentenary of Netherlands Society for Industry and Commerce.
1278 **301** 55 c. multicoloured . . . 30 10

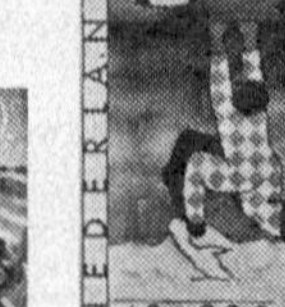

302 Man in Wheelchair and Maze of Steps **303** Risk of Drowning

1977. Anniversaries.
1279 **302** 40 c. brown, green & bl . 20 10
1280 – 45 c. multicoloured . . . 25 10
1281 – 55 c. multicoloured . . . 35 10
DESIGNS—HORIZ: 40 c. Type **302** (50th anniv of A.V.O. Nederland); 45 c. Diagram of water current (50th anniv of Delft Hydraulic Laboratory). VERT: 55 c. Teeth (centenary of dentists' training in Netherlands).

1977. Child Welfare. Dangers to Children. Mult.
1282 40 c. + 20 c. Type **303** . . . 30 20
1283 45 c. + 20 c. Medicine cabinet (poisons) 30 25
1284 55 c. + 20 c. Balls in road (traffic) 30 20
1285 75 c. + 25 c. Matches (fire) . 55 65

304 "Postcode" **305** Makkum Dish

1978. Introduction of Postcodes.
1287 **304** 40 c. red and blue . . . 20 10
1288 45 c. red and blue . . . 25 10

1978. Cultural, Health and Social Welfare Funds. Multicoloured.
1289 40 c. + 20 c. Anna Maria van Schurman (writer) 30 30
1290 45 c. + 20 c. Passage from letter by Belle de Zuylen (Mme. de Charriere) 30 25
1291 55 c. + 20 c. Delft dish . . 30 25
1292 75 c. + 25 c. Type **305** . . . 40 45

306 "Human Rights" Treaty **307** Chess

1978. European Series.
1293 **306** 45 c. grey, black and blue 25 10
1294 – 55 c. black, stone and orange 35 10
DESIGN: 55 c. Haarlem Town Hall (Europa).

1978. Sports.
1295 **307** 40 c. multicoloured . . . 50 15
1296 – 45 c. red and blue . . . 50 15
DESIGN: 45 c. The word "Korfbal".

308 Kidney Donor **309** Epaulettes

1978. Health Care. Multicoloured.
1297 **308** 40 c. black, blue and red 25 10
1298 – 45 c. multicoloured . . . 30 10
1299 – 55 c. + 25 c. red, grey and black 45 50
DESIGNS—VERT: 45 c. Heart and torch. HORIZ: 55 c. Red crosses on world map.

1978. 150th Anniv of Royal Military Academy, Breda.
1301 **309** 55 c. multicoloured . . . 30 10

310 Verkade as Hamlet

1978. Birth Centenary of Eduard Rutger Verkade (actor and producer).
1302 **310** 45 c. multicoloured . . . 30 10

311 Boy ringing Doorbell

1978. Child Welfare. Multicoloured.
1303 40 c. + 20 c. Type **311** . . . 30 20
1304 45 c. + 20 c. Child reading . 30 20
1305 55 c. + 20 c. Boy writing (vert) 30 15
1306 75 c. + 25 c. Girl and blackboard 40 60

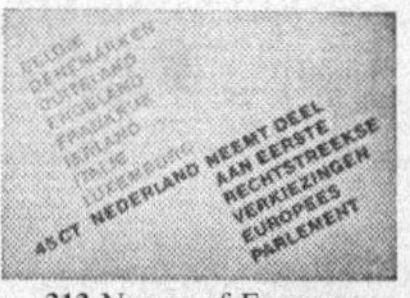

312 Clasped Hands and Arrows **313** Names of European Community Members

1979. 400th Anniv of Treaty of Utrecht.
1308 **312** 55 c. blue 35 10

1979. First Direct Elections to European Assembly.
1309 **313** 45 c. red, blue and black 40 10

314 Queen Juliana

1979. Queen Juliana's 70th Birthday.
1310 **314** 55 c. multicoloured . . . 40 10

315 Fragment of "Psalmen Trilogie" (J. Andriessen)

316 Netherlands Stamps and Magnifying Glass

1979. Cultural, Health and Social Welfare Funds.
1311 **315** 40 c. + 20 c. grey and red 30 30
1312 – 45 c. + 20 c. grey and red 30 25
1313 – 55 c. + 20 c. multicoloured 30 20
1314 – 75 c. + 25 c. multicoloured 65 45
DESIGNS AND EVENTS: 150th anniv of Musical Society; 45 c. Choir. Restoration of St. John's Church, Gouda (stained glass windows); 55 c. Mary (detail, "Birth of Christ"); 75 c. William of Orange (detail, "Relief of Leyden").

1979. Europa and 75th Anniv of Scheveningen Radio. Multicoloured.
1315 55 c. Type **316** 35 10
1316 75 c. Liner and Morse Key . 50 35

317 Map of Chambers of Commerce

318 Action Shot of Football Match

1979. 175th Anniv of First Dutch Chamber of Commerce, Maastricht.
1317 **317** 45 c. multicoloured . . . 40 15

1979. Anniversaries. Multicoloured.
1318 45 c. Type **318** (centenary of organized football) 35 15
1319 55 c. Women's suffrage meeting (60th anniv of Women's suffrage) (vert) 45 10

319 Porch of Old Amsterdam Theatre

1979. 300th Death Annivs of Joost van den Vondel (poet) and Jan Steen (painter). Multicoloured.
1320 40 c. Type **319** 20 10
1321 45 c. "Gay Company" (detail) (Jan Steen) 25 10

320 Hindustani Girl on Father's Shoulder (The Right to Love)

1979. Child Welfare. International Year of the Child
1322 **320** 40 c. + 20 c. grey, red and yellow 35 20
1323 – 45 c. + 20 c. grey, red and black 35 15
1324 – 55 c. + 20 c. grey, black and yellow 35 15
1325 – 75 c. + 25 c. black, blue and red 45 60
DESIGNS—HORIZ: 45 c. Chilean child from refugee camp (The Right to Medical Care). VERT: 55 c. Senegalese boy from Sahel area (The Right to Food); 75 c. Class from Albert Cuyp School, Amsterdam (The Right to Education).

321 A. F. de Savornin Lohman

322 Dunes

1980. Dutch Politicians. Multicoloured.
1327 45 c. Type **321** (Christian Historical Union) 25 10
1328 50 c. P. J. Troelstra (Socialist Party) 25 10
1329 60 c. P. J. Oud (Liberal Party) 35 10

1980. Cultural, Health and Social Welfare Funds. Multicoloured.
1330 45 c. + 20 c. Type **322** . . . 40 30
1331 50 c. + 20 c. Country estate (vert) 40 30
1332 60 c. + 25 c. Lake District . 50 25
1333 80 c. + 35 c. Moorland . . 65 65

323 Avro Type 683 Lancaster dropping Food Parcels

324 Queen Beatrix and New Church, Amsterdam

1980. 35th Anniv of Liberation. Multicoloured.
1334 45 c. Type **323** 40 15
1335 60 c. Anne Frank (horiz) . . 60 10

1980. Installation of Queen Beatrix.
1336 **324** 60 c. blue, red & yellow 45 10
1337 65 c. blue, red & yellow 55 10

325 Young Stamp Collectors

326 "Flight"

1980. "Jupostex 1980" Stamp Exhibition, Eindhoven, and Dutch Society of Stamp Dealers Show, The Hague.
1338 **325** 50 c. multicoloured . . 30 20

1980. Air. (Special Flights).
1339 **326** 1 g. blue and black . . . 75 45

327 Bridge Players and Cards

328 Road Haulage

1980. Sports Events. Multicoloured.
1340 50 c. Type **327** (Bridge Olympiad, Valkenburg) . . 30 10
1341 60 c. + 25 c. Sportswoman in wheelchair (Olympics for the Disabled, Arnhem and Veenendaal) 50 40

1980. Transport.
1342 **328** 50 c. multicoloured . . 25 10
1343 – 60 c. blue, brown & blk 40 10
1344 – 80 c. multicoloured . . 45 25
DESIGNS: 60 c. Rail transport; 80 c. Motorised canal barge.

329 Queen Wilhelmina

1980. Europa.
1345 **329** 60 c. black, red & blue . 35 10
1346 – 80 c. black, red & blue . 40 20
DESIGN: 80 c. Sir Winston Churchill.

330 Abraham Kuyper (first rector) and University Seal

1980. Centenary of Amsterdam Free University.
1347 **330** 50 c. multicoloured . . . 30 10

331 "Pop-up" Book

332 Saltmarsh

1980. Child Welfare. Multicoloured.
1348 45 c. + 20 c. Type **331** . . . 35 20
1349 50 c. + 20 c. Child flying on a book (vert) 35 35
1350 60 c. + 30 c. Boy reading "Kikkerkoning" (vert) . . . 45 20
1351 80 c. + 30 c. Dreaming in a book 60 65

1981. Cultural, Health and Social Welfare Funds. Multicoloured.
1353 45 c. + 20 c. Type **332** . . . 30 30
1354 55 c. + 25 c. Dyke 30 30
1355 60 c. + 25 c. Drain 35 30
1356 65 c. + 30 c. Cultivated land 40 40

333 Parcel (Parcel Post)

1981. P.T.T. Centenaries. Multicoloured.
1357 45 c. Type **333** 25 10
1358 55 c. Telephone, dish aerial and telephone directory page (public telephone service) . 30 10
1359 65 c. Savings bank books, deposit transfer card and savings bank stamps (National Savings Bank) . . 35 10

334 Huis ten Bosch Royal Palace, The Hague

1981.
1361 **334** 55 c. multicoloured . . . 35 10

335 Carillon

1981. Europa. Multicoloured.
1362 45 c. Type **335** 35 10
1363 65 c. Barrel organ 55 10

336 Council of State Emblem and Maps of 1531 and 1981

1981. 450th Anniv of Council of State.
1364 **336** 65 c. orange, deep orange and red 45 10

337 Marshalling Yard, Excavator and Ship's Screw

1981. Industrial and Agricultural Exports. Multicoloured.
1365 45 c. Type **337** 40 15
1366 55 c. Inner port, cast-iron component and weighing machine 40 15
1367 60 c. Airport, tomato and lettuce 45 40
1368 65 c. Motorway interchange, egg and cheese 55 10

338 "Integration in Society"

1981. Child Welfare. Integration of Handicapped Children. Multicoloured.
1369 45 c. + 25 c. Type **338** . . . 40 20
1370 55 c. + 20 c. "Integration in the Family" (vert) 45 45
1371 60 c. + 25 c. Child vaccinated against polio (Upper Volta project) (vert) 50 50
1372 65 c. + 30 c. "Integration among Friends" 60 20

339 Queen Beatrix

340 Agnieten Chapel and Banners

1981.
1374 **339** 65 c. brown and black . 40 10
1375 70 c. lilac and black . . 55 10
1376 75 c. pink and black . . 75 10
1377 90 c. green and black . . 1·25 10
1378 1 g. lilac and black . . . 75 10
1379 1 g. 20 bistre and black . 1·10 10
1380 1 g. 40 green and black . 1·75 10
1381 1 g. 50 lilac and black . 90 10
1382 2 g. bistre and black . . 1·50 10
1383 2 g. 50 orange and black 1·75 15
1384 3 g. blue and black . . . 2·10 10
1385 4 g. green and black . . 3·00 10
1386 5 g. blue and black . . . 3·75 10
1387 6 g. 50 lilac and black . 5·50 15
1388 7 g. blue and black . . . 5·25 10
1389 7 g. 50 green and black . 6·00 30
For this design but on uncoloured background see Nos. 1594/1605.

1982. 350th Anniv of University of Amsterdam.
1395 **340** 65 c. multicoloured . . . 50 10

341 Skater

342 Apple Blossom

1982. Centenary of Royal Dutch Skating Association.
1396 **341** 45 c. multicoloured . . . 40 20

1982. Cultural, Health and Social Welfare Funds. Multicoloured.
1397 50 c. + 20 c. Type **342** . . . 40 45
1398 60 c. + 25 c. Anemones . . 50 45
1399 65 c. + 25 c. Roses 50 45
1400 70 c. + 30 c. African violets 70 75

343 Stripes in National Colours

1982. Bicentenary of Netherlands–United States Diplomatic Relations.
1401 **343** 50 c. red, blue and black 40 10
1402 65 c. red, blue and black 60 20

344 Sandwich Tern and Eider

345 Zebra Crossing

1982. Waddenzee. Multicoloured.
1403 50 c. Type **344** 40 15
1404 70 c. Barnacle Geese 60 15

1982. 50th Anniv of Dutch Road Safety Organization.
1405 **345** 60 c. multicoloured . . . 55 15

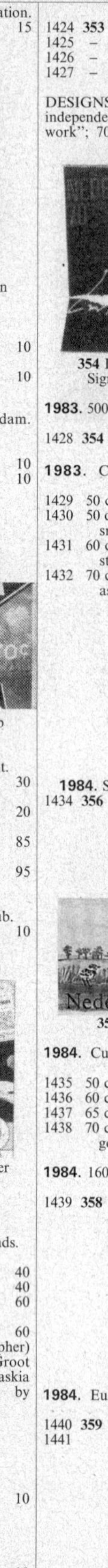

346 Ground Plan of Enkhuizen Fortifications

347 Aerial view of Palace and Liberation Monument

1982. Europa. Multicoloured.
1406 50 c. Type **346** 40 10
1407 70 c. Part of ground plan of Coevorden fortifications . . 60 10

1982. Royal Palace, Dam Square, Amsterdam. Multicoloured.
1408 50 c. Facade, ground plan and cross-section of Palace . . 40 10
1409 60 c. Type **347** 45 10

348 Great Tits and Child

349 Touring Club Activities

1982. Child Welfare. Child and Animal. Mult.
1410 50 c. + 30 c. Type **348** . . . 60 30
1411 60 c. + 20 c. Child arm-in-arm with cat 65 20
1412 65 c. + 20 c. Child with drawing of rabbit 70 85
1413 70 c. + 30 c. Child with palm cockatoo . . . . 1·00 95

1983. Centenary of Royal Dutch Touring Club.
1415 **349** 70 c. multicoloured . . . 65 10

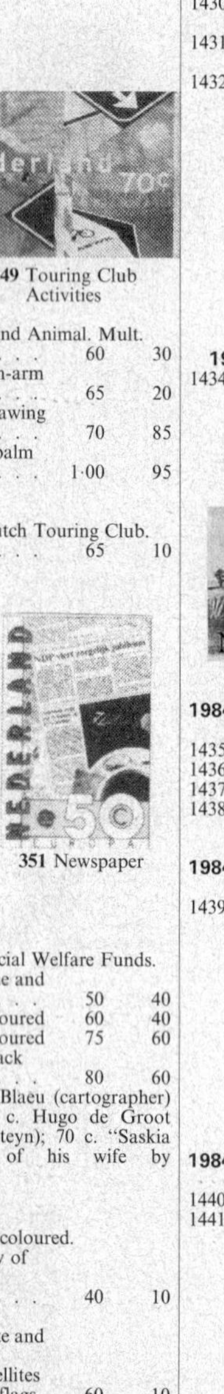

350 Johan van Oldenbarnevelt (statesman) (after J. Houbraken)

351 Newspaper

1983. Cultural, Health and Social Welfare Funds.
1416 **350** 50 c. + 20 c. pink, blue and black 50 40
1417 – 60 c. + 25 c. multicoloured 60 40
1418 – 65 c. + 25 c. multicoloured 75 60
1419 – 70 c. + 30 c. grey, black and gold 80 60
DESIGNS: 60 c. Willem Jansz Blaeu (cartographer) (after Thomas de Keijser); 65 c. Hugo de Groot (statesman) (after J. van Ravesteyn); 70 c. "Saskia van Uylenburch" (portrait of his wife by Rembrandt).

1983. Europa. Multicoloured.
1420 50 c. Type **351** (75th anniv of Netherlands Newspaper Publishers Assoc.) 40 10
1421 70 c. European Communications Satellite and European Telecommunication Satellites Organization members' flags 60 10

352 "Composition 1922" (P. Mondriaan)

353 "Geneva Conventions"

1983. De Stijl Art Movement. Multicoloured.
1422 50 c. Type **352** 40 10
1423 65 c. Contra construction from "Maison Particuliere" (C. van Eesteren and T. van Doesburg) 60 20

1983. Red Cross.
1424 **353** 50 c. + 25 c. multicoloured 45 45
1425 – 60 c. + 20 c. multicoloured 55 45
1426 – 65 c. + 25 c. multicoloured 70 45
1427 – 70 c. + 30 c. grey, black and red 80 70
DESIGNS: 60 c. Red Cross and text "charity, independence, impartiality"; 65 c. "Socio-medical work"; 70 c. Red Cross and text "For Peace".

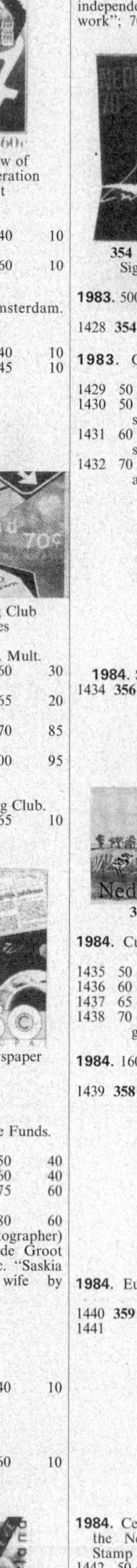

354 Luther's Signature

355 Child looking at Donkey and Ox through Window

1983. 500th Birth Anniv of Martin Luther (Protestant Reformer).
1428 **354** 70 c. multicoloured . . 40 10

1983. Child Welfare. Child and Christmas. Multicoloured.
1429 50 c. + 10 c. Type **355** . . . 50 50
1430 50 c. + 25 c. Child riding flying snowman 60 20
1431 60 c. + 30 c. Child in bed and star 75 75
1432 70 c. + 30 c. Children dressed as the three kings 80 20

356 Parliament

1984. Second Elections to European Parliament.
1434 **356** 70 c. multicoloured . . . 55 10

357 Lapwings

358 St. Servaas

1984. Cultural, Health and Social Welfare Funds. Pasture Birds. Multicoloured.
1435 50 c. + 20 c. Type **357** . . . 50 35
1436 60 c. + 25 c. Ruffs 70 35
1437 65 c. + 25 c. Redshanks (vert) 80 70
1438 70 c. + 30 c. Black-tailed godwits (vert) 85 80

1984. 1600th Death Anniv of St. Servaas (Bishop of Tongeren and Maastricht).
1439 **358** 60 c. multicoloured . . . 50 10

359 Bridge

1984. Europa. 25th Anniv of European Post and Telecommunications Conference.
1440 **359** 50 c. dp blue and blue . 40 10
1441 70 c. green and lt green 70 10

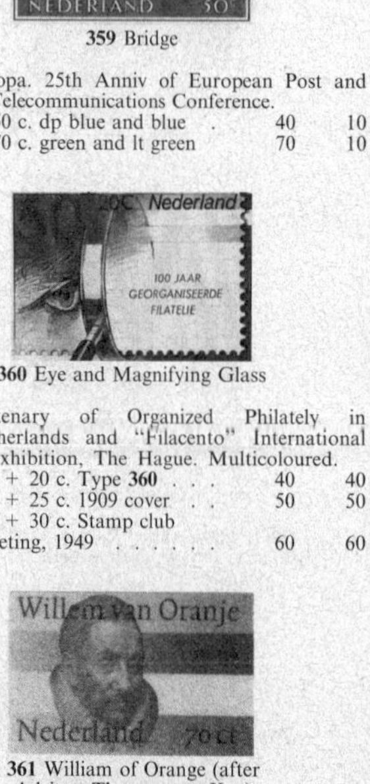

360 Eye and Magnifying Glass

1984. Centenary of Organized Philately in the Netherlands and "Filacento" International Stamp Exhibition, The Hague. Multicoloured.
1442 50 c. + 20 c. Type **360** . . . 40 40
1443 60 c. + 25 c. 1909 cover . . 50 50
1444 70 c. + 30 c. Stamp club meeting, 1949 . . . . . . 60 60

361 William of Orange (after Adriaen Thomaszoon Key)

1984. 400th Death Anniv of William of Orange.
1446 **361** 70 c. multicoloured . . 60 10

362 Giant Pandas and Globe

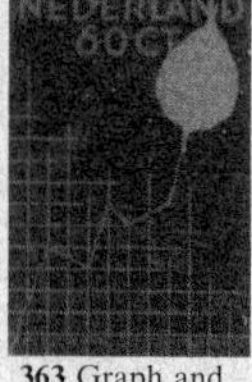

363 Graph and Leaf

1984. World Wildlife Fund.
1447 **362** 70 c. multicoloured . . . 75 10

1984. 11th International Small Business Congress, Amsterdam.
1448 **363** 60 c. multicoloured . . . 55 10

364 Violin Lesson

365 Sunny, First Dutch Guide-Dog

1984. Child Welfare. Strip Cartoons. Multicoloured.
1449 50 c. + 25 c. Type **364** . . . 40 25
1450 60 c. + 20 c. At the dentist . 75 55
1451 65 c. + 20 c. The plumber . . 85 85
1452 70 c. + 30 c. The king and money chest 65 35

1985. 50th Anniv of Royal Dutch Guide-Dog Fund.
1454 **365** 60 c. black, ochre and red 60 10

366 Plates and Cutlery on Place-mat

367 Saint Martin's Church, Zaltbommel

1985. Tourism. Multicoloured.
1455 50 c. Type **366** (centenary of Travel and Holidays Association) 40 10
1456 70 c. Kroller-Muller museum emblem, antlers and landscape (50th anniv of De Hoge Veluwe National Park) 60 10

1985. Cultural, Health and Social Welfare Funds. Religious Buildings. Multicoloured.
1457 50 c. + 20 c. Type **367** . . . 60 45
1458 60 c. + 25 c. Winterswijk synagogue and Holy Ark (horiz) 65 55
1459 65 c. + 25 c. Bolsward Baptist church 80 55
1460 70 c. + 30 c. Saint John's Cathedral, 's-Hertogenbosch (horiz) 85 35

368 Star of David, Illegal Newspapers and Rifle Practice (Resistance Movement)

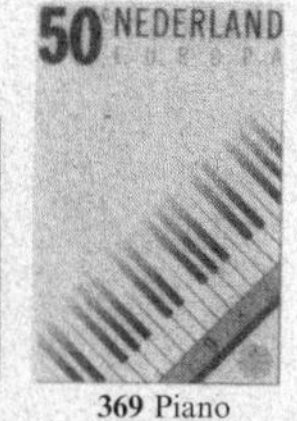

369 Piano Keyboard

1985. 40th Anniv of Liberation.
1461 **368** 50 c. black, stone & red . 50 10
1462 – 60 c. black, stone & blue . 55 10
1463 – 65 c. black, stone & orge 60 25
1464 – 70 c. black, stone & grn . 65 10
DESIGNS: 60 c. Bombers over houses, "De Vliegende Hollander" (newspaper) and soldier (Allied Forces); 65 c. Soldiers and civilians, "Parool" (newspaper) and American war cemetery, Margraten (Liberation); 70 c. Women prisoners, prison money and Burma Railway (Dutch East Indies).

1985. Europa. Music Year. Multicoloured.
1465 50 c. Type **369** 40 10
1466 70 c. Organ 60 10

370 National Museum, Amsterdam (centenary)

1985. Anniversaries and Events. Multicoloured.
1467 50 c. Type **370** 45 10
1468 60 c. Teacher with students (bicentenary of Amsterdam Nautical College) 55 10
1469 70 c. Ship's mast and rigging ("Sail '85", Amsterdam) . 70 10

371 Porpoise and Graph

1985. Endangered Animals.
1470 **371** 50 c. black, blue & red . 40 10
1471 – 70 c. black, blue & red . 85 10
DESIGN: 70 c. Seal and PCB molecule structure.

372 Ignition Key and Framed Photograph ("Think of Me")

1985. Child Welfare. Road Safety. Multicoloured.
1472 50 c. + 25 c. Type **372** . . . 60 30
1473 60 c. + 20 c. Child holding target showing speeds . . 70 70
1474 65 c. + 20 c. Girl holding red warning triangle 85 85
1475 70 c. + 30 c. Boy holding "Children Crossing" sign . 90 20

373 Penal Code Extract

1986. Centenary of Penal Code.
1477 **373** 50 c. black, yell & pur . 35 10

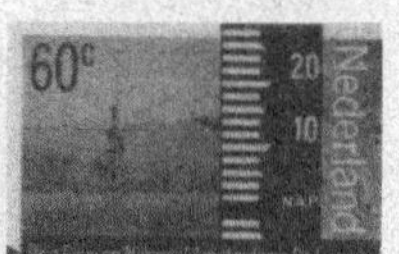

374 Surveyor with Pole and N.A.P. Water Gauge

1986. 300th Anniv of Height Gauging Marks at Amsterdam.
1478 **374** 60 c. multicoloured . . . 45 10

375 Windmill, Graph and Cloudy Sky

1986. Inaug of Windmill Test Station, Sexbierum.
1479 **375** 70 c. multicoloured . . . 60 10

376 Scales

377 Het Loo Palace Garden, Apeldoorn

1986. Cultural, Health and Social Welfare Funds. Antique Measuring Instruments. Multicoloured.
1480 50 c. + 20 c. Type **376** . . . 45 30
1481 60 c. + 25 c. Clock (vert) . . 55 30
1482 65 c. + 25 c. Barometer (vert) 70 70
1483 70 c. + 30 c. Jacob's staff . 80 80

1986. Europa. Multicoloured.
1484 50 c. Type **377** 40 10
1485 70 c. Tree with discoloured crown 70 10

MINIMUM PRICE

The minimum price quoted is 10p which represents a handling charge rather than a basis for valuing common stamps. For further notes about prices, see introductory pages.

378 Cathedral

379 Drees at Binnenhof, 1947

1986. Utrecht Events.

1486 **378** 50 c. multicoloured . . . 45 20
1487 – 60 c. blue, pink and black 65 20
1488 – 70 c. multicoloured . . . 80 10

DESIGNS—VERT: 50 c. Type **378** (completion of interior restoration); 60 c. German House (75th anniv of Heemschut Conservation Society). HORIZ: 70 c. Extract from foundation document (350th anniv of Utrecht University).

1986. Birth Centenary of Dr. Willem Drees (politician).

1489 **379** 55 c. multicoloured . . . 60 10

380 Draughts as Biscuits in Saucer

381 Map of Flood Barrier

1986. 75th Anniversary of Royal Dutch Draughts Association (1490) and Royal Dutch Billiards Association (1491). Multicoloured.

1490 75 c. Type **380** 90 15
1491 75 c. Player in ball preparing to play 90 15

1986. Delta Project Completion. Multicoloured.

1492 65 c. Type **381** 70 20
1493 75 c. Flood barrier 90 10

382 Children listening to Music (experiencing)

383 Engagement Picture

1986. Child Welfare. Child and Culture.

1494 55 c. + 25 c. Type **382** . . . 70 70
1495 65 c. + 35 c. Boy drawing (achieving) 80 60
1496 75 c. + 35 c. Children at theatre (understanding) 90 20

1987. Golden Wedding of Princess Juliana and Prince Bernhard.

1498 **383** 75 c. orange, black and gold 75 10

384 Block of Flats and Hut

1987. International Year of Shelter for the Homeless (65 c.) and Centenary of Netherlands Salvation Army (75 c.). Multicoloured.

1499 65 c. Type **384** 60 20
1500 75 c. Army officer, meeting and tramp 80 10

385 Eduard Douwes Dekker (Multatuli) and De Harmonie Club

1987. Writers' Death Annivs. Multicoloured.

1501 55 c. Type **385** (centenary) . . 55 20
1502 75 c. Constantijn Huygens and Scheveningseweg, The Hague (300th anniv) 85 10

386 Steam Pumping Station, Nijerk

1987. Cultural Health and Social Welfare Funds. Industrial Buildings.

1503 **386** 55 c. + 30 c. red, grey and black 70 75
1504 – 65 c. + 35 c. grey, black and blue 85 85
1505 – 75 c. + 35 c. grey, yellow and black 90 60

DESIGNS: 65 c. Water tower, Deventer; 75 c. Brass foundry, Joure.

387 Dance Theatre, Scheveningen (Rem Koolhaas)

1987. Europa. Architecture. Multicoloured.

1506 55 c. Type **387** 55 20
1507 75 c. Montessori School, Amsterdam (Herman Hertzberger) 85 10

388 Auction at Broek op Langedijk

1987. Centenary of Auction Sales (55, 75 c.) and 150th Anniv of Groningen Agricultural Society (65 c.). Multicoloured.

1508 55 c. Type **388** 55 20
1509 65 c. Groningen landscape and founders' signatures . . . 65 20
1510 75 c. Auction sale and clock 75 10

389 Telephone Care Circles

390 Map of Holland

1987. Dutch Red Cross. Multicoloured.

1511 55 c. + 30 c. Type **389** . . . 60 60
1512 65 c. + 35 c. Red cross and hands (Welfare work) . . 75 75
1513 75 c. + 35 c. Red cross and drip (Blood transfusion) . . . 85 45

1987. 75th Anniv of Netherlands Municipalities Union.

1514 **390** 75 c. multicoloured . . 65 10

391 Noordeinde Palace, The Hague

392 Woodcutter

1987.

1515 **391** 65 c. multicoloured . . 50 10

1987. Child Welfare. Child and Profession. Multicoloured.

1516 55 c. + 25 c. Type **392** . . . 60 60
1517 65 c. + 35 c. Woman sailor 75 55
1518 75 c. + 35 c. Woman pilot . 85 25

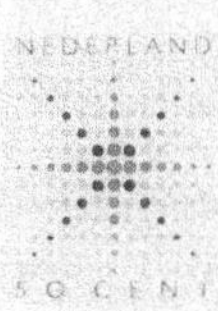
393 Star

394 "Narcissus cyclamineus" "Peeping Tom" and Extract from "I Call You Flowers" (Jan Hanlo)

1987. Christmas.

1520 **393** 50 c. red, blue and green 60 20
1521 50 c. yellow, red and blue 60 20
1522 **393** 50 c. red, blue and yellow 60 20
1523 50 c. yellow, red and green 60 20
1524 50 c. blue, green and red . 60 20

The first colour described is that of the St. George's Cross.

1988. "Filacept" European Stamp Exhibition, The Hague. Flowers. Multicoloured.

1525 55 c. + 55 c. Type **394** . . . 90 80
1526 75 c. + 70 c. "Rosa gallica" "Versicolor" and "Roses" (Daan van Golden) . . . . 1·10 1·00
1527 75 c. + 70 c. Sea holly and 1270 map of The Hague . . . . 1·10 1·00

395 Quagga

1988. Cultural, Health and Social Welfare Funds. 150th Anniv of Natura Artis Magistra Zoological Society. Multicoloured.

1528 55 c. + 30 c. Type **395** 70 70
1529 65 c. + 35 c. American manatee 80 80
1530 75 c. + 35 c. Orang-utan (vert) 90 45

396 Man's Shoulder

397 Traffic Scene with Lead Symbol crossed Through

1988. 75th Anniv of Netherlands Cancer Institute.

1531 **396** 75 c. multicoloured . . . 80 10

1988. Europa. Transport. Multicoloured.

1532 55 c. Type **397** (lead-free petrol) 50 20
1533 75 c. Cyclists reflected in car wing mirror (horiz) 75 10

398 Pendulum, Prism and Saturn

1988. 300th Anniv of England's Glorious Revolution. Multicoloured.

1534 65 c. Type **398** 50 20
1535 75 c. Queen Mary, King William III and 17th-century warship 60 10

399 "Cobra Cat" (Appel)

400 Sailing Ship and Map of Australia

1988. 40th Anniv of Founding of Cobra Painters Group. Multicoloured.

1536 55 c. Type **399** 50 50
1537 65 c. "Kite" (Corneille) . . . 55 50
1538 75 c. "Stumbling Horse" (Constant) 60 20

1988. Bicentenary of Australian Settlement.

1539 **400** 75 c. multicoloured . . . 70 10

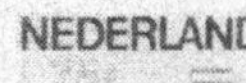

401 Statue of Erasmus, Rotterdam

402 "Rain"

1988. 75th Anniv of Erasmus University, Rotterdam (1540) and Centenary of Concertgebouw Concert Hall and Orchestra (1541).

1540 **401** 75 c. dp green & green . . 65 20
1541 – 75 c. violet 65 20

DESIGN: No. 1541, Violin and Concertgebouw concert hall.

1988. Child Welfare. Centenary of Royal Netherlands Swimming Federation. Children's drawings. Multicoloured.

1543 55 c. + 25 c. Type **402** . . . 65 60
1544 65 c. + 35 c. "Getting Ready for the Race" 85 50
1545 75 c. + 35 c. "Swimming Test" 85 30

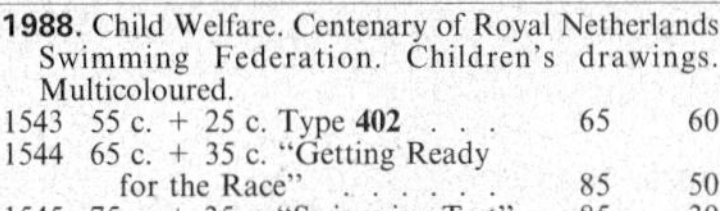

403 Stars

1988. Christmas.

1547 **403** 50 c. multicoloured . . . 50 10

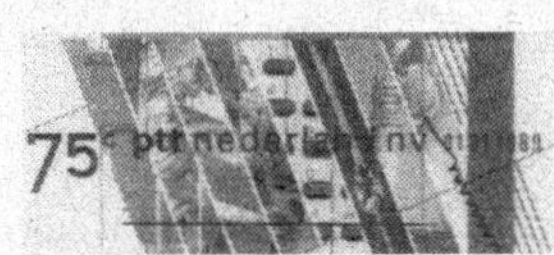
404 Postal and Telecommunications Services

1989. Privatization of Netherlands PTT.

1548 **404** 75 c. multicoloured . . . 75 10

405 "Solidarity"

406 Members' Flags

1989. Trade Unions. Multicoloured.

1549 55 c. Type **405** 40 20
1550 75 c. Talking mouths on hands 50 10

1989. 40th Anniv of N.A.T.O.

1551 **406** 75 c. multicoloured . . . 75 10

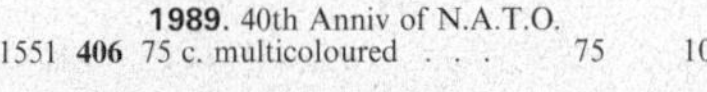
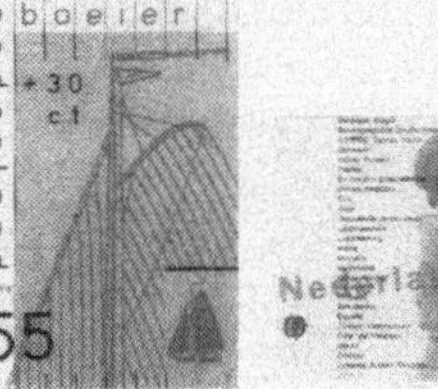
407 Boier

408 Boy with Homemade Telephone

1989. Cultural, Health and Social Welfare Funds. Old Sailing Vessels.

1552 **407** 55 c. + 30 c. grn & blk . 30 10
1553 – 65 c. + 35 c. blue & blk 35 10
1554 – 75 c. + 35 c. brn & blk . 40 10

DESIGNS: 65 c. Fishing smack; 75 c. Clipper.

1989. Europa. Children's Games. Multicoloured.

1555 55 c. Type **408** 50 20
1556 75 c. Girl with homemade telephone 75 10

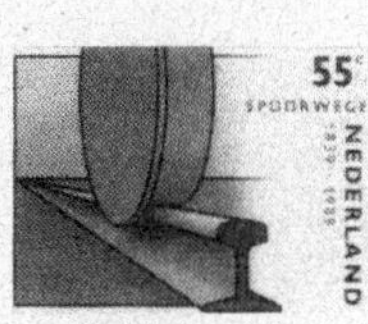
409 Wheel on Rail

410 Boy with Ball and Diagram of Goal Scored in European Championship

1989. 150th Anniv of Netherlands' Railways. Multicoloured.

1557 55 c. Type **409** 60 20
1558 65 c. Locomotives 65 20
1559 75 c. Clock and "The Kiss" (sculpture by Rodin) . . . 70 10

1989. Centenary of Royal Dutch Football Assn.

1560 **410** 75 c. multicoloured . . . 80 10

411 Map

412 Right to Housing

1989. 150th Anniv of Division of Limburg between Netherlands and Belgium.
1561 **411** 75 c. multicoloured . . . 80 10

1989. Child Welfare. 30th Anniv of Declaration of Rights of the Child. Multicoloured.
1562 55 c. + 25 c. Type **412** . . . 60 60
1563 65 c. + 35 c. Right to food . . 80 50
1564 75 c. + 35 c. Right to education 90 30

413 Candle **414** "Arms of Leiden" (tulip) and Plan of Gardens in 1601

1989. Christmas.
1566 **413** 50 c. multicoloured . . . 60 10

1990. 400th Anniv of Hortus Botanicus (botanical gardens), Leiden.
1567 **414** 65 c. multicoloured . . . 70 20

415 Pointer on Graduated Scale **416** "Self-portrait" (detail)

1990. Centenary of Labour Inspectorate.
1568 **415** 75 c. multicoloured . . . 70 10

1990. Death Centenary of Vincent van Gogh (painter). Multicoloured.
1569 55 c. Type **416** 75 20
1570 75 c. "Green Vineyard" (detail) 1·25 10

417 Summer's Day

1990. Cultural, Health and Social Welfare Funds. The Weather. Multicoloured.
1571 55 c. + 30 c. Type **417** 60 50
1572 65 c. + 35 c. Clouds and isobars (vert) 75 65
1573 75 c. + 35 c. Satellite weather picture (vert) 90 30

418 Zuiderkerk Ruins

1990. 50th Anniv of German Bombing of Rotterdam.
1574 **418** 55 c. deep brown, brown and black 55 20
1575 – 65 c. multicoloured . . . 65 10
1576 – 75 c. multicoloured . . . 85 10
DESIGNS: 65 c. City plan as stage; 75 c. Girder and plans for future construction.

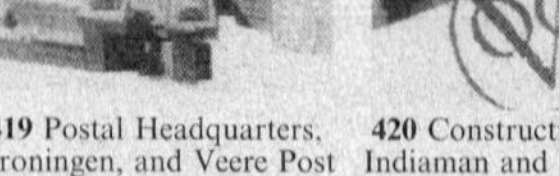
419 Postal Headquarters, Groningen, and Veere Post Office **420** Construction of Indiaman and Wreck of "Amsterdam"

1990. Europa. Post Office Buildings.
1577 – 55 c. grey, mauve & brn . 55 20
1578 **419** 75 c. blue, green & grey . 85 10
DESIGN: 55 c. As Type **419** but inscr "Postkantoor Veere".

1990. 3rd Anniv of Dutch East India Company Ships Association (replica ship project) (1579) and "Sail 90", Amsterdam (1580). Multicoloured.
1579 65 c. Type **420** 65 20
1580 75 c. Crew manning yards on sailing ship 95 10

421 Queens Emma, Wilhelmina, Juliana and Beatrix **422** Flames, Telephone Handset and Number

1990. Netherlands Queens of the House of Orange.
1581 **421** 150 c. multicoloured . . 1·50 45

1990. Introduction of National Emergency Number.
1582 **422** 65 c. multicoloured . . 60 20

423 Girl riding Horse **424** Falling Snow

1990. Child Welfare. Hobbies. Multicoloured.
1583 55 c. + 25 c. Type **423** . . . 75 60
1584 65 c. + 35 c. Girl at computer 85 50
1585 75 c. + 35 c. Young philatelist 90 30

1990. Christmas.
1587 **424** 50 c. multicoloured . . 50 10

425 Industrial Chimneys, Exhaust Pipes and Aerosol Can (Air Pollution)

1991. Environmental Protection. Multicoloured.
1588 55 c. Type **425** 55 20
1589 65 c. Outfall pipes and chemicals (sea pollution) . 70 20
1590 75 c. Agricultural chemicals, leaking drums and household landfill waste (soil pollution) 90 10

426 German Raid on Amsterdam Jewish Quarter and Open Hand

1991. 50th Anniv of Amsterdam General Strike.
1591 **426** 75 c. multicoloured . . 75 10

427 Princess Beatrix and Prince Claus on Wedding Day **428** Queen Beatrix

1991. Royal Silver Wedding Anniversary. Mult.
1592 75 c. Type **427** 95 35
1593 75 c. Queen Beatrix and Prince Claus on horseback . . . 95 35

1991.
1594 **428** 75 c. dp green & green 1·40 10
1595 80 c. brown & lt brown 60 10
1597 90 c. blue 70 10
1598 1 g. violet 75 10
1600 1 g. 30 blue and violet . 1·00 10
1601 1 g. 40 green and olive 1·00 10
1602 1 g. 60 purple & mauve 1·00 10
1603 2 g. brown . . . . . . 1·10 10
1603a 2 g. 50 purple . . . . 1·40 10
1604 3 g. blue . . . . . . 1·90 10
1605 5 g. red . . . . . . 3·25 10
1706 7 g. 50 violet . . . . 5·00 40
1708 10 g. green . . . . . 6·50 70

429 "Meadow" Farm, Wartena, Friesland **430** Gerard Philips's Experiments with Carbon Filaments

1991. Cultural, Health and Social Welfare Funds. Traditional Farmhouses. Multicoloured.
1610 55 c. + 30 c. Type **429** . . . 80 50
1611 65 c. + 35 c. "T-house" farm, Kesteren, Gelderland . . . 90 65
1612 75 c. + 35 c. "Courtyard" farm, Nuth, Limburg 95 30

1991. 75th Anniv of Netherlands Standards Institute (65 c.) and Centenary of Philips Organization (others). Multicoloured.
1615 55 c. Type **430** 45 20
1616 65 c. Wiring to Standard NEN 1010 (horiz) 55 20
1617 75 c. Laser beams reading video disc 70 10

431 Man raising Hat to Space **432** Sticking Plaster over Medal

1991. Europa. Europe in Space. Multicoloured.
1618 55 c. Type **431** 60 20
1619 75 c. Ladders stretching into space 80 10

1991. 75th Anniv of Nijmegen International Four Day Marches.
1620 **432** 80 c. multicoloured . . . 65 10

433 Jacobus Hendericus van't Hoff **434** Children and Open Book

1991. Dutch Nobel Prize Winners. Multicoloured.
1621 60 c. Type **433** (chemistry, 1901) 50 15
1622 70 c. Pieter Zeeman (physics, 1902) 60 20
1623 80 c. Tobias Michael Carel Asser (peace, 1911) 65 10

1991. Centenary (1992) of Public Libraries in the Netherlands.
1624 **434** 70 c. drab, black & mve . 60 20
1625 – 80 c. multicoloured . . . 65 10
DESIGN: 80 c. Books on shelf.

435 Girls with Doll and Robot **436** "Greetings Cards keep People in Touch"

1991. Child Welfare. Outdoor Play. Multicoloured.
1626 60 c. + 30 c. Type **435** . . . 75 50
1627 70 c. + 35 c. Bicycle race . . 85 65
1628 80 c. + 40 c. Hide and Seek . 95 30

1991. Christmas.
1630 **436** 55 c. multicoloured . . . 45 15

437 Artificial Lightning, Microchip and Oscilloscope

1992. 150th Anniv of Delft University of Technology.
1631 **437** 60 c. multicoloured . . . 50 15

438 Extract from Code **440** Tulips ("Mondrian does not like Green")

1992. Implementation of Property Provisions of New Civil Code.
1632 **438** 80 c. multicoloured . . . 65 10

1992. "Expo '92" World's Fair, Seville. Mult.
1634 70 c. Type **440** 60 20
1635 80 c. "Netherland Expo '92" . 65 10

441 Tasman's Map of Staete Landt (New Zealand)

1992. 350th Anniv of Discovery of Tasmania and New Zealand by Abel Tasman.
1636 **441** 70 c. multicoloured . . . 60 20

442 Yellow and Purple Flowers **443** Geometric Planes

1992. Cultural, Health and Social Welfare Funds. "Floriade" Flower Show, Zoetermeer. Multicoloured.
1637 60 c. + 30 c. Water lilies . . 75 50
1638 70 c. + 35 c. Orange and purple flowers 85 65
1639 80 c. + 40 c. Type **442** . . . 1·25 30

1992. 150th Anniv of Royal Association of Netherlands Architects (60 c.) and Inauguration of New States General Lower House (80 c.). Multicoloured.
1643 60 c. Type **443** 50 15
1644 80 c. Atrium and blue sky (symbolising sending of information into society) . 65 10

444 Globe and Columbus **445** Moneta (Goddess of Money)

1992. Europa. 500th Anniv of Discovery of America by Columbus.
1645 **444** 60 c. multicoloured . . . 50 15
1646 – 80 c. blk, mve & yell . . 65 10
DESIGN—VERT: 80 c. Galleon.

1992. Centenary of Royal Netherlands Numismatics Society.
1647 **445** 70 c. multicoloured . . . 60 20

446 Teddy Bear wearing Stethoscope **447** List of Relatives and Friends

1992. Centenary of Netherlands Paediatrics Society.
1648 **446** 80 c. multicoloured . . . 65 10

1992. 50th Anniv of Departure of First Deportation Train from Westerbork Concentration Camp.
1649 **447** 70 c. multicoloured . . . 55 15

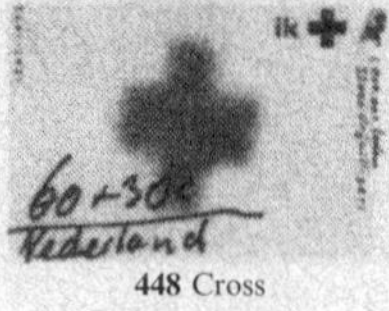
448 Cross

1992. 125th Anniv of Netherlands Red Cross. Multicoloured.
1650 60 c. + 30 c. Type **448** . . . 70 45
1651 70 c. + 35 c. Supporting injured person . . . . 1·10 55
1652 80 c. + 40 c. Red cross on dirty bandage . . . . 1·25 30

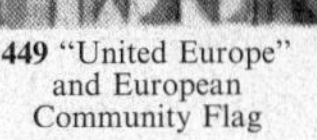

449 "United Europe" and European Community Flag

450 Queen Beatrix on Official Birthday, 1992, and at Investiture

1992. European Single Market.
1656 **449** 80 c. multicoloured . . . 60 10

1992. 12½ Years since Accession to the Throne of Queen Beatrix.
1657 **450** 80 c. multicoloured . . . 60 10

451 Saxophone Player

452 Poinsettia

1992. Child Welfare. Child and Music. Mult.
1658 60 c. + 30 c. Type **451** . . . 70 45
1659 70 c. + 35 c. Piano player . 80 55
1660 80 c. + 40 c. Double bass player 90 30

1992. Christmas.
1662 **452** 55 c. multicoloured (centre of flower silver) . . . 40 10
1663 55 c. multicoloured (centre red) 40 10

453 Cycling

1993. Centenary of Netherlands Cycle and Motor Industry Association.
1664 **453** 70 c. multicoloured . . . 55 15
1665 – 80 c. brown, grey & yell . 60 10
DESIGN: 80 c. Car.

454 Collages

455 Mouth to Mouth Resuscitation

1993. Greetings Stamps. Multicoloured.
1666 70 c. Type **454** 55 10
1667 70 c. Collages (different) . . 55 10

1993. Anniversaries. Multicoloured.
1668 70 c. Type **455** (centenary of Royal Netherlands First Aid Association) 55 10
1669 80 c. Pests on leaf (75th anniv of Wageningen University of Agriculture) 55 10
1670 80 c. Lead driver and horses (bicentenary of Royal Horse Artillery) 60 10

456 Emblems

1993. 150th Anniv of Royal Dutch Notaries Association. Each red and violet.
1671 80 c. Type **456** ("150 Jaar" reading up) 60 10
1672 80 c. As Type **456** but emblems inverted and "150 Jaar" reading down 60 10
Nos. 1671/2 were issued together in horizontal tete-beche pairs, each pair forming a composite design.

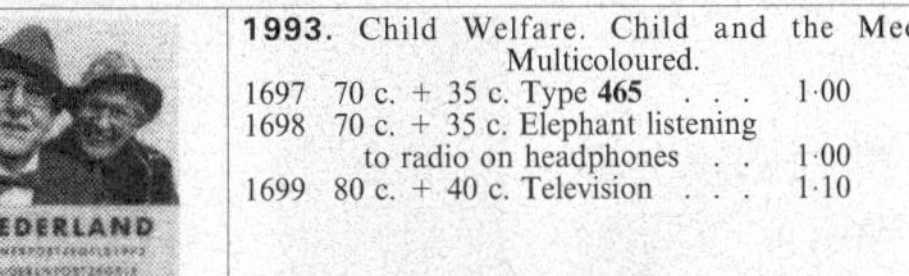

457 Large White

458 Elderly Couple

1993. Butterflies. Multicoloured.
1673 70 c. Pearl-bordered fritillary 55 15
1674 80 c. Large tortoiseshell . . 60 10
1675 90 c. Type **457** 70 20

1993. Cultural, Health and Social Welfare Funds. Senior Citizens' Independence.
1677 70 c. + 35 c. Type **458** . . . 1·00 1·00
1678 70 c. + 35 c. Elderly man . 1·00 1·00
1679 80 c. + 40 c. Elderly woman with dog . . . . 1·25 90

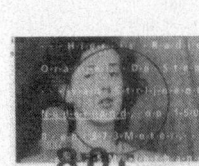

459 Radio Orange

460 Sports Pictograms

1993. Radio Orange (Dutch broadcasts from London during Second World War). Multicoloured.
1683 80 c. Type **459** 55 10
1684 80 c. Man listening to radio in secret 55 10

1993. 2nd European Youth Olympic Days. Multicoloured.
1685 70 c. Type **460** 75 15
1686 80 c. Sports pictograms (different) 80 10

461 "The Embodiment of Unity" (Wessel Couzijn)

462 Johannes Diderik van der Waals (Physics, 1910)

1993. Europa. Contemporary Art. Multicoloured.
1687 70 c. Type **461** 75 15
1688 80 c. Architectonic sculpture (Per Kirkeby) 80 10
1689 160 c. Sculpture (Naum Gabo) (vert) . . . . 1·50 1·10

1993. Nobel Prize Winners.
1690 **462** 70 c. blue, black & red . 50 15
1691 – 80 c. mauve, blk & red . 55 10
1692 – 90 c. multicoloured . . 95 15
DESIGNS: 80 c. Willem Einthoven (medicine, 1924); 90 c. Christiaan Eijkman (medicine, 1929).

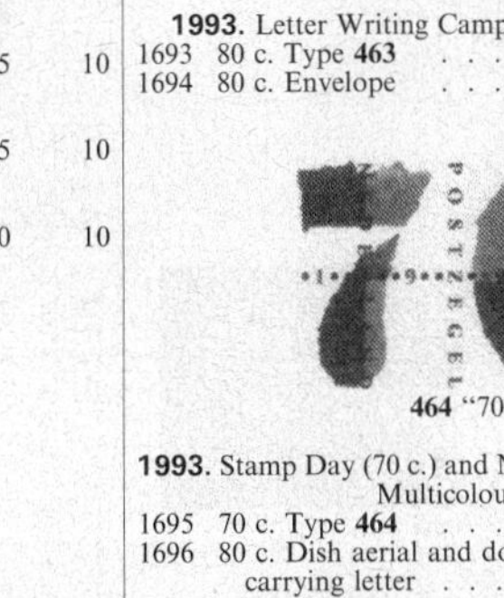

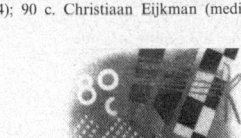

463 Pen and Pencils

1993. Letter Writing Campaign. Multicoloured.
1693 80 c. Type **463** 55 10
1694 80 c. Envelope 55 10

464 "70"

1993. Stamp Day (70 c.) and Netherlands PTT (80 c.). Multicoloured.
1695 70 c. Type **464** 50 15
1696 80 c. Dish aerial and dove carrying letter 55 10

465 Child in Newspaper Hat

1993. Child Welfare. Child and the Media. Multicoloured.
1697 70 c. + 35 c. Type **465** . . . 1·00 50
1698 70 c. + 35 c. Elephant listening to radio on headphones . . 1·00 50
1699 80 c. + 40 c. Television . . . 1·10 25

466 Candle

1993. Christmas. Multicoloured.
1711 55 c. Type **466** 45 15
1712 55 c. Fireworks 45 15
Both designs have a number of punched holes.

467 "Composition"

1994. 50th Death Anniv of Piet Mondriaan (artist). Multicoloured.
1713 70 c. "The Red Mill" (detail) 55 15
1714 80 c. Type **467** 65 10
1715 90 c. "Broadway Boogie Woogie" (detail) 70 20

468 Barnacle Goose

1994. "Fepapost 94" European Stamp Exhibition, The Hague. Multicoloured.
1716 70 c. + 60 c. Type **468** . . . 1·00 65
1717 80 c. + 70 c. Bluethroat . . . 1·25 40
1718 90 c. + 80 c. Garganey . . . 1·40 95

469 Downy Rose

1994. Wild Flowers. Multicoloured.
1719 70 c. Type **469** 55 15
1720 80 c. Daisies 65 10
1721 90 c. Wood forget-me-not . . 70 20

470 Airplane

1994. 75th Aircraft Industry Anniversaries.
1723 **470** 80 c. blue and black . . . 65 10
1724 – 80 c. grey, red and black . 65 10
1725 – 80 c. multicoloured . . . 65 10
DESIGNS: No. 1723, Type **470** (KLM (Royal Dutch Airlines)); 1724, Plan and outline of aircraft and clouds (Royal Netherlands Fokker Aircraft Industries); 1725, Airplane and clouds (National Aerospace Laboratory).

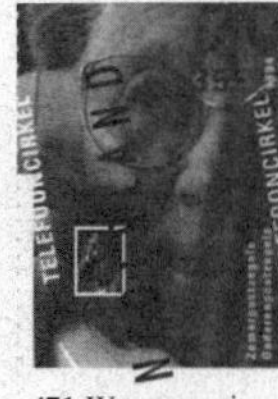

471 Woman using Telephone

472 Eisinga's Planetarium

1994. Cultural, Health and Social Welfare Funds. Senior Citizens' Security. Multicoloured.
1726 70 c. + 35 c. Type **471** . . . 85 55
1727 80 c. + 40 c. Man using telephone 95 30
1728 90 c. + 35 c. Man using telephone (different) . . . . 1·00 65

1994. Anniversaries. Multicoloured.
1732 80 c. Type **472** (250th birth anniv of Eise Eisinga) . . 65 10
1733 90 c. Astronaut and boot print on Moon surface (25th anniv of first manned Moon landing) 70 20

473 Players Celebrating

1994. World Cup Football Championship, U.S.A.
1734 **473** 80 c. multicoloured . . . 65 10

474 Stock Exchange

1994. Quotation of Netherlands PTT (KPN) on Stock Exchange.
1735 **474** 80 c. multicoloured . . . 65 15

475 Road Sign, Car and Bicycle

1994. Anniversaries and Events. Multicoloured.
1736 70 c. Type **475** (centenary of provision of road signs by Netherlands Motoring Association) 55 15
1737 80 c. Equestrian sports (World Equestrian Games, The Hague) 65 10

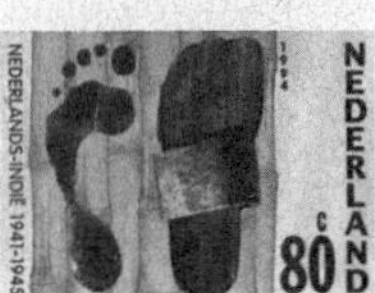

476 Footprint and Sandal

1994. Second World War. Multicoloured.
1738 80 c. Type **476** (war in Netherlands Indies, 1941–45) 65 10
1739 90 c. Soldier, children and aircraft dropping paratroops (50th anniv of Operation Market Garden (Battle of Arnhem)) (vert) 70 20

477 Brandaris Lighthouse, Terschelling

1994. Lighthouses. Multicoloured.
1740 70 c. Type **477** 55 15
1741 80 c. Ameland (vert) 65 10
1742 90 c. Vlieland (vert) 70 20

478 Decorating

479 Star and Christmas Tree

1994. Child Welfare. "Together". Multicoloured.
1744 70 c. + 35 c. Type **478** . . . 85 55
1745 80 c. + 40 c. Girl on swing knocking fruit off tree (vert) 95 30
1746 90 c. + 35 c. Girl helping boy onto roof of playhouse (vert) 1·00 65

1994. Christmas. Multicoloured.
1748 55 c. Type **479** 45 15
1749 55 c. Candle and star 45 15

480 Flying Cow

1995.
1750 **480** 100 c. multicoloured . . 80 25

481 "Prayer" (detail)

1995. Anniversary and Events.
1751 **481** 80 c. multicoloured . . . 65 10
1752 – 80 c. multicoloured . . . 65 10
1753 – 80 c. black and red . . . 65 10
DESIGNS—VERT: No. 1751, Type **481** (50th death anniv of Hendrik Werkman (graphic designer); 1752, "Mesdag Panorama" (detail) (re-opening of Mesdag Museum). HORIZ: No. 1753, Mauritius 1847 2d. "POST OFFICE" stamp (purchase by PTT Museum of remaining mint example in private hands).

482 Joriz Ivens (documentary maker)

1995. Year of the Film (centenary of motion pictures). Multicoloured.
1754 70 c. Type **482** 55 15
1755 80 c. Scene from "Turkish Delight" 65 10

483 Mahler and Score of 7th Symphony

1995. Mahler Festival, Amsterdam.
1756 **483** 80 c. black and blue . . 65 10

484 Dates and Acronym

1995. Centenaries. Multicoloured.
1757 80 c. Type **484** (Netherlands Institute of Chartered Accountants) 65 10
1758 80 c. Builders, bricklayer's trowel and saw (Netherlands Association of Building Contractors) 65 10

485 Postcard from Indonesia 486 "40 45"

1995. Cultural, Health and Social Welfare Funds. Mobility of the Elderly. Multicoloured.
1759 70 c. + 35 c. Type **485** . . 85 55
1760 80 c. + 40 c. Couple reflected in mirror 95 30
1761 100 c. + 45 c. Couple with granddaughter at zoo . . . 1·10 75

1995. 50th Anniversaries. Multicoloured.
1763 80 c. Type **486** (end of Second World War) 65 10
1764 80 c. "45 95" (liberation) . . 65 10
1765 80 c. "50" (U.N.O.) 65 10

487 Birthday Cake and Signs of the Zodiac 488 Scout

1995. Birthday Greetings.
1766 **487** 70 c. multicoloured . . 55 15

1995. Events. Multicoloured.
1767 70 c. Type **488** (World Scout Jamboree, Dronten) . . . 55 15
1768 80 c. Amsterdam harbour ("Sail '95" and finish of Tall Ships Race, Amsterdam) 65 10

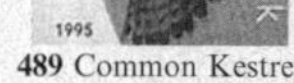

489 Common Kestrel 490 Petrus Debye (Chemistry, 1936)

1995. Birds of Prey. Multicoloured.
1769 70 c. Type **489** 55 15
1770 80 c. Face of hen harrier (horiz) 65 10
1771 100 c. Red kite (horiz) . . . 80 25

1995. Nobel Prize Winners. Multicoloured.
1773 80 c. Type **490** 65 10
1774 80 c. Frederik Zernike (Physics, 1953) 65 10
1775 80 c. Jan Tinbergen (Economics, 1969) 65 10

491 Eduard Jacobs and Jean-Louis Pisuisse

1995. Centenary of Dutch Cabaret. Multicoloured.
1776 70 c. Type **491** 55 15
1777 80 c. Wim Kan and Freek de Jonge 65 10

492 "The Schoolteacher" (Leonie Ensing) 493 Children with Stars

1995. Child Welfare. "Children and Fantasy". Children's Computer Drawings. Multicoloured.
1778 70 c. + 35 c. "Dino" (Sjoerd Stegeman) (horiz) 85 55
1779 80 c. + 40 c. Type **492** . . . 95 30
1780 100 c. + 50 c. "Children and Colours" (Marcel Jansen) (horiz) . . . . 1·10 75

1995. Christmas. Self-adhesive.
1782 **493** 55 c. red, yellow and black 45 15
1783 – 55 c. blue, yellow and black 45 15
DESIGN: No. 1783, Children looking at star through window.

494 "Woman in Blue reading a Letter" 495 Trowel, Daffodil Bulb and Glove

1996. Johannes Vermeer Exhibition, Washington and The Hague. Details of his Paintings. Multicoloured.
1784 70 c. "Lady writing a Letter with her Maid" 50 15
1785 80 c. "The Love Letter" . . 60 10
1786 100 c. Type **494** 75 20

1996. Spring Flowers. Multicoloured.
1788 70 c. Type **495** 50 15
1789 80 c. Tulips "kissing" woman 60 10
1790 100 c. Snake's-head fritillary (detail of painting, Charles Mackintosh) 75 20

496 Putting up "MOVED" sign 497 Swimming

1996. Change of Address Stamp.
1792 **496** 70 c. multicoloured . . . 50 15

1996. Cultural, Health and Social Welfare Funds. The Elderly in the Community. Multicoloured.
1793 70 c. + 35 c. Type **497** . . . 75 50
1794 80 c. + 40 c. Grandad bottle-feeding baby 90 30
1795 100 c. + 50 c. Playing piano . 1·10 75

499 Cycling

1996. Tourism. Multicoloured.
1798 70 c. Type **499** 50 15
1799 70 c. Paddling in sea 50 15
1800 80 c. Traditional architecture . 60 10
1801 100 c. Windmills 75 20

500 Parade in Traditional Costumes

1996. Bicentenary of Province of North Brabant.
1802 **500** 80 c. multicoloured . . . 60 10

501 Lighting Olympic Torch 502 Erasmus Bridge

1996. Sporting Events. Multicoloured.
1803 70 c. Type **501** (Olympic Games, Atlanta) 50 15
1804 80 c. Flag and cyclists (Tour de France cycling championship) 60 10
1805 100 c. Player, ball and Wembley Stadium (European Football Championship, England) . 75 20
1806 160 c. Olympic rings and athlete on starting block (Olympic Games, Atlanta) . . . . . 1·10 55

1996. Bridges and Tunnels. Multicoloured.
1807 80 c. Type **502** 60 10
1808 80 c. Wijker Tunnel (horiz) . 60 10
1809 80 c. Martinus Nijhoff Bridge (horiz) 60 10

503 Children in School Uniforms 504 Bert and Ernie

1996. 50th Anniv of U.N.I.C.E.F. Multicoloured.
1810 70 c. Type **503** 50 15
1811 80 c. Girl carrying platter on head 60 10

1996. "Sesame Street" (children's television programme). Multicoloured.
1812 70 c. Type **504** 50 15
1813 80 c. Bears holding Big Bird's foot 60 10

505 Petrus Plancius 506 Books and Baby

1996. 16th-century Voyages of Discovery.
1814 **505** 70 c. black, yellow and red 50 15
1815 – 80 c. multicoloured . . . 60 10
1816 – 80 c. multicoloured . . . 60 10
1817 – 100 c. multicoloured . . 75 20
DESIGNS: No. 1815, Cornelis de Houtman; 1816, Willem Barentsz; 1817, Mahu en De Cordes.

1996. Child Welfare. Multicoloured.
1818 70 c. + 35 c. Type **506** . . . 75 50
1819 80 c. + 40 c. Animals and boy 90 30
1820 80 c. + 40 c. Tools and girl . 90 30

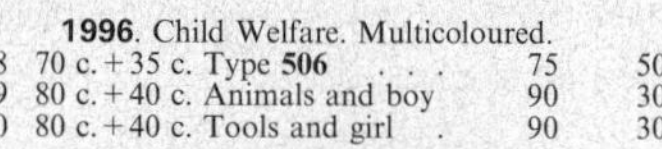

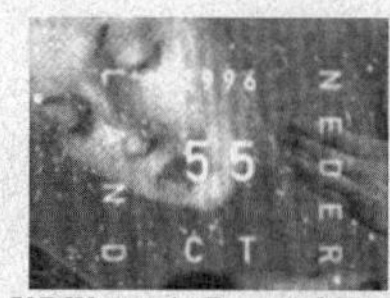

507 Woman's Face and Hand

1995. Christmas. Multicoloured. Self-adhesive.
1822 55 c. Type **507** 40 10
1823 55 c. Woman's eyes and man shouting 40 10
1824 55 c. Bird's wing, hands and detail of man's face . . . 40 10
1825 55 c. Men's faces & bird's wing 40 10
Nos. 1822/5 were issued together, se-tenant, forming a composite design.

MARINE INSURANCE STAMPS

M 22

1921.
M238 M **22** 15 c. green . . . . . 9·00 48·00
M239 60 c. red . . . . . . 11·00 55·00
M240 75 c. brown . . . . . 13·00 65·00
M241 – 1 g. 50 blue . . . . . 65·00 £500
M242 – 2 g. 25 brown £110 £700
M243 – $4\frac{1}{2}$ g. black £180 £900
M244 – $7\frac{1}{2}$ g. red £300 £1400
DESIGNS (inscr "DRIJVENDE BRANDKAST"): 1 g. 50, 2 g. 25 "Explosion"; $4\frac{1}{2}$ g., $7\frac{1}{2}$ g. Lifebelt.

OFFICIAL STAMPS

1913. Stamps of 1898 optd **ARMENWET**.
O214 **12** 1 c. red . . . . 3·75 2·75
O215 $1\frac{1}{2}$ c. blue . . . . 85 2·25
O216 2 c. brown . . . . 6·25 7·50
O217 $2\frac{1}{2}$ c. green . . . . . . 16·00 13·00
O218 **13** 3 c. green . . . . 3·75 1·25
O219 5 c. red . . . . 3·75 4·75
O220 10 c. grey . . . . 32·00 40·00

POSTAGE DUE STAMPS

D 8 D 9

1870.
D76 D **8** 5 c. brown on yellow . . 70·00 12·00
D77 10 c. purple on blue . . £160 14·50
For same stamps in other colours, see Netherlands Indies, Nos. D1/5.

1881.
D208 D **9** $\frac{1}{2}$ c. black and blue . . 15 15
D182 1 c. black and blue . . 1·25 15
D183 $1\frac{1}{2}$ c. black and blue . . 45 20
D184 $2\frac{1}{2}$ c. black and blue . . 1·75 15
D209 3 c. black and blue . . 1·50 1·00
D210 4 c. black and blue . . 1·50 1·75
D185 5 c. black and blue . . 10·00 10
D211 $6\frac{1}{2}$ c. black and blue . . 32·00 35·00
D212 $7\frac{1}{2}$ c. black and blue . . 1·75 40
D186 10 c. black and blue . . 28·00 25
D187 $12\frac{1}{2}$ c. black and blue . 23·00 1·10
D188 15 c. black and blue . . 28·00 90
D189 20 c. black and blue . . 16·00 6·50
D190 25 c. black and blue . . 35·00 45
D181 1 g. red and blue . . . 80·00 22·00
No. D181 is inscribed "EEN GULDEN".

1906. Surch.
D213 D **9** 3 c. on 1 g. red & blue 27·00 27·00
D215 4 on $6\frac{1}{2}$ c. black & blue 4·50 5·50
D216 $6\frac{1}{2}$ on 20 c. black & blue 3·50 4·50
D214 50 c. on 1 g. red & blue £130 £130

1907. De Ruyter Commem. stamps surch **PORTZEGEL** and value.

D217 **15** ½ c. on 1 c. red . . . . . 1·25 1·25
D218 1 c. on 1 c. red 75 75
D219 1½ c. on 1 c. red 75 75
D220 2½ c. on 1 c. red . . . . 1·60 1·60
D221 5 c. on 2½ c. red . . . . 1·60 75
D222 6½ c. on 2½ c. red . . . . 2·75 2·75
D223 7½ c. on ½ c. blue . . . . 1·75 1·50
D224 10 c. on ½ c. blue . . . . 1·75 95
D225 12½ c. on ½ c. blue . . . . 4·50 4·50
D226 15 c. on 2½ c. red . . . . 6·50 3·75
D227 25 c. on ½ c. blue . . . . 8·00 7·50
D228 50 c. on ½ c. blue . . . . 40·00 35·00
D229 1 g. on ½ c. blue . . . . 60·00 50·00

1912. Re-issue of Type D **9** in one colour.

D230 D **9** ½ c. blue 10 10
D231 1 c. blue 10 10
D232 1½ c. blue . . . . . . 1·50 1·50
D233 2½ c. blue 10 10
D234 3 c. blue 35 35
D235 4 c. blue 10 15
D236 4½ c. blue . . . . . . 5·00 4·75
D237 5 c. blue 10 10
D238 5½ c. blue . . . . . . 4·75 4·50
D239 7 c. blue . . . . . . 2·25 2·25
D240 7½ c. blue . . . . . . 3·25 1·50
D241 10 c. blue 50 50
D242 12½ c. blue 50 50
D453 15 c. blue 50 50
D244 20 c. blue 50 50
D245 25 c. blue . . . . . . 65·00 95
D246 50 c. blue 40 15

D 25 D 121

1921.

D442 D **25** 3 c. blue 35 15
D445 6 c. blue 35 15
D446 7 c. blue 50 50
D447 7½ c. blue 50 55
D448 8 c. blue 50 50
D449 9 c. blue 65 65
D450 11 c. blue . . . . . . 10·00 3·25
D247 12 c. blue 45 40
D455 25 c. blue 45 40
D456 30 c. blue 50 40
D458 1 g. red 60 40

1923. Surch in white figures in black circle.

D272 D **9** 1 c. on 3 c. blue 75 75
D273 2½ c. on 7 c. blue . . . 1·10 50
D274 25 c. on 1½ c. blue . . . 8·25 75
D275 25 c. on 7½ c. blue . . . 9·25 50

1924. Stamps of 1898 surch **TE BETALEN PORT** and value in white figures in black circle.

D295 **13** 4 c. on 3 c. green . . . . 1·50 1·10
D296 **12** 5 c. on 1 c. red 75 40
D297 10 c. on 1½ c. blue . . . 1·10 45
D298 **13** 12½ c. on 5 c. red . . . . 1·25 45

1947.

D656 D **121** 1 c. blue 10 10
D657 3 c. blue 10 15
D658 4 c. blue . . . . . 10·00 80
D659 5 c. blue 10 10
D660 6 c. blue 35 35
D661 7 c. blue 15 15
D662 8 c. blue 15 15
D663 10 c. blue 15 10
D664 11 c. blue 35 35
D665 12 c. blue 90 80
D666 14 c. blue 75 70
D667 15 c. blue 30 10
D668 16 c. blue 85 85
D669 20 c. blue 30 10
D670 24 c. blue . . . . . 1·25 1·25
D671 25 c. blue 30 10
D672 26 c. blue . . . . . 1·60 1·75
D673 30 c. blue 65 10
D674 35 c. blue 70 10
D675 40 c. blue 75 10
D676 50 c. blue 85 10
D677 60 c. blue . . . . . 1·00 25
D678 85 c. blue . . . . . 15·00 35
D679 90 c. blue . . . . . 2·75 40
D680 95 c. blue . . . . . 2·75 35
D681 1 g. red . . . . . 2·25 10
D682 1 g. 75 red . . . . . 5·50 25

For stamps as Types D **121**, but in violet, see under Surinam.

INTERNATIONAL COURT OF JUSTICE

Stamps specially issued for use by the Headquarters of the Court of International Justice. Nos. J1 to J36 were not sold to the public in unused condition.

1934. Optd **COUR PER- MANENTE DE JUSTICE INTER- NATIONALE.**

J1 **35** 1½ c. mauve . . . . — 40
J2 2½ c. green . . . . — 40
J3 **36** 7½ c. red . . . . — 80
J4 **68** 12½ c. blue . . . . — 25·00
J7 **36** 12½ c. blue . . . . — 18·00
J5 15 c. yellow . . . . — 1·00
J6 3 c. purple . . . . — 2·10

1940. Optd **COUR PER- MANANTE DE JUSTICE INTER- NATIONALE.**

J 9 **94** 7½ c. red . . . . — 9·00
J10 12½ c. blue . . . . — 9·00
J11 15 c. blue . . . . — 9·00
J12 30 c. bistre . . . . — 9·00

1947. Optd **COUR INTERNATIONALE DE JUSTICE.**

J13 **94** 7½ c. red . . . . — 1·00
J14 10 c. purple . . . . — 1·00
J15 12½ c. blue . . . . — 1·00
J16 20 c. violet . . . . — 1·00
J17 25 c. red . . . . — 1·00

J 3 J 4 Peace Palace, The Hague J 5 Queen Juliana

1950.

J18 J **3** 2 c. blue . . . . — 8·25
J19 4 c. green . . . . — 8·25

1951.

J20 J **4** 2 c. lake . . . . — 50
J21 3 c. blue . . . . — 50
J22 4 c. green . . . . — 50
J23 5 c. brown . . . . — 50
J24 J **5** 6 c. mauve . . . . — 2·10
J25 J **4** 6 c. green . . . . — 85
J26 7 c. red . . . . — 85
J27 J **5** 10 c. green . . . . — 15
J28 12 c. red . . . . — 1·75
J29 15 c. red . . . . — 15
J30 20 c. blue . . . . — 20
J31 25 c. brown . . . . — 20
J32 30 c. purple . . . . — 30
J33 J **4** 40 c. blue . . . . — 30
J34 45 c. red . . . . — 35
J35 50 c. mauve . . . . — 35
J36 J **5** 1 g. grey . . . . — 70

J 6 Olive Branch and Peace Palace, The Hague

1989.

J37 J **6** 5 c. black and yellow . . . 10 10
J38 10 c. black and blue . . . 10 10
J39 25 c. black and red . . . 20 20
J41 50 c. black and green . . 40 40
J42 55 c. black and mauve . . 40 40
J43 60 c. black and bistre . . 45 45
J44 65 c. black and green . . 50 50
J45 70 c. black and blue . . 55 55
J46 75 c. black and yellow . . 55 55
J47 80 c. black and green . . 60 60
J49 1 g. black and orange . . 75 75
J50 1 g. 50 black and blue . . 1·10 1·10
J51 1 g. 60 black and brown . 1·00 1·00
J54 – 5 g. multicoloured . . . . 3·25 3·25
J56 – 7 g. multicoloured . . . . 4·00 4·00

DESIGNS: 5, 7 g. Olive branch and column

NETHERLANDS ANTILLES Pt. 4

Curacao and other Netherlands islands in the Caribbean Sea. In December 1954 these were placed on an equal footing with Netherlands under the Crown.

100 cents = 1 gulden

48 Spanish Galleon

49 Alonso de Ojeda

1949. 450th Anniv of Discovery of Curacao.

306 **48** 6 c. green . . . . 3·50 1·75
307 **49** 12½ c. red . . . . 3·75 3·50
308 **48** 15 c. blue . . . . 3·75 2·25

50 Posthorns and Globe

51 Leap-frog

1949. 75th Anniv of U.P.U.

309 **50** 6 c. red . . . . 3·00 2·25
310 25 c. blue . . . . 3·00 1·10

1950. As numeral and portrait types of Netherlands but inscr "NED. ANTILLEN".

325 **118** 1 c. brown 10 10
326 1½ c. blue 10 10
327 2 c. orange 10 10
328 2½ c. green 80 15
329 3 c. violet 10 10
329a 4 c. green 45 35
330 5 c. red 10 10
310a **129** 5 c. yellow 25 25
311 6 c. purple 85 10
311a 7½ c. brown . . . . 4·00 10
312a 10 c. red 30 30
313 12½ c. green . . . . 1·75 15
314a 15 c. blue 35 35
315a 20 c. orange 70 70
316 21 c. black . . . . 2·00 1·75
316a 22½ c. green . . . . 5·00 10
317a 25 c. violet 80 80
318 27½ c. brown . . . . 5·00 1·90
319a 30 c. sepia 80 80
319b 40 c. blue 80 80
320 50 c. olive . . . . 9·00 10
321 **130** 1½ g. green . . . . 32·00 20
322 2½ g. brown . . . . 30·00 70
323 5 g. red . . . . 50·00 8·50
324 10 g. purple . . . . . . £200 50·00

1951. Child Welfare.

331 **51** 1½ c. + 1 c. violet . . . . . 1·75 2·25
332 – 5 c. + 2½ c. brown . . . . 11·00 4·50
333 – 6 c. + 2½ c. blue . . . . 11·00 4·50
334 – 12½ c. + 5 c. red . . . . 11·00 4·50
335 – 25 c. + 10 c. turquoise . . 11·00 4·50

DESIGNS: 5 c. Kite-flying; 6 c. Girl on swing; 12½ c. Girls playing "Oranges and Lemons"; 25 c. Bowling hoops.

52 Gull over Ship

54 Fort Beekenburg

1952. Seamen's Welfare Fund. Inscr "ZEEMANSWELVAREN".

336 **52** 1½ c. + 1 c. green . . . . . 1·50 75
337 – 6 c. + 4 c. brown . . . . . 8·00 3·50
338 – 12½ c. + 7 c. mauve . . . . 8·00 3·75
339 – 15 c. + 10 c. blue . . . . 10·00 4·00
340 – 25 c. + 15 c. red . . . . . 8·50 3·50

DESIGNS: 6 c. Sailor and lighthouse; 12½ c. Sailor on ship's prow; 15 c. Tanker in harbour; 25 c. Anchor and compass.

1953. Netherlands Flood Relief Fund. No. 321 surch **22½ Ct. + 7½ Ct. WATERSNOOD NEDER-LAND 1953.**

341 **130** 22½ c. + 7½ c. on 1½ g. . . 1·10 1·10

1953. 250th Anniv of Fort Beekenburg.

342 **54** 22½ c. brown . . . . 3·50 40

55 Aruba Beach

1954. 3rd Caribbean Tourist Assn Meeting.

343 **55** 15 c. blue and buff . . . . 3·50 2·50

1954. Ratification of Statute of the Kingdom. As No. 809 of Netherlands.

344 **158** 7½ c. green 70 65

56 "Anglo" Flower

1955. Child Welfare.

345 **56** 1½ c. + 1 c. blue, yellow & turquoise 40 50
346 – 7½ c. + 5 c. red, yellow and violet . . . . 3·25 2·25
347 – 15 c. + 5 c. red, grn & olive 3·25 2·50
348 – 22½ c. + 7½ c. red, yellow and blue . . . . 3·25 2·25
349 – 25 c. + 10 c. red, yellow and grey . . . . 3·25 2·50

FLOWERS: 7½ c. White Cayenne; 15 c. "French" flower; 22½ c. Cactus; 25 c. Red Cayenne.

57 Prince Bernhard and Queen Juliana

1955. Royal Visit.

350 **57** 7½ c. + 2½ c. red 20 20
351 22½ c. + 7½ c. blue 95 95

59 Oil Refinery

1955. 21st Meeting of Caribbean Commission.

352 – 15 c. blue, green & brown . 2·50 2·00
353 **59** 25 c. blue, green & brown . 4·00 2·50

DESIGN (rectangle, 36 × 25 mm): 15 c. Aruba Beach.

60 St. Anne Bay

1956. 10th Anniv of Caribbean Commission.

354 **60** 15 c. blue, red and black . 30 25

61 Lord Baden-Powell

1957. 50th Anniv of Boy Scout Movement.

355 **61** 6 c. + 1½ c. yellow 50 50
356 7½ c. + 2½ c. green 50 50
357 15 c. + 5 c. red 50 50

62 "Dawn of Health"

1957. 1st Caribbean Mental Health Congress, Aruba.

358 **62** 15 c. black and yellow . . 30 30

63 Saba

1957. Tourist Publicity. Multicoloured.

359 7½ c. Type **63** 35 35
360 15 c. St. Maarten 35 35
361 25 c. St. Eustatius 35 35

64 Footballer

65 Curacao Intercontinental Hotel

1957. 8th Central American and Caribbean Football Championships.

362 **64** 6 c. + 2½ c. orange 50 70
363 – 7½ c. + 5 c. red . . . . 1·00 1·10
364 – 15 c. + 5 c. green . . . . 1·10 1·10
365 – 22½ c. + 7½ c. blue . . . . 1·10 80

DESIGNS—HORIZ: 7½ c. Caribbean map. VERT: 15 c. Goalkeeper saving ball; 22½ c. Footballers with ball.

1957. Opening of Curacao Inter-continental Hotel.

366 **65** 15 c. blue 30 25

66 Map of Curacao

67 American Kestrel

1957. International Geophysical Year.

367 **66** 15 c. deep blue and blue . . 80 65

1958. Child Welfare. Bird design inscr "VOOR HET KIND". Multicoloured.

368 2½ c. + 1 c. Type **67** 30 25
369 7½ c. + 1½ c. Yellow oriole . . 85 65
370 15 c. + 2½ c. Scaly-breasted ground doves . . . . 1·10 80
371 22½ c. + 2½ c. Brown-throated conure . . . . 1·25 70

68 Greater Flamingoes (Bonaire)

1958. Size 33½ × 22 mm.

372 **68** 6 c. pink and green . . . 7·50 10
373 A 7½ c. yellow and brown . . 10 10
374 8 c. yellow and blue . . 10 15
375 B 10 c. yellow and grey . . 10 10
376 C 12 c. grey and green . . 15 20
377 D 15 c. blue and green . . 15 10
377a 15 c. lilac and green . . 15 10
378 E 20 c. grey and red . . . 20 10
379 A 25 c. green and blue . . 25 10
380 D 30 c. green and brown . . 30 10
381 E 35 c. pink and grey . . 35 20
382 C 40 c. green and mauve . . 40 10
383 B 45 c. blue and violet . . 50 20
384 **68** 50 c. pink and brown . . 50 10
385 E 55 c. green and red . . 65 25
386 **68** 65 c. pink and green . . 65 30
387 D 70 c. orange and purple . . 70 45
388 **68** 75 c. pink and violet . . 80 45
389 B 85 c. green and brown . . 85 60
390 E 90 c. orange and blue . . 85 70
391 C 95 c. yellow and orange . . 90 70
392 D 1 g. grey and red . . . 1·00 15
393 A 1½ g. brown and violet . . 1·40 20
394 C 2½ g. yellow and blue . . 2·50 30
395 B 5 g. mauve and brown . . 4·75 85
396 **68** 10 g. pink and blue . . . 8·50 4·00

DESIGNS: A. Dutch Colonial houses (Curacao); B. Mountain and palms (Saba); C. Town Hall (St. Maarten); D. Church tower (Aruba); E. Memorial obelisk (St. Eustatius).

For larger versions of some values see Nos. 653/6.

69

70 Red Cross Flag and Antilles Map

1958. 50th Anniv of Netherlands Antilles Radio & Telegraph Administration.

397 **69** 7½ c. lake and blue 15 15
398 15 c. blue and red 30 30

1958. Neth. Antilles Red Cross Fund. Cross in red.

399 **70** 6 c. + 2 c. brown 30 30
400 7½ c. + 2½ c. green 45 45
401 15 c. + 5 c. yellow 45 45
402 22½ c. + 7½ c. blue 45 45

71 Aruba Caribbean Hotel

1959. Opening of Aruba Caribbean Hotel.

403 **71** 15 c. multicoloured . . . 30 20

72 Zeeland

1959. Curacao Monuments Preservation Fund. Multicoloured.

404 6 c. + 1½ c. Type **72** 80 80
405 7½ c. + 2½ c. Saba Island . . 80 90
406 15 c. + 5 c. Molenplein (vert) . 80 90
407 22½ c. + 7½ c. Scharloobrug . 80 90
408 25 c. + 7½ c. Brievengat . . . 80 90

73 Water-distillation Plant

74 Antilles Flag

1959. Inauguration of Aruba Water-distillation Plant.

409 **73** 20 c. light blue and blue . 35 35

1959. 5th Anniv of Ratification of Statute of the Kingdom.

410 **74** 10 c. red, blue & lt blue . 25 25
411 20 c. red, blue and yellow . 30 30
412 25 c. red, blue and green . 30 30

75 Fokker F.XVIII "De Snip" over Caribbean

76 Mgr. Niewindt

1959. 25th Anniv of K.L.M. Netherlands-Curacao Air Service. Each yellow, deep blue and blue.

413 10 c. Type **75** 40 30
414 20 c. Fokker F.XVIII "De Snip" over globe 40 30
415 25 c. Douglas DC-7C "Seven Seas" over Handelskade (bridge), Willemstad . . . 40 15
416 35 c. Douglas DC-8 at Aruba Airport 40 40

1960. Death Centenary of Mgr. M. J. Niewindt.

417 **76** 10 c. purple 35 35
418 20 c. violet 50 50
419 25 c. olive 35 35

77 Flag and Oil-worker

78 Frogman

1960. Labour Day.

420 **77** 20 c. multicoloured . . . 30 30

1960. Princess Wilhelmina Cancer Relief Fund. Inscr "KANKERBESTRIJDING".

421 **78** 10 c. + 2 c. blue . . . . 1·10 1·10
422 – 20 c. + 3 c. multicoloured . 1·40 1·25
423 – 25 c. + 5 c. red, blue & blk . 1·40 1·25

DESIGNS—HORIZ: 20 c., 25 c. Tropical fishes (different).

79 Child on Bed

1961. Child Welfare. Inscr "voor het kind".

424 6 c. + 2 c. black and green . 25 25
425 10 c. + 3 c. black and red . . 30 30
426 20 c. + 6 c. black and yellow . 30 30
427 25 c. + 8 c. black and orange . 35 35

DESIGNS: 6 c. Type **79**; 10 c. Girl with doll; 20 c. Boy with bucket; 25 c. Children in classroom.

80 Governor's Salute to the American Naval Brig "Andrew Doria" at St. Eustatius

1961. 185th Anniv of 1st Salute to the American Flag.

428 **80** 20 c. multicoloured 70 60

1962. Royal Silver Wedding. As T **187** of Netherlands.

429 10 c. orange 15 15
430 25 c. blue 30 20

81 Jaja (nursemaid) and Child

82 Knight and World Map

1962. Cultural Series.

431 – 6 c. brown and yellow . . . 15 15
432 – 10 c. multicoloured 20 15
433 – 20 c. multicoloured 30 30
434 **81** 25 c. brown, green & blk . 35 30

DESIGNS: 6 c. Corn-masher; 10 c. Benta player; 20 c. Petji kerchief.

1962. 5th International Candidates Chess Tournament, Curacao.

436 **82** 10 c. + 5 c. green 95 60
437 20 c. + 10 c. red 95 60
438 25 c. + 10 c. blue 95 60

1963. Freedom from Hunger. No. 378 surch **TEGEN DE HONGER** wheat sprig and **+10 c.**

439 20 c. + 10 c. grey and red . . 50 50

84 Family Group

1963. 4th Caribbean Mental Health Congress, Curacao.

440 **84** 20 c. buff and blue 30 30
441 – 25 c. red and blue 30 30

DESIGN: 25 c. Egyptian Cross emblem.

85 "Freedom" 86 Hotel Bonaire

1963. Centenary of Abolition of Slavery in Dutch West Indies.

442 **85** 25 c. brown and yellow . . 25 25

1963. Opening of Hotel Bonaire.

443 **86** 20 c. brown 20 20

87 Child and Flowers

88 Test-tube and Flask

1963. Child Welfare. Child Art. Multicoloured.

444 5 c. + 2 c. Type **87** 25 35
445 6 c. + 3 c. Children and flowers 25 35
446 10 c. + 5 c. Girl with ball . . 30 35
447 20 c. + 10 c. Men with flags . 30 35
448 25 c. + 12 c. Schoolboy . . . 30 35

Nos. 445/7 are horiz.

1963. 150th Anniv of Kingdom of the Netherlands. As No. 968 of Netherlands, but smaller, size (26 × 27 mm).

449 25 c. green, red and black . . 20 20

1963. Chemical Industry, Aruba.

450 **88** 20 c. red, light green and green 45 40

89 Winged Letter

1964. 35th Anniv of 1st U.S.–Curacao Flight. Multicoloured.

451 20 c. Type **89** 30 30
452 25 c. Route map, Sikorsky S-38 flying boat and Boeing 707 40 30

90 Trinitaria

1964. Child Welfare. Multicoloured.

453 6 c. + 3 c. Type **90** 20 20
454 10 c. + 5 c. Magdalena . . . 25 25
455 20 c. + 10 c. Yellow keiki . . 30 30
456 25 c. + 11 c. Bellisima . . . 30 30

91 Caribbean Map

92 "Six Islands"

1964. 5th Caribbean Council Assembly.

457 **91** 20 c. yellow, red & blue . . 30 20

1964. 10th Anniv of Statute for the Kingdom.

458 **92** 25 c. multicoloured 20 20

93 Princess Beatrix

94 I.T.U. Emblem and Symbols

1965. Visit of Princess Beatrix.

459 **93** 25 c. red 35 30

1965. Centenary of I.T.U.

460 **94** 10 c. deep blue and blue . . 15 15

95 "Asperalla" (tanker) at Curacao

1965. 50th Anniv of Curacao's Oil Industry. Multicoloured.

461 10 c. Catalytic cracking plant (vert) 20 15
462 20 c. Type **95** 25 15
463 25 c. Super fractionating plant (vert) 25 20

96 Flag and Fruit Market, Curacao

1965.

464 **96** 1 c. blue, red & green . . . 10 10
465 – 2 c. blue, red and yellow . . 10 10
466 – 3 c. blue, red and cobalt . . 10 10
467 – 4 c. blue, red and orange . 25 10
468 – 5 c. blue, red and blue . . 10 10
469 – 6 c. blue, red and pink . . 10 10

DESIGNS (Flag and): 2 c. Divi-divi tree; 3 c. Lace; 4 c. Greater flamingoes; 5 c. Church; 6 c. Lobster. Each is inscr with a different place-name.

97 Cup Sponges

1965. Child Welfare. Marine Life. Multicoloured.

470 6 c. + 3 c. Type **97** 15 15
471 10 c. + 5 c. Cup sponges (diff) 20 20
472 20 c. + 10 c. Sea anemones on star coral 20 20
473 25 c. + 11 c. Basket sponge and "Brain" coral 30 35

98 Marine and Seascape   99 Budgerigars and Wedding Rings

1965. Tercentenary of Marine Corps.
474 **98** 25 c. multicoloured 20 15

1966. Intergovernmental Committee for European Migration (I.C.E.M.) Fund. As T **215** of Netherlands.
475 35 c. + 15 c. bistre & brown . 20 25

1966. Marriage of Crown Princess Beatrix and Herr Claus von Amsberg.
476 **99** 25 c. multicoloured 40 35

100 Admiral de Ruyter and Map

1966. 300th Anniv of Admiral de Ruyter's Visit to St. Eustatius.
477 **100** 25 c. ochre, violet & blue . 20 15

101 "Grammar"   102 Cooking

1966. 25 years of Secondary Education.
478 **101** 6 c. black, blue & yellow . 10 10
479 – 10 c. black, red & green . 10 10
480 – 20 c. black, blue & yellow 15 15
481 – 25 c. black, red and green 20 20
DESIGNS: The "Free Arts", figures representing: 10 c. "Rhetoric" and "Dialect"; 20 c. "Arithmetic" and "Geometry"; 25 c. "Astronomy" and "Music".

1966. Child Welfare. Multicoloured.
482 6 c. + 3 c. Type **102** 10 10
483 10 c. + 5 c. Nursing 10 10
484 20 c. + 10 c. Metal-work fitting 20 20
485 25 c. + 11 c. Ironing 25 25

103 "Gelderland" (cruiser)

1967. 60th Anniv of Royal Netherlands Navy League.
486 **103** 6 c. bronze and green . . 10 10
487 – 10 c. ochre and yellow . . 15 15
488 – 20 c. brown and green . . 20 15
489 – 25 c. blue and indigo . . . 20 20
SHIPS: 10 c. "Pioneer" (schooner); 20 c. "Oscilla" (tanker); 25 c. "Santa Rosa" (liner).

104 M. C. Piar   105 "Heads in Hands"

1967. 150th Death Anniv of Manuel Piar (patriot).
490 **104** 20 c. brown and red . . . 15 15

1967. Cultural and Social Relief Funds.
491 **105** 6 c. + 3 c. black & blue . 10 10
492 10 c. + 5 c. black & mve . 15 15
493 20 c. + 10 c. purple . . . 15 15
494 25 c. + 11 c. blue 15 20

106 "The Turtle and the Monkey"   107 Olympic Flame and Rings

1967. Child Welfare. "Nanzi" Fairy Tales. Mult.
495 6 c. + 3 c. "Princess Long Nose" (vert) 15 15
496 10 c. + 5 c. Type **106** 20 15
497 20 c. + 10 c. "Nanzi (spider) and the Tiger" 25 15
498 25 c. + 11 c. "Shon Arey's Balloon" (vert) 30 20

1968. Olympic Games, Mexico. Multicoloured.
499 10 c. Type **107** 20 20
500 20 c. "Throwing the discus" (statue) 20 20
501 25 c. Stadium and doves . . 20 20

108 "Dance of the Ribbons"

1968. Cultural and Social Relief Funds.
502 **108** 10 c. + 5 c. multicoloured 15 15
503 15 c. + 5 c. multicoloured 15 15
504 20 c. + 10 c. multicoloured 15 20
505 25 c. + 10 c. multicoloured 20 25

109 Boy with Goat

1968. Child Welfare Fund. Multicoloured.
506 6 c. + 3 c. Type **109** 15 15
507 10 c. + 5 c. Girl with dog . . 15 15
508 20 c. + 10 c. Boy with cat . 25 25
509 25 c. + 11 c. Girl with duck . 35 35

110 Fokker Friendship 500   111 Radio Pylon, "Waves" and Map

1968. Dutch Antillean Airlines.
510 **110** 10 c. blue, black & yellow 25 20
511 – 20 c. blue, black & brown 25 20
512 – 25 c. blue, black & pink . 25 20
DESIGNS: 20 c. Douglas DC-9; 25 c. Fokker Friendship 500 in flight and Douglas DC-9 on ground.

1969. Opening of Broadcast Relay Station, Bonaire.
513 **111** 25 c. green, dp blue & blue 20 20

112 "Code of Laws"   113 "Carnival"

1969. Centenary of Netherlands Antilles Court of Justice.
514 **112** 20 c. green, gold & lt grn 20 20
515 – 25 c. multicoloured . . . 20 20
DESIGN: 25 c. "Scales of Justice".

1969. Cultural and Social Relief Funds. Antilles' Festivals. Multicoloured.
516 10 c. + 5 c. Type **113** 30 30
517 15 c. + 5 c. "Harvest Festival" 30 30
518 20 c. + 10 c. "San Juan Day" 40 40
519 25 c. + 10 c. "New Years' Day" 40 40

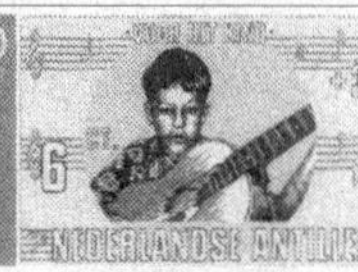

114 I.L.O. Emblem, "Koenoekoe" House and Cacti   115 Boy playing Guitar

1969. 50th Anniv of I.L.O.
520 **114** 10 c. black and blue . . . 15 15
521 25 c. black and red . . . 15 15

1969. Child Welfare.
522 **115** 6 c. + 3 c. violet & orge . 25 25
523 – 10 c. + 5 c. grn & yell . . 35 35
524 – 20 c. + 10 c. red and blue 40 40
525 – 25 c. + 11 c. brn & pink . 50 50
DESIGNS: 10 c. Girl playing recorder; 20 c. Boy playing "marimula"; 25 c. Girl playing piano.

1969. 15th Anniv of Statute of the Kingdom. As T **240** of the Netherlands, but inscr "NEDERLANDSE ANTILLEN".
526 25 c. multicoloured 25 20

117 Radio Station, Bonaire   118 St. Anna Church, Otrabanda, Curacao

1970. 5th Anniv of Trans-World Religious Radio Station, Bonaire. Multicoloured.
527 10 c. Type **117** 15 15
528 15 c. Trans-World Radio emblem 15 15

1970. Churches of the Netherlands Antilles. Mult.
529 10 c. Type **118** 20 20
530 20 c. "Mikve Israel-Emanuel" Synagogue, Punda, Curacao (horiz) 20 20
531 25 c. Pulpit Fort Church Curacao 20 20

119 "The Press"   120 Mother and Child

1970. Cultural and Social Relief Funds. "Mass-media". Multicoloured.
532 10 c. + 5 c. Type **119** 40 40
533 15 c. + 5 c. "Films" 40 40
534 20 c. + 10 c. "Radio" 45 45
535 25 c. + 10 c. "Television" . . 45 45

1970. Child Welfare. Multicoloured.
536 6 c. + 3 c. Type **120** 45 45
537 10 c. + 5 c. Child with piggy-bank 45 45
538 20 c. + 10 c. Children's Judo . 45 45
539 25 c. + 11 c. "Pick-a-back" . . 45 45

121 St. Theresia's Church, St. Nicolaas, Aruba   122 Lions Emblem

1971. 40th Anniv of St. Theresia Parish, Aruba.
540 **121** 20 c. multicoloured 20 20

1971. 25th Anniv of Curacao Lions Club.
541 **122** 25 c. multicoloured 35 25

123 Charcoal Stove   125 Admiral Brion

1971. Cultural and Social Relief Funds. Household Utensils. Multicoloured.
542 10 c. + 5 c. Type **123** 45 45
543 15 c. + 5 c. Earthenware water vessel 45 45
544 20 c. + 10 c. Baking oven . . 45 45
545 25 c. + 10 c. Kitchen implements 45 45

1971. Prince Bernhard's 60th Birthday. Design as No. 1135 of Netherlands.
546 45 c. multicoloured 45 40

1971. 150th Death Anniv of Admiral Pedro Luis Brion.
547 **125** 40 c. multicoloured . . . 30 30

126 Bottle Doll   127 Queen Emma Bridge, Curacao

1971. Child Welfare. Home-made Toys. Mult.
548 15 c. + 5 c. Type **126** 60 60
549 20 c. + 10 c. Simple cart . . 65 65
550 30 c. + 15 c. Spinning-tops . 65 65

1971. Views of the Islands. Multicoloured.
551 1 c. Type **127** 10 10
552 2 c. The Bottom, Saba 10 10
553 3 c. Greater flamingoes, Bonaire 40 10
554 4 c. Distillation plant, Aruba . 10 10
555 5 c. Fort Amsterdam, St. Maarten 10 10
556 6 c. Fort Oranje, St. Eustatius 10 10

128 Ship in Dock   129 Steel Band

1972. Inauguration of New Dry Dock Complex, Willemstad, Curacao.
557 **128** 30 c. multicoloured . . . 35 30

1972. Cultural and Social Relief Funds. Folklore. Multicoloured.
558 15 c. + 5 c. Type **129** 75 75
559 20 c. + 10 c. "Seu" festival . 75 75
560 30 c. + 15 c. "Tambu" dance 75 75

130 J. E. Irausquin   131 Dr. M. F. da Costa Gomez

1972. 10th Death Anniv of Juan Enrique Irausquin (Antilles statesman).
561 **130** 30 c. red 30 25

1972. 65th Birth Anniv of Moises F. da Costa Gomez (statesman).
562 **131** 30 c. black and green . . 30 25

132 Child playing with Earth   133 Pedestrian Crossing

1972. Child Welfare. Multicoloured.
563 15 c. + 5 c. Type **132** 85 85
564 20 c. + 10 c. Child playing in water 85 85
565 30 c. + 15 c. Child throwing ball into the air 85 85

1973. Cultural and Social Relief Funds. Road Safety.
566 **133** 12 c. + 6 c. multicoloured 90 80
567 – 15 c. + 7 c. grn, orge & red 90 80
568 – 40 c. + 20 c. multicoloured 90 80
DESIGNS: 15 c. Road-crossing patrol; 40 c. Traffic lights.

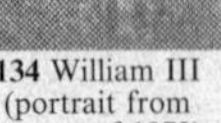

134 William III (portrait from stamp of 1873) **135** Map of Aruba, Curacao and Bonaire

1973. Stamp Centenary.
569 **134** 15 c. lilac, mauve & gold . . . 30 25
570 – 20 c. multicoloured . . . 35 30
571 – 30 c. multicoloured . . . 35 30
DESIGNS: 20 c. Antilles postman; 30 c. Postal Service emblem.

1973. Inauguration of Submarine Cable and Microwave Telecommunications Link. Multicoloured.
572 15 c. Type **135** 40 20
573 30 c. Six stars ("The Antilles") 40 40
574 45 c. Map of Saba, St. Maarten and St. Eustatius 40 40

136 Queen Juliana **137** Jan Eman

1973. Silver Jubilee of Queen Juliana's Reign.
576 **136** 15 c. multicoloured . . . 45 45

1973. 16th Death Anniv of Jan Eman (Aruba statesman).
577 **137** 30 c. black and green . . 30 25

138 "1948–1973" **139** L. B. Scott

1973. Child Welfare Fund. 25th Anniv of 1st Child Welfare Stamps.
578 **138** 15 c. + 5 c. light green, green and blue 85 70
579 – 20 c. + 10 c. brown, green and blue 85 75
580 – 30 c. + 15 c. violet, blue and light blue . . . . . . 1·25 90
DESIGNS: No. 579, Three Children; No. 580, Mother and child.

1974. 8th Death Anniv of Lionel B. Scott (St. Maarten statesman).
582 **139** 30 c. multicoloured . . . 30 30

140 Family Meal **141** Girl combing Hair

1974. Family Planning Campaign. Multicoloured.
583 6 c. Type **140** 10 103
584 12 c. Family at home 25 20
585 15 c. Family in garden 30 20

1974. Cultural and Social Relief Funds. "The Younger Generation". Multicoloured.
586 12 c. + 6 c. Type **141** . . . . 1·00 1·00
587 15 c. + 7 c. "Pop dancers" . 1·00 1·00
588 40 c. + 20 c. Group drummer 1·00 1·00

142 Desulphurisation Plant

1974. 50th Anniv of Lago Oil Co., Aruba. Multicoloured.
589 15 c. Type **142** 45 30
590 30 c. Fractionating towers . . 45 30
591 45 c. Lago refinery at night . . 45 35

143 U.P.U. Emblem **144** "A Carpenter outranks a King"

1974. Centenary of Universal Postal Union.
592 **143** 15 c. gold, green & black 40 35
593 30 c. gold, blue & black . 40 40

1974. Child Welfare. Children's Songs. Mult.
594 15 c. + 5 c. Type **144** 70 70
595 20 c. + 10 c. Footprints ("Let's Do a Ring-dance") 70 70
596 30 c. + 15 c. "Moon and Sun" 70 70

145 Queen Emma Bridge **146** Ornamental Ventilation Grid

1975. Antillean Bridges. Multicoloured.
597 20 c. Type **145** 45 40
598 30 c. Queen Juliana Bridge . 50 40
599 40 c. Queen Wilhelmina Bridge 65 50

1975. Cultural and Social Welfare Funds.
600 **146** 12 c. + 6 c. multicoloured 65 65
601 – 15 c. + 7 c. brown & stone 65 65
602 – 40 c. + 20 c. multicoloured 65 65
DESIGNS: 15 c. Knight accompanied by buglers (tombstone detail); 40 c. Foundation stone.

147 Sodium Chloride Molecules

1975. Bonaire Salt Industry. Multicoloured.
603 15 c. Type **147** 55 35
604 20 c. Salt incrustation and blocks 55 45
605 40 c. Map of salt area (vert) . 65 45

148 Fokker F.XVIII "De Snip" and Old Control Tower

1975. 40th Anniv of Aruba Airport. Mult.
606 15 c. Type **148** 45 25
607 30 c. Douglas DC-9-30 and modern control tower . . . 45 30
608 40 c. Tail of Boeing 727-200 and "Princess Beatrix" Airport buildings 45 45

149 I.W.Y. Emblem

1975. International Women's Year. Multicoloured.
609 6 c. Type **149** 20 15
610 12 c. "Social Development" . 35 20
611 20 c. "Equality of Sexes" . . 45 30

150 Children making Windmill

1975. Child Welfare. Multicoloured.
612 15 c. + 5 c. Type **150** 70 65
613 20 c. + 10 c. Child modelling clay 70 65
614 30 c. + 15 c. Children drawing pictures 70 65

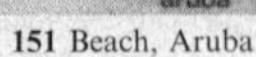

151 Beach, Aruba **152** J. A. Abraham (statesman)

1976. Tourism. Multicoloured.
615 40 c. Type **151** 60 50
616 40 c. Fish Kiosk, Bonaire . . . 60 50
617 40 c. "Table Mountain", Curacao 60 50

1976. Abraham Commemoration.
618 **152** 30 c. purple on brown . . 40 35

153 Dyke Produce **154** Arm holding Child

1976. Agriculture, Animal Husbandry and Fisheries. Multicoloured.
619 15 c. Type **153** 35 25
620 35 c. Cattle 50 40
621 45 c. Fishes 50 50

1976. Child Welfare. "Carrying the Child".
622 **154** 20 c. + 10 c. multicoloured 60 60
623 – 25 c. + 12 c. multicoloured 60 60
624 – 40 c. + 18 c. multicoloured 60 60
DESIGNS—HORIZ: 25 c. VERT: 40 c. Both similar to Type **154** showing arm holding child.

155 "Andrew Doria" (naval brig) receiving Salute **156** Carnival ostume

1976. Bicentenary of American Revolution. Multicoloured.
625 25 c. Flags and plaque, Fort Oranje 70 45
626 40 c. Type **155** 70 45
627 55 c. Johannes de Graaff, Governor of St. Eustatius . 70 70

1977. Carnival.
628 – 25 c. multicoloured 45 35
629 **156** 35 c. multicoloured 45 35
630 – 40 c. multicoloured 45 35
DESIGNS: 25 c., 40 c. Women in Carnival costumes.

157 Tortoise (Bonaire) **158** "Ace" Playing Card

1977. Rock Paintings. Multicoloured.
631 25 c. Bird (Aruba) 60 35
632 35 c. Abstract (Curacao) . . . 60 45
633 40 c. Type **157** 75 45

1977. Sixth Central American and Caribbean Bridge Championships. Multicoloured.
634 **158** 20 c. + 10 c. red & black . 50 35
635 – 25 c. + 12 c. multicoloured 50 45
636 – 40 c. + 18 c. multicoloured 65 60
DESIGNS—VERT: 25 c. "King" playing card. HORIZ: 40 c. Bridge hand.

159 "Cordia sebestena" **160** Bells outside Main Store

1977. Flowers. Multicoloured.
639 25 c. Type **159** 40 35
640 40 c. "Albizzia lebbeck" (vert) 50 45
641 55 c. "Tamarindus indica" . . 60 55

1977. 50th Anniv of Spritzer and Fuhrmann (jewellers). Multicoloured.
642 20 c. Type **160** 40 30
643 40 c. Globe basking in sun . . 50 40
644 55 c. Antillean flag and diamond ring 60 60

161 Children with Toy Animal

1977. Child Welfare. Multicoloured.
645 15 c. + 15 c. Type **161** . . . 35 25
646 20 c. + 10 c. Children with toy rabbit 40 40
647 25 c. + 12 c. Children with toy cat 50 45
648 40 c. + 18 c. Children with toy beetle 55 55

162 "The Unspoiled Queen" (Saba)

1977. Tourism. Multicoloured.
650 25 c. Type **162** 15 15
651 35 c. "The Golden Rock" (St. Eustatius) 20 20
652 40 c. "The Friendly Island" (St. Maarten) 25 25

1977. As Nos. 378, 381/2 and 385, but larger, (39 × 22 mm).
653 E 20 c. grey and red . . . . 1·00 1·00
654 35 c. pink and brown . . . 2·50 3·00
655 C 40 c. green and mauve . . 1·25 1·25
656 E 55 c. green and red . . . . 1·50 1·50

163 19th-century Chest **164** Water-skiing

1978. 150th Anniv of Netherlands Antilles' Bank. Multicoloured.
657 **163** 15 c. blue & light blue . . 10 10
658 – 20 c. orange and gold . . 10 10
659 – 40 c. green & deep green . 20 20
DESIGNS: 20 c. Bank emblem; 40 c. Strong-room door.

1978. Sports Funds. Multicoloured.
660 15 c. + 5 c. Type **164** 10 10
661 20 c. + 10 c. Yachting . . . 15 15
662 25 c. + 12 c. Football 20 20
663 40 c. + 18 c. Baseball 35 35

165 "Erythrina velutina" **166** "Polythysana rubrescens"

1978. Flora of Netherlands Antilles. Multicoloured.
664 15 c. "Delconix regia" 20 15
665 25 c. Type **165** 25 25
666 50 c. "Gualacum officinale" (horiz) 35 30
667 55 c. "Gilricidia sepium" (horiz) 45 45

1978. Butterflies. Multicoloured.
668 15 c. Type **166** 25 15
669 25 c. "Caligo sp." 40 20
670 35 c. "Prepona praeneste" . . 55 35
671 40 c. "Morpho sp." 70 50

167 "Conserve Energy" (English) **168** Red Cross

1978. Energy Conservation.
672 **167** 15 c. orange and black . . 15 15
673 – 20 c. green and black . . 20 20
674 – 40 c. red and black . . . 40 40
DESIGNS: As No. 672 but text in Dutch (20 c.) or in Papiamento (40 c.).

1978. 150th Birth Anniv of Henri Dunant (founder of Red Cross).
675 **168** 55 c. + 25 c. red & blue . 30 30

169 Curacao from Sea, and Punched Tape
170 Boy Rollerskating

1978. 70th Anniv of Antilles Telecommunications Corporation (Landsradio). Multicoloured.
677 20 c. Type **169** 25 25
678 40 c. Ship's bridge, punched tape and radio mast 35 35
679 55 c. Satellite and aerial (vert) 50 50

1978. Child Welfare. Multicoloured.
680 15 c. + 5 c. Type **170** 40 35
681 20 c. + 10 c. Boy and girl flying kite 50 40
682 25 c. + 12 c. Boy and girl playing marbles 50 45
683 40 c. + 18 c. Girl riding bicycle 60 55

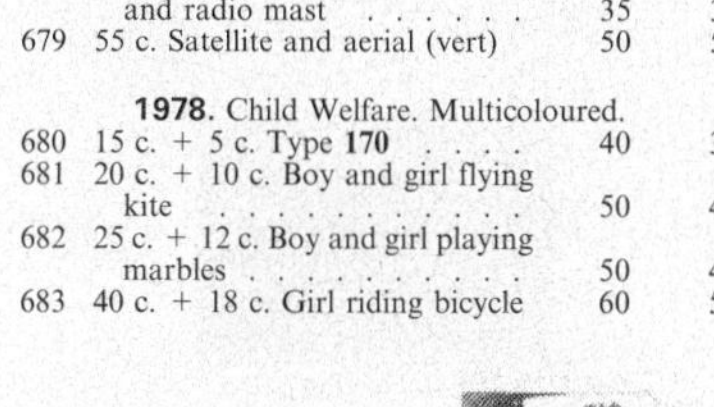

171 Ca'i Awa (pumping station)
172 Aruba Coat of Arms (float)

1978. 80th Death Anniv of Leonard Burlington Smith (entrepreneur and U.S. Consul).
685 **171** 25 c. multicoloured . . . 20 15
686 – 35 c. black, greenish yellow and yellow 25 20
687 – 40 c. multicoloured . . . 35 30
DESIGNS—VERT: 35 c. Leonard Burlington Smith. HORIZ: 40 c. Opening ceremony of Queen Emma Bridge, 1888.

1979. 25th Aruba Carnival. Multicoloured.
688 40 c. + 10 c. Float representing heraldic fantasy 40 35
689 75 c. + 20 c. Type **172** . . . 65 65

173 Goat and P.A.H.O. Emblem
174 Yacht and Sun

1979. 12th Inter-American Ministerial Meeting on Foot and Mouth Disease and Zoonosis Control, Curacao. Multicoloured.
690 50 c. Type **173** 30 30
691 75 c. Horse and conference emblem 45 45
692 150 c. Cows, flag and Pan-American Health Organization (P.A.H.O.) and W.H.O. emblems . . . . 1·00 1·00

1979. 12th International Sailing Regatta, Bonaire. Multicoloured.
694 15 c. + 5 c. Type **174** 15 15
695 35 c. + 25 c. Yachts 35 35
696 40 c. + 15 c. Yacht and globe (horiz) 50 50
697 55 c. + 25 c. Yacht, sun and flamingo 60 60

175 Corps Members
176 "Melochia tomentosa"

1979. 50th Anniv of Curacao Volunteer Corps.
699 **175** 15 c. + 10 c. blue, red and ultramarine 25 20
700 – 40 c. + 20 c. blue, violet and gold 45 40
701 – 1 g. multicoloured 70 65
DESIGNS: 40 c. Sentry in battle dress and emblem; 1 g. Corps emblem, flag and soldier in ceremonial uniform.

1979. Flowers. Multicoloured.
702 25 c. "Casearia tremula" . . . 20 15
703 40 c. "Cordia cylindrostachya" 35 30
704 1 g. 50 Type **176** . . . . . . 1·00 1·00

177 Girls reading Book
178 Dove and Netherlands Flag

1979. International Year of the Child.
705 **177** 20 c. + 10 c. multicoloured 25 25
706 – 25 c. + 12 c. multicoloured 35 30
707 – 35 c. + 15 c. violet, brown and black 50 45
708 – 50 c. + 20 c. multicoloured 60 55
DESIGNS: 25 c. Toddler and cat; 35 c. Girls carrying basket; 50 c. Boy and girl dressing-up.

1979. 25th Anniv of Statute of the Kingdom. Multicoloured.
710 65 c. Type **178** 50 40
711 1 g. 50 Dove and Netherlands Antilles flag 80 90

179 Map of Aruba and Foundation Emblem

1979. 30th Anniv of Aruba Cultural Centre Foundation. Multicoloured.
712 95 c. Type **179** 60 60
713 1 g. Foundation headquarters 70 70

180 Brass Chandelier

1980. 210th Anniv of Fort Church, Curacao.
714 **180** 20 c. + 10 c. yellow, black and brown 20 20
715 – 50 c. + 25 c. mult . . . 50 50
716 – 100 c. multicoloured . . 65 65
DESIGNS: 50 c. Pipe organ; 100 c. Cupola tower, 1910.

181 Rotary Emblem and Cogwheel

1980. 75th Anniv of Rotary International. Multicoloured.
717 45 c. Rotary emblem 35 35
718 50 c. Globe and cogwheels . . 40 40
719 85 c. Type **181** 65 65

182 Savings Box

1980. 75th Anniv of Post Office Savings Bank. Multicoloured.
721 25 c. Type **182** 20 20
722 150 c. Savings box (different) 1·00 1·00

183 Queen Juliana Accession Stamp

1980. Accession of Queen Beatrix.
723 **183** 25 c. red, green and gold 20 20
724 – 60 c. green, red and gold 40 40
DESIGN: 60 c. 1965 Royal Visit stamp.

184 Sir Rowland Hill
185 Volleyball

1980. "London 1980" International Stamp Exhibition.
725 **184** 45 c. black and green . . . 35 35
726 – 60 c. black and red 40 40
727 – 1 g. red, black and blue . . 70 70
DESIGNS: 60 c. "London 1980" logo; 1 g. Airmail label.

1980. Sports Funds.
729 – 25 c. + 10 c. red & black . 25 25
730 – 40 c. + 15 c. yellow & blk 35 35
731 **185** 45 c. + 20 c. light green, green and black 50 50
732 – 60 c. + 25 c. pink, orange and black 75 75
DESIGNS: 25 c. Gymnastics (beam exercise); 30 c. Gymnastics (horse vaulting); 60 c. Basketball.

186 White-fronted Dove

1980. Birds. Multicoloured.
734 25 c. Type **186** 25 20
735 60 c. Tropical mockingbird . . 65 45
736 85 c. Bananaquit 80 70

187 "St. Maarten Landscape"
188 Rudolf Theodorus Palm

1980. Child Welfare. Children's Drawings. Multicoloured.
737 25 c. + 10 c. Type **187** 30 30
738 30 c. + 15 c. "Bonaire House" 35 40
739 40 c. + 20 c. "Child writing on Board" 45 50
740 60 c. + 25 c. "Dancing Couple" (vert) 60 65

1981. Birth Centenary (1980) of Rudolf Theodorus Palm (musician).
742 **188** 60 c. brown and yellow . . 50 45
743 – 1 g. buff and blue . . . . 1·00 85
DESIGN: 1 g. Musical score and hands playing piano.

189 Map of Aruba and TEAM Emblem
190 Boy in Wheelchair

1981. 50th Anniv of Evangelical Alliance Mission (TEAM) in Antilles. Multicoloured.
744 30 c. Type **189** 25 20
745 50 c. Map of Curacao and emblem 50 40
746 1 g. Map of Bonaire and emblem 1·00 85

1981. International Year of Disabled Persons. Multicoloured.
747 25 c. + 10 c. Blind woman . . 35 35
748 30 c. + 15 c. Type **190** 45 45
749 45 c. + 20 c. Child in walking frame 70 70
750 60 c. + 25 c. Deaf girl 80 80

191 Tennis
192 Gateway

1981. Sports Funds. Multicoloured.
751 30 c. + 15 c. Type **191** 50 50
752 50 c. + 20 c. Swimming . . . 70 70
753 70 c. + 25 c. Boxing 90 90

1981. 125th Anniv of St. Elisabeth's Hospital. Multicoloured.
755 60 c. Type **192** 60 50
756 1 g. 50 St. Elisabeth's Hospital 1·40 1·40

193 Marinus van der Maarel (promoter)
194 Mother and Child

1981. 50th Anniv (1980) of Antillean Boy Scouts Association. Multicoloured.
757 45 c. + 20 c. Wolf Cub and leader 75 75
758 70 c. + 25 c. Type **193** . . . 1·10 1·10
759 1 g. + 50 c. Headquarters, Ronde Klip . . . . 1·60 1·60

1981. Child Welfare. Multicoloured.
761 35 c. + 15 c. Type **194** . . . 45 50
762 45 c. + 20 c. Boy and girl . . 55 60
763 55 c. + 25 c. Child with cat . . 70 75
764 85 c. + 40 c. Girl with teddy bear 1·10 1·25

195 "Jatropha gossypifolia"
196 Pilot Gig approaching Ship

1981. Flowers. Multicoloured.
766 45 c. "Cordia globosa" . . . 35 35
767 70 c. Type **195** 70 70
768 100 c. "Croton flavens" . . . 85 85

1982. Centenary of Pilotage Service. Mult.
769 70 c. Type **196** 80 80
770 85 c. Modern liner and map of Antilles . . . . 1·00 1·00
771 1 g. Pilot boarding ship . . . 1·10 1·10

197 Fencing
198 Holy Ark

1982. Sports Funds.
772 **197** 35 c. + 15 c. mauve and violet 65 50
773 – 45 c. + 20 c. blue and deep blue 85 70
774 – 70 c. + 35 c. multicoloured 1·25 95
775 – 85 c. + 40 c. brown and deep brown . . . . 1·40 1·10
DESIGNS: 45 c. Judo; 70 c. Football; 85 c. Cycling.

1982. 250th Anniv of Dedication of Mikve Israel-Emanuel Synagogue, Curacao. Mult.
777 75 c. Type **198** . . . . 1·25 90
778 85 c. Synagogue facade . . . 1·40 90
779 150 c. Tebah (raised platform) 1·75 1·40

199 Peter Stuyvesant (Governor) and Flags of Netherlands, Netherlands Antilles and United States
200 Airport Control Tower

1982. Bicentenary of Netherlands–United States Diplomatic Relations.
780 **199** 75 c. multicoloured . . . 1·00 80

1982. International Federation of Air Traffic Controllers.
782 – 35 c. black, ultramarine and blue 50 35
783 **200** 75 c. black, green and light green . . . . 1·00 75
784 – 150 c. black, orange and salmon . . . . 1·50 1·25
DESIGNS: 35 c. Radar plot trace; 150 c. Radar aerials.

201 Mail Bag

202 Brown Chromis

1982. "Philexfrance 82" International Stamp Exhibition, Paris. Multicoloured.

785 45 c. Exhibition emblem 50 40
786 85 c. Type **201** 95 75
787 150 c. Netherlands Antilles and French flags 1·40 1·25

1982. Fishes. Multicoloured.

789 35 c. Type **202** 70 40
790 75 c. Spotted trunkfish 1·25 75
791 85 c. Blue tang 1·40 1·00
792 100 c. French angelfish 1·50 1·10

203 Girl playing Accordion

1982. Child Welfare. Multicoloured.

793 35 c. + 15 c. Type **203** 80 60
794 75 c. + 35 c. Boy playing guitar 1·40 1·25
795 85 c. + 40 c. Boy playing violin 1·75 1·40

204 Saba House

1982. Cultural and Social Relief Funds. Local Houses. Multicoloured.

797 35 c. + 15 c. Type **204** 70 45
798 75 c. + 35 c. Aruba House 1·25 95
799 85 c. + 40 c. Curacao House 1·40 1·25

205 High Jumping

1983. Sports Funds. Multicoloured.

801 35 c. + 15 c. Type **205** 65 50
802 45 c. + 20 c. Weightlifting 1·00 85
803 85 c. + 40 c. Wind-surfing 1·50 1·40

206 Natural Bridge, Aruba

207 W.C.Y. Emblem and Means of Communication

1983. Tourism. Multicoloured.

804 35 c. Type **206** 60 50
805 45 c. Lac Bay, Bonaire 75 55
806 100 c. Willemstad, Curacao 1·25 1·10

1983. World Communications Year.

807 **207** 1 g. multicoloured 1·25 1·10

208 "Curacao" (paddle-steamer) and Post Office Building

209 Mango ("Mangifera indica")

1983. "Brasiliana 83" International Stamp Exhibition, Rio de Janeiro. Multicoloured.

809 45 c. Type **208** 70 60
810 55 c. Brazil flag, exhibition emblem and Netherlands Antilles flag and postal service emblem 75 65
811 100 c. Governor's Palace, Netherlands Antilles, and Sugarloaf Mountain, Rio de Janeiro 1·25 1·00

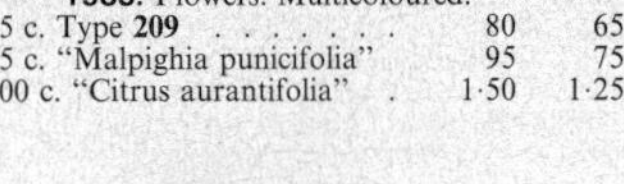

1983. Flowers. Multicoloured.

813 45 c. Type **209** 80 65
814 55 c. "Malpighia punicifolia" 95 75
815 100 c. "Citrus aurantifolia" 1·50 1·25

210 Boy and Lizard

1983. Child Welfare. Multicoloured.

816 45 c. + 20 c. Type **210** 1·00 85
817 55 c. + 25 c. Girl watching ants 1·25 1·10
818 100 c. + 50 c. Girl feeding donkey 2·00 1·75

211 Aruba Water Jar

212 Saba

1983. Cultural and Social Relief Funds. Pre-Columbian Pottery.

820 **211** 45 c. + 20 c. light blue, blue and black 1·10 1·00
821 – 55 c. + 25 c. pink, red and black 1·25 1·10
822 – 85 c. + 40 c. stone, green and black 1·50 1·25
823 – 100 c. + 50 c. light brown, brown and black 2·00 1·75

DESIGNS: 55 c. Aruba decorated bowl; 85 c. Curacao human figurine; 100 c. Fragment of Curacao female figurine.

1983. Local Government Buildings. Multicoloured.

824 20 c. Type **212** 20 20
825 25 c. St. Eustatius 25 25
826 30 c. St. Maarten 30 30
827 35 c. Aruba 1·75 35
828 45 c. Bonaire 45 45
829 55 c. Curacao 55 55
830 60 c. Type **212** 60 60
831 65 c. As No. 825 65 65
832 70 c. Type **212** 75 75
833 75 c. As No. 826 75 75
834 85 c. As No. 827 3·00 1·10
835 85 c. As No. 828 85 85
836 90 c. As No. 828 90 90
837 95 c. As No. 829 95 95
838 1 g. Type **212** 1·00 1·00
839 1 g. 50 As No. 825 1·40 1·40
841 2 g. 50 As No. 826 2·25 2·25
842 5 g. As No. 828 4·25 4·25
843 10 g. As No. 829 7·50 7·50
844 15 g. Type **212** 11·00 11·00

213 Note-taking, Type-setting and Front Page of "Amigoe"

1984. Centenary of "Amigoe de Curacao" (newspaper). Multicoloured.

845 45 c. Type **213** 65 55
846 55 c. Printing press and newspapers 75 65
847 85 c. Reading newspaper 1·25 1·10

214 W.I.A. and I.C.A.O. Emblems

1984. 40th Anniv of I.C.A.O.

848 **214** 25 c. multicoloured 40 35
849 – 45 c. violet, blue & black 75 60
850 – 55 c. multicoloured 85 70
851 – 100 c. multicoloured 1·40 1·25

DESIGNS: 45 c. I.C.A.O. anniversary emblem; 55 c. A.L.M. and I.C.A.O. emblems; 100 c. Fokker F.XIII airplane "De Snip".

215 Fielder

1984. Sports Funds. 50th Anniv of Curacao Baseball Federation. Multicoloured.

852 25 c. + 10 c. Type **215** 80 60
853 45 c. + 20 c. Batter 1·25 1·10
854 55 c. + 25 c. Pitcher 1·50 1·25
855 85 c. + 40 c. Running for base 1·75 1·50

216 Microphones and Radio

1984. Cultural and Social Relief Funds. Radio and Gramophone. Multicoloured.

857 45 c. + 20 c. Type **216** 1·25 1·10
858 55 c. + 25 c. Gramophones and record 1·50 1·40
859 100 c. + 50 c. Gramophone with horn 1·90 1·75

217 Bonnet-maker

1984. Centenary of Curacao Chamber of Commerce and Industry. Multicoloured.

860 45 c. Type **217** 1·10 85
861 55 c. Chamber emblem 1·10 90
862 1 g. "Southward" (liner) passing under bridge 1·50 1·25

No. 861 is an inverted triangle.

218 Black-faced Grassquit

219 Eleanor Roosevelt and Val-Kill, Hyde Park, New York

1984. Birds. Multicoloured.

863 45 c. Type **218** 1·10 75
864 55 c. Rufous-collared sparrow 1·50 1·00
865 150 c. Blue-tailed emerald 2·40 1·75

1984. Birth Centenary of Eleanor Roosevelt.

866 **219** 45 c. multicoloured 70 65
867 – 85 c. black, gold & bis 1·00 1·00
868 – 100 c. black, yell & red 1·10 1·10

DESIGNS: 85 c. Portrait in oval frame; 100 c. Eleanor Roosevelt with children.

220 Child Reading

221 Adult Flamingo and Chicks

1984. Child Welfare. Multicoloured.

869 45 c. + 20 c. Type **220** 1·10 1·10
870 55 c. + 25 c. Family reading 1·40 1·40
871 100 c. + 50 c. Family in church 1·75 1·75

1985. Greater Flamingoes. Multicoloured.

873 25 c. Type **221** 85 60
874 45 c. Young flamingoes 1·10 80
875 55 c. Adult flamingoes 1·40 90
876 100 c. Flamingoes in various flight positions 2·25 1·40

222 Symbols of Entered Apprentice

223 Players with Ball

1985. Bicentenary of De Vergenoeging Masonic Lodge, Curacao. Multicoloured.

877 45 c. Type **222** 1·10 75
878 55 c. Symbols of the Fellow Craft 1·40 1·10
879 100 c. Symbols of the Master Mason 2·50 1·60

1985. Sports Funds. Football. Multicoloured.

880 10 c. + 5 c. Type **223** 40 35
881 15 c. + 5 c. Dribbling ball 50 40
882 45 c. + 20 c. Running with ball 1·10 95
883 55 c. + 25 c. Tackling 1·40 1·25
884 85 c. + 40 c. Marking player with ball 1·75 1·60

224 Boy using Computer

1985. Cultural and Social Welfare Funds. International Youth Year. Multicoloured.

885 45 c. + 20 c. Type **224** 1·25 1·10
886 55 c. + 25 c. Girl listening to records 1·50 1·40
887 100 c. + 50 c. Boy break-dancing 2·25 2·00

225 U.N. Emblem

1985. 40th Anniv of U.N.O.

888 **225** 55 c. multicoloured 1·00 85
889 1 g. multicoloured 1·50 1·40

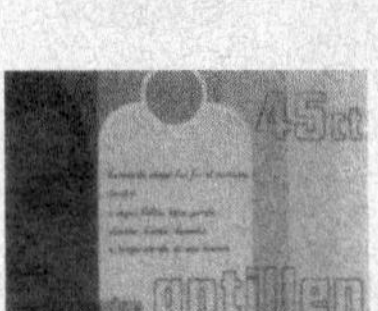
226 Pierre Lauffer and Poem

227 Eskimo

1985. Papiamentu (Creole language). Multicoloured.

890 45 c. Type **226** 50 50
891 55 c. Wave inscribe "Papiamentu" 75 75

1985. Child Welfare. Multicoloured.

892 5 c. + 5 c. Type **227** 35 20
893 10 c. + 5 c. African child 45 30
894 25 c. + 10 c. Chinese girl 65 50
895 45 c. + 20 c. Dutch girl 1·25 85
896 55 c. + 25 c. Red Indian girl 1·40 1·10

228 "Calotropis procera"

229 Courthouse

1985. Flowers. Multicoloured.

898 5 c. Type **228** 20 10
899 10 c. "Capparis flexuosa" 20 15
900 20 c. "Mimosa distachya" 45 30
901 45 c. "Ipomoea nil" 75 55
902 55 c. "Heliotropium ternatum" 90 70
903 150 c. "Ipomoea incarnata" 1·75 1·50

1986. 125th Anniv of Curacao Courthouse. Multicoloured.

904 5 c. Type **229** 15 10
905 15 c. States room (vert) 25 15
906 25 c. Court room 45 35
907 55 c. Entrance (vert) 80 70

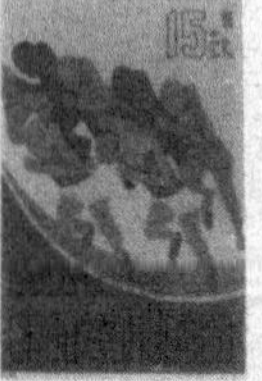
230 Sprinting

231 Girls watching Artist at work

1986. Sports Funds. Multicoloured.

908 15 c. + 5 c. Type **230** 60 35
909 25 c. + 10 c. Horse racing 85 60
910 45 c. + 20 c. Motor racing 1·25 85
911 55 c. + 25 c. Football 1·40 1·25

1986. Curacao Youth Care Foundation. Multicoloured.

912 30 c. + 15 c. Type **231** 80 55
913 45 c. + 20 c. Children watching sculptor at work 1·10 75
914 55 c. + 25 c. Children watching potter at work 1·25 1·10

232 Chained Man

1986. 25th Anniv of Amnesty International. Multicoloured.

915 45 c. Type **232** 80 55
916 55 c. Dove behind bars 90 65
917 100 c. Man behind bars 1·40 1·10

233 Post Office Mail Box **234** Boy playing Football

1986. Mail Boxes. Multicoloured.

918 10 c. Type **233** 15 10
919 25 c. Street mail box on pole 30 25
920 45 c. Street mail box in brick column 60 45
921 55 c. Street mail box 75 65

1986. Child Welfare. Multicoloured.

922 20 c. + 10 c. Type **234** 50 40
923 25 c. + 15 c. Girl playing tennis 65 55
924 45 c. + 20 c. Boy practising judo 90 75
925 55 c. + 25 c. Boy playing baseball 1·25 1·10

235 Brothers' First House and Mauritius Vliegendehond **236** Engagement Picture

1986. Centenary of Friars of Tilburg Mission. Multicoloured.

927 10 c. Type **235** 25 15
928 45 c. St. Thomas College and Mgr. Ferdinand E. C. Kieckens 80 55
929 55 c. St. Thomas College courtyard and Fr. F.S. de Beer 90 70

1987. Golden Wedding of Princess Juliana and Prince Bernhard.

930 **236** 1 g. 35 orange, blk & gold 1·75 1·40

237 Map **238** Girls playing Instruments

1987. 150th Anniv of Maduro Holding Inc. Multicoloured.

932 70 c. Type **237** 80 65
933 85 c. Group activities 90 80
934 1 g. 55 Saloman Elias Levy Maduro (founder) 1·75 1·50

1987. Cultural and Social Relief Funds.

935 **238** 35 c. + 15 c. multicoloured 70 60
936 – 45 c. + 25 c. light green, green and blue 1·00 85
937 – 85 c. + 40 c. multicoloured 1·40 1·25

DESIGNS: 45 c. Woman pushing man in wheelchair. 85 c. Bandstand.

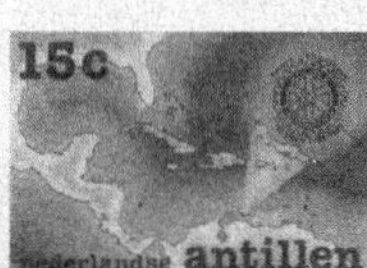

239 Map and Emblem

1987. 50th Anniv of Curacao Rotary Club. Multicoloured.

938 15 c. Type **239** 20 15
939 50 c. Zeelandia country house (meeting venue) 65 55
940 65 c. Emblem on map of Curacao 80 65

240 Octagon (house where Bolivar's sisters lived)

1987. 175th Anniv of Simon Bolivar's Exile on Curacao (60, 80 c.) and 50th Anniv of Bolivarian Society (70, 90 c.). Multicoloured.

941 60 c. Type **240** 75 65
942 70 c. Society headquarters, Willemstad, Curacao 80 70
943 80 c. Room in Octagon 1·10 90
944 90 c. Portraits of Manuel Carlos Piar, Simon Bolivar and Pedro Luis Brion 1·25 1·10

241 Baby

1987. Child Welfare. Multicoloured.

945 40 c. + 15 c. Type **241** 80 70
946 55 c. + 25 c. Child 1·25 1·10
947 115 c. + 50 c. Youth 1·75 1·60

242 White-tailed Tropic Birds

1987. 25th Anniv of Netherlands Antilles National Parks Foundation. Multicoloured.

949 70 c. Type **242** 1·00 60
950 85 c. White-tailed deer 90 75
951 155 c. Iguana 1·75 1·50

243 Printing Press and Type

1987. 175th Anniv of "De Curacaosche Courant" (periodical and printing shop). Multicoloured.

952 55 c. Type **243** 65 55
953 70 c. Keyboard and modern printing press 85 65

244 William Godden (founder)

1988. 75th Anniv of Curacao Mining Company. Multicoloured.

954 40 c. Type **244** 70 45
955 105 c. Phosphate processing plant 1·50 1·10
956 155 c. Tafelberg (source of phosphate) 2·25 1·60

245 Flags, Minutes and John Horris Sprockel (first President) **246** Bridge through "100"

1988. 50th Anniv of Netherlands Antilles Staten (legislative body). Multicoloured.

957 65 c. Type **245** 75 65
958 70 c. Ballot paper and schematic representation of extension of voting rights 75 65
959 155 c. Antilles and Netherlands flags and birds representing five Antilles islands and Aruba 1·50 1·40

1988. Cultural and Social Relief Funds. Centenary of Queen Emma Bridge, Curacao. Mult.

960 55 c. + 25 c. Type **246** 70 65
961 115 c. + 55 c. Willemstad harbour (horiz) 1·40 1·25
962 190 c. + 60 c. Leonard B. Smith (engineer) and flags (horiz) 2·50 2·40

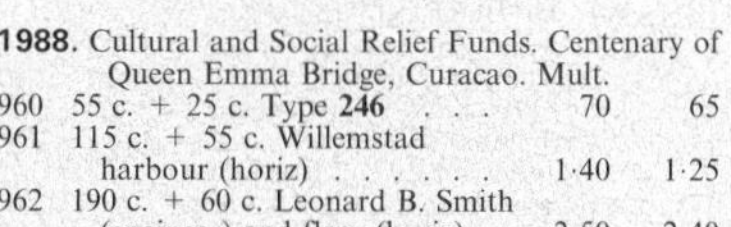

247 Broken Chain

1988. 125th Anniv of Abolition of Slavery. Mult.

963 155 c. Type **247** 1·40 1·25
964 190 c. Breach in slave wall 1·60 1·50

248 Flags and Map **249** Charles Hellmund (Bonaire councillor)

1988. 3rd Inter-American Foundation of Cities "Let us Build Bridges" Conference, Curacao. Multicoloured.

965 80 c. Type **248** 90 70
966 155 c. Bridge and globe 1·40 1·25

1988. Celebrities. Multicoloured.

967 55 c. Type **249** 55 45
968 65 c. Atthelo Maud Edwards-Jackson (founder of Saba Electric Company) 60 55
969 90 c. Nicolaas Debrot (Governor of Antilles, 1962-69) 1·00 90
970 120 c. William Charles de la Try Ellis (lawyer and politician) 1·10 1·00

250 Child watching Television **251** "Cereus hexagonus"

1988. Child Welfare. Multicoloured.

971 55 c. + 25 c. Type **250** 80 60
972 65 c. + 30 c. Boy with radio 1·10 85
973 115 c. + 55 c. Girl using computer 1·50 1·25

1988. Cacti. Multicoloured.

975 55 c. Type **251** 70 45
976 115 c. Melocactus 1·10 85
977 125 c. "Opuntia wentiana" 1·25 1·00

252 Magnifying Glass over 1936 and 1980 Stamps **253** Crested Bobwhite

1989. Cultural and Social Relief Funds. 50th Anniv of Curacao Stamp Association. Multicoloured.

978 30 c. + 10 c. Type **252** 60 40
979 55 c. + 20 c. Picking up stamp with tweezers (winning design by X. Rico in drawing competition) 85 75
980 80 c. + 30 c. Barn owl and stamp album 1·50 95

Nos. 978/80 were printed together, se-tenant, forming a composite design.

1989. 40th Anniv of Curacao Foundation for Prevention of Cruelty to Animals. Multicoloured.

981 65 c. Type **253** 1·10 55
982 115 c. Dogs and cats 1·40 90

254 "Sun Viking" in Great Bay Harbour, St. Maarten **255** Paula Clementina Dorner (teacher)

1989. Tourism. Cruise Liners. Multicoloured.

983 70 c. Type **254** 70 55
984 155 c. "Eugenio C" entering harbour, St. Annabay, Curacao 1·40 1·25

1989. Celebrities. Multicoloured.

985 40 c. Type **255** 55 35
986 55 c. John Aniseto de Jongh (pharmacist and politician) 65 45
987 90 c. Jacobo Jesus Maria Palm (musician) 95 70
988 120 c. Abraham Mendes Chumaceiro (lawyer and social campaigner) 1·25 1·00

256 Boy and Girl under Tree **257** Hand holding "7"

1989. Child Welfare. Multicoloured.

989 40 c. + 15 c. Type **256** 75 60
990 65 c. + 30 c. Two children playing on shore 1·10 85
991 115 c. + 35 c. Adult carrying child 1·60 1·40

1989. 40th Anniv of Queen Wilhelmina Foundation for Cancer Care. Multicoloured.

993 30 c. Type **257** 40 25
994 60 c. Seated figure and figure receiving radiation treatment 65 55
995 80 c. Figure exercising and Foundation emblem 80 70

258 Fireworks **259** "Tephrosia cinerea"

1989. Christmas. Multicoloured.

997 30 c. Type **258** 40 25
998 100 c. Christmas tree decorations 1·10 85

1990. Flowers. Multicoloured.

999 30 c. Type **259** 35 30
1000 55 c. "Erithalis fruticosa" 60 50
1001 65 c. "Evolvulus antillanus" 70 60
1002 70 c. "Jacquinia arborea" 80 65
1003 125 c. "Tournefortia onaphalodes" 1·40 1·25
1004 155 c. "Sesuvium portulacastrum" 1·75 1·40

260 Girl Guides **261** Nun with Child, Flag and Map

1990. Cultural and Social Relief Funds. Mult.

1005 30 c. + 10 c. Type **260** (60th anniv) 50 50
1006 40 c. + 15 c. Totolika (care of mentally handicapped organization) (17th anniv) 65 65
1007 155 c. + 65 c. Boy scout (60th anniv) 2·50 2·50

1990. Centenary of Arrival of Dominican Nuns in Netherlands Antilles. Multicoloured.

1008 10 c. Type **261** 15 10
1009 55 c. St. Rose Hospital and St. Martin's Home, St. Maarten 65 55
1010 60 c. St. Joseph School, St. Maarten 70 60

262 Goal Net, Ball and Shield **263** Carlos Nicolaas-Perez (philologist and poet)

1990. Multicoloured.

1011 65 c. + 30 c. Type **262** (65th anniv of Sport Unie Brion Trappers football club) 1·10 1·10
1012 115 c. + 55 c. Guiding addict from darkness towards sun (anti-drugs campaign) 2·25 2·25

1990. Meritorious Antilleans. Multicoloured.

1013 40 c. Type **263** 45 40
1014 60 c. Evert Kruythoff (writer) 65 55
1015 80 c. John de Pool (writer) . 90 75
1016 150 c. Joseph Sickman Corsen (poet and composer) . . . 1·75 1·40

264 Queen Emma **265** Isla Refinery

1990. Dutch Queens of the House of Orange. Multicoloured.

1017 100 c. Type **264** . . . . . . 1·10 90
1018 100 c. Queen Wilhelmina . . 1·10 90
1019 100 c. Queen Juliana . . . . 1·10 90
1020 100 c. Queen Beatrix . . . . 1·10 90

1990. 75th Anniv of Oil Refining on Curacao.

1022 **265** 100 c. multicoloured . . 1·40 1·25

266 Flower and Bees **267** Parcels

1990. Child Welfare. International Literacy Year. Designs illustrating letters of alphabet. Multicoloured.

1023 30 c. + 5 c. Type **266** 40 40
1024 55 c. + 10 c. Dolphins and sun 75 75
1025 65 c. + 15 c. Donkey with bicycle 95 95
1026 100 c. + 20 c. Goat dreaming of house . . . . 1·40 1·40
1027 115 c. + 25 c. Rabbit carrying food on yoke . . . . . . 1·60 1·60
1028 155 c. + 55 c. Lizard, moon and cactus . . . . 2·40 2·40

1990. Christmas. Multicoloured.

1029 30 c. Type **267** (25th anniv of Curacao Lions Club's Good Neighbour project) 35 30
1030 100 c. Mother and child . . . 1·10 90

268 Flag, Map and Distribution of Mail **269** Scuba Diver and French Grunt

1991. 6th Anniv of Express Mail Service.

1031 **268** 20 g. multicoloured . . . 18·00 14·00

1991. Fishes. Multicoloured.

1032 10 c. Type **269** 15 10
1033 40 c. Spotted trunkfish . . . 50 40
1034 55 c. Coppersweepers 70 60
1035 75 c. Skindiver and yellow goatfishes 90 75
1036 100 c. Blackbar soldier-fishes 1·25 1·00

270 Children and Stamps

1991. Cultural and Social Relief Funds. Mult.

1037 30 c. + 10 c. Type **270** (12th anniv of Philatelic Club of Curacao) 50 50
1038 65 c. + 25 c. St. Vincentius Brass Band (50th anniv) . . 1·10 1·10
1039 155 c. + 55 c. Games and leisure pursuits (30th anniv of FESEBAKO) (Curacao community centres) . . . . 2·40 2·40

271 "Good Luck" **272** Westpoint Lighthouse, Curacao

1991. Greetings Stamps. Multicoloured.

1040 30 c. Type **271** 35 30
1041 30 c. "Thank You" 35 30
1042 30 c. Couple and family ("Love You") 35 30
1043 30 c. Song birds ("Happy Day") 50 30
1044 30 c. Greater flamingo and medicines ("Get Well Soon") 50 30
1045 30 c. Flowers and balloons ("Happy Birthday") . . . 35 30

1991. Lighthouses. Multicoloured.

1046 30 c. Type **272** 45 40
1047 70 c. Willems Toren, Bonaire 1·00 80
1048 115 c. Klein Curacao lighthouse 1·90 1·60

273 Peter Stuyvesant College

1991. 50th Anniv of Secondary Education in Netherlands Antilles (65 c.) and "Espamer '91" Spain–Latin America Stamp Exhibition, Buenos Aires (125 c.). Multicoloured.

1049 65 c. Type **273** 75 60
1050 125 c. Dancers of Netherlands Antilles, Argentina and Portugal (vert) . . . . . 1·40 1·25

274 Octopus with Letters and Numbers **275** Nativity

1991. Child Welfare. Multicoloured.

1051 40 c. + 15 c. Type **274** . . . 90 90
1052 65 c. + 30 c. Parents teaching arithmetic . . . . 1·25 1·25
1053 155 c. + 65 c. Bird and tortoise with clock . . . . 2·50 2·50

1991. Christmas. Multicoloured.

1055 30 c. Type **275** 35 30
1056 100 c. Angel appearing to shepherds . . . . 1·25 1·00

276 Joseph Alvarez Correa (founder) and Headquarters of S.E.L. Maduro and Sons **277** Fawn

1991. 75th Anniv of Maduro and Curiel's Bank. Multicoloured.

1057 30 c. Type **276** 40 35
1058 70 c. Lion rampant (bank's emblem) and "75" 75 60
1059 155 c. Isaac Haim Capriles (Managing Director, 1954-74) and Scharloo bank branch 1·60 1·40

1992. The White-tailed Deer. Multicoloured.

1060 5 c. Type **277** (postage) . . . 10 10
1061 10 c. Young adults 10 10
1062 30 c. Stag 30 25
1063 40 c. Stag and hind in water 35 30
1064 200 c. Stag drinking (air) . . 1·75 1·40
1065 355 c. Stag calling . . . . . 2·75 2·25

278 Windsurfer **280** "Santa Maria"

1992. Cultural and Social Relief Funds. Olympic Games, Barcelona. Multicoloured.

1066 30 c. + 10 c. Type **278** (award of silver medal to Jan Boersma, 1988 Games) . . 35 35
1067 55 c. + 25 c. Globe, national flag and Olympic rings . . 65 65
1068 115 c. + 55 c. Emblem of National Olympic Committee (60th anniv) . . . . 1·40 1·40

Nos. 1066/8 were issued together, se-tenant, forming a composite design.

1992. "World Columbian Stamp Expo '92", Chicago. Multicoloured.

1070 250 c. Type **280** . . . . . . 2·00 1·60
1071 500 c. Chart and Columbus . 4·00 3·25

281 View of Dock and Town **282** Angela de Lannoy-Willems

1992. Curacao Port Container Terminal. Mult.

1072 80 c. Type **281** 60 50
1073 125 c. Crane and ship 95 80

1992. Celebrities.

1074 **282** 30 c. black, brown & grn 35 20
1075 – 40 c. black, brown & bl . 30 25
1076 – 55 c. black, brown & orge 40 35
1077 – 70 c. black, brown & red 55 45
1078 – 100 c. black, brown & bl . 75 60

DESIGNS: 30 c. Type **282** (first woman Member of Parliament); 40 c. Lodewijk Daniel Gerharts (entrepreneur on Bonaire); 55 c. Cyrus Wilberforce Wathey (entrepreneur on St. Maarten); 70 c. Christian Winkel (Deputy Governor of Antilles); 100 c. Mother Joseph (founder of Roosendaal Congregation (Franciscan welfare sisterhood)).

283 Spaceship **284** Queen Beatrix and Prince Claus

1992. Child Welfare. Multicoloured.

1079 30 c. + 10 c. Type **283** 30 30
1080 70 c. + 30 c. Robot 75 75
1081 100 c. + 40 c. Extra-terrestrial being . . . . 1·00 1·00

1992. $12\frac{1}{2}$ Years since Accession to the Throne of Queen Beatrix (100 c.) and Royal Visit to Netherlands Antilles (others). Designs showing photos of previous visits to the Antilles. Multi.

1083 70 c. Type **284** 55 45
1084 100 c. Queen Beatrix signing book 75 60
1085 175 c. Queen Beatrix and Prince Claus with girl . . . . . . 1·25 1·00

285 Crib **286** Hibiscus

1992. Christmas. Multicoloured.

1086 30 c. Type **285** 25 20
1087 100 c. Mary and Joseph searching for lodgings (vert) 75 60

1993. Flowers. Multicoloured.

1088 75 c. Type **286** 55 45
1089 90 c. Sunflower 70 60
1090 175 c. Ixora . . . . 1·25 1·00
1091 195 c. Rose . . . . 1·50 1·25

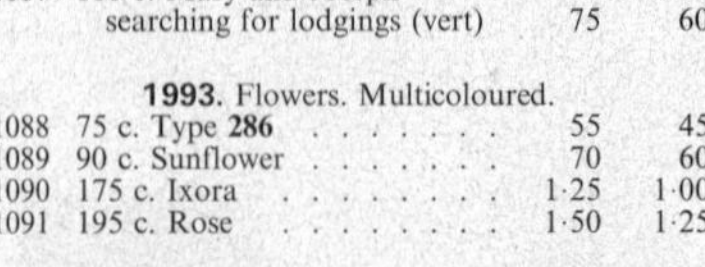

287 De Havilland Twin Otter and Flight Paths **288** Pekingese

1993. Anniversaries. Multicoloured.

1092 65 c. Type **287** (50th anniv of Princess Juliana International Airport, St. Maarten) . . . 50 40
1093 75 c. Laboratory worker and National Health Laboratory (75th anniv) 55 45
1094 90 c. De Havilland Twin Otter on runway at Princess Juliana International Airport . . . 70 60
1095 175 c. White and yellow cross (50th anniv of Princess Margriet White and Yellow Cross Foundation for District Nursing) . . . . 1·25 1·00

1993. Dogs. Multicoloured.

1096 65 c. Type **288** 50 40
1097 90 c. Standard Poodle . . . 70 70
1098 100 c. Pomeranian 75 60
1099 175 c. Papillon . . . . 1·25 1·00

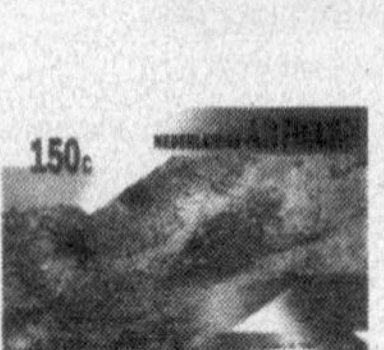

289 Cave Painting, Bonaire **290** "Sun and Sea"

1993. "Brasiliana '93" International Stamp Exhibition, Rio de Janeiro, and Admittance of Antilles to Postal Union of the Americas, Spain and Portugal. Multicoloured.

1100 150 c. Type **289** . . . . . . 1·10 90
1101 200 c. Exhibition emblem and Antilles flag . . . . 1·50 1·25
1102 250 c. Globe and hand signing U.P.A.E.P. agreement . . 1·90 1·60

1993. "Carib-Art" Exhibition, Curacao. Multicoloured.

1103 90 c. Type **290** 70 60
1104 150 c. "Heaven and Earth" . . 1·10 90

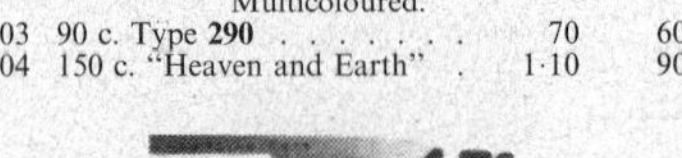

291 "Safety in the Home"

1993. Child Welfare. Child and Danger. Mult.

1105 65 c. + 25 c. Type **291** . . . 70 70
1106 90 c. + 35 c. Child using seat belt ("Safety in the Car") (vert) 95 95
1107 175 c. + 75 c. Child wearing armbands ("Safety in the Water") . . . . 1·90 1·90

292 Consulate, Curacao **293** "Mother and Child" (mosaic)

1993. Bicentenary of United States Consul General to the Antilles. Multicoloured.

1109 65 c. Type **292** 50 40
1110 90 c. Arms of Netherlands Antilles and U.S.A. . . . 70 60
1111 175 c. American bald eagle . 2·25 1·00

1993. Christmas. Works by Lucilia Engels-Boskaljon. Multicoloured.

1112 30 c. Type **293** 20 15
1113 115 c. "Madonna and Christ" (painting) 80 65

294 Basset Hound **295** Common Caracara

1994. Dogs. Multicoloured.

1114 65 c. Type **294** 45 35
1115 75 c. Pit bull terrier 55 45
1116 90 c. Cocker spaniel 65 55
1117 175 c. Chow-chow . . . . . 1·25 1·00

1994. Birds. Multicoloured.

1118 50 c. Type **295** 35 30
1119 95 c. Green peafowl 65 55
1120 100 c. Scarlet macaw 70 60
1121 125 c. Troupial 90 75

296 Joseph Husurell Lake (founder of United People's Liberation Front) **297** Players' Legs

1994. Celebrities. Multicoloured.

No.	Description	Mint	Used
1122	65 c. Type **296**	45	35
1123	75 c. Efrain Jonckheer (politician and diplomat)	55	45
1124	100 c. Michiel Martinus Romer (teacher)	70	60
1125	175 c. Carel Nicolaas Winkel (social reformer)	1·25	1·00

1994. World Cup Football Championship, U.S.A. Multicoloured.

No.	Description	Mint	Used
1126	90 c. Type **297**	60	55
1127	150 c. Foot and ball	1·10	90
1128	175 c. Referee's whistle and cards	1·25	1·00

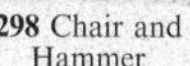

298 Chair and Hammer **299** Birds and Dolphin

1994. 75th Anniv of International Labour Organization. Multicoloured.

No.	Description	Mint	Used
1129	90 c. Type **298**	60	55
1130	110 c. Heart and "75"	80	65
1131	200 c. Tree	1·40	1·25

1994. Nature Protection. Multicoloured.

No.	Description	Mint	Used
1132	10 c. Type **299**	10	10
1133	35 c. Dolphin, magnificent frigate bird, brown pelican and troupial	25	20
1134	50 c. Coral, iguana, lobster and fish	35	30
1135	125 c. Fish, turtle, queen conch, greater flamingos and American wigeons	90	75

300 1945 $7\frac{1}{2}$ c. Netherlands Stamp **301** Mother and Child

1994. "Fepapost '94" European Stamp Exhibition, The Hague. Multicoloured.

No.	Description	Mint	Used
1137	2 g. 50 Type **300**	1·75	1·40
1138	5 g. 1933 6 c. Curacao stamp	3·50	3·00

1994. Child Welfare. International Year of the Family. Multicoloured.

No.	Description	Mint	Used
1140	35 c. + 15 c. Type **301**	35	35
1141	65 c. + 25 c. Father and daughter reading together	60	60
1142	90 c. + 35 c. Grandparents	90	90

302 Dove in Hands

1994. Christmas. Multicoloured.

No.	Description	Mint	Used
1144	30 c. Type **302**	20	15
1145	115 c. Globe and planets in hands	80	65

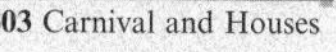

303 Carnival and Houses **304** Handicapped and Able-bodied Children

1995. Carnival. Multicoloured.

No.	Description	Mint	Used
1146	125 c. Type **303**	90	75
1147	175 c. Carnival and harbour	1·25	1·00
1148	250 c. Carnival and rural house	1·75	1·40

1995. 50th Anniv of Mgr. Verriet Institute (for the physically handicapped). Multicoloured.

No.	Description	Mint	Used
1149	65 c. Type **304**	45	35
1150	90 c. Cedric Virginie (wheelchair-bound bookbinder)	65	55

305 Dobermann

1995. Dogs. Multicoloured.

No.	Description	Mint	Used
1151	75 c. Type **305**	55	45
1152	85 c. German shepherd	60	50
1153	100 c. Bouvier	70	60
1154	175 c. St. Bernard	1·25	1·00

306 Bonaire

1995. Flags and Arms of the Constituent Islands of the Netherlands Antilles. Multicoloured.

No.	Description	Mint	Used
1155	10 c. Type **306**	10	10
1156	35 c. Curacao	25	20
1157	50 c. St. Maarten	35	30
1158	65 c. Saba	45	40
1159	75 c. St. Eustatius (also state flag and arms)	55	45
1160	90 c. Island flags and state arms	65	55

307 Monument to Slave Revolt of 1795 **309** Sealpoint Siamese

1995. Cultural and Social Relief Funds. Bicentenary of Abolition of Slavery in the Antilles (1161/2) and Children's Drawings on Philately (1163/4). Multicoloured.

No.	Description	Mint	Used
1161	30 c. + 10 c. Type **307**	30	30
1162	45 c. + 15 c. Swallow and slave bell	45	45
1163	65 c. + 25 c. "Stamps" from Curacao and Bonaire (Nicole Wever and Sabine Anthonio)	65	65
1164	75 c. + 35 c. "Stamps" from St. Maarten, St. Eustatius and Saba (Chad Jacobs, Martha Hassell and Dion Humphreys)	80	80

1995. Hurricane Relief Fund. Nos. 831, 833 and 838 surch **ORKAAN LUIS** and premium.

No.	Description	Mint	Used
1165	65 c. + 65 c. multicoloured	95	95
1166	75 c. + 75 c. multicoloured	1·10	1·10
1167	1 g. + 1 g. multicoloured	1·50	1·50

1995. Cats. Multicoloured.

No.	Description	Mint	Used
1168	25 c. Type **309**	20	15
1169	60 c. Maine coon	45	40
1170	65 c. Silver Egyptian mau	45	40
1171	90 c. Angora	65	55
1172	150 c. Blue smoke Persian	1·10	90

310 Helping Elderly Woman across Road

1995. Child Welfare. Children and Good Deeds. Multicoloured.

No.	Description	Mint	Used
1173	35 c. + 15 c. Type **310**	35	35
1174	65 c. + 25 c. Reading newspaper to blind person	65	65
1175	90 c. + 35 c. Helping younger brother	90	90
1176	175 c. + 75 c. Giving flowers to the sick	1·75	1·75

311 Wise Men on Camels **312** Serving the Community

1995. Christmas. Multicoloured.

No.	Description	Mint	Used
1177	30 c. Type **311**	20	15
1178	115 c. Fireworks over houses	85	70

1996. 50th Anniv of Curacao Lions Club. Multicoloured.

No.	Description	Mint	Used
1179	75 c. Type **312**	55	45
1180	105 c. Anniversary emblem	75	60
1181	250 c. Handshake	1·90	1·60

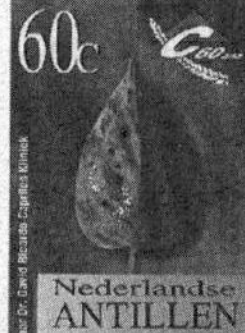

313 Disease on Half of Leaf **314** Dish Aerial and Face

1996. 60th Anniv of Capriles Psychiatric Clinic, Otrabanda on Rif. Multicoloured.

No.	Description	Mint	Used
1182	60 c. Type **313**	45	40
1183	75 c. Tornado and sun over house	55	45

1996. Centenary of Guglielmo Marconi's Patented Wireless Telegraph. Multicoloured.

No.	Description	Mint	Used
1184	85 c. Type **314**	60	50
1185	175 c. Dish aerial and morse transmitter	1·25	1·00

315 Letters and Buildings **316** Gulf Fritillary

1996. Translation of Bible into Papiamentu (Creole language). Multicoloured.

No.	Description	Mint	Used
1186	85 c. Type **315**	60	50
1187	225 c. Bible and alphabets	1·60	1·40

1996. "Capex'96" International Stamp Exhibition, Toronto, Canada. Butterflies. Multicoloured.

No.	Description	Mint	Used
1188	5 c. Type **316**	10	10
1189	110 c. "Callithea philotima"	80	65
1190	300 c. Clipper	2·25	1·90
1191	750 c. "Euphaedra francina"	5·50	4·50

317 Mary Johnson-Hassell (introducer of drawn-thread work to Saba, 57th death)

1996. Anniversaries.

No.	Type	Description	Mint	Used
1193	**317**	40 c. orange and black on grey	30	25
1194	–	50 c. green and black on grey	35	30
1195	–	75 c. red and black on grey	55	45
1196	–	80 c. blue and black on grey	60	50

DESIGNS: 50 c. Cornelius Marten (Papa Cornes) (pastor to Bonaire, 144th death); 75 c. Phelippi Chakutoe (union leader, 105th birth); 85 c. Chris Engels (physician, artist, author and fencing champion, 16th death).

318 Shire

1996. Horses. Multicoloured.

No.	Description	Mint	Used
1197	110 c. Type **318**	80	65
1198	225 c. Shetland ponies	1·60	1·40
1199	275 c. British thoroughbred	2·00	1·60
1200	350 c. Przewalski mare & foal	2·50	2·00

POSTAGE DUE STAMPS

1952. As Type D **121** of Netherlands but inscr "NEDERLANDSE ANTILLEN".

No.	Description	Mint	Used
D336	1 c. green	10	10
D337	$2\frac{1}{2}$ c. green	60	60
D338	5 c. green	20	10
D339	6 c. green	65	50
D340	7 c. green	65	50
D341	8 c. green	65	50
D342	9 c. green	65	50
D343	10 c. green	30	15
D344	$12\frac{1}{2}$ c. green	30	15
D345	15 c. green	35	25
D346	20 c. green	35	45
D347	25 c. green	65	10
D348	30 c. green	1·25	1·50
D349	35 c. green	1·50	1·50
D350	40 c. green	1·25	1·50
D351	45 c. green	1·50	1·50
D352	50 c. green	1·25	1·25

NETHERLANDS INDIES Pt. 4

A former Dutch colony, consisting of numerous settlements in the East Indies, of which the islands of Java and Sumatra and parts of Borneo and New Guinea are the most important. Renamed Indonesia in 1948, Independence was granted during 1949. Netherlands New Guinea remained a Dutch possession until 1962 when it was placed under U.N. control, being incorporated with Indonesia in 1963.

100 cents = 1 gulden

1 King William III **2**

1864. Imperf.

No.	Type	Description	Mint	Used
1	**1**	10 c. red	£275	£100

1868. Perf.

No.	Type	Description	Mint	Used
2	**1**	10 c. red	£1000	£160

1870. Perf.

No.	Type	Description	Mint	Used
27	**2**	1 c. green	3·50	1·75
28		2 c. purple	£100	90·00
29		2 c. brown	6·75	3·75
30		$2\frac{1}{2}$ c. buff	35·00	24·00
12		5 c. green	55·00	4·50
32		10 c. brown	14·50	15
51		$12\frac{1}{2}$ c. drab	45·00	19·00
34		15 c. brown	20·00	1·90
5		20 c. blue	90·00	2·75
36		25 c. purple	20·00	1·10
55		30 c. green	32·00	3·75
17		50 c. red	20·00	1·50
38		2 g. 50 green and purple	85·00	15·00

5 **6** Queen Wilhelmina

1883.

No.	Type	Description	Mint	Used
89	**5**	1 c. green	1·10	10
90		2 c. brown	1·10	10
91		$2\frac{1}{2}$ c. buff	1·10	55
92		3 c. purple	1·25	10
88		5 c. green	30·00	20·00
93		5 c. blue	11·00	10

1892.

No.	Type	Description	Mint	Used
94	**6**	10 c. brown	4·50	15
95		$12\frac{1}{2}$ c. grey	8·25	14·50
96		15 c. brown	13·00	1·25
97		20 c. blue	29·00	1·50
98		25 c. purple	27·00	1·25
99		30 c. green	40·00	1·75
100		50 c. red	25·00	1·25
101		2 g. 50 blue and brown	£110	32·00

1900. Netherlands stamps of 1898 surch **NED.-INDIE** and value.

No.	Type	Description	Mint	Used
111	**13**	10 c. on 10 c. lilac	1·75	10
112		$12\frac{1}{2}$ c. on $12\frac{1}{2}$ c. blue	2·75	80
113		15 c. on 15 c. brown	2·75	45
114		20 c. on 20 c. green	14·50	65
115		25 c. on 25 c. blue & pink	14·50	80
116		50 c. on 50 c. red & green	23·00	90
117	**11**	$2\frac{1}{2}$ g. on $2\frac{1}{2}$ g. lilac	50·00	14·50

1902. Surch.

No.	Type	Description	Mint	Used
118	**5**	$\frac{1}{2}$ on 2 c. brown	20	20
119		$2\frac{1}{2}$ on 3 c. purple	25	25

1902. As T **11/13** of Surinam but inscr "NEDERLANDSCH-INDIE".

No.	Description	Mint	Used
120	$\frac{1}{2}$ c. lilac	30	10
121	1 c. olive	30	10
122	2 c. brown	3·50	15
123	$2\frac{1}{2}$ c. green	1·75	10
124	3 c. orange	2·25	1·00
125	4 c. blue	11·50	9·25
126	5 c. red	4·50	10
127	$7\frac{1}{2}$ c. grey	3·00	25
128	10 c. slate	1·00	10
129	$12\frac{1}{2}$ c. blue	1·40	10
130	15 c. brown	8·25	1·75
131	$17\frac{1}{2}$ c. bistre	3·00	15
132	20 c. grey	1·40	1·40
133	20 c. olive	22·00	10
134	$22\frac{1}{2}$ c. olive and brown	3·50	15
135	25 c. mauve	9·25	10
136	30 c. brown	25·00	10
137	50 c. red	20·00	10
138	1 g. lilac	45·00	20
206	1 g. lilac on blue	55·00	6·50
139	$2\frac{1}{2}$ g. grey	60·00	1·25
207	$2\frac{1}{2}$ g. grey on blue	80·00	29·00

1902. No. 130 optd with horiz bars.

No.	Description	Mint	Used
140	15 c. brown	1·50	55

1905. No. 132 surch **10 cent.**

No.	Description	Mint	Used
141	10 c. on 20 c. grey	2·40	90

1908. Stamps of 1902 optd **JAVA.**

No.	Description	Mint	Used
142	$\frac{1}{2}$ c. lilac	15	20
143	1 c. olive	15	15
144	2 c. brown	2·25	1·90
145	$2\frac{1}{2}$ c. green	1·25	10
146	3 c. orange	90	1·00
147	5 c. red	2·50	10
148	$7\frac{1}{2}$ c. grey	2·25	1·90
149	10 c. slate	80	10

150 12½ c. blue 2·25 40
151 15 c. brown 2·75 2·75
152 17½ c. bistre 1·75 60
153 20 c. olive 10·00 40
154 22½ c. olive and brown 4·50 2·25
155 25 c. mauve 4·50 15
156 30 c. brown 25·00 2·25
157 50 c. red 16·00 45
158 1 g. lilac 40·00 2·50
159 2½ g. grey 55·00 42·00

1908. Stamps of 1902 optd **BUITEN BEZIT**.

160 ½ c. lilac 20 20
161 1 c. olive 25 15
162 2 c. brown 1·60 1·90
163 2½ c. green 90 15
164 3 c. orange 80 90
165 5 c. red 2·50 30
166 7½ c. grey 2·75 2·25
167 10 c. slate 75 10
168 12½ c. blue 8·25 2·00
169 15 c. brown 4·00 2·40
170 17½ c. bistre 1·90 1·50
171 20 c. olive 8·00 1·75
172 22½ c. olive and brown 6·00 3·75
173 25 c. mauve 6·50 25
174 30 c. brown 14·50 1·60
175 50 c. red 6·25 55
176 1 g. lilac 48·00 3·75
177 2½ g. grey 75·00 55·00

1912. As T **18/19** of Surinam, but inscr "NEDERLANDSCH-INDIE" (T **18**) or "NEDERL-INDIE" (T **19**).

208 **18** ½ c. lilac 10 10
209 1 c. green 15 10
210 2 c. brown 30 10
264 2 c. grey 30 10
211 2½ c. green 1·10 10
265 2½ c. pink 25 10
212 3 c. brown 30 10
266 3 c. green 1·10 10
213 4 c. blue 1·10 15
267 4 c. green 1·25 15
268 4 c. bistre 8·00 4·00
214 5 c. pink 1·25 10
269 5 c. green 1·10 10
270 5 c. blue 90 10
215 7½ c. brown 90 10
271 7½ c. bistre 90 10
216 **19** 10 c. red 1·25 10
272 **18** 10 c. lilac 1·25 10
217 **19** 12½ c. blue 1·10 10
273 12½ c. red 1·10 10
274 15 c. blue 6·50 10
218 17½ c. brown 1·10 10
219 20 c. green 1·90 10
275 20 c. blue 1·90 10
276 20 c. orange 12·00 10
220 22½ c. orange 1·90 50
221 25 c. mauve 1·90 10
222 30 c. grey 1·90 10
277 32½ c. violet and orange 1·90 15
278 35 c. brown 7·50 50
279 40 c. green 2·25 10

1913. As T **20** of Surinam but inscr "NED. INDIE".

223 50 c. green 4·50 10
280 60 c. blue 5·50 10
281 80 c. orange 4·50 10
224 1 g. brown 3·75 10
283 1 g. 75 lilac 16·00 1·75
225 2½ g. pink 12·00 35

1915. Red Cross. Stamps of 1912 surch **+5 cts.** and red cross.

243 1 c. + 5 c. green 4·50 4·50
244 5 c. + 5 c. pink 4·50 4·25
245 10 c. + 5 c. red 7·50 7·00

1917. Stamps of 1902, 1912 and 1913 surch.

246 ½ c. on 2½ c. (No. 211) 20 20
247 1 c. on 4 c. (No. 213) 45 45
250 12½ c. on 17½ c. (No. 218) 25 10
251 12½ c. on 22½ c. (No. 220) 35 10
248 17½ c. on 22½ c. (No. 134) 1·75 70
252 20 c. on 22½ c. (No. 220) 35 10
249 30 c. on 1 g. (No. 138) 6·50 1·75
253 32½ c. on 50 c. (No. 223) 1·25 10
254 40 c. on 50 c. (No. 223) 3·75 40
255 60 c. on 1 g. (No. 224) 6·00 30
256 80 c. on 1 g. (No. 224) 6·75 75

1922. Bandoeng Industrial Fair. Stamps of 1912 and 1917 optd **3de N. I. JAARBEURS BANDOENG 1922.**

285 1 c. green 6·00 5·50
286 2 c. brown 6·00 5·50
287 2½ c. pink 50·00 60·00
288 3 c. yellow 6·00 7·25
289 4 c. blue 32·00 30·00
290 5 c. green 11·00 9·00
291 7½ c. brown 7·50 5·50
292 10 c. lilac 55·00 70·00
293 12½ c. on 22½ c. orge (No. 251) 6·00 6·00
294 17½ c. brown 3·75 4·50
295 20 c. blue 6·00 4·50

Nos. 285/95 were sold at a premium for 3, 4, 5, 6, 8, 9, 10, 12½, 15, 20 and 22 c. respectively.

33

36 Fokker F.VIIa

1923. Queen's Silver Jubilee.

296 **33** 5 c. green 15 10
297 12½ c. red 15 10
298 20 c. blue 25 10
299 50 c. orange 1·25 50
300 1 g. purple 2·75 30
301 2½ g. grey 27·00 18·00
302 5 g. brown 90·00 £100

1928. Air. Stamps of 1912 and 1913 surch **LUCHTPOST**, Fokker F.VII airplane and value.

303 10 c. on 12½ c. red 1·25 1·25
304 20 c. on 25 c. mauve 2·50 2·50
305 40 c. on 80 c. orange 2·00 2·00
306 75 c. on 1 g. sepia 85 50
307 1½ g. on 2½ g. red 6·25 6·00

1928. Air.

308 **36** 10 c. purple 30 15
309 20 c. brown 75 50
310 40 c. red 1·00 50
311 75 c. green 2·00 15
312 1 g. 50 orange 4·00 50

1930. Air. Surch **30** between bars.

313 **36** 30 c. on 40 c. red 1·10 15

38 Watch-tower

40 M. P. Pattist in Flight

1930. Child Welfare. Centres in brown.

315 – 2 c. + 1 c. mauve 1·25 1·10
316 **38** 5 c. + 2½ c. green 4·50 3·00
317 – 12½ c. + 2½ c. red 3·75 75
318 – 15 c. + 5 c. blue 5·25 5·25

DESIGNS—VERT: 2 c. Bali Temple. HORIZ: 12½ c. Minangkabau Compound; 15 c. Buddhist Temple, Borobudur.

1930. No. 275 surch **12½**.

319 12½ c. on 20 c. blue 60 10

1931. Air. 1st Java–Australia Mail.

320 **40** 1 g. brown and blue 13·00 11·00

41

1931. Air.

321 **41** 30 c. red 2·25 10
322 4½ g. blue 8·00 3·00
323 7½ g. green 10·00 3·25

42 Ploughing

1931. Lepers' Colony.

324 **42** 2 c. + 1 c. brown 2·75 2·00
325 – 5 c. + 2½ c. green 4·00 3·75
326 – 12½ c. + 2½ c. red 3·25 45
327 – 15 c. + 5 c. blue 8·00 6·50

DESIGNS: 5 c. Fishing; 12½ c. Native actors; 15 c. Native musicians.

1932. Air. Surch **50** on Fokker F.VIIa/3m airplane.

328 **36** 50 c. on 1 g. 50 c. orange 2·50 35

44 Plaiting Rattan

45 William of Orange

1932. Salvation Army. Centres in brown.

329 – 2 c. + 1 c. purple 40 30
330 **44** 5 c. + 2½ c. green 2·75 2·25
331 – 12½ c. + 2½ c. red 85 25
332 – 15 c. + 5 c. blue 3·75 3·00

DESIGNS: 2 c. Weaving; 12½ c. Textile worker; 15 c. Metal worker.

1933. 400th Birth Anniv of William I of Orange.

333 **45** 12½ c. red 1·25 15

46 Rice Cultivation

47 Queen Wilhelmina

1933.

335 **46** 1 c. violet 20 10
397 2 c. purple 10 15
337 2½ c. bistre 20 10
338 3 c. green 20 15
339 3½ c. grey 15 15
340 4 c. green 75 10
401 5 c. blue 10 10
342 7½ c. violet 1·25 10
343 10 c. red 1·75 10
403 **47** 10 c. red 10 10
334 12½ c. brown 8·00 25
345 12½ c. red 25 10
404 15 c. blue 10 10
405 20 c. purple 20 10
348 25 c. green 1·90 10
349 30 c. blue 2·75 10
350 32½ c. bistre 8·00 6·50
408 35 c. violet 5·50 1·10
352 40 c. green 2·50 10
353 42½ c. yellow 2·50 20
354 50 c. blue 3·75 15
355 60 c. blue 4·50 40
356 80 c. red 5·00 60
357 1 g. violet 7·50 30
358 1 g. 75 green 16·00 13·00
414 2 g. green 26·00 13·00
359 2 g. 50 purple 20·00 1·75
415 5 g. bistre 23·00 6·25

The 50 c. to 5 g. are larger, 30×30 mm.

48 Pander S.4 Postjager

1933. Air. Special Flights.

360 **48** 30 c. blue 1·40 1·40

49 Woman and Lotus Blossom

53 Cavalryman and Wounded Soldier

1933. Y.M.C.A. Charity.

361 **49** 2 c. + 1 c. brown & purple 70 45
362 – 5 c. + 2½ c. brown & green 2·25 2·00
363 – 12½ c. + 2½ c. brown & orge 2·50 25
364 – 15 c. + 5 c. brown & blue 3·25 2·25

DESIGNS: 5 c. Symbolising the sea of life; 12½ c. Y.M.C.A. emblem; 15 c. Unemployed man.

1934. Surch.

365 **36** 2 c. on 10 c. purple 25 45
366 2 c. on 20 c. brown 20 20
367 **41** 2 c. on 30 c. red 35 75
368 **36** 42½ c. on 75 c. green 4·00 25
369 42½ c. on 1 g. 50 orange 4·00 35

1934. Anti-Tuberculosis Fund. As T **77** of Netherlands.

370 12½ c. + 2½ c. brown 1·60 45

1935. Christian Military Home.

371 – 2 c. + 1 c. brown & purple 1·40 1·50
372 **53** 5 c. + 2½ c. brown & grn 3·50 3·50
373 – 12½ c. + 2½ c. brown & orge 3·50 25
374 – 15 c. + 5 c. brown & blue 5·25 6·00

DESIGNS: 2 c. Engineer chopping wood; 12½ c. Artilleryman and volcano victim; 15 c. Infantry bugler.

54 Dinner-time

55 Boy Scouts

59 Sifting Rice

1936. Salvation Army.

375 **54** 2 c. + 1 c. purple 1·25 55
376 5 c. + 2½ c. blue 1·40 1·10
377 7½ c. + 2½ c. violet 1·40 1·40
378 12½ c. + 2½ c. orange 1·40 25
379 15 c. + 5 c. blue 2·40 2·25

Nos. 376/9 are larger, 30×27 mm.

1937. Scouts' Jamboree.

380 **55** 7½ c. + 2½ c. green 1·25 1·10
381 12½ c. + 2½ c. red 1·25 50

1937. Nos. 222 and 277 surch in figures.

382 10 c. on 30 c. slate 2·40 25
383 10 c. on 32½ c. vio & orge 2·40 25

1937. Relief Fund. Inscr "A.S.I.B.".

385 **59** 2 c. + 1 c. sepia & orange 1·25 80
386 – 3½ c. + 1½ c. grey 1·25 80
387 – 7½ c. + 2½ c. green & orge 1·40 85
388 – 10 c. + 2½ c. red & orange 1·40 20
389 – 20 c. + 5 c. blue 1·40 1·25

DESIGNS: 3½ c. Mother and children; 7½ c. Ox-team ploughing rice-field; 10 c. Ox-team and cart; 20 c. Man and woman.

1938. 40th Anniv of Coronation. As T **87** of Netherlands.

390 2 c. violet 10 15
391 10 c. red 15 10
392 15 c. blue 1·40 65
393 20 c. red 60 25

62 Douglas DC-2 Airliner

63 Nurse and Child

1938. Air Service Fund. 10th Anniv of Royal Netherlands Indies Air Lines.

394 **62** 17½ c. + 5 c. brown 85 85
395 – 20 c. + 5 c. slate 85 85

DESIGN: 20 c. As Type **62**, but reverse side of airliner.

1938. Child Welfare. Inscr "CENTRAAL MISSIE-BUREAU".

416 **63** 2 c. + 1 c. violet 65 40
417 – 3½ c. + 1½ c. green 1·10 1·10
418 – 7½ c. + 2½ c. red 80 70
419 – 10 c. + 2½ c. red 1·00 20
420 – 20 c. + 5 c. blue 1·25 80

DESIGNS—(23×23 mm): Nurse with child suffering from injuries to eye (3½ c.), arm (7½ c.), head (20 c.) and nurse bathing a baby (10 c.).

63a Group of Natives

64 European Nurse and Patient

1939. Netherlands Indies Social Bureau and Protestant Church Funds.

421 – 2 c. + 1 c. violet 25 15
422 – 3½ c. + 1½ c. green 35 20
423 **63a** 7½ c. + 2½ c. brown 25 20
424 – 10 c. + 2½ c. red 1·50 75
425 **64** 10 c. + 2½ c. red 1·50 75
426 – 20 c. + 5 c. blue 50 35

DESIGNS—VERT: 2 c. as Type **63a** but group in European clothes. HORIZ: 3½ c., 10 c. (No. 424) as Type **64**, but Native nurse and patient.

1940. Red Cross Fund. No. 345 surch **10+5 ct** and cross.

428 **47** 10 c. + 5 c. on 12½ c. red 2·75 45

68 Queen Wilhelmina

69 Netherlands Coat of Arms

1941. As T **94** of Netherlands but inscr "NED. INDIE" and T **68**.

429 – 10 c. red 20 10
430 – 15 c. blue 2·10 1·10
431 – 17½ c. orange 35 55
432 – 20 c. mauve 27·00 29·00
433 – 25 c. green 35·00 40·00
434 – 30 c. brown 3·75 1·50
435 – 35 c. purple £140 £275
436 – 40 c. green 10·00 2·50
437 – 50 c. red 2·50 65
438 – 60 c. blue 2·25 75
439 – 80 c. red 2·25 75
440 – 1 g. violet 2·25 25
441 – 2 g. green 12·50 1·40
442 – 5 g. bistre £275 £500
443 – 10 g. green 32·00 17·00
444 **68** 25 g. orange £225 £130

Nos. 429/36 measure 18×23 mm., Nos. 431/43 20½×26 mm.

1941. Prince Bernhard Fund for Dutch Forces.

453 **69** 5 c. + 5 c. blue & orange 10 15
454 10 c. + 10 c. blue and red 15 15
455 1 g. + 1 g. blue and grey 12·00 11·00

70 Doctor and Child

71 Wayangwong Dancer

1941. Indigent Mohammedans' Relief Fund.
456 70 2 c. + 1 c. green 75 50
457 – 3½ c. + 1½ c. brown 4·50 1·75
458 – 7½ c. + 2½ c. violet 3·75 2·75
459 – 10 c. + 2½ c. red 1·40 30
460 – 15 c. + 5 c. blue 11·50 5·50
DESIGNS: 3½ c. Native eating rice; 7½ c. Nurse and patient; 10 c. Nurse and children; 15 c. Basket-weaver.

1941.
461 – 2 c. red 10 15
462 – 2½ c. purple 15 20
463 – 3 c. green 15 40
464 71 4 c. green 15 35
465 – 5 c. blue 10 10
466 – 7½ c. violet 40 10
DESIGNS (dancers): 2 c. Menari; 2½ c. Nias; 3 c. Legon; 5 c. Padjoge; 7½ c. Dyak.
See also Nos. 514/16.

72 Paddyfield
73 Queen Wilhelmina

1945.
467 72 1 c. green 20 15
468 – 2 c. mauve 20 30
469 – 2½ c. purple 20 15
470 – 5 c. blue 15 10
471 – 7½ c. olive 45 10
472 73 10 c. brown 10 10
473 15 c. blue 10 10
474 17½ c. red 15 15
475 20 c. purple 15 10
476 30 c. grey 25 10
477 – 60 c. grey 60 10
478 – 1 g. green 1·00 10
479 – 2½ g. orange 3·75 45
DESIGNS: As Type 72: 2 c. Lake in W. Java; 2½ c. Medical School, Batavia; 5 c. Seashore; 7½ c. Douglas DC-2 airplane over Bromo Volcano. (30×30 mm): 60 c. to 2½ g. Portrait as Type 73 but different frame.

76 Railway Viaduct near Soekaboemi
81 Queen Wilhelmina

1946.
484 76 1 c. green 30 60
485 – 2 c. brown 10 10
486 – 2½ c. red 15 15
487 – 5 c. blue 10 10
488 – 7½ c. blue 15 10
DESIGNS: 2 c. Power station; 3 c. Minangkabau house; 5 c. Tondano scene (Celebes); 7½ c. Buddhist Stupas, Java.

1947. Surch in figures.
502 – 3 c. on 2½ c. red (No. 486) 10 10
503 – 3 c. on 7½ c. blue (No. 488) 10 10
504 76 4 c. on 1 c. green 45 1·50
505 – 45 c. on 60 c. blue (No. 355) 1·25 90
No. 505 has three bars.

1947. Optd **1947**.
506 47 12½ c. red 10 10
507 25 c. green 20 10
508 – 40 c. green (No. 436) 30 10
509 47 50 c. blue 50 25
510 80 c. red 75 55
511 – 2 g. green (No. 441) 3·25 45
512 – 5 g. brown (No. 442) 9·50 6·50

1948. Relief for Victims of the Terror. Surch **PELITA 15 + 10 Ct.** and lamp.
513 47 15 c. + 10 c. on 10 c. red 10 10

1948. Dancers. As T **71**.
514 3 c. red (Menari) 10 10
515 4 c. green (Legon) 10 10
516 7½ c. brown (Dyak) 55 55

1948.
517 81 15 c. orange 60 60
518 20 c. blue 10 10
519 25 c. green 15 10
520 40 c. green 20 10
521 45 c. mauve 35 45
522 50 c. lake 25 10
523 80 c. red 30 10
524 1 g. violet 25 10
525 10 g. green 27·00 11·00
526 25 g. orange 55·00 45·00
Nos. 524/6 are larger 21×26 mm.

1948. Queen Wilhelmina's Golden Jubilee. As T **81** but inscr "1898 1948".
528 15 c. orange 25 15
529 20 c. blue 25 10

1948. As T **126** of Netherlands.
530 15 c. red 30 15
531 20 c. blue 30 10

MARINE INSURANCE STAMPS

1921. As Type M **22** of the Netherlands, but inscribed "NED. INDIE".
M257 15 c. green 5·50 28·00
M258 60 c. red 5·50 42·00
M259 75 c. brown 5·50 48·00
M260 1 g. 50 blue 20·00 £250
M261 2 g. 25 brown 27·00 £275
M262 4½ g. black 55·00 £475
M263 7½ g. red 65·00 £550

OFFICIAL STAMPS

1911. Stamps of 1892 optd **D** in white on a black circle.
O178 6 10 c. brown 1·00 50
O179 12½ c. grey 2·25 3·75
O180 15 c. bistre 2·25 2·00
O181 20 c. blue 2·25 80
O182 25 c. mauve 8·00 7·00
O183 50 c. red 1·75 1·00
O184 2 g. 50, blue and brown 45·00 45·00

1911. Stamps of 1902 (except No. O185) optd **DIENST**.
O186 ½ c. lilac 10 30
O187 1 c. olive 15 10
O188 2 c. brown 10 10
O185 2½ c. yellow (No. 91) 50 50
O189 2½ c. green 1·10 1·00
O190 3 c. orange 30 25
O191 4 c. blue 10 10
O192 5 c. red 55 55
O193 7½ c. grey 2·00 2·25
O194 10 c. slate 15 10
O195 12½ c. blue 1·60 1·75
O196 15 c. brown 50 50
O197 15 c. brown (No. 140) 26·00
O198 17½ c. bistre 2·25 1·75
O199 20 c. olive 50 40
O200 22½ c. olive and brown 3·00 2·25
O201 25 c. mauve 1·75 1·50
O202 30 c. brown 70 40
O203 50 c. red 11·00 6·00
O204 1 g. lilac 2·25 1·00
O205 2½ g. grey 26·00 28·00

POSTAGE DUE STAMPS

1874. As Postage Due stamps of Netherlands. Colours changed.
D56 D 8 5 c. yellow £250 £225
D57 10 c. green on yellow £100 80·00
D59 15 c. orange on yellow 18·00 16·00
D60 20 c. green on blue 30·00 11·00

1882. As Type D **2** of Surinam.
D68 2½ c. black and red 30 80
D69 5 c. black and red 20 35
D65 10 c. black and red 3·00 2·25
D70 15 c. black and red 3·25 2·75
D71 20 c. black and red 85·00 35
D82 30 c. black and red 2·10 1·90
D72 40 c. black and red 1·10 1·50
D73 50 c. black and pink 1·10 75
D74 75 c. black and red 75 75

1892. As Type D **9** of Netherlands.
D102 2½ c. black and pink 40 25
D103 5 c. black and pink 2·50 10
D104b 10 c. black and pink 2·50 40
D105 15 c. black and pink 11·50 1·75
D106b 20 c. black and pink 2·10 20
D107 30 c. black and pink 16·00 5·75
D108 40 c. black and pink 12·50 1·75
D109 50 c. black and pink 9·00 65
D110 75 c. black and pink 18·00 3·75

1913. As Type D **9** of Netherlands.
D226 1 c. orange 10 95
D489 1 c. violet 50 80
D227 2½ c. orange 10 10
D527 2½ c. brown 45 75
D228 3½ c. orange 10 95
D491 3½ c. blue 50 80
D229 5 c. orange 10 10
D230 7½ c. orange 10 10
D493 7½ c. green 60 80
D231 10 c. orange 10 10
D494 10 c. mauve 60 80
D232 12½ c. orange 2·75 10
D448 15 c. orange 65 85
D234 20 c. orange 15 10
D495 20 c. blue 60 90
D235 25 c. orange 15 10
D496 25 c. yellow 75 90
D236 30 c. orange 20 20
D497 30 c. brown 80 1·00
D237 37½ c. orange 16·00 12·50
D238 40 c. orange 20 15
D498 40 c. green 1·25 1·10
D239 50 c. orange 1·75 10
D499 50 c. yellow 1·40 1·25
D240 75 c. orange 2·75 15
D500 75 c. blue 1·40 1·25
D241 1 g. orange 4·25 5·25
D452 1 g. blue 45 55
D501 100 c. green 1·40 1·25

1937. Surch **20**.
D384 D 5 20 c. on 37½ c. red 25 25

1946. Optd **TE BETALEN PORT** or surch also.
D480 2½ c. on 10 c. red (No. 429) 70 70
D481 10 c. red (No. 429) 1·75 1·75
D482 20 c. mauve (No. 432) 4·00 4·00
D483 40 c. green (No. 436) 40·00 40·00

For later issues see **INDONESIA**.

MINIMUM PRICE
The minimum price quoted is 10p which represents a handling charge rather than a basis for valuing common stamps. For further notes about prices, see introductory pages.

NETHERLANDS NEW GUINEA Pt. 4

The Western half of the island of New Guinea was governed by the Netherlands until 1962, when control was transferred to the U.N. (see West New Guinea). The territory later became part of Indonesia as West Irian (q.v.).

100 cents = 1 gulden

1950. As numeral and portrait types of Netherlands but inscr "NIEUW GUINEA".
1 118 1 c. grey 15 15
2 2 c. orange 15 15
3 2½ c. olive 15 10
4 3 c. mauve 1·50 1·25
5 4 c. green 1·50 1·00
6 5 c. blue 3·25 15
7 7½ c. brown 35 15
8 10 c. violet 1·75 15
9 12½ c. red 1·75 1·40
10 129 15 c. brown 1·75 50
11 20 c. blue 70 10
12 25 c. red 70 10
13 30 c. blue 8·00 25
14 40 c. green 1·10 10
15 45 c. brown 4·50 50
16 50 c. orange 65 10
17 55 c. grey 7·50 50
18 80 c. purple 8·00 3·00
19 130 1 g. red 11·50 15
20 2 g. brown 9·25 1·10
21 5 g. green 12·50 1·00

1953. Netherlands Flood Relief Fund. Nos. 6, 10 and 12 surch **hulp nederland 1953** and premium.
22 118 5 c. + 5 c. blue 9·00 9·00
23 129 15 c. + 10 c. brown 9·00 9·00
24 25 c. + 10 c. red 9·00 9·00

5 Lesser Bird of Paradise

6 Queen Juliana

1954.
25 5 1 c. yellow and red 30 10
26 5 c. yellow and brown 35 10
27 – 10 c. brown and blue 40 10
28 – 15 c. brown and yellow 50 10
29 – 20 c. brown and green 90 35
DESIGN: 10, 15, 20 c. Greater bird of paradise.

1954.
30 6 25 c. red 20 10
31 30 c. blue 20 10
32 40 c. orange 1·75 2·00
33 45 c. green 60 85
34 55 c. turquoise 45 10
35 80 c. grey 85 30
36 85 c. brown 90 45
37 1 g. purple 4·50 2·10

1955. Red Cross. Nos. 26/8 surch with cross and premium.
38 5 5 c. + 5 c. yellow and sepia 1·00 85
39 – 10 c. + 10 c. brown & blue 1·00 85
40 – 15 c. + 10 c. brown & lemon 1·00 85

8 Child and Native Hut

10 Papuan Girl and Beach Scene

1956. Anti-Leprosy Fund.
41 – 5 c. + 5 c. green 90 85
42 8 10 c. + 5 c. purple 90 85
43 – 25 c. + 10 c. blue 90 85
44 8 30 c. + 10 c. buff 90 85
DESIGN: 5 c., 25 c. Palm-trees and native hut.

1957. Child Welfare Fund.
51 10 5 c. + 5 c. lake 90 85
52 – 10 c. + 5 c. green 90 85
53 10 25 c. + 10 c. brown 90 85
54 – 30 c. + 10 c. blue 90 85
DESIGN: 10 c., 30 c. Papuan child and native hut.

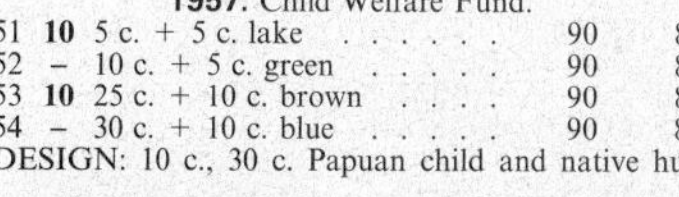

11 Red Cross and Idol
12 Papuan and Helicopter

1958. Red Cross Fund.
55 11 5 c. + 5 c. multicoloured 1·00 90
56 – 10 c. + 5 c. multicoloured 1·00 90
57 11 25 c. + 10 c. multicoloured 1·00 90
58 – 30 c. + 10 c. multicoloured 1·00 90
DESIGN: 10 c., 30 c. Red Cross and Asman-Papuan bowl in form of human figure.

1959. Stars Mountains Expedition, 1959.
59 12 55 c. brown and blue 1·10 80

13 Blue-crowned Pigeon
14 "Tecomanthe dendrophila"

1959.
60 13 7 c. purple, blue and brown 50 20
61 12 c. purple, blue & green 50 20
62 17 c. purple and blue 50 15

1959. Social Welfare. Inscr "SOCIALE ZORG".
63 14 5 c. + 5 c. red and green 65 45
64 – 10 c. + 5 c. purple, yellow and olive 65 45
65 – 25 c. + 10 c. yellow, green and red 65 45
66 – 30 c. + 10 c. green & violet 65 45
DESIGNS: 10 c. "Dendrobium attenuatum Lindley"; 25 c. "Rhododendron zoelleri Warburg"; 30 c. "Boea cf. urvillei".

1960. World Refugee Year. As T **180** of Netherlands.
67 25 c. blue 40 40
68 30 c. ochre 40 70

16 Paradise Birdwing

1960. Social Welfare Funds. Butterflies.
69 16 5 c. + 5 c. multicoloured 80 65
70 – 10 c. + 5 c. bl, blk & salmon 80 65
71 – 25 c. + 10 c. red, sep & yell 85 65
72 – 30 c. + 10 c. multicoloured 85 65
BUTTERFLIES: 10 c. Large green-banded blue; 25 c. Red lacewing; 30 c. Catops owl butterfly.

17 Council Building, Hollandia

1961. Opening of Netherlands New Guinea Council.
73 17 25 c. turquoise 20 30
74 30 c. red 20 30

18 "Scapanes australis"

19 Children's Road Crossing

1961. Social Welfare Funds. Beetles.
75 18 5 c. + 5 c. multicoloured 20 25
76 – 10 c. + 5 c. multicoloured 20 25
77 – 25 c. + 10 c. multicoloured 25 30
78 – 30 c. + 10 c. multicoloured 30 35
BEETLES: 10 c. Brenthid weevil; 25 c. "Neolamprima adolphinae" (stag beetle); 30 c. "Aspidomorpha aurata" (leaf beetle).

1962. Road Safety Campaign. Triangle in red.
79 19 25 c. blue 35 35
80 – 30 c. green (Adults at road crossing) 35 35

1962. Silver Wedding of Queen Juliana and Prince Bernhard. As T **187** of Netherlands.
81 55 c. brown 30 35

21 Shadow of Palm on Beach

22 Lobster

1962. 5th South Pacific Conference, Pago Pago. Multicoloured.
82 25 c. Type **21** 20 35
83 30 c. Palms on beach 20 35

1962. Social Welfare Funds. Shellfish. Multicoloured.
84 5 c. + 5 c. Crab (horiz) 20 20
85 10 c. + 5 c. Type **22** 20 20
86 25 c. + 10 c. Spiny lobster 25 25
87 30 c. + 10 c. Shrimp (horiz) 25 30

POSTAGE DUE STAMPS

1957. As Type D **121** of Netherlands but inscr "NEDERLANDS NIEUW GUINEA".

No.	Type	Description	Unused	Used
D45		1 c. red	10	20
D46		5 c. red	50	1·10
D47		10 c. red	1·50	2·25
D48		25 c. red	2·25	70
D49		40 c. red	2·25	85
D50		1 g. blue	3·00	3·75

For later issues see **WEST NEW GUINEA** and **WEST IRIAN**.

NEW CALEDONIA Pt. 6

A French Overseas Territory in the S. Pacific, E. of Australia, consisting of New Caledonia and a number of smaller islands.

100 centimes = 1 franc

1 Napoleon III

1860. Imperf.

No.	Type	Description	Unused	Used
1	1	10 c. black	£170	

Nos. 5/35 are stamps of French Colonies optd or surch.

1881. "Peace and Commerce" type surch **N C E** and new value. Imperf.

No.	Type	Description	Unused	Used
5	H	05 on 40 c. red on yellow	17·00	16·00
8a		5 on 40 c. red on yellow	12·00	12·00
9		5 on 75 c. red	28·00	27·00
6a		25 on 35 c. black on orge	£100	90·00
7		25 on 75 c. red	£250	£190

1886. "Peace and Commerce" (imperf) and "Commerce" types surch **N.C.E. 5c.**

No.	Type	Description	Unused	Used
10	J	5 c. on 1 f. green	11·00	11·00
11	H	5 c. on 1 f. green	£7000	£7500

1891. "Peace and Commerce" (imperf) and "Commerce" types surch **N.-C.E. 10 c.** in ornamental frame.

No.	Type	Description	Unused	Used
13	H	10 c. on 40 c. red on yell	16·00	15·00
14	J	10 c. on 40 c. red on yell	8·25	7·75

1892. "Commerce" type surch **N.-C.E. 10 centimes** in ornamental frame.

No.	Type	Description	Unused	Used
15	J	10 c. on 30 c. brn on drab	8·00	8·00

1892. Optd **NLLE CALEDONIE**. (a) "Peace and Commerce" type. Imperf.

No.	Type	Description	Unused	Used
16	H	20 c. red on green	£225	£250
17		35 c. black on orange	40·00	40·00
19		1 f. green	£170	£170

(b) "Commerce" type.

No.	Type	Description	Unused	Used
20	J	5 c. green on green	9·00	7·50
21		10 c. black on lilac	85·00	42·00
22		15 c. blue	60·00	27·00
23		20 c. red on green	60·00	35·00
24		25 c. brown on yellow	11·00	8·75
25		25 c. black on pink	60·00	8·00
26		30 c. brown on drab	45·00	38·00
27		35 c. black on orange	£160	£120
29		75 c. red on pink	£120	90·00
30		1 f. green	£100	85·00

1892. Surch **N-C-E** in ornamental scroll and new value. (a) "Peace and Commerce" type. Imperf.

No.	Type	Description	Unused	Used
31	H	10 on 1 f. green	£3500	£2750

(b) "Commerce" type.

No.	Type	Description	Unused	Used
32	J	5 on 20 c. red on green	11·00	8·25
34		5 on 75 c. red on pink	7·50	4·75
35		10 on 1 f. green	7·50	5·00

1892. "Tablet" key-type inscr "NLLE CALEDONIE ET DEPENDANCES".

No.	Type	Description	Unused	Used
37	D	1 c. black and red on blue	35	30
38		2 c. brown & blue on buff	65	40
39		4 c. brown & blue on grey	90	1·00
55		5 c. green and red	85	50
41		10 c. black & blue on lilac	3·50	2·25
56		10 c. red and blue	4·00	70
42		15 c. blue and red	11·00	80
57		15 c. grey and red	6·00	65
43		20 c. red & blue on green	9·75	6·25
44		25 c. black & red on pink	10·00	3·00
58		25 c. blue and red	8·75	5·75
45		30 c. brown & bl on drab	10·00	6·00
46		40 c. red & blue on yellow	10·00	8·25
47		50 c. red and blue on pink	38·00	16·00
59		50 c. brown & red on blue	40·00	48·00
60		50 c. brown & blue on blue	38·00	35·00
48		75 c. brown & red on orge	19·00	12·50
49		1 f. green and red	22·00	13·50

1899. Stamps of 1892 surch (a) **N-C-E** in ornamental scroll and **5**.

No.	Type	Description	Unused	Used
50	D	5 on 2 c. brown & bl on buff	11·00	8·75
51		5 on 4 c. brn & bl on grey	1·90	2·00

(b) **N.C.E.** and **15** in circle.

No.	Type	Description	Unused	Used
52	D	15 on 30 c. brown and blue on drab	2·50	2·75
53		15 on 75 c. brown and red on orange	8·50	6·25
54		15 on 1 f. green and red	13·50	12·50

1902. Surch **N.-C.E.** and value in figures.

No.	Type	Description	Unused	Used
61	D	5 on 30 c. brown and blue on drab	5·25	4·75
62		15 on 40 c. red and blue on yellow	4·00	3·75

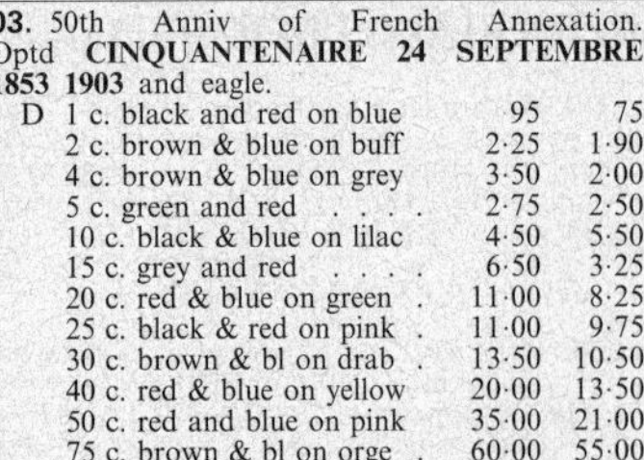

1903. 50th Anniv of French Annexation. Optd **CINQUANTENAIRE 24 SEPTEMBRE 1853 1903** and eagle.

No.	Type	Description	Unused	Used
63	D	1 c. black and red on blue	95	75
64		2 c. brown & blue on buff	2·25	1·90
65		4 c. brown & blue on grey	3·50	2·00
66		5 c. green and red	2·75	2·50
69		10 c. black & blue on lilac	4·50	5·50
70		15 c. grey and red	6·50	3·25
71		20 c. red & blue on green	11·00	8·25
72		25 c. black & red on pink	11·00	9·75
73		30 c. brown & bl on drab	13·50	10·50
74		40 c. red & blue on yellow	20·00	13·50
75		50 c. red and blue on pink	35·00	21·00
76		75 c. brown & bl on orge	60·00	55·00
77		1 f. green and red	70·00	65·00

1903. Nos. 64 etc further surch with value in figures within the jubilee opt.

No.	Type	Description	Unused	Used
78	D	1 on 2 c. brn & bl on buff	50	45
79		2 on 4 c. brn & bl on grey	1·25	1·10
80		4 on 5 c. green and red	1·25	1·10
82		10 on 15 c. grey and red	1·60	1·75
83		15 on 20 c. red and blue on green	1·75	1·60
84		20 on 25 c. black and red on pink	3·00	2·75

15 Kagu

16

17 "President Felix Faure" (barque)

1905.

No.	Type	Description	Unused	Used
85	15	1 c. black on green	15	10
86		2 c. brown	15	10
87		4 c. blue on orange	20	25
88		5 c. green	30	20
112		5 c. blue	25	30
113		10 c. green	50	45
114		10 c. red	30	35
90		15 c. lilac	40	25
91	16	20 c. brown	30	25
92		25 c. blue on green	45	20
115		25 c. red on yellow	30	20
93		30 c. brown on orange	30	40
116		30 c. red	85	90
117		30 c. orange	35	30
94		35 c. black on yellow	25	30
95		40 c. red on green	65	55
96		45 c. red	40	45
97		50 c. red on orange	1·50	1·00
118		50 c. blue	90	85
119		50 c. grey	40	35
120		65 c. blue	35	35
98		75 c. olive	35	35
121		75 c. blue	30	40
122		75 c. violet	60	50
99	17	1 f. blue on green	50	45
123		1 f. blue	90	95
100		2 f. red on blue	1·40	1·10
101		5 f. black on orange	4·00	3·75

1912. Stamps of 1892 surch.

No.	Type	Description	Unused	Used
102	D	05 on 15 c. grey and red	40	45
103		05 on 20 c. red and blue on green	40	55
104		05 on 30 c. brown and blue on drab	40	55
105		10 on 40 c. red and blue on yellow	90	95
106		10 on 50 c. brown and blue on blue	95	1·00

1915. Surch **NCE 5** and red cross.

No.	Type	Description	Unused	Used
107	15	10 c. + 5 c. red	65	60

1915. Surch **5c** and red cross.

No.	Type	Description	Unused	Used
109	15	10 c. + 5 c. red	40	50
110		15 c. + 5 c. lilac	35	45

1918. Surch **5 CENTIMES**.

No.	Type	Description	Unused	Used
111	15	5 c. on 15 c. lilac	70	70

1922. Surch **0 05**.

No.	Type	Description	Unused	Used
124	15	0.05 on 15 c. lilac	25	45

1924. Types **15/17** (some colours changed) surch.

No.	Type	Description	Unused	Used
125	15	25 c. on 15 c. lilac	30	35
126	17	25 c. on 2 f. red on blue	40	50
127		25 c. on 5 f. black on orge	40	50
128	16	60 on 75 c. green	25	35
129		65 on 45 c. purple	70	80
130		85 on 45 c. purple	90	1·00
131		90 on 75 c. red	35	45
132	17	1 f. 25 on 1 f. blue	30	35
133		1 f. 50 on 1 f. blue on blue	60	70
134		3 f. on 5 f. mauve	65	70
135		10 f. on 5 f. green on mve	4·00	4·25
136		20 f. on 5 f. red on yellow	8·50	8·50

22 Pointe des Paletuviers

23 Chief's Hut

24 La Perouse, De Bougainville and "L'Astrolabe"

1928.

No.	Type	Description	Unused	Used
137	22	1 c. blue and purple	10	20
138		2 c. green and brown	10	30
139		3 c. blue and red	15	25
140		4 c. blue and orange	15	35
141		5 c. brown and blue	15	35
142		10 c. brown and lilac	20	25
143		15 c. blue and brown	20	25
144		20 c. brown and red	20	35
145		25 c. brown and green	25	30
146	23	30 c. deep green and green	20	30
147		35 c. mauve and black	30	20
148		40 c. green and red	25	30
149		45 c. red and blue	50	60
150		45 c. green and deep green	40	50
151		50 c. brown and mauve	40	25
152		55 c. red and blue	1·90	95
153		60 c. red and blue	25	35
154		65 c. blue and brown	45	55
155		70 c. brown and mauve	30	40
156		75 c. drab and blue	80	60
157		80 c. green and purple	50	40
158		85 c. brown and green	75	55
159		90 c. pink and red	40	55
160		90 c. red and brown	50	60
161	24	1 f. pink and drab	3·75	2·00
162		1 f. carmine and red	65	75
163		1 f. green and red	40	50
164		1 f. 10 brown and green	8·75	7·50
165		1 f. 25 green and brown	55	65
166		1 f. 25 carmine and red	40	50
167		1 f. 40 red and blue	40	50
168		1 f. 50 light blue and blue	35	40
169		1 f. 60 brown and green	65	70
170		1 f. 75 orange and blue	45	45
171		1 f. 75 blue & ultramarine	45	50
172		2 f. brown and orange	40	50
173		2 f. 25 blue & ultramarine	45	50
174		2 f. 50 brown	65	70
175		3 f. brown and mauve	45	50
176		5 f. brown and blue	45	50
177		10 f. brown & pur on pink	80	80
178		20 f. brown & red on yellow	1·40	1·10

1931. "Colonial Exhibition" key-types.

No.	Type	Description	Unused	Used
179	E	40 c. green and black	2·50	2·50
180	F	50 c. mauve and black	2·50	2·50
181	G	90 c. red and black	2·50	2·50
182	H	1 f. 50 blue and black	2·50	2·50

1932. Paris-Noumea Flight. Optd with Couzinet 33 airplane and **PARIS-NOUMEA Verneilh-Deve-Munch 5 Avril 1932**.

No.	Type	Description	Unused	Used
183	23	40 c. olive and red	£300	£350
184		50 c. brown and mauve	£300	£350

1933. 1st Anniv of Paris-Noumea Flight. Optd **PARIS-NOUMEA Premiere liaison aerienne 5 Avril 1932** and Couzinet 33 airplane.

No.	Type	Description	Unused	Used
185	22	1 c. blue and purple	4·75	4·75
186		2 c. green and brown	4·75	4·75
187		4 c. blue and orange	4·75	4·75
188		5 c. brown and blue	4·75	4·75
189		10 c. brown and lilac	4·75	4·75
190		15 c. blue and brown	4·75	4·75
191		20 c. brown and red	4·75	4·75
192		25 c. brown and green	4·75	4·75
193	23	30 c. deep green and green	4·50	4·75
194		35 c. mauve and black	4·50	4·75
195		40 c. green and red	4·50	4·75
196		45 c. red and blue	4·50	4·75
197		50 c. brown and mauve	4·50	4·75
198		70 c. brown and mauve	5·25	5·50
199		75 c. drab and blue	5·25	5·50
200		85 c. brown and green	5·25	5·50
201		90 c. pink and red	5·25	5·50
202	24	1 f. pink and drab	5·25	5·50
203		1 f. 25 green and brown	5·25	5·50
204		1 f. 50 light blue & blue	5·25	5·50
205		1 f. 75 orange and blue	5·00	5·50
206		2 f. brown and orange	6·25	6·25
207		3 f. brown and mauve	5·75	6·25
208		5 f. brown and blue	5·75	6·25
209		10 f. brown & pur on pink	6·00	6·25
210		20 f. brown & red on yellow	6·00	6·25

1937. International Exhibition, Paris. As Nos. 168/73 of St.-Pierre et Miquelon.

No.	Type	Description	Unused	Used
211		20 c. violet	60	80
212		30 c. green	65	85
213		40 c. red	60	80
214		50 c. brown and blue	60	75
215		90 c. red	60	85
216		1 f. 50 blue	60	80

DESIGNS—HORIZ: 30 c. Sailing ships; 40 c. Berber, Negress and Annamite; 90 c. France extends torch of civilization; 1 f. 50, Diane de Poitiers. VERT: 50 c. Agriculture.

27 Breguet Saigon Flying Boat over Noumea

1938. Air.

No.	Type	Description	Unused	Used
217	27	65 c. violet	50	60
218		4 f. 50 red	70	70
219		7 f. green	50	50
220		9 f. blue	1·40	1·50
221		20 f. orange	85	85
222		50 f. black	1·75	1·75

1938. Int Anti-Cancer Fund. As T **22** of Mauritania.

No.	Type	Description	Unused	Used
223		1 f. 75 + 50 c. blue	5·75	7·25

1939. New York World's Fair. As T **28** of Mauritania.

No.	Type	Description	Unused	Used
224		1 f. 25 red	70	70
225		2 f. 25 blue	60	70

1939. 150th Anniv of French Revolution. As T **29** of Mauritania.

No.	Type	Description	Unused	Used
226		45 c. + 25 c. green and black (postage)	5·00	5·50
227		70 c. + 30 c. brown & black	5·00	5·50
228		90 c. + 35 c. orange & black	5·00	5·50
229		1 f. 25 + 1 f. red & black	5·00	5·50
230		2 f. 25 + 2 f. blue & black	5·50	5·00
231		4 f. 50 + 4 f. black and orange (air)	12·00	17·00

1941. Adherence to General de Gaulle. Optd **France Libre**.

No.	Type	Description	Unused	Used
232	22	1 c. blue and purple	12·50	12·50
233		2 c. green and brown	12·50	12·50
234		3 c. blue and red	12·00	12·50
235		4 c. blue and orange	12·50	12·50
236		5 c. brown and blue	11·50	12·50
237		10 c. brown and lilac	11·50	12·50
238		15 c. blue and brown	12·50	12·50
239		20 c. brown and red	12·50	12·50
240		25 c. brown and green	12·50	12·50
241	23	30 c. deep green and green	12·50	12·50
242		35 c. mauve and black	12·50	12·50
243		40 c. green and red	12·50	12·50
244		45 c. green & deep green	12·50	12·50
245		50 c. brown and mauve	12·50	12·50
246		55 c. red and blue	12·50	12·50
247		60 c. red and blue	12·50	12·50
248		65 c. blue and brown	12·50	12·50
249		70 c. brown and mauve	12·50	12·50
250		75 c. drab and blue	12·50	12·50
251		80 c. green and purple	12·50	12·50
252		85 c. brown and green	14·00	14·00
253		90 c. pink and red	14·00	14·00
254	24	1 f. carmine and red	14·00	14·00
255		1 f. 25 green and brown	14·00	14·00
256		1 f. 40 red and blue	14·00	14·00
257		1 f. 50 light blue & blue	14·00	14·00
258		1 f. 60 brown and green	14·00	14·00
259		1 f. 75 orange and blue	14·00	14·00
260		2 f. brown and orange	14·00	14·00
261		2 f. 25 blue & ultramarine	14·00	14·00
262		2 f. 50 brown	15·00	15·00
263		3 f. brown and mauve	15·00	15·00
264		5 f. brown and blue	15·00	15·00
265		10 f. brown & pur on pink	18·00	18·00
266		20 f. brown & red on yellow	20·00	20·00

29 Kagu

30 Fairey FC-1 Airliner

1942. Free French Issue. (a) Postage.

No.	Type	Description	Unused	Used
267	29	5 c. brown	20	30
268		10 c. blue	20	30
269		25 c. green	20	30
270		30 c. red	20	30
271		40 c. green	40	30
272		80 c. purple	40	30
273		1 f. mauve	50	35
274		1 f. 50 red	50	35
275		2 f. black	60	60
276		2 f. 50 blue	60	60
277		4 f. violet	70	45
278		5 f. yellow	80	60
279		10 f. brown	1·25	85
280		20 f. green	1·75	1·25

(b) Air.

No.	Type	Description	Unused	Used
281	30	1 f. orange	45	55
282		1 f. 50 red	45	55
283		5 f. purple	50	60
284		10 f. black	70	70
285		25 f. blue	70	70
286		50 f. green	95	1·00
287		100 f. red	1·40	1·25

31

32 Felix Eboue

1944. Mutual Aid and Red Cross Funds.

No.	Type	Description	Unused	Used
288	31	5 f. + 20 f. red	50	60

1945. Eboue.
289 **32** 2 f. black 40 50
290 25 f. green . . . . 1·10 1·25

1945. Surch.
291 **29** 50 c. on 5 c. brown 55 70
292 60 c. on 5 c. brown 55 70
293 70 c. on 5 c. brown 40 80
294 1 f. 20 on 5 c. brown . . . 30 40
295 2 f. 40 on 25 c. green . . . 40 50
296 3 f. on 25 c. green 40 50
297 4 f. 50 on 25 c. green . . . 60 70
298 15 f. on 2 f. 50 blue . . . . 1·00 1·25

34 "Victory"

1946. Air. Victory.
299 **34** 8 f. blue 50 70

35 Legionaries by Lake Chad

1946. Air. From Chad to the Rhine.
300 **35** 5 f. black 50 70
301 – 10 f. red 75 85
302 – 15 f. blue 70 85
303 – 20 f. brown 70 85
304 – 25 f. green . . . . 90 1·25
305 – 50 f. purple . . . . 90 1·75
DESIGNS: 10 f. Battle of Koufra; 15 f. Tank Battle, Mareth; 20 f. Normandy Landings; 25 f. Liberation of Paris; 50 f. Liberation of Strasbourg.

36 Two Kagus 37 Sud Est Languedoc Airliners over Landscape

1948. (a) Postage.
306 **36** 10 c. purple and yellow . . 10 30
307 30 c. purple and green . . 15 30
308 40 c. purple and brown . . 15 30
309 – 50 c. purple and pink . . . 15 35
310 – 60 c. brown and yellow . . . 25 35
311 – 80 c. green & light green . 25 35
312 – 1 f. violet and orange . . . 25 35
313 – 1 f. 20 brown and blue . . . 25 35
314 – 1 f. 50 blue and yellow . . . 25 35
315 – 2 f. brown and green . . . 30 25
316 – 2 f. 40 red and purple . . . 40 35
317 – 3 f. violet and orange . . . 3·50 1·00
318 – 4 f. indigo and blue 75 45
319 – 5 f. violet and red 90 60
320 – 6 f. brown and yellow . . . 90 80
321 – 10 f. blue and orange . . . 90 70
322 – 15 f. red and blue . . . . . 1·00 1·00
323 – 20 f. violet and yellow . . . 1·25 1·10
324 – 25 f. blue and orange . . . 1·75 1·60

(b) Air.
325 – 50 f. purple and orange . . 3·00 3·00
326 **37** 100 f. blue and green . . . 6·25 4·50
327 – 200 f. brown and yellow . . 10·00 8·00
DESIGNS—As T **36**: HORIZ: 50 c. to 80 c. Ducos Sanatorium; 1 f. 50, Porcupine Is; 2 f. to 4 f. Nickel foundry; 5 f. to 10 f. "The Towers of Notre Dame" Rocks. VERT: 15 f. to 25 f. Chief's hut. As T **37**: HORIZ: Sud Est Languedoc airliner over– 50 f. St. Vincent Bay; 200 f. Noumea.

38 People of Five Races, Bomber and Globe

1949. Air. 75th Anniv of U.P.U.
328 **38** 10 f. multicoloured . . . . 3·00 3·50

39 Doctor and Patient 40

1950. Colonial Welfare Fund.
329 **39** 10 f. + 2 f. pur & brn . . 2·25 2·75

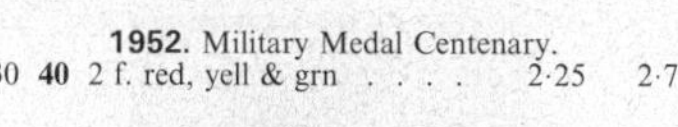

1952. Military Medal Centenary.
330 **40** 2 f. red, yell & grn . . . . 2·25 2·75

41 Admiral D'Entrecasteaux

1953. French Administration Centenary. Inscr "1853 1953".
331 **41** 1 f. 50 lake and brown . . 4·25 3·75
332 – 2 f. blue and turquoise . . 3·25 2·25
333 – 6 f. brown, blue and red . . 7·00 4·50
334 – 13 f. blue and green . . . 7·50 5·25
DESIGNS: 2 f. Mgr. Douarre and church; 6 f. Admiral D'Urville and map; 13 f. Admiral Despointes and view.

42 Normandy Landings, 1944

1954. Air. 10th Anniv of Liberation.
335 **42** 3 f. blue and deep blue . . 4·00 3·50

43 Towers of Notre-Dame (rocks) 44 Coffee

45 Transporting Nickel

1955.
336 **43** 2 f. 50 c. blue, green and sepia (postage) 80 70
337 3 f. blue, brown & green . 5·25 3·00
338 **44** 9 f. deep blue and blue . . 1·40 75
339 **45** 14 f. blue & brown (air) . 2·50 1·10

46 Dumbea Barrage 47 "Xanthostemon"

1956. Economic and Social Development Fund.
340 **46** 3 f. green and blue . . . . 1·10 65

1958. Flowers.
341 **47** 4 f. multicoloured . . . . 1·60 65
342 – 15 f. red, yellow & green . 3·50 1·25
DESIGN: 15 f. Hibiscus.

48 "Human Rights" 49 "Brachyrus zebra"

1958. 10th Anniv of Declaration of Human Rights.
343 **48** 7 f. red and blue . . . . . 1·25 95

1959.
344 **49** 1 f. brown and grey 60 45
345 – 2 f. blue, purple and green . 70 40
346 – 3 f. red, blue and green . . 85 45
347 – 4 f. purple, red and green . 70 50
348 – 5 f. bistre, blue and green . 1·40 65
349 – 10 f. multicoloured . . . . 2·00 80
350 – 26 f. multicoloured . . . . 4·25 2·75
DESIGNS—HORIZ: 2 f. Outrigger canoes racing; 3 f. "Lienardella fasciata" (fish); 5 f. Sail Rock, Noumea; 26 f. Fluorescent corals. VERT: 4 f. Fisherman with spear. 10 f. Blue sea lizard and "Spirographe" (coral).

49a The Carved Rock, Bourail

1959. Air.
351 – 15 f. green, brown & red . 3·50 1·50
352 – 20 f. brown and green . . 6·25 2·50
353 – 25 f. black, blue & purple . 6·50 2·50
354 – 50 f. brown, green & blue . 5·25 3·50
355 – 50 f. brown, green & blue . 4·25 2·50
356 – 100 f. brown, green & blue 17·00 9·00
357 **49a** 200 f. brown, green & blue 28·00 13·00
DESIGNS—HORIZ: 15 f. Fisherman with net; 20 f. New Caledonia nautilus; 25 f. Underwater swimmer shooting fish; 50 f. (No. 355), Isle of Pines; 100 f. Corbeille de Yate. VERT: 50 f. (No. 354), Yate barrage.

49b Napoleon III 49c Port-de-France, 1859

1960. Postal Centenary.
358 **15** 4 f. red 75 50
359 – 5 f. brown and lake . . . 75 50
360 – 9 f. brown and turquoise . . 90 60
361 – 12 f. black and blue . . . 90 75
362 **49b** 13 f. blue . . . . 2·50 1·60
363 **49c** 19 f. red, green & turq . . 2·75 1·10
364 – 33 f. red, green and blue . 4·00 2·25
DESIGNS—As Type **49c**: HORIZ: 5 f. Girl operating cheque-writing machine; 12 f. Telephone receiver and exchange building; 33 f. As Type **49c** but without stamps in upper corners. VERT: 9 f. Letter-box on tree.

49d Map of Pacific and Palms

1962. 5th South Pacific Conference, Pago-Pago.
365 **49d** 15 f. multicoloured . . . . 2·00 1·25

49e Map and Symbols of Meteorology

1962. 3rd Regional Assembly of World Meteorological Association, Noumea.
366 **49e** 50 f. multicoloured . . . . 7·50 4·50

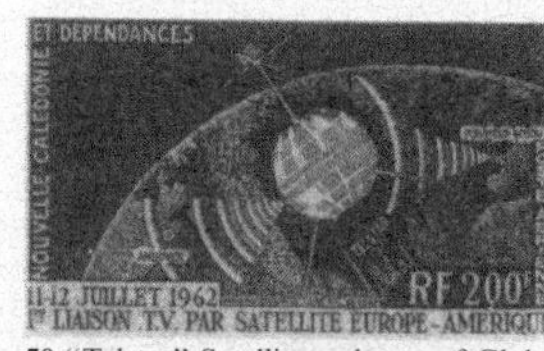
50 "Telstar" Satellite and part of Globe

1962. Air. 1st Transatlantic TV Satellite Link.
367 **50** 200 f. turquoise, brn & bl . 26·00 11·00

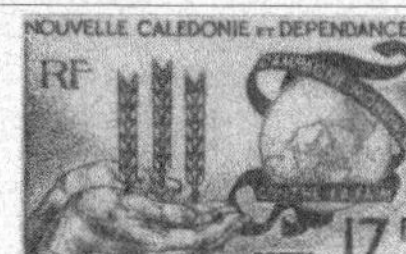
51 Emblem and Globe

1963. Freedom from Hunger.
368 **51** 17 f. blue and purple . . . 2·50 1·50

52 Relay-running 53 Centenary Emblem

1963. 1st South Pacific Games, Suva, Fiji.
369 **52** 1 f. red and green 65 60
370 – 7 f. brown and blue . . . 1·10 65
371 – 10 f. brown and green . . 1·75 1·00
372 – 27 f. blue & deep purple . 4·00 2·25
DESIGNS: 7 f. Tennis; 10 f. Football; 27 f. Throwing the javelin.

1963. Red Cross Centenary.
373 **53** 37 f. red, grey and blue . . 5·50 4·00

54 Globe and Scales of Justice 54a "Bikkia fritillarioides"

1963. 15th Anniv of Declaration of Human Rights.
374 **54** 50 f. red and blue . . . . 5·50 5·00

1964. Flowers. Multicoloured.
375 1 f. "Freycinettia" 60 40
376 2 f. Type **54a** 60 40
377 3 f. "Xanthostemon francii" . 90 70
378 4 f. "Psidiomyrtus locellatus" 1·40 80
379 5 f. "Callistemon suberosum" 1·75 1·00
380 7 f. "Montrouziera sphaeroidea" 4·75 1·40
381 10 f. "Ixora collina" . . . . 4·75 1·40
382 17 f. "Deplanchea speciosa" . 6·75 3·50
The 7 f. and 10 f. are horiz.

54b "Ascidies polycarpa" 54c "Philately"

1964. Corals and Marine Animals from Noumea Aquarium.
383 **54b** 7 f. red, brown and blue (postage) . . . . 1·10 80
384 – 10 f. red and blue . . . . 1·60 65
385 – 17 f. red, green and blue . 3·50 2·00
388 – 13 f. bistre, black and orange (air) . . . . 2·50 1·10
389 – 15 f. green, olive & blue . 3·75 1·25
390 – 25 f. blue and green . . . 6·00 3·75
386 – 27 f. multicoloured . . . 4·50 2·50
387 – 37 f. multicoloured . . . 7·00 3·75
DESIGNS—As T **54b**: VERT: 10 f. "Alcyonium catalai" (coral). HORIZ: 17 f. "Hymenocera elegans" (crab). 48 × 28 mm: 27 f. Surgeon fish; 37 f. "Phyllobranchus" (sea slug). 48 × 27 mm: 13 f. "Coris angulata" (fish) (juvenile); 15 f. "Coris angulata"; 25 f. "Coris angulata" (adult).

1964. "PHILATEC 1964" Int Stamp Exn, Paris.
391 **54c** 40 f. brown, grn & vio . . 6·00 5·50

54d Houailou Mine

1964. Air. Nickel Production at Houailou.
392 **54d** 30 f. multicoloured . . . 3·50 2·50

54e Ancient Greek Wrestling

1964. Air. Olympic Games, Tokyo.
393 **54e** 10 f. sepia, mauve & green 16·00 14·00

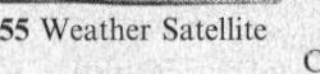

55 Weather Satellite **56** "Syncom" Communications Satellite, Telegraph Poles and Morse Key

1965. Air. World Meteorological Day.
394 **55** 9 f. multicoloured . . . . . 2·75 2·25

1965. Air. Centenary of I.T.U.
395 **56** 40 f. pur, brn & blue . . . 10·00 7·50

56a De Gaulle's Appeal of 18th June, 1940 **56b** Amedee Lighthouse

1965. 25th Anniv of New Caledonia's Adherence to the Free French.
396 **56a** 20 f. black, red & blue . . 10·00 6·00

1965. Inauguration of Amedee Lighthouse.
397 **56b** 8 f. bis., bl & green . . . 1·00 60

56c Rocket "Diamant"

1966. Air. Launching of 1st French Satellite.
398 **56c** 8 f. lake, blue & turq . . 3·00 1·50
399 – 12 f. lake, blue & turq . . 3·50 2·50
DESIGN: 12 f. Satellite "A1".

56d Games Emblem

1966. Publicity for 2nd South Pacific Games, Noumea.
400 **56d** 8 f. black, red and blue . . 1·10 70

56e Satellite "D1"

1966. Air. Launching of Satellite "D1".
401 **56e** 10 f. brown, blue and buff 2·25 1·50

57 Noumea, 1866 (after Lebreton)

1966. Air. Centenary of Renaming of Port-de-France as Noumea.
402 **57** 30 f. slate, red and blue . 4·00 2·75

58 Red-throated Parrot Finch **59** U.N.E.S.C.O. Allegory

1966. Birds. Multicoloured.
403 1 f. Type **58** (postage) . . . . 1·75 75
404 1 f. New Caledonian grass warbler . . . . 1·00 60
405 2 f. New Caledonian whistler 1·25 70
406 3 f. New Caledonian pigeon ("Notou") . . . . 3·00 1·40
407 3 f. White-throated pigeon ("Collier blanc") . . . . . 1·25 80
408 4 f. Kagu . . . . 3·00 1·10
409 5 f. Horned parakeet . . . . 5·00 1·50
410 10 f. Red-faced honeyeater . 10·00 2·75
411 15 f. New Caledonian friarbird 5·75 1·90
412 30 f. Sacred kingfisher . . . 7·75 3·75
413 27 f. Horned parakeet (diff) (air) 6·00 3·00
414 37 f. Scarlet honeyeater . . . 10·00 4·50
415 39 f. Emerald dove . . . . . 9·25 2·75
416 50 f. Cloven-feathered dove . 12·50 5·25
417 100 f. Whistling hawk . . . . 22·00 7·50
Nos. 413/14 are $26 \times 45\frac{1}{2}$ mm; Nos. 415/17 are $27\frac{1}{2} \times 48$ mm.

1966. 20th Anniv of U.N.E.S.C.O.
418 **59** 16 f. purple, ochre and green 1·50 1·00

60 High Jumping

1966. South Pacific Games, Noumea.
419 **60** 17 f. violet, green & lake . 1·75 1·10
420 – 20 f. green, purple & lake . 3·00 1·50
421 – 40 f. green, violet & lake . 3·50 2·25
422 – 100 f. purple, turq & lake . 7·50 4·50
DESIGNS: 20 f. Hurdling; 40 f. Running; 100 f. Swimming.

61 Lekine Cliffs

1967.
424 **61** 17 f. grey, green and blue . 1·75 1·00

62 Ocean Racing Yachts

1967. Air. 2nd Whangarei-Noumea Yacht Race.
425 **62** 25 f. red, blue and green . 4·50 3·00

63 Magenta Stadium

1967. Sport Centres. Multicoloured.
426 10 f. Type **63** . . . . 1·40 60
427 20 f. Ouen-Toro swimming pool 2·50 1·10

64 New Caledonian Scenery

1967. International Tourist Year.
428 **64** 30 f. multicoloured . . . . 4·00 2·00

65 19th-century Postman

1967. Stamp Day.
429 **65** 7 f. red, green & turquoise . 1·40 1·00

66 "Papilio montrouzieri"

1967. Butterflies and Moths.
430 **66** 7 f. blue, black & green (postage) . . . . 1·60 80
431 – 9 f. blue, brown and mve . 2·50 1·10
432 – 13 f. violet, purple & brn . 3·00 1·40
433 – 15 f. yellow, purple & blue . 5·00 2·50
434 19 f. orange, brown and green (air) . . . . 4·50 2·75
435 – 29 f. purple, red and blue . 6·00 4·00
436 – 85 f. brown, red & yellow . 14·00 6·75
BUTTERFLIES—As T **66**: 9 f. "Polyura clitarchus"; 13 f. Common eggfly (male), and 15 f. (female). 48×27 mm: 19 f. Orange tiger; 29 f. Silver-striped hawk moth; 85 f. "Dellas elipsis".

67 Garnierite (mineral), Factory and Jules Garnier

1967. Air. Centenary of Garnierite Industry.
437 **67** 70 f. multicoloured . . . . 6·75 4·50

67a Lifou Island

1967. Air.
438 **67a** 200 f. multicoloured . . . 11·50 7·50

67b Skier and Snow-crystal

1967. Air. Winter Olympic Games, Grenoble.
439 **67b** 100 f. brn, blue & grn . . 12·00 7·50

68 Bouquet, Sun and W.H.O. Emblem **69** Human Rights Emblem

1968. 20th Anniv of W.H.O.
440 **68** 20 f. blue, red and violet . . 2·75 1·50

1968. Human Rights Year.
441 **69** 12 f. red, green & yellow . . 1·40 1·00

70 Ferrying Mail-van across Tontouta River

1968. Stamp Day.
442 **70** 9 f. brown, blue and green . 1·75 1·00

71 Geography Cone **72** Dancers

1968. Sea Shells.
443 – 1 f. brn, grey & grn (postage) 80 45
444 – 1 f. purple and violet . . . 65 35
445 – 2 f. pur, red and blue . . . 65 60
446 – 3 f. brown and green . . . 90 45
447 – 5 f. red, brown & violet . . 1·25 65
448 **71** 10 f. brown, grey & blue . 2·00 1·10
449 – 10 f. yellow, brown & red . 2·00 80
450 – 10 f. black, brown & orge . 1·60 65
451 – 15 f. red, grey and green . 3·50 1·40
452 – 21 f. brown, sepia & green 3·75 1·25
453 – 22 f. red, brown & bl (air) 3·50 1·75
454 – 25 f. brown and red . . . 3·50 2·00
455 – 33 f. brown and blue . . . 4·50 2·50
456 – 34 f. violet, brown & orge . 4·50 2·50
457 – 39 f. brown, grey & green . 4·50 2·00
458 – 40 f. black, brown & red . 4·50 2·00
459 – 50 f. red, purple & green . 6·00 3·00
460 – 60 f. brown and green . . 9·00 4·50
461 – 70 f. brown, grey & violet . 10·00 4·00
462 – 100 f. brown, black & bl . 17·00 8·50
DESIGNS—VERT: 1 f. (No. 443) Swan conch ("Strombus epidromis"); 1 f. (No. 444) Scorpion conch ("Lambis scorpius"); 3 f. Common spider conch; 10 f. (No. 450) Variable conch ("Strombus variabilis"). 27×48 mm: 22 f. Laciniate cone; 25 f. Orange spider conch; 34 f. Vomer conch; 50 f. Chiragra spider conch. 36×22 mm: 2 f. Snipe's-bill murex; 5 f. Troschel's murex; 10 f. (No. 449) Sieve cowrie; 15 f. "Murex sp."; 21 f. Mole cowrie. 48×27 mm: 33 f. Eyed cowrie; 39 f. Lienardi's cone; 40 f. Cabrit's cone; 60 f. All-red map cowrie; 70 f. Scarlet cone; 100 f. Adusta murex.

1968. Air.
463 **72** 60 f. red, blue and green . 6·50 4·00

73 Rally Car

1968. 2nd New Caledonian Motor Safari.
464 **73** 25 f. blue, red and green . 4·50 2·00

74 Caudron C-60 "Aiglon" and Route Map

1969. Air. Stamp Day. 30th Anniv of 1st Noumea–Paris Flight by Martinet and Klein.
465 **74** 29 f. red, blue and violet . 3·50 2·00

75 Concorde in Flight

1969. Air. 1st Flight of Concorde.
466 **75** 100 f. green and light green 22·00 15·00

76 Cattle-dip

1969. Cattle-breeding in New Caledonia.
467 **76** 9 f. brown, green & blue (postage) 90 65
468 – 25 f. violet, brown & grn . 2·50 1·00
469 – 50 f. purple, red & grn (air) 4·00 2·75
DESIGNS: 25 f. Branding. LARGER 48×27 mm; 50 f. Stockman with herd.

77 Judo

1969. 3rd South Pacific Games, Port Moresby, Papua New Guinea.
470 **77** 19 f. pur, blue & red (post) 2·75 1·25
471 – 20 f. black, red & green 2·75 1·25
472 – 30 f. black & blue (air) 3·50 1·75
473 – 39 f. brn, grn and blk 5·50 2·50
DESIGNS—HORIZ: 20 f. Boxing; 30 f. Diving (38 × 27 mm). VERT: 39 f. Putting the shot (27 × 48 mm).

1969. Air. Birth Bicentenary of Napoleon Bonaparte. As T **114b** of Mauritania. Multicoloured.
474 40 f. "Napoleon in Coronation Robes" (Gerard) (vert) 15·00 8·50

78 Douglas DC-4 over Outrigger Canoe

1969. Air. 20th Anniv of Regular Noumea-Paris Air Service.
475 **78** 50 f. green, brown & blue 4·50 2·75

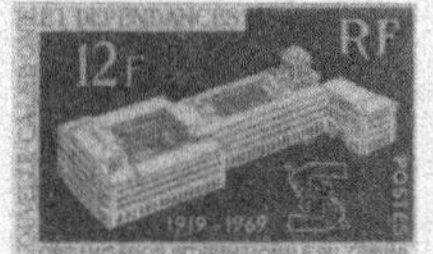

79 I.L.O. Building Geneva

1969. 50th Anniv of I.L.O.
476 **79** 12 f. brown, violet & salmon 1·10 80

80 "French Wings around the World"

1970. Air. 10th Anniv of French "Around the World" Air Service.
477 **80** 200 f. brown, blue & violet 15·00 8·50

81 New U.P.U. Building, Berne

1970. Inauguration of New U.P.U. Headquarters Building, Berne.
478 **81** 12 f. red, grey and brown 1·40 80

82 Packet Steamer "Natal", 1883

1970. Stamp Day.
479 **82** 9 f. black, green and blue 2·00 1·00

83 Cyclists on Map

1970. Air. 4th "Tour de Nouvelle Caledonie" Cycle Race.
480 **83** 40 f. brown, blue & lt bl 3·50 2·25

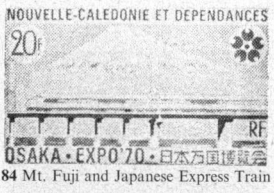

84 Mt. Fuji and Japanese Express Train

1970. Air. "EXPO 70" World Fair, Osaka, Japan. Multicoloured.
481 20 f. Type **84** 2·50 1·10
482 45 f. "EXPO" emblem, map and Buddha 3·50 1·60

85 Racing Yachts

1971. Air. One Ton Cup Yacht Race Auckland, New Zealand.
483 **85** 20 f. green, red and black 2·50 1·25

86 Dumbea Mail Train

1971. Stamp Day.
484 **86** 10 f. black, green and red 2·50 1·25

87 Ocean Racing Yachts

1971. 3rd Whangarei–Noumea Ocean Yacht Race.
485 **87** 16 f. turquoise, green and blue 3·50 1·75

88 Lieut.-Col. Broche and Theatre Map

1971. 30th Anniv of French Pacific Battalion's Participation in Second World War Mediterranean Campaign.
486 **88** 60 f. multicoloured 5·50 3·50

89 Early Tape Machine **90** Weightlifting

1971. World Telecommunications Day.
487 **89** 19 f. orange, pur & red 2·50 1·00

1971. 4th South Pacific Games, Papeete, French Polynesia.
488 **90** 11 f. brn & red (postage) 1·40 1·25
489 – 23 f. violet, red & blue 2·50 1·25
490 – 25 f. green and red (air) 2·75 2·00
491 – 100 f. blue, green and red 6·50 4·00
DESIGNS—VERT: 23 f. Basketball. HORIZ: 48 × 27 mm: 25 f. Pole-vaulting; 100 f. Archery.

91 Port de Plaisance, Noumea

1971. Air.
492 **91** 200 f. multicoloured 14·50 7·75

92 De Gaulle as President of French Republic, 1970

93 Publicity Leaflet showing De Havilland Gipsy Moth "Golden Eagle"

1971. 1st Death Anniv of General De Gaulle.
493 **92** 34 f. black and purple 6·50 2·75
494 – 100 f. black and purple 13·00 6·00
DESIGN: 100 f. De Gaulle in uniform, 1940.

1971. Air. 40th Anniv of 1st New Caledonia to Australia Flight.
495 **93** 90 f. brown, blue & orge 7·50 4·00

94 Downhill Skiing

1972. Air. Winter Olympic Games, Sapporo, Japan.
496 **94** 50 f. green, red & blue 5·00 2·50

95 St. Mark's Basilica, Venice

1972. Air. U.N.E.S.C.O. "Save Venice" Campaign.
497 **95** 20 f. brown, grn and blue 2·75 1·40

96 Commission Headquarters, Noumea

1972. Air. 25th Anniv of South Pacific Commission.
498 **96** 18 f. multicoloured 1·50 1·00

97 Couzinet 33 "Le Biarritz" and Noumea Monument

1972. Air. 40th Anniv of 1st Paris–Noumea Flight.
499 **97** 110 f. black, purple & grn 10·00 6·75

98 Pacific Island Dwelling **99** Goa Door-post

1972. Air. South Pacific Arts Festival, Fiji.
500 **98** 24 f. brown, blue & orange 2·75 1·50

1972. Exhibits from Noumea Museum.
501 **99** 1 f. red, grn & grey (post) 75 30
502 – 2 f. black, grn & dull grn 75 30
503 – 5 f. multicoloured 1·00 50
504 – 12 f. multicoloured 2·25 1·00
505 – 16 f. multicoloured (air) 1·50 1·00
506 – 40 f. multicoloured 3·00 1·50
DESIGNS: 2 f. Carved wooden pillow; 5 f. Monstrance; 12 f. Tchamba mask; 16 f. Ornamental arrowheads; 40 f. Portico, chief's house.

100 Hurdling over "H" of "MUNICH"

1972. Air. Olympic Games, Munich.
507 **100** 72 f. violet, purple & blue 6·50 3·50

101 New Head Post Office Building, Noumea

1972. Air.
508 **101** 23 f. brown, blue & green 2·25 1·00

102 J.C.I. Emblem

1972. 10th Anniv of New Caledonia Junior Chamber of Commerce.
509 **102** 12 f. multicoloured 1·25 80

103 Forest Scene

1973. Air. Landscapes of the East Coast. Multicoloured.
510 11 f. Type **103** 1·25 80
511 18 f. Beach and palms (vert) 2·50 1·25
512 21 f. Waterfall and inlet (vert) 3·00 1·40
See also Nos. 534/6.

104 Moliere and Characters

1973. Air. 300th Death Anniv of Moliere (playwright).
513 **104** 50 f. multicoloured 5·50 2·50

105 Tchamba Mask

1973.
514 **105** 12 f. purple (postage) 2·50 1·40
515 – 23 f. blue (air) 6·50 4·00
DESIGN: 23 f. Concorde in flight.

106 Liner "El Kantara" in Panama Canal

1973. 50th Anniv of Marseilles–Noumea Shipping Service via Panama Canal.
516 **106** 60 f. black, brown & green 5·50 3·00

107 Globe and Allegory of Weather

1973. Air. Centenary of World Meteorological Organization.

517 **107** 80 f. multicoloured . . . 5·50 2·75

108 DC-10 in Flight

1973. Air. Inauguration of Noumea–Paris DC-10 Air Service.

518 **108** 100 f. green, brown & blue 6·50 3·50

109 Common Egg Cowrie

1973. Marine Fauna from Noumea Aquarium. Multicoloured.

519 8 f. "Chaetodon melanotus" (daylight) . . . . 1·40 70
520 14 f. "Chaetodonmelanotus" (nocturnal) . . . . 2·00 1·10
521 3 f. Type **109** (air) 80 35
522 32 f. "Acanthurus olivaceus" (adult and young) . . . . . 4·00 1·75
523 32 f. Green-lined paper bubble ("Hydatina") . . . . 3·50 1·60
524 37 f. Pacific partridge tun ("Dolium perdix") . . . . . 3·50 1·60

111 Office Emblem

1973. 10th Anniv of Central Schools Co-operation Office.

532 **111** 20 f. blue, yellow & green 1·60 90

112 New Caledonia Mail-coach, 1880

1973. Air. Stamp Day.

533 **112** 15 f. multicoloured . . . . 1·75 1·10

1974. Air. Landscapes of the West Coast. As T **103**. Multicoloured.

534 8 f. Beach and palms (vert) . . 1·00 65
535 22 f. Trees and mountain . . . 1·75 1·10
536 26 f. Trees growing in sea . . 2·75 1·25

113 Centre Building

1974. Air. Opening of Scientific Studies Centre, Anse-Vata, Noumea.

537 **113** 50 f. multicoloured . . . 2·50 1·40

114 "Bird" embracing Flora

1974. Nature Conservation.

538 **114** 7 f. multicoloured 65 45

115 18th-century French Sailor

1974. Air. Discovery and Reconnaissance of New Caledonia and Loyalty Islands.

539 – 20 f. violet, red and blue . 1·50 80
540 – 25 f. green, brown & red 1·50 1·00
541 **115** 28 f. brown, blue & grn . 1·60 1·00
542 – 30 f. blue, brown & red . 2·25 1·40
543 – 36 f. red, brown & blue . 3·50 2·00

DESIGNS—HORIZ: 20 f. Captain Cook, H.M.S. "Endeavour" and map of Grand Terre island; 25 f. La Perouse, "L'Astrolabe" and map of Grand Terre island (reconnaissance of west coast); 30 f. Entrecasteaux, ship and map of Grand Terre island (reconnaissance of west coast); 36 f. Dumont d'Urville, "L'Astrolabe" and map of Loyalty Islands.

116 "Telecommunications"

1974. Air. Centenary of U.P.U.

544 **116** 95 f. orange, pur & grey . 5·00 3·00

117 "Art"

1974. Air. "Arphila 75" International Stamp Exhibition, Paris (1975) (1st issue).

545 **117** 80 f. multicoloured . . . 3·50 2·50
See also No. 554.

118 Hotel Chateau-Royal

1974. Air. Inauguration of Hotel Chateau Royal, Noumea.

546 **118** 22 f. multicoloured . . . 1·40 80

118a Animal Skull, Burnt Tree and Flaming Landscape

1975. "Stop Bush Fires".

547 **118a** 20 f. multicoloured . . . 1·00 65

119 "Cricket"

1975. Air. Tourism. Multicoloured.

548 3 f. Type **119** 80 45
549 25 f. "Bougna" ceremony . . 1·50 80
550 31 f. "Pilou" native dance . . 2·25 1·00

120 "Calanthe veratrifolia" 121 Global "Flower"

1975. New Caledonian Orchids. Multicoloured.

551 8 f. Type **120** (postage) . . . . 1·10 55
552 11 f. "Lyperanthus gigas" . . 1·40 65
553 42 f. "Eriaxis rigida" (air) . . 3·50 2·00

1975. Air. "Arphila 75" International Stamp Exhibition, Paris (2nd issue).

554 **121** 105 f. purple, green & bl . 5·50 3·00

122 Throwing the Discus

1975. Air. 5th South Pacific Games, Guam.

555 24 f. Type **122** . . . . 1·50 1·00
556 50 f. Volleyball . . . . 2·50 1·50

123 Festival Emblem 124 Birds in Flight

1975. "Melanesia 2000" Festival, Noumea.

557 **123** 12 f. multicoloured 80 45

1975. 10th Anniv of Noumea Ornithological Society.

558 **124** 5 f. multicoloured 65 40

125 Pres. Pompidou 127 Brown Booby

126 Concordes

1975. Pompidou Commemoration.

559 **125** 26 f. grey and green . . . 1·60 80

1976. Air. First Commercial Flight of Concorde.

560 **126** 147 f. blue and red . . . . 10·00 6·50

1976. Ocean Birds. Multicoloured.

561 1 f. Type **127** 85 40
562 2 f. Blue-faced booby . . . . 1·25 40
563 8 f. Red-footed booby (vert) . 3·00 1·00

128 Festival Emblem

1976. South Pacific Festival of Arts, Rotorua, New Zealand.

564 **128** 27 f. multicoloured . . . 1·50 1·00

129 Lion and Lions' Emblem 130 Early and Modern Telephones

1976. 15th Anniv of Lions Club, Noumea.

565 **129** 49 f. multicoloured . . . 3·00 1·75

1976. Air. Telephone Centenary.

566 **130** 36 f. multicoloured . . . 2·00 1·25

131 Capture of Penbosct

1976. Air. Bicent of American Revolution.

567 **131** 24 f. purple and brown . 1·50 1·00

132 Bandstand

1976. "Aspects of Old Noumea". Multicoloured.

568 25 f. Type **132** . . . . 1·10 55
569 30 f. Monumental fountain (vert) 1·40 80

133 Athletes

1976. Air. Olympic Games, Montreal.

570 **133** 33 f. violet, red & purple . 1·75 1·00

134 "Chick" with Magnifier

1976. Air. "Philately in Schools", Stamp Exhibition, Noumea.

571 **134** 42 f. multicoloured . . . 2·50 1·50

135 Dead Bird and Trees

1976. Nature Protection.

572 **135** 20 f. multicoloured . . . 1·40 65

136 South Pacific Heads

1976. 16th South Pacific Commission Conference.
573 **136** 20 f. multicoloured . . . 1·25 70

137 Old Town Hall, Noumea

1976. Air. Old and New Town Halls, Noumea. Mult.
574 75 f. Type **137** . . . . 3·75 2·50
575 125 f. New Town Hall . . . . 6·25 3·00

138 Water Carnival

1977. Air. Summer Festival, Noumea.
576 **138** 11 f. multicoloured . . . 80 40

139 "Pseudophyllanax imperialis" (cricket)

1977. Insects.
577 **139** 26 f. emerald, green & brn 1·25 1·00
578 – 31 f. brown, sepia and grn 2·00 1·00
DESIGN: 31 f. "Agrianome fairmairei" (long-horn beetle).

140 Miniature Roadway

1977. Air. Road Safety.
579 **140** 50 f. multicoloured . . . 2·50 1·25

141 Earth Station

1977. Earth Satellite Station, Noumea.
580 **141** 29 f. multicoloured . . . 1·40 80

142 "Phajus daenikeri"

1977. Orchids. Multicoloured.
581 22 f. Type **142** . . . . 1·25 80
582 44 f. "Dendrobium finetianum" 2·50 1·25

143 Mask and Palms

1977. La Perouse School Philatelic Exn.
583 **143** 35 f. multicoloured . . . 1·40 1·00

144 Trees

1977. Nature Protection.
584 **144** 20 f. multicoloured . . . 1·00 65

145 Palm Tree and Emblem

1977. French Junior Chambers of Commerce Congress.
585 **145** 200 f. multicoloured . . . 7·75 5·00

146 Young Bird

1977. Great Frigate Birds. Multicoloured.
586 16 f. Type **146** (postage) . . . 1·25 65
587 42 f. Adult male bird (horiz) (air) 3·75 1·75

147 Magenta Airport and Map of Internal Air Network

1977. Air. Airports. Multicoloured.
588 24 f. Type **147** . . . . 1·00 65
589 57 f. La Tontout International Airport, Noumea . . . . . 2·50 1·50

1977. Air. 1st Commercial Flight of Concorde, Paris–New York. Optd **22.11.77 PARIS NEW-YORK**.
590 **126** 147 f. blue and red . . . 11·00 9·00

149 Horse and Foal

1977. 10th Anniv of S.E.C.C. (Horse-breeding Society).
591 **149** 5 f. brown, green and blue 80 40

150 "Moselle Bay" (H. Didonna)

1977. Air. Views of Old Noumea (1st series).
592 **150** 41 f. multicoloured . . . . 2·50 1·50
593 – 42 f. purple and brown . . 2·50 1·50
DESIGN—49×27 mm: 42 f. "Settlers Valley" (J. Kreber).

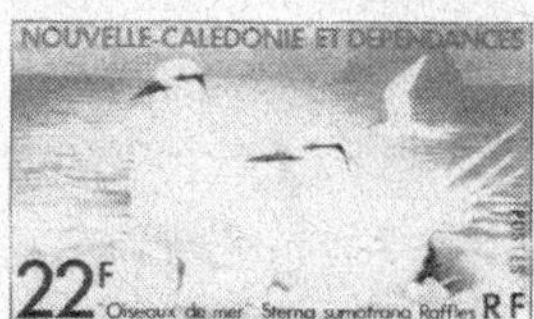

151 Black-naped Tern

1978. Ocean Birds. Multicoloured.
594 22 f. Type **151** . . . . 1·50 80
595 40 f. Sooty tern . . . . 3·00 1·50

152 "Araucaria montana" 153 "Halityle regularis"

1978. Flora. Multicoloured.
596 16 f. Type **152** (postage) . . . 55 45
597 42 f. "Amyema scandens" (horiz) (air) . . . . 2·50 1·50

1978. Noumea Aquarium.
598 **153** 10 f. multicoloured 65 30

154 Turtle

1978. Protection of the Turtle.
599 **154** 30 f. multicoloured . . . . 1·25 80

155 New Caledonian Flying Fox

1978. Nature Protection.
600 **155** 20 f. multicoloured . . . . 1·10 65

156 "Underwater Carnival"

1978. Air. Aubusson Tapestry.
601 **156** 105 f. multicoloured . . . 4·25 2·50

157 Pastor Maurice Leenhardt

1978. Birth Centenary of Pastor Maurice Leenhardt.
602 **157** 37 f. sepia, green & orge . 1·50 1·10

158 Hare chasing "Stamp" Tortoise

1978. School Philately (1st series).
603 **158** 35 f. multicoloured . . . 2·25 1·40

159 Heads, Map, Magnifying Glass and Cone Shell

1978. Air. Thematic Philately at Bourail.
604 **159** 41 f. multicoloured . . . 1·75 1·10

160 Candles 161 Footballer and League Badge

1978. 3rd New Caledonian Old People's Day.
605 **160** 36 f. multicoloured . . . 1·25 80

1978. 50th Anniv of New Caledonian Football League.
606 **161** 26 f. multicoloured . . . 1·25 65

162 "Fauberg Blanchot" (after Lacouture)

1978. Air. Views of Old Noumea.
607 **162** 24 f. multicoloured . . . 1·25 65

163 Map of Lifou, Solar Energy Panel and Transmitter Mast

1978. Telecommunications through Solar Energy.
608 **163** 33 f. multicoloured . . . 1·40 80

164 Petroglyph, Mere Region 165 Ouvea Island and Outrigger Canoe

1979. Archaeological Sites.
609 **164** 10 f. red 65 45

1979. Islands. Multicoloured.
610 11 f. Type **165** 60 40
611 31 f. Mare Island and ornaments (horiz) 85 60
See also Nos. 629 and 649.

166 Satellite Orbit of Earth

167 19th-century Barque and Modern Container Ship

1979. Air. 1st World Survey of Global Atmosphere.

612 **166** 53 f. multicoloured . . . 1·50 1·00

1979. Air. Centenary of Chamber of Commerce and Industry.

613 **167** 49 f. mauve, blue & brown 1·50 80

168 Child's Drawing

1979. Air. International Year of the Child.

614 **168** 35 f. multicoloured . . . 1·40 80

169 House at Artillery Point

1979. Views of Old Noumea.

615 **169** 20 f. multicoloured . . . 85 55

170 "Katsuwonus pelamis"

1979. Air. Sea Fishes (1st series). Multicoloured.

616 29 f. Type **170** . . . . 1·40 65

617 30 f. "Makaira indica" . . . . 1·40 70

See also Nos. 632/3 and 647/8.

171 L. Tardy de Montravel (founder) and View of Port-de-France (Noumea)

1979. Air. 125th Anniv of Noumea.

618 **171** 75 f. multicoloured . . . 2·75 1·50

172 The Eel Queen (Kanaka legend)

173 Auguste Escoffier

1979. Air. Nature Protection.

619 **172** 42 f. multicoloured . . . 2·00 1·40

1979. Auguste Escoffier Hotel School.

620 **173** 24 f. brown, green and turquoise 85 55

174 Games Emblem and Catamarans

1979. 6th South Pacific Games, Fiji.

621 **174** 16 f. multicoloured . . . 85 45

175 Children of Different Races, Map and Postmark

1979. Air. Youth Philately.

622 **175** 27 f. multicoloured . . . 90 55

176 Aerial View of Centre

1979. Air. Overseas Scientific and Technical Research Office (O.R.S.T.O.M.) Centre, Noumea.

623 **176** 25 f. multicoloured . . . 90 55

177 "Agathis ovata"

1979. Trees. Multicoloured.

624 5 f. Type **177** 50 20

625 34 f. "Cyathea intermedia" . 1·25 65

178 Rodeo Riding

1979. Pouembout Rodeo.

626 **178** 12 f. multicoloured . . . 80 40

179 Hill, 1860 10 c. Stamp and Post Office

1979. Air. Death Centenary of Sir Rowland Hill.

627 **179** 150 f. black, brn & orge . 4·50 2·50

180 "Bantamia merleti"

1980. Noumea Aquarium. Fluorescent Corals (1st issue).

628 **180** 23 f. multicoloured . . . 90 45

See also No. 646.

1980. Islands. As T **165**. Multicoloured.

629 23 f. Map of Ile des Pins and ornaments (horiz) 80 40

181 Outrigger Canoe

1980. Air.

630 **181** 45 f. blue, turq & indigo . 1·40 1·00

182 Globe, Rotary Emblem, Map and Carving

1980. Air. 75th Anniv of Rotary International.

631 **182** 100 f. multicoloured . . . 3·25 1·75

1980. Air. Sea Fishes (2nd series). As T **170**. Multicoloured.

632 34 f. Angler holding dolphin fish 1·25 80

633 39 f. Fishermen with sailfish (vert) . . . . 1·50 90

183 "Hibbertia virotii"

184 High Jumper, Magnifying Glass, Albums and Plimsoll

1980. Flowers. Multicoloured.

634 11 f. Type **183** 60 40

635 12 f. "Grevillea meisneri" . . . 60 40

1980. School Philately.

636 **184** 30 f. multicoloured 80 50

185 Scintex Super Emeraude Airplane and Map

1980. Air. Coral Sea Air Rally.

637 **185** 31 f. blue, green and brn . 1·00 80

186 Sailing Canoe

1980. Air. South Pacific Arts Festival, Port Moresby.

638 **186** 27 f. multicoloured 80 65

187 Road Signs as Road-users

1980. Road Safety.

639 **187** 15 f. multicoloured 60 25

188 "Parribacus caledonicus"

1980. Noumea Aquarium. Marine Animals (1st series). Multicoloured.

640 5 f. Type **188** 30 20

641 8 f. "Panulirus versicolor" . . 40 20

See also Nos. 668/9.

189 Kiwanis Emblem

1980. Air. 10th Anniv of Noumea Kiwanis Club.

642 **189** 50 f. multicoloured . . . . 1·50 1·00

190 Sun, Tree and Solar Panel

1980. Nature Protection. Solar Energy.

643 **190** 23 f. multicoloured 90 55

191 Old House, Poulou

1980. Air. Views of Old Noumea (4th series).

644 **191** 33 f. multicoloured . . . 90 65

192 Charles de Gaulle

193 Manta Ray

1980. Air. 10th Death Anniv of Charles de Gaulle (French statesman).

645 **192** 120 f. green, olive & blue 4·50 2·75

1981. Air. Noumea Aquarium. Fluorescent Corals (2nd series). As T **180**. Multicoloured.

646 60 f. "Trachyphyllia geoffroyi" 1·60 90

1981. Sea Fishes (3rd series). Multicoloured.

647 23 f. Type **193** 70 50

648 25 f. Grey Shark 75 50

1981. Islands. As T **165**. Multicoloured.

649 26 f. Map of Belep Archipelago and diver (horiz) 75 45

194 "Xeronema moorei"

1981. Air. Flowers. Multicoloured.

650 38 f. Type **194** 90 55

651 51 f. "Geissois pruinosa" . . 1·25 75

195 Yury Gagarin and "Vostok 1"

1981. Air. 20th Anniv of First Men in Space. Multicoloured.

652 64 f. Type **195** . . . . 1·50 1·25

653 155 f. Alan Shepard and "Freedom 7" . . . . 4·00 2·50

196 Liberation Cross, "Zealandia" (troopship) and Badge

1981. Air. 40th Anniv of Departure of Pacific Battalion for Middle East.

655 **196** 29 f. multicoloured . . . . 1·40 80

197 Rossini's Volute

198 Sail Corvette "Constantine"

1981. Shells. Multicoloured.
656 1 f. Type **197** 15 10
657 2 f. Clouded cone 25 20
658 13 f. Stolid cowrie (horiz) 65 25

1981. Ships (1st series).
659 **198** 10 f. blue, brown and red . 65 30
660 – 25 f. blue, brown and red . 1·00 65
DESIGN: 25 f. Paddle-gunboat "Le Phoque", 1853.
See also Nos. 680/1 and 725/6.

199 "Echinometra mathaei"

1981. Air. Water Plants. Multicoloured.
661 38 f. Type **199** 90 55
662 51 f. "Prionocidaris verticillata" 1·25 65

200 Broken-stemmed Rose and I.Y.D.P. Emblems

1981. International Year of Disabled Persons.
663 **200** 45 f. multicoloured . . . 1·40 80

201 25 c. Surcharged Stamp of 1881 **202** Latin Quarter

1981. Air. Stamp Day.
664 **201** 41 f. multicoloured . . . 1·10 65

1981. Air. Views of Old Noumea.
665 **202** 43 f. multicoloured . . . 1·10 65

203 Trees and Fish **204** Victor Roffey and "Golden Eagle"

1981. Nature Protection.
666 **203** 28 f. blue, green & brown 1·10 65

1981. Air. 50th Anniv of First New Caledonia–Australia Airmail Flight.
667 **204** 37 f. black, violet and blue 90 60

1982. Noumea Aquarium. Marine Animals (2nd series). As T **188**. Multicoloured.
668 13 f. "Calappa calappa" . . . 65 45
669 25 f. "Etisus splendidus" . . . 1·00 65

205 "La Rousette"

1982. Air. New Caledonian Aircraft (1st series).
670 **205** 38 f. brown, red and green 90 55
671 – 51 f. brown, orge & grn . 1·10 65
DESIGN: 51 f. "Le Cagou".
See also Nos. 712/13.

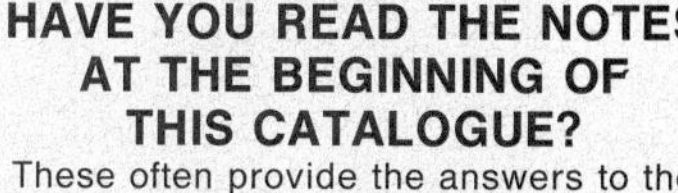

206 Chalcantite, Ouegoa

1982. Rocks and Minerals (1st series). Multicoloured.
672 15 f. Type **206** 90 65
673 30 f. Anorthosite, Blue River 1·25 65
See also Nos. 688/9.

207 De Verneilh, Deve and Munch (air crew), Couzinet 33 "Le Biarritz" and Route Map

1982. Air. 50th Anniv of First Flight from Paris to Noumea.
674 **207** 250 f. mauve, blue and black 5·50 2·75

208 Scout and Guide Badges and Map

1982. Air. 50th Anniv of New Caledonian Scout Movement.
675 **208** 40 f. multicoloured . . . 1·00 65

209 "The Rat and the Octopus" (Canaque legend)

1982. "Philexfrance 82" International Stamp Exhibition, Paris.
676 **209** 150 f. blue, mauve and deep blue . . . . 3·00 2·25

210 Footballer, Mascot and Badge

1982. Air. World Cup Football Championship, Spain.
677 **210** 74 f. multicoloured . . . 1·60 1·00

211 Savanna Trees at Niaoulis **212** Islanders, Map and Kagu

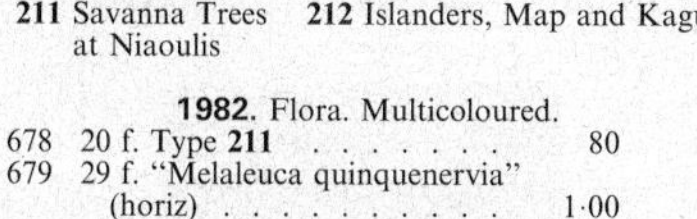

1982. Flora. Multicoloured.
678 20 f. Type **211** 80 45
679 29 f. "Melaleuca quinquenervia" (horiz) . . . . 1·00 55

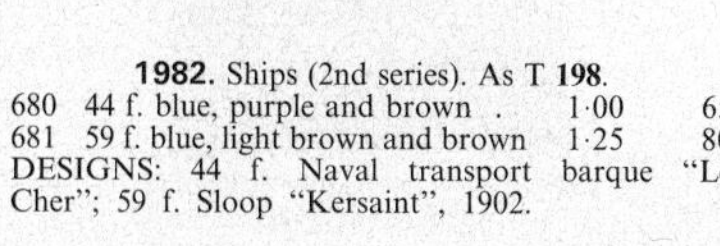

1982. Ships (2nd series). As T **198**.
680 44 f. blue, purple and brown . 1·00 65
681 59 f. blue, light brown and brown 1·25 80
DESIGNS: 44 f. Naval transport barque "Le Cher"; 59 f. Sloop "Kersaint", 1902.

1982. Air. Overseas Week.
682 **212** 100 f. brown, green & bl . 2·00 1·10

213 Ateou Tribal House **214** Grey's Fruit Dove

1982. Traditional Houses.
683 **213** 52 f. multicoloured . . . . 1·40 90

1982. Birds. Multicoloured.
684 32 f. Type **214** . . . . 1·60 70
685 35 f. Rainbow lory . . . . . . 1·60 70

215 Canoe

1982. Central Office of Education Co-operation office.
686 **215** 48 f. multicoloured . . . . 1·25 65

216 Bernheim and Library

1982. Bernheim Library, Noumea.
687 **216** 36 f. brown, purple and blk 90 50

1983. Air. Rocks and Minerals (2nd series). As T **206**. Multicoloured.
688 44 f. Paya gypsum (vert) . . . 1·10 80
689 59 f. Kone silica (vert) . . . . 1·40 90

217 "Dendrobium oppositifolium"

1983. Orchids. Multicoloured.
690 10 f. Type **217** 30 10
691 15 f. "Dendrobium munificum" 40 15
692 29 f. "Dendrobium fractiflexum" 80 35

218 W.C.Y. Emblem, Map of New Caledonia and Globe

1983. Air. World Communications Year.
693 **218** 170 f. multicoloured . . . 3·50 2·00

219 "Crinum asiaticum"

1983. Flowers. Multicoloured.
694 1 f. Type **219** 10 10
695 2 f. "Xanthostemon aurantiacum" 10 10
696 4 f. "Metrosideros demonstrans" (vert) 10 10

220 Wall Telephone and Noumea Post Office, 1890

1983. 25th Anniv of Post and Telecommunications Office. Multicoloured.
697 30 f. Type **220** 70 30
698 40 f. Telephone & Noumea Post Office, 1936 . . . . 80 30
699 50 f. Push-button telephone and Noumea Post Office, 1972 . 1·25 40

221 "Laticaudata laticaudata" **224** Volleyball

223 Bangkok Temples

1983. Noumea Aquarium. Sea Snakes. Multicoloured.
701 31 f. Type **221** 80 40
702 33 f. "Laticauda colubrina" . 1·00 40

1983. Air. New Caledonian Aircraft (2nd series). As T **205**. Each red, mauve & brown.
712 46 f. Mignet HM14 "Pou du Ciel" . . . . 1·00 65
713 61 f. Caudron C-600 "Aiglon" 1·25 80

1983. Air. "Bangkok 1983" International Stamp Exhibition.
714 **223** 47 f. multicoloured . . . 1·10 80

1983. 7th South Pacific Games, Western Samoa.
715 **224** 16 f. purple, blue and red 65 40

225 Ouehoulle

1983. Air.
716 **225** 76 f. multicoloured . . . 1·50 1·00

226 Desert and Water Drop showing Fertile Land **227** Barn Owl

1983. Water Resources.
717 **226** 56 f. multicoloured . . . 1·40 90

1983. Birds of Prey. Multicoloured.
718 34 f. Type **227** . . . . 2·10 1·00
719 37 f. Osprey . . . . 2·40 1·25

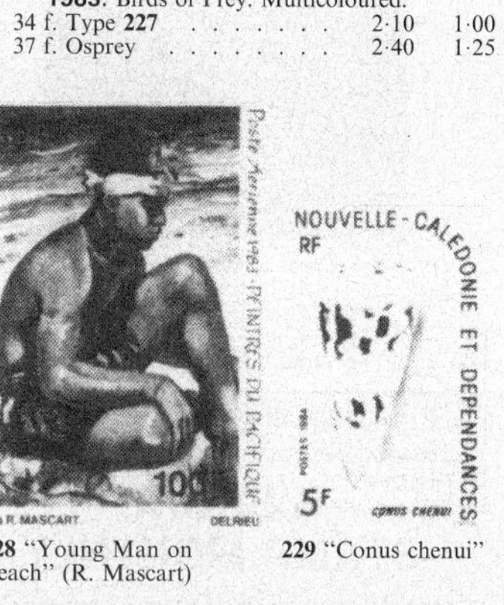

228 "Young Man on Beach" (R. Mascart) **229** "Conus chenui"

1983. Air. Paintings. Multicoloured.
720 100 f. Type **228** . . . . 2·25 1·50
721 350 f. "Man with Guitar" (P. Nielly) . . . . 7·50 4·50

1984. Sea Shells (1st series). Multicoloured.

722 5 f. Type **229** 30 10
723 15 f. Molucca cone 40 15
724 20 f. "Conus optimus" 75 40

See also Nos. 761/2 and 810/11.

230 "St. Joseph" (freighter)

1984. Ships (3rd series). Each black, red and blue.

725 18 f. Type **230** 65 40
726 31 f. "Saint Antoine" (freighter) 75 60

231 "Amphiprion clarkii"

1984. Air. Noumea Aquarium. Fishes. Multicoloured.

727 46 f. Type **231** . . . . 1·10 65
728 61 f. "Centropyge bicolor" . . 1·50 1·10

232 Arms of Noumea

233 "Araucaria columnaris"

1984.

729 **232** 35 f. multicoloured . . . 80 45

1984. Air. Trees. Multicoloured.

730 51 f. Type **233** . . . . 1·25 65
731 67 f. "Pritchardiopsis jeanneneyi" . . . . 1·40 80

234 Tourist Centres

1984. Nature Protection.

732 **234** 65 f. multicoloured . . . 1·50 80

235 Swimming

1984. Air. Olympic Games, Los Angeles. Multicoloured.

733 50 f. Type **235** . . . . 1·25 90
734 83 f. Windsurfing . . . . . . 1·75 1·25
735 200 f. Marathon . . . . 4·25 3·00

236 "Diplocaulobium ou-hinnae"

1984. Orchids. Multicoloured.

736 16 f. Type **236** 65 40
737 38 f. "Acianthus atepalus" . . 1·00 75

237 Royal Exhibition Hall, Melbourne

1984. Air. "Ausipex 84" International Stamp Exhibition, Melbourne.

738 **237** 150 f. grn, brn & mve . . 3·50 2·50

238 School and Arrow Sign-post

239 Anchor, Rope and Stars

1984. Centenary of Public Education.

740 **238** 59 f. multicoloured . . . 1·10 65

1984. Air. Armed Forces Day.

741 **239** 51 f. multicoloured . . . 1·00 65

240 "Women looking for Crabs" (Mme. Bonnet de Larbogne)

1984. Air. Art. Multicoloured.

742 120 f. Type **240** . . . . 2·50 1·50
743 300 f. "Cook discovering New Caledonia" (tapestry by Pilioko) . . . . 6·00 4·00

241 Kagu

1985.

744 **241** 1 f. blue 10 10
745 2 f. green 10 10
746 3 f. orange 10 10
747 4 f. green 15 15
748 5 f. mauve 15 15
749 35 f. red 80 45
750 38 f. red 80 60
751 40 f. red 90 35

For similar design but with "& DEPENDANCES" omitted, see Nos. 837/43.

1985. Sea Shells (2nd series). As T **229**. Multicoloured.

761 55 f. Bubble cone . . . . . . 1·25 75
762 72 f. Lambert's cone . . . . 1·50 1·00

243 Weather Station transmitting Forecast to Boeing 737 and Trawler

1985. World Meteorology Day.

763 **243** 17 f. multicoloured . . . 45 25

244 Map and Hands holding Red Cross

1985. International Medicines Campaign.

764 **244** 41 f. multicoloured 90 45

245 Electronic Telephone Exchange

1985. Inauguration of Electronic Telephone Equipment.

765 **245** 70 f. multicoloured . . . . 1·50 80

246 Marguerite la Foa Suspension Bridge

1985. Protection of Heritage.

766 **246** 44 f. brown, red and blue . 1·00 55

247 Kagu with Magnifying Glass and Stamp

1985. "Le Cagou" Stamp Club.

767 **247** 220 f. multicoloured . . . 4·00 2·50

248 Festival Emblem

1985. 4th Pacific Arts Festival, Papeete. Mult.

769 55 f. Type **248** . . . . 1·25 80
770 75 f. Girl blowing trumpet triton . . . . 1·50 1·00

249 Flowers, Barbed Wire and Starving Child

1985. International Youth Year.

771 **249** 59 f. multicoloured . . . . 1·10 55

250 "Amedee Lighthouse" (M. Hosken)

251 Tree and Seedling

1985. Electrification of Amedee Lighthouse.

772 **250** 89 f. multicoloured . . . . 1·75 1·00

1985. "Planting for the Future".

773 **251** 100 f. multicoloured . . . 2·00 1·00

252 De Havilland Dragon Rapide and Route Map

1985. Air. 30th Anniv of First Regular Internal Air Service.

774 **252** 80 f. multicoloured . . . . 1·50 1·00

253 Hands and U.N. Emblem

1985. 40th Anniv of U.N.O.

775 **253** 250 f. multicoloured . . . 4·50 2·50

254 School, Map and "Nautilus"

1985. Air. Jules Garnier High School.

776 **254** 400 f. multicoloured . . . 7·50 4·00

255 Purple Swamphen

1985. Birds. Multicoloured.

777 50 f. Type **255** . . . . 1·40 70
778 60 f. Island thrush . . . . . 1·60 90

256 Aircraft Tail Fins and Eiffel Tower

1986. Air. 30th Anniv of Scheduled Paris–Noumea Flights.

779 **256** 72 f. multicoloured . . . 1·50 90

257 "Rhinopias aphanes"

1986. Noumea Aquarium. Multicoloured.

780 10 f. "Pomacanthus imperator" 25 20
781 17 f. Type **257** 35 25

258 Kanumera Bay, Isle of Pines

1986. Landscapes (1st series). Multicoloured.

782 50 f. Type **258** . . . . 1·00 55
783 55 f. Inland village . . . . . 1·10 55

See also Nos. 795/6 and 864/5.

259 "Bavayia sauvagii"

1986. Geckos. Multicoloured.

784 20 f. Type **259** 55 25
785 45 f. "Rhacodactylus leachianus" 1·00 65

260 Players and Azteca Stadium

1986. World Cup Football Championship, Mexico.
786 **260** 60 f. multicoloured . . . 1·10 90

261 Vivarium, Nou Island

1986. Air. Protection of Heritage.
787 **261** 230 f. deep brown, blue and brown . . . . 4·50 2·75

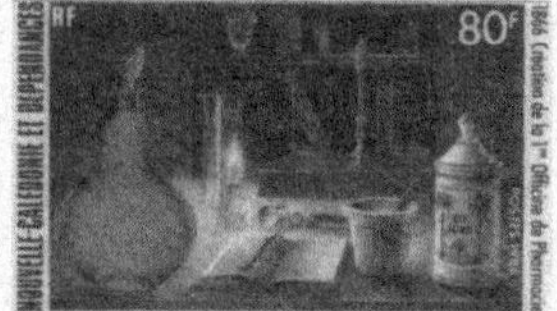

262 Pharmaceutical Equipment

1986. 120th Anniv of First Pharmacy.
788 **262** 80 f. multicoloured . . . 1·50 1·10

263 "Coelogynae licastioides"

1986. Orchids. Multicoloured.
789 44 f. Type **263** . . . . 1·00 55
790 58 f. "Calanthe langei" . . . 1·25 80

264 Black-backed Magpie

1986. "Stampex 86" National Stamp Exhibition, Adelaide.
791 **264** 110 f. multicoloured . . . 3·25 2·25

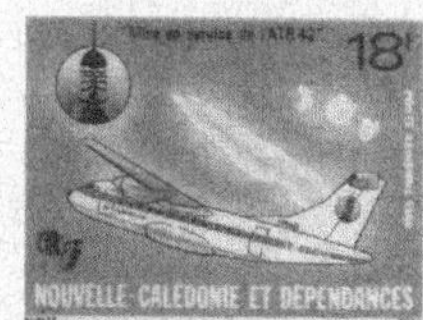

265 Airplane over New Caledonia

1986. Air. Inaugural Flight of "ATR 42".
792 **265** 18 f. multicoloured . . . 35 25

266 Emblem and 1860 Stamp

267 Arms of Mont Dore

1986. Air. "Stockholmia 86" International Stamp Exhibition.
793 **266** 108 f. black, red and lilac . 2·00 1·50

1986.
794 **267** 94 f. multicoloured . . . 1·75 1·10

1986. Landscapes (2nd series). As T **258**. Multicoloured.
795 40 f. West coast (vert) 80 40
796 76 f. South . . . . 1·50 90

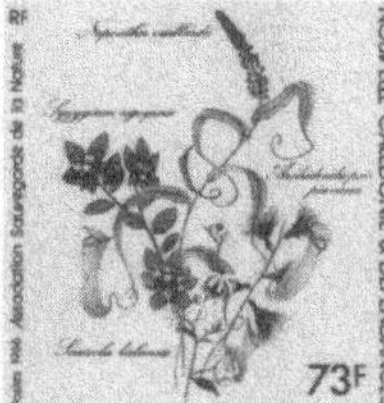

268 Wild Flowers

269 Club Banner

1986. Association for Nature Protection.
797 **268** 73 f. multicoloured . . . 1·50 90

1986. 25th Anniv of Noumea Lions Club.
798 **269** 350 f. multicoloured . . . 6·00 4·50

270 "Moret Bridge" (Alfred Sisley)

1986. Paintings. Multicoloured.
799 74 f. Type **270** . . . . 1·50 90
800 140 f. "Hunting Butterflies" (Berthe Morisot) . . . . . 2·75 1·75

271 Emblem and Sound Waves

272 "Challenge France"

1987. Air. 25th Anniv of New Caledonia Amateur Radio Association.
801 **271** 64 f. multicoloured . . . 1·25 80

1987. America's Cup Yacht Race. Multicoloured.
802 30 f. Type **272** . . . . 1·00 55
803 70 f. "French Kiss" . . . . . 1·50 1·00

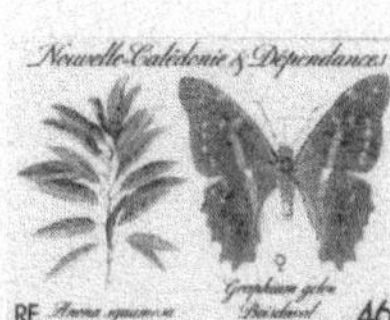

273 "Anona squamosa" and "Graphium gelon"

1987. Plants and Butterflies. Multicoloured.
804 46 f. Type **273** . . . . 1·00 65
805 54 f. "Abizzia granulosa" and "Polyura gamma" . . . . 1·25 80

274 Peaceful Landscape, Earphones and Noisy Equipment

1987. Air. Nature Protection. Campaign against Noise.
806 **274** 150 f. multicoloured . . . 3·00 1·50

275 Isle of Pines Canoe

1987. Canoes. Each brown, green and blue.
807 72 f. Type **275** . . . . 1·40 90
808 90 f. Ouvea canoe . . . . . 1·75 1·10

276 Town Hall

1987. New Town Hall, Mont Dore.
809 **276** 92 f. multicoloured . . . . 1·75 1·10

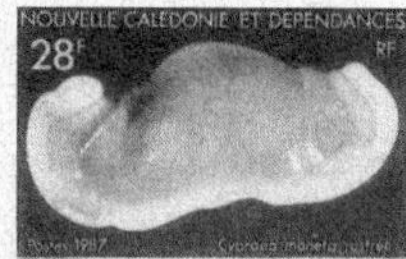

277 Money Cowrie

1987. Sea Shells (3rd series). Multicoloured.
810 28 f. Type **277** 55 45
811 36 f. Martin's cone 70 55

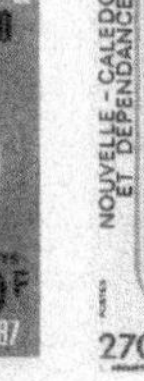

278 Games Emblem

279 Emblem

1987. 8th South Pacific Games. Noumea (1st issue).
812 **278** 40 f. multicoloured 80 55
See also Nos. 819/21.

1987. 13th Soroptimists International Convention, Melbourne.
813 **279** 270 f. multicoloured . . . 5·00 3·25

280 New Caledonia White Eye

1987. Birds. Multicoloured.
814 18 f. Type **280** 75 40
815 21 f. Peregrine falcon (vert) . . 75 45

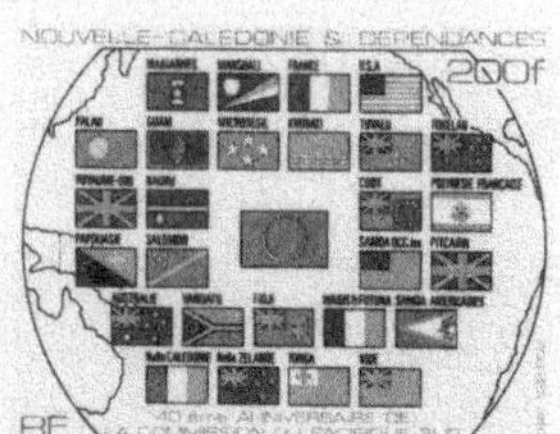

281 Flags on Globe

1987. 40th Anniv of South Pacific Commission.
816 **281** 200 f. multicoloured . . . 3·75 2·25

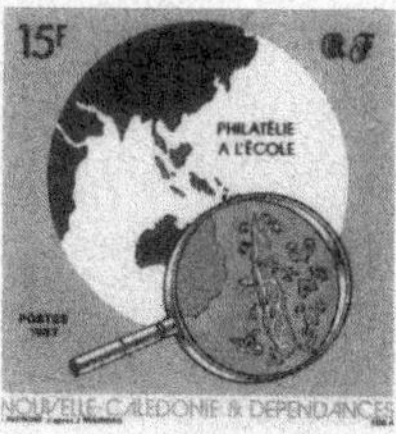

282 Globe and Magnifying Glass on Map of New Caledonia

1987. Schools Philately.
817 **282** 15 f. multicoloured 35 20

283 Cricketers

1987. Air. French Cricket Federation.
818 **283** 94 f. multicoloured . . . . 1·90 1·25

284 Golf

1987. 8th South Pacific Games, Noumea (2nd issue). Multicoloured.
819 20 f. Type **284** 40 20
820 30 f. Rugby football 60 35
821 100 f. Long jumping . . . . . 1·75 1·10

285 Arms of Dumbea

287 University

286 Route Map, "L'Astrolabe", "La Boussole" and La Perouse

1988. Air.
822 **285** 76 f. multicoloured . . . 1·40 90

1988. Bicentenary of Disappearance of La Perouse's Expedition.
823 **286** 36 f. blue, brown & red . 80 45

1988. French University of South Pacific, Noumea and Papeete.
824 **287** 400 f. multicoloured . . . 7·25 4·50

288 Zebra Angelfish

289 Mwaringou House, Canala

1988. Noumea Aquarium. Fishes. Multicoloured.
825 30 f. Type **288** 65 40
826 46 f. "Glyphidodontops cyaneus" . . . . 1·00 60

1988. Traditional Huts. Each brown, green and blue.
827 19 f. Type **289** 35 20
828 21 f. Nathalo house, Lifou (horiz) 35 20

290 Anniversary Emblem

1988. 125th Anniv of International Red Cross.
829 **290** 300 f. blue, green and red 6·00 3·25

291 "Ochrosia elliptica"

1988. Medicinal Plants. Multicoloured.
830 28 f. Type **291** (postage) . . . 60 40
831 64 f. "Rauvolfia sevenetii" (air) 1·25 80

292 "Gymnocrinus richeri"

1988.
832 **292** 51 f. multicoloured . . . 1·10 65

293 Furnished Room and Building Exterior

1988. Bourail Museum and Historical Association.
833 **293** 120 f. multicoloured . . . 2·25 1·50

294 La Perouse sighting Phillip's Fleet in Botany Bay

1988. "Sydpex 88" Stamp Exhibition, Sydney. Multicoloured.
834 42 f. Type **294** 85 70
835 42 f. Phillip sighting "La Boussole" and "L'Astrolabe" 85 70

295 Kagu

297 Laboratory Assistant, Noumea Institute and Pasteur

296 Table Tennis

1988.
837 **295** 1 f. blue 10 10
838 2 f. green 10 10
839 3 f. orange 10 10
840 4 f. green 10 10
841 5 f. mauve 15 10
842 28 f. orange 50 20
843 40 f. red 65 20

1988. Olympic Games, Seoul.
846 **296** 150 f. multicoloured . . . 2·75 1·60

1988. Centenary of Pasteur Institute, Paris.
847 **297** 100 f. red, black and blue 1·90 1·25

298 Georges Baudoux

1988. Writers.
848 **298** 72 f. brown, green and purple (postage) . . . . 1·40 80
849 – 73 f. brown, bl & blk (air) 1·40 90
DESIGN: 73 f. Jean Mariotti.

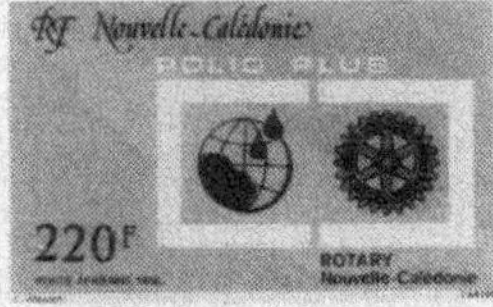
299 Map and Emblems

1988. Air. Rotary International Anti-Polio Campaign.
850 **299** 220 f. multicoloured . . . 4·00 2·75

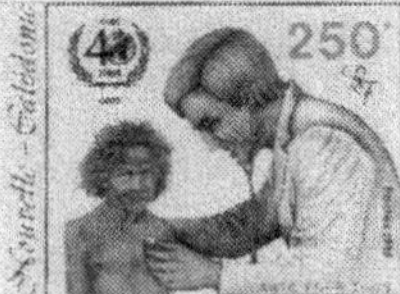
300 Doctor examining Child

1988. 40th Anniv of W.H.O.
851 **300** 250 f. multicoloured . . . 4·50 2·50

301 "Terre des Hommes" (L. Bunckley)

1988. Paintings. Multicoloured.
852 54 f. Type **301** . . . . 1·25 80
853 92 f. "Latin Quarter" (Marik) 2·00 1·25

302 Arms of Koumac

303 "Parasitaxus ustus"

1989.
854 **302** 200 f. multicoloured . . . 3·25 2·25

1989. Flowers. Multicoloured.
855 80 f. Type **303** . . . . 1·50 90
856 90 f. "Tristaniopsis guillainii" (horiz) . . . . 1·60 1·00

304 "Plesionika sp."

1989. Marine Life. Multicoloured.
857 18 f. Type **304** 45 20
858 66 f. Waspfish . . . . 1·10 80
859 110 f. Cristiate latiaxis . . . 2·00 80

305 "Liberty"

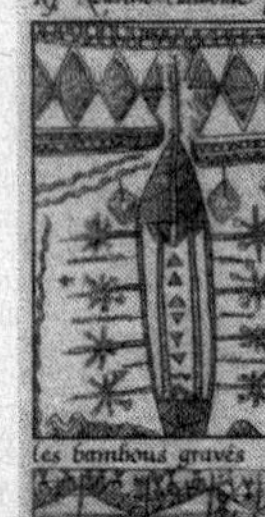
306 Canoe and Diamond Decoration

1989. Bicentenary of French Revolution and "Philexfrance 89" International Stamp Exn, Paris. Multicoloured.
860 40 f. Type **305** (postage) . . . 80 45
861 58 f. "Equality" (air) . . . . 1·10 65
862 76 f. "Fraternity" . . . . . . 1·40 90

1989. Landscapes (3rd series). As T **258**. Mult.
864 180 f. Ouaieme ferry (post) . 3·25 1·75
865 64 f. "The Broody Hen" (rocky islet), Hienghene (air) . . . 1·25 65

1989. Bamboo Decorations by C. Ohlen. Each black, bistre and orange.
866 70 f. Type **306** (postage) . . . 1·40 80
867 44 f. Animal design (air) . . 80 55

307 "Hobie Cat 14" Yachts

1989. 10th World "Hobie Cat" Class Catamaran Championship, Noumea.
868 **307** 350 f. multicoloured . . . 6·00 3·50

308 Book Title Pages and Society Members

1989. 20th Anniv of Historical Studies Society.
869 **308** 74 f. black and brown . . 1·40 90

309 Fort Teremba

1989. Protection of Heritage.
870 **309** 100 f. green, brown & blue 1·75 1·10

310 "Rochefort's Escape" (Edouard Manet)

311 Fr. Patrick O'Reilly

1989. Paintings. Multicoloured.
871 130 f. Type **310** . . . . 2·50 1·50
872 270 f. "Self-portrait" (Gustave Courbet) . . . . 4·75 3·00

1990. Writers.
873 **311** 170 f. black and mauve . . 3·00 1·75

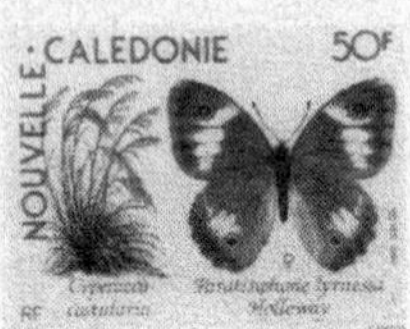
312 Grass and Female Butterfly

1990. "Cyperacea costularia" (grass) and "Paratisiphone lyrnessa" (butterfly). Multicoloured.
874 50 f. Type **312** (postage) . . . 90 55
875 18 f. Grass and female butterfly (different) (air) 35 20
876 94 f. Grass and male butterfly . 1·60 1·00

313 "Maize" Stem with Face

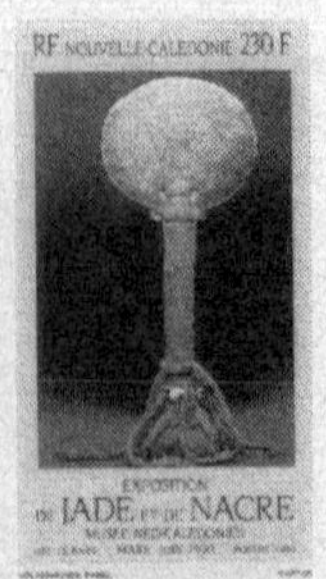
314 Exhibit

1990. Kanaka Money.
877 **313** 85 f. olive, orange & grn . 1·60 80
878 – 140 f. orange, black & grn 2·50 1·40
DESIGN: 140 f. "Rope" stem with decorative end.

1990. Jade and Mother-of-pearl Exhibition.
879 **314** 230 f. multicoloured . . . 4·00 2·40

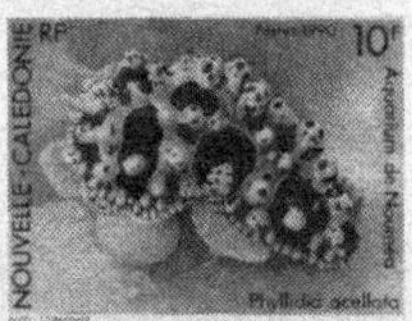
315 Ocellate Nudibranch

1990. Noumea Aquarium. Sea Slugs. Multicoloured.
880 10 f. Type **315** 25 10
881 42 f. "Chromodoris kuniei" (vert) . . . . 1·00 55

316 Head of "David" (Michelangelo) and Footballers

1990. World Cup Football Championship, Italy.
882 **316** 240 f. multicoloured . . . 4·00 2·40

317 De Gaulle

1990. Air. 50th Anniv of De Gaulle's Call to Resist.
883 **317** 160 f. multicoloured . . . 2·75 1·90

318 Neounda Site

1990. Petroglyphs.
884 **318** 40 f. brown, green and red (postage) 65 45
885 – 58 f. black, brown and blue (air) . . . . 1·00 65
DESIGN—HORIZ: 58 f. Kassducou site.

319 Map and Pacific International Meeting Centre

1990.
886 **319** 320 f. multicoloured . . . 5·00 2·40

320 New Zealand Cemetery, Bourail

321 Kagu

1990. Air. "New Zealand 1990" International Stamp Exhibition, Auckland. Multicoloured.
887 80 f. Type **320** . . . . 1·40 1·10
888 80 f. Brigadier William Walter Dove . . . . 1·40 1·10

1990.

890 **321** 1 f. blue 10 10
891 2 f. green 10 10
892 3 f. yellow 10 10
893 4 f. green 10 10
894 5 f. violet 10 10
895 9 f. grey 10 10
896 12 f. red 15 10
897 40 f. mauve 50 30
898 50 f. red 65 40
899 55 f. red 70 45

The 5 and 55 f. exist both perforated with ordinary gum and imperforate with self-adhesive gum.

For design with no value expressed see No. 994.

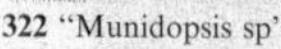

322 "Munidopsis sp"

324 "Gardenia aubryi"

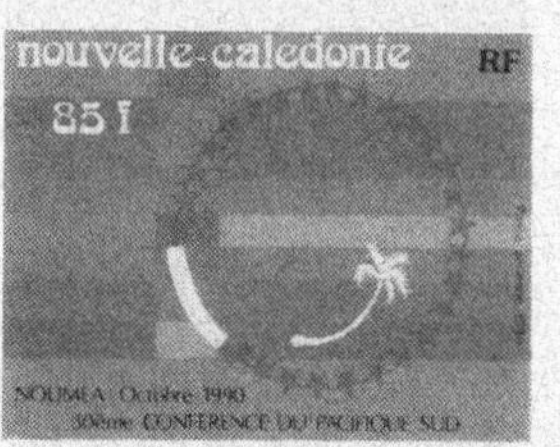

323 Emblem

1990. Air. Deep Sea Animals. Multicoloured.

900 30 f. Type **322** 55 35
901 60 f. "Lyreidius tridentatus" . 1·00 55

1990. Air. 30th South Pacific Conference, Noumea.

902 **323** 85 f. multicoloured . . . 1·40 90

1990. Flowers. Multicoloured.

903 105 f. Type **324** . . . . . . 1·60 1·10
904 130 f. "Hibbertia baudouinii" 2·00 1·40

325 De Gaulle

1990. Air. Birth Centenary of Charles de Gaulle (French statesman).

905 **325** 410 f. blue . . . . 6·75 2·75

326 "Mont Dore, Mountain of Jade" (C. Degroiselle)

1990. Air. Pacific Painters. Multicoloured.

906 365 f. Type **326** (postage) . . 5·75 3·25
907 110 f. "The Celieres House" (M. Petron) (air) . . . . 1·75 1·40

327 Fayawa-Ouvea Bay

1991. Air. Regional Landscapes. Multicoloured.

908 36 f. Type **327** 65 45
909 90 f. Coastline of Mare . . . 1·60 90

328 Louise Michel and Classroom

1991. Writers.

910 **328** 125 f. mauve and blue . . 2·00 1·25
911 – 125 f. blue and brown . . 2·00 1·25

DESIGN: No. 911, Charles B. Nething and photographer.

329 Houailou Hut

330 Northern Province

1991. Melanesian Huts. Multicoloured.

912 12 f. Type **329** 20 10
913 35 f. Hienghene hut 55 35

1991. Provinces. Multicoloured.

914 45 f. Type **330** 65 55
915 45 f. Islands Province 65 55
916 45 f. Southern Province . . . 65 55

331 "Dendrobium biflorum"

1991. Orchids. Multicoloured.

917 55 f. Type **331** 90 55
918 70 f. "Dendrobium closterium" 1·10 65

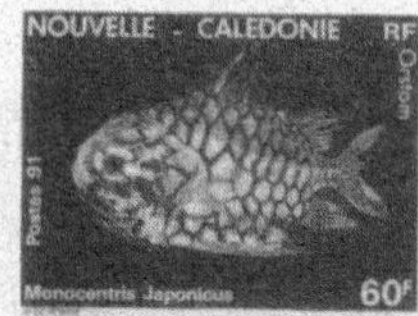

332 Pinecone Fish

1991. Fishes. Multicoloured.

919 60 f. Type **332** . . . . 1·00 55
920 100 f. "Tristigenys niphonia" 1·60 1·00

333 Research Equipment and Sites

1991. French Scientific Research Institute for Development and Co-operation.

921 **333** 170 f. multicoloured . . . 3·25 1·60

334 Emblem **336** Emblems

335 Map and Dragon

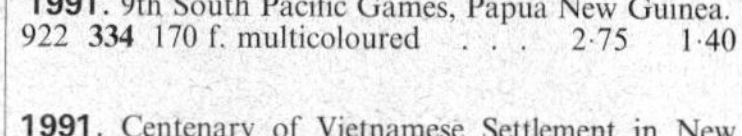

1991. 9th South Pacific Games, Papua New Guinea.

922 **334** 170 f. multicoloured . . . 2·75 1·40

1991. Centenary of Vietnamese Settlement in New Caledonia.

923 **335** 300 f. multicoloured . . . 4·50 2·75

1991. 30th Anniv of Lions International in New Caledonia.

924 **336** 192 f. multicoloured . . . 3·00 1·60

337 Map, "Camden" (missionary brig), Capt. Robert Clark Morgan and Trees

1991. 150th Anniv of Discovery of Sandalwood.

925 **337** 200 f. blue, turquoise & grn 3·00 1·75

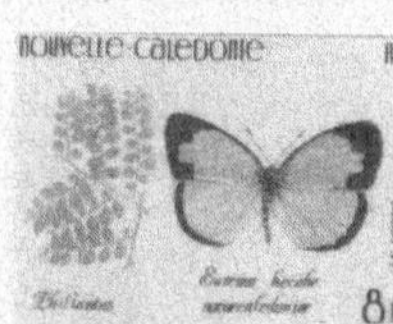

338 "Phillantus" and Common Grass Yellow

1991. "Phila Nippon '91" International Stamp Exhibition, Tokyo. Plants and Butterflies. Mult.

926 8 f. Type **338** 10 10
927 15 f. "Pipturus incanus" and "Hypolimnas octocula" . . 20 10
928 20 f. "Stachytarpheta urticaefolia" and meadow argos 30 20
929 26 f. "Malaisia scandens" and "Cyrestis telamon" 40 20

339 Nickel Processing Plant and Dam

1991. 50th Anniv of Central Economic Co-operation Bank. Multicoloured.

931 76 f. Type **339** . . . . 1·25 75
932 76 f. Housing and hotels . . . 1·25 75

340 "Caledonian Cricket" (Marcel Moutouh)

1991. Air. Pacific Painters. Multicoloured.

933 130 f. Type **340** . . . . 2·10 1·10
934 435 f. "Saint Louis" (Janine Goetz) . . . . 6·75 4·00

341 Blue River (½ size illustration)

1992. Air. Blue River National Park.

935 **341** 400 f. multicoloured . . . 5·25 3·25

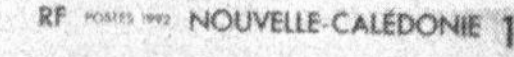

342 La Madeleine Falls

1992. Nature Protection.

937 **342** 15 f. multicoloured 20 15

343 Lapita Pot **345** "Pinta"

344 Barqueta Bridge

1992. Air. Noumea Museum.

939 **343** 25 f. black and orange . . 30 20

1992. Air. "Expo '92" World's Fair, Seville.

940 **344** 10 f. multicoloured . . . 15 10

1992. Air. "World Columbian Stamp Expo '92", Chicago. Multicoloured.

941 80 f. Type **345** . . . . 1·00 90
942 80 f. "Santa Maria" . . . . . 1·00 90
943 80 f. "Nina" . . . . 1·00 90

346 Manchurian Crane and Kagu within "100"

1992. Centenary of Arrival of First Japanese Immigrants. Multicoloured, background colours given.

945 **346** 95 f. yellow . . . . 1·25 75
946 95 f. grey . . . . 1·25 75

347 Synchronised Swimming

1992. Olympic Games, Barcelona.

947 **347** 260 f. multicoloured . . . 3·25 2·00

348 Bell Airacobra, Grumman F4F Wildcat, Barrage Balloon, Harbour and Nissen Huts

1992. 50th Anniv of Arrival of American Forces in New Caledonia.

948 **348** 50 f. multicoloured . . . 65 40

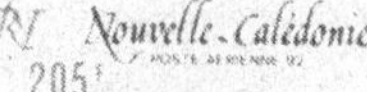

349 "Wahpa" (Paul Mascart)

1992. Air. Pacific Painters.

949 **349** 205 f. multicoloured . . . 2·50 1·50

350 Australian Cattle Dog

352 "Amalda fuscolingua"

351 Entrecasteaux and Fleet

1992. Air. Canine World Championships.
950 **350** 175 f. multicoloured . . . . 2·25 1·40

1992. Air. Navigators. Bicentenary of Landing of Admiral Bruni d'Entrecasteaux on West Coast of New Caledonia.
951 **351** 110 f. orange, blue & grn . 1·50 90

1992. Air. Shells. Multicoloured.
952 30 f. Type **352** 55 35
953 50 f. "Cassis abbotti" 85 50

353 Deole

1992. Air. "La Brousse en Folie" (comic strip) by Bernard Berger. Multicoloured.
954 80 f. Type **353** . . . . 1·00 60
955 80 f. Tonton Marcel . . . . . 1·00 60
956 80 f. Tathan . . . . 1·00 60
957 80 f. Joinville . . . . 1·00 60

354 Lagoon

1993. Lagoon Protection.
958 **354** 120 f. multicoloured . . . 1·50 90

355 Harbour (Gaston Roullet)

1993. Air. Pacific Painters.
959 **355** 150 f. multicoloured . . . 1·90 1·25

356 Symbols of New Caledonia

1993. School Philately. "Tourism my Friend".
960 **356** 25 f. multicoloured . . . 30 20

357 Still and Plantation

1993. Air. Centenary of Production of Essence of Niaouli.
966 **357** 85 f. multicoloured . . . 1·10 65

358 Planets and Copernicus

1993. Air. "Polska '93" International Stamp Exhibition, Poznan. 450th Death Anniv of Nicolas Copernicus (astronomer).
967 **358** 110 f. blue, turquoise & grey 1·40 85

359 Noumea Temple

1993. Air. Centenary of First Protestant Church in Noumea.
968 **359** 400 f. multicoloured . . . 5·25 3·25

1993. No. 898 surch **55F**.
969 **321** 55 f. on 50 f. red 70 45

361 Malabou

1993. Air. Regional Landscapes.
970 **361** 85 f. multicoloured . . . 1·10 65

362 Locomotive and Bridge

1993. Air. Centenary of Little Train of Thio.
971 **362** 115 f. red, green and lilac 1·50 90

363 Rochefort

364 "Megastylis paradoxa"

1993. Air. 80th Death Anniv of Henri Rochefort (journalist).
972 **363** 100 f. multicoloured . . . 1·40 85

1993. Air. "Bangkok 1993" International Stamp Exhibition, Thailand. Multicoloured.
973 30 f. Type **364** 40 25
974 30 f. "Vanda coerulea" . . . 40 25

365 Route Map and Boeing 737-300/500

1993. Air. 10th Anniv of Aircalin (national airline).
976 **365** 85 f. multicoloured . . . . 1·10 65

366 "Francois Arago" (cable laying ship)

1993. Air. Centenary of New Caledonia–Australia Telecommunications Cable.
977 **366** 200 f. purple, blue & turq . 2·50 1·50

367 "Oxypleurodon orbiculatus"

1993. Air. Deep-sea Life.
978 **367** 250 f. multicoloured . . . 3·25 2·00

368 Aircraft, Engine and Hangar

1993. Air. 25th Anniv of Chamber of Commerce and Industry's Management of La Tontouta Airport, Noumea.
979 **368** 90 f. multicoloured . . . . 1·25 75

369 First Christmas Mass, 1843 (stained glass window, Balade church)

1993. Air. Christmas.
980 **369** 120 f. multicoloured . . . 1·60 1·00

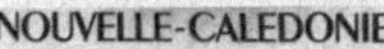

370 Bourail

1993. Town Arms. Multicoloured.
981 70 f. Type **370** . . . . 1·00 60
982 70 f. Noumea . . . . 1·00 60
983 70 f. Canala . . . . 1·00 60
984 70 f. Kone . . . . 1·00 60
985 70 f. Paita . . . . 1·10 60
986 70 f. Dumbea . . . . 1·00 60
987 70 f. Koumac . . . . 1·00 60
988 70 f. Ponerihouen . . . . . . 1·00 60
989 70 f. Kaamoo Hyehen . . . . 1·00 60
990 70 f. Mont Dore . . . . 1·00 60
991 70 f. Thio . . . . 1·00 60
992 70 f. Kaala-Gomen . . . . . 1·00 60
993 70 f. Touho . . . . 1·00 60

1994. No value expressed.
994 **321** (60 f.) red 85 55

MORE DETAILED LISTS
are given in the Stanley Gibbons Catalogues referred to in the country headings. For lists of current volumes see introduction

371 Dog, Exhibition Emblem and Chinese Horoscope Signs (New Year)

1994. Air. "Hong Kong '94" International Stamp Exhibition.
995 **371** 60 f. multicoloured . . . 85 55

372 Airbus Industrie A340

1994. Air 1st Paris–Noumea Airbus Flight. Self-adhesive.
997 **372** 90 f. multicoloured . . . 1·25 75

1994. "Philexjeunes '94" Youth Stamp Exhibition, Grenoble. No. 960 optd **PHILEXJEUNES'94 GRENOBLE 22–24 AVRIL**.
998 **356** 25 f. multicoloured . . . 35 25

374 Photograph of Canala Post Office and Post Van

1994. 50th Anniv of Noumea–Canala Postal Service.
999 **374** 15 f. brown, green and blue 20 15

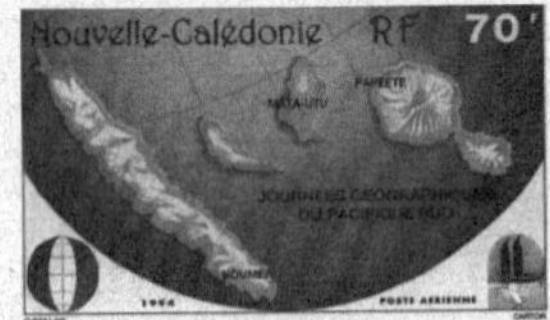

375 Pacific Islands on Globe

1994. Air. South Pacific Geographical Days.
1000 **375** 70 f. multicoloured . . . 1·00 60

376 Post Office, 1859

1994. Postal Administration Head Offices. Mult.
1001 30 f. Type **376** 40 25
1002 60 f. Posts and Telecommunications Office, 1936 . 85 55
1003 90 f. Ministry of Posts and Telecommunications, 1967 1·25 75
1004 120 f. Ministry of Posts and Telecommunications, 1993 1·60 1·00

377 "The Mask Wearer"

1994. Pacific Sculpture.
1005 **377** 60 f. multicoloured . . . 85 55

378 "Legend of the Devil Fish" (Micheline Neporon)

1994. Air. Pacific Painters.
1006 **378** 120 f. multicoloured . . . 1·60 1·00

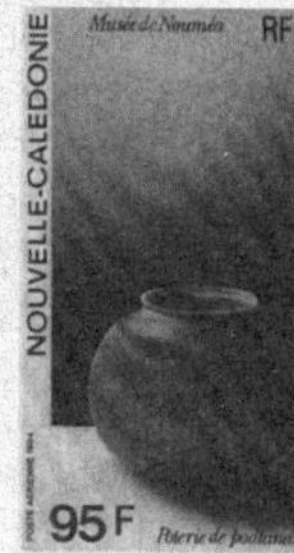
379 "Chambeyronia macrocarpa" 380 Podtanea Pot

1994.
1007 **379** 90 f. multicoloured . . . 1·25 75

1994. Air. Noumea Museum.
1008 **380** 95 f. multicoloured . . . 1·40 85

381 Trophy, U.S. Flag and Ball

1994. Air. World Cup Football Championship, U.S.A.
1009 **381** 105 f. multicoloured . . 1·50 90

1994. No. D707 with "Timbre Taxe" obliterated by black bar.
1010 D **222** 5 f. multicoloured . . 10 10

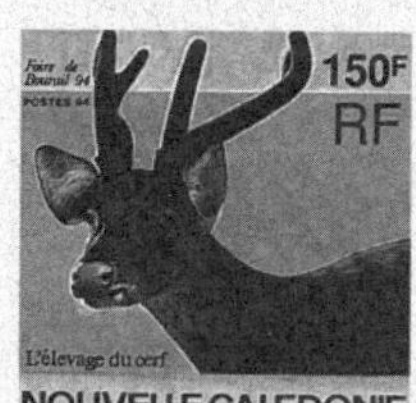
382 Timor Deer

1994. Bourail Fair.
1011 **382** 150 f. multicoloured . . 2·10 1·40

383 Korean Family

1994. Air. "Philakorea 1994" International Stamp Exhibition, Seoul. (Int Year of the Family).
1012 **383** 60 f. multicoloured . . . 85 55

384 "L'Atalante" (oceanographic research vessel)

1994. Air. Evaluation Programme of Economic Zone.
1014 **384** 120 f. multicoloured . . 1·75 1·10

385 "Nivose"

1994. Attachment of the "Nivose" (surveillance frigate) to New Caledonia. Multicoloured.
1015 30 f. Type **385** 45 30
1016 30 f. Aircraft over frigate . . 45 30
1017 30 f. Frigate moored at quay 45 30
1018 60 f. Frigate and map of New Caledonia on parchment . 85 55
1019 60 f. Ship's bell 85 55
1020 60 f. Frigate and sailor . . . 85 55

386 Driving Cattle

1994. Air. 1st European Stamp Salon, Flower Gardens, Paris. Multicoloured.
1021 90 f. Aerial view of island . 1·25 75
1022 90 f. Type **386** . . . . 1·25 75

387 Paper Darts around Girl

1994. School Philately.
1023 **387** 30 f. multicoloured . . . 45 30

388 Jaques Nervat

1994. Writers.
1024 **388** 175 f. multicoloured . . 2·50 1·50

389 Satellite transmitting to Globe and Computer Terminal

1994. Air. 50th Anniv of Overseas Scientific and Technical Research Office.
1025 **389** 95 f. multicoloured . . . . 1·40 85

390 Emblem and Temple

1994. Air. 125th Anniv of Freemasonary in New Caledonia.
1026 **390** 350 f. multicoloured . . 5·00 3·00

391 Thiebaghi Mine

1994. Air.
1027 **391** 90 f. multicoloured . . . 1·25 75

392 Place des Cocotiers, Noumea

1994. Christmas.
1028 **392** 30 f. multicoloured . . . 45 30
No. 1028 covers any one of five stamps which were issued together in horizontal se-tenant strips, the position of the bell, tree and monument differing on each stamp. The strip is stated to produce a three-dimensional image without use of a special viewer.

393 Globe and Newspapers

1994. 50th Anniv of "Le Monde" (newspaper).
1029 **393** 90 f. multicoloured . . . 1·25 75

394 1988 100 f. Pasteur Institute Stamp

1995. Death Centenary of Louis Pasteur (chemist).
1030 **394** 120 f. multicoloured . . . 1·75 1·10

395 Pictorial Map

1995. Air. Tourism.
1031 **395** 90 f. multicoloured . . . 1·25 75

396 Profile of De Gaulle (Santucci) and Cross of Lorraine

1995. 25th Death Anniv of Charles de Gaulle (French President, 1959–69).
1032 **396** 1000 f. deep blue, blue and gold . . . . 14·00 8·50

397 Emblem

1995. Pacific University Teachers' Training Institute.
1033 **397** 100 f. multicoloured . . . 1·40 85

398 "Sylviornis neo-caledoniae"

1995.
1034 **398** 60 f. multicoloured . . . 85 55

399 Swimming, Cycling and Running

1995. Triathlon.
1035 **399** 60 f. multicoloured . . . 85 55

400 Tent and Trees

1995. 50th Anniv of Pacific Franc.
1036 **400** 10 f. multicoloured . . . 15 10
No. 1036 covers any one of four stamps which were issued together in horizontal se-tenant strips, the position of the central motif rotating slightly in a clockwise direction from the left to the right-hand stamp. The strip is stated to produce a three-dimensional image without use of a special viewer.

401 Bourbon Palace (Paris), Map of New Caledonia and Chamber

1995. 50th Anniversaries. Multicoloured.
1037 60 f. Type **401** (first representation of New Caledonia at French National Assembly) 85 55
1038 90 f. National emblems, De Gaulle and Allied flags (end of Second World War) . . 1·25 75
1039 90 f. U.N. Headquarters, New York (U.N.O.) . . . . . . 1·25 75

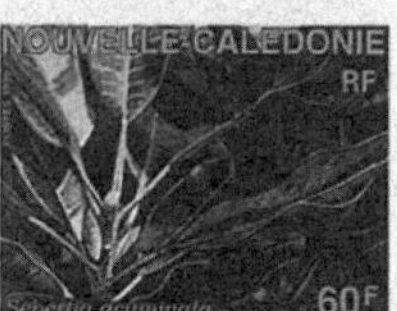
402 "Sebertia acuminata"

1995.
1040 **402** 60 f. multicoloured . . . 85 55

403 Common Noddy

1995. "Singapore'95" International Stamp Exhibition. Sea Birds. Multicoloured.
1041 5 f. Type **403** 10 10
1042 10 f. Silver gull 15 10
1043 20 f. Roseate tern 30 20
1044 35 f. Osprey 50 30
1045 65 f. Red-footed booby . . . 95 60
1046 125 f. Great frigate bird . . 1·75 1·10

404 Golf

1995. 10th South Pacific Games.
1048 **404** 90 f. multicoloured . . . 1·25 75

405 "The Lizard Man" (Dick Bone)

1995. Pacific Sculpture.
1049 **405** 65 f. multicoloured . . . 95 60

406 Venue

1995. Air. 35th South Pacific Conference.
1050 **406** 500 f. multicoloured . . 7·25 4·50

407 Silhouette of Francis Carco

1995. Writers.
1051 **407** 95 f. multicoloured . . . 1·25 75

408 Ouare

1995. Air. Kanak Dances. Multicoloured.
1052 95 f. Type **408** . . . . 1·25 75
1053 100 f. Pothe . . . . 1·40 85

409 Saw-headed Crocodilefish

1995. World of the Deep.
1054 **409** 100 f. multicoloured . . 1·40 85

410 "Mekosuchus inexpectatus"

1996. Air.
1055 **410** 125 f. multicoloured . . 1·60 1·00

411 Vessel with decorated Rim

1996. Noumea Museum.
1056 **411** 65 f. multicoloured . . . 85 55

412 "Captaincookia margaretae"

1996. Flowers. Multicoloured.
1057 65 f. Type **412** 65 55
1058 95 f. "Ixora cauliflora" . . . 1·25 75

413 Pirogue on Beach

1996. World Pirogue Championships, Noumea. Multicoloured.
1059 30 f. Type **413** 40 25
1060 65 f. Pirogue leaving shore . . 85 55
1061 95 f. Double-hulled pirogue . 1·25 75
1062 125 f. Sports pirogue . . . . 1·60 1·00
Nos. 1059/62 were issued together, se-tenant, forming a composite design.

414 Red Batfish

1996. "China'96" International Stamp Exhibition, Peking. Deep Sea Life. Multicoloured.
1063 25 f. Type **414** 35 25
1064 40 f. "Perotrochus deforgesi" (slit shell) 55 35
1065 65 f. "Mursia musorstomia" (crab) 85 55
1066 125 f. Sea lily . . . . 1·60 1·00

415 "Sarcolchilus koghiensis"

1996. "Capex'96" International Stamp Exhibition, Toronto, Canada. Orchids. Multicoloured.
1067 5 f. Type **415** 10 10
1068 10 f. "Phaius robertsii" . . . 15 10
1069 25 f. "Megastylis montana" 35 25
1070 65 f. "Dendrobium macrophyllum" 85 55
1071 95 f. "Dendrobium virotii" . . 1·25 75
1072 125 f. "Ephemerantha comata" 1·60 1·00

416 Indonesian Couple beneath Tree

417 Louis Brauquier

1996. Air. Centenary of Arrival of First Indonesian Immigrants.
1073 **416** 130 f. multicoloured . . 1·75 1·10

1996. Air. Writers.
1074 **417** 95 f. multicoloured . . . 1·25 75

1996. 50th Anniv of U.N.I.C.E.F. No. 1023 optd **unicef** and emblem.
1075 **387** 30 f. multicoloured . . . 40 25

419 Dish Aerial

1996. Air. Anniversaries. Multicoloured.
1076 95 f. Type **419** (20th anniv of New Caledonia's first Earth Station) . . . . 1·25 75
1077 125 f. Guglielmo Marconi (inventor) and telegraph masts (centenary of radio-telegraphy) . . . . 1·60 1·00

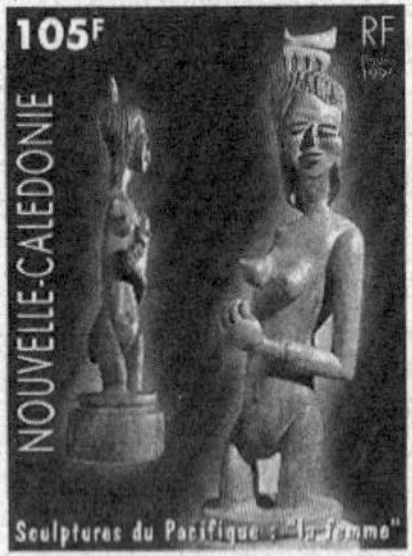

420 Tribal Dance

1996. Air. 7th South Pacific Arts Festival.
1078 **420** 100 f. multicoloured . . . 1·40 85

421 "The Woman" (Elija Trijikone)

1996. Sculptures of the Pacific.
1079 **421** 105 f. multicoloured . . . 1·40 85

422 Ordination, St. Joseph's Cathedral, Noumea

1996. 50th Anniv of Ordination of First Priests in New Caledonia.
1080 **422** 160 f. multicoloured . . . 2·10 1·40

423 "Man" (Paula Boi)

1996. Pacific Painters.
1081 **423** 200 f. multicoloured . . . 2·75 1·75

500F
RF
DANSE DE GAICA
NOUVELLE CALEDONIE

424 Gaica Dance

1996.
1082 **424** 500 f. multicoloured . . . 6·75 4·25

425 Great Reef

1996. Air. 50th Autumn Stamp Show, Paris. Multicoloured.
1083 95 f. Type **425** . . . . . . 1·25 75
1084 95 f. Mount Koghi . . . . . 1·25 75

426 Decorated Sandman

1996. Christmas.
1085 **426** 95 f. multicoloured . . . 1·25 75

OFFICIAL STAMPS

O 49 Ancestor Pole

O 110 Carved Wooden Pillow (Noumea Museum)

1958. Inscr "OFFICIEL".
O344 O **49** 1 f. yellow 45 40
O345 3 f. green 45 40
O346 4 f. purple 45 50
O347 5 f. blue 60 50
O348 9 f. black 70 70
O349 A 10 f. violet 85 70
O350 13 f. green . . . . . . 1·00 80
O351 15 f. blue . . . . . . 1·25 1·00
O352 24 f. mauve . . . . . 1·40 1·10
O353 26 f. orange . . . . . 1·50 1·25
O354 B 50 f. green . . . . . . 3·50 2·50
O355 100 f. brown . . . . . 7·50 4·00
O356 200 f. red . . . . . . 15·00 9·00
DESIGNS: A, B, Different idols.

1973.
O525 O **110** 1 f. green, blk & yell 20 20
O526 2 f. red, black & grn 20 15
O527 3 f. green, blk & brn 30 20
O528 4 f. green, blk & bl 30 20
O529 5 f. green, blk & mve 45 25
O530 9 f. green, blk & bl 55 45
O531 10 f. green, blk & orge 55 45
O532 11 f. grn, blk & mve 35 20
O533 12 f. green, blk & turq 65 45
O534 15 f. green, blk & lt grn 35 25
O535 20 f. green, blk & red 35 25
O536 23 f. green, blk & red 55 45
O537 24 f. green, blk & bl 45 35
O538 25 f. green, blk & grey 65 45
O539 26 f. green, blk & yell 55 35
O540 29 f. red, black & grn 80 55
O541 31 f. red, black & yell 65 45
O542 35 f. red, black & yell 65 45
O543 36 f. green, blk & mve 65 45
O544 38 f. red, black & brn 65 45
O545 40 f. red, black & bl 65 55
O546 42 f. green, blk & brn 65 45
O547 50 f. green, blk & bl 90 65
O548 58 f. blue, blk & grn 1·00 65
O549 65 f. red, black & mve 1·10 65
O549a 76 f. red, blk & yell 1·40 75
O550 100 f. green, blk & red 1·75 1·25
O551 200 f. green, blk & yell 3·50 2·25

PARCEL POST STAMPS

1926. Optd **Colis Postaux** or surch also.
P137 **17** 50 c. on 5 f. green on mauve 60 90
P138 1 f. blue . . . . 90 1·00
P139 2 f. red on blue . . . . . 1·25 1·40

1930. Optd **Colis Postaux**.
P179 **23** 50 c. brown and mauve . 70 70
P180 **24** 1 f. pink and drab . . . 85 85
P181 2 f. brown and orange . . 1;25 1·25

POSTAGE DUE STAMPS

1903. Postage Due stamps of French Colonies optd **CINQUANTENAIRE 24 SEPTEMBRE 1853 1903** and eagle. Imperf.
D78 U 5 c. blue . . . . 1·40 1·25
D79 10 c. brown . . . . . . 5·00 4·25
D80 15 c. green . . . . 14·00 5·50
D81 30 c. red . . . . 9·50 7·00
D82 50 c. purple . . . . . . 45·00 10·50
D83 60 c. brown on buff . . . £160 40·00
D84 1 f. pink . . . . 21·00 9·75
D85 2 f. brown £600 £650

D 18 Outrigger Canoe

D 25 Sambar Stag

D 38

1906.

D102	**D 18**	5 c. blue on blue	25	30
D103		10 c. brown on buff	35	50
D104		15 c. green	40	45
D105		20 c. black on yellow	40	45
D106		30 c. red	50	50
D107		50 c. blue on cream	80	85
D108		60 c. green on blue	75	80
D109		1 f. green on cream	1·10	1·10

1926. Surch.

D137	**D 18**	2 f. on 1 f. mauve	1·90	2·00
D138		3 f. on 1 f. brown	1·90	2·00

1928.

D179	**D 25**	2 c. brown and blue	15	30
D180		4 c. green and red	25	35
D181		5 c. grey and orange	25	35
D182		10 c. blue and mauve	20	35
D183		15 c. red and olive	25	35
D184		20 c. olive and red	40	60
D185		25 c. blue and brown	40	45
D186		30 c. olive and green	40	55
D187		50 c. red and brown	75	85
D188		60 c. red and mauve	80	80
D189		1 f. green and blue	95	1·00
D190		2 f. olive and red	1·10	1·10
D191		3 f. brown and violet	1·90	1·75

1948.

D328	**D 38**	10 c. mauve	15	30
D329		30 c. brown	20	30
D330		50 c. green	30	35
D331		1 f. brown	30	35
D332		2 f. red	30	35
D333		3 f. brown	30	35
D334		4 f. blue	45	45
D335		5 f. red	55	60
D336		10 f. green	85	85
D337		20 f. blue	1·60	1·75

D 223 New Caledonian Flying Fox

1983.

D703	**D 223**	1 f. multicoloured	10	10
D704		2 f. multicoloured	10	10
D705		3 f. multicoloured	10	10
D706		4 f. multicoloured	20	20
D707		5 f. multicoloured	20	20
D708		10 f. multicoloured	20	20
D709		20 f. multicoloured	40	40
D710		40 f. multicoloured	80	80
D711		50 f. multicoloured	90	90

NICARAGUA Pt. 15

A republic of Central America independent since 1821.

1862. 100 centavos = 1 peso (paper currency).
1912. 100 centavos de cordoba = 1 peso de cordoba (gold currency).
1925. 100 centavos = 1 cordoba.

2 Volcanoes 5

1862. Perf or roul.
13 **2** 1 c. brown 1·50 75
4 2 c. blue 2·25 75
14 5 c. black 6·00 1·25
18 10 c. red 2·25 1·40
19 25 c. green 2·25 2·40

1882.
20 **5** 1 c. green 15 20
21 2 c. red 15 20
22 5 c. blue 15 15
23 10 c. violet 15 60
24 15 c. yellow 30 1·50
25 20 c. grey 50 3·00
26 50 c. violet 70 6·00

6 Locomotive and Telegraph Key **7**

1890.
27 **6** 1 c. brown 15 25
28 2 c. red 15 25
29 5 c. blue 15 15
30 10 c. grey 15 20
31 20 c. red 15 1·50
32 50 c. violet 15 4·75
33 1 p. brown 20 6·50
34 2 p. green 20 8·50
35 5 p. red 25 16·00
36 10 p. orange 25 23·00

1891.
37 **7** 1 c. brown 15 30
38 2 c. red 15 30
39 5 c. blue 15 25
40 10 c. grey 15 35
41 20 c. lake 15 1·75
42 50 c. violet 15 3·00
43 1 p. sepia 15 4·50
44 2 p. green 15 5·00
45 5 p. red 15 12·00
46 10 p. orange 15 15·00

8 First Sight of the New World **9** Volcanoes **10**

1892. Discovery of America.
47 **8** 1 c. brown 15 25
48 2 c. red 15 25
49 5 c. blue 15 20
50 10 c. grey 15 25
51 20 c. red 15 1·75
52 50 c. violet 15 4·25
53 1 p. brown 15 4·25
54 2 p. green 15 5·00
55 5 p. red 15 14·00
56 10 p. orange 15 18·00

1893.
57 **9** 1 c. brown 15 25
58 2 c. red 15 25
59 5 c. blue 15 20
60 10 c. grey 15 25
61 20 c. brown 15 1·40
62 50 c. violet 15 3·50
63 1 p. brown 15 4·25
64 2 p. green 15 5·00
65 5 p. red 15 11·00
66 10 p. orange 15 14·00

1894.
67 **10** 1 c. brown 15 25
68 2 c. red 15 25
69 5 c. blue 15 20
70 10 c. grey 15 25
71 20 c. red 15 1·50
72 50 c. violet 15 3·50
73 1 p. brown 15 4·25
74 2 p. green 15 7·50
75 5 p. brown 15 9·00
76 10 p. orange 15 12·00

11 **12** Map of Nicaragua **13** Arms of Republic of Central America

1895.
77 **11** 1 c. brown 15 20
78 2 c. red 15 20
79 5 c. blue 15 15
80 10 c. grey 15 20
81 20 c. red 15 70
82 50 c. violet 15 3·00
83 1 p. brown 15 4·50
84 2 p. green 15 4·75
85 5 p. red 15 9·25
86 10 p. orange 15 14·50

1896. Date "1896".
90 **12** 1 c. violet 15 75
91 2 c. green 15 50
92 5 c. red 15 35
93 10 c. blue 30 65
94 20 c. brown 1·75 3·50
95 50 c. grey 35 4·75
96 1 p. black 35 6·50
97 2 p. red 35 9·00
98 5 p. blue 35 9·00

1897. As T **12**, dated "1897".
99 **12** 1 c. violet 25 35
100 2 c. green 25 35
101 5 c. red 25 20
102 10 c. blue 3·75 65
103 20 c. brown 1·50 2·25
104 50 c. grey 5·25 5·75
105 1 p. black 5·25 8·75
106 2 p. red 11·50 11·00
107 5 p. blue 11·50 25·00

1898.
108 **13** 1 c. brown 20 20
109 2 c. grey 20 20
110 4 c. lake 20 30
122 5 c. olive 15·00 15
112 10 c. purple 8·75 40
113 15 c. blue 25 1·00
114 20 c. blue 6·00 1·00
115 50 c. yellow 6·00 5·75
116 1 p. blue 30 9·50
117 2 p. brown 11·00 13·00
118 5 p. orange 15·00 19·00

14 **15** Mt. Momotombo

1899.
126 **14** 1 c. green 10 25
127 2 c. brown 10 25
128 4 c. red 20 25
129 5 c. blue 15 25
130 10 c. orange 15 25
131 15 c. brown 15 40
132 20 c. green 20 70
133 50 c. red 15 1·75
134 1 p. orange 15 5·00
135 2 p. violet 15 12·00
136 5 p. blue 15 14·50

1900.
137 **15** 1 c. red 30 10
138 2 c. orange 60 15
139 3 c. green 70 20
140 4 c. olive 90 25
184 5 c. red 75 25
185 5 c. blue 55 15
142 6 c. red 18·00 5·50
186 10 c. mauve 55 10
144 15 c. blue 9·50 35
145 20 c. brown 8·50 30
146 50 c. lake 8·50 1·50
147 1 p. yellow 18·00 6·50
148 2 p. red 7·50 75
149 5 p. black 13·00 2·50

1901. Surch **1901** and value.
151 **15** 2 c. on 1 p. yellow 7·00 6·00
169 3 c. on 6 c. red 6·50 3·75
163 4 c. on 6 c. red 5·50 3·50
173 5 c. on 1 p. yellow 9·00 4·25
168 10 c. on 2 p. red 7·00 1·75
152 10 c. on 5 p. black 12·50 10·00
153 20 c. on 2 p. red 12·50 12·50
176 20 c. on 5 p. black 4·75 3·75

1901. Postage Due stamps of 1900 optd **1901 Correos**.
177 D **16** 1 c. red 60 30
178 2 c. orange 45 30
179 5 c. blue 55 45
180 10 c. violet 55 45
181 20 c. brown 75 1·00
182 30 c. green 70 1·00
183 50 c. lake 70 1·00

1902. Surch **1902** and value.
187 **15** 15 c. on 2 c. orange 2·50 1·00
188 30 c. on 1 c. red 1·00 3·50

27 Pres. Santos Zelaya **37** Arms

1903. 10th Anniv of Revolution against Sacaza and 1st election of Pres. Zelaya.
189 **27** 1 c. black and green 25 45
190 2 c. black and red 50 45
191 5 c. black and blue 25 45
192 10 c. black and orange 25 70
193 15 c. black and lake 45 1·40
194 20 c. black and violet 45 1·40
195 50 c. black and olive 45 3·00
196 1 p. black and brown 45 3·50

1904. Surch.
205 **15** 5 c. on 10 c. mauve 75 50
200 15 c. on 10 c. mauve 5·75 3·00

1904. Surch **Vale**, value and wavy lines.
203 **15** 5 c. on 10 c. mauve 1·50 35
204 15 c. on 10 c. mauve 40 30

1905.
206 **37** 1 c. green 20 15
207 2 c. red 20 15
208 3 c. violet 25 20
280 3 c. orange 25 15
209 4 c. orange 25 20
281 4 c. violet 25 15
282 5 c. blue 25 15
211 6 c. grey 45 30
283 6 c. brown 1·75 1·10
212 10 c. brown 55 20
284 10 c. lake 60 10
213 15 c. olive 55 25
285 15 c. black 60 10
214 20 c. lake 45 25
286 20 c. olive 60 10
215 50 c. orange 1·75 1·40
287 50 c. green 70 35
216 1 p. black 90 90
288 1 p. yellow 70 35
217 2 p. green 90 1·25
289 2 p. red 70 35
218 5 p. violet 1·00 1·50

1906. Surch **Vale** (or **VALE**) and value in one line.
292 **37** 2 c. on 3 c. orange 90 75
293 5 c. on 20 c. olive 30 25
247 10 c. on 2 c. red 1·10 45
223 10 c. on 3 c. violet 30 15
248 10 c. on 4 c. orange 1·25 55
291 10 c. on 15 c. black 30 25
250 10 c. on 20 c. lake 1·90 85
252 10 c. on 50 c. orange 1·40 45
234 10 c. on 2 p. green 12·00 7·00
235 10 c. on 5 p. violet 60·00 42·00
226 15 c. on 1 c. green 30 20
229 20 c. on 2 c. red 40 25
230 20 c. on 5 c. blue 45 35
236 35 c. on 6 c. grey 1·60 1·60
232 50 c. on 6 c. grey 45 35
238 1 p. on 5 p. violet 25·00 14·50

51 **50** **64**

1908. Fiscal stamps as T **51** optd **CORREO–1908** or surch **VALE** and value also.
260 **51** 1 c. on 5 c. yellow 35 20
261 2 c. on 5 c. yellow 35 25
262 4 c. on 5 c. yellow 65 30
256 5 c. yellow 45 35
257 10 c. blue 35 20
263 15 c. on 50 c. green 45 30
264 35 c. on 50 c. green 2·50 65
258 1 p. brown 20 1·40
259 2 p. grey 20 1·50

1908. Fiscal stamps as T **50** optd **CORREOS–1908** or surch **VALE** and value also.
268 **50** 2 c. orange 2·10 1·00
269 4 c. on 2 c. orange 1·00 65
270 5 c. on 2 c. orange 1·10 45
271 10 c. on 2 c. orange 1·10 25

1909. Surch **CORREOS–1909 VALE** and value.
273 **51** 1 c. on 50 c. green 2·25 95
274 2 c. on 50 c. green 4·00 1·75
275 4 c. on 50 c. green 4·00 1·75
276 5 c. on 50 c. green 2·25 1·10
277 10 c. on 50 c. green 65 40

1910. Surch **Vale** and value in two lines.
296 **37** 2 c. on 3 c. orange 65 35
300 2 c. on 4 c. violet 25 15
301 5 c. on 20 c. olive 25 15
302 10 c. on 15 c. black 30 15
303 10 c. on 50 c. green 20 15
299 10 c. on 1 p. yellow 65 35
305 10 c. on 2 p. red 45 35

1911. Surch **Correos 1911** (or **CORREOS 1911**) and value.
307 **51** 2 c. on 5 p. blue 25 30
312 5 c. on 2 p. grey 90 70
308 5 c. on 10 p. pink 55 30
309 **51** 10 c. on 25 c. lilac 30 20
310 10 c. on 2 p. grey 30 20
311 35 c. on 1 p. brown 30 25

1911. Surch **VALE POSTAL de 1911** and value.
313 **51** 5 c. on 25 c. lilac 90 70
314 5 c. on 50 c. green 3·00 3·00
315 5 c. on 5 p. blue 4·00 4·00
317 5 c. on 50 p. red 3·00 3·00
318 10 c. on 50 c. green 70 45

1911. Railway stamps as T **64**, with fiscal surch on the front, surch on back **Vale–cts. CORREO DE 1911**.
319 **64** 2 c. on 5 c. on 2 c. blue 55 65
320 05 c. on 5 c. on 2 c. blue 30 40
321 10 c. on 5 c. on 2 c. blue 30 40
322 15 c. on 10 c. on 1 c. red 40 50

1911. Railway stamps, with fiscal surch as last, further surch on front **CORREO** and value.
323 **64** 2 c. on 10 c. on 1 c. red 80 80
324 20 c. on 10 c. on 1 c. red 4·00 4·00
325 50 c. on 10 c. on 1 c. red 7·50 7·50

1911. Railway stamps, with fiscal surch as last, surch in addition on front **Correo Vale 1911** and value.
326 **64** 2 c. on 10 c. on 1 c. red 15 15
328 5 c. on 5 c. on 2 c. blue 90 80
327 5 c. on 10 c. on 1 c. red 20 125
330 10 c. on 10 c. on 1 c. red 70 50

1911. Railway stamps, with fiscal surch on front, surch in addition **Vale CORREO DE 1911** and value on back.
331 **64** 5 c. on 10 c. on 1 c. red 18·00
332 10 c. on 10 c. on 1 c. red 7·00

70 **71**

1912.
337 **70** 1 c. green 25 15
338 2 c. red 25 15
339 3 c. brown 25 15
340 4 c. purple 25 15
341 5 c. black and blue 25 15
342 6 c. brown 25 70
343 10 c. brown 25 15
344 15 c. violet 25 15
345 20 c. brown 25 15
346 25 c. black and green 25 15
347 **71** 35 c. brown and green 1·10 1·10
348 **70** 50 c. blue 65 30
349 1 p. orange 90 1·40
350 2 p. green 90 1·75
351 5 p. black 1·60 2·10

1913. Surch **Vale 15 cts Correos 1913**.
352 **71** 15 c. on 35 c. brown & grn 30 20

1913. Surch **VALE 1913** and value in "centavos de cordoba".
A. On stamps of 1912 issue.
353 **70** ½ c. on 3 c. brown 35 25
354 ½ c. on 15 c. violet 20 15
355 ½ c. on 1 p. orange 20 15
356 1 c. on 3 c. brown 55 45
357 1 c. on 4 c. purple 20 15
358 1 c. on 50 c. blue 20 15
359 1 c. on 5 p. black 20 15
360 2 c. on 4 c. purple 25 20
361 2 c. on 20 c. brown 2·25 2·75
362 2 c. on 25 c. black & grn 25 15
363 **71** 2 c. on 35 c. brown & grn 20 35
364 **70** 2 c. on 50 c. blue 20 90
365 2 c. on 2 p. green 15 15
366 3 c. on 6 c. brown 15 10

B. On Silver Currency stamps of 1912 (Locomotive type).
367 Z **1** ½ c. on 2 c. red 1·40 1·25
368 1 c. on 3 c. brown 95 85
369 1 c. on 4 c. red 95 85
370 1 c. on 6 c. red 95 85
371 1 c. on 20 c. blue 95 85
372 1 c. on 25 c. black & grn 95 85
384 2 c. on 1 c. green 11·00 10·00
373 2 c. on 25 c. black & grn 5·00 4·50
374 5 c. on 35 c. black & grn 95 85
375 5 c. on 50 c. olive 95 85
376 6 c. on 1 p. orange 95 85
377 10 c. on 2 p. brown 95 85
378 1 p. on 5 p. green 95 85

1914. No. 352 surch with new value and **Cordoba** and thick bar over old surch.
385 **71** ½ c. on 15 c. on 35 c. 15 10
386 1 c. on 15 c. on 35 c. 20 15

1914. Official stamps of 1913 surch with new value and thick bar through "OFFICIAL".
387 **70** 1 c. on 25 c. blue 30 20
388 **71** 1 c. on 35 c. blue 30 20
389 **70** 1 c. on 1 p. blue 20 15
391 2 c. on 50 c. blue 30 15
392 2 c. on 2 p. blue 20 15
393 5 c. on 5 p. blue 20 15

79 National Palace, Managua **80** Leon Cathedral

1914. Various frames.
394 79 ½ c. blue 50 15
395 1 c. green 50 15
396 80 2 c. orange 50 15
397 79 3 c. brown 80 25
398 80 4 c. red 80 25
399 79 5 c. grey 30 10
400 80 6 c. sepia 5·25 3·25
401 10 c. yellow 55 15
402 79 15 c. violet 3·50 1·40
403 80 20 c. grey 6·50 3·25
404 79 25 c. orange 85 20
405 80 50 c. blue 85 25
See also Nos. 465/72, 617/27 and 912/24.

1915. Surch **VALE 5 cts. de Cordoba 1915.**
406 80 5 c. on 6 c. sepia 1·10 35

1918. Stamps of 1914 surch **Vale–centavos de cordoba.**
407 80 ½ c. on 6 c. sepia 2·00 75
408 ½ c. on 10 c. yellow 1·40 25
409 79 ½ c. on 15 c. violet 1·40 45
410 ½ c. on 25 c. orange 3·00 85
411 80 ½ c. on 50 c. blue 1·40 25
440 1 c. on 2 c. orange 90 20
413 79 1 c. on 3 c. brown 1·50 25
414 80 1 c. on 6 c. sepia 7·00 2·10
415 1 c. on 10 c. yellow 13·00 4·75
416 79 1 c. on 15 c. violet 2·40 55
418 80 1 c. on 20 c. grey 1·40 25
420 79 1 c. on 25 c. orange 2·40 70
421 80 1 c. on 50 c. blue 7·75 2·25
422 2 c. on 4 c. red 1·75 25
423 2 c. on 6 c. sepia 13·00 4·75
424 2 c. on 10 c. yellow 13·00 2·50
425 2 c. on 20 c. grey 7·00 2·10
426 79 2 c. on 25 c. orange 3·00 30
427 80 5 c. on 6 c. sepia 5·00 2·50
428 79 5 c. on 15 c. violet 1·75 45

1919. Official stamps of 1915 surch **Vale–centavo de cordoba** and with bar through "OFFICIAL".
444 80 ½ c. on 2 c. blue 30 15
445 ½ c. on 4 c. blue 70 15
446 79 1 c. on 3 c. blue 70 25
432 1 c. on 25 c. blue 1·10 20
433 80 2 c. on 50 c. blue 1·10 20
443a 10 c. on 20 c. blue 1·00 40

1921. Official stamps of 1913 optd **Particular** and wavy lines through "OFFICIAL".
441 70 1 c. blue 90 45
442 5 c. blue 90 35

1921. No. 399 surch **Vale medio centavo.**
447 79 ½ c. on 5 c. black 35 15

1921. Official stamp of 1915 optd **Particular R de C** and bars.
448 79 1 c. blue 3·50 1·00

1921. Official stamps of 1915 surch **Vale un centavo R de C** and bars.
449 79 1 c. on 5 c. blue 95 35
450 80 1 c. on 6 c. blue 50 20
451 1 c. on 10 c. blue 65 20
452 79 1 c. on 15 c. blue 1·10 20

90

91 Jose C. del Valle

1921. Fiscal stamps as T **23** surch **R de C Vale** and new value.
453 90 1 c. on 1 c. red and black 10 10
454 1 c. on 2 c. green and black 10 10
455 1 c. on 4 c. orange and black 10 10
456 1 c. on 15 c. blue and black 10 10
No. 456 is inscr "TIMBRE TELEGRAFICO".

1921. Independence Centenary.
457 – ½ c. black and blue 30 25
458 91 1 c. black and green 30 25
459 – 2 c. black and red 30 25
460 – 5 c. black and violet 30 25
461 – 10 c. black and orange 20 25
462 – 25 c. black and yellow 30 25
463 – 50 c. black and violet 30 25
DESIGNS: ½ c. Arce; 2 c. Larreinaga; 5 c. F. Chamorro; 10 c. Jerez; 25 c. J. P. Chamorro; 50 c. Dario.

1922. Surch **Vale un centavo R. de C.**
464 80 1 c. on 10 c. yellow 10 10

1922. As Nos. 394, etc., but colours changed.
465 79 ½ c. green 15 10
466 1 c. violet 15 10
467 80 2 c. red 15 10
468 79 3 c. olive 25 15
469 80 6 c. brown 15 15
470 79 15 c. brown 25 15
471 80 20 c. brown 35 15
472 1 cor. brown 65 35
Nos. 465/72 are size 27×22¾ mm.
For later issues of these types, see Nos. 617/27 and 912/24.

1922. Optd **R. de C.**
473 79 1 c. violet 10 10

1922. Independence issue of 1921 surch **R. de C. Vale un centavo.**
474 91 1 c. on 1 c. black and green 55 45
475 – 1 c. on 5 c. black and violet 55 55
476 – 1 c. on 10 c. black and orange 55 30
477 – 1 c. on 25 c. black and yellow 55 25
478 – 1 c. on 50 c. black and violet 25 20

94

99 F. Hernandez de Cordoba

106

1922. Surch **Nicaragua R. de C. Vale un cent.**
479 94 1 c. yellow 10 10
480 1 c. mauve 10 10
481 1 c. blue 10 10

1922. Surch thus: **Vale 0.01 de Cordoba** in two lines.
482 80 1 c. on 10 c. yellow 70 25
483 2 c. on 10 c. yellow 70 20

1923. Surch thus: **Vale 2 centavos de cordoba** in three lines.
484 79 1 c. on 5 c. black 70 15
485 80 2 c. on 10 c. yellow 70 15

1923. Optd **Sello Postal.**
486 – ½ c. black & blue (No. 457) 5·50 4·25
487 91 1 c. black and green 1·40 70

1923. Independence issue of 1921 surch **R. de C. Vale un centavo de cordoba.**
488 1 c. on 2 c. black and red 30 30
489 1 c. on 5 c. black and violet 35 15
490 1 c. on 10 c. black and orge 15 15
491 1 c. on 25 c. black and yellow 25 25
492 1 c. on 50 c. black and violet 15 10

1923. Fiscal stamp optd R. de C.
493 90 1 c. red and black 15 10

1924. Optd **R. de C. 1924** in two lines.
494 79 1 c. violet 15 15

1924. 400th Anniv of Foundation of Leon and Granada.
495 99 1 c. green 90 25
496 2 c. red 90 25
497 5 c. blue 65 25
498 10 c. brown 65 45

1925. Optd **R. de C. 1925** in two lines.
499 79 1 c. violet 15 10

1927. Optd **Resello 1927.**
525 79 ½ c. green 10 10
528 1 c. violet (No. 466) 10 10
555 1 c. violet (No. 473) 15 10
532 80 2 c. red 15 10
533 79 3 c. green 20 10
537 80 4 c. red 9·50 8·00
539 79 5 c. grey 55 20
542 80 6 c. brown 7·75 6·50
543 10 c. yellow 25 15
545 79 15 c. brown 55 25
547 80 20 c. brown 25 15
549 79 25 c. orange 30 15
551 80 50 c. blue 30 15
553 1 cor. brown 35 15

1928. Optd **Resello 1928.**
559 79 ½ c. green 20 15
560 1 c. violet 10 10
561 80 2 c. red 15 10
562 79 3 c. green 15 10
563 80 4 c. red 15 10
564 79 5 c. grey 15 10
565 80 6 c. brown 15 10
566 10 c. yellow 20 10
567 79 15 c. brown 25 20
568 80 20 c. brown 35 20
569 79 25 c. orange 55 20
570 80 50 c. blue 90 20
571 1 cor. brown 75 25

1928. Optd **Correos 1928.**
574 79 ½ c. green 15 10
575 1 c. violet 10 10
576 3 c. olive 55 20
577 80 4 c. red 25 10
578 79 5 c. grey 20 10
579 80 6 c. brown 30 15
580 10 c. yellow 35 15
581 79 15 c. brown 1·00 15
582 80 20 c. brown 1·00 15
583 79 25 c. orange 1·00 20
584 80 50 c. blue 1·00 20
585 1 cor. brown 3·00 1·50

1928. No. 577 surch **Vale 2 cts.**
586 80 2 c. on 4 c. red 90 25

1928. Fiscal stamp as T **90**, but inscr "TIMBRE TELEGRAFICO" and surch **Correos 1928 Vale** and new value.
587 90 1 c. on 5 c. blue and black 25 15
588 2 c. on 5 c. blue and black 25 15
589 3 c. on 5 c. blue and black 25 15

1928. Obligatory Tax. No. 587 additionally optd **R. de T.**
590 90 1 c. on 5 c. blue & black 45 10

1928. As Nos. 465/72 but colours changed.
591 79 ½ c. red 30 15
592 1 c. orange 30 15
593 80 2 c. green 30 15
594 79 3 c. purple 30 20
595 80 4 c. brown 30 20
596 79 5 c. yellow 30 15
597 80 6 c. blue 30 20
598 10 c. blue 65 20
599 79 15 c. red 85 35
600 80 20 c. green 85 35
601 79 25 c. purple 16·00 3·75
602 80 50 c. brown 1·90 70
603 1 cor. violet 3·75 1·75
See also Nos. 617/27 and 912/24.

1928.
604 106 1 c. purple 20 10
647 1 c. red 25 10
For 1 c. green see No. 925.

1929. Optd **R. de C.**
605 79 1 c. orange 10 10
628 1 c. olive 15 10

1929. Optd **Correos 1929.**
606 79 ½ c. green 20 15

1929. Optd **Correos 1928.**
607 99 10 c. brown 55 45

1929. Fiscal stamps as T **90**, but inscr "TIMBRE TELEGRAFICO". A. Surch **Correos 1929 R. de C. C$ 0.01** vert.
613 90 1 c. on 5 c. blue & black 10 15

B. Surch **Correos 1929** and value.
611 90 1 c. on 10 c. green and black 20 15
612 2 c. on 5 c. blue and black 20 10

C. Surch **Correos 1929** and value vert and **R. de C.** or **R. de T.** horiz.
608 90 1 c. on 5 c. blue and black (R. de T.) 20 15
609 2 c. on 5 c. blue and black (R. de T.) 15 15
610 2 c. on 5 c. blue and black (R. de C.) 13·00 70

1929. Air. Optd **Correo Aereo 1929. P.A.A.**
614 79 25 c. sepia 1·40 1·40
615 25 c. orange 1·00 1·00
616 25 c. violet 90 70

1929. As Nos. 591/603 but colours changed.
617 79 1 c. green 10 10
618 3 c. blue 25 15
619 80 4 c. blue 25 15
620 79 5 c. brown 30 15
621 80 6 c. drab 30 15
622 10 c. brown 45 15
623 79 15 c. red 65 20
624 80 20 c. orange 80 25
625 79 25 c. violet 20 10
626 80 50 c. green 35 15
627 1 cor. yellow 2·75 90
See also Nos. 912/24.

112 Mt. Momotombo

114 G.P.O. Managua

1929. Air.
629 112 15 c. purple 25 10
630 20 c. green 70 45
631 25 c. olive 50 30
632 50 c. sepia 80 45
633 1 cor. red 1·10 55
See also Nos. 926/30.

1930. Air. Surch **Vale** and value.
634 112 15 c. on 25 c. olive 40 30
635 20 c. on 25 c. olive 60 45

1930. Opening of the G.P.O., Managua.
636 114 ½ c. sepia 80 60
637 1 c. red 80 60
638 2 c. orange 65 45
639 3 c. orange 1·00 90
640 4 c. yellow 1·00 90
641 5 c. olive 1·60 1·10
642 6 c. green 1·60 1·10
643 10 c. black 1·60 1·00
644 25 c. blue 3·25 2·40
645 50 c. blue 5·25 3·50
646 1 cor. violet 15·00 7·25

1931. Optd **1931** and thick bar obliterating old overprint "1928".
648 99 10 c. brown (No. 607) 45 90

1931. No. 607 surch **C $ 0.02.**
649 99 2 c. on 10 c. brown 55 45

1931. Optd **1931** and thick bar.
650 99 2 c. on 10 c. brown (498) 55 1·75

1931. Air. Nos. 614/16 surch **1931 Vale** and value.
651 79 15 c. on 25 c. sepia 90·00 90·00
652 15 c. on 25 c. orange 45·00 45·00
653 15 c. on 25 c. violet 9·00 9·00
654 20 c. on 25 c. violet 9·00 9·00

1931. Optd **1931.**
656 79 ½ c. green 35 10
657 1 c. olive 35 10
665 1 c. orange (No. 605) 10 10
658 80 2 c. red 35 10
659 79 3 c. blue 35 15
660 5 c. yellow 2·10 1·40
661 5 c. sepia 65 20
662 15 c. orange 70 45
663 25 c. sepia 9·00 3·75
664 25 c. violet 3·50 1·50

1931. Air. Surch **1931** and value.
667 80 15 c. on 25 c. olive 4·75 4·75
668 15 c. on 50 c. sepia 36·00 36·00
669 15 c. on 1 cor. red 90·00 90·00
666 15 c. on 20 c. on 25 c. olive (No. 635) 7·50 7·50

120 G.P.O. before and after the Earthquake

1932. G.P.O. Reconstruction Fund.
670 120 ½ c. green (postage) 90 90
671 1 c. brown 1·25 1·25
672 2 c. red 90 90
673 3 c. blue 90 90
674 4 c. blue 90 90
675 5 c. brown 1·40 1·40
676 6 c. brown 1·40 1·40
677 10 c. brown 2·25 1·50
678 15 c. red 3·50 2·25
679 20 c. orange 2·10 2·10
680 25 c. violet 2·25 2·25
681 50 c. green 2·25 2·25
682 1 cor. yellow 4·50 4·50
683 15 c. mauve (air) 90 75
684 20 c. green 1·10 1·10
685 25 c. brown 5·50 5·50
686 50 c. brown 7·00 7·00
687 1 cor. red 10·50 10·50

1932. Air. Surch **Vale** and value.
688 112 30 c. on 50 c. sepia 1·40 1·40
689 35 c. on 50 c. sepia 1·40 1·40
690 40 c. on 1 cor. red 1·60 1·60
691 55 c. on 1 cor. red 1·60 1·60
For similar surcharges on these stamps in different colours see Nos. 791/4 and 931/4.

1932. Air. International Air Mail Week. Optd **Semana Correo Aereo Internacional 11-17 Septiembre 1932.**
692 112 15 c. violet 40·00 40·00

1932. Air. Inauguration of Inland Airmail Service. Surch **Inauguracion Interior 12 Octubre 1932 Vale C$0.08.**
693 112 8 c. on 1 cor. red 13·00 13·00

1932. Air. Optd **Interior–1932** or surch **Vale** and value also.
705 120 25 c. brown 4·75 4·75
706 32 c. on 50 c. brown 5·50 5·50
707 40 c. on 1 cor. red 4·25 4·25

1932. Air. Nos. 671, etc., optd **Correo Aereo Interior** in one line and **1932**, or surch **Vale** and value also.
694 120 1 c. brown 12·00 12·00
695 2 c. red 12·00 12·00
696 3 c. blue 5·50 5·50
697 4 c. blue 5·50 5·50
698 5 c. brown 5·50 5·50
699 6 c. brown 5·50 5·50
700 8 c. on 10 c. brown 5·25 5·25
701 16 c. on 20 c. orange 5·25 5·25
702 24 c. on 25 c. violet 5·25 5·25
703 50 c. green 5·25 5·25
704 1 cor. yellow 5·50 5·50

1932. Air. Surch **Correo Aereo Interior–1932** in two lines and **Vale** and value below.
710 80 1 c. on 2 c. red 40 40
711 79 2 c. on 3 c. blue 40 40
712 80 3 c. on 4 c. blue 40 40
713 79 4 c. on 5 c. sepia 40 40
714 80 5 c. on 6 c. brown 40 40
715 6 c. on 10 c. brown 40 40
716 79 8 c. on 15 c. orange 40 40
717 80 16 c. on 20 c. orange 40 40
718 79 24 c. on 25 c. violet 85 60
719 25 c. on 25 c. violet 85 60
720 80 32 c. on 50 c. green 85 75
721 40 c. on 50 c. green 95 85
722 50 c. on 1 cor. yellow 1·25 1·25
723 100 c. on 1 cor. yellow 2·50 2·50

127 Wharf, Port San Jorge

128 La Chocolata Cutting

1932. Opening of Rivas Railway.
726 127 1 c. yellow (postage) 17·00
727 – 2 c. red 17·00
728 – 5 c. sepia 17·00
729 – 10 c. brown 17·00
730 – 15 c. yellow 17·00

731 **128** 15 c. violet (air) 22·00
732 – 20 c. green 22·00
733 – 25 c. brown 22·00
734 – 50 c. sepia 22·00
735 – 1 cor. red 22·00
DESIGNS—HORIZ: 2 c. El Nacascolo Halt; 5 c. Rivas Station; 10 c. San Juan del Sur; 15 c. (No. 730), Arrival platform at Rivas; 20 c. El Nacascolo; 25 c. La Cuesta cutting; 50 c. San Juan del Sur Quay; 1 cor. El Estero.

1932. Surch **Vale** and value in words.
736 **79** 1 c. on 3 c. blue 35 15
737 **80** 2 c. on 4 c. blue 30 15

130 Railway Construction

1932. Opening of Leon–Sauce Railway.
739 – 1 c. yellow (postage) 17·00
740 – 2 c. red 17·00
741 – 5 c. sepia 17·00
742 **130** 10 c. brown 17·00
743 – 15 c. yellow 17·00
744 – 15 c. violet (air) 22·00
745 – 20 c. green 22·00
746 – 25 c. brown 22·00
747 – 50 c. sepia 22·00
748 – 1 cor. red 22·00
DESIGNS—HORIZ: 1 c. El Sauce; 2 c., 15 c. (No. 744), Bridge at Santa Lucia; 5 c. Santa Lucia; 15 c. (No. 743) Santa Lucia cutting; 20 c. Santa Lucia River Halt; 25 c. Malpaicillo Station; 50 c. Railway panorama; 1 cor. San Andres.

1933. Surch **Resello 1933 Vale** and value in words.
749 **79** 1 c. on 3 c. blue 20 15
750 1 c. on 5 c. sepia 20 15
751 **80** 2 c. on 10 c. brown 20 15

133 Flag of the Race

1933. 441st Anniv of Columbus' Departure from Palos. Roul.
753 **133** $\frac{1}{2}$ c. green (postage) 95 95
754 1 c. green 80 80
755 2 c. red 80 80
756 3 c. red 80 80
757 4 c. orange 80 80
758 5 c. yellow 95 95
759 10 c. brown 95 95
760 15 c. brown 95 95
761 20 c. blue 95 95
762 25 c. blue 95 95
763 30 c. violet 2·40 2·40
764 50 c. purple 2·40 2·40
765 1 cor. brown 2·40 2·40
766 1 c. brown (air) 90 90
767 2 c. purple 90 90
768 4 c. violet 1·50 1·40
769 5 c. blue 1·40 1·40
770 6 c. blue 1·40 1·40
771 8 c. brown 45 45
772 15 c. brown 45 45
773 20 c. yellow 1·40 1·40
774 25 c. orange 1·40 1·40
775 50 c. red 1·40 1·40
776 1 cor. green 9·00 9·00

(134) (Facsimile signatures of R. E. Deshon, Minister of Transport and J. R. Sevilla, P.M.G.)

1933. Optd with T **134**.
777 **79** $\frac{1}{2}$ c. green 30 15
778 1 c. green 15 10
779 **80** 2 c. red 40 15
780 **79** 3 c. blue 15 10
781 **80** 4 c. blue 20 15
782 **79** 5 c. brown 20 10
783 **80** 6 c. drab 25 20
784 10 c. brown 25 15
785 **79** 15 c. red 30 20
786 **80** 20 c. orange 40 30
787 **79** 25 c. violet 45 25
788 **80** 50 c. green 75 50
789 1 cor. yellow 4·00 1·60

1933. No. 605 optd with T **134**.
790 **79** 1 c. orange 25 15

1933. Air. Surch **Vale** and value.
791 **112** 30 c. on 50 c. orange 35 15
792 35 c. on 50 c. blue 45 20
793 40 c. on 1 cor. yellow 70 15
794 55 c. on 1 cor. green 70 30

135 Lake Xolotlan

1933. Air. International Airmail Week.
795 **135** 10 c. brown 90 90
796 15 c. violet 75 75
797 25 c. red 85 85
798 50 c. blue 90 90

Correo Aéreo Interior Vale C$ 0.50

(136)

1933. Air. Surch as T **136**.
799 **80** 1 c. on 2 c. green 15 15
800 **79** 2 c. on 3 c. olive 15 15
801 **80** 3 c. on 4 c. red 15 15
802 **79** 4 c. on 5 c. blue 15 15
803 **80** 5 c. on 6 c. blue 15 15
804 6 c. on 10 c. sepia 15 10
805 **79** 8 c. on 15 c. brown 20 15
806 **80** 16 c. on 20 c. brown 20 15
807 **79** 24 c. on 25 c. red 15 15
808 25 c. on 25 c. orange 30 30
809 **80** 32 c. on 50 c. violet 30 25
810 40 c. on 50 c. green 40 25
811 50 c. on 1 cor. yellow 40 30
812 1 cor. on 1 cor. red 95 80

1933. Obligatory Tax. As No. 647 optd with T **134**. Colour changed.
813 **106** 1 c. orange 25 15

1934. Air. Surch **Servicio Centroamericano Vale 10 centavos**.
814 **112** 10 c. on 20 c. green 35 35
815 10 c. on 25 c. olive 35 35
See also No. 872.

1935. Optd **Resello 1935**. (a) Nos. 778/9.
816 **79** 1 c. green 10 10
817 **80** 2 c. red 15 10

(b) No. 813 but without T **134** opt.
818 **106** 1 c. orange 15 10

1935. No. 783 surch **Vale Medio Centavo**.
819 **80** $\frac{1}{2}$ c. on 6 c. brown 35 15

1935. Optd with T **134** and **RESELLO-1935** in a box.
820 **79** $\frac{1}{2}$ c. green 20 15
821 **80** $\frac{1}{2}$ c. on 6 c. brown (No. 819) 15 10
822 **79** 1 c. green 25 10
823 **80** 2 c. red 55 10
824 2 c. red (No. 817) 30 10
825 **79** 3 c. blue 30 15
826 **80** 4 c. blue 30 15
827 **79** 5 c. brown 25 10
828 **80** 6 c. drab 30 10
829 10 c. brown 55 20
830 **79** 15 c. red 15 10
831 **80** 20 c. orange 90 25
832 **79** 25 c. violet 30 15
833 **80** 50 c. green 35 25
834 1 cor. yellow 45 35

1935. Obligatory Tax. No. 605 optd with **RESELLO-1935** in a box.
835 **79** 1 c. orange 25·00

1935. Obligatory Tax. Optd **RESELLO-1935** in a box. (a) No. 813 without T **134** opt.
836 **106** 1 c. orange 25 15

(b) No. 818.
868 **106** 1 c. orange 20 15

1935. Air. Nos. 799/812 optd with **RESELLO-1935** in a box.
839 **80** 1 c. on 2 c. green 10 10
840 **79** 2 c. on 3 c. olive 20 20
879 **80** 3 c. on 4 c. red 15 15
880 **79** 4 c. on 5 c. blue 15 15
881 **80** 5 c. on 6 c. blue 15 15
882 6 c. on 10 c. sepia 15 15
883 **79** 8 c. on 15 c. brown 15 15
884 **80** 16 c. on 20 c. brown 15 15
847 **79** 24 c. on 25 c. red 35 30
848 25 c. on 25 c. orange 25 25
849 **80** 32 c. on 50 c. violet 20 20
850 40 c. on 50 c. green 30 25
851 50 c. on 1 cor. yellow 45 35
852 1 cor. on 1 cor. red 85 40

1935. Air. Optd with **RESELLO-1935** in a box. (a) Nos. 629/33.
853 **112** 15 c. purple 30 10
873 20 c. green 40 30
855 25 c. green 40 35
856 50 c. sepia 40 35
857 1 cor. red 65 35

(b) Nos. 791/4.
858 **112** 30 c. on 50 c. orange 40 35
859 35 c. on 50 c. blue 40 25
860 40 c. on 1 cor. yellow 40 35
861 55 c. on 1 cor. green 40 30

(c) Nos. 814/5.
862 **112** 10 c. on 20 c. green £300 £300
863 10 c. on 25 c. olive 60 50

1935. Optd with **RESELLO-1935** in a box.
864 **79** $\frac{1}{2}$ c. green (No. 465) 15 10
865 1 c. green (No. 617) 20 10
866 **80** 2 c. red (No. 467) 55 10
867 **79** 3 c. blue (No. 618) 20 15

1936. Surch **Resello 1936 Vale** and value.
869 **79** 1 c. on 3 c. blue (No. 618) 15 10
870 2 c. on 5 c. brown (No. 620) 15 10

1936. Air. Surch **Servicio Centroamericano Vale diez centavos** and **RESELLO-1935** in a box.
871 **112** 10 c. on 25 c. olive 30 30

1936. Obligatory Tax. No. 818 optd **1936**.
874 **106** 1 c. orange 50 20

1936. Obligatory Tax. No. 605 optd with T **134** and **1936**.
875 **79** 1 c. orange 50 20

1936. Air. No. 622 optd **Correo Aereo Centro-Americano Resello 1936**.
876 **80** 10 c. brown 20 20

1936. Air. Nos. 799/800 and 805 optd **Resello 1936**.
885 **80** 1 c. on 2 c. green 25 20
886 **79** 2 c. on 3 c. olive 10 10
887 8 c. on 15 c. brown 25 25

1936. Optd with or without T **37**, surch **1936 Vale** and value.
888 **79** $\frac{1}{2}$ c. on 15 c. red 20 15
889 **80** 1 c. on 4 c. blue 25 15
890 **79** 1 c. on 5 c. brown 25 20
891 **80** 1 c. on 6 c. drab 45 20
892 **79** 1 c. on 15 c. red 25 20
893 **80** 1 c. on 20 c. orange 20 15
895 2 c. on 10 c. brown 30 20
896 **79** 2 c. on 15 c. red 60 50
897 **80** 2 c. on 20 c. orange 55 45
898 **79** 2 c. on 25 c. violet 35 20
900 **80** 2 c. on 50 c. green 35 25
901 2 c. on 1 cor. yellow 35 30
902 3 c. on 4 c. blue 40 30

1936. Optd **Resello 1936**.
903 **79** 3 c. blue (No. 618) 35 25
904 5 c. brown (No. 620) 30 15
905 **80** 10 c. brown (No. 784) 30 20

1936. Air. Surch **1936 Vale and value**.
906 **112** 15 c. on 50 c. brown 30 25
907 15 c. on 1 cor. red 30 25

1936. Fiscal stamps surch **RECONSTRUCCION COMUNICACIONES 5 CENTAVOS DE CORDOBA** and further surch **Vale dos centavos Resello 1936**.
908 **90** 1 c. on 5 c. green 25 10
909 2 c. on 5 c. green 25 10

1936. Obligatory Tax. Fiscal stamps surch **RECONSTRUCCION COMUNICACIONES 5 CENTAVOS DE CORDOBA** and further surch.

(a) **1936 R. de C. Vale Un Centavo**.
910 **90** 1 c. on 5 c. green 15 10

(b) **Vale un centavo R. de C. 1936**.
911 **90** 1 c. on 5 c. green 20 10

1937. Colours changed. Size 27×22$\frac{3}{4}$ mm.
912 **79** $\frac{1}{2}$ c. black 15 10
913 1 c. red 15 10
914 **80** 2 c. blue 15 10
915 **79** 3 c. brown 15 10
916 **80** 4 c. yellow 20 10
917 **79** 5 c. red 15 10
918 **80** 6 c. violet 20 10
919 10 c. green 20 10
920 **79** 15 c. green 15 10
921 **80** 20 c. brown 30 10
922 **79** 25 c. orange 30 10
923 **80** 50 c. brown 35 15
924 1 cor. blue 40 25

1937. Obligatory Tax. Colour changed.
925 **106** 1 c. green 15 10

1937. Air. Colours changed.
926 **112** 15 c. orange 20 10
927 20 c. red 20 15
928 25 c. black 25 15
929 50 c. violet 45 15
930 1 cor. orange 65 15

1937. Air. Surch **Vale** and value. Colours changed.
931 **112** 30 c. on 50 c. red 30 10
932 35 c. on 50 c. olive 35 10
933 40 c. on 1 cor. green 35 15
934 55 c. on 1 cor. blue 35 30

1937. Air. Surch **Servicio Centroamericano Vale Diez Centavos**.
949 **112** 10 c. on 1 cor. red 30 15

1937. Air. No. 805 (without T **134**) optd **1937**.
950 **79** 8 c. on 15 c. brown 50 15

142 Baseball Player

1937. Obligatory Tax. For 1937 Central American Olympic Games. Optd with ball in red under "OLIMPICO".
951 **142** 1 c. red 35 15
952 1 c. yellow 35 15
953 1 c. blue 35 15
953a 1 c. green 35 15

1937. Nos. 799/809 optd **Habilitado 1937**.
954 **80** 1 c. on 2 c. green 10 10
955 **79** 2 c. on 3 c. olive 10 10
956 **80** 3 c. on 4 c. red 10 10
957 **79** 4 c. on 5 c. blue 10 10
658 **80** 5 c. on 6 c. blue 10 10
959 6 c. on 10 c. brown 10 10
960 **79** 8 c. on 15 c. brown 10 10
661 **80** 16 c. on 20 c. brown 20 20
962 **79** 24 c. on 25 c. red 20 20
963 25 c. on 25 c. orange 20 25
664 **80** 32 c. on 50 c. violet 20 25

144 Presidential Palace, Managua

1937. Air. Inland.
965 **144** 1 c. red 15 10
966 2 c. blue 15 10
967 3 c. olive 15 10
968 4 c. black 15 10
969 5 c. purple 20 10
970 6 c. brown 20 10
971 8 c. violet 20 10
972 16 c. orange 35 25
973 24 c. yellow 20 15
974 25 c. green 50 25

145 Nicaragua

1937. Air. Abroad.
975 **145** 10 c. green 25 10
976 15 c. blue 25 10
977 20 c. yellow 30 25
978 25 c. violet 30 25
979 30 c. red 40 25
980 50 c. orange 60 25
981 1 cor. olive 65 45

146 Presidential Palace

1937. Air. Abroad. 150th Anniv of U.S. Constitution.
982 – 10 c. blue and green 1·10 70
983 **146** 15 c. blue and orange 1·10 70
984 – 20 c. blue and red 80 65
985 – 25 c. blue and brown 80 65
986 – 30 c. blue and green 80 65
987 – 35 c. blue and yellow 35 25
988 – 40 c. blue and green 55 40
989 – 45 c. blue and purple 55 40
990 – 50 c. blue and mauve 55 40
991 – 55 c. blue and green 95 60
992 – 75 c. blue and green 55 30
993 – 1 cor. red and blue 75 30
DESIGNS: 10 c. Children's Park, Managua; 20 c. S. America; 25 c. C. America; 30 c. N. America; 35 c. Lake Tiscapa; 40 c. Pan American motor-road; 45 c. Piniomi Park; 50 c. Piedrecitas Park; 55 c. San Juan del Sur; 75 c. Rio Tipitapa; 1 cor. Granada landscape.

146b Diriangen

1937. Air. Day of the Race.
993a **146b** 1 c. green (inland) 15 10
993b 4 c. lake 15 10
993c 5 c. violet 25 15
993d 8 c. blue 15 10
993e 10 c. brown (abroad) 20 10
993f 15 c. blue 20 10
993g 20 c. pink 30 15

147 Letter Carrier

1937. 75th Anniv of Postal Administration.
994 **147** ½ c. green 15 10
995 – 1 c. mauve 15 10
996 – 2 c. brown 15 10
997 – 3 c. violet 30 20
998 – 5 c. blue 30 20
999 – 7½ c. red . . . . 2·50 75
DESIGNS: 1 c. Mule transport; 2 c. Diligence; 3 c. Yacht; 5 c. Packet steamer; 7½ c. Steam mail train.

147a Gen. Tomas Martinez

1938. Air. 75th Anniv of Postal Administration.
999a **147a** 1 c. black and orange (inland) . . . 25 20
999b 5 c. black and violet . . 25 20
999c 8 c. black and blue . . 30 30
999d 16 c. black and brown . 40 35
999e – 10 c. black and green (abroad) 30 25
999f – 15 c. black and blue . . 40 35
999g – 25 c. black and violet . 25 25
999h – 50 c. black and red . . 40 30
DESIGNS: 10 c. to 50 c. Gen. Anastasio Somoza.

1938. Surch **1938** and **Vale**, new value in words and **Centavos**.
1000 **79** 3 c. on 25 c. orange . . . 10 10
1001 **80** 5 c. on 50 c. brown . . . 10 10
1002 6 c. on 1 cor. blue 15 15

149 Dario Park

150 Laka Managua

151 President Somoza

1939.
1003 **149** 1½ c. green (postage) . . 10 10
1004 2 c. red 10 10
1005 3 c. blue 10 10
1006 6 c. brown 10 10
1007 7½ c. green 10 10
1008 10 c. brown 15 10
1009 15 c. orange 15 10
1010 25 c. violet 15 15
1011 50 c. green 30 20
1012 1 cor. yellow 60 45
1013 **150** 2 c. blue (air: inland) . . 15 15
1014 3 c. olive 15 15
1015 8 c. mauve 15 15
1016 16 c. orange 25 15
1017 24 c. yellow 25 15
1018 32 c. green 35 15
1019 50 c. red 40 15
1020 **151** 10 c. brown (air: abroad) . 15 10
1021 15 c. blue 15 10
1022 20 c. yellow 15 20
1023 25 c. violet 15 15
1024 30 c. red 20 20
1025 50 c. orange 30 20
1026 1 cor. olive 45 35

1939. Nos. 920/1. Surch **Vale un Centavo 1939**.
1027 **79** 1 c. on 15 c. green . . . 10 10
1028 **80** 1 c. on 20 c. brown . . . 10 10

153 Will Rogers and Managua Airport

1939. Air. Will Rogers Commemorative. Inscr "WILL ROGERS/1931/1939".
1029 **153** 1 c. green 10 10
1030 – 2 c. red 10 10
1031 – 3 c. blue 10 10
1032 – 4 c. blue 15 10
1033 – 5 c. red 10 10
DESIGNS: 2 c. Rogers at Managua; 3 c. Rogers in P.A.A. hut; 4 c. Rogers and U.S. Marines; 5 c. Rogers and street in Managua.

156 Senate House and Pres. Somoza

1940. Air. President's Visit to U.S.A. Inscr "AEREO INTERIOR".
1034 – 4 c. brown 15 10
1035 **156** 8 c. brown 10 10
1036 – 16 c. green 15 10
1037 **156** 20 c. mauve 30 15
1038 – 32 c. red 20 20
(b) Inscr "CORREO AEREO INTERNACIONAL".
1039 – 25 c. blue 20 15
1040 – 30 c. black 20 10
1041 **156** 50 c. red 25 40
1042 – 60 c. green 30 35
1043 – 65 c. brown 30 20
1044 – 90 c. olive 40 35
1045 – 1 cor. violet 60 30
DESIGNS: 4 c., 16 c., 25 c., 30 c., 65 c., 90 c. Pres. Somoza addressing Senate; 32 c., 60 c., 1 cor. Portrait of Pres. Somoza between symbols of Nicaragua and New York World's Fair.

158 L. S. Rowe, Statue of Liberty and Union Flags

1940. Air. 50th Anniv of Pan-American Union.
1046 **158** 1 cor. 25 multicoloured . 40 35

159 First Issue of Nicaragua and Sir Rowland Hill

1941. Air. Centenary of First Adhesive Postage stamps.
1047 **159** 2 cor. brown . . . . . 2·25 75
1048 3 cor. blue . . . . . . 7·00 80
1049 5 cor. red . . . . 20·00 2·10

1941. Surch **Servicio ordinario/Vale Diez Centavos/de Cordoba**.
1050 **153** 10 c. on 1 c. green . . . 15 10

161 Rube Dario

1941. 25th Death Anniv of Ruben Dario (poet).
1051 **161** 10 c. red (postage) . . . 20 15
1052 20 c. mauve (air) 25 15
1053 35 c. green 30 20
1054 40 c. orange 35 25
1055 60 c. blue 40 35

1943. As No. 1050, but **de Cordoba** omitted.
1056 **153** 10 c. on 1 c. green . . . 10 10

162 "V" for Victory

163 Red Cross

164 Red Cross Workers and Wounded

1943. Victory.
1057 **162** 10 c. red & violet (post) . 10 10
1058 30 c. red and brown . . . 15 10
1059 40 c. red and green (air) . 15 10
1060 60 c. red and blue . . . 20 10

1944. Air. 80th Anniv of Int Red Cross Society.
1061 **163** 25 c. red 40 15
1062 – 50 c. bistre 65 35
1063 **164** 1 cor. green . . . . . . 1·25 1·00
DESIGN—VERT: 50 c. Two Hemispheres.

165 Columbus and Lighthouse

166 Columbus's Fleet and Lighthouse

1945. Honouring Columbus's Discovery of America and Erection of Columbus Lighthouse near Trujillo City, Dominican Republic.
1064 **165** 4 c. black & green (post) . 15 10
1065 6 c. black and orange . . 20 10
1066 8 c. black and red 20 15
1067 10 c. black and blue . . . 30 15
1068 **166** 20 c. grey & green (air) . 40 15
1069 35 c. black and red . . . 70 20
1070 75 c. pink and green . . . 1·25 40
1071 90 c. blue and red . . . . 1·50 60
1072 1 cor. blue and black . . 1·75 45
1073 2 cor. 50 red and blue . . 4·50 2·25

168 Roosevelt as a Stamp Collector

1946. President Roosevelt Commemorative Inscr "HOMENAJE A ROOSEVELT".
1074 **168** 4 c. green & black (post) . 15 15
1075 – 8 c. violet and black . . . 20 20
1076 – 10 c. blue and black . . . 30 25
1077 – 16 c. red and black . . . 40 30
1078 – 32 c. brown and black . . 50 25
1079 – 50 c. grey and black . . . 50 25
1080 – 25 c. orange & black (air) 20 10
1081 – 75 c. red and black . . . 25 20
1082 – 1 cor. green and black . . 30 30
1083 – 3 cor. violet and black . . 2·25 2·25
1084 – 5 cor. blue and black . . 3·00 3·00
DESIGNS — portraying Roosevelt HORIZ: 8 c., 25 c. with Churchill at the Atlantic Conference; 16 c., 1 cor. with Churchill, De Gaulle and Giraud at the Casablanca Conference; 32 c., 3 cor. with Churchill and Stalin at the Teheran Conference. VERT: 10 c., 75 c. Signing Declaration of War against Japan; 50 c., 5 cor. Head of Roosevelt

171 Managua Cathedral

172 G.P.O., Managua

1947. Managua Centenary Frames in black.
1085 **171** 4 c. red (postage) 10 10
1086 – 5 c. blue 15 10
1087 – 6 c. green 20 15
1088 – 10 c. olive 20 15
1089 – 75 c. brown 30 25
1090 – 5 c. violet (air) 10 10
1091 **172** 20 c. green 15 15
1092 – 35 c. orange 15 15
1093 – 90 c. purple 30 20
1094 – 1 cor. brown 45 35
1095 – 2 cor. 50 purple . . . . 1·00 1·10
DESIGNS—POSTAGE. (as Type **171**): 5 c. Health Ministry; 6 c. Municipal Building; 10 c. College; 75 c. G.P.O., Managua. AIR (as Type **172**): 5 c. College; 35 c. Health Ministry; 90 c. National Bank; 1 cor. Municipal Building; 2 cor. 50, National Palace.

173 San Cristobal Volcano

174 Ruben Dario Monument, Managua

1947. (a) Postage.
1096 **173** 2 c. orange and black . . 10 10
1097 – 3 c. violet and black . . 10 10
1098 – 4 c. grey and black . . . 10 10
1099 – 5 c. red and black . . . 20 10
1100 – 6 c. green and black . . 15 10
1101 – 8 c. brown and black . . 15 10
1102 – 10 c. red and black . . . 25 15
1103 – 20 c. blue and black . . 1·10 25
1104 – 30 c. purple and black . . 70 25
1105 – 50 c. red and black . . . 1·90 70
1106 – 1 cor. brown and black . 60 35
DESIGNS—as Type **173**: 3 c. Lion on Ruben Dario's tomb, Leon Cathedral; 4 c. Race Stand; 5 c. Soldiers' Monument; 6 c. Sugar cane; 8 c. Tropical fruits; 10 c. Cotton; 20 c. Horses; 30 c. Coffee plant; 50 c. Prize bullock; 1 cor. Agricultural landscape.

(b) Air.
1107 **174** 5 c. red and green . . . 10 10
1108 – 6 c. orange and black . . 10 10
1109 – 8 c. brown and red . . . 10 10
1110 – 10 c. blue and brown . . 15 10
1111 – 20 c. orange and blue . . 15 10
1112 – 25 c. green and red . . . 20 15
1113 – 35 c. brown and black . . 30 15
1114 – 50 c. black and violet . . 20 10
1115 – 1 cor. red and black . . 45 25
1116 – 1 cor. 50 green & red . . 50 45
1117 – 5 cor. red and brown . . 3·75 3·75
1118 – 10 cor. brown and violet 3·00 3·00
1119 – 25 cor. yellow and green 6·00 6·00
DESIGNS—As Type **174**: 6 c. Baird's tapir; 8 c. Highway and Lake Managua; 10 c. Genizaro Dam; 20 c. Ruben Dario Monument, Managua; 25 c. Sulphur Lagoon, Nejapa; 35 c. Managua Airport; 50 c. Mouth of Rio Prinzapolka; 1 cor. Thermal Baths, Tipitapa; 1 cor. 50, Rio Tipitapa; 5 cor. Embassy building; 10 cor. Girl carrying basket of fruit; 25 cor. Franklin D. Roosevelt Monument, Managua.

175 Soft-ball

176 Pole Vaulting

177 Tennis

178 National Stadium Managua

1949. 10th World Amateur Baseball Championships.
(a) Postage as T **175/6**.
1120 **175** 1 c. brown 10 10
1121 – 2 c. blue 50 15
1122 **176** 3 c. green 25 10
1123 – 4 c. purple 15 15
1124 – 5 c. orange 40 15
1125 – 10 c. green 40 15
1126 – 15 c. red 50 15
1127 – 25 c. blue 50 20
1128 – 35 c. green 80 20
1129 – 40 c. violet . . . . . . 1·75 30
1130 – 60 c. black . . . . . . 1·40 35
1131 – 1 cor. red . . . . 1·50 90
1132 – 2 cor. purple . . . . . . 2·75 1·50
DESIGNS—VERT: 2 c. Scout; 5 c. Cycling; 25 c. Boxing; 35 c. Basket-ball. HORIZ: 4 c. Diving; 10 c. Stadium; 15 c. Baseball; 40 c. Yachting; 60 c. Table tennis; 1 cor. Football; 2 cor. Tennis.

(b) Air as T **177**.
1133 **177** 1 c. red 10 10
1134 – 2 c. black 10 10
1135 – 3 c. red 10 10
1136 – 4 c. black 10 10

1137 – 5 c. blue 35 15
1138 – 15 c. green 65 10
1139 – 25 c. purple . . . . . . 1·25 25
1140 – 30 c. brown . . . . . . 1·00 25
1141 – 40 c. violet 50 25
1142 – 75 c. mauve . . . . . . 2·50 1·60
1143 – 1 cor. blue . . . . . . 3·00 80
1144 – 2 cor. olive . . . . . . 1·25 1·00
1145 – 5 cor. green . . . . . . 2·10 2·10

DESIGNS—SQUARE: 2 c. Football; 3 c. Table tennis; 4 c. Stadium; 5 c. Yachting; 15 c. Basketball; 25 c. Boxing; 30 c. Baseball; 40 c. Cycling; 75 c. Diving; 1 cor. Pole-vaulting; 2 cor. Scout; 5 cor. Soft-ball.

1949. Obligatory Tax stamps. Stadium Construction Fund.
1146 **178** 5 c. blue 20 10
1146a 5 c. red 20 10

179 Rowland Hill **180** Heinrich von Stephan

1950. 75th Anniv of U.P.U. Frames in black.
1147 **179** 20 c. red (postage) . . . 15 10
1148 – 25 c. green 15 10
1149 – 75 c. blue 50 50
1150 – 80 c. green 30 25
1151 – 4 cor. blue 85 80

DESIGNS—VERT: 25 c. Portrait as Type **180**; 75 c. Monument, Berne; 80 c., 4 cor. Obverse and reverse of Congress Medal.

1152 – 16 c. red (air) 15 10
1153 **180** 20 c. orange 15 10
1154 – 25 c. black 15 15
1155 – 30 c. red 25 10
1156 – 85 c. green 55 50
1157 – 1 cor. 10 brown 50 35
1158 – 2 cor. 14 green . . . . . 1·25 1·25

DESIGNS—HORIZ: 16 c. Rowland Hill; 25, 30 c. U.P.U. Offices, Berne; 85 c. Monument, Berne; 1 cor. 10, and 2 cor. 14, Obverse and reverse of Congress Medal.

181 Queen Isabella and Columbus's Fleet

182 Isabella the Catholic

1952. 500th Birth Anniv of Isabella the Catholic.
1159 – 10 c. mauve (postage) . . 10 10
1160 **181** 96 c. blue . . . . 1·00 55
1161 – 98 c. red . . . . 1·00 55
1162 – 1 cor. 20 brown 50 40
1163 **182** 1 cor. 76 purple 60 60

1164 2 cor. 30 red (air) . . . . 1·40 1·10
1165 – 2 cor. 80 orange . . . . 1·00 95
1166 – 3 cor. green . . . . . . 3·25 1·50
1167 **181** 3 cor. 30 blue . . . . . 3·25 1·75
1168 – 3 cor. 60 green . . . . . 1·50 1·25

DESIGNS—VERT: 10 c., 3 cor. 60, Queen facing right; 98 c., 3 cor. Queen and "Santa Maria"; 1 cor. 20, 2 cor. 80, Queen and Map of Americas.

183 O.D.E.C.A. Flag

1953. Foundation of Organization of Central American States.
1169 **183** 4 c. blue (postage) . . . 10 10
1170 – 5 c. green 10 10
1171 – 6 c. brown 10 10
1172 – 15 c. olive 20 15
1173 – 50 c. sepia 25 15

1174 – 20 c. red (air) 10 10
1175 **183** 25 c. blue 15 10
1176 – 30 c. brown 15 15
1177 – 60 c. green 25 20
1178 – 1 cor. purple 35 45

DESIGNS: 5 c., 1 cor. Map of C. America; 6 c., 20 c. Hands holding O.D.E.C.A. arms; 15 c., 30 c. Five Presidents of C. America; 50 c., 60 c. Charter and flags.

184 Pres. Solorzano

185 Pres. Arguello

1953. Presidential Series. Portraits in black. (a) Postage. As T **184**.
1179 **184** 4 c. red 10 10
1180 – 6 c. blue (D. M. Chamorro) 10 10
1181 – 8 c. brown (Diaz) 10 10
1182 – 15 c. red (Somoza) . . . 15 10
1183 – 50 c. grn (E. Chamorro) 20 15

(b) Air. As T **185**.
1184 **185** 4 c. red 10 10
1185 – 5 c. orange (Moncada) . 10 10
1186 – 20 c. blue (J. B. Sacasa) 10 10
1187 – 25 c. blue (Zelaya) . . . 10 10
1188 – 30 c. lake (Somoza) . . 10 10
1189 – 35 c. green (Martinez) . 20 20
1190 – 40 c. plum (Guzman) . . 20 20
1191 – 45 c. olive (Cuadra) . . 20 20
1192 – 50 c. red (P. J. Chamorro) 35 25
1193 – 60 c. blue (Zavala) . . . 40 40
1194 – 85 c. brown (Cardenas) . 40 40
1195 – 1 cor. 10 pur (Carazo) . 60 55
1196 – 1 cor. 20 bistre (R. Sacasa) 65 55

186 Sculptor and U.N. Emblem

1954. U.N.O. Inscr "HOMENAJE A LA ONU".
1197 **186** 3 c. drab (postage) . . . 10 10
1198 A 4 c. green 15 10
1199 B 5 c. green 20 10
1200 C 15 c. green 55 20
1201 D 1 cor. turquoise 45 40

1202 E 3 c. red (air) 10 10
1203 F 4 c. orange 10 10
1204 C 5 c. rd 15 10
1205 D 30 c. pink 75 15
1206 B 2 cor. red 80 70
1207 A 3 cor. brown . . . . . . 1·50 1·00
1208 **186** 5 cor. purple . . . . . . 1·75 1·40

DESIGNS: A, Detail from Nicaragua's Coat of Arms; B, Globe; C, Candle and Nicaragua's Charter; D, Flags of Nicaragua and U.N.; E, Torch; F, Trusting hands.

187 Capt. D. L. Ray

188 North American Sabre

1954. National Air Force. Frames in black. (a) Postage. Frames as T **187**.
1209 **187** 1 c. black 10 10
1210 – 2 c. black 10 10
1211 – 3 c. myrtle 10 10
1212 – 4 c. orange 15 10
1213 – 5 c. green 20 10
1214 – 15 c. turquoise 15 10
1215 – 1 cor. violet 35 25

(b) Air. Frames as T **188**.
1216 – 10 c. black 10 10
1217 **188** 15 c. black 15 10
1218 – 20 c. mauve 15 10
1219 – 25 c. red 20 10
1220 – 30 c. blue 10 10
1221 – 50 c. blue 75 50
1222 – 1 cor. green 65 35

DESIGNS—POSTAGE: 2 c. North American Sabre; 3 c. Douglas Boston; 4 c. Consolidated Liberator; 5 c. North American Texan trainer; 15 c. Pres. Somoza; 1 cor. Emblem. AIR: 10 c. D. L. Ray; 20 c. Emblem; 25 c. Hangars; 30 c. Pres. Somoza; 50 c. North American Texan trainers; 1 cor. Lockheed Lightning airplanes.

189 Rotary Slogans

190a

1955. 50th Anniv of Rotary International.
1223 **189** 15 c. orange (postage) . 10 10
1224 A 20 c. olive 15 15
1225 B 35 c. violet 15 15
1226 C 40 c. red 15 15
1227 D 90 c. black 30 25

1228 D 1 c. red (air) 10 10
1229 A 2 c. blue 10 10
1230 C 3 c. green 10 10
1231 **189** 4 c. violet 10 10
1232 B 5 c. brown 10 10
1233 25 c. turquoise 15 10
1234 **189** 30 c. black 15 10
1235 C 45 c. mauve 30 25
1236 A 50 c. green 25 20
1237 D 1 cor. blue 45 30

DESIGNS—VERT: A, Clasped hands; B, Rotarian and Nicaraguan flags; D, Paul P. Harris. HORIZ: C, World map and winged emblem.

1956. National Exhibition. Surch **Conmemoracion Exposicion Nacional Febrero 4-16, 1956** and value.
1238 5 c. on 6 c. brown (No. 1171) (postage) 10 10
1239 5 c. on 6 c. blk & blue (1180) 10 10
1240 5 c. on 8 c. brn & blk (1101) 10 10
1241 15 c. on 35 c. violet (1225) . . 15 10
1242 15 c. on 80 c. grn & blk (1150) 15 10
1243 15 c. on 90 c. black (1227) . . 15 10

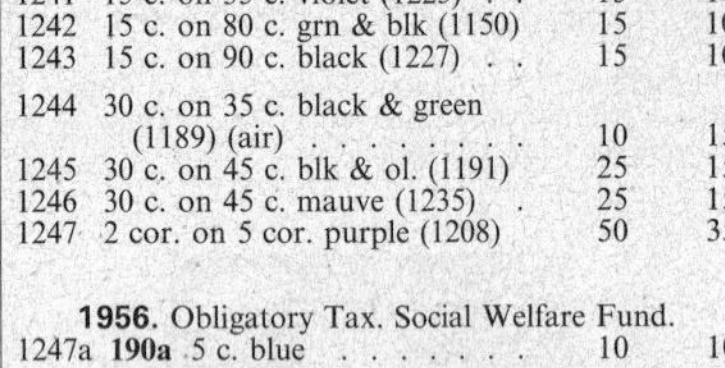

1244 30 c. on 35 c. black & green (1189) (air) 10 15
1245 30 c. on 45 c. blk & ol. (1191) 25 15
1246 30 c. on 45 c. mauve (1235) . 25 15
1247 2 cor. on 5 cor. purple (1208) 50 35

1956. Obligatory Tax. Social Welfare Fund.
1247a **190a** 5 c. blue 10 10

191 Gen. J. Dolores Estrada **192** President Somoza

1956. Cent of War of 1856. Inscr as in T **191**.
1248 – 5 c. brown (postage) . . 10 10
1249 – 10 c. lake 10 10
1250 – 15 c. grey 10 10
1251 – 25 c. red 15 15
1252 – 50 c. purple 30 20

1253 **191** 30 c. red (air) 10 10
1254 – 60 c. brown 20 15
1255 – 1 cor. 50 green 20 35
1256 – 2 cor. 50 blue 30 30
1257 – 10 cor. orange . . . . . 1·90 1·75

DESIGNS—VERT: 5 c. Gen. M. Jerez; 10 c. Gen. F. Chamorro; 50 c. Gen. J. D. Estrada; 1 cor. 50, E. Mangalo; 10 cor. Commodore H. Paulding. HORIZ: 15 c. Battle of San Jocinto; 25 c. Granada in flames; 60 c. Bas-relief; 2 cor. 50, Battle of Rivas.

1957. Air. National Mourning for Pres. G. A. Somoza. Various frames. Inscr as in T **192**. Centres in black.
1258 – 15 c. black 10 10
1259 – 30 c. blue 15 15
1260 **192** 2 cor. violet 80 70
1261 – 3 cor. olive . . . . 1·25 1·10
1262 – 5 cor. sepia . . . . 1·90 1·90

193 Scout and Badge

194 Clasped Hands, Badge and Globe

1957. Birth Centenary of Lord Baden-Powell.
1263 **193** 10 c. olive & violet (post) 10 10
1264 – 15 c. sepia and purple . . 15 15
1265 – 20 c. brown and blue . . 15 15
1266 – 25 c. brown & turquoise . 15 15
1267 – 50 c. olive and red . . . 35 35

1268 **194** 3 c. olive and red (air) . . 15 15
1269 – 4 c. blue and brown . . . 15 15
1270 – 5 c. brown and green . . 15 15
1271 – 6 c. drab and violet . . . 15 15
1272 – 8 c. red and black 15 15
1273 – 30 c. black and green . . 15 15
1274 – 40 c. black and blue . . . 15 15
1275 – 75 c. sepia and purple . . 35 35
1276 – 85 c. grey and red 40 40
1277 – 1 cor. brown and green . 40 40

DESIGNS—VERT: 4 c. Scout badge; 5 c., 15 c. Wolf cub; 6 c. Badge and flags; 8 c. Badge and emblems of scouting; 20 c. Scout; 25 c. A. Harrison; 75 c. Rover Scout; 85 c. Scout. HORIZ: 40 c. Presentation to Pres. Somoza.

195 Pres. Luis Somoza

197 Archbishop of Managua

196 Managua Cathedral

1957. Election of Pres. Somoza. Portrait in brown. (a) Postage. Oval frame.
1278 **195** 10 c. red 10 10
1279 15 c. blue 10 10
1280 35 c. purple 10 10
1281 **195** 50 c. brown 15 15
1282 75 c. green 40 40

(b) Air. Rectangular frame.
1283 – 20 c. blue 10 10
1284 – 25 c. mauve 15 10
1285 – 30 c. sepia 15 15
1286 – 40 c. turquoise 15 15
1287 – 2 cor. violet 95 95

1957. Churches and Priests. Centres in olive.
1288 **196** 5 c. green (postage) . . . 10 10
1289 – 10 c. purple 10 10
1290 **197** 15 c. blue 10 10
1291 – 20 c. sepia 15 10
1292 – 50 c. green 20 15
1293 – 1 cor. violet 30 30

1294 **197** 30 c. green (air) 10 10
1295 **196** 60 c. brown 15 15
1296 – 75 c. blue 25 25
1297 – 90 c. red 30 30
1298 – 1 cor. 50 turquoise . . . 35 35
1299 – 2 cor. purple 40 40

DESIGNS—HORIZ: As Type **196**: 20, 90 c. Leon Cathedral; 50 c., 1 cor. 50, La Merced, Granada Church. VERT: As Type **197**: 10, 75 c. Bishop of Nicaragua; 1, 2 cor. Father Mariano Dubon.

198 "Honduras" (freighter)

199 Exhibition Emblem

1957. Nicaraguan Merchant Marine Commemoration. Inscr as in T **198**.
1300 **198** 4 c. black, blue and myrtle (postage) 15 10
1301 – 5 c. violet, blue & brown 15 10
1302 – 6 c. black, blue & red . . 15 10
1303 – 10 c. black, green and sepia 20 10
1304 – 15 c. brown, blue & red . 30 10
1305 – 50 c. brown, blue & violet 30 20

1306 – 25 c. purple, blue and ultramarine (air) . . . 30 10
1307 – 30 c. grey, buff & brown 15 10
1308 – 50 c. bistre, blue & violet 20 20
1309 – 60 c. black, turquoise and purple 55 20
1310 – 1 cor. black, blue & red . 75 30
1311 – 2 cor. 50 brown, blue and black . . . . 1·75 1·00

DESIGNS: 5 c. Gen. A. Somoza, founder of Mamenic (National) Shipping Line, and "Guatemala" (freighter); 6 c. "Guatemala"; 10 c. "Salvador" (freighter); 15 c. Freighter between hemispheres; 25 c. "Managua" (freighter); 30 c. Ship's wheel and world map; 50 c. (No. 1305), Hemispheres and ship; 50 c. (No. 1308), Mamenic Shipping Line flag; 60 c. "Costa Rica" (freighter); 1 cor. "Nicarao" (freighter); 2 cor. 50, Map, freighter and flag.

1958. Air. Brussels International Exn. Inscr "EXPOSICION MUNDIAL DE BELGICA 1958".
1312 **199** 25 c. black, yell & grn . . 10 10
1313 – 30 c. multicoloured . . . 15 15
1314 – 45 c. black, ochre & blue 15 15
1315 **199** 1 cor. black, blue and dull purple 25 25
1316 – 2 cor. multicoloured . . 25 25
1317 – 10 cor. sepia, purple and blue . . . . 1·40 1·00

DESIGNS: As Type **199**: 30 c., 20 cor. Arms of Nicaragua; 45 c., 10 cor. Nicaraguan Pavilion.

200 Emblems of C. American Republics

201 Arms of La Salle

1958. 17th Central American Lions Convention. Inscr as in T **200**. Emblems (5 c., 60 c.) multicoloured; Lions badge (others) in blue, red, yellow (or orange and buff).
1318 **200** 5 c. blue (postage) . . . 10 10
1319 – 10 c. blue and orange . . 10 10
1320 – 20 c. blue and green . . . 10 10
1321 – 50 c. blue and purple . . 15 15
1322 – 75 c. blue and mauve . . 30 25
1323 – 1 cor. 50, blue, salmon and drab 45 45

1324 – 30 c. blue & orge (air) . . 10 10
1325 **200** 60 c. blue and pink . . . 20 15
1326 – 90 c. blue 25 20
1327 – 1 cor. 25 blue and olive . 35 30
1328 – 2 cor. blue and green . . 60 50
1329 – 3 cor. blue, red and violet 95 90

DESIGNS—HORIZ: 10 c., 1 cor. 25, Melvin Jones; 20, 30 c. Dr. T. A. Arias; 50, 90 c. Edward G. Barry; 75 c., 2 cor. Lions emblem; 1 cor. 50, 3 cor. Map of C. American Isthmus.

1958. Brothers of the Nicaraguan Christian Schools Commem. Inscr as in T **201**.
1330 **201** 5 c. red, blue & yellow (postage) 10 10
1331 – 10 c. sepia, blue & green 10 10
1332 – 15 c. sepia, brown & bis 10 10
1333 – 20 c. black, red & bistre 15 10

1334 – 50 c. sepia, orange & bis 15 15
1335 – 75 c. sepia, turquoise & grn 25 20
1336 – 1 cor. black, vio & bistre 40 30

1337 **201** 30 c. blue, red & yellow (air) 10 10
1338 – 60 c. sepia, purple & grey 25 20
1339 – 85 c. black, red & blue 30 25
1340 – 90 c. black, green & ochre 35 35
1341 – 1 cor. 25 black, red and ochre 50 45
1342 – 1 cor. 50 sepia, green and grey 60 55
1343 – 1 cor. 75 blk, brn & bl 65 55
1344 – 2 cor. sepia, grn & grey 65 65

DESIGNS—HORIZ: 10, 60 c. Managua Teachers Institute. VERT: 15, 85 c. De La Salle (founder); 20, 90 c. Brother Carlos; 50 c., 1 cor. 50, Brother Antonio; 75 c., 1 cor. 25, Brother Julio; 1 cor., 1 cor. 75, Brother Argeo; 2 cor. Brother Eugenio.

202 U.N. Emblem 203 204

1958. Inauguration of U.N.E.S.C.O. Headquarters Building, Paris. Inscr as in T **202**.

1345 **202** 10 c. blue & mve (postage) 10 10
1346 – 15 c. mauve and blue 10 10
1347 – 25 c. brown and green 10 10
1348 – 40 c. black and red 15 15
1349 – 45 c. mauve and blue 20 20
1350 **202** 50 c. green and brown 25 25

1351 – 60 c. blue & mauve (air) 25 15
1352 – 75 c. brown and green 25 20
1353 – 90 c. green and brown 30 25
1354 – 1 cor. mauve and blue 40 30
1355 – 3 cor. red and black 60 60
1356 – 5 cor. blue and mauve 1·00 85

DESIGNS—VERT: 15 c. Aerial view of H.Q; 25, 45 c. Facade composed of letters "UNESCO"; 40 c. H.Q. and Eiffel Tower; In oval vignettes–60 c., As 15 c; 75 c., 5 cor., As 25 c.; 90 c., 3 cor. As 40 c.; 1 cor., As Type **202**.

1959. Obligatory Tax. Consular Fiscal stamps surch Serial Nos. in red.

1357 **203** 5 c. on 50 c. blue 10 10
1358 **204** 5 c. on 50 c. blue 10 10

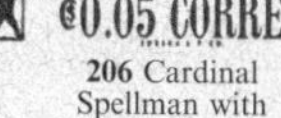

205 206 Cardinal Spellman with Pope John XXIII 207 Abraham Lincoln

1959. Obligatory Tax.

1359 **205** 5 c. blue 15 10

1959. Cardinal Spellman Commemoration.

1360 **206** 5 c. flesh & grn (postage) 10 10
1361 A 10 c. multicoloured 10 10
1362 B 15 c. red, black and grn 10 10
1363 C 20 c. yellow and blue 10 10
1364 D 25 c. red and blue 10 10

1365 E 30 c. bl, red & yellow (air) 10 10
1366 **206** 35 c. bronze and orange 10 10
1367 A 1 cor. multicoloured 30 30
1368 B 1 cor. 5 red and black 35 30
1369 C 1 cor. 50 yellow & blue 45 35
1370 D 2 cor. blue, violet & red 55 45
1371 E 5 cor. multicoloured 75 55

DESIGNS—VERT: A, Cardinal's Arms; B, Cardinal; D, Cardinal wearing sash. HORIZ: C, Cardinal and Cross; E, Flags of Nicaragua, Vatican City and U.S.A.

1960. 150th Birth Anniv of Abraham Lincoln. Portrait in black.

1372 **207** 5 c. red (postage) 10 10
1373 10 c. green 10 10
1374 15 c. orange 10 10
1375 1 cor. purple 25 25
1376 2 cor. blue 30 45

1377 30 c. blue (air) 10 10
1378 35 c. red 15 10
1379 70 c. purple 20 20
1380 1 cor. 5 green 35 35
1381 1 cor. 50 violet 50 45
1382 – 5 cor. ochre and black 55 55

DESIGN—HORIZ: 5 cor. Scroll inscr "Dar al que necesite–A. Lincoln".

1960. Air. 10th Anniv of San Jose (Costa Rica) Philatelic Society. Optd **X Aniversario Club Filatelico S. J.–C. R.**

1383 2 cor. red (No. 1206) 70 60
1384 2 cor. 50 blue (No. 1256) 75 75
1385 3 cor. green (No. 1166) 1·40 90

1960. Red Cross Fund for Chilean Earthquake Relief Nos. 1372/82 optd **Resello** and Maltese Cross. Portrait in black.

1386 **207** 5 c. red (postage) 10 10
1387 10 c. green 10 10
1388 15 c. orange 10 10
1389 1 cor. purple 25 25
1390 2 cor. blue 30 25

1391 30 c. blue (air) 25 20
1392 35 c. red 20 20
1393 **207** 70 c. purple 25 25
1394 1 cor. 5 green 30 30
1395 1 cor. 50 violet 40 35
1396 – 5 cor. ochre and black 1·00 1·00

210

1961. Air. World Refugee Year. Inscr "ANO MUNDIAL DEL REFUGIADO".

1397 – 2 cor. multicoloured 20 20
1398 **210** 5 cor. ochre, blue & grn 60 60

DESIGN: 2 cor. Procession of refugees.

211 Pres. Roosevelt, Pres. Somoza and Officer

1961. Air. 20th Anniv of Nicaraguan Military Academy.

1399 **211** 20 c. multicoloured 10 10
1400 – 25 c. red, blue and black 10 10
1401 – 30 c. multicoloured 10 10
1402 – 35 c. multicoloured 10 10
1403 – 40 c. multicoloured 10 10
1404 – 45 c. black, flesh and red 15 15
1405 **211** 60 c. multicoloured 15 15
1406 – 70 c. multicoloured 20 20
1407 – 1 cor. 5 multicoloured 25 25
1408 – 1 cor. 50 multicoloured 35 35
1409 – 2 cor. multicoloured 50 50
1410 – 5 cor. blk, flesh & grey 70 60

DESIGNS — VERT: 25, 70 c. Flags; 35 c., 1 cor. 50, Standard bearers; 40 c., 2 cor. Pennant and emblem. HORIZ: 30 c., 1 cor. 5 Group of officers; 45 c., 5 cor. Pres. Somoza and Director of Academy.

1961. Air. Consular Fiscal stamps as T **203/4** with serial Nos. in red, surch **Correo Aereo** and value.

1411 20 c. on 50 c. blue 15 10
1412 20 c. on 1 cor. olive 15 10
1413 20 c. on 2 cor. green 15 10
1414 20 c. on 3 cor. red 15 10
1415 20 c. on 5 cor. red 15 10
1416 20 c. on 10 cor. violet 15 10
1417 20 c. on 20 cor. brown 15 10
1418 20 c. on 50 cor. brown 15 10
1419 20 c. on 100 cor. lake 15 10

213 I.J.C. Emblem and Global Map of the Americas 215 R. Cabezas

1961. Air. Junior Chamber of Commerce Congress.

1420 2 c. multicoloured 10 10
1421 3 c. black and yellow 10 10
1422 4 c. multicoloured 10 10
1423 5 c. black and red 10 10
1424 6 c. multicoloured 15 10
1425 10 c. multicoloured 10 10
1426 15 c. black, green and blue 10 10
1427 30 c. black and blue 15 10
1428 35 c. multicoloured 15 10
1429 70 c. black, red and yellow 20 20
1430 1 cor. 5 multicoloured 35 30
1431 5 cor. multicoloured 70 70

DESIGNS—HORIZ: 2 c., 15 c. Type **213**; 4 c., 35 c. "J.C.I." upon Globe. VERT: 3 c., 30 c. I.J.C. emblem; 5 c., 70 c. Scroll; 6 c., 1 cor. 5, Handclasp; 10 c., 5 cor. Regional map of Nicaragua.

1961. Air. 1st Central American Philatelic Convention, San Salvador. Optd **Convencion Filatelica - Centro - America - Panama - San Salvador - 27 Julio 1961.**

1432 **158** 1 cor. 25 multicoloured 25 25

1961. Air. Birth Centenary of Cabezas.

1433 **215** 20 c. blue and orange 10 10
1434 – 40 c. purple and blue 15 15
1435 – 45 c. sepia and green 15 15
1436 – 70 c. green and brown 25 20
1437 – 2 cor. blue and pink 60 40
1438 – 10 cor. purple and turquoise 1·50 1·50

DESIGNS—HORIZ: 40 c. Map and view of Cartago; 45 c. 1884 newspaper; 70 c. Assembly outside building; 2 cor. Scroll; 10 cor. Map and view of Masaya.

216 Official Gazettes 219 "Cattleya skinneri"

1961. Centenary of Regulation of Postal Rates.

1439 **216** 5 c. brown & turquoise 10 10
1440 – 10 c. brown and green 10 10
1441 – 15 c. brown and red 10 10

DESIGNS: 10 c. Envelopes and postmarks; 15 c. Martinez and Somoza.

1961. Air. Dag Hammarskjold Commem. Nos. 1351/6 optd **Homenaje a Hammarskjold Sept. 18-1961.**

1442 60 c. blue and mauve 30 30
1443 75 c. brown and green 35 35
1444 90 c. green and brown 45 45
1445 1 cor. mauve and blue 50 50
1446 3 cor. red and black 80 80
1447 5 cor. blue and mauve 1·50 1·50

1962. Air. Surch **RESELLO C$ 1.00.**

1448 – 1 cor. on 1 cor. 10 brown (No. 1157) 30 25
1449 **207** 1 cor. on 1 cor. 5 black and green 30 25

See also Nos. 1498/1500a, 1569/70, 1608/14, 1669/76 and 1748/62.

1962. Obligatory Tax. Nicaraguan Orchids. Multicoloured.

1450 5 c. Type **219** 10 10
1451 5 c. "Bletia roezlii" 10 10
1452 5 c. "Sobralia pleiantha" 10 10
1453 5 c. "Lycaste macrophylla" 10 10
1454 5 c. "Schomburgkia tibicinus" 10 10
1455 5 c. "Maxillaria tenuifolia" 10 10
1456 5 c. "Stanhopea ecornuta" 10 10
1457 5 c. "Oncidium ascendens" and "O. cebolleta" 10 10
1458 5 c. "Cycnoches egertonianum" 10 10
1459 5 c. "Hexisia bidentata" 10 10

220 U.N.E.S.C.O. "Audience" 222 Arms of Nueva Segovia

1962. Air. 15th Anniv of U.N.E.S.C.O.

1460 **220** 2 cor. multicoloured 15 15
1461 – 5 cor. multicoloured 80 80

DESIGN: 5 cor. U.N. and U.N.E.S.C.O. emblems.

1962. Air. Malaria Eradication. Nos. 1425, 1428/31 optd with mosquito surrounded by **LUCHA CONTRA LA MALARIA.**

1462 – 10 c. 35 30
1463 – 35 c. 45 30
1464 – 70 c. 60 45
1465 – 1 cor. 5 80 65
1466 – 5 cor. 1·00 1·25

1962. Urban and Provincial Arms. Arms mult; inscr black; background colours below.

1467 **222** 2 c. mauve (postage) 10 10
1468 – 3 c. blue 10 10
1469 – 4 c. lilac 10 10
1470 – 5 c. yellow 10 10
1471 – 6 c. brown 10 10

1472 **222** 30 c. red (air) 10 10
1473 – 50 c. orange 15 10
1474 – 1 cor. green 25 20
1475 – 2 cor. grey 45 40
1476 – 5 cor. blue 75 60

ARMS: 3 c., 50 c. Leon; 4 c., 1 cor. Managua; 5 c., 2 cor. Granada; 6 c., 5 cor. Rivas.

223 Liberty Bell

1963. Air. 150th Anniv of Independence.

1477 **223** 30 c. drab, blue & black 15 10

224 Blessing

1963. Air. Death Tercentenary of St. Vincent de Paul and St. Louise de Marillac.

1478 – 60 c. black and orange 15 10
1479 **224** 1 cor. olive and orange 25 20
1480 – 2 cor. black and red 50 45

DESIGNS—VERT: 60 c. "Comfort" (St. Louise and woman). HORIZ: 2 cor. St. Vincent and St. Louise.

225 "Map Stamp" 226 Cross on Globe

1963. Air. Central American Philatelic Societies Federation Commemoration.

1481 **225** 1 cor. blue and yellow 30 20

1963. Air. Ecumenical Council, Vatican City.

1482 **226** 20 c. red and yellow 15 10

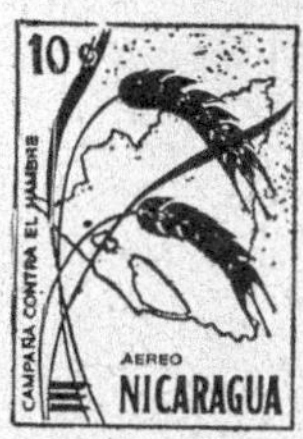

227 Ears of Wheat 228 Boxing

1963. Air. Freedom from Hunger.

1483 **227** 10 c. green & light green 10 10
1484 – 25 c. sepia and yellow 15 10

DESIGN: 25 c. Barren tree and campaign emblem.

1963. Air. Sports. Multicoloured.

1485 2 c. Type **228** 10 10
1486 3 c. Running 10 10
1487 4 c. Underwater harpooning 10 10
1488 5 c. Football 10 10
1489 6 c. Baseball 15 10
1490 10 c. Tennis 20 10
1491 15 c. Cycling 20 10
1492 20 c. Motor-cycling 20 10
1493 35 c. Chess 30 15
1494 60 c. Angling 35 20
1495 1 cor. Table-tennis 55 35
1496 2 cor. Basketball 75 55
1497 5 cor. Golf 1·90 1·10

1964. Air. Surch **Resello or RESELLO** (1500a) and value.

1498 – 5 c. on 6 c. (No. 1424) 35 15
1499 – 10 c. on 30 c. (No. 1365) 45 15
1500 **207** 15 c. on 30 c. 70 20
1500a **201** 20 c. on 30 c. 15 10

See also Nos. 1448/9, 1569/70, 1608/14 and 1669/76.

1964. Optd **CORREOS.**

1501 5 c. multicoloured (No. 1451) 10 10

231 Flags 232 "Alliance Emblem"

1964. Air. "Centro America".

1502 **231** 40 c. multicoloured 15 15

1964. Air. "Alliance for Progress". Multicoloured.

1503 5 c. Type **232** 10 10
1504 10 c. Red Cross Post 10 10
1505 15 c. Highway 10 10
1506 20 c. Ploughing 10 10
1507 25 c. Housing 15 10
1508 30 c. Presidents Somoza and Kennedy and Eugene Black (World Bank) 15 10
1509 35 c. School and adults 20 15
1510 40 c. Chimneys 25 15

Nos. 1504/10 are horiz.

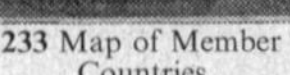

233 Map of Member Countries **235** Rescue of Wounded Soldier

1964. Air. Central-American "Common Market". Multicoloured.
1511 15 c. Type **233** 10 10
1512 25 c. Ears of wheat 10 10
1513 40 c. Cogwheels 10 10
1514 50 c. Heads of cattle 15 10

1964. Air. Olympic Games, Tokyo. Nos. 1485/7, 1489 and 1495/6 optd **OLIMPIADAS TOKYO-1964**.
1515 2 c. Type **108** 10 10
1516 3 c. Running 10 10
1517 4 c. Underwater harpooning . 10 10
1518 6 c. Baseball 10 10
1519 1 cor. Table-tennis . . . . . 1·10 1·10
1520 2 cor. Basketball . . . . . . 2·25 2·25

1965. Air. Red Cross Centenary. Multicoloured.
1521 20 c. Type **235** 10 10
1522 25 c. Blood transfusion . . . 15 10
1523 40 c. Red Cross and snowbound town 15 15
1524 10 cor. Red Cross and map of Nicaragua . . . . 1·50 1·50

236 Statuettes

1965. Air. Nicaraguan Antiquities. Multicoloured.
1525 5 c. Type **236** 10 10
1526 10 c. Totem 10 10
1527 15 c. Carved dog 10 10
1528 20 c. Composition of "objets d'art" 10 10
1529 25 c. Dish and vase 10 10
1530 30 c. Pestle and mortar . . . 10 10
1531 35 c. Statuettes (different) . . 10 10
1532 40 c. Deity 15 10
1533 50 c. Wine vessel and dish . . 15 10
1534 60 c. Bowl and dish 20 10
1535 1 cor. Urn 45 15
The 15, 25, 35 and 60 c. are horiz.

237 Pres. Kennedy **238** A. Bello

1965. Air. Pres. Kennedy Commemorative.
1536 **237** 35 c. black and green . . 15 10
1537 75 c. black and mauve . 25 15
1538 1 cor. 10 black & blue . 35 25
1539 2 cor. black & brown . . 90 55

1965. Air. Death Centenary of Andres Bello (poet and writer).
1540 **238** 10 c. black and brown . . 10 10
1541 15 c. black and blue . . 10 10
1542 45 c. black and purple . 15 10
1543 80 c. black and green . . 20 15
1544 1 cor. black and yellow . 25 20
1545 2 cor. black and grey . . 45 45

1965. 9th Central-American Scout Camporee. Nos. 1450/9 optd with scout badge and **CAMPOREE SCOUT 1965**.
1546 5 c. multicoloured 20 20
1547 5 c. multicoloured 20 20
1548 5 c. multicoloured 20 20
1549 5 c. multicoloured 20 20
1550 5 c. multicoloured 20 20
1551 5 c. multicoloured 20 20
1552 5 c. multicoloured 20 20
1553 5 c. multicoloured 20 20
1554 5 c. multicoloured 20 20
1555 5 c. multicoloured 20 20

240 Sir Winston Churchill **241** Pope John XXIII

1966. Air. Churchill Commemorative.
1556 **240** 20 c. mauve and black . . 10 10
1557 – 35 c. green and black . . 15 10
1558 – 60 c. ochre and black . . 15 15
1559 – 75 c. red 20 20
1560 – 1 cor. purple 30 25
1561 **240** 2 cor. violet, lilac & blk 60 55
1562 – 3 cor. blue and black . . 65 60
DESIGNS—HORIZ: 35 c., 1 cor. Churchill broadcasting. VERT: 60 c., 3 cor. Churchill crossing the Rhine; 75 c. Churchill in Hussars' uniform.

1966. Air. Closure of Vatican Ecumenical Council. Multicoloured.
1564 20 c. Type **241** 10 10
1565 35 c. Pope Paul VI 15 15
1566 1 cor. Archbishop Gonzalez y Robleto 30 25
1567 2 cor. St. Peter's, Rome . . 30 25
1568 3 cor. Papal arms 60 40

1967. Air. Nos. 1533/4 surch **RESELLO** and value.
1569 10 c. on 50 c. multicoloured 10 10
1570 15 c. on 60 c. multicoloured 10 10
See also Nos. 1448/9, 1498/1500a, 1608/14 and 1669/76.

243 Dario and Birthplace

1967. Air. Birth Centenary of Ruben Dario (poet). Designs showing Dario and view. Mult.
1571 5 c. Type **243** 10 10
1572 10 c. Monument, Managua . 10 10
1573 20 c. Leon Cathedral (site of Dario's tomb) 10 10
1574 40 c. Allegory of the centaurs 15 10
1575 75 c. Allegory of the swans . 2·00 75
1576 1 cor. Roman triumphal march 25 20
1577 2 cor. St. Francis and the wolf 45 40
1578 5 cor. "Faith" opposing "Death" 65 60

244 "Megalura peleus"

1967. Air. Butterflies. Multicoloured.
1580 5 c. "Heliconius petiveranua" 10 10
1581 10 c. "Colaenis julia" . . . 10 10
1582 15 c. Type **244** 10 10
1583 20 c. "Aneyluris jurgensii" . 10 10
1584 25 c. "Thecla regalis" . . . 10 10
1585 30 c. "Doriana thia" . . . 10 10
1586 35 c. "Lymnias pixae" . . . 15 10
1587 40 c. "Metamorpho dido" . 25 10
1588 50 c. "Papilio arcas" . . . 25 15
1589 60 c. "Ananea cleomestra" . 35 15
1590 1 cor. "Victorina epaphaus" 60 30
1591 2 cor. "Prepona demophon" 1·10 50
The 5, 10, 30, 35, 50 c. and 1 cor. are vert.

245 McDivitt and White

1967. Air. Space Flight of McDivitt and White. Multicoloured.
1592 5 c. Type **245** 10 10
1593 10 c. Astronauts and "Gemini 5" on launching pad . . . 10 10
1594 15 c. "Gemini 5" and White in Space 10 10
1595 20 c. Recovery operation at sea 15 10
1596 35 c. Type **245** 10 10
1597 40 c. As 10 c. 15 10
1598 75 c. As 15 c. 20 20
1599 1 cor. As 20 c. 35 25

246 National Flower of Costa Rica

1967. Air. 5th Year of Central American Economic Integration. Designs showing National Flowers of the Central-American Countries. Multicoloured.
1600 40 c. Type **246** 15 10
1601 40 c. Guatemala 15 10
1602 40 c. Honduras 15 10
1603 40 c. Nicaragua 15 10
1604 40 c. El Salvador 15 10

247 Presidents Diaz and Somoza **249** Mangoes

1968. Air. Visit of Pres. Diaz of Mexico.
1605 – 20 c. black 10 10
1606 **247** 40 c. olive 20 10
1607 – 1 cor. brown 35 20
DESIGNS—VERT: 20 c. Pres. Somoza greeting Pres. Diaz; 1 cor. Pres. Diaz of Mexico.

1968. Surch **RESELLO** and value.
1608 – 5 c. on 6 c. (No. 1180) (postage) 10 10
1609 – 5 c. on 6 c. (No. 1471) . . 10 10
1610 – 5 c. on 6 c. (No. 1424) (air) 10 10
1611 – 5 c. on 6 c. (No. 1489) . . 10 10
1612 **156** 5 c. on 8 c. (No. 1035) . . 10 10
1614 – 1 cor. on 1 cor. 50 (No. 1369) 25 20
See also Nos. 1448/9, 1498/1500a, 1569/70 and 1669/76.

1968. Air. Nicaraguan Fruits. Multicoloured.
1615 5 c. Type **249** 10 10
1616 10 c. Pineapples 10 10
1617 15 c. Oranges 10 10
1618 20 c. Pawpaws 10 10
1619 30 c. Bananas 10 10
1620 35 c. Avocado pears 15 10
1621 50 c. Water-melons 15 10
1622 75 c. Cashews 25 15
1623 1 cor. Sapodilla plums . . . 35 20
1624 2 cor. Cocoa beans 45 20

250 "The Crucifixion" (Fra Angelico)

1968. Air. Religious Paintings. Multicoloured.
1625 10 c. Type **250** 10 10
1626 15 c. "The Last Judgement" (Michelangelo) 10 10
1627 35 c. "The Beautiful Gardener" (Raphael) 15 15
1628 2 cor. "The Spoliation of Christ" (El Greco) 45 30
1629 3 cor. "The Conception" (Murillo) 60 45
Nos. 1626/9 are vert.

1968. Air. Pope Paul's Visit to Bogota. Nos. 1625/8 optd **Visita de S. S. Paulo VI C. E. de Bogota 1968**.
1631 **250** 10 c. multicoloured . . . 10 10
1632 – 15 c. multicoloured . . . 10 10
1633 – 35 c. multicoloured . . . 10 10
1634 – 2 cor. multicoloured . . . 30 20

252 Basketball

1969. Air. Olympic Games, Mexico. Mult.
1635 10 c. Type **252** 10 10
1636 15 c. Fencing 10 10
1637 20 c. High-diving 10 10
1638 35 c. Running 10 10
1639 50 c. Hurdling 15 10
1640 75 c. Weightlifting 20 15
1641 1 cor. Boxing 35 20
1642 2 cor. Football 55 55
The 15, 50 c. and 1 cor. are horiz.

253 "Cichlasoma citrinellum"

1969. Air. Fishes. Multicoloured.
1644 10 c. Type **253** 10 10
1645 15 c. "Cichlasoma nicaraguensis" 10 10
1646 20 c. "Cyprinus carpio" (Carp) 10 10
1647 30 c. "Lepisosteus tropicus" (Gar) 10 10
1648 35 c. "Xiphias gladius" (Swordfish) 10 10
1649 50 c. "Phylipuns dormitor" (vert) 15 10
1650 75 c. "Tarpon atlanticus" (Tarpon) (vert) 20 15
1651 1 cor. "Eulamia nicaraguensis" (vert) 30 15
1652 2 cor. "Istiophorus albicans" (Sailfish) (vert) 30 35
1653 3 cor. "Pristis antiquorum" (Sawfish) (vert) 60 40

1969. Air. Various stamps surch **RESELLO** and value.
1655 10 c. on 25 c. (No. 1507) . . 10 10
1656 10 c. on 25 c. (No. 1512) . . 10 10
1657 15 c. on 25 c. (No. 1529) . . 10 10
1658 50 c. on 70 c. (No. 1379) . . 15 10

255 Scenery, Tower and Emblem **258** "Minerals"

1969. Air. "Hemisfair" (1968) Exhibition.
1659 **255** 30 c. blue and red . . . 10 10
1660 35 c. purple and red . . 10 10
1661 75 c. red and blue . . . 15 10
1662 1 cor. purple and black . 30 20
1663 2 cor. purple and green . 55 40

1969. Various stamps surch. (a) Optd **CORREO**.
1665 5 c. (No. 1450) 10 10
1666 5 c. (No. 1453) 10 10
1667 5 c. (No. 1454) 10 10
1668 5 c. (No. 1459) 10 10

(b) Optd **RESELLO** and surch.
1670 10 c. on 30 c. (No. 1324) . . 10 10
1671 10 c. on 30 c. (No. 1427) . . 10 10
1669 10 c. on 25 c. (No. 1529) . . 10 10
1672 10 c. on 30 c. (No. 1530) . . 10 10
1673 15 c. on 35 c. (No. 1531) . . 10 10
1674 20 c. on 30 c. (No. 1307) . . 10 10
1675 20 c. on 30 c. (No. 1401) . . 10 10
1676 20 c. on 35 c. (No. 1509) . . 10 10

1969. Air. Nicaraguan Products. Multicoloured.
1677 5 c. Type **258** 10 10
1678 10 c. "Fish" 10 10
1679 15 c. "Bananas" 10 10
1680 20 c. "Timber" 10 10
1681 35 c. "Coffee" 10 10
1682 40 c. "Sugar-cane" 15 10
1683 60 c. "Cotton" 20 10
1684 75 c. "Rice and Maize" . . . 20 15
1685 1 cor. "Tobacco" 30 20
1686 2 cor. "Meat" 35 25

1969. 50th Anniv of I.L.O. Obligatory tax stamps. Nos. 1450/9, optd, **O.I.T. 1919-1969**.
1687 5 c. multicoloured 10 10
1688 5 c. multicoloured 10 10
1689 5 c. multicoloured 10 10
1690 5 c. multicoloured 10 10
1691 5 c. multicoloured 10 10
1692 5 c. multicoloured 10 10
1693 5 c. multicoloured 10 10
1694 5 c. multicoloured 10 10
1695 5 c. multicoloured 10 10
1696 5 c. multicoloured 10 10

260 Girl carrying Tinaja **261** Pele (Brazil)

1970. Air. 8th Inter-American Savings and Loans Conference, Managua.
1697 **260** 10 c. multicoloured . . . 10 10
1698 15 c. multicoloured . . . 10 10
1699 20 c. multicoloured . . . 10 10
1700 35 c. multicoloured . . . 15 10
1701 50 c. multicoloured . . . 15 10
1702 75 c. multicoloured . . . 20 15
1703 1 cor. multicoloured . . . 30 20
1704 2 cor. multicoloured . . 60 40

1970. World Football "Hall of Fame" Poll-winners. Multicoloured.
1705 5 c. Type **261** (postage) . . . 10 10
1706 10 c. Puskas (Hungary) . . . 10 10
1707 15 c. Matthews (England) . . 10 10
1708 40 c. Di Stefano (Argentina) 10 10
1709 2 cor. Facchetti (Italy) . . . 55 45
1710 3 cor. Yashin (Russia) . . . 70 65

1711 5 cor. Beckenbauer (West Germany) 70 90
1712 20 c. Santos (Brazil) (air) . . 10 10
1713 80 c. Wright (England) . . . 20 15
1714 1 cor. Flags of 16 World Cup Finalists 25 20
1715 4 cor. Bozsik (Hungary) . . . 90 75
1716 5 cor. Charlton (England) . . 1·10 90

262 Torii (Gate)

263 Module and Astronauts on Moon

1970. Air. EXPO 70, World Fair, Osaka, Japan.
1717 **262** 25 c. multicoloured . . . 10 10
1718 30 c. multicoloured . . . 10 10
1719 35 c. multicoloured . . . 10 10
1720 75 c. multicoloured . . . 25 15
1721 1 cor. 50 multicoloured . 35 30
1722 3 cor. multicoloured . . . 45 35

1970. Air. "Apollo 11" Moon Landing. Mult.
1724 35 c. Type **263** 10 10
1725 40 c. Module landing on Moon 10 10
1726 60 c. Astronauts with U.S. Flag 20 15
1727 75 c. As 40 c. 25 15
1728 1 cor. As 60 c. 35 20
1729 2 cor. Type **263** 40 35

264 F. D. Roosevelt

265 "The Annunciation" (Grunewald)

1970. Air. 25th Death Anniv of Franklin D. Roosevelt.
1730 **264** 10 c. black 10 10
1731 – 15 c. brown and black . 10 10
1732 – 20 c. green and black . . 10 10
1733 **264** 35 c. purple and black . 10 10
1734 – 50 c. brown 15 10
1735 **264** 75 c. blue 20 15
1736 – 1 cor. red 25 20
1737 – 2 cor. black 30 35
PORTRAITS: 15 c., 1 cor. Roosevelt with stamp collection; 20 c., 50 c., 2 cor. Roosevelt (full-face).

1970. Air. Christmas. Paintings. Multicoloured.
1738 10 c. Type **265** 10 10
1739 10 c. "The Nativity" (detail, El Greco) 10 10
1740 10 c. "The Adoration of the Magi" (detail, Durer) . . . 10 10
1741 10 c. "Virgin and Child" (J. van Hemessen) 10 10
1742 10 c. "The Holy Shepherd" (Portuguese School, 16th cent.) 10 10
1743 15 c. Type **265** 10 10
1744 20 c. As No. 1739 . . . . . 10 10
1745 35 c. As No. 1740 . . . . . 15 10
1746 75 c. As No. 1741 . . . . . 20 15
1747 1 cor. As No. 1742 . . . . . 30 20

1971. Surch **RESELLO** and new value.
1748 30 c. on 90 c. black (No. 1227) (postage) . . . . 10·00 10·00
1749 10 c. on 1 cor. 5 red, black & red (No. 1368) (air) 10 10
1750 10 c. on 1 cor. 5 mult (No. 1407) 10 10
1751 10 c. on 1 cor. 5 mult (No. 1430) 10 10
1752 15 c. on 1 cor. 50 green and red (No. 1116) 10 10
1753 15 c. on 1 cor. 50 green (No. 1255) 10 10
1754 15 c. on 1 cor. 50 yellow and blue (No. 1369) 10 10
1755 15 c. on 1 cor. 50 black and violet (No. 1381) 10 10
1756 20 c. on 85 c. black and red (No. 1276) 15 10
1757 20 c. on 85 c. black, red and blue (No. 1339) 15 10
1758 25 c. on 90 c. black, green and ochre (No. 1440) 15 15
1759 30 c. on 1 cor. 10 black and purple (No. 1195) 15 15
1760 40 c. on 1 cor. 10 brown and black (No. 1157) 65 65
1761 40 c. on 1 cor. 50 mult (No. 1408) 65 65
1762 1 cor. on 1 cor. 10 black and blue (No. 1538) . . . . . 1·60 1·60

HAVE YOU READ THE NOTES AT THE BEGINNING OF THIS CATALOGUE?
These often provide the answers to the enquiries we receive.

266 Basic Mathematical Equation

1971. Scientific Formulae. "The Ten Mathematical Equations that changed the Face of the Earth". Multicoloured.
1763 10 c. Type **266** (postage) . . 10 10
1764 15 c. Newton's Law 10 10
1765 20 c. Einstein's Law 10 10
1766 1 cor. Tsiolkovsky's Law . . 25 25
1767 2 cor. Maxwell's Law . . . 90 75
1768 25 c. Napier's Law (air) . . . 10 10
1769 30 c. Pythagoras' Law . . . 10 10
1770 40 c. Boltzmann's Law . . . 15 10
1771 1 cor. Broglie's Law 30 20
1772 2 cor. Archimedes' Law . . 55 40

267 Peace Emblem

1971. "Is There a Formula for Peace?".
1773 **267** 10 c. blue and black . . 10 10
1774 15 c. blue, black & vio . 10 10
1775 20 c. blue, black & brn . 10 10
1776 40 c. blue, black & grn . 10 10
1777 50 c. blue, black & pur . 15 10
1778 80 c. blue, black & red . 15 15
1779 1 cor. blue, black & grn 30 20
1780 2 cor. blue, black & vio 55 35

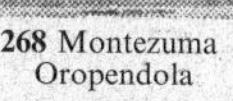

268 Montezuma Oropendola

269 "Moses with the Tablets of the Law" (Rembrandt)

1971. Air. Nicaraguan Birds. Multicoloured.
1781 10 c. Type **268** 50 15
1782 15 c. Turquoise-browed motmot 50 15
1783 20 c. White-throated magpie-jay 60 15
1784 25 c. Scissor-tailed flycatcher 60 15
1785 30 c. Spotted-breasted oriole (horiz) 80 15
1786 35 c. Rufous-naped wren . . 95 15
1787 40 c. Great kiskadee 95 15
1788 75 c. Red-legged honeycreeper (horiz) . . . . 1·75 35
1789 1 cor. Great-tailed grackle (horiz) . . . . 2·10 45
1790 2 cor. Belted kingfisher . . . 3·50 65

1971. "The Ten Commandments". Paintings. Multicoloured.
1791 10 c. Type **269** (postage) . . 10 10
1792 15 c. "Moses and the Burning Bush" (Botticelli) (1st Commandment) 10 10
1793 20 c. "Jepthah's Daughter" (Degas) (2nd Commandment) (horiz) 10 10
1794 30 c. "St. Vincent Ferrer preaching in Verona" (Morone) (3rd Commandment) (horiz) . 10 10
1795 35 c. "Noah's Drunkenness" (Michelangelo) (4th Commandment) (horiz) . 10 10
1796 40 c. "Cain and Abel" (Trevisani) (5th Commandment) (horiz) . 10 10
1797 50 c. "Joseph accused by Potiphar's Wife" (Rembrandt) (6th Commandment) 10 10
1798 60 c. "Isaac blessing Jacob" (Eeckhout) (7th Commandment) (horiz) . 15 10
1799 75 c. "Susannah and the Elders" (Rubens) (8th Commandment) (horiz) 25 20
1800 1 cor. "Bathsheba after her Bath" (Rembrandt) (9th Commandment) (air) . . 25 20
1801 2 cor. "Naboth's Vineyard" (Smetham) (10th Commandment) 40 35

270 U Thant and Pres. Somoza

1971. Air. 25th Anniv of U.N.O.
1802 **270** 10 c. brown and red . . . 10 10
1803 15 c. green and emerald . 10 10
1804 20 c. blue & light blue . . 10 10
1805 25 c. red and purple . . . 10 10
1806 30 c. brown & orange . . 10 10
1807 40 c. green and grey . . . 15 10
1808 1 cor. green & sage . . . 25 20
1809 2 cor. brown & light brown 30 35

1972. Olympic Games, Munich. Nos. 1709, 1711, 1713 and 1716 surch **OLIMPIADAS MUNICH 1972**, emblem and value or optd only (5 cor.).
1810 40 c. on 2 cor. multicoloured (postage) 10 10
1811 50 c. on 3 cor. multicoloured . 15 10
1812 20 c. on 80 c. mult (air) . . . 10 10
1813 60 c. on 4 cor. multicoloured . 15 10
1814 5 cor. multicoloured 65 65

272 Figurine and Apoyo Site on Map

1972. Air. Pre-Columbian Art. A. H. Heller's Pottery Discoveries. Multicoloured.
1815 10 c. Type **272** 10 10
1816 15 c. Cana Castilla 10 10
1817 20 c. Catarina 10 10
1818 25 c. Santa Helena 10 10
1819 30 c. Mombacho 10 10
1820 35 c. Tisma 10 10
1821 40 c. El Menco 10 10
1822 50 c. Los Placeres 15 10
1823 60 c. Masaya 15 15
1824 80 c. Granada 20 15
1825 1 cor. Las Mercedes 30 20
1826 2 cor. Nindiri 55 35

273 "Lord Peter Wimsey" (Dorothy Sayers)

1972. Air. 50th Anniv of International Criminal Police Organization (INTERPOL). Famous Fictional Detectives. Multicoloured.
1827 5 c. Type **273** 10 10
1828 10 c. "Philip Marlowe" (Raymond Chandler) . . . 10 10
1829 15 c. "Sam Spade" (D. Hammett) . . . . . . 6·00 30
1830 20 c. "Perry Mason" (Erle Stanley Gardner) . . 10 10
1831 25 c. "Nero Wolfe" (Rex Stout) 10 10
1832 35 c. "C. Auguste Dupin" (Edgar Allan Poe) 10 10
1833 40 c. "Ellery Queen" (F. Dannay and M. Lee) . . 10 10
1834 50 c. "Father Brown" (G. K. Chesterton) 10 10
1835 60 c. "Charlie Chan" (Earl D. Biggers) 15 10
1836 80 c. "Inspector Maigret" (Georges Simenon) 25 15
1837 1 cor. "Hercule Poirot" (Agatha Christie) 25 20
1838 2 cor. "Sherlock Holmes" (A. Conan Doyle) 70 70

274 "The Shepherdess and her Brothers"

1972. Air. Christmas. Scenes from Legend of the Christmas Rose. Multicoloured.
1839 10 c. Type **274** 10 10
1840 15 c. Adoration of the Wise Men 10 10
1841 20 c. Shepherdess crying . . . 10 10
1842 35 c. Angel appears to Shepherdess 10 10
1843 40 c. Christmas Rose 10 10
1844 60 c. Shepherdess thanks angel for roses 15 10
1845 80 c. Shepherdess takes roses to Holy Child 15 15
1846 1 cor. Holy Child receiving roses 20 15
1847 2 cor. Nativity Scene 45 35

275 Sir Walter Raleigh and Elizabethan Galleon

1973. Air. Causes of the American Revolution. Multicoloured.
1849 10 c. Type **275** 30 10
1850 15 c. Signing "Mayflower Compact" 10 10
1851 20 c. Acquittal of Peter Zenger (vert) 10 10
1852 25 c. Acclaiming American resistance (vert) 10 10
1853 30 c. Revenue Stamp (vert) . 10 10
1854 35 c. "Serpent" slogan–"Join or die" 10 10
1855 40 c. Boston Massacre (vert) 10 10
1856 50 c. Boston Tea-party . . . 10 10
1857 60 c. Patrick Henry on trial (vert) 15 10
1858 75 c. Battle of Bunker Hill . 20 10
1859 80 c. Declaration of Independence 20 15
1860 1 cor. Liberty Bell 30 20
1861 2 cor. US seal (vert) 90 60

1973. Nos. 1450/54, 1456 and 1458/9 optd **CORREO**.
1862 **219** 5 c. multicoloured . . . 25 10
1863 – 5 c. multicoloured . . . 25 10
1864 – 5 c. multicoloured . . . 25 10
1865 – 5 c. multicoloured . . . 25 10
1866 – 5 c. multicoloured . . . 25 10
1867 – 5 c. multicoloured . . . 25 10
1868 – 5 c. multicoloured . . . 25 10
1869 – 5 c. multicoloured . . . 25 10

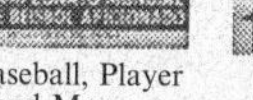

277 Baseball, Player and Map

278 Givenchy, Paris

1973. Air. 20th International Baseball Championships, Managua (1972).
1870 **277** 15 c. multicoloured . . . 10 10
1871 20 c. multicoloured . . . 10 10
1872 40 c. multicoloured . . . 10 10
1873 10 cor. multicoloured . . 1·50 90

1973. World-famous Couturiers. Mannequins. Multicoloured.
1875 1 cor. Type **278** (postage) . . 25 20
1876 2 cor. Hartnell, London . . 40 40
1877 5 cor. Balmain, Paris . . . . 1·00 90
1878 10 c. Lourdes, Nicaragua (air) 10 10
1879 15 c. Halston, New York . . 10 10
1880 20 c. Pino Lancetti, Rome . . 10 10
1881 35 c. Madame Gres, Paris . . 10 10
1882 40 c. Irene Galitzine, Rome . 10 10
1883 80 c. Pedro Rodriguez, Barcelona 15 15

279 Diet Chart

1973. Air. Child Welfare. Multicoloured.
1885 5 c. + 5 c. Type **279** 10 10
1886 10 c. + 5 c. Senora Samoza with baby, and Children's Hospital 10 10
1887 15 c. + 5 c. "Childbirth" . . 10 10
1888 20 c. + 5 c. "Immunisation" . 10 10
1889 30 c. + 5 c. Water purification 10 10
1890 35 c. + 5 c. As No. 1886 . . 10 10
1891 50 c. + 10 c. Alexander Fleming and "Antibiotics" 30 10
1892 60 c. + 15 c. Malaria control 15 10
1893 70 c. + 10 c. Laboratory analysis 15 15
1894 80 c. + 20 c. Gastro-enteritis 20 15
1895 1 cor. + 50 c. As No. 1886 . 30 25
1896 2 cor. Pediatric surgery . . . 45 35

280 Virginia and Father

1973. Christmas. "Does Santa Claus exist?" (Virginia O'Hanlon's letter to American "Sun" newspaper). Multicoloured.

1897 2 c. Type **280** (postage) 10 10
1898 3 c. Text of letter 10 10
1899 4 c. Reading the reply 10 10
1900 5 c. Type **280** 10 10
1901 15 c. As 3 c. 10 10
1902 20 c. As 4 c. 10 10

1903 1 cor. Type **280** (air) 20 15
1904 2 cor. As 3 c. 35 30
1905 4 cor. As 4 c. 75 65

281 Churchill making Speech, 1936

1974. Birth Cent of Sir Winston Churchill.

1907 **281** 2 c. multicoloured (postage) 10 10
1908 – 3 c. black, blue & brown 10 10
1909 – 4 c. multicoloured 10 10
1910 – 5 c. multicoloured 10 10
1911 – 10 c. brown, green & bl 30 10

1912 – 5 cor. multicoloured (air) 90 80
1913 – 6 cor. black, brown & bl 1·00 90

DESIGNS: 3 c. "The Four Churchills" (wartime cartoon); 4 c. Candle, cigar and "Action" stickers; 5 c. Churchill, Roosevelt and Stalin at Yalta; 10 c. Churchill landing in Normandy, 1944; 5 cor. Churchill giving "V" sign; 6 cor. "Bulldog Churchill" (cartoon).

282 Presentation of World Cup to Uruguay, 1930

1974. World Cup Football Championships. Mult.

1915 1 c. Type **282** (postage) 10 10
1916 2 c. Victorious Italian team, 1934 10 10
1917 3 c. Presentation of World Cup to Italy, 1938 10 10
1918 4 c. Uruguay's winning goal, 1950 10 10
1919 5 c. Victorious West Germany, 1954 10 10
1920 10 c. Rejoicing Brazilian players, 1958 10 10
1921 15 c. Brazilian player holding World Cup, 1962 10 10
1922 20 c. Queen Elizabeth II presenting Cup to Bobby Moore, 1966 10 10
1923 25 c. Victorious Brazilian players, 1970 10 10
1924 10 cor. Football and flags of participating countries, 1974 (air) 1·75 1·75

283 "Malachra sp."

284 Nicaraguan 7½ c. Stamp of 1937

1974. Wild Flowers and Cacti. Multicoloured.

1926 2 c. Type **283** (postage) 10 10
1927 3 c. "Paguira insignis" 10 10
1928 4 c. "Convolvulus sp." 10 10
1929 5 c. "Pereschia autumnalis" 10 10
1930 10 c. "Ipomea tuberosa" 10 10
1931 15 c. "Hibiscus elatus" 10 10
1932 20 c. "Plumeria acutifolia" 10 10

1933 1 cor. "Centrosema sp." (air) 20 20
1934 3 cor. "Hylocereus undatus" 60 55

1974. Centenary of U.P.U.

1935 **284** 2 c. red, grn & blk (postage) 10 15
1936 – 3 c. blue, green & blk 10 10
1937 – 4 c. multicoloured 10 10
1938 – 5 c. brown, mve & blk 10 10
1939 – 10 c. red, brown & blk 10 10
1940 – 20 c. green, blue & blk 10 10

1941 – 40 c. multicoloured (air) 10 10
1942 – 3 cor. green, blk & pink 50 40
1943 – 5 cor. blue, black & lilac 1·00 80

DESIGNS—VERT: 3 c. 5 c. stamp of 1937; 5 c. 2 c. stamp of 1937; 10 c. 1 c. stamp of 1937; 20 c. ½ c. stamp of 1937; 40 c. 10 c. stamp of 1961; 5 cor. 4 cor. U.P.U. stamp of 1950. HORIZ: 4 c. 10 c. air stamp of 1934; 3 cor. 85 c. U.P.U. air stamp of 1950.

1974. Air. West Germany's Victory in World Cup Football Championships. No. 1924 optd TRIUMFADOR ALEMANIA OCCIDENTAL.

1945 10 cor. multicoloured 1·75 1·60

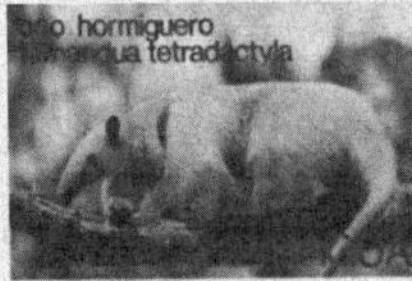

286 Tamandua

1974. Nicaraguan Fauna. Multicoloured.

1947 1 c. Type **286** (postage) 10 10
1948 2 c. Puma 10 10
1949 3 c. Common raccoon 10 10
1950 4 c. Ocelot 10 10
1951 5 c. Kinkajou 10 10
1952 10 c. Coypu 10 10
1953 15 c. Collared peccary 15 10
1954 20 c. Baird's tapir 15 10

1955 3 cor. Red brocket (air) 1·50 1·40
1956 5 cor. Jaguar 2·40 2·00

287 "Prophet Zacharias"

288 Giovanni Martinelli ("Othello")

1975. Christmas. 500th Birth Anniv of Michelangelo. Multicoloured.

1957 1 c. Type **287** (postage) 10 10
1958 2 c. "Christ amongst the Jews" 10 10
1959 3 c. "The Creation of Man" (horiz) 10 10
1960 4 c. Interior of Sistine Chapel, Rome 10 10
1961 5 c. "Moses" 10 10
1962 10 c. "Mouscron Madonna" 10 10
1963 15 c. "David" 10 10
1964 20 c. "Doni Madonna" 10 10

1965 40 c. "Madonna of the Steps" (air) 10 10
1966 80 c. "Pitti Madonna" 15 15
1967 2 cor. "Christ and Virgin Mary" 35 30
1968 5 cor. "Michelangelo" (self-portrait) 75 75

1975. Great Opera Singers. Multicoloured.

1970 1 c. Type **288** (postage) 10 10
1971 2 c. Tito Gobbi ("Simone Boccaegra") 10 10
1972 3 c. Lotte Lehmann ("Der Rosenkavalier") 10 10
1973 4 c. Lauritz Melchior ("Parsifal") 10 10
1974 5 c. Nellie Melba ("La Traviata") 10 10
1975 15 c. Jussi Bjoerling ("La Boheme") 10 10
1976 20 c. Birgit Nilsson ("Turandot") 10 10

1977 25 c. Rosa Ponselle ("Norma") (air) 10 10
1978 35 c. Guiseppe de Luca ("Rigoletto") 10 10
1979 40 c. Joan Sutherland ("La Figlia del Reggimiento") 10 10
1980 50 c. Enzio Pinza ("Don Giovanni") 10 10
1981 60 c. Kirsten Flagstad ("Tristan and Isolde") 15 10
1982 80 c. Maria Callas ("Tosca") 15 15
1983 2 cor. Fyodor Chaliapin ("Boris Godunov") 60 35
1984 5 cor. Enrico Caruso ("La Juive") 1·10 60

289 The First Station

290 "The Spirit of 76"

1975. Easter. The 14 Stations of the Cross.

1986 **289** 1 c. multicoloured (postage) 10 10
1987 – 2 c. multicoloured 10 10
1988 – 3 c. multicoloured 10 10
1989 – 4 c. multicoloured 10 10
1990 – 5 c. multicoloured 10 10
1991 – 15 c. multicoloured 10 10
1992 – 20 c. multicoloured 10 10
1993 – 25 c. multicoloured 10 10
1994 – 35 c. multicoloured 10 10

1995 – 40 c. multicoloured (air) 10 10
1996 – 50 c. multicoloured 10 10
1997 – 80 c. multicoloured 15 15
1998 – 1 cor. multicoloured 20 15
1999 – 5 cor. multicoloured 80 65

DESIGNS: 2 c. to 5 cor. Different Stations of the Cross.

1975. Bicentenary of American Independence (1st series). Multicoloured.

2000 1 c. Type **290** (postage) 10 10
2001 2 c. Pitt addressing Parliament 10 10
2002 3 c. Paul Revere's Ride (horiz) 10 10
2003 4 c. Demolishing statue of George III (horiz) 10 10
2004 5 c. Boston Massacre 10 10
2005 10 c. Tax stamp and George III 3d. coin (horiz) 10 10
2006 15 c. Boston Tea Party (horiz) 10 10
2007 20 c. Thomas Jefferson 10 10
2008 25 c. Benjamin Franklin 10 10
2009 30 c. Signing of Declaration of Independence (horiz) 10 10
2010 35 c. Surrender of Cornwallis at Yorktown (horiz) 10 10

2011 40 c. Washington's Farewell (horiz) (air) 10 10
2012 50 c. Washington addressing Congress (horiz) 10 10
2013 2 cor. Washington arriving for Presidential Inauguration (horiz) 70 30
2014 5 cor. Statue of Liberty & flags 75 45

See also Nos. 2056/71.

291 Saluting the Flag

1975. "Nordjamb 75" World Scout Jamboree, Norway. Multicoloured.

2016 1 c. Type **291** (postage) 10 10
2017 2 c. Scout canoe 10 10
2018 3 c. Scouts shaking hands 10 10
2019 4 c. Scout preparing meal 10 10
2020 5 c. Entrance to Nicaraguan camp 10 10
2021 20 c. Scouts meeting 10 10

2022 35 c. Aerial view of camp (air) 10 10
2023 40 c. Scouts making music 10 10
2024 1 cor. Camp-fire 20 15
2025 10 cor. Lord Baden-Powell 1·25 1·10

292 President Somoza

293 "Chess Players" (L. Carracci)

1975. President Somoza's New Term of Office, 1974–1981.

2027 **292** 20 c. multicoloured (postage) 10 10
2028 40 c. multicoloured 10 10

2029 1 cor. multicoloured (air) 20 20
2030 10 cor. multicoloured 1·25 1·10
2031 20 cor. multicoloured 3·25 2·75

1975. Chess. Multicoloured.

2032 1 c. Type **293** (postage) 10 10
2033 2 c. "Arabs playing Chess" (Delacroix) 10 10
2034 3 c. "Cardinals playing Chess" (V. Marais-Milton) 10 10
2035 4 c. "Duke Albrecht V of Bavaria and Anna of Austria at Chess" (H. Muelich) (vert) 10 10
2036 5 c. "Chess game" (14th-century Persian manuscript) 10 10
2037 10 c. "Origins of Chess" (India, 1602) 10 10
2038 15 c. "Napoleon playing Chess in Schonbrunn Palace in 1809" (A. Uniechowski) (vert) 10 10
2039 20 c. "The Chess Game in the House of Count Ingenheim" (J.E. Hummel) 10 10

2040 40 c. "The Chess-players" (T. Eakins) (air) 10 10
2041 2 cor. Fischer v Spassky match, Reykjavik, 1972 55 35
2042 5 cor. "William Shakespeare and Ben Jonson playing Chess" (K. van Mander) 60 50

HAVE YOU READ THE NOTES AT THE BEGINNING OF THIS CATALOGUE?
These often provide the answers to the enquiries we receive.

294 Choir of King's College Cambridge

1975. Christmas. Famous Choirs. Multicoloured.

2044 1 c. Type **294** (postage) 10 10
2045 2 c. Abbey Choir, Einsiedeln 10 10
2046 3 c. Regensburg Cathedral choir 10 10
2047 4 c. Vienna Boys' choir 10 10
2048 5 c. Sistine Chapel choir 10 10
2049 15 c. Westminster Cathedral choir 10 10
2050 20 c. Mormon Tabernacle choir 10 10

2051 50 c. School choir, Montserrat (air) 10 10
2052 1 cor. St. Florian children's choir 20 15
2053 2 cor. "Little Singers of the Wooden Cross" (vert) 45 35
2054 5 cor. Pope with choristers of Pueri Cantores 60 50

295 "The Smoke Signal" (F. Remington)

1976. Bicent of American Revolution (2nd series). "200 Years of Progress". Multicoloured.

2056 1 c. Type **295** (postage) 10 10
2057 1 c. Houston Space Centre 10 10
2058 2 c. Lighting candelabra, 1976 10 10
2059 2 c. Edison's lamp and houses 10 10
2060 3 c. "Agriculture 1776" 10 10
2061 3 c. "Agriculture 1976" 10 10
2062 4 c. Harvard College, 1776 10 10
2063 4 c. Harvard University, 1976 10 10
2064 5 c. Horse and carriage 15 10
2065 5 c. Boeing 747-100 airliner 15 10

2066 80 c. Philadelphia, 1776 (air) 25 15
2067 80 c. Washington, 1976 25 15
2068 2 cor. 75 "Bonhomme Richard" (John Paul Jones's flagship) and H.M.S. "Seraphis", Battle of Flamborough Head 1·50 70
2069 2 cor. 75 U.S.S. "Glenard Phipscomp" (nuclear submarine) 1·50 70
2070 4 cor. Wagon train 90 70
2071 4 cor. "Amtrak" express train 1·90 1·25

296 Italy, 1968

1976. Olympic Games, Victors in Rowing and Sculling. Multicoloured.

2073 1 c. Denmark 1964 (postage) 10 10
2074 2 c. East Germany 1972 10 10
2075 3 c. Type **296** 10 10
2076 4 c. Great Britain 1936 10 10
2077 5 c. France 1952 (vert) 10 10
2078 35 c. U.S.A. 1920 (vert) 10 10

2079 55 c. Russia 1956 (vert) (air) 20 10
2080 70 c. New Zealand 1972 (vert) 20 15
2081 90 c. New Zealand 1968 25 20
2082 20 cor. U.S.A. 1956 2·75 2·50

1976. Air. Olympic Games, Montreal. East German Victory in Rowing Events. No. 2082 optd **REPUBLICA DEMOCRATICA ALEMANA VENCEDOR EN 1976.**

2084 20 cor. multicoloured 2·75 2·50

299 Mauritius 1847 2d. "Post Office"

1976. Rare and Famous Stamps. Multicoloured.

2087 1 c. Type **299** (postage) 10 10
2088 2 c. Western Australia 1854 "Inverted Mute Swan" 30 10
2089 3 c. Mauritius 1847 1d. "Post Office" 10 10
2090 4 c. Jamaica 1920 1s. Inverted Frame 10 10
2091 5 c. U.S. 1918 24 c. Inverted Aircraft 10 10
2092 10 c. Swiss 1845 Basel "Dove" 10 10
2093 25 c. Canada 1959 Seaway Inverted Centre 10 10

2094 40 c. Hawaiian 1851 2 c. "Missionary" (air) 10 10
2095 1 cor. G.B. 1840 "Penny Black" 20 20

2096 2 cor. British Guiana 1850 1 c. Black on Magenta 40 35
2097 5 cor. Honduras 1925 Airmail 25 c. on 10 c. 70 50
2098 10 cor. Newfoundland 1919 "Hawker" Airmail stamp . 1·25 1·10

300 Olga Nunez de Saballos (Member of Parliament)

1977. Air. International Women's Year. Mult.
2100 35 c. Type **300** 10 10
2101 1 cor. Josefa Toledo de Aguerri (educator) 20 20
2102 10 cor. Hope Portocarreo de Samoza (President's wife) . 1·25 1·00

301 "Graf Zeppelin" in Hangar

1977. 75th Anniv of First Zeppelin Flight. Multicoloured.
2104 1 c. Type **301** (postage) . . . 10 10
2105 2 c. "Graf Zeppelin" in flight 10 10
2106 3 c. Giffard's steam-powered dirigible airship, 1852 . . . 15 10
2107 4 c. "Graf Zeppelin" in mooring hangar 15 10
2108 5 c. "Graf Zeppelin" on ground 15 10
2109 35 c. Astra airship "Ville de Paris" (air) 35 15
2110 70 c. "Schwaben" 40 20
2111 3 cor. "Graf Zeppelin" over Lake Constance . . . . . 1·00 65
2112 10 cor. LZ-2 on Lake Constance . . . . 3·75 2·25

302 Lindbergh and Map

1977. 50th Anniv of Lindbergh's Transatlantic Flight. Multicoloured.
2114 1 c. Type **302** (postage) . . . 10 10
2115 2 c. Map and "Spirit of St. Louis" 10 10
2116 3 c. Charles Lindbergh (vert) 10 10
2117 4 c. "Spirit of St. Louis" crossing Atlantic 10 10
2118 5 c. Charles Lindbergh standing by "Spirit of St. Louis" . . 10 10
2119 20 c. Lindbergh, route and "Spirit of St. Louis" . . . 20 15
2120 55 c. Lindbergh landing in Nicaragua (1928) (air) . . 20 15
2121 80 c. "Spirit of St. Louis" and route map 35 15
2122 2 cor. "Spirit of St. Louis" flying along Nicaraguan coast 65 35
2123 10 cor. Passing Momotombo (Nicaragua) . . . . 1·90 1·25

303 Christmas Festival

1977. Christmas. Scenes from Tchaikovsky's "Nutcracker" Suite. Multicoloured.
2125 1 c. Type **303** 10 10
2126 2 c. Doll's dance 10 10
2127 3 c. Clara and snowflakes . . 10 10
2128 4 c. Snow fairy and Prince . . 10 10
2129 5 c. Snow fairies 10 10
2130 15 c. Sugar fairy and prince . . 10 10
2131 40 c. Waltz of the Flowers . . 10 10
2132 90 c. Chinese dance 20 15
2133 1 cor. Senora Bonbonierre . . 20 20
2134 10 cor. Arabian dance . . . 1·40 1·25

304 "Mr. and Mrs. Andrews". (Gainsborough)

1978. Paintings. Multicoloured.
2136 1 c. Type **304** (postage) . . . 10 10
2137 2 c. "Giovanna Bacelli" (Gainsborough) 10 10
2138 3 c. "Blue Boy" (Gainsborough) 10 10
2139 4 c. "Francis I" (Titian) . . 10 10
2140 5 c. "Charles V at Battle of Muhlberg" (Titian) . . . 10 10
2141 25 c. "Sacred Love" (Titian) 10 10
2142 5 cor. "Hippopotamus and Crocodile Hunt" (Rubens) (air) 60 50
2143 10 cor. "Duke of Lerma on Horseback" (Rubens) . . 1·75 1·40

305 Gothic Portal with Rose Window, Small Basilica of St. Francis

1978. 750th Anniv of Canonisation of St. Francis of Assisi. Multicoloured.
2145 1 c. Type **305** (postage) . . . 10 10
2146 2 c. St. Francis preaching to birds 10 10
2147 3 c. Painting of St. Francis . 10 10
2148 4 c. Franciscan genealogical tree 10 10
2149 5 c. Portiuncola 10 10
2150 15 c. Autographed blessing . 10 10
2151 25 c. Windows of Large Basilica 10 10
2152 80 c. St. Francis and wolf (air) 15 10
2153 10 cor. St. Francis . . . . . 1·60 1·50

306 Passenger and Freight Locomotive

1978. Centenary of Railway. Multicoloured.
2155 1 c. Type **306** (postage) . . . 10 10
2156 2 c. Light-weight cargo locomotive 10 10
2157 3 c. American locomotive . 10 10
2158 4 c. Baldwin heavy freight locomotive 10 10
2159 5 c. Baldwin light freight and passenger locomotive . . . 10 10
2160 15 c. Presidential Pullman coach 10 10
2161 35 c. Light-weight American locomotive (air) 20 10
2162 4 cor. Baldwin locomotive . 1·75 70
2163 10 cor. Juniata locomotive . 4·75 1·75

307 Mongol Warriors ("Michael Strogoff")

1978. 150th Birth Anniv of Jules Verne. Multicoloured.
2165 1 c. Type **307** (postage) . . . 10 10
2166 2 c. Sea scene ("The Mysterious Island") 10 10
2167 3 c. Sea monsters ("Journey to the Centre of the Earth") . 10 10
2168 4 c. Balloon and African elephant ("Five Weeks in a Balloon") 20 10
2169 90 c. Submarine ("Twenty Thousand Leagues Under the Sea") (air) 40 20
2170 10 cor. Balloon, Indian, steam locomotive and elephant ("Around the World in Eighty Days") . . . . . . 5·50 3·00

308 Icarus

1978. 75th Anniv of History of Aviation. First Powered Flight. Multicoloured.
2172 1 c. Type **308** (postage) . . . 10 10
2173 2 c. Montgolfier balloon (vert) 10 10
2174 3 c. Wright Flyer I 10 10
2175 4 c. Orville Wright in Wright Type A (vert) 10 10
2176 55 c. Vought-Sikorsky VS-300 helicopter prototype (air) . 30 10
2177 10 cor. Space shuttle . . . . 2·10 1·00

309 Ernst Ocwirk and Alfredo di Stefano

310 "St. Peter" (Goya)

1978. World Cup Football Championship, Argentina. Multicoloured.
2179 20 c. Type **309** (postage) . . . 10 10
2180 25 c. Ralk Edstrom and Oswaldo Piazza 10 10
2181 50 c. Franz Beckenbauer and Dennis Law (air) 10 10
2182 5 cor. Dino Zoff and Pele . . 65 50

1978. Christmas. Multicoloured.
2184 10 c. Type **310** (postage) . . . 10 10
2185 15 c. "St. Gregory" (Goya) . 10 10
2186 3 cor. "The Apostles John and Peter" (Durer) (air) 40 30
2187 10 cor. "The Apostles Paul and Mark" (Durer) . . . . . . 1·40 1·00

311 San Cristobal

1978. Volcanoes and Lakes. Multicoloured.
2189 5 c. Type **311** (postage) . . . 10 10
2190 5 c. Lake de Cosiguina . . . 10 10
2191 20 c. Telica 10 10
2192 20 c. Lake Jiloa 10 10
2193 35 c. Cerro Negro (air) . . . 10 10
2194 35 c. Lake Masaya 10 10
2195 90 c. Momotombo 20 15
2196 90 c. Lake Asososca 20 15
2197 1 cor. Mombacho 20 15
2198 1 cor. Lake Apoyo 20 15
2199 10 cor. Concepcion . . . . . 1·60 80
2200 10 cor. Lake Tiscapa . . . . 1·60 80

312 General O'Higgins

1979. Air. Birth Bicentenary of Bernardo O'Higgins (liberation hero).
2201 **312** 20 cor. multicoloured . . 3·75 1·90

313 Ginger Plant and Broad-tailed Hummingbird

1979. Air. Flowers. Multicoloured.
2202 50 c. Type **313** . . . . 1·50 20
2203 55 c. Orchids 10 10
2204 70 c. Poinsettia 15 10
2205 80 c. "Poro poro" 15 10
2206 2 cor. "Morpho cypris" (butterfly) and Guayacan flowers 50 30
2207 4 cor. Iris 45 30

314 Children with football

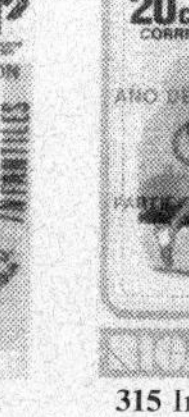

315 Indian Postal Runner

316 Einstein and Albert Schweitzer

317 Loggerhead Turtle

1980. Year of Liberation (1979) and Nicaragua's Participation in Olympic Games. Unissued stamps overprinted. (a) International Year of the Child. Multicoloured.
2208 20 c. Children on roundabout (postage) 15 15
2209 90 c. Type **314** (air) 65 65
2210 2 cor. Children with stamps albums . . . . 1·50 1·50
2211 2 cor. 20 Children playing with model train and aircraft . 3·00 2·00
2212 10 cor. Baseball . . . . . . 7·50 7·50

(b) Death Centenary of Sir Rowland Hill. Mult.
2214 20 c. Type **315** (postage) . . 20 20
2215 35 c. Pony express 40 40
2216 1 cor. Pre-stamp letter (horiz) 1·10 1·10
2217 1 cor. 80 Sir Rowland Hill examining sheet of Penny Black stamps (air) . . . . 1·90 1·90
2218 2 cor. 20 Penny Blacks (horiz) 2·40 2·40
2219 5 cor. Nicaraguan Zeppelin flight cover (horiz) . . . . 5·50 5·50

(c) Birth Centenary of Albert Einstein (physicist). Multicoloured.
2221 5 c. Type **316** (postage) . . . 15 15
2222 10 c. Einstein and equation . 25 25
2223 15 c. Einstein and 1939 World Fair pavilion 40 40
2224 20 c. Einstein and Robert Oppenheimer 50 50
2225 25 c. Einstein in Jerusalem . 65 65
2226 1 cor. Einstein and Nobel Prize medal (air) . . . . 2·50 2·50
2227 2 cor. 75 Einstein and space exploration . . . . 7·00 7·00
2228 10 cor. Einstein and Mahatma Gandhi . . . . 15·00 15·00

(d) Endangered Turtles. Multicoloured.
2230 90 c. Type **317** 70 70
2231 2 cor. Leatherback turtle . . 1·50 1·50
2232 2 cor. 30 Ridley turtle . . . 1·75 1·75
2233 10 cor. Hawksbilled turtle . . 7·50 7·50

318 Rigoberto Lopez Perez and Crowds pulling down Statue

1980. 1st Anniv of the Revolution. Multicoloured.
2235 40 c. Type **318** 10 10
2236 75 c. Street barricade 10 10
2237 1 cor. "Learn to Read" emblem (vert) 15 10
2238 1 cor. 25 German Pomares Ordonez and jungle fighters 20 15
2239 1 cor. 85 Victory celebrations (vert) 25 15
2240 2 cor. 50 Carlos Fonesca and camp-fire 35 35
2241 5 cor. Gen. Augusto Sandino and flag (vert) 70 55

1980. Literacy Year. Unissued stamps optd **1980 ANO DE LA ALFABETIZACION**. (a) International Year of the Child. As Nos. 2208/12.
2243 – 20 c. Children on roundabout (postage) . 1·00 1·00
2244 **314** 90 c. Children with football (air) . . . . 1·00 1·00
2245 – 2 cor. Children with stamp albums . . . . 1·00 1·00
2246 – 2 cor. 20 Children playing with train and airplane 2·00 2·00
2247 – 10 cor. Baseball . . . . 4·50 4·50

(b) Death Centenary of Sir Rowland Hill. Nos. 2214/16.
2249 **315** 20 c. Indian postal runner 70 70
2250 – 35 c. Pony express . . . 70 70
2251 – 1 cor. Pre-stamp letter (horiz) 70 70

(c) Birth Centenary of Albert Einstein (physicist). As Nos. 2221/8.
2253 5 c. Optd **"YURI GAGARIN/ 12/IV/1961/LER HOMBRE EN EL ESPACIO"** (postage) 1·10 1·10
2254 10 c. Optd **"LURABA 1981"** and space shuttle . . . . . 1·10 1·10

2255 15 c. Optd **"SPACE SHUTTLE"** and craft . . 1·10 1·10
2256 20 c. Optd **ANO DE LA ALFABETIZACION** . . . 1·10 1·10
2257 25 c. Optd **"16/VII/1969/LER HOMBRE A LA LUNA" and "APOLLO XI"** . . . . . 1·10 1·10
2258 1 cor. Optd As No. 2256 (air) 1·10 1·10
2259 2 cor. 75 Optd As No. 2256 . 1·10 1·10
2260 10 cor. 75 Optd **"LUNO-JOD 1"** and vehicle . . . . . . 1·10 1·10

(d) Air. Endangered Species. Turtles. As Nos. 2230/3. Multicoloured.
2262 **317** 90 c. Loggerhead turtle . 1·00 1·00
2263 – 2 cor. Leatherback turtle 1·00 1·00
2264 – 2 cor. 20 Ridley turtle . . 1·00 1·00
2265 – 10 cor. Hawksbill turtle . . 1·00 1·00

321 Footballer and El Molinon Stadium

1981. World Cup Football Championships, Spain. (1st issue). Venues. Multicoloured.
2268 5 c. Type **321** 10 10
2269 20 c. Sanchez Pizjuan, Seville 10 10
2270 25 c. San Mames, Bilbao . . 10 10
2271 30 c. Vincent Calderon, Madrid 10 10
2272 50 c. R.C.D. Espanol, Barcelona 10 10
2273 4 cor. New Stadium, Valladolid 55 35
2274 5 cor. Balaidos, Vigo 55 35
2275 10 cor. Santiago Bernabeu, Madrid . . . . 1·10 65
See also Nos. 2325/31.

322 Adult Education

1981. 2nd Anniv of Revolution. Multicoloured.
2277 50 c. Type **322** (postage) . . 10 10
2278 2 cor. 10 Workers marching (air) 30 15
2279 3 cor. Roadbuilding and container ship 65 30
2280 6 cor. Medical services . . . 50 25

323 Allegory of Revolution

1981. 20th Anniv of Sandinista National Liberation Front. Multicoloured.
2281 50 c. Type **323** (postage) . . 10 10
2282 4 cor. Sandinista guerrilla (air) 25 10

324 Postman

1981. 12th Postal Union of the Americas and Spain Congress, Managua. Multicoloured.
2283 50 c. Type **324** (postage) . . 10 10
2284 2 cor. 10 Pony Express (air) . 30 15
2285 3 cor. Postal Headquarters Managua 45 25
2286 6 cor. Government building, globe and flags of member countries 50 25

326 "Nymphaea capensis"

1981. Water Lilies. Multicoloured.
2288 50 c. Type **326** (postage) . . 10 10
2289 1 cor. "Nymphaea daubenyana" 15 10
2290 1 cor. 20 "Nymphaea Marliacea Chromat" 20 10
2291 1 cor. 80 "Nymphaea Dir. Geo. T. Moore" 25 15
2292 2 cor. "Nymphaea lotus" . . 30 15
2293 2 cor. 50 "Nymphaea B.G. Berry" 35 20
2294 10 cor. "Nymphaea Gladstoniana" (air) . . . 60 40

328 "Cheirodon axelrodi"

1981. Tropical Fishes. Multicoloured.
2296 50 c. Type **328** (postage) . . 10 10
2297 1 cor. "Poecilia reticulata" . 15 10
2298 1 cor. 85 "Anostomus anostomus" 25 15
2299 2 cor. 10 "Corydoras arculatus" 30 15
2300 2 cor. 50 "Cynolebias nigripinnis" 35 20
2301 3 cor. 50 "Petrolebias longipinnis" (air) 50 30
2302 4 cor. "Xiphophorus helleri" 55 35

330 Lineated Woodpecker

331 Satellite in Orbit

1981. Birds. Multicoloured.
2304 50 c. Type **330** (postage) . . 40 15
2305 1 cor. 20 Keel-billed toucan (horiz) 80 25
2306 1 cor. 80 Finsch's conure (horiz) 95 35
2307 2 cor. Scarlet macaw . . . . 1·25 40
2308 3 cor. Slaty-tailed trogon (air) 1·75 50
2309 4 cor. Violet sabrewing (horiz) 2·10 60
2310 6 cor. Blue-crowned motmot 3·75 1·00

1981. Satellite Communications. Multicoloured.
2311 50 c. Type **331** (postage) . . 10 10
2312 1 cor. "Intelstat IVA" . . . 15 10
2313 1 cor. 50 "Intelstat V" moving into orbit 20 15
2314 2 cor. Rocket releasing "Intelstat V" 30 20
2315 3 cor. Satellite and Space Shuttle (air) 45 25
2316 4 cor. "Intelstat V" and world maps 55 30
2317 5 cor. Tracking stations . . 70 45

332 Locomotive "El 93" at Lago Granada

1981. Locomotives. Multicoloured.
2318 50 c. Type **332** (postage) . . 15 10
2319 1 cor. Vulcan Iron Works 0-6-0 locomotive, 1946 . . . . 30 10
2320 1 cor. 20 Philadelphia Iron Works 0-6-0 locomotive, 1911 35 10
2321 1 cor. 80 Steam hoist, 1909 . 50 10
2322 2 cor. "U-10B", 1956 . . . 55 10
2323 2 cor. 50 German railbus, 1954 65 15
2324 6 cor. Japanese railbus, 1967 (air) . . . . 1·75 35

333 Heading Ball

1982. World Cup Football Championship, Spain (2nd issue). Multicoloured.
2325 5 c. Type **333** (postage) . . . 10 10
2326 20 c. Running with ball . . . 10 10
2327 25 c. Running with ball (different) 10 10
2328 2 cor. 50 Saving goal 35 20
2329 3 cor. 50 Goalkeeper diving for ball (horiz) 50 30
2330 4 cor. Kicking ball (air) . . . 55 35
2331 10 cor. Tackle (horiz) 60 40

334 Cocker Spaniel

1982. Pedigree Dogs. Multicoloured.
2333 5 c. Type **334** (postage) . . . 10 10
2334 20 c. Alsatian 10 10
2335 25 c. English setter 10 10
2336 2 cor. 50 Brittany spaniel . . 35 20
2337 3 cor. Boxer (air) 45 25
2338 3 cor. 50 Pointer 50 30
2339 6 cor. Collie 60 30

335 Satellite Communications

1982. Air. I.T.U. Congress.
2340 **335** 25 cor. multicoloured . . 2·10 1·50

336 "Dynamine myrrhina"

1982. Butterflies. Multicoloured.
2341 50 c. Type **336** (postage) . . . 20 5
2342 1 cor. 20 "Eunica alcmena" . 40 10
2343 1 cor. 50 "Callizona acesta" . 40 12
2344 2 cor. "Adelpha leuceria" . . 60 20
2345 3 cor. "Parides iphidamas" (air) 1·00 30
2346 3 cor. 50 "Consul hippona" . 1·10 35
2347 4 cor. "Morpho peleides" . . 1·25 40

337 Dog and Russian Rocket

1982. Space Exploration. Multicoloured.
2348 5 c. Type **337** (postage) . . . 10 10
2349 15 c. Satellite (vert) 10 10
2350 50 c. "Apollo-Soyuz" link . . 10 10
2351 1 cor. 50 Satellite 20 15
2352 2 cor. 50 Docking in space . . 35 20
2353 5 cor. Russian space station (air) 45 20
2354 6 cor. Space shuttle "Columbia" (vert) 60 30

338 Mailcoach

1982. Centenary of U.P.U. Membership. Multicoloured.
2355 50 c. Type **338** (postage) . . . 10 10
2356 1 cor. 20 "Victoria" (packet steamer) 60 20
2357 3 cor. 50 Railway locomotive (air) . . . . 1·50 15
2358 10 cor. Boeing 727-100 airliner 1·50 1·10

339 Cyclists

1982. 14th Central American and Caribbean Games. Multicoloured.
2359 10 c. Type **339** (postage) . . 10 10
2360 15 c. Swimming (horiz) . . . 10 10
2361 25 c. Basketball 10 10
2362 50 c. Weightlifting 10 10
2363 2 cor. 50 Handball (air) . . . 35 20
2364 3 cor. Boxing (horiz) 45 25
2365 9 cor. Football (horiz) . . . 75 45

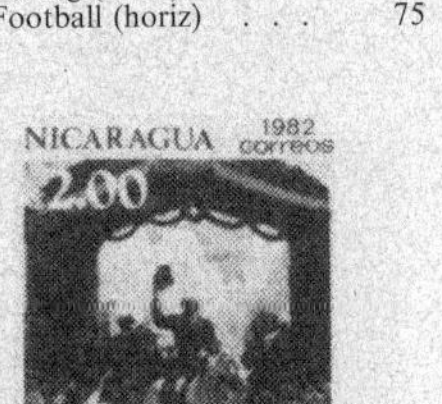

341 Washington passing through Trenton

1982. 250th Birth Anniv of George Washington. Multicoloured.
2368 50 c. Mount Vernon, Washington's house (39 × 49 mm) (postage) 10 10
2369 1 cor. Washington signing the Constitution (horiz) . . . 15 10
2370 2 cor. Type **341** 30 20
2371 2 cor. 50 Washington crossing the Delaware (horiz) (air) . 35 20
2372 3 cor. 50 Washington at Valley Forge (horiz) 50 30
2373 4 cor. Washington at the Battle of Trenton 55 35
2374 6 cor. Washington at Princeton 60 55

342 Carlos Fonseca, Dove and Flags

1982. 3rd Anniv of Revolution. Multicoloured.
2375 50 c. Type **342** (postage) . . 10 10
2376 2 cor. 50 Ribbons forming dove (vert) (air) 35 20
2377 1 cor. Augusto Sandino and dove (vert) 55 30
2378 6 cor. Dove 60 55

343 "Vase of Flowers" (R. Penalba)

1982. Paintings. Multicoloured.
2379 25 c. Type **343** (postage) . . 10 10
2380 50 c. "El Gueguense" (M. Garcia) (horiz) 10 10
2381 1 cor. "The Couple" (R. Perez) 15 10
2382 1 cor. 20 "Canales Valley" (A. Mejias) (horiz) 20 10
2383 1 cor. 85 "Portrait of Senora Castellon" (T. Jerez) . . . 25 15
2384 2 cor. "The Vendors" (L. Cerrato) 30 20
2385 9 cor. "Sitting Woman" (A. Morales) (horiz) (air) . 55 35

344 Lenin and Dimitrov, Moscow, 1921

1982. Birth Centenary of Georgi Dimitrov (Bulgarian statesman). Multicoloured.

2387 50 c. Type **344** (postage) . . 10 10

2388 2 cor. 50 Dimitrov & Todor Yikov, Sofia, 1946 (air) . . 35 20

2389 4 cor. Dimitrov and flag . . 55 35

345 Ausberto Narvaez

1982. 26th Anniv of State of Resistance Movement. Multicoloured.

2390 50 c. Type **345** (postage) . . 10 10

2391 2 cor. 50 Cornelio Silva . . . 35 20

2392 4 cor. Rigoberto Lopez Perez (air) 55 35

2393 6 cor. Edwin Castro 60 55

346 Old Ruins at Leon

1982. Tourism. Multicoloured.

2394 50 c. Type **346** (postage) . . 10 10

2395 1 cor. Ruben Dario Theatre and Park, Managua 15 10

2396 1 cor. 20 Independence Square, Granada 20 10

2397 1 cor. 80 Corn Island 25 15

2398 2 cor. Carter Santiago Volcano, Masaya 30 20

2399 2 cor. 50 El Coyotepe Fortress, Masaya (air) 35 20

2400 3 cor. 50 Luis A. Velazquez Park, Managua 50 30

347 Karl Marx and View of Trier

1982. Death Centenary of Karl Marx. Multicoloured.

2401 1 cor. Type **347** (postage) . . 15 10

2402 4 cor. Marx and grave in Highgate Cemetery (air) . . 55 35

348 Stacking Cane and Fruit

1982. World Food Day. Multicoloured.

2403 50 c. Picking Fruit (horiz) . . 10 10

2404 1 cor. Type **348** 15 10

2405 2 cor. Cutting sugar cane (horiz) 30 20

2406 10 cor. F.A.O. and P.A.N. emblems (horiz) 85 65

349 "Santa Maria"

1982. 490th Anniv of Discovery of America. Multicoloured.

2407 50 c. Type **349** (postage) . . 50 15

2408 1 cor. "Nina" . . . . 1·00 30

2409 1 cor. 50 "Pinta" . . . . . 1·40 35

2410 2 cor. Columbus and fleet . . 1·60 55

2411 2 cor. 50 Fleet and map of route (air) . . . . 1·75 55

2412 4 cor. Arrival in America . . 55 35

2413 7 cor. Death of Columbus . . 65 60

350 "Lobelia laxiflora" **351** "Micrurus lemniscatus"

1982. Woodland Flowers. Multicoloured.

2415 50 c. Type **350** (postage) . . 10 10

2416 1 cor. 20 "Bombacopsis quinata" 20 10

2417 1 cor. 80 "Mimosa albida" . . 25 15

2418 2 cor. "Epidendrum alatum" 30 20

2419 2 cor. 50 Passion flower "Passiflora foetida" wrongly inscr "Pasiflora" (air) . . 35 20

2420 3 cor. 50 "Clitoria sp." . . . 50 30

2421 5 cor. "Russelia sarmentosa" 70 45

1982. Reptiles. Multicoloured.

2422 10 c. Type **351** (postage) . . 10 10

2423 50 c. Common iguana "Iguana iguana" (horiz) 10 10

2424 2 cor. "Lachesis muta" (snake) (horiz) 30 20

2425 2 cor. 50 Hawksbill turtle "Eretmochelys imbricata" (horiz) (air) 35 20

2426 3 cor. Boa Constrictor "Constrictor constrictor" . 45 25

2427 3 cor. 50 American crocodile "Crocodilus acutus" (horiz) 50 30

2428 5 cor. Diamond-back rattlesnake "Sistrurus catenatus" (horiz) 70 45

352 Tele-cor Building, Managua

1982. Telecommunications Day. Multicoloured.

2429 1 cor. Type **352** (postage) . . 15 10

2430 50 c. Interior of radio transmission room (air) . 10 10

353 Girl with Dove

1983. Air. Non-Aligned States Conference.

2431 **353** 4 cor. multicoloured . . 55 35

354 Jose Marti and Birthplace

1983. 130th Birth Anniv of Jose Marti (Cuban revolutionary).

2432 **354** 1 cor. multicoloured . . 15 10

355 Boxing **356** "Neomarica coerulea"

1983. Olympic Games, Los Angeles (1st issue). Multicoloured.

2433 50 c. Type **355** (postage) . . 10 10

2434 1 cor. Gymnastics 15 10

2435 1 cor. 50 Running 20 15

2436 2 cor. Weightlifting 30 20

2347 4 cor. Discus (air) 55 35

2348 5 cor. Basketball 70 45

2349 6 cor. Cycling 90 55

See also Nos. 2609/15.

1983. Flowers.

2441 **356** 1 cor. blue 15 10

2442 – 1 cor. violet 15 10

2443 – 1 cor. mauve 15 10

2444 – 1 cor. brown 15 10

2445 – 1 cor. green 15 10

2446 – 1 cor. blue 15 10

2447 – 1 cor. green 15 10

2448 – 1 cor. green 15 10

2449 – 1 cor. mauve 15 10

2450 – 1 cor. red 15 10

2451 – 1 cor. grey 15 10

2452 – 1 cor. yellow 15 10

2453 – 1 cor. brown 15 10

2454 – 1 cor. purple 15 10

2455 – 1 cor. green 15 10

2456 – 1 cor. black 15 10

DESIGNS: No. 2442, "Tabebula ochraceae"; 2443, "Laella sp"; 2444, "Plumeria rubra"; 2445, "Brassavola nodosa"; 2446, "Stachytarpheta indica"; 2447, "Cochiospermum sp"; 2448, "Malvaviscus arboreus"; 2449, "Telecoma stans"; 2450, "Hibiscus rosa-sinensis"; 2451, "Cattleya lueddemanniana"; 2452, "Tagetes erecta"; 2453, "Senecio sp"; 2454, "Sobralia macrantha"; 2455, "Thumbergia alata"; 2456, "Bixa orellana".

See also Nos. 2739/54, 2838/53 and 3087/3102.

357 Momotombo Geo-thermal Electrical Plant

1983. Air. Energy.

2457 **357** 2 cor. 50 multicoloured . 35 20

358 Demonstrating Crowd

1983. Papal Visit.

2458 **358** 50 c. red, black and blue (postage) 10 10

2459 – 1 cor. multicoloured . . . 15 10

2460 – 4 cor. multicoloured (air) . . 55 35

2461 – 7 cor. multicoloured . . . 1·00 60

DESIGNS: 1 cor. Map of Nicaragua and girl picking coffee; 4 cor. Pres. Cordova Rivas and Pope John Paul II; 7 cor. Pope outside Managua Cathedral.

359 "Xilophanes chiron"

1983. Moths. Multicoloured.

2463 15 c. Type **359** (postage) . . . 10 10

2464 50 c. "Protoparce ochus" . . 15 10

2465 65 c. "Pholus lasbruscae" . . 25 10

2466 1 cor. "Amphypterus gannascus" 30 10

2467 1 cor. 50 "Pholus licaon" . . 40 15

2468 2 cor. "Agrius cingulata" . . 60 25

2469 10 cor. "Rothschildia jurulla" (vert) (air) . . . . 3·25 95

360 Subriava Church, Leon

1983. Monuments. Multicoloured.

2470 50 c. Type **360** (postage) . . . 10 10

2471 1 cor. "La Immaculada" Castle, Rio San Juan 15 10

2472 2 cor. La Recoleccion Church, Leon (vert) 30 20

2473 4 cor. Ruben Dario Monument, Managua (vert) (air) . . . 55 35

361 Passenger Coach

1983. Railway Wagons. Multicoloured.

2474 15 c. Type **361** (postage) . . 10 10

2475 65 c. Goods wagon 25 10

2476 1 cor. Tanker 30 10

2477 1 cor. 50 Ore hopper 40 15

2478 4 cor. Passenger railcar (air) . 1·10 50

2479 5 cor. Tipper truck . . . . . 1·25 60

2480 7 cor. Railbus . . . . 1·90 75

362 Aiding Flood Victims

1983. Red Cross. Multicoloured.

2481 50 c. Type **362** (postage) . . 10 10

2482 1 cor. Placing stretcher patient into ambulance 15 10

2483 4 cor. Helping earthquake victim (vert) (air) 55 35

2484 5 cor. Doctor examining wounded soldier 70 45

363 Raising Telephone Pole

1983. World Communications Year.

2485 **363** 1 cor. multicoloured . . 15 10

365 Baseball

1983. Ninth Pan-American Games. Multicoloured.

2487 15 c. Type **365** (postage) . . 10 10

2488 50 c. Water polo 10 10

2489 65 c. Running 15 10

2490 1 cor. Basketball (vert) . . . 15 10

2491 2 cor. Weightlifting (vert) . . 30 20

2492 7 cor. Fencing (air) 65 30

2493 8 cor. Gymnastics 70 40

367 Container Ship being Unloaded

1983. 4th Anniv of Revolution. Multicoloured.

2496 1 cor. Type **367** 45 15

2497 2 cor. Telcor building, Leon . 30 20

368 Carlos Fonseca **369** Simon Bolivar on Horseback

1983. Founders of Sandinista National Liberation Front. Multicoloured.

2498 50 c. Escobar, Navarro, Ubeda, Pomares and Ruiz (postage) 10 10

2499 1 cor. Santos Lopez, Borge, Buitrago and Mayorga . . 15 10

2500 4 cor. Type **368** (air) 55 35

1983. Birth Bicentenary of Simon Bolivar. Mult.
2501 50 c. Bolivar and Sandinista guerrilla . . . 10 10
2502 1 cor. Type **369** . . . 15 10

371 Movements of a Pawn

1983. Chess. Multicoloured.
2504 15 c. Type **371** (postage) . . 10 10
2505 65 c. Knight's movements . . 12 10
2506 1 cor. Bishop's movements . 15 10
2507 2 cor. Rook's movements . . 30 20
2508 4 cor. Queen's movements (air) 55 35
2509 5 cor. King's movements . . 70 45
2510 7 cor. Game in progress . . . 75 60

372 Speed Skating

1983. Winter Olympic Games, Sarajevo (1984) (1st issue). Multicoloured.
2511 50 c. Type **372** (postage) . . 10 10
2512 1 cor. Slalom . . . 15 10
2513 1 cor. 50 Luge . . . 20 15
2514 2 cor. Ski jumping . . . 30 20
2515 4 cor. Figure skating (air) . . 55 35
2516 5 cor. Downhill skiing . . . 70 45
2517 6 cor. Biathlon . . . 90 55

373 Soldiers with German Shepherd Dog **374** "Madonna of the Chair"

1983. Armed Forces.
2519 **373** 4 cor. multicoloured . . . 55 35

1983. 500th Birth Anniv of Raphael. Multicoloured.
2520 50 c. Type **374** (postage) . . 10 10
2521 1 cor. "Esterhazy Madonna" 15 10
2522 1 cor. 50 "Sistine Madonna" 20 12
2523 2 cor. "Madonna of the Linnet" 30 20
2524 4 cor. "Madonna of the Meadow" (air) . . . 55 35
2525 5 cor. "Madonna of the Garden" . . . 70 45
2526 6 cor. "Adoration of the Kings" 90 55

375 Pottery Idol

1983. Archaeological Finds. Multicoloured.
2528 50 c. Type **375** (postage) . . 10 10
2529 1 cor. Pottery dish with ornamental lid . . . 15 10
2530 2 cor. Vase with snake design 30 20
2531 4 cor. Pottery dish (air) . . . 55 35

376 Metal being poured into Moulds

1983. Nationalization of Mines. Multicoloured.
2532 1 cor. Type **376** (postage) . . 15 10
2533 4 cor. Workers and mine (air) . . 55 35

377 Radio Operator and Sinking Liner

1983. "Fracap '83" Congress of Radio Amateurs of Central America and Panama. Multicoloured.
2534 1 cor. Type **377** . . . 45 15
2535 4 cor. Congress emblem and town destroyed by earthquake . . . 55 35

378 Tobacco

1983. Agrarian Reform.
2536 **378** 1 cor. green . . . 15 10
2537 – 2 cor. orange . . . 30 20
2538 – 4 cor. brown . . . 35 35
2539 – 5 cor. blue . . . 45 45
2540 – 6 cor. lavender . . . 55 55
2541 – 7 cor. purple . . . 60 60
2542 – 8 cor. purple . . . 70 65
2543 – 10 cor. brown . . . 90 90
DESIGNS: 2 cor. Cotton; 4 cor. Maize; 5 cor. Sugar; 6 cor. Cattle; 7 cor. Rice; 8 cor. Coffee; 10 cor. Bananas.
See also Nos. 2755/62 and 2854/61.

379 Fire Engine with Ladder

1983. Fire Engines. Multicoloured.
2544 50 c. Type **379** (postage) . . 10 10
2545 1 cor. Water Tanker . . . 15 10
2546 6 cor. Crew vehicle, 1930 . . 90 55
2547 1 cor. 50 Pump with extension fire hoses (air) . . . 20 15
2548 2 cor. Pump with high-pressure tank . . . 30 20
2548a 4 cor. Water tanker . . . 60 40
2549 5 cor. Fire engine, 1910 . . 70 45

380 Jose Marti and General Sandino

1983. Nicaragua-Cuba Solidarity. Multicoloured.
2550 1 cor. Type **380** (postage) . . 15 10
2551 4 cor. Teacher, doctor and welder (air) . . . 55 35

381 "Adoration of the Shepherds" (Hugo van der Gaes) **382** Anniversary Emblem

1983. Christmas. Multicoloured.
2552 50 c. Type **381** (postage) . . 10 10
2553 1 cor. "Adoration of the Kings" (Domenico Ghirlandaio) . 15 10
2554 2 cor. "Adoration of the Shepherds" (El Greco) . . 30 20
2555 7 cor. "Adoration of the Kings" (Konrad von Soest) (air) . 65 30

1984. Air. 25th Anniv of Cuban Revolution.
2557 **382** 4 cor. red, blue and black 45 20
2558 – 6 cor. multicoloured . . 55 30
DESIGN: 6 cor. Fidel Castro and Che Guevara.

INDEX

Countries can be quickly located by referring to the index at the end of this volume.

383 Bobsleigh

1984. Winter Olympic Games, Sarajevo. Mult.
2559 50 c. Type **383** (postage) . . . 10 10
2560 50 c. Biathlon . . . 10 10
2561 1 cor. Slalom . . . 20 15
2562 1 cor. Speed skating . . . 20 15
2563 4 cor. Skiing (air) . . . 45 45
2564 5 cor. Ice dancing . . . 55 55
2565 10 cor. Ski jumping . . . 90 60

384 Chinchilla

1984. Cats. Multicoloured.
2567 50 c. Type **384** (postage) . . . 10 10
2568 50 c. Longhaired white . . . 10 10
2569 1 cor. Red tabby . . . 20 15
2570 2 cor. Tortoiseshell . . . 35 20
2571 4 cor. Burmese . . . 70 45
2572 3 cor. Siamese (air) . . . 50 35
2573 7 cor. Longhaired silver . . . 70 35

385 National Arms **386** Blanca Arauz

1984. 50th Death Anniv of Augusto Sandino. Multicoloured.
2574 1 cor. Type **385** (postage) . . 20 15
2575 4 cor. Augusto Sandino (air) . 35 20

1984. International Women's Day.
2576 **386** 1 cor. multicoloured . . . 20 15

387 Sunflower **388** "Soyuz"

1984. Agricultural Flowers. Multicoloured.
2577 50 c. Type **387** (postage) . . . 10 10
2578 50 c. "Poinsettia pulcherrima" 10 10
2579 1 cor. "Cassia alata" . 20 15
2580 2 cor. "Antigonon leptopus" . 35 20
2581 3 cor. "Bidens pilosa" (air) . 50 35
2582 4 cor. "Althaea rosea" . . 70 45
2583 5 cor. "Rivea corymbosa" . . 85 55

1984. Space Anniversaries. Multicoloured.
2584 50 c. Type **388** (15th anniv of "Soyuz 6", "7" and "8" flights) (postage) . . . 10 5
2585 50 c. "Soyuz" (different) (15th anniv of "Soyuz 6", "7" and "8" flights) . . . 10 5
2586 1 cor. "Apollo II" approaching Moon (15th anniv of 1st manned landing) . . . 20 15
2587 2 cor. "Luna I" (25th anniv of 1st Moon satellite) . . . 35 20
2588 3 cor. "Luna II" (25th anniv of 1st Moon landing) (air) . . 50 35
2589 4 cor. "Luna III" (25th anniv of 1st photographs of far side of Moon) . . . 70 45
2590 9 cor. Rocket (50th anniv of Korolev's book on space flight) . . . 1·25 75

389 "Noli me Tangere" (detail) **390** Daimler, 1886

1984. 450th Death Anniv of Correggio (artist). Multicoloured.
2591 50 c. Type **389** (postage) . . 10 10
2592 50 c. "Madonna of St. Jerome" (detail) . . . 10 10
2593 1 cor. "Allegory of Virtue" . 20 15
2594 2 cor. "Allegory of Pleasure" 35 20
2595 3 cor. "Ganymedes" (detail) (air) . . . 50 35
2596 5 cor. "The Danae" (detail) . 55 55
2597 8 cor. "Leda and the Swan" (detail) . . . 1·00 60

1984. 150th Birth Anniv of Gottlieb Daimler (automobile designer). Multicoloured.
2599 1 cor. Type **390** (postage) . . 10 10
2600 1 cor. Abadal, 1914 (horiz) . 10 10
2601 2 cor. Ford, 1903 . . . 35 20
2602 2 cor. Renault, 1899 . . . 35 20
2603 3 cor. Rolls Royce, 1910 (horiz) (air) . . . 50 35
2604 4 cor. Metallurgique, 1907 (horiz) . . . 70 45
2605 7 cor. Bugatti "Mod 40" (horiz) 75 50

392 Mail Transport

1984. Air. 19th Universal Postal Union Congress Philatelic Salon, Hamburg.
2607 **392** 15 cor. multicoloured . . 4·00 2·10

393 Basketball

1984. Olympic Games, Los Angeles (2nd issue). Multicoloured.
2609 50 c. Type **393** (postage) . . 10 10
2610 50 c. Volleyball . . . 10 10
2611 1 cor. Hockey . . . 20 15
2612 2 cor. Tennis (air) . . . 35 20
2613 3 cor. Football (horiz) . . . 50 35
2614 4 cor. Water polo (horiz) . . 70 45
2615 9 cor. Soccer (horiz) . . . 1·10 75

395 Rural Construction Site

1984. 5th Anniv of Revolution. Multicoloured.
2618 5 c. Type **395** (postage) . . . 10 10
2619 1 cor. Pacific-Atlantic Railway locomotive . . . 30 20
2620 4 cor. Ploughing with oxen and tractor (Agrarian reform) (air) . . . 40 20
2621 7 cor. State Council building 75 35

396 "Children defending Nature" (Pablo Herrera Berrios)

1984. U.N.E.S.C.O. Environmental Protection Campaign. Multicoloured.

2622	50 c. Type **396** (postage)	10	10
2623	1 cor. Living and dead forests	20	15
2624	2 cor. Fisherman and dried river bed	35	20
2625	10 cor. Hands holding plants (vert) (air)	85	75

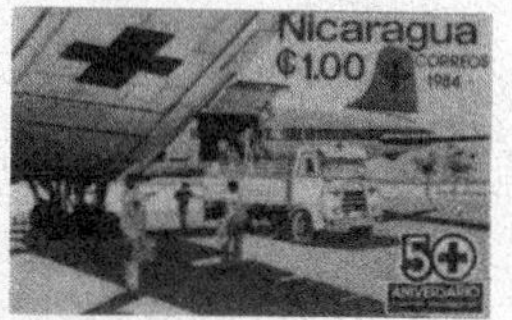

397 Red Cross Airplane and Ambulance

1984. 50th Anniv of Nicaraguan Red Cross. Multicoloured.

2626	1 cor. Type **397** (postage)	30	15
2627	7 cor. Battle of Solferino (125th anniv) (air)	90	45

399 Ventura Escalante and Dominican Republic Flag

1984. Baseball. Multicoloured.

2629	50 c. Type **399** (postage)	10	10
2630	50 c. Danial Herrera and Mexican flag	10	10
2631	1 cor. Adalberto Herrera and Venezuelan flag	20	15
2632	1 cor. Roberto Clemente and Nicaraguan flag	20	15
2633	3 cor. Carlos Colas and Cuban flag (air)	30	35
2634	4 cor. Stanley Cayasso and Argentinian flag	45	45
2635	5 cor. Babe Ruth and U.S.A. flag	55	55

400 Central American Tapir

1984. Wildlife Protection. Multicoloured.

2636	25 c. Type **400** (postage)	10	10
2637	25 c. Young tapir	10	10
2638	3 cor. Close-up of tapir (air)	15	10
2639	4 cor. Mother and young	20	15

401 Football in 1314

1985. World Cup Football Championship, Mexico (1986) (1st issue). Multicoloured.

2640	50 c. Type **401** (postage)	10	10
2641	50 c. Football in 1500	10	10
2642	1 cor. Football in 1872	10	10
2643	1 cor. Football in 1846	10	10
2644	2 cor. Football in 1883 (air)	10	10
2645	4 cor. Football in 1890	20	15
2646	6 cor. Football in 1953	30	20

See also Nos. 2731/7 and 2812/18.

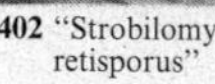

402 "Strobilomyces retisporus" **403** Postal Runner and Map

1985. Fungi. Multicoloured.

2648	50 c. Type **402** (postage)	10	10
2649	50 c. "Boletus calopus"	10	10
2650	1 cor. "Boletus luridus"	15	10
2651	1 cor. "Xerocomus illudens" (air)	15	10
2652	4 cor. "Gyrodon merulioides"	55	25
2653	5 cor. "Tylopilus plumbeoviolaceus"	65	30
2654	8 cor. "Gyroporus castaneus"	1·10	40

1985. 13th Postal Union of the Americas and Spain Congress. Multicoloured.

2655	1 cor. Type **403** (postage)	10	10
2656	7 cor. Casa Aviocar mail plane over map (air)	45	20

406 Early Steam Engine

1985. 150th Anniv of German Railway. Mult.

2659	1 cor. Type **406** (postage)	15	10
2660	1 cor. Electric locomotive	15	10
2661	9 cor. Steam locomotive No. 88 (air)	50	15
2662	9 cor. Double deck tram	50	15
2663	15 cor. Steam passenger locomotive	75	20
2664	21 cor. Mountain steam locomotive	1·10	30

407 Douglas, 1928

1985. Centenary of Motor Cycle. Multicoloured.

2666	50 c. Type **407** (postage)	10	10
2667	50 c. FN, 1928	10	10
2668	1 cor. Puch, 1938	10	10
2669	2 cor. Wanderer, 1939 (air)	10	10
2670	4 cor. Honda, 1949	10	10
2671	5 cor. BMW, 1984	10	10
2672	7 cor. Honda, 1984	40	10

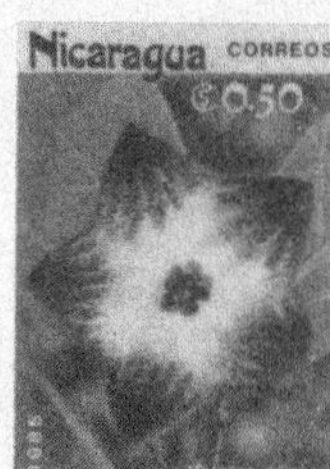

408 "Matelea quirosii" **409** "Capitulation of German Troops" (P. Krivonogov)

1985. Flowers. Multicoloured.

2673	50 c. Type **408** (postage)	10	10
2674	50 c. "Ipomea nil"	10	10
2675	1 cor. "Lysichitum americanum"	10	10
2676	2 cor. "Clusia sp." (air)	10	10
2677	4 cor. "Vanilla planifolia"	10	10
2678	7 cor. "Stemmadenia obovata"	75	40

1985. 40th Anniv of End of World War II. Mult.

2679	9 cor. 50 Type **409** (postage)	1·00	50
2680	28 cor. Woman behind barbed wire and Nuremberg trial (air)	3·00	1·50

410 Lenin and Red Flag **413** Ring-necked Pheasant

412 Victoria de Julio Sugar Factory

1985. 115th Birth Anniv of Lenin. Multicoloured.

2681	4 cor. Type **410**	10	10
2682	21 cor. Lenin addressing crowd	45	30

1985. Air. 6th Anniv of Revolution. Multicoloured.

2684	9 cor. Type **412**	20	15
2685	9 cor. Soldier and flag	20	15

1985. Domestic Birds. Multicoloured.

2686	50 c. Type **413**	50	10
2687	50 c. Hen	50	10
2688	1 cor. Helmet guineafowl	50	10
2689	2 cor. Swan goose	50	10
2690	6 cor. Ocellated turkey	1·40	15
2691	8 cor. Duck	1·75	10

414 Luis A. Delgadillo **415** Zeledon

1985. International Music Year. Multicoloured.

2692	1 cor. Type **414** (postage)	10	10
2693	1 cor. Masked dancer with floral headdress	10	10
2694	9 cor. Masked procession (air)	65	40
2695	9 cor. Crowd outside church	65	40
2696	15 cor. Masked dancer in brimmed hat	1·10	55
2697	21 cor. Procession resting	1·50	75

1985. Air. Birth Centenary of Benjamin Zeledon.

2698	**415** 15 cor. multicoloured	1·00	55

416 Dunant and Lifeboat

1985. 75th Death Anniv of Henri Dunant (founder of Red Cross). Multicoloured.

2699	3 cor. Type **416**	20	10
2700	15 cor. Dunant and Ilyushin Il-86 and Tupolev Tu-154 aircraft	1·25	55

417 Fire Engine

1985. 6th Anniv of SINACOI Fire Service. Mult.

2701	1 cor. Type **417** (postage)	10	10
2702	1 cor. Fire station	10	10
2703	1 cor. Engine with water jet	10	10
2704	3 cor. Foam tender (air)	10	10
2705	9 cor. Airport fire engine	50	15
2706	15 cor. Engine at fire	85	45
2707	21 cor. Fireman in protective clothing	1·10	75

418 Halley, Masaya Volcano and Comet

1985. Appearance of Halley's Comet. Multicoloured.

2708	1 cor. Type **418** (postage)	10	10
2709	3 cor. Armillary sphere and 1910 trajectory	10	10
2710	3 cor. "Venus" space probe and Tycho Brahe underground observatory	10	10
2711	9 cor. Habermel's astrolabe and comet's path through solar system (air)	50	15
2712	15 cor. Hale Telescope, Mt. Palomar, and Herschel's telescope	85	45
2713	21 cor. Galileo's telescope and sections through telescopes of Newton, Cassegrain and Ritchey	1·25	60

419 Tapir eating

1985. Protected Animals. Baird's Tapir. Mult.

2714	1 cor. Type **419** (postage)	10	10
2715	3 cor. Tapir in water (air)	10	10
2716	5 cor. Tapir in undergrowth	10	10
2717	9 cor. Mother and calf	20	15

420 "Rosa spinosissima"

1986. Wild Roses. Multicoloured.

2718	1 cor. Type **420**	10	10
2719	1 cor. Dog rose ("R. canina")	10	10
2720	3 cor. "R. eglanteria"	10	10
2721	5 cor. "R. rubrifolia"	10	10
2722	9 cor. "R. foetida"	20	15
2723	100 cor. "R. rugosa"	2·00	1·10

421 Crimson Topaz **422** Footballer and Statue

1986. Birds. Multicoloured.

2724	1 cor. Type **421**	15	10
2725	3 cor. Orange-billed nightingale thrush	15	10
2726	3 cor. Troupial	15	10
2727	5 cor. Painted bunting	45	15
2728	10 cor. Frantzius's nightingale thrush	90	40
2729	21 cor. Great horned owl	1·75	1·00
2730	75 cor. Great kiskadee	6·50	3·00

1986. World Cup Football Championship, Mexico (2nd issue). Multicoloured.

2731	1 cor. Type **422** (postage)	10	10
2732	1 cor. Footballer and sculptured head	10	10
2733	3 cor. Footballer and water holder with man as stem (air)	10	10
2734	3 cor. Footballer and sculpture	10	10
2735	5 cor. Footballer and sculptured head (different)	10	10
2736	9 cor. Footballer and sculpture (different)	20	15
2737	100 cor. Footballer and sculptured snake's head	3·00	1·50

1986. (a) Flowers. As Nos. 2441/56 but values changed.

2739	5 cor. blue	10	10
2740	5 cor. violet	10	10
2741	5 cor. purple	10	10
2742	5 cor. orange	10	10
2743	5 cor. green	10	10
2744	5 cor. blue	10	10
2745	5 cor. green	10	10
2746	5 cor. green	10	10
2747	5 cor. mauve	10	10
2748	5 cor. red	10	10
2749	5 cor. grey	10	10
2750	5 cor. orange	10	10
2751	5 cor. brown	10	10
2752	5 cor. brown	10	10
2753	5 cor. green	10	10
2754	5 cor. black	10	10

DESIGNS: No. 2739, Type **356**; 2740, "Tabebula ochraceae"; 2741, "Laelia sp"; 2742, Frangipani ("Plumeria rubra"); 2743, "Brassavola nodosa"; 2744, "Strachytarpheta indica"; 2745, "Cochlospermum sp"; 2746, "Malvaviscus arboreus"; 2747, "Tecoma stans"; 2748, Chinese hibiscus ("Hibiscus rosa-sinensis"); 2749, "Cattleya lueddemanniana"; 2750, African marigold ("Tagetes erecta"); 2751, "Senecio sp"; 2752, "Sobralia macrantha"; 2753, "Thumbergia alata"; 2754, "Bixa orellana".

(b) Agrarian Reform. As T **378**.

2755 1 cor. brown 10 10
2756 9 cor. violet 20 15
2757 15 cor. purple 30 20
2758 21 cor. red 45 30
2759 33 cor. orange 65 45
2760 42 cor. green 90 55
2761 50 cor. brown 1·00 65
2762 100 cor. blue 2·00 1·50

DESIGNS: 1 cor. Type **378**; 9 cor. Cotton; 15 cor. Maize; 21 cor. Sugar; 33 cor. Cattle; 42 cor. Rice; 50 cor. Coffee; 100 cor. Bananas.

423 Alfonso Cortes

1986. National Libraries. Latin American Writers. Multicoloured.

2763 1 cor. Type **423** (postage) 10 10
2764 3 cor. Azarias H. Pallais 10 10
2765 3 cor. Salomon de la Selva 10 10
2766 5 cor. Ruben Dario 10 10
2767 9 cor. Pablo Neruda 10 10
2768 15 cor. Alfonso Reyes (air) 45 25
2769 100 cor. Pedro Henriquez Urena 3·00 1·50

424 Great Britain Penny Black and Nicaragua 1929 25 c. Stamps

1986. Air. 125th Anniv of Nicaraguan Stamps. Designs showing G.B. Penny Black and Nicaragua stamps.

2770 **424** 30 cor. multicoloured 90 45
2771 – 40 cor. brown, black and grey 1·25 60
2772 – 50 cor. red, black and grey 1·50 75
2773 – 100 cor. blue, black and grey 3·00 1·50

DESIGNS: 40 c. 1903 1 p. stamp; 50 c. 1892 5 p. stamp; 1 p. 1862 2 c. stamp.

425 Sapodilla **426** Rainbow and Globe

1986. 40th Anniv of F.A.O. Multicoloured.

2774 1 cor. Type **425** (postage) 10 10
2775 1 cor. Maranon 10 10
2776 3 cor. Tree-cactus 10 10
2777 3 cor. Granadilla 10 10
2778 5 cor. Custard-apple (air) 10 10
2779 21 cor. Melocoton 65 35
2780 100 cor. Mamey 3·00 1·50

1986. Air. International Peace Year. Multicoloured.

2781 5 cor. Type **426** 10 10
2782 10 cor. Dove and globe 30 10

427 Lockheed L-1011 TriStar 500

1986. "Stockholmia 86" International Stamp Exhibition. Multicoloured.

2783 1 cor. Type **427** (postage) 10 10
2784 1 cor. Yakovlev Yak-40 10 10
2785 3 cor. B.A.C. One Eleven 10 10
2786 3 cor. Boeing 747-100 10 10
2787 9 cor. Airbus Industrie A300 (air) 30 10
2788 15 cor. Tupolev Tu-154 45 10
2789 100 cor. Concorde (vert) 3·00 1·50

428 "Pinta" and 16th-century Map

1986. 500th Anniv (1992) of Discovery of America by Columbus (1st issue). Multicoloured.

2791 1 cor. Type **428** (postage) 45 20
2792 1 cor. "Santa Maria" and "Nina" 45 20
2793 9 cor. Juan de la Cosa (air) 30 10
2794 9 cor. Christopher Columbus 30 10
2795 21 cor. King and Queen of Spain 65 35
2796 100 cor. Courtiers behind Columbus and Indians 3·00 1·50

The designs of the same value and Nos. 2795/6 were printed together in se-tenant pairs within their sheets, Nos. 2791/2 and 2795/6 forming composite designs.

See also Nos. 2903/8.

429 Fonseca and Flags

1986. Air. 25th Anniv of Sandinista Front and 10th Death Anniv of Carlos Fonseca (co-founder).

2798 **429** 15 cor. multicoloured 10 10

430 Rhinoceros **431** "Theritas coronata"

1986. Air. Endangered Animals. Multicoloured.

2799 15 cor. Type **430** 45 10
2800 15 cor. Zebra 45 10
2801 25 cor. Elephant 75 40
2802 25 cor. Giraffe 75 40
2803 50 cor. Tiger 1·50 75
2804 50 cor. Mandrill 1·50 75

1986. Butterflies. Multicoloured.

2805 10 cor. Type **431** (post) 20 10
2806 15 cor. "Salamis cacta" (air) 20 10
2807 15 cor. "Charayes nitebis" 20 10
2808 15 cor. "Papilio maacki" 20 10
2809 25 cor. "Palaeochrysophonus hippothoe" 20 10
2810 25 cor. "Euphaedro cyparissa" 20 10
2811 30 cor. "Ritra aurea" 20 10

432 Player and French Flag **433** Ernesto Mejia Sanchez

1986. Air. World Cup Football Championship, Mexico (3rd issue). Finalists. Multicoloured. Designs showing footballers and national flags.

2812 10 cor. Type **432** 10 10
2813 10 cor. Argentina 10 10
2814 10 cor. West Germany 10 10
2815 15 cor. England 10 10
2816 15 cor. Brazil 10 10
2817 25 cor. Spain 10 10
2818 50 cor. Belgium (horiz) 10 10

1987. Ruben Dario Cultural Order of Independence. Multicoloured.

2820 10 cor. Type **433** (postage) 10 10
2821 10 cor. Fernando Gordillo 10 10
2822 10 cor. Francisco Perez Estrada 10 10
2823 15 cor. Order medal (air) 10 10
2824 30 cor. Julio Cortazar 20 20
2825 60 cor. Enrique Fernandez Morales 35 25

434 Ice Hockey **435** Development

1987. Winter Olympic Games, Calgary (1988). Multicoloured.

2826 10 cor. Type **434** (postage) 10 10
2827 10 cor. Speed skating 10 10
2828 15 cor. Downhill skiing (air) 10 10
2829 15 cor. Figure skating 10 10
2830 20 cor. Shooting 15 10
2831 30 cor. Slalom 20 10
2832 40 cor. Ski jumping 25 10

1987. U.N.I.C.E.F. Child Survival Campaign. Multicoloured.

2834 10 cor. Type **435** (postage) 10 10
2835 25 cor. Vaccination (air) 75 40
2836 30 cor. Oral rehydration therapy 90 45
2837 50 cor. Breastfeeding 1·50 75

1987. (a) Flowers. As Nos. 2441/56 and 2739/54 but values changed.

2838 10 cor. blue 10 10
2839 10 cor. violet 10 10
2840 10 cor. purple 10 10
2841 10 cor. red 10 10
2842 10 cor. green 10 10
2843 10 cor. blue 10 10
2844 10 cor. green 10 10
2845 10 cor. green 10 10
2846 10 cor. mauve 10 10
2847 10 cor. red 10 10
2848 10 cor. green 10 10
2849 10 cor. orange 10 10
2850 10 cor. brown 10 10
2851 10 cor. purple 10 10
2852 10 cor. turquoise 10 10
2853 10 cor. black 10 10

DESIGNS: No. 2838, Type **356**; 2839, "Tabebula ochraceae"; 2840, "Laelia sp"; 2841, Frangipani; 2842, "Brassavola nodosa"; 2843, "Stachytarpheta indica"; 2844, "Cochlospermum sp"; 2845, "Malvaviscus arboreus"; 2846, "Tecoma stans"; 2847, Chinese hibiscus; 2848, "Cattleya lueddermanniana"; 2849, African marigold; 2850, "Senecio sp"; 2851, "Sobralla macrantha"; 2852, "Thumbergia alata"; 2853, "Bixa orellana".

(b) Agrarian Reform. As T **378**. Dated "1987".

2854 10 cor. brown 10 10
2855 10 cor. violet 10 10
2856 15 cor. purple 10 10
2857 25 cor. red 15 10
2858 30 cor. orange 20 10
2859 50 cor. brown 30 20
2860 60 cor. green 35 25
2861 100 cor. blue 65 45

DESIGNS: No. 2854, Type **378**; 2855, Cotton; 2856, Maize; 2857, Sugar; 2858, Cattle; 2859, Coffee; 2860, Rice; 2861, Bananas.

436 Flags and Buildings **438** Tennis Player

437 "Mammuthus columbi"

1987. 77th Interparliamentary Conference, Managua.

2862 **436** 10 cor. multicoloured 10 10

1987. Prehistoric Animals. Multicoloured.

2863 10 cor. Type **437** (postage) 10 10
2864 10 cor. Triceratops 10 10
2865 10 cor. Dimetrodon 10 10
2866 15 cor. Uintaterium (air) 10 10
2867 15 cor. Dinichthys 10 10
2868 30 cor. Pteranodon 60 35
2869 40 cor. Tilosaurus 85 45

1987. "Capex 87" International Stamp Exhibition, Toronto.

2870 10 cor. multicoloured (Type **438**) (postage) 10 10
2871 10 cor. multicoloured 10 10
2872 15 cor. multicoloured (male player) (air) 45 10
2873 15 cor. multicoloured (female player) 45 10
2874 20 cor. multicoloured 60 30
2875 30 cor. multicoloured 60 45
2876 40 cor. multicoloured 85 60

DESIGNS: Nos. 2871/6, Various tennis players.

439 Dobermann Pinscher **441** Levski

440 Modern Wooden Houses

1987. Dogs. Multicoloured.

2878 10 cor. Type **439** (postage) 10 10
2879 10 cor. Bull mastiff 10 10
2880 15 cor. Japanese spaniel (air) 45 10
2881 15 cor. Keeshond 45 10
2882 20 cor. Chihuahua 60 30
2883 30 cor. St. Bernard 90 45
2884 40 cor. West Gotha spitz 85 60

1987. Air. International Year of Shelter for the Homeless. Multicoloured.

2885 20 cor. Type **440** 15 10
2886 30 cor. Modern brick-built houses 20 10

1987. Air. 150th Birth Anniv of Vasil Levski (revolutionary).

2887 **441** 30 cor. multicoloured 20 10

442 "Opuntia acanthocarpa major"

1987. Cacti. Multicoloured.

2888 10 cor. Type **442** (postage) 10 10
2889 10 cor. "Lophocereus schottii" 10 10
2890 10 cor. "Echinocereus engelmanii" 10 10
2891 20 cor. Saguaros (air) 60 30
2892 20 cor. "Lemaireocereus thurberi" 60 30
2893 30 cor. "Opuntia fulgida" 90 45
2894 50 cor. "Opuntia ficus indica" 1·50 75

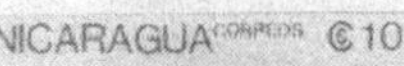

443 High Jumping

1987. 10th Pan-American Games, Indiana. Multicoloured.

2895 10 cor. Type **443** (postage) 10 10
2896 10 cor. Handball 10 10
2897 15 cor. Running (air) 45 10
2898 15 cor. Gymnastics 45 10
2899 20 cor. Baseball 60 30
2900 30 cor. Synchronised swimming (vert) 90 45
2901 40 cor. Weightlifting (vert) 1·25 60

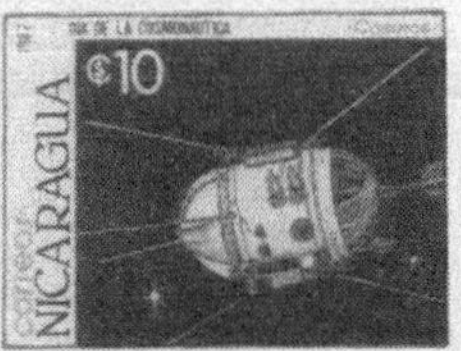

445 "Cosmos"

1987. Cosmonautics Day. Multicoloured.

2904 10 cor. Type **445** (postage) 10 10
2905 10 cor "Sputnik" 10 10
2906 15 cor. "Proton" (air) 45 10
2907 25 cor. "Luna" 75 40
2908 25 cor. "Meteor" 75 40
2909 30 cor. "Electron" 90 45
2910 50 cor. "Mars-1" 1·50 75

446 Native Huts and Terraced Hillside

1987. Air. 500th Anniv (1992) of Discovery of America by Christopher Columbus (2nd issue). Multicoloured.

2911	15 cor. Type **446**	45	20
2912	15 cor. Columbus's fleet	65	20
2913	20 cor. Spanish soldiers in native village	60	30
2914	30 cor. Mounted soldiers killing natives	90	45
2915	40 cor. Spanish people and houses	1·25	60
2916	50 cor. Church and houses	1·50	75

447 "Atractoteus tropicus gaspar"

1987. World Food Day. Fishes. Multicoloured.

2917	10 cor. Type **447** (postage)	10	10
2918	10 cor. "Tarpon atlanticus"	10	10
2919	10 cor. Cichlid	10	10
2920	15 cor. "Astyana fasciatus" (air)	45	10
2921	15 cor. Midas cichlid	45	10
2922	20 cor. Cichlid (different)	60	30
2923	50 cor. "Carcharhinus nicaraguensis"	1·50	75

448 Lenin 449 "Nativity"

1987. 70th Anniv of Russian Revolution. Mult.

2924	10 cor. Type **448** (postage)	10	10
2925	30 cor. "Aurora" (cruiser) (horiz) (air)	35	15
2926	50 cor. Russian arms	30	20

1987. Christmas. Details of Painting by L. Saenz. Multicoloured.

2927	10 cor. Type **449**	10	10
2928	20 cor. "Adoration of the Magi"	60	30
2929	25 cor. "Adoration of the Magi" (close-up detail)	75	40
2930	50 cor. "Nativity" (close-up detail)	1·50	75

1987. Surch.

2931 **435**	400 cor. on 10 cor. mult (postage)	30	15
2935 **440**	200 cor. on 20 cor. multicoloured (air)	15	10
2932 –	600 cor. on 50 cor. mult (No. 2837)	40	20
2933 –	1000 cor. on 25 cor. mult (No. 2835)	70	35
2936 –	3000 cor. on 30 cor. mult (No. 2886)	2·10	1·00
2934 –	5000 cor. on 30 cor. mult (No. 2836)	3·50	1·75

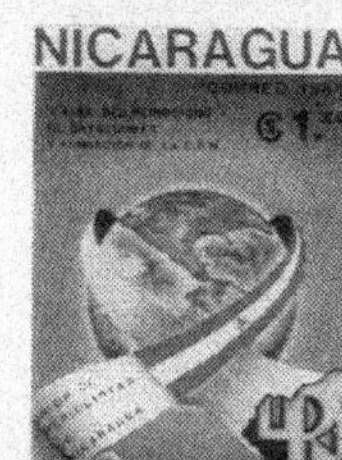

451 Cross-country Skiing 452 Flag around Globe

1988. Winter Olympic Games, Calgary. Mult.

2937	10 cor. Type **451**	10	10
2938	10 cor. Rifle-shooting (horiz)	10	10
2939	15 cor. Ice hockey	45	10
2940	20 cor. Ice skating	60	30
2941	25 cor. Downhill skiing	75	40
2942	30 cor. Ski jumping (horiz)	90	45
2943	40 cor. Slalom	1·25	60

1988. 10th Anniv of Nicaragua Journalists' Association. Multicoloured.

2945	1 cor. Type **452** (postage)	10	10
2946	5 cor. Churches of St. Francis Xavier, Sandino and Fatima, Managua, and speaker addressing journalists (42 × 27 mm) (air)	1·25	60

453 Basketball

1988. Olympic Games, Seoul. Multicoloured.

2947	10 cor. Type **453**	10	10
2948	10 cor. Gymnastics	10	10
2949	15 cor. Volleyball	45	10
2950	20 cor. Long jumping	60	30
2951	25 cor. Football	75	40
2952	30 cor. Water polo	90	45
2953	40 cor. Boxing	1·25	60

454 Brown Bear

1988. Mammals and their Young. Multicoloured.

2955	10 c. Type **454** (postage)	10	10
2956	15 c. Lion	10	10
2957	25 c. Cocker spaniel	10	10
2958	50 c. Wild boar	15	10
2959	4 cor. Cheetah (air)	55	20
2960	7 cor. Spotted hyena	1·00	40
2961	8 cor. Red fox	1·25	50

455 Slide Tackle

1988. "Essen '88" International Stamp Fair and European Football Championship, Germany. Multicoloured.

2963	50 c. Type **455** (postage)	10	10
2964	1 cor. Footballers	15	10
2965	2 cor. Lining up shot (vert) (air)	30	10
2966	3 cor. Challenging for ball (vert)	50	20
2967	4 cor. Heading ball (vert)	65	25
2968	5 cor. Tackling (vert)	80	30
2969	6 cor. Opponent winning possession	1·00	40

456 Bell JetRanger III (½-size illustration)

1988. "Finlandia 88" International Stamp Exhibition, Helsinki. Helicopters. Multicoloured.

2971	4 cor. Type **456** (postage)	15	10
2972	12 cor. MBB-Kawasaki BK-117A-3 (air)	20	10
2973	16 cor. Boeing-Vertol B-360	30	10
2974	20 cor. Agusta A.109 MR11	40	10
2975	24 cor. Sikorsky S-61N	55	20
2976	28 cor. Aerospatiale SA.365 Dauphin 2	60	25
2977	56 cor. Sikorsky S-76 Spirit	1·25	50

457 Flags and Map 458 Casimiro Sotelo Montenegro

1988. 9th Anniv of Revolution. Multicoloured.

2979	1 cor. Type **457** (postage)	20	10
2980	5 cor. Landscape and hands releasing dove (air)	80	30

1988. Revolutionaries.

2981 **458**	4 cor. blue (postage)	15	10
2982 –	12 cor. mauve (air)	20	10
2983 –	16 cor. green	30	10
2984 –	20 cor. red	45	15
2985 –	24 cor. brown	55	20
2986 –	28 cor. violet	65	25
2987 –	50 cor. red	1·25	45
2988 –	100 cor. purple	2·40	1·00

DESIGNS: 12 cor. Ricardo Morales Aviles; 16 cor. Silvio Mayorga Delgado; 20 cor. Pedro Arauz Palacios; 24 cor. Oscar A. Turcios Chavarrias; 28 cor. Julio C. Buitrago Urroz; 50 cor. Jose B. Escobar Perez; 100 cor. Eduardo E. Contreras Escobar.

459 "Acacia baileyana" 460 West Indian Fighting Conch

1988. Flowers. Multicoloured.

2989	4 cor. Type **459** (postage)	15	10
2990	12 cor. "Anigozanthos manglesii" (air)	20	10
2991	16 cor. "Telopia speciosissima"	30	10
2992	20 cor. "Eucalyptus ficifolia"	45	15
2993	24 cor. "Boronia heterophylla"	60	30
2994	28 cor. "Callistemon speciosus"	70	35
2995	30 cor. "Nymphaea caerulea" (horiz)	80	40
2996	50 cor. "Clianthus formosus"	1·25	60

1988. Molluscs. Multicoloured.

2997	4 cor. Type **460** (postage)	20	10
2998	12 cor. Painted polymita (air)	30	10
2999	16 cor. Giant sundial	40	10
3000	20 cor. Japanese baking oyster	55	10
3001	24 cor. Yoka star shell	75	20
3002	28 cor. Gawdy frog shell	80	25
3003	50 cor. Mantled top	1·75	50

461 Zapotecan Funeral Urn 462 "Chrysina macropus"

1988. 500th Anniv (1992) of Discovery of America by Columbus (3rd issue). Multicoloured.

3004	4 cor. Type **461** (postage)	15	10
3005	12 cor. Mochican ceramic seated figure (air)	20	10
3006	16 cor. Mochican ceramic head	30	10
3007	20 cor. Tainan ceramic vessel	45	10
3008	28 cor. Nazcan vessel (horiz)	65	20
3009	100 cor. Incan ritual pipe (horiz)	2·40	1·00

1988. Beetles. Multicoloured.

3011	4 cor. Type **462** (postage)	15	10
3012	12 cor. "Plusiotis victoriana" (air)	20	10
3013	16 cor. "Ceratotrupes bolivari"	30	10
3014	20 cor. "Gymnetosoma stellata"	50	15
3015	24 cor. "Euphoria lineoligera"	60	20
3016	28 cor. "Euphoria candezei"	70	30
3017	50 cor. "Sulcophanaeus chryseicollis"	1·25	50

463 Dario

1988. Air. Centenary of Publication of "Blue" by Ruben Dario.

3018 **463**	25 cor. multicoloured	60	20

464 Simon Bolivar, Jose Marti, Gen. Sandino and Fidel Castro

1989. Air. 30th Anniv of Cuban Revolution.

3019 **464**	20 cor. multicoloured	50	20

465 Pochomil Tourist Centre

1989. Tourism. Multicoloured.

3020	4 cor. Type **465** (postage)	15	10
3021	12 cor. Granada Tourist Centre (air)	20	10
3022	20 cor. Olof Palme Convention Centre	45	15
3023	24 cor. Masaya Volcano National Park	55	20
3024	28 cor. La Boquita Tourist Centre	70	25
3025	30 cor. Xiloa Tourist Centre	75	30
3026	50 cor. Managua Hotel	1·25	50

466 Footballers 467 Downhill Skiing

1989. Air. World Cup Football Championship, Italy (1990).

3028 **466**	100 cor. multicoloured	10	10
3029 –	200 cor. multicoloured	10	10
3030 –	600 cor. multicoloured	10	10
3031 –	1000 cor. multicoloured	30	10
3032 –	2000 cor. multicoloured	60	10
3033 –	3000 cor. multicoloured	90	40
3034 –	5000 cor. multicoloured	1·50	50

DESIGNS: 200 cor. to 5000 cor. Different footballers.

1989. Air. Winter Olympic Games, Albertville (1992) (1st issue). Multicoloured.

3036	50 cor. Type **467**	10	10
3037	300 cor. Ice hockey	10	10
3038	600 cor. Ski jumping	10	10
3039	1000 cor. Ice skating	30	10
3040	2000 cor. Biathlon	60	10
3041	3000 cor. Slalom	90	40
3042	5000 cor. Skiing	1·50	50

See also Nos. 3184/90.

468 Water Polo

1989. Air. Olympic Games, Barcelona (1992). Multicoloured.

3044	100 cor. Type **468**	10	10
3045	200 cor. Running	10	10
3046	600 cor. Diving	10	10
3047	1000 cor. Gymnastics	30	10
3048	2000 cor. Weightlifting	60	10
3049	3000 cor. Volleyball	90	40
3050	5000 cor. Wrestling	1·50	50

See also Nos. 3192/8.

469 Procession of States General at Versailles 470 American Anhinga

1989. "Philexfrance 89" International Stamp Exhibition, Paris, and Bicentenary of French Revolution. Multicoloured.
3052 50 cor. Type **469** (postage) 15 10
3054 300 cor. Oath of the Tennis Court (36 × 28 mm) (air) 10 10
3055 600 cor. "The 14th of July" (29 × 40 mm) 10 10
3056 1000 cor. Tree of Liberty (36 × 28 mm) 30 10
3057 2000 cor. "Liberty guiding the People" (Eugene Delacroix) (29 × 40 mm) 60 10
3058 3000 cor. Storming the Bastille (36 × 28 mm) 90 40
3059 5000 cor. Lafayette taking oath (28 × 36 mm) 1·50 50

1989. Air. "Brasiliana 89" International Stamp Exhibition, Rio de Janeiro. Birds. Multicoloured.
3060 100 cor. Type **470** 10 10
3061 200 cor. Swallow-tailed kite 10 10
3062 600 cor. Turquoise-browed motmot 10 10
3063 1000 cor. Painted redstart 30 10
3064 2000 cor. Great antshrike (horiz) 60 10
3065 3000 cor. Northern royal flycatcher 90 40
3066 5000 cor. White-flanked antwren (horiz) 1·50 50

471 Anniversary Emblem

472 Animal-shaped Vessel

1989. Air. 10th Anniv of Revolution.
3068 **471** 300 cor. multicoloured 10 10

1989. Air. America. Pre-Columbian Artefacts.
3070 **472** 2000 cor. multicoloured 60 10

Currency Reform. 150000 (old) cordoba = 1 (new) cordoba

The following issues, denominated in the old currency, were distributed by agents but were not issued (each set consists of seven values and is dated "1990"):
"London 90" International Stamp Exn. Ships
World Cup Football Championship, Italy
Olympic Games, Barcelona (1992)
Fungi
Winter Olympic Games, Albertville (1992)

473 Little Spotted Kiwi

1991. "New Zealand 1990" International Stamp Exhibition, Auckland. Birds. Multicoloured.
3071 5 c. Type **473** 10 10
3072 5 c. Takahe 10 10
3073 10 c. Red-fronted parakeet 15 10
3074 20 c. Weka rail 30 15
3075 30 c. Kagu (vert) 45 20
3076 60 c. Kea 85 45
3077 70 c. Kakapo 1·00 50

474 Jaguar

1991. 45th Anniv of Food and Agriculture Organization. Animals. Multicoloured.
3079 5 c. Type **474** 10 10
3080 5 c. Ocelot (vert) 10 10
3081 10 c. Black-handed spider monkey (vert) 15 10
3082 20 c. Baird's tapir 30 15
3083 30 c. Nine-banded armadillo 45 20
3084 60 c. Coyote 85 45
3085 70 c. Two-toed sloth 1·00 50

HAVE YOU READ THE NOTES AT THE BEGINNING OF THIS CATALOGUE?
These often provide the answers to the enquiries we receive.

475 Dr. Chamorro

476 Steam Locomotive, Peru

1991. Dr. Pedro Joaquin Chamorro (campaigner for an independent Press).
3086 **475** 2 cor. 25 multicoloured 50 20

1991. Flowers. As T **356** but with currency inscribed in "oro".
3087 – 1 cor. blue 25 10
3088 – 2 cor. green 45 20
3089 – 3 cor. brown 70 30
3090 – 4 cor. purple 95 40
3091 – 5 cor. red 1·10 45
3092 – 6 cor. green 1·40 55
3093 **356** 7 cor. blue 1·60 65
3094 – 8 cor. green 1·90 75
3095 – 9 cor. green 2·10 85
3096 – 10 cor. violet 2·25 90
3097 – 11 cor. mauve 2·50 1·00
3098 – 12 cor. yellow 2·75 1·10
3099 – 13 cor. red 3·00 1·25
3100 – 14 cor. green 3·25 1·25
3101 – 15 cor. mauve 3·50 1·40
3102 – 16 cor. black 3·75 1·50
DESIGNS: 1 cor. "Stachytarpheta indica"; 2 cor. "Cochlospermum sp."; 3 cor. "Senecio sp."; 4 cor. "Sobralia macrantha"; 5 cor. Frangipani; 6 cor. "Brassavola nodosa"; 8 cor. "Malvaviscus arboreus"; 9 cor. "Cattleya lueddemanniana"; 10 cor. "Tabebula ochraceae"; 11 cor. "Laelia sp."; 12 cor. African marigold; 13 cor. Chinese hibiscus; 14 cor. "Thumbergia alata"; 15 cor. "Tecoma stans"; 16 cor. "Bixa orellana".

1991. Steam Locomotives of South and Central America. Multicoloured.
3103 25 c. Type **476** 10 10
3104 25 c. Bolivia 10 10
3105 50 c. Argentina 10 10
3106 1 cor. 50 Chile 25 10
3107 2 cor. Colombia 35 10
3108 3 cor. Brazil 50 10
3109 3 cor. 50 Paraguay 60 10

477 Match Scene (West Germany versus Netherlands)

1991. West Germany, Winners of World Cup Football Championship (1990). Multicoloured.
3111 25 c. Type **477** 10 10
3112 25 c. Match scene (West Germany versus Colombia) (vert) 10 10
3113 50 c. West German players and referee 10 10
3114 1 cor. West German players forming wall (vert) 25 10
3115 1 cor. 50 Diego Maradona (Argentina) (vert) 35 15
3116 3 cor. Argentinian players and Italian goalkeeper (vert) 70 30
3117 3 cor. 50 Italian players 80 30

478 "Prepona praeneste"

1991. Butterflies. Multicoloured.
3119 25 c. Type **478** 10 10
3120 25 c. "Anartia fatima" 10 10
3121 50 c. "Eryphanis aesacus" 10 10
3122 1 cor. "Heliconius melpomene" 25 10
3123 1 cor. 50 "Chlosyne janais" 35 15
3124 3 cor. "Marpesia iole" 70 30
3125 3 cor. 50 Rusty-tipped page 80 30

479 Dove and Cross

1991. 700th Anniv of Swiss Confederation.
3127 **479** 2 cor. 25 red, black and yellow 50 20

480 Yellow-headed Amazon

1991. "Rainforest is Life". Fauna. Multicoloured.
3128 2 cor. 25 Type **480** 50 20
3129 2 cor. 25 Keel-billed toucan 50 20
3130 2 cor. 25 Scarlet macaw 50 20
3131 2 cor. 25 Resplendent quetzal 50 20
3132 2 cor. 25 Black-handed spider monkey 50 20
3133 2 cor. 25 White-throated capuchin 50 20
3134 2 cor. 25 Three-toed sloth 50 20
3135 2 cor. 25 Chestnut-headed oropendola 50 20
3136 2 cor. 25 Violet sabrewing 50 20
3137 2 cor. 25 Tamandua 50 20
3138 2 cor. 25 Jaguarundi 50 20
3139 2 cor. 25 Boa constrictor 50 20
3140 2 cor. 25 Common iguana 50 20
3141 2 cor. 25 Jaguar 50 20
3142 2 cor. 25 White-necked jacobin 50 20
3143 2 cor. 25 "Doxocopa clothilda" (butterfly) 50 20
3144 2 cor. 25 "Dismorphia deione" (butterfly) 50 20
3145 2 cor. 25 Golden arrow-poison frog 50 20
3146 2 cor. 25 "Callithomia hezia" (butterfly) 50 20
3147 2 cor. 25 Chameleon 50 20
Nos. 3128/47 were issued together, se-tenant, forming a composite design.

481 "Isochilus major"

1991. Orchids. Multicoloured.
3148 25 c. Type **481** 10 10
3149 25 c. "Cycnoches ventricosum" 10 10
3150 50 c. "Vanilla odorata" 10 10
3151 1 cor. "Helleriella nicaraguensis" 25 10
3152 1 cor. 50 "Barkeria spectabilis" 35 15
3153 3 cor. "Maxillaria hedwigae" 70 30
3154 3 cor. 50 "Cattleya aurantiaca" 80 30

482 Concepcion Volcano

1991. America (1990).
3156 **482** 2 cor. 25 multicoloured 50 20

483 Warehouse and Flags

1991. 30th Anniv of Central American Bank of Economic Integration.
3157 **483** 1 cor. 50 multicoloured 35 15

484 "The One-eyed Man"

1991. Death Centenary (1990) of Vincent van Gogh (painter). Multicoloured.
3158 25 c. Type **484** 10 10
3159 25 c. "Head of Countrywoman with Bonnet" 10 10
3160 50 c. "Self-portrait" 10 10
3161 1 cor. "Vase with Carnations and other Flowers" 25 10
3162 1 cor. 50 "Vase with Zinnias and Geraniums" 35 15
3163 3 cor. "Portrait of Tanguy Father" 70 30
3164 3 cor. 50 "Portrait of a Man" (horiz) 80 30

485 Painting by Rafaela Herrera (1st-prize winner)

1991. National Children's Painting Competition.
3166 **485** 2 cor. 25 multicoloured 50 20

486 Golden Pavilion

1991. "Phila Nippon '91" International Stamp Exhibition, Tokyo. Multicoloured.
3167 25 c. Type **486** 10 10
3168 50 c. Himaji Castle 10 10
3169 1 cor. Head of Bunraku doll 25 10
3170 1 cor. 50 Japanese cranes 35 15
3171 2 cor. 50 Phoenix pavilion 60 25
3172 3 cor. "The Guardian" (statue) 70 30
3173 3 cor. 50 Kabuki actor 80 30

487 Turquoise-browed Motmot

488 Columbus's Fleet

1992. Birds. Multicoloured.
3175 50 c. Type **487** 15 10
3176 75 c. Collared trogon 20 10
3177 1 cor. Broad-billed motmot 25 10
3178 1 cor. 50 Wire-tailed manakin 40 15
3179 1 cor. 75 Paradise tanager (horiz) 45 20
3180 2 cor. 25 Resplendent quetzal 60 25
3181 2 cor. 25 Black-spotted bare-eye 60 25

1992. America (1991). Voyages of Discovery.
3183 **488** 2 cor. 25 multicoloured 35 15

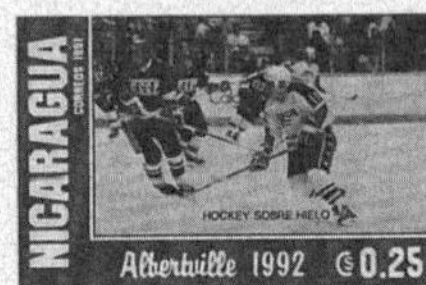

489 Ice Hockey

1992. Winter Olympic Games, Albertville (2nd issue). Multicoloured.
3184 25 c. Type **489** 10 10
3185 25 c. Four-man bobsleighing 10 10
3186 50 c. Skiing (vert) 15 10
3187 1 cor. Speed skating 25 10
3188 1 cor. 50 Cross-country skiing 40 15
3189 3 cor. Double luge 75 30
3190 3 cor. 50 Ski jumping (vert) 90 35

490 Fencing

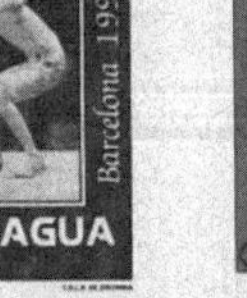

491 Ceramic Vase with Face (Lorenza Pineda Co-operative)

1992. Olympic Games, Barcelona (2nd issue) Multicoloured.
3192 25 c. Type **490** 10 10
3193 25 c. Throwing the javelin (horiz) 10 10
3194 50 c. Basketball 15 10
3195 1 cor. 50 Running 40 15
3196 2 cor. Long jumping 50 20
3197 3 cor. Running 75 30
3198 3 cor. 50 Show jumping 90 35

1992. Contemporary Arts and Crafts. Multicoloured.

3200 25 c. Type **491** 10 10
3201 25 c. Ceramic spouted vessel (Jose Oritz) (horiz) 10 10
3202 50 c. Blue-patterned ceramic vase (Elio Gutierrez) 15 10
3203 1 cor. "Christ" (Jose de los Santos) 25 10
3204 1 cor. 50 "Family" (sculpture, Erasmo Moya) 40 15
3205 3 cor. "Bird-fish" (Silvio Chavarria Co-operative) (horiz) 75 30
3206 3 cor. 50 Filigree ceramic vessel (Maria de los Angeles Bermudez) 90 35

492 "Picnic Table with Three Objects" (Alejandro Arostegui)
493 Magnificent Hummingbird

1992. Contemporary Paintings. Multicoloured.

3208 25 c. Type **492** 10 10
3209 25 c. "Prophetess of the New World" (Alberto Ycaza) 10 10
3210 50 c. "Flames of Unknown Origin" (Bernard Dreyfus) (horiz) 15 10
3211 1 cor. 50 "Owl" (Orlando Sobalvarro) (horiz) 40 15
3212 2 cor. "Pegasus at Liberty" (Hugo Palma) (horiz) 50 20
3213 3 cor. "Avocados" (Omar d'Leon) (horiz) 75 30
3214 3 cor. 50 "Gueguense" (Carlos Montenegro) 90 35

1992. 2nd U.N. Conference on Environment and Development, Rio de Janeiro. Tropical Forest Wildlife. Multicoloured.

3216 1 cor. 50 Type **493** 40 15
3217 1 cor. 50 Harpy eagle ("Aguila arpia") 40 15
3218 1 cor. 50 Orchid 40 15
3219 1 cor. 50 Toucan and morpho butterfly 40 15
3220 1 cor. 50 Quetzal 40 15
3221 1 cor. 50 Guardabarranco 40 15
3222 1 cor. 50 Howler monkey ("Mono aullador") 40 15
3223 1 cor. 50 Sloth ("Perezoso") 40 15
3224 1 cor. 50 Squirrel monkey ("Mono ardilla") 40 15
3225 1 cor. 50 Macaw ("Guacamaya") 40 15
3226 1 cor. 50 Emerald boa and scarlet tanager 40 15
3227 1 cor. 50 Poison-arrow frog 40 15
3228 1 cor. 50 Jaguar 40 15
3229 1 cor. 50 Anteater 40 15
3230 1 cor. 50 Ocelot 40 15
3231 1 cor. 50 Coati 40 15

Nos. 3216/31 were issued together, se-tenant, forming a composite design of a forest.

494 Fabretto with Children

1992. Father Fabretto, "Benefactor of Nicaraguan Children".

3232 **494** 2 cor. 25 multicoloured 60 25

495 "Nicaraguan Identity" (Claudia Gordillo)

1992. Winning Entry in Photography Competition.

3233 **495** 2 cor. 25 multicoloured 60 25

496 "The Indians of Nicaragua" (Milton Jose Cruz)

1992. Winning Entry in Children's Painting Competition.

3234 **496** 2 cor. 25 multicoloured 60 25

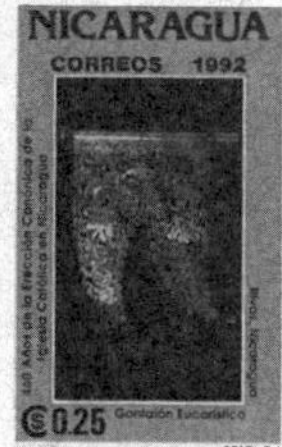

497 Eucharistical Banner
498 Rivas Cross, 1523

1993. 460th Anniv of Catholic Church in Nicaragua. Multicoloured.

3235 25 c. Type **497** 10 10
3236 50 c. "Shrine of the Immaculate Conception" 10 10
3237 1 cor. 18th-century document 20 10
3238 1 cor. 50 16th-century baptismal font 30 10
3239 2 cor. "The Immaculate Conception" 40 15
3240 2 cor. 25 Monsignor Diego Alvarez Osorio (1st Bishop of Leon) 50 20
3241 3 cor. "Christ on the Cross" 65 25

1993. America (1992). 500th Anniv of Discovery of America by Columbus.

3242 **498** 2 cor. 25 multicoloured 50 20

499 Cathedral

1993. Inauguration of Cathedral of the Immaculate Conception of Mary, Managua. Multicoloured.

3243 3 cor. Type **499** 65 25
3244 4 cor. Cross, Virgin Mary and map of Nicaragua (2nd Provincial Council) 85 35

Nos. 3243/4 were issued together, se-tenant, forming a composite design.

500 Emblem and Voters queueing outside Poll Station

1993. 23rd General Assembly of Organization of American States.

3245 **500** 3 cor. multicoloured 85 45

501 Anniversary Emblem

1993. 90th Anniv of Panamerican Health Organization.

3246 **501** 3 cor. multicoloured 85 45

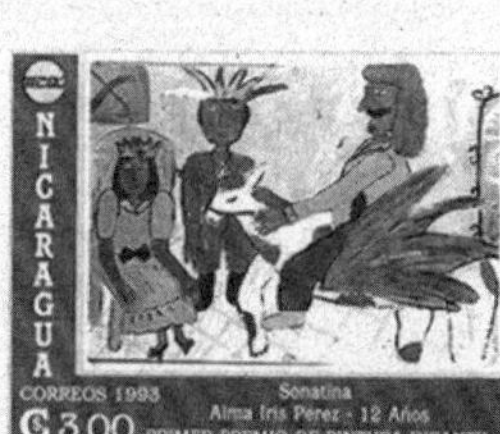

502 "Sonatina" (Alma Iris Perez)

1993. Winning Entry in Children's Painting Competition.

3247 **502** 3 cor. multicoloured 85 45

503 Red-striped Butterfly Fish ("Chaetodon lunula")

993. Butterfly Fishes. Multicoloured.

3248 1 cor. 50 Type **503** 35 20
3249 1 cor. 50 "Chaetodon rainfordi" 35 20
3250 1 cor. 50 Reticulated butterfly fish ("Chaetodon reticulatus") 35 20
3251 1 cor. 50 Threadfin butterfly fish ("Chaetodon auriga") 35 20
3252 1 cor. 50 Pennant coral fish ("Heniochus acuminatus") 35 30
3253 1 cor. 50 "Coradion fulvocinctus" 35 20
3254 1 cor. 50 "Chaetodon speculum" 35 20
3255 1 cor. 50 "Chaetodon lineolatus" 35 20
3256 1 cor. 50 Archer butterfly fish ("Chaetodon bennetti") 35 20
3257 1 cor. 50 Black-backed butterfly fish ("Chaetodon melanotus") 35 20
3258 1 cor. 50 "Chaetodon aureus" 35 20
3259 1 cor. 50 Saddleback butterfly fish ("Chaetodon ephippium") 35 20
3260 1 cor. 50 "Hemitaurichthys polylepis" 35 20
3261 1 cor. 50 "Chaetodon semeion" 35 20
3262 1 cor. 50 White-spotted butterfly fish ("Chaetodon kleinii") 35 20
3263 1 cor. 50 "Chelmon rostratus" 35 20

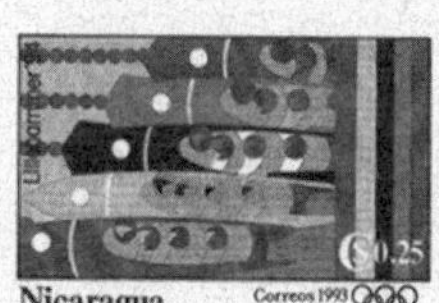

504 Four-man Bobsleighing

1993. Multicoloured. (a) Winter Olympic Games, Lillehammer, Norway (1994).

3264 25 c. Type **504** 10 10
3265 25 c. Skiing 10 10
3266 50 c. Speed skating 15 10
3267 1 cor. 50 Ski jumping 45 20
3268 2 cor. Women's figure skating 55 25
3269 3 cor. Pairs' figure skating 85 45
3270 3 cor. 50 Shooting (biathlon) 1·00 45

(b) Olympic Games, Atlanta (1996).

3271 25 c. Swimming 10 10
3272 25 c. Diving 10 10
3273 50 c. Long distance running 15 10
3274 1 cor. Hurdling 30 15
3275 1 cor. 50 Gymnastics 45 20
3276 3 cor. Throwing the javelin 85 45
3277 3 cor. 50 Sprinting 1·00 50

505 "Bromeliaceae sp."
506 Tomas Brolin (Sweden)

1994. Tropical Forest Flora and Fauna. Multicoloured.

3279 2 cor. Type **505** 50 25
3280 2 cor. Dupont's hummingbird ("Tilmatura dupontii") 50 25
3281 2 cor. "Anolis biporcatus" (lizard) 50 25
3282 2 cor. Lantern fly ("Fulgara laternaria") 50 25
3283 2 cor. Sloth ("Bradypus sp.") 50 25
3284 2 cor. Ornate hawk eagle ("Spizaetus ornatus") 50 25
3285 2 cor. Lovely cotinga ("Cotinga amabilis") 50 25
3286 2 cor. Schegel's lance-head snake ("Bothrops schlegelii") 50 25
3287 2 cor. "Odontoglossum sp." (orchid) and bee 50 25
3288 2 cor. Red-eyed tree frog ("Agalychnis callidryas") 50 25
3289 2 cor. "Heliconius sapho" (butterfly) 50 25
3290 2 cor. Passion flower ("Passiflora vitifolia") 50 25

Nos. 3279/90 were issued together, se-tenant, forming a composite design.

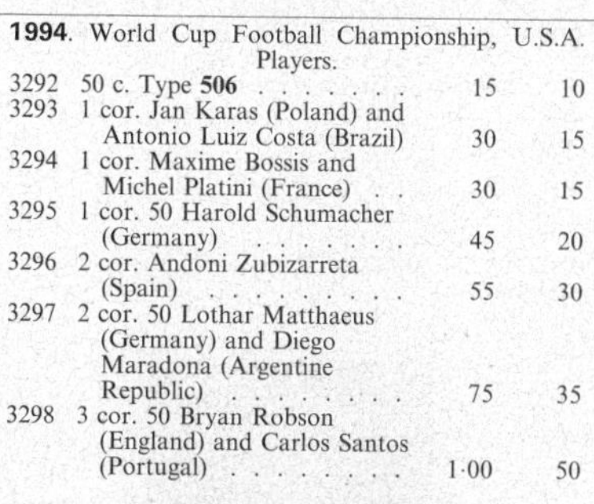

1994. World Cup Football Championship, U.S.A. Players.

3292 50 c. Type **506** 15 10
3293 1 cor. Jan Karas (Poland) and Antonio Luiz Costa (Brazil) 30 15
3294 1 cor. Maxime Bossis and Michel Platini (France) 30 15
3295 1 cor. 50 Harold Schumacher (Germany) 45 20
3296 2 cor. Andoni Zubizarreta (Spain) 55 30
3297 2 cor. 50 Lothar Matthaeus (Germany) and Diego Maradona (Argentine Republic) 75 35
3298 3 cor. 50 Bryan Robson (England) and Carlos Santos (Portugal) 1·00 50

507 "Four in One" (Julio Lopez)

1994. Contemporary Arts. Multicoloured.

3300 50 c. Rush mat (Rosalia Sevilla) (horiz) 15 10
3301 50 c. Type **507** 15 10
3302 1 cor. Ceramic church (Auxiliadora Bush) 30 15
3303 1 cor. Statuette of old woman (Indiana Robleto) 30 15
3304 2 cor. 50 "Santiago" (Jose de los Santos) 55 30
3305 3 cor. "Gueguense" (Ines Gutierrez de Chong) 85 45
3306 4 cor. Ceramic hornet's nest (Elio Gutierrez) 95 45

508 "Callicore patelina"

1994. "Hong Kong '94" International Stamp Exhibition. Butterflies. Multicoloured.

3308 1 cor. 50 Type **508** 35 15
3309 1 cor. 50 "Chlosyne narva" 35 15
3310 1 cor. 50 Giant brimstone ("Anteos maerula") 35 15
3311 1 cor. 50 Diadem ("Marpesia petreus") 35 15
3312 1 cor. 50 "Pierella helvetia" 35 15
3313 1 cor. 50 "Eurytides epidaus" 35 15
3314 1 cor. 50 Doris ("Heliconius doris") 35 15
3315 1 cor. 50 "Smyrna blomfildia" 35 15
3316 1 cor. 50 "Eueides lybia olympia" 35 15
3317 1 cor. 50 "Adelpha heraclea" 35 15
3318 1 cor. 50 "Heliconius hecale zuleika" 35 15
3319 1 cor. 50 "Parides montezuma" 35 15
3320 1 cor. 50 "Morpho polyphemus" 35 15
3321 1 cor. 50 "Eresia alsina" 35 15
3322 1 cor. 50 "Prepona omphale octavia" 35 15
3323 1 cor. 50 "Morpho grenadensis" 35 15

509 "The Holy Family" (anonymous)

1994. Christmas (1993). Paintings. Multicoloured.

3324 1 cor. Type **509** 25 15
3325 4 cor. "Nativity" (Lezamon) 95 45

510 Sculpture

1994. Chontal Culture Statuary. Multicoloured, colour of frame given.

3326	**510**	50 c. yellow	15	10
3327	–	50 c. yellow	15	10
3328	–	1 cor. emerald	30	15
3329	–	1 cor. green	30	15
3330	–	2 cor. 50 blue	55	35
3331	–	3 cor. blue	85	45
3332	–	4 cor. green	95	45

DESIGNS: 50 c. (3327) to 4 cor. Different sculptures.

511 "Virgin of Nicaragua" (Celia Lacayo)

1994. Contemporary Paintings. Multicoloured.

3334	50 c. Type **511**	15	10
3335	50 c. "Woman embroidering" (Guillermo Rivas Navas)	15	10
3336	1 cor. "Couple dancing" (June Beer)	30	15
3337	1 cor. "Song of Peace" (Alejandro Canales)	30	15
3338	2 cor. 50 "Sapodilla Plums" (Genaro Lugo) (horiz)	55	30
3339	3 cor. "Figure and Fragments" (Leonel Vanegas)	85	45
3340	4 cor. "Eruption of Agua Volcano" (Asilia Guillen) (horiz)	95	45

512 Nicolas Copernicus and Satellite

1994. Astronomers. Mutlicoloured.

3342	1 cor. 50 Type **512**	35	15
3343	1 cor. 50 Tycho Brahe and astronomers	35	15
3344	1 cor. 50 Galileo Galilei and "Galileo" space probe	35	15
3345	1 cor. 50 Sir Isaac Newton and telescope	35	15
3346	1 cor. 50 Edmond Halley, space probe and Halley's Comet	35	15
3347	1 cor. 50 James Bradley and Greenwich Observatory	35	15
3348	1 cor. 50 William Herschel and telescope	35	15
3349	1 cor. 50 John Goodricke and Algol (star)	35	15
3350	1 cor. 50 Karl Friedrich Gauss and Gottingen Observatory	35	15
3351	1 cor. 50 Friedrich Bessel and 1838 star telescope	35	15
3352	1 cor. 50 William Granch and Harvard College Observatory	35	15
3353	1 cor. 50 Sir George Airy and stellar disk	35	15
3354	1 cor. 50 Percival Lowell and Flagstaff Observatory, Arizona, U.S.A.	35	15
3355	1 cor. 50 George Halle and solar spectroscope	35	15
3356	1 cor. 50 Edwin Hubble and Hubble telescope	35	15
3357	1 cor. 50 Gerard Kuiper and Miranda (Uranus moon)	35	15

Nos. 3342/57 were issued together, se-tenant, forming a composite design.

513 1886 Benz Tricycle

1994. Automobiles. Multicoloured.

3359	1 cor. 50 Type **513**	35	15
3360	1 cor. 50 1909 Benz Blitzen	35	15
3361	1 cor. 50 1923 Mercedes Benz 24/100/140	35	15
3362	1 cor. 50 1928 Mercedes Benz SSK	35	15
3363	1 cor. 50 1934 Mercedes Benz 500K Cabriolet	35	15
3364	1 cor. 50 1949 Mercedes Benz 170S	35	15
3365	1 cor. 50 1954 Mercedes Benz W196	35	15
3366	1 cor. 50 1954 Mercedes Benz 300SL	35	15
3367	1 cor. 50 1896 Ford Quadricycle	35	15
3368	1 cor. 50 1920 Ford taxi cab	35	15
3369	1 cor. 50 1928 Ford Roadster	35	15
3370	1 cor. 50 1932 Ford V-8	35	15
3371	1 cor. 50 1937 Ford V-8 78	35	15
3372	1 cor. 50 1939 Ford 91 Deluxe Tudor Sedan	35	15
3373	1 cor. 50 1946 Ford V-8 Sedan Coupe	35	15
3374	1 cor. 50 1958 Ford Custom 300	35	15

514 Hugo Eckener and Count Ferdinand von Zeppelin

1994. Zeppelin Airships. Multicoloured.

3376	1 cor. 50 Type **514**	35	15
3377	1 cor. 50 "Graf Zeppelin" over New York, 1928	35	15
3378	1 cor. 50 "Graf Zeppelin" over Tokyo, 1929	35	15
3379	1 cor. 50 "Graf Zeppelin" over house of Randolph Hearst's villa, 1929	35	15
3380	1 cor. 50 Charles Lindbergh, Hugo Eckener and "Graf Zeppelin" at Lakehurst, 1929	35	15
3381	1 cor. 50 "Graf Zeppelin" over St. Basil's Cathedral, Moscow (wrongly inscr "Santra Sofia")	35	15
3382	1 cor. 50 "Graf Zeppelin" over Paris, 1930	35	15
3383	1 cor. 50 "Graf Zeppelin" over Cairo, Egypt, 1931	35	15
3384	1 cor. 50 "Graf Zeppelin" over Arctic Sea	35	15
3385	1 cor. 50 "Graf Zeppelin" over Rio de Janeiro, 1932	35	15
3386	1 cor. 50 "Graf Zeppelin" over St. Paul's Cathedral, London, 1935	35	15
3387	1 cor. 50 "Graf Zeppelin" over St. Peter's Cathedral, Rome	35	15
3388	1 cor. 50 "Graf Zeppelin" over Swiss Alps	35	15
3389	1 cor. 50 "Graf Zeppelin over Brandenburg Gate, Berlin	35	15
3390	1 cor. 50 Hugo Eckener piloting "Graf Zeppelin"	35	15
3391	1 cor. 50 Captain Ernest Lehman, "Graf Zeppelin" and Dornier Do-X flying boat	35	15

515 Gabriel Horvilleur

1994. Nicaraguan Philatelists. Multicoloured.

3393	1 cor. Type **515**	15	10
3394	3 cor. Jose Cauadra	85	45
3395	4 cor. Alfredo Pertz	95	45

517 "Poponjoche" (Thelma Gomez)

518 Conference Emblem

1994. 1st Nicaraguan Tree Conference.

3397	**517**	4 cor. multicoloured	95	45

1994. 2nd International Conference on New and Restored Democracies, Managua.

3398	**518**	3 cor. multicoloured	55	55

519 Pulpit, Leon Cathedral

520 Mascot and Emblem

1994. Religious Art. Multicoloured.

3399	50 c. Type **519**	15	10
3400	50 c. "St. Anna" (porcelain figure), Chinandega Church	15	10
3401	1 cor. "St. Joseph and Child" (porcelain figure), St. Peter's Church, Rivas	30	15
3402	1 cor. "St. James", Jinotepe Church	30	15
3403	2 cor. 50 Gold chalice, Subtiava Temple, Leon	55	30
3404	3 cor. Processional cross, Niquinohomo Church, Masaya	85	45
3405	4 cor. "Lord of Miracles" (crucifix), Lord of Miracles Temple, Managua	95	45

1994. 32nd World Amateur Baseball Championship.

3407	**520**	4 cor. multicoloured	1·00	1·00

SILVER CURRENCY

The following were for use in all places on the Atlantic coast of Nicaragua where the silver currency was in use. This currency was worth about 50 c. to the peso. Earlier issues (overprints on Nicaraguan stamps) were also issued for Zelaya. These are listed in the Stanley Gibbons Part 15 (Central America) Catalogue.

Z 1

1912.

Z 1	**Z 1**	1 c. green	1·25	65
Z 2		2 c. red	85	40
Z 3		3 c. brown	1·25	60
Z 4		4 c. lake	1·25	50
Z 5		5 c. blue	1·25	50
Z 6		6 c. red	6·75	3·50
Z 7		10 c. grey	1·25	50
Z 8		15 c. lilac	1·25	90
Z 9		20 c. blue	1·25	90
Z10		25 c. black and green	1·60	1·25
Z11		35 c. black and brown	2·25	1·40
Z12		50 c. green	2·25	1·40
Z13		1 p. orange	3·50	2·25
Z14		2 p. brown	6·75	4·25
Z15		5 p. green	13·50	8·75

OFFICIAL STAMPS

Overprinted **FRANQUEO OFICIAL**.

1890. Stamps of 1890.

O37	**6**	1 c. blue	15	35
O38		2 c. blue	15	35
O39		5 c. blue	15	40
O40		10 c. blue	15	45
O41		20 c. blue	15	55
O42		50 c. blue	15	75
O43		1 p. blue	20	1·10
O44		2 p. blue	20	1·60
O45		5 p. blue	20	3·50
O46		10 p. blue	20	6·75

1891. Stamps of 1891.

O47	**7**	1 c. green	15	40
O48		2 c. green	15	40
O49		5 c. green	15	40
O50		10 c. green	15	40
O51		20 c. green	15	70
O52		50 c. green	15	75
O53		1 p. green	15	90
O54		2 p. green	15	90
O55		5 p. green	15	2·25
O56		10 p. green	15	3·50

1892. Stamps of 1892.

O57	**8**	1 c. brown	15	30
O58		2 c. brown	15	30
O59		5 c. brown	15	30
O60		10 c. brown	15	30
O61		20 c. brown	15	50
O62		50 c. brown	15	70
O63		1 p. brown	15	1·10
O64		2 p. brown	15	1·75
O65		5 p. brown	15	2·75
O66		10 p. brown	15	3·50

1893. Stamps of 1893.

O67	**9**	1 c. black	15	30
O68		2 c. black	15	30
O69		5 c. black	15	30
O70		10 c. black	15	30
O71		20 c. black	15	50
O72		25 c. black	15	65
O73		50 c. black	15	70
O74		1 p. black	15	1·00
O75		2 p. black	15	1·25
O76		5 p. black	15	2·75
O77		10 p. black	15	3·50

1894. Stamps of 1894.

O78	**10**	1 c. orange	15	30
O79		2 c. orange	15	30
O80		5 c. orange	15	30
O81		10 c. orange	15	30
O82		20 c. orange	15	30
O83		50 c. orange	15	45
O84		1 p. orange	15	1·00
O85		2 p. orange	15	1·75
O86		5 p. orange	15	3·50
O87		10 p. orange	15	4·50

1895. Stamps of 1895.

O88	**11**	1 c. green	15	30
O89		2 c. green	15	30
O90		5 c. green	15	30
O91		10 c. green	15	30
O92		20 c. green	15	50
O93		50 c. green	15	80
O94		1 p. green	15	80
O95		2 p. green	15	1·25
O96		5 p. green	15	1·90
O97		10 p. green	15	2·40

1896. Stamps of 1896, dated "1896", optd **FRANQUEO OFICIAL** in oval frame.

O 99	**12**	1 c. red	1·50	1·90
O100		2 c. red	1·50	1·90
O101		5 c. red	1·50	1·90
O102		10 c. red	1·50	1·90
O103		20 c. red	1·90	1·90
O104		50 c. red	3·00	3·00
O105		1 p. red	7·25	7·25
O106		2 p. red	7·25	7·25
O107		5 p. red	9·50	9·50

1896. Nos. D99/103 handstamped **Franqueo Oficial**.
O108 **D 13** 1 c. orange — 4·25
O109 2 c. orange — 4·25
O110 5 c. orange — 3·00
O111 10 c. orange — 3·00
O112 20 c. orange — 3·00

1897. Stamps of 1897, dated "1897", optd **FRANQUEO OFICIAL** in oval frame.
O113 **12** 1 c. red 2·00 2·00
O114 2 c. red 2·00 2·00
O115 5 c. red 2·00 2·00
O116 10 c. red 1·90 2·10
O117 20 c. red 1·90 2·40
O118 50 c. red 3·00 3·00
O119 1 p. red 8·25 8·25
O120 2 p. red 9·75 9·75
O121 5 p. red 15·00 15·00

1898. Stamps of 1898 optd **FRANQUEO OFICIAL** in oval frame.
O124 **13** 1 c. red 2·00 2·00
O125 2 c. red 2·00 2·00
O126 4 c. red 2·00 2·00
O127 5 c. red 1·50 1·50
O128 10 c. red 2·40 2·40
O129 15 c. red 3·75 3·75
O130 20 c. red 3·75 3·75
O131 50 c. red 5·00 5·00
O132 1 p. red 6·50 6·50
O133 2 p. red 6·50 6·50
O134 5 p. red 6·50 6·50

1899. Stamps of 1899 optd **FRANQUEO OFICIAL** in scroll.
O137 **14** 1 c. green 15 60
O138 2 c. brown 15 60
O139 4 c. red 15 60
O140 5 c. blue 15 40
O141 10 c. orange 15 60
O142 15 c. brown 15 1·25
O143 20 c. green 15 2·00
O144 50 c. red 15 2·00
O145 1 p. orange 15 6·00
O146 2 p. violet 15 6·00
O147 5 p. blue 15 9·00

O 16

O 38

1900.
O148 **O 16** 1 c. purple 45 45
O149 2 c. orange 35 35
O150 4 c. olive 45 45
O151 5 c. blue 90 30
O152 10 c. violet 90 25
O153 20 c. brown 65 25
O154 50 c. lake 90 35
O155 1 p. blue 2·10 1·50
O156 2 p. orange 2·40 2·40
O157 5 p. black 3·00 3·00

1903. Stamps of 1900 surch **OFICIAL** and value, with or without ornaments.
O197 **15** 1 c. on 10 c. mauve 75 1·00
O198 2 c. on 3 c. green 1·00 1·25
O199 4 c. on 3 c. green 3·75 3·75
O200 4 c. on 10 c. mauve 3·75 3·75
O201 5 c. on 3 c. green 45 50

1903. Surch.
O202 **O 16** 10 c. on 20 c. brown 15 15
O203 30 c. on 20 c. brown 15 15
O204 50 c. on 20 c. brown 35 25

1905.
O219 **O 38** 1 c. green 20 20
O220 2 c. red 20 20
O221 5 c. blue 20 20
O222 10 c. brown 20 20
O223 20 c. orange 20 20
O224 50 c. olive 20 20
O225 1 p. lake 20 20
O226 2 p. violet 20 20
O227 5 p. black 20 20

1907. Surch thus: **Vale 10 c.**
O239 **O 38** 10 c. on 1 c. green 55 55
O241 10 c. on 2 c. red 15·00 11·50
O243 20 c. on 2 c. red 13·50 9·00
O245 50 c. on 1 c. green 1·10 1·10
O247 50 c. on 2 c. red 13·50 6·50

1907. Surch thus: **Vale 20 cts** or **Vale $1.00.**
O249 **O 38** 20 c. on 1 c. green 70 70
O250 $1 on 2 c. red 1·10 1·10
O251 $2 on 2 c. red 1·10 1·10
O252 $3 on 2 c. red 1·10 1·10
O253 $4 on 5 c. blue 1·40 1·40

1907. No. 206 surch **OFICIAL** and value.
O256 **49** 10 c. on 1 c. green 9·00 7·75
O257 15 c. on 1 c. green 9·00 7·75
O258 20 c. on 1 c. green 9·00 7·75
O259 50 c. on 1 c. green 9·00 7·75
O260 1 p. on 1 c. green 8·25 7·75
O261 2 p. on 1 c. green 8·25 7·75

1907. Fiscal stamps as T **50** surch thus: **10 cts. CORREOS 1907 OFICIAL 10 cts.**
O262 **50** 10 c. on 2 c. orange 10 10
O263 35 c. on 1 c. blue 10 10
O264 70 c. on 1 c. blue 10 10
O266 1 p. on 2 c. orange 10 15
O267 2 p. on 2 c. orange 10 15
O268 3 p. on 5 c. brown 10 15
O269 4 p. on 5 c. brown 15 15
O270 5 p. on 5 c. brown 15 15

1908. Stamp of 1905 surch **OFICIAL VALE** and value.
O271 **37** 10 c. on 3 c. violet 9·00 7·75
O272 15 c. on 3 c. violet 9·00 7·75
O273 20 c. on 3 c. violet 9·00 7·75
O274 35 c. on 3 c. violet 9·00 7·75
O275 50 c. on 3 c. violet 9·00 7·75

1908. Fiscal stamps as T **50** surch as last but dated 1908.
O276 **50** 10 c. on 1 c. blue 55 35
O277 10 c. on 2 c. orange 75 30
O278 35 c. on 1 c. blue 55 35
O279 35 c. on 2 c. orange 80 45
O280 50 c. on 1 c. blue 55 35
O281 50 c. on 2 c. orange 80 45
O282 70 c. on 2 c. orange 80 45
O283 1 p. on 1 c. blue 23·00 23·00
O284 1 p. on 2 c. orange 80 45
O285 2 p. on 1 c. blue 65 55
O286 2 p. on 2 c. orange 80 45

1909. Stamps of 1905 optd **OFICIAL**.
O290 **37** 10 c. lake 15 15
O291 15 c. black 45 35
O292 20 c. olive 70 55
O293 50 c. green 1·10 70
O294 1 p. yellow 1·25 90
O295 2 p. red 1·75 1·40

1911. Stamps of 1905 optd **OFICIAL** and surch **Vale** and value.
O296 **37** 5 c. on 3 c. orange 3·75 3·75
O297 10 c. on 4 c. violet 3·00 3·00

1911. Railway coupon stamp surch **Timbre Fiscal Vale 10 ctvs** further surch **Correo oficial Vale** and new value. Printed in red.
O334 **64** 10 c. on 10 c. on 1 c. 3·00 3·00
O335 15 c. on 10 c. on 1 c. 3·00 3·00
O336 20 c. on 10 c. on 1 c. 3·00 3·00
O337 50 c. on 10 c. on 1 c. 4·00 4·00
O338 $1 on 10 c. on 1 c. 4·75 7·25
O339 $2 on 10 c. on 1 c. 6·50 10·00

1911. Railway coupon stamps surch **TIMBRE FISCAL VALE 10 ctvs.** further surch **CORREO OFICIAL** and new value. Printed in red.
O340 **64** 10 c. on 10 c. on 1 c. 22·00 17·00
O341 15 c. on 10 c. on 1 c. 22·00 17·00
O342 20 c. on 10 c. on 1 c. 22·00 18·00
O343 50 c. on 10 c. on 1 c. 18·00 15·00

1911. Railway stamp with value of postal surch on back cancelled with thick bar, surch on front **Correo Oficial Vale 1911** and new value. Printed in red.
O344 **64** 5 c. on 10 c. on 1 c. 3·75 4·50
O345 10 c. on 10 c. on 1 c. 4·25 5·25
O346 15 c. on 10 c. on 1 c. 5·00 5·75
O347 20 c. on 10 c. on 1 c. 5·50 8·50
O348 50 c. on 10 c. on 1 c. 6·25 7·50

1912. Railway stamp with whole surch on back cancelled with thick bar, surch on front **Correo Oficial 1912** and new value. Printed in red.
O349 **64** 5 c. on 10 c. on 1 c. 5·50 4·75
O350 10 c. on 10 c. on 1 c. 5·50 4·75
O351 15 c. on 10 c. on 1 c. 5·50 4·75
O352 20 c. on 10 c. on 1 c. 5·50 4·75
O353 25 c. on 10 c. on 1 c. 5·50 4·75
O354 50 c. on 10 c. on 1 c. 5·50 4·75
O355 $1 on 10 c. on 1 c. 5·50 4·75

1913. Stamps of 1912 optd **OFICIAL**.
O356 **70** 1 c. blue 10 10
O357 2 c. blue 10 10
O358 3 c. blue 10 10
O359 4 c. blue 10 10
O360 5 c. blue 10 10
O361 6 c. blue 10 15
O362 10 c. blue 10 15
O363 15 c. blue 10 15
O364 20 c. blue 15 20
O365 25 c. blue 15 15
O366 **71** 35 c. blue 20 20
O367 **70** 50 c. blue 1·10 1·10
O368 1 p. blue 25 25
O369 2 p. blue 25 25
O370 5 p. blue 35 35

1915. Optd **OFICIAL**.
O406 **79** 1 c. blue 15 15
O407 **80** 2 c. blue 15 15
O408 **79** 3 c. blue 15 15
O409 **80** 4 c. blue 15 15
O410 **79** 5 c. blue 15 15
O411 **80** 6 c. blue 15 15
O412 10 c. blue 15 15
O413 **79** 15 c. blue 15 15
O414 **80** 20 c. blue 15 15
O415 **79** 25 c. blue 25 25
O416 **80** 50 c. blue 45 45

1925. Optd **Oficial** or **OFICIAL**.
O513 **79** ½ c. green 10 10
O514 1 c. violet 10 10
O515 **80** 2 c. red 10 10
O516 **79** 3 c. olive 10 10
O517 **80** 4 c. red 10 10
O518 **79** 5 c. black 10 10
O519 **80** 6 c. brown 10 10
O520 10 c. yellow 10 10
O521 **79** 15 c. brown 10 10
O522 **80** 20 c. brown 10 10
O523 **79** 25 c. orange 40 40
O524 **80** 50 c. blue 45 45

1929. Air. Official stamps of 1925 additionally optd **Correo Aereo**.
O618 **79** 25 c. orange 35 35
O619 **80** 50 c. blue 55 55

1931. Stamp of 1924 surch **OFICIAL C$ 0.05 Correos 1928**.
O651 **99** 5 c. on 10 c. brown 25 25

1931. No. 648 additionally surch **OFICIAL** and value.
O652 **99** 5 c. on 10 c. brown 25 25

1931. Stamps of 1914 optd 1931 (except 6 c., 10 c.), and also optd **OFICIAL**.
O670 **79** 1 c. olive (No. 762) 20 20
O707 **80** 2 c. red 6·50 6·50
O671 **79** 3 c. blue 20 20
O672 5 c. sepia 20 20
O673 **80** 6 c. brown 25 25
O675 10 c. brown 25 25
O674 10 c. blue (No. 697) 1·10 1·10
O710 **79** 15 c. orange 70 70
O711 25 c. sepia 70 70
O712 25 c. violet 1·75 1·75

1932. Air. Optd **Correo Aereo OFICIAL** only.
O688 **79** 15 c. orange 45 45
O689 **80** 20 c. orange 50 50
O690 **79** 25 c. violet 50 50
O691 **80** 50 c. green 60 60
O692 1 cor. yellow 60 60

1932. Air. Optd **1931. Correo Aereo OFICIAL.**
O693 **79** 25 c. sepia 25·00 25·00

1932. Optd **OFICIAL**.
O694 **79** 1 c. olive 10 10
O695 **80** 2 c. red 10 10
O696 **79** 3 c. blue 15 10
O697 **80** 4 c. blue 15 10
O698 **79** 5 c. sepia 15 15
O699 **80** 6 c. brown 20 10
O700 10 c. brown 30 25
O701 **79** 15 c. orange 40 25
O702 **80** 20 c. orange 40 30
O703 **79** 25 c. violet 1·25 50
O704 **80** 50 c. green 15 15
O705 1 cor. yellow 20 20

1933. 441st Anniv of Columbus's Departure from Palos. As T **133**, but inscr "CORREO OFICIAL". Roul.
O777 1 c. yellow 60 60
O778 2 c. yellow 60 60
O779 3 c. brown 60 60
O780 4 c. brown 60 60
O781 5 c. brown 60 60
O782 6 c. blue 75 75
O783 10 c. violet 75 75
O784 15 c. purple 75 75
O785 20 c. green 75 75
O786 25 c. green 1·75 1·75
O787 50 c. red 2·25 2·25
O788 1 cor. red 3·50 3·50

1933. Optd with T **134** and **OFICIAL**.
O814 **79** 1 c. green 10 10
O815 **80** 2 c. red 10 10
O816 **79** 3 c. blue 10 10
O817 **80** 4 c. blue 10 10
O818 **79** 5 c. brown 10 10
O819 **80** 6 c. grey 10 10
O820 10 c. brown 10 10
O821 **79** 15 c. red 15 15
O822 **80** 20 c. orange 15 15
O823 **79** 25 c. violet 15 15
O824 **80** 50 c. green 25 25
O825 1 cor. yellow 50 45

1933. Air. Optd with T **134** and **CORREO Aereo OFICIAL**.
O826 **79** 15 c. violet 20 20
O827 **80** 20 c. green 20 20
O828 **79** 25 c. olive 20 20
O829 **80** 50 c. green 35 35
O830 1 cor. red 60 50

1935. Nos. O814/25 optd **RESELLO-1935** in a box.
O864 **79** 1 c. green 10 10
O865 **80** 2 c. red 10 10
O866 **79** 3 c. blue 10 10
O867 **80** 4 c. blue 10 10
O868 **79** 5 c. brown 10 10
O869 **80** 6 c. grey 10 10
O870 10 c. brown 10 10
O871 **79** 15 c. red 15 15
O872 **80** 20 c. orange 15 15
O873 **79** 25 c. violet 15 15
O874 **80** 50 c. green 20 20
O875 1 cor. yellow 35 35

1935. Air. Nos. O826/30 optd **RESELLO-1935** in a box.
O877 **79** 15 c. violet 30 25
O878 **80** 20 c. green 30 25
O879 **79** 25 c. olive 30 30
O880 **80** 50 c. green 90 90
O881 1 cor. red 90 90

(O 141)

O 151 Islets in the Great Lake

1937. Nos. 913, etc., optd with Type O **141**.
O935 **79** 1 c. red 25 15
O936 **80** 2 c. blue 25 15
O937 **79** 3 c. brown 30 25
O938 5 c. red 35 30
O939 **80** 10 c. green 40 35
O940 **79** 15 c. green 50 40
O941 25 c. orange 60 45
O942 **80** 50 c. brown 85 50
O943 1 cor. blue 2·25 1·00

1937. Air. Nos. 926/30 optd with Type O **141**.
O944 **112** 15 c. orange 50 35
O945 20 c. red 50 35
O946 25 c. black 50 45
O947 50 c. violet 50 45
O948 1 cor. orange 50 45

1939.
O1020 **O 151** 2 c. red 15 15
O1021 3 c. blue 15 15
O1022 6 c. brown 15 15
O1023 7½ c. green 15 15
O1024 10 c. brown 15 15
O1025 15 c. orange 15 15
O1026 25 c. violet 30 30
O1027 50 c. green 45 45

O **152** Pres. Somoza

1939. Air.
O1028 **O 152** 10 c. brown 30 30
O1029 15 c. blue 30 30
O1030 20 c. yellow 30 30
O1031 25 c. violet 30 30
O1032 30 c. red 30 30
O1033 50 c. orange 40 40
O1034 1 cor. olive 75 75

O **175** Managua Airport

1947. Air.
O1120 **O 175** 5 c. brown & black 15 10
O1121 – 10 c. blue and black 15 15
O1122 – 15 c. violet & black 15 10
O1123 – 20 c. orange & black 20 10
O1124 – 25 c. blue & black 15 15
O1125 – 50 c. red & black 15 15
O1126 – 1 cor. grey & black 40 35
O1127 – 2 cor. 50 brown and black 75 90

DESIGNS: 10 c. Sulphur Lagoon, Nejapa; 15 c. Ruben Dario Monument, Managua; 20 c. Baird's tapir; 25 c. Genizaro Dam; 50 c. Thermal Baths, Tipitapa; 1 cor. Highway and Lake Managua; 2 cor. 50, Franklin D. Roosevelt Monument, Managua.

O **181** U.P.U. Offices, Berne

1950. Air. 75th Anniv of U.P.U. Inscr as in Type O **181**. Frames in black.
O1159 – 5 c. purple 10 10
O1160 – 10 c. green 10 10
O1161 – 25 c. purple 10 10
O1162 **O 181** 50 c. orange 15 10
O1163 – 1 cor. blue 35 30
O1164 – 2 cor. 60 black 2·10 1·75

DESIGNS—HORIZ: 5 c. Rowland Hill; 10 c. Heinrich von Stephan;. 25 c. Standehaus, Berne; 1 cor. Monument, Berne; 2 cor. 60, Congress Medal.

1961. Air. Consular Fiscal stamps as T **203/4** with serial Nos. in red, surch **Oficial Aereo** and value.
O1448 10 c. on 1 cor. olive 10 10
O1449 15 c. on 20 cor. brown 10 10
O1450 20 c. on 100 cor. lake 10 10
O1451 25 c. on 50 c. blue 15 10
O1452 35 c. on 50 cor. brown 15 15
O1453 50 c. on 3 cor. red 15 15
O1454 1 cor. on 2 cor. green 25 20
O1455 2 cor. on 5 cor. red 25 45
O1456 5 cor. on 10 cor. violet 60 60

POSTAGE DUE STAMPS

D 13

D 16

1896.
D 99 **D 13** 1 c. orange 45 1·10
D100 2 c. orange 45 1·10
D101 5 c. orange 45 1·10
D102 10 c. orange 45 1·10
D103 20 c. orange 45 1·10
D104 30 c. orange 45 1·10
D105 50 c. orange 45 1·40

1897.

D108	D **13**	1 c. violet	45	1·10
D109		2 c. violet	45	1·10
D110		5 c. violet	45	1·10
D111		10 c. violet	45	1·1
D112		20 c. violet	75	1·25
D113		30 c. violet	45	90
D114		50 c. violet	45	90

1898.

D124	D **13**	1 c. green	15	1·25
D125		2 c. green	15	1·25
D126		5 c. green	15	1·25
D127		10 c. green	15	1·25
D128		20 c. green	15	1·25
D129		30 c. green	15	1·25
D130		50 c. green	15	1·25

1899.

D137	D **13**	1 c. red	15	1·25
D138		2 c. red	15	1·25
D139		5 c. red	15	1·25
D140		10 c. red	15	1·25
D141		20 c. red	15	1·25
D142		50 c. red	15	1·25

1900.

D146	D **16**	1 c. red	70	
D147		2 c. orange	70	
D148		5 c. blue	70	
D149		10 c. violet	70	
D150		20 c. brown	70	
D151		30 c. green	1·40	
D152		50 c. lake	1·40	

NIGER Pt. 6; Pt. 14

Area south of the Sahara. In 1920 was separated from Upper Senegal and Niger to form a separate colony. From 1944 to 1959 used the stamps of French West Africa.

In 1958 Niger became an autonomous republic within the French Community and on 3 August 1960 an independent republic.

100 centimes = 1 franc

1921. Stamps of Upper Senegal and Niger optd **TERRITOIRE DU NIGER**.
1 **7** 1 c. violet and purple 10 30
2 2 c. purple and grey 10 30
3 4 c. blue and black 15 30
4 5 c. chocolate and brown . . . 15 30
5 10 c. green and light green . . 50 75
25 10 c. pink on blue 10 30
6 15 c. yellow and brown . . . 15 30
7 20 c. black and purple . . . 15 30
8 25 c. green and black . . . 15 30
9 30 c. carmine and red . . . 50 65
26 30 c. red and green 30 50
10 35 c. violet and red 25 40
11 40 c. red and grey 35 50
12 45 c. brown and blue 35 50
13 50 c. blue and ultramarine . . 40 60
27 50 c. blue and grey 50 70
28 60 c. red 35 55
14 75 c. brown and yellow . . . 45 85
15 1 f. purple and brown . . . 60 80
16 2 f. blue and green 65 90
17 5 f. black and violet . . . . 1·25 1·40

1922. Stamps of 1921 surch.
18 **7** 25 c. on 15 c. yellow & brown 25 40
19 25 c. on 2 f. blue and green . . 25 45
20 25 c. on 5 f. black & violet . . 25 45
21 60 on 75 c. violet on pink . . 25 45
22 65 on 45 c. brown and blue . . 75 1·40
23 85 c. on 75 c. brown & yellow 85 1·40
24 1 f. 25 on 1 f. lt blue & blue . 60 85

3 Wells

5 Zinder Fort

4 Canoe on River Niger

1926.
29 **3** 1 c. green and purple 10 25
30 2 c. red and grey 10 30
31 3 c. brown and mauve 10 30
32 4 c. black and brown 10 30
33 5 c. green and red 10 35
34 10 c. green and blue 10 20
35 15 c. light green and green . . 40 40
36 15 c. red and lilac 10 25
37 **4** 20 c. brown and blue 15 30
38 25 c. pink and black 15 30
39 30 c. light green and green . . 35 55
40 30 c. mauve and yellow . . . 20 40
41 35 c. blue and red on blue . . 15 30
42 35 c. green and deep green . . 35 50
43 40 c. grey and purple 25 40
44 45 c. mauve and yellow . . . 55 70
45 45 c. green and turquoise . . 55 55
46 50 c. green and red on green . 25 30
47 55 c. brown and red 50 70
48 60 c. brown and red 40 65
49 65 c. red and green 25 45
50 70 c. red and green 55 70
51 75 c. mauve and grn on pink 70 90
52 80 c. green and purple . . . 80 95
53 90 c. red and carmine 55 70
54 90 c. green and red 55 70
55 **5** 1 f. green and red . . . . . 3·00 3·00
56 1 f. orange and red 65 60
57 1 f. red and green 40 55
58 1 f. 10 green and brown . . . 2·25 2·00
59 1 f. 25 red and green 70 75
60 1 f. 25 orange and red . . . 50 70
61 1 f. 40 brown and mauve . . . 50 70
62 1 f. 50 light blue and blue . . 25 35
63 1 f. 60 green and brown . . . 75 95
64 1 f. 75 brown and mauve . . 1·40 1·50
65 1 f. 75 ultramarine and blue . 65 85
66 2 f. brown and orange . . . 35 50
67 2 f. 25 ultramarine and blue . 55 75
68 2 f. 50 brown 65 80
69 3 f. grey and mauve 35 45
70 5 f. black & purple on pink . 50 65
71 10 f. mauve and lilac 75 80
72 20 f. orange and green . . . 75 85

1931. "Colonial Exhibition" key types inscr "NIGER".
73 E 40 c. green . . . . 2·25 2·25
74 F 50 c. mauve . . . . . . 2·00 2·25
75 G 90 c. red . . . . 2·50 2·75
76 H 1 f. 50 blue . . . . 2·50 2·75

1937. International Exhibition, Paris. As Nos. 168/73 of St.-Pierre et Miquelon.
77 20 c. violet 60 85
78 30 c. green 60 85
79 40 c. red 55 75
80 50 c. brown and agate 50 70
81 90 c. red 55 85
82 1 f. 50 blue 55 85

1938. Int Anti-Cancer Fund. As T **22** of Mauritania.
83 1 f. 75 + 50 c. blue . . . . . 8·50 9·50

1939. Caille. As T **27** of Mauritania.
84 90 c. orange 40 55
85 2 f. violet 40 55
86 2 f. 25 blue 40 55

1939. New York World's Fair. As T **28** of Mauritania.
87 1 f. 25 red 50 60
88 2 f. 25 blue 50 60

1939. 150th Anniv of French Revolution. As T **29** of Mauritania.
89 45 c. + 25 c. green and black . 4·50 5·00
90 70 c. + 30 c. brown and black . 4·50 5·00
91 90 c. + 35 c. orange and black . 4·75 5·00
92 1 f. 25 + 1 f. red and black . 4·50 5·00
93 2 f. 25 + 2 f. blue and black . 4·50 5·00

1940. Air. As T **30** of Mauritania.
94 1 f. 90 blue 50 55
95 2 f. 90 red 45 55
96 4 f. 50 green 60 70
97 4 f. 90 olive 50 60
98 6 f. 90 orange 45 60

1941. National Defence Fund. Surch **SECOURS NATIONAL** and additional value.
98a **4** + 1 f. on 50 c. green and red on green . . . . 2·00 2·00
98b + 2 f. on 80 c. green & pur 3·00 3·00
98c **5** + 2 f. on 1 f. 50 lt blue & bl 4·25 4·25
98d + 3 f. on 2 f. brown & orge 4·25 4·25

5a Zinder Fort

5c "Vocation"

5b Weighing Baby

1942. Marshal Petain issue.
98e **5a** 1 f. green 10
98f 2 f. 50 blue 10

1942. Air. Colonial Child Welfare Fund.
98g – 1 f. 50 + 3 f. 50 green . . 20
98h – 2 f. + 6 f. brown 15
98i **5b** 3 f. + 9 f. red 15
DESIGNS: 49 × 28 mm: 1 f. 50, Maternity Hospital, Dakar; 2 f. Dispensary, Mopti.

1942. Air. Imperial Fortnight.
98j **5c** 1 f. 20 + 1 f. 80 blue & red 10

1942. Air. As T **32** of Mauritania but inscr "NIGER" at foot.
98k 50 f. red and yellow . . . . . 80 1·00

7 Giraffes

8 Carmine Bee Eater

1959. Wild Animals and Birds. Inscr "PROTECTION DE LA FAUNE".
99 – 50 c. turquoise, green and black (postage) 25 10
100 – 1 f. multicoloured 40 20
101 – 2 f. multicoloured 40 20
102 – 5 f. mauve, black & brown . 60 20
103 – 7 f. red, black and green . . 75 30
104 – 10 f. multicoloured 25 10
105 – 15 f. sepia and turquoise . . 25 10
106 – 20 f. black and violet . . . 35 10
107 **7** 25 f. multicoloured 45 10
108 30 f. brown, bistre & green . . 50 20
109 – 50 f. blue and brown . . . . 5·50 80
110 – 60 f. sepia and green . . . 7·50 1·10
111 – 85 f. brown and bistre . . . 2·50 85
112 – 100 f. bistre and green . . . 3·25 85
113 **8** 200 f. multicoloured (air) . . 26·00 7·00
114 – 500 f. green, brown & blue . 8·50 6·00
DESIGNS—As Type **7**: HORIZ: 50 c., 10 f. African manatee. VERT: 1, 2 f. Crowned Cranes; 5, 7 f. Saddle-bill Stork; 15, 20 f. Barbary sheep; 50, 60 f. Ostriches; 85, 100 f. Lion. As Type **8**: VERT: 500 f. Game animals.

1960. 10th Anniv of African Technical Co-operation Commission. As T **4** of Malagasy Republic.
115 25 f. brown and ochre 50 40

9 Conseil de l'Entente Emblem

11 Pres. Diori Hamani

1960. 1st Anniv of Conseil de l'Entente.
116 **9** 25 f. multicoloured 50 40

1960. Independence. No. 112 surch **200 F Independance 3-8-60.**
117 – 200 f. on 100 f. . . . . . . 9·00 9·00

1960.
118 **11** 25 f. black and bistre . . . 35 25

12 U.N. Emblem and Niger Flag

1961. Air. 1st Anniv of Admission into U.N.
119 **12** 25 f. red, green & orange . 40 25
120 100 f. green, red & emerald 1·40 90

1962. Air. "Air Afrique" Airline. As T **42** of Mauritania.
121 100 f. violet, black and brown . 1·50 75

1962. Malaria Eradication. As T **43** of Mauritania.
122 25 f. + 5 f. brown 45 45

13 Athletics

1962. Abidjan Games, 1961. Multicoloured.
123 15 f. Boxing and cycling (vert) 25 15
124 25 f. Basketball and football (vert) 35 20
125 85 f. Type **13** . . . . 1·10 55

1962. 1st Anniv of Union of African and Malagasy States. As T **45** of Mauritania.
126 **72** 30 f. mauve 40 30

14 Pres. Hamani and Map
15 Running

1962. 4th Anniv of Republic.
127 **14** 25 f. multicoloured 35 25

1963. Freedom from Hunger. As T **51** of Mauritania.
128 25 f. + 5 f. purple, brn & olive 55 55

1963. Dakar Games.
129 – 15 f. brown and blue . . . 25 15
130 **15** 25 f. red and brown 35 20
131 – 45 f. black and green . . . 70 40
DESIGNS—HORIZ: 15 f. Swimming. VERT: 45 f. Volleyball.

16 Agadez Mosque

1963. Air. 2nd Anniv of Admission to U.P.U. Multicoloured.
132 50 f. Type **16** 75 40
133 85 f. Gaya Bridge . . . . . . 1·25 60
134 100 f. Presidential Palace, Niamey . . . . 1·25 70

17 Wood-carving

1963. Traditional Crafts. Multicoloured.
135 5 f. Type **17** (postage) 15 15
136 10 f. Skin-tanning 20 15
137 25 f. Goldsmith 40 20
138 30 f. Mat-making 60 30
139 85 f. Potter . . . . 1·40 80
140 100 f. Canoe building (air) . . 2·00 1·10
The 10 f. and 30 f. are horiz and the 100 f. larger 47 × 27 mm.

1963. Air. African and Malagasy Posts and Telecommunications Union. As T **56** of Mauritania.
141 85 f. multicoloured 95 55

1963. Air. Red Cross Centenary. Optd with cross and **Centenaire de la Croix-Rouge** in red.
142 **12** 25 f. red, green and orange 60 40
143 100 f. green, red and emerald 1·40 85

19 Costume Museum

1963. Opening of Costume Museum, Niamey. Vert costume designs. Multicoloured.
144 15 f. Berber woman 20 15
145 20 f. Haussa woman 35 15
146 25 f. Tuareg woman 45 20
147 30 f. Tuareg man 55 20
148 60 f. Djerma woman . . . . 1·25 50
149 85 f. Type **19** . . . . 1·50 60

20 "Europafrique"

22 Man and Globe

21 Groundnut Cultivation

1963. Air. European–African Economic Convention.
150 **20** 50 f. multicoloured . . . . 2·50 2·00

1963. Air. Groundnut Cultivation Campaign.
151 **21** 20 f. blue, brown & green . 35 20
152 – 45 f. brown, blue & green . 75 25
153 – 85 f. multicoloured . . . . 1·40 65
154 – 100 f. olive, brown & blue . 1·50 90
DESIGNS: 45 f. Camel transport; 85 f. Fastening sacks; 100 f. Dispatch of groundnuts by lorry.

1963. Air. 1st Anniv of "Air Afrique" and DC-8 Service Inauguration. As T **59** of Mauritania.
155 50 f. multicoloured 70 45

1963. 15th Anniv of Declaration of Human Rights.
156 **22** 25 f. blue, brown & green . 45 25

23 "Telstar"

1964. Air. Space Telecommunications.
157 **23** 25 f. olive and violet . . . 40 20
158 – 100 f. green and purple . . 1·10 80
DESIGN: 100 f. "Relay".

24 "Parkinsonia aculeata" 25 Statue, Abu Simbel

1964. Flowers. Multicoloured.
159 5 f. Type **24** 60 30
160 10 f. "Russelia equisetiformis" 50 30
161 15 f. "Lantana Camara" . . . 1·00 45
162 20 f. "Agryeia nervosa" . . . 1·00 45
163 25 f. "Luffa Cylindrica" . . . 1·00 45
164 30 f. "Hibiscus rosa-sinensis" . 1·40 60
165 45 f. "Plumierai rubra" . . . 2·00 1·25
166 50 f. "Catharanthus roseus" . . 2·00 1·25
167 60 f. "Caesalpinia pulcherrima" 3·50 1·50
Nos. 164/7 have "REPUBLIQUE DU NIGER" at the top and the value at bottom right.

1964. Air. Nubian Monuments Preservation.
168 **25** 25 f. green and brown . . . 65 45
169 30 f. brown and blue . . . 1·00 70
170 50 f. blue and purple . . . 2·00 1·25

26 Globe and "Tiros" Satellite

1964. Air. World Meteorological Day.
171 **26** 50 f. brown, blue and green 1·10 65

27 Sun Emblem and Solar Flares 28 Convoy of Lorries

1964. International Quiet Sun Years.
172 **27** 30 f. red, violet and sepia . 50 35

1964. O.M.N.E.S. (Nigerian Mobile Medical and Sanitary Organization) Commemoration.
173 **28** 25 f. orange, olive & blue . 40 20
174 – 30 f. multicoloured 50 20
175 – 50 f. multicoloured 80 30
176 – 60 f. purple, orange & turq 90 35
DESIGNS: 30 f. Tending children; 50 f. Tending women; 60 f. Open-air laboratory.

29 Rocket, Stars and Stamp Outline

1964. Air. "PHILATEC 1964" Int Stamp Exn, Paris.
177 **29** 50 f. mauve and blue . . . 85 60

30 European, African and Symbols of Agriculture and Industry 31 Pres. Kennedy

1964. Air. 1st Anniv of European–African Economic Convention.
178 **30** 50 f. multicoloured 65 40

1964. Air. Pres. Kennedy Commemoration.
179 **31** 100 f. multicoloured . . . 1·25 1·10

32 Water-polo

1964. Air. Olympic Games, Tokyo.
180 **32** 60 f. brown, deep green and purple 60 50
181 – 85 f. brown, blue and red . 1·00 60
182 – 100 f. blue, red and green . 1·25 70
183 – 250 f. blue, brown and grn 2·50 1·75
DESIGNS—HORIZ: 85 f. Relay-racing. VERT: 100 f. Throwing the discus; 250 f. Athlete holding Olympic Torch.

1964. French, African and Malagasy Co-operation. As T **68** of Mauritania.
184 50 f. brown, orange & violet . 65 40

33 Azawak Tuareg Encampment

1964. Native Villages. Multicoloured.
185 15 f. Type **33** 20 20
186 20 f. Songhai hut 25 20
187 25 f. Wogo and Kourtey tents 30 20
188 30 f. Djerma hut 40 25
189 60 f. Sorkawa fishermen's encampment 75 30
190 85 f. Hausa urban house . . 1·25 50

34 Doctors and Patient and Microscope Slide 35 Abraham Lincoln

1964. Anti-Leprosy Campaign.
191 **34** 50 f. multicoloured 50 45

1965. Death Centenary of Abraham Lincoln.
192 **35** 50 f. multicoloured 60 50

36 Instruction by "Radio-Vision"

1965. "Human Progress". Inscr as in T **36**.
193 **36** 20 f. brown, yellow & blue 30 20
194 – 25 f. sepia, brown and green 35 20
195 – 30 f. purple, red and green 45 25
196 – 50 f. purple, blue and brown 70 35
DESIGNS: 25 f. Student; 30 f. Adult class; 50 f. Five tribesmen ("Alphabetisation").

37 Ader's Telephone 38 Pope John XXIII

1965. I.T.U. Centenary.
197 **37** 25 f. black, lake and green . 50 25
198 – 30 f. green, purple and red . 60 30
199 – 50 f. green, purple and red . 1·00 50
DESIGNS: 30 f. Wheatstone's telegraph; 50 f. "Telautographe".

1965. Air. Pope John Commemoration.
200 **38** 100 f. multicoloured . . . . 1·40 75

39 Hurdling 40 "Capture of Cancer" (the Crab)

1965. 1st African Games, Brazzaville.
201 **39** 10 f. purple, green & brown 20 15
202 – 15 f. red, brown and grey . 30 15
203 – 20 f. purple, blue & green . 40 20
204 – 30 f. purple, green & lake . 50 25
DESIGNS—VERT: 15 f. Running; 30 f. Long-jumping. HORIZ: 20 f. Pole-vaulting.

1965. Air. Campaign against Cancer.
205 **40** 100 f. brown, black & green 1·40 80

41 Sir Winston Churchill 42 Interviewing

1965. Air. Churchill Commemoration.
206 **41** 100 f. multicoloured . . . 1·40 80

1965. Radio Club Promotion.
207 **42** 30 f. brown, violet & green . 30 15
208 – 45 f. red, black and buff . . 45 25
209 – 50 f. multicoloured 55 30
210 – 60 f. purple, blue & ochre . 60 40
DESIGNS—VERT: 45 f. Recording; 50 f. Listening to broadcast. HORIZ: 60 f. Listeners debate.

43 "Agricultural and Industrial Workers" 44 Fair Scene and Flags

1965. Air. International Co-operation Year.
211 **43** 50 f. brown, black & bistre . 70 35

1965. Air. International Fair, Niamey.
212 **44** 100 f. multicoloured . . . . 1·10 70

45 Dr. Schweitzer and Diseased Hands

1966. Air. Schweitzer Commemoration.
213 **45** 50 f. multicoloured 80 45

46 "Water Distribution and Control"

1966. Int Hydrological Decade Inauguration.
214 **46** 50 f. blue, orange & violet 70 35

47 Weather Ship "France I"

1966. Air. 6th World Meteorological Day.
215 **47** 50 f. green, purple and blue 1·25 55

48 White and "Gemini" Capsule

1966. Air. Cosmonauts.
216 **48** 50 f. black, brown & green 75 40
217 – 50 f. blue, violet & orange 75 40
DESIGN: No. 217, Leonov and "Voskhod" capsule.

49 Head-dress and Carvings

1966. World Festival of Negro Arts, Dakar.
218 **49** 30 f. black, brown & green 45 25
219 – 50 f. violet, brown and blue 60 35
220 – 60 f. lake, violet & brown . 70 40
221 – 100 f. black, red & blue . . 1·25 70
DESIGNS: 50 f. Carved figures and mosaics; 60 f. Statuettes, drums and arch; 100 f. Handicrafts and church.

50 "Diamant" Rocket and Gantry 51 Goalkeeper saving Ball

1966. Air. French Space Vehicles. Multicoloured designs each showing different Satellites.
222 45 f. Type **50** 70 40
223 60 f. "A 1" (horiz) 80 45
224 90 f. "FR 1" (horiz) . . . . 1·00 50
225 100 f. "D 1" (horiz) . . . . 1·50 75

1966. World Cup Football Championships.
226 – 30 f. red, brown and blue . 55 25
227 **51** 50 f. brown, blue & green . 75 35
228 – 60 f. blue, purple and bistre 85 50
DESIGNS—VERT: 30 f. Player dribbling ball; 60 f. Player kicking ball.

52 Cogwheel Emblem and Hemispheres 53 Parachutist

1966. Air. Europafrique.
229 **52** 50 f. multicoloured 70 45

1966. 5th Anniv of National Armed Forces. Mult.
230 20 f. Type **53** 35 15
231 30 f. Soldiers with standard (vert) 45 20
232 45 f. Armoured patrol vehicle (horiz) 70 30

1966. Air. Inauguration of DC-8F Air Services. As T **87** of Mauritania.
233 30 f. olive, black and grey . . 60 25

54 Inoculating cattle

1966. Campaign for Prevention of Cattle Plague.
234 **54** 45 f. black, brown & blue . 1·00 50

55 "Voskhod 1" **56** U.N.E.S.C.O. "Tree"

1966. Air. Astronautics.
235 **55** 50 f. blue, indigo and lake . 65 35
236 – 100 f. violet, blue and lake 1·25 75
DESIGN—HORIZ: 100 f. "Gemini 6" and "7".

1966. 20th Anniv of U.N.E.S.C.O.
237 **56** 50 f. multicoloured 70 25

57 Japanese Gate, Atomic Symbol and Cancer ("The Crab") **58** Furnace

1966. Air. International Cancer Congress, Tokyo.
238 **57** 100 f. multicoloured . . . 1·40 75

1966. Malbaza Cement Works.
239 **58** 10 f. blue, orange & brown 15 10
240 – 20 f. blue and green 30 15
241 – 30 f. brown, grey and blue . 45 20
242 – 50 f. indigo, brown & blue 65 30
DESIGNS—HORIZ: 20 f. Electrical power-house; 30 f. Works and cement silos; 50 f. Installation for handling raw materials.

59 Niamey Mosque

1967. Air.
243 **59** 100 f. blue, green and grey 1·10 70

60 Durer (self-portrait)

1967. Air. Paintings. Multicoloured.
244 50 f. Type **60** 80 60
245 100 f. David (self-portrait) . . 1·50 90
246 250 f. Delacroix (self-portrait) 3·00 2·00
See also Nos. 271/2 and 277/9.

61 Red-billed Hornbill **62** Bobsleigh Course, Villard-de-Lans

1967. Birds.
247 **61** 1 f. bistre, red and green (postage) 20 20
248 – 2 f. black, brown and green 20 20
249 – 30 f. multicoloured . . . 1·10 35
249a – 40 f. purple, orange and green . . . . 1·25 60
250 – 45 f. brown, green and blue 1·60 35
250a – 65 f. yell, brown & purple 1·75 75
251 – 70 f. multicoloured . . . 2·10 95
251a – 250 f. blue, purple and green (48 × 27 mm) (air) . . . 6·25 2·10
BIRDS: 2 f. Lesser pied kingfishers; 30 f. Common gonolek; 40 f. Red bishop; 45 f., 65 f. Little masked weaver; 70 f. Chestnut-bellied sandgrouse; 250 f. Splendid glossy starlings.

1967. Grenoble–Winter Olympics Town (1968).
252 **62** 30 f. brown, blue and green 40 25
253 – 45 f. brown, blue and green 60 30
254 – 60 f. brown, blue and green 80 50
255 – 90 f. brown, blue and green 1·10 65
DESIGNS: 45 f. Ski-jump, Autrans; 60 f. Ski-jump, St. Nizier du moucherotte; 90 f. Slalom course, Chamrousse.

63 Family and Lions Emblem **64** Weather Ship

1967. 50th Anniv of Lions International.
256 **63** 50 f. blue, red and green . 60 35

1967. Air. World Meteorological Day.
257 **64** 50 f. red, black and blue . 1·25 65

65 View of World Fair

1967. Air. World Fair, Montreal.
258 **65** 100 f. black, blue & purple 1·10 50

66 I.T.Y. Emblem and Jet Airliner **67** Scouts around Campfire

1967. International Tourist Year.
259 **66** 45 f. violet, green & purple 45 35

1967. World Scout Jamboree, Idaho, U.S.A.
260 **67** 30 f. brown, lake and blue 40 20
261 – 45 f. blue, brown & orge . 60 30
262 – 80 f. lake, slate and bistre . 1·25 50
DESIGNS—HORIZ: 45 f. Jamboree emblem and scouts. VERT: 80 f. Scout cooking meal.

68 Audio-Visual Centre

1967. Air. National Audio-Visual Centre, Niamey.
263 **68** 100 f. violet, blue and green 90 50

69 Carrying Patient **70** "Europafrique"

1967. Nigerian Red Cross.
264 **69** 45 f. black, red and green . 60 20
265 – 50 f. black, red and green . 75 25
266 – 60 f. black, red and green . 1·00 35
DESIGNS: 50 f. Nurse with mother and child; 60 f. Doctor giving injection.

1967. Europafrique.
267 **70** 50 f. multicoloured 60 30

71 Dr. Konrad Adenauer **72** African Women

1967. Air. Adenauer Commemoration.
268 **71** 100 f. brown and blue . . . 1·40 70

1967. Air. 5th Anniv of African and Malagasy Post and Telecommunications Union (U.A.M.P.T.). As T **101** of Mauritania.
270 100 f. violet, green and red . . 1·10 60

1967. Air. Death Centenary of Jean Ingres (painter). Paintings by Ingres. As T **60**. Multicoloured.
271 100 f. "Jesus among the Doctors" (horiz) . . . . . . 1·60 1·00
272 150 f. "Jesus restoring the Keys to St. Peter" (vert) . . . . . 2·25 1·50

1967. U.N. Women's Rights Commission.
273 **72** 50 f. brown, yellow and blue 60 35

1967. 5th Anniv of West African Monetary Union. As T **103** of Mauritania.
274 30 f. green and purple 35 20

73 Nigerian Children **75** Allegory of Human Rights

74 O.C.A.M. Emblem

1967. Air. 21st Anniv of U.N.I.C.E.F.
275 **73** 100 f. brown, blue & green . 1·25 95

1968. Air. O.C.A.M. Conference, Niamey.
276 **74** 100 f. orange, green and blue 1·10 60

1968. Air. Paintings (self-portraits). As T **60**. Multicoloured.
277 50 f. J.-B. Corot 70 40
278 150 f. Goya . . . . 1·90 1·00
279 200 f. Van Gogh . . . . 2·50 1·50

1968. Human Rights Year.
280 **75** 50 f. indigo, brown and blue 60 30

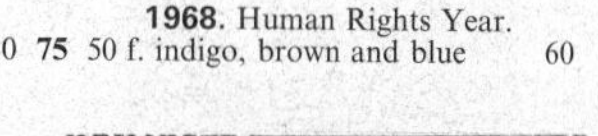

76 Breguet 27 Biplane over Lake

1968. Air. 35th Anniv of 1st France-Niger Airmail Service.
281 **76** 45 f. blue, green and mauve 95 35
282 – 80 f. slate, brown and blue 1·60 55
283 – 100 f. black, green & blue . 2·50 75
DESIGNS—Potez 25TOE biplane: 80 f. On ground; 100 f. In flight.

77 "Joyous Health"

1968. 20th Anniv of W.H.O.
284 **77** 50 f. indigo, blue and brown 60 35

78 Cyclists of 1818 and 1968

1968. Air. 150th Anniv of Bicycle.
285 **78** 100 f. green and red . . . 1·50 70

79 Beribboned Rope

1968. Air. 5th Anniv of Europafrique.
286 **79** 50 f. multicoloured 65 40

80 Fencing

1968. Air. Olympic Games, Mexico.
287 **80** 50 f. purple, violet & green 50 35
288 – 100 f. black, purple & blue 85 50
289 – 150 f. purple and orange . 1·25 70
290 – 200 f. blue, brown & green 1·75 1·25
DESIGNS—VERT: 100 f. High-diving; 150 f. Weight-lifting. HORIZ: 200 f. Horse-jumping.

81 Woodland Kingfisher **82** Mahatma Gandhi

1969. Birds. Dated "1968". Multicoloured.
292 5 f. African grey hornbill (postage) 30 10
293 10 f. Type **81** 40 20
294 15 f. Senegal coucal 85 30
295 20 f. Rose-ringed parakeets . 95 50
296 25 f. Abyssinian roller . . . . 1·40 65
297 50 f. Cattle egret . . . . . . 1·90 90
298 100 f. Violet starling (27 × 49 mm) (air) . . . . 4·25 1·75
See also Nos. 372/7, 567/8 and 714/15.

1968. Air. "Apostles of Non-Violence".
299 **82** 100 f. black and yellow . . 1·75 60
300 – 100 f. black and turquoise . 1·00 50
301 – 100 f. black and grey . . . 1·00 50
302 – 100 f. black and orange . . 1·00 50
PORTRAITS: No. 300, President Kennedy; No. 301, Martin Luther King; No. 302, Robert F. Kennedy.

1968. Air. "Philexafrique" Stamp Exhibition, Abidjan (Ivory Coast, 1969) (1st issue). As T **113a** of Mauritania. Multicoloured.
304 100 f. "Pare, Minister of the Interior" (J. L. La Neuville) 1·60 1·60

83 Arms of the Republic

1968. Air. 10th Anniv of Republic.
305 **83** 100 f. multicoloured . . . 1·00 50

1969. Air. Napoleon Bonaparte. Birth Bicentenary. As T **114b** of Mauritania. Multicoloured.
306 50 f. "Napoleon as First Consul" (Ingres) . . . 1·50 90
307 100 f. "Napoleon visiting the plague victims of Jaffa" (Gros) 2·50 1·25
308 150 f. "Napoleon Enthroned" (Ingres) . . . 3·50 1·75
309 200 f. "The French Campaign" (Meissonier) . . . 5·00 2·50

1969. Air. "Philexafrique" Stamp Exhibition, Abidjan, Ivory Coast (2nd issue). As T **114a** of Mauritania.
310 50 f. brown, blue and orange . 1·25 1·00
DESIGN: 50 f. Giraffes and stamp of 1926.

84 Boeing 707 over Rain-cloud and Anemometer

1969. Air. World Meteorological Day.
311 **84** 50 f. black, blue and green 90 35

85 Workers supporting Globe

1969. 50th Anniv of I.L.O.
312 **85** 30 f. red and green . . . 40 20
313 50 f. green and red . . . 50 35

86 Panhard and Levassor (1909)

1969. Air. Veteran Motor Cars.
314 **86** 25 f. green . . . 45 20
315 – 45 f. violet, blue and grey . 55 25
316 – 50 f. brown, ochre and grey 1·10 35
317 – 70 f. purple, red and grey . 1·50 45
318 – 100 f. green, brown and grey 1·75 65
DESIGNS: 45 f. De Dion Bouton 8 (1904); 50 f. Opel "Doktor-wagen" (1909); 70 f. Daimler (1910); 100 f. Vermorel 12/16 (1912).

87 Mother and Child

88 Mouth and Ear

1969. 50th Anniv of League of Red Cross Societies.
319 **87** 45 f. red, brown and blue . 60 25
320 – 50 f. red, grey and green . 70 25
321 – 70 f. red, brown and ochre 1·00 40
DESIGNS—VERT: 70 f. Man with Red Cross parcel. HORIZ: 50 f. Symbolic Figures, Globe and Red Crosses.

1969. First French Language Cultural Conf, Niamey.
322 **88** 100 f. multicoloured . . . 1·25 60

89 School Building

1969. National School of Administration.
323 **89** 30 f. black, green and orange 30 20

1969. Air. 1st Man on the Moon. No. 114 optd **L'HOMME SUR LA LUNE JUILLET 1969 APOLLO 11** and moon module.
324 500 f. green, brown & blue . 6·50 6·50

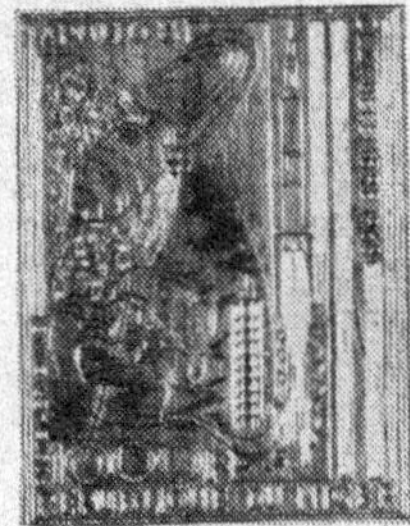
91 "Apollo 8" and Rocket

1969. Air. Moon Flight of "Apollo 8". Embossed on gold foil.
325 **91** 1,000 f. gold . . . 15·00 15·00

1969. 5th Anniv of African Development Bank. As T **122a** of Mauritania.
326 30 f. brown, green and violet 35 15

92 Child and Toys

1969. Air. International Toy Fair, Nuremburg.
327 **92** 100 f. blue, brown and green 1·50 50

93 Linked Squares

1969. Air. "Europafrique".
328 **93** 50 f. yellow, black & violet 55 30

94 Trucks crossing Sahara

1969. Air. 45th Anniv of "Croisiere Noire" Trans-Africa Expedition.
329 **94** 50 f. brown, violet and mve 75 35
330 – 100 f. violet, red and blue . 1·50 65
331 – 150 f. multicoloured . . . 2·00 1·25
332 – 200 f. green, indigo and blue 3·00 1·50
DESIGNS: 100 f. Crossing the mountains; 150 f. African children and expedition at Lake Victoria; 200 f. Route Map, European greeting African and Citroen truck.

94a Aircraft, Map and Airport

1969. 10th Anniv of Aerial Navigation Security Agency for Africa and Madagascar (A.S.E.C.N.A.).
333 **94a** 100 f. red . . . 1·50 70

95 Classical Pavilion

1970. National Museum.
334 **95** 30 f. blue, green and brown 30 15
335 – 45 f. blue, green and brown 45 25
336 – 50 f. blue, brown and green 50 25
337 – 70 f. brown, blue and green 70 40
338 – 100 f. brown, blue and grn 1·10 60
DESIGNS: 45 f. Temporary Exhibition Pavilion; 50 f. Audio-visual Pavilion; 70 f. Local Musical Instruments Gallery; 100 f. Handicrafts Pavilion.

96 Niger Village and Japanese Pagodas

97 Hypodermic "Gun" and Map

1970. Air. "EXPO 70" World Fair, Osaka, Japan (1st issue).
339 **96** 100 f. multicoloured . . . 90 45

1970. One Hundred Million Smallpox Vaccinations in West Africa.
340 **97** 50 f. blue, purple and green 70 30

98 Education Symbols

1970. Air. International Education Year.
341 **98** 100 f. slate, red and purple . 1·00 45

99 Footballer

1970. World Cup Football Competitions, Mexico.
342 **99** 40 f. green, brown and purple 60 25
343 – 70 f. purple, brown and blue 1·00 40
344 – 90 f. red and black . . . 1·25 60
DESIGNS: 70 f. Football and Globe; 90 f. Two footballers.

100 Rotary Emblems

1970. Air. 65th Anniv of Rotary International.
345 **100** 100 f. multicoloured . . . 1·25 55

101 Bay of Naples and Niger Stamp

1970. Air. 10th "Europafrique" Stamp Exn, Naples.
346 **101** 100 f. multicoloured . . . 1·00 60

102 Clement Ader's "Avion III" and Modern Airplane

1970. Air. Aviation Pioneers.
347 **102** 50 f. grey, blue and red . . 70 25
348 – 100 f. red, grey and blue . 1·50 60
349 – 150 f. lt brn, brn & grn . . 1·50 75
350 – 200 f. red, bistre and violet 2·25 1·00
351 – 250 f. violet, grey and red . 3·50 1·40
DESIGNS: 100 f. Joseph and Etienne Montgolfier balloon and rocket; 150 f. Isaac Newton and gravity diagram; 200 f. Galileo and rocket in planetary system; 250 f. Leonardo da Vinci's drawing of a "flying machine" and Chanute's glider.

103 Cathode Ray Tube illuminating Books, Microscope and Globe

1970. Air. World Telecommunications Day.
352 **103** 100 f. brown, green and red 1·25 50

1970. Inauguration of New U.P.U. Headquarters Building, Berne. As T **81** of New Caledonia.
353 30 f. red, slate and brown . . 35 20
354 60 f. violet, red and blue . . 60 30

1970. Air. Safe Return of "Apollo 13". Nos. 348 and 350 optd **Solidarite Spatiale Apollo XIII 11-17 Avril 1970.**
355 100 f. red, slate and blue . . 1·00 50
356 200 f. red, bistre and violet . . 1·75 75

105 U.N. Emblem, Man, Woman and Doves

1970. Air. 25th Anniv of U.N.O.
357 **105** 100 f. multicoloured . . . 1·00 50
358 150 f. multicoloured . . . 1·50 75

106 Globe and Heads

1970. Air. International French Language Conference, Niamey. Die-stamped on gold foil.
359 **106** 250 f. gold and blue . . 2·50 2·50

107 European and African Women

1970. Air. "Europafrique".
360 **107** 50 f. red and green . . . 55 30

108 Japanese Girls and "EXPO 70" Skyline

1970. Air. "EXPO 70" World Fair, Osaka, Japan. (2nd issue).
361 **108** 100 f. purple, orange & grn 90 40
362 – 150 f. blue, brown & green 1·25 60
DESIGN: 150 f. "No" actor and "EXPO 70" by night.

109 Gymnast on Parallel Bars

111 Beethoven, Keyboard and Manuscripts

1970. Air. World Gymnastic Championships, Ljubljana.
363 **109** 50 f. blue . . . 50 30
364 – 100 f. green . . . 1·10 55
365 – 150 f. purple . . . 1·75 75
366 – 200 f. red . . . 2·00 95
GYMNASTS—HORIZ: 100 f. Gymnast on vaulting-horse; 150 f. Gymnast in mid-air. VERT: 200 f. Gymnast on rings.

1970. Air. Moon Landing of "Luna 16". Nos. 349 and 351 surch **LUNA 16 – Sept. 1970 PREMIERS PRELEVEMENTS AUTOMATIQUES SUR LA LUNE** and value.
367 100 f. on 150 f. light brown, brown and green . . . 1·10 50
368 200 f. on 250 f. violet, grey and red . . . 2·40 1·00

1970. Air. Birth Bicentenary of Beethoven. Mult.
369 100 f. Type **111** . . . 1·40 55
370 150 f. Beethoven and allegory, "Hymn of Joy" . . . 2·25 85

112 John F. Kennedy Bridge, Niamey

1970. Air. 12th Anniv of Republic.
371 **112** 100 f. multicoloured . . . 1·10 45

1971. Birds. Designs similar to T **81**. Variously dated between 1970 and 1972. Multicoloured.
372 5 f. African grey hornbill . . . 55 25
373 10 f. Woodland kingfisher . . 70 25
374 15 f. Senegal coucal . . . . . 1·50 80
375 20 f. Rose-ringed parakeet . . 1·75 80
376 35 f. Broad-tailed paradise whydah . . . . 2·40 1·10
377 50 f. Cattle egret . . . . . . 3·00 1·50
The Latin inscription on No. 377 is incorrect, reading "Bulbucus ibis" instead of "Bubulcus ibis".
See also Nos. 714/15.

114 Pres. Nasser

1971. Air. Death of Pres. Gamal Nasser (Egyptian statesman). Multicoloured.
378 100 f. Type **114** 75 40
379 200 f. Nasser waving . . . . . 1·50 75

115 Pres. De Gaulle

1971. Air. De Gaulle Commemoration. Embossed on gold foil.
380 **115** 1000 f. gold . . . . 38·00 38·00

116 "MUNICH" and Olympic Rings

1971. Air. Publicity for 1972 Olympic Games, Munich.
381 **116** 150 f. purple, blue & green 1·25 70

117 "Apollo 14" leaving Moon

118 Symbolic Masks

1971. Air. Moon Mission of "Apollo 14".
382 **117** 250 f. green, orge & blue . 2·25 1·25

1971. Air. Racial Equality Year.
383 **118** 100 f. red, green & blue . 90 40
384 – 200 f. brown, green & blue 1·75 80
DESIGN: 200 f. "Peoples" and clover-leaf emblem.

119 Niamey on World Map

1971. 1st Anniv of French-speaking Countries Co-operative Agency.
385 **119** 40 f. multicoloured . . . 50 25

120 African Telecommunications Map

1971. Air. Pan-African Telecommunications Network.
386 **120** 100 f. multicoloured . . . 75 40

121 African Mask and Japanese Stamp

1971. Air. "PHILATOKYO 71" International Stamp Exhibition, Japan.
387 **121** 50 f. olive, purple & green 65 30
388 – 100 f. violet, red & green 1·10 45
DESIGN: 100 f. Japanese scroll painting and Niger stamp.

122 "Longwood House, St. Helena" (C. Vernet)

1971. Air. 150th Anniv of Napoleon's Death. Paintings. Multicoloured.
389 150 f. Type **122** . . . . 1·75 70
390 200 f. "Napoleon's Body on his Camp-bed" (Marryat) . . . 2·50 90

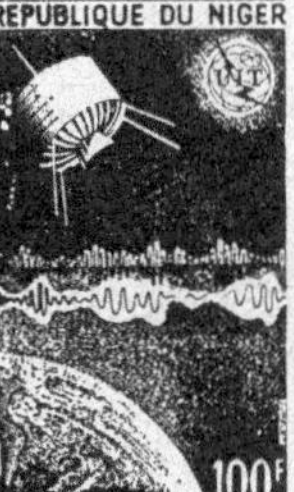

123 Satellite, Radio Waves, and Globe

125 Scout Badges and Mount Fuji

124 Pierre de Coubertin and Discus-throwers

1971. Air. World Telecommunications Day.
391 **123** 100 f. multicoloured . . . 1·10 50

1971. Air. 75th Anniv of Modern Olympic Games.
392 **124** 50 f. red and blue 50 25
393 – 100 f. multicoloured . . . 90 40
394 – 150 f. blue and purple . . 1·40 65
DESIGNS—VERT: 100 f. Male and female athletes holding torch. HORIZ: 150 f. Start of race.

1971. 13th World Scout Jamboree, Asagiri, Japan.
395 **125** 35 f. red, purple & orange 40 20
396 – 40 f. brown, plum and green 45 20
397 – 45 f. green, red and blue . 60 25
398 – 50 f. green, violet and red 70 30
DESIGNS—VERT: 40 f. Scouts and badge; 45 f. Scouts converging on Japan. HORIZ: 50 f. "Jamboree" in rope, and marquee.

126 "Apollo 15" on Moon

1971. Air. Moon Mission of "Apollo 15".
399 **126** 150 f. blue, violet & brn . 1·50 70

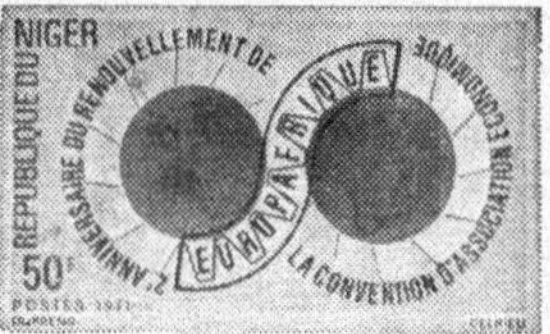

127 Linked Maps

1971. 2nd Anniv of Renewed "Europafrique" Convention, Niamey.
400 **127** 50 f. multicoloured 60 30

128 Gouroumi (Hausa)

129 De Gaulle in Uniform

1971. Musical Instruments.
401 **128** 25 f. brown, green & red . 30 10
402 – 30 f. brown, violet & grn . 35 15
403 – 35 f. blue, green & purple . 35 25
404 – 40 f. brown, orange & grn 45 25
405 – 45 f. ochre, brown & blue . 55 35
406 – 50 f. brown, red & black . 95 45
DESIGNS: 30 f. Molo (Djerma); 35 f. Garaya (Hausa); 40 f. Godjie (Djerma-Sonrai); 45 f. Inzad (Tuareg); 50 f. Kountigui (Sonrai).

1971. Air. 1st Death Anniv of Gen. Charles De Gaulle (French statesman).
407 **129** 250 f. multicoloured . . . 5·00 4·00

1971. Air. 10th Anniv of African and Malagasy Posts and Telecommunications Union. As T **139a** of Mauritania. Multicoloured.
408 100 f. U.A.M.P.T. H.Q. and rural scene 90 45

130 "Audience with Al Hariri" (Baghdad, 1237)

1971. Air. Moslem Miniatures. Multicoloured.
409 100 f. Type **130** . . . . 1·00 45
410 150 f. "Archangel Israfil" (Iraq, 14th-cent.) (vert) . . . . . . 1·50 70
411 200 f. "Horsemen" (Iraq, 1210) 2·25 1·25

131 Louis Armstrong

132 "Children of All Races"

1971. Air. Death of Louis Armstrong (American jazz musician). Multicoloured.
412 100 f. Type **131** . . . . 1·50 55
413 150 f. Armstrong playing trumpet . . . . 2·00 85

1971. 25th Anniv of U.N.I.C.E.F.
414 **132** 50 f. multicoloured 60 45

133 "Adoration of the Magi" (Di Bartolo)

1971. Air. Christmas. Paintings. Multicoloured.
415 100 f. Type **133** . . . . 1·00 45
416 150 f. "The Nativity" (D. Ghirlandaio) (vert) . . . . 1·50 70
417 200 f. "Adoration of the Shepherds" (Perugino) . . . 2·00 1·00

134 Presidents Pompidou and Hamani

1972. Air. Visit of Pres. Pompidou of France.
418 **134** 250 f. multicoloured . . . 4·75 3·50

135 Ski "Gate" and Cherry Blossom

1972. Air. Winter Olympic Games, Sapporo, Japan.
419 **135** 100 f. violet, red & green . 90 40
420 – 150 f. red, purple & violet 1·25 70
DESIGN—HORIZ: 150 f. Snow crystals and Olympic flame.

1972. Air. U.N.E.S.C.O. "Save Venice" Campaign. As T **145** of Senegal.
422 50 f. multicoloured (vert) . . 50 25
423 100 f. multicoloured (vert) . . 1·00 45
424 150 f. multicoloured (vert) . . 1·50 70
425 200 f. multicoloured . . . . . 2·00 1·00
DESIGNS: Nos. 422/5 depict various details of Guardi's painting, "The Masked Ball".

136 Johannes Brahms and Music

137 Saluting Hand

1972. Air. 75th Death Anniv of Johannes Brahms (composer).
426 **136** 100 f. green, myrtle and red 1·50 55

1972. Air. Int Scout Seminar, Cotonou, Dahomey.
427 **137** 150 f. violet, blue & orange 1·50 60

138 Star Symbol and Open Book

1972. International Book Year.
428 **138** 35 f. purple and green . . 35 20
429 – 40 f. blue and lake . . . 1·00 25
DESIGN: 40 f. Boy reading, galleon and early aircraft.

139 Heart Operation

1972. Air. World Heart Month.
430 **139** 100 f. brown and red . . . 1·50 55

140 Bleriot XI crossing the Channel, 1909

1972. Air. Milestones in Aviation History.
431 **140** 50 f. brown, blue & lake . 1·10 50
432 – 75 f. grey, brown & blue . 1·75 60
433 – 100 f. ultramarine, blue and purple . . . . 3·25 1·40
DESIGNS: 75 f. Lindbergh crossing the Atlantic in "Spirit of St. Louis"; 100 f. First flight of Concorde, 1969.

141 Satellite and Universe

1972. Air. World Telecommunications Day.
434 **141** 100 f. brown, purple & red 1·10 45

142 Boxing

1972. Air. Olympic Games, Munich. Sports and Munich Buildings.
435 **142** 50 f. brown and blue . . . 50 20
436 – 100 f. brown and green . . 75 40
437 – 150 f. brown and red . . . 1·25 60
438 – 200 f. brown and mauve . 1·75 85
DESIGNS—VERT: 100 f. Long-jumping; 150 f. Football. HORIZ: 200 f. Running.

143 A. G. Bell and Telephone

1972. Air. 50th Death Anniv of Alexander Graham Bell (inventor of telephone).
440 **143** 100 f. blue, purple and red 1·10 55

144 "Europe on Africa" Map

1972. Air. "Europafrique" Co-operation.
441 **144** 50 f. red, green and blue . 50 25

145 Herdsman and Cattle

146 Lottery Wheel

1972. Medicinal Salt-Ponds at In-Gall. Multicoloured.
442 35 f. Type **145** 50 25
443 40 f. Cattle in salt-pond . . 60 25

1972. 6th Anniv of National Lottery.
444 **146** 35 f. multicoloured . . . 35 25

147 Postal Runner

1972. Air. U.P.U. Day. Postal Transport.
445 **147** 50 f. brown, green & lake 60 25
446 – 100 f. green, blue & lake . 90 45
447 – 150 f. green, violet & lake 1·75 70
DESIGNS: 100 f. Rural mail van; 150 f. Loading Fokker Friendship mail plane.

1972. 10th Anniv of West African Monetary Union. As T **149** of Mauritania.
448 40 f. grey, violet and brown . 40 25

1972. Air. Gold Medal Winners. Munich Olympic Games. Nos. 435/8 optd with events and names, etc.
449 **142** 50 f. brown and blue . . 50 20
450 – 100 f. brown and green . 85 40
451 – 150 f. brown and red . . 1·40 60
452 – 200 f. brown and mauve . 1·75 80
OVERPRINTS: 50 f. **WELTER CORREA MEDAILLE D'OR**; 100 f. **TRIPLE SAUT SANEIEV MEDAILLE D'OR**; 150 f. **FOOTBALL POLOGNE MEDAILLE D'OR**; 200 f. **MARATHON SHORTER MEDAILLE D'OR.**

148 "The Raven and the Fox"

1972. Air. Fables of Jean de la Fontaine.
453 **148** 25 f. black, brown & grn 1·50 40
454 – 50 f. brown, green & pur 60 25
455 – 75 f. brown, green & brn 1·00 45
DESIGNS: 50 f. "The Lion and the Rat"; 75 f. "The Monkey and the Leopard".

149 Astronauts on Moon

1972. Air. Moon Flight of "Apollo 17".
456 **149** 250 f. multicoloured . . . 2·75 1·25

150 Dromedary Race

151 Pole Vaulting

1972. Niger Sports.
457 **150** 35 f. purple, red and blue 75 40
458 – 40 f. lake, brown & green 1·00 60
DESIGN: 40 f. Horse race.

1973. 2nd African Games, Lagos, Nigeria. Mult.
459 35 f. Type **151** 30 25
460 40 f. Basketball 35 25
461 45 f. Boxing 45 25
462 75 f. Football 70 45

152 "Young Athlete"

153 Knight and Pawn

1973. Air. Antique Art Treasures.
463 **152** 50 f. red 50 25
464 – 100 f. violet . . . . 1·00 40
DESIGN: 100 f. "Head of Hermes".

1973. World Chess Championships, Reykjavik, Iceland.
465 **153** 100 f. green, blue & red . 2·50 1·00

154 "Abutilon pannosum"

155 Interpol Badge

1973. Rare African Flowers. Multicoloured.
466 30 f. Type **154** 70 30
467 45 f. "Crotalaria barkae" . . . 80 30
468 60 f. "Dichrostachys cinerea" . 1·40 45
469 80 f. "Caralluma decaisneana" . 1·60 55

1973. 50th Anniv of International Criminal Police Organization (Interpol).
470 **155** 50 f. multicoloured 85 30

156 Scout with Radio

1973. Air. Scouting in Niger.
471 **156** 25 f. brown, green & red . 25 20
472 – 50 f. brown, green & red . 55 25
473 – 100 f. brown, green & red . 1·25 50
474 – 150 f. brown, green & red . 1·60 70
DESIGNS: 50 f. First Aid; 100 f. Care of animals; 150 f. Care of the environment.

157 Hansen and Microscope

158 Nurse tending Child

1973. Centenary of Dr. Hansen's Discovery of Leprosy Bacillus.
475 **157** 50 f. brown, green & blue . 85 35

1973. 25th Anniv of W.H.O.
476 **158** 50 f. brown, red and blue . 65 25

159 "The Crucifixion" (Hugo van der Goes)

1973. Air. Easter. Paintings. Multicoloured.
477 50 f. Type **159** 55 25
478 100 f. "The Deposition" (Cima de Conegliano) (horiz) . . . 1·10 50
479 150 f. "Pieta" (Bellini) (horiz) . 1·60 65

160 Douglas DC-8 and Mail Van

1973. Air. Stamp Day.
480 **160** 100 f. brown, red & green . 1·50 55

161 W.M.O. Emblem and "Weather Conditions"

1973. Air. Centenary of W.M.O.
481 **161** 100 f. brown, red & grn . 1·10 45

162 "Crouching Lioness" (Delacroix)

1973. Air. Paintings by Delacroix. Multicoloured.
482 130 f. Type **162** . . . . 2·00 1·00
483 200 f. "Tigress and Cub" . . 3·25 1·50

163 Crocodile

1973. Wild Animals from "Park W".
484 **163** 25 f. multicoloured . . . 45 20
485 – 35 f. grey, gold and black 75 30
486 – 40 f. multicoloured . . . 75 30
487 – 80 f. multicoloured . . . 1·25 50
DESIGNS: 35 f. African elephant; 40 f. Hippopotamus; 80 f. Warthog.

164 Eclipse over Mountain

1973. Total Eclipse of the Sun.
488 **164** 40 f. violet 60 30

1973. Air. 24th International Scouting Congress, Nairobi, Kenya. Nos. 473/4 optd **24 Conference Mondiale du Scoutisme NAIROBI, 1973.**
489 100 f. brown, green and red . 1·00 40
490 150 f. brown, green and red . 1·50 60

166 Palomino

1973. Horse-breeding. Multicoloured.
491 50 f. Type **166** 90 30
492 75 f. French trotter . . . . . 1·40 40
493 80 f. English thoroughbred . . 1·50 55
494 100 f. Arab thoroughbred . . 2·00 65

1973. Pan-African Drought Relief. African Solidarity. No. 436 surch **SECHERESSE SOLIDARITE AFRICAINE** and value.
495 **145** 100 f. on 35 f. multicoloured 1·40 1·00

168 Rudolf Diesel and Engine

1973. 60th Death Anniv of Rudolf Diesel (engineer).
496 **168** 25 f. blue, purple & grey . 55 35
497 – 50 f. grey, green & blue . 95 50
498 – 75 f. blue, black & mauve . 1·40 75
499 – 125 f. blue, red & green . 2·40 90
DESIGNS: 50 f. Type "BB-610 ch" diesel locomotive; 75 f. Type "060-DB" diesel locomotive; 125 f. Type "CC-72004" diesel locomotive.

1973. African and Malagasy Posts and Telecommunications Union. As T **155a** of Mauritania.
500 100 f. red, green and brown . 75 50

168a African Mask and Old Town Hall, Brussels

169 T.V. Set and Class

1973. Air. African Fortnight, Brussels.
501 **168a** 100 f. purple, blue and red 1·00 50

1973. Schools Television Service.
502 **169** 50 f. black, red and blue . 60 30

1973. 3rd International French Language and Culture Conf., Liege. No. 385 optd **3e CONFERENCE DE LA FRANCOPHONIE LIEGE OCTOBRE 1973**.
503 **110** 40 f. multicoloured . . . 50 25

171 "Apollo"  **172** Bees and Honeycomb

1973. Classical Sculptures.
504 **171** 50 f. green and brown . . 60 30
505 – 50 f. black and brown . . 60 30
506 – 50 f. brown and red . . 60 30
507 – 50 f. purple and red . . 60 30
DESIGNS: No. 505, "Atlas"; No. 506, "Hercules"; No. 507, "Venus".

1973. World Savings Day.
508 **172** 40 f. brown, red and blue . 45 25

173 "Food for the World"  **174** Copernicus and "Sputnik 1"

1973. Air. 10th Anniv of World Food Programme.
509 **173** 50 f. violet, red and blue . 60 30

1973. Air. 500th Birth Anniv of Copernicus (astonomer).
510 **174** 150 f. brown, blue and red 1·40 70

175 Pres. John Kennedy

1973. Air. 10th Death Anniv of U.S. President Kennedy.
511 **175** 100 f. multicoloured . . . 1·00 50

176 Kounta Songhai Blanket  **178** Lenin

177 Barges on River Niger

1973. Niger Textiles. Multicoloured.
513 35 f. Type **176** 50 30
514 40 f. Tcherka Snghai blanket (horiz) 70 40

1974. Air. 1st Anniv of Ascent of Niger by "Fleet of Hope".
515 **177** 50 f. blue, green and red . 75 35
516 – 75 f. purple, blue and green 1·00 45
DESIGN: 75 f. "Barban Maza" (tug) and barge.

1974. Air. 50th Death Anniv of Lenin.
517 **178** 50 c. brown 50 30

179 Slalom Skiing

1974. Air. 50th Anniv of Winter Olympic Games.
518 **179** 200 f. red, brown & blue 2·50 1·00

180 Newly-born Baby

1974. World Population Year.
519 **180** 50 f. multicoloured . . . 50 25

181 Footballers and "Global" Ball

1974. Air. World Cup Football Championships, West Germany.
520 **181** 75 f. violet, black and brn 65 35
521 – 150 f. brown, green & turq 1·40 55
522 – 200 f. blue, orange & green 1·75 1·00
DESIGNS: 150, 200 f. Football scenes similar to Type **181**.

182 "The Crucifixion" (Grunewald)

1974. Air. Easter. Paintings. Multicoloured.
524 50 f. Type **182** 50 25
525 75 f. "Avignon Pieta" (attributed to E. Quarton) 75 35
526 125 f. "The Entombment" (G. Isenmann) . . . . . . 1·25 65

183 Locomotive No. 230k (1948) and U.S.A. Loco No. 2222 (1938)

1974. Famous Railway Locomotives of the Steam Era.
527 **183** 50 f. green, black & violet 80 35
528 – 75 f. green, black & brown 1·25 45
529 – 100 f. multicoloured . . 1·75 70
530 – 150 f. brown, black & red 2·50 1·00
DESIGNS: 75 f. P.L.M. loco No. C21 (1893); 100 f. U.S.A. "220" (1866) and British "231" (1939) class locomotives; 150 f. Seguin locomotive (1821) and Stephenson's "Rocket" (1829).

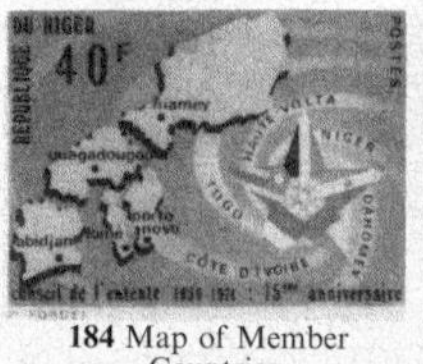

184 Map of Member Countries  **185** Knights

1974. 15th Anniv of Conseil de l'Entente.
531 **184** 40 f. multicoloured 40 20

1974. Air. 21st Chess Olympiad, Nice.
532 **185** 50 f. brown, blue & indigo 1·25 65
533 – 75 f. purple, brown & green 1·75 75
DESIGN: 75 f. Kings.

186 Marconi and "Elettra" (steam yacht)

1974. Birth Centenary of Guglielmo Marconi (radio pioneer).
534 **186** 50 f. blue, brown & mauve 50 30

187 Astronaut on Palm of Hand  **188** Tree on Palm of Hand

1974. Air. 5th Anniv of 1st Landing on Moon.
535 **187** 150 f. brown, blue & ind . 1·25 60

1974. National Tree Week.
536 **188** 35 f. turquoise, grn & brn . 40 30

189 "The Rhinoceros" (Longhi)  **190** Camel Saddle

1974. Air. Europafrique.
537 **189** 250 f. multicoloured . . . 5·00 3·00

1974. Handicrafts.
538 **190** 40 f. red, blue & brown . . 45 20
539 – 50 f. blue, red and brown . 55 30
DESIGN: 50 f. Statuettes of horses.

192 Frederic Chopin

1974. 125th Death Anniv of Frederic Chopin.
541 **192** 100 f. black, red & blue . . 1·50 55

1974. Beethoven's Ninth Symphony Commemoration. As T **192**.
542 100 f. lilac, blue and indigo . . 1·50 55
DESIGN: 100 f. Beethoven.

193 European Woman and Douglas DC-8 Airliners  **194** "Skylab" over Africa

1974. Air. Centenary of U.P.U.
543 **193** 50 f. turquoise, grn & pur 50 25
544 – 100 f. blue, mauve & ultram 1·50 60
545 – 150 f. brown, blue & indigo 1·50 80
546 – 200 f. brown, orange & red 1·60 1·25
DESIGNS: 100 f. Japanese woman and electric locomotives; 150 f. American Indian woman and liner; 200 f. African woman and road vehicles.

1974. Air. "Skylab" Space Laboratory.
547 **194** 100 f. violet, brown & blue 1·00 45

195 Don-don Drum  **197** "Virgin and Child" (Correggio)

196 Tree and Compass Rose

1974.
548 **195** 60 f. purple, green & red . 90 45

1974. 1st Death Anniv of Tenere Tree (desert landmark).
549 **196** 50 f. brown, blue and ochre 2·00 1·00

1974. Air. Christmas. Multicoloured.
550 100 f. Type **197** . . . . 1·00 35
551 150 f. "Virgin and Child, and St. Hilary" (F. Lippi) . . . . . 1·50 55
552 200 f. "Virgin and Child" (Murillo) . . . . 2·00 95

198 "Apollo" Spacecraft  **199** European and African Women

1975. Air. "Apollo–Soyuz" Space Test Project.
553 **198** 50 f. green, red and blue . 50 25
554 – 100 f. grey, red and blue . 80 40
555 – 150 f. purple, plum & blue 1·25 60
DESIGNS: 100 f. "Apollo" and "Soyuz" docked; 150 f. "Soyuz" spacecraft.

1975. Air. Europafrique.
556 **199** 250 f. brown, purple & red 2·25 1·75

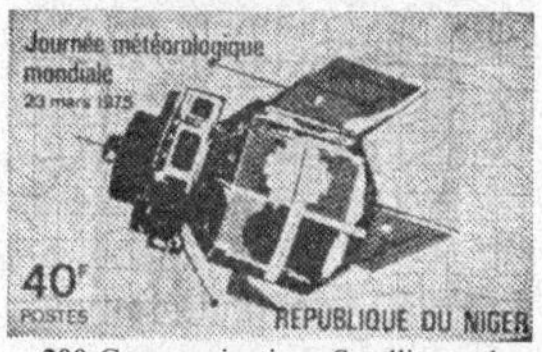

200 Communications Satellite and Weather Map

1975. World Meteorological Day.
557 **200** 40 f. red, black and blue . 40 20

201 "Christ in the Garden of Olives" (Delacroix)

1975. Air. Easter. Multicoloured.
558 75 f. Type **201** 65 35
559 125 f. "The Crucifixion" (El Greco) (vert) . . . . 1·10 50
560 150 f. "The Resurrection" (Limousin) (vert) . . . . . 1·25 75

202 Lt-Col. S. Kountche, Head of State

1975. Air. 1st Anniv of Military Coup.
561 **202** 100 f. multicoloured . . . 1·00 50

203 "City of Truro" (G.W.R., England, 1903)

1975. Famous Locomotives. Multicoloured.
562 50 f. Type **203** 85 35
563 75 f. No. 5003 (Germany, 1937) 1·10 50
564 100 f. "The General" (U.S.A., 1863) . . . . 1·75 75
565 125 f. "BB-15000" Electric (France, 1971) . . . . . 2·00 90

1975. Birds. As Nos. 296 and 298, but dated "1975". Multicoloured.
567 25 f. Abyssinian Roller (postage) 1·00 25
568 100 f. Violet Starlings (air) . . 2·25 65

205 "Zabira" Leather Bag

206 African Woman and Child

1975. Niger Handicrafts. Multicoloured.
569 35 f. Type **205** 30 20
570 40 f. Chequered rug 45 25
571 45 f. Flower pot 50 30
572 60 f. Gourd 75 35

1975. International Women's Year.
573 **206** 50 f. blue, brown & red . 75 50

207 Dr. Schweitzer and Lambarene Hospital

1975. Birth Centenary of Dr. Albert Schweitzer.
574 **207** 100 f. brown, green & blk 1·00 55

208 Peugeot, 1892

1975. Early Motor-cars.
575 **208** 50 f. blue and mauve . . . 60 30
576 – 75 f. purple and blue . . . 1·00 40
577 – 100 f. mauve and green . . 1·40 60
578 – 125 f. green and red . . . 1·50 70
DESIGNS: 75 f. Daimler, 1895; 100 f. Fiat, 1899; 125 f. Cadillac, 1903.

INDEX

Countries can be quickly located by referring to the index at the end of this volume.

209 Tree and Sun

211 Leontini Tetradrachme

210 Boxing

1975. National Tree Week.
579 **209** 40 f. green, orange and red 40 25

1975. Traditional Sports.
580 **210** 35 f. brown, orange & blk 35 20
581 – 40 f. brown, green & blk 40 20
582 – 45 f. brown, blue & black 50 25
583 – 50 f. brown, red and black 55 30
DESIGNS—VERT: 40 f. Boxing; 50 f. Wrestling. HORIZ: 45 f. Wrestling.

1975. Ancient Coins.
584 **211** 50 f. grey, blue and red . 60 20
585 – 75 f. grey, blue & mauve 85 30
586 – 100 f. grey, orange & blue 1·25 40
587 – 125 f. grey, purple & green 1·50 60
COINS: 75 f. Athens tetradrachme; 100 f. Himer diadrachme; 125 f. Gela tetradrachme.

212 Putting the Shot

1975. Air. "Pre-Olympic Year". Olympic Games, Montreal (1976).
588 **212** 150 f. brown and red . . 1·10 55
589 – 200 f. red, chestnut and brown . . . . 1·50 85
DESIGN: 200 f. Gymnastics.

213 Starving Family

1975. Pan-African Drought Relief.
590 **213** 40 f. blue, brown & orange 55 30
591 – 45 f. brown and blue . . 1·10 50
592 – 60 f. blue, green & orange 1·00 40
DESIGNS: 45 f. Animal skeletons; 60 f. Truck bringing supplies.

214 Trading Canoe crossing R. Niger

1975. Tourism. Multicoloured.
593 40 f. Type **214** 50 25
594 45 f. Boubon Camp entrance 55 25
595 50 f. Boubon Camp view . . 60 35

215 U N Emblem and Peace Dove

1975. Air. 30th Anniv of U.N.O.
596 **215** 100 f. light blue and blue 85 40

216 "Virgin of Seville" (Murillo)

1975. Air. Christmas. Multicoloured.
597 50 f. Type **216** 50 35
598 75 f. "Adoration of the Shepherds" (Tintoretto) (horiz) 75 45
599 125 f. "Virgin with Angels" (Master of Burgo d'Osma) . 1·25 75

1975. Air. "Apollo-Soyuz" Space Link. Nos. 533/5 optd **JONCTION 17 Juillet 1975.**
600 **198** 50 f. green, red and blue . 50 25
601 – 100 f. grey, red and blue 75 45
602 – 150 f. purple, plum & blue 1·25 75

218 "Ashak"

1976. Literacy Campaign. Multicoloured.
603 25 f. Type **218** 15 10
604 30 f. "Kaska" 20 15
605 40 f. "Iccee" 25 15
606 50 f. "Tuuri-nya" 30 20
607 60 f. "Lekki" 35 25

219 Ice Hockey

1976. Winter Olympic Games, Innsbruck, Austria. Multicoloured.
608 40 f. Type **219** (postage) . . . 35 20
609 50 f. Tobogganing 40 20
610 150 f. Ski-jumping . . . . . . 1·25 50
611 200 f. Figure-skating (air) . . . 1·50 75
612 300 f. Cross-country skiing . . 2·00 1·00

220 Early Telephone and Satellite

1976. Telephone Centenary.
614 **220** 100 f. orange, blue & green 85 50

221 Baby and Ambulance

1976. World Health Day.
615 **221** 50 f. red, brown & purple . 50 25

222 Washington crossing the Delaware (after Leutze)

1976. Bicentenary of American Revolution. Mult.
616 40 f. Type **222** (postage) . . . 30 15
617 50 f. First soldiers of the Revolution 40 20
618 150 f. Joseph Warren – martyr of Bunker Hill (air) . . . . . 1·10 35
619 200 f. John Paul Jones aboard the "Bonhomme Richard" . 1·50 60
620 300 f. Molly Pitcher – heroine of Monmouth . . . . 2·00 90

223 Distribution of Provisions

225 "Europafrique" Symbols

224 "Hindenburg" crossing Lake Constance

1976. 2nd Anniv of Military Coup. Multicoloured.
622 50 f. Type **223** 35 25
623 100 f. Soldiers with bulldozer (horiz) . . . . 1·10 45

1976. Air. 75th Anniv of Zeppelin Airships. Multicoloured.
624 40 f. Type **224** 40 15
625 50 f. LZ-3 over Wurzberg . . 50 25
626 150 f. L-9 over Friedrichshafen 1·40 55
627 200 f. LZ-2 over Rothenburg (vert) . . . . 1·75 70
628 300 f. "Graf Zeppelin II" over Essen . . . . 3·25 85

1976. "Europafrique".
630 **225** 100 f. multicoloured . . . 1·40 50

226 Plant Cultivation

1976. Communal Works. Multicoloured.
631 25 f. Type **226** 15 10
632 30 f. Harvesting rice 20 15

227 Boxing

1976. Olympic Games, Montreal. Multicoloured.
633 40 f. Type **227** 25 15
634 50 f. Basketball 40 20
635 60 f. Football 45 25
636 80 f. Cycling (horiz) 60 20
637 100 f. Judo (horiz) 70 30

228 Motobecane '125'

1976. Motorcycles.
639 **228** 50 f. violet, brown & turq . . . 60 25
640 – 75 f. green, red & turq . . 85 35
641 – 100 f. brown, orge & pur . 1·25 50
642 – 125 f. slate, olive & black . 1·50 75
DESIGNS: 75 f. Norton "Challenge"; 100 f. B.M.W. "903"; 125 f. Kawasaki "1000".

229 Cultivation Map

1976. Operation "Sahel Vert". Multicoloured.
643 40 f. Type **229** 30 15
644 45 f. Tending plants (vert) . . 35 20
645 60 f. Planting sapling (vert) . . 55 30

1976. International Literacy Day. Nos. 603/7 optd JOURNEE INTERNATIONALE DE L'ALPHABETISATION.
646 **218** 25 f. multicoloured . . . 15 15
647 – 30 f. multicoloured . . . 15 15
648 – 40 f. multicoloured . . . 20 15
649 – 50 f. multicoloured . . . 25 20
650 – 60 f. multicoloured . . . 30 20

231 Basket Making

1976. Niger Women's Association. Multicoloured.
651 40 f. Type **231** 35 20
652 45 f. Hairdressing (horiz) . . . 40 25
653 50 f. Making pottery 50 35

232 Wall Paintings

1976. "Archaeology". Multicoloured.
654 40 f. Type **232** 45 25
655 50 f. Neolithic statuettes . . . 50 25
656 60 f. Dinosaur skeleton . . . 90 35

233 "The Nativity" (Rubens)

234 Benin Ivory Mask

1976. Air. Christmas. Multicoloured.
657 50 f. Type **233** 50 25
658 100 f. "Holy Night" (Correggio) 1·10 45
659 150 f. "Adoration of the Magi" (David) (horiz) . . . . . . 1·50 90

1977. 2nd World Festival of Negro-African Arts, Lagos.
660 **234** 40 f. brown 40 20
661 – 50 f. blue 60 30
DESIGNS—HORIZ: 50 f. Nigerian stick dance.

235 Students in Class

236 Examining Patient

1977. Alphabetisation Campaign.
662 **235** 40 f. multicoloured . . . 30 15
663 50 f. multicoloured . . . 40 20
664 60 f. multicoloured . . . 60 20

1977. Village Health. Multicoloured.
665 40 f. Type **236** 50 20
666 50 f. Examining baby 60 30

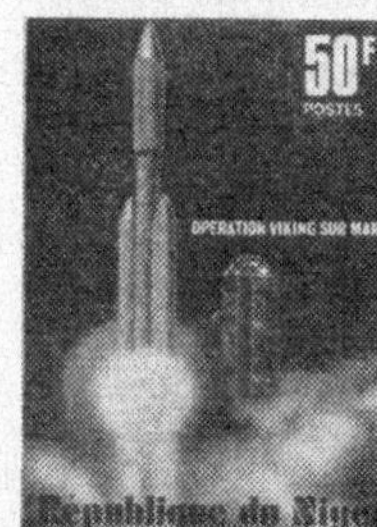
237 Rocket Launch

1977. "Viking" Space Mission. Multicoloured.
667 50 f. Type **237** (postage) . . . 45 15
668 80 f. "Viking" approaching Mars (horiz) 65 20
669 100 f. "Viking" on Mars (horiz) (air) 65 25
670 150 f. Parachute descent . . . 1·00 30
671 200 f. Rocket in flight . . . . 1·40 45

238 Marabou Stork

1977. Fauna Protection.
673 **238** 80 f. sepia, bis and red . 2·00 85
674 – 90 f. brown and turquoise 1·25 60
DESIGN: 90 f. Bushbuck.

239 Satellite and Weather Symbols

1977. World Meteorological Day.
675 **239** 100 f. blue, black & turq 1·00 50

240 Gymnastic Exercise

1977. 2nd Youth Festival, Tahoua. Multicoloured.
676 40 f. Type **240** 35 20
677 50 f. High jumping 40 25
678 80 f. Choral ensemble 70 35

241 Red Cross and Children playing

1977. World Health Day. Child Immunisation Campaign.
679 **241** 80 f. red, mauve & orange 75 35

242 Fly, Dagger, and W.H.O. Emblem in Eye

1977. Fight against Onchocerosis (blindness caused by worm infestation).
680 **242** 100 f. blue, grey and red . 1·40 55

243 Guirka Tahoua Dance

1977. "Popular Arts and Traditions". Multicoloured.
681 40 f. Type **243** 45 25
682 50 f. Maifilafili Gaya 50 20
683 80 f. Naguihinayan Loga . . . 80 45

244 Four Cavalrymen

1977. Chiefs' Traditional Cavalry. Multicoloured.
684 40 f. Type **244** 55 25
685 50 f. Chieftain at head of cavalry 65 30
686 60 f. Chieftain and cavalry . . 90 45

245 Planting Crops

1977. "Operation Green Sahel" (recovery of desert).
687 **245** 40 f. multicoloured 50 25

246 Albert John Luthuli (Peace, 1960)

1977. Nobel Prize Winners. Multicoloured.
688 50 f. Type **246** 30 15
689 80 f. Maurice Maeterlinck (Literature, 1911) 55 20
690 100 f. Allan L. Hodgkin (Medicine, 1963) 70 25
691 150 f. Albert Camus (Literature, 1957) . . . . 1·00 35
692 200 f. Paul Ehrlich (Medicine, 1908) . . . . 1·50 40

247 Mao Tse-tung

1977. 1st Death Anniv of Mao Tse-tung (Chinese leader).
694 **247** 100 f. black and red . . . 80 50

248 Vittorio Pozzo (Italy)

1977. World Football Cup Elimination Rounds. Multicoloured.
695 40 f. Type **248** 30 10
696 50 f. Vincente Feola, Spain . . 35 15
697 80 f. Aymore Moreira, Portugal 50 20
698 100 f. Sir Alf Ramsey, England 75 25
699 200 f. Helmut Schon, West Germany . . . . 1·40 45

249 Horse's Head and Parthenon

1977. U.N.E.S.C.O. Commemoration.
701 **249** 100 f. blue, red and pale blue 1·25 60

250 Carrying Water

1977. Women's Work. Multicoloured.
702 40 f. Type **250** 35 30
703 50 f. Pounding maize 40 25

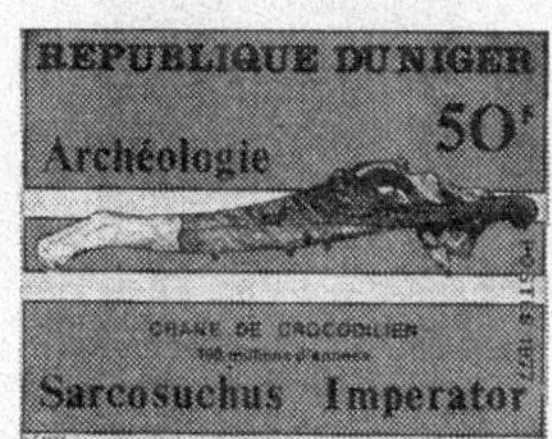
251 Crocodile Skull

1977. Archaeology. Multicoloured.
704 50 f. Type **251** 60 40
705 80 f. Neolithic tools 90 60

252 Paul Follereau and Leper

253 "The Assumption"

1978. 25th Anniv of World Leprosy Day.
706 **252** 40 f. red, blue & orange . 30 15
707 – 50 f. black, red & orange 40 20
DESIGN—HORIZ: 50 f. Follereau and two lepers.

1978. 400th Birth Anniv of Peter Paul Rubens. Paintings. Multicoloured.
708 50 f. Type **253** 30 15
709 70 f. "The Artist and his Friends" (horiz) 40 20
710 100 f. "History of Maria de Medici" 70 25
711 150 f. "Alathea Talbot" . . . 1·10 35
712 200 f. "Portrait of the Marquise de Spinola" . . . . 1·50 40

1978. As Nos. 376/7 but redrawn and background colour of 35 f. changed to blue, 35 f. undated, 50 f. dated "1978".
714 35 f. Broad-tailed paradise whydah . . . . 1·00 50
715 50 f. Cattle egret . . . . . . 2·00 60
The 50 f. is still wrongly inscribed "Balbucus".

254 Putting the Shot

1978. National Schools and University Sports Championships. Multicoloured.
716 40 f. Type **254** 20 15
717 50 f. Volleyball 30 20
718 60 f. Long-jumping 35 20
719 100 f. Throwing the javelin . . 55 35

255 Nurse assisting Patient

1978. Niger Red Cross.
720 **255** 40 f. multicoloured . . . 30 20

256 Station and Dish Aerial

1978. Goudel Earth Receiving Station.
721 **256** 100 f. multicoloured . . . 65 40

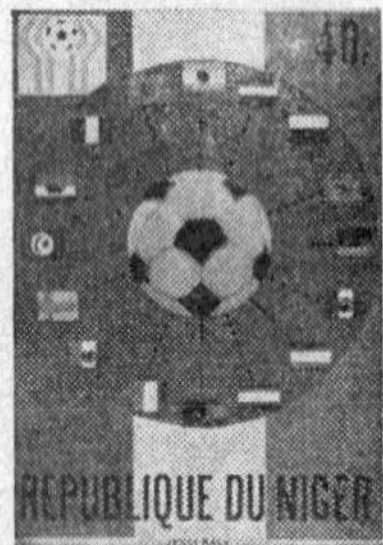

257 Football and Flags of Competing Nations

1978. World Cup Football Championship, Argentina. Multicoloured.
722 40 f. Type **257** 25 10
723 50 f. Football in net 35 15
724 100 f. Globe and goal 75 25
725 200 f. Tackling (horiz) . . . . 1·40 55

258 "Fireworks"

1978. Air. 3rd African Games, Algiers. Multicoloured.
727 40 f. Type **258** 25 20
728 150 f. Olympic rings emblem . 1·00 60

259 Niamey Post Office

1978. Niamey Post Office. Multicoloured.
729 40 f. Type **259** 25 15
730 60 f. Niamey Post Office (different) 35 25

260 Aerial View of Water-works

1978. Goudel Water-works.
731 **260** 100 f. multicoloured . . . 55 40

261 R. T. N. Emblem

1978. Air. 20th Anniv of Niger Broadcasting.
732 **261** 150 f. multicoloured . . . 90 60

262 Golden Eagle and Oldenburg 2 g. Stamp of 1859

1978. Air. "Philexafrique" Stamp Exhibition, Libreville, Gabon (1st issue) and Int Stamp Fair, Essen, West Germany. Multicoloured.
733 100 f. Type **262** . . . . 1·75 1·25
734 100 f. Giraffes and Niger 1959 2 f. stamp . . . . 1·75 1·25
See also Nos. 769/70

263 Giraffe

265 Dome of the Rock, Jerusalem

1978. Endangered Animals. Multicoloured.
735 40 f. Type **263** 45 25
736 50 f. Ostrich . . . . 1·50 30
737 70 f. Cheetah 75 35
738 150 f. Scimitar oryx (horiz) . 1·50 75
739 200 f. Addax (horiz) . . . . 2·00 95
740 300 f. Hartebeest (horiz) . . . 2·50 1·25

1978. World Cup Football Championship Finalists. Nos. 695/9 optd.
741 **248** 40 f. multicoloured . . . 30 20
742 – 50 f. multicoloured . . . 40 20
743 – 80 f. multicoloured . . . 55 25
744 – 100 f. multicoloured . . . 65 40
745 – 200 f. multicoloured . . . 1·40 75
OVERPRINTS: 40 f. **EQUIPE QUATRIEME: ITALIE**; 50 f. **EQUIPE TROISIEME: BRESIL**; 80 f. **EQUIPE SECONDE: PAYS BAS**; 100 f. **EQUIPE VAINQUEUR: ARGENTINE**. 200 f. **ARGENTINE - PAYS BAS 3 - 1.**

1978. Palestinian Welfare.
747 **265** 40 f. + 5 f. multicoloured 40 30

266 Laying Foundation Stone, and View of University

1978. Air. Islamic University of Niger.
748 **266** 100 f. multicoloured . . . 60 40

267 Tinguizi **268** "The Homecoming" (Daumier)

1978. Musicians. Multicoloured.
749 100 f. Type **267** 75 40
750 100 f. Chetima Ganga (horiz) . 75 40
751 100 f. Dan Gourmou 75 40

1979. Paintings. Multicoloured.
752 50 f. Type **268** 50 20
753 100 f. "Virgin in Prayer" (Durer) 60 20
754 150 f. "Virgin and Child" (Durer) 90 30
755 200 f. "Virgin and Child" (Durer) (different) . . . . . 1·25 40

269 Feeder Tanks

1979. Solar Energy. Multicoloured.
757 40 f. Type **269** 30 20
758 50 f. Solar panels on house roofs (horiz) 40 25

270 Langha Contestants

1979. Traditional Sports. Multicoloured.
759 40 f. Type **270** 25 15
760 50 f. Langha contestants clasping hands 35 20

271 Children with Building Bricks

1979. International Year of the Child. Multicoloured.
761 40 f. Type **271** 25 15
762 100 f. Children with book . . 60 25
763 150 f. Children with model airplane . . . . 1·25 45

272 Rowland Hill, Peugeot Mail Van and French "Ceres" Stamp of 1849

1979. Death Centenary of Sir Rowland Hill. Multicoloured.
764 40 f. Type **272** 25 15
765 100 f. Canoes and Austrian newspaper stamp, 1851 . . . 60 25
766 150 f. "DC-3" aircraft & U.S. "Lincoln" stamp, 1869 . . . 1·10 35
767 200 f. British Advanced Passenger Train and Canada 7½d. stamp, 1857 . . . . . 1·90 50

273 Zabira Decorated Bag and Niger 45 f. Stamp, 1965

1979. "Philexafrique 2" Exhibition, Gabon (2nd issue).
769 **273** 50 f. multicoloured . . . 65 40
770 – 150 f. blue, red & carmen 1·60 1·10
DESIGN: 150 f. Talking Heads, world map, satellite and U.P.U. emblem.

274 Alcock and Brown Statue and Vickers Vimy aircraft

1979. 60th Anniv of First Transatlantic Flight.
771 **274** 100 f. multicoloured . . . 1·00 35

275 Djermakoye Palace

1979. Historic Monuments.
772 **275** 100 f. multicoloured . . . 55 40

276 Bororos in Festive Headdress

1979. Annual Bororo Festival. Multicoloured.
773 45 f. Type **276** 30 20
774 60 f. Bororo women in traditional costume (vert) . 35 25

277 Boxing

1979. Pre-Olympic Year.
775 **277** 45 f. multicoloured . . . 30 15
776 – 100 f. multicoloured . . . 55 25
777 – 150 f. multicoloured . . . 85 35
778 – 250 f. multicoloured . . . 1·25 45
DESIGNS: 100 f. to 250 f. Various boxing scenes.

278 Class of Learner-drivers

1979. Driving School.
780 **278** 45 f. multicoloured . . . 30 20

279 Douglas DC-10 over Map of Niger

1979. Air. 20th Anniv of ASECNA (African Air Safety Organization).
781 **279** 150 f. multicoloured . . . 1·10 60

1979. "Apollo 11" Moon Landing. Nos. 667/8, 670/1 optd **alunissage apollo XI juillet 1969** and lunar module.
782 50 f. Type **237** (postage) . . . 30 20
783 80 f. "Viking" approaching Mars (horiz) 50 35
784 150 f. Parachute descent (air) . 90 60
785 200 f. Rocket in flight . . . . 1·25 80

281 Four-man Bobsleigh

1979. Winter Olympic Games, Lake Placid (1980). Multicoloured.
787 40 f. Type **281** 25 15
788 60 f. Downhill skiing 35 15
789 100 f. Speed skating 60 25
790 150 f. Two-man bobsleigh . . 90 35
791 200 f. Figure skating . . . . . 1·10 45

282 Le Gaweye Hotel

1980. Air.
793 **282** 100 f. multicoloured . . . 60 40

283 Sultan and Court

1980. Sultan of Zinder's Court. Multicoloured.
794 45 f. Type **283** 30 20
795 60 f. Sultan and court (different) 40 20

284 Chain Smoker and Athlete
285 Walking

1980. World Health Day. Anti-Smoking Campaign.
796 **284** 100 f. multicoloured . . . 65 40

1980. Olympic Games, Moscow. Multicoloured.
797 60 f. Throwing the javelin . . 35 15
798 90 f. Type **285** 50 20
799 100 f. High jump (horiz) . . . 55 25
800 300 f. Running (horiz) . . . . 1·50 55

1980. Winter Olympic Games Medal Winners. Nos. 787/91 optd.
802 **281** 40 f. **VAINQUEUR R.D.A.** 25 15
803 – 60 f. **VAINQUEUR STENMARK SUEDE** 30 20
804 – 100 f. **VAINQUEUR HEIDEN Etats-Unis** . . 60 30
805 – 150 f. **VAINQUEURS SCHERER-BENZ Suisse** 90 45
806 – 200 f. **VAINQUEUR COUSINS Grande Bretagne** . . . . 1·25 65

287 Village Scene

1980. Health Year.
808 **287** 150 f. multicoloured . . . 75 50

288 Shimbashi-Yokohama Steam Locomotive

1980. Steam Locomotives. Multicoloured.
809 45 f. Type **288** 50 15
810 60 f. American locomotive . . 60 20
811 90 f. German State Railway series 61 . . . . 1·00 25
812 100 f. Prussian State Railway P2 1·25 40
813 130 f. "L'Aigle" . . . . . . 1·75 50

289 Steve Biko and Map of Africa
292 U.A.P.T. Emblem

291 Footballer

1980. 4th Death Anniv of Steve Biko (South African Anti-apartheid Worker).
815 **289** 150 f. multicoloured . . . 80 60

1980. Olympic Medal Winners. Nos. 787/800 optd.
816 **285** 60 f. **KULA (URSS)** . . 35 15
817 – 90 f. **DAMILANO (IT)** . . 55 25
818 – 100 f. **WZSOLA (POL)** . 60 30
819 – 300 f. **YIFTER (ETH)** . . 1·60 90

1980. World Cup Football Championship, Spain (1982). Various designs showing Football.
821 **291** 45 f. multicoloured . . . 25 15
822 – 60 f. multicoloured . . . 30 15
823 – 90 f. multicoloured . . . 55 20
824 – 100 f. multicoloured . . . 60 25
825 – 130 f. multicoloured . . . 80 30

1980. 5th Anniv of African Posts and Telecommunications Union.
827 **292** 100 f. multicoloured . . . 55 40

293 Earthenware Statuettes

1981. Kareygorou Culture Terracotta Statuettes. Multicoloured.
828 45 f. Type **293** 25 20
829 60 f. Head (vert) 35 20
830 90 f. Head (different) (vert) . 50 30
831 150 f. Three heads 90 50

294 "Self-portrait"
295 Ostrich

1981. Paintings by Rembrandt. Multicoloured.
832 60 f. Type **294** 40 15
833 90 f. "Portrait of Hendrickje at the Window" 60 20
834 100 f. "Portrait of an Old Man" 65 25
835 130 f. "Maria Trip" 90 35
836 200 f. "Self-portrait" (different) 1·25 45
837 400 f. "Portrait of Saskia" . . 2·25 1·00

1981. Animals. Multicoloured.
839 10 f. Type **295** 75 20
840 20 f. Scimitar oryx 25 15
841 25 f. Addra gazelle 20 15
842 30 f. Arabian bustard . . . . 1·25 50
843 60 f. Giraffe 50 20
844 150 f. Addax . . . . 1·00 45

296 "Apollo 11"

1981. Air. Conquest of Space. Multicoloured.
845 100 f. Type **296** 60 25
846 150 f. Boeing 747 SCA carrying space shuttle . . . . 1·00 40
847 200 f. Rocket carrying space shuttle . . . . 1·25 40
848 300 f. Space shuttle flying over planet . . . . 3·00 1·00

297 Tanks
298 Disabled Archer

1981. 7th Anniv of Military Coup.
849 **297** 100 f. multicoloured . . . 1·00 40

1981. International Year of Disabled People.
850 **298** 50 f. dp. brown, red & brown 50 20
851 – 100 f. brown, red and green 75 40
DESIGN: 100 f. Disabled draughtsman.

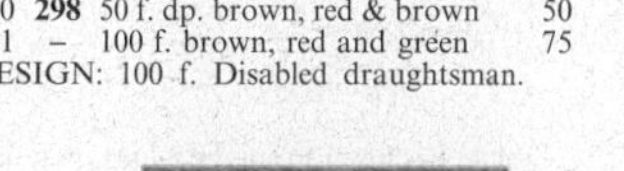

299 Ballet Mahalba

1981. Ballet Mahalba. Multicoloured.
852 100 f. Type **299** 70 35
853 100 f. Ballet Mahalba (different) 70 35

300 "Portrait of Olga in an Armchair"
301 Mosque and Ka'aba

1981. Air. Birth Centenary of Pablo Picasso (artist). Multicoloured.
854 60 f. Type **300** 40 20
855 90 f. "The Family of Acrobats" 55 25
856 120 f. "The Three Musicians" 70 35
857 200 f. "Paul on a Donkey" . 1·10 55
858 400 f. "Young Girl drawing in an Interior" (horiz) . . . . . 2·40 1·25

1981. 15th Centenary of Hejira.
859 **301** 100 f. multicoloured . . . 60 35

302 Carriage

1981. British Royal Wedding.
860 **302** 150 f. multicoloured . . . 60 35
861 – 200 f. multicoloured . . . 1·00 55
862 – 300 f. multicoloured . . . 1·25 1·00
DESIGNS: 200 f., 300 f. Similar designs showing carriages.

303 Sir Alexander Fleming
305 Crops, Cattle and Fish

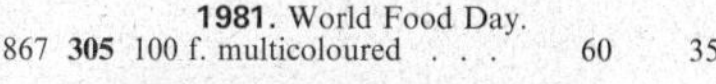

304 Pen-nibs, Envelope, Flower and U.P.U. Emblem

1981. Birth Centenary of Sir Alexander Fleming (discoverer of Penicillin).
864 **303** 150 f. blue, brown and green 1·50 60

1981. International Letter Writing Week.
865 **304** 65 f. on 45 f. blue and red 40 20
866 – 85 f. on 60 f. blue, orange and black 50 30
DESIGN: 85 f. Quill, hand holding pen and U.P.U. emblem.

1981. World Food Day.
867 **305** 100 f. multicoloured . . . 60 35

306 Tackling

1981. World Cup Football Championship, Spain (1982). Multicoloured.
868 40 f. Type **306** 25 20
869 65 f. Goal keeper fighting for ball 40 30
870 85 f. Passing ball 55 35
871 150 f. Running with ball . . . 1·00 60
872 300 f. Jumping for ball . . . 2·25 1·10

307 Peugeot, 1912

1981. 75th Anniv of French Grand Prix Motor Race. Multicoloured.
874 20 f. Type **307** 25 15
875 40 f. Bugatti, 1924 . . . . . 35 20
876 65 f. Lotus-Climax, 1962 . . . 55 30
877 85 f. Georges Boillot 75 35
878 150 f. Phil Hill . . . . 1·10 60

308 "Madonna and Child" (Botticelli)   **309** Children watering Plants

1981. Christmas. Various Madonna and Child Paintings by named artists. Multicoloured.

880 100 f. Type **308** 60 40
881 200 f. Botticini . . . . . . 1·25 75
882 300 f. Botticini (different) . . 2·00 1·10

1982. School Gardens. Multicoloured.

883 65 f. Type **309** 50 30
884 85 f. Tending plants and examining produce 60 35

310 Arturo Toscanini (conductor, 25th death anniv)

1982. Celebrities' Anniversaries. Multicoloured.

885 120 f. Type **310** . . . . . . 1·00 45
886 140 f. "Fruits on a Table" (Manet, 150th birth anniv) (horiz) 80 55
887 200 f. "L'Estaque" (Braque, birth centenary) (horiz) . . 1·25 60
888 300 f. George Washington (250th birth anniv) . . . . . . 2·00 90
889 400 f. Goethe (poet, 150th death anniv) . . . . 2·50 1·25
890 500 f. Princess of Wales (21st birthday) . . . . 2·75 1·50

311 Palace of Congresses

1982. Palace of Congresses.

892 **311** 150 f. multicoloured . . . 90 60

312 Martial Arts

1982. 7th Youth Festival, Agadez. Multicoloured.

893 65 f. Type **312** 40 30
894 100 f. Traditional wrestling . . 60 40

313 Planting a Tree

1982. National Re-afforestation Campaign. Multicoloured.

895 150 f. Type **313** . . . . . . 1·00 60
896 200 f. Forest and desert . . . 1·25 75

MINIMUM PRICE

The minimum price quoted is 10p which represents a handling charge rather than a basis for valuing common stamps. For further notes about prices, see introductory pages.

314 Scouts in Pirogue   **315** Map of Africa showing Member States

1982. 75th Anniv of Boy Scout Movement. Mult.

897 65 f. Type **314** 55 30
898 85 f. Scouts inflatable dinghy . . 65 30
899 130 f. Scouts in canoe . . . . 1·25 45
900 200 f. Scouts on raft . . . . 1·75 60

1982. Economic Community of West African States.

902 **315** 200 f. yellow, black and blue 1·25 75

316 Casting Net

1982. Niger Fishermen. Multicoloured.

903 65 f. Type **316** 55 30
904 85 f. Net fishing 70 40

1982. Birth of Prince William of Wales. Nos. 860/2 optd **NAISSANCE ROYALE 1982**.

905 **302** 150 f. multicoloured . . . 75 60
906 – 200 f. multicoloured . . . 1·00 75
907 – 300 f. multicoloured . . . 1·40 1·10

318 Hands reaching towards Mosque

1982. 13th Islamic Foreign Ministers Meeting, Niamey.

909 **318** 100 f. multicoloured . . . 60 40

319 "Flautist"

1982. Norman Rockwell Paintings. Multicoloured.

910 65 f. Type **319** 40 25
911 85 f. "Clerk" 50 25
912 110 f. "Teacher and Pupil" . . 70 35
913 150 f. "Girl Shopper" 90 50

320 World Map and Satellite

1982. I.T.U. Delegates' Conference, Nairobi.

914 **320** 130 f. blue, light blue and black . . . . 1·00 50

1982. World Cup Football Championship Winners. Nos. 868/72 optd.

915 40 f. Type **306** 25 20
916 65 f. Goal keeper fighting for ball 40 30
917 85 f. Passing ball 45 25
918 150 f. Running with ball . . 90 50
919 300 f. Jumping for ball . . . 1·75 1·10

OVERPRINTS: 40 f. **1966 VAINQUEUR GRANDE - BRETAGNE**; 65 f. **"1970 VAINQUEUR BRESIL"**; 85 f. **"1974 VAINQUEUR ALLEMAGNE (RFA)"**; 150 f. **"1978 VAINQUEUR ARGENTINE"**; 300 f. **"1982 VAINQUEUR ITALIE"**.

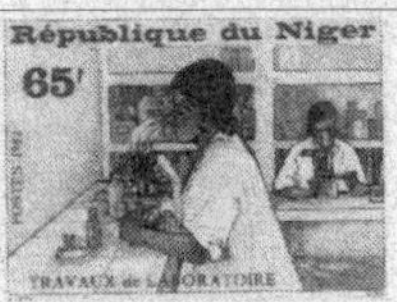

322 Laboratory Workers with Microscopes

1982. Laboratory Work. Multicoloured.

921 65 f. Type **322** 60 40
922 115 f. Laboratory workers . . 80 50

323 "Adoration of the Kings"

1982. Air. Christmas. Paintings by Rubens. Multicoloured.

923 200 f. Type **323** . . . . . . 1·25 50
924 300 f. "Mystic Marriage of St. Catherine" . . . . 2·00 75
925 400 f. "Virgin and Child" . . . 2·50 1·00

324 Montgolfier Balloon

1983. Air. Bicent of Manned Flight. Mult.

926 65 f. Type **324** 45 15
927 85 f. Charles's hydrogen balloon 60 20
928 200 f. Goodyear Aerospace airship (horiz) . . . . . . 1·25 60
929 250 f. Farman H.F.III biplane (horiz) . . . . 1·50 70
930 300 f. Concorde . . . . . . 3·00 1·40
931 500 f. "Apollo 11" spacecraft . 3·00 1·40

No. 928 is wrongly inscribed "Zeppelin".

325 Harvesting Rice   **326** E.C.A. Anniversary Emblem

1983. Self-sufficiency in Food. Multicoloured.

932 65 f. Type **325** 60 30
933 85 f. Planting rice 80 40

1983. 25th Anniv of Economic Commission for Africa.

934 **326** 120 f. multicoloured . . . 75 40
935 200 f. multicoloured . . . 1·25 70

327 "The Miraculous Draught of Fishes"

1983. 500th Birth Anniv of Raphael. Multicoloured.

936 65 f. Type **327** 70 15
937 85 f. "Grand Ducal Madonna" (vert) 50 20
938 100 f. "The Deliverance of St. Peter" 60 25
939 150 f. "Sistine Madonna" (vert) 1·00 45
940 200 f. "The Fall on the Way to Calvary" (vert) . . . . . 1·10 60
941 300 f. "The Entombment" . . 1·75 80
942 400 f. "The Transfiguration" (vert) . . . . 2·25 1·10
943 500 f. "St. Michael fighting the Dragon" (vert) . . . . . 3·00 1·40

328 Surveying

1983. The Army in the Service of Development. Multicoloured.

944 85 f. Type **328** 60 25
945 150 f. Road building . . . . 1·00 50

329 Palace of Justice

1983. Palace of Justice, Agadez.

946 **329** 65 f. multicoloured . . . 40 20

330 Javelin

1983. Air. Olympic Games, Los Angeles. Mult.

947 85 f. Type **330** 50 20
948 200 f. Shotput . . . . 1·10 60
949 250 f. Throwing the hammer (vert) . . . . 1·50 70
950 300 f. Discus . . . . 1·75 80

331 Rural Post Vehicle   **332** Dome of the Rock

1983. Rural Post Service. Multicoloured.

952 65 f. Type **331** 50 20
953 100 f. Post vehicle and map . 75 30

1983. Palestine.

954 **332** 65 f. multicoloured . . . 65 20

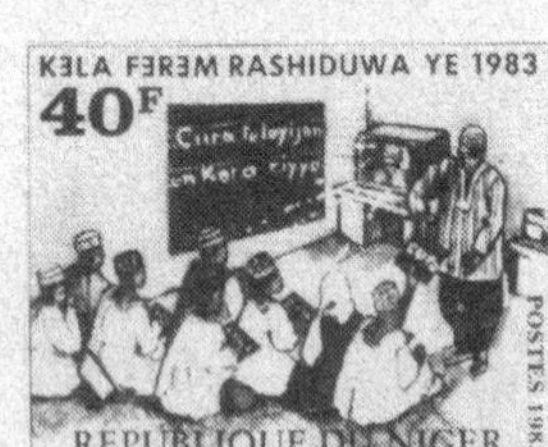

333 Class watching Television

1983. International Literacy Day. Multicoloured.

955 40 f. Type **333** 25 15
956 65 f. Teacher at blackboard (vert) 40 25
957 85 f. Learning weights (vert) . 55 30
958 100 f. Outdoor class 60 35
959 150 f. Woman reading magazine (vert) . . . . 1·00 50

334 Three Dancers

1983. Seventh Dosso Dance Festival. Multicoloured.

960 65 f. Type **334** 50 25
961 85 f. Four dancers 60 35
962 120 f. Two dancers 90 50

335 Post Van   336 Television Antenna and Solar Panel

1983. World Communications Year. Multicoloured.
963 80 f. Type **335** 60 40
964 120 f. Sorting letters 80 40
965 150 f. W.C.Y. emblem (vert) . 1·00 50

1983. Solar Energy in the Service of Television. Multicoloured.
966 85 f. Type **336** 60 30
967 130 f. Land-rover and solar panel 90 45

337 "Hypolimnas misippus"

1983. Butterflies. Multicoloured.
968 75 f. Type **337** 70 35
969 120 f. "Papilio demodocus" . 1·10 50
970 250 f. "Vanessa antiopa" . . . 2·00 90
971 350 f. "Charexes jasius" . . . 2·75 1·40
972 500 f. "Danaus chrisippus" . . 4·50 1·75

338 "Virgin and Child with Angels"   339 Samariya Emblem

1983. Air. Christmas. Paintings by Botticelli. Multicoloured.
973 120 f. Type **338** 75 40
974 350 f. "Adoration of the Magi" (horiz) . . . . 2·25 1·00
975 500 f. "Virgin of the Pomegranate" . . . . 3·00 1·25

1984. Samariya.
976 **339** 80 f. black, orange & grn . 50 30

340 Running

1984. Air. Olympic Games, Los Angeles. Mult.
977 80 f. Type **340** 40 20
978 120 f. Pole vault 60 30
979 140 f. High jump 80 30
980 200 f. Triple jump (vert) . . . 1·25 45
981 350 f. Long jump (vert) . . . 2·00 1·00

341 "Alestes bouboni"

1984. Fish.
983 **341** 120 f. multicoloured . . . 1·50 55

342 Obstacle Course

1984. Military Pentathlon. Multicoloured.
984 120 f. Type **342** 80 40
985 140 f. Shooting 95 50

343 Radio Station

1984. New Radio Station.
986 **343** 120 f. multicoloured . . . 85 40

344 Flags, Agriculture and Symbols of Unity and Growth

1984. 25th Anniv of Council of Unity.
987 **344** 65 f. multicoloured . . . 40 25
988 85 f. multicoloured . . . 50 40

345 "Paris" (early steamer)

1984. Ships. Multicoloured.
989 80 f. Type **345** 70 25
990 120 f. "Jacques Coeur" (full-rigged ship) 80 35
991 150 f. "Bosphorus" (full-rigged ship) . . . . 1·25 45
992 300 f. "Comet" (full-rigged ship) 2·25 85

346 Daimler

1984. Motor Cars. Multicoloured.
993 100 f. Type **346** 75 30
994 140 f. Renault . . . . 1·10 45
995 250 f. Delage "D 8" . . . . . 1·75 70
996 400 f. Maybach "Zeppelin" . 2·75 90

347 "Rickmer Rickmers" (full-rigged ship)

1984. Universal Postal Union Congress, Hamburg.
997 **347** 300 f. blue, brown and green 2·50 1·50

348 Cattle

1984. Ayerou Market. Multicoloured.
998 80 f. Type **348** 60 40
999 120 f. View of market 90 60

349 Viper

1984.
1000 **349** 80 f. multicoloured . . . 75 40

350 Carl Lewis (100 and 200 metres)

1984. Air. Olympic Games Medal Winners. Multicoloured.
1001 80 f. Type **350** 50 20
1002 120 f. J. Cruz (800 metres) . . 70 40
1003 140 f. A. Cova (10,000 metres) 80 45
1004 300 f. Al Joyner (Triple jump) 1·75 90

351 Emblem

1984. 10th Anniv of Economic Community of West Africa.
1006 **351** 80 f. multicoloured . . . 50 30

352 Emblem and Extract from General Kountche's Speech

1984. United Nations Disarmament Decennials.
1007 **352** 400 f. black and green . . 2·50 1·75
1008 500 f. black and blue . . 3·00 1·75

353 Football

1984. Air. Preliminary Rounds of World Cup Football Championship, Mexico.
1009 **353** 150 f. multicoloured . . . 1·00 45
1010 – 250 f. multicoloured . . . 1·75 80
1011 – 450 f. multicoloured . . . 2·50 1·25
1012 – 500 f. multicoloured . . . 3·00 1·75
DESIGNS: 250 to 500 f. Footballing scenes.

354 "The Visitation" (Ghirlandaio)

1984. Air. Christmas. Multicoloured.
1013 100 f. Type **354** 60 30
1014 200 f. "Virgin and Child" (Master of Saint Verdiana) 1·25 65
1015 400 f. "Virgin and Child" (J. Koning) . . . . 2·50 1·25

1984. Drought Relief. Nos. 895/6 optd **Aide au Sahel 84**.
1016 150 f. multicoloured . . . . . 1·00 80
1017 200 f. multicoloured . . . . . 1·25 1·10

356 Organization Emblem   357 Breast-feeding Baby

1985. 10th Anniv of World Tourism Organization.
1018 **356** 100 f. black, orange and green 70 40

1985. Infant Survival Campaign. Multicoloured.
1019 85 f. Type **357** 70 30
1020 110 f. Feeding baby and changing nappy 90 40

358 Black-necked Stilt

1985. Air. Birth Centenary of John J. Audubon (ornithologist). Multicoloured.
1021 110 f. Type **358** . . . . . . 1·25 90
1022 140 f. Greater flamingo (vert) 1·75 1·25
1023 200 f. Atlantic puffin . . . . 2·50 1·90
1024 350 f. Arctic tern (vert) . . . 4·50 2·50

360 Profile and Emblem

1985. 15th Anniv of Technical and Cultural Co-operation Agency.
1026 **360** 110 f. brown, red & vio . 65 40

361 Dancers

1985. 8th Niamey Festival. Multicoloured.
1027 85 f. Type **361** 60 40
1028 110 f. Four dancers (vert) . . 70 50
1029 150 f. Dancers (different) . . 1·00 65

362 Wolf ("White Fang") and Jack London

1985. International Youth Year. Multicoloured.
1030 85 f. Type **362** 60 25
1031 105 f. Woman with lion and Joseph Kessel 75 30
1032 250 f. Capt. Ahab harpooning white whale ("Moby Dick") 1·75 90
1033 450 f. Mowgli on elephant ("Jungle Book") . . . . . 2·75 1·50

363 Two Children on Leaf

1985. "Philexafrique" Stamp Exhibition, Lome, Togo (1st issue). Multicoloured.

1034 200 f. Type **363** . . . . 1·25 1·00
1035 200 f. Mining . . . . 1·25 1·00

See also Nos. 1064/5.

364 "Hugo with his Son Francois" (A. de Chatillon)

1985. Death Centenary of Victor Hugo (writer).

1036 **364** 500 f. multicoloured . . 3·00 1·75

365 Diesel Train, Satellite and Boeing 737 on Map

1985. Europafrique.

1037 **365** 110 f. multicoloured . . 1·25 55

366 Addax

1985. Endangered Animals. Multicoloured.

1038 50 f. Type **366** 40 15
1039 60 f. Addax (different) (horiz) 45 25
1040 85 f. Two scimitar oryxes (horiz) 55 25
1041 110 f. Oryx 75 35

367 "Oedaleus sp" on Millet

368 Cross of Agadez

1985. Vegetation Protection. Multicoloured.

1042 85 f. Type **367** 55 20
1043 110 f. "Dysdercus volkeri" (beetle) 75 35
1044 150 f. Fungi attacking sorghum and millet (horiz) . . 2·50 60
1045 210 f. Sudan golden sparrows in tree . . . . 3·50 1·60
1046 390 f. Red-billed queleas in tree 6·00 3·25

1985.

1047 **368** 85 f. green 45 15
1048 – 110 f. brown 55 15

DESIGN: 110 f. Girl carrying water jar on head.

369 Arms, Flags and Agriculture

1985. 25th Anniv of Independence.

1049 **369** 110 f. multicoloured . . 70 40

370 Baobab

371 Man watching Race

1985. Protected Trees. Multicoloured.

1050 110 f. Type **370** 80 50
1051 210 f. "Acacia albida" . . . 1·40 1·00
1052 390 f. Baobab (different) . . 3·00 1·60

1985. Niamey–Bamako Powerboat Race. Mult.

1053 110 f. Type **371** 70 45
1054 150 f. Helicopter and powerboat 1·60 85
1055 250 f. Powerboat and map . 1·75 1·25

1985. "Trees for Niger". As Nos. 1050/2 but new values and optd **DES ARBRES POUR LE NIGER**.

1056 **370** 30 f. multicoloured . . . 25 20
1057 – 85 f. multicoloured . . . 55 40
1058 – 110 f. multicoloured . . 70 55

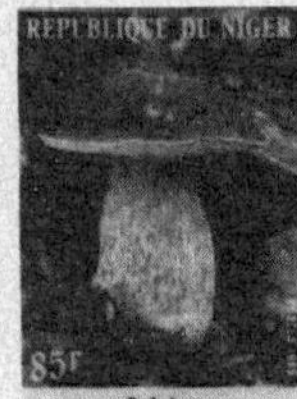

373 "Boletus"

1985. Fungi. Multicoloured.

1059 85 f. Type **373** . . . . 1·40 30
1060 110 f. "Hypholoma fasciculare" 2·10 45
1061 200 f. "Coprinus comatus" . 3·00 1·10
1062 300 f. "Agaricus arvensis" (horiz) . . . . 4·50 1·50
1063 400 f. "Geastrum fimbriatum" (horiz) . . . . 5·75 2·10

374 First Village Water Pump

1985. "Philexafrique" Stamp Exhibition, Lome, Togo (2nd issue). Multicoloured.

1064 250 f. Type **374** . . . . . . 1·75 1·25
1065 250 f. Handicapped youths playing dili (traditional game) 1·75 1·25

375 "Saving Ant" and Savings Bank Emblem

376 Gouroumi

1985. World Savings Day.

1066 **375** 210 f. multicoloured . . 1·40 85

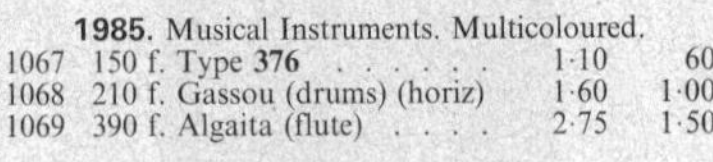

1985. Musical Instruments. Multicoloured.

1067 150 f. Type **376** . . . . . . 1·10 60
1068 210 f. Gassou (drums) (horiz) 1·60 1·00
1069 390 f. Algaita (flute) . . . . 2·75 1·50

377 "The Immaculate Conception"

379 National Identity Card

378 Comet over Paris, 1910

1985. Air. Christmas. Paintings by Murillo. Mult.

1071 110 f. "Madonna of the Rosary" 65 35
1072 250 f. Type **377** . . . . . . 1·75 90
1073 390 f. "Virgin of Seville" . . 2·50 1·25

1985. Air. Appearance of Halley's Comet. Multicoloured.

1074 110 f. Type **378** 70 35
1075 130 f. Comet over New York 85 40
1076 200 f. "Giotto" satellite . . . 1·50 70
1077 300 f. "Vega" satellite . . . . 2·25 1·00
1078 390 f. "Planet A" space probe 2·50 1·25

1986. Civil Statutes Reform. Each black, green and orange.

1079 85 f. Type **379** 65 30
1080 110 f. Civil registration emblem 75 40

380 Road Signs

381 Oumarou Ganda (film producer)

1986. Road Safety Campaign.

1081 **380** 85 f. black, yellow & red . 75 30
1082 – 110 f. black, red & green . 1·00 40

DESIGN: 110 f. Speed limit sign, road and speedometer ("Watch your speed").

1986. Honoured Artists. Multicoloured.

1083 60 f. Type **381** 35 20
1084 85 f. Idi na Dadaou 50 30
1085 100 f. Dan Gourmou 60 40
1086 130 f. Koungoui (comedian) . 80 45

382 Martin Luther King

384 Statue and F. A. Bartholdi

383 Footballer and 1970 40 f. Stamp

1986. Air. 18th Death Anniv of Martin Luther King (human rights activist).

1087 **382** 500 f. multicoloured . . . 3·25 1·90

1986. Air. World Cup Football Championship, Mexico. Multicoloured.

1088 130 f. Type **383** . . . . 1·00 30
1089 210 f. Footballer and 1970 70 f. stamp . . . . 1·25 45
1090 390 f. Footballer and 1970 90 f. stamp . . . . 2·75 1·00
1091 400 f. Footballer and Mexican figure on "stamp" . . . 2·75 1·00

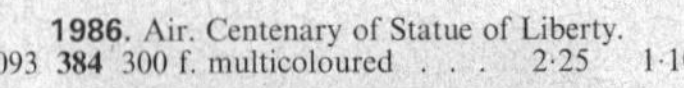

1986. Air. Centenary of Statue of Liberty.

1093 **384** 300 f. multicoloured . . . 2·25 1·10

385 Truck

1986. "Trucks of Hope". Multicoloured.

1094 85 f. Type **385** 75 30
1095 110 f. Mother and baby (vert) 1·00 40

386 Nelson Mandela and Walter Sisulu

387 Food Co-operatives

1986. International Solidarity with S. African and Namibian Political Prisoners Day. Multicoloured.

1096 200 f. Type **386** . . . . . . 1·50 80
1097 300 f. Nelson Mandela . . . 2·25 1·00

1986. 40th Anniv of F.A.O. Multicoloured.

1098 50 f. Type **387** 30 20
1099 60 f. Anti-desertification campaign 35 25
1100 85 f. Irrigation 50 35
1101 100 f. Rebuilding herds of live-stock 60 40
1102 110 f. Reafforestation . . . 75 45

388 Trees and Woman with Cooking Pots

389 "Sphodromantis sp."

1987. "For a Green Niger". Multicoloured.

1103 85 f. Type **388** 55 30
1104 110 f. Trees, woman and cooking pots (different) . . 70 40

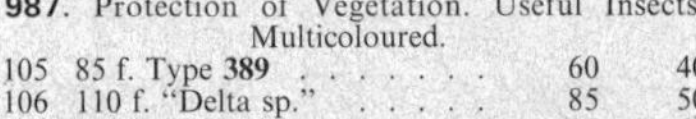

1987. Protection of Vegetation. Useful Insects. Multicoloured.

1105 85 f. Type **389** 60 40
1106 110 f. "Delta sp." 85 50
1107 120 f. "Cicindela sp." . . . 95 65

390 Transmitter, Map and Woman using Telephone

1987. Liptako–Gourma Telecommunications Network.

1108 **390** 110 f. multicoloured . . 80 50

391 Morse Key and Operator, 19th-century

1987. 150th Anniv of Morse Telegraph. Mult.

1109 120 f. Type **391** 75 40
1110 200 f. Samuel Morse (inventor) (vert) . . . . 1·25 70
1111 350 f. Morse transmitter and receiver . . . . 2·25 1·25

392 Tennis Player

1987. Olympic Games, Seoul (1988). Multicoloured.

1112 85 f. Type **392** 50 40
1113 110 f. Pole vaulter 70 40
1114 250 f. Footballer . . . . . . 1·50 90

393 Ice Hockey

1987. Winter Olympic Games, Calgary (1988) (1st issue). Multicoloured.
1116 85 f. Type **393** 60 35
1117 110 f. Speed skating 70 35
1118 250 f. Figure skating (pairs) . 1·75 90
See also Nos. 1146/9.

394 Long-distance Running

1987. African Games, Nairobi. Multicoloured.
1120 85 f. Type **394** 50 35
1121 110 f. High jumping 60 35
1122 200 f. Hurdling . . . . 1·25 70
1123 400 f. Javelin throwing . . . 2·50 1·40

395 Chief's Stool, Sceptre and Crown

1987. 10th Anniv of National Tourism Office. Multicoloured.
1124 85 f. Type **395** 50 35
1125 110 f. Nomad, caravan and sceptre handle 60 35
1126 120 f. Houses 70 40
1127 200 f. Bridge over River Niger 1·25 70

396 Yaama Mosque at Dawn

1987. Aga Khan Prize. Designs Showing Yaama mosque at various times of day.
1128 **396** 85 f. multicoloured . . . 50 35
1129 – 110 f. multicoloured . . 60 35
1130 – 250 f. multicoloured . . 1·50 90

397 Court Building

398 "Holy Family of the Sheep" (Raphael)

1987. Appeal Court, Niamey. Multicoloured.
1131 85 f. Type **397** 50 30
1132 110 f. Front entrance 60 35
1133 140 f. Side view 90 55

1987. Christmas.
1134 **398** 110 f. multicoloured . . 65 40

399 Water Drainage

1988. Health Care. Multicoloured.
1136 85 f. Type **399** 70 40
1137 110 f. Modern sanitation . . 80 40
1138 165 f. Refuse collection . . . 1·25 65

400 Singer and Band

402 New Great Market, Niamey

1988. Award of Dan-Gourmou Music Prize.
1139 **400** 85 f. multicoloured . . . 80 50

1988. Winter Olympic Games Winners. Nos. 1116/18 optd.
1140 85 f. **Medaille d'or URSS** . . 50 35
1141 110 f. **Medaille d'or 5.000-10.000 m GUSTAFSON (Suede)** . 60 40
1142 250 f. **Medaille d'or C. CORDEEVA -S. GRINKOV URSS** . . . . 1·50 90

1988.
1143 **402** 85 f. multicoloured . . . 60 40

403 Mother and Child

1988. U.N.I.C.E.F. Child Vaccination Campaign and 40th Anniv of W.H.O. Multicoloured.
1144 85 f. Type **403** 70 40
1145 110 f. Doctor and villagers . 90 50

404 Kayak

405 Emblem

1988. Air. Olympic Games, Seoul (2nd issue) and 125th Birth Anniv of Pierre de Coubertin (founder of modern Olympic Games). Multicoloured.
1146 85 f. Type **404** 50 20
1147 165 f. Rowing (horiz) . . . 90 50
1148 200 f. Two-man kayak (horiz) 1·25 70
1149 600 f. One-man kayak . . . 3·50 2·00

1988. 25th Anniv of Organization of African Unity.
1151 **405** 85 f. multicoloured . . . 50 30

406 Team working

407 Anniversary Emblem

1988. Dune Stabilisation.
1152 **406** 85 f. multicoloured . . . 60 40

1988. 125th Anniv of International Red Cross.
1153 **407** 85 f. multicoloured . . . 60 30
1154 110 f. multicoloured . . 80 40

409 Emblem

410 Couple, Globe and Laboratory Worker

1989. Niger Press Agency.
1159 **409** 85 f. black, orange & grn 45 30

1989. Campaign against AIDS.
1160 **410** 85 f. multicoloured . . . 55 30
1161 110 f. multicoloured . . 85 40

411 Radar, Tanker and Signals

412 General Ali Seybou (Pres.)

1989. 30th Anniv of International Maritime Organization.
1162 **411** 100 f. multicoloured . . . 1·25 60
1163 120 f. multicoloured . . . 1·50 80

1989. 15th Anniv of Military Coup. Mult.
1164 85 f. Type **412** 45 25
1165 110 f. Soldiers erecting flag . 65 35

413 Eiffel Tower

1989. "Philexfrance 89" International Stamp Exhibition, Paris. Multicoloured.
1166 100 f. Type **413** 60 40
1167 200 f. Flags on stamps . . . 1·25 65

414 "Planting a Tree of Liberty"

1989. Bicentenary of French Revolution.
1168 **414** 250 f. multicoloured . . . 1·50 1·00

415 Telephone Dial, Radio Mast, Map and Stamp

416 "Apollo 11" Launch

1989. 30th Anniv of West African Posts and Telecommunications Association.
1169 **415** 85 f. multicoloured . . . 45 30

1989. Air. 20th Anniv of First Manned Landing on Moon. Multicoloured.
1170 200 f. Type **416** . . . . 1·25 65
1171 300 f. Crew . . . . 2·00 1·00
1172 350 f. Astronaut and module on lunar surface . . . . 2·25 1·25
1173 400 f. Astronaut and U.S. flag on lunar surface . . . . . 2·50 1·25

417 Emblem

1989. 25th Anniv of African Development Bank.
1174 **417** 100 f. multicoloured . . . 60 30

418 Before and After Attack, and "Schistocerca gregaria"

1989. Locusts.
1175 **418** 85 f. multicoloured . . . 50 30

419 Auguste Lumiere and 1st Cine Performance, 1895

1989. 35th Death Anniv of Auguste Lumiere and 125th Birth Anniv of Louis Lumiere (photography pioneers). Multicoloured.
1176 150 f. Type **419** 90 55
1177 250 f. Louis Lumiere and first cine-camera, 1894 . . . . 1·50 85
1178 400 f. Lumiere brothers and first colour cine-camera, 1920 2·50 1·25

420 Tractor, Map and Pump

1989. 30th Anniv of Agriculture Development Council.
1179 **420** 75 f. multicoloured . . . 45 30

421 Zinder Regional Museum

422 "Russelia equisetiformis"

1989. Multicoloured.
1180 85 f. Type **421** 45 30
1182 165 f. Temet dunes 90 60

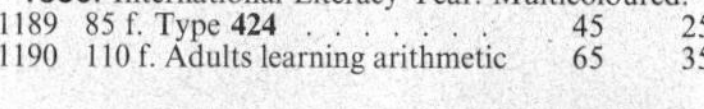

1989. Flowers. Multicoloured.
1183 10 f. Type **422** 15 10
1184 20 f. "Argyreia nervosa" . . 15 10
1185 30 f. "Hibiscus rosa-sinensis" 20 10
1186 50 f. "Catharanthus roseus" . 35 20
1187 100 f. "Cymothoe sangaris" (horiz) 75 35

423 Emblem

424 Adults learning Alphabet

1990. 10th Anniv of Pan-African Postal Union.
1188 **423** 120 f. multicoloured . . 70 40

1990. International Literacy Year. Multicoloured.
1189 85 f. Type **424** 45 25
1190 110 f. Adults learning arithmetic 65 35

425 Emblem

427 Leland and Child

426 Footballers and Florence

1990. 20th Anniv of Islamic Conference Organization.
1191 **425** 85 f. multicoloured . . . 50 30

1990. Air. World Cup Football Championship, Italy. Multicoloured.
1192 130 f. Type **426** . . . . . . 1·00 40
1193 210 f. Footballers and Verona 1·40 75
1194 500 f. Footballers and Bari . 3·25 1·75
1195 600 f. Footballers and Rome 3·75 2·00

1990. Mickey Leland (American Congressman) Commemoration.
1196 **427** 300 f. multicoloured . . 1·75 1·00
1197 500 f. multicoloured . . 3·00 1·75

428 Emblem **429** Flags and Envelopes on Map

1990. 1st Anniv of National Movement for the Development Society.
1198 **428** 85 f. multicoloured . . . 50 30

1990. 20th Anniv of Multinational Postal Training School, Abidjan.
1199 **429** 85 f. multicoloured . . . 65 30

430 Gymnastics

1990. Olympic Games, Barcelona (1992). Mult.
1200 85 f. Type **430** 40 25
1201 110 f. Hurdling 60 35
1202 250 f. Running . . . . 1·50 90
1203 400 f. Show jumping . . . . 2·75 1·40
1204 500 f. Long jumping . . . . 3·00 1·75

431 Arms, Map and Flag **432** Emblem

1990. 30th Anniv of Independence.
1206 **431** 85 f. multicoloured . . . 45 30
1207 110 f. multicoloured . . 65 40

1990. 40th Anniv of United Nations Development Programme.
1208 **432** 100 f. multicoloured . . 50 30

433 The Blusher **434** Christopher Columbus and "Santa Maria"

1991. Butterflies and Fungi. Multicoloured.
1209 85 f. Type **433** (postage) . . . 1·00 30
1210 110 f. "Graphium pylades" (female) 75 25
1211 200 f. "Pseudacraea hostilia" 1·25 55
1212 250 f. Cracked green russula . 2·50 1·10
1213 400 f. "Boletus impolitus" (air) 3·75 1·60
1214 500 f. "Precis octavia" . . . 2·75 1·25

1991. 540th Birth of Christopher Columbus. Mult.
1216 85 f. Type **434** (postage) . . . 70 25
1217 110 f. 15th-century Portuguese caravel . . . . 1·00 30
1218 200 f. 16th-century four-masted caravel . . . . 1·60 65
1219 250 f. "Estremadura" (Spanish caravel), 1511 . . . . . . 2·00 85
1220 400 f. "Vija" (Portuguese caravel), 1600 (air) . . . . 3·25 1·10
1221 500 f. "Pinta" . . . . 3·50 1·50

435 Speed Skating

1991. Winter Olympic Games, Albertville (1992). Multicoloured.
1223 110 f. Type **435** 60 25
1224 300 f. Ice-hockey . . . . . 1·25 80
1225 500 f. Women's downhill skiing 2·50 1·25
1226 600 f. Two-man luge . . . . 2·75 1·25

436 Flag and Boy holding Stone **437** Hairstyle

1991. Palestinian "Intifada" Movement.
1227 **436** 110 f. multicoloured . . 75 30

1991. Traditional Hairstyles. Multicoloured.
1228 85 f. Type **437** 20 10
1229 110 f. Netted hairstyle . . . 25 15
1230 165 f. Braided hairstyle . . . 40 20
1231 200 f. Plaited hairstyle . . . 45 25

438 Boubon Market

1991. African Tourism Year. Multicoloured.
1232 85 f. Type **438** 20 10
1233 110 f. Timia waterfalls (vert) 25 15
1234 130 f. Ruins at Assode . . . 30 15
1235 200 f. Tourism Year emblem (vert) 45 25

439 Anatoly Karpov and Gary Kasparov

1991. Anniversaries and Events. Multicoloured.
1236 85 f. Type **439** (World Chess Championship) (postage) . 20 10
1237 110 f. Ayrton Senna and Alain Prost (World Formula 1 motor racing championship) 25 15
1238 200 f. Reading of Declaration of Human Rights and Comte de Mirabeau (bicentenary of French Revolution) . . . 45 25
1239 250 f. Dwight D. Eisenhower, Winston Churchill and Field-Marshal Montgomery (50th anniv of America's entry into Second World War) . . . 60 35
1240 400 f. Charles de Gaulle and Konrad Adenauer (28th anniv of Franco-German Co-operation Agreement) (air) 95 55
1241 500 f. Helmut Kohl and Brandenburg Gate (2nd anniv of German reunification) . 1·10 60

440 Japanese "ERS-1" Satellite

1991. Satellites and Transport. Multicoloured.
1243 85 f. Type **440** (postage) . . 20 10
1244 110 f. Japanese satellite observing Aurora Borealis 25 15
1245 200 f. Louis Favre and "BB 415" diesel locomotive . . 45 25
1246 250 f. "BB-BB301" diesel locomotive 60 35
1247 400 f. "BB-BB302" diesel locomotive (air) 95 55
1248 500 f. Lockheed Stealth fighter-bomber and Concorde . . . 1·10 60

441 Crowd and Emblem on Map **443** Couple adding Final Piece to Globe Jigsaw

442 Timberless House

1991. National Conference (to determine new constitution).
1250 **441** 85 f. multicoloured . . . 20 10

1992.
1251 **442** 85 f. multicoloured . . . 20 10

1992. World Population Day. Multicoloured.
1252 85 f. Type **443** 20 10
1253 110 f. Children flying globe kite (after Robert Parker) . . . 25 15

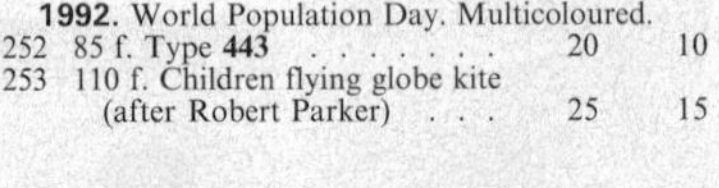

444 Columbus and Fleet

1992. 500th Anniv of Discovery of America by Columbus.
1254 **444** 250 f. multicoloured . . . 60 35

445 Zaleye

1992. 2nd Death Anniv of Hadjia Haqua Issa (Zaleye) (singer).
1255 **445** 150 f. multicoloured . . . 35 20

446 Conference Emblem **447** College Emblem

1992. International Nutrition Conference, Rome.
1256 **446** 145 f. multicoloured . . . 35 20
1257 350 f. multicoloured . . . 80 45

1993. 30th Anniv of African Meteorology and Civil Aviation College.
1258 **447** 110 f. blue, black & green 25 15

448 Girl planting Sapling

1993. Anti-desertification Campaign.
1259 **448** 85 f. multicoloured . . . 20 10
1260 165 f. multicoloured . . 40 20

449 Aerosol spraying Globe (Patricia Charets)

1993. World Population Day. Children's Drawings. Multicoloured.
1261 85 f. Type **449** 20 10
1262 110 f. Tree and person with globe as head looking at high-rise tower blocks (Mathieu Chevrault) 25 15

450 Jerusalem

1993. "Jerusalem, Holy City".
1268 **450** 110 f. multicoloured . . 30 15

451 People of Different Races

1994. Award of Nobel Peace Prize to Nelson Mandela and F. W. de Klerk (South African statesmen).
1269 **451** 270 f. multicoloured . . 70 40

OFFICIAL STAMPS

O **13** Djerma Women

1962. Figures of value in black.
O121 O **13** 1 f. violet 10 10
O122 2 f. green 10 10
O123 5 f. blue 15 10
O124 10 f. red 15 10
O125 20 f. blue 20 15
O126 25 f. orange 25 20
O127 30 f. blue 30 25
O128 35 f. green 35 30
O129 40 f. brown 35 35
O130 50 f. slate 40 40
O131 60 f. turquoise 50 45
O132 85 f. turquoise 70 40
O133 100 f. purple 85 40
O134 200 f. blue . . . . . . 1·50 80

1988. As Type O **13**, but figures of value in same colour as remainder of design.
O1155 O **13** 5 f. blue 10 10
O1156 10 f. red 10 10
O1157 15 f. yellow 10 10
O1158 20 f. blue 20 10
O1159 45 f. orange 25 20
O1160 50 f. green 30 20

POSTAGE DUE STAMPS

1921. Postage Due stamps of Upper Senegal and Niger "Figure" key-type optd **TERRITOIRE DU NIGER**.

D18 M 5 c. green . . . 15 50
D19 10 c. red . . . 15 50
D20 15 c. grey . . . 20 60
D21 20 c. brown . . . 20 60
D22 30 c. blue . . . 20 60
D23 50 c. black . . . 25 65
D24 60 c. orange . . . 30 1·00
D25 1 f. violet . . . 50 1·10

D 6 Zinder Fort

1927.

D73 D 6 2 c. red and blue . . . 10 25
D74 4 c. black and orange . . 10 25
D75 5 c. violet and yellow . . 15 25
D76 10 c. violet and red . . . 15 30
D77 15 c. orange and green . . 15 40
D78 20 c. sepia and red . . . 20 45
D79 25 c. sepia and black . . 35 50
D80 30 c. grey and violet . . 60 1·00
D81 50 c. red on green . . . 60 80
D82 60 c. orge, lilac on bl . . 60 80
D83 1 f. violet & blue on blue 60 75
D84 2 f. mauve and red . . 60 80
D85 3 f. blue and brown . . 80 1·00

D 13 Cross of Agadez

1962.

D123 D 13 50 c. green . . . 10 10
D124 1 f. violet . . . 10 10
D125 2 f. myrtle . . . 10 10
D126 A 3 f. mauve . . . 10 10
D127 5 f. green . . . 15 15
D128 10 f. orange . . . 15 15
D129 B 15 f. blue . . . 15 15
D130 20 f. red . . . 20 20
D131 50 f. brown . . . 40 40

DESIGNS: A, Cross of Iferouane; B, Cross of Tahoua.

D 450 Cross of Iferouane

1993.

D1263 D 450 5 f. multicoloured . 10 10
D1264 10 f. orange & black 10 10
D1265 – 15 f. multicoloured . 10 10
D1266 – 20 f. mve, yell & blk 10 10
D1267 – 50 f. multicoloured . 10 10

DESIGN: 15 to 50 f. Cross of Tahoua.

NORTH GERMAN CONFEDERATION Pt. 7

The North German Confederation was set up on 1st January, 1868, and comprised the postal services of Bremen, Brunswick, Hamburg Lubeck, Mecklenburg (both), Oldenburg, Prussia (including Hanover, Schleswig-Holstein with Bergedorf and Thurn and Taxis) and Saxony.

The North German Confederation joined the German Reichspost on 4th May, 1871, and the stamps of Germany were brought into use on 1st January, 1872.

Northern District: 30 groschen = 1 thaler.
Southern District: 60 kreuzer = 1 gulden.

1

3

1868. Roul or perf. (a) Northern District.

19 1 1/4 g. mauve . . . 15·00 12·00
22 1/3 g. green . . . 3·25 65
23 1/2 g. orange . . . 3·25 50
25 1 g. red . . . 2·40 30
27 2 g. blue . . . 3·25 40
29 5 g. bistre . . . 7·50 4·00

(b) Southern District.

30 – 1 k. green . . . 10·00 6·50
13 – 2 k. orange . . . 30·00 35·00
33 – 3 k. red . . . 5·50 60
36 – 7 k. blue . . . 8·50 4·00
18 – 18 k. bistre . . . 26·00 65·00

The 1 k. to 18 k. have the figures in an oval.

1869. Perf.

38 3 10 g. grey . . . £275 50·00
39 – 30 g. blue . . . £225 £100

The frame of the 30 g. is rectangular.

OFFICIAL STAMPS

O 5

1870. (a) Northern District.

O40 O 5 1/4 g. black and brown . . 22·00 45·00
O41 1/3 g. black and brown . . 14·00 17·00
O42 1/2 g. black and brown . . 2·00 2·50
O43 1 g. black and brown . . 2·50 35
O44 2 g. black and brown . . 5·00 2·75

(b) Southern District.

O45 1 k. black and grey . . 32·00 £225
O46 2 k. black and grey . . 85·00 £800
O47 3 k. black and grey . . 28·00 35·00
O48 7 k. black and grey . . 38·00 £250

NORTH INGERMANLAND Pt. 10

Stamps issued during temporary independence of this Russian territory, which adjoins Finland.

100 pennia = 1 mark

1 18th-century Arms of Ingermanland

4 Gathering Crops

1920.

1 1 5 p. green . . . 2·25 3·75
2 10 p. red . . . 2·25 3·75
3 25 p. brown . . . 2·25 3·75
4 50 p. blue . . . 2·25 3·75
5 1 m. black and red . . . 20·00 27·00
6 5 m. black and purple . . . 65·00 £110
7 10 m. black and brown . . . £130 £180

1920. Inscr as in T **2**.

8 – 10 p. blue and green . . . 3·00 5·00
9 – 30 p. green and brown . . . 3·00 5·00
10 – 50 p. brown and blue . . . 3·00 5·00
11 – 80 p. grey and red . . . 3·00 5·00
12 4 1 m. grey and red . . . 15·00 28·00
13 – 5 m. red and violet . . . 10·00 15·00
14 – 10 m. violet and brown . . . 11·00 17·00

DESIGNS—VERT: 10 p. Arms; 30 p. Reaper; 50 p. Ploughing; 80 p. Milking. HORIZ: 5 m. Burning church; 10 m. Zither players.

NORTH WEST RUSSIA Pt. 10

Issues made for use by the various Anti-bolshevist Armies during the Russian Civil War, 1918–20.

100 kopeks = 1 rouble

NORTHERN ARMY

1 "OKCA" = Osobiy Korpus Severnoy Army.—(trans "Special Corps, Northern Army")

1919. As T **1** inscr "OKCA".

1 1 5 k. purple . . . 10 25
2 10 k. blue . . . 10 25
3 15 k. yellow . . . 10 25
4 20 k. red . . . 10 25
5 50 k. green . . . 10 25

NORTH-WESTERN ARMY

(2)

1919. Arms types of Russia optd as T **2**. Imperf or perf.

6 22 2 k. green . . . 2·50 6·00
16 3 k. red . . . 1·75 5·50
7 5 k. lilac . . . 2·50 6·00
8 23 10 k. blue . . . 3·50 8·00
9 10 15 k. blue and purple . . . 3·25 6·00
10 14 20 k. red and blue . . . 4·50 7·00
11 10 20 k. on 14 k. red and blue £200
12 25 k. mauve and green . . . 6·00 11·00
13 14 50 k. green and purple . . . 6·00 11·00
14 15 1 r. orange & brn on brn . . 12·00 22·00
17 11 3 r. 50 green and red . . . 25·00 35·00
18 22 5 r. blue on green . . . 14·00 22·00
19 11 7 r. pink and green . . . 75·00 £140
15 20 10 r. grey and red on yell . . 40·00 70·00

1919. No. 7 surch.

20 22 10 k. on 5 k. red . . . 3·00 5·00

WESTERN ARMY

1919. Stamps of Latvia optd with Cross of Lorraine in circle with plain background. Imperf. (a) Postage stamps.

21 1 3 k. lilac . . . 22·00 40·00
22 5 k. red . . . 22·00 40·00
23 10 k. blue . . . £110 £190
24 20 k. orange . . . 22·00 40·00
25 25 k. grey . . . 22·00 40·00
26 35 k. brown . . . 22·00 40·00
27 50 k. violet . . . 22·00 40·00
28 75 k. green . . . 24·00 55·00

(b) Liberation of Riga issue.

29 4 5 k. red . . . 15·00 35·00
30 15 k. green . . . 15·00 35·00
31 35 k. brown . . . 15·00 35·00

1919. Stamps of Latvia optd with Cross of Lorraine in circle with burele background and characters **3. A** (= "Z. A."). Imperf (a) Postage stamps.

32 1 3 k. lilac . . . 4·00 8·00
33 5 k. red . . . 4·00 8·00
34 10 k. blue . . . 90·00 £170
35 20 k. orange . . . 8·00 16·00
36 25 k. grey . . . 22·00 45·00
37 35 k. brown . . . 14·00 24·00
38 50 k. violet . . . 14·00 24·00
39 75 k. green . . . 14·00 24·00

(b) Liberation of Riga issue.

40 4 5 k. red . . . 2·75 6·50
41 15 k. green . . . 2·75 6·50
42 35 k. brown . . . 2·75 6·50

1919. Arms type of Russia surch with Cross of Lorraine in ornamental frame and **LP** with value in curved frame. Imperf or perf.

43 22 10 k. on 2 k. green . . . 4·50 6·00
54 20 k. on 3 k. red . . . 48·00 75·00
44 23 30 k. on 4 k. red . . . 4·50 7·00
45 22 40 k. on 5 k. red . . . 4·50 7·00
46 23 50 k. on 10 k. blue . . . 4·50 6·00
47 10 70 k. on 15 k. blue & purple 4·50 6·00
48 14 90 k. on 20 k. red & blue . . 4·50 7·00
49 10 1 r. on 25 k. mauve & grn . 4·50 6·00
50 1 r. 50 on 35 k. green & pur 35·00 55·00
51 14 2 r. on 50 k. green & pur . . 6·00 10·00
52 10 4 r. on 70 k. orange & brn 16·00 24·00
53 15 6 r. on 1 r. orange & brown . 16·00 25·00
56 11 10 r. on 3 r. 50 green & pur 38·00 48·00

NORWAY Pt. 11

In 1814 Denmark ceded Norway to Sweden, from 1814 to 1905 the King of Sweden was also King of Norway after which Norway was an independent Kingdom.

1855. 120 skilling = 1 speciedaler.
1877. 100 ore = 1 krone.

1

3 King Oscar I

1855. Imperf.

1 1 4 s. blue . . . £4250 75·00

1856. Perf.

4 3 2 s. yellow . . . £300 75·00
6 3 s. lilac . . . £225 45·00
7 4 s. blue . . . £120 5·00
11 8 s. red . . . £500 18·00

4

5

1863.

12 4 2 s. yellow . . . £350 £100
13 3 s. lilac . . . £325 £250
16 4 s. blue . . . 50·00 4·50
17 8 s. pink . . . £425 30·00
18 24 s. brown . . . 20·00 70·00

1867.

21 5 1 s. black . . . 55·00 27·00
23 2 s. buff . . . 10·00 27·00
26 3 s. lilac . . . £190 55·00
27 4 s. blue . . . 35·00 3·25
29 8 s. red . . . £250 21·00

6

10 With background shading

A

1872. Value in "Skilling".

33 6 1 s. green . . . 4·00 19·00
36 2 s. blue . . . 6·50 35·00
39 3 s. red . . . 30·00 3·00
42 4 s. mauve . . . 7·00 30·00
44 6 s. brown . . . £225 25·00
45 7 s. brown . . . 23·00 30·00

1877. Letters without serifs as Type A. Value in "ore".

47 10 1 ore brown . . . 3·25 3·50
83 2 ore brown . . . 1·75 2·25
84c 3 ore orange . . . 35·00 2·75
51 5 ore blue . . . 20·00 3·00
85d 5 ore green . . . 27·00 70
86a 10 ore red . . . 26·00 40
55 12 ore green . . . 60·00 12·00
75b 12 ore brown . . . 15·00 11·00
76 20 ore brown . . . 50·00 7·50
87 20 ore blue . . . 35·00 75
88 25 ore mauve . . . 9·00 7·50
61 35 ore green . . . 9·00 8·00
62 50 ore purple . . . 24·00 5·50
63 60 ore blue . . . 22·00 6·50

9 King Oscar II

1878.

68 9 1 k. green and light green . . 16·00 5·00
69 1 k. 50 blue and ultramarine 30·00 23·00
70 2 k. brown and pink . . . 20·00 16·00

1888. Surch **2 Ore.**

89a 6 2 ore on 12 ore brown . . . 90 1·00

D

1893. Letters with serifs as Type D.

133 10 1 ore drab . . . 15 25
134 2 ore brown . . . 15 15
135 3 ore orange . . . 20 10
136 5 ore green . . . 2·25 10

529	10	5 ore purple	10	10
138		7 ore green	30	10
139		10 ore red	2·75	10
140		10 ore green	4·00	10
529a		10 ore grey	10	10
141		12 ore violet	45	50
530		15 ore brown	20	10
143		15 ore blue	2·50	10
144		20 ore blue	4·50	10
145		20 ore green	4·00	10
146		25 ore mauve	22·00	15
147		25 ore red	4·00	75
531		25 ore blue	20	10
148		30 ore grey	5·00	15
149		30 ore blue	4·75	1·90
119		35 ore green	6·00	4·00
150		35 ore brown	6·00	25
151		40 ore green	2·00	25
152		40 ore blue	16·00	15
531ab		50 ore purple	10	10
154		60 ore blue	15·00	20
531ac		60 ore orange	10	10
531ad		70 ore orange	20	10
531ae		80 ore brown	20	10
531af		90 ore brown	20	10

See also Nos. 279 etc and 1100/3.

1905. Surch.

122	5	1 k. on 2 s. buff	20·00	20·00
123		1 k. 50 on 2 s. buff	40·00	40·00
124		2 k. on 2 s. buff	35·00	30·00

1906. Surch.

162	10	5 ore on 25 ore mauve	20	30
125	6	15 ore on 4 s. mauve	1·75	2·50
126		30 ore on 7 s. brown	4·50	4·75

15 King Haakon VII 16

1907.

127	15	1 k. green	20·00	22·00
128		1½ k. blue	55·00	55·00
129		2 k. red	70·00	70·00

1910.

155a	16	1 k. green	25	10
156		1½ k. blue	1·00	40
157		2 k. red	1·25	40
158		5 k. violet	2·25	2·50

17 Constitutional Assembly (after O. Wergeland)

19

1914. Centenary of Independence.

159	17	5 ore green	40	15
160		10 ore red	80	15
161		20 ore blue	5·50	2·75

1922.

163	19	10 ore green	6·00	10
164		20 ore purple	8·00	10
165		25 ore red	18·00	50
166		45 ore blue	85	50

20 21 22

1925. Air. Amundsen's Polar Flight.

167	20	2 ore brown	1·50	1·75
168		3 ore orange	2·50	2·75
169		5 ore mauve	4·50	5·50
170		10 ore green	6·00	6·00
171		15 ore blue	5·50	6·50
172		20 ore mauve	9·00	10·00
173		25 ore red	1·50	1·75

1925. Annexation of Spitzbergen.

183	21	10 ore green	3·00	3·50
184		15 ore blue	2·50	2·50
185		20 ore purple	3·50	60
186		45 ore blue	3·00	3·00

1926. Size 16 × 19½ mm.

187	22	10 ore green	40	10
187a		14 ore orange	90	1·25
188		15 ore brown	55	10
189		20 ore purple	15·00	10
189a		20 ore red	45	10
190		25 ore red	6·50	1·25
190a		25 ore brown	60	15
190b		30 ore blue	75	10
191		35 ore brown	45·00	15
191a		35 ore violet	1·50	20
192		40 ore blue	1·75	60
193		40 ore grey	1·50	10
194		50 ore pink	1·50	15
195		60 ore blue	1·50	15

For stamps as Type **22** but size 17 × 21 mm, see Nos. 284, etc.

1927. Surcharged with new value and bar.

196	22	20 ore on 25 ore red	1·00	80
197	19	30 ore on 45 ore blue	7·00	80
198	21	30 ore on 45 ore blue	1·50	2·00

24 Akershus Castle

25 Ibsen

28 Abel

1927. Air.

199a	24	45 ore blue (with frame-lines)	2·25	1·25
323		45 ore blue (without frame-lines)	40	15

1928. Ibsen Centenary.

200	25	10 ore green	4·00	1·50
201		15 ore brown	1·75	1·75
202		20 ore red	1·75	35
203		30 ore blue	2·75	2·00

1929. Postage Due stamps optd **Post Frimerke** (204/6 and 211) or **POST** and thick bar (others).

204	D 12	1 ore brown	25	60
205		4 ore purple (No. D96a)	20	30
206		10 ore green	1·25	1·25
207		15 ore brown	1·75	2·00
208		20 ore purple	80	35
209		40 ore blue	1·25	40
210		50 ore purple	4·75	5·00
211		100 ore yellow	2·00	1·25
212		200 ore violet	3·50	2·00

1929. Death Cent of N. H. Abel (mathematician).

213	28	10 ore green	1·25	40
214		15 ore brown	1·50	1·25
215		20 ore red	70	15
216		30 ore blue	1·75	1·25

1929. Surch **14 ORE 14**.

217	5	14 ore on 2 s. buff	1·90	2·50

30 St. Olaf (sculpture, Brunlanes Church)

31 Nidaros Trondhjem Cathedral

32 Death of St. Olaf (after P. N. Arbo)

1930. 9th Death Centenary of St. Olaf.

219	30	10 ore green	5·50	25
220	31	15 ore sepia and brown	60	30
221	30	20 ore red	70	15
222	32	30 ore blue	2·25	1·25

33 North Cape and "Bergensfjord" (liner)

1930. Norwegian Tourist Association Fund. Size 35½ × 21½ mm.

223	33	15 ore + 25 ore brown	2·00	3·25
224		20 ore + 25 ore red	20·00	23·00
225		30 ore + 25 ore blue	65·00	75·00

For smaller stamps in this design see Nos. 349/51 (1938), 442/66 and 464/6.

34 Radium Hospital

1931. Radium Hospital Fund.

226	34	20 ore + 10 ore red	4·00	3·00

35 Bjornson

36 L. Holberg

1932. Birth Cent of Bjornstjerne Bjornson (writer).

227	35	10 ore green	6·00	25
228		15 ore brown	75	85
229		20 ore red	65	15
230		30 ore blue	1·50	1·25

1934. 250th Birth Anniv of Holberg (writer).

231	36	10 ore green	1·10	25
232		15 ore brown	50	40
233		20 ore red	8·00	15
234		30 ore blue	1·75	1·25

37 Dr. Nansen

38 No background shading

38b King Haakon VII

1935. Nansen Refugee Fund.

235	37	10 ore + 10 ore green	1·50	1·60
236		15 ore + 10 ore brown	6·50	7·50
237		20 ore + 10 ore red	85	90
238		30 ore + 10 ore blue	6·50	7·00

See also Nos. 275/8.

1937.

279	38	1 ore green	10	10
280		2 ore brown	10	10
281		3 ore orange	10	10
282		5 ore mauve	20	10
283		7 ore green	30	10
413		10 ore grey	30	10
285		12 ore violet	70	80
414		15 ore green	1·75	10
415		15 ore brown	40	10
416		20 ore brown	4·00	1·50
417		20 ore green	40	10

1937. As T **22**, but size 17 × 21 mm.

284	22	10 ore green	15	10
286		14 ore orange	1·40	1·40
287		15 ore green	30	10
288a		20 ore red	20	10
289		25 ore brown	1·00	15
289a		25 ore red	30	10
290		30 ore blue	1·00	15
290a		30 ore grey	7·00	20
291		35 ore violet	1·50	10
292		40 ore grey	60	10
292a		40 ore blue	2·25	10
293		50 ore purple	70	10
293a		55 ore orange	19·00	10
294		60 ore blue	70	10
294a		80 ore brown	17·00	10

1937.

255	38b	1 k. green	15	20
256		1 k. 50 blue	70	1·50
257		2 k. red	70	3·50
258		5 k. purple	3·75	30·00

39 Reindeer

41 Joelster in Sunnfjord

1938. Tourist Propaganda.

262	39	15 ore brown	50	30
263	–	20 ore red	20	10
264	41	30 ore blue	25	10

DESIGN—As T **39** but VERT: 20 ore, Stave Church, Borgund.

1938. Norwegian Tourist Association Fund. As T **33**, but reduced to 27 × 21 mm.

349	33	15 ore + 25 ore brown	90	1·25
350		20 ore + 25 ore red	1·10	2·00
351		30 ore + 25 ore blue	1·60	2·50

42 Queen Maud

43 Lion Rampant

44 Dr. Nansen

1939. Queen Maud Children's Fund.

267	42	10 ore + 5 ore green	45	3·50
268		15 ore + 5 ore brown	45	3·50
269		20 ore + 5 ore red	45	3·50
270		30 ore + 5 ore blue	45	3·50

1940.

271	43	1 k. green	60	10
272		1½ k. blue	1·00	25
273		2 k. red	1·25	1·10
274		5 k. purple	2·75	2·75

See also Nos. 318/21.

1940. National Relief Fund.

275	44	10 ore + 10 ore green	2·00	2·00
276		15 ore + 10 ore brown	2·00	2·75
277		20 ore + 10 ore red	60	70
278		30 ore + 10 ore blue	1·25	1·50

46 Fernboring (fishing boat) and Iceberg

47 Colin Archer (founder) and Lifeboat "Colin Archer"

1941. Haalogaland Exhibition and Fishermen's Families Relief Fund.

295	46	15 ore + 10 ore blue	1·00	3·25

1941. 50th Anniv of National Lifeboat Institution.

296	47	10 ore + 10 ore green	1·00	1·25
297		15 ore + 10 ore brown	1·25	1·60
298	–	20 ore + 10 ore red	60	60
299	–	30 ore + 10 ore blue	2·75	3·75

DESIGN—VERT: 20 ore, 30 ore, "Osloskoyta" (lifeboat).

48 Soldier and Flags

51 Oslo University

1941. Norwegian Legion Support Fund.

300	48	20 ore + 80 ore red	21·00	48·00

1941. Stamps of 1937 optd **V** (= Victory).

301	38	1 ore green	15	2·00
302		2 ore brown	15	2·75
303		3 ore orange	15	2·25
304		5 ore mauve	15	20
305		7 ore green	40	2·00
306	22	10 ore green	15	15
307	38	12 ore violet	40	9·00
308	22	14 ore orange	75	8·00
309		15 ore green	15	70
310		20 ore red	15	10
311		25 ore brown	15	30
312		30 ore blue	40	1·00
313		35 ore violet	40	50
314		40 ore grey	20	40
315		50 ore purple	50	1·50
316		60 ore blue	40	90
317	43	1 k. green	40	30
318		1½ k. blue	1·75	10·00
319		2 k. red	5·50	35·00
320		5 k. purple	9·50	55·00

1941. As No. 413, but with "V" incorporated in the design.

321	10 ore green	40	6·50

1941. Centenary of Foundation of Oslo University Building.

322	51	1 k. green	13·00	30·00

52 Queen Ragnhild's Dream

53 Stiklestad Battlefield

1941. 700th Death Anniv of Snorre Sturlason (historian).

324	52	10 ore green	15	10
325	–	15 ore brown	20	30
326	–	20 ore red	15	10
327	–	30 ore blue	90	1·60
328	–	50 ore violet	60	1·25
329	53	60 ore blue	60	1·00

DESIGNS (illustrations from "Sagas of Kings")—As T **53**: 15 ore Einar Tambarskjelve at Battle of Svolder; 30 ore King Olav II sails to his wedding; 50 ore Svipdag's men enter Hall of the Seven Kings. As T **52**: 20 ore Snorre Sturlason.

55 Vidkun Quisling

1942. (a) Without opt.

330	55	20 ore + 30 ore red	2·50	9·50

(b) Optd **1-2-1942**.

331	55	20 ore + 30 ore red	2·50	9·50

See also No. 336.

56 Rikard Nordraak

57 Embarkation of the Viking Fleet

1942. Birth Centenary of Rikard Nordraak (composer).

332	56	10 ore green	1·25	1·25
333	57	15 ore brown	1·25	1·60
334	56	20 ore red	1·25	1·25
335	–	30 ore blue	1·25	1·25

DESIGN—As Type **57**: 30 ore Mountains across sea and two lines of the National Anthem.

1942. War Orphans' Relief Fund. As T **55** but inscr "RIKSTINGET 1942".

336	20 ore + 30 ore red	30	2·25

58 J. H. Wessel   59 Reproduction of Types 55 and 1

1942. Birth Bicentenary of Wessel (poet).
337 **58** 15 ore brown 15 15
338 20 ore red 15 15

1942. Inaug of European Postal Union, Vienna.
339 **59** 20 ore red 20 50
340 30 ore blue . . . . 20 1·10

60 Destroyer "Sleipner"   61 Edvard Grieg

1943.
341 **60** 5 ore purple 10 20
342 – 7 ore green 20 20
343 **60** 10 ore green 10 10
344 – 15 ore green 25 40
345 – 20 ore red 10 10
346 – 30 ore blue 85 85
347 – 40 ore green 40 60
348 – 60 ore blue 40 60
DESIGNS: 7 ore, 30 ore Merchant ships in convoy; 15 ore Airman; 20 ore "Vi Vil Vinne" (We will win) written on the highway; 40 ore Soldiers on skis; 60 ore King Haakon VII.

For use on correspondence posted at sea on Norwegian merchant ships and (in certain circumstances) from Norwegian camps in Gt. Britain during the German Occupation of Norway. After liberation all values were put on sale in Norway.

1943. Birth Centenary of Grieg (composer).
352 **61** 10 ore green 30 25
353 20 ore red 30 25
354 40 ore green 30 35
355 60 ore blue 30 35

62 Soldier's Emblem   63 Fishing Station

1943. Soldiers' Relief Fund.
356 **62** 20 ore + 30 ore red . . . 30 2·75

1943. Winter Relief Fund.
357 **63** 10 ore + 10 ore green . . 70 4·25
358 – 20 ore + 10 ore red . . . 60 3·75
359 – 40 ore + 10 ore grey . . . 60 3·75
DESIGNS: 20 ore Mountain scenery; 40 ore Winter landscape.

64 Sinking of "Baroy" (freighter)   65 Gran's Bleriot XI "Nordsjoen"

1944. Shipwrecked Mariners' Relief Fund.
360 **64** 10 ore + 10 ore green . . 70 4·25
361 – 15 ore + 10 ore brown . . 70 4·25
362 – 20 ore + 10 ore red . . . 70 4·25
DESIGNS—HORIZ: 15 ore Cargo liner "Sanct Svithun" attacked by Bristol Blenheim airplane. VERT: 20 ore Sinking of freighter "Irma".

1944. 30th Anniv of First North Sea Flight, by Tryggve Gran.
363 **65** 40 ore blue . . . . 30 2·00

66 Girl Spinning   67 Arms   68 Henrik Wergeland

1944. Winter Relief Fund. Inscr as in T **66**.
364 **66** 5 ore + 10 ore mauve . . 30 3·75
365 – 10 ore + 10 ore green . . 30 3·75
366 – 15 ore + 10 ore purple . . 30 3·75
367 – 20 ore + 10 ore red . . . 30 3·75
DESIGNS: 10 ore Ploughing; 15 ore Tree felling; 20 ore Mother and children.

1945.
368 **67** $1\frac{1}{2}$ k. blue . . . . 1·10 40

1945. Death Centenary of Wergeland (poet).
369 **68** 10 ore green 25 20
370 15 ore brown 80 80
371 20 ore red 20 10

69 Red Cross Sister   70 Folklore Museum Emblem

1945. Red Cross Relief Fund and Norwegian Red Cross Jubilee.
372 **69** 20 ore + 10 ore red . . . 50 50

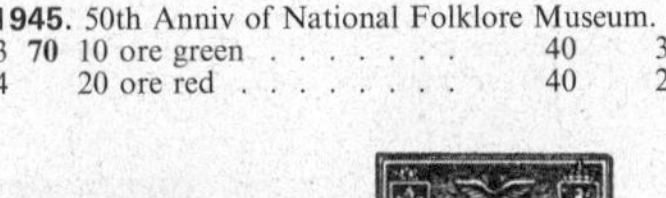

1945. 50th Anniv of National Folklore Museum.
373 **70** 10 ore green 40 30
374 20 ore red 40 20

71 Crown Prince Olav   72 "R.N.A.F."

1946. National Relief Fund.
375 **71** 10 ore + 10 ore green . . 30 30
376 15 ore + 10 ore brown . . 30 30
377 20 ore + 10 ore red . . . 30 30
378 30 ore + 10 ore blue . . . 1·00 1·00

1946. Honouring Norwegian Air Force Trained in Canada.
379 **72** 15 ore red 45 40

73 King Haakon VII   74 Fridjof of Nansen, Roald Amundsen and "Fram"

1946.
380 **73** 1 k. green . . . . 1·25 10
381 $1\frac{1}{2}$ k. blue . . . . 4·00 20
382 2 k. brown . . . . 27·00 10
383 5 k. violet . . . . 18·00 35

1947. Tercentenary of Norwegian Post Office.
384 – 5 ore mauve 30 10
385 – 10 ore green 30 10
386 – 15 ore brown 55 10
387 – 25 ore red 30 10
388 – 30 ore grey . . . . 1·10 30
389 – 40 ore blue . . . . 1·60 15
390 – 45 ore violet . . . . . . 3·25 50
391 – 50 ore brown . . . . . . 2·50 15
392 **74** 55 ore orange . . . . . . 4·50 20
393 – 60 ore grey . . . . 2·00 80
394 – 80 ore brown . . . . . . 2·00 30
DESIGNS: 5 ore Hannibal Sehested (founder of postal service) and Akershus Castle; 10 ore "Postal-peasant"; 15 ore Admiral Tordenskiold and 18th-century warship; 25 ore Christian M. Falsen; 30 ore Cleng Peerson and "Restaurationen" (emigrant sloop); 40 ore "Constitutionen" (paddle-steamer); 45 ore First Norwegian steam locomotive "Caroline"; 50 ore Svend Foyn and "Spes et Fides" (whale catcher); 60 ore Coronation of King Haakon and Queen Maud in Nidaros Cathedral; 80 ore King Haakon and Oslo Town Hall.

75 Petter Dass   76 King Haakon VII

1947. Birth Tercentenary of Petter Dass (poet).
395 **75** 25 ore red 35 35

1947. 75th Birthday of King Haakon VII.
396 **76** 25 ore orange 35 35

77 Axel Heiberg   80 A. L. Kielland

1948. 50th Anniv of Norwegian Forestry Society and Birth Centenary of Axel Heiberg (founder).
397 **77** 25 ore red 40 30
398 80 ore brown . . . . 1·00 30

1948. Red Cross. Surch **25 + 5** and bars.
399 **69** 25 + 5 ore on 20 + 10 ore red 40 50

1949. Stamps of 1937 surch.
400 **22** 25 ore on 20 ore red . . . 50 10
401 45 ore on 40 ore blue . . . 2·25 30

1949. Birth Centenary of Alexander L. Kielland (author).
402 **80** 25 ore red 80 15
403 40 ore blue 80 25
404 80 ore brown . . . . 1·25 50

81 Symbolising Universe   82 Pigeon and Globe

1949. 75th Anniv of U.P.U.
405 **81** 10 ore green and purple . . 50 40
406 **82** 25 ore red 30 15
407 – 40 ore blue 30 30
DESIGN—37 × 21 mm: 40 ore Dove, globe and signpost.

84 King Harald Haardraade and Oslo Town Hall   85 Child with Flowers

1950. 900th Anniv of Founding of Oslo.
408 **84** 15 ore green 45 60
409 25 ore red 30 15
410 45 ore blue 40 50

1950. Infantile Paralysis Fund.
411 **85** 25 ore + 5 ore red . . . . 1·25 1·25
412 45 ore + 5 ore blue . . . . 3·50 3·75

87 King Haakon VII   88 Arne Garborg (after O. Rusti)

1950.
418 **87** 25 ore red 45 10
419 25 ore grey . . . . 12·00 10
419a 25 ore green 85 10
420 30 ore grey . . . . 6·50 45
421 30 ore red 50 10
422 35 ore red . . . . 9·00 10
422a 35 ore red . . . . 4·00 10
422b 40 ore purple . . . . . . 1·50 10
423 45 ore blue . . . . 1·40 85
424 50 ore brown . . . . 1·50 10
425 55 ore orange . . . . . . 1·40 70
426 55 ore blue . . . . 1·25 30
427 60 ore blue . . . . 8·00 10
427a 65 ore blue . . . . 1·25 15
427b 70 ore brown . . . . 13·00 15
428 75 ore purple . . . . . . 1·90 15
429 80 ore brown . . . . 1·75 10
430 90 ore orange . . . . . . 1·50 15

1951. Birth Centenary of Garborg (author).
431 **88** 25 ore red 30 20
432 45 ore blue . . . . 1·25 1·25
433 80 ore brown . . . . 1·75 1·10
"NOREG" on the stamps was the spelling advocated by Arne Garborg.

89 Ice Skater   92 King Haakon VII

1951. 6th Winter Olympic Games. Inscr "OSLO 1952".
434 **89** 15 ore + 5 ore green . . . 1·90 1·90
435 – 30 ore + 10 ore red . . . 1·90 1·90
436 – 55 ore + 20 ore blue . . . 6·50 6·50
DESIGNS—As T **89**: 30 ore Ski jumping. 38 × 21 mm: 55 ore Winter landscape.

1951. Surch in figures.
440 **88** 20 ore on 15 ore green . . 40 15
437 **87** 30 ore on 25 ore red . . . 40 10

1952. 80th Birthday of King Haakon.
438 **92** 30 ore scarlet and red . . . 20 15
439 55 ore blue and grey . . . 60 60

94 "Supplication"   95 Medieval Sculpture

1953. Anti-Cancer Fund.
441 **94** 30 ore + 10 ore red and cream . . . . 85 1·10

1953. Norwegian Tourist Association Fund. As T **33** but smaller ($27\frac{1}{2} \times 21$ mm).
442 **33** 20 ore + 10 ore green . . 8·00 8·00
464 25 ore + 10 ore green . . 4·50 4·50
443 30 ore + 15 ore red . . . 8·00 8·00
465 35 ore + 15 ore red . . . 6·00 6·00
444 55 ore + 25 ore blue . . . 13·50 13·50
466 65 ore + 25 ore blue . . . 4·50 4·50

1953. 8th Cent of Archbishopric of Nidaros.
445 **95** 30 ore red 30 25

96 1st Railway Steam Locomotive "Caroline" and Horse-drawn Sledge   97 C. T. Nielsen (first Director)

1954. Centenary of Norwegian Railways.
446 **96** 20 ore green 80 30
447 – 30 ore red 80 15
448 – 55 ore blue . . . . 1·50 1·25
DESIGNS: 30 ore Diesel express train; 55 ore Engine driver.

1954. Centenary of Telegraph Service.
449 **97** 20 ore black and green . . 30 30
450 – 30 ore red 30 15
451 – 55 ore blue . . . . 1·25 1·00
DESIGNS: 30 ore Radio masts at Tryvannshogda; 55 ore Telegraph lineman on skis.

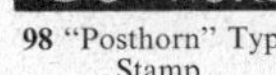

98 "Posthorn" Type Stamp   100 King Haakon and Queen Maud

1955. Norwegian Stamp Centenary.
452 – 20 ore blue and green . . . 15 20
453 **98** 30 ore deep red and red . . 15 10
454 – 55 ore blue & grey 25 40
DESIGNS: 20 ore Norway's first stamp; 55 ore "Lion" type stamp.

1955. Stamp Cent and Int Stamp Exn, Oslo. Nos. 452/4 with circular opt **OSLO NORWEX**.
455 – 20 ore blue and green . . . 6·50 8·00
456 **98** 30 ore deep red and red . . 6·50 8·00
457 – 55 ore blue and grey . . . 6·50 8·00
Nos. 455/7 were only on sale at the Exhibition P.O. at face + 1 k. entrance fee.

1955. Golden Jubilee of King Haakon.
458 **100** 30 ore red 30 15
459 55 ore blue 40 40

101 Crown Princess Martha   101a Whooper Swans

1956. Crown Princess Martha Memorial Fund.
460 **101** 35 ore + 10 ore red . . . 75 1·00
461 65 ore + 10 ore blue . . 1·50 2·00

1956. Northern Countries' Day.
462 **101a** 35 ore red . . . . 1·00 50
463 65 ore blue . . . . 1·00 75

102 Jan Mayen Island (after aquarell, H. Mohn) **103** Map of Spitzbergen

1957. Int Geophysical Year. Inscr "INTERN. GEOFYSISK AR 1957–1958".

No.	Type	Description	Unused	Used
467	102	25 ore green	40	25
468	103	35 ore red and grey	40	10
469	–	65 ore green and blue	50	40

DESIGN—VERT: 65 ore Map of Antarctica showing Queen Maud Land.

104 King Haakon VII **105** King Olav V **106**

1957. 85th Birthday of King Haakon.

No.	Type	Description	Unused	Used
470	104	35 ore red	15	10
471		65 ore blue	35	35

1958.

No.	Type	Description	Unused	Used
472	105	25 ore light green	80	10
473		30 ore violet	1·25	10
474		35 ore red	80	10
474a		35 ore green	2·25	10
475		40 ore red	80	10
475a		40 ore grey	2·50	70
476		45 ore red	1·00	10
477		50 ore brown	4·00	10
478		50 ore red	5·00	10
479		55 ore grey	1·50	35
480		60 ore violet	3·75	45
481		65 ore blue	1·75	25
482		80 ore brown	7·00	30
483		85 ore brown	1·25	15
484		90 ore orange	1·10	10
485	106	1 k. green	50	10
486		1 k. 50 blue	1·25	10
487		2 k. red	1·50	10
488		5 k. purple	25·00	10
489		10 k. orange	2·75	10

107 Asbjorn Kloster (founder) **108** Society's Centenary Medal

1959. Cent of Norwegian Temperance Movement.

No.	Type	Description	Unused	Used
490	107	45 ore brown	30	25

1959. 150th Anniv of Royal Norwegian Agricultural Society.

No.	Type	Description	Unused	Used
491	108	45 ore brown and red	25	25
492		90 ore grey and blue	85	1·00

109 Sower **110** White Anemone

1959. Centenary of Norwegian Royal College of Agriculture.

No.	Type	Description	Unused	Used
493	109	45 ore black and brown	25	25
494	–	90 ore black and blue	60	70

DESIGN—VERT: 90 ore Ears of Corn.

1960. Tuberculosis Relief Funds.

No.	Type	Description	Unused	Used
495	110	45 ore + 10 ore yellow, green and red	90	1·00
496	–	90 ore + 10 ore mult	2·50	3·00

DESIGN: 90 ore Blue anemone.

111 Society's Original Seal **112** Refugee Mother and Child

1960. Bicentenary of Royal Norwegian Society of Scientists.

No.	Type	Description	Unused	Used
497	111	45 ore red on grey	25	15
498		90 ore blue on grey	65	80

1960. World Refugee Year.

No.	Type	Description	Unused	Used
499	112	45 ore + 25 ore black and pink	1·50	2·00
500		90 ore + 25 ore black and blue	3·00	4·50

113 Viking Longship

1960. Norwegian Ships.

No.	Type	Description	Unused	Used
501	113	20 ore black and grey	1·00	80
502	–	25 ore black and green	1·00	80
503	–	45 ore black and red	1·00	15
504	–	55 ore black and brown	2·00	2·00
505	–	90 ore black and blue	1·25	90

SHIPS: 25 ore Hanse kogge; 45 ore "Skomvaer" (barque); 55 ore "Dalfon" (tanker); 90 ore "Bergensfjord" (liner).

113a Conference Emblem **113b** Douglas DC-8

1960. Europa.

No.	Type	Description	Unused	Used
506	113a	90 ore blue	35	35

1961. 10th Anniv of Scandinavian Airlines System (SAS).

No.	Type	Description	Unused	Used
507	113b	90 ore blue	30	30

114 Throwing the Javelin **115** Haakonshallen Barracks and Rosencrantz Tower

1961. Centenary of Norwegian Sport.

No.	Type	Description	Unused	Used
508	114	20 ore brown	40	40
509	–	25 ore green	40	40
510	–	45 ore red	40	15
511	–	90 ore mauve	70	80

DESIGNS: 25 ore Ice skating; 45 ore Ski jumping; 90 ore Yachting.

1961. 700th Anniv of Haakonshallen, Bergen.

No.	Type	Description	Unused	Used
512	115	45 ore black and red	30	15
513		1 k. black and green	40	25

116 Oslo University **117** Nansen

1961. 150th Anniv of Oslo University.

No.	Type	Description	Unused	Used
514	116	45 ore red	25	10
515		1 k. 50 blue	45	20

1961. Birth Centenary of Fridtjof Nansen (polar explorer).

No.	Type	Description	Unused	Used
516	117	45 ore black and red	25	15
517		90 ore black and blue	50	50

118 Amundsen, "Fram" and Dog-team **119** Frederic Passy and Henri Dunant (winners in 1901)

1961. 50th Anniv of Amundsen's Arrival at South Pole.

No.	Type	Description	Unused	Used
518	118	45 ore red and grey	50	15
519	–	90 ore deep blue and blue	90	55

DESIGN: 90 ore Amundsen's party and tent at South Pole.

1961. Nobel Peace Prize.

No.	Type	Description	Unused	Used
520	119	45 ore red	30	10
521	–	1 k. green	55	20

120 Prof. V. Bjerknes **121** Etrich/Rumpler Taube Monoplane "Start"

1962. Birth Centenary of Prof. Vilhelm Bjerknes (physicist).

No.	Type	Description	Unused	Used
522	120	45 ore black and red	25	10
523		1 k. 50 black and blue	45	25

1962. 50th Anniv of Norwegian Aviation.

No.	Type	Description	Unused	Used
524	121	1 k. 50 brown and blue	70	40

122 Branch of Fir, and Cone **123** Europa "Tree"

1962. Cent of State Forestry Administration.

No.	Type	Description	Unused	Used
525	122	45 ore grey, black & red	50	35
526		1 k. grey, black & green	2·50	20

1962. Europa.

No.	Type	Description	Unused	Used
527	123	50 ore red	30	10
528		90 ore blue	70	70

125 Reef Knot **126** Camilla Collett **127** Boatload of Wheat

1962.

No.	Type	Description	Unused	Used
531ag	–	25 ore green	90	10
532	–	30 ore drab	2·25	1·60
532a	–	30 ore green	30	10
533	125	35 ore green	40	10
533a	–	40 ore red	1·40	10
534	–	40 ore green	30	10
534a	–	45 ore green	40	25
535	125	50 ore red	2·75	10
535a		50 ore grey	30	10
536	–	55 ore brown	30	20
536a	125	60 ore green	6·50	15
537		60 ore red	60	10
537b	–	65 ore violet	2·00	10
538	125	65 ore red	30	10
538a		70 ore brown	30	10
539	–	75 ore green	30	10
539a	–	80 ore purple	2·50	1·00
539b	–	80 ore brown	35	10
540	–	85 ore brown	45	15
540a	–	85 ore buff	40	15
540b	–	90 ore blue	35	10
541	–	100 ore violet	60	10
541a	–	100 ore red	50	10
542	–	110 ore red	45	15
542a	–	115 ore brown	60	20
543	–	120 ore blue	40	20
543a	–	125 ore red	40	10
544	–	140 ore blue	60	35
544a	–	750 ore brown	80	10

DESIGNS: 25, 40, 90, 100(2), 110, 120, 125 ore, Runic drawings; 30, 45, 55, 75, 85 ore, Ear of wheat and fish; 65 (537b), 80, 140 ore, "Stave" (wooden) church and Aurora Borealis; 115 ore Fragment of Urnes stave-church; 750 ore Sigurd Farnesbane (the Dragon killer) and Regin (the blacksmith), portal from Hylestad stave-church.

1963. 150th Birth Anniv of Camilla Collett (author).

No.	Type	Description	Unused	Used
545	126	50 ore red	20	10
546		90 ore blue	55	60

1963. Freedom from Hunger.

No.	Type	Description	Unused	Used
547	127	25 ore bistre	20	30
548		35 ore green	30	30
549	–	50 ore red	30	10
550	–	90 ore blue	60	70

DESIGN—$37\frac{1}{2} \times 21$ mm: 50, 90 ore Birds carrying food on cloth.

128 River Mail Boat **129** Ivar Aasen

1963. Tercentenary of Southern-Northern Norwegian Postal Services.

No.	Type	Description	Unused	Used
551	128	50 ore red	90	25
552	–	90 ore blue	1·50	2·00

DESIGN: 90 ore Femboring (Northern sailing vessel).

1963. 150th Birth Anniv of Ivar Aasen (philologist).

No.	Type	Description	Unused	Used
533	129	50 ore red and grey	20	10
554		90 ore blue and grey	45	55

The note after No. 433 re "NOREG" also applies here.

HAVE YOU READ THE NOTES AT THE BEGINNING OF THIS CATALOGUE?

These often provide the answers to the enquiries we receive.

130 "Co-operation" **131** "Herringbone" Pattern

1963. Europa.

No.	Type	Description	Unused	Used
555	130	50 ore orange and purple	30	10
556		90 ore green and blue	1·00	1·00

1963. 150th Anniv of Norwegian Textile Industry.

No.	Type	Description	Unused	Used
557	131	25 ore green and bistre	30	35
558		35 ore ultramarine and blue	40	55
559		50 ore purple and red	30	20

132 Edvard Munch (self-portrait) **133** Eilert Sundt (founder)

1963. Birth Centenary of Edvard Munch (painter and engraver).

No.	Type	Description	Unused	Used
560	132	25 ore black	20	15
561	–	35 ore green	20	25
562	–	50 ore brown	20	10
563	–	90 ore blue and indigo	50	65

DESIGNS (woodcuts)—HORIZ: 35 ore "Fecundity"; 50 ore "The Solitaries". VERT: 90 ore "The Girls on the Bridge".

1964. Centenary of Oslo Workers' Society.

No.	Type	Description	Unused	Used
564	133	25 ore green	20	25
565	–	50 ore purple	20	10

DESIGN: 50 ore Beehive emblem of O.W.S.

134 C. M. Guldberg and P. Waage (chemists) **135** Eidsvoll Manor

1964. Centenary of Law of Mass Action.

No.	Type	Description	Unused	Used
566	134	35 ore green	40	30
567		55 ore stone	1·00	1·00

1964. 150th Anniv of Norwegian Constitution.

No.	Type	Description	Unused	Used
568	135	50 ore grey and red	20	10
569	–	90 ore black and blue	60	60

DESIGN: 90 ore Storting (Parliament House), Oslo.

On 1st June, 1964, a stamp depicting the U.N. refugee emblem and inscr "PORTO BETALT ... LYKKEBREVET 1964" was put on sale. It had a franking value of 50 ore but was sold for 2 k. 50, the balance being for the Refugee Fund. In addition, each stamp bore a serial number representing participation in a lottery which took place in September. The stamp was on sale until 15th July and had validity until 10th August.

136 Harbour Scene **137** Europa "Flower"

1964. Cent of Norwegian Seamen's Mission.

No.	Type	Description	Unused	Used
570	136	25 ore green and yellow	30	25
571		90 ore blue and cream	80	80

1964. Europa.

No.	Type	Description	Unused	Used
572	137	90 ore deep blue & blue	75	75

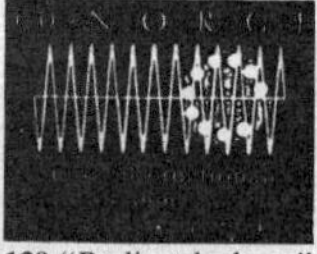

138 H. Anker and O. Arvesen (founders) **139** "Radio-telephone"

1964. Cent of Norwegian Folk High Schools.

No.	Type	Description	Unused	Used
573	138	50 ore pink	25	10
574		90 ore blue	1·00	1·00

The note after No. 433 re "NOREG" also applies here.

1965. Cent of I.T.U.

No.	Type	Description	Unused	Used
575	139	60 ore purple	25	10
576	–	90 ore grey	60	60

DESIGN: 90 ore "T.V. transmission".

140 Dove of Peace and Broken Chain

1965. 20th Anniv of Liberation.
577 **140** 30 ore + 10 ore brown, green and sepia 25 25
578 – 60 ore + 10 ore blue and red 25 20
DESIGN: 60 ore Norwegian flags.

141 Mountain Landscapes **142** Europa "Sprig"

1965. Centenary of Norwegian Red Cross.
579 **141** 60 ore brown and red . . 20 10
580 – 90 ore blue and red . . . 1·60 1·75
DESIGN: 90 ore Coastal view.

1965. Europa.
581 **142** 60 ore red 25 10
582 90 ore blue 60 60

143 St. Sunniva and Bergen Buildings **144** Rondane Mountains (after H. Sohlberg)

1965. Bicentenary of Harmonien Philharmonic Society.
583 – 30 ore black and green . . 25 20
584 **143** 90 ore black and blue . . 50 50
DESIGN—VERT: 30 ore St. Sunniva.

1965. Rondane National Park.
585 **144** 1 k. 50 blue 70 15

145 "Rodoy Skier" (rock carving) **146** "The Bible"

1966. World Skiing Championships, Oslo. Inscr "VM OSLO 1966".
586 **145** 40 ore brown 50 50
587 – 55 ore green . . . . 1·25 1·25
588 – 60 ore brown 50 15
589 – 90 ore blue 90 75
DESIGNS—HORIZ: 55 ore Ski jumper; 60 ore Cross-country skier. VERT: 90 ore Holmenkollen ski jumping tower, Oslo.

1966. 150th Anniv of Norwegian Bible Society.
590 **146** 60 ore red 25 15
591 90 ore blue 45 55

147 Guilloche Pattern **148** J. Sverdrup (after C. Krohg)

1966. 150th Anniv of Bank of Norway.
592 **147** 30 ore green 35 30
593 – 60 ore red (Bank building) 25 15
No. 593 is size $27\frac{1}{2} \times 21$ mm.

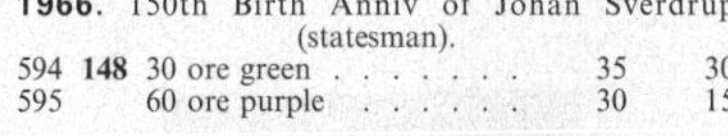
1966. 150th Birth Anniv of Johan Sverdrup (statesman).
594 **148** 30 ore green 35 30
595 60 ore purple 30 15

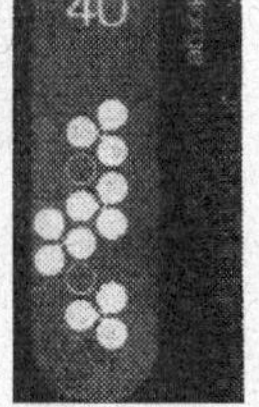

149 Europa "Ship" **150** Molecules in Test-tube

1966. Europa.
596 **149** 60 ore red 30 10
597 90 ore blue 60 60

1966. Birth Centenaries of S. Eyde (industrialist) (1966) and K. Birkeland (scientist) (1967), founders of Norwegian Nitrogen Industry.
598 **150** 40 ore blue and lt blue . 75 60
599 – 55 ore mauve and red . . 1·00 90
DESIGN: 55 ore Ear of wheat and conical flask.

151 E.F.T.A. Emblem **152** "Owl" and Three Swords

1967. European Free Trade Association.
600 **151** 60 ore red 20 10
601 90 ore blue . . . . 80 1·00

1967. 150th Anniv of Higher Military Training.
602 **152** 60 ore brown 40 20
603 90 ore green . . . . . . 1·50 1·25

153 Cogwheels **154** Johanne Dybwad

1967. Europa.
604 **153** 60 ore deep plum, plum and purple 25 10
605 90 ore deep violet, violet and blue 75 65

1967. Birth Centenary of J. Dybwad (actress).
606 **154** 40 ore blue 20 20
607 60 ore red 20 10

155 I. Skrefsrud (missionary and founder) **156** Climbers on Mountain-top

1967. Centenary of Norwegian Santal Mission.
608 **155** 60 ore brown 20 10
609 – 90 ore blue 50 50
DESIGN—HORIZ: 90 ore Ebenezer Church, Benagaria, Santal, India.

1968. Centenary of Norwegian Mountain Touring Association.
610 **156** 40 ore brown 50 45
611 – 60 ore red 40 15
612 – 90 ore blue 80 60
DESIGNS: 60 ore Mountain cairn and scenery; 90 ore Glitretind peak.

157 "The Blacksmiths" **158** Vinje

1968. Norwegian Handicrafts.
613 **157** 65 ore brown, black & red 25 10
614 90 ore brown, black & bl 55 60

1968. 150th Birth Anniv of Aasmund Vinje (poet).
615 **158** 50 ore brown 20 20
616 65 ore red 20 10
See note below No. 433.

159 Cross and Heart **160** Cathinka Guldberg (first deaconess)

1968. Centenary of Norwegian Lutheran Home Mission Society.
617 **159** 40 ore red and green . . 1·25 1·00
618 65 ore red and violet . . 25 10

1968. Centenary of Deaconess House, Oslo.
619 **160** 50 ore blue 20 20
620 65 ore red 20 10

161 K. P. Arnoldson and F. Bajer **161a** Viking Ships (from old Swedish coin)

1968. Nobel Peace Prize Winners of 1908.
621 **161** 65 ore brown 30 15
622 90 ore blue 60 50

1969. 50th Anniv of Northern Countries' Union.
623 **161a** 65 ore red 20 10
624 90 ore blue 40 45

162 Transport

1969. Centenary of "Rutebok for Norge" ("Communications of Norway") and Road Safety Campaign.
625 **162** 50 ore green 60 40
626 – 65 ore red and green . . . 25 10
DESIGN: 65 ore Pedestrian-crossing.

163 Colonnade

1969. Europa.
627 **163** 65 ore black and red . . . 25 10
628 90 ore black and blue . . 45 55

164 J. Hjort and Fish Egg **165** Traena Islands

1969. Birth Centenary of Professor Johan Hjort (fisheries pioneer).
629 **164** 40 ore brown and blue . . 50 40
630 – 90 ore blue and green . . 90 80
DESIGN: 90 ore Hjort and polyp.

1969.
631 **165** 3 k. 50 black 60 10

166 King Olav V **167** "Mother and Child"

1969.
632 **166** 1 k. green 45 10
633 1 k. 50 blue 45 10
634 2 k. red 50 10
635 5 k. blue 60 10
636 10 k. brown . . . . . . 1·00 10
637 20 k. brown . . . . . . 2·00 10
637a 50 k. green . . . . . . 5·00 25

1969. Birth Centenary of Gustav Vigeland (sculptor).
638 **167** 65 ore black and red . . . 30 10
639 – 90 ore black and blue . . 70 60
DESIGN: 90 ore "Family" (sculpture).

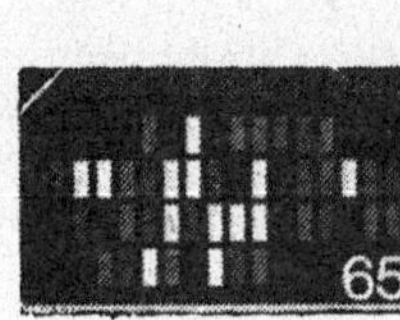

168 Punched Cards **169** Queen Maud

1969. Bicentenary of 1st National Census. Mult.
640 65 ore Type **168** 30 10
641 90 ore "People" (diagram) . . 70 60

1969. Birth Centenary of Queen Maud.
642 **169** 65 ore purple 30 10
643 90 ore blue 70 55

INDEX

Countries can be quickly located by referring to the index at the end of this volume.

170 Wolf **171** "V" Symbol

1970. Nature Conservation Year.
644 **170** 40 ore brown and blue . . 80 35
645 – 60 ore grey and brown . . 80 80
646 – 70 ore brown and blue . . 1·00 15
647 – 100 ore brown and blue . 2·25 1·00
DESIGNS—VERT: 60 ore Pale pasque flower; 70 ore Voringsfossen Falls. HORIZ: 100 ore White-tailed sea eagle.

1970. 25th Anniv of Liberation.
648 **171** 70 ore red and violet . . 1·00 25
649 – 100 ore blue and green . . 1·00 1·00
DESIGN—HORIZ: 100 ore Merchant ships in convoy.

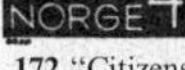

172 "Citizens" **173** Hands reaching for Globe

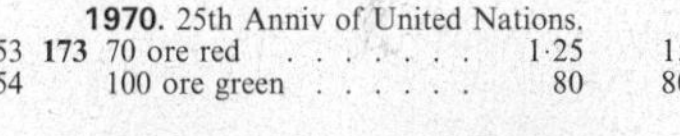
1970. 900th Anniv of Bergen.
650 **172** 40 ore green 70 50
651 – 70 ore purple . . . . . . 1·40 20
652 – 1 k. blue . . . . 1·00 80
DESIGNS: 70 ore "City between the Mountains"; 1 k. "Ships".

1970. 25th Anniv of United Nations.
653 **173** 70 ore red . . . . 1·25 15
654 100 ore green 80 80

174 G. O. Sars **175** Ball-game

1970. Norwegian Zoologists.
655 **174** 40 ore brown 50 60
656 – 50 ore lilac 60 50
657 – 70 ore brown 70 15
658 – 100 ore blue 70 70
ZOOLOGISTS: 50 ore Hans Strom; 70 ore J. E. Gunnerus; 100 ore Michael Sars.

1970. Centenary of Central School of Gymnastics, Oslo.
659 **175** 50 ore brown and blue . . 45 25
660 – 70 ore brown and red . . 55 10
DESIGN—HORIZ: 70 ore "Leapfrog" exercise.

176 Tonsberg's Seal c. 1340

1971. 1100th Anniv of Tonsberg.
661 **176** 70 ore red 30 10
662 100 ore blue 50 45

177 Parliament House, Oslo

1971. Centenary of Introduction of Annual Parliamentary Sessions.
663 **177** 70 ore lilac and red . . . 30 10
664 100 ore green and blue . . 50 40

178 "Helping Hand"

1971. "Help for Refugees".
665 **178** 50 ore green & black . . 40 30
666 70 ore red & black . . . 30 10

179 "Hauge addressing Followers" (A. Tidemand)

1971. Birth Centenary of Hans Nielson Hauge (church reformer).
667 **179** 60 ore black 35 30
668 70 ore brown 25 10

180 Bishop welcoming Worshippers

1971. 900th Anniv of Oslo Bishopric.
669 – 70 ore black and red . . . 30 10
670 **180** 1 k. black and blue . . . 95 80
DESIGN—VERT: 70 ore Masons building first church.

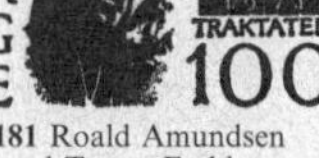

181 Roald Amundsen and Treaty Emblem
182 "The Preacher and the King"

1971. 10th Anniv of Antarctic Treaty.
671 **181** 100 ore red and blue . . . 1·90 1·25

1971. Norwegian Folk Tales. Drawings by Erik Werenskiold.
672 – 40 ore black and green . . . 35 10
673 **182** 50 ore black and blue . . 40 15
674 – 70 ore black and purple . . 55 10
DESIGNS—VERT: 40 ore "The Farmer and the Woman"; 70 ore "The Troll and the Girl".

183 Anniversary Symbol
184 3 s. "Posthorn" Stamp

1972. 150th Anniv of Norwegian Savings Banks.
675 **183** 80 ore gold and red . . . 40 10
676 1 k. 20 gold and blue . . 50 45

1972. Centenary of Norwegian "Posthorn" Stamps.
677 **184** 80 ore red and brown . . 30 10
678 1 k. blue and violet . . . 40 30

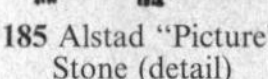

185 Alstad "Picture" Stone (detail)
186 King Haakon VII

1972. 1100th Anniv of Norway's Unification. Relics.
680 **185** 50 ore green 45 40
681 – 60 ore brown 70 65
682 – 80 ore red . . . . 1·00 50
683 – 1 k. 20 blue 70 70
DESIGNS: 60 ore Portal, Hemsedal Church (detail); 80 ore Figurehead of Oseberg Viking ship; 1 k. 20, Sword-hilt (Lodingen).

1972. Birth Centenary of King Haakon VII.
684 **186** 80 ore red 70 10
685 1 k. 20 blue 55 55

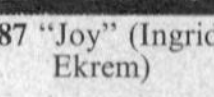

187 "Joy" (Ingrid Ekrem)
189 "Maud"

1972. "Youth and Leisure".
686 **187** 80 ore mauve 35 10
687 – 1 k. 20 blue 60 60
DESIGN: 1 k. 20, "Solidarity" (Ole Instefjord).

1972. "Interjunex 1972" Stamp Exhibition, Oslo. Nos. 686/7 optd **INTERJUNEX 72**.
688 **187** 80 ore mauve . . . . . . 1·50 2·00
689 – 1 k. 20 blue . . . . 1·50 2·00

1972. Norwegian Polar Ships.
690 **189** 60 ore olive and green . . 1·10 60
691 – 80 ore red and black . . 1·10 10
692 – 1 k. 20 blue and red . . . 1·10 80
DESIGNS: 80 ore "Fram" (Amundsen and Nansen's ship); 1 k. 20, "Gjoa".

190 "Little Man"
191 Dr. Hansen and Bacillus Diagram

1972. Norwegian Folk Tales. Drawings of Trolls by Th. Kittelsen.
693 **190** 50 ore black and green . . 30 10
694 – 60 ore black and blue . . 40 35
695 – 80 ore black and pink . . 30 10
TROLLS: 60 ore "The troll who wonders how old he is"; 80 ore "Princess riding on a bear".

1973. Centenary of Hansen's Identification of Leprosy Bacillus.
696 **191** 1 k. red and blue 60 10
697 – 1 k. 40 blue and red . . . 80 70
DESIGN: 1 k. 40, As Type **191** but bacillus as seen in modern microscope.

192 Europa "Posthorn"
193 King Olav V

1973. Europa.
698 **192** 1 k. red, scarlet and carmine 75 10
699 1 k. 40 emerald, green and blue 55 55

1973. Nordic Countries' Postal Co-operation. As T **214** of Sweden.
700 1 k. multicoloured 65 10
701 1 k. 40 multicoloured 60 55

1973. King Olav's 70th Birthday.
702 **193** 1 k. brown and purple . . 40 10
703 1 k. 40 brown and blue . 40 50

194 J. Aall
195 Bone Carving

1973. Birth Centenary of Jacob Aall (industrialist).
704 **194** 1 k. purple 40 10
705 1 k. 40 blue 40 40

1973. Lapp Handicrafts.
706 **195** 75 ore brown and cream . 40 25
707 – 1 k. red and cream . . . 55 10
708 – 1 k. 40 black and blue . . 65 50
DESIGNS: 1 k. Detail of weaving; 1 k. 40, Detail of tin-ware.

196 Yellow Wood Violet
197 Land Surveying

1973. Mountain Flowers. Multicoloured.
709 65 ore Type **196** 40 10
710 70 ore Rock speedwell . . . 50 40
711 1 k. Mountain heath 50 10

1973. Bicentenary of Norwegian Geographical Society.
712 **197** 1 k. red 50 10
713 – 1 k. 40 blue 75 55
DESIGN: 1 k. 40, Old map of Hestbraepiggene (mountain range).

198 Lindesnes
199 "Bridal Procession on Hardanger Fjord" (A. Tidemand and H. Gude)

1974. Norwegian Capes.
714 **198** 1 k. green 50 15
715 – 1 k. 40 blue . . . . 1·00 95
DESIGN: 1 k. 40, North Cape.

1974. Norwegian Paintings. Multicoloured.
716 1 k. Type **199** 40 10
717 1 k. 40, "Stugunoset from Filefjell" (J. Dahl) 60 60

200 Gulating Law Manuscript, 1325
201 Trees and Saw Blade

1974. 700th Anniv of King Magnus Lagaboter National Legislation.
718 **200** 1 k. red and brown 30 10
719 – 1 k. 40 blue and brown . . 35 40
DESIGN: 1 k. 40, King Magnus Lagaboter (sculpture in Stavanger Cathedral).

1974. Industrial Accident Prevention.
720 **201** 85 ore green, deep green and emerald . . . . 1·50 1·10
721 – 1 k. carmine, red and orange 1·00 15
DESIGN: 1 k. Flower and cogwheel.

202 J. H. L. Vogt
203 Buildings of the World

1974. Norwegian Geologists.
722 **202** 65 ore brown and green . 30 25
723 – 85 ore brown and purple 85 75
724 – 1 k. brown and orange . . 45 10
725 – 1 k. 40 brown and blue . . 65 60
DESIGNS: 85 ore V. M. Goldschmidt; 1 k. Th. Kjerulf; 1 k. 40, W. C. Brogger.

1974. Centenary of Universal Postal Union.
726 **203** 1 k. brown and green . . . 30 10
727 – 1 k. 40 blue and brown . . 35 45
DESIGN: 1 k. 40, People of the World.

204 Detail of Chest of Drawers
205 Woman Skier, 1900

1974. Norwegian Folk Art. Rose Painting. Mult.
728 85 ore Type **204** 45 45
729 1 k. Detail of cupboard . . . 30 10

1975. Norwegian Skiing.
730 **205** 1 k. red and green 75 15
731 – 1 k. 40 blue and brown . . 75 55
DESIGN: 1 k. 40, Skier making telemark turn.

206 "Three Women with Ivies" Gate, Vigeland Park, Oslo
207 Nusfjord Fishing Harbour, Lofoten Islands

1975. International Women's Year.
732 **206** 1 k. 25 violet and purple . 50 10
733 1 k. 40 ultramarine and blue 50 50

1975. European Architectural Heritage Year.
734 **207** 1 k. green 50 35
735 – 1 k. 25 red 40 10
736 – 1 k. 40 blue 50 50
DESIGNS. 1 k. 25, Old Stavanger; 1 k. 40, Roros.

208 Norwegian 1 k. Coin, 1875 (Monetary Convention)

1975. Cent of Monetary and Metre Conventions.
737 **208** 1 k. 25 red 30 10
738 – 1 k. 40 blue 50 40
DESIGN: 1 k. 40, O. J. Broch (original Director of the International Bureau of Weights and Measures) (Metre Convention).

209 Camping and Emblem

1975. World Scout Jamboree, Lillehammer. Mult.
739 1 k. 25 Type **209** 45 15
740 1 k. 40 Skiing and emblem . . 80 60

210 Colonist's Peat House

1975. 150th Anniv of First Emigrations to America.
741 **210** 1 k. 25 brown 80 15
742 – 1 k. 40 blue 70 50
DESIGNS: 1 k. 40, C. Peerson and extract from letter to America, 1874.

211 "Templet" (Temple Mountain), Tempelfjord, Spitzbergen
212 "Television Screen" (T. E. Johnsen)

1975. 50th Anniv of Norwegian Administration of Spitzbergen.
743 **211** 1 k. grey 50 25
744 – 1 k. 25 purple 50 10
745 – 1 k. 40 blue . . . . 1·50 1·00
DESIGNS: 1 k. 25, Miners leaving pit; 1 k. 40, Polar bear.

1975. 50th Anniv of Norwegian Broadcasting System. Multicoloured.
746 1 k. 25 Type **212** 30 10
747 1 k. 40 Telecommunications antenna (N. Davidsen) (vert) 50 35

213 "The Annunciation"
214 "Halling" (folk dance)

1975. Paintings from "Altaket" (wooden vault from "Al" (Stave Church), Hallingdal).
748 80 ore Type **213** 30 10
749 1 k. "The Visitation" 30 25
750 1 k. 25 "The Nativity" (30 × 38 mm) 30 10
751 1 k. 40 "The Adoration" (30 × 38 mm) 60 45

1976. Norwegian Folk Dances. Multicoloured.
752 80 ore Type **214** 45 25
753 1 k. "Springar" 45 25
754 1 k. 25 "Gangar" 45 10

215 Silver Sugar Caster, Stavanger, 1770
217 "The Pulpit", Lyse Fjord

216 Bishop's "Mitre" Bowl, 1760

1976. Centenary of Oslo Museum of Applied Art.
755 **215** 1 k. 25 brown, red & pink 20 10
756 – 1 k. 40 lilac, blue and azure 35 40
DESIGN: 1 k. 40, Goblet, Nostetangen Glass-works, 1770.

1976. Europa. Early Products of Herrebo Potteries, Halden.
757 **216** 1 k. 25 red and mauve . . 20 10
758 – 1 k. 40 ultramarine & blue 30 40
DESIGN: 1 k. 40, Decorative plate, 1760.

1976. Norwegian Scenery. Multicoloured.
759 1 k. Type **217** 50 25
760 1 k. 25 Peak of Gulleplet ("The Golden Apple"), Balestrand, Sognefjord 50 10

218 Social Development Graph
219 Olav Duun and Cairn, Dun Mountain, Joa Island, Namsen Fjord

1976. Cent of Norwegian Central Bureau of Statistics.
761 **218** 1 k. 25 red 20 10
762 – 2 k. blue 30 20
DESIGN: 2 k. National productivity graph.

1976. Birth Centenary of Olav Duun (novelist).
763 **219** 1 k. 25 multicoloured . . 20 10
764 1 k. 40 multicoloured . . 25 30

220 "Slindebirkin" (T. Fearnley)
221 Details of "April"

1976. Norwegian Paintings. Multicoloured.
765 1 k. 25 Type **220** 20 10
766 1 k. 40 "Gamle Furutraer" (L. Hertervig) 25 35

1976. Tapestry from Baldishol Stave Church. Mult.
767 80 ore Type **221** 20 15
768 1 k. Detail of "May" 20 25
769 1 k. 25 "April" and "May" section of tapestry (48 × 30 mm) 20 15

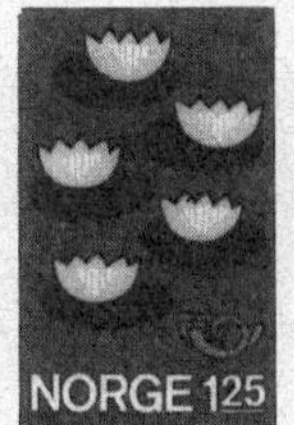

222 Five Water-lilies

1977. Nordic Countries Co-operation in Nature Conservation and Environment Protection.
770 **222** 1 k. 25 multicoloured . . 25 10
771 1 k. 40 multicoloured . . 25 35

223 Akershus Castle, Oslo
224 Hamnoy, Lofoten Islands

1977.
772 – 1 k. green 15 10
773 – 1 k. 10 purple 45 15
774 **223** 1 k. 25 red 20 10
775 – 1 k. 30 brown 30 10
776 – 1 k. 40 lilac 45 10
777 – 1 k. 50 red 20 10
778 – 1 k. 70 green 30 15
779 – 1 k. 75 green 30 10
780 – 1 k. 80 blue 50 10
781 – 2 k. red 30 10
782 – 2 k. 20 blue 30 15
783 – 2 k. 25 violet 30 15
784 – 2 k. 50 red 30 10
785 – 2 k. 75 red 40 30
786 – 3 k. blue 40 10
787 – 3 k. 50 violet 55 15
DESIGNS—HORIZ: 1 k. Austraat Manor; 1 k. 10, Trondenes Church, Harstad; 1 k. 30, Steinviksholm Fortress, Asen Fjord; 1 k. 40, Ruins of Hamar Cathedral; 2 k. 20, Tromsdalen Church; 2 k. 50, Loghouse, Breiland; 2 k. 75, Damsgard Palace, Laksevag, near Bergen; 3 k. Ruins of Selje Monastery; 3 k. 50, Lindesnes lighthouse. VERT: 1 k. 50, Stavanger Cathedral; 1 k. 70, Rosenkrantz Tower, Bergen; 1 k. 75, Seamen's commemoration hall, Stavern; 1 k. 80, Torungen lighthouses, Arendal; 2 k. Tofte royal estate, Dovre; 2 k. 25, Oscarshall (royal residence), Oslofjord.

1977. Europa. Multicoloured.
795 1 k. 25 Type **224** 40 10
796 1 k. 80 Huldrefossen, Nordfjord (vert) 40 40

225 Spruce
226 Paddle-Steamer "Constitutionen" at Arendal

1977. Norwegian Trees.
797 **225** 1 k. green 20 25
798 – 1 k. 25 brown 20 15
799 – 1 k. 80 black 30 35
DESIGNS: 1 k. 25, Fir; 1 k. 80, Birch.
See note below No. 433.

1977. Norwegian Coastal Routes.
800 **226** 1 k. brown 40 25
801 – 1 k. 25 red 60 10
802 – 1 k. 30 green . . . . . . 1·25 1·10
803 – 1 k. 80 blue 60 65
DESIGNS: 1 k. 25, "Vesteraalen" (freighter) off Bodo; 1 k. 30, Ferries "Kong Haakon" and "Dronningen" at Stavanger, 1893; 1 k. 80, "Nordstjernen" and "Harald Jarl" (ferries).

227 "From the Herring Fishery" (after photo by S. A. Borretzen)
228 "Saturday Evening" (H. Egedius)

1977. Fishing Industry.
804 **227** 1 k. 25 brown on orange . . 20 10
805 – 1 k. 80 blue on blue . . . 30 35
DESIGN: 1 k. 80, Coley and fish hooks.
See note below No. 433.

1977. Norwegian Paintings. Multicoloured.
806 1 k. 25 Type **228** 20 10
807 1 k. 80 "Forest Lake in Lower Telemark" (A. Cappelen) . . 30 40

229 "David with the Bells"
230 "Peer and the Buck Reindeer" (after drawing by P. Krohg for "Peer Gynt")

1977. Miniatures from the Bible of Aslak Bolt. Multicoloured.
808 80 ore Type **229** 20 10
809 1 k. "Singing Friars" 20 20
810 1 k. 25 "The Holy Virgin with the Child" (34 × 27 mm) 20 10

1978. 150th Birth Anniv of Henrik Ibsen (dramatist).
811 **230** 1 k. 25 black and stone . . 20 10
812 – 1 k. 80 multicoloured . . 25 30
DESIGN: 1 k. 80, Ibsen (after E. Werenskiold).

231 Heddal Stave Church, Telemark
232 Lenangstindene and Jaegervasstindene, Troms

1978. Europa.
813 **231** 1 k. 25 brown & orange . . 25 10
814 – 1 k. 80 green and blue . . 30 40
DESIGN: 1 k. 80, Borgund stave church, Sogn.

1978. Norwegian Scenery. Multicoloured.
815 1 k. Type **232** 30 15
816 1 k. 25 Gaustatoppen, Telemark 35 30

233 King Olav in Sailing-boat

1978. 75th Birthday of King Olav V.
817 **233** 1 k. 25 brown 20 10
818 – 1 k. 80 violet 30 35
DESIGN—VERT: 1 k. 80, King Olav delivering royal speech at opening of Parliament.

234 Amundsen's Polar Flight Stamp of 1925

1978. "Norwex 80" International Stamp Exhibition.
819 **234** 1 k. 25 green and grey . . 85 90
820 1 k. 25 blue and grey . . . 85 90
821 – 1 k. 25 green and grey . . 85 90
822 – 1 k. 25 blue and grey . . . 85 90
823 **234** 1 k. 25 purple and grey . . 85 90
824 1 k. 25 red and grey . . . 85 90
825 – 1 k. 25 purple and grey . . 85 90
826 – 1 k. 25 blue and grey . . . 85 90
DESIGNS: Nos. 821/2, 825/6, Annexation of Spitzbergen stamp of 1925.
On Nos. 819/26 each design incorporates a different value of the 1925 issues.

235 Willow Pipe Player
236 Wooden Doll, c. 1830

1978. Musical Instruments.
827 **235** 1 k. green 30 10
828 – 1 k. 25 red 30 10
829 – 1 k. 80 blue 30 30
830 – 7 k. 50 grey . . . . 1·25 25
831 – 15 k. brown . . . . 1·75 15
DESIGNS: 1 k. 25, Norwegian violin; 1 k. 80, Norwegian zither; 7 k. 50, Ram's horn; 15 k. Jew's harp.
See note below No. 433.

1978. Christmas. Antique Toys from Norwegian Folk Museum. Multicoloured.
835 80 ore Type **236** 20 10
836 1 k. Toy town, 1896/7 . . . . 20 20
837 1 k. 25 Wooden horse from Torpo, Hallingdal 20 10

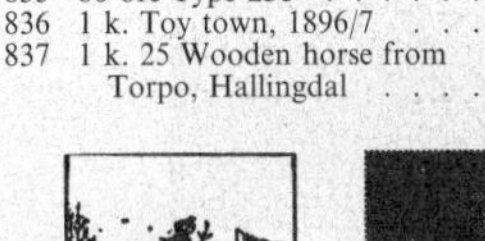

237 Ski Jumping at Huseby, 1879
238 "Portrait of Girl" (M. Stoltenberg)

1979. Centenary of Skiing Competitions at Huseby and Holmenkollen.
838 **237** 1 k. green 30 15
839 – 1 k. 25 red 30 10
840 – 1 k. 80 blue 35 35
DESIGNS: 1 k. 25, Crown Prince Olav ski jumping at Holmenkollen, 1922; 1 k. 80, Cross-country skiing at Holmenkollen, 1976.

1979. International Year of the Child. Mult.
841 1 k. 25 Type **238** 25 10
842 1 k. 80 "Portrait of Boy" (H. C. F. Hosenfelder) 30 30

239 Road to Briksdal Glacier
240 Falkberget (after Harald Dal)

1979. Norwegian Scenery. Multicoloured.
843 1 k. Type **239** 25 15
844 1 k. 25 Skjernoysund, near Mandal 25 10

1979. Birth Centenary of Johan Falkberget (novelist).
845 **240** 1 k. 25 brown 20 10
846 – 1 k. 80 blue 25 35
DESIGN: 1 k. 80, "Ann-Magritt and the Hovi Bullock" (statue by Kristofer Leirdal).

242 Kylling Bridge, Verma, Romsdal
243 Glacier Buttercup

1979. Norwegian Engineering.
848 **242** 1 k. 25 black and brown . . 40 10
849 – 2 k. black and blue 35 20
850 – 10 k. brown and bistre . . 1·90 35
DESIGNS: 2 k. Vessingsjo Dam, Nea, Sor-Trondelag; 10 k. Statfjord A offshore oil drilling and production platform.

1979. Flowers. Multicoloured.
851 80 ore Type **243** 20 10
852 1 k. Alpine cinquefoil 25 20
853 1 k. 25 Purple saxifrage . . . 25 10
See also Nos. 867/8.

244 Leaf and Emblems
245 Oystercatcher Chick ("Haematopus ostralegus")

1980. Centenary of Norwegian Christian Youth Association. Multicoloured.
854 1 k. Type **244** 15 10
855 1 k. 80 Plant and emblems . . 20 30

1980. Birds (1st series). Multicoloured.
856 1 k. Type **245** 35 15
857 1 k. Mallard chick ("Anas platyrhynchos") 35 15
858 1 k. 25 Dipper ("Cinclus cinclus") 35 15
859 1 k. 25 Great tit ("Parus major") 35 15
See also Nos. 869/72, 894/5 and 914/15.

246 Telephone and Dish Aerial

1980. Centenary of Norwegian Telephone Service.
860 **246** 1 k. 25 brown, pur & bl . . 20 10
861 – 1 k. 80 multicoloured . . 30 35
DESIGN: 1 k. 80, Erecting a telephone pole.

248 "Vulcan as an Armourer" (Hassel Jerverk after Bech)

1980. Nordic Countries' Postal Co-operation. Cast-iron Stove Ornaments.
863 **248** 1 k. 25 brown 15 10
864 – 1 k. 80 violet 20 30
DESIGN: 1 k. 80, "Hercules at a burning Altar" (Moss Jerverk after Henrich Bech).

249 "Jonsokbal" (N. Astrup)

1980. Norwegian Paintings. Multicoloured.
865 1 k. 25 Type **249** 15 10
866 1 k. 80 "Seljefloyten" (C. Skredsvig) 25 30

1980. Flowers. As T **243**. Multicoloured.
867 80 ore Rowan berries 15 10
868 1 k. Dog rose hips 15 10

1981. Birds (2nd series). As T **245**. Multicoloured.
869 1 k. 30 Lesser white-fronted goose ("Anser erythropus") 30 20
870 1 k. 30 Peregrine falcon ("Falco peregrinus") 30 20
871 1 k. 50 Atlantic puffin ("Fratercula arctica") . . . 50 10
872 1 k. 50 Black guillemot ("Cepphus grylle") 50 10

250 Cow
251 "The Mermaid" (painting by Kristen Aanstad on wooden dish from Hol)

1981. Centenary of Norwegian Milk Producers' National Association. Multicoloured.
873 1 k. 10 Type **250** 15 15
874 1 k. 50 Goat 20 10
See note below No. 433.

1981. Europa. Multicoloured.

875 1 k. 50 Type **251** 30 10
876 2 k. 20 "The Proposal" (painting by Ola Hansson on box from Nes) 40 45

See note below No. 433.

252 Weighing Anchor

253 Paddle Steamer "Skibladner"

1981. Sailing Ship Era.

877 **252** 1 k. 30 green 40 30
878 – 1 k. 50 red 35 15
879 – 2 k. 20 blue 70 45

DESIGNS—VERT: 1 k. 50, Climbing the rigging. HORIZ: 2 k. 20, Cadet ship "Christian Radich".

1981. Norwegian Lake Shipping.

880 **253** 1 k. 10 brown 20 20
881 – 1 k. 30 green 20 30
882 – 1 k. 50 red 20 10
883 – 2 k. 30 blue 40 30

DESIGNS: 1 k. 30, "Victoria" (ferry); 1 k. 50, "Faemund II" (ferry); 2 k. 30, "Storegut" (train ferry).

254 Handicapped People as Part of Community

1981. International Year of Disabled Persons.

884 **254** 1 k. 50 pink, red & blue . 20 10
885 – 2 k. 20 blue, deep blue and red 30 35

DESIGN: 2 k. 20, Handicapped and non-handicapped people walking together.

255 "Interior in Blue" (Harriet Backer)

256 Hajalmar Branting and Christian Lange

1981. Norwegian Paintings. Multicoloured.

886 1 k. 50 Type **255** 20 10
887 1 k. 70 "Peat Moor on Jaeren" (Kitty Lange Kielland) . . . 30 35

1981. Nobel Peace Prize Winners of 1921.

888 **256** 5 k. black 70 35

257 "One of the Magi" (detail from Skjak tapestry, 1625)

258 Ski Sticks

1981. Tapestries. Multicoloured.

889 1 k. 10 Type **257** 20 10
890 1 k. 30 "Adoration of Christ" (detail, Skjak tapestry, 1625) 20 15
891 1 k. 50 "Marriage in Cana" (pillow slip from Storen, 18th century) (29 × 36 mm) . . . 20 10

1982. World Ski Championships, Oslo.

892 **258** 2 k. red and blue 30 10
893 – 3 k. blue and red 50 35

DESIGN: 3 k. Skis.

1982. Birds (3rd series). As T **245**. Multicoloured.

894 2 k. Bluethroat ("Luscinia svecica") 40 20
895 2 k. European robin ("Erithacus rubecula") 40 20

259 Nurse

260 King Haakon VII disembarking from "Heimdal" after Election, 1905

1982. Anti-tuberculosis Campaign. Mult.

896 2 k. Type **259** 25 10
897 3 k. Microscope 35 35

See note below No. 433.

1982. Europa.

898 **260** 2 k. brown 40 10
899 – 3 k. blue 50 35

DESIGN: 3 k. Crown Prince Olav greeting King Haakon VII after liberation, 1945.

261 "Girls from Telemark" (Erik Werenskiold)

1982. Norwegian Paintings. Multicoloured.

900 1 k. 75 Type **261** 25 25
901 2 k. "Tone Veli by Fence" (Henrik Sorenson) 25 10

See note below No. 433.

262 Consecration Ceremony, Nidaros Cathedral, Trondheim

1982. 25th Anniv of King Olav V's Reign.

902 **262** 3 k. violet 35 40

263 "Bjornstjerne Bjornson on Balcony at Aulestad" (Erik Werenskiold)

1982. Writers' Birth Anniversaries. Multicoloured.

903 1 k. 75 Type **263** (150th anniv) 25 25
904 2 k. "Sigrid Undset" (after A. C. Svarstad) (birth centenary) 25 10

264 Construction of Letter "A"

265 Fridtjof Nansen

1982. Centenary of Graphical Union of Norway.

905 **264** 2 k. yellow, green and black 25 15
906 – 3 k. multicoloured . . . 35 35

DESIGN: 3 k. Offset litho printing rollers.

1982. 1922 Nobel Peace Prize-Winner.

907 **265** 3 k. blue 40 35

See note below No. 433.

266 "Christmas Tradition" (Adolf Tidemand)

267 Buhund (farm dog)

1982. Christmas.

908 **266** 1 k. 75 multicoloured . . 25 15

1983. Norwegian Dogs. Multicoloured.

909 2 k. Type **267** 40 25
910 2 k. 50 Elkhound 35 15
911 3 k. 50 Lundehund (puffin hunter) 40 40

See note below No. 433.

268 Mountain Scenery

269 Edvard Grieg with Concerto in A minor

1983. Nordic Countries' Postal Co-operation. "Visit the North". Multicoloured.

912 2 k. 50 Type **268** 25 10
913 3 k. 50 Fjord scenery 35 35

1983. Birds (4th series). As T **245**. Mult.

914 2 k. 50 Barnacle goose ("Branta leucopsis") 50 25
915 2 k. 50 Little auk ("Alle alle") 50 25

1983. Europa.

916 **269** 2 k. 50 red 50 10
917 – 3 k. 50 blue & green . . . 50 35

DESIGN—VERT: 3 k. 50, Statue of Niels Henrik Abel (mathematician) by Gustav Vigeland.

270 Arrows forming Posthorn

271 King Olav V and Royal Birch, Molde

1983. World Communications Year. Multicoloured.

918 2 k. 50 Type **270** 25 10
919 3 k. 50 Arrows circling globe . 35 35

1983. 80th Birthday of King Olav V.

920 **271** 5 k. green 65 25

272 Lie

273 Northern Femboring

1983. 150th Birth Anniv of Jonas Lie (author).

921 **272** 2 k. 50 red 30 10

1983. North Norwegian Ships.

922 **273** 2 k. blue and brown . . . 50 20
923 – 3 k. brown and blue . . . 60 40

DESIGNS: 3 k. Jekt.

See note below No. 433.

274 "The Sleigh Ride" (Axel Ender)

275 Post Office Counter

1983. Christmas. Multicoloured.

924 2 k. Type **274** 20 10
925 2 k. 50 "The Guests are arriving" (Gustav Wendel) 25 10

1984. Postal Work. Multicoloured.

926 2 k. Type **275** 25 20
927 2 k. 50 Postal sorting 30 10
928 3 k. 50 Postal delivery 40 35

276 Freshwater Fishing

277 Magnetic Meridians and Parallels

1984. Sport Fishing.

929 **276** 2 k. 50 red 30 10
930 – 3 k. green 35 40
931 – 3 k. 50 blue 85 50

DESIGNS: 3 k. Salmon fishing; 3 k. 50, Sea fishing.

1984. Birth Bicentenary of Christopher Hansteen (astronomer and geophysicist).

932 **277** 3 k. 50 blue 40 30
933 – 5 k. red 60 30

DESIGN—VERT: 5 k. Portrait of Hansteen by Johan Gorbitz.

278 Bridge

279 Vegetables, Fruit and Herbs

1984. Europa. 25th Anniv of European Post and Telecommunications Conference.

934 **278** 2 k. 50 multicoloured . . 30 10
935 3 k. 50 multicoloured . . 40 40

1984. Centenary of Norwegian Horticultural Society. Multicoloured.

936 2 k. Type **279** 25 15
937 2 k. 50 Rose and garland of flowers 30 10

280 Honey Bees

281 Holberg (after J. M. Bernigeroth)

1984. Centenaries of Norwegian Beekeeping Society and Norwegian Poultry-breeding Society. Mult.

938 2 k. 50 Type **280** 30 10
939 2 k. 50 Leghorn cock 30 10

See note below No. 433.

1984. 300th Birth Anniv of Ludvig Holberg (writer).

940 **281** 2 k. 50 red 30 10

282 Children reading

284 Karius and Baktus (tooth decay bacteria)

283 Entering Parliamentary Chamber, 2 July 1884

1984. 150th Anniv of "Norsk Penning-Magazin" (1st weekly magazine in Norway).

941 **282** 2 k. 50 purple, blue and red 25 10
942 – 3 k. 50 orange and violet . 35 35

DESIGN: 3 k. 50, 1st edition of "Norsk Penning-Magazin".

1984. Cent. of Norwegian Parliament.

943 **283** 7 k. 50 brown 80 45

1984. Characters from Stories by Thorbjorn Egner. Multicoloured.

944 2 k. Type **284** 30 15
945 2 k. The tree shrew playing guitar 30 15
946 2 k. 50 Kasper, Jesper and Jonatan (Rovers) in Kardemomme Town . . . 80 25
947 2 k. 50 Chief Constable Bastian 40 15

285 Mount Sagbladet (Saw Blade)

286 Return of Crown Prince Olav, 1945

1985. Antarctic Mountains. Multicoloured.

948 2 k. 50 Type **285** 35 15
949 3 k. 50 Mount Hoggestabben (Chopping Block) 45 40

1985. 40th Anniv of Liberation.

950 **286** 3 k. 50 red and blue . . . 60 35

287 Kongsten Fort

1985. 300th Anniv of Kongsten Fort.

951 **287** 2 k. 50 multicoloured . . 30 10

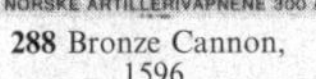

288 Bronze Cannon, 1596 — 289 "Boy and Girl" (detail)

1985. Artillery Anniversaries. Multicoloured.
952 3 k. Type **288** (300th anniv of Artillery) 35 30
953 4 k. Cannon on sledge carriage, 1758 (bicentenary of Artillery Officers Training School) . . 45 35

1985. International Youth Year. Sculptures in Vigeland Park, Oslo. Multicoloured.
954 2 k. Type **289** 20 20
955 3 k. 50 Bronze fountain (detail) 40 40
See note below No. 433.

290 Torgeir Augundsson (fiddler) — 291 Workers at Glomfjord

1985. Europa. Music Year.
956 **290** 2 k. 50 red 50 10
957 – 3 k. 50 blue 60 40
DESIGN: 3 k. 50, Ole Bull (composer and violinist).

1985. Centenary of Electricity in Norway.
958 **291** 2 k. 50 red and scarlet . . . 35 10
959 – 4 k. blue and green . . . 45 40
DESIGN: 4 k. Men working on overhead cable.

293 Carl Deichman on Book Cover — 294 Wreath

1985. Bicentenary of Public Libraries.
961 **293** 2 k. 50 sepia and brown . 35 10
962 – 10 k. green . . . . 1·25 50
DESIGN—HORIZ: 10 k. Library interior.

1985. Christmas. Multicoloured.
963 2 k. Type **294** 35 10
964 2 k. 50 Bullfinches 50 10

295 Dredger "Berghavn" — 296 Sun

1985. 250th Anniv of Port Authorities and Bicentenary of Hydrography in Norway.
965 **295** 2 k. 50 purple, orange & bl 35 10
966 – 5 k. blue, green & brown . 60 40
DESIGN: 5 k. Sextant and detail of chart No. 1 of Lt. F.C. Grove showing Trondheim sealane, 1791.

1986.
967 **296** 2 k. 10 orange and brown 25 10
968 – 2 k. 30 green and blue . . 35 10
969 – 2 k. 70 pink and red . . . 35 10
970 – 4 k. blue and green . . . 40 10
DESIGNS: 2 k. 30, Fishes; 2 k. 70, Flowers; 4 k. Star ornaments.

297 Marksman in Prone Position

1986. World Biathlon Championships. Mult.
977 2 k. 50 Type **297** 35 10
978 3 k. 50 Marksman standing to take aim 45 35

298 Industry and Countryside — 299 Stone Cutter

1986. Europa. Multicoloured.
979 2 k. 50 Type **298** 50 10
980 3 k. 50 Dead and living forest, mountains and butterflies . 60 35

1986. Centenary of Norwegian Craftsmen's Federation.
981 **299** 2 k. 50 lake and red . . . 35 10
982 – 7 k. blue and red 80 50
DESIGN: 7 k. Carpenter.

300 Moss

1986. Nordic Countries' Postal Co-operation. Twinned Towns. Multicoloured.
983 2 k. 50 Type **300** 50 15
984 4 k. Alesund 75 55
See note below No. 433.

301 Han Polson Egede (missionary) and Map — 303 "Olav Kyrre founds Diocese in Nidaros"

1986. Birth Anniversaries.
985 **301** 2 k. 10 brown and red . . 30 30
986 – 2 k. 50 red, green & blue 35 10
987 – 3 k. brown and red . . . 45 40
988 – 4 k. purple and lilac . . . 55 40
DESIGNS: 2 k. 10, Type **301** (300th anniv); 2 k. 50, Herman Wildenvey (poet) and poem carved in wall at Stavern (centenary); 3 k. Tore Ojasaeter (poet) and old cupboard from Skjak (centenary); 4 k. Engebret Soot (engineer) and lock gates, Orje (centenary).
See note below No. 433.

1986. Christmas. Stained Glass Windows by Gabriel Kielland in Nidaros Cathedral, Trondheim. Multicoloured.
990 2 k. 10 Type **303** 30 20
991 2 k. 50 "The King and the Peasant at Sul" 30 15

304 Doves — 305 Numeral

1986. International Peace Year.
992 **304** 15 k. red, blue & green . 1·75 75

1987.
993 **305** 3 k. 50 yellow, red & blue 60 20
994 4 k. 50 blue, yellow & grn 65 15

306 Wooden Building

1987. Europa. Multicoloured.
1000 2 k. 70 Type **306** 55 10
1001 4 k. 50 Building of glass and stone 70 20

307 The Final Vote — 309 Funnel-shaped Chanterelle ("Cantharellus tubaeformis")

1987. 150th Anniv of Laws on Local Councils (granting local autonomy).
1002 **307** 12 k. green . . . . 1·60 55

1987. Fungi (1st series). Multicoloured.
1004 2 k. 70 Type **309** 75 15
1005 2 k. 70 The gypsy ("Rozites caperata") 75 15
See also Nos. 1040/1 and 1052/3.

310 Bjornstad Farm from Vaga

1987. Centenary of Sandvig Collections, Maihaugen.
1006 **310** 2 k. 70 sepia and brown . 50 15
1007 – 3 k. 50 purple and blue . 60 40
DESIGN: 3 k. 50, "Horse and Rider" (wooden carving, Christen Erlandsen Listad).

311 Valevag Churchyard

1987. Birth Centenary of Fartein Valen (composer).
1008 **311** 2 k. 30 blue and green . . 50 30
1009 – 4 k. 50 brown 90 35
DESIGN—VERT: 4 k. 50, Farten Valen.
See note below No. 433.

312 "Storm at Sea" (Christian Krohg)

1987. Paintings. Multicoloured.
1010 2 k. 70 Type **312** 50 15
1011 5 k. "The Farm" (Gerhard Munthe) . . . . 1·00 50

314 Cat with Children making Decorations

1987. Christmas. Multicoloured.
1013 2 k. 30 Type **314** 45 15
1014 2 k. 70 Dog with children making gingersnaps 55 15

315 Dales Pony — 316 Capercaillie

1987. Native Ponies.
1015 **315** 2 k. 30 deep brown, green and brown 55 20
1016 – 2 k. 70 buff, brown & bl . 65 15
1017 – 4 k. 50 brown, red and blue 90 45
DESIGNS: 2 k. 70, Fjord pony; 4 k. 50, Nordland pony.
See note below No. 433.

1988. Animals.
1018 – 2 k. 60 deep brown, brown and green 45 10
1019 **316** 2 k. 90 black, brn & grn . 45 15
1020 – 3 k. brown, grey & grn . 55 10
1021 – 3 k. 20 ultramarine, green and blue 60 20
1022 – 3 k. 80 brown, bl & blk . 55 10
1023 – 4 k. brown, red & green 70 10
1024 – 4 k. 50 brown, grn & bl . 90 10
1025 – 5 k. 50 brown, grey & grn 1·10 25
1026 – 6 k. 40 brown, blk & grn 1·25 50
DESIGNS: 2 k. 60, Fox; 3 k. Stoat; 3 k. 20, Mute swan; 3 k. 80, Reindeer; 4 k. Eurasian red squirrel; 4 k. 50, Beaver; 5 k. 50, Lynx; 6 k. 40, Tengmalm's owl.

317 Band

1988. Centenary of Salvation Army in Norway. Multicoloured.
1035 2 k. 90 Type **317** 45 15
1036 4 k. 80 Othilie Tonning (early social worker) and Army nurse 80 40

318 Building Fortress

1988. Military Anniversaries.
1037 **318** 2 k. 50 green 50 20
1038 – 2 k. 90 brown 55 15
1039 – 4 k. 60 blue 90 35
DESIGNS: 2 k. 50, Type **318** (300th anniv of Defence Construction Service); 2 k. 90, Corps members in action (centenary of Army Signals corps); 4 k. 60, Making pontoon bridge (centenary of Engineer Corps).

1988. Fungi (2nd series). As T **309**. Mult.
1040 2 k. 90 Wood blewits 75 15
1041 2 k. 90 Milk caps 75 15

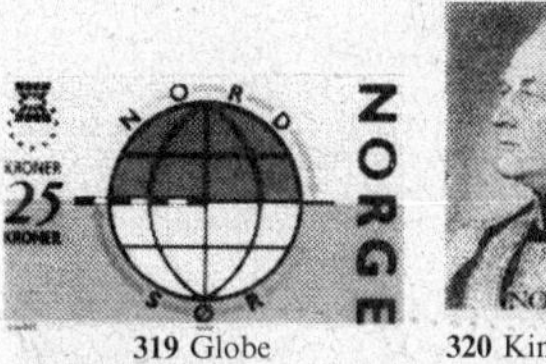

319 Globe — 320 King Olav V

1988. European Campaign for Interdependence and Solidarity of North and South.
1042 **319** 25 k. multicoloured . . . 3·50 75

1988. 85th Birthday of King Olav V.
1043 **320** 2 k. 90 multicoloured . . 70 10

321 "Prinds Gustav" (paddle-steamer) — 322 King Christian IV

1988. Europa. Transport and Communications.
1045 **321** 2 k. 90 black, red & blue 85 10
1046 – 3 k. 80 blue, red & yell . 1·00 60
DESIGN: 3 k. 80, Heroybrua Bridge.

1988. 400th Anniv of Christian IV's Accession to Danish and Norwegian Thrones.
1047 **322** 2 k. 50 black, stone & vio 60 10
1048 – 10 k. multicoloured . . . 2·40 45
DESIGN: 10 k. 1628 silver coin and extract from decree on mining in Norway.

324 Ludvig with Ski Stick — 325 Start and Finish of Race

1988. Christmas. Multicoloured.
1050 2 k. 90 Type **324** 70 10
1051 2 k. 90 Ludvig reading letter 70 10

1989. Fungi (3rd series). As T **309**. Multicoloured.
1052 3 k. Chanterelle ("Cantharellus cibarius") 80 20
1053 3 k. Butter mushroom ("Suillus luteus") 80 20

1989. World Cross-country Championship, Stavanger.
1054 **325** 5 k. multicoloured . . . 1·10 25

326 Vardo 327 Setesdal Woman

1989. Town Bicentenaries.
1055 **326** 3 k. blue, red & lt blue . . 60 10
1056 – 4 k. purple, blue & orge . . 1·00 35
DESIGN: 4 k. Hammerfest.

1989. Nordic Countries' Postal Co-operation. Traditional Costumes. Multicoloured.
1057 3 k. Type **327** 60 10
1058 4 k. Kautokeino man . . . . 1·00 45

328 Children making Snowman 329 Rooster and Cover of 1804 First Reader

1989. Europa. Children's Games. Multicoloured.
1059 3 k. 70 Type **328** 85 50
1060 5 k. Cat's cradle . . . . . . 1·50 50
See note below No. 433.

1989. 250th Anniv of Primary Schools.
1061 **329** 2 k. 60 multicoloured . . 85 45
1062 – 3 k. brown 60 10
DESIGN: 3 k. Pocket calculator and child writing.

332 Arnulf Overland (poet, centenary) 333 Star Decoration

1989. Writers' Birth Anniversaries.
1065 **332** 3 k. red and blue 60 10
1066 – 25 k. blue, orange & green 4·50 70
DESIGN: 25 k. Hanna Winsnes (pseudonym Hugo Schwartz) (bicentenary).

1989. Christmas. Tree Decorations. Mult.
1067 3 k. Type **333** 60 10
1068 3 k. Bauble 60 10

334 Larvik Manor 335 Emblem

1989. Manor Houses.
1069 **334** 3 k. brown 60 10
1070 – 3 k. green 60 10
DESIGN: No. 1070, Rosendal Barony.

1990. Winter Cities Events, Tromso.
1071 **335** 5 k. multicoloured . . . 1·00 35

336 Common Spotted Orchid ("Dactylorhiza fuchsii") 337 Merchant Navy, Airforce, Home Guard, "Moses" (coastal gun) and Haakon VII's Monogram

1990. Orchids (1st series). Multicoloured.
1072 3 k. 20 Type **336** 60 10
1073 3 k. 20 Dark red helleborine ("Epipactis atrorubens") 60 10
See also Nos. 1141/2.

1990. 50th Anniv of Norway's Entry into Second World War. Multicoloured.
1074 3 k. 20 Type **337** 60 10
1075 4 k. Second Battle of Narvik, 1940 . . . . 1·00 45

339 Trondheim Post Office 340 "Tordenskiold" (from print by J. W. Tegner after Balthazar Denner)

1990. Europa. Post Office Buildings. Mult.
1077 3 k. 20 Type **339** 75 10
1078 4 k. Longyearbyen Post Office 85 45

1990. 300th Birth Anniv of Admiral Tordenskiold (Peter Wessel). Multicoloured.
1079 3 k. 20 Type **340** 75 10
1080 5 k. Tordenskiold's coat-of-arms . . . . 1·00 45

341 Svendsen 343 "Children and Snowman" (Ragni Engstrom Nilsen)

1990. 150th Birth Anniv of Johan Svendsen (composer and conductor).
1081 **341** 2 k. 70 black and red . . 85 50
1082 – 15 k. brown & yellow . 2·75 50
DESIGN: 15 k. Svendsen Monument (Stinius Fredriksen), Oslo.

1990. Christmas. Children's Prize-winning Drawings. Multicoloured.
1084 3 k. 20 Type **343** 60 10
1085 3 k. 20 "Christmas Church" (Jorgen Ingier) 60 10

344 Nobel Medal and Soderblom

1990. 60th Anniv of Award of Nobel Peace Prize to Nathan Soderblom, Archbishop of Uppsala.
1086 **344** 30 k. brown, blue & red 5·50 70

345 Plan and Elevation of Container Ship and Propeller 346 Satellite transmitting to Tromso

1991. Centenaries of Federation of Engineering Industries (1989) and Union of Iron and Metal Workers.
1087 **345** 5 k. multicoloured . . . 1·00 45

1991. Europa. Europe in Space. Mult.
1088 3 k. 20 Type **346** 60 10
1089 4 k. Rocket leaving Andoya rocket range 90 25
See note below No. 433.

347 Christiansholm Fortress (late 17th-century) 348 Fountain, Vigeland Park, Oslo

1991. 350th Anniv of Kristiansand. Each black, blue and red.
1090 3 k. 20 Type **347** 60 15
1091 5 k. 50 Present day view of Christiansholm Fortress . 1·10 60

1991. Nordic Countries' Postal Co-operation. Tourism. Multicoloured.
1092 3 k. 20 Type **348** 60 10
1093 4 k. Globe, North Cape Plateau 85 45

349 "Skomvaer III" (lifeboat) 352 Posthorn

1991. Centenary of Norwegian Society for Sea Rescue.
1094 **349** 3 k. 20 brown, black & grn 60 25
1095 – 27 k. brown, grey & purple 5·00 2·25
DESIGN—VERT: 27 k. "Colin Archer" (first lifeboat).

1991.
1098 **352** 1 k. black and orange . . 20 10
1099 2 k. red and green 35 10
1100 3 k. green and blue . . . 55 10
1101 4 k. red and orange . . . 75 10
1102 5 k. blue and green . . . 90 10
1103 6 k. red and green . . . . 1·10 25
1104 7 k. blue and brown . . . 1·25 25
1105 8 k. green and purple . . 1·50 35
1106 9 k. brown and blue . . . 1·60 45

353 Guisers with Goat Head

1991. Christmas. Guising. Multicoloured.
1120 3 k. 20 Type **353** 60 10
1121 3 k. 20 Guisers with lantern . 60 10

354 Queen Sonja 355 King Harald 356 King Harald

1992.
1122 **354** 2 k. 80 lake, purple & red 50 10
1123 3 k. green, deep green and turquoise 55 10
1124 **355** 3 k. 30 blue, ultramarine and light blue 60 10
1125 3 k. 50 black and grey . . 65 10
1127 4 k. 50 deep red and red . 90 10
1128 5 k. 50 brn, sepia & blk . 1·00 25
1129 5 k. 60 orange, red and vermilion . . . . . . 1·00 25
1131 6 k. 50 emerald, green and turquoise . . . . . . 1·25 25
1132 6 k. 60 maroon, purple and brown . . . . 1·25 25
1133 7 k. 50 violet, lilac and purple . . . . 1·50 60
1134 8 k. 50 chestnut, deep brown and brown . . . 1·75 70
1135 **356** 10 k. green 90 45
1137 20 k. violet . . . . . . 3·75 85
1138 30 k. blue . . . . . . 6·00 2·40
1139 50 k. green . . . . . . 9·25 1·25

1992. Orchids (2nd series). As T **336**. Mult.
1141 3 k. 30 Lady's slipper orchid ("Cypripedium calceolus") . 60 10
1142 3 k. 30 Fly orchid ("Ophrys insectifera") 60 10

358 "Restauration" (emigrant sloop)

1992. Europa. 500th Anniv of Discovery of America by Columbus. Transatlantic Ships. Multicoloured.
1144 3 k. 30 Type **358** 70 15
1145 4 k. 20 "Stavangerfjord" (liner) and American skyline . . . 1·25 35
See note below No. 433.

359 Norwegian Pavilion, Rainbow and Ship 360 Molde

1992. "Expo '92" World's Fair, Seville. Mult.
1146 3 k. 30 Type **359** 70 10
1147 5 k. 20 Mountains, rainbow, fish and oil rig . . . . . 1·25 25

1992. 250th Anniversaries of Molde and Kristiansund.
1148 **360** 3 k. 30 blue, green & brn 70 10
1149 – 3 k. 30 blue, brown & lt bl 70 10
DESIGN: No. 1149, Kristiansund.

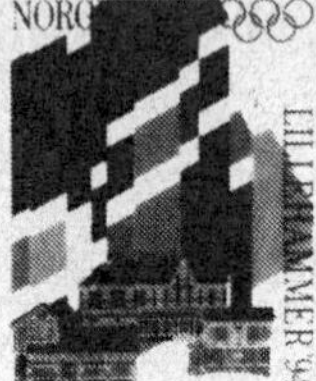

361 Banners and Lillehammer Buildings 363 Gnomes below Pillar Box

1992. Winter Olympic Games, Lillehammer (1994) (1st issue). Multicoloured.
1150 3 k. 30 Type **361** 60 10
1151 4 k. 20 Flags 75 35
See also Nos. 1169/70 and 1175/80.

1992. Christmas. Christmas card designs by Otto Moe. Multicoloured.
1153 3 k. 30 Type **363** 60 10
1154 3 k. 30 Gnome posting letter 60 10

364 Orange-tip ("Anthocaris cardamines") 366 Grieg

1993. Butterflies (1st series). Multicoloured.
1155 3 k. 50 Type **364** 65 10
1156 3 k. 50 Small tortoiseshell ("Aglais urticae") 65 10
See also Nos. 1173/4.

1993. 150th Birth Anniv of Edvard Grieg (composer). Multicoloured.
1158 3 k. 50 Type **366** 65 10
1159 5 k. 50 "Spring" . . . . . . 1·00 25

367 Two-man Kayak on Lake 368 Richard With (founder) and "Vesteraalen"

1993. Nordic Countries' Postal Co-operation. Tourist Activities. Multicoloured.
1160 4 k. Type **367** 75 45
1161 4 k. 50 White-water rafting . 85 55

1993. Centenary of Express Coaster Service.
1162 **368** 3 k. 50 blue, vio & red . . 65 10
1163 – 4 k. 50 multicoloured . . 85 25
DESIGN: 4 k. 50, Modern vessel.

369 Handball 370 Johann Castberg (politician)

1993. Sports Events. Multicoloured.
1164 3 k. 50 Type **369** (Women's World Championship, Norway) 65 10
1165 5 k. 50 Cycling (World Championships, Oslo and Hamar) . . . . 1·00 40

1993. Centenary of Workforce Protection Legislation.
1166 **370** 3 k. 50 brown and blue . . 65 10
1167 – 12 k. blue and brown . . 2·25 90
DESIGN: 12 k. Betzy Kjelsberg (first woman factory inspector).

372 Torch Bearer on Skis 373 Store Mangen Chapel

1993. Winter Olympic Games, Lillehammer (1994) (2nd issue). Morgedal–Lillehammer Torch Relay. Multicoloured.
1169 3 k. 50 Type **372** 65 10
1170 3 k. 50 Lillehammer 65 10
Nos. 1169/70 were issued together, se-tenant, forming a composite design.

1993. Christmas. Multicoloured.
1171 3 k. 50 Type **373** 65 10
1172 3 k. 50 Stamnes church, Sandnessjoen 65 10

1994. Butterflies (2nd series). As T **364**. Mult.
1173 3 k. 50 Northern clouded yellow ("Colias hecla") 65 10
1174 3 k. 50 Freya's fritillary ("Clossiana freija") 65 10

374 Flags **375** Cross-country Skiing

1994. Winter Olympic Games, Lillehammer (3rd issue). Multicoloured.
1175 3 k. 50 Type **374** 65 10
1176 3 k. 50 Flags (different) . . . 65 10
1177 3 k. 50 Lillehammer (church) and rings 65 10
1178 3 k. 50 Lillehammer (ski jump) and rings 65 10
1179 4 k. 50 Flags of European countries 85 25
1180 5 k. 50 Flags of non-European countries . . . . 1·00 40
Nos. 1175/8 were issued together, se-tenant, forming a composite design.

1994. Paralympic Games, Lillehammer. Mult.
1181 4 k. 50 Type **375** 80 20
1182 5 k. 50 Downhill skiing . . . 1·00 40

376 King Christian VII's Signature and Seal

1994. Bicentenary of Tromso.
1183 **376** 3 k. 50 red, bistre & brn . 65 10
1184 – 4 k. 50 blue, yellow and light blue 85 25
DESIGN: 4 k. 50, Tromsdalen church.

377 Mount Floy Incline Railway, Bergen

1994. Tourism. Multicoloured.
1185 4 k. Type **377** 70 25
1186 4 k. 50 "Svolvaer Goat" (rock formation), Lofoten . . . 85 25
1187 5 k. 50 Beacon, World's End, Tjome . . . . 1·00 40

378 Osterdal Farm Buildings

1994. Cent of Norwegian Folk Museum, Bygdoy.
1188 **378** 3 k. multicoloured . . . 60 10
1189 – 3 k. 50 blue, yellow and purple 70 10
DESIGN: 3 k. 50, Horse-drawn sleigh, 1750 (Torsten Hoff).

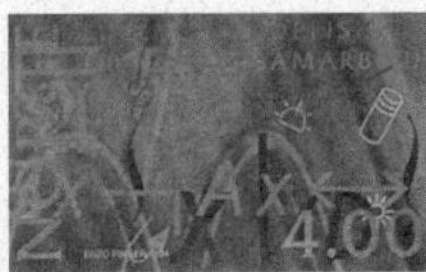

379 Technological Symbols and Formula ("Glass Flasks")

1994. EUREKA (European technology co-operation organization) Conference of Ministers, Lillehammer. Multicoloured.
1190 4 k. Type **379** 80 20
1191 4 k. 50 Technological symbols ("Electronic Chips") . . . 90 25

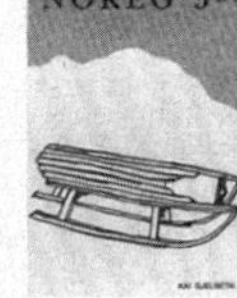

380 Tram and Street Plan of Oslo, 1894 **382** Sledge

1994. Centenary of Electric Trams. Multicoloured.
1192 3 k. 50 Type **380** 70 10
1193 12 k. Modern tram and Oslo route map . . . . 2·40 95

1994. Christmas.
1195 **382** 3 k. 50 red and black . . 70 10
1196 – 3 k. 50 ultramarine, blue and black 70 10
DESIGN: No. 1196, Kick-sledge.

383 Cowberry **384** Swan Pharmacy, Bergen ("Vaccinium vitis-idaea")

1995. Wild Berries (1st Series). Multicoloured.
1197 3 k. 50 Type **383** 70 10
1198 3 k. 50 Bilberry ("Vaccinium myrtillus") 70 10
See also Nos. 1224/5.

1995. 400th Anniv of Norwegian Pharmacies.
1199 **384** 3 k. 50 green and brown 70 10
1200 – 25 k. multicoloured . . 5·00 2·00
DESIGN: 25 k. Scales, pestle and mortar and ingredients.

385 German Commander saluting Terje Rollem (Home Guard commander)

1995. 50th Anniv of Liberation of Norway.
1201 **385** 3 k. 50 silver, green and black 70 10
1202 – 4 k. 50 silver, blue and black 90 35
1203 – 5 k. 50 silver, red and black 1·10 45
DESIGNS: 4 k. 50, King Haakon VII and family returning to Norway; 5 k. 50, Children waving Norwegian flags.

386 Old Moster Church **387** Skudeneshavn

1995. Millenary of Christianity in Norway. Multicoloured.
1204 3 k. 50 Type **386** 70 10
1205 15 k. Slettebakken Church, Bergen . . . . 3·00 1·25

1995. Nordic Countries' Postal Co-operation. Tourism. Multicoloured.
1206 4 k. Type **387** 80 20
1207 4 k. 50 Hole in the Hat (coastal rock formation) 90 35

388 Flagstad as Isolde **389** Disputants in Conflict

1995. Birth Centenary of Kirsten Flagstad (opera singer). Multicoloured.
1208 3 k. 50 Type **388** 70 10
1209 5 k. 50 Flagstad in scene from "Lohengrin" (Wagner) . . 1·10 40

1995. Bicentenary of Conciliation Boards. Multicoloured.
1210 7 k. Type **389** . . . . 1·40 55
1211 12 k. Disputants in conciliation with mediator . . . . . . 2·50 1·00

390 Letter and Vice-regent Hannibal Sehested (founder)

1995. 350th Anniv (1997) of Norwegian Postal Service (1st issue). Multicoloured.
1212 3 k. 50 Type **390** (letter post, 1647) 70 10
1213 3 k. 50 Wax seal (registered post, 1745) 70 10
1214 3 k. 50 Postmarks (1845) . . 70 10
1215 3 k. 50 Banknotes, coins and money orders (transfer of funds, 1883) 70 10
1216 3 k. 50 Editions of "Norska Intelligenz-Sedler" and "Arkiv" (newspapers and magazines, 1660) 70 10
1217 3 k. 50 Address label, cancellations and steamship (parcel post, 1827) 70 10
1218 3 k. 50 Stamps (1855) . . . 70 10
1219 3 k. 50 Savings book (Post Office Savings Bank, 1950) 70 10
The dates are those of the introduction of the various services.
See also Nos. 1237/44.

391 Trygve Lie (first Secretary-General) and Emblem **392** Woolly Hat

1995. 50th Anniv of U.N.O. Multicoloured.
1220 3 k. 50 Type **391** 70 10
1221 5 k. 50 Relief worker, water pump and emblem . . . . 1·10 40

1995. Christmas. Multicoloured.
1222 3 k. 50 Type **392** 70 10
1223 3 k. 50 Mitten 70 10

1996. Wild Berries (2nd series). As T **383**. Multicoloured.
1224 3 k. 50 Wild strawberries ("Fragaria vesca") 70 10
1225 3 k. 50 Cloudberries ("Rubus chamaemorus") 70 10

393 Advent Bay **394** Cross-country Skier (Hakon Paulsen)

1996. Svalbard Islands. Multicoloured.
1226 10 k. Type **393** . . . . 1·90 75
1227 20 k. Polar bear . . . . . . 3·75 1·50

1996. Centenary of Modern Olympic Games. Children's Drawings. Multicoloured.
1228 3 k. 50 Type **394** 65 10
1229 5 k. 50 Athlete (Emil Tanem) 1·10 40

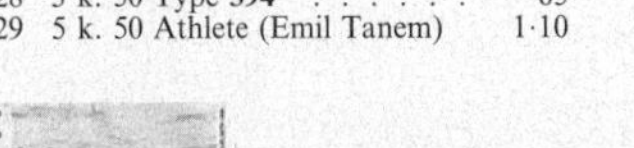

395 Besseggen **396** Urskog–Holand Line

1996. Tourism. U.N.E.S.C.O. World Heritage Sites. Multicoloured.
1230 4 k. Type **395** 75 20
1231 4 k. 50 Stave church, Urnes . 85 30
1232 5 k. 50 Rock carvings, Alta . 1·10 40

1996. Railway Centenaries. Multicoloured.
1233 3 k. Type **396** 65 10
1234 4 k. 50 Setesdal line 85 30

397 Location Map and Height Indicator

1996. Natural Gas Production at Troll, near Bergen. Multicoloured.
1235 3 k. 50 Type **397** 65 10
1236 25 k. Planned route map of pipelines to Europe for next 200 years . . . . 4·75 1·90

398 Postal Courier crossing Mountains

1996. 350th Anniv (1997) of Postal Service (2nd issue). Multicoloured.
1237 3 k. 50 Type **398** 65 10
1238 3 k. 50 "Framnaes" (fjord steamer) 65 10
1239 3 k. 50 Postal truck in Oslo . 65 10
1240 3 k. 50 Taking mail on board "Ternen" (seaplane) on Jonsvatn Lake, Trondheim 65 10
1241 3 k. 50 Loading mail train at East Station, Oslo 65 10
1242 3 k. 50 Rural postman at Mago farm, Nittedal 65 10
1243 3 k. 50 Serving customer, Elverum post office . . . 65 10
1244 3 k. 50 Computer, letters and globe 65 10

399 Leif Juster, Sean Connery, Liv Ullmann and Olsen Gang

1996. Centenary of Motion Pictures. Multicoloured.
1245 3 k. 50 Type **399** 65 10
1246 5 k. 50 Wenche Foss, Jack Fjeldstad, Marilyn Monroe, blood and gun . . . . . . 1·10 40
1247 7 k. Charlie Chaplin in "Modern Times", Ottar Gladvedt, Laurel and Hardy and Marlene Dietrich . . . 1·40 55

400 Left detail **401** Skram

1996. Christmas. Embroidery Details from Telemark Folk Costume. Multicoloured.
1248 3 k. 50 Type **400** 65 10
1249 3 k. 50 Right detail 65 10
Nos. 1248/9 were issued together, se-tenant, forming a composite design.

1996. 150th Birth Anniv of Amalie Skram (writer).
1250 **401** 3 k. 50 red 65 10
1251 – 15 k. violet and red . . . 3·00 1·10
DESIGN: 15 k. Scene from dramatisation of "People of Hellemyr".

OFFICIAL STAMPS

O 22 O 36

1925.
O187 O 22 5 ore mauve 20 40
O188 10 ore green 20 15
O189 15 ore blue 60 95
O190 20 ore purple 20 10
O191 30 ore grey . . . . . 1·60 2·50
O192 40 ore blue 45 35
O193 60 ore blue . . . . . 2·00 2·50

1929. Surch **2 2**.
O219 O 22 2 ore on 5 ore mauve . 20 40

1933.
O231 O 36 2 ore brown 30 60
O243 5 ore purple 40 60
O233 7 ore orange . . . . 3·25 2·75
O245 10 ore green 30 15
O235 15 ore green 30 25
O247 20 ore red 30 10
O237 25 ore brown 40 40
O238 30 ore blue 40 30
O248 35 ore violet 40 30
O249 40 ore grey 40 15
O250 60 ore blue 40 25
O241 70 ore brown . . . . . 80 1·25
O242 100 ore blue . . . . . 90 1·00

O 39

O 58 Quisling Emblem

1937.

O267 O 39 5 ore mauve 15 10
O268 7 ore orange 30 15
O257 10 ore green 15 10
O270 15 ore brown 30 15
O271 20 ore red 15 10
O260 25 ore brown 40 50
O273 25 ore red 20 10
O261 30 ore blue 40 30
O275 30 ore grey 50 20
O276 35 ore purple 15 10
O277 40 ore grey 20 10
O278 40 ore blue . . . . . 2·00 20
O279 50 ore lilac 50 10
O280 60 ore blue 30 10
O281 100 ore blue 30 10
O282 200 ore orange . . . . 1·60 20

1942.

O336 O 58 5 ore mauve 20 60
O337 7 ore orange 20 60
O338 10 ore green 10 15
O339 15 ore brown . . . . 1·25 6·00
O340 20 ore red 10 15
O341 25 ore brown . . . . 2·25 13·00
O342 30 ore blue . . . . . 1·50 11·00
O343 35 ore purple . . . . 1·50 9·00
O344 40 ore grey 15 20
O345 60 ore blue . . . . . 1·25 6·00
O346 1 k. blue . . . . 1·25 7·50

1949. Surch **25** and bar.

O402 O 39 25 ore on 20 ore red . 30 15

O 89

O 99

1951.

O434 O 89 5 ore mauve 40 15
O435 10 ore grey 40 10
O436 15 ore brown 50 20
O437 30 ore red 40 10
O438 35 ore brown 60 40
O439 60 ore blue 60 15
O440 100 ore violet . . . . 1·25 25

1955.

O458 O 99 5 ore purple 15 10
O459 10 ore grey 15 10
O460 15 ore brown 50 60
O461 20 ore green 20 10
O736 25 ore green 20 15
O463 30 ore red 80 40
O464 30 ore green 55 15
O465 35 ore red 30 10
O466 40 ore lilac 60 10
O467 40 ore green 50 15
O468 45 ore red 65 10
O469 50 ore brown . . . . 1·50 25
O470 50 ore red 80 10
O471 50 ore blue 30 10
O738 50 ore grey 30 10
O739 60 ore blue 80 85
O473 60 ore red 60 10
O475 65 ore red 60 10
O476 70 ore brown . . . . 1·75 60
O477 70 ore red 30 10
O478 75 ore purple . . . . 6·50 6·50
O479 75 ore green 60 50
O481 80 ore brown 40 10
O741 80 ore red 30 10
O482 85 ore brown 60 80
O483 90 ore orange 60 15
O484 1 k. violet 50 10
O485 1 k. red 30 10
O486 1 k. 10 red 55 30
O744 1 k. 25 red 45 10
O745 1 k. 30 purple 45 30
O746 1 k. 50 red 30 10
O747 1 k. 75 green 60 40
O748 2 k. green 55 10
O749 2 k. red 55 10
O750 3 k. violet 75 20
O488 5 k. violet . . . . . . 3·00 35
O752 5 k. blue . . . . 1·00 20

POSTAGE DUE STAMPS

D 12

1889. Inscr "at betale" and "PORTOMAERKE".

D95 D 12 1 ore green 30 40
D96a 4 ore mauve 65 35
D97 10 ore red . . . . . . 1·90 25
D98 15 ore brown 75 40
D99 20 ore blue . . . . . 1·10 25
D94 50 ore purple . . . . 1·90 1·25

1922. Inscr "a betale" and "PORTOMERKE".

D162 D 12 4 ore purple . . . . . 3·50 3·50
D163 10 ore green . . . . 1·25 85
D164 20 ore purple . . . . 2·50 2·00
D165 40 ore blue . . . . . 4·50 40
D166 100 ore yellow . . . 14·00 7·50
D167 200 ore violet . . . . 38·00 17·50

NOSSI-BE Pt. 6

An island north-west of Madagascar, declared a French protectorate in 1840. In 1901 it became part of Madagascar and Dependencies.

100 centimes = 1 franc

1889. Stamp of French Colonies, "Peace and Commerce" type, surch.

8 H 25 c. on 40 c. red on yellow . £1400 £500

1889. Stamps of French Colonies, "Commerce" type, surch.

4 J 5 c. on 10 c. black on lilac . . £1600 £550
2 5 c. on 20 c. red on green . . £1800 £700
6 15 on 20 c. red on green . . . £1500 £550
7 25 on 30 c. brown on drab . . £1400 £425
9 25 on 40 c. red on yellow . . £1400 £400

1890. Stamps of French Colonies, "Commerce" type, surch (a) **N S B 0 25**.

10 J 0.25 on 20 c. red on green . . £225 £160
11 0 25 on 75 c. red on pink . . £225 £160
12 0 25 on 1 f. green £225 £160

(b) **N S B 25 c.**

13 J 25 c. on 20 c. red on green . £225 £160
14 25 c. on 75 c. red on pink . . £225 £160
15 25 c. on 1 f. green £225 £160

(c) **N S B 25** in frame.

16 J 25 on 20 c. red on green . . £575 £375
17 25 on 75 c. red on pink . . . £575 £375
18 25 on 1 f. green £575 £375

1893. Stamps of French Colonies, "Commerce" type, surch **NOSSI-BE** and bar over value in figures.

36 J 25 on 20 c. red on green . . 23·00 18·00
37 50 on 10 c. black on lilac . . 25·00 18·00
38 75 on 15 c. blue £160 £120
39 1 f. on 5 c. green . . . . . . 60·00 50·00

1893. Stamps of French Colonies, "Commerce" type, optd **Nossi Be**.

40 J 10 c. black on lilac . . . . . 8·00 4·50
41 15 c. blue . . . . 8·50 7·00
42 20 c. red on green . . . . . 60·00 30·00

1894. "Tablet" key-type inscr "NOSSI-BE" in red (1, 5, 15, 25, 75 c., 1 f.) or blue (others).

44 D 1 c. black on blue 60 60
45 2 c. brown on buff 85 75
46 4 c. brown on grey . . . . 1·25 75
47 5 c. green on green . . . . 1·40 85
48 10 c. black on lilac . . . . 3·00 1·90
49 15 c. blue . . . . 4·75 2·25
50 20 c. red on green . . . . . 5·25 3·00
51 25 c. black on pink . . . . 6·00 4·25
52 30 c. brown on drab . . . . 8·25 5·00
53 40 c. red on yellow . . . . 9·00 7·75
54 50 c. red on pink . . . . . 9·00 6·25
55 75 c. brown on orange . . . 23·00 17·00
56 1 f. green . . . . 12·00 9·00

POSTAGE DUE STAMPS

1891. Stamps of French Colonies, "Commerce" type, surch **NOSSI-BE chiffre-taxe A PERCEVOIR** and value.

D19 J 0.20 on 1 c. black on blue . £210 £160
D20 0.30 on 2 c. brown on buff £210 £160
D21 0.35 on 4 c. brown on grey £225 £170
D22 0.35 on 20 c. red on green . £250 £170
D23 0.50 on 30 c. brn on drab 70·00 55·00
D24 1 f. on 35 c. blk on orge £160 £110

1891. Stamps of French Colonies, "Commerce" type, surch **Nossi-Be A PERCEVOIR** and value.

D25 J 5 c. on 20 c. red on green . £160 £110
D26 10 c. on 15 c. blue on blue £140 £140
D33 0.10 on 5 c. green . . . . 10·00 8·25
D27 15 c. on 10 c. blk on lilac 90·00 90·00
D34 0.15 on 20 c. red on green 12·50 11·00
D28 25 c. on 5 c. green on grn 90·00 90·00
D35 0.25 on 75 c. red on pink . £375 £350

NYASSA COMPANY Pt. 9

In 1894 Portugal granted a charter to the Nyassa Company to administer an area in the Northern part of Mozambique, including the right to issue its own stamps. The lease was terminated in 1929 and the administration was transferred to Mozambique whose stamps were used there.

1898. 1000 reis = 1 milreis.
1913. 100 centavos = 1 escudo.

1898. "Figures" and "Newspaper" key-types inscr "MOCAMBIQUE" optd **NYASSA**.

1 V 2½ r. brown 85 85
2 R 5 r. orange 85 85
3 10 r. mauve 85 85
4 15 r. brown 85 85
5 20 r. lilac 85 85
6 25 r. green 85 85
7 50 r. blue 85 85
8 75 r. pink . . . . 1·25 1·00
9 80 r. green . . . . 1·25 1·00
10 100 r. brown on buff . . . . 1·25 1·00
11 150 r. red on pink . . . . . 2·75 2·75
12 200 r. blue on blue . . . . . 1·90 1·90
13 300 r. blue on brown . . . . 1·90 1·90

1898. "King Carlos" key-type inscr "MOCAMBIQUE" optd **NYASSA**.

14 S 2½ r. grey 60 50
15 5 r. red 60 50
16 10 r. green 60 50
17 15 r. brown 85 60
18 20 r. lilac 85 60
19 25 r. green 85 60
20 50 r. blue 85 60
21 75 r. pink 85 60
22 80 r. mauve . . . . 1·00 85
23 100 r. blue on blue . . . . 1·00 85
24 150 r. brown on yellow . . 1·00 85
25 200 r. purple on pink . . . 1·00 85
26 300 r. blue on pink . . . . 1·00 85

2 Giraffe

3 Dromedaries

1901.

27 2 2½ r. brown and black . . . 50 25
28 5 r. violet and black . . . 50 25
29 10 r. green and black . . . 50 25
30 15 r. brown and black . . . 50 25
31 20 r. red and black 50 25
32 25 r. orange and black . . . 50 25
33 50 r. blue and black 50 25
34 3 75 r. red and black 60 25
35 80 r. bistre and black . . . 60 25
36 100 r. brown and black . . . 60 45
37 150 r. brown and black . . . 60 45
38 200 r. green and black . . . 60 45
39 300 r. green and black . . . 60 45

1903. (a) Surch in figures and words.

40 3 65 r. on 80 r. mauve & blk . 50 40
41 115 r. on 150 r. brown & blk 50 40
42 130 r. on 300 r. green & blk . 50 40

(b) Optd **PROVISORIO**.

43 2 15 r. brown and black . . . 50 45
44 25 r. orange and black . . . 50 45

1910. Optd **PROVISORIO** and surch in figures and words.

50 2 5 r. on 2½ r. brown and black 50 50
51 3 50 r. on 100 r. bistre & black 50 50

9 Dromedaries

12 Vasco de Gama's Flagship "Sao Gabriel"

1911. Optd **REPUBLICA**.

53 9 2½ r. violet and black . . . 40 25
54 5 r. black 40 25
55 10 r. green and black . . . 40 25
56 – 20 r. red and black 40 25
57 – 25 r. brown and black . . . 40 25
58 – 50 r. blue and black 40 25
59 – 75 r. brown and black . . . 40 25
60 – 100 r. brown & black on green 40 35
61 – 200 r. green & black on orge 50 50
62 12 300 r. black on blue . . . . 1·25 90
63 400 r. brown and black . . 1·40 1·00
64 500 r. violet and green . . . 1·75 1·40

DESIGNS—HORIZ: 20, 25, 50 r. Common zebra. VERT: 75, 100, 200 r. Giraffe.

1918. Surch **REPUBLICA** and value in figures.

(a) Stamps of 1901.

65 2 ¼ c. on 2½ c. brown and black 22·00 13·00
66 ½ c. on 5 r. violet and black . 22·00 13·00
67 1 c. on 10 r. green and black 22·00 13·00
68 1½ c. on 15 r. brown & black 1·00 50
69 2 c. on 20 r. red and black . 60 50
70 3½ c. on 25 r. orange & black 60 50
71 5 c. on 50 r. blue and black . 60 50
72 3 7½ c. on 75 r. red and black . 60 50
73 8 c. on 80 r. mauve and black 60 50
74 10 c. on 100 r. bistre & black 60 50
75 15 c. on 150 r. brown & black 1·00 90
76 20 c. on 200 r. green & black 80 90
77 30 c. on 300 r. green & black 1·50 1·25

(b) Nos. 43/4 and 40/2.

78 2 1½ c. on 15 r. brown & black 2·00 1·50
79 3½ c. on 25 r. orange & blk . 70 50
80 3 40 c. on 65 r. on 80 r. . . . 4·50 4·50
81 50 c. on 115 r. on 150 r. . . 1·25 1·00
82 1 c. on 130 r. on 300 r. . . . 1·25 1·00

1921. Stamps of 1911 surch in figures and words.

83 9 ¼ c. on 2½ r. violet & black . 60 60
85 ½ c. on 5 r. black 60 60
86 1 c. on 10 r. green & black . 60 60
87 12 1½ c. on 300 r. black on blue 60 60
88 – 2 c. on 20 r. red and black . 60 60
89 – 2½ c. on 25 r. brown & black 60 60
90 12 3 c. on 400 r. brown & black 60 60
91 – 5 c. on 50 r. blue and black 60 60
92 – 7½ c. on 75 r. brown & black 60 60
93 – 10 c. on 100 r. brown and black on green 60 60
94 12 12 c. on 500 r. violet & green 60 60
95 – 20 c. on 200 r. green and black on orange 60 60

16 Giraffe

19 Common Zebra

1921.

96 16 ¼ c. purple 40 30
97 ½ c. blue 40 30
98 1 c. black and green . . . 40 30
99 1½ c. orange and black . . 40 30
100 – 2 c. black and red 40 30
101 – 2½ c. green and black . . . 40 30
102 – 4 c. red and black 40 30
103 – 5 c. black and blue 40 30
104 – 6 c. violet and black . . . 40 30
123 – 7½ c. brown and black . . . 40 30
124 – 8 c. green and black . . . 40 30
125 – 10 c. brown and black . . 40 30
126 – 15 c. red and black 40 30
127 – 20 c. blue and black . . . 50 40
110 19 30 c. brown and black . . 65 40
111 40 c. blue and black . . . 65 40
112 50 c. green and black . . . 65 40
113 1 e. brown and black . . . 85 40
114 – 2 e. black and brown . . . 2·00 1·25
115 – 5 e. brown and blue . . . . 1·60 1·10

DESIGNS—As Type **16**: 2 c. to 6 c. Vasco da Gama; 7½ c. to 20 c. Vasco da Gama's flagship "Sao Gabriel". As Type **19**: 2, 5 e. Native dhow.

CHARITY TAX STAMPS

The notes under this heading in Portugal also apply here.

1925. Marquis de Pombal Commem. Nos. C327/9 of Mozambique optd **NYASSA**.

C141 C 22 15 c. brown . . . . . 3·75 3·75
C142 – 15 c. brown . . . . . 3·75 3·75
C143 C 25 15 c. brown . . . . . 3·75 3·75

POSTAGE DUE STAMPS

D 21 "Sao Gabriel"

1924.

D132 – ½ c. green . . . . 1·10 85
D133 – 1 c. blue . . . . 1·10 85
D134 – 2 c. red . . . . 1·10 85
D135 – 3 c. red . . . . 1·10 85
D136 D 21 5 c. brown . . . . . . 1·75 1·25
D137 6 c. brown . . . . . . 1·75 1·25
D138 10 c. purple . . . . . . 1·75 1·25
D139 – 20 c. red . . . . 1·10 85
D140 – 50 c. purple . . . . . . 1·10 85

DESIGNS: ½ c., 1 c. Giraffe; 2 c., 3 c. Common Zebra; 20 c., 50 c. Vasco da Gama.

1925. De Pombal stamps of Mozambique, Nos. D327/9, optd **NYASSA**.

D144 C 22 30 c. brown . . . . . 5·00 5·00
D145 – 30 c. brown . . . . . 5·00 5·00
D146 C 25 30 c. brown . . . . . 5·00 5·00

OBOCK Pt. 6

A port and district on the Somali Coast. During 1894 the administration was moved to Djibouti, the capital of French Somali Coast, and the Obock post office was closed.

1892. Stamps of French Colonies, "Commerce" type, optd **OBOCK**.

1 J 1 c. black on blue . . . . . 18·00 16·00
2 2 c. brown on buff . . . . . 21·00 18·00
12 4 c. brown on grey . . . . . 11·00 9·50
13 5 c. green on green . . . . . 11·00 9·25
14 10 c. black on lilac . . . . . 11·50 11·00
15 15 c. blue . . . . 12·00 10·50
16 20 c. red on green . . . . . 25·00 20·00
17 25 c. black on pink . . . . . 10·00 8·25
8 35 c. black on orange . . . £250 £250
18 40 c. red on buff . . . . . 30·00 25·00
19 75 c. red on pink £190 £160
20 1 f. green . . . . 40·00 35·00

1892. Nos. 14, 15, 17 and 20 surch.

39 J 1 on 25 c. black on red . . . 6·00 5·50
40 2 on 10 c. black on lilac . . . 40·00 25·00
41 2 on 15 c. blue . . . . . . 6·25 6·75
42 4 on 15 c. blue . . . . . . 7·00 6·75
43 4 on 25 c. black on red . . . 7·75 7·00
44 5 on 25 c. black on red . . . 11·00 8·25
45 20 on 10 c. black on lilac . . 50·00 42·00
46 30 on 10 c. black on lilac . . 65·00 55·00
47 35 on 25 c. black on red . . 50·00 45·00
48 75 on 1 f. olive . . . . . . 65·00 60·00
49 5 f. on 1 f. olive £525 £475

1892. "Tablet" key-type inscr "OBOCK" in red (1, 5, 15, 25, 75 c., 1 f.) or blue (others).

50 D 1 c. black on blue . . . . 1·40 1·25
51 2 c. brown on buff 60 65
52 4 c. brown on grey . . . . 1·50 1·25
53 5 c. green on green . . . . 2·25 1·50
54 10 c. black on lilac . . . . 3·75 2·25
55 15 c. blue . . . . 7·75 5·00
56 20 c. red on green . . . . 15·00 12·50
57 25 c. black on pink . . . . 14·00 12·50
58 30 c. brown on drab . . . 11·00 9·00
59 40 c. red on yellow . . . . 11·00 8·00
60 50 c. red on pink . . . . . 12·50 8·25
61 75 c. brown on orange . . . 16·00 8·25
62 1 f. green . . . . 22·00 18·00

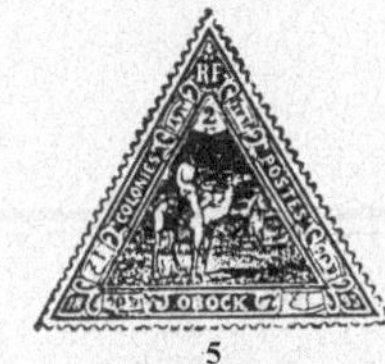

5

1893.

63 5 2 f. grey . . . . 30·00 29·00
64 5 f. red . . . . 80·00 75·00

The 5 f. stamp is larger than the 2 f.

6

7

1894.

65 6 1 c. black and red 60 95
66 2 c. red and green 90 95
67 4 c. red and orange . . . . 50 1·00
68 5 c. green and brown . . . . 1·00 85
69 10 c. black and green . . . 3·50 3·75
70 15 c. blue and red . . . . . 4·00 2·00
71 20 c. orange and purple . . 4·50 2·25
72 25 c. black and blue . . . . 5·00 3·00
73 30 c. yellow and green . . . 11·00 7·50
74 40 c. orange and green . . . 8·25 4·75
75 50 c. red and blue . . . . . 6·50 5·00
76 75 c. lilac and orange . . . 6·50 5·50
77 1 f. olive and purple . . . . 7·50 6·00
78 7 2 f. orange and lilac . . . . 75·00 65·00
79 5 f. red and blue . . . . . . 60·00 55·00
80 10 f. lake and red . . . . . £100 90·00
81 25 f. blue and brown £575 £525
82 50 f. green and lake £625 £625

Length of sides of Type **7**: 2 f. 37 mm; 5 f. 42 mm; 10 f. 46 mm; 25, 50 f. 49 mm.

POSTAGE DUE STAMPS

1892. Postage Due stamps of French Colonies optd **OBOCK**.

D25 U 1 c. black . . . . 28·00 28·00
D26 2 c. black . . . . 22·00 22·00
D27 3 c. black . . . . 22·00 22·00
D28 4 c. black . . . . 15·00 16·00
D29 5 c. black . . . . 6·00 6·00
D30 10 c. black . . . . . . 16·00 16·00
D31 15 c. black . . . . . . 11·00 10·00
D32 20 c. black . . . . . . 14·00 14·00
D33 30 c. black . . . . . . 16·00 16·00
D34 40 c. black . . . . . . 28·00 28·00
D35 60 c. black . . . . . . 45·00 45·00
D36 1 f. brown £130 £130
D37 2 f. brown £130 £130
D38 5 f. brown £275 £275

For later issues see **DJIBOUTI**.

OCEANIC SETTLEMENTS Pt. 6

Scattered French islands in the E. Pacific Ocean, including Tahiti and the Marquesas.

In 1957 the Oceanic Settlements were renamed French Polynesia.

1892. "Tablet" key-type.

1 D 1 c. black and red on blue . . 65 60
2 2 c. brown & blue on buff . . 90 85
3 4 c. brown & blue on grey . . 1·75 1·25
14 5 c. green and red 80 65
5 10 c. black & blue on lilac . . 12·00 5·00
15 10 c. red and blue 80 60
6 15 c. blue and red . . . . . 10·50 4·75
16 15 c. grey and red . . . . . 1·75 1·40
7 20 c. red & blue on green . . 9·25 4·00
8 25 c. black & red on pink . . 27·00 12·50
17 D 25 c. blue and red . . . . . 7·50 3·25
9 30 c. brown & blue on drab . 8·00 6·00
18 35 c. black & red on yellow . 2·50 2·00
10 40 c. red & blue on yellow . 65·00 45·00
19 45 c. black & red on green . 2·75 1·60
11 50 c. red and blue on pink . 4·50 3·25
20 50 c. brown & red on blue . £140 £110
12 75 c. brown & red on orge . 6·00 4·00
13 1 f. green and red . . . . . 8·25 6·25

2 Tahitian Woman

3 Kanakas

4 Valley of Fautaua

1913.

21 2 1 c. brown and violet 10 25
22 2 c. grey and brown 15 25
23 4 c. blue and orange 15 30
25 5 c. light green and green . . 30 45
46 5 c. black and blue 30 40
25 10 c. orange and red 40 50
47 10 c. light green and green . 35 50
48 10 c. purple & red on blue . 60 70
25a 15 c. black and orange . . . 30 35
26 20 c. violet and black 25 35
49 20 c. green 35 50
50 20 c. brown and red 65 70
27 3 25 c. blue and ultramarine . . 45 50
51 25 c. red and violet 50 60
28 30 c. brown and grey . . . . 1·75 1·60
52 30 c. red and carmine 75 90
53 30 c. red and black 40 55
54 30 c. green and blue 65 80
29 35 c. red and green 35 40
30 40 c. green and black 40 45
31 45 c. red and orange 35 45
32 50 c. black and brown . . . 7·25 5·50
55 50 c. blue and ultramarine . . 45 60
56 50 c. blue and grey 45 60
57 60 c. black and green 35 45
58 65 c. mauve and brown . . . 1·25 1·40
33 75 c. violet and purple . . . 1·00 85
59 90 c. mauve and red . . . . 8·25 8·25
34 4 1 f. black and red . . . . . 1·40 1·00
60 1 f. 10 brown and mauve . . 85 85
61 1 f. 40 violet and brown . . 2·00 2·00
62 1 f. 50 light blue and blue . . 8·00 8·00
35 2 f. green and brown . . . . 2·25 2·00
36 5 f. blue and violet . . . . . 5·00 5·00

1915. "Tablet" key-type optd **E F O 1915** and bar.

37 D 10 c. red . . . . 1·90 1·90

1915. Red Cross. No. 37 surch **5c** and red cross.

38 D 10 c. + 5 c. red . . . . 12·00 13·50

1915. Red Cross. Surch **5c** and red cross.

41 2 10 c. + 5 c. orange and red . 1·10 1·25

1916. Surch.

42 2 10 c. on 15 c. black & orange 70 75
67 4 25 c. on 2 f. green & brown . 50 60
68 25 c. on 5 f. blue and violet . 50 60
63 3 60 c. on 75 c. brown and blue 20 35
64 4 65 on 1 f. brown and blue . . 80 80
65 85 on 1 f. brown and blue . . 75 80
66 3 90 on 75 c. mauve and red . . 75 80
69 4 1 f. 25 on 1 f. ultramarine & bl 50 60
70 1 f. 50 on 1 f. lt blue & blue . 1·00 1·25
71 20 f. on 5 f. mauve and red . 12·50 10·00

1921. Surch **1921** and new value.

43 2 05 on 2 c. grey and brown . . 17·00 17·00
44 3 10 on 45 c. red and orange . . 17·00 17·00
45 2 25 on 15 c. black and orange . 3·75 4·00

1924. Surch **45 c. 1924**.

72 2 45 c. on 10 c. orange and red 95 95

1926. Surch in words.

73 4 3 f. on 5 f. blue and grey . . 1·10 90
74 10 f. on 5 f. black and green . 3·00 2·50

13 Papetoia Bay

1929.

75 13 3 f. sepia and green . . . . 4·00 4·00
76 5 f. sepia and blue . . . . 6·25 6·75
77 10 f. sepia and red . . . . . 18·00 20·00
78 20 f. sepia and mauve . . . 22·00 23·00

1931. "International Colonial Exhibition", Paris, key-types.

79 E 40 c. black and green . . . . 3·50 3·00
80 F 50 c. black and mauve . . . 3·50 3·25
81 G 90 c. black and red . . . . 3·50 3·25
82 H 1 f. 50 black and blue . . . 3·50 3·50

14 Spearing Fish

15 Tahitian Girl

16 Native Gods

1934.

83 14 1 c. black 15 30
84 2 c. red 15 30
85 3 c. blue 15 30
86 4 c. orange 15 35
87 5 c. mauve 35 45
88 10 c. brown 15 30
89 15 c. green 25 35
90 20 c. red 15 30
91 15 25 c. blue 35 45
92 30 c. green 65 70
93 30 c. orange 25 35
94 16 35 c. green . . . . 1·90 1·90
95 15 40 c. mauve 30 35
96 45 c. red . . . . 4·75 4·50
97 45 c. green 35 45
98 50 c. violet 15 30
99 55 c. blue . . . . 2·75 2·75
100 60 c. black 25 35
101 65 c. brown . . . . 1·60 1·60
102 70 c. pink 40 45
103 75 c. olive . . . . 4·00 4·00
104 80 c. purple 70 65
105 90 c. red 40 45
106 16 1 f. brown 40 50
107 1 f. 25 purple . . . . . . 4·75 4·75
108 1 f. 25 red 40 50
109 1 f. 40 orange 40 50
110 1 f. 50 blue 45 50
111 1 f. 60 violet 40 50
112 1 f. 75 green . . . . . . 3·25 3·00
113 2 f. red 35 40
114 2 f. 25 blue 40 50
115 2 f. 50 black 55 60
116 3 f. orange 50 60
117 5 f. mauve 50 70
118 10 f. green . . . . 1·50 1·60
119 20 f. brown . . . . 2·00 2·00

17 Flying Boat

1934. Air.

120 17 5 f. green 50 60

1937. International Exhibition, Paris. As Nos. 168/73 of St.-Pierre et Miquelon.

121 20 c. violet . . . . 1·10 1·10
122 30 c. green . . . . 1·10 1·10
123 40 c. red . . . . 1·40 1·40
124 50 c. brown . . . . 1·25 1·60
125 90 c. red . . . . 1·40 1·90
126 1 f. 50 blue . . . . 1·75 2·75

1938. Int Anti-Cancer Fund. As T **33** of Mauritania.

127 1 f. 75 + 50 c. blue . . . . . 8·50 8·75

1939. New York World's Fair. As T **28** of Mauritania.

128 1 f. 25 red . . . . 1·10 1·10
129 2 f. 25 blue . . . . 1·10 1·10

1939. 150th Anniv of French Revolution. As T **29** of Mauritania.

130 45 c. + 25 c. green and black (postage) . . . . 8·75 8·75
131 70 c. + 30 c. brown & black . 8·75 8·75
132 90 c. + 35 c. orange & black . 8·75 8·75
133 1 f. 25 + 1 f. red and black . 8·75 8·75
134 2 f. 25 + 2 f. blue and black . 8·75 8·75
135 5 f. + 4 f. black & orge (air) . 17·00 17·00

1941. Adherence to General de Gaulle. Optd **FRANCE LIBRE**. (a) Nos. 75/8.

136 13 3 f. brown and green . . . 3·25
137 5 f. brown and blue . . . 3·25
138 10 f. brown and red . . . 9·00
139 20 f. brown and mauve . . 65·00

(b) Nos. 106 and 115/19.

140 16 1 f. brown . . . . 2·25 2·75
141 2 f. 50 black . . . . 2·50 3·50
142 3 f. red . . . . 2·75 3·50
143 5 f. mauve . . . . 3·25 3·50
144 10 f. green . . . . 35·00
145 20 f. brown . . . . 32·00

(c) Air stamp of 1934.

146 17 5 f. green . . . . 1·90 1·90

19 Polynesian Travelling Canoe

1942. Free French Issue. (a) Postage.

147	**19**	5 c. brown	15	30
148		10 c. blue	15	30
149		25 c. green	15	30
150		30 c. red	15	30
151		40 c. green	15	30
152		80 c. purple	15	30
153		1 f. mauve	20	35
154		1 f. 50 red	25	35
155		2 f. black	25	30
156		2 f. 50 blue	60	1·10
157		4 f. violet	40	55
158		5 f. yellow	50	70
159		10 f. brown	75	85
160		20 f. green	90	90

(b) Air. As T **30** of New Caledonia.

161	1 f. orange	40	50
162	1 f. 50 red	40	50
163	5 f. purple	50	60
164	10 f. black	75	80
165	25 f. blue	1·10	1·25
166	50 f. green	1·10	1·25
167	100 f. red	1·00	1·25

1944. Mutual Aid and Red Cross Funds. As T **31** of New Caledonia.

168	5 f. + 20 f. blue	65	80

1945. Surch in figures.

169	**19**	50 c. on 5 c. brown	25	35
170		60 c. on 5 c. brown	25	35
171		70 c. on 5 c. brown	25	35
172		1 f. 20 on 5 c. brown	25	35
173		2 f. 40 on 25 c. green	60	70
174		3 f. on 25 c. green	35	45
175		4 f. 50 on 25 c. green	70	85
176		15 f. on 2 f. 50 blue	95	1·10

1945. Eboue. As T **32** of New Caledonia.

177	2 f. black	30	40
178	25 f. green	95	1·10

1946. Air. Victory. As T **34** of New Caledonia.

179	8 f. green	75	1·10

1946. Air. From Chad to the Rhine. As Nos. 300/5 of New Caledonia.

180	5 f. red	1·00	1·10
181	10 f. brown	1·00	1·10
182	15 f. green	1·00	1·10
183	20 f. red	1·50	1·50
184	25 f. purple	1·60	1·90
185	50 f. black	2·00	2·25

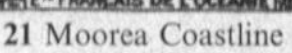

21 Moorea Coastline 22 Tahitian Girl

23 Wandering Albatross over Moorea

1948. (a) Postage as T **21/22**.

186	**21**	10 c. brown	15	30
187		30 c. green	15	30
188		40 c. blue	15	30
189	–	50 c. lake	30	40
190	–	60 c. olive	30	40
191	–	80 c. blue	30	40
192	–	1 f. lake	30	40
193	–	1 f. 20 blue	30	40
194	–	1 f. 50 blue	30	40
195	**22**	2 f. brown	50	60
196		2 f. 40 lake	65	70
197		3 f. violet	5·00	1·50
198		4 f. blue	65	65
199	–	5 f. brown	75	70
200	–	6 f. blue	90	75
201	–	9 f. brown, black and red	6·00	5·00
202	–	10 f. olive	2·75	1·25
203	–	15 f. red	3·00	1·50
204	–	20 f. blue	3·50	1·90
205	–	25 f. brown	2·75	2·50

(b) Air. As T **23**.

206	–	13 f. light blue and deep blue	6·00	3·75
207	**23**	50 f. lake	18·00	10·00
208	–	100 f. violet	8·50	5·50
209	–	200 f. blue	45·00	18·00

DESIGNS: As T **22**: 50 c. to 80 c. Kanaka fishermen; 9 f. Bora-Bora girl; 1 f. to 1 f. 50, Faa village; 5 f., 6 f., 10 f. Bora-Bora and Pandanus pine; 15 f. to 25 f. Polynesian girls. As T **23**: 13 f. Pahia Peak and palms; 100 f. Airplane over Moorea; 200 f. Wandering albatross over Maupiti Island.

1949. Air. 75th Anniv of U.P.U. As T **38** of New Caledonia.

210	10 f. blue	7·50	9·00

1950. Colonial Welfare. As T **39** of New Caledonia.

211	10 f. + 2 f. green and blue	2·50	2·75

1952. Centenary of Military Medals. As T **40** of New Caledonia.

212	3 f. violet, yellow and green	5·25	5·50

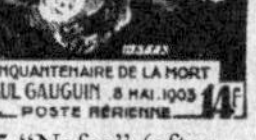

25 "Nafea" (after Gauguin) 26 Schooner in Dry Dock, Papeete

1953. Air. 50th Death Anniv of Gauguin (painter).

213	**25**	14 f. sepia, red and turquoise	55·00	55·00

1954. Air. 10th Anniv of Liberation. As T **42** of New Caledonia.

214	3 f. green and turquoise	2·75	2·50

1956. Economic and Social Development Fund.

215	**26**	3 f. turquoise	1·40	1·00

POSTAGE DUE STAMPS

1926. Postage Due stamps of France surch **Etabts Francais de l'Oceanie 2 francs a percevoir** (No. D80) or optd **Etablissements Francais de l'Oceanie** (others).

D73	**D 11**	5 c. blue	25	45
D74		10 c. brown	25	45
D75		20 c. olive	65	70
D76		30 c. red	65	70
D77		40 c. red	1·40	1·40
D78		60 c. green	1·40	1·40
D79		1 f. red on yellow	1·25	1·40
D80		2 f. on 1 f. red	1·90	1·90
D81		3 f. mauve	5·50	5·50

D 14 Fautaua Falls D 24

1929.

D82	**D 14**	5 c. brown and blue	35	40
D83		10 c. green and orange	35	40
D84		30 c. red and brown	80	80
D85		50 c. brown and green	65	70
D86		60 c. green and violet	1·90	2·00
D87	–	1 f. mauve and blue	1·25	1·40
D88	–	2 f. brown and red	80	80
D89	–	3 f. green and blue	90	95

DESIGN: 1 to 3 f. Polynesian man.

1948.

D210	**D 24**	10 c. green	15	30
D211		30 c. brown	25	30
D212		50 c. red	25	30
D213		1 f. blue	30	35
D214		2 f. green	50	55
D215		3 f. red	65	70
D216		4 f. violet	75	85
D217		5 f. mauve	1·10	1·25
D218		10 f. blue	2·00	2·25
D219		20 f. lake	2·50	2·75

For later issues see **FRENCH POLYNESIA**.

OLDENBURG Pt. 7

A former Grand Duchy in North Germany. In 1867 it joined the North German Federation.

72 grote = 1 thaler

1 2 3

1852. Imperf.

1	**1**	1/3 sgr. black on green	£1000	£1000
2		1/30 th. black on blue	£300	20·00
5		1/15 th. black on red	£650	75·00
8		1/10 th. black on yellow	£700	80·00

1859. Imperf.

17	**2**	1/4 g. yellow	£225	£4500
10		1/3 g. black on green	£1900	£2750
19		1/3 g. green	£375	£750
21		1/2 g. brown	£350	£425
11		1 g. black on blue	£550	30·00
23		1 g. blue	£180	£120
15		2 g. black on red	£800	£550
26		2 g. red	£375	£400
16		3 g. black on yellow	£800	£500
28		3 g. yellow	£375	£400

1862. Roul.

30	**3**	1/3 g. green	£190	£170
32		1/2 g. orange	£170	95·00
42		1 g. red	5·00	35·00
36		2 g. blue	£170	35·00
39		3 g. bistre	£170	40·00

OMAN (SULTANATE) Pt. 19

In Jan. 1971, the independent Sultanate of Muscat and Oman was renamed Sultanate of Oman.

NOTE. Labels inscribed "State of Oman" or "Oman Imamate State" are said to have been issued by a rebel administration under the Imam of Oman. There is no convincing evidence that these labels had any postal use within Oman and they are therefore omitted. They can be found, however, used on covers which appear to emanate from Amman and Baghdad.

1971. 1000 baizas = rial saidi.
1972. 1000 baizas = 1 rial omani.

1971. Nos. 110/21 of Muscat and Oman optd **SULTANATE of OMAN** in English and Arabic.

122	**12**	5 b. purple	10	10
142		10 b. brown	20	10
124		20 b. brown	40	25
125	A	25 b. black and violet	50	25
126		30 b. black and blue	70	40
127		40 b. black and orange	95	50
128	**14**	50 b. mauve and blue	1·25	65
129	B	75 b. green and brown	1·60	90
130	C	100 b. blue and orange	1·90	1·25
131		1/4 r. brown and green	6·25	3·75
132	E	1/2 r. violet and red	12·50	6·25
133	F	1 r. red and violet	24·00	14·00

19 Sultan Qabus and Buildings ("Land Development")

1971. National Day. Multicoloured.

134	10 b. Type **19**	35	25
135	40 b. Sultan in military uniform and Omanis ("Freedom")	95	65
136	50 b. Doctors and patients ("Health Services")	1·25	1·00
137	100 b. Children at school ("Education")	2·50	1·90

1971. No. 94 of Muscat and Oman surch **SULTANATE of OMAN 5** in English and Arabic.

138	5 b. on 3 b. purple	20·00	8·25

21 Child in Class

1971. 25th Anniv of U.N.I.C.E.F.

139	**21**	50 b. + 25 b. multicoloured	2·50	2·50

22 Book Year Emblem

1972. International Book Year.

140	**22**	25 b. multicoloured	3·25	1·25

سلطنة عمان
25 B ٢٥ ب
(24)

26 Matrah, 1809

1972. Nos. 102 of Muscat and Oman and 127 of Oman optd with T **24**.

144	25 b. on 1 r. blue and orange	21·00	13·00
145	25 b. on 40 b. black and orange	21·00	13·00

1972.

158	**26**	5 b. multicoloured	15	10
147		10 b. multicoloured	15	10
148		20 b. multicoloured	25	10
149		25 b. multicoloured	25	10
150	–	30 b. multicoloured	40	25
151	–	40 b. multicoloured	50	30
152	–	50 b. multicoloured	65	45
153	–	75 b. multicoloured	90	55
154	–	100 b. multicoloured	1·25	85
155	–	1/4 r. multicoloured	3·25	1·40
156	–	1/2 r. multicoloured	6·25	3·50
157	–	1 r. multicoloured	14·00	6·50

DESIGNS—26 × 21 mm: 30 b. to 75 b. Shinas, 1809. 42 × 25 mm: 100 b. to 1 r. Muscat, 1809.

29 Government Buildings

1973. Opening of Ministerial Complex.

170	**29**	25 b. multicoloured	45	35
171		100 b. multicoloured	1·90	1·25

30 Oman Crafts (dhow building)

1973. National Day. Multicoloured.

172	15 b. Type **30**	40	25
173	50 b. Seeb International Airport	2·25	1·25
174	65 b. Dhow and tanker	2·25	1·25
175	100 b. "Ship of the Desert" (camel)	3·25	1·90

31 Aerial View of Port

1974. Inaug of Port Qabus.

176	**31**	100 b. multicoloured	2·75	2·00

32 Map on Open Book

1974. Illiteracy Eradication Campaign. Mult.

177	25 b. Type **32**	60	30
178	100 b. Hands reaching for open book (vert)	2·40	1·60

33 Sultan Qabus bin Said and Emblems

1974. Centenary of U.P.U.

179	**33**	100 b. multicoloured	1·75	1·25

34 Arab Scribe

1975. "Eradicate Illiteracy".

180 **34** 25 b. multicoloured . . . . . 3·50 95

35 New Harbour, Mina Raysoot

1975. National Day. Multicoloured.

181 30 b. Type **35** 25 25
182 50 b. Stadium and map . . . 65 40
183 75 b. Water Desalination Plant 65 65
184 100 b. Television Station . . . 1·00 75
185 150 b. Satellite Earth Station and map . . . . 1·25 1·25
186 250 b. Telecommunications symbols and map . . . . . 2·50 2·00

36 Arab Woman and Child with Nurse

1975. International Women's Year. Mult.

187 75 b. Type **36** 70 65
188 150 b. Mother and children (vert) 1·25 1·25

37 Presenting Colours and Opening of Seeb–Nizwa Highway

1976. National Day. Multicoloured.

201 25 b. Type **37** 25 20
202 40 b. Parachutists and harvesting 90 45
203 75 b. Agusta-Bell AB-212 helicopters and Victory Day procession . . . . 1·75 90
204 150 b. Road construction and Salalah T.V. Station . . . . 2·00 1·50

38 Great Bath, Moenjodaro

1977. "Save Moenjodaro" Campaign.

205 **38** 125 b. multicoloured . . . . 2·25 1·90

39 A.P.U. Emblem **40** Coffee Pots

1977. 25th Anniv of Arab Postal Union.

206 **39** 30 b. multicoloured 65 40
207 75 b. multicoloured . . . . 1·90 1·10

1977. National Day. Multicoloured.

208 40 b. Type **40** 60 40
209 75 b. Earthenware pots . . . 1·10 50
210 100 b. Khor Rori inscriptions . 1·25 75
211 150 b. Silver jewellery . . . . 2·25 1·25

1978. Surch in English and Arabic.

212 40 b. on 150 b. mult (No. 185) 12·00 12·00
213 50 b. on 150 b. mult (No. 188) 15·00 15·00
214 75 b. on 250 b. mult (No. 186) 24·00 24·00

42 Mount Arafat, Pilgrims and Kaaba

1978. Pilgrimage to Mecca.

215 **42** 40 b. multicoloured . . . 1·75 1·40

43 Jalali Fort

1978. National Day. Forts. Multicoloured.

216 20 b. Type **43** 25 20
217 25 b. Nizwa Fort 30 25
218 40 b. Rostaq Fort 70 40
219 50 b. Sohar Fort 80 50
220 75 b. Bahla Fort . . . . . . 1·00 80
221 100 b. Jibrin Fort . . . . . . 1·50 1·00

44 World Map, Koran and Symbols of Arab Achievements

1979. The Arabs.

222 **44** 40 b. multicoloured . . . 45 40
223 100 b. multicoloured . . . 1·60 1·25

45 Child on Swing

1979. International Year of the Child.

224 **45** 40 b. multicoloured . . . 1·90 1·50

46 Gas Plant

1979. National Day. Multicoloured.

225 25 b. Type **46** 95 45
226 75 b. Dhow and modern trawler 1·50 1·25

47 Sultan Qabus on Horseback

1979. Armed Forces Day. Multicoloured.

227 40 b. Type **47** . . . . 2·25 75
228 100 b. Soldier . . . . 3·00 1·90

48 Mosque, Mecca

1980. 1400th Anniv of Hegira. Multicoloured.

229 50 b. Type **48** 60 50
230 150 b. Mosque and Kaaba . 2·25 1·60

49 Bab Alkabir

1980. National Day. Multicoloured.

231 75 b. Type **49** 55 50
232 100 b. Corniche 90 80
233 250 b. Polo match . . . . . . 2·50 2·25
234 500 b. Omani women . . . . 4·25 4·00

50 Sultan and Naval Patrol Boat

1980. Armed Forces Day. Multicoloured.

235 150 b. Type **50** . . . . 1·60 1·50
236 750 b. Sultan and mounted soldiers . . . . 7·00 7·00

51 Policewoman helping Children across Road

1981. National Police Day. Multicoloured.

237 50 b. Type **51** 70 50
238 100 b. Police bandsmen . . . 1·25 1·00
239 150 b. Mounted police . . . . 1·75 1·50
240 ½ r. Police headquarters . . . . 5·50 4·75

1981. Nos. 231, 234 and 235/6 surch **POSTAGE** and new value in English and Arabic.

241 **50** 20 b. on 150 b. multicoloured 50 30
242 – 30 b. on 750 b. multicoloured 75 40
243 **49** 50 b. on 75 b. multicoloured 1·25 75
244 – 100 b. on 500 b. multicoloured 2·75 1·75

53 Sultan's Crest

1981. Welfare of Blind.

245 **53** 10 b. black, blue and red . 40 25

54 Palm Tree, Fishes and Wheat

1981. World Food Day.

246 **54** 50 b. multicoloured . . . . 1·50 1·00

55 Pilgrims at Prayer

1981. Pilgrimage to Mecca.

247 **55** 50 b. multicoloured . . . . 1·60 75

56 Al Razha

1981. National Day. Multicoloured.

248 160 b. Type **56** . . . . 1·50 1·50
249 300 b. Sultan Qabus bin Said 2·50 2·50

57 Muscat Port, 1981

1981. Retracing the Voyage of Sinbad. Mult.

250 50 b. Type **57** 50 50
251 100 b. The "Sohar" (replica of medieval dhow) . . . . . . 1·25 1·25
252 130 b. Map showing route of voyage . . . . 1·60 1·60
253 200 b. Muscat Harbour, 1650 2·25 2·25

58 Parachute-drop

1981. Armed Forces Day. Multicoloured.

255 100 b. Type **58** . . . . 1·40 85
256 400 b. Missile-armed corvettes 4·75 4·75

59 Police Launch

1982. National Police Day. Multicoloured.

257 50 b. Type **59** . . . . 1·25 60
258 100 b. Royal Oman Police Band at Cardiff . . . . 1·60 1·10

60 "Nerium mascatense"

1982. Flora and Fauna. Multicoloured.

259 5 b. Type **60** 10 10
260 10 b. "Dionysia mira" 10 10
261 20 b. "Teucrium mascatense" 15 10
262 25 b. "Geranium mascatense" 15 15
263 30 b. "Cymatium boschi" (horiz) 25 20
264 40 b. Eloise's acteon (horiz) 25 20
265 50 b. Teulere's cowrie (horiz) 30 25
266 75 b. Lovely cowrie (horiz) 45 40
267 100 b. Arabian chukar (25 × 33 mm) . . . . 1·50 70
268 ¼ r. Hoopoe (25 × 33 mm) . . 4·00 2·75
269 ½ r. Arabian tahr (25 × 39 mm) 4·25 3·75
270 1 r. Arabian oryx (25 × 39 mm) 8·00 7·50

Nos. 259/62 show flowers, Nos. 263/6 shells, Nos. 267/8 birds and Nos. 269/70 animals.

61 Palm Tree

1982. Arab Palm Tree Day. Multicoloured.

271 40 b. Type **61** 90 50
272 100 b. Palm tree and nuts . . 2·10 1·25

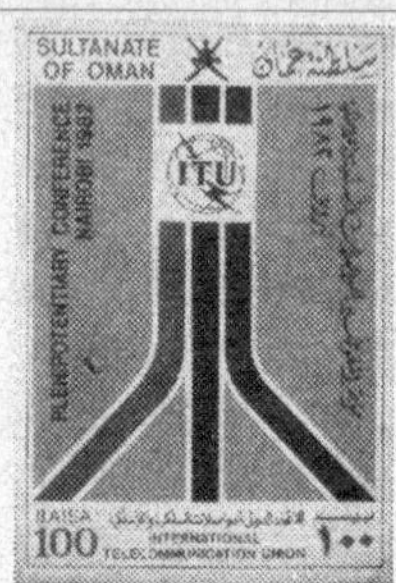

62 I.T.U. Emblem

1982. I.T.U. Delegates Conference, Nairobi.
273 **62** 100 b. multicoloured . . . . 2·00 1·25

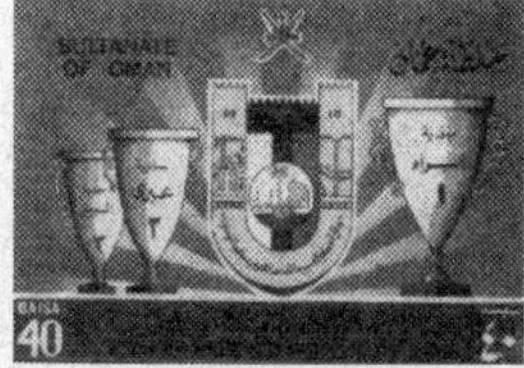

63 Emblem and Cups

1982. Municipalities Week.
274 **63** 40 b. multicoloured . . . . 1·50 70

64 State Consultative Council Inaugural Session

1982. National Day. Multicoloured.
275 40 b. Type **64** 50 45
276 100 b. Petroleum refinery . . 1·75 1·25

65 Sultan meeting Troops

1982. Armed Forces Day. Multicoloured.
277 50 b. Type **65** 75 50
278 100 b. Mounted army band . 2·00 1·25

66 Police Motorcyclist and Headquarters

1983. National Police Day.
279 **66** 50 b. multicoloured . . . . 1·60 1·00

67 Satellite, W.C.Y. Emblem and Dish Aerial

1983. World Communications Year.
280 **67** 50 b. multicoloured . . . . 1·60 1·00

68 Bee Hives

1983. Bee-keeping. Multicoloured.
281 50 b. Type **68** . . . . 1·25 1·00
282 50 b. Bee collecting nectar . . 1·25 1·00
Nos. 281/2 were issued together, se-tenant, each pair forming a composite design.

69 Pilgrims at Mudhalfa

1983. Pilgrimage to Mecca.
283 **69** 40 b. multicoloured . . . 1·90 1·00

70 Emblem, Map and Sultan

1983. Omani Youth Year.
284 **70** 50 b. multicoloured . . . 1·40 70

71 Sohar Copper Mine

1983. National Day. Multicoloured.
285 50 b. Type **71** 90 50
286 100 b. Sultan Qabus University and foundation stone . . . 1·50 1·00

72 Machine Gun Post

1983. Armed Forces Day.
287 **72** 100 b. multicoloured . . . 2·25 1·25

73 Police Cadets Parade

1984. National Police Day.
288 **73** 100 b. multicoloured . . . 1·90 1·25

74 Footballers and Cup

1984. 7th Arabian Gulf Cup Football Tournament. Multicoloured.
289 40 b. Type **74** 60 40
290 50 b. Emblem and pictograms of footballers . . . . 1·00 65

75 Stoning the Devil

1984. Pilgrimage to Mecca.
291 **75** 50 b. multicoloured . . . 1·60 90

76 New Central Post Office and Automatic Sorting Machine

1984. National Day. Multicoloured.
292 130 b. Type **76** . . . . 1·25 1·10
293 160 b. Map of Oman with telecommunications symbols 1·90 1·75

77 Scouts reading Map

1984. 16th Arab Scouts Conference, Muscat. Multicoloured.
294 50 b. Scouts pegging tent . . . 45 40
295 50 b. Type **77** 45 40
296 130 b. Scouts assembled round flag . . . . 1·25 1·10
297 130 b. Scout, cub, guide, brownie and scout leaders . . . . . 1·25 1·10

78 Sultan, Jet Fighters and "Al Munassir" (landing craft)

1984. Armed Forces Day.
298 **78** 100 b. multicoloured . . . 1·50 1·25

79 Bell 214ST Helicopter lifting Man from Tanker

1985. National Police Day.
299 **79** 100 b. multicoloured . . . 2·50 1·40

80 Al-Khaif Mosque and Tent, Mina

1985. Pilgrimage to Mecca.
300 **80** 50 b. multicoloured . . . . 1·00 50

81 I.Y.Y. Emblem and Youth holding Olive Branches

1985. International Youth Year. Mult.
301 50 b. Type **81** 50 50
302 100 b. Emblem and young people at various activities 90 90

82 Palace before and after Restoration

1985. Restoration of Jabrin Palace. Mult.
303 100 b. Type **82** 75 70
304 250 b. Restored ceiling . . . 2·75 2·50

83 Drummers

1985. International Omani Traditional Music Symposium.
305 **83** 50 b. multicoloured . . . . 1·00 55

84 Scenes of Child Care and Emblem

1985. U.N.I.C.E.F. Child Health Campaign.
306 **84** 50 b. multicoloured . . . . 1·00 55

85 Flags around Map of Gulf

1985. 6th Supreme Council Session of Gulf Co-operation Council, Muscat. Multicoloured.
307 40 b. Type **85** 60 50
308 50 b. Portraits of rulers of Council member countries . 80 60

86 Sultan Qabus University and Students

1985. National Day. Multicoloured.
309 20 b. Type **86** 20 15
310 50 b. Tractor and oxen ploughing field 45 40
311 100 b. Port Qabus cement factory and Oman Chamber of Commerce 90 80
312 200 b. Road bridge, Douglas DC-10 airliner and communications centre . . 2·25 1·50
313 250 b. Portrait of Sultan Qabus (vert) . . . . 1·75 1·60

87 Military Exercise at Sea

1985. Armed Forces Day.
314 **87** 100 b. multicoloured . . . 1·50 1·00

88 "Chaetodon collaris"

1985. Marine Life. Multicoloured.
315 20 b. Type **88** 20 15
316 50 b. "Chaetodon melapterus" 45 40
317 100 c. "Chaetodon gardineri" 90 80
318 150 b. "Scomberomorus commerson" (horiz) . . . . 1·40 1·25
319 200 b. Lobster (horiz) . . . . 1·60 1·50

89 Frankincense Tree

1985. Frankincense Production.

320 **89** 100 b. multicoloured . . . 60 50
321 3 r. multicoloured . . . . 20·00 14·00

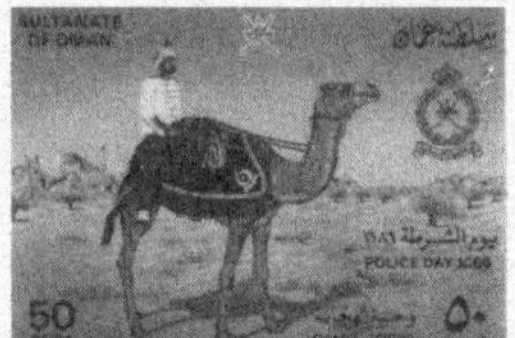

90 Camel Corps Member

1986. National Police Day.

322 **90** 50 b. multicoloured 95 65

91 Cadet Barquentine "Shabab Oman", 1986

1986. Participation of "Shabab Oman" in Statue of Liberty Centenary Celebrations. Multicoloured.

323 50 b. "Sultana" (full-rigged sailing ship), 1840 . . . . . 50 40
324 100 b. Type **91** . . . . 1·25 90

92 Crowd around Holy Kaaba

1986. Pilgrimage to Mecca.

326 **92** 50 b. multicoloured 85 40

93 Scouts erecting Tent

1986. 17th Arab Scout Camp, Salalah. Multicoloured.

327 50 b. Type **93** 55 35
328 100 b. Scouts making survey . 1·10 65

94 Sports Complex

1986. Inauguration of Sultan Qabus Sports Complex.

329 **94** 100 b. multicoloured . . . 1·10 75

95 Mother and Baby, Emblem and Tank on Globe

1986. International Peace Year.

330 **95** 130 b. multicoloured . . . 1·25 90

96 Al-Sahwa Tower

1986. National Day. Multicoloured.

331 50 b. Type **96** 50 30
332 100 b. Sultan Qabus University (inauguration) . . . . . . 1·10 65
333 130 b. 1966 stamps and F.D.C. cancellation (20th anniv of first Oman stamp issue) (57 × 27 mm) . . . . 1·40 95

97 Camel Corps

1987. National Police Day.

334 **97** 50 b. multicoloured . . . 85 60

98 Family

1987. Arabian Gulf Social Work Week.

335 **98** 50 b. multicoloured . . . 85 45

99 Aqueduct

101 Examples of Work and Hand holding Cup

1987. International Environment Day. Mult.

336 50 b. Greater flamingoes . . 1·75 55
337 130 b. Type **99** . . . . 1·25 80

100 Crowd around Holy Kaaba

1987. Pilgrimage to Mecca. Multicoloured.

338 50 b. Type **100** 60 50
339 50 b. Al-Khaif Mosque and tents, Mina 60 50
340 50 b. Stoning the Devil . . . 60 50
341 50 b. Pilgrims at Mudhalfa . 60 50
342 50 b. Pilgrims at prayer . . . 60 50
343 50 b. Mount Arafat, pilgrims and Kaaba 60 50

1987. 3rd Municipalities Month.

344 **101** 50 b. multicoloured . . . 75 50

102 Marine Science and Fisheries Centre

1987. National Day. Multicoloured.

345 50 b. Type **102** 40 30
346 130 b. Royal Hospital . . . . 1·10 85

103 Radio Operators

1987. 15th Anniv of Royal Omani Amateur Radio Society.

347 **103** 130 b. multicoloured . . . 95 80

104 Weaver

1988. Traditional Crafts. Multicoloured.

348 50 b. Type **104** 35 30
349 100 b. Potter 60 50
350 150 b. Halwa maker 85 75
351 200 b. Silversmith . . . . . . 1·00 85

105 Show Jumping

106 Emblem

1988. Olympic Games, Seoul. Multicoloured.

353 100 b. Type **105** 55 50
354 100 b. Hockey 55 50
355 100 b. Football 55 50
356 100 b. Running 55 50
357 100 b. Swimming 55 50
358 100 b. Shooting 55 50

1988. 40th Anniv of W.H.O. "Health for All".

360 **106** 100 b. multicoloured . . . 75 65

107 Tending Land and Crops

1988. National Day. Agriculture Year. Mult.

361 100 b. Type **107** 70 70
362 100 b. Livestock 70 70

108 Dhahira Region (woman's)

1989. Costumes. Multicoloured.

363 30 b. Type **108** 15 10
364 40 b. Eastern region (woman's) 20 15
365 50 b. Batinah region (woman's) 25 20
366 100 b. Interior region (woman's) 55 45
367 130 b. Southern region (woman's) 70 60
368 150 b. Muscat region (woman's) 80 70
369 200 b. Dhahira region (man's) 1·10 95
370 ¼ r. Eastern region (man's) . . 1·40 1·25
371 ½ r. Southern region (man's) . . 2·75 2·40
372 1 r. Muscat region (man's) . . 5·25 4·50

109 Fishing

1989. National Day. Agriculture Year. Mult.

375 100 b. Type **109** 65 55
376 100 b. Agriculture 65 55

110 Flags and Omani State Arms

1989. 10th Supreme Council Session of Arab Co-operation Council, Muscat. Multicoloured.

377 50 b. Type **110** 30 25
378 50 b. Council emblem and Sultan Qabus 30 25

111 Emblem and Map

1990. 5th Anniv (1989) of Gulf Investment Corporation.

379 **111** 50 b. multicoloured . . . 30 25
380 130 b. multicoloured . . . 80 70

112 Emblem and Douglas DC-10 Airliner

113 Map

1990. 40th Anniv of Gulf Air.

381 **112** 80 b. multicoloured . . . 50 45

1990. Omani Ophiolite Symposium, Muscat.

382 **113** 80 b. multicoloured . . . 60 50
383 150 b. multicoloured . . . 1·25 1·10

114 Ahmed bin Na'aman al-Ka'aby (envoy), "Sultana" and Said bin Sultan al-Busaidi

1990. 150th Anniv of First Omani Envoy's Journey to U.S.A.

384 **114** 200 b. multicoloured . . . 1·25 1·10

115 Sultan Qabus Rose

1990. 20th Anniv of Sultan Qabus's Accession.

385 **115** 200 b. multicoloured . . . 1·25 1·10

116 National Day Emblem

1990. National Day.

386 **116** 100 b. red and green on gold foil 60 50
387 – 200 b. green and red on gold foil . . . . 1·25 1·10

DESIGN: 200 b. Sultan Qabus.

117 Donor and Recipient

1991. Blood Donation.

389 **117** 50 b. multicoloured . . . 35 30
390 200 b. multicoloured . . . 1·50 1·25

118 Industrial Emblems

1991. National Day and Industry Year. Mult.

391 100 b. Type **118** 70 60
392 200 b. Sultan Qabus . . . . . 1·25 1·10

119 Weapons, Military Transport and Sultan Qabus

1991. Armed Forces Day.

394 **119** 100 b. multicoloured . . . 70 60

120 Interior of Museum and National Flags

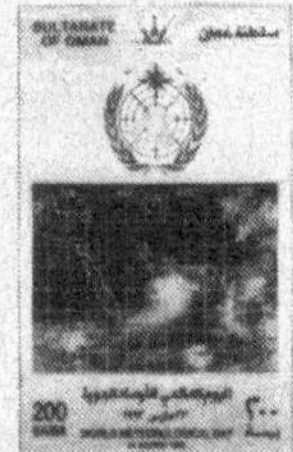

121 Satellite Picture of Asia

1992. Inaug of Omani-French Museum, Muscat.

395 **120** 100 b. multicoloured . . . 65 55

1992. World Meteorological Day.

397 **121** 220 b. multicoloured . . . 1·40 1·25

122 Emblem and Hands

123 Emblem and Hands protecting Handicapped Child

1992. World Environment Day.

398 **122** 100 b. multicoloured . . . 65 55

1992. Welfare of Handicapped Children.

399 **123** 70 b. multicoloured . . . 50 45

124 Sultan Qabus and Books

1992. Publication of Sultan Qabus "Encyclopedia of Arab Names".

400 **124** 100 b. multicoloured . . 60 50

125 Sultan Qabus, Factories and Industry Year Emblem

1992. National Day. Multicoloured.

401 100 b. Type **125** 60 50
402 200 b. Sultan Qabus and Majlis As'shura (Consultative Council) emblem . . . . . 1·25 1·10

126 Mounted Policemen and Sultan Qabus

1993. National Police Day.

403 **126** 80 b. multicoloured . . . 50 45

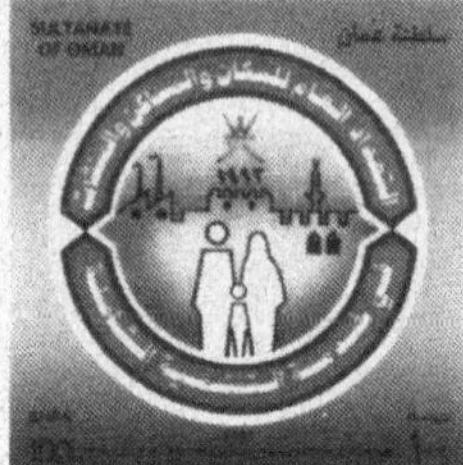

127 Census Emblem

1993. Population, Housing and Establishments Census.

404 **127** 100 b. multicoloured . . 55 50

128 Frigate and Sultan Qabus presenting Colours

1993. Navy Day.

405 **128** 100 b. multicoloured . . 55 50

129 Youth Year Emblem

1993. National Day and Youth Year. Multi.

406 100 b. Type **129** 55 50
407 200 b. Sultan Qabus . . . . . 1·10 95

130 Scout Headquarters and Emblem

1993. 61st Anniv of Scouting in Oman (408) and 10th Anniv of Sultan Qabus as Chief Scout (409). Multicoloured.

408 100 b. Type **130** 35 30
409 100 b. Scout camp and Sultan Qabus 35 30

Nos. 408/9 were issued together, se-tenant, forming a composite design.

131 Sei Whale and School of Dolphins

1993. Whales and Dolphins in Omani Waters. Multicoloured.

410 100 b. Type **131** 55 45
411 100 b. Sperm whale and dolphins 55 45

Nos. 410/11 were issued together, se-tenant, forming a composite design.

132 Water Drops and Falaj (ancient water system)

133 Municipality Building

1994. World Water Day.

413 **132** 50 b. multicoloured . . . 30 25

1994. 70th Anniv of Muscat Municipality.

414 **133** 50 b. multicoloured . . . 30 25

134 Centenary Emblem and Sports Pictograms

1994. Centenary of International Olympic Committee.

415 **134** 100 b. multicoloured . . . 55 50

135 Emblem

1994. National Day. Multicoloured.

416 50 b. Type **135** 15 10
417 50 b. Sultan Qabus 15 10

136 Airplane and Emblem

1994. 50th Anniv of I.C.A.O.

418 **136** 100 b. multicoloured . . . 30 25

137 Arms

139 Emblem and National Colours

138 Meeting

1994. 250th Anniv of Al-Busaid Dynasty. Multicoloured.

419 50 b. Type **137** dated "1744–1775" 15 10
420 50 b. Type **137** dated "1775–1779" 15 10
421 50 b. Type **137** dated "1779–1792" 15 10
422 50 b. Type **137** dated "1792–1804 . . . . 15 10
423 50 b. Type **137** dated "1804–1807" 15 10
424 50 b. Said bin Sultan (1807–1856) 15 10
425 50 b. Type **137** dated "1856–1866" 15 10
426 50 b. Type **137** dated "1866–1868" 15 10
427 50 b. Type **137** dated "1868–1871" 15 10
428 50 b. Turki bin Said (1871–1888) 15 10
429 50 b. Feisal bin Turki (1888–1913) 15 10
430 50 b. Taimur bin Feisal (1913–1932) 15 10
431 50 b. Arms, Sultan Qabus and family tree 15 10
432 50 b. Said bin Taimur (1932–1970) 15 10
433 50 b. Sultan Qabus (1970–) . 15 10

1995. Open Parliament.

435 **138** 50 b. multicoloured . . . 15 10

1995. 50th Anniv of Arab League.

436 **139** 100 b. multicoloured . . . 30 25

140 Anniversary Emblem

1995. 50th Anniv of U.N.O.

437 **140** 100 b. multicoloured . . . 30 25

141 Sultan Qabus in Robes

1995. National Day. Multicoloured.

438 50 b. Type **141** 15 10
439 100 b. Sultan Qabus in military uniform 30 25

142 Council Emblem

1995. 16th Supreme Council Session of Gulf Co-operation Council, Oman. Multicoloured.
441 100 b. Type **142** 30 25
442 200 b. Sultan Qabus, members' flags and map 65 55

PAKHOI Pt. 17

An Indo-Chinese Post Office in China, closed in 1922.

1903. Stamps of Indo-China, "Tablet" key-type, surch **PACKHOI** and value in Chinese.
1 D 1 c. black and red on blue . 3·75 3·75
2 2 c. brown and blue on buff 2·25 2·50
3 4 c. brown and blue on grey 2·00 2·00
4 5 c. green and red . . . . . 1·75 2·00
5 10 c. red and blue . . . . . 1·75 1·75
6 15 c. grey and red . . . . . 1·75 1·75
7 20 c. red and blue on green . 3·75 3·75
8 25 c. blue and red . . . . . 2·50 2·50
9 25 c. black and red on pink . 3·75 3·75
10 30 c. brown and blue on drab 3·75 3·75
11 40 c. red and blue on yellow 27·00 27·00
12 50 c. red and blue on pink . £200 £200
13 50 c. brown and red on blue 35·00 35·00
14 75 c. brown and red on orange 35·00 35·00
15 1 f. green and red . . . . . 38·00 38·00
16 5 f. mauve and blue on lilac 60·00 60·00

1906. Stamps of Indo-China surch **PAK-HOI** and value in Chinese.
17 **8** 1 c. olive 70 65
18 2 c. red on yellow 70 65
19 4 c. purple on grey 70 65
20 5 c. green 70 65
21 10 c. red 70 65
22 15 c. brown on blue . . . . 2·75 2·75
23 20 c. red on green . . . . . 1·90 1·90
24 25 c. blue . . . . 1·75 1·75
25 30 c. brown on cream . . . 1·90 1·75
26 35 c. black on yellow . . . . 1·90 1·90
27 40 c. black on grey . . . . . 1·90 1·90
28 50 c. olive on green . . . . 3·50 3·50
29 D 75 c. brown on orange . . . 25·00 25·00
30 **8** 1 f. green . . . . 13·50 13·50
31 2 f. brown on yellow . . . . 22·00 22·00
32 D 5 f. mauve on lilac . . . . 55·00 55·00
33 **8** 10 f. red on green . . . . . 65·00 70·00

1908. Stamps of Indo-China (Native types) surch **PAKHOI** and value in Chinese.
34 **10** 1 c. black and olive 25 30
35 2 c. black and brown . . . 35 40
36 4 c. black and blue 40 45
37 5 c. black and green 55 60
38 10 c. black and red 55 60
39 15 c. black and violet . . . 75 75
40 **11** 20 c. black and violet . . . 75 75
41 25 c. black and blue 90 90
42 30 c. black and brown . . . 1·40 1·50
43 35 c. black and green . . . 1·50 1·50
44 40 c. black and brown . . . 1·40 1·50
45 50 c. black and red . . . . 1·50 1·50
46 **12** 75 c. black and orange . . 2·75 2·75
47 – 1 f. black and red . . . . . 3·50 3·50
48 – 2 f. black and green . . . . 8·00 8·25
49 – 5 f. black and blue . . . . 48·00 50·00
50 – 10 f. black and violet . . . 75·00 75·00

1919. As last surch in addition in figures and words.
51 **10** $\frac{2}{5}$ c. on 1 c. black and olive 40 40
52 $\frac{4}{5}$ c. on 2 c. black and brown 40 45
53 $1\frac{3}{5}$ c. on 4 c. black and blue 40 45
54 2 c. on 5 c. black and green 55 55
55 4 c. on 10 c. black and red . 1·50 1·50
56 6 c. on 15 c. black & violet 55 55
57 **11** 8 c. on 20 c. black & violet 1·50 1·50
58 10 c. on 25 c. black & blue 1·75 1·75
59 12 c. on 30 c. black & purple 70 65
60 14 c. on 35 c. black & green 45 45
61 16 c. on 40 c. black & brown 1·10 1·10
62 20 c. on 50 c. black and red 70 65
63 **12** 30 c. on 75 c. black & orge 1·10 1·10
64 – 40 c. on 1 f. black and red . 5·25 5·25
65 – 80 c. on 2 f. black & green . 2·25 2·00
66 – 2 pi. on 5 f. black & blue . 5·50 5·50
67 – 4 pi. on 10 f. black & violet 11·50 11·50

PALAU Pt. 22

Formerly part of the United States Trust Territory of the Pacific Islands, Palau became an autonomous republic on 1 January 1981. Until 1983 it continued to use United States stamps.

Palau became an independent republic on 1 October 1994.

100 cents = 1 dollar

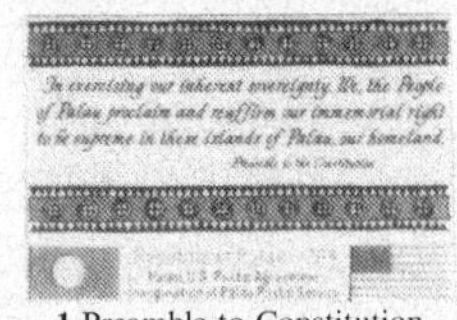
1 Preamble to Constitution

1983. Inaug of Postal Independence. Mult.
1 20 c. Type **1** 60 45
2 20 c. Natives hunting (design from Koror meeting house) 60 45
3 20 c. Preambule to Constitution (different) 60 45
4 20 c. Three fishes (design from Koror meeting house) 60 45

2 Palau Fruit Dove

3 Map Cowrie

1983. Birds. Multicoloured.
5 20 c. Type **2** 55 40
6 20 c. Morning bird 55 40
7 20 c. Palau white eye (inscr "Giant White-eye") 55 40
8 20 c. Palau fantail 55 45

1983. Marine Life. Multicoloured.
9 1 c. Sea fan 10 10
10 3 c. Type **3** 10 10
11 5 c. Jellyfish 15 10
12 10 c. Hawksbill turtle 20 10
13 13 c. Giant clam 25 15
14 14 c. Trumpet triton 30 25
15 20 c. Parrotfish 40 25
16 22 c. Bumphead parrotfish . . 40 30
17 25 c. Soft coral and damsel fish 40 30
17a 28 c. Chambered nautilus . . . 55 40
18 30 c. Dappled sea cucumber . . 55 40
18a 33 c. Sea anemone and clownfish 55 40
19 37 c. Sea urchin 75 40
19a 39 c. Green sea turtle 75 60
19b 44 c. Pacific sailfish 85 70
20 50 c. Starfish . . . . 1·00 60
21 $1 Common squid . . . . . . 2·00 1·00
22 $2 Dugong . . . . 3·75 2·25
23 $5 Pink sponge . . . . 8·50 5·50
24 $10 Spinner dolphin . . . . . 15·00 11·00

4 Humpback Whale

1983. World Wildlife Fund. Whales. Mult.
25 20 c. Type **4** 70 45
26 20 c. Blue whale 70 45
27 20 c. Fin whale 70 45
28 20 c. Sperm whale 70 45

5 "Spear fishing at New Moon"

6 King Abba Thulle

1983. Christmas. Paintings by Charlie Gibbons. Mult.
29 20 c. Type **5** 55 35
30 20 c. "Taro Gardening" 55 35
31 20 c. "First Child Ceremony" . 55 35
32 20 c. "Traditional Feast at the Bai" 55 35
33 20 c. "Spear Fishing from Red Canoe" 55 35

1983. Bicentenary of Captain Henry Wilson's Voyage to Palau.
34 **6** 20 c. brown, blue & dp blue . 50 35
35 – 20 c. brown, blue & dp blue . 50 35
36 – 20 c. brown, blue & dp blue . 50 35
37 – 20 c. brown, blue & dp blue . 50 35
38 – 20 c. brown, blue & dp blue . 50 35
39 – 20 c. brown, blue & dp blue . 50 35
40 – 20 c. brown, blue & dp blue . 50 35
41 – 20 c. brown, blue & dp blue . 50 35
DESIGNS—VERT: No. 37, Ludec (King Abba Thulle's wife); 38, Capt. Henry Wilson; 41, Prince Lee Boo. HORIZ: (47 × 20 mm): 35, Mooring in Koror; 36, Village scene in Pelew Islands; 39, Approaching Pelew; 40, Englishman's camp on Ulong.

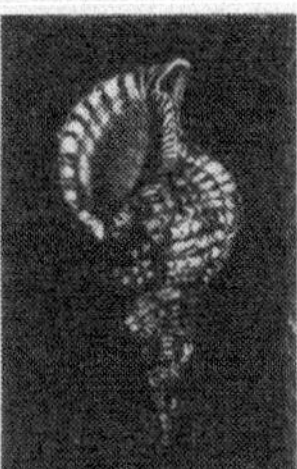
7 Triton Trumpet

1984. Sea Shells (1st series). Multicoloured.
42 20 c. Type **7** 50 40
43 20 c. Horned helmet 50 40
44 20 c. Giant clam 50 40
45 20 c. Laciniate conch 50 40
46 20 c. Royal cloak scallop . . . 50 40
47 20 c. Triton trumpet (different) 50 40
48 20 c. Horned helmet (different) 50 40
49 20 c. Giant clam (different) . . 50 40
50 20 c. Laciniate conch (different) 50 40
51 20 c. Royal cloak scallop (diff) 50 40
Nos. 43/6 have mauve backgrounds, Nos. 48/51 blue backgrounds.

See also Nos. 145/9, 194/8, 231/5, 256/60 and 515/19.

8 White-tailed Tropic Bird

1984. Air. Birds. Multicoloured.
52 40 c. Type **8** . . . . 1·00 75
53 40 c. White tern (inscr "Fairy Tern") . . . . 1·00 75
54 40 c. White-capped noddy (inscr "Black Noddy") . . . . . . 1·00 75
55 40 c. Black-naped tern . . . . 1·00 75

9 "Oroolong" (Wilson's schooner)

1984. 19th Universal Postal Union Congress Philatelic Salon, Hamburg. Multicoloured.
56 40 c. Type **9** . . . . 1·00 75
57 40 c. Missionary ship "Duff" . 1·00 75
58 40 c. German expeditionary steamer "Peiho" . . . . 1·00 75
59 40 c. German gunboat "Albatros" 1·00 75

10 Spear Fishing

1984. "Ausipex 84" International Stamp Exhibition, Melbourne. Fishing. Multicoloured.
60 20 c. Type **10** 55 35
61 20 c. Kite fishing 55 35
62 20 c. Underwater spear fishing 55 35
63 20 c. Net fishing 55 35

11 Mountain Apple

1984. Christmas. Multicoloured.
64 20 c. Type **11** 55 35
65 20 c. Beach morning glory . . 55 35
66 20 c. Turmeric 55 35
67 20 c. Plumeria 55 35

12 Chick

1985. Birth Bicentenary of John J. Audubon (ornithologist). Designs showing Audubon's Shearwater. Multicoloured.
68 22 c. Type **12** (postage) 65 45
69 22 c. Head of shearwater . . . 65 45
70 22 c. Shearwater flying 65 45
71 22 c. Shearwater on lake . . . 65 45
72 44 c. "Audubon's Shearwater" (Audubon) (air) . . . . . . 1·00 70

13 Borotong (cargo canoe)

1985. Traditional Canoes and Rafts. Multicoloured.
73 22 c. Type **13** 60 45
74 22 c. Kabeki (war canoe) . . . 60 45
75 22 c. Olechutel (bamboo raft) . 60 45
76 22 c. Kaeb (racing/sailing canoe) 60 45

14 Boy with Guitar

16 Mother cuddling Child

15 Raising German Flag at Palau, 1885, and German 1880 20 pf. Stamp

1985. International Youth Year. Multicoloured.
77 44 c. Type **14** 80 60
78 44 c. Boy with fishing rod . . . 80 60
79 44 c. Boy with baseball bat . . 80 60
80 44 c. Boy with spade 80 60
Nos. 77/80 were issued together se-tenant, each block forming a composite design showing a ring of children of different races.

1985. Air. Centenary of Vatican Treaty (granting German trading privileges in Caroline Islands). Multicoloured.
81 44 c. Type **15** . . . . 1·00 75
82 44 c. Early German trading post, Angaur, and Marshall Islands 1899 5 pf. overprinted stamp 1·00 75
83 44 c. Abai (village meeting house) and Caroline Islands 1901 5 m. yacht stamp . . . . 1·00 75
84 44 c. "Cormoran" (German cruiser), 1914, and Caroline Islands 1901 40 pf. yacht stamp 1·00 75

1985. Christmas. Multicoloured.
85 14 c. Mother with child on lap . 30 15
86 22 c. Type **16** 45 30
87 33 c. Mother supporting child in arms 70 50
88 44 c. Mother lifting child in air 80 70

17 Consolidated Catalina Amphibian over Natural Bridge

1985. Air. 50th Anniv of First Trans-Pacific Airmail Flight. Multicoloured.
89 44 c. Type **17** . . . . 1·00 65
90 44 c. Douglas DC-6B approaching Airai-Koror Passage . . . . 1·00 65
91 44 c. Grumman Albatross flying boat over Airai Village . . . 1·00 65
92 44 c. Douglas DC-4 landing at Airai . . . . 1·00 65

18 Comet and Kaeb, 1758

1985. Appearance of Halley's Comet. Multicoloured.
94 44 c. Type **18** . . . . 1·10 75
95 44 c. Comet and U.S.S. "Vincennes", 1835 . . . . . 1·10 75
96 44 c. Comet and "Scharnhorst" (German cruiser), 1910 . . . 1·10 75
97 44 c. Comet and tourist cabin cruiser, 1986 . . . . 1·10 75

19 Palau Myiagra Flycatchers

1986. Songbirds. Multicoloured.
98 44 c. Type **19** (inscr "Mangrove Flycatchers") . . . . 1·00 75
99 44 c. Cardinal honeyeaters . . 1·00 75
100 44 c. Blue-faced parrot finches 1·00 75
101 44 c. Grey-brown white eye (inscr "Dusky White-eye") and bridled white eye . . . . . 1·00 75

20 Spear Fisherman

1986. "Ameripex '86" International Stamp Exhibition, Chicago. Sea and Reef World. Multicoloured.
102 14 c. Type **20** 90 55
103 14 c. Olechutel (native raft) . 90 55
104 14 c. Kaebs (sailing canoes) . 90 55
105 14 c. Rock islands and sailfish 90 55
106 14 c. Inter-island ferry and flying fishes 90 55
107 14 c. Bone fishes 90 55
108 14 c. Common jacks 90 55
109 14 c. Mackerel 90 55
110 14 c. Sailfishes 90 55
111 14 c. Barracuda 90 55
112 14 c. Trigger fishes 90 55
113 14 c. Dolphin fishes 90 55
114 14 c. Spear fisherman with grouper 90 55
115 14 c. Manta ray 90 55
116 14 c. Marlin 90 55
117 14 c. Parrotfishes 90 55
118 14 c. Wrasse 90 55
119 14 c. Red snappers 90 55
120 14 c. Herring 90 55
121 14 c. Dugongs 90 55
122 14 c. Surgeonfishes 90 55
123 14 c. Leopard ray 90 55
124 14 c. Hawksbill turtle 90 55
125 14 c. Needlefishes 90 55
126 14 c. Tuna 90 55
127 14 c. Octopus 90 55
128 14 c. Clown fishes 90 55
129 14 c. Squid 90 55
130 14 c. Groupers 90 55
131 14 c. Moorish idols 90 55
132 14 c. Queen conch and starfish 90 55
133 14 c. Squirrel fishes 90 55
134 14 c. Starfish and sting rays . 90 55
135 14 c. Lion fish 90 55
136 14 c. Angel fishes 90 55
137 14 c. Butterfly fishes 90 55
138 14 c. Spiny lobster 90 55
139 14 c. Mangrove crab 90 55
140 14 c. Giant clam ("Tridacna gigas") 90 55
141 14 c. Moray eel 90 55
Nos. 102/41 are each inscribed on the back (over the gum) with the name of the subject featured on the stamp.
Nos. 102/41 were printed together, se-tenant, forming a composite design.

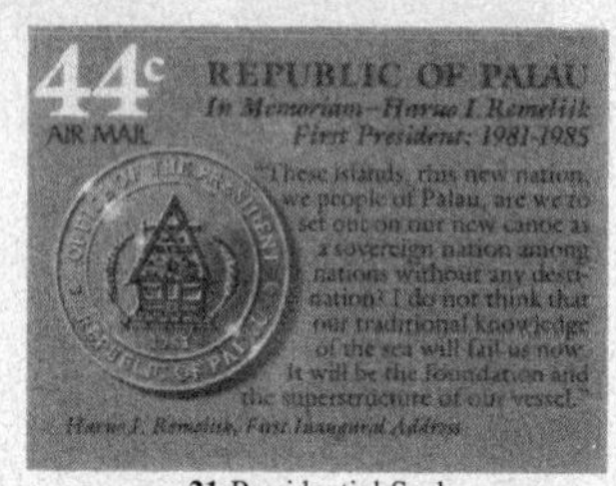

21 Presidential Seal

1986. Air. Haruo I. Remeliik (first President) Commemoration. Multicoloured.
142 44 c. Type **21** 90 60
143 44 c. Kabeki (war canoe) passing under Koror-Babeldaob Bridge 90 60
144 44 c. Presidents Reagan and Remeliik 90 60

1986. Sea Shells (2nd series). As T **7**. Multicoloured.
145 22 c. Commercial trochus . . 55 40
146 22 c. Marble cone 55 40
147 22 c. Fluted giant clam . . . 55 40
148 22 c. Bullmouth helmet . . . 55 40
149 22 c. Golden cowrie 55 40

23 Crab inhabiting Soldier's rusting Helmet

1986. International Peace Year. Multicoloured.
150 22 c. Type **23** (postage) . . . 55 40
151 22 c. Marine life inhabiting airplane 55 40
152 22 c. Rusting tank behind girl 55 40
153 22 c. Abandoned assault landing craft, Airai 55 40
154 22 c. Statue of Liberty, New York (centenary) (air) . . . 1·00 70

24 Gecko

1986. Reptiles. Multicoloured.
155 22 c. Type **24** 60 45
156 22 c. Emerald tree skink . . . 60 45
157 22 c. Estuarine crocodile . . . 60 45
158 22 c. Leatherback turtle . . . 60 45

25 Girl with Guitar and Boy leading Child on Goat

26 Tailed Jay on Soursop

1986. Christmas. Multicoloured.
159 22 c. Type **25** 45 35
160 22 c. Boys singing and girl carrying flowers 45 35
161 22 c. Mother holding baby . . 45 35
162 22 c. Children carrying baskets of fruit 45 35
163 22 c. Girl with white terns . . 45 35
Nos. 159/63 were issued together, se-tenant, forming a composite design.

1987. Butterflies (1st series). Multicoloured.
164 44 c. Type **26** . . . . 1·10 75
165 44 c. Common mormon on sweet orange . . . . 1·10 75
166 44 c. Common eggfly on swamp cabbage . . . . 1·10 75
167 44 c. Oleander butterfly on fig 1·10 75
See also Nos. 223/6.

27 Bat flying

28 "Ixora casei"

1987. Air. Palau Fruit Bat. Multicoloured.
168 44 c. Type **27** 95 70
169 44 c. Bat hanging from branch 95 70
170 44 c. Bat feeding 95 70
171 44 c. Head of bat 95 70

1987. Flowers. Multicoloured.
172 1 c. Type **28** 10 10
173 3 c. "Lumnitzera littorea" . . 10 10
174 5 c. "Sonneratia alba" 10 10
175 10 c. Woody vine 15 10
176 14 c. "Bikkia palauensis" . . . 20 10
177 15 c. "Limophila aromatica" . 20 10
178 22 c. "Bruguiera gymnorhiza" 30 20
179 25 c. "Fragraea ksid" 30 20
180 36 c. "Ophiorrhiza palauensis" 45 35
181 39 c. "Cerbera manghas" . . . 60 40
182 44 c. "Samadera indica" . . . 65 45
183 45 c. "Maesa canfieldiae" . . . 55 45
184 50 c. "Dolichandrone spathacea" 80 55
185 $1 "Barringtonia racemosa" . 1·50 1·10
186 $2 "Nepenthes mirabilis" . . 2·50 2·00
187 $5 Orchid . . . . 6·00 4·50
188 $10 Bouquet of mixed flowers . 12·00 9·00

29 Babeldaob

1987. "Capex '87" International Stamp Exhibition, Toronto. Multicoloured.
190 22 c. Type **29** 40 30
191 22 c. Floating Garden Islands . 40 30
192 22 c. Rock Island 40 30
193 22 c. Koror 40 30

1987. Sea Shells (3rd series). As T **7**. Multicoloured.
194 22 c. Black-striped triton . . . 50 35
195 22 c. Tapestry turban 50 35
196 22 c. Adusta murex 50 35
197 22 c. Little fox mitre 50 35
198 22 c. Cardinal mitre 50 35

31 "The President shall be the chief executive ..."

1987. Bicentenary of United States of America Constitution. Multicoloured.
199 14 c. Type **31** 25 20
200 14 c. Palau and U.S. Presidents' seals (24 × 37 mm) 25 20
201 14 c. "The executive power shall be vested ..." 25 20
202 22 c. "The legislative power of Palau ..." 35 25
203 22 c. Palau Olbiil Era Kelulau and U.S. Senate seals (24 × 37 mm) 35 25
204 22 c. "All legislative powers herein granted ..." 35 25
205 44 c. "The judicial power of Palau ..." 70 60
206 44 c. Palau and U.S. Supreme Court seals (24 × 37 mm) . 70 60
207 44 c. "The judicial power of the United States ..." 70 60
The three designs of the same value were printed together in se-tenant strips, the top stamp of each strip bearing extracts from the Palau Constitution and the bottom stamp extracts from the U.S. Constitution.

32 Japanese Mobile Post Office and 1937 Japan ½ s. Stamp

1987. Links with Japan. Multicoloured.
208 14 c. Type **32** 40 30
209 22 c. Phosphate mine and Japan 1942 5 s. stamp 70 50
210 33 c. Douglas DC-2 flying over Badrulchau monuments and Japan 1937 2 s. + 2 s. stamp 85 60
211 44 c. Japanese Post Office, Koror, and Japan 1927 10 s. stamp . . . . 1·10 80

33 Huts, White Tern and Outrigger Canoes

34 Snapping Shrimp and Goby

1987. Christmas. Multicoloured.
213 22 c. Type **33** 45 35
214 22 c. Flying white tern carrying twig 45 35
215 22 c. Holy family in kaeb . . 45 35
216 22 c. Angel and kaeb 45 35
217 22 c. Outrigger canoes and hut 45 35
Nos. 213/17 were issued together, se-tenant, forming a composite design; each stamp bears a verse of the carol "I Saw Three Ships".

1987. 25th Anniv of World Ecology Movement. Multicoloured.
218 22 c. Type **34** 50 40
219 22 c. Mauve vase sponge and sponge crab 50 40
220 22 c. Pope's damsel fish and cleaner wrasse 50 40
221 22 c. Clown anemone fishes and sea anemone 50 40
222 22 c. Four-coloured nudibranch and banded coral shrimp . 50 40

1988. Butterflies (2nd series). As T **26**.
223 44 c. Orange tiger on "Tournefotia argentia" . . 65 55
224 44 c. Swallowtail on "Citrus reticulata" 65 55
225 44 c. Lemon migrant on "Crataeva speciosa" 65 55
226 44 c. "Appias ada" (wrongly inscr "Colias philodice") on "Crataeva speciosa" 65 55

35 Whimbrel 37 Baseball

1988. Ground-dwelling Birds. Multicoloured.

227	44 c. Type **35**	65	55
228	44 c. Chinese little bittern	65	55
229	44 c. Rufous night heron	65	55
230	44 c. Banded rail	65	55

1988. Sea Shells (4th series). As T **7**. Mult.

231	25 c. Striped engina	50	35
232	25 c. Ivory cone	50	35
233	25 c. Plaited mitre	50	35
234	25 c. Episcopal mitre	50	35
235	25 c. Isabelle cowrie	50	35

1988. Olympic Games, Seoul. Multicoloured.

237	25 c. + 5 c. Type **37**	45	40
238	25 c. + 5 c. Running	45	40
239	45 c. + 5 c. Diving	80	65
240	45 c. + 5 c. Swimming	80	65

39 Angel Violinist and Singing Cherubs 41 Nicobar Pigeon

1988. Christmas. Multicoloured.

242	25 c. Type **39**	40	30
243	25 c. Angels and children singing	40	30
244	25 c. Children adoring child	40	30
245	25 c. Angels and birds flying	40	30
246	25 c. Running children and angels playing trumpets	40	30

Nos. 242/6 were issued together, se-tenant, forming a composite design.

1989. Endangered Birds. Multicoloured.

248	45 c. Type **41**	1·10	75
249	45 c. Palau ground dove	1·10	75
250	45 c. Marianas scrub hen	1·10	75
251	45 c. Palau scops owl	1·10	75

42 Gilled Auricularia

1989. Fungi. Multicoloured.

252	45 c. Type **42**	1·10	75
253	45 c. Rock mushroom	1·10	75
254	45 c. Polyporous	1·10	75
255	45 c. Veiled stinkhorn	1·10	75

43 Robin Redbreast Triton

1989. Sea Shells (5th series). Multicoloured.

256	25 c. Type **43**	60	45
257	25 c. Hebrew cone	60	45
258	25 c. Tadpole triton	60	45
259	25 c. Lettered cone	60	45
260	25 c. Rugose mitre	60	45

44 Cessna 207 Stationair 7 46 Jettison of Third Stage

1989. Air. Airplanes. Multicoloured.

261	36 c. Type **44**	50	40
262	39 c. Embraer Bandeirante	60	50
264	45 c. Boeing 727	70	60

No. 261 is wrongly inscribed "Skywagon"

1989. 20th Anniv of First Manned Landing on Moon. Multicoloured.

267	25 c. Type **46**	40	30
268	25 c. Command Module adjusting position	40	30
269	25 c. Lunar Excursion Module "Eagle" docking	40	30
270	25 c. Space module docking	40	30
271	25 c. Propulsion for entry into lunar orbit	40	30
272	25 c. Third stage burn	40	30
273	25 c. Command Module orbiting Moon	40	30
274	25 c. Command Module and part of "Eagle"	40	30
275	25 c. Upper part of "Eagle" on Moon	40	30
276	25 c. Descent of "Eagle"	40	30
277	25 c. Nose of rocket	40	30
278	25 c. Reflection in Edwin "Buzz" Aldrin's visor	40	30
279	25 c. Neil Armstrong and flag on Moon	40	30
280	25 c. Footprints and astronaut's oxygen tank	40	30
281	25 c. Upper part of astronaut descending ladder	40	30
282	25 c. Launch tower and body of rocket	40	30
283	25 c. Survival equipment on Aldrin's space suit	40	30
284	25 c. Blast off from lunar surface	40	30
285	25 c. View of Earth and astronaut's legs	40	30
286	25 c. Leg on ladder	40	30
287	25 c. Lift off	40	30
288	25 c. Spectators at launch	40	30
289	25 c. Capsule parachuting into Pacific	40	30
290	25 c. Re-entry	40	30
291	25 c. Space Module jettison	40	30
292	$2.40 "Buzz" Aldrin on Moon (photo by Neil Armstrong) (34×47 mm)	3·50	2·50

Nos. 267/91 were issued together, se-tenant, forming a composite design.

47 Girl as Astronaut 48 Bridled Tern

1989. Year of the Young Reader. Multicoloured.

293	25 c. Type **47**	45	35
294	25 c. Boy riding dolphin	45	35
295	25 c. Cheshire Cat in tree	45	35
296	25 c. Mother Goose	45	35
297	25 c. Baseball player	45	35
298	25 c. Girl reading	45	35
299	25 c. Boy reading	45	35
300	25 c. Mother reading to child	45	35
301	25 c. Girl holding flowers listening to story	45	35
302	25 c. Boy in baseball strip	45	35

1989. "World Stamp Expo '89" International Stamp Exhibition, Washington D.C. Stilt Mangrove. Multicoloured.

303	25 c. Type **48**	45	35
304	25 c. Lemon migrant (inscr "Sulphur Butterfly")	45	35
305	25 c. Palau myiagra flycatcher (inscr "Mangrove Flycatcher")	45	35
306	25 c. White-collared kingfisher	45	35
307	25 c. Fruit bat	45	35
308	25 c. Estuarine crocodile	45	35
309	25 c. Rufous night heron	45	35
310	25 c. Stilt mangrove	45	35
311	25 c. Bird's nest fern	45	35
312	25 c. Beach hibiscus tree	45	35
313	25 c. Common eggfly (butterfly)	45	35
314	25 c. Dog-faced watersnake	45	35
315	25 c. Mangrove jingle shell	45	35
316	25 c. Palau bark cricket	45	35
317	25 c. Periwinkle and mangrove oyster	45	35
318	25 c. Jellyfish	45	35
319	25 c. Striped mullet	45	35
320	25 c. Mussels, sea anemones and algae	45	35
321	25 c. Cardinalfish	45	35
322	25 c. Snappers	45	35

Nos. 303/22 are each inscribed on the back (over the gum) with the name of the subject featured on the stamp.

Nos. 303/22 were issued together, se-tenant, forming a composite design.

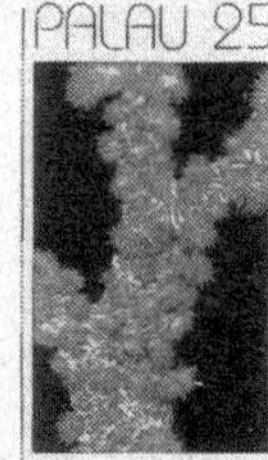

49 Angels, Sooty Tern and Audubon's Shearwater 50 Pink Coral

1989. Christmas. Carol of the Birds. Mult.

323	25 c. Type **49**	45	35
324	25 c. Palau fruit dove and angel	45	35
325	25 c. Madonna and child, cherub and birds	45	35
326	25 c. Angel, blue-faced parrot finch, Palau myiagra flycatcher and cardinal honeyeater	45	35
327	25 c. Angel, Palau myiagra flycatcher and black-headed gulls	45	35

Nos. 323/7 were printed together, se-tenant, forming a composite design.

1990. Soft Corals. Multicoloured.

328	25 c. Type **50**	50	35
329	25 c. Mauve coral	50	35
330	25 c. Yellow coral	50	35
331	25 c. Orange coral	50	35

See also Nos. 392/5.

51 Siberian Rubythroat

1990. Forest Birds. Multicoloured.

332	45 c. Type **51**	90	65
333	45 c. Palau bush warbler	90	65
334	45 c. Micronesian starling	90	65
335	45 c. Slender-billed greybird (inscr "Cicadabird")	90	65

52 Prince Lee Boo, Capt. Henry Wilson and H.M.S. "Victory"

1990. "Stamp World London 90" International Stamp Exhibition. Prince Lee Boo's Visit to England, 1784, and 150th Anniv of the Penny Black. Multicoloured.

336	25 c. Type **52**	30	20
337	25 c. St. James's Palace	30	20
338	25 c. Rotherhithe Docks	30	20
339	25 c. Oroolong House, Devon (Capt. Wilson's home)	30	20
340	25 c. Vincenzo Lunardi's balloon	30	20
341	25 c. St. Paul's Cathedral	30	20
342	25 c. Prince Lee Boo's grave	30	20
343	25 c. St. Mary's Church, Rotherhithe	30	20
344	25 c. Memorial tablet to Prince Lee Boo	30	20

53 "Corymborkis veratrifolia" 55 White Tern, American Golden Plover and Sanderling

54 Plane Butterfly on Beach Sunflower

1990. "Expo 90" International Garden and Greenery Exposition, Osaka. Orchids. Multicoloured.

346	45 c. Type **53**	55	40
347	45 c. "Malaxis setipes"	55	40
348	45 c. "Dipodium freycinetianum"	55	40
349	45 c. "Bulbophyllum micronesiacum"	55	40
350	45 c. "Vanda teres"	55	40

1990. Butterflies. Multicoloured.

351	45 c. Type **54**	70	55
352	45 c. Painted lady on coral tree	70	55
353	45 c. "Euploea nemertes" on sorcerer's flower	70	55
354	45 c. Meadow argus (inscr "Buckeye") on beach pea	70	55

1990. Lagoon Life. Multicoloured.

355	25 c. Type **55**	30	20
356	25 c. Bidekill fisherman	30	20
357	25 c. Yacht and insular halfbeaks	30	20
358	25 c. Palauan kaebs	30	20
359	25 c. White-tailed tropic bird	30	20
360	25 c. Spotted eagle ray	30	20
361	25 c. Great barracudas	30	20
362	25 c. Reef needlefish	30	20
363	25 c. Reef blacktip shark	30	20
364	25 c. Hawksbill turtle	30	20
365	25 c. Sixfeeler threadfins and octopus	30	20
366	25 c. Batfish and sixfeeler threadfins	30	20
367	25 c. Lionfish and sixfeeler threadfins	30	20
368	25 c. Snowflake moray and sixfeeler threadfins	30	20
369	25 c. Inflated and uninflated porcupine fishes and sixfeeler threadfins	30	20
370	25 c. Regal angelfish, blue-streak cleaner wrasse, blue sea star and corals	30	20
371	25 c. Clown triggerfish and spotted garden eels	30	20
372	25 c. Spotted garden eels	30	20
373	25 c. Blue-lined sea bream, blue-green chromis and sapphire damselfish	30	20
374	25 c. Orangespine unicornfish and whitetipped soldierfish	30	20
375	25 c. Slatepencil sea urchin and leopard sea cucumber	30	20
376	25 c. Pacific partridge tun shell	30	20
377	25 c. Mandarinfish	30	20
378	25 c. Tiger cowrie	30	20
379	25 c. Feather starfish and orange-fin anemone fish	30	20

Nos. 355/79 were printed together, se-tenant, forming a composite design.

56 "Delphin", 1890, and Card

1990. Pacifica. Mail Transport. Multicoloured.

380	45 c. Type **56**	55	45
381	45 c. Right-hand half of card flown on 1951 inaugural U.S. civilian airmail flight and forklift unloading mail from Boeing 727 airplane	55	45

Nos. 380/1 were issued together, se-tenant, forming a composite design.

57 Girls singing and Boy with Butterfly

1990. Christmas. Multicoloured.

382	25 c. Type **57**	30	20
383	25 c. White terns perching on girl's songbook	30	20
384	25 c. Girl singing and boys playing flute and guitar	30	20
385	25 c. Couple with baby	30	20
386	25 c. Three girls singing	30	20

58 Consolidated B-24S Liberator Bombers over Peleliu

1960. 46th Anniv of U.S. Action in Palau Islands during Second World War.

387	45 c. Type **58**	55	45
388	45 c. Landing craft firing rocket barrage	55	45
389	45 c. 1st Marine division attacking Peleliu	55	45
390	45 c. U.S. Infantryman and Palauan children	55	45

1991. Hard Corals. As T **50**.

392 30 c. Staghorn coral 40 30
393 30 c. Velvet leather coral . . . 40 30
394 30 c. Van Gogh's cypress coral 40 30
395 30 c. Violet lace coral 40 30

59 Statue of Virgin Mary, Nkulangelul Point

1991. Angaur, The Phosphate Island. Mult.

396 30 c. Type **59** 40 30
397 30 c. Angaur Post Office opening day cancellation and kaeb (sailing canoe) (41 × 27 mm) 40 30
398 30 c. Swordfish and Caroline Islands 40 pf. "Yacht" stamp (41 × 27 mm) 40 30
399 30 c. Locomotive at phosphate mine 40 30
400 30 c. Lighthouse Hill and German copra freighter . . 40 30
401 30 c. Dolphins and map showing phosphate mines (41 × 27 mm) 40 30
402 30 c. Estuarine crocodile (41 × 27 mm) 40 30
403 30 c. Workers cycling to phosphate plant 40 30
404 30 c. Freighter loading phosphate 40 30
405 30 c. Hammerhead shark and German overseer (41 × 27 mm) 40 30
406 30 c. Angaur cancellation and Marshall Islands 10 pf. "Yacht" stamp (41 × 27 mm) 40 30
407 30 c. Rear Admiral Graf von Spee and "Scharnhorst" (German cruiser) 40 30
408 30 c. "Emden" (German cruiser) and Capt. Karl von Muller . 40 30
409 30 c. Crab-eating macaque (41 × 27 mm) 40 30
410 30 c. Sperm whale (41 × 27 mm) 40 30
411 30 c. H.M.A.S. "Sydney" (cruiser) shelling radio tower 40 30

Nos. 396/411 were issued together, se-tenant, with the centre block of eight stamps forming a composite design of a map of the island.

60 Moorhen

61 Pope Leo XIII and 19th-century Spanish and German Flags

1991. Birds. Multicoloured.

412 1 c. Palau bush warbler 10 10
413 4 c. Type **60** 10 10
414 6 c. Banded rail 10 10
415 19 c. Palau fantail 25 15
416 20 c. Palau myiagra (inscr "Mangrove") flycatcher . . 25 15
417 23 c. Purple swamphen 30 20
418 29 c. Palau fruit dove 40 30
419 35 c. Crested tern 45 30
420 40 c. Eastern reef herons (inscr "Pacific Reef-Heron") . . . 55 40
421 45 c. Micronesian pigeon . . . 60 45
422 50 c. Great frigate bird 65 45
423 52 c. Little pied cormorant . . 70 50
424 75 c. Jungle nightjar . . . . . 1·00 75
425 95 c. Cattle egret . . . . . . 1·25 90
426 $1.34 Sulphur-crested cockatoo 1·75 1·25
427 $2 Blue-faced parrot finch . . 2·75 2·00
428 $5 Eclectus parrots . . . . . 6·75 5·00
429 $10 Palau bush warblers feeding chicks (51 × 28 mm) . . . . 13·00 9·75

1991. Centenary of Christianity in Palau Islands. Multicoloured.

432 29 c. Type **61** 40 30
433 29 c. Ibedul Ilengelekei and Church of the Sacred Heart, Koror, 1920 . . . . 40 30
434 29 c. Marino de la Hoz, Emilio Villar and Elias Fernandez (Jesuit priests executed in Second World War) 40 30
435 29 c. Centenary emblem and Fr. Edwin G. McManus (compiler of Palauan-English dictionary) 40 30
436 29 c. Present Church of the Sacred Heart, Koror 40 30
437 29 c. Pope John Paul II and Palau and Vatican flags . . 40 30

62 Pacific White-sided Dolphin

1991. Pacific Marine Life. Multicoloured.

438 29 c. Type **62** 40 30
439 29 c. Common dolphin 40 30
440 29 c. Rough-toothed dolphin . . 40 30
441 29 c. Bottle-nosed dolphin . . 40 30
442 29 c. Common (inscr "Harbor") porpoise 40 30
443 29 c. Head and body of killer whale 40 30
444 29 c. Tail of killer whale, spinner dolphin and yellowfin tuna 40 30
445 29 c. Dall's porpoise 40 30
446 29 c. Finless porpoise 40 30
447 29 c. Map of Palau Islands and bottle-nosed dolphin . . . 40 30
448 29 c. Dusky dolphin 40 30
449 29 c. Southern right whale dolphin 40 30
450 29 c. Striped dolphin 40 30
451 29 c. Fraser's dolphin 40 30
452 29 c. Peale's dolphin 40 30
453 29 c. Spectacled porpoise . . 40 30
454 29 c. Spotted dolphin 40 30
455 29 c. Hourglass dolphin . . . 40 30
456 29 c. Risso's dolphin 40 30
457 29 c. Hector's dolphin 40 30

63 McDonnell Douglas Wild Weasel Fighters

1991. Operation Desert Storm (liberation of Kuwait). Multicoloured.

458 20 c. Type **63** 25 20
459 20 c. Lockheed Stealth fighter-bomber 25 20
460 20 c. Hughes Apache helicopter 25 20
461 20 c. "M-109 TOW" missile on "M998 HMMWV" vehicle 25 20
462 20 c. President Bush of U.S.A. 25 20
463 20 c. M2 "Bradley" tank . . 25 20
464 20 c. U.S.S. "Ranger" (aircraft carrier) 25 20
465 20 c. PHM-1 (patrol boat) . . 25 20
466 20 c. U.S.S. "Wisconsin" (battleship) 25 20
467 $2.90 Sun, dove and yellow ribbon . . . . 3·75 2·75

64 Bai Gable

66 "Silent Night, Holy Night!"

65 Bear's-paw Clam, China Clam, Fluted Giant Clam and "Tridacna derasa"

1991. 10th Anniv of Republic of Palau and Palau-Pacific Women's Conference, Koror. Bai (community building) Decorations. Mult. Imperf (self-adhesive) (50 c.) perf (others).

469 29 c. Type **64** (postage) . . . 40 30
470 29 c. Interior of bai (left side) (32 × 48 mm) 40 30
471 29 c. Interior of bai (right side) (32 × 48 mm) 40 30
472 29 c. God of construction . . 40 30
473 29 c. Bubuu (spider) (value at left) (30 × 23 mm) 40 30
474 29 c. Delerrok, the money bird (facing right) (31 × 23 mm) 40 30
475 29 c. Delerrok (facing left) (31 × 23 mm) 40 30
476 29 c. Bubuu (value at right) (30 × 23 mm) 40 30
477 50 c. Bai gable (as in Type **64**) (24 × 51 mm) (air) 65 45

Nos. 469/76 were issued together, se-tenant, Nos. 470/1 forming a composite design.

1991. Conservation and Cultivation of Giant Clams. Multicoloured.

478 50 c. Type **65** 70 50
479 50 c. Symbiotic relationship between giant clam and "Symbiodinium microadriaticum" 70 50
480 50 c. Hatchery 70 50
481 50 c. Diver measuring clams in sea-bed nursery 70 50
482 50 c. Micronesian Mariculture Demonstration Center, Koror (108 × 16 mm) 70 50

1991. Christmas. Multicoloured.

483 29 c. Type **66** 40 30
484 29 c. "All is calm, all is bright;" 40 30
485 29 c. "Round yon virgin mother and child!" 40 30
486 29 c. "Holy Infant, so tender and mild," 40 30
487 29 c. "Sleep in heavenly peace." 40 30

Nos. 483/7 were issued together, se-tenant, forming a composite design.

67 Flag, Islands and Children

1991. 25th Anniv of Presence of United States Peace Corps in Palau. Children's paintings.

488 29 c. Type **67** 40 30
489 29 c. Volunteers arriving by airplane 40 30
490 29 c. Health care 40 30
491 29 c. Fishing 40 30
492 29 c. Agriculture 40 30
493 29 c. Education 40 30

68 "Zuiho Maru" (trochus shell breeding and marine research)

1991. "Phila Nippon '91" International Stamp Exhibition, Tokyo. Japanese Heritage in Palau. Multicoloured.

494 29 c. Type **68** 40 30
495 29 c. Man carving story board (traditional arts) 40 30
496 29 c. Tending pineapple crop (agricultural training) . . . 40 30
497 29 c. Klidm (stone carving), Koror (archaeological research) 40 30
498 29 c. Teaching carpentry and building design 40 30
499 29 c. Kawasaki "Mavis" flying boat (air transport) 40 30

69 Mitsubishi Zero-Sen attacking Shipping at Pearl Harbor

70 "Troides criton"

1991. Pacific Theatre in Second World War (1st issue). Multicoloured.

501 29 c. Type **69** 40 30
502 29 c. U.S.S. "Nevada" underway from Pearl Harbor 40 30
503 29 c. U.S.S. "Shaw" exploding at Pearl Harbor 40 30
504 29 c. Douglas Dauntless dive bombers attacking Japanese carrier "Akagi" 40 30
505 29 c. U.S.S. "Wasp" sinking off Guadalcanal 40 30
506 29 c. Battle of Philippine Sea . 40 30
507 29 c. Landing craft storming Saipan Beach 40 30
508 29 c. U.S. 1st Cavalry on Leyte 40 30
509 29 c. Battle of Bloody Nose Ridge, Peleliu 40 30
510 29 c. U.S. troops landing at Iwo Jima 40 30

See also Nos. 574/83, 601/10 and 681/90.

1992. Butterflies. Multicoloured.

511 50 c. Type **70** 65 45
512 50 c. "Alcides zodiaca" 65 45
513 50 c. "Papilio poboroi" 65 45
514 50 c. "Vindula arsinoe" 65 45

71 Common Hairy Triton

73 "And darkness was upon the face of the deep ..."

72 Christopher Columbus

1992. Sea Shells (6th series). Multicoloured.

515 29 c. Type **71** 50 35
516 29 c. Eglantine cowrie 50 35
517 29 c. Sulcate swamp cerith . . 50 35
518 29 c. Black-spined murex . . 50 35
519 29 c. Black-mouth moon . . . 50 35

1992. Age of Discovery from Columbus to Drake. Multicoloured.

520 29 c. Type **72** 40 30
521 29 c. Ferdinand Magellan . . 40 30
522 29 c. Sir Francis Drake . . . 40 30
523 29 c. Cloud blowing northerly wind 40 30
524 29 c. Compass rose 40 30
525 29 c. Dolphin and "Golden Hind" (Drake's ship) . . . 40 30
526 29 c. Corn cobs and "Santa Maria" (Columbus's ship) . 40 30
527 29 c. Mythical fishes 40 30
528 29 c. Betel palm, cloves and black pepper 40 30
529 29 c. "Vitoria" (Magellan's ship), Palau Islands, Audubon's shearwater and crested tern 40 30
530 29 c. White-tailed tropic bird, bicolour parrotfish, pineapple and potatoes 40 30
531 29 c. Compass 40 30
532 29 c. Mythical sea monster . . 40 30
533 29 c. Paddles and astrolabe . . 40 30
534 29 c. Parallel ruler, divider and Inca gold treasure 40 30
535 29 c. Backstaff 40 30
536 29 c. Cloud blowing southerly wind 40 30
537 29 c. Amerigo Vespucci . . . 40 30
538 29 c. Francisco Pizarro . . . 40 30
539 29 c. Vasco Nunez de Balboa . 40 30

With the exception of Nos. 523 and 536 each stamp is inscribed on the back (over the gum) with the names of the subject featured on the stamp.

Nos. 520/39 were issued together, se-tenant, the backgrounds forming a composite design of the hemispheres.

1992. 2nd U.N. Conference on Environment and Development, Rio de Janeiro. The Creation of the World from the Book of Genesis, Chapter 1. Multicoloured.

540 29 c. Type **73** 40 30
541 29 c. Sunlight 40 30
542 29 c. "Let there be a firmament in the midst of the waters, ..." 40 30
543 29 c. Sky and clouds 40 30
544 29 c. "Let the waters under the heaven..." 40 30
545 29 c. Tree 40 30
546 29 c. Waves and sunlight (no inscr) 40 30
547 29 c. Waves and sunlight ("... and it was good.") 40 30
548 29 c. Waves and clouds (no inscr) 40 30
549 29 c. Waves and clouds ("... and it was so.") 40 30
550 29 c. Plants on river bank (no inscr) 40 30
551 29 c. Plants on river bank ("... and it was good.") 40 30
552 29 c. "Let there be lights in the firmament..." 40 30
553 29 c. Comet, planet and clouds 40 30
554 29 c. "Let the waters bring forth abundantly the moving creature..." 40 30
555 29 c. Great frigate bird and red-tailed tropic bird flying and collared lory on branch . . 40 30
556 29 c. "Let the earth bring forth the living creature after his kind..." 40 30
557 29 c. Woman, man and rainbow 40 30
558 29 c. Mountains ("... and it was good.") 40 30
559 29 c. Sun and hills 40 30
560 29 c. Whale and fishes 40 30
561 29 c. Fishes ("... and it was good.") 40 30
562 29 c. Elephants and squirrel . 40 30
563 29 c. Orchard and cat ("... and it was very good.") 40 30

Nos. 540/63 were issued together, se-tenant, forming six composite designs each covering four stamps.

75 Presley and Dove

1992. 15th Death Anniv of Elvis Presley (entertainer). Multicoloured.

565 29 c. Type **75** 40 30
566 29 c. Presley and dove's wing . 40 30
567 29 c. Presley in yellow cape . . 40 30
568 29 c. Presley in white and red shirt (¾ face) 40 30
569 29 c. Presley singing into microphone 40 30
570 29 c. Presley crying 40 30
571 29 c. Presley in red shirt (¾ face) 40 30
572 29 c. Presley in purple shirt (full face) 40 30
573 29 c. Presley (left profile) . . . 40 30

76 Grumman Avenger

1992. Air. Pacific Theatre in Second World War (2nd issue). Aircraft. Multicoloured.

574 50 c. Type **76** 65 45
575 50 c. Curtiss P-40C of the Flying Tigers 65 45
576 50 c. Mitsubishi Zero-Sen . . 65 45
577 50 c. Hawker Hurricane Mk I 65 45
578 50 c. Consolidated Catalina flying boat 65 45
579 50 c. Curtiss Hawk 75 . . . . 65 45
580 50 c. Boeing Flying Fortress . 65 45
581 50 c. Brewster Buffalo 65 45
582 50 c. Vickers Supermarine Walrus flying boat 65 45
583 50 c. Curtiss Kittyhawk I . . 65 45

77 "Thus Every Beast"

1992. Christmas. "The Friendly Beasts" (carol). Multicoloured.

584 29 c. Type **77** 40 30
585 29 c. "By Some Good Spell" . 40 30
586 29 c. "In the Stable Dark was Glad to Tell" 40 30
587 29 c. "of the Gift He Gave Emanuel" (angel on donkey) 40 30
588 29 c. "The Gift He Gave Emanuel" (Palau fruit doves) 40 30

78 Dugong

1993. Animals. Multicoloured.

589 50 c. Type **78** 65 45
590 50 c. Blue-faced (inscr "Masked") booby 65 45
591 50 c. Crab-eating macaque . . 65 45
592 50 c. New Guinea crocodile . 65 45

79 Giant Deepwater Crab

1993. Seafood. Multicoloured.

593 29 c. Type **79** 40 30
594 29 c. Scarlet shrimp 40 30
595 29 c. Smooth nylon shrimp . . 40 30
596 29 c. Armed nylon shrimp . . 40 30

80 Oceanic Whitetip Shark

1993. Sharks. Multicoloured.

597 50 c. Type **80** 65 45
598 50 c. Great hammerhead shark 65 45
599 50 c. Leopard shark 65 45
600 50 c. Reef blacktip shark . . . 65 45

81 U.S.S. "Tranquility" (hospital ship) **82** Girl with Goat

1993. Pacific Theatre in Second World War (3rd issue). Multicoloured.

601 29 c. Capture of Guadalcanal 40 30
602 29 c. Type **81** 40 30
603 29 c. New Guineans drilling . 40 30
604 29 c. Americans land in New Georgia 40 30
605 29 c. U.S.S. "California" (battle ship) 40 30
606 29 c. Douglas Dauntless dive bombers over Wake Island 40 30
607 29 c. Flame-throwers on Tarawa 40 30
608 29 c. American advance on Makin 40 30
609 29 c. North American B-25 Mitchells bomb Simpson Harbour, Rabaul 40 30
610 29 c. Aerial bombardment of Kwajelein 40 30

1992. Christmas. Multicoloured.

611 29 c. Type **82** 40 30
612 29 c. Children with garlands and goats 40 30
613 29 c. Father Christmas . . . 40 30
614 29 c. Musicians and singer . . 40 30
615 29 c. Family carrying food . 40 30

83 Pterosaur

85 Flukes of Whale's Tail

84 "After Child-birth Ceremony" (Charlie Gibbons)

1993. Monsters of the Pacific. Multicoloured.

616 29 c. Type **83** 40 30
617 29 c. Outrigger canoe 40 30
618 29 c. Head of plesiosaur . . . 40 30
619 29 c. Pterosaur and neck of plesiosaur 40 30
620 29 c. Pterosaur (flying towards left) 40 30
621 29 c. Giant crab 40 30
622 29 c. Tentacles of kraken and two sharks 40 30
623 29 c. Hammerhead shark, tentacle of kraken and neck of plesiosaur 40 30
624 29 c. Head of lake serpent . . 40 30
625 29 c. Hammerhead shark and neck of serpent 40 30
626 29 c. Squid ("Kraken") . . . 40 30
627 29 c. Ray, tentacles of kraken and body of plesiosaur . . 40 30
628 29 c. Three fishes and body of plesiosaur 40 30
629 29 c. Butterfly fishes and serpent's claw 40 30
630 29 c. Octopus and body of serpent 40 30
631 29 c. Giant nautilus and body of plesiosaur 40 30
632 29 c. Striped angel fishes . . 40 30
633 29 c. Lion fish 40 30
634 29 c. Squid 40 30
635 29 c. Shark and body of kronosaur 40 30
636 29 c. Striped shark and sea-bed 40 30
637 29 c. Squid and sea-bed . . . 40 30
638 29 c. Giant nautilus and tail of serpent 40 30
639 29 c. Head of kronosaur . . . 40 30
640 29 c. Lion fish, body of kronosaur and sea-bed . . 40 30

Nos. 616/40 were issued together, se-tenant, forming a composite design.

1993. International Year of Indigenous Peoples. Multicoloured.

641 29 c. Type **84** 40 30
642 29 c. "Village in Early Palau" (Charlie Gibbons) 40 30

1993. Jonah and The Whale. Multicoloured.

644 29 c. Type **85** 40 30
645 29 c. Bird and part of fluke . . 40 30
646 29 c. Two birds 40 30
647 29 c. Kaeb (canoe) 40 30
648 29 c. Sun, birds and dolphin . 40 30
649 29 c. Shark and whale's tail . . 40 30
650 29 c. Shoal of brown fishes and part of whale 40 30
651 29 c. Hammerhead shark, shark's tail and fishes 40 30
652 29 c. Two species of fish and shark's head 40 30
653 29 c. Dolphin and fishes . . . 40 30
654 29 c. Small brown and large striped fishes and part of whale 40 30
655 29 c. Two turtles swimming across whale's body 40 30
656 29 c. Shoal of pink fishes and whale's back 40 30
657 29 c. Rays, fishes and top of whale's head 40 30
658 29 c. Two large and shoal of small brown fishes 40 30
659 29 c. Jellyfish and blue fish . . 40 30
660 29 c. Fishes and whale's dorsal fin 40 30
661 29 c. Whale's eye and corner of mouth 40 30
662 29 c. Opened mouth 40 30
663 29 c. Jonah 40 30
664 29 c. Yellow and black striped fish and corals on sea bed . 40 30
665 29 c. Three fishes and sea anenome 40 30
666 29 c. Blue-striped fish and corals on sea bed 40 30
667 29 c. Brown and red striped fish, corals and part of whale's jaw 40 30
668 29 c. Spotted fishes on sea bed 40 30

Nos. 644/68 were issued together, se-tenant, forming a composite design.

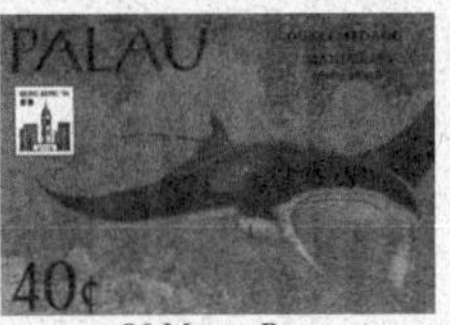

86 Manta Ray

1994. "Hong Kong '94" International Stamp Exhibition. Rays. Multicoloured.

669 40 c. Type **86** 50 35
670 40 c. Spotted eagle ray 50 35
671 40 c. Coachwhip ray 50 35
672 40 c. Black-spotted ray 50 35

87 Crocodile's Head

1994. The Estuarine Crocodile. Multicoloured.

673 20 c. Type **87** 25 15
674 20 c. Hatchling and eggs . . . 25 15
675 20 c. Crocodile swimming underwater 25 15
676 20 c. Crocodile half-submerged 25 15

88 Red-footed Booby

1994. Sea Birds. Multicoloured.

677 50 c. Type **88** 65 45
678 50 c. Great frigate bird 65 45
679 50 c. Brown booby 65 45
680 50 c. Little pied cormorant . . 65 45

89 U.S. Marines capture Kwajalein

1994. Pacific Theatre in Second World War (4th issue). Multicoloured.

681 29 c. Type **89** 35 25
682 29 c. Aerial bombardment of Japanese airbase, Truk . . . 35 25
683 29 c. U.S.S. "284 Tullibee" (Operation Desecrate) . . . 35 25
684 29 c. Landing craft storming Saipan beach 35 25
685 29 c. Shooting down Japanese Zeros, Mariana Islands . . . 35 25
686 29 c. Liberated civilians, Guam 35 25
687 29 c. U.S. troops taking Peleliu 35 25
688 29 c. Securing Angaur 35 25
689 29 c. General MacArthur . . . 35 25
690 29 c. U.S. Army memorial . . 35 25

90 Allied Warships

1994. 50th Anniv of D-day (Allied Landings in Normandy). Multicoloured.

691 50 c. C-47 transport aircraft dropping paratroopers . . . 65 45
692 50 c. Type **90** 65 45
693 50 c. Troops disembarking from landing craft 65 45
694 50 c. Tanks coming ashore . . 65 45
695 50 c. Sherman tank crossing minefield 65 45
696 50 c. Aircraft attacking German positions 65 45
697 50 c. Gliders dropping paratroops behind lines . . 65 45
698 50 c. Pegasus Bridge 65 45
699 50 c. Allied forces pushing inland 65 45
700 50 c. Beach at end of 6 June, 1944 65 45

91 Baron Pierre de Coubertin (founder of modern games)

1994. Centenary of International Olympic Committee. Multicoloured.

701 **91** 29 c. multicoloured . . . 40 30

92 Top of "Saturn V" Rocket and Command and Lunar Modules joined

93 Sailfin Goby

1994. 25th Anniv of First Manned Moon Landing. Multicoloured.

703 29 c. Type **92** 40 30
704 29 c. Lunar module preparing to land (side view) 40 30
705 29 c. Lunar module leaving surface (top view) 40 30
706 29 c. Command module (view of circular end) 40 30
707 29 c. Earth viewed from Moon 40 30
708 29 c. "Saturn V" third stage . 40 30
709 29 c. Neil Armstrong descending ladder to lunar surface . . 40 30
710 29 c. Footprint in lunar surface 40 30
711 29 c. Alan Shepard and lunar module on Moon 40 30
712 29 c. Command module separating from service module 40 30
713 29 c. "Saturn V" second stage (rocket inscr "USA USA") . 40 30
714 29 c. Rear view of "Apollo 17" astronaut at Splitrock Valley of Taurus-Littrow 40 30
715 29 c. Lunar module reflected in visor of Edwin Aldrin . . . 40 30
716 29 c. James Irwin and David Scott raising flag on "Apollo 15" mission 40 30
717 29 c. Command module descending with parachutes deployed 40 30
718 29 c. "Saturn V" lifting off from Kennedy Space Centre . . . 40 30
719 29 c. "Apollo 17" astronaut Harrison Schmitt collecting lunar surface samples with shovel 40 30
720 29 c. "Apollo 16" astronaut John Young and lunar rover vehicle 40 30
721 29 c. "Apollo 12" astronaut Charles Conrad collecting samples with machine . . . 40 30
722 29 c. Command module after splashdown 40 30

Nos. 703/22 were issued together, se-tenant, forming a composite design.

1994. "Philakorea 1994" International Stamp Exhibition, Seoul. Philatelic Fantasies. Designs showing named animal with various postal items. Multicoloured.

723 29 c. Type **93** (postage) . . . 40 30
724 29 c. Sharpnose puffers . . . 40 30
725 29 c. Lightning butterfly fish . 40 30
726 29 c. Clown anemonefish . . 40 30
727 29 c. Parrotfish 40 30
728 29 c. Batfish 40 30
729 29 c. Clown triggerfish . . . 40 30
730 29 c. Twinspot wrasse 40 30
731 40 c. Palau fruit bat 50 35
732 40 c. Crocodile 50 35
733 40 c. Dugong 50 35
734 40 c. Banded sea snake . . . 50 35

735 40 c. Bottle-nosed dolphin . . 50 35
736 40 c. Hawksbill turtle 50 35
737 40 c. Octopus 50 35
738 40 c. Manta ray 50 35
739 50 c. Palau fantail and chicks (air) 65 45
740 50 c. Banded crake 65 45
741 50 c. Grey-rumped ("Island") swiftlets 65 45
742 50 c. Micronesian kingfisher . 65 45
743 50 c. Red-footed booby . . . 65 45
744 50 c. Great frigate bird 65 45
745 50 c. Palau scops owl 65 45
746 50 c. Palau fruit dove 65 45

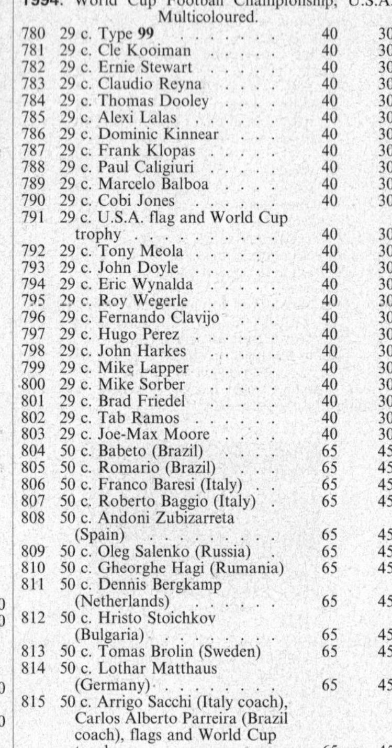

95 Micronesian Monument (Henrik Starcke), U.N. Headquarters

97 Tebruchel in Mother's Arms

96 Mickey and Minnie Mouse at Airport

1994. Attainment of Independence. Multicoloured.
748 29 c. Type **95** 40 30
749 29 c. Presidential seal 40 30
750 29 c. Pres. Kuniwo Nakamura of Palau and Pres. William Clinton of United States shaking hands (56 × 41 mm) 40 30
751 29 c. Palau and United States flags 40 30
752 29 c. Score of "Belau Er Kid" (national anthem) 40 30
Nos. 748/52 were issued together, se-tenant, forming a composite design.

1994. Tourism. Walt Disney cartoon characters. Multicoloured.
753 29 c. Type **96** 40 30
754 29 c. Goofy on way to hotel . 40 30
755 29 c. Donald Duck on beach . 40 30
756 29 c. Minnie Mouse and Daisy Duck learning Ngloik (dance) 40 30
757 29 c. Mickey and Minnie rafting to natural bridge 40 30
758 29 c. Uncle Scrooge finding stone money in Babeldaob Jungle 40 30
759 29 c. Goofy and napoleon wrasse after collision 40 30
760 29 c. Minnie visiting clam garden 40 30
761 29 c. Grandma Duck weaving basket 40 30

1994. International Year of the Family. Illustrating story of Tebruchel. Multicoloured.
763 20 c. Type **97** 25 15
764 20 c. Tebruchel's father (kneeling on beach) 25 15
765 20 c. Tebruchel as youth . . . 25 15
766 20 c. Tebruchel's wife (standing on beach) 25 15
767 20 c. Tebruchel with catch of fish 25 15
768 20 c. Tebruchel's pregnant wife sitting in house 25 15
769 20 c. Tebruchel's aged mother in dilapidated house 25 15
770 20 c. Tebruchel's aged father (standing) 25 15
771 20 c. Tebruchel holding first child 25 15
772 20 c. Tebruchel's wife (sitting on beach mat) 25 15
773 20 c. Tebruchel with aged mother 25 15
774 20 c. Tebruchel's father (sitting cross-legged) and wife holding child 25 15
Nos. 763/74 were issued together, se-tenant, forming a composite design.

98 Wise Men and Cherubs

99 Bora Milutinovic (coach)

1994. Christmas. "O Little Town of Bethlehem" (carol). Multicoloured.
775 29 c. Type **98** 40 30
776 29 c. Angel, shepherds with sheep and cherub 40 30
777 29 c. Angels and Madonna and Child 40 30
778 29 c. Angels, Bethlehem and shepherd with sheep . . . 40 30
779 29 c. Cherubs and Palau fruit doves 40 30
Nos. 775/9 were issued together, se-tenant, forming a composite design.

1994. World Cup Football Championship, U.S.A. Multicoloured.
780 29 c. Type **99** 40 30
781 29 c. Cle Kooiman 40 30
782 29 c. Ernie Stewart 40 30
783 29 c. Claudio Reyna 40 30
784 29 c. Thomas Dooley 40 30
785 29 c. Alexi Lalas 40 30
786 29 c. Dominic Kinnear 40 30
787 29 c. Frank Klopas 40 30
788 29 c. Paul Caligiuri 40 30
789 29 c. Marcelo Balboa 40 30
790 29 c. Cobi Jones 40 30
791 29 c. U.S.A. flag and World Cup trophy 40 30
792 29 c. Tony Meola 40 30
793 29 c. John Doyle 40 30
794 29 c. Eric Wynalda 40 30
795 29 c. Roy Wegerle 40 30
796 29 c. Fernando Clavijo . . . 40 30
797 29 c. Hugo Perez 40 30
798 29 c. John Harkes 40 30
799 29 c. Mike Lapper 40 30
800 29 c. Mike Sorber 40 30
801 29 c. Brad Friedel 40 30
802 29 c. Tab Ramos 40 30
803 29 c. Joe-Max Moore 40 30
804 50 c. Babeto (Brazil) 65 45
805 50 c. Romario (Brazil) . . . 65 45
806 50 c. Franco Baresi (Italy) . . 65 45
807 50 c. Roberto Baggio (Italy) . . 65 45
808 50 c. Andoni Zubizarreta (Spain) 65 45
809 50 c. Oleg Salenko (Russia) . 65 45
810 50 c. Gheorghe Hagi (Rumania) 65 45
811 50 c. Dennis Bergkamp (Netherlands) 65 45
812 50 c. Hristo Stoichkov (Bulgaria) 65 45
813 50 c. Tomas Brolin (Sweden) . 65 45
814 50 c. Lothar Matthaus (Germany) 65 45
815 50 c. Arrigo Sacchi (Italy coach), Carlos Alberto Parreira (Brazil coach), flags and World Cup trophy 65 45

100 Cube Trunkfish

101 Presley

1995. Fishes. Multicoloured.
816 1 c. Type **100** 10 10
817 2 c. Lionfish 10 10
818 3 c. Long-jawed squirrelfish . 10 10
819 4 c. Longnose filefish 10 10
820 5 c. Ornate butterfly fish . . 10 10
821 10 c. Yellow seahorse 15 10
822 20 c. Magenta dottyback (22 × 30 mm) 25 15
836 20 c. Magenta dottyback ($17\frac{1}{2}$ × 21 mm) 25 15
823 32 c. Reef lizardfish (22 × 30 mm) 40 30
837 32 c. Reef lizardfish ($17\frac{1}{2}$ × 21 mm) 40 30
824 50 c. Multi-barred goatfish . 65 45
825 55 c. Barred blenny 70 50
826 $1 Fingerprint sharpnose puffer 1·25 90
827 $2 Longnose hawkfish . . . 2·50 1·75
828 $3 Mandarinfish . . . . . 3·75 2·75
829 $5 Blue surgeonfish . . . . 6·50 4·75
830 $10 Coral grouper (47 × 30 mm) 13·00 9·75

1995. 60th Birth Anniv of Elvis Presley (entertainer). Multicoloured.
838 32 c. Type **101** 40 30
839 32 c. Presley wearing white shirt and blue jacket 40 30
840 32 c. Presley with microphone and flower 40 30
841 32 c. Presley wearing blue shirt and jumper 40 30
842 32 c. Presley with rose . . . 40 30
843 32 c. Presley with brown hair wearing white shirt 40 30
844 32 c. Presley wearing blue open-necked shirt 40 30
845 32 c. Presley (in green shirt) singing 40 30
846 32 c. Presley as boy (with fair hair) 40 30

102 "Pteranodon sternbergi"

1995. 25th Anniv of Earth Day. Prehistoric Winged Animals. Multicoloured.
847 32 c. Type **102** 40 30
848 32 c. "Pteranodon ingens" . . 40 30
849 32 c. Pterodactyls 40 30
850 32 c. Dorygnathus 40 30
851 32 c. Dimorphodon 40 30
852 32 c. Nyctosaurus 40 30
853 32 c. "Pterodactylus kochi" . . 40 30
854 32 c. Ornithodesmus 40 30
855 32 c. Diatryma 40 30
856 32 c. Archaeopteryx 40 30
857 32 c. Campylognathoides . . . 40 30
858 32 c. Gallodactylus 40 30
859 32 c. Batrachognathus 40 30
860 32 c. Scaphognathus 40 30
861 32 c. Peteinosaurus 40 30
862 32 c. Ichthyornis 40 30
863 32 c. Ctenochasma 40 30
864 32 c. Rhamphorhynchus . . . 40 30
Nos. 847/64 were issued together, se-tenant, forming a composite design.

103 Grey-rumped ("Palau") Swiftlets

1995. Air. Birds. Multicoloured.
865 50 c. Type **103** 65 45
866 50 c. Barn swallows 65 45
867 50 c. Jungle nightjar 65 45
868 50 c. White-breasted wood swallow 65 45

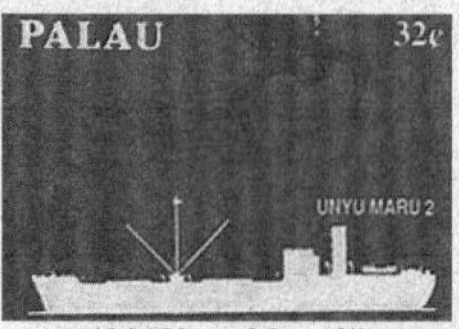

104 "Unyu Maru 2"

1995. Japanese Fleet Sunk off Rock Islands (1944). Multicoloured.
869 32 c. Type **104** 40 30
870 32 c. "Wakatake" (destroyer) . 40 30
871 32 c. "Teshio Maru" 40 30
872 32 c. "Raizan Maru" 40 30
873 32 c. "Chuyo Maru" 40 30
874 32 c. "Shinsei Maru" 40 30
875 32 c. "Urakami Maru" 40 30
876 32 c. "Ose Maru" 40 30
877 32 c. "Iro" 40 30
878 32 c. "Shosei Maru" 40 30
879 32 c. Patrol Boat 31 . . . . . 40 30
880 32 c. "Kibi Maru" 40 30
881 32 c. "Amatsu Maru" 40 30
882 32 c. "Gozan Maru" 40 30
883 32 c. "Matuei Maru" 40 30
884 32 c. "Nagisan Maru" 40 30
885 32 c. "Akashi" 40 30
886 32 c. "Kamikazi Maru" 40 30
Nos. 869/86 were issued together, se-tenant, forming a composite design.

105 Fairey Delta 2

1995. Research and Experimental Jet-propelled Aircraft. Multicoloured.
887 50 c. Type **105** 65 45
888 50 c. B-70 Valkyrie 65 45
889 50 c. Douglas X-3 Stiletto . . 65 45
890 50 c. Northrop/Nasa HL-10 . . 65 45
891 50 c. Bell XS-1 . . . . 65 45
892 50 c. Tupolev Tu-144 . . . . 65 45
893 50 c. Bell X-1 . . . . 65 45
894 50 c. Boulton Paul P.111 . . . 65 45
895 50 c. EWR VJ 101C 65 45
896 50 c. Handley Page HP-115 . . 65 45
897 50 c. Rolls Royce TMR "Flying Bedstead" 65 45
898 50 c. North American X-15 . . 65 45

106 Scuba Gear

1995. Submersibles. Multicoloured.
900 32 c. Type **106** 40 30
901 32 c. Cousteau diving saucer "Denise" 40 30
902 32 c. Jim suit 40 30
903 32 c. "Beaver IV" 40 30
904 32 c. "Ben Franklin" 40 30
905 32 c. U.S.S. "Nautilus" (submarine) 40 30
906 32 c. Deep Rover 40 30
907 32 c. Beebe bathysphere . . . 40 30
908 32 c. "Deep Star IV" 40 30
909 32 c. U.S. Navy Deep Submergence Rescue Vehicle 40 30
910 32 c. Aluminaut (aluminium submarine) 40 30
911 32 c. "Nautile" 40 30
912 32 c. "Cyana" 40 30
913 32 c. F.N.R.S. bathyscaphe . 40 30
914 32 c. Woods Hole Oceanographic Institute's "Alvin" 40 30
915 32 c. "Mir I" 40 30
916 32 c. "Archimede" 40 30
917 32 c. "Trieste" 40 30
Nos. 900/917 were issued together, se-tenant, forming a composite design.

107 Dolphins, Diver and Spiny Puffer

1995. "Singapore'95" International Stamp Exhibition. Marine Life. Multicoloured.
918 32 c. Type **107** 40 30
919 32 c. Turtle and diver 40 30
920 32 c. Fishes and crab on sea-bed (emblem on right) 40 30
921 32 c. Parrotfish, sergeant major fish and scorpion fish (emblem on left) 40 30

108 Dove in Helmet (Peace)

1995. 50th Annivs of U.N.O. and F.A.O. Mult.
922 60 c. Type **108** 80 60
923 60 c. Ibedul Gibbons (Palau chief) in flame (human rights) 80 60
924 60 c. Palau atlas in open book (education) 80 60
925 60 c. Bananas in tractor (agriculture) 80 60
Nos. 922/5 were issued together, se-tenant, the centre of each block forming a composite design of the U.N. emblem.

109 Palau Fruit Doves

1995. 1st Anniv of Independence. Each showing Palau national flag. Multicoloured.
927 20 c. Type **109** 25 15
928 20 c. Rock Islands 25 15
929 20 c. Map of Palau islands . . 25 15
930 20 c. Orchid and hibiscus . . 25 15
931 32 c. Fishes and conch shell . . 40 30

110 "Preparing Tin-Fish" (William Draper)

1995. 50th Anniv of the End of Second World War. Multicoloured.
932 32 c. Type **110** 40 30
933 32 c. "Hellcat's Take-off into Palau's Rising Sun" (Draper) 40 30
934 32 c. "Dauntless Dive Bombers over Malakal Harbor" (Draper) 40 30
935 32 c. "Planes Return from Palau" (Draper) 40 30

936 32 c. "Communion Before Battle" (Draper) 40 30
937 32 c. "The Landing" (Draper) 40 30
938 32 c. "First Task Ashore" (Draper) 40 30
939 32 c. "Fire Fighters save Flak-torn Pilot" (Draper) 40 30
940 32 c. "Young Marine Headed for Peleliu" (Tom Lea) 40 30
941 32 c. "Peleliu" (Lea) 40 30
942 32 c. "Last Rites" (Lea) . . . 40 30
943 32 c. "The Thousand Yard Stare" (Lea) 40 30
944 60 c. "Admiral Chester W. Nimitz" (Albert Murray) (vert) 80 60
945 60 c. "Admiral William F. Halsey" (Murray) (vert) . . 80 60
946 60 c. "Admiral Raymond A. Spruance" (Murray) (vert) . 80 60
947 60 c. "Vice-Admiral Marc A. Mitscher" (Murray) (vert) . . 80 60
948 60 c. "General Holland M. Smith" (Murray) (vert) . . . 80 60

111 Angel with Animals

1995. Christmas. "We Three Kings of Orient Are" (carol). Multicoloured.
950 32 c. Type **111** 40 30
951 32 c. Two wise men 40 30
952 32 c. Shepherd at crib 40 30
953 32 c. Wise man and shepherd . 40 30
954 32 c. Children with goat . . . 40 30
Nos. 950/4 were issued together, se-tenant, forming a composite design.

112 Mother and Young in Feeding Area

1995. Year of the Sea Turtle. Multicoloured.
955 32 c. Type **112** 40 30
956 32 c. Young adult females meeting males 40 30
957 32 c. Sun, cockerel in tree and mating area 40 30
958 32 c. Woman and hatchlings . 40 30
959 32 c. Couple and nesting area 40 30
960 32 c. House and female swimming to lay eggs . . . 40 30
Nos. 955/60 were issued together, se-tenant, forming a composite design of the turtle's life cycle.

113 Lennon

114 Rats leading Procession

1995. 15th Death Anniv of John Lennon (entertainer).
961 **113** 32 c. multicoloured 40 30

1996. Chinese New Year. Year of the Rat. Multicoloured.
962 10 c. Type **114** 10 10
963 10 c. Three rats playing instruments 10 10
964 10 c. Rats playing tuba and banging drum 10 10
965 10 c. Family of rats outside house 10 10
Nos. 962/5 were issued together, se-tenant, forming a composite design of a procession.

115 Girls

116 Fairy Basslet and Vermiculate Parrotfish ("P")

1996. 50th Anniv of U.N.I.C.E.F. Each showing three children. Multicoloured.
967 32 c. Type **115** 40 30
968 32 c. Girl in centre wearing lei around neck 40 30
969 32 c. Girl in centre wearing headscarf 40 30
970 32 c. Boy in centre and girls holding bunches of grass . 40 30
Nos. 967/70 were issued together, se-tenant, forming a composite design of the children around a globe and the U.N.I.C.E.F. emblem.

1996. Underwater Wonders. Illuminated letters spelling out PALAU. Multicoloured.
971 32 c. Type **116** 40 30
972 32 c. Yellow cardinalfishes ("A") 40 30
973 32 c. Pair of Merten's butterflyfish ("L") 40 30
974 32 c. Starry moray and slate-pencil sea urchin ("A") . . 40 30
975 32 c. Cleaner wrasse and coral grouper ("U") 40 30

117 Ferdinand Magellan and "Vitoria"

1996. "CAPEX'96" International Stamp Exhibition, Toronto, Canada. Circumnavigators. Multicoloured.
976 32 c. Type **117** (postage) . . 40 30
977 32 c. Charles Wilkes and U.S.S. "Vincennes" (sail frigate) . 40 30
978 32 c. Joshua Slocum and "Spray" (yacht) 40 30
979 32 c. Ben Carlin and "Half-Safe" (land and sea vehicle) . . . 40 30
980 32 c. Edward Beach and U.S.S. "Triton" (submarine) . . . 40 30
981 32 c. Naomi James and "Express Crusader" (yacht) 40 30
982 32 c. Sir Ranulf Fiennes and snow vehicle 40 30
983 32 c. Rick Hansen and wheelchair 40 30
984 32 c. Robin Knox-Johnson and "Enza New Zealand" (catamaran) 40 30
986 60 c. Lowell Smith and Douglas world cruiser seaplanes (air) 40 30
987 60 c. Ernst Lehmann and "Graf Zeppelin" (dirigible airship) 40 30
988 60 c. Wiley Post and Lockheed Vega "Winnie Mae" . . . 40 30
989 60 c. Yury Gagarin and "Vostok I" (spaceship) 40 30
990 60 c. Jerrie Mock and Cessna 180 "Spirit of Columbus" . . . 40 30
991 60 c. H. Ross Perot Jnr. and Bell Longranger III helicopter "Spirit of Texas" 40 30
992 60 c. Brooke Knapp and Gulfstream III "The American Dream" 40 30
993 60 c. Jeana Yeager and Dick Rutan and "Voyager" . . . 40 30
994 60 c. Fred Lasby and Piper Commanche 40 30

118 Simba, Nala and Timon ("The Lion King")

1996. Disney Sweethearts. Multicoloured.
995 1 c. Type **118** 10 10
996 2 c. Georgette, Tito and Oliver ("Oliver & Company") . . . 10 10
997 3 c. Duchess, O'Malley and Marie ("The Aristocats") . 10 10
998 4 c. Bianca, Jake and Polly ("The Rescuers Down Under") 10 10
999 5 c. Tod, Vixey and Copper ("The Fox and the Hound") 10 10
1000 6 c. Thumper, Flower and their Sweethearts ("Bambi") . . 10 10
1001 60 c. As No. 995 . . . . . . 75 55
1002 60 c. Bernard, Bianca and Mr. Chairman ("The Rescuers") 75 55
1003 60 c. As No. 996 . . . . . . 75 55
1004 60 c. As No. 997 . . . . . . 75 55
1005 60 c. As No. 998 . . . . . . 75 55
1006 60 c. As No. 999 . . . . . . 75 55
1007 60 c. Robin Hood, Maid Marian and Alan-a-Dale ("Robin Hood") 75 55
1008 60 c. As No. 1000 . . . . . . 75 55
1009 60 c. Pongo, Perdita and the Puppies ("101 Dalmatians") 75 55

119 Hakeem Olajuwan (basketball)

1996. Centenary of Modern Olympic Games and Olympic Games, Atlanta. Multicoloured.
1011 32 c. Type **119** 40 30
1012 32 c. Pat McCormick (gymnastics) 40 30
1013 32 c. Jim Thorpe (pentathlon and decathlon) 40 30
1014 32 c. Jesse Owens (athletics) . 40 30
1015 32 c. Tatyana Gutsu (gymnastics) 40 30
1016 32 c. Michael Jordan (basketball) 40 30
1017 32 c. Fu Mingxia (diving) . . 40 30
1018 32 c. Robert Zmelik (decathlon) 40 30
1019 32 c. Ivan Pedroso (long jumping) 40 30
1020 32 c. Nadia Comaneci (gymnastics) 40 30
1021 32 c. Jackie Joyner-Kersee (long jumping) 40 30
1022 32 c. Michael Johnson (running) 40 30
1023 32 c. Kristin Otto (swimming) 40 30
1024 32 c. Vitai Scherbo (gymnastics) 40 30
1025 32 c. Johnny Weissmuller (swimming) 40 30
1026 32 c. Babe Didrikson (track and field athlete) 40 30
1027 32 c. Eddie Tolan (track athlete) 40 30
1028 32 c. Krisztina Egerszegi (swimming) 40 30
1029 32 c. Sawao Kato (gymnastics) 40 30
1030 32 c. Aleksandr Popov (swimming) 40 30
1031 40 c. Fanny Blankers-Koen (track and field athlete) (vert) 40 30
1032 40 c. Bob Mathias (decathlon) (vert) 40 30
1033 60 c. Torchbearer entering Wembley Stadium, 1948 . . 40 30
1034 60 c. Entrance to Olympia Stadium, Athens, and flags 40 30
Nos. 1011/30 were issued together, se-tenant, forming a composite design of the athletes and olympic rings.

120 The Creation

1996. 3000th Anniv of Jerusalem. Illustrations by Guy Rowe from "In Our Image: Character Studies from the Old Testament". Mult..
1035 20 c. Type **120** 25 15
1036 20 c. Adam and Eve 25 15
1037 20 c. Noah and his Wife . . . 25 15
1038 20 c. Abraham 25 15
1039 20 c. Jacob's Blessing 25 15
1040 20 c. Jacob becomes Israel . . 25 15
1041 20 c. Joseph and his Brethren 25 15
1042 20 c. Moses & Burning Bush . 25 15
1043 20 c. Moses and the Tablets . 25 15
1044 20 c. Balaam 25 15
1045 20 c. Joshua 25 15
1046 20 c. Gideon 25 15
1047 20 c. Jephthah 25 15
1048 20 c. Samson 25 15
1049 20 c. Ruth and Naomi . . . 25 15
1050 20 c. Saul anointed 25 15
1051 20 c. Saul denounced 25 15
1052 20 c. David and Jonathan . . 25 15
1053 20 c. David and Nathan . . . 25 15
1054 20 c. David mourns 25 15
1055 20 c. Solomon praying . . . 25 15
1056 20 c. Solomon judging 25 15
1057 20 c. Elijah 25 15
1058 20 c. Elisha 25 15
1059 20 c. Job 25 15
1060 20 c. Isaiah 25 15
1061 20 c. Jeremiah 25 15
1062 20 c. Ezekiel 25 15
1063 20 c. Nebuchadnezzar's Dream 25 15
1064 20 c. Amos 25 15

121 Rufous Night Heron

1996. Birds over Palau Lagoon. Multicoloured.
1065 50 c. Eclectus parrot (female) ("Iakkotsiang") 60 45
1066 50 c. Type **121** 60 45
1067 50 c. Micronesian pigeon ("Belochel") 60 45
1068 50 c. Eclectus parrot (male) ("Iakkotsiang") 60 45
1069 50 c. White tern ("Sechosech") 60 45
1070 50 c. Common noddy ("Mechadelbedaoch") . . . 60 45
1071 50 c. Nicobar pigeon ("Laib") 60 45
1072 50 c. Chinese little bittern ("Cheloteachel") 60 45
1073 50 c. Little pied cormorant ("Deroech") 60 45
1074 50 c. Black-naped tern ("Kerkirs") 60 45
1075 50 c. White-tailed tropic bird ("Dudek") 60 45
1076 50 c. Sulphur-crested cockatoo ("Iakkotsiang") (white bird) 60 45
1077 50 c. White-capped noddy ("Bedaoch") 60 45
1078 50 c. Bridled tern ("Bedebedchakl") 60 45
1079 50 c. Eastern reef heron (grey) ("Sechou") 60 45
1080 50 c. Grey-rumped sandpiper ("Kekereielderariik") . . . 60 45
1081 50 c. Eastern reef heron (white) ("Sechou") 60 45
1082 50 c. Audubon's shearwater ("Ochaieu") 60 45
1083 50 c. Black-headed gull ("Oltirakladial") 60 45
1084 50 c. Turnstone ("Omechederiibabad") . . 60 45
Nos. 1065/84 were issued together, se-tenant, forming a composite design.

122 Lockheed U-2

1996. Spy Planes. Multicoloured.
1085 40 c. Type **122** 50 35
1086 40 c. General Dynamics EF-111A 50 35
1087 40 c. Lockheed YF-12A . . . 50 35
1088 40 c. Lockheed SR-71 . . . 50 35
1089 40 c. Teledyne Ryan Tier II Plus 50 35
1090 40 c. Lockheed XST 50 35
1091 40 c. Lockheed ER-2 . . . . 50 35
1092 40 c. Lockheed F-117A Nighthawk 50 35
1093 40 c. Lockheed EC-130E . . 50 35
1094 40 c. Ryan Firebee 50 35
1095 40 c. Lockheed Martin/Boeing Darkstar 50 35
1096 40 c. Boeing E-3A Sentry . . 50 35

123 "In the Blue Shade of Trees"

1996. 2nd Anniv of Independence. Illustrations from "Kirie" by Koh Sekiguchi. Multicoloured.
1098 20 c. Type **123** 25 15
1099 20 c. "The Birth of a New Nation" 25 15

124 Pandanus

1996. Christmas. "O Tannenbaum" (carol). Decorated Trees. Multicoloured.
1100 32 c. Type **124** 40 30
1101 32 c. Mangrove 40 30
1102 32 c. Norfolk Island pine . . 40 30
1103 32 c. Papaya 40 30
1104 32 c. Casuarina 40 30
Nos. 1100/4 were issued together, se-tenant, forming a composite design.

125 "Viking I" in Orbit ($\frac{1}{2}$-size illustration)

1996. Space Missions to Mars. Multicoloured.
1105 32 c. Type **125** 40 30
1106 32 c. "Viking I" emblem (top half) 40 30
1107 32 c. "Mars Lander" firing de-orbit engines 40 30
1108 32 c. "Viking I" emblem (bottom half) 40 30
1109 32 c. Phobos (Martian moon) 40 30
1110 32 c. "Mars Lander" entering Martian atmosphere . . . 40 30
1111 32 c. "Mariner 9" (first mission, 1971) 40 30
1112 32 c. Parachute opens for landing and heat shield jettisons 40 30
1113 32 c. Projected U.S./Russian manned spacecraft, 21st century (top half) 40 30
1114 32 c. "Lander" descent engines firing 40 30
1115 32 c. Projected U.S./Russian spacecraft (bottom half) . . 40 30
1116 32 c. "Viking I Lander" on Martian surface, 1976 . . . 40 30
Nos. 1105/16 were issued together, se-tenant, forming several composite designs.

126 Northrop XB-35 Bomber

1996. Oddities of the Air. Aircraft Designs. Multicoloured.
1118 60 c. Type **126** 75 55
1119 60 c. Leduc O.21 . . . . . . 75 55
1120 60 c. Convair Model 118 flying car 75 55
1121 60 c. Blohm und Voss BV 141 75 55
1122 60 c. Vought V-173 . . . . . 75 55
1123 60 c. McDonnell XF-85 Goblin 75 55
1124 60 c. North American F-82B Twin Mustang fighter . . . 75 55
1125 60 c. Lockheed XFV-1 vertical take-off fighter 75 55
1126 60 c. Northrop XP-79B . . . 75 55
1127 60 c. Saunders Roe SR/A1 flying boat fighter 75 55
1128 60 c. "Caspian Sea Monster" hovercraft 75 55
1129 60 c. Grumman X-29 demonstrator 75 55

PANAMA Pt. 15

Country situated on the C. American isthmus. Formerly a State or Department of Colombia, Panama was proclaimed an independent republic in 1903.

1878. 100 centavos = 1 peso.
1906. 100 centesimos = 1 balboa.

1 Coat of Arms **3** Map

1878. Imperf. The 50 c. is larger.
1 **1** 5 c. green . . . . 15·00 13·50
2 10 c. blue . . . . 38·00 35·00
3 20 c. red . . . . 24·00 21·00
4 50 c. yellow . . . . 9·75

1887. Perf.
5 **3** 1 c. black on green 50 65
6 2 c. black on pink . . . . 1·25 1·00
7 5 c. black on blue 90 35
7a 5 c. black on grey . . . . 1·50 45
8 10 c. black on yellow . . . 90 45
9 20 c. black on lilac . . . 90 45
10 50 c. brown . . . . 1·50 75

5 Map of Panama **38**

1892.
12a **5** 1 c. green 15 15
12b 2 c. red 20 20
12c 5 c. blue 90 45
12d 10 c. orange 20 20
12e 20 c. violet 25 25
12f 50 c. brown 30 25
12g 1 p. lake . . . . 3·75 2·40

1894. Surch **HABILITADO 1894** and value.
13 **5** 1 c. on 2 c. red 35 35
15 **3** 5 c. on 20 c. black on lilac . 1·50 1·00
18 10 c. on 50 c. brown . . . . 1·90 1·90

1903. Optd **REPUBLICA DE PANAMA**.
70 **5** 1 c. green . . . . 1·25 75
36 2 c. red 55 55
37 5 c. blue . . . . 1·25 55
38 10 c. orange . . . . 1·25 1·25
39 20 c. violet . . . . 2·40 2·40
75 **3** 50 c. brown . . . . 14·00 14·00
40 **5** 50 c. brown . . . . 6·00 4·25
41 1 p. lake . . . . 29·00 24·00

1903. Optd **PANAMA** twice.
53 **5** 1 c. green 25 25
54 2 c. red 25 25
55 5 c. blue 30 30
56 10 c. orange 30 30
64 20 c. violet 90 90
65 50 c. brown . . . . 1·50 1·50
66 1 p. lake . . . . 3·50 2·75

1904. Optd **Republica de Panama**.
94 **5** 1 c. green 35 35
97 2 c. red 45 45
98 5 c. blue 45 45
99 10 c. orange 45 45
100 20 c. violet 45 45
103 **3** 50 c. brown . . . . 1·75 1·75
104 **5** 1 p. lake . . . . 9·50 8·25

1905.
151 **38** $\frac{1}{2}$ c. orange 55 45
136 1 c. green 55 40
137 2 c. red 70 55

1906. Surch **PANAMA** twice and new value and thick bar.
138 **5** 1 c. on 20 c. violet 25 25
139 2 c. on 50 c. brown 25 25
140 5 c. on 1 p. lake 55 45

41 Panamanian Flag **42** Vasco Nunez de Balboa

43 F. de Cordoba **44** Arms of Panama

45 J. Arosemena **46** M. J. Hurtado **47** J. de Obaldia

1906.
142 **41** $\frac{1}{2}$ c. multicoloured 40 35
143 **42** 1 c. black and green 40 35
144 **43** 2 c. black and red 55 35
145 **44** $2\frac{1}{2}$ c. red 55 35
146 **45** 5 c. black and blue . . . . 1·00 35
147 **46** 8 c. black and purple . . . 55 40
148 **47** 10 c. black and violet . . . 55 35
149 – 25 c. black and brown . . . 1·50 60
150 – 50 c. black . . . . 3·75 2·10
DESIGNS: 25 c. Tomas Herrera; 50 c. Jose de Fabrega.

48 Balboa **49** De Cordoba **50** Arms

51 Arosemena **52** Hurtado **53** Obaldia

1909.
152 **48** 1 c. black and green 65 50
153 **49** 2 c. black and red 65 30
154 **50** $2\frac{1}{2}$ c. red 90 30
155 **51** 5 c. black and blue . . . . 1·10 30
156 **52** 8 c. black and purple . . . 4·25 2·50
157 **53** 10 c. black and purple . . . 2·10 1·10

56 Balboa viewing Pacific Ocean **57** Balboa reaches the Pacific

1913. 400th Anniv of Discovery of Pacific Ocean.
160 **56** $2\frac{1}{2}$ c. yellow and green . . . 45 40

1915. Panama Exhibition and Opening of Canal.
161 – $\frac{1}{2}$ c. black and olive 45 35
162 – 1 c. black and green 55 35
163 **57** 2 c. black and red 65 35
164 – $2\frac{1}{2}$ c. black and red 65 35
165 – 3 c. black and violet . . . . 1·00 35
166 – 5 c. black and blue . . . . 1·50 50
167 – 10 c. black and orange . . . 1·50 50
168 – 20 c. black and brown . . . 7·25 2·40
DESIGNS: $\frac{1}{2}$ c. Chorrera Falls; 1 c. Relief Map of Panama Canal; $2\frac{1}{2}$ c. Cathedral Ruins, Old Panama; 3 c. Palace of Arts, National Exhibition; 5 c. Gatun Locks; 10 c. Culebra Cut; 20 c. Archway, S. Domingo Monastery.

62 Balboa Docks

1918. Views on Panama Canal.
178 – 12 c. black and violet . . . 17·00 5·50
179 – 15 c. black and blue . . . 10·00 2·75
180 – 24 c. black and brown . . . 24·00 7·50
181 **62** 50 c. black and orange . . . 25·00 16·00
182 – 1 b. black and violet . . . 35·00 19·00
DESIGNS: 12 c. "Panama" (cargo liner) in Gaillard Cut, north; 15 c. "Panama" in Gaillard Cut, south; 24 c. "Cristobal" (cargo liner) in Gatun Lock; 1 b. "Nereus" (U.S. Navy collier) in San Pedro Miguel Locks.

1919. 400th Anniv of Founding of City of Panama. No. 164 surch **1519 1919 2 CENTESIMOS 2**.
183 2 c. on $2\frac{1}{2}$ c. black and red . . . 45 45

MINIMUM PRICE

The minimum price quoted is 10p which represents a handling charge rather than a basis for valuing common stamps. For further notes about prices, see introductory pages.

64 Arms of Panama **65** Vallarino

68 Bolivar's Speech **70** Hurtado

1921. Independence Cent. Dated "1821 1921".
184 **64** $\frac{1}{2}$ c. orange 55 30
185 **65** 1 c. green 55 25
186 – 2 c. red ("Land Gate", Panama City) 70 30
187 **65** $2\frac{1}{2}$ c. (Bolivar) 95 75
188 – 3 c. violet (Cervantes statue) 95 75
189 **68** 5 c. blue 90 45
190 **65** 8 c. olive (Carlos Ycaza) . 3·50 2·10
191 – 10 c. violet (Government House 1821-1921) . . . 2·40 85
192 – 15 c. blue (Balboa statue) . 3·00 1·25
193 – 20 c. brown (Los Santos Church) . . . . 5·00 2·40
194 **65** 24 c. sepia (Herrera) . . . 5·00 3·00
195 – 50 c. black (Fabrega) . . . 8·75 4·50

1921. Birth Centenary of Manuel Jose Hurtado (writer).
196 **70** 2 c. green 55 35

1923. No. 164 surch **1923 2 CENTESIMOS 2**.
197 2 c. on $2\frac{1}{2}$ c. black and red . . 35 35

72 **73** Simon Bolivar

74 Statue of Bolivar **75** Congress Hall, Panama

1924.
198 **72** $\frac{1}{2}$ c. orange 20 10
199 1 c. green 20 10
200 2 c. red 25 10
201 5 c. blue 35 15
202 10 c. violet 40 20
203 12 c. olive 45 45
204 15 c. blue 55 45
205 24 c. brown . . . . 2·25 65
206 50 c. orange . . . . 3·75 90
207 1 b. black . . . . 5·50 2·25

1926. Bolivar Congress.
208 **73** $\frac{1}{2}$ c. orange 35 15
209 1 c. green 35 15
210 2 c. red 40 25
211 4 c. grey 40 25
212 5 c. blue 65 40
213 **74** 8 c. purple 75 65
214 10 c. violet 60 60
215 12 c. olive 90 90
216 15 c. blue . . . . 1·25 1·10
217 20 c. brown . . . . 2·40 1·25
218 **75** 24 c. slate . . . . 3·00 1·50
219 50 c. black . . . . 7·00 3·50

78 "Spirit of St. Louis" over Map

1928. Lindbergh's Flying Tour.
222 – 2 c. red on rose 55 35
223 **78** 5 c. blue on green 75 55
DESIGN—VERT: 2 c. "Spirit of St. Louis" over Old Panama with opt **HOMENAJE A LINDBERGH**.

1928. 25th Anniv of Independence. Optd **1903. NOV 3 BRE 1928**.
224 **70** 2 c. green 30 20

1929. Air. No. E226 surch with Fokker Universal airplane and **CORREO AEREO 25 25 VEINTICINCO CENTESIMOS**.
225 E **81** 25 c. on 10 c. orange . . 1·10 90

1929. Air. Nos. E226/7 optd **CORREO AEREO** or additionally surch with new value in **CENTESIMOS**.
238 E **81** 5 c. on 10 c. orange . . . 55 55
228 10 c. orange 55 55
268 10 c. on 20 c. brown . . 90 55
229 15 c. on 10 c. orange . . 55 55
269 20 c. brown 90 55
230 25 c. on 20 c. brown . . 1·25 1·10

83 87

1930. Air.
231 **83** 5 c. blue 20 10
232 5 c. orange 35 10
233 7 c. red 35 10
234 8 c. black 35 10
235 15 c. green 45 10
236 20 c. red 50 10
237 25 c. blue 55 55

1930. No. 182 optd with airplane and **CORREO AEREO**.
239 1 b. black and violet . . . . 18·00 14·00

1930. Air.
244 **87** 5 c. blue 20 10
245 10 c. orange 35 25
246 30 c. violet . . . . 6·75 4·00
247 50 c. red . . . . 1·25 35
248 1 b. black . . . . 6·75 4·25

1930. Bolivar's Death Cent. Surch **1830-1930 17 DE DICIEMBRE UN CENTESIMO**.
249 **73** 1 c. on 4 c. grey 25 20

89 Seaplane over old Panama **92** Manuel Amador Guerrero

1931. Air. Opening of service between Panama City and western provinces.
250 **89** 5 c. blue . . . . 1·00 90

1932. Optd **HABILITADA** or surch also.
251 **64** ½ c. orange (postage) . . . 35 20
252 **73** ½ c. orange 20 20
253 1 c. green 25 20
270 **68** 1 c. on 5 c. blue 45 35
254 **73** 2 c. red 20 20
255 5 c. blue 45 30
256 – 10 c. violet (No. 191) . . . 70 35
258 **74** 10 c. on 12 c. olive 75 40
259 10 c. on 15 c. blue 70 35
257 20 c. brown . . . . 1·00 1·10
260 **83** 20 c. on 25 c. blue (air) . . 4·00 55

1932. Birth Centenary of Dr. Guerrero (first president of republic).
261 **92** 2 c. red 45 20

95 National Institute

1934. 25th Anniv of National Institute.
262 – 1 c. green 55 55
263 – 2 c. red 55 55
264 – 5 c. blue 75 60
265 **95** 10 c. brown . . . . 2·10 1·00
266 – 12 c. green . . . . 3·50 1·50
267 – 15 c. blue . . . . 4·75 1·75
DESIGNS—VERT: 1 c. J. D. de Obaldia; 2 c. E. A. Morales; 5 c. Sphinx and Quotation from Emerson. HORIZ: 12 c. J. A. Facio; 15 c. P. Arosemena.

(98)

100 Urraca Monument

99 Custom House Ruins, Portobelo

1936. Birth Cent of Pablo Arosemena. (a) Postage. Surch as T **98**, but without **CORREO AEREO**.
271 **72** 2 c. on 24 c. brown . . . 55 45

(b) Air. Surch with T **98**.
272 **72** 5 c. on 50 c. orange . . . 60 50

1936. 4th Spanish-American Postal Congress (1st issue). Inscr "IV CONGRESO POSTAL AMERICO–ESPANOL".
273 **99** ½ c. orange (postage) . . . 40 25
274 – 1 c. green 40 25
275 – 2 c. red 40 25
276 – 5 c. blue 45 30
277 – 10 c. violet 75 45
278 – 15 c. blue 75 60
279 – 20 c. red . . . . 95 1·00
280 – 25 c. brown . . . . 1·50 1·40
281 – 50 c. orange . . . . 8·00 2·75
282 – 1 b. black . . . . 9·00 7·00
DESIGNS: 1 c. "Panama" (Old tree); 2 c. "La Pollera" (woman in costume); 5 c. Bolivar; 10 c. Ruins of Old Panama Cathedral; 15 c. Garcia y Santos; 20 c. Madden Dam; 25 c. Columbus;. 50 c. "Resolute" (liner) in Gaillard Cut; 1 b. Panama Cathedral.

283 **100** 5 c. blue (air) 70 40
284 – 10 c. orange 90 65
285 – 20 c. red . . . . 1·25 1·00
286 – 30 c. violet . . . . 2·10 1·90
287 – 50 c. red . . . . 22·00 15·00
288 – 1 b. black . . . . 9·00 6·50
DESIGNS—HORIZ: 10 c. "Man's Genius Uniting the Oceans"; 20 c. Panama; 50 c. San Pedro Miguel Locks; 1 b. Courts of Justice. VERT: 10 c. Balboa Monument.

1937. 4th Spanish-American Postal Congress (2nd issue). Nos. 273/88 optd **UPU**.
289 **99** ½ c. orange (postage) . . . 35 20
290 – 1 c. green 45 20
291 – 2 c. red 45 20
292 – 5 c. blue 45 30
293 – 10 c. violet 75 45
294 – 15 c. blue . . . . 4·75 2·40
295 – 20 c. red . . . . 1·10 1·10
296 – 25 c. brown . . . . 1·75 90
297 – 50 c. orange . . . . 7·00 4·25
298 – 1 b. black . . . . 8·75 7·50

299 **99** 5 c. blue (air) 45 45
300 – 10 c. orange 70 55
301 – 20 c. red 95 75
302 – 30 c. violet . . . . 3·50 2·40
303 – 50 c. red . . . . 18·00 18·00
304 – 1 b. black . . . . 11·50 9·50

1937. Optd **1937-38**.
305 **73** ½ c. orange 50 45
306 **65** 1 c. green 30 25
307 **73** 1 c. green 30 25
308 **70** 2 c. green 35 25
309 **73** 2 c. red 35 30

1937. Surch **1937-38** and value.
310 **73** 2 c. on 4 c. grey 45 30
311 **78** 2 c. on 8 c. olive 45 30
312 **74** 2 c. on 8 c. purple 45 30
313 2 c. on 10 c. violet 45 30
314 2 c. on 12 c. olive 45 30
315 – 2 c. on 15 c. (No. 192) . . 45 30
316 **65** 2 c. on 24 c. sepia 45 30
317 2 c. on 50 c. black 45 30

1937. Air. Optd **CORREO AEREO** or surch also.
318 **73** 5 c. blue 45 45
319 **74** 5 c. on 15 c. blue 45 45
320 5 c. on 20 c. brown 45 45
321 **75** 5 c. on 24 c. slate 45 45
322 **62** 5 c. on 1 b. black & violet 2·50 1·25
323 – 10 c. on 10 c. violet (191) . 1·40 90
324 **75** 10 c. on 50 c. black . . . 1·40 90

105 Fire-Engine

106 Firemen's Monument **107** Fire-Brigade Badge

1937. 50th Anniv of Fire Brigade.
325 – ½ c. orange (postage) . . 45 25
326 – 1 c. green 45 25
327 – 2 c. red 45 30
328 **105** 5 c. blue 65 30
329 **106** 10 c. violet . . . . 1·10 65
330 – 12 c. green . . . . 1·50 1·10
331 **107** 5 c. blue (air) 55 35
332 – 10 c. orange 70 45
333 – 20 c. red 90 55
DESIGNS—VERT: ½ c. R. Arango; 1 c. J. A. Guizado; 10 c. (No. 332), F. Arosemena; 12 c. D. H. Brandon; 20 c. J. G. Duque. HORIZ: 2 c. House on fire.

108 Basketball Player **111** Old Panama Cathedral and Statue of Liberty

1938. Air. C. American and Caribbean Olympic Games.
334 **108** 1 c. red 80 30
335 – 2 c. green (Baseball player) 80 15
336 – 7 c. grey (Swimmer) . . . 1·10 35
337 – 8 c. brown (Boxers) . . . 1·10 35
338 – 15 c. blue (Footballer) . . 2·60 1·10
The 1 c. and 15 c. are vert, the rest horiz.

1938. Opening of Aguadulce Normal School, Santiago. Optd **NORMAL DE SANTIAGO JUNIO 5 1938** or surch also.
340 **72** 2 c. red (postage) 30 25
341 **87** 7 c. on 30 c. violet (air) . . 45 45
342 **83** 8 c. on 15 c. green 45 45

1938. 150th Anniv of U.S. Constitution. Flags in red, white and blue.
343 **111** 1 c. black & green (post) . 45 20
344 2 c. black and red 55 25
345 5 c. black and blue 60 45
346 12 c. black and olive . . . 1·10 65
347 15 c. black and blue . . . 1·40 75

348 7 c. black and grey (air) . 50 30
349 8 c. black and blue 70 30
350 15 c. black and brown . . 90 70
351 50 c. black and orange . . 12·00 9·00
352 1 b. black . . . . 12·00 9·00
Nos. 343/7 are without the Douglas DC-3 airliner.

112 Pierre and Marie Curie **113** Gatun Lock

1939. Obligatory Tax. Cancer Research Fund. Dated "1939".
353 **112** 1 c. red 55 15
354 1 c. green 55 15
355 1 c. orange 55 15
356 1 c. blue 55 15

1939. 25th Anniv of Opening of Panama Canal.
357 **113** ½ c. yellow (postage) . . . 1·25 1·25
358 – 1 c. green . . . . 1·50 1·50
359 – 2 c. red 55 15
360 – 5 c. blue . . . . 1·50 20
361 – 10 c. violet . . . . 2·00 50
362 – 12 c. olive 75 55
363 – 15 c. blue 75 70
364 – 50 c. orange . . . . 1·75 1·25
365 – 1 b. brown . . . . 3·50 2·25
DESIGNS: 1 c. "Santa Elena" (liner) in Pedro Miguel Locks; 2 c. Allegory of canal construction; 5 c. "Rangitata" (liner) in Culebra Cut; 10 c. Panama canal ferry; 12 c. Aerial view; 15 c. Gen. Gorgas; 50 c. M. A. Guerrero; 1 b. Woodrow Wilson.

366 – 1 c. red (air) 35 10
367 – 2 c. green 35 15
368 – 5 c. blue 55 20
369 – 10 c. violet 70 25
370 – 15 c. blue 95 35
371 – 20 c. red . . . . 2·50 95
372 – 50 c. brown . . . . 3·00 90
373 – 1 b. black . . . . 6·00 4·00
PORTRAITS: 1 c. B. Porras; 2 c. Wm. H. Taft; 5 c. P. J. Sosa; 10 c. L. B. Wise; 15 c. A. Reclus; 20 c. Gen. Goethals; 50 c. F. de Lesseps; 1 b. Theodore Roosevelt.

115 Flags of American Republics **120a** "Liberty"

1940. Air. 50th Anniv of Pan-American Union.
374 **115** 15 c. blue 45 30

1940. Air. No. 370 surch **55**.
375 5 c. on 15 c. blue 25 25

No. 363 surch **AEREO SIETE**.
376 7 c. on 15 c. blue 40 30

No. 371 surch **SIETE**.
377 7 c. on 20 c. red 40 30

No. 374 surch **8–8**.
378 **115** 8 c. on 15 c. blue 40 30

1941. Obligatory Tax. Cancer Research Fund. Optd **LUCHA CONTRA EL CANCER**.
379 **72** 1 c. green . . . . 1·40 1·10

1941. Enactment of New Constitution (a) Postage. Optd **CONSTITUCION 1941**.
380 **72** ½ c. orange 35 20
381 1 c. green 35 20
382 2 c. red 35 25
383 5 c. blue 45 20
384 10 c. violet 65 45
385 15 c. blue . . . . 1·00 65
386 50 c. orange . . . . 5·50 2·50
387 1 b. black . . . . 13·00 4·50
(b) Air. Surch **CONSTITUCION 1941 AEREO** and value in figures.
388 E **81** 7 c. on 10 c. orange . . 65 65
389 **72** 15 c. on 24 c. brown . . 2·25 1·50

(c) Air. Optd **CONSTITUCION 1941**.
390 **83** 20 c. red . . . . 3·25 2·25
391 **87** 50 c. red . . . . 7·50 4·25
392 1 b. black . . . . 17·00 9·00

1941. Obligatory Tax. Cancer Research Fund. Dated "1940".
393 **112** 1 c. red 45 10
394 1 c. green 45 10
395 1 c. orange 45 10
396 1 c. blue 45 10

1942. Telegraph stamps as T **120a** optd or surch. (a) Optd **CORREOS 1942** and (No. 397) surch **2c**.
397 2 c. on 5 c. blue 70 55
398 10 c. violet 90 70

(b) Air. Optd **CORREO AEREO 1942**.
399 20 c. brown . . . . 1·75 1·50

123 Flags of Panama and Costa Rica

1942. 1st Anniv of Revised Frontier Agreement between Panama and Costa Rica.
400 **123** 2 c. red (postage) 30 25
401 15 c. green (air) 60 15

1942. Obligatory Tax. Cancer Research Fund. Dated "1942".
402 **112** 1 c. violet 45 15

127 Balboa reaches Pacific

129 J. D. Arosemena Normal School **131** A. G. Melendez

1942. (a) Postage stamps.
403 – ½ c. red, blue and violet . 10 10
404 – ½ c. blue, orange and red . 15 10
405 – 1 c. green 10 10
406 – 1 c. red 10 10
407 – 2 c. red ("ACARRERO") . . 20 10
408 – 2 c. red ("ACARREO") . . 45 10
409 – 2 c. black and red 15 10
410 **127** 5 c. black and blue . . . 20 10
411 – 5 c. blue 30 10
412 – 10 c. orange and red . . . 45 20
413 – 10 c. orange and purple . . 35 20
414 – 15 c. black and blue . . . 35 55
415 – 15 c. black 35 20
416 – 50 c. black and red . . . 85 60
417 – 1 b. black . . . . 1·75 70
DESIGNS—VERT: ½ c. National flag; 1 c. Farm girl; 10 c. Golden Altar, Church of St. Jose; 50 c. San Blas Indian woman and child. HORIZ: 2 c. Oxen drawing sugar cart; 15 c. St. Thomas's Hospital; 1 b. National highway.

(b) Air.
418 – 2 c. red 45 10
419 – 7 c. red 55 20
420 – 8 c. black and brown . . . 20 10
421 – 10 c. black and blue . . . 20 15
422 – 15 c. violet 30 10
423 – 15 c. grey 35 15
424 **129** 20 c. brown 35 10
425 20 c. green 35 20

426 – 50 c. green . . . . 1·25 45
427 – 50 c. red . . . . 3·50 2·60
428 – 50 c. blue 60 40
429 – 1 b. orange, yellow & black 1·40 65
DESIGNS—HORIZ: 2 c., 7 c. Sword-fish; 8 c., 10 c. Gate of Glory, Portobelo; 15 c. Taboga Is; 50 c. Fire Brigade H.Q., Panama City; 1 b. Idol (Golden Beast).

1943. Obligatory Tax. Cancer Research Fund. Dated "1943".
433 **112** 1 c. green 45 15
434 1 c. red 45 15
435 1 c. orange 45 15
436 1 c. blue 45 15

1943. Air.
437 **131** 3 b. grey . . . . 5·50 5·50
438 – 5 b. blue (T. Lefevre) . . 8·50 7·00

1945. Obligatory Tax. Cancer Research Fund. Dated "1945".
439 **112** 1 c. red 45 20
440 1 c. green 45 20
441 1 c. orange 45 20
442 1 c. blue 45 20

1946. Obligatory Tax. Cancer Research Fund. Surch **CANCER B/.0.01 1947**.
443 **72** 1 c. on ½ c. orange 55 15
444 1 c. on 1 c. green 55 15
445 – 1 c. on ½ c. red, blue and violet (No. 403) 45 10
446 **72** 1 c. on 12 c. olive 45 15
447 1 c. on 24 c. brown 45 15

1947. Air. Surch **AEREO 1947** and value.
448 – 5 c. on 7 c. red (No. 419) . 20 20
449 **83** 5 c. on 8 c. black 20 20
450 – 5 c. on 8 c. black and brown (No. 420) 20 20
451 **83** 10 c. on 15 c. green 55 35
452 – 10 c. on 15 c. violet (422) . 30 25

134 Flag of Panama
135 National Theatre

1947. 2nd Anniv of National Constitutional Assembly.
453 **134** 2 c. red, deep red and blue (postage) 15 10
454 – 5 c. blue 20 20
455 **135** 8 c. violet (air) 45 30
DESIGN—As Type **134**: 5 c. Arms of Panama.

1947. Cancer Research Fund. Dated "1947".
456 **112** 1 c. red 45 10
457 1 c. green 45 10
458 1 c. orange 45 10
459 1 c. blue 45 10

1947. Surch **HABILITADA CORREOS** and value.
460 **83** ½ c. on 8 c. black 10 10
461 – ½ c. on 8 c. black and brown (No. 420) 10 10
462 – 1 c. on 7 c. red (No. 419) . 15 15
463 **135** 2 c. on 8 c. violet 20 15

1947. Surch **Habilitada CORREOS B/.0.50**.
464 **72** 50 c. on 24 c. brown . . . 65 65

138 J. A. Arango
140 Firemen's Monument

1948. Air. Honouring members of the Revolutionary Junta of 1903.
465 – 3 c. black and blue . . . 35 25
466 **138** 5 c. black and brown . . 35 25
467 – 10 c. black and orange . . 35 25
468 – 15 c. black and red . . . 35 55
469 – 20 c. black and red . . . 40 40
470 – 50 c. black . . . . 1·75 70
471 – 1 b. black and green . . . 3·00 2·75
472 – 2 b. black and yellow . . . 7·00 6·00
PORTRAITS—HORIZ: 3 c. M. A. Guerrero; 10 c. F. Boyd; 15 c. R. Arias. VERT: 20 c. M. Espinosa; 50 c. C. C. Arosemena (engineer); 1 b. N. de Obarrio; 2 b. T. Arias.

1948. 50th Anniv of Colon Fire Brigade.
473 **140** 5 c. black and red 20 15
474 – 10 c. black and orange . . 35 20
475 – 20 c. black and blue . . . 70 40
476 – 25 c. black and brown . . 70 55
477 – 50 c. black and violet . . 90 55
478 – 1 b. black and green . . . 1·50 90
DESIGNS—HORIZ: 10 c. Fire engine; 20 c. Fire hose; 25 c. Fire Brigade Headquarters. VERT: 50 c. Commander Walker; 1 b. First Fire-Brigade Commander.

142 F. D. Roosevelt and J. D. Arosemena
144 Roosevelt Monument, Panama

1948. Air. Homage to F. D. Roosevelt.
479 **142** 5 c. black and red 20 15
480 – 10 c. orange 30 30
481 **144** 20 c. green 35 35
482 – 50 c. black and blue . . . 40 35
483 – 1 b. black 90 75
DESIGNS—HORIZ: 10 c. Woman with palm symbolizing "Four Freedoms"; 50 c. Map of Panama Canal. VERT: 1 b. Portrait of Roosevelt.

147 Cervantes
148 Monument to Cervantes

1948. 400th Birth Anniv of Cervantes.
484 **147** 2 c. black and red (post.) 30 15
485 **148** 5 c. black and blue (air) . 20 10
486 – 10 c. black and mauve . . 35 30
DESIGN—HORIZ: 10 c. Don Quixote and Sancho Panza (inscr as Type **148**).

1949. Air. Jose Gabriel Duque (philanthropist). Birth Centenary No. 486 optd **"CENTENARIO DE/JOSE GABRIEL DUQUE/"18 de Enero de 1949"**.
487 10 c. black & mauve 40 40

1949. Obligatory Tax. Cancer Research Fund. Surch **LUCHA CONTRA EL CANCER** and value.
488 **142** 1 c. on 5 c. black and red 35 10
489 – 1 c. on 10 c. orange (No. 480) 35 10

1949. Incorporation of Chiriqui Province Cent. Stamps of 1930 and 1942 optd **1849-1949 CHIRIQUI CENTENARIO**. (a) On postage stamps as No. 407. (i) Without surcharge.
491 – 2 c. red 20 10

(ii) Surch **1 UN CENTESIMO 1** also.
490 – 1 c. on 2 c. red 20 10

(b) Air.
492 – 2 c. red (No. 418) 20 20
493 **83** 5 c. blue 30 30
494 – 15 c. grey (No. 423) . . . 40 40
495 – 50 c. red (No. 427) . . . . 1·75 1·75

1949. 75th Anniv of U.P.U. Stamps of 1930 and 1942/3 optd **1874 1949 U.P.U.** No. 625 is also surch. **B/0.25**.
496 – 1 c. grn (No. 405) (postage) 20 10
497 – 2 c. red (No. 407) 30 15
498 **127** 5 c. blue 45 25
499 – 2 c. red (No. 418) (air) . 20 20
500 **83** 5 c. orange 55 35
501 – 10 c. black and blue (No. 421) 20 20
502 **131** 25 c. on 3 b. grey 30 30
503 – 50 c. red (No. 427) . . . . 1·60 1·60

1949. Cancer Research Fund. Dated "1949".
504 **112** 1 c. brown 45 10

153 Father Xavier
154 St. Xavier University

1949. Bicentenary of Founding of St. Xavier University.
505 **153** 2 c. black & red (postage) 25 15
506 **154** 5 c. black & blue (air) . . 35 15

155 Dr. Carlos J. Finlay
156 "Aedes aegypti"

1950. Dr. Finlay (medical research worker).
507 **155** 2 c. black & red (postage) 35 15
508 **156** 5 c. black & blue (air) . . 85 40

1950. Death Cent of San Martin. Optd **CENTENARIO del General (or Gral.) Jose de San Martin 17 de Agosto de 1950** or surch also. The 50 c. is optd **AEREO** as well.
509 – 1 c. grn (No. 405) (postage) 15 10
510 – 2 c. on ½ c. (No. 404) . . . 20 10
511 **127** 5 c. black and blue 25 20
512 – 2 c. red (No. 418) (air) . . 35 30
513 **83** 5 c. orange 35 35
514 – 10 c. black & blue (No. 421) 55 45
515 **83** 25 c. blue 90 70
516 – 50 c. black & violet (No. 477) 1·40 1·00

158 Badge
159 Stadium

1950. Obligatory Tax. Physical Culture Fund. Dated "1950".
517 – 1 c. black and red 70 20
518 **158** 1 c. black and blue 70 20
519 **159** 1 c. black and green . . . 70 20
520 – 1 c. black and orange . . . 70 20
521 – 1 c. black and violet . . . 70 20
DESIGNS—VERT: No. 520, as Type **159** but medallion changed and incorporating four "F"s; No. 521, Discus thrower. HORIZ: No. 517, as Type **159** but front of Stadium.

1951. Birth Tercent of Jean-Baptiste de La Salle (educational reformer). Optd **Tercer Centenario del Natalicio de San Juan Baptista de La Salle. 1651-1951.**
522 2 c. black and red (No. 409) . 15 10
523 5 c. blue (No. 411) 25 15

1952. Air. Surch **AEREO 1952** and value.
524 2 c. on 10 c. black & blue (No. 421) 20 15
525 5 c. on 10 c. black & blue (No. 421) 25 10
526 1 b. on 5 b. blue (No. 438) . . 23·00 23·00

1952. Surch **1952** and figure of value.
527 1 c. on ½ c. (No. 404) 15 10

Air. Optd **AEREO** also.
528 5 c. on 2 c. (No. 408) 15 10
529 25 c. on 10 c. (No. 413) . . . 70 65

164 Isabella the Catholic
167 Masthead of "La Estrella"

1952. 500th Birth Anniv of Isabella the Catholic.
530 **164** 1 c. black & grn (postage) 10 10
531 2 c. black and red 15 10
532 5 c. black and blue 20 15
533 10 c. black and violet . . . 25 20
534 4 c. black and orange (air) 10 10
535 5 c. black and olive . . . 15 10
536 10 c. black and buff . . . 35 30
537 25 c. black and slate . . . 55 35
538 50 c. black and brown . . 75 45
539 1 b. black . . . . 3·00 3·00

1953. Surch **B/.0.01 1953**.
540 1 c. on 10 c. (No. 413) 10 10
541 1 c. on 15 c. black (No. 415) . 15 10

1953. Air. No. 421 surch **5 1953**.
542 5 c. on 10 c. black and blue . . 35 10

1953. Air. Centenary of "La Estrella de Panama", Newspaper.
543 **167** 5 c. red 20 15
544 10 c. blue 25 25

168 Pres. and Senora Amador Guerrero

1953. 50th Anniv of Panama Republic.
545 – 2 c. violet (postage) . . . 15 10
546 **168** 5 c. orange 20 10
547 – 12 c. purple 35 15
548 – 20 c. indigo 65 25
549 – 50 c. yellow 90 65
550 – 1 b. blue . . . . 2·25 1·00
DESIGNS—VERT: 2 c. Blessing the flat; 50 c. Old Town Hall. HORIZ: 12 c. J. A. Santos and J. De La Ossa; 20 c. Revolutionary council; 1 b. Obverse and reverse of coin.
551 – 2 c. blue (air) 10 10
552 – 5 c. green 15 10
553 – 7 c. grey 20 15
554 – 25 c. black . . . . 1·40 70
555 – 50 c. brown 65 70
556 – 1 b. orange . . . . 2·25 1·00
DESIGNS—VERT: 2 c. Act of Independence. HORIZ: 5 c. Pres. and Senora Remon Cantera; 7 c. Girl in national costume; 25 c. National flower; 50 c. Salazar, Huertas and Domingo; 1 b. National dance.

1954. Surch in figures.
557 – 3 c. on 1 c. red (No. 406) (postage) 10 10
558 **167** 1 c. on 5 c. red (air) . . . 10 10
559 1 c. on 10 c. blue 10 10

170 Gen. Herrera at Conference Table

1954. Death Centenary of Gen. Herrera.
560 – 3 c. violet (postage) . . . 20 10
561 **170** 6 c. green (air) 15 10
562 – 1 b. black and red . . . . 2·25 2·10
DESIGNS—VERT: 3 c. Equestrian statue. HORIZ: 1 b. Cavalry charge.

171 Rotary Emblem and Map

1955. Air. 50th Anniv of Rotary International.
563 **171** 6 c. violet 15 10
564 21 c. red 55 35
565 1 b. black . . . . 3·50 1·90

172 Tocumen Airport
173 President Remon Cantera

1955.
566 **172** ½ c. brown 10 10

1955. National Mourning for Pres. Remon Cantera.
567 **173** 3 c. blk & pur (postage) . 15 10
568 6 c. black & violet (air) . 20 15

174 V. de la Guardia y Azala and M. Chiaria
175 F. de Lesseps

1955. Centenary of Cocle Province.
569 **174** 5 c. violet 20 10

1955. 150th Birth Anniv of De Lesseps (engineer).
570 **175** 3 c. lake on pink (postage) 30 10
571 – 25 c. blue on blue . . . . 2·25 1·25
572 – 50 c. violet on lilac . . . 90 60
573 – 5 c. myrtle on green (air) . 20 10
574 – 1 b. black and mauve . . 2·75 1·75
DESIGNS—VERT: 5 c. P. J. Sosa; 50 c. T. Roosevelt. HORIZ: 25 c. First excavations for Panama Canal; 1 b. "Ancon I" (first ship to pass through canal) and De Lesseps.

1955. Air. No. 564 surch.
575 **171** 15 c. on 21 c. red 45 35

177 Pres. Eisenhower (United States)
178 Bolivar Statue

1956. Air. Pan-American Congress, Panama and 30th Anniv of First Congress.
576 – 6 c. black and blue . . . 30 20
577 – 6 c. black and bistre . . 30 20
578 – 6 c. black and green . . 30 20
579 – 6 c. sepia and green . . 30 20
580 – 6 c. green and yellow . . 30 20
581 – 6 c. green and violet . . 30 20
582 – 6 c. blue and lilac . . . 30 20

583 – 6 c. green and purple . . 30 20
584 – 6 c. blue and olive 30 20
585 – 6 c. sepia and yellow . . . 30 20
586 – 6 c. blue and sepia 30 20
587 – 6 c. green and mauve . . 30 20
588 – 6 c. sepia and red 30 20
589 – 6 c. green and blue . . . 30 20
590 – 6 c. sepia and blue 30 20
591 – 6 c. black and orange . . 30 20
592 – 6 c. sepia and grey 30 20
593 – 6 c. black and pink . . . 30 20
594 **177** 6 c. blue and red 70 35
595 – 6 c. blue and grey 30 20
596 – 6 c. green and brown . . 30 20
597 **178** 20 c. grey 40 55
598 – 50 c. green 75 75
599 – 1 b. sepia . . . . 1·50 95

PRESIDENTIAL PORTRAITS as Type **177**: No. 576, Argentina; 577, Bolivia; 578, Brazil; 579, Chile; 580, Colombia; 581, Costa Rica; 582, Cuba; 583, Dominican Republic; 584, Ecuador; 585, Guatemala; 586, Haiti; 587, Honduras; 588, Mexico; 589, Nicaragua; 590, Panama; 591, Paraguay; 592, Peru; 593, Salvador; 595, Uruguay; 596, Venezuela. As Type **178**—HORIZ: No. 598, Bolivar Hall. VERT: No. 599, Bolivar Medallion.

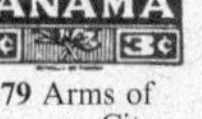

179 Arms of Panama City

180 Pres. Carlos A. Mendoza

1956. 6th Inter-American Congress of Municipalities, Panama City.
600 **179** 3 c. green (postage) . . . 15 10
601 – 25 c. red (air) 55 35
602 – 50 c. black 65 55

DESIGNS: 25 c. Stone bridge, Old Panama; 50 c. Town Hall, Panama.

1956. Birth Centenary of Pres. Carlos A. Mendoza.
604 **180** 10 c. green and red . . . 20 15

182 Dr. Belisario Porras

1956. Birth Centenary of Dr. Porras.
605 – 15 c. grey (postage) . . . 45 20
606 **182** 25 c. blue and red 65 45
607 – 5 c. green (air) 10 10
608 – 15 c. red 30 25

DESIGNS—HORIZ: 15 c. (No. 605), National Archives; 15 c. (No. 608), St. Thomas's Hospital. VERT: 5 c. Porras Monument.

183 Isthmus Highway

185 Manuel E. Batista

1957. 7th Pan-American Highway Congress.
609 **183** 3 c. green (postage) . . . 15 10
610 – 10 c. black (air) 20 15
611 – 20 c. black and blue . . . 35 35
612 – 1 b. green . . . . 1·75 1·75

DESIGNS—VERT: 10 c. Highway under construction; 20 c. Darien Forest; 1 b. Map of Pan-American Highway.

1957. Air. Surch **1957 X 10 C X**.
614 **173** 10 c. on 6 c. black & violet 20 20

1957. Birth Centenary of Manuel Espinosa Batista (independence leader).
615 **185** 5 c. blue and green . . . 15 10

186 Portobelo Castle

189 U.N. Emblem

1957. Air. Buildings. Centres in black.
616 **186** 10 c. grey 25 15
617 – 10 c. purple 25 15
618 – 10 c. violet 25 15
619 – 10 c. grey and green . . . 25 15
620 – 10 c. blue 25 15
621 – 10 c. brown 25 15
622 – 10 c. orange 25 15
623 – 10 c. light blue 25 15
624 – 1 b. red . . . . 2·10 95

DESIGNS—HORIZ: No. 617, San Jeronimo Castle; No. 618, Portobelo Customs-house; No. 619, Panama Hotel; No. 620, Pres. Remon Cantera Stadium; No. 621, Palace of Justice; No. 622, Treasury; No. 623, San Lorenzo Castle. VERT: No. 624, Jose Remon Clinics.

1957. Surch **1957** and value.
625 **172** 1 c. on ½ c. brown 10 10
626 3 c. on ½ c. brown 10 10

1958. Air. Surch **1958** and value.
627 **170** 5 c. on 6 c. green 20 10

1958. Air. 10th Anniv of U.N.O.
628 **189** 10 c. green 20 10
629 21 c. blue 45 35
630 50 c. orange 45 45
631 – 1 b. red, blue and grey . 1·75 1·40

DESIGN: 1 b. Flags of Panama and United Nations.

1958. No. 547 surch **3 c 1958**.
633 3 c. on 12 c. purple 10 10

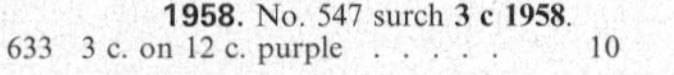

191 Flags Emblem

192 Brazilian Pavilion

1958. 10th Anniv of Organization of American States. Emblem (T **191**) multicoloured within yellow and black circular band; background colours given below.
634 **191** 1 c. grey (postage) . . . 10 10
635 2 c. green 10 10
636 3 c. red 15 10
637 7 c. blue 25 10
638 5 c. blue (air) 15 10
639 10 c. red 20 15
640 – 50 c. black, yellow & grey 35 35
641 **191** 1 b. black . . . . 1·75 1·40

DESIGN—VERT: 50 c. Headquarters building.

1958. Brussels International Exhbition.
642 **192** 1 c. green & yell (postage) 10 10
643 – 3 c. green and blue . . . 15 10
644 – 5 c. slate and brown . . 15 10
645 – 10 c. brown and blue . . 20 20
646 – 15 c. violet and grey (air) 35 35
647 – 50 c. brown and slate . . 60 60
648 – 1 b. turquoise and lilac . 1·25 1·25

DESIGNS—PAVILIONS: As Type **192**: 3 c. Argentina; 5 c. Venezuela; 10 c. Great Britain; 15 c. Vatican City; 50 c. United States; 1 b. Belgium.

193 Pope Pius XII

194 Children on Farm

1959. Pope Pius XII Commemoration.
650 **193** 3 c. brown (postage) . . 15 10
651 – 5 c. violet (air) 15 15
652 – 30 c. mauve 30 25
653 – 50 c. grey 75 60

PORTRAITS (Pope Pius XII): 5 c. when Cardinal; 30 c. wearing Papal tiara; 50 c. enthroned.

1959. Obligatory Tax. Youth Rehabilitation Institute. Size 35 × 24 mm.
655 **194** 1 c. grey and red 15 10

195 U.N. Headquarters, New York

197 J. A. Facio

1959. 10th Anniv of Declaration of Human Rights.
656 **195** 3 c. olive & brown (postage) 10 10
657 – 15 c. green and orange . 35 25
658 – 5 c. blue and green (air) . 15 10
659 – 10 c. brown and grey . . 20 15
660 – 20 c. slate and brown . . 35 35
661 – 50 c. blue and green . . . 60 60
662 **195** 1 b. blue and red . . . . . 1·40 1·25

DESIGNS: 5 c., 15 c. Family looking towards light; 10 c., 20 c. U.N. emblem and torch; 50 c. U.N. flag.

1959. 8th Latin-American Economic Commission Congress. Nos. 656/61 optd **8A REUNION C.E.P.A.L. MAYO 1959** or surch also.
663 **195** 3 c. olive and brown (postage) 10 10
664 – 15 c. green and orange . . 35 20
665 – 5 c. blue and green (air) . 10 10
666 – 10 c. brown and grey . . . 25 15
667 – 20 c. slate and brown . . . 45 35
668 – 1 b. on 50 c. blue and green 1·60 1·60

1959. 50th Anniv of National Institute.
670 – 3 c. red (postage) 10 10
671 – 13 c. green 30 15
672 – 21 c. blue 40 30
673 **197** 5 c. black (air) 10 10
674 – 10 c. black 20 10

DESIGNS—VERT: 3 c. E. A. Morales (founder); 10 c. Ernesto de la Guardia, Nr; 13 c. A. Bravo. HORIZ: 21 c. National Institute Bldg.

1959. Obligatory Tax. Youth Rehabilitation Institute. As No. 655, but colours changed and inscr "1959".
675 **194** 1 c. green and black . . . 10 10
676 1 c. blue and black 10 10
See also No. 690.

198 Football

200 Administration Building

1959. 3rd Pan-American Games, Chicago. Inscr "III JUEGOS DEPORTIVOS PANAMERICANOS".
677 **198** 1 c. green & grey (postage) 10 10
678 – 3 c. brown and blue . . . 15 10
679 – 20 c. brown and green . . 50 45
680 – 5 c. brown and black (air) 15 10
681 – 10 c. brown and grey . . . 25 20
682 – 50 c. brown and blue . . . 45 40

DESIGNS: 3 c. Swimming; 5 c. Boxing; 10 c. Baseball; 20 c. Hurdling; 50 c. Basketball.

1960. Air. World Refugee Year. Nos. 554/6 optd **NACIONES UNIDAS ANO MUNDIAL, REFUGIADOS. 1959-1960.**
683 25 c. black 35 35
684 50 c. brown 70 55
685 1 b. orange . . . . 1·50 1·10

1960. Air. 25th Anniv of National University.
686 **200** 10 c. green 15 15
687 – 21 c. blue 30 20
688 – 25 c. blue 50 35
689 – 30 c. black 55 40

DESIGNS: 21 c. Faculty of Science; 25 c. Faculty of Medicine; 30 c. Statue of Dr. Octavio Mendez Pereira (first rector) and Faculty of Law.

1960. Obligatory Tax. Youth Rehabilitation Institute. As No. 655 but smaller (32 × 22 mm) and inscr "1960".
690 **194** 1 c. grey and red 10 10

202 Fencing

204 "Population"

1960. Olympic Games.
691 **202** 3 c. purple & vio (postage) 10 10
692 – 5 c. green & turquoise 20 10
693 – 5 c. red and orange (air) . 10 10
694 – 10 c. black and bistre . . . 20 15
695 – 25 c. deep blue and blue . 45 40
696 – 50 c. black and brown . . 60 45

DESIGNS—VERT: 5 c. (No. 692), Football; (No. 693), Basketball; 25 c. Javelin-throwing; 50 c. Runner with Olympic Flame. HORIZ: 10 c. Cycling.

1960. Air. 6th National Census (5 c.) and Central American Census.
698 **204** 5 c. black 10 10
699 – 10 c. brown 20 15

DESIGN: 10 c. Two heads and map.

205 Boeing 707 Airliner

1960. Air.
700 **205** 5 c. blue 15 10
701 10 c. green 40 20
702 20 c. brown 85 40

206 Pastoral Scene

1961. Agricultural Census (16th April).
703 **206** 3 c. turquoise 10 10

207 Helen Keller School

1961. 25th Anniv of Lions Club.
705 – 3 c. blue (postage) 10 10
706 **207** 5 c. black (air) 10 10
707 – 10 c. green 20 10
708 – 21 c. blue, red and yellow 40 30

DESIGNS: 3 c. Nino Hospital; 10 c. Children's Colony, Verano; 21 c. Lions emblem, arms and slogan.

1961. Air. Obligatory Tax. Youth Rehabilitation Fund. Surch **1 c "Rehabilitacion de Menores"**.
709 – 1 c. on 10 c. black and bistre (No. 694) 10 10
710 **205** 1 c. on 10 c. green 10 10

1961. Air. Surch **HABILITAD en** and value.
712 **200** 1 c. on 10 c. green 10 10
713 – 1 b. on 25 c. blue and blue (No. 695) . . . . 1·25 1·25

210 Flags of Costa Rica and Panama

1961. Meeting of Presidents of Costa Rica and Panama.
715 **210** 3 c. red & blue (postage) . 15 10
716 – 1 b. black and gold (air) . 1·25 75

DESIGN: 1 b. Pres. Chiari of Panama and Pres. Echandi of Costa Rica.

211 Girl using Sewing-machine

212 Campaign Emblem

1961. Obligatory Tax. Youth Rehabilitation Fund.
717 **211** 1 c. violet 10 10
718 1 c. yellow 10 10
719 1 c. green 10 10
720 1 c. blue 10 10
721 1 c. purple 10 10
722 – 1 c. mauve 10 10
723 – 1 c. grey 10 10
724 – 1 c. blue 10 10
725 – 1 c. orange 10 10
726 – 1 c. red 10 10

DESIGN: Nos. 722/6, Boy sawing wood.

1961. Air. Malaria Eradication.
727 **212** 5 c. + 5 c. red 60 30
728 10 c. + 10 c. blue 60 30
729 15 c. + 15 c. green . . . 60 30

213 Dag Hammarskjold

214 Arms of Panama

1961. Air. Death of Dag Hammarskjold.
730 **213** 10 c. black and grey . . . 20 15

1962. Air. (a) Surch **"Vale B/.0.15"**.
731 **200** 15 c. on 10 c. green . . . 30 20

(b) No. 810 surch **"XX"** over old value and **"VALE B/.1.00"**.
732 – 1 b. on 25 c. deep blue and blue 1·25 75

1962. 3rd Central American Inter-Municipal Co-operation Assembly.
733 **214** 3 c. red, yellow and blue (postage) 10 10
734 – 5 c. black and blue (air) . 20 10
DESIGN—HORIZ: 5 c. City Hall, Colon.

215 Mercury on Cogwheel
217 Social Security Hospital

1962. 1st Industrial Census.
735 **215** 3 c. red 10 10

1962. Surch **VALE** and value with old value obliterated.
736 **212** 10 c. on 5 c. + 5 c. red . 90 45
737 20 c. on 10 c. + 10 c. blue 1·50 90

1962. Opening of Social Security Hospital, Panama City.
738 **217** 3 c. black and red 10 10

218 Colon Cathedral
221 Col. Glenn and Capsule "Friendship 7"

220 Thatcher Ferry Bridge nearing Completion

1962. "Freedom of Worship". Inscr "LIBERTAD DE CULTOS". Centres in black.
739 – 1 c. red and blue (postage) 10 10
740 – 2 c. red and cream 10 10
741 – 3 c. blue and cream . . . 10 10
742 – 5 c. red and green . . . 10 10
743 – 10 c. green and cream . . 20 15
744 – 10 c. mauve and blue . . 20 15
745 – 15 c. blue and green . . 30 20
746 **218** 20 c. red and pink . . . 35 25
747 – 25 c. green and pink . . 45 35
748 – 50 c. blue and pink . . . 60 55
749 – 1 b. violet and cream . . 1·75 1·40
DESIGNS—HORIZ: 1 c. San Francisco de Veraguas Church; 3 c. David Cathedral; 25 c. Orthodox Greek Temple; 1 b. Colon Protestant Church. VERT: 2 c. Panama Old Cathedral; 5 c. Nata Church; 10 c. Don Bosco Temple; 15 c. Virgin of Carmen Church; 50 c. Panama Cathedral.
750 – 5 c. violet and flesh (air) . . 10 10
751 – 7 c. lt mauve and mauve . . 15 10
752 – 8 c. violet and blue . . . 15 10
753 – 10 c. violet and salmon . . . 20 10
754 – 10 c. green and light purple . 20 20
755 – 15 c. red and orange . . . 25 20
756 – 21 c. sepia and blue . . . 35 30
757 – 25 c. blue and pink . . . 45 35
758 – 30 c. mauve and blue . . . 50 45
759 – 50 c. purple and green . . . 70 70
760 – 1 b. blue and salmon . . . . 1·25 1·10
DESIGNS—HORIZ: 5 c. Cristo Rey Church; 7 c. San Miguel Church; 21 c. Canal Zone Synagogue; 25 c. Panama Synagogue; 50 c. Canal Zone Protestant Church. VERT: 8 c. Santuario Church; 10 c. Los Santos Church; 15 c. Santa Ana Church; 30 c. San Francisco Church; 1 b. Canal Zone Catholic Church.

1962. Air. 9th Central American and Caribbean Games, Jamaica. Nos. 693 and 695 optd **"IX JUEGOS C.A. y DEL CARIBE KINGSTON - 1962"** or surch also.
762 5 c. red and orange 15 15
764 10 c. on 25 c. dp blue and blue 55 50
765 15 c. on 25 c. dp blue and blue 40 35
766 20 c. on 25 c. dp blue and blue 45 45
763 25 c. deep blue and blue . . 55 50

1962. Opening of Thatcher Ferry Bridge, Canal Zone.
767 **220** 3 c. black & red (postage) 10 10
768 – 10 c. black and blue (air) . 20 15
DESIGN: 10 c. Completed bridge.

1962. Air. Col. Glenn's Space Flight.
769 **221** 5 c. red 10 10
770 – 10 c. yellow 20 20
771 – 31 c. blue 45 40
772 – 50 c. green 65 65
DESIGNS—HORIZ: "Friendship": 10 c. Over Earth; 31 c. In space. VERT: 50 c. Col Glenn.

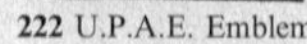

222 U.P.A.E. Emblem
225 F.A.O. Emblem

223 Water Exercise

1963. Air. 50th Anniv of Postal Union of Americas and Spain.
774 **222** 10 c. multicoloured . . . 20 15

1963. 75th Anniv of Panama Fire Brigade.
775 **223** 1 c. blk & green (postage) 10 10
776 – 3 c. black and blue . . . 10 10
777 – 5 c. black and red . . . 10 10
778 – 10 c. black & orge (air) . 15 15
779 – 15 c. black and purple . . 20 20
780 – 21 c. blue, gold and red . 50 45
DESIGNS: 3 c. Brigade officers; 5 c. Brigade president and advisory council; 10 c. "China" pump in action, 1887; 15 c. "Cable 14" station and fire-engine; 21 c. Fire Brigade badge.

1963. Air. Red Cross Cent (1st issue). Nos. 769/71 surch with red cross **1863 1963** and premium.
781 **215** 5 c. + 5 c. red . . . . . 1·40 1·40
782 – 10 c. + 10 c. yellow . . 2·75 2·75
783 – 31 c. + 15 c. blue . . . 2·75 2·75
See also No. 797.

1963. Air. Freedom from Hunger.
784 **225** 10 c. red and green . . . 20 20
785 15 c. red and blue . . . 30 25

1963. Air. 22nd Central American Lions Convention. Optd **"XXII Convencion Leonistica Centroamericana Panama 18-21 Abril 1963"**.
786 **207** 5 c. black 10 10

1963. Air. Surch **HABILITADO Vale B./0.04.**
789 **200** 4 c. in 10 c. green 10 10

1963. Air. Nos. 743 and 769 optd **AEREO** vert.
790 10 c. green and cream . . . 20 15
791 20 c. brown and green . . . 30 25

1963. Air. Freedom of the Press. No. 693 optd **LIBERTAD DE PRENSA 20-VIII-63.**
792 5 c. red and orange 10 10

1963. Air. Visit of U.S. Astronauts to Panama. Optd **"Visita Astronautas Glenn-Schirra Sheppard Cooper a Panama"** or surch also.
793 **221** 5 c. red . . . . 2·50 2·50
794 10 c. on 5 c. red . . . . 3·25 3·25

1963. Air. Surch **HABILITADO 10 c.**
796 **221** 10 c. on 5 c. red . . . . 5·50 5·50

1963. Air. Red Cross Centenary (2nd issue). No. 781 surch **"Centenario Cruz Roja Internacional 10 c."** with premium obliterated.
797 **221** 10 c. on 5 c. + 5 c. red . 6·00 6·00

1963. Surch **VALE** and value.
798 **217** 4 c. on 3 c. black and red (postage) 15 10
799 – 4 c. on 3 c. black, blue and cream (No. 741) . . . 15 10
800 **220** 4 c. on 3 c. black & red . 15 10
801 – 4 c. on 3 c. black and blue (No. 776) 15 10
802 **182** 10 c. on 25 c. blue & red 35 15
803 – 10 c. on 25 c. blue (No. 688) (air) 20 15

234 Pres. Orlich (Costa Rica) and Flags
236 Vasco Nunez de Balboa

235 Innsbruck

1963. Presidential Reunion, San Jose (Costa Rica). Multicoloured. Presidents and flags of their countries.
804 1 c. Type **234** (postage) 10 10
805 2 c. Somoza (Nicaragua) . . . 15 15
806 3 c. Villeda (Honduras) 20 15
807 4 c. Chiari (Panama) 25 20
808 5 c. Rivera (El Salvador) (air) . 30 30
809 10 c. Ydigoras (Guatemala) . . 55 45
810 21 c. Kennedy (U.S.A.) . . . . 1·60 1·40

1963. Winter Olympic Games, Innsbruck.
811 ½ c. red and blue (postage) . . 10 10
812 1 c. red, brown and turquoise . 10 10
813 3 c. red and blue 25 15
814 4 c. red, brown and green . . 35 20
815 5 c. red, brown & mauve (air) . 45 25
816 15 c. red, brown and blue . . 1·10 90
817 21 c. red, brown and myrtle . . 2·25 1·90
818 31 c. red, brown and blue . . 3·00 2·25
DESIGNS: ½ c. (expressed "B/0.005"); 3 c. Type **235**: 1 c., 4 c. Speed-skating; 5 c. to 31 c. Skiing (slalom).

1964. 450th Anniv of Discovery of Pacific Ocean.
820 **236** 4 c. grn on flesh (postage) 10 10
821 10 c. violet on pink (air) . 20 20

237 Boy Scout
238 St. Paul's Cathedral, London

1964. Obligatory Tax for Youth Rehabilitation, Institute.
822 **237** 1 c. red 10 10
823 1 c. grey 10 10
824 1 c. light blue 10 10
825 1 c. olive 10 10
826 1 c. violet 10 10
827 – 1 c. brown 10 10
828 – 1 c. orange 10 10
829 – 1 c. turquoise 10 10
830 – 1 c. violet 10 10
831 – 1 c. yellow 10 10
DESIGN: Nos. 827/31, Girl guide.

1964. Air. Ecumenical Council, Vatican City (1st issue). Cathedrals. Centres in black.
832 21 c. red (Type **238**) 55 35
833 21 c. blue (Kassa, Hungary) . 55 35
834 21 c. green (Milan) 55 35
835 21 c. black (St. John's, Poland) 55 35
836 21 c. brown (St. Stephen's, Vienna) 55 35
837 21 c. brown (Notre Dame, Paris) 55 35
838 21 c. violet (Moscow) 55 35
839 21 c. violet (Lima) 55 35
840 21 c. red (Stockholm) 55 35
841 21 c. mauve (Cologne) 55 35
842 21 c. bistre (New Delhi) . . . 55 35
843 21 c. deep turquoise (Basel) . . 55 35
844 21 c. green (Toledo) 55 35
845 21 c. red (Metropolitan, Athens) 55 35
846 21 c. olive (St. Patrick's, New York) 55 35
847 21 c. green (Lisbon) 55 35
848 21 c. turquoise (Sofia) 55 35
849 21 c. deep brown (New Church, Delft, Netherlands) 55 35
850 21 c. deep sepia (St. George's Patriarchal Church, Istanbul) 55 35
851 21 c. blue (Basilica, Guadalupe, Mexico) 55 35
852 1 b. blue (Panama) . . . . . 1·75 1·75
853 2 b. green (St. Peter's, Rome) . 3·00 3·00
See Nos. 882, etc.

1964. As Nos. 749 and 760 but colours changed and optd **HABILITADA**.
855 1 b. blk, red & blue (postage) . 1·75 1·60
856 1 b. blk, green & yellow (air) . 1·75 1·25

1964. Air. No. 756 surch **VALE B/.0.50.**
857 50 c. on 21 c. black, sepia and blue 65 40

241 Discus-thrower

1964. Olympic Games, Tokyo.
858 ½ c. ("B/0.005") purple, red, brown and green (postage) . 10 10
859 1 c. multicoloured 10 10
860 5 c. black, red and olive (air) . 35 25
861 10 c. black, red and yellow . . 70 45
862 21 c. multicoloured . . . . . 1·40 90
863 50 c. multicoloured . . . . . 2·75 1·75
DESIGNS: ½ c. Type **241**; 1 c. Runner with Olympic Flame; 5 c. to 50 c. Olympic Stadium, Tokyo, and Mt. Fuji.

1964. Air. Nos. 692 and 742 surch **Aereo B/.0.10.**
865 10 c. on 5 c. green & turquoise 20 15
866 10 c. on 5 c. black, red and green 20 15

243 Space Vehicles (Project "Apollo")

1964. Space Exploration. Multicoloured.
867 ½ c. ("B/0.005") Type **243** (postage) 10 10
868 1 c. Rocket and capsule (Project "Gemini") 10 10
869 5 c. W.M. Schirra (air) . . . 20 20
870 10 c. L.G. Cooper 30 30
871 21 c. Schirra's capsule 75 75
872 50 c. Cooper's capsule . . . . 3·25 3·00

1964. No. 687 surch **Correos B/.0.10.**
874 10 c. on 21 c. blue 15 15

245 Water-skiing

1964. Aquatic Sports. Multicoloured.
875 ½ c. ("B/0.005") Type **245** (postage) 10 10
876 1 c. Underwater-swimming . . 10 10
877 5 c. Fishing (air) 20 10
878 10 c. Sailing (vert) . . . . . 1·50 60
879 21 c. Speedboat racing . . . . 2·75 1·50
880 31 c. Water polo at Olympic Games, 1964 . . . . 3·50 1·75

1964. Air. Ecumenical Council, Vatican City (2nd issue). Stamps of 1st issue optd **1964**. Centres in black.
882 21 c. red (No. 832) 70 50
883 21 c. green (No. 834) 70 50
884 21 c. olive (No. 836) 70 50
885 21 c. deep sepia (No. 850) . . 70 50
886 1 b. blue (No. 852) . . . . . 2·75 2·00
887 2 b. green (No. 853) . . . . . 5·50 4·50

247 General View
248 Eleanor Roosevelt

1964. Air. New York's World Fair.
889 **247** 5 c. black and yellow . . 30 25
890 – 10 c. black and red . . . 75 60
891 – 15 c. black and green . . 1·25 80
892 – 21 c. black and blue . . . 1·90 1·50
DESIGNS: 10 c., 15 c. Fair pavilions (different); 21 c. Unisphere.

1964. Mrs. Eleanor Roosevelt Commemoration.
894 **248** 4 c. black and red on yellow (postage) 15 10
895 20 c. black and green on buff (air) 50 45

249 Dag Hammarskjold **250** Pope John XXIII

1964. Air. U.N. Day.

897	249	21 c. black and blue	70	50
898	–	21 c. blue and black	70	50

DESIGN: No. 898, U.N. Emblem.

1964. Air. Pope John Commemoration.

900	250	21 c. black and bistre	70	50
901	–	21 c. mult (Papal Arms)	70	50

251 Slalom Skiing Medals

1964. Winter Olympic Winners' Medals. Medals in gold, silver and bronze.

903	251	½ c. ("B/0.005") turquoise (postage)	10	10
904	–	1 c. deep blue	10	10
905	–	2 c. brown	20	15
906	–	3 c. mauve	25	15
907	–	4 c. lake	35	20
908	–	5 c. violet (air)	45	25
909	–	6 c. blue	55	30
910	–	7 c. violet	65	35
911	–	10 c. green	90	50
912	–	21 c. red	1·40	95
913	–	31 c. blue	2·50	1·40

DESIGNS—Medals for: 1 c., 7 c. Speed-skating; 2 c., 21 c. Bobsleighing; 3 c., 10 c. Figure-skating; 4 c. Ski-jumping; 5 c., 6 c., 31 c. Cross-country skiing. Values in the same design show different medal-winners and country names.

252 Cuvier's Toucan

1965. Birds. Multicoloured.

915	1 c. Type **252** (postage)	80	10
916	2 c. Scarlet macaw	80	10
917	3 c. Black-cheeked woodpecker	1·25	15
918	4 c. Blue-grey tanager (horiz)	1·25	25
919	5 c. Troupial (horiz) (air)	1·60	35
920	10 c. Crimson-backed tanager (horiz)	3·00	50

253 Snapper

1965. Marine Life. Multicoloured.

921	1 c. Type **253** (postage)	10	10
922	2 c. Dolphin	10	10
923	3 c. Shrimp (air)	20	15
924	12 c. Hammerhead	25	20
925	13 c. Atlantic sailfish	30	25
926	25 c. Seahorse (vert)	30	25

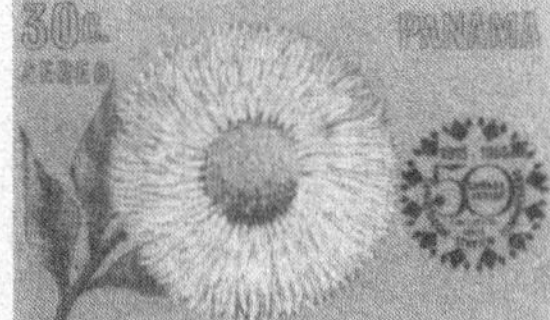

254 Double Daisy and Emblem

1966. Air. 50th Anniv of Junior Chamber of Commerce. Flowers. Multicoloured: background colour given.

927	254	30 c. mauve	55	45
928	–	30 c. flesh (Hibiscus)	55	45
929	–	30 c. olive (Mauve orchid)	55	45
930	–	40 c. green (Water lily)	60	55
931	–	40 c. blue (Gladiolus)	60	55
932	–	40 c. pink (White orchid)	60	55

Each design incorporates the Junior Chamber of Commerce Emblem.

1966. Surch (a) Postage.

933	13 c. on 25 c. (No. 747)	30	20

(b) Air.

934	3 c. on 5 c. (No. 680)	10	10
935	13 c. on 25 c. (No. 695)	30	25

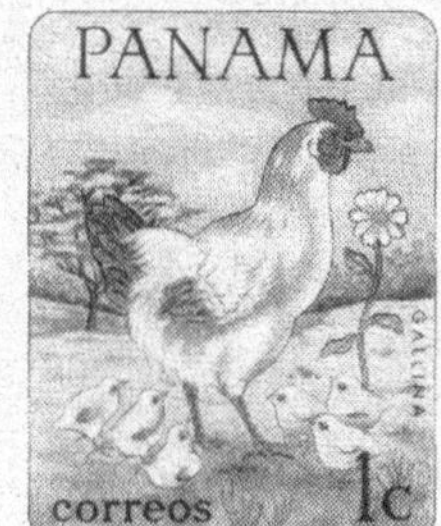

256 Chicken

1967. Domestic Animals. Multicoloured.

936	1 c. Type **256** (postage)	10	10
937	3 c. Cockerel	10	10
938	5 c. Pig (horiz)	10	10
939	8 c. Cow (horiz)	15	10
940	10 c. Pekingese dog (air)	25	20
941	13 c. Zebu (horiz)	30	20
942	30 c. Cat	60	50
943	40 c. Horse (horiz)	75	60

257 American Anhinga

1967. Wild Birds. Multicoloured.

944	½ c. Type **257**	55	10
945	1 c. Resplendent quetzal	55	10
946	3 c. Turquoise-browed motmot	70	15
947	4 c. Red-necked aracari (horiz)	85	20
948	5 c. Chestnut-fronted macaw	1·10	20
949	13 c. Belted kingfisher	2·40	50

258 "Deer" (F. Marc)

1967. Wild Animals. Paintings. Multicoloured.

950	1 c. Type **258** (postage)	10	10
951	3 c. "Cougar" (F. Marc)	10	10
952	5 c. "Monkeys" (F. Marc)	10	10
953	8 c. "Fox" (F. Marc)	20	10
954	10 c. "St. Jerome and the Lion" (Durer) (air)	20	15
955	13 c. "The Hare" (Durer)	30	20
956	20 c. "Lady with the Ermine" (Da Vinci)	45	25
957	30 c. "The Hunt" (Delacroix)	65	45

The 3, 10, 13 and 20 are vert.

259 Map of Panama and People

1969. National Population Census.

958	259	5 c. blue	10	10
959	–	10 c. purple	20	15

DESIGN—VERT: 10 c. People and map of the Americas.

260 Cogwheel

1969. 50th Anniv of Rotary Int in Panama.

960	260	13 c. black, yellow & blue	20	20

261 Cornucopia and Map **262** Tower and Map

1969. 1st Anniv of 11 October Revolution.

961	261	10 c. multicoloured	20	10

1969.

962	262	3 c. black and orange	10	10
963	–	5 c. green	10	10
964	–	8 c. brown	20	15
965	–	13 c. black and green	25	15
966	–	20 c. brown	35	25
967	–	21 c. yellow	35	25
968	–	25 c. green	45	30
969	–	30 c. black	50	45
970	–	34 c. brown	55	45
971	–	38 c. blue	60	45
972	–	40 c. yellow	65	45
973	–	50 c. black and purple	85	65
974	–	59 c. purple	1·00	60

DESIGNS—HORIZ: 5 c. Peasants; 13 c. Hotel Continental; 25 c. Del Rey Bridge; 34 c. Panama Cathedral; 38 c. Municipal Palace; 40 c. French Plaza; 50 c. Thatcher Ferry Bridge; 59 c. National Theatre. VERT: 8 c. Nata Church; 20 c. Virgin of Carmen Church; 21 c. Altar, San Jose Church; 30 c. Dr. Arosemena statue.

263 Discus-thrower and Stadium

1970. 11th Central American and Caribbean Games, Panama (1st series).

975	263	1 c. multicoloured (postage)	10	10
976		2 c. multicoloured	10	10
977		3 c. multicoloured	10	10
978		5 c. multicoloured	10	10
979		10 c. multicoloured	20	15
980		13 c. multicoloured	25	15
981	–	13 c. multicoloured	25	15
982	263	25 c. multicoloured	45	35
983		30 c. multicoloured	55	45
984	–	13 c. multicoloured (air)	70	20
985	–	30 c. multicoloured	60	45

DESIGNS—VERT: No. 981, "Flor del Espirited Santo" (flowers); No. 985, Indian girl. HORIZ: No. 984, Thatcher Ferry Bridge and palm.

See also Nos. 986/94.

264 J. D. Arosemena and Stadium

1970. Air. 11th Central American and Caribbean Games, Panama (2nd series). Multicoloured.

986	1 c. Type **264**	10	10
987	2 c. Type **264**	10	10
988	3 c. Type **264**	10	10
989	5 c. Type **264**	10	10
990	13 c. Basketball	20	15
991	13 c. New Gymnasium	20	15
992	13 c. Revolution Stadium	20	15
993	13 c. Panamanian couple in festive costume	20	15
994	30 c. Eternal Flame and stadium	45	35

265 A. Tapia and M. Sosa (first comptrollers)

1971. 40th Anniv of Panamanian Comptroller-General's Office. Multicoloured.

996	3 c. Comptroller-General's Building (1970) (vert)	10	10
997	5 c. Type **265**	10	10
998	8 c. Comptroller-General's emblem (vert)	15	10
999	13 c. Comptroller-General's Building (1955–70)	30	15

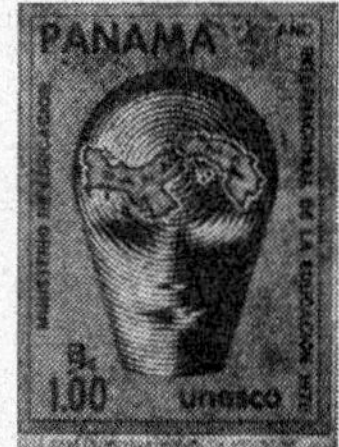

266 "Man and Alligator" **267** Map of Panama on I.E.Y. Emblem

1971. Indian Handicrafts.

1000	266	8 c. multicoloured	20	15

1971. International Education Year.

1001	267	1 b. multicoloured	1·50	1·50

268 Astronaut on Moon **269** Panama Pavilion

1971. Air. "Apollo 11" and "Apollo 12" Moon Missions. Multicoloured.

1002	13 c. Type **268**	35	25
1003	13 c. "Apollo 12" astronauts	35	25

1971. Air. "EXPO 70", World Fair, Osaka, Japan.

1004	269	10 c. multicoloured	15	15

270 Conference Text and Emblem

1971. 9th Inter-American Loan and Savings Association Conference, Panama City.

1005	270	25 c. multicoloured	60	35

271 Panama Flag

1971. Air. American Tourist Year. Multicoloured.

1006	5 c. Type **271**	10	10
1007	13 c. Map of Panama and Western Hemisphere	30	20

272 New U.P.U. H.Q. Building

1971. Inauguration of New U.P.U. Headquarters Building, Berne. Multicoloured.

1008	8 c. Type **272**	20	10
1009	30 c. U.P.U. Monument, Berne (vert)	60	35

273 Cow and Pig

1971. 3rd Agricultural Census.

1010	273	3 c. multicoloured	10	10

274 Map and "4S" Emblem

1971. "4S" Programme for Rural Youth.
1011 **274** 2 c. multicoloured . . . 10 10

275 Gandhi

276 Central American Flags

1971. Air. Birth Centenary (1969) of Mahatma Gandhi.
1012 **275** 10 c. multicoloured . . . 20 15

1971. Air. 150th Anniv of Central American States' Independence from Spain.
1013 **276** 13 c. multicoloured . . . 30 20

277 Early Panama Stamp

278 Altar, Nata Church

1971. Air. 2nd National, Philatelic and Numismatic Exhibition, Panama.
1014 **277** 8 c. blue, black & red . . 20 15

1972. Air. 450th Anniv of Nata Church.
1015 **278** 40 c. multicoloured . . . 50 45

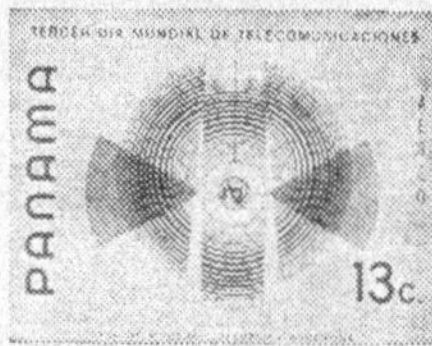

279 Telecommunications Emblem

1972. Air. World Telecommunications Day.
1016 **279** 13 c. black, blue & lt blue 20 15

280 "Apollo 14" Badge

1972. Air. Moon Flight of "Apollo 14".
1017 **280** 13 c. multicoloured . . . 60 25

281 Children on See-saw

1972. 25th Anniv (1971) of U.N.I.C.E.F. Multicoloured.
1018 1 c. Type **281** (postage) . . . 10 10
1019 5 c. Boy sitting by kerb (vert) (air) . . . 10 10
1020 8 c. Indian mother and child (vert) . . . 15 10
1021 50 c. U.N.I.C.E.F. emblem (vert) . . . 70 45

282 Tropical Fruits

1972. Tourist Publicity. Multicoloured.
1023 1 c. Type **282** (postage) . . . 10 10
1024 2 c. "Isle of Night" . . . 10 10
1025 3 c. Carnival float (vert) . . 10 10
1026 5 c. San Blas textile (air) . . 10 10
1027 8 c. Chaquira (beaded collar) 20 10
1028 25 c. Ruined fort, Portobelo 35 30

283 Map and Flags

284 Baseball Players

1973. Obligatory Tax. Panama City Post Office Building Fund. 7th Bolivar Games.
1030 **283** 1 c. black 10 10

1973. Air. 7th Bolivar Games.
1031 **284** 8 c. red and yellow . . . 15 10
1032 – 10 c. black and blue . . 20 15
1033 – 13 c. multicoloured . . 30 20
1034 – 25 c. black, red & green 55 30
1035 – 50 c. multicoloured . . 1·25 55
1036 – 1 b. multicoloured . . . 2·50 1·10
DESIGNS—VERT: 10 c. Basketball; 13 c. Flaming torch. HORIZ: 25 c. Boxing; 50 c. Panama map and flag, Games emblem and Bolivar; 1 b. Games' medals.

1973. U.N. Security Council Meeting, Panama City. Various stamps surch **O.N.U.** in laurel leaf and **CONSEJO DE SEGURIDAD 15-21 Marzo 1973** and value.
1037 8 c. on 59 c. (No. 974) (postage) 10 10
1038 10 c. on 1 b. (No. 1001) . . 15 15
1039 13 c. on 30 c. (No. 969) . . 20 15
1040 13 c. on 40 c. (No. 1015) (air) 25 15

286 Farming Co-operative

1973. Obligatory Tax. Post Office Building Fund.
1041 **286** 1 c. green and red . . . 10 10
1042 – 1 c. grey and red . . . 10 10
1043 – 1 c. yellow and red . . . 10 10
1044 – 1 c. orange and red . . 10 10
1045 – 1 c. blue and red . . . 10 10
DESIGNS: No. 1042, Silver coins; No. 1043, V. Lorenzo; No. 1044, Cacique Urraca; No. 1045, Post Office building.
See also Nos. 1061/2.

287 J. D. Crespo (educator)

290 Women's upraised Hands

1973. Famous Panamanians. Multicoloured.
1046 3 c. Type **287** (postage) . . . 10 10
1047 5 c. Isabel Obaldia (educator) (air) . . . 10 10
1048 8 c. N. V. Jaen (educator) . 20 15
1049 10 c. "Forest Scene" (Roberto Lewis, painter) . . . 20 15
1050 13 c. R. Miro (poet) . . . 35 20
1051 13 c. "Portrait of a Lady" (M. E. Amador, painter) . 35 20
1052 20 c. "Self-Portrait" (Isaac Benitez, painter) . . . 55 20
1053 21 c. M. A. Guerrero (statesman) . . . 55 25
1054 25 c. Dr. B. Porras (statesman) 55 30
1055 30 c. J. D. Arosemena (statesman) . . . 70 35
1056 34 c. Dr. O. M. Pereira (writer) 90 45
1057 38 c. Dr. R. J. Alfaro (writer) 1·10 50

1973. Air. 50th Anniv of Isabel Obaldia Professional School. Nos. 1047, 1054 and 1056 optd **1923 1973 Godas de Oro Escuela Profesional Isabel Herrera Obaldia** and EP emblem.
1058 5 c. multicoloured . . . 15 10
1059 25 c. multicoloured . . . 55 30
1060 34 c. multicoloured . . . 60 55

1974. Obligatory Tax. Post Office Building Fund. As Nos. 1044/5.
1061 1 c. orange 10 10
1062 2 c. blue 10 10

1974. Surch **VALE** and value.
1063 5 c. on 30 c. black (No. 969) (postage) . . . 10 10
1064 10 c. on 34 c. brown (No. 970) 15 10
1065 13 c. on 21 c. yellow (No. 967) 20 15
1066 1 c. on 25 c. mult (No. 1028) (air) . . . 10 10
1067 3 c. on 20 c. mult (No. 1052) 10 10
1068 8 c. on 38 c. mult (No. 1057) 15 10
1069 10 c. on 34 c. mult (No. 1056) 15 15
1070 13 c. on 21 c. mult (No. 1053) 20 15

1975. Air. International Women's Year.
1071 **290** 17 c. multicoloured . . . 45 20

291 Bayano Dam

1975. Air. 7th Anniv of October 1968 Revolution.
1073 **291** 17 c. black, brown & blue 20 15
1074 – 27 c. blue and green . . . 30 25
1075 – 33 c. multicoloured . . . 1·10 30
DESIGNS—VERT: 27 c. Victoria sugar plant, Veraguas, and sugar cane. HORIZ: 33 c. Tocumen International Airport.

1975. Obligatory Tax. Various stamps surch **VALE PRO EDIFICIO** and value.
1076 – 1 c. on 30 c. black (No. 969) (postage) . . . 10 10
1077 – 1 c. on 40 c. yellow (No. 972) . . . 10 10
1078 – 1 c. on 50 c. black & purple (No. 973) . . . 10 10
1079 – 1 c. on 30 c. mult (No. 1009) 10 10
1080 **282** 1 c. on 1 c. multicoloured 10 10
1081 – 1 c. on 2 c. multicoloured (No. 1024) . . . 10 10
1082 **278** 1 c. on 40 c. mult (air) . . 10 10
1083 – 1 c. on 25 c. mult (No. 1028) 10 10
1084 – 1 c. on 25 c. mult (No. 1052) 10 10
1085 – 1 c. on 20 c. mult (No. 1054) 10 10
1086 – 1 c. on 30 c. mult (No. 1055) 10 10

1975. Obligatory Tax. Post Office Building Fund. As No. 1045.
1087 1 c. red 10 10

294 Bolivar and Thatcher Ferry Bridge

295 "Evibacus princeps"

1976. 150th Anniv of Panama Congress (1st issue). Multicoloured.
1088 6 c. Type **294** (postage) . . . 10 10
1089 23 c. Bolivar Statue (air) . . . 30 25
1090 35 c. Bolivar Hall, Panama City (horiz) . . . 50 30
1091 41 c. Bolivar and flag . . . 60 40

1976. Marine Fauna. Multicoloured.
1092 2 c. Type **295** (postage) . . . 10 10
1093 3 c. "Ptitosarcus sinuosus" (vert) . . . 10 10
1094 4 c. "Acanthaster planci" . . 10 10
1095 7 c. "Oreaster reticulatus" . . 10 10
1096 17 c. "Diodon hystrix" (vert) (air) . . . 25 15
1097 27 c. "Pocillopora damicornis" 40 25

296 "Simon Bolivar"

1976. 150th Anniv of Panama Congress (2nd issue). Designs showing details of Bolivar Monument or flags of Latin-American countries. Multicoloured.
1099 20 c. Type **296** . . . 30 20
1100 20 c. Argentina . . . 30 20
1101 20 c. Bolivia . . . 30 20
1102 20 c. Brazil . . . 30 20
1103 20 c. Chile . . . 30 20
1104 20 c. "Battle scene" . . . 30 20
1105 20 c. Colombia . . . 30 20
1106 20 c. Costa Rica . . . 30 20
1107 20 c. Cuba . . . 30 20
1108 20 c. Ecuador . . . 30 20
1109 20 c. El Salvador . . . 30 20
1110 20 c. Guatemala . . . 30 20
1111 20 c. Guyana . . . 30 20
1112 20 c. Haiti . . . 30 20
1113 20 c. "Congress assembly" . . 30 20
1114 20 c. "Liberated people" . . 30 20
1115 20 c. Honduras . . . 30 20
1116 20 c. Jamaica . . . 30 20
1117 20 c. Mexico . . . 30 20
1118 20 c. Nicaragua . . . 30 20
1119 20 c. Panama . . . 30 20
1120 20 c. Paraguay . . . 30 20
1121 20 c. Peru . . . 30 20
1122 20 c. Dominican Republic . . 30 20
1123 20 c. "Bolivar and standard-bearer" . . . 30 20
1124 20 c. Surinam . . . 30 20
1125 20 c. Trinidad and Tobago . 30 20
1126 20 c. Uruguay . . . 30 20
1127 20 c. Venezuela . . . 30 20
1128 20 c. "Indian Delegation" . . 30 20

297 Nicanor Villalaz (designer of Panama Arms)

298 National Lottery Building, Panama City

1976. Villalaz Commemoration.
1130 **297** 5 c. blue 10 10

1976. "Progressive Panama".
1131 **298** 6 c. multicoloured . . . 10 10

299 Cerro Colorado, Copper Mine

1976. Air.
1132 **299** 23 c. multicoloured . . . 30 20

300 Contadora Island

1977. Tourism.
1133 **300** 3 c. multicoloured . . . 10 10

301 Secretary-General of Pan-American Union, A. Orfila

1978. Signing of Panama–U.S.A. Treaty. Mult.
1134 3 c. Type **301** 10 10
1135 23 c. Treaty signing scene (horiz) . . . 30 25
1136 40 c. President Carter . . . 55 30
1137 50 c. Gen. O. Torrijos of Panama . . . 70 50
Nos. 1134 and 1136/7 were issued together se-tenant in horizontal stamps of three showing Treaty signing as No. 1135.

302 Signing Ratification of Panama Canal Treaty

1978. Ratification of Panama Canal Treaty.
1138 **302** 3 c. multicoloured . . . 10 10
1139 – 5 c. multicoloured . . . 10 10
1140 – 35 c. multicoloured . . . 50 25
1141 – 41 c. multicoloured . . . 60 30
DESIGNS: 5 c., 35 c., 41 c. As Type **302**, but with the design of the Ratification Ceremony spread over the three stamps, issued as a se-tenant strip in the order 5 c. (29 × 39 mm), 41 c. (44 × 39 mm), 35 c. (29 × 39 mm).

303 Colon Harbour and Warehouses

1978. 30th Anniv of Colon Free Zone.
1142 **303** 6 c. multicoloured . . . 10 10

304 Children's Home and Melvin Jones

1978. Birth Centenary of Melvin Jones (founder of Lions International).
1143 **304** 50 c. multicoloured . . . 70 55

305 Pres. Torrijos, "Flavia" (liner) and Children

1979. Return of Canal Zone. Multicoloured.
1144 3 c. Type **305** 10 10
1145 23 c. Presidents Torrijos and Carter, liner and flags of Panama and U.S.A. . . . 40 20

306 "75" and Bank Emblem

1979. 75th Anniv of National Bank.
1146 **306** 6 c. black, red and blue . 10 10

307 Rotary Emblem **308** Children inside Heart

1979. 75th Anniv of Rotary International.
1147 **307** 17 c. blue and yellow . . 25 20

1979. International Year of the Child.
1148 **308** 50 c. multicoloured . . . 70 45

309 U.P.U. Emblem and Globe **310** Colon Station

1979. 18th Universal Postal Union Congress, Rio de Janeiro.
1149 **309** 35 c. multicoloured . . . 50 30

1980. Centenary of Trans-Panamanian Railway.
1150 **310** 1 c. purple and lilac . . . 10 25

311 Postal Headquarters, Balboa (inauguration) **318** Boys in Children's Village

1980. Anniversaries and Events.
1151 **311** 3 c. multicoloured . . . 10 10
1152 – 6 c. multicoloured . . . 10 10
1153 – 17 c. multicoloured . . . 25 20
1154 – 23 c. multicoloured . . . 30 20
1155 – 35 c. blue, black and red 50 30
1156 – 41 c. pink and black . . . 60 40
1157 – 50 c. multicoloured . . . 70 45
DESIGNS—HORIZ: 17 c. Map of Central America and flags (census of the Americas); 23 c. Tourism and Convention Centre (opening); 35 c. Bank emblem (Inter-American Development Bank, 25th anniv); 41 c. F. de Lesseps (Panama Canal cent); 50 c. Olympic Stadium, Moscow (Olympic Games). VERT: 6 c. National flag (return of Canal Zone).

1980. Olympic Games, Lake Placid and Moscow. (a) Optd **1980 LAKE PLACID MOSCU** and venue emblems.
1158 20 c. (No. 1099) 80 80
1160 20 c. (1101) 80 80
1162 20 c. (1103) 80 80
1164 20 c. (1105) 80 80
1166 20 c. (1107) 80 80
1168 20 c. (1109) 80 80
1170 20 c. (1111) 80 80
1172 20 c. (1113) 80 80
1174 20 c. (1115) 80 80
1176 20 c. 1117) 80 80
1178 20 c. (1119) 80 80
1180 20 c. (1121) 80 80
1182 20 c. (1123) 80 80
1184 20 c. (1125) 80 80
1186 20 c. (1127) 80 80

(b) Optd with Lake Placid Olympic emblems and medals total of country indicated.
1159 20 c. **"ALEMANIA D."** (1101) 80 80
1161 20 c. **"AUSTRIA"** (1102) . . 80 80
1163 20 c. **"SUECIA"** (1104) . . 80 80
1165 20 c. **"U.R.S.S."** (1106) . . 80 80
1167 20 c. **"ALEMANIA F."** (1108) 80 80
1169 20 c. **"ITALIA"** (1110) . . . 80 80
1171 20 c. **"U.S.A."** (1112) . . . 80 80
1173 20 c. **"SUIZA"** (1114) . . . 80 80
1175 20 c. **"CANADA/GRAN BRETANA"** (1116) . . . 80 80
1177 20 c. **"NORUEGA"** (1118) . . 80 80
1179 20 c. **"LICHTENSTEIN"** (1120) 80 80
1181 20 c. **"HUNGRIA/ BULGARIA"** (1122) . . . 80 80
1183 20 c. **"FINLANDIA"** (1124) 80 80
1185 20 c. **"HOLANDA"** (1126) . . 80 80
1187 20 c. **"CHECOSLOVAQUIA/ FRANCIA"** (1128) 80 80
Footnote 1158 etc. occur on 1st, 3rd and 5th rows and Nos. 1160 etc. occur in other rows.

(a) Lake Placid and Moscow and venue with Olympic rings.
1188 20 c. (No. 1099) 80 80
1190 20 c. (1101) 80 80
1192 20 c. (1103) 80 80
1194 20 c. (1105) 80 80
1196 20 c. (1107) 80 80
1198 20 c. (1109) 80 80
1200 20 c. (1111) 80 80
1202 20 c. (1113) 80 80
1204 20 c. (1115) 80 80
1206 20 c. (1117) 80 80
1208 20 c. (1119) 80 80
1210 20 c. (1121) 80 80
1212 20 c. (1123) 80 80
1214 20 c. (1125) 80 80
1216 20 c. (1127) 80 80

(b) Optd with country names as indicated.
1189 20 c. **"RUSIA/ALEMANIA D."** (1101) 80 80
1191 20 c. **"SUECIA/FINLANDIA"** (1102) 80 80
1193 20 c. **"GRECIA/BELGICA/ INDIA"** (1104) 80 80
1195 20 c. **"BULGARIA/CUBA"** (1106) 80 80
1197 20 c. **"CHECOSLOVAQUIA/ YUGOSLAVIA"** (1108) . . 80 80
1199 20 c. **"ZIMBAWE/COREA DEL NORTE/ MONGOLIA"** (1110) . . 80 80
1201 20 c. **"ITALIA/HUNGRIA"** (1112) 80 80
1203 20 c. **"AUSTRALIA/ DINAMARCA"** (1114) . . 80 80
1205 20 c. **"TANZANIA/MEXICO/ HOLANDA"** (1116) . . 80 80
1207 20 c. **"RUMANIA/FRANCIA"** (1118) 80 80
1209 20 c. **"BRASIL/ETIOPIA"** (1120) 80 80
1211 20 c. **"IRLANDA/UGANDA/ VENEZUELA"** (1122) . . 80 80
1213 20 c. **"GRAN BRETANA/ POLONIA"** (1124) . . . 80 80
1215 20 c. **"SUIZA/ESPANA/ AUSTRIA"** (1126) . . . 80 80
1217 20 c. **"JAMAICA/LIBANO/ GUYANA"** (1128) 80 80
Footnote Nos. 1188, etc., occur on 1st, 3rd and 5th rows and Nos. 1189 etc., on the others.

1980. Medal Winners at Winter Olympic Games, Lake Placid. (a) Optd with 1980, medals and venue emblems.
1219 20 c. 1980 medals and venue and emblems (No. 1099) . . . 80 80
1221 20 c. As No. 1219 (1101) . . 80 80
1223 20 c. As No. 1219 (1103) . . 80 80
1225 20 c. As No. 1219 (1105) . . 80 80
1227 20 c. As No. 1219 (1107) . . 80 80
1229 20 c. As No. 1219 (1109) . . 80 80
1231 20 c. As No. 1219 (1111) . . 80 80
1233 20 c. As No. 1219 (1113) . . 80 80
1235 20 c. As No. 1219 (1115) . . 80 80
1237 20 c. As No. 1219 (1117) . . 80 80
1239 20 c. As No. 1219 (1119) . . 80 80
1241 20 c. As No. 1219 (1121) . . 80 80
1243 20 c. As No. 1219 (1123) . . 80 80
1245 20 c. As No. 1219 (1125) . . 80 80
1247 20 c. As No. 1219 (1127) . . 80 80

(b) Optd with 1980 medals and venue emblems and Olympic torch and country indicated.
1220 20 c. **"ALEMANIA D."** (1100) 80 80
1222 20 c. **"AUSTRIA"** (1102) . . 80 80
1224 20 c. **"SUECIA"** (1104) . . 80 80
1226 20 c. **"U.R.S.S."** (1106) . . 80 80
1228 20 c. **"ALEMANIA F."** (1108) 80 80
1230 20 c. **"ITALIA"** (1110) . . . 80 80
1232 20 c. **"U.S.A."** (1112) . . . 80 80
1234 20 c. **"SUIZA"** (1114) . . . 80 80
1236 20 c. **"CANADA/GRAN BRETANA"** (1116) . . . 80 80
1238 20 c. **"NORUEGA"** (1118) . . 80 80
1240 20 c. **"LICHTENSTEIN"** (1120) 80 80
1242 20 c. **"HUNGRIA/ BULGARIA"** (1122) . . . 80 80
1244 20 c. **"FINLANDIA"** (1124) 80 80
1246 20 c. **"HOLANDIA"** (1126) . . 80 80
1248 20 c. **"CHECOSLOVAQUIA/ FRANCIA"** (1128) 80 80
Footnote Nos. 1219, etc., occur in 1st, 3rd and 5th rows and Nos. 1220 occur in others.

1980. World Cup Football Championship, Argentina (1978) and Spain (1980). Optd with:
A. Football cup emblems.
B. **"ESPAMER 80"** and "Argentina '78" emblems and inscriptions **"ESPANA '82/CAMPEONATO/ MUNDIAL DE FUTBOL"**.
C. World Cup Trophy and **"ESPANA '82."**.
D. **"ESPANA 82/Football/ Argentina '78/BESPAMER '80 MADRID"**.
E. FIFA globes emblem and **"ESPANA '82/ ARGENTINAA '78/ESPANA '82"**.
F. With ball and inscription as for B.
1249 20 c. No. 1099 (A, C, E) . . . 80 80
1250 20 c. No. 1100 (B, D, F) . . . 80 80
1251 20 c. No. 1101 (A, C, E) . . . 80 80
1252 20 c. No. 1102 (B, D, F) . . . 80 80
1253 20 c. No. 1103 (A, C, E) . . . 80 80
1254 20 c. No. 1104 (B, D, F) . . . 80 80
1255 20 c. No. 1105 (A, C, E) . . . 80 80
1256 20 c. No. 1106 (B, D, F) . . . 80 80
1257 20 c. No. 1107 (A, C, E) . . . 80 80
1258 20 c. No. 1108 (B, D, F) . . . 80 80
1259 20 c. No. 1109 (A, C, E) . . . 80 80
1260 20 c. No. 1110 (B, D, F) . . . 80 80
1261 20 c. No. 1111 (A, C, E) . . . 80 80
1262 20 c. No. 1112 (B, D, F) . . . 80 80
1263 20 c. No. 1113 (A, C, E) . . . 80 80
1264 20 c. No. 1114 (B, D, F) . . . 80 80
1265 20 c. No. 1115 (A, C, E) . . . 80 80
1266 20 c. No. 1116 (B, D, F) . . . 80 80
1267 20 c. No. 1117 (A, C, E) . . . 80 80
1268 20 c. No. 1118 (B, D, F) . . . 80 80
1269 20 c. No. 1119 (A, C, E) . . . 80 80
1270 20 c. No. 1120 (B, D, F) . . . 80 80
1271 20 c. No. 1121 (A, C, E) . . . 80 80
1272 20 c. No. 1122 (B, D, F) . . . 80 80
1273 20 c. No. 1123 (A, C, E) . . . 80 80
1274 20 c. No. 1124 (B, D, F) . . . 80 80
1275 20 c. No. 1125 (A, C, E) . . . 80 80
1276 20 c. No. 1126 (B, D, F) . . . 80 80
1277 20 c. No. 1127 (A, C, E) . . . 80 80
1278 20 c. No. 1128 (B, D, F) . . . 80 80

1980. Obligatory Tax. Children's Village. Multicoloured.
1280 2 c. Type **318** 10 10
1281 2 c. Boy with chicks 10 10
1282 2 c. Working in the fields . . 10 10
1283 2 c. Boys with pig 10 10

319 Jean Baptiste de la Salle and Map showing La Salle Schools **320** Louis Braille

1981. Education in Panama by the Christian Schools.
1285 **319** 17 c. blue, black and red . 25 20

1981. International Year of Disabled People.
1286 **320** 23 c. multicoloured . . . 30 20

321 Statue of the Virgin

1981. 150th Anniv of Apparition of Miraculous Virgin to St. Catharine Laboure.
1287 **321** 35 c. multicoloured . . . 50 35

322 Crimson-backed Tanager

1981. Birds. Multicoloured.
1288 3 c. Type **322** 65 10
1289 6 c. Chestnut-fronted macaw (vert) 80 30
1290 41 c. Violet sabrewing (vert) . 3·25 1·90
1291 50 c. Keel-billed toucan . . . 4·25 2·10

323 "Boy feeding Donkey" (Ricardo Morales) **324** Banner

1981. Obligatory Tax. Christmas. Children's Village. Multicoloured.
1292 2 c. Type **323** 10 10
1293 2 c. "Nativity" (Enrique Daniel Austin) 10 10
1294 2 c. "Bird in Tree" (Jorge Gonzalez) 10 10
1295 2 c. "Church" (Eric Belgrane) 10 10

1981. National Reaffirmation.
1297 **324** 3 c. multicoloured . . . 10 10

325 General Herrera **326** Ricardo J. Alfaro

1982. 1st Death Anniv of General Omar Torrijos Herrera. Multicoloured.
1298 5 c. Aerial view of Panama (postage) 10 10
1299 6 c. Colecito army camp . . 10 10
1300 17 c. Bayano river barrage . 25 20
1301 50 c. Felipillo engineering works 70 45
1302 23 c. Type **325** (air) 35 25
1303 35 c. Security Council reunion 50 30
1304 41 c. Gen. Omar Torrijos airport . . . . 1·25 45

1982. Birth Centenary of Ricardo J. Alfaro (statesman).
1306 **326** 3 c. black, mauve and blue (postage) 10 10
1307 – 17 c. black and mauve (air) 25 15
1308 – 23 c. multicoloured . . . 30 20
DESIGNS: 17 c. Profile of Alfaro wearing spectacles (as humanist); 23 c. Portrait of Alfaro (as lawyer).

328 Pig Farming **329** Pele (Brazilian footballer)

1982. Obligatory tax. Christmas. Children's Village. Multicoloured.
1309 2 c. Type **328** 10 10
1310 2 c. Gardening 10 10
1311 2 c. Metalwork (horiz) . . . 10 10
1312 2 c. Bee-keeping (horiz) . . . 10 10

1982. World Cup Football Championship, Spain. Multicoloured.
1314 50 c. Italian team (horiz) (postage) 70 45
1315 23 c. Football emblem and map of Panama (air) 30 20
1316 35 c. Type **329** 50 30
1317 41 c. World Cup Trophy . . 60 35

330 Chamber of Trade Emblem

1983. "Expo Comer" Chamber of Trade Exhibition.
1319 **330** 17 c. lt blue, blue, & gold 25 15

331 Dr. Nicolas Solano

332 Pope John Paul II giving Blessing

1983. Air. Birth Centenary (1982) of Dr. Nicolas Solano (anti-tuberculosis pioneer).
1320 **331** 23 c. brown 35 20

1983. Papal Visit. Multicoloured.
1321 6 c. Type **332** (postage) . . . 10 10
1322 17 c. Pope John Paul II . . . 25 15
1323 35 c. Pope and map of Panama (air) 50 30

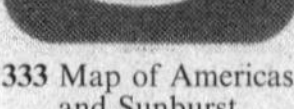

333 Map of Americas and Sunburst
334 Simon Bolivar

1983. 24th Assembly of Inter-American Development Bank Governors.
1324 **333** 50 c. light blue, blue and gold 70 45

1983. Birth Bicentenary of Simon Bolivar.
1325 **334** 50 c. multicoloured 70 45

335 Postal Union of the Americas and Spain Emblem
336 Moslem Mosque

1983. World Communications Day. Mult.
1327 30 c. Type **335** 45 25
1328 40 c. W.C.Y. Emblem 60 40
1329 50 c. Universal Postal Union emblem 70 45
1330 60 c. "Flying Dove" (Alfredo Sinclair) 85 55

1983. Freedom of Worship. Multicoloured.
1332 3 c. Type **336** 10 10
1333 5 c. Bahai temple 10 10
1334 6 c. Church of St. Francis of the Mountains, Veraguas 10 10
1335 17 c. Shevet Ahim synagogue 25 15

337 "The Annunciation" (Dagoberto Moran)
338 Ricardo Miro (writer)

1983. Obligatory Tax. Christmas. Children's Village. Multicoloured.
1336 2 c. Type **337** 10 10
1337 2 c. Church and houses (Leonidas Molinar) (vert) 10 10
1338 2 c. Bethlehem and star (Colon Olmedo Zambrano) (vert) 10 10
1339 2 c. Flight into Egypt (Hector Ulises Velasquez) (vert) 10 10

1983. Famous Panamanians. Multicoloured.
1341 1 c. Type **338** 10 10
1342 3 c. Richard Newman (educationalist) 10 10
1343 5 c. Cristobal Rodriguez (politician) 10 10
1344 6 c. Alcibiades Arosemena (politician) 10 10
1345 35 c. Cirilo Martinez (educationalist) 50 30

339 "Rural Architecture" (Juan Manuel Cedero)

1983. Paintings. Multicoloured.
1346 1 c. Type **339** 10 10
1347 1 c. "Large Nude" (Manuel Chong Neto) 10 10
1348 3 c. "On another Occasion" (Spiros Vamvas) 10 10
1349 6 c. "Punta Chame" (Guillermo Trujillo) 10 10
1350 28 c. "Neon Light" (Alfredo Sinclair) 30 20
1351 35 c. "The Prophet" (Alfredo Sinclair) (vert) 50 30
1352 41 c. "Highland Girls" (Al Sprague) (vert) 60 40
1353 1 b. "One Morning" (Ignacio Mallol Pibernat) 1·40 75

340 Tonosi Double Jug

1984. Archaeological Finds. Multicoloured.
1354 30 c. Type **340** 35 10
1355 40 c. Dish on stand 60 20
1356 50 c. Jug decorated with human face (vert) 70 25
1357 60 c. Waisted bowl (vert) 85 35

341 Boxing
342 Roberto Duran

1984. Olympic Games, Los Angeles. Mult.
1359 19 c. Type **341** 35 25
1360 19 c. Baseball 35 25
1361 19 c. Basketball (vert) 35 25
1362 19 c. Swimming (vert) 35 25

1984. Roberto Duran (boxer) Commem.
1363 **342** 26 c. multicoloured 45 30

343 Shooting

1984. Olympic Games, Los Angeles (2nd series). Multicoloured.
1364 6 c. Type **343** (postage) 15 10
1366 30 c. Weightlifting (air) 50 30
1367 37 c. Wrestling 65 45
1368 1 b. Long jump 1·25 90

344 "Pensive Woman" (Manuel Chong Neto)
345 Map, Pres. Torrijos Herrera and Liner in Canal Lock

1984. Paintings. Multicoloured.
1369 1 c. Type **344** 10 10
1370 3 c. "The Child" (Alfredo Sinclair) (horiz) 10 10
1371 6 c. "A Day in the Life of Rumalda" (Brooke Alfaro) (horiz) 15 10
1372 30 c. "Highlanders" (Al Sprague) 50 10
1373 37 c. "Ballet Interval" (Roberto Sprague) (horiz) 65 15
1374 44 c. "Wood on Chame Head" (Guillermo Trujillo) (horiz) 75 25
1375 50 c. "La Plaza Azul" (Juan Manuel Cedeno) (horiz) 60 25
1376 1 b. "Ira" (Spiros Vamvas) (horiz) 1·25 90

1984. 5th Anniv of Canal Zone Postal Sovereignty.
1377 **345** 19 c. multicoloured 25 25

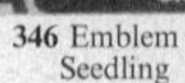

346 Emblem as Seedling
347 Boy

1984. Air. World Food Day.
1378 **346** 30 c. red, green and blue 50 45

1984. Obligatory Tax. Christmas. Children's Village. Multicoloured.
1379 2 c. Type **347** 10 10
1380 2 c. Boy in tee-shirt 10 10
1381 2 c. Boy in checked shirt 10 10
1382 2 c. Cub scout 10 10

348 American Manatee

1984. Animals. Each in black.
1384 3 c. Type **348** (postage) 10 10
1385 30 c. "Tayra" (air) 60 25
1386 44 c. Jaguarundi 85 40
1387 50 c. White-lipped peccary 90 40

349 Copper One Centesimo Coins, 1935

1985. Coins. Multicoloured.
1389 3 c. Type **349** (postage) 10 10
1390 3 c. Silver ten centesimo coins, 1904 10 10
1391 3 c. Silver five centesimo coins, 1916 10 10
1392 30 c. Silver 50 centesimo coins, 1904 (air) 50 30
1393 37 c. Silver half balboa coins, 1962 65 45
1394 44 c. Silver balboa coins, 1953 75 50

350 Figures on Map reaching for Dove
351 Tanker in Dock

1985. Contadora Peace Movement.
1395 **350** 10 c. multicoloured 15 10
1396 20 c. multicoloured 30 20
1397 30 c. multicoloured 40 25

1985. 70th Anniv of Panama Canal.
1399 **351** 19 c. multicoloured 70 20

352 Scouts with Statue of Christ
354 Boys in Cab of Crane

353 "40" on Emblem

1985. Obligatory Tax. Christmas. Children's Village. Multicoloured.
1400 2 c. Type **352** 10 10
1401 2 c. Children holding cards spelling "Feliz Navidad" 10 10
1402 2 c. Children holding balloons 10 10
1403 2 c. Group of cub scouts 10 10

1986. 40th Anniv (1985) of U.N.O.
1405 **353** 23 c. multicoloured 30 20

1986. International Youth Year (1985).
1406 **354** 30 c. multicoloured 40 25

355 "Awaiting Her Turn" (Al Sprague)
356 Atlapa Convention Centre

1986. Paintings. Multicoloured.
1407 3 c. Type **355** 10 10
1408 5 c. "Aerobics" (Guillermo Trujillo) (horiz) 10 10
1409 19 c. "House of Cardboard" (Eduardo Augustine) 30 20
1410 30 c. "Tierra Gate" (Juan Manuel Cedeno) (horiz) 40 25
1411 36 c. "Supper for Three" (Brood Alfaro) 50 30
1412 42 c. "Tenderness" (Alfredo Sinclair) 60 40
1413 50 c. "Lady of Character" (Manuel Chong Neto) 70 45
1414 60 c. "Calla Lilies No. 1" (Maigualida de Diaz) (horiz) 80 55

1986. Miss Universe Contest. Multicoloured.
1415 23 c. Type **356** 30 20
1416 60 c. Emblem 80 55

357 Comet and Globe
358 Angels

1986. Appearance of Halley's Comet.
1417 **357** 23 c. multicoloured 25 15
1418 30 c. blue, brown and yellow 35 25
DESIGN: 30 c. Panama la Vieja Cathedral tower.

1986. Obligatory Tax. 20th Anniv of Children's Village. Children's drawings. Multicoloured.
1420 2 c. Type **358** 10 10
1421 2 c. Cupids 10 10
1422 2 c. Indians 10 10
1423 2 c. Angels (different) 10 10

359 Basketball
360 Argentina Player

1986. 15th Central American and Caribbean Games, Santiago. Multicoloured.
1425 20 c. Type **359** 20 10
1426 23 c. Sports 25 15

1986. World Cup Football Championship, Mexico. Multicoloured.
1427 23 c. Type **360** 25 15
1428 30 c. West Germany player 35 25
1429 37 c. West Germany and Argentina players 45 30

361 Crib
362 Dove and Globe

1986. Christmas. Multicoloured.
1431 23 c. Type **361** 25 15
1432 36 c. Tree and presents 40 25
1433 42 c. As No. 1432 45 30

1986. International Peace Year. Multicoloured.
1434 8 c. Type **362** 10 10
1435 19 c. Profiles and emblem 20 10

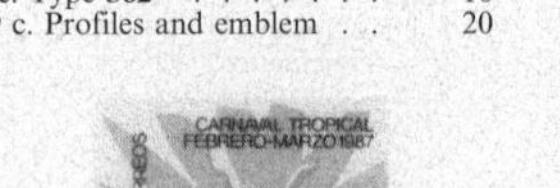

363 Mask

1987. Tropical Carnival. Multicoloured.
1436 20 c. Type **363** 20 10
1437 35 c. Sun with eye mask 40 25

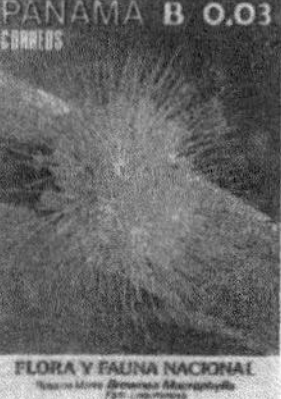
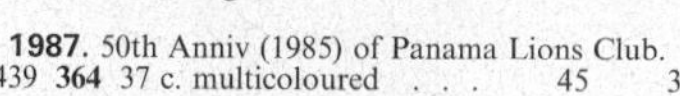

364 Headquarters Building **365** Mountain Rose

1987. 50th Anniv (1985) of Panama Lions Club.
1439 **364** 37 c. multicoloured . . . 45 30

1987. Flowers and Birds. Multicoloured.
1440 3 c. Type **365** 10 10
1441 5 c. Blue-grey tanager (horiz) 50 15
1442 8 c. Golden cup 10 10
1443 15 c. Tropical kingbird (horiz) 90 15
1444 19 c. "Barleria micans" (flower) 20 10
1445 23 c. Brown pelican (horiz) . 1·10 20
1446 30 c. "Cordia dentata" (flower) 35 25
1447 36 c. Rufous pigeon (horiz) . 1·50 35

366 Octavio Menendez Pereira (founder) and Anniversary Monument

1987. 50th Anniv (1986) of Panama University.
1448 **366** 19 c. multicoloured . . . 20 10

367 Emblem in "40" **368** Heinrich Schutz

1987. 40th Anniv (1985) of F.A.O.
1449 **367** 10 c. brown, yellow and black 10 10
1450 45 c. brown, green and black 50 30

1987. Composers and 7th Anniv (1986) of National Theatre.
1451 **368** 19 c. multicoloured . . . 20 10
1452 – 30 c. green, mve & brn . 35 25
1453 – 37 c. brown, blue and deep blue 45 30
1454 – 60 c. green, yell & blk . . 70 45
DESIGNS—HORIZ: 30 c. National Theatre. VERT: 37 c. Johann Sebastian Bach; 60 c. Georg Friedrich Handel.

369 Development Projects **370** Horse-drawn Fire Pump, 1887, and Modern Appliance

1987. 25th Anniv (1986) of Inter-American Development Bank.
1455 **369** 23 c. multicoloured . . . 25 15

1987. Centenary of Fire Service. Mult.
1456 25 c. Type **370** 30 20
1457 35 c. Fireman carrying boy . 40 25

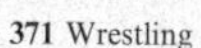

371 Wrestling **372** "Adoration of the Magi" (Albrecht Nentz)

1987. 10th Pan-American Games, Indianapolis. Multicoloured.
1458 15 c. Type **371** 20 10
1459 25 c. Tennis (vert) 25 15
1460 30 c. Swimming 35 25
1461 41 c. Basketball (vert) 45 30
1462 60 c. Cycling (vert) 70 45

1987. Christmas. Multicoloured.
1464 22 c. Type **372** 25 15
1465 35 c. "The Virgin adored by Angels" (Matthias Grunewald) 40 25
1466 37 c. "Virgin and Child" (Konrad Witz) 45 30

373 Distressed Family and Poor Housing **374** Heart falling into Crack

1987. International Year of Shelter for the Homeless. Multicoloured.
1467 45 c. Type **373** 50 30
1468 50 c. Happy family and stylized modern housing 50 30

1988. Anti-Drugs Campaign.
1469 **374** 10 c. red and orange . . 10 10
1470 17 c. red and green . . . 20 10
1471 25 c. red and blue . . . 30 20

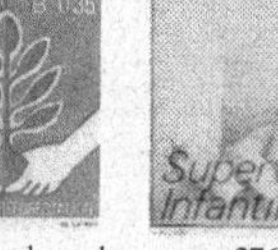

375 Hands and Sapling **376** Breastfeeding

1988. Reafforestation Campaign.
1472 **375** 35 c. deep green and green 40 25
1473 40 c. red and purple . . 45 30
1474 45 c. brown and bistre . 50 30

1988. U.N.I.C.E.F. Infant Survival Campaign. Multicoloured.
1475 20 c. Type **376** 25 15
1476 31 c. Vaccination 35 25
1477 45 c. Children playing by lake (vert) 50 30

377 Rock Beauty

1988. Fishes. Multicoloured.
1478 7 c. Type **377** 10 10
1479 35 c. French angelfish . . . 40 25
1480 60 c. Black bar soldier fish . 70 45
1481 1 b. Spotted drum fish . . . 1·25 90

378 Emblem and Clasped Hands **379** "Virgin with Donors"

1988. 75th Anniv of Girl Guide Movement.
1482 **378** 35 c. multicoloured . . 35 25

1988. Christmas. Anonymous Paintings from Museum of Colonial Religious Art. Mult.
1483 17 c. Type **379** (postage) . . 20 10
1484 45 c. "Virgin of the Rosary with St. Dominic" 50 30
1485 35 c. "St. Joseph with the Child" (air) 35 25

380 Athletes and Silver Medal (Brazil) **381** St. John Bosco

1989. Seoul Olympic Games Medals. Mult.
1486 17 c. Type **380** (postage) . . 20 10
1487 25 c. Wrestlers and gold medal (Hungary) 30 20
1488 60 c. Weightlifter and gold medal (Turkey) 70 45
1490 35 c. Boxers and bronze medal (Colombia) (air) 35 25

1989. Death Centenary of St. John Bosco (founder of Salesian Brothers). Multicoloured.
1491 10 c. Type **381** 15 10
1492 20 c. Menor Basilica and St. John with people 25 15

382 Anniversary Emblem **383** "Ancon I" (first ship through Canal)

1989. 125th Anniv of Red Cross Movement.
1493 **382** 40 c. black and red . . . 50 30
1494 – 1 b. multicoloured . . . 1·50 90
DESIGN: 1 b. Red Cross workers putting patient in ambulance.

1989. Air. 75th Anniv of Panama Canal.
1495 **383** 35 c. red, black & yellow 60 40
1496 – 60 c. multicoloured . . . 1·00 80
DESIGN: 60 c. Modern tanker.

384 Barriles Ceremonial Statue **385** "March of the Women on Versailles" (engraving)

1989. America. Pre-Columbian Artefacts. Multicoloured.
1497 20 c. Type **384** 25 15
1498 35 c. Ceramic vase 45 30

1989. Bicent of French Revolution. Mult.
1499 25 c. Type **385** (postage) . . . 30 20
1500 35 c. "Storming the Bastille" (air) 45 30
1501 45 c. Birds 55 35

386 "Holy Family"

1989. Christmas. Multicoloured.
1502 17 c. Type **386** 20 10
1503 35 c. 1988 crib in Cathedral . 45 30
1504 45 c. "Nativity" 55 35
The 17 and 45 c. show children's paintings.

387 "Byrsonima crassifolia" **388** Sinan

1990. Fruit. Multicoloured.
1505 20 c. Type **387** 20 10
1506 35 c. "Bactris gasipaes" . . . 40 25
1507 40 c. "Anacardium occidentale" 40 25

1990. 88th Birthday of Rogelio Sinan (writer).
1508 **388** 23 c. brown and blue . . 25 15

389 Pond Turtle

1990. Reptiles. Multicoloured.
1509 35 c. Type **389** 40 25
1510 45 c. Olive loggerhead turtle . 50 35
1511 60 c. Red-footed tortoise . . 65 40

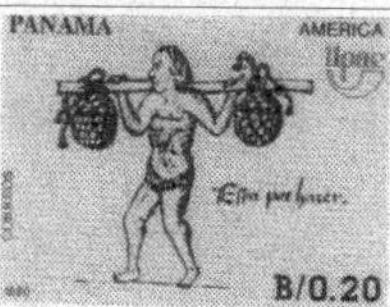

390 Carrying Goods on Yoke (after Oviedo)

1990. America.
1512 **390** 20 c. brown, light brown and gold 20 10
1513 – 35 c. multicoloured . . . 70 50
DESIGN—VERT: 35 c. Warrior wearing gold chest ornament and armbands.

391 Dr. Guillermo Patterson, jun., "Father of Chemistry" **393** St. Ignatius

392 In Sight of Land

1990. Chemistry in Panama.
1514 **391** 25 c. black & turquoise . 25 15
1515 – 35 c. multicoloured . . . 40 25
1516 – 45 c. multicoloured . . . 50 35
DESIGNS: 35 c. Evaporation experiment; 45 c. Books and laboratory equipment.

1991. America. 490th Anniv of Discovery of Panama Isthmus by Rodrigo Bastidas.
1517 **392** 35 c. multicoloured . . . 50 35

1991. 450th Anniv of Society of Jesus and 500th Birth Anniv of St. Ignatius de Loyola (founder).
1518 **393** 20 c. multicoloured . . . 30 20

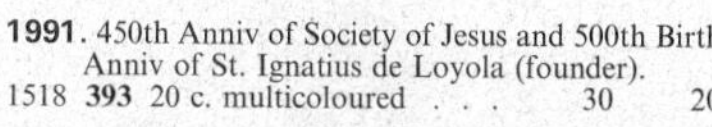

394 Declaration of Women's Right to Vote

1991. 50th Anniv of First Presidency of Dr. Arnulfo Arias Madrid.
1519 **394** 10 c. brown, stone & gold 15 10
1520 – 10 c. brown, stone & gold 15 10
DESIGN: No. 1520, Department of Social Security headquarters.

395 "Glory to God..." (Luke 2:14) and Score of "Gloria in Excelsis"

1991. Christmas. Multicoloured.
1521 35 c. Type **395** 50 35
1522 35 c. Nativity 50 35

396 Adoration of the Kings

1992. Epiphany.
1523 **396** 10 c. multicoloured . . . 15 10

INDEX

Countries can be quickly located by referring to the index at the end of this volume.

397 Family and Housing Estate

1992. "New Lives" Housing Project.
1524 **397** 5 c. multicoloured . . . 10 10

398 Costa Rican and Panamanian shaking Hands

1992. 50th Anniv (1991) of Border Agreement with Costa Rica. Multicoloured.
1525 20 c. Type **398** 30 20
1526 40 c. Map showing Costa Rica and Panama 55 35
1527 50 c. Presidents Calderon and Arias and national flags . . 70 45

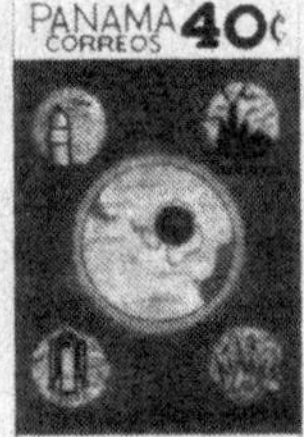

399 Pollutants and Hole over Antarctic

1992. "Save the Ozone Layer".
1528 **399** 40 c. multicoloured . . . 55 35

400 Exhibition Emblem

1992. "Expocomer 92" 10th International Trade Exhibition, Panama City.
1529 **400** 10 c. multicoloured . . . 15 10

401 Portrait

402 Maria Olimpia de Obaldia

1992. 1st Death Anniv of Dame Margot Fonteyn (ballet dancer). Portraits by Pietro Annigoni. Multicoloured.
1530 35 c. Type **401** 50 35
1531 45 c. On stage 60 40

1992. Birth Centenary of Maria Olimpia de Obaldia (poet).
1532 **402** 10 c. multicoloured . . . 15 10

403 Athletics Events and Map of Spain

1992. Olympic Games, Barcelona.
1533 **403** 10 c. multicoloured . . . 15 10

404 Paca

1992. Endangered Animals.
1534 **404** 5 c. brown, stone & blk 10 10
1535 – 10 c. black, brn & stone 15 10
1536 – 15 c. brown, blk & stone 20 15
1537 – 20 c. multicoloured . . 30 20
DESIGNS: 10 c. Harpy eagle; 15 c. Jaguar; 20 c. Iguana.

405 Zion Baptist Church, Bocas del Toro

1992. Centenary of Baptist Church in Panama.
1538 **405** 20 c. multicoloured . . 30 20

406 Columbus's Fleet

1992. America. 500th Anniv of Discovery of America by Columbus. Multicoloured.
1539 20 c. Type **406** 30 20
1540 35 c. Columbus planting flag 50 35

407 Flag and Map of Europe

408 Mascot

1992. European Single Market.
1541 **407** 10 c. multicoloured . . 15 10

1992. "Expo '92" World's Fair, Seville.
1542 **408** 10 c. multicoloured . . 15 10

409 Occupations

1992. American Workers' Health Year.
1543 **409** 15 c. multicoloured . . 20 15

410 Angel and Shepherds

1992. Christmas. Multicoloured.
1544 20 c. Type **410** 30 20
1545 35 c. Mary and Joseph arriving at Bethlehem 50 35

411 Jesus lighting up the Americas

1993. 500th Anniv (1992) of Evangelization of the American Continent.
1546 **411** 10 c. multicoloured . . . 15 10

412 Woman on Crutches and Wheelchair-bound Man

413 Herrera (bust)

1993. National Day of Disabled Persons.
1547 **412** 5 c. multicoloured 10 10

1993. 32nd Death Anniv of Dr. Jose de la Cruz Herrera (essayist).
1548 **413** 5 c. multicoloured 10 10

414 Nutritious Foods and Emblems

1993. International Nutrition Conference, Rome.
1549 **414** 10 c. multicoloured . . . 15 10

415 Caravel and Columbus in Portobelo Harbour

1994. 490th Anniv (1992) of Columbus's Fourth Voyage and Exploration of the Panama Isthmus.
1550 **415** 50 c. multicoloured . . . 65 45

416 Panama Flag and Greek Motifs

418 Chinese Family and House

1995. 50th Anniv of Greek Community in Panama.
1551 **416** 20 c. multicoloured . . . 25 15

1995. Various stamps surch.
1553 – 20 c. on 23 c. multicoloured (1459) . 25 15
1554 **373** 25 c. on 45 c. multicoloured 30 20
1555 – 30 c. on 45 c. multicoloured (1510) . 40 25
1556 **375** 35 c. on 45 c. brown and bistre 45 30
1557 – 35 c. on 45 c. multicoloured (1477) . 45 30
1558 – 40 c. on 41 c. multicoloured (1461) . 50 35
1559 – 50 c. on 60 c. multicoloured (1511) . 65 45
1560 – 1 b. on 50 c. multicoloured (1480) . . . . . . 1·25 85

1996. Chinese Presence in Panama. 142nd Anniv of Arrival of First Chinese Immigrants.
1561 **418** 60 c. multicoloured . . . 75 50

419 The King's Bridge from the North (16th century)

1996. 475th Anniv (1994) of Founding by the Spanish of Panama City. Multicoloured.
1563 15 c. Type **419** 20 15
1564 20 c. City arms, 1521 (vert) . 25 15
1565 25 c. Plan of first cathedral . 30 20
1566 35 c. Present-day ruins of Cathedral of the Assumption of Our Lady 45 30

420 "60", Campus and Emblem

1996. 60th Anniv of Panama University.
1567 **420** 40 c. multicoloured . . . 50 35

421 Anniversary Emblem

1996. 75th Anniv of Panama Chapter of Rotary International.
1568 **421** 5 b. multicoloured . . . 6·25 4·25

422 Great Tinamou

1996. America (1993). Endangered Species.
1569 **422** 20 c. multicoloured . . . 25 15

423 Northern Coati

1996. Mammals. Multicoloured.
1570 25 c. Type **423** 30 20
1571 25 c. Collared anteater ("Tamandua mexicana") . 30 20
1572 25 c. Two-toed anteater ("Cyclopes didactylus") . . 30 20
1573 25 c. Puma 30 20

424 De Lesseps

425 "50" and Emblem

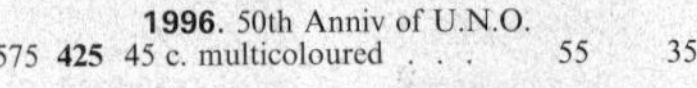
1996. Death Centenary of Ferdinand, Vicomte de Lesseps (builder of Suez Canal).
1574 **424** 35 c. multicoloured . . . 45 30

1996. 50th Anniv of U.N.O.
1575 **425** 45 c. multicoloured . . . 55 35

426 Emblem and Motto

427 Bello

1996. 25th Anniv (1993) of Panama Chapter of Kiwanis International.
1576 **426** 40 c. multicoloured . . . 50 35

1996. 25th Anniv (1995) of Andres Bello Covenant for Education, Science, Technology and Culture.
1577 **427** 35 c. multicoloured . . . 45 30

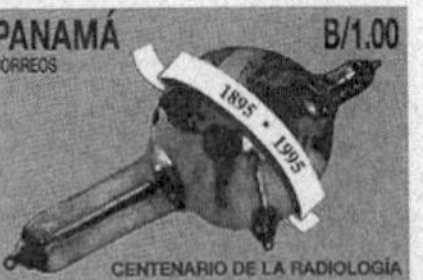

428 World Map on X-ray Equipment

1996. Centenary of Discovery of X-rays by Wilhelm Rontgen.
1578 **428** 1 b. multicoloured . . . 1·25 85

429 Madonna and Child

1996. Christmas.
1579 **429** 35 c. multicoloured . . . 45 30

ACKNOWLEDGEMENT OF RECEIPT STAMPS

1898. Handstamped **A. R. COLON COLOMBIA.**
AR24 **5** 5 c. blue . . . . 4·50 3·75
AR25 10 c. orange . . . . . . 8·00 8·00

1902. Handstamped **AR** in circle.
AR32 **5** 5 c. blue . . . . 3·00 3·00
AR33 10 c. orange . . . . . . 6·00 6·00

1903. No. AR169 of Colombia handstamped **AR** in circle.
AR34 **AR 60** 5 c. red . . . . . . 11·00 11·00

AR 37

1904.
AR135 **AR 37** 5 c. blue 90 90

1916. Optd **A.R.**
AR177 **50** $2\frac{1}{2}$ c. red 90 90

EXPRESS LETTER STAMPS

1926. Optd **EXPRESO.**
E220 **57** 10 c. black and orange . 4·25 2·10
E221 20 c. black and brown . 5·50 2·10

E **81** Cyclist Messenger

1929.
E226 **E 81** 10 c. orange 90 70
E227 20 c. brown . . . . . 1·75 1·10

INSURANCE STAMPS

1942. Surch **SEGURO POSTAL HABILITADO** and value.
IN430 5 c. on 1 b. black (No. 373) 45 35
IN431 10 c. on 1 b. brown (No. 365) 70 55
IN432 25 c. on 50 c. brown (No. 372) 1·25 1·25

POSTAGE DUE STAMPS

D **58** San Geronimo Castle Gate, Portobelo

1915.
D169 **D 58** 1 c. brown . . . . . 1·90 30
D170 – 2 c. brown . . . . . 2·75 25
D171 – 4 c. brown . . . . . 3·75 55
D172 – 10 c. brown . . . . . 2·75 1·10
DESIGNS—VERT: 2 c. Statue of Columbus. HORIZ: 4 c. House of Deputies. VERT: 10 c. Pedro J. Sosa.

No. D169 is wrongly inscr "CASTILLO DE SAN LORENZO CHAGRES".

D 86

1930.
D240 **D 86** 1 c. green 70 25
D241 2 c. red 70 20
D242 4 c. blue 75 30
D243 10 c. violet 75 40

REGISTRATION STAMPS

R 4

1888.
R12 **R 4** 10 c. black on grey . . 6·00 4·00

1897. Handstamped **R COLON** in circle.
R22 **5** 10 c. orange . . . . 4·25 4·00

R 15

1900.
R29 **R 15** 10 c. black on blue . . . 2·50 2·10
R30 10 c. red . . . . 18·00 15·00

1902. No. R30 surch by hand.
R31 **R 15** 20 c. on 10 c. red . . . 15·00 12·00

1903. Type R **85** of Colombia optd **REPUBLICA DE PANAMA.**
R42 20 c. red on blue . . . . 27·00
R43 20 c. blue on blue . . . . . . 27·00

1903. Nos. R42/3 surch.
R46 10 c. on 20 c. red on blue . . 50·00 50·00
R47 10 c. on 20 c. blue on blue . . 50·00 50·00

1904. Optd **PANAMA.**
R60 **5** 10 c. orange . . . . 2·10 2·10

1904. Type R **6** of Colombia surch **Panama 10** and bar.
R67 10 c. on 20 c. red on blue . . 38·00 35·00
R68 10 c. on 20 c. blue on blue . . 38·00 35·00

1904. Type R **85** of Colombia optd **Republica de Panama.**
R106 20 c. red on blue . . . . . . 5·00 5·00

R 35

1904.
R133 **R 35** 10 c. green 70 30

1916. Stamps of Panama surch **R 5 cts.**
R175 **46** 5 c. on 8 c. black & purple 2·10 1·40
R176 **52** 5 c. on 8 c. black & purple 2·10 50

TOO LATE STAMPS

1903. Too Late stamp of Colombia optd **REPUBLICA DE PANAMA.**
L44 **L 86** 5 c. violet on red . . . . 7·50 5·50

L 36

1904.
L134 **L 36** $2\frac{1}{2}$ c. red 70 40

1910. Typewritten optd **Retardo.**
L158 **50** $2\frac{1}{2}$ c. red . . . . 75·00 75·00

1910. Optd **RETARDO.**
L159 **50** $2\frac{1}{2}$ c. red . . . . 38·00 30·00

1916. Surch **RETARDO UN CENTESIMO.**
L174 **38** 1 c. on $\frac{1}{2}$ c. orange . . . . 15·00 12·00

APPENDIX

The following stamps have either been issued in excess of postal needs or have not been available to the public in a reasonable quantities at face value. Such stamps may later be given full listing if there is evidence of regular postal use.

1964.
Satellites. Postage $\frac{1}{2}$, 1 c.; Air 5, 10, 21, 50 c.

1965.
Tokyo Olympic Games Medal Winners. Postage $\frac{1}{2}$, 1, 2, 3, 4 c.; Air 5, 6, 7, 10, 21, 31 c.

Space Research. Postage $\frac{1}{2}$, 1, 2, 3 c.; Air 5, 10, 11, 31 c.

400th Birth Anniv of Galileo. Air 10, 21 c.

Peaceful Uses of Atomic Energy. Postage $\frac{1}{2}$, 1, 4 c.; Air 6, 10, 21 c.

Nobel Prize Medals. Air 10, 21 c.

Pres. John Kennedy. Postage $\frac{1}{2}$, 1 c.; Air 10 + 5 c., 21 + 10 c., 31 + 15 c.

1966.
Pope Paul's Visit to U.N. in New York. Postage $\frac{1}{2}$, 1 c.; Air 5, 10, 21, 31 c.

Famous Men. Postage $\frac{1}{2}$ c.; Air 10, 31 c.

Famous Paintings. Postage $\frac{1}{2}$ c.; Air 10, 31 c.

World Cup Football Championships. Postage $\frac{1}{2}$, $\frac{1}{2}$ c.; Air 10, 10, 21, 21 c.

Italian Space Research. Postage $\frac{1}{2}$, 1 c.; Air 5, 10, 21 c.

Centenary of I.T.U. Air. 31 c.

World Cup Winners. Optd on 1966 World Cup Issue. Postage $\frac{1}{2}$, $\frac{1}{2}$ c.; Air. 10, 10, 21, 21 c.

Religious Paintings. Postage $\frac{1}{2}$, 1, 2, 3 c.; Air 21, 21 c.

Churchill and Space Research. Postage $\frac{1}{2}$ c.; Air 10, 31 c.

3rd Death Anniv of Pres. John Kennedy. Postage $\frac{1}{2}$, 1 c.; Air 10, 31, c.

Jules Verne and Space Research. Postage $\frac{1}{2}$, 1 c.; Air 5, 10, 21, 31 c.

1967.
Religious Paintings. Postage $\frac{1}{2}$, 1 c.; Air 5, 10, 21, 31 c.

Mexico Olympics. Postage $\frac{1}{2}$, 1 c.; Air 5, 10, 21, 31 c.

Famous Paintings. Postage 5 c. × 3; Air 21 c. × 3.

Goya's Paintings. Postage 2, 3, 4 c.; Air 5, 8, 10, 13, 21 c.

1968.
Religious Paintings. Postage 1, 1, 3 c.; Air 4, 21, 21 c.

Mexican President's Visit. Air 50 c., 1 b.

Winter Olympic Games, Grenoble. Postage $\frac{1}{2}$, 1 c.; Air 5, 10, 21, 31 c.

Butterflies. Postage $\frac{1}{2}$, 1, 3, 4 c.; Air 5, 13 c.

Ship Paintings. Postage $\frac{1}{2}$, 1, 3, 4 c.; Air 5, 13 c.

Fishes. Postage $\frac{1}{2}$, 1, 3, 4 c.; Air 5, 13 c.

Winter Olympic Medal Winners. Postage 1, 2, 3, 4, 5, 6, 8 c.; Air 13, 30 c.

Paintings of Musicians. 5, 10, 15, 20, 25, 30 c.

Satellite Transmissions from Panama T.V. (a) Olympic Games, Mexico. Optd on 1964 Satellites issue. Postage $\frac{1}{2}$ c.; Air 50 c. (b) Pope Paul's Visit to Latin America. Postage $\frac{1}{2}$ c.; Air 21 c. (c) Panama Satellite Transmissions. Inauguration (i) optd on Space Research issue of 1965. Postage 5 c.; Air 31 c. (ii) optd on Churchill and Space Research issue of 1966. Postage $\frac{1}{2}$ c.; Air 10 c.

Hunting Paintings. Postage 1, 3, 5, 10 c.; Air 13, 30 c.

Horses and Jockeys. Postage 5, 10, 15, 20, 25, 30 c.

Mexico Olympics. Postage 1, 2, 3, 4, 5, 6, 8 c.; Air 13, 30 c.

1969.
1st International Philatelic and Numismatic Exhibition. Optd on 1968 Issue of Mexican President's Visit. Air 50 c., 1 b.

Telecommunications Satellites. Air 5, 10, 15, 20, 25, 30 c.

Provisionals. Surch "Decreto No. 112 (de 6 de marzo de 1969)" and new values on No. 781 and 10 c. + 5 c. and 21 c. + 10 c. of 1965 Issue of 3rd Death Anniv of Pres. John Kennedy. Air 5 c. on 5 c. + 5 c., 5 c. on 10 c. + 5 c., 10 c. on 21 c. + 10 c.

Pope Paul VI. Visit to Latin America. Religious Paintings. Postage 1, 2, 3, 4, 5 c.; Air 6, 7, 8, 10 c.

PAPAL STATES — Pt. 8

Parts of Italy under Papal rule till 1870 when they became part of the Kingdom of Italy.

1852. 100 bajocchi = 1 scudo.
1866. 100 centesimi = 1 lira.

1

2

1852. Papal insignia as in T **1** and **2** in various shapes and frames. Imperf.
1 $\frac{1}{2}$ b. black on grey . . . . . . £200 45·00
5 $\frac{1}{2}$ b. black on lilac . . . . . . 12·00 75·00
10 1 b. black on green . . . . . . 20·00 24·00
11 2 b. black on green . . . . . . 42·00 3·25
14 2 b. black on white . . . . . . 1·75 22·00
15 3 b. black on brown . . . . . 75·00 17·00
16 3 b. black on yellow . . . . . 7·50 80·00
17 4 b. black on brown . . . . . £1200 24·00
18 4 b. black on yellow . . . . . 65·00 20·00
21 5 b. black on pink . . . . . . 85·00 4·00
22 6 b. black on lilac . . . . . . £250 60·00
23 6 b. black on grey . . . . . . £200 12·00
25 7 b. black on blue . . . . . . £400 24·00
26 8 b. black on white . . . . . . £150 12·00
27 50 b. blue £7000 £1000
29 1 s. pink £1000 £2000

1867. Same types. Imperf.
30 2 c. black on green . . . . . . 60·00 £100
32 3 c. black on grey £400 £1000
33 5 c. black on blue . . . . . . 70·00 £140
34 10 c. black on red . . . . . . £400 20·00
35 20 c. black on red . . . . . . 60·00 21·00
36 40 c. black on yellow £100 £160
37 80 c. black on pink . . . . . . 90·00 £400

1868. Same types. Perf.
42 2 c. black on green . . . . . . 3·50 24·00
43 3 c. black on grey . . . . . . 18·00 £2500
45 5 c. black on blue . . . . . . 5·50 18·00
46 10 c. black on orange . . . . 1·25 6·00
49 20 c. black on mauve . . . . . 2·00 10·00
50 20 c. black on red . . . . . . 1·25 10·00
52 40 c. black on yellow . . . . . 1·75 60·00
55 80 c. black on pink . . . . . . 11·00 £250

INDEX

Countries can be quickly located by referring to the index at the end of this volume.

PARAGUAY Pt. 20

A republic in the centre of S. America independent since 1811.

1870. 8 reales = 1 peso.
1878. 100 centavos = 1 peso.
1944. 100 centimos = 1 guarani.

1 7

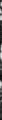

1870. Various frames. Values in "reales". Imperf.
1 **1** 1 r. red . . . 2·25 2·25
3 2 r. blue . . . 27·00 27·00
4 3 r. black . . . 65·00 65·00

1878. Handstamped with large **5**. Imperf.
5 **1** 5 c. on 1 r. red . . . 25·00 25·00
9 5 c. on 2 r. blue . . . £120 £110
13 5 c. on 3 r. black . . . 85·00 85·00

1879. Prepared for use but not issued (wrong currency). Values in "reales". Perf.
14 **7** 5 r. orange . . . 40
15 10 r. brown . . . 50

1879. Values in "centavos". Perf.
16 **7** 5 c. brown . . . 70 70
17 10 c. green . . . 95 95

1881. Handstamped with large figures.
18 **7** 1 on 10 c. green . . . 3·50 3·50
19 2 on 10 c. green . . . 3·50 3·50

1881. As T **1** (various frames), but value in "centavos". Perf.
20 **1** 1 c. blue . . . 40 40
21a 2 c. red . . . 30 40
22 4 c. brown . . . 40 50

1884. No. 1 handstamped with large **1**. Imperf.
23 **1** 1 c. on 1 r. red . . . 1·50 1·40

13 24

1884. Perf.
24 **13** 1 c. green . . . 30 15
25 2 c. red . . . 40 15
26 5 c. blue . . . 40 15

1887.
32 **24** 1 c. green . . . 15 15
33a 2 c. red . . . 15 15
34 5 c. blue . . . 30 20
35 7 c. brown . . . 30 25
36 10 c. mauve . . . 45 30
37 15 c. orange . . . 45 30
38 20 c. pink . . . 45 30
50 40 c. blue . . . 1·50 70
51 60 c. orange . . . 60 30
52 80 c. blue . . . 55 30
53 1 p. green . . . 60 30

25 27 C. Rivarola

1889. Imperf or perf.
40 **25** 15 c. purple . . . 95 95

1892.
42 **27** 1 CENTAVOS grey . . . 15 10
54 1 CENTAVO grey . . . 15 10
43 – 2 c. green . . . 15 10
44 – 4 c. red . . . 10 10
57 – 5 c. purple . . . 15 10
46 – 10 c. violet . . . 30 25
47 – 14 c. brown . . . 30 30
48 – 20 c. red . . . 50 30
49 – 30 c. green . . . 75 30
84 – 1 p. blue . . . 40 25
PORTRAITS: 2 c. S. Jovellano; 4 c. J. Bautista Gil; 5 c. H. Uriarte; 10 c. C. Barreiro; 14 c. Gen. B. Caballero; 20 c. Gen. P. Escobar; 30 c. J. Gonzales; 1 p. J. B. Egusquisa.

1892. 400th Anniv of Discovery of America. No. 46 optd **1492 12 DE OCTUBRE 1892** in oval.
41 10 c. violet . . . 3·50 1·50

1895. Surch **PROVISORIO 5**.
59 **24** 5 c. on 7 c. brown . . . 30 30

30 39

1896. Telegraph stamps as T **30** surch **CORREOS 5 CENTAVOS** in oval.
60 **30** 5 c. on 2 c. brown, blk & grey 45 20
61 5 c. on 4 c. orange, blk & grey 45 20

1898. Surch **Provisorio 10 Centavos**.
63 **24** 10 c. on 15 c. orange . . . 35 35
62 10 c. on 40 c. blue . . . 25 25

1900. Telegraph stamps as T **30** surch with figures of value twice and bar.
64 **30** 5 c. on 30 c. green, black and grey . . . 95 70
65 10 c. on 50 c. lilac, black and grey . . . 2·25 1·50

1900.
76 **39** 1 c. green . . . 10 10
67 2 c. grey . . . 10 10
73 2 c. pink . . . 20 15
68 3 c. brown . . . 10 10
78 4 c. blue . . . 15 10
69 5 c. green . . . 10 10
74 5 c. brown . . . 20 10
79 5 c. lilac . . . 25 10
80 8 c. brown . . . 20 15
70 10 c. red . . . 20 15
71 24 c. blue . . . 45 20
82 28 c. orange . . . 25 35
83 40 c. blue . . . 25 10

1902. Surch **Habilitado en** and new values.
88 – 1 c. on 14 c. brown (No. 47) 30 20
91 – 1 c. on 1 p. blue (No. 84) . 20 15
86 **39** 5 c. on 8 c. brown (No. 80) 35 20
87 5 c. on 28 c. orange (No. 82) 20 30
89 **24** 5 c. on 60 c. orange (No. 51) 20 25
90 5 c. on 80 c. blue (No. 52) . 30 25
85 **39** 20 c. on 24 c. blue (No. 72) 35 20

46 47 48

1903.
92 **46** 1 c. grey . . . 20 15
93 2 c. green . . . 25 20
94a 5 c. blue . . . 25 10
95 10 c. brown . . . 45 20
96 20 c. red . . . 45 25
97 30 c. blue . . . 50 25
98 60 c. violet . . . 75 30

1903.
99 **47** 1 c. green . . . 15 10
100 2 c. orange . . . 15 10
101 5 c. blue . . . 20 15
102 10 c. violet . . . 30 20
103 20 c. green . . . 50 25
104 30 c. blue . . . 60 30
105 60 c. brown . . . 60 35

1904.
106 **48** 10 c. blue . . . 35 20

1904. End of successful Revolt against Govt. (begun in August). Surch **PAZ 12 Dic. 1904. 30 centavos.**
107 **48** 30 c. on 10 c. blue . . . 50 35

50

51 National Palace, Asuncion

1905.
108 **50** 1 c. orange . . . 15 10
109 1 c. red . . . 15 10
110 1 c. blue . . . 15 10
112 2 c. green . . . 23·00
113 2 c. red . . . 15 10
114 5 c. blue . . . 15 10
116 5 c. yellow . . . 15 10
117 10 c. brown . . . 15 10
118 10 c. green . . . 15 10
119 10 c. blue . . . 15 10
120 20 c. lilac . . . 45 35
121 20 c. brown . . . 45 35
122 20 c. green . . . 35 20
123 30 c. blue . . . 45 20
124 30 c. grey . . . 45 20
125 30 c. lilac . . . 50 35
126 60 c. brown . . . 35 25
128 60 c. pink . . . 2·75 95
129 **51** 1 p. black and red . . . 95 80
130 1 p. black and brown . . . 35 35
131 1 p. black and green . . . 35 35
132 2 p. black and blue . . . 35 25
133 2 p. black and red . . . 35 25
134 2 p. black and brown . . . 40 30
135 **51** 5 p. black and red . . . 60 35
136 5 p. black and blue . . . 60 35
137 5 p. black and green . . . 60 35
138 10 p. black and brown . . . 55 35
139 10 p. black and blue . . . 55 35
141 20 p. black and green . . . 1·40 1·25
142 20 p. black and yellow . . . 1·40 1·25
143 20 p. black and purple . . . 1·40 1·25

1907. Surch **Habilitado en** and value and bars.
159 **50** 5 c. on 1 c. blue . . . 10 10
160 5 c. on 2 c. red . . . 15 10
145 5 c. on 2 c. green . . . 40 25
172 **39** 5 c. on 28 c. orange . . . 95 35
173 5 c. on 40 c. blue . . . 30 25
163 **50** 5 c. on 60 c. brown . . . 15 10
162 5 c. on 60 c. pink . . . 20 15
175 20 c. on 1 c. blue . . . 20 15
180 **24** 20 c. on 2 c. red . . . 1·90 1·50
177 **50** 20 c. on 2 c. red . . . 2·75 2·25
178 20 c. on 30 c. blue . . . 1·10 1·10
179 20 c. on 30 c. lilac . . . 30 30

1907. Official stamps surch **Habilitado en** and value and bars. Where not otherwise stated, the design is as T **50** but with "OFICIAL" below the lion.
164 – 5 c. on 10 c. green . . . 30 20
149 – 5 c. on 10 c. brown . . . 30 20
150 – 5 c. on 10 c. lilac . . . 30 20
181 **24** 5 c. on 15 c. orange (No. O63) 1·90 1·40
182 5 c. on 20 c. pink (No. O64) 30·00 25·00
166 – 5 c. on 20 c. brown . . . 30 25
151 – 5 c. on 20 c. green . . . 30 20
167 – 5 c. on 20 c. pink . . . 30 25
152 – 5 c. on 20 c. lilac . . . 30 20
157 **46** 5 c. on 30 c. blue (No. O104) 95 85
154 – 5 c. on 30 c. blue . . . 50 50
169 – 5 c. on 30 c. yellow . . . 10 10
168 – 5 c. on 30 c. grey . . . 20 15
183 **24** 5 c. on 50 c. grey (No. O65) 13·50 9·50
158 **46** 5 c. on 60 c. violet (No. O105) 35 25
155 – 5 c. on 60 c. brown . . . 20 15
171 – 5 c. on 60 c. blue . . . 20 10
184 **24** 20 c. on 5 c. blue (No. O60) 1·10 95
174 **46** 20 c. on 5 c. blue (No. O101) 95 75

1907. Official stamps, as T **50** and **51** with "OFICIAL" added, optd **Habilitado** and one bar.
146 5 c. grey . . . 30 20
148 5 c. blue . . . 25 15
185 1 p. black and orange . . . 35 35
186 1 p. black and red . . . 30 25

1907. Official stamps, as T **51** with "OFFICIAL" added, surch **Habilitado. 1908 UN CENTAVO** and bar.
188 1 c. on 1 p. black and red . . 20 20
189 1 c. on 1 p. black and brown . 70 50

1908. Optd **1908**.
190 **50** 1 c. green . . . 10 10
191 5 c. yellow . . . 10 10
192 10 c. brown . . . 10 10
193 20 c. orange . . . 10 10
194 30 c. red . . . 40 30
195 60 c. mauve . . . 30 30
196 **51** 1 p. blue . . . 15 15

1909. Optd **1909**.
197 **50** 1 c. blue . . . 10 10
198 1 c. red . . . 10 10
199 5 c. green . . . 10 10
200 5 c. orange . . . 10 10
201 10 c. red . . . 20 15
202 10 c. brown . . . 20 15
203 20 c. lilac . . . 20 20
204 20 c. yellow . . . 10 10
205 30 c. brown . . . 45 30
206 30 c. blue . . . 45 30

62 63 65

1910.
207 **62** 1 c. brown . . . 10 10
208 5 c. lilac . . . 10 10
209 5 c. green . . . 10 10
210 5 c. blue . . . 10 10
211 10 c. green . . . 10 10
212 10 c. violet . . . 10 10
213 10 c. red . . . 10 10
214 20 c. red . . . 10 10
215 50 c. red . . . 45 20
216 75 c. blue . . . 15 10

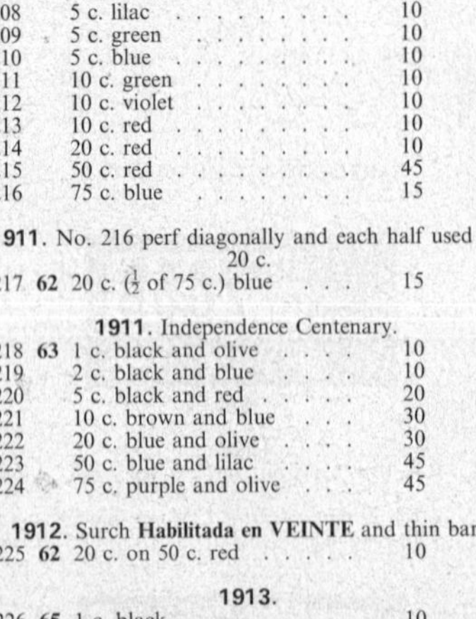

1911. No. 216 perf diagonally and each half used as 20 c.
217 **62** 20 c. (½ of 75 c.) blue . . . 15 10

1911. Independence Centenary.
218 **63** 1 c. black and olive . . . 10 10
219 2 c. black and blue . . . 10 10
220 5 c. black and red . . . 20 10
221 10 c. brown and blue . . . 30 15
222 20 c. blue and olive . . . 30 15
223 50 c. blue and lilac . . . 45 30
224 75 c. purple and olive . . . 45 30

1912. Surch **Habilitada en VEINTE** and thin bar.
225 **62** 20 c. on 50 c. red . . . 10 10

1913.
226 **65** 1 c. black . . . 10 10
227 2 c. orange . . . 10 10
228 5 c. mauve . . . 10 10
229 10 c. green . . . 10 10
230 20 c. red . . . 10 10
231 40 c. red . . . 10 10
232 75 c. blue . . . 10 10
233 **65** 80 c. yellow . . . 10 10
234 1 p. blue . . . 10 10
235 1 p. 25 blue . . . 30 10
236 3 p. green . . . 30 10

1918. No. D242 surch **HABILITADO EN 0.05 1918** and bar.
237 5 c. on 40 c. brown . . . 10 10

1918. Nos. D239/42 optd **HABILITADO 1918**.
238 5 c. brown . . . 10 10
239 10 c. brown . . . 10 10
240 20 c. brown . . . 10 10
241 40 c. brown . . . 15 10

1918. Surch **HABILITADO EN 0.30 1918** and bar.
242 **65** 30 c. on 40 c. red . . . 10 10

1920. Surch **HABILITADO en**, value and **1920**.
243 **65** 50 c. on 80 c. yellow . . . 15 10
244 1 p. 75 on 3 p. green . . . 60 50

1920. Nos. D243/4 optd **HABILITADO 1920** or surch also.
245 1 p. brown . . . 20 10
246 1 p. on 1 p. 50 brown . . . 35 10

72 Parliament House, Asuncion

1920. Jubilee of Constitution.
247 **72** 50 c. black and red . . . 30 20
248 1 p. black and blue . . . 50 40
249 1 p. 75 black and blue . . . 20 15
250 3 p. black and yellow . . . 75 25

1920. Surch **50**.
251 **65** 50 on 75 c. blue . . . 45 10

1921. Surch **50** and two bars.
252 **62** 50 on 75 c. blue . . . 10 10
253 **65** 50 on 75 c. blue . . . 25 10

75

1922.
254 **75** 50 c. blue and red . . . 10 10
255 1 p. brown and blue . . . 10 10

Between 1922 and 1936 many regular postage stamps were overprinted **C** (= Campana—country), these being used at post offices outside Asuncion but not for mail sent abroad. The prices quoted are for whichever is the cheapest.

77 Starting-point of Conspirators

80 Map

1922. Independence.
256 **77** 1 p. blue . . . 20 10
258 1 p. blue and red . . . 30 10
259 1 p. grey and purple . . . 30 10
260 1 p. grey and orange . . . 30 10
257 5 p. purple . . . 30 25
261 5 p. brown and blue . . . 30 25
262 5 p. black and green . . . 30 25
263 5 p. blue and red . . . 30 25

1924. Surch **Habilitado en** value and **1924**.
265 **65** 50 c. on 75 c. blue . . . 10 10
266 $1 on 1 p. 25 blue . . . 10 10
267 – $1 on 1 p. 50 brown (No. D244) . . . 10 10

1924.
268 **80** 1 p. blue . . . 10 10
269 2 p. red . . . 15 10
270 4 p. blue . . . 30 10

81 Gen. Jose E. Diaz

82 Columbus

1925.
271 **81** 50 c. red . . . 10 10
272 1 p. blue . . . 10 10
273 1 p. green . . . 10 10

1925.
274 **82** 1 p. blue . . . 15 10

1926. Surch **Habilitado en** and new value.
275 **62** 1 c. on 5 c. blue 10 10
276 $0.02 on 5 c. blue 10 10
277 **65** 7 c. on 40 c. red 10 10
278 15 c. on 75 c. blue 10 10
279 **50** $0.50 on 60 c. purple (No. 195) 10 10
280 – $0.50 on 75 c. blue (No. O243) 10 10
281 – $1.50 on 1 p. 50 brown (No. D244) 15 10
282 **80** $1.50 on 4 p. blue 10 10

86

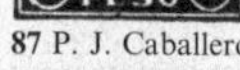
87 P. J. Caballero

88 Paraguay

89 Cassel Tower, Asuncion

90 Columbus

92 Arms of De Salazarde Espinosa, founder of Asuncion

1927.
283 **86** 1 c. red 10 10
284 2 c. orange 10 10
285 7 c. lilac 10 10
286 7 c. green 10 10
287 10 c. green 10 10
288 10 c. red 10 10
290 10 c. blue 10 10
291 20 c. blue 10 10
292 20 c. purple 10 10
293 20 c. violet 10 10
294 20 c. pink 10 10
295 50 c. blue 10 10
296 50 c. red 10 10
323 50 c. orange 10 10
326 50 c. green 10 10
299 50 c. mauve 10 10
300 50 c. pink 10 10
301 70 c. blue 10 10
328 **87** 1 p. green 10 10
329 1 p. red 10 10
330 1 p. purple 10 10
331 1 p. blue 10 10
304 1 p. orange 10 10
332 1 p. violet 10 10
333 **88** 1 p. 50 brown 10 10
334 1 p. 50 lilac 10 10
307 1 p. 50 pink 10 10
335 1 p. 50 blue 10 10
308 – 2 p. 50 bistre 10 10
337 – 2 p. 50 violet 10 10
338 – 3 p. grey 10 10
310 – 3 p. red 10 10
311 – 3 p. violet 10 10
312 **89** 5 p. brown 25 20
340 5 p. violet 10 10
314 5 p. orange 10 10
315 **90** 10 p. red 35 35
317 10 p. blue 35 35
318 **88** 20 p. red . . . . . 1·10 85
319 20 p. green . . . . . 1·10 85
320 20 p. purple . . . . . 1·10 85
DESIGNS—As Type **87**: 2 p. 50, Fulgencio Yegros; 3 p. V. Ignacio Yturbe.

1928. Foundation of Asuncion, 1537.
342 **92** 10 p. purple 95 70

93 Pres. Hayes of U.S.A. and Villa Hayes

1928. 50th Anniv of Hayes's Decision to award Northern Chaco to Paraguay.
343 **93** 10 p. brown . . . . . 2·50 1·10
344 10 p. grey . . . . . 2·50 1·10

1929. Air. Surch **Correo Aereo Habilitado en** and value.
357 **86** $0.95 on 7 c. lilac 20 20
358 $1.90 on 20 c. blue 20 20
345 – $2.85 on 5 c. purple (No. O239) 60 70
348 – $3.40 on 3 p. grey (No. 338) 1·40 85
359 **80** $3.40 on 4 p. blue 30 30
360 $4.75 on 4 p. blue 55 30
346 – $5.65 on 10 c. green (No. O240) 35 45
361 – $6.80 on 3 p. grey (No. 338) 35 35
349 **80** $6.80 on 4 p. blue . . . . 1·40 85
347 – $11.30 on 50 c. red (No. O242) 60 50
350 **89** $17 on 5 p. brown (A) . . 1·40 85
362 $17 on 5 p. brown (B) . . 1·10 1·10
On No. 350 (A) the surcharge is on four lines, and on No. 362 (B) it is in three lines.

95

1929. Air.
352 **95** 2.85 p. green 35 30
353 – 5.65 p. brown 60 30
354 – 5.65 p. red 40 35
355 – 11.30 purple 70 55
356 – 11.30 blue 35 35
DESIGNS: 5.65 p. Carrier pigeon; 11.30 p. Stylized airplane.

1930. Air. Optd **CORREO AEREO** or surch also in words.
363 **86** 5 c. on 10 c. green 10 10
364 5 c. on 70 c. blue 10 10
365 10 c. green 10 10
366 20 c. blue 20 20
367 **87** 20 c. on 1 p. red 30 30
368 **86** 40 c. on 50 c. orange . . . 15 10
369 **87** 1 p. green 35 35
370 – 3 p. grey (No. 338) 35 35
371 **90** 6 p. on 10 p. red 60 50
372 **88** 10 p. on 20 p. red . . . . 2·25 2·10
373 10 p. on 20 p. purple . . . 2·25 2·10

101

103

1930. Air.
374 **101** 95 c. blue on blue 40 35
375 95 c. red on pink 40 35
376 – 1 p. 90 purple on blue . . 40 35
377 – 1 p. 90 red on pink . . . 40 35
378 **103** 6 p. 80 black on blue . . 40 35
379 6 p. 80 green on pink . . 45 40
DESIGN: 1 p. 90, Asuncion Cathedral.

104 Declaration of Independence

105

1930. Air. Independence Day.
380 **104** 2 p. 85 blue 40 35
381 3 p. 40 green 35 25
382 4 p. 75 purple 35 25

1930. Red Cross Fund.
383 **105** 1 p. 50 + 50 c. blue . . 75 70
384 1 p. 50 + 50 c. red . . . 75 70
385 1 p. 50 + 50 c. lilac . . . 75 70

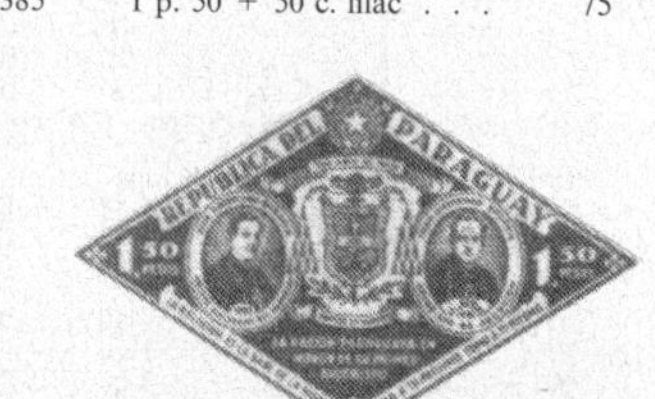
106 Portraits of Archbishop Bogarin

1930. Consecration of Archbishop Bogarin.
386 **106** 1 p. 50 blue 75 60
387 1 p. 50 red 75 60
388 1 p. 50 violet 75 60

1930. Surch **Habilitado en CINCO**.
389 **86** 5 c. on 7 c. green 10 10

108 Planned Agricultural College at Ypacarai

1931. Agricultural College Fund.
390 **108** 1 p. 50 + 50 c. blue on red 30 30

109 Arms of Paraguay

1931. 60th Anniv of First Paraguay Postage Stamps.
391 **109** 10 p. brown 30 25
392 10 p. red on blue 35 25
393 10 p. blue on red 35 25
395 10 p. grey 50 20
396 10 p. blue 20 20

110 Gunboat "Paraguay"

1931. Air. 60th Anniv of Constitution and Arrival of new Gunboats.
397 **110** 1 p. red 20 20
398 1 p. blue 20 20
399 2 p. orange 25 25
400 2 p. brown 25 25
401 3 p. green 50 40
402 3 p. blue 50 45
403 3 p. red 45 40
404 6 p. green 60 60
405 6 p. mauve 75 65
406 6 p. blue 55 50
407 10 p. red . . . . . 1·60 1·40
408 10 p. green . . . . . 2·00 1·90
409 10 p. blue . . . . . 1·10 1·00
410 10 p. brown . . . . . 1·75 1·60
411 10 p. pink . . . . . 1·60 1·40

1931. As T **110**.
412 – 1 p. 50 violet 70 35
413 – 1 p. 50 blue 10 10
DESIGN: Gunboat "Humaita".
No. 413 is optd with large **C**.

112 War Memorial

113 Orange Tree and Yerba Mate

114 Yerba Mate

115 Palms

116 Yellow-headed Caracara

1931. Air.
414 **112** 5 c. blue 15 10
415 5 c. green 15 10
416 5 c. red 20 10
417 5 c. purple 15 10
418 **113** 10 c. violet 15 10
419 10 c. red 10 10
420 10 c. brown 10 10
421 10 c. blue 10 10
422 **114** 20 c. red 15 10
423 20 c. blue 20 10
424 20 c. green 20 15
425 20 c. brown 15 10
426 **115** 40 c. green 20 10
426a 40 c. blue 15 10
426b 40 c. red 20 10
427 **116** 80 c. blue 70 15
428 80 c. green 80 20
428a 80 c. red 70 15

1931. Air. Optd with airship "Graf Zeppelin" and **Correo Aereo "Graf Zeppelin"** or surch also.
429 **80** 3 p. on 4 p. blue . . . . 4·50 3·75
430 4 p. blue . . . . . 3·50 3·00

118 Farm Colony

1931. 50th Anniv of Foundation of San Bernardino.
431 **118** 1 p. green 35 20
432 1 p. red 10 10

1931. New Year. Optd **FELIZ ANO NUEVO 1932**.
433 **106** 1 p. 50 blue 60 60
434 1 p. 50 red 60 60

120 "Graf Zeppelin"

1932. Air.
435 **120** 4 p. blue . . . . . 1·40 1·75
436 8 p. red . . . . . 2·40 2·00
437 12 p. green . . . . . 1·90 1·75
438 16 p. purple . . . . . 3·75 3·00
439 20 p. brown . . . . . 4·00 3·75

121 Red Cross H.Q.

122 (Trans: "Has been, is and will be")

1932. Red Cross Fund.
440 **121** 50 c. + 50 c. pink 25 25

1932. Chaco Boundary Dispute.
441 **122** 1 p. purple 20 10
442 1 p. 50 pink 10 10
443 1 p. 50 brown 10 10
444 1 p. 50 green 10 10
445 1 p. 50 blue 10 10
Nos. 443/5 are optd with a large **C**.

1932. New Year. Surch **CORREOS FELIZ ANO NUEVO 1933** (trans: "Happy New Year 1933") and value.
446 **120** 50 c. on 4 p. blue 35 30
447 1 p. on 8 p. red 35 30
448 1 p. 50 on 12 p. green . . 35 30
449 2 p. on 16 p. purple . . . 35 30
450 5 p. on 20 p. brown . . . 95 75

124 "Graf Zeppelin" over Paraguay

125 "Graf Zeppelin" over Atlantic

1933. Air. "Graf Zeppelin" issue.
451 **124** 4 p. 50 blue 95 75
452 9 p. red . . . . . 1·90 1·50
453 13 p. 50 green . . . . . 1·90 1·50
454 **125** 22 p. 50 brown . . . . 4·75 3·75
455 45 p. violet . . . . . 6·75 6·75

126 Columbus's Fleet

1933. 441st Anniv of Departure of Columbus from Palos. Maltese Crosses in violet.
456 **126** 10 c. olive and red 35 15
457 20 c. blue and lake 35 15
458 50 c. red and green . . . 55 30
459 1 p. brown and blue . . . 40 35
460 1 p. 50 green and blue . . 40 35
461 2 p. green and sepia . . . 1·25 65
462 5 p. lake and olive . . . 2·50 1·25
463 10 p. sepia and blue . . . 2·50 1·25

127 G.P.O., Asuncion

1934. Air.
464 **127** 33 p. 75 blue . . . . . . 1·10 95
468 33 p. 75 red 95 95
466 33 p. 75 green . . . . . . 1·10 95
467 33 p. 75 brown . . . . . 1·10 95

1934. Air. Optd **1934.**
469 **124** 4 p. 50 blue . . . . 1·75 1·75
470 9 p. red . . . . 2·25 2·25
471 13 p. 50 green . . . . . . 6·50 6·50
472 **125** 22 p. 50 brown . . . . . 5·25 5·25
473 45 p. violet . . . . 11·00 11·00

1935. Air. Optd **1935.**
474 **124** 4 p. 50 red . . . . 2·25 2·25
475 9 p. green . . . . 3·25 3·25
476 13 p. 50 brown . . . . . . 9·25 9·25
477 **125** 22 p. 50 purple . . . . . 8·75 8·75
478 45 p. blue . . . . 23·00 23·00

131 Tobacco Plant

1935. Air.
479 **131** 17 p. brown . . . . . . 3·75 3·00
480 17 p. red . . . . 6·75 5·00
481 17 p. blue . . . . 4·25 3·50
482 17 p. green . . . . 2·10 1·75

132 Church of the Incarnation

1935. Air.
483 **132** 102 p. red . . . . 2·25 1·75
485 102 p. blue . . . . 1·50 1·50
486 102 p. brown . . . . . . 1·50 1·50
487 102 p. violet 75 75
487a 102 p. orange 65 65

1937. Air. Surch **Habilitado en** and value in figures.
488 **127** $24 on 33 p. 75 blue . . . 40 50
489 **132** $65 on 102 p. grey 95 70
490 $84 on 102 p. green 95 60

134 Arms of Asuncion **135** Monstrance

1937. 4th Centenary of Asuncion (1st issue).
491 **134** 50 c. purple and violet . . 10 10
492 1 p. green and bistre . . . 10 10
493 3 p. blue and red 10 10
494 10 p. yellow and red . . . 15 10
495 20 p. grey and blue . . . 20 20

1937. 1st National Eucharistic Congress.
496 **135** 1 p. red, yellow and blue . 10 10
497 3 p. red, yellow and blue . 10 10
498 10 p. red, yellow and blue 15 10

136 Oratory of the Virgin of Asuncion **137** Asuncion

1938. 4th Centenary of Asuncion (2nd issue).
499 **136** 5 p. olive 25 10
500 5 p. red 35 10
501 11 p. brown 25 10

1939. Air.
502 **137** 3 p. 40 blue 75 45
503 3 p. 40 green 75 45
504 3 p. 40 brown 75 45

138 J. E. Diaz

1939. Reburial in National Pantheon of Ashes of C. A. Lopez and J. E. Diaz.
505 **138** 2 p. brown and blue . . 25 15
506 – 2 p. brown and blue . . 25 15
DESIGN—VERT: No. 506, C. A. Lopez.

139 Pres. Caballero and Senator Decoud

1939. 50th Anniv of Asuncion University.
507 – 50 c. blk & orge (postage) 10 10
508 – 1 p. black and blue . . . 15 10
509 – 2 p. black and red . . . 25 10
510 **139** 5 p. black and blue . . . 35 20
511 28 p. black & red (air) . . 2·50 2·50
512 90 p. black & green . . . 3·00 3·00
DESIGN: Nos. 507/9, Pres. Escobar and Dr. Zubizarreta.

140 Coats of Arms **141** Pres. Baldomir and Flags of Paraguay and Uruguay

1939. Chaco Boundary Peace Conference, Buenos Aires (1st issue).
513 **140** 50 c. blue (postage) . . . 15 10
514 **141** 1 p. olive 15 10
515 A 2 p. green 20 10
516 B 3 p. brown 35 25
517 C 5 p. orange 25 20
518 D 6 p. violet 40 30
519 E 10 p. brown 50 35
520 F 1 p. brown (air) 10 10
521 **140** 3 p. blue 10 10
522 E 5 p. olive 10 15
523 D 10 p. violet 15 15
524 C 30 p. orange 25 15
525 B 50 p. brown 15 25
526 A 100 p. green 25 25
527 **41** 200 p. green . . . . . . 1·50 95
528 – 500 p. black . . . . . . 3·75 3·75
DESIGNS (flag on right is that of country named): A, Benavides (Peru); B, Eagle (USA); C, Alessandri (Chile); D, Vargas (Brazil); E, Ortiz (Argentina); F, Figure of "Peace" (Bolivia); 500 p. (30×40 mm), Map of Chaco frontiers.
See also Nos. 536/43.

143 Arms of New York **144** Asuncion–New York Air Route

1939. New York World's Fair.
529 **143** 5 p. red (postage) 20 15
530 10 p. blue 40 30
531 11 p. green 25 45
532 22 p. grey 35 30
533 **144** 30 p. brown (air) . . . . 1·50 1·10
534 80 p. orange . . . . . . 1·75 1·75
535 90 p. violet . . . . . . 3·00 3·00

145 Soldier **147** Waterfall

1940. Chaco Boundary Peace Conference, Buenos Aires (2nd issue). Inscr "PAZ DEL CHACO".
536 **145** 50 c. orange 15 10
537 – 1 p. purple 15 15
538 – 3 p. green 25 20
539 – 5 p. brown 10 25
540 – 10 p. mauve 35 20
541 – 20 p. blue 30 25
542 – 50 p. green 70 35
543 **147** 100 p. black . . . . . . 1·50 1·10
DESIGNS: As Type **145**: VERT: 1 p. Water-carrier; 5 p. Ploughing with oxen. HORIZ: 3 p. Cattle Farming. As Type **147**: VERT: 10 p. Fishing in the Paraguay River. HORIZ: 20 p. Bullock-cart; 50 p. Cattle-grazing.

148 Western Hemisphere **149** Reproduction of Paraguay No. 1

1940. 50th Anniv of Pan-American Union.
544 **148** 50 c. orange (postage) . . 10 10
545 1 p. green 10 10
546 5 p. blue 25 10
547 10 p. brown 30 30
548 20 p. red (air) 35 25
549 70 p. blue 35 30
550 100 p. green 40 40
551 500 p. violet . . . . 1·75 1·40

1940. Cent of First Adhesive Postage Stamps. Inscr "CENTENARIO DEL SELLO POSTAL 1940".
552 **149** 1 p. purple and green . . . 40 35
553 – 5 p. brown and green . . . 50 45
554 – 6 p. blue and brown . . . 1·10 50
555 – 10 p. black and red . . . 1·10 85
DESIGNS: 5 p. Sir Rowland Hill; 6 p., 10 p. Early Paraguayan stamps.

1940. National Mourning for Pres. Estigarribia. Surch **7-IX-40/DUELO NACIONAL/5 PESOS** in black border.
556 **145** 5 p. on 50 c. orange . . . 25 25

152 Dr. Francia **154** Our Lady of Asuncion

1940. Death Centenary of Dr. Francia (dictator).
557 **152** 50 c. red 15 10
558 – 50 c. purple 15 10
559 **152** 1 p. green 15 10
560 – 5 p. blue 15 10
PORTRAIT: Nos. 558 and 560, Dr. Francia seated in library.

1941. Visit of President Vargas of Brazil. Optd **Visita al Paraguay/Agosto de 1941.**
560a 6 p. violet (No. 518) 25 25

1941. Mothers' Fund.
561 **154** 7 p. + 3 p. brown 35 25
562 7 p. + 3 p. violet 35 25
563 7 p. + 3 p. red 35 25
564 7 p. + 3 p. blue 35 25

1942. Nos. 520/2 optd **Habilitado** and bar(s).
565 – 1 p. brown 15 10
566 **140** 3 p. blue 20 10
567 – 5 p. olive 25 10

156 Arms of Paraguay **158** Irala's Vision

1942.
568 **156** 1 p. green 10 10
569 1 p. orange 10 10
570 7 p. blue 10 10
571 7 p. brown 10 10
For other values as Type **156** see Nos. 631, etc.

1942. 4th Centenary of Asuncion.
572 – 2 p. green (postage) . . . 50 40
573 **158** 5 p. red 50 40
574 – 7 p. blue 50 35
575 – 20 p. purple (air) 40 30
576 **158** 70 p. brown . . . . 1·10 85
577 – 500 p. olive . . . . 3·00 2·75
DESIGNS—VERT: 2 p., 20 p. Indian hailing ships; 7 p., 500 p. Irala's Arms.

160 Columbus sighting America **161** Pres. Morinigo and Symbols of Progress

1943. 450th Anniv of Discovery of America by Columbus.
578 **160** 50 c. violet 25 20
579 1 p. brown 20 10
580 5 p. green 35 20
581 7 p. blue 35 10

1943. Three Year Plan.
582 **161** 7 p. blue 10 10

NOTE: From No. 583 onwards, the currency having been changed, the letter "c" in the value description indicates "centimos" instead of "centavos".

1944. St. Juan Earthquake Fund. Surch **U.P.A.E. Adhesion victimas San Juan y Pueblo Argentino centimos** and bar.
583 – 10 c. on 10 p. brown (No. 519) 40 25

1944. No. 311 surch **Habilitado en un centimo.**
584 1 c. on 3 p. violet 10 10

1944. Surch **1944/5 centimos 5.**
585 **160** 5 c. on 7 p. blue 15 10
586 **161** 5 c. on 7 p. blue 15 10

164 Primitive Indian Postmen **181** Jesuit Relics of Colonial Paraguay

1944.
587 **164** 1 c. black (postage) . . . 10 10
588 – 2 c. brown 15 10
589 – 5 c. olive 20 10
590 – 7 c. blue 15 20
591 – 10 c. green . . . . 1·00 45
592 – 15 c. blue 40 25
593 – 50 c. black 35 35
594 – 1 g. red 70 40
DESIGNS—HORIZ: 2 c. Ruins of Humaita Church; 7 c. Marshal Francisco S. Lopez; 1 g. Ytororo Heroes' Monument. VERT: 5 c. First Paraguayan railway locomotive; 10 c. "Tacuary" (paddle-steamer); 15 c. Port of Asuncion; 50 c. Meeting place of Independence conspirators.
595 – 1 c. blue (air) 15 15
596 – 2 c. green 10 10
597 – 3 c. purple 50 20
598 – 5 c. green 20 10
599 – 10 c. violet 20 15
600 – 20 c. brown 15 10
601 – 30 c. blue 25 25
602 – 40 c. olive 15 15
603 – 70 c. red 25 20
604 **181** 1 g. orange 55 40
605 – 2 g. brown 65 55
606 – 5 g. brown . . . . 1·50 1·50
607 – 10 g. blue . . . . 3·50 3·50
DESIGNS—HORIZ: 1 c. Port of Asuncion; 2 c. First telegraphic apparatus in S. America; 3 c. Paddle-steamer "Tacuary"; 5 c. Meeting Place of Independence Conspirators; 10 c. Antequera Monument; 20 c. First Paraguayan railway locomotive; 40 c. Government House. VERT: 30 c. Ytororo Heroes' Monument; 70 c. As Type **164** but vert: 2 g. Ruins of Humaita Church; 5 g. Oratory of the Virgin; 10 g. Marshal Francisco S. Lopez.
See also Nos. 640/51.

1945. No. 590 surch with figure **5** over ornaments deleting old value.
608 5 c. on 7 c. blue 10 10

186 Clasped Hands and Flags

1945. President Morinigo's Goodwill Visits. Designs of different sizes inscr "CONFRATERNIDAD" between crossed flags of Paraguay and another American country, mentioned in brackets. (a) Postage.
609 **186** 1 c. green (Panama) . . . 10 10
610 3 c. red (Venezuela) . . . 10 10
611 5 c. grey (Ecuador) . . . 10 10
612 2 g. brown (Peru) 85 60

(b) Air.
613 20 c. orange (Colombia) . 10 30
614 40 c. olive (Bolivia) . . . 10 25
615 70 c. red (Mexico) 10 10
616 1 g. blue (Chile) 25 25
617 2 g. violet (Brazil) 30 30
618 5 g. green (Argentina) . . 45 45
619 10 g. brown (U.S.A.) . . . 2·25 2·25
The 5 and 10 g. are larger: 32×28 and $33\frac{1}{2}$×30 mm respectively.

1945. Surch **1945 5 Centimos 5.**
620 **160** 5 c. on 7 p. blue 25 20
621 **161** 5 c. on 7 p. blue 20 20
622 – 5 c. on 7 p. blue (No. 590) 10 20

1945. Surch **1945** and value.
623 **154** 2 c. on 7 p. + 3 p. brown 10 10
624 2 c. on 7 p. + 3 p. violet 10 10
625 2 c. on 7 p. + 3 p. red . 10 10
626 2 c. on 7 p. + 3 p. blue . 10 10
627 5 c. on 7 p. + 3 p. brown 20 10
628 5 c. on 7 p. + 3 p. violet 20 10
629 5 c. on 7 p. + 3 p. red . 20 10
630 5 c. on 7 p. + 3 p. blue . 20 10

1946. As T **156** but inscr "U.P.U." at foot.
631 **156** 5 c. grey 10 10
631a 5 c. pink 10 10
631b 5 c. brown 10 10
686 10 c. blue 10 10
687 10 c. pink 10 10
631c 30 c. green 10 10
631d 30 c. brown 10 10
775 45 c. green 10 10
631e 50 c. mauve 10 10
776 50 c. purple 10 10
858 70 c. brown 10 10
777 90 c. blue 10 10
778 1 g. violet 10 10
860 1 g. 50 mauve 10 10
814 2 g. ochre 10 10
780 2 g. 20 mauve 10 10
781 3 g. brown 10 10
782 4 g. 20 green 10 10
862 4 g. 50 blue 15 10
816 5 g. red 10 10
689 10 g. orange 20 30
784 10 g. green 20 15
818 12 g. 45 green 20 10
819 15 g. orange 25 15
786 20 g. blue 40 30
820 30 g. bistre 20 30
812 50 g. brown 30 25
821 100 g. blue 65 50
See also Nos. 1037/49.

1946. Surch **1946 5 Centimos 5**.
632 **154** 5 c. on 7 p. + 3 p. brown 25 35
633 5 c. on 7 p. + 3 p. violet . 25 35
634 5 c. on 7 p. + 3 p. red . . 25 35
635 5 c. on 7 p. + 3 p. blue . 25 35

1946. Air. Surch **1946 5 Centimos 5**.
636 5 c. on 20 c. brown (No. 600) 30 30
637 5 c. on 30 c. blue (No. 601) . 30 30
638 5 c. on 40 c. olive (No. 602) . 30 30
639 5 c. on 70 c. red (No. 603) . . 30 30

1946. As Nos. 587/607 but colours changed and some designs smaller.
640 – 1 c. red (postage) 15 15
641 – 2 c. violet 10 10
642 **164** 5 c. blue 10 10
643 – 10 c. orange 10 10
644 – 15 c. olive 15 15
645 **181** 50 c. green 25 10
646 – 1 g. blue 50 30
DESIGNS—VERT: 1 c. Paddle-steamer "Tacuary"; 1 g. Meeting place of Independence Conspirators. HORIZ: 2 c. First telegraphic apparatus in S. America; 10 c. Antequera Monument; 15 c. Ytororo Heroes' Monument.
647 – 10 c. red (air) 10 10
648 – 20 c. green 40 20
649 – 1 g. brown 25 25
650 – 5 g. purple 70 70
651 – 10 g. red . . . . 1·90 1·90
DESIGNS—VERT: 10 c. Ruins of Humaita Church. HORIZ: 20 c. Port of Asuncion; 1 g. Govt. House; 5 g. Marshal Francisco S. Lopez; 10 g. Oratory of the Virgin.

189 Marshal Francisco Lopez

190 Archbishop of Paraguay

1947. Various frames.
652 **189** 1 c. violet (postage) . . . 10 10
653 2 c. red 10 10
654 5 c. green 10 10
655 15 c. blue 10 10
656 50 c. green 40 40
657 32 c. red (air) 10 10
658 64 c. brown 25 25
659 1 g. blue 40 40
660 5 g. purple and blue . . . 60 60
661 10 g. green and red . . . 95 95

1947. 50th Anniv of Archbishopric of Paraguay.
662 **190** 2 c. grey (postage) 10 10
663 – 5 c. red 10 10
664 – 10 c. black 10 10
665 – 15 c. green 25 15
666 – 20 c. black (air) 10 10
667 – 30 c. grey 10 10
668 – 40 c. mauve 15 10
669 **190** 70 c. red 25 25
670 – 1 g. lake 30 30
671 – 2 g. red 40 40
672 **190** 5 g. slate and red 70 70
673 – 10 g. brown and green . . . 95 95
DESIGNS: 5, 20 c., 10 g. Episcopal Arms; 10, 30, 1 g. Sacred Heart Monument; 15 c., 40 c., 2 g. Vision of projected monument.

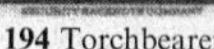
194 Torchbearer

195 C. A. Lopez, J. N. Gonzalez and "Paraguari" (freighter)

1948. Honouring the "Barefeet" (political party). Badge in red and blue.
674 **194** 5 c. red (postage) 10 10
675 15 c. orange 15 10
676 69 c. green (air) 40 40
677 5 g. blue . . . . 1·50 1·50

1948. Centenary of Paraguay's Merchant Fleet. Centres in black, red and blue.
678 **195** 2 c. orange 10 10
679 5 c. blue 15 10
680 10 c. black 20 10
681 15 c. violet 30 10
682 50 c. green 40 20
683 1 g. red 60 25

1949. Air. National Mourning for Archbishop of Paraguay. Surch **DUELO NACIONAL 5 CENTIMOS 5**.
684 **190** 5 c. on 70 c. red 15 15

1949. Air. Aid to Victims of Ecuadorean Earthquake. No. 667 surch **AYUDA AL ECUADOR 5 + 5** and two crosses.
685 5 c. + 5 c. on 30 c. slate . . 10 10

198 "Postal Communications"

199 President Roosevelt

1950. Air. 75th Anniv of U.P.U.
691 **198** 20 c. violet and green . . 30 30
692 30 c. brown and purple . 10 10
693 50 c. green and grey . . . 10 10
694 1 g. brown and blue . . . 10 10
695 5 g. black and red . . . 30 30

1950. Air. Honouring F. D. Roosevelt. Flags in red and blue.
696 **199** 20 c. orange 10 10
697 30 c. black 10 10
698 50 c. purple 15 10
699 1 g. green 25 25
700 5 g. blue 30 30

1951. 1st Economic Congress of Paraguay. Surch **PRIMER CONGRESO DE ENTIDADES ECONOMICAS DEL PARAGUAY 18-IV-1951** and shield over a block of four stamps.
700a **156** 5 c. pink 20 10
700b 10 c. blue 35 25
700c 30 c. green 50 40
Prices are for single stamps. Prices for blocks of four, four times single prices.

200 Columbus Lighthouse

201 Urn

1952. Columbus Memorial Lighthouse.
701 **200** 2 c. brown (postage) . . 10 10
702 5 c. blue 10 10
703 10 c. pink 10 10
704 15 c. blue 10 10
705 20 c. purple 10 10
706 50 c. orange 15 10
707 1 g. green 25 25
708 **201** 10 c. blue (air) 10 10
709 20 c. green 10 10
710 30 c. purple 10 10
711 40 c. pink 10 10
712 50 c. bistre 10 10
713 1 g. blue 15 10
714 2 g. orange 25 20
715 5 g. lake 25 40

202 Isabella the Catholic

203 S. Pettirossi (aviator)

1952. Air. 500th Birth Anniv of Isabella the Catholic.
716 **202** 1 g. blue 10 10
717 2 g. brown 20 20
718 5 g. green 40 40
719 10 g. purple 40 40

1954. Pettirossi Commemoration.
720 **203** 5 c. blue (postage) 10 10
721 20 c. red 10 10
722 50 c. purple 10 10
723 60 c. violet 15 10
724 40 c. brown (air) 10 10
725 55 c. green 10 10
726 80 c. blue 10 10
727 1 g. 30 grey 35 35

204 San Roque Church, Asuncion

1954. Air. San Roque Church Centenary.
728 **204** 20 c. red 10 10
729 30 c. purple 10 10
730 50 c. blue 10 10
731 1 g. purple and brown . . 10 10
732 1 g. black and brown . . . 10 10
733 1 g. green and brown . . . 10 10
734 1 g. orange and brown . . 10 10
735 5 g. yellow and brown . . 20 20
736 5 g. olive and brown . . . 20 20
737 5 g. violet and brown . . 20 20
738 5 g. buff and brown . . . 20 20

205 Marshal Lopez, C. A. Lopez and Gen. Caballero

1954. National Heroes.
739 **205** 5 c. violet (postage) . . . 10 10
740 20 c. blue 10 10
741 50 c. mauve 10 10
742 1 g. brown 10 10
743 2 g. green 15 10
744 5 g. violet (air) 20 15
745 10 g. olive 35 35
746 20 g. grey 35 30
747 50 g. pink 75 75
748 100 g. blue . . . . 2·50 2·50

206 Presidents Stroessner and Peron

1955. Visit of President Peron. Flags in red and blue.
749 **206** 5 c. brown & buff (postage) 10 10
750 10 c. lake and buff 10 10
751 50 c. grey 10 10
752 1 g. 30 lilac and buff . . . 10 10
753 2 g. 20 blue and buff . . . 20 10
754 60 c. olive and buff (air) . 10 10
755 2 g. green 10 10
756 3 g. red 20 10
757 4 g. 10 mauve and buff . . 30 20

207 Trinidad Campanile

1955. Sacerdotal Silver Jubilee of Mgr. Rodriguez.
758 **207** 5 c. brown (postage) . . . 10 10
759 – 20 c. brown 10 10
760 – 50 c. brown 10 10
761 – 2 g. 50 green 10 10
762 – 5 g. brown 15 10
763 – 15 g. green 30 20
764 – 25 g. green 35 35
765 **207** 2 g. blue (air) 10 10
766 – 3 g. green 10 10
767 – 4 g. green 10 10
768 – 6 g. brown 10 10
769 – 10 g. red 20 10
770 – 20 g. brown 30 10
771 – 30 g. green 25 40
772 – 50 g. blue 25 25
DESIGNS—HORIZ: 20 c., 3 g. Cloisters in Trinidad; 5, 10 g. San Cosme Portico; 15, 20 g. Church of Jesus. VERT: 50 c., 4 g. Cornice in Santa Maria; 2 g. 50, 6 g. Santa Rosa Tower; 25, 30 g. Niche in Trinidad; 50 g. Trinidad Sacristy.

208 Angel and Marching Soldiers

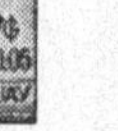
209 Soldier and Flags

1957. Chaco Heroes. Inscr "HOMENAJE A LOS HEROES DEL CHACO". Flags in red, white and blue.
787 **208** 5 c. green (postage) . . . 10 10
788 10 c. red 10 10
789 15 c. blue 10 10
790 20 c. purple 10 10
791 25 c. black 10 10
792 – 30 c. blue 10 10
793 – 40 c. black 10 10
794 – 50 c. lake 10 10
795 – 1 g. turquoise 10 10
796 – 1 g. 30 blue 10 10
797 – 1 g. 50 purple 10 10
798 – 2 g. green 10 10
799 **209** 10 c. blue (air) 10 10
800 15 c. purple 10 10
801 20 c. red 10 10
802 25 c. blue 10 10
803 50 c. turquoise 10 10
804 1 g. red 10 10
805 – 1 g. 30 purple 10 10
806 – 1 g. 50 blue 10 10
807 – 2 g. green 10 10
808 – 4 g. 10 vermilion and red . 10 10
809 – 5 g. black 10 10
810 – 10 g. turquoise 15 15
811 – 25 g. blue 40 15
DESIGNS—HORIZ: Nos. 792/8, Man, woman and flags; Nos. 805/11, "Paraguay" and kneeling soldier.

212 R. Gonzalez and St. Ignatius

213 President Stroessner

1958. 4th Centenary of St. Ignatius of Loyola.
822 **212** 50 c. green 10 10
823 – 50 c. brown 10 10
824 – 1 g. 50 violet 10 10
825 – 3 g. blue 10 10
826 **212** 6 g. 25 red 15 10
DESIGNS—VERT: 50 c. brown; 3 g. Statue of St. Ignatius. HORIZ: 1 g. 50, Jesuit Fathers' house, Antigua.
See also Nos. 1074/81.

1958. Re-election of Pres. Stroessner. Portrait in black.
827 **213** 10 c. red (postage) 10 10
828 15 c. violet 10 10
829 25 c. green 10 10
830 30 c. lake 10 10
831 50 c. mauve 10 10
832 75 c. blue 10 10
833 5 g. turquoise 10 10
834 10 g. brown 10 15
835 12 g. mauve (air) 40 35
836 18 g. orange 25 40
837 23 g. brown 40 40
838 36 g. green 40 40
839 50 g. olive 50 50
840 65 g. grey 75 75

1959. Nos. 758/72 surch with star enclosed by palm leaves and value.
841 1 g. 50 c. on 5 c. ochre (postage) 10 10
842 1 g. 50 c. on 20 c. brown . . 10 10
843 1 g. 50 c. on 50 c. purple . . 10 10
844 3 g. on 2 g. 50 c. olive . . . 10 10
845 6 g. 25 c. on 5 g. brown . . 10 10
846 20 g. on 15 g. turquoise . . . 35 35
847 30 g. on 25 g. green 50 50
848 4 g. on 2 g. blue (air) 10 10
849 12 g. 45 c. on 3 g. olive . . . 25 20
850 18 g. 15 c. on 6 g. brown . . 35 30
851 23 g. 40 c. on 10 g. red . . . 25 35
852 34 g. 80 c. on 20 g. bistre . . 40 50
853 36 g. on 4 g. green 40 30
854 43 g. 95 c. on 30 g. green . . 50 35
855 100 g. on 50 g. blue . . . . 1·10 75

215 U.N. Emblem

216 U.N. Emblem and Map of Paraguay

1959. Air. Visit of U.N. Secretary-General.
856 **215** 5 g. blue and orange . . . 40 30

1959. Air. U.N. Day.
857 **216** 12 g. 45 orange & blue . . 25 20

217 Football 218 "Uprooted Tree"

1960. Olympic Games, Rome. Inscr "1960".
863 217 30 c. red & grn (postage) 10 10
864 50 c. purple and blue 10 10
865 75 c. green and orange 10 10
866 1 g. 50 violet and green 10 10

867 – 12 g. 45 blue and red (air) 25 25
868 – 18 g. 15 green and purple 35 35
869 – 36 g. red and green 30 30
DESIGN—AIR: Basketball.

1960. World Refugee Year (1st issue).
870 218 25 c. pink & grn (postage) 10 10
871 50 c. green and red 10 10
872 70 c. brown and mauve 30 25
873 1 g. 50 blue & deep blue 30 30
874 3 g. grey and brown 40 35

875 – 4 g. pink and green (air) 35 50
876 – 12 g. 45 green and blue 70 50
877 – 18 g. 15 orange and red 95 60
878 – 23 g. 40 blue and red 95 1·10
DESIGN—AIR. As Type **218** but with "ANO MUNDIAL" inscr below tree.
See also Nos. 971/7.

219 U.N. Emblem 220 U.N. Emblem and Flags

1960. "Human Rights". Inscr "DERECHOS HUMANOS".
879 219 1 g. red & blue (postage) 10 10
880 – 3 g. orange and blue 10 10
881 – 6 g. orange and green 10 10
882 – 20 g. yellow and red 15 15

883 219 40 g. blue and red (air) 30 30
884 – 60 g. red and green 40 40
885 – 100 g. red and blue 50 50
DESIGNS: 3 g., 60 g. Hand holding scales; 6 g. Hands breaking chain; 20 g., 100 g. "Freedom flame".

1960. U.N. Day. Flags and inscr in blue and red.
886 220 30 c. blue (postage) 10 10
887 75 c. yellow 10 10
888 90 c. mauve 10 10

889 3 g. orange (air) 10 10
890 4 g. green 10 10

221 Bridge with Arms of Brazil and Paraguay 222 Timber Truck

1961. Inauguration of International Bridge between Brazil and Paraguay.
891 221 15 c. green (postage) 10 10
892 30 c. blue 10 10
893 50 c. orange 10 10
894 75 c. blue 10 10
895 1 g. violet 10 10

896 – 3 g. red (air) 15 10
897 – 12 g. 45 lake 30 25
898 – 18 g. 15 green 35 30
899 – 36 g. blue 30 25
DESIGN—HORIZ: Nos. 896/9, Aerial view of bridge.

1961. Paraguayan Progress. Inscr "PARAGUAY EN MARCHA".
900 222 25 c. red & grn (postage) 10 10
901 – 90 c. yellow and blue 10 10
902 – 1 g. red and orange 10 10
903 – 2 g. green and pink 10 10
904 – 5 g. violet and green 15 10

905 222 12 g. 45 blue and buff (air) 40 25
906 – 18 g. 15 violet and buff 55 35
907 – 22 g. blue and orange 30 40
908 – 36 g. yellow, green & blue 60 50
DESIGNS: 90 c., 2 g., 18 g. 15, Motorised timber barge; 1, 5, 22 g. Radio mast; 36 g. Boeing 707 jetliner.

223 P. J. Caballero, J. G. R. de Francia and F. Yegros 224 "Chaco Peace"

1961. 150th Anniv of Independence. (a) 1st issue.
909 223 30 c. green (postage) 10 10
910 50 c. mauve 10 10
911 90 c. violet 10 10
912 1 g. 50 blue 10 10
913 3 g. bistre 10 10
914 4 g. blue 10 10
915 5 g. brown 10 10

916 – 12 g. 45 red (air) 20 15
917 – 18 g. 15 blue 30 25
918 – 23 g. 40 green 40 30
919 – 30 g. violet 45 35
920 – 36 g. red 30 50
921 – 44 g. brown 40 35
DESIGN: Nos. 916/21, Declaration of Independence.

(b) 2nd issue. Inscr "PAZ DEL CHACO".
922 224 25 c. red (postage) 10 10
923 30 c. green 10 10
924 50 c. brown 10 10
925 1 g. violet 10 10
926 2 g. blue 10 10

927 – 3 g. blue (air) 20 15
928 – 4 g. purple 20 20
929 – 100 g. green 70 60
DESIGN: Nos. 927/9, Clasped hands.

225 Puma 226 Arms of Paraguay

(c) 3rd issue.
930 225 75 c. violet (postage) 10 10
931 1 g. 50 brown 10 10
932 4 g. 50 green 15 10
933 10 g. blue 25 20

934 – 12 g. 45 purple (air) 50 40
935 – 18 g. 15 blue 50 50
936 – 34 g. 80 brown 95 95
DESIGN: Nos. 934/6, Brazilian tapir.

(d) 4th issue.
937 226 15 c. blue (postage) 10 10
938 25 c. red 10 10
939 75 c. green 10 10
940 1 g. red 10 10

941 3 g. brown (air) 10 10
942 12 g. 45 mauve 25 25
943 36 g. turquoise 30 30
The air stamps have a background pattern of horiz lines.

227 Grand Hotel, Guarani 228 Racquet, Net and Balls

(e) 5th issue.
944 227 50 c. grey (postage) 10 10
945 1 g. green 10 10
946 4 g. 50 violet 10 10

947 – 3 g. brown (air) 10 10
948 – 4 g. blue 10 10
949 – 18 g. 15 orange 40 35
950 – 36 g. red 30 50
The air stamps are similar to Type **227** but inscr "HOTEL GUARANI" in upper left corner.
See also Nos. 978/85 and 997/1011.

1961. 28th South American Tennis Championships. Asuncion (1st issue). Centres multicoloured; border colours given.
951 228 35 c. pink (postage) 10 10
952 75 c. yellow 10 10
953 1 g. 50 blue 10 10
954 2 g. 25 turquoise 10 10
955 4 g. grey 15 10

956 12 g. 45 orange (air) 40 40
957 20 g. orange 35 70
958 50 g. orange 75 1·75
See also Nos. 978/85.

229

1961. "Europa".
959 229 50 c. red, blue and mauve 10 10
960 75 c. red, blue and green 10 10
961 1 g. red, blue and brown 10 10
962 1 g. 50 red, blue & lt blue 10 10
963 4 g. 50 red, blue & yellow 20 20

230 Comm. Alan Shepard and Solar System 231

1961. Commander Shepard's Space Flight.
964 – 10 c. brn & blue (postage) 10 10
965 – 25 c. mauve and blue 10 10
966 – 50 c. orange and blue 10 10
967 – 75 c. green and blue 10 10

968 230 18 g. 15 blue & green (air) 4·50 3·25
969 36 g. blue and orange 4·50 3·25
970 50 g. blue and mauve 7·00 3·50
DESIGN—HORIZ: Nos. 964/7, Comm. Shepard.

1961. World Refugee Year (2nd issue).
971 231 10 c. deep blue and blue (postage) 10 10
972 25 c. purple and orange 10 10
973 50 c. mauve and pink 10 10
974 75 c. blue and green 10 10

975 – 18 g. 15 red and brown (air) 25 25
976 – 36 g. green and red 55 55
977 – 50 g. orange and green 70 70
Nos. 975/7 have a different background and frame.

232 Tennis-player 233 Scout Bugler

1962. 150th Anniv of Independence (6th issue) and 28th South American Tennis Championships, Asuncion (2nd issue).
978 232 35 c. blue (postage) 10 10
979 75 c. violet 10 10
980 1 g. 50 brown 10 10
981 2 g. 25 green 10 10

982 – 4 g. red (air) 10 10
983 – 12 g. 45 purple 30 30
984 – 20 g. turquoise 25 25
985 – 50 g. brown 40 40
Nos. 982/5 show tennis-player using backhand stroke.

1962. Boy Scouts Commemoration.
986 233 10 c. grn & pur (postage) 10 10
987 20 c. green and red 10 10
988 25 c. green and brown 10 10
989 30 c. green and emerald 10 10
990 50 c. green and blue 10 10

991 – 12 g. 45 mauve & bl (air) 20 40
992 – 36 g. mauve and green 60 90
993 – 50 g. mauve and yellow 75 90
DESIGN: Nos. 991/3, Lord Baden-Powell.

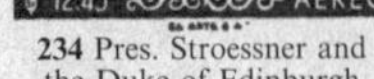

234 Pres. Stroessner and the Duke of Edinburgh 235 Map of the Americas

1962. Air. Visit of Duke of Edinburgh.
994 234 12 g. 45 blue, buff & grn 20 15
995 18 g. 15 blue, pink & red 30 25
996 36 g. blue, yellow & brn 25 45

1962. 150th Anniv of Independence (7th issue) and Day of the Americas.
997 235 50 c. orange (postage) 10 10
998 75 c. blue 10 10
999 1 g. violet 10 10
1000 1 g. 50 green 10 10
1001 4 g. 50 red 10 10

1002 – 20 g. mauve (air) 30 20
1003 – 50 g. orange 30 50
DESIGN: 20 g., 50 g. Hands supporting Globe.

236 U.N. Emblem

1962. 150th Anniv of Independence (8th issue).
1004 236 50 c. brown (postage) 10 10
1005 75 c. purple 10 10
1006 1 g. blue 10 10
1007 2 g. brown 10 10

1008 – 12 g. 45 violet (air) 35 35
1009 – 18 g. 15 green 25 25
1010 – 23 g. 40 red 35 35
1011 – 30 g. red 40 40
DESIGN: Nos. 1008/11, U.N. Headquarters, New York.

237 Mosquito and W.H.O. Emblem

1962. Malaria Eradication.
1012 237 30 c. black, blue and pink (postage) 10 10
1013 50 c. black, grn & bistre 10 10
1014 – 75 c. black, bistre & red 10 10
1015 – 1 g. black, bistre & grn 10 10
1016 – 1 g. 50 black, bis & brn 10 10

1017 237 3 g. black, red & bl (air) 10 10
1018 4 g. black, red & green 10 10
1019 – 12 g. 45 blk, grn & brn 25 10
1020 – 18 g. 15 black, red and purple 50 15
1021 – 36 g. black, blue & red 75 85
DESIGN: Nos. 1014/16, 1019/21, Mosquito on U.N. emblem, and microscope.

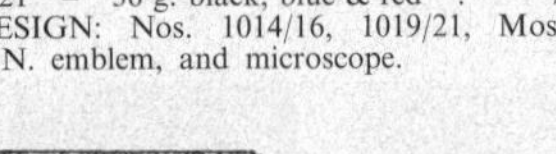

238 Football Stadium 239 "Lago Ypoa" (freighter)

1962. World Football Championships, Chile.
1022 238 15 c. brn & yell (postage) 10 10
1023 25 c. brown and green 10 10
1024 30 c. brown and violet 10 10
1025 40 c. brown & orange 10 10
1026 50 c. brown and green 10 10

1027 – 12 g. 45 black, red and violet (air) 50 25
1028 – 18 g. 15 black, brn & vio 40 45
1029 – 36 g. black, grey & brn 85 80
DESIGN—HORIZ: Nos. 1027/9, Footballers and Globe.

1962. Paraguayan Merchant Marine Commemoration.
1030 239 30 c. brown (postage) 10 10
1031 – 90 c. blue 10 10
1032 – 1 g. 50 purple 15 10
1033 – 2 g. green 25 15
1034 – 4 g. 20 blue 35 20

1035 – 12 g. 45 red (air) 30 15
1036 – 44 g. blue 30 45
DESIGNS—HORIZ: 90 c. Freighter; 1 g. 50, "Olympo" (freighter); 2 g. Freighter (diff); 4 g. 20, "Rio Apa" (freighter). VERT: 12 g. 45, 44 g. Ship's wheel.

1962. As Nos. 631, etc., but with taller figures of value.
1037 156 50 c. blue 10 10
1038 70 c. lilac 10 10
1039 1 g. 50 violet 10 10
1040 3 g. blue 10 10
1041 4 g. 50 brown 10 10
1042 5 g. mauve 10 10
1043 10 g. mauve 20 10
1044 12 g. 45 blue 20 10
1045 15 g. 45 red 25 10
1046 18 g. 15 purple 10 15
1047 20 g. brown 10 15
1048 50 g. brown 25 30
1049 100 g. grey 55 30

241 Gen. A. Stroessner

242 Popes Paul VI, John XXIII and St. Peter's

1963. Re-election of Pres. Stroessner to Third Term of Office.
1050 **241** 50 c. brn & drab (postage) 10 10
1051 75 c. brown & pink . . . 10 10
1052 1 g. 50 brown & mve . . . 10 10
1053 3 g. brown and green . . 10 10
1054 12 g. 45 red and pink (air) 25 20
1055 18 g. 15 green and pink . . 35 30
1056 36 g. violet and pink . . 60 40

1964. Popes Paul VI and John XXIII.
1057 **242** 1 g. 50 yell & red (postage) 10 10
1058 3 g. green and red . . . 10 10
1059 4 g. brown and red . . . 10 10
1060 – 12 g. 45 olive & grn (air) 35 20
1061 – 18 g. 15 green & violet . 20 30
1062 – 36 g. green and blue . . 75 60
DESIGNS: Nos. 1060/2, Cathedral, Asuncion.

243 Arms of Paraguay and France
245 Map of the Americas

1964. Visit of French President.
1063 **243** 1 g. 50 brown (postage) . 10 10
1064 – 3 g. blue 10 10
1065 **243** 4 g. grey 10 10
1066 – 12 g. 45 violet (air) . . . 25 20
1067 **243** 18 g. 15 green 40 30
1068 – 36 g. red 75 60
DESIGNS: 3, 12 g. 45, 36 g. Presidents Stroessner and De Gaulle.

1965. 6th Reunion of the Board of Governors of the Inter-American Development Bank. Optd **Centenario de la Epopeya Nacional 1,864-1,870** as in T **245**.
1069 **245** 1 g. 50 green (postage) . 10 10
1070 3 g. pink 10 10
1071 4 g. blue 10 10
1072 12 g. 45 brown (air) . . . 20 10
1073 36 g. violet 40 45
The overprint refers to the National Epic of 1864-70, the war with Argentina, Brazil and Uruguay and this inscription occurs on many other issues from 1965 onwards. Nos. 1069/73 without the overprint were not authorised.

246 R. Gonzalez and St. Ignatius
247 Ruben Dario

1966. 350th Anniv of Founding of San Ignacio Guazu Monastery.
1074 **246** 15 c. blue (postage) . . . 10 10
1075 25 c. blue 10 10
1076 75 c. blue 10 10
1077 90 c. blue 10 10
1078 – 3 g. brown (air) 10 10
1079 – 12 g. 45, brown 10 10
1080 – 18 g. 15, brown 20 10
1081 – 23 g. 40 brown 35 25
DESIGNS: Nos. 1078/81, Jesuit Fathers' house, Antigua.
For similar stamps with different inscriptions, see Nos. 822, 824 and 826.

1966. 50th Death Anniv of Ruben Dario (poet).
1082 **247** 50 c. blue 10 10
1083 70 c. brown 10 10
1084 1 g. 50 lake 10 10
1085 3 g. violet 10 10
1086 4 g. turquoise 10 10
1087 5 g. black 10 10
1088 – 12 g. 45 blue (air) 10 10
1089 – 18 g. 15 violet 10 10
1090 – 23 g. 40 brown 35 10
1091 – 36 g. green 50 25
1092 – 50 g. red 50 25
DESIGNS: Nos. 1088/92, Open book inscr "Paraguay de Fuego ..." by Dario.

248 Lions' Emblem on Globe

249 W.H.O. Emblem

1967. 50th Anniv of Lions International.
1093 **248** 50 c. violet (postage) . . 10 10
1094 70 c. blue 10 10
1095 – 1 g. 50 blue 10 10
1096 – 3 g. brown 10 10
1097 – 4 g. blue 10 10
1098 – 5 g. brown 10 10
1099 – 12 g. 45 brown (air) . . 10 10
1100 – 18 g. 15 violet 15 10
1101 – 23 g. 40 purple 20 10
1102 – 36 g. blue 25 25
1103 – 50 g. red 25 25
DESIGNS—VERT: 1 g. 50, 3 g. M. Jones; 4, 5 g. Lions headquarters, Chicago. HORIZ: 12 g. 45, 18 g. 15, Library–"Education"; 23 g. 40, 36 g., 50 g. Medical laboratory–"Health".

1968. 20th Anniv of W.H.O.
1104 **249** 3 g. turquoise (postage) . 10 10
1105 4 g. purple 10 10
1106 5 g. brown 10 10
1107 10 g. violet 10 10
1108 – 36 g. brown (air) 40 25
1109 – 50 g. red 45 30
1110 – 100 g. blue 60 35
DESIGN—VERT: Nos. 1108/10, W.H.O. emblem on scroll.

250

251

1969. World Friendship Week.
1111 **250** 50 c. red 10 10
1112 70 c. blue 10 10
1113 1 g. 50 brown 10 10
1114 3 g. mauve 10 10
1115 4 g. green 10 10
1116 5 g. violet 10 10
1117 10 g. purple 20 10

1969. Air. Campaign for Houses for Teachers.
1118 **251** 36 g. blue 40 45
1119 50 g. brown 50 70
1120 100 g. red . . . . 95 1·00

252 Pres. Lopez

253 Paraguay 2 r. Stamp of 1870

1970. Death Centenary of Pres. F. Solano Lopez.
1121 **252** 1 g. brown (postage) . . 10 10
1122 2 g. violet 10 10
1123 3 g. pink 10 10
1124 4 g. red 10 10
1125 5 g. blue 10 10
1126 10 g. green 10 10
1127 15 g. blue (air) 10 10
1128 20 g. brown 20 10
1129 30 g. green 30 20
1130 40 g. purple 35 25

1970. Centenary of First Paraguayan Stamps.
1131 **253** 1 g. red (postage) . . . 10 10
1132 A 2 g. blue 10 10
1133 B 3 g. brown 10 10
1134 **253** 5 g. violet 10 10
1135 A 10 g. lilac 20 10
1136 B 15 g. purple (air) 30 25
1137 **253** 30 g. green 35 50
1138 A 36 g. red 40 30
DESIGNS: First Paraguay stamps. A, 1 r. B, 3 r.

254 Teacher and Pupil

255 U.N.I.C.E.F. Emblem

1971. Int Education Year–U.N.E.S.C.O.
1139 **254** 3 g. blue (postage) . . . 10 10
1140 5 g. lilac 10 10
1141 10 g. green 10 10
1142 20 g. red (air) 20 10
1143 25 g. mauve 25 15
1144 30 g. brown 25 20
1145 50 g. green 40 35

1972. 25th Anniv of U.N.I.C.E.F.
1146 **255** 1 g. brown (postage) . . 10 10
1147 2 g. blue 10 10
1148 3 g. red 10 10
1149 4 g. purple 10 10
1150 5 g. green 10 10
1151 10 g. purple 10 10
1152 20 g. blue (air) 20 10
1153 25 g. green 25 15
1154 30 g. brown 25 20

256 Acaray Dam

1972. Tourist Year of the Americas.
1155 **256** 1 g. brown (postage) . . 10 10
1156 – 2 g. brown 10 10
1157 – 3 g. blue 10 10
1158 – 5 g. red 10 10
1159 – 10 g. green 10 10
1160 – 20 g. red (air) 25 10
1161 – 25 g. grey 30 15
1162 – 50 g. lilac . . . . 1·00 45
1163 – 100 g. mauve 55 40
DESIGNS: 2 g. Statue of Lopez; 3 g. Friendship Bridge; 5 g. Rio Tebicuary Bridge; 10 g. Grand Hotel, Guarani; 20 g. Motor coach; 25 g. Social Service Institute Hospital; 50 g. Liner "Presidente Stroessner"; 100 g. Lockheed Electra airliner.

257 O.E.A. Emblem

258 Exhibition Emblem

1973. 25th Anniv of Organization of American States (O.E.A.).
1164 **257** 1 g. mult. (postage) . . . 10 10
1165 2 g. multicoloured 10 10
1166 3 g. multicoloured 10 10
1167 4 g. multicoloured 10 10
1168 5 g. multicoloured 10 10
1169 10 g. multicoloured . . . 10 10
1170 20 g. multicoloured (air) . 20 10
1171 25 g. multicoloured . . . 30 15
1172 50 g. multicoloured . . . 25 35
1173 100 g. multicoloured . . 55 40

1973. Int Industrial Exhibition, Paraguay.
1174 **258** 1 g. brown (postage) . . 10 10
1175 2 g. red 10 10
1176 3 g. blue 10 10
1177 4 g. green 10 10
1178 5 g. lilac 10 10
1179 20 g. mauve (air) 20 10
1180 25 g. red 25 10

259 Carrier Pigeon with Letter

1975. Centenary of U.P.U.
1181 **259** 1 g. vio & blk (postage) . 10 10
1182 2 g. red and black . . . 10 10
1183 3 g. blue and black . . . 10 10
1184 5 g. blue and black . . . 10 10
1185 10 g. purple and black . . 10 10
1186 20 g. brown & blk (air) . 25 15
1187 25 g. green and black . . 30 20

260 Institute Buildings

1976. Inauguration (1974) of Institute of Higher Education.
1188 **260** 5 g. violet, red and black (postage) 10 10
1189 10 g. blue, red & black . 10 10
1190 30 g. brn, red & blk (air) 25 15

261 Rotary Emblem

1976. 70th Anniv of Rotary International.
1191 **261** 3 g. blue, bistre and black (postage) 10 10
1192 4 g. blue, bistre and mauve 10 10
1193 25 g. blue, bistre and green (air) 30 15

262 Woman and I.W.Y. Emblem

1976. International Women's Year.
1194 **262** 1 g. brown & bl (postage) 10 10
1195 2 g. brown and red . . . 10 10
1196 20 g. brown & green (air) 25 10

263 Black Palms

1977. Flowering Plants and Trees. Multicoloured.
1197 2 g. Type **263** (postage) . . . 10 10
1198 3 g. Mburucuya flowers . . 10 10
1199 20 g. Marsh rose (tree) (air) . 35 25

264 Nanduti Lace

265 F. S. Lopez

1977. Multicoloured.
1200 1 g. Type **264** (postage) . . . 10 10
1201 5 g. Nanduti weaver 10 10
1202 25 g. Lady holding jar (air) . 40 25

1977. 150th Birth Anniv of Marshal Francisco Solano Lopez.
1203 **265** 10 g. brown (postage) . . 10 10
1204 50 g. blue (air) 40 50
1205 100 g. green 75 60

266 General Bernardino Caballero National College

1978. Cent of National College of Asuncion.
1206 **266** 3 g. red (postage) 10 10
1207 4 g. blue 10 10
1208 5 g. violet 10 10
1209 20 g. brown (air) 20 15
1210 25 g. purple 25 20
1211 30 g. green 35 25

267 Marshal Jose F. Estigarribia, Trumpeter and Flag
268 Congress Emblem

1978. "Salon de Bronce" Commemoration.
1212 **267** 3 g. purple, blue and red (postage) 10 10
1213 5 g. violet, blue and red . 10 10
1214 10 g. grey, blue and red . 10 10
1215 20 g. green, bl & red (air) 25 15
1216 25 g. violet, blue and red 30 20
1217 30 g. purple, blue & red . 35 25

1979. 22nd Latin American Tourism Congress, Asuncion.
1218 **268** 10 g. black, blue and red (postage) 10 10
1219 50 g. black, blue and red (air) 30 40

269 Spanish Colonial House, Pilar

1980. Bicentenary of Pilar City.
1220 **269** 5 g. mult (postage) . . . 10 10
1221 25 g. multicoloured (air) . 30 20

270 Boeing 707

1980. Inauguration of Paraguayan Airlines Boeing 707 Service.
1222 **270** 20 g. mult (postage) . . . 30 10
1223 100 g. multicoloured (air) . 1·40 70

271 Seminary, Communion Cup and Bible

1981. Air. Centenary of Metropolitan Seminary, Asuncion.
1224 **271** 5 g. blue 10 10
1225 10 g. brown 10 10
1226 25 g. green 30 20
1227 50 g. black 30 40

272 U.P.U. Monument, Berne

1981. Centenary of Admission to U.P.U.
1228 **272** 5 g. red and black (postage) 10 10
1229 10 g. mauve and black . 10 10
1230 20 g. green and black (air) 25 15
1231 25 g. red and black . . . 30 20
1232 50 g. blue and black . . 30 40

273 St. Maria Mazzarello
275 Sun and Map of Americas

274 Stroessner and Bridge over River Itaipua

1981. Air. Death Centenary of Mother Maria Mazzarello (founder of Daughters of Mary).
1233 **273** 20 g. green and black . 25 15
1234 25 g. red and black . . 30 20
1235 50 g. violet and black . 30 40

1983. 25th Anniv of President Stroessner City.
1236 **274** 3 g. grn, bl & blk (postage) 10 10
1237 5 g. red, blue and black 10 10
1238 10 g. violet, blue & blk . 10 10
1239 20 g. grey, blue & blk (air) 25 15
1240 25 g. purple, blue & blk 30 20
1241 50 g. blue, grey & black 30 40

1985. Air. 25th Anniv of Inter-American Development Bank.
1242 **275** 3 g. orange, yell & pink 10 10
1243 5 g. orange, yell & mauve 10 10
1244 10 g. orange, yell & mauve 10 10
1245 50 g. orange, yell & brown 10 10
1246 65 g. orange, yellow & bl 15 10
1247 95 g. orange, yell & green 20 15

276 U.N. Emblem
277 1886 1 c. Stamp

1986. Air. 40th Anniv of U.N.O.
1248 **276** 5 g. blue and brown . . 10 10
1249 10 g. blue and grey . . 10 10
1250 50 g. blue and black . . 10 10

1986. Centenary of First Official Stamp.
1251 **277** 5 g. deep blue, brown and blue (postage) 10 10
1252 15 g. deep blue, brown and blue 10 10
1253 40 g. deep blue, brown and blue 10 10
1254 – 65 g. blue, green and red (air) 15 15
1255 – 100 g. blue, green and red 25 25
1256 – 150 g. blue, green and red 40 40
DESIGNS: 65, 100, 150 g. 1886 7 c. stamp.

278 Integration of the Nations Monument, Colmena

1986. Air. 50th Anniv of Japanese Immigration. Multicoloured.
1257 5 g. La Colmena vineyards (horiz) 10 10
1258 10 g. Flowers of cherry tree and lapacho (horiz) 10 10
1259 20 g. Type **278** 10 10

279 Caballero, Stroessner and Road

1987. Centenary of National Republican Association (Colorado Party).
1260 **279** 5 g. multicoloured (postage) 10 10
1261 10 g. multicoloured . . . 10 10
1262 25 g. multicoloured . . . 10 10
1263 – 150 g. multicoloured (air) 25 40
1264 – 170 g. multicoloured . . 30 20
1265 – 200 g. multicoloured . . 35 25
DESIGN: 150 to 200 g. Gen. Bernardino Caballero (President 1881–86 and founder of party), Pres. Alfredo Stroessner and electrification of countryside.

280 Emblem of Visit
281 Silver Mate

1988. Visit of Pope John Paul II.
1266 **280** 10 g. blue and black (postage) 10 10
1267 20 g. blue and black . . . 10 10
1268 50 g. blue and black . . . 15 10
1269 – 100 g. multicoloured (air) 30 20
1270 – 120 g. multicoloured . . 35 25
1271 – 150 g. multicoloured . . 45 35
DESIGN—HORIZ: 100 to 150 g. Pope and Caacupe Basilica.

1988. Air. Centenary of New Germany Colony. Multicoloured.
1272 90 g. Type **281** 25 10
1273 105 g. Mate ("Ilex paraguayensis") plantation . 30 20
1274 120 g. As No. 1273 . . . . . 35 25

1988. Air. 75th Anniv of Paraguay Philatelic Centre. No. 1249 optd ***75o ANIVERSARIO DE FUNDACION CENTRO FILATELICO DEL PARAGUAY 15 JUNIO-1913 - 1988.**
1275 **276** 10 g. blue and grey . . . 10 10

283 Pres. Stroessner and Government Palace

1988. Air. Re-election of President Stroessner.
1276 **283** 200 g. multicoloured . . 30 25
1277 500 g. multicoloured . . 75 90
1278 1000 g. multicoloured . . 1·50 1·50

1989. "Parafil 89" Stamp Exhibition. Nos. 1268 and 1270 optd **PARAFIL 89.**
1279 **280** 50 g. blue and black (postage) 15 10
1280 – 120 g. multicoloured (air) 35 25

285 Green-winged Macaw

1989. Birds. Multicoloured.
1281 50 g. Type **285** (postage) . . . 20 10
1282 100 g. Brazilian merganser (horiz) (air) 20 10
1283 300 g. Greater rhea (horiz) . . 60 20
1284 500 g. Toco toucan (horiz) . . 95 45
1285 1000 g. Bare-faced curassow (horiz) . . . . 2·00 1·00
1286 2000 g. Caninde macaw and blue and yellow macaw . . 3·75 2·00

286 Anniversary Emblem

1990. Centenary of Organization of American States. Multicoloured.
1287 50 g. Type **286** 10 10
1288 100 g. Organization and anniversary emblems (vert) 10 10
1289 200 g. Map of Paraguay . . . 45 15

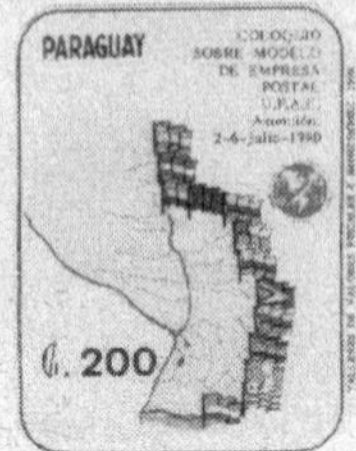

287 Basket
288 Flags on Map

1990. America. Pre-Columbian Life. Mult.
1290 150 g. Type **287** (postage) . . 15 10
1291 500 g. Guarani post (air) . . 1·10 95

1990. Postal Union of the Americas and Spain Colloquium. Multicoloured.
1292 200 g. Type **288** 20 15
1293 250 g. First Paraguay stamp 25 15
1294 350 g. Paraguay 1990 America first day cover (horiz) . . 35 25

289 Planned Building

1990. Centenary of National University. Mult.
1295 300 g. Type **289** 70 55
1296 400 g. Present building . . . 95 75
1297 600 g. Old building . . . . . 1·40 1·10

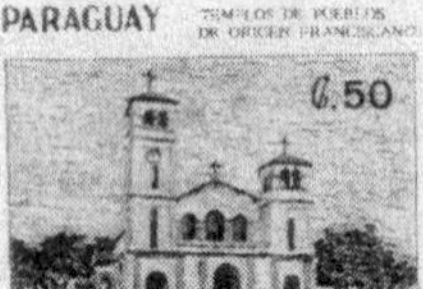

290 Guarambare Church

1990. Franciscan Churches. Multicoloured.
1298 50 g. Type **290** 10 10
1299 100 g. Yaguaron Church . . 25 20
1300 200 g. Ita Church 45 35

1991. Visit of King and Queen of Spain. Nos. 1290/1 optd **Vista de sus Majestades Los Reyes de Espana 22-24 Octubre 1990.**
1301 **287** 150 g. mult (postage) . . 15 10
1302 – 500 g. multicoloured (air) 1·10 95

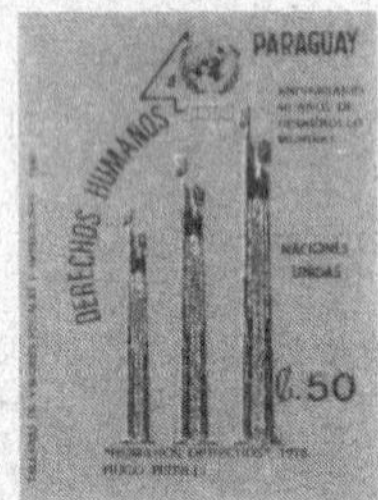

292 "Human Rights" (Hugo Pistilli)

1991. 40th Anniv of United Nations Development Programme. Multicoloured.
1303 50 g. Type **292** 10 10
1304 100 g. "United Nations" (sculpture, Hermann Guggiari) 10 20
1305 150 f. First Miguel de Cervantes prize, awarded to Augusto Roa Bastos, 1989 . . . . 15 10

294 Hands and Ballot Box (free elections)

1991. Democracy. Multicoloured.
1308 50 g. Type **294** (postage) . . 10 10
1309 100 g. Sun (State and Catholic Church) (vert) 10 10
1310 200 g. Arrows and male and female symbols (human rights) (vert) 15 10
1311 300 g. Dove and flag (freedom of the press) (vert) (air) . . 25 20
1312 500 g. Woman and child welcoming man (return of exiles) 35 25
1313 3000 g. Crowd with banners (democracy) . . . . 2·25 1·75

295 Julio Manuel Morales (gynaecologist)

1991. Medical Professors.
1314 **295** 50 g. mult (postage) . . . 10 10
1315 – 100 g. multicoloured . . 10 10
1316 – 200 g. multicoloured . . 15 10
1317 – 300 g. brown, blk & grn . 25 20
1318 – 350 g. brown, black and green (air) 25 20
1319 – 500 g. multicoloured . . 35 25
DESIGNS: 100 g. Carlos Gatti (surgeon); 200 g. Gustavo Gonzalez (symptomatologist); 300 g. Juan Max Boettner (physician and musician); 350 g. Juan Boggino (pathologist); 500 g. Andres Barbero (founder of Paraguayan Red Cross).

1991. "Espamer '91" Spain-Latin America Stamp Exhibition, Buenos Aires. Nos. 1298/1300 optd **ESPAMER 91 BUENOS AIRES 5 14 Jul** and Conquistador in oval.
1323 50 g. multicoloured 10 10
1324 100 g. multicoloured 10 10
1325 200 g. multicoloured 15 10

298 Ruy Diaz de Guzman (historian)

1991. Writers and Musicians. Multicoloured.
1326 50 g. Type **298** (postage) . . 10 10
1327 100 g. Maria Talavera (war chronicler) (vert) 10 10
1328 150 g. Augusto Roa Bastos (writer and 1989 winner of Miguel de Cervantes Prize) (vert) 10 10
1329 200 g. Jose Asuncion Flores (composer of "La Guarania") (vert) (air) 15 10
1330 250 g. Felix Perez Cardozo (harpist and composer) . . 20 15
1331 300 g. Juan Carlos Moreno Gonzalez (composer) . . . 25 20

299 Battle of Tavare **300** "Compass of Life" (Alfredo Moraes)

1991. America. Voyages of Discovery. Mult.
1332 100 g. Type **299** (postage) . . 10 10
1333 300 g. Arrival of Domingo Martinez de Irala in Paraguay (air) 25 20

1991. Paintings. Multicoloured.
1334 50 g. Type **300** (postage) . . 10 10
1335 100 g. "Callejon Illuminated" (Michael Burt) 10 10
1336 150 g. "Arete" (Lucy Yegros) 10 10
1337 200 g. "Itinerants" (Hugo Bogado Barrios) (air) . . . 15 10
1338 250 g. "Travellers without a Ship" (Bernardo Ismachoviez) 20 15
1339 300 g. "Guarani" (Lotte Schulz) 25 20

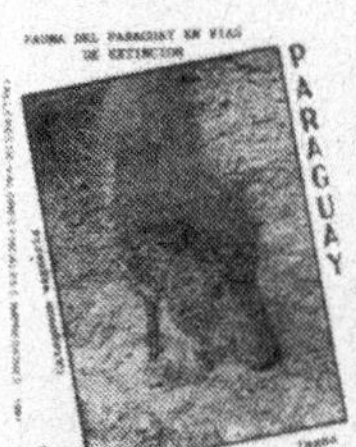

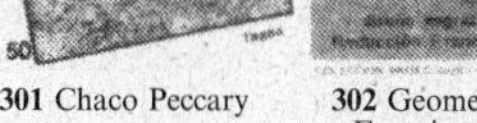

301 Chaco Peccary **302** Geometric Design, Franciscan Church, Caazapa

1992. Endangered Mammals. Multicoloured.
1340 50 g. Type **301** 10 10
1341 100 g. Ocelot (horiz) 10 10
1342 150 g. Brazilian tapir 10 10
1343 200 g. Maned wolf 15 10

1992. 500th Anniv of Discovery of America by Columbus (1st series). Church Roof Tiles. Mult.
1344 50 g. Type **302** 10 10
1345 100 g. Church, Jesuit church, Trinidad 10 10
1346 150 g. Missionary ship, Jesuit church, Trinidad 10 10
1347 200 g. Plant, Franciscan church, Caazapa 15 10
See also Nos. 1367/71.

1992. "Granada '92" International Thematic Stamp Exhibition. Nos. 1344/7 optd **GRANADA '92** and emblem.
1348 50 g. multicoloured 10 10
1349 100 g. multicoloured 10 10
1350 150 g. multicoloured 10 10
1351 200 g. multicoloured 10 10

304 Malcolm L. Norment (founder) and Emblem **305** Southern Hemisphere and Ecology Symbols on Hands

1992. 68th Anniv of Paraguay Leprosy Foundation. Multicoloured.
1352 50 g. Type **304** 10 10
1353 250 g. Gerhard Hansen (discoverer of leprosy bacillus) 20 15

1992. 2nd United Nations Conference on Environment and Development, Rio de Janeiro. Multicoloured.
1354 50 g. Type **305** 10 10
1355 100 g. Butterfly and chimneys emitting smoke 10 10
1356 250 g. Tree and map of South America on globe 20 15

306 Factories and Cotton (economy)

1992. National Population and Housing Census. Multicoloured.
1357 50 g. Type **306** 10 10
1358 200 g. Houses (vert) 15 10
1359 250 g. Numbers and stylized people (population) (vert) 20 15
1360 300 g. Abacus (education) . 25 20

307 Football

1992. Olympic Games, Barcelona. Multicoloured.
1361 50 g. Type **307** 10 10
1362 100 g. Tennis 10 10
1363 150 g. Running 10 10
1364 200 g. Swimming (horiz) . . 15 10
1365 250 g. Judo 20 15
1366 350 g. Fencing (horiz) . . . 25 20

308 Brother Luis Bolanos

1992. 500th Anniv of Discovery of America by Columbus (2nd series). Evangelists. Multicoloured.
1367 50 g. Type **308** (translator of Catechism into Guarani and founder of Guarani Christian settlements) 10 10
1368 100 g. Brother Juan de San Bernardo (Franciscan and first Paraguayan martyr) . 10 10
1369 150 g. St. Roque Gonzalez de Santa Cruz (Jesuit missionary and first Paraguayan saint) 10 10
1370 200 g. Fr. Amancio Gonzalez (founder of Melodia settlement) 15 10
1371 250 g. Mgr. Juan Sinforiano Bogarin (first Archbishop of Asuncion) (vert) 20 15

309 Fleet approaching Shore

1992. America. 500th Anniv of Discovery of America by Columbus. Multicoloured.
1372 150 g. Type **309** (postage) . . 10 10
1373 350 g. Christopher Columbus (vert) (air) 25 20

1992. 30th Anniv of United Nations Information Centre in Paraguay. Nos. 1354/6 optd **NACIONES UNIDAS 1992 - 30 AÑOS CENTRO INFORMACION ONU EN PARAGUAY.**
1374 50 g. multicoloured 10 10
1375 100 g. multicoloured 10 10
1376 250 g. multicoloured 20 15

1992. Christmas. Nos. 1367/9 optd **Navidad 92.**
1377 50 g. multicoloured 10 10
1378 100 g. multicoloured 10 10
1379 150 g. multicoloured 10 10

1992. "Parafil 92" Paraguay-Argentina Stamp Exhibition, Buenos Aires. Nos. 1372/3 optd **PARAFIL 92.**
1380 150 g. mult (postage) 10 10
1381 350 g. multicoloured (air) . . 25 20

313 Planting and Hoeing

1992. 50th Anniv of Pan-American Agricultural Institute. Multicoloured.
1382 50 g. Type **313** 10 10
1383 100 g. Test tubes 10 10
1384 200 g. Cotton plant in cupped hands 15 10
1385 250 g. Cattle and maize plant 20 15

314 Yolanda Bado de Artecona

1992. Centenary of Paraguayan Writers' College. Multicoloured.
1386 50 g. Type **314** 10 10
1387 100 g. Jose Ramon Silva . . . 10 10
1388 150 g. Abelardo Brugada Valpy 10 10
1389 200 g. Tomas Varela 15 10
1390 250 g. Jose Livio Lezcano . . 20 15
1391 300 g. Francisco I. Fernandez 25 20

315 Members' Flags and Map of South America **316** Orange Flowers (Gilda Hellmers)

1993. 1st Anniv (1992) of Treaty of Asuncion forming Mercosur (common market of Argentina, Brazil, Paraguay and Uruguay). Multicoloured.
1392 50 g. Type **315** 10 10
1393 350 g. Flags encircling globe showing map of South America 25 20

1993. 50th Anniv of St. Isabel Leprosy Association. Flower paintings by artists named. Multicoloured.
1394 50 g. Type **316** 10 10
1395 200 g. Luis Alberto Balmelli 15 10
1396 250 g. Lili del Monico . . . 20 15
1397 350 g. Brunilde Guggiari . . 25 20

317 Goethe (after J. Lips) and Manuscript of Poem

1993. Centenary of Goethe College.
1398 **317** 50 g. brown, black & bl . 10 10
1399 – 200 g. multicoloured . . 15 10
DESIGN: 200 g. Goethe (after J. Tischbein).

1993. "Brasiliana 93" International Stamp Exhibition, Rio de Janeiro. Nos. 1398/9 optd **BRASILIANA 93.**
1400 50 g. brown, black and blue . 10 10
1401 200 g. multicoloured 15 10

319 Palace (Michael Burt)

1993. Centenary (1992) of Los Lopez (Government) Palace, Asuncion. Paintings of palace by artists named. Multicolured.
1402 50 g. Type **319** 10 10
1403 100 g. Esperanza Gill 10 10
1404 200 g. Emili Aparici 15 10
1405 250 g. Hugo Bogado Barrios (vert) 15 10

320 Couple sitting on Globe and Emblem

1993. 35th Anniv of World Friendship Crusade.
1406 **320** 50 g. black, blue and mauve 10 10
1407 – 100 g. multicoloured . . 10 10
1408 – 200 g. multicoloured . . 15 10
1409 – 250 g. multicoloured . . 15 10
DESIGNS: 100 g. Dr. Ramon Artemio Bracho (founder), map of Americas and emblem; 200 g. Children and sun emerging from cloud; 250 g. Couple hugging and emblem.

1993. Inauguration of President Juan Carlos Wasmosy. Nos. 1402/5 optd **TRANSMISION DEL MANDO PRESIDENCIAL GRAL. ANDRES RODRIGUEZ ING. JUAN C. WASMOSY 15 DE AGOSTO 1993.**
1410 50 g. multicoloured 10 10
1411 100 g. multicoloured 10 10
1412 200 g. multicoloured 15 10
1413 250 g. multicoloured 15 10

322 "Church of the Incarnation" (Juan Guerra Gaja)

1993. Centenary of Church of the Incarnation. Paintings. Multicoloured.
1414 50 g. Type **322** 10 10
1415 350 g. "Church of the Incarnation" (Hector Blas Ruiz) (horiz) 25 20

323 Bush Dog

1993. America. Endangered Animals. Multicoloured.

1416 250 g. Type **323** (postage) . . 15 10

1417 50 g. Great anteater (air) . . 10 10

1993. 80th Anniv of World Food Programme. Nos. 1383/4 optd **'30 ANOS DEL PROGRAMA MUNDIAL DE ALIMENTOS'** and emblem.

1418 100 g. multicoloured 10 10

1419 200 g. multicoloured 15 10

325 Children Carol-singing

1993. Christmas. Multicoloured.

1420 50 g. Type **325** 10 10

1421 250 g. Wise men following star 15 10

326 Boy and Girl Scouts

1993. 80th Anniv of Paraguay Scouts Association. Multicoloured.

1422 50 g. Type **326** 10 10

1423 100 g. Boy scouts in camp . . 10 10

1424 200 g. Lord Robert Baden-Powell (founder of Scouting movement) 15 10

1425 250 g. Girl scout with flag . . 15 10

327 Cecilio Baez

1994. Centenary of First Graduation of Lawyers from National University, Asuncion.

1426 **327** 50 g. red and crimson . . 10 10

1427 – 100 g. yellow and orange 10 10

1428 – 250 g. yellow and green . 15 10

1429 – 500 g. blue and deep blue 30 20

DESIGNS—VERT: 100 g. Benigno Riquelme. HORIZ: 250 g. Emeterio Gonzalez; 500 g. J. Gaspar Villamayor.

328 Basketball **329** Penalty Kick

1994. 50th Anniv of Phoenix Sports Association. Multicoloured.

1430 50 g. Type **328** 10 10

1431 200 g. Football 15 10

1432 250 g. Pedro Andres Garcia Arias (founder) and tennis (horiz) 15 10

1994. World Cup Football Championship, U.S.A. Multicoloured.

1433 250 g. Type **329** 15 10

1434 500 g. Tackle 30 20

1435 1000 g. Dribbling ball past opponent 65 50

330 Runner

1994. Centenary of International Olympic Committee. Multicoloured.

1436 350 g. Type **330** 25 20

1437 400 g. Athlete lighting Olympic Flame 25 20

331 World Map and Emblem

1994. World Congress of International Federation for Physical Education, Asuncion. Multicoloured.

1438 200 g. Type **331** 15 10

1439 1000 g. Family exercising and flag (vert) 65 50

1994. Brazil, Winners of World Cup Football Championship. Nos. 1433/5 optd **BRASIL Campeon Mundial de Futbol Estados Unidos '94.**

1440 250 g. multicoloured 15 10

1441 500 g. multicoloured 30 20

1442 1000 g. multicoloured . . . 65 50

1994. 25th Anniv of First Manned Moon Landing. No. 1407 optd **25 Anos, Conquista de la Luna por el hombre 1969 - 1994.**

1443 100 g. multicoloured 10 10

334 Barrios

1994. 50th Death Anniv of Agustin Pio Barrios Mangore (guitarist). Multicoloured.

1444 250 g. Type **334** 15 10

1445 500 g. Barrios wearing casual clothes and a hat 30 20

335 Police Commandant, 1913

1994. 151st Anniv of Police Force. Multicoloured.

1446 50 g. Type **335** 10 10

1447 250 g. Carlos Bernardino Cacabelos (first Commissioner) and Pedro Nolasco Fernandez (first Chief of Asuncion Police Dept) 15 10

336 Maguari Stork

1994. "Parafil 94" Stamp Exhibition. Birds. Multicoloured.

1448 100 g. Type **336** 10 10

1449 150 g. Yellow-billed cardinal . 10 10

1450 400 g. Green kingfisher (vert) 25 20

1451 500 g. Jabiru (vert) 30 20

337 Nicolas Copernicus and Eclipse **339** Mother and Child

338 Steam Locomotive

1994. Total Eclipse of the Sun, November 1994. Astronomers. Multicoloured.

1452 50 g. Type **337** 10 10

1453 200 g. Johannes Kepler and sun dial, St. Cosmas and Damian Jesuit settlement 15 10

1994. America. Postal Transport. Multicoloured.

1454 100 g. Type **338** 10 10

1455 1000 g. Express mail motor cycle 65 50

1994. International Year of the Family. Details of paintings by Olga Blinder. Multicoloured.

1456 50 g. Type **339** 10 10

1457 250 g. Mother and children . 15 10

340 Holy Family and Angels

1994. Christmas. Ceramic Figures. Multicoloured.

1458 150 g. Type **340** 10 10

1459 700 g. Holy Family (vert) . . 45 20

341 Red Cross Workers and Dr. Andres Barbero (founder)

1994. 75th Anniv of Paraguay Red Cross. Multicoloured.

1460 150 g. Scouts, anniversary emblem and Henri Dunant (founder of International Red Cross) 10 10

1461 700 g. Type **341** 45 20

342 Sculpture by Herman Guggiari and Pope John Paul II

1994. 90th Anniv of San Jose College. Multicoloured.

1462 200 g. Type **342** 15 10

1463 250 g. College entrance and Pope John Paul II 15 10

343 Pasteur and Hospital Facade **344** Couple

1995. Paraguayan Red Cross. Death Centenary of Louis Pasteur (chemist) and Centenary of Clinical Hospital.

1464 **343** 1000 g. multicoloured . 65 50

1995. Anti-AIDS Campaign. Multicoloured.

1465 500 g. Type **344** 30 20

1466 1000 g. Sad and happy blood droplets 65 50

345 Jug and Loaf

1995. 50th Anniv of F.A.O. Paintings by Hernan Miranda. Multicoloured.

1467 950 g. Type **345** 60 45

1468 2000 g. Melon and leaf . . . 1·25 1·00

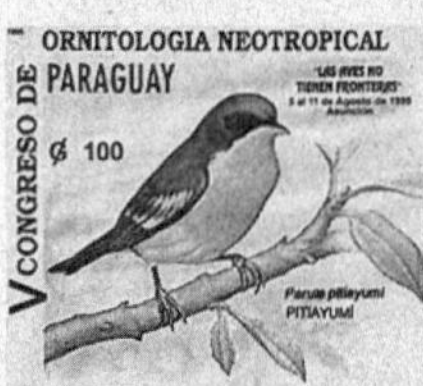

346 Olive-backed Warbler

1995. 5th Neo-tropical Ornithological Congress, Asuncion. Multicoloured.

1469 100 g. Type **346** 10 10

1470 200 g. Swallow-tailed manakin 15 10

1471 600 g. Troupial 40 30

1472 1000 g. Hooded siskin . . . 65 50

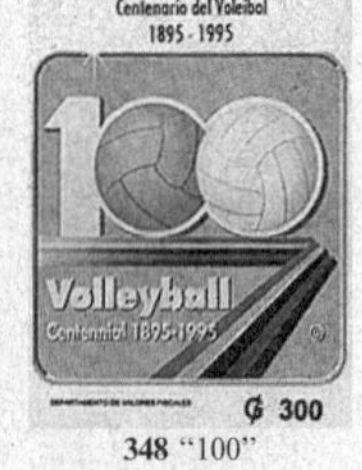

347 River Monday Rapids **348** "100"

1995. 5th International Town, Ecology and Tourism Symposium. Multicoloured.

1473 1150 g. Type **347** 75 60

1474 1300 g. Aregua railway station 85 65

1995. Centenary of Volleyball.

1475 **348** 300 g. multicoloured . . 20 15

1476 – 600 g. blue and black . . 40 30

1477 – 1000 g. multicoloured . 65 50

DESIGNS: 600 g. Ball hitting net; 1000 g. Hands, ball and net.

349 Macizo, Acahay

1995. America. Environmental Protection. Multicoloured.

1478 950 g. Type **349** 60 45

1479 2000 g. Tinfunque Reserve, Chaco (vert) . . . . . . 1·25 1·00

MINIMUM PRICE

The minimum price quoted is 10p which represents a handling charge rather than a basis for valuing common stamps. For further notes about prices, see introductory pages.

350 Anniversary Emblem

1995. 50th Anniv of U.N.O. Multicoloured.

1480	200 g. Type **350**	15	10
1481	3000 g. Stylised figures supporting emblem	1·90	1·50

351 Couple holding Star

1995. Christmas. Multicoloured.

1482	200 g. Type **351**	15	10
1483	1000 g. Crib	65	50

352 Marti and "Hedychium coronarium"

1995. Birth Centenary of Jose Marti (revolutionary). Multicoloured.

1484	200 g. Type **352**	10	10
1485	1000 g. Marti, Cuban national flag and "Hedychium coronarium" (horiz)	65	50

353 "Railway Station"

1996. 25th Latin American and Caribbean Forum of Lions International. Paintings by Esperanza Gill. Multicoloured.

1486	200 g. Type **353**	10	10
1487	1000 g. "Viola House"	60	45

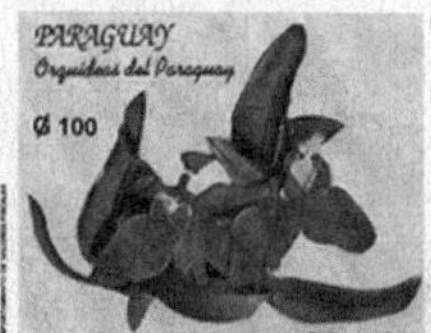

354 "Cattleya nobilior"

1996. Orchids. Multicoloured.

1488	100 g. Type **354**	10	10
1489	200 g. "Oncidium varicosum"	10	10
1490	1000 g. "Oncidium jonesianum" (vert)	60	45
1491	1150 g. "Sophronitis cernua"	70	55

355 Emblems and Gymnast on "Stamp"

1996. Centenary of Modern Olympic Games and Olympic Games, Atlanta. Multicoloured.

1492	500 g. Type **355**	30	20
1493	1000 g. Emblems and runner on "stamp"	60	45

OFFICIAL STAMPS

O 14

O 19

O 20

O 37

1886. Various types as O **14**, O **19** and O **20** optd **OFICIAL**. (a) Imperf.

O32	1 c. orange	2·25	2·25
O33	2 c. violet	2·25	2·25
O34	5 c. orange	2·25	2·25
O35	7 c. green	2·25	2·25
O36	10 c. brown	2·25	2·25
O37	15 c. blue	2·25	2·25
O38	20 c. lake	2·25	2·25

(b) New colours. Perf.

O39	1 c. green	40	40
O40	2 c. red	40	40
O41	5 c. blue	40	40
O42	7 c. orange	40	40
O43	10 c. lake	40	40
O44	15 c. brown	40	40
O45	20 c. blue	40	40

1889. Stamp of 1889 surch **OFICIAL** and value. Perf.

O47	**25**	1 on 15 c. purple	1·10	75
O48		2 on 10 c. purple	1·10	75

1889. Stamp of 1889 surch **OFICIAL** and value. Imperf.

O49	**25**	3 on 15 c. purple	1·10	75
O50		5 on 15 c. brown	1·10	75

1890. Stamps of 1887 optd **OFICIAL** or **Oficial**.

O58	**24**	1 c. green	10	10
O59		2 c. red	15	10
O60		5 c. blue	15	10
O61		7 c. brown	1·40	75
O55		10 c. mauve	20	15
O63		15 c. orange	20	15
O64		20 c. pink	25	15
O65		50 c. grey	15	15
O86		1 p. green	10	10

1901.

O73	O **37**	1 c. blue	30	30
O74		2 c. red	10	10
O75		4 c. brown	10	10
O76		5 c. green	10	10
O77		8 c. brown	10	10
O78		10 c. red	10	10
O79		20 c. blue	20	15

1903. Stamps of 1903, optd **OFICIAL**.

O 99	**46**	1 c. grey	10	10
O100		2 c. green	10	10
O101		5 c. blue	15	10
O102		10 c. brown	10	10
O103		20 c. red	10	10
O104		30 c. blue	10	10
O105		60 c. violet	20	20

1904. As T **50**, but inscr "OFICIAL".

O106	1 c. green	20	10
O107	1 c. olive	30	10
O108	1 c. orange	35	15
O109	1 c. red	30	20
O110	2 c. orange	20	10
O111	2 c. green	20	10
O112	2 c. red	60	40
O113	2 c. grey	50	30
O114	5 c. blue	25	20
O116	5 c. grey	1·10	75
O117	10 c. lilac	15	10
O118	20 c. lilac	50	30

1913. As T **65**, but inscr "OFICIAL".

O237	1 c. grey	10	10
O238	2 c. orange	10	10
O239	5 c. purple	10	10
O240	10 c. green	10	10
O241	20 c. red	10	10
O242	50 c. red	10	10
O243	75 c. blue	10	10
O244	1 p. blue	10	10
O245	2 p. yellow	20	20

1935. Optd **OFICIAL**.

O474	**86**	10 c. blue	10	10
O475		50 c. mauve	10	10
O476	**87**	1 p. orange	10	10
O477	**122**	1 p. 50 green	10	10
O478	–	2 p. 50 violet (No. 337)	10	10

1940. 50th Anniv of Asuncion University. As T **139**, inscr "SERVICIO OFICIAL", but portraits of Pres. Escobar and Dr. Zubizarreta.

O513	50 c. black and red	10	10
O514	1 p. black and red	10	10
O515	2 p. black and blue	10	10
O516	5 p. black and blue	10	10
O517	10 p. black and blue	10	10
O518	50 p. black and orange	40	10

POSTAGE DUE STAMPS

D 48

1904.

D106	D **48**	2 c. green	30	30
D107		4 c. green	30	30
D108		10 c. green	30	30
D109		20 c. green	30	30

1913. As T **65**, but inscr "DEFICIENTE".

D237	1 c. brown	10	10
D238	2 c. brown	10	10
D239	5 c. brown	10	10
D240	10 c. brown	10	10
D241	20 c. brown	10	10
D242	40 c. brown	10	10
D243	1 p. brown	10	10
D244	1 p. 50 brown	10	10

APPENDIX

The following stamps have either been issued in excess of postal needs or have not been available to the public in reasonable quantities at face value. Such stamps may later be given full listing if there is evidence of regular postal use.

1962.

Manned Spacecraft. Postage 15, 25, 30, 40, 50 c.; Air 12 g. 45, 18 g. 15, 36 g.

Previous Olympic Games. (First series). Vert designs. Postage 15, 25, 30, 40, 50 c.; Air 12 g. 45, 18 g. 15, 36 g.

Vatican Council. Postage 50, 70 c., 1 g. 50, 2, 3 g.; Air 5, 10 g., 12 g. 45, 18 g. 15, 23 g. 40, 36 g.

Europa. Postage 4 g.; Air 36 g.

Solar System. Postage 10, 20, 25, 30, 50 c.; Air 12 g. 45, 36 g., 50 g.

1963.

Previous Olympic Games. (Second series). Horiz designs. Postage 15, 25, 30, 40, 50 c.; Air 12 g. 45, 18 g. 15, 36 g.

Satellites and Space Flights. Vert designs. Postage 10, 20, 25, 30, 50 c.; Air 12 g. 45, 36 g., 50 g.

Previous Winter Olympic Games. Postage 10, 20, 25, 30, 50 c.; Air 12 g. 45, 36 g., 50 g.

Freedom from Hunger. Postage 10, 25, 50, 75 c.; Air 18 g. 15, 36 g., 50 g.

"Mercury" Space Flights. Postage 15, 25, 30, 40, 50 c.; Air 12 g. 45, 18 g. 15, 50 g.

Winter Olympic Games. Postage 15, 25, 30, 40, 50 c.; Air 12 g. 45, 18 g. 15, 50 g.

1964.

Tokyo Olympic Games. Postage 15, 25, 30, 40, 50 c.; Air 12 g. 45, 18 g. 15, 50 g.

Red Cross Cent. Postage 10, 25, 30, 50 c.; Air 18 g. 15, 36 g., 50 g.

"Gemini", "Telstar" and "Apollo" Projects. Postage 15, 25, 30, 40, 50 c.; Air 12 g. 45, 18 g. 15, 50 g.

Spacecraft Developments. Postage 15, 25, 30, 40, 50 c.; Air 12 g. 45, 18 g. 15, 50 g.

United Nations. Postage 15, 25, 30, 40, 50 c.; Air 12 g. 45, 18 g. 15, 50 g.

American Space Research. Postage 10, 15, 20, 30, 40 c.; Air 12 g. 45 + 6 g., 18 g. 15 + 9 g., 20 g. + 20 g.

Eucharistic Conference. Postage 20 g. + 10 g., 30 g. + 15 g., 50 g. + 25 g., 100 g. + 50 g.

Pope John Memorial Issue. Postage 20 g. + 10 g., 30 g. + 15 g., 50 g. + 25 g., 100 g. + 50 g.

1965.

Scouts. Postage 10, 15, 20, 30, 50 c.; Air 12 g. 45, 18 g. 15, 36 g.

Tokyo Olympic Games Medals. Postage 15, 25, 30, 40, 50 c.; Air 12 g. 45, 18 g. 15, 50 g.

Famous Scientists. Postage 10, 15, 20, 30, 40 c.; Air 12 g. 45 + 6 g., 18 g. 15 + 9 g., 20 g. + 20 g.

Orchids and Trees. Postage 20, 30, 90 c., 1 g. 50, 4 g. 50.; Air 3 g., 4 g., 66 g.

Kennedy and Churchill. Postage 15, 25, 30, 40, 50 c.; Air 12 g. 45, 18 g. 15, 50 g.

I.T.U. Cent. Postage 10, 15, 20, 30, 40 c.; Air 12 g. 45 + 6 g., 18 g. 15 + 9 g., 20 g. + 10 g.

Pope Paul VI. Visit to United Nations. Postage 10, 15, 20, 30, 50 c.; Air 12 g. 45, 18 g. 15, 36 g.

1966.

"Gemini" Space Project. Postage 15, 25, 30, 40, 50 c.; Air 12 g. 45, 18 g. 15, 50 g.

Events of 1965. Postage 10, 15, 20, 30, 50 c.; Air 12 g. 45, 18 g. 15, 36 g.

Mexico Olympic Games. Postage 10, 15, 20, 30, 50 c.; Air 12 g. 45, 18 g. 15, 36 g.

German Space Research. Postage 10, 15, 20, 30, 50 c.; Air 12 g. 45, 18 g. 15, 36 g.

Famous Writers. Postage 10, 15, 20, 30, 50 c.; Air 12 g. 45, 18 g. 15, 36 g.

Italian Space Research. Postage 10, 15, 20, 30, 50 c.; Air 12 g. 45, 18 g. 15, 36 g.

Moon Missions. Postage 10, 15, 20, 30, 50 c.; Air 12 g. 45, 18 g. 15, 36 g.

Sports Commemorative Issue. Postage 10, 15, 20, 30, 50 c.; Air 12 g. 45, 18 g. 15, 36 g.

3rd Death Anniv of Pres. John Kennedy. Postage 10, 15, 20, 30, 50 c.; Air 12 g. 45, 18 g. 15, 36 g.

Famous Paintings. Postage 10, 15, 20, 30, 50 c.; Air 12 g. 45, 18 g. 15, 36 g.

1967.

Religious Paintings. Postage 10, 15, 20, 30, 50 c.; Air 12 g. 45, 18 g. 15, 36 g.

16th Cent. Religious Paintings. Postage 10, 15, 20, 30, 50 c.; Air 12 g. 45, 18 g. 15, 36 g.

Impressionist Paintings. Postage 10, 15, 20, 30, 50 c.; Air 12 g. 45, 18 g. 15, 36 g.

European Paintings of 17th and 18th Cent. Postage 10, 15, 20, 25, 30, 50 c.; Air 12 g. 45, 18 g. 15, 36 g.

Birth Anniv of Pres. John Kennedy. Postage 10, 15, 20, 25, 30, 50 c.; Air 12 g. 45, 18 g. 15, 36 g.

Sculpture. Postage 10, 15, 20, 25, 30, 50 c.; Air 12 g. 45, 18 g. 15, 50 g.

Mexico Olympic Games. Archaeological Relics. Postage 10, 15, 20, 25, 30, 50 c.; Air 12 g. 45, 18 g. 15, 36 g.

1968.

Religious Paintings. Postage 10, 15, 20, 25, 30, 50 c.; Air 12 g. 45, 18 g. 15, 36 g.

Winter Olympic Games, Grenoble. Paintings. Postage 10, 15, 20, 25, 30, 50 c.; Air 12 g. 45, 18 g. 15, 36 g.

Paraguayan Stamps from 1870-1970. Postage 10, 15, 20, 25, 30, 50 c.; Air 12 g. 45, 18 g. 15, 36 g.

Mexico Olympic Games, Paintings of Children. Postage 10, 15, 20, 25, 30, 50 c.; Air 12 g. 45, 18 g. 15, 36 g. (Sailing ship and Olympic Rings).

Visit of Pope Paul VI to Eucharistic Congress. Religious Paintings. Postage 10, 15, 20, 25, 30, 50 c.; Air 12 g. 45, 18 g. 15, 36 g.

Important Events of 1968. Postage 10, 15, 20, 25, 30, 50 c.; Air 12 g. 45, 18 g. 15, 50 g.

1969.

Gold Medal Winners of 1968 Mexico Olympic Games. Postage 10, 15, 20, 25, 30, 50 c.; Air 12 g. 45, 18 g. 15, 50 g.

Int. Projects in Outer Space. Postage 10, 15, 20, 25, 30, 50 c.; Air 12 g. 45, 18 g. 15, 50 g.

Latin American Wildlife. Postage 10, 10, 15, 15, 20, 20, 25, 25, 30, 30, 50, 50, 75, 75 c; Air 12 g. 45 × 2, 18 g. 15 × 2.

Gold Medal Winners in Olympic Football, 1900-1968. Postage 10, 15, 20, 25, 30, 50, 75 c.; Air 12 g. 45, 18 g. 15.

Paraguayan Football Champions, 1930-1966. Postage 10, 15, 20, 25, 30, 50, 75 c.; Air 12 g. 45, 18 g. 15.

Paintings by Goya. Postage 10, 15, 20, 25, 30, 50, 75 c.; Air 12 g. 45, 18 g. 15.

Christmas. Religious Paintings. Postage 10, 15, 20, 25, 30, 50, 75 c.; Air 12 g. 45, 18 g. 15.

1970.

Moon Walk. Postage 10, 15, 20, 25, 30, 50, 75 c.; Air 12 g. 45, 18 g. 15.

Easter. Paintings. Postage 10, 15, 20, 25, 30, 50, 75 c.; Air 12 g. 45, 18 g. 15.

Munich, Olympic Games. Postage 10, 15, 20, 25, 30, 50, 75 c.; Air 12 g. 45, 18 g. 15.

Paintings from the Pinakothek Museum in Munich. Postage 10, 15, 20, 25, 30, 50, 75 c.; Air 12 g. 45, 18 g. 15.

"Apollo" Space Programme. Postage 10, 15, 20, 25, 30, 50, 75 c.; Air 12 g. 45, 18 g. 15.

Space Projects in the Future. Postage 10, 15, 20, 25, 30, 50, 75 c.; Air 12 g. 45, 18 g. 15.

"Expo 70" World Fair, Osaka, Japan. Japanese Paintings. Postage 10, 15, 20, 25, 30, 50, 75 c.; Air 12 g. 45, 18 g. 15, 50 g.

Flower Paintings. Postage 10, 15, 20, 25, 30, 50, 75 c.; Air 12 g. 45, 18 g. 15, 50 g.

Paintings from Prado Museum, Madrid. Postage 10, 15, 20, 25, 30, 50, 75 c.; Air 12 g. 45, 18 g. 15, 50 g.

Paintings by Durer. Postage 10, 15, 20, 25, 30, 50, 75 c.; Air 12 g. 45, 18 g. 15, 50 g.

1971.

Christmas 1970/71. Religious Paintings. Postage 10, 15, 20, 25, 30, 50, 75 c.; Air 12 g. 45, 18 g. 15, 50 g.

Munich Olympic Games 1972. Postage 10, 15, 20, 25, 30, 50, 75 c.; Air 12 g. 45, 18 g. 15, 50 g.

Paintings of Horses and Horsemen. Postage 10, 15, 20, 25, 30, 50, 75 c.; Air 12 g. 45, 18 g. 15, 50 g.

Famous Paintings from the Louvre, Paris. Postage 10, 15, 20, 25, 30, 50, 75 c.; Air 12, g. 45, 18 g. 15, 50 g.

Paintings in the National Museum, Asuncion. Postage 10, 15, 20, 25, 30, 50, 75 c.; Air 12 g. 45, 18 g. 15, 50 g.

Hunting Paintings. Postage 10, 15, 20, 25, 30, 50, 75 c.; Air 12 g. 45, 18 g. 15, 50 g.

Philatokyo '71, Stamp Exhibition, Tokyo. Japanese Paintings. Postage 10, 15, 20, 25, 30, 50, 75 c.; Air 12 g. 45, 18 g. 15, 50 g.

Winter Olympic Games, Sapporo 1972. Japanese Paintings. Postage 10, 15, 20, 25, 30, 50, 75 c.; Air 12 g. 45, 18 g. 15, 50 g.

150th Death Anniv of Napoleon. Paintings. Postage 10, 15, 20, 25, 30, 50, 75 c.; Air 12 g. 45, 18 g. 15, 50 g.

Famous Paintings from the Dahlem Museum, Berlin. Postage 10, 15, 20, 25, 30, 50, 75 c.; Air 12 g. 45, 18 g. 15, 50 g.

1972.

Locomotives (1st series). Postage 10, 15, 20, 25, 30, 50, 75 c.; Air 12 g. 45, 18 g. 15, 50 g.

Winter Olympic Games, Sapporo. Postage 10, 15, 20, 25, 30, 50, 75 c.; Air 12 g. 45, 18 g. 15, 50 g.

Racing Cars. Postage 10, 15, 20, 25, 30, 50, 75 c.; Air 12 g. 45, 18 g. 15, 50 g.

Famous Sailing Ships. Postage 10, 15, 20, 25, 30, 50, 75 c.; Air 12 g. 45, 18 g. 15, 50 g.

Famous Paintings from the Vienna Museum. Postage 10, 15, 20, 25, 30, 50, 75 c.; Air 12 g. 45, 18 g. 15, 50 g.

Famous Paintings from the Asuncion Museum. Postage 10, 15, 20, 25, 30, 50, 75 c.; Air 12 g. 45, 18 g. 15, 50 g.

Visit of the Argentine President to Paraguay. Postage 10, 15, 20, 25, 30, 50, 75 c.; Air 12 g. 45, 18 g. 15.

Visit of President of Paraguay to Japan. Postage 10, 15, 20, 25, 30, 50, 75 c.; Air 12 g. 45, 18 g. 15.

Paintings of Animals and Birds. Postage 10, 15, 20, 25, 30, 50, 75 c.; Air 12 g. 45, 18 g. 15.

Locomotives (2nd series). Postage 10, 15, 20, 25, 30, 50, 75 c.; Air 12 g. 45, 18 g. 15.

South American Fauna. Postage 10, 15, 20, 25, 30, 50, 75 c., Air 12 g. 45, 18 g. 15.

1973.

Famous Paintings from the Florence Museum. Postage 10, 15, 20, 25, 30, 50, 75 c.; Air 5, 10, 20 g.

South American Butterflies. Postage 10, 15, 20, 25, 30, 50, 75 c.; Air 5, 10, 20 g.

Cats. Postage 10, 15, 20, 25, 30, 50, 75 c.; Air 5, 10, 20 g.

Portraits of Women. Postage 10, 15, 20, 25, 30, 50, 75 c.; Air 5, 10, 20 g.

World Cup Football Championships, West Germany (1974) (1st issue). Postage 10, 15, 20, 25, 30, 50, 75 c.; Air 5, 10, 20 g.

Paintings of Women. Postage 10, 15, 20, 25, 30, 50, 75 c.; Air 5, 10, 20 g.

Birds. Postage 10, 15, 20, 25, 30, 50, 75 c.; Air 5, 10, 20 g.

"Apollo" Moon Missions and Future Space Projects. Postage 10, 15, 20, 25, 30, 50, 75 c.; Air 5, 10, 20 g.

Visit of Pres. Stroessner to Europe and Morocco. Air 5, 10, 25, 50, 150 g.

Folk Costume. 25, 50, 75 c., 1 g., 1 g. 50, 1 g. 75, 2 g. 25.

Flowers. 10, 20, 25, 30, 40, 50, 75 c.

1974.

World Cup Football Championships, West Germany (2nd issue). Air 5, 10, 20 g.

Roses. 10, 15, 20, 25, 30, 50, 75 c.

Famous Paintings from the Gulbenkian Museum, New York. Postage 10, 15, 20, 25, 30, 50, 75 c; Air 5, 10, 20 g.

U.P.U. Cent Postage 10, 15, 20, 25, 30, 50, 75 c.; Air 5, 10, 20 g.

Famous Masterpieces. Postage 10, 15, 20, 25, 30, 50, 75 c.; Air 5, 10, 20 g.

Visit of Pres. Stroessner to France. Air 100 g.

World Cup Football Championships, West Germany (3rd issue). Air 4, 5, 10 g.

Ships. Postage 5, 10, 15, 20, 25, 35, 40, 50 c.

Events of 1974. Air 4 g. (U.P.U.), 5 g. (President of Chile's visit), 10 g. (Pres. Stroessner's visit to South Africa).

Centenary of U.P.U. Air 4, 5, 10, 20 g.

1975.

Paintings. 5, 10, 15, 20, 25, 35, 40, 50 c.

Christmas. (1974) 5, 10, 15, 20, 25, 35, 40, 50 c.

"Expo '75" Okinawa, Japan. Air 4, 5, 10 g.

Paintings from National Gallery, London. 5, 10, 15, 20, 25, 35, 40, 50 c.

Dogs. 10, 15, 20, 25, 35, 40, 50 c.

South American Fauna. 5, 10, 15, 20, 25, 35, 40, 50 c.

"Espana '75". Air 4, 5, 10 g.

500th Birth Anniv of Michelangelo. Postage 5, 10, 15, 20, 25, 35, 40, 50 c.; Air 4, 5, 10 g.

Winter Olympic Games, Innsbruck (1976). Postage 1, 2, 3, 4, 5 g.; Air 10, 15, 20 g.

Olympic Games, Montreal (1976). Gold borders. Postage 1, 2, 3, 4, 5 g.; Air 10, 15, 20 g.

Various Commemorations. Air 4 g. (Zeppelin), 5 g. (1978 World Cup), 10 g. (Nordposta Exhibition).

Bicent. (1976) of American Revolution (1st issue). Paintings of Sailing Ships. 5, 10, 15, 20, 25, 35, 40, 50 c.

Bicent. (1976) of American Revolution (2nd issue). Paintings. 5, 10, 15, 20, 25, 35, 40, 50 c.

Bicent. (1976) of American Revolution (3rd issue). Lunar Rover and American Cars. Air 4, 5, 10 g.

Various Commemorations. Air 4 g. (Concorde), 5 g. (Lufthansa), 10 g. ("Exfilmo" and "Espamer" Stamp Exhibitions).

Paintings by Spanish Artists. Postage 1, 2, 3, 4, 5 g.; Air 10, 15, 20 g.

1976.

Holy Year. Air 4, 5, 10 g.

Cats. 5, 10, 15, 20, 25, 35, 40, 50 c.

Railway Locomotives. Postage 1, 2, 3, 4, 5 g.; Air 10, 15, 20 g.

Butterflies. 5, 10, 15, 20, 25, 35, 40, 50 c.

Domestic Animals. Postage 1, 2, 3, 4, 5 g.; Air 10, 15, 20 g.

Bicentenary of American Revolution (4th issue) and U.S. Postal Service. Postage 1, 2, 3, 4, 5 g.; Air 10, 15, 20 g.

"Paintings and Planets". Postage 1, 2, 3, 4, 5 g.; Air 10, 15, 20 g.

Ship Paintings. Postage 1, 2, 3, 4, 5 g.; Air 10, 15, 20 g.

German Ship Paintings (1st issue). Postage 1, 2, 3, 4, 5 g.; Air 10, 15, 20 g.

Bicentenary of American Revolution (5th issue). Paintings of Cowboys and Indians. Postage 1, 2, 3, 4, 5 g.; Air 10, 15, 20 g.

Gold Medal Winners. Olympic Games, Montreal. Postage 1, 2, 3, 4, 5 g.; Air 10, 15, 20 g.

Paintings by Titian. Postage 1, 2, 3, 4, 5 g.; Air 10, 15, 20 g.

History of the Olympics. Postage 1, 2, 3, 4, 5 g.; Air 10, 15, 20 g.

1977.

Paintings by Rubens (1st issue). Postage 1, 2, 3, 4, 5 g.; Air 10, 15, 20 g.

Bicentenary of American Revolution (6th issue). Astronautics. Postage 1, 2, 3, 4, 5 g.; Air 10, 15, 20 g.

"Luposta 77" Stamp Exn. Zeppelin and National Costumes. Postage 1, 2, 3, 4, 5 g.; Air 10, 15, 20 g.

History of Aviation. Postage 1, 2, 3, 4, 5 g.; Air 10, 15, 20 g.

Paintings. Postage 1, 2, 3, 4, 5 g.; Air 10, 15, 20 g.

German Ship Paintings (2nd issue). Postage 1, 2, 3, 4, 5 g.; Air 10, 15, 20 g.

Nobel Prize-winners for Literature. Postage 1, 2, 3, 4, 5 g.; Air 10, 15, 20 g.

History of World Cup (1st issue). Postage 1, 2, 3, 4, 5 g.; Air 10, 15, 20 g.

History of World Cup (2nd issue). Postage 1, 2, 3, 4, 5 g.; Air 10, 15, 20 g.

1978.

Paintings by Rubens (2nd issue). Postage 1, 2, 3, 4, 5 g.; Air 10, 15, 20 g.

Chess Olympiad, Buenos Aires. Paintings of Chess Games. Postage 1, 2, 3, 4, 5 g.; Air 10, 15, 20 g.

Paintings by Jordaens. Postage 3, 4, 5, 6, 7, 8, 20 g.; Air 10, 25 g.

450th Death Anniv of Durer (1st issue). Postage 3, 4, 5, 6, 7, 8, 20 g.; Air 10, 25 g.

Paintings by Goya. Postage 3, 4, 5, 6, 7, 8, 20 g.; Air 10, 25 g.

Astronautics of the Future. Postage 3, 4, 5, 6, 7, 8, 20 g.; Air 10, 25 g.

Racing Cars. Postage 3, 4, 5, 6, 7, 8, 20 g.; Air 10, 25 g.

Paintings by Rubens (3rd issue). Postage 3, 4, 5, 6, 7, 8, 20 g.; Air 10, 25 g.

25th Anniv of Queen Elizabeth's Coronation (reproduction of stamps). Postage 3, 4, 5, 6, 7, 8, 20 g.; Air 10, 25 g.

Paintings and Stamp Exhibition Emblems. Postage 3, 4, 5, 6, 7, 8, 20 g.; Air 10, 25 g.

Various Commemorations. Air 75 g. (Satellite Earth Station), 500 g. (Coat of Arms), 1000 g. (Pres. Stroessner).

International Year of the Child (1st issue). Snow White and the Seven Dwarfs. Postage 3, 4, 5, 6, 7, 8, 20 g.; Air 10, 25 g.

Military Uniforms. Postage 3, 4, 5, 6, 7, 8, 20 g.; Air 10, 25 g.

1979.

World Cup Football Championship, Argentina. Postage 3, 4, 5, 6, 7, 8, 20 g.; Air 10, 25 g.

Christmas (1978). Paintings of Madonnas. Postage 3, 4, 5, 6, 7, 8, 20 g.; Air 10, 25 g.

History of Aviation. Postage 3, 4, 5, 6, 7, 8, 20 g.; Air 10, 25 g.

450th Death Anniv of Durer (2nd issue). Postage 3, 4, 5, 6, 7, 8, 20 g.; Air 10, 25 g.

Death Centenary of Sir Rowland Hill (1st issue). Reproduction of Stamps. Postage 3, 4, 5, 6, 7, 8, 20 g.; Air 10, 25 g.

International Year of the Child (2nd issue). Cinderella. Postage 3, 4, 5, 6, 7, 8, 20 g.; Air 10, 25 g.

Winter Olympic Games, Lake Placid (1980). Postage 3, 4, 5, 6, 7, 8, 20 g.; Air 10, 25 g.

Sailing Ships. Postage 3, 4, 5, 6, 7, 8, 20 g.; Air 10, 25 g.

International Year of the Child (3rd issue). Cats. Postage 3, 4, 5, 6, 7, 8, 20 g.; Air 10, 25 g.

International Year of the Child (4th issue). Little Red Riding Hood. Postage 3, 4, 5, 6, 7, 8, 20 g.; Air 10, 25 g.

Olympic Games, Moscow (1980). Greek Athletes. Postage 3, 4, 5, 6, 7, 8, 20 g.; Air 10, 25 g.

Centenary of Electric Locomotives. Postage 3, 4, 5, 6, 7, 8, 20 g.; Air 10, 25 g.

1980.

Death Centenary of Sir Rowland Hill (2nd issue). Military Aircraft. Postage 3, 4, 5, 6, 7, 8, 20 g; Air 10, 25 g.

Death Centenary of Sir Rowland Hill (3rd issue). Stamps. Postage 3, 4, 5, 6, 7, 8, 20 g.; Air 10, 25 g.

Winter Olympic Games Medal Winners (1st issue). Postage 3, 4, 5, 6, 7, 8, 20 g.; Air 10, 25 g.

Composers. Scenes from Ballets. Postage 3, 4, 5, 6, 7, 8, 20 g.; Air 20, 25 g.

International Year of the Child (1979) (5th issue). Christmas. Postage 3, 4, 5, 6, 7, 8, 20 g.; Air 10, 25 g.

Exhibitions. Paintings of Ships. Postage 3, 4, 5, 6, 7, 8, 20 g.; Air 10, 25 g.

World Cup Football Championship, Spain (1982) (1st issue). Postage 3, 4, 5, 6, 7, 8, 20 g.; Air 10, 25 g.

World Chess Championship, Merano. Postage 3, 4, 5, 6, 7, 8, 20 g.; Air 10, 25 g.

1981.

Winter Olympic Games Medal Winners (2nd issue). Postage 25, 50 c., 1, 2, 3, 4, 5 g.; Air 5, 10, 30 g.

International Year of the Child (1979) (6th issue). Children and Flowers. Postage 10, 25, 50, 100, 200, 300, 400 g.; Air 75, 500, 1000 g.

"WIPA 1981" International Stamp Exhibition, Vienna. 1980 Composers stamp optd. Postage 4 g.; Air 10 g.

Wedding of Prince of Wales (1st issue). Postage 25, 50 c., 1, 2, 3, 4, 5 g.; Air 5, 10, 30 g.

Costumes and Treaty of Itaipu. 10, 25, 50, 100, 200, 300, 400 g.

Paintings by Rubens. 25, 50 c., 1, 2, 3, 4, 5 g.

Anniversaries and Events. Air 5 g. (250th birth anniv of George Washington), 10 g. (80th birthday of Queen Mother), 30 g. ("Philatokyo '81").

Flight of Space Shuttle. Air. 5, 10, 30 g.

Birth Bicentenary of Ingres. 25, 50 c., 1, 2, 3, 4, 5 g.

World Cup Football Championship, Spain (1982) (2nd issue). Air 5, 10, 30 g.

Birth Centenary of Picasso. 25, 50 c., 1, 2, 3, 4, 5 g.

"Philatelia '81" International Stamp Exhibition, Frankfurt. Picasso Stamps optd. 25, 50 c., 1, 2, 3, 4 g.

"Espamer '81" International Stamp Exhibition. Picasso stamps optd. 25, 50 c., 1, 2, 3, 4 g.

Wedding of Prince of Wales (2nd issue). Postage 25, 50 c., 1, 2, 3, 4, 5 g.; Air 5, 10, 30 g.

International Year of the Child (1979) (7th issue). Christmas. 25, 50 c., 1, 2, 3, 4, 5 g.

Christmas. Paintings. Air 5, 10, 30 g.

1982.

International Year of the Child (1979) (8th issue). Puss in Boots. 25, 50 c., 1, 2, 3, 4, 5 g.

World Cup Football Championship, Spain (3rd issue). Air 5, 10, 30 g.

75th Anniv of Boy Scout Movement and 125th birth Anniv of Lord-Baden Powell (founder). Postage 25, 50 c., 1, 2, 3, 4, 5 g.; Air 5, 10, 30 g.

"Essen 82" International Stamp Exhibition. 1981 International Year of the Child (7th issue) Christmas stamps optd. 25, 50 c., 1, 2, 3, 4 g.

Cats. 25, 50 c., 1, 2, 3, 4, 5 g.

Chess paintings. Air 5, 10, 30 g.

"Philexfrance 82" International Stamp Exhibition. 1981 Ingres stamps optd. 25, 50 c., 1, 2, 3 g.

World Cup Football Championship, Spain (4th issue). Postage 25, 50 c., 1, 2, 3, 4, 5 g.; Air 5, 10, 30 g.

"Philatelia 82" International Stamp Exhibition, Hanover. 1982 Cats issue optd. 25, 50 c., 1, 2, 3, 4, 5 g.

500th Birth Anniv of Raphael (1st issue). 25, 50 c., 1, 2, 3, 4, 5 g.

500th Birth Anniv of Raphael (2nd issue) and Christmas (1st issue). 25, 50 c., 1, 2, 3, 4, 5 g.

World Cup Football Championship Results. Air 5, 10, 30 g.

Christmas (2nd issue). Paintings by Rubens. Air 5, 10, 30 g.

Paintings by Durer. Life of Christ. 25, 50 c., 1, 2, 3, 4, 5 g.

500th Birth Anniv of Raphael (3rd issue) and Christmas (3rd issue). Air 5, 10, 30 g.

1983.

Third International Railways Congress, Malaga (1982). 25, 50 c., 1, 2, 3, 4, 5 g.

Racing Cars. 25, 50 c., 1, 2, 3, 4, 5 g.

Paintings by Rembrandt. Air 5, 10, 30 g.

German Astronautics. Air 5, 10, 30 g.

Winter Olympic Games, Sarajevo (1984). 25, 50 c., 1, 2, 3, 4, 5 g.

Bicentenary of Manned Flight. Air 5, 10, 30 g.

Pope John Paul II. 25, 50 c., 1, 2, 3, 4, 5 g.

Olympic Games, Los Angeles (1984). Air 5, 10, 30 g.

Veteran Cars. Postage 25, 50 c., 1, 2, 3, 4, 5 g.; Air 5, 10, 30 g.

"Brasiliana '83" International Stamp Exhibition and 52nd F.I.P. Congress (1st issue). 1982 World Cup (4th issue) stamps optd. 25, 50 c., 1, 2, 3, 4 g.

"Brasiliana '83" International Stamp Exhibition and 52nd F.I.P. Congress (2nd issue). 1982 Raphael/Christmas stamps optd. 25, 50 c., 1, 2, 3, 4 g.

Aircraft Carriers. 25, 50 c., 1, 2, 3, 4, 5 g.

South American Flowers. Air 5, 10, 30 g.

South American Birds. 25, 50 c., 1, 2, 3, 4, 5 g.

25th Anniv of International Maritime Organization. Air 5, 10, 30 g.

"Philatelia '83" International Stamp Exhibition, Dusseldorf. 1983 International Railway Congress stamps optd. 25, 50 c., 1, 2, 3, 4 g.

"Exfivia - 83" International Stamp Exn, Bolivia. 1982 Durer paintings optd. 25, 50 c., 1, 2, 3, 4 g.

Flowers 10, 25 g.; Chaco soldier 50 g.; Dams, Postage 75 g. Air 100 g.; President, Air 200 g.

1984.

Bicentenary of Manned Flight. 25, 50 c., 1, 2, 3, 4, 5 g.

World Communications Year. Air 5, 10, 30 g.

Dogs. 25, 50 c., 1, 2, 3, 4, 5 g.

Olympic Games, Los Angeles. Air 5, 10, 30 g.

Animals. 10, 25, 50, 75 g.

1983 Anniversaries. Air 100 g. (birth bicentenary of Bolivar), 200 g. (76th anniv of boy scout movement).

Christmas (1983) and New Year. 25, 50 c., 1, 2, 3, 4, 5 g.

Winter Olympic Games, Sarajevo. Air 5, 10, 30 g.

Troubador Knights. 25, 50 c., 1, 2, 3, 4, 5 g.

World Cup Football Championships, Spain (1982) and Mexico (1986). Air 5, 10, 30 g.

International Stamp Fair, Essen. 1983 Racing Cars stamps optd. 25, 50 c., 1, 2, 3, 4 g.

Extinct Animals. 25, 50 c., 1, 2, 3, 4, 5 g.

60th Anniv of International Chess Federation. Air 5, 10, 30 g.

19th Universal Postal Union Congress Stamp Exhibition, Hamburg (1st issue). Sailing Ships. 25, 50 c., 1, 2, 3, 4, 5 g.

19th Universal Postal Union Congress Stamp Exhibition, Hamburg (2nd issue). Troubadour Knights stamp optd. 5 g.

Leaders of the World. British Railway Locomotives. 25, 50 c., 1, 2, 3, 4, 5 g.

50th Anniv of First Lufthansa Europe-South America Direct Mail Flight. Air 5, 10, 30 g.

30th Anniv of Presidency of Alfredo Stroessner. Dam stamp optd. Air 100 g.

"Ausipex 84" International Stamp Exhibition, Melbourne. 1974 U.P.U. Centenary stamps optd. 10, 15, 20, 25, 30, 50, 75 c.

"Phila Korea 1984" International Stamp Exhibition, Seoul. Olympic Games, Los Angeles, and Extinct Animals stamps optd. Postage 5 g.; Air 30 g.

German National Football Championship and Sindelfingen Stamp Bourse. 1974 World Cup stamps (1st issue) optd. 10, 15, 20, 25, 30, 50, 75 c.

Cats. 25, 50 c., 1, 2, 3, 4, 5 g.

Winter Olympic Games Medal Winners. Air 5, 10, 30 g.

Centenary of Motor Cycle. Air 5, 10, 30 g.

1985.

Olympic Games Medal Winners. 25, 50 c., 1, 2, 3, 4, 5 g.

Christmas (1984). Costumes. Air 5, 10, 30 g.

Fungi. 25, 50 c., 1, 2, 3, 4, 5 g.

Participation of Paraguay in Preliminary Rounds of World Cup Football Championship. Air 5, 10, 30 g.

"Interpex 1985" and "Stampex 1985" Stamp Exhibitions. 1981 Queen Mother's Birthday stamp optd. 10 g. × 2.

International Federation of Aero-Philatelic Societies Congress, Stuttgart. 1984 Lufthansa Europe-South America Mail Flight stamp optd. Air 10 g.

Paraguayan Animals and Extinct Animals. 25, 50 c., 1, 2, 3, 4, 5 g.

"Olymphilex 85" Olympic Stamps Exhibition, Lausanne. 1984 Winter Olympics Games Medal Winners stamp optd. 10 g.

"Israphil 85" International Stamp Exhibition, Tel Aviv. 1982 Boy Scout Movement stamp optd. 5 g.

Music Year. Air 5, 10, 30 g.

Birth Bicentenary of John J. Audubon (ornithologist). Birds. 25, 50 c., 1, 2, 3, 4, 5 g.

Railway Locomotives. Air 5, 10, 30 g.

"Italia '85" International Stamp Exhibition, Rome (1st issue). 1983 Pope John Paul II stamp optd. 5 g.

50th Anniv of Chaco Peace (1st issue). 1972 Visit of Argentine President stamp optd. 30 c.

"Mophila 85" Stamp Exhibition, Hamburg. 1984 U.P.U. Congress Stamp Exhibition (1st issue) stamp optd. 5 g.

"Lupo 85" Stamp Exhibition, Lucerne. 1984 Bicentenary of Manned Flight stamp optd. 5 g.

"Expo 85" World's Fair, Tsukuba. 1981 "Philatokyo '81" stamp optd. Air 30 g.

International Youth Year. Mark Twain. 25, 50 c., 1, 2, 3, 4, 5 g.

75th Death Anniv of Henri Dunant (founder of Red Cross). Air 5, 10, 30 g.

150th Anniv of German Railways (1st issue). 25, 50 c., 1, 2, 3, 4, 5 g.

International Chess Federation Congress, Graz. Air 5, 10, 30 g.

50th Anniv of Chaco Peace (2nd issue) and Government Achievements. Postage 10, 25, 50, 75 g.; Air 100, 200 g.

Paintings by Rubens. 25, 50 c., 1, 2, 3, 4, 5 g.

Explorers and their Ships. Air 5, 10, 30 g.

"Italia '85" International Stamp Exhibition, Rome (2nd issue). Paintings. Air 5, 10, 30 g.

1986.

Paintings by Titian. 25, 50 c., 1, 2, 3, 4, 5 g.

International Stamp Fair, Essen. 1985 German Railways stamps optd. 25, 50 c., 1, 2, 3, 4 g.

Fungi. 25, 50 c., 1, 2, 3, 4, 5 g.

"Ameripex '86" International Stamp Exhibition, Chicago. Air 5, 10, 30 g.

Lawn Tennis (1st issue). Inscriptions in black or red. Air 5, 10, 30 g.

Centenary of Motor Car. 25, 50 c., 1, 2, 3, 4, 5 g.

Appearance of Halley's Comet. Air 5, 10, 30 g.

Qualification of Paraguay for World Cup Football Championship Final Rounds, Mexico (1st issue). 25, 50 c., 1, 2, 3, 4, 5 g.

Tenth Pan-American Games, Indianapolis (1987). 1985 Olympic Games Medal Winners stamp optd. 5 g.

Maybach Cars. 25, 50 c., 1, 2, 3, 4, 5 g.

Freight Trains. Air 5, 10, 30 g.

Qualification of Paraguay for World Cup Football Championship Final Rounds (2nd issue). Air 5, 10, 30 g.

Winter Olympic Games, Calgary (1988) (1st issue). 1983 Winter Olympic Games stamp optd. 5 g.

Centenary of Statue of Liberty. 25, 50 c., 1, 2, 3, 4, 5 g.

Dogs. 25, 50 c., 1, 2, 3, 4, 5 g.

150th Anniv of German Railways (2nd issue). Air 5, 10, 30 g.

Lawn Tennis (2nd issue). 25, 50 c., 1, 2, 3, 4, 5 g.

Visit of Prince Hitachi of Japan. 1972 Visit of President of Paraguay to Japan stamps optd. 10, 15, 20, 25, 30, 50, 75 c.

International Peace Year. Paintings by Rubens. Air 5, 10, 30 g.

Olympic Games, Seoul (1988) (1st issue). 25, 50 c., 1, 2, 3, 4, 5 g.

27th Chess Olympiad, Dubai. 1982 Chess Paintings stamp optd. Air 10 g.

1987.

World Cup Football Championships, Mexico (1986) and Italy (1990). Air 5, 10, 20, 25, 30 g.

12th Spanish American Stamp and Coin Exhibition, Madrid, and 500th Anniv of Discovery of America by Columbus. 1975 South American Fauna and 1983 25th Anniv of I.M.O. stamps optd. Postage 15, 20, 25, 35, 40 g.; Air 10 g.

Tennis as Olympic Sport. 1986 Lawn Tennis (1st issue) stamps optd. Air 10, 30 g.

Olympic Games, Barcelona (1992). 1985 Olympic Games Medal Winners stamps optd. 25, 50 c., 1, 2, 3, 4 g.

"Olymphilex '87" Olympic Stamps Exhibition, Rome. 1985 Olympic Games Medal Winners stamp optd. 5 g.

Cats. 1, 2, 3, 5, 60 g.

Paintings by Rubens (1st issue). 1, 2, 3, 5, 60 g.

Saloon Cars. Air 5, 10, 20, 25, 30 g.

National Topics. Postage 10 g. (steel plant), 25 g. (Franciscan monk), 50 g. (400th anniv of Ita and Yaguaron), 75 g. (450th Anniv of Asuncion); Air 100 g. (airliner), 200 g. (Pres. Stroessner).

"Capex 87" International Stamp Exhibition, Toronto. Cats stamps optd. 1, 2, 3, 5 g.

500th Anniv of Discovery of America by Columbus. 1, 2, 3, 5, 60 g.

Winter Olympic Games, Calgary (1988) (2nd issue). Air 5, 10, 20, 25, 30 g.

Centenary of Colorado Party. National Topics and 1978 Pres. Stroessner stamps optd. Air 200, 1000 g.

750th Anniv of Berlin (1st issue) and "Luposta '87" Air Stamps Exhibition, Berlin. 1, 2, 3, 5, 60 g.

Olympic Games, Seoul (1988) (2nd issue). Air 5, 10, 20, 25, 30 g.

Rally Cars. 1, 2, 3, 5, 60 g.

"Exfivia 87" Stamp Exhibition, Bolivia. National Topics stamps optd. Postage 75 g.; Air 100 g.

"Olymphilex '88" Olympic Stamps Exhibition, Seoul. 1986 Olympic Games, Seoul (1st issue) stamps optd. 2, 3, 4, 5 g.

"Philatelia '87" International Stamp Exhibition, Cologne. 1986 Lawn Tennis (2nd issue) stamps optd. 25, 50 c., 1, 2, 3, 4 g.

Italy-Argentina Match at Zurich to Launch 1990 World Cup Football Championship, Italy. 1986 Paraguay Qualification (2nd issue) stamps optd. Air 10, 30 g.

"Exfilna '87" Stamp Exhibition, Gerona. 1986 Olympic Games, Seoul (1st issue) stamps optd. 25, 50 c.

Spanish Ships. 1, 2, 3, 5, 60 g.

Paintings by Rubens (2nd issue). Air 5, 10, 20, 25, 30 g.

Christmas. Air 5, 10, 20, 25, 30 g.

Winter Olympic Games, Calgary (1988) (3rd issue). 1, 2, 3, 5, 60 g.

1988.

150th Anniv of Austrian Railways. Air 5, 10, 20, 25, 30 g.

"Aeropex 88" Air Stamps Exhibition, Adelaide. 1987 750th Anniv of Berlin and "Luposta '87" stamps optd. 1, 2, 3, 5 g.

"Olympex" Stamp Exhibition, Calgary. 1987 Winter Olympic Games (3rd issue) stamps optd. 1, 2, 3 g.

Olympic Games, Seoul (3rd issue). Equestrian Events. 1, 2, 3, 5, 60 g.

Space Projects. Air 5, 10, 20, 25, 30 g.

750th Anniv of Berlin (2nd issue). Paintings. 1, 2, 3, 5, 60 g.

Visit of Pope John Paul II. 1, 2, 3, 5, 60 g.

"Lupo Wien 88" Stamp Exhibition, Vienna. 1987 National Topics stamp optd. Air 100 g.

World Wildlife Fund. Extinct Animals. 1, 2, 3, 5 g.

Paintings in West Berlin State Museum. Air 5, 10, 20, 25, 30 g.

Bicentenary of Australian Settlement. 1981 Wedding of Prince of Wales (1st issue) optd. 25, 50 c., 1, 2 g.

History of World Cup Football Championship (1st issue). Air 5, 10, 20, 25, 30 g.

New Presidential Period, 1988-1993. 1985 Chaco Peace and Government Achievements issue optd. Postage 10, 25, 50, 75 g.; Air 100, 200 g.

Olympic Games, Seoul (4th issue). Lawn Tennis and Medal. 1, 2, 3, 5, 60 g.

Calgary Winter Olympics Gold Medal Winners. Air 5, 10, 20, 25, 30 g.

History of World Cup Football Championship (2nd issue). Air 5, 10, 20, 25, 30 g.

"Prenfil '88" International Philatelic Press Exhibition, Buenos Aires. "Ameripex '86" stamp optd. Air 30 g.

"Philexfrance 89" International Stamp Exhibition, Paris. 1985 Explorers stamp optd. Air 30 g.

PARMA — Pt. 8

A former Grand Duchy of N. Italy, united with Sardinia in 1860 and now part of Italy.

100 centesimi = 1 lira

1 Bourbon "fleur-de-lis"

2

3

1852. Imperf.
1 **1** 5 c. black on yellow . . . . . 38·00 65·00
11 5 c. yellow £2750 £500
4 10 c. black . . . . 38·00 65·00
6 15 c. black on pink . . . . . £950 22·00
13 15 c. red . . . . £3500 70·00
7 25 c. black on purple . . . . £5500 90·00
14 25 c. brown £6500 £150
9 40 c. black on blue £950 £160

1857. Imperf.
17 **2** 15 c. red £100 £300
19 25 c. purple . . . . £180 80·00
20 40 c. blue . . . . 25·00 £300

1859. Imperf.
28 **3** 5 c. green £850 £2750
30 10 c. brown £200 £375
31 20 c. blue £400 £150
33 40 c. red £300 £5500
35 80 c. yellow £3250

NEWSPAPER STAMPS

1853. As T **3**. Imperf.
N1 **3** 6 c. black on pink £170 £200
N3 9 c. black on blue . . . . . 80·00 £16000

PERU — Pt. 20

A republic on the N.W. coast of S. America independent since 1821.

1857. 8 reales = 1 peso.
1858. 100 centavos = 10 dineros = 5 pesetas = 1 peso.
1874. 100 centavos = 1 sol.
1985. 100 centimos = 1 inti.
1991. 100 centimos = 1 sol.

7

8

10 Vicuna

1858. T **7** and similar designs with flags below arms. Imperf.
8 **7** 1 d. blue . . . . 75·00 5·00
13 1 peseta red . . . . 90·00 11·00
5 ½ peso yellow £1300 £225

1862. Various frames. Imperf.
14 **8** 1 d. red . . . . 10·00 1·75
20 1 d. green . . . . 10·00 2·10
16 1 peseta, brown . . . . . . 55·00 17·00
22 1 peseta, yellow . . . . . . 70·00 21·00

1866. Various frames. Perf.
17 **10** 5 c. green . . . . 5·00 60
18 – 10 c. red . . . . 5·00 1·10
19 – 20 c. brown . . . . 17·00 3·50
See also No. 316.

13

14

1871. 20th Anniv of First Railway in Peru (Lima–Chorillos–Callao). Imperf.
21a **13** 5 c. red . . . . £110 24·00

1873. Roul by imperf.
23 **14** 2 c. blue . . . . 25·00 £200

15 Sun-god

16

20

21

1874. Various frames. Perf.
24 **15** 1 c. orange 40 40
25a **16** 2 c. violet 40 40
26 5 c. blue 70 25
27 10 c. green 15 15
28 20 c. red . . . . 1·60 40
29 **20** 50 c. green . . . . 7·50 2·10
30 **21** 1 s. pink . . . . 1·25 1·25
For further stamps in these types, see Nos. 278, 279/84 and 314/5.

(24)

(**27**) Arms of Chile

1880. Optd with T **24**.
36 **15** 1 c. green 40 40
37 **16** 2 c. red 85 45
39 5 c. blue . . . . 1·60 70
40 **20** 50 c. green . . . . 23·00 14·50
41 **21** 1 s. red . . . . 60·00 38·00

1881. Optd as T **24**, but inscr "LIMA" at foot instead of "PERU".
42 **15** 1 c. green 60 30
43 **16** 2 c. red . . . . 12·00 7·50
44 5 c. blue . . . . 1·25 45
286 10 c. green 40 50
45 **20** 50 c. green £375 £200
46 **21** 1 s. red . . . . 70·00 45·00

1881. Optd with T **27**.
57 **15** 1 c. orange 30 85
58 **16** 2 c. violet . . . . 30 3·50
59 2 c. red . . . . 1·40 15·00
60 5 c. blue . . . . 45·00 50·00
61 10 c. green . . . . 30 1·50
62 20 c. red . . . . 65·00 £100

(28)

(28a)

1882. Optd with T **27** and **28**.
63 **15** 1 c. green 45 65
64 **16** 5 c. blue 45 65
66 **20** 50 c. red . . . . 1·40 1·60
67 **21** 1 s. blue . . . . 2·75 3·75

1883. Optd with T **28** only.
200 **15** 1 c. green . . . . 1·00 1·00
201 **16** 2 c. red . . . . 1·00 3·25
202 5 c. blue . . . . 1·60 1·60
203 **20** 50 c. pink . . . . 48·00
204 **21** 1 s. blue . . . . 25·00

1883. Handstamped with T **28a** only.
206 **15** 1 c. orange 65 65
210 **16** 5 c. blue . . . . 6·25 4·25
211 10 c. green 65 65
216 **20** 50 c. green . . . . 5·75 3·00
220 **21** 1 s. red . . . . 8·25 5·00

1883. Optd with T **24** and **28a**, the inscription in oval reading "PERU".
223 **20** 50 c. green . . . . £100 50·00
225 **21** 1 s. red . . . . £120 75·00

1883. Optd with T **24** and **28a**, the inscription in oval reading "LIMA".
227 **15** 1 c. green . . . . 3·25 3·25
228 **16** 2 c. red . . . . 3·25 3·25
232 5 c. blue . . . . 5·50 5·00
234 **20** 50 c. green . . . . £120 75·00
236 **21** 1 s. red £130 £100

1883. Optd with T **28** and **28a**.
238 **15** 1 c. green 85 65
241 **16** 2 c. red 85 60
246 5 c. blue . . . . 1·00 65

1884. Optd **CORREOS LIMA** and sun.
277 **16** 5 c. blue 35 25

1886. Re-issue of 1866 and 1874 types.
278 **15** 1 c. violet 25 20
314 1 c. red 30 20
279 **16** 2 c. green 60 10
315 2 c. blue 25 20
280 5 c. orange 30 10
316 **10** 5 c. lake . . . . 1·00 35
281 **16** 10 c. black 15 10
317 – 10 c. orange (Llamas) . . . 35 25
282 **16** 20 c. blue . . . . 4·25 35
318 – 20 c. blue (Llamas) . . . . 5·00 1·10
283 **20** 50 c. red . . . . 1·25 35
284 **21** 1 s. brown . . . . 1·00 35

(**71** Pres. R. M. Bermudez)

73

1894. Optd with T **71**.
294 **15** 1 c. orange 50 25
295 1 c. green 20 20
296c **16** 2 c. violet 15 15
297 2 c. red 25 20
298 5 c. blue . . . . 2·10 1·50
299 10 c. green 25 20
300 **20** 50 c. green . . . . 1·10 1·00

1894. Optd with T **28** and **71**.
301 **16** 2 c. red 20 20
302 5 c. blue 85 30
303 **20** 50 c. red . . . . 35·00 25·00
304 **21** 1 s. blue . . . . 85·00 75·00

1895. Installation of Pres. Nicolas de Pierola.
328 **73** 1 c. violet . . . . 1·00 75
329 2 c. green . . . . 1·00 75
330 5 c. yellow . . . . 1·00 75
331 10 c. blue . . . . 1·00 75
332 – 20 c. orange . . . . 1·00 80
333 – 50 c. blue . . . . 6·00 3·75
334 – 1 s. lake . . . . 32·00 21·00
Nos. 332/4 are larger (30×36 mm) and the central device is in a frame of laurel.
See also Nos. 352/4.

75 Atahualpa

76 Pizarro

77 General de la Mar

1896.
335 **75** 1 c. blue 25 15
336 1 c. green 25 10
337 2 c. blue 20 15
338 2 c. red 20 10
341 **76** 5 c. blue 60 10
340 5 c. green 60 10
342 10 c. yellow 85 20
343 10 c. black 85 10
344 20 c. orange . . . . 1·60 25
345 **77** 50 c. red . . . . 4·25 50
346 1 s. red . . . . 6·25 85
347 2 s. lake . . . . 1·90 65

1897. No. D31 optd **FRANQUEO**.
348 D **22** 1 c. brown 25 25

82 Suspension Bridge at Paucartambo

83 Pres. D. Nicolas de Pierola

1897. Opening of New Postal Building. Dated "1897".
349 **82** 1 c. blue 40 30
350 – 2 c. brown 40 25
351 **83** 5 c. red 85 30
DESIGN: 2 c. G.P.O. Lima.

1899. As Nos. 328/34, but vert inscr replaced by pearl ornaments.
352 **73** 22 c. green 30 15
353 – 5 s. red . . . . 1·40 1·40
354 – 10 s. green £350 £275

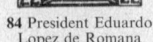

84 President Eduardo Lopez de Romana

85 Admiral Grau

1900.
357 **84** 22 c. black and green . . . 6·75 70

1901. Advent of the Twentieth Century.
358 **85** 1 c. black and green . . . 70 25
359 – 2 c. black and red 70 25
360 – 5 c. black and lilac . . . . 1·00 25
PORTRAITS: 2 c. Col. Bolognesi; 5 c. Pres. Romana.

90 Municipal Board of Health Building

1905.
361 **90** 12 c. black and blue . . . 70 25

1907. Surch.
362 **90** 1 c. on 12 c. black & blue . 25 20
363 2 c. on 12 c. black & blue . 50 35

97 Bolognesi Monument

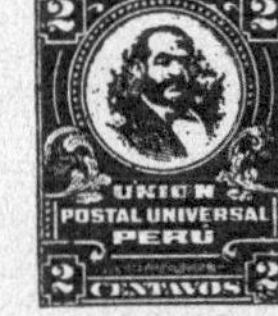
98 Admiral Grau

99 Llama

101 Exhibition Buildings

103 G.P.O., Lima

107 Columbus

1907.
364 **97** 1 c. black and green . . . 25 15
365 **98** 2 c. purple and red . . . 25 15
366 **99** 4 c. olive . . . . 4·50 60
367 – 5 c. black and blue . . . 40 10
368 **101** 10 c. black and brown . . 1·00 25
369 – 20 c. black and green . . 19·00 50
370 **103** 50 c. black . . . . 19·00 70
371 – 1 s. green and violet . . . £100 2·10
372 – 2 s. black and blue . . . £100 85·00
DESIGNS—VERT: As Type **98**: 5 c. Statue of Bolivar. (24×33 mm): 2 c. Columbus Monument. HORIZ: As Type **101**: 20 c. Medical School, Lima. (33×24 mm): 1 s. Grandstand, Santa Beatrice Race-course, Lima.

1909. Portraits.
373 – 1 c. grey (Manco Capac) . 15 15
374 **107** 2 c. green 15 15
375 – 4 c. red (Pizarro) 40 15
376 – 5 c. purple (San Martin) . 15 10
377 – 10 c. blue (Bolivar) . . . 55 15
378 – 12 c. blue (de la Mar) . . 85 25
379 – 20 c. brown (Castilla) . . 90 40
380 – 50 c. orange (Grau) . . . 4·25 30
381 – 1 s. black and lake (Bolognesi) . . . . . . 8·50 30
See also Nos. 406/13, 431/5, 439/40 and 484/9.

1913. Surch **UNION POSTAL 8 Cts. Sud Americana** in oval.
382 **90** 8 c. on 12 c. black & blue . 55 20

1915. As 1896, 1905 and 1907, surch **1915**, and value.
383 **75** 1 c. on 1 c. green . . . . 13·50 10·50
384 **97** 1 c. on 1 c. black & green 70 50
385 **98** 1 c. on 2 c. purple & red . 1·00 85
386 **76** 1 c. on 10 c. black . . . 85 60
387 **99** 1 c. on 4 c. green . . . . 1·60 1·40
388 **101** 1 c. on 10 c. black & brn 35 20
389 2 c. on 10 c. black & brn 85·00 70·00
390 **90** 2 c. on 12 c. black & blue 25 15
391 – 2 c. on 20 c. black and green (No. 369) . . . . . . 12·00 10·00
392 **103** 2 c. on 50 c. black . . . 1·60 1·60

1916. Surch **VALE**, value and **1916**.
393 1 c. on 12 c. blue (378) . . . 15 15
394 1 c. on 20 c. brown (379) . . 15 15
395 1 c. on 50 c. orange (380) . . 15 15
396 2 c. on 4 c. red (375) 15 15
397 10 c. on 1 s. black & lake (381) 40 25

1916. Official stamps of 1909 optd **FRANQUEO 1916** or surch **VALE 2 Cts** also.
398 O **108** 1 c. red 15 15
399 2 c. on 50 c. olive . . . 15 15
400 10 c. brown 20 15

1916. Postage Due stamps of 1909 surch **FRANQUEO VALE 2 Cts. 1916**.
401 D **109** 2 c. on 1 c. brown . . 40 40
402 2 c. on 5 c. brown . . 15 15
403 2 c. on 10 c. brown . . 15 15
404 2 c. on 50 c. brown . . 15 15

1917. Surch **Un Centavo**.
405 1 c. on 4 c. (No. 375) 20 15

1918. Portraits as T **107**.
406 1 c. black & orge (San Martin) 10 10
407 2 c. black & green (Bolivar) . 15 10
408 4 c. black and red (Galvez) . . 25 10
409 5 c. black and blue (Pardo) . . 15 10
410 8 c. black and brown (Grau) . 50 25
411 10 c. black & blue (Bolognesi) 35 10
412 12 c. black & lilac (Castilla) . 70 15
413 20 c. black & green (Caceres) . 85 15

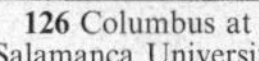

126 Columbus at Salamanca University **129** A. B. Leguia

1918.
414 **126** 50 c. black and brown . . 4·25 35
415a – 1 s. black and green . . . 10·50 50
416 – 2 s. black and blue . . . 18·00 55
DESIGNS: 1 s. Funeral of Atahualpa; 2 s. Battle of Arica.

1920. New Constitution.
417 **129** 5 c. black and blue . . . 15 15
418 5 c. black and brown . . 15 15

130 San Martin **131** Oath of Independence

132 Admiral Cochrane **137** J. Olaya

1921. Centenary of Independence.
419 **130** 1 c. brown (San Martin) . 25 15
420 2 c. green (Arenales) . . . 25 15
421 4 c. red (Las Heras) . . . 85 50
422 **131** 5 c. brown 35 15
423 **132** 7 c. violet 70 35
424 **130** 10 c. blue (Guisse) 70 35
425 12 c. black (Vidal) . . . . 2·00 40
426 20 c. blk & red (Leguia) . 2·00 70
427 50 c. violet and purple (S. Martin Monument) . 6·00 2·00
428 **131** 1 s. green and red (San Martin and Leguia) . . 10·00 3·00

1923. Surch **CINCO Centavos 1923**.
429 5 c. on 8 c. black and brown (No. 410) 40 20

1924. Surch **CUATRO Centavos 1924**.
430 4 c. on 5 c. (No. 409) 25 15

1924. Portraits as T **107**. Size $18\frac{1}{2}\times23$ mm.
431 2 c. olive (Rivadeneyra) . . . 10 10
432 4 c. green (Melgar) 10 10
433 8 c. black (Iturregui) . . . . . 1·60 1·60
434 10 c. red (A. B. Leguia) . . . 15 10
435 15 c. blue (De la Mar) 50 15
439 1 s. brown (De Saco) . . . . 7·50 85
440 2 s. blue (J. Leguia) . . . . . 19·00 4·25

1924. Monuments.
436 **137** 20 c. blue 70 10
437 20 c. yellow . . . . 1·25 15
438 – 50 c. purple (Bellido) . . . 4·25 35
See also Nos. 484/9.

139 Simon Bolivar **140**

1924. Centenary of Battle of Ayacucho. Portraits of Bolivar.
441 – 2 c. olive 35 10
442 **139** 4 c. green 40 10
443 5 c. black 85 10
444 **140** 10 c. red 40 10
445 – 20 c. blue 85 15
446 – 50 c. lilac . . . . 3·00 50
447 – 1 s. brown . . . . 8·50 2·00
448 – 2 s. blue . . . . 17·00 8·25

1925. Surch **DOS Centavos 1925**.
449 **137** 2 c. on 20 c. blue 85 50

1925. Optd **Plebiscito**.
450 10 c. red (No. 434) 70 70

143 The Rock of Arica

1925. Obligatory Tax. Tacna-Arica Plebiscite.
451 **143** 2 c. orange 25 10
452 5 c. blue . . . . 1·25 50
453 5 c. red 65 40
454 5 c. green 60 40
455 – 10 c. brown . . . . . . 2·50 85
456 – 50 c. green . . . . . . 16·00 7·50
DESIGNS—HORIZ: 39 × 30 mm: 10 c. Soldiers with colours. VERT: 27 × 33 mm: 50 c. Bolognesi Statue.

146 The Rock of Arica

1927. Obligatory Tax. Figures of value not encircled.
457 **146** 2 c. orange 50 15
458 2 c. brown 50 15
459 2 c. blue 50 15
460 2 c. violet 35 15
461 2 c. green 35 15
462 20 c. red . . . . 2·10 85

1927. Air. Optd **Servicio Aereo**.
463 **9** 50 c. purple (No. 438) . . . 35·00 25·00

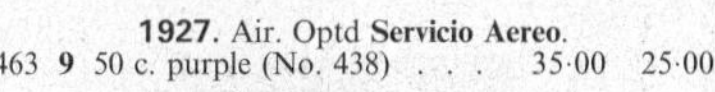

148 Pres. A. B. Leguia **149** The Rock of Arica

1928. Air.
464 **148** 50 c. green 70 35

1928. Obligatory Tax. Plebiscite Fund.
465 **149** 2 c. mauve 15 10

1929. Surch **Habilitada 2 Cts. 1929**.
466 – 2 c. on 8 c. (No. 410) . . 50 50
468 **137** 15 c. on 20 c. (No. 437) . 70 70

1929. Surch **Habilitada 2 centavos 1929**.
467 2 c. on 8 c. (No. 410) 70 70

1930. Optd **Habilitada Franqueo**.
469 **149** 2 c. mauve 30 30

1930. Surch **Habilitada 2 Cts. 1930**.
470 **137** 2 c. on 20 c. yellow . . . 25 25

1930. Surch **Habilitada Franqueo** 2 Cts. 1930.
471 **148** 2 c. on 50 c. green . . . 25 25

156 Arms of Peru **157** Lima Cathedral

1930. 6th (inscribed "seventh") Pan-American Child Congress.
472 **156** 2 c. green 60 55
473 **157** 5 c. red . . . . 1·40 1·00
474 – 10 c. blue 90 85
475 – 50 c. brown . . . . . . 15·00 10·00
DESIGNS—HORIZ: 10 c. G.P.O., Lima. VERT: 50 c. Madonna and Child.

1930. Fall of Leguia Govt. No. 434 optd with Arms of Peru or surch with new value in four corners also.
477 2 c. on 10 c. red 10 10
478 4 c. on 10 c. red 20 20
479 10 c. red 15 10
476 15 c. on 10 c. red 20 15

159 Simon Bolivar **161** Pizarro

162 The Old Stone Bridge, Lima

1930. Death Centenary of Bolivar.
480 **159** 2 c. brown 35 20
481 4 c. red 70 30
482 10 c. green 35 25
483 15 c. grey 70 50

1930. As T **107** and **137** but smaller 18 × 22 mm.
484 – 2 c. olive (Rivadeneyra) . . 15 10
485 – 4 c. green (Melgar) 15 10
486 – 15 c. blue (De la Mar) . . . 50 10
487 **137** 20 c. yellow (Olaya) . . . 1·00 20
488 – 50 c. purple (Bellido) . . . 1·00 25
489 – 1 s. brown (De Saco) . . . 1·60 35

1931. Obligatory Tax. Unemployment Fund. Surch **Habilitada Pro Desocupados 2 Cts**.
490 **159** 2 c. on 4 c. red 70 35
491 2 c. on 10 c. green 50 35
492 2 c. on 15 c. grey 50 35

1931. 1st Peruvian Philatelic Exhibition.
493 **161** 2 c. slate . . . . 1·40 1·10
494 4 c. brown . . . . 1·40 1·10
495 **162** 10 c. red . . . . 1·40 1·10
496 10 c. green and mauve . . 1·40 1·10
497 **161** 15 c. green . . . . 1·40 1·10
498 **162** 15 c. red and grey . . . . 1·40 1·10
499 15 c. blue and orange . . . 1·40 1·10

163 Manco Capac **164** Oil Well **170**

1931.
500 **163** 2 c. olive 20 10
501 **164** 4 c. green 40 30
502 – 10 c. orange 85 10
503 – 15 c. blue . . . . 1·25 25
504 – 20 c. yellow . . . . 5·50 40
505 – 50 c. lilac . . . . 5·00 40
506 – 1 s. brown . . . . 11·00 85
DESIGNS—VERT: 10 c. Sugar Plantation; 15 c. Cotton Plantation; 50 c. Copper Mines. 1 s. Llamas. HORIZ: 20 c. Guano Islands.

1931. Obligatory Tax. Unemployment Fund.
507 **170** 2 c. green 10 10
508 2 c. red 10 10

171 Arms of Piura **172** Parakas

1932. 4th Centenary of Piura.
509 **171** 10 c. blue (postage) . . . 5·00 5·00
510 15 c. violet . . . . 5·00 5·00
511 50 c. red (air) . . . . . . 17·00 16·00

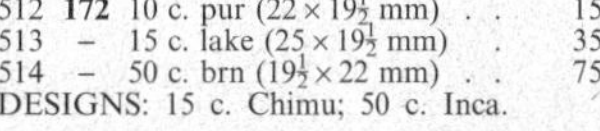

1932. 400th Anniv of Spanish Conquest of Peru. Native designs.
512 **172** 10 c. pur ($22\times19\frac{1}{2}$ mm) . . 15 10
513 – 15 c. lake ($25\times19\frac{1}{2}$ mm) . . 35 10
514 – 50 c. brn ($19\frac{1}{2}\times22$ mm) . . 75 15
DESIGNS: 15 c. Chimu; 50 c. Inca.

175 Arequipa and El Misti **176** Pres. Sanchez Cerro

1932. 1st Anniv of Constitutional Government.
515 **175** 2 c. blue 15 10
527 2 c. black 15 10
528 2 c. green 15 10
516 4 c. brown 15 10
529 4 c. orange 15 10
517 **176** 10 c. red . . . . 11·00 8·25
530 – 10 c. red 50 10
518 – 15 c. blue 35 10
531 – 15 c. mauve 35 10
519 – 20 c. lake 50 10
532 – 20 c. violet 50 15
520 – 50 c. green 70 15
521 – 1 s. orange . . . . 5·00 35
533 – 1 s. brown . . . . 6·25 40
DESIGNS—VERT: 10 c. (No. 530), Statue of Liberty; 15 c. to 1 s. Bolivar Monument, Lima.

178 Blacksmith **179** Monument of 2nd May to Battle of Callao

1932. Obligatory Tax. Unemployment Fund.
522 **178** 2 c. grey 10 10
523 2 c. violet 10 10

1933. Obligatory Tax. Unemployment Fund.
524 **179** 2 c. violet 15 10
525 2 c. orange 15 10
526 2 c. purple 15 10

181 Hawker Hart Bomber **184** F. Pizarro

185 Coronation of Huascar **186** The Inca

1934. Air.
534 **181** 2 s. blue . . . . 4·50 35
535 5 s. brown . . . . 9·50 70

1934. Obligatory Tax. Unemployment Fund. Optd **Pro-Desocupados**. (a) In one line.
536 **176** 2 c. green 10 10
585 – 2 c. purple (No. 537) . . 10 10

(b) In two lines.
566 – 2 c. purple (No. 537) . . . 10 10

1934.
537 – 2 c. purple 10 10
538 – 4 c. green 15 10
539 **184** 10 c. red 15 10
540 15 c. blue 50 10
541 **185** 20 c. blue . . . . 1·00 15
542 50 c. brown . . . . 1·00 15
543 **186** 1 s. violet . . . . 2·40 35
DESIGNS: 2, 4 c. show the scene depicted in Type **189**.

187 Lake of the Marvellous Cure **188** Grapes

1935. Tercentenary of Founding of Ica.
544 – 4 c. black 65 65
545 **187** 5 c. red 25 65
546 **188** 10 c. mauve . . . . 2·75 1·40
547 **187** 20 c. green . . . . 1·00 1·00
548 – 35 c. red . . . . 5·50 3·25
549 – 50 c. brown and orange . 3·75 3·25
550 – 1 s. red and violet . . . . 11·00 8·25
DESIGNS—HORIZ: 4 c. City of Ica; 50 c. Don Diego Lopez and King Philip IV of Spain. VERT: 35 c. Cotton blossom; 1 s. Supreme God of the Nazcas.

189 Pizarro and "The Thirteen"

192 Funeral of Atahualpa

1935. 4th Centenary of Founding of Lima.
551 **189** 2 c. brown (postage) . . . 35 20
552 – 4 c. violet 50 35
553 – 10 c. red 50 20
554 – 15 c. blue 85 40
555 **189** 20 c. grey . . . . 1·10 50
556 – 50 c. green . . . . 1·60 1·25
557 – 1 s. blue . . . . 3·75 2·40
558 – 2 s. brown . . . . 8·75 6·75
DESIGNS—HORIZ: 4 c. Lima Cathedral. VERT: 10 c., 50 c. Miss L. S. de Canevaro; 15 c., 2 s. Pizarro; 1 s. The "Tapada" (a veiled woman).

559 **192** 5 c. green (air) 35 20
560 – 35 c. brown 75 35
561 – 50 c. yellow . . . . 1·25 70
562 – 1 s. purple . . . . 1·75 75
563 – 2 s. orange . . . . 1·50 1·50
564 **192** 5 s. purple . . . . 6·25 4·25
565 **189** 10 s. blue . . . . 23·00 19·00
DESIGNS—HORIZ: 35 c. Airplane near San Cristobal Hill; 50 c., 1 s. Airplane over Avenue of Barefoot Friars. VERT: 2 s. Palace of Torre Tagle.

207 "San Cristobal" (caravel)

1936. Callao Centenary.
567 **207** 2 c. black (postage) . . . 90 20
568 – 4 c. green 45 15
569 – 5 c. brown 45 15
570 – 10 c. blue 45 20
571 – 15 c. green . . . . 1·40 25
572 – 20 c. brown 45 25
573 – 50 c. lilac 90 45
574 – 1 s. olive . . . . 18·00 1·60
575 – 2 s. purple . . . . 11·00 5·00
576 – 5 s. red . . . . 15·00 11·50
577 – 10 s. brown and red . . . 38·00 29·00

578 – 35 c. slate (air) . . . . . 6·00 3·00
DESIGNS—HORIZ: 4 c. La Punta Naval College; 5 c. Independence Square, Callao; 10 c. Aerial view of Callao; 15 c. "Reina del Pacifico" (liner) in Callao Docks and Custom House; 20 c. Plan of Callao, 1746; 35 c. "La Callao" (early locomotive); 1 s. Gunboat "Sacramento"; 10 s. Real Felipe Fortifications. VERT: 50 c. D. Jose de la Mar; 2 s. Don Jose de Velasco; 5 s. Fort Maipo and miniature portraits of Galvez and Nunez.

1936. Obligatory Tax. St. Rosa de Lima Cathedral Construction Fund. Optd **"Ley 8310"**.
579 **179** 2 c. purple 10 10

1936. Surch **Habilitado** and value in figures and words.
580 – 2 c. on 4 c. green (No. 538) (postage) 10 10
581 **185** 10 c. on 20 c. blue 15 15
582 **186** 10 c. on 1 s. violet 20 20

583 **181** 5 c. on 2 s. blue (air) . . . 35 15
584 25 c. on 5 s. brown . . . 70 25

211 Guanay Cormorants **217** Mail Steamer "Inca" on Lake Titicaca

1936.
586 **211** 2 c. brown (postage) . . . 1·75 15
616 2 c. green . . . . 1·50 15
587 – 4 c. brown 50 25
617 – 4 c. black 25 15
618 – 10 c. red 10 10
619 – 15 c. blue 20 10
590 – 20 c. black 70 15
620 – 20 c. brown 25 15
591 – 50 c. yellow . . . . 2·10 50
621 – 50 c. grey 70 15
592 – 1 s. purple . . . . 4·25 70
622 – 1 s. blue . . . . 1·40 35
593 – 2 s. blue . . . . 9·00 2·00
623 – 2 s. violet . . . . 3·00 35
594 – 5 s. blue . . . . 9·00 3·00
595 – 10 s. brown and violet . . 50·00 19·00
DESIGNS—VERT: 4 c. Oil well; 10 c. Inca postal runner; 1 s. G.P.O., Lima; 2 s. M. de Amat y Junyent; 5 s. J. A. de Pando y Riva; 10 s. J. D. Condemarin. HORIZ: 15 c. Paseo de la Republica, Lima; 20 c. Municipal Palace and Natural History Museum; 50 c. University of San Marcos, Lima.

596 – 5 c. green (air) 25 10
625 **217** 15 c. blue 70 15
598 – 20 c. grey 90 15
626 – 20 c. green 85 15
627 – 25 c. red 40 10
628 – 30 c. brown 80 15
600 – 35 c. brown . . . . 1·60 1·40
601 – 50 c. yellow 25 35
629 – 50 c. red 40 20
630 – 70 c. green . . . . 1·25 50
603 – 80 c. black . . . . 5·00 3·00
631 – 80 c. green . . . . 1·25 30
604 – 1 s. blue . . . . 9·50 1·50
632 – 1 s. brown . . . . 4·25 40
605 – 1 s. 50 brown . . . . . . 8·00 5·50
633 – 1 s. 50 orange . . . . . . 5·50 40
606 – 2 s. blue . . . . 15·00 6·50
634 – 2 s. green . . . . 11·00 70
607 – 5 s. green . . . . 20·00 3·25
608 – 10 s. brown and red . . . 85·00 65·00
DESIGNS—HORIZ: 5 c. La Mar Park; 20 c. Native recorder player and llama; 30 c. Chuquibambilla ram; 25, 35 c. J. Chavez; 50 c. Mining Area; 70 c. Ford "Tin Goose" airplane over La Punta; 1 s. Steam train at La Cima; 1 s. 50, Aerodrome at Las Palmas, Lima. 2 s. Douglas DC-2 mail plane; 5 s. Valley of R. Inambari. VERT: 80 c. Infiernillo Canyon, Andes; 10 s. St. Rosa de Lima.

223 St. Rosa de Lima

1937. Obligatory Tax. St. Rosa de Lima Construction Fund.
609 **223** 2 c. red 15 10

1937. Surch **Habilit.** and value in figures and words.
(a) Postage.
610 1 s. on 2 s. blue (593) . . . . 2·10 2·10

(b) Air.
611 15 c. on 30 c. brown (599) . . 45 40
612 15 c. on 35 c. brown (600) . . 45 25
613 15 c. on 70 c. green (630) . . 2·75 2·25
614 25 c. on 80 c. black (603) . . 2·75 2·25
615 1 s. on 2 s. blue (606) . . . . 4·25 3·00

225 Bielovucic over Lima **226** Jorge Chavez

1937. Air. Pan-American Aviation Conf.
635 **225** 10 c. violet 40 10
636 **226** 15 c. green 50 10
637 – 25 c. brown 40 10
638 – 1 s. black . . . . 1·90 1·00
DESIGNS—As T **225**: 25 c. Limatambo Airport; 1 s. Peruvian air routes.

229 "Protection" (by John Q. A. Ward) **230** Children's Holiday Camp

1938. Obligatory Tax. Unemployment Fund.
757c **229** 2 c. brown 10 10

1938. Designs as T **230**.
693 **230** 2 c. green 10 10
694 – 4 c. brown 10 10
642 – 10 c. red 20 10
696 – 15 c. blue 10 10
727 – 15 c. turquoise 10 10
644 – 20 c. purple 15 10
740 – 20 c. violet 10 10
698 – 50 c. blue 15 10
741 – 50 c. brown 15 10
699 – 1 s. purple 85 10
742 – 1 s. brown 25 10
700 – 2 s. green . . . . 2·50 10
731 – 2 s. blue 55 10
701 – 5 s. brown and violet . . . 5·75 35
732 – 5 s. purple and blue . . . 75 35
702 – 10 s. blue and black . . . 10·00 50
733 – 10 s. black and green . . . 2·50 70
DESIGNS—VERT: 4 c. Chavin pottery; 10 c. Auto-mobile roads in Andes; 20 c. (2) Industrial Bank of Peru; 1 s. (2) Portrait of Toribio de Luzuriaga; 5 s. (2) Chavin Idol. HORIZ: 15 c. (2) Archaeological Museum, Lima; 50 c. (2) Labourers' homes at Lima; 2 s. (2) Fig Tree; 10 s. (2) Mt. Huascaran.

240 Monument on Junin Plains **248** Seal of City of Lima

1938. Air. As T **240**.
650 – 5 c. brown 15 10
743 – 5 c. green 10 10
651 **240** 15 c. brown 15 10
652 – 20 c. red 40 10
653 – 25 c. green 20 10
654 – 30 c. orange 20 10
735 – 30 c. red 15 10
655 – 50 c. green 35 30
736 – 70 c. blue . . . . 1·50 10
657 – 80 c. green 60 10
737 – 80 c. red 55 15
658 – 1 s. green . . . . 4·50 2·10
705 – 1 s. 50 violet 45 35
738 – 1 s. 50 purple 45 30
660 – 2 s. red and blue . . . . . 1·60 50
661 – 5 s. purple . . . . 8·25 70
662 – 10 s. blue and green . . . 32·00 20·00
DESIGNS—VERT: 20 c. Rear-Admiral M. Villar; 70 c. Infiernillo Canyon; 2 s. Stele from Chavin Temple. HORIZ: 5 c. People's restaurant, Callao; 25 c. View of Tarma; 30 c. Ica River irrigation system; 50 c. Port of Iquitos; 80 c. Mountain roadway; 1 s. Plaza San Martin, Lima; 1 s. 50, Nat. Radio Station, San Miguel; 5 s. Ministry of Public Works; 10 s. Heroe's Crypt, Lima.

1938. 8th Pan-American Congress, Lima.
663 – 10 c. grey (postage) . . . 50 20
664 **248** 15 c. gold, blue, red & blk 85 25
665 – 1 s. brown . . . . 1·60 85
DESIGNS (39×32½ mm): 10 c. Palace and Square, 1864; 1 s. Palace, 1938.

666 – 25 c. blue (air) 55 50
667 – 1 s. 50 lake . . . . 1·50 1·25
668 – 2 s. black 90 45
DESIGNS—VERT: 26×37 mm: 25 c. Torre Tagle Palace. HORIZ: 39×32½ mm: 1 s. 50, National Congress Building, Lima; 2 s. Congress Presidents, Ferreyros, Paz Soldan and Arenas.

1940. No. 642 surch **Habilitada 5 cts.**
669 5 c. on 10 c. red 15 10

251 National Broadcasting Station

1941. Optd **FRANQUEO POSTAL**.
670 **251** 50 c. yellow . . . . 1·60 15
671 1 s. violet . . . . 1·60 20
672 2 s. green . . . . 3·25 50
673 5 s. brown . . . . 19·00 5·50
674 10 s. mauve . . . . 29·00 4·25

1942. Air. No. 653 surch **Habilit 0.15**.
675 15 c. on 25 c. green 85 10

253 Map of S. America showing R. Amazon **254** Francisco de Orellana

255 Francisco Pizarro **257** Samuel Morse

1943. 400th Anniv of Discovery of R. Amazon.
676 – 2 c. red 10 10
677 **254** 4 c. grey 15 10
678 **255** 10 c. brown 20 10
679 **253** 15 c. blue 50 20
680 – 20 c. olive 20 15
681 – 25 c. orange . . . . 1·40 35
682 **254** 30 c. red 35 20
683 **253** 50 c. green 35 40
685 – 70 c. violet . . . . 2·00 70
686 – 80 c. blue . . . . 2·00 70
687 – 1 s. brown . . . . 3·25 70
688 **255** 5 s. black . . . . 6·75 3·25
DESIGNS—As Type **254**: 2, 70 c. Portraits of G. Pizarro and Orellana in medallion; 20, 80 c. G. Pizarro. As Type **253**: 25 c., 1 s. Orellana's Discovery of the R. Amazon.

1943. Surch with Arms of Peru (as Nos. 483, etc) above **10 CTVS**.
689 10 c. on 10 c. red (No. 642) . . 15 10

1944. Centenary of Invention of Telegraphy.
691 **257** 15 c. blue 15 15
692 30 c. brown 50 20

1946. Surch **Habilitada S/o 0.20**.
706 20 c. on 1 s. purple (No. 699) . 25 10

259

261

1947. 1st National Tourist Congress, Lima. Unissued designs inscr "V Congreso Pan Americano de Carretas 1944" optd **Habilitada I Congreso Nac. de Turismo Lima—1947**.
707 **259** 15 c. black and red . . . 25 15
708 – 1 s. brown 35 20
709 – 1 s. 35 green 35 25
710 **261** 3 s. blue 85 50
711 – 5 s. green . . . . 1·75 1·25
DESIGNS—VERT: 1 s. Mountain road; 1 s. 35, Forest road. HORIZ: 5 s. Road and house.

1947. Air. 1st Peruvian Int Airways Lima–New York Flight. Optd with PIA badge and **PRIMER VUELO LIMA—NUEVA YORK**.
712 5 c. brown (No. 650) 10 10
713 50 c. green (No. 655) 15 10

263 Basketball Players

1948. Air. Olympic Games.
714 – 1 s. blue . . . . 1·25 1·25
715 **263** 2 s. brown . . . . 1·60 1·60
716 – 5 s. green . . . . 2·75 2·75
717 – 10 s. yellow . . . . 3·25 3·25
DESIGNS: 1 s. Map showing air route from Peru to Great Britain; 5 s. Discus thrower; 10 s. Rifleman.

No. 714 is inscr "AEREO" and Nos. 715/17 are optd **AEREO**.

The above stamps exist overprinted **MELBOURNE 1956** but were only valid for postage on one day.

1948. Air. Nos. 653, 736 and 657 surch **Habilitada S/o.** and value.
722 5 c. on 25 c. green 10 10
723 10 c. on 25 c. green 10 10
718 10 c. on 70 c. blue 40 15
719 15 c. on 70 c. blue 50 15
720 20 c. on 70 c. blue 40 15
724 30 c. on 80 c. green 55 15
721 55 c. on 70 c. blue 60 15

263a **263b**

1949. Anti-Tuberculosis Fund. Surch **Decreto Ley No. 18** and value.
724a **263a** 3 c. on 4 c. blue 55 10
724b **263b** 3 c. in 10 c. blue 55 10

264 Statue of Admiral Grau **264a** "Education"

1949.
726 **264** 10 c. blue and green . . . 10 10

1950. Obligatory Tax. National Education Fund.
851 **264a** 3 c. lake (16½×21 mm) . 10 10
897 3 c. lake (18×21½ mm) . 15 10

265 Park, Lima

268 Obrero Hospital, Lima

1951. Air. 75th Anniv of U.P.U. Unissued stamps inscr "VI CONGRESO DE LA UNION POSTAL DE LAS AMREICAS Y ESPANA-1949" optd **U.P.U. 1874-1949**.

745 **265** 5 c. green 10 10
746 – 30 c. red and black 15 10
747 – 55 c. green 15 10
748 – 95 c. turquoise 20 15
749 – 1 s. 50 red 30 25
750 – 2 s. blue 35 30
751 – 5 s. red 2·10 2·10
752 – 10 s. violet 2·75 3·00
753 – 20 s. blue and brown 4·50 4·50

DESIGNS: 30 c. Peruvian flag; 55 c. Huancayo Hotel; 95 c. Ancash Mtns; 1 s. 50, Arequipa Hotel; 2 s. Coaling Jetty; 5 s. Town Hall, Miraflores; 10 s. Congressional Palace; 20 s. Pan-American flags.

1951. Air Surch **HABILITADA S/O.0.25.**

754 25 c. on 30 c. red (No. 735) 15 10

1951. Surch **HABILITADA S/.** and figures.

755 1 c. on 2 c. (No. 693) 10 10
756 5 c. on 15 c. (No. 727) 10 10
757 10 c. on 15 c. (No. 727) 10 10

1951. 5th Pan-American Highways Congress. Unissued "VI CONGRESO DE LA UNION POSTAL" stamps, optd **V Congreso Panamericano de Carreteras 1951**.

758 – 2 c. green 10 10
759 **268** 4 c. red 10 10
760 – 15 c. grey 15 10
761 – 20 c. brown 10 10
762 – 50 c. purple 15 10
763 – 1 s. blue 20 10
764 – 2 s. blue 30 10
765 – 5 s. red 1·00 1·00
766 – 10 s. brown 1·75 85

DESIGNS—HORIZ: 2 c. Aguas Promenade; 50 c. Archiepiscopal Palace, Lima; 1 s. National Judicial Palace; 2 s. Municipal Palace; 5 s. Lake Llanganuco, Ancash. VERT: 15 c. Inca postal runner; 20 c. Old P.O., Lima; 10 s. Machu-Picchu ruins.

269 Father Tomas de San Martin and Capt. J. de Aliaga

1951. Air. 4th Cent of S. Marcos University.

767 **269** 30 c. black 10 10
768 – 40 c. blue 15 10
769 – 50 c. mauve 20 10
770 – 1 s. 20 green 30 15
771 – 2 s. grey 35 15
772 – 5 s. multicoloured 90 20

DESIGNS: 40 c. San Marcos University; 50 c. Santo Domingo Convent; 1 s. 20, P. de Peralto Barnuevo, Father Tomas de San Martin and Jose Baquijano; 2 s. Toribio Rodriguez, Jose Hipolito Unanue and Jose Cayetano Heredia; 5 s. University Arms in 1571 and 1735.

270 Engineer's School

1952. (a) Postage.

774 – 2 c. purple 10 10
775 – 5 c. green 15 10
776 – 10 c. green 25 10
777 – 15 c. grey 10 10
777a – 15 c. brown 90 20
829 – 20 c. brown 20 10
779 **270** 25 c. red 15 10
779a 25 c. green 30 10
780 – 30 c. blue 10 10
780a – 30 c. red 15 10
830 – 30 c. mauve 15 10
924 – 50 c. green 10 10
831 – 50 c. purple 15 10
782 – 1 s. brown 30 10
782a – 1 s. blue 30 10
783 – 2 s. turquoise 40 10
783a – 2 s. grey 55 15

DESIGNS—As Type **270**: HORIZ: 2 c. Hotel, Tacna; 5 c. Tuna fishing boat and indigenous fish; 10 c. View of Matarani; 15 c. Steam train; 30 c. Public Health and Social Assistance. VERT: 20 c. Vicuna. Larger (35 × 25 mm): HORIZ: 50 c. Inca maize terraces; 1 s. Inca ruins, Paramonga Fort; 2 s. Agriculture Monument, Lima.

(b) Air.

784 – 40 c. green 30 10
785 – 75 c. brown 2·00 25
834 – 80 c. red 1·75 10
786 – 1 s. 25 blue 25 10
787 – 1 s. 50 red 20 10
788 – 2 s. 20 blue 65 15
789 – 3 s. brown 75 25
835 – 3 s. green 50 30
836 – 3 s. 80 orange 85 35
790 – 5 s. brown 50 15
791 – 10 s. brown 1·50 35
838 – 10 s. red 1·00 45

DESIGNS—As Type **270**. HORIZ: 40 c. Gunboat "Maranon"; 1 s. 50, Housing Complex. VERT: 75 c., 80 c. Colony of Guanay cormorants. Larger (25 × 25 mm.): HORIZ: 1 s. 25, Corpac-Limatambo Airport; 2 s. 20, 3 s. 80, Inca Observatory, Cuzco; 5 s. Garcilaso (portrait). VERT: 3 s. Tobacco plant, leaves and cigarettes; 10 s. Manco Capac Monument (25 × 37 mm).

See also Nos. 867, etc.

271 Isabella the Catholic

272 "Santa Maria", "Pinta" and "Nina"

273

1953. Air. 500th Birth Anniv of Isabella the Catholic.

792 **271** 40 c. red 20 10
793 **272** 1 s. 25 green 1·40 30
794 **271** 2 s. 15 purple 35 25
795 **272** 2 s. 20 black 3·25 55

1954. Obligatory Tax. National Marian Eucharistic Congress Fund. Roul.

796 **273** 5 c. blue and red 25 10

274 Gen. M. Perez Jimenez

275 Arms of Lima and Bordeaux

1956. Visit of President of Venezuela.

797 **274** 25 c. brown 10 10

1957. Air. Exn of French Products, Lima.

798 **275** 40 c. lake, blue and green 10 10
799 – 50 c. black, brown & grn 15 10
800 – 1 s. 25 deep blue, green and blue 1·25 35
801 – 2 s. 20 brown and blue 40 30

DESIGNS—HORIZ: 50 c. Eiffel Tower and Lima Cathedral; 1 s. 25, Admiral Dupetit-Thouars and frigate "La Victorieuse"; 2 s. 20, Exhibition building, Pres. Prado and Pres. Coty.

276 1857 Stamp

277 Carlos Paz Soldan (founder)

1957. Air. Centenary of First Peruvian Postage Stamp.

802 – 5 c. black and grey 10 10
803 **276** 10 c. turquoise and mauve 10 10
804 – 15 c. brown and green 10 10
805 – 25 c. blue and yellow 10 10
806 – 30 c. brown & chocolate 10 10
807 – 40 c. ochre and black 15 10
808 – 1 s. 25 brown and blue 35 25
809 – 2 s. 20 red and blue 50 30
810 – 5 s. red and mauve 1·00 1·00
811 – 10 s. violet and green 1·60 1·50

DESIGNS: 5 c. Pre-stamp Postmarks; 15 c. 1857 2 r. stamp; 25 c. 1 d. 1858; 30 c. 1 p. 1858 stamp; 40 c. ½ peso 1858 stamp; 1 s. 25, J. Davila Condemarin, Director of Posts, 1857; 2 s. 20, Pres. Ramon Castilla; 5 s. Pres. D. M. Prado; 10 s. Various Peruvian stamps in shield.

1958. Air. Centenary of Lima–Callao Telegraph Service.

812 **277** 40 c. brown and red 10 10
813 – 1 s. green 15 10
814 – 1 s. 25 blue and purple 25 15

DESIGNS—VERT: 1 s. Marshal Ramon Castilla. HORIZ: 1 s. 25, Pres. D. M. Prado and view of Callao; No. 814 also commemorates the political centenary of the Province of Callao.

278 Flags of France and Peru

279 Father Martin de Porras Velasquez

1958. Air. "Treasures of Peru" Exhibition, Paris.

815 **278** 50 c. red, blue & dp blue 10 10
816 – 65 c. multicoloured 10 10
817 – 1 s. 50 brown, purple & bl 25 10
818 – 2 s. 50 purple, turq and green 35 20

DESIGNS—HORIZ: 65 c. Lima Cathedral and girl in national costume; 1 s. 50, Caballero and ancient palace. VERT: 2 s. 50, Natural resources map of Peru.

1958. Air. Birth Centenary of D. A. Carrion Garcia (patriot).

819 **279** 60 c. multicoloured 10 10
820 – 1 s. 20 multicoloured 15 10
821 – 1 s. 50 multicoloured 25 10
822 – 2 s. 20 black 30 20

DESIGNS—VERT: 1 s. 20, D. A. Carrion Garcia. 1 s. 50, J. H. Unanue Pavon. HORIZ: 2 s. 20, First Royal School of Medicine (now Ministry of Government Police, Posts and Telecommunications).

280 Gen. Alvarez Thomas

281 Association Emblems

1958. Air. Death Centenary of Gen. Thomas.

823 **280** 1 s. 10 purple, red & bistre 20 15
824 1 s. 20 black, red & bistre 25 15

1958. Air. 150th Anniv of Advocates' College, Lima. Emblems in bistre and blue.

825 **281** 80 c. green 10 10
826 1 s. 10 red 15 10
827 1 s. 20 blue 15 10
828 1 s. 50 purple 20 10

282 Piura Arms and Congress Emblem

283

1960. Obligatory Tax. 6th National Eucharistic Congress Fund.

839 **282** 10 c. multicoloured 20 10
839a 10 c. blue and red 20 10

1960. Air. World Refugee Year.

840 **283** 80 c. multicoloured 30 30
841 4 s. 30 multicoloured 50 50

284 Sea Bird bearing Map

285 Congress Emblem

1960. Air. International Pacific Fair, Lima.

842 **284** 1 s. multicoloured 40 15

1960. 6th National Eucharistic Congress, Piura.

843 **285** 50 c. red, black & blue 15 10
844 – 1 s. mult (Eucharistic symbols) 25 10

286 1659 Coin

1961. Air. 1st National Numismatic Exhibition, Lima.

845 – 1 s. grey and brown 20 10
846 **286** 2 s. grey and blue 25 15

DESIGNS: 1 s. 1659 coin.

287 "Amazonas"

1961. Air. Centenary of World Tour of Cadet Sailing Ship "Amazonas".

847 **287** 50 c. green and brown 25 10
848 80 c. red and purple 35 10
849 1 s. black and green 50 10

288 Globe, Moon and Stars

289 Olympic Torch

1961. Air. I.G.Y.

850 **288** 1 s. multicoloured 15 15

1961. Air. Olympic Games, 1960.

852 **289** 5 c. blue and black 40 35
853 10 s. red and black 70 60

290 "Balloon"

291 Fair Emblem

1961. Christmas and New Year.

854 **290** 20 c. blue 30 10

1961. Air. 2nd International Pacific Fair, Lima.

855 **291** 1 s. multicoloured 20 15

292 Symbol of Eucharist

293 Sculptures "Cahuide" and "Cuauhtemoc"

1962. Obligatory Tax. 7th National Eucharistic Congress Fund. Roul.

857 **292** 10 c. blue and yellow 10 10

1962. Air. Peruvian Art Treasures Exhibition, Mexico. 1960. Flags red and green.

859 **293** 1 s. red 15 10
860 – 2 s. turquoise 25 15
861 – 3 s. brown 30 15

DESIGNS: 2 s. Tupac-Amaru and Hidalgo; 3 s. Presidents Prado and Lopez.

294 Frontier Maps

1962. Air. 20th Anniv of Ecuador–Peru Border Agreement.
862 **294** 1 s. 30 blk & red on grey . 25 15
863 1 s. 50 multicoloured . . . 25 15
864 2 s. 50 multicoloured . . . 30 30

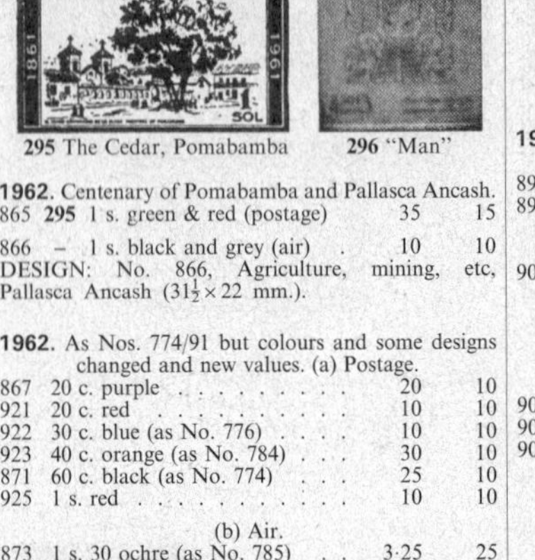

295 The Cedar, Pomabamba **296** "Man"

1962. Centenary of Pomabamba and Pallasca Ancash.
865 **295** 1 s. green & red (postage) 35 15
866 – 1 s. black and grey (air) . 10 10
DESIGN: No. 866, Agriculture, mining, etc, Pallasca Ancash (31½ × 22 mm.).

1962. As Nos. 774/91 but colours and some designs changed and new values. (a) Postage.
867 20 c. purple 20 10
921 20 c. red 10 10
922 30 c. blue (as No. 776) 10 10
923 40 c. orange (as No. 784) . . . 30 10
871 60 c. black (as No. 774) . . . 25 10
925 1 s. red 10 10

(b) Air.
873 1 s. 30 ochre (as No. 785) . . 3·25 25
874 1 s. 50 purple 35 10
875 1 s. 80 blue (as No. 777) . . . 45 15
876 2 s. green 40 15
926 2 s. 60 green (as No. 783) . . 30 15
877 3 s. purple 40 15
927 3 s. 60 purple (as No. 789) . . 45 20
878 4 s. 30 orange 55 30
928 4 s. 60 orange (as No. 788) . . 35 25
879 5 s. green 55 35
880 10 s. blue . . . . 1·00 40

1963. Air. Chavin Excavations Fund. Pottery.
881 – 1 s. + 50 c. grey & pink . 15 15
882 – 1 s. 50 + 1 s. grey & blue 15 15
883 – 3 s. + 2 s. 50 grey & green 50 50
884 **296** 4 s. 30 + 3 s. grey and green 85 65
885 – 6 s. + 4 s. grey and olive . 95 85
FIGURES—HORIZ: 1 s. "Griffin"; 1 s. 50, "Eagle"; 3 s. "Cat". VERT: 6 s. "Deity".

297 Campaign and Industrial Emblems

298 Henri Dunant and Centenary Emblem

1963. Freedom from Hunger.
886 **297** 1 s. bistre & red (postage) 15 10
887 4 s. 30 bistre & grn (air) . 40 40

1964. Air. Red Cross Centenary.
888 **298** 1 s. 30 + 70 c. multicoloured 25 25
889 4 s. 30 + 1 s. 70 mult . . 55 55

299 Chavez and Wing

300 Alliance Emblem

1964. Air. 50th Anniv of Jorge Chavez's Trans-Alpine Flight.
890 **299** 5 s. blue, purple and brn . 75 35

1964. "Alliance for Progress". Emblem black, green and blue.
891 **300** 40 c. blk & yell (postage) . 10 10
892 – 1 s. 30 black & mauve (air) 15 10
893 **300** 3 s. black and blue 30 25
DESIGN—HORIZ: 1 s. 30, As Type **300**, but with inscription at right.

301 Fair Poster

302 Net, Flag and Globe

1965. Air. 3rd International Pacific Fair, Lima.
894 **301** 1 s. multicoloured 10 10

1965. Air. Women's World Basketball Championships, Lima.
895 **302** 1 s. 30 violet and red . . . 30 15
896 4 s. 30 bistre and red . . . 45 30

303 St. Martin de Porras (anonymous)

304 Fair Emblem

1965. Air. Canonisation of St. Martin de Porras (1962). Paintings. Multicoloured.
898 1 s. 30 Type **303** 15 10
899 1 s. 80 "St. Martin and the Miracle of the Animals" (after painting by Camino Brent) 25 10
900 4 s. 30 "St. Martin and the Angels" (after painting by Fausto Conti) 50 25
Porras is wrongly spelt "Porres" on the stamps.

1965. 4th International Pacific Fair, Lima.
901 **304** 1 s. 50 multicoloured . . 15 10
902 2 s. 50 multicoloured . . 20 10
903 3 s. 50 multicoloured . . 30 20

305 Father Christmas and Postmarked Envelope

312 2nd May Monument and Battle Scene

1965. Christmas.
904 **305** 20 c. black and red . . . 15 10
905 50 c. black and green . . 20 10
906 1 s. black and blue . . . 30 10
The above stamps were valid for postage only on November 2nd. They were subsequently used as postal employees' charity labels.

1966. Obligatory Tax. Journalists' Fund. (a) Surch **HABILITADO "Fondo del Periodista Peruano" Ley 16078 S/o.0.10.**
907 **264a** 10 c. on 3 c. (No. 897) . 65 10
(b) Surch **Habilitado "Fondo del Periodista Peruano" Ley 16078 S/. 0.10.**
909 **264a** 10 c. on 3 c. (No. 897) . 25 10

1966. Obligatory Tax. Journalists' Fund. No. 857 optd **Periodista Peruano Ley 16078**.
910 **292** 10 c. blue and yellow . . 10 10

1966. Nos. 757c, 851 and 897 surch **XX Habilitado S/. 0.10.**
911 **229** 10 c. on 2 c. brown . . 10 10
912 **264a** 10 c. on 3 c. lake (No. 897) 10 10
912b 10 c. on 3 c. lake (No. 851) 2·00 70

1966. Air. Centenary of Battle of Callao. Mult.
913 1 s. 90 Type **312** 30 20
914 3 s. 60 Monument and sculpture 45 30
915 4 s. 60 Monument and Jose Galvez 50 40

313 Funerary Mask

1966. Gold Objects of Chimu Culture. Multicoloured.
916 1 s. 90 + 90 c. Type **313** . . 35 35
917 2 s. 60 + 1 s. 30 Ceremonial knife (vert) 40 40
918 3 s. 60 + 1 s. 80 Ceremonial urn 60 60
919 4 s. 60 + 2 s. 30 Goblet (vert) 85 85
920 20 s. + 10 s. Ear-ring . . . . 3·25 3·25

314 Civil Guard Emblem

1966. Air. Civil Guard Centenary Multicoloured.
929 90 c. Type **314** 10 10
930 1 s. 90 Emblem and activities of Civil Guard 20 10

INDEX

Countries can be quickly located by referring to the index at the end of this volume.

315 Map and Mountains

1966. Opening of Huinco Hydro-electric Scheme.
931 **315** 70 c. black, deep blue and blue (postage) 10 10
932 1 s. 90 black, blue and violet (air) 20 15

316 Globe

1967. Air. Peruvian Photographic Exhibition, Lima.
933 – 2 s. 60 red and black . . . 25 15
934 – 3 s. 60 black and blue . . 35 25
935 **316** 4 s. 60 multicoloured . . . 40 30
DESIGNS: 2 s. 60, "Sun" carving; 3 s. 60, Map of Peru within spiral.

317 Symbol of Construction

1967. Six-year Construction Plan.
936 **317** 90 c. black, gold and mauve (postage) 10 10
937 1 s. 90 black, gold and ochre (air) 15 15

318 "St. Rosa" (from painting by A. Medoro)

319 Vicuna within Figure "5"

1967. Air. 350th Death Anniv of St. Rosa of Lima. Designs showing portraits of St. Rosa by artists given below. Multicoloured.
938 1 s. 90 Type **318** 30 15
939 2 s. 60 C. Maratta 40 15
940 3 s. 60 Anon., Cusquena School 55 25

1967. 5th International Pacific Fair, Lima.
941 **319** 1 s. black, green and gold (postage) 10 10
942 1 s. purple, black and gold (air) 10 10

320 Pen-nib made of Newspaper

321 Wall Reliefs (fishes)

1967. Obligatory Tax. Journalists' Fund.
943 **320** 10 c. black and red 10 10

1967. Obligatory Tax. Chan-Chan Excavation Fund.
944 **321** 20 c. black and blue . . . 10 10
945 – 20 c. black and mauve . . 10 10
946 – 20 c. black and brown . . 10 10
947 – 20 c. multicoloured 10 10
948 – 20 c. multicoloured 10 10
949 – 20 c. black and green . . . 10 10
DESIGNS: No. 945, Ornamental pattern; No. 946, Carved "bird"; No. 947, Temple on hillside; No. 948, Corner of Temple; No. 949, Ornamental pattern (birds).

322 Lions' Emblem

323 Nazca Jug

1967. Air. 50th Anniv of Lions International.
950 **322** 1 s. 60 violet, blue & grey 15 10

1968. Air. Ceramic Treasures of Nazca Culture. Designs showing painted pottery jugs. Mult.
951 1 s. 90 Type **323** 15 15
952 2 s. 60 Falcon 20 15
953 3 s. 60 Round jug decorated with bird 25 20
954 4 s. 60 Two-headed snake . . 30 25
955 5 s. 60 Sea Bird 40 35

324 Alligator **325** "Antarqui" (Airline Symbol)

1968. Gold Sculptures of Mochica Culture. Mult.
956 1 s. 90 Type **324** 15 10
957 2 s. 60 Bird 15 10
958 3 s. 60 Lizard 25 15
959 4 s. 60 Bird 30 15
960 5 s. 60 Jaguar 35 20
Nos. 957 and 959 are vert.

1968. Air. 12th Anniv of APSA (Peruvian Airlines).
961 **325** 3 s. 60 multicoloured . . 30 15
962 – 5 s. 60 brown, black & red 45 20
DESIGN: 5 s. 60, Alpaca and stylized Boeing 747.

326 Human Rights Emblem

327 "The Discus-thrower"

1968. Air. Human Rights Year.
963 **326** 6 s. 50 red, green & brn . 25 20

1968. Air. Olympic Games, Mexico.
964 **327** 2 s. 30 brown, blue & yell 15 10
965 3 s. 50 blue, red & green . 20 15
966 5 s. black, blue and pink . 25 15
967 6 s. 50 purple, brown & bl 35 20
968 8 s. blue, mauve and lilac 40 25
969 9 s. violet, green & orge . 45 30

328 **331** Indian's Head and Wheat

1968. Obligatory Tax. Unissued stamps surch as in T **328**.
970 **328** 20 c. on 50 c. violet, orange and black 40 40
971 20 c. on 1 s. blue, orange and black 40 40

1968. Obligatory Tax. Journalists' Fund. No. 897 surch **Habilitado Fondo Periodista Peruano Ley 17050 S/.** and value.
972 **264a** 20 c. on 3 c. lake 10 10

1968. Christmas. No. 900 surch **PRO NAVIDAD Veinte Centavos R.S. 5-11-68.**
973 20 c. on 4 s. 30 multicoloured 25 20

1969. Unissued Agrarian Reform stamps, surch as in T **331**. Multicoloured.
974 2 s. 50 on 90 c. Type **331** (postage) 15 10
975 3 s. on 90 c. Man digging . . 15 15
976 4 s. on 90 c. As No. 975 . . . 25 15
977 5 s. 50 on 1 s. 90 Corn-cob and hand scattering cobs (air) . . 30 15
978 6 s. 50 on 1 s. 90 As No. 977 . 40 20

333 First Peruvian Coin (obverse and reverse)

1969. Air. 400th Anniv of 1st Peruvian Coinage.
979 **333** 5 s. black, grey and yellow 25 15
980 5 s. black, grey and green 25 15

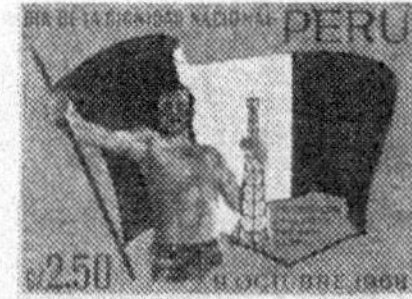

334 Worker holding Flag and Oil Derrick

1969. Nationalization of International Petroleum Company's Oilfields and Refinery (9 October, 1968).
981 **334** 2 s. 50 multicoloured . . . 15 10
982 3 s. multicoloured 20 10
983 4 s. multicoloured 25 15
984 5 s. 50 multicoloured . . . 30 20

335 Castilla Monument **336** Boeing 707, Globe and "Kon Tiki" (replica of balsa raft)

1969. Air. Death Centenary of President Ramon Castilla.
985 **335** 5 s. blue and green 30 15
986 – 10 s. brown and purple . . 70 30
DESIGN—(21 × 37 mm): 10 s. President Castilla.

1969. 1st A.P.S.A. (Peruvian Airlines) Flight to Europe.
987 **336** 2 s. 50 mult (postage) . . 20 10
988 3 s. multicoloured (air) . . 30 10
989 4 s. multicoloured 40 10
990 5 s. 50 multicoloured . . . 50 15
991 6 s. 50 multicoloured . . . 60 25

337 Dish Aerial, Satellite and Globe

1969. Air. Inauguration of Lurin Satellite Telecommunications Station, Lima.
992 **337** 20 s. multicoloured . . . 1·00 60

338 Captain Jose A. Quinones Gonzales (military aviator)

1969. Quinones Gonzales Commemoration.
994 **338** 20 s. mult (postage) . . . 1·00 70
995 20 s. multicoloured (air) . 1·00 45

339 W.H.O. Emblem

1969. Air. 20th Anniv (1968) of W.H.O.
996 **339** 5 s. multicoloured 15 15
997 6 s. 50 multicoloured . . . 20 15

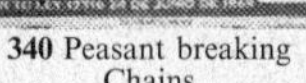

340 Peasant breaking Chains **341** Arms of the Inca Garcilaso de la Vega (historian)

1969. Agrarian Reform Decree.
998 **340** 2 s. 50 deep blue, blue and red (postage) 10 10
999 3 s. purple, lilac and black (air) 10 10
1000 4 s. brown & lt brown . 15 10

1969. Air. Garcilaso de la Vega Commem.
1001 **341** 2 s. 40 black, silver & grn 10 10
1002 – 3 s. 50 black, buff & blue 15 10
1003 – 5 s. multicoloured . . . 20 15
DESIGNS: 3 s. 50, Title page, "Commentarios Reales", Lisbon, 1609; 5 s. Inca Garcilaso de la Vega.

342 Admiral Grau and Ironclad Warship "Huascar"

1969. Navy Day.
1005 **342** 50 s. multicoloured . . . 3·50 1·75

343 "6" and Fair Flags

1969. 6th International Pacific Fair, Lima.
1006 **343** 2 s. 50 mult (postage) . 10 10
1007 3 s. multicoloured (air) . 15 10
1008 4 s. multicoloured . . . 15 10

344 Father Christmas and Greetings Card **345** Col. F. Bolognesi and Soldier

1969. Christmas.
1009 **344** 20 c. black and red . . . 10 10
1010 20 c. black and orange . 10 10
1011 20 c. black and brown . 10 10

1969. Army Day.
1012 **345** 1 s. 20 black, gold and blue (postage) 10 10
1013 50 s. black, gold and brown (air) . . . . 2·50 1·10

346 Arms of Amazonas

1970. Air. 150th Anniv (1971) of Republic (1st issue).
1014 **346** 10 s. multicoloured . . . 35 30
See also Nos. 1066/70, 1076/80 and 1081/90.

347 I.L.O. Emblem on Map

1970. Air. 50th Anniv of I.L.O.
1015 **347** 3 s. deep blue and blue . 15 10

348 "Motherhood"

1970. Air. 24th Anniv of U.N.I.C.E.F.
1016 **348** 5 s. black and yellow . . 25 15
1017 6 s. 50 black and pink . . 35 20

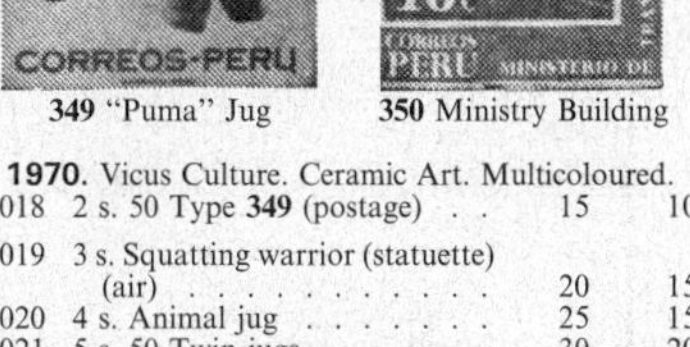

349 "Puma" Jug **350** Ministry Building

1970. Vicus Culture. Ceramic Art. Multicoloured.
1018 2 s. 50 Type **349** (postage) . . 15 10
1019 3 s. Squatting warrior (statuette) (air) 20 15
1020 4 s. Animal jug 25 15
1021 5 s. 50 Twin jugs 30 20
1022 6 s. 50 Woman with jug (statuette) 40 25

1970. Ministry of Transport and Communications.
1023 **350** 40 c. black and purple . . 10 10
1024 40 c. black and yellow . . 10 10
1025 40 c. black and grey . . . 10 10
1026 40 c. black and red . . . 10 10
1027 40 c. black and brown . . 10 10

351 Anchovy **352** Telephone and Skyline

1970. Fishes. Multicoloured.
1028 2 s. 50 Type **351** (postage) . . 15 10
1029 2 s. 50 Hake 15 10
1030 3 s. Swordfish (air) 15 10
1031 3 s. Yellowfin tuna 15 10
1032 5 s. 50 Wolf-fish 40 15

1970. Air. Nationalization of Lima Telephone Service.
1033 **352** 5 s. multicoloured 30 15
1034 10 s. multicoloured . . . 55 25

353 "Soldier and Farmer" **354** U.N. Headquarters and Dove

1970. Unity of Armed Forces and People.
1035 **353** 2 s. 50 multicoloured (postage) 15 10
1036 3 s. multicoloured (air) . 25 10
1037 5 s. 50 multicoloured . . 35 15

1970. Air. 25th Anniv of U.N.O.
1038 **354** 3 s. blue and light blue . 15 10

355 Rotary Emblem

1970. Air. 50th Anniv of Lima Rotary Club.
1039 **355** 10 s. gold, red and black . 75 25

356 Military Parade (Army Staff College, Chorrillos)

1970. Military, Naval and Air Force Academies. Multicoloured.
1040 2 s. 50 Type **356** 35 20
1041 2 s. 50 Parade, Naval Academy, La Punta 35 20
1042 2 s. 50 Parade, Air Force Officer Training School, Las Palmas 35 20

357 Puruchuco, Lima

1970. Tourism. Multicoloured.
1043 2 s. 50 Type **357** (postage) . 15 10
1044 3 s. Chan-Chan-Trujillo, La Libertad (air) 15 10
1045 4 s. Sacsayhuaman, Cuzco . 25 10
1046 5 s. 50 Lake Titicaca, Pomata, Puno 30 15
1047 10 s. Machu-Picchu, Cuzco . 60 30
Nos. 1045/7 are vert.

358 Festival Procession

1970. Air. October Festival, Lima. Multicoloured.
1049 3 s. Type **358** 15 10
1050 4 s. "The Cock-fight" (T. Nunez Ureta) 25 10
1051 5 s. 50 Altar, Nazarenas Shrine (vert) 30 20
1052 6 s. 50 "The Procession" (J. Vinatea Reinoso) . . . 35 25
1053 8 s. "The Procession" (Jose Sabogal) (vert) 50 20

359 "The Nativity" (Cuzco School)

1970. Christmas. Paintings by Unknown Artists. Multicoloured.
1054 1 s. 20 Type **359** 10 10
1055 1 s. 50 "The Adoration of the Magi" (Cuzquena School) 10 10
1056 1 s. 80 "The Adoration of the Shepherds" (Peruvian School) 10 10

360 "Close Embrace" (petroglyph)

1971. Air. "Gratitude for World Help in Earthquake of May 1970".
1057 **360** 4 s. olive, black and red . 25 15
1058 5 s. 50 blue, flesh and red 35 15
1059 6 s. 50 grey, blue and red 40 20

361 "St. Rosa de Lima" (F. Laso)

1971. 300th Anniv of Canonisation of St. Rosa de Lima.
1060 **361** 2 s. 50 multicoloured . . 15 10

362 Tiahuanaco Fabric

1971. Ancient Peruvian Textiles.

No.	Type	Description		
1061	**362**	1 s. 20 mult (postage)	15	10
1062	–	2 s. 50 multicoloured	25	10
1063	–	3 s. multicoloured (air)	30	10
1064	–	4 s. pink, green & dp grn	40	10
1065	–	5 s. 50 multicoloured	55	15

DESIGNS—HORIZ: 2 s. 50, Chancay fabric; 4 s. Chancay lace. VERT: 3 s. Chancay tapestry; 5 s. 50, Paracas fabric.

363 M. Garcia Pumacahua **364** "Cojinova" (Nazca Culture)

1971. 150th Anniv of Independence (2nd issue). National Heroes.

No.	Type	Description		
1066	**363**	1 s. 20 blk & red (postage)	10	10
1067	–	2 s. 50 black and blue	15	10
1068	–	3 s. black & mve (air)	15	10
1069	–	4 s. black and green	15	10
1070	–	5 s. 50 black and brown	25	15

DESIGNS: 2 s. 50, F. Antonio de Zela; 3 s. T. Rodriguez de Mendoza; 4 s. J. P. Viscardo y Guzman; 5 s. 50, J. G. Condorcanqui, Tupac Amani.

See also Nos. 1076/80 and Nos. 1081/90.

1971. "Traditional Fisheries of Peru". Piscatorial Ceramics. Multicoloured.

No.	Description		
1071	1 s. 50 Type **364** (postage)	15	10
1072	3 s. 50 "Bonito" (Chimu Inca) (air)	30	10
1073	4 s. "Anchoveta" (Mochica)	40	10
1074	5 s. 50 "Merluza" (Chimu)	60	15
1075	8 s. 50 "Machete" (Nazca)	80	25

1971. 150th Anniv of Independence. National Heroes (3rd issue). As T **363**. Multicoloured.

No.	Description		
1076	1 s. 20 M. Melgar (postage)	10	10
1077	2 s. 50 J. Baquijano y Carrillo	15	10
1078	3 s. J. de la Riva Aguero (air)	15	10
1079	4 s. H. Unanue	15	10
1080	5 s. 50 F. J. de Luna Pizarro	25	15

366 Liberation Expedition Monument **367** R. Palma (author and poet)

1971. 150th Anniv of Independence (4th issue). As T **366**. Multicoloured.

No.	Description		
1081	1 s. 50 M. Bastidas (post.)	10	10
1082	2 s. J. F. Sanchez Carrion	10	10
1083	2 s. 50 M. J. Guise	15	10
1084	3 s. F. Vidal (air)	15	10
1085	3 s. 50 J. de San Martin	15	15
1086	4 s. 50 Type **366**	20	15
1087	6 s. "Surrender of the 'Numancia Battalion'" (horiz) (42 × 35 mm)	30	15
1088	7 s. 50 Alvarez de Arenales Monument (horiz) (42 × 39 mm)	35	20
1089	9 s. Monument to Founders of the Republic, Lima (horiz) (42 × 39 mm)	40	20
1090	10 s. "Proclamation of Independence" (horiz) (46 × 35 mm)	50	20

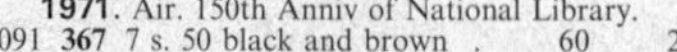

1971. Air. 150th Anniv of National Library.

No.	Type	Description		
1091	**367**	7 s. 50 black and brown	60	25

368 Weightlifting **369** "Gongora portentosa"

1971. Air. 25th World Weightlifting Championships, Huampani, Lima.

No.	Type	Description		
1092	**368**	7 s. 50 black and blue	60	25

1971. Peruvian Flora (1st series). Orchids. Mult.

No.	Description		
1093	1 s. 50 Type **369**	25	10
1094	2 s. "Odontoglossum cristatum"	30	10
1095	2 s. 50 "Mormolyca peruviana"	35	10
1096	3 s. "Trichocentrum pulchrum"	45	15
1097	3 s. 50 "Oncidium sanderae"	35	20

See also Nos. 1170/4 and 1206/10.

370 Family and Flag **371** Schooner "Sacramento" of 1821

1971. Air. 3rd Anniv of October 3rd Revolution.

No.	Type	Description		
1098	**370**	7 s. 50 black, red & blue	50	30

1971. Air. 150th Anniv of Peruvian Navy and "Order of the Peruvian Sun".

No.	Type	Description		
1100	**371**	7 s. 50 blue & lt blue	1·00	30
1101	–	7 s. 50 multicoloured	50	25

DESIGN: No. 1101, Order of the Peruvian Sun.

372 "Development and Liberation" (detail)

1971. 2nd Ministerial Meeting of "The 77" Group.

No.	Type	Description		
1102	**372**	1 s. 20 multicoloured (postage)	10	10
1103	–	3 s. 50 multicoloured	25	10
1104	–	50 s. mult (air)	2·50	1·25

DESIGNS—As Type **372**: 3 s. 50, 50 s. Detail from the painting "Development and Liberation".

373 "Plaza de Armas, 1843" (J. Rugendas)

1971. "Exfilima" Stamp Exhibition, Lima.

No.	Type	Description		
1105	**373**	3 s. black & green	30	10
1106	–	3 s. 50 black and pink	40	15

DESIGN: 3 s. 50, "Plaza de Armas, 1971" (C. Zeiter).

374 Fair Emblem **375** Army Crest

1971. Air. 7th International Pacific Fair, Lima.

No.	Type	Description		
1107	**374**	4 s. 50 multicoloured	20	15

1971. 150th Anniv of Peruvian Army.

No.	Type	Description		
1108	**375**	8 s. 50 multicoloured	60	20

376 "The Flight into Egypt"

1971. Christmas. Multicoloured.

No.	Description		
1109	1 s. 80 Type **376**	20	10
1110	2 s. 50 "The Magi"	25	10
1111	3 s. "The Nativity"	35	10

377 "Fishermen" (J. Ugarte Elespuru) **378** Chimu Idol

1971. Social Reforms. Paintings. Mulicoloured

No.	Description		
1112	3 s. 50 Type **377**	35	10
1113	4 s. "Threshing Grain in Cajamarca" (Camilo Blas)	45	10
1114	6 s. "Hand-spinning Huanca Native Women" (J. Sabogal)	60	15

1972. Peruvian Antiquities. Multicoloured.

No.	Description		
1115	3 s. 90 Type **378**	35	15
1116	4 s. Chimu statuette	35	15
1117	4 s. 50 Lambayeque idol	45	15
1118	5 s. 40 Mochica collar	55	15
1119	6 s. Lambayeque "spider" pendant	60	15

379 "Pseudopriacanthus serrula"

1972. Peruvian Fishes. Multicoloured.

No.	Description		
1120	1 s. 20 Type **379** (postage)	15	10
1121	1 s. 50 "Trachichthys mento"	15	10
1122	2 s. 50 "Trachurus symmetricus murphyi"	25	10
1123	3 s. "Pontinus furcirhinus" (air)	30	10
1124	5 s. 50 "Bodianus eclancheri"	55	15

380 "Peruvian Family" (T. Nunez Ureta)

1972. Air. Education Reforms.

No.	Type	Description		
1125	**380**	6 s. 50 multicoloured	35	20

381 Mochica Warrior **382** White-tailed Trogon

1972. Peruvian Art (1st series). Mochica Ceramics. Multicoloured.

No.	Description		
1126	1 s. 20 Type **381**	15	10
1127	1 s. 50 Warrior's head	15	10
1128	2 s. Kneeling deer	25	10
1129	2 s. 50 Warrior's head (different)	35	10
1130	3 s. Kneeling warrior	40	15

See also Nos. 1180/4.

1972. Air. Peruvian Birds. Multicoloured.

No.	Description		
1131	2 s. Type **382**	90	30
1132	2 s. 50 Amazonian umbrellabird	1·10	30
1133	3 s. Andean cock of the rock	1·25	35
1134	6 s. 50 Cuvier's toucan	2·50	65
1135	8 s. 50 Blue-crowned motmot	3·00	90

383 "The Harvest" (July) **384** "Quipu" on Map

1972. 400th Anniv of G. Poma de Ayala's "Inca Chronicles". Woodcuts.

No.	Type	Description		
1136	**383**	2 s. 50 black and red	35	10
1137	–	3 s. black and green	60	10
1138	–	2 s. 50 black and pink	30	10
1139	–	3 s. black and blue	50	10
1140	–	2 s. 50 black & orange	50	10
1141	–	3 s. black and lilac	50	10
1142	–	2 s. 50 black and brown	35	10
1143	–	3 s. black and green	50	10
1144	–	2 s. 50 black and blue	35	10
1145	–	3 s. black and orange	50	10
1146	–	2 s. 50 black & mauve	35	10
1147	–	3 s. black and yellow	50	10

DESIGNS: No. 1137, "Land Purification" (August); No. 1138, "Sowing" (September); No. 1139, "Invocation of the Rains" (October); No. 1140, "Irrigation" (November); No. 1141, "Rite of the Nobility" (December); No. 1142, "Maize Cultivation Rights" (January); No. 1143, "Ripening of the Maize" (February); No. 1144, "Birds in the Maize" (March); No. 1145, "Children as camp-guards" (April); No. 1146, "Gathering the harvest" (May); No. 1147, "Removing the harvest" (June).

1972. Air. "Exfibra 72" Stamp Exn, Rio de Janeiro.

No.	Type	Description		
1148	**384**	5 s. multicoloured	25	15

385 "The Messenger" **386** Catacaos Woman

1972. Air. Olympic Games, Munich.

No.	Type	Description		
1149	**385**	8 s. multicoloured	55	20

1972. Air. Provincial Costumes (1st series). Mult.

No.	Description		
1150	2 s. Tupe girl	15	10
1151	3 s. 50 Type **386**	30	10
1152	4 s. Conibo Indian	40	10
1153	4 s. 50 Agricultural worker playing "quena" and drum	40	15
1154	5 s. "Moche" (Trujillo) girl	40	15
1155	6 s. 50 Ocongate (Cuzco) man and woman	55	40
1156	8 s. "Chucupana" (Ayacucho) girl	60	50
1157	8 s. 50 "Cotuncha" (Junin) girl	70	55
1158	10 s. "Pandilla" dancer	60	60

See also Nos. 1248/9.

387 Ruins of Chavin (Ancash)

1972. Air. 25th Death Anniv Julio C. Tello (archaeologist). Multicoloured.

No.	Description		
1159	1 s. 50 "Stone of the 12 Angles", Cuzco (vert)	15	10
1160	3 s. 50 Type **387**	30	10
1161	4 s. Burial-tower, Sillustani (Puno) (vert)	30	10
1162	5 s. Gateway, Chavin (Ancash)	45	15
1163	8 s. "Wall of the 3 Windows", Machu Picchu (Cuzco)	55	25

388 "Territorial Waters"

1972. 4th Anniv of Armed Forces Revolution. Mult.

No.	Description		
1164	2 s. Agricultural Workers ("Agrarian Reform") (vert)	10	10
1165	2 s. 50 Type **388**	15	10
1166	3 s. Oil rigs ("Nationalisation of Petroleum Industry") (vert)	20	10

389 "The Holy Family" (wood-carving) **390** "Ipomoea purpurea"

1972. Christmas. Multicoloured.

No.	Description		
1167	1 s. 50 Type **389**	15	10
1168	2 s. "The Holy Family" (carved Huamanga stone) (horiz)	15	10
1169	2 s. 50 "The Holy Family" (carved Huamanga stone)	20	10

1972. Peruvian Flora (2nd series). Multicoloured.
1170 1 s. 50 Type **390** 15 10
1171 2 s. 50 "Amaryllis ferreyrae" 20 10
1172 3 s. "Liabum excelsum" . . . 30 10
1173 3 s. 50 "Bletia catenulata" . . 30 10
1174 5 s. "Cantua buxifolia cantuta" 35 20

391 Inca Poncho
392 Mochica Cameo and Cups

1973. Air. Ancient Inca Textiles.
1175 **391** 2 s. multicoloured . . . 15 10
1176 – 3 s. 50 multicoloured . . 25 10
1177 – 4 s. multicoloured . . . 25 10
1178 – 5 s. multicoloured . . . 30 12
1179 – 8 s. multicoloured . . . 55 25
DESIGNS: Nos. 1176/9, similar to T **391**.

1973. Air. Peruvian Art (2nd series). Jewelled Antiquities. Multicoloured.
1180 1 s. 50 Type **392** 10 10
1181 2 s. 50 Gold-plated arms and hands (Lambayeque) . . . 15 10
1182 4 s. Bronze effigy (Mochica) . 25 10
1183 5 s. Gold pendants (Nazca) . 30 15
1184 8 s. Gold cat (Mochica) . . . 60 25

393 Andean Condor
394 "The Macebearer" (J. Sabogal)

1973. Air. Fauna Protection (1st series). Mult.
1185 2 s. 50 Lesser rhea . . . . . 1·75 40
1186 3 s. 50 Giant otter 45 10
1187 4 s. Type **393** . . . . 2·25 45
1188 5 s. Vicuna 60 15
1189 6 s. Chilian flamingo . . . . 2·75 55
1190 8 s. Spectacled bear 70 25
1191 8 s. 50 Bush dog (horiz) . . . 60 25
1192 10 s. Short-tailed chinchilla (horiz) 75 30
See also Nos. 1245/6.

1973. Air. Peruvian Paintings. Multicoloured.
1193 1 s. 50 Type **394** 10 10
1194 8 s. "Yananacu Bridge" (E. C. Brent) (horiz) . . . 30 15
1195 8 s. 50 "Portrait of a Lady" (D. Hernandez) 35 15
1196 10 s. "Peruvian Birds" (T. N. Ureta) . . . . . . 3·00 50
1197 20 s. "The Potter" (F. Laso) . 1·10 40
1198 50 s. "Reed Boats" (J. V. Reinoso) (horiz) . . 2·75 1·00

395 Basketball Net and Map

1973. Air. 1st World Basketball Festival.
1199 **395** 5 s. green 35 10
1200 20 s. purple 90 40

396 "Spanish Mayor on Horseback"
398 Fair Emblem (poster)

1973. 170th Birth Anniv of Pancho Fierro (painter). Multicoloured.
1201 1 s. 50 Type **396** 10 10
1202 2 s. "Peasants" 15 10
1203 2 s. 50 "Father Abregu" . . 20 10
1204 3 s. 50 "Dancers" 30 10
1205 4 s. 50 "Esteban Arredondo on horseback" 45 20

1973. Air. Peruvian Flora (3rd series). Orchids. As T **390**. Multicoloured.
1206 1 s. 50 "Lycaste reichenbachii" 20 10
1207 2 s. 50 "Masdevallia amabilis" 30 10
1208 3 s. "Sigmatostalix peruviana" 40 10
1209 3 s. 50 "Porrogossum peruvianum" 40 10
1210 8 s. "Oncidium incarum" . . 60 25

1973. Air. 8th International Pacific Fair, Lima.
1211 **398** 8 s. red, black and grey . 60 20

399 Symbol of Flight

1973. Air. 50th Anniv of Air Force Officers' School.
1212 **399** 8 s. 50 multicoloured . . 60 15

400 "The Presentation of the Child"

1973. Christmas. Paintings of the Cuzco School. Multicoloured.
1213 1 s. 50 Type **400** 10 10
1214 2 s. "The Holy Family" (vert) 15 10
1215 2 s. 50 "The Adoration of the Kings" 15 10

401 Freighter "Ilo"

1973. Air. National Development. Multicoloured.
1216 1 s. 50 Type **401** 40 15
1217 2 s. 50 Trawlers 60 15
1218 8 s. B.A.C. One Eleven 200 airliner and seagull . . . 1·00 25

402 House of the Mulberry Tree, Arequipa

1974. Air. "Landscapes and Cities". Mult.
1219 1 s. 50 Type **402** 10 10
1220 2 s. 50 El Misti (peak), Arequipa 15 10
1221 5 s. Giant puya, Cordillera Blanca, Ancash (vert) . . 30 15
1222 6 s. Huascaran (peak), Cordillera Blanca, Ancash 35 15
1223 8 s. Lake Querococha, Cordillera Blanca, Ancash 55 20

403 Peruvian 2 c. Stamp of 1873
405 Church of San Jeronimo, Cuzco

404 Room of the Three Windows, Machu Picchu

1974. Stamp Day and 25th Anniv of Peruvian Philatelic Association.
1224 **403** 6 s. blue and grey . . . 40 15

1974. Air. Archaeological Discoveries. Mult. (a) Cuzco Relics.
1225 3 s. Type **404** 15 10
1226 5 s. Baths of Tampumacchay 25 15
1227 10 s. "Kencco" 45 25

(b) Dr. Tello's Discoveries at Chavin de Huantar. Stone carvings.
1228 3 s. Mythological jaguar . . . 15 10
1229 5 s. Rodent ("Vizcacha") . . 25 15
1230 10 s. Chavin warrior 45 25
Nos. 1228/30 are vert designs.

1974. Air. Architectural Treasures. Multicoloured.
1231 1 s. 50 Type **405** 10 10
1232 3 s. 50 Cathedral of Santa Catalina, Cajamarca . . . 20 10
1233 5 s. Church of San Pedro, Zepita, Puno (horiz) . . . 25 10
1234 6 s. Cuzco Cathedral 30 15
1235 8 s. 50 Wall of the Coricancha, Cuzco 55 20

406 "Colombia" Bridge, Tarapoto–Juanjui Highway

1974. "Structural Changes". Multicoloured.
1236 2 s. Type **406** 15 10
1237 8 s. Tayacaja hydro-electric scheme 40 20
1238 10 s. Tablachaca dam 50 25

407 "Battle of Junin" (F. Yanez)

1974. 150th Anniv of Battle of Junin.
1239 **407** 1 s. 50 mult (postage) . . 10 10
1240 2 s. 50 multicoloured . . 10 10
1241 6 s. multicoloured (air) . 30 10

408 "Battle of Ayacucho" (F. Yanez)

1974. 150th Anniv of Battle of Ayacucho.
1242 **408** 2 s. mult (postage) . . . 10 10
1243 3 s. multicoloured 15 10
1244 7 s. 50 mult (air) 45 15

1974. Air. Fauna Protection (2nd series). As T **393**. Multicoloured.
1245 8 s. Red uakari 50 15
1246 20 s. As 8 s. 85 50

409 Chimu Gold Mask

1974. Air. 8th World Mining Congress, Lima.
1247 **409** 8 s. multicoloured 45 15

1974. Air. Provincial Costumes (2nd series). As T **386**. Multicoloured.
1248 5 s. Horseman in "chalan" (Cajamarca) 35 15
1249 8 s. 50 As 5 s. 60 15

410 Pedro Paulet and Spacecraft

1974. Air. Centenary of U.P.U. and Birth Centenary of Pedro E. Paulet (aviation scientist).
1250 **410** 8 s. violet and blue . . . 40 15

411 Copper Smelter, La Oroya

1974. Expropriation of Cerro de Pasco Mining Complex.
1251 **411** 1 s. 50 blue & deep blue 10 10
1252 3 s. red and brown . . . 15 10
1253 4 s. 50 green and grey . . 25 15

412 "Capitulation of Ayacucho" (D. Hernandez)
413 "Madonna and Child"

1974. Air. 150th Anniv of Spanish Forces' Capitulation at Ayacucho.
1254 **412** 3 s. 50 multicoloured . . 20 10
1255 8 s. 50 multicoloured . . 60 20
1256 10 s. multicoloured . . . 55 25

1974. Christmas. Paintings of the Cuzco Shool. Multicoloured.
1257 1 s. 50 Type **413** (postage) . 10 10
1258 6 s. 50 "Holy Family" (air) . 30 15

414 "Andean Landscape" (T. Nunez Ureta)
415 Map and Civic Centre, Lima

1974. Air. Andean Pact Communications Ministers' Meeting, Cali, Colombia.
1259 **414** 6 s. 50 multicoloured . . 35 15

1975. Air. 2nd General Conference of U.N. Organization for Industrial Development.
1260 **415** 6 s. black, red and grey . 25 15

1975. Air. Various stamps surch.
1261 – 1 s. 50 on 3 s. 60 purple (No. 927) 10 10
1262 – 2 s. on 2 s. 60 green (No. 926) 15 10
1263 – 2 s. on 3 s. 60 purple (No. 927) 15 10
1263a – 2 s. on 3 s. 60 black and blue (No. 934) . . . 10 10
1264 – 2 s. on 4 s. 30 orange (No. 878) 10 10
1265 – 2 s. on 4 s. 30 multicoloured (No. 900) 15 10
1266 – 2 s. on 4 s. 60 orange (No. 928) 10 10
1267 – 2 s. 50 on 4 s. 60 orange (No. 928) 25 10
1268 – 3 s. on 2 s. 60 green (No. 926) 15 10
1294 – 3 s. 50 on 4 s. 60 orange (No. 928) 20 10
1269 – 4 s. on 2 s. 60 green (No. 926) 20 10
1270 – 4 s. on 3 s. 60 purple (No. 927) 20 10
1271 – 4 s. on 4 s. 60 orange (No. 928) 15 10
1295 – 4 s. 50 on 3 s. 80 orange (No. 836) 20 10
1272 – 5 s. on 3 s. 60 purple (No. 927) 20 10
1273 – 5 s. on 3 s. 80 orange (No. 836) 35 10
1296 – 5 s. on 4 s. 30 orange (No. 878) 30 10
1297 – 6 c. on 4 s. 60 orange (No. 928) 40 15
1277 **316** 6 s. on 4 s. 60 multicoloured (No. 935) 45 10
1278 – 7 s. on 4 s. 30 orange (No. 878) 40 15
1279 – 7 s. 50 on 3 s. 60 purple (No. 927) 50 15
1280 – 8 s. on 3 s. 60 purple (No. 927) 50 15
1281 **271** 10 s. on 2 s. 15 purple (No. 794) 40 25
1298 – 10 s. on 2 s. 60 green (No. 926) 60 20
1282 – 10 s. on 3 s. 60 purple (No. 927) 60 25
1283 – 10 s. on 3 s. 60 multicoloured (No. 940) 50 25
1284 – 10 s. on 4 s. 30 orange (No. 878) 25 25
1285 – 10 s. on 4 s. 60 orange (No. 928) 60 25
1286 – 20 s. on 3 s. 60 purple (No. 927) 40 15
1287 – 24 s. on 3 s. 60 multicoloured (No. 953) 1·40 45
1288 – 28 s. on 4 s. 60 multicoloured (No. 954) 85 55
1289 – 32 s. on 5 s. 60 multicoloured (No. 955) 85 65
1290 – 50 s. on 2 s. 60 green (No. 926) . . . . 2·10 1·00
1299 – 50 s. on 3 s. 60 purple (No. 927) . . . . 1·60 1·50
1292 – 100 s. on 3 s. 80 orange (No. 836) . . . . . . 1·60 1·50

417 Lima on World Map

1975. Air. Conference of Non-aligned Countries' Foreign Ministers, Lima.

1311 **417** 6 s. 50 multicoloured . . 40 15

418 Maria Parado de Bellido

1975. "Year of Peruvian Women" and International Women's Year. Multicoloured.

1312 1 s. 50 Type **418** 15 10
1313 2 s. Micaela Bastidas (vert) . 15 10
1314 2 s. 50 Juana Alarco de Dammert 20 10
1315 3 s. I.W.Y. emblem (vert) . . 35 10

419 Route Map of Flight **420** San Juan Macias

1975. Air. First "Aero–Peru" Flight, Rio de Janeiro–Lima–Los Angeles.

1316 **419** 8 s. multicoloured . . . 30 15

1975. Canonisation of St. Juan Macias.

1317 **420** 5 s. multicoloured . . . 30 10

421 Fair Poster **422** Col. F. Bolognesi

1975. Air. 9th International Pacific Fair, Lima.

1318 **421** 6 s. red, brown & black . 50 15

1975. Air. 159th Birth Anniv of Colonel Francisco Bolognesi.

1319 **422** 20 s. multicoloured . . . 65 35

423 "Nativity" **424** Louis Braille

1976. Air. Christmas (1975).

1320 **423** 6 s. multicoloured . . . 35 15

1976. 150th Anniv of Braille System for Blind.

1321 **424** 4 s. 50 red, black & grey 30 10

426 Inca Postal Runner **427** Map on Riband

1976. Air. 11th UPAE Congress, Lima.

1322 **426** 5 s. black, brown and red 50 10

1976. Air. Re-incorporation of Tacna.

1323 **427** 10 s. multicoloured . . . 30 15

428 Peruvian Flag **429** Police Badge

1976. 1st Anniv of Second Phase of Revolution.

1324 **428** 5 s. red, black and grey . 15 10

1976. Air. 54th Anniv of Peruvian Special Police.

1325 **429** 20 s. multicoloured . . . 55 40

430 "Tree of Badges" **431** Chairman Pal Losonczi

1976. Air. 10th Anniv of Bogota Declaration.

1326 **430** 10 s. multicoloured . . . 30 20

1976. Air. Visit of Hungarian Head of State.

1327 **431** 7 s. black and blue . . . 40 15

432 "St. Francis of Assisi" (El Greco) **434** "Nativity"

433 Map and National Colours

1976. 750th Death Anniv of St. Francis of Assisi.

1328 **432** 5 s. brown and gold . . 35 10

1976. Air. Meeting of Presidents of Peru and Brazil.

1329 **433** 10 s. multicoloured . . . 30 20

1976. Christmas.

1330 **434** 4 s. multicoloured . . . 30 10

435 Military Monument and Symbols

1977. Air. Army Day.

1331 **435** 20 s. black, buff and red 40 40

436 Map and Scroll **437** Printed Circuit

1977. Air. Visit of Peruvian President to Venezuela.

1332 **436** 12 s. multicoloured . . . 60 25

1977. Air. World Telecommunications Day.

1333 **437** 20 s. red, black & silver 55 40

438 Inca Postal Runner **439** Petrochemical Plant, Map and Tanker

1977.

1334 **438** 6 s. black and turquoise (postage) 40 15
1335 8 s. black and red 40 15
1336 10 s. black and blue . . . 55 25
1337 12 s. black and green . . 55 35
1338 24 s. black and red (air) . 55 50
1339 28 s. black and blue . . . 1·10 50
1340 32 s. black and brown . . 65 70

1977. Air. Bayovar Petrochemical Complex.

1341 **439** 14 s. multicoloured . . . 1·25 30

440 Arms of Arequipa **441** President Videla

1977. Air. "Gold of Peru" Exhibition, Arequipa.

1342 **440** 10 s. multicoloured . . . 20 10

1977. Air. Visit of President Videla of Argentina.

1343 **441** 36 s. multicoloured . . . 75 25

1977. Various stamps surch **FRANQUEO** and new value.

1344 **325** 6 s. on 3 s. 60 multicoloured 40 15
1345 8 s. on 3 s. 60 multicoloured 45 15
1346 – 10 s. on 5 s. 60 brown, black and red (No. 962) . . . 50 25
1347 **305** 10 s. on 50 c. black & grn 30 10
1348 20 s. on 20 c. black and red 50 20
1349 30 s. on 1 s. black and blue 70 35

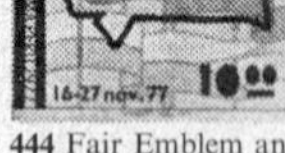

444 Fair Emblem and Flags **445** Republican Guard Badge

1977. 10th International Pacific Fair.

1350 **444** 10 s. multicoloured . . . 20 10

1977. 58th Anniv of Republican Guard.

1351 **445** 12 s. multicoloured . . . 25 15

446 Admiral Miguel Grau **447** "The Holy Family"

1977. Air. Navy Day.

1352 **446** 28 s. multicoloured . . . 35 25

1977. Christmas. Multicoloured.

1353 8 s. Type **447** (postage) . . . 10 10
1354 20s. "The adoration of the Shepherds" (air) 50 20

448 Open Book of Flags **449** Inca Head

1978. Air. 8th Meeting of Education Ministers.

1355 **448** 30 s. multicoloured . . . 40 25

1978.

1356 **449** 6 s. green (postage) . . . 10 10
1357 10 s. red 15 10
1358 16 s. brown 20 20
1359 24 s. mauve (air) 30 25
1360 30 s. pink 40 30
1361 65 s. blue 90 70
1362 95 s. blue . . . . 1·00 1·00

450 Emblem and Flags of West Germany, Argentina, Austria and Brazil

1978. World Cup Football Championship, Argentina (1st issue). Multicoloured.

1367 10 s. Type **450** 20 10
1368 10 s. Emblem and flags of Hungary, Iran, Italy and Mexico 20 10
1369 10 s. Emblem and flags of Scotland, Spain, France and Netherlands 20 10
1370 10 s. Emblem and flags of Peru, Poland, Sweden and Tunisia 20 10

See also Nos. 1412/15.

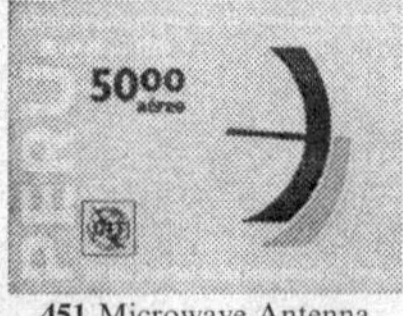

451 Microwave Antenna

1978. Air. 10th World Telecommunications Day.

1371 **451** 50 s. grey, deep blue and blue 75 50

1978. Various stamps surch **Habilitado Dif.-Porte** and value (Nos. 1372/4), **Habilitado R.D. No. 0118** and value (Nos. 1377/8, 1381, 1384, 1390) or with value only (others).

1372 **229** 2 s. on 2 c. brown (postage) 10 10
1373 4 s. on 2 c. brown . . . 10 10
1374 5 s. on 2 c. brown . . . 10 10
1375 **313** 20 s. on 1 s. 90 + 90 c. multicoloured 75 60
1376 – 30 s. on 2 s. 60 + 1 s. 30 mult (No. 917) . . . 60 60
1377 **229** 35 s. on 2 c. brown . . . 25 20
1378 50 s. on 2 c. brown . . . 1·60 1·60
1379 – 55 s. on 3 s. 60 + 1 s. 80 mult (No. 918) 85 85
1380 – 65 s. on 4 s. 60 + 2 s. 30 mult (No. 919) 85 85
1381 – 80 s. on 5 s. 60 mult (No. 960) 60 40
1382 – 85 s. on 20 s. + 10 s. mult (No. 920) . . . . . . 1·25 1·25
1383 – 25 s. on 4 s. 60 mult (No. 954) (air) 20 15
1384 **316** 34 s. on 4 s. 60 mult . . 25 15
1385 **302** 40 s. on 4 s. 30 bistre and red 50 20
1386 **449** 45 s. on 28 s. green . . . 45 25
1387 – 70 s. on 2 s. 60 green (No. 926) 50 40
1388 **449** 75 s. on 28 s. green . . . 75 40
1389 – 105 s. on 5 s. 60 mult (No. 955) . . . . 1·00 85
1390 – 110 s. on 3 s. 60 purple (No. 927) 75 60
1391 – 265 s. on 4 s. 30 mult (No. 900) . . . . 1·90 1·50

The 28 s. value as Type **449** was not issued without a surcharge.

1978. Surch **SOBRE TASA OFICIAL** and value.

1400 **229** 3 s. on 2 s. brown . . . 10 10
1401 6 s. on 2 c. brown . . . 15 10

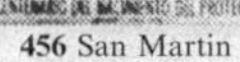

456 San Martin **457** Elmer Faucett and Stinson-Faucett F-19 and Boeing 727-200 Aircraft

1978. Air. Birth Bicentenary of General Jose de San Martin.

1410 **456** 30 s. multicoloured . . . 40 30

1978. 50th Anniv of Faucett Aviation.

1411 **457** 40 s. multicoloured . . . 50 30

1978. World Cup Football Championship, Argentina (2nd issue). Multicoloured.

1412 16 s. As Type **450** 15 10
1413 16 s. As No. 1368 . . . . . 15 10
1414 16 s. As No. 1369 . . . . . 15 10
1415 16 s. As No. 1370 . . . . . 15 10

458 Nazca Bowl

459 Peruvian Nativity

1978.

1416 **458** 16 s. blue 15 10
1417 20 s. green 15 10
1418 25 s. green 20 15
1419 35 s. red 35 15
1420 45 s. brown 40 25
1421 50 s. black 50 25
1422 55 s. mauve 50 25
1423 70 s. mauve 60 35
1424 75 s. blue 55 40
1425 80 s. brown 55 40
1426 200 s. violet . . . . . . 1·40 1·00

1978. Christmas.
1436 **459** 16 s. multicoloured . . . 15 10

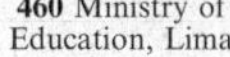
460 Ministry of Education, Lima

461 Queen Sophia and King Juan Carlos

1979. National Education.
1437 **460** 16 s. multicoloured . . . 15 10

1979. Air. Visit of King and Queen of Spain.
1438 **461** 75 s. multicoloured . . . 60 25

462 Red Cross Emblem

1979. Centenary of Peruvian Red Cross Society.
1439 **462** 16 s. multicoloured . . . 10 10

463 "Naval Battle of Iquique" (E. Velarde)

1979. Pacific War Centenary. Multicoloured.
1440 14 s. Type **463** 20 10
1441 25 s. "Col. Jose Joaquin Inclan" (vert) 30 15
1442 25 s. "Arica Blockade-runner, the Corvette "Union" . . . 40 15
1443 25 s. "Heroes of Angamos" . 40 15
1444 25 s. "Lt. Col. Pedro Ruiz Gallo" (vert) 30 15
1445 85 s. "Marshal Andres H. Caceres" (vert) 45 40
1446 100 s. "Battle of Angamos" (T. Castillo) . . . . 1·40 60
1447 100 s. "Battle of Tarapaca" . 55 45
1448 115 s. "Admiral Miguel Grau" (vert) . . . . 1·00 50
1449 200 s. "Bolognesi's Reply" (Leppiani) . . . . 3·25 2·50
1450 200 s. "Col. Francisco Bolognesi" (vert) . . . . . 1·00 85
1451 200 s. "Col. Alfonso Ugarte" (Morizani) . . . . 1·00 85
A similar 200 s. value, showing the Crypt of the Fallen was on sale for a very limited period only.

464 Billiard Balls and Cue

465 Arms of Cuzco

1979. 34th World Billiards Championship, Lima.
1456 **464** 34 s. multicoloured . . . 30 15

1979. Inca Sun Festival, Cuzco.
1457 **465** 50 s. multicoloured . . . 35 20

466 Flag and Arch

468 Exposition Emblem

1979. 50th Anniv of Re-incorporation of Tacna into Peru.
1458 **466** 16 s. multicoloured . . . 15 10

1979. Surch in figures only.
1459 **229** 7 s. on 2 c. brown . . . 10 10
1460 9 s. on 2 c. brown . . . 10 10
1461 15 s. on 2 c. brown . . 15 10

1979. 3rd World Telecommunications Exhibition, Geneva.
1467 **468** 15 s. orange, blue & grey 10 10

469 Caduceus

470 Fair Emblem on World Map

1979. Int Stomatology Congress, Lima, and 50th Anniv of Peruvian Academy of Stomatology.
1468 **469** 25 s. gold, black & turq 20 15

1979. 11th International Pacific Fair.
1469 **470** 55 s. multicoloured . . . 40 30

471 Regalia of Chimu Chief (Imperial period)

472 Angel with Lute

1979. Rafael Larco Herrera Museum of Archaeology.
1470 **471** 85 s. multicoloured . . . 60 40

1980. Christmas.
1471 **472** 25 s. multicoloured . . . 20 10

1980. Various stamps surch.
1472 **466** 20 s. on 16 s. multicoloured (postage) 15 10
1473 **463** 25 s. on 14 s. multicoloured 30 15
1474 **464** 65 s. on 34 s. multicoloured 45 35
1475 **458** 80 s. on 70 s. mauve . . 55 40
1476 **449** 35 s. on 24 s. mauve (air) 25 15
1477 **438** 45 s. on 32 s. black and brown 30 20

474 "Respect and Comply with the Constitution"

475 Ceramic Vase (Chimu Culture)

1980. Citizens' Duties.
1478 **474** 15 s. turquoise 10 10
1479 – 20 s. red 15 10
1480 – 25 s. blue 20 15
1481 – 30 s. mauve 20 15
1482 – 35 s. black 25 20
1483 – 45 s. green 30 25
1484 – 50 s. brown 35 25
INSCRIPTIONS: 20 s. "Honour your country and protect your interests"; 25 s. "Comply with the elective process"; 30 s. "Comply with your military service"; 35 s. "Pay your taxes"; 45 s. "Work and contribute to national progress"; 50 s. "Respect the rights of others".

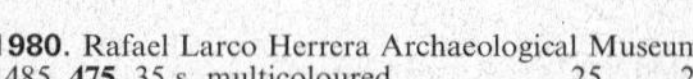
1980. Rafael Larco Herrera Archaeological Museum.
1485 **475** 35 s. multicoloured . . . 25 20

476 "Liberty" and Map of Peru

1980. Return to Democracy.
1486 **476** 25 s. black, buff and red . 20 15
1487 – 35 s. black and red . . . 25 20
DESIGN: 35 s. Handshake.

477 Machu Picchu

478 Rebellion Memorial, Cuzco (Joaquin Ugarte)

1980. World Tourism Conference, Manila.
1488 **477** 25 s. multicoloured . . . 20 15

1980. Bicentenary of Tupac Amaru Rebellion.
1489 **478** 25 s. multicoloured . . . 20 15
See also No. 1503.

479 Nativity

1980. Christmas.
1490 **479** 15 s. multicoloured . . . 10 10

480 Bolivar and Flags

482 Presidential Badge of Office, Laurel Leaves and Open Book

1981. 150th Death Anniv of Simon Bolivar.
1491 **480** 40 s. multicoloured . . . 30 20

1981. Various stamps surch.
1492 – 25 s. on 35 s. black and red (No. 1487) 20 15
1493 **482** 40 s. on 25 s. multicoloured 30 20
1494 **458** 85 s. on 200 s. violet . . 60 45
1495 – 100 s. on 115 s. mult (No. 1448) 70 50
1496 **482** 130 s. on 25 s. mult . . . 25 15
1497 140 s. on 25 s. mult . . . 25 15

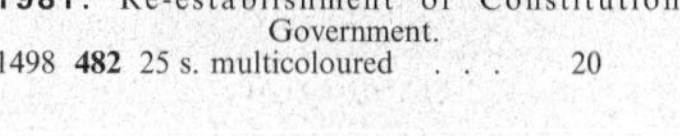
1981. Re-establishment of Constitutional Government.
1498 **482** 25 s. multicoloured . . . 20 15

483 Stone Head, Pallasca

1981.
1499 **483** 30 s. violet 20 15
1500 – 40 s. blue 30 20
1501 – 100 s. mauve 70 45
1502 – 140 s. green 95 60
DESIGNS—VERT: 40 s. Stone head, Huamachuco; 100 s. Stone head (Chavin culture). HORIZ: 140 s. Stone puma head (Chavin culture).

484 Tupac Amaru and Micaela Bastidas (sculptures by Miguel Boca Rossi)

485 Post Box, 1859

1981. Bicentenary of Revolution of Tupac Amaru and Micaela Bastidas.
1503 **484** 60 s. multicoloured . . . 40 30

1981. 50th Anniv of Postal and Philatelic Museum, Lima.
1504 **485** 130 s. multicoloured . . 50 60

486 Map of Peru and I.Y.D.P. Emblem

487 Victor Raul Haya de la Torre (President of Constitutional Assembly)

1981. International Year of Disabled Persons.
1505 **486** 100 s. violet, mauve and gold 70 45

1981. Constitution.
1506 **487** 30 s. violet and grey . . 20 15

1981. No. 801 surch.
1507 30 s. on 2 s. 20 brown & blue 20 15
1508 40 s. on 2 s. 20 brown & blue 30 20

1981. 12th International Pacific Fair. No. 801 surch with **12 Feria Internacional del Pacifico 1981 140**.
1509 140 s. on 2 s. 20 brown & blue 95 70

490 Inca Messenger (drawing by Guaman Ponce de Ayala)

493 Inca Pot

1981. Christmas.
1510 **490** 30 s. black and mauve . 20 10
1511 40 s. black and red . . . 35 10
1512 130 s. black and green . 45 35
1513 140 s. black and blue . . 45 40
1514 200 s. black and brown . 65 60

1982. Various stamps surch **Habilitado Franq. Postal** and value (Nos. 1520/1) or with value only (others).
1515 **229** 10 s. on 2 c. brown (postage) 15 10
1516 – 10 s. on 10 c. red (No. 642) 10 10
1517 **292** 40 s. on 10 c. blue and yellow 15 10
1518 **273** 70 s. on 5 c. blue and red 35 20
1519 **264a** 80 s. on 3 c. lake . . . 30 15
1520 D **109** 80 s. on 10 c. green . . 30 15
1521 O **108** 80 s. on 10 c. brown . . 30 15
1522 **292** 100 s. on 10 c. blue and yellow 40 20
1523 – 140 s. on 50 c. brown, yellow and red . . . 50 25
1524 – 140 s. on 1 s. mult . . . 50 25
1525 **264a** 150 s. on 3 c. lake . . . 40 20
1526 180 s. on 3 c. lake . . . 55 30
1527 200 s. on 3 c. lake . . . 40 40
1528 **273** 280 s. on 5 c. blue and red 60 55
1529 – 40 s. on 1 s. 25 blue and purple (No. 814) (air) 30 15
1530 – 100 s. on 2 s. 20 brown and blue (No. 801) . . . 40 20
1531 – 240 s. on 1 s. 25 blue and purple (No. 814) . . 50 60
Nos. 1523/4 are surcharged on labels for the Seventh Eucharistic Congress which previously had no postal validity.

1982. Indian Ceramics.
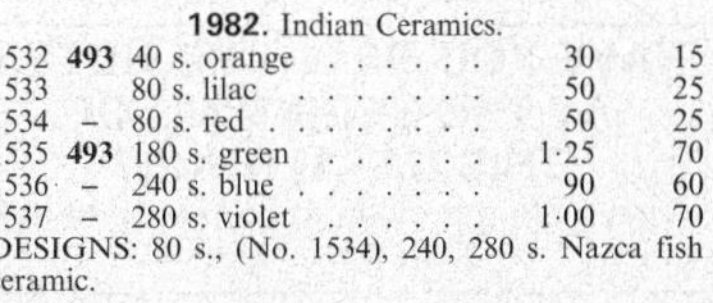
1532 **493** 40 s. orange 30 15
1533 80 s. lilac 50 25
1534 – 80 s. red 50 25
1535 **493** 180 s. green . . . . . . 1·25 70
1536 – 240 s. blue 90 60
1537 – 280 s. violet 100 70
DESIGNS: 80 s., (No. 1534), 240, 280 s. Nazca fish ceramic.

494 Jorge Basadre (after Oscar Lopez Aliaga)

1982. Jorge Basadre (historian) Commemoration.

1538 **494** 100 s. black and green . . 25 20

495 Julio C. Tello (bust, Victoria Macho)

1982. Birth Centenary of Julio C. Tello (archaeologist).

1539 **495** 200 s. green and blue . . 45 30

496 Championship Emblem **497** Disabled Person in Wheelchair

1982. 9th World Women's Volleyball Championship, Peru.

1540 **496** 80 s. red and black . . . 20 15

1982. Rights for the Disabled Year.

1541 **497** 200 s. blue and red . . . 50 30

498 Andres A. Caceres Medallion

1982. Centenary of Brena Campaign.

1542 **498** 70 s. brown and grey . . 20 15

499 Footballers **500** Congress Emblem

1982. World Cup Football Championship, Spain.

1543 **499** 80 s. multicoloured . . . 20 15

1982. 16th Int Latin Notaries Congress, Lima.

1544 **500** 500 s. black, gold and red 75 50

501 Bull (clay jar) **502** Pedro Vilcapaza

1982. Handicrafts Year.

1545 **501** 200 s. red, brown and black 50 30

1982. Death Bicentenary of Pedro Vilcapaza (Indian leader).

1546 **502** 240 s. brown and black . 35 35

503 Jose Davila Condemarin (after J. Y. Pastor) **504** "Nativity" (Hilario Mendivil)

1982. Death Centenary of Jose Davila Condemarin (Director General of Posts).

1547 **503** 150 s. black and blue . . 40 25

1982. Christmas.

1548 **504** 280 s. multicoloured . . 40 30

505 Centre Emblem and Hand holding Potatoes

1982. 10th Anniv of International Potato Centre.

1549 **505** 240 s. brown and grey . 35 35

506 Arms of Piura

1982. 450th Anniv of San Miguel de Piura.

1550 **506** 280 s. multicoloured . . 40 40

507 Microscope

1982. Centenary of Discovery of Tubercule Bacillus.

1551 **507** 240 s. green 35 35

508 "St. Theresa of Avila" (Jose Espinoza de los Monteros) **509** Civil Defence Badge and Interlocked Hands

1983. 400th Death Anniv of St. Theresa of Avila.

1552 **508** 100 s. multicoloured . . 25 15

1983. 10th Anniv of Civil Defence System.

1553 **509** 100 s. blue, orange & blk 25 15

510 Silver Shoe

1983. "Peru, Land of Silver".

1554 **510** 250 s. silver, black & bl . 55 35

511 Map of Signatories and 200 Mile Zone

1983. 30th Anniv of Santiago Declaration.

1555 **511** 280 s. brown, blue & blk 40 40

512 Boeing 747-200 **513** "75"

1983. 25th Anniv of Lima-Bogota Airmail Service.

1556 **512** 150 s. multicoloured . . . 60 25

1983. 75th Anniv of Lima and Callao State Lotteries.

1557 **513** 100 s. blue and purple . . 20 15

514 Cruiser "Almirante Grau"

1983. Peruvian Navy. Multicoloured.

1558 150 s. Type **514** 75 20

1559 350 s. Submarine "Ferre" . . 1·00 50

1983. Various stamps surch.

1560 **493** 100 s. on 40 s. orange . . 20 15

1561 **498** 100 s. on 70 s. brown and grey 20 15

1562 **496** 100 s. on 80 s. red and black 20 15

1563 **502** 100 s. on 240 s. brown and black 20 15

1564 **505** 100 s. on 240 s. ochre, deep brown and brown . . . 20 15

1565 **507** 100 s. on 240 s. green . . 20 15

1566 **506** 150 s. on 280 s. mult . . 30 15

1567 **511** 150 s. on 280 s. brown, blue and black 30 15

1568 **504** 200 s. on 280 s. mult . . 40 25

1569 **493** 300 s. on 180 s. green . . 55 35

1570 400 s. on 180 s. green . . 75 50

1571 **499** 500 s. on 80 s. mult . . . 95 65

516 Simon Bolivar **517** "Virgin and Child" (Cuzquena School)

1983. Birth Bicentenary of Simon Bolivar.

1572 **516** 100 s. blue and black . . 20 15

1983. Christmas.

1573 **517** 100 s. multicoloured . . . 20 10

518 Fair Emblem **519** W.C.Y. Emblem

1983. 14th International Pacific Fair.

1574 **518** 350 s. multicoloured . . . 65 40

1984. World Communications Year.

1575 **519** 700 s. multicoloured . . . 1·00 70

520 Leoncio Prado **521** Container Ship at Wharf

1984. Death Centenary (1983) of Colonel Leoncio Prado.

1576 **520** 150 s. bistre and brown . 15 10

1984. Peruvian Industry.

1577 **521** 200 s. purple 40 25

1578 – 300 s. blue 60 25

DESIGN: 300 s. Container ship.

522 Ricardo Palma **523** Pistol Shooting

1984. 150th Birth Anniv (1983) of Ricardo Palma (writer).

1579 **522** 200 s. violet 15 10

1984. Olympic Games, Los Angeles.

1580 **523** 500 s. mauve and black . 45 25

1581 – 750 s. red and black . . 60 30

DESIGN: 750 s. Hurdling.

524 Arms of Callao **525** Water Jar

1984. Town Arms.

1582 **524** 350 s. grey 25 15

1583 – 400 s. brown 30 25

1584 – 500 s. brown 40 30

DESIGNS: 400 s. Cajamarca; 500 s. Ayacucho.

1984. Wari Ceramics (1st series).

1585 **525** 100 s. brown 10 10

1586 – 150 s. brown 15 10

1587 – 200 s. brown 20 10

DESIGNS: 150 s. Llama; 200 s. Vase.

See also Nos. 1616/18.

526 Hendee's Woolly Monkeys **527** Signing Declaration of Independence

1984. Fauna.

1588 **526** 1000 s. multicoloured . . 45 40

1984. Declaration of Independence.

1589 **527** 350 s. black, brown & red 25 15

528 General Post Office, Lima **529** "Canna edulis"

1984. Postal Services.

1590 **528** 50 s. olive 10 10

1984. Flora.

1591 **529** 700 s. multicoloured . . 45 25

530 Grau (after Pablo Muniz) **531** Hipolito Unanue

1984. 150th Anniv of Admiral Miguel Grau. Mult.

1592 600 s. Type **530** 35 20

1593 600 s. Battle of Angamos (45 × 35 mm) 70 30

1594 600 s. Grau's seat, National Congress 35 20

1595 600 s. "Battle of Iquique" (Guillermo Spier) (45 × 35 mm) 70 30

1984. 150th Death Anniv (1983) of Hipolito Unanue (founder of School of Medicine).

1596 **531** 50 s. green 10 10

532 Destroyer "Almirante Guise"

1984. Peruvian Navy.
1597 **532** 250 s. blue 25 15
1598 – 400 s. turquoise & blue . 55 20
DESIGN: 400 s. River gunboat "America".

533 "The Adoration of the Shepherds" **534** Belaunde

1984. Christmas.
1599 **533** 1000 s. multicoloured . . 40 15

1984. Birth Centenary (1983) of Victor Andres Belaunde (diplomat).
1600 **534** 100 s. purple 15 10

535 Street in Cuzco **536** Fair Emblem

1984. 450th Anniv of Founding of Cuzco by the Spanish.
1601 **535** 1000 s. multicoloured . . 40 25

1984. 15th International Pacific Fair, Lima.
1602 **536** 1000 s. blue and red . . 40 25

537 "Foundation of Lima" (Francisco Gonzalez Gamarra) **538** Pope John Paul II

1985. 450th Anniv of Lima.
1603 **537** 1500 s. multicoloured . . 55 30

1985. Papal Visit.
1604 **538** 2000 s. multicoloured . . . 45 35

539 Dish Aerial, Huancayo **540** Jose Carlos Mariategui

1985. 15th Anniv (1984) of Entel Peru (National Telecommunications Enterprise).
1605 **539** 1100 s. multicoloured . . 25 15

1985. 60th Death Anniv (1984) of Jose Carlos Mariategui (writer).
1606 **540** 800 s. red 20 15

541 Emblem

1985. 25th Meeting of American Airforces Co-operation System.
1607 **541** 400 s. multicoloured . . 15 10

542 Captain Quinones

1985. 44th Death Anniv of Jose Abelardo Quinones Gonzales (airforce captain).
1608 **542** 1000 s. multicoloured . 25 15

543 Arms of Huancavelica **544** Globe and Emblem

1985.
1609 **543** 700 s. orange 15 15
See also Nos. 1628/9.

1985. 14th Latin-American Air and Space Regulations Days, Lima.
1610 **544** 900 s. blue 25 15

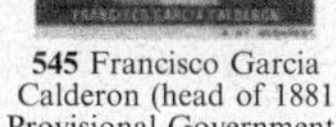

545 Francisco Garcia Calderon (head of 1881 Provisional Government) **546** Cross, Flag and Map

1985. Personalities.
1611 **545** 500 s. green 20 10
1612 – 800 s. green 35 15
DESIGN: 800 s. Oscar Miro Quesada (philosopher and jurist).

1985. 1st Anniv of Constitucion City.
1613 **546** 300 s. multicoloured . . 15 10

547 General Post Office Lima **548** Society Emblem, Satellite and Radio Equipment

1985. Postal Services.
1614 **547** 200 s. grey 10 10

1985. 55th Anniv of Peruvian Radio Club.
1615 **548** 1300 s. blue and orange 35 20

549 Robles Moqo Style Cat Vase **550** St. Francis's Monastry, Lima

1985. Wari Ceramics (2nd series).
1616 **549** 500 s. brown 15 10
1617 – 500 s. brown 15 10
1618 – 500 s. brown 15 10
DESIGNS: No. 1617, Cat, Huaura Style; No. 1618, Llama's head, Robles Moqo style.

1985. Tourism Day.
1619 **550** 1300 s. multicoloured . 30 15

551 Title Page of "Doctrina Christiana" **552** Emblem and Curtiss "Jenny" Airplane

1985. 400th Anniv of First Book printed in South America.
1620 **551** 300 s. black and stone . . 15 10

1985. 40th Anniv of I.C.A.O.
1621 **552** 1100 s. black, blue & red 40 15

553 Humboldt Penguin **554** "Virgin and Child" (Cuzquena School)

1985. Fauna.
1622 **553** 1500 s. multicoloured . . 1·75 55

1985. Christmas.
1623 **554** 2 i. 50 multicoloured . . 20 10

555 Postman lifting Child **556** Cesar Vallejo

1985. Postal Workers' Christmas and Children's Restaurant Funds.
1624 **555** 2 i. 50 multicoloured . . 30 20

1986. Poets.
1625 **556** 800 s. blue 20 10
1626 – 800 s. brown 20 10
DESIGN: No. 1626, Jose Santos Chocano.

557 Arms

1986. 450th Anniv of Trujillo.
1627 **557** 3 i. multicoloured 30 15

1986. Town Arms. As T **543**.
1628 700 s. blue 15 10
1629 900 s. brown 25 15
DESIGNS: 700 s. Huanuco; 900 s. Puno.

558 Stone Carving of Fish **559** "Hymenocallis amancaes"

1986. Restoration of Chan-Chan.
1630 **558** 50 c. multicoloured . . . 10 10

1986. Flora.
1631 **559** 1100 s. multicoloured . . 25 15

560 Alpaca and Textiles **561** St. Rosa de Lima (Daniel Hernandez)

1986. Peruvian Industry.
1632 **560** 1100 s. multicoloured . . 25 15

1986. 400th Birth Anniv of St. Rosa de Lima.
1633 **561** 7 i. multicoloured . . . 70 40

562 Daniel Alcides Carrion **563** Emblems and "16"

1986. Death Centenary (1985) of Daniel Alcides Carrion.
1634 **562** 50 c. brown 10 10

1986. 16th International Pacific Fair, Lima.
1635 **563** 1 i. multicoloured . . . 10 10

564 Woman Handspinning and Boy in Reed Canoe **565** Pedro Vilcapaza

1986. International Youth Year.
1636 **564** 3 i. 50 multicoloured . . 55 20

1986. 205th Anniv of Vilcapaza Rebellion.
1637 **565** 50 c. brown 10 10

566 U.N. Building, New York **567** Fernando and Justo Albujar Fayaque and Manuel Guarniz

1986. 40th Anniv (1985) of U.N.O.
1638 **566** 3 i. 50 multicoloured . . 30 20

1986. National Heroes.
1639 **567** 50 c. brown 10 10

568 Nasturtium **569** Submarine "Casma (R-1)", 1926

1986. Flora.
1640 **568** 80 c. multicoloured . . . 10 10

1986. Peruvian Navy. Each blue.
1641 1 i. 50 Type **569** 45 15
1642 2 i. 50 Submarine "Abtao", 1954 . . . . 80 25

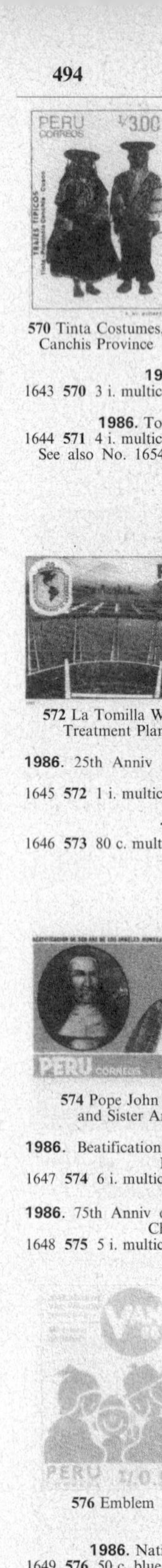

570 Tinta Costumes, Canchis Province **571** Sacsayhuaman Fort, Cuzco

1986. Costumes.
1643 **570** 3 i. multicoloured 30 20

1986. Tourism Day (1st issue).
1644 **571** 4 i. multicoloured 40 30
See also No. 1654.

572 La Tomilla Water Treatment Plant **573** "Datura candida"

1986. 25th Anniv of Inter-American Development Bank.
1645 **572** 1 i. multicoloured 10 10

1986. Flora.
1646 **573** 80 c. multicoloured . . . 10 10

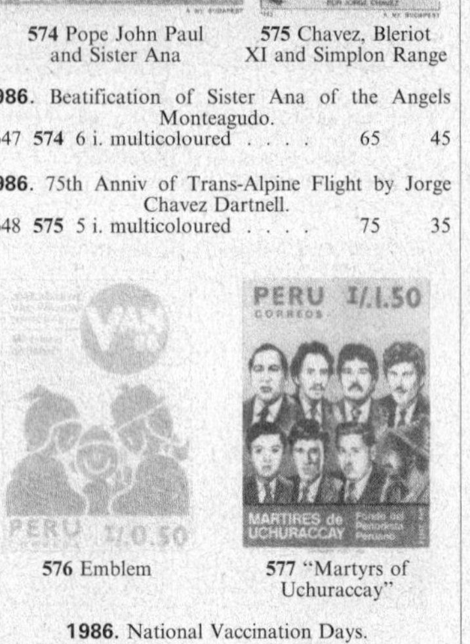

574 Pope John Paul and Sister Ana **575** Chavez, Bleriot XI and Simplon Range

1986. Beatification of Sister Ana of the Angels Monteagudo.
1647 **574** 6 i. multicoloured 65 45

1986. 75th Anniv of Trans-Alpine Flight by Jorge Chavez Dartnell.
1648 **575** 5 i. multicoloured 75 35

576 Emblem **577** "Martyrs of Uchuraccay"

1986. National Vaccination Days.
1649 **576** 50 c. blue 10 10

1986. Peruvian Journalists' Fund.
1650 **577** 1 i. 50 black and blue . . 15 10

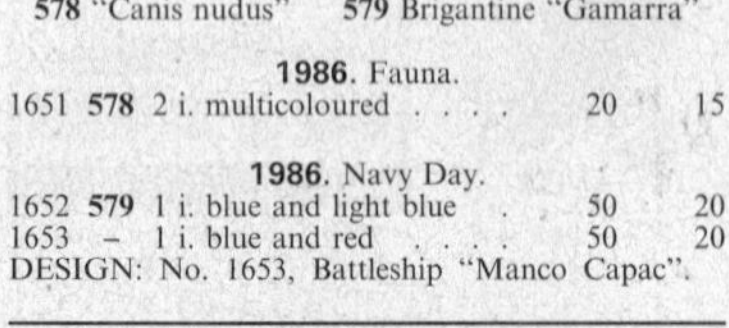

578 "Canis nudus" **579** Brigantine "Gamarra"

1986. Fauna.
1651 **578** 2 i. multicoloured 20 15

1986. Navy Day.
1652 **579** 1 i. blue and light blue . . 50 20
1653 – 1 i. blue and red 50 20
DESIGN: No. 1653, Battleship "Manco Capac".

580 Intihuatana Cuzco

1986. Tourism Day (2nd issue).
1654 **580** 4 i. multicoloured . . . 40 30

581 Institute Building

1986. 35th Anniv (1985) of Institute of Higher Military Studies.
1655 **581** 1 i. multicoloured . . . 15 10

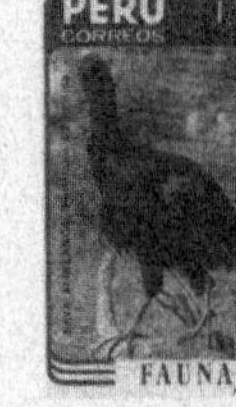

582 Children **583** White-winged Guan

1986. Postal Workers' Christmas and Children's Restaurant Funds.
1656 **582** 2 i. 50 black and brown 30 20

1986. Fauna.
1657 **583** 2 i. multicoloured . . . 1·75 30

584 Galvez **585** "St. Joseph and Child" (Cuzquena School)

1986. Birth Centenary (1985) of Jose Galvez Barrenechea (poet).
1658 **584** 50 c. brown 10 10

1986. Christmas.
1659 **585** 5 i. multicoloured . . . 50 30

586 Flags, and Hands holding Cogwheel **587** Shipibo Costumes

1986. 25th Anniv of "Senati" (National Industrial Training Organization).
1660 **586** 4 i. multicoloured . . . 40 30

1987. Christmas.
1661 **587** 3 i. multicoloured . . . 30 25

588 Harvesting Mashua **589** Dr. Reiche and Diagram of Nazca Lines

1987. World Food Day.
1662 **588** 50 c. multicoloured . . 10 10

1987. Dr. Maria Reiche (Nazca Lines researcher).
1663 **589** 8 i. multicoloured . . . 80 60

590 Santos **591** Show Jumping

1987. Mariano Santos (Hero of War of the Pacific).
1664 **590** 50 c. violet 10 10

1987. 50th Anniv of Peruvian Horse Club.
1665 **591** 3 i. multicoloured 30 25

592 Salaverry

1987. 150th Death Anniv (1986) of General Felipe Santiago Salaverry (President, 1835–36).
1666 **592** 2 i. multicoloured 20 15

593 Colca Canyon **594** 1857 1 & 2 r. Stamps

1987. "Arequipa 87" National Stamp Exhibition.
1667 **593** 6 i. multicoloured 50 30

1987. "Amifil 87" National Stamp Exhibition, Lima.
1668 **594** 1 i. brown, blue and grey 10 10

595 Arguedas **596** Carving, Emblem and Nasturtium

1987. 75th Birth Anniv (1986) of Jose Maria Arguedas (writer).
1669 **595** 50 c. brown 10 10

1987. Centenary of Arequipa Chamber of Commerce and Industry.
1670 **596** 2 i. multicoloured 20 15

597 Vaccinating Child **598** De la Riva Aguero

1987. Child Vaccination Campaign.
1671 **597** 50 c. red 10 10

1987. Birth Centenary (1985) of Jose de la Riva Aguero (historian).
1672 **598** 80 c. brown 10 10

599 Porras Barrenechea **600** Footballers

1987. 90th Birth Anniv of Raul Porras Barrenechea (historian).
1673 **599** 80 c. brown 10 10

1987. World Cup Football Championship, Mexico (1986).
1674 **600** 4 i. multicoloured . . . 20 15

601 Stone Carving of Man

1987. Restoration of Chan-Chan.
1675 **601** 50 c. multicoloured . . . 10 10

602 Comet and "Giotto" Space Probe

1987. Appearance of Halley's Comet (1986).
1676 **602** 4 i. multicoloured . . . 20 15

603 Chavez **604** Osambela Palace

1987. Birth Centenary of Jorge Chavez Dartnell (aviator).
1677 **603** 2 i. brown, ochre & gold 10 10

1987. 450th Birth Anniv of Lima.
1678 **604** 2 i. 50 multicoloured . . 15 10

605 Machu Picchu

1987. 75th Anniv (1986) of Discovery of Machu Picchu.
1679 **605** 9 i. multicoloured . . . 40 30

606 St. Francis's Church

1987. Cajamarca, American Historical and Cultural Site.
1680 **606** 2 i. multicoloured . . . 10 10

607 National Team, Emblem and Olympic Rings

1988. 50th Anniv (1986) of First Peruvian Participation in Olympic Games (at Berlin).
1681 **607** 1 i. 50 multicoloured . . 10 10

608 Children

1988. 150th Anniv of Ministry of Education.
1682 **608** 1 i. multicoloured 10 10

609 Statue and Pope

1988. Coronation of Virgin of Evangelization, Lima.
1683 **609** 10 i. multicoloured . . . 40 30

610 Emblems

611 Postman and Lima Cathedral

1988. Rotary International Anti-Polio Campaign.
1684 **610** 2 i. blue, gold and red . . 10 10

1988. Postal Workers' Christmas and Children's Restaurant Funds.
1685 **611** 9 i. blue 30 20

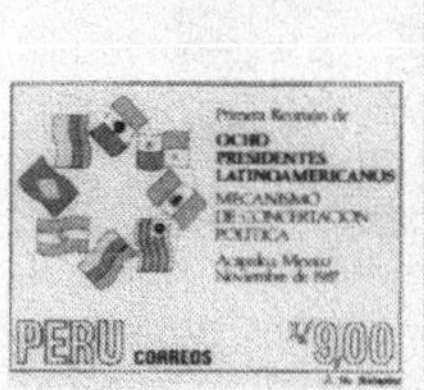

612 Flags

613 St. John Bosco

1988. 1st Meeting of Eight Latin American Presidents of Contadora and Lima Groups, Acapulco, Mexico.
1686 **612** 9 i. multicoloured 30 20

1988. Death Centenary of St. John Bosco (founder of Salesian Brothers).
1687 **613** 5 i. multicoloured 20 15

614 Supply Ship "Humboldt" and Globe

1988. 1st Peruvian Scientific Expedition to Antarctica.
1688 **614** 7 i. multicoloured 70 20

615 Clay Wall

1988. Restoration of Chan-Chan.
1689 **615** 4 i. brown and black . . 15 10

616 Vallejo (after Picasso)

617 Journalists at Work

1988. 50th Death Anniv of Cesar Vallejo (poet).
1690 **616** 25 i. black, yellow & brn 50 40

1988. Peruvian Journalists' Fund.
1691 **617** 4 i. blue and brown . . . 10 10

618 1908 2 s. Columbus Monument Stamp

619 "17" and Guanaco

1988. "Exfilima 88" Stamp Exhibition, Lima, and 500th Anniv of Discovery of America by Christopher Columbus.
1692 **618** 20 i. blue, pink & black 20 10

1988. 17th International Pacific Fair, Lima.
1693 **619** 4 i. multicoloured . . . 10 10

620 "Village Band"

621 Dogs

1988. Birth Centenary of Jose Sabogal (painter).
1694 **620** 12 i. multicoloured . . . 15 10

1988. "Canino '88" International Dog Show, Lima.
1695 **621** 20 i. multicoloured . . . 20 10

622 Silva and Score of "Splendour of Flowers"

623 Pope

1988. 50th Death Anniv (1987) of Alfonso de Silva (composer).
1696 **622** 20 i. grey, deep brown and brown 20 10

1988. 2nd Visit of Pope John Paul II.
1697 **623** 50 i. multicoloured . . . 35 25

624 Volleyball

625 Volleyball

1988. Olympic Games, Seoul.
1698 **624** 25 i. multicoloured . . . 20 10

1988. Postal Workers' Christmas and Children's Restaurant Funds. Unissued stamp surch as in T **625**.
1699 **625** 95 i. on 300 s. black and red 60 50

626 Ceramic Vase

627 Map

1988. Chavin Culture. Unissued stamps surch as in T **626**.
1700 **626** 40 i. on 100 s. red . . . 30 20
1701 80 i. on 10 s. black . . . 25 15

1989. Forest Boundary Road. Unissued stamp surch as in T **627**.
1702 **627** 70 i. on 80 s. green, black and blue 40 30

628 Arm

629 Huari Weaving

1989. Laws of the Indies. Unissued stamp surch as in T **628**.
1703 **628** 230 i. on 300 s. brown . . 40 15

1989. Centenary of Credit Bank of Peru.
1704 **629** 500 i. multicoloured . . . 60 20

630 Special Postal Services Emblem

631 Newspaper Offices

1989. Postal Services.
1705 **630** 50 i. blue and green . . . 10 10
1706 – 100 i. red and pink . . . 10 10
DESIGN: 100 i. National Express Post emblem.

1989. 150th Anniv of "El Comercio" (newspaper).
1707 **631** 600 i. multicoloured . . . 50 10

632 Garcilaso de la Vega

1989. 450th Birth Anniv of Garcilaso de la Vega (writer).
1708 **632** 300 i. multicoloured . . . 10 10

633 Emblem

1989. Express Mail Service.
1709 **633** 100 i. red, blue & orange 10 10

634 Dr. Luis Loli Roca (founder of Journalists' Federation)

1989. Peruvian Journalists' Fund.
1710 **634** 100 i. blue, deep blue and black 10 10

635 Relief of Birds

1989. Restoration of Chan-Chan.
1711 **635** 400 i. multicoloured . . . 35 10

636 Old Map of South America

1989. Centenary of Lima Geographical Society.
1712 **636** 600 i. multicoloured . . 95 20

637 Painting

1989. 132nd Anniv of Society of Founders of Independence.
1713 **637** 300 i. multicoloured . . 10 10

638 Lake Huacachina

1989. 3rd Meeting of Latin American Presidents of Contadora and Lima Groups, Ica.
1714 **638** 1300 i. multicoloured . . 1·10 60

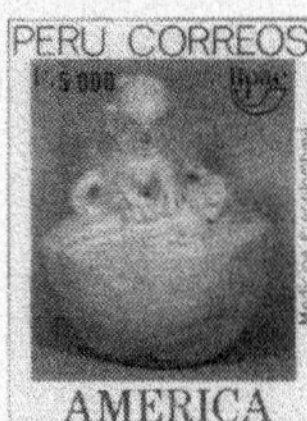

639 Children buying Stamps for Commemorative Envelopes

641 Vessel with Figure of Doctor examining Patient

640 "Corryocactus huincoensis"

1989. Postal Workers' Christmas and Children's Restaurant Funds.
1715 **639** 1200 i. multicoloured . . 30 20

1989. Cacti. Multicoloured.
1716 500 i. Type **640** 15 10
1717 500 i. "Haagocereus clavispinus" (vert) 15 10
1718 500 i. "Loxanthocereus acanthurus" 15 10
1719 500 i. "Matucana cereoides" (vert) 15 10
1720 500 i. "Trichocereus peruvianus" (vert) 15 10

1989. America. Pre-Columbian Ceramics. Mult.
1721 5000 i. Type **641** . . . . . . 1·60 1·00
1722 5000 i. Vessel with figure of surgeon performing cranial operation . . . . 1·60 1·00

642 Bethlehem Church

1990. Cajamarca, American Historical and Cultural Site.
1723 **642** 600 i. multicoloured . . 15 10

643 Climber in Andes

644 Pope and Virgin of Evangelization

1990. Huascaran National Park. Multicoloured.

1724 900 i. Type **643** 20 15
1725 900 i. Llanganuco Lake (horiz) 20 15
1726 1000 i. "Puya raimondi" (plant) 25 20
1727 1000 i. Snow-covered mountain peak (horiz) 25 20
1728 1100 i. Huascaran Mountain (horiz) 30 25
1729 1100 i. Andean condor over mountain slopes (horiz) . . 1·00 55

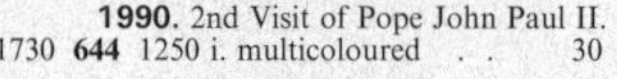

1990. 2nd Visit of Pope John Paul II.

1730 **644** 1250 i. multicoloured . . 30 25

645 "Agrias beata" (female)

1990. Butterflies. Multicoloured.

1731 1000 i. Type **645** 35 25
1732 1000 i. "Agrias beata" (male) 35 25
1733 1000 i. "Agrias amydon" (female) 35 25
1734 1000 i. "Agrias sardanapalus" (female) 35 25
1735 1000 i. "Agrias sardanapalus" (male) 35 25

646 Victor Raul Haya de la Torre (President of Constituent Assembly)

647 Emblem

1990. 10th Anniv of Political Constitution.

1736 **646** 2100 i. multicoloured . . 45 10

1990. 40th Anniv of Peruvian Philatelic Association.

1737 **647** 300 i. brown, blk & cream 10 10

648 Globe and Exhibition Emblem

1990. "Prenfil '88" International Philatelic Literature Exhibition, Buenos Aires.

1738 **648** 300 i. multicoloured . . . 10 10

649 "Republic" (Antoine-Jean Gros)

1990. Bicentenary of French Revolution. Paintings. Multicoloured.

1739 2000 i. Type **649** 40 10
1740 2000 i. "Storming the Bastille" (Hubert Robert) 40 10
1741 2000 i. "Lafayette at the Festival of the Republic" (anon) 40 10
1742 2000 i. "Jean Jacques Rousseau and Symbols of the Revolution" (E. Jeaurat) . 40 10

650 "Founding Arequipa" (Teodoro Nunez Ureta)

1990. 450th Anniv of Arequipa.

1734 **650** 50000 i. multicoloured . 10 10

651 Pelado Island Lighthouse

1990. Peruvian Navy. Unissued stamps, each light blue and blue, surch as in T **651**.

1744 110000 i. on 200 i. Type **651** 40 25
1745 230000 i. on 400 i. "Morona" (hospital ship) . . . . . . 1·25 60

652 Games Mascot

653 1857 1 r. Stamp and Container Ship

1990. 4th South American Games (1st issue). Multicoloured.

1746 110000 i. Type **652** 25 20
1747 280000 i. Shooting . . . . . 1·10 60
1748 290000 i. Athletics (horiz) . 1·25 65
1749 300000 i. Football . . . . . 1·25 65

See also Nos. 1753/6.

1990. 150th Anniv of Pacific Steam Navigation Company. Multicoloured. Self-adhesive.

1750 250000 i. Type **653** . . . . . 1·25 65
1751 350000 i. 1857 2 r. stamp and container ship . . . . . . 1·75 85

654 Postal Van

1990. Postal Workers' Christmas and Children's Restaurant Funds.

1752 **654** 310000 i. multicoloured . 75 70

1991. 4th South American Games (2nd issue). As T **652**. Multicoloured.

1753 560000 i. Swimming . . . . 1·90 1·10
1754 580000 i. Show jumping (vert) 2·00 1·25
1755 600000 i. Yachting (vert) . . 2·50 1·40
1756 620000 i. Tennis (vert) . . . 2·10 1·40

655 Maria Jesus Castaneda de Pardo

1991. Red Cross. Unissued stamp surch.

1757 **655** 0.15 i/m. on 2500 i. red . 50 25

Note. "i/m" on No. 1757 onwards indicates face value in million intis.

656 Adelie Penguins, Scientist and Station

1991. 2nd Peruvian Scientific Expedition to Antarctica. Unissued stamps surch. Multicoloured.

1758 0.40 i/m. on 50000 i. Type **656** 50 20
1759 0.45 i/m. on 80000 i. Station and Pomarine skua 50 20
1760 0.50 i/m. on 100000 i. Whale, map and station . . . . . 1·60 10

657 "Siphoonandra elliptica" (plant No. 1 in University herbarium)

658 "Virgin of the Milk"

1991. 300th Anniv of National University of St. Anthony Abad del Cusco. Multicoloured.

1761 10 c. Type **657** 15 10
1762 20 c. Bishop Manuel de Mollinedo y Angulo (first Chancellor) 25 20
1763 1 s. University arms . . . . . 2·00 1·00

1991. Postal Workers' Christmas and Children's Restaurant Funds. Paintings by unknown artists. Multicoloured.

1764 70 c. Type **658** . . . . 1·25 10
1765 70 c. "Divine Shepherdess" . 1·25 10

659 Lake

1991. America (1990). The Natural World. Mult.

1766 0.50 i/m. Type **659** 90 10
1767 0.50 i/m. Waterfall (vert) . . 90 10

660 Sir Rowland Hill and Penny Black

1992. 150th Anniv (1990) of the Penny Black.

1768 **660** 0.40 i/m. black, grey & bl 70 10

661 Arms and College

662 Arms

1992. 150th Anniv (1990) of Our Lady of Guadalupe College.

1769 **661** 0.30 i/m. multicoloured . . 55 10

1992. 80th Anniv (1991) of Entre Nous Society, Lima (literature society for women).

1770 **662** 10 c. multicoloured . . . 10 10

663 Map

1992. Bolivia–Peru Presidential Meeting, Ilo.

1771 **663** 20 c. multicoloured . . . 15 10

664 Tacaynamo Idol

665 Raimondi

1992. Restoration of Chan-Chan.

1772 **664** 0.15 i/m. multicoloured . 10 10

See note below No. 1757.

1992. Death Centenary of Jose Antonio Raimondi (naturalist).

1773 **665** 0.30 i/m. multicoloured . 25 20

See note below No. 1757.

666 First Issue

1992. Bicentenary (1990) of "Diario de Lima" (newspaper).

1774 **666** 35 c. black and yellow . 35 15

667 Melgar

1992. Birth Bicentenary (1990) of Mariano Melgar (poet).

1775 **667** 60 c. multicoloured . . . 50 25

668 1568 Eight Silver Reales Coin

1992. First Peruvian Coinage.

1776 **668** 70 c. multicoloured . . . 70 35

669 Emblem

1992. 75th Anniv of Catholic University of Peru.

1777 **669** 90 c. black and stone . . 70 35

670 Emblem

672 "Virgin of the Spindle" (painting, Santa Clara Monastery, Cuzco)

1992. 90th Anniv of Pan-American Health Organization. Self-adhesive. Imperf.

1778 **670** 3 s. multicoloured . . . 3·00 1·10

1992. Various stamps surch.

1779 – 40 c. on 500 i. multicoloured (1717) . 30 15
1780 – 40 c. on 500 i. multicoloured (1718) . 30 15
1781 – 40 c. on 500 i. multicoloured (1719) . 30 15
1782 – 40 c. on 500 i. multicoloured (1720) . 30 15

1783 **493** 50 c. on 180 s. green . . 40 20
1784 **648** 50 c. on 300 i. mult . . . 40 20
1785 **645** 50 c. on 1000 i. mult . . 40 20
1786 – 50 c. on 1000 i. mult (1732) 40 20
1787 – 50 c. on 1000 i. mult (1733) 40 20
1788 – 50 c. on 1000 i. mult (1734) 40 20
1789 – 50 c. on 1000 i. mult (1735) 40 20
1790 **647** 1 s. on 300 i. brown, black and cream 80 40
1791 **644** 1 s. on 1250 i. mult . . . 80 40
1792 **638** 1 s. on 1300 i. mult . . . 80 40

1993. Self-adhesive. Imperf.
1793 **672** 80 c. multicoloured . . . 65 30

673 Gold Figures

1993. Sican Culture (1st series). Multicoloured. Self-adhesive. Imperf.
1794 2 s. Type **673** . . . . 2·75 80
1795 5 s. Gold foil figure (vert) . . 5·00 2·00
See also Nos. 1814/15.

674 Incan Gold Decoration and Crucifix on Chancay Robe

1993. 500th Anniv of Evangelization of Peru.
1796 **674** 1 s. multicoloured . . . 80 40

675 "The Marinera" (Monica Rojas)
676 "Madonna and Child" (statue)

1993. Paintings of Traditional Scenes. Multicoloured. Self-adhesive. Imperf.
1797 1 s. 50 Type **675** . . . . . . 1·50 60
1798 1 s. 50 "Fruit Sellers" (Angel Chavez) . . . . 1·50 60

1993. Centenary (1991) of Salesian Brothers in Peru. Self-adhesive. Imperf.
1799 **676** 70 c. multicoloured . . . 95 25

677 Francisco Pizarro and Spanish Galleon

1993. America (1991). Voyages of Discovery. Multicoloured.
1800 90 c. Type **677** 95 25
1801 1 s. Spanish galleon and route map of Pizarros' second voyage . . . . 1·00 30
Nos. 1800/1 were issued together, se-tenant, forming a composite design.

678 Gold Mask

1993. Jewels from Funerary Chamber of "Senor of Sipan" (1st series).
1802 **678** 50 c. multicoloured . . . 55 15
See also Nos. 1830/1.

679 Escriva
680 Cherry Blossom and Nazca Lines Hummingbird

1993. 1st Anniv of Beatification of Josemaria Escriva (founder of Opus Dei). Self-adhesive. Imperf.
1803 **679** 30 c. multicoloured . . 45 10

1993. 120th Anniv of Diplomatic Relations and Peace, Friendship, Commerce and Navigation Treaty with Japan. Multicoloured.
1804 1 s. 50 Type **680** . . . . . . 1·75 45
1805 1 s. 70 Peruvian and Japanese children and Mts. Huascaran (Peru) and Fuji (Japan) . 1·90 55

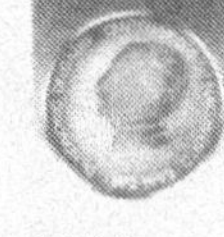

681 Sea Lions
682 Delgado

1993. Stamp Exhibitions. Multicoloured.
1806 90 c. Type **681** ("Amifil '93" National Stamp Exhibition, Lima) 85 25
1807 1 s. Blue and yellow macaw ("Brasiliana '93" International Stamp Exhibition, Rio de Janeiro) (vert) 90 30

1993. Birth Centenary of Dr. Honorio Delgado (psychiatrist and neurologist). Self-adhesive. Imperf.
1808 **682** 50 c. brown 30 15

683 Morales Macedo
684 "The Sling" (Quechua Indians)

1993. Birth Centenary of Rosalia de Lavalle de Morales Macedo (founder of Society for Protection of Children and of Christian Co-operation Bank). Self-adhesive. Imperf.
1809 **683** 80 c. orange 50 25

1993. Ethnic Groups (1st series). Statuettes by Felipe Lettersten. Multicoloured. Self-adhesive. Imperf.
1810 2 s. Type **684** . . . . 1·25 60
1811 3 s. 50 "Fire" (Orejon Indians) 2·25 1·10
See also Nos. 1850/1.

685 "20" on Stamp
686 "Virgin of Loreta"

1993. 20th International Pacific Fair.
1812 **685** 1 s. 50 multicoloured . . 95 45

1993. Christmas.
1813 **686** 1 s. multicoloured . . . 60 30

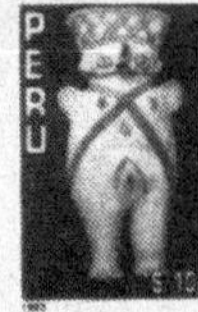

687 Artefacts from Tomb, Poma
688 Ceramic Figure

1993. Sican Culture (2nd series). Multicoloured. Self-adhesive. Imperf.
1814 2 s. 50 Type **687** . . . . . . 1·50 75
1815 4 s. Gold mask . . . . 2·50 1·25

1993. Chancay Culture. Multicoloured. Self-adhesive. Imperf.
1816 10 s. Type **688** . . . . 6·25 3·00
1817 20 s. Textile pattern (horiz) . 12·50 6·25

689 "With AIDS There is No Tomorrow"
690 Computer Graphics

1993. International AIDS Day.
1818 **689** 1 s. 50 multicoloured . . 95 45

1994. 25th Anniv of National Council for Science and Technology. Self-adhesive. Imperf.
1819 **690** 1 s. multicoloured . . . . 1·40 25

691 "The Bridge" (woodcut from "New Chronicle and Good Government" by Poma de Ayala)
692 Engraved Mate Dish

1994. Self-adhesive. Imperf.
1820 **691** 20 c. blue 35 10
1821 40 c. orange 55 10
1822 50 c. violet 70 15
For similar design see Nos. 1827/9.

1994. Multicoloured. Self-adhesive. Imperf.
1823 1 s. 50 Type **692** . . . . . . 2·00 40
1824 1 s. 50 Engraved silver and mate vessel (vert) . . . . 2·00 40
1825 3 s. Figure of bull from Pucara 3·75 85
1826 3 s. Glazed plate decorated with fishes . . . . 3·75 85

693 "The Bridge" (Poma de Ayala)
694 Gold Trinkets

1994.
1827 **693** 30 c. brown 45 10
1828 40 c. black 60 10
1829 50 c. red 70 15

1994. Jewels from Funerary Chamber of Senor de Sipan (2nd series). Multicoloured.
1830 3 s. Type **694** . . . . 3·75 85
1831 5 s. Gold mask (vert) . . . . 6·50 1·25

695 El Brujo

1994. Archaeology. El Brujo Complex, Trujillo.
1832 **695** 70 c. multicoloured . . . 40 20

696 "Baby Emmanuel" (Cuzco sculpture)
697 Brazilian Player

1995. Christmas (1994). Multicoloured.
1833 1 s. 80 Type **696** . . . . . . 1·00 50
1834 2 s. "Nativity" (Huamanga ceramic) . . . . 1·10 55

1995. World Cup Football Championship, U.S.A. (1994). Multicoloured.
1835 60 c. Type **697** 35 15
1836 4 s. 80 Mascot, pitch and flags 2·75 1·25

698 Jauja–Huancayo Road

1995. 25th Anniv (1994) of Ministry of Transport, Communications, Housing and Construction.
1837 **698** 20 c. multicoloured . . . 10 10

699 Mochican Pot (Rafael Larco Herrera Museum of Archaeology)
700 Juan Parra del Reigo (poet) (after David Alfaro)

1995. Museum Exhibits. Multicoloured.
1838 40 c. Type **699** 20 10
1839 80 c. Mochican gold and gemstone ornament of man with slingshot (Rafael Larco Herrera Museum of Archaeology, Lima) . . . 45 20
1840 90 c. Vessel in shape of beheaded man (National Museum) 50 25

1995. Writers' Birth Centenaries (1994). Mult.
1841 90 c. Type **700** 50 25
1842 90 c. Jose Carlos Mariategui 50 25

701 Church
702 Violoncello and Music Stand

1995. 350th Anniv (1993) of Carmelite Monastery, Lima.
1843 **701** 70 c. multicoloured . . . 40 20

1995. Musical Instruments. Multicoloured.
1844 20 c. Type **702** 10 10
1845 40 c. Andean drum 20 10

703 Steam-powered Fire Engine

1995. Volunteer Firemen. Multicoloured.
1846 50 c. Type **703** 25 10
1847 90 c. Modern fire engine . . 50 25

704 Union Club and Plaza de Armas

1995. World Heritage Site. Lima. Multicoloured.
1848 90 c. Type **704** 50 25
1849 1 s. Cloisters of Dominican Monastery 55 25

705 "Bora Child"

1995. Ethnic Groups (2nd series). Statuettes by Felipe Lettersten. Multicoloured.
1850 1 s. Type **705** 55 25
1851 1 s. 80 "Aguaruna Man" . . 1·00 50

706 Woman fishing

1995. 30th Anniv (1993) of World Food Programme.
1852 **706** 1 s. 80 multicoloured . . 1·00 50

707 Potato Plant **708** Reed Sailing Canoe

1995. The Potato. Multicoloured.
1853 1 s. 80 Type **707** . . . . . . 1·00 50
1854 2 s. Mochican ceramic of potato tubers . . . . 1·10 55

1995. Tourism and Ecology. Lake Titicaca.
1855 **708** 2 s. multicoloured . . . 1·10 55

709 Great Horned Owl **710** Anniversary Emblem

1995. Endangered Animals. Multicoloured.
1856 1 s. Type **709** 55 25
1857 1 s. 80 Jaguar on branch (horiz) . . . . 1·00 50

1995. 25th Anniv of Andean Development Corporation.
1858 **710** 5 s. multicoloured . . . 2·75 1·25

711 Ollantaytambo

1995. World Tourism Day.
1859 **711** 5 s. 40 multicoloured . . 3·00 1·50

712 Ancient Letterbox, Head Post Office

1995. World Post Day.
1860 **712** 1 s. 80 multicoloured . . 1·00 50

713 Columbus landing on Beach

1995. America (1992 and 1993). Multicoloured.
1861 1 s. 50 Type **713** (500th anniv of discovery of America) . . . 80 40
1862 1 s. 70 Guanaco (vert) . . . 95 45

714 Cart **715** Lima Cathedral (rear entrance)

1995. America (1994). Postal Transport. Mult.
1863 1 s. 80 Type **714** . . . . . . 1·00 50
1864 2 s. Post vans . . . . 1·10 55

1995. Doorways. Multicoloured.
1865 30 c. Type **715** 15 10
1866 70 c. St. Francis's Church (side entrance) 40 20

716 Peruvian Delegation, San Francisco Conference, 1945

1995. 50th Anniv of U.N.O.
1867 **716** 90 c. multicoloured . . 50 25

717 Ceramic Church (National Culture Museum) **718** Lady Olave Baden-Powell (Girl Guides)

1995. Museum Exhibits. Multicoloured.
1868 20 c. Type **717** 10 10
1869 20 c. "St. John the Apostle" (figurine) (Riva Aguero Institute Museum of Popular Art) 10 10
1870 40 c. "Allegory of Asia" (alabaster figurine) (National Culture Museum) 20 10
1871 50 c. "Archangel Moro" (figurine) (Riva Aguero Institute Museum of Popular Art) 25 10

1995. Scouting. Multicoloured.
1872 80 c. Type **718** 45 20
1873 1 s. Lord Robert Baden Powell (founder of Boy Scouts) . 55 25
Nos. 1872/3 were issued together, se-tenant, forming a composite design.

719 "Festejo" **720** Stream in Sub-tropical Forest

1995. Folk Dances. Multicoloured.
1874 1 s. 80 Type **719** . . . . . . 1·00 50
1875 2 s. "Marinera Limena" (horiz) 1·10 55

1995. Manu National Park, Madre de Dios. Multicoloured.
1876 50 c. Type **720** 25 10
1877 90 c. American chamaeleon (horiz) 50 25

721 Toma de Huinco **722** St. Toribio de Mogrovejo (Archbishop of Lima)

1995. Electricity and Development. Multicoloured.
1878 20 c. Type **721** 10 10
1879 40 c. Antacoto Lake 20 10

1995. Saints. Multicoloured.
1880 90 c. Type **722** 50 25
1881 1 s. St. Francisco Solano (missionary) 55 25

723 Cultivating Crops

1996. 50th Anniv (1995) of F.A.O.
1882 **723** 60 c. multicoloured . . 30 15

724 Crib

1996. Christmas (1995). Porcelain Figures. Multicoloured.
1883 30 c. Type **724** 15 10
1884 70 c. Three Wise Men (horiz) 35 15

725 Lachay National Park

1996. America (1995). Environmental Protection. Multicoloured.
1885 30 c. Type **725** 15 10
1886 70 c. Blackcaiman 35 15

726 "21" **727** Rifle Shooting

1996. 21st International Pacific Fair, Lima.
1887 **726** 60 c. multicoloured . . . 30 15

1996. Olympic Games, Barcelona (1992). Multicoloured.
1888 40 c. Type **727** 20 10
1889 40 c. Tennis 20 10
1890 60 c. Swimming 30 15
1891 60 c. Weightlifting 30 15
Nos. 1888/91 were issued together, se-tenant, forming a composite design of the sports around the games emblem.

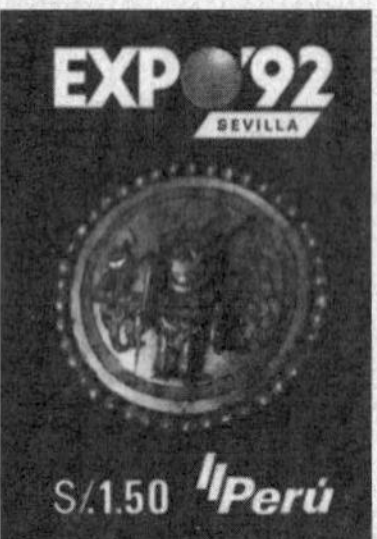

728 Archaeological Find from Sipan

1996. "Expo'92" World's Fair, Seville.
1892 **728** 1 s. 50 multicoloured . . 75 35

729 Vallejo (after Gaston Garreu)

1996. Birth Centenary of Cesar Vallejo (writer).
1893 **729** 50 c. black 25 10

730 Avenue of the Descalzos

1996. U.N.E.S.C.O. World Heritage Site. Lima.
1894 **730** 30 c. brown and stone . . 15 10

EXPRESS LETTER STAMPS

1908. Optd **EXPRESO**.
E373 **76** 10 c. black . . . . . . 17·00 12·50
E382 – 10 c. blue (No. 377) . . 21·00 11·50
E383 **101** 10 c. black and brown . 11·50 10·00

OFFICIAL STAMPS

1890. Stamps of 1866 optd **GOBIERNO** in frame.
O287 **15** 1 c. violet . . . . 1·10 1·10
O324 1 c. red . . . . 7·00 7·00
O288 **16** 2 c. green . . . . 1·10 1·10
O325 2 c. blue . . . . 7·00 7·00
O289 5 c. orange . . . . . . 1·60 1·60
O326 **10** 5 c. lake . . . . 5·50 5·50
O290 **16** 10 c. black 85 45
O291 20 c. blue . . . . 2·50 1·60
O327 20 c. blue (as T **10**) . . . 5·50 5·50
O292 **20** 50 c. red . . . . 3·50 1·75
O293 **21** 1 s. brown . . . . 4·25 3·75

1894. Stamps of 1894 (with "Head" optd) optd **GOBIERNO** in frame.
O305 **15** 1 c. orange (No. 294) . . 19·00 19·00
O306 1 c. green (No. 295) . . 1·10 1·10
O307 **16** 2 c. violet (No. 296) . . 1·10 1·10
O308 2 c. red (No. 297) . . . 90 90
O309 5 c. blue (No. 298) . . . 8·50 7·50
O310 10 c. green (No. 299) . . 3·00 3·00
O311 **20** 50 c. green (No. 300) . . 4·25 4·25

1894. Stamps of 1894 (with "Head" and "Horseshoe" optd) optd **GOBIERNO** in frame.
O312 **16** 2 c. red (No. 301) . . . 1·60 1·60
O313 5 c. blue (No. 302) . . . 1·60 1·60

1896. Stamps of 1896 optd **GOBIERNO**.
O348 **75** 1 c. blue 10 10
O349 **76** 10 c. yellow . . . . . . 1·00 25
O350 10 c. black 10 10
O351 **77** 50 c. red 25 20

O 108

1909.
O382 O **108** 1 c. red 10 10
O572 10 c. brown 40 30
O385 10 c. purple 15 10
O573 50 c. green 35 20

1935. Optd **Servicio Oficial**.
O567 **184** 10 c. red 10 10

PARCEL POST STAMPS.

P 79

1895. Different frames.
P348 P **79** 1 c. purple . . . . . . 1·90 1·60
P349 2 c. brown . . . . . . 2·10 1·90
P350 5 c. blue . . . . . . 8·50 5·50
P351 10 c. brown . . . . . 11·50 8·25
P352 20 c. pink . . . . . . 14·50 12·00
P353 50 c. green . . . . . 38·00 32·00

1903. Surch in words.
P361 P **79** 1 c. on 20 c. pink . . . 10·00 8·25
P362 1 c. on 50 c. green . . 10·00 8·25
P363 5 c. on 10 c. brown . . 65·00 55·00

POSTAGE DUE STAMPS

D 22 D 23 D 109

1874.
D31 D **22** 1 c. brown 10 10
D32 D **23** 5 c. red 15 15
D33 10 c. orange 15 15
D34 20 c. blue 30 30
D35 50 c. brown . . . . . 7·50 3·00

1881. Optd with T **24** "LIMA" at foot instead of "PERU").
D47 D **22** 1 c. brown . . . . . . 3·00 2·00
D48 D **23** 5 c. red . . . . 5·50 5·00
D49 10 c. orange . . . . . 5·50 5·50
D50 20 c. blue . . . . . . 21·00 17·00
D51 50 c. brown . . . . . 45·00 42·00

1881. Optd **LIMA CORREOS** in double-lined circle.
D52 D **22** 1 c. brown . . . . . . 4·25 4·25
D53 D **23** 5 c. red . . . . 5·50 5·00
D54 10 c. orange . . . . . 6·75 5·50
D55 20 c. blue . . . . . . 21·00 17·00
D56 50 c. brown . . . . . 65·00 55·00

1883. Optd with T **24** (inscr "LIMA" instead of "PERU") and also with T **28a**.

D247	D **22**	1 c. brown	4·25	3·00
D250	D **23**	5 c. red	6·25	5·75
D253		10 c. orange	6·25	5·75
D256		20 c. blue	£375	£375
D258		50 c. brown	45·00	35·00

1884. Optd with T **28a** only.

D259	D **22**	1 c. brown	40	40
D262	D **23**	5 c. red	20	20
D267		10 c. orange	25	25
D269		20 c. blue	85	35
D271		50 c. brown	2·50	75

1894. Optd **LIMA CORREOS** in double-lined circle and with T **28a**.

D275	D **22**	1 c. brown	10·50	9·25

1896. Optd **DEFICIT**.

D348	D **22**	1 c. brown (D31) . . .	15	15
D349	D **23**	5 c. red (D32)	15	15
D350		10 c. orange (D33) . .	45	15
D351		20 c. blue (D34) . . .	55	20
D352	**20**	50 c. red (283)	60	20
D353	**21**	1 s. brown (284) . . .	85	35

1899. As T **73**, but inscr "DEFICIT" instead of "FRANQUEO".

D355	5 s. green	85	4·25
D356	10 s. brown	60·00	60·00

1902. Surch **DEFICIT** and value in words.

D361	1 c. on 10 s. (D356)	85	50
D362	5 c. on 10 s. (354)	50	40

1902. Surch **DEFICIT** and value in words.

D363	D **23**	1 c. on 20 c. (D34) . .	50	40
D364		5 c. on 20 c. (D34) . .	1·25	1·00

1909.

D382	D **109**	1 c. brown	35	15
D419		1 c. purple	15	15
D420		2 c. purple	15	15
D570		2 c. brown	15	15
D383		5 c. brown	35	15
D421		5 c. purple	25	20
D384		10 c. brown	40	15
D422		10 c. purple	40	15
D571		10 c. green	40	15
D385		50 c. brown	60	20
D423		50 c. purple	1·40	50
D424		1 s. purple	10·00	3·00
D425		2 s. purple	19·00	6·75

1935. Optd **Deficit**.

D568	–	2 c. purple (No. 537) . .	40	40
D569	**184**	10 c. red	50	40

PHILIPPINES Pt. 9; Pt. 22; Pt. 21

A group of islands in the China Sea, E. of Asia, ceded by Spain to the United States after the war of 1898. Under Japanese Occupation from 1941 until 1945. The Philippines became fully independent in 1946. An independent Republic since 1946.

1854. 20 cuartos = 1 real; 8 reales = 1 peso plata fuerte.
1864. 100 centimos = 1 peso plata fuerte.
1871. 100 centimos = 1 escudo (= $\frac{1}{2}$ peso).
1872. 100 centimos = 1 peseta (= $\frac{1}{5}$ peso).
1876. 1000 milesimas = 100 centavos or centimos = 1 peso.
1899. 100 cents = 1 dollar.
1906. 100 centavos = 1 peso.
1962. 100 sentimos = 1 piso.

SPANISH ADMINISTRATION

1 4 5
Queen Isabella II

1854. Imperf.
1 1 5 c. red £1200 £180
3 10 c. red £400 £120
5 1 r. blue £450 £130
7a 2 r. green £650 £120
On the 1 r. the inscriptions are reversed.

1859. Imperf.
13 4 5 c. red 10·00 4·00
14 10 c. pink 10·00 12·00

1861. Larger lettering. Imperf.
17 5 5 c. red 23·00 7·50

7 8

1863. Imperf.
19 7 5 c. red 9·00 3·75
20 10 c. red 27·00 28·00
21 1 r. mauve £500 £325
22 2 r. blue £400 £275

1863. Imperf.
25 8 1 r. green £100 38·00

1864. As T **14** of Spain, but value in "centimos de peso". Imperf.
26 $3\frac{1}{8}$ c. black on buff 2·50 1·40
27 $6\frac{2}{8}$ c. green on pink 2·50 70
28 $12\frac{4}{8}$ c. blue on pink 5·00 70
29 25 c. red on pink 10·00 4·00
30 25 c. red on white 7·00 2·00

1868. Optd **HABILITADO POR LA NACION.**
(a) On 1854 to 1863 issues of Philippines.
41 7 5 c. red 42·00 27·00
53 4 10 c. pink 85·00 45·00
36 8 1 r. green 42·00 12·00
42 7 1 r. mauve £425 £275
52 1 1 r. blue £2000 £1000
43 7 2 r. blue £400 £180

(b) On 1864 issues of Philippines.
31 $3\frac{1}{8}$ c. black on buff 15·00 3·00
32 $6\frac{2}{8}$ c. green on pink 15·00 3·00
33 $12\frac{4}{8}$ c. blue on pink 40·00 18·00
34 25 c. red 18·00 10·00

(c) On Nos. 10/11a of Cuba (as T **8** of Philippines).
44 1 r. green £130 60·00
45 2 r. red £170 65·00

12 13 King Amadeo

1871.
37 12 5 c. blue 42·00 4·50
38 10 c. green 6·00 3·75
39 20 c. brown 48·00 26·00
40 40 c. red 65·00 14·00

1872.
46 13 12 c. pink 9·50 3·50
47 16 c. blue 95·00 25·00
48a 25 c. grey 7·50 3·50
49 62 c. mauve 23·00 6·50
50a 1 p. 25 brown 42·00 20·00

14

1874.
54 14 12 c. grey 11·00 3·25
55 25 c. blue 3·75 1·40
56 62 c. pink 32·00 3·25
57 1 p. 25 brown £160 48·00

15 16

1875. With rosettes each side of "FILIPINAS".
58 15 2 c. pink 1·50 50
59 2 c. blue £140 65·00
60 6 c. orange 7·50 1·75
61 10 c. blue 2·00 45
62 12 c. mauve 2·10 45
63 20 c. brown 9·50 2·25
64 25 c. green 7·50 45

1878. Without rosettes.
65 16 25 m. black 1·90 30
66 25 m. green 45·00 21·00
67 50 m. purple 22·00 8·50
68a ($62\frac{1}{2}$ m.) 0.0625 lilac 40·00 13·00
69 100 m. red 75·00 32·00
70 100 m. green 7·00 2·00
71 125 m. blue 3·50 30
72 200 m. pink 23·00 4·75
74 250 m. brown 8·50 2·00

1877. Surch **HABILITADO 12 CS. PTA**. in frame.
75 15 12 c. on 2 c. pink 65·00 22·00
76 16 12 c. on 25 m. black 65·00 22·00

1879. Surch **CONVENIO UNIVERSAL DE CORREOS HABILITADO** and value in figures and words.
78 16 2 c. on 25 m. green 35·00 7·50
79 8 c. on 100 m. red 28·00 5·50

1880. "Alfonso XII" key-type inscr "FILIPINAS".
97 X 1 c. green 30 10
82a 2 c. red 60 1·25
83 $2\frac{1}{2}$ c. brown 6·00 1·25
95 $2\frac{4}{8}$ c. blue 30 10
99 50 m. bistre 30 15
85 5 c. grey 60 1·25
100 6 c. brown 8·00 1·25
87 $6\frac{2}{8}$ c. green 4·75 7·50
88 8 c. brown 27·00 14·00
89a 10 c. brown 2·50 1·25
90 10 c. purple 5·00 10·00
91 10 c. green £300 £180
92 $12\frac{4}{8}$ c. pink 1·25 1·25
93 20 c. brown 2·50 1·25
94 25 c. brown 3·25 1·25

1881. "Alfonso XII" key-type inscr "FILIPINAS" with various circular surcharges.
(a) **HABILITADO U. POSTAL** and value.
111 X 1 c. on $2\frac{4}{8}$ c. blue 60 40
102 10 c. on $2\frac{4}{8}$ c. blue 6·00 1·25

(b) **HABILITADO CORREOS 2 CENTS. DE PESO.**
101 X 2 c. on $2\frac{1}{2}$ c. brown 3·00 1·15

(c) **HABILITADO PA. U. POSTAL 8 CMOS.**
106 X 8 c. on 2 c. red 6·00 1·40

(d) **HABILITADO PA. CORREOS DE** and value.
107 X 10 c. cuartos on 2 c. red 3·50 1·40
112 16 cuartos on $2\frac{4}{8}$ c. blue 8·50 2·00
103 20 c. on 8 c. brown 8·25 2·50
113 1 r. on 2 c. red 5·50 2·00
109 1 r. on 5 c. lilac 5·00 2·25
110 1 r. on 8 c. brown 9·50 3·00
105 2 r. on $2\frac{4}{8}$ c. blue 5·00 1·40

25 29 30

31 34

1881. Fiscal and telegraph stamps (a) with circular surch **HABILITADO CORREOS**, **HABILITADO PARA CORREOS**, **HABILITADO PA. U. POSTAL** or **HABILITADO PA. CORREOS** and value in figures and words.
115 25 2 c. on 10 cuartos bistre 21·00 13·50
129 29 2 c. on 200 m. green 4·75 2·25
116 25 $2\frac{4}{8}$ c. on 10 cuartos bistre 3·00 65
117 $2\frac{4}{8}$ c. on 2 r. blue £150 65·00
124 $6\frac{2}{8}$ c. on $12\frac{4}{8}$ c. lilac 4·75 2·75
118 8 c. on 2 r. blue 8·50 2·25
119 8 c. on 10 c. brown £170 £130
123 16 cmos. on 2 r. blue 5·75 2·40
137 31 20 c. on 150 m. blue 25·00 21·00
134 20 c. on 250 m. blue 95·00 80·00
127 25 1 r. on 10 cuartos bistre 10·00 3·50
121 1 r. on $12\frac{4}{8}$ c. lilac 7·00 3·00
130 29 1 r. on 200 m. green 55·00 35·00
131 1 r. on 1 peso green 28·00 13·50
132 30 1 r. on 10 pesetas bistre 40·00 21·00
133 31 2 r. on 250 m. blue 9·00 3·00

(b) With two circular surcharges as above, showing two different values.
128 25 8 c. on 2 r. on 2 r. blue 20·00 12·00
136 31 1 r. on 20 c. on 250 m. bl 9·00 4·50

(c) Optd **HABILITADO PARA CORREOS** in straight lines.
122 25 10 cuartos bistre £150 65·00
126 1 r. green 85·00 65·00

1887. Various stamps with oval surch **UNION GRAL. POSTAL HABILITADO** (No. 142) or **HABILITADO PARA COMMUNICACIONES** and new value. (a) "Alfonso XII" key-type inscr "FILIPINAS".
138 X $2\frac{4}{8}$ c. on 1 c. green 1·90 1·00
139 $2\frac{4}{8}$ c. on 5 c. lilac 1·25 50
140 $2\frac{4}{8}$ c. on 50 m. bistre 1·75 1·10
141 $2\frac{4}{8}$ c. on 10 c. green 1·25 65
142 8 c. on $2\frac{4}{8}$ c. blue 75 40

(b) "Alfonso XII" key-type inscr "FILIPAS-IMPRESOS".
143 X $2\frac{4}{8}$ c. on $\frac{1}{8}$ c. green 40 15

(c) Fiscal and telegraph stamps.
144 29 $2\frac{4}{8}$ c. on 200 m. green 3·50 1·25
145 $2\frac{4}{8}$ c. on 20 c. brown 10·00 4·75
146 34 $2\frac{4}{8}$ c. on 1 c. bistre 75 50

1889. Various stamps with oval surch **RECARGO DE CONSUMOS HABILITADO** and new value. (a) "Alfonso XII" key-type inscr "FILIPINAS".
147 X $2\frac{4}{8}$ c. on 1 c. green 15 15
148 $2\frac{4}{8}$ c. on 2 c. red 10 10
149 $2\frac{4}{8}$ c. on $2\frac{4}{8}$ c. blue 10 10
150 $2\frac{4}{8}$ c. on 5 c. lilac 10 10
151 $2\frac{4}{8}$ c. on 50 m. bistre 10 10
152 $2\frac{4}{8}$ c. on $12\frac{4}{8}$ c. pink 60 60

(b) "Alfonso XII" key-type inscr "FILIPAS-IMPRESOS".
160 X $2\frac{4}{8}$ c. on $\frac{1}{8}$ c. green 15 15

(c) Fiscal and telegraph stamps.
153 34 $2\frac{4}{8}$ c. on 1 c. bistre 30 30
154 $2\frac{4}{8}$ c. on 2 c. red 30 30
155 $2\frac{4}{8}$ c. on $2\frac{4}{8}$ c. brown 10 10
156 $2\frac{4}{8}$ c. on 5 c. blue 10 10
157 $2\frac{4}{8}$ c. on 10 c. green 10 10
158 $2\frac{4}{8}$ c. on 10 c. mauve 60 65
159 $2\frac{4}{8}$ c. on 20 c. mauve 20 20
161 – $17\frac{4}{8}$ c. on 5 p. green 70·00
No. 161 is a fiscal stamp inscribed "DERECHO JUDICIAL" with a central motif as T **43** of Spain.

1890. "Baby" key-type inscr "FILIPINAS".
176 Y 1 c. violet 40 15
188 1 c. red 13·00 6·50
197 1 c. green 1·75 60
162 2 c. red 10 10
177 2 c. violet 10 10
190 2 c. brown 10 10
198 2 c. blue 25 25
163 $2\frac{4}{8}$ c. blue 40 10
178 $2\frac{4}{8}$ c. grey 15 10
165 5 c. blue 30 10
163 5 c. green 40 10
199 5 c. brown 7·50 3·25
181 6 c. purple 20 10
192 6 c. red 1·40 70
166 8 c. green 20 10
182 8 c. blue 40 20
193 8 c. red 65 20
167 10 c. green 1·40 20
172 10 c. pink 50 10
202 10 c. brown 50 10
173 $12\frac{4}{8}$ c. green 15 10
184 $12\frac{4}{8}$ c. orange 50 10
185 15 c. brown 50 20
195 15 c. red 1·60 70
203 15 c. green 1·75 1·75
169 20 c. red 55·00 29·00
186 20 c. brown 1·50 25
196 20 c. purple 13·00 6·50
204 20 c. orange 3·75 1·75
170 25 c. brown 4·25 75
175 25 c. blue 1·50 15
205 40 c. purple 18·00 5·00
206 80 c. red 26·00 14·50

1897. Surch **HABILITADO CORREOS PARA 1897** and value in frame.
(a) "Baby" key-type inscr "FILIPINAS".
212 Y 5 c. on 5 c. green 3·00 2·00
208 15 c. on 15 c. red 3·00 2·00
213 15 c. on 15 c. brown 3·50 2·00
209 20 c. on 20 c. purple 15·00 8·00
214 20 c. on 20 c. brown 5·00 3·50
210 20 c. on 25 c. brown 10·00 8·00

(b) "Alfonso XII" key-type inscr "FILIPINAS".
215 X 5 c. on 5 c. lilac 4·00 2·25

1898. "Curly Head" key-type inscr "FILIPNAS 1898 y 99".
217 Z 1 m. brown 15 15
218 2 m. brown 15 15
219 3 m. brown 15 15
220 4 m. brown 6·00 1·25
221 5 m. brown 15 15
222 1 c. purple 15 15
223 2 c. green 15 15
224 3 c. brown 15 15
225 4 c. orange 12·00 7·50
226 5 c. red 15 15
227 6 c. blue 75 45
228 8 c. brown 35 15
229 10 c. red 1·25 75
230 15 c. grey 1·25 65
231 20 c. purple 1·25 90
232 40 c. lilac 75 60
233 60 c. black 3·25 2·25
234 80 c. brown 4·00 2·25
235 1 p. green 9·50 9·25
236 2 p. blue 22·00 12·00

STAMPS FOR PRINTED MATTER

1886. "Alfonso XII" key-type inscr "FILIPAS-IMPRESOS".
P138 X 1 m. red 20 10
P139 $\frac{1}{8}$ c. green 20 10
P140 2 m. blue 20 10
P141 5 m. brown 20 10

1890. "Baby" key-type inscr "FILIPAS-IMPRESOS".
P171 Y 1 m. purple 10 10
P172 $\frac{1}{8}$ c. purple 10 10
P173 2 m. purple 10 10
P174 5 m. purple 10 10

1892. "Baby" key-type inscr "FILIPAS-IMPRESOS".
P192 Y 1 m. green 1·40 40
P193 $\frac{1}{8}$ c. green 80 15
P194 2 m. green 2·00 40
P191 5 m. green £190 40·00

1894. "Baby" key-type inscr "FILIPAS-IMPRESOS".
P197 Y 1 m. grey 20 20
P198 $\frac{1}{8}$ c. brown 20 20
P199 2 m. grey 20 20
P200 5 m. grey 20 20

1896. "Baby" key-type inscr "FILIPAS-IMPRESOS".
P205 Y 1 m. blue 25 15
P206 $\frac{1}{8}$ c. blue 75 60
P207 2 m. brown 25 15
P208 5 m. blue 2·25 1·40

UNITED STATES ADMINISTRATION

1899. United States stamps of 1894 (No. 267 etc) optd **PHILIPPINES**.
252 – 1 c. green 2·50 65
253 – 2 c. red 1·25 50
255 – 3 c. violet 4·00 1·60
256 – 4 c. brown 17·00 4·75
257 – 5 c. blue 4·00 1·00
258 – 6 c. purple 20·00 6·00
259 – 8 c. brown 22·00 6·00
260 – 10 c. brown 15·00 3·00
262 – 15 c. green 26·00 6·50
263 83 50 c. orange 90·00 38·00
264 – $1 black £325 £190
266 – $2 blue £500 £275
267 – $5 green £1200 £850

1903. United States stamps of 1902 optd **PHILIPPINES**.
268 103 1 c. green 3·00 30
269 104 2 c. red 5·00 1·25
270 105 3 c. violet 55·00 14·00
271 106 4 c. brown 60·00 20·00
272 107 5 c. blue 8·50 70
273 108 6 c. lake 65·00 18·00
274 109 8 c. violet 28·00 12·00
275 110 10 c. brown 18·00 2·50
276 111 13 c. purple 23·00 13·00
277 112 15 c. olive 42·00 8·00
278 113 50 c. orange £100 30·00
279 114 $1 black £425 £200
280 115 $2 blue £1300 £800
281 116 $5 green £1500 £1000

1904. United States stamp of 1903 optd **PHILIPPINES**.
282 117 2 c. red 3·75 1·50

45 Rizal 46 Arms of Manila

1906. Various portraits as T **45** and T **46**.
337 45 2 c. green 10 10
338 – 4 c. red (McKinley) 10 10
339 – 6 c. violet (Magellan) 30 10
340 – 8 c. brown (Legaspi) 25 10
341 – 10 c. blue (Lawton) 20 10
288 – 12 c. red (Lincoln) 4·00 1·75
342 – 12 c. orange (Lincoln) 45 15
289 – 16 c. black (Sampson) 3·50 15
298 – 16 c. green (Sampson) 2·00 10
344 – 16 c. olive (Dewey) 1·00 15
290 – 20 c. brown (Washington) 3·50 20
345 – 20 c. yellow (Washington) 35 10
291 – 26 c. brown (Carriedo) 4·50 1·75
346 – 26 c. green (Carriedo) 65 30
292 – 30 c. green (Franklin) 4·75 90
313 – 30 c. blue (Franklin) 2·75 35
347 – 30 c. grey (Franklin) 45 10
293 46 1 p. orange 18·00 5·00
363a 1 p. violet 3·50 3·50
294 2 p. black 23·00 1·00
364 2 p. brown 9·00 9·00
350 4 p. blue 20·00 25
351 10 p. green 55·00 4·40
Nos. 288, 289, 298, 290, 291, 292, 313, 293 and 294 exist perf only, the other values perf or imperf.

1926. Air. Madrid–Manila Flight. Stamps as last, optd **AIR MAIL 1926 MADRID-MANILA** and aeroplane propeller.
368 45 2 c. green 4·00 3·25
369 4 c. red 5·00 3·75
370 – 6 c. violet 25·00 8·00
371 – 8 c. brown 25·00 9·50
372 – 10 c. blue 25·00 9·50
373 – 12 c. orange 27·00 14·00
374 – 16 c. green (Sampson) £1100 £1000
375 – 16 c. olive (Dewey) 28·00 13·50
376 – 20 c. yellow 28·00 13·50
377 – 26 c. green 28·00 13·50
378 – 30 c. grey 28·00 13·50
383 46 1 p. violet £100 65·00
379 2 p. brown £250 £180
380 4 p. blue £425 £275
381 10 p. green £650 £450

49 Legislative Palace

1926. Inauguration of Legislative Palace.
384 **49** 2 c. black and green . . . 40 25
385 4 c. black and red . . . 40 30
386 16 c. black and olive . . . 60 50
387 18 c. black and brown . . . 1·00 55
388 20 c. black and orange . . 1·25 80
389 24 c. black and grey . . . 1·00 50
390 1 p. black and mauve . . . 45·00 25·00

1928. Air. London–Orient Flight by British Squadron of Seaplanes. Stamps of 1906 optd **L.O.F.** (= London Orient Flight) **1928** and Fairey IIID seaplane.
402 **45** 2 c. green 35 20
403 – 4 c. red 40 30
404 – 6 c. violet . . . . 2·40 1·60
405 – 8 c. brown . . . . 2·40 2·00
406 – 10 c. blue . . . . 2·40 2·00
407 – 12 c. orange . . . . . . 4·00 2·40
408 – 16 c. olive (Dewey) . . . . 3·75 2·40
409 – 20 c. yellow . . . . 4·00 2·40
410 – 26 c. green . . . . 7·50 5·50
411 – 30 c. grey . . . . 7·50 5·50
412 **46** 1 p. violet . . . . 32·00 32·00

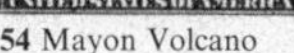
54 Mayon Volcano

57 Vernal Falls, Yosemite National Park, California, wrongly inscr "PAGSANJAN FALLS"

1932.
424 **54** 2 c. green 75 30
425 – 4 c. red 30 20
426 – 12 c. orange 60 50
427 **57** 18 c. red . . . . 24·00 7·00
428 – 20 c. yellow 70 45
429 – 24 c. violet . . . . . . 1·25 55
430 – 32 c. brown . . . . . . 1·25 65
DESIGNS—HORIZ: 4 c. Post Office, Manila; 12 c. Freighters at Pier No. 7, Manila Bay; 20 c. Rice plantation; 24 c. Rice terraces; 32 c. Baguio Zigzag.

1932. No. 350 surch in words in double circle.
431 **46** 1 p. on 4 p. blue . . . . 1·50 30
432 2 p. on 4 p. blue . . . . 3·00 55

1932. Air. Nos. 424/30 optd with Dornier Do-J flying boat "Gronland Wal" and **ROUND-THE-WORLD FLIGHT VON GRONAU 1932**.
433 2 c. green 30 30
434 4 c. red 30 30
435 12 c. orange 40 40
436 18 c. red . . . . 3·00 2·50
437 20 c. yellow . . . . 1·75 1·50
438 24 c. violet . . . . 1·75 1·50
439 32 c. brown . . . . 1·75 1·50

1933. Air. Stamps of 1906 optd **F. REIN MADRID - MANILA FLIGHT - 1933** under propeller.
440 **45** 2 c. green 30 30
441 – 4 c. red 35 35
442 – 6 c. violet 60 60
443 – 8 c. brown . . . . . . 1·60 1·25
444 – 10 c. blue . . . . . . 1·40 90
445 – 12 c. orange . . . . . 1·25 90
446 – 16 c. olive (Dewey) . . . 1·25 90
447 – 20 c. orange . . . . . 1·25 90
448 – 26 c. green . . . . . . 1·60 1·10
449 – 30 c. grey . . . . . . 2·00 1·25

1933. Air. Nos. 337 and 425/30 optd with **AIR MAIL** on wings of airplane.
450 2 c. green 40 30
451 4 c. red 15 10
452 12 c. orange 25 10
453 20 c. yellow 25 15
454 24 c. violet 35 15
455 32 c. brown 40 25

66 Baseball

1934. 10th Far Eastern Championship Games.
456 **66** 2 c. brown . . . . 1·50 60
457 – 6 c. blue 45 20
458 – 16 c. purple . . . . . . 1·25 80
DESIGNS—VERT: 6 c. Tennis; 16 c. Basketball.

69 Dr. J. Rizal

70 Pearl Fishing

1935. Designs as T **69/70** in various sizes (sizes in millimetres).
459 2 c. red (19 × 22) 10 10
460 4 c. green (34 × 22) 10 10
461 6 c. brown (22½ × 28) 15 10
462 8 c. violet (34 × 22) 20 15
463 10 c. red (34 × 22) 30 15
464 12 c. black (34 × 22) 25 20
465 16 c. blue (34 × 22) 35 15
466 20 c. bistre (19 × 22) 25 10
467 26 c. blue (34 × 22) 40 20
468 30 c. red (34 × 22) 40 30
469 1 p. black & orge (37 × 27) . . 2·40 90
470 2 p. black & brn (37 × 27) . . 4·00 1·25
471 4 p. black & blue (37 × 27) . . 4·00 2·50
472 5 p. black & grn (27 × 37) . . 9·50 1·75
DESIGNS: 4 c. Woman, Carabao and Ricestalks; 6 c. Filipino girl; 10 c. Fort Santiago; 12 c. Salt springs; 16 c. Magellan's landing; 20 c. "Juan de la Cruz"; 26 c. Rice terraces; 30 c. Blood Compact; 1 p. Barasoain Church; 2 p. Battle of Manila Bay; 4 p. Montalban Gorge; 5 p. George Washington (after painting by John Faed).

COMMONWEALTH OF THE PHILIPPINES

83 "Temples of Human Progress"

1935. Inauguration of Commonwealth of the Philippines.
483 **83** 2 c. red 15 15
484 6 c. violet 20 15
485 16 c. blue 20 15
486 36 c. green 40 25
487 50 c. brown 60 50

1935. Air. "China Clipper" Trans-Pacific Air Mail Flight. Optd **P.I.U.S. INITIAL FLIGHT December-1935** and Martin M-130 flying boat.
488 10 c. red (No. 463) 25 20
489 30 c. red (No. 468) 30 35

85 J. Rizal y Mercado

89 Manuel L. Quezon

1936. 75th Birth Anniv of Rizal.
490 **85** 2 c. yellow 10 15
491 6 c. blue 15 15
492 36 c. brown 60 45

1936. Air. Manila-Madrid Flight by Arnaiz and Calvo. Stamps of 1906 surch **MANILA-MADRID ARNACAL FLIGHT-1936** and value.
493 **45** 2 c. on 4 c. red 10 10
494 6 c. on 12 c. orange . . . 15 10
495 16 c. on 26 c. green . . . 20 15

1936. Stamps of 1935 (Nos. 459/72) optd **COMMON-WEALTH** (2 c., 6 c., 20 c.) or **COMMONWEALTH** (others).
496 2 c. red 10 10
497 4 c. green 50 40
526 6 c. brown 10 10
527 8 c. violet 10 10
528 10 c. red 10 10
529 12 c. black 10 10
530 16 c. blue 20 10
531 20 c. bistre 20 10
532 26 c. blue 30 20
505 30 c. red 30 15
534 1 p. black and orange 50 15
535 2 p. black and brown . . . . 4·00 75
508 4 p. black and blue . . . . 17·00 2·50
509 5 p. black and green . . . . 2·40 1·25

1936. 1st Anniv of Autonomous Government.
510 **89** 2 c. brown 10 10
511 6 c. green 10 10
512 12 c. blue 15 15

90 Philippine Is

92 Arms of Manila

1937. 33rd International Eucharistic Congress.
513 **90** 2 c. green 10 10
514 6 c. brown 15 10
515 12 c. blue 20 10
516 20 c. orange 25 10
517 36 c. violet 35 30
518 50 c. red 45 25

1937.
522 **92** 10 p. grey . . . . 3·50 1·50
523 20 p. brown . . . . 1·75 1·10

1939. Air. 1st Manila Air Mail Exhibition. Surch **FIRST AIR MAIL EXHIBITION Feb 17 to 19, 1939** and value.
548a – 8 c. on 26 c. green (346) . 60 35
549 **92** 1 p. on 10 p. grey . . . . 3·00 2·40

1939. 1st National Foreign Trade Week. Surch **FIRST FOREIGN TRADE WEEK MAY 21-27, 1939** and value.
551 – 2 c. on 4 c. green (460) . . 10 10
552a **45** 6 c. on 26 c. green (346) . 20 15
553 **92** 50 c. on 20 p. brown . . . 90 85

101 Triumphal Arch

102 Malacanan Palace

103 Pres. Quezon taking Oath of Office

1939. 4th Anniv of National Independence.
554 **101** 2 c. green 10 10
555 6 c. red 15 10
556 12 c. blue 20 10
557 **102** 2 c. green 10 10
558 6 c. orange 15 10
559 12 c. red 20 10
560 **103** 2 c. orange 10 10
561 6 c. green 15 10
562 12 c. violet 30 15

104 Jose Rizal

105 Filipino Vinta and Boeing 314 Flying Boat

1941.
563 **104** 2 c. green 10 10
623 – 2 c. brown 10 10
In No. 623 the head faces to the right.

1941. Air.
566 **105** 8 c. red 80 75
567 20 c. blue . . . . 1·00 50
568 60 c. green . . . . 1·50 85
569 1 p. sepia 75 60

For Japanese Occupation issues of 1941–45 see **JAPANESE OCCUPATION OF PHILIPPINE ISLANDS**.

1945. Victory issue. Nos. 496, 525/31, 505, 534 and 522/3 optd **VICTORY**.
610 2 c. red 10 10
611 4 c. green 10 10
612 6 c. brown 15 10
613 8 c. violet 20 15
614 10 c. red 20 10
615 12 c. black 25 15
616 16 c. blue 40 15
617 20 c. bistre 40 10
618 30 c. red 70 50
619 1 p. black and orange . . . . 1·40 30
620 10 p. grey . . . . 40·00 14·00
621 20 p. brown . . . . 35·00 16·00

INDEPENDENT REPUBLIC

111 "Independence"

113 Bonifacio Monument

1946. Proclamation of Independence.
625 **111** 2 c. red 30 30
626 6 c. green 45 30
627 12 c. blue 70 45

1946. Optd **PHILIPPINES 50TH ANNIVERSARY MARTYRDOM OF RIZAL 1896-1946**.
628 **104** 2 c. brown (No. 623) . . . 30 20

1947.
629 – 4 c. brown 15 10
630 **113** 10 c. red 20 10
631 – 12 c. blue 25 10
632 – 16 c. grey . . . . 1·50 90
633 – 20 c. brown 45 15
634 – 50 c. green . . . . 1·10 75
635 – 1 p. violet . . . . 2·25 55
DESIGNS—VERT: 4 c. Rizal Monument; 50 c., 1 p. Avenue of Palm Trees. HORIZ: 12 c. Jones Bridge; 16 c. Santa Lucia Gate; 20 c. Mayon Volcano.

115 Manuel L. Quezon

117 Presidents Quezon and Roosevelt

116 Pres. Roxas taking Oath of Office

1947.
636 **115** 1 c. green 15 10

1947. 1st Anniv of Independence.
638 **116** 4 c. red 20 15
639 6 c. green 50 50
640 16 c. purple . . . . 1·10 75

1947. Air.
641 **117** 6 c. green 60 60
642 40 c. orange . . . . 1·10 1·10
643 80 c. blue . . . . 3·00 3·00

119 United Nations Emblem

121 General MacArthur

1947. Conference of Economic Commission for Asia and Far East, Baguio. Imperf or perf.
648 **119** 4 c. red and pink . . . . 1·50 1·40
649 6 c. violet & light violet . . 2·10 2·10
650 12 c. blue & light blue . . 2·50 2·50

1948. 3rd Anniv of Liberation.
652 **121** 4 c. violet 50 20
653 6 c. red . . . . 1·00 65
654 16 c. blue . . . . 1·50 65

122 Threshing Rice

125 Dr. Jose Rizal

1948. United Nations Food and Agriculture Organization Conference, Baguio.
655 **122** 2 c. green & yell (postage) 85 55
656 6 c. brown and stone . . 1·00 80
657 18 c. blue & light blue . . 2·75 2·10

658 40 c. red and pink (air) . 14·00 7·50

1948.
662 **125** 2 c. green 15 10

126 Pres. Manuel Roxas

127 Scout and Badge

128 Sampaguita, National Flower

1948. President Roxas Mourning Issue.
663 **126** 2 c. black 25 15
664 4 c. black 35 25

1948. 25th Anniv of Philippine Boy Scouts. Perf or imperf.
665 **127** 2 c. green and brown . . . 1·10 55
666 4 c. pink and brown . . . 1·40 80

1948. Flower Day.
667 **128** 3 c. green and black . . . 35 30

130 Santos, Tavera and Kalaw

131 "Doctrina Christiana" (first book published in Philippines)

1949. Library Rebuilding Fund.
671 **130** 4 c. + 2 c. brown . . . . 1·00 75
672 **131** 6 c. + 4 c. violet . . . . 3·00 2·00
673 – 18 c. + 7 c. blue . . . . 4·00 3·50
DESIGN—VERT: 18 c. Title page of Rizal's "Noli Me Tangere".

132 U.P.U. Monument, Berne

1949. 75th Anniv of U.P.U.
674 **132** 4 c. green 20 10
675 6 c. violet 20 10
676 18 c. blue 80 25

133 General del Pilar at Tirad Pass **134** Globe

1949. 50th Death Anniv of Gen. Gregorio del Pilar.
678 **133** 2 c. brown 15 15
679 4 c. green 35 30

1950. 5th International Congress of Junior Chamber of Commerce.
680 **134** 2 c. violet (postage) . . . 20 10
681 6 c. green 30 10
682 18 c. blue 65 20
683 30 c. orange (air) 50 20
684 50 c. red 90 25

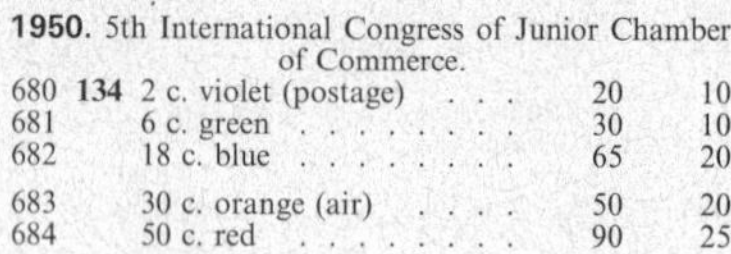

135 Red Lauan Trees **136** Franklin D. Roosevelt

1950. 15th Anniv of Forestry Service.
685 **135** 2 c. green 30 20
686 4 c. violet 70 25

1950. 25th Anniv of Philatelic Association.
687 **136** 4 c. brown 35 25
688 6 c. pink 50 35
689 18 c. blue . . . . 1·25 90

137 Lions Emblem **138** President Quirino taking Oath of Office

1950. "Lions" International Convention, Manila.
691 **137** 2 c. orange (postage) . . . 60 60
692 4 c. lilac 95 95
693 30 c. green (air) . . . . . 1·00 70
694 50 c. blue . . . . 1·10 95

1950. Pres. Quirino's Inauguration.
696 **138** 2 c. red 10 10
697 4 c. purple 15 10
698 6 c. green 25 15

1950. Surch **ONE CENTAVO**.
699 **125** 1 c. on 2 c. green 15 10

140 Dove and Map **141** War Widow and Children

1950. Baguio Conference.
701 **140** 5 c. green 30 25
702 6 c. red 30 25
703 18 c. blue 70 50

1950. Aid to War Victims.
704 **141** 2 c. + 2 c. red 10 10
705 – 4 c. + 4 c. violet 40 40
DESIGN: 4 c. Disabled veteran.

142 Arms of Manila **143** Soldier and Peasants

1950. As T **142**. Various arms and frames. (a) Arms inscr "MANILA".
706 5 c. violet 60 45
707 6 c. grey 45 35
708 18 c. blue 60 45

(b) Arms inscr "CEBU".
709 5 c. red 60 45
710 6 c. brown 45 35
711 18 c. violet 60 45

(c) Arms inscr "ZAMBOANGA".
712 5 c. green 60 45
713 6 c. brown 45 35
714 18 c. blue 60 45

(d) Arms inscr "ILOILO".
715 5 c. green 60 45
716 6 c. violet 45 35
717 18 c. blue 60 45

1951. Guarding Peaceful Labour. Perf or imperf.
718 **143** 5 c. green 20 10
719 6 c. purple 35 35
720 18 c. blue 90 90

144 Philippines Flag and U.N. Emblem **145** Statue of Liberty

1951. U.N. Day.
721 **144** 5 c. red 75 35
722 6 c. green 60 35
723 18 c. blue . . . . 1·50 1·00

1951. Human Rights Day.
724 **145** 5 c. green 50 25
725 6 c. orange 65 50
726 18 c. blue . . . . 1·50 75

146 Schoolchildren **147** M. L. Quezon

1952. 50th Anniv of Philippine Educational System.
727 **146** 5 c. orange 60 50

1952. Portraits.
728 **147** 1 c. brown 10 10
729 – 2 c. black (J. Abad Santos) 10 10
730 – 3 c. red (A. Mabini) . . . 10 10
731 – 5 c. red (M. H. del Pilar) 10 10
732 – 10 c. blue (Father J. Burgos) 15 10
733 – 20 c. red (Lapu-Lapu) . . 30 10
734 – 25 c. green (Gen. A. Luna) 45 20
735 – 50 c. red (C. Arellano) . 85 25
736 – 60 c. red (A. Bonifacio) . 1·00 45
737 – 2 p. violet (G. L. Jaena) . 3·25 1·00

149 Aurora A. Quezon

1952. Fruit Tree Memorial Fund.
742 **149** 5 c. + 1 c. blue 15 15
743 6 c. + 2 c. pink 40 40
See also No. 925.

150 Milkfish and Map of Oceania

1952. Indo-Pacific Fisheries Council.
744 **150** 5 c. brown . . . . 1·10 65
745 6 c. blue 70 50

151 "A Letter from Rizal"

1952. Pan-Asiatic Philatelic Exhibition, Manila.
746 **151** 5 c. blue (postage) 60 15
747 6 c. brown 60 20
748 30 c. red (air) . . . . . . 1·25 1·00

152 Wright Park, Baguio City **153** F. Baltazar (poet)

1952. 3rd Lions District Convention.
749 **152** 5 c. red 90 90
750 6 c. green . . . . 1·25 1·00

1953. National Language Week.
751 **153** 5 c. bistre 50 35

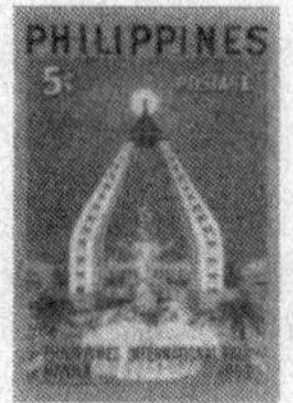

154 "Gateway to the East" **155** Pres. Quirino and Pres. Sukarno

1953. International Fair, Manila.
752 **154** 5 c. turquoise 30 15
753 6 c. red 35 15

1953. Visit of President to Indonesia. Flags in yellow, blue and red.
754 **155** 5 c. blue, yellow & black . 20 10
755 6 c. green, yellow & black . 25 25

156 Doctor examining patient

1953. 50th Anniv of Philippines Medical Association.
756 **156** 5 c. mauve 30 25
757 6 c. blue 35 35

1954. Optd **FIRST NATIONAL BOY SCOUTS JAMBOREE APRIL 23-30, 1954** or surch also.
758 5 c. red (No. 731) . . . . . 1·25 1·00
759 18 c. on 50 c. green (No. 634) . 2·00 1·50

158 Stamp of 1854, Magellan and Manila P.O.

1954. Stamp Centenary. Central stamp in orange.
760 **158** 5 c. violet (postage) . . . 75 50
761 18 c. blue . . . . 1·50 1·25
762 30 c. green . . . . 3·50 2·10
763 10 c. brown (air) . . . . . 1·50 1·25
764 20 c. green . . . . 2·50 2·00
765 50 c. red . . . . 5·00 4·25

159 Diving **161** "Independence"

1954. 2nd Asian Games, Manila.
766 – 5 c. blue on blue (Discus) 85 60
767 **159** 18 c. green on green . . . 1·40 1·00
768 – 30 c. red on pink (Boxing) 2·00 1·90

1954. Surch **MANILA CONFERENCE OF 1954** and value.
769 **113** 5 c. on 10 c. red 20 15
770 – 18 c. on 20 c. brown (No. 633) 75 65

1954. Independence Commemoration.
771 **161** 5 c. red 30 25
772 18 c. blue 90 50

162 "The Immaculate Conception" (Murillo) **163** Mayon Volcano and Filipino Vinta

1954. Marian Year.
773 **162** 5 c. blue 50 35

1955. 50th Anniv of Rotary International.
774 **163** 5 c. blue (postage) 40 15
775 18 c. red . . . . 1·25 70
776 50 c. green (air) . . . . . 2·50 1·10

164 "Labour" **165** Pres. Magsaysay

1955. Labour-Management Congress, Manila.
777 **164** 5 c. brown . . . . 1·50 60

1955. 9th Anniv of Republic.
778 **165** 5 c. blue 25 20
779 20 c. red 70 70
780 30 c. green . . . . 1·25 1·25

166 Lt. J. Gozar

1955. Air. Air Force Heroes.
781 **166** 20 c. violet 80 15
782 – 30 c. red (Lt. C. F. Basa) 1·10 20
783 **166** 50 c. green . . . . 1·25 25
784 – 70 c. bl (Lt. C. F. Basa) . 2·10 1·25

167 Liberty Well

1956. Artesian Wells for Rural Areas.
785 **167** 5 c. violet 35 35
786 20 c. green 80 65

1956. 5th Conference of World Confederation of Organizations of the Teaching Profession. No. 731 optd **WCOTP CONFERENCE MANILA.**
787 5 c. red 35 35

169 Nurse and War Victims **170** Monument (landing marker) in Leyte

1956. 50th Anniv of Philippines Red Cross.
788 **169** 5 c. violet and red 50 45
789 20 c. brown and red . . . 65 50

1956. Liberation Commem. Perf or imperf.
790 **170** 5 c. red 15 15

171 St. Thomas's University

172 Statue of the Sacred Heart

1956. University of St. Thomas.

791 **171** 5 c. brown and red . . . 35 25
792 60 c. brown and mauve . 1·50 1·40

1956. 2nd National Eucharistic Congress and Centenary of the Feast of the Sacred Heart.

793 **172** 5 c. green 35 30
794 20 c. pink 80 75

1956. Surch **5 5.**

795 5 c. on 6 c. brown (No. 710) . 15 15
796 5 c. on 6 c. brown (No. 713) . 15 15
797 5 c. on 6 c. violet (No. 716) . 15 15

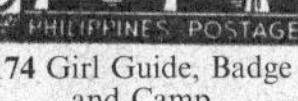

174 Girl Guide, Badge and Camp

175 Pres. Ramon Magsaysay

1957. Girl Guides' Pacific World Camp, Quezon City, and Birth Centenary of Lord Baden-Powell. Perf or imperf.

798 **174** 5 c. blue 45 45

1957. Death of Pres. Magsaysay.

799 **175** 5 c. black 15 10

176 Sergio Osmena (Speaker) and First Philippine Assembly

1957. 50th Anniv of First Philippine Assembly.

800 **176** 5 c. green 15 15

177 "The Spoliarium" after Juan Luna

1957. Birth Centenary of Juan Luna (painter).

801 **177** 5 c. red 15 10

1957. Inauguration of President C. P. Garcia and Vice-President D. Macapagal. Nos. 732/3 surch **GARCIA-MACAPAGAL INAUGURATION DEC. 30, 1957** and value.

802 5 c. on 10 c. blue 20 20
803 10 c. on 20 c. red 30 30

179 University of the Philippines

1958. Golden Jubilee of University of the Philippines.

804 **179** 5 c. red 35 15

180 Pres. Garcia

181 Main Hospital Building, Quezon Institute

1958. 12th Anniv of Republic.

805 **180** 5 c. multicoloured 15 10
806 20 c. multicoloured . . . 55 40

1958. Obligatory Tax. T.B. Relief Fund.

807 **181** 5 c. + 5 c. green and red 20 20
808 10 c. + 5 c. violet and red 40 40

182 The Immaculate Conception and Manila Cathedral

1958. Inauguration of Manila Cathedral.

809 **182** 5 c. multicoloured 25 15

1959. Surch **One Centavo.**

810 1 c. on 5 c. red (No. 731) . . 15 10

1959. 14th Anniv of Liberation. Nos. 704/5 surch.

812 **141** 1 c. on 2 c. + 2 c. red . . 10 10
813 – 6 c. on 4 c. + 4 c. violet . 15 15

186 Philippines Flag

187 Bulacan Seal

1959. Adoption of Philippine Constitution.

814 **186** 6 c. red, blue and yellow . 15 10
815 20 c. red, blue and yellow 25 20

1959. Provincial Seals. (a) Bulacan Seal and 60th Anniv of Malolos Constitution.

816 **187** 6 c. green 15 10
817 20 c. red 30 20

(b) Capiz Seal and 11th Death Anniv of Pres. Roxas.

818 6 c. brown 10 10
819 25 c. violet 30 30

The shield within the Capiz seal bears the inset portrait of Pres. Roxas.

(c) Bacolod Seal.

820 6 c. green 25 15
821 10 c. purple 35 25

188 Scout at Campfire

190 Bohol Sanatorium

1959. 10th World Scout Jamboree, Manila.

822 **188** 6 c. + 4 c. red on yellow (postage) 15 15
823 6 c. + 4 c. red 35 35
824 – 25 c. + 5 c. blue on yell . 60 60
825 – 25 c. + 5 c. blue 75 75
826 – 30 c. + 10 c. green (air) . 60 60
827 – 70 c. + 20 c. brown . . 1·25 1·25
828 – 80 c. + 20 c. violet . . . 1·90 1·90

DESIGNS: 25 c. Scout with bow and arrow; 30 c. Scout cycling; 70 c. Scout with model airplane; 80 c. Pres. Garcia with scout.

1959. Obligatory Tax. T.B. Relief Fund. Nos. 807/8 surch **HELP FIGHT T B** with Cross of Lorraine and value and new design (T **190**).

830 **181** 3 c. + 5 c. on 5 c. + 5 c. 20 20
831 6 c. + 5 c. on 10 c. + 5 c. 20 20
832 **190** 6 c. + 5 c. green and red 20 20
833 25 c. + 5 c. blue and red 45 35

191 Pagoda and Gardens at Camp John Hay

1959. 50th Anniv of Baguio.

834 **191** 6 c. green 15 10
835 25 c. red 35 25

1959. U.N. Day. Surch **6c UNITED NATIONS DAY.**

836 **132** 6 c. on 18 c. blue 15 10

193 Maria Cristina Falls

196 Dr. Jose Rizal

195

1959. World Tourist Conference, Manila.

837 **193** 6 c. green and violet . . . 15 15
838 30 c. green and brown . . 55 40

1959. No. 629 surch **One** and bars.

839 1 c. on 4 c. brown 15 10

1959. Centenary of Manila Athenaeum (school).

840 **195** 6 c. blue 10 10
841 30 c. red 45 35

1959.

842 **196** 6 c. blue 15 10

197 Book of the Constitution

1960. 25th Anniv of Philippines Constitution.

844 **197** 6 c. brn & gold (postage) . 15 10
845 30 c. blue & silver (air) . . 40 30

198 Congress Building

1960. 5th Anniv of Manila Pact.

846 **198** 6 c. green 10 10
847 25 c. orange 40 30

199 Sunset, Manila Bay

1960. World Refugee Year.

848 **199** 6 c. multicoloured 15 15
849 25 c. multicoloured 40 30

200 North American F-86 Sabre and Boeing P-12 Fighters

1960. Air. 25th Anniv of Philippine Air Force.

850 **200** 10 c. red 30 15
851 20 c. blue 55 35

1960. Surch.

852 **134** 1 c. on 18 c. blue 10 10
853 **161** 5 c. on 18 c. blue 25 20
854 **163** 5 c. on 18 c. red 30 15
855 **158** 10 c. on 18 c. orange & bl 25 15
856 **140** 10 c. on 18 c. blue 25 20

202 Lorraine Cross

204 Pres. Quezon

1960. 50th Anniv of Philippine Tuberculosis Society. Lorraine Cross and wreath in red and gold.

857 **202** 5 c. green 15 10
858 6 c. blue 15 10

1960. Obligatory Tax. T.B. Relief Fund. Surch **6 + 5 HELP PREVENT TB.**

859 **181** 6 c. + 5 c. on 5 c. + 5 c. green and red 20 15

1960.

860 **204** 1 c. green 15 10

205 Basketball

1960. Olympic Games.

861 **205** 6 c. brn & grn (postage) . 15 10
862 – 10 c. brown and purple . 20 15
863 – 30 c. brn and orge (air) . 60 50
864 – 70 c. purple and blue . . 1·25 1·00

DESIGNS: 10 c. Running; 30 c. Rifle-shooting; 70 c. Swimming.

206 Presidents Eisenhower and Garcia

1960. Visit of President Eisenhower.

865 **206** 6 c. multicoloured 25 15
866 20 c. multicoloured . . . 50 25

207 "Mercury" and Globe

1961. Manila Postal Conference.

867 **207** 6 c. multicoloured (postage) 15 10
868 30 c. multicoloured (air) . 35 25

1961. Surch **20 20.**

869 20 c. on 25 c. grn (No. 734) . 25 15

1961. 2nd National Scout Jamboree, Zamboanga. Nos. 822/5 surch **2nd National Boy Scout Jamboree Pasonanca Park** and value.

870 10 c. on 6 c. + 4 c. red on yellow 15 15
871 10 c. on 6 c. + 4 c. red . . . 50 50
872 30 c. on 25 c. + 5 c. blue on yellow 40 40
873 30 c. on 25 c. + 5 c. blue . . 50 50

210 La Salle College

1961. 50th Anniv of La Salle College.

874 **210** 6 c. multicoloured 15 10
875 10 c. multicoloured . . . 25 10

211 Rizal when Student, School and University Buildings

1961. Birth Centenary of Dr. Jose Rizal.
876 **211** 5 c. multicoloured 10 10
877 – 6 c. multicoloured 10 10
878 – 10 c. brown and green . . 20 20
879 – 20 c. turquoise and brown 30 30
880 – 30 c. multicoloured . . . 45 35
DESIGNS: 6 c. Rizal and birthplace at Calamba, Laguna; 10 c. Rizal, mother and father; 20 c. Rizal extolling Luna and Hidalgo at Madrid; 30 c. Rizal's execution.

1961. 15th Anniv of Republic. Optd **IKA 15 KAARAWAN Republika ng Pilipinas Hulyo 4, 1961.**
881 **198** 6 c. green 25 25
882 25 c. orange 40 40

213 Roxas Memorial T.B. Pavilion
214 Globe, Plan Emblem and Supporting Hand

1961. Obligatory Tax. T.B. Relief Fund.
883 **213** 6 c. + 5 c. brown and red 20 15

1961. 7th Anniv of Admission of Philippines to Colombo Plan.
884 **214** 5 c. multicoloured 10 10
885 6 c. multicoloured 10 10

1961. Philippine Amateur Athletic Federation's Golden Jubilee. Surch with P.A.A.F. monogram and **6c PAAF GOLDEN JUBILEE 1911 1961.**
886 **200** 6 c. on 10 c. red 25 20

216 Typist

1961. Government Employees' Association.
887 **216** 6 c. violet and brown . . 15 10
888 10 c. blue and brown . . 35 20

1961. Inauguration of Pres. Macapagal and Vice-Pres. Pelaez. Surch **MACAPAGAL-PELAEZ DEC. 30, 1961 INAUGURATION 6 c.**
889 6 c. on 25 c. vio (No. 819) . . 20 10

1962. Cross obliterated by Arms and surch **6 s.**
890 **181** 6 c. on 5 c. + 5 c. green and red 15 15

220 Waling-Waling
221 A. Mabini (statesman)

1962. Orchids. Multicoloured.
892 5 c. Type **220** 10 10
893 6 c. White Mariposa 15 15
894 10 c. "Dendrobium sanderii" . 20 20
895 20 c. Sanggumay 35 35

1962. New Currency.
896 – 1 s. brown 10 10
897 **221** 3 s. red 10 10
898 – 5 s. red 10 10
899 – 6 s. brown 15 10
900 – 6 s. blue 15 10
901 – 10 s. purple 15 10
902 – 20 s. blue 25 10
903 – 30 s. red 50 15
904 – 50 s. violet 80 15
905 – 70 s. blue . . . . 1·00 45
906 – 1 p. green . . . . 2·00 40
907 – 1 p. orange 65 35
PORTRAITS: 1 s. M. L. Quezon; 5 s. M. H. del Pilar; 6 s. (2) J. Rizal (different); 10 s. Father J. Burgos; 20 s. Lapu-Lapu; 30 s. Rajah Soliman; 50 s. C. Arellano; 70 s. S. Osmena; 1 p. (No. 906) E. Jacinto; 1 p. (No. 907) J. M. Panganiban.

225 Pres. Macapagal taking Oath

1962. Independence Day.
915 **225** 6 s. multicoloured 15 10
916 10 s. multicoloured . . . 20 15
917 30 s. multicoloured . . . 35 20

226 Valdes Memorial T.B. Pavilion

1962. Obligatory Tax Stamps. T.B. Relief Fund. Cross in red.
918 **226** 6 s. + 5 s. purple 15 15
919 30 s. + 5 s. blue 45 30
920 70 s. + 5 s. blue . . . . 1·00 80

227 Lake Taal

1962. Malaria Eradication.
921 **227** 6 s. multicoloured 15 15
922 10 s. multicoloured . . . 20 15
923 70 s. multicoloured . . . 1·40 1·00

1962. Bicentenary of Diego Silang Revolt. No. 734 surch **1762 1962 BICENTENNIAL Diego Silang Revolt 20.**
924 20 s. on 25 c. green 30 20

1962. No. 742 with premium obliterated.
925 **149** 5 c. blue 20 15

230 Dr. Rizal playing Chess

1962. Rizal Foundation Fund.
926 **230** 6 s. + 4 s. green & mauve 25 25
927 – 30 s. + 5 s. blue & purple 50 50
DESIGN: 30 s. Dr. Rizal fencing.

1963. Surch.
928 **221** 1 s. on 3 s. red 15 10
929 – 5 s. on 6 s. brown (No. 899) 15 10

1963. Diego Silang Bicentenary Art and Philatelic Exhibition, G.P.O., Manila. No. 737 surch **1763 1963 DIEGO SILANG BICENTENNIAL ARPHEX** and value.
930 6 c. on 2 p. violet 20 15
931 20 c. on 2 p. violet 25 25
932 70 c. on 2 p. violet 80 65

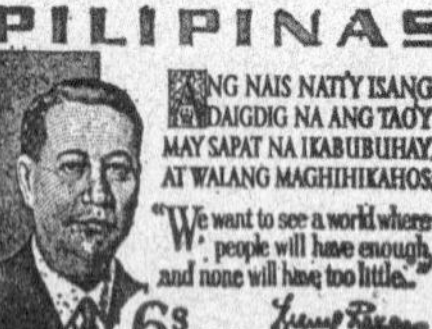

233 "We want to see ..." (Pres. Roxas)

1963. Presidential Sayings (1st issue).
933 **233** 6 s. blue and black . . . 15 10
934 30 s. brown and black . . 50 15
See also Nos. 959/60, 981/2, 1015/16, 1034/5, 1055/6, 1148/9 and 1292/3.

MINIMUM PRICE

The minimum price quoted is 10p which represents a handling charge rather than a basis for valuing common stamps. For further notes about prices, see introductory pages.

234 Lorraine Cross on Map

1963. Obligatory Tax. T.B. Relief Fund. Cross in red.
935 **234** 6 s. + 5 s. pink & violet . 15 10
936 10 s. + 5 s. pink & green . 15 15
937 50 s. + 5 s. pink & brown 65 45

235 Globe and Flags
236 Centenary Emblem

1963. 1st Anniv of Asian-Oceanic Postal Union.
938 **235** 6 s. multicoloured 15 15
939 20 s. multicoloured 20 15

1963. Red Cross Centenary. Cross in red.
940 **236** 5 s. grey and violet 15 10
941 6 s. grey and blue 15 10
942 20 s. grey and green . . . 40 25

237 Tinikling (dance)

1963. Folk Dances. Multicoloured.
943 5 s. Type **237** 20 20
944 6 s. Pandanggo sa Ilaw . . . 20 20
945 10 s. Itik-Itik 20 20
946 20 s. Singkil 35 30

238 Pres. Macapagal and Philippine Family

1963. President's Social-Economic Programme.
947 **238** 5 s. multicoloured 15 10
948 6 s. multicoloured 15 15
949 20 s. multicoloured 30 25

239 Presidents' Meeting
240 Bonifacio and Flag

1963. Visit of President Mateos of Mexico.
950 **239** 6 s. multicoloured 20 15
951 30 s. multicoloured 40 15

1963. Birth Cent of Andres Bonifacio (patriot).
952 **240** 5 s. multicoloured 15 10
953 6 s. multicoloured 15 10
954 25 s. multicoloured 30 25

241 Harvester
242 Bamboo Organ, Catholic Church, Las Pinas

1963. Freedom from Hunger.
956 **241** 6 s. multicoloured (postage) 15 10
957 30 s. multicoloured (air) . 55 40
958 50 s. multicoloured . . . 90 45

1963. Presidential Sayings (2nd issue). As T **233** but with portrait and saying changed.
959 6 s. black and violet 15 10
960 30 s. black and green 35 15
PORTRAIT AND SAYING: Pres. Magsaysay, "I believe ...".

1964. Las Pinas Organ Commemoration.
961 **242** 5 s. multicoloured 15 10
962 6 s. multicoloured 15 10
963 20 s. multicoloured . . . 40 25

243 A. Mabini (patriot)
245 S.E.A.T.O. Emblems and Flags

244 Negros Oriental T.B. Pavilion

1964. Birth Centenary of A. Mabini.
964 **243** 6 s. gold and violet . . . 15 10
965 10 s. gold and brown . . 15 15
966 30 s. gold and green . . . 25 15

1964. Obligatory Tax. T.B. Relief Fund. Cross in red.
967 **244** 5 s. + 5 s. purple 15 10
968 5 s. + 5 s. blue 15 10
969 30 s. + 5 s. brown 45 30
970 70 s. + 5 s. green 80 75

1964. 10th Anniv of S.E.A.T.O.
971 **245** 6 s. multicoloured 15 10
972 10 s. multicoloured . . . 20 15
973 25 s. multicoloured . . . 25 20

246 President signing the Land Reform Code
247 Basketball

1964. Agricultural Land Reform Code. President and inscr at foot in brown, red and sepia.
974 **246** 3 s. green (postage) . . . 15 10
975 6 s. blue 15 10
976 30 s. brown (air) 30 25

1964. Olympic Games, Tokyo. Sport in brown. Perf or imperf.
977 **247** 6 s. blue and gold 15 15
978 – 10 s. pink and gold . . . 25 15
979 – 20 s. yellow and gold . . 45 25
980 – 30 s. green and gold . . . 60 45
SPORTS: 10 s. Relay-racing; 20 s. Hurdling; 30 s. Football.

1965. Presidential Sayings (3rd issue). As T **233** but with portrait and saying changed.
981 6 s. black and green 15 10
982 30 s. black and purple 35 15
PORTRAIT AND SAYING: Pres. Quirino, "So live ...".

248 Presidents Luebke and Macapagal

1965. Visit of President of German Federal Republic.
983 **248** 6 s. multicoloured 15 10
984 10 s. multicoloured . . . 20 10
985 25 s. multicoloured . . . 35 30

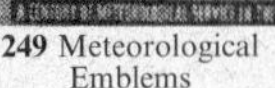

249 Meteorological Emblems
250 Pres. Kennedy

1965. Cent of Philippines Meteorological Services.
986 **249** 6 s. multicoloured 15 10
987 20 s. multicoloured . . . 15 15
988 50 s. multicoloured . . . 50 30

1965. John F. Kennedy (U.S. President) Commemoration.
989 **250** 6 s. multicoloured 20 10
990 10 s. multicoloured . . . 20 15
991 30 s. multicoloured . . . 45 25

251 King Bhumibol and Queen Sirikit, Pres. Macapagal and Wife

1965. Visit of King and Queen of Thailand.
992 **251** 2 s. multicoloured 10 10
993 6 s. multicoloured 15 10
994 30 s. multicoloured . . . 45 25

252 Princess Beatrix and Mrs. Macapagal

1965. Visit of Princess Beatrix of the Netherlands.
995 **252** 2 s. multicoloured 10 10
996 6 s. multicoloured 15 10
997 10 s. multicoloured . . . 20 15

1965. Obligatory Tax. T.B. Relief Fund. Surch.
998 **244** 1 s. + 5 s. on 6 s. + 5 s. . 15 10
999 3 s. + 5 s. on 6 s. + 5 s. . 20 15

254 Hand holding Cross and Rosary
256 Signing Agreement

1965. 400th Anniv of Philippines Christianisation. Multicoloured.
1000 3 s. Type **254** (postage) . . . 15 10
1001 6 s. Legaspi-Urdaneta, monument 20 10
1002 30 s. Baptism of Filipinos by Father Urdaneta, Cebu (air) 50 30
1003 70 s. "Way of the Cross"–ocean map of Christian voyagers' route, Spain to the Philippines 1·10 65
Nos. 1002/3 are horiz, 48 × 27 mm.

1965. "MAPILINDO" Conference, Manila.
1005 **256** 6 s. blue, red & yellow . 15 10
1006 10 s. multicoloured . . . 15 15
1007 25 s. multicoloured . . . 40 25
The above stamps depict Pres. Sukarno of Indonesia, former Pres. Macapagal of the Philippines and Prime Minister Tunku Abdul Rahman of Malaysia.

257 Cyclists and Globe
259 Dr. A. Regidor

1965. 2nd Asian Cycling Championships, Philippines.
1008 **257** 6 s. multicoloured . . . 10 10
1009 10 s. multicoloured . . . 20 15
1010 25 s. multicoloured . . . 40 25

1965. Inauguration of Pres. Marcos and Vice-Pres. Lopez. Nos. 926/7 surch **MARCOS-LOPEZ INAUGURATION DEC. 30, 1965** and value.
1011 **230** 10 s. on 6 s. + 4 s. . . 20 20
1012 – 30 s. on 30 s. + 5 s. . . 50 50

1966. Regidor (patriot) Commemoration.
1013 **259** 6 s. blue 15 10
1014 30 s. brown 25 25

1966. Presidential Sayings (4th issue). As T **233** but with portrait and saying changed.
1015 6 s. black and red 15 10
1016 30 s. black and blue 35 15
PORTRAIT AND SAYING: Pres. Aguinaldo, "Have faith ...".

1966. Campaign Against Smuggling. No. 900 optd **HELP ME STOP SMUGGLING Pres. MARCOS.**
1017 6 s. blue 20 15

261 Girl Scout

1966. Silver Jubilee of Philippines Girl Scouts.
1018 **261** 3 s. multicoloured . . . 10 10
1019 6 s. multicoloured . . . 15 10
1020 20 s. multicoloured . . . 40 25

262 Pres. Marcos taking Oath

1966. Inauguration (1965) of Pres. Marcos.
1021 **262** 6 s. multicoloured . . . 15 10
1022 20 s. multicoloured . . . 15 15
1023 30 s. multicoloured . . . 25 25

263 Manila Seal and Historical Scenes

1966. Introduction of New Seal for Manila.
1024 **263** 6 s. multicoloured . . . 15 15
1025 30 s. multicoloured . . . 25 15

264 Bank Facade and 1-peso Coin

1966. 50th Anniv of Philippines National Bank. Mult.
1026 6 s. Type **264** 15 10
1027 10 s. Old and new bank buildings 15 15

266 Bank Building

1966. 60th Anniv of Postal Savings Bank.
1029 **266** 6 s. violet, yellow & grn . 15 10
1030 10 s. red, yellow & grn . . 15 15
1031 20 s. blue, yellow & grn . 40 20

1966. Manila Summit Conference. Nos. 1021 and 1023 optd **MANILA SUMMIT CONFERENCE 1966 7 NATIONS** and emblem.
1032 **262** 6 s. multicoloured . . . 15 15
1033 30 s. multicoloured . . . 35 25

1966. Presidential Sayings (5th issue). As T **233** but with portrait and saying changed.
1034 6 s. black and brown 15 10
1035 30 s. black and blue 35 15
PORTRAIT AND SAYING: Pres. Laurel; "No one can love the Filipinos better ...".

1967. 50th Anniv of Lions International. Nos. 977/80 optd with Lions emblem and **50th ANNIVERSARY LIONS INTERNATIONAL 1967.** Imperf.
1036 **247** 6 c. blue and gold . . . 15 15
1037 – 10 c. pink and gold . . 20 15
1038 – 20 c. yellow and gold . . 40 25
1039 – 30 c. green and gold . . 60 60

269 "Succour" (after painting by F. Amorsolo)

1967. 25th Anniv of Battle of Bataan.
1040 **269** 5 s. multicoloured 15 10
1041 20 s. multicoloured . . . 25 15
1042 2 p. multicoloured . . . 2·10 1·25

1967. Nos. 900 and 975 surch.
1043 – 4 s. on 6 s. blue 15 10
1044 **246** 5 s. on 6 s. blue 15 10

271 Stork-billed Kingfisher

1967. Obligatory Tax. T.B. Relief Fund. Birds. Multicoloured.
1045 1 s. + 5 s. Type **271** 15 10
1046 5 s. + 5 s. Rufous hornbill . 65 15
1047 10 s. + 5 s. Philippine eagle . 1·25 30
1048 30 s. + 5 s. Great-billed parrot 1·90 55
See also Nos. 1113/16.

272 Gen. MacArthur and Paratroopers landing on Corregidor

1967. 25th Anniv of Battle of Corregidor.
1049 **272** 6 s. multicoloured 10 10
1050 5 p. multicoloured . . . 4·00 3·25

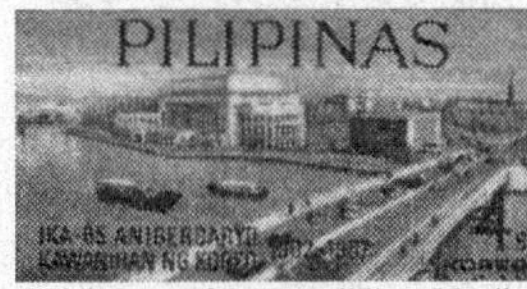

273 Bureau of Posts Building, Manila

1967. 65th Anniv of Philippines Bureau of Posts.
1051 **273** 4 s. multicoloured 20 20
1052 20 s. multicoloured . . . 20 10
1053 50 s. multicoloured . . . 50 40

274 Escaping from Eruption

1967. Obligatory Tax. Taal Volcano Eruption (1965) (1st issue).
1054 **274** 70 s. multicoloured . . . 90 75
For compulsory use on foreign air mail where the rate exceeds 70 s. in aid of Taal Volcano Rehabilitation Committee.
See also No. 1071.

1967. Presidential Sayings (6th issue). As T **233** but with portrait and saying changed.
1055 10 s. black and blue 15 10
1056 30 s. black and violet 35 15
PORTRAIT AND SAYING: Pres. Quezon. "Social justice is far more beneficial ...".

275 "The Holy Family" (Filipino version)

1967. Christmas.
1057 **275** 10 s. multicoloured . . . 15 15
1058 40 s. multicoloured . . . 50 35

276 Pagoda, Pres. Marcos and Chiang Kai-shek

1967. China–Philippines Friendship.
1059 **276** 5 s. multicoloured . . . 10 10
1060 – 10 s. multicoloured . . . 15 15
1061 – 20 s. multicoloured . . . 20 15
DESIGNS (with portraits of Pres. Marcos and Chiang Kai-shek): 10 s. Gateway, Chinese Garden, Rizal Park, Luneta; 20 s. Chinese Garden, Rizal Park, Luneta.

277 Ayala Avenue, Manila, Inaugural Ceremony and Rotary Badge

1968. 1st Anniv of Makati Centre Post Office, Manila.
1062 **277** 10 s. multicoloured . . . 10 10
1063 20 s. multicoloured . . . 25 25
1064 40 s. multicoloured . . . 50 50

1968. Surch.
1065 – 5 s. on 6 s. (No. 981) . . 10 10
1066 – 5 s. on 6 s. (No. 1034) . . 10 10
1067 **244** 10 s. on 6 s. + 5 s. . . . 10 10

280 Calderon, Barasoain Church and Constitution

1068. Birth Centenary of Felipe G. Calderon (lawyer and author of Malolos Constitution).
1068 **280** 10 s. multicoloured . . . 15 10
1069 40 s. multicoloured . . . 60 40
1070 75 s. multicoloured . . . 1·10 1·00

281 Eruption
282 "Philcomsat" Earth Station and Globe

1968. Taal Volcano Eruption (1965) (2nd issue).
1071 **281** 70 s. multicoloured . . . 90 90

Two issues were prepared by an American Agency under a contract signed with the Philippine postal authority but at the last moment this contract was cancelled by the Philippine Government. In the meanwhile the stamps had been on sale in the U.S.A. but they were never issued in the Philippines and they had no postal validity.

They comprise a set for the Mexican Olympic Games in the values 1, 2, 3 and 15 s. postage and 50, 75 s., 1, 2. p. airmail and a set in memory of J. F. Kennedy and Robert Kennedy in the values 1, 2, 3 s. postage and 5, 10 p. airmail.

1968. Inauguration of "Philcomsat"–POTC Earth Station, Tanay, Rizal, Luzon.
1072 **282** 10 s. multicoloured . . . 20 15
1073 40 s. multicoloured . . . 50 45
1074 75 s. multicoloured . . . 95 80

283 "Tobacco Production" (mural)

1968. Philippines Tobacco Industry.
1075 **283** 10 s. multicoloured . . . 15 15
1076 40 s. multicoloured . . . 60 50
1077 70 s. multicoloured . . . 1·00 85

284 "Kudyapi"

1968. St. Cecilia's Day. Musical Instruments. Mult.

1078 10 s. Type **284** 15 10
1079 20 s. "Ludag" 15 15
1080 30 s. "Kulintangan" 35 30
1081 50 s. "Subing" 50 50

285 Concordia College **286** Children singing Carols

1968. Centenary of Concordia Women's College.

1082 **285** 10 s. multicoloured 15 15
1083 20 s. multicoloured 20 15
1084 70 s. multicoloured 65 50

1968. Christmas.

1085 **286** 10 s. multicoloured 15 15
1086 40 s. multicoloured 50 45
1087 75 s. multicoloured 90 75

287 Philippine Tarsier

1969. Philippines Fauna. Multicoloured.

1088 2 s. Type **287** 15 15
1089 10 s. Tamarau 15 15
1090 20 s. Water buffalo 25 20
1091 75 s. Greater Malay chevrotain 1·25 1·00

288 President Aguinaldo and Cavite Building

1969. Birth Centenary of President Amilio Aguinaldo.

1092 **288** 10 s. multicoloured 20 15
1093 40 s. multicoloured 55 35
1094 70 s. multicoloured 1·00 80

289 Rotary Emblem and "Bastion of San Andres"

1969. 50th Anniv of Manila Rotary Club.

1095 **289** 10 s. mult (postage) 15 15
1096 40 s. multicoloured (air) 40 30
1097 75 s. multicoloured 90 70

290 Senator C. M. Recto **292** Jose Rizal College

1969. Recto Commemoration.

1098 **290** 10 s. purple 15 10

1969. Philatelic Week. No. 1051 optd **PHILATELIC WEEK NOV. 24-30, 1968.**

1099 **273** 4 s. multicoloured 20 10

1969. 50th Anniv of Jose Rizal College, Mandaluyong, Rizal.

1100 **292** 10 s. multicoloured 15 15
1101 40 s. multicoloured 60 40
1102 50 s. multicoloured 75 65

1969. 4th National Boy Scout Jamboree, Palayan City. No. 1019 surch **4th NATIONAL BOY SCOUT JAMBOREE PALAYAN CITY — MAY, 1969 5 s.**

1103 **261** 5 s. on 6 s. multicoloured 20 15

294 Red Cross Emblems and Map **295** Pres. and Mrs. Marcos harvesting Rice

1969. 50th Anniv of League of Red Cross Societies.

1104 **294** 10 s. red, blue and grey 15 10
1105 40 s. red, blue and cobalt 50 30
1106 75 s. red, brown & buff 80 70

1969. "Rice for Progress".

1107 **295** 10 s. multicoloured 15 10
1108 40 s. multicoloured 50 35
1109 75 s. multicoloured 80 70

296 "The Holy Child of Leyte" (statue)

1969. 80th Anniv of Return of the "Holy Child of Leyte" to Tacloban.

1110 **296** 5 s. mult (postage) 10 10
1111 10 s. multicoloured 15 15
1112 40 s. multicoloured (air) 45 35

1969. Obligatory Tax. T.B. Relief Fund. Birds as T **271**.

1113 1 s. + 5 s. Golden-backed three-toed woodpecker 10 10
1114 5 s. + 5 s. Philippine trogon 50 15
1115 10 s. + 5 s. Johnstone's (inscr "Mt. Apo") lorikeet 1·40 35
1116 40 s. + 5 s. Scarlet (inscr "Johnstone's") minivet 1·90 50

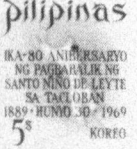

297 Bank Building

1969. Inauguration of Philippines Development Bank, Makati, Rizal.

1117 **297** 10 s. black, blue & green 15 10
1118 40 s. black, purple & green 85 40
1119 75 s. black, brown & grn 1·25 90

298 "Philippine Birdwing"

1969. Philippine Butterflies. Multicoloured.

1120 10 s. Type **298** 25 15
1121 20 s. Tailed jay 30 20
1122 30 s. Red Helen 55 30
1123 40 s. Birdwing 80 45

299 Children of the World

1969. 15th Anniv of Universal Children's Day.

1124 **299** 10 s. multicoloured 15 10
1125 20 s. multicoloured 15 15
1126 30 s. multicoloured 25 20

300 Memorial and Outline of Landing **303** Melchora Aquino

301 Cultural Centre

1969. 25th Anniv of U.S. Forces' Landing on Leyte.

1127 **300** 5 s. multicoloured 15 10
1128 10 s. multicoloured 15 15
1129 40 s. multicoloured 50 30

1969. Cultural Centre, Manila.

1130 **301** 10 s. blue 15 15
1131 30 s. purple 35 25

1969. Philatelic Week. Nos. 943/6 (Folk Dances) optd **1969 PHILATELIC WEEK** or surch also.

1132 5 s. multicoloured 15 15
1133 5 s. on 6 s. multicoloured 15 15
1134 10 s. multicoloured 20 20
1135 10 s. on 20 s. multicoloured 25 20

1969. 50th Death Anniv of Melchora Aquino, "Tandang Sora" (Grand Old Woman of the Revolution).

1136 **303** 10 s. multicoloured 15 10
1137 20 s. multicoloured 25 15
1138 30 s. multicoloured 40 25

1969. 2nd-term Inaug of President Marcos. Surch **PASINAYA, IKA-2 PANUNUNGKULAN PANGULONG FERDINAND E. MARCOS DISYEMBRE 30, 1969.**

1139 **262** 5 s. on 6 s. multicoloured 25 10

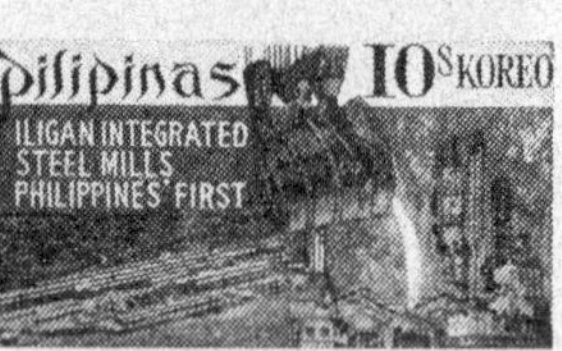

305 Ladle and Steel Mills

1970. Iligan Integrated Steel Mills.

1140 **305** 10 s. multicoloured 20 10
1141 20 s. multicoloured 40 20
1142 30 s. multicoloured 60 30

1970. Nos. 900, 962 and 964 surch.

1143 – 4 s. on 6 s. blue 15 10
1144 **242** 5 s. on 6 s. multicoloured 15 10
1145 **243** 5 s. on 6 s. multicoloured 15 10

307 New U.P.U. Headquarters Building

1970. New U.P.U. Headquarters Building, Berne.

1146 **307** 10 s. ultramarine, yellow and blue 15 10
1147 30 s. blue, yellow and green 50 30

1970. Presidential Sayings (7th issue). As T **233** but with portrait and saying changed.

1148 10 s. black and purple 10 10
1149 40 s. black and green 35 15

PORTRAIT AND SAYING: Pres. Osmena, "Ante todo el bien de nuestro pueblo" ("The well-being of our nation comes above all").

308 Dona Julia V. de Ortigas and T.B. Society Headquarters

1970. Obligatory Tax. T.B. Relief Fund.

1150 **308** 1 s. + 5 s. multicoloured 15 10
1151 5 s. + 5 s. multicoloured 20 20
1152 30 s. + 5 s. multicoloured 70 70
1153 70 s. + 5 s. multicoloured 90 90

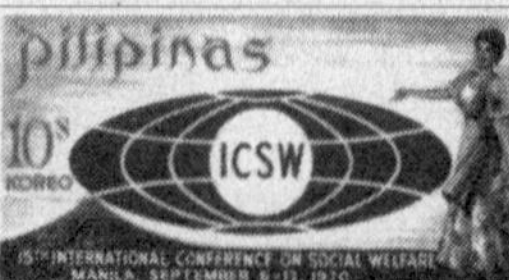

309 I.C.S.W. Emblem

1970. 15th Int Conference on Social Welfare.

1154 **309** 10 s. multicoloured 15 15
1155 20 s. multicoloured 30 20
1156 30 s. multicoloured 50 25

310 "Crab" (after sculpture by A. Calder)

1970. "Fight Cancer" Campaign.

1157 **310** 10 s. multicoloured 20 15
1158 40 s. multicoloured 45 25
1159 50 s. multicoloured 65 35

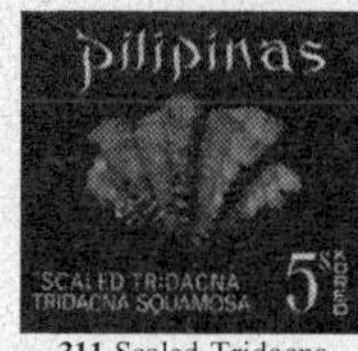

311 Scaled Tridacna

1970. Sea Shells. Multicoloured.

1160 5 s. Type **311** 10 10
1161 10 s. Royal spiny oyster 25 10
1162 20 s. Venus comb murex 40 15
1163 40 s. Glory-of-the-sea cone 85 40

1970. Nos. 986, 1024 and 1026 surch with new values in figures and words.

1164 **249** 4 s. on 6 s. 15 10
1165 **263** 4 s. on 6 s. 15 10
1166 **264** 4 s. on 6 s. 15 10

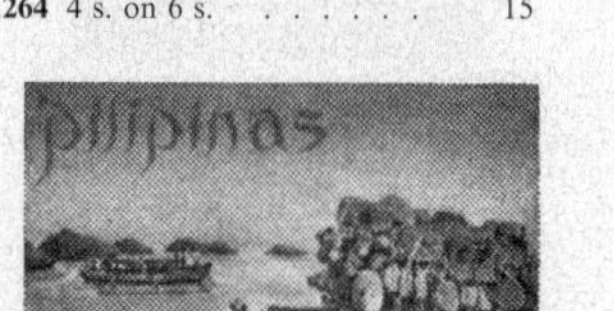

313 The "Hundred Islands" and Ox-cart

1970. Tourism (1st series). Multicoloured.

1167 10 s. Type **313** 15 15
1168 20 s. Tree-house, Pasonanca Park, Zamboanga City 20 15
1169 30 s. "Filipino" (statue) and sugar plantation, Negros Island 30 25
1170 2 p. Calesa (horse-carriage) and Miagao Church, Iloilo 1·90 1·10

See also Nos. 1186/9, 1192/5 and 1196/9.

314 Map of the Philippines

1970. Golden Jubilee of Philippine Pharmaceutical Association.

1171 **314** 10 s. multicoloured 15 10
1172 50 s. multicoloured 65 35

1970. U.P.U./A.O.P.U. Regional Seminar, Manila. No. 938 surch **UPU-AOPU REGIONAL SEMINAR NOV. 23–DEC. 5, 1970 TEN 10s.**

1173 **235** 10 s. on 6 s. multicoloured 15 15

1970. Philatelic Week. No. 977 surch **1970 PHILATELIC WEEK 10s TEN.**

1174 **247** 10 s. on 6 s. brown, blue and gold 15 10

317 Pope Paul VI and Map

1970. Pope Paul's Visit to the Philippines.
1175 **317** 10 s. mult (postage) . . . 15 10
1176 30 s. multicoloured . . . 30 20
1177 40 s. multicoloured (air) . 35 25

318 Mariano Ponce
320 "PATA" Horse and Carriage

1970.
1178 **318** 10 s. red 15 10
1179 – 15 s. brown 15 10
1180 – 40 s. red 35 10
1181 – 1 p. blue 90 35
DESIGNS: 15 s. Josefa Llanes Escoda; 40 s. Gen. Miguel Malvar; 1 p. Julian Felipe.

1971. 20th PATA Conference and Workshop, Manila.
1183 **320** 5 s. multicoloured . . . 10 10
1184 10 s. multicoloured . . . 15 15
1185 70 s. multicoloured . . . 50 35

1971. Tourism (2nd series). Views as T **313**. Multicoloured.
1186 10 s. Nayong Pilipino resort . 10 10
1187 20 s. Fish farm, Iloilo 15 10
1188 30 s. Pagsanjan Falls 20 15
1189 5 p. Watch-tower, Punta Cruz 1·60 1·60

321 Emblem and Family

1971. Regional Conference of International Planned Parenthood Federation for South-East Asia and Oceania.
1190 **321** 20 s. multicoloured . . . 15 10
1191 40 s. multicoloured . . . 25 15

1971. Tourism (3rd series). As T **313**. Mult.
1192 10 s. Aguinaldo pearl farm . . 15 10
1193 20 s. Coral-diving, Davao . . 20 15
1194 40 s. Taluksengay Mosque . . 25 20
1195 1 p. Ifugao woman and Banaue rice-terraces 60 50

1971. Tourism (4th series). As T **313**. Mult.
1196 10 s. Cannon and Filipino vintas, Fort del Pilar . . . 15 10
1197 30 s. Magellan's Cross, Cebu City 15 15
1198 50 s. "Big Jar", Calamba, Laguna (Rizal's birthplace) 25 25
1199 70 s. Mayon Volcano and diesel train . . . . 1·75 50

1971. Surch **FIVE 5s.**
1200 **264** 5 s. on 6 s. multicoloured 15 10

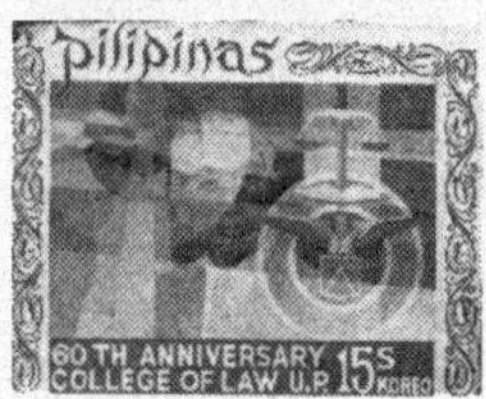

323 G. A. Malcolm (founder) and Law Symbols

1971. 60th Anniv of Philippines College of Law.
1201 **323** 15 s. mult (postage) . . . 15 15
1202 1 p. multicoloured (air) . 75 70

324 Commemorative Seal

1971. 400th Anniv of Manila.
1203 **324** 10 s. multicoloured (postage) 15 15
1204 1 p. multicoloured (air) . 1·10 75

325 Arms of Faculties

1971. Centenaries of Faculties of Medicine and Surgery, and of Pharmacy, Santo Tomas University.
1205 **325** 5 s. mult (postage) . . . 15 10
1206 2 p. multicoloured (air) . 1·50 1·40

1971. University Presidents' World Congress, Manila. Surch **MANILA MCMLXXI CONGRESS OF UNIVERSITY PRESIDENTS 5s FIVE** and emblem.
1207 **266** 5 s. on 6 s. violet, yellow and green 15 10

327 "Our Lady of Guia"

1971. 400th Anniv of "Our Lady of Guia", Ermita, Manila.
1208 **327** 10 s. multicoloured . . . 15 15
1209 75 s. multicoloured . . . 60 50

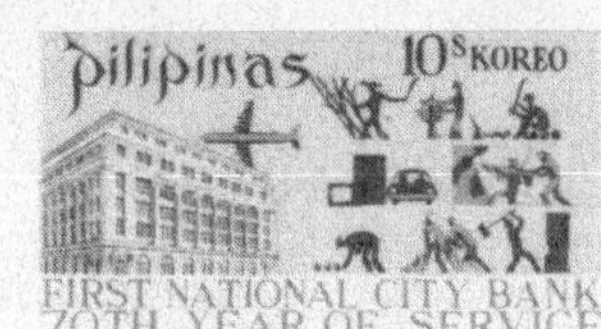

328 Bank and "Customers"

1971. 70th Anniv of First National City Bank.
1210 **328** 10 s. multicoloured . . . 15 10
1211 30 s. multicoloured . . . 30 25
1212 1 p. multicoloured . . . 65 50

1971. Surch in figure and word.
1213 **259** 4 s. on 6 s. blue 15 10
1214 5 s. on 6 s. blue 15 10

1971. Philatelic Week. Surch **1971 - PHILATELIC WEEK 5s FIVE.**
1215 **266** 5 s. on 6 s. violet, yellow and green 15 10

331 Dish Aerial and Events

1972. 6th Asian Electronics Conference, Manila (1971) and Related Events.
1216 **331** 5 s. multicoloured . . . 15 10
1217 40 s. multicoloured . . . 50 35

332 Fathers Burgos, Gomez and Zamora

1972. Centenary of Martyrdom of Fathers Burgos, Gomez and Zamora.
1218 **332** 5 s. multicoloured . . . 10 10
1219 60 s. multicoloured . . . 40 40

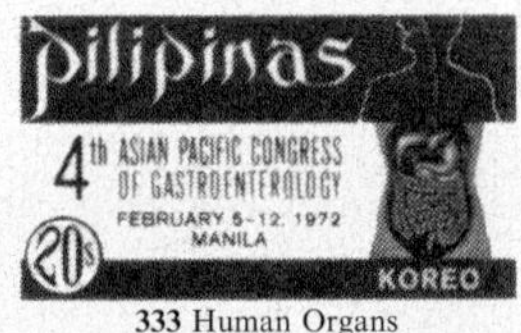

333 Human Organs

1972. 4th Asian-Pacific Gastro-enterological Congress, Manila.
1220 **333** 20 s. mult (postage) . . 20 15
1221 40 s. multicoloured (air) 40 35

1972. Surch **5s FIVE.**
1222 **263** 5 s. on 6 s. multicoloured 15 10

1972. No. O914 with optd **G.O.** obliterated by bars.
1223 50 s. violet 40 25

1972. Surch.
1224 **245** 10 s. on 6 s. multicoloured 15 10
1225 **251** 10 s. on 6 s. multicoloured 15 10
1226 – 10 s. on 6 s. black & red (No. 1015) 15 10

336 Memorial Gardens, Manila

1972. Tourism. "Visit Asean Lands" Campaign.
1227 **336** 5 s. multicoloured 15 10
1228 50 s. multicoloured . . . 85 25
1229 60 s. multicoloured . . . 1·10 35

337 "KKK" Flag

1972. Evolution of Philippines' Flag.
1230 **337** 30 s. red and blue 30 25
1231 – 30 s. red and blue 30 25
1232 – 30 s. red and blue 30 25
1233 – 30 s. black and blue . . . 30 25
1234 – 30 s. red and blue 30 25
1235 – 30 s. red and blue 30 25
1236 – 30 s. red and blue 30 25
1237 – 30 s. red and blue 30 25
1238 – 30 s. black, red and blue . 30 25
1239 – 30 s. yellow, red & blue . 30 25
FLAGS: No. 1231, Three "K"s in pyramid; No. 1232, Single "K"; No. 1233, "K", skull and crossbones; No. 1234, Three "K"s and sun in triangle; No. 1235, Sun and three "K"s; No. 1236, Ancient Tagalog "K" within sun; No. 1237, Face in sun; No. 1238, Tricolor; No. 1239, Present national flag—sun and stars within triangle, two stripes.

338 Mabol, Santol and Papaya

1972. Obligatory Tax. T.B. Relief Fund. Fruits. Mult.
1240 1 s. + 5 s. Type **338** 10 10
1241 10 s. + 5 s. Bananas, balimbang and mangosteen 15 15
1242 40 s. + 5 s. Guava, mango, duhat and susongkalabac . 30 30
1243 1 p. + 5 s. Orange, pineapple, lanzones and sirhuelas . . . 60 60

339 "Scarus frenatus"

1972. Fishes. Multicoloured.
1244 5 s. Type **339** (postage) . . . 10 10
1245 10 s. "Chaetodon kleini" . . 15 10
1246 20 s. "Zanclus cornutus" . . 25 15
1247 50 s. "Holacanthus bispinosus" (air) 70 35

340 Bank Headquarters

1972. 25th Anniv of Philippines Development Bank.
1248 **340** 10 s. multicoloured . . . 15 10
1249 20 s. multicoloured . . . 15 10
1250 60 s. multicoloured . . . 50 35

341 Pope Paul VI

1972. 1st Anniv of Pope Paul's Visit to Philippines.
1251 **341** 10 s. mult (postage) . . 10 10
1252 50 s. multicoloured . . . 40 35
1253 60 s. multicoloured (air) 50 50

1972. Various stamps surch.
1254 **240** 10 s. on 6 s. (No. 953) . 15 10
1255 – 10 s. on 6 s. (No. 959) . 15 10
1256 **250** 10 s. on 6 s. (No. 989) . 15 10

343 "La Barca de Aqueronte" (Hidalgo)

1972. 25th Anniv of Stamps and Philatelic Division, Philippines Bureau of Posts. Filipino Paintings. Multicoloured.
1257 5 s. Type **343** 10 10
1258 10 s. "Afternoon Meal of the Rice Workers" (Amorsolo) 10 10
1259 30 s. "Espana y Filipinas" (Luna) (27 × 60 mm) . . . 25 25
1260 70 s. "The Song of Maria Clara" (Amorsolo) 50 50

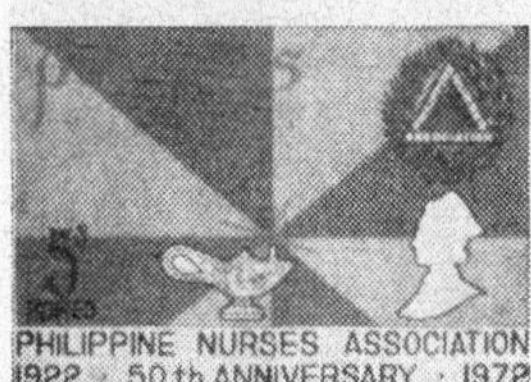

344 Lamp, Emblem and Nurse

1972. 50th Anniv of Philippine Nurses Assn.
1261 **344** 5 s. multicoloured . . . 10 10
1262 10 s. multicoloured . . . 10 10
1263 70 s. multicoloured . . . 40 35

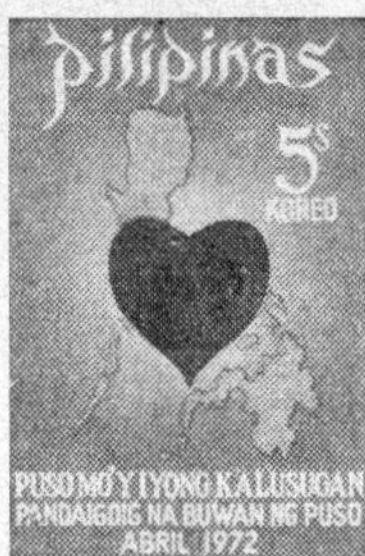

345 Heart on Map

1972. World Heart Month.
1264 **345** 5 s. red, green & violet . 10 10
1265 10 s. red, green & blue . 10 10
1266 30 s. red, blue & green . 25 20

346 "The First Mass" (C. V. Francisco)

1972. 450th Anniv of 1st Mass in Limasawa (1971).
1267 **346** 10 s. mult (postage) . . 15 15
1268 60 s. multicoloured (air) 45 40

1972. Asia–Pacific Scout Conference, Manila. Various stamps surch **ASIA PACIFIC SCOUT CONFERENCE NOV, 1972** and value.
1269 **233** 10 s. on 6 s. (No. 933) . 15 10
1270 **240** 10 s. on 6 s. (No. 953) . 15 10
1271 – 10 s. on 6 s. (No. 981) . 15 10

348 Olympic Emblems and Torch

1972. Olympic Games, Munich.

1272 **348** 5 s. multicoloured 10 10
1273 10 s. multicoloured 10 10
1274 70 s. multicoloured 50 40

1972. Philatelic Week. Nos. 950 and 983 surch **1972 PHILATELIC WEEK TEN 10s.**

1275 **239** 10 s. on 6 s. multicoloured 15 10
1276 **248** 10 s. on 6 s. multicoloured 15 10

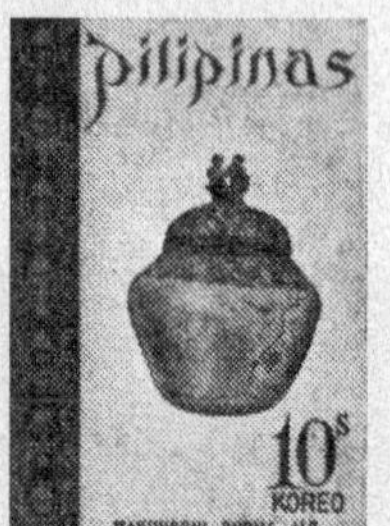

350 Manunggul Burial Jar

1972. Philippine Archaeological Discoveries. Multicoloured.

1277 10 s. Type **350** 15 10
1278 10 s. Ritual earthenware vessel 15 10
1279 10 s. Metal pot 15 10
1280 10 s. Earthenware vessel 15 10

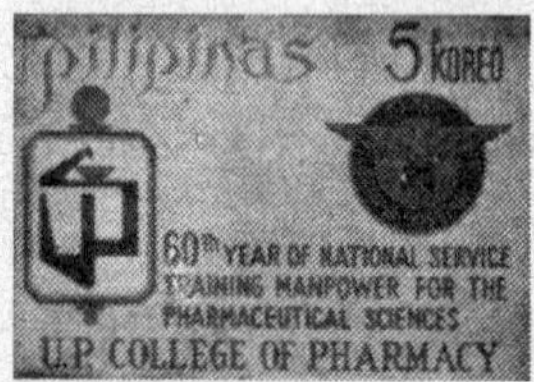

351 Emblems of Pharmacy and University of the Philippines

1972. 60th Anniv of National Training for Pharmaceutical Sciences, University of the Philippines.

1281 **351** 5 s. multicoloured 10 10
1282 10 s. multicoloured 10 10
1283 30 s. multicoloured 25 15

352 "The Lantern-makers" (J. Pineda)

1972. Christmas.

1284 **352** 10 s. multicoloured 10 10
1285 30 s. multicoloured 25 15
1286 50 s. multicoloured 40 35

353 President Roxas and Wife

1972. 25th Anniv of Philippines Red Cross.

1287 **353** 5 s. multicoloured 10 10
1288 20 s. multicoloured 15 15
1289 30 s. multicoloured 25 20

1973. Nos. 948 and 1005 surch **10s.**

1290 **238** 10 s. on 6 s. multicoloured 15 10
1291 **256** 10 s. on 6 s. blue. red and yellow 15 10

1973. Presidential Sayings (8th issue). As T **233** but with portrait and saying changed.

1292 10 s. black and bistre 15 10
1293 30 s. black and mauve 35 15

PORTRAIT AND SAYING: 10 s., 30 s. Pres. Garcia, "I would rather be right than successful".

355 University Building

1973. 60th Anniv of St. Louis University, Baguio City.

1294 **355** 5 s. multicoloured 10 10
1295 10 s. multicoloured 10 10
1296 75 s. multicoloured 50 45

356 Col. J. Villamor and Air Battle

1973. Villamor Commemoration.

1297 **356** 10 s. multicoloured 15 10
1298 2 p. multicoloured 1·40 1·25

1973. Various stamps surch.

1299 **252** 5 s. on 6 s. multicoloured 10 10
1300 **266** 5 s. on 6 s. violet, yellow and green 10 10
1301 **318** 15 s. on 10 s. red (No. O1182) 15 10

359 Actor and Stage Performance

1973. 1st "Third-World" Theatre Festival, Manila.

1302 **359** 5 s. multicoloured 10 10
1303 10 s. multicoloured 10 10
1304 50 s. multicoloured 35 20
1305 70 s. multicoloured 55 30

1973. President Marcos's Anti-Smuggling Campaign. No. 1017 surch **5s.**

1306 5 s. on 6 s. blue 15 10

1973. 10th Death Anniv of John F. Kennedy. No. 989 surch **5s.**

1307 5 s. on 6 s. multicoloured 15 10

1973. Compulsory Tax Stamps. T.B. Relief Fund. Nos. 1241/2 surch.

1308 15 s. + 5 s. on 10 s. + 5 s. multicoloured 15 15
1309 60 s. + 5 s. on 40 s. + 5 s. multicoloured 40 40

363 Proclamation Scenes

1973. 75th Anniv of Philippine Independence.

1310 **363** 15 s. multicoloured 10 10
1311 45 s. multicoloured 25 25
1312 90 s. multicoloured 55 55

364 M. Agoncillo (maker of first national flag) 365 Imelda Marcos

1973. Perf or imperf.

1313 – 15 s. violet 15 10
1314 **364** 60 s. brown 35 35
1315 – 90 s. blue 50 25
1316 – 1 p. 10 blue 65 30
1317 – 1 p. 50 red 90 75
1318 – 1 p. 50 brown 90 35
1319 – 1 p. 80 green 1·00 95
1320 – 5 p. blue 2·75 2·75

DESIGNS: 15 s. Gabriela Silang (revolutionary); 90 s. Teodoro Yangco (businessman); 1 p. 10, Pio Valenzuela (physician); 1 p. 50 (No. 1317), Pedro Paterno (revolutionary); 1 p. 50 (No. 1318), Teodora Alonso (mother of Jose Rizal); 1 p. 80, E. Evangelista (revolutionary); 5 p. F. M. Guerrero (writer).

For similar designs see Nos. 1455/8.

1973. Projects Inaugurated by Sra Imelda Marcos.

1321 **365** 15 s. multicoloured 10 10
1322 50 s. multicoloured 30 30
1323 60 s. multicoloured 35 35

366 Malakanyang Palace

1973. Presidential Palace, Manila.

1324 **366** 15 s. mult (postage) 10 10
1325 50 s. multicoloured 25 25
1326 60 s. multicoloured (air) 35 35

367 Interpol Emblem 368 Scouting Activities

1973. 50th Anniv of International Criminal Police Organization (Interpol).

1327 **367** 15 s. multicoloured 15 10
1328 65 s. multicoloured 35 20

1973. Golden Jubilee of Philippine Boy Scouts. Perf or imperf.

1329 **368** 15 s. bistre and green 15 10
1330 – 65 s. blue and yellow 35 30

DESIGN: 65 s. Scouts reading brochure.

369 Bank Emblem, Urban and Agricultural Landscapes

1974. 25th Anniv of Central Bank of the Philippines. Multicoloured.

1331 15 s. Type **369** 15 10
1332 60 s. Bank building, 1949 35 20
1333 1 p. 50 Bank complex, 1974 90 50

370 "Maria Clara" Costume 373 Map of South-East Asia

1974. Centenary of U.P.U. Philippine Costumes. Multicoloured.

1334 15 s. Type **370** 15 10
1335 60 s. "Balintawak" 35 20
1336 80 s. "Malong" 50 30

1974. Philatelic Week (1973). No. 1303 surch **1973 PHILATELIC WEEK 15s.**

1337 **359** 15 s. on 10 s. multicoloured 15 10

1974. 25th Anniv of Philippine "Lionism". Nos. 1297 and 1180 surch **PHILIPPINE LIONISM 1949-1974 15s** and Lion emblem.

1338 **356** 15 s. on 10 s. multicoloured 15 10
1339 – 45 s. on 40 s. red 25 20

1974. Asian Paediatrics Congress, Manila. Perf or imperf.

1340 **373** 30 s. red and blue 15 15
1341 1 p. red and green 55 35

374 Gen. Valdes and Hospital

1974. Obligatory Tax. T.B. Relief Fund. Perf or imperf.

1342 **374** 15 s. + 5 s. green & red 15 15
1343 1 p. 10 + 5 s. blue & red 25 15

1974. Nos. 974, 1024 and 1026 surch.

1344 **246** 5 s. on 3 s. green 15 10
1345 **263** 5 s. on 6 s. mult 15 10
1346 **264** 5 s. on 6 s. mult 15 10

378 W.P.Y. Emblem

1974. World Population Year. Perf or imperf.

1347 **378** 5 s. black and orange 10 10
1348 2 p. blue and green 1·00 55

379 Red Feather Emblem

1974. 25th Anniv of Community Chest Movement in the Philippines. Perf or imperf.

1349 **379** 15 s. red and blue 10 10
1350 40 s. red and green 25 15
1351 45 s. red and brown 35 15

381 Sultan Mohammad Kudarat, Map, Malayan Prau and Order

1975. Sultan Kudarat of Mindanao Commem.

1352 **381** 15 s. multicoloured 15 10

382 Association Emblem 383 Rafael Palma

1975. 25th Anniv of Philippine Mental Health Association. Perf or imperf.

1353 **382** 45 s. green and orange 20 15
1354 1 p. green and purple 45 35

1975. Birth Centenary of Rafael Palma (educationalist and statesman). Perf or imperf (15 s.), perf (30 s.).

1355 **383** 15 s. green 15 10
1436 30 s. brown 15 10

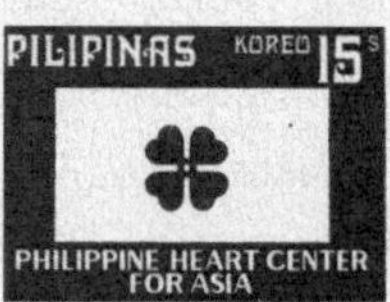

384 Heart Centre Emblem

1975. Inauguration of Philippine Heart Centre for Asia, Quezon City. Perf or imperf.

1356 **384** 15 s. red and blue 15 10
1357 50 s. red and green 20 20

385 Cadet in Full Dress, and Academy Building

1975. 70th Anniv of Philippine Military Academy.
1358 **385** 15 s. multicoloured . . . 15 10
1359 45 s. multicoloured . . . 40 25

387/9, 392/4 "Helping the Disabled"

1975. 25th Anniv (1974) of Philippines Orthopaedic Association. Perf or imperf.
1360 – 45 s. green (inscr at left and top) 20 15
1361 **387** 45 s. green 20 15
1362 **388** 45 s. green 20 15
1363 **389** 45 s. green 20 15
1364 – 45 s. green (inscr at top and right) 20 15
1365 – 45 s. green (inscr at left and bottom) 20 15
1366 **392** 45 s. green 20 15
1367 **393** 45 s. green 20 15
1368 **394** 45 s. green 20 15
1369 – 45 s. green (inscr at bottom and right) 20 15
DESIGNS—23 × 30 mm: Nos. 1360, 1364/5, 1369, Details of corners of the mural.
Nos. 1360/9 were issued together, se-tenant, forming a composite design.

1975. Nos. 1153 and 1342/3 surch.
1370 **374** 5 s. on 15 s. + 5 s. green and red 10 10
1371 **308** 60 s. on 70 s. + 5 s. multicoloured 25 25
1372 **374** 1 p. on 1 p. 10 + 5 s. blue and red 30 25

397 Planting Sapling

398 Jade Vine

1975. Forest Conservation. Multicoloured.
1373 45 s. Type **397** 25 15
1374 45 s. Sapling and tree-trunks 25 15

1975.
1375 **398** 15 s. multicoloured . . . 15 10

399 Imelda Marcos and I.W.Y. Emblem

400 Commission Badge

1975. International Women's Year. Perf or imperf.
1376 **399** 15 s. black, blue & dp bl 15 15
1377 80 s. black, blue and pink 45 35

1975. 75th Anniv of Civil Service Commission. Perf or imperf.
1378 **400** 15 s. multicoloured . . . 15 15
1379 50 s. multicoloured . . . 25 15

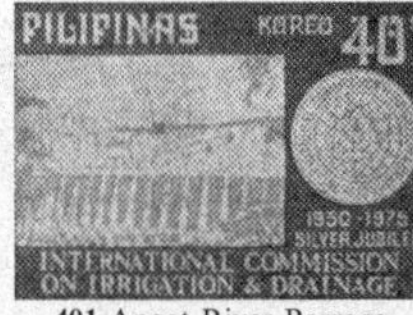

401 Angat River Barrage

1975. 25th Anniv of International Irrigation and Drainage Commission. Perf or imperf.
1380 **401** 40 s. blue and orange . . 15 15
1381 1 p. 50 blue and mauve . 50 40

402 "Welcome to Manila"

403 N. Romualdez (legislator and writer)

1975. Centenary of Hong Kong and Shanghai Banking Corporation's Service in the Philippines.
1382 **402** 1 p. 50 multicoloured . . 1·25 35

1975. Birth Centenaries. Perf or imperf.
1383 **403** 60 s. lilac 15 10
1384 – 90 s. mauve 35 15
DESIGN: 90 s. General G. del Pilar.

405 Boeing 747-100 Airliner and Martin M-130 Flying Boat

1975. 40th Anniv of First Trans-Pacific China Clipper Airmail Flight. San Francisco–Manila.
1385 **405** 60 s. multicoloured . . . 35 20
1386 1 p. 50 multicoloured . 90 55

1975. Airmail Exn. Nos. 1314 and 1318 optd **AIRMAIL EXHIBITION NOV 22-DEC 9.**
1387 **364** 60 s. brown 25 25
1388 – 1 p. 50 brown 55 55

407 APO Emblem

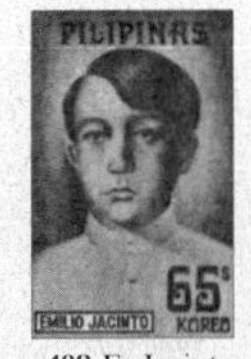

408 E. Jacinto

1975. 25th Anniv of APO Philatelic Society. Perf or imperf.
1389 **407** 5 s. multicoloured . . . 15 10
1390 1 p. multicoloured . . . 45 35

1975. Birth Centenary of Emilio Jacinto (military leader). Perf or imperf.
1391 **408** 65 s. mauve 20 10

409 San Agustin Church

410 "Conducting" Hands

1975. Holy Year. Churches. Perf or imperf.
1392 **409** 20 s. blue 15 15
1393 – 30 s. black and yellow . . 15 15
1394 – 45 s. red, pink and black 20 20
1395 – 60 s. bistre, yell & blk . 25 20
DESIGNS—HORIZ: 30 s. Morong Church; 45 s. Taal Basilica. VERT: 60 s. San Sebastian Church.

1976. 50th Anniv of Manila Symphony Orchestra.
1396 **410** 5 s. multicoloured . . . 10 10
1397 50 s. multicoloured . . . 35 25

411 Douglas DC-3 and DC-10

1976. 30th Anniv of Philippines Airlines (PAL).
1398 **411** 60 s. multicoloured . . . 30 15
1399 1 p. 50 multicoloured . . 1·10 55

412 Felipe Agoncillo (statesman)

413 University Building

1976. Felipe Agoncillo Commemoration.
1400 **412** 1 p. 60 black 90 25

1976. 75th Anniv of National University.
1401 **413** 45 s. multicoloured . . . 20 15
1402 60 s. multicoloured . . . 35 20

414 "Foresight Prevents Blindness"

415 Emblem on Book

1976. World Health Day.
1403 **414** 15 s. multicoloured . . . 15 10

1976. 75th Anniv of National Archives.
1404 **415** 1 p. 50 multicoloured . . 80 65

416 College Emblem and University Tower

1976. 50th Anniv of Colleges of Education and Science, Saint Thomas's University.
1405 **416** 15 s. multicoloured . . . 15 10
1406 50 s. multicoloured . . . 25 20

417 College Building

1976. 50th Anniv of Maryknoll College.
1407 **417** 15 s. multicoloured . . . 15 10
1408 1 p. 50 multicoloured . . 75 55

1976. Olympic Games, Montreal. Surch **15s Montreal 1976 21st OLYMPICS, CANADA** and emblem.
1409 **348** 15 s. on 10 s. mult. . . . 15 10

419 Constabulary Headquarters, Manila

1976. 75th Anniv of Philippine Constabulary. Perf or imperf.
1410 **419** 15 s. multicoloured . . . 15 15
1411 60 s. multicoloured . . . 35 20

420 Land and Aerial Surveying

1976. 75th Anniv of Lands Bureau.
1412 **420** 80 s. multicoloured . . . 35 35

422 Badges of Banking Organizations

1976. International Monetary Fund and World Bank joint Board of Governors Annual Meeting, Manila.
1414 **422** 60 s. multicoloured . . . 25 20
1415 1 p. 50 multicoloured . . 75 55

423 Virgin of Antipolo

426 Facets of Education

425 "Going to Church"

1976. 350th Anniv of "Virgin of Antipolo".
1416 **423** 30 s. multicoloured . . . 15 15
1417 90 s. multicoloured . . . 35 25

1976. Philatelic Week. Surch **1976 PHILATELIC WEEK 30s**.
1418 **355** 30 s. on 10 s. mult . . . 15 15

1976. Christmas.
1419 **425** 15 s. multicoloured . . . 10 10
1420 30 s. multicoloured . . . 20 10

1976. 75th Anniv of Philippine Educational System.
1421 **426** 30 s. multicoloured . . . 15 10
1422 75 s. multicoloured . . . 35 25

1977. Surch.
1423 1 p. 20 on 1 p. 10 blue (No. 1316) 55 35
1424 3 p. on 5 p. blue (No. 1320) . 1·10 1·00

428 Jose Rizal

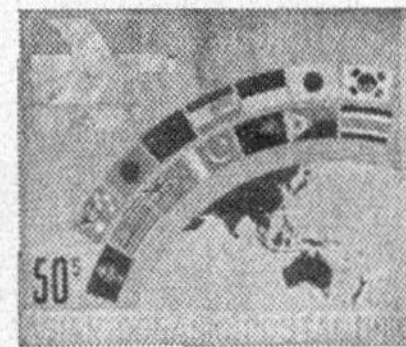

429 Flags, Map and Emblem

1977. Famous Filipinos. Multicoloured.
1425 30 s. Type **428** 15 10
1426 2 p. 30 Dr. Galicano Apacible 90 60

1977. 15th Anniv of Asian-Oceanic Postal Union.
1427 **429** 50 s. multicoloured . . . 15 10
1428 1 p. 50 multicoloured . . 55 45

430 Worker and Cogwheels

431 Commission Emblem

1977. 10th Anniv of Asian Development Bank.
1429 **430** 90 s. multicoloured . . . 45 35
1430 2 p. 30 multicoloured . . 90 75

1977. National Rural Credit Commission.
1431 **431** 30 s. multicoloured . . . 15 10

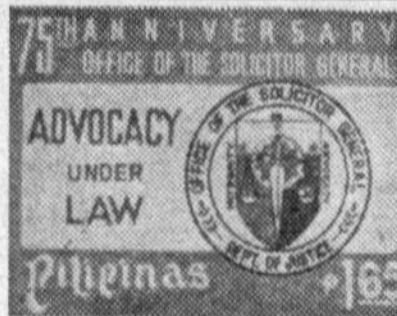

433 Solicitor-General's Emblem

1977. 75th Anniv of Office of Solicitor-General.
1433 **433** 1 p. 65 multicoloured . . 40 25

434 Conference Emblem

1977. World Law Conference, Manila.
1434 **434** 2 p. 20 multicoloured . . 70 25

435 A.S.E.A.N. Emblem

1977. 10th Anniv of Association of South East Asian Nationals (A.S.E.A.N.).
1435 **435** 1 p. 50 multicoloured . . 60 35

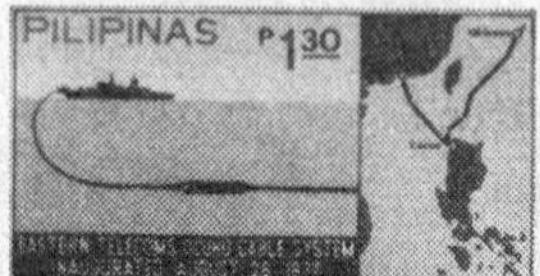

436 Cable Ship "Mercury" and Map

1977. Inauguration of OLUHO Cable (Okinawan–Luzon–Hong Kong).
1437 **436** 1 p. 30 multicoloured . . 55 35

437 President Marcos

1977. 60th Birthday of President Marcos.
1438 **437** 30 s. multicoloured . . . 15 10
1439 2 p. 30 multicoloured . . 95 60

438 People raising Flag

439 Bishop Gregorio Aglipay (founder)

1977. 5th Anniv of "New Society".
1440 **438** 30 s. multicoloured . . . 15 10
1441 2 p. 30 multicoloured . . 95 60

1977. 75th Anniv of Aglipayan Church.
1442 **439** 30 s. multicoloured . . . 10 10
1443 90 s. multicoloured . . . 35 20

441 Fokker F.7 Trimotor "General New" and World Map

1977. 50th Anniv of 1st Pan-Am International Air Service.
1445 **441** 2 p. 30 multicoloured . . 90 55

442 Eight-pointed Star and Children

445 University Badge

444 Scouts and Map of Philippines

1977. Christmas.
1446 **442** 30 s. multicoloured . . . 15 10
1447 45 s. multicoloured . . . 25 15

1977. Philatelic Week. Surch **90s 1977 PHILATELIC WEEK**.
1448 **407** 90 s. on 1 p. multicoloured 35 20

1977. National Scout Jamboree.
1449 **444** 30 s. multicoloured . . . 35 15

1978. 50th Anniv of Far Eastern University.
1450 **445** 30 s. multicoloured . . . 15 10

446 Sipa Player

1978. "Sipa" (Filipino ball game).
1451 **446** 5 s. multicoloured . . . 10 10
1452 – 10 s. multicoloured . . . 10 10
1453 – 40 s. multicoloured . . . 20 10
1454 – 75 s. multicoloured . . . 40 15
DESIGNS: Nos. 1452/4, Different players.
Nos. 1451/4 were issued together, se-tenant, forming a composite design.

447 Jose Rizal

448 Arms of Meycauayan

1978.
1455 **447** 30 s. blue 15 10
1456 – 30 s. mauve 15 10
1457 – 90 s. green 20 10
1458 – 1 p. 20 red 35 15
DESIGNS: No. 1456, Rajah Kalantiaw (Panay chief); 1457, Lope K. Santos ("Father of Filipino grammar"); 1458, Gregoria de Jesus (patriot).

1978. 400th Anniv of Meycauayan.
1459 **448** 1 p. 05 multicoloured . 35 20

449 Horse-drawn Mail Cart

1978. "CAPEX 78" International Stamp Exhibition, Toronto. Multicoloured.
1460 2 p. 50 Type **449** . . . . . 1·00 65
1461 5 p. Filipino vinta (sailing canoe) . . . . 2·75 2·00

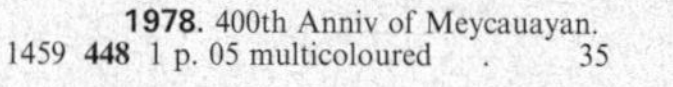

450 Andres Bonifacio Monument (Guillermo Tolentino)

1978. Andres Bonifacio Monument.
1463 **450** 30 s. multicoloured . . . 15 10

451 Knight, Rook and Globe

1978. World Chess Championship, Baguio City.
1464 **451** 30 s. red and violet . . . 15 10
1465 2 p. red and violet . . . 50 35

452 Miner

1978. 75th Anniv of Benguet Consolidated Mining Company.
1466 **452** 2 p. 30 multicoloured . . 1·25 50

453 Pres. Quezon

455 Pres. Osmena

454 Law Association and Conference Emblems

1978. Birth Centenary of Manuel L. Quezon (former President).
1467 **453** 30 s. multicoloured . . . 15 10
1468 1 p. multicoloured . . . 35 15

1978. 58th Int Law Association Conf, Manila.
1469 **454** 2 p. 30 multicoloured . . 80 55

1978. Birth Centenary of Sergio Osmena (former President).
1470 **455** 30 s. multicoloured . . . 15 10
1471 1 p. multicoloured . . . 35 15

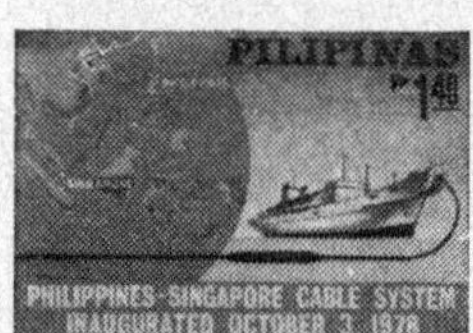

456 Map of Cable Route and Cable Ship "Mercury"

1978. Inauguration of Philippines–Singapore Submarine Cable.
1472 **456** 1 p. 40 multicoloured . . 65 25

457 Basketball

1978. 8th Men's World Basketball Championship, Manila.
1473 **457** 30 s. multicoloured . . . 15 10
1474 2 p. 30 multicoloured . . 80 55

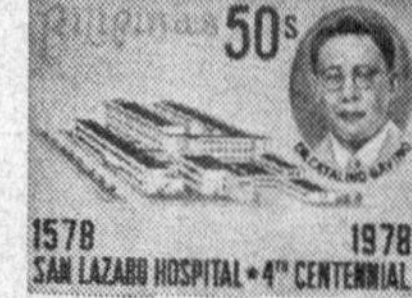

458 Dr. Catalino Gavino and Hospital

1978. 400th Anniv of San Lazaro Hospital.
1475 **458** 50 s. multicoloured . . . 20 10
1476 90 s. multicoloured . . . 35 15

459 Nurse vaccinating Child

461 Man on Telephone, Map and Satellite

1978. Global Eradication of Smallpox.
1477 **459** 30 s. multicoloured . . . 15 10
1478 1 p. 50 multicoloured . . 60 35

1978. Philatelic Week. No. 1391 surch **1978 PHILATELIC WEEK 60s**.
1479 **408** 60 s. on 65 s. mauve . . 25 10

1978. 50th Anniv of Philippine Long Distance Telephone Company. Multicoloured.
1480 30 s. Type **461** 20 10
1481 2 p. Woman on telephone and globe 65 45
Nos. 1480/1 were issued together, se-tenant, forming a composite design.

462 Family travelling in Ox-drawn Cart

1978. Decade of the Filipino Child.
1482 **462** 30 s. multicoloured . . . 10 10
1483 1 p. 35 multicoloured . . 55 20

463 Spanish Colonial Church and Arms

1978. 400th Anniv of Agoo Town.
1484 **463** 30 s. multicoloured . . . 15 10
1485 45 s. multicoloured . . . 20 15

464 Church and Arms

1978. 400th Anniv of Balayan Town.
1486 **464** 30 s. multicoloured . . . 10 10
1487 90 s. multicoloured . . . 35 15

465 Dr. Sison

466 Family and Houses

1978. Dr. Honoria Acosta Sison (first Filipino woman physician) Commemoration.
1488 **465** 30 s. multicoloured . . . 15 10

1978. 30th Anniv of Declaration of Human Rights.
1489 **466** 30 s. multicoloured . . . 10 10
1490 3 p. multicoloured . . . 1·10 65

467 "Chaetodon trifasciatus"

1978. Fishes. Multicoloured.
1491 30 s. Type **467** 10 10
1492 1 p. 20 "Balistoides niger" . 45 15
1493 2 p. 20 "Rhinecanthus aculeatus" 75 35
1494 2 p. 30 "Chelmon rostratus" 80 45
1495 5 p. "Chaetodon mertensi" . 1·75 95
1496 5 p. "Euxiphipops xanthometapon" . . . . . 1·75 95

468 Carlos P. Romulo

1979. 80th Anniv of Carlos P. Romulo (1st Asian President of U.N. General Assembly).
1497 **468** 30 s. multicoloured . . . 10 10
1498 2 p. multicoloured . . . 90 45

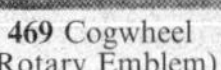

469 Cogwheel (Rotary Emblem) **470** Rosa Sevilla de Alvero

1979. 60th Anniv of Manila Rotary Club.
1499 **469** 30 s. multicoloured . . . 15 10
1500 2 p. 30 multicoloured . . 95 35

1979. Birth Centenary of Rosa Sevilla de Alvero (writer and educator).
1501 **470** 30 s. mauve 15 10

471 Burning-off Gas and Map

1979. 1st Oil Production. Nido Complex, Palawan.
1502 **471** 30 s. multicoloured . . . 20 10
1503 45 s. multicoloured . . . 30 15

472 Merrill's Fruit Dove

1979. Birds. Multicoloured.
1504 30 s. Type **472** 30 15
1505 1 p. 20 Brown tit-babbler . . 55 45
1506 2 p. 20 Mindoro zone-tailed (inscr "Imperial") pigeon . 1·00 50
1507 2 p. 30 Steere's pitta . . . . 1·10 55
1508 5 p. Koch's pitta and red-breasted pitta . . . . . . 2·40 1·25
1509 5 p. Great eared nightjar . . 2·40 1·25

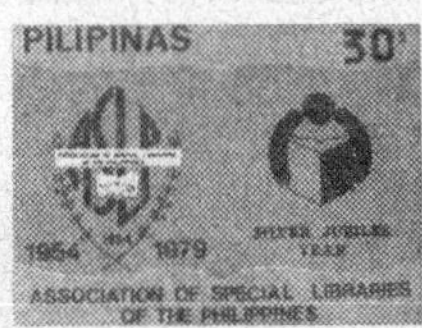

473 Association Emblem

1979. 25th Anniv of Association of Special Libraries of the Philippines.
1510 **473** 30 s. green, black & yell . 10 10
1511 75 s. green, black & yell . 25 10
1512 1 p. green, black & orge . 40 15

474 Conference Emblem

1979. 5th U.N. Conference on Trade and Development, Manila.
1513 **474** 1 p. 20 multicoloured . 35 15
1514 2 p. 30 multicoloured . 90 35

475 Malay Civet

1979. Animals. Multicoloured.
1515 30 s. Type **475** 10 10
1516 1 p. 20 Crab-eating macaque 45 20
1517 2 p. 20 Javan pig 75 40
1518 2 p. 30 Leopard cat 80 45
1519 5 p. Oriental small-clawed otter 1·75 95
1520 5 p. Malayan pangolin . . . 1·75 95

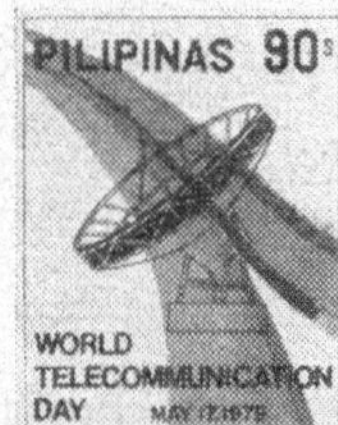

476 Dish Aerial

1979. World Telecommunications Day. Mult.
1521 90 s. Type **476** 30 10
1522 1 p. 30 Hemispheres 40 15

477 Mussaenda "Dona Evangelina"

1979. Cultivated Mussaendas. Multicoloured.
1523 30 s. Type **477** 10 10
1524 1 p. 20 "Dona Esperanza" . 45 15
1525 2 p. 20 "Dona Hilaria" . . 75 35
1526 2 p. 30 "Dona Aurora" . . 80 45
1527 5 p. "Gining Imelda" . . . 1·75 95
1528 5 p. "Dona Trining" . . . . 1·75 95

478 Manila Cathedral

1979. 400th Anniv of Archdiocese of Manila.
1529 **478** 30 s. multicoloured . . . 10 10
1530 75 s. multicoloured . . . 25 10
1531 90 s. multicoloured . . . 35 15

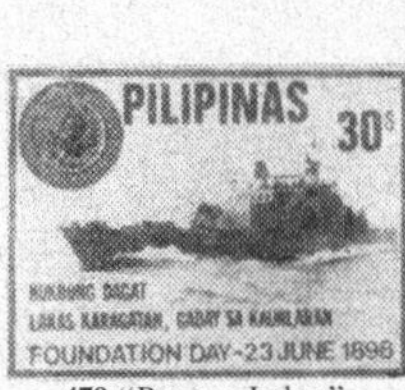

479 "Bagong Lakas" (patrol boat) **481** Drug Addict breaking Manacles

1979. Philippine Navy Foundation Day.
1532 **479** 30 s. multicoloured . . . 25 10
1533 45 s. multicoloured . . . 35 15

1979. Air. 1st Scout Philatelic Exhibition and 25th Anniv of 1st National Jamboree. Surch **1ST SCOUT PHILATELIC EXHIBITION JULY 4.14, 1979 QUEZON CITY AIRMAIL 90s.**
1534 **188** 90 s. on 6 c. + 4 c. red on yellow 30 30

1979. "Fight Drug Abuse" Campaign.
1536 **481** 30 s. multicoloured . . . 10 10
1537 90 s. multicoloured . . . 35 15
1538 1 p. 05 multicoloured . 40 20

482 Afghan Hound

1979. Cats and Dogs. Multicoloured.
1539 30 s. Type **482** 10 10
1540 90 s. Tabby cats 35 15
1541 1 p. 20 Dobermann pinscher . 45 20
1542 2 p. 20 Siamese cats 80 25
1543 2 p. 30 German shepherd dog 90 75
1544 5 p. Chinchilla cats . . . . . 1·75 90

483 Children flying Kites

1979. International Year of the Child. Paintings by Rod Dayao. Multicoloured.
1545 15 s. Type **483** 10 10
1546 20 s. Boys fighting with catapults 15 10
1547 25 s. Girls dressing-up 15 10
1548 1 p. 20 Boy playing policeman 35 15

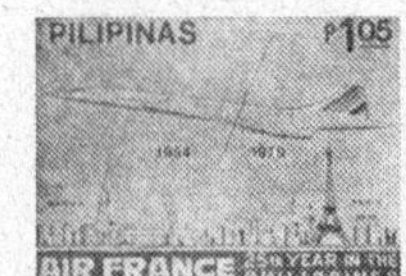
484 Hands holding Emblems **485** Anniversary Medal and 1868 Coin

1979. 80th Anniv of Methodism in the Philippines.
1549 **484** 30 s. multicoloured . . . 15 10
1550 1 p. 35 multicoloured . . 45 15

1979. 50th Anniv of Philippine Numismatic and Antiquarian Society.
1551 **485** 30 s. multicoloured . . . 15 10

486 Concorde over Manila and Paris

1979. 25th Anniv of Air France Service to the Philippines. Multicoloured.
1552 1 p. 05 Type **486** 60 30
1553 2 p. 20 Concorde over monument . . . . 1·40 55

1979. Philatelic Week. Surch **1979 PHILATELIC WEEK 90s.**
1554 **412** 90 s. on 1 p. 60 black . . 35 15

488 "35" and I.A.T.A. Emblem

1979. 35th Annual General Meeting of International Air Transport Association, Manila.
1555 **488** 75 s. multicoloured . . . 30 15
1556 2 p. 30 multicoloured . . 85 60

489 Bureau of Local Government Emblem **490** Christmas Greetings

1979. Local Government Year.
1557 **489** 30 s. multicoloured . . . 15 10
1558 45 s. multicoloured . . . 20 15

1979. Christmas. Multicoloured.
1559 30 s. Type **490** 15 10
1560 90 s. Stars 40 25

491 Rheumatism Victim **492** Birthplace and MacArthur Memorial Foundation

1980. 4th Congress of Southeast Asia and Pacific Area League Against Rheumatism, Manila.
1561 **491** 30 s. multicoloured . . . 20 10
1562 90 s. multicoloured . . . 45 25

1980. Birth Centenary of General Douglas MacArthur (U.S. Army Chief of Staff). Multicoloured.
1563 30 s. Type **492** 15 10
1564 75 s. General MacArthur . . 35 15
1565 2 p. 30 Hat, pipe and glasses 1·10 70

493 Columbus and Emblem **495** Tirona, Benitez and University

494 Soldiers and Academy Emblem

1980. 75th Anniv of Knights of Columbus Organization in Philippines.
1567 **493** 30 s. multicoloured . . . 20 10
1568 1 p. 35 multicoloured . . 75 40

1980. 75th Anniv of Philippine Military Academy.
1569 **494** 30 s. multicoloured . . . 20 10
1570 1 p. 20 multicoloured . . 65 30

1980. 60th Anniv of Philippine Women's University.
1571 **495** 30 s. multicoloured . . . 20 10
1572 1 p. 05 multicoloured . . 55 25

496 Boats and Burning City

1980. 75th Anniv of Rotary International. Details of painting by Carlos Francisco. Multicoloured.
1573 30 s. Type **496** 20 10
1574 30 s. Priest with cross, swordsmen and soldier . . 20 10
1575 30 s. "K K K" flag and group around table 20 10
1576 30 s. Man in midst of spearmen and civilian scenes . . . 20 10
1577 30 s. Reading the Constitution, soliders and U.S. and Philippine flags 20 10
1578 2 p. 30 Type **496** . . . . . . 1·25 55
1579 2 p. 30 As No. 1574 . . . . 1·25 55
1580 2 p. 30 As No. 1575 . . . . 1·25 55
1581 2 p. 30 As No. 1576 . . . . 1·25 55
1582 2 p. 30 As No. 1577 . . . . 1·25 55

Nos. 1573/7 and 1578/82 were issued together in se-tenant strips of five, each strip forming a composite design.

497 Mosque and Koran **498** Hand stubbing out Cigarette

1980. 600th Anniv of Islam in the Philippines.
1583 **497** 30 s. multicoloured . . . 20 10
1584 1 p. 30 multicoloured . . 65 30

1980. World Health Day. Anti-Smoking Campaign.
1585 **498** 30 s. multicoloured . . . 20 10
1586 75 s. multicoloured . . . 35 20

499 Scouting Activities and Badge

1980. 40th Anniv of Girl Scouting in the Philippines.
1587 **499** 30 s. multicoloured . . . 20 10
1588 2 p. multicoloured . . . 55 25

500 Jeepney **502** Association Emblem

1980. Philippine Jeepneys (decorated jeeps). Multicoloured.
1589 30 s. Type **500** 20 10
1590 1 p. 20 Side view of Jeepney . 60 30

1980. 82nd Anniv of Independence. Surch **PHILIPPINE INDEPENDENCE 82ND ANNIVERSARY 1898 1980.**
1591 **412** 1 p. 35 on 1 p. 60 black . 80 40
1592 1 p. 50 on 1 p. 80 green (No. 1319) 90 45

1980. 7th General Conference of International Association of Universities, Manila.
1593 **502** 30 s. multicoloured . . . 80 40
1594 2 p. 30 multicoloured . . 1·25 1·10

503 Map and Emblems **504** Filipinos and Emblem

1980. 46th Congress of International Federation of Library Associations and Institutions, Manila.
1595 **503** 30 s. green and black . . 20 10
1596 75 s. blue and black . . . 40 25
1597 2 p. 30 red and black . . 1·40 75

1980. 5th Anniv of Kabataang Barangay (national council charged with building the "New Society").
1598 **504** 30 s. multicoloured . . . 20 10
1599 40 s. multicoloured . . . 25 10
1600 1 p. multicoloured . . . 55 30

1980. Nos. 1433, 1501, 1536, 1557 and 1559 surch.
1601 **470** 40 s. on 30 s. mauve . . 25 10
1602 **481** 40 s. on 30 s. multicoloured 25 10
1603 **489** 40 s. on 30 s. multicoloured 25 10
1604 **490** 40 s. on 30 s. multicoloured 25 10
1605 **433** 2 p. on 1 p. 65 mult . . 1·25 60

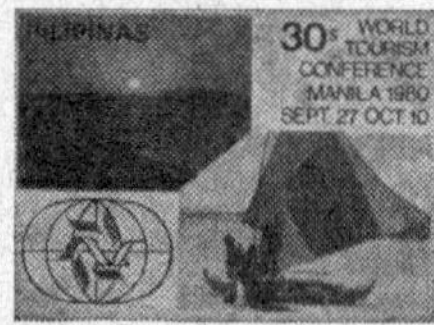

506 Sunset, Filipino Vinta and Conference Emblem

1980. World Tourism Conference, Manila.
1606 **506** 30 s. multicoloured . . . 25 10
1607 2 p. 30 multicoloured . . 1·25 80

507 Magnifying Glass and Stamps **508** U.N. Headquarters and Philippines Flag

1980. Postage Stamp Day.
1608 **507** 40 s. multicoloured . . . 25 10
1609 1 p. multicoloured . . . 60 30
1610 2 p. multicoloured . . . 1·25 60

1980. 35th Anniv of U.N.O.
1611 40 s. Type **508** 25 10
1612 3 p. 20 U.N. Headquarters and U.N. and Philippines flags 1·75 1·25

509 Alabaster Murex **510** Interpol Emblem on Globe

1980. Shells. Multicoloured.
1613 40 s. Type **509** 25 10
1614 60 s. Giant frog shell 35 20
1615 1 p. 20 Zambo's murex . . . 65 30
1616 2 p. Pallid carrier shell . . . 1·25 55

1980. 49th General Assembly of Interpol, Manila.
1617 **510** 40 s. multicoloured . . . 25 10
1618 1 p. multicoloured . . . 60 25
1619 3 p. 20 multicoloured . 1·75 1·25

511 University and Faculty Emblems **513** Christmas Tree and Presents

1980. 75th Anniv of Central Philippine University. Multicoloured, background colour given.
1620 **511** 40 s. blue 20 10
1621 3 p. 20 green . . . . . 1·75 1·25

1980. Philatelic Week. No. 1377 surch **1980 PHILATELIC WEEK P1. 20.**
1622 **399** 1 p. 20 on 80 s. black, blue and pink 60 30

1980. Christmas.
1623 **513** 40 s. multicoloured . . . 20 10

1981. Various stamps surch.
1624 **244** 10 s. on 6 s. + 5 s. blue 15 10
1625 **462** 10 s. on 30 s. mult . . . 10 10
1626 **408** 40 s. on 65 s. mauve . . 25 10
1627 **458** 40 s. on 90 s. mult . . . 25 10
1628 **481** 40 s. on 90 s. mult . . . 25 10
1629 – 40 s. on 90 s. mult (No. 1560) 25 10
1630 **448** 40 s. on 1 p. 05 mult . . 25 10
1631 **462** 40 s. on 1 p. 35 mult . . 25 10
1632 **399** 85 s. on 80 s. black, blue and pink 45 25
1633 **408** 1 p. on 65 s. mauve . . 65 30
1634 **401** 1 p. on 1 p. 50 blue and mauve 60 25
1635 **422** 1 p. on 1 p. 50 mult . . 65 30
1636 – 1 p. 20 on 1 p. 50 brown (No. 1318) 65 35
1637 **433** 1 p. 20 on 1 p. 65 mult . 65 35
1638 – 1 p. 20 on 1 p. 80 grn (No. 1319) 65 35
1639 **401** 2 p. on 1 p. 50 blue and mauve . . . . . . 1·25 50
1640 **434** 3 p. 20 on 2 p. 20 mult . 1·75 95

1981. 30th Anniv of APO Philatelic Society. Surch **NOV. 30, 1980 APO PHILATELIC SOCIETY PEARL JUBILEE 40s.**
1641 **455** 40 s. on 30 s. mult . . . 25 10

517 Von Stephan and U.P.U. Emblem

1981. 150th Birth Anniv of Heinrich von Stephan (founder of U.P.U.).
1642 **517** 3 p. 20 multicoloured . 1·75 90

1981. Girl Scouts Camp. No. 1589 surch **GSP RJASIA-PACIFIC REGIONAL CAMP PHILIPPINES DECEMBER 23, 1980 40s.**
1643 **500** 40 s. on 30 s. mult . . . 25 10

518 Pope John Paul II **519** Parliamentary Debate

1981. Papal Visit. Multicoloured.
1644 90 s. Type **518** 45 25
1645 1 p. 20 Pope and cardinals . . 60 30
1646 2 p. 30 Pope blessing crowd (horiz) . . . . 1·25 60
1647 3 p. Pope and Manila Cathedral (horiz) . . . . 1·60 75

1981. Interparliamentary Union Meeting, Manila.
1649 **519** 2 p. multicoloured . . . 1·25 55
1650 3 p. 20 multicoloured . . 1·75 1·00

520 Monument **521** President Aguinaldo's Car

1981. Jose Rizal Monument, Luneta Park.
1651 **520** 40 s. black, yellow & brn 20 10

1981. 50th Anniv of Philippine Motor Association. Multicoloured.
1652 40 s. Type **521** 25 10
1653 40 s. 1930 model car 25 10
1654 40 s. 1937 model car 25 10
1655 40 s. 1937 model car (different) 25 10

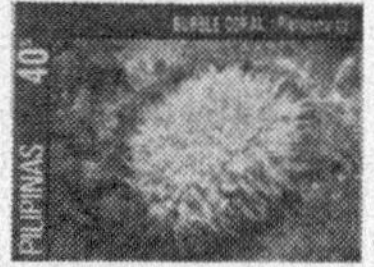

522 Bubble Coral

1981. Corals. Multicoloured.
1656 40 s. Type **522** 25 10
1657 40 s. Branching corals 25 10
1658 40 s. Brain coral 25 10
1659 40 s. Table coral 25 10

523 President Marcos and Flag

1981. Inauguration of President Marcos. Perf or imperf.
1660 **523** 40 s. multicoloured . . . 25 10

524 St. Ignatius de Loyola (founder)

1981. 400th Anniv of Jesuits in the Philippines. Mult.
1662 40 s. Type **524** 25 10
1663 40 s. Dr. Jose P. Rizal and Intramuros Ateneo 25 10
1664 40 s. Father Frederico Faura (director) and Manila Observatory 25 10
1665 40 s. Father Saturnino Urios (missionary) and map of Mindanao 25 10

525 F. R. Castro **526** Pres. Ramon Magsaysay

1981. Chief Justice Fred Ruiz Castro.
1667 **525** 40 s. multicoloured . . . 25 10

1981.
1668 – 1 p. brown and black . . 65 25
1669 **526** 1 p. 20 brown and black . 65 35
1670 – 2 p. purple and black . . 1·25 50
DESIGNS: 1 p. General Gregorio del Pilar; 2 p. Ambrosio R. Bautista.

See also Nos. 1699/1704, 1807 etc and 2031/3.

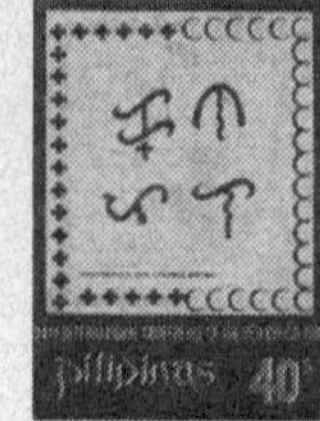

527 Man in Wheelchair **528** Early Filipino Writing

1981. International Year of Disabled Persons.
1671 **527** 40 s. multicoloured . . . 25 10
1672 3 p. 20 multicoloured . . 1·75 1·00

1981. 24th International Red Cross Conference.
1673 **528** 40 s. black, red and bistre 20 10
1674 2 p. black and red . . . 1·25 45
1675 3 p. 20 black, red and mauve . . . . 1·75 85

529 Isabel II Gate, Manila

1981.
1676 **529** 40 s. black 25 10

530 Concert in Park

1981. Opening of Concert at Park 200.
1677 **530** 40 s. multicoloured . . . 25 10

1981. Philatelic Week. No. 1435 surch **P1 20 1981 PHILATELIC WEEK.**
1678 **435** 1 p. 20 on 1 p. 50 mult . 65 35

532 Running

1981. 11th South-east Asian Games, Manila.
1679 **532** 40 s. yellow, green & brn 25 10
1680 – 1 p. multicoloured . . . 65 25
1681 – 2 p. multicoloured . . . 1·40 50
1682 – 2 p. 30 multicoloured . . 1·40 65
1683 – 2 p. 80 multicoloured . . 1·75 75
1684 – 3 p. 20 violet and blue . 1·75 95
DESIGNS: 1 p. Cycling; 2 p. President Marcos and Juan Antonio Samaranch (president of International Olympic Committee); 2 p. 30, Football; 2 p. 80, Shooting; 3 p. 20, Bowling.

533 Manila Film Centre

1982. Manila International Film Festival. Mult.
1685 40 s. Type **533** 25 10
1686 2 p. Front view of trophy . . 1·40 50
1687 3 p. 20 Side view of trophy . 1·90 95

534 Carriedo Fountain **535** Lord Baden-Powell (founder)

1982. Centenary of Manila Metropolitan Waterworks and Sewerage System.
1688 **534** 40 s. blue 25 10
1689 1 p. 20 brown 65 35

1982. 75th Anniv of Boy Scout Movement. Mult.
1690 40 s. Type **535** 25 10
1691 2 p. Scout . . . . 1·40 50

536 Embroidered Banner

1982. 25th Anniv of Children's Museum and Library Inc. Multicoloured.
1692 40 s. Type **536** 25 10
1693 1 p. 20 Children playing . . 65 35

537 President Marcos presenting Sword of Honour

1982. Military Academy.
1694 **537** 40 s. multicoloured . . . 25 10
1695 1 p. multicoloured . . . 65 30

538 Soldier and Memorial

1982. Bataan Day. Multicoloured.
1696 40 s. Type **538** 25 10
1697 2 p. Doves and rifle . . . . 1·40 50

1982. Portraits. As T **526**.
1699 40 s. blue 25 10
1700 1 p. red 65 30
1701 1 p. 20 brown 65 35
1702 2 p. mauve . . . . 1·25 50
1703 2 p. 30 purple . . . . 1·40 55
1704 3 p. 20 blue . . . . 1·50 95
DESIGNS: 40 s. Isabelo de los Reyes (founder of first workers' union); 1 p. Aurora Aragon Quezon (social worker and former First Lady); 1 p. 20, Francisco Dagohoy; 2 p. Juan Sumulong (politician); 2 p. 30, Professor Nicanor Abelardo (composer); 3 p. 20, General Vicente Lim.
For these designs in other values, see Nos. 1811/15.

539 Worker with Tower Award
541 Green Turtle

1982. Tower Awards (for best "Blue Collar" Workers). Multicoloured.
1705 40 s. Type **539** (inscr "MANGGAGAWA") . . 25 10
1705d 40 s. Type **539** (inscr "MANGAGAWA" 25 10
1706 1 p. 20 Cogwheel and tower award (inscr "MANGGAGAWA") . . 65 35
1706b 1 p. 20 As No. 1706 but inscr "Mangagawa" 65 35

1982. 10th Anniv of United Nations Environment Programme. Multicoloured.
1707 40 s. Type **541** 25 10
1708 3 p. 20 Philippine eagle . . . 3·25 95

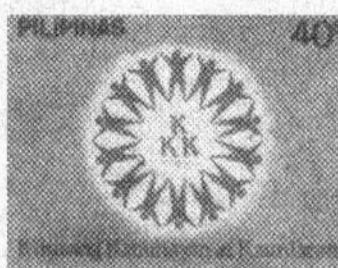

542 K.K.K. Emblem

1982. Inauguration of Kilusang Kabuhayan at Kaunlaran (national livelihood movement).
1709 **542** 40 s. green, light green and black 25 10
1816 60 s. green, light green and black 15 10
1817 60 s. green, red and black 15 15

543 Chemistry Apparatus and Emblem

1982. 50th Anniv of Adamson University.
1710 **543** 40 s. multicoloured . . . 25 10
1711 1 p. 20 multicoloured . 65 35

544 Dr. Fernando G. Calderon and Emblems

1982. 75th Anniv of College of Medicine, University of the Philippines.
1712 **544** 40 s. multicoloured . . . 25 10
1713 3 p. 20 multicoloured . 1·75 95

545 President Marcos
546 Hands supporting Family

1982. 65th Birthday of President Ferdinand Marcos.
1714 **545** 40 s. multicoloured . . . 25 10
1715 3 p. 20 multicoloured . 1·75 95

1982. 25th Anniv of Social Security System.
1717 **546** 40 s. black, orange & blue 25 10
1718 1 p. 20 black, orange and green 65 35

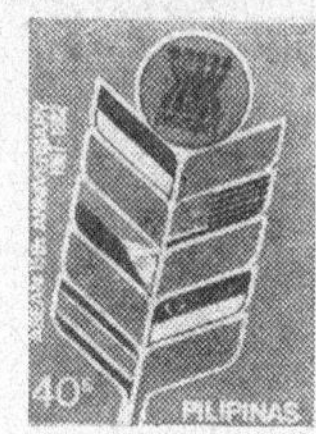

547 Emblem and Flags forming Ear of Wheat

1982. 15th Anniv of Association of South East Asian Nations.
1719 **547** 40 s. multicoloured . . . 25 10

548 St. Theresa of Avila

1982. 400th Death Anniv of St. Theresa of Avila. Multicoloured.
1720 40 s. Type **548** 25 10
1721 1 p. 20 St. Theresa and map of Europe, Africa and Asia . 65 35
1722 2 p. As 1 p. 20 . . . . . . 1·40 50

549 St. Isabel College

1982. 350th Anniv of St. Isabel College.
1723 **549** 40 s. multicoloured . . . 25 10
1724 1 p. multicoloured . . . 65 30

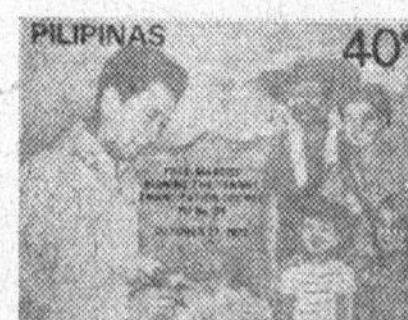

550 President Marcos signing Decree and Tenant Family

1982. 10th Anniv of Tenant Emancipation Decree.
1725a **550** 40 s. green, brown and black (37 × 27 mm) . 25 10
1726 40 s. green, brown and black (32 × 22½ mm) . 20 10

551 "Reading Tree"

1982. Literacy Campaign.
1727 **551** 40 s. multicoloured 25 10
1728 2 p. 30 multicoloured . . 1·40 50

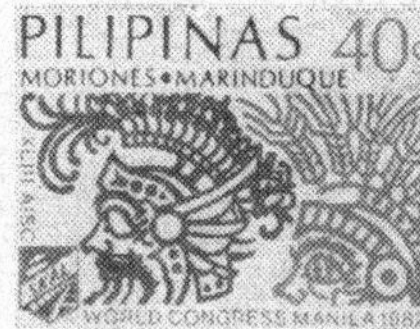

552 Helmeted Heads

1982. 43rd World Congress of Skal Clubs, Manila.
1729 40 s. Type **552** 25 10
1730 2 p. Head in feathered head-dress . . . . 1·40 50

553 Dancers with Parasols

1982. 25th Anniv of Bayanihan Folk Arts Centre. Multicoloured.
1731 40 s. Type **553** 35 10
1732 2 p. 80 Dancers (different) . . 1·50 70

554 Dr. Robert Koch and Bacillus

1982. Cent of Discovery of Tubercule Bacillus.
1733 **554** 40 s. red, blue & black . . 25 10
1734 2 p. 80 multicoloured . . 1·75 75

555 Father Christmas in Sleigh

1982. Christmas.
1735 **555** 40 s. multicoloured . . . 25 10
1736 1 p. multicoloured . . . 65 30

556 Presidential Couples and Flags

1982. State Visit of Pres. Marcos to United States.
1737 **556** 40 s. multicoloured . . . 20 10
1738 3 p. 20 multicoloured . . 1·40 85

557 Woman with Sewing Machine
559 Eulogio Rodriguez

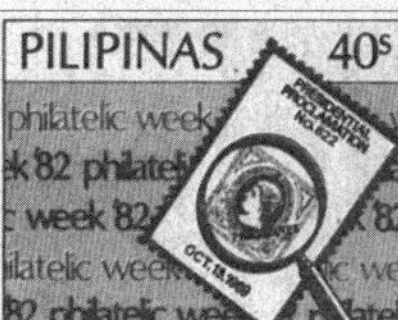

558 Stamp and Magnifying Glass

1982. U.N. World Assembly on Ageing.
1740a **557** 1 p. 20 green & orange 65 35
1741a – 2 p. pink and blue . . . 1·40 50
DESIGN: 2 p. Man with carpentry tools.

1983. Philatelic Week.
1742 **558** 40 s. multicoloured . . . 25 10
1743 1 p. multicoloured . . . 65 30

1983. Birth Centenary of Eulogio Rodriguez (former President of Senate).
1744a **559** 40 s. multicoloured . . 25 10
1745 1 p. 20 multicoloured . 65 35

560 Symbolic Figure and Film Frame

1983. Manila International Film Festival.
1746a **560** 40 s. multicoloured . . 25 10
1747a 3 p. 20 multicoloured . 1·50 90

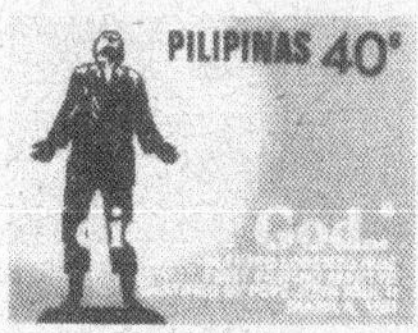

561 Monument

1983. 2nd Anniv of Beatification of Lorenzo Ruiz.
1748 **561** 40 s. yellow, red & blk . 25 10
1749 1 p. 20 multicoloured . . 70 35

562 Early Printing Press
563 Emblem and Ship

1983. 390th Anniv of First Local Printing Press.
1750 **562** 40 s. green and black . . 25 10

1983. 25th Anniv of International Maritime Organization.
1751 **563** 40 s. red, black & blue . 25 10

1983. 7th National Scout Jamboree. No. 1709 optd **7TH BSP NATIONAL JAMBOREE 1983**.
1752 **542** 40 s. green, light green and black 25 10

1983. Nos. 1360/9 surch **40s**.
1753 – 40 s. on 45 c. green . . . 25 10
1754 **387** 40 s. on 45 c. green . . . 25 10
1755 **388** 40 s. on 45 c. green . . . 25 10
1756 **389** 40 s. on 45 c. green . . . 25 10
1757 – 40 s. on 45 c. green . . . 25 10
1758 – 40 s. on 45 c. green . . . 25 10
1759 **392** 40 s. on 45 c. green . . . 25 10
1760 **393** 40 s. on 45 c. green . . . 25 10
1761 **394** 40 s. on 45 c. green . . . 25 10
1762 – 40 s. on 45 c. green . . . 25 10

566 Calculator Keys

1983. 11th International Organization of Supreme Audit Institutions Congress.
1763 **566** 40 s. blue, light blue and silver 25 10
1764 – 2 p. 80 multicoloured . . 1·75 75
DESIGN: 2 p. 80, Congress emblem.

HAVE YOU READ THE NOTES AT THE BEGINNING OF THIS CATALOGUE?
These often provide the answers to the enquiries we receive.

567 Smiling Children　　568 Detail of Statue

1983. 75th Anniv of Philippine Dental Association.

1766 **567** 40 s. green, mauve & brn 20 15

1983. 75th Anniv of University of the Philippines.

1767 **568** 40 s. brown and green 20 15

1768 – 1 p. 20 multicoloured 60 30

DESIGN: 1 p. 20, Statue and diamond.

569 Yasuhiro Nakasone and Pres. Marcos

1983. Visit of Japanese Prime Minister.

1769 **569** 40 s. multicoloured 20 15

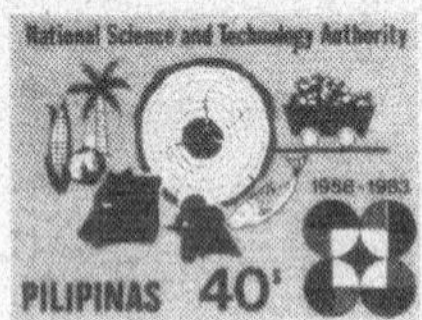

570 Agriculture and Natural Resources

1983. 25th Anniv of National Science and Technology Authority. Multicoloured.

1770 40 s. Type **570** 35 15

1771 40 s. Heart, medical products and food (Health and nutrition) 35 15

1772 40 s. Industrial complex and air (Industry and energy) 35 15

1773 40 s. House, scientific equipment and book (Sciences and social science) 35 15

571 Globes and W.C.Y. Emblem

1983. World Communication Year.

1774 **571** 3 p. 20 multicoloured 1·75 85

572 Postman　　573 Woman with Tambourine

1983. Bicent of Philippine Postal System.

1775 **572** 40 s. multicoloured 20 15

1983. Christmas. Multicoloured.

1776 40 s. Type **573** 20 15

1777 40 s. Man turning spit (left side) 20 15

1778 40 s. Pig on spit 20 15

1779 40 s. Man turning spit (right side) 20 15

1780 40 s. Man with guitar 20 15

Nos. 1776/80 were issued together, se-tenant, forming a composite design.

574 University Activities

1983. 50th Anniv of Xavier University.

1782 **574** 40 s. multicoloured 20 15

1783 60 s. multicoloured 35 15

575 Woman casting Vote　　576 Workers

1983. 50th Anniv of Female Suffrage.

1784 **575** 40 s. multicoloured 20 15

1785 60 s. multicoloured 30 15

1983. 50th Anniv of Ministry of Labour and Employment.

1786 **576** 40 s. multicoloured 20 15

1787 60 s. multicoloured 30 15

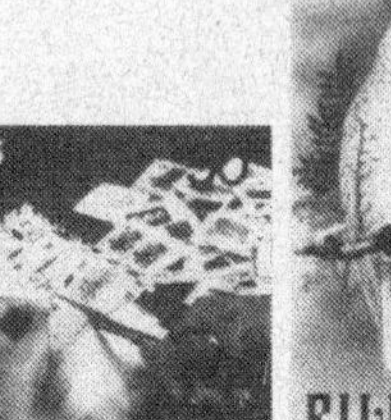

577 Cutting Stamp from Envelope　　578 Red-vented Cockatoo

1983. Philatelic Week. Multicoloured.

1788 50 s. Type **577** 45 20

1789 50 s. Sorting stamps 45 20

1790 50 s. Soaking stamps 45 20

1791 50 s. Hinging stamp 45 20

1792 50 s. Mounting stamp in album 45 20

1984. Parrots. Multicoloured.

1793 40 s. Type **578** 15 10

1794 2 p. 30 Guaiabero 65 35

1795 2 p. 80 Mountain racket-tailed parrot 85 35

1796 3 p. 20 Great-billed parrot 1·00 40

1797 3 p. 60 Muller's parrot 1·10 40

1798 5 p. Philippine hanging parrot 1·50 60

579 Princess Tarhata Kiram　　580 Nun and Congregation

1984. 5th Death Anniv of Princess Tarhata Kiram.

1799 **579** 3 p. deep green, green and red 65 25

1984. 300th Anniv of Religious Congregation of the Virgin Mary.

1800 **580** 40 s. multicoloured 15 15

1801 60 s. multicoloured 15 15

581 Dona Concha Felix de Calderon　　583 Manila

1984. Birth Centenary of Dona Concha Felix de Calderon.

1802 **581** 60 s. green and black 10 10

1803 3 p. 60 green and red 50 15

1984. Various stamps surch.

1804 **545** 60 s. on 40 s. multicoloured 15 10

1805 **558** 60 s. on 40 s. multicoloured 15 10

1806 – 3 p. 60 on 3 p. 20 blue (No. 1704) 80 30

1984. As Nos. 1700/4 but values changed, and new designs as T **526**.

1807 60 s. brown and black 15 10

1808 60 s. violet and black 15 10

1809 60 s. black 15 10

1913 60 s. blue 15 10

1889 60 s. brown 20 10

1914 60 s. red 15 10

1811 1 p. 80 blue 25 15

1812 2 p. 40 purple 35 15

1813 3 p. brown 35 15

1814 3 p. 60 red 45 15

1815 4 p. 20 purple 50 25

DESIGNS: No. 1807, General Artemio Ricarte; 1808, Teodoro M. Kalaw (politician); 1809, Carlos P. Garcia (4th President); 1913, Quintin Paredes (senator); 1889, Dr. Deogracias V. Villadolid; 1914, Santiago Fonacier (former Senator and army chaplain); 1811, General Vicente Lim; 1812, Professor Nicanor Abelardo; 1813, Francisco Dagohoy; 1814, Aurora Aragon Quezon; 1815, Juan Sumulong.

1984. 150th Anniv of Ayala Corporation.

1818 **583** 70 s. multicoloured 20 10

1819 3 p. 60 multicoloured 50 15

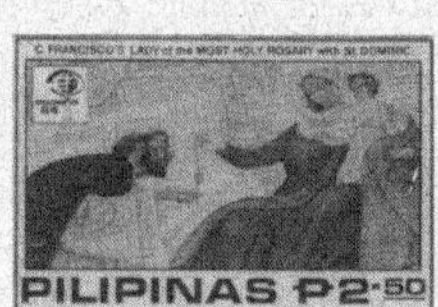

584 "Lady of the Most Holy Rosary with St. Dominic" (C. Francisco)　　585 Maria Paz Mendoza Guazon

1984. "Espana 84" International Stamp Exhibition, Madrid. Multicoloured.

1820 2 p. 50 Type **584** 35 15

1821 5 p. "Spoliarum" (Juan Luna) 75 35

1984. Birth Centenary of Dr. Maria Paz Mendoza Guazon.

1823 **585** 60 s. red and blue 15 10

1824 65 s. red, black and blue 15 10

586 "Adolias amlana"

1984. Butterflies. Multicoloured.

1825 60 s. Type **586** 20 10

1826 2 p. 40 "Papilio daedalus" 55 25

1827 3 p. "Prothoe franckii semperi" 70 25

1828 3 p. 60 Philippine birdwing 85 30

1829 4 p. 20 Lurcher 1·00 40

1830 5 p. "Chilasa idaeoides" 1·10 45

1984. National Children's Book Day. Stamp from miniature sheet ("The Monkey and the Turtle") surch **7-17-84 NATIONAL CHILDREN'S BOOK DAY 20**. Perf or imperf.

1831 7 p. 20 on 7 p. 50 multicoloured 1·40 80

1984. 420th Anniv of Philippine–Mexican Friendship. Stamp from miniature sheet (Virgin of Manila) surch **420TH PHIL-MEXICAN FRIENDSHIP 8-3-84 20**. Perf or imperf.

1832 7 p. 20 on 7 p. 50 multicoloured 1·40 80

589 Running　　590 The Mansion

1984. Olympic Games, Los Angeles. Multicoloured.

1833 60 s. Type **589** 10 10

1834 2 p. 40 Boxing 40 25

1835 6 p. Swimming 1·10 55

1836 7 p. 20 Windsurfing 1·40 75

1837 8 p. 40 Cycling 1·60 80

1838 20 p. Running (woman athlete) 3·75 2·00

1984. 75th Anniv of Baguio City.

1840 **590** 1 p. 20 multicoloured 25 15

1984. 300th Anniv of Our Lady of Holy Rosary Parish. Stamp from miniature sheet ("Lady of the Most Holy Rosary") surch **9-1-84 300th YR O.L. HOLY ROSARY PARISH 20**. Perf or imperf.

1841 7 p. 20 on 7 p. 50 multicoloured 1·40 80

592 Electric Train on Viaduct

1984. Light Railway Transit.

1842 **592** 1 p. 20 multicoloured 20 15

593 Australian and Philippine Stamps and Koalas

1984. "Ausipex 84" International Stamp Exhibition, Melbourne.

1843 **593** 3 p. multicoloured 55 25

1844 3 p. 60 multicoloured 65 30

1984. National Museum Week. Stamp from miniature sheet (as No. 1821) surch **NATIONAL MUSEUM WEEK 10-5-84 20**. Perf or imperf.

1846 7 p. 20 on 7 p. 50 multicoloured 1·40 80

1984. Asia Regional Conference of Rotary International. No. 1728 surch **14-17 NOV. 84 R.I. ASIA REGIONAL CONFERENCE P.1. 20.**

1847 **551** 1 p. 20 on 2 p. 30 mult 20 15

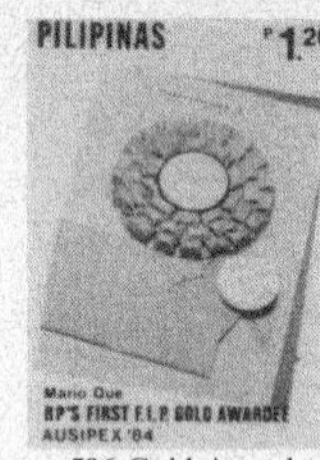

596 Gold Award

1984. Philatelic Week. Gold Award at "Ausipex 84" to Mario Que. Multicoloured.

1848 1 p. 20 Type **596** 25 15

1849 3 p. Page of Que's exhibit 35 15

597 Caracao

1984. Water Transport. Multicoloured.

1850 60 s. Type **597** 10 10

1851 1 p. 20 Chinese junk 25 10

1852 6 p. Spanish galleon 1·10 55

1853 7 p. 20 Casco (Filipino cargo prau) 1·40 65

1854 8 p. 40 Early paddle-steamer 1·60 80

1855 20 p. Modern liner 3·75 1·75

599 Anniversary Emblem

1984. 125th Anniv of Ateneo de Manila University.

1857 **599** 60 s. blue and gold 20 10

1858 1 p. 20 blue and silver 35 25

600 Virgin and Child　　602 Abstract

601 Manila–Dagupan Steam Locomotive, 1892

1984. Christmas. Multicoloured.
1859 60 s. Type **600** 20 10
1860 1 p. 20 Holy Family 35 25

1984. Rail Transport. Multicoloured.
1861 60 s. Type **601** 15 10
1862 1 p. 20 Light Railway Transit train, 1984 25 10
1863 6 p. Bicol express, 1955 1·10 55
1864 7 p. 20 Electric tram, 1905 1·40 65
1865 8 p. 40 Commuter train, 1972 1·60 80
1866 20 p. Horse-drawn tram, 1898 3·75 1·75

1984. 10th Anniv of Philippine Jaycees' Ten Outstanding Young Men Awards. Abstracts by Raul Isidro. Multicoloured.
1867 60 s. brown background in circle 20 10
1868 60 s. Type **602** 20 10
1869 60 s. red background 20 10
1870 60 s. blue and purple background 20 10
1871 60 s. orange and brown background 20 10
1872 3 p. As No. 1867 40 25
1873 3 p. Type **602** 40 25
1874 3 p. As No. 1869 40 25
1875 3 p. As No. 1870 40 25
1876 3 p. As No. 1871 40 25

603 Tobacco Plant and Dried Leaf

1985. 25th Anniv of Philippine Virginia Tobacco Administration.
1877 **603** 60 s. multicoloured 15 10
1878 3 p. multicoloured 55 25

1985. Philatelic Week, 1984. Nos. 1848/9 optd **Philatelic Week, 1984.**
1879 **596** 1 p. 20 multicoloured 20 15
1880 – 3 p. multicoloured 50 35

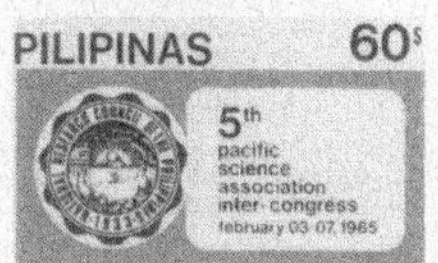

605 National Research Council Emblem

1985. 5th Pacific Science Association Congress.
1881 **605** 60 s. black, blue and light blue 15 10
1882 1 p. 20 black, blue and orange 40 20

606 "Carmona retusa"

1985. Medicinal Plants. Multicoloured.
1883a 60 s. Type **606** 10 10
1884 1 p. 20 "Orthosiphon aristatus" 20 15
1885 2 p. 40 "Vitex negundo" 45 30
1886 3 p. "Aloe barbadensis" 50 35
1887 3 p. 60 "Quisqualis indica" 65 45
1888 4 p. 20 "Blumea balsamifera" 75 45

607 "Early Bird" Satellite

1985. 20th Anniv of International Telecommunications Satellite Organization.
1896 **607** 60 s. multicoloured 15 10
1897 3 p. multicoloured 55 25

608 Piebalds

1985. Horses. Multicoloured.
1898 60 s. Type **608** 15 10
1899 1 p. 20 Palominos 25 10
1900 6 p. Bays 1·25 55
1901 7 p. 20 Browns 1·40 70
1902 8 p. 40 Greys 1·50 80
1903 20 p. Chestnuts 3·75 1·75

609 Emblem

1985. 25th Anniv of National Tax Research Centre.
1905 **609** 60 s. multicoloured 20 10

610 Transplanting Rice

1985. 25th Anniv of International Rice Research Institute, Los Baños. Multicoloured.
1906 60 s. Type **610** 15 10
1907 3 p. Paddy fields 35 10

611 Image of Holy Child of Cebu

1985. 420th Anniv of Filipino–Spanish Treaty. Mult.
1908 1 p. 20 Type **611** 25 15
1909 3 p. 60 Rajah Tupas and Miguel Lopez de Lagazpi signing treaty 40 15

613 Early Anti-TB Label

1985. 75th Anniv of Philippine Tuberculosis Society. Multicoloured.
1911 60 s. Screening for TB, laboratory work, health education and inoculation 15 10
1912 1 p. 20 Type **613** 25 15

1985. 45th Anniv of Girl Scout Charter. No. 1409 surch **45th ANNIVERSARY GIRL SCOUT CHARTER**, emblem and new value.
1917 **348** 2 p. 40 on 15 s. on 10 s. multicoloured 30 25
1918 4 p. 20 on 15 s. on 10 s. multicoloured 55 25
1919 7 p. 20 on 15 s. on 10 s. multicoloured 90 45

616 "Our Lady of Fatima"

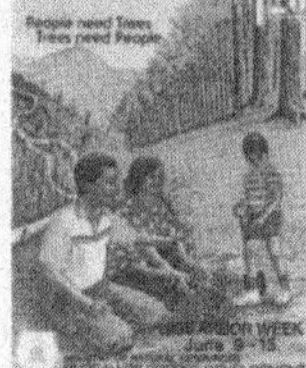

617 Family planting Tree

1985. Marian Year. 2000th Birth Anniversary of Virgin Mary. Multicoloured.
1920 1 p. 20 Type **616** 25 15
1921 2 p. 40 "Our Lady of Beaterio" (Juan Bueno Silva) 30 15
1922 3 p. "Our Lady of Penafrancia" 35 20
1923 3 p. 60 "Our Lady of Guadalupe" 45 25

1985. Tree Week. International Year of the Forest.
1924 **617** 1 p. 20 multicoloured 25 15

618 Battle of Bessang Pass

619 Vicente Orestes Romualdez

1985. 40th Anniv of Bessang Pass Campaign.
1925 **618** 1 p. 20 multicoloured 25 15

1985. Birth Centenary of Vicente Orestes Romualdez (lawyer).
1926a **619** 60 s. blue 20 10
1927a 2 p. mauve 35 20

620 Fishing

1985. International Youth Year. Children's Paintings. Multicoloured.
1928 2 p. 40 Type **620** 30 15
1929 3 p. 60 Picnic 45 15

621 Banawe Rice Terraces

1985. World Tourism Organization Congress, Sofia, Bulgaria.
1930 **621** 2 p. 40 multicoloured 30 20

622 Export Graph and Crane lifting Crate

624 Emblem and Dove with Olive Branch

1985. Export Promotion Year.
1931 **622** 1 p. 20 multicoloured 25 15

1985. No. 1815 surch **P3 60.**
1932 3 p. 60 on 4 p. 20 purple 65 35

1985. 40th Anniv of U.N.O.
1933 **624** 3 p. 60 multicoloured 45 25

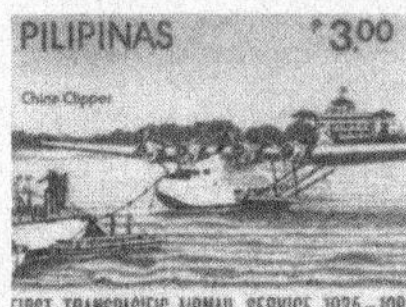

625 Martin M-130 Flying Boat "China Clipper"

1985. 50th Anniv of First Trans-Pacific Commercial Flight (San Francisco–Manila). Multicoloured.
1934 3 p. Type **625** 35 20
1935 3 p. 60 Route map, "China Clipper" and anniversary emblem 45 25

1985. Philatelic Week. Nos. 1863/4 surch **PHILATELIC WEEK 1985**, No. 1937 further optd **AIRMAIL**.
1936 60 s. on 6 p. mult (postage) 15 10
1937 3 p. on 7 p. 20 mult (air) 55 30

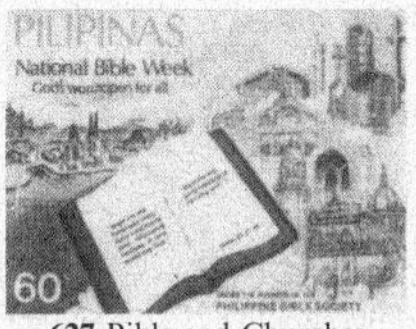

627 Bible and Churches

1985. National Bible Week.
1938 **627** 60 s. multicoloured 15 10
1939 3 p. multicoloured 55 25

628 Panuluyan (enactment of search for an inn)

1985. Christmas. Multicoloured.
1940 60 s. Type **628** 15 10
1941 3 p. Pagdalaw (nativity) 55 25

629 Justice holding Scales **630** Rizal and "Noli Me Tangere"

1986. 75th Anniv of College of Law.
1942 **629** 60 s. mauve and black 15 10
1943 3 p. green, purple & blk 55 25
See also No. 2009.

1986. Centenary of Publication of "Noli Me Tangere" (Jose Rizal's first book).
1944 **630** 60 s. violet 10 10
1945 – 1 p. 20 green 25 20
1946 – 3 p. 60 brown 65 30
DESIGNS: 1 p. 20, 3 p. 60, Rizal, "To the Flowers of Heidelberg" (poem) and Heidelberg University.

631 Douglas DC-3, 1946

632 Oil Refinery, Manila Bay

1986. 45th Anniv of Philippine Airlines. Each red, black and blue.
1947 60 s. Type **631** 10 10
1948 60 s. Douglas DC-4 Skymaster, 1946 15 10
1949 60 s. Douglas DC-6, 1948 15 10
1950 60 s. Vickers Viscount 784, 1957 15 10
1951 2 p. 40 Fokker F.27 Friendship, 1960 45 25
1952 2 p. 40 Douglas DC-8-50, 1962 45 25
1953 2 p. 40 B.A.C. One Eleven 500, 1964 45 25
1954 2 p. 40 Douglas DC-10-30, 1974 45 25
1955 3 p. 60 Beech 18, 1941 65 30
1956 3 p. 60 Boeing 747-200, 1980 65 30
See also No. 2013.

1986. 25th Anniv of Bataan Refinery Corporation.
1957 **632** 60 s. silver and green 15 10
1958 – 3 p. silver and blue 55 25
DESIGN—HORIZ: 3 p. Refinery (different).

633 Emblem

1986. "Expo 86" World's Fair, Vancouver.
1959 **633** 60 s. multicoloured 15 10
1960 3 p. multicoloured 55 25

634 Emblem and Industrial and Agricultural Symbols

1986. 25th Anniv of Asian Productivity Organization.
1961 **634** 60 s. black, green & orge 15 10
1962 3 p. black, green & orge 55 25
1963 3 p. brown (30 × 22 mm) 55 25

635 1906 2 c. Stamp

637 Corazon Aquino, Salvador Laurel and Hands

1986. "Ameripex 86" Int Stamp Exhibition, Chicago.
1964 **635** 60 s. green, black & yell 15 10
1965 – 3 p. bistre, black & grn 55 25
DESIGN: 3 p. 1935 20 c. stamp.
See also No. 2006.

1986. "People Power". Multicoloured.
1966 60 s. Type **637** 10 10
1967 1 p. 20 Radio antennae, helicopter and people . . . 30 10
1968 2 p. 40 Religious procession . 40 20
1969 3 p. Crowds around soldiers in tanks 50 25

638 Monument and Paco and Taft Schools

1986. 75th Anniv of First La Salle School in Philippines.
1971 **638** 60 s. black, lilac and green 10 10
1972 – 2 p. 40 black, blue & grn 40 20
1973 – 3 p. black, yellow & grn . 50 25
DESIGNS: 2 p. 40, St. Miguel Febres Cordero and Paco School; 3 p. St. Benilde and Taft school; 7 p. 20, Founding brothers of Paco school.

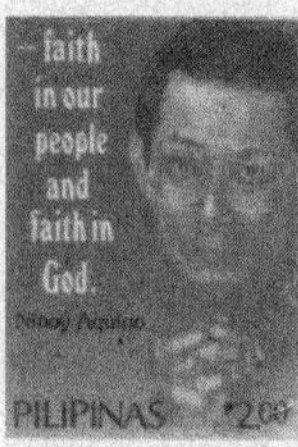

639 Aquino praying **640** "Vanda sanderiana"

1986. 3rd Death Anniv of Benigno S. Aquino, jun.
1975 – 60 s. green 10 10
1976 **639** 2 p. multicoloured . . . 30 15
1977 – 3 p. 60 multicoloured . . 60 25
DESIGNS—27 × 36 mm (as T **526**): 60 s. Aquino. HORIZ (as T **639**): 3 p. 60, Aquino (different).
See also No. 2007.

1986. Orchids. Multicoloured.
1979 60 s. Type **640** 10 10
1980 1 p. 20 "Epigeneium lyonii" . 20 10
1981 2 p. 40 "Paphiopedilum philippinense" 40 20
1982 3 p. "Amesiella philippinense" 50 25

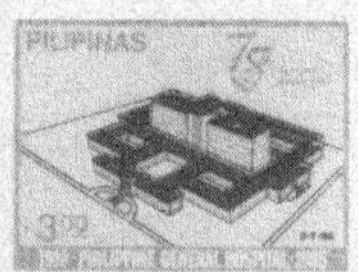

641 "Christ carrying the Cross" **642** Hospital

1986. 400th Anniv of Quiapo District.
1983 **641** 60 s. red, black and mauve 10 10
1984 – 3 p. 60 blue, blk & grn 60 25
DESIGN—HORIZ: 3 p. 60, Quiapo Church.

1986. 75th Anniv of Philippine General Hospital.
1985 **642** 60 s. multicoloured . . . 10 10
1986 3 p. multicoloured . . . 50 25
2012 5 p. brown . . . . 1·00 60

643 Comet and Earth

1986. Appearance of Halley's Comet. Multicoloured.
1987 60 s. Type **643** 10 10
1988 2 p. 40 Comet, Moon and Earth 40 25

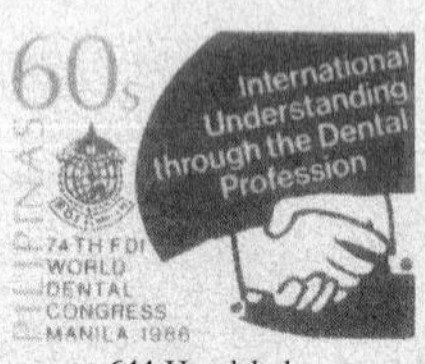

644 Handshake **645** Emblem

1986. 74th International Dental Federation Congress, Manila. Multicoloured.
1989 60 s. Type **644** 15 10
1990 3 p. Jeepney, Manila 65 35
See also Nos. 2008 and 2011.

1986. 75th Anniv of Manila Young Men's Christian Association.
1991 **645** 2 p. blue 35 15
1992 3 p. 60 red 65 30
2058 4 p. blue 65 30

646 Old and New Buildings

1986. 85th Anniv of Philippine Normal College.
1993 – 60 s. multicoloured . . . 15 10
1994 **646** 3 p. 60 yellow, brn & bl 80 40
DESIGN: 60 s. Old and new buildings (different).

647 Butterfly and Beetles

1986. Philatelic Week and International Peace Year.
1995 **647** 60 s. multicoloured . . . 15 10
1996 – 1 p. blue and black . . 25 10
1997 – 3 p. multicoloured . . . 65 35
DESIGNS—VERT: 1 p. Peace Year emblem. HORIZ: 3 p. Dragonflies.

648 Mother and Child **651** Emblem

650 Manila Hotel, 1912

1986. Christmas. Multicoloured.
1998 60 s. Type **648** 15 10
1999 60 s. Couple with child and cow 15 10
2000 60 s. Mother and child with doves 15 10
2001 1 p. Mother and child receiving gifts (horiz) 25 10
2002 1 p. Mother and child beneath arch (horiz) 25 10
2003 1 p. Madonna and shepherd adoring child (horiz) . . . 25 10
2004 1 p. Shepherds and animals around child in manger (horiz) 25 10

1987. No. 1944 surch **P1 00**.
2005 **630** 1 p. on 60 s. violet . . . 15 10

1987. As previous issues but smaller, 22 × 30 mm, 30 × 22mm or 32 × 22 mm (5 p. 50), and values and colours changed.
2006 – 75 s. green (As No. 1965) 10 10
2007 – 1 p. blue (As No. 1975) 25 10
2008 **644** 3 p. 25 green 65 40
2009 **629** 3 p. 50 brown 75 45
2011 – 4 p. 75 green (As No. 1990) 85 40
2013 – 5 p. 50 blue (As No. 1956) 95 45

1987. 75th Anniv of Manila Hotel.
2014 **650** 1 p. bistre and black . . 25 15
2015 – 4 p. multicoloured . . . 65 35
2016 – 4 p. 75 multicoloured . . 85 40
2017 – 5 p. 50 multicoloured . 95 45
DESIGNS: 4 p. Hotel; 4 p. 75, Lobby; 5 p. 50, Staff in ante-lobby.

1987. 50th Anniv of International Eucharistic Congress, Manila. Multicoloured.
2018 75 s. Type **651** 10 10
2019 1 p. Emblem (different) (horiz) 15 10

652 Pres. Cory Aquino taking Oath

1987. Ratification of New Constitution.
2020 **652** 1 p. multicoloured . . . 25 15
2021 – 5 p. 50 blue & brown . 1·10 55
2060 – 5 p. 50 green & brown (22 × 31 mm) 65 30
DESIGN: 5 p. 50, Constitution on open book and dove.

653 Dr. Jose P. Laurel (founder) and Tower

1987. 35th Anniv of Lyceum.
2022 **653** 1 p. multicoloured . . . 10 10
2023 2 p. multicoloured . . . 20 15

654 City Seal, Man with Philippine Eagle and Woman with Fruit

1987. 50th Anniv of Davao City.
2024 **654** 1 p. multicoloured . . . 35 10

655 Salary and Policy Loans **656** Emblem and People in Hand

1987. 50th Anniv of Government Service Insurance System. Multicoloured.
2025 1 p. Type **655** 25 15
2026 1 p. 25 Disability and medicare 25 15
2027 2 p. Retirement benefits . . . 35 20
2028 3 p. 50 Survivorship benefits . 65 30

1987. 50th Anniv of Salvation Army in Philippines.
2029 **656** 1 p. multicoloured . . . 15 10

657 Woman, Ballot Box and Map **659** Man with Outstretched Arm

658 Map and Flags as Leaves

1987. 50th Anniv of League of Women Voters.
2030 **657** 1 p. blue and mauve . . . 15 10

1987. As T **526**.
2031 1 p. green 15 10
2032 1 p. blue 15 10
2033 1 p. red 15 10
2034 1 p. purple and red 15 10
DESIGNS: No. 2031, Gen. Vicente Lukban; 2032, Wenceslao Q. Vinzons; 2033, Brigadier-General Mateo M. Capinpin; 2034, Jesus Balmori.

1987. 20th Anniv of Association of South-East Asian Nations.
2035 **658** 1 p. multicoloured . . . 15 10

1987. Exports.
2036 **659** 1 p. multicoloured . . . 10 10
2037 – 2 p. green, yell & brn . . 20 15
2059 – 4 p. 75 blue and black . . 55 30
DESIGN: 2 p., 4 p. 75, Man, cogwheel and factory.

660 Nuns, People and Crucifix within Flaming Heart **661** Statue and Stained Glass Window

1967. 125th Anniv of Daughters of Charity in the Philippines.
2038 **660** 1 p. blue, red and black . 15 10

1987. Canonisation of Blessed Lorenzo Ruiz de Manila (first Filipino saint). Multicoloured.
2039 1 p. Type **661** 25 15
2040 5 p. 50 Lorenzo Ruiz praying before execution 75 35

1987. No. 2012 surch **P4.75**.
2042 **642** 4 p. 75 on 5 p. brown . 60 30

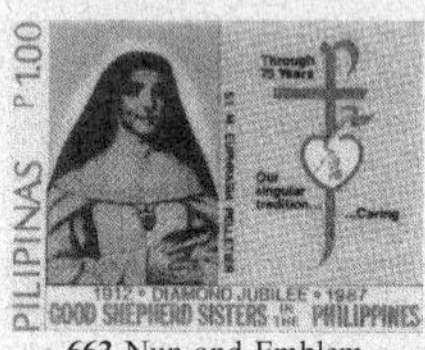

663 Nun and Emblem

1987. 75th Anniv of Good Shepherd Sisters in Philippines.
2043 **663** 1 p. multicoloured . . . 15 10

664 Founders

1987. 50th Anniv of Philippines Boy Scouts.
2044 **664** 1 p. multicoloured . . . 15 10

665 Family with Stamp Album

1987. 50th Anniv of Philippine Philatelic Club.
2045 **665** 1 p. multicoloured . . . 15 10

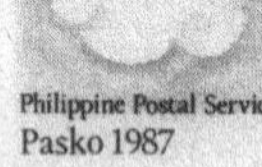

666 Monks, Church and Wrecked Galleon **668** Dove with Letter

667 Flags

1987. 400th Anniv of Dominican Order in Philippines.
2046 **666** 1 p. black, blue and orange 25 15
2047 – 4 p. 75 multicoloured . . 60 30
2048 – 5 p. 50 multicoloured . . 75 35
DESIGNS: 4 p. 75, J. A. Jeronimo Guerrero, Diego de Sta. Maria and Letran Dominican college; 5 p. 50, Pope and monks.

1987. 3rd Association of South-east Asian Nations Summit Meeting.
2049 **667** 4 p. multicoloured . . . 45 25

1987. Christmas. Multicoloured.
2050 1 p. Type **668** 25 15
2051 1 p. People and star decoration 25 15
2052 4 p. Crowd going to church . 45 25
2053 4 p. 75 Mother and children exchanging gifts 55 25
2054 5 p. 50 Children and bamboo cannons 65 30
2055 8 p. Children at table bearing festive fare 90 45
2056 9 p. 50 Woman at table . . . 1·10 55
2057 11 p. Woman having Christmas meal . . . . 1·25 65

669 Emblem, Headquarters and Dr. Rizal

1987. 75th Anniv of Grand Lodge of Philippine Masons.
2061 **669** 1 p. multicoloured . . . 15 10

670 Foodstuffs in Split Globe

1987. 40th Anniv of U.N.O. Multicoloured.
2062 1 p. Type **670** (International Fund for Agricultural Development) 15 10
2063 1 p. Means of transport and communications (Asian and Pacific Transport and Communications Decade) . 15 10
2064 1 p. People and hands holding houses (International Year of Shelter for the Homeless) . 15 10
2065 1 p. Happy children playing musical instruments (World Health Day: U.N.I.C.E.F. child vaccination campaign) 15 10

671 Official Seals and Gavel

1988. Opening Session of 1987 Congress. Mult.
2066 1 p. Type **671** 15 10
2067 5 p. 50 Congress in session and gavel (horiz) 65 40

672 Children and Bosco

1988. Death Centenary of St. John Bosco (founder of Salesian Brothers).
2068 **672** 1 p. multicoloured . . . 15 10
2069 5 p. 50 multicoloured . . 65 40

673 Emblem **675** Envelope with Coded Addresses

1988. Buy Philippine-Made Movement Month.
2070 **673** 1 p. multicoloured . . . 15 15

1988. Various stamps surch **P 3.00**.
2071 – 3 p. on 3 p. 60 brown (No. 1946) 45 25
2072 **645** 3 p. on 3 p. 60 red . . . 45 25
2073 – 3 p. on 3 p. 60 mult (No. 1977) 45 25
2074 – 3 p. on 3 p. 60 blue, black & green (No. 1984) . . . 45 25
2075 **646** 3 p. on 3 p. 60 yellow, brown and blue . . . 45 25

1988. Postal Codes.
2076 **675** 60 s. multicoloured . . . 15 10
2077 1 p. multicoloured . . . 15 10

676 "Vesbius purpureus" (soldier bug) **677** Solar Eclipse

1988. Insect Predators. Multicoloured.
2078 1 p. Type **676** 15 10
2079 5 p. 50 "Campsomeris aurulenta" (dagger wasp) . 60 40

1988.
2080 **677** 1 p. multicoloured . . . 15 10
2081 5 p. 50 multicoloured . . . 15 10

678 Teodoro **679** Emblem

1988. 101st Birth Anniv of Toribio Teodoro (industrialist).
2082 **678** 1 p. cinnamon, brn & red 15 10
2083 1 p. 20 blue, brown & red 15 10

1988. 75th Anniv of College of Holy Spirit.
2084 **679** 1 p. brn, gold and blk . 15 10
2085 – 4 p. brown, green & blk 55 25
DESIGN: 4 p. Arnold Janssen (founder) and Sister Edelwina (director, 1920–47).

680 Emblem **681** Luna and Hidalgo

1988. Newly Restored Democracies International Conference.
2086 **680** 4 p. blue, ultram & blk . 55 30

1988. National Juan Luna and Felix Resurreccion Hidalgo Memorial Exhibition.
2087 **681** 1 p. black, yellow & brn 15 10
2088 5 p. 50 black, cinnamon and brown 70 35

682 Magat Dam, Ramon, Isabela

1988. 25th Anniv of National Irrigation Administration.
2089 **682** 1 p. multicoloured . . . 15 10
2090 5 p. 50 multicoloured . 70 45

683 Scuba Diving, Siquijor

1988. Olympic Games, Seoul (1st issue). Multicoloured. Perf or imperf.
2091 1 p. Type **683** 20 10
2092 1 p. 20 Big game fishing, Aparri, Cagayan 20 15
2093 4 p. Yachting, Manila Central 70 45
2094 5 p. 50 Mountain climbing, Mt. Apo, Davao 95 65
2095 8 p. Golfing, Cebu City . . 1·40 90
2096 11 p. Cycling (Tour of Mindanao), Marawi City . 1·90 1·25
See also Nos. 2113/18.

684 Headquarters, Plaza Santa Cruz, Manila **686** Balagtas

1988. Banking Anniversaries. Multicoloured.
2097 1 p. Type **684** (50th anniv of Philippine International Commercial Bank) 15 10
2098 1 p. Family looking at factory and countryside (25th anniv of Land Bank) 15 10
2099 5 p. 50 Type **684** 75 50
2100 5 p. 50 As No. 2098 . . . . 75 50

1988. Various stamps surch.
2101 1 p. 90 on 2 p. 40 mult (No. 1968) 30 15
2102 1 p. 90 on 2 p. 40 black, blue and green (No. 1972) . . . 30 15
2103 1 p. 90 on 2 p. 40 mult (No. 1981) 30 15
2104 1 p. 90 on 2 p. 40 mult (No. 1988) 30 15

1988. Birth Bicentenary of Francisco Balagtas Baltasco (writer). Each green, brown and yellow.
2105 1 p. Type **686** 15 10
2106 1 p. As Type **686** but details reversed 15 10

687 Hospital **688** Brown Mushroom

1988. 50th Anniv of Quezon Institute (tuberculosis hospital).
2107 **687** 1 p. multicoloured . . . 15 10
2108 5 p. 50 multicoloured . . 80 55

1988. Fungi. Multicoloured.
2109 60 s. Type **688** 20 10
2110 1 p. Rat's ear fungus 40 15
2111 2 p. Abalone mushroom . . . 65 25
2112 4 p. Straw mushroom . . . . 1·40 45

689 Archery **691** Red Cross Work

690 Department of Justice

1988. Olympic Games, Seoul (2nd issue). Multicoloured. Perf or imperf.
2113 1 p. Type **689** 20 10
2114 1 p. 20 Tennis 20 15
2115 4 p. Boxing 60 30
2116 5 p. 50 Athletics 80 40
2117 8 p. Swimming . . . . 1·10 60
2118 11 p. Cycling . . . . 1·60 80

1988. Law and Justice Week.
2120 **690** 1 p. multicoloured . . . 15 10

1988. 125th Anniv of Red Cross.
2121 **691** 1 p. multicoloured . . . 15 10
2122 5 p. 50 multicoloured . . 75 50

692 Girl and Boy **693** Map and Shrimps

1988. 50th Anniv of Christian Children's Fund.
2123 **692** 1 p. multicoloured . . . 15 10

1988. 50th Anniv of Bacolod City Charter.
2124 **693** 1 p. multicoloured . . . 15 10

694 Breastfeeding **695** A. Aragon Quezon

1988. Child Survival Campaign. Multicoloured.
2125 1 p. Type **694** 15 10
2126 1 p. Growth monitoring . . 15 10
2127 1 p. Immunization 15 10
2128 1 p. Oral rehydration 15 10
2129 1 p. Access for the disabled (U.N. Decade of Disabled Persons) 15 10

1988. Birth Centenary of Aurora Aragon Quezon.
2130 **695** 1 p. multicoloured . . . 15 10
2131 5 p. 50 multicoloured . . 80 55

696 Post Office **697** Sampaloc Branch Transmitter

1988. Philatelic Week. Multicoloured.
2132 1 p. Type **696** (inscr "1938") 20 15
2132b 1 p. Type **696** (inscr "1988") 35 15
2133 1 p. Stamp counter 20 15
2134 1 p. Fern and stamp displays 20 15
2135 1 p. People looking at stamp displays 20 15

1988. 10 Years of Technological Improvements by Philippine Long Distance Telephone Company.
2136 **697** 1 p. multicoloured . . . 15 10

698 Clasped Hands and Dove **699** Crowd with Banners

1988. Christmas. Multicoloured.
2137 75 s. Type **698** 15 10
2138 1 p. Children making decorations (horiz) 15 15
2139 2 p. Man carrying decorations on yoke (horiz) 30 20
2140 3 p. 50 Christmas tree . . . 55 25
2141 4 p. 75 Candle and stars . . 75 35
2142 5 p. 50 Reflection of star forming heart (horiz) . . . 85 45

1988. Commission on Human Rights (2143) and 40th Anniv of Universal Declaration of Human Rights (2144). Multicoloured.
2143 1 p. Type **699** 15 10
2144 1 p. Doves escaping from cage 15 10

700 Church, 1776 **701** Statue and School

1988. 400th Anniv of Malate. Multicoloured.
2145 1 p. Type **700** 15 10
2146 1 p. Our Lady of Remedies Church anniversary emblem and statue of Virgin (Eduardo Castrillo) 15 10
2147 1 p. Church, 1880 . . . . . 15 10
2148 1 p. Church, 1988 . . . . . 15 10

1988. 50th Anniv of University of Santo Tomas Graduate School.
2149 **701** 1 p. multicoloured . . . 15 10

702 Order's Activities **703** Miguel Ver (first leader)

1989. 50th Anniv of Oblates of Mary Immaculate.
2150 **702** 1 p. multicoloured . . . 15 10

1989. 47th Anniv of Recognition of Hunters ROTC Guerrilla Unit (formed by Military Academy and University students). Mult.
2151 1 p. Type **703** 15 10
2152 1 p. Eleuterio Adevoso (leader after Ver's death) 15 10

704 Foodstuffs and Paulino Santos — 705 Sinulog

1989. 50th Anniv of General Santos City.
2153 **704** 1 p. multicoloured . . . 15 10

1989. "Fiesta Islands '89" (1st series). Mult.
2154 4 p. 75 Type **705** 80 35
2155 5 p. 50 Cenaculo (Lenten festival) 85 45
2156 6 p. 25 Iloilo Paraw Regatta . 1·00 55
See also Nos. 2169/71, 2177/9, 2194/6 and 2210.

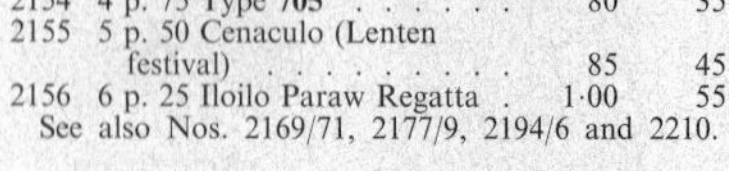

706 Tomas Mapua — 707 Adventure Pool

1989. Birth Centenaries. Multicoloured.
2157 1 p. Type **706** 20 10
2158 1 p. Camilo Osias 20 10
2159 1 p. Dr. Olivia Salamanca . . 20 10
2160 1 p. Dr. Francisco Santiago . 20 10
2161 1 p. Leandro Fernandez . . . 20 10

1989. 26th International Federation of Landscape Architects World Congress, Manila. Mult.
2162 1 p. Type **707** 15 10
2163 1 p. Paco Park 15 10
2164 1 p. Street improvements in Malacanang area 15 10
2165 1 p. Erosion control on upland farm 15 10

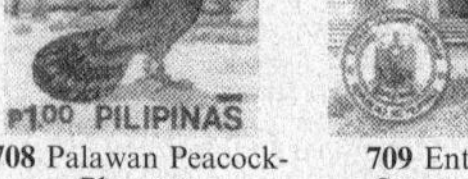

708 Palawan Peacock-Pheasant — 709 Entrance and Statue of Justice

1989. Environment Month. Multicoloured.
2166 1 p. Type **708** 60 10
2167 1 p. Palawan bear cat 15 10

1989. Supreme Court.
2168 **709** 1 p. multicoloured . . . 25 15

1989. "Fiesta Islands '89" (2nd series). As T **705**. Multicoloured.
2169 60 s. Turumba 10 10
2170 75 s. Pahiyas 15 10
2171 3 p. 50 Independence Day . . 50 25

710 Birds, Quill, "Noli Me Tangere" and Flags

1989. Bicentenary of French Revolution and Decade of Philippine Nationalism.
2172 **710** 1 p. multicoloured . . . 15 10
2173 5 p. 50 multicoloured . . 80 55

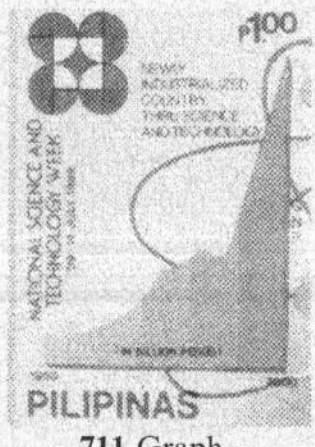

711 Graph — 713 Monument, Flag, Civilian and Soldier

1989. National Science and Technology Week. Multicoloured.
2174 1 p. Type **711** 15 10
2175 1 p. "Man" (Leonardo da Vinci) and emblem of Philippine Science High School) 15 10

1989. New Constitution stamp of 1987 surch **P4 75**.
2176 4 p. 75 on 5 p. 50 green and brown (2060) 70 45

1989. "Fiesta Island 89" (3rd series). As T **705**.
2177 1 p. Pagoda Sa Wawa (carnival float) 30 15
2178 4 p. 75 Cagayan de Oro Fiesta 75 35
2179 5 p. 50 Penafrancia Festival 85 45

1989. 50th Anniv of National Defence Department.
2180 **713** 1 p. multicoloured . . . 25 10

714 Map and Satellite — 715 Annunciation

1989. 10th Anniv of Asia–Pacific Telecommunity.
2181 **714** 1 p. multicoloured . . . 25 15

1989. Christmas. Multicoloured.
2182 60 s. Type **715** 10 10
2183 75 s. Mary and Elizabeth . . 10 10
2184 1 p. Mary and Joseph travelling to Bethlehem 15 10
2185 2 p. Search for an inn . . . 30 20
2186 4 p. Magi and star 60 40
2187 4 p. 75 Adoration of shepherds 70 50

716 Lighthouse, Liner and Lifebelt

1989. International Maritime Organization.
2188 **716** 1 p. multicoloured . . . 25 10

717 Spanish Philippines 1854 5 c. and Revolutionary Govt 1898 2 c. Stamps

1989. "World Stamp Expo '89" International Stamp Exhibition, Washington D.C. Multicoloured.
2189 1 p. Type **717** 15 10
2190 4 p. U.S. Administration 1899 50 c. and Commonwealth 1935 6 c. stamps 70 45
2191 5 p. 50 Japanese Occupation 1942 2 c. and Republic 1946 6 c. stamps 80 55

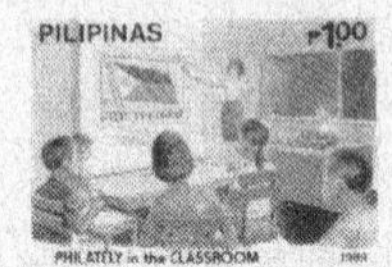

718 Teacher using Stamp as Teaching Aid

1989. Philatelic Week. Philately in the Classroom. Multicoloured.
2192 1 p. Type **718** 15 10
2193 1 p. Children working with stamps 15 10

1989. "Fiesta Islands '89" (4th series). As T **705**.
2194 1 p. Masked festival, Negros 15 10
2195 4 p. 75 Grand Canao, Baguio 75 35
2196 5 p. 50 Fireworks 85 45

719 Heart

1990. 11th World Cardiology Congress, Manila.
2197 **719** 5 p. 50 red, blue & black 85 45

720 Glasses of Beer

1990. Centenary of San Miguel Brewery.
2198 **720** 1 p. multicoloured . . . 15 10
2199 5 p. 50 multicoloured . 85 45

721 Houses and Family

1990. Population and Housing Census. Multicoloured, colours of houses given.
2200 **721** 1 p. blue 15 10
2201 1 p. pink 15 10

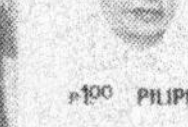

722 Scouts — 723 Claro Recto (politician)

1990. 50th Anniv of Philippine Girl Scouts.
2202 **722** 1 p. multicoloured . . . 15 10
2203 1 p. 20 multicoloured . . 15 10

1990. Birth Centenaries. Multicoloured.
2204 1 p. Type **723** 15 10
2205 1 p. Manuel Bernabe (poet) . 15 10
2206 1 p. Guillermo Tolentino (sculptor) 15 10
2207 1 p. Elpidio Quirino (President 1948–53) 15 10
2208 1 p. Dr. Bienvenido Gonzalez (University President, 1937–51) 15 10

724 Badge and Globe

1990. 50th Anniv of Legion of Mary.
2209 **724** 1 p. multicoloured . . . 15 10

1990. "Fiesta Islands '89" (5th series). As No. 2179 but new value.
2210 4 p. multicoloured 60 40

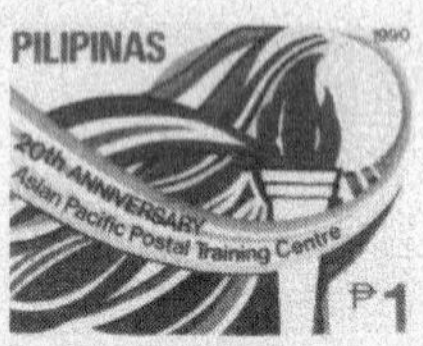

725 Torch

1990. 20th Anniv of Asian–Pacific Postal Training Centre.
2211 **725** 1 p. multicoloured . . . 15 10
2212 4 p. multicoloured . . . 60 40

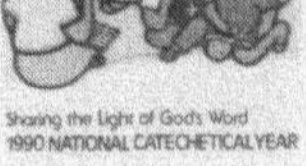

726 Catechism Class — 727 Waling Waling Flowers

1990. National Catechetical Year.
2213 **726** 1 p. multicoloured . . . 15 10
2214 3 p. 50 multicoloured . . 50 35

1990. 29th Orient and South-East Asian Lions Forum, Manila. Multicoloured.
2215 1 p. Type **727** 20 10
2216 4 p. Sampaguita flowers . . . 65 30

728 Areas for Improvement

1990. 40th Anniv of United Nations Development Programme.
2217 **728** 1 p. multicoloured . . . 15 10
2218 5 p. 50 multicoloured . . 80 55

729 Letters of Alphabet

1990. International Literacy Year.
2219 **729** 1 p. green, orange & blk 15 10
2220 5 p. 50 green, yell & blk 80 55

730 "Laughter" (A. Magsaysay-Ho)

1990. Philatelic Week. Multicoloured.
2221 1 p. "Family" (F. Amorsolo) (horiz) 25 15
2222 4 p. 75 "The Builders" (V. Edades) . . . . 1·10 55
2223 5 p. 50 Type **730** . . . . . . 1·25 65

731 Star

1990. Christmas. Multicoloured.
2224 1 p. Type **731** 15 10
2225 1 p. Stars within stars (blue background) 15 10
2226 1 p. Red and white star . . . 15 10
2227 1 p. Gold and red star (green background) 15 10
2228 5 p. 50 Geometric star (Paskuhan Village, San Fernando) 80 55

732 Figures

1990. International White Cane Safety Day.
2229 **732** 1 p. black, yellow & blue 25 15

733 La Solidaridad in 1990 and 1890 and Statue of Rizal

1990. Centenary of Publication of "Filipinas Dentro de Cien Anos" by Jose Rizal.
2230 **733** 1 p. multicoloured . . . 25 15

734 Crowd before Figure of Christ — 735 Tailplane and Stewardess

1991. 2nd Plenary Council of the Philippines.
2231 **734** 1 p. multicoloured . . . 25 15

1991. 50th Anniv of Philippine Airlines.
2232 **735** 1 p. mult (postage) . . . 15 10
2233 5 p. 50 multicoloured (air) 85 55

736 Gardenia 737 Sheepshank

1991. Flowers. Multicoloured.
2234 60 s. Type **736** 10 10
2235 75 s. Yellow bell 10 10
2475 1 p. Yellow bell 10 10
2236 1 p. Yellow plumeria 15 10
2237 1 p. Red plumeria 15 10
2238 1 p. Pink plumeria 15 10
2239 1 p. White plumeria 15 10
2240 1 p. 20 Nerium 15 10
2241 3 p. 25 Ylang-ylang 55 35
2242 4 p. Pink ixora 55 35
2243 4 p. White ixora 55 35
2244 4 p. Yellow ixora 55 35
2245 4 p. Red ixora 55 35
2246 4 p. 75 Orange bougainvillea 65 40
2247 4 p. 75 Purple bougainvillea . 65 40
2248 4 p. 75 White bougainvillea . 65 40
2249 4 p. 75 Red bougainvillea . . 65 40
2250 5 p. Canna 65 45
2251 5 p. 50 Red hibiscus 90 60
2252 5 p. 50 Yellow hibiscus . . . 90 60
2253 5 p. 50 White hibiscus . . . 90 60
2254 5 p. 50 Pink hibiscus 90 60
See also Nos. 2322/41.

1991. 12th Asia–Pacific and 9th National Boy Scouts Jamboree. Multicoloured.
2255 1 p. Reef knot 20 10
2256 4 p. Type **737** 55 25
2257 4 p. 75 Granny knot 60 30

738 Jorge Vargas 739 "Antipolo" (Carlos Francisco) and Score

1991. Birth Centenaries. Multicoloured.
2259 1 p. Type **738** 15 10
2260 1 p. Ricardo Paras 15 10
2261 1 p. Jose Laurel 15 10
2262 1 p. Vicente Fabella 15 10
2263 1 p. Maximo Kalaw 15 10

1991. 400th Anniv of Antipolo.
2264 **739** 1 p. multicoloured . . . 25 15

740 Philippine Eagle

1991. Endangered Species. The Philippine Eagle. Multicoloured.
2265 1 p. Type **740** 15 10
2266 4 p. 75 Eagle on branch . . . 65 45
2267 5 p. 50 Eagle in flight . . . 75 50
2268 8 p. Eagle feeding chick . . . 1·10 70

741 Emblem

1991. Centenary of Founding of Society of Lawyers (from 1904 Philippine Bar Association).
2269 **741** 1 p. multicoloured . . . 25 15

742 Flags and Induction Ceremony 743 First Regular Division Emblem

1991. 50th Anniv of Induction of Philippine Reservists into United States Army Forces in the Far East. Background colours given where necessary in brackets.
2270 **742** 1 p. multicoloured . . . 25 15
2272 **743** 2 p. red, black and yellow 20 15
2273 – 2 p. multicoloured (yellow) (2nd Regular) 20 15
2274 – 2 p. multicoloured (yellow) (11th) 20 15
2275 – 2 p. blue, yellow and black (yellow) (21st) 20 15
2276 **743** 2 p. red and black . . . 20 15
2277 – 2 p. black, blue and red (2nd Regular) 20 15
2278 – 2 p. multicoloured (white) (11th) 20 15
2279 – 2 p. blue, yellow and black (white) (21st) 20 15
2280 – 2 p. multicoloured (yellow) (31st) 20 15
2281 – 2 p. multicoloured (yellow) (41st) 20 15
2282 – 2 p. multicoloured (yellow) (51st) 20 15
2283 – 2 p. multicoloured (yellow) (61st) 20 15
2284 – 2 p. red, blue and black (31st) 20 15
2285 – 2 p. multicoloured (white) (41st) 20 15
2286 – 2 p. blue, black and red (51st) 20 15
2287 – 2 p. multicoloured (white) (61st) 20 15
2288 – 2 p. multicoloured (yellow) (71st) 20 15
2289 – 2 p. multicoloured (yellow) (81st) 20 15
2290 – 2 p. multicoloured (yellow) (91st) 20 15
2291 – 2 p. multicoloured (yellow) (101st) 20 15
2292 – 2 p. multicoloured (white) (71st) 20 15
2293 – 2 p. multicoloured (white) (81st) 20 15
2294 – 2 p. multicoloured (white) (91st) 20 15
2295 – 2 p. multicoloured (white) (101st) 20 15
2296 – 2 p. blue, black & yellow (Bataan Force) . . . 20 15
2297 – 2 p. yellow, red & blk (yellow) (Philippine) . . 20 15
2298 – 2 p. multicoloured (yellow) (Air Corps) 20 15
2299 – 2 p. black, blue & yellow (Offshore Patrol) . . 20 15
2300 – 2 p. blue and black (Bataan Force) 20 15
2301 – 2 p. yellow, red & black (white) (Philippine) . . 20 15
2302 – 2 p. multicoloured (white) (Air Corps) 20 15
2303 – 2 p. black and blue (Offshore Patrol) . . 20 15
Nos. 2272/2303 (all as T **743**) show divisional emblems.

744 Basilio 745 St. John of the Cross

1991. Centenary of Publication of "El Filibusterismo" by Jose Rizal. Characters from the novel. Each red, blue and black.
2304 1 p. Type **744** 15 10
2305 1 p. Simoun 15 10
2306 1 p. Father Florentino . . . 15 10
2307 1 p. Juli 15 10

1991. 400th Death Anniv of St. John of the Cross.
2308 **745** 1 p. multicoloured . . . 25 15

746 Faces (Children's Fund)

1991. United Nations Agencies.
2310 **746** 1 p. multicoloured . . . 15 10
2311 – 4 p. multicoloured . . . 55 25
2312 – 5 p. 50 black, red & blue 75 35
DESIGNS: 4 p. Hands supporting boatload of people (High Commissioner for Refugees); 5 p. 50, 1951 15 c. and 1954 3 c. U.N. stamps (40th anniv of Postal Administration).

747 "Bayanihan" (Carlos "Botong" Francisco)

1991. Philatelic Week. Multicoloured.
2313 2 p. Type **747** 30 15
2314 7 p. "Sari-Sari Vendor" (Mauro Malang Santos) 95 45
2315 8 p. "Give Us This Day" (Vicente Manansala) . . . 1·10 55

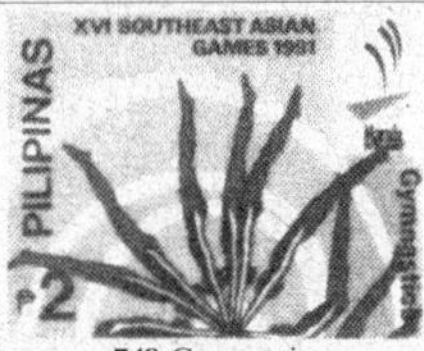

748 Gymnastics

1991. 16th South-East Asian Games, Manila. Multicoloured.
2316 2 p. Type **748** 20 15
2317 2 p. Gymnastics (emblem at bottom) 20 15
2318 6 p. Arnis (martial arts) (emblem at left) (vert) . . . 65 45
2319 6 p. Arnis (emblem at right) (vert) 65 45
Designs of the same value were issued together, se-tenant, each pair forming a composite design.

1991. Flowers. As T **736**. Multicoloured.
2322 1 p. 50 Type **736** 15 15
2323 2 p. Yellow plumeria 20 10
2324 2 p. Red plumeria 20 10
2325 2 p. Pink plumeria 20 10
2326 2 p. White plumeria 20 10
2327 3 p. Nerium 30 15
2328 5 p. Ylang-ylang 50 35
2329 6 p. Pink ixora 55 40
2330 6 p. White ixora 55 40
2331 6 p. Yellow ixora 55 40
2332 6 p. Red ixora 55 40
2333 7 p. Orange bougainvillea . . 65 45
2334 7 p. Purple bougainvillea . . 65 45
2335 7 p. White bougainvillea . . 65 45
2336 7 p. Red bougainvillea . . . 65 45
2337 8 p. Red hibiscus 75 55
2338 8 p. Yellow hibiscus 75 55
2339 8 p. White hibiscus 75 55
2340 8 p. Pink hibiscus 75 55
2341 10 p. Canna 95 70

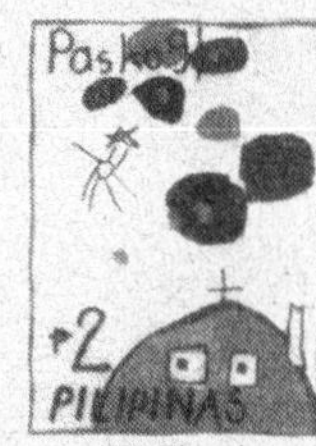

750 Church 751 Player

1991. Christmas. Children's Paintings. Mult.
2342 2 p. Type **750** 20 15
2343 6 p. Christmas present 60 40
2344 7 p. Santa Claus and tree . . 70 50
2345 8 p. Christmas tree and star . . 80 55

1991. Centenary of Basketball. Multicoloured.
2346 2 p. Type **751** 25 15
2347 6 p. Basketball player and map (issue of first basketball stamp, 1934) (horiz) 65 30
2348 7 p. Girls playing basketball (introduction of basketball in Philippines, 1904) (horiz) . 75 35
2349 8 p. Players 85 45

752 Monkey firing Cannon

1991. New Year. Year of the Monkey.
2351 **752** 2 p. multicoloured . . . 25 15
2352 6 p. multicoloured . . . 65 30

753 Pres. Aquino and Mailing Centre Emblem

1992. Kabisig Community Projects Organization. Multicoloured.
2353 2 p. Type **753** 25 15
2354 6 p. Housing 65 30
2355 7 p. Livestock 75 35
2356 8 p. Handicrafts 85 45

754 "Curcuma longa"

1992. Asian Medicinal Plants Symposium, Los Banos, Laguna. Multicoloured.
2357 2 p. Type **754** 25 15
2358 6 p. "Centella asiatica" . . . 65 30
2359 7 p. "Cassia alata" 75 35
2360 8 p. "Ervatamia pandacaqui" 85 45

755 "Mahal Kita", Envelopes and Map

1992. Greetings Stamps. Multicoloured.
2361 2 p. Type **755** 20 15
2362 2 p. As No. 2361 but inscr "I Love You" 20 15
2363 6 p. Heart and doves ("Mahal Kita") 65 35
2364 6 p. As No. 2363 but inscr "I Love You" 65 35
2365 7 p. Basket of flowers ("Mahal Kita") 75 35
2366 7 p. As No. 2365 but inscr "I Love You" 75 35
2367 8 p. Cupid ("Mahal Kita") . . 85 45
2368 8 p. As No. 2367 but inscr "I Love You" 85 45

756 Philippine Pavilion and Couple Dancing 757 "Our Lady of the Sun" (icon)

1992. "Expo '92" World's Fair, Seville. Mult.
2369 2 p. Type **756** 25 15
2370 8 p. Pavilion, preacher and conquistador holding globe 85 45

1992. 300th Anniv of Apparition of Our Lady of the Sun at Gate, Vaga Cavite.
2372 **757** 2 p. multicoloured . . . 25 15
2373 8 p. multicoloured . . . 85 45

758 Fish Farming

1992. 75th Anniv of Department of Agriculture. Multicoloured.
2374 2 p. Type **758** 20 15
2375 2 p. Pig farming 20 15
2376 2 p. Sowing seeds 20 15

759 Race Horses and Emblem 760 Manuel Roxas (President, 1946-48)

1992. 125th Anniv of Manila Jockey Club.
2377 **759** 2 p. multicoloured . . . 25 15

1992. Birth Centenaries. Multicoloured.
2379 2 p. Type **760** 20 15
2380 2 p. Natividad Almeda-Lopez (judge) 20 15
2381 2 p. Roman Ozaeta (judge) . 20 15
2382 2 p. Engracia Cruz-Reyes (women's rights campaigner and environmentalist) . . 20 15
2383 2 p. Fernando Amorsolo (artist) 20 15

761 Queen, Bishop and 1978 30 s. Stamp

1992. 30th Chess Olympiad, Manila. Mult.
2384 2 p. Type **761** 20 15
2385 6 p. King, queen and 1962 6 s. + 4 s. stamp 60 40

762 Bataan Cross

1992. 50th Anniv of Pacific Theatre in Second World War. Multicoloured.
2387 2 p. Type **762** 20 15
2388 6 p. Map inside "W" 60 40
2389 8 p. Corregidor eternal flame 85 55

763 President Aquino and President-elect Ramos

1992. Election of Fidel Ramos to Presidency.
2391 **763** 2 p. multicoloured . . . 30 15

764 "Dapitan Shrine" (Cesar Legaspi)

1992. Centenary of Dr. Jose Rizal's Exile to Dapitan. Multicoloured.
2392 2 p. Type **764** 20 15
2393 2 p. Portrait (after Juan Luna) (vert) 20 15

765 "Spirit of ASEAN" (Visit Asean Year) **766** Member of the Katipunan

1992. 25th Anniv of Association of South-East Asian Nations. Multicoloured.
2394 2 p. Type **765** 20 15
2395 2 p. "ASEAN Sea" (25th Ministerial Meeting and Postal Ministers' Conf) . . 20 15
2396 6 p. Type **765** 60 40
2397 6 p. As No. 2395 . . . . . . 60 40

1992. Centenary of Katipunan ("KKK") (revolutionary organization). Multicoloured.
2398 2 p. Type **766** 20 15
2399 2 p. Revolutionaries 20 15
2400 2 p. Plotting (horiz) 20 15
2401 2 p. Attacking (horiz) 20 15

767 Dr. Jose Rizal, Text and Quill

1992. Centenary of La Liga Filipina.
2402 **767** 2 p. multicoloured . . . 25 15

768 Swimming

1992. Olympic Games, Barcelona. Multicoloured.
2403 2 p. Type **768** 20 15
2404 7 p. Boxing 70 45
2405 8 p. Hurdling 80 55

769 School, Emblem and Students

1992. Centenaries. Multicoloured.
2407 2 p. Type **769** (Sisters of the Assumption in the Philippines) 20 15
2408 2 p. San Sebastian's Basilica, Manila (centenary (1991) of blessing of fifth construction) (vert) 25 15

770 Masonic Symbols

1992. Centenary of Nilad Lodge (first Filipino Masonic Lodge).
2409 **770** 2 p. black and green . . . 20 15
2410 – 6 p. multicoloured . . . 60 40
2411 – 8 p. multicoloured . . . 80 55
DESIGNS: 6 p. Antonio Luna and symbols; 8 p. Marcelo del Pilar ("Father of Philippine Masonry") and symbols.

771 Ramos taking Oath

1992. Swearing in of President Fidel Ramos. Mult.
2412 2 p. Type **771** 25 15
2413 8 p. President taking oath in front of flag 85 45

772 Flamingo Guppy

1992. Freshwater Aquarium Fishes (1st series). Multicoloured.
2414 1 p. 50 Type **772** 15 10
2415 1 p. 50 Neon tuxedo guppy . 15 10
2416 1 p. 50 King cobra guppy . 15 10
2417 1 p. 50 Red-tailed guppy . . 15 10
2418 1 p. 50 Tiger lacetail guppy . 15 10
2419 2 p. Pearl scale goldfish . . 25 15
2420 2 p. Red cap goldfish . . . 25 15
2421 2 p. Lionhead goldfish . . . 25 15
2422 2 p. Black moor 25 15
2423 2 p. Bubble-eye 25 15
2424 4 p. Delta topsail variaties . 45 25
2425 4 p. Orange spotted hi-fin platy 45 25
2426 4 p. Red lyretail swordtail . 45 25
2427 4 p. Bleeding heart hi-fin platy 45 25
See also Nos. 2543/56.

774 Couple

1992. Greetings Stamps. "Happy Birthday". Multicoloured.
2430 2 p. Type **774** 20 15
2431 6 p. Type **774** 60 40
2432 7 p. Balloons and candles on birthday cake 70 50
2433 8 p. As No. 2432 . . . . . 80 55

775 Melon, Beans, Tomatoes and Potatoes

1992. 500th Anniv of Discovery of America by Columbus. Multicoloured.
2434 2 p. Type **775** 20 15
2435 6 p. Maize and sweet potatoes 60 40
2436 8 p. Pineapple, cashews, avocado and water melon . 80 55

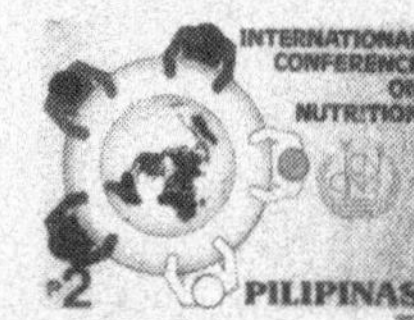

777 Figures around World Map

1992. International Nutrition Conference, Rome.
2438 **777** 2 p. multicoloured . . . 20 15

778 Mother and Child **780** Family and Canoe

1992. Christmas.
2439 **778** 2 p. multicoloured . . . 20 15
2440 – 6 p. multicoloured . . . 60 40
2441 – 7 p. multicoloured . . . 70 50
2442 – 8 p. multicoloured . . . 80 55
DESIGNS: 6 p. to 8 p. Various designs showing mothers and children.

1992. Anti-drugs Campaign. Multicoloured.
2444 2 p. Type **780** 20 15
2445 8 p. Man carrying paddle, children and canoe 80 55

781 Damaged Trees **782** Red Junglefowl

1992. Mt. Pinatubo Fund (for victims of volcanic eruption). Multicoloured.
2446 25 s. Type **781** 10 10
2447 1 p. Mt. Pinatubo erupting . 10 10
2448 1 p. Cattle in ash-covered field 10 10
2449 1 p. Refugee settlement . . . 10 10
2450 1 p. People shovelling ash . . 10 10

1992. New Year. Year of the Cock. Mult.
2451 2 p. Type **782** 20 15
2452 6 p. Maranao Sarimanok (mythical bird) 60 40

784 Badges of 61st and 71st Divisions, Cebu Area Command **785** "Family" (Cesar Legaspi) (family ties)

1992. Philippine Guerrilla Units of Second World War (1st series). Multicoloured.
2455 2 p. Type **784** 20 15
2456 2 p. Vinzon's Guerrillas and badges of 48th Chinese Guerrilla Squadron and 101st Division 20 15
2457 2 p. Anderson's Command, Luzon Guerrilla Army Forces and badge of Bulacan Military Area 20 15
2458 2 p. President Quezon's Own Guerrillas and badges of Marking's Fil-American Troops and Hunters ROTC Guerrillas 20 15
See also Nos. 2594/7, 2712/15 and 2809/12.

1992. Philatelic Week. Multicoloured.
2459 2 p. Type **785** 10 10
2460 6 p. "Pounding Rice" (Nena Saguil) (hard work and industry) 30 20
2461 7 p. "Fish Vendors" (Romeo Tabuena) (flexibility and adaptability) 40 25

786 Black Shama

1992. Endangered Birds. Multicoloured. (a) As T **786**.
2462 2 p. Type **786** 20 15
2463 2 p. Blue-headed fantail . . 20 15
2464 2 p. Mindoro zone-tailed (inscr "Imperial") pigeon 20 15
2465 2 p. Sulu hornbill 20 15
2466 2 p. Red-vented (inscr "Philippine") cockatoo . . 20 15

(b) Size 29 × 39 mm.
2467 2 p. Philippine trogon . . . 20 15
2468 2 p. Rufous hornbill 20 15
2469 2 p. White-bellied black woodpecker 20 15
2470 2 p. Spotted wood kingfisher 20 15

(c) Size 36 × 26½ mm.
2471 2 p. Brahminy kite 20 15
2472 2 p. Philippine falconet . . . 20 15
2473 2 p. Eastern reef heron . . . 20 15
2474 2 p. Philippine duck (inscr "Mallard") 20 15

787 Flower (Jasmine) **788**

1993. National Symbols. Multicoloured. (a) As T **787**. "Pilipinas" in brown at top.
2476 1 p. Type **787** 10 10
2571 2 p. Flag 15 10
2478 6 p. Leaf (palm) 50 30
2479 7 p. Costume 60 35
2480 8 p. Fruit (mango) 70 60

(b) As T **788**. "Pilipinas" in red at foot.
2481 60 s. Tree 10 10
2512 1 p. Flag 10 10
2513 1 p. House 10 10
2514 1 p. Costume 10 10
2515 1 p. As No. 2481 . . . . . 10 10
2516 1 p. Type **788** 10 10
2517 1 p. Fruit 10 10
2518 1 p. Leaf 10 10
2519 1 p. Fish 10 10
2520 1 p. Animal (water buffalo) . 10 10
2521 1 p. Bird (Philippine trogons) 10 10
2482 1 p. 50 As No. 2519 . . . . 10 10
2565 2 p. Hero (Dr. Jose Rizal) . 15 10
2566 2 p. As No. 2513 . . . . . 15 10
2567 2 p. As No. 2514 . . . . . 15 10
2568 2 p. Dance ("Tinikling") . . 15 10
2569 2 p. Sport (Sipa) 15 10
2570 2 p. As No. 2521 . . . . . 15 10
2572 2 p. As No. 2520 . . . . . 15 10
2573 2 p. Type **788** 15 10
2574 2 p. As No. 2481 . . . . . 15 10
2575 2 p. As No. 2517 . . . . . 15 10
2576 2 p. As No. 2518 . . . . . 15 10
2577 2 p. As No. 2519 . . . . . 15 10
2578 2 p. As No. 2512 . . . . . 15 10
2644 3 p. As No. 2520 . . . . . 15 10
2645 5 p. As No. 2521 . . . . . 25 15
2646 6 p. As No. 2518 . . . . . 30 15
2647 7 p. As No. 2514 . . . . . 35 20
2486 8 p. As No. 2517 . . . . . 70 40
2649 10 p. As No. 2513 . . . . . 50 25
For similar designs but with blue barcode at top, see Nos. 2781 etc.

789 "Euploea mulciber dufresne"

1993. Butterflies. Multicoloured. (a) As T **789**.
2488 2 p. Type **789** 20 10
2489 2 p. "Cheritra orpheus" . . 20 10
2490 2 p. "Delias henningia" . . . 20 10
2491 2 p. "Mycalesis ita" 20 10
2492 2 p. "Delias diaphana" . . . 20 10

(b) Size 28 × 35 mm.
2493 2 p. "Papilio rumanzobia" . . 20 10
2494 2 p. "Papilio palinurus" . . 20 10
2495 2 p. "Trogonoptera trojana" . 20 10
2496 2 p. Tailed jay ("Graphium agamemnon") 20 10
Nos. 2488/92 were issued together, se-tenant, forming a composite design.

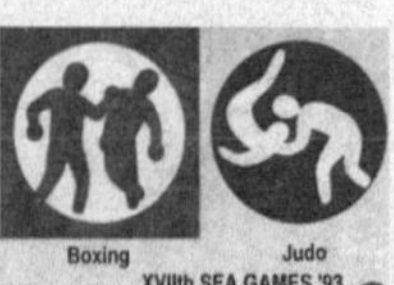

791 Nicanor Abelardo **792** Boxing and Judo

1993. Birth Centenaries. Multicoloured.
2499 2 p. Type **791** 20 10
2500 2 p. Pilar Hidalgo-Lim . . . 20 10
2501 2 p. Manuel Viola Gallego . 20 10
2502 2 p. Maria Ylagan-Orosa . . 20 10
2503 2 p. Eulogio B. Rodriguez . . 20 10

1993. 17th South-East Asian Games, Singapore. Multicoloured.
2504 2 p. Weightlifting, archery, fencing and shooting (79 × 29 mm) 20 10
2505 2 p. Type **792** 20 10
2506 2 p. Athletics, cycling, gymnastics and golf (79 × 29 mm) 20 10
2507 6 p. Table tennis, football, volleyball and badminton (79 × 29 mm) 50 25
2508 6 p. Billiards and bowling . . 50 25
2509 6 p. Swimming, water polo, yachting and diving (79 × 29 mm) 50 25

794 "Spathoglottis chrysantha"

1993. Orchids. Multicoloured.
2522 2 p. Type **794** 15 10
2523 2 p. "Arachnis longicaulis" . 15 10
2524 2 p. "Phalaenopsis mariae" . 15 10
2525 2 p. "Coelogyne marmorata" 15 10
2526 2 p. "Dendrobium sanderae" 15 10
2527 3 p. "Dendrobium serratilabium" 20 10
2528 3 p. "Phalaenopsis equestris" 20 10
2529 3 p. "Vanda merrillii" . . . 20 10
2530 3 p. "Vanda luzonica" . . . 20 10
2531 3 p. "Grammatophyllum martae" 20 10

796 Dog in Window ("Thinking of You")

1993. Greetings Stamps. Multicoloured.
2534 2 p. Type **796** 15 10
2535 2 p. As No. 2534 but inscr "Naaalala Kita" 15 10
2536 6 p. Dog looking at clock ("Thinking of You") . . . 40 20
2537 6 p. As No. 2536 but inscr "Naaalala Kita" 40 20
2538 7 p. Dog looking at calendar ("Thinking of You") . . . 50 25
2539 7 p. As No. 2538 but inscr "Naaalala Kita" 50 25
2540 8 p. Dog with pair of slippers ("Thinking of You") . . . 55 30
2541 8 p. As No. 2540 but inscr "Naaalala Kita" 55 30

797 Palms and Coconuts **799** Map and Emblem

798 Albino Ryukin Goldfish

1993. "Tree of Life".
2542 **797** 2 p. multicoloured . . . 15 10

1993. Freshwater Aquarium Fishes (2nd series). Multicoloured. (a) As T **798**.
2543 2 p. Type **798** 15 10
2544 2 p. Black oranda goldfish . 15 10
2545 2 p. Lionhead goldfish . . . 15 10
2546 2 p. Celestial-eye goldfish . . 15 10
2547 2 p. Pompon goldfish 15 10
2548 2 p. Paradise fish 15 10
2549 2 p. Pearl gourami 15 10
2550 2 p. Red-tailed black shark . 15 10
2551 2 p. Tiger barb 15 10
2552 2 p. Cardinal tetra 15 10

(b) Size 29 × 39 mm.
2553 2 p. Pearl-scale angel fish . . 15 10
2554 2 p. Zebra angel fish 15 10
2555 2 p. Marble angel fish . . . 15 10
2556 2 p. Black angel fish 15 10

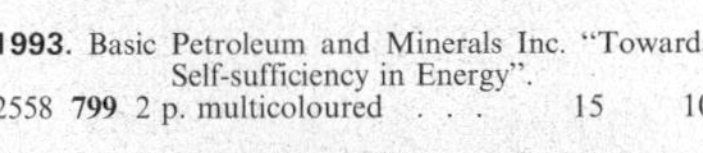
1993. Basic Petroleum and Minerals Inc. "Towards Self-sufficiency in Energy".
2558 **799** 2 p. multicoloured . . . 15 10

801 Globe, Scales, Book and Gavel

1993. 16th Int Law Conference, Manila. Mult.
2560 2 p. Type **801** 10 10
2561 6 p. Globe, scales, gavel and conference emblem on flag of Philippines (vert) 30 15
2562 7 p. Woman holding scales, conference building and globe 35 15
2563 8 p. Fisherman pulling in nets and emblem (vert) 40 20

802 Our Lady of La Naval (statue) and Galleon

1993. 400th Anniv of Our Lady of La Naval.
2564 **802** 2 p. multicoloured . . . 15 10

803 Woman and Terraced Hillside

1993. International Year of Indigenous Peoples. Women in traditional costumes. Multicoloured.
2579 2 p. Type **803** 15 10
2580 6 p. Woman, plantation and mountain 30 15
2581 7 p. Woman and mosque . . 70 35
2582 8 p. Woman and vintas (boats) 1·40 70

804 Trees

1993. Philatelic Week. "Save the Earth". Multicoloured.
2583 2 p. Type **804** 15 10
2584 6 p. Marine flora and fauna 30 15
2585 7 p. Dove and irrigation system 70 35
2586 8 p. Effects of industrial pollution . . . . 1·40 70

805 1949 6 c. + 4 c. Stamp and Symbols **806** Moon-buggy and Society Emblem

1993. 400th Anniv of Publication of "Doctrina Christiana" (first book published in Philippines).
2587 **805** 2 p. multicoloured . . . 10 10

1993. 50th Anniv of Filipino Inventors Society. Multicoloured.
2588 2 p. Type **806** 10 10
2589 2 p. Rice-harvesting machine 10 10
Nos. 2588/9 were issued together, se-tenant, forming a composite design.

807 Holy Family **808** Northern Luzon

1993. Christmas. Multicoloured.
2590 2 p. Type **807** 10 10
2591 6 p. Church goers 30 15
2592 7 p. Cattle and baskets of food 70 35
2593 8 p. Carol-singers . . . . . . 1·40 70

1993. Philippine Guerrilla Units of Second World War (2nd series). Multicoloured.
2594 2 p. Type **808** 10 10
2595 2 p. Bohol Area Command . 10 10
2596 2 p. Leyte Area Command . . 10 10
2597 2 p. Palawan Special Battalion and Sulu Area Command . 10 10

809 Dove over City (peace and order)

1993. "Philippines 2000" (development plan). Multicoloured.
2598 2 p. Type **809** 10 10
2599 6 p. Means of transport and communications 30 15
2600 7 p. Offices, roads and factories (infrastructure and industry) 70 35
2601 8 p. People from different walks of life (people empowerment) 1·40 70

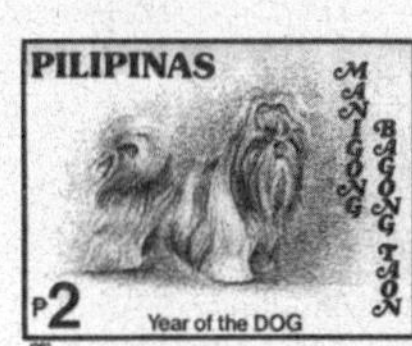

810 Shih Tzu

1993. New Year. Year of the Dog. Multicoloured.
2603 2 p. Type **810** 10 10
2604 6 p. Chow 30 15

811 Jamboree Emblem and Flags

1993. 1st Association of South-East Asian Nations Scout Jamboree, Makiling. Multicoloured.
2606 2 p. Type **811** 10 10
2607 6 p. Scout at camp-site, flags and emblem 30 15

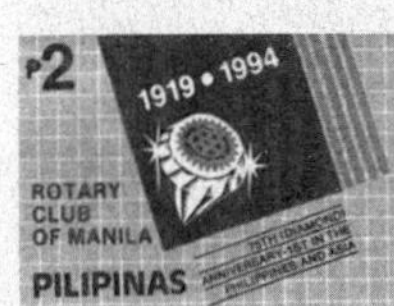

812 Club Emblem on Diamond

1994. 75th Anniv of Manila Rotary Club.
2609 **812** 2 p. multicoloured . . . 10 10

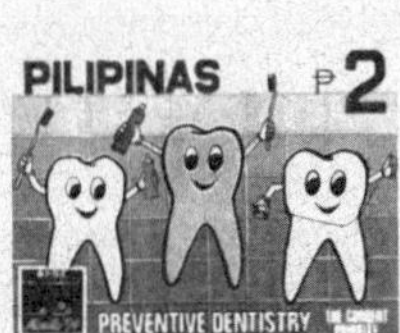

813 Teeth and Dental Hygiene Products

1994. 17th Asian–Pacific Dental Congress, Manila. Multicoloured.
2610 2 p. Type **813** 10 10
2611 6 p. Teeth, flags of participating countries and teeth over globe with Philippines circled (vert) 30 15

814 "Acropora micropthalma"

1994. Corals. Multicoloured.
2612 2 p. Type **814** 10 10
2613 2 p. "Seriatopora hystrix" . 10 10
2614 2 p. "Acropora latistella" . . 10 10
2615 2 p. "Millepora tenella" . . 10 10
2616 2 p. "Millepora tenella" (different) 10 10
2617 2 p. "Pachyseris valenciennesi" 10 10
2618 2 p. "Pavona decussata" . . 10 10
2619 2 p. "Galaxea fascicularis" . 10 10
2620 2 p. "Acropora formosa" . . 10 10
2621 2 p. "Acropora humilis" . . 10 10
2622 2 p. "Isis sp." (vert) 10 10
2623 2 p. "Plexaura sp." (vert) . . 10 10
2624 2 p. "Dendronepthya sp." (vert) 10 10
2625 2 p. "Heteroxenia sp." (vert) 10 10

815 New Year Stamps of 1991 and 1992 bearing Exhibition Emblem

1994. "Hong Kong '94" Stamp Exhibition. Multicoloured.
2627 2 p. Type **815** 10 10
2628 6 p. 1993 New Year stamps . 30 15

816 Class of 1944 Emblem **817** Airplane over Harbour, Man and Cogwheel and Emblem

1994. 50th Anniv of Philippine Military Academy Class of 1944.
2630 **816** 2 p. multicoloured . . . 10 10

1994. Federation of Filipino–Chinese Chambers of Commerce and Industry.
2632 **817** 2 p. multicoloured . . . 10 10

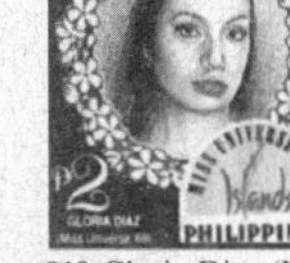

818 Stork carrying Baby ("Binabati Kita") **819** Gloria Diaz (Miss Universe 1969)

1994. Greetings Stamps. Multicoloured.
2633 2 p. Type **818** 10 10
2634 2 p. As No. 2633 but inscr "Congratulations" 10 10
2635 2 p. Bouquet ("Binabati Kita") 10 10
2636 2 p. As No. 2635 but inscr "Congratulations" 10 10
2637 2 p. Mortar board, scroll and books ("Binabati Kita") . 10 10
2638 2 p. As No. 2637 but inscr "Congratulations" 10 10
2639 2 p. Bouquet, doves and heads inside heart ("Binabati Kita") 10 10
2640 2 p. As No. 2639 but inscr "Congratulations" 10 10

1994. Miss Universe Beauty Contest. Multicoloured.
2653 2 p. Type **819** 10 10
2654 2 p. Margie Moran (Miss Universe 1973) 10 10
2655 6 p. Crown 30 15
2656 7 p. Contestant 35 20

820 Antonio Molina (composer) **821** Map, Forest and Emblem (Baguio City)

1994. Birth Centenaries. Multicoloured.
2658 2 p. Type **820** 10 10
2659 2 p. Jose Yulo (Secretary of Justice) 10 10
2660 2 p. Josefa Jara-Martinez (social worker) 10 10
2661 2 p. Nicanor Reyes (accountant) 10 10
2662 2 p. Sabino Padilla (judge) . 10 10

1994. Export Processing Zones. Multicoloured.
2664 2 p. Type **821** 10 10
2665 2 p. Cross on hilltop (Bataan) 10 10
2666 2 p. Octagonal building (Mactan) 10 10
2667 2 p. Aguinaldo Shrine (Cavite) 10 10
2668 7 p. Map and products . . . 35 20
2669 8 p. Globe and products . . 40 20
Nos. 2264/7 and 2668/9 repectively were issued together, se-tenant, forming composite designs.

822 Cross through "ILLEGAL RECRUITMENT"

1994. Anti-illegal Recruitment Campaign.
2670 **822** 2 p. multicoloured . . . 10 10

823 Palawan Bearcat

1994. Mammals. Multicoloured.
2671 6 p. Type **823** 30 15
2672 6 p. Philippine tarsier 30 15
2673 6 p. Malayan pangolin (inscr "Scaly Anteater") 30 15
2674 6 p. Indonesian ("Palawan") porcupine 30 15

824 Glory of the Sea Cone ("Conus gloriamaris")

1994. "Philakorea 1994" International Stamp Exhibition, Seoul. Shells. Multicoloured.
2676 2 p. Type **824** 10 10
2677 2 p. Striate cone ("Conus striatus") 10 10
2678 2 p. Geography cone ("Conus geographus") 10 10
2679 2 p. Textile cone ("Conus textile") 10 10

825 Sergio Osmena, Snr.

1994. 50th Anniv of Leyte Gulf Landings. Multicoloured.
2682 2 p. Type **825** 10 10
2683 2 p. Soldiers landing at Palo . 10 10
2684 2 p. "Peace - A Better World" emblem 10 10
2685 2 p. Carlos Romulo 10 10
Nos. 2682/5 were issued together, se-tenant, forming a composite design.

826 Family (International Year of the Family)

1994. Anniversaries and Event. Multicoloured.
2686 2 p. Type **826** 10 10
2687 6 p. Workers (75th anniv of I.L.O.) 30 15
2688 7 p. Aircraft and symbols of flight (50th anniv of I.C.A.O.) 35 20

827 Blue-naped Parrot

1994. "Aseanpex '94" Stamp Exhibition, Penang, Malaysia. Birds. Muilticoloured.
2689 2 p. Type **827** 10 10
2690 2 p. Luzon bleeding heart ("Bleeding Heart Pigeon") 10 10
2691 2 p. Palawan peacock-pheasant 10 10
2692 2 p. Koch's pitta 10 10

828 Presidents Fidel Ramos and W. Clinton

1994. Visit of United States President William Clinton to Philippines.
2694 **828** 2 p. multicoloured . . . 10 10
2695 8 p. multicoloured . . . 40 20

829 Convention Emblem

830 "Soteranna Puson y Quintos de Ventenilla" (Dionisio de Castro)

1994. Association of South-East Asian Nations Eastern Business Convention, Davao City.
2696 **829** 2 p. multicoloured . . . 10 10
2697 6 p. multicoloured . . . 30 15

1994. Philatelic Week. Portraits. Multicoloured.
2698 2 p. Type **830** 10 10
2699 6 p. "Quintina Castor de Sadie" (Simon Flores y de la Rosa) 30 15
2700 7 p. "Portrait of the Artist's Mother" (Felix Hidalgo y Padilla) 35 20
2701 8 p. "Una Bulaquena" (Juan Luna y Novicio) 40 20

831 Wreath

1994. Christmas. Multicoloured.
2703 2 p. Type **831** 10 10
2704 6 p. Angels 30 15
2705 7 p. Bells 35 20
2706 8 p. Christmas basket . . . 40 20

832 Piggy Bank

1994. New Year. Year of the Pig. Multicoloured.
2707 2 p. Type **832** 10 10
2708 6 p. Pig couple 30 15

833 Raid on Prison

1994. 50th Anniversaries of Raid by Hunters ROTC Guerrillas on Psew Bilibi Prison and of Mass Escape by Inmates. Multicoloured.
2710 2 p. Type **833** 10 10
2711 2 p. Inmates fleeing 10 10
Nos. 2710/11 were issued together, se-tenant, forming a composite design.

834 East Central Luzon Guerrilla Area

835 Ribbon on Globe

1994. Philippine Guerrilla Units of Second World War (3rd series). Multicoloured.
2712 2 p. Type **834** 10 10
2713 2 p. Mindoro Provincial Battalion and Marinduque Guerrilla Force 10 10
2714 2 p. Zambales Military District and Masbate Guerrilla Regiment 10 10
2715 2 p. Samar Area Command . 10 10

1994. National AIDS Awareness Campaign.
2716 **835** 2 p. multicoloured . . . 10 10

836 Flag

1994. Centenary of Declaration of Philippine Independence. Multicoloured.
2717 2 p. Type **836** 10 10
2718 2 p. Present state flag 10 10
2719 2 p. Anniversary emblem . . 10 10
Nos. 2717/19 were issued together, se-tenant, forming a composite design.

837 Pope John Paul II and Manila Cathedral

1995. Papal Visit. Multicoloured.
2720 2 p. Type **837** (400th anniv of Manila Archdiocese) . . . 10 10
2721 2 p. Pope and Cebu Cathedral (400th anniv of Diocese) . . 10 10
2722 2 p. Pope and Caceres Cathedral (400th anniv of Diocese) 10 10
2723 2 p. Pope and Nueva Segovia Cathedral (400th anniv of Diocese) 10 10
2724 2 p. Pope, globe and Pope's arms 10 10
2725 6 p. Pope and Federation of Asian Bishops emblem (6th Conference, Manila) . . . 30 15
2726 8 p. Pope, youths and emblem (10th World Youth Day) . 40 20

839 Landing Craft and Map

1995. 50th Anniv of Lingayen Gulf Landings. Multicoloured.
2729 2 p. Type **839** 10 10
2730 2 p. Map and emblems of 6th, 37th, 40th and 43rd army divisions 10 10
Nos. 2729/30 were issued together, se-tenant, forming a composite design.

840 Monument (Peter de Guzman) and Ruins of Intramuros (½-size illustration)

1995. 50th Anniv of Battle for the Liberation of Manila. Multicoloured.
2731 2 p. Type **840** 10 10
2732 8 p. Monument and ruins of Legislative Building and Department of Agriculture . 40 20

841 Diokno

1995. 8th Death Anniv of Jose Diokno (politician).
2733 **841** 2 p. multicoloured . . . 10 10

842 Anniversary Emblem and Ethnic Groups

1995. 75th Anniv of International School, Manila. Multicoloured.
2734 2 p. Type **842** 10 10
2735 8 p. Globe and cut-outs of children 40 20

843 Greater Malay Mouse Deer

1995. Mammals. Multicoloured.
2736 2 p. Type **843** 10 10
2737 2 p. Tamarau 10 10
2738 2 p. Visayan warty pig . . . 10 10
2739 2 p. Palm civet 10 10

844 Nasugbu Landings

1995. 50th Anniversaries. Multicoloured.
2741 2 p. Type **844** 10 10
2742 2 p. Tagaytay Landings . . . 10 10
2743 2 p. Battle of Nichols Airbase and Fort McKinley . . . 10 10
Nos. 2741/2 were issued together, se-tenant, forming a composite design.

845 Memorial

1995. 50th Anniv of Liberation of Baguio.
2744 **845** 2 p. multicoloured . . . 10 10

846 Cabanatuan Camp

847 Victorio Edades (artist)

1995. 50th Anniv of Liberation of Internment and Prisoner of War Camps. Multicoloured.
2745 2 p. Type **846** 10 10
2746 2 p. Entrance to U.S.T. camp 10 10
2747 2 p. Los Banos camp 10 10
Nos. 2746/7 are wrongly inscribed "Interment".

1995. Birth Centenaries. Multicoloured.
2748 2 p. Type **847** 10 10
2749 2 p. Jovita Fuentes (opera singer) 10 10
2750 2 p. Candido Africa (medical researcher) 10 10
2751 2 p. Asuncion Arriola-Perez (politician) 10 10
2752 2 p. Eduardo Quisumbing (botanist) 10 10

848 Emblems and Bible

1995. 50th Anniv of Philippine Catholic Bishops' Conference, Manila.
2754 **848** 2 p. multicoloured . . . 10 10

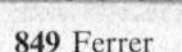
849 Ferrer 850 Neolithic Burial Jar, Manunggul

1995. 8th Death Anniv of Jaime Ferrer (administrator).
2755 **849** 2 p. multicoloured . . . 10 10

1995. Archaeology. Multicoloured.
2756 2 p. Type **850** 10 10
2757 2 p. Iron age secondary burial jar, Ayub Cave, Mindanao 10 10
2758 2 p. Iron age secondary burial jar (different), Ayub Cave . 10 10
2759 2 p. Neolithic ritual drinking vessel, Leta-Leta Cave, Palawan 10 10

852 Right Hand supporting Wildlife

1995. Association of South-East Asian Nations Environment Year. Multicoloured.
2762 2 p. Type **852** 10 10
2763 2 p. Left hand supporting wildlife 10 10
Nos. 2762/3 were issued together, se-tenant, forming a composite design.

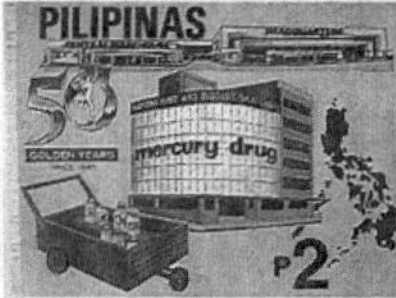

853 Anniversary Emblem, Buildings and Trolley

1995. 50th Anniv of Mercury Drug Corporation.
2765 **853** 2 p. multicoloured . . . 10 10

854 Parish Church

1995. 400th Anniv of Parish of Saint Louis Bishop, Lucban.
2766 **854** 2 p. multicoloured . . . 10 10

855 Instructor and Pupils

1995. 25th Anniv of Asian-Pacific Postal Training Centre, Bangkok.
2768 **855** 6 p. multicoloured . . . 30 15

856 Crops and Child drinking from Well 857 Carlos Romulo

1995. 50th Anniv of F.A.O.
2769 **856** 8 p. multicoloured . . . 40 20

1995. 50th Anniv of U.N.O. Multicoloured.
2770 2 p. Jose Bengzon (inscr "Cesar Bengzon") 10 10
2771 2 p. Rafael Salas (Assistant Secretary General) 10 10
2772 2 p. Salvador Lopez (Secretary) 10 10
2773 2 p. Jose Ingles (Under-secretary) 10 10
2775 2 p. Type **857** 10 10
No. 2770 depicts Jose Bengzon in error for his brother Cesar.

858 Anniversary Emblem 859 Eclipse

1995. 50th Anniv of Manila Overseas Press Club.
2779 **858** 2 p. multicoloured . . . 10 10

1995. Total Solar Eclipse.
2780 **859** 2 p. multicoloured . . . 10 10

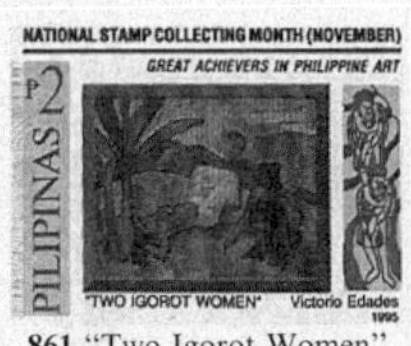

860 Flag 861 "Two Igorot Women" (Victorio Edades)

1995. National Symbols. With blue barcode at top. Variously dated. Multicoloured.
2822 1 p. Flower (jasmine) . . . 10 10
2823 1 p. 50 Fish 10 10
2781 2 p. Flag ("Pilipinas" at top) 10 10
2782 2 p. Hero (Jose Rizal) . . . 10 10
2783 2 p. House 10 10
2784 2 p. Costume 10 10
2785 2 p. Dance 10 10
2786 2 p. Sport 10 10
2787 2 p. Bird (Philippine eagle) . 10 10
2788 2 p. Type **860** 10 10
2789 2 p. Animal (water buffalo) . 10 10
2790 2 p. Flower (jasmine) . . . 10 10
2791 2 p. Tree 10 10
2792 2 p. Fruit (mango) 10 10
2793 2 p. Leaf (palm) 10 10
2794 2 p. Fish 10 10
2824 3 p. Animal (water buffalo) . 15 10
2825 4 p. Flag ("Pilipinas" at top) 20 10
2826 4 p. Hero (Jose Rizal) . . . 20 10
2827 4 p. House 20 10
2828 4 p. Costume 20 10
2829 4 p. Dance 20 10
2830 4 p. Sport 20 10
2831 4 p. Bird (Philippine eagle) . 20 10
2832 4 p. Type **860** 20 10
2833 4 p. Animal (head of water buffalo) (dated "1995") . 20 10
2834 4 p. Flower (jasmine) . . . 20 10
2835 4 p. Tree 20 10
2836 4 p. Fruit (mango) 20 10
2837 4 p. Leaf (palm) 20 10
2838 4 p. Fish 20 10
2839 4 p. Animal (water buffalo) (dated "1996") 20 10
2840 5 p. Bird (Philippine eagle) . 25 15
2842 7 p. Costume 35 20
2843 8 p. Fruit (mango) 40 20
2844 10 p. House 50 25

1995. National Stamp Collecting Month (1st issue). Paintings by Filipino artists. Multicoloured.
2795 2 p. Type **861** 10 10
2796 6 p. "Serenade" (Carlos Francisco) 30 15
2797 7 p. "Tuba Drinkers" (Vicente Manansala) 35 20
2798 8 p. "Genesis" (Hernando Ocampo) 40 20

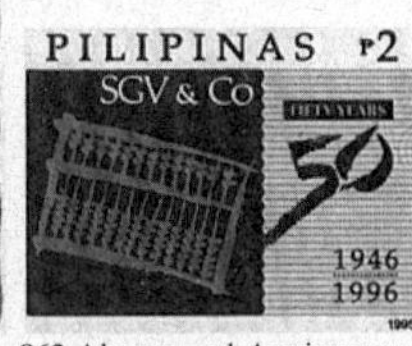

862 Tambourine 863 Abacus and Anniversary Emblem

1995. Christmas. Musical instruments and Lines from Carols. Multicoloured.
2800 2 p. Type **862** 10 10
2801 6 p. Maracas 30 15
2802 7 p. Guitar 35 20
2803 8 p. Drum 40 20

1995. 50th Anniv of Sycip Gorres Velayo & Co. (accountants).
2804 **863** 2 p. multicoloured . . . 10 10

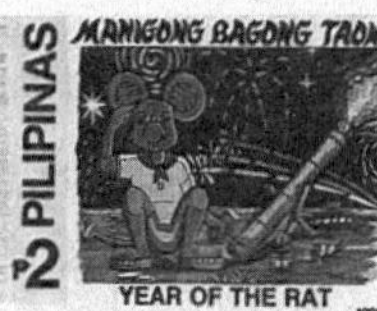

865 Rat and Fireworks

1995. New Year. Year of the Rat. Multicoloured.
2806 2 p. Type **865** 10 10
2807 6 p. Model of rat 35 15

866 Badge of Fil-American Irregular Troops Veterans Legion

1995. Philippine Guerrilla Units of Second World War (4th series). Multicoloured.
2809 2 p. Type **866** 10 10
2810 2 p. Badge of Bicol Brigade Veterans 10 10
2811 2 p. Map of Fil-American Guerrilla forces (Cavite) and Hukbalahap unit (Pampanga) 10 10
2812 2 p. Map of South Tarlac military district and Northwest Pampanga . . . 10 10

867 Liberation of Panay and Romblon

1995. 50th Anniversaries. Multicoloured.
2813 2 p. Type **867** 10 10
2814 2 p. Liberation of Cebu . . . 10 10
2815 2 p. Battle of Ipo Dam . . . 10 10
2816 2 p. Battle of Bessang Pass . . 10 10
2817 2 p. Surrender of General Yamashita 10 10

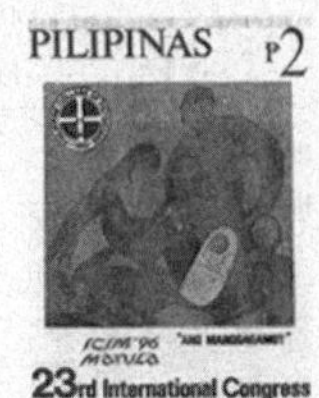

868 Jose Rizal 870 "Treating Patient" (Manuel Baldemor)

1995. Centenary of Declaration of Philippine Independence Revolutionaries. Multicoloured.
2818 2 p. Type **868** 10 10
2819 2 p. Andres Bonifacio 10 10
2820 2 p. Apolinario Mabini . . . 10 10

1996. 23rd International Congress of Internal Medicine, Manila.
2856 **870** 2 p. multicoloured . . . 10 10

871 Walled City of Intramuros

1996. Centenary of Sun Life of Canada (insurance company). Multicoloured.
2857 2 p. Type **871** 10 10
2858 8 p. Manila Bay sunset . . . 40 20

872 Pair of Lovebirds on Branch ("I Love You") 873 University Building and Map of Islands on Grid

1996. Greetings Stamps. Multicoloured.
2859 2 p. Type **872** 10 10
2860 2 p. Pair of lovebirds ("Happy Valentine") . . . 10 10
2861 6 p. Cupid holding banner ("I Love You") 30 15
2862 6 p. Cupid holding banner ("Happy Valentine") . . . 30 15
2863 7 p. Box of chocolates ("I Love You") 35 20
2864 7 p. Box of chocolates ("Happy Valentine") 35 20
2865 8 p. Butterfly and roses ("I Love You") 40 20
2866 8 p. Butterfly and roses ("Happy Valentine") . . . 40 20
Nos. 2861/2 were issued together, se-tenant, forming a composite design.

1996. 50th Anniv of Gregorio Araneta University Foundation.
2867 **873** 2 p. multicoloured . . . 10 10

874 Hospital

1996. 50th Anniv of Santo Tomas University Hospital.
2868 **874** 2 p. multicoloured . . . 10 10

875 Racoon Butterflyfish

1996. Fishes (1st series). Multicoloured.
2869 4 p. Type **875** 20 10
2870 4 p. Clown trigger fish . . . 20 10
2871 4 p. Regal angel fish 20 10
2872 4 p. Mandarin fish 20 10
2873 4 p. Emperor angel fish . . . 20 10
2874 4 p. Powder brown tang . . . 20 10
2875 4 p. Majestic angel fish . . . 20 10
2876 4 p. Blue tang 20 10
2877 4 p. Moorish idol 20 10
2878 4 p. Two-banded anemone fish 20 10
See also Nos. 2885/94.

877 Francisco Ortigas

1996.
2882 **877** 4 p. multicoloured . . . 20 10

878 Mother Francisca and Convent

1996. 300th Anniv of Dominican Sisters of St. Catherine of Siena.
2883 **878** 4 p. multicoloured . . . 20 10

879 Nuclear Reactor

1996. Centenary of Discovery of Radioactivity by Antoine Henri Becquerel.

2884	**879**	4 p. multicoloured	20	10

1996. Fishes (2nd series). As T **875**. Multicoloured.

2885	4 p. Spotted boxfish	20	10
2886	4 p. Saddleback butterfly fish	20	10
2887	4 p. Sailfin tang	20	10
2888	4 p. Harlequin tuskfish	20	10
2889	4 p. Gaimard's ("Clown") wrasse	20	10
2890	4 p. Blue-faced angel fish	20	10
2891	4 p. Long-horned cowfish	20	10
2892	4 p. Queen angel fish	20	10
2893	4 p. Longnose butterfly fish	20	10
2894	4 p. Yellow tang	20	10

OFFICIAL STAMPS

1926. Commemorative issue of 1926 optd **OFFICIAL**.

O391	**49**	2 c. black and green	1·50	80
O392		4 c. black and red	1·50	80
O393		18 c. black and brown	5·50	4·50
O394		20 c. black and orange	4·50	1·50

1931. Stamps of 1906 optd **O.B.**

O413	2 c. green (No. 337)	10	10
O414	4 c. red (No. 338)	10	10
O415	6 c. violet (No. 339)	10	10
O416	8 c. brown (No. 340)	10	10
O417	10 c. blue (No. 341)	55	10
O418	12 c. orange (No. 342)	30	15
O419	16 c. olive (No. 344)	30	10
O420	20 c. orange (No. 345)	40	10
O421	26 c. green (No. 346)	50	40
O422	30 c. grey (No. 347)	40	30

1935. Nos. 459/68 optd **O.B.**

O473	2 c. red	10	10
O474	4 c. green	10	10
O475	6 c. brown	10	10
O476	8 c. violet	15	15
O477	10 c. red	15	10
O478	12 c. black	20	15
O479	16 c. blue	20	15
O480	20 c. bistre	20	15
O481	26 c. blue	40	35
O482	30 c. red	45	40

1936. Stamps of 1935 Nos. 459/68 optd **O. B. COMMON-WEALTH** (2, 6, 20 c.) or **O. B. COMMONWEALTH** (others).

O538	2 c. red	10	10
O539	4 c. green	10	10
O540	6 c. brown	15	10
O541	8 c. violet	15	10
O542	10 c. red	15	10
O543	12 c. black	15	15
O544	16 c. blue	25	10
O545	20 c. bistre	40	40
O546	26 c. blue	45	45
O547	30 c. red	45	45

1941. Nos. 563 and 623 optd **O. B.**

O565	**104**	2 c. green	10	10
O624	–	2 c. brown	10	10

1948. Various stamps optd **O.B.**

O738	**147**	1 c. brown	10	10
O668	**125**	2 c. green	45	10
O659	–	4 c. brown (No. 629)	15	10
O739	–	5 c. red (No. 731)	15	10
O843	–	6 c. blue (No. 842)	15	10
O660	**113**	10 c. red	25	10
O740	–	10 c. blue (No. 732)	25	10
O661	–	16 c. grey (No. 632)	1·60	60
O669	–	20 c. brown (No. 633)	60	15
O741	–	20 c. red (No. 733)	45	15
O670	–	50 c. green (No. 634)	1·00	60

1950. Surch **ONE CENTAVO.**

O700	**125**	1 c. on 2 c. grn (No. O668)	15	10

1959. No. 810 optd **O B.**

O811	1 c. on 5 c. red	10	10

1962. Nos. 898/904 optd **G. O.**

O908	5 s. red	10	10
O909	6 s. brown	15	10
O910	6 s. blue	15	10
O911	10 s. purple	20	15
O912	20 s. blue	30	15
O913	30 s. red	35	25
O914	50 s. violet	45	35

1970. Optd **G.O.**

O1182	**318**	10 s. red	15	10

OFFICIAL SPECIAL DELIVERY STAMP

1931. No. E353b optd **O.B.**

EO423	20 c. violet	50	35

POSTAGE DUE STAMPS

1899. Postage Due stamps of United States of 1894 optd **PHILIPPINES.**

D268	**D 87**	1 c. red	3·25	1·50
D269		2 c. red	3·25	1·25
D270		3 c. red	12·00	7·00
D271		5 c. red	8·00	2·50
D272		10 c. red	10·00	4·00
D273		30 c. red	£180	85·00
D274		50 c. red	£140	80·00

D 51 Post Office Clerk

D 118

1928.

D395	**D 51**	4 c. red	15	15
D396		6 c. red	25	25
D397		8 c. red	25	25
D398		10 c. red	25	25
D399		12 c. red	25	25
D400		16 c. red	30	30
D401		20 c. red	25	25

1937. Surch **3 CVOS. 3.**

D521	**D 51**	3 c. on 4 c. red	20	15

1947.

D644	**D 118**	3 c. red	15	15
D645		4 c. blue	35	30
D646		6 c. green	45	45
D647		10 c. orange	55	55

SPECIAL DELIVERY STAMPS

1901. Special Delivery stamp of United States of 1888 optd **PHILIPPINES.**

E268	**E 46**	10 c. blue (No. E283)	85·00	90·00

1907. Special Delivery stamp of United States optd **PHILIPPINES.**

E29	**E 117**	10 c. blue	£1500	

E 47 Messenger running

1919. Perf (E353), perf or imperf (E353b).

E353	**E 47**	20 c. blue	45	20
E353b		20 c. violet	45	15

1939. Optd **COMMONWEALTH.** Perf.

E550	**E 47**	20 c. violet	30	20

1945. Optd **VICTORY.**

E622	**E 47**	20 c. vio. (No. E550)	50	50

E 120 Cyclist Messenger and Post Office

1947.

E651	**E 120**	20 c. purple	60	40

E 219 G.P.O. Manila

1962.

E891	**E 219**	20 c. mauve	35	30

POLAND Pt. 5

A country lying between Russia and Germany, originally independent, but divided between Prussia, Austria and Russia in 1772/95. An independent republic since 1918. Occupied by Germany from 1939 to 1945.

1860. 100 kopeks = 1 rouble.
1918. 100 pfennig = 1 mark.
1918. 100 halerzy = 1 korona.
100 fenigow = 1 marka.
1924. 100 groszy = 1 zloty.

1 Russian Arms

2 Sigismund III Vasa Column, Warsaw

1860.
1b 1 10 k. blue and red £475 £160

1918. Surch **POCZTA POLSKA** and value in fen. as in T **2**.
2 2 5 f. on 2 g. brown 70 60
3 – 10 f. on 6 g. green 60 50
4 – 25 f. on 10 g. red . . . . . 1·90 1·25
5 – 50 f. on 20 g. blue . . . . . 4·25 3·00
DESIGNS: 6 g. Arms of Warsaw; 10 g. Polish eagle; 20 g. Jan III Sobieski Monument, Warsaw.

1918. Stamps of German Occupation of Poland optd **Poczta Polska** or surch also.
9 10 3 pf. brown . . . . 9·00 6·00
10 5 pf. green 40 40
6 24 5 on 2½ pf. grey 25 25
7 10 5 on 3 pf. brown . . . . . . 2·25 1·25
11 10 pf. red 15 15
12 24 15 pf. violet 20 15
13 10 20 pf. blue 20 20
8 24 25 on 7½ pf. orange 40 30
14 10 30 pf. black & orge on buff . 15 15
15 40 pf. black and red 30 30
16 60 pf. mauve 30 30

1918. Stamps of Austro-Hungarian Military Post (Nos. 69/71) optd **POLSKA POCZTA** and Polish eagle.
17 10 h. green . . . . 5·75 5·25
18 20 h. red . . . . 5·75 5·25
19 45 h. blue . . . . 5·75 5·25

1918. As stamps of Austro-Hungarian Military Post of 1917 optd **POLSKA POCZTA** and Polish eagle or surch also.
20b 3 h. on 3 h. olive . . . . . . 18·00 12·50
21 3 h. on 15 h. red . . . . . . 3·75 2·00
22 10 h. on 30 h. green . . . . . 3·75 2·00
23 25 h. on 40 h. olive . . . . . 6·00 2·75
24 45 h. on 60 h. red . . . . . 5·50 2·75
25 45 h. on 80 h. blue . . . . . 6·00 2·75
28 50 h. green . . . . 38·00 21·00
26 50 h. on 60 h. red . . . . . 5·50 2·75
29 90 h. violet . . . . 5·50 3·00

1919. Stamps of Austria optd **POCZTA POLSKA**, No. 49 also surch **25**.
30 49 3 h. violet £170 £130
31 5 h. green £170 £130
32 6 h. orange . . . . 18·00 12·50
33 10 h. purple £170 £140
34 12 h. blue . . . . 18·00 12·00
35 60 15 h. red . . . . 5·25 4·25
36 20 h. green . . . . 60·00 55·00
37 25 h. blue £600 £550
49 51 25 on 80 h. brown . . . . 2·10 1·90
38 60 30 h. violet . . . . £120 85·00
39 51 40 h. green . . . . 12·00 9·50
40 50 h. green . . . . 4·25 3·50
41 60 h. blue . . . . 3·25 3·25
42 80 h. brown . . . . 3·50 3·50
43 90 h. purple £500 £400
44 1 k. red on yellow . . . . 6·75 4·50
45 52 2 k. blue . . . . 3·75 3·75
46 3 k. red . . . . 45·00 38·00
47 4 k. green . . . . 65·00 50·00
48a 10 k. violet £3000 £2500

11

1919. Imperf.
50 11 2 h. grey 35 45
51 3 h. violet 35 45
52 5 h. green 25 30
53 6 h. orange . . . . 12·00 15·00
54 10 h. red 25 30
55 15 h. brown 25 30
56 20 h. olive 35 45
57 25 h. red 15 15
58 50 h. blue 25 30
59 70 h. blue 35 45
60 1 k. red and grey 60 75

15

16

17 Agriculture

18 Ploughing in peace

19 Polish Uhlan

1919. For Southern Poland. Value in halerzy or korony. Imperf or perf.
68 15 3 h. brown 10 10
69 5 h. green 10 10
70 10 h. orange 10 10
71 15 h. red 10 10
72 16 20 h. brown 10 10
85 25 h. blue 10 10
86 50 h. brown 10 10
75 17 1 k. green 10 10
88 1 k. 50 brown 90 25
89 2 k. blue . . . . 1·10 25
90 18 2 k. 50 purple . . . . . . 1·10 50
91 19 5 k. blue . . . . 1·75 90

1919. For Northern Poland. Value in fenigow or marki. Imperf or perf.
104 15 3 f. brown 10 10
105 5 f. green 10 10
179 5 f. blue 10 10
106 10 f. purple 10 10
129 10 f. brown 10 10
107 15 f. red 10 10
108 16 20 f. blue 10 10
181 20 f. red 10 10
109 25 f. green 10 10
110 50 f. green 10 10
183 50 f. orange 10 10
137 17 1 m. violet 20 10
112 1 m. 50 green 60 25
138 2 m. brown 60 10
114 18 2 m. 50 brown . . . . . . 1·00 60
139 3 m. brown 30 10
140 19 5 m. purple 10 10
141 6 m. red 10 10
142 10 m. red 25 15
143 20 m. green 50 25

1919. 1st Polish Philatelic Exhibition and Polish White Cross Fund. Surch **I POLSKA WYSTAWA MAREK**, cross and new value. Imperf or perf.
116 15 5+5 f. green 15 15
117 10+5 f. purple 30 15
118 15+5 f. red 15 15
119 16 25+5 f. olive 20 15
120 50+5 f. green 50 30

20

21 Prime Minster Paderewski

22 A. Trampczynski

23 Eagle and Ship

24

1919. 1st Session of Parliament in Liberated Poland. Dated "1919".
121 20 10 f. mauve 15 10
122 21 15 f. red 15 10
123 22 20 f. brown (21 × 25 mm) . 55 30
124 20 f. brown (17 × 20 mm) . 1·10 65
125 – 25 f. green . . . . 1·10 65
126 23 50 f. blue 35 15
127 – 1 m. violet 40 15
DESIGN—As Type **21**: 25 f. Gen. Pilsudski; As Type **23**: 1 m. Griffin and fasces.

1920.
146 24 40 f. violet 10 10
182 40 f. brown 10 10
184 75 f. green 10 10

1920. As T **15**, but value in marks ("Mk").
147 15 1 m. red 10 10
148 2 m. green 10 10
149 3 m. blue 10 10
150 4 m. red 10 10
151 5 m. purple 10 10
152 8 m. brown 25 20

1921. Surch **3 Mk**, and bars.
153 24 3 m. on 40 f. violet 10 10

1921. Red Cross Fund. Surch with cross and **30MK**.
154 19 5 m. + 30 m. purple . . . 3·75 8·00
155 6 m. + 30 m. red . . . . 3·75 8·00
156 10 m. + 30 m. red . . . . 8·00 13·00
157 20 m. + 30 m. green . . . 30·00 27·00

28 Sun of Peace

29 Agriculture

1921. New Constitution.
158 28 2 m. green . . . . 1·50 1·25
159 3 m. blue . . . . 1·50 1·25
160 4 m. red 70 40
161 29 6 m. red 70 40
162 10 m. green . . . . 1·10 40
163 – 25 m. violet . . . . 2·25 1·25
164 – 50 m. green and buff . . . 1·50 90
DESIGN: 25, 50 m. "Peace" (Seated women.)

31 Sower

32

1921. Peace Treaty with Russia.
165 31 10 m. blue 20 10
166 15 m. brown 25 10
167 20 m. red 20 10

1921.
170 32 25 m. violet and buff . . . 10 10
171 50 m. red and buff 10 10
172 100 m. brown and orange . 10 10
173 200 m. pink and black . . . 10 15
174 300 m. green 15 10
175 400 m. brown 15 10
176 500 m. purple 15 10
177 1000 m. orange 15 10
178 2000 m. violet 15 10

33 Silesian Miner

1922.
185 33 1 m. black 10 10
186 1 m. 25 green 10 10
187 2 m. red 10 10
188 3 m. green 10 10
189 4 m. blue 10 10
190 5 m. brown 10 10
191 6 m. orange 10 25
192 10 m. brown 10 10
193 20 m. purple 10 10
194 50 m. olive 10 70
195 80 m. red . . . . 40 1·00
196 100 m. violet . . . . . . 40 1·00
197 200 m. orange . . . . . . 80 1·50
198 300 m. blue . . . . 2·10 3·25

34 Copernicus

39

1923. 450th Birth Anniv of Copernicus (astronomer) and 150th Death Anniv of Konarski (educationist).
199 34 1,000 m. slate 60 25
200 – 3,000 m. brown 35 25
201 34 5,000 m. red 60 35
DESIGN: 3,000 m. Konarski.

1923. Surch.
202 32 10 TYSIECY (= 10000) on 25 m. violet and buff 15 10
206 15 20,000 m. on 2 m. green (No. 148) 35 15
204 31 25,000 m. on 20 m. red . . 15 10
205 50,000 m. on 10 m. blue . . 15 10
207 15 100,000 m. on 5 m. purple (No. 151) 15 10

1924.
208 39 10,000 m. purple 25 30
209 20,000 m. green 15 10
210 30,000 m. red 80 30
211 50,000 m. green 85 30
212 100,000 m. brown 60 25
213 200,000 m. blue 60 15
214 300,000 m. mauve 60 30
215 500,000 m. brown . . . . 60 1·50
216 1,000,000 m. pink . . . . 60 3·25
217 2,000,000 m. green . . . 95 12·00

40

41 President Wojciechowski

42

1924. New Currency.
218 40 1 g. brown 45 40
219 2 g. brown 45 10
220 3 g. orange 55 10
221 5 g. green 75 10
222 10 g. green 75 10
223 15 g. red 75 10
224 20 g. blue . . . . 3·00 10
225 25 g. red . . . . 4·00 15
226 30 g. violet . . . . 16·00 10
227 40 g. blue . . . . 4·50 30
228 50 g. purple . . . . 3·50 15
229 41 1 z. red . . . . 32·00 1·40

1925. National Fund.
230 42 1 g. + 50 g. brown . . . . 17·00 20·00
231 2 g. + 50 g. brown . . . . 17·00 20·00
232 3 g. + 50 g. orange . . . . 17·00 20·00
233 5 g. + 50 g. green . . . . 17·00 20·00
234 10 g. + 50 g. green . . . . 17·00 20·00
235 15 g. + 50 g. red . . . . 17·00 20·00
236 20 g. + 50 g. blue . . . . 17·00 20·00
237 25 g. + 50 g. red . . . . 17·00 20·00
238 30 g. + 50 g. violet . . . . 17·00 20·00
239 40 g. + 50 g. blue . . . . 17·00 20·00
240 50 g. + 50 g. purple . . . . 17·00 20·00

43 Holy Gate, Vilna

44 Town Hall, Pozan

48 Galleon

1925.
241 43 1 g. brown 25 10
242 – 2 g. olive 50 25
243a – 3 g. blue . . . . 1·40 10
244a 44 5 g. green . . . . 1·40 10
245a – 10 g. violet . . . . 1·40 10
246 – 15 g. red . . . . 1·50 10
247 48 20 g. red . . . . 3·00 10
248 43 24 g. blue . . . . 8·00 60
249 – 30 g. blue . . . . 3·25 10
250 – 40 g. blue . . . . 3·25 10
251 48 45 g. mauve . . . . 10·00 40
DESIGNS—As Type **43**: VERT: 2, 30 g. Jan III Sobieski Statue, Lwow. As Type **44**: 3, 10 g. King Sigismund Vasa Column, Warsaw. HORIZ: 15, 40 g. Wawel Castle, Cracow.

49 LVG Schneider Biplane

50 Chopin

1925. Air.
252 49 1 g. blue . . . . 65 2·25
253 2 g. orange . . . . 65 2·25
254 3 g. brown . . . . 65 2·25
255 5 g. brown 65 50
256 10 g. green . . . . 1·75 60
257 15 g. mauve . . . . 2·25 75
258 20 g. olive . . . . 12·00 3·50
259 30 g. red . . . . 8·00 1·75
260 45 g. lilac . . . . 11·00 3·75

1927.
261 50 40 g. blue . . . . 13·00 1·25

51 Marshal Pilsudski

52 Pres. Moscicki

53

1927.
262 51 20 g. red . . . . 2·10 10
262a 25 g. brown . . . . 2·10 15

1927.
263 52 20 g. red . . . . 5·25 35

1927. Educational Funds.
264 53 10 g. + 5 g. purple on green 8·50 10·00
265 20 g. + 5 g. blue on yellow . 8·50 10·00

54 Dr. Karl Kaczkowski

55 J. Slowacki (poet)

1927. 4th Int Military Medical Congress, Warsaw.
266 54 10 g. green . . . . 3·00 1·00
267 25 g. red . . . . 6·00 2·75
268 40 g. blue . . . . 8·00 2·25

1927. Transfer of Slowacki's remains to Cracow.
269 **55** 20 g. red . . . . 5·25 40

56 Marshal Pilsudski — **57** Pres. Moscicki — **58** Gen. Joseph Bem

1928.
272 **56** 50 g. grey . . . . 3·25 15
272a 50 g. green . . . . 9·00 15
273 **57** 1 z. black on cream . . . 8·75 15

1928.
271 **58** 25 g. red . . . . 3·00 20

59 H. Sienkiewicz — **60** Slav God, "Swiatowit"

1928. Henryk Sienkiewicz (author).
274 **59** 15 g. blue . . . . 1·90 15

1929. National Exhibition Poznan.
275 **60** 25 g. brown . . . . 2·40 15

61 — **62** King Jan III Sobieski — **63**

1929.
276 **61** 5 g. violet 20 10
277 10 g. green 60 10
278 25 g. brown 40 10

1930. Birth Tercentenary of Jan III Sobieski.
279 **62** 75 g. purple . . . . 5·25 20

1930. Centenary of "November Rising" (29th Nov., 1830).
280 **63** 5 g. purple 75 10
281 15 g. blue . . . . 3·00 20
282 25 g. lake . . . . 1·75 10
283 30 g. red . . . . 10·00 3·25

64 Kosciusko, Washington and Pulaski — **65**

1932. Birth Bicentenary of George Washington.
284 **64** 30 g. brown on cream . . . 2·75 25

1932.
284a **65** 5 g. violet 15 10
285 10 g. green 15 10
285a 15 g. red 15 10
286 20 g. grey 50 10
287 25 g. bistre 50 10
288 30 g. red . . . . 3·00 10
289 60 g. blue . . . . 2·50 10

67 Town Hall, Torun — **68** Franciszek Zwirko (airman) and Stanislaw Wigura (aircraft designer)

1933. 700th Anniv of Torun.
290 **67** 60 g. blue on cream . . . . 30·00 45

1933. Victory in Flight round Europe Air Race, 1932.
292 **68** 30 g. green . . . . 15·00 1·50

1933. Torun Philatelic Exhibition.
293 **67** 60 g. red on cream . . . . 17·00 15·00

69 Altar-piece, St. Mary's Church, Cracow

1933. 4th Death Centenary of Veit Stoss (sculptor).
294 **69** 80 g. brown on cream . . 13·00 1·40

70 "Liberation of Vienna" by J. Matejko

1933. 250th Anniv of Relief of Vienna.
295 **70** 1 z. 20 blue on cream . . 32·00 12·00

71 Cross of Independence — **73** Marshal Pilsudski and Legion of Fusiliers Badge

1933. 15th Anniv of Proclamation of Republic.
296 **71** 30 g. red . . . . 7·75 30

1934. Katowice Philatelic Exhibition. Optd **Wyst. Filat. 1934 Katowice**.
297 **65** 20 g. grey . . . . 38·00 26·00
298 30 g. red . . . . 38·00 26·00

1934. 20th Anniv of Formation of Polish Legion.
299 **73** 25 g. blue 95 20
300 30 g. brown . . . . 2·40 30

1934. Int Air Tournament. Optd **Challenge 1934**.
301 **49** 20 g. olive . . . . 14·00 8·50
302 **68** 30 g. green . . . . 8·00 2·00

1934. Surch in figures.
303 **69** 25 g. on 80 g. brown on cream 5·25 45
304 **65** 55 g. on 60 g. blue . . . . 5·00 25
305 **70** 1 z. on 1 z. 20 blue on cream 17·00 4·00

77 Marshal Pilsudski

1935. Mourning Issue.
306 **77** 5 g. black 70 10
307 15 g. black 70 25
308 25 g. black . . . . 1·10 10
309 45 g. black . . . . 3·00 1·40
310 1 z. black . . . . 5·00 3·00

1935. Optd **Kopiec Marszalka Pilsudskiego**.
311 **65** 15g. red 70 65
312 **73** 25 g. blue . . . . 2·50 1·60

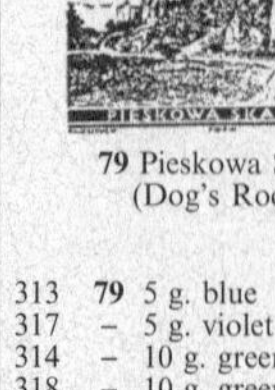

79 Pieskowa Skala (Dog's Rock) — **80** Pres. Moscicki

1935.
313 **79** 5 g. blue 40 10
317 – 5 g. violet 15 10
314 – 10 g. green 40 10
318 – 10 g. green 75 10
315 – 15 g. blue . . . . 3·25 10
319 – 15 g. lake 30 10
316 – 20 g. black 90 10
320 – 20 g. orange 45 10
321a – 25 g. green 80 10
322 – 30 g. red . . . . 1·75 15
323a – 45 g. mauve . . . . 1·75 15
324a – 50 g. black . . . . 2·25 15
325 – 55 g. blue . . . . 6·50 40
326 – 1 z. brown . . . . 4·00 90
327 **80** 3 z. brown . . . . 2·50 2·25
DESIGNS: 5 g. (No. 317) Monastery of Jasna Gora, Czestochowa; 10 g. (314) Lake Morskie Oko; 10 g. (318) "Batory" (liner) at sea passenger terminal, Gdynia; 15 g. (315) "Pilsudski" (liner); 15 g. (319) University, Lwow; 20 g. (316) Pieniny-Czorsztyn; 20 g. (320) Administrative Buildings, Katowice; 25 g. Belvedere Palace, Warsaw; 30 g. Castle at Mir; 45 h. Castle at Podhorce; 50 g. Cloth Hall, Cracow; 55 g. Raczynski Library, Poznan; 1 z. Vilna Cathedral.

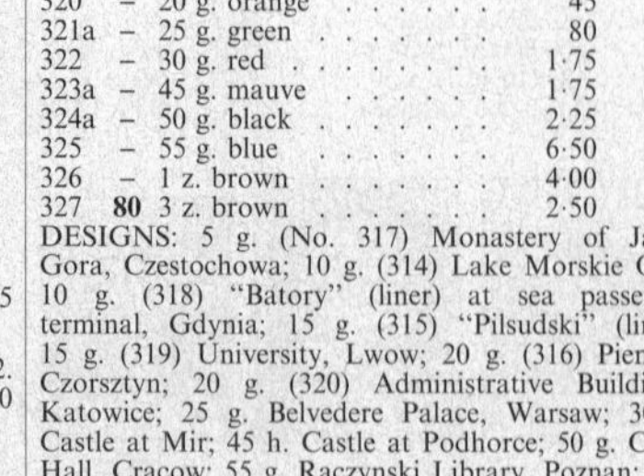

1936. 10th Anniv of Moscicki Presidency. As T **57** but inscr "1926. 3. VI. 1936" below design.
328 **57** 1 z. blue . . . . 6·00 5·50

1936. Gordon-Bennett Balloon Race. Optd **GORDON-BENNETT 30. VIII. 1936.**
329 30 g. red (No. 322) . . . . . 10·50 5·00
330 55 g. blue (No. 325) . . . . 10·50 5·00

82 Marshal Smigly-Rydz — **83** Pres. Moscicki

1937.
331 **82** 25 g. blue 35 10
332 55 g. blue 50 10
For 25 g. brown see note after No. 273.

1938. President's 70th Birthday.
333 **83** 15 g. grey 20 10
334 30 g. purple 40 10

84 Kosciuszko, Paine and Washington

1938. 150th Anniv of U.S. Constitution.
335 **84** 1 z. blue . . . . 1·60 1·40

85a — **86** Marshal Pilsudski

1938. 20th Anniv of Independence.
336 – 5 g. orange 10 10
337 – 10 g. green 10 10
338 **85a** 15 g. brown (A) 15 15
357 15 g. brown (B) 25 20
339 – 20 g. blue 35 10
340 – 25 g. purple 10 10
341 – 30 g. red 55 10
342 – 45 g. black 85 15
343 – 50 g. mauve . . . . 1·90 10
344 – 55 g. blue 45 10
345 – 75 g. green . . . . 2·75 1·40
346 – 1 z. orange . . . . 2·75 1·40
347 – 2 z. red . . . . 9·00 7·00
348 **86** 3 z. blue . . . . 9·00 13·00
DESIGNS—VERT: 5 g. Boleslaw the Brave; 10 g. Casimir the Great; 20 g. Casimir Jagiellon; 25 g. Sigismund August; 30 g. Stefan Batory; 45 g. Chodkiewicz and Zolkiewski; 50 g. Jan III Sobieski; 55 g. Symbol of Constitution of May 3rd, 1791; 75 g. Kosciuszko, Poniatowski and Dabrowski; 1 z. November Uprising 1830–31; 2 z. Romuald Traugutt.
(A) Type **85a**. (B) as Type **85a** but crossed swords omitted.

87 Teschen comes to Poland — **88** "Warmth"

1938. Acquisition of Teschen.
349 **87** 25 g. purple . . . . 1·40 35

1938. Winter Relief Fund.
350 **88** 5 g.+5 g. orange . . . . 40 1·70
351 25 g.+10 g. purple . . . . 85 1·60
352 55 g.+15 g. blue . . . . 1·60 2·50

89 Tatra Mountaineer

1939. International Ski Championship, Zakopane.
353 **89** 15 g. brown . . . . 1·00 70
354 25 g. purple . . . . 1·50 80
355 30 g. red . . . . 2·00 90
356 55 g. blue . . . . 7·00 4·50

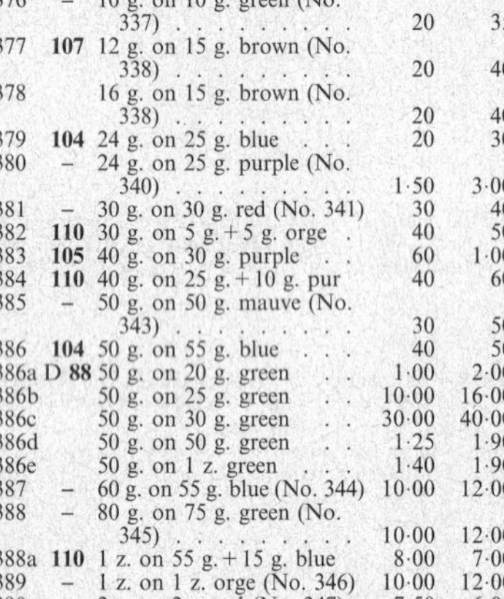

90 Pilsudski and Polish Legionaries

1939. 25th Anniv of 1st Battles of Polish Legions.
358 **90** 25 g. purple 80 40

1939–1945. GERMAN OCCUPATION.

1939. T **94** of Germany surch **Deutsche Post OSTEN** and value.
359 **94** 6 g. on 3 pf. brown 15 40
360 8 g. on 4 pf. blue 15 45
361 12 g. on 6 pf. green . . . 15 35
362 16 g. on 8 pf. red . . . . 40 1·10
363 20 g. on 10 pf. brown . . . 15 30
364 24 g. on 12 pf. red 15 20
365 30 g. on 15 pf. purple . . . 65 85
366 40 g. on 20 pf. blue 50 40
367 50 g. on 25 pf. blue 60 65
368 60 g. on 30 pf. green . . . 60 40
369 80 g. on 40 pf. mauve . . 60 80
370 1 z. on 50 pf. black & grn . 1·50 1·40
371 2 z. on 100 pf. black & yell 3·50 3·25

1940. Surch **General-Gouvernement**, Nazi emblem and value.
372 – 2 g. on 5 g. orge (No. 336) 20 35
373 – 4 g. on 5 g. orge (No. 336) 20 35
374 – 6 g. on 10 g. grn (No. 337) 20 35
375 – 8 g. on 10 g. grn (No. 337) 20 40
376 – 10 g. on 10 g. green (No. 337) 20 35
377 **107** 12 g. on 15 g. brown (No. 338) 20 40
378 16 g. on 15 g. brown (No. 338) 20 40
379 **104** 24 g. on 25 g. blue . . . 20 30
380 – 24 g. on 25 g. purple (No. 340) . . . . 1·50 3·00
381 – 30 g. on 30 g. red (No. 341) 30 40
382 **110** 30 g. on 5 g.+5 g. orge . 40 50
383 **105** 40 g. on 30 g. purple . . 60 1·00
384 **110** 40 g. on 25 g.+10 g. pur 40 60
385 – 50 g. on 50 g. mauve (No. 343) 30 50
386 **104** 50 g. on 55 g. blue . . . 40 50
386a D **88** 50 g. on 20 g. green . . 1·00 2·00
386b 50 g. on 25 g. green . . 10·00 16·00
386c 50 g. on 30 g. green . . 30·00 40·00
386d 50 g. on 50 g. green . . 1·25 1·90
386e 50 g. on 1 z. green . . . 1·40 1·90
387 – 60 g. on 55 g. blue (No. 344) 10·00 12·00
388 – 80 g. on 75 g. green (No. 345) . . . . 10·00 12·00
388a **110** 1 z. on 55 g.+15 g. blue 8·00 7·00
389 – 1 z. on 1 z. orge (No. 346) 10·00 12·00
390 – 2 z. on 2 z. red (No. 347) 7·50 6·00
391 **108** 3 z. on 3 z. blue . . . . 7·50 6·00
Nos. 386a/e are all postage stamps.

93 Copernicus Memorial, Cracow — **95**

1940.
392 – 6 g. brown 25 60
393 – 8 g. brown 25 60
394 – 8 g. black 15 40
395 – 10 g. green 15 20
396 **93** 12 g. green . . . . 2·50 35
397 12 g. violet 30 15
398 – 20 g. brown 10 10
399 – 24 g. red 10 10
400 – 30 g. violet 10 15
401 – 30 g. purple 20 30
402 – 40 g. black 20 15
403 – 48 g. brown . . . . 70 1·00
404 – 50 g. blue 20 15
405 – 60 g. green 20 20
406 – 80 g. violet 25 25
407 – 1 z. purple . . . . 2·00 1·10
408 – 1 z. green 45 40
DESIGNS: 6 g. Florian gate, Cracow; 8 g. Castle Keep, Cracow; 10 g. Cracow Gate, Lublin; 20 g. Church of the Dominicans, Cracow; 24 g. Wawel Castle, Cracow; 30 g. Old Church in Lublin; 40 g. Arcade, Cloth Hall, Cracow; 48 g. Town Hall, Sandomir; 50 g. Town Hall, Cracow; 60 g. Courtyard of Wawel Castle, Cracow; 80 g. St. Mary's Church, Cracow; 1 z. Bruhl Palace, Warsaw.

1940. Red Cross Fund. As last, new colours, surch with Cross and premium in figures.
409 12 g.+8 g. green . . . . . 2·00 3·50
410 24 g.+16 g. green . . . . . 2·00 3·50
411 50 g.+50 g. green . . . . . 3·00 4·50
412 80 g.+80 g. green . . . . . 3·00 4·50

1940. 1st Anniv of German Occupation.
413 **95** 12 g.+38 g. green on yellow 1·75 3·00
414 – 24 g.+26 g. red on yellow 1·75 3·00
415 – 30 g.+20 g. violet on yellow 3·00 6·00
DESIGNS: 24 g. Woman with scarf; 30 g. Fur-capped peasant as Type **96**.

96

1940. Winter Relief Fund.
416 **96** 12 g. + 8 g. green . . . . . 65 1·10
417 24 g. + 16 g. red . . . . . 85 1·75
418 30 g. + 30 g. brown . . . . 1·00 2·25
419 50 g. + 50 g. blue . . . . . 1·50 3·00

97 Cracow

1941.
420 **97** 10 z. grey and red . . . . 1·00 2·25

98 The Barbican, Cracow

99 Adolf Hitler

1941.
421 **98** 2 z. blue 35 60
422 – 4 z. green . . . . 40 1·00
DESIGN: 4 z. Tyniec Monastery.
See also Nos. 465/8.

1941.
423 **99** 2 g. grey 10 20
424 6 g. brown 10 20
425 8 g. blue 10 20
426 10 g. green 10 10
427 12 g. violet 10 10
428 16 g. orange 35 40
429 20 g. brown 10 15
430 24 g. red 10 10
431 30 g. purple 30 15
432 32 g. green 15 35
433 40 g. blue 10 15
434 48 g. brown 40 40
435 50 g. blue 10 15
436 60 g. green 10 15
437 80 g. purple 10 15
441 1 z. green 30 40
442 1 z. 20 brown 35 45
443 1 z. 60 blue 45 60

1942. Hitler's 53rd Birthday. As T **99**, but premium inserted in design.
444 30 g. + 1 z. purple on yellow . 30 60
445 50 g. + 1 z. blue on yellow . . 30 60
446 1 z. 20 + 1 z. brown on yellow 30 60

100 Modern Lublin

1942. 600th Anniv of Lublin.
447 – 12 g. + 8 g. purple 10 20
448 **100** 24 g. + 6 g. brown 10 20
449 – 50 g. + 50 g. blue 15 30
450 **100** 1 z. + 1 z. green . . . . . 50 1·10
DESIGN: 12, 50 g. Lublin, after an ancient engraving.

101 Copernicus

102 Adolf Hitler

1942. 3rd Anniv of German Occupation.
451 – 12 g. + 18 g. violet 10 25
452 – 24 g. + 26 g. red 10 25
453 – 30 g. + 30 g. purple . . . 10 25
454 – 50 g. + 50 g. blue 10 35
455 **101** 1 z. + 1 z. green 30 55
DESIGNS: 12 g. Veit Stoss (Vit Stvosz); 24 g. Hans Durer; 30 g. J. Schuch; 50 g. J. Elsner.

1943. Hitler's 54th Birthday.
456 **102** 12 g. + 1 z. violet 15 30
457 24 g. + 1 z. red 15 30
458 84 g. + 1 z. green 30 60

1943. 400th Death Anniv of Nicolas Copernicus (astronomer). As No. 455, colour changed, optd **24. MAI 1543 24. MAI 1943.**
459 **101** 1 z. + 1 z. purple . . . . . 50 1·00

103 Cracow Gate, Lublin

103a Lwow

1943. 3rd Anniv of Nazi Party in German-occupied Poland.
460 **103** 12 g. + 38 g. green 10 15
461 – 24 g. + 76 g. red 10 15
462 – 30 g. + 70 g. purple . . . 10 15
464 – 1 z. + 2 z. grey 15 25
DESIGNS: 24 g. Cloth Hall, Cracow; 30 g. Administrative Building, Radom; 50 g. Bruhl Palace, Warsaw; 1 z. Town Hall, Lwow.

1943.
465 – 2 z. green 15 20
466 – 4 z. violet 15 35
467 **103a** 6 z. brown 25 60
468 – 10 z. grey and brown . . 35 60
DESIGNS: 2 z. The Barbican, Cracow; 4 z. Tyniec Monastery; 10 z. Cracow.

104 Adolf Hitler

105 Konrad Celtis

1944. Hitler's 55th Birthday.
469 **104** 12 z. + 1 z. green 10 20
470 24 z. + 1 z. brown 10 20
471 84 z. + 1 z. violet 15 35

1944. Culture Funds.
472 **105** 12 g. + 18 g. green 10 10
473 – 24 g. + 26 g. red 10 10
474 – 30 g. + 30 g. purple . . . 10 10
475 – 50 g. + 50 g. blue 20 25
476 – 1 z. + 1 z. brown 20 25
PORTRAITS: 24 g. Andreas Schluter; 30 g. Hans Boner; 50 g. Augustus the Strong; 1 z. Gottlieb Pusch.

105a Cracow Castle

1944. 5th Anniv of German Occupation.
477a **105a** 10 z. + 10 z. black & red 6·00 10·00

1941–45. ISSUES OF EXILED GOVERNMENT IN LONDON.

For correspondence on Polish sea-going vessels and, on certain days, from Polish Military camps in Great Britain.

106 Ruins of Ministry of Finance, Warsaw

107 Vickers-Armstrong Wellington and Hawker Hurricanes used by Poles in Great Britain

1941.
478 – 5 g. violet 15 60
479 **106** 10 g. green 20 70
480 – 25 g. grey . . . . 40 1·25
481 – 55 g. blue . . . . 70 1·75
482 – 75 g. olive . . . . 2·50 4·00
483 – 80 g. red . . . . 2·50 4·00
484 **107** 1 z. blue . . . . 6·00 5·00
485 – 1 z. 50 brown . . . . . 6·00 5·00
DESIGNS—VERT: 5 g. Ruins of U.S. Embassy, Warsaw; 25 g. Destruction of Mickiewicz Monument, Cracow; 1 z. 50, Polish submarine "Orzel". HORIZ: 55 g. Ruins of Warsaw; 75 g. Polish machine-gunners in Great Britain; 80 g. Polish tank in Great Britain.

108 Vickers-Armstrong Wellington and U-boat

109 Merchant Navy

1943.
486 **108** 5 g. red . . . . 1·00 85
487 **109** 10 g. green 60 90
488 – 25 g. violet 60 90
489 – 55 g. blue . . . . 65 1·25
490 – 75 g. brown . . . . 1·40 2·00
491 – 80 g. red . . . . 1·75 2·25
492 – 1 z. olive . . . . 3·00 3·00
493 – 1 z. 50 black . . . . . . 2·00 4·00
DESIGNS—VERT: 25 g. Anti-tank gun in France; 55 g. Poles at Narvik; 1 z. Saboteurs damaging railway line. HORIZ: 75 g. The Tobruk road; 80 g. Gen. Sikorski visiting Polish troops in Middle East; 1 z. 50, Underground newspaper office.

1944. Capture of Monte Casino. Nos. 482/5 surch **MONTE CASSINO 18 V 1944** and value and bars.
494 – 45 g. on 75 g. olive . . . . 10·00 13·00
495 – 55 g. on 80 g. red . . . . 10·00 13·00
496 **107** 80 g. on 1 z. blue . . . . 10·00 13·00
497 – 1 z. 20 on 1 z. 50 brown . 10·00 13·00

111 Polish Partisans

112 Romuald Traugutt

1945. Relief Fund for Survivors of Warsaw Rising.
498 **111** 1 z. + 2 z. green . . . . . 5·25 7·00

1944. INDEPENDENT REPUBLIC.

1944. National Heroes.
499 **112** 25 g. red . . . . 42·00 55·00
500 – 50 g. green . . . . 48·00 65·00
501 – 1 z. blue . . . . 50·00 55·00
PORTRAITS: 50 g. Kosciuszko; 1 z. H. Dabrowski.

113 White Eagle

114 Grunwald Memorial, Cracow

1944.
502 **113** 25 g. red 50 25
503 **114** 50 g. green 50 15

1944. No. 502 surch with value **31.XII. 1943** or **1944** and **K.R.N.**, **P.K.W.N.** or **R.T.R.P.**
504 **113** 1 z. on 25 g. red . . . . . 1·75 2·00
505 2 z. on 25 g. red . . . . . 1·75 2·00
506 3 z. on 25 g. red . . . . . 1·75 2·00

1945. 82nd Anniv of 1863 Revolt against Russia. Surch with value and **22.I.1863.**
507 **112** 5 z. on 25 g. brown . . . 40·00 55·00

1945. Liberation. No. 502 surch **3 zl.** with town names and dates as indicated.
508 3 z. on 25 g. Bydgoszcz 23.1.1945 4·25 5·00
509 3 z. on 25 g. Czestochowa 17.1.1945 . . . . 4·25 5·00
510 3 z. on 25 g. Gniezno 22.1.1945 4·25 5·00
511 3 z. on 25 g. Kalisz 24.1.1945 . 4·25 5·00
512 3 z. on 25 g. Kielce 15.1.1945 . 4·25 5·00
513 3 z. on 25 g. Lodz 19.1.1945 . 4·25 5·00
515 3 z. on 25 g. Radom 16.1.1945 4·25 5·00
516 3 z. on 25 g. Warszawa 17.1.1945 10·50 14·00
517 3 z. on 25 g. Zakopane 29.1.1945 6·50 6·50

120 Flag-bearer and War Victim

121 Lodz Factories

123 Grunwald Memorial Cracow

1945. Liberation of Warsaw.
518 **120** 5 z. red . . . . 2·00 2·00

1945. Liberation of Lodz.
519 **121** 1 z. blue 65 20

1945. 151st Anniv of Kosciuszko's Oath of Allegiance. No. 500 surch **5 zl. 24.III.1794.**
520 5 z. on 50 g. green . . . . . 9·00 14·00

1945. Cracow Monuments. Inscr "19.1.1945".
521 **123** 50 g. purple 15 10
522 – 1 z. brown 20 10
523 – 2 z. blue 75 15
524 – 3 z. violet 85 25
525 – 5 z. green . . . . 5·00 7·00
DESIGNS—VERT: 1 z. Kosciuszko Statue; 3 z. Copernicus Memorial. HORIZ: 2 z. Cloth Hall; 5 z. Wawel Castle.

125 H.M.S. "Dragon" (cruiser)

1945. 25th Anniv of Polish Maritime League.
526 **125** 50 g. + 2 z. orange . . . . 8·50 6·50
527 – 1 z. + 3 z. blue . . . . . 4·50 6·50
528 – 2 z. + 4 z. red . . . . . 3·50 5·50
529 – 3 z. + 5 z. olive . . . . . 3·50 5·50
DESIGNS—VERT: 1 z. "Dar Pomorza" (full-rigged cadet ship); 2 z. Naval ensigns. HORIZ: 3 z. Crane and tower, Gdansk.

126 Town Hall, Poznan

1945. Postal Employees Congress.
530 **126** 1 z. + 5 z. green . . . . . 18·00 23·00

127 Kosciuszko Memorial, Lodz

128 Grunwald, 1410

1945.
531 **127** 3 z. purple 70 25

1945. 535th Anniv of Battle of Grunwald.
532 **128** 5 z. blue . . . . 8·00 9·00

129 Eagle and Manifesto

1945. 1st Anniv of Liberation.
533 **129** 3 z. red . . . . 10·00 13·00

130 Westerplatte

1945. 6th Anniv of Defence of Westerplatte.
534 **130** 1 z. + 9 z. slate . . . . . 20·00 24·00

1945. Surch with new value and heavy bars.
535 **114** 1 z. on 50 g. green 45 15
536a **113** 1 z. 50 on 25 g. red . . . 45 15

133 Crane Tower, Gdansk

1945. Liberation of Gdansk (Danzig). Perf or imperf.
537 **133** 1 z. olive 10 10
538 – 2 z. blue 20 10
539 – 3 z. purple 50 10
DESIGNS—VERT: 2 z. Stock Exchange, Gdansk. HORIZ: 3 z. High Gate, Gdansk.

135 St. John's Cathedral

1945. "Warsaw, 1939–1945". Warsaw before and after destruction. Imperf.

540 – 1 z. 50 red 20 10
541 **135** 3 z. blue 25 10
542 – 3 z. 50 green . . . . . . 1·10 30
543 – 6 z. grey 25 15
544 – 8 z. brown . . . . 3·00 30
545 – 10 z. purple 65 20

DESIGNS: 1 z. 50, Royal Castle; 3 z. 50, City Hall; 6 z. G.P.O.; 8 z. War Ministry; 10 z. Church of the Holy Cross.

136 United Workers

1945. Trades' Union Congress.

546 **136** 1 z. 50+8 z. 50 grey . . . 7·25 8·00

137 Soldiers of 1830 and Jan III Sobieski Statue

1945. 115th Anniv of 1830 Revolt against Russia.

547 **137** 10 z. grey . . . . 8·50 10·50

1946. 1st Anniv of Warsaw Liberation. Nos. 540/5 optd **WARSZAWA WOLNA 17 Styczen 1945-1946**. Imperf.

548 1 z. 50 red . . . . 1·75 2·50
549 3 z. blue . . . . 1·75 2·50
550 3 z. 50 green . . . . 1·75 2·50
551 6 z. grey . . . . 1·75 2·50
552 8 z. brown . . . . 1·75 2·50
553 10 z. purple . . . . 1·75 2·50

139 Insurgent

1946. 83rd Anniv of 1863 Revolt.

554 **139** 6 z. blue . . . . 6·75 8·00

140 Lisunov Li-2 over Ruins of Warsaw

1946. Air.

555 **140** 5 z. grey 35 10
556 10 z. purple 45 15
557 15 z. blue . . . . 2·50 20
558 20 z. purple . . . . 1·10 15
559 25 z. green . . . . 2·00 35
560 30 z. red . . . . 3·00 45

141 Fighting in Spain

1946. Polish Legion in the Spanish Civil War.

561 **141** 3 z.+5 z. red . . . . . . 4·00 3·75

142 Bydgoszcz **143** "Death" over Majdanek Concentration Camp

1946. 600th Anniv of City of Bydgoszcz.

562 **142** 3 z+2 z. grey . . . . . 6·50 6·00

1946. Majdanek Concentration Camp.

563 **143** 3 z.+5 z. green . . . . . 3·00 3·00

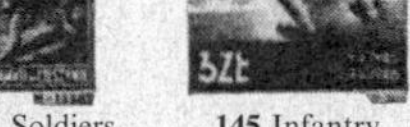

144 Shield and Soldiers **145** Infantry

1946. Uprisings in Upper Silesia (1919–23) and Silesian Campaign against the Germans (1939–45).

564 **144** 3 z.+7 z. brown 90 65

1946. 1st Anniv of Peace.

565 **145** 3 z. brown 40 25

146 Polish Coastline **148** Bedzin Castle

147 Pres. Bierut, Premier O. Morawski and Marshal Zymierski

1946. Maritime Festival.

566 **146** 3 z.+7 z. blue . . . . . 1·75 2·25

1946. 2nd Anniv of Polish Committee of National Liberation Manifesto.

567 **147** 3 z. violet . . . . 3·25 3·75

1946. Imperf (5z., 10z.) or perf (6 z.).

568 **148** 5 z. olive 15 10
568a 5 z. brown 20 10
569 – 6 z. black 35 10
570 – 10 z. blue 70 15

DESIGNS—VERT: 6 z. Tombstone of Henry IV. HORIZ: 10 z. Castle at Lanckorona.

149 Crane, Monument and Crane Tower, Gdansk

1946. The Fallen in Gdansk.

571 **149** 3 z.+12 z. grey . . . . . 2·00 2·00

150 Schoolchildren at Desk

1946. Polish Work for Education and Fund for International Bureau of Education.

571a **150** 3 z.+22 z. red . . . . . 25·00 42·00
571b – 6 z.+24 z. blue . . . . . 25·00 42·00
571c – 11 z.+19 z. green . . . 25·00 42·00

DESIGNS: 6 z. Court of Jagiellonian University, Cracow; 11 z. Gregory Piramowicz (1735–1801), founder of the Education Commission.

152 Stojalowski, Bojko, Stapinski and Witos

1946. 50th Anniv of Peasant Movement and Relief Fund.

572 **152** 5 z.+10 z. green . . . . . 1·25 1·40
573 5 z.+10 z. blue . . . . . 1·25 1·40
574 5 z.+10 z. olive . . . . . 1·25 1·40

1947. Opening of Polish Parliament. Surch **+7 SEJM USTAWODAWCZY 19.1.1947.**

575 **147** 3 z.+7 z. violet . . . . . 7·25 7·75

1947. 22nd National Ski Championships, Zakopane. Surch **5+15 zl XXII MISTRZOSTWA NARCIARSKIE POLSKI 1947.**

576 **113** 5+15 z. on 25 g. red . . . 3·25 4·00

1947. No. 569 surch **5 ZL** in outlined figure and capital letters between stars.

577 5 z. on 6 z. black 60 25

156 Home of Emil Zegadlowicz **157** Frederic Chopin (musician)

158 Boguslawski, Modrzejewska and Jaracz (actors) **159** Wounded Soldier, Nurse and Child

1947. Emil Zegadlowicz Commemoration.

578 **156** 5 z.+15 z. green . . . . . 1·10 1·40

1947. Polish Culture. Imperf or perf.

579 – 1 z. blue 20 15
580 – 1 z. grey 20 15
581 – 2 z. brown 25 15
582 – 2 z. orange 15 15
583 **157** 3 z. green 80 20
584 3 z. olive . . . . 1·75 30
585 **158** 5 z. black 55 15
586 5 z. brown 20 15
587 – 6 z. grey 90 20
588 – 6 z. red 35 15
589 – 10 z. grey . . . . 1·50 40
590 – 10 z. blue . . . . 1·40 25
591 – 15 z. violet . . . . . . 1·50 40
592 – 15 z. brown . . . . . . 1·00 35
593 – 20 z. black . . . . . . 2·25 60
594 – 20 z. purple . . . . . . 1·00 50

PORTRAITS—HORIZ: 1 z. Matejko, Malczewski and Chelmonski (painters); 6 z. Swietochowski, Zeromski and Prus (writers); 15 z. Wyspianski, Slowacki and Kasprowicz (poets). VERT: 2 z. Brother Albert of Cracow; 10 z. Marie Curie (scientist); 20 z. Mickiewicz (poet).

1947. Red Cross Fund.

595 **159** 5 z.+5 z. grey and red . . 2·40 3·50

161 Steelworker **163** Brother Albert of Cracow

1947. Occupations.

596 **161** 5 z. lake . . . . 1·00 30
597 – 10 z. green 30 15
598 – 15 z. blue 60 25
599 – 20 z. black . . . . 1·00 30

DESIGNS: 10 z. Harvester; 15 z. Fisherman; 20 z. Miner.

1947. Air. Surch **LOTNICZA** bars and value.

600 **114** 40 z. on 50 g. green . . . 2·00 50
602 **113** 50 z. on 25 g. red . . . 3·00 1·75

1947. Winter Relief Fund.

603 **163** 2 z.+18 z. violet . . . . . 1·10 2·40

164 Sagittarius **165** Chainbreaker

1948. Air.

604 **164** 15 z. violet . . . . 1·90 25
605 25 z. blue . . . . 1·25 15
606 30 z. brown . . . . . . 1·25 40
607 50 z. green . . . . . . 2·40 45
608 75 z. black . . . . . . 2·40 60
609 100 z. orange . . . . . 2·40 60

1948. Revolution Centenaries.

610 **165** 15 z. brown 35 15
611 – 30 z. brown . . . . 1·25 35
612 – 35 z. green . . . . 2·75 60
613 – 60 z. red . . . . 1·50 70

PORTRAITS—HORIZ: 30 z. Generals H. Dembinski and J. Bem; 35 z. S. Worcell, P. Sciegienny and E. Dembowski; 60 z. F. Engels and K. Marx.

167 Insurgents **168** Wheel and Streamers

1948. 5th Anniv of Warsaw Ghetto Revolt.

614 **167** 15 z. black . . . . 1·10 1·40

1948. Warsaw–Prague Cycle Race.

615 **168** 15 z. red and blue . . . . 3·00 1·10

169 Cycle Race **170** "Oliwa" under Construction

1948. 7th Circuit of Poland Cycle Race.

616 **169** 3 z. black . . . . 2·00 1·75
617 6 z. brown . . . . 2·00 1·75
618 15 z. green . . . . 2·75 2·50

1948. Merchant Marine.

619 **170** 6 z. violet . . . . 1·90 1·25
620 – 15 z. red . . . . 2·25 2·00
621 – 35 z. grey . . . . 3·50 3·25

DESIGNS—HORIZ: 15 z. Freighter at wharf; 35 z. "General M. Zaruski" (cadet ketch).

173 Firework Display **174** "Youth"

1948. Wroclaw Exhibition.

622 **173** 6 z. blue 40 30
623 15 z. red 65 20
624 18 z. red . . . . 1·10 40
625 35 z. brown . . . . 1·10 40

1948. International Youth Conf, Warsaw.

626 **174** 15 z. blue 50 25

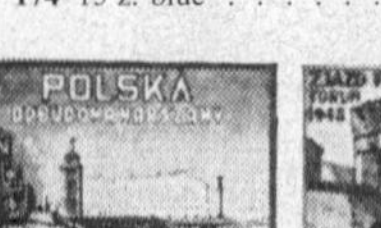

175 Roadway, St. Anne's Church and Palace **176** Torun Ramparts and Mail Coach

1948. Warsaw Reconstruction Fund.

627 **175** 15 z.+5 z. green 25 25

1948. Philatelic Congress, Torun.

628 **176** 15 z. brown 65 25

177 Steam Locomotive, Clock and Winged Wheel **178** President Bierut

1948. European Railway Conference.

629 **177** 18 z. blue . . . . 5·50 7·75

1948.

629a **178** 2 z. orange 10 10
629b 3 z. green 10 10
630 5 z. brown 10 10
631 6 z. black 60 15
631a 10 z. violet 15 10
632 15 z. red 50 10
633 18 z. green 70 20
634 30 z. blue . . . . 1·25 20
635 35 z. purple . . . . 2·00 40

179 Workers and Flag

1948. Workers' Class Unity Congress, (a) Dated "8 XII 1948".

636 **179** 5 z. red 80 50
637 – 15 z. violet 80 50
638 – 25 z. brown 80 50

(b) Dated "XII 1948".

639 **179** 5 z. plum . . . . 2·25 1·75
640 – 15 z. blue . . . . 2·25 1·75
641 – 25 z. green . . . . 3·00 2·00

DESIGNS: 15 z. Flags and portraits of Engels, Marx, Lenin and Stalin; 25 z. Workers marching and portrait of L. Warynski.

180 Baby

180a Pres. Franklin D. Roosevelt

1948. Anti-tuberculosis Fund. Portraits of babies as T **180**.

642 **180** 3 z.+2 z. green . . . . . 3·00 2·50
643 – 5 z.+5 z. brown . . . . . 3·00 2·50
644 – 6 z.+4 z. purple . . . . . 1·50 2·50
645 – 15 z.+10 . red . . . . . 1·25 1·75

1948. Air. Honouring Presidents Roosevelt, Pulaski and Kosciuszko.

645a **180a** 80 z. violet . . . . . . 22·00 28·00
645b – 100 z. purple (Pulaski) . 24·00 22·00
645c – 120 z. blue (Kosciuszko) 24·00 22·00

181 Workers

1949. Trades' Union Congress, Warsaw.

646 **181** 3 z. red 90 90
647 – 5 z. blue 90 90
648 – 15 z. green . . . . 1·25 1·25

DESIGNS: 5 z. inscr "PRACA" (Labour), Labourer and tractor; 15 z. inscr "POKOJ" (Peace), Three labourers.

182 Banks of R. Vistula

183 Pres. Bierut

1949. 5th Anniv of National Liberation Committee.

649 **182** 10 z. black . . . . 2·00 1·50
650 **183** 15 z. mauve . . . . 2·00 1·50
651 – 35 z. blue . . . . 2·00 1·50

DESIGN—VERT: 35 z. Radio station, Rasyn.

184 Mail Coach and Map

185 Worker and Tractor

1949. 75th Anniv of U.P.U.

652 **184** 6 z. violet . . . . 1·00 1·25
653 – 30 z. blue (liner) . . . . 1·75 1·60
654 – 80 z. green (airplane) . . . 3·50 3·50

1949. Congress of Peasant Movement.

655 **185** 5 z. red 85 20
656 10 z. red 20 10
657 15 z. green 20 10
658 35 z. brown . . . . 1·00 70

186 Frederic Chopin

187 Mickiewicz and Pushkin

188 Postman

1949. National Celebrities.

659 – 10 z. purple . . . . . . 2·00 1·50
660 **186** 15 z. red . . . . 2·75 1·50
661 – 35 z. blue . . . . 2·00 1·50

PORTRAITS: 10 z. Adam Mickiewicz; 35 z. Julius Slowacki.

1949. Polish–Russian Friendship Month.

662 **187** 15 z. violet . . . . 2·40 2·40

1950. 3rd Congress of Postal Workers.

663 **188** 15 z. purple . . . . . . 2·00 1·40

189 Mechanic, Hangar and Aeroplane

190 President Bierut

195a

1950. Air.

664 **189** 500 z. lake . . . . 5·00 6·75

1950. (a) With frame.

665 **190** 15 z. red 50 15

(b) Without frame. Values in "zloty".

673 **195a** 5 z. green 10 10
674 10 z. red 10 10
675 15 z. blue 85 10
676 20 z. violet 35 10
677 25 z. brown 35 10
678 30 z. red 50 10
679 40 z. brown 70 10
680 50 z. olive . . . . 1·40 20

For values in "groszy" see Nos. 687/94.

191 J. Marchlewski

192 Workers

1950. 25th Death Anniv of Julian Marchlewski (patriot).

666 **191** 15 z. black 65 40

1950. Reconstruction of Warsaw.

667 **192** 5 z. brown 10 10

See also No.695.

193 Worker and Flag

194 Statue

1950. 60th Anniv of May Day Manifesto.

668 **193** 10 z. mauve . . . . . . 1·60 30
669 – 15 z. olive . . . . 1·60 15

DESIGN—VERT: 15 z. Three workers and flag.

1950. 23rd International Fair, Poznan.

670 **194** 15 z. brown 25 15

195 Dove and Globe

196 Industrial and Agricultural Workers

1950. International Peace Conference.

671 **195** 10 z. green 70 20
672 15 z. brown 30 15

1950. Six Year Reconstruction Plan.

681 **196** 15 z. blue 20 10

See also Nos. 696/e.

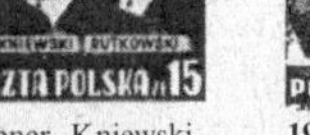

197 Hibner, Kniewski, Rutkowski

198 Worker and Dove

1950. 25th Anniv of Revolutionaries' Execution.

682 **197** 15 z. grey . . . . 2·00 60

1950. 1st Polish Peace Congress.

683 **198** 15 z. green 30 10

REVALUATION SURCHARGES. Following a revaluation of the Polish currency, a large number of definitive and commemorative stamps were locally overprinted "Groszy" or "gr". There are 37 known types of overprint and various colours of overprint. We do not list them as they had only local use, but the following is a list of the stamps which were duly authorised for overprinting:—Nos. 579/94, 596/615 and 619/58. Overprints on other stamps are not authorised.

Currency Revalued: 100 old zlotys = 1 new zloty.

199 Dove (after Picasso)

1950. 2nd World Peace Congress, Warsaw.

684 **199** 40 g. blue . . . . 1·60 35
685 45 g. red 30 10

200 General Bem and Battle of Piski

1950. Death Centenary of General Bem.

686 **200** 45 g. blue . . . . 2·75 1·75

1950. As T **195a**. Values in "groszy".

687 **195a** 5 g. violet 10 10
688 10 g. green 10 10
689 15 g. olive 10 10
690 25 g. red 15 10
691 30 g. red 20 10
692 40 g. orange 20 10
693 45 g. blue . . . . 1·25 20
694 75 g. brown 70 10

1950. As No. 667 but value in "groszy".

695 **192** 15 g. green 10 10

1950. As No. 681 but values in "groszy" or "zlotys".

696 **196** 45 g. blue 15 10
696b 75 g. brown 20 10
696d 1 z. 15 green 50 15
696e 1 z. 20 red 35 15

201 Woman and Doves

202 Battle Scene and J. Dabrowski

1951. Women's League Congress.

697 **201** 45 g. red 40 20

1951 80th Anniv of Paris Commune.

698 **202** 45 g. green 30 10

1951. Surch **45gr.**

699 **199** 45 g. on 15 z. red 50 15

204 Worker with Flag

205 Smelting Works

1951. Labour Day.

700 **204** 45 g. red 40 10

1951.

701 **205** 40 g. blue 15 10
702 45 g. black 15 10
702a 60 g. brown 20 10
702c 90 g. lake 55 10

206 Pioneer and Badge

207 St. Staszic

1951. Int Children's Day. Inscr "I-VI-51"

703 **206** 30 g. olive . . . . 1·00 60
704 – 45 g. blue (Boy, girl and map) . . . . 5·75 60

1951. 1st Polish Scientific Congress. Inscr "KONGRES NAUKI POLSKIEJ"

705 **207** 25 g. red . . . . 2·75 2·75
706 – 40 g. blue 60 20
707 – 45 g. violet . . . . . . 7·75 65
708 – 60 g. green 60 20
709 – 1 z. 15 purple 90 50
710 – 1 z. 20 grey . . . . . . 1·75 20

DESIGNS—As Type **207**: 40 g. Marie Curie; 60 g. M. Nencki; 1 z. 15, Copernicus; 1 z. 20, Dove and book. HORIZ—36×21 mm: 45 g. Z. Wroblewski and Olszewski.

209 F. Dzerzhinsky

210 Pres. Bierut, Industry and Agriculture

1951. 25th Death Anniv of Dzerzhinsky (Russian politician).

711 **209** 45 g. brown 25 15

1951. 7th Anniv of People's Republic.

712 **210** 45 g. red 60 15
713 60 g. green . . . . 15·00 5·75
714 90 g. blue . . . . 3·50 70

211 Young People and Globe

213 Sports Badge

1951. 3rd World Youth Festival, Berlin.

715 **211** 40 g. blue 85 25

1951. Surch **45 gr.**

716 **195a** 45 g. on 35 z. orange . . 25 15

1951. Spartacist Games.

717 **213** 45 g. green . . . . 1·10 40

214 Stalin

215 Chopin and Moniuszko

1951. Polish–Soviet Friendship.

718 **214** 45 g. red 15 10
719 90 g. black 35 20

1951. Polish Musical Festival.

720 **215** 45 g. black 30 10
721 90 g. red 90 50

216 Mining Machinery

217 Building Modern Flats

1951. Six Year Plan (Mining).

722 **216** 90 g. brown 25 10
723 1 z. 20 blue 30 10
724 1 z. 20+15 g. orange . . . 25 15

1951. Six Year Plan (Reconstruction).

725 **217** 30 g. green 10 10
726 30 g.+15 g. red 20 10
727 1 z. 15 purple 25 10

218 Installing Electric Cables

219 M. Nowotko

1951. Six Year Plan (Electrification).

728 **218** 30 g. black 10 10
729 45 g. red 15 10
730 45 g.+15 g. brown . . . 50 15

1952. 10th Anniv of Polish Workers' Coalition.
731 **219** 45 g.+15 g. lake 15 10
732 – 90 g. brown 30 15
733 – 1 z. 15 orange 30 15
PORTRAITS: 90 g. P. Finder; 1 z. 15, M. Fornalska.

220 Women and Banner

1952. International Women's Day.
734 **220** 45 g.+15 g. brown . . . 35 10
735 1 z. 20 red 45 20

221 Gen. Swierczewski **222** Ilyushin Il-12 over Farm

1952. 5th Death Anniv of Gen. Swierczewski.
736 **221** 45 g.+15 g. brown . . . 35 10
737 90 g. blue 45 25

1952. Air. Aeroplanes and views.
738 – 55 g. blue (Tug and freighters) 40 25
739 **222** 90g. green 35 30
740 – 1 z. 40 purple (Warsaw) . 50 30
741 – 5 z. black (Steelworks) . . 1·50 40

223 President Bierut **224** Cyclists and City Arms

1952. Pres. Bierut's 60th Birthday.
742 **223** 45 g.+15 g. red 30 25
743 90 g. green 55 60
744 1 z. 20+15 g. blue 70 25

1952. 5th Warsaw–Berlin–Prague Peace Cycle Race.
745 **224** 40 g. blue . . . . 1·50 80

225 Workers and Banner

1952. Labour Day.
746 **225** 45 g.+15 g. red 15 10
747 75 g. green 40 25

226 Kraszewski **227** Maria Konopnicka

1952. 140th Birth Anniv of Jozef Ignacy Kraszewski (writer).
748 **226** 25 g. purple 40 25

1952. 110th Birth Anniv of Maria Konopnicka (poet).
749 **227** 30 g.+15 g. green 45 15
750 1 z. 15 brown 65 45

INDEX

Countries can be quickly located by referring to the index at the end of this volume.

228 H. Kollataj **229** Leonardo da Vinci **231** N. V. Gogol

230 President Bierut and Children

1952. 140th Death Anniv of Hugo Kollataj (educationist and politician).
751 **228** 45 g.+15 g. brown . . . 15 10
752 1 z. green 25 15

1952. 500th Birth Anniv of Leonardo da Vinci (artist).
753 **229** 30 g.+15 g. blue 75 35

1952. International Children's Day.
754 **230** 45 g.+15 g. blue . . . . 2·25 60

1952. Death Centenary of Nikolai Gogol (Russian writer).
755 **231** 25 g. green 60 25

232 Cement Works **233** Swimmers

1952. Construction of Concrete Works, Wierzbica.
756 **232** 3 z. black . . . . 1·25 35
757 10 z. red . . . . 1·60 30

1952. Sports Day.
758 **233** 30 g.+15 g. blue . . . . 4·50 1·00
759 – 45g.+15 g. violet . . . . 1·60 15
760 – 1 z. 15 green . . . . . . 1·40 1·40
761 – 1 z. 20 red 85 55
DESIGNS: 45 g. Footballers; 1 z. 15, Runners; 1 z. 20, High jumper.

234 Yachts

1952. Shipbuilders' Day.
762 **234** 30 g.+15 g. green . . . . 3·00 85
763 – 45 g.+15 g. blue 75 20
764 – 90 g. plum 75 75
DESIGNS—VERT: 45 g. Full-rigged cadet ship "Dar Pomorza"; 90 g. Shipbuilding worker.

235 Young Workers **236** "New Constitution"

1952. Youth Festival, Warsaw.
765 **235** 30 g.+15 g. green 35 25
766 – 45 g.+15 g. red 60 15
767 – 90 g. brown 35 30
DESIGNS—HORIZ: 45 g. Girl and boy students; 90 g. Boy bugler.

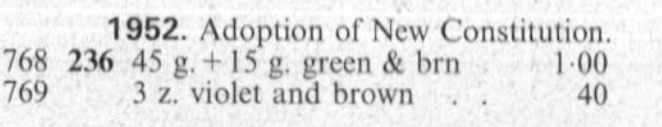

1952. Adoption of New Constitution.
768 **236** 45 g.+15 g. green & brn . . 1·00 15
769 3 z. violet and brown . . 40 35

237 L. Warynski **238** Jaworzno Power Station

1952. 70th Anniv of Party "Proletariat".
770 **237** 30 g.+15 g. red 45 15
771 45 g.+15 g. brown . . . 45 15

1952. Electricity Power Station, Jaworzno.
772 **238** 45 g.+15 g. red 65 10
773 1 z. black 60 40
774 1 z. 50 green 60 15

239 Frydman **240** Pilot and Glider

1952. Pleniny Mountain Resorts.
775 **239** 45 g.+15 g. purple 45 10
776 – 60 g. green (Grywald) . . 30 40
777 – 1 z. red (Niedzica) 90 10

1952. Aviation Day.
778 **240** 3 g.+15 g. green . . . . . 1·40 20
779 – 45 g.+15 g. red . . . . . 2·25 70
780 – 90 g. blue 40 30
DESIGNS: 45 g. Pilot and Yakovlev Yak-18U; 90 g. Parachutists descending.

241 Avicenna **242** Victor Hugo **243** Shipbuilding

1952. Birth Millenary of Avicenna (Arab physician).
781 **241** 75 g. red 30 15

1952. 150th Birth Anniv of Victor Hugo (French author).
782 **242** 90 g. brown 30 15

1952. Gdansk Shipyards.
783 **243** 5 g. green 15 10
784 15 g. red 15 10

244 H. Sienkiewicz (author) **245** Assault on Winter Palace, Petrograd

1952.
785 **244** 45 g.+15 g. brown 25 10

1952. 35th Anniv of Russian Revolution. Perf or Imperf.
786 **245** 45 g.+15 g. red . . . . . 1·00 20
787 60 g. brown 40 30

246 Lenin **247** Miner **248** H. Wieniawski (violinist)

1952. Polish-Soviet Friendship Month.
788 **246** 30 g.+15 g. purple 30 15
789 45 g.+15 g. brown 55 25

1952. Miners' Day.
790 **247** 45 g.+15 g. black 15 10
791 1 z. 20+15 g. brown . . . 55 30

1952. 2nd Wieniawski Int Violin Competition.
792 **248** 30 g.+15 g. green . . . . 1·00 40
793 45 g.+15 g. violet . . . . 2·75 50

249 Car Factory, Zeran **250** Dove of Peace

1952.
800 – 30 g.+15 g. blue 20 10
794 **249** 45 g.+15 g. green 15 10
801 – 60 g.+20 g. purple 20 10
795 **249** 1 z. 15 brown 55 25
DESIGN: 30, 60 g. Lorry factory, Lublin.

1952. Peace Congress, Vienna.
796 **250** 30 g. green 70 25
797 60 g. blue . . . . 1·25 35

251 Soldier and Flag **253** Karl Marx **254** Globe and Flag

1952. 10th Anniv of Battle of Stalingrad.
798 **251** 60 g. red and green . . . 5·00 1·50
799 80 g. red and grey 60 30

1953. 70th Death Anniv of Marx.
802 **253** 60 g. blue . . . . 17·00 10·00
803 80 g. brown . . . . 1·25 30

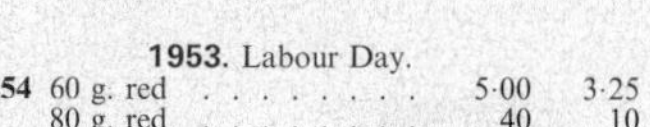

1953. Labour Day.
804 **254** 60 g. red . . . . 5·00 3·25
805 80 g. red 40 10

255 Cyclists and Arms of Warsaw **256** Boxer

1953. 6th International Peace Cycle Race.
806 – 80 g. green 70 25
807 **255** 80 g. brown 70 25
808 – 80 g. red . . . . 13·00 7·00
DESIGNS: As Type **255**, but Arms of Berlin (No. 806) or Prague (No. 808).

1953. European Boxing Championship, Warsaw. Inscr "17-24. V. 1953".
809 **256** 40 g. lake . . . . 1·00 25
810 80 g. orange . . . . 9·00 5·00
811 – 95 g. purple . . . . 1·00 90
DESIGN: 95 g. Boxers in ring.

257 Copernicus (after Matejko) **258** "Dalmor" (trawler)

1953. 480th Birth Anniv of Copernicus, (astronomer).
812 **257** 20 g. brown . . . . . . 1·00 30
813 – 80 g. blue . . . . 9·00 8·00
DESIGN—VERT: 80 g. Copernicus and diagram.

1953. Merchant Navy Day.
814 **258** 80 g. green . . . . 1·75 15
815 – 1 z. 35 blue . . . . 1·75 3·00
DESIGN: 1 z. 35 "Czech" (freighter).

259 Warsaw Market-place **260** Students' Badge **261** Nurse Feeding Baby

1953. Polish National Day.
816 **259** 20 g. lake 20 10
817 2 z. 35 blue . . . . 3·75 3·00

1953. 3rd World Students' Congress, Warsaw. Inscr "III SWIATOWY KONGRESS STUDENTOW". (a) Postage. Perf.
818 – 40 g. brown 15 10
819 **260** 1 z. 35 green 50 10
820 – 1 z. 50 blue . . . . 2·25 1·60

(b) Air. Imperf.
821 **260** 55 g. plum . . . . 1·50 40
822 75 g. red 75 75
DESIGNS—HORIZ: 40 g. Students and globe. VERT: 1 z. 50, Woman and dove.

1953. Social Health Service.
823 **261** 80 g. red . . . . 8·00 4·75
824 – 1 z. 75 green 25 15
DESIGN: 1 z. 75, Nurse, mother and baby.

262 M. Kalinowski **263** Jan Kochanowski (poet)

1953. 10th Anniv of Polish People's Army.
825 **262** 45 g. brown 3·00 2·75
826 – 80 g. red 60 10
827 – 1 g. 75 olive 60 10
DESIGNS—HORIZ: 80 g. Russian and Polish soldiers. VERT: 1 z. 75, R. Pazinski.

1953. "Renaissance" Commemoration. Inscr "ROK ODRODZENIA".
828 **263** 20 g. brown 10 10
829 – 80 g. purple 30 10
830 – 1 z. 35 blue 1·50 1·25
DESIGNS—HORIZ: 80 g. Wawel Castle. VERT: 1 z. 35, Mikolaj Rej (writer).

264 Palace of Science and Culture **265** Dunajec Canyon, Pieniny Mts

1953. Reconstruction of Warsaw. Inscr "WARSZAWA".
831 **264** 80 g. red 7·25 1·00
832 – 1 z. 75 blue 1·25 25
833 – 2 z. purple 4·00 2·00
DESIGNS: 1 z. 75, Constitution Square; 2 z. Old City Market, Warsaw.

1953. Tourist Series.
834 – 20 g. lake and blue 15 10
835 – 80 g. lilac and green 2·50 1·50
836 **265** 1 z. 75 green and brown 70 15
837 – 2 z. black and red 1·00 10
DESIGNS—HORIZ: 20 g. Krynica Spa; 2 z. Clechocinek Spa. VERT: 80 g. Morskie Oko Lake, Tatra Mts.

266 Skiing **267** Infants playing

1953. Winter Sports.
838 – 80 g. blue 1·25 25
839 **266** 95 g. green 1·50 25
840 – 2 z. 85 red 4·00 1·90
DESIGNS—VERT: 80 g. Ice-skating; 2 z. 85, Ice-hockey.

1953. Children's Education.
841 **267** 10 g. violet 50 10
842 – 80 g. red 75 25
843 – 1 z. 50 green 5·00 2·75
DESIGNS: 80 g. Girls and school; 1 z. 50, Two Schoolgirls writing.

268 Electric Locomotive **269** Mill Girl

1954. Electrification of Railways.
844 – 60 g. blue 9·00 4·00
845 **268** 80 g. brown 1·00 25
DESIGN: 60 g. Electric commuter train.

1954. International Women's Day.
846 **269** 20 g. green 2·00 1·75
847 – 40 g. blue 50 10
848 – 80 g. brown 50 10
DESIGNS: 40 g. Postwoman; 80 g. Woman driving tractor.

270 Flags and Mayflowers **271** "Warsaw–Berlin–Prague"

1954. Labour Day.
849 **270** 40 g. brown 55 30
850 60 g. blue 55 15
851 80 g. red 60 15

1954. 7th Int Peace Cycle Race. Inscr "2–17 MAJ 1954".
852 **271** 80 g. brown 70 20
853 – 80 g. blue (Dove and cycle wheel) 70 20

272 Symbols of Labour **273** Glider and Flags

1954. 3rd Trades' Union Congress, Warsaw.
854 **272** 25 g. blue 60 25
855 80 g. lake 25 10

1954. International Gliding Competition.
856 – 45 g. green 60 15
857 **273** 60 g. violet 1,75 70
858 60 g. brown 1·25 15
859a – 1 z. 35 blue 1·90 25
DESIGNS: 45 g. Glider and clouds in frame; 1 z. 35, Glider and sky.

274 Paczkow **275** Fencing

1954. Air. Inscr "POCZTA LOTNICZA".
860 **274** 60 g. green 25 10
861 – 80 g. red 30 15
862 – 1 z. 15 black 1·40 1·50
863 – 1 z. 50 red 70 10
864 – 1 z. 55 blue 70 10
865 – 1 z. 95 brown 85 15
DESIGNS—Ilyushin Il-12 airplane over: 80 g. Market-place, Kazimierz Dolny; 1 z. 15, Wawel Castle, Cracow; 1 z. 50, Town Hall, Wroclaw; 1 z. 55, Lazienki Palace, Warsaw; 1 z. 95, Cracow Tower, Lublin.

1954. 2nd Spartacist Games (1st issue). Inscr "II OGOLNOPOLSKA SPARTAKIADA".
866 **275** 25 g. purple 1·25 35
867 – 60 g. turquoise 1·25 20
868 – 1 z. blue 2·40 40
DESIGNS—VERT: 60 g. Gymnastics. HORIZ: 1 z. Running.

276 Spartacist Games Badge **277** Battlefield

1954. 2nd Spartacist Games (2nd issue).
869 **276** 60 g. brown 1·00 20
870 1 z. 55 grey 1·00 30

1954. 10th Anniv of Liberation and Battle of Studzianki.
871 **277** 60 g. green 1·50 40
872 – 1 z. blue 5·00 2·75
DESIGN—HORIZ: 1 z. Soldier, airman and tank.

278 Steel Works

1954. 10th Anniv of Second Republic.
873 – 10 g. sepia and brown 90 10
874 – 20 g. green and red 45 10
876 **278** 25 g. black and buff 1·50 10
877 – 40 g. brown and yellow 70 10
878 – 45 g. purple and mauve 70 10
880 – 60 g. purple and green 75 10
881 – 1 z. 15 black & turquoise 3·75 20
882 – 1 z. 40 brown and orange 14·00 2·50
883 – 1 z. 55 blue and indigo 3·25 55
884 – 2 z. 10 blue and cobalt 5·00 1·50
DESIGNS: 10 g. Coal mine; 20 g. Soldier and flag; 40 g. Worker on holiday; 45 g. House-builders; 60 g. Tractor and binder; 1 z. 15, Lublin Castle; 1 z. 40, Customers in bookshop; 1 z. 55,"Soldek" (freighter) alongside wharf; 2 z. 10, Battle of Lenino.

279 Signal **280** Picking Apples

1954. Railway Workers' Day.
885 **279** 40 g. blue 3·25 50
886 – 60 g. black 2·50 40
DESIGN: 60 g. Night train.

1954. Polish–Russian Friendship.
887 **280** 40 g. violet 1·25 60
888 60 g. black 50 15

281 Elblag **282** Chopin and Grand Piano

1954. 500th Anniv of Return of Pomerania to Poland.
889 **281** 20 g. red on blue 1·50 60
890 – 45 g. brown on yellow 15 10
891 – 60 g. green on yellow 20 10
892 – 1 z. 40 blue on pink 50 15
893 – 1 z. 55 brown on cream 75 10
VIEWS: 45 g. Gdansk; 60 g. Torun; 1 z. 40, Malbork; 1 z. 55, Olsztyn.

1954. 5th International Chopin Piano Competition, Warsaw (1st issue).
894 **282** 45 g. brown 40 10
895 60 g. green 85 10
896 1 z. blue 2·50 1·40
See also Nos. 906/7.

283 Battle Scene

1954. 160th Anniv of Kosciuszko's Insurrection.
897 **283** 40 g. olive 40 15
898 – 60 g. brown 60 10
899 – 1 z. 40 black 1·50 70
DESIGNS: 60 g. Kosciuszko on horseback, with insurgents; 1 z. 40, Street battle.

284 European Bison **285** "The Liberator"

1954. Protected Animals.
900 **284** 45 g. brown and green 45 15
901 – 60 g. brown and green 45 15
902 – 1 z. 90 brown and blue 90 15
903 – 3 z. brown and turquoise 1·40 60
ANIMALS: 60 g. Elk; 1 z. 90, Chamois; 3 z. Eurasian beaver.

1955. 10th Anniv of Liberation of Warsaw.
904 **285** 40 g. brown 1·40 30
905 – 60 g. blue 1·40 50
DESIGN: 60 g. "Spirit of Poland".

286 Bust of Chopin (after L. Isler) **287** Mickiewicz Monument

1955. 5th International Chopin Piano Competition (2nd issue).
906 **286** 40 g. brown 30 10
907 60 g. blue 90 20

1955. Warsaw Monuments.
908 – 5 g. green on yellow 10 10
909 – 10 g. purple on yellow 10 10
910 – 15 g. black on green 10 10
911 – 20 g. blue on pink 10 10
912 – 40 g. violet on lilac 30 10
913 – 45 g. brown on orange 65 20
914 **287** 60 g. blue on grey 10 10
915 – 1 z. 55 green on grey 1·00 25
MONUMENTS: 5 g. "Siren"; 10 g. Dzerzhinski Statue; 15 g. King Sigismund III Statue; 20 g. "Brotherhood in Arms"; 40 g. Copernicus; 45 g. Marie Curie Statue; 1 z. 55, Kilinski Statue.

288 Flags and Tower **289**

1955. 10th Anniv of Russo–Polish Treaty of Friendship.
916 **288** 40 g. red 20 10
917 40 g. brown 50 35
918 – 60 g. brown 20 10
919 – 60 g. turquoise 20 10
DESIGN: 60 g. Statue of "Friendship".

1955. 8th International Peace Cycle Race.
920 **289** 40 g. brown 45 20
921 – 60 g. blue 25 10
DESIGN: 60 g. "VIII" and doves.

290 Town Hall, Poznan **291** Festival Emblem

1955. 24th International Fair, Poznan.
922 **290** 40 g. blue 25 10
923 60 g. red 15 10

1955. Cracow Festival.
924 **291** 20 g. multicoloured 50 20
925 – 40 g. multicoloured 25 15
926 **291** 60 g. multicoloured 1·00 25
No. 925 is as T **291** but horiz and inscr "FESTIWAL SZTUKI", etc.

292 "Peace" **293** Motor Cyclists

1955. 5th International Youth Festival, Warsaw.
927 – 25 g. brown, pink & yellow 20 10
928 – 40 g. grey and blue 20 10
929 – 45 g. red, mauve & yellow 35 10
930 **292** 60 g. ultramarine and blue 30 10
931 – 60 g. black and orange 30 10
932 **292** 1 z. purple and blue 70 50
DESIGNS: 25, 45 g. Pansies and dove; 40, 60 g. (No. 931) Dove and tower.

1955. 13th International Tatra Mountains Motor Cycle Race.
933 **293** 40 g. brown 30 10
934 60 g. green 20 10

294 Stalin Palace of Culture and Science, Warsaw **295** Athletes

1955. Polish National Day.
935 **294** 60 g. blue 15 10
936 60 g. grey 15 10
937 75 g. green 50 20
938 75 g. brown 50 20

1955. 2nd International Games. Imperf or perf.
939 **295** 20 g. brown 15 10
940 – 40 g. purple 20 10
941 – 60 g. blue 35 10
942 – 1 z. red 50 10
943 – 1 z. 35 lilac 70 10
944 – 1 z. 55 green 1·40 50
DESIGNS—VERT: 40 g. Throwing the hammer; 1 z. Net-ball; 1 z. 35, Sculling; 1 z. 55, Swimming. HORIZ: 60 g. Stadium.

296 Szczecin **297** Peasants and Flag

1955. 10th Anniv of Return of Western Territories.
945 **296** 25 g. green 15 10
946 – 40 g. red (Wroclaw) . . . 25 10
947 – 60 g. blue (Zielona Gora) . 45 10
948 – 95 g. black (Opole) . . . 1·25 50

1955. 50th Anniv of 1905 Revolution.
949 **297** 40 g. brown 25 15
950 60 g. red 15 10

298 Mickiewicz **299** Statue

1955. Death Cent of Adam Mickiewicz (poet).
951 **298** 20 g. brown 20 10
952 **299** 40 g. brown and orange . 20 10
953 – 60 g. brown and green . . 30 10
954 – 95 g. black and red . . . 1·25 50
DESIGNS—As Type **299**: 60 g. Sculptured head; 95 g. Statue.

300 Teacher and Pupil **301** Rook and Hands

1955. 50th Anniv of Polish Teachers' Union.
955 **300** 40 g. brown . . . . 1·25 30
956 – 60 g. blue . . . . 2·25 65
DESIGN: 60 g. Open book and lamp.

1956. 1st World Chess Championship for the Deaf and Dumb, Zakopane.
957 **301** 40 g. red . . . . 4·00 1·00
958 – 60 g. blue . . . . 2·50 10
DESIGNS: 60 g. Knight and hands.

302 Ice Skates **304** Racing Cyclist

303 Officer and "Kilinski" (freighter)

1956. 11th World Students' Winter Sports Championship.
959 **302** 20 g. black and blue . . . 4·00 1·60
960 – 40 g. blue and green . . . 1·00 10
961 – 60 g. red and mauve . . . 1·00 10
DESIGNS: 40 g. Ice-hockey sticks and puck; 60 g. Skis and ski sticks.

1956. Merchant Navy.
962 **303** 5 g. green 15 10
963 – 10 g. red 20 10
964 – 20 g. blue 30 10
965 – 45 g. brown 85 40
966 – 60 g. blue 50 10
DESIGNS: 10 g. Tug and barges; 20 g. "Pokoj" (freighter) in dock; 45 g. Building "Marceli Nowatka" (freighter); 60 g. "Fryderyk Chopin" (freighter) and "Radunia" (trawler).

1956. 9th International Peace Cycle Race.
967 **304** 40 g. blue . . . . 1·10 30
968 60 g. green 20 10

305 Lodge, Tatra Mountains **307** Ghetto Heroes' Monument

1956. Tourist Propaganda.
969 **305** 30 g. green 15 10
970 – 40 g. brown 15 10
971 – 60 g. blue . . . . 1·40 70
972 – 1 z. 15 purple 50 10
DESIGNS: 40 g. Compass, rucksack and map; 60 g. Canoe and map; 1 z. 15, Skis and mountains.

1956. No. 829 surch.
973 10 g. on 80 g. purple 40 20
974 40 g. on 80 g. purple 25 10
975 60 g. on 80 g. purple 25 10
976 1 z. 35 on 80 g. purple . . . 1·25 90

1956. Warsaw Monuments.
977 **307** 30 g. black 15 10
978 – 40 g. brown on green . . 50 15
979 – 1 z. 55 purple on pink . . 40 15
STATUES: 40 g. Statue of King Jan III Sobieski; 1 z. 55, Statue of Prince Joseph Poniatowski.

308 "Economic Co-operation" **309** Ludwika Wawrzynska (teacher)

1956. Russo-Polish Friendship Month.
980 – 40 g. brown and pink . . 40 20
981 **308** 60 g. red and bistre . . . 25 15
DESIGN: 40 g. Polish and Russian dancers.

1956. Ludwika Wawrzynska Commemoration.
982 **309** 40 g. brown . . . . . . 1·75 25
983 60 g. blue 25 10

310 "Lady with a Weasel" (Leonardo da Vinci) **311** Honey Bee and Hive

1956. International Campaign for Museums.
984 – 40 g. green . . . . 2·25 1·40
985 – 60 g. violet . . . . 1·00 15
986 **310** 1 z. 55 brown . . . . . 2·00 20
DESIGNS: 40 g. Niobe (bust); 60 g. Madonna (Vit Stvosz).

1956. 50th Death Anniv of Jan Dzierzon (apiarist).
987 **311** 40 g. brown on yellow . . 85 30
988 – 60 g. brown on yellow . . 20 10
DESIGN: 60 g. Dr. J. Dzierzon.

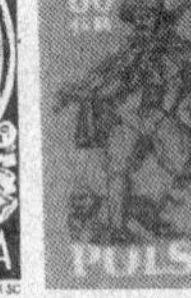

312 Fencing **313** 15th-century Postman

1956. Olympic Games. Inscr "MELBOURNE 1956".
989 **312** 10 g. brown and grey . . 15 10
990 – 20 g. lilac and brown . . 20 10
991 – 25 g. black and blue . . 60 15
992 – 40 g. brown and green . . 30 10
993 – 60 g. brown and red . . 50 10
994 – 1 z. 55 brown and violet . 2·50 1·00
995 – 1 z. 55 brown & orange . 1·00 25
DESIGNS: No. 990, Boxing; No. 991, Rowing; No. 992, Steeplechase; No. 993, Javelin throwing; No. 994, Gymnastics. No. 995, Long jumping (Elizabeth Dunska-krzesinska's gold medal).

1956. Re-opening of Postal Museum, Wroclaw.
996 **313** 60 g. black on blue . . . 85 75

314 Snow Crystals and Skier of 1907 **315** Apple Tree and Globe

1957. 50 Years of Skiing in Poland.
997 **314** 40 g. blue 30 10
998 – 60 g. green 30 10
999 – 1 z. purple 70 20
DESIGNS (with snow crystals)—VERT: 60 g. Skier jumping. HORIZ: 1 z. Skier standing.

1957. U.N.O. Commemoration.
1000 **315** 5 g. red and turquoise . 25 15
1001 – 15 g. blue and grey . . 40 15
1002 – 40 g. green and grey . . 70 50
DESIGNS—VERT: 15 g. U.N.O. emblem; 40 g. U.N.O. Headquarters, New York.

316 Skier **317** Winged Letter

1957. 12th Death Annivs of Bronislaw Czech and Hanna Marusarzowna (skiers).
1003 **316** 60 g. brown 90 25
1004 60 g. blue 50 15

1957. Air. 7th Polish National Philatelic Exhibition, Warsaw.
1005 **317** 4 z.+2 z. blue . . . . . 2·75 2·75

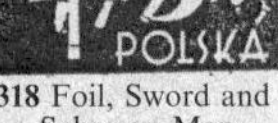
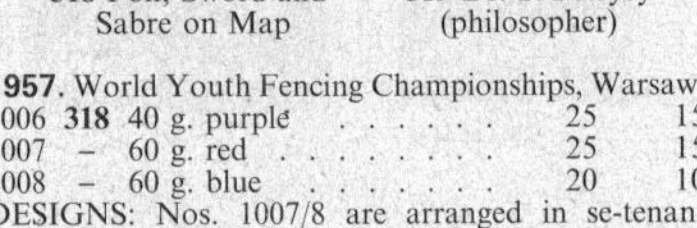

318 Foil, Sword and Sabre on Map **319** Dr. S. Petrycy (philosopher)

1957. World Youth Fencing Championships, Warsaw.
1006 **318** 40 g. purple 25 15
1007 – 60 g. red 25 15
1008 – 60 g. blue 20 10
DESIGNS: Nos. 1007/8 are arranged in se-tenant pairs in the sheet and together show two fencers duelling.

1957. Polish Doctors.
1009 **319** 10 g. brown and blue . . 10 10
1010 – 20 g. lake and green . . 10 10
1011 – 40 g. black and red . . 10 10
1012 – 60 g. purple and blue . . 40 20
1013 – 1 z. blue and yellow . . 20 10
1014 – 1 z. 35 brown and green . 15 10
1015 – 2 z. 50 violet and red . . 35 10
1016 – 3 z. brown and violet . . 45 10
PORTRAITS: 20 g. Dr. W. Oczko; 40 g. Dr. J. Sniadecki; 60 g. Dr. T. Chalubinski; 1 z. Dr. W. Bieganski; 1 z. 35, Dr. J. Dietl; 2 z. 50, Dr. B. Dybowski; 3 z. Dr. H. Jordan.

320 Cycle Wheel and Flower **321** Fair Emblem

1957. 10th International Peace Cycle Race.
1017 **320** 60 g. blue 30 15
1018 – 1 z. 50 red (Cyclist) . . 40 15

1957. 26th International Fair, Poznan.
1019 **321** 60 g. blue 20 10
1020 2 z. 50 green 20 10

322 Carline Thistle **323** Fireman

1957. Wild Flowers.
1021 **322** 60 g. yellow, green & grey 45 10
1022 – 60 g. green and blue . . 45 10
1023 – 60 g. olive and grey . . 45 10
1024 – 60 g. purple and green . . 80 10
1025 – 60 g. purple and green . . 45 10
FLOWERS—VERT: No. 1022, Sea holly; No. 1023, Edelweiss; No. 1024, Lady's slipper orchid; No. 1025, Turk's cap lily.

1957. International Fire Brigades Conference, Warsaw. Inscr "KONGRES C.T.I.F. WARSZAWA 1957".
1026 **323** 40 g. black and red . . . 15 10
1027 – 60 g. green and red . . 15 10
1028 – 2 z. 50 violet and red . . 45 15
DESIGNS: 60 g. Flames enveloping child; 2 z. 50, Ear of corn in flames.

324 Town Hall, Leipzig **325** "The Letter" (after Fragonard)

1957. 4th Int Trade Union Congress, Leipzig.
1029 **324** 60 g. violet 20 10

1957. Stamp Day.
1030 **325** 2 z. 50 green 50 15

326 Red Banner **327** Karol Libelt (founder) **328** H. Wieniawski (violinist)

1957. 40th Anniv of Russian Revolution.
1031 **326** 60 g. red and blue . . . 10 10
1032 – 2 z. 50 brown & black . 20 10
DESIGN: 2 z. 50, Lenin Monument, Poronin.

1957. Cent of Poznan Scientific Society.
1033 **327** 60 g. red 15 10

1957. 3rd Wieniawski Int Violin Competition.
1034 **328** 2 z. 50 blue 25 15

329 Ilyushin Il-14P over Steel Works **330a** J. A. Komensky (Comenius)

1957. Air.
1035 **329** 90 g. black and pink . . 15 10
1036 – 1 z. 50 brown & salmon 15 10
1037 – 3 z. 40 sepia and buff . 45 10
1038 – 3 z. 90 brown & yellow 90 55
1039 – 4 z. blue and green . . 45 10
1039a – 5 z. lake and lavender . 55 15
1039b – 10 z. brown & turquoise 90 30
1040 – 15 z. violet and blue . 1·60 35
1040a – 20 z. violet & yellow . 1·75 80
1040b – 30 z. olive and buff . . 2·75 1·00
1040c – 50 z. blue and drab . 7·00 1·90
DESIGNS—Ilyushin Il-14P over: 1 z. 50, Castle Square, Warsaw; 3 z. 40, Market, Cracow; 3 z. 90, Szczecin; 4 z. Karkonosze Mountains; 5 z. Old Market, Gdansk; 10 z. Liw Castle; 15 z. Lublin; 20 z. Cable railway, Kasprowy Wierch; 30 z. Porabka Dam; 50 z. "Batory" (liner).
For stamp as No. 1039b, but printed in purple only, see No.1095.

1957. 300th Anniv of Publication of Komensky's "Opera Didactica Omnia".
1041 **330a** 2 z. 50 red 25 10

331 A. Strug **332** Joseph Conrad and Full-rigged Sailing Ship "Torrens"

1957. 20th Death Anniv of Andrzej Strug (writer).
1042 **331** 2 z. 50 brown 25 10

1957. Birth Centenary of Joseph Conrad (Korzeniowski) (author).
1043 **332** 60 g. brown on green . . 30 10
1044 2 z. 50 blue on pink . . 1·10 10

333 Postman of 1558 **334** Town Hall, Biecz

1958. 400th Anniv of Polish Postal Service (1st issue).
1045 **333** 2 z. 50, purple and blue . 25 10
For similar stamps see Nos. 1063/7.

1958. Ancient Polish Town Halls.
1046 **334** 20 g. green 10 10
1047 – 40 g. brown (Wroclaw) . 10 10
1048 – 60 g. blue (Tarnow) (horiz) 10 10
1049 – 2 z. 10 lake (Gdansk) . . 15 10
1050 – 2 z. 50 violet (Zamosc) . . 55 25

335 Perch 336 Warsaw University

1958. Fishes.
1051 **335** 50 g. yellow, black & blue . . 15 10
1052 – 60 g. blue, indigo & green 25 10
1053 – 2 z. 10 multicoloured . . 40 10
1054 – 2 z. 50 green, blk & vio . 1·25 30
1055 – 6 z. 40 multicoloured . . 1·10 40
DESIGNS—VERT: 60 g. Salmon; 2 z. 10, Pike; 2 z. 50, Trout. HORIZ 6 z. 40, Grayling.

1958. 140th Anniv of Warsaw University.
1056 **336** 2 z. 50 blue 25 10

337 Fair Emblem 338

1958. 27th International Fair, Poznan.
1057 **337** 2z. 50 red and black . . 30 10

1958. 7th International Gliding Championships.
1058 **338** 60 g. black and blue . . 10 10
1059 – 2 z. 50 black and grey . . 30 10
DESIGN: 2 z. 50, As Type **338** but design in reverse.

339 Armed Postman 340 Polar Bear on Iceberg

1958. 19th Anniv of Defence of Gdansk Post Office.
1060 **339** 60 g. blue 25 10

1958. I.G.Y. Inscr as in T **340**.
1061 **340** 60 g. black 15 10
1062 – 2 z. 50 blue 70 15
DESIGN: 2 z. 50, Sputnik and track of rocket.

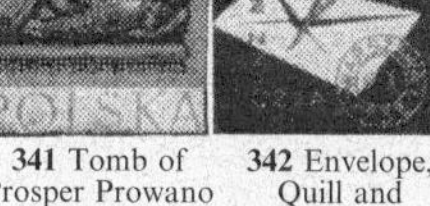

341 Tomb of Prosper Prowano (First Polish Postmaster) 342 Envelope, Quill and Postmark 343 Partisans' Cross

1958. 400th Anniv of Polish Postal Service (2nd issue).
1063 **341** 40 g. purple and blue . . 40 10
1064 – 60 g. black and lilac . . 10 10
1065 – 95 g. violet and yellow . 10 10
1066 – 2 z. 10 blue and grey . . 60 25
1067 – 3 z. 40 brown & turquoise 35 20
DESIGNS: 60 g. Mail coach and Church of Our Lady, Cracow; 95 g. Mail coach (rear view); 2 z. 10, 16th-century postman; 3 z. 40, Kogge.
Nos. 1064/7 show various forms of modern transport in clear silhouette in the background.

1958. Stamp Day.
1068 **342** 60 g. green, red & black . 55 40

1958 15th Anniv of Polish People's Army. Polish decorations.
1069 **343** 40 g. buff, black & green 15 10
1070 – 60 g. multicoloured . . 15 10
1071 – 2 z. 50 multicoloured . . 55 15
DESIGNS: 60 g. Virtuti Military Cross; 2 z. 50, Grunwald Cross.

344 "Mail Coach in the Kielce District" (after painting by A. Kedzierskiego)

1958. Polish Postal Service 400th Anniv Exhibition.
1072 **344** 2 z. 50 black on buff . . 85 55

345 Galleon 346 U.N.E.S.C.O Headquarters, Paris

1958. 350th Anniv of Polish Emigration to America.
1073 **345** 60 g. green 15 10
1074 – 2 z. 50 red (Polish emigrants) 30 15

1958. Inauguration of U.N.E.S.C.O. Headquarters Building, Paris.
1075 **346** 2 z. 50 black and green . 55 15

347 S. Wyspianski (dramatist and painter) 348 "Human Rights"

1958. Famous Poles.
1076 **347** 60 g. violet 10 15
1077 – 2 z. 50 green 45 15
PORTRAIT: 2 z. 50, S. Moniuszko (composer).

1958. 10th Anniv of Declaration of Human Rights.
1078 **348** 2 z. 50 lake & brown . . 55 15

349 Party Flag 350 Yacht

1958. 40th Anniv of Polish Communist Party.
1079 **349** 60 g. red and purple . . 10 10

1959. Sports.
1080 **350** 40 g. ultramarine & blue 35 10
1081 – 60 g. purple and salmon 35 10
1082 – 95 g. purple and green . 70 20
1083 – 2 z. blue and green . . . 35 20
DESIGNS: 60 g. Archer; 95 g. Footballers; 2 z. Horseman.

351 The "Guilding Hand" 352 Death Cap

1959. 3rd Polish United Workers' Party Congress.
1084 **351** 40 g. black, brown & red 10 10
1085 – 60 g. multicoloured . . 10 10
1086 – 1 z. 55 multicoloured . . 40 10
DESIGNS—HORIZ: 60 g. Hammer and ears of corn. VERT: 1 z. 55, Nowa Huta foundry.

1959. Mushrooms.
1087 **352** 20 g. yellow, brn & grn . 2·10 25
1088 – 30 g. multicoloured . . 40 10
1089 – 40 g. multicoloured . . 70 10
1090 – 60 g. multicoloured . . 1·00 10
1091 – 1 z. multicoloured . . . 1·25 10
1092 – 2 z. 50 brown, grn & bl 2·00 30
1093 – 3 z. 40 multicoloured . . 2·25 35
1094 – 5 z. 60 brown, grn & yell 5·75 1·75
MUSHROOMS: 30 g. Butter mushroom; 40 g. Cep; 60 g. Saffron milk cap; 1 z. Chanterelle; 2 z. 50, Fieldmushroom; 3 z. 40, Fly agaric; 5 z. 60, Brown beech bolete.

1959. Air. 65 Years of Philately in Poland and 6th Polish Philatelic Assn. Congress Warsaw. As No. 1039b but in one colour only.
1095 10 z. purple . . . . 2·75 2·75

353 "Storks" (after Chelmonski) 354 Miner

1959. Polish Paintings.
1096 **353** 40 g. green 15 10
1097 – 60 g. purple 30 10
1098 – 1 z. black 30 10
1099 – 1 z. 50 brown 70 25
1100 – 6 z. 40 blue . . . . . . 2·75 1·00
PAINTINGS—VERT: 60 g. "Motherhood" (Wyspianski); 1 z. "Madame de Romanet" (Roda-kowski); 1 z. 50, "Death" (Maiczewski). HORIZ: 6 z. 40, "The Sandmen" (Gierymski).

1959. 3rd Int Miners' Congress, Katowice.
1101 **354** 2 z. 50 multicoloured . . 40 15

355 Sheaf of Wheat ("Agriculture") 356 Dr L. Zamenhof 357 "Flowering Pink" (Map of Austria)

1959. 15th Anniv of People's Republic.
1102 **355** 40 g. green and black . . 10 10
1103 – 60 g. red and black . . . 10 10
1104 – 1 z. 50 blue and black . . 20 10
DESIGNS: 60 g. Crane ("Building"); 1 z. 50, Corinthian column, and book ("Culture and Science").

1959. Int Esperanto Congress, Warsaw and Birth Centenary of Dr. Ludwig Zamenhof (inventor of Esperanto).
1105 **356** 60 g. black & grn on grn 10 10
1106 1 z. 50 green, red and violet on grey 60 20
DESIGNS: 1 z. 50, Esperanto Star and globe.

1959. 7th World Youth Festival, Vienna.
1107 **357** 60 g. multicoloured . . . 10 10
1108 2 z. 50 multicoloured . . . 35 15

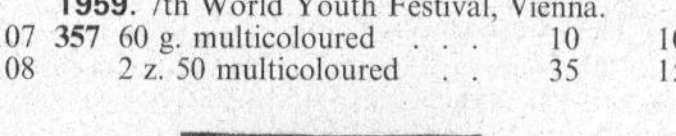

358

1959. 30th Anniv of Polish Airlines "LOT".
1109 **358** 60 g. blue, violet & black 15 10

359 Parliament House, Warsaw

1959. 48th Inter-Parliamentary Union Conf, Warsaw.
1110 **359** 60 g. green, red & black . 10 10
1111 2 z. 50 purple, red & blk . 40 15

1959. Baltic States' International Philatelic Exhibition, Gdansk. No. 890 optd **BALPEX I-GDANSK 1959**.
1112 45 g. brown on lemon . . . 60 50

361 Dove and Globe 362 Nurse with Bag

1959. 10th Anniv of World Peace Movement.
1113 **361** 60 g. grey and blue . . . 35 10

1959. 40th Anniv of Polish Red Cross. Cross in red.
1114 **362** 40 g. black and green . . 15 10
1115 – 60 g. brown 15 10
1116 – 2 z. 50 black and red . . 60 30
DESIGNS—VERT: 60 g. Nurse with bottle and bandages. SQUARE—23×23 mm: 2 z. 50, J. H. Dunant.

363 Emblem of Polish-Chinese Friendship Society 364

1959. Polish–Chinese Friendship.
1117 **363** 60 g. multicoloured . . . 35 15
1118 2 z. 50 multicoloured . . 25 10

1959. Stamp Day.
1119 **364** 60 g. red, green & turq . 15 10
1120 2 z. 50 blue, grn and red . 30 10

365 Sputnik "3"

1959. Cosmic Flights.
1121 **365** 40 g. black and blue . . 15 10
1122 – 60 g. black and lake . . 30 10
1123 – 2 z. 50 blue and green . 1·25 50
DESIGNS: 60 g. Rocket "Miecza" encircling Sun; 2 z. 50, Moon rocket "Lunik 2".

366 Schoolgirl 367 Darwin

1959. "1000 Schools for Polish Millennium". Inscr as in T **366**.
1124 **366** 40 g. brown and green . 10 10
1125 – 60 g. red, black & blue . 10 10
DESIGN: 60 g. Children going to school.

1959. Famous Scientists.
1126 **367** 20 g. blue 10 10
1127 – 40 g. olive (Mendeleev) . 10 10
1128 – 60 g. purple (Einstein) . 15 10
1129 – 1 z. 50 brn (Pasteur) . . 20 10
1130 – 1 z. 55 grn (Newton) . . 50 10
1131 – 2 z. 50 violet (Copernicus) 80 50

368 Costumes of Rzeszow 369

1959. Provincial Costumes (1st series).
1132 **368** 20 g. black and green . . 10 10
1133 **369** 20 g. black and green . . 10 10
1134 – 60 g. brown and pink . . 15 10
1135 – 60 g. brown and pink . . 15 10
1136 – 1 z. red and blue 20 10
1137 – 1 z. red and blue 20 10
1138 – 2 z. 50 green and grey . 40 10
1139 – 2 z. 50 green and grey . 40 10
1140 – 5 z. 60 blue and yellow . 1·60 40
1141 – 5 z. 60 blue and yellow . 1·60 40
DESIGNS—Male and female costumes of: Nos. 1134/5, Kurpic; Nos. 1136/7, Silesia; Nos. 1138/9, Mountain regions; Nos. 1140/1, Szamotuly.
See also Nos. 1150/9.

370 Piano 371 Polish 10 k. Stamp of 1860 and Postmark

1960. 150th Birth Anniv of Chopin and Chopin Music Competition, Warsaw.
1142 **370** 60 g. black and violet . . 45 15
1143 – 1 z. 50 black, red & blue 70 15
1144 – 2 z. 50 brown . . . . . 2·00 1·25
DESIGNS—As Type **370**: 1 z. 50, Portion of Chopin's music, 25×39½ mm: 2 z. 50, Portrait of Chopin.

1960. Stamp Centenary.
1145 **371** 40 g. red, blue and black 15 10
1146 – 60 g. blue, black & violet 25 10
1147 – 1 z. 35 blue, red and grey 65 35
1148 – 1 z. 55 red, black & green 80 25
1149 – 2 z. 50 green, black & ol 1·40 60
DESIGNS: 1 z. 35, Emblem inscr "1860 1960". Reproductions of Polish stamps: 60 g. No. 356; 1 z. 55, No. 533; 2 z. 50, No. 1030. With appropriate postmarks.

1960. Provincial Costumes (2nd series). As T **368/69**.
1150 40 g. red and blue 10 10
1151 40 g. red and blue 10 10
1152 2 z. blue and yellow 25 10
1153 2 z. blue and yellow 25 10
1154 3 z. 10 turquoise and green . 40 15
1155 3 z. 10 turquoise and green . 40 15
1156 3 z. 40 brown and turquoise 50 20
1157 3 z. 40 brown and turquoise 50 20
1158 6 z. 50 violet and green . . 1·60 40
1159 6 z. 50 violet and green . . 1·60 40
DESIGNS—Male and female costumes of: Nos. 1150/1, Cracow; Nos. 1152/3, Lowicz; Nos. 1154/5, Kujawy; Nos. 1156/7, Lublin; Nos. 1158/9, Lubusz.

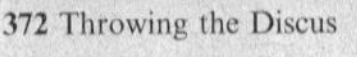

372 Throwing the Discus 373 King Wladislaw Jagiello's Tomb, Wawel Castle

1960. Olympic Games, Rome. Rings and inscr in black.
1160 60 g. blue (T **372**) 15 15
1161 60 g. mauve (Running) . . . 15 15
1162 60 g. violet (Cycling) 15 15
1163 60 g. turq (Show jumping) . . 15 15
1164 2 z. 50 blue (Trumpeters) . . 70 25
1165 2 z. 50 brown (Boxing) . . . 70 25
1166 2 z. 50 red (Olympic flame) . 70 25
1167 2 z. 50 green (Long jump) . . 70 25
Stamps of the same value were issued together, se-tenant, forming composite designs illustrating a complete circuit of the stadium track.

1960. 550th Anniv of Battle of Grunwald.
1168 **373** 60 g. brown 25 15
1169 – 90 g. green 55 30
1170 – 2 z. 50 black . . . . . . 2·25 1·25
DESIGNS—As Type **373**: 90 g. Proposed Grunwald Monument. HORIZ: 78 × 35½ mm; 2 z. 50, "Battle of Grunwald" (after Jan Matejko).

374 1860 Stamp and Postmark 375 Lukasiewicz (inventor of petrol lamp)

1960. International Philatelic Exn, Warsaw.
1171 **374** 10 z. + 10 z. red, black and blue . . . . 7·75 7·75

1960. Lukasiewicz Commemoration and 5th Pharmaceutical Congress. Poznan.
1172 **375** 60 g. black and yellow . 15 10

376 "The Annunciation" 377 Paderewski

1960. Altar Wood Carvings of St. Mary's Church, Cracow, by Veit Stoss.
1173 **376** 20 g. blue 20 10
1174 – 30 g. brown 15 10
1175 – 40 g. violet 20 10
1176 – 60 g. green 20 10
1177 – 2 z. 50 red 90 30
1178 – 5 z. 60 brown . . . . . 5·50 3·75
DESIGNS: 30 g. "The Nativity"; 40 g. "Homage of the Three Kings"; 60 g. "The Resurrection"; 2 z. 50, "The Ascension"; 5 z. 60, "The Descent of the Holy Ghost".

1960. Birth Centenary of Paderewski.
1179 **377** 2 z. 50 black 35 15

1960. Stamp Day. Optd **DZIEN ZNACZKA 1960**.
1180 **371** 40 g. red, blue & black . 1·40 55

379 Gniezno 380 Great Bustard

1960. Old Polish Towns as T **379**.
1181 5 g. brown 10 10
1182 10 g. green 10 10
1183 20 g. brown 10 10
1184 40 g. red 10 10
1185 50 g. violet 10 10
1186 60 g. lilac 10 10
1187 60 g. blue 10 10
1188 80 g. blue 15 10
1189 90 g. brown 15 10
1190 95 g. green 30 10
1191 1 z. red and lilac 15 10
1192 1 z. 15 green and orange . . 30 10
1193 1 z. 35 mauve and green . . 15 10
1194 1 z. 50 brown and blue . . . 30 10
1195 1 z. 55 lilac and yellow . . 30 10
1196 2 z. blue and lilac 20 10
1197 2 z. 10 brown and yellow . . 20 10
1198 2 z. 50 violet and green . . 25 10
1199 3 z. 10 red and grey 30 20
1200 5 z. 60 grey and green . . . 60 25
TOWNS: 10 g. Cracow; 20 g. Warsaw; 40 g. Poznan; 50 g. Plock; 60 g. mauve, Kalisz; 60 g. blue, Tczew; 80 g. Frombork; 90 g. Torum; 95 g. Puck; 1 z. Slupsk; 1 z. 15, Gdansk; 1 z. 35, Wroclaw; 1 z. 50, Szczecin; 1 z. 55, Opole; 2 z. Kolobrzeg; 2 z. 10, Legnica; 2 z. 50, Katowice; 3 z. 10, Lodz; 5 z. 60, Walbrzych.

1960. Birds. Multicoloured.
1201 10 g. Type **380** 20 10
1202 20 g. Raven 20 10
1203 30 g. Common cormorant . . 20 10
1204 40 g. Black stork 35 10
1205 50 g. Eagle owl 65 15
1206 60 g. White-tailed sea eagle . 65 15
1207 75 g. Golden eagle 70 15
1208 90 g. Short-toed eagle . . . 75 25
1209 2 z. 50 Rock thrush . . . . 4·00 1·40
1210 4 z. Common kingfisher . . . 3·25 1·00
1211 5 z. 60 Wallcreeper . . . . 5·50 1·10
1212 6 z. 50 Common roller . . . 8·00 2·00

381 Front page of Newspaper "Proletaryat" (1883) 382 Ice Hockey

1961. 300th Anniv of Polish Newspaper Press.
1213 – 40 g. green, blue & black 50 25
1214 **381** 60 g. yellow, red & black 50 25
1215 – 2 z. 50 blue, violet & blk 2·75 2·50
DESIGNS—Newspaper front page: 40 g. "Mercuriusz" (first issue, 1661); 2 z. 50, "Rzeczpospolita" (1944).

1961. 1st Winter Military Spartakiad.
1216 **382** 40 g. black, yellow & lilac 40 10
1217 – 60 g. multicoloured . . 1·00 30
1218 – 1 z. multicoloured . . . 5·50 1·90
1219 – 1 z. 50 black, yell & turq 90 30
DESIGNS: 60 g. Ski jumping; 1 z. Rifle-shooting; 1 z. 50, Slalom.

383 Congress Emblem 384 Yury Gagarin

1961. 4th Polish Engineers' Conference.
1220 **383** 60 g. black and red . . 15 10

1961. World's 1st Manned Space Flight.
1221 **384** 40 g. black, red and brown 75 20
1222 – 60 g. red, black and blue 75 25
DESIGN: 60 g. Globe and star.

385 Fair Emblem

1961. 30th International Fair, Poznan.
1223 **385** 40 g. black, red and blue 10 10
1224 1 z. 50 black, blue & red 20 10

386 King Mieszko I

1961. Famous Poles (1st issue).
1225 **386** 60 g. black and blue . . 10 10
1226 – 60 g. black and red . . 10 10
1227 – 60 g. black and green . 10 10
1228 – 60 g. black and violet . 70 20
1229 – 60 g. black and brown . 10 10
1230 – 60 g. black and olive . . 10 10
PORTRAITS: No. 1226, King Casimire the Great; No. 1227, King Casmir Jagiellon; No. 1228, Copernicus; No. 1229, A.F. Modrzewski; No. 1230, Kosciuszko.
See also Nos. 1301/6 and 1398/1401.

387 "Leskov" (trawler support ship)

1961. Shipbuilding Industry. Multicoloured.
1231 60 g. Type **387** 25 10
1232 1 z. 55 "Severodvinsk" (depot ship) 40 15
1233 2 z. 50 "Rambutan" (coaster) 70 30
1234 3 z. 40 "Krynica" (freighter) . 1·00 40
1235 4 z. "B 54" freighter . . . . 1·75 70
1236 5 z. 60 "Bavsk" (tanker) . . . 4·50 1·75
SIZES: 2 z. 50, As Type **387**; 5 z. 60 108 × 21 mm; Rest, 81 × 21 mm.

388 Posthorn and Telephone Dial 389 Opole Seal

1961. Communications Minsters' Conference, Warsaw.
1237 **388** 40 g. red, green & blue . 10 10
1238 – 60 g. violet, yellow & purple 15 10
1239 – 2 z. 50 ultram, blue & bis 50 20
DESIGNS: 60 g. Posthorn and radar screen; 2 z. 50, Posthorn and conference emblem.

1961. Polish Western Provinces.
1240 40 g. brown on buff 10 10
1241 40 g. brown on buff 10 10
1242 60 g. violet on pink 10 10
1243 60 g. violet on pink 10 10
1243a 95 g. green on blue 15 10
1243b 95 g. green on blue 15 10
1244 2 z. 50 sage on green . . . 30 15
1245 2 z. 50 sage on green . . . 30 15
DESIGNS—VERT: No. 1240, Type **389**; No. 1242, Henry IV's tomb; No. 1243a, Seal of Conrad II; No. 1244, Prince Barnim's seal. HORIZ: No. 1241, Opole cement works; No. 1243, Wroclaw apartment-house; No. 1243b, Factory interior, Zielona Gora; No. 1245, Szczecin harbour.
See also Nos. 1308/13.

390 Beribboned Paddle 391 Titov and Orbit within Star

1961. 6th European Canoeing Championships. Multicoloured.
1246 40 g. Two canoes within letter "E" 15 10
1247 60 g. Two four-seater canoes at finishing post 15 10
1248 2 z. 50 Type **390** . . . . . . 1·25 40
The 40 g. and 60 g. are horiz.

1961. 2nd Russian Manned Space Flight.
1249 **391** 40 g. black, red and pink 40 10
1250 – 60 g. blue and black . . 40 10
DESIGN: 60 g. Dove and spaceman's orbit around globe.

392 Monument 393 P.K.O. Emblem and Ant

1961. 40th Anniv of 3rd Silesian Uprising.
1251 **392** 60 g. grey and green . . . 10 10
1252 – 1 z. 55 grey and blue . . 20 10
DESIGN: 1 z. 55, Cross of Silesian uprisers.

1961. Savings Month.
1253 – 40 g. red, yellow & blk . 15 10
1254 **393** 60 g. brown, yell & blk . 15 10
1255 – 60 g. blue, violet & pink . 15 10
1256 – 60 g. green, red & blk . . 15 10
1257 – 2 z. 50 mauve, grey & blk 2·40 1·25
DESIGNS: No. 1253, Savings Bank motif; No. 1255, Bee; No. 1256, Squirrel; No. 1257, Savings Bank book.

394 "Mail Cart" (after J. Chelmonski)

1961. Stamp Day and 40th Anniv of Postal Museum.
1258 **394** 60 g. brown 25 10
1259 60 g. green 25 10

395 Congress Emblem 396 Emblem of Kopasyni Mining Family, 1284

1961. 5th W.F.T.U. Congress, Moscow.
1260 **395** 60 g. black 10 10

1961. Millenary of Polish Mining Industry.
1261 **396** 40 g. purple and orange . 15 10
1262 – 60 g. grey and blue . . . 15 10
1263 – 2 z. 50 green and black . 60 25
DESIGNS: 60 g. 14th-century seal of Bytom; 2 z. 50, Emblem of Int Mine Constructors' Congress, Warsaw, 1958.

397 Child and Syringe 398 Cogwheel and Wheat

1961. 15th Anniv of U.N.I.C.E.F.
1264 **397** 40 g. black and blue . . 10 10
1265 – 60 g. black and orange . 10 10
1266 – 2 z. 50 black & turquoise 60 25
DESIGNS—HORIZ: 60 g. Children of three races. VERT: 2 z. 50, Mother and child, and feeding bottle.

1961. 15th Economic Co-operative Council Meeting, Warsaw.
1267 **398** 40 g. red, yellow & blue . 15 10
1268 – 60 g. red, blue & ultram 15 10
DESIGN: 60 g. Oil pipeline map, E. Europe.

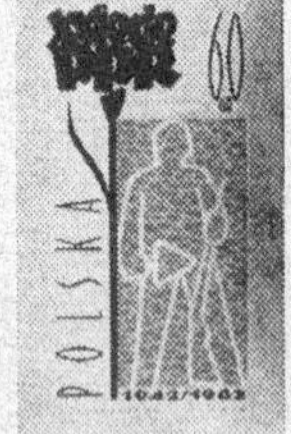

399 Caterpillar-hunter 400 Worker with Flag and Dove

1961. Insects. Multicoloured.
1269 20 g. Type **399** 20 10
1270 30 g. Violet ground beetle . . 20 10
1271 40 g. Alpine longhorn beetle 20 10
1272 50 g. "Cerambyx cerdo" (longhorn beetle) 20 10
1273 60 g. "Carabus auronitens" (ground beetle) 20 10
1274 80 g. Stag beetle 35 10
1275 1 z. 15 Clouded apollo (butterfly) 70 15
1276 1 z. 35 Death's-head hawk moth 45 15
1277 1 z. 50 Scarce swallowtail (butterfly) 90 15
1278 1 z. 55 Apollo (butterfly) . . 90 15
1279 2 z. 50 Red wood ant . . . 1·50 40
1280 5 z. 60 White-tailed bumble bee 8·00 4·25
Nos. 1275/80 are square, 36½ × 36½ mm.

1962. 20th Anniv of Polish Workers' Coalition.
1281 **400** 60 g. brown, blk & red . 15 10
1282 – 60 g. bistre, black & red 15 10
1283 – 60 g. blue, black & red . 15 10
1284 – 60 g. grey, black & red . 15 10
1285 – 60 g. blue, black & red . 15 10
DESIGNS: No. 1282, Steersman; No. 1283, Worker with hammer; No. 1284, Soldier with weapon; No. 1285, Worker with trowel and rifle.

401 Two Skiers Racing

1962. F.I.S. Int. Ski Championships, Zakopane.
1286 **401** 40 g. blue, grey and red . 10 10
1287 40 g. blue, brown & red 1·00 20
1288 – 60 g. blue, grey and red . 20 10
1289 – 60 g. blue, brown & red . 1·25 70

1290 – 1 z. 50 blue, grey and red 35 10
1291 – 1 z. 50 violet, grey & red 1·75 1·25
DESIGNS—HORIZ: 60 g. Skier racing. VERT: 1 z. 50, Ski jumper.

402 Majdanek Monument

1962. Concentration Camp Monuments.
1292 – 40 g. blue 10 10
1293 **402** 60 g. black 30 10
1294 – 1 z. 50 violet 40 15
DESIGNS—VERT: (20×31 mm): 40 g. Broken carnations and portion of prison clothing (Auschwitz camp); 1 z. 50, Treblinka monument.

403 Racing Cyclist

1962. 15th International Peace Cycle Race.
1295 **403** 60 g. black and blue 20 10
1296 – 2 z. 50 black and yellow 40 10
1297 – 3 z. 40 black and violet 70 25
DESIGNS—74½×22 mm: 2 z. 50, Cyclists & "XV". As Type **403**: 3 z. 40, Arms of Berlin, Prague and Warsaw, and cycle wheel.

405 Lenin Walking
406 Gen. K. Swierczewski-Walter (monument)

1962. 50th Anniv of Lenin's Sojourn in Poland.
1298 **405** 40 g. green & lt green 35 10
1299 – 60 g. lake and pink 15 10
1300 – 2 z. 50 brown & yellow 35 10
DESIGNS: 60 g. Lenin; 2 z. 50, Lenin wearing cap, and St. Mary's Church, Cracow.

1962. Famous Poles (2nd issue). As T **386**.
1301 60 g. black and green 10 10
1302 60 g. black and brown 10 10
1303 60 g. black and blue 50 10
1304 60 g. black and bistre 10 10
1305 60 g. black and purple 10 10
1306 60 g. black and turquoise 10 10
PORTRAITS: No. 1301, A. Mickiewicz (poet); 1302, J. Slowacki (poet); 1303, F. Chopin (composer); 1304, R. Traugutt (patriot); 1305, J. Dabrowski (revolutionary); 1306, Maria Konopnicka (poet).

1962. 15th Death Anniv of Gen. K. Swierczewski-Walter (patriot).
1307 **406** 60 g. black 10 10

1962. Polish Northern Provinces. As T **389**.
1308 60 g. blue and grey 10 10
1309 60 g. blue and grey 10 10
1310 1 z. 55 brown and yellow 20 10
1311 1 z. 55 brown and yellow 20 10
1312 2 z. 50 slate and grey 50 15
1313 2 z. 50 slate and grey 50 15
DESIGNS—VERT: No. 1308, Princess Elizabeth's seal; No. 1310, Gdansk Governor's seal; No. 1312, Frombork Cathedral. HORIZ: No. 1309, Insulators factory, Szczecinek; No. 1311, Gdansk shipyard; No. 1313, Laboratory of Agricultural College, Kortowo.

407 "Crocus scepusiensis" (Borb)
408 "The Poison Well", after J. Malczewski

1962. Polish Protected Plants. Plants in natural colours.
1314 **407** 60 g. yellow 20 10
1315 A 60 g. brown 80 30
1316 B 60 g. pink 20 10
1317 C 90 g. green 25 10
1318 D 90 g. olive 25 10
1319 E 90 g. green 25 10
1320 F 1 z. 50 blue 35 15
1321 G 1 z. 50 green 45 15
1322 H 1 z. 50 turquoise 35 15
1323 I 2 z. 50 green 90 50
1324 J 2 z. 50 turquoise 90 50
1325 K 2 z. 50 blue 1·25 60
PLANTS: A, "Platanthera bifolia" (Rich); B, "Aconitum callibotryon" (Rchb.); C, "Gentiana clusii" (Perr. et Song); D, "Dictamnus albus" (L.); E, "Nymphaca alba" (L.); F, "Daphne mezereum" (L.); G, "Pulsatilla vulgaris" (Mill.); H, "Anemone silvestris" (L.); I, "Trollius europaeus" (L.); J, "Galanthus nivalis" (L.); K, "Adonis vernalis" (L.).

1962. F.I.P. Day ("Federation Internationale de Philatelie").
1326 **408** 60 g. black on cream 30 10

409 Pole Vault

1962. 7th European Athletic Championships, Belgrade. Multicoloured.
1327 40 g. Type **409** 10 10
1328 60 g. 400-metres relay 10 10
1329 90 g. Throwing the javelin 10 10
1330 1 z. Hurdling 10 10
1331 1 z. 50 High-jumping 15 10
1332 1 z. 55 Throwing the discus 15 10
1333 2 z. 50 100-metres final 45 15
1334 3 z. 40 Throwing the hammer 1·10 25

410 "Anopheles sp."
411 Cosmonauts "in flight"

1962. Malaria Eradication.
1335 **410** 60 g. brown & turquoise 10 10
1336 – 1 z. 50 multicoloured 15 10
1337 – 2 z. 50 multicoloured 55 20
DESIGNS: 1 z. 50, Malaria parasites in blood; 2 z. 50, Cinchona plant.

1962. 1st "Team" Manned Space Flight.
1338 **411** 60 g. green, black & violet 15 10
1339 – 2 z. 50 red, black and turquoise 35 15
DESIGN: 2 z. 50, Two stars (representing space-ships) in orbit.

412 "A Moment of Determination" (after painting by A. Kamienski)
413 Mazovian Princes' Mansion, Warsaw

1962. Stamp Day.
1340 **412** 60 g. black 10 10
1341 2 z. 50 brown 45 20

1962. 25th Anniv of Polish Democratic Party.
1342 **413** 60 g. black on red 15 10

414 Cruiser "Aurora"

1962. 45th Anniv of Russian Revolution.
1343 **414** 60 g. blue and red 30 10

415 J. Korczak (bust after Dunikowski)

1962. 20th Death Anniv of Janusz Korczak (child educator).
1344 **415** 40 g. sepia, bistre & brn 15 10
1345 – 60 g. multicoloured 15 10
1346 – 90 g. multicoloured 30 15
1347 – 1 z. multicoloured 30 10
1348 – 2 z. 50 multicoloured 70 40
1349 – 5 z. 60 multicoloured 2·10 90
DESIGNS: 60 g. to 5 z. 60, Illustrations from Korczak's children's books.

416 Old Town, Warsaw

1962. 5th T.U. Congress, Warsaw.
1350 **416** 3 z. 40 multicoloured 45 15

417 Master Buncombe
418 R. Traugutt (insurgent leader)

1962. Maria Konopnicka's Fairy Tale "The Dwarfs and Orphan Mary". Multicoloured.
1351 40 g. Type **417** 45 10
1352 60 g. Lardie the Fox and Master Buncombe 2·25 1·25
1353 1 z. 50 Bluey the Frog making music 60 15
1354 1 z. 55 Peter's kitchen 60 20
1355 2 z. 50 Saraband's concert in Nightingale Valley 75 35
1356 3 z. 40 Orphan Mary and Subearthy 2·40 1·50

1963. Centenary of January (1863) Rising.
1357 **418** 60 g. black, pink & turq 10 10

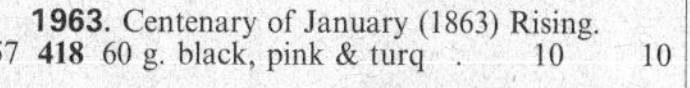

419 Tractor and Wheat

1963. Freedom from Hunger. Multicoloured.
1358 40 g. Type **419** 10 10
1359 60 g. Millet and hoeing 60 25
1360 2 z. 50 Rice and mechanical harvester 55 15

420 Cocker Spaniel

1963. Dogs.
1361 **420** 20 g. red, black & lilac 15 10
1362 – 30 g. black and red 15 10
1363 – 40 g. ochre, black & lilac 20 10
1364 – 50 g. ochre, black & blue 35 10
1365 – 60 g. black and blue 35 10
1366 – 1 z. black and green 90 30
1367 – 2 z. 50 brown, yell & blk 1·40 40
1368 – 3 z. 40 black and red 3·00 1·40
1369 – 6 z. 50 black and yellow 6·00 3·75
DOGS—HORIZ: 30 g. Sheep-dog; 40 g. Boxer; 2 z. 50, Gun-dog "Ogar"; 6 z. 50, Great dane. VERT: 50 g. Airedale terrier; 60 g. French bulldog; 1 z. French poodle; 3 z. 40, Podhale sheep-dog.

421 Egyptian Galley (15th-century B.C.)
422 Insurgent

1963. Sailing Ships (1st series).
1370 **421** 5 g. brown on bistre 10 10
1371 – 10 g. turquoise on green 15 10
1372 – 20 g. blue on grey 15 10
1373 – 30 g. black on olive 20 10
1374 – 40 g. blue on blue 20 10
1375 – 60 g. purple on brown 35 10
1376 – 1 z. black on blue 40 10
1377 – 1 z. 15 green on pink 65 10
SHIPS: 10 g. Phoenician merchantman (15th cent B.C.); 20 g. Greek trireme (5th cent B.C.); 30 g. Roman merchantman (3rd cent A.D.); 40 g. "Mora" (Norman ship, 1066); 60 g. Hanse kogge (14th cent); 1 z. Hulk (16th cent); 1 z. 15, Carrack (15th cent).
See also Nos. 1451/66.

1963. 20th Anniv of Warsaw Ghetto Uprising.
1378 **422** 2 z. 50 brown and blue 25 10

423 Centenary Emblem
424 Lizard

1963. Red Cross Centenary.
1379 **423** 2 z. 50 red, blue & yellow 60 20

1963. Protected Reptiles and Amphibians. Reptiles in natural colours: inscr in black: background colours given.
1380 **424** 30 g. green 10 10
1381 – 40 g. olive 10 10
1382 – 50 g. brown 15 10
1383 – 60 g. grey 15 10
1384 – 90 g. green 15 10
1385 – 1 z. 15 grey 20 10
1386 – 1 z. 35 blue 20 10
1387 – 1 z. 50 turquoise 45 20
1388 – 1 z. 55 pale blue 40 10
1389 – 2 z. 50 lavender 40 25
1390 – 3 z. green 1·00 30
1391 – 3 z. 40 purple 2·50 1·75
DESIGNS: 40 g. Copperhead (snake); 50 g. Marsh tortoise; 60 g. Grass snake; 90 g. Blindworm; 1 z. 15, Tree toad; 1 z. 35, Mountain newt; 1 z. 50, Crested newt; 1 z. 55, Green toad; 2 z. 50, "Bombina" toad; 3 z. Salamander; 3 z. 40, "Natterjack" (toad).

425 Epee, Foil, Sabre and Knight's Helmet

1963. World Fencing Championships, Gdansk.
1392 **425** 20 g. yellow and brown 10 10
1393 – 40 g. light blue and blue 15 10
1394 – 60 g. vermilion and red 15 10
1395 – 1 z. 15 lt green & green 20 10
1396 – 1 z. 55 red and violet 50 15
1397 – 6 z. 50 yellow, pur & bis 1·60 75
DESIGNS—HORIZ: Fencers with background of: 40 g. Knights jousting; 60 g. Dragoons in sword-fight; 1 z. 15, 18th-century duellists; 1 z. 55, Old Gdansk. VERT: 6 z. 50, Inscription and Arms of Gdansk.

1963. Famous Poles (3rd issue) As T **386**.
1398 60 g. black and brown 10 10
1399 60 g. black and brown 10 10
1400 60 g. black and turquoise 35 10
1401 60 g. black and green 10 10
PORTRAITS: No. 1398, L. Warynski (patriot); No. 1399, L. Krzywicki (economist); No. 1400, M. Sklodowska-Curie (scientist); No. 1401, K. Swierczewski (patriot).

426 Bykovsky and "Vostok 5"

1963. 2nd "Team" Manned Space Flights.
1402 **426** 40 g. black, green & blue 15 10
1403 – 60 g. black, blue & green 15 10
1404 – 6 z. 50 multicoloured 1·10 45
DESIGNS: 60 g. Tereshkova and "Vostok 6"; 6 z. 50, "Vostoks 5 and 6" in orbit.

427 Basketball

1963. 13th European (Men's) Basketball Championships, Wroclaw.
1405 **427** 40 g. multicoloured 10 10
1406 – 50 g. green, black & pink 10 10
1407 – 60 g. black, green & red 10 10
1408 – 90 g. multicoloured 10 10
1409 – 2 z. 50 multicoloured 30 10
1410 – 5 z. 60 multicoloured 1·50 35
DESIGNS: 50 g. to 2 z. 50, As Type **427** but with ball, players and hands in various positions; 5 z. 60, Hands placing ball in net.

428 Missile

1963. 20th Anniv of Polish People's Army. Multicoloured.
1411 20 g. Type **428** 10 10
1412 40 g. "Blyskawica" (destroyer) 15 10
1413 60 g. PZL-106 Kruk (airplane) 15 10
1414 1 z. 15 Radar scanner 15 10
1415 1 z. 35 Tank 20 10
1416 1 z. 55 Missile carrier 30 10
1417 2 z. 50 Amphibious troop carrier 40 10
1418 3 z. Ancient warrior, modern soldier and two swords . . 50 30

429 "A Love Letter" (after Czachorski)

1963. Stamp Day.
1419 **429** 60 g. brown 45 30

1963. Visit of Soviet Cosmonauts to Poland. Nos. 1402/4 optd **23-28 X. 1963** and **w Polsce** together with Cosmonauts names.
1420 **426** 40 g. black, green & blue 25 10
1421 – 60 g. black, blue & green 40 10
1422 – 6 z. 50 multicoloured . . 1·60 1·00

431 Tsiolkovsky's Rocket and Formula

432 Mazurian Horses

1963. "The Conquest of Space". Inscr in black.
1423 **431** 30 g. turquoise 10 10
1424 – 40 g. olive 10 10
1425 – 50 g. violet 10 10
1426 – 60 g. brown 10 10
1427 – 1 z. turquoise 10 10
1428 – 1 z. 50 red 15 10
1429 – 1 z. 55 blue 15 10
1430 – 2 z. 50 purple 30 10
1431 – 5 z. 60 green 90 25
1432 – 6 z. 50 turquoise . . . . 1·50 40
DESIGNS: 40 g. "Sputnik 1"; 50 g. "Explorer 1"; 60 g. Banner carried by "Lunik 2"; 1 z. "Lunik 3"; 1 z. 50, "Vostok 1"; 1 z. 55, "Friendship 7"; 2 z. 50, "Vostoks 3 and 4"; 5 z. 60, "Mariner 2"; 6 z. 50, "Mars 1".

1963. Polish Horse-breeding. Multicoloured.
1433 20 g. Arab stallion "Comet" . 10 10
1434 30 g. Wild horses 10 10
1435 40 g. Sokolski horse 15 10
1436 50 g. Arab mares and foals . 15 10
1437 60 g. Type **432** 15 10
1438 90 g. Steeplechasers 25 10
1439 1 z. 55 Arab stallion "Witez II" 50 15
1440 2 z. 50 Head of Arab horse (facing right) 95 15
1441 4 z. Mixed breeds . . . . . 2·25 55
1442 6 z. 50 Head of Arab horse (facing left) . . . . . . 3·25 2·00
SIZES—TRIANGULAR (55 × 27½ mm): 20, 30 g., 40 g. HORIZ: (75 × 26 mm): 50, 90 g., 4 z. VERT: as Type **432**: 1 z. 55, 2 z. 50, 6 z. 50.

433 Ice Hockey

1964. Winter Olympic Games, Innsbruck. Mult.
1443 20 g. Type **433** 10 10
1444 30 g. Slalom 10 10
1445 40 g. Downhill skiing 10 10
1446 60 g. Speed skating 10 10
1447 1 z. Ski-jumping 20 10
1448 2 z. 50 Tobogganing 50 10
1449 5 z. 60 Cross-country skiing . 90 25
1450 6 z. 50 Pairs, figure skating . 1·90 70

1964. Sailing Ships (2nd series). As T **421** but without coloured backgrounds. Some new designs.
1451 **421** 5 g. brown 10 10
1452 – 10 g. green 10 10
1453 – 20 g. blue 15 10
1454 – 30 g. bronze 20 10
1455 – 40 g. blue 20 10
1456 – 60 g. purple 20 10
1457 – 1 z. brown 40 10
1458 – 1 z. 15 brown 40 10
1459 – 1 z. 35 blue 40 10
1460 – 1 z. 50 purple 40 10
1461 – 1 z. 55 black 40 10
1462 – 2 z. violet 40 10
1463 – 2 z. 10 green 40 10
1464 – 2 z. 50 mauve 45 10
1465 – 3 z. olive 70 10
1466 – 3 z. 40 brown . . . . . 1·00 10
SHIPS—HORIZ: 10 g. to 1 z. 15, As Nos. 1370/7; 1 z. 50, "Ark Royal" (English galleon, 1587); 2 z. 10, Ship of the line (18th cent); 2 z. 50, Sail frigate (19th cent); 3 z. "Flying Cloud" (clipper, 19th cent). VERT: 1 z. 35, Columbus's "Santa Maria"; 1 z. 55, "Wodnik" (Polish warship, 17th cent); 2 z. Dutch fleute (17th cent); 3 z. 40, "Dar Pomorza" (cadet ship).

434 "Flourishing Tree"

1964. 20th Anniv of People's Republic (1st issue).
1467 **434** 60 g. multicoloured . . 10 10
1468 – 60 g. black, yellow & red 10 10
DESIGN: No. 1468, Emblem composed of symbols of agriculture and industry.
See also Nos. 1497/1506.

435 European Cat

436 Casimir the Great (founder)

1964. Domestic Cats. As T **435**.
1469 30 g. black and yellow . . . 20 10
1470 40 g. multicoloured 20 10
1471 50 g. black, turquoise & yell 20 10
1472 60 g. multicoloured 40 10
1473 90 g. multicoloured 30 10
1474 1 z. 35 multicoloured . . . 30 10
1475 1 z. 55 multicoloured . . . 60 10
1476 2 z. 50 yellow, black & violet 90 50
1477 3 z. 40 multicoloured . . . 2·00 1·00
1478 6 z. 50 multicoloured . . . 4·00 1·75
CATS—European: 30, 40, 60 g., 1 z. 55, 2 z. 50, 6 z. 50, Siamese: 50 g. Persian: 90 g., 1 z. 35, 3 z. 40. Nos. 1472/5 are horiz.

1964. 600th Anniv of Jagiellonian University, Cracow.
1479 **436** 40 g. purple 10 10
1480 – 40 g. green 10 10
1481 – 60 g. violet 10 10
1482 – 60 g. blue 10 10
1483 – 2 z. 50 sepia 60 15
PORTRAITS: No. 1480, Hugo Kollataj (educationist and politician); No. 1481, Jan Dlugosz (geographer and historian); No. 1482, Copernicus (astronomer); No. 1483 (36 × 37 mm), King Wladislaw Jagiello and Queen Jadwiga.

437 Lapwing

1964. Birds. Multicoloured.
1484 30 g. Type **437** 20 10
1485 40 g. Bluethroat 20 10
1486 50 g. Black-tailed godwit . . 20 10
1487 60 g. Osprey 30 10
1488 90 g. Grey heron 40 10
1489 1 z. 35 Little gull 70 10
1490 1 z. 55 Common shoveler . . 70 15
1491 5 z. 60 Black-throated diver 1·40 50
1492 6 z. 50 Great crested grebe . 2·00 70
Nos. 1487/9 are vert, 35 × 48 mm.

438 Red Flag on Brick Wall

1964. 4th Polish United Workers' Party Congress, Warsaw. Inscr "PZPR". Multicoloured.
1493 60 g. Type **438** 10 10
1494 60 g. Beribboned hammer . . 10 10
1495 60 g. Hands reaching for Red Flag 10 10
1496 60 g. Hammer and corn emblems 10 10

439 Factory and Cogwheel

440 Gdansk Shipyard

441 Battle Scene

1964. 20th Anniv of People's Republic (2nd issue).
1497 **439** 60 g. black and blue . . . 10 10
1498 – 60 g. black and green . . 10 10
1499 – 60 g. red and orange . . 10 10
1500 – 60 g. blue and grey . . . 10 10
1501 **440** 60 g. blue and green . . . 10 10
1502 – 60 g. violet and mauve . . 10 10
1503 – 60 g. brown and violet . . 10 10
1504 – 60 g. bronze and green . . 10 10
1505 – 60 g. purple and red . . . 10 10
1506 – 60 g. brown and yellow . . 10 10
DESIGNS—As Type **439**: No. 1498, Tractor and ear of wheat; No. 1499, Mask and symbols of the arts; No. 1500, Atomic symbol and book. As Type **440**: No. 1502, Lenin Foundry, Nowa Huta; No. 1503, Cement Works, Chelm; No. 1504, Turoszow power station; No. 1505, Petro-chemical plant, Plock; No. 1506, Tarnobrzeg sulphur mine.

1964. 20th Anniv of Warsaw Insurrection.
1507 **441** 60 g. multicoloured . . . 15 10

442 Relay-racing

443 Congress Emblem

1964. Olympic Games, Tokyo. Multicoloured.
1508 20 g. Triple-jumping 10 10
1509 40 g. Rowing 10 10
1510 60 g. Weightlifting 10 10
1511 90 g. Type **442** 10 10
1512 1 z. Boxing 15 10
1513 2 z. 50 Football 35 10
1514 5 z. 60 High jumping (women) 1·00 40
1515 6 z. 50 High-diving . . . . . 1·50 75
SIZES: DIAMOND—20 g. to 60 g. SQUARE—90 g. to 2 z. 50. VERT: (23½ × 36 mm)—5 z. 60, 6 z. 50.

1964. 15th Int Astronautical Congress, Warsaw.
1516 **443** 2 z. 50 black and violet . 40 15

444 Hand holding Hammer

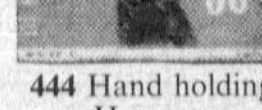

445 S. Zeromski

1964. 3rd Congress of Fighters for Freedom and Democracy Association, Warsaw.
1517 **444** 60 g. red, black & green . 10 10

1964. Birth Cent of Stefan Zeromski (writer).
1518 **445** 60 g. brown 10 10

446 Globe and Red Flag

448 Eleanor Roosevelt

447 18th-century Stage Coach (after Brodowski)

1964. Centenary of "First International".
1519 **446** 60 g. black and red . . . 10 10

1964. Stamp Day.
1520 **447** 60 g. green 20 10
1521 60 g. brown 20 10

1964. 80th Birth Anniv of Eleanor Roosevelt.
1522 **448** 2 z. 50 brown 25 10

449 Battle of Studzianki (after S. Zoltowski)

1964. "Poland's Struggle" (World War II) (1st issue).
1523 – 40 g. black 10 10
1524 – 40 g. violet 10 10
1525 – 60 g. blue 15 10
1526 – 60 g. green 15 10
1527 **449** 60 g. bronze 15 10
DESIGNS—VERT: No. 1523, Virtuti Militari Cross; 1524, Westerplatte Memorial, Gdansk; 1525, Bydogoszez Memorial. HORIZ: No. 1526, Soldiers crossing the Oder (after S. Zoltowski).
See also Nos. 1610/12.

450 Cyclamen

451 Spacecraft of the Future

1964. Garden Flowers. Multicoloured.
1528 20 g. Type **450** 10 10
1529 30 g. Freesia 10 10
1530 40 g. Rose 10 10
1531 50 g. Peony 10 10
1532 60 g. Lily 10 10
1533 90 g. Poppy 15 10
1534 1 z. 35 Tulip 15 10
1535 1 z. 50 Narcissus 65 25
1536 1 z. 55 Begonia 25 10
1537 2 z. 50 Carnation 60 15
1538 3 z. 40 Iris 90 30
1539 5 z. 60 Japanese camelia . . 1·50 70
Nos. 1534/9 are smaller, 26½ × 37 mm.

1964. Space Research. Multicoloured.
1540 20 g. Type **451** 10 10
1541 30 g. Launching rocket . . . 10 10
1542 40 g. Dog "Laika" and rocket 10 10
1543 60 g. "Lunik 3" and Moon . 10 10
1544 1 z. 55 Satelite 20 10
1545 2 z. 50 "Elektron 2" 50 10
1546 5 z. 60 "Mars 1" . . . . . 1·25 50
1547 6 z. 50 + 2 z. Gagarin seated in Capsule . . . . 1·75 85

452 "Siren of Warsaw"

1965. 20th Anniv of Liberation of Warsaw.
1548 **452** 60 g. green 10 10

453 Edaphosaurus

1965. Prehistoric Animals (1st series). Multicoloured.
1549 20 g. Type **453** 15 10
1550 30 g. Cryptocleidus 15 10
1551 40 g. Brontosaurus 15 10
1552 60 g. Mesosaurus 15 10
1553 90 g. Stegosaurus 15 10
1554 1 z. 15 Brachiosaurus 20 10
1555 1 z. 35 Styracosaurus 25 10
1556 3 z. 40 Corythosaurus 70 20
1557 5 z. 60 Rhamphorhynchus . . 1·75 50
1558 6 z. 50 Tyrannosaurus . . . 2·50 60
The 30 g., 60 g., 1 z. 15, 3 z. 40, and 5 z. 60, are vert.
See also Nos. 1639/47.

454 Petro-chemical Works, Plock, and Polish and Soviet Flags

1965. 20th Anniv of Polish-Soviet Friendship Treaty. Multicoloured.
1559 60 g. Seal (vert, 27 × 38½ mm) 10 10
1560 60 g. Type **454** 10 10

455 Polish Eagle and Civic Arms

1965. 20th Anniv of Return of Western and Northern Territories to Poland.
1561 **455** 60 g. red 10 10

456 Dove of Peace **457** I.T.U. Emblem

1965. 20th Anniv of Victory.
1562 **456** 60 g. red and black . . . 10 10

1965. Centenary of I.T.U.
1563 **457** 2 z. 50 black, violet & bl 45 15

458 Clover-leaf Emblem and "The Friend of the People" (journal) **459** "Dragon" Class Yachts

1965. 70th Anniv of Peasant Movement. Mult.
1564 40 g. Type **458** 10 10
1565 60 g. Ears of corn and industrial plant (horiz) 10 10

1965. World Finn Class Sailing Championships, Gdynia. Multicoloured.
1566 30 g. Type **459** 10 10
1567 40 g. "5.5 m." class 10 10
1568 50 g. "Finn" class 15 10
1569 60 g. "V" class 15 10
1570 1 z. 35 "Cadet" class 20 10
1571 4 z. "Star" class 90 30
1572 5 z. 60 "Flying Dutchman" class 1·50 60
1573 6 z. 50 "Amethyst" class . . 2·25 75
The 50 g., 1 z. 35, 4 z. and 6 z. 50, are horiz.

460 Marx and Lenin **461** 17th-Cent Arms of Warsaw

1965. Postal Ministers' Congress, Peking.
1574 **460** 60 g. black on red . . . 15 10

1965. 700th Anniv of Warsaw.
1575 **461** 5 g. red 10 10
1576 – 10 g. green 10 10
1577 – 20 g. blue 10 10
1578 – 40 g. brown 10 10
1579 – 60 g. orange 10 10
1580 – 1 z. 50 black 15 10
1581 – 1 z. 55 blue 20 10
1582 – 2 z. 50 purple 35 10
DESIGNS—VERT: 10 g. 13th-cent antiquities. HORIZ: 20 g. Tombstone of last Masovian dukes; 40 g. Old Town Hall; 60 g. Barbican; 1 z. 50, Arsenal; 1 z. 55, National Theatre; 2 z. 50, Staszic Palace.

463 I.Q.S.Y. Emblem **464** "Odontoglossum grande"

1965. International Quiet Sun Year. Multicoloured. Background colours given.
1584 **463** 60 g. blue 10 10
1585 60 g. violet 10 10
1586 – 2 z. 50 red 35 10
1587 – 2 z. 50 brown 35 10
1588 – 3 z. 40 orange 45 20
1589 – 3 z. 40 olive 45 20
DESIGNS: 2 z. 50, Solar scanner; 3 z. 40, Solar System.

1965. Orchids. Multicoloured.
1590 20 g. Type **464** 15 10
1591 30 g. "Cypripedium hibridum" 15 10
1592 40 g. "Lycaste skinneri" . . 15 10
1593 50 g. "Cattleya warzewicza" 15 10
1594 60 g. "Vanda sanderiana" . 15 10
1595 1 z. 35 "Cypripedium hibridum" 40 10
1596 4 z. "Sobralia" 70 40
1597 5 z. 60 "Disa grandiflora" . 1·75 50
1598 6z. 50 "Cattleya labiata" . . 2·75 1·00
The 30 g. and 1 z. 35, are different designs.

465 Weightlifting **466** "The Post Coach" (after P. Michalowski)

1965. Olympic Games, Tokyo. Polish Medal Winners. Multicoloured.
1599 30 g. Type **465** 10 10
1600 40 g. Boxing 10 10
1601 50 g. Relay-racing 10 10
1602 60 g. Fencing 10 10
1603 90 g. Hurdling (women's 80 m) 10 10
1604 3 z. 40 Relay-racing (women's) 50 10
1605 6 z. 50 "Hop, step and jump" 90 60
1606 7 z. 10 Volleyball (women's) 1·10 50

1965. Stamp Day.
1607 **466** 60 g. brown 15 10
1608 – 2 z. 50 green 25 10
DESIGN: 2 z. 50, "Coach about to leave" (after P. Michalowski).

467 U.N. Emblem **468** Memorial, Holy Cross Mountains

1965. 20th Anniv of U.N.O.
1609 **467** 2 z. 50 blue 30 10

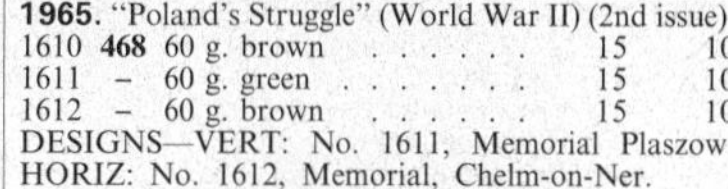
1965. "Poland's Struggle" (World War II) (2nd issue).
1610 **468** 60 g. brown 15 10
1611 – 60 g. green 15 10
1612 – 60 g. brown 15 10
DESIGNS—VERT: No. 1611, Memorial Plaszow. HORIZ: No. 1612, Memorial, Chelm-on-Ner.

469 Wolf

1965. Forest Animals. Multicoloured.
1613 20 g. Type **469** 10 10
1614 30 g. Lynx 10 10
1615 40 g. Red fox 10 10
1616 50 g. Eurasian badger 10 10
1617 60 g. Brown bear 10 10
1618 1 z. 50 Wild boar 70 10
1619 2 z. 50 Red deer 70 15
1620 5 z. 60 European bison . . . 1·60 45
1621 7 z. 10 Elk . . . . 2·50 1·00

470 Gig

1965. Horse-drawn Carriages in Lancut Museum. Multicoloured.
1622 20 g. Type **470** 10 10
1623 40 g. Coupe 10 10
1624 50 g. Ladies' "basket" (trap) . 10 10
1625 60 g. "Vis-a-vis" 10 10
1626 90 g. Cab 15 10
1627 1 z. 15 Berlinka 20 10
1628 2 z. 50 Hunting brake 50 10
1629 6 z. 50 Barouche . . . . . . 1·40 45
1630 7 z. 10 English brake . . . . 2·00 1·00
Nos. 1627/9 are 77 × 22 mm and No. 1630 is 104 × 22 mm.

471 Congress Emblem and Industrial Products

1966. 5th Polish Technicians' Congress, Katowice.
1631 **471** 60 g. multicoloured . . . 15 10

1966. 20th Anniv of Industrial Nationalisation. Designs similar to T **471**. Multicoloured.
1632 60 g. Pithead gear (vert) . . . 15 10
1633 60 g. Freighter 15 10
1634 60 g. Petro-chemical works, Plock 15 10
1635 60 g. Combine-harvester . . . 15 10
1636 60 g. Electric train 20 10
1637 60 g. Exhibition Hall, 35th Poznan Fair 15 10
1638 60 g. Crane (vert) 15 10

1966. Prehistoric Animals (2nd series). As T **453**. Multicoloured.
1639 20 g. Dinichthys 15 10
1640 30 g. Eusthenopteron 15 10
1641 40 g. Ichthyostega 15 10
1642 50 g. Mastodonsaurus 15 10
1643 60 g. Cynognathus 25 10
1644 2 z. 50 Archaeopteryx (vert) . 40 10
1645 3 z. 40 Brontotherium 60 10
1646 6 z. 50 Machairodus 95 50
1647 7 z. 10 Mammuthus . . . . . 2·00 95

472 H. Sienkiewicz (novelist) **473** Footballers (Montevideo, 1930)

1966. 50th Death Anniv of Henryk Sienkiewicz.
1648 **472** 60 g. black on buff . . . 15 10

1966. World Cup Football Championship. Mult.
1649 20 g. Type **473** 10 10
1650 40 g. Rome, 1934 . . . . . . 10 10
1651 60 g. Paris, 1938 . . . . . . 10 10
1652 90 g. Rio de Janeiro, 1950 . . 10 10
1653 1 z. 50 Berne, 1954 . . . . . 65 15
1654 3 z. 40 Stockholm, 1958 . . . 65 15
1655 6 z. 50 Santiago, 1962 . . . 1·25 65
1656 7 z. 10 "London", 1966 (elimination match, Glasgow, 1965) . . . . 1·75 1·25
Football scenes represent World Cup finals played at the cities stated.

475 Soldier with Flag, and Dove of Peace **476** Women's Relay-racing

1966. 21st Anniv of Victory Day.
1658 **475** 60 g. red and black on silver 10 10

1966. 8th European Athletic Championships, Budapest. Multicoloured.
1659 20 g. Runner starting race . 10 10
1660 40 g. Type **476** 10 10
1661 60 g. Throwing the javelin . 10 10
1662 90 g. Women's hurdles . . . 10 10
1663 1 z. 35 Throwing the discus . 15 10
1664 3 z. 40 Finish of race 55 10
1665 6 z. 50 Throwing the hammer 95 35
1666 7 z. 10 High-jumping . . . . 1·25 60
The 20 g., 60 g., 1 z. 35, and 6 z. 50, are vert.

478 White Eagle **479** Flowers and Produce

1966. Polish Millenary (1st issue). Each red and black on gold.
1668 60 g. Type **478** 10 10
1669 60 g. Polish flag 10 10
1670 2 z. 50 Type **478** 30 15
1671 2 z. 50 Polish flag 30 15
See also Nos. 1717/18.

1966. Harvest Festival. Multicoloured.
1672 40 g. Type **479** 25 10
1673 60 g. Woman and loaf . . . 25 10
1674 3 z. 40 Festival bouquet . . 65 30
The 3 z. 40, is 49 × 48 mm.

480 Chrysanthemum **481** Tourist Map

1966. Flowers. Multicoloured.
1675 10 g. Type **480** 10 10
1676 20 g. Poinsettia 10 10
1677 30 g. Centaury 10 10
1678 40 g. Rose 10 10
1679 60 g. Zinnia 10 10
1680 90 g. Nasturtium 15 10
1681 5 z. 60 Dahlia 90 35
1682 6 z. 50 Sunflower . . . . . 1·25 45
1683 7 z. 10 Magnolia . . . . . . 2·00 50

1966. Tourism.
1684 **481** 10 g. red 10 10
1685 – 20 g. olive 10 10
1686 – 40 g. blue 10 10
1687 – 60 g. brown 10 10
1688 – 60 g. black 10 10
1689 – 1 z. 15 green 10 10
1690 – 1 z. 35 red 20 10
1691 – 1 z. 55 violet 20 10
1692 – 2 z. green 40 10
DESIGNS: 20 g. Hela Lighthouse; 40 g. Yacht; 60 g. (No. 1687); Poniatowski Bridge, Warsaw; 60 g. (No. 1688), Mining Academy, Kielce; 1 z. 15, Dunajec Gorge; 1 z. 35, Old oaks, Rogalin; 1 z. 55, Silesian Planetarium; 2 z. "Batory" (liner).

482 Roman Capital

1966. Polish Culture Congress.
1693 **482** 60 g. red and brown . . 10 10

483 Stable-man with Percherons

1966. Stamp Day.
1694 **483** 60 g. brown 15 10
1695 – 2 z. 50 green 25 10
DESIGNS: 2 z. 50, Stablemen with horses and dogs.

484 Soldier in Action

1966. 30th Anniv of Jaroslav Dabrowski Brigade.
1696 **484** 60 g. black, green & red . 15 10

485 Woodland Birds

1966. Woodland Birds. Multicoloured.
1697 10 g. Type **485** 25 10
1698 20 g. Green woodpecker . . 25 10
1699 30 g. Jay 30 10
1700 40 g. Golden oriole 30 10
1701 60 g. Hoopoe 30 10
1702 2 z. 50 Redstart 70 40
1703 4 z. Siskin . . . . 2·25 50
1704 6 z. 50 Chaffinch . . . . . 2·40 80
1705 7 z. 10 Great tit . . . . . 2·60 85

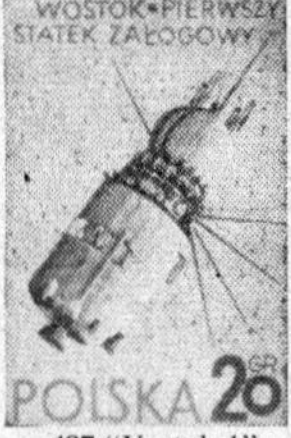

486 Ram (ritual statuette) 487 "Vostok 1"

1966. Polish Archaeological Research.
1706 **486** 60 g. blue 15 10
1707 – 60 g. green 15 10
1708 – 60 g. brown 15 10
DESIGNS—VERT: No. 1707, Plan of Biskupin settlement. HORIZ: No. 1708, Brass implements and ornaments.

1966. Space Research. Multicoloured.
1709 20 g. Type **487** 10 10
1710 40 g. "Gemini" 10 10
1711 60 g. "Ariel 2" 10 10
1712 1 z. 35 "Proton 1" 15 10
1713 1 z. 50 "FR 1" 25 10
1714 3 z. 40 "Alouette" 40 10
1715 6 z. 50 "San Marco 1" . . . 1·25 25
1716 7 z. 10 "Luna 9" . . . . . . 1·50 40

488 Polish Eagle and Hammer

1966. Polish Millenary (2nd issue).
1717 **488** 40 g. purple, lilac & red . 10 10
1718 – 60 g. purple, green & red 10 10
DESIGN: 60 g. Polish eagle and agricultural and industrial symbols.

489 Dressage

1967. 150th Anniv of Racehorse Breeding in Poland. Multicoloured.
1719 10 g. Type **489** 20 10
1720 20 g. Cross-country racing . 20 10
1721 40 g. Horse-jumping 20 10
1722 60 g. Jumping fence in open country 30 10
1723 90 g. Horse-trotting 35 10
1724 5 z. 90 Playing polo . . . . 1·00 20
1725 6 z. 60 Stallion "Ofir" . . . 1·40 60
1726 7 z. Stallion "Skowronek" . 2·25 85

490 Striped Butterfly

1967. Exotic Fishes. Multicoloured.
1727 5 g. Type **490** 10 10
1728 10 g. Imperial angelfish . . 10 10
1729 40 g. Banded butterfly . . . 10 10
1730 60 g. Spotted triggerfish . . 10 10
1731 90 g. Undulate triggerfish . . 15 10
1732 1 z. 50 Picasso fish 25 10
1733 4 z. 50 Black-eyed butterfly . 80 30
1734 6 z. 60 Blue angelfish . . . 1·10 60
1735 7 z. Saddleback butterfly . . 1·40 80

491 Auschwitz Memorial

1967. Polish Martyrdom and Resistance, 1939–45.
1736 **491** 40 g. brown 10 10
1737 – 40 g. black 10 10
1738 – 40 g. violet 10 10
DESIGNS—VERT: No. 1737, Auschwitz-Monowitz Memorial; No. 1738, Memorial guide's emblem.
See also Nos. 1770/2, 1798/9 and 1865/9.

492 Cyclists

1967. 20th International Peace Cycle Race.
1739 **492** 60 g. multicoloured . . 15 10

493 Running

1967. Olympic Games (1968). Multicoloured.
1740 20 g. Type **493** 10 10
1741 40 g. Horse-jumping 10 10
1742 60 g. Relay-running 10 10
1743 90 g. Weight-lifting 10 10
1744 1 z. 35 Hurdling 10 10
1745 3 z. 40 Gymnastics 45 15
1746 6 z. 60 High-jumping . . . 60 25
1747 7 z. Boxing . . . . 1·10 65

494 Socialist Symbols

1967. Polish Trade Unions Congress, Warsaw.
1749 **494** 60 g. multicoloured . . 10 10

495 "Arnica montana"

1967. Protected Plants. Multicoloured.
1750 40 g. Type **495** 10 10
1751 60 g. "Aquilegia vulgaris" . . 10 10
1752 3 z. 40 "Gentiana punctata" . 40 10
1753 4 z. 50 "Lycopodium clavatum" 45 10
1754 5 z. "Iris sibirica" 65 15
1755 10 z. "Azalea pontica" . . . 1·25 20

496 Katowice Memorial 497 Marie Curie

1967. Inauguration of Katowice Memorial.
1756 **496** 60 g. multicoloured . . . 10 10

1967. Birth Centenary of Marie Curie.
1757 **497** 60 g. lake 15 10
1758 – 60 g. brown 15 10
1759 – 60 g. violet 15 10
DESIGNS: No. 1758, Marie Curie's Nobel Prize diploma; No. 1759, Statue of Marie Curie, Warsaw.

498 "Fifth Congress of the Deaf" (sign language)

1967. 5th World Federation of the Deaf Congress, Warsaw.
1760 **498** 60 g. black and blue . . . 15 10

499 Bouquet

1967. "Flowers of the Meadow". Multicoloured.
1761 20 g. Type **499** 10 10
1762 40 g. Red poppy 10 10
1763 60 g. Field bindweed 10 10
1764 90 g. Wild pansy 15 10
1765 1 z. 15 Tansy 15 10
1766 2 z. 50 Corn cockle 25 10
1767 3 z. 40 Field seabious 50 25
1768 4 z. 50 Scarlet pimpernel . . 1·60 40
1769 7 z. 90 Chicory . . . . . . 1·75 65

1967. Polish Martyrdom and Resistance, 1939–45 (2nd series). As T **491**.
1770 40 g. blue 10 10
1771 40 g. green 10 10
1772 40 g. black 10 10
DESIGNS—HORIZ: No. 1770, Stutthof Memorial. VERT: No. 1771, Walez Memorial; No. 1772, Lodz-Radogoszez Memorial.

500 "Wilanow Palace" (from painting by W. Kasprzycki)

1967. Stamp Day.
1773 **500** 60 g. brown and blue . . 15 10

501 Cruiser "Aurora"

1967. 50th Anniv of October Revolution. Each black, grey and red.
1774 60 g. Type **501** 30 10
1775 60 g. Lenin 30 10
1776 60 g. "Luna 10" 30 10

502 Peacock 503 Kosciuszko

1967. Butterflies. Multicoloured.
1777 10 g. Type **502** 15 10
1778 20 g. Swallowtail 15 10
1779 40 g. Small tortoiseshell . . 15 10
1780 60 g. Camberwell beauty . . 20 10
1781 2 z. Purple emperor 35 10
1782 2 z. 50 Red admiral 45 10
1783 3 z. 40 Pale clouded yellow . 45 15
1784 4 z. 50 Marbled white . . . 2·00 80
1785 7 z. 90 Large blue . . . . . 2·25 80

1967. 150th Death Anniv of Tadeusz Kosciuszko (national hero).
1786 **503** 60 g. chocolate & brown . 10 10
1787 2 z. 50 green and red . . 20 10

504 "The Lobster" (Jean de Heem)

1967. Famous Paintings.
1788 – 20 g. multicoloured . . . 20 10
1789 – 40 g. multicoloured . . . 10 10
1790 – 60 g. multicoloured . . . 10 10
1791 – 2 z. multicoloured . . . 25 15
1792 – 2 z. 50 multicoloured . . 30 15
1793 – 3 z. 40 multicoloured . . 55 15
1794 **504** 4 z. 50 multicoloured . . 1·00 50
1795 – 6 z. 60 multicoloured . . 1·25 60
DESIGNS (Paintings from the National Museums, Warsaw and Cracow). VERT: 20 g. "Lady with a Weasel" (Leonardo da Vinci); 40 g. "The Polish Lady" (Watteau); 60 g. "Dog fighting Heron" (A. Hondius); 2 z. "Fowler tuning Guitar" (J. B. Greuze); 2 z. 50, "The Tax Collectors" (M. van Reymerswaele); 3 z. 40, "Daria Fiodorowna" (F. S. Rokotov). HORIZ: 6 z. 60, "Parable of the Good Samaritan" (landscape, Rembrandt).

505 W. S. Reymont

1967. Birth Centenary of W. S. Reymont (novelist).
1796 **505** 60 g. brown, red & ochre 10 10

506 J. M. Ossolinski (medallion), Book and Flag

1967. 150th Anniv of Ossolineum Foundation.
1797 **506** 60 g. brown, red & blue . 10 10

1967. Polish Martyrdom and Resistance, 1939-45 (3rd series). As T **491**.
1798 40 g. red 10 10
1799 40 g. brown 10 10
DESIGNS—VERT: No. 1798, Zagan Memorial. HORIZ: No. 1799, Lambinowice Memorial.

507 Ice Hockey 508 "Puss in Boots"

1968. Winter Olympic Games, Grenoble. Mult.
1800 40 g. Type **507** 10 10
1801 60 g. Ski-jumping 10 10
1802 90 g. Slalom 15 10
1803 1 z. 35 Speed-skating 15 10
1804 1 z. 55 Ski-walking 15 10
1805 2 z. Tobogganing 25 10
1806 7 z. Rifle-shooting on skis . 60 40
1807 7 z. 90 Ski-jumping (different) 1·10 50

1968. Fairy Tales. Multicoloured.
1808 20 g. Type **508** 10 10
1809 40 g. "The Raven and the Fox" 10 10
1810 60 g. "Mr. Twardowski" . . 15 10
1811 2 z. "The Fisherman and the Fish" 25 10
1812 2 z. 50 "Little Red Riding Hood" 35 10
1813 3 z. 40 "Cinderella" 50 10
1814 5 z. 50 "The Waif" . . . . . 1·25 50
1815 7 z. "Snow White" . . . . . 1·50 65

509 "Passiflora quadrangularis" **510** "Peace" (poster by H. Tomaszewski)

1968. Flowers. Multicoloured.
1816 10 g. "Clianthus dampieri" . 10 10
1817 20 g. Type **509** 10 10
1818 30 g. "Strelitzia reginae" . . 10 10
1819 40 g. "Coryphanta vivipara" 10 10
1820 60 g. "Odontonia" 10 10
1821 90 g. "Protea cyneroides" . . 15 10
1822 4 z.+2 z. "Abutilon" 75 40
1823 8 z.+4 z. "Rosa polyantha" . 1·90 85

1968. 2nd Int Poster Biennale, Warsaw. Mult.
1824 60 g. Type **510** 10 10
1825 2 z. 50 Gounod's "Faust" (poster by Jan Lenica) . . . 20 10

511 Zephyr Glider

1968. 11th World Gliding Championships, Leszno. Gliders. Multicoloured.
1826 60 g. Type **511** 10 10
1827 90 g. Stork 10 10
1828 1 z. 50 Swallow 20 10
1829 3 z. 40 Fly 50 20
1830 4 z. Seal . . . . 1·00 30
1831 5 z. 50 Pirate . . . . 1·25 35

512 Child with "Stamp" **513** Part of Monument

1968. "75 years of Polish Philately". Multicoloured.
1832 60 g. Type **512** 10 10
1833 60 g. Balloon over Poznan . . . 10 10

1968. Silesian Insurrection Monument, Sosnowiec.
1834 **513** 60 g. black and purple . 10 10

514 Relay-racing

1968. Olympic Games, Mexico. Multicoloured.
1835 30 g. Type **514** 10 10
1836 40 g. Boxing 10 10
1837 60 g. Basketball 10 10
1838 90 g. Long-jumping 10 10
1839 2 z. 50 Throwing the javelin . 20 10
1840 3 z. 40 Gymnastics 35 10
1841 4 z. Cycling 45 30
1842 7 z. 90 Fencing 80 40
1843 10 z.+5 z. Torch runner and Aztec bas-relief . . . . 2·00 1·25
The 10 z. is larger, 56×45 mm.

515 "Knight on a Bay Horse" (P. Michalowski)

1968. Polish Paintings. Multicoloured.
1844 40 g. Type **515** 10 10
1845 60 g. "Fisherman" (L. Wyczolkowski) 10 10
1846 1 z. 15 "Jewish Woman with Lemons" (A. Gierymski) . 10 10
1847 1 z. 35 "Eliza Parenska" (S. Wyspianski) 15 10
1848 1 z. 50 "Manifesto" (W. Weiss) 40 20
1849 4 z. 50 "Stanczyk" (Jan Matejko) 40 25
1850 5 z. "Children's Band" (T. Makowski) 65 20
1851 7 z. "Feast II" (Z. Waliszewski) 70 45
The 4 z. 50, 5 z. and 7 z. are horiz.

516 "September, 1939" (Bylina)

1968. 25th Anniv of Polish People's Army. Designs show paintings.
1852 40 g. violet & olive on yellow 10 10
1853 40 g. blue & violet on lilac . 10 10
1854 40 g. green & blue on grey . 10 10
1855 40 g. black & brown on orge 10 10
1856 40 g. purple & green on green 10 10
1857 60 g. brown & ultram on bl 15 10
1858 60 g. purple and grn on grn 15 10
1859 60 g. olive and red on pink . 15 10
1860 60 g. green & brown on red 30 10
1861 60 g. blue & turq on blue . . 20 10
PAINTINGS AND PAINTERS: No. 1852, Type **516**; 1853, "Partisans" (Maciag); 1854, "Lenino" (Bylina); 1855, "Monte Cassino" (Boratynski); 1856, "Tanks before Warsaw" (Garwatowski); 1857, "Neisse River" (Bylina); 1858, "On the Oder" (Mackiewicz); 1859, "In Berlin" (Bylina); 1860, "Blyskawica" (destroyer) (Mokwa); 1861, "Pursuit" (Mikoyan Gurevich MiG-17 aircraft) (Kulisiewicz).

517 "Party Members" (F. Kowarski)

1968. 5th Polish United Workers' Party Congress, Warsaw. Multicoloured designs showing paintings.
1862 60 g. Type **517** 10 10
1863 60 g. "Strike" (S. Lentz) . . 10 10
1864 60 g. "Manifesto" (W. Weiss) 10 10
Nos. 1863/4 are vert.

1968. Polish Martyrdom and Resistance, 1939–45 (4th series). As T **491**.
1865 40 g. grey 10 10
1866 40 g. brown 10 10
1867 40 g. brown 10 10
1868 40 g. blue 10 10
1869 40 g. brown 10 10
DESIGNS—HORIZ: No. 1865, Tomb of Unknown Soldier, Warsaw; No. 1866, Guerillas' Monument, Kartuzy. VERT: No. 1867, Insurgents' Monument, Poznan; No. 1868, People's Guard Insurgents' Monument, Polichno; No. 1869, Rotunda, Zamosc.

518 "Start of Hunt" (W. Kossak)

1968. Paintings. Hunting Scenes. Multicoloured.
1870 20 g. Type **518** 10 10
1871 40 g. "Hunting with Falcon" (J. Kossak) 10 10
1872 60 g. "Wolves' Raid" (A. Wierusz-Kowalski) . . 10 10
1873 1 z. 50 "Home-coming with a Bear" (J. Falat) 40 10
1874 2 z. 50 "The Fox-hunt" (T. Sutherland) 30 10
1875 3 z. 40 "The Boar-hunt" (F. Snyders) 40 15
1876 4 z. 50 "Hunters' Rest" (W. G. Pierow) . . . . . 1·50 50
1877 8 z. 50 "Hunting a Lion in Morocco" (Delacroix) . . 1·40 70

519 Maltese Terrier **520** House Sign

1969. Pedigree Dogs. Multicoloured.
1878 20 g. Type **519** 20 10
1879 40 g. Wire-haired fox-terrier . 30 15
1880 60 g. Afghan hound 30 20
1881 1 z. 50 Rough-haired terrier . 30 20
1882 2 z. 50 English setter 60 20
1883 3 z. 40 Pekinese 75 25
1884 4 z. 50 Alsatian . . . . 1·60 50
1885 8 z. 50 Pointer . . . . 3·00 1·00
Nos. 1879, 1884 and 1885 are vert.

1969. 9th Polish Democratic Party Congress.
1886 **520** 60 g. red, black & grey . 10 10

521 "Dove" and Wheat-ears **522** Running

1969. 5th Congress of United Peasant's Party.
1887 **521** 60 g. multicoloured . . . 10 10

1969. 75th Anniv of International Olympic Committee and 50th Anniv of Polish Olympic Committee. Multicoloured.
1888 10 g. Type **522** 10 10
1889 20 g. Gynmastics 10 10
1890 40 g. Weightlifting 10 10
1891 60 g. Throwing the javelin . . 10 10
1892 2 z. 50+50 g. Throwing the discus 20 10
1893 3 z. 40+1 z. Running 30 15
1894 4 z.+1 z. 50 Wrestling . . . 75 25
1895 7 z.+2 z. Fencing . . . . . . 1·40 35

523 Pictorial Map of Swietokrzyski National Park

1969. Tourism (1st series). Multicoloured.
1896 40 g. Type **523** 10 10
1897 60 g. Niedzica Castle (vert) . 10 10
1898 1 z. 35 Kolobrzeg Lighthouse and yacht 30 10
1899 1 z. 50 Szczecin Castle and Harbour 30 10
1900 2 z. 50 Torun and Vistula River 25 10
1901 3 z. 40 Klodzko, Silesia (vert) 35 10
1902 4 z. Sulejow 55 25
1903 4 z. 50 Kazimierz Dolny market-place (vert) 60 25
See also Nos. 1981/5.

524 Route Map and "Opty"

1969. Leonid Teliga's World Voyage in Yacht "Opty".
1904 **524** 60 g. multicoloured . . . 30 10

525 Copernicus (after woodcut by T. Stimer) and Inscription **526** "Memory" Flame and Badge

1969. 500th Birth Anniv (1973) of Copernicus (1st issue).
1905 **525** 40 g. brown, red & yellow 15 10
1906 – 60 g. blue, red & green . 20 10
1907 – 2 z. 50 olive, red & pur . 50 15
DESIGNS: 60 g. Copernicus (after J. Falck) and 15th-century globe; 2 z. 50, Copernicus (after painting by J. Matejko) and diagram of heliocentric system.
See also Nos. 1995/7, 2069/72, 2167/70, 2213/14 and 2217/21.

1969. 5th National Alert of Polish Boy Scout Association.
1908 **526** 60 g. black, red & blue . 10 10
1909 – 60 g. red, black & green 10 10
1910 – 60 g. black, green and red 10 10
DESIGN: No. 1909, "Defence" eagle and badge; No. 1910, "Labour" map and badge.

528 Coal-miner

1969. 25th Anniv of Polish People's Republic. Multicoloured.
1911 60 g. Frontier guard and arms 10 10
1912 60 g. Plock Petro-chemical Plant 10 10
1913 60 g. Combine-harvester . . 10 10
1914 60 g. Grand Theatre, Warsaw 10 10
1915 60 g. Curie statue and University, Lublin 10 10
1916 60 g. Type **528** 10 10
1917 60 g. Sulphur-worker 10 10
1918 60 g. Steel-worker 10 10
1919 60 g. Shipbuilder 10 10
Nos. 1911/5 are vert and have white arms embossed in the top portion of the stamps.

529 Astronauts and Module on Moon

1969. 1st Man on the Moon.
1920 **529** 2 z. 50 multicoloured . . 65 35

530 "Motherhood" (S. Wyspianski)

1969. Polish Paintings. Multicoloured.
1921 20 g. Type **530** 10 10
1922 40 g. "Hamlet" (J. Malczewski) 10 10
1923 60 g. "Indian Summer" (J. Chelmonski) 10 10
1924 2 z. "Two Girls" (Olga Bonznanska) (vert) 25 10
1925 2 z. 50 "The Sun of May" (J. Mehoffer) (vert) 15 10
1926 3 z. 40 "Woman combing her Hair" (W. Slewinski) . . . 30 20
1927 5 z. 50 "Still Life" (J. Pankiewicz) 65 30
1928 7 z. "Abduction of the King's Daughter" (W. Wojtkiewicz) 1·25 35

531 "Nike" statue **533** Krzczonow (Lublin) Costumes

532 Majdanek Memorial

1969. 4th Congress of Fighters for Freedom and Democracy Association.
1929 **531** 60 g. red, black & brown 10 10

1969. Inaug of Majdanek Memorial.
1930 **532** 40 g. black and mauve . 15 10

1969. Provincial Costumes. Multicoloured.
1931 40 g. Type **533** 10 10
1932 60 g. Lowicz (Lodz) 10 10
1933 1 z. 15 Rozbasrk (Katowice) 15 10
1934 1 z. 35 Lower Silesia (Wroclaw) 15 10
1935 1 z. 50 Opoczno (Lodz) . . . 30 10
1936 4 z. 50 Sacz (Cracow) . . . 60 15
1937 5 z. Highlanders, Cracow . . 50 35
1938 7 z. Kurple (Warsaw) 70 35

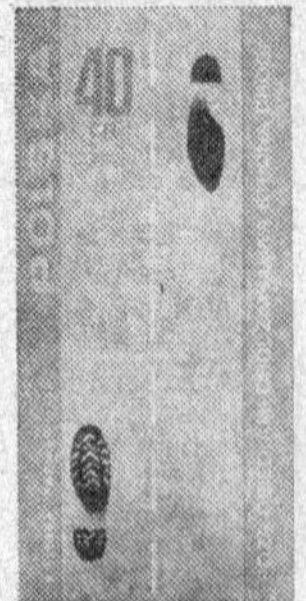

534 "Pedestrians Keep Left" **535** "Welding" and I.L.O. Emblem

1969. Road Safety. Multicoloured.

1939 40 g. Type **534** 10 10
1940 60 g. "Drive Carefully" (horses on road) 10 10
1941 2 z. 50 "Do Not Dazzle" (cars on road at night) 30 15

1969. 50th Anniv of I.L.O.

1942 **535** 2 z. 50 blue and gold . . 25 10

536 "The Bell-founder" **537** "Angel" (19th-century)

1969. Miniatures from Behem's Code of 1505. Multicoloured.

1943 40 g. Type **536** 10 10
1944 60 g. "The Painter" 10 10
1945 1 z. 35 "The Woodcarver" . 15 10
1946 1 z. 55 "The Shoemaker" . . 20 10
1947 2 z. 50 "The Cooper" 25 10
1948 3 z. 40 "The Baker" 30 10
1949 4 z. 50 "The Tailor" 60 30
1950 7 z. "The Bowyer" . . . . . 1·00 40

1969. Polish Folk Sculpture. Multicoloured.

1951 20 g. Type **537** 10 10
1952 40 g. "Sorrowful Christ" (19th-century) 10 10
1953 60 g. "Sorrowful Christ" (19th-cent.) (different) 10 10
1954 2 z. "Weeping Woman" (19th-century) 20 10
1955 2 z. 50 "Adam and Eve" (F. Czajkowski) 20 10
1956 3 z. 40 "Girl with Birds" (L. Kudla) 35 10
1957 5 z. 50+1 z. 50 "Choir" (A. Zegadlo) 80 30
1958 7 z.+1 z. "Organ-grinder" (Z. Skretowicz) 90 50

Nos. 1957/8 are larger, size 25×35 mm.

538 Leopold Staff

1969. Modern Polish Writers.

1959 **538** 40 g. black, olive & green 10 10
1960 – 60 g. black, red and pink 10 10
1961 – 1 z. 35 black, deep blue and blue 10 10
1962 – 1 z. 50 black, vio & lilac 10 10
1963 – 1 z. 55 black, deep green and green 15 10
1964 – 2 z. 50 black, deep blue and blue 20 10
1965 – 3 z. 40 blk, brn and flesh 30 20

DESIGNS: 60 g. Wladyslaw Broniewski; 1 z. 35, Leon Kruczkowski; 1 z. 50, Julian Tuwim; 1 z. 55, Konstanty Ildefons Galczynski; 2 z. 50, Maria Dabrowska; 3 z. 40, Zofia Nalkowska.

539 Nike Monument

1970. 25th Anniv of Liberation of Warsaw.

1966 **539** 60 g. multicoloured . . . 25 10

540 Early Printing Works and Colour Dots

1970. Centenary of Printers' Trade Union.

1967 **540** 60 g. multicoloured . . 10 10

541 Mallard

1970. Game Birds. Multicoloured.

1968 40 g. Type **541** 25 10
1969 60 g. Ring-necked pheasant . 45 10
1970 1 z. 15 Woodcock 35 10
1971 1 z. 35 Ruff 45 10
1972 1 z. 50 Wood pigeon 45 15
1973 3 z. 40 Black grouse 50 15
1974 7 z. Grey partridge . . . . 2·75 1·00
1975 8 z. 50 Capercaillie . . . . 3·00 1·00

542 Lenin at Desk

1970. Birth Centenary of Lenin.

1976 **542** 40 g. grey and red . . . 10 10
1977 – 60 g. brown and red . . 10 10
1978 – 2 z. 50 black and red . . 20 10

DESIGNS: 60 g. Lenin addressing meeting; 2 z. 50, Lenin at Party conference.

543 Polish and Russian Soldiers in Berlin

1970. 25th Anniv of Liberation.

1980 **543** 60 g. multicoloured . . 15 10

1970. Tourism (2nd series). As T **523**, but with imprint "PWPW 70". Multicoloured.

1981 60 g. Town Hall, Wroclaw (vert) 15 10
1982 60 g. View of Opol 15 10
1983 60 g. Legnica Castle 15 10
1984 60 g. Bolkow Castle 15 10
1985 60 g. Town Hall, Brzeg . . 15 10

544 Polish "Flower"

1970. 25th Anniv of Return of Western Territories.

1986 **544** 60 g. red, silver and green 15 10

545 Movement Flag **546** U.P.U. Emblem and New Headquarters

1970. 75th Anniv of Peasant Movement.

1987 **545** 60 g. multicoloured . . . 10 10

1970. New U.P.U. Headquarters Building, Berne.

1988 **546** 2 z. 50 blue and turquoise 20 10

547 Footballers **548** Hand with "Lamp of Learning"

1970. Gornik Zabrze v. Manchester City, Final of European Cup-winners Cup Championship.

1989 **547** 60 g. multicoloured . . . 20 10

1970. 150th Anniv of Plock Scientific Society.

1990 **548** 60 g. olive, red and black 10 10

549 "Olympic Runners" (from Greek amphora)

1970. 10th Session of Int Olympic Academy.

1991 **549** 60 g. red, yellow & black 10 10
1992 – 60 g. violet, blue & black 10 10
1993 – 60 g. multicoloured . . . 10 10

DESIGNS: No. 1992, "The Archer"; No. 1993, Modern runners.

550 Copernicus (after miniature by Bacciarelli) and Bologna

1970. 500th Birth Anniv (1973) of Copernicus. (2nd issue).

1995 **550** 40 g. green, orange & lilac 15 10
1996 – 60 g. lilac, green & yellow 15 10
1997 – 2 z. 50 brn, blue and green 50 10

DESIGNS: 60 g. Copernicus (after miniature by Lesseur) and Padua; 2 z. 50, Copernicus (by N. Zinck, after lost Goluchowska portrait) and Ferrara.

551 "Aleksander Orlowski" (self-portrait)

1970. Polish Miniatures. Multicoloured.

1998 20 g. Type **551** 10 10
1999 40 g. "Jan Matejko" (self-portrait) 10 10
2000 60 g. "Stefan Batory" (unknown artist) 10 10
2001 2 z. "Maria Leszczynska" (unknown artist) 10 10
2002 2 z. 50 "Maria Walewska" (Marie-Victorie Jacquetot) . 20 10
2003 3 z. 40 "Tadeusz Kosciuszko" (Jan Rustem) 25 10
2004 5 z. 50 "Samuel Linde" (G. Landolfi) 70 40
2005 7 z. "Michal Oginski" (Nanette Windisch) . . . . 1·40 55

552 U.N. Emblem within "Eye"

1970. 25th Anniv of United Nations.

2006 **552** 2 z. 50 multicoloured . . 25 10

553 Piano Keyboard and Chopin's Signature **554** Population Pictograph

1970. 8th International Chopin Piano Competition.

2007 **553** 2 z. 50 black & violet . . 25 10

1970. National Census. Multicoloured.

2008 40 g. Type **554** 10 10
2009 60 g. Family in "house" . . 15 10

555 Destroyer "Piorun" (½-size illustration)

1970. Polish Warships, World War II.

2010 **555** 40 g. brown 25 10
2011 – 60 g. black 40 15
2012 – 2 z. 50 brown . . . . . 1·00 30

DESIGNS: 60 g. "Orzel" (submarine); 2 z. 50, H.M.S. "Garland" (destroyer loaned to Polish Navy).

556 "Expressions" (Maria Jarema)

1970. Stamp Day. Contemporary Polish Paintings. Multicoloured.

2013 20 g. "The Violin-cellist" (J. Nowosielski) (vert) . . 10 10
2014 40 g. "View of Lodz" (B. Liberski) (vert) 10 10
2015 60 g. "Studio Concert" (W. Taranczewski) (vert) . 10 10
2016 1 z. 50 "Still Life" (Z. Pronaszko) (vert) . . . 10 10
2017 2 z. "Hanging-up Washing" (A. Wroblewski) (vert) . . 15 10
2018 3 z. 40 Type **556** 25 10
2019 4 z. "Canal in the Forest" (P. Potworowski) 55 20
2020 8 z. 50 "The Sun" (W. Strzeminski) . . . . . 1·10 50

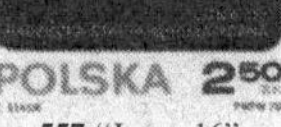

557 "Luna 16" landing on Moon **558** "Stag" (detail from "Daniel" tapestry)

1970. Moon Landing of "Luna 16".

2021 **557** 2 z. 50 multicoloured . . 35 15

1970. Tapestries in Wawel Castle. Multicoloured.

2022 60 g. Type **558** 10 10
2023 1 z. 15 "White Stork" (detail) 30 10
2024 1 z. 35 "Panther fighting Dragon" 15 10
2025 2 z. "Man's Head" (detail "Deluge" tapestry) 20 10
2026 2 z. 50 "Child with Bird" (detail "Adam Tilling the Soil" tapestry) 25 10
2027 4 z. "God, Adam and Eve" (detail "Happiness in Paradise" tapestry) 50 25
2028 4 z. 50 Royal Monogram tapestry 80 35

559 Cadet ship "Dar Pomorza"

1971. Polish Ships. Multicoloured.

2030 40 g. Type **559** 15 10
2031 60 g. Liner "Stefan Batory" . 15 10
2032 1 z. 15 Ice-breaker "Perkun" 25 10

2033 1 z. 35 Lifeboat "R-1" . . . 35 10
2034 1 z. 50 Bulk carrier "Ziemia Szczecinska" 40 10
2035 2 z. 50 Tanker "Beskidy" . . 50 10
2036 5 z. Freighter "Hel" . . . . 1·00 20
2037 8 z. 50 Ferry "Gryf" . . . . 2·10 50

560 Checiny Castle

1971. Polish Castles. Multicoloured.
2038 20 g. Type **560** 10 10
2039 40 g. Wisnicz 10 10
2040 60 g. Bedzin 10 10
2041 2 z. Ogrodzieniec 15 10
2042 2 z. 50 Niedzica 15 10
2043 3 z. 40 Kwidzyn 30 10
2044 4 z. Pieskowa Skala 35 15
2045 8 z. 50 Lidzbark Warminski . 80 60

561 Battle of Pouilly, J. Dabrowski and W. Wroblewski

1971. Centenary of Paris Commune.
2046 **561** 60 g. brown, blue & red . 15 10

562 Plantation **563** "Bishop Marianos"

1971. Forestry Management. Multicoloured.
2047 40 g. Type **562** 10 10
2048 60 g. Forest (27×47 mm) . . 10 10
2049 1 z. 50 Tree-felling 30 10

1971. Fresco Discoveries made by Polish Expedition at Faras, Nubia. Multicoloured.
2050 40 g. Type **563** 10 10
2051 60 g. "St. Anne" 10 10
2052 1 z. 15 "Archangel Michael" 10 10
2053 1 z. 35 "The Hermit, Anamon" 10 10
2054 1 z. 50 "Head of Archangel Michael" 15 10
2055 4 z. 50 "Evangelists' Cross" . 35 10
2056 5 z. "Christ protecting a nobleman" 55 25
2057 7 z. "Archangel Michael" (half-length) 65 40

564 Revolutionaries

1971. 50th Anniv of Silesian Insurrection.
2058 **564** 60 g. brown and gold . . 15 10

565 "Soldiers"

1971. 25th Anniv of U.N.I.C.E.F. Children's Drawings. Multicoloured.
2060 20 g. "Peacock" (vert) . . . 10 10
2061 40 g. Type **565** 10 10
2062 60 g. "Lady Spring" (vert) . 10 10
2063 2 z. "Cat and Ball" 15 10
2064 2 z. 50 "Flowers in Jug" (vert) 20 10
2065 3 z. 40 "Friendship" 30 10
2066 5 z. 50 "Clown" (vert) . . . 70 35
2067 7 z. "Strange Planet" 90 40

566 Fair Emblem **567** Copernicus's House, Torun

1971. 40th International Fair, Poznan.
2068 **566** 60 g. multicoloured . . 10 10

1971. 500th Birth Anniv (1973) of Copernicus (3rd issue). Multicoloured.
2069 40 g. Type **567** 10 10
2070 60 g. Collegium Naius, Jagiellonian University, Cracow (horiz) 10 10
2071 2 z. 50 Olsztyn Castle (horiz) 20 10
2072 4 z. Frombork Cathedral . . 60 25

568 Folk Art Pattern **569** "Head of Worker" (X. Dunikowski)

1971. Folk Art. "Paper Cut-outs" showing various patterns.
2073 **568** 20 g. black, green & bl . 10 10
2074 – 40 g. blue, green & cream 10 10
2075 – 60 g. brown, blue & grey 10 10
2076 – 1 z. 15 purple, brn & buff 10 10
2077 – 1 z. 35 green, red & yell 20 10

1971. Modern Polish Sculpture. Multicoloured.
2078 40 g. Type **569** 10 10
2079 40 g. "Foundryman" (X. Dunikowski) 10 10
2080 60 g. "Miners" (M. Wiecek) 15 10
2081 60 g. "Harvester" (S. Horno-Poplawski) 15 10

570 Congress Emblem and Computer Tapes

1971. 6th Polish Technical Congress, Warsaw.
2083 **570** 60 g. violet and red . . 15 10

571 "Angel" (J. Mehoffer) **573** PZL P-11C Fighters

572 "Mrs. Fedorowicz" (W. Pruszkowski)

1971. Stained Glass Windows. Multicoloured.
2084 20 g. Type **571** 10 10
2085 40 g. "Lillies" (S. Wyspianski) 10 10
2086 60 g. "Iris" (S. Wyspianski) 10 10
2087 1 z. 35 "Apollo" (S. Wyspianski) 15 10
2088 1 z. 55 "Two Wise Men" (14th-century) 15 10
2089 3 z. 40 "The Flight into Egypt" (14th-century) 30 20
2090 5 z. 50 "Jacob" (14th-century) 60 25
2091 8 z. 50+4 z. "Madonna" (15th-century) 90 50

1971. Contemporary Art from National Museum, Cracow. Multicoloured.
2092 40 g. Type **572** 10 10
2093 50 g. "Woman with Book" (T. Czyzeski) 10 10
2094 60 g. "Girl with Chrysanthemums" (O. Boznanska) 10 10
2095 2 z. 50 "Girl in Red Dress" (J. Pankiewicz) (horiz) . . . 15 10
2096 3 z. 40 "Reclining Nude" (L. Chwistek) (horiz) . . . 30 15
2097 4 z. 50 "Strange Garden" (J. Mehoffer) 45 15
2098 5 z. "Wife in White Hat" (Z. Pronaszko) 55 15
2099 7 z.+1 z. "Seated Nude" (W. Weiss) 75 50

1971. Polish Aircraft of World War II. Multicoloured.
2100 90 g. Type **573** 15 10
2101 1 z. 50 PZL 23A Karas fighters 25 10
2102 3 z. 40 PZL P-37 Los bomber 40 10

574 Royal Castle, Warsaw (pre-1939)

1971. Reconstruction of Royal Castle, Warsaw.
2103 **574** 60 g. black, red and gold 15 10

575 Astronauts in Moon Rover **576** "Lunokhod 1"

1971. Moon Flight of "Apollo 15".
2104 **575** 2 z. 50 multicoloured . . 45 15

1971. Moon Flight of "Lunik 17" and "Lunokhod 1".
2106 **576** 2 z. 50 multicoloured . . 45 15

577 Worker at Wheel **578** Ship-building

1971. 6th Polish United Workers' Party Congress (a) Party Posters.
2108 **577** 60 g. red, blue & grey . . 10 10
2109 60 g. red and grey (Worker's head) 10 10

(b) Industrial Development. Each in gold and red.
2110 60 g. Type **578** 10 10
2111 60 g. Building construction . 10 10
2112 60 g. Combine-harvester . . . 10 10
2113 60 g. Motor-car production . 10 10
2114 60 g. Pit-head 10 10
2115 60 g. Petro-chemical plant . . 10 10

579 "Prunus cerasus"

1971. Flowers of Trees and Shrubs. Multicoloured.
2117 10 g. Type **579** 10 10
2118 20 g. "Malusniedzwetzskyana" 10 10
2119 40 g. "Pyrus L." 10 10
2120 60 g. "Prunus persica" . . . 10 10
2121 1 z. 15 "Magnolia kobus" . . 15 10
2122 1 z. 35 "Crategus oxyacantha" 15 10
2123 2 z. 50 "Malus M." 20 10
2124 3 z. 40 "Aesculus carnea" . . 30 10
2125 5 z. "Robinia pseudacacia" . 1·00 25
2126 8 z. 50 "Prunus avium" . . . 1·90 60

580 "Worker" (sculpture, J. Januszkiewicz)

1972. 30th Anniv of Polish Workers' Coalition.
2127 **580** 60 g. black and red . . . 15 10

581 Luge

1972. Winter Olympic Games, Sapporo, Japan. Multicoloured.
2128 40 g. Type **581** 10 10
2129 60 g. Slalom (vert) 10 10
2130 1 z. 65 Biathlon (vert) . . . 30 10
2131 2 z. 50 Ski jumping 45 20

582 "Heart" and Cardiogram Trace **583** Running

1972. World Heart Month.
2133 **582** 2 z. 50 multicoloured . . 20 10

1972. Olympic Games, Munich. Multicoloured.
2134 20 g. Type **583** 10 10
2135 30 g. Archery 10 10
2136 40 g. Boxing 10 10
2137 60 g. Fencing 10 10
2138 2 z. 50 Wrestling 15 10
2139 3 z. 40 Weightlifting 20 10
2140 5 z. Cycling 75 30
2141 8 z. 50 Shooting . . . . . . 1·25 45

584 Cyclists **585** Polish War Memorial, Berlin

1972. 25th International Peace Cycle Race.
2143 **584** 60 g. multicoloured . . . 20 10

1972. "Victory Day, 1945".
2144 **585** 60 g. green 15 10

586 "Rodlo" Emblem **587** Polish Knight of 972 A.D

1972. 50th Anniv of Polish Posts in Germany.
2145 **586** 60 g. ochre, red & green 15 10

1972. Millenary of Battle of Cedynia.
2146 **587** 60 g. multicoloured . . . 15 10

588 Cheetah

1972. Zoo Animals. Multicoloured.

2147		20 g. Type **588**	15	10
2148		40 g. Giraffe (vert)	20	10
2149		60 g. Toco toucan	30	10
2150		1 z. 35 Chimpanzee	20	10
2151		1 z. 65 Common gibbon	30	10
2152		3 z. 40 Crocodile	40	10
2153		4 z. Red kangaroo	70	15
2154		4 z. 50 Tiger (vert)	2·75	1·00
2155		7 z. Mountain zebra	3·00	1·25

589 L. Warynski. (founder)

590 F. Dzerzhinsky

1972. 90th Anniv of Proletarian Party.

2156	**589**	60 g. multicoloured	15	10

1972. 95th Birth Anniv of Feliks Dzerzhinsky (Russian politician).

2157	**590**	60 g. black and red	15	10

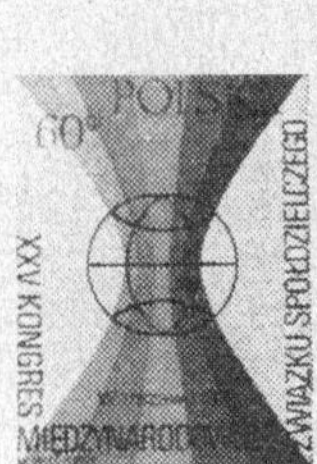

591 Global Emblem

592 Scene from "In Barracks" (ballet)

1972. 25th Int Co-operative Federation Congress.

2158	**591**	60 g. multicoloured	15	10

1972. Death Centenary of Stanislaus Moniuszko (composer). Scenes from Works.

2159	**592**	10 g. violet and gold	10	10
2160	–	20 g. black and gold	10	10
2161	–	40 g. green and gold	10	10
2162	–	60 g. blue and gold	15	10
2163	–	1 z. 15 blue and gold	15	10
2164	–	1 z. 35 blue and gold	15	10
2165	–	1 z. 55 green and gold	15	15
2166	–	2 z. 50 brown and gold	50	25

DESIGNS: 20 g. "The Countess" (opera); 40 g. "The Haunted Manor" (opera); 60 g. "Halka" (opera); 1 z. 15, "New Don Quixote" (ballet); 1 z. 35, "Verbum Nobile"; 1 z. 55, "Ideal" (operetta); 2 z. 50, "Pariah" (opera).

593 "Copernicus the Astronomer"

1972. 500th Birth Anniv (1973) of Nicolas Copernicus. (4th issue).

2167	**593**	40 g. black and blue	10	10
2168	–	60 g. black and orange	15	10
2169	–	2 z. 50 black and red	50	10
2170	–	3 z. 40 black and green	60	30

DESIGNS: 60 g. Copernicus and Polish eagle; 2 z. 50, Copernicus and Medal; 3 z. 40, Copernicus and page of book.

594 "The Amazon" (P. Michalowski)

1972. Stamp Day. Polish Paintings. Multicoloured.

2172		30 g. Type **594**	10	10
2173		40 g. "Ostafi Laskiewicz" (J. Metejko)	10	10
2174		60 g. "Summer Idyll" (W. Gerson)	10	10
2175		2 z. "The Neapolitan Woman" (A. Kotsis)	15	10
2176		2 z. 50 "Girl Bathing" (P. Szyndler)	20	10
2177		3 z. 40 "The Princess of Thum" (A. Grottger)	30	10
2178		4 z. "Rhapsody" (S. Wyspianski)	1·25	45
2179		8 z. 50+4 z. "Young Woman" (J. Malczewski) (horiz)	1·50	75

1972. Nos. 1578/9 surch.

2180		50 g. on 40 g. brown	10	10
2181		90 g. on 40 g. brown	15	10
2182		1 z. on 40 g. brown	10	10
2183		1 z. 50 on 60 g. orange	10	10
2184		2 z. 70 on 40 g. brown	20	10
2185		4 z. on 60 g. orange	30	10
2186		4 z. 50 on 60 g. orange	30	10
2187		4 z. 90 on 60 g. orange	50	15

596 "The Little Soldier" (E. Piwowarski)

1972. Children's Health Centre.

2188	**596**	60 g. black and pink	15	10

597 "Royal Castle, Warsaw". (E. J. Dahlberg, 1656)

598 Chalet, Chocholowska Valley

1972. Restoration of Royal Castle, Warsaw.

2189	**597**	60 g. black, violet & bl	15	10

1972. Tourism. Mountain Chalets. Multicoloured.

2190		40 g. Type **598**	10	10
2191		60 g. Hala Ornak (horiz)	10	10
2192		1 z. 55 Hala Gasienicowa	10	10
2193		1 z. 65 Valley of Five Lakes (horiz)	20	10
2194		2 z. 50 Morskie Oko	35	10

599 Trade Union Banners

600 Congress Emblem

1972. 7th Polish Trade Union Congresses.

2195	**599**	60 g. multicoloured	15	10

1972. 5th Socialist Youth Union Congress.

2196	**600**	60 g. multicoloured	15	10

601 Japanese Azalea

1972. Flowering Shrubs. Multicoloured.

2197		40 g. Type **601**	10	10
2198		50 g. Alpine rose	10	10
2199		60 g. Pomeranian honeysuckle	10	10
2200		1 z. 65 Chinese quince	10	10
2201		2 z. 50 Korean cranberry	20	10
2202		3 z. 40 Pontic azalea	30	10
2203		4 z. Delavay's white syringa	70	25
2204		8 z. 50 Common lilac ("Massena")	1·50	65

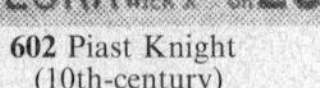

602 Piast Knight (10th-century)

603 Copernicus

1972. Polish Cavalry Through the Ages. Mult.

2205		20 g. Type **602**	10	10
2206		40 g. 13th-century knight	10	10
2207		60 g. Knight of Wladyslaw Jagiello's Army (15th-century) (horiz)	10	10
2208		1 z. 35 17th-century hussar	10	10
2209		4 z. Lancer of National Guard (18th-century)	60	15
2210		4 z. 50 "Congress Kingdom" cavalry officer	65	20
2211		5 z. Trooper of Light Cavalry (1939) (horiz)	1·25	35
2212		7 z. Trooper of People's Army (1945)	1·40	50

1972. 500th Birth Anniv (1973) of Copernicus (5th issue).

2213	**603**	1 z. brown	15	10
2214		1 z. 50 ochre	20	10

604 Couple with Hammer and Sickle

605 "Copernicus as Young Man" (Bacciarelli)

1972. 50th Anniv of U.S.S.R. Multicoloured.

2215		40 g. Type **604**	10	10
2216		60 g. Red star and globe	10	10

1973. 500th Birth Anniv of Copernicus (6th issue). Multicoloured.

2217		1 z. Type **605**	15	10
2218		1 z. 50 "Copernicus" (anon)	15	10
2219		2 z. 70 "Copernicus" (Zinck Nor)	25	10
2220		4 z. "Copernicus" (from Strasbourg clock)	50	25
2221		4 z. 90 "Copernicus" (Jan Matejko) (horiz)	65	35

606 Coronation Sword

607 Statue of Lenin

1973. Polish Art. Multicoloured.

2222		50 g. Type **606**	10	10
2223		1 z. Kruzlowa Madonna (detail)	10	10
2224		1 z. Armour of hussar	10	10
2225		1 z. 50 Carved head from Wavel Castle	10	10
2226		1 z. 50 Silver cockerel	10	10
2227		2 z. 70 Armorial eagle	25	10
2228		4 z. 90 Skarbimierz Madonna	65	35
2229		8 z. 50 "Portrait of Tenczynski" (anon.)	1·00	50

1973. Unveiling of Lenin's Statue, Nowa Huta.

2230	**607**	1 z. multicoloured	15	10

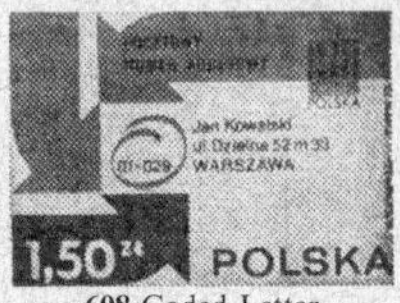

608 Coded Letter

1973. Introduction of Postal Codes.

2231	**608**	1 z. multicoloured	15	10

609 Wolf

1973. International Hunting Council Congress and 50th Anniv of Polish Hunting Association. Game Animals. Multicoloured.

2232		50 g. Type **609**	10	10
2233		1 z. Mouflon	10	10
2234		1 z. 50 Elk	10	10
2235		2 z. 70 Capercaillie	40	10
2236		3 z. Roe deer	30	10
2237		4 z. 50 Lynx	65	20
2238		4 z. 90 Red deer	1·75	35
2239		5 z. Wild boar	2·00	45

610 "Salyut"

611 Open Book and Flame

1973. Cosmic Research. Multicoloured.

2240		4 z. 90 Type **610**	45	25
2241		4 z. 90 "Copernicus" (U.S. satellite)	45	25

1973. 2nd Polish Science Congress, Warsaw.

2242	**611**	1 z. 50 multicoloured	15	10

612 Ancient Seal of Poznan

613 M. Nowotko

1973. "Polska 73" Philatelic Exhibition, Poznan. Multicoloured.

2243		1 z. Type **612**	10	10
2244		1 z. 50 Tombstone of N. Tomicki	10	10
2245		2 z. 70 Kalisz paten	25	10
2246		4 z. Bronze gates, Gniezno Cathedral (horiz)	40	20

1973. 80th Birth Anniv of Marceli Nowotko (party leader).

2249	**613**	1 z. 50 black and red	15	10

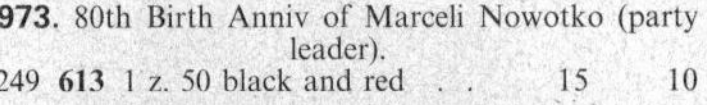

614 Cherry Blossom

1973. Protection of the Environment. Multicoloured.

2250		50 g. Type **614**	10	10
2251		90 g. Cattle in meadow	10	10
2252		1 z. White stork on nest	70	10
2253		1 z. 50 Pond life	15	10
2254		2 z. 70 Meadow flora	25	10
2255		4 z. 90 Ocean fauna	55	30
2256		5 z. Forest life	3·50	45
2257		6 z. 50 Agricultural produce	1·75	50

615 Motor-cyclist

1973. World Speedway Race Championships, Chorzow.
2258 **615** 1 z. 50 multicoloured . . 15 10

616 "Copernicus" (M. Bacciarelli)

1973. Stamp Day.
2259 **616** 4 z.+2 z. multicoloured . 50 25

617 Tank

1973. 30th Anniv of Polish People's Army. Mult.
2260 1 z. Type **617** 15 10
2261 1 z. Mikoyan Gurevich MiG-21D airplane 20 10
2262 1 z. 50 Guided missile 20 10
2263 1 z. 50 Missile boat 25 10

618 G. Piramowicz and Title Page

1973. Bicent of Nat Educational Commission.
2264 **618** 1 z. brown and yellow . . 10 10
2265 – 1 z. 50 green, & lt green . 15 10
DESIGN: 1 z. 50, J. Sniadecki, H. Kollataj and J. U. Niemcewicz.

619 Pawel Strzelecki (explorer) and Red Kangaroo

1973. Polish Scientists. Multicoloured.
2266 1 z. Type **619** 15 10
2267 1 z. Henryk Arctowski (Polar explorer) and Adelie penguins 45 10
2268 1 z. 50 Stefan Rogozinski (explorer) and "Lucy-Margaret" (schooner) . . . 30 10
2269 1 z. 50 Benedykt Dybowski (zoologist) and sable, Lake Baikal 20 10
2270 2 z. Bronislaw Malinowski (anthropologist) and New Guinea dancers 25 10
2271 2 z. 70 Stefan Drzewiecki (oceanographer) and submarine 35 10
2272 3 z. Edward Strasburger (botanist) and classified plants 35 15
2273 8 z. Ignacy Domeyko (geologist) and Chilean desert landscape 1·40 50

HAVE YOU READ THE NOTES AT THE BEGINNING OF THIS CATALOGUE?
These often provide the answers to the enquiries we receive.

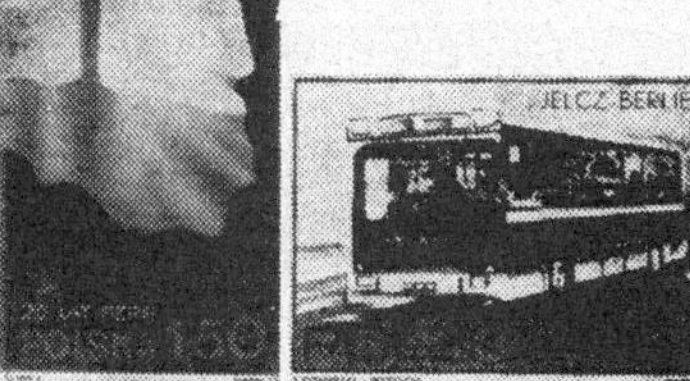

620 Polish Flag **621** Jelcz-Berliet Coach

1973. 25th Anniv of Polish United Workers' Party.
2274 **620** 1 z. 40 red, blue and gold 15 10

1973. Polish Motor Vehicles. Multicoloured.
2275 50 g. Type **621** 10 10
2276 90 g. Jelcz "316" truck . . . 10 10
2277 1 z. Polski-Fiat "126p" saloon 10 10
2278 1 z. 50 Polski-Fiat "125p" saloon and mileage records 10 10
2279 4 z. Nysa "M-521" utility van 40 40
2280 4 z. 50 Star "660" truck . . 75 50

622 Iris **623** Cottage, Kurpie

1974. Flowers. Drawings by S. Wyspianski.
2281 **622** 50 g. purple 10 10
2282 – 1 z. green 10 10
2283 – 1 z. 50 red 10 10
2284 – 3 z. violet 35 10
2285 – 4 z. blue 40 10
2286 – 4 z. 50 green 60 25
FLOWERS: 1 z. Dandelion; 1 z. 50, Rose; 3 z. Thistle; 4 z. Cornflower; 4 z. 50, Clover.

1974. Wooden Architecture. Multicoloured.
2287 1 z. Type **623** 10 10
2288 1 z. 50 Church, Sekowa . . 10 10
2289 4 z. Town Hall, Sulmierzycc 30 10
2290 4 z. 50 Church, Lachowice . 35 10
2291 4 z. 90 Windmill, Sobienie Jeziory 55 20
2292 5 z. Orthodox Church, Ulucz 60 30

624 19th-century Mail Coach **625** Cracow Motif

1974. Centenary of Universal Postal Union.
2293 **624** 1 z. 50 multicoloured . . 15 10

1974. "SOCPHILEX IV" Int Stamp Exn, Katowice. Regional Floral Embroideries. Multicoloured.
2294 50 g. Type **625** 10 10
2295 1 z. 50 Lowicz motif 10 10
2296 4 z. Silesian motif 35 15

626 Association Emblem **627** Soldier and Dove

1974. 5th Congress of Fighters for Freedom and Democracy Association, Warsaw.
2298 **626** 1 z. 50 red 15 10

1974. 29th Anniv of Victory over Fascism in Second World War.
2299 **627** 1 z. 50 multicoloured . . 15 10

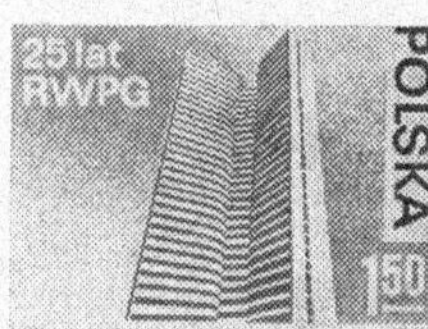

628 "Comecon" Headquarters, Moscow

1974. 25th Anniv of Council for Mutual Economic Aid.
2300 **628** 1 z. 50 brown, red & blue 15 10

629 World Cup Emblem

1974. World Cup Football Championships, West Germany. Multicoloured.
2301 4 z. 90 Type **629** 50 20
2302 4 z. 90 Players and Olympic Gold Medal of 1972 . . . 50 20

630 Model of 16th-century Galleon **631** Title page of "Chess" by J. Kochanowski

1974. Sailing Ships. Multicoloured.
2304 1 z. Type **630** 25 10
2305 1 z. 50 Sloop "Dal" (1934) . 25 10
2306 2 z. 70 Yacht "Opty" (Teliga's circumnavigation, 1969) . . 35 10
2307 4 z. Cadet ship "Dar Pomorza", 1972 . . . . 65 25
2308 4 z. 90 Yacht "Polonez" (Baranowski's circumnavigation, 1973) 95 35

1974. 10th Inter-Chess Festival, Lublin. Mult.
2309 1 z. Type **631** 20 10
2310 1 z. 50 "Education" (18th-century engraving, D. Chodowiecki) 30 10

632 Lazienkowska Road Junction

1974. Opening of Lazienkowska Flyover.
2311 **632** 1 z. 50 multicoloured . . 15 10

633 Face and Map of Poland **634** Strawberries

1974. 30th Anniv of Polish People's Republic.
2312 **633** 1 z. 50 black, gold & red . 15 10
2313 – 1 z. 50 multicoloured (silver background) 15 10
2314 – 1 z. 50 multicoloured (red background) 15 10
DESIGN—31×43 mm: Nos. 2313/14, Polish "Eagle".

1974. 19th Int Horticultural Congress, Warsaw. Fruits, Vegetables and Flowers. Multicoloured.
2316 50 g. Type **634** 10 10
2317 90 g. Blackcurrants 10 10
2318 1 z. Apples 10 10
2319 1 z. 50 Cucumbers 15 10
2320 2 z. 70 Tomatoes 25 10
2321 4 z. 50 Green Peas 60 20
2322 4 z. 90 Pansies 90 25
2323 5 z. Nasturtiums . . . . . . 1·25 30

635 Civic Militia and Security Service Emblem **636** "Child in Polish Costume" (L. Orlowski)

1974. 30th Anniv of Polish Civic Militia and Security Service.
2324 **635** 1 z. 50 multicoloured . . 15 10

1974. Stamp Day. "The Child in Polish Costume" Painting. Multicoloured.
2325 50 g. Type **636** 10 10
2326 90 g. "Girl with Pigeon" (anon) 10 10
2327 1 z. "Portrait of a Girl" (S. Wyspianski) 10 10
2328 1 z. 50 "The Orphan from Poronin" (W. Slewinski) . 10 10
2329 3 z. "Peasant Boy" (K. Sichulski) 25 10
2330 4 z. 50 "Florence Page" (A. Gierymski) 40 10
2331 4 z. 90 "Tadeusz and Dog" (P. Michalowski) 50 25
2332 6 z. 50 "Boy with Doe" (A. Kotsis) 70 40

637 "The Crib", Cracow

1974. Polish Art. Multicoloured.
2333 1 z. Type **637** 10 10
2334 1 z. 50 "The Flight to Egypt" (15th-century polyptych) . 15 10
2335 2 z. "King Sigismund III Vasa" (16th-century miniature) . 20 10
2336 4 z. "King Jan Olbracht" (16th-century title-page) 80 25

638 Angler and Fish **639** "Pablo Neruda" (O. Guayasamin)

1974. Polish Folklore. 16th-century Woodcuts (1st series).
2337 **638** 1 z. black 10 10
2338 – 1 z. 50 blue 15 10
DESIGN: 1 z. 50, Hunter and wild animals.
See also Nos. 2525/6.

1974. 70th Birth Anniv of Pablo Neruda (Chilean poet).
2339 **639** 1 z. 50 multicoloured . . 15 10

640 "Nike" Memorial and National Opera House

1975. 30th Anniv of Warsaw Liberation.
2340 **640** 1 z. 50 multicoloured . . 15 10

641 Male Lesser Kestrel **642** Broken Barbed Wire

1975. Birds of Prey. Multicoloured.
2341 1 z. Type **641** 30 10
2342 1 z. Lesser kestrel (female) . 30 10
2343 1 z. 50 Red-footed falcon (male) 40 10
2344 1 z. 50 Red-footed falcon (female) 40 10
2345 2 z. European hobby 55 10
2346 3 z. Common kestrel 90 10
2347 4 z. Merlin . . . . 2·50 70
2348 8 z. Peregrine falcon . . . . 3·50 1·40

1975. 30th Anniv of Auschwitz Concentration Camp Liberation.
2349 **642** 1 z. 50 black and red . . 20 10

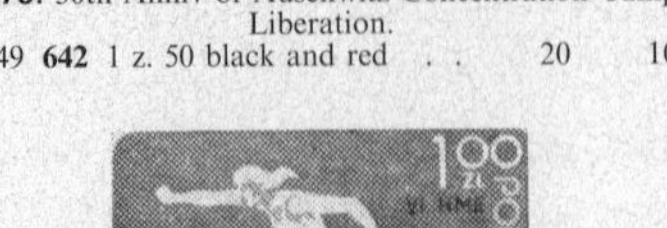

643 Hurdling

1975. 6th European Indoor Athletic Championships, Katowice. Multicoloured.
2350 1 z. Type **643** 10 10
2351 1 z. 50 Pole vault 15 10
2352 4 z. Triple jump 30 10
2353 4 z. 90 Running 35 15

644 "St. Anne" (Veit Stoss)

1975. "Arphila 1975" International Stamp Exhibition, Paris.
2355 **644** 1 z. 50 multicoloured . . 15 10

645 Globe and "Radio Waves"

1975. International Amateur Radio Union Conference, Warsaw.
2356 **645** 1 z. 50 multicoloured . . 15 10

646 Stone, Pine and Tatra Mountains

647 Hands holding Tulips and Rifle

1975. Centenary of Mountain Guides' Association. Multicoloured.
2357 1 z. Type **646** 10 10
2358 1 z. Gentians and Tatra Mountains 10 10
2359 1 z. 50 Sudety Mountains (horiz) 15 10
2360 1 z. 50 Branch of yew (horiz) 15 10
2361 4 z. Beskidy Mountains . . . 40 15
2362 4 z. Arnica blossoms 40 15

1975. 30th Anniv of Victory over Fascism.
2363 **647** 1 z. 50 multicoloured . . 15 10

648 Flags of Member Countries

1975. 20th Anniv of Warsaw Treaty Organization.
2364 **648** 1 z. 50 multicoloured . . 15 10

649 Hens

1975. 26th European Zoo-technical Federation Congress, Warsaw. Multicoloured.
2365 50 g. Type **649** 10 10
2366 1 z. Geese 10 10
2367 1 z. 50 Cattle 15 10
2368 2 z. Cow 15 10
2369 3 z. Wielkopolska horse . . 30 10
2370 4 z. Pure-bred Arab horses . 35 10
2371 4 z. 50 Pigs . . . . 1·25 40
2372 5 z. Sheep . . . . 1·75 60

650 "Apollo" and "Soyuz" Spacecraft linked

651 Organization Emblem

1975. "Apollo-Soyuz" Space Project. Multicoloured.
2373 1 z. 50 Type **650** 15 10
2374 4 z. 90 "Apollo" spacecraft . 50 20
2375 4 z. 90 "Soyuz" spacecraft . 50 20

1975. National Health Protection Fund.
2377 **651** 1 z. 50 blue, blk & silver 15 10

652 U.N. Emblem

1975. 30th Anniv of U.N.O.
2378 **652** 4 z. multicoloured . . . 35 15

653 Polish Flag within "E" for Europe

1975. European Security and Co-operation Conference, Helsinki.
2379 **653** 4 z. red, blue and black . 35 15

654 "Bolek and Lolek"

1975. Children's Television Characters. Mult.
2380 50 g. Type **654** 10 10
2381 1 z. "Jacek" and "Agatka" . 15 10
2382 1 z. 50 "Reksio" (dog) . . . 15 10
2383 4 z. "Telesfor" (dragon) . . 55 15

655 Institute Emblem

656 Women's Faces

1975. 40th Session of International Statistics Institute.
2384 **655** 1 z. 50 multicoloured . . 15 10

1975. International Women's Year.
2385 **656** 1 z. 50 multicoloured . . 15 10

657 Albatros Biplane

1975. 50th Anniv of First Polish Airmail Stamps. Multicoloured.
2386 2 z. 40 Type **657** 20 10
2387 4 z. 90 Ilyushin Il-62 airplane 45 15

658 "Mary and Margaret" and Polish Settlers

659 Frederic Chopin

1975. Bicentenary of American Revolution. Poles in American Life. Multicoloured.
2388 1 z. Type **658** 20 10
2389 1 z. 50 Polish glass-works, Jamestown 15 10
2390 2 z. 70 Helena Modrzejewska (actress) 15 10
2391 4 z. K. Pulaski (soldier) . . . 30 10
2392 6 z. 40 T. Kosciuzko (soldier) 70 30

1975. 9th International Chopin Piano Competition.
2394 **659** 1 z. 50 black, lilac & gold 15 10

660 "Self-portrait"

661 Market Place, Kazimierz Dolny

1975. Stamp Day. Birth Centenary of Xawery Dunikowski (sculptor). Multicoloured.
2395 50 g. Type **660** 10 10
2396 1 z. "Breath" 10 10
2397 1 z. 50 "Maternity" 15 10
2398 8 z. + 4 z. "Silesian Insurrectionists" 90 45

1975. European Architectural Heritage Year.
2399 **661** 1 z. green 10 10
2400 – 1 z. 50 brown 15 10
DESIGN—VERT: 1 z. 50, Town Hall, Zamosc.

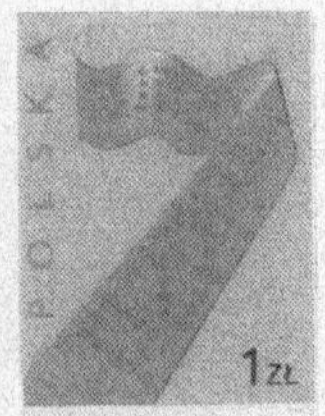

662 "Lodz" (W. Strzeminski)

664 Symbolised Figure "7"

663 Henry IV's Eagle Gravestone Head (14th-century)

1975. "Lodz 75" National Stamp Exhibition.
2401 **662** 4 z. 50 multicoloured . . 40 15

1975. Piast Dynasty of Silesia.
2403 **663** 1 z. green 10 10
2404 – 1 z. 50 brown 10 10
2405 – 4 z. violet 35 15
DESIGNS: 1 z. 50, Seal of Prince Boleslaw of Legnica; 4 z. Coin of last Prince, Jerzy Wilhelm.

1975. 7th Congress of Polish United Workers Party.
2406 **664** 1 z. multicoloured 10 10
2407 – 1 z. 50 red, blue & silver . 15 10
DESIGN: 1 z. 50, Party initials "PZPR".

665 Ski Jumping

1976. Winter Olympic Games, Innsbruck. Mult.
2408 50 g. Type **665** 10 10
2409 1 z. Ice hockey 15 10
2410 1 z. 50 Skiing 20 10
2411 2 z. Skating 20 10
2412 4 z. Tobogganing 35 10
2413 6 z. 40 Biathlon 50 25

666 R. Trevithick's Steam Railway Locomotive, 1803

1976. History of the Railway Locomotive. Mult.
2414 50 g. Type **666** 15 10
2415 1 z. Murray and Blenkinsop's steam locomotive, 1810 . . 15 10
2416 1 z. 50 George Stephenson's locomotive "Rocket", 1829 25 10
2417 1 z. 50 Polish "Universal" Type ET-22 electric locomotive, 1969 . . . . 25 10
2418 2 z. 70 Robert Stephenson's locomotive "North Star", 1837 . . . . 30 10
2419 3 z. Joseph Harrison's steam locomotive, 1840 . . . . . 45 10
2420 4 z. 50 Thomas Roger's steam locomotive, 1855 . . . . 2·00 45
2421 4 z. 90 Polish Chrzanow Works steam locomotive, 1922 . . 2·00 45

667 Flags of Member Countries

1976. 20th Anniv of Institute for Nuclear Research (C.M.E.A.).
2422 **667** 1 z. 50 multicoloured . . 15 10

668 Early Telephone, Satellite and Radar

1976. Telephone Centenary.
2423 **668** 1 z. 50 multicoloured . . 15 10

669 Jantar Glider

670 Player

1976. Air. Contemporary Aviation.
2424 **669** 5 z. blue 30 15
2425 – 10 z. brown 60 30
2425a – 20 z. olive . . . . . . 1·25 40
2425b – 50 z. lake . . . . 3·00 1·50
DESIGN: 10 z. Mil Mi-6 helicopter; 20 z. PZL-106A agricultural airplane; 50 z. PZL-Mielec TS-11 Iskra jet trainer over Warsaw Castle.

1976. World Ice Hockey Championships, Katowice. Multicoloured.
2426 1 z. Type **670** 10 10
2427 1 z. 50 Player (different) . . 15 10

671 Polish U.N. Soldier

1976. Polish Troops in U.N. Sinai Force.
2428 **671** 1 z. 50 multicoloured . . 15 10

672 "Glory to the Sappers" (S. Kulon)

673 "Interphil 76"

1976. War Memorials. Multicoloured.

2429 1 z. Type **672** 15 10
2430 1 z. 1st Polish Army Monument, Sandau, Laba (B. Koniuszy) 15 10

1976. "Interphil '76" Int Stamp Exn, Philadelphia.

2431 **673** 8 z. 40 multicoloured . . 60 20

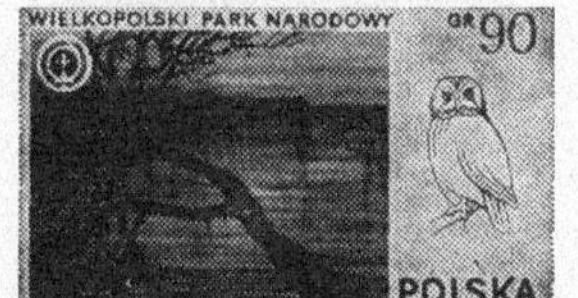

674 Wielkopolski Park and Tawny Owl

1976. National Parks. Multicoloured.

2432 90 g. Type **674** 60 15
2433 1 z. Wolinski Park and white-tailed sea eagle 60 15
2434 1 z. 50 Slowinski Park and seagull 65 15
2435 4 z. 50 Bieszezadzki Park and lynx 40 15
2436 5 z. Ojcowski Park and bat . . 40 15
2437 6 z. Kampinoski Park and elk 50 25

675 Peace Dove within Globe

1976. 25th Anniv of U.N. Postal Administration.

2438 **675** 8 z. 40 multicoloured . . 60 20

676 Fencing

677 National Theatre

1976. Olympic Games, Montreal. Multicoloured.

2439 50 g. Type **676** 10 10
2440 1 z. Cycling 10 10
2441 1 z. 50 Football 10 10
2442 4 z. 20 Boxing 40 10
2443 6 z. 90 Weightlifting 65 15
2444 8 z. 40 Athletics 75 25

1976. Cent of National Theatre, Poznan.

2446 **677** 1 z. 50 green & orange . 15 10

678 Aleksander Czekanowski and Baikal Landscape

679 "Sphinx"

1976. Death Centenary of Aleksander Czekanowski (geologist).

2447 **678** 1 z. 50 multicoloured . . 15 10

1976. Stamp Day. Corinthian Vase Paintings (7th century B.C.). Multicoloured.

2448 1 z. Type **679** 10 10
2449 1 z. 50 "Siren" (horiz) . . . 10 10
2450 2 z. "Lion" (horiz) 15 10
2451 4 z. 20 "Bull" (horiz) 30 10
2452 4 z. 50 "Goat" (horiz) . . . 35 20
2453 8 z.+4 z. "Sphinx" (different) 1·10 50

680 Warszawa "M 20"

1976. 25th Anniv of Zeran Motor-car Factory, Warsaw. Multicoloured.

2454 1 z. Type **680** 10 10
2455 1 z. 50 Warszawa "223" . . 10 10
2456 2 z. Syrena "104" 15 10
2457 4 z. 90 Polski - Fiat "125P" 40 20

681 Molten Steel Ladle

1976. Huta Katowice Steel Works.

2459 **681** 1 z. 50 multicoloured . . 15 10

682 Congress Emblem

683 "Wirzbieto Epitaph" (painting on wood, 1425)

1976. 8th Polish Trade Unions Congress.

2460 **682** 1 z. 50 orange, bistre and brown 15 10

1976. Polish Art. Multicoloured.

2461 1 z. Type **683** 10 10
2462 6 z. "Madonna and Child" (painted carving, c.1410) . 35 15

684 Tanker "Zawrat" at Oil Terminal, Gdansk

1976. Polish Ports. Multicoloured.

2463 1 z. Type **684** 20 10
2464 1 z. Ferry "Gryf" at Gdansk 20 10
2465 1 z. 50 Loading container ship "General Bem", Gdynia . . 40 10
2466 1 z. 50 Liner "Stefan Batory" leaving Gdynia 40 10
2467 2 z. Bulk carrier "Ziemia Szczecinska" loading at Szczecin 55 10
2468 4 z. 20 Loading coal, Swinoujscie 70 15
2469 6 z. 90 Pleasure craft, Kolobrzeg 90 25
2470 8 z. 40 Coastal map . . . . 1·40 35

685 Nurse and Patient

686 Order of Civil Defence Service

1977. Polish Red Cross.

2471 **685** 1 z. 50 multicoloured . . 15 10

1977. Polish Civil Defence.

2472 **686** 1 z. 50 multicoloured . . 15 10

687 Ball in Road

1977. Child Road Safety Campaign.

2473 **687** 1 z. 50 multicoloured . . 15 10

688 Dewberries

689 Computer Tape

1977. Wild Fruits. Multicoloured.

2474 50 g. Type **688** 10 10
2475 90 g. Cowberries 10 10
2476 1z. Wild strawberries 10 10
2477 1 z. 50 Bilberries 15 10
2478 2 z. Raspberries 20 10
2479 4 z. 50 Sloes 40 15
2480 6 z. Rose hips 50 15
2481 6 z. 90 hazelnuts 60 25

1977. 30th Anniv of Russian-Polish Technical Co-operation.

2482 **689** 1 z. 50 multicoloured . . 15 10

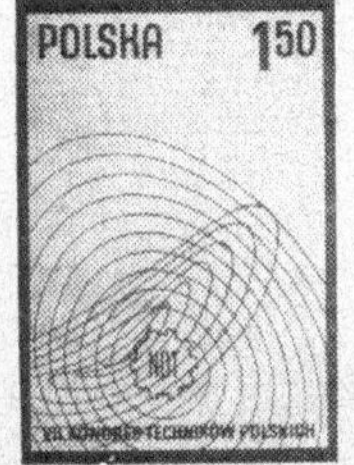

690 Pendulum Traces and Emblem

1977. 7th Polish Congress of Technology.

2483 **690** 1 z. 50 multicoloured . . 15 10

691 "Toilet of Venus"

1977. 400th Birth Anniv of Peter Paul Rubens. Multicoloured.

2484 1 z. Type **691** 10 10
2485 1 z. 50 "Bathsheba at the Fountain" 10 10
2486 5 z. "Helena Fourment with Fur Coat" 40 20
2487 6 z. "Self-portrait" 55 35

692 Dove

694 Wolf

693 Cyclist

1977. World Council of Peace Congress.

2489 **692** 1 z. 50 blue, yellow & blk 15 10

1977. 30th International Peace Cycle Race.

2490 **693** 1 z. 50 multicoloured . . 15 10

1977. Endangered Animals. Multicoloured.

2491 1 z. Type **694** 10 10
2492 1 z. 50 Great bustard . . . 65 15
2493 1 z. 50 Common kestrel . . . 65 15
2494 6 z. European otter 50 20

695 "The Violinist" (J. Toorenvliet)

697 H. Wieniawski and Music Clef

696 Midsummer's Day Bonfire

1977. "Amphilex 77" Stamp Exhibition, Amsterdam.

2495 6 z. Type **695** Multicoloured. . 40 25

1977. Folk Customs. 19th-century Wood Engravings. Multicoloured.

2496 90 g. Type **696** 10 10
2497 1 z. Easter cock (vert) . . . 10 10
2498 1 z. 50 "Smigus" (dousing of women on Easter Monday, Miechow district) (vert) . . 10 10
2499 3 z. Harvest Festival, Sandomierz district (vert) . 25 10
2500 6 z. Children with Christmas crib (vert) 50 15
2501 8 z. 40 Mountain wedding dance 70 20

1977. Wieniawski International Music Competitions, Poznan.

2502 **697** 1 z. 50 black, red & gold 20 10

698 Apollo ("Parnassius apollo")

1977. Butterflies. Multicoloured.

2503 1 z. Type **698** 20 10
2504 1 z. Large tortoiseshell ("Nymphalis polychloros") 20 10
2505 1 z. 50 Camberwell beauty ("Nymphalis antiopa") . . 25 10
2506 1 z. 50 Swallowtail ("Papilio machaon") 25 10
2507 5 z. High brown fritillary . . 75 15
2508 6 z. 90 Silver-washed fritillary 1·40 65

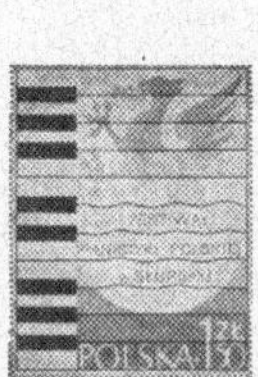

699 Keyboard and Arms of Slupsk

700 Feliks Dzerzhinsky

1977. Piano Festival, Slupsk.

2509 **699** 1 z. 50 mauve, blk & grn 15 10

1977. Birth Centenary of Feliks Dzerzhinsky (Russian politician).

2510 **700** 1 z. 50 brown and ochre 15 10

701 "Sputnik" circling Earth

702 Silver Dinar (11th century)

1977. 60th Anniv of Russian Revolution and 20th Anniv of 1st Artificial Satellite (1st issue).

2511 **701** 1 z. 50 red and blue . . 15 10

See also No. 2527.

1977. Stamp Day. Polish Coins. Multicoloured.

2513 50 g. Type **702** 10 10
2514 1 z. Cracow grosz, 14th-century 10 10
2515 1 z. 50 Legnica thaler, 17th-century 10 10
2516 4 z. 20 Gdansk guilder, 18th-century 35 10
2517 4 z. 50 Silver 5 z. coin, 1936 35 10
2518 6 z. Millenary 100 z. coin, 1966 60 25

703 Wolin Gate, Kamien Pomorski — 704 "Sputnik 1" and "Mercury" Capsule

1977. Architectural Monuments. Multicoloured.

2519	1 z. Type **703**	10	10
2520	1 z. Larch church, Debno	10	10
2521	1 z. 50 Monastery, Przasnysz (horiz)	10	10
2522	1 z. 50 Plock cathedral (horiz)	10	10
2523	6 z. Kornik castle (horiz)	40	10
2524	6 z. 90 Palace and garden, Wilanow (horiz)	50	25

1977. Polish Folklore. 16th-century woodcuts (2nd series). As T **638**.

2525	4 z. sepia	25	10
2526	4 z. 50 brown	30	10

DESIGNS: 4 z. Bird snaring; 4 z. 50, Bee-keeper and hives.

1977. 20th Anniv of 1st Space Satellite (2nd issue).

2527	**704**	6 z. 90 multicoloured	45	35

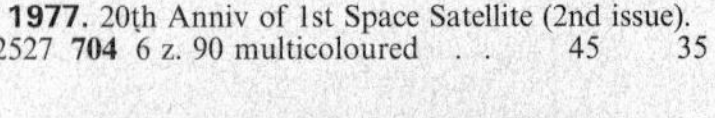

705 DN Category Iceboats

1978. 6th World Ice Sailing Championships.

2528	**705**	1 z. 50 black, grey & blue	15	10
2529	–	1 z. 50 black, grey & blue	15	10

DESIGN: No. 2529, Close-up of DN iceboat.

706 Electric Locomotive and Katowice Station

1978. Railway Engines. Multicoloured.

2530	50 g. Type **706**	10	10
2531	1 z. Py 27 Steam locomotive (Znin-Gasawa narrow-gauge railway)	15	10
2532	1 z. Pm 36 Steam locomotive and Cegielski's factory, Poznan	15	10
2533	1 z. 50 Electric locomotive and Otwock station	15	10
2534	1 z. 50 Steam locomotive and Warsaw Stalowa station	15	10
2535	4 z. 50 Steam locomotive Ty 51 and Gdynia station	35	10
2536	5 z. Tr 21 and steam locomotive factory, Chrzanow	40	15
2537	6 z. Cockerill steam locomotive and Vienna station	60	25

707 Czeslaw Tanski and Glider

1978. Aviation History and 50th Anniv of Polish Aero Club. Multicoloured.

2538	50 g. Type **707**	10	10
2539	1 z. Franciszek Zwirko and Stanislaw Wigura with RWD-6 aircraft (vert)	10	10
2540	1 z. 50 Stanislaw Skarzynski and RWD-5 bis monoplane (vert)	15	10
2541	4 z. 20 Mil Mi-2 helicopter (vert)	25	10
2542	6 z. 90 PZL-104 Wilga 35 monoplane	90	20
2543	8 z. 40 SZD-45 Ogar powered glider	80	20

708 Tackle

1978. World Cup Football Championship, Argentina. Multicoloured.

2544	1 z. 50 Type **708**	10	10
2545	6 z. 90 Ball on field (horiz)	45	20

709 Biennale Emblem

1978. 7th International Poster Biennale, Warsaw.

2546	**709**	1 z. 50 mauve, yell & vio	10	10

711 Polonez Saloon Car

1978. Car Production.

2548	**711**	1 z. 50 multicoloured	15	10

712 Fair Emblem — 713 Miroslaw Hermaszewski

1978. 50th International Fair, Poznan.

2549	**712**	1 z. 50 multicoloured	10	10

1978. First Pole in Space. Multicoloured. With or without date.

2550	1 z. 50 Type **713**	15	10
2551	6 z. 90 M. Hermaszewski and globe	55	15

714 Globe containing Face

1978. 11th World Youth and Students Festival, Havana.

2552	**714**	1 z. 50 multicoloured	10	10

716 Mosquito and Malaria Organisms — 717 Pedunculate Oak

1978. 4th International Congress of Parasitologists, Warsaw and Cracow. Multicoloured.

2554	1 z. 50 Type **716**	15	10
2555	6 z. Tsetse fly and sleeping sickness organism	40	20

1978. Environment Protection. Trees. Multicoloured.

2556	50 g. Norway Maple	10	10
2557	1 z. Type **717**	10	10
2558	1 z. 50 White Poplar	10	10
2559	4 z. 20 Scots Pine	30	10
2560	4 z. 50 White Willow	30	10
2561	6 z. Birch	45	20

719 Communications

1978. 20th Anniv of Socialist Countries Communications Organization.

2563	**719**	1 z. 50 red, lt blue & bl	10	10

720 "Peace" (Andre Le Brun)

1978.

2564	**720**	1 z. violet	10	10
2565		1 z. 50 turquoise	15	10
2565a		2 z. brown	15	10
2565b		2 z. 50 blue	20	10

721 Polish Unit of U.N. Middle East Force

1978. 35th Anniv of Polish People's Army. Multicoloured.

2566	1 z. 50 Colour party of Tadeusz Kosciuszko 1st Warsaw Infantry Division	15	10
2567	1 z. 50 Mechanised Unit colour party	15	10
2568	1 z. 50 Type **721**	15	10

722 "Portrait of a Young Man" (Raphael)

1978. Stamp Day.

2569	**722**	6 z. multicoloured	35	20

723 Janusz Korczak with Children — 724 Wojciech Boguslawski

1978. Birth Centenary of Janusz Korczak (pioneer of children's education).

2570	**723**	1 z. 50 multicoloured	15	10

1978. Polish Dramatists. Multicoloured.

2571	50 g. Type **724**	10	10
2572	1 z. Aleksander Fredro	10	10
2573	1 z. 50 Juliusz Slowacki	15	10
2574	2 z. Adam Mickiewicz	15	10
2575	4 z. 50 Stanislaw Wyspianski	30	10
2576	6 z. Gabriela Zapolska	50	20

725 Polish Combatants' Monument and Eiffel Tower

1978. Monument to Polish Combatants in France, Paris.

2577	**725**	1 z. 50 brown, blue & red	15	10

726 Przewalski Horses

1978. 50th Anniv of Warsaw Zoo. Multicoloured.

2578	50 g. Type **726**	10	10
2579	1 z. Polar bears	10	10
2580	1 z. 50 Indian elephants	20	10
2581	2 z. Jaguars	25	10
2582	4 z. 20 Grey seals	30	10
2583	4 z. 50 Hartebeests	30	10
2584	6 z. Mandrills	45	25

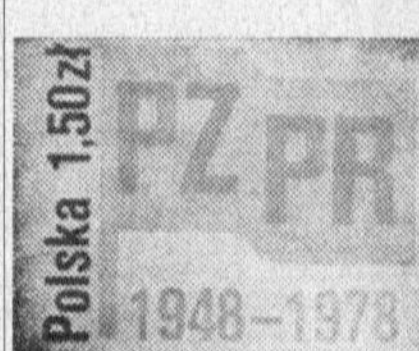

727 Party Flag — 728 Stanislaw Dubois

1978. 30th Anniv of Polish Workers' United Party.

2585	**727**	1 z. 50 red, gold and black	10	10

1978. Leaders of Polish Workers' Movement.

2586	**728**	1 z. 50 blue and red	10	10
2587	–	1 z. 50 lilac and red	10	10
2588	–	1 z. 50 olive and red	10	10
2589	–	1 z. 50 brown and red	10	10

DESIGNS: No. 2587, Aleksander Zawadzki; No. 2588, Julian Lenski; No. 2589, Aldolf Warski.

729 Ilyushin Il-62M and Fokkerb.VIIb/3m

1979. 50th Anniv of LOT Polish Airlines.

2590	**729**	6 z. 90 multicoloured	60	20

730 Train

1979. International Year of the Child. Children's Paintings. Multicoloured.

2591	50 g. Type **730**	15	10
2592	1 z. "Mother with Children"	10	10
2593	1 z. 50 Children playing	15	10
2594	6 z. Family Group	45	15

731 "Portrait of Artist's Wife with Foxgloves" (Karol Mondrala)

1979. Contemporary Graphics.

2595	–	50 g. lilac	10	10
2596	**731**	1 z. green	10	10
2597	–	1 z. 50 blue	10	10
2598	–	4 z. 50 brown	30	10

DESIGNS—HORIZ: 50 g. "Lightning" (Edmund Bartlomiejczyk). VERT: 1 z. 50, "The Musicians" (Tadeusz Kulisiewicz); 4 z. 50, "Head of a Young Man" (Wladyslaw Skoczylas).

732 A. Frycz Modrzewski (political writer), King Stefan Batory and Jan Zamoyski (chancellor)

1979. 400th Anniv (1978) of Royal Tribunal in Piotrkow Trybunalski.

2599	**732**	1 z. 50 brown and deep brown	15	10

733 Pole Vaulting

1979. 60th Anniv of Polish Olympic Committee. Multicoloured.

2600	1 z. Type **733**	10	10
2601	1 z. 50 High jump	10	10
2602	6 z. Skiing	40	15
2603	8 z. 40 Horse riding	60	25

734 Flounder

1979. Centenary of Polish Angling. Multicoloured.

2605	50 g. Type **734**	10	10
2606	90 g. Perch	10	10
2607	1 z. Greyling	10	10
2608	1 z. 50 Salmon	10	10
2609	2 z. Trout	15	10
2610	4 z. 50 Pike	25	10
2611	5 z. Carp	40	10
2612	6 z. Catfish	45	20

735 "30 Years of RWPG"

1979. 30th Anniv of Council of Mutual Economic Aid.

2613 **735** 1 z. 50 red, ultram and blue 15 10

736 Soldier, Civilian and Congress Emblem

738 Pope and Auschwitz Concentration Camp Memorial

737 St. George's Church, Sofia

1979. 6th Congress of Association of Fighters for Liberty and Democracy.

2614 **736** 1 z. 50 red and black 15 10

1979. "Philaserdica 79" International Stamp Exhibition, Sofia, Bulgaria.

2615 **737** 1 z. 50 orge, brn & red 15 10

1979. Visit of Pope John Paul II. Multicoloured.

2616	1 z. 50 Pope and St. Mary's Church, Cracow	25	10
2617	8 z. 40 Type **738**	65	30

739 River Paddle-steamer "Ksiaze Ksawery" and Old Warsaw

1979. 150th Anniv of Vistula River Navigation. Multicoloured.

2619	1 z. Type **739**	20	10
2620	1 z. 50 River paddle-steamer "General Swierczewski" and Gdansk	25	10
2621	4 z. 50 River tug "Zubr" and Plock	70	10
2622	6 z. Passenger launch "Syrena" and modern Warsaw	1·25	20

740 Statue of Tadeusz Kosciuszko (Marian Konieczny)

741 Mining Machinery

1979. Monument to Tadeusz Kosciuszko in Philadelphia.

2623 **740** 8 z. 40 multicoloured 50 20

1979. Wieliczka Salt Mine.

2624	**741**	1 z. brown and black	10	10
2625	–	1 z. 50 turquoise & black	10	10

DESIGN: 1 z. 50, Salt crystals.

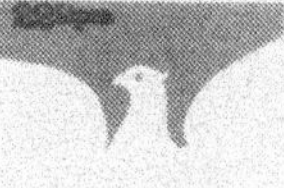

742 Heraldic Eagle

743 Rowland Hill and 1860 Stamp

1979. 35th Anniv of Polish People's Republic.

2626	–	1 z. 50 red, silver and black	15	10
2627	**742**	1 z. 50 red, silver and blue	15	10

DESIGN: No. 2626, Girl and stylized flag.

1979. Death Centenary of Sir Rowland Hill.

2629 **743** 6 z. blue, black & orange 45 15

745 Wojciech Jastrzebowski

746 Monument (Wincenty Kucma)

1979. 7th Congress of International Ergonomic Association, Warsaw.

2631 **745** 1 z. 50 multicoloured 15 10

1979. Unveiling of Monument to Defenders of Polish Post, Gdansk, and 40th Anniv of German Occupation.

2632 **746** 1 z. 50 multicoloured 15 10

747 Radio Mast and Telecommunications Emblem

1979. 50th Anniv of International Radio Communication Advisory Committee.

2634 **747** 1 z. 50 multicoloured 15 10

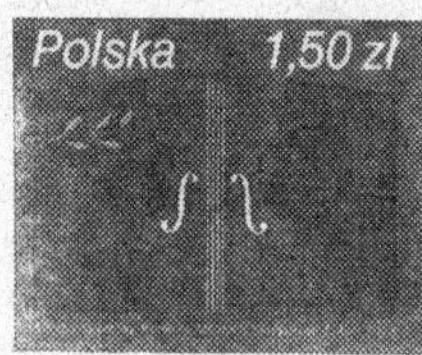

748 Violin

1979. Wieniawski Young Violinists' Competition, Lublin.

2635 **748** 1 z. 50 blue, orange & grn 15 10

749 Statue of Kazimierz Pulaski, Buffalo (K. Danilewicz)

750 Franciszek Jozwiak (first Commander)

1979. Death Bicentenary of Kazimierz Pulaski (American Revolution Hero).

2636 **749** 8 z. 40 multicoloured 60 20

1979. 35th Anniv of Civic Militia and Security Force.

2637 **750** 1 z. 50 blue and gold 15 10

INDEX

Countries can be quickly located by referring to the index at the end of this volume.

751 Post Office in Rural Area

1979. Stamp Day. Multicoloured.

2638	1 z. Type **751**	10	10
2639	1 z. 50 Parcel sorting machinery	10	10
2640	4 z. 50 Loading containers on train	40	10
2641	6 z. Mobile post office	50	20

752 "The Holy Family" (Ewelina Peksowa)

753 "Soyuz 30-Salyut 6" Complex and Crystal

1979. Polish Folk Art. Glass Paintings. Mult.

2642	2 z. Type **752**	15	10
2643	6 z. 90 "The Nativity" (Zdzislaw Walczak)	55	20

1979. Space Achievements. Multicoloured.

2644	1 z. Type **753** (1st anniv of 1st Pole in space)	10	10
2645	1 z. 50 "Kopernik" and "Copernicus" satellites	15	10
2646	2 z. "Lunik 2" and "Ranger 7" spacecraft (20th anniv of 1st unmanned Moon landing)	15	10
2647	4 z. 50 Yuri Gagarin and "Vostok 1"	40	10
2648	6 z. 90 Neil Armstrong, lunar module and "Apollo 11" (10th anniv of first man on Moon)	50	20

754 Coach and Four

755 Slogan on Map of Poland

1980. 150th Anniv of Sierakow Stud Farm. Mult.

2650	1 z. Type **754**	15	10
2651	2 z. Horse and groom	20	10
2652	2 z. 50 Sulky racing	25	10
2653	3 z. Hunting	30	10
2654	4 z. Horse-drawn sledge	40	10
2655	6 z. Haywain	60	15
2656	6 z. 50 Grooms exercising horses	70	15
2657	6 z. 90 Show jumping	80	20

1980. 8th Polish United Workers' Party Congress. Multicoloured.

2658	2 z. 50 Type **755**	20	10
2659	2 z. 50 Janusz Stann (26 × 46 mm)	20	10

756 Horse Jumping

1980. Olympic Games, Moscow and Winter Olympic Games, Lake Placid. Multicoloured.

2660	2 z. Type **756**	15	10
2661	2 z. 50 Archery	20	10
2662	6 z. 50 Skiing	45	15
2663	8 z. 40 Volleyball	60	25

757 Town Plan and Old Town Hall

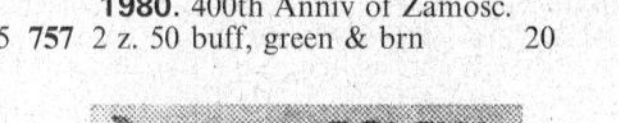
1980. 400th Anniv of Zamosc.

2665 **757** 2 z. 50 buff, green & brn 20 10

759 Seals of Poland and Russia

1980. 35th Anniv of Soviet-Polish Friendship Treaty.

2667 **759** 2 z. 50 multicoloured 20 10

760 "Lenin in Cracow" (Zbigniew Pronaszko)

1980. 110th Birth Anniv of Lenin.

2668 **760** 2 z. 50 multicoloured 20 15

761 Workers with Red Flag

1980. 75th Anniv of Revolution of 1905.

2669 **761** 2 z. 50 red, black & yell 20 10

762 Dove

763 Shield with Crests of Member Nations

1980. 35th Anniv of Liberation.

2670 **762** 2 z. 50 multicoloured 20 10

1980. 25th Anniv of Warsaw Pact.

2671 **763** 2 z. grey and red 20 10

764 Speleological Expedition, Cuba

1980. Polish Scientific Expeditions. Multicoloured.

2672	2 z. Type **764**	15	10
2673	2 z. Antarctic	30	10
2674	2 z. 50 Archaeology, Syria	25	10
2675	2 z. 50 Ethnology, Mongolia	25	10
2676	6 z. 50 Mountaineering, Nepal	45	20
2677	8 z. 40 Paleontology, Mongolia	60	25

765 School and Arms

766 "Clathrus ruber"

1980. 800th Anniv of Malachowski School, Plock.

No.	Type	Description	Mint	Used
2678	765	2 z. green and black	20	10

1980. Fungi. Multicoloured.

No.	Type	Description	Mint	Used
2679		2 z. Type **766**	40	10
2680		2 z. "Xerocomus parasiticus"	40	10
2681		2 z. 50 Old man of the woods ("Strobilomyces floccopus")	50	10
2682		2 z. 50 "Phallus hadriani"	50	10
2683		8 z. Cauliflower fungus	85	20
2684		10 z. 50 Giant puff-ball	1·25	40

767 T. Ziolowski and "Lwow"

1980. Polish Merchant Navy School. Cadet Ships and their Captains.

No.	Type	Description	Mint	Used
2685	767	2 z. black, mauve and violet	30	10
2686	–	2 z. 50 black, light blue and blue	35	10
2687	–	6 z. black, pale green and green	55	15
2688	–	6 z. 50 black, yellow and grey	65	15
2689	–	6 z. 90 black, grey and green	85	20
2690	–	8 z. 40 black, blue and green	90	25

DESIGNS: 2 z. 50, A. Garnuszewski and "Antoni Garnuszewski"; 6 z. A. Ledochowski and "Zenit"; 6 z. 50, K. Porebski and "Jan Turleski"; 6 z. 90, G. Kanski and "Horyzont"; 8 z. 40, Maciejewicz and "Dar Pomorza".

768 Town Hall

769 "Atropa belladonna"

1980. Millenary of Sandomir.

No.	Type	Description	Mint	Used
2691	768	2 z. 50 brown and black	20	10

1980. Medicinal Plants. Multicoloured.

No.	Type	Description	Mint	Used
2692		2 z. Type **769**	20	10
2693		2 z. 50 "Datura innoxia"	25	10
2694		3 z. 40 "Valeriana officinalis"	35	10
2695		5 z. "Menta piperita"	45	10
2696		6 z. 50 "Calendula officinalis"	55	15
2697		8 z. "Salvia officinalis"	70	30

770 Jan Kochanowski

771 U.N. General Assembly

1980. 450th Birth Anniv of Jan Kochanowski (poet).

No.	Type	Description	Mint	Used
2698	770	2 z. 50 multicoloured	20	10

1980. 35th Anniv of U.N.O.

No.	Type	Description	Mint	Used
2703	771	8 z. 40 brown, blue & red	70	25

772 Chopin and Trees

1980. 10th International Chopin Piano Competition, Warsaw.

No.	Type	Description	Mint	Used
2704	772	6 z. 90 multicoloured	50	15

773 Postman emptying Post Box

1980. Stamp Day. Multicoloured.

No.	Type	Description	Mint	Used
2705		2 z. Type **773**	20	10
2706		2 z. 50 Mail sorting	20	10
2707		6 z. Loading mail onto aircraft	50	15
2708		6 z. 50 Letter boxes	55	15

774 Child embracing Dove

1980. United Nations Declaration on the Preparation of Societies for Life in Peace.

No.	Type	Description	Mint	Used
2710	774	8 z. 40 multicoloured	70	20

775 "Battle of Olszynka Grochowska" (Wojciech Kossak)

1980. 150th Anniv of Battle of Olszynka Grochowska.

No.	Type	Description	Mint	Used
2711	775	2 z. 50 multicoloured	20	10

776 Fire Engine

1980. Warsaw Horse-drawn Vehicles. Mult.

No.	Type	Description	Mint	Used
2712		2 z. Type **776**	15	10
2713		2 z. 50 Omnibus	20	10
2714		3 z. Brewery dray	25	10
2715		5 z. Sledge-cab	40	10
2716		6 z. Tram	45	20
2717		6 z. 50 Droshky cab	60	30

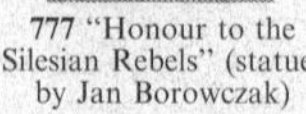
777 "Honour to the Silesian Rebels" (statue by Jan Borowczak)

778 Picasso

1981. 60th Anniv of Silesian Rising.

No.	Type	Description	Mint	Used
2718	777	2 z. 50 green	15	10

1981. Birth Centenary of Pablo Picasso (artist).

No.	Type	Description	Mint	Used
2719	778	8 z. 40 multicoloured	90	25

779 Balloon of Pilatre de Rozier and Romain, 1785

780 "Iphigenia" (Anton Maulbertsch)

1981. Balloons. Multicoloured.

No.	Type	Description	Mint	Used
2721		2 z. Type **779**	20	10
2722		2 z. Balloon of J. Blanchard and J. Jeffries, 1785	20	10
2723		2 z. 50 Eugene Godard's quintuple "acrobatic" balloon, 1850	25	10
2724		3 z. F. Hynek and Z. Burzynski's "Kosciuszko", 1933	30	10
2725		6 z. Z. Burzynski and N. Wyescki's "Polonia II" 1935	55	15
2726		6 z. 50 Ben Abruzzo, Max Anderson and Larry Newman's "Double Eagle II", 1978	55	20

1981. "WIPA 1981" International Stamp Exhibition, Vienna.

No.	Type	Description	Mint	Used
2728	780	10 z. 50 multicoloured	90	35

781 Wroclaw, 1493

782 Sikorski

1981. Towns.

No.	Type	Description	Mint	Used
2729	–	4 z. violet	30	10
2730	–	5 z. green	50	15
2731	–	6 z. orange	60	15
2732	781	6 z. 50 brown	60	20
2733	–	8 z. blue	70	25

DESIGNS—VERT: 4 z. Gdansk, 1652; 5 z. Cracow, 1493. HORIZ: 6 z. Legnica, 1744; 8 z. Warsaw, 1618.

1981. Birth Centenary of General Wladyslaw Sikorski (statesman).

No.	Type	Description	Mint	Used
2744	782	6 z. 50 multicoloured	55	20

783 Faience Vase

784 Congress Emblem

1981. Pottery. Multicoloured.

No.	Type	Description	Mint	Used
2745		1 z. Type **783**	15	10
2746		2 z. Porcelain cup and saucer in "Baranowka" design	25	10
2747		2 z. 50 Porcelain jug Korzec manufacture	25	10
2748		5 z. Faience plate with portrait of King Jan III Sobieski by Thiele	50	15
2749		6 z. 50 Faience "Secession" vase	65	20
2750		8 z. 40 Porcelain dish, Cmielow manufacture	80	30

1981. 14th International Architects' Union Congress, Warsaw.

No.	Type	Description	Mint	Used
2751	784	2 z. yellow, blk and red	20	10

785 Wild Boar, Rifle and Oak Leaves

786 European Bison

1981. Game Shooting. Multicoloured.

No.	Type	Description	Mint	Used
2752		2 z. Type **785**	25	10
2753		2 z. Elk, rifle and fir twigs	25	10
2754		2 z. 50 Red fox, shotgun, cartridges and fir branches	30	10
2755		2 z. 50 Roe deer, feeding rack, rifle and fir branches	30	10
2756		6 z. 50 Mallard, shotgun, basket and reeds	1·10	30
2757		6 z. 50 Barnacle goose, shotgun and reeds (horiz)	1·10	30

1981. Protection of European Bison. Mult.

No.	Type	Description	Mint	Used
2758		6 z. 50 Type **786**	75	25
2759		6 z. 50 Two bison, one grazing	75	25
2760		6 z. 50 Bison with calf	75	25
2761		6 z. 50 Calf Feeding	75	25
2762		6 z. 50 Two bison, both looking towards right	75	25

787 Tennis Player

1981. 60th Anniv of Polish Tennis Federation.

No.	Type	Description	Mint	Used
2763	787	6 z. 50 multicoloured	55	15

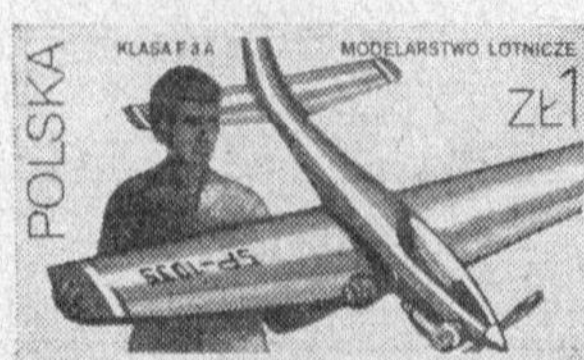
788 Boy with Model Airplane

1981. Model Making. Multicoloured.

No.	Type	Description	Mint	Used
2764		1 z. Type **788**	15	10
2765		2 z. Model of "Atlas 2" tug	30	10
2766		2 z. 50 Cars	30	10
2767		4 z. 20 Man with gliders	35	15
2768		6 z. 50 Racing cars	70	15
2769		8 z. Boy with yacht	80	25

789 Disabled Pictogram

791 H. Wieniawski and Violin Head

790 17th-cent Flint-lock Pistol

1981. International Year of Disabled Persons.

No.	Type	Description	Mint	Used
2770	789	8 z. 40 green, light green and black	75	20

1981. Stamp Day. Antique Weapons. Mult.

No.	Type	Description	Mint	Used
2771		2 z. 50 Type **790**	25	10
2772		8 z. 40 17th-century gala sabre	70	20

1981. Wieniawski Young Violinists' Competition.

No.	Type	Description	Mint	Used
2773	791	2 z. 50 multicoloured	25	15

792 Bronislaw Wesolowski

793 F.A.O. Emblem and Globe

1981. Activists of Polish Workers' Movement.

No.	Type	Description	Mint	Used
2774	792	50 g. green and black	10	10
2775	–	2 z. blue and black	15	10
2776	–	2 z. 50 brown and black	20	10
2777	–	6 z. 50 mauve and black	60	25

DESIGNS: 2 z. Malgorzata Fornalska; 2 z. 50, Maria Koszutska; 6 z. 50, Marcin Kasprzak.

1981. World Food Day.

No.	Type	Description	Mint	Used
2778	793	6 z. 90 brn, orge & yell	55	25

794 Helena Modrzejewska (actress)

1981. Bicentenary of Cracow Old Theatre.

No.	Type	Description	Mint	Used
2779	794	2 z. purple, grey and vio	15	10
2780	–	2 z. 50 blue, stone & brn	20	10
2781	–	6 z. 50 violet, bl and grn	50	20
2782	–	8 z. brown, green & red	80	20

DESIGNS: 2 z. 50, Stanislaw Kozmian (politician, writer and theatre director); 6 z. 50, Konrad Swinarski (stage manager and scenographer); 8 z. Old Theatre building.

796 Gdansk Memorial

797 "Epiphyllopsis gaertneri"

1981. Memorials to the Victims of the 1970 Uprisings.
2784 **796** 2 z. 50+1 z. grey, black and red 50 20
2785 – 6 z. 50+1 z. grey, black and blue . . . . 1·10 90
DESIGN: 6 z. 50, Gdynia Memorial.

1981. Succulent Plants. Multicoloured.
2786 90 g. Type **797** 15 10
2787 1 z. "Cereus tonduzii" 15 10
2788 2 z. "Cylindropuntia leptocaulis" 15 10
2789 2 z. 50 "Cylindropuntia fulgida" 20 10
2790 2 z. 50 "Coralluma lugardi" . 20 10
2791 6 z. 50 "Nopalea cochenillifera" 60 20
2792 6 z. 50 "Lithops helmutii" . . 60 20
2793 10 z. 50 "Cylindropuntia spinosior" . . . . 1·00 35

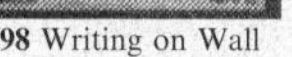

798 Writing on Wall **799** Faience Plate

1982. 40th Anniv of Polish Workers' Coalition.
2794 **798** 2 z. 50 pink, red and black 25 10

1982. Polish Ceramics. Multicoloured.
2795 1 z. Type **799** 15 10
2796 2 z. Porcelain cup and saucer, Korzec 20 10
2797 2 z. 50 Porcelain tureen and sauce-boat, Barnowka . . 25 10
2798 6 z. Porcelain inkpot, Horodnica 60 20
2799 8 z. Faience "Hunter's Tumbler", Lubartow . . . 75 20
2800 10 z. 50 Faience figurine of nobleman, Biala Podlaska . 1·10 40

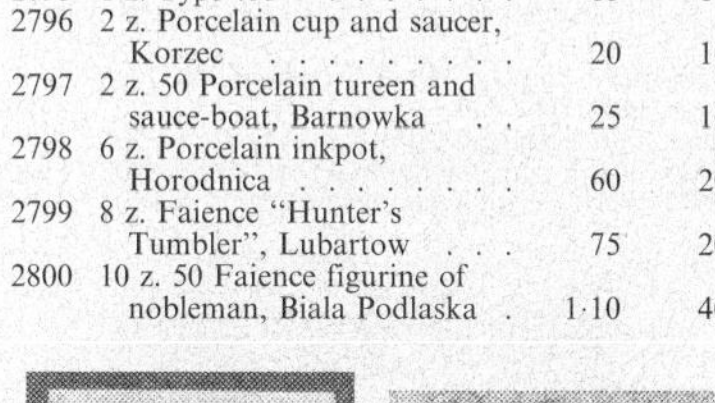

800 Ignacy Lukasiewicz and Lamp **801** Karol Szymanowski

1982. Death Centenary of Ignacy Lukasiewicz (inventor of petroleum lamp).
2801 **800** 1 z. multicoloured . . . 15 10
2802 – 2 z. multicoloured . . . 20 10
2803 – 2 z. 50 multicoloured . . 30 10
2804 – 3 z. 50 multicoloured . . 35 15
2805 – 9 z. multicoloured . . . 90 25
2806 – 10 z. multicoloured . . . 95 30
DESIGNS: 2 z. to 10 z. Different designs showing lamps.

1982. Birth Centenary of Karol Szymanowski (composer).
2807 **801** 2 z. 50 brown and gold . 25 10

802 RWD 6, 1932

1982. 50th Anniv of Polish Victory in Tourist Aircraft Challenge Competition. Multicoloured.
2808 27 z. Type **802** . . . . 1·50 1·25
2809 31 z. RWD 9 (winner of 1934 Challenge) . . . . 1·90 1·75

803 Henryk Sienkiewicz (literature, 1905) **804** Football as Globe

1982. Polish Nobel Prize Winners.
2811 **803** 3 z. green and black . . 15 10
2812 – 15 z. brown and black . 65 25
2813 – 25 z. blue . . . . . . 1·50 30
2814 – 31 z. grey and black . . 1·25 70
DESIGNS: 15 z. Wladyslaw Reymont (literature, 1924); 25 z. Marie Curie (physics, 1903, and chemistry, 1911); 31 z. Czeslaw Milosz (literature, 1980).

1982. World Cup Football Championship, Spain. Multicoloured.
2815 25 z. Type **804** . . . . . 1·10 40
2816 27 z. Bull and football (35×28 mm) . . . . 1·25 70

806 Stanislaw Sierakowski and Boleslaw Domanski (former Association presidents) **807** Text around Globe

1982. 60th Anniv of Association of Poles in Germany.
2818 **806** 4 z. 50 red and green . . 55 15

1982. 2nd U.N. Conference on the Exploration and Peaceful Uses of Outer Space, Vienna.
2819 **807** 31 z. multicoloured . . 90 35

1982. No. 2732 surch **10** °°.
2820 10 z. on 6 z. 50 brown . . . 25 10

809 Father Augustyn Kordecki (prior) **810** Marchers with Banner

1982. 600th Anniv of "Black Madonna" (icon) of Jasna Gora. Multicoloured.
2821 2 z. 50 Type **809** 10 10
2822 25 z. "Siege of Jasna Gora by Swedes, 1655" (detail) (horiz) 40 20
2823 65 z. "Black Madonna" . . 1·25 60

1982. Centenary of Proletarian Party.
2825 **810** 6 z. multicoloured . . . 40 10

811 Norbert Barlicki **812** Dr. Robert Koch

1982. Activists of Polish Workers' Movement.
2826 **811** 5 z. light blue, blue and black 15 10
2827 – 6 z. deep green, green and black 20 15
2828 – 15 z. pink, red and black 35 20
2829 – 20 z. mauve, violet and black 60 30
2830 – 29 z. light brown, brown and black 75 45
DESIGNS: 6 z. Pawel Finder; 15 z. Marian Buczek; 20 z. Cezaryna Wojnarowska; 29 z. Ignacy Daszynski.

1982. Centenary of Discovery of Tubercle Bacillus. Multicoloured.
2831 10 z. Type **812** 25 10
2832 25 z. Dr. Odo Bujwid . . . 85 20

813 Carved Head of Woman **813a** Head of Ruler

1982. Carved Heads from Wawel Castle.
2835 **813a** 3 z. 50 brown 15 10
2836 – 5 z. green 20 10
2837 – 5 z. red 20 10
2838 – 10 z. blue 25 10
2839 – 15 z. brown 15 10
2840 – 20 z. grey 45 15
2841 **813a** 20 z. blue 15 10
2842 – 40 z. brown 75 25
2833 **813** 60 z. orange and brn . 1·50 50
2843 – 60 z. green 15 10
2834 – 100 z. ochre & brown 3·00 1·00
2843a – 200 z. black . . . . . 3·75 1·75
DESIGNS—As T **813**: 100 z. Man. As T **813a**: 5 z. (2836), Warrior; 5 z. (2837); 15 z. Woman wearing chaplet; 10 z. Man in cap; 20 z. (2840), Thinker; 40 z. Man in beret; 60 z. Young man; 200 z. Man.

814 Maximilian Kolbe (after M. Koscielniak) **815** Polar Research Station

1982. Sanctification of Maximilian Kolbe (Franciscan concentration camp victim).
2844 **814** 27 z. multicoloured . . . 90 50

1982. 50th Anniv of Polish Polar Research.
2845 **815** 27 z. multicoloured . . . 2·50 60

816 "Log Floats on Vistula River" (drawing by J. Telakowski) **817** Stanislaw Zaremba

1982. Views of the Vistula River.
2846 **816** 12 z. blue 25 10
2847 – 17 z. blue 30 15
2848 – 25 z. blue 40 20
DESIGNS: 17 z. "Kazimierz Dolny" (engraving by Andriollo); 25 z. "Danzig" (18th-cent engraving).

1982. Mathematicians.
2849 **817** 5 z. lilac, blue and black . 25 10
2850 – 6 z. orange, violet and black 25 10
2851 – 12 z. blue, brown and black 40 10
2852 – 15 z. yellow, brown and black 60 20
DESIGNS: 6 z. Waclaw Sierpinski; 12 z. Zygmunt Janiszewski; 15 z. Stefan Banach.

818 Military Council Medal

1982. 1st Anniv of Military Council.
2853 **818** 2 z. 50 multicoloured . . 25 15

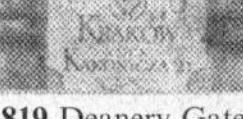

819 Deanery Gate **820** Bernard Wapowski Map, 1526

1982. Renovation of Cracow Monuments (1st series).
2854 **819** 15 z. black, olive & grn . 50 15
2855 – 25 z. black, purple & mve 65 20
DESIGN: 25 z. Gateway of Collegium.
See also Nos. 2904/5, 2968/9, 3029/30, 3116 and 3153.

1982. Polish Maps.
2857 **820** 5 z. multicoloured 15 10
2858 – 6 z. brown, black and red 20 10
2859 – 8 z. multicoloured 25 10
2860 – 25 z. multicoloured . . . 70 25
DESIGNS: 6 z. Map of Prague, 1839; 8 z. Map of Poland from Eugen Romer's Atlas, 1908; 25 z. Plan of Cracow by A. Buchowiecki, 1703, and Astrolabe.

821 "The Last of the Resistance" (Artur Grottger)

1983. 120th Anniv of January Uprising.
2861 **821** 6 z. brown 15 10

822 "Grand Theatre, Warsaw, 1838" (Maciej Zaleski)

1983. 150th Anniv of Grand Theatre, Warsaw.
2862 **822** 6 z. multicoloured . . . 15 10

823 Wild Flowers

1983. Environmental Protection. Multicoloured.
2863 5 z. Type **823** 20 10
2864 6 z. Mute swan and river fishes 50 10
2865 17 z. Hoopoe and trees . . . 1·50 30
2866 30 z. Sea fishes . . . . . . 1·10 45
2867 31 z. European bison and roe deer . . . . 1·10 50
2868 38 z. Fruit . . . . 1·10 60

824 Karol Kurpinski (composer)

1983. Celebrities.
2869 **824** 5 z. lt brown and brown 20 10
2870 – 6 z. purple and violet . . 25 10
2871 – 17 z. lt green and green . 60 20
2872 – 25 z. lt brown and brown 75 20
2873 – 27 z. lt blue and blue . . 80 25
2874 – 31 z. lilac and violet . . 90 25
DESIGNS: 6 z. Maria Jasnorzewska Pawlikowska (poetess); 17 z. Stanislaw Szober (linguist); 25 z. Tadeusz Banachiewicz (astronomer and mathematician); 27 z. Jaroslaw Iwaskiewicz (writer); 31 z. Wladyslaw Tatarkiewicz (philosopher and historian).

825 3000 Metres Steeplechase

1983. Sports Achievements.
2875 **825** 5 z. pink and violet . . . 20 10
2876 – 6 z. pink, brown & blk . 20 10
2877 – 15 z. yellow and green . 45 15
2878 – 27 z.+5 z. light blue, blue and black . . . . . . 1·00 30
DESIGNS: 6 z. Show jumping; 1 z. Football; 27 z.+5 z. Pole Vault.

826 Ghetto Heroes Monument (Natan Rappaport) **827** Customs Officer and Suitcases

1983. 40th Anniv of Warsaw Ghetto Uprising.
2879 **826** 5 z. lt brown & brown . 15 10

1983. 30th Anniv of Customs Co-operation Council.
2880 **827** 5 z. multicoloured . . . 15 10

828 John Paul II and Jasna Gora Sanctuary — **829** Dragoons

1983. Papal Visit. Multicoloured.

2881 31 z. Type **828** . . . . . . 1·00 30
2882 65 z. Niepokalanow Church and John Paul holding crucifix . 2·25 80

1983. 300th Anniv of Polish Relief of Vienna (1st issue). Troops of King Jan III Sobieski. Multicoloured.

2884 5 z. Type **829** 20 10
2885 5 z. Armoured cavalryman . 20 10
2886 6 z. Infantry non-commissioned officer and musketeer . . . 30 10
2887 15 z. Light cavalry lieutenant 40 20
2888 27 z. "Winged" hussar and trooper with carbine . . . 1·00 40

See also Nos. 2893/6.

830 Arrow piercing "E"

1983. 50th Anniv of Deciphering "Enigma" Machine Codes.

2889 **830** 5 z. red, grey and black . 15 15

831 Torun

1983. 750th Anniv of Torun.

2890 **831** 6 z. multicoloured . . . 30 15

832 Childs Painting

1983. "Order of the Smile" (Politeness Publicity Campaign).

2892 **832** 6 z. multicoloured . . . 15 10

833 King Jan III Sobieski

1983. 300th Anniv of Relief of Vienna (2nd issue). Multicoloured.

2893 5 z. Type **833** 20 10
2894 6 z. King Jan III Sobieski (different) 20 10
2895 6 z. "King Jan III Sobieski on Horseback" (Francesco Trevisani) 20 10
2896 25 z. "King Jan III Sobieski" (Jerzy Eleuter) 90 35

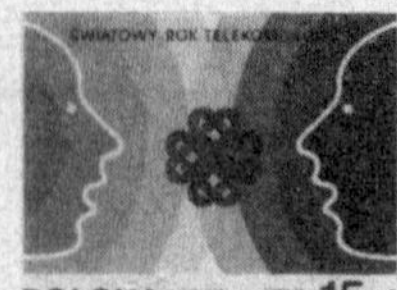

834 Wanda Wasilewska — **835** Profiles and W.C.Y. Emblem

1983. 40th Anniv of Polish People's Army. Multicoloured.

2898 **834** 5 z. multicoloured . . . 15 10
2899 – 5 z. deep green, green and black 15 10
2900 – 6 z. multicoloured . . . 25 10
2901 – 6 z. multicoloured . . . 25 10

DESIGNS—VERT: No. 2899, General Zygmunt Berling; 2900, "The Frontier Post" (S. Poznanski). HORIZ: No. 2901, "Taking the Oath" (S. Poznanski).

1983. World Communications Year.

2902 **835** 15 z. multicoloured . . 45 20

836 Boxing

1983. 60th Anniv of Polish Boxing Federation.

2903 **836** 6 z. multicoloured . . . 20 10

1983. Renovation of Cracow Monuments (2nd series). As T **819**.

2904 5 z. brown, purple & blk . . 20 10
2905 6 z. black, green and blue . 20 15

DESIGNS—HORIZ: 5 z. Cloth Hall. VERT: 6 z. Town Hall tower.

837 Biskupiec Costume — **838** Hand with Sword (poster by Zakrzewski and Krolikowski, 1945)

1983. Women's Folk Costumes. Multicoloured.

2906 5 z. Type **837** 20 10
2907 5 z. Rozbark 20 10
2908 6 z. Warmia & Mazuria . . 25 10
2909 6 z. Cieszyn 25 10
2910 25 z. Kurpie . . . . 1·10 30
2911 38 z. Lubusk . . . . 1·60 60

1983. 40th Anniv of National People's Council.

2912 **838** 6 z. multicoloured . . . 20 10

839 Badge of "General Bem" Brigade — **840** Dulcimer

1983. 40th Anniv of People's Army.

2913 **839** 5 z. multicoloured . . . 20 10

1984. Musical Instruments (1st series). Mult.

2914 5 z. Type **840** 20 10
2915 6 z. Kettle drum and tambourine 25 10
2916 10 z. Accordion 40 10
2917 15 z. Double bass 50 20
2918 17 z. Bagpipe 60 20
2919 29 z. Country band (wood carvings by Tadeusz Zak) 1·00 30

841 Wincenty Witos — **842** "Clematis lanuginosa"

1984. 110th Birth Anniv of Wincenty Witos (leader of Peasants' Movement).

2920 **841** 6 z. brown and green . . 20 10

1984. Clematis. Multicoloured.

2921 5 z. Type **842** 20 10
2922 6 z. "C. tangutica" 25 10
2923 10 z. "C. texensis" 30 15
2924 17 z. "C. alpina" 50 25
2925 25 z. "C. vitalba" . . . . . . 1·00 30
2926 27 z. "C. montana" . . . . . 1·10 35

843 "The Ecstasy of St. Francis" (El Greco)

1984. "Espana 84" International Stamp Exhibition, Madrid.

2927 **843** 27 z. multicoloured . . . 90 25

844 Handball

1984. Olympic Games, Los Angeles, and Winter Olympics, Sarajevo. Multicoloured.

2928 5 z. Type **844** 15 10
2929 6 z. Fencing 20 10
2930 15 z. Cycling 50 15
2931 16 z. Janusz Kusocinski winning 10,000 metres race, 1932 Olympics, Los Angeles . . 70 20
2932 17 z. Stanislawa Walasiewiczowna winning 100 metres race, 1932 Olympics, Los Angeles . . 70 20
2933 31 z. Women's slalom (Winter Olympics) . . . . 1·10 35

845 Monte Cassino Memorial Cross and Monastery — **846** "German Princess" (Lucas Cranach)

1984. 40th Anniv of Battle of Monte Cassino.

2935 **845** 15 z. olive and red . . . 45 15

1984. 19th U.P.U. Congress, Hamburg.

2936 **846** 27 z. + 10 z. multicoloured 1·10 50

847 "Warsaw from the Praga Bank" (Canaletto)

1984. Paintings of Vistula River. Multicoloured.

2937 5 z. Type **847** 20 10
2938 6 z. "Trumpet Festivity" (A. Gierymski) 25 10
2939 25 z. "The Vistula near Bielany District" (J. Rapacki) . . 90 30
2940 27 z. "Steamship Harbour in the Powisle District" (F. Kostrzewski) . . . . . 1·00 35

848 Order of Grunwald Cross — **849** Group of Insurgents

1984. 40th Anniv of Polish People's Republic. Multicoloured.

2941 5 z. Type **848** 20 10
2942 6 z. Order of Revival of Poland 20 10
2943 10 z. Order of Banner of Labour, First Class . . . 30 10
2944 16 z. Order of Builders of People's Poland 55 25

1984. 40th Anniv of Warsaw Uprising. Multicoloured.

2946 4 z. Type **849** 20 10
2947 5 z. Insurgent on postal duty 20 10
2948 6 z. Insurgents fighting . . . 20 10
2949 25 z. Tending wounded . . . 90 35

850 Defence of Oksywie Holm and Col. Stanislaw Dabek

1984. 45th Anniv of German Invasion. Multicoloured.

2950 5 z. Type **850** 20 10
2951 6 z. Battle of Bzura River and Gen. Tadeusz Kutrzeba . . 25 10

See also Nos. 3004/5, 3062, 3126/8, 3172/4 and 3240/3.

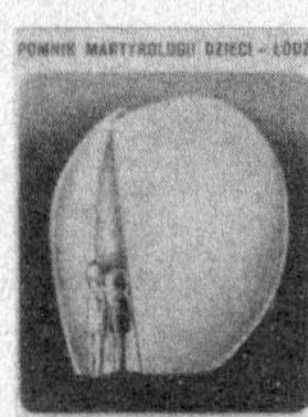

851 "Broken Heart" (monument, Lodz Concentration Camp)

1984. Child Martyrs.

2952 **851** 16 z. brown, blue and deep brown 45 15

852 Militiaman and Ruins

1984. 40th Anniv of Security Force and Civil Militia. Multicoloured.

2953 5 z. Type **852** 20 10
2954 6 z. Militiaman in control centre 25 10

853 First Balloon Flight, 1784 (after Chostovski)

1984. Polish Aviation.

2955 **853** 5 z. black, green & mve . 20 10
2956 – 5 z. multicoloured . . . 20 10
2957 – 6 z. multicoloured . . . 20 10
2958 – 10 z. multicoloured . . . 30 15
2959 – 16 z. multicoloured . . . 40 20

2960 – 27 z. multicoloured . . . 90 40
2961 – 31 z. multicoloured . . . 1·10 50
DESIGNS: No. 2956, Michal Scipio del Campo and biplane (1st flight over Warsaw, 1911); 2957, Balloon "Polonez" (winner, Gordon Bennett Cup, 1983); 2958, PWS 101 and Jantar gliders (Lilienthal Medal winners); 2959, PZL-104 Wilga airplane (world precise flight champion, 1983); 2960, Jan Nagorski and Farman M.F.7 floatplane (Arctic zone flights, 1914); 2961, PZL P-37 Los and PZL P-7 aircraft.

854 Weasel

1984. Fur-bearing Animals. Multicoloured.
2962 4 z. Type **854** 20 10
2963 5 z. Stoat 20 10
2964 5 z. Beech marten 25 10
2965 10 z. Eurasian beaver 30 15
2966 10 z. Eurasian otter 30 15
2967 65 z. Alpine marmot . . . . 2·40 75

1984. Renovation of Cracow Monuments (3rd series). As T **819**.
2968 5 z. brown, black and green . 20 10
2969 15 z. blue, brown and black . 40 15
DESIGNS—VERT: 5 z. Wawel cathedral. HORIZ: 15 z. Wawel castle (royal residence).

855 Protestant Church, Warsaw

1984. Religious Architecture. Multicoloured.
2970 5 z. Type **855** 15 10
2971 10 z. Saint Andrew's Roman Catholic church, Krakow . 30 10
2972 15 z. Greek Catholic church, Rychwald 45 20
2973 20 z. St. Maria Magdalena Orthodox church, Warsaw 60 20
2974 25 z. Tykocin synagogue, Kaczorow (horiz) 75 25
2975 31 z. Tatar mosque Kruszyiany (horiz) 95 40

856 Steam Fire Hose (late 19th century)

1985. Fire Engines. Multicoloured.
2976 4 z. Type **856** 15 10
2977 10 z. "Polski Fait" 1930s . . 30 10
2978 12 z. "Jelcz 315" fire engine . 35 15
2979 15 z. Manual fire hose, 1899 . 45 15
2980 20 z. "Magirus" fire ladder on "Jelcz" chassis 60 25
2981 30 z. Manual fire hose (early 18th century) . . . . 1·00 45

857 "Battle of Raclawice" (Jan Styka and Wojciech Kossak)

1985.
2982 **857** 27 z. multicoloured . . . 70 25

858 Wincenty Rzymowski

859 Badge on Denim

1985. 35th Death Anniv of Wincenty Rzymowski (founder of Polish Democratic Party).
2983 **858** 10 z. violet and red . . 25 10

1985. International Youth Year.
2984 **859** 15 z. multicoloured . . 40 15

860 Boleslaw III, the Wry-mouthed, and Map

1985. 40th Anniv of Return of Western and Northern Territories to Poland. Multicoloured.
2985 5 z. Type **860** 10 10
2986 10 z. Wladyslaw Gomulka (vice-president of first postwar government) and map . . 35 10
2987 20 z. Piotr Zaremba (Governor of Szczecin) and map . . 60 20

861 "Victory, Berlin 1945" (Joesf Mlynarski)

1985. 40th Anniv of Victory over Fascism.
2988 **861** 5 z. multicoloured . . . 15 10

862 Warsaw Arms and Flags of Member Countries

864 Cadet Ship "Iskra"

863 Wolves in Winter

1985. 30th Anniv of Warsaw Pact.
2989 **862** 5 z. multicoloured . . . 15 10

1985. Protected Animals. The Wolf. Mult.
2990 5 z. Type **863** 30 10
2991 10 z. She-wolf with cubs . . 70 10
2992 10 z. Close-up of wolf . . . 70 10
2993 20 z. Wolves in summer . . 1·40 20

1985. Musical Instruments (2nd series). As T **840**. Multicoloured.
2994 5 z. Rattle and tarapata . . 15 10
2995 10 z. Stick rattle and berlo . 30 10
2996 12 z. Clay whistles 35 15
2997 20 z. Stringed instruments . 55 20
2998 25 z. Cow bells 75 30
2999 31 z. Wind instruments . . . 90 40

1985. 40th Anniv of Polish Navy.
3000 **864** 5 z. blue and yellow . . 40 10

865 Tomasz Nocznicki

1985. Leaders of Peasants' Movement.
3001 **865** 10 z. green 25 10
3002 – 20 z. brown 50 20
DESIGN: 20 z. Maciej Rataj.

866 Hockey Players

1985. 60th Anniv (1986) of Polish Field Hockey Association.
3003 **866** 5 z. multicoloured 15 10

1985. 46th Anniv of German Invasion. As T **850**. Multicoloured.
3004 5 z. Defence of Wizna and Capt. Wladyslaw Raginis 20 10
3005 10 z. Battle of Mlawa and Col. Wilhelm Liszka-Lawicz . . 60 15

867 Goods Wagon Type "20 K"

1985. PAFAWAG Railway Rolling Stock. Multicoloured.
3006 5 z. Type **867** 20 10
3007 10 z. Electric locomotive, type "201 E" 40 15
3008 17 z. Two-axle coal car, type "OMMK" 65 25
3009 20 z. Passenger car, type "111 A" 85 35

869 Green-winged Teal

1985. Wild Ducks. Multicoloured.
3011 5 z. Type **869** 20 10
3012 5 z. Garganey 20 10
3013 10 z. Tufted duck 45 10
3014 15 z. Goldeneye 60 15
3015 25 z. Eider . . . . 1·00 30
3016 29 z. Red-crested pochard . . 1·40 40

870 U.N. Emblem and "Flags"

1985. 40th Anniv of U.N.O.
3017 **870** 27 z. multicoloured . . . 70 25

871 Ballerina 872 "Marysia and Burek in Ceylon"

1985. Bicentenary of Polish Ballet.
3018 **871** 5 z. green, orange & red . 15 10
3019 – 15 z. brown, violet & orge 45 10
DESIGN: 15 z. Male dancer.

1985. Birth Centenary of Stanislaw Ignacy Witkiewicz (artist). Multicoloured.
3020 5 z. Type **872** 15 10
3021 10 z. "Woman with Fox" (horiz) 30 10
3022 10z. "Self-portrait" 30 10
3023 20 z. "Compositions (1917–20)" 55 25
3024 25 z. "Nena Stachurska" . . 70 30

874 Human Profile

1986. Congress of Intellectuals for Defence of Peaceful Future of the World, Warsaw.
3026 **874** 10 z. ultramarine, violet and blue 25 10

875 Michal Kamienski and Planetary and Comet's Orbits

1985. Appearance of Halley's Comet.
3027 **875** 25 z. blue and brown . . 60 25
3028 – 25 z. deep blue, blue and brown 60 25
DESIGN: No. 3028, "Vega", "Planet A", "Giotto" and "Ice" space probes and comet.

1986. Renovation of Cracow Monuments (4th series). As T **819**.
3029 5 z. dp brown, brown & blk 10 10
3030 10 z. green, brown & black . 30 10
DESIGNS: 5 z. Collegium Maius (Jagiellonian University Museum); 10 z. Kazimierz Town Hall.

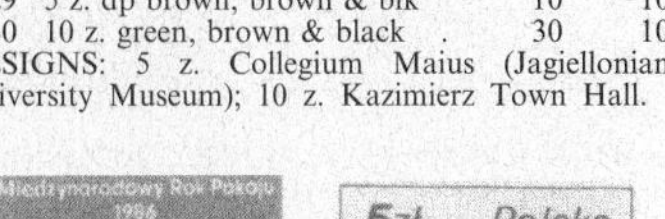

876 Sun

877 Grey Partridge

1986. International Peace Year.
3031 **876** 25 z. yellow, light blue and blue 55 20

1986. Game. Multicoloured.
3032 5 z. Type **877** 70 20
3033 5 z. Common rabbit 15 10
3034 10 z. Ring-necked pheasants (horiz) . . . . 1·10 20
3035 10 z. Fallow deer (horiz) . . 30 10
3036 20 z. Hare 60 20
3037 40 z. Argali . . . . 1·25 45

878 Kulczynski 880 Paderewski (composer)

879 "Warsaw Fire Brigade, 1871" (detail, Jozef Brodowski)

1986. 10th Death Anniv (1985) of Stanislaw Kulczynski (politician).
3038 **878** 10 z. light brown and brown 25 10

1986. 150th Anniv of Warsaw Fire Brigade.
3039 **879** 10 z. dp brown & brown 25 10

1986. "Ameripex '86" International Stamp Exhibition, Chicago.
3040 **880** 65 z. blue, black & grey . 1·50 70

881 Footballers

1986. World Cup Football Championship, Mexico.
3041 **881** 25 z. multicoloured . . . 50 20

882 "Wilanow"

1986. Passenger Ferries. Multicoloured.
3042 10 z. Type **882** 55 20
3043 10 z. "Wawel" 55 20
3044 15 z. "Pomerania" 70 30
3045 25 z. "Rogalin" . . . . . . 1·25 50

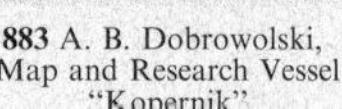

883 A. B. Dobrowolski, Map and Research Vessel "Kopernik"

885 "The Paulinite Church on Skalka in Cracow" (detail), 1627

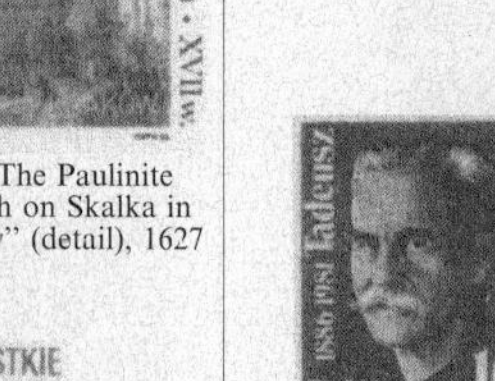

884 Workers and Emblem

1986. 25th Anniv of Antarctic Agreement.
3047 **883** 5 z. green, black & red . 40 25
3048 – 40 z. lavender, violet and orange . . . . 3·50 85
DESIGN: 40 z. H. Arctowski, map and research vessel "Professor Siedlecki".

1986. 10th Polish United Workers' Party Congress, Warsaw.
3049 **884** 10 z. blue and red . . . 25 10

1986. Treasures of Jasna Gora Monastery. Mult.
3050 5 z. Type **885** 15 10
3051 5 z. "Tree of Jesse", 17th-century 15 10
3052 20 z. Chalice, 18th-century . 40 20
3053 40 z. "Virgin Mary" (detail, chasuble column), 15th-century . . . . 1·00 40

886 Precision Flying (Waclaw Nycz)

1986. 1985 Polish World Championship Successes. Multicoloured.
3054 5 z. Type **886** 20 10
3055 10 z. Windsurfing (Malgorzata Palasz-Piasecka) 50 10
3056 10 z. Glider areobatics (Jerzy Makula) 40 10
3057 15 z. Wrestling (Bogdan Daras) 40 15
3058 20 z. Individual road cycling (Lech Piasecki) 60 20
3059 30 z. Women's modern pentathlon (Barbara Kotowska) . . . . 1·00 35

887 "Bird" in National Costume carrying Stamp

888 Schweitzer

1986. "Stockholmia '86" International Stamp Exhibition.
3060 **887** 65 z. multicoloured . . . 1·50 55

1986. 47th Anniv of German Invasion. As T **850**. Multicoloured.
3062 10 z. Battle of Jordanow and Col. Stanislaw Maczek . . 25 10

1986. 10th Death Anniv (1985) of Albert Schweitzer (medical missionary).
3063 **888** 5 z. brown, lt brown & bl 10 10

889 Airliner and Postal Messenger

890 Basilisk

1986. World Post Day.
3064 **889** 40 z. brown, blue & red 80 35

1986. Folk Tales. Multicoloured.
3066 5 z. Type **890** 15 10
3067 5 z. Duke Popiel (vert) . . . 15 10
3068 10 z. Golden Duck 25 10
3069 10 z. Boruta the Devil (vert) 25 10
3070 20 z. Janosik the Robber (vert) 40 20
3071 50 z. Lajkonik (vert) . . . . 1·10 50

891 Kotarbinski

892 20th-century Windmill, Zygmuntow

1986. Birth Centenary of Tadeusz Kotarbinski (philosopher).
3072 **891** 10 z. deep brown and brown 20 10

1986. Wooden Architecture. Multicoloured.
3073 5 z. Type **892** 10 10
3074 5 z. 17th-century church Baczal Dolny 10 10
3075 10 z. 19th-century Oravian cottage, Zubrzyca Gorna . 25 10
3076 15 z. 18th-century Kashubian arcade cottage, Wdzydze . 30 15
3077 25 z. 19th-century barn, Grzawa 60 20
3078 30 z. 19th-century watermill Siolkowice Stare 90 30

893 Mieszko (Mieczyslaw) I

1986. Polish Rulers (1st series). Drawings by Jan Matejko.
3079 **893** 10 z. brown & green . . 20 10
3080 – 25 z. black and purple . 50 20
DESIGN: 25 z. Queen Dobrawa (wife of Mieszko I).

See also Nos. 3144/5, 3193/4, 3251/2, 3341/2, 3351/2, 3387/8, 3461/4, 3511/12 and 3641/4.

894 Star

1986. New Year.
3081 **894** 25 z. multicoloured . . 45 35

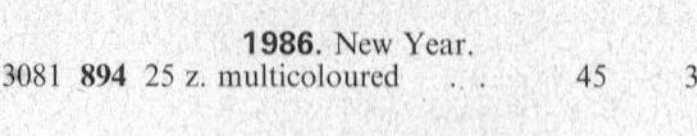

895 Trip to Bielany, 1887

1986. Centenary of Warsaw Cyclists' Society.
3082 **895** 5 z. multicoloured . . . 10 10
3083 – 5 z. brown, light brown and black 10 10
3084 – 10 z. multicoloured . . 25 10
3085 – 10 z. multicoloured . . 25 10
3086 – 30 z. multicoloured . . 60 25
3087 – 50 z. multicoloured . . 1·10 40
DESIGNS: No. 3083, Jan Stanislaw Skrodaki (1895 touring record holder); 3084, Dynasy (Society's headquarters, 1892–1937); 3085, Mieczyslaw Baranski (1896 Kingdom of Poland road cycling champion); 3086, Karolina Kociecka; 3087, Henryk Weiss (Race champion).

896 Lelewel

1986. Birth Bicentary of Joachim Lelewel (historian).
3088 **896** 10 z. + 5 z. multicoloured 30 15

897 Krill and "Antoni Garnuszewski" (cadet freighter)

1987. 10th Anniv of Henryk Arctowski Antarctic Station, King George Island, South Shetlands. Multicoloured.
3089 5 z. Type **897** 10 10
3090 5 z. "Nototenia marmurkowa", "Notothenia rossi" (fishes) and "Zulawy" (supply ship) 10 10
3091 10 z. Southern fulmar and "Pogoria" (cadet brigantine) 75 30
3092 10 z. Adelie penguin and "Gedania" (yacht) 75 30
3093 30 z. Fur seal and "Dziunia" (research vessel) 70 25
3094 40 z. Leopard seals and "Kapitan Ledochowski" (research vessel) 90 35

898 "Portrait of a Woman"

1987. 50th Death Anniv (1986) of Leon Wyczolkowski (artist). Multicoloured.
3095 5 z. "Cineraria Flowers" (horiz) 10 10
3096 10 z. Type **898** 20 10
3097 10 z. "Wooden Church" (horiz) 20 10
3098 25 z. "Beetroot Lifting" . . . 45 20
3099 30 z. "Wading Fishermen" (horiz) 50 25
3100 40 z. "Self-portrait" (horiz) . 70 40

899 "Ravage" (from "War Cycle") and Artur Grottger

1987. 150th Birth Anniv of Artur Grottger (artist).
3101 **899** 15 z. brown and stone . . 20 10

900 Swierczewski

901 Strzelecki

1987. 90th Birth Anniv of General Karol Swierczewski.
3102 **900** 15 z. green and olive . . 20 10

1987. 190th Birth Anniv of Pawel Edmund Strzelecki (scientist and explorer of Tasmania).
3103 **901** 65 z. green 95 45

902 Emblem and Banner

1987. 2nd Patriotic Movement for National Revival Congress.
3104 **902** 10 z. red, blue and brown 15 10

903 CWS "T-1" Motor Car, 1928

1987. Polish Motor Vehicles. Multicoloured.
3105 10 z. Type **903** 15 10
3106 10 z. Saurer-Zawrat bus, 1936 15 10
3107 15 z. Ursus-A lorry, 1928 . . 25 10
3108 15 z. Lux-Sport motor car, 1936 25 10
3109 25 z. Podkowa "100" motor cycle, 1939 . . . . 35 20
3110 45 z. Sokol "600 RT" motor cycle, 1935 . . . . 65 50

904 Royal Palace, Warsaw

1987.
3111 **904** 50 z. multicoloured . . . 75 35

905 Pope John Paul II

1987. 3rd Papal Visit. Multicoloured.
3112 15 z. Type **905** 30 10
3113 45 z. Pope and signature . . 70 35

906 Polish Settler at Kasubia, Ontario

1987. "Capex '87" International Stamp Exhibition, Toronto.
3115 **906** 50 z. + 20 z. multicoloured 95 45

1987. Renovation of Cracow Monuments (5th series). As T **819**.
3116 10 z. lilac, black and green . 15 10
DESIGN: 10 z. Barbican.

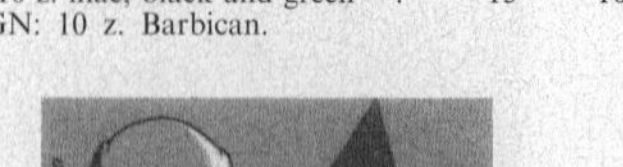

907 Ludwig Zamenhof (inventor) and Star

1987. Cent of Esperanto (invented language).
3117 **907** 5 z. brown, green & blk . 80 30

908 "Poznan Town Hall" (Stanislaw Wyspianski) **909** Queen Bee

1987. "Poznan 87" National Stamp Exhibition.
3118 **908** 15 z. brown and orange . 20 10

1987. "Apimondia 87" International Bee Keeping Congress, Warsaw. Multicoloured.
3119 10 z. Type **909** 20 10
3120 10 z. Worker bee 20 10
3121 5 z. Drone 25 15
3122 15 z. Hive in orchard 25 15
3123 40 z. Worker bee on clover flower 70 30
3124 50 z. Forest bee keeper collecting honey 90 50

1987. 48th Anniv of German Invasion. As T **850**. Multicoloured.
3126 10 z. Battle of Mokra and Col. Julian Filipowicz 20 10
3127 10 z. Fighting at Oleszyce and Brig-Gen. Jozef Rudolf Kustron 20 10
3128 15 z. PZL P-7 aircraft over Warsaw and Col. Stefan Pawlikowsi 40 15

911 Hevelius and Sextant **912** High Jump (World Acrobatics Championships, France)

1987. 300th Death Anniv of Jan Hevelius (astronomer). Multicoloured.
3129 15 z. Type **911** 30 15
3130 40 z. Hevelius and map of constellations (horiz) . . . 70 25

1987. 1986 Polish World Championship Successes. Multicoloured.
3131 10 z. Type **912** 15 10
3132 15 z. Two-man canoe (World Canoeing Championships, Canada) 25 10
3133 20 z. Marksman (Free pistol event, World Marksmanship Championships, East Germany) 40 15
3134 25 z. Wrestlers (World Wrestling Championships, Hungary) 50 20

914 Warsaw Post Office and Ignacy Franciszek Przebendowski (Postmaster General)

1987. World Post Day.
3136 **914** 15 z. green and red . . . 20 10

915 "The Little Mermaid" **916** Col. Stanislaw Wieckowski (founder)

1987. "Hafnia 87" International Stamp Exhibition, Copenhagen. Hans Christain Andersen's Fairy Tales. Multicoloured.
3137 10 z. Type **915** 15 10
3138 10 z. "The Nightingale" . . . 15 10
3139 20 z. "The Wild Swans" . . 30 15
3140 20 z. "The Little Match Girl" 30 15
3141 30 z. "The Snow Queen" . . 50 25
3142 40 z. "The Tin Soldier" . . . 70 30

1987. 50th Anniv of Democratic Clubs.
3143 **916** 15 z. black and blue . . 20 10

1987. Polish Rulers (2nd series). As T **893**. Drawings by Jan Matejko.
3144 10 z. green and blue 10 10
3145 15 z. blue and ultramarine . . 25 10
DESIGNS: 10 z. Boleslaw I, the Brave; 15 z. Mieszko (Mieczyslaw) II.

917 Santa Claus with Christmas Trees

1987. New Year.
3146 **917** 15 z. multicoloured . . 20 10

918 Emperor Dragonfly

1988. Dragonflies. Multicoloured.
3147 10 z. Type **918** 20 10
3148 15 z. Four-spotted libellula ("Libellula quadrimaculata") (vert) 35 10
3149 15 z. Banded agrion ("Calopteryx splendens") . 35 10
3150 20 z. "Condulegaster annulatus" (vert) 35 10
3151 30 z. "Sympetrum pedemontanum" 50 15
3152 50 z. "Aeschna viridis" (vert) 90 25

1988. Renovation of Cracow Monuments (6th series). As T **819**.
3153 15 z. yellow, brown & black 15 10
DESIGN: 15 z. Florianska Gate.

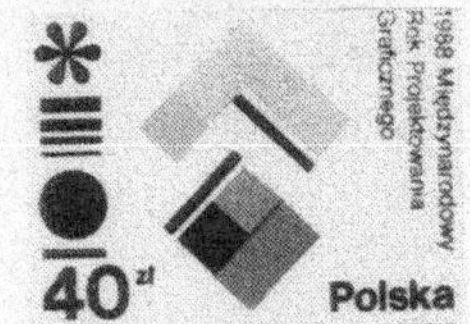

919 Composition

1988. International Year of Graphic Design.
3154 **919** 40 z. multicoloured . . 45 15

920 17th-century Friesian Wall Clock with Bracket Case

1988. Clocks and Watches. Multicoloured.
3155 10 z. Type **920** 15 10
3156 10 z. 20th-century annual clock (horiz) 15 10
3157 15 z. 18th-century carriage clock 20 10
3158 15 z. 18th-century French rococo bracket clock . . . 20 10
3159 20 z. 19th-century pocket watch (horiz) 25 10
3160 40 z. 17th-cent tile-case clock from Gdansk by Benjamin Zoll (horiz) 50 25

921 Salmon and Reindeer

1988. "Finlandia 88" International Stamp Exhibition, Helsinki.
3161 **921** 45 z. + 30 z. multicoloured 85 30

922 Triple Jump **924** Wheat as Graph on VDU

1988. Olympic Games, Seoul. Multicoloured.
3162 15 z. Type **922** 20 10
3163 20 z. Wrestling 25 10
3164 20 z. Canoeing 25 10
3165 25 z. Judo 30 15
3166 40 z. Shooting 50 25
3167 55 z. Swimming 65 35

1988. 16th European Conference of Food and Agriculture Organization, Cracow. Multicoloured.
3169 15 z. Type **924** 20 10
3170 40 z. Factory in forest 45 20

925 PZL P-37 Los Bomber

1988. 70th Anniv of Polish Republic (1st issue). 60th Anniv of Polish State Aircraft Works.
3171 **925** 45 z. multicoloured . . . 80 20
See also Nos. 3175, 3177, 3181/88 and 3190/2.

1988. 49th Anniv of German Invasion. As T **850**. Multicoloured.
3172 15 z. Battle of Modlin and Brig.-Gen. Wiktor Thommee 20 10
3173 20 z. Battle of Warsaw and Brig.-Gen. Walerian Czuma 20 10
3174 20 z. Battle of Tomaszow Lubelski and Brig.-Gen. Antoni Szylling 20 10

1988. 70th Anniv of Polish Republic (2nd issue). 50th Anniv of Stalowa Wola Ironworks. As T **925**. Multicoloured.
3175 15 z. View of plant 15 10

926 Postal Emblem and Tomasz Arciszewski (Postal Minister,1918–19) **927** On the Field of Glory Medal

1988. World Post Day.
3176 **926** 20 z. multicoloured . . . 20 10

1988. 70th Anniv of Polish Republic (3rd issue). 60th Anniv of Military Institute for Aviation Medicine. As T **925**. Multicoloured.
3177 20 z. Hanriot XIV hospital aircraft (38 × 28 mm) . . . 30 10

1988. Polish People's Army Battle Medals (1st series). Multicoloured.
3178 20 z. Type **927** 25 10
3179 20 z. Battle of Lenino Cross . 25 10
See also Nos. 3249/50.

928 "Stanislaw Malachowski" and "Kazimierz Nestor Sapieha"

1988. Bicentenary of Four Years Diet (political and social reforms). Paintings of Diet Presidents by Jozef Peszko.
3180 **928** 20 z. multicoloured . . . 20 10

929 Ignacy Daszynski (politician) **930** Snowman

1988. 70th Anniv of Polish Republic (4th issue). Personalities.
3181 **929** 15 z. green, red & black . 10 10
3182 – 15 z. green, red & black . 10 10
3183 – 20 z. brown, red & black 20 10
3184 – 20 z. brown, red & black 20 10
3185 – 20 z. brown, red & black 20 10
3186 – 200 z. purple, red & black 1·75 50
3187 – 200 z. purple, red & black 1·75 50
3188 – 200 z. purple, red & black 1·75 50
DESIGNS: No. 3182, Wincenty Witos (politician); 3183, Julian Marchlewski (trade unionist and economist); 3184, Stanislaw Wojciechowski (politician); 3185, Wojciech Korfanty (politician); 3186, Ignacy Paderewski (musician and politician); 3187; Marshal Jozef Pilsudski; 3188, Gabriel Narutowicz (President, 1922).

1988. 70th Anniv of Polish Republic (5th issue). As T **925**. Multicoloured.
3190 15 z. Coal wharf, Gdynia Port (65th anniv) (38 × 28 mm) 10 10
3191 20 z. Hipolit Cegielski (founder) and steam locomotive (142nd anniv of H. Cegielski Metal Works, Poznan) (38 × 28 mm) 20 10
3192 40 z. Upper Silesia Tower (main entrance) (60th anniv of International Poznan Fair) 45 20

1988. Polish Rulers (3rd series). Drawings by Jan Matejko. As T **893**.
3193 10 z. deep brown & brown . 10 10
3194 15 z. deep brown & brown . 15 10
DESIGNS: 10 z. Queen Rycheza; 15 z. Kazimierz (Karol Odnowiciel) I.

1988. New Year.
3195 **930** 20 z. multicoloured . . . 20 10

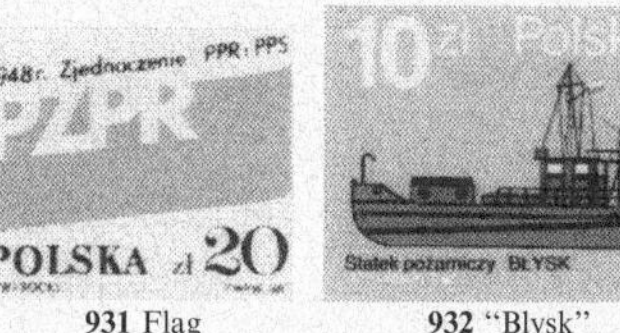

931 Flag **932** "Blysk"

1988. 40th Anniv of Polish United Workers' Party.
3196 **931** 20 z. red and black . . . 20 10

1988. Fire Boats. Multicoloured.
3197 10 z. Type **932** 15 10
3198 15 z. "Plomien" 25 10
3199 15 z. "Zar" 25 10
3200 20 z. "Strazak II" 40 10
3201 20 z. "Strazak 4" 40 10
3202 45 z. "Strazak 25" 80 50

933 Ardennes **934** Wire-haired Dachshund

1989. Horses. Multicoloured.
3203 15 z. Lippizaner (horiz) . . . 10 10
3204 15 z. Type **933** 10 10
3205 20 z. English thoroughbred (horiz) 20 10
3206 20 z. Arab 20 10
3207 30 z. Great Poland race-horse (horiz) 35 10
3208 70 z. Polish horse 75 50

1989. Hunting Dogs. Multicoloured.
3209 15 z. Type **934** 10 10
3210 15 z. Cocker spaniel 10 10
3211 20 z. Czech fousek pointer . 15 10
3212 20 z. Welsh terrier 15 10
3213 25 z. English setter 20 10
3214 45 z. Pointer 40 25

935 Gen. Wladyslaw Anders and Plan of Battle **936** Marianne

1989. 45th Anniv of Battle of Monte Cassino.
3215 **935** 80 z. multicoloured . . . 45 20
See also Nos. 3227, 3247, 3287 and 3327.

1989. Bicentenary of French Revolution.
3216 **936** 100 z. black, red & blue . 60 30

937 Polonia House

1989. Opening of Polonia House (cultural centre), Pultusk.
3218 **937** 100 z. multicoloured . . 60 30

938 Monument (Bohdan Chmielewski)

1989. 45th Anniv of Civic Militia and Security Force.
3219 **938** 35 z. blue and brown . . 70 25

939 Xaweri Dunikowski (artist) 941 Firemen

940 Astronaut

1989. Recipients of Order of Builders of the Republic of Poland. Multicoloured.
3220 35 z. Type **939** 25 10
3221 35 z. Stanislaw Mazur (farmer) 25 10
3222 35 z. Natalia Gasiorowska (historian) 25 10
3223 35 z. Wincenti Pstrowski (initiator of worker performance contests) . . . 25 10

1989. 20th Anniv of First Manned Landing on Moon.
3224 **940** 100 z. multicoloured . . 60 30

1989. World Fire Fighting Congress, Warsaw.
3226 **941** 80 z. multicoloured . . . 45 20

1989. 45th Anniv of Battle of Falaise. As T **935**. Multicoloured.
3227 165 z. Plan of battle and Gen. Stanislaw Maczek (horiz) . 90 45

942 Daisy 943 Museum Emblem

1989. Plants. (a) Perf.
3229 **942** 40 z. green 10 10
3230 – 60 z. violet 15 10
3231 **942** 150 z. red 20 10
3232 – 500 z. mauve 25 15
3233 – 700 z. green 15 10
3234 – 1000 z. blue 80 30

(b) Self-adhesive. Imperf.
3297 – 2000 z. green . . . . 1·00 50
3298 – 5000 z. violet . . . . 2·50 75
DESIGNS: 60 z. Juniper; 500 z. Wild rose; 700 z. Lily of the valley; 1000 z. Blue cornflower; 2000 z. Water lily; 5000 z. Iris.

1989. 50th Anniv of German Invasion. As T **850**.
3240 25 z. grey, orange & black . . 15 10
3241 25 z. multicoloured 15 10
3242 35 z. multicoloured 25 10
3243 35 z. multicoloured 25 10
DESIGNS: No. 3240, Defence of Westerplatte and Captain Franciszek Dabrowski; 3241, Defence of Hel and Captain B. Przybyszewski; 3242, Battle of Kock and Brig.-Gen. Franciszek Kleeberg; 3243, Defence of Lwow and Brig.-Gen. Wladyslaw Langner.

1989. Caricature Museum.
3244 **943** 40 z. multicoloured . . . 15 10

944 Rafal Czerwiakowski (founder of first university Surgery Department) 945 Emil Kalinski (Postal Minister, 1933–39)

1989. Polish Surgeons' Society Centenary Congress, Cracow.
3245 **944** 40 z. blue and black . . 20 10
3246 – 60 z. green and black . . 25 10
DESIGN: 60 z. Ludwik Rydygier (founder of Polish Surgeons' Society).

1989. 45th Anniv of Landing at Arnhem. As T **935**. Multicoloured.
3247 210 z. Gen. Stanislaw Sosabowski and plan of battle 80 40

1989. World Post Day.
3248 **945** 60 z. multicoloured . . 15 10

1989. Polish People's Army Battle Medals (2nd series). As T **927**. Multicoloured.
3249 60 z. "For Participation in the Struggle for the Rule of the People" 20 10
3250 60 z. Warsaw 1939–45 Medal 20 10

1989. Polish Rulers (4th series). As T **893**. Drawings by Jan Matejko.
3251 20 z. black and grey 10 10
3252 30 z. sepia and brown . . . 10 10
DESIGNS: 20 z. Boleslaw II, the Bold; 30 z. Wladyslaw I Herman.

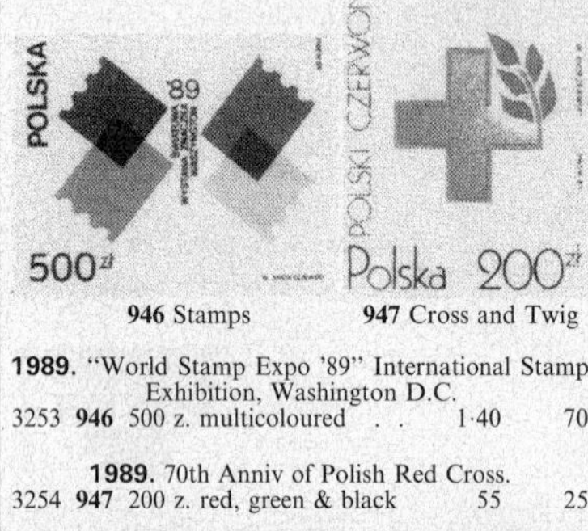

946 Stamps 947 Cross and Twig

1989. "World Stamp Expo '89" International Stamp Exhibition, Washington D.C.
3253 **946** 500 z. multicoloured . . 1·40 70

1989. 70th Anniv of Polish Red Cross.
3254 **947** 200 z. red, green & black 55 25

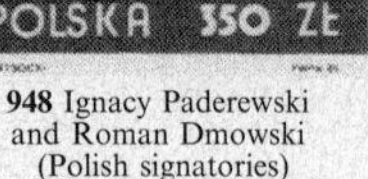

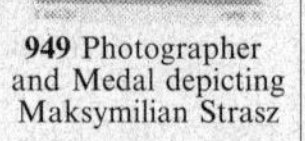

948 Ignacy Paderewski and Roman Dmowski (Polish signatories) 949 Photographer and Medal depicting Maksymilian Strasz

1989. 70th Anniv of Treaty of Versailles.
3255 **948** 350 z. multicoloured . . 95 45

1989. 150th Anniv of Photography. Multicoloured.
3256 40 z. Type **949** 15 10
3257 60 z. Lens shutter as pupil of eye (horiz) 20 10

1989. No. 2729 surch **500**.
3258 500 z. on 4 z. violet . . . . 1·40 70

951 Painting by Jan Ciaglinski

1989. Flower Paintings by Artists Named. Multicoloured.
3259 25 z. Type **951** 10 10
3260 30 z. Wojciech Weiss 10 10
3261 35 z. Antoni Kolasinski . . . 15 10
3262 50 z. Stefan Nacht-Samborski 15 10
3263 60 z. Jozef Pankiewicz . . . 20 10
3264 85 z. Henryka Beyer 30 10
3265 110 z. Wladyslaw Slewinski . 40 20
3266 190 z. Czeslaw Wdowiszewski 50 30

952 Christ

1989. Icons (1st series). Multicoloured.
3267 50 z. Type **952** 20 15
3268 60 z. Two saints with books 20 15
3269 90 z. Three saints with books 30 20
3270 150 z. Displaying scriptures (vert) 60 30
3271 200 z. Madonna and child (vert) 70 30
3272 350 z. Christ with saints and angels (vert) 80 40
See also Nos. 3345/50.

1990. No. 2839 surch **350 zl.**
3273 350 z. on 15 z. brown 15 10

954 Krystyna Jamroz 955 High Jumping

1990. Singers. Multicoloured.
3274 100 z. Type **954** 10 10
3275 150 z. Wanda Werminska . . 10 10
3276 350 z. Ada Sari 15 10
3277 500 z. Jan Kiepura 20 10

1990. Sports. Multicoloured.
3278 100 z. Yachting 20 10
3279 200 z. Football 20 10
3280 400 z. Type **955** 20 10
3281 500 z. Ice skating 25 10
3282 500 z. Diving 25 10
3283 1000 z. Gymnastics 40 20

956 Kozlowski

1990. Birth Centenary (1989) of Roman Kozlowski (palaeontologist).
3284 **956** 500 z. brown and red . . 25 10

957 John Paul II 959 Ball and Colosseum

1990. 70th Birthday of Pope John Paul II.
3285 **957** 1000 z. multicoloured . . 45 20

1990. 50th Anniv of Battle of Narvik. As T **935**. Multicoloured.
3287 1500 z. Gen. Zygmunt Bohusz-Szyszko and plan of battle . 45 20

1990. World Cup Football Championship, Italy.
3288 **959** 1000 z. multicoloured . . 70 30

1990. No. 3230 surch **700 zl.**
3289 700 z. on 60 z. violet 35 15

961 Memorial 963 Stagnant Pond Snail

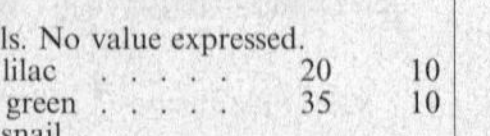

962 People and "ZUS"

1990. 34th Anniv of 1956 Poznan Uprising.
3290 **961** 1500 z. multicoloured . . 70 30

1990. 70th Anniv of Social Insurance.
3291 **962** 1500 z. blue, mve & yell . 70 30

1990. Shells. No value expressed.
3292 – B (500 z.) lilac 20 10
3293 **963** A (700 z.) green 35 10
DESIGN: B, River snail.

964 Cross

1990. 50th Anniv of Katyn Massacre.
3294 **964** 1500 z. black and red . . 70 30

965 Weather Balloon

1990. Polish Hydrology and Meteorology Service. Multicoloured.
3295 500 z. Type **965** 20 10
3296 700 z. Water-height gauge . 35 10

966 Women's Kayak Pairs

1990. 23rd World Canoeing Championships. Multicoloured.
3305 700 z. Type **966** 30 20
3306 1000 z. Men's kayak singles . 50 20

967 Victory Sign 968 Jacob's Ladder

1990. 10th Anniv of Solidarity Trade Union.
3307 **967** 1500 z. grey, black & red 70 30

1990. Flowers. Multicoloured.
3308 200 z. Type **968** 10 10
3309 700 z. Floating heart water fringe ("Nymphoides peltata") 30 15
3310 700 z. Dragonhead ("Dracocephalum ruyschiana") 30 15
3311 1000 z. "Helleborus purpurascens" 50 20
3312 1500 z. Daphne cneorum . . 90 30
3313 1700 z. Campion . . . . . . 1·25 40

969 Serving Dish, 1870–87

1990. Bicentenary of Cmieow Porcelain Works. Multicoloured.
3314 700 z. Type **969** 30 15
3315 800 z. Plate, 1887–90 (vert) . 40 20
3316 1000 z. Cup and saucer, 1887 50 20
3317 1000 z. Figurine of dancer, 1941–44 (vert) 50 20
3318 1500 z. Chocolate box, 1930–90 90 30
3319 2000 z. Vase, 1979 (vert) . . 1·00 40

970 Little Owl 972 Collegiate Church, Tum (12th century)

971 Walesa

1990. Owls. Multicoloured.
3320 200 z. Type **970** 25 10
3321 500 z. Tawny owl (value at left) 40 15
3322 500 z. Tawny owl (value at right) 40 15
3323 1000 z. Short-eared owl . . . 75 30
3324 1500 z. Long-eared owl . . . 1·10 40
3325 2000 z. Barn owl . . . . . . 1·60 55

1990. Lech Walesa, 1984 Nobel Peace Prize Winner and new President.
3326 **971** 1700 z. multicoloured . . 80 40

1990. 50th Anniv of Battle of Britain. As T **935**. Multicoloured.
3327 1500 z. Emblem of 303 Squadron, Polish Fighter Wing R.A.F. and Hawker Hurricane 70 30

1990. Historic Architecture. Multicoloured.
3328 700 z. Type **972** 30 15
3329 800 z. Reszel castle (11th century) 40 20
3330 1500 z. Chelmno Town Hall (16th century) 90 30
3331 1700 z. Church of the Nuns of the Visitation, Warsaw (18th century) . . . . 1·00 40

973 "King Zygmunt II August" (anon)
974 Silver Fir

1991. Paintings. Multicoloured.
3332 500 z. Type **973** 10 10
3333 700 z. "Adoration of the Magi" (Pultusk Codex) 15 10
3334 1000 z. "St Matthew" (Pultusk Codex) 20 10
3335 1500 z. "Expelling of Merchants from Temple" (Nikolai Haberschrack) 30 15
3336 1700 z. "The Annunciation" (miniature) 35 15
3337 2000 z. "Three Marys" (Nikolai Haberschrack) 40 20

1991. Cones. Multicoloured.
3338 700 z. Type **974** 15 10
3339 1500 z. Weymouth pine . . . 30 15
See also Nos. 3483/4.

975 Radziwill Palace
977 Chmielowski

1991. Admission of Poland into European Postal and Telecommunications Conference.
3340 **975** 1500 z. multicoloured . . 30 15

1991. Polish Rulers (5th series). Drawings by Jan Matejko. As T **893** but surch.
3341 1000 z. on 40 z. black & grn . 25 10
3342 1500 z. on 50 z. black & red . 40 15
DESIGNS: 1000 z. Boleslaw III, the Wry Mouthed; 1500 z. Wladyslaw II, the Exile.
Nos. 3341/2 were not issued unsurcharged.

1991. 75th Death Anniv of Adam Chmielowski ("Brother Albert") (founder of Albertine Sisters).
3343 **977** 2000 z. multicoloured . . 50 15

978 Battle (detail of miniature, Schlackenwerth Codex, 1350)

1991. 750th Anniv of Battle of Legnica.
3344 **978** 1500 z. multicoloured . . 35 15

1991. Icons (2nd series). As T **952**. Mult.
3345 500 z. "Madonna of Nazareth" 10 10
3346 700 z. "Christ the Acheirophyte" 15 10
3347 1000 z. "Madonna of Vladimir" 25 10
3348 1500 z. "Madonna of Kazan" 35 15
3349 2000 z. "St. John the Baptist" 50 20
3350 2200 z. "Christ the Pentocrator" 60 25

1991. Polish Rulers (6th series). Drawings by Jan Matejko. As T **893**.
3351 1000 z. black and red . . . 25 10
3352 1500 z. black and blue . . . 35 15
DESIGNS: 1000 z. Boleslaw IV, the Curly; 1500 z. Mieszko (Mieczyslaw) III, the Old.

979 Title Page of Constitution
980 Satellite in Earth Orbit

1991. Bicentenary of 3rd May Constitution.
3353 **979** 2000 z. brown, buff & red 50 20
3354 – 2500 z. brown, stone & red 60 25
DESIGNS: 2500 z. "Administration of Oath by Gustav Taubert" (detail, Johann Friedrich Bolt).

1991. Europa. Europe in Space.
3356 **980** 1000 z. multicoloured . 25 10

981 Map and Battle Scene

1991. 50th Anniv of Participation of "Piorun" (destroyer) in Operation against "Bismarck" (German battleship).
3357 **981** 2000 z. multicoloured . 50 20

982 Arms of Cracow
983 Pope John Paul II

1991. European Security and Co-operation Conference Cultural Heritage Symposium, Cracow.
3358 **982** 2000 z. purple and blue . 50 20

1991. Papal Visit. Multicoloured.
3359 1000 z. Type **983** 25 10
3360 2000 z. Pope in white robes . 50 20

984 Chinstrap Penguin
985 Making Paper

1991. 30th Anniv of Antarctic Treaty.
3361 **984** 2000 z. multicoloured . 85 25

1991. 500th Anniv of Paper Making in Poland.
3362 **985** 2500 z. blue and red . . 60 25

986 Prisoner

1991. Commemoration of Victims of Stalin's Purges.
3363 **986** 2500 z. red and black . 60 25

988 Ball and Basket

1991. Centenary of Basketball.
3365 **988** 2500 z. multicoloured . . 60 25

989 "Self-portrait" (Leon Wyczolkowski)

1991. "Bydgoszcz '91" National Stamp Exn.
3366 **989** 3000 z. green & brown . 70 30

990 Twardowski

1991. 125th Birth Anniv of Kazimierz Twardowski (philosopher).
3368 **990** 2500 z. black and grey . . 50 20

991 Swallowtail

1991. Butterflies and Moths. Multicoloured.
3369 1000 z. Type **991** 20 10
3370 1000 z. Dark crimson underwing ("Mormonia sponsa") 20 10
3371 1500 z. Painted lady ("Vanessa cardui") 30 15
3372 1500 z. Scarce swallowtail ("Iphiclides podalirius") . . 30 15
3373 2500 z. Scarlet tiger moth ("Panaxia dominula") . . . 50 25
3374 2500 z. Peacock ("Nymphalis io") 50 25

992 "The Shepherd's Bow" (Francesco Solimena)

1991. Christmas.
3376 **992** 1000 z. multicoloured . . 20 10

993 Gen. Stanislaw Kopanski and Battle Map

1991. 50th Anniv of Participation of Polish Troops in Battle of Tobruk.
3377 **993** 2000 z. multicoloured . . 45 20

994 Brig.-Gen. Michal Tokarzewski-Karaszewicz
995 Lord Baden-Powell (founder)

1991. World War II Polish Underground Army Commanders.
3378 **994** 2000 z. black and red . . 50 20
3379 – 2500 z. red and violet . . 60 20
3380 – 3000 z. violet and mauve 70 25
3381 – 5000 z. brown and green 1·25 40
3382 – 6500 z. dp brown & brn 1·60 50
DESIGNS: 2500 z. Gen. Broni Kazimierz Sosnkowski; 3000 z. Lt.-Gen. Stefan Rowecki; 5000 z. Lt.-Gen. Tadeusz Komorowski; 6500 z. Brig.-Gen. Leopold Okulicki.

1991. 80th Anniv of Scout Movement in Poland.
3383 **995** 1500 z. yellow and green 35 10
3384 – 2000 z. blue and yellow . 50 20
3385 – 2500 z. violet and yellow 60 20
3386 – 3500 z. brown & yellow . 75 25
DESIGNS: 2000 z. Andrzej Malkowski (Polish founder); 2500 z. "Watch on the Vistula" (Wojciech Kossak); 3500 z. Polish scout in Warsaw Uprising, 1944.

1992. Polish Rulers (7th series). As T **893**.
3387 1500 z. brown and green . . 35 10
3388 2000 z. black and blue . . . 50 20
DESIGNS: 1500 z. Kazimierz II, the Just; 2000 z. Leszek I, the White.

996 Sebastien Bourdon

1992. Self-portraits. Multicoloured.
3389 700 z. Type **996** 15 10
3390 1000 z. Sir Joshua Reynolds 20 10
3391 1500 z. Sir Godfrey Kneller . 25 10
3392 2000 z. Bartolome Esteban Murillo 40 15
3393 2200 z. Peter Paul Rubens . 45 15
3394 3000 z. Diego de Silva y Velazquez 60 25

997 Skiing
998 Manteuffel

1992. Winter Olympic Games, Albertville. Mult.
3395 1500 z. Type **997** 25 10
3396 2500 z. Ice hockey 45 15

1992. 90th Birth Anniv of Tadeusz Manteuffel (historian).
3397 **998** 2500 z. brown 45 15

999 Nicolas Copernicus (astronomer)

1992. Famous Poles. Multicoloured.
3398 1500 z. Type **999** 25 10
3399 2000 z. Frederic Chopin (composer) 40 15
3400 2500 z. Henryk Sienkiewicz (writer) 45 15
3401 3500 z. Marie Curie (physicist) 65 25

1000 Columbus and Left-hand Detail of Map

1992. Europa. 500th Anniv of Discovery of America by Christopher Columbus. Multicoloured.
3403 1500 z. Type **1000** 25 10
3404 3000 z. "Santa Maria" and right-hand detail of Juan de la Costa map, 1500 . . . . . 50 25
Nos. 3403/4 were issued together, se-tenant, forming a composite design.

1001 River Czarna Wiselka

1003 Family and Heart

1002 Prince Jozef Poniatowski

1992. Environmental Protection. River Cascades. Multicoloured.

3405 2000 z. Type **1001** 40 15
3406 2500 z. River Swider 45 15
3407 3000 z. River Tanew 60 20
3408 3500 z. Mickiewicz waterfall . 65 30

1992. Bicentenary of Order of Military Virtue. Multicoloured.

3409 1500 z. Type **1002** 25 10
3410 3000 z. Marshal Jozef Pilsudski 50 25

1992. Children's Drawings. Multicoloured.

3412 1500 z. Type **1003** 25 10
3413 3000 z. Butterfly, sun, bird and dog 50 25

1004 Fencing

1992. Olympic Games, Barcelona. Multicoloured.

3414 1500 z. Type **1004** 25 10
3415 2000 z. Boxing 40 15
3416 2500 z. Running 45 20
3417 3000 z. Cycling 55 25

1006 Statue of Korczak

1992. 50th Death Anniv of Janusz Korczak (educationist).

3419 **1006** 1500 z. black, brn & yell 30 10

1007 Flag and "V"

1008 Wyszinski

1992. 5th Polish Veterans World Meeting.

3420 **1007** 3000 z. multicoloured . 60 30

1992. 11th Death Anniv of Stefan Wyszinski (Primate of Poland) (3421) and 1st Anniv of World Youth Day (3422). Multicoloured.

3421 1500 z. Type **1008** 30 10
3422 3000 z. Pope John Paul II embracing youth 60 30

1009 National Colours encircling World Map

1992. World Meeting of Expatriate Poles, Cracow.

3423 **1009** 3000 z. multicoloured . 60 30

1010 Polish Museum, Adampol

1011 18th-century Post Office Sign, Slonim

1992. 150th Anniv of Polish Settlement at Adampol, Turkey.

3424 **1010** 3500 z. multicoloured . 65 35

1992. World Post Day.

3425 **1011** 3500 z. multicoloured . 65 35

1012 "Dedication" (self-portrait)

1992. Birth Centenary of Bruno Schulz (writer and artist).

3426 **1012** 3000 z. multicoloured . 60 30

1013 "Seated Girl" (Henryk Wicinski)

1992. Polish Sculptures. Multicoloured.

3427 2000 z. Type **1013** 40 15
3428 2500 z. "Portrait of Tytus Czyzewski" (Zbigniew Pronaszko) 45 20
3429 3000 z. "Polish Nike" (Edward Wittig) 60 30
3430 3500 z. "The Nude" (August Zamoyski) 65 35

1014 "10th Theatrical Summer in Zamosc" (Jan Mlodozeniec)

1992. Poster Art (1st series). Multicoloured.

3432 1500 z. Type **1014** 25 10
3433 2000 z. "Red Art" (Franciszek Starowieyski) 40 15
3434 2500 z. "Circus" (Waldemar Swierzy) 45 20
3435 3500 z. "Mannequins" (Henryk Tomaszewski) 65 35

See also Nos. 3502/3, 3523/4 and 3585/6.

1015 Girl skipping with Snake

1992. "Polska '93" International Stamp Exn, Poznan (1st issue). Multicoloured.

3436 1500 z. Type **1015** 25 10
3437 2000 z. Boy on rocking horse with upside-down runners . 40 15
3438 2500 z. Boy firing bird from bow 45 20
3439 3500 z. Girl placing ladder against clockwork giraffe . 65 35

See also Nos. 3452, 3453/6 and 3466/9.

1016 Medal and Soldiers

1992. 50th Anniv of Formation of Polish Underground Army. Multicoloured.

3440 1500 z. Type **1016** 25 10
3441 3500 z. Soldiers 65 35

1017 Church and Star

1018 Wheat

1992. Christmas.

3443 **1017** 1000 z. multicoloured . . 20 10

1992. International Nutrition Conference, Rome. Multicoloured.

3444 1500 z. Type **1018** 25 10
3445 3500 z. Glass, bread, vegetables and jug on table 60 30

1019 Arms of Sovereign Military Order

1020 Arms, 1295

1992. Postal Agreement with Sovereign Military Order of Malta.

3446 **1019** 3000 z. multicoloured . . 50 25

1992. History of the White Eagle (Poland's arms). Each black, red and yellow.

3447 2000 z. Type **1020** 30 10
3448 2500 z. 15th-century arms . . 40 15
3449 3000 z. 18th-century arms . . 50 25
3450 3500 z. Arms, 1919 . . . . . 60 30
3451 5000 z. Arms, 1990 . . . . . 80 35

1021 Exhibition Emblem and Stylised Stamp

1022 Amber

1992. Centenary of Polish Philately and "Polska '93" International Stamp Exhibition, Poznan (2nd issue).

3452 **1021** 1500 z. multicoloured . . 20 10

1993. "Polska '93" International Stamp Exhibition, Poznan (3rd issue). Amber. Multicoloured.

3453 1500 z. Type **1022** 20 10
3454 2000 z. Pinkish amber . . . 30 10
3455 2500 z. Amber in stone . . . 40 25
3456 3000 z. Amber containing wasp 50 30

1023 Downhill Skier

1024 Flower-filled Heart

1993. Winter University Games, Zakopane.

3458 **1023** 3000 z. multicoloured . 50 30

1993. St. Valentine's Day. Multicoloured.

3459 1500 z. Type **1024** 20 15
3460 3000 z. Heart in envelope . . 50 30

1993. Polish Rulers (8th series). As T **983** showing drawings by Jan Matejko.

3461 1500 z. brown and green . . 20 15
3462 2000 z. black and mauve . . 30 20
3463 2500 z. black and green . . 40 25
3464 3000 z. dp brown & brown . . 50 30

DESIGNS: 1500 z. Wladyslaw Laskonogi; 2000 z. Henryk I; 2500 z. Konrad I of Masovia; 3000 z. Boleslaw V, the Chaste.

1025 Arsenal

1993. 50th Anniv of Attack by Szare Szeregi (formation of Polish Scouts in the resistance forces) on Warsaw Arsenal.

3465 **1025** 1500 z. multicoloured . . 20 15

1026 Jousters with Lances

1993. "Polska '93" International Stamp Exhibition, Poznan (4th issue). Jousting at Golub Dobrzyn. Designs showing a modern and a medieval jouster. Multicoloured.

3466 1500 z. Type **1026** 20 15
3467 2000 z. Jousters 30 20
3468 2500 z. Jousters with swords . 40 25
3469 3500 z. Officials 60 30

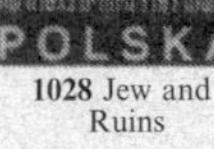

1027 Szczecin

1028 Jew and Ruins

1993. 750th Anniv of Granting of Town Charter to Szczecin.

3470 **1027** 1500 z. multicoloured . 20 15

1993. 50th Anniv of Warsaw Ghetto Uprising.

3471 **1028** 4000 z. black, yell & bl 65 40

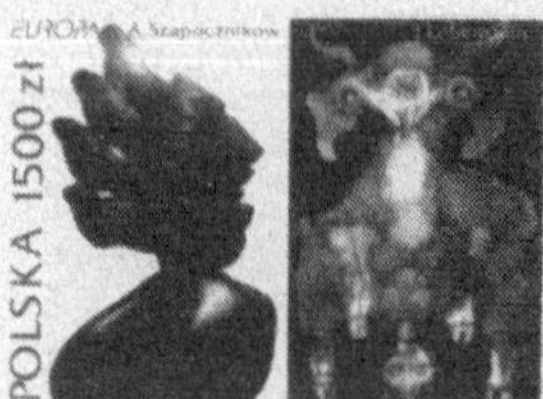

1029 Works by A. Szapocznikow and J. Lebenstein

1993. Europa. Contemporary Art. Multicoloured.

3472 1500 z. Type **1029** 20 15
3473 4000 z. "CXCIX" (S. Gierawski) and "Red Head" (B. Linke) 65 40

1030 "King Alexander Jagiellonczyk in the Sejm" (Jan Laski, 1505)

1993. 500th Anniv of Parliament.
3474 **1030** 2000 z. multicoloured . 30 20

1031 Nullo 1033 Cap

1993. 130th Death Anniv of Francesco Nullo (Italian volunteer in January 1863 Rising).
3475 **1031** 2500 z. multicoloured . 40 25

1993. 3rd World Congress of Cadets of the Second Republic.
3477 **1033** 2000 z. multicoloured . 30 15

1034 Copernicus and Solar System

1993. 450th Death Anniv of Nicolas Copernicus (astronomer).
3478 **1034** 2000 z. multicoloured . 30 15

1035 Fiki Miki and Lion

1993. 40th Death Anniv of Kornel Makuszynski (writer of children's books). Multicoloured.
3479 1500 z. Type **1035** 25 15
3480 2000 z. Billy goat 35 20
3481 3000 z. Fiki Miki 50 30
3482 5000 z. Billy goat riding ostrich 80 45

1993. Cones. As T **974**. Multicoloured.
3483 10000 z. Arolla pine . . . . 1·60 80
3484 20000 z. Scots pine . . . . . 3·25 1·60

1036 Tree Sparrow

1993. Birds. Multicoloured.
3485 1500 z. Type **1036** 25 10
3486 2000 z. Pied wagtail 35 15
3487 3000 z. Syrian woodpecker . 50 25
3488 4000 z. Goldfinch 70 30
3489 5000 z. Common starling . . 80 40
3490 6000 z. Bullfinch . . . . . . 1·00 50

1037 Soldiers Marching

1993. Bicentenary of Dabrowski's "Mazurka" (national anthem) (1st issue).
3491 **1037** 1500 z. multicoloured . 15 10
See also Nos. 3526, 3575 and 3639

1038 "Madonna and Child" (St. Mary's Basilica, Lesna Podlaska)

1993. Sanctuaries to St. Mary. Multicoloured.
3492 1500 z. Type **1038** 15 10
3493 2000 z. "Madonna and Child" (St. Mary's Church, Swieta Lipka) 20 15

1039 Handley Page Halifax and Parachutes

1993. The Polish Rangers (Second World War air troop).
3494 **1039** 1500 z. multicoloured . 15 10

1040 Trumpet Player

1993. "Jazz Jamboree '93" International Jazz Festival, Warsaw.
3495 **1040** 2000 z. multicoloured . 20 15

1041 Postman 1042 St. Jadwiga (miniature, Schlackenwerther Codex)

1993. World Post Day.
3496 **1041** 2500 z. brown, grey and blue 25 15

1993. 750th Death Anniv of St. Jadwiga of Silesia.
3497 **1042** 2500 z. multicoloured . 15 10

1044 Golden Eagle and Crown 1045 St. Nicholas

1993. 75th Anniv of Republic.
3499 **1044** 4000 z. multicoloured . 40 25

1993. Christmas.
3501 **1045** 1500 z. multicoloured . 15 10

1993. Poster Art (2nd series). As T **1014**. Mult.
3502 2000 z. "Come and see Polish Mountains" (M. Urbaniec) 20 15
3503 5000 z. Production of Alban Berg's "Wozzeck" (J. Lenica) 50 30

INDEX

Countries can be quickly located by referring to the index at the end of this volume.

1046 Daisy shedding Petals 1047 Cross-country Skiing

1994. Greetings Stamp.
3504 **1046** 1500 z. multicoloured . . 15 10

1994. Winter Olympic Games, Lillehammer, Norway. Multicoloured.
3505 2500 z. Type **1047** 25 10
3506 5000 z. Ski jumping 50 30

1048 Bem and Cannon

1994. Birth Bicentenary of General Jozef Bem.
3508 **1048** 5000 z. multicoloured . . 50 30

1049 Jan Zamojski (founder) 1050 Cracow Battalion Flag and Scythes

1994. 400th Anniv of Zamojski Academy, Zamosc.
3509 **1049** 5000 z. grey, black and brown 50 30

1994. Bicentenary of Tadeusz Kosciuszko's Insurrection.
3510 **1050** 2000 z. multicoloured . . 20 10

1994. Polish Rulers (9th series). Drawings by Jan Matejko. As T **893**.
3511 2500 z. black and blue . . . 25 10
3512 5000 z. black, deep violet and violet 50 30
DESIGN: 2500 z. Leszek II, the Black; 5000 a. Przemysl II.

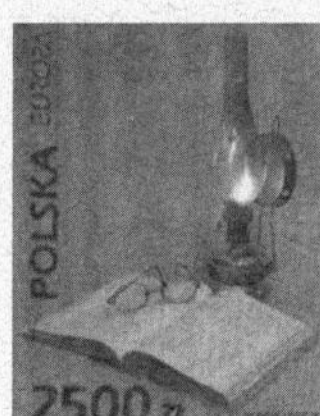

1051 Oil Lamp, Open Book and Spectacles 1052 "Madonna and Child"

1994. Europa. Inventions and Discoveries. Multicoloured.
3513 2500 z. Type **1051** (invention of modern oil lamp by Ignacy Lukasiewicz) 25 10
3514 6000 z. Illuminated filament forming "man in the moon" (astronomy) 60 40

1994. St. Mary's Sanctuary, Kalwaria Zebrzydowska.
3515 **1052** 4000 z. multicoloured . . 40 25

1053 Abbey Ruins and Poppies

1994. 50th Anniv of Battle of Monte Cassino.
3516 **1053** 6000 z. multicoloured . . 60 40

1054 Mazurka

1994. Traditional Dances. Multicoloured.
3517 3000 z. Type **1054** 30 20
3518 4000 z. Coralski 40 25
3519 9000 z. Krakowiak 90 60

1055 Cogwheels

1994. 75th Anniv of International Labour Organization.
3520 **1055** 6000 z. deep blue, blue and black 60 40

1056 Optic Fibre Cable

1994. 75th Anniv of Polish Electricians Association.
3521 **1056** 4000 z. multicoloured . 40 25

1057 Map of Americas on Football

1994. World Cup Football Championship, U.S.A.
3522 **1057** 6000 z. multicoloured . 60 40

1994. Poster Art (3rd series). As T **1014**. Mult.
3523 4000 z. "Monsieur Fabre" (Wiktor Gorka) 40 25
3524 6000 z. "8th OISTAT Congress" (Hurbert Hilscher) (horiz) 60 40

1058 Znaniecki 1059 Polish Eagle and Ribbon

1994. 36th Death Anniv of Professor Florian Znaniecki.
3525 **1058** 9000 z. green, bis & yellow 90 60

1994. Bicentenary of Dabrowski's Mazurka (2nd issue). As T **1037**. Multicoloured.
3526 2500 z. Troops preparing to charge 25 10

1994. 50th Anniv of Warsaw Uprising.
3527 **1059** 2500 z. multicoloured . 25 10

1060 "Stamp" protruding from Pocket 1061 Basilica of St. Brigida, Gdansk

1994. "Philakorea 1994" International Stamp Exhibition, Seoul.
3528 **1060** 4000 z. multicoloured . . 25 10

1994. Sanctuaries.
3529 **1061** 4000 z. multicoloured . 25 10

1062 "Nike" (goddess of Victory)

1994. Centenary of International Olympic Committee.
3530 **1062** 4000 z. multicoloured . 25 10

1063 Komeda and Piano Keys

1994. 25th Death Anniv of Krzysztof Komeda (jazz musician).
3531 **1063** 6000 z. multicoloured . 35 15

1064 Catfish ("Ancistrus dolichopterus")

1065 Arms of Polish Post, 1858

1994. Fishes. Multicoloured.
3532 4000 z. Type **1064** 20 10
3533 4000 z. Angel fish ("Pterophyllum scalare") . 20 10
3534 4000 z. Green swordtail ("Xiphophorus helleri") and neon tetra ("Paracheirodon innesi") 20 10
3535 4000 z. Rainbowfish ("Poecilia reticulata") 20 10
Nos. 3532/5 were issued together, se-tenant, forming a composite design.

1994. World Post Day.
3536 **1065** 4000 z. multicoloured . 20 10

1066 Kolbe

1994. Maximilian Kolbe (concentration camp victim) Year.
3537 **1066** 2500 z. multicoloured . 15 10

1067 Pigeon

1994. Pigeons. Multicoloured.
3538 4000 z. Type **1067** 20 10
3539 4000 z. Friar pigeon 20 10
3540 6000 z. Silver magpie pigeon . 35 15
3541 6000 z. Danzig pigeon (black) 35 15

1068 Musicians playing Carols

1994. Christmas.
3543 **1068** 2500 z. multicoloured . 15 10

1069 Landscape and E.U. Flag

1994. Application by Poland for Membership of European Union.
3544 **1069** 6000 z. multicoloured . 35 15

Currency reform. 10000 (old) zlotys = 1 (new) zloty

1070 "I Love You" on Pierced Heart

1995. Greetings Stamp.
3545 **1070** 35 g. red and blue . . 20 10

1071 Rain, Sun and Water

1995. 75th Anniv of Hydrological-Meteorological Service.
3546 **1071** 60 g. multicoloured . . 30 10

1072 Flag and Sea

1073 St. John

1995. 75th Anniv of Poland's "Marriage to the Sea" (symbolic ceremony commemorating renewal of access to sea).
3547 **1072** 45 g. multicoloured . . 25 10

1995. Polish Rulers (10th series). As T **893** showing drawings by Jan Matejko.
3548 35 g. deep brown, brown and light brown 20 10
3549 45 g. olive, deep green and green 25 10
3550 60 g. brown and ochre . . . 30 10
3551 80 g. black and blue 45 15
DESIGNS: 35 g. Waclaw II; 45 g. Wladyslaw I; 60 g. Kazimierz III, the Great; 80 g. Ludwik Wegierski.

1995. 500th Birth Anniv of St. John of God (founder of Order of Hospitallers).
3552 **1073** 60 g. multicoloured . . 30 10

1074 Eggs

1995. Easter. Decorated Easter eggs. Multicoloured, background colours given.
3553 **1074** 35 g. red 20 10
3554 – 35 g. lilac 20 10
3555 – 45 g. blue 25 10
3556 – 45 g. green 25 10

1995. Cones. As T **974**. Multicoloured.
3557 45 g. European larch 25 10
3558 80 g. Mountain pine 45 15

1075 Polish Officer's Button and Leaf

1995. Katyn Commemoration Year.
3559 **1075** 80 g. multicoloured . . 40 15

1076 Rose and Barbed Wire

1995. Europa. Peace and Freedom. Multicoloured.
3560 35 g. Type **1076** (liberation of concentration camps) . . . 20 10
3561 80 g. Flowers in helmet . . . 40 15

1077 Commom Cranes

1995. 50th Anniv of Return of Western Territories.
3562 **1077** 45 g. multicoloured . . . 25 10

1078 Pope and Wadowice Church Font

1995. 75th Birthday of Pope John Paul II.
3563 **1078** 80 g. multicoloured . . . 40 15

1079 Puppets under Spotlight ("Miromagia")

1995. 50th Anniv of Groteska Fairy Tale Theatre. Multicoloured.
3564 35 g. Type **1079** 20 10
3565 35 g. Puppets in scene from play 20 10
3566 45 g. Puppet leaning on barrel ("Thomas Fingerchen") (vert) 25 10
3567 45 g. Clown ("Bumstara Circus") 25 10

1080 Locomotive "Cockerill", Warsaw–Vienna, 1845

1995. 150th Anniv of Polish Railways. Multicoloured.
3568 35 g. Type **1080** 15 10
3569 60 g. "Lux-Torpedo" railcar, 1927 . . . . 30 10
3570 80 g. Electric locomotive drawing freight train, 1936 . 40 15
3571 1 z. EuroCity "Sobieski" train, Warsaw–Vienna line, 1992 . 50 20

1081 Symbols of Nations

1995. 50th Anniv of U.N.O.
3572 **1081** 80 g. multicoloured . . . 40 15

1082 Bank

1995. 125th Anniv of Warsaw Commercial Bank.
3573 **1082** 45 g. multicoloured . . 25 10

1083 Loaf and Four-leaved Clover

1995. Centenary of Peasant Movement.
3574 **1083** 45 g. multicoloured . . 25 10

1995. Bicentenary of Dabrowski's "Mazurka" (3rd issue). As T **1037**. Multicoloured.
3575 35 g. Mounted troops . . . 20 10

1084 Rowan Berries

1085 Madonna and Child

1995. Fruits of Trees. No value expressed. Multicoloured.
3576 A (35 g.) Type **1084** 20 10
3577 B (45 g.) Acorns and sessile oak leaves 25 10

1995. Basilica of the Holy Trinity, Lezajsk.
3578 **1085** 45 g. multicoloured . . 25 10

1086 Marshal Josef Pilsudski

1995. 75th Anniv of Defence of Warsaw and of Riga Peace Conference.
3579 **1086** 45 g. multicoloured . . 25 10

1087 Dressage

1995. World Carriage Driving Championships, Poznan. Multicoloured.
3580 60 g. Type **1087** 30 10
3581 80 g. Cross-country event . . 40 15

1088 Warsaw Technical University

1089 Russian Space Station and U.S. Spacecraft

1995. "Warsaw '95" National Stamp Exhibition.
3582 **1088** 35 g. multicoloured . . 20 10

1995. 11th World Cosmonauts Congress, Warsaw.
3584 **1089** 80 g. multicoloured . . 40 15

1995. Poster Art (4th series). As T **1014**. Multicoloured.
3585 35 g. "The Crazy Locomotive" (Jan Sawka) 20 10
3586 45 g. "The Wedding" (Eugeniusz Get Stankiewicz) 25 10

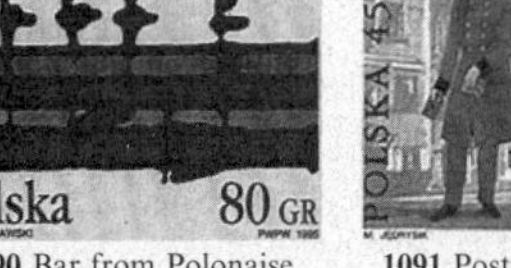

1090 Bar from Polonaise (Frederic Chopin) 1091 Postman

1995. 13th International Chopin Piano Competition.
3587 **1090** 80 g. multicoloured . . 40 15

1995. Post Day. Multicoloured.
3588 45 g. Type **1091** 25 10
3589 80 g. Feather fixed to envelope by seal 40 15

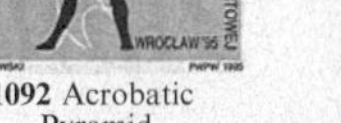

1092 Acrobatic Pyramid 1094 Crib

1093 Groszkowski and Formula

1995. World Acrobatic Sports Championships, Wroclaw.
3590 **1092** 45 g. multicoloured . . 25 10

1995. 11th Death Anniv of Professor Janusz Groszkowski (radio-electronic scientist).
3591 **1093** 45 g. multicoloured . . 25 10

1995. Christmas. Multicoloured.
3592 35 g. Type **1094** 20 10
3593 45 g. Wise men, Christmas tree and star of Bethlehem . . 25 10
Nos. 3592/3 were issued together, se-tenant, forming a composite design.

1095 Blue Tit

1995. Song Birds. Multicoloured.
3594 35 g. Type **1095** 20 10
3595 45 g. Long-tailed tit 25 10
3596 60 g. Great grey shrike . . . 30 10
3597 80 g. Hawfinch 40 15

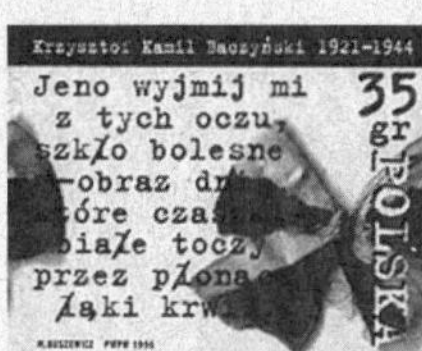

1096 Extract from Poem and Bow

1996. 75th Birth Anniv of Krzysztof Kamil Baczynski (poet).
3598 **1096** 35 g. multicoloured . . 20 10

1097 Cherries and "I love you" 1098 Romanesque-style Inowlodz Church

1996. Greetings Stamp.
3599 **1097** 40 g. multicoloured . . 20 10

1996. Architectural Styles. Multicoloured.
3600 40 g. Type **1098** 20 10
3601 55 g. Gothic-style St. Mary the Virgin's Church, Cracow . 30 10
3602 70 g. Renaissance-style St. Sigismund's Chapel, Wawel Castle 35 15
3603 1 z. Baroque-style Church of the Order of the Holy Sacrament, Warsaw 50 20

1099 "Oceania"

1996. Sailing Ships. Multicoloured.
3604 40 g. Type **1099** 20 10
3605 55 g. "Zawisza Czarny" (schooner) 25 10
3606 70 g. "General Zaruski" (cadet ketch) 30 10
3607 75 g. "Fryderyk Chopin" (brig) 35 15

1100 16th-century Warsaw 1101 Bull (Taurus)

1996. 400th Anniv of Warsaw.
3608 **1100** 55 g. multicoloured . . 25 10

1996. Signs of the Zodiac. Multicoloured.
3609 5 g. Workman in water (Aquarius) 10 10
3610 10 g. "Fish-person" holding fish (Pisces) 10 10
3611 20 g. Type **1101** 10 10
3612 25 g. Twins looking through keyhole (Gemini) 10 10
3613 30 g. Crab smoking pipe (Cancer) 15 10
3614 40 g. Maid and cogwheels (Virgo) 20 10
3615 50 g. Lion in military uniform (Leo) 20 10
3616 55 g. Couple with head and shoulders as scales (Libra) 25 10
3617 70 g. Ram with ram-head (Aries) 30 10
3618 1 z. Woman with scorpion's tail hat (Scorpio) 45 15
3619 2 z. Archer on motor cycle (Sagittarius) 90 30
3620 5 z. Office worker shielding face with paper mask (Capricorn) 2·25 75

1102 Hanka Ordonowna (singer)

1996. Europa. Famous Women. Multicoloured.
3621 40 g. Type **1102** 20 10
3622 1 z. Pola Negri (actress) . . 45 15

1103 Flag of Osiek and Old Photographs forming "1921"

1996. 75th Anniv of Silesian Uprising.
3623 **1103** 55 g. red, green and black 25 10

1104 "On Bergamuty Islands"

1996. 50th Anniv of U.N.I.C.E.F. Scenes from Fairy Tales by Jan Brzechwa. Multicoloured.
3624 40 g. Type **1104** 20 10
3625 40 g. Waiters carrying trays of apples (nursery rhyme) . . . 20 10
3626 55 g. Vegetable characters ("At the Market Stall") 25 10
3627 55 g. Chef holding duck ("Wacky Duck") 25 10
3628 70 g. Woman and birdchild ("The Fibber") 30 10
3629 70 g. Red fox ("The Impishness of Witalis Fox") 30 10

1105 "City Walls and Building"

1996. Paintings by Stanislaw Noakowski. Multicoloured.
3630 40 g. Type **1105** 20 10
3631 55 g. "Renaissance Bedroom" 25 10
3632 70 g. "Rural Gothic Church" 30 10
3633 1 z. "Renaissance Library" . 45 15

1106 Discus on Ribbon

1996. Olympic Games, Atlanta, and Centenary of Modern Olympic Games. Multicoloured.
3634 40 g. Type **1106** (gold medal, Halina Konopacka, 1928) . 20 10
3635 55 g. Tennis ball (horiz) . . . 25 10
3636 70 g. Polish Olympic Committee emblem (horiz) 30 10
3637 1 z. Bicycle wheel 45 15

1107 Tweezers holding Stamp showing Emblem 1108 St. Mary of Przeczycka

1996. "Olymphilex '96" International Sports Stamp Exhibition, Atlanta.
3638 **1107** 1 z. multicoloured . . . 45 15

1996. Bicentenary of Dabrowski's Mazurka (4th issue). As T **1037**. Multicoloured.
3639 40 g. Charge of Polish cavalry at Somosierra 20 10

1996. St. Mary's Church, Przeczycka.
3640 **1108** 40 g. multicoloured . . . 20 10

1996. Polish Rulers (11th series). As T **893**.
3641 40 g. brown and bistre . . . 20 10
3642 55 g. lilac and mauve 25 10
3643 70 g. deep grey and grey . . . 30 10
3644 1 z. deep green, green and yellow 45 15
DESIGNS: 40 g. Queen Jadwiga (wife of Wladyslaw II); 55 g. Wladyslaw II Jagiello; 70 g. Wladyslaw III Warnenczyk; 1 z. Kazimierz IV Jagiellonczyk.

1109 Mt. Giewont and Edelweiss

1996. The Tatra Mountains. Multicoloured.
3645 40 g. Type **1109** 20 10
3646 40 g. Mt. Krzesanica and spring gentian 20 10
3647 55 g. Mt. Koscielec and leopard's bane 25 10
3648 55 g. Mt. Swinica and clusius gentian 25 10
3649 70 g. Mt. Rysy and ragwort . . 30 10
3650 70 g. Mieguszowieckie peaks and pine trees 30 10

1110 Seifert

1996. 50th Birth Anniv of Zbigniew Seifert (jazz musician).
3651 **1110** 70 g. multicoloured . . 30 10

1111 "Changing of Horses at Post Station" (detail, Mieczyslaw Watorski)

1996. World Post Day. 75th Anniv of Post and Telecommunications Museum, Wroclaw. Paintings.
3652 **1111** 40 g. multicoloured . . 20 10

1112 Father Christmas on Horse-drawn Sleigh 1113 Head of Male

1996. Christmas. Multicoloured.
3654 40 g. Type **1112** 20 10
3655 55 g. Carol singers with star lantern 25 10

1996. The European Bison. Multicoloured.
3656 55 g. Type **1113** 25 10
3657 55 g. Head of female 25 10
3658 55 g. Pair of bison 25 10
3659 55 g. Male 25 10

1114 Wislawa Szymborska

1996. Award of Nobel Prize for Literature to Wislawa Szymborska (poet).
3660 **1114** 1 z. multicoloured . . . 45 15

MILITARY POST

I. Polish Corps in Russia, 1918.

1918. Stamps of Russia optd **POCZTA Pol. Korp.** and eagle. Perf or imperf. (70 k.).

No.	Type	Description		
M 1	22	3 k. red	40·00	38·00
M 2	23	4 k. red	40·00	38·00
M 3	22	5 k. red	13·00	10·50
M 4	23	10 k. blue	13·00	10·50
M 5	22	10 k. on 7 k. bl (No.151)	£400	£450
M 6	10	15 k. blue and purple	2·75	2·50
M 7	14	20 k. red and blue	5·25	3·75
M 8	10	25 k. mauve and green	65·00	50·00
M 9		35 k. green and purple	2·75	2·50
M10	14	40 k. green and purple	10·00	7·50
M11	10	70 k. orange and brown (No. 166)	£180	£150

1918. Stamps of Russia surch **Pol. Korp.**, eagle and value. (a) Perf on Nos. 92/4.

No.	Type	Description		
M12A	22	10 k. on 3 k. red	2·50	2·50
M13A		35 k. on 1 k. orange	40·00	40·00
M14A		50 k. on 2 k. green	2·75	2·75
M15A		1 r. on 3 k. red	50·00	50·00

(b) Imperf on Nos. 155/7.

No.	Type	Description		
M12B	22	10 k. on 3 k. red	90	90
M13B		35 k. on 1 k. orange	40	40
M14B		50 k. on 2 k. green	90	90
M15B		1 r. on 3 k. red	1·90	1·90

II. Polish Army in Russia, 1942.

M 3 "We Shall Return"

1942.

No.	Type	Description		
M16	M 3	50 k. brown	£130	£300

NEWSPAPER STAMPS

1919. Newspaper stamps of Austria optd **POCZTA POLSKA**. Imperf.

No.	Type	Description		
N50	N 53	2 h. brown	10·00	10·00
N51		4 h. green	2·40	2·40
N52		6 h. blue	2·40	2·40
N53		10 h. orange	38·00	38·00
N54		30 h. red	6·00	6·00

OFFICIAL STAMPS

O 24 O 70

1920.

No.	Type	Description		
O128	O 24	3 f. red	10	10
O129		5 f. red	10	10
O130		10 f. red	10	10
O131		15 f. red	10	10
O132		25 f. red	10	10
O123		50 f. red	10	10
O134		100 f. red	25	25
O135		150 f. red	30	30
O136		200 f. red	40	40
O137		300 f. red	35	35
O138		600 f. red	50	50

1933. (a) Inscr "ZWYCZAJNA".

No.	Type	Description		
O295	O 70	(No value) mauve	75	15
O306		(No value) blue	10	10

(b) Inscr "POLECONA".

No.	Type	Description		
O307	O 70	(No value) red	20	10

O 93

1940. (a) Size 31 × 23 mm.

No.	Type	Description		
O392	O 93	6 g. brown	1·00	1·50
O393		8 g. grey	1·00	1·50
O394		10 g. green	1·00	1·50
O395		12 g. green	1·25	1·75
O396		20 g. brown	1·25	3·00
O397		24 g. red	18·00	1·00
O398		30 g. red	1·50	3·50
O399		40 g. violet	1·50	6·00
O400		48 g. green	7·50	7·00
O401		50 g. blue	2·00	2·50
O402		60 g. green	1·25	2·00
O403		80 g. purple	1·25	2·00

(b) Size 35 × 26 mm.

No.	Type	Description		
O404	O 93	1 z. purple and grey	4·00	5·00
O405		3 z. brown and grey	4·00	5·00
O406		5 z. orange and grey	4·00	6·00

(c) Size 21 × 16 mm.

No.	Type	Description		
O407	O 93	6 g. brown	90	1·25
O408		8 g. grey	1·25	1·75
O409		10 g. green	1·50	2·00
O410		12 g. green	1·50	2·00
O411	O 93	20 g. brown	1·00	1·25
O412		24 g. red	75	85
O413		30 g. red	1·25	2·00
O414		40 g. violet	1·75	2·00
O415		50 g. blue	1·75	2·00

O 102 O 128 O 277

1943.

No.	Type	Description		
O456	O 102	6 g. brown	10	20
O457		8 g. blue	10	20
O458		10 g. green	10	20
O459		12 g. violet	25	20
O460		16 g. orange	10	30
O461		20 g. green	15	20
O462		24 g. red	25	20
O463		30 g. purple	15	20
O464		40 g. blue	15	20
O465		60 g. green	15	20
O466		80 g. purple	20	20
O467		100 g. grey	25	60

1945. No value. (a) With control number below design. Perf or imperf.

No.	Type	Description		
O534	O 128	(5 z.) blue	15	10
O535		(10 z.) red	25	15

(b) Without control number below design. Perf.

No.	Type	Description		
O748	O 128	(60 g.) pale blue	25	10
O805		(60 g.) indigo	65	30
O806		(1.55 z.) red	40	15

The blue and indigo stamps are inscr "ZWYKLA" (Ordinary) and the red stamps "POLECONA" (Registered).

1954. No value.

No.	Type	Description		
O871	O 277	(60 g.) blue	20	10
O872		(1.55 z.) red ("POLECONA")	40	15

POSTAGE DUE STAMPS

1991. Postage Due Stamps of Austria optd **POCZTA POLSKA**.

No.	Type	Description		
D50	D 55	5 h. red	5·75	5·25
D51		10 h. red	£1100	£1200
D52		15 h. red	2·40	2·00
D53		20 h. red	£300	£300
D54		25 h. red	14·00	13·00
D55		30 h. red	£550	£475
D56		40 h. red	£150	£120
D57	D 56	1 k. blue	£1700	£1700
D58		5 k. blue	£1700	£1700
D59		10 k. blue	£6000	£5500

1919. Postage Due Provisionals of Austria optd **POCZTA POLSKA**.

No.	Type	Description		
D60	50	15 on 36 h. (No. D287)	£180	£120
D61		50 on 42 h. (No. D289)	19·00	19·00

D 20 D 28 D 63

1919. Sold in halerzy or fenigow.

No.	Type	Description		
D 92	D 20	2 h. blue	10	10
D 93		4 h. blue	10	10
D 94		5 h. blue	10	10
D 95		10 h. blue	10	10
D 96		20 h. blue	10	10
D 97		30 h. blue	10	10
D 98		50 h. blue	10	10
D145		100 h. blue	20	20
D146		200 f. blue	40	30
D147		500 h. blue	25	20

The 20, 100 and 500 values were sold in both currencies.

1919. Sold in fenigow.

No.	Type	Description		
D128	D 20	2 f. red	25	30
D129		4 f. red	10	10
D130		5 f. red	10	10
D131		10 f. red	10	10
D132		20 f. red	10	10
D133		30 f. red	10	10
D134		50 f. red	10	10
D135		100 f. red	50	30
D136		500 f. red	1·40	70

1921. Stamps of 1919 surch with new value and **doplata**. Imperf.

No.	Type	Description		
D154	11	6 m. on 15 h. brown	75	75
D155		6 m. on 25 h. red	50	50
D156		20 m. on 10 h. red	95	95
D157		20 m. on 50 h. blue	1·25	1·60
D158		35 m. on 70 h. blue	10·00	12·00

1921. Value in marks. (a) Size 17 × 22 mm.

No.	Type	Description		
D159	D 28	1 m. blue	20	10
D160		2 m. blue	20	10
D161		4 m. blue	20	10
D162		6 m. blue	20	10
D163		8 m. blue	20	10
D164		20 m. blue	20	10
D165		50 m. blue	20	10
D166		100 m. blue	40	10

(b) Size 19 × 24 mm.

No.	Type	Description		
D199	D 28	50 m. blue	10	10
D200		100 m. blue	10	10
D201		200 m. blue	10	10
D202		500 m. blue	10	10
D203	D 28	1000 m. blue	10	10
D204		2000 m. blue	10	10
D205		10,000 m. blue	10	10
D206		20,000 m. blue	10	10
D207		30,000 m. blue	10	10
D208		50,000 m. blue	20	10
D209		100,000 m. blue	25	10
D210		200,000 m. blue	30	10
D211		300,000 m. blue	30	20
D212		500,000 m. blue	50	15
D213		1,000,000 m. blue	95	40
D214		2,000,000 m. blue	1·75	40
D215		3,000,000 m. blue	1·90	50

1923. Surch.

No.	Type	Description		
D216	D 28	10,000 on 8 m. blue	25	10
D217		20,000 on 20 m. blue	25	20
D218		50,000 on 2 m. blue	1·50	50

1924. As Type D **28** but value in "groszy" or "zloty". (a) Size 20 × 25½ mm.

No.	Type	Description		
D229	D 28	1 g. brown	15	15
D230		2 g. brown	15	15
D231		4 g. brown	15	15
D232		6 g. brown	25	15
D233		10 g. brown	3·25	15
D234		15 g. brown	3·00	20
D235		20 g. brown	6·50	20
D236		25 g. brown	4·50	20
D237		30 g. brown	85	20
D238		40 g. brown	1·10	20
D239		50 g. brown	1·10	20
D240		1 z. brown	85	30
D241		2 z. brown	85	30
D242		3 z. brown	1·10	1·25
D243		5 z. brown	1·10	50

(b) Size 19 × 24 mm.

No.	Type	Description		
D290	D 28	1 g. brown	20	10
D291		2 g. brown	20	10
D292		10 g. brown	1·00	20
D293		15 g. brown	1·40	10
D294		20 g. brown	3·00	10
D295		25 g. brown	27·00	10

1930.

No.	Type	Description		
D280	D 63	5 g. brown	50	15

1934. Nos. D 79/84 surch.

No.	Type	Description		
D301	D 28	10 g. on 2 z. brown	20	15
D302		15 g. on 2 z. brown	20	15
D303		20 g. on 1 z. brown	20	15
D304		20 g. on 5 z. brown	1·90	40
D305		25 g. on 40 g. brown	50	40
D306		30 g. on 40 g. brown	70	40
D307		50 g. on 40 g. brown	70	40
D308		50 g. on 3 z. brown	1·90	70

1934. No. 273 surch **DOPLATA** and value.

No.	Type	Description		
D309		10 g. on 1 z. black on cream	80	10
D310		20 g. on 1 z. black on cream	1·75	45
D311		25 g. on 1 z. black on cream	80	20

D 88 D 97

1938.

No.	Type	Description		
D350	D 88	5 g. green	15	10
D351		10 g. green	15	10
D352		15 g. green	15	10
D353		20 g. green	40	15
D354		25 g. green	15	10
D355		30 g. green	20	15
D356		50 g. green	55	70
D357		1 z. green	2·10	1·40

1940. German Occupation.

No.	Type	Description		
D420	D 97	10 g. orange	35	90
D421		20 g. orange	35	1·00
D422		30 g. orange	35	1·00
D423		50 g. orange	1·25	1·60

D 126 D 190

1945. Size 26 × 19½ mm. Perf.

No.	Type	Description		
D530	D 126	1 z. brown	10	10
D531		2 z. brown	10	10
D532		3 z. brown	15	15
D533		5 z. brown	20	15

1946. Size 29 × 21½ mm. Perf or imperf.

No.	Type	Description		
D646	D 126	1 z. brown	10	10
D647		2 z. brown	10	10
D572		3 z. brown	10	10
D573		5 z. brown	10	10
D574		6 z. brown	10	10
D575		10 z. brown	15	10
D649		15 z. brown	20	15
D577		25 z. brown	30	15
D651		100 z. brown	75	25
D652		150 z. brown	1·40	25

1950.

No.	Type	Description		
D665	D 190	5 z. red	15	10
D666		10 z. red	15	10
D667		15 z. red	15	10
D668		20 z. red	15	10
D669		25 z. red	25	15
D670		50 z. red	40	15
D671		100 z. red	70	45

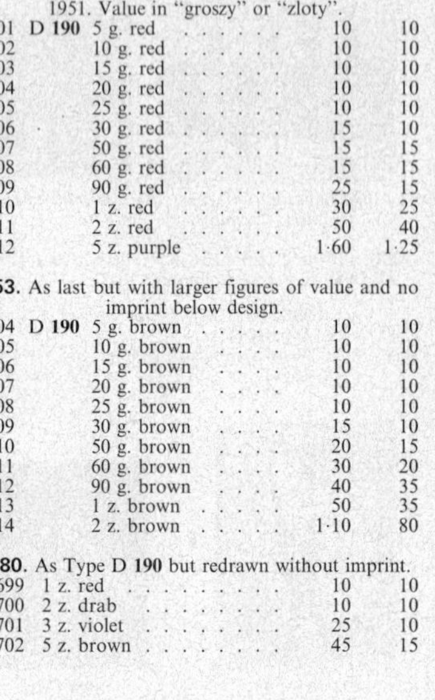

1951. Value in "groszy" or "zloty".

No.	Type	Description		
D701	D 190	5 g. red	10	10
D702		10 g. red	10	10
D703		15 g. red	10	10
D704		20 g. red	10	10
D705		25 g. red	10	10
D706		30 g. red	15	10
D707		50 g. red	15	15
D708		60 g. red	15	15
D709		90 g. red	25	15
D710		1 z. red	30	25
D711		2 z. red	50	40
D712		5 z. purple	1·60	1·25

1953. As last but with larger figures of value and no imprint below design.

No.	Type	Description		
D804	D 190	5 g. brown	10	10
D805		10 g. brown	10	10
D806		15 g. brown	10	10
D807		20 g. brown	10	10
D808		25 g. brown	10	10
D809		30 g. brown	15	10
D810		50 g. brown	20	15
D811		60 g. brown	30	20
D812		90 g. brown	40	35
D813		1 z. brown	50	35
D814		2 z. brown	1·10	80

1980. As Type D **190** but redrawn without imprint.

No.	Type	Description		
D2699		1 z. red	10	10
D2700		2 z. drab	10	10
D2701		3 z. violet	25	10
D2702		5 z. brown	45	15

POLISH POST IN DANZIG Pt. 5

For Polish post in Danzig, the port through which Poland had access to the sea between the two Great Wars.

100 groszy = 1 zloty

Stamps of Poland optd **PORT GDANSK**.

1925. Issue of 1924.
R 1 **40** 1 g. brown 30 60
R 2 2 g. brown 35 1·60
R 3 3 g. orange 35 60
R 4 5 g. green 8·75 3·75
R 5 10 g. green 3·00 1·25
R 6 15 g. red 18·00 3·00
R 7 20 g. blue 1·00 60
R 8 25 g. red 1·00 60
R 9 30 g. violet 1·25 60
R10 40 g. blue 1·25 60
R11 50 g. purple 3·25 80

1926. Issues of 1925–28.
R14 **44** 5 g. green 1·25 1·00
R15 – 10 g. violet (No. 245a) 1·25 1·00
R16 – 15 g. red (No. 246) 2·40 2·25
R17 **48** 20 g. red 1·90 1·40
R18 **51** 25 g. brown 2·75 90
R19 **57** 1 z. black and cream 18·00 18·00

1929. Issues of 1928/9.
R21 **61** 5 g. violet 95 80
R22 10 g. green 95 80
R23 **59** 15 g. blue 1·75 2·40
R24 **61** 25 g. brown 1·60 80

1933. Stamp of 1928 with vert opt.
R25 **57** 1 z. black on cream 48·00 60·00

1934. Issue of 1932.
R26 **65** 5 g. violet 1·90 2·25
R27 10 g. green 20·00 65·00
R28 15 g. red 1·90 2·25

1936. Issue of 1935.
R29 **79** 5 g. blue (No.313) 2·00 1·75
R31 – 5 g. violet (No.317) 65 1·00
R30 – 15 g. blue (No.315) 2·00 2·75
R32 – 15 g. lake (No.319) 65 1·00
R33 – 25 g. green (No.321a) 2·00 1·25

R 6 Port of Danzig

1938. 20th Anniv of Polish Independence.
R34 R **6** 5 g. orange 35 55
R35 15 g. brown 35 55
R36 25 g. purple 35 95
R37 55 g. blue 85 1·75

POLISH POST OFFICE IN TURKEY Pt. 5

Stamps used for a short period for franking correspondence handed in at the Polish Consulate, Constantinople.

100 fenigow = 1 marka

1919. Stamps of Poland of 1919 optd **LEVANT**. Perf.
1 **15** 3 f. brown 1·40
2 5 f. green 1·40
3 10 f. purple 1·40
4 15 f. red 1·40
5 20 f. blue 1·40
6 25 f. olive 1·40
7 50 f. green 1·40
8 **17** 1 m. violet 1·40
9 1 m. 50 green 1·40
10 2 m. brown 1·40
11 **18** 2 m. 50 brown 1·40
12 **19** 5 m. purple 1·40

PONTA DELGADA Pt. 9

A district of the Azores, whose stamps were used from 1868, and again after 1905.

1000 reis = 1 milreis

1892. As T **26** of Portugal but inscr "PONTA DELGADA".
6 5 r. yellow 2·25 1·50
7 10 r. mauve 2·25 1·50
8 15 r. brown 2·75 2·25
9 20 r. lilac 2·75 2·25
3 25 r. green 5·75 1·00
12 50 r.blue 5·75 3·25
25 75 r. pink 5·75 5·25
14 80 r. green 9·00 9·00
15 100 r. brown on yellow 9·00 5·25
28 150 r. red on pink 45·00 29·00
16 200 r. blue on blue 48·00 42·00
17 300 r. blue on brown 48·00 42·00

1897. "King Carlos" key-types inscr "PONTA DELGADA".
29 S 2½ r grey 45 35
30 5 r. orange 45 35
31 10 r. green 45 35
32 15 r. brown 5·75 5·75
45 15 r. green 1·50 1·10
33 20 r. lilac 1·60 1·10
34 25 r. green 2·25 1·10
46 25 r. red 1·25 40
35 50 r. blue 2·40 1·10
48 65 r. blue 1·00 45
36 75 r. pink 5·00 1·10
49 75 r. brown on yellow 10·00 6·00
37 80 r. mauve 1·25 1·10
38 100 r. blue on blue 2·75 1·10
50 115 r. brown k 1·60 1·25
51 130 r. brown on cream 1·60 1·25
39 150 r. brown on yellow 1·60 1·25
52 180 r. grey on pink 1·60 1·25
40 200 r. purple on pink 5·25 5·00
41 300 r. blue on pink 5·25 5·00
42 500 r. black on blue 11·00 9·75

PORT LAGOS Pt. 6

French Post Office in the Turkish Empire. Closed in 1898.

25 centimes = 1 piastre

1893. Stamps of France optd **Port-Lagos** and the three higher values surch also in figures and words.
75 **10** 5 c. green 13·50 10·00
76 10 c. black on lilac 27·00 19·00
77 15 c. blue 55·00 45·00
78 1 p. on 25 c. black on pink 40·00 35·00
79 2 p. on 50 c. red £120 70·00
80 4 p. on 1 f. green 65·00 60·00

PORT SAID Pt. 6

French Post Office in Egypt. Closed 1931.

1902. 100 centimes = 1 franc.
1921. 10 milliemes = 1 piastre.

1899. Stamps of France optd **PORT SAID**.
101 **10** 1 c. black on blue 40 50
102 2 c. brown on buff 50 60
103 3 c. grey 75 70
104 4 c. brown on grey 50 80
105 5 c. green 1·25 2·00
107 10 c. black on lilac 4·00 3·50
109 15 c. blue 2·50 4·00
110 20 c. red on green 3·25 4·50
111 25 c. black on pink 1·00 55
112 30 c. brown 4·75 5·00
113 40 c. red on yellow 7·25 4·50
115 50 c. red 9·50 6·00
116 1 f. green 13·00 7·75
117 2 f. brown on blue 42·00 35·00
118 5 f. mauve on lilac 50·00 50·00

1899. No. 107 surch. (a) **25c VINGT-CINQ**.
119 **10** 25 c. on 10 c. blk on lilac £275 £110

(b) **VINGT-CINQ** only.
121 **10** 25 c on 10 c blk on lilac 75·00 14·50

1902. "Blanc", "Mouchon" and "Merson" key-types inscr "PORT SAID".
122 A 1 c. grey 10 40
123 2 c. purple 15 35
124 3 c. red 15 20
125 4 c. brown 20 20
126a 5 c. green 65 30
127 B 10 c. red 30 45
128 15 c. red 75 85
128a 15 c. orange 1·10 90
129 20 c. brown 35 60
130 25 c. blue 30 15
131 30 c. mauve 1·75 1·50
132 C 40 c. red and blue 1·25 2·00
133 50 c. brown and lilac 1·00 1·25
134 1 f. red and green 4·25 3·50
135 2 f. lilac and buff 3·75 6·00
136 5 f. blue and buff 14·00 15·00

1915. Red Cross. Surch **5c** and red cross.
137 B **10** c. + 5 c. red 25 80

1921. Surch with value in figures and words (without bars).
151a A 1 m. on 1 c. grey 40 45
152 2 m. on 5 c. green 40 50
153 B 4 m. on 10 c. red 60 95
166a A 5 m. on 1 c. grey 4·00 4·50
167 5 m. on 2 c. purple 6·25 6·25
154 5 m. on 3 c. red 3·75 4·00
141 5 m. on 4 c. brown 4·75 4·75
155 B 6 m. on 15 c. orange 85 1·00
156 6 m. on 15 c. red 5·50 5·50
157 8 m. on 20 c. brown 75 90
168 A 10 m. on 2 c. purple 6·00 6·25
142 10 m. on 4 c. brown 9·50 9·50
158 B 10 m. on 25 c. blue 1·40 1·40
159 10 m. on 30 c. mauve 2·75 3·25
144 12 m. on 30 c. mauve 16·00 16·00
145 A 15 m. on 4 c. brown 3·50 3·75
169 B 15 m. on 15 c. red 27·00 27·00
170 15 m. on 20 c. brown 27·00 27·00
146 C 15 m. on 40 c. red & bl 25·00 25·00
160 15 m. on 50 c. brown and lilac 2·00 2·50
161 B 15 m. on 50 c. blue 2·50 2·00
162 30 m. on 1 f. red & green 1·50 3·00
171 C 30 m. on 50 c. brown & lilac £160 £160
172 60 m. on 50 c. brown and lilac £170 £170
149 60 m. on 2 f. lilac & buff 48·00 48·00
164 60 m. on 2 f. red & green 4·00 4·75
173 150 m. on 50 c. brown and lilac £200 £200
165 150 m. on 5 f. blue & buff 3·75 4·00

1925. Surch with value in figures and words and bars over old value.
174 A 1 m. on 1 c. grey 35 50
175 2 m. on 5 c. green 35 50
176 B 4 m. on 10 c. red 35 50
177 A 5 m. on 3 c. red 40 50
178 B 6 m. on 15 c. orange 60 70
179 8 m. on 20 c. brown 35 60
180 10 m. on 25 c. blue 60 70
181 15 m. on 50 c. blue 70 70
182 C 30 m. on 1 f. red & green 70 95
183 60 m. on 2 f. red & green 70 1·10
184 150 m. on 5 f. bl & buff 1·25 1·27

1927. Altered key-types. Inscr 'Mm' below value.
185 A 3 m. orange 60 75
186 B 15 m. blue 65 75
187 20 m. mauve 90 1·00
188 C 50 m. red and green 1·75 1·90
189 100 m. blue and yellow 2·00 2·50
190 250 m. green and red 4·00 4·25

1927. "French Sinking Fund" issue. As No. 186 (colour changed) surch **+5 Mm Caisse d'Amortissement**.
191 B 15 m. + 5 m. orange 1·25 1·50
192 15 m. + 5 m. mauve 1·25 1·50
193 15 m. + 5 m. brown 1·25 1·50
194 15 m. + 5 m. lilac 1·75 2·75

POSTAGE DUE STAMPS

1921. Postage Due stamps of France surch in figures and words.
D174 D **11** 2 m. on 5 c. blue 25·00 25·00
D175 4 m. on 10 c. brown 25·00 25·00
D176 10 m. on 30 c. red 25·00 25·00
D166 12 m. on 10 c. brown 28·00 28·00
D167 15 m. on 5 c. blue 30·00 30·00
D177 15 m. on 50 c. purple 35·00 35·00
D168 30 m. on 20 c. olive 35·00 35·00
D169 30 m. on 50 c. purple £170 £170
For 1928 issues, see Alexandria.

PORTUGAL Pt. 9

A country on the S.W. coast of Europe, a kingdom till 1910, when it became a republic.

1853. 1000 reis = 1 milreis.
1912. 100 centavos = 1 escudo.

1 Queen Maria II 5 King Pedro V 9 King Luis

1853. Various frames. Imperf.
1 **1** 5 r. brown £2500 £850
4 25 r. blue £800 16·00
6 50 r. green £2750 £850
8 100 r. lilac £25000 £1800

1855. Various frames. Imperf.
18a **5** 5 r. brown £350 60·00
21 25 r. blue £350 12·50
22 25 r. pink £250 4·50
13 50 r. green £450 65·00
15 100 r. lilac £650 85·00

1862. Various frames. Imperf.
24 **9** 5 r. brown £120 24·00
28 10 r. yellow £120 42·00
30 25 r. pink 90·00 4·25
32 50 r. green £650 70·00
34 100 r. lilac £700 85·00

14 King Luis 15

1866. With curved value labels. Imperf.
35 **14** 5 r. black £100 8·50
36 10 r. yellow £190 £140
38 20 r. bistre £160 60·00
39 25 r. pink £190 7·50
41 50 r. green £225 65·00
43 80 r. orange £225 65·00
45 100 r. purple £250 £110
46 120 r. blue £250 65·00

1867. With curved value labels. Perf.
52 **14** 5 r. black £110 40·00
54 10 r. yellow £225 £100
56 20 r. bistre £250 £100
57 25 r. pink 60·00 6·25
60 50 r. green £225 £100
61 80 r. orange £300 £100
62 100 r. lilac £225 £100
64 120 r. blue £250 65·00
67 240 r. lilac £850 £400

1870. With straight value labels. Perf.
69 **15** 5 r. black 50·00 5·00
70 10 r. yellow 70·00 26·00
158 10 r. green £100 29·00
74 15 r. brown 95·00 26·00
76 20 r. bistre 70·00 23·00
143 20 r. red £275 45·00
80 25 r. red 26·00 3·00
115 50 r. green £130 19·00
117 50 r. blue £275 50·00
148 80 r. orange £110 18·00
153 100 r. mauve 65·00 11·50
93 120 r. blue £250 70·00
95 150 r. blue £300 £110
155 150 r. yellow £110 12·50
99 240 r. lilac £1400 £1000
156 300 r. mauve £110 27·00
128 1000 r. black £200 60·00

16 King Luis 17

1880. Various frames for T **16**.
185 **16** 5 r. black 25·00 3·75
188 25 r. grey 26·00 3·00
190 25 r. brown 26·00 3·00
180 **17** 25 r. grey £275 26·00
184 **16** 50 r. blue £275 14·00

19 King Luis 26 King Carlos

1882. Various frames.
229 **19** 5 r. black 12·50 1·25
231 10 r. green 32·00 3·75
232 20 r. red 40·00 16·00
205 25 r. brown 26·00 2·25
234 25 r. mauve 26·00 2·75
236 50 r. blue 40·00 2·75
216 500 r. black £450 £275
217 500 r. mauve £250 50·00

1892.
271 **26** 5 r. orange 11·00 1·90
239 10 r. mauve 26·00 5·00
256 15 r. brown 26·00 3·75
242 20 r. lilac 30·00 8·25
275 25 r. green 25·00 1·90
244 50 r. blue 30·00 8·50
245 75 r. red 55·00 7·50
262 80 r. green 80·00 48·00
248 100 r. brown on buff 60·00 6·00
265 150 r. red on pink £140 50·00
252 200 r. blue on blue £150 40·00
267 300 r. blue on brown £160 60·00

1892. Optd **PROVISORIO**.
284 **19** 5 r. black 12·50 6·50
283 10 r. green 14·50 8·25
297 **15** 15 r. brown 14·50 12·50
290 **19** 20 r. red 35·00 21·00
291 25 r. mauve 12·50 4·75
292 50 r. blue 70·00 55·00
293 **15** 80 r. orange 95·00 85·00

1893. Optd **1893 PROVISORIO** or surch also.
302 **19** 5 r. black 24·00 21·00
303 10 r. green 22·00 19·00
304 20 r. red 40·00 32·00
309 20 r. on 25 r. mauve 50·00 45·00
305 25 r. mauve £100 95·00
306 50 r. blue £100 £100
310 **15** 50 r. on 80 r. orange £110 £100
312 75 r. on 80 r. orange 70·00 65·00
308 80 r. orange £100 85·00

32 Prince Henry in his Caravel and Family Motto

1894. 500th Birth Anniv of Prince Henry the Navigator.
314 **32** 5 r. orange 3·00 1·00
315 10 r. red 3·00 1·00
316 15 r. brown 7·50 2·50
317 20 r. lilac 7·50 3·00
318 – 25 r. green 7·50 1·10
319 – 50 r. blue 18·00 5·00
320 – 75 r. red 35·00 9·00
321 – 80 r. green 35·00 11·00
322 – 100 r. brown on buff 29·00 9·00
323 – 150 r. red 70·00 22·00
324 – 300 r. blue on buff 85·00 25·00
325 – 500 r. purple £200 55·00
326 – 1000 r. black on buff £350 75·00
DESIGNS: 25 r. to 100 r. Prince Henry directing movements of his fleet; 150 r. to 1000 r. Prince Henry's studies.

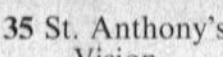

35 St. Anthony's Vision
37 St. Anthony ascending into Heaven

1895. 700th Birth Anniv of St. Anthony (Patron Saint). With a prayer in Latin printed on back.

No.	Type	Description	Unused	Used
327	35	2½ r. black	4·25	1·25
328	–	5 r. orange	4·25	1·25
329	–	10 r. mauve	12·50	7·50
330	–	15 r. brown	14·00	7·50
331	–	20 r. lilac	14·00	8·25
332	–	25 r. purple and green	12·00	1·25
333	37	50 r. brown and blue	30·00	21·00
334		75 r. brown and red	45·00	35·00
335		80 r. brown and green	55·00	55·00
336		100 r. black and brown	50·00	28·00
337	–	150 r. red and bistre	£150	95·00
338	–	200 r. blue and bistre	£140	95·00
339	–	300 r. grey and bistre	£200	£110
340	–	500 r. brown and green	£350	£225
341	–	1000 r. lilac and green	£600	£300

DESIGNS—HORIZ: 5 r. to 25 r. St. Anthony preaching to fishes. VERT: 150 r. to 1000 r. St. Anthony from picture in Academy of Fine Arts, Paris.

39 King Carlos

1895. Numerals of value in red (Nos. 354 and 363) or black (others).

No.	Type	Description	Unused	Used
342	39	2½ r. grey	20	10
343		5 r. orange	20	10
344		10 r. green	40	10
345		15 r. green	35·00	2·10
346		15 r. brown	70·00	3·50
347		20 r. lilac	50	30
348		25 r. green	50·00	25
349		25 r. red	30	10
351		50 r. blue	40	25
352		65 r. blue	40	25
353		75 r. red	85·00	4·25
354		75 r. brown on yellow	1·10	65
355		80 r. mauve	1·75	1·10
356		100 r. blue on blue	75	40
357		115 r. brown on pink	3·75	2·50
358		130 r. brown on cream	2·75	1·25
359		150 r. brown on yellow	£110	21·00
360		180 r. grey on pink	12·00	8·50
361		200 r. puple on pink	4·50	1·00
362		300 r. blue on pink	3·00	1·90
363		500 r. black on blue	8·00	4·25

40 Departure of Fleet

43 Muse of History
44 Da Gama and Camoens and "Sao Gabriel" (flagship)

1898. 4th Centenary of Discovery of Route to India by Vasco da Gama.

No.	Type	Description	Unused	Used
378	40	2½ r. green	1·25	35
379	–	5 r. red	1·25	35
380	–	10 r. purple	7·25	1·40
381	43	25 r. green	4·00	45
382	44	50 r. blue	8·50	2·50
383	–	75 r. brown	35·00	10·00
384	–	100 r. brown	25·00	10·00
385	–	150 r. brown	50·00	26·00

DESIGNS—HORIZ: 5 r. Arrival at Calicut; 10 r. Embarkation at Rastello; 100 r. Flagship "Sao Gabriel"; 150 r. Vasco da Gama. VERT: 75 r. Archangel Gabriel, Patron Saint of the Expedition.

48 King Manoel II 49

1910.

No.	Type	Description	Unused	Used
390	48	2½ r. lilac	20	15
391		5 r. black	20	15
392		10 r. green	30	15
393		15 r. brown	2·50	1·25
394		20 r. red	80	70
395		25 r. brown	60	20
396		50 r. blue	1·40	65
397		75 r. brown	8·75	4·50
398		80 r. grey	2·40	2·10
399		100 r. brown on green	10·00	2·75
400		200 r. green on orange	5·75	3·75
401		300 r. black on blue	6·75	4·50
402	49	500 r. brown and green	12·50	10·50
403		1000 r. black and blue	27·00	22·00

1910. Optd **REPUBLICA**.

No.	Type	Description	Unused	Used
404	48	2½ r. lilac	30	10
405		5 r. black	30	10
406		10 r. green	2·50	1·10
407		15 r. brown	1·00	80
408		20 r. red	4·00	1·40
409		25 r. brown	80	15
410		50 r. blue	5·75	1·90
411		75 r. brown	8·75	3·50
412		80 r. grey	3·00	2·25
413		100 r. brown on green	1·90	70
414		200 r. green on orange	2·25	1·60
415		300 r. black on blue	3·50	2·50
416	49	500 r brown and green	9·00	8·00
417		1000 r. black and blue	23·00	17·00

1911. Optd **REPUBLICA** or surch also.

No.	Type	Description	Unused	Used
441	40	2½ r. green	40	15
442a	D 48	5 r. black	60	20
443a		10 r. mauve	85	45
444	–	15 r. on 5 r. red (No. 379)	65	35
445a	D 48	20 r. orange	4·25	2·75
446	43	25 r. green	40	20
447	44	50 r. blue	2·50	1·75
448	–	75 r. brown (No. 383)	35·00	29·00
449	–	80 r. on 150 r. (No. 385)	5·25	4·25
450	–	100 r. brown (No. 384)	5·25	2·40
451	D 48	200 r. brown on buff	85·00	60·00
452		300 r. on 50 r. grey	60·00	38·00
453		500 r. on 100 r. red on pink	32·00	22·00
454	–	1000 r. on 10 r. (No. 380)	50·00	35·00

1911. Vasco da Gama stamps of Madeira optd **REPUBLICA** or surch also.

No.	Description	Unused	Used
455	2½ r. green	9·75	8·00
456	15 r. on 5 r. red	2·10	2·10
457	25 r. green	4·75	4·75
458	50 r. blue	8·75	8·25
459	75 r. brown	8·75	5·25
460	80 r. on 150 r. brown	10·00	10·00
461	100 r. brown	29·00	7·75
462	1000 r. on 10 r. purple	29·00	22·00

56 Ceres

60 Presidents of Portugal and Brazil and Airmen Gago Coutinho and Sacadura Cabral

1912.

No.	Type	Description	Unused	Used
484	56	¼ c. brown	15	10
485		½ c. black	15	10
486		1 c. green	95	35
515		1 c. brown	20	10
488		1½ c. brown	6·00	2·40
516		1½ c. green	25	20
490		2 c. red	6·00	1·50
517		2 c. yellow	20	10
702		2 c. brown	15	10
492		2½ c. lilac	35	15
521		3 c. red	25	15
703		3 c. blue	15	10
495		3½ c. green	25	15
523		4 c. green	20	10
704		4 c. orange	15	10
497		5 c. blue	5·50	50
705		5 c. brown	15	10
527		6 c. purple	20	10
706		6 c. brown	15	10
815		6 c. red	30	20
500		7½ c. brown	7·25	1·50
529		7½ c. blue	30	20
530		8 c. grey	40	30
531		8 c. green	60	50
532		8 c. orange	45	40
503		10 c. brown	12·50	50
707		10 c. red	15	10
504		12 c. blue	1·25	60
534		12 c. green	50	35
535		13½ c. blue	1·25	90
481		14 c. blue on yellow	2·00	1·40
536		14 c. purple	55	50
505		15 c. brown	1·90	75
708		15 c. black	25	75
709		16 c. blue	25	15
474		20 c. brown on green	15·00	1·50
475		20 c. brown on buff	17·00	3·50
539		20 c. brown	55	30
540		20 c. green	35	35
541		20 c. grey	50	40
542		24 c. blue	50	15
543		25 c. pink	35	15
710		25 c. grey	25	25
819		25 c. green	50	25
476		30 c. brown on pink	£110	10·00
477		30 c. brown on yellow	10·00	2·00
545		30 c. brown	50	30
820		32 c. green	50	25
548		36 c. red	1·75	35
549		40 c. blue	1·00	60
550		40 c. brown	55	35
712		40 c. green	35	15
713		48 c. pink	1·00	80
478		50 c. orange on orange	14·00	1·25
553		50 c. yellow	1·25	60

No.	Type	Description	Unused	Used
824	56	50 c. red	1·50	75
554		60 c. blue	1·50	60
715		64 c. blue	1·75	1·50
826		75 c. red	1·50	75
510		80 c. pink	1·50	1·00
558		80 c. lilac	1·00	50
827		80 c. green	1·50	75
559		90 c. blue	1·75	60
717		96 c. red	2·00	1·00
480		1 e. green on blue	8·00	1·25
561		1 e. lilac	2·50	40
565		1 e. blue	5·00	2·00
566		1 e. purple	1·60	80
829		1 e. red	35·00	75
562		1 e. 10 brown	4·00	1·75
563		1 e. 20 green	2·25	1·25
830		1 e. 20 brown	2·75	90
831		1 e. 25 blue	2·25	90
568		1 e. 50 lilac	15·00	3·50
720		1 e. 60 blue	2·10	50
721		2 e. green	13·50	90
833		2 e. mauve	14·50	5·00
572		2 e. 40 green	£180	£140
573		3 e. pink	£180	£140
722		3 e. 20 green	5·00	90
723		4 e. 50 yellow	5·00	90
575		5 e. green	40·00	9·75
724		5 e. brown	70·00	2·50
725		10 e. red	7·25	1·60
577		20 e. blue	£300	£180

1923. Portugal–Brazil Trans-Atlantic Flight.

No.	Type	Description	Unused	Used
578	60	1 c. brown	15	25
579		2 c. orange	15	25
580		3 c. blue	15	25
581		4 c. green	20	25
582		5 c. brown	20	25
583		10 c. brown	20	25
584		15 c. black	25	25
585		20 c. green	25	25
586		25 c. red	30	25
587		30 c. brown	80	90
588		40 c. brown	25	25
589		50 c. yellow	35	35
590		75 c. purple	35	45
591		1 e. blue	45	90
592		1 e. 50 grey	75	1·10
593		2 e. green	80	2·75

62 Camoens at Ceuta

63 Saving the "Lusiad"

1924. 400th Birth Anniv of Camoens (poet). Value in black.

No.	Type	Description	Unused	Used
600	62	2 c. blue	15	15
601		3 c. orange	15	15
602		4 c. grey	15	15
603		5 c. green	15	15
604		6 c. red	15	15
605	63	8 c. brown	15	15
606		10 c. violet	15	15
607		15 c. green	15	15
608		16 c. purple	15	15
609		20 c. orange	30	15
610	–	25 c. violet	30	15
611	–	30 c. brown	30	15
612	–	32 c. green	70	70
613	–	40 c. blue	25	15
614	–	48 c. red	1·10	1·10
615	–	50 c. red	1·25	90
616	–	64 c. green	1·25	90
617	–	75 c. lilac	1·25	90
618	–	80 c. brown	1·00	85
619	–	96 c. red	1·00	85
620	–	1 e. turquoise	1·00	75
621	–	1 e. 20 brown	5·00	4·50
622	–	1 e 50 red	1·10	90
623	–	1 e. 60 blue	1·10	90
624	–	2 e. green	4·75	4·75
625	–	2 e. 40 green on green	3·25	2·50
626	–	3 e. blue on blue	1·50	90
627	–	3 e. 20 black on turquoise	1·50	90
628	–	4 e. 50 black on yellow	3·75	2·75
629	–	10 e. brown on pink	8·50	5·75
630	–	20 e. violet on mauve	8·75	7·00

DESIGNS—VERT: 25 c. to 48 c. Luis de Camoens; 50 c. to 96 c. 1st Edition of "Lusiad"; 20 e. Monument to Camoens. HORIZ: 1 e. to 2 e. Death of Camoens; 2 e. 40 to 10 e. Tomb of Camoens.

65 Branco's House at S.Miguel de Seide

67 Camilo Castelo Branco

1925. Birth Centenary of Camilo Castelo Branco (novelist). Value in black.

No.	Type	Description	Unused	Used
631	65	2 c. orange	15	15
632		3 c. green	15	15
633		4 c. blue	15	15
634		5 c. red	15	15
635		6 c. purple	15	15
636		8 c. brown	15	15
637	A	10 c. blue	15	15
638	67	15 c. green	15	15
639	A	16 c. orange	30	30
640		20 c. violet	30	30
641	67	25 c. red	30	30
642	A	30 c. bistre	30	30
643		32 c. green	1·00	1·00
644	67	40 c. black and green	60	60
645	A	48 c. red	2·75	2·75
646	B	50 c. green	60	60
647		64 c. brown	2·75	2·75
648		75 c. grey	55	55
649	67	80 c. brown	55	55
650	B	96 c. red	1·40	1·40
651		1 e. lilac	1·25	1·25
652		1 e. 20 green	1·40	1·40
653	C	1 e. 50 blue on blue	24·00	12·50
654	67	1 e. 60 blue	4·25	3·50
655	C	2 e. green on green	5·75	3·75
656		2 e. 40 red on orange	50·00	29·00
657		3 e. red on blue	60·00	38·00
658		3 e. 20 black on green	29·00	29·00
659	67	4 e. 50 black and red	11·50	3·50
660	C	10 e. brown on buff	11·50	3·50
661	D	20 e. black on orange	11·50	3·50

DESIGNS—HORIZ: A, Branco's study. VERT: B, Teresa de Albuquerque; C, Mariana and Joao da Cruz; D, Simao de Botelho. Types B/D shows characters from Branco's "Amor de Peredicao".

76 Afonso I, first King of Portugal, 1140

80 Goncalo Mendes da Maia

77 Battle of Aljubarrota

1926. 1st Independence issue. Dated 1926. Centres in black.

No.	Type	Description	Unused	Used
671	76	2 c. orange	15	15
672	–	3 c. blue	15	15
673	76	4 c. green	15	15
674	–	5 c. brown	15	15
675	76	6 c. orange	15	15
676	–	15 c. green	15	15
677	76	16 c. blue	70	70
678	77	20 c. violet	70	70
679	–	25 c. red	70	70
680	77	32 c. green	90	90
681	–	40 c. brown	50	50
682	–	46 c. red	2·75	2·75
683	–	50 c. bistre	2·75	2·75
684	–	64 c. green	3·75	3·75
685	–	75 c. brown	3·75	3·75
686	–	96 c. red	6·50	6·50
687	–	1 e. violet	6·50	6·50
688	77	1 e. 60 blue	9·00	9·00
689	–	3 e. purple	25·00	25·00
690	–	4 e. 50 green	32·00	32·00
691	77	10 e. red	50·00	50·00

DESIGNS—VERT: 25, 40, 50, 75 c. Philippa de Vilhena arms her sons; 64 c., 1 e. Don Joao IV, 1640; 96 c. 3, 4 e. 50, Independence Monument, Lisbon. HORIZ: 3, 5, 15, 46 c. Monastery of D. Joao I.

1926. 1st Independence issue surch. Centres in black.

No.	Description	Unused	Used
692	2 c. on 5 c. brown	1·10	1·10
693	2 c. on 46 c. red	1·00	1·00
694	2 c. on 64 c. green	1·25	1·25
695	3 c. on 75 c. brown	1·10	1·10
696	3 c. on 96 c. red	1·90	1·90
697	3 c. on 1 e. violet	1·60	1·60
698	4 c. on 1 e. 60 blue	10·50	10·50
699	4 c. on 3 e. purple	3·75	3·75
700	6 c. on 4 e. 50 green	3·75	3·75
701	6 c. on 10 e. red	3·75	3·75

1927. 2nd Independence issue. Dated 1927. Centres in black.

No.	Type	Description	Unused	Used
726	80	2 c. brown	15	15
727	–	3 c. blue	15	15
728	80	4 c. orange	15	15
729	–	5 c. brown	15	15
730	–	6 c. brown	15	15
731	–	15 c. brown	35	35
732	–	16 c. blue	1·00	85
733	80	25 c. grey	1·00	1·00
734	–	32 c. green	2·25	1·50
735	–	40 c. green	50	50
736	80	48 c. red	10·50	9·25
737	–	80 c. violet	7·50	6·25
738	–	96 c. red	13·50	12·00
739	–	1 e. 60 blue	14·50	14·00
740	–	4 e. 50 brown	21·00	20·00

DESIGNS—HORIZ: 3, 15, 80 c. Gulmaraes Castle; 6, 32 c. Battle of Montijo. VERT: 5, 16 c., 1 e. 50, Joao das Regras; 40, 96 c. Brites de Aimelda; 4 e. 50, J. P. Ribeiro.

1928. Surch.

No.	Type	Description	Unused	Used
742	56	4 c. on 8 c. orange	40	30
743		4 c. on 30 c. brown	40	30
744		10 c. on ¼ c. brown	40	30
745		10 c. on ½ c. black	50	40
746		10 c. on 1 c. brown	50	30
747		10 c. on 4 c. green	35	30
748		10 c. on 4 c. orange	35	35

749	56	10 c. on 5 c. brown	35	35
751		15 c. on 16 c. blue	1·00	75
752		15 c. on 20 c. brown	30·00	30·00
753		15 c. on 20 c. grey	40	30
754		15 c. on 24 c. blue	2·00	1·00
755		15 c. on 25 c. pink	40	25
756		15 c. on 25 c. grey	40	25
757		16 c. on 32 c. green	80	75
758		40 c. on 2 c. yellow	40	25
760		40 c. on 2 c. brown	35	25
761		40 c. on 3 c. blue	40	30
762		40 c. on 50 c. yellow	30	25
763		40 c. on 60 c. blue	85	60
764		40 c. on 64 c. blue	85	75
765		40 c. on 75 c. pink	80	70
766		40 c. on 80 c. lilac	60	50
767		40 c. on 90 c. blue	4·00	3·00
768		40 c. on 1 e. grey	75	70
769		40 c. on 1 e. 10 brown	80	75
770		80 c. on 6 c. purple	75	60
771		80 c. on 6 c. brown	75	60
772		80 c. on 48 c. pink	1·10	1·00
773		80 c. on 1 e. 50 lilac	1·75	1·10
774		96 c. on 1 e. 20 green	3·25	2·25
775		96 c. on 1 e. 20 buff	3·25	2·50
777		1 e. 60 on 2 e. green	32·00	25·00
778		1 e. 60 on 3 e. 20 green	10·00	6·75
779		1 e. 60 on 20 e. blue	12·50	8·50

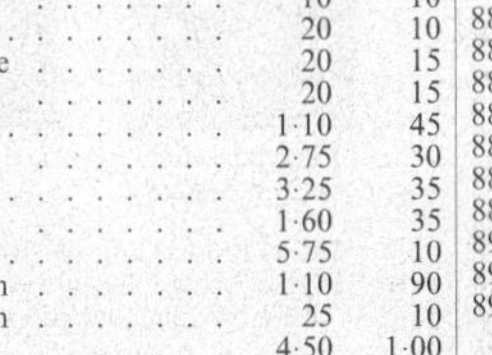
84 Storming of Santarem

1928. 3rd Independence issue. Dated 1928. Centres in black.

780	–	2 c. blue	15	15
781	84	3 c. green	15	15
782	–	4 c. red	15	15
783	–	5 c. green	15	15
784	–	6 c. brown	15	15
785	84	15 c. grey	75	75
786	–	16 c. purple	75	75
787	–	25 c. blue	75	75
788	–	32 c. green	3·25	3·00
789	–	40 c. brown	65	55
790	–	50 c. red	9·00	5·25
791	84	80 c. grey	9·00	6·75
792	–	96 c. red	17·00	14·50
793	–	1 e. mauve	26·00	25·00
794	–	1 e. 60 blue	11·50	10·50
795	–	4 e. 50 yellow	12·50	12·00

DESIGNS—VERT: 2, 25 c., 1 e. 60, G. Paes; 6, 32, 96 c. Joana de Gouveia; 4 e. 50, Matias de Albuquerque. HORIZ: 4, 16, 50 c. Battle of Rolica; 5, 40 c., 1 e. Battle of Atoleiros.

1929. Optd **Revalidado**.

805	56	10 c. red	40	25
806		15 c. black	40	25
807		40 c. brown	60	50
808		40 c. green	50	40
810		96 c. red	5·00	4·00
811		1 e. 60 blue	20·00	15·00

1929. Telegraph stamp surch **CORREIO 1$60** and bars.

812	–	1 e. 60 on 5 c. brown	13·50	9·50

88 Camoens, Poem "Lusiad" 89 St. Anthony's Birthplace

1931.

835	88	4 c. brown	20	10
836		5 c. brown	10	10
837		6 c. grey	20	10
838		10 c. mauve	20	15
839		15 c. black	20	15
840		16 c. blue	1·10	45
841		25 c. green	2·75	30
841a		25 c. blue	3·25	35
841b		30 c. green	1·60	35
842		40 c. red	5·75	10
843		48 c. brown	1·10	90
844		50 c. brown	25	10
845		75 c. red	4·50	1·00
846		80 c. green	35	10
846a		95 c. red	14·00	5·75
847		1 e. purple	28·00	10
848		1 e. 20 green	2·00	85
849		1 e. 25 blue	1·75	20
849a		1 e. 60 blue	28·00	3·75
849b		1 e. 75 blue	60	25
850		2 e. mauve	50	20
851		4 e. 50 orange	1·40	20
852		5 e. green	1·40	20

1931. 700th Death Anniv of St. Anthony.

853	89	15 c. purple	60	25
854	–	25 c. myrtle and green	75	25
855	–	40 c. brown and buff	50	25
856	–	75 c. pink	21·00	13·00
857	–	1 e. 25 grey and blue	48·00	28·00
858	–	4 e. 50 purple and mauve	24·00	3·00

DESIGNS—VERT: 25 c. Saint's baptismal font; 40 c. Lisbon Cathedral; 75 c. St. Anthony; 1 e. 25, Santa Cruz Cathedral, Coimbra. HORIZ: 4 e. 50, Saint's tomb, Padua.

90 Don Nuno Alvares Pereira 94 President Carmona

1931. 5th Death Centenary of Pereira.

859	90	15 c. black	1·00	1·00
860		25 c. green and black	10·00	1·00
861		40 c. orange	2·50	50
862		75 c. red	20·00	20·00
863		1 e. 25 light blue and blue	25·00	19·00
864		4 e. 50 green and brown	£120	48·00

1933. Pereira issue of 1931 surch.

865	90	15 c. on 40 c. orange	50	40
866		40 c. on 15 c. black	2·75	2·25
867		40 c. on 25 c. green & blk	65	55
868		40 c. on 75 c. red	7·00	3·75
869		40 c. on 1 e. 25 light blue and blue	7·00	3·75
870		40 c. on 4 e. 50 green and brown	3·00	2·00

1933. St. Anthony issue of 1931 surch.

871	–	15 c. on 40 c. brown and buff	75	35
872	89	40 c. on 15 c. purple	1·75	1·00
873	–	40 c. on 25 c. myrtle and green	1·40	65
874	–	40 c. on 75 c. pink	7·00	4·50
875	–	40 c. on 1 e. 25 grey and blue	7·00	4·75
876	–	40 c. on 4 e. 50 purple and mauve	7·00	4·75

1934.

877	94	40 c. violet	17·00	30

95 96 Queen Maria

1934. Colonial Exhibition.

878	95	25 c. brown	2·75	75
879		40 c. red	17·00	30
880		1 e. 60 blue	28·00	12·50

1935. 1st Portuguese Philatelic Exhibition.

881	96	40 c. red	1·25	25

97 Temple of Diana at Evora 98 Prince Henry the Navigator

99 "All for the Nation" 100 Coimbra Cathedral

1935.

882	97	4 c. black	40	15
883		5 c. blue	45	15
884		6 c. brown	70	25
885	98	10 c. green	65	10
886		15 c. red	25	10
887	99	25 c. blue	5·50	35
888		40 c. brown	1·90	10
889		1 e. red	8·75	40
890	100	1 e. 75 blue	70·00	1·10
890a	99	10 e. grey	20·00	2·25
890b		20 e. blue	28·00	2·00

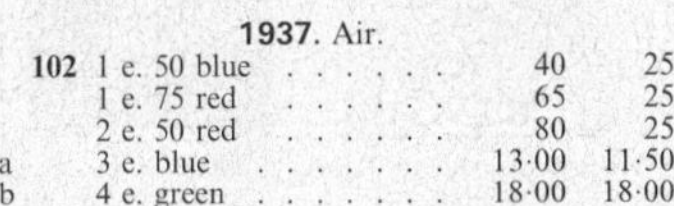
102 Shield and Propeller 103 Symbol of Medicine

1937. Air.

891	102	1 e. 50 blue	40	25
892		1 e. 75 red	65	25
893		2 e. 50 red	80	25
893a		3 e. blue	13·00	11·50
893b		4 e. green	18·00	18·00
894	102	5 e. red	1·60	1·00
895		10 e. purple	2·75	1·00
895a		15 e. orange	11·50	6·75
896		20 e. brown	8·25	2·40
896a		50 e. purple	£150	70·00

1937. Centenary of Medical and Surgical Colleges at Lisbon and Oporto.

897	103	25 c. blue	9·75	85

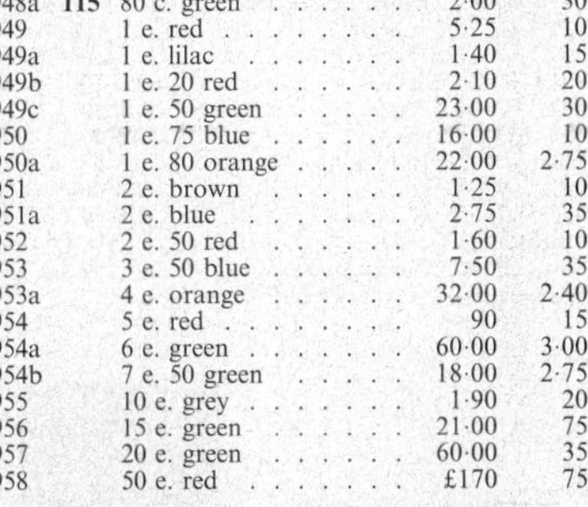
104 Gil Vicente 106 Grapes 107 Cross of Avis

1937. 400th Death Anniv of Gil Vicente (poet).

898	104	40 c. brown	18·00	10
899		1 e. red	2·40	10

1938. Wine and Raisin Congress.

900	106	15 c. violet	1·10	55
901		25 c. brown	2·40	1·50
902		40 c. mauve	9·75	35
903		1 e. 75 blue	28·00	24·00

1940. Portuguese Legion.

904	107	5 c. buff	30	10
905		10 c. violet	30	10
906		15 c. blue	30	10
907		25 c. brown	16·00	1·00
908		40 c. green	28·00	15
909		80 c. green	1·60	40
910		1 e. red	40·00	3·00
911		1 e. 75 blue	5·50	5·25

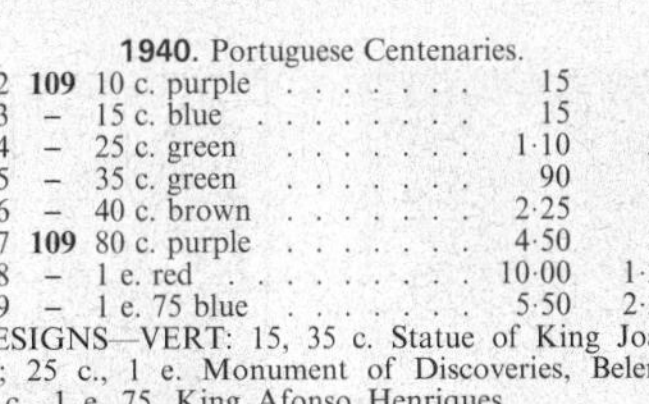
109 Portuguese World Exhibition 113 Sir Rowland Hill

1940. Portuguese Centenaries.

912	109	10 c. purple	15	15
913	–	15 c. blue	15	15
914	–	25 c. green	1·10	25
915	–	35 c. green	90	30
916	–	40 c. brown	2·25	10
917	109	80 c. purple	4·50	30
918	–	1 e. red	10·00	1·25
919	–	1 e. 75 blue	5·50	2·25

DESIGNS—VERT: 15, 35 c. Statue of King Joao IV; 25 c., 1 e. Monument of Discoveries, Belem; 40 c., 1 e. 75, King Afonso Henriques.

1940. Cent of First Adhesive Postage Stamps.

920	113	15 c. purple	25	15
921		25 c. red	30	15
922		35 c. green	30	15
923		40 c. purple	35	15
924		50 c. green	14·50	3·75
925		80 c. blue	1·60	1·00
926		1 e. red	17·00	3·00
927		1 e. 75 blue	5·00	3·00

114 Fish-woman of Nazare

115 Caravel

1941. Costumes.

932	114	4 c. green	20	15
933	–	5 c. brown	20	15
934	–	10 c. purple	2·50	1·00
935	–	15 c. green	20	15
936	–	25 c. purple	1·60	55
937	–	40 c. green	20	15
938	–	80 c. blue	2·75	1·90
939	–	1 e. red	7·25	1·25
940	–	1 e. 75 blue	7·25	3·75
941	–	2 e. orange	30·00	20·00

DESIGNS: 5 c. Woman from Coimbra; 10 c. Vine-grower of Saloio; 15 c. Fish-woman of Lisbon; 25 c. Woman of Olhao; 40 c. Woman of Aveiro; 80 c. Shepherdess of Madeira; 1 e. Spinner of Viana do Castelo; 1 e. 75, Horsebreeder of Ribatejo; 2 e. Reaper of Alentejo.

1943.

942	115	5 c. black	10	10
943		10 c. brown	10	10
944		15 c. grey	10	10
945		20 c. violet	10	10
946		30 c. purple	10	10
947		35 c. green	10	10
948		50 c. purple	10	10
948a	115	80 c. green	2·00	30
949		1 e. red	5·25	10
949a		1 e. lilac	1·40	15
949b		1 e. 20 red	2·10	20
949c		1 e. 50 green	23·00	30
950		1 e. 75 blue	16·00	10
950a		1 e. 80 orange	22·00	2·75
951		2 e. brown	1·25	10
951a		2 e. blue	2·75	35
952		2 e. 50 red	1·60	10
953		3 e. 50 blue	7·50	35
953a		4 e. orange	32·00	2·40
954		5 e. red	90	15
954a		6 e. green	60·00	3·00
954b		7 e. 50 green	18·00	2·75
955		10 e. grey	1·90	20
956		15 e. green	21·00	75
957		20 e. green	60·00	35
958		50 e. red	£170	75

116 Labourer

117 Mounted Postal Courier

1943. 1st Agricultural Science Congress.

959	116	10 c. blue	70	25
960		50 c. red	1·10	30

1944. 3rd National Philatelic Exn, Lisbon.

961	117	10 c. brown	20	10
962		50 c. violet	20	10
963		1 e. red	2·40	55
964		1 e. 75 blue	2·40	1·40

118 Felix Avellar Brotero

120 Vasco da Gama

1944. Birth Bicentenary of Avellar Brotero (botanist).

965	118	10 c. brown	20	10
966	–	50 c. green	1·25	10
967	–	1 e. red	5·00	1·10
968	118	1 e. 75 blue	4·50	2·25

DESIGN: 50 c., 1 e. Brotero's statue, Coimbra.

1945. Portuguese Navigators.

969	–	10 c. brown	10	10
970	–	30 c. orange	10	10
971	–	35 c. green	30	15
972	120	50 c. green	1·00	25
973	–	1 e. red	2·40	60
974	–	1 e. 75 blue	3·00	2·00
975	–	2 e. black	3·50	2·25
976	–	3 e. 50 red	7·00	3·50

PORTRAITS: 10 c. Gil Eanes; 30 c. Joao Goncalves Zarco; 35 c. Bartolomeu Dias; 1 e. Pedro Alvares Cabral; 1 e. 75, Fernao de Magalhaes (Magellan); 2 e. Frey Goncalo Velho; 3 e. 50, Diogo Cao.

121 President Carmona

122

1945.

977	121	10 c. violet	25	10
978		30 c. brown	25	10
979		35 c. green	25	10
980		50 c. green	30	10
981		1 e. red	7·25	1·10
982		1 e. 75 blue	6·00	3·25
983		2 e. purple	32·00	4·25
984		3 e. 50 grey	21·00	6·50

1945. Naval School Centenary.

985	122	10 c. brown	10	10
986		50 c. green	20	10
987		1 e. red	2·50	60
988		1 e. 75 blue	2·50	2·50

123 Almourol Castle

1946. Portuguese Castles.
989 – 10 c. purple 10 10
990 – 30 c. brown 10 10
991 – 35 c. green 10 10
992 – 50 c. grey 30 10
993 **123** 1 e. red . . . . 15·00 90
994 – 1 e. 75 blue . . . . 8·75 2·25
995 – 2 e. green . . . . 27·00 3·50
996 – 3 e. 50 brown . . . . . . 14·50 4·50
DESIGNS: Castles at Silves (10 c.); Leiria (30 c.); Feira (35 c.); Guimaraes (50 c.); Lisbon (1 e. 75); Braganza (2 e.) and Ourem (3 e. 50).

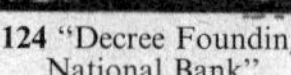

124 "Decree Founding National Bank" **125** Madonna and Child

1946. Centenary of Bank of Portugal.
997 **124** 50 c. blue 45 20

1946. Tercentenary of Proclamation of St. Mary of Castile as Patron Saint of Portugal.
998 **125** 30 c. grey 15 10
999 50 c. green 15 10
1000 1 e. red . . . . 2·00 95
1001 1 e. 75 blue . . . . . . 3·75 1·90

126 Caramulo Shepherdess **127** Surrender of the Keys of Lisbon

1947. Regional Costumes.
1002 **126** 10 c. mauve 10 10
1003 – 30 c. red 10 10
1004 – 35 c. green 15 10
1005 – 50 c. brown 25 15
1006 – 1 e. red . . . . 8·50 50
1007 – 1 e. 75 blue . . . . . . 8·50 3·50
1008 – 2 e. blue . . . . 32·00 4·00
1009 – 3 e. 50 green . . . . . . 22·00 1·90
COSTUMES: 30 c. Malpique timbrel player; 35 c. Monsanto flautist; 50 c. Woman of Avintes; 1 e. Maia field labourer; 1 e. 75, Woman of Algarve; 2 e. Miranda do Douro bastonet player; 3 e. 50, Woman of the Azores.

1947. 800th Anniv of Recapture of Lisbon from the Moors.
1010 **127** 5 c. green 10 10
1011 20 c. red 10 10
1012 50 c. violet 10 10
1013 1 e. 75 blue . . . . . . 3·75 3·75
1014 2 e. 50 brown . . . . . . 5·50 5·50
1015 3 e. 50 black . . . . . . 9·00 9·00

128 St. Joao de Brito

1948. Birth Tercentenary of St. Joao de Brito.
1016 **128** 30 c. green 10 10
1017 – 50 c. brown 10 10
1018 **128** 1 e. red . . . . 5·75 1·50
1019 – 1 e. 75 blue . . . . . . 7·00 2·40
DESIGN: 50 c., 1 e. 75, St. Joao de Brito (different).

130 "Architecture and Engineering" **131** King Joao I

1948. Exhibition of Public Works and National Congress of Engineering and Architecture.
1020 **130** 50 c. purple 45 20

1949. Portraits.
1021 **131** 10 c. violet and buff . . 15 10
1022 – 30 c. green and buff . . 15 10
1023 – 35 c. green and olive . . 25 10
1024 – 50 c. blue and light blue . 60 10
1025 – 1 e. lake and red 70 10
1026 – 1 e. 75 black and grey . . 12·50 7·75
1027 – 2 e. blue and light blue . 7·00 1·60
1028 – 3 e. 50 chocolate & brown 25·00 20·00
PORTRAITS: 30 c. Queen Philippa; 35 c. Prince Fernando; 50 c. Prince Henry the Navigator; 1 e. Nun Alvares; 1 e. 75, Joao da Regras; 2 e. Fernao Lopes; 3 e. 50, Afonso Domingues.

132 Statue of Angel **133** Hands and Letter

1949. 16th Congress of the History of Art.
1029 **132** 1 e. red . . . . 6·75 10
1030 5 e. brown . . . . 1·25 15

1949. 75th Anniv of U.P.U.
1031 **133** 1 e. lilac 20 10
1032 2 e. blue 55 20
1033 2 e. 50 green . . . . . 3·25 1·00
1034 4 e. brown . . . . . . 8·75 3·25

134 Our Lady of Fatima **135** Saint and Invalid

1950. Holy Year.
1035 **134** 50 c. green 30 15
1036 1 e. brown . . . . . . 1·60 30
1037 2 e. blue . . . . 3·50 1·60
1038 5 e. lilac . . . . 50·00 25·00

1950. 400th Death Anniv of San Juan de Dios.
1039 **135** 20 c. violet 15 10
1040 50 c. red 25 20
1041 1 e. green 85 30
1042 1 e. 50 orange . . . . . 7·00 2·40
1043 2 e. blue . . . . 6·00 2·00
1044 4 e. brown . . . . . . 25·00 7·00

136 G. Junqueiro **137** Fisherman

1951. Birth Centenary of Junqueiro (poet).
1045 **136** 50 c. brown . . . . . . 2·75 20
1046 1 e. blue 75 30

1951. Fisheries Congress.
1047 **137** 50 c. green on buff . . . 2·25 40
1048 1 e. purple on buff . . . 60 10

138 Dove and Olive Branch **139** 15th-century Colonists

1951. Termination of Holy Year.
1049 **138** 20 c. brown and buff . . 20 15
1050 90 c. green and yellow . 5·00 1·50
1051 – 1 e. purple and pink . . 5·00 25
1052 – 2 e. 30 green and blue . 6·50 1·90
PORTRAIT: 1 e., 2 e. 30, Pope Pius XII.

1951. 500th Anniv of Colonization of Terceira, Azores.
1053 **139** 50 c. blue on flesh . . . 1·10 35
1054 1 e. brown on buff . . . 85 35

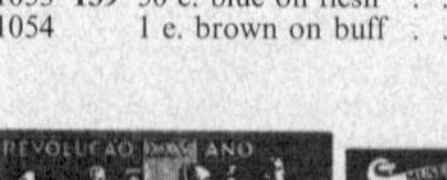

140 Revolutionaries **141** Coach of King Joao VI

1951. 25th Anniv of National Revolution.
1055 **140** 1 e. brown . . . . 2·00 15
1056 2 e. 30 blue . . . . . . 1·75 1·00

1952. National Coach Museum.
1057 – 10 c. purple 10 10
1058 **141** 20 c. green 10 10
1059 – 50 c. green 35 10
1060 – 90 c. green . . . . . . 1·50 1·40
1061 – 1 e. orange 60 10
1062 – 1 e. 40 pink . . . . . 3·75 3·50
1063 **141** 1 e. 50 brown . . . . . 4·00 21·00
1064 – 2 e. 30 blue . . . . . 1·90 1·90
DESIGNS (coaches of): 10, 90 c. King Felippe II; 50 c., 1 e. 40, Papal Nuncio to Joao V; 1, 2 e. 30, King Jose.

142 "N.A.T.O." **143** Hockey Players

1952. 3rd Anniv of N.A.T.O.
1065 **142** 1 e. green and deep green 5·50 10
1066 3 e. 50 grey and blue . . £130 19·00

1952. 8th World Roller-skating Hockey Championship.
1067 **143** 1 e. black and blue . . . 2·25 10
1068 3 e. 50 black and brown . 3·25 2·00

144 Teixeira **145** Marshal Carmona Bridge

1952. Birth Centenary of Prof. Gomes Teixeira (mathematician).
1069 **144** 1 e. mauve and pink . . . 55 10
1070 2 e. 30 dp blue and blue . 4·25 3·75

1952. Centenary of Ministry of Public Works.
1071 **145** 1 e. brown on stone . . . 35 10
1072 – 1 e. 40 lilac on stone . . 7·00 4·50
1073 – 2 e. green on stone . . . 4·00 2·25
1074 – 3 e. 50 blue on stone . . 7·25 3·50
DESIGNS: 1 e. 40, 28th May Stadium, Braga; 2 e. Coimbra University; 3 e. 50, Salazar Barrage.

146 St. Francis Xavier **147** Medieval Knight

1952. 4th Death Centenary of St. Francis Xavier.
1075 **146** 1 e. blue 35 15
1076 2 e. purple . . . . 1·00 35
1077 3 e. 50 blue . . . . . . 13·50 11·00
1078 5 e. lilac . . . . 25·00 3·25

1953.
1079 **147** 5 c. green on yellow . . 10 10
1080 10 c. grey on pink . . . 10 10
1081 20 c. orange on yellow . 10 10
1081a 30 c. purple on buff . . 10 10
1082 50 c. black 10 10
1083 90 c. green on yellow . . 5·75 50
1084 1 e. brown on pink . . . 20 10
1085 1 e. 40 red . . . . . . 6·00 80
1086 1 e. 50 red on yellow . . 25 10
1087 2 e. black 25 10
1088 2 e. 30 blue . . . . . . 9·00 70
1089 2 e. 50 black on pink . . 50 10
1089a 2 e. 50 green on yellow . 50 10
1090 5 e. purple on yellow . . 50 10
1091 10 e. blue on yellow . . 1·10 20
1091a 10 e. green on yellow . . 2·25 10
1092 20 e. brown on yellow . . 3·00 25
1093 50 e. lilac . . . . 2·75 30

148 St. Martin of Dume **149** G. Gomes Fernandes

1953. 14th Centenary of Landing of St. Martin of Dume on Iberian Peninsula.
1094 **148** 1 e. black and grey . . . 85 10
1095 3 e. 50 brown and yellow . 7·50 5·00

1953. Birth Centenary of Fernandes (fire-brigade chief).
1096 **149** 1 e. purple and cream . . 40 10
1097 2 e. 30 blue and cream . 6·75 5·00

150 Club Emblems, 1903 and 1953 **151** Princess St. Joan

1953. 50th Anniv of Portuguese Automobile Club.
1098 **150** 1 e. deep green and green 40 10
1099 3 e. 50 brown and buff . 8·25 5·00

1953. 5th Centenary of Birth of Princess St. Joan.
1100 **151** 1 e. black and green . . 1·10 10
1101 3 e. 50 deep blue and blue 8·00 6·00

152 Queen Maria II

1953. Centenary of First Portuguese Stamps. Bottom panel in gold.
1102 **152** 50 c. red 10 10
1103 1 e. brown 10 10
1104 1 e. 40 purple . . . . . 1·10 70
1105 2 e. 30 blue . . . . . . 2·50 1·75
1106 3 e. 50 blue . . . . . . 2·50 1·75
1107 4 e. 50 green . . . . . 1·60 1·25
1108 5 e. green . . . . 4·25 1·40
1109 20 e. violet . . . . . . 38·00 7·25

153 **154**

1954. 150th Anniv of Trade Secretariat.
1110 **153** 1 e. blue and light blue . 40 10
1111 1 e. 50 brown and buff . 1·75 60

1954. People's Education Plan.
1112 **154** 50 c. blue and turquoise . 15 10
1113 1 e. red and pink 15 10
1114 2 e. deep green and green 14·50 1·00
1115 2 e. 50 brown and light brown . . . . 12·50 1·10

155 Cadet and College Banner **156** Father Manuel da Nobrega

1954. 150th Anniv of Military College.
1116 **155** 1 e. brown and green . . 95 10
1117 3 e. 50 blue and green . 4·00 2·50

1954. 400th Anniv of Sao Paulo.
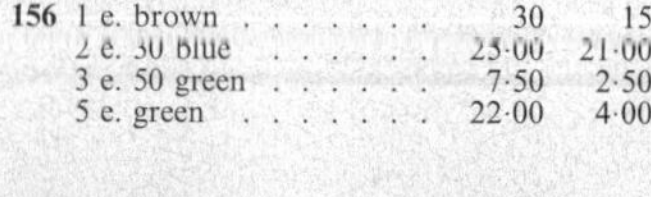
1118 **156** 1 e. brown 30 15
1119 2 e. 30 blue . . . . . . 25·00 21·00
1120 3 e. 50 green . . . . . . 7·50 2·50
1121 5 e. green . . . . 22·00 4·00

157 King Sancho I, 1154–1211 **158** Telegraph Poles

1955. Portuguese Kings.

1122 – 10 c. purple 15 10
1123 157 20 c. green 15 10
1124 – 50 c. blue 25 15
1125 – 90 c. green . . . . 1·90 1·25
1126 – 1 e. brown 80 15
1127 – 1 e. 40 red . . . . 5·00 2·75
1128 – 1 e. 50 green . . . . . . 2·10 1·00
1129 – 2 e. red . . . . 6·25 2·75
1130 – 2 e. 30 blue . . . . . . 5·25 2·50

KINGS: 10 c. Afonso I; 50 c. Afonso II; 90 c. Sancho II; 1 e. Afonso III; 1 e. 40, Diniz; 1 e. 50, Afonso IV; 2 e. Pedro I; 2 e. 30, Fernando.

1955. Centenary of Electric Telegraph System in Portugal.

1131 158 1 e. red and brown . . . 30 10
1132 2 e. 30 blue and green . . 11·00 3·50
1133 3 e. 50 green and yellow . 11·00 2·75

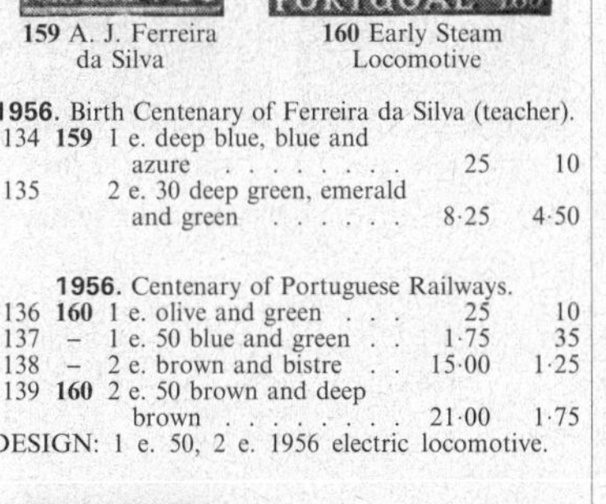

159 A. J. Ferreira da Silva — 160 Early Steam Locomotive

1956. Birth Centenary of Ferreira da Silva (teacher).

1134 159 1 e. deep blue, blue and azure 25 10
1135 2 e. 30 deep green, emerald and green . . . . . . 8·25 4·50

1956. Centenary of Portuguese Railways.

1136 160 1 e. olive and green . . . 25 10
1137 – 1 e. 50 blue and green . . 1·75 35
1138 – 2 e. brown and bistre . . 15·00 1·25
1139 160 2 e. 50 brown and deep brown . . . . 21·00 1·75

DESIGN: 1 e. 50, 2 e. 1956 electric locomotive.

161 Madonna and Child — 162 Almeida Garrett (after Barata Feyo)

1956. Mothers' Day.

1140 161 1 e. sage and green . . . 20 10
1141 1 e. 50 lt brown & brown 60 20

1957. Almeida Garrett (writer) Commem.

1142 162 1 e. brown 40 10
1143 2 e. 30 lilac . . . . . . 20·00 9·25
1144 3 e. 50 green . . . . . . 4·50 1·10
1145 5 e. red . . . . 32·00 9·25

163 Cesario Verde — 164 Exhibition Emblem

1957. Cesario Verde (poet) Commem.

1146 163 1 e. brown, buff & green 35 10
1147 3 e. 30 black, olive and green . . . . 1·60 95

1958. Brussels International Exhibition.

1148 164 1 e. multicoloured . . . 35 10
1149 3 e. 30 multicoloured . . 1·60 1·25

165 St. Elizabeth — 166 Institute of Tropical Medicine, Lisbon

1958. St. Elizabeth and St. Teotonio Commem.

1150 165 1 e. red and cream . . . 20 10
1151 – 2 e. green and cream . . 50 35
1152 165 2 e. 50 violet and cream . 3·50 75
1153 – 5 e. brown and cream . . 4·25 85

PORTRAIT: 2, 5 e. St. Teotonio.

1958. 6th Int Congress of Tropical Medicine.

1154 166 1 e. green and grey . . . 1·25 15
1155 2 e. 50 blue and grey . . 5·25 1·25

167 Liner — 168 Queen Leonora

1958. 2nd National Merchant Navy Congress.

1156 167 1 e. brown, ochre & sepia 4·00 20
1157 4 e. 50 violet, lilac & bl . 3·50 1·90

1958. 500th Birth Anniv of Queen Leonora. Frames and ornaments in bistre, inscriptions and value tablet in black.

1158 168 1 e. blue and brown . . 15 10
1159 1 e. 50 turquoise & blue 3·00 60
1160 2 e. 30 blue and green . 2·75 1·10
1161 4 e. 10 blue and grey . . 2·75 1·50

169 Arms of Aveiro — 170

1959. Millenary of Aveiro.

1162 169 1 e. multicoloured . . . 85 15
1163 5 e. multicoloured . . . 9·25 1·60

1960. 10th Anniv of N.A.T.O.

1164 170 1 e. black and lilac . . . 30 10
1165 3 e. 50 green and grey . 3·00 1·75

171 "Doorway to Peace" — 172 Glider

1960. World Refugee Year. Symbol in black.

1166 171 20 c. yellow, lemon & brn 10 10
1167 1 e. yellow, green & blue 45 10
1168 1 e. 80 yellow and green 1·00 90

1960. 50th Anniv of Portuguese Aero Club. Multicoloured.

1169 1 e. Type 172 . . . . . . 15 10
1170 1 e. 50 Light monoplane . . 55 25
1171 2 e. Airplane and parachutes 1·10 65
1172 2 e. 50 Model glider . . . . 2·50 1·10

173 Padre Cruz (after M. Barata) — 174 University Seal

1960. Death Centenary of Padre Cruz.

1173 173 1 e. brown 25 10
1174 4 e. 30 blue . . . . . . 7·00 6·25

1960. 400th Anniv of Evora University.

1175 174 50 c. blue 10 10
1176 1 e. brown and yellow . 20 10
1177 1 e. 40 purple . . . . . 2·25 1·40

175 Prince Henry's Arms — 175a Conference Emblem

1960. 5th Death Centenary of Prince Henry the Navigator. Multicoloured.

1178 1 e. Type 175 . . . . 15 10
1179 2 e. 50 Caravel . . . . . . 1·75 30
1180 3 e. 50 Prince Henry the Navigator . . . . 2·10 1·25
1181 5 e. Motto . . . . 4·50 60
1182 8 e. Barketta 85 60
1183 10 e. Map showing Sagres . 7·25 2·00

1960. Europa.

1184 175a 1 e. light blue and blue . 25 10
1185 3 e. 50 red and lake . . 3·00 1·75

176 Emblems of Prince Henry and Lisbon

1960. 5th National Philatelic Exhibition, Lisbon.

1186 176 1 e. blue, black and green 30 10
1187 3 e. 30 blue, black and light blue . . . . 4·25 3·50

177 Portuguese Flag — 178 King Pedro V

1960. 50th Anniv of Republic.

1188 177 1 e. multicoloured 25 10

1961. Cent of Lisbon University Faculty of Letters.

1189 178 1 e. green and brown . . 25 10
1190 6 e. 50 brown and blue . 2·50 85

179 Arms of Setubal — 180

1961. Centenary of Setubal City.

1191 179 1 e. multicoloured 25 10
1192 4 e. 30 multicoloured . . 8·00 5·25

1961. Europa.

1193 180 1 e. light blue, blue and deep blue 10 10
1194 1 e. 50 light green, green and deep green . . . . 1·25 1·25
1195 3 e. 50 pink, red and lake 1·60 1·60

181 Tomar Gateway — 182 National Guardsman

1961. 800th Anniv of Tomar.

1196 – 1 e. multicoloured 15 10
1197 181 3 e. 50 multicoloured . . 1·25 1·10

DESIGN: 1 e. As Type 181 but without ornamental background.

1962. 50th Anniv of National Republican Guard.

1198 182 1 e. multicoloured 10 10
1199 2 e. multicoloured . . . . 1·60 75
1200 2 e. 50 multicoloured . . 1·60 60

183 St. Gabriel (Patron Saint of Telecommunications) — 184 Scout Badge and Tents

1962. St. Gabriel Commem.

1201 183 1 e. brown, green and olive 70 10
1202 3 e. 50 green, brown & ol 40 40

1962. 18th Int Scout Conference (1961).

1203 184 20 c. multicoloured . . . 10 10
1204 50 c. multicoloured . . . 10 10
1205 1 e. multicoloured 40 10
1206 2 e. 50 multicoloured . . 2·75 55
1207 3 e. 50 mulitcoloured . . 60 55
1208 6 e. 50 multicoloured . . 60 55

185 Children with Ball — 186 Europa "Honeycomb"

1962. 10th International Paediatrics Congress, Lisbon. Centres in black.

1209 – 50 c. yellow and green . 10 10
1210 – 1 e. yellow and grey . . 65 10
1211 185 2 e. 80 yellow & brown . 1·60 85
1212 – 3 e. 50 yellow & purple . 3·00 1·90

DESIGNS: 50 c. Children with book; 1 e. Inoculating child; 3 e. 50, Weighing baby.

1962. Europa. "EUROPA" in gold.

1213 186 1 e. ultramarine, light blue and blue 15 10
1214 1 e. 50 deep green, light green and green . . . 1·25 60
1215 3 e. 50 purple, pink and claret . . . . 1·50 1·50

187 St. Zenon (the Courier) — 188 Benfica Emblem and European Cup

1962. Stamp Day. Saint in yellow and pink.

1216 187 1 e. black and purple . . 15 10
1217 2 e. black and green . . 85 75
1218 2 e. 80 black and bistre . 1·75 1·60

1963. Benfica Club's Double Victory in European Football Cup Championship (1961–62).

1219 188 1 e. multicoloured . . . 60 10
1220 4 e. 30 multicoloured . . 1·25 1·25

189 Campaign Emblem

1963. Freedom from Hunger.

1221 189 1 e. multicoloured . . . 10 10
1222 3 e. 30 multicoloured . . 1·00 1·00
1223 3 e. 50 multicoloured . . 1·00 1·00

190 Mail Coach — 191 St. Vincent de Paul

1963. Centenary of Paris Postal Conference.

1224 190 1 e. blue, light blue and grey 20 10
1225 1 e. 50 multicoloured . . 1·60 45
1226 5 e. brown, lilac and light brown 40 35

1963. 300th Death Anniv of St. Vincent de Paul. Inscr in gold.

1227 191 20 c. ultram and blue . . 10 10
1228 1 e. blue and grey . . . 25 10
1229 2 e. 80 black and green . 2·50 1·75
1230 5 e. grey and mauve . . 2·40 1·10

192 Medieval Knight

1963. 800th Anniv of Military Order of Avis.

1231 192 1 e. multicoloured . . . 10 10
1232 1 e. 50 multicoloured . . 45 20
1233 2 e. 50 mulitcoloured . . 1·25 85

193 Europa "Dove"

1963. Europa.

1234 193 1 e. grey, blue and black 25 10
1235 2 e. 50 grey, green & blk 1·90 1·10
1236 3 e. 50 grey, red & black 3·25 2·10

194 Supersonic Flight **195** Pharmacist's Jar

1963. 10th Anniv of T.A.P. Airline.
1237 **194** 1 e. blue and deep blue . 15 10
1238 2 e. 50 lt green & green . 1·10 55
1239 3 e. 50 orange and red . 1·60 1·10

1964. 400th Anniv of Publication of "Coloquios dos Simples" (Dissertation on Indian herbs and drugs) by Dr. G. d'Orta.
1240 **195** 50 c. brown, black & bis 10 10
1241 1 e. purple, black & red . 25 10
1242 4 e. 30 blue, blk & grey . 4·50 3·75

196 Bank Emblem **197** Sameiro Shrine (Braga)

1964. Centenary of National Overseas Bank.
1243 **196** 1 e. yellow, green & blue 10 10
1244 2 e. 50 yellow, olive & grn 2·00 95
1245 3 e. 50 yellow, green & brn 1·60 1·00

1964. Centenary of Sameiro Shrine.
1246 **197** 1 e. yellow, brown & red 10 10
1247 2 e. yellow, light brown and brown . . . . 1·40 70
1248 5 e. yellow, grn & blue . 1·75 1·00

198 Europa "Flower" **199** Sun and Globe

1964. Europa.
1249 **198** 1 e. deep blue, light blue and blue 25 10
1250 3 e. 50 brown, light brown and purple . . . . . . 1·75 1·10
1251 4 e. 30 deep green, light green and green . . . 3·75 3·25

1964. International Quiet Sun Years.
1252 **199** 1 e. mulitcoloured . . . 20 10
1253 8 e. multicoloured . . . 1·00 1·00

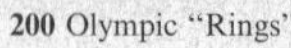

200 Olympic "Rings" **201** E. Coelho (founder)

1964. Olympic Games, Tokyo.
1254 **200** 20 c. multicoloured . . . 10 10
1255 1 e. multicoloured . . . 10 10
1256 1 e. 50 multicoloured . . 1·40 1·00
1257 6 e. 50 multicoloured . . 2·10 1·75

1964. Centenary of "Diario de Noticias" (newspaper).
1258 **201** 1 e. multicoloured . . . 25 10
1259 5 e. mutlicoloured . . . 1·50 90

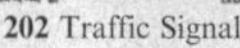

202 Traffic Signals **203** Dom Fernando (second Duke of Braganza)

1965. 1st National Traffic Congress Lisbon.
1260 **202** 1 e. yellow, red & green . 20 10
1261 3 e. 30 green, red & yellow 4·75 3·75
1262 3 e. 50 red, yellow & grn 3·00 1·10

1965. 500th Anniv of Braganza.
1263 **203** 1 e. red and black . . . 15 10
1264 10 e. green and black . . 1·60 75

204 Angel and Gateway **205** I.T.U. Emblem

1965. 900th Anniv of Capture of Coimbra from the Moors.
1265 **204** 1 e. multicoloured . . . 10 10
1266 2 e. 50 multicoloured . . 2·00 1·40
1267 5 e. multicoloured . . . 2·00 2·00

1965. Centenary of I.T.U.
1268 **205** 1 e. green and brown . . 10 10
1269 3 e. 50 purple and green 1·25 1·25
1270 6 e. 50 blue and green . 1·00 1·00

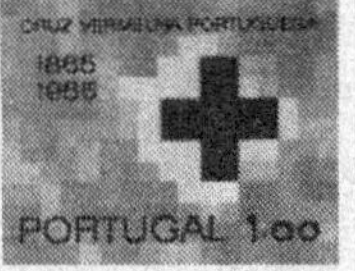

206 C. Gulbenkian **207** Red Cross Emblem

1965. 10th Death Anniv of Calouste Gulbenkian (oil industry pioneer and philanthropist).
1271 **206** 1 e. multicoloured . . . 55 10
1272 8 e. multicoloured . . . 55 45

1965. Centenary of Portuguese Red Cross.
1273 **207** 1 e. red, green & black . 20 10
1274 4 e. red, green and black 1·60 1·00
1275 4 e. 30 red, lt red & black 8·25 7·75

208 Europa "Sprig" **209** North American F-86 Sabre Jet Fighter

1965. Europa.
1276 **208** 1 e. lt blue, black & blue 15 10
1277 3 e. 50 flesh, brn & red . 3·50 1·60
1278 4 e. 30 light green, black and green . . . . . . 9·75 6·75

1965. 50th Anniv of Portuguese Air Force.
1279 **209** 1 e. red, green and olive 15 10
1280 2 e. red, green & brown 1·00 70
1281 5 e. red, green and blue . 2·10 1·60

210 **211** Monogram of Christ

1965. 500th Birth Anniv of Gil Vicente (poet and dramatist). Designs depicting characters from Vicente's poems.
1282 **210** 20 c. multicoloured . . 10 10
1283 – 1 e. multicoloured . . . 35 10
1284 – 2 e. 50 multicoloured . . 2·50 50
1285 – 6 e. 50 multicoloured . . 75 65

1966. International Committee for the Defence of Christian Civilisation Congress, Lisbon.
1286 **211** 1 e. violet, gold & bistre 25 10
1287 3 e. 30 black, gold & pur 5·00 3·50
1288 5 e. black, gold and red 3·00 1·10

212 Emblems of Agriculture, Construction and Industry **213** Giraldo the "Fearless"

1966. 40th Anniv of National Revolution.
1289 **212** 1 e. black, blue & grey . 15 10
1290 3 e. 50 brown, light brown and bistre . . . . . . 1·60 1·25
1291 4 e. purple, red and pink 1·60 1·10

1966. 800th Anniv of Reconquest of Evora.
1292 **213** 1 e. multicoloured . . . 30 10
1293 8 e. multicoloured . . . 85 65

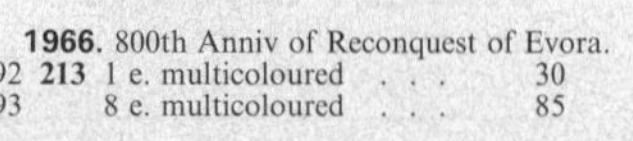

214 Salazar Bridge **215** Europa "Ship"

1966. Inauguration of Salazar Bridge, Lisbon.
1294 **214** 1 e. red and gold 30 10
1295 2 e. 50 blue and gold . . 1·00 70
1296 – 2 e. 80 blue and silver . . 2·00 1·60
1297 – 4 e. 30 green and silver . 2·00 1·60
DESIGN—VERT: 2 e. 80, 4 e. 30, Salazar Bridge (different view).

1966. Europa.
1298 **215** 1 e. multicoloured 20 10
1299 3 e. 50 multicoloured . . 4·50 1·75
1300 4 e. 50 multicoloured . . 4·50 3·00

216 C. Pestana (bacteriologist) **217** Bocage

1966. Portuguese Scientists. Portraits in brown and bistre; background colours given.
1301 **216** 20 c. green 10 10
1302 – 50 c. orange 10 10
1303 – 1 e. yellow 20 10
1304 – 1 e. 50 brown 20 10
1305 – 2 e. brown . . . . 1·50 15
1306 – 2 e. 50 green . . . . . . 1·75 45
1307 – 2 e. 80 orange . . . . . 1·75 1·50
1308 – 4 e. 30 blue . . . . 2·75 2·75
SCIENTISTS: 50 c. E. Moniz (neurologist); 1 e. E. A. P. Coutinho (botanist); 1 e. 50, J. C. da Serra (botanist); 2 e. R. Jorge (hygienist and anthropologist); 2 e. 50, J. L. de Vasconcelos (ethnologist); 2 e. 80, M. Lemos (medical historian); 4 e. 30, J. A. Serrano (anatomist).

1966. Birth Bicentenary (1965) of Manuel M. B. du Bocage (poet).
1309 **217** 1 e. black, green & bistre 10 10
1310 2 e. black, green & brn . 60 40
1311 6 e. black, green & grey . 1·10 75

218 Cogwheels **219** Adoration of the Virgin

1967. Europa.
1312 **218** 1 e. blue, black & light blue 20 10
1313 3 e. 50 brown, black and orange . . . . 3·25 1·10
1314 4 e. 30 green, black and light green . . . . . . 5·75 2·25

1967. 50th Anniv of Fatima Apparitions. Mult.
1315 1 e. Type **219** 10 10
1316 2 e. 80 Fatima Church . . . 55 50
1317 3 e. 50 Virgin of Fatima . . . 35 25
1318 4 e. Chapel of the Apparitions 35 35

220 Roman Senators **221** Lisnave Shipyard

1967. New Civil Law Code.
1319 **220** 1 e. red and gold 10 10
1320 2 e. 50 blue and gold . . 1·75 1·10
1321 4 e. 30 green and gold . . 1·10 1·10

1967. Inauguration of Lisnave Shipyard, Lisbon.
1322 **221** 1 e. multicoloured 10 10
1323 – 2 e. 80 multicoloured . . 1·90 1·10
1324 **221** 3 e. 50 multicoloured . . 1·00 65
1325 – 4 e. 30 multicoloured . . 1·60 1·10
DESIGN: 2 e. 80, 4 e. 30, Section of ship's hull and location map.

222 Serpent Symbol **223** Flags of EFTA Countries

1967. 6th European Rheumatological Congress. Lisbon.
1326 **222** 1 e. multicoloured . . . 10 10
1327 2 e. multicoloured . . . 1·00 50
1328 5 e. multicoloured . . . 1·60 1·25

1967. European Free Trade Association.
1329 **223** 1 e. multicoloured . . . 10 10
1330 3 e. 50 multicoloured . . 1·00 1·00
1331 4 e. 30 multicoloured . . 3·00 3·00

224 Tombstones **225** Bento de Goes

1967. Centenary of Abolition of Death Penalty in Portugal.
1332 **224** 1 e. green 10 10
1333 2 e. brown . . . . 1·00 80
1334 5 e. green . . . . 1·75 1·75

1968. Bento de Goes Commem.
1335 **225** 1 e. blue, brown and green 50 10
1336 8 e. purple, green & brn 90 65

226 Europa "Key" **227** "Maternal Love"

1968. Europa.
1337 **226** 1 e. multicoloured . . . 10 10
1338 3 e. 50 multicoloured . . 3·25 1·50
1339 4 e. 30 multicoloured . . 6·00 3·25

1968. 30th Anniv of Organization of Mothers for National Education (O.M.E.N.).
1340 **227** 1 e. black, orange & grey 10 10
1341 2 e. black, orange & pink 1·25 65
1342 5 e. black, orange & blue 2·50 1·50

228 "Victory over Disease"

1968. 20th Anniv of W.H.O.
1343 **228** 1 e. multicoloured . . . 10 10
1344 3 e. 50 multicoloured . . 1·00 55
1345 4 e. 30 multicoloured . . 5·75 5·50

229 Vineyard, Girao

1968. "Lubrapex 1968" Stamp Exhibition. Madeira—"Pearl of the Atlantic" Multicoloured.
1346 50 c. Type **229** 10 10
1347 1 e. Firework display 20 10
1348 1 e. 50 Landscape 25 10
1349 2 e. 80 J. Fernandes Vieira (liberator of Pernambuco) 1·75 1·60
1350 3 e. 50 Embroidery . . . . . 1·25 1·00
1351 4 e. 30 J. Goncalves Zarco (navigator) . . . . . . 6·75 6·75
1352 20 e. "Muschia aurea" . . . 3·00 1·10
The 2 e. 80 to 20 e. are vert.

230 Pedro Alvares Cabral (from medallion)

1969. 500th Birth Anniv of Pedro Alvares Cabral (explorer).
1353 **230** 1 e. blue 15 10
1354 – 3 e. 50 purple . . . . . 3·50 2·40
1355 – 6 e. 50 multicoloured . . 2·00 1·60
DESIGNS—VERT: 3 e. 50, Cabral's arms. HORIZ: 6 e. 50, Cabral's fleet (from contemporary documents).

231 Colonnade **232** King Joseph I

1969. Europa.
1356 **231** 1 e. multicoloured . . . 15 10
1357 3 e. 50 multicoloured . . 3·50 1·75
1358 4 e. 30 multicoloured . . 6·75 3·75

1969. Centenary of National Press
1359 **232** 1 e. multicoloured . . . 10 10
1360 2 e. multicoloured . . . 1·00 55
1361 8 e. multicoloured . . . 90 80

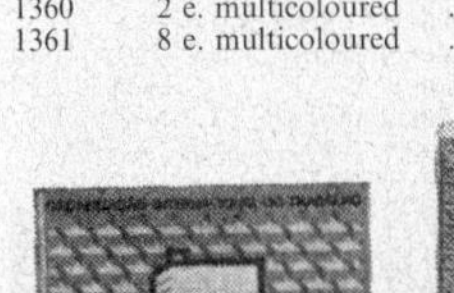

233 I.L.O. Emblem **234** J. R. Cabrilho (navigator and coloniser)

1969. 50th Anniv of I.L.O.
1362 **233** 1 e. multicoloured . . . 10 10
1363 3 e. 50 multicoloured . . 1·25 80
1364 4 e. 30 multicoloured . . 2·10 1·75

1969. Bicentenary of San Diego, California.
1365 **234** 1 e. dp green, yell & grn . 10 10
1366 1 e. 50 brown, light brown and blue . . . . 1·25 55
1367 6 e. 50 deep brown, green and brown . . . . . . 1·50 1·10

235 Vianna da Motta (from painting by C. B. Pinheiro)

1969. Birth Centenary (1968) of Jose Vianna da Motta (concert pianist).
1368 **235** 1 e. multicoloured . . . 70 10
1369 9 e. multicoloured . . . 75 75

236 Coutinho and Fairey IIID Seaplane

1969. Birth Centenary of Gago Coutinho (aviator). Multicoloured.
1370 1 e. Type **236** 15 10
1371 2 e. 80 Coutinho and sextant 1·50 1·25
1372 3 e. 30 Type **236** . . . . . . 1·90 1·75
1373 4 e. 30 As No. 1371 . . . . 1·90 1·75

237 Vasco da Gama

1969. 500th Birth Anniv of Vasco da Gama. Multicoloured.
1374 1 e. Type **237** 15 10
1375 2 e. 50 Arms of Vasco da Gama 2·50 2·25
1376 3 e. 50 Route map (horiz) . . 1·75 1·00
1377 4 e. Vasca da Gama's fleet (horiz) . . . . 1·60 80

238 "Flaming Sun" **239** Distillation Plant and Pipelines

1970. Europa.
1378 **238** 1 e. cream and blue . . 20 10
1379 3 e. 50 cream and brown . 3·75 1·10
1380 4 e. 30 cream and green 6·75 3·75

1970. Inauguration of Porto Oil Refinery.
1381 **239** 1 e. blue and light blue . 10 10
1382 – 2 e. 80 black and green . 2·10 1·90
1383 **239** 3 e. 30 green and olive . 1·40 1·25
1384 – 6 e. brown & light brown 1·00 90
DESIGN: 2 e. 80, 6 e. Catalytic cracking plant and pipelines.

240 Marshal Carmona (from sculpture by L. de Almeida)

1970. Birth Centenary of Marshal Carmona.
1385 **240** 1 e. green and black . . 10 10
1386 2 e. 50 blue, red & black 1·50 75
1387 7 e. blue and black . . . 1·25 1·10

241 Station Badge

1970. 25th Anniv of Plant-breeding Station.
1388 **241** 1 e. multicoloured . . . 10 10
1389 2 e. 50 multicoloured . . 1·00 40
1390 5 e. multicoloured . . . 1·40 75

242 Emblem within Cultural Symbol

1970. Expo 70. Multicoloured.
1391 1 e. Compass (postage) . . . 10 10
1392 5 e. Christian symbol . . . 1·10 1·10
1393 6 e. 50 symbolic initials . . 2·75 2·75
1394 3 e. 50 Type **242** (air) . . . 65 35

243 Wheel and Star

1970. Centenaries of Covilha (Nos. 1395/6) and Santarem (Nos. 1397/8). Multicoloured.
1395 1 e. Type **243** 10 10
1397 1 e. Castle 10 10
1396 2 e. 80 Ram and weaving frame 2·25 2·25
1398 4 e. Two knights . . . . . 1·25 95

244 "Great Eastern" laying Cable

1970. Centenary of Portugal–England Submarine Telegraph Cable.
1399 **244** 1 e. black, blue & green 15 10
1400 2 e. 50 black, green & buff 1·40 40
1401 – 2 e. 80 multicoloured . . 2·75 2·75
1402 – 4 e. multicoloured . . . 1·25 75
DESIGN: 2 e. 80, 4 e. Cable cross-section.

245 Harvesting Grapes **246** Mountain Windmill, Bussaco Hills

1970. Port Wine Industry. Multicoloured.
1403 50 c. Type **245** 10 10
1404 1 e. Harvester and jug 10 10
1405 3 e. 50 Wine-glass and wine barge 65 15
1406 7 e. Wine-bottle and casks . . 65 60

1971. Portuguese Windmills.
1407 **246** 20 c. brown, black & sepia 10 10
1408 – 50 c. brown, black & blue 10 10
1409 – 1 e. purple, black and grey 15 10
1410 – 2 e. red, black and mauve 70 15
1411 – 3 e. 30 chocolate, black and brown . . . . 2·10 2·10
1412 – 5 e. brown, black & green 1·75 65
WINDMILLS: 50 c. Beira Litoral Province; 1 e. "Saloio" type Estremadura Province; 2 e. St. Miguel Azores; 3 e. 30, Porto Santo, Madeira; 5 e. Pico, Azores.

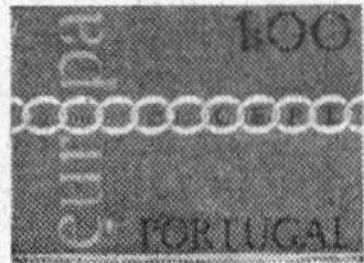

247 Europa Chain **248** F. Franco

1971. Europa.
1413 **247** 1 e. green, blue & black . 10 10
1414 3 e. 50 yellow, brn & blk 2·75 55
1415 7 e. 50 brown, grn & blk . 5·50 1·90

1971. Portuguese Sculptors.
1416 **248** 20 c. black 10 10
1417 – 1 e. red 25 10
1418 – 1 e. 50 brown 50 45
1419a – 2 e. 50 blue 80 40
1420 – 3 e. 50 mauve . . . . . 1·00 55
1421 – 4 e. green . . . . 2·10 1·75
DESIGNS: 1 e. A. Lopes; 1 e. 50, A. de Costa Mota; 2 e. 50, R. Gameiro; 3 e. 50, J. Simoes de Almeida (the Younger); 4 e. F. dos Santos.

249 Pres. Salazar **250** Wolframite

1971. Pres. Antonio Salazar Commemoration
1422 **249** 1 e. brown, green & orge 10 10
1423 5 e. brown, pur & orge . 1·00 40
1424 10 e. brown, blue & orge 2·00 1·10

1971. 1st Spanish–Portuguese–American Congress of Economic Geology. Multicoloured.
1425 1 e. Type **250** 10 10
1426 2 e. 50 Arsenopyrite . . . . 1·60 50
1427 3 e. 50 Beryllium 50 40
1428 6 e. 50 Chalcopyrite 95 45

251 Town Gate **252** Weather Equipment

1971. Bicentenary of Castelo Branco. Mult.
1429 1 e. Type **251** 10 10
1430 3 e. Town square and monument . . . . 1·10 65
1431 12 e. 50 Arms of Castelo Branco (horiz) 95 65

1971. 25th Anniv of Portuguese Meteorological Service. Multicoloured.
1432 1 e. Type **252** 10 10
1433 4 e. Weather balloon . . . . 1·75 1·10
1434 6 e. 50 weather satellite . . . 1·10 55

253 Drowning Missionaries **254** Man and his Habitat

1971. 400th Anniv of Martyrdom of Brazil Missionaries.
1435 **253** 1 e. black, blue & grey . 10 10
1436 3 e. 30 black, pur & brn 1·60 1·40
1437 4 e. 80 black, grn & olive 1·60 1·40

1971. Nature Conservation. Multicoloured.
1438 1 e. Type **254** 10 10
1439 3 e. 30 Horses and trees ("Earth") 50 30
1440 3 e. 50 Birds ("The Atmosphere") 50 30
1441 4 e. 50 Fishes ("Water") . . 2·10 1·60

255 Clerigos Tower, Oporto

1972 Buildings and Views.
1442 – 5 c. grey, black & green 10 10
1443 – 10 c. black, green & blue 10 10
1444 – 30 c. sepia, brown & yell 10 10
1445 – 50 c. blue, orange & blk 15 10
1446p **255** 1 e. black, brown & grn 45 10
1447 – 1 e. 50 brown, bl & blk 15 10
1448p – 2 e. black, brown & pur 45 10
1449p – 2 e. 50 brown, light brown and grey 15 10
1450 – 3 e. yellow, blk & brn . 15 10
1451p – 3 e. 50 green, orge & brn 15 10
1452 – 4 e. black, yellow & bl . 55 10
1453 – 4 e. 50 black, brn & grn 80 10
1454 – 5 e. green, brown & blk 5·25 10
1455 – 6 e. bistre, green & blk . 2·00 15
1456 – 7 e. 50 black, orge & grn 1·10 10
1457 – 8 e. bistre, black & grn 1·25 15
1458 – 10 e. multicoloured . . 50 10
1459 – 20 e. multicoloured . . 3·25 10
1460 – 50 e. multicoloured . . 3·50 20
1461 – 100 e. multicoloured . . 5·25 50
DESIGNS—As T **255**: 5 c. Aguas Livres aqueduct, Lisbon; 10 c. Lima Bridge; 30 c. Monastery interior, Alcobaca; 50 c. Coimbra University; 1 e. 50, Belem Tower, Lisbon; 2 e. Domus Municipalis, Braganza; 2 e. 50, Castle, Vila de Feira; 3 e. Misericord House, Viana do Castelo; 3 e. 50, Window, Tomar Convent; 4 e. Gateway, Braga; 4 e. 50, Dolmen of Carrazeda; 5 e. Roman Temple, Evora; 6 e. Monastery, Leca do Balio; 7 e. 50, Almourol Castle; 8 e. Ducal Palace, Guimaraes. 31×22 mm; 10 e. Cape Girao, Madeira; 20 e. Episcopal Garden, Castelo Branco; 50 e. Town Hall, Sintra; 100 e. Seven Cities' Lake, Sao Miguel. Azores.

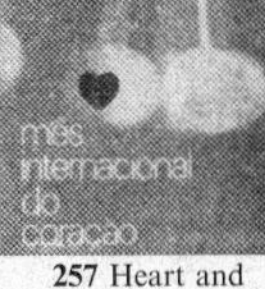

256 Arms of Pinhel **257** Heart and Pendulum

1972. Bicentenary of Pinhel's Status as a City. Multicoloured.
1464 1 e. Type **256** 10 10
1465 2 e. 50 Balustrade (vert) . . 1·25 35
1466 7 e. 50 Lantern on pedestal (vert) . . . . 1·10 60

1972 World Heart Month.
1467 **257** 1 e. red and lilac . . . 10 10
1468 – 4 e. red and brown . . . 2·50 1·10
1469 – 9 e. red and brown . . . 1·10 70
DESIGNS: 4 e. Heart in spiral; 9 e. Heart and cardiogram trace.

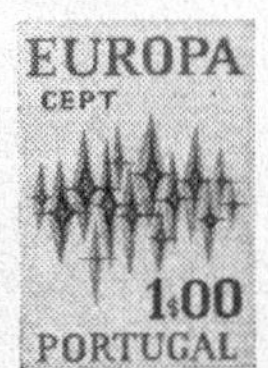

258 "Communications" **259** Container Truck

1972. Europa.
1470 **258** 1 e. multicoloured . . . 20 10
1471 3 e. 50 multicoloured . . 1·25 35
1472 6 e. multicoloured . . . 4·50 1·50

1972. 13th International Road Transport Union Congress, Estoril. Multicoloured.
1473 1 e. Type **259** 10 10
1474 4 e. 50 Roof of taxi-cab . . . 1·60 1·00
1475 8 e. Motor-coach . . . . . . 1·25 95

260 Football

1972. Olympic Games, Munich. Multicoloured.
1476 50 c. Type **260** 10 10
1477 1 e. Running 10 10
1478 1 e. 50 Show jumping 25 20
1479 3 e. 50 Swimming 65 40
1480 4 e. 50 Yachting 95 95
1481 5 e. Gymnastics . . . . . . 1·75 1·00

261 Marquis de Pombal **262** Tome de Sousa

1972. Pombaline University Reforms. Multicoloured.
1482 1 e. Type **261** 10 10
1483 2 e. 50 "The Sciences" (emblems) . . . . 1·25 85
1484 8 e. Arms of Coimbra Univesity 1·25 1·10

1972. 150th Anniv of Brazilian Independence. Multicoloured.
1485 1 e. Type **262** 10 10
1486 2 e. 50 Jose Bonifacio 60 30
1487 3 e. 50 Dom Pedro IV 60 30
1488 6 e. Dove and globe . . . . 1·25 75

263 Sacadura Cabral, Gago Coutinho and Fairey IIID Seaplane

1972. 50th Anniv of 1st Lisbon–Rio de Janeiro Flight. Multicoloured.
1489 1 e. Type **263** 10 10
1490 2 e. 50 Route map 60 35
1491 2 e. 80 Type **263** 90 85
1492 3 e. 80 As 2 e. 50 . . . . . 1·25 1·10

264 Camoens

1972. 400th Anniv of Camoens' "Lusiads" (epic poem).
1493 **264** 1 e. yellow, brown & black 10 10
1494 – 3 e. blue, green & black . 1·00 65
1495 – 10 e. brown, purple & blk 1·25 90
DESIGNS: 3 e. "Saved from the Sea"; 10 e. "Encounter with Adamastor".

265 Graph and Computer Tapes

1973. Portuguese Productivity Conference, Lisbon. Multicoloured.
1496 1 e. Type **265** 10 10
1497 4 e. Computer scale . . . . 1·00 65
1498 9 e. Graphs 95 55

266 Europa "Posthorn" **268** Child Running

267 Pres. Medici and Arms

1973. Europa.
1499 **266** 1 e. multicoloured . . . 25 10
1500 4 e. multicoloured . . . 4·75 95
1501 6 e. multicoloured . . . 5·50 1·90

1973. Visit of Pres. Medici of Brazil. Mult.
1502 1 e. Type **267** 10 10
1503 2 e. 80 Pres. Medici and globe 65 60
1504 3 e. 50 Type **267** 65 60
1505 4 e. 80 As No. 1503 . . . . 65 60

1973. "For the Child".
1506 **268** 1 e. dp blue, blue & brn 10 10
1507 – 4 e. purple, mauve & brn 1·10 60
1508 – 7 e. 50 orange, ochre and brown . . . . 1·10 1·00
DESIGNS: 4 e. Child running (to right); 7 e. 50, Child jumping.

269 Transport and Weather Map **270** Child and Written Text

1973. 25th Anniv of Ministry of Communications. Multicoloured.
1509 1 e. Type **269** 35 10
1510 3 e. 80 "Telecommunications" 30 30
1511 6 e. "Postal Services" . . . 90 60

1973. Bicentenary of Primary State School Education. Multicoloured.
1512 1 e. Type **270** 10 10
1513 4 e. 50 Page of children's primer 1·10 40
1514 5 e. 30 "Schooldays" (child's drawing) (horiz) 85 65
1515 8 e. "Teacher and children" (horiz) . . . . 3·00 1·40

271 Early Tram-car **272** League Badge

1973. Centenary of Oporto's Public Transport System. Multicoloured.
1516 1 e. Horse-drawn tramcar . 25 10
1517 3 e. 50 Modern bus . . . . 1·60 1·25
1518 7 e. 50 Type **271** . . . . . 1·75 1·10
Nos. 1516/17 are 31½×31½ mm.

1973. 50th Anniv of Servicemen's League. Multicoloured.
1519 1 e. Type **272** 10 10
1520 2 e. 50 Servicemen . . . . . 1·75 70
1521 11 e. Awards and medals . . 3·00 55

273 Death of Nuno Goncalves **274** Damiao de Gois (after Durer)

1973. 600th Anniv of Defence of Faria Castle by the Alcaide, Nuno Goncalves.
1522 **273** 1 e. green and yellow . . 15 10
1523 10 e. purple and yellow . 1·40 1·00

1974. 400th Death Anniv of Damiao de Gois (scholar and diplomat). Multicoloured.
1524 1 e. Type **274** 10 10
1525 4 e. 50 Title-page of "Chronicles of Prince Dom Joao" . . 1·90 60
1526 7 e. 50 Lute and "Dodecahordon" score . . 95 50

275 "The Exile" (A. Soares dos Reis) **276** Light Emission

1974. Europa
1527 **275** 1 e. green, blue and olive 35 10
1528 4 e. green, red and yellow 6·50 65
1529 6 e. dp green, green & bl 7·75 1·25

1974. Inauguration of Satellite Communications Station Network.
1530 **276** 1 e. 50 green 10 10
1531 – 4 e. 50 blue . . . . 1·10 60
1532 – 5 e. 30 purple . . . . . 1·60 1·00
DESIGNS: 4 e. 50, Spiral Waves; 5 e. 30, Satellite and Earth.

277 "Diffusion of Hertzian Radio Waves"

1974. Birth Centenary of Guglielmo Marconi (radio pioneer). Multicoloured.
1533 1 e. 50 Type **277** 10 10
1534 3 e. 30 "Radio waves across Space" . . . . 1·75 80
1535 10 e. "Radio waves for Navigation" 90 50

278 Early Post-boy and Modern Mail Van

1974. Centenary of U.P.U. Multicoloured.
1536 1 e. 50 Type **278** 10 10
1537 2 e. Hand with letters 60 10
1538 3 e. 30 Sailing packet and modern liner 30 15
1539 4 e. 50 Dove and airliner . . 1·10 50
1540 5 e. 30 Hand with letter . . . 35 35
1541 20 e. Early and modern railway locomotives . . . . 2·50 1·50

279 Luisa Todi **280** Arms of Beja

1974. Portuguese Musicians.
1543 **279** 1 e. 50 purple 10 10
1544 – 2 e. red . . . . 1·00 30
1545 – 2 e. 50 brown 70 15
1546 – 3 e. blue 65 35
1547 – 5 e. 30 green 75 50
1548 – 11 e. red 75 50
PORTRAITS: 2 e. Joao Domingos Bomtempo; 2 e. 50, Carlos Seixas; 3 e. Duarte Lobo; 5 e. 30, Joao de Sousa Carvalho; 11 e. Marcos Portugal.

1974. Bimillenary of Beja. Multicoloured.
1549 1 e. 50 Type **280** 10 10
1550 3 e. 50 Beja's inhabitants through the ages . . . . . 1·90 1·00
1551 7 e. Moorish arches . . . . . 2·00 1·10

281 "The Annunciation" **282** Rainbow and Dove

1974. Christmas. Multicoloured.
1552 1 e. 50 Type **281** 10 10
1553 4 e. 50 "The Nativity" . . . 2·50 55
1554 10 e. "The Flight into Egypt" 2·00 85

1974. Portuguese Armed Forces Movement of 25 April.
1555 **282** 1 e. 50 multicoloured . . 10 10
1556 3 e. 50 multicoloured . . 2·50 1·50
1557 5 e. multicoloured . . . 1·60 60

283 Egas Moniz **284** Farmer and Soldier

1974. Birth Centenary of Professor Egas Moniz (brain surgeon).
1558 **283** 1 e. 50 brown & orange . 15 10
1559 – 3 e. 30 orange & brown . . 80 50
1560 – 10 e. grey and blue . . . 3·25 75
DESIGNS: 3 e. 30, Nobel Medicine and Physiology Prize medal, 1949; 10 e. Cerebral angiograph, 1927.

1975. Portuguese Cultural Progress and Citizens' Guidance Campaign.
1561 **284** 1 e. 50 multicoloured . . 10 10
1562 3 e. multicoloured . . . 1·60 60
1563 4 e. 50 multicoloured . . 2·40 1·00

285 Hands and Dove of Peace **286** "The Hand of God"

1975. 1st Anniv of Portuguese Revolution. Multicoloured.
1564 1 e. 50 Type **285** 10 10
1565 4 e. 50 Hands and peace dove 2·10 65
1566 10 e. Peace dove and emblem 2·50 1·00

1975. Holy Year. Multicoloured.
1567 1 e. 50 Type **286** 10 10
1568 4 e. 50 Hand with cross . . . 2·50 95
1569 10 e. Peace dove . . . . . . 3·25 1·00

287 "The Horseman of the Apocalypse" (detail of 12th-cent manuscript)

1975. Europa. Multicoloured.
1570 1 e. 50 Type **287** 40 10
1571 10 e. "Fernando Pessoa" (poet) (A. Negreiros) . . . . . . 8·75 95

288 Assembly Building

1975. Opening of Portuguese Constituent Assembly.
1572 **288** 2 e. black, red & yellow . 25 10
1573 20 e. black, green & yell 4·50 1·25

289 Hiking

1975. 36th International Camping and Caravanning Federation Rally. Multicoloured.
1574 2 e. Type **289** 80 15
1575 4 e. 50 Boating and swimming 2·10 1·00
1576 5 e. 30 Caravanning . . . . 1·10 1·00

290 Planting Tree

1975. 30th Anniv of U.N.O. Multicoloured.

1577	2 e. Type **290**	30	10
1578	4 e. 50 Releasing peace dove	1·25	50
1579	20 c. Harvesting corn	2·75	1·25

291 Lilienthal Glider and Modern Space Rocket

1975. 26th International Astronautical Federation Congress, Lisbon. Multicoloured.

1580	2 e. Type **291**	40	10
1581	4 e. 50 "Apollo" – "Soyuz" space link	1·60	80
1582	5 e. 30 R. H. Goddard, R. E. Pelteric, H. Oberth and K. E. Tsiolkovsky (space pioneers)	80	80
1583	10 e. Astronaut and spaceships (70 × 32 mm)	6·25	2·75

292 Surveying the Land

1975 Centenary of National Geographical Society, Lisbon. Multicoloured.

1584	2 e. Type **292**	20	10
1585	8 e. Surveying the sea	1·00	65
1586	10 e. Globe and people	2·40	1·10

293 Symbolic Arch **294** Nurse in Hospital Ward

1975. European Architectural Heritage Year.

1587	**293**	2 e. grey, blue & dp blue	20	10
1588	–	8 e. grey and red	1·90	60
1589	–	10 e. multicoloured	2·10	90

DESIGNS: 8 e. Stylized building plan; 10 e. Historical building being protected from development.

1975 International Women's Year. Multicoloured

1590	50 c. Type **294**	10	10
1591	2 e. Woman farm worker	75	30
1592	3 e. 50 Woman office worker	75	50
1593	8 e. Woman factory worker	1·40	1·10

295 Pen-nib as Plough Blade

1976. 50th Anniv of National Writers Society.

1595	**295**	3 e. blue and red	25	10
1596		20 e. red and blue	3·00	1·10

296 First Telephone Set

1976. Telephone Centenary.

1597	**296**	3 e. black, grn & dp grn	75	10
1598	–	10 e. 50 black, red and pink	2·40	80

DESIGNS: 10 e. 50, Alexander Graham Bell.

297 "Industrial Progress" **298** Carved Olive-wood Spoons

1976. National Production Campaign.

1599	**297**	50 c. red	25	10
1600	–	1 e. green	35	10

DESIGN: 1 e. Consumer goods.

1976. Europa. Multicoloured.

1601	3 e. Type **298**	1·50	1·00
1602	20 e. Gold ornaments	22·00	5·75

299 Stamp Designing

1976. "Interphil 76" International Stamp Exhibition, Philadelphia. Multicoloured.

1603	3 e. Type **299**	20	10
1604	7 e. 50 Stamp being hand-cancelled	80	60
1605	10 e. Stamp printing	1·25	60

300 King Fernando promulgating Law

1976. 600th Anniv of Law of "Sesmarias" (uncultivated land). Multicoloured.

1606	3 e. Type **300**	15	10
1607	5 e. Plough and farmers repelling hunters	1·40	35
1608	10 e. Corn harvesting	1·75	80

301 Athlete with Olympic Torch

1976. Olympic Games, Montreal. Multicoloured.

1610	3 e. Type **301**	20	10
1611	7 e. Women's relay	1·25	1·10
1612	10 e. 50 Olympic flame	2·00	1·00

302 "Speaking in the Country"

1976. Literacy Campaign. Multicoloured.

1613	3 e. Type **302**	50	10
1614	3 e. "Speaking at Sea"	50	10
1615	3 e. "Speaking in Town"	50	10
1616	3 e. "Speaking at Work"	60	10

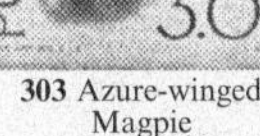

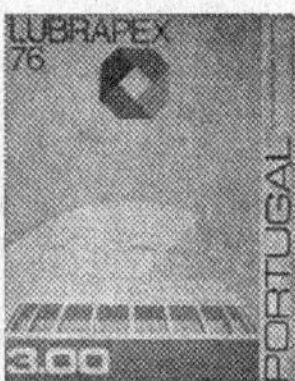

303 Azure-winged Magpie **304** "Lubrapex" Emblem and Exhibition Hall

1976. "Portucale 77" Thematic Stamp Exhibition, Oporto (1st issue). Flora and Fauna. Multicoloured.

1618	3 e. Type **303**	60	10
1619	5 e. Lynx	1·10	25
1620	7 e. Portuguese laurel cherry and blue tit	1·50	75
1621	10 e. 50 Little wild carnation and lizard	1·25	1·10

See also Nos 1673/8.

1976. "Lubrapex 1976" Luso-Brazilian Stamp Exhibition. Multicoloured.

1622	3 e. Type **304**	25	10
1623	20 e. "Lubrapex" emblem and "stamp"	2·10	1·40

305 Bank Emblem

1976. Centenary of National Trust Fund Bank.

1625	**305**	3 e. multicoloured	10	10
1626		7 e. multicoloured	1·25	80
1627		15 e. multicoloured	2·10	1·10

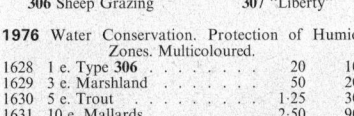

306 Sheep Grazing **307** "Liberty"

1976 Water Conservation. Protection of Humid Zones. Multicoloured.

1628	1 e. Type **306**	20	10
1629	3 e. Marshland	50	20
1630	5 e. Trout	1·25	30
1631	10 e. Mallards	2·50	90

1976. Consolidation of Democratic Institutions.

1632	**307**	3 e. grey, green and red	60	10

308 Examining Child's Eyes

1976. World Health Day. Detection and Prevention of Blindness. Multicoloured.

1633	3 e. Type **308**	20	10
1634	5 e. Welder wearing protective goggles	1·60	25
1635	10 e. 50 Blind person reading Braille	1·25	1·00

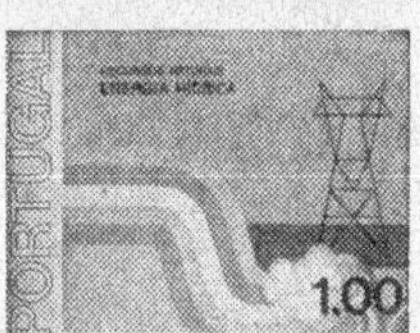

309 Hydro-electric Power

1976. Uses of Natural Energy. Multicoloured.

1636	1 e. Type **309**	10	10
1637	4 e. Fossil fuel (oil)	45	15
1638	5 e. Geo-thermic sources	60	25
1639	10 e. Wind power	1·10	70
1640	15 e. Solar energy	2·10	1·40

310 Map of Member Countries

1977. Admission of Portugal to the Council of Europe.

1641	**310**	8 e. 50 multicoloured	1·10	1·10
1642		10 e. multicoloured	1·10	1·10

311 Bottle inside Human Body

1977. 10th Anniv of Portuguese Anti-Alcoholic Society. Multicoloured.

1643	3 e. Type **311**	10	10
1644	5 e. Broken body and bottle	60	40
1645	15 e. Sun behind prison bars and bottle	1·50	1·10

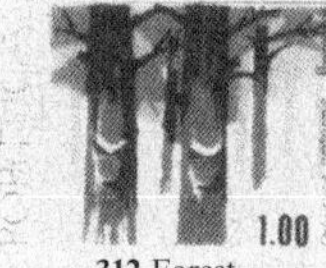

312 Forest

1977. Natural Resources. Forests. Multicoloured.

1646	1 e. Type **312**	10	10
1647	4 e. Cork oaks	50	25
1648	7 e. Logs and trees	1·40	1·10
1649	15 e. Trees by the sea	1·40	1·25

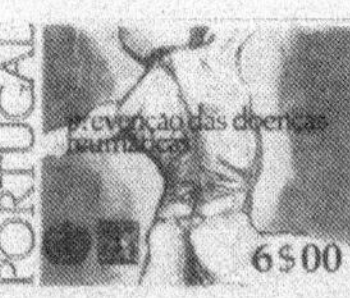

313 Exercising

1977. International Rheumatism Year.

1650	–	4 e. orange, brown & blk	15	10
1651	**313**	6 e. ultramarine, blue and black	1·00	95
1652	–	10 e. red, mauve & black	1·00	60

DESIGNS: 4 e. Rheumatism victim; 10 e. Group exercising.

314 Southern Plains **315** John XXI Enthroned

1977. Europa. Multicoloured.

1653	4 e. Type **314**	15	10
1654	8 e. 50 Northern terraced mountains	1·10	65

1977. 7th Death Centenary of Pope John XXI. Multicoloured.

1656	4 e. Type **315**	20	10
1657	15 e. Pope as doctor	55	35

316 Compass

1977. Camoes Day.

1658	**316**	4 e. multicoloured	20	10
1659		8 e. 50 multicoloured	1·00	1·00

317 Child and Computer

1977. Permanent Education. Multicoloured.

1660	4 e. Type **317**	35	10
1661	4 e. Flautist and dancers	35	10
1662	4 e. Farmer and tractor	35	10
1663	4 e. Students and atomic construction	35	10

318 Pyrite

1977. Natural Resources. The Subsoil. Mult.

1665	4 e. Type **318**	15	10
1666	5 e. Marble	60	30
1667	10 e. Iron ore	70	45
1668	20 e. Uranium	1·60	1·10

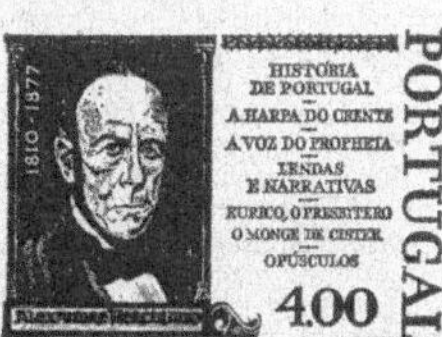

319 Alexandre Herculano

1977. Death Centenary of Alexandre Herculano (writer and politician).

1669	**319**	4 e. multicoloured	20	10
1670		15 e. multicoloured	1·25	50

320 Early Locomotive and Peasant Cart (ceramic panel, J. Colaco)

1977. Centenary of Railway Bridge over River Douro. Multicoloured.

1671	4 e. Type **320**	25	10
1672	10 e. Maria Pia bridge (Eiffel)	1·75	1·60

321 Poviero (Northern coast)

1977. "Portucale 77" Thematic Stamp Exhibition, Oporto (2nd issue). Coastal Fishing Boats. Multicoloured.

1673 2 e. Type **321** 40 10
1674 3 e. Sea-going rowing boat, Furadouro 25 10
1675 4 e. Rowing boat from Nazare 25 10
1676 7 e. Caicque from Algarve . . 35 15
1677 10 e. Tunny fishing boat, Algarve 70 55
1678 15 e. Boat from Buarcos . . 1·10 80

322 "The Adoration" (Maria do Sameiro A. Santos)

1977. Christmas. Children's Paintings. Mult.

1680 4 e. Type **322** 20 10
1681 7 e. "Star over Bethlehem" (Paula Maria L. David) . . 90 35
1682 10 e. "The Holy Family" (Carla Maria M. Cruz) (vert) . . 95 60
1683 20 e. "Children following the Star" (Rosa Maria M. Cardoso) (vert) . . . . . . 2·10 1·00

323 Medical Equipment and Operating Theatre **324** Mediterranean Soil

1978. (a) Size 22 × 17 mm.

1684 **323** 50 c. green, blk & red . . 10 10
1685 – 1 e. blue, orange and black 10 10
1686 – 2 e. blue, green & brn . 10 10
1687 – 3 e. brown, green and black 10 10
1688 – 4 e. green, blue & brn . 10 10
1689 – 5 e. blue, green & brn . 15 10
1690 – 5 e. 50 brown, buff and green 15 10
1691 – 6 e. brown, yell & grn . 15 10
1692 – 6 e. 50 blue, deep blue and green 15 10
1693 – 7 e. black, grey and blue 15 10
1694 – 8 e. ochre, brown and grey 15 10
1694a – 8 e. 50 brown, blk & lt brn 15 10
1695 – 9 e. yellow, brn & blk . 20 10
1696 – 10 e. brown, blk & grn . 20 10
1697 – 12 e. 50 blue, red and black 25 10
1698 – 16 e. brown, black and violet 25 10

(b) Size 30 × 21 mm.

1699 – 20 e. multicoloured . . . 45 10
1700a – 30 e. multicoloured . . . 55 20
1701 – 40 e. multicoloured . . . 60 25
1702 – 50 e. multicoloured . . . 95 15
1703 – 100 e. multicoloured . . 1·75 35
1703a – 250 e. multicoloured . . 4·00 65

DESIGNS: 1 e. Old and modern kitchen equipment; 2 e. Telegraph key and masts, microwaves and dish aerial; 3 e. Dressmaking and ready-to-wear clothes; 4 e. Writing desk and computer; 5 e. Tunny fishing boats and modern trawler; 5 e. 50, Manual and mechanical weaver's looms; 6 e. Plough and tractor; 6 e. 50, Monoplane and B.A.C. One Eleven airliner; 7 e. Hand press and modern printing press; 8 e. Carpenter's hand tools and mechanical tool; 8 e. 50, Potter's wheel and modern ceramic machinery; 9 e. Old cameras and modern cine and photo cameras; 10 e. Axe, saw and mechanical saw; 12 e. 50, Navigation and radar instruments; 16 e. Manual and automatic mail sorting; 20 e. Hand tools and building site; 30 e. Hammer, anvil, bellows and industrial complex; 40 e. Peasant cart and lorry; 50 e. Alembic, retorts and modern chemical plant; 100 e. Carpenter's shipyard, modern shipyard and tanker; 250 e. Survey instruments.

1978. Natural Resources. The Soil. Mult.

1704 4 e. Type **324** 25 10
1705 5 e. Rock formation 30 10
1706 10 e. Alluvial soil 80 55
1707 20 e. Black soil . . . . 2·10 75

325 Pedestrian on Zebra Crossing

1978. Road Safety.

1708 **325** 1 e. blue, black & orge . 10 10
1709 – 2 e. blue, black & grn . 20 10
1710 – 2 e. 50 blue, blk & lt bl . 45 10
1711 – 5 e. blue, black & red . 85 20
1712 – 9 e. blue, blk & ultram . 1·50 60
1713 – 12 e. 50 blue and black . 2·25 1·60

DESIGNS: 2 e. Motor cyclist; 2 e. 50, Children in back of car; 5 e. Driver in car; 9 e. View of road from driver's seat; 12 e. 50, Road victim ("Don't drink and drive").

326 Roman Tower of Centum Cellas, Belmonte **327** Roman Bridge, Chaves

1978. Europa. Multicoloured.

1714 10 e. Type **326** 85 20
1715 40 e. Belem Monastery, Lisbon 2·40 1·10

1978. 19th Century of Chaves (Aquae Flaviae). Multicoloured.

1717 5 e. Type **327** 30 15
1718 20 e. Inscribed tablet from bridge . . . . 1·75 50

328 Running

1978. Sport for All. Multicoloured.

1719 5 e. Type **328** 15 10
1720 10 e. Cycling 30 20
1721 12 e. 50 Swimming 90 90
1722 15 e. Football . . . . 1·10 1·10

329 Pedro Nunes

1978. 400th Death Anniv of Pedro Nunes (cosmographer). Multicoloured.

1723 5 e. Type **329** 20 10
1724 20 e. Nonio (navigation instrument) and diagram . 85 35

330 Trawler, Crates of Fish and Lorry

1978. Natural Resources. Fishes. Multicoloured.

1725 5 e. Type **330** 15 10
1726 9 e. Trawler and dockside cranes 30 20
1727 12 e. 50 Trawler, radar and lecture 85 85
1728 15 e. Trawler with echo-sounding equipment and laboratory . . . . 1·10 1·10

331 Post Rider

1978. Introduction of Post Code. Multicoloured.

1729 5 e. Type **331** 25 10
1730 5 e. Pigeon with letter . . . 25 10
1731 5 e. Sorting letters 25 10
1732 5 e. Pen nib and post codes . 25 10

332 Symbolic Figure

1978. 30th Anniv of Declaration of Human Rights. Multicoloured.

1733 14 e. Type **332** 50 30
1734 40 e. Similar symbolic figure, but facing right . . . . . . 1·40 1·00

333 Sebastiao Magalhaes Lima

1978. 50th Death Anniv of Magalhaes Lima (journalist and pacifist).

1736 **333** 5 e. multicoloured 25 10

334 Portable Post Boxes and Letter Balance

1978. Centenary of Post Museum. Multicoloured.

1737 4 e. Type **334** 25 10
1738 5 e. Morse equipment 20 10
1739 10 e. Printing press and Portuguese stamps of 1853 (125th anniv) 50 15
1740 14 e. Books, bookcase and entrance to Postal Library (centenary) . . . . 1·75 1·60

335 Emigrant at Railway Station

1979. Portuguese Emigrants. Multicoloured.

1742 5 e. Type **335** 30 10
1743 14 e. Emigrants at airport . . 55 40
1744 17 e. Man greeting child at railway station . . . . . . 1·10 1·00

336 Traffic **337** N.A.T.O. Emblem

1979. Fight Against Noise. Multicoloured.

1745 4 e. Type **336** 10 10
1746 5 e. Pneumatic drill 45 10
1747 14 e. Loud hailer . . . . . . 1·00 60

1979. 30th Anniv of N.A.T.O.

1748 **337** 5 e. blue, red & brown . . 25 10
1749 50 e. blue, yellow and red 2·50 2·10

338 Door-to-door Delivery

1979. Europa. Multicoloured.

1751 14 e. Postal messenger delivering letter in cleft stick 45 25
1752 40 e. Type **338** . . . . 1·10 1·00

339 Children playing Ball

1979. International Year of the Child. Multicoloured.

1754 5 e. 50 Type **339** 20 10
1755 6 e. 50 Mother, baby and dove 25 10
1756 10 e. Child eating 35 35
1757 14 e. Children of different races 95 85

340 Saluting the Flag

1979. Camoes Day.

1759 **340** 6 e. 50 multicoloured . . 35 10

341 Pregnant Woman

1979. The Mentally Handicapped. Multicoloured.

1761 6 e. 50 Type **341** 25 10
1762 17 e. Boy sitting in cage . . 60 40
1763 20 e. Face, and hands holding hammer and chisel 85 75

342 Children reading Book

1979. 50th Anniv of International Bureau of Education. Multicoloured.

1764 6 e. 50 Type **342** 30 10
1765 17 e. Teaching a deaf child . 1·00 85

343 Water Cart, Caldas de Monchique

1979. "Brasiliana 79" International Stamp Exhibition. Portuguese Country Carts. Mult.

1766 2 e. 50 Type **343** 15 10
1767 5 e. 50 Wine sledge, Madeira 15 10
1768 6 e. 50 Wine cart, Upper Douro 20 10
1769 16 e. Covered cart, Alentejo 70 65
1770 19 e. Cart, Mogadouro . . . 95 1·00
1771 20 e. Sand cart, Murtosa . . 95 30

344 Aircraft flying through Storm Cloud

1979. 35th Anniv of TAP National Airline. Multicoloured.

1772 16 e. Type **344** . . . . . . 1·00 50
1773 19 e. Aircraft and sunset . . 1·10 75

345 Antonio Jose de Almeida **346** Family Group

1979. Republican Personalities (1st series).

1774 **345** 5 e. 50 mauve, grey and red 25 10
1775 – 6 e. 50 red, grey and carmine 25 10
1776 – 10 e. brown, grey & red . 35 10
1777 – 16 e. blue, grey and red . 60 55
1778 – 19 e. 50 green, grey and red 95 95
1779 – 20 e. purple, grey and red 85 40

DESIGNS: 6 e. Afonso Costa; 10 e. Teofilo Braga; 16 e. Bernardino Machado; 19 e. 50, Joao Chagas; 20 e. Elias Garcia.

See also Nos. 1787/92.

1979. Towards a National Health Service. Mult.

1780 6 e. 50 Type **346** 25 10
1781 20 e. Doctor examining patient 1·10 50

347 "The Holy Family"

1979. Christmas. Tile Pictures. Multicoloured.
1782 5 e. 50 Type **347** 30 20
1783 6 e. 50 "Adoration of the Shepherds" 35 20
1784 16 e. "Flight into Egypt" . . 1·00 80

348 Rotary Emblem and Globe

1980. 75th Anniv of Rotary International. Mult.
1785 16 e. Type **348** 85 60
1786 50 e. Rotary emblem and torch 2·25 1·60

349 Jaime Cortesao

1980. Republican Personalities (2nd series).
1787 – 3 e. 50 orange & brown . 20 10
1788 – 5 e. 50 green, olive and deep olive 25 10
1789 – 6 e. 50 lilac and violet . . 25 10
1790 **349** 11 e. multicoloured . . . 1·10 1·00
1791 – 16 e. ochre and brown . 85 60
1792 – 20 e. green, blue & lt bl . 75 35
DESIGNS: 3 e. 50, Alvaro de Castro; 5 e. 50, Antonio Sergio; 6 e. 50, Norton de Matos; 16 e. Teixeira Gomes; 20 e. Jose Domingues dos Santos.

350 Serpa Pinto

1980. Europa, Multicoloured.
1793 16 e. Type **350** 55 35
1794 60 e. Vasco da Gama . . . . 1·75 1·00

351 Barn Owl

1980. Protection of Species. Animals in Lisbon Zoo. Multicoloured.
1796 6 e. 50 Type **351** . . . . . . 1·00 20
1797 16 e. Red fox . . . . 1·00 30
1798 19 e. 50 Wolf . . . . 1·25 55
1799 20 e. Golden eagle . . . . . 2·25 55

352 Luis Vaz de Camoes

354 Lisbon and Statue of St. Vincent (Jeronimos Monastery)

353 Pinto in Japan

1980. 400th Death Anniv of Luis Vaz de Camoes (poet).
1801 **352** 6 e. 50 multicoloured . . 40 10
1802 20 e. multicoloured . . . 90 55

1980. 400th Anniv of Fernao Mendes Pinto's "A Peregrinacao" (The Pilgrimage). Multicoloured.
1803 6 e. 50 Type **353** 30 10
1804 10 e. Sea battle 70 45

1980. World Tourism Conference, Manila, Philippines. Multicoloured.
1805 6 e. 50 Type **354** 25 10
1806 8 e. Lantern Tower, Evora Cathedral 25 25
1807 11 e. Mountain village and "Jesus with Top-hat" (Mirando do Douro Cathedral) 50 45
1808 16 e. Canicada dam and "Lady of the Milk" (Braga Cathedral) 90 60
1809 19 e. 50 Aveiro River and pulpit from Santa Cruz Monastery, Coimbra 90 75
1810 20 e. Rocha beach and ornamental chimney, Algarve 1·00 55

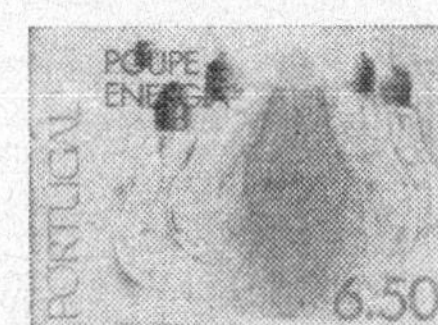

355 Caravel

1980. "Lubrapex 80" Portuguese–Brazilian Stamp Exhibition, Lisbon. Multicoloured.
1811 6 e. 50 Type **355** 25 10
1812 8 e. Nau 45 40
1813 16 e. Galleon 90 45
1814 19 e. 50 Early paddle-steamer with sails . . . . 1·10 60

356 Lightbulbs

1980. Energy Conservation. Multicoloured.
1816 6 e. 50 Type **356** 25 10
1817 16 e. Speeding car . . . . . 1·10 65

357 Duke of Braganca and Open Book

1980. Bicentenary of Academy of Sciences, Lisbon. Multicoloured.
1818 6 e. 50 Type **357** 25 10
1819 19 e. 50 Uniformed academician, Academy and sextant . . . . 1·10 60

358 Cigarette contaminating Lungs

1980. Anti-Smoking Campaign. Multicoloured.
1820 6 e. 50 Type **358** 25 10
1821 19 e. 50 Healthy figure pushing away hand with cigarette . 1·10 95

359 Head and Computer Punch-card

1981. National Census. Multicoloured.
1822 6 e. 50 Type **359** 25 10
1823 16 e. Houses and punch-card . 1·10 90

360 Fragata, River Tejo

1981. River Boats. Multicoloured.
1824 8 e. Type **360** 25 15
1825 8 e. 50 Rabelo, River Douro 25 15
1826 10 e. Moliceiro, Aveiro River 35 15
1827 16 e. Barco, River Lima . . . 50 30
1828 19 e. 50 Carocho, River Minho 60 45
1829 20 e. Varino, River Tejo . . . 70 35

361 "Rajola" Tile from Setubal Peninsula (15th century)

1981. Tiles (1st series).
1830 **361** 8 e. 50 multicoloured . . 55 10
See also Nos. 1843, 1847, 1862, 1871, 1885, 1893, 1902, 1914, 1926, 1935, 1941, 1952, 1970, 1972, 1976, 1983, 1993, 2020 and 2031.

362 Agua Dog

1981. 50th Anniv of Kennel Club of Portugal. Multicoloured.
1832 7 e. Type **362** 25 15
1833 8 e. 50 Serra de Aires 25 15
1834 15 e. Perdigueiro 55 15
1835 22 e. Podengo 80 50
1836 25 e. 50 Castro Laboreiro . . 1·10 90
1837 33 e. 50 Serra de Estrela . . . 1·75 70

363 "Agriculture"

364 Dancer and Tapestry

1981. May Day. Multicoloured.
1838 8 e. 50 Type **363** 25 10
1839 25 e. 50 "Industry" . . . . . 1·10 80

1981. Europa. Multicoloured.
1840 22 e. Type **364** . . . . 1·00 40
1841 48 e. Painted boat prow, painted plate and shipwright with model boat . . . . 2·10 1·25

1981. Tiles (2nd series). Horiz design as T **361**.
1843 8 e. 50 multicoloured 55 10
DESIGN: 8 e. 50, Tracery-pattern tile from Seville (16th century).

365 St. Anthony Writing

1981. 750th Death Anniv of St. Anthony of Lisbon. Multicoloured.
1845 8 e. 50 Type **365** 30 10
1846 70 e. St. Anthony giving blessing . . . . 3·00 95

1981. Tiles (3rd series). As T **361**. Mult.
1847 8 e. 50 Arms of Jaime, Duke of Braganca (Seville, 1510) . . 55 10

366 King Joao II and Caravels

1981. 500th Anniv of King Joao II's Accession. Multicoloured.
1849 8 e. 50 Type **366** 30 10
1850 27 e. King Joao II on horseback 1·75 80

367 "Dom Luiz" 1862

1981. 125th Anniv of Portuguese Railways. Multicoloured.
1851 8 e. 50 Type **367** 45 10
1852 19 e. Pacific type steam locomotive, 1925 . . . . . 1·25 90
1853 27 e. "Alco 1550" diesel locomotive, 1948 . . . . . 1·25 95
1854 33 e. 50 Alsthom "BB2600" electric locomotive, 1974 . . 1·75 75

368 "Perrier" Pump, 1856

369 "Virgin and Child"

1981. Portuguese Fire Engines. Multicoloured.
1855 7 e. Type **368** 30 10
1856 8 e. 50 Ford fire engine, 1927 45 25
1857 27 e. Renault fire pump, 1914 1·25 90
1858 33 e. 50 Ford "Snorkel" combined hoist and pump, 1978 . . . . 1·90 90

1981. Christmas. Crib Figures. Multicoloured.
1859 7 e. Type **369** 40 30
1860 8 e. 50 "Nativity" 50 20
1861 27 e. "Flight into Egypt" . . 1·60 1·25

1981. Tiles (4th series). As T **361**. Multicoloured.
1862 8 e. 50 "Pisana" tile, Lisbon (16th century) 55 10

370 St. Francis with Animals

371 Flags of E.E.C. Members

1982. 800th Birth Anniv of St. Francis of Assisi. Multicoloured.
1865 8 e. 50 Type **370** 30 10
1866 27 e. St. Francis helping to build church . . . . 1·60 1·25

1982. 25th Anniv of European Economic Community.
1867 **371** 27 e. multicoloured . . . 1·10 65

372 Fort St. Catherina, Lighthouse and Memorial Column

1982. Centenary of Figueira da Foz City. Mult.
1869 10 e. Type **372** 40 10
1870 19 e. Tagus Bridge, shipbuilding yard and trawler . . . . . 1·25 85

1982. Tiles (5th series). As T **361**. Multicoloured.
1871 10 e. Italo-Flemish pattern tile (17th century) 55 10

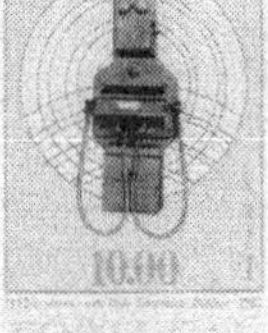

373 "Sagres I" (cadet barque)

374 Edison Gower Bell Telephone, 1883

1982. Sporting Events. Multicoloured.
1873 27 e. Type **373** (Lisbon sailing races) . . . . 1·00 75
1874 33 e. 50 Roller hockey (25th World Championship) . . 1·25 1·00
1875 50 e. "470 Class" racing yachts (World Championships) . 1·90 1·25
1876 75 e. Football (World Cup Football Championship, Spain) . . . . 3·25 1·50

1982. Centenary of Public Telephone Service. Multicoloured.

1877 10 e. Type **374** 30 10
1878 27 e. Consolidated telephone, 1887 . . . . 1·00 90

375 Embassy of King Manuel to Pope Leo X

1982. Europa.

1879 **375** 33 e. 50 multicoloured . 1·75 70

376 Pope John Paul II and Shrine of Fatima **377** Dunlin

1982. Papal Visit. Multicoloured.

1881 10 e. Type **376** 30 10
1882 27 e. Pope and Sameiro Sanctuary . . . . 1·50 1·00
1883 33 e. 50 Pope and Lisbon Cathedral . . . . 1·75 1·00

1982. Tiles (6th series). As T **361**. Multicoloured.

1885 10 e. Altar front panel depicting oriental tapestry (17th century) 55 10

1982. "Philexfrance 82" International Stamp Exhibition, Paris. Birds. Multicoloured.

1887 10 e. Type **377** 35 10
1888 19 e. Red-crested pochard . . 1·00 50
1889 27 e. Greater flamingo . . . 1·10 75
1890 33 e. 50 Black-winged stilt . . 1·40 90

378 Dr. Robert Koch

1982. Centenary of Discovery of Tubercle Bacillus. Multicoloured.

1891 27 e. Type **378** . . . . 1·10 1·00
1892 33 e. 50 Lungs . . . . 1·40 1·00

1982. Tiles (7th series). As T **361**. Multicoloured.

1893 10 e. Polychromatic quadrilobate pattern, 1630–40 55 10

379 Wine Glass and Stop Sign

1982. "Don't Drink and Drive".

1895 **379** 10 e. multicoloured . . . 40 10

380 Fairey IIID Seaplane "Lusitania"

1982. "Lubrapex 82" Brazilian–Portuguese Stamp Exhibition, Curitiba. Multicoloured.

1896 10 e. Type **380** 25 10
1897 19 e. Dornier Do-J Wal flying boat "Argus" 65 60
1898 33 e. 50 Douglas DC-7C "Seven Seas" airliner . . . . . . 1·25 65
1899 50 e. Boeing 747-282B jetliner 1·75 1·00

381 Marquis de Pombal

1982. Death Bicentenary of Marquis de Pombal (statesman and reformer).

1901 **381** 10 e. multicoloured . . 40 10

1982. Tiles (8th series). As T **361**. Multicoloured.

1902 10 e. Monochrome quadrilobate pattern, 1670–90 . . . . . 55 10

382 Gallic Cock and Tricolour

1983. Centenary of French Alliance (French language teaching association).

1905 **382** 27 e. multicoloured . . 1·10 65

383 Lisnave Shipyard

1983. 75th Anniv of Port of Lisbon Administration.

1906 **383** 10 e. multicoloured . . 45 15

384 Export Campaign Emblem

1983. Export Promotion.

1907 **384** 10 e. multicoloured . . 40 10

385 Midshipman, 1782, and Frigate "Vasco da Gama" **386** W.C.Y. Emblem

1983. Naval Uniforms. Multicoloured.

1908 12 e. 50 Type **385** 35 10
1909 25 e. Seaman and steam corvette "Estefania", 1845 . . . . 95 30
1910 30 e. Marine sergeant and cruiser "Adamastor", 1900 1·00 45
1911 37 e. 50 Midshipman and frigate "Joao Belo", 1982 . . . . 1·25 65

1983. World Communications Year. Mult.

1912 10 e. Type **386** 40 15
1913 33 e. 50 E.C.Y. emblem (diff) 1·60 1·00

1983. Tiles (9th series). As T **361**. Multicoloured.

1914 12 e. 50 Hunter killing white bull (tile from Saldanha Palace, Lisbon, 17/18th century) 65 10

387 Portuguese Helmet (16th century)

1983. "Expo XVII" Council of Europe Exhibition. Multicoloured.

1916 11 e. Type **387** 30 15
1917 12 e. 50 Astrolabe (16th century) 45 10
1918 25 e. Portuguese caravels (from 16-century Flemish tapestry) 95 50
1919 30 e. Carved capital (12th century) . . . . 1·10 55
1920 37 e. 50 Hour glass (16th century) . . . . 1·50 85
1921 40 e. Detail from Chinese panel painting (16th-17th century) 1·60 75

388 Egas Moniz (Nobel Prize winner and brain surgeon)

1983. Europa.

1923 **388** 37 e. 50 multicoloured . . 1·40 65

389 Passenger in Train

1983. European Ministers of Transport Conference.

1925 **389** 30 e. blue, deep blue and silver . . . . 1·75 65

1983. Tiles (10th series). As T **361**. Multicoloured.

1926 12 e. 50 Tiles depicting birds (18th century) 65 10

390 Mediterranean Monk Seal

1983. "Brasiliana 83" International Stamp Exhibition, Rio de Janeiro. Marine Mammals. Multicoloured.

1928 12 e. 50 Type **390** 60 15
1929 30 e. Common dolphin . . . 1·40 40
1930 37 e. 50 Killer whale . . . . 1·60 1·00
1931 80 e. Humpback whale . . . 3·00 1·00

391 Assassination of Spanish Administrator by Prince John

1983. 600th Anniv of Independence. Mult.

1933 12 e. 50 Type **391** 50 15
1934 30 e. Prince John proclaimed King of Portugal . . . . . 2·10 1·10

1983. Tiles (11th series). As T **361**. Multicoloured.

1935 12 e. 50 Flower pot by Gabriel del Barco (18th century) . . 65 10

392 Bartolomeu de Gusmao and Model Balloon, 1709 **393** "Adoration of the Magi"

1983. Bicentenary of Manned Flight. Mult.

1937 16 e. Type **392** 55 15
1938 51 e. Montgolfier balloon, 1783 1·40 85

1983. Christmas. Stained Glass Windows from Monastery of Our Lady of Victory, Batalha. Multicoloured.

1939 12 e. 50 Type **393** 35 10
1940 30 e. "The Flight into Egypt" 1·40 75

1983. Tiles (12th series). As T **361**. Multicoloured.

1941 12 e. 50 Turkish horseman (18th century) 65 10

394 Siberian Tiger

1983. Centenary of Lisbon Zoo. Multicoloured.

1944 16 e. Type **394** . . . . 1·00 15
1945 16 e. Cheetah . . . . 1·00 15
1946 16 e. Blesbok . . . . 1·00 15
1947 16 e. White rhino . . . . . 1·00 15

395 Fighter Pilot and Hawker Hurricane Mk II, 1954

1983. Air Force Uniforms. Multicoloured.

1948 16 e. Type **395** 35 10
1949 35 e. Pilot in summer uniform and Republic F-84G Thunderjet, 1960 . . . . . 1·40 45
1950 40 e. Paratrooper in walking-out uniform and Nord 250ID Noratlas military transport plane, 1966 . . . . 1·50 60
1951 51 e. Pilot in normal uniform and Vought A-70 Corsair II bomber, 1966 . . . . . . 2·00 85

1984. Tiles (13th series). As T **361**. Multicoloured.

1952 16 e. Coat of arms of King Jose I (late 18th century) . 70 15

396 "25" on Crate (25th Lisbon International Fair)

1984. Events.

1954 35 e. Type **396** . . . . 1·25 50
1955 40 e. Wheat rainbow and globe (World Food Day) . . . . 1·40 60
1956 51 e. Hand holding stylised flower (15th World Congress of International Rehabilitation) (vert) . . . 2·00 80

397 National Flag

1984. 10th Anniv of Revolution.

1957 **397** 16 e. multicoloured . . . 1·00 15

398 Bridge

1984. Europa.

1958 **398** 51 e. multicoloured . . . 1·75 1·00

399 "Panel of St. Vincent"

1984. "Lubrapex 84" Portuguese–Brazilian Stamp Exhibition. Multicoloured.

1960 16 e. Type **399** 50 15
1961 40 e. "St. James" (altar panel) 1·40 55
1962 51 e. "View of Lisbon" (painting) . . . . 2·00 85
1963 66 e. "Head of Youth" (Domingos Sequeira) . . . 2·10 1·10

400 Fencing

1984. Olympic Games, Los Angeles and 75th Anniv of Portuguese Olympic Committee. Multicoloured.

1965 35 e. Type 400 . . . . 1·00 25
1966 40 e. Gymnastics . . . . . . 1·10 50
1967 51 e. Running . . . . 1·60 90
1968 80 e. Pole vaulting . . . . . 2·10 1·00

1984. Tiles (14th series). As T **361**. Multicoloured.

1970 16 e. Pictorial tile from Pombal Palace, Lisbon (late 18th century) 65 10

1984. Tiles (15th series). As T **361**. Multicoloured.

1972 16 e. Four art nouveau tiles (late 19th century) 65 10

401 Gil Eanes

1984. Anniversaries. Multicoloured.

1974 16 e. Type **401** (550th anniv of rounding of Cape Bojador) 40 10
1975 51 e. King Pedro IV of Portugal and I of Brazil (150th death anniv) . . . . 1·90 90

1984. Tiles (16th series). As T **361**. Multicoloured.

1976 16 e. Grasshoppers and wheat (R. Bordalo Pinheiro, 19th century) 65 10

402 Infantry Grenadier, 1740, and Regiment in Formation

1985. Army Uniforms. Multicoloured.

1979 20 e. Type **402** 40 10
1980 46 e. Officer, Fifth Cavalry, 1810, and cavalry charge . 1·00 40
1981 60 e. Artillery corporal, 1891, and Krupp 9 mm gun and crew . . . . 1·60 75
1982 100 e. Engineer in chemical protection suit, 1985, and bridge-laying armoured car 2·25 1·10

1985. Tiles (17th series). As T **361**. Multicoloured.

1983 20 e. Detail of panel by Jorge Barrados in Lisbon Faculty of Letters (20th century) . . . 65 10

403 Calcada R. dos Santos Kiosk

1985. Lisbon Kiosks. Multicoloured.

1985 20 e. Type **403** 90 10
1986 20 e. Tivoli kiosk, Avenida da Liberdade 90 10
1987 20 e. Porto de Lisboa kiosk . 90 10
1988 20 e. Rua de Artilharia Um kiosk 90 10

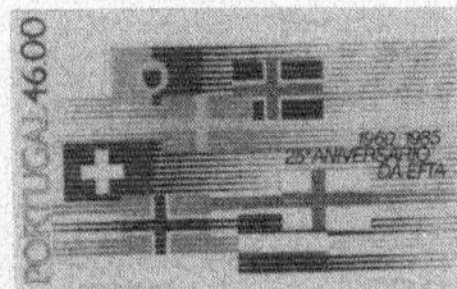

404 Flags of Member Countries

1985. 25th Anniv of European Free Trade Assn.

1989 **404** 46 e. multicoloured . . . 1·10 50

405 Profiles

1985. International Youth Year.

1990 **405** 60 e. multicoloured . . 1·40 75

406 Woman holding Adufe (tambourine)

1985. Europa.

1991 **406** 60 e. multicoloured . . 2·10 90

1985. Tiles (18th series). As T **361**. Multicoloured.

1993 20 e. Detail of panel by Maria Keil on Avenida Infante Santo (20th century) . . . 65 10

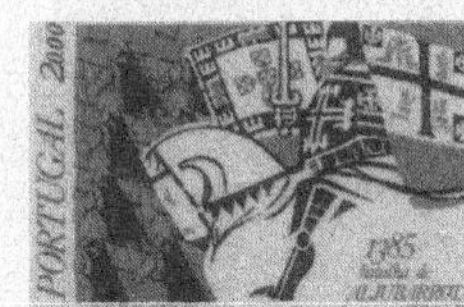

407 Knight on Horseback

1985. Anniversaries. Multicoloured.

1995 20 e. Type **407** (600th anniv of Battle of Aljubarrota) . . 65 15
1996 46 e. Queen Leonor and hospital (500th anniv of Caldas da Rainha thermal hospital) . . . . 1·50 60
1997 60 e. Pedro Reinel (500th anniversary of first Portuguese sea-chart) . . 1·75 90

408 Farmhouse, Minho

409 Aquilino Ribeiro (writer)

1985. Architecture.

1998 – 50 c. black, bistre & blue 10 10
1999 – 1 e. black, yellow & grn 10 10
2000 – 1 e. 50 black, green and emerald 10 10
2001 – 2 e. 50 brown, orge & bl 10 10
2002 – 10 e. black, pur & pink . 15 10
2003 **408** 20 e. brown, yellow and deep yellow 25 10
2004 – 22 e. 50 brown, blue and ochre 25 10
2005 – 25 e. brown, yellow & grn 30 10
2006 – 27 e. black, green and yellow 40 10
2007 – 29 e. black, yellow & orge 40 10
2008 – 30 e. black, blue & brown 40 10
2009 – 40 e. black, yellow & grn 60 10
2010 – 50 e. black, blue & brown 70 10
2011 – 55 e. black, yellow & grn 70 15
2012 – 60 e. black, orange & bl 95 15
2013 – 70 e. black, yellow & orge 95 15
2014 – 80 e. brown, green & red 1·00 25
2015 – 90 e. brown, yellow & grn 1·10 25
2016 – 100 e. brown, yellow & bl 1·40 30
2017 – 500 e. black, grey & blue 5·75 70

DESIGNS: 50 e. Saloia house, Estremadura; 1 e. Beira inland house; 1 e. 50, Ribatejo house; 2 e. 50, Tras-os-montes houses; 10 e. Minho and Douro coast house; 22 e. 50, Alentejo houses; 25 e. Sitio house, Algarve; 27 e. Beira inland house (different); 29 e. Tras-os-montes house; 30 e. Algarve house; 40 e. Beira inland house (different); 50 e. Beira coast house; 55 e. Tras-os-montes house (different); 60 e. Beira coast house (different); 70 e. South Estramadura and Alentejo house; 80 e. Estremadura house; 90 e. Minho house; 100 e. Monte house, Alentejo; 500 e. Terraced houses, East Algarve.

1985. Tiles (19th series). As T **361**. Multicoloured.

2020 20 e. Head of woman by Querubim Lapa (20th century) 65 10

1985. Anniversaries. Multicoloured.

2022 20 e. Type **409** (birth centenary) 60 10
2023 46 e. Fernando Pessoa (poet 50th death anniv) . . . . 1·25 55

410 Berlenga National Reserve

1985. National Parks and Reserves. Multicoloured.

2024 20 e. Type **410** 50 15
2025 40 e. Estrela Mountains National Park . . . . . . 1·00 45
2026 46 e. Boquilobo Marsh National Reserve . . . . . 1·50 75
2027 80 e. Formosa Lagoon National Reserve . . . . 1·75 85

411 "Nativity"

412 Post Rider

1985. Christmas. Illustrations from "Book of Hours of King Manoel I". Multicoloured.

2029 20 e. Type **411** 50 10
2030 46 e. "Adoration of the Three Wise Men" . . . . 1·40 55

1985. Tiles (20th series). As T **361**. Multicoloured.

2031 20 e. Detail of panel by Manuel Cargaleiro (20th century) 65 10

1985. No value expressed.

2034 **412** (–) green and deep green . 60 10

413 Map and Flags of Member Countries

1985. Admission of Portugal and Spain to European Economic Community. Multicoloured.

2035 20 e. Flags of Portugal and Spain uniting with flags of other members 55 10
2036 57 e. 50 Type **413** . . . . . . 1·60 75

414 Feira Castle

1986. Castles (1st series). Multicoloured.

2037 22 e. 50 Type **414** 70 15
2038 22 e. 50 Beja Castle 70 15

See also Nos. 2040/1, 2054/5, 2065/6, 2073/4, 2086/7, 2093/4, 2102/3 and 2108/9.

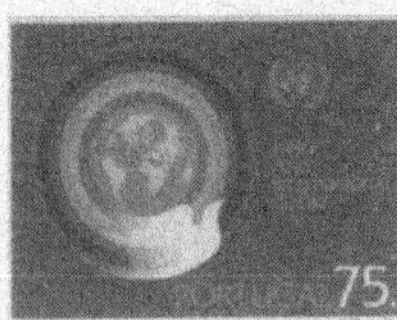

415 Globe and Dove

1986. International Peace Year.

2039 **415** 75 e. multicoloured . . . 1·90 95

1986. Castles (2nd series). As T **414**. Multicoloured.

2040 22 e. 50 Braganca Castle . . 70 15
2041 22 e. 50 Guimaraes Castle . . 70 15

INDEX

Countries can be quickly located by referring to the index at the end of this volume.

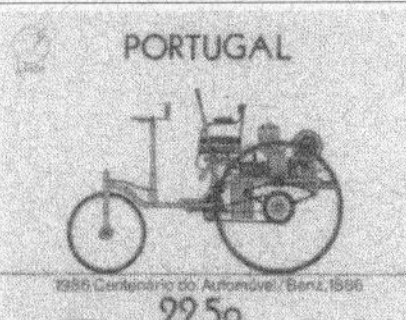

416 Benz Motor Tricycle, 1886

1986. Centenary of Motor Car. Multicoloured.

2042 22 e. 50 Type **416** 90 10
2043 22 e. 50 Daimler motor car, 1886 . . . . 90 10

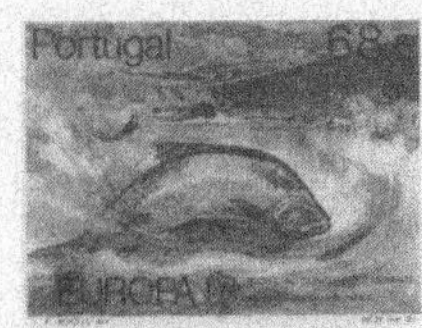

417 Shad

1986. Europa.

2044 **417** 68 e. 50 multicoloured . 1·75 80

418 Alter

1986. "Ameripex 86" International Stamp Exn, Chicago. Thoroughbred Horses. Multicoloured.

2046 22 e. 50 Type **418** 50 15
2047 47 e. 50 Lusitano . . . . . 1·25 65
2048 52 e. 50 Garrano . . . . . . 1·50 80
2049 68 e. 50 Sorraia . . . . . . 1·75 90

420 Diogo Cao (navigator) and Monument

1986. Anniversaries. Multicoloured.

2051 22 c. 50 Type **420** (500th anniv of 2nd expedition to Africa) 50 10
2052 52 e. 50 Passos Manuel (Director) and capital (150th anniv of National Academy of Fine Arts, Lisbon) . . . 1·25 60
2053 52 e. 50 Joao Baptista Ribeiro (painter and Oporto Academy Director) and drawing (150th anniv of Portuguese Academy of Fine Arts, Oporto) . . . . . . 1·25 60

1986. Castles (3rd series). As T **414**. Multicoloured.

2054 22 e. 50 Belmonte Castle . . 70 15
2055 22 e. 50 Montemor-o-Velho Castle 70 15

421 Hand writing on Postcard

1986. Anniversaries. Multicoloured.

2057 22 e. 50 Type **421** (centenary of first Portuguese postcards) 60 10
2058 47 e. 50 Guardsman and houses (75th anniv of National Republican Guard) . . . . 1·10 460
2059 52 e. 50 Calipers, globe and banner (50th anniv of Order of Engineers) . . . . . . 1·25 60

422 Seasonal Mill, Douro

1986. "Luprapex 86" Portuguese–Brazilian Stamp Exhibition, Rio de Janeiro. Multicoloured.

2060 22 e. 50 Type **422** 50 10
2061 47 e. 50 Seasonal mill, Coimbra 1·10 70
2062 52 e. 50 Overshot bucket mill, Gerez . . . . 1·25 80
2063 90 e. Permanent stream mill, Braga . . . . 1·75 85

1987. Castles (4th series). As T **414**. Mult.
2065 25 e. Silves Castle 70 15
2066 25 e. Evora-Monte Castle . . 70 15

423 Houses on Stilts, Tocha

1987. 75th Anniv (1986) of Organized Tourism. Multicoloured.
2067 25 e. Type **423** 55 15
2068 57 e. Fishing boats, Espinho . 1·40 70
2069 98 e. Fountain, Arraiolos . . 1·90 85

424 Hand, Sun and Trees

1987. European Environment Year. Multicoloured.
2070 25 e. Type **424** 50 15
2071 57 e. Hands and flower on map of Europe . . . . 1·25 65
2072 74 e. 50 Hand, sea, purple dye murex shell, moon and rainbow . . . . 1·75 85

1987. Castles (5th series). As T **414**. Multicoloured.
2073 25 e. Leiria Castle 70 10
2074 25 e. Trancoso Castle 70 10

425 Bank Borges and Irmao Agency, Vila do Conde (Alvaro Siza)

1987. Europa. Architecture.
2075 **425** 74 e. 50 multicoloured . 1·60 55

426 Cape Mondego

427 Souza-Cardoso (self-portrait)

1987. "Capex '87" International Stamp Exhibition Toronto. Portuguese Lighthouses. Multicoloured.
2077 25 e. Type **426** 55 15
2078 25 e. Berlenga 55 15
2079 25 e. Aveiro 55 15
2080 25 e. Cape St. Vincent . . . 55 15

1987. Birth Centenary of Amadeo de Souza-Cardoso (painter)
2081 **427** 74 e. 50 multicoloured . 1·40 70

428 Clipped 400 Reis Silver Coin

1987. 300th Anniv of Portuguese Paper Currency.
2082 **428** 100 e. multicoloured . . 1·90 70

429 Dias's Fleet leaving Lisbon

1987. 500th Anniv of Bartolomeu Dias's Voyages (1st issue). Multicoloured.
2083 25 e. Type **429** 70 20
2084 25 e. Ships off coast of Africa 70 20
Nos. 2083/4 were printed together, se-tenant, each pair forming a composite design.
See also Nos. 2099/2100.

430 Library

1987. 150th Anniv of Portuguese Royal Library, Rio de Janeiro.
2085 **430** 125 e. multicoloured . . 2·25 1·00

1987. Castles (6th series). As T **414**. Multicoloured.
2086 25 e. Marvao Castle 70 10
1087 25 e. St. George's Castle, Lisbon 70 10

432 Angels around Baby Jesus, Tree and Kings (Jose Manuel Coutinho)

1987. Christmas. Children's Paintings. Mult.
2089 25 e. Type **432** 60 10
2090 57 e. Children dancing around sunburst (Rosa J. Leitao) . 1·10 60
2091 74 e. 50 Santa Claus flying on dove (Sonya Alexandra Hilario) . . . . 1·40 90

1988. Castles (7th series). As T **414**. Multicoloured.
2093 27 e. Fernandine Walls, Oporto 70 10
2094 27 e. Almourol Castle . . . 70 10

433 Lynx

1988. Iberian Lynx. Multicoloured.
2095 27 e. Type **433** 80 10
2096 27 e. Lynx carrying rabbit . 80 10
2097 27 e. Pair of lynxes 80 10
2098 27 e. Mother with young . . 80 10

434 King Joao II sending Pero da Covilha on Expedition

1988. 500th Anniv of Voyages of Bartolomeu Dias (2nd issue) (2099/2100) and Pero da Covilha (2101). Multicoloured.
2099 27 e. Dias's ships in storm off Cape of Good Hope . . . 65 10
2100 27 e. Contemporary map . . 85 85
2101 105 e. Type **434** 85 85
Nos. 2099/2100 are as T **429**.

1988. Castles (8th series). As T **414**. Multicoloured.
2102 27 e. Palmela Castle 70 10
2103 27 e. Vila Nova da Cerveira Castle 70 10

435 19th-century Mail Coach

1988. Europa. Transport and Communications.
2104 **435** 80 e. multicoloured . . 1·60 70

436 Map of Europe and Monnet

1988. Birth Centenary of Jean Monnet (statesman). "Europex 88" Stamp Exhibition.
2106 **436** 60 e. multicoloured . . 1·10 50

1988. Castles (9th series). As T **414**. Multicoloured.
2108 27 e. Chaves Castle 70 10
2109 27 e. Penedono Castle 70 10

438 "Part of a Viola" (Amadeo de Souza-Cardoso)

1988. 20th-century Portuguese Paintings (1st series). Multicoloured.
2110 27 e. Type **438** 50 10
2111 60 e. "Acrobats" (Almada Negreiros) . . . . 1·10 60
2112 80 e. "Still Life with Viola" (Eduardo Viana) . . . . . 1·50 80
See also Nos. 2121/3, 2131/3, 2148/50, 2166/8 and 2206/8.

439 Archery

1988. Olympic Games, Seoul Multicoloured.
2114 27 e. Type **439** 50 10
2115 55 e. Weightlifting . . . . . 1·10 60
2116 60 e. Judo . . . . 1·25 80
2117 80 e. Tennis . . . . 1·75 80

440 "Winter" (House of the Fountains, Coimbra)

1988. Roman Mosaics of 3rd Century. Mult.
2119 27 e. Type **440** 50 10
2120 80 e. "Fish" (Baths, Faro) . . 1·40 60

1988. 20th Century Portuguese Paintings (2nd series). As T **438**. Multicoloured.
2121 27 e. "Internment" (Mario Eloy) 50 10
2122 60 e. "Lisbon Houses" (Carlos Botelho) . . . . 1·10 60
2123 80 e. "Avejao Lirico" (Antonio Pedro) . . . . 1·40 65

441 Braga Cathedral

442 "Greetings"

1989. Anniversaries. Multicoloured.
2126 30 e. Type **441** (900th anniv) . 60 25
2127 55 e. Caravel, Fischer's lovebird and S. Jorge da Mina Castle (505th anniv) . . . . 1·10 60
2128 60 e. Sailor using astrolabe (500th anniv of South Atlantic voyages) . . . . . 1·40 70
Nos. 2127/8 also have the "India 89" Stamp Exhibition, New Delhi, emblem.

1989. Greetings Stamps. Multicoloured.
2129 29 e. Type **442** 50 10
2130 60 e. Airplane distributing envelopes inscribed "with Love" 80 45

1989. 20th-Century Portuguese Paintings (3rd series). As T **438**. Multicoloured.
2131 29 e. "Antithesis of Calm" (Antonio Dacosta) 50 10
2132 60 e. "Unskilled Mason's Lunch" (Julio Pomar) . . . 1·10 55
2133 87 e. "Simumis" (Vespeira) . 1·40 80

443 Flags in Ballot Box

444 Boy with Spinning Top

1989. 3rd Direct Elections to European Parliament.
2135 **443** 60 e. multicoloured . . . 1·10 55

1989. Europa. Children's Games and Toys.
2136 **444** 80 e. multicoloured . . . 1·50 70

445 Cable Railway

1989. Lisbon Transport. Multicoloured.
2138 29 e. Type **445** 50 10
2139 65 e. Electric tram-car . . . 1·25 65
2140 87 e. Santa Justa lift . . . . 1·40 90
2141 100 e. Bus . . . . 1·90 80

446 Gyratory Mill, Ansiao

1989. Windmills. Multicoloured.
2143 29 e. Type **446** 50 10
2144 60 e. Stone mill, Santiago do Cacem . . . . 1·25 65
2145 87 e. Post mill, Afife . . . . 1·50 80
2146 100 e. Wooden mill, Caldas da Rainha . . . . 1·75 90

1989. 20th-Century Portuguese Paintings (4th series). As T **438**.
2148 29 e. blue, green and black . 45 10
2149 60 e. multicoloured . . . . . 1·10 50
2150 87 e. multicoloured . . . . . 1·40 80
DESIGNS: 29 e. "046-72" (Fernando Lanhas); 60 e. "Spirals" (Nadir Afonso); 87 e. "Sim" (Carlos Calvet).

448 Luis I (death centenary) and Ajuda Palace, Lisbon

449 "Armeria pseudarmeria"

1989. National Palaces (1st series). Multicoloured.
2153 29 e. Type **448** 45 10
2154 60 e. Queluz Palace . . . . 1·40 85
See also Nos. 2211/14.

1989. Wild Flowers. Multicoloured.
2155 29 e. Type **449** 30 15
2156 60 e. "Santolina impressa" . 90 50
2157 87 e. "Linaria lamarckii" . . 1·25 75
2158 100 e. "Limonium multiflorum" . . . . 1·75 1·00

450 Blue and White Plate

1990. Portuguese Faience (1st series). Mult.
2159 33 e. Type **450** 45 10
2160 33 e. Blue and white plate with man in centre 45 10
2161 35 e. Vase decorated with flowers 45 10
2162 60 e. Fish-shaped jug . . . . 1·00 20
2163 60 e. Blue and white plate with arms in centre . . . . . . 1·00 20
2164 60 e. Blue and white dish with lid . . . . 1·00 20
See also Nos. 2221/6 and 2262/7.

1990. 20th-Century Portuguese Paintings (5th series). As T **438**. Multicoloured.
2166 32 e. "Aluenda-Tordesillas" (Joaquim Rodrigo) 45 10
2167 60 e. "Painting" (Luis Noronha da Costa) 90 40
2168 95 e. "Painting" (Vasco Costa) 1·40 85

504 Mounted Knight and Explorer with Model Caravel

1994. Europa. Discoveries.
2367 **504** 100 e. multicoloured . . 90 50

505 Emblem

1994. International Year of the Family.
2369 **505** 45 e. red, black and lake 35 20
2370 140 e. red, black and green 1·25 60

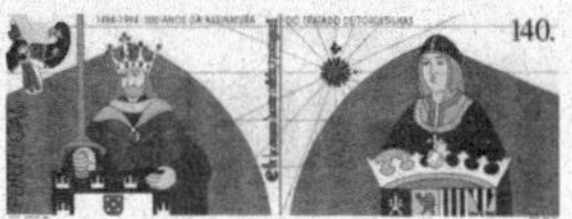

506 Footballer kicking Ball and World Map

1994. World Cup Football Championship, U.S.A. Multicoloured.
2371 100 e. Type **506** 90 45
2372 140 e. Ball and footballers' legs 1·25 60

507 King Joao II of Portugal and King Fernando of Spain (½-size illustration)

1994. 500th Anniv of Treaty of Tordesillas (defining Portuguese and Spanish spheres of influence).
2373 **507** 140 e. multicoloured . . 1·25 60

508 Music

1994. Lisbon, European Capital of Culture. Multicoloured.
2374 45 e. Type **508** 35 20
2375 75 e. Photography and cinema 60 30
2376 100 e. Theatre and dance . . 80 40
2377 140 e. Art . . . . 1·10 55

509 Emblem

1994. Portuguese Road Safety Year.
2379 **509** 45 e. red, green and black 35 20

1994. Sculptures (2nd series). As T **491**. Mult.
2380 45 e. Carved stonework from Citania de Briteiros (1st century) (horiz) 35 20
2381 75 e. Visigothic pilaster (7th century) 60 30
2382 80 e. Capital from Amorim Church (horiz) 65 35
2383 100 e. Laying Christ's body in tomb (attr Joao de Ruao) (Monastery Church of Santa Cruz de Coimbra) (horiz) . 80 40
2384 140 e. Carved wood reliquary (Santa Maria Monastery, Alcobaca) (horiz) . . . . 1·10 55
2385 180 e. Relief of Writers (Leopoldo de Almeida) (Lisbon National Library) (horiz) . . . . 1·40 70

510 Falconer, Peregrine Falcon and Dog

1994. Falconry. Designs showing a peregrine falcon in various hunting scenes. Multicoloured.
2387 45 e. Type **510** 35 20
2388 75 e. Falcon chasing duck . 65 35
2389 100 e. Falconer approaching falcon with dead duck . . 85 45
2390 140 e. Falcons . . . . 1·25 70

511 "Maria Arminda"

1994. Trawlers (2nd series). Multicoloured.
2392 45 e. Type **511** 35 20
2393 75 e. "Bom Pastor" 60 30
2394 100 e. Aladores trawler with triplex haulers 80 40
2395 140 e. "Sueste" . . . . . . 1·10 55

512 19th-century Horse-drawn Wagon

1994. Postal Transport. Multicoloured.
2396 45 e. Type **512** 35 20
2397 75 e. Travelling Post Office sorting carriage No. C7, 1910 60 30
2398 100 e. Mercedes mail van, 1910 80 40
2399 140 e. Volkswagen mail van, 1950 . . . . 1·10 55

513 Multiple Car Unit, Sintra Suburban Railway (½-size illustration)

1994. Modern Electric Locomotives (1st series). Multicoloured.
2401 45 e. Type **513** 35 20
2402 75 e. Locomotive Series "5600" (national network) 60 30
2403 140 e. Lisbon Underground train . . . . 1·10 55
See also No. 2465.

514 Medal

1994. 150th Anniv of Montepio Geral Savings Bank (45 e.) and World Savings Day (100 e.). Mult.
2404 45 e. Type **514** 35 20
2405 100 e. Coins and bee 80 40

515 St. Philip's Fort, Setubal

1994. Pousadas (hotels) in Historic Buildings. Multicoloured.
2406 45 e. Type **515** 35 20
2407 75 e. Obidos Castle 60 30
2408 100 e. Convent of Loios, Evora 80 40
2409 140 e. Santa Marinha Monastery, Guimaraes . . 1·10 55

516 Businessman and Tourist

1994. American Society of Travel Agents World Congress, Lisbon.
2410 **516** 140 e. multicoloured . . . 1·10 55

517 Statuette of Missionary, Mozambique

1994. Evangelization by Portuguese Missionaries. Multicoloured.
2411 45 e. Type **517** 35 20
2412 75 e. "Child Jesus the Good Shepherd" (carving), India . 60 30
2413 100 e. Chalice, Macao 80 40
2414 140 e. Carving of man in frame, Angola (horiz) . . . . . . 1·10 55

518 Africans greeting Portuguese

1994. 550th Anniv of First Portuguese Landing in Senegal.
2415 **518** 140 e. multicoloured . . . 1·10 55

521 Great Bustard

1995. European Nature Conservation Year. Multicoloured.
2418 42 e. Type **521** 35 20
2419 90 e. Osprey 75 35
2420 130 e. Schreiber's green lizard 1·00 50

522 St. John and Sick Man

1995. 500th Birth Anniv of St. John of God (founder of Order of Hospitallers).
2422 **522** 45 e. multicoloured . . . 35 20

523 Electrico No. 22, 1895

1995. Centenaries of Trams and Motor Cars in Portugal. Multicoloured.
2423 90 e. Type **523** 70 35
2424 130 e. Panhard and Levassor motor car . . . . 1·00 50

524 Bread Seller

1995. 19th-century Itinerant Trades. Multicoloured.
2425 1 e. Type **524** 10 10
2426 3 e. Broker 10 10
2431 20 e. Spinning-wheel and spoon seller 15 10
2435 45 e. General street trader . 35 20
2436 47 e. Hot chestnut seller . . 40 20
2437 50 e. Fruit seller 40 20
2439 75 e. Whitewasher 60 30
2440 78 e. Cloth seller 60 30
2441 100 e. Mussels seller 80 40
2443 250 e. Water seller . . . . . 2·00 1·00

526 Emblem

1995. 50th Anniv of U.N.O. Multicoloured.
2449 75 e. Type **526** 60 30
2450 135 e. Clouds and emblem . 1·10 55

527 Evacuees from Gibraltar arriving at Madeira (½-size illustration)

1995. Europa. Peace and Freedom. Portuguese Neutrality during Second World War. Mult.
2452 95 e. Type **527** 75 40
2453 95 e. Refugees waiting at Lisbon for transatlantic ship and Aristides de Sousa Mendes (Portuguese Consul in Bordeaux) 75 40

528 "St. Antony holding Child Jesus" (painting)

1995. 800th Birth Anniv of St. Antony of Padua (Franciscan preacher). Multicoloured.
2454 45 e. Type **528** 35 20
2455 75 e. St. Antony with flowers (vert) 60 30
2456 135 e. "St. Antony holding Child Jesus" (statue) 1·10 55

529 Carpenters with Axes and Women with Water, 1395

1995. 600th Anniv of Fire Service in Portugal. Multicoloured.
2458 45 e. Type **529** 35 20
2459 80 e. Fire cart and men carrying barrels of water, 1834 . . 65 35
2460 95 e. Merryweather steam-powered fire engine, 1867 . 75 40
2461 135 e. Zoost fire engine No. 1, 1908 . . . . 1·10 55

530 Coronation

1995. 500th Anniv of Acession of King Manoel I.
2463 **530** 45 e. brown, yellow and red 35 20

1995. Modern Electric Locomotives (2nd series). As T **513**.
2465 80 e. multicoloured 65 35
DESIGN: 80 e. Electric railcar.

1995. Sculptures (3rd series). As T **491**. Multicoloured.
2466 45 e. "Warrior" (castle statue) 35 20
2467 75 e. Double-headed fountain 60 30
2468 80 e. "Truth" (monument to Eca de Queiros by Antonio Teixeira Lopes) 65 35
2469 95 e. First World War memorial, Abrantes (Ruy Gameiro) 75 40
2470 135 e. "Fernao Lopes" (Martins Correia) . . . . 1·10 55
2471 190 e. " Fernando Pessoa" (Lagoa Henriques) . . . . 1·50 75

531 "Portugal's Guardian Angel" (sculpture, Diogo Pires)

533 Archangel Gabriel

532 Queiroz

1995. Art of the Period of Discoveries (15th–16th centuries). Multicoloured.
2473 45 e. Type **531** 35 20
2474 75 e. Reliquary of Queen Leonor (Master Joao) . . . 60 30
2475 80 e. "Don Manuel" (sculpture, Nicolas Chanterenne) . . . 65 35
2476 95 e."St. Antony" (painting, Nuno Goncalves) 75 40
2477 135 e. "Adoration of the Three Wise Men" (painting, Grao Vasco) . . . . 1·10 55
2478 190 e. "Christ on the Way to Calvary" (painting, Jorge Afonso) . . . . 1·50 75

1995. 150th Birth Anniv of Eca de Queiroz (writer).
2480 **532** 135 e. multicoloured . . 1·10 55

1995. Christmas. Multicoloured. (a) With country name at foot.
2481 **533** 80 e. multicoloured . . 65 35

(b) With country name omitted.
2483 80 e. Type **533** 80 50

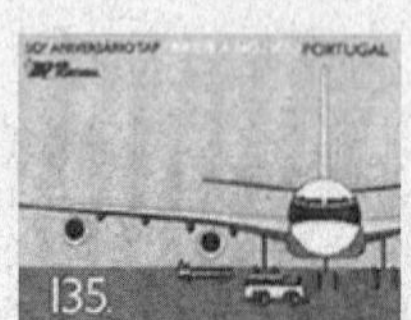

534 Airbus Industrie A340/300

1995. 50th Anniv of TAP Air Portugal.
2485 **534** 135 e. multicoloured . . 1·10 55

535 King Carlos I of Portugal (½-size illustration)

1996. Centenary of Oceanographic Expeditions. Multicoloured.
2486 95 e. Type **535** 75 40
2487 135 e. Prince Albert I of Monaco . . . . 1·10 55

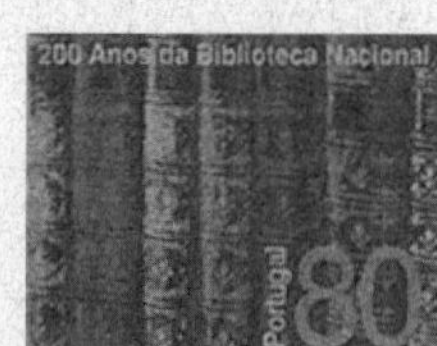

536 Books

1996. Anniversaries. Multicoloured.
2488 80 e. Type **536** (bicentenary of National Library) 65 35
2489 200 e. Hand writing with quill pen (700th anniv of adoption of Portuguese as official language) . . . . 1·60 80

537 Joao de Deus (poet and author of reading primer)

1996. Writers' Anniversaries. Multicoloured.
2490 78 e. Type **537** (death centenary) 60 30
2491 140 e. Joao de Barros (historian, philosopher and grammarian, 500th birth) . . . . 1·10 55

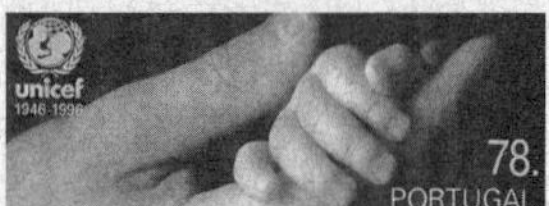

538 Holding Child's Hand (½-size illustration)

1996. 50th Anniv of U.N.I.C.E.F. Multicoloured.
2492 78 e. Type **538** 60 30
2493 140 e. Children of different races . . . . 1·10 55

539 Helena Vieira da Silva (artist, self-portrait)

1996. Europa. Famous Women.
2494 **539** 98 e. multicoloured . . 80 40

540 Match Scene

1996. European Football Championship, England. Multicoloured.
2496 78 e. Type **540** 60 30
2497 140 e. Match scene (different) 1·10 55

541 Caravel and Arms (½-size illustration)

1996. 500th Death Anniv of Joao Vaz Corte-Real (explorer).
2499 **541** 140 e. multicoloured . . 1·10 55

542 Wrestling

1996. Olympic Games, Atlanta. Multicoloured.
2501 47 e. Type **542** 40 20
2502 78 e. Show jumping 65 35
2503 98 e. Boxing 80 40
2504 140 e. Running . . . . . . 1·10 55

543 Hilario and Guitar

1996. Death Centenary of Augusto Hilario (fado singer).
2506 **543** 80 e. multicoloured . . 65 35

544 Antonio Silva (actor)

1996. Centenary of Motion Pictures. Multicoloured.
2507 47 e. Type 544 . . . . 40 20
2508 78 e. Vasco Santana (actor) . 65 35
2509 80 e. Laura Alves (actress) . . 65 35
2510 98 e. Auelio Pais dos Reis (director) 80 40
2511 100 e. Leitao de Barros (director) 80 40
2512 140 e. Antonio Lopes Ribeiro (director) . . . . 1·10 55

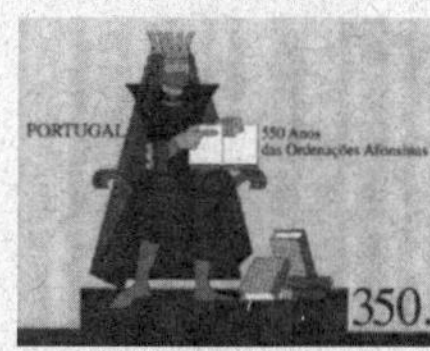

545 King Afonso V

1996. 550th Anniv of Alphonsine Collection of Statutes.
2515 **545** 350 e. multicoloured . . 2·75 1·40

546 Perdigao

1996. Birth Centenary of Jose de Azeredo Perdigao (lawyer and Council of State member).
2516 **546** 47 e. multicoloured . . . 40 20

547 Aveiro

1996. District Arms. Multicoloured.
2517 47 e. Type **547** 40 20
2518 78 e. Beja 65 35
2519 80 e. Braga 65 35
2520 98 e. Braganca 80 40
2521 100 e. Castelo Branco 80 40
2522 140 e. Coimbra . . . . 1·10 55

548 Henry of Burgundy (governor of Portucale) and his Wife Theresa

1996. 900th Anniv of Foundation of County of Portucale by King Afonso VI of Leon and Castille.
2524 **548** 47 e. multicoloured . . . 40 20

549 Rojoes (Pork dish)

1996. Traditional Portuguese Dishes. Multicoloured.
2525 47 e. Type **549** 40 20
2526 78 e. Boticas trout 65 35
2527 80 e. Oporto tripe 65 35
2528 98 e. Baked cod with jacket potatoes 80 40
2529 100 e. Aveiro eel 80 40
2530 140 e. Peniche lobster . . . . 1·10 55

550 Lisbon Postman, 1821

1996. 175th Anniv of Home Delivery Postal Service. Multicoloured.
2531 47 e. Type **550** 40 20
2532 78 e. Postman, 1854 . . . . 65 35
2533 98 e. Rural postman, 1893 . . . 80 40
2534 100 e. Postman, 1939 . . . . 80 40
2535 140 e. Modern postman, 1992 1·10 55

551 King Manuel I in Shipyard

1996. 500th Anniv (1997) of Discovery of Sea-route to India by Vasco da Gama. Multicoloured.
2536 47 e. Type **551** 40 20
2537 78 e. Departure from Lisbon 65 35
2538 98 e. Fleet in Atlantic Ocean 80 40
2539 140 e. Sailing around Cape of Good Hope . . . . 1·10 55

552 "Banknote"

1996. 150th Anniv of Bank of Portugal.
2541 **552** 78 e. multicoloured . . 65 35

553 East Timorese Couple

1996. Right of People of East Timor. Award of 1996 Nobel Peace Prize to Don Carlos Ximenes Belo and Jose Ramos Horton.
2542 **553** 140 e. multicoloured . . 1·10 55

CHARITY TAX STAMPS

Used on certain days of the year as an additional postal tax on internal letters. Other values in some of the types were for use on telegrams only. The proceeds were devoted to public charities. If one was not affixed in addition to the ordinary postage, postage due stamps were used to collect the deficiency and the fine.

1911. Optd **ASSISTENCIA**.
C455 **48** 10 r. green (No. 406) . . 8·25 2·10
C484 **56** 1 c. green (No. 486) . . . 5·75 1·60

C 57 "Lisbon" C 58 "Charity"

1913. Lisbon Festival.
C485 C **57** 1 c. green 85 65

1915. For the Poor.
C486 C **58** 1 c. red 35 30
C669 15 c. red 35 35

1924. Surch **15 ctvs.**
C594 C **58** 15 c. on 1 c. red . . . 1·10 15

C 71 Muse of History C 81 Hurdler

C 73 Monument to De Pombal C 75 Marquis de Pombal

1925. Portuguese Army in Flanders, 1484 and 1918.
C662 C **71** 10 c. red . . . . 1·00 1·00
C663 10 c. green . . . . . . 1·00 1·00
C664 10 c. blue . . . . . . 1·00 1·00
C665 10 c. brown . . . . . 1·00 1·00

1925. Marquis de Pombal Commemoration.
C666 C **73** 15 c. blue and black . 30 30
C667 – 15 c. blue and black . 1·10 70
C668 C **75** 15 c. blue and black . 1·10 70
DESIGN: No. C677, Planning reconstruction of Lisbon.

1928. Olympic Games.
C741 C **81** 15 c. black and red . . 3·50 2·50

NEWSPAPER STAMPS

N 16 N 17

1876.
N180 N **16** 2 r. black . . . . . . 20·00 13·00
N178 N **17** 2½ r. green . . . . . . 13·00 1·10
N187 2½ r. brown . . . . . 13·00 1·10

OFFICIAL STAMPS

1938. Optd **OFICIAL**.
O900 **99** 40 c. brown 45 10

O 144

1952. No value.
O1069 O **144** (1 e.) black & stone . 45 10
O1070 (1 e.) black & stone . 55 10
On No. O1069 "CORREIO DE PORTUGAL" is in stone on a black background, on No. O1070 it is in black on the stone background.

PARCEL POST STAMPS

P 59

1920.
P578 P **59** 1 c. brown 25 25
P579 2 c. orange 25 25
P580 5 c. brown 25 25
P581 10 c. brown 25 25
P582 20 c. blue 30 25
P583 40 c. red 35 25
P584 50 c. black 60 50
P585 60 c. blue 50 50
P586 70 c. brown . . . . . 3·00 2·00
P587 80 c. blue . . . . . . 3·25 3·25
P588 90 c. violet . . . . . 3·25 2·25
P589 1 e. green . . . . . . 3·75 3·25
P591 2 e. lilac . . . . . . 10·50 3·50
P592 3 e. green . . . . . . 20·00 4·00
P593 4 e. blue . . . . . . 40·00 7·00
P594 5 e. lilac . . . . . . 50·00 4·50
P595 10 e. brown . . . . . 75·00 8·50

P 101

1936.
P891 P **101** 50 c. grey 65 55
P892 1 e. brown 65 55
P893 1 e. 50 violet 65 55
P894 2 e. purple . . . . . 2·50 55
P895 2 e. 50 green . . . . 2·50 55
P896 4 e. 50 purple . . . . 5·50 55
P897 5 e. violet . . . . . 9·00 55
P898 10 e. orange . . . . 11·00 1·50

POSTAGE DUE STAMPS

D 48 Da Gama received by the Zamorin of Calicut D 49

1898.
D386 D **48** 5 r. black . . . . . . 2·25 1·25
D387 10 r. mauve . . . . . 3·50 1·60
D388 20 r. orange . . . . . 5·75 2·50
D389 50 r. grey . . . . . . 45·00 10·00
D390 100 r. red on pink . . 80·00 40·00
D391 200 r. brown on buff 80·00 55·00

1904.
D392 D **49** 5 r. brown 40 40
D393 10 r. orange . . . . . 2·75 95
D394 20 r. mauve . . . . . 7·50 4·00
D395 30 r. green . . . . . 5·00 2·75
D396 40 r. lilac . . . . . . 5·75 2·75
D397 50 r. red . . . . . . 48·00 4·25
D398 100 r. blue . . . . . 7·50 6·00

1911. Optd **REPUBLICA**.
D418 D **49** 5 r. brown 40 30
D419 10 r. orange 40 30
D420 20 r. mauve . . . . . 1·25 1·00
D421 30 r. green . . . . . 1·10 30
D422 40 r. lilac . . . . . . 1·10 30
D423 50 r. red . . . . . . 5·25 4·25
D424 100 r. blue . . . . . 5·50 4·75

1915. As Type D **49** but value in centavos.
D491 D **49** ½ c. brown 60 60
D498 1 c. orange 60 60
D493 2 c. purple 60 60
D499 3 c. green 60 60
D500 4 c. lilac 60 60
D501 5 c. red 60 60
D497 10 c. blue 90 90

1921.
D578 D **49** ½ c. green 40 40
D579 4 c. green 40 40
D580 8 c. green 40 40
D581 10 c. green 40 40
D582 12 c. green 50 50
D583 16 c. green 50 50
D584 20 c. green 50 50
D585 24 c. green 50 50
D586 32 c. green 60 60
D587 36 c. green . . . . . 1·10 1·10
D588 40 c. green . . . . . 1·10 1·10
D589 48 c. green 65 65
D590 50 c. green 65 65
D591 60 c. green 65 65
D592 72 c. green 65 65
D593 80 c. green . . . . . 6·25 6·25
D594 1 e. 20 green . . . . 3·50 3·50

D 72 D 82

1925. Portuguese Army in Flanders, 1484 and 1918.
D662 D **72** 20 c. brown 50 40

1925. De Pombal types optd **MULTA**.
D663 C **73** 30 c. blue . . . . . . 1·00 1·00
D664 – 30 c. blue . . . . . . 1·00 1·00
D665 C **75** 30 c. blue . . . . . . 1·00 1·00

1928. Olympic Games.
D741 D **82** 30 e. black and red . . 1·60 1·60

D 91 D 108 D 218

1932.
D865 D **91** 5 c. buff 50 45
D866 10 c. blue 50 45
D867 20 c. pink . . . . . . 1·10 1·00
D868 30 c. blue . . . . . . 1·40 1·00
D869 40 c. green . . . . . 1·40 1·00
D870 50 c. grey . . . . . . 1·60 1·00
D871 60 c. pink . . . . . . 3·25 1·75
D872 80 c. purple . . . . . 7·75 3·50
D873 1 e. 20 green . . . . 12·50 11·50

1940.
D912 D **108** 5 c. brown 40 35
D913 10 c. lilac 30 25
D914 20 c. red 30 25
D925 30 c. violet 30 25
D916 40 c. mauve 30 25
D917 50 c. blue 30 25
D928 60 c. green 30 25
D929 80 c. red 30 25
D930 1 e. brown 70 25
D921 2 e. mauve . . . . . 1·25 65
D922 5 e. orange . . . . . 10·50 8·50

1967.
D1312 D **218** 10 c. brown, yellow and orange 10 10
D1313 20 c. purple, yellow and brown 10 10
D1314 30 c. brown, light yellow and yellow . 10 10
D1315 40 c. purple, yellow and bistre 10 10
D1316 50 c. indigo, blue and light blue 10 10
D1317 60 e. olive, blue and turquoise 10 10
D1318 80 c. indigo, blue and light blue 10 10
D1319 1 e. indigo, bl & ultram 10 10
D1320 2 e. olive, light green and green 10 10
D1321 3 e. deep green, light green and green . 10 10
D1322 4 e. deep green, green and turquoise . . 10 10
D1323 5 e. brown, mauve and purple 10 10
D1324 9 e. deep lilac, lilac and violet 15 10
D1325 10 e. deep purple, grey and purple 15 10
D1326 20 e. maroon, grey and purple 45 30
D1327 40 e. lilac, grey and mauve . . . . . . 1·10 40
D1328 50 e. maroon, grey and purple . . . . . 1·10 50

D 481

1992. Inscr "CORREIOS DE PORTUGAL".
D2305 D **481** 1 e. blue, deep blue and black 10 10
D2306 2 e. light green, green and black 10 10
D2307 5 e. yellow, brown and black 10 10
D2308 10 e. red, orange and black 10 10
D2309 20 e. green, violet and black 20 10
D2310 50 e. yellow, green and black 50 25
D2311 100 e. orange, red and black 95 45
D2312 200 e. mauve, violet and black . . . . 1·90 1·00

1995. Inscr "CTT CORREIOS".
D2445 D **481** 3 e. multicoloured . 10 10
D2446 4 e. multicoloured . 10 10
D2447 9 e. multicoloured . 10 10
D2448 40 e. multicoloured . 30 15

PORTUGUESE COLONIES Pt.9

General issues for the Portuguese possessions in Africa; Angola, Cape Verde Islands, Guinea, Lourenco Marques, Mozambique, Congo, St. Thomas and Prince Islands and Zambezia.

1898. 1000 reis = 1 milreis.
1919. 100 centavos = 1 escudo.

1898. 400th Anniv of Vasco da Gama's Discovery of Route to India. As Nos. 378/85 of Portugal but inscr "AFRICA".
1 2½ r. green 40 30
2 5 r. red 40 30
3 10 r. purple 30 20
4 25 r. green 30 20
5 50 r. blue 40 40
6 75 r. brown . . . . 2·10 2·00
7 100 r. brown . . . . 2·10 1·50
8 150 r. brown . . . . 2·75 1·50

CHARITY TAX STAMP

C 1

1919. Fiscal stamps optd **TAXA DE GUERRA**.
C1 C **1** 1 c. black and green . . . 30 30
C2 5 c. black and green . . . 30 30

POSTAGE DUE STAMPS

D 1

1945. Value in black.
D1 D **1** 10 c. purple 10 10
D2 20 c. purple 10 10
D3 30 c. blue 10 10
D4 40 c. brown 15 15
D5 50 c. lilac 15 15
D6 1 e. brown 40 40
D7 2 e. green 85 85
D8 3 e. red . . . . 1·50 1·50
D9 5 e. yellow . . . . . . 2·10 2·10

PORTUGUESE CONGO Pt.9

The area known as Portuguese Congo, now called Cabinda, was the part of Angola north of the River Congo. It issued its own stamps from 1894 until 1920.

1894. 1000 reis = 1 milreis.
1913. 100 centavos = 1 escudo.

1894. "Figures" key-type inscr "CONGO".
8 R 5 r. orange 35 30
9 10 r. mauve . . . . 1·00 35
10 15 r. brown . . . . 1·60 1·25
12 20 r. lilac . . . . 1·60 1·25
13 25 r. green 40 40
22 50 r. blue . . . . 1·60 1·00
5 75 r. pink . . . . 2·50 2·40
6 80 r. green . . . . 4·00 3·75
16 100 r. brown on yellow . . 2·25 1·90
17 150 r. red on pink . . . . 4·00 3·75
18 200 r. blue on blue . . . 4·00 3·75
19 300 r. blue on brown . . . 5·00 4·50

1898. "King Carlos" key-type inscr "CONGO".
24 S 2½ r. grey 15 10
25 5 r. red 15 10
26 10 r. green 25 20
27 15 r. brown 75 60
66 15 r. green 45 30
28 20 r. lilac 55 40
29 25 r. green 95 60
67 25 r. red 45 25
30 50 r. blue . . . . 1·00 85
68 50 r. brown . . . . 1·00 65
69 65 r. blue . . . . 2·75 2·50
31 75 r. pink . . . . 1·60 1·50
70 75 r. purple . . . . 1·10 1·00
32 80 r. mauve . . . . 1·60 1·50
33 100 r. blue on blue . . . 1·25 1·00
71 115 r. brown on pink . . 2·75 2·25
72 130 r. brown on yellow . . 3·25 3·25
34 150 r. brown on yellow . . 1·90 1·60
35 200 r. purple on pink . . 2·10 2·00
36 300 r. blue on pink . . . 2·00 1·60
73 400 r. blue on cream . . 3·00 2·75
37 500 r. black on blue . . . 5·75 4·00
38 700 r. mauve on yellow . . 9·50 6·25

1902. Surch.
74 S 50 r. on 65 r. blue . . . . 1·50 1·00
40 R 65 r. on 15 r. brown . . . 1·50 1·10
41 65 r. on 20 r. lilac . . . . 1·50 1·10
44 65 r. on 25 r. green . . . 1·25 1·00
46 65 r. on 300 r. blue on brn . 1·60 1·60
50 V 115 r. on 2½ r. brown . . . 1·25 1·00
47 R 115 r. on 10 r. mauve . . . 1·25 1·00
48 115 r. on 50 r. blue . . . 1·50 1·00
53 130 r. on 5 r. orange . . . 1·25 1·00
54 130 r. on 75 r. pink . . . . 1·50 1·00
57 130 r. on 100 r. brn on yell . 1·50 1·10
58 400 r. on 80 r. green . . . 60 50
60 400 r. on 150 r. red on pink 60 40
61 400 r. on 200 r. blue on blue 60 40

1902. "King Carlos" key-type of Portuguese Congo optd **PROVISORIO**.
62 S 15 r. brown . . . 75 15
63 25 r. green . . . 75 15
64 50 r. blue . . . 75 15
65 75 r. pink . . . 1·75 1·25

1911. "King Carlos" key-type of Angola, optd **REPUBLICA** and **CONGO** with bar (200 r. also surch).
75 S 2½ r. grey . . . 50 40
76 5 r. red . . . 75 55
77 10 r. green . . . 75 55
78 15 r. green . . . 75 55
79 25 r. on 200 r. purple on pink 1·10 90

1911. "King Carlos" key-type of Portuguese Congo optd **REPUBLICA**.
80 S 2½ r. grey . . . 10 10
81 5 r. orange . . . 15 10
82 10 r. green . . . 15 10
83 15 r. green . . . 15 10
84 20 r. lilac . . . 15 15
85 25 r. red . . . 15 15
86 50 r. brown . . . 15 15
87 75 r. purple . . . 30 25
88 100 r. blue on blue . . . 30 25
89 115 r. brown on pink . . . 50 40
90 130 r. brown on yellow . . 50 40
143 200 r. purple on pink . . . 65 55
92 400 r. blue on cream . . . 80 75
93 500 r. black on blue . . . 1·10 80
94 700 r. mauve on yellow . . 1·10 80

1913. Surch **REPUBLICA CONGO** and value on "Vasco da Gama" stamps of (a) Portuguese Colonies.
95 ¼ c. on 2½ r. green . . . 50 45
96 ½ c. on 5 r. red . . . 50 45
97 1 c. on 10 r. purple . . . 35 35
98 2½ c. on 25 r. green . . . 35 35
99 5 c. on 50 r. blue . . . 50 45
100 7½ c. on 75 r. brown . . . 80 65
101 10 c. on 100 r. brown . . . 50 45
102 15 c. on 150 r. brown . . . 50 45

(b) Macao.
103 ¼ c. on ½ a. green . . . 60 50
104 ½ c. on 1 a. red . . . 60 50
105 1 c. on 2 a. purple . . . 50 45
106 2½ c. on 4 a. green . . . 50 45
107 5 c. on 8 a. blue . . . 60 50
108 7½ c. on 12 a. brown . . . 90 80
109 10 c. on 16 a. brown . . . 85 65
110 15 c. on 24 a. brown . . . 75 50

(c) Timor.
111 ¼ c. on ½ a. green . . . 70 60
112 ½ c. on 1 a. red . . . 70 60
113 1 c. on 2 a. purple . . . 55 50
114 2½ c. on 4 a. green . . . 55 50
115 5 c. on 8 a. blue . . . 70 60
116 7½ c. on 12 a. brown . . . 1·00 65
117 10 c. on 16 a. brown . . . 90 60
118 15 c. on 24 a. brown . . . 75 50

1914. "Ceres" key-type inscr "CONGO".
135 U ¼ c. green . . . 20 15
120 ½ c. black . . . 25 15
121 1 c. green . . . 80 55
122 1½ c. brown . . . 55 30
136 2 c. red . . . 20 15
124 2½ c. violet . . . 15 15
125 5 c. blue . . . 25 25
126 7½ c. brown . . . 40 35
127 8 c. grey . . . 50 40
128 10 c. red . . . 50 40
129 15 c. purple . . . 55 40
130 20 c. green . . . 55 50
131 30 c. brown on green . . . 1·00 75
132 40 c. brown on pink . . . 1·00 75
133 50 c. orange on orange . . 1·10 75
134 1 c. green on blue . . . 1·60 1·00

1914. "King Carlos" key-type of Portuguese Congo optd **PROVISORIO** and **REPUBLICA**.
146 S 15 r. brown (No. 62) . . . 20 20
147 50 r. blue (No. 64) . . . 20 20
140 75 r. pink (No. 65) . . . 65 45

1914. Provisional stamps of 1902 optd **REPUBLICA**.
148 S 50 r. on 65 r. blue . . . 20 20
150 V 115 r. on 2½ r. brown . . . 30 10
151 R 115 r. on 10 r. mauve . . . 20 15
154 115 r. on 50 r.blue . . . 50 10
156 130 r. on 5 r. orange . . . 50 10
157 130 r. on 75 r. pink . . . 50 30
160 130 r. on 100 r. brown on yellow . . . 30 20

NEWSPAPER STAMP

1894. "Newspaper" key-type inscr "CONGO".
N24 V 2½ r. brown . . . 35 30

PORTUGUESE GUINEA Pt. 9

A former Portuguese territory, on the west coast of Africa, with adjacent islands. Used stamps of Cape Verde Islands from 1877 until 1881. In September 1974 the territory became independent and was renamed Guinea-Bissau.

1881. 1000 reis = 1 milreis.
1913. 100 centavos = 1 escudo.

1881. "Crown" key-type inscr "CABO VERDE" and optd **GUINE**.
19 P 5 r. black . . . 1·40 1·25
20 10 r. yellow . . . 45·00 38·00
31 10 r. green . . . 2·50 1·60
21 20 r. bistre . . . 1·25 80
32 20 r. red . . . 2·50 1·60
13 25 r. pink . . . 80 60
28 25 r. lilac . . . 1·25 75
23 40 r. blue . . . 42·00 32·00
29 P 40 r. yellow . . . 75 65
24 50 r. green . . . 50·00 32·00
30 50 r. blue . . . 1·90 85
16 100 r. lilac . . . 2·25 1·90
17 200 r. orange . . . 3·75 3·00
18 300 r. brown . . . 5·00 3·75

3

1886.
35 3 5 r. black . . . 1·50 85
36 10 r. green . . . 2·00 1·40
37 20 r. red . . . 3·00 1·90
38 25 r. purple . . . 3·00 2·10
46 40 r. brown . . . 2·00 1·90
40 50 r. blue . . . 5·00 1·75
47 80 r. grey . . . 4·25 3·25
48 100 r. brown . . . 4·25 3·25
43 200 r. lilac . . . 11·00 7·00
44 300 r. orange . . . 12·50 10·00

1893. "Figures" key-type inscr 'GUINE".
50 R 5 r. yellow . . . 60 50
51 10 r. mauve . . . 60 55
52 15 r. brown . . . 75 60
53 20 r. lilac . . . 75 60
54 25 r. green . . . 75 60
55 50 r. blue . . . 1·40 85
57 75 r. pink . . . 3·75 3·00
58 80 r. green . . . 3·75 3·00
59 100 r. brown on buff . . . 3·75 3·00
60 150 r. red on pink . . . 4·75 4·00
61 200 r. blue on blue . . . 4·75 4·00
62 300 r. blue on brown . . . 6·00 4·50

1898. "King Carlos" key-type inscr "GUINE".
65 S 2½ r. grey . . . 15 15
66 5 r. red . . . 20 15
67 10 r. green . . . 20 15
68 15 r. brown . . . 1·10 90
114 15 r. green . . . 60 40
69 20 r. lilac . . . 50 30
70 25 r. green . . . 80 40
115 25 r. red . . . 35 25
71 50 r. blue . . . 1·10 50
116 50 r. brown . . . 60 50
117 65 r. blue . . . 2·50 2·10
72 75 r. pink . . . 5·00 2·75
118 75 r. purple . . . 1·00 75
73 80 r. mauve . . . 1·50 90
74 100 r. blue on blue . . . 1·00 50
119 115 r. brown on pink . . . 2·50 1·90
120 130 r. brown on yellow . . . 2·50 1·90
75 150 r. brown on yellow . . . 3·00 1·50
76 200 r. purple on pink . . . 3·00 1·50
77 300 r. blue on pink . . . 2·50 1·50
121 400 r. blue on yellow . . . 2·50 1·90
78 500 r. black on blue . . . 4·25 2·50
79 700 r. mauve on yellow . . . 6·50 4·25

1902. Surch.
122 S 50 r. on 65 r. blue . . . 1·40 1·10
81 3 65 r. on 10 r. green . . . 2·25 1·50
84 R 65 r. on 10 r. mauve . . . 1·90 1·25
85 65 r. on 15 r. brown . . . 1·90 1·25
82 3 65 r. on 20 r. red . . . 2·25 1·50
86 R 65 r. on 20 r. lilac . . . 1·90 1·25
83 3 65 r. on 25 r. purple . . . 2·25 1·50
88 R 65 r. on 50 r. blue . . . 1·00 85
97 V 115 r. on 2½ r. brown . . . 1·90 1·25
93 R 115 r. on 5 r. yellow . . . 1·60 1·10
95 115 r. on 25 r. green . . . 1·90 1·10
89 3 115 r. on 40 r. brown . . . 1·90 1·25
91 115 r. on 50 r. blue . . . 1·90 1·25
92 115 r. on 300 r. orange . . . 2·50 1·90
98 130 r. on 80 r. grey . . . 2·50 2·00
100 130 r. on 100 r. brown . . . 2·75 2·00
102 R 130 r. on 150 r. red on pink 2·00 1·10
103 130 r. on 200 r. blue on blue 2·25 1·40
104 130 r. on 300 r. bl on brn . 2·25 1·40
105 3 400 r. on 5 r. black . . . 9·00 6·75
107 R 400 r. on 75 r. pink . . . 1·25 1·10
108 400 r. on 80 r. green . . . 85 70
109 400 r. on 100 r. brn on buff 85 70
106 3 400 r. on 200 r. lilac . . . 4·25 2·75

1902. "King Carlos" key-type of Portuguese Guinea optd **PROVISORIO**.
110 S 15 r. brown . . . 85 55
111 25 r. green . . . 85 55
112 50 r. blue . . . 1·00 75
113 75 r. pink . . . 1·60 1·40

1911. "King Carlos" key-type of Portuguese Guinea optd **REPUBLICA**.
123 S 2½ r. grey . . . 25 15
124 5 r. red . . . 25 15
125 10 r. green . . . 25 15
126 15 r. green . . . 25 15
127 20 r. lilac . . . 25 15
128 25 r. red . . . 25 15
129 50 r. brown . . . 25 15
130 75 r. purple . . . 25 15
131 100 r. blue on blue . . . 45 25
132 115 r. brown on pink . . . 45 25
133 130 r. brown on yellow . . . 45 25
134 200 r. purple on pink . . . 2·50 1·25
135 400 r. blue on yellow . . . 75 45
136 500 r. black on blue . . . 75 45
137 700 r. mauve on yellow . . . 1·25 70

1913. Surch **REPUBLICA GUINE** and value on "Vasco da Gama" stamps of (a) Portuguese Colonies.
138 ¼ c. on 2½ r. green . . . 70 70
139 ½ c. on 5 r. red . . . 70 70
140 1 c. on 10 r. purple . . . 60 60
141 2½ c. on 25 r. green . . . 60 60
142 5 c. on 50 r. blue . . . 70 70
143 7½ c. on 75 r. brown . . . 1·25 1·25
144 10 c. on 100 r. brown . . . 70 50
145 15 c. on 150 r. brown . . . 1·50 1·40

(b) Macao.
146 ¼ c. on ½ a. green . . . 80 70
147 ½ c. on 1 a. red . . . 80 70
148 1 c. on 2 a. purple . . . 70 60
149 2½ c. on 4 a. green . . . 70 60
150 5 c. on 8 a. blue . . . 80 70
151 7½ c. on 12 a. brown . . . 1·25 95
152 10 c. on 16 a. brown . . . 1·25 1·10
153 15 c. on 24 a. brown . . . 1·25 85

(c) Timor.
154 ¼ c. on ½ a. green . . . 80 70
155 ½ c. on 1 a. red . . . 80 70
156 1 c. on 2 a. purple . . . 70 60
157 2½ c. on 4 a. green . . . 70 60
158 5 c. on 8 a. blue . . . 80 70
159 7½ c. on 12 a. brown . . . 1·25 90
160 10 c. on 16 a. brown . . . 1·25 1·00
161 15 c. on 24 a. brown . . . 1·25 90

1913. "King Carlos" key-type of Portuguese Guinea optd **PROVISORIO** and **REPUBLICA**.
184 S 15 r. brown . . . 30 25
185 50 r. blue . . . 30 25
164 75 r. pink . . . 2·50 2·25

1914. "Ceres" key-type inscr "GUINE". Name and value in black.
204 U ¼ c. green . . . 10 10
209 ½ c. black . . . 10 10
210 1 c. green . . . 10 10
211 1½ c. brown . . . 10 10
212 2 c. red . . . 10 10
213 2 c. grey . . . 10 10
214 2½ c. violet . . . 10 10
215 3 c. orange . . . 10 10
216 4 c. red . . . 10 10
217 4½ c. grey . . . 10 10
218 5 c. blue . . . 10 10
219 6 c. mauve . . . 10 10
220 7 c. blue . . . 10 10
221 7½ c. brown . . . 10 10
222 8 c. grey . . . 10 10
223 10 c. red . . . 10 10
224 12 c. green . . . 20 15
225 15 c. red . . . 25 10
226 20 c. green . . . 10 10
227 24 c. blue . . . 75 55
228 25 c. brown . . . 75 55
180 30 c. brown on green . . . 2·10 1·60
229 30 c. green . . . 30 15
181 40 c. brown on pink . . . 1·00 80
230 40 c. turquoise . . . 30 15
182 50 c. orange on orange . . . 1·25 80
231 50 c. mauve . . . 65 35
232 60 c. blue . . . 65 35
233 60 c. red . . . 65 35
234 80 c. red . . . 70 35
183 1 e. green on blue . . . 1·25 80
235 1 e. blue . . . 85 55
236 1 e. pink . . . 85 55
237 2 e. purple . . . 1·00 60
238 5 e. bistre . . . 5·00 3·50
239 10 e. pink . . . 8·75 6·25
240 20 e. green . . . 22·00 15·00

1915. Provisional stamps of 1902 optd **REPUBLICA**.
186 S 50 r. on 65 r. blue . . . 30 25
187 V 115 r. on 2½ r. brown . . . 45 35
190 R 115 r. on 5 r. yellow . . . 35 30
191 115 r. on 25 r. green . . . 35 30
192 3 115 r. on 40 r. brown . . . 35 30
194 115 r. on 50 r. blue . . . 35 30
196 130 r. on 80 r. grey . . . 1·00 75
197 130 r. on 100 r. brown . . . 85 75
199 R 130 r. on 150 r. red on pink 35 30
200 130 r. on 200 r. blue on blue 35 30
201 130 r. on 300 r. blue on brn 35 30

1920. Surch.
241 U 4 c. on ½ c. green . . . 1·50 1·00
242 6 c. on ½ c. black . . . 1·50 1·00
243 S 12 c. on 115 r. brown on pink (No. 132) . . . 2·10 1·75

1925. Stamps of 1902 (Nos. 107/9) surch **Republica** and new value.
244 R 40 c. on 400 r. on 75 r. pink 45 35
245 40 c. on 400 r. on 80 r. grn 40 35
246 40 c. on 400 r. on 100 r. brown on buff . . . 40 35

1931. "Ceres" key-type of Portuguese Guinea surch.
247 U 50 c. on 60 c. red . . . 75 50
248 70 c. on 80 c. red . . . 1·25 80
249 1 e. 40 on 2 e. purple . . . 1·90 1·40

24 Ceres

31 Cacheu Castle

1933.
251 24 1 c. brown . . . 10 10
252 5 c. brown . . . 10 10
253 10 c. mauve . . . 10 10
254 15 c. black . . . 10 10
255 20 c. grey . . . 10 10
256 30 c. green . . . 10 10
257 40 c. red . . . 15 10
258 45 c. turquoise . . . 30 20
259 50 c. brown . . . 30 20
260 60 c. green . . . 30 20
261 70 c. brown . . . 30 20
262 80 c. green . . . 50 25
263 85 c. red . . . 90 45
264 1 e. purple . . . 45 30
265 1 e. 40 blue . . . 1·75 1·00
266 2 e. mauve . . . 80 55
267 24 5 e. green . . . 3·00 1·90
268 10 e. brown . . . 5·50 3·75
269 20 e. orange . . . 19·00 10·00

1938. As T **54** and **56** of Macao but inscr "GUINE".
270 54 1 c. green (postage) . . . 10 10
271 5 c. brown . . . 10 10
272 10 c. red . . . 10 10
273 15 c. purple . . . 10 10
274 20 c. grey . . . 15 10
275 – 30 c. purple . . . 15 10
276 – 35 c. green . . . 20 15
277 – 40 c. brown . . . 20 15
278 – 50 c. mauve . . . 20 15
279 – 60 c. black . . . 20 15
280 – 70 c. violet . . . 20 15
281 – 80 c. orange . . . 30 20
282 – 1 e. red . . . 35 15
283 – 1 e. 75 blue . . . 50 35
284 – 2 e. red . . . 1·50 50
285 – 5 e. green . . . 1·90 75
286 – 10 e. blue . . . 3·50 1·00
287 – 20 e. brown . . . 10·00 2·00
288 56 10 c. red (air) . . . 20 15
289 20 c. violet . . . 20 15
290 50 c. orange . . . 20 15
291 1 e. blue . . . 40 25
292 2 e. red . . . 3·00 1·75
293 3 e. green . . . 65 40
294 5 e. brown . . . 1·75 60
295 9 e. red . . . 2·00 1·25
296 10 e. mauve . . . 5·00 1·50
DESIGNS (postage): 30 c. to 50 c. Mousinho de Albuquerque; 60 c. to 1 e. Dam; 1 e. 75 to 5 e. Prince Henry the Navigator; 10, 20 e. Afonso de Albuquerque.

1946. 500th Anniv of Discovery of Portuguese Guinea.
297 31 30 c. black and grey . . . 35 25
298 – 50 c. green and light green 15 15
299 – 50 c. purple and claret . . 15 15
300 – 1 e. 75 blue and light blue . 1·10 40
301 – 3 e. 50 red and pink . . . 1·75 70
302 – 5 e. brown and chocolate . 4·75 2·25
303 – 20 e. violet and mauve . . 8·00 4·00
DESIGNS—VERT: 50 c. Nuno Tristao; 1 e. 75, President Grant; 3 e. 50, Teixeiro Pinto; 5 e. Honorio Barreto. HORIZ: 20 e. Church at Bissau.

32 Native Huts

34 Letter and Globe

1948.
304 32 5 c. brown . . . 10 10
305 – 10 c. purple . . . 6·00 2·50
306 – 20 c. mauve . . . 25 20
307 – 35 c. green . . . 35 20
308 – 50 c. red . . . 15 10
309 – 70 c. blue . . . 25 15
310 – 80 c. green . . . 35 15
311 – 1 e. red . . . 35 15
312 – 1 e. 75 blue . . . 5·50 2·75
313 – 2 e. blue . . . 6·50 70
314 – 3 e. 50 brown . . . 1·50 70
315 – 5 e. grey . . . 2·40 1·50
316 – 20 e. violet . . . 10·00 3·75
DESIGNS: 10 c. Crowned crane; 20 c., 3 e. 50, Youth; 35 c., 5 e. Woman; 50 c. Musician; 70 c. Man; 80 c., 20 e. Girl; 1, 2 e. Drummer; 1 e. 75, Bushbuck.

1948. Statue of Our Lady of Fatima. As T **62** of Macao.
317 50 c. green . . . 2·75 2·75

1949. 75th Anniv of U.P.U.
318 34 2 e. orange . . . 3·75 1·90

1950. Holy Year. As Nos. 425/6 of Macao.
319 1 e. purple . . . 1·25 90
320 3 e. green . . . 2·00 1·10

1951. Termination of Holy Year. As T **69** of Macao.
321 1 e. brown and buff . . . 55 40

37 Doctor examining Patient

39 Exhibition Entrance

1952. 1st Tropical Medicine Congress, Lisbon.
322 37 50 c. brown and purple . . 30 25

1953. Missionary Art Exhibition.
323 39 10 c. red and green . . . 10 10
324 50 c. blue and brown . . . 40 25
325 3 e. black and orange . . . 1·10 65

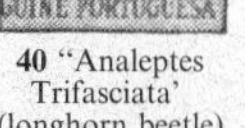

40 "Analeptes Trifasciata' (longhorn beetle)

43 Arms of Cape Verde Islands and Portuguese Guinea

1953. Bugs and Beetles. Multicoloured.
326 5 c. Type **40** 10 10
327 10 c. "Callidea panaethiopica kirk" (shieldbug) 10 10
328 30 c. "Craspedophorus brevicollis" (ground beetle) . 10 10
329 50 c. "Anthia nimrod" (ground beetle) 10 10
330 70 c. "Platypria luctuosa" (leaf beetle) 20 10
331 1 e. "Acanthophorus maculatus" (longhorn beetle) 20 10
332 2 e. "Cordylomera nitidipennis" (longhorn beetle) 55 15
333 3 e. "Lycus latissimus" (powder-post beetle) . . . . 1·10 20
334 5 e. "Cicindeia brunet" (tiger beetle) . . . . 2·25 55
335 10 e. "Calliurus dimidiata" (ground beetle) . . . . . . 3·50 1·90

1953. Portuguese Stamp Cent. As T **75** of Macao.
336 50 c. multicoloured 55 55

1954. 4th Cent of Sao Paulo. As T **76** of Macao.
337 1 e. multicoloured 20 15

1955. Presidential Visit.
338 **43** 1 e. multicoloured 25 15
339 2 e. 50 mulitcoloured . . . 55 25

44 Exhibition Emblem Globe and Arms

46 Statue of Barreto at Bissau

1958. Brussels International Exhibition.
340 **44** 2 e. 50 green 40 35

1958. 6th International Congress of Tropical Medicine. As T **79** of Macao.
341 5 e. multicoloured . . . . . . 2·00 1·00
DESIGN: 5 e. "Maytenus senegalensis" (plant).

1959. Death Centenary of Honorio Barreto (statesman).
342 **46** 2 e. 50 multicoloured . . . 20 15

47 Astrolabe

48 "Medical Service"

1960. 500th Death Anniv of Prince Henry the Navigator.
343 **47** 2 e. 50 multicoloured . . . 15 10

1960. 10th Anniv of African Technical Co-operation Commission.
344 **48** 1 e. 50 multicoloured . . . 20 15

1962. Sports. As T **82** of Macao. Multicoloured.
345 50 c. Motor racing 10 10
346 1 e. Tennis 55 20
347 1 e. 50 Putting the shot . . . 25 15
348 2 e. 50 Wrestling 30 20
349 3 e. 50 Shooting 30 20
350 15 e. Volleyball . . . . 1·25 1·00

1962. Malaria Eradication. Mosquito design as T **83** of Macao. Multicoloured.
351 2 e. 50 "Anopheles gambiae" . 45 30

51 Common Spitting Cobra

52 Map of Africa, Boeing 707 and Lockheed L.1049G Super Constellation

1963. Snakes. Multicoloured.
352 20 c. Type **51** 15 10
353 35 c. African rock python . . 15 10
354 70 c. Boomslang 40 25
355 80 c. West African mamba . 30 20
356 1 e. 50 Symthe's watersnake . 40 10
357 2 e. Common night adder . . 25 10
358 2 e. 50 Green swampsnake . 1·25 25
359 3 e. 50 Brown house snake . 30 20
360 4 e. Spotted wolfsnake . . . 40 25
361 5 e. Common puff adder . . 50 25
362 15 e. Striped beauty snake . 1·25 80
363 20 e. African egg-eating snake 2·00 1·00
The 2 e. and 20 e. are horiz.

1963. 10th Anniv of Transportes Aereos Portugueses (airline).
364 **52** 2 e. 50 multicoloured . . . 45 25

1964. Centenary of National Overseas Bank. As T **84** of Macao, but portrait of J. de A. Corvo.
365 2 e. 50 multicoloured 40 20

1965. Centenary of I.T.U. As T **85** of Macao.
366 2 e. 50 multicoloured . . . . 1·00 55

55 Soldier, 1548

63 Pres. Tomas

1966. Portuguese Military Uniforms. Multicoloured.
367 25 c. Type **55** 10 10
368 40 c. Arquebusier, 1578 . . . 15 10
369 60 c. Arquebusier, 1640 . . . 25 10
370 1 e. Grenadier, 1721 . . . . 25 10
371 2 e. 50 Captain of Fusiliers, 1740 50 10
372 4 e. 50 Infantryman, 1740 . . 1·10 25
373 7 e. 50 Sergeant-major, 1762 . 1·90 1·00
374 10 e. Engineers' officer, 1806 . 2·50 1·25

1966. 40th Anniv of Portuguese National Revolution. As T **86** of Macao, but showing different buildings. Multicoloured.
375 2 e. 50 B.C. Lopes School and Bissau Hospital 30 20

1967. Centenary of Military Naval Assn. As T **88** of Macao. Multicoloured.
376 50 e. O. Muzanty and cruiser "Republica" 15 10
377 1 e. A. de Cerqueira and destroyer "Guadiana" . . . 50 30

1967. 50th Anniv of Fatima Apparitions. As T **89** of Macao.
378 50 c. multicoloured 15 10
DESIGN: 50 c. Chapel of the Apparitions and Monument of the Holy Spirit.

1968. Visit of President Tomas of Portugal.
396 **63** 1 e. multicoloured 15 10

1968. 500th Birth Anniv of Pedro Cabral (explorer). As T **90** of Macao. Multicoloured.
397 2 e. 50 Cabral's arms 45 20

1969. Birth Centenary of Admiral Gago Coutinho. As T **91** of Macao. Multicoloured.
409 1 e. Admiral Coutinho's astrolabe (horiz) 30 15

1969. 500th Birth Anniv of Vasco da Gama (explorer). As T **92** of Macao. Multicoloured.
410 2 e. 50 Arms of Vasco da Gama 25 15

1969. Centenary of Overseas Administrative Reforms. As T **93** of Macao.
411 50 c. multicoloured 15 15

1969. 500th Birth Anniv of Manoel I. As T **95** of Macao. Multicoloured.
412 2 e. Arms of Manoel I . . . 40 15

70 Ulysses Grant and Square, Bolama

73 Camoens

1970. Centenary of Arbitral Judgment on Sovereignty of Bolama.
413 **70** 2 e. 50 multicoloured . . . 25 15

1970. Birth Centenary of Marshal Carmona. As T **96** of Macao.
414 1 e. 50 Portrait wearing cap and cloak 15 10

1972. 400th Anniv of Camoens' "The Lusiads" (epic poem).
422 **73** 50 c. multicoloured 20 15

74 Weightlifting and Hammer-throwing

1972. Olympic Games, Munich.
423 **74** 2 e. 50 multicoloured . . . 20 15

75 Fairey IIID Seaplane "Lusitania" taking-off from Lisbon

1972. 50th Anniv of 1st Lisbon–Rio de Janeiro Flight.
424 **75** 1 e. multicoloured 15 15

1973. Centenary of I.M.O./W.M.O. As T **102** of Macao.
425 2 e. multicoloured 20 15

CHARITY TAX STAMPS

The notes under this heading in Portugal also apply here.

C 16

1919. Fiscal stamp optd **REPUBLICA TAXA DE GUERRA**.
C241 C **16** 10 r. brown, buff & blk 11·00 15·00

1925. Marquis de Pombal Commem stamps of Portugal but inscr "GUINE".
C247 C **73** 15 c. black and red . . 35 30
C248 – 15 c. black and red . . 35 30
C249 C **75** 15 c. black and red . . 35 30

C 26

1934.
C270 C **26** 50 c. purple and green . 3·75 2·25

C 29a Arms

C 59

C 60

1938.
C297 C **29a** 50 c. yellow . . . . . 3·25 2·25
C298 50 c. brown & green . 3·25 2·25

1942. As Type **C29a** but smaller $20\frac{1}{2}$ x 25 mm.
C299 **C29a** 50c black and brown 10 10
C300 50 c. black & yellow . 85 50
C301 50 c. brown & yellow 90 75
C302 2 e. 50 black & blue . 20 20
C303 5 e. black and green . 35 10
C304 10 e. black and blue . 75 35
Nos. C302/4 were used at several small post offices as ordinary postage stamps during a temporary shortage.

1967. National Defence. No gum.
C379 C **59** 50 c. red, pink and black 40 25
C380 1 e. red, green & blk . 55 40
C381 5 e. red, grey & black . 1·10 1·00
C382 10 e. red, blue & blk . 3·25 3·25
50 e. in the same design was for fiscal use only.

1967. National Defence. No gum.
C383 C **60** 50 c. red, pink & black 15 15
C384 1 e. red, green & black 15 15
C385 5 e. red, grey & black . 40 30
C386 10 e. red, blue & black 90 65

C 61 Carved Statuette of Woman

C 65 Hands grasping Sword

1967. Guinean Artifacts from Bissau Museum. Multicoloured.
C387 50 c. Type C **61** 10 10
C388 1 e. "Tree of life"(carving) (horiz) 10 10
C389 2 e. Cow-headed statuette . 15 10
C390 2 e. 50 "The Magistrate" (statuette) 30 30
C391 5 e. "Kneeling Servant" (statuette) 40 30
C392 10 e. Stylized pelican (carving) 65 65

1968. No. C389 but inscr "TOCADOR DE BOMBOLON" surch.
C394 50 c. on 2 e. multicoloured . 15 15
C395 1 e. on 2 e. multicoloured 15 15

1969. National Defence.
C398 C **65** 50 c. multicoloured . . 15 15
C399 1 e. multicoloured . . 15 15
C400 2 e. multicoloured . . 15 15
C401 2 e. 50 multicoloured . 15 15
C402 3 e. multicoloured . . 15 15
C403 4 e. multicoloured . . 20 20
C404 5 e. multicoloured . . 25 25
C405 8 e. multicoloured . . 40 40
C406 9 e. multicoloured . . 50 50
C407 10 e. multicoloured . . 55 55
C408 15 e. multicoloured . . 90 90
NOTE—30, 50 and 100 e. stamps in the same design were for fiscal use only.

C 72 Mother and Children

1971.
C415 C **72** 50 c. multicoloured . . 10 10
C416 1 e. multicoloured . . 10 10
C417 2 e. multicoloured . . 10 10
C418 3 e. multicoloured . . 15 10
C419 4 e. multicoloured . . 20 10
C420 5 e. multicoloured . . 25 15
C421 10 e. multicoloured . . 50 30
Higher values were intended for fiscal use.

NEWSPAPER STAMP

1983. "Newspaper" key-type inscr "GUINE".
N50 V $2\frac{1}{2}$ r. brown 30 25

POSTAGE DUE STAMPS

1904. "Due" key-type inscr "GUINE". Name and value in black.
D122 W 5 r. green 40 15
D123 10 r. grey 40 15
D124 20 r. brown 40 15
D125 30 r. orange 45 35
D126 50 r. brown 45 35
D127 60 r. brown . . . . . . 1·25 90
D128 100 r. mauve . . . . . 1·25 90
D129 130 r. blue . . . . . . 1·95 90
D130 200 r. red . . . . . . 1·90 1·50
D131 500 r. lilac . . . . . . 4·50 2·25

1911. "Due" key-type of Portuguese Guinea optd **REPUBLICA**.
D138 W 5 r. green 10 10
D139 10 r. grey 10 10
D140 20 r. brown 15 10
D141 30 r. orange 15 10
D142 50 r. brown 15 10

D143 60 r. brown 40 30
D208 100 r. mauve 60 50
D145 130 r. blue 75 60
D146 200 r. red 75 60
D147 500 r. lilac 55 45

1921. "Due" key-type of Portuguese Guinea. Currency changed.
D244 W ½ c. green 15 15
D245 1 c. grey 15 15
D246 2 c. brown 15 15
D247 3 c. orange 15 15
D248 5 c. brown 15 15
D249 6 c. brown 15 15
D250 10 c. mauve 20 20
D251 13 c. blue 20 20
D252 20 c. red 20 20
D253 50 c. grey 20 20

1925. Marquis de Pombal stamps, as Nos. C247/9 optd **MULTA**.
D254 C **73** 30 c. black and red 35 30
D255 – 30 c. black and red 35 30
D256 C **75** 30 c. black and red 35 30

1952. As Type D **70** of Macao, but inscr "GUINE PORTUGUESA". Numerals in red, name in black (except 2 e. in blue).
D323 10 c. green and pink 15 15
D324 30 c. violet and grey 15 15
D325 50 c. green and lemon 15 15
D326 1 e. blue and grey 15 15
D327 2 e. black and olive 20 20
D328 5 e. brown and orange 25 25

PORTUGUESE INDIA Pt. 9

Portuguese territories on the west coast of India, consisting of Goa, Damao and Diu. Became part of India in December 1961.

1871. 1000 reis = 1 milreis.
1882. 12 reis = 1 tanga; 16 tangas = 1 rupia.
1959. 100 centavos = 1 escudo.

1 9

1871. Perf.
35 **1** 10 r. black 3·75 2·75
33a 15 r. pink 6·75 5·25
26 20 r. red 6·00 4·75
21 40 r. blue 13·50 32·00
22 100 r. green 48·00 40·00
23 200 r. yellow £130 £120
27 300 r. purple 65·00 55·00
28 600 r. purple 80·00 75·00
29 900 r. purple 80·00 75·00

1877. Star above value. Imperf (241/3) or perf (others).
241 **9** 1½ r. black 1·00 80
242 4½ r. green 10·00 8·00
243 6 r. green 10·00 7·50
48 10 r. black 25·00 22·00
49 15 r. pink 27·00 25·00
50 20 r. red 6·75 5·75
51 40 r. blue 11·50 9·25
52 100 r. green 60·00 55·00
53 200 r. yellow 65·00 60·00
54 300 r. purple 75·00 65·00
55 600 r. purple 75·00 65·00
56 900 r. purple 75·00 65·00

1877. "Crown" key-type inscr "INDIA PORTUGUEZA". Perf.
65 P 5 r. black 3·25 2·75
58 10 r. buff 8·00 6·00
78 10 r. green 7·50 6·00
67 20 r. bistre 5·25 4·00
68 25 r. pink 7·50 5·25
79 25 r. grey 32·00 27·00
80 25 r. purple 23·00 17·00
69 40 r. blue 10·00 8·00
81 40 r. yellow 30·00 23·00
70b 50 r. green 25·00 12·00
82 50 r. blue 15·00 13·50
71 100 r. lilac 9·50 8·00
64 200 r. orange 17·00 15·00
73 300 r. brown 20·00 17·00
See also Nos. 204/10.

1881. Surch in figures.
213 **1** 1½ on 10 r. black — £250
215 **9** 1½ on 10 r. black — £225
90 **1** 1½ on 20 r. red 65·00 50·00
91 **9** 1½ on 20 r. red £120 85·00
217 **1** 4½ on 40 r. blue 17·00 17·00
223 4½ on 100 r. green 30·00 26·00
96 5 on 10 r. black 4·00 4·00
98 **9** 5 on 10 r. black 27·00 22·00
101 **1** 5 on 15 r. pink 1·90 1·90
106 5 on 20 r. red 1·60 1·60
108 **9** 5 on 20 r. red 3·75 3·25
224 **1** 6 on 20 r. red
228 6 on 100 r. green £150 £110
231 6 on 200 r. yellow — £120
233 **9** 6 on 200 r. yellow £250 £210

1881. "Crown" key-type of Portuguese India surch in figures.
199 P 1½ on 4½ on 5 r. black 23·00 22·00
109 1½ on 5 r. black 1·00 85
200 1½ on 6 on10 r. green 38·00 35·00
110 1½ on 10 r. green 1·00 85
111 1½ on 20 r. bistre 8·75 6·75
157 1½ on 25 r. grey 23·00 22·00
158 1½ on 100 r. lilac 40·00 35·00
200a 1½ on 1 t. on 20 r. bistre — £100
201 2 on 4 t. on 50 r. green 50·00 40·00
114 4½ on 5 r. black 6·00 5·00
115 4½ on 10 r. green 90·00 85·00
116 4½ on 20 r. bistre 2·40 2·00
162 4½ on 25 r. purple 7·25 6·00
118 4½ on 100 r. lilac 70·00 60·00
119a 6 on 10 r. buff 24·00 22·00
120 6 on 10 r. green 6·00 5·00
121 6 on 20 r. bistre 10·00 8·00
167 6 on 25 r. grey 20·00 15·00
168 6 on 25 r. purple 2·00 1·75
169 6 on 40 r. blue 50·00 38·00
170 6 on 40 r. yellow 28·00 23·00
171 6 on 50 r. green 32·00 28·00
127 6 on 50 r. blue 40·00 32·00
202 6 on 1 t. on 10 r. green £100
128 1 t. on 10 r. green 70·00 70·00
129 1 t. on 20 r. bistre 32·00 28·00
175 1 t. on 25 r. grey 23·00 17·00
176 1 t. on 25 r. purple 8·00 5·75
132 1 t. on 40 r. blue 13·50 10·00
178 1 t. on 50 r. green 35·00 32·00
134 1 t. on 50 r. blue 17·00 12·00
136 1 t. on 100 r. lilac 17·00 10·00
137 1 t. on 200 r. orange 28·00 23·00
139 2 t. on 25 r. purple 8·00 6·75
182 2 t. on 25 r. grey 23·00 20·00
184 2 t. on 40 r. blue 27·00 20·00
141 2 t. on 40 r. yellow 28·00 25·00
142a 2 t. on 50 r. green 11·00 8·00
143 2 t. on 50 r. blue 55·00 45·00
144 2 t. on 100 r. lilac 8·00 6·75
188 2 t. on 200 r. orange 23·00 20·00
189 2 t. on 300 r. brown 23·00 20·00
190 P 4 t. on 10 r. green 10·00 8·00
191 4 t. on 50 r. green 8·75 7·00
148 4 t. on 200 r. orange 28·00 20·00
193 8 t. on 20 r. bistre 23·00 17·00
194 8 t. on 25 r. pink £100 85·00
151 8 t. on 40 r. blue 28·00 23·00
196 8 t. on 100 r. lilac 32·00 25·00
197 8 t. on 200 r. orange 23·00 18·00
198 8 t. on 300 r. brown 27·00 23·00

1882. "Crown" key-type of Portuguese India.
204 P 1½ r. black 40 35
205 4½ r. green 40 35
206 6 r. green 40 35
207 1 t. pink 40 35
208 2 t. blue 40 35
209 4 t. purple 2·10 1·75
210 8 t. orange 2·10 1·75

1886. "Embossed" key-type inscr "INDIA PORTUGUEZA".
244 Q 1½ r. black 1·25 1·00
245 4½ r. olive 1·60 1·10
246 6 r. green 2·10 1·25
247 1 t. red 2·75 2·40
248 2 t. blue 5·75 3·50
249 4 t. lilac 5·75 3·50
257 8 t. orange 4·75 3·50

1895. "Figures" key-type inscr "INDIA".
271 R 1½ r. black 70 40
259 4½ r. orange 70 40
273 6 r. green 70 40
274 9 r. lilac 2·75 2·10
260 1 t. blue 95 70
261 2 t. red 95 40
262 4 t. blue 1·10 70
270 8 t. lilac 2·00 1·50

1898. As Vasco da Gama stamps of Portugal T **40** etc, but inscr "INDIA".
275 1½ r. green 65 55
276 4½ r. red 65 55
277 6 r. purple 70 60
278 9 r. green 80 70
279 1 t. blue 1·10 1·00
280 2 t. brown 1·25 1·25
281 4 t. brown 1·50 1·40
282 8 t. brown 2·75 2·50
DESIGNS—HORIZ: 1½ r. Departure of fleet; 4½ r. Arrival at Calicut; 6 r. Embarkation at Rastello; 4 t. Flagship "Sao Gabriel"; 8 t. Vasco da Gama. VERT: 9 r. Muse of History; 1 t. Flagship "Sao Gabriel" and portraits of Da Gama and Camoens; 2 t. Archangel Gabriel, patron saint of the expedition.

1898. "King Carlos" key-type inscr "INDIA". Value in red (No. 292) or black (others).
323 S 1 r. grey 25 20
283 1½ r. orange 25 20
324 1½ r. grey 30 20
325 2 r. orange 25 20
326 2½ r. brown 30 20
327 3 r. blue 30 20
284 4½ r. green 55 40
285 6 r. brown 55 40
328 6 r. green 30 20
286 9 r. lilac 55 40
287 1 t. green 55 40
329 1 t. red 45 20
288 2 t. blue 70 40
330 2 t. brown 1·25 70
331 2½ t. blue 4·75 3·00
289 4 t. blue on blue 1·25 85
332 5 t. brown on yellow 1·60 1·00
290 8 t. purple on pink 1·25 85
291 12 t. blue on pink 2·00 1·25
334 12 t. green on pink 3·25 1·60
292 1 rp. black on blue 4·25 2·75
335 1 rp. blue on yellow 6·75 3·00
293 2 rp. mauve on yellow 6·75 4·00
336 2 rp. black on yellow 10·00 10·50

1900. No. 288 surch **1½ Reis.**
295 S 1½ r. on 2 t. blue 1·00 70

1902. Surch.
299 R 1 r. on 6 r. green 30 25
298 Q 1 r. on 2 t. blue 40 30
300 2 r. on 4½ r. olive 30 25
301 R 2 r. on 8 t. lilac 30 25
302 Q 2½ r. on 6 r. green 35 25
303 R 2½ r. on 9 r. lilac 30 25
305 3 r. on 4½ r. orange 1·00 60
304 Q 3 r. on 1 t. red 30 25
306 R 3 r. on 1 t. blue 60 60
337 S 2 t. on 2½ t. blue and black 1·25 1·10
307 Q 2½ t. on 1½ r. black 1·10 85
310 R 2½ t. on 1½ r. black 1·00 85
309 Q 2½ t. on 4 t. lilac 95 70
315 R 5 t. on 2 t. red 1·00 70
317 5 t. on 4 t. blue 1·00 70
314 Q 5 t. on 8 t. orange 70 40

1902. 1898 "King Carlos" stamps optd **PROVISORIO**.
319 S 6 r. brown and black 1·25 1·00
320 1 t. green and black 1·25 1·00
321 2 t. blue and black 1·25 1·00

1911. 1898 "King Carlos" stamps optd **REPUBLICA**. Value in black.
338 S 1 r. grey 20 20
339 1½ r. grey 20 20
340 2 r. orange 20 20
341 2½ r. brown 25 20
342 3 r. blue 25 20
343 4½ r. green 25 20
344 6 r. green 25 20
345 9 r. lilac 25 20
346 1 t. red 40 20
347 2 t. brown 40 20
348 4 t. blue on blue 90 85
349 5 t. brown on yellow 1·00 85
350 8 t. purple on pink 3·00 1·75
402 12 t. green on pink 2·00 1·75
352 1 rp. blue on yellow 4·25 3·25
405 2 rp. black on yellow 5·75 5·00
404 2 rp. mauve on yellow 6·50 5·00

Both unused and used prices for the following issue (Nos. 371 etc.) are for entire stamps showing both halves.

1911. Various stamps bisected by vertical perforation, and each half surch.
(a) On 1898 "King Carlos" key-type
371 S 1 r. on 2 r. orange and black 15 15
372 1 r. on 1 t. red and black 15 15
378 1 r. on 5 t. brown and black on yellow 1·00 90
374 1½ r. on 2½ r. brown and black 25 20
354 1½ r. on 4½ r. green and black 3·25 2·50
355 1½ r. on 9 r. lilac and black 15 15
356 1½ r. on 4 t. blue and black on blue 15 15
375 2 r. on 2½ r. brown and black 25 20
357 2 r. on 4 t. blue and black on blue 25 15
376 3 r. on 2½ r. brown and black 25 20
377 3 r. on 2 t. brown and black 25 20
358 6 r. on 4½ r. green and black 25 20
359d 6 r. on 9 r. lilac and black 25 20
379 6 r. on 8 t. purple and black on pink 50 40

(b) On1902 Provisional issue
360 R 1 r. on 5 t. on 2 t. red 2·00 1·75
361 1 r. on 5 t. on 4 t. blue 1·75 1·60
363 Q 1 r. on 5 t. on 8 t. orange 60 40
364 2 r. on 2½ r. on 6 r. green 90 70
365 R 2 r. on 2½ r. on 9 r. lilac 5·00 4·75
366 3 r. on 5 t. on 2 t. red 1·75 1·60
367 3 r. on 5 t. on 4 t. blue 1·75 1·60
370 Q 3 r. on 5 t. on 8 t. orange 50 30

(c) On 1911 issue (optd **REPUBLICA**).
380 S 1 r. on 1 r. grey and black 15 15
381 1 r. on 2 r. orange and black 15 15
382 1 r. on 1 t. red and black 15 15
383 1 r. on 5 t. brown and black on yellow and black 15 15
384 1½ r. on 4½ r. green and black 15 15
419 3 r. on 2 t. brown and black 80 75
420 6 r. on 4½ r. green and black 30 30
386 6 r. on 9 r. lilac and black 20 20
422 6 r. on 8 t. purple and black on pink 50 40

1913. Nos. 275/82 optd **REPUBLICA**.
389 1½ r. green 30 25
390 4½ r. red 35 25
391 6 r. purple 40 35
392 9 r. green 40 35
393 1 t. blue 70 40
394 2 t. brown 1·25 95
395 4 t. brown 80 60
396 8 t. brown 1·40 85

1914. Stamps of 1902 optd **REPUBLICA**.
406 R 2 r. on 8 t. lilac 4·00 3·25
407 Q 2½ r. on 6 r. green 65 50
415 S 1 t. green and black (No. 320) 5·25 3·50
458 2 t. blue and black (No. 321) 80 80
459 2 t. on 2½ t. blue and black 1·25 80
408 R 5 t. on 2 t. red 2·00 1·60
410 5 t. on 4 t. blue 2·00 1·60
460 Q 5 t. on 8 t. orange 1·40 1·10

1914. "King Carlos" key-type of Portuguese India optd **REPUBLICA** and surch.
423 S 1½ r. on 4½ r. green and black 30 30
424 1½ r. on 9 r. lilac and black 30 30
425 1½ r. on 12 t. green and black on pink 50 40
426 3 r. on 1 t. red and black 30 30
427 3 r. on 2 t. brown and black 1·25 1·10
428 3 r. on 8 t. purple and black on pink 1·00 90
429 3 r. on 1 rp. blue and black on yellow 50 40
430 3 r. on 2 rp. black on yellow 55 50

1914. Nos. 390 and 392/6 surch.
433 1½ on 4½ r. red 30 30
434 1½ r. on 9 r. green 30 30
435 3 r. on 1 t. blue 30 30
436 3 r. on 2 t. brown 55 40
437 3 r. on 4 t. brown 30 30
438 3 r. on 8 t. brown 1·00 90

1914. "Ceres" key-type inscr "INDIA". Name and value in black.
439 U 1 r. green 45 35
440 1½ r. green 45 35
441 2 r. black 60 35
442 2½ r. green 60 35
443 3 r. lilac 60 35
474 4 r. blue 1·00 80
444 4½ r. red 60 35
445 5 r. green 60 35
446 6 r. brown 60 35
447 9 r. blue 60 35
448 10 r. red 75 45
449 1 t. violet 1·10 45
481 1½ t. green 90 90
450 2 t. blue 1·25 45
483 2½ t. turquoise 80 70
451 3 t. brown 1·60 65
484 3 t. 4 brown 4·00 2·50
452 4 t. grey 1·25 80
453 8 t. purple 3·25 3·00
454 12 t. brown on green 3·00 3·00
455 1 rp. brown on pink 12·50 9·25
487 1 rp. brown 13·50 11·00
456 2 rp. orange on orange 8·50 6·75
488 2 rp. yellow 13·50 11·00
457 3 rp. green on blue 10·50 7·00
489 3 rp. green 20·00 18·00
490 5 rp. red 21·00 20·00

1922. "Ceres" key-type of Portuguese India surch with new value.
496 U 1½ r. on 8 t. purple and black 70 50
492 1½ r. on 2 r. black 40 30
497 2½ t. on 3 t. 4 brown and black 10·50 8·25

34 Vasco da Gama and Flagship "Sao Gabriel"

1925. 400th Death Anniv of Vasco da Gama. No gum.
493 **34** 6 r. brown 3·25 1·75
494 1 t. purple 3·25 2·00

36 The Signature of Francis

40 "Portugal" and Galeasse

1931. St. Francis Xavier Exhibition.
498 – 1 r. green 85 65
499 **36** 2 r. brown 85 65
500 – 6 r. purple 1·00 65
501 – 1½ t. brown 3·25 2·50
502 – 2 t. blue 5·25 4·75
503 – 2½ t. red 7·75 4·75
DESIGNS—VERT: 1 r. Monument to St. Francis; 6 r. St. Francis's surplice and cassock; 1½ t. St. Francis and Cross; 2½ t. St. Francis's Tomb. HORIZ: 2 t. Bom Jesus Church, Goa.

1933.
504 **40** 1 r. brown 20 15
505 2 r. brown 20 15
506 4 r. mauve 20 15
507 6 r. green 20 15
508 8 r. black 35 30
509 1 t. grey 35 30
510 1½ t. red 35 30
511 2 t. brown 35 30
512 2½ t. blue 1·10 50
513 3 t. turquoise 1·10 50
514 5 t. red 1·10 50
515 1 rp. green 4·00 1·75
516 2 rp. purple 7·00 3·50
517 3 rp. orange 8·75 5·50
518 5 rp. green 20·00 17·00

1938. As T **54** and **56** of Macao, but inscr "ESTADO DA INDIA".
519 **54** 1 r. green (postage) 25 25
520 2 r. brown 25 25
521 3 r. violet 25 25
522 6 r. green 25 25
523 – 10 r. red 35 30
524 – 1 t. mauve 35 30
525 – 1½ t. red 35 30
526 – 2 t. orange 35 30
527 – 2½ t. blue 35 30
528 – 3 t. grey 95 30
529 – 5 t. purple 1·10 40
530 – 1 rp. red 3·00 75
531 – 2 rp. green 5·00 2·25
532 – 3 rp. blue 8·00 4·25
533 – 5 rp. brown 18·00 5·50
DESIGNS: 10 r. to 1½t. Mousinho de Albuquerque; 2 t. to 3 t. Prince Henry the Navigator; 5 t. to 2 rp. Dam; 3, 5 rp. Afonso de Albuquerque.

534 **56** 1 t. red (air) 60 35
535 2½ t. violet 700 35
536 3½ t. orange 70 35
537 4½ t. blue 1·00 40
538 7 t. red 1·00 50
539 7½ t. green 1·75 60
540 9 t. brown 3·75 1·10
541 11 t. mauve 4·00 1·10

1942. Surch.
549 40 1 r. on 8 r. black 70 70
546 1 r. on 5 t. red 70 70
550 2 r. on 8 r. black 70 70
547 3 r. on 1½ t. red 70 70
551 3 r. on 2 t. brown 70 70
552 3 r. on 3 rp. orange 1·60 1·50
553 6 r. on 2½ t. blue 1·60 1·50
554 6 r. on 3 t. turquoise 1·60 1·50
542 1 t. on 1½ t. red 3·00 1·75
548 1 t. on 2 t. brown 2·00 1·50
543 1 t. on 1 rp. green 3·00 1·75
544 1 t. on 2 rp. purple 3·00 1·75
545 1 t. on 5 rp. green 3·00 1·75

48 St. Francis Xavier — **50** D. Joao de Castro

1946. Portraits and View.
555 48 1 r. black and grey 35 25
556 – 2 r. purple and pink 35 25
557 – 6 r. bistre and buff 35 25
558 – 7 r. violet and mauve 1·25 70
559 – 9 r. brown and buff 1·25 70
560 – 1 t. green and light green 1·10 65
561 – 3½ t. blue and light blue 1·25 1·10
562 – 1 rp. purple and bistre 4·00 1·10
DESIGNS: 2 r. Luis de Camoens; 6 r. Garcia de Orta; 7 r. Beato Joao Brito; 9 r. Vice-regal Archway; 1 t. Afonso de Albuquerque; 3½ t. Vasco da Gama; 1 rp. D. Francisco de Almeida.

1948. Portraits.
564 50 3 r. blue and light blue 85 55
565 – 1 t. green and light green 1·40 70
566 – 1½ t. purple and mauve 1·75 1·00
567 – 2½ t. red and orange 2·40 1·50
568 – 7½ t. purple and brown 4·00 2·00
PORTRAITS: 1 t. St. Francis Xavier; 1½ t. P. Jose Vaz; 2½ t. D. Luis de Ataide; 7½ t. Duarte Pacheco Pereira.

1948. Statue of Our Lady of Fatima. As T **62** of Macao.
570 1 t. green 2·75 2·50

53 Our Lady of Fatima — **59** Father Jose Vaz

1949. Statue of Our Lady of Fatima.
571 53 1 r. light blue and blue 75 70
572 3 r. yellow, orange and lemon 75 70
573 9 r. red and mauve 1·75 1·25
574 2 t. green and light green 3·50 1·50
575 9 t. red and vermilion 4·00 1·60
576 2 rp. brown and purple 6·25 3·00
577 5 rp. black and green 12·00 5·00
578 8 rp. blue and violet 25·00 10·00

1949. 75th Anniv of U.P.U. As T **64** of Macao.
579 2½ t. red 2·75 2·00

1950. Holy Year. As Nos. 425/6 of Macao.
580 65 1 r. bistre 1·00 40
588 1 r. red 40 25
589 2 r. green 40 25
590 – 3 r. brown 40 25
591 65 6 r. grey 40 25
592 – 9 r. mauve 1·00 60
593 65 1 t. blue 1·00 60
581 – 2 t. green 1·25 60
594 – 2 t. yellow 1·00 60
595 65 4 t. brown 1·00 60

1950. Nos. 523 and 527 surch.
582 1 real on 10 r. red 40 30
583 1 real on 2½ t. blue 40 30
584 2 reis on 10 r. red 40 30
585 3 reis on 2½ t. blue 40 30
586 6 reis on 2½ t. blue 40 30
587 1 tanga on 2½ t. blue 40 30

1951. Termination of Holy Year. As T **69** of Macao.
596 1 rp. blue and grey 1·00 60

1951. 300th Birth Anniv of Jose Vaz.
597 59 1 r. grey and slate 20 15
598 – 2 r. orange and brown 20 15
599 59 3 r. grey and black 50 20
600 – 1 t. blue and indigo 30 20
601 59 2 t. purple and maroon 30 20
602 – 3 t. green and black 50 20
603 59 9 t. violet and blue 55 25
604 – 10 t. violet and mauve 1·50 90
605 – 12 t. brown and black 5·00 2·75
DESIGNS: 2 r., 1, 3, 10 t. Sancoale Church Ruins; 12 t. Veneravel Altar.

60 Goa Medical School

1952. 1st Tropical Medicine Congress, Lisbon.
606 60 4½ t. turquoise and black 3·00 1·90

1952. 4th Death Cent of St. Francis Xavier. As Nos. 452/4 of Macao but without lined background.
607 6 r. multicoloured 25 15
608 2 t. multicoloured 1·75 55
609 5 t. green, silver and mauve 2·75 85

62 St. Francis Xavier — **63** Stamp of 1871 — **64** The Virgin

1952. Philatelic Exhibition, Goa.
612 63 3 t. black 8·00 8·00
613 62 5 t. black and lilac 8·00 8·00

1953. Missionary Art Exhibition.
614 64 6 r. black and blue 25 20
615 1 t. brown and buff 1·00 70
616 3 t. lilac and yellow 2·40 1·25

1953. Portuguese Postage Stamp Centenary. As T **75** of Macao.
617 1 t. multicoloured 90 80

66 Dr. Gama Pinto — **67** Academy Buildings

1954. Birth Centenary of Dr. Gama Pinto.
618 66 3 r. green and grey 25 20
619 2 t. black and blue 40 25

1954. 4th Cent of Sao Paulo. As T **76** of Macao.
620 2 t. multicoloured 50 30

1954. Centenary of Afonso de Albuquerque National Academy.
621 67 9 t. multicoloured 85 25

68 Mgr. Dalgado — **71** M. A. de Sousa

72 F. de Almeida — **73** Map of Bacaim

1955. Birth Centenary of Mgr. Dalgado.
622 68 1 r. multicoloured 15 15
623 1 t. multicoloured 35 15

1956 450th Anniv of Portuguese Settlements in India. Multicoloured. (a) Famous Men. As T **71**.
624 6 r. Type **71** 30 20
625 1½ t. F. N. Xavier 30 20
626 4 t. A. V. Lourenco 30 20
627 8 t. Father Jose Vaz 50 25
628 9 t. M. G. de Heredia 50 25
629 2 rp. A. C. Pacheco 1·50 1·00

(b) Viceroys. As T **72**.
630 3 r. Type **72** 25 15
631 9 r. A. de Albuquerque 30 20
632 1 t. Vasco da Gama 30 20
633 3 t. N. da Cunha 45 20
634 10 t. J. de Castro 40 25
635 3 rp. C. de Braganca 1·75 1·10

(c) Settlements. As T **73**.
636 2 t. Type **73** 3·25 1·75
637 2½ t. Mombaim 1·75 1·00
638 3½ t. Damao 1·75 1·00
639 5 t. Diu 1·00 55
640 12 t. Cochim 1·25 70
641 1 rp. Goa 2·75 1·25

74 Map of Damao. Dadra and Nagar Aveli Districts — **75** Arms of Vasco da Gama

1957. Centres multicoloured.
642 74 3 r. grey 15 10
643 6 r. green 15 10
644 3 t. pink 25 20
645 6 t. blue 25 20
646 11 t. bistre 80 55
647 2 rp. lilac 1·10 80
648 3 rp. yellow 1·75 1·10
649 5 rp. red 2·10 1·60

1958. Heraldic Arms of Famous Men. Multicoloured.
650 2 r. Type **75** 20 10
651 6 r. Lopo Soares de Albergaria 20 10
652 9 r. D. Francisco de Almeida 20 10
653 1 t. Garcia de Noronha 20 10
654 4 t. D. Afonso de Albuquerque 30 20
655 5 t. D. Joao de Castro 35 20
656 11 t. D. Luis de Ataide 80 55
657 1 rp. Nuno da Cunha 80 55

1958. 6th International Congress of Tropical Medicine. As T **79** of Macao.
658 5 t. multicoloured 70 50
DESIGN: 5 t. "Holarrhena antidysenterica" (plant).

1958. Brussels Int Exn. As T **78** of Macao.
659 1 rp. multicoloured 45 30

1959. Surch in new currency.
660 – 5 c. on 2 r. (No. 650) 25 15
661 74 10 c. on 3 r. grey 25 15
662 – 15 c. on 6 r. (No. 651) 25 15
663 – 20 c. on 9 r. (No. 652) 25 15
664 – 30 c. on 1 t. (No. 653) 25 15
681 – 40 c. on 1½ t. (No. 566) 30 20
682 – 40 c. on 1½ t. (No. 625) 30 20
683 – 40 c. on 2 t. (No. 620) 50 40
665 73 40 c. on 2 t. 30 20
666 – 40 c. on 2½ t. (No. 637) 40 20
667 – 40 c. on 3½ t. (No. 638) 30 20
668 74 50 c. on 3 t. pink 30 20
684 64 80 c. on 3 t. lilac and yellow 30 20
669 – 80 c. on 3 t. (No. 633) 30 20
685 – 80 c. on 3½ t. (No. 561) 30 20
686 – 80 c. on 5 t. (No. 658) 35 20
670 – 80 c. on 10 t. (No. 634) 60 50
687 – 80 c. on 1 rp. (No. 659) 85 50
671 – 80 c. on 3 rp. (No. 635) 70 60
672 – 1 e. on 4 t. (No. 654) 30 20
673 – 1 e. 50 on 5 t. (No. 655) 30 20
674 74 2 e. on 6 t. blue 30 20
675 2 e. 50 on 11 t. bistre 35 20
676 – 4 e. on 11 t. (No. 656) 35 35
677 – 4 e. 50 on 1 rp. (No. 657) 55 35
678 74 5 e. on 2 rp. lilac 55 30
679 10 e. on 3 rp. yellow 1·00 75
680 30 e. on 5 rp. red 2·75 1·10

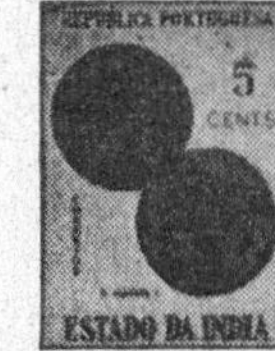

78 Coin of Manoel I — **79** Prince Henry's Arms

1959. Portuguese Indian Coins. Designs showing both sides of coins of various rulers. Multicoloured.
688 5 c. Type **78** 25 10
689 10 c. Joao III 25 10
690 15 c. Sebastiao 25 10
691 30 c. Filipe I 25 10
692 40 c. Filipe II 25 10
693 50 c. Filipe III 25 10
694 60 c. Joao IV 25 10
695 80 c. Afonso VI 25 10
696 1 e. Pedro II 25 10
697 1 e. 50 Joao V 25 10
698 2 e. Jose I 50 30
699 2 e. 50 Maria I 50 30
700 3 e. Prince Regent Joao 50 30
701 4 e. Pedro IV 60 40
702 4 e. 40 Miguel 60 40
703 5 e. Maria II 60 40
704 10 e. Pedro V 1·00 70
705 20 e. Luis 2·75 2·00
706 30 e. Carlos 3·50 2·75
707 50 e. Portuguese Republic 5·00 4·25

1960. 500th Death Anniv of Prince Henry the Navigator.
708 79 3 e. multicoloured 70 50

The 1962 sports set and malaria eradication stamp similar to those for the other territories were ready for issue when Portuguese India was occupied, but they were not put on sale there.

CHARITY TAX STAMPS.

The notes under this heading in Portugal also apply here.

1919. Fiscal stamp. Type C **1** of Portuguese Africa optd **TAXA DE GUERRA**.
C491 Rps. 0:00:05, 48 green 2·00 1·60
C492 Rps. 0:02:03, 43 green 4·00 2·50

1925. Marquis de Pombal Commem stamps of Portugal, but inscr "INDIA".
C495 C 73 6 r. pink 35 35
C496 – 6 r. pink 35 35
C497 C 75 6 r. pink 35 35

C 52 Mother and Child — **C 69** Mother and Child

1948. (a) Inscr "ASSISTENCIA PUBLICA".
C571 C 52 6 r. green 2·00 1·75
C572 6 r. yellow 2·25 2·00
C573 1 t. red 2·00 1·75
C574 1 t. orange 1·75 1·00
C575 1 t. green 3·50 2·10

(b) Inscr "PROVEDORIA DE ASSISTENCIA PUBLICA".
C607 C 52 1 t. grey 2·00 1·25

1951. Surch **1 tanga**.
C606 C 52 1 t. on 6 r. red 1·75 1·40

1953. Optd **"Revalidado" P. A. P.** and dotted line.
C617 C 52 1 t. red 5·00 3·75

1953. Surch as in Type C **69**.
C624 C 69 1 t. on 4 t. blue 7·50 6·25

C 70 Mother and Child — **C 80** Arms and People

1956.
C625 C 70 1 t. black, green & red 70 45
C626 1 t. blue, orange & grn 60 45

1957. Surch **6 reis**.
C650 C 70 6 r. on 1 t. black, green and red 70 50

1959. Surch.
C688 C 70 20 c. on 1 t. blue, orange and green 40 40
C689 40 c. on 1 t. blue, orange and green 40 40

1960.
C709 C 80 20 e. brown and red 40 40

POSTAGE DUE STAMPS

1904. "Due" key-type inscr "INDIA".
D337 W 2 r. green 40 40
D338 3 r. green 40 40
D339 4 r. orange 40 40
D340 5 r. grey 40 40
D341 6 r. grey 40 40
D342 9 r. brown 50 45
D343 1 t. red 50 45
D344 2 t. brown 1·00 80
D345 5 t. blue 2·00 1·75
D346 10 t. red 2·00 2·00
D347 1 rp. lilac 6·75 5·25

1911. Nos. D337/47 optd **REPUBLICA**.
D354 W 2 r. green 25 15
D355 3 r. green 25 15
D356 4 r. orange 25 15
D357 5 r. grey 25 15
D358 6 r. grey 25 20
D359 9 r. brown 25 20
D360 1 t. red 25 20
D361 2 t. brown 55 40
D362 5 t. blue 95 95
D363 10 t. red 2·00 1·60
D364 1 rp. lilac 2·75 2·50

1925. Marquis de Pombal stamps, as Nos. C495/7 optd **MULTA**.
D495 C 73 1 t. pink 35 35
D496 – 1 t. pink 35 35
D497 C 75 1 t. pink 35 35

1943. Stamps of 1933 surch **Porteado** and new value.
D549 40 3 r. on 2½ t. blue 40 35
D550 6 r. on 3 t. turquoise 55 40
D551 1 t. on 5 t. red 1·00 90

1945. As Type D **1** of Portuguese Colonies, but optd **ESTADO DA INDIA**.
D555 2 r. black and red 1·00 70
D556 3 r. black and blue 1·00 70
D557 4 r. black and yellow 1·00 70
D558 6 r. black and green 1·00 70

D559 1 t. black and brown 1·00 70
D560 2 t. black and brown 1·00 70

1951. Surch **Porteado** and new value and bar.
D588 2 rs. on 7 r. (No. 558) 50 30
D589 3 rs. on 7 r. (No. 558) 50 30
D590 1 t. on 1 rp. (No. 562) 50 30
D591 2 t. on 1 rp. (No. 562) 50 30

1952. As Type D **70** of Macao, but inscr "INDIA PORTUGUESA". Numerals in red, name in black.
D606 2 r. olive and brown 20 10
D607 3 r. black and green 20 10
D608 6 r. blue and turquoise 20 10
D609 1 t. red and grey 30 20
D610 2 t. orange, green and grey 60 40
D611 10 t. blue, green and yellow 2·00 1·75

1959. Nos. D606/8 and D610/11 surch in new currency.
D688 5 c. on 2 r. multicoloured 20 20
D689 10 c. on 3 r. multicoloured 20 20
D690 15 c. on 6 r. multicoloured 20 20
D691 60 c. on 2 t. multicoloured 70 70
D692 60 c. on 10 t. multicoloured 1·40 1·25

PRUSSIA Pt. 7

Formerly a kingdom in the N. of Germany. In 1867 it became part of the North German Confederation.

1850. 12 pfennig = 1 silbergroschen;
30 silbergroschen = 1 thaler.
1867. 60 kreuzer = 1 gulden.

1 Friedrich Wilhelm IV — 3 — 4

1850. Imperf.
14 1 4 pf. green 65·00 24·00
4 6 pf. red 70·00 40·00
22 ½ sgr. (=6 pf.) red £100 90·00
5 1 sgr. black on pink 80·00 4·75
16 1 sgr. pink 35·00 1·50
6 2 sgr. black on blue 85·00 10·00
18 2 sgr. blue 90·00 11·00
8 3 sgr. black on yellow 85·00 10·00
21 3 sgr. yellow 70·00 11·00

1861. Roul.
24 3 3 pf. lilac 17·00 30·00
26 4 pf. green 8·00 5·50
28 6 pf. orange 6·50 12·00
31 4 1 sgr. pink 3·25 30
35 2 sgr. blue 7·00 80
36 3 sgr. yellow 7·00 1·25

5 — 7

1866. Printed in reverse on back of specially treated transparent paper. Roul.
38 5 10 sgr. pink 60·00 65·00
39 – 30 sgr. blue 75·00 £170
The 30 sgr. has the value in a square.

1867. Roul.
40 7 1 k. green 20·00 38·00
42 2 k. orange 38·00 85·00
43 3 k. pink 20·00 18·00
45 6 k. blue 20·00 40·00
46 9 k. bistre 24·00 45·00

PUERTO RICO Pt. 9; Pt. 22

A West Indian island ceded by Spain to the United States after the war of 1898. Until 1873 stamps of Cuba were in use. Now uses stamps of the U.S.A.

1873. 100 centimos = 1 peseta.
1881. 1000 milesimas = 100 centavos = 1 peso.
1898. 100 cents = 1 dollar.

A. SPANISH OCCUPATION

(2)

1873. Nos. 53/5 of Cuba optd with T **2**.
1 25 c. de p. lilac 30·00 80
3 50 c. de p. brown 80·00 4·00
4 1 p. brown £180 16·00

1874. No. 57 of Cuba with opt similar to T **2** (two separate characters).
5 25 c. de p. blue 27·00 1·90

1875. Nos. 61/3 of Cuba with opt similar to T **2** (two separate characters).
6 25 c. de p. blue 18·00 1·90
7 50 c. de p. green 26·00 2·25
8 1 p. brown 95·00 11·00

1876. Nos. 65a and 67 of Cuba with opt similar to T **2** (two separate characters).
9 25 c. de p. lilac 3·25 1·40
10 50 c. de p. blue 6·75 2·50
11 1 p. black 32·00 8·75

1876. Nos. 65a and 67 of Cuba with opt as last, but characters joined.
12 25 c. de p. lilac 25·00 70
13 1 p. black 50·00 8·25

1877. As T **45** of Spain, but inscr "PTO-RICO 1877".
14 5 c. brown 5·25 1·75
15 10 c. red 16·00 2·25
16 15 c. green 24·00 9·25
17 25 c. blue 9·50 1·50
18 50 c. bistre 16·00 3·75

1878. As T **45** of Spain, but inscr "PTO-RICO 1878".
19 5 c. grey 12·00 12·00
20 10 c. brown £190 70·00
21 25 c. green 1·50 85
22 50 c. blue 5·00 2·00
23a 1 p. bistre 9·50 4·00

1879. As T **45** of Spain, but inscr "PTO-RICO 1879".
24 5 c. red 10·00 4·25
25 10 c. brown 10·00 4·25
26 15 c. grey 10·00 4·25
27 25 c. blue 3·50 1·50
28 50 c. green 10·00 4·25
29 1 p. lilac 48·00 19·00

1880. "Alfonso XII" key-type inscr "PUERTO-RICO 1880".
30 X ½ c. green 21·00 15·00
31 ½ c. red 5·50 2·00
32 1 c. purple 9·50 8·00
33 2 c. grey 5·50 3·75
34 3 c. buff 5·50 3·75
35 4 c. black 5·50 3·75
36 5 c. green 2·75 1·40
37 10 c. red 3·25 1·90
38 15 c. brown 5·50 2·75
39 25 c. lilac 2·75 1·40
40 40 c. grey 11·00 1·40
41 50 c. brown 21·00 12·50
42 1 p. bistre 75·00 16·00

1881. "Alfonso XIII" key-type inscr "PUERTO-RICO 1881".
43 X ½ m. red 20 10
45 1 m. violet 40 30
46 2 m. red 40 30
47 4 m. green 70 20
48 6 m. purple 70 40
49 8 m. blue 1·60 1·00
50 1 c. green 2·75 1·00
51 2 c. red 3·50 2·75
52 3 c. brown 7·25 4·25
53 5 c. lilac 2·50 30
54 8 c. brown 2·40 1·25
55 10 c. grey 22·00 7·00
56 20 c. bistre 28·00 12·50

1882. "Alfonso XII" key-type inscr "PUERTO-RICO".
57 X ½ m. red 15 10
74 1 m. red 15 10
75 1 m. orange 15 10
59 2 m. mauve 20 15
60 4 m. purple 20 15
61 6 m. brown 35 15
62 8 m. green 35 15
63 1 c. green 15 15
64 2 c. red 1·00 15
65 3 c. yellow 3·50 2·00
76 3 c. brown 3·50 65
77 5 c. lilac 13·00 1·00
67 8 c. brown 3·25 10
68 10 c. green 3·25 20
69 20 c. grey 4·75 20
70 40 c. blue 35·00 13·00
71 80 c. bistre 50·00 18·00

1890. "Baby" key-type inscr "PUERTO-RICO".
80 Y ½ m. black 15 10
95 ½ m. grey 15 10
111 ½ m. brown 15 15
124 ½ m. purple 15 10
81 1 m. green 25 10
96 1 m. purple 15 10
112 1 m. blue 15 15
125 1 m. brown 15 10
82 2 m. red 15 10
97 2 m. purple 15 10
126 2 m. green 15 10
83 4 m. black 9·75 5·50
98 4 m. blue 15 10
114 4 m. brown 15 15
127 4 m. green 85 30
84 6 m. brown 32·00 13·00
99 6 m. red 15 10
85 8 m. bistre 25·00 18·00
100 8 m. green 15 10
86 1 c. brown 20 10
101 1 c. green 50 10
115 1 c. purple 5·25 40
128 1 c. red 60 10
87 2 c. purple 85 80
102 2 c. pink 80 10
116 Y 2 c. lilac 1·90 40
129 2 c. brown 60 10
88 3 c. blue 6·50 85
103 3 c. orange 80 10
117 3 c. grey 5·25 40
131 3 c. brown 20 10
118 4 c. blue 1·25 40
132 4 c. brown 65 10
89 5 c. purple 10·50 40
104 5 c. green 80 10
133 5 c. blue 20 10
120 6 c. orange 40 15
134 6 c. lilac 20 10
90 8 c. blue 13·50 1·60
105 8 c. brown 15 10
121 8 c. purple 11·00 4·50
135 8 c. red 2·40 1·25
106 10 c. red 1·25 10
122 20 c. red 1·40 40
107 20 c. lilac 1·90 45
136 20 c. grey 6·00 1·25
93 40 c. orange 85·00 42·00
108 40 c. blue 5·00 3·25
137 40 c. red 6·00 1·25
94 80 c. green £400 £140
109 80 c. red 13·00 10·00
138 80 c. black 24·00 19·00

13 Landing of Columbus

1893. 400th Anniv of Discovery of America by Columbus.
110 13 3 c. green £160 40·00

1898. "Curly Head" key-type inscr "PTO RICO 1898 y 99".
139 Z 1 m. brown 10 10
140 2 m. brown 10 10
141 3 m. brown 10 10
142 4 m. brown 1·25 50
143 5 m. brown 10 10
144 1 c. purple 10 10
145 2 c. green 10 10
146 3 c. brown 10 10
147 4 c. orange 1·25 85
148 5 c. pink 10 10
149 6 c. blue 10 10
150 8 c. brown 10 10
151 10 c. red 10 10
152 15 c. grey 10 10
153 20 c. purple 1·50 50
154 40 c. lilac 1·10 1·25
155 60 c. black 1·10 1·25
156 80 c. brown 4·00 4·50
157 1 p. green 9·00 8·75
158 2 p. blue 21·00 12·00

1898. "Baby" key-type inscr "PUERTO RICO" and optd **Habilitado PARA 1898 y '99**.
159 Y ½ m. purple 10·00 5·50
160 1 m. brown 40 20
161 2 m. green 40 20
162 4 m. green 40 20
163 1 c. purple 40 20
164 2 c. brown 30 15
165 3 c. blue 18·00 8·50
166 3 c. brown 40 20
167 4 c. brown 35 25
168 4 c. blue 11·00 7·00
169 5 c. blue 40 25
170 5 c. green 5·50 4·00
172 6 c. lilac 40 20
173a 8 c. red 60 30
174 20 c. grey 75 40
175 40 c. red 3·00 50
176 80 c. black 19·00 14·50

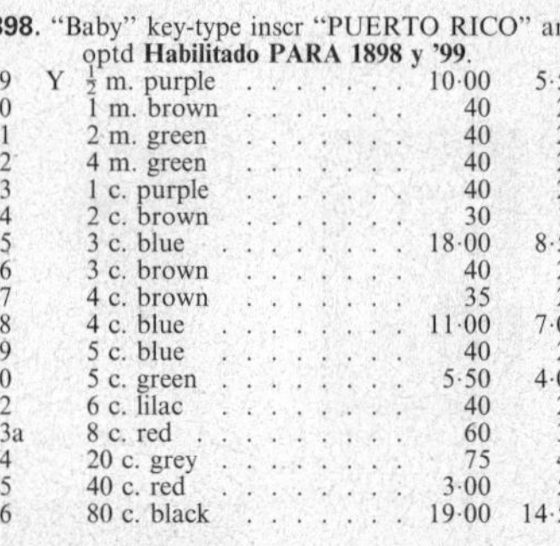

WAR TAX STAMPS

1898. 1890 and 1898 stamps optd **IMPUESTO DE GUERRA** or surch also.
W177 Y 1 m. blue 2·40 1·75
W178 1 m. brown 6·50 4·75
W179 2 m. red 12·50 8·00
W180 2 m. green 6·50 4·75
W181 4 m. green 10·00 10·00
W182a 1 c. brown 6·50 4·00
W183 1 c. purple 11·00 10·00
W184 2 c. purple 35 20
W185 2 c. pink 35 20
W186 2 c. lilac 85 85
W187 2 c. brown 85 20
W192 2 c. on 2 m. red 40 25
W193c 2 c. on 5 c. green 2·00 1·75
W188 3 c. orange 12·00 10·00
W194 3 c. on 10 c. red 12·00 9·50
W195 4 c. on 20 c. red 12·00 9·50
W189 5 c. green 25 15
W196a 5 c. on ½ m. brown 4·75 3·25
W197 5 c. on 1 m. purple 35 25
W198 5 c. on 1 m. blue 40 40
W199 Z 5 c. on 1 m. brown 6·50 4·50
W200 Y 5 c. on 5 c. green 3·25 2·50
W191 8 c. purple 19·00 16·00

MORE DETAILED LISTS
are given in the Stanley Gibbons Catalogues referred to in the country headings. For lists of current volumes see introduction

B. UNITED STATES OCCUPATION

1899. 1894 stamps of United States (No. 267 etc) optd **PORTO RICO**.
202 1 c. green 6·00 1·25
203 2 c. red 5·50 1·00
204 5 c. blue 8·50 1·75
205 8 c. brown 25·00 12·00
206 10 c. brown 18·00 3·75

1900. 1894 stamps of United States (No. 267 etc) optd **PUERTO RICO**.
210 1 c. green 5·00 1·25
212 2 c. red 4·50 90

POSTAGE DUE STAMPS

1899. Postage Due stamps of United States of 1894 optd **PORTO RICO**.
D207 D 87 1 c. red 18·00 6·00
D208 2 c. red 14·00 4·50
D209 10 c. red £130 42·00

QATAR Pt. 19

An independent Arab Shaikhdom with British postal administration until May 23, 1963, issues for which are listed in Volume 3. Later issues by the Qatar Post Department.

1964. 100 naye paise = 1 rupee.
1966. 100 dirhams = 1 riyal.

1964. Olympic Games, Tokyo. Optd **1964**, Olympic rings and Arabic inscr or surch also.
38 9 50 n.p. brown 1·75 1·25
39 – 75 n.p. blue (No. 33) 2·50 1·75
40 – 1 r. on 10 r. black (No. 37) 1·10 1·00
41 11 2 r. blue 2·50 2·00
42 5 r. green (No. 36) 7·00 6·00

1964. Pres. Kennedy Commem. Optd **John F Kennedy 1917–1963** in English and Arabic or surch also.
43 9 50 n.p. brown 1·75 1·25
44 – 75 n.p. blue (No. 33) 2·50 1·75
45 – 1 r. on 10 r. black (No. 37) 1·10 1·00
46 11 2 r. blue 2·50 2·00
47 – 5 r. green (No. 36) 7·00 5·00

15 Colonnade, Temple of Isis — 16 Scouts on Parade

1965. Nubian Monuments Preservation. Mult.
48 1 n.p. Type **15** 10 15
49 2 n.p. Temple of Isis, Philac 10 15
50 3 n.p. Trajan's Kiosk, Philac 10 15
51 1 r. As 3 n.p. 1·25 30
52 1 r. 50 As 2 n.p. 2·10 50
53 2 r. Type **15** 2·50 50

1965. Qatar Scouts.
54 – 1 n.p. brown and green 20 15
55 – 2 n.p. blue and brown 20 15
56 – 3 n.p. blue and green 20 15
57 – 4 n.p. brown and blue 20 15
58 – 5 n.p. blue and turquoise 20 15
59 16 30 n.p. multicoloured 50 40
60 40 n.p. multicoloured 65 50
61 1 r. multicoloured 1·60 1·10
DESIGNS—TRIANGULAR (60×30 mm): 1, 4 n.p. Qatar Scout badge; 2, 3, 5 n.p. Ruler, badge, palms and camp.

17 "Telstar" and Eiffel Tower

1965. I.T.U. Centenary.
62 17 1 n.p. brown and blue 20 15
63 – 2 n.p. brown and blue 20 15
64 – 3 n.p. violet and green 20 15
65 – 4 n.p. blue and brown 20 15
66 17 5 n.p. brown and violet 20 15
67 – 40 n.p. black and red 50 30
68 – 50 n.p. brown and green 60 40
69 – 1 r. red and green 1·25 80
DESIGNS: 2 n.p., 1 r. "Syncom 3" and pagoda; 3, 40 n.p. "Relay" and radar scanner; 4, 50 n.p. Post Office Tower (London), globe and satellites.

18 Triggerfish

1965. Fish of the Arabian Gulf. Multicoloured.
70 1 n.p. Type **18** 10 10
71 2 n.p. Butterfly sweetlip 10 10
72 3 n.p. Saddle-spot butterfly fish 10 10
73 4 n.p. Threadfin butterfly fish 10 10
74 5 n.p. Mahomet's lancet fish 10 10
75 15 n.p. Paradise fish 30 10
76 20 n.p. Sailfin tang 35 10
77 30 n.p. Thousand-spotted grouper 45 10
78 40 n.p. Regal angelfish 60 15
79 50 n.p. As 2 n.p 90 30
80 75 n.p. Type **18** 1·50 35
81 1 r. As 30 n.p. 2·25 35
82 2 r. As 20 n.p. 4·50 90
83 3 r. As 15 n.p. 6·50 1·75
84 4 r. As 5 n.p. 8·00 2·25
85 5 r. As 4 n.p. 8·50 3·00
86 10 r. As 3 n.p. 14·00 6·50

19 Basketball

1966. Pan-Arab Games, Cairo (1965).
87 **19** 1 r. black, grey and red 90 60
88 – 1 r. brown and green 90 60
89 – 1 r. red and blue 90 60
90 – 1 r. green and blue 90 60
91 – 1 r. blue and brown 90 60
SPORTS: No. 88, Horse-jumping; No. 89, Running; No. 90, Football; No. 91, Weightlifting.

1966. Space Rendezvous. Nos. 62/9 optd with two space capsules and **SPACE RENDEZVOUS 15th. DECEMBER 1965** in English and Arabic.
92 **17** 1 n.p. brown and blue 15 10
93 – 2 n.p. brown and blue 15 10
94 – 3 n.p. violet and green 15 10
95 – 4 n.p. blue and brown 15 10
96 **17** 5 n.p. brown and violet 15 10
97 – 40 n.p. black and red 90 25
98 – 50 n.p. brown and green 90 30
99 – 1 r. red and green 1·90 55

21 Shaikh Ahmed

1966. Gold and Silver Coinage. Circular designs embossed on gold (G) or silver (S) foil, backed with "Walsall Security Paper" inscr in English and Arabic. Imperf. (a) Diameter 42 mm.
101 **21** 1 n.p. bistre and purple (S) 15 15
102 – 3 n.p. black and orange (S) 15 15
103 **21** 4 n.p. violet and red (G) 15 15
104 – 5 n.p. green and mauve (G) 15 15

(b) Diameter 55 mm.
105 **21** 10 n.p. brown & violet (S) 25 15
106 – 40 n.p. red and blue (S) 50 25
107 **21** 70 n.p. blue & ultram (G) 85 45
108 – 80 n.p. mauve and green (G) 85 45

(c) Diameter 64 mm.
109 **21** 1 r. mauve and black (S) 1·50 60
110 – 2 r. green and purple (S) 3·00 1·40
111 **21** 5 r. purple and orange (G) 7·00 3·00
112 – 10 r. blue and red (G) 14·00 6·00

The 1, 4, 10, 70 n.p. and 1 and 5 r. each show the obverse side of the coins as Type **21**. The remainder show the reverse side of the coins (Shaikh's seal).

22 I.C.Y. and U.N. Emblem

1966. International Co-operation Year
113 **22** 40 n.p. brn, violet & blue 1·10 65
114 A 40 n.p. violet, brn & turq 1·10 65
115 B 40 n.p. blue, brn & violet 1·10 65
116 C 40 n.p. turq, violet & bl 1·10 65
DESIGNS: A, Pres. Kennedy, I.C.Y. emblem and U.N. Headquarters; B, Dag Hammarskjold and U.N. General Assembly; C, Nehru and dove.
Nos. 113/16 were issued together in blocks of four, each sheet containing four blocks separated by gutter margins. Subsequently the sheets were reissued perf and imperf with the opt **U.N. 20TH ANNIVERSARY** on the stamps. The gutter margins were also printed in various designs, face values and overprints.

23 Pres. Kennedy and New York Skyline

1966. Pres. Kennedy Commem. Multicoloured.
118 10 n.p. Type **23** 20 15
119 30 n.p. Pres. Kennedy and Cape Kennedy 40 20
120 60 n.p. Pres. Kennedy and Statue of Liberty 65 40
121 70 n.p. Type **23** 70 55
122 80 n.p. As 30 n.p. 80 55
123 1 r. As 60 n.p. 1·50 95

24 Horse-jumping

1966. Olympic Games Preparation (Mexico). Multicoloured.
125 1 n.p. Type **24** 15 15
126 4 n.p. Running 15 15
127 5 n.p. Throwing the javelin 15 15
128 70 n.p. Type **24** 85 45
129 80 n.p. Running 85 50
130 90 n.p. Throwing the javelin 90 70

25 J. A. Lovell and Capsule

1966. American Astronauts. Each design showing spacecraft and astronaut. Multicoloured.
132 5 n.p. Type **25** 15 15
133 10 n.p. T. P. Stafford 15 15
134 15 n.p. A. B. Shepard 15 15
135 20 n.p. J. H. Glenn 15 15
136 30 n.p. M. Scott Carpenter 30 20
137 40 n.p. W. M. Schirra 30 20
138 50 n.p. V. I. Grissom 45 35
139 60 n.p. L. G. Cooper 65 45
Nos. 132/4 are diamond-shaped as Type **25**, the remainder are horiz designs (56 × 25 mm).

1966. Various stamps with currency names changed to dirhams and riyals by overprinting in English and Arabic.

(i) Nos. 27/37 (Definitives).
141 **8** 5 d. on 5 n.p. red 25 10
142 15 d. on 15 n.p. black 35 10
143 20 d. on 20 n.p. purple 35 15
144 30 d. on 30 n.p. green 65 25
145 **9** 40 d. on 40 n.p. red 1·50 30
146 50 d. on 50 n.p. brown 1·90 40
147 – 75 d. on 75 n.p. blue 2·25 55
148 **11** 1 r. on 1 r. red 2·50 50
149 2 r. on 2 r. blue 5·50 2·25
150 – 5 r. on 5 r. green 12·50 7·00
151 – 10 r. on 10 r. black 21·00 10·00

(ii) Nos. 70/86 (Fish). Multicoloured.
152 1 d. on 1 n.p. 10 10
153 2 d. on 2 n.p. 10 10
154 3 d. on 3 n.p. 10 10
155 4 d. on 4 n.p. 10 10
156 5 d. on 5 n.p. 10 10
157 15 d. on 15 n.p. 30 10
158 20 d. on 20 n.p. 40 10
159 30 d. on 30 n.p. 50 15
160 40 d. on 40 n.p. 75 20
161 50 d. on 50 n.p. 95 30
162 75 d. on 75 n.p. 1·75 55
163 1 r. on 1 r. 2·00 70
164 2 r. on 2 r. 4·00 1·90
165 3 r. on 3 r. 6·50 3·25
166 4 r. on 4 r. 9·00 4·75
167 5 r. on 5 r. 11·00 5·50
168 10 r. on 10 r. 20·00 11·00

27 National Library, Doha

1966. Education Day. Multicoloured.
169 2 n.p. Type **27** 10 10
170 3 n.p. School and playing field 15 10
171 5 n.p. School and gardens 15 10
172 1 r. Type **27** 2·75 90
173 2 r. As 3 n.p 4·25 2·00
174 3 r. As 5 n.p 6·00 2·75

28 Palace, Doha 29 Hands holding Jules Rimet Trophy

1966. Currency expressed in naye paise and rupees. Multicoloured.
175 2 n.p. Type **28** 10 10
176 3 n.p. Gulf Street, Shahra Al-Khalij 10 10
177 10 n.p. Doha airport 30 10
178 15 n.p. Garden, Rayan 20 10
179 20 n.p. Head Post Office, Doha 25 10
180 30 n.p. Mosque Doha (vert) 40 15
181 40 n.p. Shaikh Ahmad 80 20
182 50 n.p. Type **28** 90 35
183 60 n.p. As 3 n p. 1·40 50
184 70 n.p. As 10 n p. 2·00 75
185 80 n.p. As 15 n p. 1·90 85
186 90 n.p. As 20 n p. 2·25 1·40
187 1 r. As 30 n.p. (vert) 2·40 1·50
188 2 r. As 40 n.p. 5·00 3·75

1966. World Cup Football Championship, England.
189 **29** 60 n.p. mult (postage) 85 65
190 – 70 n.p. multicoloured 1·00 80
191 – 80 n.p. multicoloured 1·40 1·00
192 – 90 n.p. multicoloured 1·50 1·10
193 – 1 n.p. blue (air) 15 15
194 – 2 n.p. blue 15 15
195 – 3 n.p. blue 25 25
196 – 4 n.p. blue 30 30
DESIGNS: No. 190, Jules Rimet Trophy and "football" globe; No. 191, Footballers and globe; No. 192, Wembley stadium; Nos. 193/6, Jules Rimet Trophy.

30 A.P.U. Emblem 32 Traffic Lights

31 Astronauts on Moon

1967. Admission of Qatar to Arab Postal Union.
198 **30** 70 d. brown and violet 1·10 60
199 80 d. brown and blue 1·40 85

1967. U.S. "Apollo" Space Missions. Mult.
200 5 d. Type **31** 10 10
201 10 d. "Apollo" spacecraft 10 10
202 20 d. Landing module on Moon 15 10
203 30 d. Blast-off from Moon 25 15
204 40 d. "Saturn 5" rocket 35 20
205 70 d. Type **31** 75 45
206 80 d. As 10 d. 85 60
207 1 r. As 20 d. 90 80
208 1 r. 20 As 30 d. 1·50 1·25
209 2 r. As 40 d. 2·10 1·75

1967. Traffic Day.
211 **32** 20 d. multicoloured 35 15
212 30 d. multicoloured 70 30
213 50 d. multicoloured 1·10 50
214 1 r. multicoloured 3·00 1·75

33 Brownsea Island and Jamboree Camp, Idaho

1967. Diamond Jubilee of Scout Movement and World Scout Jamboree, Idaho. Multicoloured.
215 1 d. Type **33** 15 10
216 2 d. Lord Baden-Powell 15 10
217 3 d. Pony-trekking 15 10
218 5 d. Canoeing 20 10
219 15 d. Swimming 60 25
220 75 d. Rock-climbing 1·50 85
221 2 r. World Jamboree emblem 4·75 2·40

34 Norman Ship (from Bayeux Tapestry)

1967. Famous Navigators' Ships. Multicoloured.
222 1 d. Type **34** 15 10
223 2 d. "Santa Maria" (Columbus) 20 10
224 3 d. "Sao Gabriel" (Vasco da Gama) 20 10
225 75 d. "Vitoria" (Magellan) 1·60 1·25
226 1 r. "Golden Hind" (Drake) 2·50 1·25
227 2 r. "Gipsy Moth IV" (Chichester) 5·25 2·10

35 Arab Scribe

1968. 10th Anniv of Qatar Postage Stamps. Multicoloured.
228 1 d. Type **35** 15 10
229 2 d. Pigeon post (vert) 15 10
230 3 d. Mounted postman 15 10
231 60 d. Rowing boat postman (vert) 1·25 85
232 1 r. 25 Camel postman 2·25 1·50
233 2 r. Letter-writing and Qatar 1 n.p. stamp of 1957 3·75 2·75

36 Human Rights Emblem and Barbed Wire

1968. Human Rights Year. Multicoloured designs embodying Human Rights emblem.
234 1 d. Type **36** 15 10
235 2 d. Arab refugees 15 10
236 3 d. Scales of justice 15 10
237 60 d. Opening doors 85 50
238 1 r. 25 Family (vert) 1·40 1·25
239 2 r. Human figures 2·40 1·75

37 Shaikh Ahmad 39

38 Dhow

1968.
240 **37** 5 d. green and blue 15 10
241 10 d. brown and blue 15 10
242 20 d. red and black 30 10
243 25 d. green and purple 50 15
244 **38** 35 d. green, blue and pink 1·00 20
245 – 40 d. purple, blue & orange 1·00 20
246 – 60 d. brown, blue & violet 2·25 45

247 – 70 d. black, blue and green 1·60 55
248 – 1 r. blue, yellow and green 1·90 60
249 – 1 r. 25 blue, pink and light blue 3·50 75
250 – 1 r. 50 green, blue & purple 5·50 1·00
251 39 2 r. blue, brown & cinnamon 5·25 1·25
252 5 r. purple, green and light green 11·00 4·50
253 10 r. brown, ultram & blue 22·00 7·50

DESIGNS—As Type **38**: 40 d. Water purification plant; 60 d. Oil jetty; 70 d. Qatar mosque; 1 r. Palace Doha; 1 r. 25, Doha fort; 1 r. 50, Peregrine falcon.

41 Maternity Ward

1968. 20th Anniv of W.H.O. Multicoloured.

258 1 d. Type **41** 15 10
259 2 d. Operating theatre 15 10
260 3 d. Dental surgery 15 10
261 60 d. X-ray examination table 90 50
262 1 r. 25 Laboratory 2·50 1·50
263 2 r. State Hospital Qatar 3·25 4·00

42 Throwing the Discus

1968. Olympic Games, Mexico. Multicoloured.

264 1 d. Type **42** 15 10
265 2 d. Olympic Flame and runner 15 10
266 3 d. "68", Rings and gymnast 15 10
267 60 d. Weightlifting and Flame 1·25 65
268 1 r. 25 "Flame" in mosaic pattern (vert) 2·40 1·00
269 2 r. "Cock" emblem 3·50 1·60

43 U.N. Emblem and Flags

1968. United Nations Day. Multicoloured.

270 1 d. Type **43** 15 10
271 4 d. Dove of Peace and world map 15 10
272 5 d. U. N. Headquarters and flags 15 10
273 60 d. Teacher and class 1·25 65
274 1 r. 50 Agricultural workers 2·40 1·00
275 2 r. U. Thant and U.N. Assembly 3·50 1·60

44 Trawler "Ross Rayyan"

1969. Progress in Qatar. Multicoloured.

276 1 d. Type **44** 10 10
277 4 d. Primary school 10 10
278 5 d. Doha International Airport 10 10
279 60 d. Cement factory and road-making 1·40 50
280 1 r. 50 Power station and pylon 2·75 1·25
281 2 r. Housing estate 3·75 1·90

45 Armoured Cars

1969. Qatar Security Forces. Multicoloured.

282 1 d. Type **45** 10 10
283 2 d. Traffic control 10 10
284 3 d. Military helicopter 10 10
285 60 d. Section of military band 1·50 70
286 1 r. 25 Field gun 2·75 1·50
287 2 r. Mounted police 4·25 2·10

46 Tanker "Sivella" at Mooring

1969. Qatar's Oil Industry. Multicoloured.

288 1 d. Type **46** 10 10
289 2 d. Training school 10 10
290 3 d. "Sea Shell" (oil rig) and "Shell Dolphin" (supply vessel) 10 10
291 60 d. Storage tanks, Halul 1·50 85
292 1 r. 50 Topping plant 3·50 1·90
293 2 r. Various tankers, 1890-1968 6·00 2·50

47 "Guest-house" and Dhow-building

1969. 10th Scout Jamboree, Qatar. Multicoloured.

294 1 d. Type **47** 10 10
295 2 d. Scouts at work 10 10
296 3 d. Review and March Past 10 10
297 60 d. Interior gateway 1·50 70
298 1 r. 25 Camp entrance 2·75 1·50
299 2 r. Hoisting flag, and Shaikh Ahmad 4·00 2·10

48 Neil Armstrong

1969. 1st Man on the Moon. Multicoloured.

301 1 d. Type **48** 10 10
302 2 d. Edward Aldrin 10 10
303 3 d. Michael Collins 10 10
304 60 d. Astronaut on Moon 90 45
305 1 r. 25 Take-off from Moon 1·75 1·00
306 2 r. Splashdown (horiz) 3·75 2·00

49 Douglas DC-8 and Mail Van

1970. Admission to U.P.U. Multicoloured.

307 1 d. Type **49** 10 10
308 2 d. Liner "Oriental Empress" 10 10
309 3 d. Loading mail-van 10 10
310 60 d. G.P.O., Doha 1·00 65
311 1 r. 25 U.P.U. Building, Berne 2·40 1·50
312 2 r. U.P.U. Monument, Berne 3·00 1·60

50 League Emblem, Flag and Map

1970. Silver Jubilee of Arab League.

313 50 35 d. multicoloured 45 25
314 60 d. multicoloured 70 45
315 1 r. 25 multicoloured 1·75 85
316 1 r. 50 multicoloured 2·25 1·40

51 Vickers VC-10 on Runway

1970. 1st Gulf Aviation Vickers VC-10 Flight, Doha–London. Multicoloured.

317 1 d. Type **51** 10 10
318 2 d. Peregrine falcon and VC-10 85 10
319 3 d. Tail view of VC-10 15 10
320 60 d. Gulf Aviation emblem on map 1·00 85
321 1 r. 25 VC-10 over Doha 3·50 1·60
322 2 r. Tail assembly of VC-10 4·50 2·25

52 "Space Achievements"

1970. International Education Year.

323 52 35 d. multicoloured 65 25
324 60 d. multicoloured 1·40 50

53 Freesias **55** Globe, "25" and U.N. Emblem

54 Toyahama Fishermen with Giant "Fish"

1970. Qatar Flowers. Multicoloured.

325 1 d. Type **53** 10 10
326 2 d. Azalieas 10 10
327 3 d. Ixias 10 10
328 60 d. Amaryllises 1·00 50
329 1 r. 25 Cinerarias 2·25 1·10
330 2 r. Roses 3·00 1·50

1970. "EXPO 70" World Fair, Osaka. Multicoloured.

331 1 d. Type **54** 10 10
332 2 d. Expo emblem and map of Japan 10 10
333 3 d. Fisherman on Shikoku beach 15 10
334 60 d. Expo emblem and Mt. Fuji 1·40 60
335 1 r. 50 Gateway to Shinto Shrine 2·00 1·00
336 2 r. Expo Tower and Mt. Fuji 3·25 2·75

Nos. 333, 334 and 336 are vert.

1970. 25th Anniv of U.N.O. Multicoloured.

337 1 d. Type **55** 10 10
338 2 d. Flowers in gun-barrel 10 10
339 3 d. Anniversary cake 10 10
340 35 d. "The U.N. Agencies" 1·25 45
341 1 r. 50 "Trumpet fanfare" 2·25 1·00
342 2 r. "World friendship" 3·50 2·00

56 Al Jahiz (philosopher) and Ancient Globe

1971. Famous Men of Islam. Multicoloured.

343 1 d. Type **56** 10 10
344 2 d. Saladin (soldier), palace and weapons 10 10
345 3 d. Al Farabi (philosopher and musician), felucca and instruments 10 10
346 35 d. Ibn Al Haithum (scientist), palace and emblems 75 40
347 1 r. 50 Al Motanabbi (poet), symbols and desert 3·25 2·00
348 2 r. Ibn Sina (Avicenna) (physician and philosopher), medical instruments and ancient globe 4·50 2·40

57 Common Cormorant and Water Plants

1971. Qatar Fauna and Flora. Multicoloured.

349 1 d. Type **57** 40 10
350 2 d. Lizard and prickly pear 20 10
351 3 d. Greater flamingos and palms 40 10
352 60 d. Arabian oryx and yucca 1·40 80
353 1 r. 25 Mountain gazelle and desert dandelion 3·50 1·75
354 2 r. Dromedary, palm and bronzed chenopod 4·75 2·50

58 Satellite Earth Station, Goonhilly

1971. World Telecommunications Day. Mult.

355 1 d. Type **58** 10 10
356 2 d. Cable ship "Ariel" 10 10
357 3 d. Post Office Tower and T.V. control-room 10 10
358 4 d. Modern telephones 10 10
359 5 d. Video-phone equipment 10 10
360 35 d. As 3 d. 65 35
361 75 d. As 5 d. 1·00 85
362 3 r. Telex machine 5·75 3·25

59 Arab Child reading Book **60** A.P.U. Emblem

1971. 10th Anniv of Education Day.

363 59 35 d. multicoloured 40 20
364 55 d. multicoloured 80 40
365 75 d. multicoloured 1·25 65

1971. 25th Anniv of Arab Postal Union.

366 60 35 d. multicoloured 50 20
367 55 d. multicoloured 75 45
368 75 d. multicoloured 1·10 65
369 1 r. 25 multicoloured 1·75 1·40

61 "Hammering Racism"

1971. Racial Equality Year. Multicoloured.

370 1 d. Type **61** 10 10
371 2 d. "Pushing back racism" 10 10
372 3 d. War-wounded 10 10
373 4 d. Working together (vert) 10 10
374 5 d. Playing together (vert) 10 10
375 35 d. Racial "tidal-wave" 60 30
376 75 d. Type **61** 1·60 95
377 3 r. As 2 d. 4·50 3·25

62 Nurse and Child

1971. 25th Anniv of U.N.I.C.E.F. Multicoloured.

378 1 d. Mother and child (vert) 10 10
379 2 d. Child's face 10 10
380 3 d. Child with book (vert) 10 10
381 4 d. Type **62** 10 10
382 5 d. Mother and baby 10 10
383 35 d. Child with daffodil (vert) 60 30
384 75 d. As 3 d. 1·60 95
385 3 r. As 1 d. 4·50 3·25

63 Shaikh Ahmad, and Flags of Arab League and Qatar

1971. Independence.

386 63 35 d. multicoloured 40 15
387 – 75 d. multicoloured 95 55
388 – 1 r. 25 black, pink & brown 1·50 90
389 – 3 r. multicoloured 4·25 2·75

DESIGNS—HORIZ: 75 d. As Type **63**, but with U.N. flag in place of Arab League flag. VERT: 1 r. 25, Shaikh Ahmad; 3 r. Handclasp.

64 Common Roller **66** Shaikh Khalifa bin Hamad al-Thani

1972. Birds. Multicoloured.

No.	Description	Mint	Used
391	1 d. Type **64**	10	10
392	2 d. Common kingfisher	10	10
393	3 d. Rock thrush	10	10
394	4 d. Caspian tern	15	10
395	5 d. Hoopoe	15	10
396	35 d. European bee eater	1·00	35
397	75 d. Golden oriole	2·75	1·25
398	3 r. Peregrine falcon	9·00	5·00

1972. Nos. 328/30 surch with value in English and Arabic.

No.	Description	Mint	Used
399	10 d. on 60 d. multicoloured	1·00	15
400	1 r. on 1 r. 25 multicoloured	4·25	85
401	5 r. on 2 r. multicoloured	8·50	4·00

1972.

No.	Type	Description	Mint	Used
402	**66**	5 d. blue and violet	15	10
403		10 d. red and brown	15	10
404		35 d. green and orange	55	15
405		55 d. mauve and green	95	35
406		75 d. mauve and blue	1·50	50
407	–	1 r. black and brown	1·75	50
408	–	1 r. 25 black and green	2·75	70
409	–	5 r. black and blue	10·00	3·50
410	–	10 r. black and red	17·00	6·00

The rupee values are larger, 27 × 32 mm.

For similar design but with Shaikh's head turned slightly to right, see Nos. 444a/b.

67 Book Year Emblem

1972. International Book Year.

No.	Type	Description	Mint	Used
411	**67**	35 d. black and blue	50	30
412		55 d. black and brown	75	45
413		75 d. black and green	1·10	75
414		1 r. 25 black and lilac	2·00	1·25

68 Football

1972. Olympic Games, Munich. Designs depicting sportsmen's hands or feet. Multicoloured.

No.	Description	Mint	Used
415	1 d. Type **68**	10	10
416	2 d. Running (foot on starting block)	10	10
417	3 d. Cycling (hand)	10	10
418	4 d. Gymnastics (hand)	10	10
419	5 d. Basketball (hand)	15	10
420	35 d. Discus (hand)	55	30
421	75 d. Type **68**	1·40	90
422	3 r. As 2 d.	4·50	3·25

69 Underwater Pipeline Construction

1972. "Oil from the Sea". Multicoloured.

No.	Description	Mint	Used
424	1 d. Drilling (vert)	10	10
425	4 d. Type **69**	10	10
426	5 d. Offshore rig "Sea Shell"	10	10
427	35 d. Underwater "prospecting" for oil	80	35
428	75 d. As 1 d.	1·75	85
429	3 r. As 5 d.	7·50	3·75

70 Administrative Building

1972. Independence Day. Multicoloured.

No.	Description	Mint	Used
430	10 d. Type **70**	25	10
431	35 d. Handclasp and Arab League flag	65	30
432	75 d. Handclasp and U.N. flag	1·10	70
433	1 r. 25 Shaikh Khalifa	2·00	1·25

71 Dish Aerial, Satellite and Telephone (I.T.U.)

1972. United Nations Day. Multicoloured.

No.	Description	Mint	Used
435	1 d. Type **71**	10	10
436	2 d. Archaeological team (U.N.E.S.C.O.)	10	10
437	3 d. Tractor, produce and helicopter (F.A.O.)	10	10
438	4 d. Children with books (U.N.I.C.E.F.)	10	10
439	5 d. Weather satellite (W.M.O.)	10	10
440	25 d. Construction workers (I.L.O.)	70	30
441	55 d. Child care (W.H.O.)	1·75	65
442	1 r. Airliner and van (U.P.U.)	3·25	1·10

72 Emblem and Flags **72a** Shaikh Khalifa

1972. 10th Session of Arab States Civil Aviation Council, Qatar.

No.	Type	Description	Mint	Used
443	**72**	25 d. multicoloured	70	35
444		30 d. multicoloured	95	50

1972.

No.	Type	Description	Mint	Used
444a	**72a**	10 d. red and brown	25·00	25·00
444b		25 d. green and purple	25·00	25·00

73 Shaikh Khalifa **74** Clock Tower, Doha

1973.

No.	Type	Description	Mint	Used
445	**73**	5 d. multicoloured	15	10
446		10 d. multicoloured	15	10
447		20 d. multicoloured	35	10
448		25 d. multicoloured	35	10
449		35 d. multicoloured	60	15
450		55 d. multicoloured	1·00	35
451	**74**	75 d. purple, green and blue	2·25	65
452	**73**	1 r. multicoloured	2·25	55
453		5 r. multicoloured	8·25	2·40
454		10 r. multicoloured	16·00	5·75

Nos. 452/4 are larger, 27 × 32 mm.

75 Housing Development

1973. 1st Anniv of Shaikh Khalifa's Accession. Multicoloured.

No.	Description	Mint	Used
455	2 d. Road construction	10	10
456	3 d. Type **75**	10	10
457	4 d. Hospital operating theatre	10	10
458	5 d. Telephone exchange	10	10
459	15 d. School classroom	25	10
460	20 d. Television studio	30	10
461	35 d. Shaikh Khalifa	50	15
462	55 d. Gulf Hotel, Doha	95	45
463	1 r. Industrial plant	1·75	80
464	1 r. 35 Flour mills	2·25	1·40

76 Aerial Crop-spraying

1973. 25th Anniv of W.H.O. Multicoloured.

No.	Description	Mint	Used
465	2 d. Type **76**	10	10
466	3 d. Drugs and syringe	10	10
467	4 d. Woman in wheelchair (Prevention of polio)	10	10
468	5 d. Mosquito (Malaria control)	10	10
469	55 d. Mental patient (Mental Health Research)	1·60	80
470	1 r. Dead trees (Anti-pollution)	3·00	1·60

77 Weather Ship

1973. Centenary of World Meteorological Organization. Multicoloured.

No.	Description	Mint	Used
471	2 d. Type **77**	10	10
472	3 d. Launching radio-sonde balloon	10	10
473	4 d. Hawker Siddeley H.S.125 weather plane	10	10
474	5 d. Meteorological station	10	10
475	10 d. Met airplane taking-off	20	10
476	1 r. "Nimbus 1"	2·00	95
477	1 r. 55 Rocket on launch-pad	3·50	1·75

78 Handclasp

1973. Independence Day. Multicoloured.

No.	Description	Mint	Used
478	15 d. Type **78**	10	10
479	35 d. Agriculture	20	10
480	55 d. Government building	60	30
481	1 r. 35 View of Doha	1·50	70
482	1 r. 55 Illuminated fountain	1·75	1·10

79 Child planting Sapling (U.N.E.S.C.O.)

1973. United Nations Day. Multicoloured.

No.	Description	Mint	Used
483	2 d. Type **79**	10	10
484	4 d. U.N. Headquarters, New York, and flags	10	10
485	5 d. Building construction (I.L.O.)	10	10
486	35 d. Nurses in dispensary (W.H.O.)	35	10
487	1 r. 35 Radar control (I.T.U.)	1·75	95
488	3 r. Inspection of wheat and cattle (F.A.O.)	4·00	2·50

80 "Open Gates"

1973. 25th Anniv of Declaration of Human Rights. Multicoloured.

No.	Description	Mint	Used
489	2 d. Type **80**	10	10
490	4 d. Freedom marchers	10	10
491	5 d. "Equality of Man"	10	10
492	35 d. Primary education	35	15
493	1 r. 35 General Assembly, U.N.	1·75	70
494	3 r. Flame emblem (vert)	4·00	2·25

81 New Flyover, Doha

1974. 2nd Anniv of Shaikh Khalifa's Accession. Mult.

No.	Description	Mint	Used
495	2 d. Type **81**	10	10
496	3 d. Education symbol	10	10
497	5 d. Gas plant	10	10
498	35 d. Gulf Hotel, Doha	40	20
499	1 r. 55 Space communications station	2·00	95
500	2 r. 25 Shaikh Khalifa	3·00	1·75

82 Camel Caravan and Articulated Mail Van

1974. Centenary of U.P.U. Multicoloured.

No.	Description	Mint	Used
501	2 d. Type **82**	10	10
502	3 d. Early mail wagon and modern express train	10	10
503	10 d. "Hindoostan" (paddle-steamer) and "Iberia" (liner)	40	20
504	35 d. Early (Handley Page H.P.42) and modern (Vickers VC-10) mail planes	55	35
505	75 d. Manual and mechanised mail-sorting	1·10	70
506	1 r. 25 Early and modern P.O. sales counters	1·75	1·25

83 Doha Hospital

1974. World Population Year. Multicoloured.

No.	Description	Mint	Used
507	5 d. Type **83**	10	10
508	10 d. W.P.Y. emblem	15	10
509	15 d. Emblem within wreath	15	10
510	35 d. World population map	40	20
511	1 r. 75 New-born infants and clock ("a birth every minute")	2·00	90
512	2 r. 25 "Ideal Family" group	2·50	1·50

84 Television Station

1974. Independence Day. Multicoloured.

No.	Description	Mint	Used
513	5 d. Type **84**	10	10
514	10 d. Doha palace	15	10
515	15 d. Teachers' College	20	10
516	75 d. Clock tower and Mosque	85	40
517	1 r. 55 Roundabout and surroundings	1·75	1·00
518	2 r. 25 Shaikh Khalifa	2·50	1·50

85 Operating Theatre (W.H.O.)

1974. United Nations Day.

No.	Type	Description	Mint	Used
519	**85**	5 d. orange, purple & black	10	10
520	–	10 d. orange, red & black	15	10
521	–	20 d. blue, green & black	25	10
522	–	25 d. blue, brown & black	35	15
523	–	1 r. 75 blue, mauve & black	1·90	1·25
524	–	2 r. blue, orange & black	2·75	1·60

DESIGNS: 10 d. Satellite earth station (I.T.U.); 20 d. Tractor (F.A.O.); 25 d. Classroom (U.N.E.S.C.O.); 1 r. 75, African open-air court (Human Rights); 2 r. U.P.U. and U.N. emblems (U.P.U.).

86 Vickers VC-10 Airliner

1974. Arab Civil Aviation Day.

525 86 20 d. multicoloured 60 20
526 – 25 d. blue, green & yellow . 70 30
527 – 30 d. multicoloured . . . . 1·10 40
528 – 50 d. red, green & purple . 2·50 90

DESIGNS: 25 d. Doha airport; 30, 50 d. Flags of Qatar and the Arab League.

87 Clock Tower, Doha

1974. Tourism. Multicoloured.

529 5 d. Type 87 . . . . 20 10
530 10 d. White-cheeked terns, hoopoes and Shara'o Island (horiz) . . . . 1·60 20
531 15 d. Fort Zubara (horiz) . . 30 10
532 35 d. Yachts and Gulf Hotel (horiz) 50 20
533 55 d. Qatar by night (horiz) 85 35
534 75 d. Arabian oryx (horiz) . . 1·60 50
535 1 r. 25 Khor-al-Udeid (horiz) 1·90 95
536 1 r. 75 Ruins Wakrah (horiz) 2·10 1·50

88 Traffic Roundabout, Doha

1975. 3rd Anniv of Shaikh Khalifa's Accession. Multicoloured.

537 10 d. Type 88 . . . . 20 10
538 35 d. Oil pipelines 60 20
539 55 d. Laying offshore pipelines 90 35
540 1 r. Oil refinery . . . . 1·60 65
541 1 r. 35 Shaikh Khalifa (vert) . 2·40 1·10
542 1 r. 55 As 1 r. 35 . . . . . . 3·00 1·60

89 Flintlock Pistol

1975. Opening of National Museum. Multicoloured.

543 2 d. Type 89 . . . . 10 10
544 3 d. Arabesque-pattern mosaic 10 10
545 35 d. Museum buildings . . . 65 35
546 75 d. Museum archway (vert) 1·50 80
547 1 r. 25 Flint tools . . . . . 2·25 1·40
548 3 r. Gold necklace and pendant (vert) . . . . 4·50 3·50

90 Policeman and Road Signs

1975. Traffic Week. Multicoloured.

549 5 d. Type 90 . . . . 35 15
550 15 d. Traffic arrows and signal lights 90 30
551 35 d. Type 90 . . . . 2·00 50
552 55 d. As 15 d. . . . . 3·50 1·40

91 Flag and Emblem

1975. 10th Anniv of Arab Labour Charter.

553 91 10 d. multicoloured . . . 25 15
554 35 d. multicoloured . . . 1·00 40
555 1 r. multicoloured . . . . 2·75 2·00

92 Government Building, Doha

1975. 4th Anniv of Independence. Multicoloured.

556 5 d. Type 92 . . . . 10 10
557 15 d. Museum and clock tower, Doha 30 10
558 35 d. Constitution – Arabic text (vert) 55 15
559 55 d. Ruler and flag (vert) . . 80 40
560 75 d. Constitution – English text (vert) . . . . 1·10 70
561 1 r. 25 As 55 d. . . . . 2·25 1·25

93 Telecommunications Satellite (I.T.U.)

1975. 30th Anniv of U.N.O. Multicoloured.

562 5 d. Type 93 . . . . 10 10
563 15 d. U.N. Headquarters, New York 15 10
564 35 d. U.P.U. emblem and map 40 15
565 1 r. Doctors tending child (U.N.I.C.E.F.) . . . . . . 1·00 55
566 1 r. 25 Bulldozer (I.L.O.) . . 1·60 90
567 2 r. Students in class (U.N.E.S.C.O.) . . . . . . 2·75 1·50

94 Fertilizer Plant

1975. Qatar Industry. Multicoloured.

568 5 d. Type 94 . . . . 15 10
569 10 d. Flour mills (vert) . . . 25 10
570 35 d. Natural gas plant . . . 50 15
571 75 d. Oil refinery . . . . . . 1·40 70
572 1 r. 25 Cement works . . . . 2·00 1·25
573 1 r. 55 Steel mills . . . . . . 2·50 1·50

95 Modern Building, Doha

1976. 4th Anniv of Shaikh Khalifa's Accession.

574 95 5 d. multicoloured 10 10
575 – 10 d. multicoloured . . . 10 10
576 – 35 d. multicoloured . . . 40 10
577 – 55 d. multicoloured . . . 70 30
578 – 75 d. multicoloured . . . 90 50
579 – 1 r. 55 multicoloured . . . 2·75 1·90

DESIGNS: Nos. 575/6 and 579 show public buildings; Nos. 577/8 show Shaikh Khalifa with flag.

96 Tracking Aerial 97 Early and Modern Telephones

1976. Opening of Satellite Earth Station. Mult.

580 35 d. Type 96 . . . . 65 15
581 55 d. "Intelsat" satellite . . . 90 35
582 75 d. Type 96 . . . . 1·50 70
583 1 r. As 55 d. . . . . 1·90 90

1976. Telephone Centenary.

584 97 1 r. multicoloured . . . . 1·40 80
585 1 r. 35 multicoloured . . . 1·90 1·00

98 Tournament Emblem 100 Football

99 Qatar Dhow

1976. 4th Arabian Gulf Football Cup Tournament. Multicoloured.

586 5 d. Type 98 . . . . 10 10
587 10 d. Qatar Stadium 15 10
588 35 d. Type 98 . . . . 75 15
589 55 d. Two players with ball . . 1·25 35
590 75 d. Player with ball . . . . 1·75 60
591 1 r. 25 As 10 d. . . . . 3·25 1·40

1976. Dhows.

592 99 10 d. multicoloured 25 10
593 – 35 d. multicoloured 70 15
594 – 80 d. multicoloured . . . . 1·60 40
595 – 1 r. 25 multicoloured . . . 2·50 1·40
596 – 1 r. 50 multicoloured . . . 3·25 1·75
597 – 2 r. multicoloured . . . . . 4·75 2·25

DESIGNS: 35 d. to 2 r. Various craft.

1976. Olympic Games, Montreal, Multicoloured.

598 5 d. Type 100 . . . . 10 10
599 10 d. Yachting 25 10
600 35 d. Show jumping 55 15
601 80 d. Boxing . . . . 1·40 50
602 1 r. 25 Weightlifting . . . . 2·25 1·25
603 1 r. 50 Basketball . . . . . . 2·50 2·10

101 Urban Housing Development

1976. United Nations Conference on Human Settlements. Multicoloured.

604 10 d. Type 101 . . . . 10 10
605 35 d. U.N. and conference emblems 40 15
606 80 d. Communal housing development . . . . 1·10 50
607 1 r. 25 Shaikh Khalifa . . . . 2·25 1·25

102 Kentish Plover

1976. Birds. Multicoloured.

608 5 d. Type 102 . . . . 35 10
609 10 d. Common cormorant . . 35 10
610 35 d. Osprey . . . . 1·60 30
611 80 d. Greater flamingo (vert) . 3·25 70
612 1 r. 25 Rock thrush (vert) . . 4·50 1·50
613 2 r. Saker falcon (vert) . . . . 6·50 2·00

103 Shaikh Khalifa and Flag 105 Shaikh Khalifa

104 U.N. Emblem

1976. 5th Anniv of Independence. Multicoloured.

614 5 d. Type 103 . . . . 10 10
615 10 d. Type 103 . . . . 20 10
616 40 d. Doha buildings (horiz) . 35 15
617 80 d. As 40 d 70 30
618 1 r. 25 "Dana" (oil rig) (horiz) 2·00 1·10
619 1 r. 50 United Nations and Qatar emblems (horiz) . . . 2·10 1·50

1976. United Nations Day.

620 104 2 r. multicoloured . . . . 3·00 1·75
621 3 r. multicoloured . . . . 3·75 2·25

1977. 5th Anniv of Amir's Accession.

622 105 20 d. multicoloured . . . 25 10
623 1 r. 80 multicoloured . . 2·75 2·10

106 Shaikh Khalifa 107 Envelope and A.P.U. Emblem

1977.

624 106 5 d. multicoloured 15 10
625 10 d. multicoloured . . . 20 10
626 35 d. multicoloured . . . 60 15
627 80 d. multicoloured . . . 1·10 35
628 1 r. multicoloured . . . . 1·40 50
629 5 r. multicoloured . . . . 6·75 3·25
630 10 r. multicoloured . . . 12·00 5·50

Nos. 628/30 are larger, size 25×31 mm.

1977. 25th Anniv of Arab Postal Union.

631 107 35 d. multicoloured . . . 35 15
632 1 r. 35 multicoloured . . 1·75 1·25

108 Shaikh Khalifa and Sound Waves

1977. International Telecommunications Day.

633 108 35 d. multicoloured . . . 35 15
634 1 r. 80 multicoloured . . 2·25 1·90

108a Shaikh Khalifa 109 Parliament Building, Doha

1977.

634a 108a 5 d. multicoloured . . . 15 15
634c 10 d. multicoloured . . 25 25
634d 35 d. multicoloured . . 60 60
634e 80 d. multicoloured . . 1·90 1·90

1977. 6th Anniv of Independence. Multicoloured.

635 80 d. Type 109 . . . . 1·10 75
636 80 d. Main business district, Doha . . . . 1·10 75
637 80 d. Motorway, Doha . . . 1·10 75

110 U.N. Emblem

1977. United Nations Day.

638	110	20 d. multicoloured	25	10
639		1 r. multicoloured	1·75	1·25

111 Steel Mill

1978. 6th Anniv of Amir's Accession. Mult.

640	20 d. Type **111**	20	10
641	80 d. Operating theatre	80	30
642	1 r. Children's classroom	1·00	50
643	5 r. Shaikh Khalifa	3·75	2·75

112 Oil Refinery

1978. 7th Anniv of Independence. Multicoloured.

644	35 d. Type **112**	30	15
645	80 d. Apartment buildings	70	30
646	1 r. 35 Town centre, Doha	1·50	1·00
647	1 r. 80 Shaikh Khalifa	2·00	1·40

113 Man reading Alphabet

1978. International Literacy Day.

648	113	35 d. multicoloured	30	15
649		80 d. multicoloured	85	60

115 "Human Rights Flame" 116 I.Y.C. Emblem

1978. 30th Anniv of Declaration of Human Rights. Multicoloured.

652	35 d. Type **115**	30	15
653	80 d. Type **115**	50	40
654	1 r. 25 Flame and scales of justice	85	70
655	1 r. 80 As 1 r. 25	1·25	90

1979. International Year of the Child.

656	116	35 d. mauve, blue & blk	30	15
657		1 r. 80 green, blue & blk	1·25	90

117 Shaikh Khalifa 118 Shaikh Khalifa and Laurel Wreath

1979.

658	117	5 d. multicoloured	10	10
659		10 d. multicoloured	10	10
660		20 d. multicoloured	25	10
661		25 d. multicoloured	25	10
662		35 d. multicoloured	45	15
663		60 d. multicoloured	80	15
664		80 d. multicoloured	1·00	20
665		1 r. multicoloured	1·10	20
666		1 r. 25 multicoloured	1·40	30
667		1 r. 35 multicoloured	1·60	40
668		1 r. 80 multicoloured	2·00	55
669		5 r. multicoloured	5·00	1·90
670		10 r. multicoloured	8·50	2·75

Nos. 665/70 are larger, size 27 × 32½ mm.

1979. 7th Anniv of Amir's Accession.

671	118	35 d. multicoloured	25	10
672		80 d. multicoloured	50	25
673		1 r. multicoloured	65	35
674		1 r. 25 multicoloured	90	75

119 Wave Pattern and Television Screen

1979. World Telecommunications Day.

675	119	2 r. multicoloured	1·25	90
676		2 r. 80 multicoloured	1·50	1·25

120 Two Children supporting Globe

1979. 50th Anniv of Int Bureau of Education.

677	120	35 d. multicoloured	35	15
678		80 d. multicoloured	75	35

121 Rolling Mill 122 U.N. Emblem and Flag of Qatar

1979. 8th Anniv of Independence. Multicoloured.

679	5 d. Type **121**	10	10
680	10 d. Aerial view of Doha	10	10
681	1 r. 25 Qatar flag	85	60
682	2 r. Shaikh Khalifa	1·40	1·10

1979. United Nations Day.

683	122	1 r. 25 multicoloured	1·25	65
684		2 r. multicoloured	2·25	1·60

123 Mosque Minaret and Crescent Moon

1979. Third World Conference on the Prophet's Seera and Sunna.

685	123	35 d. multicoloured	40	15
686		1 r. 80 multicoloured	2·10	1·60

124 Shaikh Khalifa

1980. 8th Anniv of Amir's Accession.

687	124	20 d. multicoloured	20	10
688		60 d. multicoloured	60	25
689		1 r. 25 multicoloured	1·40	95
690		2 r. multicoloured	2·25	1·75

125 Emblem

1980. 6th Congress of Arab Towns Organization, Doha.

691	125	2 r. 35 multicoloured	2·50	1·75
692		2 r. 80 multicoloured	3·00	2·25

126 Oil Refinery

1980. 9th Anniv of Independence. Multicoloured.

693	10 d. Type **126**	15	10
694	35 d. Doha	40	15
695	2 r. Oil Rig	2·25	1·60
696	2 r. 35 Hospital	2·50	1·75

127 Figures supporting O.P.E.C. Emblem

1980. 20th Anniv of Organization of Petroleum Exporting Countries.

697	127	1 r. 35 multicoloured	90	60
698		2 r. multicoloured	1·60	90

128 U.N.Emblem 129 Mosque and Kaaba, Mecca

1980. United Nations Day.

699	128	1 r. 35 blue, light blue and purple	90	60
700		1 r. 80 turquoise, green and black	1·90	1·40

1980. 1400th Anniv of Hegira.

701	129	10 d. multicoloured	10	10
702		35 d. multicoloured	40	20
703		1 r. 25 multicoloured	90	65
704		2 r. 80 multicoloured	2·40	1·75

130 I.Y.D.P. Emblem

1981. International Year of Disabled Persons.

705	130	2 r. multicoloured	1·90	1·25
706		3 r. multicoloured	3·00	1·75

131 Student 132 Shaikh Khalifa

1981. 20th Anniv of Education Day.

707	131	2 r. multicoloured	1·90	1·10
708		3 r. multicoloured	2·75	1·60

1981. 9th Anniv of Amir's Accession.

709	132	10 d. multicoloured	10	10
710		35 d. multicoloured	45	25
711		80 d. multicoloured	75	45
712		5 r. multicoloured	3·75	2·40

133 I.T.U. and W.H.O. Emblems and Ribbons forming Caduceus 134 Torch

1981. World Telecommunications Day.

713	133	2 r. multicoloured	2·00	95
714		2 r. 80 multicoloured	2·75	1·25

1981. 30th International Military Football Championship.

715	134	1 r. 25 multicoloured	1·75	85
716		2 r. 80 multicoloured	3·50	2·25

135 Qatar Flag

1981. 10th Anniv of Independence.

717	135	5 d. multicoloured	10	10
718		60 d. multicoloured	70	30
719		80 d. multicoloured	1·00	50
720		5 r. multicoloured	5·25	3·50

136 Tractor gathering Crops

1981. World Food Day.

721	136	2 r. multicoloured	2·10	1·40
722		2 r. 80 multicoloured	3·25	1·90

137 Red Crescent

1982. Qatar Red Crescent.
723 **137** 20 d. multicoloured . . . 40 10
724 2 r. 80 multicoloured . . . 4·25 2·75

138 Shaikh Khalifa

1982. 10th Anniv of Amir's Accession.
725 **138** 10 d. multicoloured . . . 10 10
726 20 d. multicoloured . . . 25 10
727 1 r. 25 multicoloured . . . 1·40 80
728 2 r. 80 multicoloured . . . 3·25 2·00

139 Hamad General Hospital 140 Shaikh Khalifa

1982. Hamad General Hospital.
729 **139** 10 d. multicoloured . . . 10 10
730 2 r. 35 multicoloured . . . 2·50 1·90

1982.
731 **140** 5 d. multicoloured 10 10
732 10 d. multicoloured 10 10
733 15 d. multicoloured 40 10
734 20 d. multicoloured 15 10
735 25 d. multicoloured 20 15
736 35 d. multicoloured 30 15
737 60 d. multicoloured 50 15
738 80 d. multicoloured 60 15
739 – 1 r. multicoloured . . . . 1·00 20
740 – 1 r. 25 multicoloured . . . 1·00 25
741 – 2 r. multicoloured . . . . 1·40 65
742 – 5 r. multicoloured . . . . 4·00 1·60
743 – 10 r. multicoloured . . . 8·00 3·50
744 – 15 r. multicoloured . . . 9·75 4·75
DESIGNS—25 × 32 mm: 1 r. to 2 r. Oil refinery; 5 r. to 15 r. Doha clock tower.

142 Container Ship

1982. 6th Anniv of United Arab Shipping Company.
745 **142** 20 d. multicoloured . . . 40 15
746 2 r. 35 multicoloured . . . 3·25 2·25

143 A.P.U. Emblem 144 National Flag

1982. 30th Anniv of Arab Postal Union.
747 **143** 35 d. multicoloured . . . 50 15
748 2 r. 80 multicoloured . . . 3·25 2·25

1982. 11th Anniv of Independence.
749 **144** 10 d. multicoloured . . . 10 10
750 80 d. multicoloured . . . 80 30
751 1 r. 25 multicoloured . . . 1·25 75
752 2 r. 80 multicoloured . . . 3·00 1·90

145 W.C.Y. Emblem 147 Arabic Script

146 Conference Emblem

1983. World Communications Year.
753 **145** 35 d. multicoloured . . . 50 15
754 2 r. 80 multicoloured . . . 3·00 2·10

1983. 2nd Gulf Postal Organization Conference.
755 **146** 1 r. multicoloured . . . . 1·25 50
756 1 r. 35 multicoloured . . . 1·90 75

1983. 12th Anniv of Independence.
757 **147** 10 d. multicoloured . . . 10 10
758 35 d. multicoloured . . . 35 20
759 80 d. multicoloured . . . 75 40
760 2 r. 80 multicoloured . . . 2·75 2·10

148 Council Emblem

1983. 4th Session of Gulf Co-operation Council Supreme Council.
761 **148** 35 d. multicoloured . . . 40 15
762 2 r. 80 multicoloured . . . 2·25 1·90

149 Globe and Human Rights Emblem

1983. 35th Anniv of Declaration of Human Rights. Multicoloured.
763 1 r. 25 Type **149** . . . . . . 1·75 70
764 2 r. 80 Globe and emblem in balance . . . . 3·75 1·90

150 Harbour 151 Shaikh Khalifa

1984.
765 **150** 15 d. multicoloured . . . 10 10
765a **151** 25 d. mult (22 × 27 mm) . . 20 15
766 **150** 40 d. multicoloured . . . 30 20
767 50 d. multicoloured . . . 40 25
767a **151** 75 d. mult (22 × 27 mm) . . 45 35
768 1 r. multicoloured 75 35
769 1 r. 50 multicoloured . . 1·25 55
769a 2 r. multicoloured . . . . 1·25 90
770 2 r. 50 multicoloured . . 1·90 85
771 3 r. multicoloured . . . 2·50 1·25
772 5 r. multicoloured . . . 4·00 2·00
773 10 r. multicoloured . . . 7·75 5·25

152 Flag and Shaikh Khalifa

1984. 13th Anniv of Independence.
774 **152** 15 d. multicoloured . . . 15 10
775 1 r. multicoloured 85 35
776 2 r. 50 multicoloured . . 2·10 1·10
777 3 r. 50 multicoloured . . 3·00 1·60

153 Teacher and Blackboard 154 I.C.A.O. Emblem

1984. International Literacy Day. Multicoloured, background colour behind board given.
778 **153** 1 r. mauve 90 40
779 1 r. orange 90 40

1984. 40th Anniv of I.C.A.O.
780 **154** 20 d. multicoloured . . . 25 10
781 3 r. 50 multicoloured . . . 3·25 1·90

155 I.Y.Y. Emblem 156 Crossing the Road

1985. International Youth Year.
782 **155** 50 d. multicoloured . . . 65 30
783 1 r. multicoloured . . . . 1·40 45

1985. Traffic Week. Multicoloured, frame colour given.
784 **156** 1 r. red . . . . 1·25 40
785 1 r. blue . . . . 1·25 40

157 Emblem

1985. 40th Anniv of League of Arab States.
786 **157** 50 d. multicoloured . . . 50 20
787 4 r. multicoloured . . . . 3·50 2·25

158 Doha

1985. 14th Anniv of Independence. Multicoloured.
788 40 d. Type **158** 30 25
789 50 d. Dish aerials and microwave tower 45 30
790 1 r. 50 Oil refinery . . . . . 1·25 1·00
791 4 r. Cement works . . . . . 3·25 2·75

159 O.P.E.C. Emblem in "25"

1985. 25th Anniv of Organization of Petroleum Exporting Countries. Multicoloured, background colours given.
792 **159** 1 r. red . . . . 1·25 70
793 1 r. green . . . . 1·25 70

160 U.N. Emblem

1985. 40th Anniv of U.N.O.
794 **160** 1 r. multicoloured 80 70
795 3 r. multicoloured . . . . 2·00 1·90

161 Emblem

1986. Population and Housing Census.
796 **161** 1 r. multicoloured 70 60
797 3 r. multicoloured . . . . 2·00 1·75

162 "Qatari ibn al-Fuja'a" (container ship)

1986. 10th Anniv of United Arab Shipping Company. Multicoloured.
798 1 r. 50 Type **162** 90 80
799 4 r. "Al Wajda" (container ship) 2·40 2·25

163 Flag and Shaikh Khalifa

1986. 15th Anniv of Independence.
800 **163** 40 d. multicoloured . . . 25 20
801 50 d. multicoloured . . . 35 25
802 1 r. multicoloured 65 55
803 4 r. multicoloured . . . . 2·40 2·25

164 Shaikh Khalifa 165 Palace

1987.
804 **164** 15 r. multicoloured . . . 7·25 6·50
805 20 r. multicoloured . . . 9·75 8·50
806 30 r. multicoloured . . . 14·00 12·50

1987. 15th Anniv of Amir's Accession.
807 **165** 50 d. multicoloured . . . 35 25
808 1 r. multicoloured 60 30
809 1 r. 50 multicoloured . . 80 70
810 4 r. multicoloured . . . . 2·25 1·90

166 Emblem 167 Emblem

1987. 35th Anniv of Arab Postal Union.
811 **166** 1 r. yellow, green and black 50 45
812 1 r. 50 multicoloured . . 1·00 70

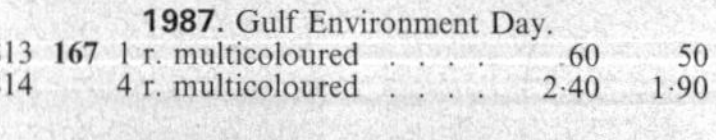
1987. Gulf Environment Day.
813 **167** 1 r. multicoloured 60 50
814 4 r. multicoloured . . . . 2·40 1·90

168 Modern Complex

1987. 16th Anniv of Independence.
815 25 d. Type **168** 20 10
816 75 d. Aerial view of city . . . 50 35
817 2 r. Modern building . . . . 1·25 90
818 4 r. Oil refinery . . . . 2·40 2·00

169 Pens in Fist 170 Anniversary Emblem

1987. International Literacy Day.

819 169 1 r. 50 multicoloured . . . 90 80
820 4 r. multicoloured . . . . 2·40 1·90

1988. 40th Anniv of W.H.O.

821 170 1 r. 50 yellow, black & bl . . 90 80
822 2 r. yellow, black & pink . 1·40 95

171 State Arms, Shaikh Khalifa and Flag

1988. 17th Anniv of Independence.

823 171 50 d. multicoloured . . . 30 25
824 75 d. multicoloured . . . 45 35
825 1 r. 50 multicoloured . . . 85 70
826 2 r. multicoloured . . . . 1·10 90

172 Post Office

1988. Opening of New Doha General Post Office.

827 172 1 r. 50 multicoloured . . . 75 65
828 4 r. multicoloured . . . . 1·90 1·75

173 Housing Development

1988. Arab Housing Day.

829 173 1 r. 50 multicoloured . . . 75 70
830 4 r. multicoloured . . . . 2·00 1·75

174 Hands shielding Flame 175 Dish Aerials and Arrows

1988. 40th Anniv of Declaration of Human Rights.

831 174 1 r. 50 multicoloured . . . 75 65
832 2 r. multicoloured . . . . 1·00 90

1989. World Telecommunications Day.

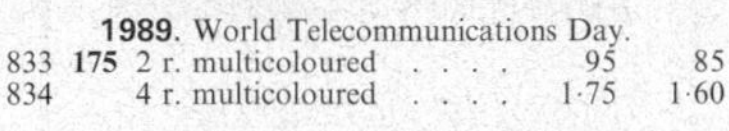

833 175 2 r. multicoloured 95 85
834 4 r. multicoloured . . . . 1·75 1·60

176 Headquarters

1989. 10th Anniv of Qatar Red Crescent Society.

835 176 4 r. multicoloured . . . . 1·90 1·60

177 Palace

1989. 18th Anniv of Independence.

836 177 75 d. multicoloured . . . 35 25
837 1 r. multicoloured 60 55
838 1 r. 50 multicoloured . . 75 65
839 2 r. multicoloured 90 85

178 Anniversary Emblem

1990. 40th Anniv of Gulf Air.

840 178 50 d. multicoloured . . . 35 30
841 75 d. multicoloured . . . 50 45
842 4 r. multicoloured . . . . 2·50 2·25

179 Map and Rising Sun

1990. 19th Anniv of Independence. Multicoloured.

843 50 d. Type **179** 35 30
844 75 d. Map and sunburst . . . 50 45
845 1 r. 50 Musicians and sword dancer . . . . 1·00 90
846 2 r. As No. 845 . . . . 2·00 1·75

180 Anniversary Emblem 181 Emblem and Dhow

1990. 30th Anniv of Organization of Petroleum Exporting Countries. Multicoloured.

847 50 d. Type **180** 35 30
848 1 r. 50 Flags of member nations 1·00 90

1990. 11th Session of Supreme Council of Gulf Co-operation Council. Multicoloured.

849 50 d. Type **181** 35 30
850 1 r. Council heads of state and emblem 65 55
851 1 r. 50 State flag and Council emblem . . . . 1·00 90
852 2 r. State and Council emblems 1·25 1·10

182 "Glossonema edule" 183 Emblem

1991. Plants. Multicoloured.

853 10 d. Type **182** 10 10
854 25 d. "Lycium shawii" . . . 15 10
855 50 d. "Acacia tortilis" 35 30
856 75 d. "Acacia ehrenbergiana" . 50 45
857 1 r. "Capparis spinosa" . . 65 55
858 4 r. "Cymbopogon parkeri" . 2·50 2·25

No. 858 is wrongly inscribed "Cymhopogon".

1991. 20th Anniv of Independence. Multicoloured.

859 25 d. Type **183** 15 10
860 75 d. As Type **183** but different Arabic inscription 50 45
861 1 r. View of Doha (35 × 32 mm) 65 55
862 1 r. 50 Palace (35 × 32 mm) . 1·00 90

184 Two-banded Porgy 185 Shaikh Khalifa

1991. Fishes. Multicoloured.

863 10 d. Type **184** 10 10
864 15 d. Feather-fin bullfish . . . 10 10
865 25 d. Scarlet-fin soldierfish . . 15 10
866 50 d. Black-tip tope 35 30
867 75 d. Japanese silver bream . . 50 45
868 1 r. Golden trevally 65 55
869 1 r. 50 White-spotted spinefoot 1·00 90
870 2 r. Semi-circle anglefish . . . 1·25 1·10

1992. Multicoloured. (a) Size 22 × 28 or 28 × 22 mm.

871 10 d. Type **185** 10 10
872 25 d. North Field gas project . 15 10
873 50 d. Map of Qatar 25 20
874 75 d. Petrochemical factory (horiz) 30 25
875 1 r. Oil refinery (horiz) 40 35

(b) Size 25 × 32 or 32 × 25 mm.

876 1 r. 50 As No. 872 . . . . . . 65 60
877 2 r. As No. 873 . . . . 85 75
878 3 r. As No. 874 . . . . 1·40 1·25
879 4 r. As No. 875 . . . . 1·75 1·50
880 5 r. As No. 873 . . . . 2·10 1·75
881 10 r. As No. 875 . . . . 4·25 3·75
882 15 r. Shaikh Khalifa (different frame) . . . . 6·75 6·00
883 20 r. As No. 882 . . . . 8·75 7·75
884 30 r. As No. 882 . . . . 13·50 12·00

186 Shaikh Khalifa and Gateway 187 Heart in Centre of Flower

1992. 20th Anniv of Amir's Accession. Mult.

885 25 d. Type **186** 15 10
886 50 d. Type **186** 25 20
887 75 d. Archway and "20" . . . 40 35
888 1 r. 50 As No 887 . . . . . . 75 65

1992. World Health Day. "Heartbeat, the Rhythm of Health". Multicoloured.

889 50 d. Type **187** 25 20
890 1 r. 50 Heart on clockface and cardiograph (horiz) 75 65

188 Women dancing

1992. Children's Paintings. Multicoloured.

891 25 d. Type **188** 15 10
892 50 d. Children's playground . . 25 20
893 75 d. Boat race 40 35
894 1 r. 50 Fishing fleet 75 65

189 Runner and Emblems

1992. Olympic Games, Barcelona. Multicoloured.

896 50 d. Type **189** 25 20
897 1 r. 50 Footballer and emblems 75 65

190 Shaikh Khalifa and Script

1992. 21st Anniv of Independence. Multicoloured.

898 50 d. Type **190** 25 20
899 50 d. Shaikh Kalifa and "21" in English and Arabic 25 20
900 1 r. Oil well, pen and dhow (42 × 42 mm) 50 45
901 1 r. Dhow in harbour (42 × 42 mm) 50 45

191 Ball, Flag and Emblem

1992. 11th Arabian Gulf Football Championship. Multicoloured.

902 50 d. Type **191** 25 20
903 1 r. Ball bursting goal net (vert) 50 45

192 Emblems and Globe

1992. International Nutrition Conference, Rome. Multicoloured.

904 50 d. Type **192** 25 20
905 1 r. Cornucopia (horiz) . . . 50 45

193 Mosque

1993. Old Mosques. Each sepia, yellow and brown.

906 1 r. Type **193** 55 45
907 1 r. Mosque (minaret without balcony) 55 45
908 1 r. Mosque (minaret with wide balcony) 55 45
909 1 r. Mosque (minaret with narrow balcony) 55 45

194 Presenter and Dish Aerial

1993. 25th Anniv of Qatar Broadcasting. Mult.

910 25 d. Type **194** 15 10
911 50 d. Rocket and satellite . . 30 25
912 75 d. Broadcasting House . . 40 35
913 1 r. Journalists 55 45

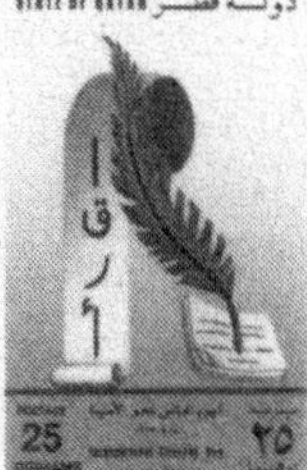

195 Oil Refinery and Sea 196 Scroll, Quill and Paper

1993. 22nd Anniv of Independence. Multicoloured.

915 25 d. Type **195** 15 10
916 50 d. Flag and clock tower, Doha 30 25
917 75 d. "22" in English and Arabic 40 35
918 1 r. 50 Flag and fort 80 70

1993. International Literacy Day. Multicoloured.

919 25 d. Type **196** 15 10
920 50 d. Fountain pen and flags spelling "Qatar" 30 25
921 75 d. Fountain pen and Arabic characters 40 35
922 1 r. 50 Arabic text on scroll and fountain pen 80 70

197 Girls playing

1993. Children's Games. Multicoloured.

923	25 d. Type **197**	15	10
924	50 d. Boys playing with propeller (vert)	30	25
925	75 d. Wheel and stick race (vert)	40	35
926	1 r. 50 Skipping	80	70

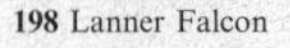

198 Lanner Falcon **199** Headquarters

1993. Falcons. Multicoloured.

928	25 d. Type **198**	15	10
929	50 d. Saker falcon	30	25
930	75 d. Barbary falcon	40	35
931	1 r. 50 Peregrine falcon	80	70

1994. 30th Anniv of Qatar Insurance Company. Multicoloured.

933	50 d. Type **199**	25	20
934	1 r. 50 Company emblem and international landmarks	70	60

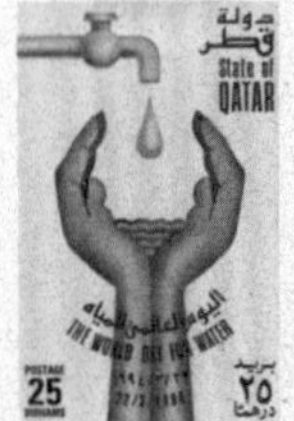

200 Hands catching Drops from Tap **201** Gavel, Scales and National Flag

1994. World Water Day. Mulicoloured.

935	25 d. Type **200**	10	10
936	1 r. Hands catching raindrop, water tower, crops and United Nations emblem	50	45

1994. Qatar International Law Conference. Multicoloured.

937	75 d. Type **201**	35	30
938	2 r. Gavel and scales suspended from flag	1·00	90

202 Society Emblem **203** Anniversary Emblem

1994. Qatar Society for Welfare and Rehabilitation of the Handicapped. Multicoloured.

939	25 d. Type **202**	10	10
940	75 d. Handicapped symbol and hands	35	30

1994. 75th Anniv of I.L.O. Multicoloured.

941	25 d. Type **203**	10	10
942	2 r. Anniversary emblem and cogwheel	1·00	90

204 Family and Emblem **205** Scroll

1994. International Year of the Family.

943	**204**	25 d. blue and black	10	10
944	–	1 r. multicoloured	50	45

DESIGN: 1 r. I.Y.F. emblem and stylized family standing on U.N. emblem.

1994. 23rd Anniv of Independence. Multicoloured.

945	25 d. Type **205**	10	10
946	75 d. Oasis	35	30
947	1 r. Industry	50	45
948	2 r. Scroll (different)	1·00	90

206 Map, Airplane and Emblem

1994. 50th Anniv of I.C.A.O. Multicoloured.

949	25 d. Type **206**	10	10
950	75 d. Anniversary emblem	35	30

207 Ship like Carvings

1995. Rock Carvings, Jabal Jusasiyah. Multicoloured.

951	1 r. Type **207**	40	35
952	1 r. Circular and geometric patterns	40	35
953	1 r. Six irregular-shaped carvings	40	35
954	1 r. Carvings including three multi-limbed creatures	40	35
955	1 r. Nine multi-limbed creatures	40	35
956	1 r. Fishes	40	35

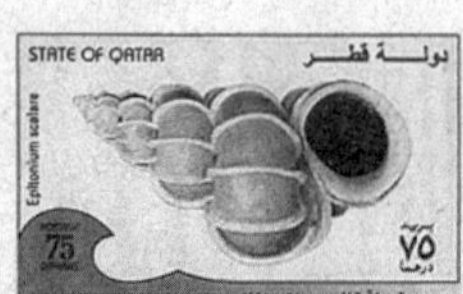

208 Precious Wentletrap ("Epitonium scalare")

1995. Gulf Environment Day. Sea Shells. Multicoloured.

957	75 d. Type **208**	35	30
958	75 d. Feathered cone ("Conus pennaceus")	35	30
959	75 d. "Cerithidea cingulata"	35	30
960	75 d. "Hexaplex kuesterianus"	35	30
961	1 r. Giant spider conch ("Lambis truncata sebae")	40	35
962	1 r. Woodcock murex ("Murex scolopax")	40	35
963	1 r. "Thais mutabilis"	40	35
964	1 r. Spindle shell ("Fusinus arabicus")	40	35

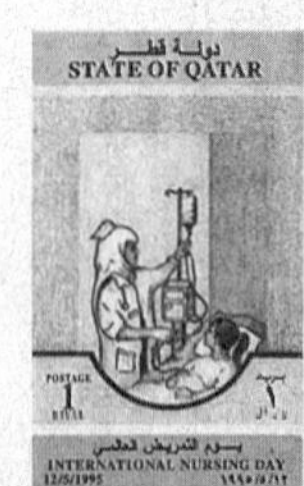

209 Nursing Patient **211** Anniversary Emblem

210 Schoolchildren

1995. International Nursing Day. Multicoloured.

965	1 r. Type **209**	40	35
966	1 r. 50 Vaccinating child	60	55

1995. 24th Anniv of Independence. Multicoloured.

967	1 r. Type **210**	35	30
968	1 r. Palm trees	35	30
969	1 r. 50 Port	55	45
970	1 r. 50 Doha	55	45

Nos. 967/70 were issued together, se-tenant, forming a composite design.

1995. 50th Anniv of U.N.O.

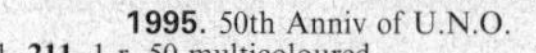

971	**211**	1 r. 50 multicoloured	55	45

212 Addra Gazelle

1996. Mammals. Multicoloured.

972	25 d. Type **212**	10	10
973	50 d. Beira antelope	15	10
974	75 d. "Gazella dorcas pelzelni"	25	20
975	1 r. Dorcas gazelle	35	30
976	1 r. 50 Speke's gazelle	50	40
977	2 r. Soemmerring's gazelle	70	55

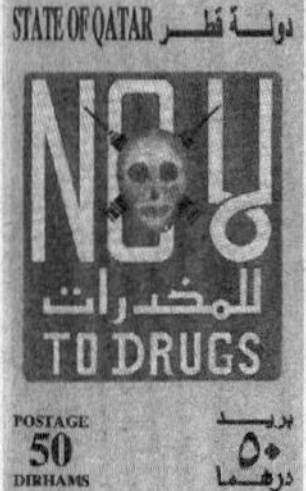

213 Syringes through Skull **214** Map of Qatar and Games Emblem

1996. International Day against Drug Abuse. Multicoloured.

979	50 d. Type **213**	15	10
980	1 r. "No entry" sign over syringes in hand	35	30

1996. Olympic Games, Atlanta. Multicoloured.

981	10 d. Type **214**	10	10
982	15 d. Rifle shooting	10	10
983	25 d. Bowling	10	10
984	50 d. Table tennis	15	10
985	1 r. Running	35	30
986	1 r. 50 Yachting	50	40

Nos. 981/6 were issued together, se-tenant, forming a composite design.

215 Map, National Flag and Shaikh Hamad

1996. 25th Anniv of Independence.

987	**215**	1 r. 50 multicoloured	50	40
988		2 r. multicoloured	70	55

216 Shaikh Hamad **217**

1996.

990	**216**	25 d. multicoloured	10	10
991		50 d. multicoloured	15	10
992		75 d. multicoloured	25	20
993		1 r. multicoloured	35	30
994	**217**	1 r. 50 multicoloured	50	40
995		2 r. multicoloured	70	55
997		4 r. multicoloured	1·40	1·10
998		5 r. multicoloured	1·75	1·40
999		10 r. multicoloured	3·50	2·75
1001		20 r. multicoloured	6·75	5·50
1002		30 r. multicoloured	10·00	8·00

218 Doha Clock Tower, Dove and Heads of State **219** Children and U.N.I.C.E.F. Emblem

1996. 17th Session of Gulf Co-operation Council Supreme Council, Doha. Multicoloured.

1004	1 r. Type **218**	35	30
1005	1 r. 50 Council emblem, dove and national flag	50	40

1996. 50th Anniv of U.N.I.C.E.F. Multicoloured.

1006	75 d. Type **219**	25	20
1007	75 d. Children and emblem	25	20

220 Al-Wajbah

1997. Forts. Multicoloured.

1008	25 d. Type **220**	10	10
1009	75 d. Al-Zubarah (horiz)	25	20
1010	1 r. Al-Kout Fort, Doha (horiz)	35	30
1011	3 r. Umm Salal Mohammed (horiz)	1·00	80

POSTAGE DUE STAMPS

D **40**

1968.

D254	D **40**	5 d. blue	13·50	13·50
D255		10 d. red	16·00	16·00
D256		20 d. green	20·00	20·00
D257		30 d. lilac	21·00	21·00

QUELIMANE Pt. 9

A district of Portuguese E. Africa, now part of Mozambique, whose stamps it now uses.

100 centavos = 1 escudo

1913. Surch **REPUBLICA QUELIMANE** and new value on "Vasco da Gama" stamps of (a) Portuguese Colonies.

1 ¼ c. on 2½ r. green 60 35
2 ½ c. on 5 r. red 60 35
3 1 c. on 10 r. purple 60 35
4 2½ c. on 25 r. green 60 35
5 5 c. on 50 r. blue 60 35
6 7½ c. on 75 r. brown 70 60
7 10 c. on 100 r. brown 50 35
8 15 c. on 150 r. brown 50 35

(b) Macao.

9 ¼ c. on ½ a. green 60 35
10 ½ c. on 1 a. red 60 35
11 1 c. on 2 a. purple 60 35
12 2½ c. on 4 a. green 60 35
13 5 c. on 8 a. blue 60 35
14 7½ c. on 12 a. brown 70 60
15 10 c. on 16 a. brown 50 35
16 15 c. on 24 a. brown 50 35

(c) Timor.

17 ¼ c. on ½ a. green 60 35
18 ½ c. on 1 a. red 60 35
19 1 c. on 2 a. purple 60 35
20 2½ c. on 2 a. green 60 35
21 5 c. on 8 a. blue 60 35
22 7½ c. on 12 a. brown 70 60
23 10 c. on 16 a. brown 50 35
24 15 c. on 24 a. brown 50 35

1914. "Ceres" key-type inscr "QUELIMANE".

25 U ¼ c. green 25 25
26 ½ c. black 50 35
42 1 c. green 45 45
28 1½ c. brown 60 40
29 2 c. red 50 50
30 2½ c. violet 25 15
31 5 c. blue 40 35
43 7½ c. brown 45 45
33 8 c. grey 50 40
44 10 c. red 45 45
35 15 c. purple 70 65
45 20 c. green 45 45
37 30 c. brown on green . . . 1·10 85
38 40 c. brown on pink . . . . 1·10 85
39 50 c. orange on orange . . 1·10 85
40 1 e. green on blue . . . . . 1·10 85

RAS AL KHAIMA Pt. 19

Arab Shaikhdom in the Arabian Gulf.
Ras al Khaima joined the United Arab Emirates in February, 1972 and U.A.E. stamps were used in the shaikhdom from 1st January, 1973.

1964. 100 naye paise = 1 rupee.
1966. 100 dirhams = 1 riyal.

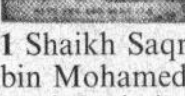
1 Shaikh Saqr bin Mohamed al-Qasimi

3 Dhow

1964.

1 **1** 5 n.p. brown and black . . . 15 15
2 15 n.p. blue and black 15 15
3 – 30 n.p. brown and black . . . 15 15
4 – 40 n.p. blue and black . . . 25 20
5 – 75 n.p. red and black . . . 60 50
6 **3** 1 r. brown and green . . . . 1·50 90
7 2 r. brown and violet . . . . 2·50 1·90
8 5 r. brown and blue . . . . . 5·50 5·00

DESIGNS—As Type **1**: 30 n.p. to 75 n.p. Seven palms.

3a Pres. Kennedy inspecting "Friendship 7"

1965. Pres. Kennedy Commemoration.

9 **3a** 2 r. blue and brown . . . . 1·00 95
10 – 3 r. blue and brown . . . . 1·25 1·25
11 – 4 r. blue and brown . . . . 1·75 1·75

DESIGNS—HORIZ: 3 r. Kennedy and wife. VERT: 4 r. Kennedy and flame of remembrance.

MORE DETAILED LISTS

are given in the Stanley Gibbons Catalogues referred to in the country headings. For lists of current volumes see introduction

4 Sir Winston Churchill and Houses of Parliament

1965. Churchill Commemoration.

12 **4** 2 r. blue and brown 90 90
13 – 3 r. blue and brown . . . . 1·25 1·25
14 – 4 r. blue and brown . . . . 1·90 1·75

DESIGNS—HORIZ: 3 r. Churchill and Pres. Roosevelt; 4 r. Churchill, and Heads of State at his funeral.

1965. Olympic Games, Tokyo (1964). Optd **OLYMPIC TOKYO 1964** in English and Arabic and Olympic "rings".

15 **3** 1 r. brown and green 40 40
16 2 r. brown and violet 90 90
17 5 r. brown and blue . . . . 2·50 2·50

1965. Death Centenary of Abraham Lincoln. Optd **ABRAHAM LINCOLN 1809–1865** in English and Arabic.

18 **3** 1 r. brown and green 40 40
19 2 r. brown and violet 90 90
20 5 r. brown and blue . . . . 2·50 2·50

1965. 20th Death Anniv of Pres. Roosevelt. Optd **FRANKLIN D. ROOSEVELT 1882–1945** in English and Arabic.

21 **3** 1 r. brown and green 40 40
22 2 r. brown and violet 90 90
23 5 r. brown and blue . . . . 2·50 2·50

8 Satellite and Tracking Station

1966. I.T.U. Centenary. Multicoloured.

24 15 n.p. Type **8** 15 10
25 50 n.p. Post Office Tower, London, "Telstar" and tracking gantry 30 15
26 85 n.p. Rocket on launching-pad and "Relay" 60 20
27 1 r. Type **8** 70 30
28 2 r. As 50 n.p. . . . . 1·25 35
29 3 r. As 85 n.p. . . . . 1·50 65

9 Swimming

10 Carpenter

1966. Pan-Arab Games, Cairo (1965).

31 A 1 n.p. brown, pink & green 10 10
32 B 2 n.p. black, grey & green . 10 10
33 C 3 n.p. brown, pink & green 10 10
34 D 4 n.p. brown, pink & purple 10 10
35 A 5 n.p. black, grey & orange 10 10
36 **9** 10 n.p. brown, pink & blue 15 10
37 B 25 n.p. brown, pink and cinnamon 15 10
38 C 50 n.p. black, grey & violet 35 15
39 D 75 n.p. black, grey & blue . 55 15
40 **9** 1 r. black, grey & green 70 30

DESIGNS: A, Running; B, Boxing; C, Football; D, Fencing.

1966. American Astronauts.

42 **10** 25 n.p. black, gold & purple 15 10
43 – 50 n.p. black, silver & brown 25 15
44 – 75 n.p. black, silver & blue 35 20
45 – 1 r. black, silver & bistre . 55 35
46 – 2 r. black, silver & mauve . 90 70
47 – 3 r. black, gold and green . 1·50 1·10
48 – 4 r. black, gold and red . . 1·75 1·25
49 – 5 r. black, gold and blue . . 2·10 1·60

ASTRONAUTS: 50 n.p. Glenn; 75 n.p. Shepard; 1 r. Cooper; 2 r. Grissom; 3 r. Schirra; 4 r. Stafford; 5 r. Lovell.

11 Shaikh Sabah of Kuwait and Shaikh Saqr of Ras al Khaima

1966. International Co-operation Year.

51 **11** 1 r. black and red 50 20
52 A 1 r. black and lilac 50 20
53 B 1 r. black and pink 50 20
54 C 1 r. black and green 50 20
55 D 1 r. black and green 50 20
56 E 1 r. black and yellow 50 20
57 F 1 r. black and orange 50 20
58 G 1 r. black and blue 50 20

SHAIKH SAQR AND WORLD LEADERS: A, Shaikh Ahmad of Qatar; B, Pres. Nasser; C, King Hussein; D, Pres. Johnson; E, Pres. De Gaulle; F, Pope Paul VI; G, Prime Minister Harold Wilson.

NEW CURRENCY SURCHARGES. During the latter half of 1966 various issues appeared surcharged in dirhams and riyals. The 1964 definitives with this surcharge are listed below as there is considerable evidence of their postal use. Nos. 24/58 also exist with these surcharges.

In August 1966 Nos. 1/14, 24/9 and 51/8 appeared surcharged in fils and rupees. As Ras Al Khaima did not adopt this currency their status is uncertain.

1966. Nos. 1/8 with currency names changed to dirhams and riyals by overprinting in English and Arabic

60 **1** 5 d. on 5 n.p. brown and black 20 15
60a – 5 d. on 75 n.p. red & black . 20 15
64b **3** 5 d. on 5 r. brown & blue . . 20 15
61 **1** 15 d. on 15 n.p. blue & black 30 15
62 – 30 d. on 30 n.p. brown and black 55 20
63 – 40 d. on 40 n.p. blue & blk 70 30
64 – 75 d. on 75 n.p. red & blk . 80 35
65 **3** 1 r. on 1 r. brown & green . 90 45
66 2 r. on 2 r. brown & violet . 2·00 1·75
67 5 r. on 5 r. brown & blue . . 4·50 3·00

15 W.H.O. Building and Flowers

1966. Inauguration of W.H.O. Headquarters, Geneva.

68 **15** 15 d. multicoloured (postage) 20 10
69 – 35 d. multicoloured 40 15
70 **15** 50 d. multicoloured (air) . . 50 25
71 – 3 r. multicoloured . . . . . 1·75 65

DESIGN: 35 d., 3 r. As Type **15** but with red instead of yellow flowers at left.

16 Queen Elizabeth II presenting Jules Rimet Cup to Bobby Moore, Captain of England Team

1966. Air. England's Victory in World Cup Football Championships. Multicoloured.

73 1 r. Wembley Stadium 50 15
74 2 r. Goalkeeper saving ball . . . 1·00 30
75 3 r. Footballers with ball . . . 1·50 50
76 4 r. Type **16** . . . . 1·75 1·00

17 Shaikh Saqr

18 Oil Rig

1971.

78 **17** 5 d. multicoloured . . . . .
79 **18** 20 d. multicoloured . . . .
80 **17** 30 d. multicoloured . . . .

For later issues see **UNITED ARAB EMIRATES.**

APPENDIX

The following stamps have either been issued in excess of postal needs or have not been available to the public in reasonable quantities at face value. Such stamps may later be given full listing if there is evidence of regular postal use.

1967.

"The Arabian Nights". Paintings. Air 30, 70 d., 1, 2, 3 r.
Cats. Postage 1, 2, 3, 4, 5 d.: Air 3 r.
Arab Paintings. 1, 2, 3, 4, 10, 20, 30 d.
European Paintings. Air 60, 70 d., 1, 2, 3, 5, 10 r.
50th Birth Anniv of Pres. John F. Kennedy. Optd on 1965 Pres. Kennedy Commem. 2, 3, 4 r.
World Scout Jamboree, Idaho. Postage 1, 2, 3, 4 d.; Air 35, 75 d., 1 r.
U.S. "Apollo" Disaster. Optd on 1966 American Astronauts issue. 25 d. on 25 n.p., 50 d. on 50 n.p., 75 d. on 75 n.p., 1, 2, 3, 4, 5 r.
Summer Olympics Preparation, Mexico 1968. Postage 10, 20, 30, 40 d.; Air 1, 2 r.
Winter Olympics Preparation, Grenoble 1968. Postage 1, 2, 3, 4, 5 d.; Air 85 d., 2, 3 r.

1968.

Mothers' Day. Paintings. Postage 20, 30, 40, 50 d.; Air 1, 2, 3, 4 r.
International Human Rights Year. 2 r. × 3.
International Museum Campaign. Paintings. 15, 15, 20, 25, 35, 40, 45, 60, 70, 80, 90 d.; 1, 1 r. 25, 1 r. 50, 2 r. 50, 2 r. 75.
Winter Olympic Medal Winners, Grenoble. 50 d., 1, 1 r. 50, 2, 2 r. 50, 3 r.
Olympic Games, Mexico. Air 1, 2, 2, 3, 3, 4 r.
5th Death Anniv of Pres. John F. Kennedy. Air. 2, 3 r.
Christmas. Religious Paintings. Postage 20, 30, 40, 50, 60 d., 1 r.; Air 2, 3, 4 r.

1969.

Famous Composers (1st series). Paintings. 25, 50, 75 d., 1 r. 50, 2 r. 50.
Famous Operas. 20, 40, 60, 80 d., 1, 2 r.
Famous Men. Postage 20, 30, 50 d.; Air 1 r. 50, 2, 3, 4, 5 r.
International Philatelic Exhibition, Mexico 1968 (EFIMEX). Postage 10, 10, 25, 35, 40, 50, 60, 70d.; Air 1, 2, 3, 5, 5 r.
Int Co-operation in Olympics. 1, 2, 3, 4 r.
International Co-operation in Space. Air 1 r. 50, 2 r. 50, 3 r. 50, 4 r. 50.
Birth Bicentenary of Napoleon. Paintings. Postage 1 r. 75, 2 r. 75, 3 r. 75; Air 75 d.
"Apollo" Moon Missions. Air 2, 2 r. 50, 3, 3 r. 50, 4, 4 r. 50, 5, 5 r. 50.
"Apollo 11" Astronauts. Air 2 r. 25, 3 r. 25, 4 r. 25, 5 r. 25.
"Apollo 12" Astronauts. Air 60 d., 2 r. 60, 3 r. 60, 4 r. 60, 5 r. 60.

1970.

Christmas 1969. Religious Paintings. Postage 50 d.; Air 3, 3 r. 50.
World Cup, Mexico. Air 1, 2, 3, 4, 5, 6 r.
Easter. Religious Paintings. Postage 50 d.; Air 3, 3 r. 50.
Paintings by Titian and Tiepolo. Postage 50, 50 d.; Air 3, 3, 3 r. 50, 3 r. 50.
Winter Olympics, Sapporo 1972. Air 1, 2, 3, 4, 5, 6 r.
Olympic Games, Munich 1972. Air 1, 2, 3, 4, 5, 6 r.
Paul Gauguin's Paintings. Postage 50 d.; Air 3, 3 r. 50.
Christmas. Religious Paintings. Postage 50 d.; Air 3, 3 r. 50.
"World Cup Champions, Brazil". Optd on Mexico World Cup issue. Air 1, 2, 3, 4, 5, 6 r.
"EXPO 70" World Fair, Osaka, Japan (1st issue). Postage 40, 45, 50, 55, 60, 65, 70, 75 d.; Air 80, 85, 90, 95 d., 1 r. 60, 1 r. 65, 1 r. 85, 2 r.
"EXPO 70" World Fair, Osaka, Japan (2nd issue). Postage 55, 65, 75 d.; Air 25, 85, 95 d., 1 r. 50, 1 r. 75.
Space Programmes. Air 1 r. × 6, 2 r. × 6, 4 r. × 6.
Famous Frenchmen. Air 1 r. × 4, 2 r. × 4, 2 r. 50 × 2, 3 r. × 2, 4 r. × 4, 5 r. 50 × 2.
Int Philatelic Exhib (Philympia '70). Air 1 r. × 4, 1 r. 50 × 4, 2 r. 50 × 4, 3 r. × 4, 4 r. × 4.
Events in the Life of Christ. Religious Paintings. 5, 10, 25, 50 d., 1, 2, 5 r.
"Stages of the Cross". Religious Paintings. 10, 20, 30, 40, 50, 60, 70, 80 d., 1, 1 r. 50, 2, 2 r. 50, 3, 3 r. 50.
The Life of Mary. Religious Paintings. 10, 15, 30, 60, 75 d., 3, 4 r.

1971.

Easter. "Stages of the Cross" (1970) but with additional inscr "EASTER". 10, 20, 30, 40, 50, 60, 70, 80 d., 1, 1 r. 50, 2, 2 r. 50, 3, 3 r. 50.
Charles de Gaulle Memorial. Postage 50 d.; Air 1, 1 r. 50, 2, 3, 4 r.
Safe Return of "Apollo 14". Postage 50 d.; Air 1, 1 r. 50, 2, 3, 4 r.
U.S.A.–Japan Baseball Friendship. Postage 10, 25, 30, 80 d.; Air 50, 70 d., 1, 1r. 50.
Munich Olympics, 1972. Postage 50 d.; Air 1, 1 r. 50, 2, 3, 4 r.
Cats. 35, 60, 65, 110, 120, 160 d.
13th World Jamboree, Japan. Postage 30, 50, 60, 75 d.; Air 1, 1 r. 50, 3, 4 r.
Sapporo Olympic Gold Medal Winners. Optd on 1970 Winter Olympics, Sapporo 1972, issue. Air 1, 2, 3, 4, 5, 6 r.
Munich Olympic Medal Winners. Optd on 1970 Summer Olympics, Munich 1972, issue. Air 1, 2, 3, 4, 5, 6 r.
Japanese Locomotives. Postage 30, 35, 75 d.; Air 90 d., 1, 1 r. 75.

"Soyuz 11" Russian Cosmonauts Memorial. Air 1, 2, 3, 4 r.
"Apollo 15". Postage 50 d.; Air 1, 1 r. 50, 2, 3, 4 r.
Dogs. 5, 20, 75, 85, 185, 200 d.
Durer's Paintings. Postage 50 d.; Air 1, 1 r. 50 2, 3, 4 r.
Famous Composers (2nd series). Postage 50 d.; Air 1, 1 r. 50, 2, 3, 4 r.
"Soyuz 11" and "Salyut" Space Projects. Postage 50 d.; Air 1, 1 r. 50, 2, 3, 4 r.
Butterflies. Postage 15, 20, 70 d.; Air 1 r. 25, 1 r. 50, 1 r. 70.
Wild Animals. 10, 40, 80 d.; 1 r. 15, 1 r. 30, 1 r. 65.
Fishes. 30, 50, 60, 90 d., 1 r. 45, 1 r. 55.
Ludwig van Beethoven. Portraits. Postage 50 d.; Air 1, 1 r. 50, 2, 3, 4 r.

1972.

Birds. 50, 55, 80, 100, 105, 190 d.
Winter Olympics, Sapporo (1st issue). Postage 20, 30, 50 d., Air 70, 90 d., 2 r. 50
Winter Olympics, Sapporo (2nd issue). Postage 5, 60, 80, 90 d.; Air 1 r. 10, 1 r. 75
Mozart. Portraits. Postage 50 d.; Air 1, 1 r. 50, 2, 3, 4 r.
Olympic Games, Munich. Postage 50 d.; Air 1, 1 r. 50, 2, 3, 4 r.
"In Memory of Charles de Gaulle". Optd on 1971 Charles de Gaulle memorial issue. Postage 50 d.; Air 1, 1 r. 50, 2, 3, 4 r.
Winter Olympics, Sapporo (3rd issue). Postage 15, 45 d.; Air 65, 75 d., 1 r. 20, 1 r. 25.
Horses. Postage 10, 25, 30 d.; Air 1 r. 40, 1 r. 80, 1 r. 95.
Parrots. 40, 45, 70, 95 d., 1 r. 35, 1 r. 75.
"Apollo 16". Postage 50 d.; Air 1, 1 r. 50, 2, 3, 4 r.
European Footballers. Postage 50 d.; Air 1, 1 r. 50, 2, 3, 4 r.

A number of issues on gold or silver foil also exist, but it is understood that these were mainly for presentation purposes, although valid for postage.

In common with the other states of the United Arab Emirates the Ras al Khaima stamp contract was terminated on 1st August 1972, and any further new issues released after that date were unauthorised.

REUNION — Pt. 6

An island in the Indian Ocean, E. of Madagascar, now an overseas department of France.

100 centimes = 1 franc

1

1852. Imperf. No gum.

1 **1** 15 c. black on blue £20000 £11000
2 30 c. black on blue £20000 £11000

1885. Stamps of French Colonies surch **R** and value in figures. Imperf.

5 D 5 c. on 30 c. brown . . . . 30·00 28·00
7 H 5 c. on 30 c. brown . . . . 3·50 4·50
3 A 5 c. on 40 c. orange £225 £200
6 F 5 c. on 40 c. orange . . . . 26·00 18·00
8 H 5 c. on 40 c. red on yellow . 65·00 55·00
9 10 c. on 40 c. red on yellow 6·50 4·50
10 20 c. on 30 c. brown . . . 42·00 35·00
4 **A** 25 c. on 40 c. orange . . . 30·00 25·00

1891. Stamps of French Colonies optd **REUNION**. Imperf (Types F and H) or perf (Type J).

17 J 1 c. black on blue . . . . . 1·40 1·60
18 2 c. brown on buff . . . . . 2·25 1·00
19 4 c. brown on grey . . . . . 3·00 3·00
20 5 c. green on green . . . . . 4·50 2·25
21 10 c. black on lilac . . . . . 19·00 1·75
22 15 c. blue on blue . . . . . 28·00 1·75
23 20 c. red on green . . . . . 18·00 2·50
24 25 c. black on pink . . . . . 20·00 2·50
13 H 30 c. brown . . . . 23·00 21·00
25 J 35 c. black on yellow . . . . 16·00 11·50
11 F 40 c. orange £300 £290
14 H 40 c. red on yellow . . . . . 17·00 14·00
26 J 40 c. red on buff . . . . . 45·00 35·00
15 H 75 c. red £225 £225
27 J 75 c. red on pink £400 £325
12 F 80 c. pink . . . . 35·00 30·00
16 H 1 f. green . . . . 25·00 23·00
28 J 1 f. green £300 £300

1891. Stamps of French Colonies surch **REUNION** and new value.

29 J 02 c. on 20 c. red on green . . 4·50 3·75
31 2 on 20 c. red on green . . . 1·75 1·75
30 15 c. on 20 c. red on green 5·50 5·00

1892. "Tablet" key-type inscr "REUNION".

34 D 1 c. black and red on blue . . 50 50
35 2 c. brown & blue on buff 50 45
36 4 c. brown & blue on grey 1·10 60
50 5 c. green and red 70 40
38 10 c. black & blue on lilac 4·00 1·00
51 10 c. red and blue 80 35
39 15 c. blue and red . . . . 11·50 75
52 15 c. grey and red . . . . 2·75 35
40 20 c. red & blue on green 4·50 5·00
41 25 c. black & red on pink 8·25 1·00
53 25 c. blue and red . . . . 9·75 9·50
42 30 c. brown & bl on drab 9·25 4·75
43 40 c. red & blue on yellow 14·00 9·00
44 50 c. red and blue on pink 42·00 21·00
54 50 c. brown & red on blue 23·00 21·00
55 D 50 c. brown & blue on blue 30·00 26·00
45 75 c. brown & red on orge 38·00 24·00
46 1 f. green and red . . . . 28·00 15·00

1893. Stamp of French Colonies, "Commerce" type, surch **2 c.**

47 J 2 c. on 20 c. red on green . 1·00 95

1901. "Tablet" key-type surch in figures.

56 D 5 c. on 40 c. red and blue on yellow . . . . 1·25 2·25
57 5 c. on 50 c. red and blue on pink . . . . 2·75 2·75
58 15 c. on 75 c. brown and red on orange . . . . . . 8·00 8·00
59 15 c. on 1 f. green and red 7·00 7·00

16 Map of Reunion

17 View of Saint-Denis and Arms of the Colony

18 View of St. Pierre and Crater Dolomieu

1907.

60 **16** 1 c. red and lilac 10 10
61 2 c. blue and brown . . . 10 10
62 4 c. red and green 10 10
63 5 c. red and green 25 10
92 5 c. violet and yellow . . . 20 15
64 10 c. green and red 90 10
93 10 c. turquoise and green . 20 15
94 10 c. red and lake on blue 35 15
65 15 c. blue and black . . . 30 10
95 15 c. turquoise and green . 20 25
96 15 c. red and blue 25 35
66 **17** 20 c. green and olive . . . 25 25
67 25 c. brown and blue . . . 1·40 50
97 25 c. blue and brown . . . 20 10
68 30 c. green and brown . . 35 55
98 30 c. pink and red 30 50
99 30 c. red and grey 15 25
100 30 c. light green and green 55 70
69 35 c. blue and brown . . . 55 35
101 40 c. brown and green . . 35 15
70 45 c. pink and violet . . . 55 70
102 45 c. red and purple . . . 35 50
103 45 c. red and mauve . . . 90 1·25
71 50 c. blue and brown . . . 1·40 75
104 50 c. ultramarine and blue 25 25
105 50 c. violet and yellow . . 20 15
106 60 c. brown and blue . . . 15 30
107 65 c. blue and violet . . . 55 70
72 75 c. pink and red 45 35
108 75 c. purple and brown . . 1·00 1·00
109 90 c. pink and red . . . . 3·50 3·50
78 **18** 1 f. blue and brown . . . 40 45
110 1 f. blue 50 65
111 1 f. lilac and brown . . . 50 50
112 1 f. 10 mauve and brown . 55 60
113 1 f. 50 lt blue & blue on bl 6·00 4·50
74 2 f. green and red . . . . 2·25 1·60
114 3 f. mauve on pink . . . . 6·25 4·75
75 5 f. brown and pink . . . 3·50 3·00

1912. "Tablet" key-type surch.

76 D 05 on 2 c. brown and red on buff 20 25
77 05 on 15 c. grey and red . 40 50
78 05 on 20 c. red and blue on green 65 75
79 05 on 25 c. black and red on pink 35 60
80 05 on 30 c. brown and blue on drab 35 55
81 10 on 40 c. red and blue on yellow 30 50
82 10 on 50 c. brown and blue on blue . . . . 75 1·60
83 10 on 75 c. brown and red on orange . . . . 2·50 5·00

1915. Red Cross Surch **5c** and red cross.

90 **16** 10 c. + 5 c. green and red . . 50 80

1917. Surch in figures.

91 **16** 0.01 on 4 c. red and green 70 70
124 **18** 25 c. on 5 f. brown & red . 40 60
115 **17** 40 on 20 c. yellow & green 30 40
116 50 on 45 c. red and purple 50 65
117 50 on 45 c. red and mauve £160 £160
118 50 on 65 c. blue and violet 45 60
119 60 on 75 c. carmine and red 25 25
120 **16** 65 on 15 c. blue and black 65 75
121 85 on 15 c. blue and black 60 75
122 **17** 85 on 75 c. pink and red 70 80
123 90 on 75 c. pink and red 85 90
125 **18** 1 f. 25 on 1 f. blue 35 45
126 1 f. 50 on 1 f. light blue and blue on blue 35 35
127 3 f. on 5 f. blue and red . 1·25 1·25
128 10 f. on 5 f. red & green . 8·75 7·25
129 20 f. on 5 f. pink & brown 11·00 9·00

1931. "Colonial Exhibition" key-types inscr "REUNION".

130 E 40 c. green and black . . . 1·50 1·60
131 F 50 c. mauve and black . . 1·90 2·00
132 G 90 c. red and black . . . . 2·00 2·00
133 H 1 f. 50 blue and black . . . 2·00 2·00

30 Cascade, Salazie

31 Anchain Peak, Salazie

32 Leon Dierx Museum

34 Caudron C-600 "Aiglon"

1933.

134 **30** 1 c. purple 10 30
135 2 c. brown 10 20
136 3 c. mauve 10 25
137 4 c. olive 10 30
138 5 c. orange 10 20
139 10 c. blue 10 25
140 15 c. black 10 15
141 20 c. blue 20 25
142 25 c. brown 15 25
143 30 c. green 15 20
144 **31** 35 c. green 30 40
145 40 c. blue 25 35
146 40 c. brown 20 35
147 45 c. mauve 45 55
148 45 c. green 25 35
149 50 c. red 25 15
150 55 c. orange 55 55
151 60 c. blue 20 35
152 65 c. olive 70 65
153 70 c. olive 35 40
154 75 c. brown . . . . 2·50 2·25
155 80 c. black 35 50
156 90 c. red . . . . 1·25 1·00
157 90 c. purple 50 45
158 1 f. green . . . . 1·00 65
159 1 f. red 65 60
160 1 f. black 25 35
161 **32** 1 f. 25 brown 35 50
162 1 f. 25 red 50 50
163 **30** 1 f. 40 blue 50 45
164 **32** 1 f. 50 blue 15 15
165 **30** 1 f. 60 red 45 45
166 **32** 1 f. 75 olive 35 35
167 **30** 1 f. 75 blue 45 55
168 **32** 2 f. red 25 40
169 **30** 2 f. 25 blue 85 80
170 2 f. 50 brown 55 55
171 **32** 3 f. violet 30 30
172 5 f. mauve 30 35
173 10 f. blue 40 45
174 20 f. brown 70 75

1937. Air. Pioneer Flight from Reunion to France by Laurent, Lenier and Touge. Optd **REUNION – FRANCE par avion "ROLAND GARROS"**.

174a **31** 50 c. red £170 £160

1937. International Exhibition, Paris. As Nos. 168/73 of St.-Pierre et Miquelon.

175 20 c. violet 85 95
176 30 c. green . . . . 95 1·10
177 40 c. red . . . . 90 1·10
178 50 c. brown and agate . . . 90 1·10
179 90 c. red . . . . 95 1·10
180 1 f. 50 blue . . . . 95 1·25

1938. Air.

181 **34** 3 f. 65 blue and red 60 85
182 6 f. 65 brown and red . . . 60 85
183 9 f. 65 red and blue 60 85
184 12 f. 65 brown and green . 1·00 1·40

1938. Int Anti-Cancer Fund. As T **22** of Mauritania.

185 1 f. 75 + 50 c. blue . . . . . 5·50 7·50

1939. New York World's Fair. As T **28** of Mauritania.

186 1 f. 25 red 50 60
187 2 f. 25 blue 55 60

1939. 150th Anniv of French Revolution. As T **29** of Mauritania.

188 45 c. + 25 c. green and black (postage) . . . . 4·75 5·00
189 70 c. + 30 c. brown & black . 4·75 5·00
190 90 c. + 35 c. orange & black . 4·50 5·00
191 1 f. 25 + 1 f. red and black . 4·75 5·00
192 2 f. 25 + 2 f. blue and black . 4·75 5·00
193 3 f. 65 + 4 f. blk & orge (air) . 9·50 11·50

1943. Surch **1f.**

194 **31** 1 f. on 65 c. green 55 55

1943. Optd **France Libre**.

198 **30** 1 c. purple (postage) 50 55
199 2 c. brown 40 55
200 3 c. purple 40 55
195 **16** 4 c. red and green . . . . . 1·25 1·90
201 **30** 4 c. green 40 55
202 **30** 5 c. red 40 55
203 10 c. blue 40 55
204 15 c. black 40 55
205 20 c. blue 40 55
206 25 c. brown 40 55
207 30 c. green 40 55
208 **31** 35 c. green 35 55
209 40 c. blue 40 55
210 40 c. brown 40 55
211 45 c. mauve 40 55
212 45 c. green 40 55
213 50 c. red 45 65
214 55 c. orange 40 55
215 60 c. blue . . . . 1·40 1·40
216 65 c. green 40 55
217 70 c. green 85 90
196 **17** 75 c. pink and red 65 70
218 **31** 75 c. brown . . . . 1·50 1·60
219 80 c. black 40 55
220 90 c. purple 40 55
221 1 f. green 40 55
222 1 f. red 40 55
223 1 f. black . . . . 95 1·00
240 1 f. on 65 c. green (No. 194) 65 75
224 **32** 1 f. 25 brown 40 55
225 1 f. 25 red 85 90
238 – 1 f. 25 red (No. 186) . . . 1·25 1·40
226 **30** 1 f. 40 blue 75 90
227 **32** 1 f. 50 blue 35 55
228 **30** 1 f. 60 red . . . . 85 1·00
229 **32** 1 f. 75 green 40 55
230 **30** 1 f. 75 blue . . . . 2·00 2·25
231 **32** 2 f. red 35 55
239 – 2 f. 25 blue (No. 187) . . . 1·40 1·40
232 **30** 2 f. 25 blue 85 90
233 2 f. 50 brown . . . . . . 3·00 3·00
234 **32** 3 f. violet 45 55
197 **18** 5 f. brown and pink . . . 27·00 27·00
235 **32** 5 f. mauve 85 90
236 10 f. blue . . . . 3·50 3·75
237 20 f. brown . . . . 5·75 5·75
241 **34** 3 f. 65 blue and red (air) . 2·00 2·00
242 6 f. 65 brown and red . . 2·00 2·00
243 9 f. 65 red and blue . . . 2·00 2·00
244 12 f. 65 brown and green . 2·00 2·00

37 Chief Products

1943. Free French Issue.

245 **37** 5 c. brown 10 25
246a 10 c. blue 20 25
247 25 c. green 10 25
248 30 c. red 10 25
249 40 c. green 10 25
250 80 c. mauve 10 30
251 1 f. purple 15 30
252 1 f. 50 red 15 35
253 2 f. black 20 35
254 2 f. 50 blue 25 40
255 4 f. violet 15 30
256 5 f. yellow 20 30
257 10 f. brown 25 70
258 20 f. green 30 80

1944. Air. Free French Administration. As T **30** of New Caledonia.

259 1 f. orange 20 30
260 1 f. 50 red 30 35
261 5 f. purple 30 35
262 10 f. black 40 45
263 25 f. blue 40 45
264 50 f. green 40 50
265 100 f. red 60 70

1944. Mutual Air and Red Cross Funds. As T **31** of New Caledonia.

266 5 f. + 20 f. black 55 55

1945. Eboue. As T **32** of New Caledonia.

267 2 f. black 45 45
268 25 f. green 55 55

1945. Surch.

269 **37** 50 c. on 5 c. brown 25 35
270 60 c. on 5 c. brown 25 35
271 70 c. on 5 c. brown 25 35
272 1 f. 20 on 5 c. brown . . . 35 50
273 2 f. 40 on 25 c. green . . . 35 50
274 3 f. on 25 c. green 35 50
275 4 f. 50 on 25 c. green . . . 45 60
276 15 f. on 2 f. 50 blue . . . 45 65

1946. Air. Victory. As T **34** of New Caledonia.

277 8 f. grey 40 55

1946. Air. From Chad to the Rhine. As Nos. 300/305 of New Caledonia.

278 5 f. red 60 85
279 10 f. violet 60 85
280 15 f. black 60 80
281 20 f. red 70 90
282 25 f. blue 70 85
283 50 f. green 70 90

39 Cliffs

40 Banana Tree and Cliff

41 Mountain Landscape

42 Shadow of Airplane over Coast

1947.
284 **39** 10 c. orange & grn (postage) 10 30
285 30 c. orange and blue . . . 10 30
286 40 c. orange and brown . . 10 30
287 – 50 c. brown and green . . 15 30
288 – 60 c. brown and blue . . . 15 10
289 – 80 c. green and brown . . 15 40
290 – 1 f. purple and blue . . . 30 20
291 – 1 f. 20 grey and green . . . 35 50
292 – 1 f. 50 purple and orange . 35 50
293 **40** 2 f. blue and green . . . 25 30
294 3 f. purple and green . . . 35 55
295 3 f. 60 pink and red . . . 35 55
296 4 f. blue and brown . . . 35 55
297 **41** 5 f. mauve and brown . . . 35 50
298 6 f. blue and brown . . . 50 60
299 10 f. orange and blue . . . 80 85
300 – 15 f. purple and blue . . . 1·75 1·90
301 – 20 f. blue and orange . . 2·25 2·25
302 – 25 f. brown and mauve . . 2·75 2·75
303 **42** 50 f. green and grey (air) . 3·75 3·75
304 – 100 f. orange and brown . 5·75 5·75
305 – 200 f. blue and orange . . 7·50 7·75
DESIGNS—20 × 37 mm: 50 c. to 80 c. Cutting sugar cane; 1 f. to 1 f. 50, Cascade. 28 × 50 mm: 100 f. Douglas DC-4 airplane over Reunion. 37 × 20 mm: 15 f. to 25 f. "Ville de Strasbourg" (liner) approaching Reunion. 50 × 28 mm: 200 f. Reunion from the air.

1949. Stamps of France surch **CFA** and value. (a) Postage. (i) Ceres.
306 **218** 50 c. on 1 f. red 15 30
307 60 c. on 2 f. green . . . . 2·25 1·40
(ii) Nos. 972/3 (Arms).
308 10 c. on 30 c. black, red and yellow (Alsace) 10 30
309 30 c. on 50 c. brown, yellow and red (Lorraine) 25 40
(iii) Nos. 981, 979 and 982/a (Views).
310 5 f. on 20 f. blue (Finistere) . 1·75 50
311 7 f. on 12 f. red (Luxembourg Palace) . . . . 2·50 1·25
312 8 f. on 25 f. blue (Nancy) . . 6·00 1·90
313 10 f. on 25 f. brn (Nancy) . . 1·00 70
(iv) Marianne.
314 **219** 1 f. on 3 f. mauve 40 30
315 2 f. on 4 f. green 75 50
316 2 f. on 5 f. green . . . . 3·25 3·25
317 2 f. on 5 f. violet 60 50
318 2 f. 50 on 5 f. blue . . . . 7·50 6·75
319 3 f. on 6 f. red 90 30
320 3 f. on 6 f. green . . . . 1·60 1·40
321 4 f. on 10 f. violet 85 40
322 6 f. on 12 f. blue . . . . 2·25 75
323 6 f. on 12 f. orange . . . . 1·90 1·25
324 9 f. on 18 f. red . . . . 2·75 2·75
(v) Conques Abbey.
325 **263** 11 f. on 18 f. blue . . . . 2·00 1·90
(b) Air. (i) Nos. 967/70 (Mythology).
326 – 20 f. on 40 f. green . . . 1·50 1·00
327 **236** 25 f. on 50 f. pink . . . 1·75 80
328 **237** 50 f. on 100 f. blue . . . 3·75 2·50
329 – 100 f. on 200 f. red . . . 25·00 12·50
(ii) Nos. 1056 and 1058/9 (Cities).
330 100 f. on 200 f. green (Bordeaux) 65·00 28·00
331 200 f. on 500 f. red (Marseilles) 24·00 16·00
332 500 f. on 1000 f. purple and black on blue (Paris) £170 £130

1950. Stamps of France surch **CFA** and value. (a) Nos. 1050 and 1052 (Arms).
342 10 c. on 50 c. yellow, red and blue (Guyenne) 15 30
343 1 f. on 2 f. red, yellow & green (Auvergne) . . . . 3·00 2·50
(b) On Nos. 1067/8 and 1068b (Views).
344 – 5 f. on 20 f. red (Comminges) 2·75 50
345 **284** 8 f. on 25 f. blue (Wandrille) 1·60 50
346 – 15 f. on 30 f. blue (Arbois) 85 60

1951. Nos. 1123/4 of France (Arms) surch **CFA** and value.
347 50 c. on 1 f. red, yellow and blue (Bearn) 30 35
348 1 f. on 2 f. yellow, blue and red (Touraine) 35 35

1952. Nos. 1138 and 1144 of France surch **CFA** and value.
349 **323** 5 f. on 20 f. violet (Chambord) 60 50
350 **317** 8 f. on 40 f. violet (Bigorre) 2·75 35

1953. Stamps of France surch **CFA** and value. (a) Nos. 1162, 1168 and 1170 (Literary Figures and National Industries).
351 3 f. on 6 f. lake and red (Gargantua) 40 35
352 8 f. on 40 f. brown and chocolate (Porcelain) . . . . 1·50 25
353 20 f. on 75 f. red and carmine (Flowers) . . . . 1·50 50
(b) Nos. 1181/2 (Arms).
354 50 c. on 1 f. yellow, red and black (Poitou) 45 60
355 1 f. on 2 f. yellow, blue and brown (Champagne) . . . 60 55

1954. Stamps of France surch **CFA** and value. (a) Postage. (i) Nos. 1188 and 1190 (Sports).
356 8 f. on 40 f. blue and brown (Canoeing) . . . . 10·00 5·00
357 20 f. on 75 f. red and orange (Horse jumping) . . . . . 35·00 23·00
(ii) Nos. 1205/8 and 1210/11 (Views).
358 2 f. on 6 f. indigo, blue and green (Lourdes) 45 45
359 3 f. on 8 f. green and blue (Andelys) 50 55
360 4 f. on 10 f. brown and blue (Royan) 65 70
361 6 f. on 12 f. lilac and violet (Quimper) 90 80
362 9 f. on 18 f. indigo, blue and green (Cheverny) . . . . . 2·25 2·75
363 10 f. on 20 f. brown, chestnut & blue (Ajaccio) . . . . . . 1·60 90
(iii) No. 1229 (Arms).
364 1 f. on 2 f. yellow, red and black (Angoumois) 30 30
(b) Air. Nos. 1194/7 (Aircraft).
365 50 f. on 100 f. brown and blue (Mystere IV) . . . . 1·00 75
366 100 f. on 200 f. purple and blue (Noratlas) . . . . 2·00 1·25
367 200 f. on 500 f. red and orange (Magister) . . . . 10·00 9·25
368 500 f. on 1000 f. indigo, purple and blue (Provence) . . . . 11·00 8·25

1955. Stamps of France surch **CFA** and value. (a) Nos. 1262/5, 1266, 1268 and 1268b (Views).
369 2 f. on 6 f. red (Bordeaux) . . 70 65
370 3 f. on 8 f. blue (Marseilles) . . 80 80
371 4 f. on 10 f. blue (Nice) . . . 55 50
372 5 f. on 12 f. brown and grey (Cahors) 60 50
373 6 f. on 18 f. blue and green (Uzerche) 60 50
374 10 f. on 25 f. brown and chestnut (Brouage) 65 50
375 17 f. on 70 f. black and green (Cahors) . . . . 2·75 2·00
(b) No. 1273 (Arms).
376 50 c. on 1 f. yellow, red and blue (Comtat Venaissin) 20 25

1956. Nos. 1297/1300 of France (Sports) surch **CFA** and value.
377 8 f. on 30 f. black and grey (Basketball) . . . . 1·25 45
378 9 f. on 40 f. purple and brown (Pelota) . . . . 1·90 1·10
379 15 f. on 50 f. violet and purple (Rugby) . . . . 2·75 1·25
380 20 f. on 75 f. green, black and blue (Climbing) . . . . . . 1·90 1·25

1957. Stamps of France surch **CFA** and value. (a) Postage. (i) Harvester.
381 **344** 2 f. on 6 f. brown 25 15
382 4 f. on 12 f. purple . . . 1·75 65
383 5 f. on 10 f. green . . . . 1·25 55
(ii) France.
384 **362** 10 f. on 20 f. blue 55 15
385 12 f. on 25 f. red . . . . 2·00 30
(iii) No. 1335 (Le Quesnoy).
386 7 f. on 15 f. black and green . 80 40
(iv) Nos. 1351, 1352/3, 1354/5 and 1356a (Tourist Publicity).
387 3 f. on 10 f. chocolate and brown (Elysee) 55 20
388 6 f. on 18 f. brown and blue (Beynac) 65 55
389 9 f. on 25 f. brown and grey (Valencay) 70 60
390 17 f. on 35 f. mauve and red (Rouen) . . . . 1·60 1·00
391 20 f. on 50 f. brown and green (St. Remy) 80 40
392 25 f. on 85 f. purple (Evian-les-Bains) . . . . 2·25 1·00
(b) Air. Nos. 1319/20 (Aircraft).
393 200 f. on 500 f. black and blue (Caravelle) . . . . 10·50 6·00
394 500 f. on 1000 f. black, violet and brown (Alouette II) . . . . 15·00 8·75

1960. Nos. 1461, 1464 and 1467 of France (Tourist Publicity) surch **CFA** and value.
395 7 f. on 15 c. indigo and blue (Laon) 65 45
396 20 f. on 50 c. purple and green (Tlemcen) . . . . 12·00 3·25
397 50 f. on 1 f. violet, green and blue (Cilaos) . . . . 1·60 55

1961. Harvester and Sower stamps of France (in new currency) surch **CFA** and value.
398 **344** 5 f. on 10 c. green . . . 30 20
400 **453** 10 f. on 20 c. red and turquoise 20 10

1961. "Marianne" stamp of France surch **12 f. CFA.**
401 **463** 12 f. on 25 c. grey & purple 20 10

1961. Nos. 1457, 1457b and 1459/60 of France (Aircraft) surch **CFA** and value.
402 100 f. on 2 f. purple and blue (Noratlas) . . . . 3·50 1·00
403 100 f. on 2 f. indigo and blue (Mystere Falcon 20) . . . 1·25 50
404 200 f. on 5 f. black and blue (Caravelle) . . . . 4·50 2·00
405 500 f. on 10 f. black, violet and brown (Alouette II) . . . . 11·50 4·00

1962. Red Cross stamps of France (Nos. 1593/4) surch **CFA** and value.
409 10 f. + 5 f. on 20 c. + 10 c. . 1·75 1·50
410 12 f. + 5 f. on 25 c. + 10 c. . 1·75 1·50

1962. Satellite Link stamps of France surch **CFA** and value.
411 12 f. on 25 c. (No. 1587) . . . 60 50
412 25 f. on 50 c. (No. 1588) . . . 60 50

1963. Nos. 1541 and 1545 of France (Tourist Publicity) surch **CFA** and value.
413 7 f. on 15 c. grey, purple and blue (St. Paul) 20 15
414 20 f. on 45 c. brown, green and blue (Sully) 80 30

1963. Nos. 1498b/9b and 1499e/f of France (Arms) surch **CFA** and value.
415 1 f. on 2 c. yellow, green and blue (Gueret) 10 10
416 2 f. on 5 c. mult (Oran) . . . 10 10
417 2 f. on 5 c. red, yellow and blue (Armiens) 10 10
418 5 f. on 10 c. blue, yellow and red (Troyes) 10 10
419 6 f. on 18 c. multicoloured (St. Denis) 15 15
420 15 f. on 30 c. red and blue (Paris) 20 10

1963. Red Cross stamps of France (Nos. 1627/8) surch **CFA** and value.
421 10 f. + 5 f. on 20 c. + 10 c. . 2·50 2·25
422 12 f. + 5 f. on 25 c. + 10 c. . 2·50 2·25

1964. 'PHILATEC 1964' International Stamp Exhibition stamp of France surch **CFA** and value.
423 12 f. on 25 c. (No. 1629) . . . 85 60

1964. Nos. 1654/5 of France (Tourist Publicity) surch **CFA** and value.
431 20 f. on 40 c. chocolate, green and brown (Ronchamp) . . . 60 45
432 35 f. on 70 c. purple, green and blue (Provins) 80 65

1964. Red Cross stamps of France. (Nos. 1665/6) surch **CFA** and value.
433 10 f. + 5 f. on 20 c. + 10 c. . 1·10 1·00
434 12 f. + 5 f. on 25 c. + 10 c. . 1·10 1·00

1965. No. 1621 of France (Saint Flour) surch **3F CFA.**
435 30 f. on 60 c. red, green & bl . 80 65

1965. Nos 1684/5 and 1688 of France (Tourist Publicity) surch **CFA** and value.
436 25 f. on 50 c. blue, green and bistre (St. Marie) 50 25
437 30 f. on 60 c. brown and blue (Aix les Bains) 65 45
438 50 f. on 1 f. grey, green and brown (Carnac) . . . . . . 1·10 90

1965. Tercent of Colonisation of Reunion. As No. 1692 of France, but additionally inscr 'CFA'.
439 15 f. blue and red 45 30

1965. Red Cross stamps of France (Nos. 1698/9) surch **CFA** and value.
440 12 f. + 5 f. on 25 c. + 10 c. . 1·00 1·00
441 15 f. + 5 f. on 30 c. + 10 c. . 1·00 1·00

1966. "Marianne" stamp of France surch **10f CFA.**
442 **476** 10 f. on 20 c. red & blue . 1·00 50

1966. Launching of 1st French Satellite. Nos. 1696/7 (plus se-tenant label) of France surch **CFA** and value.
443 15 f. on 30 c. blue, turquoise and light blue 60 50
444 30 f. on 60 c. blue, turquoise and light blue 80 70

1966. Red Cross stamps of France (Nos. 1733/4) surch **CFA** and value.
445 12 f. + 5 f. on 25 c. + 10 c. . 90 70
446 15 f. + 5 f. on 30 c. + 10 c. . 90 70

1967. World Fair Montreal. No. 1747 of France surch **CFA** and value.
447 30 f. on 60 c. 90 65

1967. No. 1700 of France (Arms of Auch) surch **2fCFA.**
448 2 f. on 5 c. red and blue . . . 15 10

1967. 50th Anniv of Lions Int. No. 1766 of France surch **CFA** and value.
449 20 f. on 40 c. . . . . 1·10 90

1967. Red Cross. Nos. 1772/3 of France surch **CFA** and value.
450 12 f. + 5 f. on 25 c. + 10 c. . 2·50 2·50
451 15 f. + 5 f. on 30 c. + 10 c. . 2·50 2·50

1968. French Polar Exploration. No. 1806 of France surch **CFA** and value.
452 20 f. on 40 c. 75 65

1968. Red Cross stamps of France (Nos. 1812/13) surch **CFA** and value.
453 12 f. + 5 f. on 25 c. + 10 c. . 1·25 1·10
454 15 f. + 5 f. on 30 c. + 10 c. . 1·25 1·10

1969. Stamp Day. No. 1824 of France surch **CFA** and value.
455 15 f. + 5 f. on 30 c. + 10 c. . 80 80

1969. "Republique" stamps of France surch **CFA** and value.
456 **604** 15 f. on 30 c. green 45 35
457 20 f. on 40 c. mauve 45 25

1969. No. 1735 of France (Arms of Saint-Lo) surch **10F CFA.**
458 10 f. on 20 c. multicoloured . . 25 25

1969. Birth Bicent of Napoleon Bonaparte. No. 1845 of France surch **CFA** and value.
459 35 f. on 70 c. green, violet & bl 1·10 90

1969. Red Cross stamps of France (Nos. 1853/4) surch **CFA** and value.
460 20 f. + 7 f. on 40 c. + 15 c. . 1·00 1·00
461 20 f. + 7 f. on 40 c. + 15 c. . 1·00 1·00

1970. Stamp Day. No. 1866 of France surch **CFA** and value.
462 20 f. + 5 f. on 40 c. + 10 c. . 90 65

1970. Red Cross. Nos. 1902/3 of France surch **CFA** and value.
463 20 f. + 7 f. on 40 c. + 15 c. . 2·25 1·75
464 20 f. + 7 f. on 40 c. + 15 c. . 2·25 1·75

1971. "Marianne" stamp of France surch **25f CFA.**
465 **668** 25 f. on 50 c. mauve . . . 45 10

1971. Stamp Day. No. 1919 of France surch **CFA** and value.
466 25 f. + 5 f. on 50 c. + 10 c. . 90 35

1971. "Antoinette". No. 1920 of France surch **CFA** and value.
467 40 f. on 80 c. . . . . 1·10 90

1971. No. 1928 of France (Rural Aid) surch **CFA** and value.
468 **678** 15 f. on 40 c. 55 45

1971. Nos. 1931/2 of France (Tourist Publicity) surch **CFA** and value.
469 45 f. on 90 c. brown, green and ochre (Riquewihr) 65 45
470 50 f. on 1 f. 10 brown, blue and green (Sedan) 90 55

1971. 40th Anniv of 1st Meeting of Crafts Guilds Association. No. 1935 of France surch **CFA** and value.
471 **680** 45 c. on 90 c. purple & red 80 60

63 Reunion Chameleon

65 King Penguin, Map and Exploration Ships

1971. Nature Protection.
472 **63** 25 f. green, brn & yellow . 80 55

1971. De Gaulle Commem. As T **92** of New Caledonia but with face value in CFA francs.
473 25 f. black . . . . 1·10 1·10
474 25 f. blue . . . . 1·10 1·00
475 25 f. red . . . . 1·10 1·10
476 25 f. black . . . . 1·10 1·10
DESIGNS: No. 473, De Gaulle in uniform (June, 1940); No. 474, De Gaulle at Brazzaville, 1944; No. 475, De Gaulle in Paris, 1944; No. 476, De Gaulle as President of the French Republic, 1970 (T **92**).

1971. Nos. 1942/3 of France (Red Cross Fund) surch **CFA** and value.
477 15 f. + 5 f. on 30 c. + 10 c. . 90 90
478 25 f. + 5 f. on 50 c. + 10 c. . 90 90

1972. Bicentenary of Discovery of Crozet Islands and Kerguelen (French Southern and Antarctic Territories).
479 **65** 45 f. black, blue & brown . 2·00 1·50

1972. No. 1956 of France surch **CFA** and value.
480 **688** 25 f. + 5 f. on 50 c. + 10 c. blue, drab and yellow . 65 65

1972. No. 1966 of France (Blood Donors) surch **CFA** and value.
481 **692** 15 f. on 40 c. red 45 30

1972. Air. No 1890 of France (Daurat and Vanier) surch **CFA** and value.
482 **662** 200 f. on 5 f. brn, grn and bl 3·50 1·50

1972. Postal Codes. Nos. 1969/70 of France surch **CFA** and value.
483 **695** 15 f. on 30 c. red, black and green 40 25
484 25 f. on 50 c. yellow, blk & red 40 25

1972. Red Cross Fund. Nos. 1979/80 of France surch **CFA** and value.
485 **701** 15 f. + 5 f. on 30 c. + 10 c. 75 75
486 25 f. + 5 f. on 50 c. + 10 c. 90 90

1973. Stamp Day. No. 1996 of France surch **CFA** and value.
487 **707** 25 f. + 5 f. on 50 c. + 10 c. 1·10 90

1973. No. 2011 of France surch **CFA** and value.
488 **714** 45 f. on 90 c. green, violet and blue . . . . . . 1·25 1·00

1973. No. 2008 of France surch **CFA** and value.
489 50 f. on 1 f. green, brown & bl 75 55

1973. No. 1960 of France surch **CFA** and value.
490 100 f. on 2 f. purple & green . 1·50 90

1973. No. 2021/2 of France surch **CFA** and value.
491 **721** 15 f. + 5 f. on 30 c. + 10 c. green and red . . . . . 1·00 1·00
492 25 f. + 5 f. on 50 c. + 10 c. red and black . . . . . 1·10 1·10

1973. No. 2026 of France surch **CFA** and value.
494 **725** 25 f. on 50 c. brown, blue and purple 55 35

1974. Stamp Day. No. 2031 surch **FCFA** and value.
495 **727** 25 f. + 5 f. on 50 c. + 10 c. 55 55

1974. French Art. Nos. 2033/6 surch **FCFA** and value.
496 100 f. on 2 f. multicoloured 1·75 1·50
497 100 f. on 2 f. multicoloured 1·75 1·50
498 100 f. on 2 f. brown and blue 2·00 1·50
499 100 f. on 2 f. multicoloured 2·00 1·50

1974. French Lifeboat Service. No. 2040 surch **FCFA** and value.
500 **731** 45 f. on 90 c. blue, red and brown . . . . 1·10 90

1974. Centenary of Universal Postal Union. No. 2057 surch **FCFA** and value.
501 **741** 60 f. on 1 f. 20 green, red and blue . . . . 1·10 1·00

1974. "Marianne" stamps of France surch **FCFA** and value.
502 **668** 30 f. on 60 c. green . . . 1·40 1·25
503 40 f. on 80 c. red . . . . 1·60 1·40

1974. Red Cross Fund. "The Seasons". Nos. 2059/60 surch **FCFA** and value.
504 **743** 30 f. + 7 f. on 60 c. + 15 c. 1·00 1·00
505 – 40 f. + 7 f. on 80 c. + 15 c. 1·10 1·10

From 1st January 1975 the CFA franc was replaced by the French Metropolitan franc, and Reunion subsequently used unsurcharged stamps of France.

PARCEL POST STAMPS

P 5 P 20

1890.
P11 **P 5** 10 c. black on yellow (black frame) £200 £120
P13 10 c. black on yellow (blue frame) . . . . 14·50 12·50

1907. Receipt stamps surch as in Type **P 20**.
P76 **P 20** 10 c. brown and black . . 9·00 6·50
P77 10 c. brown and red . . . 9·00 10·00

POSTAGE DUE STAMPS

D 4 D 19

1889. Imperf.
D11 **D 4** 5 c. black . . . . 11·50 5·50
D12 10 c. black . . . . 14·50 4·75
D13 15 c. black . . . . 29·00 17·00
D14 20 c. black . . . . 25·00 9·00
D15 30 c. black . . . . 23·00 9·00

1907.
D76 **D 19** 5 c. red on yellow . . . 10 20
D77 10 c. blue on blue . . . 15 25
D78 15 c. black on grey . . . 15 40
D79 20 c. pink 15 35
D80 30 c. green on green . . 20 65
D81 50 c. red on green . . . 20 75
D82 60 c. pink on blue . . . 25 75
D83 1 f. lilac . . . . 75 1·40

1927. Surch.
D130 **D 19** 2 f. on 1 f. red . . . . 3·25 5·00
D131 3 f. on 1 f. brown . . 3·25 5·00

D 33 Arms of Reunion **D 43**

1933.
D175 **D 33** 5 c. purple 10 25
D176 10 c. green 10 25
D177 15 c. brown 10 25
D178 20 c. orange 15 25
D179 30 c. olive 15 30
D180 50 c. blue 20 45
D181 60 c. brown 25 45
D182 1 f. violet 20 40
D183 2 f. blue 25 40
D184 3 f. red 25 45

1947.
D306 **D 43** 10 c. mauve 10 30
D307 30 c. brown 10 25
D308 50 c. green 10 30
D309 1 f. brown 15 30
D310 2 f. red 20 30
D311 3 f. brown 20 30
D312 4 f. blue 20 60
D313 5 f. red 20 60
D314 10 f. green 25 60
D315 20 f. blue 30 75

1949. As Type **D 250** of France, but inscr "TIMBRE TAXE" surch **CFA** and value.
D333 10 c. on 1 f. blue 10 30
D334 50 c. on 2 f. blue 10 30
D335 1 f. on 3 f. red 30 50
D336 2 f. on 4 f. violet 60 80
D337 3 f. on 5 f. pink . . . . . 1·50 1·75
D338 5 f. on 10 f. red . . . . . 85 1·00
D339 10 f. on 20 f. brown . . . . 1·25 1·50
D340 20 f. on 50 f. green . . . . 3·25 2·75
D341 50 f. on 100 f. green . . . . 11·00 9·50

1962. Wheat Sheaves Type of France surch **CFA** and value.
D406 **D 457** 1 f. on 5 c. mauve . 1·00 75
D407 10 f. on 20 c. brown 2·50 1·50
D408 20 f. on 50 c. green . 15·00 10·00

1964. Nos. D1650/4 and D1656/7 of France surch **CFA** and value.
D424 – 1 f. on 5 c. 10 10
D425 – 5 f. on 10 c. 10 10
D426 **D 539** 7 f. on 15 c. 20 20
D427 – 10 f. on 20 c. . . . . 1·25 60
D428 – 15 f. on 30 c. 35 30
D429 – 20 f. on 50 c. 45 40
D430 – 50 f. on 1 f. . . . . 1·25 1·00

RIAU-LINGGA ARCHIPELAGO Pt. 21

A group of islands E of Sumatra and S of Singapore. Part of Indonesia.

100 cents or sen = 1 rupiah

1954. Optd **RIAU**. (a) On stamps of Indonesia.
1 **96** 5 s. red . . . . 28·00 19·00
2 7½ s. green 20 35
3 10 s. blue . . . . 32·00 40·00
4 15 s. violet 80 80
5 20 s. red . . . . 95 1·10
6 25 s. green . . . . 65·00 22·00
7 **97** 30 s. red . . . . 2·40 1·60
8 35 s. violet 20 35
9 40 s. green 20 35
10 45 s. purple 25 35
11 50 s. brown . . . . £190 32·00
12 **98** 60 s. brown 20 35
13 70 s. grey 60 65
14 75 s. blue . . . . 3·25 1·60
15 80 s. purple . . . . 50 1·90
16 90 s. green . . . . 50 1·10

(b) On Netherlands Indies Nos. 566/71.
17 – 1 r. violet . . . . 6·25 1·60
18 – 2 r. green . . . . 65 1·90
19 – 3 r. purple . . . . 95 1·90
20 – 5 r. brown . . . . 95 1·90
21 – 10 r. black . . . . 1·25 2·40
22 – 25 r. brown . . . . 1·25 2·40

1958. Stamps of Indonesia optd **RIAU**.
26 **115** 5 s. blue 20 35
27 10 s. brown (No. 714) . . 40 35
28 15 s. purple (No. 715) . . 40 1·50
29 – 20 s. green (No. 716) . . 40 35
30 – 25 s. brown (No. 717) . . 40 35
31 – 30 s. orange (No. 718) . . 40 35
32 – 50 s. brown (No. 722) . . 40 35

1960. Stamps of Indonesia optd **RIAU**.
33 **99** 1 r. 25 orange . . . . . 95 3·25
34 1 r. 50 brown . . . . . 95 3·25
35 2 r. 50 brown . . . . . 1·25 4·75
36 4 r. green . . . . . 25 4·75
37 6 r. mauve . . . . . 25 4·75
38 15 r. stone . . . . . 25 4·75
39 20 r. purple . . . . . 25 6·25
40 40 r. green . . . . . 25 7·00
41 50 r. violet . . . . . 35 7·50

RIO DE ORO Pt. 9

A Spanish territory on the West Coast of North Africa, renamed Spanish Sahara in 1924.

100 centimos = 1 peseta

1905. "Curly Head" key-type inscr "COLONIA DE RIO DE ORO".
1 Z 1 c. green . . . . 3·00 2·40
2 2 c. red . . . . 3·00 2·40
3 3 c. black . . . . 3·00 2·40
4 4 c. brown . . . . 3·00 2·40
5 5 c. red . . . . 3·00 2·40
6 10 c. brown . . . . 3·00 2·40
7 15 c. brown . . . . 3·00 2·40
8 25 c. blue . . . . 60·00 26·00
9 50 c. green . . . . 29·00 10·50
10 75 c. violet . . . . 29·00 14·50
11 1 p. brown . . . . 19·00 6·50
12 2 p. orange . . . . 65·00 40·00
13 3 p. lilac . . . . 42·00 14·50
14 4 p. green . . . . 42·00 14·50
15 5 p. blue . . . . 60·00 30·00
16 10 p. red £140 £100

1906. "Curly Head" key-type surch **HABILITADO PARA 15 CENTS** in circle.
17 Z 15 c. on 25 c. blue . . . . £170 55·00

3 7 11

1907.
18 **3** 1 c. purple . . . . 2·40 1·90
19 2 c. black . . . . 2·40 1·90
20 3 c. brown . . . . 2·40 1·90
21 4 c. red . . . . 2·40 1·90
22 5 c. brown . . . . 2·40 1·90
23 10 c. brown . . . . 2·40 1·90
24 15 c. blue . . . . 2·40 1·90
25 25 c. green . . . . 6·00 1·90
26 50 c. purple . . . . 6·00 1·90
27 75 c. brown . . . . 6·00 1·90
28 1 p. buff . . . . 10·50 1·90
29 2 p. lilac . . . . 3·75 1·90
30 3 p. green . . . . 3·75 1·90
31 4 p. blue . . . . 6·00 3·50
32 5 p. red . . . . 6·00 3·50
33 10 p. green . . . . 6·00 9·00

1907. Nos. 9/10 surch **1907 10 Cens**.
34 Z 10 c. on 50 c. green . . . . 60·00 23·00
35 10 c. on 75 c. violet . . . . 45·00 23·00

1908. Nos. 12 and 26 surch **1908** and value.
36 Z 2 c. on 2 p. orange . . . . . 38·00 23·00
37 **3** 10 c. on 50 c. purple . . . . 17·00 3·75

1908. Surch **HABILITADO PARA 15 CENTS** in circle.
38 **3** 15 c. on 25 c. green . . . . . 21·00 4·00
39 15 c. on 75 c. brown . . . . 28·00 7·00
40 15 c. on 1 p. buff . . . . . 28·00 7·00
71 15 c. on 3 p. green . . . . . £120 21·00
72 15 c. on 5 p. red . . . . . 8·75 8·00

1908. Large Fiscal stamp inscr "TERRITORIOS ESPAÑOLES DEL AFRICA OCCIDENTAL" surch **HABILITADO PARA CORREOS RIO DE ORO 5 CENS.** Imperf.
45 5 c. on 50 c. green . . . . . . 55·00 23·00

1909.
47 **7** 1 c. orange 55 40
48 2 c. orange 55 40
49 5 c. green 55 40
50 10 c. red 55 40
51 15 c. green 55 40
52 20 c. purple . . . . 1·50 65
53 25 c. blue . . . . 1·50 65
54 30 c. red . . . . 1·50 65
55 40 c. brown . . . . 1·50 65
56 50 c. purple . . . . 2·75 65
57 1 p. brown . . . . 3·75 3·25
58 4 p. red . . . . 4·25 4·50
59 10 p. purple . . . . 9·50 7·50

1910. Nos. 13/16 surch **1910** and value.
60 Z 10 c. on 5 p. blue . . . . . 14·00 12·50
62 10 c. on 10 p. red . . . . . 12·00 7·00
65 15 c. on 3 p. lilac . . . . . 12·00 7·00
66 15 c. on 4 p. green . . . . . 12·00 7·00

1911. Surch with value in figures and words.
67 **3** 2 c. on 4 p. blue . . . . . 8·75 7·00
68 5 c. on 10 p. green . . . . . 23·00 7·00
69 10 c. on 2 p. lilac . . . . . 11·50 7·00
70 10 c. on 3 p. green . . . . . £140 42·00

1912.
73 **11** 1 c. pink 20 15
74 2 c. lilac 20 15
75 5 c. green 20 15
76 10 c. red 20 15
77 15 c. brown 20 15
78 20 c. brown 20 15
79 25 c. blue 20 15
80 30 c. lilac 20 15
81 40 c. green 20 15
82 50 c. purple 20 15
83 1 p. red . . . . 2·00 55
84 4 p. red . . . . 4·50 2·75
85 10 p. brown . . . . 6·50 4·25

12 14 15

1914.
86 **12** 1 c. brown 25 15
87 2 c. purple 25 15
88 5 c. green 25 15
89 10 c. red 25 15
90 15 c. red 25 15
91 20 c. red 25 15
92 25 c. blue 25 15
93 30 c. green 25 15
94 40 c. orange 25 15
95 50 c. brown 25 15
96 1 p. lilac . . . . 2·25 2·40
97 4 p. red . . . . 5·25 2·40
98 10 p. violet . . . . 7·00 7·00

1917. Nos. 73/85 optd **1917**.
99 **11** 1 c. pink . . . . 8·25 1·10
100 2 c. lilac . . . . 8·25 1·10
101 5 c. green . . . . 2·25 1·10
102 10 c. red . . . . 2·25 1·10
103 **11** 15 c. brown . . . . 2·25 1·10
104 20 c. brown . . . . 2·25 1·10
105 25 c. blue . . . . 2·25 1·10
106 30 c. lilac . . . . 2·25 1·10
107 40 c. green . . . . 2·25 1·10
108 50 c. purple . . . . 2·25 1·10
109 1 p. red . . . . 11·00 4·75
110 4 p. red . . . . 14·50 6·75
111 10 p. brown . . . . 25·00 11·00

1919.
112 **14** 1 c. brown 60 40
113 2 c. purple 60 40
114 5 c. green 60 40
115 10 c. red 60 40
116 15 c. red 60 40
117 20 c. orange 60 40
118 25 c. blue 60 40
119 30 c. green 60 40
120 40 c. orange 60 40
121 50 c. brown 60 40
122 1 p. lilac . . . . 4·25 2·75
123 4 p. red . . . . 7·00 5·25
124 10 p. violet . . . . 11·00 8·00

1920.
125 **15** 1 c. purple 55 35
126 2 c. pink 55 35
127 5 c. red 55 35
128 10 c. purple 55 35
129 15 c. brown 55 35
130 20 c. green 55 35
131 25 c. orange 55 35
132 30 c. blue . . . . 3·25 3·25
133 40 c. orange . . . . 1·90 1·40
134 50 c. purple . . . . 1·90 1·40
135 1 p. green . . . . 1·90 1·40
136 4 p. red . . . . 3·75 3·25
137 10 p. brown . . . . 9·00 8·00

1921. As T **2** of La Aguera but inscr "RIO DE ORO".
138 1 c. yellow 55 40
139 2 c. brown 55 40
140 5 c. green 55 40
141 10 c. red 55 40
142 15 c. green 55 40
143 20 c. blue 55 40
144 25 c. blue 55 40
145 30 c. pink . . . . 1·10 95
146 40 c. violet . . . . 1·10 95
147 50 c. orange . . . . 1·10 95
148 1 p. mauve . . . . 3·25 1·75
149 4 p. purple . . . . 5·50 4·00
150 10 p. brown . . . . 9·50 9·00

For later issues see **SPANISH SAHARA**.

RIO MUNI Pt. 9

A coastal settlement between Cameroun and Gabon, formerly using the stamps of Spanish Guinea. On 12 October 1968 it became independent and joined Fernando Poo to become Equatorial Guinea.

100 centimos = 1 peseta

1 Native Boy reading Book

2 Cactus

1960.
1 **1** 25 c. grey 10 10
2 50 c. brown 10 10
3 75 c. purple 10 10
4 1 p. red 10 10
5 1 p. 50 green 10 10
6 2 p. purple 15 10
7 3 p. blue 30 10
8 5 p. brown 65 10
9 10 p. green . . . . 1·25 20

1960. Child Welfare Fund.
10 **2** 10 c. + 5 c. purple 10 10
11 – 15 c. + 5 c. brown 10 10
12 – 35 c. green 10 10
13 **2** 80 c. green 10 10

DESIGNS: 15 c. Sprig with berries; 35 c. Star-shaped flowers.

3 Bishop Juan de Ribera

4 Mandrill with Banana

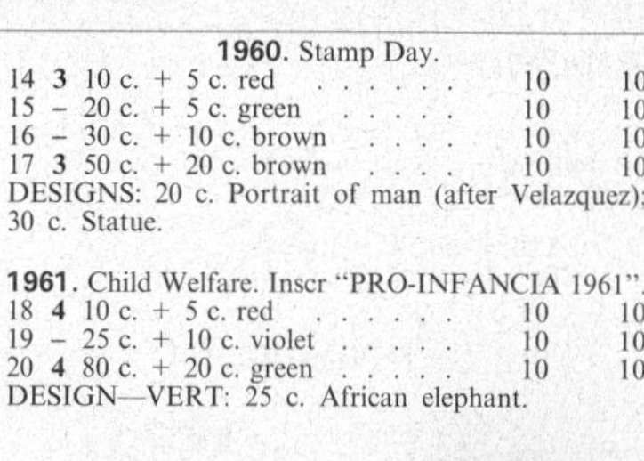

1960. Stamp Day.
14 **3** 10 c. + 5 c. red 10 10
15 – 20 c. + 5 c. green 10 10
16 – 30 c. + 10 c. brown 10 10
17 **3** 50 c. + 20 c. brown 10 10
DESIGNS: 20 c. Portrait of man (after Velazquez); 30 c. Statue.

1961. Child Welfare. Inscr "PRO-INFANCIA 1961".
18 **4** 10 c. + 5 c. red 10 10
19 – 25 c. + 10 c. violet 10 10
20 **4** 80 c. + 20 c. green 10 10
DESIGN—VERT: 25 c. African elephant.

5

6 Statuette

1961. 25th Anniv of Gen. Franco as Head of State.
21 – 25 c. grey 30 10
22 **5** 50 c. brown 10 10
23 – 70 c. green 10 10
24 **5** 1 p. red 10 10
DESIGNS: 25 c. Map; 70 c. Govt building.

1961. Stamp Day. Inscr "DIA DEL SELLO 1961".
25 **6** 10 c. + 5 c. red 10 10
26 – 25 c. + 10 c. purple 10 10
27 **6** 30 c. + 10 c. brown 10 10
28 – 1 p. + 10 c. orange 10 10
DESIGN: 25 c., 1 p. Figure holding offering.

7 Girl wearing Headdress

8 African Buffalo

1962. Child Welfare. Inscr "PRO-INFANCIA 1962".
29 **7** 25 c. violet 10 10
30 – 50 c. green 10 10
31 **7** 1 p. brown 10 10
DESIGN: 50 c. Native mask.

1962. Stamp Day. Inscr "DIA DEL SELLO 1962".
32 **8** 15 c. green 10 10
33 – 35 c. purple 10 10
34 **8** 1 p. red 15 10
DESIGN—VERT: 35 c. Gorilla.

9 Statuette

10 "Blessing"

1963. Seville Flood Relief.
35 **9** 50 c. green 10 10
36 1 p. brown 10 10

1963. Child Welfare. Inscr "PRO-INFANCIA 1963".
37 – 25 c. violet 10 10
38 **10** 50 c. green 10 10
39 – 1 p. red 10 10
DESIGN: 25 c., 1 p. Priest.

11 Chid at Prayer

12 Copal Flower

1963. "For Barcelona".
40 **11** 50 c. green 10 10
41 1 p. brown 10 10

1964. Stamp Day. Inscr "DIA DEL SELLO 1963".
42 **12** 25 c. violet 10 10
43 – 50 c. turquoise 10 10
44 **12** 1 p. red 10 10
FLOWER—HORIZ: 50 c. Cinchona blossom.

13 Giant Ground Pangolin

1964. Child Welfare. Inscr "PRO-INFANCIA 1964".
45 **13** 25 c. violet 10 10
46 – 50 c. green (Chameleon) . . 10 10
47 **13** 1 p. brown 10 10

1964. Wild Life. As T **13** but without "PRO INFANCIA" inscription.
48 15 c. brown 10 10
49 25 c. violet 10 10
50 50 c. green 10 10
51 70 c. green 10 10
52 1 p. brown 55 10
53 1 p. 50 green 55 10
54 3 p. blue . . . . 1·10 10
55 5 p. brown . . . . 3·00 35
56 10 p. green . . . . 5·50 65
ANIMALS: 15, 70 c., 3 p. Crocodile; 25 c., 1, 5 p. Leopard; 50 c., 1 p. 50, 10 p. Black rhinoceros.

14 "Goliath" Frog

15 Woman

1964. Stamp Day.
57 **14** 50 c. green 10 10
58 – 1 p. red 45 10
59 **14** 1 p. 50 green 10 10
DESIGN—VERT: 1 p. Helmet guineafowl.

1965. 25th Anniv of End of Spanish Civil War.
60 **15** 50 c. green 10 10
61 – 1 p. red 10 10
62 – 1 p. 50 turquoise 10 10
DESIGNS: 1 p. Nurse; 1 p. 50, Logging.

16 Goliath Beetle

1965. Child Welfare. Insects.
63 **16** 50 c. green 10 10
64 – 1 p. brown 10 10
65 **16** 1 p. 50 black 20 15
DESIGN: 1 p. "Acridoxena hewaniana".

17 Leopard and Arms of Rio Muni

1965. Stamp Day.
66 – 50 c. grey 50 10
67 **17** 1 p. brown 30 10
68 – 2 p. 50 violet . . . . 2·75 50
DESIGN—VERT: 50 c., 2 p. 50, Ring-necked pheasant.

18 African Elephant and Grey Parrot

1966. Child Welfare.
69 **18** 50 c. brown 30 10
70 1 p. lilac 30 10
71 – 1 p. 50 blue 25 10
DESIGN: 1 p. 50, African and lion.

19 Water Chevrotain

20 Floss Flowers

1966. Stamp Day.
72 **19** 10 c. brown and ochre . . . 10 10
73 – 40 c. brown and yellow . . 10 10
74 **19** 1 p. 50 violet and red . . . 10 10
75 – 4 p. blue and green 15 10
DESIGN—VERT: 40 c., 4 p. Giant ground pangolin.

1967. Child Welfare.
76 **20** 10 c. yellow, olive & green . 10 10
77 – 40 c. green, black & mve . . 10 10
78 **20** 1 p. 50 red and blue 10 10
79 – 4 p. black and green 15 10
DESIGNS: 40 c., 4 p. Ylang-ylang (flower).

21 Bush Pig

1967. Stamp Day.
80 **21** 1 p. chestnut and brown . . 10 10
81 – 1 p. 50 brown and green . . 10 10
82 – 3 p. 50 brown and green . . 15 10
DESIGNS—VERT: 1 p. 50, Potto. HORIZ: 3 p. 50, African golden cat.

1968. Child Welfare. Signs of the Zodiac. As T **56a** of Spanish Sahara.
83 1 p. mauve on yellow 10 10
84 1 p. 50 brown on pink 10 10
85 2 p. 50 violet on yellow . . . 15 10
DESIGNS: 1 p. Cancer (crab); 1 p. 50, Taurus (bull); 2 p. 50, Gemini (twins).

ROMAGNA Pt. 8

One of the Papal states, now part of Italy. Stamps issued prior to union with Sardinia in 1860.

100 bajocchi = 1 scudo

1

1859. Imperf.
2 **1** ½ b. black on buff . . . . . 10·00 £250
3 1 b. black on grey . . . . . 10·00 £110
4 2 b. black on buff . . . . . 16·00 £110
5 3 b. black on green . . . . . 21·00 £225
6 4 b. black on brown £475 £110
7 5 b. black on lilac . . . . . 26·00 £300
8 6 b. black on green £2500 £6000
9 8 b. black on pink £200 £1400
10 20 b. black on green £160 £2000

ROUAD ISLAND (ARWAD) Pt. 6

An island in the E. Mediterranean off the coast of Syria. A French P.O. was established there during 1916.

25 centimes = 1 piastre

1916. "Blanc" and "Mouchon" key-types inscr "LEVANT" and optd **ILE ROUAD** (vert).
1 A 5 c. green £300 £130
2 B 10 c. red £300 £130
3 1 pi. on 25 c. blue £300 £130

1916. "Blanc" "Mouchon" and "Merson" key-types inscr "LEVANT" and optd **ILE ROUAD** horiz.
4 A 1 c. grey 30 30
5 2 c. purple 30 35
6 3 c. red 30 35
7 5 c. green 35 40
8 B 10 c. red 40 40
9 15 c. red 60 70
10 20 c. brown . . . . 1·00 1·00
11 1 p. on 25 c. blue . . . . . 1·00 1·00
12 30 c. lilac . . . . 1·00 1·00
13 C 40 c. red and blue . . . . . 2·00 2·00
14 2 p. on 50 c. brown & lav . . 3·25 3·25
15 4 p. on 1 f. red and yellow . 4·75 5·50
16 30 p. on 5 f. blue & yellow . 17·00 20·00

RUANDA-URUNDI Pt. 4

Part of German E. Africa, including Ruanda and Urundi, occupied by Belgian forces during the war of 1914-18 and a Trust Territory administered by Belgium until 1 July 1962. The territory then became two separate independent states, named Rwanda and Burundi.

100 centimes = 1 franc

1916. Nos. 70/77 of Belgian Congo optd. (a) **RUANDA**.
1 **32** 5 c. black and green . . . . 15·00
2 **33** 10 c. black and red . . . . . 15·00
3 **13** 15 c. black and green . . . . 26·00
4 **34** 25 c. black and blue . . . . 15·00
5 **14** 40 c. black and red . . . . . 15·00
6 – 50 c. black and red . . . . . 18·00
7 – 1 f. black and brown . . . . 55·00
7a – 5 f. black and orange £2000

(b) **URUNDI**.
8 **32** 5 c. black and green . . . 15·00
9 **33** 10 c. black and red . . . . 15·00
10 **13** 15 c. black and green . . . 26·00
11 **34** 25 c. black and blue . . . 15·00
12 **14** 40 c. black and red . . . . 15·00
13 – 50 c. black and red . . . . 18·00
14 – 1 f. black and brown . . . 55·00
14a – 5 f. black and orange . . . £2000

1916. Stamps of Belgian Congo of 1915 optd **EST AFRICAIN ALLEMAND OCCUPATION BELGE. DUITSCH OOST AFRIKA BELGISCHE BEZETTING**.
15 **32** 5 c. black and green 25 20
16 **33** 10 c. black and red 40 30
17 **13** 15 c. black and green . . . 30 20
18 **34** 25 c. black and blue . . . . 1·75 95
19 **14** 40 c. black and lake . . . . 5·00 4·00
20 – 50 c. black and lake . . . . 5·50 4·00
21 – 1 f. black and olive 60 40
22 – 5 f. black and orange . . . 85 75

1918. Belgian Congo Red Cross stamps of 1918 optd **A. O.**.
23 **32** 5 c. + 10 c. blue & green . 20 20
24 **33** 10 c. + 15 c. blue and red . 20 20
25 **13** 15 c. + 20 c. blue & green . 20 20
26 **34** 25 c. + 25 c. blue 20 20
27 **14** 40 c. + 40 c. blue and lake . 25 25
28 – 50 c. + 50 c. blue and lake . 50 1·50
29 – 1 f. + 1 f. blue and olive . . 1·25 1·25
30 – 5 f. + 5 f. blue and orange . 6·00 6·00
31 – 10 f. + 10 f. blue & green . 50·00 60·00

1922. Stamps of 1916 surch.
32 – 5 c. on 50 c. black & lake . 35 1·50
33 **32** 10 c. on 5 c. black & green . 30 20
34a **14** 25 c. on 40 c. black & lake . 2·00 90
35 **33** 30 c. on 10 c. black & red . 30 20
36 **34** 50 c. on 25 c. black & blue . 30 20

1924. Belgian Congo stamps of 1923 optd **RUANDA URUNDI**.
37 A 5 c. yellow 15 15
38 B 10 c. green 15 15
39 C 15 c. brown 15 15
40 D 20 c. green 15 15
41 E 20 c. green 15 15
42 F 25 c. brown 25 15
43 **46** 30 c. pink 20 20
44 30 c. green 20 15
66 35 c. green 20 15
45 D 40 c. purple 25 25
46 G 50 c. blue 25 20
47 50 c. orange 25 20
48 E 75 c. orange 25 25
49 75 c. blue 35 25
67 **46** 75 c. pink 30 25
50 H 1 f. brown 40 50
51 1 f. blue 45 20
68 1 f. pink 45 30
69 D 1 f. 50 blue 50 35
71 1 f. 75 blue 95 60
52 I 3 f. brown . . . . 2·50 1·90
53 J 5 f. grey . . . . 5·00 4·00
54 K 10 f. black . . . . 19·00 10·00

1925. Stamp of Belgian Congo optd **RUANDA-URUNDI**. Inscriptions in French or in Flemish.
61 **55** 25 c. + 25 c. black and red . 20 30

1925. Native cattle type of Belgian Congo optd **RUANDA-URUNDI**.
62 **56** 45 c. purple 30 30
63 60 c. red 35 30

1927. Belgian Congo stamps of 1923 optd **RUANDA URUNDI** in two lines, wide apart.
64 B 10 c. green 20 20
65 C 15 c. brown 80 60
66 **46** 35 c. green 20 15
67 75 c. red 30 25
68 H 1 f. red 45 30
69 D 1 f. 25 blue 50 40
70 1 f. 50 blue 50 35
71 1 f. 75 blue 95 60

1927. No. 144 of Belgian Congo optd **RUANDA URUNDI**.
72 1 f. 75 on 1 f. 50 blue 50 35

1930. Native Fund stamps of Belgian Congo (Nos. 160/8), optd **RUANDA URUNDI**.
73 10 c. + 5 c. red 30 30
74 20 c. + 10 c. brown 65 65
75 35 c. + 15 c. green . . . . . 1·25 1·25
76 60 c. + 30 c. purple . . . . . 1·50 1·50
77 1 f. + 50 c. red . . . . 2·10 2·10
78 1 f. 75 + 75 c. blue . . . . . 2·50 2·50
79 3 f. 50 + 1 f. 50 lake . . . . 5·00 5·00
80 5 f. + 2 f. 50 brown . . . . . 4·00 4·00
81 10 f. + 5 f. black . . . . . . 4·75 4·75

1931. Nos. 68 and 71 surch.
82 H 1 f. 25 on 1 f. red . . . . . 2·25 1·25
83 D 2 f. on 1 f. 75 blue . . . . 3·00 1·75

10 Mountain Scenery

11 King Albert I

1931.
84 – 5 c. red 10 10
85 **10** 10 c. grey 10 10
86 – 15 c. red 15 15
87 – 25 c. purple 10 10
88 – 40 c. green 30 30

89 – 50 c. violet 15 10
90 – 60 c. red 10 10
91 – 75 c. black 10 10
92 – 1 f. red 10 10
93 – 1 f. 25 brown 15 10
94 – 1 f. 50 purple 20 15
95 – 2 f. blue 20 15
96 – 2 f. 50 blue 20 20
97 – 3 f. 25 purple 20 15
98 – 4 f. red 30 30
99 – 5 f. grey 35 35
100 – 10 f. purple 70 45
101 – 20 f. brown . . . . 2·00 1·75

DESIGNS—HORIZ: 15 c. Warrior; 25 c. Chieftain's kraal; 50 c. Head of African buffalo; 1 f. Wives of Urundi chiefs; 1 f. 50, 2 f. Wooden pot hewer; 2 f. 50, 3 f. 25, Workers making tissues from ficus bark; 4 f. Hutu Potter. VERT: 5, 60 c., Native porter; 40 c. Two cowherds; 75 c. Native greeting; 1 f. 25, Mother and child; 5 f. Ruanda dancer; 10 f. Warriors; 20 f. Native prince of Urundi

1934. King Albert Mourning stamp.
102 **11** 1 f. 50 black 50 50

11a Queen Astrid and Children

14a "Belgium shall rise Again"

1936. Charity. Queen Astrid Fund.
103 **11a** 1 f. 25 + 5 c. brown . . . 50 50
104 1 f. 50 + 10 c. red 50 50
105 2 f. 50 + 25 c. blue . . . 70 70

1941. Stamps of Belgian Congo optd **RUANDA URUNDI**.
106 **78** 10 c. grey . . . . 5·50 5·50
107 1 f. 75 orange . . . . . . 3·75 3·75
108 2 f. 75 blue . . . . 3·75 3·75

1941. Ruanda-Urundi stamps of 1931 surch.
109 – 5 c. on 40 c. green . . . . . 3·00 3·00
110 – 60 c. on 50 c. violet . . . . 2·00 2·00
111 – 2 f. 50 on 1 f. 50 purple . . 2·00 2·00
112 – 3 f. 25 on 2 f. blue . . . . . 9·00 9·00

1941. Stamps of Belgian Congo optd **RUANDA URUNDI** and surch also.
113 – 5 c. on 1 f. 50 black and brown (No. 222) 10 10
114 – 75 c. on 90 c. brown and red (No. 221) 90 75
115 **78** 2 f. 50 on 10 f. red . . . . . 1·50 1·25

1942. War Relief.
116 **14a** 10 f. + 40 f. red . . . . . 1·75 1·75
117 10 f. + 40 f. blue . . . . . 1·75 1·75

On No. 116 the French slogan is above the Flemish, on No. 117 vice versa.

1942. Nos. 107/8 of Ruanda-Urundi surch.
118 **78** 75 c. on 1 f. 75 orange . . . 85 85
119 2 f. 50 on 2 f. 75 blue . . . . 3·25 3·25

15a Head of Warrior

17 Seated Figure

1942.
120 A 5 c. red 10 10
121 10 c. green 10 10
122 15 c. brown 10 10
123 20 c. blue 10 10
124 25 c. purple 10 10
125 30 c. blue 10 10
126 50 c. green 10 10
127 60 c. brown 10 10
128 **15a** 75 c. black and lilac . . . 15 10
129 1 f. black and brown . . . 15 10
130 1 f. 25 black and red . . . 20 15
131 B 1 f. 75 brown 75 45
132 2 f. orange 75 30
133 2 f. 50 red 75 15
134 C 3 f. 50 green 40 25
135 5 f. orange 40 25
136 6 f. blue 40 25
137 7 f. black 40 30
138 10 f. brown 65 40
139 – 20 f. black and brown . . 1·50 95
140 – 50 f. black and red . . . 1·75 1·10
141 – 100 f. black and green . . 3·50 2·75

DESIGNS—As Type **15a** (various frames): A, Oil palms; C, Askari sentry; 20 f. Head of zebra. 35 × 24 mm: B, Leopard. 29 × 34 mm: 50 f. Askari sentry; 100 f. Head of warrior.

1944. Red Cross Fund. Nos. 126, 130, 131 and 134 surch **Au profit de la Croix Rouge Ten voordeele van het Roode Kruis** (50 c., 1 f. 75) or with Flemish and French reversed (others) and premium.
147 50 c. + 50 f. green 75 90
148 1 f. 25 + 100 f. black & red . . 1·10 1·40
149 1 f. 75 + 100 f. brown . . . 75 90
150 3 f. 50 + 100 f. green . . . . 1·10 1·40

1948. Native Carvings.
151 **17** 10 c. orange 10 10
152 A 15 c. blue 10 10
153 B 20 c. blue 20 10
154 C 25 c. red 40 15
155 D 40 c. purple 20 10
156 **17** 50 c. brown 20 10
157 A 70 c. green 20 10
158 B 75 c. purple 25 15
159 C 1 f. purple and orange . . 25 10
160 D 1 f. 25 red and blue . . . 25 15
161 E 1 f. 50 red and green . . . 90 40
162 **17** 2 f. red and vermilion . . . 30 10
163 A 2 f. 50 green and brown . . 30 10
164 B 3 f. 50 green and blue . . 40 20
165 C 5 f. red and bistre 85 20
166 D 6 f. green and orange . . . 85 15
167 E 10 f. brown and violet . . 1·25 20
168 F 20 f. brown and red . . . 1·90 35
169 E 50 f. black and brown . . 3·75 1·00
170 F 100 f. black and red . . . 6·00 2·50

DESIGNS: A, Seated figure (different); B, Kneeling figure; C, Double mask; D, Mask; E, Mask with tassels; F, Mask with horns.

1949. Surch.
171 3 f. on 2 f. 50 (No. 163) . . . 40 15
172 4 f. on 6 f. (No. 166) 40 15
173 6 f. 50 on 6 f. (No. 166) . . . 40 25

18a St. Francis Xavier

19 "Dissotis"

1953. 400th Death Anniv of St. Francis Xavier.
174 **18a** 1 f. 50 black and blue . . 40 40

1953. Flowers Multicoloured.
175 10 c. Type **19** 15 10
176 15 c. "Protea" 15 10
177 20 c. "Vellozia" 15 10
178 25 c. "Littonia" 15 10
179 40 c. "Ipomoea" 15 10
180 50 c. "Angraecum" 15 10
181 60 c. "Euphorbia" 15 10
182 75 c. "Ochna" 15 10
183 1 f. "Hibiscus" 25 10
184 1 f. 25 "Protea" 90 40
185 1 f. 50 "Schizoglossum" . . . 20 10
186 2 f. "Ansellia" . . . . . . 2·25 20
187 3 f. "Costus" 55 10
188 4 f. "Nymphaea" 55 15
189 5 f. "Thunbergia" 80 15
190 7 f. "Gerbera" 95 30
191 8 f. "Gloriosa" . . . . . . 1·40 45
192 10 f. "Silene" . . . . 2·50 35
193 20 f. "Aristolochia" . . . . . 5·00 60

20 King Baudouin and Mountains

20a Mozart when a Child

1955.
194 **20** 1 f. 50 black and red . . . 50 15
195 – 3 f. black and green . . . 40 15
196 – 4 f. 50 black and blue . . 50 20
197 – 6 f. 50 black and purple . . 60 30

DESIGNS: 3 f. Forest; 4 f. 50, River; 6 f. 50, Grassland.

1956. Birth Bicentenary of Mozart.
198 **20a** 4 f. 50 + 1 f. 50 violet . . 1·50 1·00
199 – 6 f. 50 + 2 f. 50 purple . . 4·50 2·00

DESIGN—52 × 36 mm: 6 f. 50, Queen Elizabeth and Mozart sonata.

20b Nurse with Children

21 Gorilla

1957. Red Cross Fund.
200 **20b** 3 f. + 50 c. blue 55 20
201 – 4 f. 50 + 50 c. green . . . 70 30
202 – 6 f. 50 + 50 c. brown . . 95 50

DESIGNS: 4 f. 50, Doctor inoculating patient; 6 f. 50, Nurse in tropical kit bandaging patient.

1959. Fauna.
203 10 c. black, red and brown . . 10 10
204 20 c. black and green 10 10
205 40 c. black, olive & mauve . . 10 10
206 50 c. brown, yellow & green . . 10 10
207 1 f. black, blue and brown . . 10 10
208 1 f. 50 black and orange . . . 15 10
209 2 f. black, brown & turquoise . 20 10
210 3 f. black, red and brown . . . 40 10
211 5 f. multicoloured 40 15
212 6 f. 50 brown, yell & red . . . 25 10
213 8 f. black, mauve & blue . . . 70 30
214 10 f. multicoloured 70 20

DESIGNS—VERT: 10 c., 1 f. Type **21**: 40 c., 2 f. Eastern black and white colobus. HORIZ: 20 c. 1 f. 50, African buffaloes; 50 c., 6 f. 50, Impala; 3, 8 f. African elephants; 5, 10 f. Eland and common zebras.

22 African Resources

1960. 10th Anniv of African Technical Co-operation Commission. Inscr in French or Flemish.
222 **22** 3 f. salmon and blue . . . 20 15

23 High Jumping

1960. Child Welfare Fund. Olympic Games, Rome.
223 50 c. + 25 c. blue and red . . 10 10
224 1 f. 50 + 50 c. lake & black . 15 15
225 2 f. + 2 f. black and red . . . 15 15
226 3 f. + 1 f. 25 red and green . . 95 85
227 6 f. 50 + 3 f. 50 green and red . 95 85

DESIGNS: 50 c. Type **23**: 1 f. 50, Hurdling; 2 f. Football; 3 f. Throwing the javelin; 6 f. 50, Throwing the discus.

1960. No. 210 surch.
228 3 f. 50 on 3 f. black, red and brown 30 10

25 Leopard

1961.
229 **25** 20 f. multicoloured 85 35
230 – 50 f. multicoloured . . . . 1·90 85

DESIGN: 50 f. Lion and lioness.

26 Usumbura Cathedral

1961. Usumbura Cathedral Fund.
231 **26** 50 c. + 25 c. brown & buff . 10 10
232 – 1 f. + 50 c. dp green & grn . 10 10
233 – 1 f. 50 + 75 c. multicoloured . 10 10
234 **26** 3 f. 50 + 1 f. 50 bl & lt bl . . 10 10
235 – 5 f. + 2 f. red and orange . . 20 20
236 – 6 f. 50 + 3 f. multicoloured . 40 30

DESIGNS: 1, 5 f. Side view of Cathedral; 1 f. 50, 6 f. 50, Stained glass windows.

POSTAGE DUE STAMPS

1924. Postage Due stamps of Belgian Congo optd **RUANDA URUNDI**.
D55 D **54** 5 c. brown 15 15
D56 10 c. red 15 15
D57 15 c. violet 20 20
D58 30 c. green 30 30
D59 50 c. blue 40 35
D60 1 f. grey 45 50

1943. Postage Due stamps of Belgian Congo optd **RUANDA URUNDI**.
D142 D **86** 10 c. olive 10 10
D143 20 c. blue 10 10
D144 50 c. green 10 10
D145 1 f. brown 20 20
D146 2 f. orange 25 25

1959. Postage Due stamps of Belgian Congo optd **RUANDA URUNDI**.
D215 D **99** 10 c. brown 10 10
D216 20 c. purple 10 10
D217 50 c. green 10 10
D218 1 f. blue 15 15
D219 2 f. red 20 20
D220 4 f. violet 50 40
D221 6 f. blue 60 50

For later issues see **BURUNDI** and **RWANDA**.

RUMANIA Pt. 3

A republic in S.E. Europe bordering on the Black Sea originally a kingdom formed by the union of Moldavia and Wallachia.

1858. 40 parale = 1 piastre.
1867. 100 bani = 1 leu.

MOLDAVIA

1

2

1858. Imperf.
1 **1** 27 p. black on red £13000 £5000
2 54 p. blue on green £5000 £2250
3 81 p. blue on blue £13000 £15000
4 108 p. blue on pink £9000 £5000

1858. Imperf.
15 **2** 5 p. black £120
13 40 p. blue £120 £130
14 80 p. red £350 £200

RUMANIA

4

1862. Imperf.
29 **4** 3 p. yellow . . . . 55·00 £170
30 6 p. red . . . . 50·00 £130
31 30 p. blue . . . . 40·00 40·00

5 Prince Alexander Cuza

6 Prince Carol 7

1865. Imperf.
49a **5** 2 p. orange . . . . 40·00 £160
46 5 p. blue . . . . 30·00 £190
48 20 p. red . . . . 18·00 26·00

1866. Imperf.
60 **6** 2 p. black on yellow . . . . 16·00 65·00
61 5 p. black on blue . . . . . 40·00 £400
62 20 p. black on red . . . . . 18·00 15·00

1868. Imperf.
71 **7** 2 b. orange . . . . 30·00 21·00
72 3 b. mauve . . . . 32·00 28·00
66c 4 b. blue . . . . 40·00 26·00
67 18 b. red . . . . £160 20·00

8

9

10

1869. Without beard. Imperf.
74 **8** 5 b. orange . . . . 55·00 32·00
75 10 b. blue . . . . 30·00 26·00
76d 15 b. red . . . . 27·00 23·00
77c 25 b. blue and orange . . . 32·00 23·00
78 50 b. red and blue . . . . . £130 35·00

1871. With beard. Imperf.
83 **9** 5 b. red . . . . 27·00 23·00
84 10 b. orange . . . . 45·00 27·00
99 10 b. blue . . . . 35·00 40·00
86 15 b. red £130 £130
87 25 b. brown . . . . 30·00 28·00
100 50 b. red and blue £140 £160

1872. Perf.
93 **9** 5 b. red . . . . 50·00 35·00
94 10 b. blue . . . . 42·00 35·00
95 25 b. brown . . . . 32·00 35·00

1872. Perf.
112 **10** $1\frac{1}{2}$ b. green . . . . . . 5·00 2·10
124 $1\frac{1}{2}$ b. black . . . . 5·00 1·40
105 3 b. green . . . . 21·00 3·00
125 3 b. olive . . . . 10·00 7·50
106 5 b. bistre . . . . 3·00 2·00
126 5 b. green . . . . 4·00 1·60
107 10 b. blue . . . . 11·50 3·25
127c 10 b. red . . . . 10·50 1·60
115 15 b. brown . . . . 50·00 7·50

128a **10** 15 b. red 32·00 10·00
110 25 b. orange 75·00 15·00
130 25 b. blue £110 15·00
116 30 b. red £130 42·00
111 50 b. red 80·00 30·00
131 50 b. bistre 75·00 16·00

11 King Carol 12 14

1880.

146a **11** 15 b. brown 10·00 1·40
147 25 b. blue 16·00 2·00

1885. On white or coloured papers.

161 **12** 1½ b. black 2·75 1·40
163 3 b. green 4·00 1·40
165a 3 b. violet 4·00 1·40
166 5 b. green 4·00 1·40
168 10 b. red 4·00 1·40
169 15 b. brown 11·50 1·75
171 25 b. blue 11·50 3·25
186 50 b. brown 55·00 15·00

1890.

271 **14** 1½ b. lake 1·40 65
272a 3 b. mauve 1·00 1·00
273 5 b. green 2·00 1·00
254 10 b. red 8·25 1·00
255 15 b. brown 10·00 85
306 25 b. blue 6·50 95
307 50 b. orange 21·00 10·00

15 17 19

1891. 25th Anniv of Reign.

300 **15** 1½ b. lake 4·00 4·25
293 3 b. mauve 4·00 4·25
294 5 b. green 5·25 5·00
295 10 b. red 5·25 5·00
303 15 b. brown 5·25 5·00

1893. Various frames as T **17** and **19**.

316 1 BANI brown 1·00 35
426 1 BAN brown 1·00 20
317 1½ b. black 50 15
533 3 b. brown 1·10 10
319 5 b. blue 1·40 40
534 5 b. green 2·00 15
320 10 b. green 2·00 15
535 10 b. red 1·60 10
332 15 b. pink 2·00 15
400 15 b. black 2·00 15
430 15 b. brown 2·00 15
545 15 b. violet 2·00 10
322 25 b. mauve 3·00 15
701 25 b. blue 35 10
421 40 b. green 6·75 50
324 50 b. orange 8·25 1·00
325 1 l. pink and brown 16·00 1·60
326 2 l. brown and orange 20·00 2·50

See also Nos. 532 etc.

25 Four-in-hand Postal Coach **26** New Post Office, Bucharest

1903. Opening of New Post Office in 1901.

464 **25** 1 b. brown 1·40 80
465 3 b. red 2·50 75
466 5 b. green 5·00 1·60
467 10 b. red 4·00 1·60
468 15 b. black 4·00 2·00
472 **26** 15 b. black 3·25 2·50
469 **25** 25 b. blue 14·00 7·25
473 **26** 25 b. blue 8·25 5·00
470 **25** 40 b. green 20·00 8·25
474 **26** 40 b. green 11·50 6·50
471 **25** 50 b. orange 25·00 1·50
475 **26** 50 b. orange 11·50 6·50
476 1 l. brown 11·50 6·50
477 2 l. red 90·00 50·00
478 5 l. lilac £110 70·00

See also No. 1275.

1905. Various frames as T **17** and **19**.

532 1 ban black 1·00 10
625b 1½ b. yellow 1·60 1·10
703 40 b. brown 1·00 50
705 50 b. pink 1·00 45
432 1 l. black and green 20·00 2·40
706 1 l. green 1·60 30
433 2 l. black and brown 16·00 2·25
707 2 l. orange 1·75 45

27 Queen of Rumania spinning **28** Queen of Rumania weaving

1906. Welfare Fund.

481 **27** 3 b. (+7) brown 5·00 3·25
482 5 b. (+10) green 5·00 3·25
483 10 b. (+10) red 26·00 13·00
484 15 b. (+10) purple 16·00 6·50

1906. Welfare Fund.

485 **28** 3 b. (+7) brown 5·00 3·25
486 5 b. (+10) green 5·00 3·25
487 10 b. (+10) red 26·00 13·00
488 15 b. (+10) lilac 16·00 6·50

29 Queen of Rumania nursing wounded Soldier **30**

1906. Welfare Fund.

489 **29** 3 b. (+7) brown 5·00 3·25
490 5 b. (+10) green 5·00 3·25
491 10 b. (+10) red 26·00 13·00
492 15 b. (+10) purple 16·00 6·50

1906. 25th Anniv of Kingdom.

493 **30** 1 b. black and bistre 65 25
494 3 b. black and brown 1·60 65
495 5 b. black and green 1·00 50
496 10 b. black and red 1·00 50
497 15 b. black and violet 1·00 50
498 25 b. black and blue 9·50 5·00
499 40 b. black and brown 2·75 80
500 50 b. black and brown 2·75 1·00
501 1 l. black and red 2·75 80
502 2 l. black and orange 1·50 80

31 Prince Carol at Battle of Calafat **32**

1906. 40 Years' Rule of Prince and King. Dated "1906".

503 – 1 b. black and bistre 20 25
504 – 3 b. black and brown 65 30
505 **31** 5 b. black and green 75 25
506 – 10 b. black and red 30 15
507 – 15 b. black and violet 30 15
508 – 25 b. black and blue 4·00 3·25
508a – 25 b. black and green 4·00 6·50
509 – 40 b. black and brown 1·00 70
510 – 50 b. black and brown 1·10 70
511 – 1 l. black and red 1·00 75
512 – 2 l. black and orange 1·40 1·40

DESIGNS—HORIZ: 1 b. Prince Carol taking oath of allegiance in 1866; 3 b. Prince in carriage; 10 b. Meeting of Prince and Osman Pasha, 1878; 15 b. Carol when Prince in 1866 and King in 1906; 25 b. Rumanian Army crossing Danube, 1877; 40 b. Triumphal entry into Bucharest, 1878; 50 b. Prince at head of Army in 1877; 1 l. King Carol at Cathedral in 1896; 2 l. King at shrine of S. Nicholas, 1904.

1906. Charity.

513 **32** 3 b. (+7) brown, bistre and blue 2·50 1·60
514 5 b. (+10) green, red and bistre 1·50 1·60
515 10 b. (+10) red, bistre and blue 5·00 3·25
516 15 b. (+10) violet, bistre and blue 13·00 5·00

33 Peasant ploughing and Angel

1906. Jubilee Exhibition, Bucharest.

517 **33** 5 b. black and green 3·00 1·00
518 10 b. black and red 3·00 1·00
519 – 15 b. black and violet 5·00 1·60
520 – 25 b. black and blue 5·00 1·65
521 – 30 b. brown and red 6·00 1·50
522 – 40 b. brown and green 7·25 1·75
523 – 50 b. black and orange 6·00 2·40
524 – 75 b. sepia and brown 6·00 2·40
525 – 1 l. 50 brown and mauve 65·00 32·00
526 – 2 l. 50 brown and yellow 25·00 20·00
527 – 3 l. brown and orange 16·00 20·00

DESIGNS—HORIZ: 15, 25 b. Exhibition Building. VERT: 30, 40 b. Farmhouse; 50, 75 b. (different), Royal Family pavilion; 1 l. 50, 2 l. 50, King Carol on horseback; 3 l. Queen Elizabeth (Carmen Sylva).

34 Princess Maria and her Children receiving Poor Family conducted by an Angel

1907. Welfare Fund.

528 **34** 3 b. (+7) brown 6·50 3·25
529 5 b. (+10) brown & green 3·25 1·60
530 10 b. (+10) brown & red 3·25 1·60
531 15 b. (+10) brown & blue 3·25 2·00

35 37

1908.

575 **35** 5 b. green 1·25 20
562 10 b. red 30 10
577 15 b. violet 7·25 2·00
564 25 b. blue 75 10
579 40 b. green 40 15
702 40 b. brown 3·25 2·00
566 50 b. orange 40 10
705 50 b. red 1·25 45
581 1 l. brown 1·10 25
582 2 l. red 6·50 2·00

1908.

583 **37** 1 b. black 15 10
590 3 b. brown 50 10
585 5 b. green 20 10
592 10 b. red 35 10
599 15 b. violet 10·00 8·25
594 15 b. olive 45 10
692 15 b. brown 50 30

38 **39** Troops crossing Danube

1913. Acquisition of Southern Dobruja.

626 – 1 b. black 65 25
627 **38** 3 b. brown and grey 1·60 50
628 **39** 5 b. black and green 1·40 15
629 – 10 b. black and orange 55 15
630 – 15 b. violet and brown 1·60 65
631 – 25 b. brown and blue 2·25 1·00
632 **39** 40 b. red and brown 3·25 1·75
633 **38** 50 b. blue and yellow 4·25 3·25
634 1 l. brown and blue 11·50 8·25
635 2 l. red and red 15·00 10·00

DESIGNS—VERT: (As Type **38**): 1 b. "Dobruja" holding flag. HORIZ: (As Type **39**): 10 b. Town of Constanza; 25 b. Church and School in Dobruja (24 × 16 mm); 15 b. "Mircea the Great and King Carol".

1918. Surch **25. BANI**.

657 **37** 25 b. on 1 b. black 35 30

1918. Optd **1918**.

662 **37** 5 b. green 40 25
663 10 b. red 45 25

TRANSYLVANIA

The Eastern portion of Hungary. Union with Rumania proclaimed in December 1918 and the final frontiers settled by the Treaty of Trianon 4th June, 1920.

The following issues for Transylvania (Nos. 747/858) were valid throughout Rumania.

BANI (42) Bani (43)

(The "F" stands for King Ferdinand and "P.T.T." for Posts Telegraphs and Telephones).

The values "BANI", "LEU" or "LEI" appear above or below the monogram.

A. Issues for Cluj (Kolozsvar or Klausenburg).

1919. Various stamps of Hungary optd as T **42**. (a) Flood Relief Charity stamps of 1913.

747 **7** 1 l. on 1 f. grey 11·50 11·50
748 1 l. on 2 f. yellow 50·00 50·00
749 1 l. on 3 f. orange 26·00 26·00
750 1 l. on 5 f. green 1·00 1·00
751 1 l. on 10 f. red 1·00 1·00
752 1 l. on 12 f. lilac on yellow 3·75 3·75
753 1 l. on 16 f. green 2·00 2·00
754 1 l. on 25 f. blue 26·00 26·00
755 1 l. on 35 f. purple 2·00 2·00
756 **8** 1 l. on 1 k. red 32·00 32·00

(b) War Charity stamps of 1916.

757 **20** 10 (+2) b. red 15 15
758 – 15 (+2) b. violet 15 15
759 **22** 40 (+2) b. lake 15 15

(c) Harvesters and Parliament Types.

760 **18** 2 b. brown 15 15
761 3 b. red 15 15
762 5 b. green 15 15
763 6 b. blue 15 15
764 10 b. red 65·00 65·00
765 15 b. violet (No. 244) 2·50 2·50
766 15 b. violet 15 15
767 25 b. blue 15 15
768 35 b. brown 15 15
769 40 b. olive 15 15
770 **19** 50 b. purple 15 15
771 75 b. blue 15 15
772 80 b. green 15 15
773 1 l. lake 15 15
774 2 l. brown 20 20
775 3 l. grey and violet 1·75 1·75
776 5 l. brown 1·40 1·40
777 10 l. lilac and brown 1·75 1·75

(d) Karl and Zita stamps.

778 **27** 10 b. red 13·50 13·50
779 15 b. violet 5·00 5·00
780 20 b. brown 15 15
781 25 b. blue 30 30
782 **28** 40 b. olive 15 15

B. Issues for Oradea (Nagyvarad, Grosswardein).

1919. Various stamps of Hungary optd as T **43**. (a) "Turul" Type.

794 **7** 2 b. yellow 2·75 2·75
795 3 b. orange 4·75 4·75
796 6 b. drab 25 25
797 16 b. green 8·50 8·50
798 50 b. lake on blue 40 40
799 70 b. brown and green 10·00 10·00

(b) Flood Relief Charity stamps of 1913.

800 **7** 1 l. on 1 f. grey 40 40
801 1 l. on 2 f. yellow 2·00 2·00
802 1 l. on 3 f. orange 45 45
803 1 l. on 5 f. green 15 15
804 1 l. on 6 f. drab 40 40
805 1 l. on 10 f. red 15 15
806 1 l. on 12 f. lilac on yellow 23·00 23·00
807 1 l. on 16 f. green 50 50
808 1 l. on 20 f. brown 3·00 3·00
809 1 l. on 25 f. blue 2·00 2·00
810 1 l. on 35 f. purple 2·00 2·00

(c) War Charity stamp of 1915.

811 **7** 5 + 2 b. green (No. 173) 5·00 5·00

(d) War Charity stamps of 1916.

812 **20** 10 (+2) b. red 20 20
813 – 15 (+2) b. violet 15 15
814 **22** 40 (+2) b. lake 15 15

(e) Harvesters and Parliament Types.

815 **18** 2 b. brown 15 15
816 3 b. red 15 15
817 5 b. green 15 15
818 6 b. blue 35 35
819 10 b. red 65 65
820 15 b. violet (No. 244) 65·00 65·00
821 15 b. violet 15 15
822 20 b. brown 6·00 6·00
823 25 b. blue 15 15
824 35 b. brown 15 15
825 40 b. olive 15 15
826 **19** 50 b. purple 15 15
827 75 b. blue 15 15
828 80 b. green 15 15
829 1 l. lake 20 20
830 2 l. brown 15 15
831 3 l. grey and violet 2·50 2·50
832 5 l. brown 1·75 1·75
833 10 l. lilac and brown 1·00 1·00

(f) Charles and Zita stamps.

834 **27** 10 b. red 1·40 1·40
835 20 b. brown 15 15
836 25 b. blue 20 20
837 40 b. olive 25 25

The following (Nos. 838/58) are also optd **KOZTARSASAG**.

(g) Harvesters and Parliament Types.

838 **18** 2 b. brown 75 75
839 3 b. red 15 15
840 4 b. grey 15 15
841 5 b. green 15 15
842 6 b. blue 1·00 1·00
843 10 b. red 8·25 8·25
844 20 b. brown 85 85
845 40 b. olive 15 15
846 **19** 1 l. lake 15 15
847 3 l. grey and violet 35 35
848 5 l. brown 2·40 2·40

(h) Charles and Zita stamps.

849 **27** 10 b. red 80·00 80·00
850 20 b. brown 1·40 1·40
851 25 b. blue 20 20
852 **28** 50 b. purple 15 15

(k) Harvesters and Parliament Types inscr "MAGYAR POSTA".

853 **18** 5 b. green 15 15
854 20 b. red 15 15
855 20 b. brown 15 15
856 25 b. blue 25 25
857 40 b. olive 30 40
858 **19** 5 l. brown 4·00 4·00

(44) King Ferdinand's Monogram — 45 King Ferdinand 46

1919. Recovery of Transylvania and Return of King of Rumania to Bucharest. Optd with T **44**.

No.	Type	Description	Unused	Used
873	**37**	1 b. black	20	15
874		5 b. green	30	20
878a		10 b. red	10	10

1920.

No.	Type	Description	Unused	Used
891	**45**	1 b. black	10	10
892		5 b. green	10	10
893		10 b. red	10	10
882		15 b. brown	30	15
895		25 b. blue	20	10
896		25 b. brown	20	10
910		40 b. brown	45	20
898		50 b. pink	20	10
887		1 l. green	40	10
900		1 l. red	30	10
889		2 l. orange	45	25
902		2 l. blue	45	10
903		2 l. red	1·75	1·40

1922.

No.	Type	Description	Unused	Used
923	**46**	3 b. black	15	10
924		5 b. black	10	10
925		10 b. green	10	10
926		25 b. brown	10	10
927		25 b. red	15	10
928		30 b. violet	15	10
929		50 b. yellow	10	10
930		60 b. green	75	40
931		1 l. violet	15	10
932		2 l. red	55	10
933a		2 l. green	20	10
934		3 l. blue	1·00	65
935a		3 l. brown	1·00	65
937		3 l. red	35	10
936a		3 l. pink	25	10
938		5 l. green	1·50	65
939b		5 l. brown	20	10
940		6 l. blue	1·75	1·00
941		6 l. red	4·25	2·40
942		6 l. olive	1·75	45
943		7 l. 50 blue	1·50	25
944		10 l. blue	1·50	20

47 Cathedral of Alba Julia — 48 King Ferdinand — 49 State Arms

51 Michael the Brave and King Ferdinand

1922. Coronation.

No.	Type	Description	Unused	Used
1032	**47**	5 b. black	15	15
1033	**48**	25 b. brown	75	20
1034	**49**	50 b. green	75	50
1035	–	1 l. olive	90	60
1036	**51**	2 l. red	90	60
1037	–	3 l. blue	1·75	1·00
1050	–	6 l. violet	6·50	6·00

DESIGNS—As Type **48**: 1 l. Queen Marie as a nurse; 3 l. Portrait of King but rectangular frame. Larger (21 × 33 mm): 6 l. Queen Marie in coronation robes.

54 King Ferdinand — 55 Map of Rumania

1926. King's 60th Birthday. Imperf or perf.

No.	Type	Description	Unused	Used
1051	**54**	10 b. green	20	20
1052		25 b. orange	15	15
1053		50 b. brown	15	15
1054		1 l. violet	15	15
1055		2 l. green	15	15
1056		3 l. red	15	15
1057		5 l. brown	15	15
1058		6 l. olive	15	15
1059		9 l. grey	15	15
1060		10 l. blue	15	15

1927. 50th Anniv of Rumanian Geographical Society.

No.	Type	Description	Unused	Used
1061	**55**	1 + 9 l. violet	2·25	1·40
1062	–	2 + 8 l. green	2·25	1·40
1063	–	3 + 7 l. red	2·25	1·40
1064	–	5 + 5 l. blue	2·25	1·40
1065	–	6 + 4 l. olive	4·75	2·00

DESIGNS: 2 l. Stephen the Great; 3 l. Michael the Brave; 5 l. Carol and Ferdinand; 6 l. Adam Clisi Monument.

60 King Carol and King Ferdinand

1927. 50th Anniv of Independence.

No.	Type	Description	Unused	Used
1066	**60**	25 b. red	25	15
1067	–	30 b. black	20	15
1068	–	50 b. green	25	15
1069	**60**	1 l. blue	20	15
1070	–	2 l. green	20	20
1071	–	3 l. purple	20	25
1072	–	4 l. brown	45	30
1073	–	4 l. 50 brown	1·60	1·25
1074	–	5 l. brown	23	25
1075	–	6 l. red	80	80
1076	**60**	7 l. 50 blue	30	25
1077		10 l. blue	1·60	50

DESIGNS—HORIZ: 30 b., 2, 3, 5 l. King Ferdinand. VERT: 50 b., 4 l, 4 l. 50, 6 l. King Ferdinand as in Type **60**.

63 King Michael 64

1928.

No.	Type	Description	Unused	Used
1080	**63**	25 b. black	20	10
1081		30 b. pink	50	10
1082		50 b. olive	20	10
		(a) Size 19 × 25 mm.		
1083	**64**	1 l. purple	20	10
1084		2 l. green	40	10
1085		3 l. red	50	10
1086		5 l. brown	1·00	10
1087		7 l. 50 blue	6·00	45
1088		10 l. blue	5·00	15
		(b) Size 18 × 23 mm.		
1129	**64**	1 l. purple	25	10
1130		2 l. green	60	15
1131		3 l. red	1·40	10
1132		7 l. 50 blue	2·50	1·00
1133		10 l. blue	7·50	6·75

65 Bessarabian Parliament House

1928. 10th Anniv of Annexation of Bessarabia.

No.	Type	Description	Unused	Used
1092	**65**	1 l. green	1·10	65
1093		2 l. brown	1·10	65
1094	–	3 l. sepia	1·10	65
1095	–	5 l. lake	1·50	85
1096	–	7 l. 50 blue	1·50	85
1097	–	10 l. blue	3·50	2·00
1098	–	20 l. violet	4·75	2·75

DESIGNS: 3, 5, 20 l. Hotin Fortress; 7 l. 50, 10 l. Alba Fortress.

66 Bleriot SPAD 33 Biplane

1928. Air.

No.	Type	Description	Unused	Used
1099	**66**	1 l. brown	5·50	3·25
1100		2 l. blue	5·50	3·25
1101		5 l. red	5·50	3·25

67 King Carol and King Michael

1928. 50th Anniv of Acquisition of Northern Dobruja.

No.	Type	Description	Unused	Used
1102	**67**	1 l. green	75	30
1103	–	2 l. brown	75	30
1104	**67**	3 l. grey	90	30
1105	–	5 l. mauve	1·25	35
1106	–	7 l. 50 blue	1·50	50
1107	–	10 l. blue	3·25	1·40
1108	–	20 l. red	4·50	1·75

DESIGNS: 2 l. Constanza Harbour and Carol Lighthouse; 5 l., 7 l. 50, Adam Clisi Monument; 10, 20 l. Cernavoda Bridge over the Danube.

68 — 69 The Union

1929. 10th Anniv of Union of Rumania and Transylvania.

No.	Type	Description	Unused	Used
1109	**68**	1 l. purple	1·75	1·40
1110	**69**	2 l. green	1·75	1·40
1111	–	3 l. brown	2·50	1·40
1112	–	4 l. red	2·50	1·60
1113	–	5 l. orange	2·75	1·75
1114	–	10 l. blue	3·75	3·50

DESIGNS—HORIZ: 1 l. Ferdinand I, Stephen the Great, Michael the Brave, Hunyadi and Brancoveanu; 10 l. Ferdinand I. VERT: 2 l. Union; 3 l. Avram Jancu; 4 l. King Michael the Brave; 5 l. Bran Castle.

1930. Stamps of King Michael optd **8 IUNIE 1930** (Accession of Carol II).

No.	Type	Description	Unused	Used
1134	**63**	25 b. black (postage)	30	10
1135		30 b. pink	50	10
1136		50 b. olive	45	10
1142	**64**	1 l. purple (No. 1129)	50	10
1143		2 l. green (No. 1130)	50	10
1144		3 l. red (No. 1131)	70	10
1137		5 l. brown	70	10
1140		7 l. 50 blue (No. 1087)	2·75	1·25
1145		7 l. 50 blue (No. 1132)	2·10	55
1138		10 l. blue (No. 1088)	4·50	1·40
1146		10 l. blue (No. 1133)	1·75	65
1147	**66**	1 l. brown (air)	12·00	6·50
1148		2 l. blue	12·00	6·50
1149		5 l. red	12·00	6·50

72 — 73 King Carol II — 76

1930.

No.	Type	Description	Unused	Used
1172	**72**	25 b. black	25	10
1173		50 b. brown	60	30
1174		1 l. violet	30	10
1175		2 l. green	50	10
1176	**73**	3 l. red	1·10	10
1177		4 l. orange	1·25	10
1178		6 l. red	1·40	10
1179		7 l. 50 blue	1·60	15
1180	–	10 l. blue	4·00	10
1181	–	16 l. green	9·00	15
1182	–	20 l. yellow	12·00	40

DESIGN: 10 l. to 20 l. Portrait as Type **72**, but in plain circle, with "ROMANIA" at top.

1930. Air.

No.	Type	Description	Unused	Used
1183	**76**	1 l. violet on blue	2·50	2·00
1184		2 l. green on blue	3·00	2·00
1185		5 l. brown on blue	6·00	2·75
1186		10 l. blue on blue	12·00	6·00

77 Map of Rumania — 78 Woman with Census Paper — 79 King Carol II

1930. National Census.

No.	Type	Description	Unused	Used
1187	**77**	1 l. violet	1·25	30
1188	**78**	2 l. green	2·25	35
1189		4 l. orange	2·50	30
1190		6 l. red	5·50	35

1931.

No.	Type	Description	Unused	Used
1191	**79**	30 l. blue and olive	1·10	50
1192		50 l. blue and red	2·40	1·25
1193		100 l. blue and green	4·50	2·40

80 King Carol II

81 King Carol I — 82 Kings Carol II, Ferdinand I & Carol I

1931. 50th Anniv of Rumanian Monarchy.

No.	Type	Description	Unused	Used
1200	**80**	1 l. violet	2·25	1·75
1201	**81**	2 l. green	4·00	1·75
1202	–	6 l. red	9·00	2·75
1203	**82**	10 l. blue	13·50	5·00
1204	–	20 l. orange	15·00	6·75

DESIGNS—As Type **80**: 6 l. King Carol II, facing right. As Type **81**: 20 l. King Ferdinand I.

83 Naval Cadet Ship "Mircea"

1931. 50th Anniv of Rumanian Navy.

No.	Type	Description	Unused	Used
1205	**83**	6 l. red	5·50	3·25
1206	–	10 l. blue	7·25	3·75
1207	–	12 l. green	27·00	4·00
1208	–	20 l. orange	10·50	7·50

DESIGNS: 10 l. Monitors "Lascar Catargiu" and "Mihail Kogalniceanu"; 16 l. Monitor "Ardeal"; 20 l. Destroyer "Regele Ferdinand".

84 Bayonet Attack — 87 King Carol I

88 Infantry Attack — 89 King Ferdinand I

1931. Centenary of Rumanian Army.

No.	Type	Description	Unused	Used
1209	**84**	25 b. black	1·75	1·00
1210	–	50 b. brown	2·25	1·40
1211	–	1 l. violet	2·75	1·75
1212	**87**	2 l. green	4·50	2·00
1213	**88**	3 l. red	10·00	6·00
1214	**89**	7 l. 50 blue	12·00	13·50
1215	–	16 l. green	15·00	6·00

DESIGNS: 50 b. Infantryman, 1870, 20 × 33 mm: 1 l. Infantry and drummer, 1830, 23 × 36 mm: 16 l. King Carol II in uniform with plumed helmet, 21 × 34 mm.

91 Scouts' Encampment — 92a Farman F.121 Jaribu

1931. Rumanian Boy Scouts' Exhibition Fund.

No.	Type	Description	Unused	Used
1221	**91**	1 l. + 1 l. red	4·00	3·25
1222	–	2 l. + 2 l. green	4·75	4·00
1223	–	3 l. + 3 l. blue	6·50	5·00
1224	–	4 l. + 4 l. brown	8·50	6·50
1225	–	6 l. + 6 l. brown	11·00	6·75

DESIGNS—VERT: As Type **91**: 3 l. Recruiting, 22 × 37½ mm; 2 l. Rescue work, 22 × 41½ mm; 4 l. Prince Nicholas; 6 l. King Carol II in scoutmaster's uniform.

1931. Air.

No.	Type	Description	Unused	Used
1226	**92a**	2 l. green	1·05	90
1227	–	3 l. red	2·00	1·25
1228	–	5 l. brown	3·00	1·50
1229	–	10 l. blue	7·50	3·25
1230	–	20 l. violet	17·00	5·00

DESIGNS—As T **92a**: 3 l. Farman F.300; 5 l. Farman F.60 Goliath; 10 l. Fokker F.XII. 34 × 20 mm: 20 l. Three aircraft flying in formation.

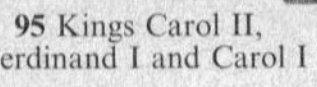

95 Kings Carol II, Ferdinand I and Carol I — 96 Alexander the Good

1931.

No.	Type	Description	Unused	Used
1231	**95**	16 l. green	13·00	50

1932. 500th Death Centenary of Alexander I, Prince of Moldavia.

No.	Type	Description	Unused	Used
1232	**96**	6 l. red	12·00	10·00

97 King Carol II

98 Semaphore Signaller

1932.

1248 **97** 10 l. blue . . . . 13·00 30

1932. Boy Scouts' Jamboree Fund.

1256 – 25 b. + 25 b. green . . . 3·50 1·75
1257 **98** 50 b. + 50 b. blue . . . . 4·00 3·50
1258 – 1 l. + 1 l. green . . . . . 5·50 5·00
1259 – 2 l. + 2 l. red . . . . . . 9·00 6·75
1260 – 3 l. + 3 l. blue . . . . . 22·00 13·50
1261 – 6 l. + 6 l. brown . . . . 24·00 17·00

DESIGNS—VERT: As Type **98**: 25 b. Scouts in camp; 1 l. On the trail; 3 l. King Carol II; 6 l. King Carol and King Michael when a Prince. HORIZ: 20 × 15 mm: 2 l. Camp fire.

99 Cantacuzino and Gregory Chika

1932. 9th Int Medical Congress.

1262 **99** 1 l. red . . . . 7·50 6·75
1263 – 6 l. orange . . . . 21·00 10·00
1264 – 10 l. blue . . . . 35·00 17·00

DESIGNS: 6 l. Congress in session; 10 l. Hygeia and Aesculapius.

100 Tuberculosis Sanatorium

1932. Postal Employees' Fund.

1265 **100** 4 l. + 1 l. green . . . . 5·50 3·25
1266 – 6 l. + 1 l. brown . . . . 6·75 4·00
1267 – 10 l. + 1 l. blue . . . . 12·00 6·75

DESIGNS—VERT: 6 l. War Memorial tablet. HORIZ: 10 l. Convalescent home.

102 "Bull's head"

103 Dolphins

104 Arms

1932. 75th Anniv of First Moldavian Stamps. Imperf.

1268 **102** 25 b. black . . . . 1·25 20
1269 – 1 l. purple . . . . 2·00 65
1270 **103** 2 l. green . . . . 2·50 80
1271 – 3 l. red . . . . 2·50 1·00
1272 **104** 6 l. red . . . . 3·25 1·10
1273 – 7 l. 50 blue . . . . 4·00 1·75
1274 – 10 l. blue . . . . 6·00 2·75

DESIGNS—As Type **103**: 1 l. Lion rampant and bridge; 3 l. Eagle and castles; 7 l. 50, Eagle; 10 l. Bull's head.

1932. 30th Anniv of Opening of G.P.O. Bucharest. As T **25** but smaller.

1275 16 l. green . . . . 11·50 6·75

105 Ruins of Trajan's Bridge, Arms of Turnu-Severin and Towers of Severus

1933. Centenary of Founding of Turnu-Severin.

1279 **105** 25 b. green 65 20
1280 – 50 b. blue . . . . 1·00 30
1281 – 1 l. brown . . . . 1·75 45
1282 – 2 l. green . . . . 2·50 1·00

DESIGNS: 50 b. Trajan at the completion of bridge over the Danube; 1 l. Arrival of Prince Carol at Turnu-Severin; 2 l. Trajan's Bridge.

107 Carmen Sylva and Carol I

1933. 50th Anniv of Construction of Pelesch Castle, Sinaia.

1283 **107** 1 l. violet . . . . 2·10 1·75
1284 – 3 l. brown . . . . 2·40 2·00
1285 – 6 l. red . . . . 3·25 2·40

DESIGNS: 3 l. Eagle and medallion portraits of Kings Carol I, Ferdinand I and Carol II; 6 l. Pelesch Castle.

108 Wayside Shrine

110 King Carol II

1934. Rumanian Women's Exhibition. Inscr "L.N.F.R. MUNCA NOASTRA ROMANEASC".

1286 **108** 1 l. + 1 l. brown . . . 2·00 1·75
1287 – 2 l. + 1 l. blue . . . . 2·50 2·00
1288 – 3 l. + 1 l. green . . . . 3·75 3·00

DESIGNS—HORIZ: 2 l. Weaver. VERT: 3 l. Spinner.

1934. Mamaia Jamboree Fund. Nos. 1256/61 optd **MAMAIA 1934** and Arms of Constanza.

1289 – 26 b. + 25 b. green . . . 4·00 3·25
1290 **98** 50 b. + 50 b. blue . . . 5·75 4·00
1291 – 1 l. + 1 l. green . . . . 7·75 6·25
1292 – 2 l. + 2 l. red . . . . . 8·75 7·75
1293 – 3 l. + 3 l. blue . . . . . 19·00 12·50
1294 – 6 l. + 6 l. brown . . . . 22·00 16·00

1934.

1295 – 50 b. brown . . . . . . 1·00 30
1296 **110** 2 l. green . . . . 2·00 30
1297 4 l. orange . . . . . . 2·75 45
1298 – 6 l. lake . . . . 6·25 30

DESIGNS: 50 b. Profile portrait of King Carol II in civilian clothes; 6 l. King Carol in plumed helmet.

112 "Grapes for Health"

113 Crisan, Horia and Closca

1934. Bucharest Fruit Exhibition.

1299 **112** 1 l. green . . . . 4·00 2·75
1300 – 2 l. brown . . . . 4·00 2·75

DESIGN: 2 l. Woman with fruit.

1935. 150th Anniv of Death of Three Rumanian Martyrs. Portraits inscr "MARTIR AL NEAMULUI 1785".

1301 **113** 1 l. violet 50 30
1302 – 2 l. green (Crisan) . . . 1·00 45
1303 – 6 l. brown (Closca) . . . 2·75 1·25
1304 – 10 l. blue (Horia) . . . 4·50 2·40

114 Boy Scouts

1935. 5th Anniv of Accession of Carol II.

1305 – 25 b. black . . . . . . 3·25 2·75
1306 – 1 l. violet . . . . 6·00 4·75
1307 **114** 2 l. green . . . . 6·75 6·75
1308 – 6 l. + 1 l. brown . . . 8·50 8·50
1309 – 10 l. + 2 l. blue . . . . 20·00 20·00

DESIGNS—VERT: 25 b. Scout saluting; 1 l. Bugler; 6 l. King Carol II. HORIZ: 10 l. Colour party.

1935. Portraits as T **110** but additionally inscr "POSTA".

1310 – 25 b. black 10 10
1311 – 50 b. brown 10 10
1312 – 1 l. violet 15 10
1313 **110** 2 l. green 35 10
1315 – 3 l. red 70 15
1316 – 3 l. blue . . . . 1·25 15
1317 **110** 4 l. orange . . . . . . 1·50 10
1318 – 5 l. red . . . . 1·25 55
1319 – 6 l. lake . . . . 1·75 10
1320 – 7 l. 50 blue . . . . . . 1·90 35
1321 – 8 l. purple . . . . . . 1·90 35
1322 **110** 9 l. blue . . . . 2·75 65
1323 – 10 l. blue . . . . 1·25 20
1324 – 12 l. blue . . . . 1·75 85
1325 – 15 l. brown . . . . . . 1·75 50
1326 – 16 l. green . . . . . . 2·25 30
1327 – 20 l. orange . . . . . . 1·50 40
1328 – 24 l. red . . . . 2·25 50

PORTRAITS—IN PROFILE: 25 b., 15 l. In naval uniform; 50 b., 3, 8, 10 l. In civilian clothes. THREE-QUARTER FACE: 1, 5, 7 l. 50, In civilian clothes. FULL FACE: 6, 12, 16, 20, 24 l. In plumed helmet.

118 King Carol II

119 Oltenia Peasant Girl

1936. Bucharest Exhibition and 70th Anniv of Hohenzollern–Sigmaringen Dynasty.

1329 **118** 6 l. + 1 l. red . . . . . 1·40 80

1936. 6th Anniv of Accession of Carol II Inscr "O.E.T.R. 8 IUNIE 1936".

1330 **119** 50 b. + 50 b. brown . . 1·25 50
1331 – 1 l. + 1 l. violet 75 55
1332 – 2 l. + 1 l. green 95 85
1333 – 3 l. + 1 l. red . . . . . 1·40 1·00
1334 – 4 l. + 2 l. red . . . . . 1·75 80
1335 – 6 l. + 3 l. grey . . . . . 2·25 1·40
1336 – 10 l. + 5 l. blue . . . . 3·50 2·75

DESIGNS (costumes of following districts)—VERT: 1 l. Banat; 4 l. Gori; 6 l. Neamz. HORIZ: 2 l. Saliste; 3 l. Hateg; 10 l. Suceava (Bukovina).

120 Brasov Jamboree Badge

121 Liner "Transylvania"

1936. National Scout Jamboree, Brasov.

1337 – 1 l. + 1 l. blue . . . . . 6·00 5·75
1338 – 3 l. + 3 l. grey . . . . . 7·50 5·75
1339 **120** 6 l. + 6 l. red . . . . . 9·50 5·75

DESIGNS: 1 l. National Scout Badge; 3 l. Tenderfoot Badge.

1936. 1st Marine Exhibition, Bucharest.

1343 – 1 l. + 1 l. violet . . . . 5·25 3·75
1344 – 3 l. + 2 l. blue . . . . . 5·25 4·00
1345 **121** 6 l. + 3 l. red . . . . . 6·75 5·75

DESIGNS: 1 l. Submarine "Delfinul"; 3 l. Naval cadet ship "Mircea"

1936. 18th Anniv of Annexation of Transylvania and 16th Anniv of Foundation of "Little Entente". Nos. 1320 and 1323 optd **CEHOSLOVACIA YUGOSLAVIA 1920-1936**.

1346 7 l. 50 blue . . . . 4·00 4·00
1347 10 l. blue . . . . 4·00 4·00

123 Creanga's Birthplace

1937. Birth Centenary of Ion Creanga (poet).

1348 **123** 2 l. green . . . . 1·10 50
1349 – 3 l. red . . . . 1·40 55
1350 **123** 4 l. violet . . . . . . 1·75 95
1351 – 6 l. brown . . . . 4·00 2·00

DESIGN: 3, 6 l. Portrait of Creanga, 37 × 22 mm.

124 Footballers

1937. 7th Anniv of Accession of Carol II.

1352 **124** 25 b. + 25 b. olive . . . 1·00 20
1353 – 50 b. + 50 b. brown . . 1·00 25
1354 – 1 l. + 50 b. violet . . . 1·25 40
1355 – 2 l. + 1 l. green . . . . 1·40 45
1356 – 3 l. + 1 l. red . . . . . 2·50 50
1357 – 4 l. + 1 l. red . . . . . 4·00 60
1358 – 6 l. + 2 l. brown . . . . 6·00 1·10
1359 – 10 l. + 4 l. blue . . . . 6·50 1·75

DESIGNS—HORIZ: 50 b. Swimmer; 3 l. King Carol II hunting; 10 l. U.F.S.R. Inaugural Meeting. VERT: 1 l. Javelin thrower; 2 l. Skier; 4 l. Rowing; 6 l. Steeplechaser.

Premium in aid of the Federation of Rumanian Sports Clubs (U.F.S.R.).

127 Curtea de Arges Cathedral

128 Hurdling

1937. "Little Entente".

1360 **127** 7 l. 50 blue . . . . 1·75 80
1361 10 l. blue . . . . 2·40 45

1937 8th Balkan Games, Bucharest. Inscr as in T **115**.

1362 – 1 l. + 1 l. violet . . . . 1·10 65
1363 – 2 l. + 1 l. green . . . . 1·50 90
1364 **128** 4 l. + 1 l. red . . . . . 1·75 1·50
1365 – 6 l. + 1 l. brown . . . . 2·10 1·75
1366 – 10 l. + 1 l. blue . . . . 6·50 3·00

DESIGNS: 1 l. Sprinting; 2 l. Throwing the javelin; 6 l. Breasting the tape; 10 l. High jumping.

129 Arms of Rumania, Greece, Turkey and Yugoslavia

130 King Carol II

1938. Balkan Entente.

1368 **129** 7 l. 50 blue . . . . . . 1·50 90
1369 10 l. blue . . . . 2·00 75

1938. New Constitution. Profile portraits of King inscr "27 FEBRUARIE 1938". 6 l. shows Arms also.

1370 **130** 3 l. red 80 50
1371 – 6 l. brown . . . . 1·25 50
1372 – 10 l. blue . . . . 1·90 1·00

131 King Carol II and Provincial Arms

132 Dimitrie Cantemir

1938. Fund for Bucharest Exhibition celebrating 20th Anniv of Union of Provinces.

1373 **131** 6 l. + 1 l. mauve . . . . 1·00 35

1938. Boy Scouts' Fund. 8th Anniv of Accession of Carol II. Inscr "STRAJA TARII 8 IUNIE 1938".

1374 **132** 25 b. + 25 b. olive . . . 35 20
1375 – 50 b. + 50 b. brown . . 80 20
1376 – 1 l. + 1 l. violet 90 25
1377 – 2 l. + 2 l. green 80 25
1378 – 3 l. + 2 l. mauve 85 30
1379 – 4 l. + 2 l. red 90 35
1380 – 6 l. + 2 l. brown . . . . 1·10 40
1381 – 7 l. 50 blue . . . . . . 1·50 40
1382 – 10 l. blue . . . . 1·60 50
1383 – 16 l. green . . . . 2·40 2·00
1384 – 20 l. red . . . . 3·50 2·00

PORTRAITS: 50 b. Maria Doamna; 1 l. Mircea the Great; 2 l. Constantin Brancoveanu; 3 l. Stephen the Great; 4 l. Prince Cuza; 6 l. Michael the Brave; 7 l. 50, Queen Elisabeth; 10 l. King Carol II; 16 l. King Ferdinand I; 20 l. King Carol I.

134 "The Spring"

135 Prince Carol in Royal Carriage

1938. Birth Centenary of Nicholas Grigorescu (painter).

1385 **134** 1 l. + 1 l. blue . . . . . 1·25 50
1386 – 2 l. + 1 l. green . . . . 1·75 1·10
1387 – 4 l. + 1 l. red . . . . . 1·75 1·25
1388 – 6 l. + 1 l. red . . . . . 1·90 1·60
1389 – 10 l. + 1 l. blue . . . . 2·75 2·10

DESIGNS—HORIZ: 2 l. "Escorting Prisoners" (Russo-Turkish War 1877–78); 4 l. "Returning from Market". VERT: 6 l. "Rodica, the Water Carrier"; 10 l. Self-portrait.

1939. Birth Centenary of King Carol I.

1390 **135** 25 b. black 10 10
1391 – 50 b. brown 10 10
1392 – 1 l. violet 20 10
1393 – 1 l. 50 green 10 10
1394 – 2 l. blue 10 10
1395 – 3 l. red 10 10
1396 – 4 l. red 10 10
1397 – 5 l. black 10 10
1398 – 7 l. black 10 10
1399 – 8 l. blue 25 15
1400 – 10 l. mauve 30 15
1401 – 12 l. blue 30 20
1402 – 15 l. blue 35 15
1403 – 16 l. green . . . . . . 1·00 60

DESIGNS—HORIZ 50 b. Prince Carol at Battle of Calafat; 1 l. 50, Sigmaringen and Pelesch Castles; 5 l. Carol I, Queen Elizabeth and Arms of Rumania. VERT: 1 l. Examining plans for restoring Curtea de Arges Monastery; 2 l. Carol I and Queen Elizabeth; 3 l. Carol I at age of 8; 4 l. In 1866; 5 l. In 1877; 7 l. Equestrian statue; 8 l. Leading troops in 1878; 10 l. In General's uniform; 12 l. Bust; 16 l. Restored Monastery of Curtea de Arges.

136 Rumanian Pavilion N.Y. World's Fair

137 Michael Eminescu, after painting by Joano Basarab

1939. New York World's Fair.
1407 136 6 l. lake 80 30
1408 – 12 l. blue 80 30
DESIGN: 12 l. Another view of Pavilion.

1939. 50th Death Anniv of Michael Eminescu (poet).
1409 137 5 l. black 80 40
1410 – 7 l. red 80 40
DESIGN: 7 l. Eminescu in later years.

138 St. George and Dragon

139 Railway Locomotives of 1869 and 1939

1939. 9th Anniv of Accession of Carol II and Boy Scouts' Fund.
1411 138 25 b. + 25 b. grey . . . 60 35
1412 50 b. + 50 b. brown . . 60 35
1413 1 l. + 1 l. blue 65 35
1414 2 l. + 2 l. green 75 35
1415 3 l. + 2 l. purple 90 35
1416 4 l. + 2 l. orange . . . . 1·40 45
1417 6 l. + 2 l. red . . . . . 1·50 45
1418 8 l. grey . . . . 1·50 50
1419 10 l. blue . . . . 1·60 50
1420 12 l. blue . . . . 2·00 1·40
1421 16 l. green . . . . 2·40 1·50

1939. 70th Anniv of Rumanian Railways.
1422 139 1 l. violet . . . . 1·25 55
1423 – 4 l. red . . . . 1·25 65
1424 – 5 l. grey . . . . 1·10 85
1425 – 7 l. mauve . . . . 1·40 90
1426 – 12 l. blue . . . . 2·25 1·25
1427 – 15 l. green . . . . . . 2·50 2·00
DESIGNS—HORIZ: 4 l. Steam train crossing railway-bridge; 15 l. Railway Headquarters, Budapest. VERT: 5 l., 7 l. Steam train leaving station; 12 l. Diesel train crossing railway bridge.

1940. Balkan Entente. As T 103 of Yugoslavia, but with Arms rearranged.
1428 12 l. blue 90 70
1429 16 l. blue 90 70

141 King Carol II

142 King Carol II

1940. Aviation Fund.
1430 141 1 l. + 50 b. green . . . 20 15
1431 2 l. 50 + 50 b. green . . 25 20
1432 3 l. + 1 l. red 35 25
1433 3 l. 50 + 50 b. brown . . 35 30
1434 4 l. + 1 l. orange 45 35
1435 6 l. + 1 l. blue 95 20
1436 9 l. + 1 l. blue . . . . . 1·10 95
1437 14 l. + 1 l. green . . . . 1·25 1·10

1940. 10th Anniv of Carol II and Aviation Fund. Royal portraits.
1438 142 1 l. + 50 b. purple . . . 75 25
1439 4 l. + 1 l. brown 75 35
1440 – 6 l. + 1 l. blue 75 45
1441 – 8 l. red . . . . 1·00 85
1442 – 16 l. blue . . . . 1·25 1·00
1443 – 32 l. brown . . . . . . 2·40 1·75
PORTRAITS: 6, 16 l. In steel helmet; 8 l. In military uniform; 32 l. In flying helmet.

144 The Iron Gates of the Danube

1940. Charity. 10th Anniv of Accession of Carol II and Boy Scouts' Fund. Inscr "STRAJA TARII 8 IUNIE 1940".
1444 144 1 l. + 1 l. violet 60 40
1445 – 2 l. + 1 l. brown 60 45
1446 – 3 l. + 1 l. green 65 50
1447 – 4 l. + 1 l. black 75 55
1448 – 5 l. + 1 l. orange 85 65
1449 – 8 l. + 1 l. red . . . . . 1·00 70
1450 – 12 l. + 2 l. blue . . . . 1·25 1·00
1451 – 16 l. + 2 l. grey . . . . 2·50 2·00
DESIGNS—HORIZ: 3 l. Hotin Fortress; 4 l. Hurez Monastery. VERT: 2 l. Greco-Roman ruins; 5 l. Church in Suceava; 8 l. Alba Julia Cathedral; 12 l. Village Church, Transylvania; 16 l. Triumphal Arch, Bucharest.

145 King Michael 146

1940.
1455 145 25 b. green 10 10
1456 50 b. olive 10 10
1457 1 l. violet 10 10
1458 2 l. orange 10 10
1608 3 l. brown 10 10
1609 3 l. 50 brown 10 10
1459 4 l. grey 10 10
1611 4 l. 50 brown 10 10
1460 5 l. pink 10 10
1613 6 l. 50 violet 10 10
1461 7 l. blue 10 10
1615 10 l. mauve 10 10
1616 11 l. blue 10 10
1463 12 l. blue 10 10
1464 13 l. purple 10 10
1618 15 l. blue 10 10
1619 16 l. blue 10 10
1620 20 l. brown 10 10
1621 29 l. blue 85 70
1467 30 l. green 15 10
1468 50 l. brown 15 10
1469 100 l. brown 30 10

1940. Aviation Fund.
1470 146 1 l. + 50 b. green . . . 10 10
1471 2 l. + 50 b. green . . . 10 10
1472 2 l. 50 + 50 b. green . . 10 10
1473 3 l. + 1 l. violet 10 10
1474 3 l. 50 + 50 b. pink . . 15 15
1475 4 l. + 50 b. red 10 10
1476 4 l. + 1 l. brown 10 10
1477 5 l. + 1 l. red 80 25
1478 6 l. + 1 l. blue 10 10
1479 7 l. + 1 l. green 20 10
1480 8 l. + 1 l. violet 15 10
1481 12 l. + 1 l. brown . . . 20 10
1482 14 l. + 1 l. blue 25 15
1483 19 l. + 1 l. mauve . . . 75 20

147 Codreanu (founder) 148

1940. "Iron Guard" Fund.
1484 147 7 l. + 30 l. grn (postage) 4·50 4·00
1485 148 20 l. + 5 l. green (air) . 2·00 2·50

149 Ion Mota

150 Library

1941. Marin and Mota (legionaries killed in Spain).
1486 – 7 l. + 7 l. red . . . . . 2·25 3·25
1487 149 15 l. + 15 l. blue . . . 3·75 5·00
PORTRAIT: 7 l. Vasile Marin.

1941. Carol I Endowment Fund. Inscr "1891 1941".
1488 – 1 l. 50 + 43 l. 50 violet 1·50 1·75
1489 150 2 l. + 43 l. red . . . . 1·50 1·75
1490 – 7 l. + 38 l. red . . . . 1·50 1·75
1491 – 10 l. + 35 l. green . . . 1·50 1·75
1492 – 16 l. + 29 l. brown . . . 1·50 1·75
DESIGNS: 1 l. 50, Ex-libris; 7 l. Foundation building and equestrian statue; 10 l. Foundation stone; 16 l. King Michael and Carol I.

1941. Occupation of Cernauti. Nos. 1488/92 optd **CERNAUTI 5 Iulie 1941.**
1493 – 1 l. 50 + 43 l. 50 violet 2·50 3·25
1494 150 2 l. + 43 l. red . . . . 2·50 3·25
1495 – 7 l. + 38 l. red . . . . 2·50 3·25
1496 – 10 l. + 35 l. green . . . 2·50 3·25
1497 – 16 l. + 29 l. brown . . . 2·50 3·25

1941. Occupation of Chisinau. Nos. 1488/92 optd **CHISINAU 16 Iulie 1941.**
1498 – 1 l. 50 + 43 l. 1.50 violet 2·50 3·25
1499 150 2 l. + 43 l. red . . . . 2·50 3·25
1500 – 7 l. + 38 l. red . . . . 2·50 3·25
1501 – 10 l. + 35 l. green . . . 2·50 3·25
1502 – 16 l. + 29 l. brown . . . 2·50 3·25

153 "Charity"

154 Prince Voda

1941. Red Cross Fund. Cross in red.
1503 153 1 l. 50 + 38 l. 50 violet . 1·00 75
1504 2 l. + 38 l. red . . . . . 1·00 75
1505 5 l. + 35 l. olive . . . . 1·00 75
1506 7 l. + 33 l. brown . . . . 1·00 75
1507 10 l. + 30 l. blue . . . . 1·25 1·40

1941. Conquest of Transdniestria.
1572 154 3 l. orange 30 65
1509 6 l. brown 30 35
1510 12 l. violet 50 60
1511 24 l. blue . . . . 70 1·00

155 King Michael and Stephen the Great

1941. Anti-Bolshevik Crusade. Inscr "RAZBOIUL SFANT CONTRA BOLSE-VISMULUI".
1512 155 10 l. + 30 l. blue . . . . 1·50 3·25
1513 – 12 l. + 28 l. red . . . . 1·50 3·25
1514 – 16 l. + 24 l. brown . . . 2·10 3·25
1515 – 20 l. + 20 l. violet . . . 2·10 3·25
DESIGNS: 12 l. Hotin and Akkerman Fortresses; 16 l. Arms and helmeted soldiers; 20 l. Bayonet charge and Arms of Rumania.

1941. Fall of Odessa. Nos. 1512/15 optd **ODESA/16 Oct. 1941.**
1517 155 10 l. + 30 l. blue . . . . 1·50 3·25
1518 – 12 l. + 28 l. red . . . . 1·50 3·25
1519 – 16 l. + 24 l. brown . . . 2·10 3·25
1520 – 20 l. + 20 l. violet . . . 2·10 3·25

157 Hotin

1941. Restoration of Bessarabia and Bukovina (Suceava). Inscr "BASARABIA" or "BUCOVINA".
1522 – 25 b. red 10 10
1523 157 50 b. brown 10 10
1524 – 1 l. violet 10 10
1525 – 1 l. 50 green 10 10
1526 – 2 l. brown 10 10
1527 – 3 l. olive 15 10
1528 – 5 l. olive 20 10
1529 – 5 l. 50 brown 20 15
1530 – 6 l. 50 mauve 50 40
1531 157 9 l. 50 grey 50 50
1532 – 10 l. purple 35 15
1533 – 13 l. blue 50 20
1534 – 17 l. brown 60 15
1535 – 26 l. green 95 30
1536 – 39 l. blue . . . . 1·40 40
1537 – 130 l. yellow . . . . . . 5·00 3·50
VIEWS—VERT: 25 b., 5 l. Paraclis Hotin; 3 l. Dragomirna; 13 l. Milisauti. HORIZ: 1, 17 l. Sucevita; 1 l. 50, Soroca; 2, 5 l. 50, Tighina; 6 l. 50, Cetatea Alba; 10, 130 l. Putna; 26 l. St. Nicolae, Suceava; 39 l. Monastery. Rughi.

1941. Winter Relief Fund. Inscr "BASARABIA" or "BUCOVINA".
1538 – 3 l. + 50 b. red 20 20
1539 – 5 l. 50 + 50 b. orange . . 55 30
1540 – 5 l. 50 + 1 l. black . . . 55 30
1541 – 6 l. 50 + 1 l. brown . . . 60 40
1542 – 8 l. + 1 l. blue 60 25
1543 – 9 l. 50 + 1 l. blue 75 45
1544 – 10 l. 50 + 1 l. blue . . . 75 25
1545 – 16 l. + 1 l. mauve 85 55
1546 157 25 l. + 1 l. grey . . . . 1·10 60
VIEWS—HORIZ: 3 l. Sucevita; 5 l. 50, (1539), Monastery, Rughi; 5 l. 50, (1540), Tighina; 6 l. 50, Soroca; 8 l. St. Nicolae, Suceava; 10 l. 50, Putna; 16 l. Cetatea Alba. VERT: 8 l. 50, Milisauti.

158 Titu Maiorescu

159 Coat-of-Arms of Bukovina

1942. Prisoners of War Relief Fund through International Education Office, Geneva.
1549 158 9 l. + 11 l. violet . . . 50 65
1550 20 l. + 20 l. brown . . . 1·90 1·90
1551 20 l. + 30 l. blue . . . . 2·00 2·00

1942. 1st Anniv of Liberation of Bukovina.
1553 159 9 l. + 4 l. red . . . . . 2·25 3·25
1554 – 18 l. + 32 l. blue . . . . 2·25 3·25
1555 – 20 l. + 30 l. red . . . . 2·25 3·25
ARMORIAL DESIGNS: 18 l. Castle; 20 l. Mounds and crosses.

INDEX

Countries can be quickly located by referring to the index at the end of this volume.

160 Map of Bessarabia, King Michael, Antonescu, Hitler and Mussolini

161 Statue of Miron Costin

1942. 1st Anniv of Liberation of Bessarabia.
1556 160 9 l. + 41 l. brown . . . 2·00 3·25
1557 – 18 l. + 32 l. olive . . . 2·00 3·25
1558 – 20 l. + 30 l. blue . . . 2·00 3·25
DESIGNS—VERT: 18 l. King Michael and Marshall Antonescu below miniature of King Stephen. HORIZ: 20 l. Marching soldiers and miniature of Marshal Antonescu.

1942. 1st Anniv of Incorporation of Transdniestria.
1559 161 6 l. + 44 l. brown . . . 1·50 2·50
1560 12 l. + 38 l. violet . . . 1·50 2·50
1561 24 l. + 26 l. blue . . . . 1·50 2·50

162 Andrei Muresanu

163 Statue of Avram Iancu

1942. 80th Death Anniv of A. Muresanu (novelist).
1562 162 5 l. + 5 l. violet 90 90

1943. Fund for Statue of Iancu (national hero).
1563 163 16 l. + 4 l. brown . . . 90 1·25

164 Nurse and wounded Soldier

165 Sword and Shield

1943. Red Cross Charity. Cross in red.
1564 164 12 l. + 88 l. red 75 75
1565 16 l. + 84 l. blue 75 75
1566 20 l. + 80 l. olive 75 75

1943. Charity. 2nd Year of War. Inscr "22 JUNIE 1941 22 JUNIE 1943".
1568 165 36 l. + 164 l. brown . . 2·10 2·40
1569 – 62 l. + 138 l. blue . . . 2·10 2·40
1570 – 76 l. + 124 l. red . . . 2·10 2·40
DESIGNS: 62 l. Sword severing chain; 76 l. Angel protecting soldier and family.

167 P. Maior

169 King Michael and Marshal Antonescu

1943. Transylvanian Refugees' Fund (1st issue).
1576 167 16 l. + 134 l. red . . . 40 65
1577 – 32 l. + 118 l. blue . . . 40 65
1578 – 36 l. + 114 l. purple . . 40 65
1579 – 62 l. + 138 l. red . . . 40 65
1580 – 91 l. + 109 l. brown . . 40 65
PORTRAITS—VERT: 32 l. G. Sincai; 36 l. T. Cipariu; 91 l. G. Cosbuc. HORIZ: 62 l. Horia, Closca and Crisan.
See also Nos. 1584/8.

1943. 3rd Anniv of King Michael's Reign.
1581 169 16 l. + 24 l. blue . . . . 1·50 2·50

170 Sports Shield

171 Calafat, 1877

1943. Charity. Sports Week.
1582 170 16 l. + 24 l. blue 45 45
1583 16 l. + 24 l. brown . . . 45 45

1943. Transylvanian Refugees' Fund (2nd issue) Portraits as T **167**.
1584 16 l. + 134 l. mauve 40 65
1585 51 l. + 99 l. orange 40 65
1586 56 l. + 144 l. red 40 65
1587 76 l. + 124 l. blue 40 65
1588 77 l. + 123 l. brown 40 65
PORTRAITS—VERT: 16 l. S. Micu; 51 l. G. Lazar; 56 l. O. Goga; 76 l. S. Barnutiu; 77 l. A. Saguna.

1943. Centenary of National Artillery.
1596 **171** 1 l. + 1 l. brown 30 30
1597 – 2 l. + 2 l. violet 30 30
1598 – 3 l. 50 + 3 l. 50 blue 30 30
1599 – 4 l. + 4 l. mauve 30 30
1600 – 5 l. + 5 l. orange 50 50
1601 – 6l. 50 + 6 l. 50 blue 50 50
1602 – 7 l. + 7 l. purple 75 1·00
1603 – 20 l. + 20 l. red 1·25 1·75
DESIGNS—HORIZ: (1 l. to 7 l. inscr battle scenes): 2 l. "1916–1918"; 3 l. 50, Stalingrad; 4 l. Crossing R. Tisza; 5 l. Odessa; 6 l. 50, Caucasus; 7 l. Sevastopol; 20 l. Bibescu and King Michael.

172 Association Insignia

1943. 25th Anniv of National Engineers' Assn.
1624 **172** 21 l. + 29 l. brown 1·00 85

173 Motor-cycle and Delivery Van

1944. Postal Employees' Relief Fund and Bicent of National Postal Service. (a) Without opt.
1625 **173** 1 l. + 49 l. red 2·00 2·00
1626 – 2 l. + 48 l. mauve 2·00 2·00
1627 – 4 l. + 46 l. blue 2·00 2·00
1628 – 10 l. + 40 l. purple 2·00 2·00

(b) Optd **1744 1944**.
1631 **173** 1l + 49 l. red 3·75 4·25
1632 – 2 l. + 48 l. mauve 3·75 4·25
1633 – 4 l. + 46 l. blue 3·75 4·25
1634 – 10 l. + 40 l. purple 3·75 4·25
DESIGNS—HORIZ: 2 l. Mail van and eight horses; 4 l. Chariot. VERT: 10 l. Horseman and Globe.

174 Dr. Cretzulescu **175** Rugby Player

1944. Cent of Medical Teaching in Rumania.
1637 **174** 35 l. + 65 l. blue 90 90

1944. 30th Anniv of Foundation of National Rugby Football Association.
1638 **175** 16 l. + 184 l. red 3·25 4·25

176 Stefan Tomsa Church, Radaseni **177** Fruit Pickers

1944. Cultural Fund. Town of Radaseni. Inscr "RADASENI".
1639 **176** 5 l. + 145 l. blue 60 85
1640 – 12 l. + 138 l. red 60 85
1641 **177** 15 l. + 135 l. orange 60 85
1642 – 32 l. + 118 l. brown 60 85
DESIGNS—HORIZ: 12 l. Agricultural Institution; 32 l. School.

178 Queen Helen

179 King Michael and Carol I Foundation, Bucharest

1945. Red Cross Relief Fund. Portrait in black on yellow and Cross in red.
1643 **178** 4 l. 50 + 5 l. 50 violet 15 20
1644 10 l. + 40 l. brown 25 30
1645 15 l. + 75 l. blue 40 50
1646 20 l. + 80 l. red 95 75

1945. King Carol I Foundation Fund.
1647 **179** 20 l. + 180 l. orange 25 30
1648 25 l. + 175 l. slate 25 30
1649 35 l. + 165 l. brown 25 30
1650 76 l. + 125 l. violet 25 30

180 A. Saguna **181** A Muresanu

1945. Liberation of Northern Transylvania. Inscr "1944".
1652 **180** 25 b. red 50 50
1653 **181** 50 b. orange 15 15
1654 – 4 l. 50 brown 20 20
1655 – 11 l. blue 20 20
1656 – 15 l. green 20 20
1657 – 31 l. violet 20 20
1658 – 35 l. grey 20 20
1659 – 41 l. olive 1·00 1·00
1660 – 55 l. brown 20 20
1661 – 61 l. mauve 20 20
1662 – 75 l. + 75 l. brown 40 40
DESIGNS—HORIZ: 4 l. 50, Samuel Micu; 31 l. George Lazar; 55 l. Three Heroes; 61 l. Petru Maior; 75 l. King Ferdinand and King Michael. VERT: 11 l. George Sincai; 15 l. Michael the Brave; 35 l. Avram Iancu; 41 l. Simeon Barnutiu.

182 King Michael **183**

184 King Michael **185**

1945.
1663 **182** 50 b. grey 10 10
1664 **183** 1 l. brown 10 10
1665 2 l. violet 10 10
1666 **182** 2 l. brown 10 10
1667 **183** 4 l. green 10 10
1668 **184** 5 l. mauve 10 10
1669 **182** 10 l. blue 10 10
1670 10 l. brown 10 10
1671 **183** 10 l. brown 10 10
1672 **182** 15 l. mauve 10 10
1673 20 l. blue 10 10
1674 20 l. lilac 10 10
1675 **184** 20 l. purple 10 10
1676 25 l. red 10 10
1677 35 l. brown 10 10
1678 40 l. red 10 10
1679 **183** 50 l. blue 10 10
1680 55 l. red 10 10
1681 **184** 75 l. green 10 10
1682 **185** 80 l. orange 10 10
1683 80 l. blue 10 10
1684 **182** 80 l. blue 10 10
1685 **185** 100 l. brown 10 10
1686 **182** 137 l. green 15 10
1687 **185** 160 l. green 10 10
1688 160 l. violet 10 10
1689 200 l. green 20 15
1690 200 l. red 10 10
1691 **183** 200 l. red 10 10
1692 **185** 300 l. blue 10 10
1693 360 l. brown 15 10
1694 400 l. violet 10 10
1695 **183** 400 l. red 10 10
1696 **185** 480 l. brown 15 10
1697 **182** 500 l. mauve 15 10
1698 **185** 600 l. green 10 10
1699 **184** 860 l. brown 20 15
1700 **185** 1000 l. green 10 10
1701 **182** 1500 l. green 10 10
1702 **185** 2400 l. lilac 25 10
1703 **183** 1500 l. blue 15 10
1704 **185** 3700 l. blue 25 10
1705 **182** 5000 l. grey 10 10
1706 8000 l. green 25 10
1707 **185** 10000 l. brown 40 20

186 N. Jorga

187 Books and Torch

1945. War Victims' Relief Fund.
1708 – 12 l. + 188 l. blue 65 65
1709 – 16 l. + 184 l. brown 65 65
1710 **186** 20 l. + 180 l. brown 65 65
1711 – 32 l. + 168 l. red 65 65
1712 – 35 l. + 165 l. blue 65 65
1713 – 36 l. + 164 l. violet 70 80
PORTRAITS: 12 l. I. G. Duca; 16 l. Virgil Madgearu; 32 l. Ilie Pintilie; 35 l. Bernath Andrei; 36 l. Filimon Sarbu.

1945. Charity. 1st Rumanian–Soviet Congress Fund. Inscr "ARLUS".
1715 **187** 20 l. + 80 l. olive 30 30
1716 – 35 l. + 165 l. red 30 30
1717 – 75 l. + 225 l. blue 30 30
1718 – 80 l. + 420 l. brown 30 30
DESIGNS: 35 l. Soviet and Rumanian flags; 75 l. Drawn curtain revealing Kremlin; 80 l. T. Vladimirescu and A. Nevsky.

188 Karl Marx

189 Postman

1945. Trade Union Congress, Bucharest. Perf or imperf.
1720 **188** 75 l. + 425 l. red 3·00 3·00
1723 75 l. + 425 l. blue 8·50 8·50
1721 – 120 l. + 380 l. blue 3·00 3·00
1724 – 120 l. + 380 l. brown 8·50 8·50
1722 – 155 l. + 445 l. brown 3·00 3·00
1725 – 155 l. + 445 l. red 8·50 8·50
PORTRAITS: 120 l. Engels; 155 l. Lenin.

1945. Postal Employees. Inscr "MUNCA P.T.T.".
1726 **189** 100 l. brown 50 50
1727 100 l. olive 50 50
1728 – 150 l. brown 1·00 1·00
1729 – 150 l. red 1·00 1·00
1730 – 250 l. olive 1·60 1·60
1731 – 250 l. blue 1·60 1·60
1732 – 500 l. mauve 13·50 13·50
DESIGNS: 150 l. Telegraphist; 250 l. Lineman; 500 l. Post Office, Bucharest.

190 Throwing the Discus

192 Agricultural and Industrial Workers

1945. Charity. With shield inscr "O.S.P." Perf or imperf.
1733 **190** 12 l. + 188 l. olive (post) 2·50 2·40
1738 – 12 l. + 188 l. orange 2·50 2·40
1734 – 16 l. + 184 l. blue 2·50 2·40
1739 – 16 l. + 184 l. purple 2·50 2·40
1735 – 20 l. + 180 l. green 2·50 2·40
1740 – 20 l. + 180 l. violet 2·50 2·40
1736 – 32 l. + 168 l. mauve 2·50 2·40
1741 – 32 l. + 168 l. green 2·50 2·40
1737 – 35 l. + 165 l. blue 2·50 2·40
1742 – 35 l. + 165 l. olive 2·50 2·40

1743 – 200 l. + 1000 l. bl (air) 13·00 15·00
DESIGNS—As T **190**: 16 l. Diving; 20 l. Skiing; 32 l. Volleyball; 35 l. "Sport and work". 36 × 50 mm: 200 l. Airplane and bird.

1945. 1st Anniv of Rumanian Armistice with Russia.
1744 **192** 100 l. + 400 l. red 75 60
1745 – 200 l. + 800 l. blue 75 60
DESIGN: 200 l. King Michael, "Agriculture" and "Industry".

193 T. Vladimirescu

194 Destitute Children

1945. Charity. Patriotic Defence Fund. Inscr "APARAREA PATRIOTICA".
1746 – 20 l. + 580 l. brown 10·00 12·50
1747 – 20 l. + 580 l. mauve 10·00 12·50
1748 – 40 l. + 560 l. blue 10·00 12·50
1749 – 40 l. + 560 l. green 10·00 12·50
1750 – 55 l. + 545 l. red 10·00 12·50
1751 – 55 l. + 545 l. brown 10·00 12·50
1752 **193** 60 l. + 540 l. blue 10·00 12·50
1753 60 l. + 540 l. brown 10·00 12·50
1754 – 80 l. + 520 l. red 10·00 12·50
1755 – 80 l. + 520 l. mauve 10·00 12·50
1756 – 100 l. + 500 l. green 10·00 12·50
1757 – 100 l. + 500 l. brown 10·00 12·50
DESIGNS—HORIZ: 20 l. "Political Amnesty"; 40 l. "Military Amnesty"; 55 l. "Agrarian Amnesty"; 100 l. King Michael and "Recontruction". VERT: 80 l. Nicholas Horia.

1945. Child Welfare Fund.
1758 **194** 40 l. blue 20 15

195 I. Ionescu, G. Titeica, A. G. Idachimescu and V. Cristescu

1945. 50th Anniv of Founding of Journal of Mathematics.
1759 **195** 2 l. brown 10 10
1760 – 80 l. grey 60 60
DESIGN: 80 l. Allegory of Learning.

196 Cernavoda Bridge

1945. 50th Anniv of Cernavoda Bridge.
1761 **196** 80 l. black 35 25

197 German Electric Train

198

1945. Charity. 16th Congress of Rumanian Engineers. Perf or imperf. (a) Postage.
1762 **197** 10 l. + 490 l. olive 1·40 1·50
1763 10 l. + 490 l. blue 1·40 1·50
1764 – 20 l. + 480 l. brown 65 65
1765 – 20 l. + 480 l. violet 65 65
1766 – 25 l. + 475 l. purple 65 65
1767 – 25 l. + 475 l. green 90 1·25
1768 – 55 l. + 445 l. blue 65 65
1769 – 55 l. + 445 l. grey 65 65
1770 – 100 l. + 400 l. brown 65 65
1771 – 100 l. + 400 l. mauve 65 65

(b) Air. Symbolical design as T **198**. Imperf.
1772 **198** 80 l. + 420 l. grey 1·50 1·50
1773 200 l. + 800 l. blue 1·50 1·50
DESIGNS—As Type **197**: 20 l. Coats of Arms; 25 l. Arterial road; 55 l. Oil wells; 100 l. "Agriculture".

199 Globe and Clasped Hands

1945. Charity. World Trade Union Congress, Paris. Symbolical designs inscr "CONFERINTA MONDIAL LA SINDICALA DIN-PARIS 25 SEPTEMVRE 1945".
1776 **199** 80 l. + 920 l. mauve 17·00 17·00
1777 – 160 l. + 1840 l. brown 17·00 17·00
1778 – 320 l. + 1680 l. violet 17·00 17·00
1779 – 440 l. + 2560 l. green 17·00 17·00
DESIGNS: 160 l. Globe and Dove of Peace; 320 l. Hand and hammer; 440 l. Scaffolding and flags.

1946. Nos 1444/5 surch in figures.
1780 10 l. + 90 l. on 100 l. + 400 l. 95 1·90
1781 10 l. + 90 l. on 200 l. + 800 l. 95 1·90
1782 20 l. + 80 l. on 100 l. + 400 l. 95 1·90
1783 20 l. + 80 l. on 200 l. + 800 l. 95 1·90
1784 80 l. + 120 l. on 100 l. + 400 l. 95 1·90

1785 80 l. + 120 l. on 200 l. + 800 l. 95 1·90
1786 100 l. + 150 l. on 100 l. + 400 l. 95 1·90
1787 100 l. + 150 l. on 200 l. + 800 l. 95 1·90

200 Sower

201 Distribution of Title Deeds

1946. Agrarian Reform. Inscr "REFORMA AGRARA".
1788 – 80 l. blue 20 20
1789 **200** 50 l. + 450 l. red 20 20
1790 **201** 100 l. + 900 l. purple 20 20
1791 – 200 l. + 800 l. orange 20 20
1792 – 400 l. + 1600 l. green 25 25
DESIGNS—VERT: 80 l. Blacksmith and ploughman. HORIZ: 200 l. Ox-drawn farm wagon; 400 l. Plough and tractor.

202

1946. 25th Anniv of Philharmonic Orchestra.
1794 **202** 10 l. blue 10 10
1795 – 20 l. brown 10 10
1796 – 55 l. green 10 10
1797 – 80 l. violet 20 15
1798 – 160 l. orange 10 10
1799 **202** 200 l. + 800 l. red 1·00 1·00
1800 – 350 l. + 1650 l. blue 1·25 1·25
DESIGNS: 20 l., 55 l., 160 l. "XXV" and musical score; 80 l., 350 l. G. Enescu.

203 Building Worker

205 Sower

1946. Labour Day. Designs of workers inscr "ZIUA MUNCII".
1803 **203** 10 l. red 10 10
1804 10 l. green 40 50
1805 20 l. blue 40 50
1806 20 l. brown 10 10
1807 200 l. red 15 15

1946. Youth Issue.
1809 **205** 10 l. + 100 l. red & brn 10 10
1810 – 10 l. + 200 l. pur & blue 1·50 1·50
1811 – 80 l. + 200 l. brn & pur 10 10
1812 – 80 l. + 300 l. mve & brn 10 10
1813 – 200 l. + 400 l. red & grn 15 15
DESIGNS: No. 1810, Hurdling; No. 1811, Student; No. 1812, Worker and factory; No. 1813, Marching with flag.

206 Aviator and Aeroplanes

207 Football

1946. Air. Youth Issue.
1814 – 200 l. blue and green 3·00 3·00
1815 **206** 500 l. blue and orange 3·00 3·00
DESIGN: 200 l. Aeroplane grounded.

1946. Sports, designs inscr "O.S.P." Perf or imperf.
1816 **207** 10 l. blue (postage) 30 30
1817 – 20 l. red 30 30
1818 – 50 l. violet 30 30
1819 – 80 l. brown 30 30
1820 – 160 l. + 1340 l. green 30 30
1821 – 300 l. red (air) 90 1·50
1822 – 300 l. + 1200 l. blue 90 1·50
DESIGNS: 20 l. Diving; 50 l. Running; 80 l. Mountaineering; 160 l. Ski-jumping; 300 l., 300 l. + 1200 l. Flying.

208 "Traditional Ties"

209 Banat Girl holding Distaff

1946. Rumanian–Soviet Friendship Pact.
1824 **208** 80 l. brown 10 10
1825 – 100 l. blue 10 10
1826 – 300 l. grey 10 10
1827 – 300 l. + 1200 l. red 60 60
DESIGNS: 100 l. "Cultural ties"; 300 l. "Economic ties"; 300 l. + 1200 l. Dove.
No. 1827 also exists imperf.

1946. Charity. Women's Democratic Federation.
1829 – 80 l. olive 10 10
1830 **209** 80 l. + 320 l. red 15 15
1831 – 140 l. + 360 l. orange 15 15
1832 – 300 l. + 450 l. green 20 20
1833 – 600 l. + 900 l. blue 35 30
DESIGNS: 80 l. Girl and handloom; 140 l. Wallachian girl and wheatsheaf; 300 l. Transylvanian horsewoman; 600 l. Moldavian girl carrying water.

211 King Michael and Food Transport

1947. Social Relief Fund.
1845 – 300 l. olive 15 15
1846 **211** 600 l. mauve 20 20
1847 – 1500 l. + 3500 l. orange 20 20
1848 – 3700 l. + 5300 l. violet 20 20
DESIGNS—VERT: 300 l. Loaf of bread and hungry child; 1500 l. Angel bringing food and clothing to destitute people; 3700 l. Loaf of bread and starving family.

213 King Michael and Chariot

214 Symbols of Labour and Clasped Hands

1947. Peace.
1850 **213** 300 l. purple 20 20
1851 – 600 l. brown 20 20
1852 – 3000 l. blue 20 20
1853 – 7200 l. green 20 20
DESIGNS—VERT: 600 l. Winged figure of Peace; 300 l. Flags of four Allied Nations; 7200 l. Dove of Peace.

1947. Trades Union Congress.
1854 **214** 200 l. blue (postage) 45 45
1855 300 l. orange 45 45
1856 600 l. red 45 45
1857 – 1100 l. blue (air) 85 85
DESIGN—22×37mm: 1100 l. As Type **214** with Lockheed Super Electra airplane at top.

216 Worker and Torch

219 King Michael

1947. Air. Trades Union Congress. Imperf.
1858 **216** 300 l. + 7000 l. brown 85 85

1947.
1865 **219** 1000 l. blue 15 10
1869 3000 l. blue 20 10
1866 5500 l. green 25 10
1870 7200 l. mauve 20 10
1871 15000 l. blue 30 10
1867 20000 l. brown 40 20
1872 21000 l. mauve 30 20
1873 36000 l. violet 60 25
1868 50000 l. orange 70 25
Nos. 1865/8 are size 18×21½ mm and Nos. 1869/73 are 25×30mm.

218 Symbolical of "Learning"

1947. Charity. People's Culture.
1859 – 200 l. + 200 l. blue 10 15
1860 – 300 l. + 300 l. brown 10 15
1861 – 600 l. + 600 l. green 10 15
1862 – 1200 l. + 1200 l. blue 10 15
1863 **218** 1500 l. + 1500 l. red 10 15
DESIGNS—HORIZ: 200 l. Boys' reading class; 300 l. Girls' school; 600 l. Engineering classroom; 1200 l. School building.

220 N. Grigorescu

221 Lisunov Li-2 over Land

1947. Charity. Institute of Rumanian–Soviet Studies.
1874 – 1500 l. + 1500 l. purple (postage) 20 20
1875 – 1500 l. + 1500 l. orange 20 20
1876 – 1500 l. + 1500 l. green 20 20
1877 **220** 1500 l. + 1500 l. blue 20 20
1878 – 1500 l. + 1500 l. blue 20 20
1879 – 1500 l. + 1500 l. lake 20 20
1880 – 1500 l. + 1500 l. red 20 20
1881 – 1500 l. + 1500 l. brown 20 20
1882 **221** 15000 l. + 15000 l. green (air) 60 75
PORTRAITS: No. 1874, Petru Movila; No. 1875, V. Babes; No. 1876, M. Eminescu; No. 1878, P. Tchaikovsky; No. 1879, M. Lomonosov; No. 1880, A. Pushkin; No. 1881, I. Y. Repin.
No. 1882 is imperf.

222 Miner

224 Lockheed Super Electra over Black Sea

1947. Charity. Labour Day.
1883 **222** 1000 l. + 1000 l. olive 25 30
1884 – 1500 l. + 1500 l. brown 20 25
1885 – 2000 l. + 2000 l. blue 20 25
1886 – 2500 l. + 2500 l. mauve 20 25
1887 – 3000 l. + 3000 l. red 25 30
DESIGNS: 1500 l. Peasant; 2000 l. Peasant woman; 2500 l. Intellectual; 3000 l. Factory worker.

1947. Air. Labour Day.
1888 – 3000 l. red 30 25
1889 – 3000 l. green 30 25
1890 – 3000 l. brown 30 25
1891 **224** 3000 l. + 12,000 l. bl 30 25
DESIGNS—24½×30 mm: No. 1888, Four parachutes; No. 1889, Air Force Monument; No. 1890, Douglas DC-4 over landscape.

(New currency 1 (new) leu = 100 (old) lei.)

223 King Michael and Timber Barges

227

1947. Designs with medallion portrait of King Michael.
1892 – 50 b. orange 10 10
1893 **225** 1 l. brown 10 10
1894 – 2 l. blue 10 10
1895 – 3 l. red 20 10
1896 – 5 l. blue 20 10
1897 – 10 l. blue 40 10
1898 – 12 l. violet 60 20
1899 – 15 l. blue 1·00 20
1900 – 20 l. brown 1·60 25
1901 – 32 l. brown 4·75 2·25
1902 – 36 l. lake 4·00 1·60
DESIGNS: 50 b. Harvesting; 2 l. River Danube; 3 l. Reshitza Industries; 5 l. Curtea de Arges Cathedral; 10 l. Royal Palace, Bucharest; 12, 36 l. Cernavoda Bridge; 15, 32 l. Port of Constantza; 20 l. Oil Wells, Prahova.

1947. Balkan Games. Surch **2 + 3 LEI C.B.A. 1947** and bar.
1903 **219** 2 + 3 l. on 36,000 l. vio 90 90

1947. 17th Congress of General Assn of Rumanian Engineers. With monogram as in T **227**.
1904 **227** 1 l. + 1 l. red (post) 10 10
1905 – 2 l. + 2 l. brown 10 10
1906 – 3 l. + 3 l. violet 20 20
1907 – 4 l. + 4 l. olive 20 20
1908 – 5 l. + 5 l. blue (air) 55 55
DESIGNS: 2 l. Sawmill; 3 l. Refinery; 4 l. Steel mill; 5 l. Gliders over mountains.

1947. Charity. Soviet–Rumanian Amity. As No. 1896 surch **ARLUS 1-7 XI 1947 + 5**. Imperf.
1909 **5** l. + 5 l. blue 85 50

229 Beehive

230 Food Convoy

1947. Savings Day.
1910 **229** 12 l. red 15 15

1947. Patriotic Defence.
1911 **230** 1 l. + 1 l. blue 15 15
1912 – 2 l. + 2 l. brown 15 15
1913 – 3 l. + 3 l. red 15 15
1914 – 4 l. + 4 l. blue 20 20
1915 – 5 l. + 5 l. red 35 35
SYMBOLIC DESIGNS—HORIZ: 2 l. Soldiers' parcels; 3 l. Modern hospital; 4 l. Hungry children. VERT: 5 l. Manacled wrist and flag.

231 Allegory of work

1947. Charity. Trades Union Congress, Bucharest. Inscr "C.G.M. 1947".
1916 – 2 l. + 10 l. red (post) 15 15
1917 **231** 7 l. + 10 l. black 20 20
1918 – 11 l. red and blue (air) 40 40
DESIGNS—As T **231**: 2 l. Industrial and agricultural workers. 23×18 mm: 11 l. Lisunov Li-2 airplane over demonstration.

233 Map of Rumania

1948. Census of 1948.
1925 **233** 12 l. blue 25 15

234 Printing Works and Press

235 Discus Thrower

1948. 75th Anniv of Rumanian State Stamp Printing Works.
1926 **234** 6 l. violet 1·25 75
1927 7 l. 50 green 65 10

1948. Balkan Games, 1947. Inscr as in T **235**. Imperf or perf.
1928 **235** 1 l. + 1 l. brown (post) 50 50
1929 – 2 l. + 2 l. red 65 65
1930 – 5 l. + 5 l. blue 1·00 1·00
1931 – 7 l. + 7 l. violet (air) 1·00 75
1932 – 10 l. + 10 l. green 1·50 1·00
DESIGNS: 2 l. Runner; 5 l. Heads of two young athletes; 7, 10 l. Airplane over running track.

1948. Nos. 1892/1902 optd **RPR** (Republica Populara Romana).
1933 50 b. orange 25 20
1934 1 l. brown 15 10
1935 2 l. blue 70 15
1936 3 l. red 85 15
1937 5 l. blue 1·40 15
1938 10 l. blue 1·60 15
1939 12 l. violet 2·00 30
1940 15 l. blue 2·00 40
1941 20 l. brown 1·75 30
1942 32 l. brown 8·50 3·75
1943 36 l. lake 6·50 2·50

237 Industrial Worker

1948. Young Workers' Union. Imperf or perf.
1954 **237** 2 l. + 2 l. blue (post) . . 40 40
1955 – 3 l. + 3 l. green 35 25
1956 – 5 l. + 5 l. brown 40 30
1957 – 8 l. + 8 l. red 45 40

1958 – 12 l. + 12 l. blue (air) . 1·40 90
DESIGNS—As Type **237**: 3 l. Peasant girl and wheatsheaf; 5 l. Student and book. TRIANGULAR: 8 l. Youths bearing Filimon Sarbu banner. 36 × 23 mm: 12 l. Airplane and barn swallows.

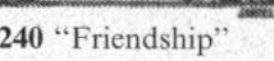
240 "Friendship" 241 "New Constitution"

1948. Rumanian–Bulgarian Amity.
1959 **240** 32 l. brown . . . . . . 1·00 20

1948. New Constitution.
1960 **241** 1 l. red 30 20
1961 2 l. orange 65 50
1962 12 l. blue . . . . 2·00 80

242 Globe and Banner 243 Aviator and Heinkel He 116A

1948. Labour Day.
1963 **242** 8 l. + 8 l. red (postage) . 1·50 2·50
1964 – 10 l. + 10 l. green . . . 2·50 3·25
1965 – 12 l. + 12 l. brown . . . 3·25 4·25

1966 **243** 20 l. + 20 l. blue (air) . 5·25 5·75
DESIGNS—HORIZ: 10 l. Peasants and mountains. VERT: 12 l. Worker and factory.

244 Barbed Wire Entanglement

1948. Army Day.
1967 – 1 l. 50 + 1 l. 50 red (postage) 35 35
1968 **244** 2 l. + 2 l. purple 35 35
1969 – 4 l. + 4 l. brown 70 70
1970 – 7 l. 50 + 7 l. 50 black . . 1·40 1·40
1971 – 8 l. + 8 l. violet . . . . 1·50 1·50

1972 – 3 l. + 3 l. blue (air) . . . 5·50 5·50
1973 – 5 l. + 5 l. blue . . . . . 8·00 8·00
DESIGNS—VERT: 1 l. 50, Infantry; 3 l. Ilyushin Stormovik fighter; 5 l. Petlyakov Pe-2 dive bomber. HORIZ: 4 l. Artillery; 7 l. 50, Tank; 8 l. Destroyer.

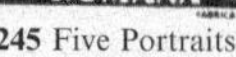

245 Five Portraits 246 Proclamation of Islaz

1948. Cent of 1848 Revolution. Dated "1848 1948".
1974 – 2 l. + 2 l. purple 35 30
1975 **245** 5 l. + 5 l. violet 45 40
1976 **246** 11 l. red 60 15
1977 – 10 l. + 10 l. green . . . 60 60
1978 – 36 l. + 18 l. blue . . . . 1·90 1·50
DESIGS—22 × 38 mm. HORIZ: 10 l. Balcescu, Petofi, Iancu, Barnutiu Baritiu and Murcu. VERT: 2 l. Nicolas Balcescu; 36 l. Balcescu, Kogalniceanu, Alecsandri and Cuza.

247 Emblem of Republic

1948.
2023 **247** 50 b. red 50 50
1980 0.50 l. red 40 40
1981 1 l. brown 15 10
1982 2 l. green 20 10
1983 3 l. grey 35 10
1984 4 l. brown 30 10
1985 5 l. blue 30 10
2028 5 l. violet 60 10
1986 10 l. blue . . . . 1·40 15
No. 2023 is inscribed "BANI 0.50" (= $\frac{1}{2}$ bani) and in No. 1980 this was corrected to "LEI 0.50".

248 Monimoa Gliders 249 Yachts

1948. Air Force and Navy Day. (a) Air Force (vert).
1987 **248** 2 l. + 2 l. blue . . . . 1·25 1·25
1988 – 5 l. + 5 l. violet . . . . 1·25 1·25
1989 – 8 l. + 8 l. red . . . . 1·90 1·90
1990 – 10 l. + 10 l. brown . . . 2·50 2·50

(b) Navy (horiz).
1991 **249** 2 l. + 2 l. green . . . . 1·25 1·25
1992 – 5 l. + 5 l. grey . . . . 1·25 1·25
1993 – 8 l. + 8 l. blue . . . . 1·90 1·90
1994 – 10 l. + 10 l. red . . . . 2·50 2·50
DESIGNS—AIR FORCE. 5 l. Vlaicu's No. 1 "Crazy Fly"; 8 l. Lisunov Li-2 airplane and tractor; 10 l. Lisunov Li 2 airplane. NAVY. 5 l. "Mircea" (cadet ship) 1882; 8 l. "Romana Mare" (Danube river steamer); 10 l. "Transylvania" (liner).

1948. Surch.
1995 **240** 31 l. on 32 l. brown . . 60 20

251 Newspapers and Torch 252 Soviet Soldiers' Monument

1948. Press Week. Imperf or perf.
1996 **251** 5 l. + 5 l. red 20 10
1997 10 l. brown 65 65
1998 – 10 l. + 10 l. violet . . . 1·00 1·00
1999 – 15 l. + 15 l. blue . . . 1·40 1·40
DESIGNS—HORIZ: 10 l. (No. 1998), Flag, torch and ink-well. VERT: 15 l. Alexander Sahia (journalist).

1948. Rumanian–Russian Amity.
2000 **252** 10 l. red (postage) . . . 65 65
2001 – 10 l. + 10 l. green . . . 2·75 2·75
2002 – 15 l. + 15 l. blue . . . 3·25 3·25

2003 – 20 l. + 20 l. blue (air) . 9·75 6·00
DESIGNS—VERT: 10 l. (No. 2001), Badge of Arlus; 15 l. Kremlin. HORIZ: 20 l. Twin-engined aircraft.

255 Emblem of Republic

1948. Air. Designs showing aircraft.
2004 **255** 30 l. red 50 10
2005 – 50 l. green 75 25
2006 – 100 l. blue . . . . . . 4·00 3·25
DESIGNS: 50 l. Workers in a field; 100 l. Forms of transport (steam train, liner, etc.).

256 Lorry

1948. Work on Communications.
2007 – 1 l. + 1 l. black & green 60 60
2008 **256** 3 l. + 3 l. black & brown 70 60
2009 – 11 l. + 11 l. black & blue 2·75 2·10
2010 – 15 l. + 15 l. black & red 5·50 3·75
DESIGNS: 1 l. Dockers loading freighter; 11 l. Lisunov Li-2 airplane; 15 l. Steam train.

257 Nicolas Balcescu 258 Hands breaking Chain

1948.
2012 **257** 20 l. red 65 15

1948. 1st Anniv of People's Republic.
2013 **258** 5 l. red 25 15

259 Runners 260 Lenin

1948. National Sports Organization. Imperf or perf.
2014 **259** 5 l. + 5 l. green (postage) 3·25 3·25
2017 5 l. + 5 l. brown . . . . 3·25 3·25
2015 – 10 l. + 10 l. violet . . . 5·00 5·00
2018 – 10 l. + 10 l. red . . . . 5·00 5·00

2016 – 20 l. + 20 l. blue (air) . . 17·00 17·00
2019 – 20 l. + 20 l. green . . . 17·00 17·00
DESIGNS—HORIZ: 10 l. Parade of athletes with flags. VERT: 20 l. Boy flying model airplane.

1949. 25th Death Anniv of Lenin. Perf or imperf.
2020 **260** 20 l. black 30 15

261 Dancers

1949. 90th Anniv of Union of Rumanian Principalities.
2021 **261** 10 l. blue 40 15

262 I. C. Frimu and Revolutionaries 263 Pushkin

1949. 30th Death Anniv of I. C. Frimu. Perf or imperf.
2022 **262** 20 l. red 30 15

1949. 150th Birth Anniv of A. S. Pushkin (Russian poet).
2030 **263** 11 l. red 75 15
2031 30 l. green 90 25

264 Globe and Posthorn 265 Forms of Transport

1949. 75th Anniv of U.P.U.
2032 **264** 20 l. brown . . . . 1·75 1·75
2033 **265** 30 l. blue . . . . 3·25 3·25

266 Russians entering Bucharest

1949. 5th Anniv of Russian Army's Entry into Bucharest. Perf or imperf.
2034 **266** 50 l. brown on green . . 85 60

267 "Rumanian–Soviet Amity"

1949. Rumanian–Soviet Friendship Week. Perf or imperf.
2035 **267** 20 l. red 65 40

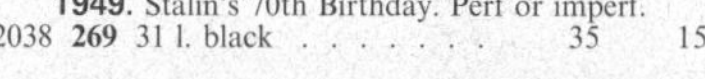
268 Forms of Transport 269 Joseph Stalin

1949. International Congress of Transport Unions. Perf or imperf.
2036 **268** 11 l. blue . . . . 1·10 1·00
2037 20 l. red . . . . 1·40 1·25

1949. Stalin's 70th Birthday. Perf or imperf.
2038 **269** 31 l. black 35 15

270 "The Third Letter" 271 Michael Eminescu

1950. Birth Centenary of Eminescu (poet).
2040 **270** 11 l. green . . . . 1·00 20
2041 – 11 l. brown . . . . . . 1·75 45
2042 – 11 l. red . . . . 1·00 20
2043 – 11 l. violet . . . . . . 1·00 20
2044 **271** 11 l. blue . . . . 1·00 25
DESIGNS (Scenes representing poems): No. 2041, "Angel and Demon"; No. 2042, "Ruler and Proletariat"; No. 2043, "Life".

272 "Dragaica Fair"

1950. Birth Centenary of Andreescu (painter).
(a) Perf.
2045 **272** 5 l. olive . . . . 1·00 50
2047 – 20 l. brown . . . . . . 1·75 90
(b) Perf or imperf.
2046 – 11 l. blue . . . . 1·50 65
DESIGNS—VERT: 11 l. I. Andreescu. HORIZ: 20 l. "The Village Well".

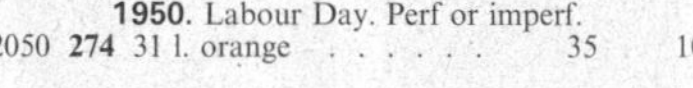
273 Factory and Graph 274 Worker and Flag

1950. State Plan, 1950. Inscr "PLANUL DU STAT 1950".
2048 **273** 11 l. red 30 15
2049 – 31 l. violet . . . . 1·00 50
DESIGN: 31 l. Tractor and factories.
No. 2048 exists imperf.

1950. Labour Day. Perf or imperf.
2050 **274** 31 l. orange 35 10

275 Emblem of Republic 276 Trumpeter and Drummer

1950.
2051 **275** 50 b. black 20 15
2052 1 l. red 10 10
2053 2 l. grey 10 10
2054 3 l. purple 15 10
2055 4 l. mauve 10 10

2056 **275** 5 l. red 15 10
2057 6 l. green 15 10
2058 7 l. brown 20 10
2059 7 l. 50 blue 25 10
2060 10 l. brown 65 10
2061 11 l. red 65 10
2062 15 l. blue 35 10
2063 20 l. green 35 10
2064 31 l. green 50 10
2065 36 l. brown . . . . . . 1·40 45
For stamps as Type **275** but with inscriptions in white, see Nos. 2240, etc., and Nos. 2277/8.

1950. 1st Anniv of Rumanian Pioneers Organization.
2074 **276** 8 l. blue . . . . 1·40 45
2075 – 11 l. purple . . . . . . 1·75 1·00
2076 – 31 l. red . . . . 3·00 2·00
DESIGNS: 11 l. Children reading; 31 l. Youth parade.

277 Engineer **278** A. Vlaicu and No. 1 "Crazy Fly"

1950. Industrial Nationalization.
2077 **277** 11 l. red 35 25
2078 11 l. blue 80 15
2079 11 l. brown 80 25
2080 11 l. olive 35 10

1950. 40th Anniv of 1st Flight by Aurel Vlaicu.
2081 **278** 3 l. green 45 10
2082 6 l. blue 50 15
2083 8 l. blue 60 20

279 Mother and Child

1950. Peace Congress, Bucharest.
2084 **279** 11 l. red 20 15
2085 – 20 l. brown 25 15
DESIGN: 20 l. Lathe operator.

280 Statue and Flags **282** Young People and Badge

1950. Rumanian–Soviet Amity.
2086 **280** 30 l. brown 65 15

1950. Rumanian–Hungarian Amity. Optd **TRAIASCA PRIETENIA ROMANO-MAGHIARA!.**
2087 **275** 15 l. blue 85 20

1950. G.M.A. Complex Sports Facilities. Designs incorporating badge.
2088 – 3 l. red . . . . 1·40 1·40
2089 **282** 5 l. brown . . . . . . 1·00 1·00
2090 5 l. blue . . . . 1·00 1·00
2091 – 11 l. green . . . . . . 1·00 1·00
2092 – 31 l. olive . . . . . . 2·40 2·40
DESIGNS: 3 l. Agriculture and Industry; 11 l. Runners; 31 l. Gymnasts.

283

284 Ski-jumper

1950. 3rd Congress of "ARLUS".
2093 **283** 11 l. red 30 20
2094 11 l. blue 30 20

1951. Winter Sports.
2095 **284** 4 l. brown . . . . . . 1·00 15
2096 – 5 l. red . . . . 1·40 25
2097 – 11 l. blue . . . . . . 2·00 25
2098 – 20 l. brown . . . . . . 2·00 1·40
2099 – 31 l. green . . . . . . 3·25 1·50
DESIGNS: 5 l. Skater; 11 l. Skier; 20 l. Ice-hockey; 31 l. Tobogganing.

286 Peasant and Tractor

1951. Agricultural and Industrial Exhibition.
2100 – 11 l. brown 20 10
2101 **286** 31 l. blue 65 20
DESIGN—VERT: 11 l. Engineer and machine.

287 Star of the Republic **288** Youth Camp

1951. Orders and Medals. Perf or imperf.
2102 – 2 l. grey 20 15
2103 – 4 l. blue 25 20
2104 – 11 l. red 40 30
2105 **287** 35 l. brown 60 45
DESIGNS: 2 l. Medal of Work; 4 l. As Type **287** but with different centre to star and with ribbon at top; 11 l. Order of Work.

1951. 2nd Anniv of Rumanian Pioneer Organization.
2106 **288** 1 l. green . . . . . . 1·00 65
2107 – 11 l. blue . . . . . . 1·00 65
2108 – 35 l. red . . . . 1·40 1·00
DESIGNS—VERT: 11 l. Children meeting Stalin. HORIZ: 35 l. Decorating boy on parade.

289 Woman and Flags **290** Ion Negulici

1951. International Women's Day. Perf or imperf.
2109 **289** 11 l. brown 25 10

1951. Death Centenary of Negulici (painter).
2110 **290** 35 l. red . . . . 3·00 2·40

291 Cyclists

292 F. Sarbu

1951. Rumanian Cycle Race.
2111 **291** 11 l. brown . . . . . . 1·90 75

1951. 10th Death Anniv of Sarbu (patriot).
2112 **292** 11 l. brown 30 15

293 "Revolutionary Rumania"

294 Students

1951. Death Centenary of Rosenthal (painter).
2113 **293** 11 l. green . . . . . . 1·60 50
2114 11 l. orange . . . . . . 1·60 65
2115 – 11 l. brown . . . . . . 1·60 50
2116 – 11 l. violet . . . . . . 1·60 65
DESIGN—VERT: Nos 2115/16, Portrait of a woman.

1951. 3rd World Youth Festival, Berlin.
2117 **294** 1 l. red 35 20
2118 – 5 l. blue 65 20
2119 – 11 l. purple 95 45
DESIGNS: 5 l. Girl, boy and flag; 11 l. Young people around globe.

295 "Scanteia" Building

296 Soldier and Pithead

1951. 20th Anniv of "Scanteia" (Communist newspaper).
2120 **295** 11 l. blue 65 20

1951. Miners' Day.
2121 **296** 5 l. blue 40 20
2122 – 11 l. mauve 75 15
DESIGN: 11 l. Miner and pithead.

297 Order of Defence

298 Oil Refinery

1951. Liberation Day.
2123 **297** 10 l. red 35 20

1951. Five-Year Plan. Dated "1951 1955".
2124 **298** 1 l. olive (postage) . . . 20 10
2125 – 2 l. red 30 15
2126 – 3 l. red 55 25
2127 – 4 l. brown 35 15
2128 – 5 l. green 55 10
2129 – 6 l. blue . . . . 1·60 1·00
2130 – 7 l. green . . . . . . 1·00 35
2131 – 8 l. brown 65 25
2132 – 11 l. blue 75 10
2133 – 35 l. violet 80 45
2134 – 30 l. green (air) . . . . 3·25 2·75
2135 – 50 l. brown . . . . . . 5·00 3·50
DESIGNS: 2 l. Miner and pithead; 3 l. Soldier and pylons; 4 l. Steel furnace; 5 l. Combine-harvester; 6 l. Canal construction; 7 l. Threshing machine; 8 l. Sanatorium; 11 l. Dam and pylons; 30 l. Potato planting; 35 l. Factory; 50 l. Liner, locomotive and Lisunov Li-2 airplane.

299 Orchestra and Dancers **300** Soldier and Arms

1951. Music Festival.
2136 **299** 11 l. brown 45 20
2137 – 11 l. blue (Mixed choir) . . 60 40
2138 – 11 l. mauve (Lyre and dove) (vert) 45 25

1951. Army Day.
2139 **300** 11 l. blue 40 10

301 Arms of U.S.S.R. and Rumania **302** P. Tcancenco

1951. Rumanian–Soviet Friendship.
2140 **301** 4 l. brown on buff . . . 20 20
2141 35 l. orange 65 65

1951. 25th Death Anniv of Tcancenco (revolutionary).
2142 **302** 10 l. olive 65 15

303 Open Book "1907" **304** I. L. Caragiale

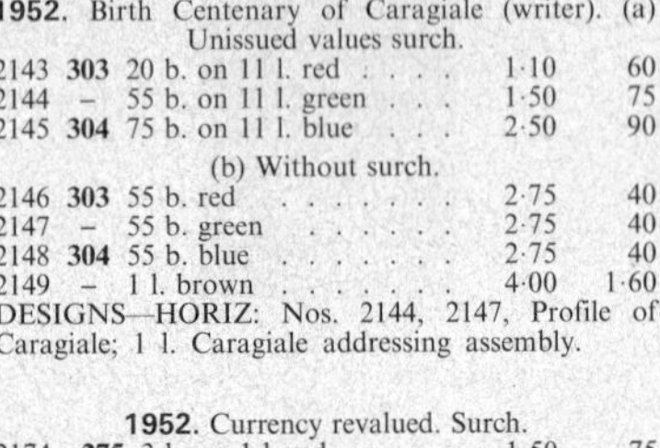

1952. Birth Centenary of Caragiale (writer). (a) Unissued values surch.
2143 **303** 20 b. on 11 l. red . . . . 1·10 60
2144 – 55 b. on 11 l. green . . . 1·50 75
2145 **304** 75 b. on 11 l. blue . . . 2·50 90
(b) Without surch.
2146 **303** 55 b. red . . . . 2·75 40
2147 – 55 b. green . . . . . . 2·75 40
2148 **304** 55 b. blue . . . . . . 2·75 40
2149 – 1 l. brown . . . . . . 4·00 1·60
DESIGNS—HORIZ: Nos. 2144, 2147, Profile of Caragiale; 1 l. Caragiale addressing assembly.

1952. Currency revalued. Surch.
2174 **275** 3 b. on 1 l. red . . . . 1·50 75
2175 3 b. on 2 l. grey . . . . 1·25 65
2176 3 b. on 4 l. mauve . . . 1·50 75
2177 3 b. on 5 l. red . . . . 1·25 65
2178 3 b. on 7 l. 50 blue . . . 1·25 75
2179 3 b. on 10 l. brown . . . 1·25 65
2157a **255** 3 b. on 30 l. red . . . . 3·75 2·75
2158 – 3 b. on 50 l. (No. 2005) 1·50 75
2159 – 3 b. on 100 l. (No. 2006) 4·00 3·00
2191 **278** 10 b. on 3 l. green . . . 2·40 75
2218 **301** 10 b. on 4 l. brown on buff 2·10 1·10
2192 **278** 10 b. on 6 l. blue . . . 2·40 75
2193 10 b. on 8 l. blue . . . 2·40 75
2220 **302** 10 b. on 10 l. olive . . . 2·10 75
2160 **263** 10 b. on 11 l. red . . . 3·75 1·50
2164 **270** 10 b. on 11 l. green . . . 3·75 1·50
2165 – 10 b. on 11 l. (No. 2041) 2·75 1·90
2166 – 10 b. on 11 l. (No. 2042) 2·75 1·90
2167 – 10 b. on 11 l. (No. 2043) 2·75 1·90
2168 **271** 10 b. on 11 l. blue . . . 2·75 1·90
2161 **263** 10 b. on 30 l. green . . . 3·75 1·50
2219 **301** 10 b. on 35 l. orange . . 2·10 1·10
2199 – 20 b. on 2 l. (No. 2102) 4·25 2·10
2200 – 20 b. on 4 l. (No. 2103) 4·25 2·10
2171 **273** 20 b. on 11 l. red . . . 4·25 2·10
2201 – 20 b. on 11 l. (No. 2104) 4·25 2·10
2194 – 20 b. on 20 l. (No. 2085) 3·00 1·50
2172 – 20 b. on 31 l. (No. 2049) 3·25 1·25
2202 **287** 20 b. on 35 l. brown . . 2·75 1·50
2206 **298** 35 b. on 1 l. olive . . . 1·90 65
2207 – 35 b. on 2 l. (No. 2125) 3·00 3·00
2208 – 35 b. on 3 l. (No. 2126) 3·75 1·90
2209 – 35 b. on 4 l. (No. 2127) 3·00 1·50
2210 – 35 b. on 5 l. (No. 2128) 3·75 3·75
2151 **241** 50 b. on 12 l. blue . . . 1·90 1·25
2180 **275** 55 b. on 50 b. black . . 5·00 1·25
2181 55 b. on 3 l. purple . . 5·00 1·25
2195 – 55 b. on 3 l. (No. 2088) 17·00 11·00
2169 **272** 55 b. on 5 l. olive . . . 9·25 3·00
2204 **295** 55 b. on 5 l. blue . . . 3·00 2·50
2182 **275** 55 b. on 6 l. green . . . 5·00 1·25
2183 55 b. on 7 l. brown . . . 5·00 1·25
2188 **276** 55 b. on 8 l. blue . . . 7·50 3·75
2205 **297** 55 b. on 10 l. red . . . 5·00 2·50
2170 – 55 b. on 11 l. (No. 2046) 9·25 3·00
2189 – 55 b. on 11 l. (No. 2075) 5·00 2·50
2150 **233** 55 b. on 12 l. blue . . . 3·75 1·25
2184 **275** 55 b. on 15 l. blue . . . 7·50 1·25
2185 55 b. on 20 l. green . . . 5·00 1·25
2196 – 55 b. on 20 l. (No. 2098) 30·00 13·50
2186 **275** 55 b. on 31 l. green . . . 5·00 1·25
2173 **274** 55 b. on 31 l. orange . . 4·50 3·00
2190 – 55 b. on 31 l. (No. 2076) 5·00 3·25
2197 – 55 b. on 31 l. (No. 2099) 30·00 13·50
2198 **286** 55 b. on 31 l. blue . . . 5·00 3·25
2203 – 55 b. on 35 l. (No. 2108) 7·50 4·25
2187 **275** 55 b. on 36 l. brown . . 7·50 1·25
2211 – 1 l. on 6 l. (No. 2129) 5·50 2·10
2212 – 1 l. on 7 l. (No. 2130) 5·50 5·50
2213 – 1 l. on 8 l. (No. 2131) 5·50 4·25
2214 – 1 l. on 11 l. (No. 2132) 5·50 2·75
2216 – 1 l. on 30 l. (No. 2134) 9·25 2·10
2215 – 1 l. on 35 l. (No. 2133) 7·50 2·10
2217 – 1 l. on 50 l. (No. 2135) 8·50 4·50
2152 – 1 l. 75 on 2 l. + 2 l. purple (No. 1974) . . . . . . 13·50 4·50
2153 **245** 1 l. 75 on 5 l. + 5 l. violet 13·50 4·50
2154 **246** 1 l. 75 on 11 l. red . . . 13·50 4·50
2155 – 1 l. 75 on 10 l. + 10 l. (No. 1977) . . . . . . 13·50 4·50
2156 – 1 l. 75 on 36 l. + 18 l. (No. 1978) . . . . . . 13·50 4·50

1952. Air. Surch with airplane, **AERIANA** and value.
2162 **264** 3 l. on 20 l. brown . . . 25·00 18·00
2163 **265** 5 l. on 30 l. blue . . . . 32·00 23·00

307 Railwayman

308 Gogol and character from "Taras Bulba"

1952. Railway Day.
2229 **307** 55 b. brown . . . . . . 2·40 30

1952. Death Centenary of Gogol (Russian writer).
2230 **308** 55 b. blue . . . . . . 1·75 15
2231 – 1 l. 75 green . . . . . 3·00 40
DESIGN—VERT: 1 l. 75, Gogol and open book.

309 Maternity Medal

310 I. P. Pavlov

1952. International Women's Day.
2232 **309** 20 b. blue and purple . . 85 15
2233 – 55 b. brown & chestnut . 1·50 20
2234 – 1 l. 75 brown and red . . 4·25 40
MEDALS: 55 b. "Glory of Maternity" medal; 1 l. 75, "Mother Heroine" medal.

1952. Rumanian–Soviet Medical Congress.
2235 **310** 11 l. brown . . . . . . 2·75 15

311 Hammer and Sickle Medal **312** Boy and Girl Pioneers

1952. Labour Day.
2236 **311** 55 b. brown . . . . . . 2·40 15

1952. 3rd Anniv of Rumanian Pioneers Organization.
2237 **312** 20 b. brown . . . . . . 1·40 10
2238 – 55 b. green . . . . . . 3·25 15
2239 – 1 l. 75 blue . . . . . . 6·75 30
DESIGNS—VERT: 55 b. Pioneer nature-study group. HORIZ: 1 l. 75, Worker and pioneers.

1952. As T **275** but with figures and inscriptions in white. Bani values size $20\frac{1}{4} \times 24\frac{1}{4}$ mm, lei values size $24\frac{1}{2} \times 29\frac{1}{2}$ mm.
2240 **275** 3 b. orange 40 20
2241 5 b. red 60 10
2242 7 b. green 65 25
2243 10 b. brown 85 10
2244 20 b. blue . . . . . . 1·25 10
2245 35 b. brown . . . . . . 2·40 10
2246 50 b. green . . . . . . 2·50 10
2247 55 b. violet . . . . . . 6·00 10
2248 1 l. 10 brown . . . . . 5·00 20
2249 1 l. 75 violet . . . . . 22·00 35
2250 2 l. olive . . . . . . 5·75 25
2251 2 l. 35 brown . . . . . 6·75 35
2252 2 l. 55 orange . . . . . 8·25 40
2253 3 l. green . . . . . . 8·75 35
2254 5 l. red . . . . 11·00 85
For similar stamps with star added at top of emblem, see Nos. 2277/8.

314 "Smirdan" (after Grigorescu) **315** Leonardo da Vinci

1952. 75th Anniv of Independence.
2255 **314** 50 b. lake . . . . 1·00 10
2256 – 1 l. 10 b. blue . . . . . 1·40 30
DESIGN—HORIZ: 1 l. 10, Rumanian and Russian soldiers.

1952. 500th Anniv of Birth of Leonardo da Vinci.
2257 **315** 55 b. violet . . . . 4·75 25

316 Miner **317** Students' Union Badge

1952. Miners' Day.
2258 **316** 20 b. red . . . . 2·00 25
2259 55 b. violet . . . . 2·00 20

1952. Int Students' Union Council, Bucharest.
2260 **317** 10 b. blue 25 10
2261 – 20 b. orange . . . . . . 2·75 20
2262 – 55 b. green . . . . . . 2·75 15
2263 – 1 l. 75 red . . . . . . 5·00 1·00
DESIGNS—HORIZ: 20 b. Student in laboratory ($35\frac{1}{2} \times 22$ mm). 1 l. 75, Six students dancing, (30×24 mm). VERT: 55 b. Students playing football, (24×30 mm).

318 Soldier, Sailor and Airman

1952. Army Day.
2264 **318** 55 b. blue . . . . . . 1·60 15

319 Statue and Flags **320** Workers and Views of Russia and Rumania (after N. Parlius)

1952. Rumanian-Soviet Friendship.
2265 **319** 55 b. red . . . . 1·10 10
2266 **320** 1 l. 75 brown . . . . . 3·00 30

321 Rowing **322** N. Balcescu (after C. Tattarescu)

1952. Physical Culture.
2267 **321** 20 b. blue . . . . . . 4·00 20
2268 – 1 l. 75 red (Athletes) . . 9·25 90

1952. Death Centenary of Balcescu (revolutionary).
2269 **322** 55 b. grey . . . . 3·25 10
2270 1 l. 75 olive . . . . . . 8·25 90

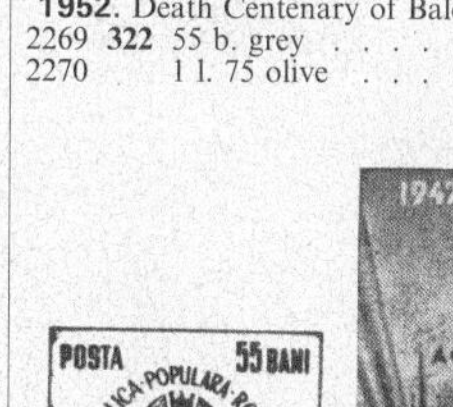

323 Emblem and Flags **324**

1952. New Constitution.
2271 **323** 55 b. green . . . . . . 1·60 15

1952. 5th Anniv of People's Republic.
2272 **324** 55 b. multicoloured . . 3·00 30

325 Millo, Caragiale and Mme. Romanescu **326** Foundry Worker

1953. Centenary of Caragiale National Theatre.
2273 **325** 55 b. blue . . . . 3·25 15

1953. 3rd Industrial and Agricultural Congress.
2274 **326** 55 b. green . . . . . . 1·00 15
2275 – 55 b. orange 90 30
2276 – 55 b. brown . . . . . . 1·40 15
DESIGNS—HORIZ: No. 2275, Farm workers and tractor; No. 2276, Workman, refinery and oil wells.

1953. As Nos. 2240 etc., but with star added at top of emblem.
2277 **275** 5 b. red 70 10
2278 55 b. purple . . . . . . 1·40 10

327 "The Strikers of Grivitsa" (after Nazarev)

1953. 20th Anniv of Grivitsa Strike.
2279 **327** 55 b. brown . . . . . . 2·75 15

328

1953. 5th Anniv of Treaty of Friendship with Russia.
2280 **328** 55 b. brown on blue . . 2·75 20

329 Table Tennis Badge **330** Oltenian Carpet

1953. 20th World Table Tennis Championship, Bucharest.
2281 **329** 55 b. green . . . . 6·75 1·00
2282 55 b. brown . . . . . . 6·75 1·00

1953. Rumanian Art.
2283 – 10 b. green . . . . 1·40 10
2284 – 20 b. brown . . . . 2·00 10
2285 – 35 b. violet . . . . 2·40 15
2286 – 55 b. blue . . . . 4·25 10
2287 **330** 1 l. purple . . . . 8·25 25
DESIGNS—VERT: 10 b. Pottery; 20 b. Campulung peasant girl; 55 b. Apuseni Mountains peasant girl. HORIZ: 35 b. National dance.

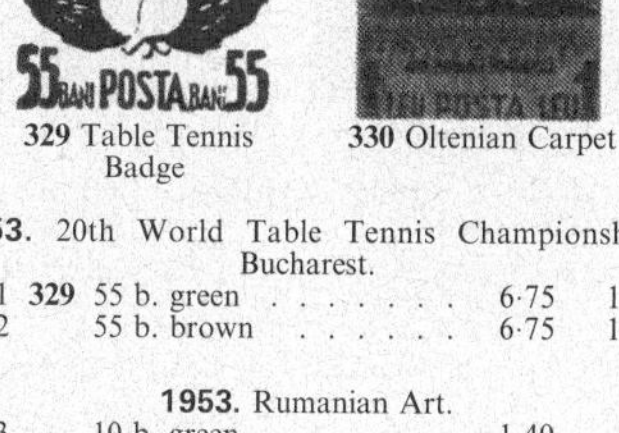

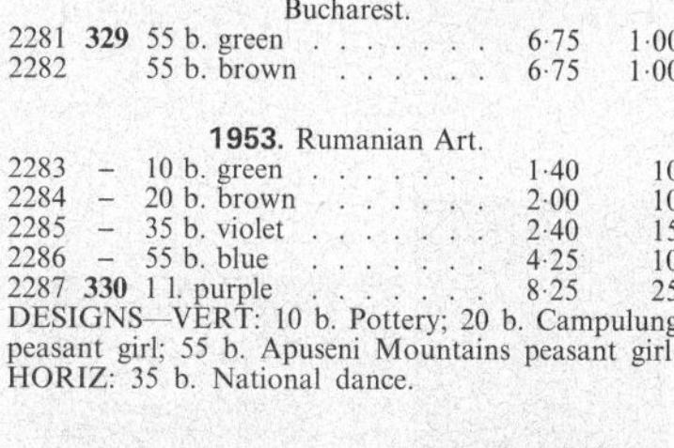

331 Karl Marx **332** Pioneers planting Tree

1953. 70th Death Anniv of Karl Marx.
2288 **331** 1 l. 55 brown . . . . . . 3·25 25

1953. 4th Anniv of Rumanian Pioneer Organization.
2289 **332** 35 b. green . . . . 1·60 15
2290 – 55 b. blue . . . . 2·00 15
2291 – 1 l. 75 brown . . . . . . 4·75 40
DESIGNS—VERT: 55 b. Boy and girl flying model gliders. HORIZ: 1 l. 75, Pioneers and instructor.

333 Women and Flags

1953. 3rd World Congress of Women.
2292 **333** 55 b. brown . . . . . . 2·00 15

334 **335** Cornfield and Forest

1953. 4th World Youth Festival.
2293 **334** 20 b. orange . . . . . . 1·00 10
2294 – 55 b. blue . . . . 1·60 10
2295 – 65 b. red . . . . 2·40 30
2296 – 1 l. 75 purple . . . . . . 6·75 45
DESIGNS—VERT: 55 b. Students releasing dove over globe. HORIZ: 65 b. Girl presenting bouquet; 1 l. 75, Folk dancers.

1953. Forestry Month.
2297 – 20 b. blue . . . . 1·00 15
2298 **335** 38 b. green . . . . 3·25 90
2299 – 55 b. brown . . . . . . 4·00 15
DESIGNS—VERT: 20 b. Waterfall and trees; 55 b. Forestry worker.

336 V.V. Mayakovsky **337** Miner

1953. 60th Birth Anniv of Mayakovsky (Russian poet).
2300 **336** 55 b. brown . . . . . . 2·40 20

1953. Miners' Day.
2301 **337** 1 l. 55 black . . . . . . 3·75 20

338 Telephonist, G.P.O. and P.O. Worker **339**

1953. 50th Anniv of Construction of G.P.O.
2302 **338** 20 b. brown 25 10
2303 – 55 b. olive 45 10
2304 – 1 l. blue . . . . 1·60 15
2305 – 1 l. 55 lake . . . . . . 2·40 35
DESIGNS: 55 b. Postwoman and G.P.O.; 1 l. G.P.O. radio-transmitter and map; 1 l. 55, Telegraphist, G.P.O. and teletypist.

1953. 9th Anniv of Liberation.
2306 **339** 55 b. brown . . . . . . 1·00 15

340 Soldier and Flag

1953. Army Day.
2307 **340** 55 b. olive . . . . 1·60 15

341 Girl and Model Glider

1953. Aerial Sports.
2308 **341** 10 b. green and orange . 2·75 25
2309 – 20 b. olive and brown . . 5·50 15
2310 – 55 b. purple and red . . 10·00 35
2311 – 1 l. 75 brown & purple . 12·00 75
DESIGNS: 20 b. Parachutists; 55 b. Glider and pilot; 1 l. 75, Monoplane.

342 Workman, Girl and Flags

1953. Rumanian-Soviet Friendship.
2312 **342** 55 b. brown 70 15
2313 – 1 l. 55 lake . . . . . . 2·00 25
DESIGN: 1 l. 55, Spasski Tower and Volga-Don canal.

343 "Unity"

1953. 3rd World Trades' Union Congress.
2314 **343** 55 b. olive 85 15
2315 – 1 l. 25 red . . . . . . 2·00 30
DESIGN—VERT: 1 l. 25, Workers, flags and globe.

344 C. Porumbescu **345** Agricultural Machinery

1953. Birth Centenary of Porumbescu (composer).
2316 **344** 55 b. lilac . . . . 8·25 20

1953. Agricultural designs.
2317 **345** 10 b. olive 25 10
2318 – 35 b. green 40 10
2319 – 2 l. 55 brown . . . . . 4·00 70
DESIGNS: 35 b. Tractor drawing disc harrows; 2 l. 55, Cows grazing

346 A. Vlaicu **347** Lenin

1953. 40th Death Anniv of Vlaicu (pioneer aviator).
2320 **346** 50 b. blue . . . . 1·75 20

1954. 30th Death Anniv of Lenin.
2321 **347** 55 b. brown . . . . . . 2·00 15

348 Red Deer **349** Calimanesti

1954. Forestry Month.
2322 **348** 20 b. brown on yellow . 3·25 45
2323 – 55 b. violet on yellow . . 2·75 45
2324 – 1 l. 75 blue on yellow . . 4·00 85
DESIGNS: 55 b. Pioneers planting tree; 1 l. 75, Forest.

1954. Workers' Rest Homes.
2325 **349** 5 b. black on yellow . . 40 10
2326 – 1 l. 55 black on blue . . 2·00 15
2327 – 2 l. green on pink . . . 3·25 20
2328 – 2 l. 35 brown on green . 3·00 1·00
2329 – 2 l. 55 brown on green . 4·25 1·40
DESIGNS: 1 l. 55, Siniai; 2 l. Predeal; 2 l. 35, Tusnad; 2 l. 55, Govora.

350 O. Bancila **351** Child and Dove of Peace

1954. 10th Death Anniv of Bancila (painter).
2330 **350** 55 b. green and brown . 4·00 2·00

1954. International Children's Day.
2331 **351** 55 b. brown . . . . . . 1·60 15

352 Girl Pioneer feeding Calf **353** Stephen the Great

1954. 5th Anniv of Rumanian Pioneer Organization.
2332 **352** 20 b. black 30 15
2333 – 55 b. blue 85 15
2334 – 1 l. 75 red . . . . . . 2·75 65
DESIGNS: 55 b. Girl Pioneers harvesting; 1 l. 75, Young Pioneers examining globe.

1954. 450th Death Anniv of Stephen the Great.
2335 **353** 55 b. brown . . . . . . 2·75 20

354 Miner operating Coal-cutter **355** Dr. V. Babes

1954. Miners' Day.
2336 **354** 1 l. 75 black . . . . . . 2·75 40

1954. Birth Centenary of Babes (pathologist).
2337 **355** 55 b. red . . . . 1·75 15

356 Sailor and Flag **357** Dedication Tablet

1954. Navy Day.
2338 **356** 55 b. blue . . . . 1·75 20

1954. 5th Anniv of Mutual Aid Organization.
2339 – 20 b. violet 35 15
2340 **357** 55 b. brown 85 15
DESIGN: 20 b. Man receiving money from counter clerk.

358 Liberation Monument **359** Recreation Centre

1954. 10th Anniv of Liberation.
2341 **358** 55 b. lilac and red . . . 1·40 15

1954. Liberation Anniv Celebrations.
2342 **359** 20 b. blue 30 10
2343 – 38 b. violet 90 25
2344 – 55 b. purple . . . . . . 1·00 10
2345 – 1 l. 55 brown . . . . . 2·40 30
DESIGNS—38 × 22 mm: 55 b. "Scanteia" offices. $24\frac{1}{2} \times 29\frac{1}{2}$ mm: 38 b. Opera House, Bucharest; 1 l. 55, Radio Station.

360 Airman **361** Chemical Plant and Oil Derricks

1954. Aviation Day.
2346 **360** 55 b. blue . . . . 2·00 15

1954. International Chemical and Petroleum Workers Conference, Bucharest.
2347 **361** 55 b. black . . . . . . 2·40 30

362 Dragon Pillar, Peking **363** T. Neculuta

1954. Chinese Culture Week.
2348 **362** 55 b. black on yellow . . 2·40 30

1954. 50th Death Anniv of Neculuta (poet).
2349 **363** 55 b. violet . . . . . . 2·00 15

364 ARLUS Badge **365** Friendship

1954. 10th Anniv of "ARLUS" and Rumanian-Russian Friendship.
2350 **364** 55 b. red 65 15
2351 **365** 65 b. purple . . . . . . 1·00 20

366 G. Tattarescu **367** B. Iscovescu

1954. 60th Death Anniv of Tattarescu (painter).
2352 **366** 55 b. red . . . . 2·50 15

1954. Death Centenary of Iscovescu (painter).
2353 **367** 1 l. 75 brown . . . . . . 3·25 45

368 Teleprinter **369** Wild Boar

1954. Cent of Telecommunications in Rumania.
2354 **368** 50 b. lilac . . . . 1·50 20

1955. Forestry Month. Inscr "LUNA PADURII 1955".
2355 **369** 35 b. brown . . . . . . 1·60 20
2356 – 65 b. blue . . . . 2·10 25
2357 – 1 l. 20 red . . . . . . 4·75 50
DESIGNS: 65 b. Tree planting; 1 l. 20, Logging.

370 Airman **371** Clasped Hands

1955. Occupations.
2358 – 3 b. blue 25 10
2359 – 5 b. violet 15 10
2360 **370** 10 b. brown 30 10
2361 – 20 b. mauve 40 10
2362 – 30 b. blue . . . . 1·00 10
2363 – 35 b. turquoise 60 10
2364 – 40 b. blue . . . . 1·40 15
2365 – 55 b. olive . . . . 1·40 10
2366 – 1 l. violet . . . . 2·00 10
2367 – 1 l. 55 lake . . . . . . 3·25 10
2368 – 2 l. 35 buff . . . . . . 4·75 60
2369 – 2 l. 55 green . . . . . . 6·75 40
DESIGNS: 3 b. Scientist; 5 b. Foundryman; 20 b. Miner; 30 b. Tractor driver; 35 b. Schoolboy; 40 b. Girl student; 55 b. Bricklayer; 1 l. Sailor; 1 l. 55, Millgirl; 2 l. 35, Soldier; 2 l. 55, Telegraph linesman.

1955. International Conference of Postal Municipal Workers, Vienna.
2370 **371** 25 b. red 65 20

372 Lenin **373** Dove and Globe

1955. 85th Birth Anniv of Lenin. Portraits of Lenin.
2371 **372** 20 b. brown and bistre . 65 15
2372 – 55 b. brown (full face) . . 1·40 20
2373 – 1 l. lake and red (half length) . . . . 2·00 25

1955. Peace Congress, Helsinki.
2374 **373** 55 b. blue . . . . 1·60 15

374 War Memorial, Berlin **375** Children and Dove

1955. 10th Anniv of Victory over Germany.
2375 **374** 55 b. blue . . . . 1·40 15

1955. International Children's Day.
2376 **375** 55 b. brown . . . . . . 1·50 15

376 "Service" **377** People's Art Museum

1955. European Volley-ball Championships.
2377 – 55 b. purple on pink . . 5·00 1·00
2378 **376** 1 l. 75 red on yellow . . 11·50 1·00
DESIGN: 55 b. Volley-ball players.

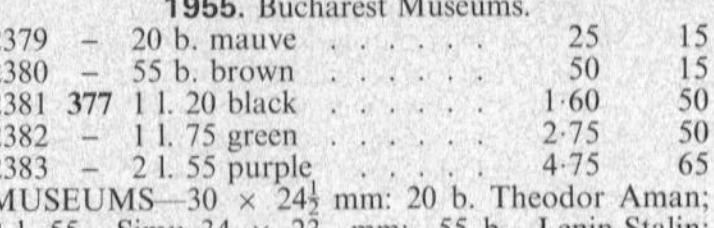

1955. Bucharest Museums.
2379 – 20 b. mauve 25 15
2380 – 55 b. brown 50 15
2381 **377** 1 l. 20 black . . . . . . 1·60 50
2382 – 1 l. 75 green . . . . . . 2·75 50
2383 – 2 l. 55 purple . . . . . 4·75 65
MUSEUMS—30 × $24\frac{1}{2}$ mm: 20 b. Theodor Aman; 2 l. 55, Simu 34 × 23 mm: 55 b. Lenin-Stalin; 1 l. 75, Republican Art.

378 Mother and Child **379** "Nature Study"

1955. 1st World Mothers' Congress, Lausanne.
2384 **378** 55 b. blue . . . . 1·60 20

1955. 5th Anniv of Pioneer Headquarters, Bucharest.
2385 – 10 b. blue 60 10
2386 **379** 20 b. green . . . . . . 1·40 10
2387 – 55 b. purple . . . . . . 3·00 20
DESIGNS: 10 b. Model railway; 55 b. Headquarters building.

380 Coxed Four **381** A. Pann

1955. Women's European Rowing Championships, Snagov.
2388 **380** 55 b. green . . . . . . 8·25 1·00
2389 – 1 l. blue (Woman sculler) 13·00 1·00

1955. Rumanian Writers.
2390 – 55 b. blue . . . . 1·40 25
2391 – 55 b. grey . . . . 1·40 25
2392 **381** 55 b. olive . . . . . . 1·40 25
2393 – 55 b. violet . . . . . . 1·40 25
2394 – 55 b. purple . . . . . . 1·40 25
PORTRAITS—No. 2390 D. Cantemir; No. 2391 M. Dosoftei; No. 2393 S. C. Cantacuzino; No. 2394 E Vacarescu.

382 Marksman **383** Fire Engine

1955. European Sharpshooting Championships, Bucharest.
2395 **382** 1 l. brown & lt brown . . 6·00 65

1955. Firemen's Day.
2396 **383** 55 b. red . . . . 1·90 25

384 **385** Spraying Fruit Trees

1955. 10th Anniv of W.F.T.U.
2397 **384** 55 b. olive 50 10
2398 – 1 l. blue 85 25
DESIGN: 1 l. Workers and flag.

1955. Fruit and Vegetable Cultivation.
2399 **385** 10 b. green 40 15
2400 – 20 b. red 50 35
2401 – 55 b. blue . . . . 1·60 45
2402 – 1 l. lake . . . . 3·75 1·10
DESIGNS: 20 b. Fruit picking; 55 b. Harvesting grapes; 1 l. Gathering vegetables.

386 **387** Michurin

1955. 4th ARLUS Congress.
2403 **386** 20 b. blue and buff . . . 1·00 15

1955. Birth Cent of Michurin (Russian botanist).
2404 **387** 55 b. blue . . . . 1·60 20

388 Cotton

389 Sheep and Shepherd blowing Bucium

1955.

2405 – 10 b. pur (Sugar beet) . . 45 15
2406 **388** 20 b. grey 85 15
2407 – 55 b. blue (Linseed) . . . 2·10 60
2408 – 1 l. 55 brown (Sunflower) 4·25 1·10

1955.

2409 **389** 5 b. brown and green . . 1·00 15
2410 – 10 b. violet and bistre . . 1·40 15
2411 – 35 b. brown and salmon . 2·75 45
2412 – 55 b. brown and bistre . 5·00 75
DESIGNS: 10 b. Pigs and farm girl; 35 b. Cows and dairy maid; 55 b. Horses and groom.

390 Schiller

391 Bank and Book

1955. Famous Writers.

2413 – 20 b. blue 25 10
2414 – 55 b. blue . . . . 1·10 15
2415 **390** 1 l. grey . . . . 2·00 20
2416 – 1 l. 55 brown . . . . . 4·00 1·00
2417 – 1 l. 75 violet . . . . . 5·00 1·00
2418 – 2 l. lake . . . . 5·75 1·60
PORTRAITS: 20 b. Hans Andersen; 55 b. Mickiewicz; 1 l. 55, Montesquieu; 1 l. 75, Walt Whitman; 2 l. Cervantes.

1955. Savings Bank.

2419 **391** 55 b. blue . . . . 2·00 25
2420 55 b. violet . . . . 6·75 4·00

392 Family

393 Brown Hare

1956. National Census.

2421 – 55 b. orange 30 10
2422 **392** 1 l. 75 brown and green . 2·00 65
DESIGNS: 55 b. "21 FEBRUARIE 1956" in circle.

1956. Wild Life

2423 **393** 20 b. black and green . . 2·00 2·00
2424 – 20 b. black and olive . . 2·75 2·00
2425 – 35 b. black and blue . . 2·00 2·00
2426 – 50 b. brown and blue . . 2·00 2·00
2427 – 55 b. green and bistre . . 3·00 2·00
2428 – 55 b. brown & turquoise . 2·50 2·00
2429 – 1 l. lake and green . . . 4·00 4·00
2430 – 1 l. 55 lake and blue . . 4·50 4·50
2431 – 1 l. 75 brown and green . 6·00 5·00
2432 – 2 l. brown and blue . . 20·00 20·00
2433 – 3 l. 25 black and green . 20·00 20·00
2434 – 4 l. 25 brown & salmon . 20·00 20·00
DESIGNS—VERT: No. 2424, Great bustard; 35 b. Trout; 1 l. 55, Eurasian red squirrel; 1 l. 75, Capercaillie; 4 l. 25, Red deer. HORIZ: 50 b. Wild boar; No. 2427, Ringed-necked pheasant; No. 2428, Brown bear; 1 l. Lynx; 2 l. Chamois; 3 l. 25, Pintail.
See also Nos. 2474/85.

394 Insurgents

395 Boy and Globe

1956. 85th Anniv of Paris Commune.

2435 **394** 55 b. red . . . . 1·60 50

1956. International Children's Day.

2436 **395** 55 b. violet . . . . 1·90 20

396 Red Cross Nurse

397 Tree

1956. 2nd Rumanian Red Cross Congress.

2437 **396** 55 b. olive and red . . . 2·75 20

1956. Forestry Month.

2438 **397** 20 b. grey on green . . 1·40 20
2439 – 55 b. black on green . . 4·00 30
DESIGN: 55 b. Lumber train.

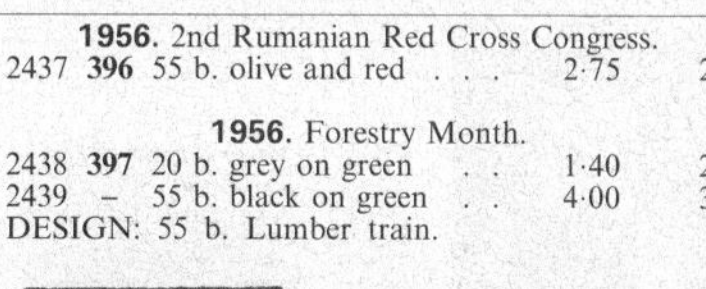

398 Woman Speaking

399 Academy Buildings

1956. International Women's Congress, Bucharest.

2440 **398** 55 b. green . . . . . . 1·60 20

1956. 90th Anniv of Rumanian People's Academy.

2441 **399** 55 b. green and buff . . 1·60 20

400 Vuia, Vuia No. 1 Biplane and Yakovlev Yak-25 Fighters

1956. 50th Anniv of 1st Flight by Traian Vuia (pioneer airman).

2442 **400** 55 b. brown and olive . 2·00 35

401 Georgescu and Statues

402 Farm Girl

1956. Birth Centenary of Georgescu (sculptor).

2443 **401** 55 b. green & brown . . 2·75 20

1956. Collective Farming. (a) Inscr "1951–1956".

2444 **402** 55 b. plum . . . . . . 10·00 10·00

(b) Inscr "1949-1956".

2445 **402** 55 b. plum . . . . . . 1·50 20

403 "Aporia crataegi"

404 Striker

1956. Insect Pests.

2446 **403** 10 b. cream, black and violet . . . . 3·25 30
2447 – 55 b. orange & brown . 5·00 60
2448 – 1 l. 75 lake and olive . 13·50 10·00
2449 – 1 l. 75 brown and olive . 10·50 1·10
PESTS: 55 b. "Leptinotarsa decemlineata"; 1 l. 75, (2) "Melontha melontha".

1956. 50th Anniv of Dockers Strike at Galatz.

2450 **404** 55 b. brown on pink . . 1·60 20

405

406 Maxim Gorky

1956. 25th Anniv of Newspaper "Scanteia".

2451 **405** 55 b. blue . . . . 1·40 20

1956. 20th Death Anniv of Maxim Gorky.

2452 **406** 55 b. brown . . . . . . 1·40 20

407 T. Aman

408 Snowdrops and Polyanthus

1956. 125th Birth Anniv of Aman (painter).

2453 **407** 55 b. grey . . . . 2·75 65

1956. Flowers. Designs multicoloured. Colours of backgrounds given.

2454 **408** 5 b. blue 55 15
2455 – 55 b. black . . . . 2·75 60
2456 – 1 l. 75 blue . . . . . . 6·75 85
2457 – 3 l. green . . . . 10·00 1·25
FLOWERS: 55 b. Daffodil and violets; 1 l. 75, Antirrhinums and campanulas; 3 l. Poppies and lilies of the valley.

409 Janos Hunyadi

410 Olympic Flame

1956. 500th Death Anniv of Hunyadi.

2458 **409** 55 b. violet . . . . 2·00 25

1956. Olympic Games.

2459 **410** 20 b. red 65 15
2460 – 55 b. blue . . . . 1·00 20
2461 – 1 l. mauve . . . . 2·40 25
2462 – 1 l. 55 turquoise . . . . 3·25 30
2463 – 1 l. 75 violet . . . . . . 4·25 65
DESIGNS: 55 b. Water-polo; 1 l. Ice-skating; 1 l. 55, Canoeing; 1 l. 75, High-jumping.

411 George Bernard Shaw

412 Ilyushin Il-18 over City

1956. Cultural Anniversaries.

2464 – 20 b. blue (Franklin) . . 30 10
2465 – 35 b. red (Toyo Oda) . . 40 15
2466 **411** 40 b. brown 45 15
2467 – 50 b. brown (I. Franko) 55 10
2468 – 55 b. olive (Curie) 95 10
2469 – 1 l. turquoise (Ibsen) . . 1·50 15
2470 – 1 l. 55 violet (Dostoevsky) 2·10 15
2471 – 1 l. 75 blue (Heine) . . . 2·75 15
2472 – 2 l. 55 pur (Mozart) . . . 3·75 25
2473 – 3 l. 25 blue (Rembrandt) 4·00 65

1956. Wild Life. As Nos. 2423/34 but colours changed. Imperf.

2474 20 b. brown and green . . . 5·00 5·00
2475 20 b. black and blue . . . . 5·00 5·00
2476 35 b. black and blue . . . . 5·00 5·00
2477 50 b. black and brown . . . 5·00 5·00
2478 55 b. black and violet . . . 5·00 5·00
2479 55 b. brown and green . . . 5·00 5·00
2480 1 l. brown and blue . . . . 5·00 5·00
2481 1 l. 55 brown and bistre . . 5·00 5·00
2482 1 l. 75 purple and green . . 5·00 5·00
2483 2 l. black and blue . . . . 5·00 5·00
2484 3 l. 25 brown and green . . 8·00 8·00
2485 4 l. 25 brown and violet . . 10·00 10·00

1956. Air. Multicoloured designs embodying airplanes and views.

2486 20 b. Type **412** 45 20
2487 55 b. Mountains 95 15
2488 1 l. 75 Cornfield . . . . . . 3·00 25
2489 2 l. 55 Seashore . . . . . . 4·00 75

413 Georgi Enescu

414 "Rebels" (after O. Bancila)

1956. 75th Birth Anniv of Enescu (musician).

2490 – 55 b. blue . . . . 1·25 20
2491 **413** 1 l. 75 purple . . . . . . 2·75 30
DESIGN: 55 b. Enescu when a child, holding violin.

1957. 50th Anniv of Peasant Revolt.

2492 **414** 55 b. slate . . . . 1·60 20

415 Stephen the Great

416 Dr. G. Marinescu and Institute of Medicine

1957. 500th Anniv of Accession of Stephen the Great.

2493 **415** 55 b. brown . . . . . . 1·40 25
2494 55 b. olive . . . . 1·40 25

1957. National Congress of Medical Sciences, Bucharest and Centenary of Medical and Pharmaceutical Teaching in Bucharest (11.75).

2495 **416** 20 b. green 40 15
2496 – 35 b. brown 50 20
2497 – 55 b. purple . . . . . . 1·00 50
2498 – 1 l. 75 red and blue . . 4·25 1·60
DESIGNS: 35 b. Dr. I. Cantacuzino and Cantacuzino Institute; 55 b. Dr. V. Babes and Babes Institute; 1 l. 75, (66 × 23 mm) Drs. N. Kretzulescu and C. Dairla, and Faculty of Medicine, Bucharest.

417 Gymnast and Spectator

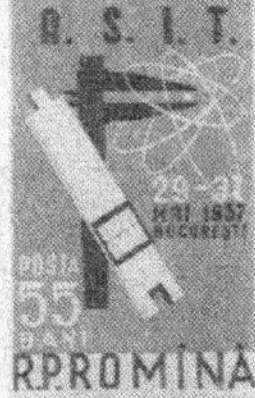

418 Emblems of Atomic Energy

1957. 1st European Women's Gymnastic Championships, Bucharest.

2499 **417** 20 b. green 65 15
2500 – 35 b. red . . . . 1·00 15
2501 – 55 b. blue . . . . 2·00 50
2502 – 1 l. 75 purple . . . . . 5·75 85
DESIGNS—HORIZ: 35 b. On asymmetric bars; 55 b. Vaulting over horse. VERT: 1 l. 75, On beam.

1957. 2nd A.S.I.T. Congress.

2503 **418** 55 b. brown . . . . . . 1·40 15
2504 55 b. blue . . . . 1·60 20

419 Dove and Handlebars

420 Rhododendron

1957. 10th International Cycle Race.

2505 **419** 20 b. blue 50 15
2506 – 55 b. brown . . . . . . 1·40 20
DESIGN: 55 b. Racing cyclist.

1957. Flowers of the Carpathian Mountains.

2513 **420** 5 b. red and grey 35 10
2514 – 10 b. green and grey . . 50 10
2515 – 20 b. orange and grey . . 60 10
2516 – 35 b. olive and grey . . 90 15
2517 – 55 b. blue and grey . . . 1·25 15
2518 – 1 l. red and grey . . . . 3·75 30
2519 – 1 l. 55 yellow and grey . 3·75 35
2520 – 1 l. 75 violet and grey . 6·75 35
FLOWERS: 10 b. Daphne; 20 b. Lily; 35 b. Edelweiss; 55 b. Gentian; 1 l. Dianthus; 1 l. 55, Primula; 1 l. 75, Anemone.

421 N. Grigorescu

1957. 50th Death Anniv of Grigorescu (painter).

2521 – 20 b. green . . . . . . 1·00 10
2522 **421** 55 b. brown . . . . . . 2·40 20
2523 – 1 l. 75 blue . . . . . . 6·75 85
DESIGNS—HORIZ: 20 b. Country scene; 1 l. 75, Battle scene.

422 Festival Visitors 423 Festival Emblem

1957. 6th World Youth Festival, Moscow.
2524 **422** 20 b. purple 15 10
2525 – 55 b. green 45 10
2526 **423** 1 l. orange . . . . . . 1·10 40
2527 – 1 l. 75 blue . . . . 2·00 20
DESIGNS: 55 b. Girl with flags; (22 × 38 mm) 1 l. 75, Dancers (49 × 20 mm).

424 Destroyer "Stalingrad" 425 "The Trumpeter" (after N. Grigorescu)

1957. Navy Day.
2528 **424** 1 l. 75 blue . . . . 1·75 20

1957. 80th Anniv of War of Independence.
2529 **425** 20 b. violet . . . . 1·60 15

426 Soldiers Advancing 427 Child with Dove

1957. 40th Anniv of Battle of Marasesti.
2530 **426** 1 l. 75 brown . . . . . . 2·00 20

1957. Red Cross.
2531 **427** 55 b. green and red . . . 1·60 20

428 Sprinter and Bird 429 Ovid

1957. Int Athletic Championships, Bucharest.
2532 **428** 20 b. black and blue . . 65 10
2533 – 55 b. black and yellow . 1·40 15
2534 – 1 l. 75 black and red . . 4·75 60
DESIGNS: 55 b. Javelin-thrower and bull; 1 l. 75, Runner and stag.

1957. Birth Bimillenary of Ovid (Latin poet).
2535 **429** 1 l. 75 blue . . . . 3·25 65

430 Congress Emblem 431 Oil Refinery, 1957

1957. 4th W.F.T.U. Congress, Leipzig.
2536 **430** 55 b. blue 90 15

1957. Centenary of Rumanian Petroleum Industry.
2537 **431** 20 b. brown 35 10
2538 20 b. blue 35 10
2539 – 55 b. purple 85 30
DESIGN: 55 b. Oil production, 1857: horse-operated borer.

432 Lenin, Youth and Girl 433 Artificial Satellite encircling Globe

1957. 40th Anniv of Russian Revolution.
2540 **432** 10 b. red 20 10
2541 – 35 b. purple 65 10
2542 – 55 b. brown . . . . . 1·00 20
DESIGNS—HORIZ: 35 b. Lenin and flags; 55 b. Statue of Lenin.

1957. Air. Launching of Artificial Satellite by Russia. Inscr "SATELITII ARTIFICIALI".
2543 **433** 25 b. green 35 15
2545 25 b. blue 35 15
2544 – 3 l. 75 green . . . . . 3·25 35
2546 – 3 l. 75 blue . . . . . 3·25 35
DESIGN: 3 l. 75 (2), Satellite's orbit around Globe. See also Nos. 2593/6.

434 Peasant Soldiers 435 Endre Ady

1957. 520th Anniv of Bobilna Revolution.
2547 **434** 50 b. purple 35 15
2548 – 55 b. grey 45 20
DESIGN—VERT: 55 b. Bobilna Memorial.

1957. 80th Birth Anniv of Endre Ady (Hungarian poet).
2549 **435** 55 b. olive . . . . 1·40 15

436 "Laika" and Satellite 437 Black-winged Stilt

1957. Launching of Dog "Laika" in artificial satellite.
2550 **436** 1 l. 20 brown and green 4·75 85
2551 1 l. 20 brown and blue . 4·75 85

1957. Fauna of the Danube Delta
2552 **437** 5 b. grey & brn (postage) 50 10
2553 – 10 b. orange and green 70 10
2554 – 20 b. orange and red . . 90 15
2555 – 50 b. orange and green . 65 10
2556 – 55 b. blue and purple . 1·00 10
2557 – 1 l. 30 orange and violet 2·75 20
2558 – 3 l. 30 grey & blue (air) 4·75 90
2559 – 5 l. orange and red . . 6·50 1·40
DESIGNS—VERT: 10 b. Great egret; 20 b. White spoonbill; 50 b. Fish. HORIZ: 55 b. Stoat; 1 l. 30, Eastern white pelican; 3 l. 30, Black-headed gull; 5 l. White-tailed sea eagle.

438 Emblem of Republic and Flags

1957. 10th Anniv of People's Republic.
2560 **438** 25 b. buff, red and blue 20 10
2561 – 55 b. yellow 75 25
2562 – 1 l. 20 red . . . . 1·40 35
DESIGNS: 55 b. Emblem, Industry and Agriculture; 1 l. 20, Emblem, the Arts and Sports.

439 Republican Flag

1958. 25th Anniv of Strike at Grivitsa.
2563 **439** 1 l. red & brown on buff 1·00 20
2564 1 l. red & blue on buff . 1·00 20

440 "Telecommunications"

1958. Communist Postal Conference, Moscow.
2565 **440** 55 b. violet 35 20
2566 – 1 l. 75 purple . . . . . 1·10 15
DESIGN: 1 l. 75, Telegraph pole and pylons carrying lines.

441 N. Balcescu 442 Fencer

1958. Rumanian Writers.
2567 **441** 5 b. blue 30 15
2568 – 10 b. black (Ion Creanga) 35 15
2569 – 35 b. blue (Vlahuta) . . . 40 15
2570 – 55 b. brown (Eminescu) 75 15
2571 – 1 l. 75 brown (Alecsandri) 1·10 30
2572 – 2 l. myrtle (Delavrancea) 2·75 30

1958. World Youth Fencing Championships, Bucharest.
2573 **442** 1 l. 75 mauve . . . . . . 2·00 20

443 Symbols of Medicine and Sport 444

1958. 25th Anniv of Sports Doctors' Service.
2574 **443** 1 l. 20 red and green . . 2·00 20

1958. 4th Int Congress of Democratic Women.
2575 **444** 55 b. blue . . . . 1·10 15

445 Linnaeus 446 "Lepiota procera"

1958. Cultural Celebrities. Inscr "MARILE ANIVERSARI CULTURALE 1957".
2576 **445** 10 b. green 20 10
2577 – 20 b. brown (Comte) . . 35 10
2578 – 40 b. purple (Blake) . . 50 15
2579 – 55 b. blue (Glinka) . . . 1·25 10
2580 – 1 l. plum (Longfellow) . 1·50 20
2581 – 1 l. 75 bl (Goldoni) . . 2·25 25
2582 – 2 l. brown (Comenius) . 4·00 30

1958. Mushrooms. As T **446**.
2583 **446** 5 b. brn, light brn & blue 10 10
2584 – 10 b. brown, buff and bronze 20 10
2585 – 20 b. red yellow & grey . 45 10
2586 – 30 b. brown, orge and green 60 30
2587 – 35 b. brown, lt brn & bl . 65 10
2588 – 55 b. brown, red & green 1·10 15
2589 – 1 l. brn, buff & turquoise 1·90 20
2590 – 1 l. 55 pink, drab & grey 3·25 35
2591 – 1 l. 75 brown, buff and green . . . . 4·75 50
2592 – 2 l. yellow, brown and turquoise . . . . . . 5·75 55
MUSHROOMS: 10 b. "Clavaria aurea"; 20 b. "Amanita caesarea"; 30 b. "Lactarius deliciosus"; 35 b. "Armillaria mellea"; 55 b. "Coprinus comatus"; 1 l. "Morchella conica"; 1 l. 55, "Psalliota campestris"; 1 l. 75, "Boletus edulis"; 2 l. "Cantharellus cibarins".

1958. Brussels International Exhib. Nos. 2543/4 and 2545/6 optd **EXPOZITIA BRUXELLES 1958** and star or with star only.
2593 **433** 25 b. green . . . . . . 3·25 2·00
2594 25 b. blue . . . . . . 20·00 11·50
2595 – 3 l. 75 green . . . . . 3·25 2·00
2596 – 3 l. 75 blue . . . . . . 20·00 11·50

448 Emil Racovita (scientist), Antarctic Map and "Belgica"

1958. Racovita Commem. Inscr "1868 1947".
2597 **448** 55 b. indigo and blue . . 3·25 40
2598 – 1 l. 20 violet and olive . . 2·75 30
DESIGN: 1 l. 20, Racovita and grotto.

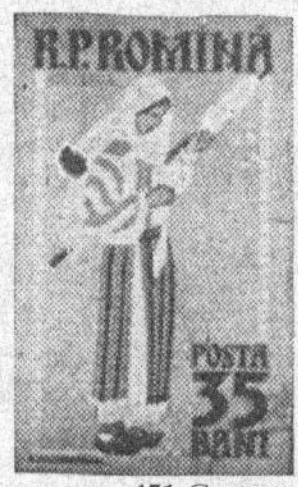

449 Sputnik encircling Globe 450 Servicemen's Statue

1958. Air. Launching of Third Artificial Satellite by Russia.
2599 **449** 3 l. 25 buff and blue . . 5·00 1·40

1958. Army Day.
2600 **450** 55 b. brown (postage) . 25 10
2601 – 75 b. purple 45 15
2602 – 1 l. 75 blue . . . . . . 1·10 20
2603 – 3 l. 30 violet (air) . . . . 2·00 65
DESIGNS: 75 b. Soldier guarding industrial plant; 1 l. 75, Sailor hoisting flag; 3 l. 30, Pilot and Mikoyan Gurevich MiG-17 jet fighters.

451 Costumes of Oltenia 452

1958. Provincial Costumes. Female and male costumes as T **451/2**.
2604 **451** 35 b. red and black on yellow 30 15
2605 **452** 35 b. red and black on yellow 30 15
2606 – 40 b. red and brown on grey 40 20
2607 – 40 b. red and brown on grey 40 20
2608 – 50 b. red and brown on lilac 45 15
2609 – 50 b. red and brown on lilac 45 15
2610 – 55 b. red and brown on grey 55 15
2611 – 55 b. red and brown on grey 55 15
2612 – 1 l. red & brown on pink 1·50 20
2613 – 1 l. red & brown on pink 1·50 20
2614 – 1 l. 75 red and brown on blue . . . . 2·00 35
2615 – 1 l. 75 red and brown on blue . . . . 2·00 35
PROVINCES: Nos. 2606/7, Tara Oasului; Nos. 2608/9, Transylvania; Nos. 2610/11, Muntenia; Nos. 2612/3, Banat; Nos. 2614/5, Moldova.

453 Stamp Printer 454 Runner

1958. Rumanian Stamp Centenary. Inscr "1858 1958".
2617 **453** 35 b. blue 35 10
2618 – 55 b. brown 45 10
2619 – 1 l. 20 blue . . . . . 1·40 25
2620 – 1 l. 30 plum . . . . . 1·50 40
2621 – 1 l. 55 brown . . . . . 2·00 20
2622 – 1 l. 75 red . . . . . . 2·40 25
2623 – 2 l. violet . . . . . . 3·00 65
2624 – 3 l. 30 brown . . . . . 5·00 1·00
DESIGNS: 55 b. Scissors and Moldavian stamps of 1858; 1 l. 20, Driver with whip and mail coach; 1 l. 30, Postman with horn and mounted courier; 1 l. 55, to 3 l. 30, Moldavian stamps of 1858 (Nos. 1/4).

1958. 3rd Youth Spartacist Games.
2627 **454** 1 l. brown . . . . 1·40 20

455 Revolutionary Emblem 456 Boy Bugler

1958. 40th Anniv of Workers' Revolution.
2628 **455** 55 b. red 85 15

1958. 10th Anniv of Education Reform.
2629 **456** 55 b. red 65 15

457 Alexander Cuza 458 First Cosmic Rocket

1959. Centenary of Union of Rumanian Provinces.
2630 **457** 1 l. 75 b. blue . . . . . 1·60 15

1959. Air. Launching of 1st Cosmic Rocket.
2631 **458** 3 l. 25 b. blue on salmon 13·50 1·50

459 Charles Darwin **460** Maize

1959. Cultural Anniversaries.
2633 **459** 55 b. black (postage) . . 55 10
2634 – 55 b. blue (Robert Burns) 55 15
2635 – 55 b. red (Popov) 55 10
2636 – 55 b. purple (Sholem Aleichem) 55 10
2637 – 55 b. brown (Handel) . . 55 15

2638 – 3 l. 25 b. blue (Joliot-Curie) (air) . . . . 4·75 50

1959. 10th Anniv of Collective Farming in Rumania.
2639 **460** 55 b. green 35 10
2640 – 55 b. orange 35 20
2641 – 55 b. purple 35 20
2642 – 55 b. olive 35 20
2643 – 55 b. brown 35 20
2644 – 55 b. bistre 35 20
2645 – 55 b. blue 35 20
2646 – 55 b. bistre 35 20
2647 – 5 l. red . . . . 5·00 75
DESIGNS—VERT: No. 2640, Sunflower with bee; No. 2641, Sugar beet. HORIZ: No. 2642, Sheep; No. 2643, Cattle; No. 2644, Rooster and hens; No. 2645, Farm tractor; No. 2646, Farm wagon and horses; No. 2647, (38 × 26½ mm), Farmer and wife, and wheatfield within figure "10".

461 Rock Thrush **462**

1959. Air. Birds in natural colours. Inscriptions in grey. Colours of value tablets and backgrounds given.
2648 **461** 10 b. grey on buff . . . 20 15
2649 – 20 b. grey on grey . . . 20 15
2650 – 35 b. grey on deep grey . 25 15
2651 – 40 b. red on pink . . . 40 40
2652 – 55 b. grey on green . . . 50 15
2653 – 55 b. grey on cream . . . 50 15
2654 – 55 b. green on azure . . 50 15
2655 – 1 l. red on yellow . . . 1·60 35
2656 – 1 l. 55 red on pink . . . 2·10 35
2657 – 5 l. grey on green . . . 8·25 2·00
BIRDS—HORIZ: No. 2649, Golden oriole; No. 2656, Long-tailed tit; No. 2657, Wallcreeper. VERT: No. 2650, Lapwing; No. 2651, Barn swallow; No. 2652, Great spotted woodpecker; No. 2653, Goldfinch; No. 2654, Great tit; No. 2655, Bullfinch.

1959. 7th World Youth Festival, Vienna. Inscr "26 VII-4 VIII 1959".
2658 **462** 1 l. blue 85 20
2659 – 1 l. 60 red 90 20
DESIGN: 1 l. 60, Folk-dancer in national costume.

463 Workers and Banners (**466**)

1959. 15th Anniv of Liberation.
2660 **463** 55 b. multicoloured . . . 45 15

1959. Air. Landing of Russian Rocket on the Moon. Surch **h. 00.02'.24" 14-IX-1959 PRIMA RACHETA COSMICA IN LUNA 5 LEI** in red.
2662 **458** 5 l. on 3 l. 25 blue on salmon . . . . 17·00 4·00

1959. 8th Balkan Games. Optd with T **466** in silver.
2663 **454** 1 l. brown . . . . 17·00 17·00

467 Prince Vlad Tepes and Charter

1959. 500th Anniv of Bucharest.
2664 **467** 20 b. black and blue . . 1·00 20
2665 – 40 b. black and brown . 1·75 25
2666 – 55 b. black and bistre . 2·40 25
2667 – 55 b. black and purple . 2·75 25
2668 – 1 l. 55 black and lilac . 6·00 1·10
2669 – 1 l. 75 black & turquoise 6·75 1·40
DESIGNS—HORIZ: 40 b. Peace Buildings, Bucharest; 55 b. (No. 2666), Atheneum; 55 b. (No 2667), "Scanteia" Printing House; 1 l. 55, Opera House; 1 l. 75, "23 August" Stadium.

468 Football **469** Atomic Icebreaker "Lenin"

1959. International Sport. Multicoloured.
2671 20 b. Type **468** (postage) . . 25 15
2672 35 b. Motor-cycle racing . . 35 10
2673 40 b. Ice-hockey 45 15
2674 55 b. Handball 50 10
2675 1 l. Horse-jumping . . . . . 1·00 10
2676 1 l. 50 Boxing . . . . 2·00 15
2677 1 l. 55 Rugby football . . . 2·10 10
2678 1 l. 60 Tennis . . . . 2·50 25

2679 2 l. 80 Hydroplaning (air) . 3·00 90
The 35, 40 b., 1 l. 55, 1 l. 60, and 2 l. 80, are horiz.

1959. Launching of Atomic Icebreaker "Lenin".
2680 **469** 1 l. 75 violet . . . . . . 2·50 30

470 Stamp Album and Magnifier

1959. Stamp Day.
2681 **470** 1 l. 60 (+40 b.) blue . . 1·60 1·00

471 Foxglove **472** Cuza University

1959. Medicinal Flowers. Multicoloured.
2682 20 b. Type **471** 25 10
2683 40 b. Peppermint 40 20
2684 55 b. Camomile 55 10
2685 55 b. Cornflower 65 15
2686 1 l. Autumn crocus 85 15
2687 1 l. 20 Monk's-hood . . . . 1·10 20
2688 1 l. 55 Red poppy . . . . . 1·40 25
2689 1 l. 60 Linden . . . . 1·90 30
2690 1 l. 75 Wild rose . . . . . 2·00 35
2691 3 l. 20 Adonis . . . . 4·00 45

1959. Centenary of Cuza University, Jassy.
2692 **472** 55 b. brown 65 20

473 Rocket, Dog and Rabbit **474** G. Cosbuc

1959. Air. Cosmic Rocket Flight.
2693 **473** 1 l. 55 blue . . . . . . 4·00 30
2694 – 1 l. 60 blue on cream . . 5·00 40
2695 – 1 l. 75 blue . . . . . . 5·00 45
DESIGNS—HORIZ: (52 × 29½ mm): 1 l. 60, Picture of "invisible" side of the Moon, with lists of place-names in Rumanian and Russian. VERT—(As Type **473**): 1 l. 75, Lunik 3's trajectory around the Moon.

1960. Rumanian Authors.
2696 **474** 20 b. blue 20 15
2697 – 40 b. purple 65 20
2698 – 50 b. brown 85 15
2699 – 55 b. purple 85 15
2700 – 1 l. violet . . . . 1·50 20
2701 – 1 l. 55 blue . . . . . . 2·50 35
PORTRAITS: 40 b. I. L. Caragiale; 50 b. G. Alexandrescu; 55 b. A. Donici; 1 l. C. Negruzzi; 1 l. 55, D. Bolintineanu.

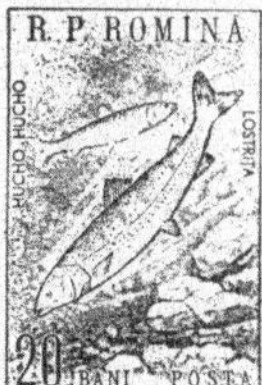

475 Huchen (Danube salmon) **476**

1960. Rumanian Fauna.
2702 **475** 20 b. blue (postage) . . . 30 10
2703 – 55 b. brn (Tortoise) . . . 55 10
2704 – 1 l. 20 lilac (Common shelduck) . . . . 2·50 35

2705 – 1 l. 30 blue (Golden eagle) (air) . . . . 3·00 35
2706 – 1 l. 75 grn (Black grouse) 3·25 35
2707 – 2 l. red (Lammergeier) . . 3·50 50

1960. 50th Anniv of International Women's Day.
2708 **476** 55 b. blue . . . . 1·00 50

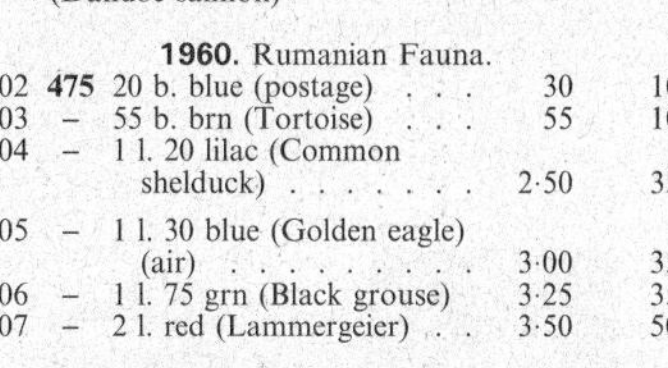

477 Lenin (after painting by M. A. Gerasimov) **478** "Victory"

1960. 90th Birth Anniv of Lenin.
2709 **477** 40 b. purple 45 15
2710 – 55 b. blue (Statue of Lenin by Boris Carogea) . . . 60 15

1960. 15th Anniv of Victory.
2712 **478** 40 b. blue 50 10
2714 40 b. purple . . . . . . 3·75 4·00
2713 – 55 b. blue 50 10
2715 – 55 b. purple . . . . . . 3·75 4·00
DESIGN: 55 b. Statue of soldier with flag.

479 Rocket Flight

1960. Air. Launching of Soviet Rocket.
2716 **479** 55 b. blue . . . . 3·75 25

480 Diving **481** Gymnastics

1960. Olympic Games, Rome (1st issue). Multicoloured.
2717 40 b. Type **480** . . . . 2·00 2·00
2718 55 b. Gymnastics . . . . . . 2·00 2·00
2719 1 l. 20 High-jumping . . . . 2·00 2·00
2720 1 l. 60 Boxing . . . . 3·25 3·25
2721 2 l. 45 Canoeing . . . . . . 3·25 3·25
2722 3 l. 70 Canoeing . . . . . . 6·75 4·00
Nos. 2717/9 and 2720/1 are arranged together in 'brickwork' fashion, se tenant in sheets forming complete overall patterns of the Olympic rings.
No. 2722 is imperf.

1960. Olympic Games, Rome (2nd issue).
2723 – 20 b. blue 20 15
2724 **481** 40 b. purple 65 15
2725 – 55 b. blue . . . . 1·00 15
2726 – 1 l. red . . . . 1·40 10
2727 – 1 l. 60 purple . . . . . 2·00 30
2728 – 2 l. lilac . . . . 3·00 65
DESIGNS: 20 b. Diving; 55 b. High-jumping; 1 l. Boxing; 1 l. 60, Canoeing; 2 l. Football.

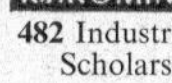

482 Industrial Scholars **483** Vlaicu and No. 1 "Crazy Fly"

484 I.A.R. 817 Flying Ambulance **485** Pilot and Mikoyan Gurevich MiG-17 Jet Fighters

1960.
2731 **482** 3 b. mauve (postage) . . 10 10
2732 – 5 b. brown 25 10
2733 – 10 b. purple 10 10
2734 – 20 b. blue 15 10
2735 – 30 b. red 20 10
2736 – 35 b. red 20 10
2737 – 40 b. bistre 25 10
2738 – 50 b. violet 25 10
2739 – 55 b. blue 30 10
2740 – 60 b. green 30 10
2741 – 75 b. olive 50 10
2742 – 1 l. red 50 10
2743 – 1 l. 20 black 55 10
2744 – 1 l. 50 purple 75 10
2745 – 1 l. 55 turquoise 90 10
2746 – 1 l. 60 blue 80 10
2747 – 1 l. 75 brown . . . . . 1·00 10
2748 – 2 l. brown . . . . 1·40 20
2749 – 2 l. 40 violet . . . . . 1·50 15
2750 – 3 l. blue . . . . 1·50 15

2751 – 3 l. 20 blue (air) . . . . 3·25 10
DESIGNS—VERT: 5 b. Diesel train; 10 b. Dam; 20 b. Miner; 30 b. Doctor; 35 b. Textile worker; 50 b. Children at play; 55 b. Timber tractor; 1 l. Atomic reactor; 1 l. 20, Petroleum refinery; 1 l. 50, Iron-works; 1 l. 75, Mason; 2 l. Road-roller; 2 l. 40, Chemist; 3 l. Radio communications and television. HORIZ: 40 b. Grand piano and books; 60 b. Combine harvester; 75 b. Cattle-shed; 1 l. 55, Dock scene; 1 l. 60, Runner; 3 l. 20, Baneasa Airport, Bucharest.

1960. 50th Anniv of 1st Flight by A. Vlaicu and Aviation Day.
2752 **483** 10 b. brown and yellow . 20 10
2753 – 20 b. brown and orange 30 10
2754 **484** 35 b. red 35 10
2755 – 40 b. violet 55 10
2756 **485** 55 b. blue 70 10
2757 – 1 l. 60 multicoloured . . 1·75 50
2758 – 1 l. 75 multicoloured . . 2·25 55
DESIGNS—As T **483**: 20 b. Vlaicu in flying helmet and his No. 2 airplane; 40 b. Antonov An-2 biplane spraying crops. 59 × 22 mm: 1 l. 60, Ilyushin Il-18 airliner and airport control tower; 1 l. 75, Parachute descents.

486 Worker and Emblem

1960. 3rd Workers' Party Congress.
2759 **486** 55 b. orange and red . . 1·00 15

487 Tolstoy **488** Tomis (Constantza)

1960. Cultural Anniversaries.
2760 10 b. purple (T **487**) 10 10
2761 20 b. olive (Mark Twain) . . 15 10
2762 35 b. blue (K. Hokusai) . . 20 10
2763 40 b. green (De Musset) . . 25 15
2764 55 b. brown (Defoe) 45 10
2765 1 l. turquoise (J. Bolyai) . . 1·40 20
2766 1 l. 20 red (Chekhov) . . . 1·50 10
2767 1 l. 55 grey (R. Koch) . . . 2·00 15
2768 1 l. 75 brown (Chopin) . . . 2·75 30

1960. Black Sea Resorts. Multicoloured.
2769 20 b. Type **488** (postage) . . 20 10
2770 35 b. Constantza 40 10
2771 40 b. Vasile Roaita 45 10
2772 55 b. Mangalia 85 15
2773 1 l. Eforie . . . . 1·40 25
2774 1 l. 60 Eforie (different) . . . 1·50 20

2775 2 l. Mamaia (air) . . . . . . 2·75 65

INDEX

Countries can be quickly located by referring to the index at the end of this volume.

489 Globe and Flags **490** "Saturnia pyri" (moth)

1960. Int Puppet Theatre Festival, Bucharest. Designs ($24 \times 28\frac{1}{2}$ mm, except 20 b.) show puppets. Multicoloured.
2776 20 b. Type **489** 25 10
2777 40 b. Petrushka 30 10
2778 55 b. Punch 40 10
2779 1 l. Kaspar 60 15
2780 1 l. 20 Tindarica 80 20
2781 1 l. 75 Vasilache . . . . . . 1·25 15

1960. Air. Butterflies and Moths. Multicoloured.
2782 10 b. Type **490** 30 10
2783 20 b. "Limenitus populi" . . . 35 10
2784 40 b "Chrisophanus virgaureae" 40 10
2785 55 b. "Papilio machaon" . . 70 15
2786 1 l. 60 "Acherontia atropus" 2·10 30
2787 1 l. 75 "Apatura iris" . . . . 2·75 30
SIZES: TRIANGULAR—$36\frac{1}{2} \times 21\frac{1}{2}$ mm: 20, 40 b. VERT—$23\frac{1}{2} \times 34$ mm: 55 b., 1 l. 60. HORIZ—$34 \times 23\frac{1}{2}$ mm: 1 l. 75.

491 Children tobagganing

1960. Village Children's Games. Multicoloured.
2788 20 b. Type **491** 15 10
2789 35 b. "Oina" (ball-game) . . 20 10
2790 55 b. Ice-skating 30 10
2791 1 l. Running 65 15
2792 1 l. 75 Swimming . . . . . 1·75 20
The 20 b. and 1 l. are vert and the rest horiz.

492 Striker and Flag

1960. 40th Anniv of General Strike.
2793 **492** 55 b. red and lake 65 25

493 Compass Points and Ilyushin Il-18 Airliner

1960 Air. Stamp Day.
2794 **493** 55 b. (+ 45 b.) blue . . 85 25

494 "XV" Globe and "Peace" Riband **496** Woman tending Vine (Cotnari)

495 Herrings

1960. 15th Anniv of World Democratic Youth Federation.
2795 **494** 55 b. yellow and blue . . 65 10

1960. Fish Culture. Fish in actual colours. Background colours given.
2796 – 10 b. turquoise 15 10
2797 – 20 b. blue 25 10
2798 – 40 b. yellow 45 10
2799 **495** 55 b. grey 85 10
2800 – 1 l. red . . . . 1·50 15
2801 – 1 l. 20 blue . . . . . . 2·00 20
2802 – 1 l. 60 olive . . . . . . 2·75 25
FISHES: 10 b. Carp; 20 b. Coal-fish; 40 b. Turbot; 1 l. Silurus; 1 l. 20, Sturgeon; 1 l. 60, Cod.

1960. Rumanian Vineyards. Multicoloured.
2803 20 b. Dragasani 15 10
2804 30 b. Dealul Mare (horiz) . 25 10
2805 40 b. Odobesti (horiz) . . . 40 10
2806 55 b. Type **496** 65 10
2807 75 b. Tirnave . . . . . . 1·40 15
2808 1 l. Minis . . . . 2·10 25
2809 1 l. 20 Murfatlar . . . . . 2·75 40

497 "Furnaceman" (after I. Irimescu) **498** Slalom Racer

1961. Rumanian Sculptures.
2811 **497** 5 b. red 10 10
2812 – 10 b. violet 15 10
2813 – 20 b. black 20 10
2814 – 40 b. bistre 25 10
2815 – 50 b. brown 40 10
2816 – 55 b. red 75 10
2817 – 1 l. purple . . . . . . 1·10 15
2818 – 1 l. 55 blue . . . . . 1·75 15
2819 – 1 l. 75 green . . . . . 2·40 20
SCULPTURES—VERT: 10 b. "Gh. Doja" (I. Vlad); 20 b. "Reunion" (B. Caragea); 40 b. "Enescu" (G. Anghel); 50 b. "Eminescu" (C. Baraschi); 1 l. "Peace" (I. Jalea); 1 l. 55, "Constructive Socialism" (C. Medrea); 1 l. 75, "Birth of an idea" (A. Szobotka). HORIZ: 55 b. "Peasant Uprising, 1907" (M. Constantinescu).

1961. Air. 50th Anniv of Rumanian Winter Sports. (a) Perf.
2820 – 10 b. olive and grey . . 10 10
2821 **498** 20 b. red and grey . . . 25 10
2822 – 25 b. turquoise and grey 40 10
2823 – 40 b. violet and grey . . 50 10
2824 – 55 b. blue and grey . . 65 10
2825 – 1 l. red and grey . . . . 1·25 15
2826 – 1 l. 55 brown and grey . 2·25 20

(b) Imperf.
2827 – 10 b. blue and grey . . 10 10
2828 **498** 20 b. brown and grey . . 20 10
2829 – 25 b. olive and grey . . 30 15
2830 – 40 b. red and grey . . 65 25
2831 – 55 b. turquoise & grey . 90 70
2832 – 1 l. violet and grey . . 1·40 1·25
2833 – 1 l. 55 red and grey . . 2·40 2·25
DESIGNS—HORIZ: Skier: racing (10 b.), jumping (55 b.), walking (1 l. 55). VERT: 25 b. Skiers climbing slope; 40 b. Toboggan; 1 l. Rock-climber.

499 P. Poni (chemist) **500** Yury Gagarin in Capsule

1961. Rumanian Scientists. Inscr "1961". Portraits in sepia.
2834 **499** 10 b. brown and pink . 10 10
2835 – 20 b. purple and yellow 25 10
2836 – 55 b. red and blue . . . 40 10
2837 – 1 l. 55 violet & orange . 1·60 30
PORTRAITS: 20 b. A. Saligny (engineer); 55 b. C. Budeanu (electrical engineer); 1 l. 55, G. Titeica (mathematician).

1961. Air. World's First Manned Space Flight. Inscr "12 IV 1961". (a) Perf.
2838 – 1 l. 35 blue . . . . . . 1·00 20
2839 **500** 3 l. 20 blue . . . . . . 2·40 70

(b) Imperf.
2840 **500** 3 l. 20 red . . . . . . 8·50 2·75
DESIGN—VERT: 1 l. 35, Yury Gagarin.

501 Freighter "Galati"

1961. Merchant Navy. Multicoloured.
2841 20 b. Type **501** 35 10
2842 40 b. Liner "Oltenita" . . . 60 10
2843 55 b. Water-bus "Tomis" . . 60 10
2844 1 l. Freighter "Arad" . . . 1·00 15
2845 1 l. 55 Tug "N. Cristea" . . 1·60 15
2846 1 l. 75 Freighter "Dobrogea" 1·90 25

502 Red Flag with Marx, Engels and Lenin

1961. 40th Anniv of Rumanian Communist Party.
2847 **502** 35 b. multicoloured . . . 65 10
2848 – 55 b. multicoloured . . . 1·00 10
DESIGN: 55 b. Two bill-posters.

503 Eclipse over Scanteia Building and Observatory **504** Roe Deer

1961. Air. Solar Eclipse.
2850 – 1 l. 60 blue . . . . 1·50 15
2851 **503** 1 l. 75 blue . . . . 1·75 15
DESIGN: 1 l. 60, Eclipse over Palace Square, Bucharest.

1961. Forest Animals. Inscr "1961". Multicoloured.
2852 10 b. Type **504** 15 15
2853 20 b. Lynx (horiz) 20 15
2854 35 b. Wild boar (horiz) . . . 40 15
2855 40 b. Brown bear (horiz) . . 70 25
2856 55 b. Red deer 90 25
2857 75 b. Red fox (horiz) . . . 1·10 20
2858 1 l. Chamois . . . . 1·50 25
2859 1 l. 55 Brown hare . . . . 2·10 35
2860 1 l. 75 Eurasian badger . . . 2·50 45
2861 2 l. Roe deer . . . . 3·75 70

505 George Enescu

1961. 2nd International George Enescu Festival.
2862 **505** 3 l. lavender and brown . 2·40 35

506 Gagarin and Titov **507** Iris

1961. Air. 2nd Soviet Space Flight.
2863 – 55 b. blue 50 10
2864 – 1 l. 35 violet 90 25
2865 **506** 1 l. 75 red . . . . 1·75 30
DESIGNS—VERT: 55 b. "Vostock-2" in flight; 1 l. 35, G. S. Titov.

1961. Centenary of Bucharest Botanical Gardens. Flowers in natural colours. Background and inscription colours given. Perf or imperf.
2866 – 10 b. yellow and brown . 15 10
2867 – 20 b. green and red . . 15 10
2869 – 35 b. lilac and grey . . . 30 10
2870 **507** 40 b. yellow and violet . 40 10
2871 – 55 b. blue & ultramarine . 60 10
2872 – 1 l. orange and blue . . . 1·40 10
2873 – 1 l. 20 blue and brown . 1·50 10
2874 – 1 l. 55 brown and lake . . 2·00 15
FLOWERS—HORIZ: 10 b. Primula; 35 b. Opuntia; 1 l. Hepatica. VERT: 20 b. Dianthus; 25 b. Peony; 55 b. Ranunculus; 1 l. 20, Poppy; 1 l. 55, Gentian.

508 Cobza Player **509** Heraclides

1961. Musicians. Multicoloured.
2876 10 b. Pan piper 10 10
2877 20 b. Alpenhorn player . . . 15 10
2878 40 b. Flautist 40 10
2879 55 b. Type **508** 60 10
2880 60 b. Bagpiper 80 10
2881 1 l. Cembalo player . . . . 1·40 20
The 20 b. is horiz and the rest vert.

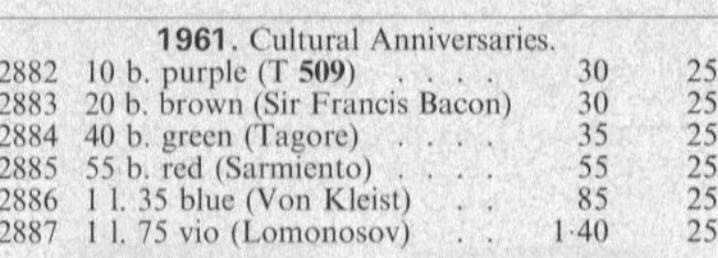

1961. Cultural Anniversaries.
2882 10 b. purple (T **509**) 30 25
2883 20 b. brown (Sir Francis Bacon) 30 25
2884 40 b. green (Tagore) 35 25
2885 55 b. red (Sarmiento) 55 25
2886 1 l. 35 blue (Von Kleist) . . 85 25
2887 1 l. 75 vio (Lomonosov) . . 1·40 25

510 Olympic Flame **512** Tower Building, Republic Palace Square, Bucharest

511 "Stamps Round the World"

1961. Olympic Games 1960. Gold Medal Awards. Inscr "MELBOURNE 1956" or "ROMA 1960". Perf or imperf.
2888 – 10 b. turq and ochre . . 20 10
2889 **510** 20 b. red 25 10
2890 – 20 b. grey 25 10
2891 – 35 b. brown and ochre . 35 10
2892 – 40 b. purple and ochre . 40 10
2893 – 55 b. blue 50 15
2894 – 55 b. blue 50 15
2895 – 55 b. red and ochre . . . 50 15
2896 – 1 l. 35 blue and ochre . . 1·90 15
2897 1 l. 75 red and ochre . . . . 2·75 20
DESIGNS (Medals)—DIAMOND: 10 b. Boxing; 35 b. Pistol-shooting; 40 b. Rifle-shooting; 55 b. (No. 2895), Wrestling; 1 l. 35, High-jumping. VERT: as Type **510**: 20 b. (No. 2890), Diving; 55 b. (No. 2893), Water-polo; 55 b. (No. 2894), Women's high-jumping. HORIZ—45×33 mm: 1 l. 75, Canoeing.

1961. Air. Stamp Day.
2899 **511** 55 b. (+ 45 b.) blue, brown and red . . . . 1·60 65

1961. Air. Modern Rumanian Architecture. Mult.
2900 20 b. Type **512** 30 10
2901 40 b. Constantza Railway Station . . . . 1·00 15
2902 55 b. Congress Hall, Republic Palace, Bucharest 50 10
2903 75 b. Rolling mill, Hunedoara 55 10
2904 1 l. Apartment blocks, Bucharest 75 15
2905 1 l. 20 Circus Building, Bucharest 80 30
2906 1 l. 75 Workers' Club, Mangalia 1·50 20
The 40 b. to 1 l. 75 are horiz.

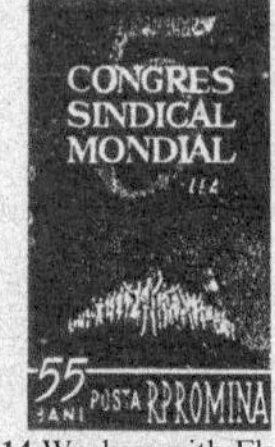

513 U.N. Emblem **514** Workers with Flags

1961. 15th Anniv of U.N.O. Perf or imperf.
2907 – 20 b. multicoloured . . . 20 10
2908 – 40 b. multicoloured . . . 65 15
2909 **513** 55 b. multicoloured . . . 1·00 20
DESIGNS (bearing U.N. emblem): 20 b. Peace dove over Eastern Europe; 40 b. Peace dove and youths of three races.

1961. 5th W.F.T.U. Congress, Moscow.
2910 **514** 55 b. red . . . . 1·00 15

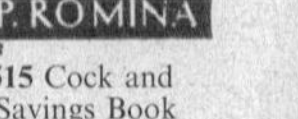

515 Cock and Savings Book **516** Footballer

1962. Savings Day. Inscr "1962". Multicoloured.
2911 40 b. Type **515** 25 10
2912 55 b. Savings Bank book, bee and honeycombs 65 15

1962. European Junior Football Competition, Bucharest.
2913 **516** 55 b. brown and green . 1·40 20

517 Ear of Corn, Map and Tractor

518 Handball Player

1962. Completion of Agricultural Collectivisation Project. Inscr "1962".
2914 **517** 40 b. red and orange . . 20 10
2915 – 55 b. lake and yellow . . 25 10
2916 – 1 l. 55 yellow, red & blue 65 20
DESIGNS: 55 b. Commemorative medal. 1 l. 55, Wheatsheaf, and hammer and sickle emblem.

1962. Women's World Handball Championships Bucharest
2917 **518** 55 b. violet and yellow . 1·40 20

519 Canoe Race

520 J. J. Rousseau

1962. Boating and Sailing. Inscr "1962". (a) Perf.
2918 **519** 10 b. blue and mauve . . 20 10
2919 – 20 b. blue and olive . . . 25 10
2920 – 40 b. blue and brown . . 30 10
2921 – 55 b. blue & ultramarine 40 15
2922 – 1 l. blue and red . . . . 1·00 15
2923 – 1 l. 20 blue and purple . 1·25 15
2924 – 1 l. 55 blue and orange . 1·50 15
2925 – 3 l. blue and violet . . . 2·50 30
(b) Imperf. Colours changed.
2926 **519** 10 b. blue & ultramarine 25 15
2927 – 20 b. blue and mauve . . 30 20
2928 – 40 b. blue and orange . . 50 30
2929 – 55 b. blue and olive . . 65 45
2930 – 1 l. blue and brown . . . 1·40 60
2931 – 1 l. 20 blue and violet . . 1·50 1·00
2932 – 1 l. 55 blue and red . . . 1·90 1·10
2933 – 3 l. blue and purple . . . 4·00 1·90
DESIGNS: 20 b. Kayak; 40 b. Racing "eight"; 55 b. Sculling; 1 l. Yachting; 1 l. 20, Motor-boats; 1 l. 55, Sailing; 3 l. Canoe slalom.

1962. Cultural Anniversaries (writers).
2934 **520** 40 b. olive 20 10
2935 – 55 b. lake 25 15
2936 – 1 l. 75 blue 95 15
WRITERS: 55 b. I. L. Caragiale; 1 l. 75, A. I. Herzen.

521 Flags and Globes

522 T. Vuia (aviator)

1962. World Youth Festival. Helsinki.
2938 **521** 55 b. multicoloured . . . 1·00 15

1962. Rumanian Celebrities.
2939 **522** 15 b. brown 15 10
2940 – 20 b. red 20 10
2941 – 35 b. purple 25 10
2942 – 40 b. blue 35 15
2943 – 55 b. blue 40 10
2944 – 1 l. blue . . . . 1·00 10
2945 – 1 l. 20 red . . . . . . 1·25 20
2946 – 1 l. 35 turquoise . . . . 1·40 20
2947 – 1 l. 55 violet . . . . . 1·50 15
PORTRAITS: 20 b. A. Davila (writer); 35 b. V. Pirvan (archaeologist); 40 b. I. Negullei (painter); 55 b. G. Cobilcescu (geologist); 1 l. Dr. G. Marinescu; 1 l. 20, Dr. I. Cantacuzino; 1 l. 35, Dr. V. Babes; 1 l. 55, Dr. C. Levaditi.

523 Anglers by Pond

1962. Fishing Sport. Multicoloured.
2948 10 b. Rod-fishing in fishing punts 10 10
2949 25 b. Line-fishing in mountain pool 15 10
2950 40 b. Type **523** 25 10
2951 55 b. Anglers on beach . . . 35 10
2952 75 b. Line-fishing in mountain stream 50 10
2953 1 l. Shore-fishing 60 20
2954 1 l. 75 Freshwater-fishing . . 1·25 15
2955 3 l. 25 Fishing in Danube delta 2·10 20

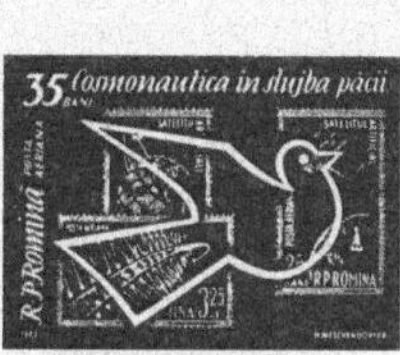

524 Dove and "Space" Stamps of 1957/58

527 "Vostok 3" and "4" in Orbit

1962. Air. Cosmic Flights.
2956 **524** 35 b. brown 20 10
2957 – 55 b. green 30 10
2958 – 1 l. 35 blue 90 10
2959 – 1 l. 75 red . . . . . . 1·40 25
DESIGNS—Dove and: 55 b. "Space" stamps of 1959; 1 l. 35, "Space" stamps of 1957 ("Laika"), 1959 and 1960; 1 l. 75, "Spacemen" stamps of 1961.

1962. Rumanian Victory in European Junior Football Competition, Bucharest. Surch **1962. Campioana Europeana 2 lei**.
2961 **516** 2 l. on 55 b. brown & grn 2·00 2·25

1962. Rumanian Victory in Women's World Handball Championships, Bucharest. Surch **Campioana Mondiala 5 lei**.
2962 **518** 5 l. on 55 b. violet and yellow . . . . 7·50 5·00

1962. Air. 1st "Team" Manned Space Flight.
2963 – 55 b. violet 50 10
2964 **527** 1 l. 60 blue . . . . . . 1·50 25
2965 – 1 l. 75 purple . . . . . 1·90 30
DESIGNS: 55 b. Cosmonaut Nikolaev; 1 l. 75, Cosmonaut Popovich.

528 Child and Butterfly

529 Pottery

1962. Children.
2966 **528** 20 b. blue, brown & red 20 10
2967 – 30 b. yellow, blue & red 25 10
2968 – 40 b. blue, red & turq . 30 10
2969 – 55 b. olive, blue and red 60 10
2970 – 1 l. 20 red, brown & blue 1·25 20
2971 – 1 l. 55 ochre, blue & red 2·10 20
DESIGNS—VERT: 30 b. Girl feeding dove; 40 b. Boy with model yacht; 1 l. 20, Boy violinist and girl pianist. HORIZ: 55 b. Girl teaching boy to write; 1 l. 55, Pioneers around camp-fire.

1962. 4th Sample Fair. Bucharest. Inscr "AL IV — LEA PAVILION DE MOSTRE — BUCURESTI 1962". Multicoloured.
2972 5 b. Type **529** (postage) . . 35 15
2973 10 b. Preserved foodstuffs . 40 15
2974 20 b. Chemical products . . 40 15
2975 40 b. Ceramics 50 10
2976 55 b. Leather goods 70 10
2977 75 b. Textiles 85 10
2978 1 l. Furniture and fabrics . . 1·40 10
2979 1 l. 20 Office equipment . . 1·75 10
2980 1 l. 55 Needlework . . . . 2·10 10
2981 1 l. 60 Fair pavillion (air) . . 2·75 15
The 1 l. 60 is horiz, the rest vert.

530 Lenin and Red Flag

1962. 45th Anniv of Russian Revolution.
2982 **530** 55 b. brown, red & blue 1·00 15

531 "The Coachmen" (after Szatmay)

1962. Air. Stamp Day and Centenary of 1st Rumanian Stamps.
2983 **531** 55 b. (+ 45 b.) black and blue . . . . 1·50 35

532 Lamb

1962. Prime Farm Stock.
2984 **532** 20 b. black and blue . . . 15 10
2985 – 40 b. brown, yell & blue . 15 10
2986 – 55 b. green, buff and orange 30 10
2987 – 1 l. brown, buff & grey . 40 10
2988 – 1 l. 35 brown, blk & grn . 60 15
2989 – 1 l. 55 brown, blk & red . 70 20
2990 – 1 l. 75 brown, cream & blue 1·40 35
DESIGNS—HORIZ: 40 b. Ram; 1 l. 55, Heifer; 1 l. 75, Sows. VERT: 55 b. Bull; 1 l. Pig; 1 l. 35, Cow.

533 Arms, Industry and Agriculture

1962. 15th Anniv of People's Republic.
2991 **533** 1 l. 55 multicoloured . . 1·60 20

534 Strikers

1963. 30th Anniv of Grivitsa Strike.
2992 **534** 1 l. 75 multicoloured . . 1·75 30

535 Tractor-driver

1963. Freedom from Hunger.
2993 **535** 40 b. blue 20 10
2994 – 55 b. brown 35 10
2995 – 1 l. 55 red . . . . 1·00 15
2996 – 1 l. 75 green . . . . . . 1·25 20
DESIGNS (each with F.A.O. emblem): 55 b. Girl harvester; 1 l. 55, Child with beaker of milk; 1 l. 75, Girl vintager.

1963. Air. Rumanian Philatelists' Conference, Bucharest. No. 2983, optd **A.F.R.** surrounded by **CONFERINTA PE TARA BUCURESTI 30-III-1963** in diamond shape.
2997 **531** 55 b. (+ 45 b.) black and blue . . . . 5·00 4·00
The opt is applied in the middle of the se-tenant pair—stamp and 45 b. label.

537 Sighisoara Glass Factory

538 Tomatoes

1963. Air. "Socialist Achievements".
2998 **537** 30 b. blue and red 30 10
2999 – 40 b. green and violet . . 40 15
3000 – 55 b. red and blue 65 15
3001 – 1 l. violet and brown . . 95 15
3002 – 1 l. 55 red and blue . . . 1·25 15
3003 – 1 l. 75 blue and purple . 1·25 15
DESIGNS: 40 b. Govora soda works; 55 b. Tirgul-Jiu wood factory; 1 l. Savinesti chemical works; 1 l. 55, Hunedoara metal works; 1 l. 75, Brazi thermic power station.

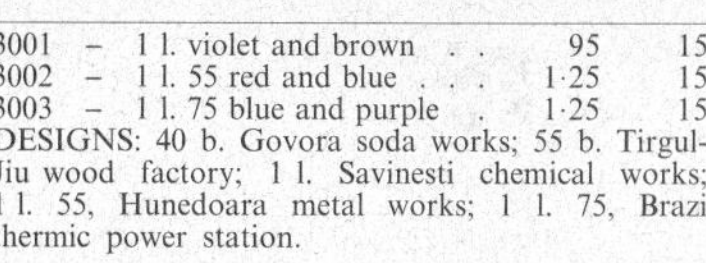

1963. Vegetable Culture. Multicoloured.
3004 35 b. Type **538** 20 10
3005 40 b. Hot peppers 35 10
3006 55 b. Radishes 40 10
3007 75 b. Aubergines 60 15
3008 1 l. 20 Mild peppers 85 15
3009 3 l. 25 Cucumbers (horiz) . . 2·00 25

539 Moon Rocket "Luna 4"

540 Chick

1963. Air. Launching of Soviet Moon Rocket "Luna 4". The 1 l. 75 is imperf.
3010 **539** 55 b. red and blue . . . 35 15
3011 1 l. 75 red and violet . . 1·40 10

1963. Domestic Poultry.
3012 **540** 20 b. yellow and blue . . 20 10
3013 – 30 b. red, blue & brown 25 10
3014 – 40 b. blue, orge & brn 35 10
3015 – 55 b. multicoloured . . . 40 10
3016 – 70 b. blue, red & purple 45 10
3017 – 1 l. red, grey and blue . 50 10
3018 – 1 l. 35 red, blue & ochre 60 10
3019 – 3 l. 20 multicoloured . . 1·50 25
POULTRY: 30 b. Cockerel; 40 b. Duck; 55 b. White Leghorn; 70 b. Goose; 1 l. Rooster; 1 l. 35, Turkey (cock); 3 l. 20, Turkey (hen).

541 Diving

542 Congress Emblem

1963. Swimming. Bodies in drab.
3020 **541** 25 b. green and brown . 15 10
3021 – 30 b. yellow and olive . 20 10
3022 – 55 b. red and turquoise . 25 10
3023 – 1 l. red and green . . . 45 10
3024 – 1 l. 35 mauve and blue . 55 10
3025 – 1 l. 55 orange and violet 1·25 10
3026 – 2 l. yellow and mauve . 1·25 15
DESIGNS—HORIZ: 30 b. Crawl; 55 b. Butterfly; 1 l. Back stroke; 1 l. 35, Breast stroke. VERT: 1 l. 55, Swallow diving; 2 l. Water polo.

1963. International Women's Congress, Moscow.
3027 **542** 55 b. blue 65 15

543 Bykovsky and Globe

1963. Air. 2nd "Team" Manned Space Flights.
3028 **543** 55 b. blue 35 15
3029 – 1 l. 75 red . . . . 1·60 25
DESIGN: 1 l. 75, Tereshkova and globe.

544 Steam Locomotive

1963. Air. Transport. Multicoloured.
3031 40 b. Type **544** 65 15
3032 55 b. Diesel freight locomotive 65 15
3033 75 b. Trolley bus 65 25
3034 1 l. 35 "Oltenita" (Danube passenger vessel) . . . . . 1·90 30
3035 1 l. 75 Ilyushin Il-18 airplane 1·75 20

545 W. M. Thackeray (writer)

1963. Cultural Anniversaries. Inscr "MARILE ANNIVERSARI CULTURALE 1963".
3036 545 40 b. black and lilac . . 20 15
3037 – 50 b. black and brown . 35 15
3038 – 55 b. black and olive . . 50 15
3039 – 1 l. 55 black and red . . 1·10 15
3040 – 1 l. 75 black and blue . . 1·25 20
PORTRAITS: 50 b. E. Delacroix (painter); 55 b. G. Marinescu (physician); 1 l. 55, G. Verdi (composer); 1 l. 75, K. Stanislavsky (theatrical producer).

546 Walnuts

548 Volleyball

1963. Fruits and Nuts. Multicoloured.
3041 10 b. Type 546 . . . . 30 15
3042 20 b. Plums 30 10
3043 40 b. Peaches 60 10
3044 55 b. Strawberries 70 10
3045 1 l. Grapes 80 10
3046 1 l. 55 Apples . . . . 1·40 15
3047 1 l. 60 Cherries . . . . . . 1·40 15
3048 1 l. 75 Pears . . . . 2·00 20

1963. Air. 50th Death Anniv of Aurel Vlaicu (aviation pioneer). No. 2752 surch **1913-1963. 50 ani de la moarte 1,75 lei**.
3049 483 1 l. 75 on 10 b. brown and yellow . . . . 3·00 1·10

1963. European Volleyball Championships.
3050 548 5 b. mauve and grey . . 20 10
3051 – 40 b. blue and grey . . . 20 10
3052 – 55 b. turquoise and grey . 65 10
3053 – 1 l. 75 brown and grey . 1·40 15
3054 – 3 l. 20 violet and grey . . 2·00 25
DESIGNS: 40 b. to 1 l. 75, Various scenes of play at net; 3 l. 20, European Cup.

549 Rumanian 1 l. 55 "Centenary" Stamp of 1958

1963. Air. Stamp Day and 15th U.P.U. Congress. Inscr "AL XV-LEA CONGRESS", etc.
3055 549 20 b. brown & light blue 15 10
3056 – 40 b. blue and mauve . . 20 10
3057 – 55 b. lake and blue . . . 25 10
3058 – 1 l. 20 violet and buff . . 50 15
3059 – 1 l. 55 olive and red . . 70 15
3060 – 1 l. 60 + 50 b. mult . . 1·60 40
DESIGNS (Rumanian stamps): 40 b. (1 l. 20) "Laika", 1957 (blue); 55 b. (3 l. 20) "Gagarin", 1961; 1 l. 20, (55 b.) "Nikolaev" and (1 l. 75) "Popovich", 1962; 1 l. 55, (55 b.) "Postwoman", 1953; 1 l. 60, U.P.U. Monument, Berne, globe, map of Rumania and aircraft (76 × 27 mm).

551 Ski Jumping

1963. Winter Olympic Games, Innsbruck, 1964. (a) Perf.
3061 551 10 b. blue and red . . . 50 15
3062 – 20 b. brown and blue . . 65 15
3063 – 40 b. brown and green . 85 10
3064 – 55 b. brown and violet . 1·00 10
3065 – 60 b. blue and brown . 1·40 15
3066 – 75 b. blue and mauve . . 1·50 20
3067 – 1 l. blue and ochre . . . 2·00 20
3068 – 1 l. 20 blue & turquoise . 2·75 35

(b) Imperf. Colours changed.
3069 551 10 b. brown and green . 1·50 1·25
3070 – 20 b. brown and violet . 1·50 1·25
3071 – 40 b. blue and red . . . 1·50 1·25
3072 – 55 b. brown and blue . . 1·50 1·25
3073 – 60 b. blue & turquoise . 1·50 1·25
3074 – 75 b. blue and ochre . . 1·50 1·25
3075 – 1 l. blue and mauve . . . 1·50 1·25
3076 – 1 l. 20 blue & brown . . 1·50 1·25
DESIGNS: 20 b. Ice skating; 40 b. Ice hockey; 55 b. Figure skating; 60 b. Slalom; 75 b. Rifle shooting on skis; 1 l. Bobsleigh; 1 l. 20, Skiing.

552 Cone, Fern and Conifer

553 Silkworm Moth

1963. 18th Anniv of Reafforestation Campaign.
3078 552 55 b. green 20 10
3079 – 1 l. 75 blue 65 15
DESIGN: 1 l. 75, Chestnut trees.

1963. Bee-keeping and Silkworm-breeding. Multicoloured.
3080 10 b. Type 553 . . . . . . 25 10
3081 20 b. Moth emerging from chrysalis 35 10
3082 40 b. Silkworm 45 10
3083 55 b. Bee 60 10
3084 60 b. Bee extracting nectar from various flowers . . . . . 1·00 20
3085 1 l. 20 As No. 3084 (different) 1·40 25
3086 1 l. 35 As No. 3084 (different) 1·60 35
3087 1 l. 60 As No. 3084 (different) 2·00 40
The 55 b. to 1 l. 60, are horiz.

554 Carved Pillar

556 G. Stephanescu

555 Gagarin

1963. Village Museum, Bucharest.
3088 554 20 b. purple 25 10
3089 – 40 b. blue 30 10
3090 – 55 b. violet 40 10
3091 – 75 b. green 50 10
3092 – 1 l. red and brown . . . 1·00 10
3093 – 1 l. 20 green . . . . . 1·25 10
3094 – 1 l. 75 blue and brown . 2·00 10
DESIGNS: Various Rumanian peasant houses. The 40 b. and 55 b. are horiz, the rest vert.

1964. Air. "Space Navigation". Soviet flag, red and yellow; U.S. flag, red and blue; backgrounds, light blue; portrait and inscription colours below.

(a) Perf.
3095 555 5 b. blue 25 10
3096 – 10 b. violet 35 10
3097 – 20 b. bronze 40 10
3098 – 35 b. grey 45 10
3099 – 40 b. violet 50 15
3100 – 55 b. violet 65 15
3101 – 60 b. brown 65 20
3102 – 75 b. blue 75 20
3103 – 1 l. purple . . . . . . 1·00 25
3104 – 1 l. 40 purple . . . . . 1·50 50

(b) Imperf. Colours changed.
3105 555 5 b. violet 10 10
3106 – 10 b. blue 15 10
3107 – 20 b. grey 30 15
3108 – 35 b. bronze 60 35
3109 – 40 b. purple 85 40
3110 – 55 b. purple . . . . . . 1·10 50
3111 – 60 b. blue . . . . 1·10 75
3112 – 75 b. brown . . . . . . 1·50 1·00
3113 – 1 l. violet . . . . . . 1·75 1·25
3114 – 1 l. 40 violet . . . . . 2·40 1·90
PORTRAITS (with flags of their countries)—As Type 555: 10 b. G. Titov; 20 b. J. Glenn; 35 b. S. Carpenter; 60 b. W. Schirra; 75 b. G. Cooper. SQUARE (35 × 34 mm): 40 b. A. Nikolaev; 55 b. P. Popovich; 1 l. V. Bykovsky; 1 l. 40, V. Tereshkova.

1964. Rumanian Opera Singers and their stage roles. Portraits in brown.
3116 556 10 b. olive 35 10
3117 – 20 b. blue 45 10
3118 – 35 b. green 50 10
3119 – 40 b. light blue 55 10
3120 – 55 b. mauve 65 10
3121 – 75 b. violet 70 10
3122 – 1 l. blue 80 10
3123 – 1 l. 35 violet 90 15
3124 – 1 l. 55 red . . . . . . 1·40 20
SINGERS: 20 b. Elena Teodorini; 35 b. I. Bajenaru; 40 b. D. Popovici; 55 b. Hariclea Darclee; 75 b. G. Folescu; 1 l. J. Athanasiu; 1 l. 35, T. Grosavescu; 1 l. 55, N. Leonard.

557 Prof. G. M. Murgoci

558 "Ascalaphus macaronius" (moth)

1964. 80th International Soil Congress, Bucharest.
3125 557 1 l. 60 indigo, ochre and blue . . . . 1·00 20

1964. Rumanian Insects. Multicoloured.
3126 5 b. Type 558 . . . . 20 10
3127 10 b. "Ammophila sabulosa" (flying ant) 25 10
3128 35 b. "Scolia maculata" (wasp) 30 10
3129 40 b. "Rhyparioides metelkana" (moth) 45 10
3130 55 b. "Lymantria dispar" (moth) 60 10
3131 1 l. 20 "Kanetisa circe" (butterfly) 85 15
3132 1 l. 55 "C. Fabricii malachiticus" (beetle) . . . 90 20
3133 1 l. 75 "Procerus gigas" (horned beetle) . . . . 1·50 20

559 "Nicotiana alata"

560 Cross Country

1964. Rumanian Flowers. Multicoloured.
3134 10 b. Type 559 . . . . 25 10
3135 20 b. "Pelargonium" 25 10
3136 40 b. "Fuchsia gracilis" . . . 35 15
3137 55 b. "Chrysanthemum indicum" 40 10
3138 75 b. "Dahlia hybrida" . . . 45 10
3139 1 l. "Lilium croceum" 75 10
3140 1 l. 25 "Hosta ovata" 90 20
3141 1 l. 55 "Tagetes erectus" . . . 1·40 15

1964. Horsemanship.
3142 – 40 b. multicoloured . . . 30 10
3143 560 55 b. brown, red & lilac . 40 10
3144 – 1 l. 35 brown, red & grn . 1·00 15
3145 – 1 l. 55 mauve, blue & bis . 1·60 20
DESIGNS—HORIZ: 40 b. Dressage; 1 l. 55, Horse race. VERT: 1 l. 35, Show jumping.

561 Scorpionfish

562 M. Eminescu (poet)

1964. Constantza Aquarium. Fish designs. Mult.
3146 5 b. Type 561 . . . . 10 10
3147 10 b. Blenny 10 10
3148 20 b. Mackerel 15 10
3149 40 b. Nisetru sturgeon 30 10
3150 50 b. Seahorse 40 15
3151 55 b. Gurnard 50 10
3152 1 l. Bekuga sturgeon 70 10
3153 3 l. 20 Sting ray . . . . . . 2·75 25

1964. Cultural Anniversaries. Portraits in brown.
3154 5 b. green (Type 562) 10 10
3155 20 b. lake (I. Creanga) . . . 15 10
3156 35 b. red (E. Girleanu) . . . 25 10
3157 55 b. bistre (Michelangelo) . . 30 10
3158 1 l. 20 blue (Galileo) 85 15
3159 1 l. 75 violet (Shakespeare) . 1·40 20
Nos. 3154/5 commemorate 75th anniv of death; No. 3156, 50th anniv of death; No. 3157, 400th anniv of death; Nos. 3158/9, 400th anniv of birth. Creanga and Girleanu were writers.

563 Cheile Bicazului (gorge)

564 High Jumping

1964. Mountain Resorts.
3160 563 40 b. lake 25 10
3161 – 55 b. blue 40 10
3162 – 1 l. purple 55 10
3163 – 1 l. 35 brown 65 10
3164 – 1 l. 75 green . . . . . . 1·40 10
DESIGNS—VERT: 55 b. Cabin on Lake Bilea; 1 l. Poiana Brasov ski-lift; 1 l. 75, Alpine Hotel. HORIZ: 1 l. 35, Lake Bicaz.

1964. Balkan Games. Multicoloured.
3165 30 b. Type 564 . . . . 15 10
3166 40 b. Throwing the javelin . . 15 10
3167 55 b. Running 30 10
3168 1 l. Throwing the discus . . 60 10
3169 1 l. 20 Hurdling 60 10
3170 1 l. 55 Flags of competing countries (24 × 44 mm) . . 70 15

565 Arms and Flag

1964. 20th Anniv of Liberation. Multicoloured.
3171 55 b. Type 565 . . . . 25 10
3172 60 b. Industrial plant 25 10
3173 75 b. Harvest scene 35 15
3174 1 l. 20 Apartment houses . . 60 15
Nos. 3172/4 are horiz.

566 High Jumping

1964. Olympic Games, Tokyo. Multicoloured. (a) Perf.
3176 20 b. Type 566 . . . . 25 10
3177 30 b. Wrestling 40 15
3178 35 b. Volley ball 45 20
3179 40 b. Canoeing 50 25
3180 55 b. Fencing . . . . 1·00 15
3181 1 l. 20 Gymnastics . . . . . 1·40 25
3182 1 l. 35 Football . . . . . . 1·60 40
3183 1 l. 55 Rifle-shooting . . . . 2·00 75

(b) Imperf. Colours changed and new values.
3184 20 b. Type 566 . . . . 45 10
3185 30 b. Wrestling 50 20
3186 35 b. Volleyball 85 20
3187 40 b. Canoeing 85 20
3188 55 b. Fencing . . . . 1·40 50
3189 1 l. 60 Gymnastics . . . . . 3·00 1·25
3190 2 l. Football . . . . 3·50 1·75
3191 2 l. 40 Rifle-shooting . . . 4·25 2·50

567 George Enescu

568 Python

1964. 3rd International George Enescu Festival.
3193 567 10 b. green 25 10
3194 – 55 b. purple 40 10
3195 – 1 l. 60 purple . . . . . 1·00 35
3196 – 1 l. 75 blue . . . . . . 1·60 20
DESIGNS (Portraits of Enescu): 55 b. At piano; 1 l. 60, Medallion; 1 l. 75, When an old man.

1964. Bucharest Zoo. Multicoloured.
3197 5 b. Type 568 . . . . 10 10
3198 10 b. Black swans 65 10
3199 35 b. Ostriches 85 10
3200 40 b. Crowned cranes . . . 1·00 15
3201 55 b. Tigers 75 10
3202 1 l. Lions . . . . 1·10 20
3203 1 l. 55 Grevy's zebras . . . 1·60 20
3204 2 l. Bactrian camels . . . . 2·40 30

569 Brincoveanu, Cantacuzino, Lazar and Academy

570 Soldier

1964. Anniversaries. Multicoloured.
3205 20 b. Type **569** 10 10
3206 40 b. Cuza and seal 15 10
3207 55 b. Emblems and the Arts (vert) 25 10
3208 75 b. Laboratory workers and class 30 10
3209 1 l. Savings Bank building 50 25
EVENTS, etc: 20 b. 270th Anniv of Domneasca Academy; 40 b. and 75 b. Bucharest University centenary; 55 b. "Fine Arts" centenary (emblems are masks, curtain, piano keyboard, harp, palette and brushes); 1 l. Savings Bank centenary.

1964. Centenary of Army Day.
3210 **570** 55 b. blue and lt blue 45 15

571 Post Office of 19th and 20th Centuries

1964. Air. Stamp Day.
3211 **571** 1 l. 60 + 40 b. blue, red and yellow 1·60 25
No. 3211 is a two-part design, the two parts being arranged vert imperf between.

572 Canoeing Medal (1956) **573** Strawberries

1964. Olympic Games-Rumanian Gold Medal Awards. Medals in brown and bistre (Nos. 3218/19 and 3226/7 in sepia and gold). (a) Perf.
3212 **572** 20 b. red and blue 50 15
3213 – 30 b. green and blue 50 15
3214 – 35 b. turquoise and blue 75 25
3215 – 40 b. lilac and blue 90 35
3216 – 55 b. orange and blue 1·10 20
3217 – 1 l. 20 green and blue 1·40 35
3218 – 1 l. 35 brown and blue 2·00 45
3219 – 1 l. 55 mauve and blue 2·40 50

(b) Imperf. Colours changed and new values.
3220 **572** 20 b. orange and blue 15 20
3221 – 30 b. turquoise and blue 40 30
3222 – 35 b. green and blue 40 30
3223 – 40 b. green and blue 50 40
3224 – 55 b. red and blue 1·10 50
3225 – 1 l. 60 lilac and blue 2·50 2·00
3226 – 2 l. mauve and blue 3·75 2·75
3227 – 2 l. 40 brown and blue 4·50 3·50
MEDALS: 30 b. Boxing (1956); 35 b. Pistol-shooting (1956); 40 b. High-jumping (1960); 55 b. Wrestling (1960); 1 l. 20, 1 l. 60, Rifle-shooting (1960); 1 l. 35, 2 l. High-jumping (1964); 1 l. 55, 2 l. 40, Throwing the javelin (1964).

1964. Forest Fruits. Multicoloured.
3229 5 b. Type **573** 15 10
3230 35 b. Blackberries 25 10
3231 40 b. Raspberries 30 10
3232 55 b. Rosehips 40 10
3233 1 l. 20 Blueberries 75 15
3234 1 l. 35 Cornelian cherries 85 15
3235 1 l. 55 Hazel nuts 1·25 10
3236 2 l. 55 Cherries 1·40 20

574 "Syncom 3" **575** U.N. Headquarters, New York

1965. Space Navigation. Multicoloured.
3237 30 b. Type **574** 20 10
3238 40 b. "Syncom 3" (different view) 25 10
3239 55 b. "Ranger 7" 45 10
3240 1 l. "Ranger 7" (different view) 50 15
3241 1 l. 20 "Voskhod 1" 90 10
3242 5 l. Feoktistov, Komarov and Yegorov, and "Voskhod 1" (52½×29½ mm) 2·75 75
Nos. 3239/42 are horiz.

1965. 20th Anniv of U.N.O.
3243 **575** 55 b. gold, blue & red 30 10
3244 – 1 l. 60 multicoloured 1·00 20
DESIGN: 1 l. 60, Arms and U.N. emblem on Rumanian flag.

576 Tortoise ("Testudo graeca")

1965. Reptiles. Multicoloured.
3245 5 b. Type **576** 15 10
3246 10 b. "Lacerta taurica" 15 10
3247 20 b. "Lacerta trilineata" 20 10
3248 40 b. "Alepharus kitaibelii" 25 10
3249 55 b. "Anguis fragilis" 30 10
3250 60 b. "Vipera ammodytes" 45 10
3251 1 l. "Eremias arguta" 55 10
3252 1 l. 20 "Vipera ursinii" 65 10
3253 1 l. 35 "Coluber jugularis" 85 15
3254 3 l. 25 "Elaphe quatuorlineata" 2·75 40

577 Tabby Cat **579** Ion Bianu (philologist)

1965. Domestic Cats. Multicoloured.
3255 5 b. Type **577** 10 10
3256 10 b. Ginger tomcat 15 10
3257 40 b. White Persians 25 10
3258 55 b. Kittens with shoe 40 10
3259 60 b. Kitten with ball of wool 60 10
3260 75 b. Cat and two kittens 75 10
3261 1 l. 35 Siamese 1·40 15
3262 3 l. 25 Heads of three cats (62×29 mm) 3·00 40
Nos. 3257/61 are vert.

1965. Space Flight of "Ranger 9" (24.3.65). No. 3240 surch **RANGER 9 24-3-1965 5 Lei** and floral emblem over old value.
3263 5 l. on 1 l. multicoloured 29·00 29·00

1965. Cultural Anniversaries. Portraits in sepia.
3264 **579** 40 l. blue 15 10
3265 – 55 b. ochre 20 10
3266 – 60 b. purple 25 10
3267 – 1 l. red 60 15
3268 – 1 l. 35 olive 50 20
3269 – 1 l. 75 red 80 25
PORTRAITS, etc: 40 b. (30th death anniv); 55 b. A. Bacalbasa (writer: birth cent); 60 b. V. Conta (philosopher: 120th birth anniv); 1 l. Jean Sibelius (composer: birth cent); 1 l. 35, Horace (poet: birth bimillenary); 1 l. 75, Dante (poet: 700th birth anniv).

580 I.T.U. Emblem and Symbols

1965. Centenary of I.T.U.
3270 **580** 1 l. 75 blue 1·25 20

581 Derdap Gorge (The Iron Gate)

1965. Inaug of Derdap Hydro Electric Project.
3271 **581** 30 b. (25 d.) green and grey 15 10
3272 – 55 b. (50 d.) red and grey 30 10
DESIGN: 55 b. Derdap Dam.
Nos. 3271/72 were issued simultaneously in Yugoslavia.

582 Rifleman **583** "Fat-Frumos and the Beast"

1965. European Shooting Championships, Bucharest. Multicoloured. (a) Perf.
3274 20 b. Type **582** 15 10
3275 40 b. Prone rifleman 25 10
3276 55 b. Pistol shooting 30 10
3277 1 l. "Free" pistol shooting 60 10
3278 1 l. 60 Standing rifleman 85 15
3279 2 l. Various marksmen 1·40 35

(b) Imperf. Colours changed and new values.
3280 40 b. Prone rifleman 20 10
3281 55 b. Pistol shooting 25 15
3282 1 l. "Free" pistol shooting 45 25
3283 1 l. 60 Standing rifleman 65 50
3284 3 l. 25 Type **582** 1·60 90
3285 5 l. Various marksmen 2·75 1·00
Apart from Type **582** the designs are horiz, the 2 l. and 5 l. being larger 51½×28½ mm.

1965. Rumanian Fairy Tales. Multicoloured.
3286 20 b. Type **583** 25 10
3287 40 b. "Fat-Frumos and Ileana Cosinzeana" 25 10
3288 55 b. "Harap Alb" (horseman and bear) 30 10
3289 1 l. "The Moralist Wolf" 60 10
3290 1 l. 35 "The Ox and the Calf" 90 10
3291 2 l. "The Bear and the Wolf" (drawing a sledge) 1·25 25

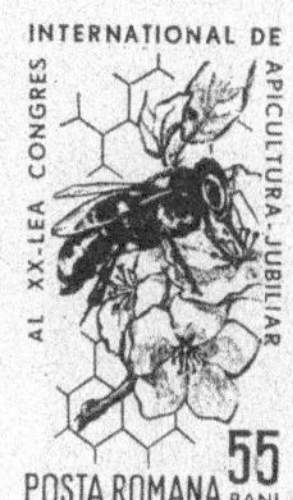

584 Bee on Flowers **585** Belyaev, Leonov, "Voskhod 2" and Leonov in Space

1965. 20th International Bee-keeping Association Federation ("Apimondia") Congress, Bucharest.
3292 **584** 55 b. black, red & yellow 35 10
3293 – 1 l. 60 multicoloured 1·25 15
DESIGN—HORIZ: 1 l. 60, Congress Hall.

1965. Space Achievements. Multicoloured.
3294 5 b. "Proton 1" 15 10
3295 10 b. "Sonda 3" (horiz) 20 15
3296 15 b. "Molnia 1" 25 20
3297 1 l. 75 Type **585** 1·10 15
3298 2 l. 40 "Early Bird" satellite 1·60 20
3299 3 l. 20 "Gemini 3" and astronauts in capsule 3·00 25
3300 3 l. 25 "Mariner 4" 3·75 40
3301 5 l. "Gemini 5" (horiz) 5·75 1·40

586 Marx and Lenin **588** V. Alecsandri

587 Common Quail

1965. Postal Ministers' Congress, Peking.
3302 **586** 55 b. multicoloured 50 15

1965. Migratory Birds. Multicoloured.
3303 5 b. Type **587** 20 10
3304 10 b. Woodcock 35 10
3305 20 b. Common snipe 50 10
3306 40 b. Turtle dove 50 15
3307 55 b. Mallard 60 15
3308 60 b. White fronted goose 75 15
3309 1 l. Common crane 1·00 20
3310 1 l. 20 Glossy ibis 1·40 20
3311 1 l. 25 Mute swan 1·60 20
3312 3 l. 25 Eastern white pelican 5·25 70
The 3 l. 25, is vert 32×73 mm.

1965. 75th Death Anniv of Vasile Alecsandri (poet).
3313 **588** 55 b. multicoloured 50 15

589 "Nymphaea zanzibariensis"

1965. Cluj Botanical Gardens. Multicoloured.
3314 5 b. "Strelitzia reginae" (crane flower) 10 10
3315 10 b. "Stanhopea tigrina" (orchid) 15 10
3316 20 b. "Paphiopedilum insigne" (orchid) 15 10
3317 30 b. Type **589** 30 10
3318 40 b. "Ferocactus glaucescens" (cactus) 40 10
3319 55 b. "Gossypium arboreum" 35 10
3320 1 l. "Hibiscus rosa sinensis" 25 15
3321 1 l. 35 "Gloxinia hibrida" 1·00 15
3322 1 l. 75 "Victoria amazonica" (Victoria Regis lily) 1·60 15
3323 2 l. 30 Hibiscus, crane flower, water lily and botanical building (52×29½ mm) 2·00 40
The 5, 10, 20 b. and 1 l. 35, are vert.

590 Running **592** Pigeon on TV Aerial

591 Pigeon and Horseman

1965. Spartacist Games. Multicoloured.
3324 55 b. Type **590** 25 15
3325 1 l. 55 Football 1·00 20
3326 1 l. 75 Diving 1·00 20
3327 2 l. Mountaineering (inscr "TURISM") 1·40 25
3328 5 l. Canoeing (inscr "CAMPIONATELLE EUROPENE 1965") (horiz) 3·00 50

1965. Stamp Day.
3329 **591** 55 b. + 45 b. blue and mauve 40 10
3330 **592** 1 l. brown and green 40 20
3331 – 1 l. 75 brown and green 1·40 25
DESIGN: As Type **592**. 1 l. 75, Pigeon in flight.

593 Chamois

1965. "Hunting Trophies".
3332 **593** 55 b. brown, yell & mve 50 15
3333 – 1 l. brown, green & red 90 15
3334 – 1 l. 60 brown, bl & orge 1·75 30
3335 – 1 l. 75 brown, red & grn 2·25 35
3336 – 3 l. 20 multicoloured 3·00 75
DESIGNS—37×23 mm: 1 l. Brown bear; 1 l. 60, Roe deer; 1 l. 75, Wild boar. 49×37½ mm: 3 l. 20, Trophy and antlers.

594 Dachshund

1965. Hunting Dogs. Multicoloured.
3337 5 b. Type **594** 10 10
3338 10 b. Spaniel 10 10
3339 40 b. Retriever with woodcock 75 10
3340 55 b. Fox terrier 40 10
3341 60 b. Red setter 55 10
3342 75 b. White setter . . . . . 1·00 15
3343 1 l. 55 Pointers . . . . 2·00 20
3344 3 l. 25 Duck–shooting with retriever . . . . 3·75 1·50
SIZES—DIAMOND. 47½ × 47½ mm: 10 b. to 75 b. HORIZ—43½ × 29 mm: 1 l. 55, 3 l. 25.

595 Pawn and Globe

596 Tractor, Corn and Sun

1966. 17th Chess Olympiad, Havana. Mult.
3345 20 b. Type **595** 35 10
3346 40 b. Jester and bishop (chess piece) 45 10
3347 55 b. Knight on horseback and rook (chess piece) 70 10
3348 1 l. As No. 3347 . . . . . . 95 10
3349 1 l. 60 Type **595** . . . . . 2·00 20
3350 3 l. 25 As No. 3346 . . . . . 4·00 1·50

1966. Co-operative Farming Union Congress.
3351 **596** 55 b. green and yellow . 45 15

597 G. Gheorghiu-Dej

598 Congress Emblem

1966. Death Anniv of G. Gheorghiu-Dej (Head of State).
3352 **597** 55 b. black and gold . . 40 15

1966. Communist Youth Union Congress.
3354 **598** 55 b. red and yellow . . 40 15

599 Dance of Moldova

1966. Rumanian Folk-dancing.
3355 **599** 30 b. black and purple . 30 10
3356 – 40 b. black and red . . . 50 20
3357 – 55 b. black & turquoise . 65 10
3358 – 1 l. black and lake . . . 85 10
3359 – 1 l. 60 black and blue . . 1·25 15
3360 – 2 l. black and green . . . 3·00 1·60
DANCES OF: 40 b. Oltenia; 55 b. Maramures; 1 l. Muntenia; 1 l. 60, Banat; 2 l. Transylvania.

600 Footballers

601 "Agriculture and Industry"

1966. World Cup Football Championships.
3361 **600** 5 b. multicoloured . . . 15 10
3362 – 10 b. multicoloured . . . 25 10
3363 – 15 b. multicoloured . . . 35 10
3364 – 55 b. multicoloured . . . 95 10
3365 – 1 l. 75 multicoloured . . 2·25 25
3366 – 4 l. multicoloured . . . . 5·00 3·25
DESIGNS: 10 b. to 1 l. 75, Various footballers as Type **600**; 4 l. Jules Rimet Cup.

1966. Trade Union Congress, Bucharest.
3368 **601** 55 b. multicoloured . . . 35 15

602 Red–breasted Flycatcher

603 "Venue 3"

1966. Song Birds. Multicoloured.
3369 5 b. Type **602** 30 10
3370 10 b. Red crossbill 40 10
3371 15 b. Great reed warbler . . 75 10
3372 20 b. Redstart 80 10
3373 55 b. European robin . . . 1·10 10
3374 1 l. 20 Bluethroat . . . . . 1·75 15
3375 1 l. 55 Yellow wagtail . . . 2·75 20
3375 3 l. 20 Penduline tit . . . . 4·25 2·25

1966. Space Achievements. Multicoloured.
3377 10 b. Type **603** 25 10
3378 20 b. "FR 1" satellite . . . 30 10
3379 1 l. 60 "Luna 9" . . . . . 2·00 20
3380 5 l. "Gemini 6" and "7" . . 4·75 1·60

604 U. Nestor (birth cent)

606 "Hottonia palustris"

605 "House" (after Petrascu)

1966. Cultural Anniversaries.
3381 – 5 b. blue, black & green 10 10
3382 – 10 b. green, black & red 15 10
3383 **604** 20 b. purple, black & grn 10 10
3384 – 40 b. brown, black & bl 15 10
3385 – 55 b. green, black & brn 20 10
3386 – 1 l. violet, black & bistre 45 15
3387 – 1 l. 35 olive, black & bl 70 20
3388 – 1 l. 60 purple, blk & grn 1·50 45
3389 – 1 l. 75 purple, blk & orge 95 20
3390 – 3 l. 25 lake, black & bl . 1·60 40
PORTRAITS: 5 b. G. Cosbuc (birth cent); 10 b. G. Sincai (150th death anniv); 40 b. A. Pumnul (death cent); 55 b. S. Luchian (50th death anniv); 1 l. Sun Yat-sen (birth cent); 1 l. 35, G. W. Leibnitz (250th death anniv); 1 l. 60, R. Rolland (birth cent); 1 l. 75, I. Ghica (150th birth anniv); 3 l. 25, S. C. Cantacuzino (250th death anniv).

1966. Paintings in National Gallery, Bucharest. Multicoloured.
3391 5 b. Type **605** 20 10
3392 10 b. "Peasant Girl" (Grigorescu) 25 10
3393 20 b. "Midday Rest" (Rescu) 40 15
3394 55 b. "Portrait of a Man" (Van Eyck) . . . . 1·40 25
3395 1 l. 55 "The 2nd Class Compartment" (Daumier) 5·25 60
3396 3 l. 25 "The Blessing" (El Greco) . . . . 7·50 5·25
The 10, 55 b. and 3 l. 25, are vert.

1966. Aquatic Flora. Multicoloured.
3397 5 b. Type **606** 15 10
3398 10 b. "Ceratophyllum submersum" 20 10
3399 20 b. "Aldrovanda vesiculosa" 25 10
3400 40 b. "Callitriche verna" . . 45 10
3401 55 b. "Vallisneria spiralis" . 45 10
3402 1 l. "Elodea canadensis" . . 1·25 15
3403 1 l. 55 "Hippuris vulgaris" . 1·50 20
3404 3 l. 25 "Myriophyllum spicatum" (28 × 49½ mm) . 3·50 1·60

607 Diagram showing one metre in relation to quadrant of Earth

608 Putna Monastery

1966. Centenary of Metric System in Rumania.
3405 **607** 55 b. blue and brown . . 30 10
3406 – 1 l. violet and green . . . 50 20
DESIGN: 1 l. Metric abbreviations and globe.

1966. 500th Anniv of Putna Monastery.
3407 **608** 2 l. multicoloured . . . . 1·40 30

609 "Medicine"

1966. Centenary of Rumanian Academy.
3408 **609** 40 b. multicoloured . . . 20 10
3409 – 55 b. multicoloured . . . 25 10
3410 – 1 l. brown, gold & blue . 40 10
3411 – 3 l. brown, gold & yellow 1·75 1·00
DESIGNS—As Type **609**: 55 b. "Science" (formula). 22½ × 33½ mm: 1 l. Gold medal. 67 × 27 mm: 3 l. I. Radulescu, M. Kogalniceanu and T. Savulescu.

610 Crayfish

1966. Crustaceans and Molluscs. Mult.
3412 5 b. Type **610** 15 10
3413 10 b. Netted nassa (vert) . . . 20 10
3414 20 b. Marbled rock crab . . . 25 10
3415 40 b. "Campylaea trizona" (snail) 40 10
3416 55 b. Lucorum helix 60 10
3417 1 l. 35 Mediterranean blue mussel . . . . 1·50 15
3418 1 l. 75 Stagnant pond snail . 1·75 20
3419 3 l. 25 Swan mussel . . . . . 3·75 1·60

611 Bucharest and Mail Coach

1966. Stamp Day.
3420 **611** 55 b. + 45 b. mult. . . . 1·00 25
No. 3420 is a two-part design arranged horiz imperf between.

612 "Ursus spelaeus"

1966. Prehistoric Animals.
3421 **612** 5 b. blue, brown & green 20 10
3422 – 10 b. violet, bistre & grn . 20 10
3423 – 15 b. brown, purple & grn 25 10
3424 – 55 b. violet, bistre & grn . 70 10
3425 – 1 l. 55 blue, brown & grn 2·00 15
3426 – 4 l. mauve, bistre & green 3·75 1·75
ANIMALS: 10 b. "Mamuthus trogontherii"; 15 b. "Bison priscus"; 55 b. "Archidiscodon"; 1 l. 55, "Megaceros eurycerus". (43 × 27 mm): 4 l. "Deinotherium gigantissimum".

613 "Sputnik 1" orbiting Globe

1967. 10 Years of Space Achievements. Mult.
3427 10 b. Type **613** (postage) . . 15 10
3428 20 b. Gagarin and "Vostok 1" 15 10
3429 25 b. Tereshkova ("Vostok 6") 20 10
3430 40 b. Nikolaiev and Popovich ("Vostok 3" and "4") . . 35 10
3431 55 b. Leonov in space ("Voskhod 2") 45 10
3432 1 l. 20 "Early Bird" (air) . . 1·25 15
3433 1 l. 55 Photo transmission ("Mariner 4") . . . . . . 1·60 20
3434 3 l. 25 Space rendezvous ("Gemini 6" and "7") . . . 2·25 40
3435 5 l. Space link up ("Gemini 8") 3·25 2·75

614 Barn Owl

1967. Birds of Prey. Multicoloured.
3442 10 b. Type **614** 60 10
3443 20 b. Eagle owl 95 10
3444 40 b. Saker falcon 85 10
3445 55 b. Egyptian vulture . . . 1·90 15
3446 75 b. Osprey . . . . 1·25 15
3447 1 l. Griffon vulture . . . . . 1·90 15
3448 1 l. 20 Lammergeier . . . . 3·25 25
3449 1 l. 75 European black vulture 3·75 1·90

615 "Washerwoman" (after I. Steriadi)

1967. Paintings.
3450 – 10 b. blue, gold and red . 20 10
3451 **615** 20 b. green, gold & ochre 25 15
3452 – 40 b. red, gold and blue . 40 20
3453 – 1 l. 55 purple, gold & blue 95 30
3454 – 3 l. 20 brown, gold & brn 3·25 40
3455 – 5 l. brown, gold & orge . 4·75 2·75
PAINTINGS—VERT: 10 b. "Model in Fancy Dress" (I. Andreescu); 40 b. "Peasants Weaving" (S. Dimitrescu); 1 l. 55, "Venus and Cupid" (L. Cranach); 5 l. "Haman beseeching Esther" (Rembrandt). HORIZ: 3 l. 20, "Hercules and the Lion" (Rubens).

616 Woman's Head

618 "Infantryman" (after Grigorescu)

617 Copper and Silver Coins of 1867

1967. 10th Anniv of C. Brancusi (sculptor). Sculptures.
3456 **616** 5 b. brown, yellow & red 15 10
3457 – 10 b. black, grn & violet 20 10
3458 – 20 b. black, green & red 20 10
3459 – 40 b. black, red & green 25 10
3460 – 55 b. black, olive & blue 50 20
3461 – 1 l. 20 brown, violet and orange . . . . 1·75 20
3462 – 3 l. 25 black, green and mauve . . . . 3·25 1·75
DESIGNS—HORIZ: 10 b. Sleeping muse; 40 b. "The Kiss"; 3 l. 25, Gate of Kisses, Targujiu. VERT: 20 b. "The Endless Column"; 55 b. Seated woman; 1 l. 20, "Miss Pogany".

1967. Centenary of Rumanian Monetary System.
3463 **617** 55 b. multicoloured . . . 30 15
3464 – 1 l. 20 multicoloured . . 60 55
DESIGN: 1 l. 20 Obverse and reverse of modern silver coin (1966).

1967. 90th Anniv of Independence.
3465 **618** 55 b. multicoloured . . . 1·60 1·60

MINIMUM PRICE

The minimum price quoted is 10p which represents a handling charge rather than a basis for valuing common stamps. For further notes about prices, see introductory pages.

619 Peasants attacking (after O. Bancila)

620 "Centaurea pinnatifida"

1967. 60th Anniv of Peasant Rising.
3466 **619** 40 b. multicoloured . . . 50 70
3467 – 1 l. 55 multicoloured . . 1·40 1·40
DESIGN—HORIZ: 1 l. 55, Peasants marching (after S. Luchian).

1967. Carpathian Flora. Multicoloured.
3468 20 b. Type **620** 15 10
3469 40 b. "Erysimum transsilvanicum" 20 10
3470 55 b. "Aquilegia transsilvanica" 25 10
3471 1 l. 20 "Viola alpina" . . . . 1·00 10
3472 1 l. 75 "Campanula carpatica" 1·10 10
3473 4 l. "Dryas octopetala" (horiz) 3·25 1·60

621 Towers, Sibiu

1967. Historic Monuments and International Tourist Year. Multicoloured.
3474 20 b. Type **621** 20 10
3475 40 b. Castle at Cris 25 10
3476 55 b. Wooden church, Plopis 50 10
3477 1 l. 60 Ruins, Neamtului . . 85 20
3478 1 l. 75. Mogosoaia Palace, Bucharest . . . . 1·40 20
3479 2 l. 25 Church, Voronet . . . 2·00 1·40
No. 3479 is horiz, $48\frac{1}{2} \times 36$ mm.

623 "The Marasesti Attack" (from painting by E. Stoica)

1967. 50th Anniv of Battles of Marasesti, Marasti and Oituz.
3481 **623** 55 b. brown, blue & grey 70 25

624 D. Lipatti (composer and pianist: 50th birth anniv)

625 Wrestling

1967. Cultural Anniversaries.
3482 **624** 10 b. violet, blue & black 15 10
3483 – 20 b. blue, brown & black 15 10
3484 – 40 b. brown, turq & blk . 15 10
3485 – 55 b. brown, red & black 25 10
3486 – 1 l. 20 bowrn, olive & blk 40 15
3487 – 1 l. 75 green, blue & blk . 1·00 1·00
DESIGNS: 20 b. A. Orascu (architect: 150th birth anniv); 40 b. G. Antipa (zoologist: birth cent); 55 b. M. Kogalniceanu (politician: 150th birth anniv); 1 l. 20, Jonathan Swift (300th birth anniv); 1 l. 75, Marie Curie (birth cent).

1967. World Wrestling Championships, Bucharest. Designs showing wrestlers and globes.
3488 **625** 10 b. multicoloured . . . 10 10
3489 – 20 b. mult (horiz) . . . 15 10
3490 – 55 b. multicoloured . . . 25 10
3491 – 1 l. 20 multicoloured . . 1·00 15
3492 – 2 l. mult (horiz) . . . . 1·60 80

626 Inscription on Globe

1967. International Linguists' Congress, Bucharest.
3493 **626** 1 l. 60 ultramarine, red and blue . . . . 1·40 20

627 Academy

1967. Centenary of Book Academy, Bucharest.
3494 **627** 55 b. grey, brown & blue 1·00 20

628 Dancing on Ice

629 Curtea de Arges Monastery

1967. Winter Olympic Games, Grenoble. Mult.
3495 20 b. Type **628** 10 10
3496 40 b. Skiing 15 10
3497 55 b. Bobsleighing 25 10
3498 1 l. Downhill skiing 45 15
3499 1 l. 55 Ice hockey 70 15
3500 2 l. Games emblem 90 25
3501 2 l. 30 Ski–jumping . . . . 1·60 1·00

1967. 450th Anniv of Curtea de Arges Monastery.
3503 **629** 55 b. multicoloured . . 65 20

630 Karl Marx and Title Page

631 Lenin

1967. Centenary of Karl Marx's "Das Kapital".
3504 **630** 40 b. black, yell & red . 30 15

1967. 50th Anniv of October Revolution.
3505 **631** 1 l. 20 black, gold & red 60 15

632 Arms of Rumania

633 Telephone Dial and Map

1967. (a) T **632**.
3506 **632** 40 b. blue 30 10
3506 55 b. yellow 40 10
3507 1 l. 60 red . . . . 1·00 10

(b) T **633** and similar designs.
3509 – 5 b. green 10 10
3510 – 10 b. red 10 10
3511 – 20 b. grey 40 10
3512 – 35 b. blue 20 10
3513 – 40 b. blue 20 10
3514 – 50 b. orange 25 10
3515 – 55 b. red 40 10
3516 – 60 b. brown 40 10
3517 – 1 l. green 40 10
3518 – 1 l. 20 violet 45 10
3519 – 1 l. 35 blue 75 10
3520 – 1 l. 50 red 70 10
3521 – 1 l. 55 brown 75 10
3522 – 1 l. 75 green 85 10
3523 – 2 l. yellow 90 10
3524 – 2 l. 40 blue 95 10
3525 **633** 3 l. turquoise . . . . . 1·10 10
3526 – 3 l. 20 ochre . . . . . . 1·50 10
3527 – 3 l. 25 blue . . . . 1·75 10
3528 – 4 l. mauve . . . . 2·50 15
3529 – 5 l. violet . . . . 2·00 15
DESIGNS—23 × 17 mm: 5 b. "Carpati" lorry; 20 b. Railway T.P.O. coach; 35 b. Zlin Z-226A Akrobat airplane; 60 b. Electric parcels truck. As Type **633** (29 × 23 mm): 1 l. 20, Motor-coach; 1 l. 35, Mil Mi-4 helicopter. 1 l. 75, Lakeside highway; 2 l. Postal van; 3 l. 20, Ilyushin Il-18 airliner; 4 l. Electric train; 5 l. Telex instrument and world map. 17 × 23 mm: 10 b. Posthorn and telephone emblem; 40 b. Power pylons; 50 b. Telephone handset; 55 b. Dam. 23 × 29 mm: 1 l. Diesel train; 1 l. 50, Trolley bus; 1 l. 55, Radio station; 2 l. 40, T.V. relay station; 3 l. 25, Liner "Transylvania".
No. 3525 also commemorates the 40th anniv of the automatic telephone service.
For Nos. 3517/29 in smaller format see Nos. 3842/57.

634 "Crossing the River Buzau" (lithograph by Raffet) ($\frac{1}{2}$-size illustration)

1967. Stamp Day.
3530 **634** 55 b. + 45 b. blue and ochre . . . . 1·00 30

635 Monorail Train and Globe

636 Arms and Industrial Scene

1967. World Fair, Montreal. Multicoloured.
3531 55 b. Type **635** 30 10
3532 1 l. Expo emblem within atomic symbol 35 10
3533 1 l. 60 Gold cup and world map 70 15
3534 2 l. Expo emblem . . . . . . 1·10 75

1967. 20th Anniv of Republic. Multicoloured.
3535 40 b. Type **636** 15 10
3536 55 b. Arms of Rumania . . . 15 10
3537 1 l. 60 Rumanian flag 40 15
3538 1 l. 75 Arms and cultural emblems . . . . 1·40 75
The 1 l. 60 is 34 × 48 mm.

637 I.A.R. 817 Flying Ambulance

1968. Air. Rumanian Aviation.
3539 – 40 b. multicoloured . . . 15 10
3540 **637** 55 b. multicoloured . . . 35 10
3541 – 1 l. multicoloured 40 10
3542 – 2 l. 40 multicoloured . . 1·10 55
DESIGNS—VERT: 40 b. Antonov An-2 biplane spraying crops; 1 l. "Aviasan" emblem and airliner; 2 l. 40, Mircea Zorileanu (pioneer aviator) and biplane.

638 "Angelica and Medor" (S. Ricci)

1968. Paintings in Rumanian Galleries. Mult.
3543 40 b. "Young Woman" (Misu Pop) 40 20
3544 55 b. "Little Girl in Red Scarf" (N. Grigorescu) 55 25
3545 1 l. "Old Nicholas, the Cobza-player" (S. Luchian) . . . 1·25 30
3546 1 l. 60 "Man with Skull" (Dierick Bouts) . . . . . . 1·60 35
3547 2 l. 40 Type **638** . . . . . . 2·10 50
3548 3 l. 20 "Ecce Homo" (Titian) 6·75 6·00
Nos. 3543/6 and 3548 are vert.
See also Nos. 3583/8, 3631/6, 3658/63, 3756/61 and 3779/84.

640 Human Rights Emblem

641 W.H.O. Emblem

1968. Human Rights Year.
3551 **640** 1 l. multicoloured . . . . 1·00 15

1968. 20th Anniv of W.H.O.
3552 **641** 1 l. 60 multicoloured . . 1·40 15

642 "The Hunter" (after N. Grigorescu)

1968. Hunting Congress, Mamaia.
3553 **642** 1 l. 60 multicoloured . . 1·60 25

643 Pioneers and Liberation Monument

1968. Young Pioneers. Multicoloured.
3554 5 b. Type **643** 10 10
3555 40 b. Receiving scarves . . . 15 10
3556 55 b. With models 25 10
3557 1 l. Operating radio sets . . 40 10
3558 1 l. 60 Folk-dancing 70 15
3559 2 l. 40 In camp . . . . . . 1·10 45

644 Prince Mircea

645 Ion Ionescu de la Brad (scholar)

1968. 550th Death Anniv of Prince Mircea (the Old).
3560 **644** 1 l. 60 multicoloured . . 1·40 25

1968. Cultural Anniversaries.
3561 **645** 40 b. multicoloured . . . 15 15
3562 – 55 b. multicoloured . . . 30 15
PORTRAITS AND ANNIVS: 40 b. Type **645** (150th birth anniv); 55 b. Emil Racovita (scientist: birth cent).

646 "Pelargonium zonale, Ait"

648 Throwing the Javelin

647 "Nicolae Balcescu" (G. Tattarescu)

1968. Garden Geraniums. Multicoloured.
3563 10 b. Type **646** 15 10
3564 20 b. "Pelargonium zonale Ait" 15 10
3565 40 b. "Pelargonium zonale Ait" 20 10
3566 55 b. "Pelargonium zonale Ait" 20 10
3567 60 b. "Pelargonium grandiflorum Hort" 35 10
3568 1 l. 20 "Pelargonium peltatum Hort" 40 10

3569 1 l. 35 "Pelargonium peltatum Hort" . . . 50 15
3570 1 l. 60 "Pelargonium grandiflorum Hort" . . . 1·00 50

Nos. 3563/6, 3567 and 3570, 3568/9 respectively are different varieties of the same species.

1968. 120th Anniv of 1848 Revolution. Paintings. Multicoloured.

3571 55 b. Type **647** . . . 30 10
3572 1 l. 20 "Avram Iancu" (B. Iscovescu) . . . 35 15
3573 1 l. 60 "Vasile Alecsandri" (N. Livaditti) . . . 1·60 85

1968. Olympic Games, Mexico. Multicoloured.

3574 10 b. Type **648** . . . 10 10
3575 20 b. Diving . . . 15 10
3576 40 b. Volleyball . . . 15 10
3577 55 b. Boxing . . . 25 10
3578 60 b. Wrestling . . . 25 10
3579 1 l. 20 Fencing . . . 65 15
3580 1 l. 35 Punting . . . 85 15
3581 1 l. 60 Football . . . 1·40 1·00

1968. Paintings in the Fine Arts Museum, Bucarest. Multicoloured.

3583 10 b. "The Awakening of Rumania" (G. Tattarescu) (28×49 mm) . . . 10 10
3584 20 b. "Composition" (Teodorescu Sionion) . . . 15 10
3585 35 b. "The Judgement of Paris" (H. van Balen) . . . 20 10
3586 60 b. "The Mystical Betrothal of St. Catherine" (L. Sustris) . . . 35 15
3587 1 l.75 "Mary with the Child Jesus" (J. van Bylert) . . . 1·40 25
3588 3 l. "The Summer" (J. Jordaens) . . . 3·25 1·60

649 F.I.A.P. Emblem within "Lens" — **650** Academy and Harp

1968. 20th Anniv of International Federation of Photographic Art (F.I.A.P.).

3589 **649** 1 l. 60 multicoloured . . . 1·40 20

1968. Centenary of Georgi Enescu Philharmonic Academy.

3590 **650** 55 b. multicoloured . . . 70 15

651 Triumph of Trajan (Roman metope)

1968. Historic Monuments.

3591 **651** 10 b. green, blue & red . . . 10 10
3592 – 40 b. blue, brown & red . . . 20 10
3593 – 55 b. violet, brown & grn . . . 25 10
3594 – 1 l. 20 purple, grey and ochre . . . 45 15
3595 – 1 l. 55 blue, green & pur . . . 1·00 20
3596 – 1 l. 75 brown, bistre and orange . . . 1·40 50

DESIGNS—HORIZ: 40 b. Monastery Church, Moldovita; 55 b. Mon. Church, Cozia; 1 l. 20, Tower and Church, Tirgoviste; 1 l. 55, Palace of Culture, Jassy; 1 l. 75, Corvinus Castle, Hunedoara.

652 Old Bucharest (18th-cent painting) (Illustration reduced. Actual size 76×28 mm)

1968. Stamp Day.

3597 **652** 55 b. + 45 b. multicoloured . . . 1·40 70

653 Mute Swan — **655** Neamtz Costume (female)

654 "Entry of Michael the Brave into Alba Julia" (E. Stoica)

1968. Fauna of Nature Reservations. Multicoloured.

3598 10 b. Type **653** . . . 60 10
3599 20 b. Black-winged stilt . . . 70 10
3600 40 b. Common shelduck . . . 85 10
3601 55 b. Great egret . . . 1·00 30
3602 60 b. Golden eagle . . . 1·25 15
3603 1 l. 20 Great bustard . . . 1·50 30
3604 1 l. 35 Chamois . . . 80 25
3605 1 l. 60 European bison . . . 1·00 1·40

1968. 50th Anniv of Union of Transylvania with Rumania. Multicoloured.

3606 55 b. Type **654** . . . 25 10
3607 1 l. "Union Dance" (T. Aman) . . . 40 10
3608 1 l. 75 "Alba Julia Assembly" . . . 1·00 30

1968. Provincial Costumes (1st series). Multicoloured.

3610 5 b. Type **655** . . . 10 10
3611 40 b. Neamtz (male) . . . 20 10
3612 55 b. Hunedoara (female) . . . 30 10
3613 1 l. Hunedoara (male) . . . 50 10
3614 1 l. 60 Brasov (female) . . . 80 20
3615 2 l. 40 Brasov (male) . . . 1·25 1·00

See also Nos. 3617/22.

656 Earth, Moon and Orbital Track of "Apollo 8" — **657** Fencing

1969. Air. Flight of "Apollo 8" around the Moon.

3616 **656** 3 l. 30 black, sil & bl . . . 2.75 2.75

1969. Provincial Costumes (2nd series). As T **655**. Multicoloured.

3617 5 b. Doli (female) . . . 10 10
3618 40 b. Doli (male) . . . 20 10
3619 55 b. Arges (female) . . . 30 10
3620 1 l. Arges (male) . . . 50 20
3621 1 l. 60 Timisoara (female) . . . 80 25
3622 2 l. 40 Timisoara (male) . . . 1·25 1·00

1969. Sports.

3623 **657** 10 b. grey, black & brn . . . 10 10
3624 – 20 b. grey, black & vio . . . 10 10
3625 – 40 b. grey, black & blue . . . 10 10
3626 – 55 b. grey, black & red . . . 20 10
3627 – 1 l. grey, black & green . . . 30 10
3628 – 1 l. 20 grey, black & bl . . . 35 10
3629 – 1 l. 60 grey, black & red . . . 1·40 20
3630 – 2 l. 40 grey, black & grn . . . 1·00 50

DESIGNS: 20 b. Throwing the javelin; 40 b. Canoeing; 55 b. Boxing; 1 l. Volleyball; 1 l. 20, Swimming; 1 l. 60, Wrestling; 2 l. 40, Football.

1969. Nude Paintings in the National Gallery. As T **638**. Multicoloured.

3631 10 b. "Nude" (C. Tattarescu) . . . 10 10
3632 20 b. "Nude" (T. Pallady) . . . 10 10
3633 35 b. "Nude" (N. Tonitza) . . . 15 10
3634 60 b. "Venus and Cupid" (Flemish School) . . . 40 10
3635 1 l. 75 "Diana and Endymion" (M. Liberi) . . . 1·60 65
3636 3 l. "The Three Graces" (J. H. von Achen) . . . 3·25 1·60

SIZES—36×49 mm: 10 b., 35 b., 60 b., 1 l. 75. 27×49 mm: 3 l. 49×36 mm: 20 b.

658 "Soyuz 4" and "Soyuz 5" — **659** I.L.O. Emblem

1969. Air. Space Link-up of "Soyuz 4" and "Soyuz 5".

3638 **658** 3 l. 30 multicoloured . . . 2·75 2·75

1969. 50th Anniv of International Labour Office.

3639 **659** 55 b. multicoloured . . . 65 15

660 Stylised Head — **662** Referee introducing Boxers

661 Posthorn

1969. Inter-European Cultural Economic Co-operation.

3640 **660** 55 b. multicoloured . . . 65 65
3641 1 l. 50 multicoloured . . . 1·40 1·40

1969. Postal Ministers' Conference, Bucharest.

3642 **661** 55 b. dp blue and blue . . . 35 15

1969. European Boxing Championships, Bucharest. Multicoloured.

3643 35 b. Type **662** . . . 15 10
3644 40 b. Sparring . . . 20 10
3645 55 b. Leading with punch . . . 30 10
3646 1 l. 75 Declaring the winner . . . 1·40 50

663 "Apollo 9" and Module over Earth

1969. Air. "Apollo" Moon Flights. Multicoloured.

3647 60 b. Type **663** . . . 15 10
3648 2 l. 40 "Apollo 10" and module approaching Moon (vert) . . . 1·40 15

664 "Apatura ilia" — **665** Astronaut and Module on Moon

1969. Butterflies. Multicoloured.

3649 5 b. Type **664** . . . 10 10
3650 10 b. "Prosperpinus prosperina" . . . 10 10
3651 20 b. "Colias erate" . . . 15 10
3652 40 b. "Pericallia matronula" . . . 20 10
3653 55 b. "Argynnis laodice" . . . 30 10
3654 1 l. "Callimorpha quadripunctaria" . . . 65 10
3655 1 l. 20 "Anthocaris cardamines" . . . 85 20
3656 2 l. 40 "Meleageria daphnis" . . . 1·75 1·00

1969. Air. First Man on the Moon.

3657 **665** 3 l. 30 multicoloured . . . 2·00 2·00

1969. Paintings in the National Gallery, Bucharest. Multicoloured. As T **638**.

3658 10 b. "Venetian Senator" (School of Tintoretto) . . . 10 10
3659 20 b. "Sofia Kretzulescu" (G. Tattarescu) . . . 10 10
3660 35 b. "Philip IV" (Velasquez) . . . 20 10
3661 35 b. "Man Reading" (Memling) . . . 40 10
3662 1 l. 75 "Lady D'Aguesseau" (Vigee-Lebrun) . . . 1·00 20
3663 3 l. "Portrait of a Woman" (Rembrandt) . . . 2·40 1·40

666 Communist Flag — **667** Symbols of Learning

1969. 10th Rumanian Communist Party Congress.

3665 **666** 55 b. multicoloured . . . 60 15

1969. National "Economic Achievements" Exhibition, Bucharest. Multicoloured.

3666 35 b. Type **667** . . . 10 10
3667 40 b. Symbols of Agriculture and Science . . . 15 10
3668 1 l. 75 Symbols of Industry . . . 1·00 15

668 Liberation Emblem — **669** Juggling on Trick-cycle

1969. 25th Anniv of Liberation. Multicoloured.

3669 10 b. Type **668** . . . 10 10
3670 55 b. Crane and trowel . . . 15 10
3671 60 b. Flags on scaffolding . . . 25 10

1969. Rumanian State Circus. Multicoloured.

3672 10 b. Type **669** . . . 10 10
3673 20 b. Clown . . . 10 10
3674 35 b. Trapeze artists . . . 25 10
3675 60 b. Equestrian act . . . 35 10
3676 1 l. 75 High-wire act . . . 65 10
3677 3 l. Performing tiger . . . 1·60 60

670 Forces' Memorial

1969. "Army Day" and 25th Anniv of People's Army.

3678 **670** 55 b. black, gold & red . . . 40 15

671 Trains of 1869 and 1969

1969. Centenary of Rumanian Railways.

3679 **671** 55 b. multicoloured . . . 60 15

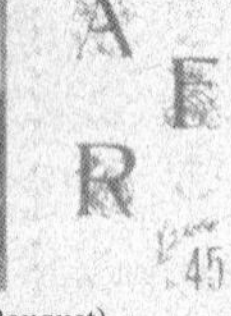

672 "Courtyard" (M. Bouquet) (2/3-size illustration)

1969. Stamp Day.

3680 **672** 55 b. + 45 b. multicoloured . . . 75 65

673 Branesti Mask — **674** "Apollo 12" above Moon

1969. Folklore Masks. Multicoloured.

3681 40 b. Type **673** . . . 15 10
3682 55 b. Tudora mask . . . 20 10
3683 1 l. 55 Birsesti mask . . . 50 10
3684 1 l. 75 Rudaria mask . . . 65 10

1969. Moon Landing of "Apollo 12".

3685 **674** 1 l. 50 multicoloured . . . 1·10 75

675 "Three Kings" (Voronet Monastery)

1969. Frescoes from Northern Moldavian Monasteries (1st series). Multicoloured.

3686 10 b. Type **675** 10 10
3687 20 b. "Three Kings" (Sucevita) 15 10
3688 35 b. "Holy Child in Manger" (Voronet) 20 10
3689 60 b. "Ship" (Sucevita) 35 10
3690 1 l. 75 "Walled City" (Moldovita) 1·25 20
3691 3 l. "Pastoral Scene" (Voronet) 2·40 1·40

The 60 b. and 3 l. are vert.
See also Nos. 3736/42 and 3872/8.

676 "Old Mother Goose", Capra

1969. New Year. Children's Celebrations. Multicoloured.

3692 40 b. Type **676** 15 10
3693 55 b. Decorated tree, Sorcova 20 10
3694 1 l. 50 Drummers, Buhaiul 75 10
3695 2 l. 40 Singer and bellringer, Plugusorul 1·00 45

677 Hockey players and Emblem
678 "Pulsatilla pratensis"

1970. World Ice Hockey Championships. Mult.

3696 20 b. Type **677** 10 10
3697 55 b. Goalkeeper 15 10
3698 1 l. 20 Two players 45 10
3699 2 l. 40 Goal mouth melee 1·00 40

1970. Flowers. Multicoloured.

3700 5 b. Type **678** 10 10
3701 10 b. "Adonis vernalis" 10 10
3702 20 b. "Carduus nutans" 10 10
3703 40 b. "Amygdalus nana" 10 10
3704 55 b. "Iris pumilla" 10 10
3705 1 l. "Linum hirsutum" 25 10
3706 1 l. 20 "Salvia aethiopis" 40 10
3707 2 l. 40 "Paeonia tenuifolia" 3·00 80

679 Japanese Woodcut
681 Lenin

680 B.A.C One Eleven 475

1970. World Fair, Osaka, Japan. Expo 70. Mult.

3714 20 b. Type **679** 20 10
3715 1 l. Japanese pagoda (29×92 mm) 1·00 65

1970. 50th Anniv of Rumanian Civil Aviation. Multicoloured.

3717 60 b. Type **680** 25 10
3718 2 l. Tail of B.A.C. One Eleven 475 75 25

1970. Birth Centenary of Lenin.

3719 **681** 40 b. multicoloured 40 10

682 "Camille" (Monet) and Maximum Card
683 "Prince Alexander Cuza" (Szathmary)

1970. Maximafila Franco-Rumanian Philatelic Exn, Bucharest.

3720 **682** 1 l. 50 multicoloured 1·40 30

1970. 150th Birth Anniv of Prince Alexander Cuza.

3721 **683** 55 b. multicoloured 55 15

684 "Co-operation" Map
685 Victory Monument, Bucharest

1970. Inter-European Cultural and Economic Co-operation.

3722 **684** 40 b. green, brn & blk 45 45
3723 – 1 l. 50 blue, brown & blk 1·40 1·40

1970. 25th Anniv of Liberation.

3724 **685** 55 b. multicoloured 65 15

686 Greek Silver Drachma. 5th cent B.C.

1970. Ancient Coins.

3725 **686** 10 b. black and blue 15 10
3726 – 20 b. black and red 20 10
3727 – 35 b. bronze and green 25 10
3728 – 60 b. black and brown 35 10
3729 – 1 l. 75 black and blue 85 10
3730 – 3 l. black and red 2·00 1·00

DESIGNS—HORIZ: 20 b. Getic-Dacian silver didrachm, 2nd–1st-cent B.C.; 35 b. Copper sestertius of Trajan, 106 A.D.; 60 b. Mircea ducat, 1400; 1 l. 75, Silver groschen of Stephen the Great, 1460. VERT: 3 l. Brasov klippe-thaler, 1601.

687 Footballers and Ball

1970. World Cup Football Championships, Mexico.

3731 **687** 40 b. multicoloured 15 10
3732 – 55 b. multicoloured 20 10
3733 – 1 l. 75 multicoloured 70 15
3734 – 3 l. 30 multicoloured 1·60 50

DESIGNS: Nos. 3732/4, various football scenes as Type **687**.

1970. Frescoes from Northern Moldavian Monasteries (2nd series). As T **675**. Multicoloured.

3736 10 b. "Prince Petru Rares and Family" (Moldovita) 10 10
3737 20 b. "Metropolitan Grigore Rosca" (Voronet) 15 10
3738 40 b. "Alexander the Good and Family" (Sucevita) 20 10
3739 55 b. "The Last Judgement" (Voronet) (vert) 35 10
3740 1 l. 75 "The Last Judgement" (Voronet) (different) 90 20
3741 3 l. "St. Anthony" (Voronet) 2·50 1·40

The 20 b. is smaller, 28×48 mm.

688 "Apollo 13" Spashdown
689 Engels

1970. Air. Space Flight of "Apollo 13".

3743 **688** 1 l. 50 multicoloured 65 65

1970. 150th Birth Anniv of Friedrich Engels.

3744 **689** 1 l. 50 multicoloured 1·00 15

690 Exhibition Hall

1970. National Events. Multicoloured.

3745 35 b. "Iron Gates" Dam 15 10
3746 55 b. Freighter and flag 45 10
3747 1 l. 50 Type **690** 85 15

EVENTS: 35 b. Danube navigation projects; 55 b. 75th anniv of Rumanian Merchant Marine; 1 l. 50, 1st International Fair, Bucharest.

691 New Headquarters Building

1970. New U.P.U. Headquarters Building, Berne.

3748 **691** 1 l. 50 green and blue 1·10 15

692 Education Year Emblem
693 "Iceberg"

1970. International Education Year.

3749 **692** 55 b. plum, black & red 65 15

1970. Roses. Multicoloured.

3750 20 b. Type **693** 10 10
3751 35 b. "Wiener Charme" 10 10
3752 55 b. "Pink Lustre" 20 10
3753 1 l. "Piccadilly" 60 10
3754 1 l. 50 "Orange Delbard" 75 10
3755 2 l. 40 "Sibelius" 1·50 55

694 "Spaniel and Pheasant" (J. B. Oudry)
695 Refugee Woman and Child

1970. Paintings in Rumanian Galleries. Multicoloured. Sizes in millimetres.

3756 10 b. "The Hunt" (D. Brandi) (38×50) 10 10
3757 20 b. Type **694** 10 10
3758 35 b. "The Hunt" (Jan Fyt) (38×50) 15 10
3759 60 b. "After the Chase" (Jordaens) (As T **694**) 40 10
3760 1 l. 75 "The Game Dealer" (F. Snyders) (50×38) 90 20
3761 3 l. "The Hunt" (A. de Gryeff) (As T **694**) 2·40 1·40

1970. Danube Flood Victims (1st issue).

3763 **695** 55 b. black, blue and green (postage) 25 10
3764 – 1 l. 50 multicoloured 60 15
3765 – 1 l. 75 multicoloured 90 65
3766 – 60 b. black, drab and blue (air) 50 10

DESIGNS: 60 b. Helicopter rescue; 1 l. 50, Red Cross post; 1 l. 75, Building reconstruction.
See also No. 3777.

696 U.N. Emblem
698 Beethoven

697 Arab Horse

1970. 25th Anniv of United Nations.

3767 **696** 1 l. 50 multicoloured 1·10 15

1970. Horses. Multicoloured.

3768 20 b. Type **697** 10 10
3769 35 b. American trotter 10 10
3770 55 b. Ghidran 15 10
3771 1 l. Hutul 50 10
3772 1 l. 50 Thoroughbred 75 15
3773 2 l. 40 Lippizaner 2·25 1·40

1970. Birth Bicentenary of Beethoven.

3774 **698** 55 b. multicoloured 1·25 15

699 "Mail-cart in the Snow" (E. Volkers) (½-size illustration)

1970. Stamp Day.

3775 **699** 55 b. + 45 b. mult 1·40 1·00

700 Henri Coanda's Turbine-powered Model Airplane

1970. Air. 60th Anniv of First Experimental Rocket-powered Flight.

3776 **700** 60 b. multicoloured 75 15

701 "The Flood" (abstract, Joan Miro)

1970. Danube Flood Victims (2nd issue).

3777 **701** 3 l. multicoloured 3·25 3·25

702 "Sight" (G. Coques)

1970. Paintings from the Bruckenthal Museum, Sibiu. Multicoloured.

3779 10 b. Type **702** 10 10
3780 20 b. "Hearing" 10 10
3781 35 b. "Smell" 15 10
3782 60 b. "Taste" 25 10
3783 1 l. 75 "Touch" 50 10
3784 3 l. Bruckenthal Museum 1·60 85

Nos. 3779/84 show a series of pictures by Coques entitled "The Five Senses".

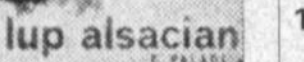

703 T. Vladimirescu (T. Aman) **705** Alsatian

704 "Three Races"

1971. 150th Death Anniv of Tudor Vladimirescu (Wallachian revolutionary).
3786 **703** 1 l. 50 multicoloured . . . 90 15

1971. Racial Equality Year.
3787 **704** 1 l. 50 multicoloured . . . 1·10 15

1971. Dogs. Multicoloured.
3788 20 b. Type **705** 10 10
3789 35 b. Bulldog 15 10
3790 55 b. Fox terrier 20 10
3791 1 l. Setter 50 10
3792 1 l. 50 Cocker spaniel 75 20
3793 2 l. 40 Poodle . . . . 3·25 1·60

706 "Luna 16" leaving Moon **707** Proclamation of the Commune

1971. Air. Moon Missions of "Luna 16" and "Luna 17". Multicoloured.
3794 3 l. 30 Type **706** . . . . . . 1·60 1·60
3795 3 l. 30 "Lunokhod 1" on Moon 1·60 1·60

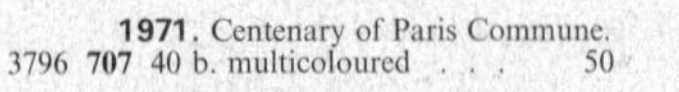

1971. Centenary of Paris Commune.
3796 **707** 40 b. multicoloured . . . 50 15

708 Astonaut and Moon Trolley

1971. Air. Moon Mission of "Apollo 14".
3797 **708** 3 l. 30 multicoloured . . . 1·60 1·60

709 "Three Fists" Emblem and Flags **710** "Toadstool" Rocks, Babele

1971. Trade Union Congress, Bucharest.
3798 **709** 55 b. multicoloured . . . 65 15

1971. Tourism. Multicoloured.
3799 10 b. Gorge, Cheile Bicazului (vert) 10 10
3800 40 b. Type **710** 10 10
3801 55 b. Winter resort, Poiana Brasov 15 10
3802 1 l. Holiday scene, Danube delta 45 10
3803 1 l. 50 Hotel, Baile Sovata . . 85 15
3804 2 l. 40 Venus, Jupiter and Neptune Hotels, Black Sea (77 × 29 mm) . . . . 1·25 85

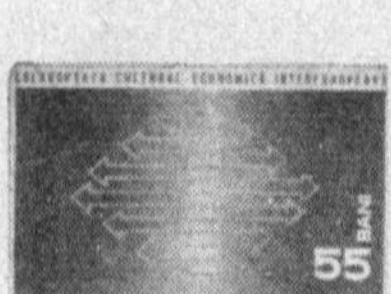

711 "Arrows" **712** Museum Building

1971. Inter-European Cultural Economic Co-operation. Multicoloured.
3805 55 b. Type **711** . . . . . . 1·50 1·50
3806 1 l. 75 Stylised map of Europe 2·75 2·40

1971. Historical Museum, Bucharest.
3807 **712** 55 b. multicoloured . . 40 10

713 "The Secret Printing-press" (S. Szonyi) **714** "Motra Tone" (K. Idromeno)

1971. 50th Anniv of Rumanian Communist Party. Multicoloured.
3808 35 b. Type **713** 10 10
3809 40 b. Emblem and red flags (horiz) 15 10
3810 55 b. "The Builders" (A. Anastasiu) 25 15

1971. "Balkanfila III". International Stamp Exhibition, Bucharest. Multicoloured.
3811 1 l. 20 + 60 b. Type **714** . . 1·25 1·25
3812 1 l. 20 + 60 b. "Maid" (V. Dimitrov-Maystora) . . . 1·25 1·25
3813 1 l. 20 + 60 b. "Rosa Botzaris" (J. Stieler) . . . . . 1·25 1·25
3814 1 l. 20 + 60 b. "Portrait of a Lady" (K. Ivanovic) . . . 1·25 1·25
3815 1 l. 20 + 60 b. "Agreseanca" (C. Popp de Szathmary) . . 1·25 1·25
3816 1 l. 20 + 60 b. "Woman in Modern Dress" (C. Ibrahim) 1·25 1·25
Each stamp has a premium carrying "tab" as shown in Type **714**.

715 "Punica granatum"

1971. Flowers. Multicoloured.
3818 20 b. Type **715** 10 10
3819 35 b. "Calceolus speciosum" . . 10 10
3820 55 b. "Life jagra" 10 10
3821 1 l. "Mimulus luteus" . . . 40 10
3822 1 l. 50 "Convolvulus tricolor" 60 20
3823 2 l. 40 "Phyllocactus phyllanthoides" (horiz) . . 1·75 20

716 "Nude" (J. Iser)

1971. Paintings of Nudes. Multicoloured.
3824 10 b. Type **716** 10 10
3825 20 b. "Nude" (C. Ressu) . . 10 10
3826 35 b. "Nude" (N. Grigorescu) 10 10
3827 60 b. "Odalisque" (Delacroix) (horiz) 10 10
3828 1 l. 75 "Nude in a Landscape" (Renoir) . . . . 1·00 20
3829 3 l. "Venus and Cupid" (Il Vecchio) (horiz) . . . . . 2·00 1·00
The 20 b. is smaller, 29 × 50 mm.

718 Astronauts and Lunar Rover on Moon

1971. Air. Moon Flight of "Apollo 15".
3833 **718** 1 l. 50 multicoloured (blue background) . . . . . 2·40 2·40
No. 3833 also exists imperforate, with background colour changed to green, from a restricted printing.

719 "Fishing Boats" (M. W. Arnold)

1971. Marine Paintings. Multicoloured.
3835 10 b. "Coastal Storm" (B. Peters) 10 10
3836 20 b. "Seascape" (I. Backhuysen) 10 10
3837 35 b. "Boat in Stormy Seas" (A. van de Eertvelt) 15 10
3838 60 b. Type **719** 25 10
3839 1 l. 75 "Seascape" (I. K. Aivazovsky) 65 20
3840 3 l. "Fishing boats, Braila" (J. A. Steriadi) . . . . . . 1·75 40

1971. As Nos. 3517/29 and three new designs but in smaller format, 17 × 23 or 23 × 17 mm.
3842 1 l. green 45 10
3843 1 l. 20 violet 40 10
3844 1 l. 35 blue 75 10
3845 1 l. 50 red 50 10
3846 1 l. 55 brown 50 10
3847 1 l. 75 green 55 10
3848 2 l. green 65 10
3849 2 l. 40 blue 75 10
3850 3 l. blue 95 10
3851 3 l. 20 brown . . . . 1·50 10
3852 3 l. 25 blue . . . . 1·50 10
3853 3 l. 60 blue . . . . 1·25 10
3854 4 l. mauve . . . . 1·50 10
3855 4 l. 80 blue . . . . 1·50 10
3856 5 l. violet . . . . 1·75 10
3857 6 l. mauve . . . . 1·90 10
NEW DESIGNS—VERT: 3 l. 60, Clearing letter box; 4 l. 80, Postman on round; 6 l. Postal Ministry, Bucharest.

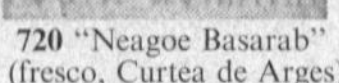

720 "Neagoe Basarab" (fresco, Curtea de Arges) **721** "T. Pallady" (self portrait)

1971. 450th Death Anniv of Prince Neagoe Basarab, Regent of Wallachia.
3858 **720** 60 b. multicoloured . . . 45 15

1971. Artists Anniversaries.
3859 **721** 40 b. multicoloured . . . 10 10
3860 – 55 b. black, stone & gold 15 10
3861 – 1 l. 50 black, stone & gold 40 10
3862 – 2 l. 40 multicoloured . . 1·10 25
DESIGNS: 40 b. (birth centenary); 55 b. "B. Cellini" (400th death anniv); 1 l. 50, "Watteau" (self-portrait) (250th death anniv); 2 l. 40, "Durer" (self-portrait) (500th birth anniv).

722 Persian Text and Seal **723** Figure Skating

1971. 2500th Anniv of Persian Empire.
3863 **722** 55 b. multicoloured . . . 50 10

1971. Winter Olympic Games, Sapporo, Japan (1972). Multicoloured.
3864 10 b. Type **723** 10 10
3865 20 b. Ice-hockey 10 10
3866 40 b. Biathlon 10 10
3867 55 b. Bobsleighing 10 10
3868 1 l. 75 Downhill skiing . . . 65 20
3869 3 l. Games emblem . . . . . 1·60 1·00

724 "Lady with Letter" (Sava Hentia)

1971. Stamp Day.
3871 **724** 1 l. 10 + 90 b. mult . . 1·50 1·00

1971. Frescoes from Northern Moldavian Monasteries (3rd series). As T **675**. Multicoloured.
3872 10 b. "St. George and The Dragon" (Moldovita) (vert) 10 10
3873 20 b. "Three Kings and Angel" (Moldovita) (vert) . . . 10 10
3874 40 b. "The Crucifixion" (Moldovita) (vert) 10 10
3875 55 b. "Trial" (Voronet) (vert) 15 10
3876 1 l. 75 "Death of a Martyr" (Voronet) (vert) . . . . 1·00 20
3877 3 l. "King and Court" (Arborea) . . . . 2·00 1·40

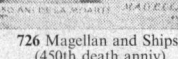

725 Matei Millo (dramatist, 75th death anniv) **726** Magellan and Ships (450th death anniv)

1971. Famous Rumanians. Multicoloured.
3879 55 b. Type **725** 20 10
3880 1 l. Nicolae Iorga (historian, birth cent) 35 15

1971. Scientific Anniversaries.
3881 **726** 40 b. mauve, blue & grn 40 10
3882 – 55 b. blue, green & lilac . 20 10
3883 – 1 l. multicoloured . . . 50 10
3884 – 1 l. 50 green, bl & brn . 65 20
DESIGNS AND ANNIVERSARIES: 55 b. Kepler and observatory (400th birth anniv); 1 l. Gagarin, rocket and Globe (10th anniv of first manned space flight); 1 l. 50, Lord Rutherford and atomic symbol (Birth cent).

727 Lynx Cubs

1972. Young Wild Animals. Multicoloured.

3885 20 b. Type **727** 10 10
3886 35 b. Red fox cubs 10 10
3887 55 b. Roe deer fawns 20 10
3888 1 l. Wild piglets 50 20
3889 1 l. 50 Wolf cubs 85 20
3890 2 l. 40 Brown bear cubs . . . 2·75 1·00

728 U.T.C. Emblem

730 Stylised Map of Europe

729 Wrestling

1972. 50th Anniv of Communist Youth Union (U.T.C.).

3891 **728** 55 b. multicoloured . . . 30 15

1972. Olympic Games, Munich (1st issue). Multicoloured.

3892 10 b. Type **729** 10 10
3893 20 b. Canoeing 10 10
3894 55 b. Football 15 10
3895 1 l. 55 High-jumping 45 10
3896 2 l. 90 Boxing . . . . 1·10 15
3897 6 l. 70 Volleyball . . . . . . 2·75 1·50

See also Nos. 3914/19 and 3926.

1972. Inter-European Cultural and Economic Co-operation.

3899 **730** 1 l. 75 gold, black & pur 1·40 1·40
3900 – 2 l. 90 gold, black & grn 2·50 2·00

DESIGN: 2 l. 90, "Crossed arrows" symbol.

731 Astronauts in Lunar Rover

732 Modern Trains and Symbols

1972. Air. Moon Flight of "Apollo 16".

3901 **731** 3 l. blue, green & pink . 2·00 2·00

1972. 50th Anniv of Int Railway Union.

3902 **732** 55 b. multicoloured . . . 70 15

734 "Paeonia romanica"

1972. Scarce Rumanian Flowers.

3904 **734** 20 b. multicoloured . . . 10 10
3905 – 40 b. purple, grn & brn . 15 10
3906 – 55 b. brown and blue . . 25 10
3907 – 60 b. red, green and light green 30 10
3908 – 1 l. 35 multicoloured . . 65 15
3909 – 2 l. 90 multicoloured . . 1·50 35

DESIGNS: 40 b. "Dianthus callizonus"; 55 b. "Leontopodium alpinum"; 60 b. "Nigritella rubra"; 1 l. 35, "Narcissus stellaris"; 2 l. 90, "Cypripedium calceolus".

735 Saligny Bridge, Cernavoda

1972. Danube Bridges. Multicoloured.

3910 1 l. 35 Type **735** 80 10
3911 1 l. 75 Giurgeni Bridge, Vadul Oii 85 20
3912 2 l. 75 Prieteniel Bridge, Giurgiu–Ruse . . . . . . 2·75 60

736 North Railway Station, Bucharest, 1872

1972. Cent of North Railway Station, Bucharest.

3913 **736** 55 b. multicoloured . . 70 15

737 Water-polo

1972. Olympic Games, Munich (2nd issue). Multicoloured.

3914 10 b. Type **737** 10 10
3915 20 b. Pistol-shooting 15 10
3916 55 b. Throwing the discus . 15 10
3917 1 l. 55 Gymnastics 45 10
3918 2 l. 75 Canoeing . . . . . . 1·40 15
3919 6 l. 40 Fencing . . . . . . 2·75 1·40

738 Rotary Stamp-printing Press

739 "E. Stoenescu" (S. Popescu)

1972. Centenary of State Stamp-printing Works.

3921 **738** 55 b. multicoloured . . 50 10

1972. Rumanian Art. Portraits and Self-portraits. Multicoloured.

3922 55 b. Type **739** 10 10
3923 1 l. 75 "O. Bancila" (self-portrait) 30 10
3924 2 l. 90 "Gh. Petrascu" (self-portrait) 60 10
3925 6 l. 50 "I. Andreescu" (self-portrait) . . . . 2·00 35

740 Runner with Torch

1972. Olympic Games, Munich (3rd issue). Olympic Flame.

3926 **740** 55 b. pur & blue on silver 1·00 45

741 Aurel Vlaicu and No. 1 "Crazy Fly"

1972. Air. Rumanian Aviation Pioneers. Mult.

3927 60 b. Type **741** 20 10
3928 3 l. Traian Vuja and Vuia No. 1 machine . . . . 1·25 45

MORE DETAILED LISTS

are given in the Stanley Gibbons Catalogues referred to in the country headings. For lists of current volumes see introduction

742 Cluj Cathedral

743 Satu Mare

1972.

3929 **742** 1 l. 85 violet (postage) . . 35 10
3930 – 2 l. 75 grey 45 10
3931 – 3 l. 35 red 55 10
3932 – 3 l. 45 green 65 10
3933 – 5 l. 15 blue 90 10
3934 – 5 l. 60 blue 95 10
3935 – 6 l. 20 mauve . . . . . 1·00 10
3936 – 6 l. 40 brown . . . . . 1·25 10
3937 – 6 l. 80 red . . . . . . 1·25 10
3938 – 7 l. 05 black . . . . . 1·10 10
3939 – 8 l. 45 red . . . . . . 1·50 10
3940 – 9 l. 05 green . . . . . 1·40 10
3941 – 9 l. 10 blue . . . . . . 1·40 15
3942 – 9 l. 85 green . . . . . 1·40 15
3943 – 10 l. brown . . . . . . 1·50 20
3944 – 11 l. 90 blue . . . . . 2·00 20
3945 – 12 l. 75 violet . . . . 1·90 25
3946 – 13 l. 30 red . . . . . 2·00 25
3947 – 16 l. 20 green . . . . 2·40 25
3948 – 14 l. 60 blue (air) . . . 3·50 25

DESIGNS—HORIZ: (As Type **742**): 2 l. 75, Sphinx Rock, Mt. Bucegi; 3 l. 45, Sinaia Castle; 5 l. 15, Hydro-electric power station, Arges; 6 l. 40, Hunidoara Castle; 6 l. 80, Bucharest Polytechnic complex; 9 l. 05, Coliseum, Sarmisegtetuza; 9 l. 10, Hydro-electric power station, Iron Gates. (29 × 21 mm). 11 l. 90, Palace of the Republic, Bucharest; 13 l. 30, City Gate, Alba Julia; 14 l. 60, Otopeni Airport, Bucharest. VERT: (As Type **742**): 3 l. 35, Heroes' Monument, Bucharest; 5 l. 60, Iasi-Biserica; 6 l. 20, Bran Castle; 7 l. 05, Black Church, Brasova; 8 l. 45, Atheneum, Bucharest; 9 l. 85, Decebal's statue, Cetatea Deva. (20 × 30 mm): 10 l. City Hall Tower, Sibiu; 12 l. 75, T.V. Building, Bucharest; 16 l. 20, Clock Tower, Sighisoara.

1972. Millenium of Satu Mare.

3949 **743** 55 b. multicoloured . . . 50 10

744 Davis Cup on Racquet

1972. Final of Davis Cup Championships 1972, Bucharest.

3950 **744** 2 l. 75 multicoloured . . 1·50 40

745 "Venice" (G. Petrascu)

1972. Paintings of Venice. Multicoloured.

3951 10 b. Type **745** 10 10
3952 20 b. "Marina" (Darascu) . . 10 10
3953 55 b. "Moliberi Palace" (Petrascu) 15 10
3954 1 l. 55 "Venice" (Bunescu) . . 45 10
3955 2 l. 75 "Venetian Palace" (Darascu) . . . . 1·10 15
3956 6 l. 40 "Venice" (Bunesca) (different) . . . . 2·75 1·40

746 Fencing and Bronze Medal

748 Flags and "25"

747 "Travelling Romanies" (E. Volkers) (⅔-size illustration)

1972. Munich Olympic Games, Medals.

3958 **746** 10 b. multicoloured . . . 10 10
3959 – 20 b. multicoloured . . . 15 10
3960 – 35 b. multicoloured . . . 20 10
3961 – 1 l. 45 grey, purple & pink 50 10
3962 – 2 l. 75 grey, brn & ochre 1·25 15
3963 – 6 l. 20 multicoloured . . 3·75 1·50

DESIGNS: 20 b. Handball and bronze medal; 35 b. Boxing and silver medal; 1 l. 45, Hurdling and silver medal; 2 l. 75, Pistol shooting, silver and bronze medals; 6 l. 20, Wrestling and two gold medals.

1972. Stamp Day.

3965 **747** 1 l. 10 + 90 b. mult . . 1·60 1·00

1972. 25th Anniv of Proclamation of Republic. Multicoloured.

3966 55 b. Type **748** 20 10
3967 1 l. 20 Arms and "25" . . . 30 10
3968 1 l. 75 Industrial scene and "25" 75 20

749 "Apollo 1, 2, 3"

750 European Bee Eater

1972. "Apollo" Moon Flights. Multicoloured.

3969 10 b. Type **749** 10 10
3970 35 b. Grissom, Chaffee and White 10 10
3971 40 b. "Apollo 4, 5, 6" . . . 15 10
3972 55 b. "Apollo 7, 8" 20 10
3973 1 l. "Apollo 9, 10" 30 10
3974 1 l. 20 "Apollo 11, 12" . . . 40 10
3975 1 l. 85 "Apollo 13, 14" . . . 50 15
3976 2 l. 75 "Apollo 15, 16" . . . 90 15
3977 3 l. 60 "Apollo 17" . . . . . 2·00 1·40

1973. Protection of Nature. Multicoloured. (a) Birds.

3979 1 l. 40 Type **750** . . . . . 1·25 15
3980 1 l. 85 Red breasted goose . 1·40 20
3981 2 l. 75 Peduline tit . . . . . 2·25 40

(b) Flowers.

3982 1 l. 40 Marsh marigold . . . 40 10
3983 1 l. 85 Martagon lily 50 15
3984 2 l. 75 Gentian 75 25

751 Copernicus

752 Suceava Costume (female)

1973. 500th Birth Anniv of Copernicus.

3985 **751** 2 l. 75 multicoloured . . 1·40 35

1973. Regional Costumes. Multicoloured.

3986 10 b. Type **752** 10 10
3987 40 b. Suceava (male) 10 10
3988 55 b. Harghila (female) . . . 15 10
3989 1 l. 75 Harghila (male) . . . 45 10
3990 2 l. 75 Gorj (female) 75 15
3991 6 l. 40 Gorj (male) . . . . . 1·50 1·00

753 D. Paciurea (sculptor)

754 Map of Europe

1973. Cultural Celebrities. Multicoloured.

3992 10 b. Type **753** 10 10
3993 40 b. I. Slavici (writer) . . . 10 10
3994 55 b. G. Lazar (writer) . . . 15 10
3995 6 l. 40 A. Flechtenmacher (composer) . . . . 2·00 1·00

1973. Inter-European Cultural and Economic Co-operation.
3996 **754** 3 l. 35 gold, blue & purple 1·40 1·40
3997 – 3 l. 60 gold and purple . 2·50 2·00
DESIGN: 3 l. 60, Symbol of collaboration.

756 Hand with Hammer and Sickle

757 W.M.O. Emblem and Weather Satellite

1973. Anniversaries. Multicoloured.
3999 40 b. Type **756** 30 10
4000 55 b. Flags and bayonets . . 40 10
4001 1 l. 75 Prince Cuza . . . . . 1·00 15
EVENTS: 40 b. 25th anniv of Rumanian Workers and Peasant Party; 55 b. 40th anniv of National Anti-Fascist Committee; 1 l. 75, Death cent of Prince Alexander Cuza.

1973. Centenary of I.M.O./W.M.O.
4002 **757** 2 l. multicoloured 90 20

758 "Dimitri Ralet" (anon)

759 Prince Dimitri Cantemir

1973. "Socfilex III" Stamp Exhibition, Bucharest. Portrait Paintings. Multicoloured.
4003 40 b. Type **758** 10 10
4004 60 b. "Enacheta Vacarescu" (A. Chladek) 15 10
4005 1 l. 55 "Dimitri Aman" (C. Lecca) 30 10
4006 4 l. + 2l. "Barbat at his Desk" (B. Iscovescu) . . . . . . 2·00 1·00

1973. 300th Birth Anniv of Dimitri Cantemir, Prince of Moldavia (writer). Multicoloured.
4008 **759** 1 l. 75 multicoloured . . 1·00 20

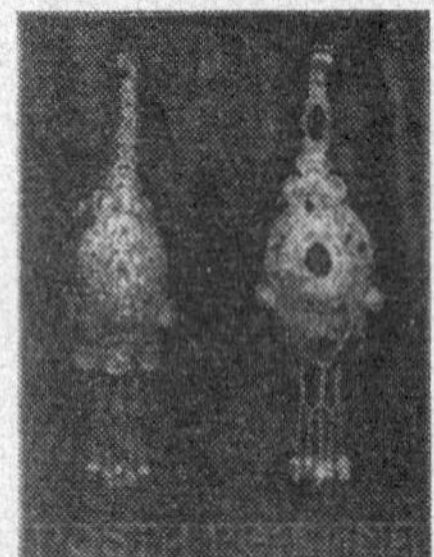
760 Fibular Brooches

1973. Treasures of Pietroasa. Multicoloured.
4010 10 b. Type **760** 10 10
4011 20 b. Golden figurine and bowl (horiz) 10 10
4012 55 b. Gold oil flask 15 10
4013 1 l. 55 Brooch and bracelets (horiz) 60 10
4014 2 l. 75 Gold platter 90 10
4015 6 l. 80 Filgree cup holder (horiz) 2·40 1·00

762 Oboga Jar
763 "Postilion" (A. Verona)

1973. Rumanian Ceramics. Multicoloured.
4018 10 b. Type **762** 10 10
4019 20 b. Vama dish and jug . . 10 10
4020 55 b. Maginea bowl 10 10
4021 1 l. 55 Sibiu Saschiz jug and dish 60 10
4022 2 l. 75 Pisc pot and dish . . 85 15
4023 6 l. 80 Oboga "bird" vessel . 2·10 45

1973. Stamp Day.
4024 **763** 1 l. 10 + 90 b. mult . . 1·10 1·10

764 "Textile Workers" (G. Saru)

765 Town Hall, Craiova

1973. Paintings showing Workers. Multicoloured.
4025 10 b. Type **764** 10 10
4026 20 b. "Construction Site" (M. Bunescu) (horiz) . . . 10 10
4027 55 b. "Shipyard Workers" (H. Catargi) (horiz) . . . 15 10
4028 1 l. 55 "Working Man" (H. Catargi) 40 10
4029 2 l. 75 "Miners" (A. Phoebus) 1·00 15
4030 6 l. 80 "The Spinner" (N. Grigorescu) . . . . . 2·00 85

1974. (a) Buidings.
4032 **765** 5 b. red 10 10
4033 – 10 b. blue 10 10
4034 – 20 b. orange 10 10
4035 – 35 b. green 10 10
4036 – 40 b. violet 10 10
4037 – 50 b. blue 10 10
4038 – 55 b. brown 10 10
4039 – 60 b. red 10 10
4040 – 1 l. blue 15 10
4041 – 1 l. 20 green 20 10

(b) Ships.
4042 – 1 l. 35 black 30 10
4043 – 1 l. 45 blue 30 10
4044 – 1 l. 50 red 30 10
4045 – 1 l. 55 blue 40 10
4046 – 1 l. 75 green 50 10
4047 – 2 l. 20 blue 55 10
4048 – 3 l. 65 lilac 80 10
4049 – 4 l. 70 purple . . . . . . 1·25 15
DESIGNS—VERT: 10 b. "Column of Infinity", Tirgu Jiu; 40 b. Romanesque church, Densus; 50 b. Reformed Church, Dej; 1 l. Curtea de Arges Monastery. HORIZ: 20 b. Heroes' Monument, Marasesti; 35 b. Citadel, Risnov; 55 b. Castle, Maldarasti; 60 b. National Theatre, Jassy; 1 l. 20, Fortress and church, Tirgu Mures; 1 l. 35, Danube Tug "Impingator"; 1 l. 45, Freighter "Dimbovita"; 1 l. 50, Danube passenger vessel "Muntenia"; 1 l. 55, Cadet barque "Mircea"; 1 l. 75, Liner "Transylvania"; 2 l. 20, Bulk carrier "Oltul"; 3 l. 65, Trawler "Mures"; 4 l. 70, Tanker "Arges".

767 "Boats at Honfleur" (Monet)

1974. Impressionist Paintings. Multicoloured.
4056 20 b. Type **767** 10 10
4057 40 b. "Moret Church" (Sisley) (vert) 10 10
4058 55 b. "Orchard in Blossom" (Pissarro) 15 10
4059 1 l. 75 "Jeanne" (Pissarro) (vert) 35 10
4060 2 l. 75 "Landscape" (Renoir) 60 15
4061 3 l. 60 "Portrait of a Girl" (Cezanne) (vert) . . . . . 1·60 35

768 Trotting with Sulky

769 Nicolas Titulescu (Rumanian League of Nations Delegate)

1974. Cent of Horse-racing in Rumania. Mult.
4063 40 b. Type **768** 10 10
4064 55 b. Three horses racing . . 15 10
4065 60 b. Horse galloping . . . 20 10
4066 1 l. 55 Two trotters racing . . 40 10
4067 2 l. 75 Three trotters racing . 75 10
4068 3 l. 45 Two horses racing . . 1·25 35

1974. Interparliamentary Congress Session, Bucharest.
4069 **769** 1 l. 75 multicoloured . . 50 20

771 "Anniversary Parade" (Pepene Cornelia)

1974. 25th Anniv of Young Pioneers Organization.
4071 **771** 55 b. multicoloured . . . 50 10

772 "Europe"

1974. Inter-European Cultural and Economic Co-operation. Multicoloured.
4072 2 l. 20 Type **772** . . . . . . 1·50 1·50
4073 3 l. 45 Satellite over Europe . 2·40 2·00

1974. Rumania's Victory in World Handball Championships. No. 3959 surch **ROMANIA CAMPIOANA MONDIALA 1974** and value.
4074 1 l. 75 on 20 b. multicoloured 3·25 2·25

774 Postal Motor Boat

1974. U.P.U. Centenary. Multicoloured.
4075 20 b. Type **774** 10 10
4076 40 b. Loading mail train . . . 40 10
4077 55 b. Loading Ilyushin Il-62M mail plane 10 10
4078 1 l. 75 Rural postman delivering letter 45 10
4079 2 l. 75 Town postman delivering letter 50 15
4080 3 l. 60 Young stamp collectors 90 25

775 Footballers

776 Anniversary Emblem

1974. World Cup Football Championships, West Germany.
4082 **775** 20 b. multicoloured . . . 10 10
4083 – 40 b. multicoloured . . . 10 10
4084 – 55 b. multicoloured . . . 10 10
4085 – 1 l. 75 multicoloured . . 30 10
4086 – 2 l. 75 multicoloured . . 65 15
4087 – 3 l. 60 multicoloured . . 90 20
DESIGNS: Nos. 4083/7, Football scenes similar to Type **775**.

1974. 25th Anniv of Council for Mutual Economic Aid.
4089 **776** 55 b. multicoloured . . . 45 15

777 U.N. and World Population Emblems
778 Emblem on Map of Europe

1974. World Population Year Conference, Bucharest.
4090 **777** 2 l. multicoloured 65 15

1974. "Euromax 1974" International Stamp Exhibition, Bucharest.
4091 **778** 4 l. + 3 l. yell, bl & red . 2·40 35

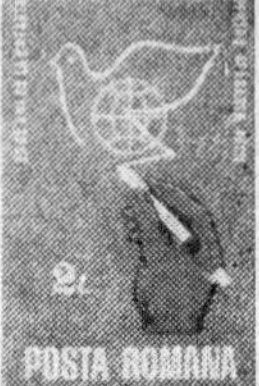

779 Hand drawing Peace Dove

780 Prince John of Wallachia (400th birth anniv)

1974. 25th Anniv of World Peace Movement.
4092 **779** 2 l. multicoloured . . . 50 10

1974. Anniversaries.
4093 **780** 20 b. blue 10 10
4094 – 55 b. red 10 10
4095 – 1 l. blue 25 10
4096 – 1 l. 10 brown 20 10
4097 – 1 l. 30 purple 35 10
4098 – 1 l. 40 violet 40 10
DESIGNS AND ANNIVERSARIES—VERT: 1 l. Iron and Steel Works, Hunedoara (220th anniv); 1 l. 10, Avram Iancu (150th anniv); 1 l. 30, Dr. C. I. Parhon (birth cent); 1 l. 40, Dosoftel (savant) (350th birth anniv). HORIZ: 55 b. Soldier and Installations (Rumanian Army Day. 30th anniv).

781 Rumanian and Soviet Flags as "XXX"

783 "Centaurea nervosa"

1974. 30th Anniv of Liberation. Multicoloured.
4099 40 b. Type **781** 15 10
4100 55 b. Citizens and flags (horiz) 15 10

1974. "Save Nature". Wild Flowers. Multicoloured.
4102 20 b. Type **783** 10 10
4103 40 b. "Fritillaria montana" . 10 10
4104 55 b. "Taxus baccata" . . . 20 10
4105 1 l. 75 "Rhododendron kotschyi" 40 10
4106 2 l. 75 "Eritrichium nanum" 55 20
4107 3 l. 60 "Dianthus spiculifolius" 85 25

784 Bust of Isis

1974. Rumanian Archaeological Finds. Sculpture. Multicoloured.
4108 20 b. Type **784** 10 10
4109 40 b. Glykon serpent 15 10
4110 55 b. Head of Emperor Decius 15 10
4111 1 l. 75 Rumanian Woman . 30 10
4112 2 l. 75 Mithras 50 15
4113 3 l. 60 Roman senator . . . 1·10 25

785 Sibiu Market Place

1974. Stamp Day.
4114 **785** 2 l. 10 + 1 l. 90 mult . . 1·50 35

1974. "Nationala 74" Stamp Exhibition. No. 4114 optd **EXPOZITIA FILATELICA "NATIONALA '74" 15-24 noiembrie Bucuresti**.
4115 **786** 2 l. 10 + 1 l. 90 mult . . 2·75 2·75

MINIMUM PRICE

The minimum price quoted is 10p which represents a handling charge rather than a basis for valuing common stamps. For further notes about prices, see introductory pages.

787 Party Emblem

1974. 11th Rumanian Communist Party Congress, Bucharest.

4116 **787** 55 b. multicoloured . . . 10 10
4117 – 1 l. multicoloured 15 10

DESIGN: 1 l. Similar to Type **787**, showing party emblem and curtain.

788 "The Discus-thrower" (Myron)

1974. 60th Anniv of Rumanian Olympic Committee.

4118 **788** 2 l. multicoloured . . . . 1·00 25

789 "Skylab" **790** Dr. Albert Schweitzer

1974. "Skylab" Space Laboratory.

4119 **789** 2 l. 50 multicoloured . . 1·25 1·10

1974. Birth Centenary of Dr. Albert Schweitzer.

4120 **790** 40 b. brown 25 10

791 Handball **793** Torch and Inscription

792 "Rocks and Birches"

1975. World Universities Handball Championships, Rumania.

4121 **791** 55 b. multicoloured . . . 15 10
4122 – 1 l. 75 multicoloured (vert) 30 10
4123 – 2 l. 20 multicoloured . . 55 20

DESIGNS: 1 l. 75, 2 l. 20, similar designs to Type **791**.

1975. Paintings by Ion Andreescu. Multicoloured.

4124 20 b. Type **792** 10 10
4125 40 b. "Peasant Woman with Green Kerchief" 10 10
4126 55 b. "Winter in the Forest" 15 10
4127 1 l. 75 "Winter in Barbizon" (horiz) 35 10
4128 2 l. 75 Self-portrait 60 20
4129 3 l. 50 "Main Road" (horiz) . 1·40 35

1975. 10th Anniv of Socialist Republic.

4130 **793** 40 b. multicoloured . . . 25 10

794 "Battle of the High Bridge" (O. Obedeanu)

1975. 500th Anniv of Victory over the Ottomans at High Bridge.

4131 **794** 55 b. multicoloured . . 40 10

795 "Peasant Woman Spinning" (N. Grigorescu) **796** "Self-portrait"

1975. International Women's Year.

4132 **795** 55 b. multicoloured . . 30 10

1975. 500th Birth Anniv of Michelangelo.

4133 **796** 5 l. multicoloured . . . 1·60 25

798 Mitsui Children's Science Pavilion, Okinawa

1975. International Exposition, Okinawa.

4135 **798** 4 l. multicoloured . . . 1·50 30

799 "Peonies" (N. Tonitza)

1975. Inter-European Cultural and Economic Co-operation. Multicoloured.

4136 2 l. 20 Type **799** . . . . . . 1·50 1·50
4137 3 l. 45 "Chrysanthemums" (St. Luchian) . . . . 2·00 2·00

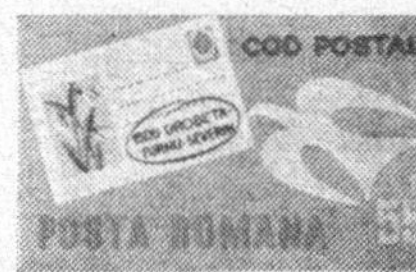

800 Dove with Coded Letter

1975. Introduction of Postal Coding.

4138 **800** 55 b. multicoloured . . 30 10

801 Convention Emblem on "Globe"

1975. Centenary of International Metre Convention.

4139 **801** 1 l. 85 multicoloured . . 85 20

802 Mihail Eminescu and Museum

1975. 125th Birth Anniv of Mihail Eminescu (poet).

4110 **802** 55 b. multicoloured . . 30 10

803 Roman Coins and Stone Inscription **805** Ana Ipatescu

1975. Bimillenary of Alba Julia.

4141 **803** 55 b. multicoloured . . . 30 10

1975. Death Centenary of Ana Ipatescu (revolutionary).

4143 **805** 55 b. mauve 30 10

806 Turnu-Severin

1975. European Architectural Heritage Year. Roman Antiquities.

4144 – 55 b. black and brown . . 10 10
4145 – 1 l. 20 black, light blue and blue 25 15
4146 – 1 l. 55 black and green . 50 15
4147 – 1 l. 75 black and red . . 60 20
4148 **806** 2 l. black and ochre . . . 70 25
4149 – 2 l. 25 black and blue . . 90 55

DESIGNS—VERT: 55 b. Emperor Trajan; 1 l. 20, Trajan's Column, Rome; 1 l. 55, Decebalus (sculpture); 10 l. Roman remains, Gradiste. HORIZ: 1 l. 75, Imperial monument, Adam Clissi; 2 l. 25, Trajan's Bridge.

807 "Apollo" and "Soyuz" Spacecraft

1975. Air. "Apollo-Soyuz" Space Link. Mult.

4151 1 l. 75 Type **807** . . . . . . 1·40 1·40
4152 3 l. 25 "Apollo" and "Soyuz" linked together . . . . . . 1·60 1·60

808 "Michael the Brave" (A. Sadeler)

1975. 375th Anniv of First Political Union of Rumanian States. Multicoloured.

4153 55 b. Type **808** 10 10
4154 1 l. 20 "Ottoman Envoys bringing gifts to Michael the Brave" (T. Aman) (horiz) . 25 10
4155 2 l. 75 "Michael the Brave at Calugareni" (T. Aman) . . 55 20

810 "Delphinium consolida" **812** Policeman using Walkie–talkie

1975. Flowers. Multicoloured.

4157 20 b. Type **810** 10 10
4158 40 b. "Papaver dubium" . . . 10 10
4159 55 b. "Xeranthemum annuum" 15 10
4160 1 l. 75 "Helianthemum nummularium" 35 10
4161 2 l. 75 "Salvia pratensis" . . 65 15
4162 3 l. 60 "Cichorium intybus" . 85 25

1975. International Philatelic Fair, Riccione (Italy). Optd **Tîrg international de mârci postale Riccione — Italia 23-25 August 1975.**

4163 **796** 5 l. multicoloured . . . . 5·00 5·00

1975. Road Safety.

4164 **812** 55 b. blue 40 10

813 Text on Map of Pelendava

1975. 1750th Anniv of First Documentary Attestations of Daco-Getian Settlements of Pelendava and 500th Anniv of Craiova. Multicoloured.

4165 20 b. Type **813** 10 10
4166 55 b. Map showing location of Pelendava and Craiova (horiz) 15 10
4167 1 l. Text on map of Pelendava 25 10

814 Muntenia Carpet

1975. Rumanian Carpets. Multicoloured.

4168 20 b. Type **814** 10 10
4169 40 b. Banat 10 10
4170 55 b. Oltenia 15 10
4171 1 l. 75 Moldova 50 10
4172 2 l. 75 Oltenia (different) . . 65 20
4173 3 l. 60 Maramures 80 30

815 T.V. "12M" Minibus

1975. Rumanian Motor Vehicles. Multicoloured.

4174 20 b. Type **815** 10 10
4175 40 b. L.K.W. "19 A.L.P." Oil tanker 15 10
4176 55 b. A.R.O. "240" Field car 15 10
4177 1 l. 75 L.K.W. "R 8135 F" Truck 50 10
4178 2 l. 75 P.K.W. "Dacia 1300" Saloon car 65 20
4179 3 l. 60 L.K.W. "R 19215 D.F.K." Tipper truck . . 85 35

816 Postal Transit Centre, Bucharest

1975. Stamp Day. Multicoloured.

4180 1 l. 50 + 1 l. 50 Type **816** . 1·40 60
4181 2 l. 10 + 1 l. 90 Aerial view of P.T.C. . . . . 2·40 85

818 Toboganning

1976. Winter Olympics Games, Innsbruck. Multicoloured.

4183 20 b. Type **818** 10 10
4184 40 b. Rifle-shooting (biathlon) (vert) 15 10
4185 55 b. Downhill skiing (slalom) 25 10
4186 1 l. 75 Ski-jumping 45 20
4187 2 l. 75 Figure-skating (women's) 70 30
4188 3 l. 60 Ice-hockey . . . . . 1·25 60

819 "Washington at Valley Forge" (W. Trego)

1976. Bicent of American Revolution. Mult.

4190 20 b. Type **819** 10 10
4191 40 b. "Washington at Trenton" (Trumbull) (vert) 10 10
4192 55 b. "Washington crossing the Delaware" (Leutze) 25 10
4193 1 l. 75 "Capture of the Hessians" (Trumbull) . . . 55 20
4194 2 l. 75 "Jefferson" (Sully) (vert) 85 25
4195 3 l. 60 "Surrender of Cornwallis at Yorktown" (Trumbull) 1·25 40

820 "Prayer"

1976. Birth Centenary of C. Brancusi (sculptor). Multicoloured.

4197 55 b. Type **820** 15 10
4198 1 l. 75 Architectural Assembly, Tg. Jiu 35 15
4199 3 l. 60 C. Brancusi 90 35

821 Anton Davidoglu (mathematician) (birth cent) **823** Dr. Carol Davila

822 Inscribed Tablets, Tibiscum (Banat)

1976. Anniversaries. Multicoloured.

4200 40 b. Type **821** 10 10
4201 55 b. Prince Vlad Tepes (500th death anniv) 15 10
4202 1 l. 20 Costache Negri (patriot-death centenary) 25 10
4203 1 l. 75 Gallery, Archives Museum (50th anniv) . . . 30 20

1976. Daco-Roman Archaeological Finds. Mult.

4204 20 b. Type **822** 10 10
4205 40 b. Roman sculptures . . . 15 10
4206 55 b. Dacian coins and pottery 25 10
4207 1 l. 75 Dacian pottery 50 10
4208 2 l. 75 Roman altar and spears 65 15
4209 3 l. 60 Vase and spears . . . 95 35

1976. Centenary of Rumanian Red Cross. Mult.

4211 55 b. Type **823** (postage) . . 10 10
4212 1 l. 75 Nurse and patient . . 30 10
4213 2 l. 20 First aid 40 10
4214 3 l. 35 Blood donors (air) . . 75 25

824 King Decebalus Vase **825** Rumanian Arms

1976. Inter-European Cultural and Economic Collaboration. Multicoloured.

4215 2 l. 20 Type **824** 65 75
4216 3 l. 45 Vase with portrait of King Michael the Brave . . 2·00 2·00

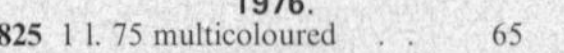

1976.

4217 **825** 1 l. 75 multicoloured . . 65 10

826 De Havilland D.H.9C

1976. 50th Anniv of TAROM (State airline).

4218 20 b. Type **826** 10 10
4219 40 b. I.C.A.R. Comercial . . 20 10
4220 60 b. Douglas DC-3 . . . . 30 10
4221 1 l. 75 Antonov An-24 . . . 70 10
4222 2 l. 75 Ilyushin Il-62 . . . . 90 15
4223 3 l. 60 Boeing 707 . . . . . 1·40 45

827 Gymnastics **828** Spiru Haret

1976. Olympic Games, Montreal. Multicoloured.

4224 20 b. Type **827** 10 10
4225 40 b. Boxing 15 10
4226 55 b. Handball 30 10
4227 1 l. 75 Rowing (horiz) . . . 45 15
4228 2 l. 75 Gymnastics (different) (horiz) 70 20
4229 3 l. 60 Canoeing (horiz) . . 1·25 30

1976. 125th Birth Anniv of Spiru Haret (mathematician).

4231 **828** 20 b. brown, orge & blue 25 10

829 Daco-Getian Sculpture on Map of Buzau

1976. 1600th Anniv of Buzau State.

4232 **829** 55 b. multicoloured . . 30 10

1976. Philatelic Exhibition, Bucharest. No. 4199 surch **+1.80 EXPOZITIA FILATELICA BUCURESTI. 12-19 IX 1976.**

4233 3 l. 60 + 1 l. 80 multicoloured 8·25 8·25

831 Red Deer

1976. Endangered Animals. Multicoloured.

4234 20 b. Type **831** 10 10
4235 40 b. Brown bear 20 10
4236 55 b. Chamois 35 10
4237 1 l. 75 Wild boar 50 10
4238 2 l. 75 Red fox 95 25
4239 3 l. 60 Lynx . . . . 1·25 35

832 Cathedral, Milan

1976. "Italia '76" International Philatelic Exhibition, Milan.

4240 **832** 4 l. 75 multicoloured . . 1·50 35

833 D. Grecu (gymnast) and Bronze Medal

1976. Olympic Games, Montreal. Rumanian Medal Winners. Multicoloured.

4241 20 b. Type **833** 10 10
4242 40 b. Fencing (Bronze Medal) 15 10
4243 55 b. Javelin (Bronze Medal) . 20 10
4244 1 l. 75 Handball (Silver Medal) 35 10
4245 2 l. 75 Boxing (Silver and Bronze Medals) (horiz) . . 60 20
4246 3 l. 60 Wrestling (Silver and Bronze Medals) (horiz) . . 1·10 30
4247 5 l. 70 Nadia Comaneci (gymnastics – 3 Gold, 1 Silver and 1 Bronze Medals) (27×42 mm) . . . . 3·25 1·50

834 "Carnations and Oranges"

1976. Floral Paintings by Stefan Luchian. Multicoloured.

4249 20 b. Type **834** 10 10
4250 40 b. "Flower Arrangement" . 10 10
4251 55 b. "Immortelles" 10 10
4252 1 l. 75 "Roses in Vase" . . . 35 15
4253 2 l. 75 "Cornflowers" 45 15
4254 3 l. 60 "Carnations in Vase" . 90 35

835 "Elena Cuza" (T. Aman) **836** Arms of Alba

1976. Stamp Day.

4255 **835** 2 l. 10 + 1 l. 90 mult . . 1·90 1·50

1976. Rumanian Districts' Coats of Arms (1st series). Multicoloured.

4256 55 b. Type **836** 15 10
4257 55 b. Arad 15 10
4258 55 b. Arges 15 10
4259 55 b. Bacau 15 10
4260 55 b. Bihor 15 10
4261 55 b. Bistrita Nasaud 15 10
4262 55 b. Botosani 15 10
4263 55 b. Brasov 15 10
4264 55 b. Braila 15 10
4265 55 b. Buzau 15 10
4266 55 b. Caras-Severin 15 10
4267 55 b. Cluj 15 10
4268 55 b. Constanta 15 10
4269 55 b. Covasna 15 10
4270 55 b. Dimbovita 15 10

See also Nos. 4307/31, 4496/520 and 4542/63.

837 "Ox Cart"

1977. Paintings by Nicola Grigorescu. Multicoloured.

4271 55 b. Type **837** 15 10
4272 1 l. "Self-portrait" (vert) . . . 20 10
4273 1 l. 50 "Shepherdess" 30 10
4274 2 l. 15 "Girl with Distaff" . . 40 15
4275 3 l. 40 "Shepherd" (vert) . . 50 25
4276 4 l. 80 "Halt at the Well" . . 1·00 40

838 Telecommunications Station, Cheia

1977.

4277 **838** 55 b. multicoloured . . . 20 10

839 I.C.A.R.1

1977. Air. Rumanian Gliders. Multicoloured.

4278 20 b. Type **839** 10 10
4279 40 b. IS-3d 15 10
4280 55 b. RG-5 . . . . 20 10
4281 1 l. 50 IS-11 . . . . 40 10
4282 3 l. IS-29D 65 15
4283 3 l. 40 IS-28B . . . . 1·10 40

840 Red Deer

1977. Protected Animals. Multicoloured.

4284 55 b. Type **840** 20 10
4285 1 l. 50 Mute swan 60 15
4286 1 l. 50 Egyptian vulture . . . 90 25
4287 2 l. 15 European bison . . . 1·10 10
4288 3 l. 40 White-headed duck . 1·75 35
4289 4 l. 80 Common kingfisher . 2·00 50

841 "The Infantryman" (O. Obedeanu)

1977. Cent of Independence. Paintings. Mult.

4290 55 b. Type **841** 15 10
4291 1 l. "Artillery Battery at Calafat" (S. Hentia) (horiz) 20 10
4292 1 l. 50 "Soldiers Attacking" (S. Luchian) 30 10
4293 2 l. 15 "Battle of Plevna" (N. Grigorescu) (horiz) . . 45 10
4294 3 l. 40 "The Artillerymen" (N. Grigorescu) (horiz) . . 65 20
4295 4 l. 80 + 2l. "Battle of Rahova" (horiz) . . . . 1·75 65

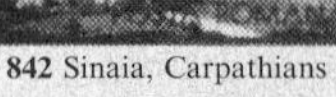

842 Sinaia, Carpathians **843** Petro Rares (monarch) (450th birth anniv)

1977. Inter-European Cultural and Economic Co-operation. Multicoloured.

4297 2 l. Type **842** 50 50
4298 2 l. 40 Auroa, Black Sea . . 65 65

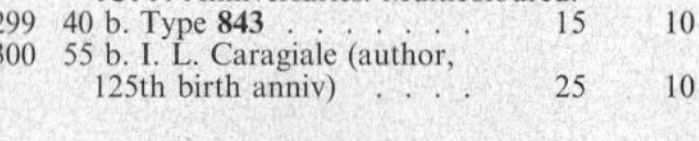

1977. Anniversaries. Multicoloured.

4299 40 b. Type **843** 15 10
4300 55 b. I. L. Caragiale (author, 125th birth anniv) 25 10

844 Nurse with Children and Emblems

1977. 23rd Int Red Cross Conference, Bucharest.

4301 **844** 1 l. 50 multicoloured . . 40 15

845 Triumphal Arch, Bucharest

1977. 60th Anniv of Battles of Marasti, Marasesti and Oituz.

4302 **845** 2 l. 15 multicoloured . . 70 30

847 Postwoman and Letters

1977. Air.

4304 20 l. Type **847** . . . . 5·00 1·40
4305 30 l. Douglas DC-10 airliner and mail . . . . 7·50 2·00

848 Mount Titano Castle, San Marino

1977. Centenary of San Marino Postage Stamps.

4306 **848** 4 l. multicoloured . . . . 1·40 25

1977. Rumanian District Coats of Arms (2nd series). As T **836**. Multicoloured.

4307 55 b. Dolj 15 10
4308 55 b. Galati 15 10
4309 55 b. Gorj 15 10
4310 55 b. Harghita 15 10
4311 55 b. Hunedoara 15 10
4312 55 b. Ialomita 15 10
4313 55 b. Iasi 15 10
4314 55 b. Ilfov 15 10
4315 55 b. Maramures 15 10
4316 55 b. Mehedinti 15 10
4317 55 b. Mures 15 10
4318 55 b. Neamt 15 10
4319 55 b. Olt 15 10
4320 55 b. Prahova 15 10
4321 55 b. Salaj 15 10
4322 55 b. Satu Mare 15 10
4323 55 b. Sibiu 15 10
4324 55 b. Suceava 15 10
4325 55 b. Teleorman 15 10
4326 55 b. Timis 15 10
4327 55 b. Tulcea 15 10
4328 55 b. Vaslui 15 10
4329 55 b. Vilcea 15 10
4330 55 b. Vrancea 15 10
4331 55 b. Rumanian postal emblem 15 10

849 Gymnast on Vaulting Horse

850 Dispatch Rider and Army Officer

1977. Gymnastics. Multicoloured.

4332 20 b. Type **849** 10 10
4333 40 b. Floor exercise 10 10
4334 55 b. Gymnast on parallel bars 15 10
4335 1 l. Somersault on bar . . . 25 10
4336 2 l. 15 Gymnast on rings . . 40 15
4337 4 l. 80 Gymnastic exercise . . 1·60 55

1977. Stamp Day.

4338 **850** 2 l. 10 + 1 l. 90 mult . . 1·40 1·25

MORE DETAILED LISTS

are given in the Stanley Gibbons Catalogues referred to in the country headings. For lists of current volumes see introduction

851 Two Dancers with Sticks

1977. Calusarii Folk Dance. Multicoloured.

4339 20 b. Type **851** 10 10
4340 40 b. Leaping dancer with stick 10 10
4341 55 b. Two dancers 20 10
4342 1 l. Dancer with stick . . . 30 10
4343 2 l. 15 Leaping dancers . . . 50 15
4344 4 l. 80 Leaping dancer . . . 1·60 1·10

852 "Carpati" at Cazane

1977. European Navigation on the Danube. Multicoloured.

4346 55 b. Type **852** 30 10
4347 1 l. Passenger vessel "Mircesti" near Orsova 40 10
4348 1 l. 50 Passenger vessel "Oltenita" near Calafat . 60 15
4349 2 l. 15 Hydrofoil at Giurgiu port 65 25
4350 3 l. Passenger vessel "Herculani" at Tulcea . . 80 30
4351 3 l. 40 Passenger vessel "Muntenia" at Sulina . . 95 35
4352 4 l. 80 Map of Danube delta 2·25 80

853 Arms and Flag of Rumania

1977. 30th Anniv of Rumanian Republic. Multicoloured.

4354 55 b. Type **853** 10 10
4355 1 l. 20 Rumanian-built computers 20 10
4356 1 l. 75 National Theatre, Craiova 35 20

854 Firiza Dam

1978. Rumanian Dams and Hydro-electric Installations. Multicoloured.

4357 20 b. Type **854** 10 10
4358 40 b. Negovanu dam 15 10
4359 55 b. Piatra Neamt power station 25 10
4360 1 l. Izvorul Montelui Bicaz dam 30 10
4361 2 l. 15 Vidraru dam 45 15
4362 4 l. 80 Danube barrage and navigation system, Iron Gates 90 40

855 LZ-1 over Lake Constance

1978. Air. Airships. Multicoloured.

4363 60 b. Type **855** 15 10
4364 1 l. Santos Dumont's "Ballon No. 6" over Paris 25 10
4365 1 l. 50 Beardmore R-34 over Manhattan Island 35 10
4366 2 l. 15 N.4 "Italia" at North Pole 50 10
4367 3 l. 40 "Graf Zeppelin" over Brasov 70 15
4368 4 l. 80 "Graf Zeppelin" over Sibiu . . . . 1·40 45

856 Footballers and Emblem

1978. World Cup Football Championship, Argentina.

4370 **856** 55 b. blue 10 10
4371 – 1 l. orange 15 10
4372 – 1 l. 50 yellow 25 10
4373 – 2 l. 15 red 40 10
4374 – 3 l. 40 green 65 15
4375 – 4 l. 80 mauve . . . . . . 1·40 25

DESIGNS: Nos. 4371/5, Footballers and emblem, similar to Type **856**.

857 King Decebalus of Dacia

858 Worker and Factory

1978. Inter-European Cultural and Economic Co-operation. Multicoloured.

4377 1 l. 30 Type **857** 65 75
4378 3 l. 40 Prince Mircea the Elder 2·75 2·75

1978. 30th Anniv of Nationalization of Industry.

4379 **858** 55 b. multicoloured . . . 20 10

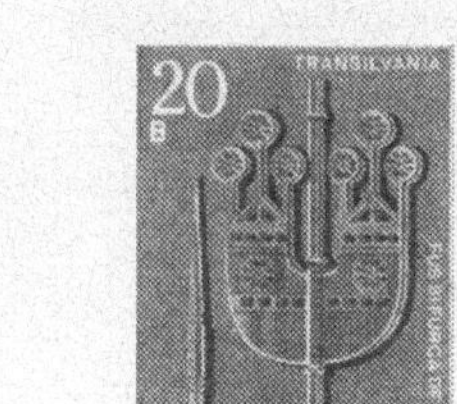

859 Spindle and Fork Handle, Transylvania

1978. Wood-carving. Multicoloured.

4380 20 b. Type **859** 10 10
4381 40 b. Cheese mould, Muntenia 15 10
4382 55 b. Spoons, Oltenia 20 10
4383 1 l. Barrel, Moldavia 25 10
4384 2 l. 15 Ladle and mug, Transylvania 40 10
4385 4 l. 80 Water bucket, Oltenia . 80 35

860 Danube Delta

1978. Tourism. Multicoloured.

4386 55 b. Type **860** . . . . . . 1·00 15
4387 1 l. Bran Castle (vert) 20 10
4388 1 l. 50 Moldavian village . . 25 10
4389 2 l. 15 Muierii caves 45 10
4390 3 l. 40 Cable car at Boiana Brasov 60 15
4391 4 l. 80 Mangalia (Black Sea resort) 90 30

861 MC-6 Electron Microscope **862** Polovraci Cave

1978. Rumanian Industry. Multicoloured.

4393 20 b. Type **861** 10 10
4394 40 b. Hydraulic excavator . . 10 10
4395 55 b. Power station control room 15 10
4396 1 l. 50 Oil drillheads 25 10
4397 3 l. C-12 combine harvester (horiz) 45 15
4398 3 l. 40 Petro-chemical combine, Pitesti 55 25

1978. Caves and Caverns. Multicoloured.

4399 55 b. Type **862** 10 10
4400 1 l. Topolnita 20 10
4401 1 l. 50 Ponoare 25 10
4402 2 l. 15 Ratei 35 10
4403 3 l. 40 Closani 60 15
4404 4 l. 80 Epuran . . . . 1·10 30

863 Gymnastics

865 Symbols of Equality

864 Zoomorphic Gold Plate

1978. "Daciada" Rumanian Games. Multicoloured.

4405 55 b. Type **863** 10 10
4406 1 l. Running 15 10
4407 1 l. 50 Skiing 20 10
4408 2 l. 15 Horse jumping . . . 30 10
4409 3 l. 40 Football 55 15
4410 4 l. 80 Handball . . . . . . 1·10 25

1978. Daco-Roman Archaeology. Multicoloured.

4411 20 b. Type **864** 10 10
4412 40 b. Gold torque 10 10
4413 55 b. Gold cameo ring . . . 15 10
4414 1 l. Silver bowl 25 10
4415 2 l. 15 Bronze eagle (vert) . . 45 15
4416 4 l. 80 Silver bracelet 55 30

1978. International Anti-Apartheid Year.

4418 **865** 3 l. 40 black, yell & red . 65 60

867 Ptolemaic Map of Dacia (2000th anniv of first record of Ziridava)

1978. Anniversaries in the History of Arad. Multicoloured.

4420 40 b. Type **867** 10 10
4421 55 b. Meeting place of National Council (60th anniv of unified Rumania) 10 10
4422 1 l. 75 Ceramic pots (950th anniv of first documentary evidence of Arad) 25 15

868 Dacian Warrior

1978. Stamp Day.

4423 **868** 6 l. + 3 l. multicoloured 2·00 1·40

No. 4423 was issued se-tenant with a premium carrying tab as shown in Type **868**.

869 Assembly at Alba Julia

871 Dacian Warrior

870 Wright Brothers and Wright Type A

1979. 60th Anniv of National Unity. Mult.
4424 55 b. Type **869** 10 10
4425 1 l. Open book, flag and sculpture 20 10

1979. Air. Pioneers of Aviation. Multicoloured.
4426 55 b. Type **870** 15 10
4427 1 l. Louis Bleriot and Bleriot XI 25 10
4428 1 l. 50 Anthony Fokker and "Josephine Ford" 30 10
4429 2 l. 15 A. N. Tupolev and Tupolev ANT-25 . . . . . 50 10
4430 3 l. Otto Lilienthal and Lilienthal monoplane glider 55 15
4431 3 l. 40 Traian Vuia and Vuia No. 1 . . . . 70 15
4432 4 l. 80 Aurel Vlaicu and No. 1 "Crazy Fly" 90 30

1979. 2050th Anniv of Independent Centralised Dacian State. Multicoloured.
4434 5 b. Type **871** 15 10
4435 1 l. 50 Decian warrior on horseback 25 20

872 "The Heroes from Vaslui" **873** Championship Emblem

1979. International Year of the Child (1st issue). Children's Paintings. Multicoloured.
4436 55 b. Type **872** 10 10
4437 1 l. "Tica's Folk Music Band" 15 10
4438 1 l. 50 "Buildingsite" 20 10
4439 2 l. 15 "Industrial Landscape" (horiz) 30 10
4440 3 l. 40 "Winter Holiday" (horiz) 45 15
4441 4 l. 80 "Pioneers' Celebration" (horiz) 65 25
See also Nos. 4453/6.

1979. European Junior Ice Hockey Championship, Miercurea-Ciuc, and World Championship, Galati. Multicoloured.
4442 1 l. 30 Type **873** 25 10
4443 3 l. 40 Championship emblem (different) 45 15

874 "Erythronium dens-canis" **876** Oil Derrick

875 Street with Mail-coach and Post-rider

1979. Protected Flowers. Multicoloured.
4444 55 b. Type **874** 10 10
4445 1 l. "Viola alpina" 15 10
4446 1 l. 50 "Linum borzaeanum" 20 10
4447 2 l. 15 "Convolvulus persicus" 30 10
4448 3 l. 40 "Primula auricula serratifolia" 45 15
4449 4 l. 80 "Aquilegia transsylvanica" 65 25

1979. Inter-European Cultural and Economic Co-operation.
4450 1 l. 30 Type **875** (postage) . . 45 45
4451 3 l. 40 Boeing 707 and motorcycle postman (air) . 55 55

1979. International Petroleum Congress, Bucharest.
4452 **876** 3 l. 40 multicoloured . . 50 15

877 Children with Flowers **878** Young Pioneer

1979. International Year of the Child (2nd issue). Multicoloured.
4453 40 b. Type **877** 10 10
4454 1 l. Children at creative play 20 10
4455 2 l. Children with hare . . . 35 10
4456 4 l. 60 Young pioneers . . . 70 20

1979. 30th Anniv of Young Pioneers.
4457 **878** 55 b. multicoloured . . 10 10

879 "Woman in Garden" **881** Stefan Gheorghiu

880 Brasov University

1979. Paintings by G. Tattarescu. Multicoloured.
4458 20 b. Type **879** 10 10
4459 40 b. 'Muntenian Woman" . . 10 10
4460 55 b. "Muntenian Man" . . 10 10
4461 1 l. "General G. Magheru" . 20 10
4462 2 l. 15 "The Artist's Daughter" 40 10
4463 4 l. 80 "Self-portrait" . . . 1·00 20

1979. Contemporary Architecture. Multicoloured.
4464 20 b. State Theatre, Tirgu Mures 10 10
4465 40 b. Type **880** 10 10
4466 55 b. Administration Centre, Baia Mare 10 10
4467 1 l. Stefan Gheorghiu Academy, Bucharest 15 10
4468 2 l. 15 Adminstration Centre, Botosani 30 10
4469 4 l. 80 House of Culture, Tirgoviste 70 20

1979. Anniversaries and Events. Multicoloured.
4470 40 b. Type **881** (birth cent) . 10 10
4471 55 b. Statue of Gheorghe Lazar (poet) (birth bicent) . . 10 10
4472 2 l. 15 Fallen Workers monument (Strike at Lupeni. 50th anniv) 30 10

882 Moldavian and Wallachian Women and Monuments to Union **883** Party and National Flags

1979. 120th Anniv of Union of Moldavia and Wallachia.
4473 **882** 4 l. 60 multicoloured . . 1·00 25

1979. 35th Anniv of Liberation. Multicoloured.
4474 55 b. Type **883** 10 10
4475 1 l. "Workers' Militia" (L. Suhar) (horiz) 20 10

884 Freighter "Galati" **885** "Snapdragons"

1979. Ships. Multicoloured.
4476 55 b. Type **884** 15 10
4477 1 l. Freighter "Buchuresti" . . 20 10
4478 1 l. 50 Bulk carrier "Resita" . 30 10
4479 2 l. 15 Bulk carrier "Tomis" . 35 15
4480 3 l. 40 Tanker "Dacia" . . . 55 20
4481 4 l. 80 Tanker "Independenta" 75 40

1979. "Socfilex 79" Stamp Exhibition, Bucharest. Flower Paintings by Stefan Luchian. Multicoloured.
4482 40 b. Type **885** 10 10
4483 60 b. "Carnations" 10 10
4484 1 l. 55 "Flowers on a Stairway" 25 10
4485 4 l. + 2 l. "Flowers of the Field" . . . . 1·10 1·10

888 Olympic Stadium, Melbourne (1956 Games)

1979. Olympic Games, Moscow (1980). Olympic Stadia. Multicoloured.
4489 55 b. Type **888** 10 10
4490 1 l. Rome (1960) 15 10
4491 1 l. 50 Tokyo (1964) 25 10
4492 2 l. 15 Mexico City (1968) . . 30 10
4493 3 l. 40 Munich (1972) 45 10
4494 4 l. 80 Montreal (1978) . . . 70 25

1979. Municipal Coats of Arms. As T **836**. Mult.
4496 1 l. 20 Alba Julia 20 10
4497 1 l. 20 Arad 20 10
4498 1 l. 20 Bacau 20 10
4499 1 l. 20 Baia Mare 20 10
4500 1 l. 20 Birlad 20 10
4501 1 l. 20 Botosani 20 10
4502 1 l. 20 Brasov 20 10
4503 1 l. 20 Braila 20 10
4504 1 l. 20 Buzau 20 10
4505 1 l. 20 Calarasi 20 10
4506 1 l. 20 Cluj 20 10
4507 1 l. 20 Constanta 20 10
4508 1 l. 20 Craiova 20 10
4509 1 l. 20 Dej 20 10
4510 1 l. 20 Deva 20 10
4511 1 l. 20 Drobeta Turnu Severin 20 10
4512 1 l. 20 Focsani 20 10
4513 1 l. 20 Galati 20 10
4514 1 l. 20 Gheorghe Gheorghiu Dej 20 10
4515 1 l. 20 Giurgiu 20 10
4516 1 l. 20 Hunedoara 20 10
4517 1 l. 20 Iasi 20 10
4518 1 l. 20 Lugoj 20 10
4519 1 l. 20 Medias 20 10
4520 1 l. 20 Odorheiu Secuiesc . . 20 10

889 Costumes of Maramures (female) **891** Figure Skating

890 Post Coding Desks

1979. National Costumes. Multicoloured.
4521 20 b. Type **889** 10 10
4522 40 b. Maramures (male) . . . 15 10
4523 55 b. Vrancea (female) . . . 15 10
4524 1 l. 50 Vrancea (male) 30 10
4525 3 l. Padureni (female) 55 15
4526 3 l. 40 Padureni (male) . . . 60 30

1979. Stamp Day.
4527 **890** 2 l. 10 + 1 l. 90 mult . . 75 30

1979. Winter Olympic Games, Lake Placid (1980). Multicoloured.
4528 55 b. Type **891** 10 10
4529 1 l. Downhill skiing 10 10
4530 1 l. 50 Biathlon 15 10
4531 2 l. 15 Bobsleighing 30 10
4532 3 l. 40 Speed skaing 50 10
4533 4 l. 80 Ice hockey 70 20

892 Locomotive No. 43 "Calugareni" **893** Dacian Warrior

1979. International Transport Exhibition, Hamburg. Multicoloured.
4535 55 b. Type **892** 15 10
4536 1 l. Locomotive No. 458 "Orleans" 35 10
4537 1 l. 50 Locomotive No. 1059 40 10
4538 2 l. 15 Locomotive No. 15021 55 15
4539 3 l. 40 Locomotive No. 231085 "Pacific" type 90 15
4550 4 l. 80 Electric locomotive "060-EA" . . . . 1·90 25

1980. Arms (4th series). As T **836**. Multicoloured.
4542 1 l. 20 Oradea 20 10
4543 1 l. 20 Petrosani 20 10
4544 1 l. 20 Piatra Neamt 20 10
4545 1 l. 20 Pitesti 20 10
4546 1 l. 20 Ploiesti 20 10
4547 1 l. 20 Resita 20 10
4548 1 l. 20 Rimnicu Vilcea . . . 20 10
4549 1 l. 20 Roman 20 10
4550 1 l. 20 Satu Mare 20 10
4551 1 l. 20 Sibiu 20 10
4552 1 l. 20 Sighetu Marmatiei . . 20 10
4553 1 l. 20 Sighisoara 20 10
4554 1 l. 20 Suceava 20 10
4555 1 l. 20 Tecuci 20 10
4556 1 l. 20 Timisoara 20 10
4557 1 l. 20 Tirgoviste 20 10
4558 1 l. 20 Tirgu Jiu 20 10
4559 1 l. 20 Tirgu-Mures 20 10
4560 1 l. 20 Tulcea 20 10
4561 1 l. 20 Turda 20 10
4562 1 l. 20 Turnu Magurele . . . 20 10
4563 1 l. 20 Bucharest 20 10

1980. 2050th Anniv of Independent Centralised Dacian State under Burebista.
4564 55 b. Type **893** 10 10
4565 1 l. 50 Dacian fighters with flag 20 10

894 Common Kingfisher

1980. European Nature Protection Year. Multicoloured.
4566 55 b. Type **894** 60 15
4567 1 l. Great egret (vert) 85 15
4568 1 l. 50 Red-breasted goose . 1·00 25
4569 2 l. 15 Red deer (vert) 45 15
4570 3 l. 40 Roe deer fawn 70 20
4571 4 l. 80 European bison (vert) . 1·10 30

895 "Vallota purpurea" **896** Tudor Vladimirescu

1980. Exotic Flowers from Bucharest Botanical Gardens. Multicoloured.
4573 55 b. Type **895** 10 10
4574 1 l. "Eichhornia crasipes" . . . 20 10
4575 1 l. 50 "Sprekelia formosissima" 25 10
4576 2 l. 15 "Hypericum calycinum" 35 10
4577 3 l. 40 "Camellia japonica" . . 45 25
4578 4 l. 80 "Nelumbo nucifera" . . 70 25

1980. Anniversaries. Multicoloured.
4579 40 b. Type **896** (revolutionary leader)–(birth bicent) . . . 10 10
4580 55 b. Mihail Sadoveanu (writer)–(birth cent) . . . 10 10
4581 1 l. 50 Battle of Posada (650th anniv) 25 10
4582 2 l. 15 Tudor Arghezi (poet)–(birth cent) 35 10
4583 3 l. Horea (leader, Transylvanian uprising)–(250th birth anniv) 50 15

898 Dacian Fruit Dish

899 Throwing the Javelin

1980. Bimillenary of Dacian Fortress, Petrodava (now Piatra Neamt).

4585	898	1 l. multicoloured	15	10

1980. Olympic Games, Moscow. Multicoloured.

4586	55 b. Type 899	10	10
4587	1 l. Fencing	15	10
4588	1 l. 50 Pistol shooting	20	10
4589	2 l. 15 Single kayak	30	10
4590	3 l. 40 Wrestling	45	10
4591	4 l. 80 Single skiff	90	15

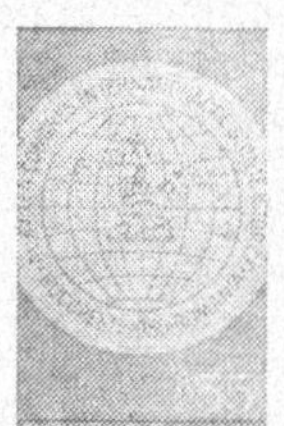
901 Congress Emblem

902 Fireman carrying Child

1980. 15th International Congress of Historical Sciences.

4594	901	55 b. deep blue & blue	10	10

1980. Firemen's Day.

4595	902	55 b. multicoloured	10	10

903 Chinese and Rumanian Stamp Collectors

906 Dacian Warrior

905 Rooks and Chessboard

1980. Rumanian–Chinese Stamp Exhibition, Bucharest.

4596	903	1 l. multicoloured	15	10

1980. 24th Chess Olympiad, Malta. Multicoloured.

4598	55 b. Knights and chessboard	15	10
4599	1 l. Type 905	25	10
4600	2 l. 15 Male head and chessboard	50	15
4601	4 l. 80 Female head and chessboard	95	35

1980. Military Uniforms. Multicoloured.

4602	20 b. Type 906	10	10
4603	40 b. Moldavian soldier (15th century)	10	10
4604	55 b. Wallachian horseman (17th century)	15	10
4605	1 l. Standard bearer (19th century)	20	10
4606	1 l. 50 Infantryman (19th century)	25	10
4607	2 l. 15 Lancer (19th century)	35	15
4608	4 l. 80 Hussar (19th century)	90	20

907 Burebista (sculpture, P. Mercea)

908 George Oprescu

1980. Stamp Day.

4609	907	2 l. multicoloured	25	10

1981. Celebrities' Birth Anniversaries. Multicoloured.

4610	1 l. 50 Type 908 (historian and art critic, centenary)	25	10
4611	2 l. 15 Marius Bunescu (painter, centenary)	35	10
4612	3 l. 40 Ion Georgescu (sculptor, 120th anniv)	55	25

909 St. Bernard

1981. Dogs. Multicoloured.

4613	40 b. Mountain sheepdog (horiz)	10	10
4614	55 b. Type 909	15	10
4615	1 l. Fox terrier (horiz)	20	10
4616	1 l. 50 Alsatian (horiz)	30	10
4617	2 l. 15 Boxer (horiz)	45	10
4618	3 l. 40 Dalmatian (horiz)	65	15
4619	4 l. 80 Poodle	85	30

910 Paddle-steamer "Stefan cel Mare"

1981. 125th Anniv of European Danube Committee. Multicoloured.

4620	55 b. Type 910	20	10
4621	1 l. Danube Commission steam launch	30	15
4622	1 l. 50 Paddle-steamer "Tudor Vladimirescu"	45	15
4623	2 l. 15 Dredger "Sulina"	55	25
4624	3 l. 40 Paddle-steamer "Republica Populara Romana"	80	30
4625	4 l. 80 Freighter in Sulina Channel	1·00	40

911 Bare-neck Pigeon

912 Party Flag and Oak Leaves

1981. Pigeons. Multicoloured.

4627	40 b. Type 911	15	10
4628	55 b. Orbetan pigeon	10	10
4629	1 l. Craiova chestnut pigeon	20	10
4630	1 l. 50 Timisoara pigeon	30	10
4631	2 l. 15 Homing pigeon	45	15
4632	3 l. 40 Salonta giant pigeon	70	40

1981. 60th Anniv of Rumanian Communist Party.

4633	912	1 l. multicoloured	15	10

914 "Soyuz 40"

1981. Air. Soviet–Rumanian Space Flight. Mult.

4635	55 b. Type 914	15	10
4636	3 l. 40 "Soyuz"–"Salyut" link-up	55	15

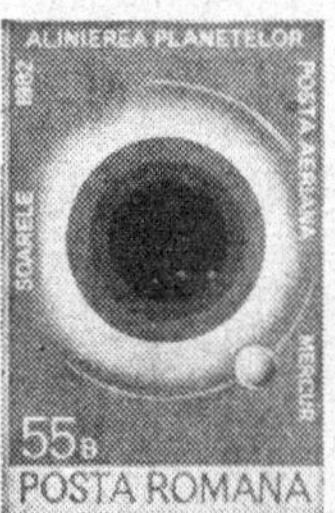
915 Sun and Mercury

916 Industrial Symbols

1981. The Planets. Multicoloured.

4638	55 b. Type 915	15	10
4639	1 l. Venus, Earth and Mars	25	15
4640	1 l. 50 Jupiter	35	20
4641	2 l. 15 Saturn	50	25
4642	3 l. 40 Uranus	75	30
4643	4 l. 80 Neptune and Pluto	1·10	45

1981. "Singing Rumania" National Festival. Multicoloured.

4645	55 b. Type 916	15	10
4646	1 l. 50 Science	30	10
4647	2 l. 15 Agriculture	40	15
4648	3 l. 40 Culture	65	30

917 Book and Flag

918 "Woman in an Interior"

1981. "Universiada" Games, Bucharest. Multicoloured.

4649	1 l. Type 917	20	10
4650	2 l. 15 Games emblem	40	20
4651	4 l. 80 Stadium (horiz)	1·00	1·00

1981. 150th Birth Anniv of Theodor Aman (painter). Multicoloured.

4652	40 b. "Self-portrait"	10	10
4653	55 b. "Battle of Giurgiu" (horiz)	15	10
4654	1 l. "Family Picnic" (horiz)	20	10
4655	1 l. 50 "The Painter's Studio" (horiz)	30	10
4656	2 l. 15 Type 918	40	15
4657	3 l. 10 Aman Museum, Bucharest (horiz)	60	35

919 "The Thinker of Cernavoda" (polished stone sculpture)

920 Blood Donation

1981. 16th Science History Congress, Bucharest.

4658	919	3 l. 40 multicoloured	65	65

1981. Blood Donor Publicity.

4659	920	55 b. multicoloured	20	15

921 Central Military Hospital

1981. 150th Anniv of Central Military Hospital, Bucharest.

4660	921	55 b. multicoloured	15	10

922 Paul Constantinescu

923 Children at Stamp Exhibition

1981. Rumanian Musicians. Multicoloured.

4661	40 b. George Enescu	15	10
4662	55 b. Type 922	15	10
4663	1 l. Dinu Lipatti	25	10
4664	1 l. 50 Ionel Perlea	35	10
4665	2 l. 15 Ciprian Porumbescu	45	15
4666	3 l. 40 Mihail Jora	70	40

1981. Stamp Day.

4667	923	2 l. multicoloured	35	15

924 Hopscotch

925 Football Players

1981. Children's Games and Activities. Multicoloured.

4668	40 b. Type 924 (postage)	10	10
4669	55 b. Football	15	10
4670	1 l. Children with balloons and hobby horse	20	15
4671	1 l. 50 Fishing	30	15
4672	2 l. 15 Dog looking through school window at child	45	15
4673	3 l. Child on stilts	55	20
4674	4 l. Child tending sick dog	75	25
4675	4 l. 80 Children with model gliders (air)	1·00	75

Nos. 4671/15 are from illustrations by Norman Rockwell.

1981. World Cup Football Championship, Spain (1982). Multicoloured.

4676	55 b. Type 925	15	10
4677	1 l. Goalkeeper saving ball	20	10
4678	1 l. 50 Player heading ball	30	15
4679	2 l. 15 Player kicking ball over head	40	20
4680	3 l. 40 Goalkeeper catching ball	65	65
4681	4 l. 80 Player kicking ball	90	90

926 Alexander the Good, Prince of Moldavia

927 Entrance to Union Square Station

1982. Anniversaries. Multicoloured.

4683	1 l. Type 926 (550th death anniv)	20	10
4684	1 l.50 Bogdan P. Hasdeu (historian, 75th death anniv)	30	10
4685	2 l. 15 Nicolae Titulescu (diplomat and politician, birth centenary)	50	25

1982. Inauguration of Bucharest Underground Railway. Multicoloured.

4686	60 b. Type 927	15	10
4687	2 l. 40 Platforms and train at Heroes' Square station	75	25

928 Dog rescuing Child from Sea

1982. Dog, Friend of Mankind. Multicoloured.

4688	55 b. Type 928	15	10
4689	1 l. Shepherd and sheepdog (vert)	20	10
4690	3 l. Gundog (vert)	55	15
4691	3 l. 40 Huskies	65	20
4692	4 l. Dog carrying woman's basket (vert)	75	20
4693	4 l. 80 Dog guiding blind person (vert)	85	35
4694	5 l. Dalmatian and child with doll	90	40
4695	6 l. St. Bernard	1·10	55

929 Dove, Banner and Crowd

1982. 60th Anniv of Communist Youth Union. Multicoloured.

4696	1 l. Type 929	20	10
4697	1 l. 20 Construction worker	25	10
4698	1 l. 50 Farm workers	30	15
4699	2 l. Laboratory worker and students	40	15
4700	2 l. 50 Labourers	55	20
4701	3 l. Choir, musicians and dancers	65	25

932 Harvesting Wheat

1982. 20th Anniv of Agricultural Co-operatives. Multicoloured.

No.	Description	Mint	Used
4704	50 b. Type **932** (postage)	15	10
4705	1 l. Cows and milking equipment	25	10
4706	1 l. 50 Watering apple trees	30	15
4707	2 l. 50 Cultivator in vineyard	55	20
4708	3 l. Watering vegetables	65	25
4709	4 l. Helicopter spraying cereal crop (air)	1·00	40

933 Vladimir Nicolae's Standard 1 Hang-glider

1982. Air. Hang-gliders. Multicoloured.

No.	Description	Mint	Used
4711	50 b. Type **933**	15	10
4712	1 l. Excelsior D	35	10
4713	1 l. 50 Dedal-1	40	15
4714	2 l. 50 Entuziast	75	25
4715	4 l. AK-22	1·10	50
4716	5 l. Grifrom	1·40	50

934 Baile Felix

936 Vlaicu Monument, Banesti-Prahova

935 "Legend"

1982. Spas and Health Resorts. Multicoloured.

No.	Description	Mint	Used
4717	50 b. Type **934**	15	10
4718	1 l. Predeal (horiz)	25	10
4719	1 l. 50 Baile Herculane	30	15
4720	2 l. 50 Eforie Nord (horiz)	55	20
4721	3 l. Olimp (horiz)	65	20
4722	5 l. Neptun (horiz)	1·00	40

1982. Paintings by Sabin Balasa. Multicoloured.

No.	Description	Mint	Used
4723	1 l. Type **935**	25	10
4724	1 l. 50 "Contrasts"	35	15
4725	2 l. 50 "Peace Relay"	75	30
4726	4 l. "Genesis of the Rumanian People" (vert)	85	35

1982. Air. Birth Centenary of Aurel Vlaicu (aviation pioneer). Multicoloured.

No.	Description	Mint	Used
4727	50 b. Vlaicu's glider, 1909 (horiz)	15	10
4728	1 l. Type **936**	30	10
4729	2 l. 50 Air Heroes' Monument	70	25
4730	3 l. Vlaicu's No. 1 "Crazy Fly", 1910 (horiz)	80	30

938 Central Exhibition Pavilion

1982. "Tib '82" International Fair, Bucharest.

No.	Type	Description	Mint	Used
4732	**938**	2 l. multicoloured	45	10

MINIMUM PRICE

The minimum price quoted is 10p which represents a handling charge rather than a basis for valuing common stamps. For further notes about prices, see introductory pages.

939 Young Pioneer with Savings Book and Books

940 Postwoman delivering Letters

1982. Savings Week. Multicoloured.

No.	Description	Mint	Used
4733	1 l. Type **939**	25	10
4734	2 l. Savings Bank advertisement (Calin Popovici)	45	10

1982. Stamp Day. Multicoloured.

No.	Description	Mint	Used
4735	1 l. Type **940**	25	10
4736	2 l. Postman	40	15

941 "Brave Young Man and the Golden Apples" (Petre Ispirescu)

942 Symbols of Industry, Party Emblem and Programme

1982. Fairy Tales. Multicoloured.

No.	Description	Mint	Used
4737	50 b. Type **941**	15	10
4738	1 l. "Bear tricked by the Fox" (Ion Creanga)	25	10
4739	1 l. 50 Warrior fighting bird ("Prince of Tears" (Mihai Eminescu))	35	10
4740	2 l. 50 Hen with bag ("Bag with Two Coins" (Ion Creanga))	55	20
4741	3 l. Rider fighting three-headed dragon ("Ileana Simziana" (Petre Ispirescu))	65	25
4742	5 l. Man riding devil ("Danila Prepeleac" (Ion Creanga))	1·10	35

1982. Rumanian Communist Party National Conference, Bucharest. Multicoloured.

No.	Description	Mint	Used
4743	1 l. Type **942**	30	25
4744	2 l. Wheat symbols of industry and Party emblem and open programme	60	55

943 Wooden Canteen from Suceava

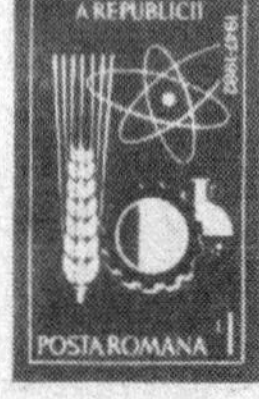

944 Wheat, Cogwheel, Flask and Electricity Emblem

1982. Household Utensils.

No.	Type	Description	Mint	Used
4745	**943**	50 b. red	10	10
4746	–	1 l. blue	20	10
4747	–	1 l. 50 orange	35	10
4748	–	2 l. blue	45	10
4749	–	3 l. green	65	10
4750	–	3 l. 50 green	75	10
4751	–	4 l. brown	90	10
4752	–	5 l. blue	1·10	10
4753	–	6 l. blue	1·40	10
4754	–	7 l. purple	1·50	10
4755	–	7 l. 50 mauve	1·60	10
4756	–	8 l. green	1·75	10
4757	–	10 l. red	2·10	10
4758	–	20 l. violet	4·25	15
4759	–	30 l. blue	6·50	15
4760	–	50 l. brown	10·50	15

DESIGNS: As T 943—VERT: 1 l. Ceramic plates from Radauti; 2 l. Jug and plate from Vama-Maramures; 3 l. Wooden churn and pail from North Moldavia; 4 l. Wooden spoons and ceramic plate from Cluj; 5 l. Ceramic bowl and pot from Marginea-Suceava. HORIZ: 1 l. 50, Wooden dipper from Valea Mare; 3 l. 50, Ceramic plates from Leheceni-Crisana. 29 × 23 mm: 10 l. Wooden tubs from Hunedoara and Suceava; 30 l. Wooden spoons from Alba. 23 × 29 mm: 6 l. Ceramic pot and jug from Bihor; 7 l. Distaff and spindle from Transylvania; 7 l. 50, Double wooden pail from Suceava; 8 l. Pitcher and ceramic plate from Oboga and Horezu; 20 l. Wooden canteen and six glasses from Horezu; 50 l. Ceramic plates from Horezu.

1982. 35th Anniv of People's Republic. Mult.

No.	Description	Mint	Used
4767	1 l. Type **944**	25	10
4768	2 l. National flag and oakleaves	45	15

945 H. Coanda and Diagram of Jet Engine

1983. Air. 25 Years of Space Exploration. Mult.

No.	Description	Mint	Used
4769	50 b. Type **945**	15	10
4770	1 l. H. Oberth and diagram of rocket	25	10
4771	1 l. 50 "Sputnik 1", 1957 (first artificial satellite)	40	15
4772	2 l. 50 "Vostok 1", (first manned flight)	70	15
4773	4 l. "Apollo 11, 1969 (first Moon landing)	1·10	30
4774	5 l. Space shuttle "Columbia"	1·40	50

946 Rombac One Eleven

947 Matei Millo in "The Discontented" by Vasile Alecsandri

1983. Air. First Rumanian-built Jet Airliner.

No.	Type	Description	Mint	Used
4776	**946**	11 l. blue	3·50	15

1983. Rumanian Actors.

No.	Type	Description	Mint	Used
4777	**947**	50 b. red and black	15	10
4778	–	1 l. green and black	30	10
4779	–	1 l. 50 violet and black	40	10
4780	–	2 l. brown and black	55	15
4781	–	2 l. 50 green & black	70	20
4782	–	3 l. blue and black	80	25
4783	–	4 l. green and black	1·10	30
4784	–	5 l. lilac and black	1·40	35

DESIGNS: 1 l. Mihail Pascaly in "Director Millo", by Vasile Alecsandri; 1 l. 50, Aristizza Romanescu in "The Dogs" by H. Lecca; 2 l. C. I. Nottara in "Blizzard" by B. S. Delavrancea; 2 l. 50, Grigore Manolescu in "Hamlet" by William Shakespeare; 3 l. Agatha Birsescu in "Medea" by Lebouvet; 4 l. Ion Brezeanu in "The Lost Letter" by I. L. Caragiale. 5 l. Aristide Demetriad in "The Despotic Prince" by Vasile Alecsandri.

948 Hugo Grotius

949 Aro "10"

1983. 400th Birth Anniv of Hugo Grotius (Dutch jurist).

No.	Type	Description	Mint	Used
4785	**948**	2 l. brown	55	15

1983. Rumanian-built Vehicles. Multicoloured.

No.	Description	Mint	Used
4786	50 b. Type **949**	15	10
4787	1 l. Dacia "1300" Break	30	10
4788	1 l. 50 Aro "242"	45	10
4789	2 l. 50 Aro "244"	70	20
4790	4 l. Dacia "1310"	1·10	30
4791	5 l. Oltcit "Club"	1·40	35

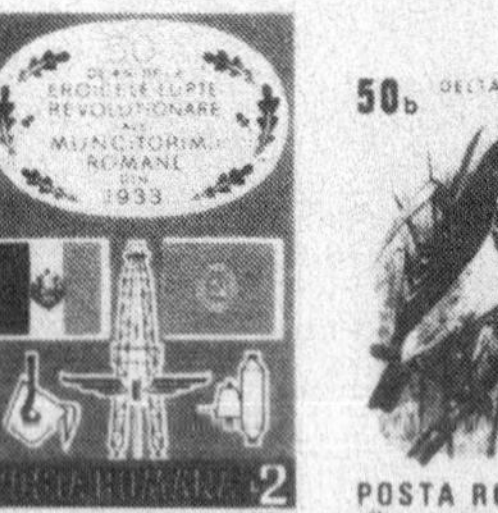

951 National and Communist Party Flags

953 Bluethroat

952 Loading Mail

1983. 50th Anniv of 1933 Workers' Revolution.

No.	Type	Description	Mint	Used
4793	**951**	2 l. multicoloured	55	15

1983. Air. World Communications Year.

No.	Type	Description	Mint	Used
4794	**952**	2 l. multicoloured	75	15

1983. Birds of the Danube Delta. Multicoloured.

No.	Description	Mint	Used
4795	50 b. Type **953**	25	10
4796	1 l. Rose-coloured starling	60	25
4797	1 l. 50 Common roller	75	30
4798	2 l. 50 European bee eater	1·40	50
4799	4 l. Reed bunting	2·25	90
4800	5 l. Lesser grey shrike	2·50	1·10

954 Kayak

1983. Water Sports. Multicoloured.

No.	Description	Mint	Used
4801	50 b. Type **954**	15	10
4802	1 l. Water polo	30	10
4803	1 l. 50 Canoeing	40	15
4804	2 l. 50 Diving	70	20
4805	4 l. Rowing	1·10	35
4806	5 l. Swimming (start of race)	1·40	90

955 Postman on Bicycle

1983. Stamp Day. Multicoloured.

No.	Description	Mint	Used
4807	1 l. Type **955**	30	10
4808	3 l. 50 (+ 3 l.) National flag as stamp	1·75	1·75

No. 4808 was issued with premium carrying label attached.

956 "Geum reptans"

1983. European Flora and Fauna. Multicoloured.

No.	Description	Mint	Used
4810	1 l. Type **956**	40	25
4811	1 l. "Papaver dubium"	40	25
4812	1 l. "Carlina acaulis"	40	25
4813	1 l. "Paeonia peregrina"	40	25
4814	1 l. "Gentiana excisa"	40	25
4815	1 l. Eurasian red squirrel	40	25
4816	1 l. "Grammia quenselii" (butterfly)	60	30
4817	1 l. Middle spotted woodpecker	1·50	40
4818	1 l. Lynx	40	25
4819	1 l. Wallcreeper	1·50	40

957 "Girl with Feather"

958 Flag and Oak Leaves

1983. Paintings by C. Baba. Multicoloured.

No.	Description	Mint	Used
4820	1 l. Type **957**	30	10
4821	2 l. "Congregation"	55	15
4822	3 l. "Farm Workers"	80	25
4823	4 l. "Rest in the Fields" (horiz)	1·10	35

1983. 65th Anniv of Union of Transylvania and Rumania. Multicoloured.

No.	Description	Mint	Used
4824	1 l. Type **958**	30	10
4825	2 l. National and Communist Party Flags and Parliament building, Bucharest	55	15

959 Postman and Post Office

961 Cross-country Skiing

1983. "Balkanfila IX '83" Stamp Exhibition, Bucharest. Multicoloured.
4826 1 l. Type **959** 30 10
4827 2 l. Postwoman and Athenaeum Concert Hall 55 15

1984. Winter Olympic Games, Sarajevo. Multicoloured.
4830 50 b. Type **961** 15 10
4831 1 l. Biathlon 25 20
4832 1 l. 50 Ice skating 40 30
4833 2 l. Speed skating 50 40
4834 3 l. Ice hockey 75 65
4835 3 l. 50 Bobsleighing 90 80
4836 4 l. Luge . . . . 1·00 90
4837 5 l. Downhill skiing . . . . . 1·25 1·10

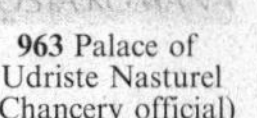

963 Palace of Udriste Nasturel (Chancery official)

967 Flowering Rush

966 Sunflower

1984. Anniversaries.
4839 50 b. green, pink and silver . 15 10
4840 1 l. violet, green and silver . 30 10
4841 1 l. 50 multicoloured 40 15
4842 2 l. brown, blue and silver . . 65 15
4843 3 l. 50 multicoloured 95 30
4844 4 l. multicoloured . . . . . 1·10 35
DESIGNS: 50 b. Type **963** (325th death anniv); 1 l. Miron Costin (poet, 350th birth anniv); 1 l. 50, Crisan (Giurgiu Marcu) (leader of peasant revolt, 250th birth anniv); 2 l. Simion Barnutiu (scientist, 175th birth anniv); 3 l. 50, Diuliu Zamfirescu (writer, 125th birth anniv); 4 l. Nicolae Milescu at Great Wall of China (explorer, 275th death anniv).

1984. Protection of Environment. Multicoloured.
4847 1 l. Type **966** 30 10
4848 2 l. Red deer 55 20
4849 3 l. Fish 80 25
4850 4 l. Jay . . . . 2·40 45

1984. Flowers of the Danube. Multicoloured.
4851 50 b. Arrowhead 15 10
4852 1 l. Yellow iris 30 10
4853 1 l. 50 Type **967** 40 15
4854 3 l. White water lily 80 25
4855 4 l. Fringed water lily (horiz) 1·10 35
4856 5 l. Yellow water lily (horiz) . 1·40 50

968 Crowd with Banners

970 Congress Emblem

969 High Jumping

1984. 45th Anniv of Anti-Fascist Demonstration.
4857 **968** 2 l. multicoloured 55 15

1984. Olympic Games, Los Angeles (1st issue). Multicoloured.
4858 50 b. Type **969** 15 10
4859 1 l. Swimming 25 20
4860 1 l. 50 Running 40 30
4861 3 l. Handball 75 65
4862 4 l. Rowing . . . . 1·00 90
4863 5 l. Canoeing . . . . 1·25 1·10
See also Nos. 4866/73.

1984. 25th Ear, Nose and Throat Association Congress, Bucharest.
4864 **970** 2 l. multicoloured 55 15

1984. Olympic Games, Los Angeles (2nd issue). As T **969**. Multicoloured.
4866 50 b. Boxing 15 10
4867 1 l. Rowing 25 20
4868 1 l. Handball 40 30
4869 2 l. Judo 50 40
4870 3 l. Wrestling 75 65
4871 3 l. 50 Fencing 90 80
4872 4 l. Kayak . . . . 1·00 90
4873 5 l. Swimming . . . . 1·25 1·10

972 Mihai Ciuca (bacteriologist, cent)

974 Flags, Flame and Power Station

973 Lockhead Super Electra

1984. Birth Anniversaries. Dated "1983".
4874 **972** 1 l. purple, blue and silver 30 10
4875 – 2 l. brown and silver . . 55 15
4876 – 3 l. green, brown and silver 80 25
4877 – 4 l. violet, green and silver 1·10 35
DESIGNS: 2 l. Petre S. Aurelian (agronomist, 150th anniv); 3 l. Alexandru Vlahuta (writer, 125th anniv); 4 l. Dimitrie Leonida (engineer, centenary).

1984. Air. 40th Anniv of International Civil Aviation Organization. Multicoloured.
4878 50 b. Type **973** 15 10
4879 1 l. 50 Britten Norman Islander 50 15
4880 3 l. Rombac One Eleven . . 1·00 35
4881 6 l. Boeing 707 . . . . . . 2·00 80

1984. 40th Anniv of Liberation.
4882 **974** 2 l. multicoloured . . . 55 15

975 Lippizaner

1984. Horses. Multicoloured.
4883 50 b. Type **975** 15 10
4884 1 l. Hutul 30 10
4885 1 l. 50 Bukovina 40 15
4886 2 l. 50 Nonius 70 20
4887 4 l. Arab . . . . 1·10 35
4888 5 l. Rumanian half-breed . . 1·40 50

977 Memorial, Alba Julia

978 "Portrait of a Child" (Th. Aman)

1984. Bicentenary of Horea, Closa and Crisan Uprisings.
4890 **977** 2 l. multicoloured . . . 55 15

1984. Paintings of Children. Multicoloured.
4891 50 b. Type **978** 15 10
4892 1 l. "The Little Shepherd" (N. Grigorescu) 30 15
4893 2 l. "Lica with an Orange" (St. Luchian) 55 15
4894 3 l. "Portrait of a Child" (N. Tonitza) 80 25
4895 4 l. "Portrait of a Boy" (S. Popp) . . . . 1·10 35
4896 5 l. "Portrait of Young Girl" (I. Tuculescu) . . . . . 1·40 50

979 Stage Coach and Rumanian Philatelic Association Emblem

1984. Stamp Day.
4897 **979** 2 l. (+ 1 l.) multicoloured 80 65
No. 4897 was issued with premium carrying label attached.

981 Dalmatian Pelicans

982 Dr. Petru Groza (former President)

1984. Protected Animals. Dalmatian Pelicans. Multicoloured.
4899 50 b. Type **981** 30 15
4900 1 l. Pelican on nest 65 25
4901 1 l. Pelicans on lake 65 25
4902 2 l. Pelicans roosting . . . . 1·10 70

1984. Anniversaries. Multicoloured.
4903 50 b. Type **982** (birth centenary) 15 10
4904 1 l. Alexandru Odobescu (writer) (150th birth anniv) 30 10
4905 2 l. Dr. Carol Davila (physician) (death centenary) 55 15
4906 3 l. Dr. Nicolae Gh. Lupu (physician) (birth centenary) 80 25
4907 4 l. Dr. Daniel Danielopolu (physician) (birth centenary) 1·10 35
4908 5 l. Panait Istrati (writer) (birth centenary) . . . . . . 1·40 50

983 Generator

985 August Treboniu Laurian (linguist and historian)

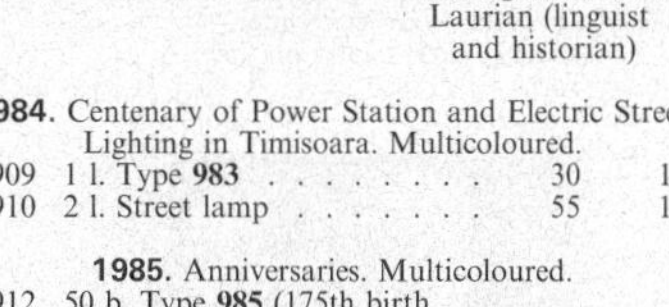
1984. Centenary of Power Station and Electric Street Lighting in Timisoara. Multicoloured.
4909 1 l. Type **983** 30 10
4910 2 l. Street lamp 55 15

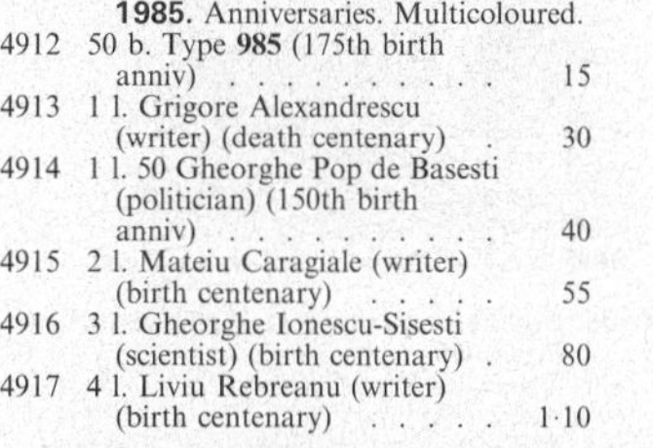
1985. Anniversaries. Multicoloured.
4912 50 b. Type **985** (175th birth anniv) 15 10
4913 1 l. Grigore Alexandrescu (writer) (death centenary) . 30 10
4914 1 l. 50 Gheorghe Pop de Basesti (politician) (150th birth anniv) 40 15
4915 2 l. Mateiu Caragiale (writer) (birth centenary) 55 15
4916 3 l. Gheorghe Ionescu-Sisesti (scientist) (birth centenary) . 80 25
4917 4 l. Liviu Rebreanu (writer) (birth centenary) . . . . 1·10 35

986 Students in Science Laboratory

987 Racoon Dog

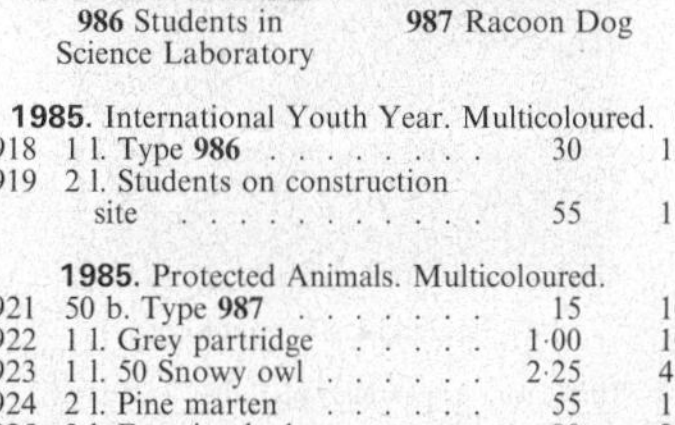
1985. International Youth Year. Multicoloured.
4918 1 l. Type **986** 30 10
4919 2 l. Students on construction site 55 15

1985. Protected Animals. Multicoloured.
4921 50 b. Type **987** 15 10
4922 1 l. Grey partridge . . . . 1·00 10
4923 1 l. 50 Snowy owl . . . . . 2·25 45
4924 2 l. Pine marten 55 15
4925 3 l. Eurasian badger 80 25
4926 3 l. 50 Eurasian otter . . . 90 30
4927 4 l. Capercaillie . . . . . . 3·50 65
4928 5 l. Great bustard . . . . . 4·00 80

988 Flags and Victory Monument, Bucharest

989 Union Emblem

1985. 40th Anniv of Victory in Europe Day.
4929 **988** 2 l. multicoloured . . . 55 15

1985. Communist Youth Union Congress.
4930 **989** 2 l. multicoloured . . . 55 15

990 Route Map and Canal

1985. Danube–Black Sea Canal. Multicoloured.
4931 1 l. Type **990** 30 10
4932 2 l. Canal and bridge, Cernavoda 70 25
4933 3 l. Road over Canal, Medgidia 90 25
4934 4 l. Canal control tower, Agigea 1·25 35

991 Brown Pelican

992 "Fire"

1985. Birth Bicentenary of John J. Audubon (ornithologist). Multicoloured.
4936 50 b. American robin (horiz) 25 10
4937 1 l. Type **991** 50 15
4938 1 l. 50 Yellow-crowned night heron 90 30
4939 2 l. Northern oriole . . . . 1·25 35
4940 3 l. Red-necked grebe . . . 1·90 50
4941 4 l. Mallard (horiz) . . . . 2·50 65

1985. Paintings by Ion Tuculescu. Multicoloured.
4942 1 l. Type **992** 30 10
4943 2 l. "Circulation" 55 15
4944 3 l. "Interior of Peasant's Home" (horiz) 80 25
4945 4 l. "Sunset" (horiz) . . . . 1·10 35

993 "Inachis io"

1985. Butterflies and Moths. Multicoloured.
4946 50 b. Type **993** 20 10
4947 1 l. "Papilio machaon" . . . 45 10
4948 2 l. "Vanessa atalanta" . . . 70 20
4949 3 l. "Saturnia pavonia" . . . 1·00 30
4950 4 l. "Ammobiota festiva" . . 1·40 45
4951 5 l. "Smerinthus ocellata" . . 1·75 60

994 Transfagarasan Mountain Road

1985. 20th Anniv of Election of General Secretary Nicolae Ceausescu and 9th Communist Party Congress. Multicoloured.
4952 1 l. Type **994** 30 10
4953 2 l. Danube–Black Sea Canal 55 15
4954 3 l. Bucharest underground railway 80 25
4955 4 l. Irrigating fields . . . . . 1·10 35

995 Rumanian Crest, Symbols of Agriculture and "XX" — **997** "Senecio glaberrimus"

1985. 20th Anniv of Rumanian Socialist Republic. Multicoloured.

4956	1 l. Type **995**	30	10
4957	2 l. Crest, symbols of industry and "XX"	55	15

1985. 50th Anniv of Retezat National Park. Multicoloured.

4959	50 b. Type **997**	15	15
4960	1 l. Chamois	30	10
4961	2 l. "Centaurea retezatensis"	55	15
4962	3 l. Violet	80	25
4963	4 l. Alpine marmot	1·10	35
4964	5 l. Golden eagle	3·75	75

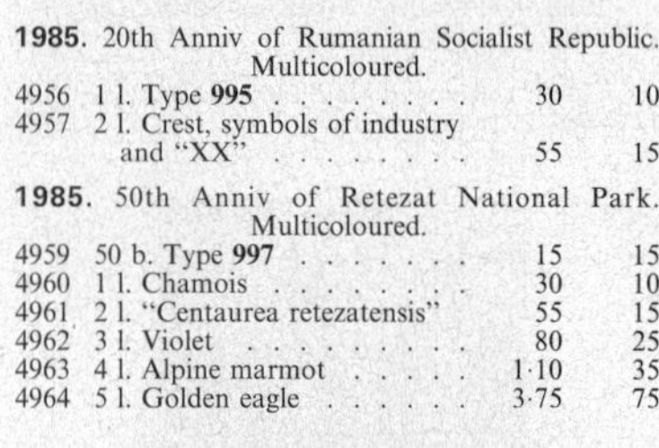

998 Universal "530 DTC"

1985. Rumanian Tractors. Multicoloured.

4966	50 b. Type **998**	15	10
4967	1 l. Universal "550 M HC"	30	10
4968	1 l. 50 Universal "650 Super"	40	15
4969	2 l. Universal "850"	55	15
4970	3 l. Universal "S 1801 IF" tracked front loader	80	25
4971	4 l. Universal "A 3602 IF" front loader	1·10	35

999 Costume of Muscel (female)

1985. Costumes (1st series). Multicoloured.

4972	50 b. Type **999**	15	10
4973	50 b. Muscel (male)	15	10
4974	1 l. 50 Bistrita-Nasaud (female)	40	15
4975	1 l. 50 Bistrita-Nasaud (male)	40	15
4976	2 l. Vrancea (female)	55	15
4977	2 l. Vrancea (male)	55	15
4978	3 l. Vilcea (female)	80	25
4979	3 l. Vilcea (male)	80	25

See also Nos. 5143/5150.

1000 Footballer attacking Goal

1985. World Cup Football Championship, Mexico (1986) (1st issue). Multicoloured.

4980	50 b. Type **1000**	15	10
4981	1 l. Player capturing ball	30	10
4982	1 l. 50 Player heading ball	40	15
4983	2 l. Player about to tackle	55	15
4984	3 l. Player heading ball and goal keeper	80	25
4985	4 l. Player kicking ball over head	1·10	35

See also Nos. 5038/43.

1001 U.N. Emblem and "40" — **1002** Copper

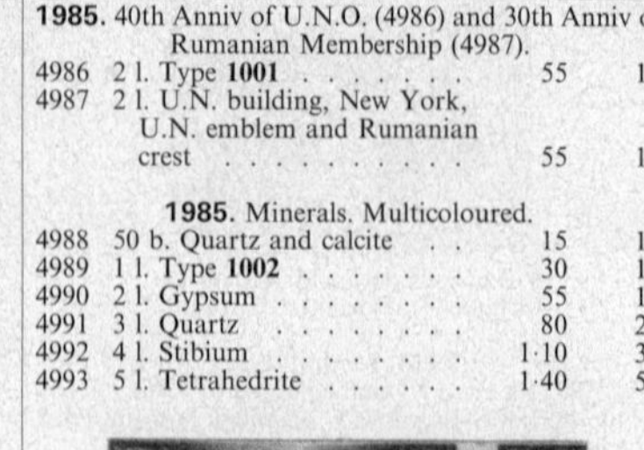

1985. 40th Anniv of U.N.O. (4986) and 30th Anniv of Rumanian Membership (4987).

4986	2 l. Type **1001**	55	15
4987	2 l. U.N. building, New York, U.N. emblem and Rumanian crest	55	15

1985. Minerals. Multicoloured.

4988	50 b. Quartz and calcite	15	10
4989	1 l. Type **1002**	30	10
4990	2 l. Gypsum	55	15
4991	3 l. Quartz	80	25
4992	4 l. Stibium	1·10	35
4993	5 l. Tetrahedrite	1·40	50

1003 Posthorn

1985. Stamp Day.

4994	**1003** 2 l. (+ 1 l.) multicoloured	80	70

1004 Goofy as Hank waking to find himself at Camelot

1985. 150th Birth of Mark Twain (writer). Scenes from "A Connecticut Yankee in King Arthur's Court" (film). Multicoloured.

4995	50 b. Type **1004**		
4996	50 b. Hank at the stake and Merlin (Mickey Mouse)	2·00	2·00
4997	50 b. Hank being hoisted onto horseback in full armour	2·00	2·00
4998	50 b. Pete as Sir Sagramoor on horseback	2·00	2·00

1985. Birth Bicentenaries of Grimm Brothers (folklorists). Scenes from "The Three Brothers". As T **1004**. Multicoloured.

5000	1 l. Father (Donald Duck) bidding farewell to the brothers (Huey, Louie and Dewey)	4·25	4·25
5001	1 l. Louie as fencing master brother	4·25	4·25
5002	1 l. Louie keeping rain off his father with sword	4·25	4·25
5003	1 l. Huey as blacksmith brother shoeing galloping horse	4·25	4·25
5004	1l. Dewey as barber brother shaving Brer Rabbit on the run	4·25	4·25

1005 Wright Brothers (aviation pioneers)

1985. Explorers and Pioneers. Multicoloured.

5006	1 l. Type **1005**	35	10
5007	1 l. 50 Jacques Yves Cousteau (undersea explorer)	60	15
5008	2 l. Amelia Earhart Putnam (first woman trans-Atlantic flyer)	70	15
5009	3 l. Charles Lindbergh (first solo trans-Atlantic flyer)	90	25
5010	3 l. 50 Sir Edmund Hillary (first man to reach summit of Everest)	90	30
5011	4 l. Robert Edwin Peary and Emil Racovita (polar explorers)	1·10	35
5012	5 l. Richard Evelyn Byrd (polar explorer and aviator)	2·00	55
5013	6 l. Neil A. Armstrong (first man on Moon)	1·40	50

1006 Edmond Halley and Comet

1986. Air. Appearance of Halley's Comet.

5014	2 l. Type **1006**	55	15
5015	4 l. Comet, orbit and space probes	1·10	35

No. 5014 is wrongly inscr "Edmund".

1007 "Nina in Green" — **1010** Hotel Diana, Baile Herculane

1009 Goofy playing Clarinet

1986. Paintings by Nicolae Tonitza. Multicoloured.

5016	1 l. Type **1007**	25	10
5017	2 l. "Irina"	55	20
5018	3 l. "Forester's Daughter"	80	35
5019	4 l. "Woman on Veranda"	1·10	55

1986. 50th Anniv of Colour Animation. Scenes from "Band Concert" (cartoon film). Multicoloured.

5021	50 b. Type **1009**	2·00	2·00
5022	50 b. Clarabelle playing flute	2·00	2·00
5023	50 b. Mickey Mouse conducting	2·00	2·00
5024	50 b. Paddy and Peter Pig playing euphonium and trumpet	2·00	2·00
5025	1 l. Conductor Mickey and flautist Donald Duck	4·25	4·25
5026	1 l. Donald caught in trombone slide	4·25	4·25
5027	1 l. Horace playing drums	4·25	4·25
5028	1 l. Donald selling ice cream	4·25	4·25
5029	1 l. Mickey and euphonium caught in tornado	4·25	4·25

1986. Spa Hotels. Multicoloured.

5031	50 b. Type **1010**	15	10
5032	1 l. Hotel Termal, Baile Felix	25	10
5033	2 l. Hotels Delfin, Meduza and Steaua de Mare, North Eforie	55	15
5034	3 l. Hotel Caciulata, Calimanesti-Caciulata	80	25
5035	4 l. Villa Palas, Slanic Moldova	1·10	35
5036	5 l. Hotel Bradet, Sovata	1·25	45

1011 Ceausescu and Red Flag

1986. 65th Anniv of Rumanian Communist Party

5037	**1011** 2 l. multicoloured	55	15

1012 Italy v. Bulgaria

1986. World Cup Football Championship, Mexico (2nd issue). Multicoloured.

5038	50 b. Type **1012**	15	10
5039	1 l. Mexico v. Belgium	25	10
5040	2 l. Canada v. France	55	15
5041	3 l. Brazil v. Spain	80	25
5042	4 l. Uruguay v. W. Germany	1·10	35
5043	5 l. Morocco v. Poland	1·25	45

1014 "Tulipa gesneriana"

1986. Flowers. Multicoloured.

5045	50 b. Type **1014**	15	10
5046	1 l. "Iris hispanica"	25	10
5047	2 l. "Rosa hybrida"	55	15
5048	3 l. "Anemone coronaria"	80	25
5049	4 l. "Freesia refracta"	1·10	35
5050	5 l. "Chrysanthemum indicum"	1·25	45

1015 Mircea the Great and Horsemen

1986. 600th Anniv of Mircea the Great's Accession.

5051	**1015** 2 l. multicoloured	55	15

1016 Thatched House with Veranda, Alba

1986. 50th Anniv of Museum of Historic Dwellings, Bucharest. Multicoloured.

5052	50 b. Type **1016**	15	10
5053	1 l. Stone-built house, Arges	25	10
5054	2 l. House with veranda, Constanta	55	15
5055	3 l. House with tiled roof and steps, Timis	80	25
5056	4 l. House with ramp to veranda, Neamt	1·10	35
5057	5 l. Two storey house with first floor veranda, Gorj	1·25	45

1017 Julius Popper (Tierra del Fuego, 1886–93)

1986. Polar Research. Multicoloured.

5058	50 b. Type **1017**	15	10
5059	1 l. Bazil Gh. Assan (Spitzbergen, 1896)	50	10
5060	2 l. Emil Racovita (Antarctic, 1897–99)	75	15
5061	3 l. Constantin Dumbrava (Greenland, 1927–28)	80	25
5062	4 l. Rumanian participation in 17th Soviet Antarctic Expedition, 1971–72	2·25	40
5063	5 l. 1977 "Sinoe" and 1979–80 "Tirnava" krill fishing expeditions	1·50	45

1019 The Blusher — **1020** Group of Cyclists

1986. Fungi. Multicoloured.

5065	50 b. Type **1019**	45	10
5066	1 l. "Boletus luridus"	65	15
5067	2 l. "Lactarius piperatus"	1·25	35
5068	3 l. "Lepiota clypeolaria"	1·75	50
5069	4 l. "Russula cyanoxantha"	2·75	70
5070	5 l. "Tremiscus helvelloides"	3·25	95

1986. Cycle Tour of Rumania. Multicoloured.
5071 1 l. Type **1020** 25 10
5072 2 l. Motor cycle following cyclist 55 15
5073 3 l. Jeep following cyclists . . 80 25
5074 4 l. Winner . . . . 1·10 35

1021 Emblem

1022 Petru Maior (historian) (225th birth anniv)

1986. 40th Anniv of U.N. and 30th Anniv of Rumanian Membership.
5076 **1021** 4 l. multicoloured . . . 1·10 35

1986. Birth Anniversaries.
5077 **1022** 50 b. purple, gold and green 15 10
5078 – 1 b. green, gold and mauve 25 10
5079 – 2 l. red, gold and blue . 55 15
5080 – 3 l. blue, gold and brown 80 25
DESIGNS: 1 l. George Topirceanu (writer, centenary); 2 l. Henri Coanda (engineer, centenary); 3 l. Constantin Budeanu (engineer, centenary).

1023 Coach and Horses

1024 F 300 Oil Drilling Rigs

1986. Stamp Day.
5081 **1023** 2 l. (+ 1 l.) multicoloured 80 25
No. 5081 was issued se-tenant with premium-carrying tab.

1986. Industry. Multicoloured.
5082 50 b. Type **1024** 15 10
5083 1 l. "Promex" excavator (horiz) 25 10
5084 2 l. Petrochemical refinery, Pitesti 55 15
5085 3 l. Tipper "110 t" (horiz) . . 80 25
5086 4 l. "Coral" computer . . . 1·10 35
5087 5 l. 350 m.w. turbine (horiz) . 1·25 45

1025 "Goat"

1026 Tin Can and Motor Car ("recycle metals")

1986. Folk Customs. Multicoloured.
5088 50 b. Type **1025** 15 10
5089 1 l. Sorcova 25 10
5090 2 l. Plugusorul 55 15
5091 3 l. Buhaiul 80 25
5092 4 l. Caiutii . . . . 1·10 35
5093 5 l. Uratorii . . . . 1·25 45

1986. "Save Waste Materials".
5094 **1026** 1 l. red and orange . . 25 10
5095 – 2 l. light green and green 55 15
DESIGN: 2 l. Trees and hand with newspaper ("recycle waste paper").

1027 Flags and Young People

1028 Anniversary Emblem

1987. 65th Anniv of Communist Youth Union. Multicoloured.
5096 1 l. Type **1027** 15 10
5097 2 l. Anniversary emblem . . 20 10
5098 3 l. Flags and young people (different) 40 10

1987. 25th Anniv of Agricultural Co-operatives.
5099 **1028** 2 l. multicoloured . . . 20 10

1030 "Birch Trees by Lake" (I. Andreescu)

1987. Paintings. Multicoloured.
5101 50 b. Type **1030** 10 10
5102 1 l. "Young Peasant Girls spinning" (N. Grigorescu) 25 10
5103 2 l. "Washerwoman" (St. Luchian) 55 10
5104 3 l. "Interior" (St. Dimitrescu) 80 10
5105 4 l. "Winter Landscape" (Al. Ciucurencu) . . . . 1·10 15
5106 5 l. "Winter in Bucharest" (N. Tonitza) (vert) . . . . . . 1·40 20

1031 "1907" and Peasants

1987. 80th Anniv of Peasant Uprising.
5107 **1031** 2 l. multicoloured . . . 55 10

1032 Players

1033 1 Leu Coin

1987. 10th Men's World Handball Championship. Various match scenes.
5108 **1032** 50 b. multicoloured . . 10 10
5109 – 1 l. multicoloured (horiz) 10 10
5110 – 2 l. multicoloured . . . 55 10
5111 – 3 l. multicoloured (horiz) 80 10
5112 – 4 l. multicoloured . . . 1·10 15
5113 – 5 l. multicoloured (horiz) 1·40 20

1987. Currency.
5114 **1033** 1 l. multicoloured . . . 10 10

1034 Eastern White Pelicans in the Danube Delta

1987. Tourism. Multicoloured.
5116 50 b. Type **1034** 30 20
5117 1 l. Cable car above Transfagarasan mountain road 30 10
5118 2 l. Cheile Bicazului 55 10
5119 3 l. Ceahlau mountains . . . 80 10
5120 4 l. Lake Capra, Fagaras, mountains . . . . 1·10 15
5121 5 l. Borsa orchards . . . . 1·40 20

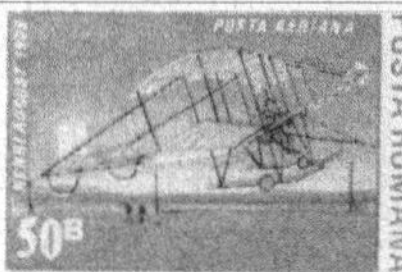

1035 Henri August's Glider, 1909

1987. Air. Aircraft. Multicoloured.
5122 50 b. Type **1035** 15 10
5123 1 l. Sky-diver jumping from IS-28 B2 glider 20 10
5124 2 l. IS-29 D2 glider 35 10
5125 3 l. IS-32 glider 65 15
5126 4 l. I.A.R.35 light airplane . . 90 25
5127 5 l. IS-28 M2 aircraft . . . . 1·10 30

1036 Youth on Winged Horse

1987. Fairy Tales by Petre Ispirescu. Multicoloured.
5128 50 b. Type **1036** 10 10
5129 1 l. King and princesses ("Salt in the Food") 30 10
5130 2 l. Girl on horse fighting lion ("Ileana Simziana") 20 10
5131 3 l. Youth with bow and arrow aiming at bird ("The Youth and the Golden Apples") . 80 10
5132 4 l. "George the Brave" . . . 1·10 15
5133 5 l. Girl looking at sleeping youth ("The Enchanted Pig") 1·40 20

1037 Class "L 45H" Diesel Shunter

1987. Railway Locomotives. Multicoloured.
5135 50 b. Type **1037** 15 10
5136 1 l. Class "LDE 125" 20 10
5137 2 l. Class "LDH 70" 30 10
5138 3 l. Class "LDE 2100" . . . 65 10
5139 4 l. Class "LDE 3000" . . . 90 15
5140 5 l. Class "LE 5100" . . . . 1·10 20
The 5 l. is an electric locomotives the rest are diesel.

1987. Costumes (2nd series). As T **999**. Multicoloured.
5143 1 l. Tirnave (female) 30 10
5144 1 l. Tirnave (male) 30 10
5145 2 l. Buzau (female) 50 10
5146 2 l. Buzau (male) 50 10
5147 3 l. Dobrogea (female) . . . 70 10
5148 3 l. Dobrogea (male) 70 10
5149 4 l. Ilfov (female) 95 15
5150 4 l. Ilfov (male) 95 15

1040 Postal Services (½-size illustration)

1987. Stamp Day.
5151 **1040** 2 l. (+ 1 l.) multicoloured 75 10
No. 5151 was issued se-tenant with premium carrying tab.

1041 Bee on Flower

1987. Bee-keeping. Multicoloured.
5152 1 l. Type **1041** 15 10
5153 2 l. Bee, sunflowers and hives 60 10
5154 3 l. Hives in Danube delta . . 70 10
5155 4 l. Apiculture Complex, Bucharest 95 15

1042 Car behind Boy on Bicycle

1987. Road Safety. Multicoloured.
5156 50 b. Type **1042** 10 10
5157 1 l. Children using school crossing 10 10
5158 2 l. Driver carelessly opening car door 25 10
5159 3 l. Hand holding crossing sign and children using zebra crossing 70 10
5160 4 l. Speedometer and crashed car 95 15
5161 5 l. Child's face and speeding car . . . . 1·10 25

1043 Red Flag and Lenin

1987. 70th Anniv of Russian Revolution.
5162 **1043** 2 l. multicoloured . . . 55 10

1044 Biathlon

1045 Crest and National Colours

1987. Winter Olympic Games, Calgary (1988). Multicoloured.
5163 50 b. Type **1044** 10 10
5164 1 l. Slalom 25 10
5165 1 l. 50 Ice hockey 20 10
5166 2 l. Luge 25 10
5167 3 l. Speed skating 40 10
5168 3 l. 50 Figure skating 80 10
5169 4 l. Downhill skiing 90 15
5170 5 l. Two-man bobsleigh . . . 1·10 25

1987. 40th Anniv of People's Republic.
5171 **1045** 2 l. multicoloured . . . 55 10

1046 Pres. Ceausescu and Flags

1988. 70th Birthday and 55 Years of Revolutionary Activity of Pres. Ceausescu.
5172 **1046** 2 l. multicoloured . . . 55 10

1047 Wide-necked Pot, Marginea

1988. Pottery. Multicoloured.
5173 50 b. Type **1047** 10 10
5174 1 l. Flask, Oboga 15 10
5175 2 l. Jug and saucer, Horezu . 25 10

5176 3 l. Narrow-necked pot, Curtea de Arges 70 10
5177 4 l. Jug, Birsa 95 15
5178 5 l. Jug and plate, Vama . . 1·10 25

1049 Ceramic Clock

1051 Constantin Brincoveanu

1988. Clocks in Ploiesti Museum. Multicoloured.
5180 50 b. Type **1049** 10 10
5181 1 l. 50 Gilt clock with sun at base 20 10
5182 2 l. Clock with pastoral figure 25 10
5183 3 l. Gilt clock surmounted by figure 70 10
5184 4 l. Vase-shaped clock . . . 95 15
5185 5 l. Clock surmounted by porcelain figures . . . . . 1·10 25

1988. 300th Anniv of Election of Constantin Brincoveanu as Ruler of Wallachia.
5187 **1051** 2 l. multicoloured . . . 55 10

1052 Gymnastics

1988. Olympic Games, Seoul (1st issue). Mult.
5188 50 b. Type **1052** 10 10
5189 1 l. 50 Boxing 20 10
5190 2 l. Lawn tennis 25 10
5191 3 l. Judo 70 10
5192 4 l. Running 95 15
5193 5 l. Rowing . . . . 1·10 25
See also Nos. 5197/5204.

1053 Emblems and Roses

1988. Rumanian–Chinese Stamp Exhibition.
5194 **1053** 2 l. multicoloured . . . 55 10

1056 Running

1988. Olympic Games, Seoul (2nd issue). Mult.
5197 50 b. Type **1056** 10 10
5198 1 l. Canoeing 25 10
5199 1 l. 50 Gymnastics 20 10
5200 2 l. Double kayak 25 10
5201 3 l. Weightlifting 70 10
5202 3 l. 50 Swimming 80 10
5203 4 l. Fencing 90 15
5204 5 l. Rowing . . . . 1·10 25

1058 Past and Present Postal Services (½-size illustration)

1988. Stamp Day.
5206 **1058** 2 l. (+ 1 l.) multicoloured 70 10
No. 5206 was issued with se-tenant premium-carrying label, as shown in T **1058**.

1060 State Arms

1988. 70th Anniv of Union of Transylvania and Rumania.
5208 **1060** 2 l. multicoloured . . . 55 10

1061 Athenaeum Concert Hall, Bucharest (centenary)

1988. Rumanian History. Multicoloured.
5209 50 b. Type **1061** 15 10
5210 1 l. 50 Roman coin showing Drobeta Bridge 20 10
5211 2 l. Ruins (600th anniv of Suceava as capital of Moldavian feudal state) . 25 10
5212 3 l. Scroll, arms and town (600th anniv of first documentary reference to Pitesti) . . . 70 10
5213 4 l. Dacian warriors from Trajan's Column 95 15
5214 5 l. Thracian gold helmet from Cotofenesti-Prahova . . . 1·10 25

1062 Zapodeni, 17th century

1989. Traditional House Architecture. Mult.
5215 50 b. Type **1062** 15 10
5216 1 l. 50 Berbesti, 18th century 20 10
5217 2 l. Voitinel, 18th century . 30 10
5218 3 l. Chiojdu Mic, 18th century 70 10
5219 4 l. Cimpanii de Sus, 19th century 95 15
5220 5 l. Naruja, 19th century . . 1·10 25

1063 Red Cross Worker

1989. Life-saving Services. Multicoloured.
5221 50 b. Type **1063** 15 10
5222 1 l. Red Cross orderlies giving first aid to girl (horiz) . . 15 10
5223 1 l. 50 Fireman carrying child 20 10
5224 2 l. Rescuing child from earthquake damaged building 30 10
5225 3 l. Mountain rescue team transporting casualty on sledge (horiz) 70 10
5226 3 l. 50 Rescuing climber from cliff face 85 15
5227 4 l. Rescuing child from river 95 15
5228 5 l. Life-guard in boat and children playing in sea (horiz) 1·10 25

1064 Tasca Bicaz Cement Factory

1989. Industrial Achievements. Multicoloured.
5229 50 b. Type **1064** 15 10
5230 1 l. 50 Railway bridge, Cernavoda 20 10
5231 2 l. Synchronous motor, Resita 30 10
5232 3 l. Bucharest underground . 40 10
5233 4 l. Mangalia-Constanta ferry 95 15
5234 5 l. "Gloria" oil drilling platform . . . . 1·10 25

1065 Flags and Symbols of Industry and Agriculture

1989. 50th Anniv of Anti-Fascist Demonstration.
5235 **1065** 2 l. multicoloured . . . 55 10

1068 Ion Creanga (writer, death centenary)

1989. Anniversaries. Multicoloured.
5239 1 l. Type **1068** 15 10
5240 2 l. Mihai Eminescu (poet, death centenary) 30 10
5241 3 l. Nicolae Teclu (150th birth anniv) 75 10

1069 Flags and Symbols of Industry and Agriculture

1989. 45th Anniv of Liberation.
5242 **1069** 2 l. multicoloured . . . 55 10

1070 "Pin-Pin"

1989. Rumanian Cartoon Films. Multicoloured.
5243 50 b. Type **1070** 10 10
5244 1 l. "Maria" 15 10
5245 1 l. 50 "Gore and Grigore" . 20 10
5246 2 l. "Pisoiul Balanel, Manole, Monk 30 10
5247 3 l. "Gruia lui Novac" . . . 75 10
5248 3 l. 50 "Mihaela" 901 5
5249 4 l. "Harap Alb" . . . . . . 1·00 15
5250 5 l. "Homo Sapiens" . . . . 1·25 25

1071 Globe, Letter and Houses (½-size illustration)

1989. Stamp Day.
5251 **1071** 2 l. (+ 1.) multicoloured 75 10
No. 521 was issued se-tenant with premium-carrying tab as illustrated in T **1071**.

1072 Storming of the Bastille

1989. Bicentenary of French Revolution. Mult.
5252 50 b. Type **1072** 15 10
5253 1 l. 50 Street boy and Marianne 20 10
5254 2 l. Robespierre 30 10
5255 3 l. Rouget de Lisle singing "Marseillaise" 75 10
5256 4 l. Diderot (writer) . . . . 1·00 15
5257 5 l. Crowd . . . . 1·25 25

1073 Conrad Haas and Diagram

1989. Air. Space Pioneers. Multicoloured.
5259 50 b. Type **1073** 10 10
5260 1 l. 50 K. Tsiolkovski and diagram 40 10
5261 2 l. Hermann Oberth and equation 55 10
5262 3 l. Robert Goddard and diagram 80 10
5263 4 l. Sergei Pavlovich Korolev, Earth and satellite . . . . 1·10 10
5264 5 l. Wernher von Braun and landing module . . . . . 1·40 10

1075 Flags and Emblem

1076 Date, Flag, Victory Sign and Candles

1989. 14th Communist Party Congress.
5266 **1075** 2 l. multicoloured . . . 55 10

1990. Popular Uprising (1st issue).
5268 **1076** 2 l. multicoloured . . . 55 10
See also Nos. 594/5301.

1077 Flags and Footballers

1990. World Cup Football Championship, Italy (1st issue). Designs showing flags and footballers.
5269 **1077** 50 b. multicoloured . . 15 10
5270 – 1 l. 50 multicoloured . 40 10
5271 – 2 l. multicoloured . . . 55 10
5272 – 3 l. multicoloured . . . 80 15
5273 – 4 l. multicoloured . . . 1·10 25
5274 – 5 l. multicoloured . . . 1·40 25
See also Nos. 5276/83.

1079 Footballers

1990. World Cup Football Championship, Italy (2nd issue).
5276 **1079** 50 b. multicoloured . . 15 10
5277 – 1 l. multicoloured . . . 25 10
5378 – 1 l. 50 multicoloured . 40 10
5379 – 2 l. multicoloured . . . 55 10
5380 – 3 l. multicoloured . . . 80 15
5381 – 3 l. 50 multicoloured . 95 20
5382 – 4 l. multicoloured . . . 1·10 25
5383 – 5 l. multicoloured . . . 1·40 25
DESIGNS: 1 to 5 l. Different football scenes.

1080 German Shepherds

1990. International Dog Show, Brno. Multicoloured.

5284	50 b. Type **1080**	10	10
5285	1 l. English setter	25	10
5286	1 l. 50 Boxers	35	10
5287	2 l. Beagles	45	10
5288	3 l. Dobermann pinschers	70	15
5289	3 l. 50 Great danes	80	15
5290	4 l. Afghan hounds	90	15
5291	5 l. Yorkshire terriers	1·10	20

1081 Fountain

1990. "Riccione 90" International Stamp Fair.

5292 **1081**	2 l. multicoloured	45	10

1082 Bucharest Athenaeum and Chinese Temple

1990. Rumanian–Chinese Stamp Exhibition, Bucharest.

5293 **1082**	2 l. multicoloured	45	10

1083 Republic Palace ablaze, Bucharest

1990. Popular Uprising (2nd issue). Multicoloured.

5294	50 b. + 50 b. Type **1083**	25	10
5295	1 l. + 1 l. Crowd in Opera Square, Timisoara	45	10
5296	1 l. 50 + 1 l. Soldiers joining crowd in Town Hall Square, Tirgu Mures	60	10
5297	2 l. + 1 l. Soldiers and crowd before television headquarters, Bucharest (vert)	70	10
5298	3 l. + 1 l. Mourners at funeral, Timisoara	90	10
5299	3 l. 50 + 1 l. Crowd celebrating, Brasov (vert)	1·00	15
5300	4 l. + 1 l. Crowd, Sibiu	1·00	15
5301	5 l. + 2 l. Cemetery, Bucharest	1·60	20

1084 "Nicolae Cobzarul" (St. Luchian)

1990. Paintings. Multicoloured.

5303	50 b. Type **1084**	10	10
5304	1 l. 50 "Woman in White" (I. Andreescu)	35	10
5305	2 l. "Florist" (St. Luchian)	45	10
5306	3 l. "Vase of Flowers" (Jan Brueghel, the elder)	70	15
5307	4 l. "Spring" (Pieter Brueghel, the elder) (horiz)	95	15
5308	5 l. "Madonna and Child" (G. B. Paggi)	1·10	20

1085 Flag Stamps encircling Globe

1990. Stamp Day.

5309 **1085**	2 l. (+ 1 l.) multicoloured	70	30

No. 5309 was issued with se-tenant premium-carrying label.

1086 Prince Constantin Cantacuzino (350th birth anniv)

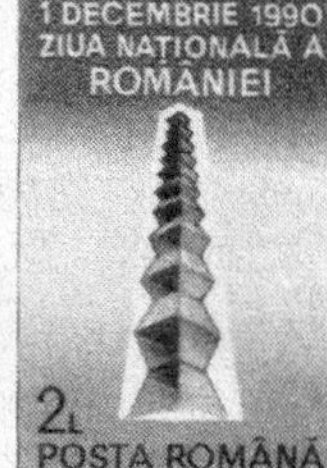

1087 Column of Infinity

1990. Anniversaries.

5310	**1086**	50 b. brown and blue	10	10
5311	–	1 l. 50 green and mauve	35	10
5312	–	2 l. red and blue	45	10
5313	–	3 l. blue and brown	65	10
5314	–	4 l. brown and blue	90	15
5315	–	5 l. violet and green	1·10	20

DESIGNS: 1 l. 50, Ienachita Vacarescu (annalist, 250th birth anniv); 2 l. Titu Maiorescu (writer, 150th birth anniv); 3 l. Nicolae Iorga (historian, 50th death anniv); 4 l. Martha Bibescu (birth centenary); 5 l. Stefan Procupiu (scientist, birth centenary).

1990. National Day.

5316 **1087**	2 l. multicoloured	45	10

1990. 1st Anniv of Popular Uprising. No. 5268 surch **L4 UN AN DE LA VICTORIA REVOLUTIEI**.

5317 **1076**	4 l. on 2 l. multicoloured	90	10

1089 "Irises"

1991. Death Centenary of Vincent van Gogh (painter). Multicoloured.

5318	50 b. Type **1089**	10	10
5319	2 l. "The Artist's Room"	10	10
5320	3 l. "Illuminated Coffee Terrace" (vert)	25	10
5321	3 l. 50 "Ochard in Blossom"	30	10
5322	5 l. "Sunflowers" (vert)	40	10

1090 Great Black-backed Gull

1091 Crucifixion

1991. Water Birds.

5323	**1090**	50 b. blue	10	10
5324	–	1 l. green	10	10
5325	–	1 l. 50 bistre	15	10
5326	–	2 l. blue	20	10
5327	–	3 l. green	30	15
5328	–	3 l. 50 green	35	15
5329	–	4 l. violet	40	20
5330	–	5 l. brown	50	25
5331	–	6 l. brown	60	30
5332	–	7 l. blue	70	35

DESIGNS: 1 l. Common tern; 1 l. 50, Avocet; 2 l. Pomarine skua; 3 l. Lapwings; 3 l. 50, Red-breasted merganser; 4 l. Little egret; 5 l. Dunlin; 6 l. Black-tailed godwit; 7 l. Whiskered tern.

1991. Easter.

5333 **1091**	4 l. multicoloured	30	10

1092 "Eutelsat 1" Communications Satellite

1093 Posthorn

1991. Europa. Europe in Space.

5334 **1092**	4 l. 50 multicoloured	35	10

1991.

5335 **1093**	4 l. 50 blue	35	10

1094 Rings Exercise

1095 Curtea de Arges Monastery

1991. Gymnastics. Multicoloured.

5336	1 l. Type **1094**	10	10
5337	1 l. Parallel bars	10	10
5338	4 l. 50 Vaulting	40	10
5339	4 l. 50 Asymmetric bars	40	10
5340	8 l. Floor exercises	65	10
5341	9 l. Beam	75	10

1991. Monasteries. Multicoloured.

5342	1 l. Type **1095**	10	10
5343	1 l. Putna	10	10
5344	4 l. 50 Varatec	40	10
5345	4 l. 50 Agapia (horiz)	40	10
5346	8 l. Golia (horiz)	65	10
5347	9 l. Sucevita (horiz)	75	10

1096 Hotel Continental, Timisoara

1097 Gull and Sea Shore

1991. Hotels.

5349	**1096**	1 l. blue	10	10
5350	–	2 l. green	15	10
5352	–	4 l. red	25	10
5353	–	5 l. violet	40	10
5354	–	6 l. brown	35	10
5356	–	8 l. brown	45	10
5357	–	9 l. red	75	10
5358	–	10 l. green	85	10
5360	–	18 l. red	1·00	10
5361	–	20 l. orange	1·10	10
5362	–	25 l. blue	1·40	10
5363	–	30 l. purple	1·60	10
5365	–	45 l. blue	2·50	10
5367	–	60 l. green	3·25	10
5369	–	80 l. violet	4·50	10
5371	–	120 l. blue and grey	2·75	10
5372	–	160 l. red and pink	3·75	10
5374	–	250 l. blue and grey	5·50	10
5376	–	400 l. brown and ochre	9·00	10
5377	–	500 l. dp green & green	11·00	10
5379	–	800 l. mauve and pink	18·00	10

DESIGNS—As T **1096**: HORIZ: 2 l. Valea Caprei Chalet, Mt. Fagaras; 5 l. Hotel Lebada, Crisan; 6 l. Muntele Rosu Chalet, Mt. Ciucas; 8 l. Transsilvania Hotel, Cluj-Napoca; 9 l. Hotel Orizont, Predeal; 20 l. Alpin Hotel, Poiana Bra, Psov; 25 l. Constanta Casino; 30 l. Miorita Chalet, Mt. Bucegi; 45 l. Sura Dacilor Chalet, Poiana Brasov; 60 l. Valea Draganului Tourist Complex; 80 l. Hotel Florica, Venus. VERT: 4 l. Intercontinental Hotel, Bucharest; 10 l. Hotel Roman, Baile Herculcane; 18 l. Rarau Chalet, Mt. Rarau. 26 × 40 mm: 120 l. International Complex, Baile Felix; 160 l. Hotel Egreta, Tulcea. 40 × 26 mm: 250 l. Valea de Pesti Motel, Jiului Valley; 400 l. Baisoara Tourist Complex; 500 l. Bradul Hotel, Covasna; 800 l. Gorj Hotel, Jiu.

Nos. 5367/79 have no frame.

1991. "Riccione 91" Stamp Exhibition, Italy.

5381 **1097**	4 l. multicoloured	20	10

1098 Vase

1099 Emblem

1991. Rumanian–Chinese Stamp Exhibition. Mult.

5382	5 l. Type **1098**	40	10
5383	5 l. Vase with peony decoration	40	10

1991. 125th Anniv of Rumanian Academy.

5384 **1099**	1 l. blue	10	10

1100 "Flowers" (Nicu Enea)

1102 Map with House and People

1991. "Balcanfila '91" Stamp Exhibition, Bacau. Multicoloured.

5385	4 l. Type **1100**	35	10
5386	5 l. (+ 2 l.) "Peasant Girl of Vlasca" (Georghe Tattarescu)	60	15

1991. Population and Housing Census.

5389 **1102**	5 l. multicoloured	40	20

1103 Bridge

1991. "Phila Nippon '91" International Stamp Exhibition, Tokyo.

5390	**1103**	10 l. ochre, brown & red	10	10
5391	–	10 l. multicoloured	10	10

DESIGN: No. 5391, Junk.

1105 Running

1991. World Athletics Championships, Tokyo. Multicoloured.

5393	1 l. Type **1105**	10	10
5394	4 l. Long jumping	35	10
5395	5 l. High jumping	45	10
5396	5 l. Athlete in starting blocks	45	10
5397	9 l. Hurdling	75	10
5398	10 l. Throwing the javelin	85	10

1106 Mihail Kogalniceanu (policitian, death cent)

1991. Anniversaries.

5399	**1106**	1 l. brown, blue & dp bl	10	10
5400	–	4 l. green, lilac & violet	35	10
5401	–	5 l. brown, dp blue & bl	45	10
5402	–	5 l. blue, brown & red	45	10
5403	–	9 l. red, blue & dp blue	75	10
5404	–	10 l. black, lt brn & brn	85	10

DESIGNS: No. 5400, Nicolae Titulescu (politician, 50th death anniv); 5401, Andrei Mureseanu (writer, 175th birth anniv); 5402, Aron Pumnul (writer, 125th death anniv); 5403, George Bacovia (writer, 110th birth anniv); 5404, Perpessicius (literature critic, birth centenary).

1107 Library Building

1991. Centenary of Central University Library.
5405 **1107** 8 l. brown 65 10

1108 Coach and Horses
(⅔-size illustration)

1991. Stamp Day.
5406 **1108** 8 l. (+ 2 l.) multicoloured 85 15
No. 5406 was issued se-tenant with premium-carrying label as illustrated in Type **1108**.

1109 "Nativity" (17th-century icon)
1110 Shooting (biathlon)

1991. Christmas.
5407 **1109** 8 l. multicoloured . . . 65 10

1992. Winter Olympic Games, Albertville. Mult.
5408 4 l. Type **1110** 10 10
5409 5 l. Downhill skiing 15 10
5410 8 l. Cross-country skiing . . 25 10
5411 10 l. Two-man luge 30 10
5412 20 l. Speed skating 55 10
5413 25 l. Ski-jumping 70 10
5414 30 l. Ice hockey 85 10
5415 45 l. Men's figure skating . . 1·25 10

1112 Jug, Plate, Tray and Bowl

1992. Rumanian Porcelain. Multicoloured.
5419 4 l. Type **1112** 10 10
5420 5 l. Tea set 10 10
5421 8 l. Jug and goblet (vert) . . 10 10
5422 30 l. Tea set (different) . . . 65 10
5423 45 l. Vase (vert) . . . . . . 1·00 10

1113 Mackerels

1992. Fishes. Multicoloured.
5424 4 l. Type **1113** 10 10
5425 5 l. Tench 10 10
5426 8 l. Speckled trout 10 10
5427 10 l. Riffle perch 10 10
5428 30 l. Undermouth 65 10
5429 45 l. Blunt-snouted mullet . . 1·25 10

1114 Vase
1115 Gymnast on Beam

1992. Apollo Art Gallery. Unissued stamp surch.
5430 **1114** 90 l. on 5 l. multicoloured 2·10 10

1992. Individual Gymnastic Championships, Paris. Unissued stamp surch.
5431 **1115** 90 l. on 5 l. multicoloured 2·10 10

1116 Dressage
1118 "Descent into Hell" (icon)

1992. Horses. Multicoloured.
5432 6 l. Type **1116** 15 10
5433 7 l. Racing (horiz) 15 10
5434 10 l. Rearing 20 10
5435 25 l. Jumping gate 55 10
5436 30 l. Stamping foot (horiz) . 65 10
5437 50 l. Winged horse . . . . . 1·10 10

1992. Easter.
5440 **1118** 10 l. multicoloured . . 25 10

1120 "Tower and Hand Pump"

1992. Centenary of Bucharest Fire Tower.
5441 **1120** 10 l. multicoloured . . 25 10

1121 Filipino Vinta and Rook

1992. 30th Chess Olympiad, Manila. Mult.
5442 10 l. Type **1121** 25 10
5443 10 l. Exterior of venue and chessmen 25 10

1122 Post Rider approaching Town

1992. Stamp Day.
5445 **1122** 10 l. + 4 l. pink, violet and blue 15 10

1123 Pistol shooting
1124 Ion Bratianu

1992. Olympic Games, Barcelona. Multicoloured.
5446 6 l. Type **1123** 10 10
5447 7 l. Weightlifting 10 10
5448 9 l. Two-man kayak racing (horiz) 10 10
5449 10 l. Handball 10 10
5450 25 l. Wrestling (horiz) . . . 30 10
5451 30 l. Fencing (horiz) 35 10
5452 50 l. Running 60 10
5453 55 l. Boxing (horiz) 65 10

1992. 130th Anniv of Foreign Ministry. Designs showing former Ministers.
5455 **1124** 10 l. violet, green and deep green 10 10
5456 – 25 l. purple, bl & dp bl . 20 10
5457 – 30 l. blue, purple & brn . 25 10
DESIGNS: 25 l. Ion Duca; 30 l. Grigore Gafencu.

1125 Sculpture

1992. "Expo 92" World's Fair, Seville. "Era of Discovery". Multicoloured.
5458 6 l. Type **1125** 10 10
5459 7 l. Roman bridge, Turnu-Severin 10 10
5460 10 l. House on stilts 10 10
5461 25 l. Railway bridge, Cernavoda 10 10
5462 30 l. Vuia No. 1 (airplane) . . 20 10
5463 55 l. Rocket 35 15

1126 Doves posting Letters in Globe

1992. World Post Day.
5465 **1126** 10 l. multicoloured . . . 10 10

1127 "Santa Maria" and Bust of Columbus

1992. 500th Anniv of Discovery of America by Columbus. Multicoloured.
5466 6 l. Type **1127** 10 10
5467 10 l. "Nina" 10 10
5468 25 l. "Pinta" 20 10
5469 55 l. Columbus claiming New World 40 10

1128 Post Office Emblem

1992. 1st Anniv of Establishment of R.A. Posta Romana (postal organization).
5471 **1128** 10 l. multicoloured . . . 10 10

1129 Jacob Negruzzi (writer, 150th birth anniv)
1130 American Bald Eagle

1992. Anniversaries.
5472 **1129** 6 l. green and violet . . 10 10
5473 – 7 l. mauve, purple and green 10 10
5474 – 9 l. blue and mauve . . 10 10
5475 – 10 l. lt brown, brown and ultramarine 10 10
5476 – 25 l. blue and brown . . 15 10
5477 – 30 l. green and lbue . . 20 10
DESIGNS: 7 l. Grigore Antipa (zoologist, 125th birth anniv); 9 l. Alexe Mateevici (poet, 75th death anniv); 10 l. Cezar Petrescu (writer, birth centenary); 25 l. Octav Onicescu (mathematician, birth centenary); 30 l. Ecaterina Teodoroiu (first world war fighter, 75th death anniv).

1992. Animals. Multicoloured.
5478 6 l. Type **1130** 10 10
5479 7 l. Spotted owl 10 10
5480 9 l. Brown bear 10 10
5481 10 l. American black oystercatcher (horiz) 10 10
5482 25 l. Wolf (horiz) 20 10
5483 30 l. White-tailed deer (horiz) 20 10
5484 55 l. Elk (horiz) 40 10

1131 Arms
1133 Nativity

1132 Buildings and Street, Galea Victoriei

1992. New State Arms.
5486 **1131** 15 l. multicoloured . . 10 10

1992. Anniversaries. Multicoloured.
5487 7 l. Type **1132** (300th anniv) 10 10
5488 9 l. College building and statue, Roman (600th anniv) . . . 10 10
5489 10 l. Prince Basarab, monastery and Princess Despina (475th anniv of Curtea de Arges monastery) 10 10
5490 25 l. Bucharest School of Architecture (80th anniv) . 10 10

1992. Christmas.
5491 **1133** 15 l. multicoloured . . 10 10

1134 Globe and Key-pad on Telephone

1992. New Telephone Number System.
5492 **1134** 15 l. black, red & blue . 10 10

1136 Mihai Voda Monastery

1993. Bucharest Buildings. Multicoloured.
5494 10 l. Type **1136** 10 10
5495 15 l. Vacaresti Monastery . . 10 10
5496 25 l. Unirii Hall 15 10
5497 30 l. Mina Minovici Medico-legal Institute 20 10

1137 Parseval Sigsfeld Kite-type Observation Balloon

1993. Air. Balloons. Multicoloured.
5498 30 l. Type **1137** 20 10
5499 90 l. Caquot observation balloon 55 10

1138 Crucifixion
1139 Hawthorn

1993. Easter.
5500 **1138** 15 l. multicoloured . . 10 10

1993. Medicinal Plants. Multicoloured.
5501 10 l. Type **1139** 10 10
5502 15 l. Gentian 10 10

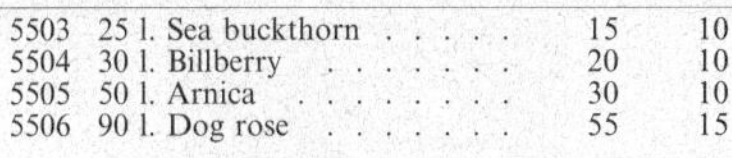

5503 25 l. Sea buckthorn 15 10
5504 30 l. Billberry 20 10
5505 50 l. Arnica 30 10
5506 90 l. Dog rose 55 15

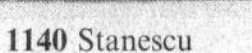

1140 Stanescu 1141 Mounted Courier

1993. 60th Birth Anniv of Nichita Stanescu (poet).
5507 **1140** 15 l. multicoloured . . . 10 10

1993. Stamp Day.
5508 **1141** 15 l. + 10 l. multicoloured 10 10

1143 Magpie

1993. Birds.
5510 **1143** 5 l. black and green . . 10 10
5511 – 10 l. black and red . . . 10 10
5512 – 15 l. black and red . . . 10 10
5513 – 20 l. black and brown . 10 10
5514 – 25 l. black and red . . . 15 10
5515 – 50 l. black and yellow . 30 10
5516 – 65 l. black and red . . . 40 10
5517 – 90 l. black and red . . . 55 15
5518 – 160 l. black and blue . . 95 30
5519 – 250 l. black & mauve . 1·50 50
DESIGNS—HORIZ: 10 l. Golden eagle. VERT: 15 l. Bullfinch; 20 l. Hoopoe; 25 l. Great spotted woodpecker; 50 l. Golden oriole; 65 l. White winged crossbill; 90 l. Barn swallows; 160 l. Azure tit; 250 l. Rose-coloured starling.

1144 Long-hair 1147 Pine Marten

1146 Adder

1993. Cats. Multicoloured.
5520 10 l. Type **1144** 10 10
5521 15 l. Tabby-point long-hair . 10 10
5522 30 l. Red long-hair 15 10
5523 90 l. Blue persian 40 10
5524 135 l. Tabby 60 20
5525 160 l. Long-haired white Persian 70 20

1993. Protected Animals. Multicoloured.
5527 10 l. Type **1146** 10 10
5528 15 l. Lynx (vert) 10 10
5529 25 l. Common shelduck . . . 10 10
5530 75 l. Danube salmon 25 10
5531 105 l. Poplar admiral 35 10
5532 280 l. Alpine longthorn beetle 1·00 30

1993. Mammals.
5533 **1147** 10 l. black and yellow . 10 10
5534 – 15 l. black and brown . 10 10
5535 – 20 l. red and black . . . 10 10
5536 – 25 l. black and brown . 10 10
5537 – 30 l. black and red . . . 10 10
5538 – 40 l. black and red . . . 15 10
5539 – 75 l. black and yellow . 25 10
5540 – 105 l. black & brown . 35 10
5541 – 150 l. black & orange . 50 15
5542 – 280 l. black & yellow . 95 30
DESIGNS—HORIZ: 15 l. Common rabbit; 30 l. Red fox; 150 l. Stoat; 280 l. Egyptian mongoose. VERT: 20 l. Eurasian red squirrel; 25 l. Chamois; 40 l. Argali; 75 l. Small spotted genet; 105 l. Garden dormouse.

1148 Brontosaurus

1993. Prehistoric Animals. Multicoloured.
5543 29 l. Type **1148** 10 10
5544 46 l. Plesiosaurus 15 10
5545 85 l. Triceratops 30 10
5546 171 l. Stegosaurus 60 20
5547 216 l. Tyannosaurus 75 20
5548 319 l. Archaeopteryx . . . . 1·10 35

1150 Stefan the Great, Prince of Moldavia 1151 Mounted Officers

1993. Icons. Multicoloured.
5550 75 l. Type **1150** 10 10
5551 171 l. Prince Costantin Brancoveanu of Wallachia with his sons Constantin, Stefan, Radu and Matei and Adviser Ianache Vacarescu 30 10
5552 216 l. St. Antim Ivireanul, Metropolitan of Wallachia 70 20

1993. Centenary of Rural Gendarmeric Law.
5553 **1151** 29 l. multicoloured . . 10 10

1993. "Riccione 93" International Stamp Fair. No. 5292 surch **Riccione '93 3-5 septembrie 171 L.**
5554 **1081** 171 l. on 2 l. multicoloured 70 20

1154 George Baritiu

1993. Anniversaries.
5556 **1154** 29 l. flesh, black & lilac 10 10
5557 – 46 l. flesh, black & blue 15 10
5558 – 85 l. flesh, black & grn 30 10
5559 – 171 l. flesh, black & pur 60 20
5560 – 216 l. flesh, black & bl 75 25
5561 – 319 l. flesh, black and grey 1·10 35
DESIGNS: 29 l. Type **1154** (politician and journalist, death centenary); 46 l. Horia Creanga (architect, 50th death anniv); 85 l. Armand Calinescu (leader of Peasant National Party, birth centenary); 171 l. Dr. Dumitru Bagdasar (neurosurgeon, birth centenary); 216 l. Constantin Brailoiu (musician, birth centenary); 319 l. Iuliu Maniu (politician, 40th death anniv).

1993. 35th Annivs of Rumanian Philatelic Association and Rumanian Philatelic Federation. No. 5445 surch **35 ANI DE ACTIVITATE AFR-FFR 1958–1993 70L+45L.**
5562 **1122** 70 l. + 45 l. on 10 l. + 4 l. pink, violet and blue 40 10

1157 Iancu Flondor (Bukovinan politician)

1993. 75th Anniv of Union of Bessarabia, Bukovina and Transylvania with Rumania.
5564 **1157** 115 l. brown, blue and black 30 10
5565 – 245 l. violet, yellow and green 55 15
5566 – 255 l. multicoloured . . 65 20
5567 – 325 l. brown, pink and deep brown 95 30
DESIGNS: 245 l. Ionel Bratianu (Prime Minister 1918–19, 1922–26 and 1927); 255 l. Iuliu Maniu (Prime Minister, 1927–30 and 1932–33); 325 l. Panteleimon Halippa (Bessarabian politician).

1158 Emblem

1993. Anniversaries. Multicoloured.
5569 115 l. Type **1158** (75th anniv of General Association of Rumanian Engineers) . . . 30 10
5570 245 l. Statue of Johannes Honterus (450th anniv of Rumanian Humanist School) 55 15
5571 255 l. Bridge, arms on book spine and seal (625th anniv of first documentary reference to Slatina) 65 20
5572 325 l. Map and town arms (625th anniv of first documentary reference to Braila) 95 30

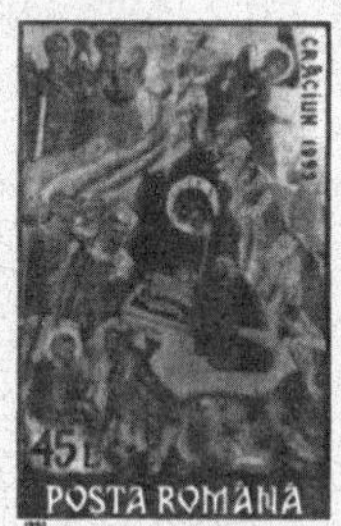

1159 "Nativity" (17th-century icon)

1993. Christmas.
5573 **1159** 45 l. multicoloured . . . 30 10

1160 "Clivina subterranea"

1993. Movile Cave Animals. Multicoloured.
5574 29 l. Type **1160** 10 10
5575 46 l. "Nepa anophthalma" . . 25 10
5576 85 l. "Haemopis caeca" . . . 45 15
5577 171 l. "Lascona cristiani" . . 65 20
5578 216 l. "Semisalsa dobrogica" . 75 25
5579 319 l. "Armadilidium tabacarui" . . . . 1·40 45

1161 Prince Alexandru Ioan Cuza and Seal

1994. 130th Anniv of Court of Accounts.
5581 **1161** 45 l. multicoloured . . . 20 10

1162 Opera House

1994. Destroyed Buildings of Bucharest. Mult.
5582 115 l. Type **1162** 25 10
5583 245 l. Vacaresti Church (vert) 55 15
5584 255 l. St. Vineri's Church . . 65 20
5585 325 l. Vacaresti Monastery . 90 30

1164 Speed Skating 1165 Sarichioi Windmill, Tulcea

1994. Winter Olympic Games, Lillehammer, Norway. Multicoloured.
5588 70 l. Type **1164** 10 10
5589 115 l. Downhill skiing . . . 15 10
5590 125 l. Bobsleighing 20 10
5591 245 l. Cross-country skiing . 45 15
5592 255 l. Ski jumping 55 15
5593 325 l. Figure skating 70 20

1994. Mills. Multicoloured.
5595 70 l. Type **1165** 10 10
5596 115 l. Nucarilor Valley windmill, Tulcea 10 10
5597 125 l. Caraorman windmill, Tulcea 25 10
5598 245 l. Romanii de Jos watermill, Valcea 50 15
5599 255 l. Enisala windmill, Tulcea (horiz) 60 20
5600 325 l. Nistoresti watermill, Vrancea 75 25

1166 Calin the Backward 1167 "Resurrection of Christ" (17th-century icon)

1994. Fairy Tales. Multicoloured.
5601 70 l. Type **1166** 10 10
5602 115 l. Ileana Cosanzeana flying 15 10
5603 125 l. Ileana Cosanzeana seated 25 10
5604 245 l. Ileana Cosanzeana and castle 50 15
5605 255 l. Agheran the Brave . . 60 20
5606 325 l. The Enchanted Wolf carrying Ileana Cosanzeana 75 25

1994. Easter.
5607 **1167** 60 l. multicoloured . . 40 10

1168 "Struthiosaurus transylvanicus"

1994. Dinosaurs. Multicoloured.
5608 90 l. Type **1168** 15 10
5609 130 l. Megalosaurus 25 10
5610 150 l. Parasaurolophus . . . 50 10
5611 280 l. Stenonychosaurus . . . 45 15
5612 500 l. Camarasaurus 85 25
5613 635 l. Gallimimus . . . . . 1·10 35

1170 Silver Fir 1171 Players and Flags of U.S.A., Switzerland, Colombia and Rumania

1994. Trees. Each green and black.
5615 15 l. Type **1170** 10 10
5616 35 l. Scots pine 10 10
5617 45 l. White poplar 10 10
5618 60 l. Pedunculate oak 15 10
5619 70 l. European larch 20 10
5620 125 l. Beech 25 10
5621 350 l. Sycamore 40 10

5622 940 l. Ash . . . . 1·25 40
5623 1440 l. Norway spruce . . . 1·75 55
5624 3095 l. Large-leaved lime . . 3·25 1·00

1994. World Cup Football Championship, U.S.A. Designs showing various footballing scenes and flags of participating countries. Multicoloured.

5625 90 l. Type **1171** 10 10
5626 130 l. Brazil, Russia, Cameroun and Sweden 15 10
5627 150 l. Germany, Bolivia, Spain and South Korea 20 10
5628 280 l. Argentina, Greece, Nigeria and Bulgaria . . . 35 10
5629 500 l. Italy, Ireland, Norway and Mexico 75 25
5630 635 l. Belgium, Morocco, Netherlands and Saudi Arabia 95 30

1172 Torch-bearer and Centenary Emblem

1994. Centenary of International Olympic Committee. Multicoloured.

5632 150 l. Type **1172** 20 10
5633 280 l. Athlete and International Sports Year emblem . . . 35 10
5634 500 l. Wrestlers and Olympic Peace emblem 75 25
5635 635 l. Athlete and "Paris 1994" centenary congress emblem 95 30

1173 National History Museum

1176 Tuning Fork

1175 Traian Vuia's Airplane No. 1, 1906

1994. Stamp Day.

5637 **1173** 90 l. + 60 l. multicoloured 40 10

1994. Air. 50th Anniv of I.C.A.O.

5639 **1175** 110 l. brown, black & bl 25 10
5640 – 350 l. multicoloured . . 65 20
5641 – 500 l. multicoloured . . 95 30
5642 – 635 l. black, ultramarine and blue . . . . . . 1·25 40

DESIGNS: 350 l. ROMBAC One Eleven; 500 l. Boeing 737-300; 635 l. Airbus Industrie A310.

1994. "Philakorea 1994" International Stamp Exhibition, Seoul.

5643 **1176** 60 l. multicoloured . . . 45 15

1177 Great Sturgeon

1994. Environmental Protection of Danube Delta. Multicoloured.

5645 150 l. Type **1177** 20 10
5646 280 l. Orsini's viper 25 10
5647 500 l. White-tailed sea eagle . 75 25
5648 635 l. European mink 95 30

1994. Victory of Rumanian Team in European Gymnastics Championships, Stockholm. Nos. 5338/9 surch **Echipa Romaniei Compioana Europeana Stockholm 1994** and value.

5650 150 l. on 4 l. 50 multicoloured 10 10
5651 525 l. on 4 l. 50 multicoloured 40 10

1179 Elephant

1994. The Circus. Multicoloured.

5652 90 l. Type **1179** 10 10
5653 130 l. Balancing bear (vert) . 10 10
5654 150 l. Cycling monkeys . . . 10 10
5655 280 l. Tiger jumping through hoop 20 10
5656 500 l. Clown balancing dogs on tight-rope 30 10
5657 635 l. Clown on horseback . 45 15

1994. World Post Day. No. 5465 surch **150LEI 1994 Posta - cea mai buna alegere**.

5658 **1126** 150 l. on 10 l. mult . . 10 10

1181 Emblem

1183 Snake

1182 Sterlet

1994. 20th International Fair, Bucharest.

5659 **1181** 525 l. multicoloured . . 40 10

1994. Sturgeons.

5660 150 l. Type **1182** 10 10
5661 280 l. Russian sturgeon . . 20 10
5662 500 l. Starred sturgeon . . . 35 10
5663 635 l. Common sturgeon . . 45 15

1994. Rumanian–Chinese Stamp Exhibition, Timisoara and Cluj-Napoca. Multicoloured.

5664 150 l. Type **1183** 10 10
5665 1135 l. Dragon 80 25

1184 Steam Locomotive

1994. 125th Anniv of Rumanian Railway Administration.

5666 **1184** 90 l. multicoloured . . 10 10

1185 Alexandru Orascu (architect and mathematician)

1994. Anniversaries. Multicoloured.

5667 30 l. Type **1185** (death centenary) 10 10
5668 60 l. Gheorghe Polizu (physician, 175th birth anniv) 10 10
5669 150 l. Iulia Hasdeu (writer, 125th birth anniv) 10 10
5670 280 l. S. Mehedinti (scientist, 125th birth anniv) 20 10
5671 350 l. Camil Petrescu (writer, birth centenary) 25 10
5672 500 l. N. Paulescu (physician, 125th birth anniv) 35 10
5673 940 l. L. Grigorescu (painter, birth centenary) 70 20

See also No. 5684.

1186 Nativity

1994. Christmas.

5674 **1186** 60 l. multicoloured . . . 10 10

1187 St. Mary's Church, Cleveland, U.S.A.

1994.

5675 **1187** 610 l. multicoloured . . 45 15

1188 Anniversary Emblem

1994. 20th Anniv of World Tourism Organization.

5676 **1188** 525 l. blue, orge & blk . 40 10

1190 Kittens

1191 Emblem

1994. Young Domestic Animals. Multicoloured.

5678 90 l. Type **1190** 10 10
5679 130 l. Puppies 10 10
5680 150 l. Kid 10 10
5681 280 l. Foal 20 10
5682 500 l. Rabbit kittens 35 10
5683 635 l. Lambs 45 15

1994. Death Centenary of Gheorghe Tattarescu (painter). As T **1185**. Multicoloured.

5684 90 l. Tattarescu 10 10

1995. Save the Children Organization.

5685 **1191** 60 l. blue 10 10

1192 Tanar

1995. Brasov Youth. Neighbourhood Group Leaders. Multicoloured.

5686 40 l. Type **1192** 10 10
5687 60 l. Batran 10 10
5688 150 l. Curcan 10 10
5689 280 l. Dorobant 20 10
5690 350 l. Brasovechean 25 10
5691 500 l. Rosior 35 10
5692 635 l. Albior 45 15

1193 Hand and Barbed Wire

1995. 50th Anniv of Liberation of Concentration Camps.

5693 **1193** 960 l. black and red . . 65 20

1194 Emblems of French and Rumanian State Airlines

1995. Air. 75th Anniv of Founding of Franco–Rumanian Air Company.

5694 **1194** 60 l. blue and red . . . 10 10
5695 – 960 l. blue and black . 65 20

DESIGN: 960 l. Potez IX biplane and Paris–Bucharest route map.

1195 Ear of Wheat

1995. 50th Anniversaries. Multicoloured.

5696 675 l. Type **1195** (F.A.O.) . . 45 15
5697 960 l. Anniversary emblem (U.N.O.) 65 20
5698 1615 l. Hand holding pen showing members' flags (signing of U.N. Charter) . 1·10 35

1196 "Resurrection" (icon)

1995. Easter.

5699 **1196** 60 l. multicoloured . . 10 10

1197 Immortal King on Horse

1995. Fairy Tales. Multicoloured.

5700 90 l. Type **1197** 10 10
5701 130 l. Girl with mythical creatures (vert) 10 10
5702 150 l. The prince with the golden hair 10 10
5703 280 l. Son of the Red King . 20 10
5704 500 l. Praslea the Brave and the Golden Apples (vert) . . . 35 10
5705 635 l. King Dafin (drawn by golden horses) 40 10

1198 Enescu

1995. 40th Death Anniv of George Enescu (composer).

5706 **1198** 960 l. orange and black 65 20

1199 Dove with Section of Rainbow

1200 Blaga

1995. Europa. Peace and Freedom. Multicoloured.

5707 150 l. Type **1199** 10 10
5708 4370 l. Dove wings forming "EUROPA" around rainbow 2·75 90

1995. Birth Centenary of Lucian Blaga (poet).
5709 **1200** 150 l. multicoloured . . 10 10
See also Nos. 5745/9.

1201 Bucharest Underground Railway, 1979

1995. Transport.
5712 **1201** 470 l. yellow and black (postage) 30 10
5713 – 630 l. red and blue . . . 25 10
5714 – 675 l. red and black . . 45 15
5716 – 755 l. blue and black . . 30 10
5720 – 1615 l. green and black . 70 20
5723 – 2300 l. green and black . 1·50 50
5726 – 2550 l. black and red . . 1·60 50
5728 – 285 l. green and black (air) 15 10
5729 – 965 l. black and blue . . 65 20
5730 – 1575 l. green and black . 65 20
5732 – 3410 l. blue and black . 2·25 75
DESIGNS—HORIZ: 285 l. I.A.R. 80 aircraft; 630 l. "Masagerul" (post boat); 715 l. "Razboueni" (container ship); 965 l. Sud Aviation SA 330 Puma helicopter; 1575 l. I.A.R. 818H flying boat; 2300 l. Trolleybus, 1904; 2550 l. Steam locomotive, 1869; 3410 l. Boeing 737-300 (75th anniv of Rumanian air transport). VERT: 675 l. Cable-car, Brasov; 1615 l. Electric tram, 1894.

1202 "Dacia" (liner) **1203** Fallow Deer

1995. Centenary of Rumanian Maritime Service. Multicoloured.
5735 90 l. Type **1202** 10 10
5736 130 l. "Imparatul Traian" (Danube steamer) (horiz) . 10 10
5737 150 l. "Romania" (Danube steamer) (horiz) 10 10
5738 280 l. "Costinesti" (tanker) (horiz) 20 10
5739 960 l. "Caransebes" (container ship) (horiz) 65 20
5740 3410 l. "Tutova" (car ferry) (horiz) . . . . 2·25 75

1995. European Nature Conservation Year. Multicoloured.
5741 150 l. Type **1203** 10 10
5742 280 l. Great bustard 25 10
5743 960 l. "Cypripedium calceolus" (orchid) 60 20
5744 1615 l. Stalagmites . . . . . 1·00 30

1995. Anniversaries. As T **1200**. Multicoloured.
5745 90 l. D. Rosca (birth centenary) 10 10
5746 130 l. Vasile Conta (150th birth anniv) 10 10
5747 280 l. Ion Barbu (birth centenary) 20 10
5748 960 l. Iuliu Hatieganu (110th birth anniv) 60 20
5749 1650 l. Dimitrie Brandza (botanist) (death centenary) 1·00 30

1204 Youths and Torch-bearer

1995. European Youth Olympic Days.
5750 **1204** 1650 l. multicoloured . . 1·00 30

1205 Post Wagon (⅓-size illustration)

1995. Stamp Day. Centenary of Upper Rhine Local Post.
5751 **1205** 960 l. (+ 715 l.) mult . 1·10 35
No. 5751 was issued se-tenant with premium-carrying tab, as shown in Type **1205**.

1206 Cernavoda Bridge

1995. Centenary of Cernavoda Bridge.
5752 **1206** 675 l. multicoloured . . 45 15

1207 Mallard **1208** General Dr. Victor Anastasiu

1995. Domestic Birds. Multicoloured.
5753 90 l. Type **1207** 10 10
5754 130 l. Red junglefowl (hen) . 10 10
5755 150 l. Helmet guineafowl . . 10 10
5756 280 l. Common turkey . . . 20 10
5757 960 l. Greylag goose 60 20
5758 1650 l. Red junglefowl (cock) 1·00 30

1995. 75th Anniv of Institute of Aeronautics Medicine.
5759 **1208** 960 l. ultramarine, blue and red 60 20

1209 Battle Scene

1995. 400th Anniv of Battle of Calugareni.
5760 **1209** 100 l. multicoloured . . 10 10

1210 Giurgiu Castle

1995. Anniversaries. Multicoloured.
5761 250 l. Type **1210** (600th anniv) 15 10
5762 500 l. Neamtului Castle (600th anniv) 30 10
5763 960 l. Sebes-Alba Mill (700th anniv) 60 20
5764 1615 l. Dorohoi Church (500th anniv) . . . . 1·00 30
5765 1650 l. Military observatory, Bucharest (centenary) . . 1·00 30

1211 Moldovita Monastery **1212** Racket

1995. U.N.E.S.C.O. World Heritage Sites. Multicoloured.
5766 675 l. Type **1211** 40 10
5767 960 l. Hurez Monastery . . 60 20
5768 1615 l. Biertan Castle (horiz) 1·00 30

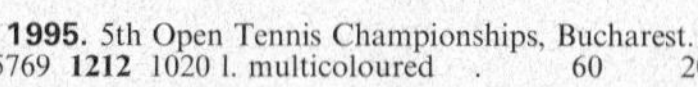

1995. 5th Open Tennis Championships, Bucharest.
5769 **1212** 1020 l. multicoloured . 60 20

1213 Ion Ionescu (editor)

1995. Centenary of Mathematics Gazette.
5770 **1213** 100 l. pink and brown 10 10

1214 "Albizzia julibrissin"

1995. Plants from Bucharest Botanical Garden. Multicoloured.
5771 50 l. Type **1214** 10 10
5772 100 l. Yew 10 10
5773 150 l. "Paulownia tomentosa" 10 10
5774 500 l. Bird of Paradise flower 30 10
5775 960 l. "Victoria amazonica" . 60 20
5776 2300 l. "Rhododendron indicum" . . . . 1·40 45

1215 St. John's Church **1216** George Apostu (sculptor, 110th death (1996))

1995. 600th Anniv of Piatra-Neamt.
5777 **1215** 250 l. multicoloured . . 15 10

1995. Anniversaries.
5778 **1216** 150 l. green and black . . 10 10
5779 – 250 l. blue and black . . 15 10
5780 – 500 l. light brown, brown and black 25 10
5781 – 960 l. rose, purple and black 50 15
5782 – 1650 l. brown and black 90 30
DESIGNS: 250 l. Emil Cioran (philosopher, death centenary); 500 l. Eugen Ionescu (writer, death centenary (1994)); 960 l. Elena Vacarescu (poetess, 130th birth (1996)); 1650 l. Mircea Eliade (philosopher, 110th death (1996)).

1217 Running

1995. Olympic Games, Atlanta (1996) (1st issue). Multicoloured.
5783 50 l. Type **1217** 10 10
5784 100 l. Gymnastics 10 10
5785 150 l. Canoeing 10 10
5786 500 l. Fencing 20 10
5787 960 l. Rowing 40 10
5788 2300 l. Boxing . . . . 1·10 35
See also Nos. 5829/33.

1218 Nativity

1995. Christmas.
5790 **1218** 100 l. multicoloured . . 10 10

1219 Masked Person

1996. Folk Masks.
5791 **1219** 250 l. multicoloured . 10 10
5792 – 500 l. multicoloured . 20 10
5793 – 960 l. multicoloured (vert) 35 10
5794 – 1650 l. multicoloured (vert) 60 20
DESIGNS: 500 l. to 1650 l. Different masks.

1220 Tristan Tzara **1221** "Resurrection" (icon)

1996. Writers' Birth Anniversaries. Multicoloured.
5795 150 l. Type **1220** (centenary) 10 10
5796 1500 l. Anton Pann (bicentenary) 55 15

1996. Easter.
5797 **1221** 150 l. multicoloured . 10 10

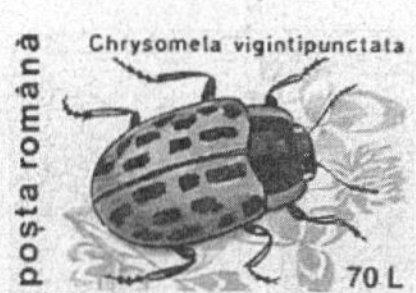

1223 Leaf Beetle

1996. Beetles.
5799 **1223** 70 l. yellow and black 10 10
5800 – 220 l. red and black . 10 10
5801 – 370 l. brown and black 15 10
5802 – 650 l. black, red & grey 25 10
5803 – 700 l. red, black & green 25 10
5804 – 740 l. black and yellow 25 10
5805 – 960 l. black and red . 35 10
5806 – 1000 l. yellow and black 35 10
5807 – 1500 l. black and brown 55 15
5808 – 2500 l. red, black & green 95 30
DESIGNS: 220 l. Longhorn beetle; 370 l. "Entomoscelis adonidis"; 650 l. Ladybird; 700 l. Ground beetle; 740 l. "Hedobia imperialis"; 960 l. European rhinocerus beetle; 1000 l. Bee chafer; 1500 l. Longhorn beetle (different); 2500 l. "Anthaxia salicis".

1225 Arbore Church

1996. U.N.E.S.C.O. World Heritage Sites. Multicoloured.
5810 150 l. Type **1225** 10 10
5811 1500 l. Voronet Monastery . 55 15
5812 2550 l. Humor Monastery . 95 30

1226 Ana Aslan (doctor)

1996. Europa. Famous Women. Multicoloured.
5813 370 l. Type **1226** 15 10
5814 4140 l. Lucia Bulandra (actress) . . . . 1·50 50

1227 "Mother and Children" (Oana Negoita)

1996. 50th Anniv of U.N.I.C.E.F. Prize-winning Children's Paintings. Multicoloured.
5815 370 l. Type **1227** 15 10
5816 740 l. "Winter Scene" (Badea Cosmin) 25 10
5817 1500 l. "Children and Sun over House" (Nicoleta Georgescu) 55 15
5818 2550 l. "House on Stilts" (Biborka Bartha) (vert) . . 95 30

1228 Goalkeeper with Ball

1996. European Football Championship, England. Multicoloured.
5819 220 l. Type **1228** 10 10
5820 370 l. Player with ball 15 10
5821 740 l. Two players with ball . . 25 10
5822 1500 l. Three players with ball 55 15
5823 2550 l. Player dribbling ball . 95 30
Nos. 5819/23 were issued together, se-tenant, forming a composite design of the pitch and stadium.

1229 Metropolitan Toronto Convention Centre (venue) 1232 Boxing

1230 Factory

1996. "Capex'96" International Stamp Exhibition, Toronto, Canada.
5825 **1229** 150 l. multicoloured . . 10 10

1996. 225th Anniv of Resita Works.
5827 **1230** 150 l. brown 10 10

1996. 5th Anniv of Establishment of R. A. Posta Romana (postal organization). No. 5471 surch **1996 - 5 ANI DE LA INFIINTARE L150.**
5828 **1128** 150 l. on 10 l. multicoloured 10 10

1996. Centenary of Modern Olympic Games and Olympic Games, Atlanta (2nd issue). Multicoloured.
5829 220 l. Type **1232** 10 10
5830 370 l. Running 15 10
5831 740 l. Rowing 25 10
5832 1500 l. Judo 55 15
5833 2550 l. Gymnastics 95 30

1233 Postman, Keyboard and Stamp under Magnifying Glass (2/3-size illustration)

1996. Stamp Day.
5835 **1233** 1500 l. (+ 650 l.) mult . 80 25
No. 5835 was issued se-tenant with a premium-carrying tab, as shown in Type **1233**.

1234 White Spruce

1996. Coniferous Trees. Multicoloured.
5836 70 l. Type **1234** 10 10
5837 150 l. Serbian spruce 10 10
5838 220 l. Blue Colorado spruce 10 10
5839 740 l. Sitka spruce 25 10
5840 1500 l. Scots pine 55 15
5841 3500 l. Maritime pine . . . 1·25 40

1235 Grass Snake 1236 Madonna and Child

1996. Animals. Multicoloured.
5842 70 l. Type **1235** 10 10
5843 150 l. Hermann's tortoise . . 10 10
5844 220 l. Sky lark (horiz) . . . 10 10
5845 740 l. Red fox (horiz) . . . 25 10
5846 1500 l. Common porpoise . 55 15
5847 3500 l. Golden eagle (horiz) 1·25 40

1996. Christmas.
5848 **1236** 150 l. multicoloured . . 10 10

1237 Stan Golestan (composer, 40th)

1996. Death Anniversaries.
5849 **1237** 100 l. pink and black . 10 10
5850 – 150 l. purple and black 10 10
5851 – 370 l. orange and black 15 10
5852 – 1500 l. red and black . 55 15
DESIGNS: 150 l. Corneliu Coposu (politician, 1st); 370 l. Horia Vintila (writer, 4th); 1500 l. Alexandru Papana (test pilot, 50th).

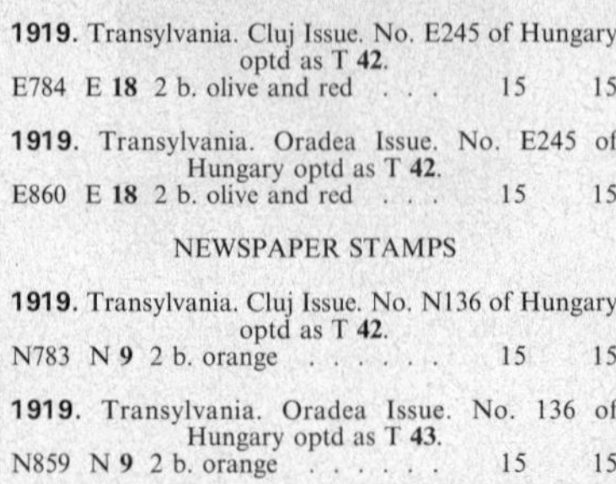

EXPRESS LETTER STAMPS

1919. Transylvania. Cluj Issue. No. E245 of Hungary optd as T **42**.
E784 E **18** 2 b. olive and red . . . 15 15

1919. Transylvania. Oradea Issue. No. E245 of Hungary optd as T **42**.
E860 E **18** 2 b. olive and red . . . 15 15

NEWSPAPER STAMPS

1919. Transylvania. Cluj Issue. No. N136 of Hungary optd as T **42**.
N783 N **9** 2 b. orange 15 15

1919. Transylvania. Oradea Issue. No. 136 of Hungary optd as T **43**.
N859 N **9** 2 b. orange 15 15

OFFICIAL STAMPS

O 71 Rumanian Eagle and National Flag O 80

1929.
O1115 O **71** 25 b. orange 10 10
O1116 50 b. brown 10 15
O1117 1 l. violet 10 10
O1118 2 l. green 10 10
O1119 3 l. red 30 10
O1120 4 l. olive 25 15
O1221 6 l. blue 35 25
O1222 10 l. blue 35 25
O1223 25 l. red . . . . . . 1·50 90
O1224 50 l. violet . . . . . 4·50 2·40

1930. Optd **8 IUNIE 1930**.
O1150 O **71** 25 b. orange 15 10
O1151 50 b. brown 15 10
O1152 1 l. violet 10 10
O1153 2 l. green 10 10
O1165 3 l. red 40 15
O1154 4 l. olive 40 15
O1160 6 l. blue 30 20
O1161 10 l. blue 50 15
O1156 25 l. red . . . . . . 2·10 1·10
O1157 50 l. violet . . . . . 3·50 2·50

1931.
O1194 O **80** 25 b. black 15 10
O1195 1 l. purple 20 15
O1196 2 l. green 30 20
O1197 3 l. red 35 25
O1247 6 l. red 75 40

PARCEL POST STAMPS

1895. As Type D **12** but inscr at top "TAXA DE FACTAGIU".
P353 25 b. brown . . . . 10·00 1·75
P479 25 b. red . . . . 7·50 1·00

1928. Surch **FACTAJ 5 LEI**.
P1078 **46** 5 l. on 10 b. green . . . . 1·40 25

POSTAGE DUE STAMPS

A. Ordinary Postage Due Stamps

D 12 D 38

1881.
D152 D **12** 2 b. brown . . . . . . 3·25 1·75
D153 5 b. brown . . . . . . 16·00 2·75
D200 10 b. brown . . . . . 6·50 65
D201 30 b. brown . . . . . 6·50 65
D156 50 b. brown . . . . . 13·00 3·25
D157 60 b. brown . . . . . 16·00 4·00

1887.
D448 D **12** 2 b. green 50 20
D449 5 b. green 35 10
D450 10 b. green 25 10
D451 30 b. green 35 10
D452 50 b. green . . . . . . 1·50 65
D453 60 b. green . . . . . . 3·25 1·75

1911.
D617 D **38** 2 b. blue on yellow . . 15 10
D618 5 b. blue on yellow . . 15 10
D619 10 b. blue on yellow . 15 10
D604 15 b. blue on yellow . 20 10
D621 20 b. blue on yellow . 15 10
D622 30 b. blue on yellow . 50 15
D623 50 b. blue on yellow . 50 15
D624 60 b. blue on yellow . 55 15
D609 2 l. blue on yellow . . 1·00 50

1918. Optd **TAXA DE PLATA**.
D675 **37** 5 b. green . . . . 1·10 65
D676 10 b. red . . . . 1·10 65

1918. Re-issue of Type D **38**. On greenish or white paper.
D1001 D **38** 5 b. black 10 10
D 722 10 b. black 10 10
D 734a 20 b. black 15 10
D 735 30 b. black 15 15
D 736 50 b. black 25 35
D 998 60 b. black 15 10
D1007 D **38** 1 l. black 25 10
D1010 2 l. black 30 10
D 991 3 l. black 15 10
D 992 6 l. black 25 10
D1547 50 l. black 20 15
D1548 100 l. black 30 20

1919. Transylvania. Cluj Issue. No. D190 etc. of Hungary optd as T **42**.
D786 D **9** 1 b. red and green . . £160 £160
D787 2 b. red and green . . 15 15
D788 5 b. red and green . . 30·00 30·00
D789 10 b. red and green . . 15 15
D790 15 b. red and green . . 6·00 6·00
D791 20 b. red and green . . 15 15
D792 30 b. red and green . . 10·00 10·00
D793 50 b. red and green . . 10·00 10·00

1919. Transylvania. Oradea Issue. No. D190, etc. of Hungary optd as T **43**.
D861 D **9** 1 b. red and green . . 17·00 17·00
D862 2 b. red and green . . 10 10
D863 5 b. red and green . . 2·50 2·50
D865 10 b. red and green . . 15 15
D866 12 b. red and green . . 20 20
D867 15 b. red and green . . 20 20
D868 20 b. red and green . . 10 10
D869 30 b. red and green . . 25 25

1930. Optd **8 IUNIE 1930**.
D1168 D **38** 1 l. black 15 10
D1169 2 l. black 20 10
D1170 3 l. black 25 15
D1171 6 l. black 65 25

D 98 D 233

1932.
D1249 D **98** 1 l. black 10 10
D1250 2 l. black 10 10
D1251 3 l. black 10 10
D1252 6 l. black 15 10
D1835 20 l. black 10 10
D1839 50 l. black 15 10
D1840 80 l. black 25 15
D1841 100 l. black 35 20
D1842 200 l. black 55 35
D1843 500 l. black 80 50
D1844 5000 l. black . . . . 1·75 1·00

1947. Type D **233** (without opts) perforated down centre.
Un. pair
D1919 2 l. red 25
D1920 4 l. blue 65
D1921 5 l. black . . . . 1·00
D1922 10 l. brown . . . . 1·60
The left half of Nos. D1919/22, showing Crown, served as a receipt and was stuck in the postman's book and so does not come postally used.

1948. Nos. D1919/22, optd as in Type D **233**.
Un. pair Us. pair
D1944 2 l. red 20 15
D1945 4 l. blue 30 20
D1946 5 l. black 50 30
D1947 10 l. brown . . . . 1·40 45

D 276
Badge Postwoman

1950.
Un. pair Us. pair
D2066 D **276** 2 l. red 40 40
D2067 4 l. blue 50 50
D2068 5 l. green . . . . . 1·00 1·00
D2069 10 l. brown . . . . 1·40 1·40

1952. Currency revalued. Nos. D2066/9 surch thus: **4 Bani** on each half.
Un. pair Us. pair
D2221 D **276** 4 b. on 2 l. red . . 35 35
D2222 10 b. on 4 l. blue . 35 35
D2223 20 b. on 5 l. green . 1·00 1·00
D2224 50 b. on 10 l. brown 1·10 1·10

D 420
G.P.O. Bucharest Posthorn

1957.
Un. pair Us. pair
D2507 D **420** 3 b. black 15 10
D2508 5 b. orange 15 10
D2509 10 b. purple 15 10
D2510 20 b. red 15 10
D2511 40 b. green 40 20
D2512 1 l. blue . . . . . . 1·75 25

D 614

1967.

			Un. pair	Us. pair
D3436	D 614	3 b. green	10	10
D3437		5 b. blue	10	10
D3438		10 b. mauve	10	10
D3439		20 b. red	15	10
D3440		40 b. brown	20	10
D3441		1 l. violet	40	15

D 766 Postal Emblems and Postman

1974.

			Un. pair	Us. pair
D4050	D 766	5 b. blue	10	10
D4051		10 b. green	10	10
D4052	–	20 b. red	10	10
D4053	–	40 b. violet	15	10
D4054	–	50 b. brown	30	10
D4055	–	1 l. orange	40	10

DESIGNS: 20 b., 40 b. Dove with letter and Hermes with posthorn. 50 b., 1 l. G.P.O., Bucharest and emblem with mail van.

1982. As Type **D 766**.

D4761	–	25 b. violet	10	10
D4762	D 766	50 b. yellow	15	10
D4763	–	1 l. red	25	10
D4764	–	2 l. green	45	10
D4765	D 766	3 l. brown	65	15
D4766	–	4 l. blue	90	15

DESIGNS: 25 b., 1 l. Dove with letter and Hermes with posthorn; 2, 4 l. G.P.O., Bucharest and emblem with mail van.

D 1111

1992.

D5417	D 1111	4 l. red	10	10
D5418		8 l. blue	10	10

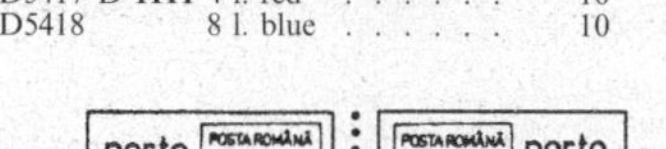

D 1163

1994.

D5586	D 1163	10 l. brown	10	10
D5587		45 l. orange	10	10

B. Postal Tax Due Stamps

1915. Optd **TIMBRU DE AJUTOR**.

TD643	D 38	5 b. blue on yellow	35	15
TD644		10 b. blue on yellow	30	15

TD 42 TD 106

1917. Green or white paper.

TD655	TD 42	5 b. brown	55	25
TD743		5 b. red	15	15
TD654		10 b. red	35	25
TD741		10 b. brown	25	30

1918. Optd **TAXA DE PLATA**.

TD680	T 41	5 b. black	65	25
TD681		10 b. brown	1·00	65

1922. As Type **TD 42** but inscr "ASSISTENTA SOCIALA". On green or white paper.

TD1028	10 b. brown	10	10
TD1029	20 b. brown	10	10
TD1030	25 b. brown	10	10
TD1031	50 b. brown	10	10

1931. Aviation Fund. Optd **TIMBRUL AVIATIEI**.

TD1219	D 38	1 l. black	10	10
TD1220		2 l. black	10	10

1932.

TD1278	TD 106	3 l. black	1·10	60

POSTAL TAX STAMPS

The following stamps were for compulsory use at certain times on inland mail to raise money for various funds. In some instances where the stamps were not applied the appropriate Postal Tax Postage Due stamps were applied.

Other demominations exist but these were purely for revenue purposes and were not applied to postal matter.

Soldiers Families Fund

1915. Optd **TIMBRU DE AJUTOR**.

T638	37	5 b. green	20	15
T639		10 b. red	30	15

T 41 The Queen Weaving **T 47** "Charity"

1916.

T649	T 41	5 b. black	20	15
T710		5 b. green	50	15
T650		10 b. brown	25	15
T711		10 b. black	50	15

The 50 b. and 1, 2, 5 and 50 l. in similar designs were only used fiscally.

1918. Optd **1918**.

T671	37	5 b. green (No. T638)	30·00	30·00
T667	T 41	5 b. black	50	35
T672	37	10 b. red (No. T639)	30·00	30·00
T668	T 41	10 b. brown	1·00	30

1921. Social Welfare.

T978	T 47	10 b. green	10	10
T979		25 b. black	10	10

Aviation Fund

T 91 T 98

1931.

T1216	T 91	50 b. green	30	10
T1217		1 l. brown	85	10
T1218		2 l. blue	1·00	20

1932.

T1253	T 98	50 b. green	15	10
T1254		1 l. purple	50	10
T1255		2 l. blue	65	10

Stamps as Type **98** but inscr "FONDUL AVIATIEI" were only for fiscal use. Nos. T **1252/4** could only be used fiscally after 1937.

T 105 **T 121** "Aviation"

1932. Cultural Fund.

T1276	T 105	2 l. blue	80	40
T1277		2 l. brown	70	30

These were for compulsory use on postcards.

1936.

T1340	T 121	50 b. green	15	10
T1341		1 l. brown	15	10
T1342		2 l. blue	25	10

Other stamps inscr "FONDUL AVIATIEI" were only for fiscal use.

T 171 King Michael

1943.

T1589	T 171	50 b. orange	10	10
T1590		1 l. lilac	10	10
T1591		2 l. brown	10	10
T1592		4 l. blue	10	10
T1593		5 l. violet	10	10
T1594		8 l. green	10	10
T1595		10 l. brown	10	10

1947. Fiscal stamps ($22 \times 18\frac{1}{2}$ mm), perf vert through centre surch **IOVR** and value.

T1923	1 l. on 2 l. red	15	15
T1924	5 l. on 1 l. green	50	45

1948. Vert designs (approx $18\frac{1}{2} \times 22$ mm). Inscr "I.O.V.R.".

T1948	1 l. red	15	20
T1949	1 l. violet	40	30
T1950	2 l. blue	60	40
T1951	5 l. yellow	3·25	2·00

SAVINGS BANK STAMPS

1919. Transylvania. Cluj Issue. No. B199 of Hungary optd as T **42**.

B785	B 17	10 b. purple	15	15

1919. Transylvania. Oradea Issue. No. B199 of Hungary optd as T **43**.

B861	B 17	10 b. purple	15	15

RUMANIAN OCCUPATION OF HUNGARY Pt. 2

A. BANAT BACSKA

The following stamps were issued by the Temesvar postal authorities between the period of the Serbian evacuation and the Rumanian occupation. This area was later divided, the Western part going to Yugoslavia and the Eastern part going to Rumania.

100 filler = 1 korona

1919. Stamps of Hungary optd **Banat Bacska 1919**. (a) "Turul" Type.
1 **7** 50 f. red on blue . . . . 10·00 10·00

(b) War Charity stamps of 1916.
2 **20** 10 f. (+ 2 f.) red 40 40
3 – 15 f. (+ 2 f.) violet 40 40
4 **22** 40 f. (+ 2 f.) red 40 40

(c) Harvesters and Parliament Types.
5 **18** 2 f. brown 40 40
6 3 f. purple 40 40
7 5 f. green 40 40
8 6 f. blue 40 40
9 15 f. purple 40 40
10 35 f. brown . . . . 11·00 11·00
11 **19** 50 f. purple . . . . 10·00 10·00
12 75 f. blue 40 40
13 80 f. green 40 40
14 1 k. red 40 40
15 2 k. brown 40 40
16 2 k. grey and violet . . . . 15·00 15·00
17 5 k. light brown and brown . 75 75
18 10 k. mauve and brown . . 2·25 2·25

(d) Charles and Zita stamps.
19 **27** 10 f. pink 40 40
20 20 f. brown 40 40
21 25 f. blue 40 40
22 **28** 40 f. green 40 40
23 50 f. violet 40 40

(e) Harvesters Type inscr "MAGYAR POSTA".
24 **18** 10 f. red . . . . 10·00 10·00
25 20 f. brown . . . . 10·00 10·00
26 25 f. blue . . . . 12·00 12·00

(f) Various Types optd **KOZTARSASAG**.
(i) Harvesters and Parliament Types.
27 **18** 4 f. grey 40 40
28 5 f. green 40 40
29 6 f. blue 40 40
30 10 f. red . . . . 9·00 9·00
31 20 f. brown . . . . 7·00 7·00
32 40 f. green 40 40
33 **19** 1 k. red 40 40
34 2 k. brown . . . . 7·50 7·50
35 3 k. grey and violet . . . . 7·50 7·50
36 5 k. light brown and brown . 7·50 7·50
37 10 k. mauve and brown . . 7·50 7·50

(iii) Charles portrait stamps.
38 **27** 15 f. purple . . . . 2·50 2·50
39 25 f. blue . . . . 1·90 1·90

(g) Serbian Occupation of Temesvar stamps.
40 **18** 10 f. on 2 f. brown 50 50
41 **20** 45 f. on 10 f. (+ 2 f.) red . . 50 50
42 **18** 1 k. 50 on 15 f. purple . . . 1·25 1·25

EXPRESS LETTER STAMP

1919. No. E245 of Hungary optd **Banat Bacska 30 FILLER 1919**.
E44 **E 18** 30 f. on 2 f. green and red 1·40 1·40

NEWSPAPER STAMPS

1919. No. N136 of Hungary optd **Banat Bacska 1919**.
N43 **N 9** (2 f.) orange 40 40

POSTAGE DUE STAMPS

1919. Nos. D191 etc. optd as above.
D46 **D 9** 2 f. red and green . . . 40 40
D47 10 f. red and green . . . 40 40
D48 15 f. red and green . . . 11·00 11·00
D49 20 f. red and green . . . 40 40
D50 30 f. red and green . . . 10·00 10·00
D51 50 f. black and green . . . 12·00 12·00

SAVINGS BANK STAMP

1919. No. B199 of Hungary surch **Banat Bacska 50 FILLER 1919**.
B45 **B 17** 50 f. on 10 f. purple . . . 1·40 1·40

B. DEBRECEN

This area was later returned to Hungary.

100 filler = 1 korona

1

1919. Stamps of Hungary optd with T **1** or surch in addition. (a) "Turul" Type.
1 **7** 2 f. yellow . . . . 25·00 25·00
2 3 f. orange . . . . 35·00 35·00
3 6 f. brown . . . . 7·50 7·50

(b) War Charity stamps of 1915.
4 **7** 2 f. + 2 f. yellow (No. 171) . 40·00 40·00
5 3 f. + 2 f. orange (No. 172) . 40·00 40·00

(c) War Charity stamps of 1916.
6 **20** 10 f. (+ 2 f.) red 40 40
7 – 15 f. (+ 2 f.) lilac . . . . . 3·00 3·00
8 **22** 40 f. (+ 2 f.) red . . . . . 1·40 1·40

(d) Harvesters and Parliament Types.
9 **18** 2 f. brown 30 10
10 3 f. purple 10 10
11 **18** 5 f. green 60 60
12 6 f. blue 30 30
13 10 f. red (No. 243) . . . . 30·00 30·00
14 15 f. violet (No. 244) . . . 20·00 20·00
15 15 f. purple 10 15
16 20 f. brown . . . . 22·00 22·00
17 25 f. blue 60 60
18 35 f. brown . . . . 7·00 7·00
19 35 f. on 3 f. purple 65 65
20 40 f. green 50 50
21 45 f. on 2 f. brown 30 30
22 **19** 50 f. purple 65 65
23 75 f. blue 35 35
24 80 f. green 60 60
25 1 k. red 75 75
26 2 k. brown 30 30
27 3 k. grey and violet . . . . 6·50 6·50
28 3 k. on 75 f. blue . . . . . 1·40 1·40
29 5 k. light brown and brown . 6·00 6·00
30 5 k. on 75 f. blue 65 65
31 10 k. mauve and brown . . 45·00 45·00
32 10 k. on 80 f. green . . . . 1·10 1·10

(e) Charles and Zita stamps.
33 **27** 10 f. pink . . . . 8·00 8·00
34 15 f. purple . . . . 20·00 20·00
35 20 f. brown 55 55
36 25 f. blue . . . . 1·00 1·00
37 **28** 40 f. green 60 60
38 50 f. purple . . . . 5·50 5·50

(f) Harvesters and Parliament Types inscr "MAGAR POSTA".
39 **18** 5 f. green 10 10
40 6 f. blue . . . . 3·75 3·75
41 10 f. red 10 10
42 20 f. brown 10 10
43 25 f. blue 20 20
44 45 f. orange . . . . 3·50 3·50
45 **19** 5 k. brown £325

(g) Various Types optd **KOZTARSASAG**.
(i) Harvesters and Parliament Types.
46 **18** 2 f. brown 60 60
47 3 f. purple . . . . 7·00 7·00
48 4 f. grey 30 30
49 5 f. green 10 10
50 10 f. red . . . . 6·00 6·00
51 20 f. brown 50 50
52 40 f. green 30 30
53 **19** 1 k. red 35 35
54 2 k. brown . . . . 10·00 10·00
55 3 k. grey and violet . . . . 1·00 1·00
56 5 k. light brown and brown 70·00 70·00

(ii) War Charity stamps of 1916.
57 **20** 10 f. (+ 2 f.) red . . . . . 7·00 7·00
58 – 15 f. (+ 2 f.) lilac . . . . . 30·00 30·00
59 **22** 40 f. (+ 2 f.) red . . . . . 6·50 6·50

(iii) Charles and Zita stamps.
60 **27** 10 f. pink . . . . 5·00 5·00
61 15 f. purple . . . . 8·00 8·00
62 20 f. brown . . . . 1·75 1·75
63 25 f. blue 45 45
64 **28** 50 f. purple 60 60

2

4

1920. Types **2** and **4** and similar design, optd with inscr as T **1** but in circle.
65 **2** 2 f. brown 40 40
66 3 f. brown 60 60
67 4 f. violet 40 40
68 5 f. green 10 10
69 6 f. grey 40 40
70 10 f. red 10 10
71 15 f. violet 50 50
72 20 f. brown 10 10
73 – 25 f. blue 40 40
74 – 30 f. brown 10 10
75 – 35 f. purple 30 30
76 – 40 f. green 30 30
77 – 45 f. red 30 30
78 – 50 f. mauve 30 30
79 – 60 f. green 30 30
80 – 75 f. blue 30 30
81 **4** 80 f. green 30 30
82 1 k. red . . . . 1·00 1·00
83 1 k. 20 orange . . . . . . 5·50 5·50
84 2 k. brown 50 50
85 3 k. brown 65 65
86 5 k. brown 65 65
87 10 k. purple 65 65

DESIGN: Nos. 73/80, Horseman using lasso.

5

1920. War Charity. Type **5** with circular opt, and "Segely belyeg" at top.
88 **5** 20 f. green 40 40
89 20 f. green on blue . . . . 1·25 1·25
90 50 f. brown 60 60
91 50 f. brown on mauve . . . 70 70
92 1 k. green 60 60
93 1 k. green on green 70 70
94 2 k. green 60 60

EXPRESS LETTER STAMP

1919. No. E245 of Hungary optd with T **1**.
E66 **E 18** 2 f. green and red . . . 40 40

NEWSPAPER STAMP

1919. No. N136 of Hungary optd with T **1**.
N65 **N 9** 2 f. orange 25 25

POSTAGE DUE STAMPS

1919. (a) Nos. D190 etc. of Hungary optd with T **1**.
D68 **D 9** 1 f. red and green . . . . 9·00 9·00
D69 2 f. red and green 30 30
D70 5 f. red and green . . . . 60·00 60·00
D71 6 f. red and green . . . . 15·00 15·00
D72 10 f. red and green . . . 10 10
D73 12 f. red and green . . . 26·00 26·00
D74 15 f. red and green . . . 3·00 3·00
D75 20 f. red and green . . . 85 85
D76 30 f. red and green . . . 2·50 2·50

(b) With **KOZTARSASAG** opt.
D77 **D 9** 2 f. red and green . . . . 6·00 6·00
D78 3 f. red and green . . . . 6·00 6·00
D79 10 f. red and green . . . 6·00 6·00
D80 20 f. red and green . . . 6·00 6·00
D81 40 f. red and green . . . 6·00 6·00
D82 50 f. red and green . . . 6·00 6·00

D 6

1920.
D95 **D 6** 5 f. green 30 30
D96 10 f. green 30 30
D97 20 f. green 30 30
D98 30 f. green 30 30
D99 40 f. green 30 30

SAVINGS BANK STAMP

1919. No. B199 of Hungary optd with T **1**.
B67 **B 17** 10 f. purple . . . . . . 8·00 8·00

C. TEMESVAR

After being occupied by Serbia this area was then occupied by Rumania. It later became part of Rumania and was renamed Timisoara.

100 filler = 1 korona

1919. Stamps of Hungary surch.
(a) Harvesters Type.
6 **18** 30 on 2 f. brown 10 10
7 1 k. on 4 f. grey (optd **KOZTARSASAG** 10 10
8 150 on 3 f. purple 10 10
9 150 on 5 f. green 15 15

(b) Express Letter Stamp.
10 **E 18** 3 KORONA on 2 f. green and red 20 20

POSTAGE DUE STAMPS

1919. Charity stamp of Hungary surch **PORTO 40**.
D11 40 on 15 + (2 f.) lilac (No. 265) 35 35

(D 8)

1919. Postage Due stamps of Hungary surch with Type **D 8**.
D12 **D 9** 60 on 2 f. red and green . 1·00 1·00
D13 60 on 10 f. red and green 30 30

RUMANIAN POST OFFICES ABROAD Pt. 16

Rumanian P.O.s in the Turkish Empire including Constantinople. Now closed.

I. IN TURKISH EMPIRE

40 paras = 1 piastre

1896. Stamps of Rumania of 1893 surch in "PARAS".
9 10 pa. on 5 b. blue (No. 319) . 10·00 10·00
10 20 pa. on 10 b. grn (No. 320) . 10·00 10·00
11 1 pi. on 25 b. mauve (No. 322) . 10·00 10·00

II. IN CONSTANTINOPLE

100 bani = 1 leu

1

1919. Stamps of Rumania of 1893–1908 optd with T **1**.
10 **37** 5 b. green 30 35
6 10 b. red 40 50
7 **37** 15 b. brown 50 55
13 – 25 b. blue (No. 701) 55 75
14 – 40 b. brown (No. 703) . . . 1·75 1·75

1919. 1916 Postal Tax stamp of Rumania optd with T **1**.
16 **T 41** 5 b. green . . . . 1·00 1·00

RUSSIA Pt. 10

A country in the E. of Europe and N. Asia.

An empire until 1917 when the Russian Socialist Federal Soviet Republic was formed. In 1923 this became the Union of Soviet Socialist Republics (U.S.S.R.), eventually comprising 15 constituent republics.

In 1991 the U.S.S.R. was dissolved and subsequent issues were used in the Russian Federation only.

100 kopeks = 1 rouble

1

5

8

9

10

11

1858. Imperf.
1 **1** 10 k. blue and brown £2000 £375

1858. Perf.
21 **1** 10 k. blue and brown . . . . 35·00 50
22 20 k. orange and blue . . . 70·00 10·00
23 30 k. green and red . . . . 95·00 27·00

1863.
8 **5** 5 k. black and blue . . . . . 18·00 £250

No. 8 was first issued as a local but was later authorised for general use.

1864.
18 **9** 1 k. black and yellow . . . 3·25 65
30 2 k. black and red . . . . 8·50 65
19b 3 k. black and green . . . . 6·00 1·00
20 5 k. black and lilac . . . . 8·00 65

1875.
31 **8** 7 k. red and grey . . . . . 8·00 40
32 8 k. red and grey . . . . . 10·00 65
33 10 k. blue and brown . . . . 24·00 3·00
34 20 k. orange and blue . . . 35·00 2·50

12 No thunderbolts

1883. Posthorns in design without thunderbolts, as T **12**.
38 **9** 1 k. orange . . . . 3·00 65
40 2 k. green . . . . 5·00 65
41 3 k. red . . . . 5·00 65
42b 5 k. purple . . . . 4·00 40
43c 7 k. blue . . . . 5·00 15
44b **10** 14 k. red and blue . . . . 10·00 25
45 35 k. green and purple . . 32·00 5·00
46 70 k. orange and brown . . 70·00 5·00
47 **11** 3 r. 50 k. grey and black . . £500 £425
48 7 r. yellow and black . . . £500 £500

14

15

13 With thunderbolts

1889. Posthorns in design with thunderbolts as T **13**. Perf.
50 **9** 1 k. orange 20 10
51a 2 k. green 20 10
52 3 k. red 20 10
53 **14** 4 k. red 30 10
54 **9** 5 k. purple 60 10
55 7 k. blue 30 10
56 **14** 10 k. blue 60 10
114 **10** 14 k. red and blue 10 10
100 15 k. blue and purple . . . 10 10
116 **14** 20 k. red and blue 10 10
102 **10** 25 k. violet and green . . . 10 10
103 35 k. green and purple . . 10 10

119 14 50 k. green and purple 10 10
120 10 70 k. orange and brown 10 10
121A 15 1 r. orange and brown 10 10
79 11 3 r. 50 grey and black 10·00 2·75
122A 3 r. 50 green and red 20 30
80 7 r. yellow and black 8·50 5·00
124bA 7 r. pink and green 20 50
For imperf stamps, see Nos. 107B/125aB.

16 Monument to Admiral Kornilov at Sevastopol

1905. War Orphans Fund (Russo-Japanese War).
88 16 3 (6) k. brown, red & green 3·25 3·25
82 – 5 (8) k. purple and yellow 2·50 2·50
83 – 7 (10) k. blue, lt blue & pink 3·25 3·25
87 – 10 (13) k. blue & lt bl & yell 3·75 3·75
DESIGNS: 5 (8) k. Monument to Minin and Pozharsky, Moscow; 7 (10) k. Statue of Peter the Great, St. Petersburg; 10 (13) k. Moscow Kremlin.

22 23 20

1906.
107 22 1 k. orange 10 10
93 2 k. green 10 10
94 3 k. red 10 10
95 23 4 k. red 10 10
96 22 5 k. red 10 10
97 7 k. blue 10 10
98a 23 10 k. blue 10 10
123aA 20 5 r. blue and green 30 30
125aA 10 r. grey, red & yellow 60 65
For imperf stamps, see Nos. 107B/125aB.

25 Nicholas II

26 Elizabeth

27 The Kremlin

1913. Tercentenary of Romanov Dynasty. Views as T 27 and portraits as T 25/26.
126 1 k. orange (Peter I) 30 15
127 2 k. green (Alexander II) 40 15
128 3 k. red (Alexander III) 40 15
129 4 k. red (Peter I) 40 15
130 7 k. brown (Type 25) 40 15
131 10 k. blue (Nicholas II) 50 15
132 14 k. green (Katherine II) 50 15
133 15 k. brown (Nicholas I) 75 65
134 20 k. olive (Alexander I) 1·00 65
135 25 k. red (Alexei Michaelovich) 1·50 85
136 35 k. green & violet (Paul I) 1·50 1·00
137 50 k. grey and brown (T 26) 1·75 1·25
138 70 k. brown and green (Michael Feodorovich) 2·00 1·40
139 1 r. green (Type 27) 5·00 4·00
140 2 r. brown 6·75 6·00
141 3 r. violet 13·50 3·25
142 5 r. brown 17·00 13·50
DESIGNS—As T 27: 2 r. Winter Palace; 3 r. Castle Romanov. 23 × 29 mm: 5 r. Nicholas II.

31 Russian hero, Ilya Murometz

1914. War Charity.
143 31 1 (2) k. green & red on yell 65 1·60
144 – 3 (4) k. green & red on red 65 1·60
145 – 7 (8) k. green and brown on buff 65 3·25
161 – 10 (11) k. brown and blue on blue 3·25 6·75
DESIGNS: 3 k. Cossack shaking girl's hand; 7 k. Symbolical of Russia surrounded by her children; 10 k. St. George and Dragon.

1915. As last. Colours changed.
155 31 1 (2) k. grey and brown 1·40 2·00
156 – 3 (4) k. black and red 1·40 2·75
158 – 10 (11) k. brown and blue 1·00 2·40

35

39

1
КОПѢЙКА.
Имѣетъ
хожденіе на-
равнѣ съ мѣд-
ной монетой.
41

45 Cutting the Fetters

1915. Nos. 131, 133 and 134 printed on card with inscriptions on back as T 35.
165 10 k. blue 75 4·75
166 15 k. brown 75 4·75
167 20 k. olive 75 4·75

1916. Various types surch.
168 – 10 k. on 7 k. brown (No. 130) 30 15
170 22 10 k. on 7 k. blue 30 15
169 – 20 k. on 14 k. green (No. 132) 30 20
171 10 20 k. on 14 k. red and blue 30 15

1917. Various earlier types, but imperf.
107B 22 1 k. orange 10 10
108bB 2 k. green 10 10
109B 3 k. red 10 10
110B 23 4 k. red 15 25
111B 22 5 k. lilac 10 10
113B 23 10 k. blue 13·50 35·00
115dB 10 15 k. blue & pur (No. 100) 10 10
116B 14 20 k. red and blue 15 30
117dB 10 25 k. vio & grn (No. 102) 1·00 4·00
118B 35 k. grn & pur (No. 103) 15 25
119B 14 50 k. green and purple 15 25
120B 10 70 k. orange and brown (No. 120) 10 30
121B 15 1 r. orange and brown 10 10
122B 11 3 r. 50k. green and red 20 30
123aB 20 5 r. blue and green 30 60
124aB 11 7 r. pink and green 85 1·00
125aB 20 10 r. grey, red & yellow 40·00 40·00

1916. Types of 1913 printed on card with surch on back as T 39 or 41, or optd with figure "1" or "2" in addition on front.
172 39 1 k. orange (No. 126) 17·00 27·00
175 1 on 1 k. orange (No. 126) 40 5·00
177 41 1 on 1 k. orange (No. 126) 75 4·50
175 39 2 k. green (No. 127) 27·00 35·00
176 2 on 2 k. green (No. 127) 40 5·00
178 41 2 on 2 k. green (No. 127) 75 4·75
174 39 3 k. red (No. 128) 1·00 4·00
179 41 3 k. red (No. 128) 35 2·75

1917.
187 45 35 k. blue 1·75 17·00
188 70 k. brown 1·40 17·00

46 Agriculture and Industry

47 Triumph of Revolution

MINIMUM PRICE
The minimum price quoted is 10p which represents a handling charge rather than a basis for valuing common stamps. For further notes about prices, see introductory pages.

48 Agriculture

49 Industry

55 Science and Arts

56

64 Industry

1921. Imperf.
195 48 1 r. orange 1·40 20·00
196 2 r. brown 1·40 20·00
197 49 5 r. blue 1·40 20·00
198 46 20 r. blue 2·50 6·75
199a 47 40 r. blue 3·50 6·75
214 48 100 r. yellow 10 10
215 200 r. brown 10 25
216 55 250 r. lilac 10 10
217 48 300 r. green 15 40
218 49 500 r. blue 15 45
219 1000 r. red 10 10
256 64 5000 r. violet 40 85
257 46 7500 r. blue 20 30
259 7500 r. blue on buff 20 35
258 64 10,000 r. blue 5·00 4·75
260 22,500 r. purple on buff 35 50

1921. 4th Anniv of October Revolution. Imperf.
227 56 100 r. yellow 50 2·75
228 250 r. violet 50 2·75
229 1000 r. red 50 2·75

57 Famine Relief Work

58

Р. С. Ф. С. Р.
ГОЛОДАЮЩИМ
250 р.+250 р.
(62)

1921. Charity. Volga Famine. Imperf.
230 57 2250 r. green 8·25 13·50
231 2250 r. red 5·00 10·00
232 2250 r. brown 4·00 11·50
235 58 2250 r. blue 4·75 7·25

1922. Surch. Imperf.
234 48 5000 r. on 1 r. orange 1·40 2·75
240 5000 r. on 2 r. brown 1·40 2·75
236 49 5000 r. on 5 r. blue 1·60 2·75
242 46 5000 r. on 20 r. blue 2·50 3·25
243 47 10,000 r on 40 r. blue 1·75 3·25

1922. Famine Relief. Surch as T 62. Perf.
245 45 100 r. + 100 r. on 70 k. brown 85 2·00
247 250 r. + 250 r. on 25 k. bl 85 2·00

(63)

1922. Surch as T 63. Imperf.
250 55 7500 r. on 250 r. lilac 10 10
251 100,000 r. on 250 r. lilac 10 20

65

1922. Obligatory Tax. Rostov-on-Don issue. Famine Relief. Various sizes. Without gum. Imperf.
261 65 2 T. (2000 r.) green 40·00 £225
262 – 2 T. (2000 r.) red 32·00 £225
263 – 4 T. (4000 r.) red 55·00 £225
264 – 6 T. (6000 r.) green 40·00 £225
DESIGNS: 2 T. red, Worker and family (35 × 42 mm); 4 T. Clasped hands (triangular, 57 mm each side); 6 T. Sower (29 × 59 mm).

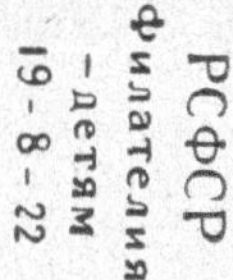

(70 "Philately for the children")

1922. Optd with T 70. Perf or imperf.
278 22 1 k. orange £350 £425
274 2 k. green 32·00 50·00
275 3 k. red 13·50 23·00
276 5 k. red 10·00 23·00
277 23 10 k. blue 10·00 23·00

71

73

1922. 5th Anniv of October Revolution. Imperf.
279 71 5 r. black and yellow 50 45
280 10 r. black and brown 50 45
281 25 r. black and purple 2·00 1·40
282 27 r. black and red 5·00 4·00
283 45 r. black and blue 3·25 2·75

1922. Air. Optd with airplane. Imperf.
284 71 45 r. black and green 20·00 48·00

1922. Famine Relief. Imperf.
285 73 20 r. + 5 r. mauve 30 2·50
286 – 20 r. + 5 r. violet 40 2·50
287 – 20 r. + 5 r. blue 50 2·50
288 – 20 r. + 5 r. blue 3·00 15·00
DESIGNS—HORIZ: No. 286, Freighter; No. 287, Steam train. VERT: No. 288, Airplane.

(77)

78 Worker

79 Soldier

1922. Surch as T 77. Imperf or perf.
289 14 5 r. on 20 k. red & blue 3·25 17·00
290 10 20 r. on 15 k. blue & purple 3·25 17·00
291 20 r. on 70 k. orange and brown 15 30
292a 14 30 r. on 50 k. green & pur 35 35
293 10 40 r. on 15 k. blue & pur 15 15
294 100 r. on 15 k. blue & pur 15 20
295 200 r. on 15 k. blue & pur 15 20

1922. Imperf or perf.
303 78 10 r. blue 10 10
304 79 50 r. brown 10 10
305 70 r. purple 10 10
310 100 r. red 15 15

1 мая
1923 г. Филателия—
Трудящимся,
1 р.+1 р.
(80)

1923. Charity. Surch as T 80. Imperf.
315 71 1 r. + 1 r. on 10 r. black and brown 50·00 70·00
317b 55 2 r. + 2 r. on 250 r. violet 50·00 70·00
318 64 4 r. + 4 r. on 5000 r. vio 70·00 85·00

83 Worker **84** Peasant **85** Soldier

1923. Perf.

320 **85** 3 r. red 10 10
321 **83** 4 r. brown 10 10
322 **84** 5 r. blue 10 10
323 **85** 10 r. grey 15 15
324 20 r. purple 25 25

86 Reaper **88** Tractor

1923. Agricultural Exn, Moscow. Imperf or perf.

325 **86** 1 r. brown . . . . 2·50 6·75
326 – 2 r. green . . . . 2·50 6·75
327 **88** 5 r. blue . . . . 2·50 6·75
328 – 7 r. red . . . . 2·50 6·75

DESIGNS: As Type **86**: 2 r. Sower; 7 r. Exhibition buildings.

90 Worker **91** Peasant **92** Soldier **93**

94 **95**

1923. Perf (some values also imperf).

335 **90** 1 k. yellow 30 15
359 **91** 2 k. green 30 15
360 **92** 3 k. brown 35 15
361 **90** 4 k. red 35 15
434 5 k. purple 55 15
363 **91** 6 k. blue 55 15
364 **92** 7 k. brown 55 15
437 **90** 8 k. olive 90 15
366 **91** 9 k. red . . . . 1·00 40
341 **92** 10 k. blue 55 15
385 **90** 14 k. grey . . . . 1·00 20
386 **91** 15 k. yellow . . . . 1·25 90
442 **92** 18 k. violet . . . . 2·40 55
443 **90** 20 k. green . . . . 2·00 30
444 **91** 30 k. violet . . . . 3·75 40
445 **92** 40 k. grey . . . . 4·75 60
343 **91** 50 k. brown . . . . 2·00 1·75
447 **92** 1 r. red and brown . . . . 6·00 1·10
375 **93** 2 r. green and red . . . . 8·25 3·50
449 **94** 3 r. green and brown . . . 18·00 4·75
450 **95** 5 r. brown and blue . . . . 23·00 5·75

96 Lenin **97**

1924. Lenin Mourning. Imperf or perf.

413 **96** 3 k. black and red . . . . 2·75 1·10
414 6 k. black and red . . . . 3·75 2·00
411 12 k. black and red . . . . 5·25 1·00
412 20 k. black and red 2·75 85

1924. Air. Surch. Imperf.

417 **97** 5 k. on 3 r. blue . . . . . 3·75 2·10
418 10 k. on 5 r. green . . . . 3·75 1·50
419 15 k. on 1 r. brown . . . . 3·00 1·25
420 20 k. on 10 r. red . . . . . 3·00 1·40

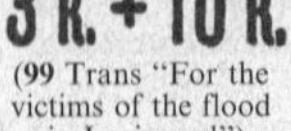

(**99** Trans "For the victims of the flood in Leningrad")

102 Lenin Mausoleum, Moscow

1924. Leningrad Flood Relief. Surch as T **99**. Imperf.

421 **48** 3 + 10 k. on 100 r. yellow 2·00 1·40
422 7 + 20 k. on 200 r. brown 2·00 1·40
423 14 + 30 k. on 300 r. green 2·75 2·50
424 **49** 12 + 40 k. on 500 r. blue 2·75 2·75
425 20 + 50 k. on 1000 r. red 2·75 2·50

1925. 1st Death Anniv of Lenin. Imperf or perf.

426 **102** 7 k. blue . . . . 4·00 3·00
427 14 k. olive . . . . 6·00 4·00
428 20 k. red . . . . 6·00 4·00
429 40 k. brown . . . . . . 8·00 4·00

104 Lenin **106** Prof. Lomonosov and Academy of Sciences, Leningrad

1925.

451 **104** 1 r. brown . . . . 10·00 3·25
452 2 r. brown . . . . 8·25 3·25
850 3 r. green . . . . 1·90 1·40
851 5 r. brown . . . . 3·25 2·00
852 10 r. blue . . . . 8·00 4·75

1925. Bicentenary of Academy of Sciences.

456b **106** 3 k. brown . . . . . . 4·00 2·00
457 15 k. olive . . . . 6·00 3·75

107 A. S. Popov **110** Moscow Barricade

1925. 30th Anniv of Popov's Radio Discoveries.

458 **107** 7 k. blue . . . . 2·25 1·75
459 14 k. olive . . . . 4·00 2·25

1925. 20th Anniv of 1905 Rebellion. Imperf or perf.

463b – 3 k. green . . . . 4·00 2·00
464c – 7 k. brown . . . . 6·00 4·00
465a **110** 14 k. red . . . . 4·00 2·75

DESIGNS—VERT: 3 k. Postal rioters; 7 k. Orator and mob.

111 Decembrist Exiles **112** Senate Square, St. Petersburg, 1825

1925. Centenary of Decembrist Rebellion. Imperf or perf.

466 **111** 3 k. green . . . . 3·25 2·75
467 **112** 7 k. brown . . . . 5·00 4·00
468 – 14 k. red . . . . 5·00 5·00

DESIGN—VERT: 14 k. Medallion with heads of Pestel, Ryleev, Bestuzhev-Ryumin, Muravev-Apostol and Kakhovsky.

114

1926. 6th International Proletarian Esperanto Congress.

471 **114** 7 k. red and green . . . 5·75 3·00
472 14 k. violet and green . . 6·00 2·00

115 Waifs **116** Lenin when a Child

1926. Child Welfare.

473 **115** 10 k. brown . . . . 1·00 45
474 **116** 20 k. blue . . . . 2·75 95

1927. Same type with new inscriptions.

475 **115** 8 k. + 2 k. green 80 35
476 **116** 18 k. + 2 k. red . . . . . 1·75 65

ПОЧТОВАЯ
МАРКА
КОП. 8 КОП.
(**117**)

1927. Postage Due stamps surch with T **117**.

491 D **104** 8 k. on 1 k. red . . . 1·75 3·50
492 8 k. on 2 k. violet . . 1·75 3·50
493 8 k. on 3 k. blue . . . 1·75 3·50
494 8 k. on 7 k. yellow . . 1·75 3·50
494b 8 k. on 8 k. green . . 1·75 3·50
494d 8 k. on 10 k. blue . . 1·75 3·50
494f 8 k. on 14 k. brown . 1·75 3·50

1927. Various types of 7 k. surch (some values imperf or perf).

495 **92** 8 k. on 7 k. brown . . . . 10·00 10·00
523 **107** 8 k. on 7 k. blue . . . . . 5·00 3·25
524 – 8 k. on 7 k. brown (No. 464c) . . . . 8·25 8·25
527 **112** 8 k. on 7 k. brown . . . . 8·25 6·75
526 **114** 8 k. on 7 k. red & green . 15·00 13·50

119 Dr. Zamenhof

1927. 40th Anniv of Publication of Zamenhof's "Langue Internationale" (Esperanto).

498 **119** 14 k. green and brown . . 3·75 1·75

120

1927. 1st Int Air Post Congress, The Hague.

499 **120** 10 k. blue and brown . . . 13·50 6·75
500 15 k. red and olive . . . 17·00 11·50

121 Worker, Soldier and Peasant **124** Sailor and Worker

122 Allegory of Revolution

1927. 10th Anniv of October Revolution.

501 **121** 3 k. red . . . . 2·50 75
502 **122** 5 k. brown . . . . 6·00 2·00
503 – 7 k. green . . . . 8·00 2·50
504 **124** 8 k. black and brown . . . 4·25 85
505 – 14 k. red and blue . . . . 6·00 1·25
506 – 18 k. blue . . . . 4·25 1·00
507 – 28 k. brown . . . . 13·50 8·00

DESIGNS—HORIZ: (As Type **122**): HORIZ: 7 k. Smolny Institute; 14 k. Map of Russia inscr "C.C.C.P."; 18 k. Various Russian races; 28 k. Worker, soldier and peasant.

128 Worker **129** Peasant **130** Lenin

1927.

508 **128** 1 k. orange 90 50
509 **129** 2 k. green 90 20
510 **128** 4 k. blue 90 20
511 **129** 5 k. brown 90 20
512 7 k. red . . . . 4·75 1·00
513 **128** 8 k. green . . . . 2·50 20
514 **128** 10 k. brown . . . . 2·00 20
515 **130** 14 k. green . . . . 2·25 45
516 18 k. olive . . . . 3·00 40
517 18 k. blue . . . . 4·50 70
518 **129** 20 k. olive . . . . 2·50 35
519 **128** 40 k. red . . . . 5·00 60
520 **129** 50 k. blue . . . . 6·00 1·00
521 **128** 70 k. olive . . . . 10·00 1·40
522 **129** 80 k. orange . . . . . . 22·00 5·25

131 Infantryman, Lenin Mausoleum and Kremlin

1928. 10th Anniv of Red Army.

529 **131** 8 k. brown . . . . 2·00 45
530 – 14 k. blue . . . . 2·75 50
531 – 18 k. red . . . . 2·75 1·75
532 – 28 k. green . . . . 4·00 4·00

DESIGNS: 14 k. Sailor and cruiser "Aurora"; 18 k. Cavalryman; 28 k. Airman.

135 Young Factory Workers **137** Trumpeter sounding the Assembly

1929. Child Welfare.

536 **135** 10 k. + 2 k. brn & sepia . 3·00 1·10
537 – 20 k. + 2 k. blue & brown 3·25 3·25

DESIGN: 20 k. Children in harvest field.

See also Nos. 567/8.

1929. 1st All-Union Gathering of Pioneers.

538 **137** 10 k. brown . . . . . . 8·25 8·25
539 14 k. blue . . . . 5·00 5·00

138 Worker **139** Factory Girl **140** Peasant

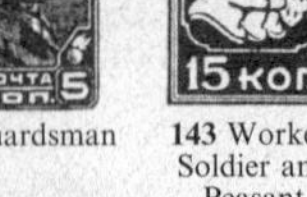

141 Farm Girl **142** Guardsman **143** Worker, Soldier and Peasant

144 Lenin **242a** Miner **242b** Steel foundryman

242c Infantryman **242d** Airman **242e** Arms of U.S.S.R

149 Central Telegraph Office, Moscow

150 Lenin Hydro-electric Power Station

743a Farm Girl 743b Architect 744 Furnaceman

1929. Perf, but some values exist imperf.

541 138 1 k. yellow 65 15
542 139 2 k. green 85 10
543 140 3 k. blue 85 10
544 141 4 k. mauve 85 15
545 142 5 k. brown 90 10
847a 242a 5 k. red 20 10
546 143 7 k. red 2·00 50
547 138 10 k. grey 1·75 10
727f 139 10 k. blue 60 15
1214b 10 k. black 80 15
554 144 14 k. blue 1·40 55
548 143 15 k. blue 2·00 30
847b 242b 15 k. blue 1·00 30
847c 242c 15 k. green 50 15
549 140 20 k. green and blue 2·75 20
727h 141 20 k. green 1·00 25
2252a 743a 20 k. olive 80 30
2252b 743b 25 k. brown 65 45
550 139 30 k. violet and lilac 4·00 50
847d 242d 30 k. blue 1·40 20
727l 144 40 k. blue 1·50 40
727m 141 50 k. brown and buff 1·25 40
847f 242e 60 k. red 1·50 30
2253 744 60 k. red 1·00 20
2253a 60 k. blue 3·00 1·00
552 142 70 k. red and pink 6·75 1·40
553 140 80 k. brown & yellow 6·75 1·75
561 149 1 r. blue 2·50 85
562 150 3 r. brown and green 20·00 6·75

Nos. 727f, 1214b and 550 show the factory girl without factory in background. Nos. 549, 727m, 552, 553 have designs like those shown but with unshaded background.

151 Industry

153 "More metal more machines"

1929. Industrial Loan Propaganda.

563 151 5 k. brown 2·00 1·50
564 – 10 k. olive 2·75 2·00
565 153 20 k. green 10·00 3·50
566 – 28 k. violet 5·75 4·00

DESIGNS—HORIZ: 10 k. Tractors. VERT: 28 k. Blast furnace and graph of pig-iron output.

1930. Child Welfare.

567 135 10 k. + 2 k. olive 2·00 2·00
568 – 20 k. + 2 k. green (as No. 537) 3·00 4·00

155

1930. 10th Anniv of 1st Red Cavalry.

569 155 2 k. green 2·10 1·75
570 – 5 k. brown 2·10 1·75
571 – 10 k. olive 5·00 3·00
572 – 14 k. blue and red 3·00 2·50

DESIGNS: 5 k. Cavalry charge; 10 k. Cavalry charging; 14 k. Cavalry and map.

159 Group of Soviet Pupils

1930. Educational Exhibition, Leningrad.

573 159 10 k. olive 2·00 1·00

160

1930. Air. "Graf-Zeppelin" Flight to Moscow.

574 160 40 k. blue 27·00 18·00
575 80 k. red 40·00 25·00

162 "Potemkin"

1930. 25th Anniv of 1905 Rebellion. Imperf or perf.

576 162 3 k. red 1·75 50
577 – 5 k. blue 2·00 60
578 – 10 k. red and green 3·25 1·10

DESIGNS—HORIZ: 5 k. Barricade and rebels. VERT: 10 k. Red flag at Presnya barricade.

165 From the Tundra (reindeer) to the Steppes (camel)

166 Above Dnieprostroi Dam

1931. Airship Construction Fund. Imperf or perf.

579 165 10 k. violet 8·25 3·50
580 166 15 k. blue 27·00 12·00
581a – 20 k. red 10·00 5·00
582b – 50 k. brown 7·00 7·00
583 – 1 r. green 8·25 5·50

DESIGNS—As Type **165**. VERT: 20 k. Above Lenin's Mausoleum. HORIZ: 1 r. Airship construction. As Type **166**: 50 k. Above the North Pole.

See also No. E592.

170 Ice breaker "Malygin"

1931. Air. "Graf Zeppelin" North Pole Flight. Imperf or perf.

584 170 30 k. purple 28·00 17·00
585 35 k. green 28·00 17·00
586 1 r. black 28·00 17·00
587 2 r. blue 28·00 17·00

171 Polar Region and Ice-breaker "Sibiriakov"

1932. Air. 2nd Int Polar Year and Franz Joseph's Land to Archangel Flight.

588 171 50 k. red 50·00 25·00
589a 1 r. green 70·00 40·00

172 Maksim Gorky

173 Storming the Winter Palace

1932. 40th Anniv of Publication of "Makar Chadra".

590 172 15 k. brown 6·00 4·00
591 35 k. blue 22·00 16·00

1932. 15th Anniv of October Revolution.

593 – 3 k. violet 1·40 50
594 173 5 k. brown 1·40 50
595 – 10 k. blue 3·25 1·60
596 – 15 k. green 2·40 1·60
597 – 20 k. red 5·50 1·75
598 – 30 k. grey 13·50 2·40
599 – 35 k. brown 70·00 70·00

DESIGNS—HORIZ: 10 k. Dnieper Dam; 15 k. Harvesting with combines; 20 k. Industrial Works, Magnitogorsk; 30 k. Siberians listening to Moscow broadcast. VERT: 3 k. Lenin's arrival in Petrograd; 35 k. People of the World hailing Lenin.

INDEX

Countries can be quickly located by referring to the index at the end of this volume.

175 "Liberation"

1932. 10th Anniv of International Revolutionaries' Relief Organization.

600 175 50 k. red 15·00 6·00

176 Museum of Fine Arts

1932. 1st All-Union Philatelic Exn, Moscow.

601 176 15 k. brown 23·00 13·50
602 35 k. blue 70·00 35·00

177 Trier, Marx's Birthplace

1933. 50th Death Anniv of Marx.

603 177 3 k. green 5·00 90
604 – 10 k. brown 8·50 1·40
605 – 35 k. purple 13·50 12·50

DESIGNS—VERT: 10 k. Marx's grave, Highgate Cemetery; 35 k. Marx.

1933. Leningrad Philatelic Exhibition. Surch **LENINGRAD 1933** in Russian characters and premium.

606 176 15 k. + 30 k. blk & brn £100 60·00
607 35 k. + 70 k. blue £120 60·00

182

183

1933. Ethnographical Issue. Racial types.

608 – 1 k. brown (Kazakhs) 1·50 40
609 183 2 k. blue (Lesgins) 1·50 40
610 – 3 k. green (Crimean Tatars) 1·25 40
611 – 4 k. brown (Jews of Birobidzhan) 90 60
612 – 5 k. red (Tungusians) 1·00 40
613 – 6 k. blue (Buryats) 90 40
614 – 7 k. brown (Chechens) 90 40
615 – 8 k. red (Abkhazians) 1·25 55
616 – 9 k. blue (Georgians) 2·75 60
617 – 10 k. brn (Samoyedes) 3·25 2·00
618 – 14 k. green (Yakuts) 2·75 40
619 – 15 k. purple (Ukrainians) 4·25 1·00
620 – 15 k. black (Uzbeks) 3·00 80
621 – 15 k. blue (Tadzhiks) 3·50 75
622 – 15 k. brown (Transcaucasians) 4·00 75
623 – 15 k. green (Byelorussians) 3·75 60
624 – 15 k. orange (Great Russians) 3·25 80
625 – 15 k. red (Turkmens) 4·25 1·00
626 – 20 k. blue (Koryaks) 6·75 2·00
627 – 30 k. red (Bashkirs) 8·00 2·00
628 182 35 k. brown (Chuvashes) 13·50 2·75

SIZES: Nos. 608, 610/11, 614/17, 626/7, As T **182**: Nos. 612/13, 618. As T **183**: Nos. 619/24, 48 × 22 mm. No. 625, 22 × 48 mm.

186 V. V. Vorovsky

1933. Communist Party Activists. Dated "1933", "1934" or "1935".

629 186 1 k. green 65 50
718 – 2 k. violet 5·75 25
630 – 3 k. blue 1·60 60
719 – 4 k. purple 11·50 45
631 – 5 k. brown 3·75 1·90
632 – 10 k. blue 20·00 6·00
633 – 15 k. red 48·00 20·00
720 – 40 k. brown 11·50 6·75

DESIGNS: 2 k. M. Frunze; 3 k. V. M. Volodarsky; 4 k. N. E. Bauman; 5 k. M. S. Uritsky; 10 k. Iacov M. Sverdlov; 15 k. Viktor P. Nogin; 40 k. S. M. Kirov.

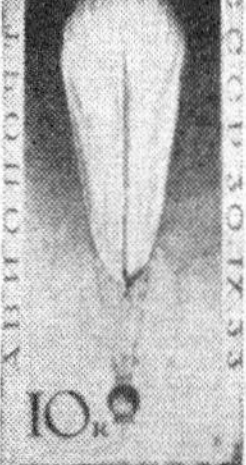
187 Stratosphere Balloon "U.S.S.R.–1" over Moscow

188 Massed Standard Bearers

1933. Air. Stratosphere record (19,000 metres).

634 187 5 k. blue 90·00 19·00
635 10 k. red 55·00 9·00
636 20 k. violet 32·00 6·75

1933. 15th Anniv of Order of Red Banner.

637 188 20 k. red, yellow & black 3·25 2·40

189 Commissar Shaumyan

190 Tupolev ANT-9 PS9 over Oilfield

1934. 15th Death Anniv of 26 Baku Commissars.

688 189 4 k. brown 6·75 1·60
639 – 5 k. black 6·75 1·60
640 – 20 k. violet 5·00 85
641 – 35 k. blue 20·00 6·75
642 – 40 k. red 18·00 8·50

DESIGNS: 5 k. Commissar Dzhaparidze. HORIZ: 20 k. The 26 condemned commissars; 35 k. Monument in Baku; 40 k. Workman, peasant and soldier dipping flags in salute.

1934. Air. 10th Anniv of Soviet Civil Aviation and U.S.S.R. Airmail Service.

643 – 5 k. blue 17·00 5·00
644 190 10 k. green 17·00 5·00
645 – 20 k. red 30·00 8·50
646 – 50 k. blue 32·00 10·00
647 – 80 k. violet 20·00 8·25

DESIGNS: Tupolev ANT-9 PS9 airplane over: 5 k. Furnaces at Kuznetsk; 20 k. Harvesters; 50 k. Volga-Moscow Canal; 80 k. Ice breaker "OB" in the Arctic.

191 New Lenin Mausoleum

1934. 10th Death Anniv of Lenin.

648 191 5 k. brown 2·40 1·00
649 10 k. blue 8·25 2·75
650 15 k. red 6·75 2·00
651 20 k. green 1·75 2·00
652 35 k. brown 6·75 3·00

192 Fedorov Monument, Moscow, between Hand and Rotary Presses

1934. 350th Death Anniv of Ivan Fedorov (first Russian printer).

653 192 20 k. red 8·25 5·00
654 40 k. blue 10·00 5·00

194 Dmitri Mendeleev

195 A. V. Vasenko and Stratosphere Balloon "Osoaviachim"

1934. Birth Centenary of Dmitri Mendeleev (chemist).

655 – 5 k. green 6·00 1·60
656 194 10 k. brown 17·00 4·75
657 15 k. red 13·50 4·00
658 – 20 k. blue 8·25 3·25

DESIGN—VERT: 5 k., 20 k. Mendeleev seated.

1934. Air. Stratosphere Disaster Victims.
659 – 5 k. purple . . . . 27·00 5·75
660 **195** 10 k. brown . . . . . . 55·00 6·00
661 – 20 k. violet . . . . 85·00 10·00
1042 – 1 r. green . . . . 8·50 2·75
1043 **195** 1 r. green . . . . 8·50 2·75
1044 – 1 r. blue . . . . 8·50 2·75
DESIGNS: 5 k., 1 r. (No. 1042). I. D. Usyskin; 20 k., 1 r. (No. 1044), P. F. Fedoseenko.
The 1 r. values issued in 1944, commemorated the 10th anniv of the disaster.

196 Airship "Pravda"

1934. Air. Airship Travel Propaganda.
662 **196** 5 k. red . . . . 13·50 2·75
663 – 10 k. lake . . . . 13·50 2·75
664 – 15 k. brown . . . . 40·00 20·00
665 – 20 k. black . . . . 20·00 13·50
666 – 30 k. blue . . . . 70·00 28·00
DESIGNS—HORIZ: 10 k. Airship landing; 15 k. Airship "Voroshilov"; 30 k. Airship "Lenin" and route map. VERT: 20 k. Airship's gondolas and mooring mast.

199 Stalin and Marchers inspired by Lenin **200** "War Clouds"

1934. "Ten years without Lenin". Portraits inscr "1924–1934".
667 – 1 k. black and blue . . . 1·50 1·40
668 – 3 k. black and blue . . . 1·50 1·40
669 – 5 k. black and blue . . . 3·25 2·00
670 – 10 k. black and blue . . . 2·25 2·00
671 – 20 k. blue and orange . . 6·75 3·25
672 **199** 30 k. red and orange . . . 28·00 6·75
DESIGN—VERT: 1 k. Lenin aged 3; 3 k. Lenin as student; 5 k. Lenin as man; 10 k. Lenin as orator. HORIZ: 20 k. Red demonstration, Lenin Mausoleum.

1935. Anti-War. Inscr "1914–1934".
673 **200** 5 k. black . . . . 3·25 90
674 – 10 k. blue . . . . 8·25 4·00
675 – 15 k. green . . . . 20·00 10·00
676 – 20 k. brown . . . . 13·50 4·00
677 – 35 k. red . . . . 30·00 13·50
DESIGNS: 10 k. "Flight from a burning village"; 15 k. "Before war and afterwards"; 20 k. "Ploughing with the sword"; 35 k. "Fraternisation".

202 Capt. Voronin and "Chelyuskin"

1935. Air. Rescue of "Chelyuskin" Expedition.
678 **202** 1 k. orange . . . . 4·25 1·00
679 – 3 k. red . . . . 5·00 1·40
680 – 5 k. green . . . . 5·00 1·40
681 – 10 k. brown . . . . 6·75 2·40
682 – 15 k. black . . . . 8·50 2·50
683 – 20 k. purple . . . . . . 13·50 2·50
684 – 25 k. blue . . . . 40·00 20·00
685 – 30 k. green . . . . 50·00 25·00
686 – 40 k. violet . . . . 28·00 5·00
687 **202** 50 k. blue . . . . 40·00 9·00
DESIGNS—HORIZ: 3 k. Prof. Schmidt and Schmidt Camp; 50 k. Schmidt Camp deserted. VERT: 5 k. A. V. Lyapidevsky; 10 k. S. A. Levanevsky; 15 k. M. G. Slepnev; 20 k. I. V. Doronin; 25 k. M. V. Vodopyanov; 30 k. V. S. Molokov; 40 k. N. P. Kamanin.

205 Underground Station

1935. Opening of Moscow Underground.
688 – 5 k. orange . . . . 8·00 3·25
689 – 10 k. blue . . . . 9·00 3·25
690 **205** 15 k. red . . . . 70·00 24·00
691 – 20 k. green . . . . 15·00 9·00
DESIGNS—As Type **205**: 5 k. Excavating tunnel; 10 k. Section of roadway, escalator and station. 48½ × 23 mm: 20 k. Train in station.

207 Rowing

1935. Spartacist Games.
692 – 1 k. blue and orange . . . 3·25 1·40
693 – 2 k. blue and black . . . 3·25 1·40
694 **207** 3 k. brown and green . . 6·75 3·25
695 – 4 k. blue and red . . . . 3·25 1·75
696 – 5 k. brown and violet . . 3·25 1·75
697 – 10 k. purple and red . . 17·00 3·25
698 – 15 k. brown and black . . 32·00 8·25
699 – 20 k. blue and brown . . 23·00 6·75
700 – 35 k. brown and blue . . 32·00 15·00
701 – 40 k. red and brown . . 27·00 8·25
DESIGNS: 1 k. Running; 2 k. Diving; 4 k. Football; 5 k. Skiing; 10 k. Cycling; 15 k. Lawn tennis; 20 k. Skating; 35 k. Hurdling; 40 k. Parade of athletes.

208 Friedrich Engels **210** A "Lion Hunt" from a Sassanian Silver Plate

1935. 40th Death Anniv of F. Engels.
702 **208** 5 k. red . . . . 6·75 1·40
703 10 k. green . . . . 3·25 2·00
704 15 k. blue . . . . 10·00 2·75
705 20 k. black . . . . 6·00 5·00

1935. Air. Moscow–San Francisco via North Pole Flight. Surch in Russian characters.
706 1 r. on 10 k. brown (No. 681) £300 £400

1935. 3rd International Congress of Persian Art and Archaeology, Leningrad.
707 **210** 5 k. orange . . . . 8·25 1·40
708 10 k. green . . . . 8·25 2·00
709 15 k. purple . . . . 10·00 4·25
710 35 k. brown . . . . 17·00 6·00

211 M. I. Kalinin **212** Tolstoi

1935. Pres. Kalinin's 60th Birthday. Autographed portraits inscr "1875–1935".
711 – 3 k. purple . . . . 1·00 20
712 – 5 k. green . . . . 2·00 25
713 – 10 k. blue . . . . 1·60 60
714 **211** 20 k. brown . . . . 2·75 2·00
DESIGNS: 3 k. Kalinin as machine worker; 5 k. Harvester; 10 k. Orator.
See also No. 1189.

1935. 25th Death Anniv of Tolstoi (writer).
715 – 3 k. violet and black . . . 1·10 50
716 **212** 10 k. brown and blue . . 1·90 1·00
717 – 20 k. brown and green . . 4·00 2·75
DESIGNS: 3 k. Tolstoi in 1860; 20 k. Monument in Moscow.

213 Pioneers securing Letter-box

1936. Pioneer Movement.
721 **213** 1 k. green . . . . 1·60 30
722 2 k. red . . . . 1·00 70
723 – 3 k. blue . . . . 3·25 2·25
724 – 5 k. red . . . . 3·00 85
725 – 10 k. blue . . . . 3·25 4·00
726 – 15 k. brown . . . . 8·50 4·00
DESIGNS: 3, 5 k. Pioneer preventing another from throwing stones; 10 k. Pioneers disentangling kite line from telegraph wires; 15 k. Girl pioneer saluting.

214 N. A. Dobrolyubov **215** A. S. Pushkin

1936. Birth Cent of Dobrolyubov (author and critic).
727 **214** 10 k. purple . . . . 7·00 1·50

1937. Death Centenary of A. S. Pushkin (poet).
728 **215** 10 k. brown 55 30
729 20 k. green 60 30
730 40 k. red . . . . 1·60 50
731 – 50 k. blue . . . . 2·75 35
732a – 80 k. red . . . . 3·25 1·00
733a – 1 r. green . . . . 4·75 1·60
DESIGN: 50 k. to 1 r. Pushkin's Monument.

217 Meyerhold Theatre **218** F. E. Dzerzhinsky

1937. 1st Soviet Architectural Congress.
734 **217** 3 k. red . . . . 1·60 20
735 – 5 k. lake . . . . 1·75 20
736 **217** 10 k. brown . . . . 2·10 25
737 – 15 k. black . . . . 2·75 25
738 – 20 k. olive . . . . 1·50 40
739 – 30 k. black . . . . 2·00 70
740 – 40 k. violet . . . . 2·00 25
741 – 50 k. brown . . . . 4·00 4·00
DESIGNS—As T **217**: 5, 15 k. G.P.O.; 20, 50 k. Red Army Theatre. 45 × 27 mm: 30 k. Hotel Moscow; 40 k. Palace of Soviets.

1937. 10th Death Anniv of F. E. Dzerzhinsky.
742 **218** 10 k. brown 40 20
743 20 k. green 55 55
744 40 k. red . . . . 2·10 1·00
745 80 k. red . . . . 3·25 1·75

219 Yakovlev Ya-7 Air 7

1937. Air. Air Force Exhibition.
746 **219** 10 k. black and brown . . 2·40 70
747 – 20 k. black and green . . . 2·40 70
748 – 30 k. black and brown . . 4·75 85
749 – 40 k. black and purple . . 6·75 1·40
750 – 50 k. black and violet . . 9·25 2·50
751 – 80 k. brown and blue . . . 11·50 2·50
752 – 1 r. black, orange & brn . 13·50 5·00
DESIGNS—As T **219**: 20 k. Tupolev ANT-9; 30 k. Tupolev ANT-6; 40 k. O.S.G.A. 101 flying boat; 50 k. Tupolev ANT-4 TB-1. 60 × 26 mm: 80 k. Tupolev ANT-20 "Maksim Gorki"; 1 r. Tupolev ANT-14 "Pravda".

220 Arms of Ukraine **221** Arms of U.S.S.R.

1937. New U.S.S.R. Constitution. Arms of Constituent Republics.
753 – 20 k. blue (Armenia) . . . 2·40 65
754 – 20 k. purple (Azerbaijan) . 2·40 65
755 – 20 k. brown (Byelorussia) . 2·40 65
756 – 20 k. red (Georgia) . . . . 2·40 65
757 – 20 k. grn (Kazakhstan) . . 2·40 65
758 – 20 k. red (Kirghizia) . . . 2·40 65
759 – 20 k. red (Tadzhikistan) . 2·40 65
760 – 20 k. red (Turkmenistan) . 2·40 65
761 **220** 20 k. red (Ukraine) . . . . 2·40 65
762 – 20 k. orge (Uzbekistan) . . 2·40 65
763 – 20 k. blue (R.S.F.S.R.) . . 2·40 65
764 **221** 40 k. red . . . . 6·75 1·60

222 Sculptured Group on Pavilion **223** Russian Pavilion, Paris Exhibition

1938. Paris International Exhibition.
765 **222** 5 k. red . . . . 1·00 40
766 **223** 20 k. red . . . . 2·50 40
767 **222** 50 k. blue . . . . 4·00 1·40

224 Shota Rustaveli

1938. 750th Anniv of Poem "Knight in Tiger Skin".
768 **224** 20 k. green . . . . 2·00 65

225 Route of North Pole Flight **227** Infantryman

1938. North Pole Flight.
769 **225** 10 k. black and brown . . 2·75 30
770 20 k. black and grey . . . 3·75 30
771 – 40 k. red and green . . . 10·00 2·40
772 – 80 k. red and deep red . . 3·00 2·00
DESIGN: 40 k., 80 k. Soviet Flag at North Pole.

1938. 20th Anniv of Red Army.
773 **227** 10 k. black and red . . . 50 20
774 – 20 k. black and red . . . 85 25
775 – 30 k. black, red and blue . 1·25 25
776 – 40 k. black, red and blue . 1·75 1·10
777 – 50 k. black and red . . . 2·25 1·10
778a – 80 k. black and red . . . 5·00 1·10
779 – 1 r. black and red . . . 3·25 1·10
DESIGNS—VERT: 20 k. Tank driver; 30 k. Sailor; 40 k. Airman; 50 k. Artilleryman. HORIZ: 80 k. Stalin reviewing cavalry; 1 r. Machine gunners.

229 Polar Flight Heroes **230**

1938. 1st Polar Flight.
780 **229** 10 k. red and black . . . 2·10 50
781 20 k. red and black . . . 2·50 1·00
782 40 k. red and brown . . . 5·00 1·90
783 50 k. red and purple . . . 8·50 2·40

1938. 2nd Polar Flight.
784 **230** 10 k. purple . . . . 4·75 45
785 20 k. black . . . . 4·50 1·40
786 50 k. purple . . . . 7·50 2·00

231 Ice-breaker "Murman" approaching Survivors

1938. Rescue of Papanin's North Pole Meteorological Party.
787 **231** 10 k. purple . . . . 4·00 50
788 20 k. blue . . . . 4·00 70
789 – 30 k. brown . . . . 7·00 1·25
790 – 50 k. blue . . . . 8·00 1·50
DESIGNS—VERT: 30, 50 k. Papanin survivors.

233 Nurse weighing Baby 234 Children visiting Statue of Lenin

1938. Soviet Union Children.

791 **233** 10 k. blue . . . . 1·25 30
792 **234** 15 k. blue . . . . 1·25 35
793 – 20 k. purple . . . . 1·50 35
794 – 30 k. red . . . . 1·60 45
795 – 40 k. brown . . . . 2·75 1·25
796 – 50 k. blue . . . . 5·50 1·50
797 – 80 k. green . . . . 7·00 1·90

DESIGNS—HORIZ: 20, 40 k. Biology class; 30 k. Health camp; 50, 80 k. Young inventors at play.

235 Crimean landscape

1938. Views of Crimea and Caucasus.

798 **235** 5 k. black . . . . 2·00 65
799 A 5 k. brown . . . . 2·00 65
800 B 10 k. green . . . . 3·25 85
801 C 10 k. brown . . . . 3·25 1·00
802 D 15 k. black . . . . 6·75 1·00
803 A 15 k. black . . . . 6·75 1·40
804 E 20 k. brown . . . . 7·50 1·50
805 C 30 k. black . . . . 8·50 1·60
806 F 40 k. brown . . . . 8·50 2·00
807 G 50 k. green . . . . 10·00 2·75
808 H 80 k. brown . . . . 13·50 3·25
809 I 1 r. green . . . . 17·00 6·75

DESIGNS—HORIZ: A, Yalta (two views); B, Georgian military road; E, Crimean resthouse; F, Alupka; H, Crimea; I, Swallows' Nest Castle. VERT: C, Crimea (two views); D, Swallows' Nest Castle; G, Gurzuf Park.

236 Schoolchildren and Model Tupolev ANT-6

1938. Aviation.

810 **236** 5 k. purple . . . . 2·00 1·00
811 – 10 k. brown . . . . 2·00 1·00
812 – 15 k. red . . . . 2·75 1·00
813 – 20 k. blue . . . . 2·75 1·00
814 – 30 k. red . . . . 5·00 2·00
815 – 40 k. blue . . . . 8·25 2·00
816 – 50 k. green . . . . 11·50 2·75
817 – 80 k. brown . . . . 10·00 3·25
818 – 1 r. green . . . . 13·50 3·25

DESIGNS—HORIZ: 10 k. Glider in flight; 40 k. Yakovlev VT-2 seaplane landing; 1 r. Tupolev ANT-6 airplane. VERT: 15 k. Captive observation balloon; 20 k. Airship "Osoaviachim" over Kremlin; 30 k. Parachutists; 30 k. Balloon in flight; 80 k. Stratosphere balloon.

237 Underground Railway

1938. Moscow Underground Railway Extension.

819 – 10 k. violet . . . . 2·00 85
820 – 15 k. brown . . . . 2·50 85
821 – 20 k. black . . . . 3·00 1·00
822 – 30 k. violet . . . . 3·25 1·25
823 **237** 40 k. black . . . . 3·50 1·75
824 – 50 k. brown . . . . 5·00 5·00

DESIGNS—VERT: 10 k. Mayakovsky Square station; 15 k. Sokol Terminus station; 20 k. Kiev station. HORIZ: 30 k. Dynamo Stadium station; 50 k. Revolution Square station.

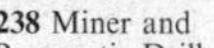

238 Miner and Pneumatic Drill 239 Diving

1936. 20th Anniv of Federation of Young Lenin Communists.

825 – 20 k. blue . . . . 1·10 85
826 **238** 30 k. purple . . . . 1·75 85
827 – 40 k. purple . . . . 2·40 85
828 – 50 k. red . . . . 3·25 90
829 – 80 k. blue . . . . 6·50 1·50

DESIGNS—VERT: 20 k. Girl parachutist; 50 k. Students and University. HORIZ: 40 k. Harvesting; 80 k. Airman, sailor and battleship "Marat".

1938. Soviet Sports.

830 **239** 5 k. red . . . . 2·75 30
831 – 10 k. black . . . . 3·75 1·00
832 – 15 k. brown . . . . 4·75 1·10
833 – 20 k. green . . . . 5·00 1·50
834 – 30 k. purple . . . . 9·00 1·75
835 – 40 k. green . . . . 11·50 2·40
836 – 50 k. blue . . . . 9·00 2·75
837 – 80 k. blue . . . . 10·00 5·00

DESIGNS: 10 k. Discus throwing; 15 k. Tennis; 20 k. Motor cycling; 30 k. Skiing; 40 k. Sprinting; 50 k. Football; 80 k. Athletic parade.

241 Council of People's Commissars Headquarters and Hotel Moscow

1939. New Moscow. Architectural designs as T **241**.

838 – 10 k. brown 85 70
839 **241** 20 k. green . . . . 1·10 70
840 – 30 k. purple . . . . 1·40 1·00
841 – 40 k. blue . . . . 3·25 1·50
842 – 50 k. red . . . . 5·00 2·00
843 – 80 k. olive . . . . 5·00 2·00
844 – 1 r. blue . . . . 9·50 2·75

DESIGNS—HORIZ: 10 k. Gorky Avenue; 30 k. Lenin Library; 40 k. Suspension and 50 k. Arched Bridges over River Moskva; 80 k. Khimki River Station. VERT: 1 r. Dynamo Underground Station.

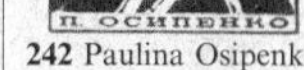

242 Paulina Osipenko 243 Russian Pavilion, N.Y. World's Fair

1939. Women's Moscow–Far East Flight.

845 **242** 15 k. green . . . . 2·10 80
846 – 30 k. purple . . . . 2·10 1·60
847 – 60 k. red . . . . 5·00 2·00

PORTRAITS: 30 k. Marina Raskova; 60 k. Valentina Grisodubova.

1939. New York World's Fair.

848 – 30 k. red and black . . . 3·25 85
849 **243** 50 k. brown and blue . . 5·00 1·40

DESIGN—VERT: (26 × 41½ mm): 30 k. Statue over Russian pavilion.

244 T. G. Shevchenko in early Manhood 245 Milkmaid

1939. 125th Birth Anniv of Shevchenko (Ukrainian poet and painter).

853 **244** 15 k. black and brown . 2·50 85
854 – 30 k. black and red . . . 3·00 1·10
855 – 60 k. brown and green . 6·75 2·75

DESIGNS: 30 k. Last portrait of Shevchenko; 60 k. Monument to Shevchenko, Kharkov.

1939. All Union Agricultural Fair.

856 **245** 10 k. red . . . . 1·00 25
857 – 15 k. red . . . . 1·00 15
858a – 20 k. grey . . . . 1·00 40
859 – 30 k. orange . . . . 1·40 25
860 – 30 k. violet . . . . 1·40 25
861 – 45 k. green . . . . 2·40 35
862 – 50 k. brown . . . . 2·75 65
863a – 60 k. violet . . . . 2·50 85
864 – 80 k. violet . . . . 2·75 85
865 – 1 r. blue . . . . 5·00 1·50

DESIGNS—HORIZ: 15 k. Harvesting; 20 k. Sheep farming; 30 k. (No. 860) Agricultural Fair Pavilion. VERT: 30 k. (No. 859) Agricultural Fair Emblem; 45 k. Gathering cotton; 50 k. Thoroughbred horses; 60 k. "Agricultural Wealth"; 80 k. Girl with sugar beet; 1 r. Trapper.

18 АВГУСТА
ДЕНЬ АВИАЦИИ СССР
(247)

1939. Aviation Day. As Nos. 811, 814/16 and 818 (colours changed) optd with T **247**.

866 10 k. red . . . . 2·40 55
867 30 k. blue . . . . 2·40 55
868 40 k. green . . . . 3·25 55
869 50 k. violet . . . . 5·00 2·75
870 1 r. brown . . . . 8·25 5·25

1939. Surch.

871 **141** 30 k. on 4 k. mauve . . . 17·00 10·00

249 Saltykov-Shchedrin 250 Kislovodsk Sanatorium

1939. 50th Death Anniv of M. E. Saltykov-Shchedrin (writer and satirist).

872 **249** 15 k. red 85 15
873 – 30 k. green . . . . 1·25 20
874 **249** 45 k. brown . . . . 1·50 65
874 – 60 k. blue . . . . 2·00 1·00

DESIGN: 30, 60 k. Saltykov-Shchedrin in later years.

1939. Caucasian Health Resorts.

876 **250** 5 k. brown 65 15
877 – 10 k. red 70 20
878 – 15 k. green 75 30
879 – 20 k. green . . . . 1·40 60
880 – 30 k. blue . . . . 1·50 60
881 – 50 k. black . . . . 2·40 1·25
882 – 60 k. purple . . . . 2·75 1·50
883 – 80 k. red . . . . 3·25 2·00

DESIGNS: 10, 15, 30, 50, 80 k. Sochi Convalescent Homes; 20 k. Abkhazia Sanatorium; 60 k. Sukumi Rest Home.

251 M. I. Lermontov 252 N. G. Chernyshevsky

1939. 125th Birth Anniv of Lermontov (poet and novelist).

884 **251** 15 k. brown and blue . . . 1·40 30
885 – 30 k. black and green . . . 3·00 85
886 – 45 k. blue and red . . . . 3·00 1·75

1939. 50th Death Anniv of N. G. Chernyshevsky (writer and politician).

887 **252** 15 k. green 50 30
888 30 k. violet . . . . 1·40 65
889 60 k. green . . . . 3·00 1·00

253 A. P. Chekhov 254 Welcoming Soviet Troops

1940. 80th Birth Anniv of Chekhov (writer).

890 **253** 10 k. green 30 15
891 15 k. blue 30 15
892 – 20 k. violet 60 30
893 – 30 k. brown . . . . 1·40 55

DESIGN: 20, 30 k. Chekhov with hat on.

1940. Occupation of Eastern Poland.

893a **254** 10 k. red . . . . 1·40 35
894 – 30 k. green . . . . 1·40 35
895 – 50 k. black . . . . 1·50 1·40
896 – 60 k. blue . . . . 2·40 1·40
897 – 1 r. red . . . . 5·00 2·00

DESIGNS: 30 k. Villagers welcoming tank crew; 50, 60 k. Soldier distributing newspapers to crowd; 1 r. People waving to column of tanks.

255 Ice-breaker "Georgy Sedov" and Badigin and Trofimov

1940. Polar Research.

898 – 15 k. green . . . . 2·25 40
899 **255** 30 k. violet . . . . 3·00 70
900 – 50 k. brown . . . . 4·00 1·75
901 – 1 r. blue . . . . 8·50 2·25

DESIGNS: 15 k. Ice-breaker "Iosif Stalin" and portraits of Papanin and Belousov; 50 k. Badgin and Papanin meeting. LARGER. (46 × 26 mm): 1 r. Route of drift of "Georgy Sedov".

256 V. Mayakovsky

1940. 10th Death Anniv of Mayakovsky (poet).

902 **256** 15 k. red 30 15
903 30 k. brown 85 20
904 – 60 k. violet . . . . 1·10 45
905 – 80 k. blue . . . . 1·60 45

DESIGN—VERT: 60, 80 k. Mayakovsky in profile wearing a cap.

257 Timiryazev 258 Relay Runner

1940. 20th Death Anniv of K. A. Timiryazev (scientist).

906 – 10 k. blue 85 20
907 – 15 k. violet 85 50
908 **257** 30 k. brown . . . . 1·10 85
909 – 60 k. green . . . . 3·25 1·60

DESIGNS—HORIZ: 10 k. Miniature of Timiryazev and Academy of Agricultural Sciences, Moscow; 15 k. Timiryazev in laboratory. VERT: 60 k. Timiryazev's statue (by S. Merkurov), Moscow.

1940. 2nd All Union Physical Culture Festival.

910 **258** 15 k. red . . . . 1·60 35
911a – 30 k. purple . . . . 2·50 30
912a – 50 k. blue . . . . 3·25 85
913 – 60 k. blue . . . . 4·25 60
914 – 1 r. green . . . . 5·50 1·40

DESIGNS—HORIZ: 30 k. Girls parade; 60 k. Skiing; 1 r. Grenade throwing. VERT: 50 k. Children and sports badges.

259 Tchaikovsky and Passage from his "Fourth Symphony" 260 Central Regions Pavilion

1940. Birth Cent of Tchaikovsky (composer).

915 – 15 k. green . . . . 1·75 20
916 **259** 20 k. brown . . . . 1·75 20
917 30 k. blue . . . . 1·75 50
918 – 50 k. red . . . . 2·50 85
919 – 60 k. red . . . . 3·25 1·10

DESIGNS: 15, 50 k. Tchaikovsky's house at Klin; 60 k. Tchaikovsky and excerpt from "Eugene Onegin".

920 ПАВИЛЬОН «ПОВОЛЖЬЕ»
921 ПАВИЛЬОН «ДАЛЬНИЙ ВОСТОК»
922 ПОРТАЛ ПАВИЛЬОНА „ЛЕНИНГРАД И СЕВЕРО-ВОСТОК РСФСР"
923 ПАВИЛЬОН МОСКОВСКОЙ, РЯЗАНСКОЙ И ТУЛЬСКОЙ ОБЛ.
924 ПАВИЛЬОН УКРАИНСКОЙ ССР
925 ПАВИЛЬОН БЕЛОРУССКОЙ ССР
926 ПАВИЛЬОН АЗЕРБАЙДЖАНСКОЙ ССР
927 ПАВИЛЬОН ГРУЗИНСКОЙ ССР
928 ПАВИЛЬОН АРМЯНСКОЙ ССР
929 „У ВХОДА В ПАВИЛЬОН УЗБЕКСКОЙ ССР"
930 ПАВИЛЬОН ТУРКМЕНСКОЙ ССР
931 ПАВИЛЬОН ТАДЖИКСКОЙ ССР
932 ПАВИЛЬОН КИРГИЗСКОЙ ССР
933 ПАВИЛЬОН КАРЕЛО-ФИНСКОЙ ССР
934 ПАВИЛЬОН КАЗАХСКОЙ ССР
935 ГЛАВНЫЙ ПАВИЛЬОН
936 ПАВИЛЬОН МЕХАНИЗАЦИИ

(211a)

1940. All Union Agricultural Fair, Coloured reproductions of Soviet Pavilions in green frames as T **260**. Inscriptions at foot as illustrated.

920 10 k. Volga provinces (RSFSR) (horiz) . . . . 3·00 1·00
921 15 k. Far East . . . . 1·40 1·00
922 30 k. Leningrad and North East RSFSR . . . . 1·90 1·10
923 30 k. Three Central Regions (RSFSR) . . . . 1·90 1·10
924 30 k. Ukrainian SSR . . . . 1·90 1·10
925 30 k. Byelorussian SSR . . . 1·90 1·10
926 30 k. Azerbaijan SSR . . . . 1·90 1·10
927 30 k. Georgian SSR (horiz) . 1·90 1·10
928 30 k. Armenian SSR . . . . 1·90 1·10
929 30 k. Uzbek SSR . . . . . . 1·90 1·10
930 30 k. Turkmen SSR (horiz) . 1·90 1·10
931 30 k. Tadzhik SSR . . . . . 1·90 1·10

932 30 k. Kirgiz SSR . . . . . . 1·90 1·10
933 30 k. Karelo-Finnish SSR . . 2·75 1·10
934 30 k. Kazakh SSR . . . . . . 1·90 1·10
935 50 k. Main Pavilion . . . . . . 3·00 2·00
936 60 k. Mechanization Pavilion and the statue of Stalin . . 8·00 1·90

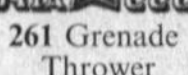

261 Grenade Thrower **262** Railway Bridge and Moscow–Volga Canal

1940. 20th Anniv of Wrangel's Defeat at Perekop (Crimea). Perf or imperf.
937 – 10 k. green . . . . 1·10 30
938 **261** 15 k. red 45 15
939 – 30 k. brown and red . . . 85 30
940 – 50 k. purple . . . . 1·00 50
941 – 60 k. blue . . . . 1·75 1·00
942 – 1 r. black . . . . 4·25 2·40
DESIGNS—VERT: 10 k. Red Army Heroes Monument; 30 k. Map of Perekop and portrait of M. V. Frunze; 1 r. Victorious soldier. HORIZ: 50 k. Soldiers crossing R. Sivash; 60 k. Army H.Q. at Stroganovka.

1941. Industrial and Agricultural Records.
943 – 10 k. blue 30 15
944a – 15 k. mauve 30 15
945a **262** 20 k. blue . . . . . . 1·75 70
946 – 30 k. brown . . . . . . 1·75 70
947 – 50 k. brown 60 15
948 – 60 k. brown . . . . . . 1·25 55
949 – 1 r. green . . . . 1·60 80
DESIGNS—VERT: 10 k. Coal-miners and pithead; 15 k. Blast furnace; 1 r. Derricks and petroleum refinery. HORIZ: 30 k. Locomotives; 50 k. Harvesting; 60 k. Ball-bearing vehicles.

263 Red Army Ski Corps **264** N. E. Zhukovsky and Air Force Academy

1941. 23rd Anniv of Red Army. Designs with Hammer, Sickle and Star Symbol.
950a **263** 5 k. violet . . . . . . 1·60 15
951 – 10 k. blue . . . . 1·25 15
952 – 15 k. green 85 15
953a – 20 k. red 85 15
954a – 30 k. brown 45 15
955a – 45 k. green . . . . . . 2·40 1·00
956 – 50 k. blue . . . . 1·00 1·10
957 – 1 r. green . . . . 1·00 1·10
957b – 3 r. green . . . . 7·50 3·00
DESIGNS—VERT: 10 k. Sailor; 20 k. Cavalry; 30 k. Automatic Rifle Squad; 50 k. Airman; 1, 3 r. Marshal's star. HORIZ: 15 k. Artillery; 45 k. Clearing a hurdle.

1941. 20th Death Anniv of Zhukovsky (scientist).
958 – 15 k. blue 85 50
959 **264** 30 k. red . . . . 1·75 65
960 – 50 k. red . . . . 2·50 85
DESIGNS—VERT: 15 k. Zhukovsky; 50 k. Zhukovsky lecturing.

265 Thoroughbred Horses **266** Arms of Karelo-Finnish S.S.R

1941. 15th Anniv of Kirghiz S.S.R.
961 **265** 15 k. brown . . . . . . 3·00 85
962a – 30 k. violet . . . . . . 4·00 1·25
DESIGN: 30 k. Coal miner and colliery.

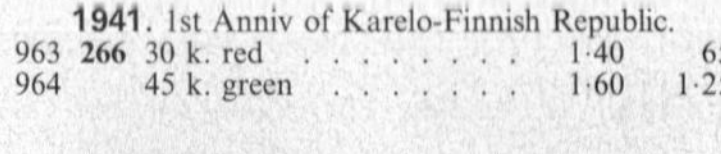

1941. 1st Anniv of Karelo-Finnish Republic.
963 **266** 30 k. red . . . . 1·40 65
964 45 k. green . . . . 1·60 1·25

267 Marshal Suvorov **268** Spassky Tower, Kremlin

1941. 150th Anniv of Battle of Izmail.
965 – 10 k. green 75 30
966 – 15 k. red 75 40
967 **267** 30 k. blue . . . . 1·40 65
968 1 r. brown . . . . 3·00 1·60
DESIGN: 10, 15 k. Storming of Izmail.

1941.
970 **268** 1 r. red . . . . 2·50 85
971 – 2 r. orange . . . . 5·00 1·60
DESIGN—HORIZ: 2 r. Kremlin Palace.

269 "Razin on the Volga"

1941. 25th Death Anniv of Surikov (artist).
972 – 20 k. black . . . . 2·00 1·60
973 **269** 30 k. red . . . . 4·00 2·00
974 – 50 k. purple . . . . . . 8·50 8·50
975 **269** 1 r. green . . . . 11·50 10·00
976 – 2 r. brown . . . . 20·00 11·50
DESIGNS—VERT: 20, 50 k. "Suvorov's march through Alps, 1799"; 2 r. Surikov.

270 Lenin Museum (interior) **271** Lermontov

1941. 5th Anniv of Lenin Museum.
977 **270** 15 k. red . . . . 2·75 2·75
978 – 30 k. violet on mauve . . 22·00 20·00
979 **270** 45 k. green . . . . . . 5·00 5·00
980 – 1 r. red on rose . . . . . 23·00 23·00
DESIGN: 30 k., 1 r. Exterior of Lenin Museum.

1941. Death Centenary of M. Yu. Lermontov (poet and novelist).
981 **271** 15 k. grey . . . . 7·25 6·75
982 30 k. violet . . . . 10·50 13·50

272 Reproduction of Poster **273** Mass Enlistment

1941. Mobilization.
983a **272** 30 k. red . . . . 17·00 17·00

1941. National Defence.
984 **273** 30 k. blue . . . . 70·00 70·00

274 Alishir Navoi **275** Lt. Talalikhin ramming Enemy Airplane

289a Five Heroes

1942. 5th Centenary of Uzbek poet Mir Ali Shir (Alishir Navoi).
985 **274** 30 k. brown . . . . . . 22·00 22·00
986 1 r. purple . . . . . . 22·00 22·00

1942. Russian Heroes (1st issue).
987 **275** 20 k. blue 50 15
988 A 30 k. grey 60 25
989 B 30 k. black 60 15
990 C 30 k. black 60 15
991 D 30 k. black 60 30
1048c **275** 30 k. grey . . . . . . 1·50 65
1048d A 30 k. blue . . . . . . 1·50 65
1048e C 30 k. green . . . . . . 1·50 65
1048f D 30 k. purple . . . . . . 1·50 65
1048g **289a** 30 k. blue . . . . . . 1·50 65
992 C 1 r. green . . . . 5·75 5·00
993 D 2 r. green . . . . 11·50 10·00
DESIGNS: A, Capt. Gastello and burning airplane diving into enemy petrol tanks; B, Maj-Gen. Dovator and Cossack cavalry in action; C, Shura Chekalin guerilla fighting; D, Zoya Kosmodemyanskaya being led to death.
See also Nos. 1072/6.

276 Anti-tank Gun

1942. War Episodes (1st series).
994 **276** 20 k. brown . . . . 2·00 1·10
995 – 30 k. blue . . . . 2·00 1·10
996 – 30 k. green . . . . 2·00 1·10
997 – 30 k. red . . . . 2·00 1·10
998 – 60 k. grey . . . . 2·75 2·00
999 – 1 r. brown . . . . 5·75 5·00
DESIGNS—HORIZ: 30 k. (No. 996), Guerrillas attacking train; 30 k. (No. 997), Munition worker; 1 r. Machine gunners. VERT: 30 k. (No. 995), Signallers; 60 k. Defenders of Leningrad.

277 Distributing Gifts to Soldiers

1942. War Episodes (2nd series).
1000 **277** 20 k. blue . . . . 1·50 1·10
1001 – 20 k. purple . . . . . . 1·75 1·10
1002 – 30 k. purple . . . . . . 1·75 1·40
1003 – 45 k. red . . . . 4·00 3·25
1004 – 45 k. blue . . . . 5·00 4·75
DESIGNS—VERT: No. 1001, Bomber destroying tank; No. 1002, Food packers; No. 1003, Woman sewing; No. 1004, Anti-aircraft gun.
See also Nos. 1013/17.

278 Munition Worker

1943. 25th Anniv of Russian Revolution.
1005 **278** 5 k. brown 85 25
1006 – 10 k. brown 80 15
1007 – 15 k. blue 65 20
1008 – 20 k. blue 65 20
1009 – 30 k. brown . . . . . . 1·25 20
1010 – 60 k. brown . . . . . . 1·75 1·00
1011 – 1 r. red . . . . 2·40 1·60
1012 – 2 r. brown . . . . . . 4·25 2·50
DESIGNS: 10 k. Lorry convoy; 15 k. Troops supporting Lenin's banner; 20 k. Leningrad seen through an archway; 30 k. Spassky Tower, Lenin and Stalin; 60 k. Tank parade; 1 r. Lenin speaking; 2 r. Star of Order of Lenin.

279 Nurses and Wounded Soldier

1943. War Episodes (3rd series).
1013 **279** 30 k. green . . . . 1·75 1·50
1014 – 30 k. green (Scouts) . . . . 1·75 1·50
1015 – 30 k. brown (Mine-thrower) 1·75 1·50
1016 – 60 k. green (Anti-tank troops) . . . . 2·00 1·50
1017 – 60 k. blue (Sniper) . . . 2·00 1·50

280 Routes of Bering's Voyages

1943. Death Bicent of Vitus Bering (explorer).
1018 – 30 k. blue . . . . 1·60 1·00
1019 **280** 60 k. grey . . . . 3·25 1·00
1020 – 1 r. green . . . . 4·50 1·00
1021 **280** 2 r. brown . . . . 7·50 3·50
DESIGN: 30 k., 1 r. Mt. St. Ilya.

281 Gorky

1943. 75th Birth Anniv of Maksim Gorky (novelist).
1022 **281** 30 k. green . . . . . . 1·25 15
1023 60 k. blue . . . . 1·50 15

282 Order of the Great Patriotic War **(a)** Order of Suvorov

1943. War Orders and Medals (1st series). Medals with ribbon attached.
1024 **282** 1 r. black . . . . 2·50 2·50
1025 **a** 10 r. olive . . . . 11·50 11·50
See also Nos. 1051/8, 1089/94, 1097/99a, 1172/86, 1197/1204 and 1776/80a.

283 Karl Marx **284** Naval Landing Party

1943. 125th Birth Anniv of Marx.
1026 **283** 30 k. blue . . . . 1·75 20
1027 60 k. green . . . . 2·50 35

1943. 25th Anniv of Red Army and Navy.
1028 **284** 20 k. brown 30 20
1029 – 30 k. green 35 15
1030 – 60 k. green . . . . 1·00 40
1031 **284** 3 r. blue . . . . 3·00 90
DESIGNS: 30 k. Sailors and anti-aircraft gun; 60 k. Tanks and infantry.

285 Ivan Turgenev **286** Loading a Gun

1943. 125th Birth Anniv of Ivan Turgenev (novelist).
1032 **285** 30 k. green . . . . . . 17·00 17·00
1032a 60 k. violet . . . . . . 25·00 25·00

1943. 25th Anniv of Young Communist League.
1033 **286** 15 k. blue 55 15
1034 – 20 k. orange 55 15
1035 – 30 k. brown and red . . 70 15
1036 – 1 r. green . . . . 1·00 35
1037 – 2 r. green . . . . 2·25 1·00
DESIGNS—As T **286**: 20 k. Tank and banner; 1 r. Infantrymen; 2 r. Grenade thrower. $22\frac{1}{2} \times 28\frac{1}{2}$ mm: 30 k. Bayonet fighter and flag.

287 V. V. Mayakovsky **288** Memorial Tablet and Allied Flags

1943. 50th Birth Anniv of Mayakovsky (poet).
1038 **287** 30 k. orange 65 65
1039 60 k. blue . . . . 1·25 1·00

1943. Teheran Three Power Conference and 26th Anniv of Revolution.
1040 **288** 30 k. black . . . . . . 1·40 50
1041 3 r. blue . . . . 4·75 1·25

289 Defence of Odessa

1944. Liberation of Russian Towns.
1045 – 30 k. brown and red . . 65 25
1046 – 30 k. blue 65 25
1047 – 30 k. green 65 25
1048 **289** 30 k. green 65 25
DESIGNS: No. 1045, Stalingrad; No. 1046, Sevastopol; No. 1047, Leningrad.

АВИАПОЧТА
1944 г.
1 РУБЛЬ
(290)

291 Order of Kutusov

(b) Order of Patriotic War

(c) Order of Aleksandr Nevsky

(d) Order of Suvorov

(e) Order of Kutusov

1944. Air. Surch with T **290**.

1049	**275**	1 r. on 30 k. grey	2·50	85
1050	A	1 r. on 30 k. blue (No. 1048d)	2·50	85

1944. War Orders and Medals (2nd series). Various Stars without ribbons showing as Types **b** to **e**. Perf or imperf. (a) Frames as T **291**.

1051	**b**	15 k. red	50	50
1052	**c**	20 k. blue	50	50
1053	**d**	30 k. green	1·40	1·40
1054	**e**	60 k. red	1·50	1·50
		(b) Frames as T **282**.		
1055	**b**	1 r. black	80	30
1056	**c**	3 r. blue	4·25	2·10
1057	**e**	5 r. green	5·25	2·00
1058	**d**	10 r. red	7·00	3·75

293 Lenin Mausoleum and Red Square, Moscow

1944. "Twenty Years without Lenin". As Nos. 667/72, but inscr "1924–1944", and T **293**.

1059	–	30 k. black and blue	65	10
1060	**199**	30 k. red and orange	65	10
1061	–	45 k. black and blue	65	15
1062	–	50 k. black and blue	70	15
1063	–	60 k. black and blue	85	50
1064	**293**	1 r. brown and blue	2·00	75
1065	**199**	3 r. black and orange	4·75	2·10

DESIGNS—VERT: Lenin at 3 years of age (No. 1059): at school (45 k.); as man (50 k.); as orator (60 k.).

294 Allied Flags

295 Rimsky-Korsakov and Bolshoi Theatre

1944. 14 June (Allied Nations' Day).

1066	**294**	60 k. black, red & blue	1·60	65
1067		3 r. blue and red	6·00	2·50

1944. Birth Centenary of Rimsky-Korsakov (composer). Imperf or perf.

1068	**295**	30 k. grey	40	10
1069		60 k. green	60	10
1070		1 r. green	1·00	20
1071		3 r. violet	2·50	50

296 Nuradilov and Machine-gun

297 Polivanova and Kovshova

298 S. A. Chaplygin

1944. War Heroes (3rd issue).

1072	**296**	30 k. green	45	45
1073	–	60 k. violet	85	45
1074	–	60 k. blue	85	45
1075	**297**	60 k. green	1·50	45
1076	–	60 k. black	1·75	45

DESIGNS—HORIZ: No. 1073, Matrosov defending a snow-trench; No. 1074, Luzak hurling a hand grenade. VERT: No. 1076, B. Safonev, medals and aerial battle over the sea.

1944. 75th Birth Anniv of S. A. Chaplygin (scientist).

1077	**298**	30 k. grey	30	10
1078		1 r. brown	1·40	1·40

299 V. I. Chapaev

300 Ilya Yefimovich Repin

301 "Reply of the Cossacks to Sultan Mahmoud IV"

302 I. A. Krylov

1944. Heroes of 1918 Civil War.

1079	**299**	30 k. green	1·00	25
1080	–	30 k. black (N. Shchors)	1·00	25
1081	–	30 k. green (S. Lazo)	1·00	25

For 40 k. stamp as Type **299**, see No. 1531.
See also Nos. 1349/51.

1944. Birth Centenary of I. Y. Repin (artist). Imperf or perf.

1082	**300**	30 k. green	1·40	20
1083	**301**	50 k. green	1·40	20
1084		60 k. blue	1·40	20
1085	**300**	1 r. brown	2·00	40
1086	**301**	2 r. violet	4·00	1·25

1944. Death Centenary of Krylov (fabulist).

1087	**302**	30 k. brown	1·00	10
1088		1 r. blue	2·00	50

(f) Partisans' Medal

(g) Medal for Bravery

(h) Order of Bogdan Chmielnitsky

(j) Order of Victory

(k) Order of Ushakov

(l) Order of Nakhimov

1945. War Orders and Medals (3rd series). Frame as T **291** with various centres as Types **f** to **l**. Perf or imperf.

1089	**f**	15 k. black	75	15
1090	**g**	30 k. blue	1·50	20
1091	**h**	45 k. blue	1·50	40
1092	**j**	60 k. red	1·75	45
1093	**k**	1 r. blue	2·25	1·00
1094	**l**	1 r. green	2·25	1·00

303 Griboedov (after P. Karatygin)

305 Soldier

1945. 150th Birth Anniv of Aleksander S. Griboedov (author).

1095	**303**	30 k. green	1·50	35
1096		60 k. brown	2·00	50

1945. War Orders and Medals (4th series). Frames as T **282**. Various centres.

1097	**g**	1 r. black	1·40	65
1098	**h**	2 r. black	3·00	1·75
1098a		2 r. purple	40·00	15·00
1098b		2 r. olive	6·00	2·00
1099	**j**	3 r. red	4·75	1·40
1099a		3 r. purple	6·75	3·25

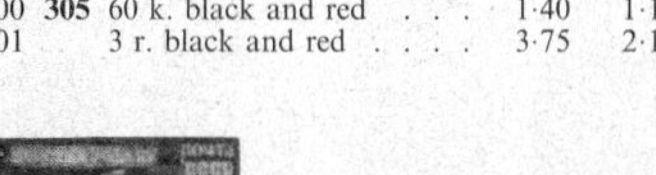

1945. Relief of Stalingrad.

1100	**305**	60 k. black and red	1·40	1·10
1101		3 r. black and red	3·75	2·10

306 Standard Bearer

308 Attack

1945. Red Army Victories.

1102	**306**	20 k. green, red & black	40	15
1103	–	30 k. black and red	40	40
1104	–	1 r. green and red	2·10	2·10

DESIGN—HORIZ: 30 k. Infantry v. Tank; 1 r. Infantry charge.

1945. Liberation of Russian Soil.

1105	**308**	30 k. blue	40	60
1106	–	60 k. red	1·00	1·00
1107	–	1 r. green	2·10	2·10

DESIGNS: 60 k. Welcoming troops; 1 r. Grenade thrower.

309 Badge and Guns

310 Barricade

1945. Red Guards Commemoration.

1108	**309**	60 k. red	2·75	1·00

1945. Battle of Moscow.

1109	–	30 k. blue	40	50
1110	**310**	60 k. black	80	50
1111	–	1 r. black	1·50	1·00

DESIGNS: 30 k. Tanks in Red Square, Moscow. 1 r. Aerial battle and searchlights.

311 Prof. Lomonosov and Academy of Sciences, Leningrad

312 Popov

1945. 220th Anniv of Academy of Sciences.

1112	–	30 k. blue	1·00	50
1113	**311**	2 r. black	3·00	80

DESIGN—VERT: 30 k. Moscow Academy, inscr "1725–1945".

1945. 50th Anniv of Popov's Radio Discoveries.

1114	**312**	30 k. blue	35	40
1115		60 k. red	1·40	60
1116	–	1 r. brown (Popov)	2·40	1·10

314 Motherhood Medal 315

1945. Orders and Medals of Motherhood. Imperf or perf.

1117	**314**	20 k. brown on blue	30	20
1118	–	30 k. brown on green	45	20
1119	–	60 k. red	1·50	70
1120	**315**	1 r. black on green	1·00	20
1121	–	2 r. blue	2·40	30
1122	–	3 r. red on blue	3·25	1·40

DESIGNS: 30 k., 2 r. Order of Motherhood Glory; 60 k., 3 r. Order of Heroine-Mother.

316 Petlyakov Pe-2 Dive Bombers

317 Ilyushin Il-2M3 Stormovik Fighters

318 Petlyakov Pe-8 TB-7 Bomber

1945. Air. Aviation Day.

1123	**316**	1 r. brown	3·00	75
1124	**317**	1 r. brown	3·00	75
1125	–	1 r. red	3·00	75
1126	–	1 r. black	3·00	75
1127	–	1 r. blue	3·00	75
1128	–	1 r. green	3·00	75
1129	**318**	1 r. grey	3·00	75
1130	–	1 r. brown	3·00	75
1131	–	1 r. red	3·00	75

DESIGNS—As Type **317**: No. 1125, Lavochkin-La7 fighter shooting tail off Focke Wulf Fw 190 plane; 1126, Ilyushin Il-4 DB-3 bombers dropping bombs; 1127, Tupolev ANT-60 Tu-2 bombers in flight; 1128, Polikarpov Po-2 biplane. As Type **318**: No. 1130, Yakovlev-3 fighter destroying enemy fighter; 1131, Yakovlev Yak-9 fighter destroying Henschel Hs 129B plane.
See also Nos. 1163/71.

ПРАЗДНИК
ПОБЕДЫ

9 мая
1945 года
(319)

1945. VE Day. No. 1099 optd with T **319**.

1132	–	3 r. red	4·25	1·50

320 Lenin

321 Lenin

1945. 75th Birth Anniv of Lenin.

1133	**320**	30 k. blue	50	20
1134	–	50 k. brown	85	20
1135	–	60 k. red	85	30
1136	**321**	1 r. black	1·40	60
1137	–	3 r. brown	3·25	1·75

DESIGNS—VERT: (inscr "1870–1945"). 50 k. Lenin at desk; 60 k. Lenin making a speech; 3 r. Portrait of Lenin.

322 Kutuzov (after R. Volkov)

323 A. I. Herzen

1945. Birth Bicentenary of Mikhail Kutuzov (military leader).

1138	**322**	30 k. blue	80	40
1139		60 k. brown	1·50	60

1945. 75th Death Anniv of Herzen (author and critic).

1140	**323**	30 k. brown	1·00	15
1141		2 r. black	1·90	65

324 I. I. Mechnikov

325 Friedrich Engels

1945. Birth Centenary of Mechnikov (biologist).

1142	**324**	30 k. brown	85	15
1143		1 r. black	1·60	30

1945. 125th Birth Anniv of Engels.
1144 **325** 30 k. brown 80 15
1145 60 k. green . . . . 1·25 60

326 Observer and Guns 327 Heavy Guns

1945. Artillery Day.
1146 **326** 30 k. brown . . . . . . 1·10 1·00
1147 **327** 60 k. black . . . . 3·25 3·25

328 Tank Production

1945. Home Front.
1148 **328** 20 k. blue and brown . . 1·75 35
1149 – 30 k. black and brown . 1·50 40
1150 – 60 k. brown and green . 2·50 1·40
1151 – 1 r. blue and brown . . . 3·25 1·60
DESIGNS: 30 k. Harvesting; 60 k. Aircraft designing; 1 r. Firework display.

329 Victory Medal 330 Soldier with Victory Flag

1946. Victory Issue.
1152 **329** 30 k. violet 30 15
1153 30 k. brown 30 15
1154 60 k. black 55 20
1155 60 k. brown 55 20
1156 **330** 60 k. black and red . . . 1·75 85

331 Arms of U.S.S.R. 332 Kremlin, Moscow

1946. Supreme Soviet Elections.
1157 **331** 30 k. red 30 10
1158 **332** 45 k. red 50 30
1159 **331** 60 k. green . . . . 2·75 1·00

333 Tank Parade

334 Infantry Parade

1946. 28th Anniv of Red Army and Navy.
1160 **333** 60 k. brown . . . . . . 1·00 15
1161 2 r. violet . . . . 2·00 50
1162 **334** 3 r. black and red . . . 5·00 1·40

1946. Air. As Nos. 1123/31.
1163 – 5 k. violet (as No. 1130) . 40 60
1164 **316** 10 k. red 40 60
1165 **317** 15 k. red 40 60
1166 **318** 15 k. green 40 60
1167 – 20 k. black (as No. 1127) 40 60
1168 – 30 k. vio (as No. 1127) . 85 50
1169 – 30 k. brown (as No. 1128) 90 50
1170 – 50 k. blue (as No. 1125) . 1·40 65
1171 – 60 k. blue (as No. 1131) . 2·75 85

A B C D

E F G H

J K L M

N O P

1946. War Orders with Medals (5th series). Frames as T **291** with various centres as Types A to P.
1172 A 60 k. red . . . . 1·00 1·40
1173 B 60 k. red . . . . 1·00 1·40
1174 C 60 k. green . . . . . . 1·00 1·40
1175 D 60 k. green . . . . . . 1·00 1·40
1176 E 60 k. green . . . . . . 1·00 1·40
1177 F 60 k. blue . . . . 1·00 1·40
1178 G 60 k. blue . . . . 1·00 1·40
1179 H 60 k. violet . . . . . . 1·00 1·40
1180 J 60 k. purple . . . . . . 1·00 1·40
1181 K 60 k. brown . . . . . . 1·00 1·40
1182 L 60 k. brown . . . . . . 1·00 1·40
1183 M 60 k. purple . . . . . . 1·00 1·40
1184 N 60 k. red . . . . 1·00 1·40
1185 O 60 k. blue . . . . 1·00 1·40
1186 P 60 k. purple . . . . . . 1·00 1·40

336 P. L. Chebyshev 337 Gorky

1946. 125th Birth Anniv of Chebyshev (mathematician).
1187 **336** 30 k. brown 50 20
1188 60 k. black . . . . . . 1·00 30

1946. Death of President Kalinin. As T **211**, but inscr "3-VI-1946".
1189 20 k. black . . . . 1·90 1·00

1946. 10th Death Anniv of Maksim Gorky (novelist).
1190 **337** 30 k. brown 40 10
1191 – 60 k. green 70 20
DESIGN: 60 k. Gorky and laurel leaves.

338 Gagy

1946. Health Resorts.
1192 – 15 k. brown 40 15
1193 **338** 30 k. green 60 15
1194 – 30 k. green 70 15
1195 – 45 k. brown . . . . . . 1·10 35
DESIGNS—HORIZ: 15 k. Sukumi; 45 k. Novy Afon. VERT: 30 k. (No. 1194) Sochi.

339 Stalin and Parade of Athletes R

1946. Sports Festival.
1196 **339** 30 k. green . . . . 6·75 4·75

1946. War Medals (6th series). Frames as T **282** with various centres.
1197 R 1 r. red . . . . 1·90 1·10
1198 B 1 r. green . . . . 1·90 1·10
1199 C 1 r. brown . . . . 1·90 1·10
1200 D 1 r. blue . . . . 1·90 1·10
1201 G 1 r. grey . . . . 1·90 1·10
1202 H 1 r. red . . . . 1·90 1·10
1203 K 1 r. purple . . . . 1·90 1·10
1204 L 1 r. red . . . . 1·90 1·10

341 Moscow Opera House 342 Tanks in Red Square

1946. Moscow Buildings.
1205 – 5 k. brown 30 15
1206 **341** 10 k. grey 35 15
1207 – 15 k. brown 30 15
1208 – 20 k. brown 60 20
1209 – 45 k. green 70 30
1210 – 50 k. brown 80 85
1211 – 60 k. violet . . . . . . 1·40 1·10
1212 – 1 r. brown . . . . 2·00 1·60
DESIGNS—VERT: 5 k. Church of Ivan the Great and Kremlin; 1 r. Spassky Tower (larger). HORIZ: 15 k. Hotel Moscow; 20 k. Theatre and Sverdlov Square; 45 k. As 5 k. but horiz; 50 k. Lenin Museum; 60 k. St. Basil's Cathedral and Spassky Tower (larger).

1946. Heroes of Tank Engagements.
1213 **342** 30 k. green . . . . 2·00 2·00
1214 60 k. brown . . . . . . 3·00 3·00

343 "Iron" 345 Lenin and Stalin

344 Soviet Postage Stamps

1946. 4th Stalin "Five-Year Reconstruction Plan". Agriculture and Industry.
1215 – 5 k. olive 30 10
1216 – 10 k. green 30 10
1217 – 15 k. brown 50 10
1218 – 20 k. violet 80 10
1219 **343** 30 k. brown . . . . . . 1·40 25
DESIGNS—HORIZ: 5 k. "Agriculture"; 15 k. "Coal". VERT: 10 k. "Oil"; 20 k. "Steel".

1946. 25th Anniv of Soviet Postal Services.
1220 – 15 k. black and red . . 1·50 40
1221 – 30 k. brown and green . . 2·40 1·40
1222 **344** 60 k. black and green . . 3·75 1·60
DESIGNS: 15 k. ($48\frac{1}{2} \times 23$ mm). Stamps on map of U.S.S.R.; 30 k. ($33 \times 22\frac{1}{2}$ mm). Reproduction of Type **47**.

1946. 29th Anniv of Russian Revolution. Imperf or Perf.
1223 **345** 30 k. orange . . . . . . 2·75 2·75
1224 30 k. green . . . . 2·75 2·75

346 N. A. Nekrasov 347 Stalin Prize Medal

1946. 125th Birth Anniv of Nekrasov (poet).
1225 **346** 30 k. black 85 10
1226 60 k. brown . . . . . . 1·40 60

1946. Stalin Prize.
1227 **347** 30 k. brown . . . . 2·75 1·00

348 Dnieperprostroi Dam

1946. Restoration of Dnieperprostroi Hydro-electric Power Station.
1228 **348** 30 k. black . . . . . . 1·50 65
1229 60 k. blue . . . . 2·75 1·00

349 A. Karpinsky 350 N. E. Zhukovsky

1947. Birth Centenary of Karpinsky (geologist).
1230 **349** 30 k. green 80 85
1231 50 k. black . . . . . . 3·00 90

1947. Birth Centenary of Zhukovsky (scientist).
1232 **350** 30 k. black . . . . 1·50 85
1233 60 k. blue . . . . 2·50 1·25

351 Lenin Mausoleum 352 Lenin

1947. 23rd Death Anniv of Lenin.
1234 **351** 30 k. green 65 50
1235 30 k. blue 65 50
1236 **352** 50 k. brown . . . . . . 3·25 1·00
For similar designs inscr "1924/1948" see Nos. 1334/6.

353 Nikolai M. Przhevalsky 354 Arms of R.S.F.S.R

356 Arms of U.S.S.R

1947. Centenary of Soviet Geographical Society.
1237 – 20 k. brown . . . . . . 2·00 50
1238 – 20 k. blue . . . . 2·00 50
1239 **353** 60 k. olive . . . . 3·50 1·40
1240 – 60 k. brown . . . . . . 3·50 1·40
DESIGN: 20 k. Miniature portrait of F. P. Litke and full rigged ship "Senyavin".

1947. Supreme Soviet Elections. Arms of Constituent Republics. As T **354**.
1241 **354** 30 k. red (Russian Federation) 75 65
1242 – 30 k. brown (Armenia) . . 75 65
1243 – 30 k. bistre (Azerbaijan) 75 65
1244 – 30 k. green (Byelorussia) 75 65
1245 – 30 k. grey (Estonia) . . 75 65
1246 – 30 k. brown (Georgia) . 75 65
1247 – 30 k. purple (Karelo-Finnish S.S.R.) 75 65
1248 – 30 k. orange (Kazakhstan) 75 65
1249 – 30 k. purple (Kirgizia) . 75 65
1250 – 30 k. brown (Latvia) . . 75 65
1251 – 30 k. green (Lithuania) . 75 65
1252 – 30 k. purple (Moldavia) . 75 65
1253 – 30 k. green (Tadzhikistan) 75 65
1254 – 30 k. black (Turkmenistan) 75 65
1255 – 30 k. blue (Ukraine) . . 75 65
1256 – 30 k. brown (Uzbekistan) 75 65
1257 **356** 1r. multicoloured . . . . 2·75 85
A Hammer and Sickle in the centre of No. 1247 and at the base of No. 1249 should assist identification.

357 Russian Soldier

359 A. S. Pushkin

1947. 29th Anniv of Soviet Army. Perf or imperf.

1258	357	20 k. black	45	10
1259	–	30 k. blue	50	15
1260	–	30 k. brown	55	15

DESIGNS—VERT: No. 1259, Military cadet. HORIZ: No. 1260, Soldier, sailor and airman.

1947. 110th Death Anniv of Pushkin (poet).

1261	359	30 k. black	65	30
1262		50 k. green	1·00	1·10

360 Schoolroom

1947. International Women's Day.

1263	360	15 k. blue	3·25	1·60
1264	–	30 k. red	5·00	3·00

DESIGN—$26\frac{1}{2} \times 39\frac{1}{2}$ mm: 30 k. Women students and banner.

362 Moscow Council Building

364 Soviet Yakovlev Yak-9 Aircraft and Flag

363 May Day Procession

1947. 30th Anniv of Moscow Soviet. Perf or imperf.

1265	362	30 k. red, blue & blk	2·00	1·60

1947. May Day.

1266	363	30 k. red	1·75	1·60
1267		1r. green	3·75	3·75

1947. Air Force Day.

1268	364	30 k. violet	80	15
1269		1r. blue	2·00	85

365 Yakhromsky Lock

1947. 10th Anniv of Volga-Moscow Canal.

1270	–	30 k. black	70	10
1271	365	30 k. lake	70	10
1272	–	45 k. red	65	25
1273	–	50 k. blue	1·25	30
1274	–	60 k. red	1·25	85
1275	–	1r. violet	2·75	1·10

DESIGNS—HORIZ: 30 k. (No. 1270), Karamyshevsky Dam; 45 k. Yakhromsky Pumping Station; 50 k. Khimki Pier; 1 r. Lock No. 8. VERT: 60 k. Map of Volga-Moscow Canal.

800 лет Москвы
1147—1947 гг.

(366)

367 Izmailovsky Station

1947. 800th Anniv of Moscow (1st issue). Optd as T **366**.

1276	20 k. brown (No. 1208)	55	15
1277	50 k. brown (No. 1210)	90	35
1278	60 k. violet (No. 1211)	1·40	60
1279	1 r. brown (No. 1212)	3·75	1·75

See also Nos. 1286/1300.

1947. Opening of New Moscow Underground Stations. Inscr "M".

1280	367	30 k. blue	60	15
1281	–	30 k. brown	60	15
1282	–	45 k. brown	85	35
1283	–	45 k. violet	85	35
1284	–	60 k. green	2·00	50
1285	–	60 k. red	2·00	50

DESIGNS—HORIZ: No. 1281, Power House; No. 1282, Falcon Station; No. 1283, Stalinsky Station; No. 1284, Kiev Station. VERT: No. 1285, Mayakovsky Station.

368 Crimea Bridge, Moscow

1947. 800th Anniv of Moscow (2nd issue).

1286	368	5 k. brown and blue	50	10
1287	–	10 k. black and brown	30	10
1288	–	30 k. grey	1·25	25
1289	–	30 k. blue	1·25	25
1290	–	30 k. brown	55	25
1291	–	30 k. green	55	25
1292	–	30 k. green	55	25
1293	–	50 k. green	1·25	70
1294	–	60 k. blue	2·00	55
1295	–	60 k. black and brown	2·00	55
1296	–	1 r. purple	3·25	80
		Centre in yellow, red and blue.		
1297	–	1 r. blue	5·00	85
1298	–	2 r. red	6·75	2·00
1299	–	3 r. blue	11·00	2·75
1300	–	5 r. blue	18·00	6·00

DESIGNS—VERT: 10 k. Gorky Street, Moscow; 30 k. (No. 1292), Pushkin Place; 60 k. (No. 1294), 2 r. Kremlin; 1 r. (No. 1296), "Old Moscow" after A. M. Vasnetsov; 1 r. (No. 1279), St. Basil Cathedral. HORIZ: 30 k. (No. 1288), Kiev railway station; 30 k. (No. 1289), Kazan railway station; 30 k. (No. 1290), Central Telegraph Offices; 30 k. (No. 1291), Kaluga Street; 50 k. Kremlin; 3 r. Kremlin; 5 r. Government Buildings. ($54\frac{1}{2} \times 24\frac{1}{2}$ mm): 60 k. (No. 1295), Bridge and Kremlin.

369 "Ritz", Gagry

370 "Zapadugol", Sochi

1947. U.S.S.R. Health Resorts. (a) Vertical.

1301	369	30 k. green	55	15
1302	–	30 k. green (Sukhumi)	55	15
		(b) Horizontal.		
1303	370	30 k. black	55	15
1304	–	30 k. brown ("New Riveria", Sochi)	55	15
1305	–	30 k. purple ("Voroshilov", Sochi)	55	15
1306	–	30 k. violet ("Gulripsh", Sukhumi)	55	15
1307	–	30 k. blue ("Kemeri", Riga)	55	15
1308	–	30 k. brown ("Abkhazia", Novy Afon)	55	15
1309	–	30 k. bistre ("Krestyansky", Livadia)	55	15
1310	–	30 k. blue ("Kirov", Kislovodsk)	55	15

371 1917 Revolution

1947. 30th Anniv of Revolution. Perf or imperf.

1311	371	30 k. black and red	30	15
1312	–	50 k. blue and red	1·25	20
1313	371	60 k. black and red	1·00	30
1314	–	60 k. brown and red	1·00	30
1315	–	1 r. black and red	2·25	50
1316	–	2 r. green and red	3·75	1·00

DESIGNS: 50 k., 1 r. "Industry"; 60 k. (No. 1314), 2 r. "Agriculture".

372 Metallurgical Works

373 Spassky Tower, Kremlin

1947. Post-War Five Year Plan. Horiz industrial designs. All dated "1947" except No. 1324. Perf or imperf.

1317	372	15 k. brown	40	20
1318	–	20 k. brown (Foundry)	50	30
1319	372	30 k. purple	1·00	30
1320	–	30 k. green (Harvesting machines)	75	50
1321	–	30 k. brown (Tractor)	1·00	30
1322	–	30 k. brown (Tractors)	75	30
1323	–	60 k. bistre (Harvesting machines)	1·50	1·00
1324	–	60 k. purple (Builders)	1·50	1·00
1325	–	1 r. orange (Foundry)	3·00	2·00
1326	–	1 r. red (Tractor)	3·00	2·00
1327	–	1 r. violet (Tractors)	3·00	2·00

1947.

1328	373	60 k. red	10·00	8·25
1329a		1 r. red	1·10	35

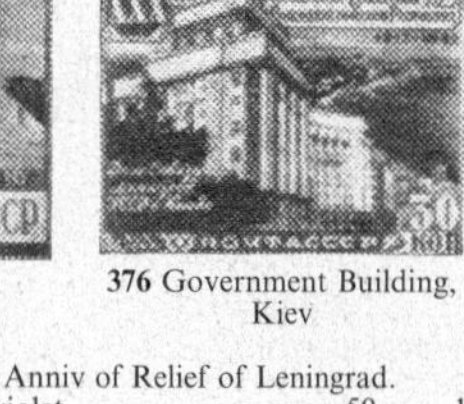

374 Peter I Monument

376 Government Building, Kiev

1948. 4th Anniv of Relief of Leningrad.

1330	–	30 k. violet	50	15
1331	374	50 k. green	1·10	30
1332	–	60 k. black	1·60	50
1333	–	1 r. violet	2·10	1·10

DESIGNS—HORIZ: 30 k. Winter Palace; 60 k. Peter and Paul Fortress; 1 r. Smolny Institute.

1948. 24th Death Anniv of Lenin. As Issue of 1947, but dated "1924–1948".

1334	351	30 k. red	65	50
1355		60 k. blue	1·40	85
1336	352	60 k. green	3·00	1·40

1948. 30th Anniversary of Ukrainian S.S.R. Various designs inscr "XXX" and "1917–1947".

1337	376	30 k. blue	55	15
1338	–	50 k. violet	1·10	75
1339	–	60 k. brown	1·50	75
1340	–	1 r. brown	2·40	1·90

DESIGNS: 50 k. Dnieper hydro-electric power station; 60 k. Wheatfield and granary; 1 r. Metallurgical works and colliery.

377 Vasily I. Surikov

378 Skiing

1948. Birth Centenary of Surikov (artist).

1341	377	30 k. brown	1·40	65
1342		60 k. green	2·40	1·40

1948. R.S.F.S.R. Games.

1343	378	15 k. blue	2·00	25
1344	–	20 k. blue	3·25	50

DESIGN—VERT: 20 k. Motor cyclist crossing stream.

379 Artillery

381 Karl Marx and Friedrich Engels

380 Bulganin and Military School

1948. 30th Anniv of Founding of Soviet Defence Forces and of Civil War. (a) Various designs with arms and inscr "1918 XXX 1948".

1345	379	30 k. brown	1·25	60
1346	–	30 k. grey	1·25	60
1347	–	30 k. blue	1·10	60
1348	380	60 k. brown	2·75	1·10

DESIGNS—VERT: No. 1346, Navy. HORIZ: No. 1347, Air Force.

(b) Portraits of Civil War Heroes as Nos. 1079/81.

1349	299	60 k. brown (Chapaev)	1·60	1·60
1350	–	60 k. green (Shchors)	1·60	1·60
1351	–	60 k. blue (Lazo)	1·60	1·60

1948. Centenary of Publication of "Communist Manifesto".

1352	381	30 k. black	40	25
1353		50 k. brown	85	25

382 Miner

384b Arms of U.S.S.R

384d Spassky Tower, Kremlin

1948.

1354	382	5 k. black	1·90	80
1355	–	10 k. violet (Sailor)	1·90	80
1356	–	15 k. blue (Airman)	3·75	2·50
1361i	382	15 k. black	1·10	65
1357	–	20 k. brown (Farm girl)	4·25	2·40
1361j	–	20 k. green (Farm girl)	1·25	65
1361ka	–	25 k. bl (Airman)	1·40	65
1358	384b	30 k. brown	6·75	3·75
1361l	–	30 k. brown (Scientist)	1·40	65
1361n	384b	40 k. red	2·10	50
1359	–	45 k. violet (Scientist)	7·50	5·75
1361f	384d	50 k. blue	9·25	3·25
1361	–	60 k. grn (Soldier)	15·00	12·50

385 Parade of Workers

1948. May Day.

1362	385	30 k. red	1·10	1·00
1363		60 k. blue	2·50	1·10

386 Belinsky (after K. Gorbunov)

1948. Death Centenary of Vissarion Grigorievich Belinsky (literary critic and journalist).

1364	386	30 k. brown	1·00	40
1365		50 k. green	1·50	90
1366		60 k. violet	2·00	1·90

387 A. N. Ostrovsky 388

1948. 125th Birth Anniv of Ostrovsky (dramatist).

1367	387	30 k. green	75	60
1368	388	60 k. brown	1·40	1·10
1369		1 r. violet	3·25	2·50

389 I. I. Shishkin (after I. Kramskoi)

391 Factories

390 "Rye Field"

1948. 50th Death Anniv of Shishkin (landscape painter).

1370	389	30 k. brown and green	1·60	20
1371	390	50 k. yellow, red & blue	2·75	35
1372	–	60 k. multicoloured	4·00	1·00
1373	389	1 r. blue and brown	5·00	1·50

DESIGN—HORIZ: 60 k. "Morning in the Forest".

1948. Leningrad Workers' Four-Year Plan.
1374 **391** 15 k. brown and red . . . 2·50 1·00
1375 – 30 k. black and red . . . 2·00 2·00
1376 **391** 60 k. brown and red . . 6·50 3·75
DESIGN—HORIZ (40 × 22 mm): 30 k. Proclamation to Leningrad workers.

392 Arms and People of the U.S.S.R

393 Caterpillar drawing Seed Drills

1948. 25th Anniv of U.S.S.R.
1377 **392** 30 k. black and red . . . 1·10 1·00
1378 60 k. olive and red . . . 3·25 3·00

1948. Five-Year Agricultural Plan.
1379 **393** 30 k. red 55 50
1380 30 k. green 65 50
1381 – 45 k. brown . . . . . . 1·40 1·10
1382 **393** 50 k. black . . . . 2·10 1·10
1383 – 60 k. green . . . . 1·60 1·40
1384 – 60 k. green . . . . 1·60 1·40
1385 – 1 r. violet . . . . 5·25 2·25
DESIGNS: 30 k. (No. 1380), 1 r. Harvesting sugar beet; 45, 60 k. (No. 1383), Gathering cotton; 60 k. (No. 1384), Harvesting machine.

(394)

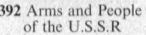

395 Miners

396 A. Zhdanov

1948. Air Force Day. Optd with T **394**.
1386 **364** 30 k. violet . . . . 4·25 2·40
1387 1 r. blue . . . . 4·25 2·40

1948. Miners' Day.
1388 **395** 30 k. blue 70 40
1389 – 60 k. violet . . . . 1·75 1·00
1390 – 1 r. green . . . . 3·25 1·90
DESIGNS: 60 k. Inside a coal mine; 1 r. Miner's emblem.

1948. Death of A. A. Zhdanov (statesman).
1391 **396** 40 k. blue . . . . 2·50 1·50

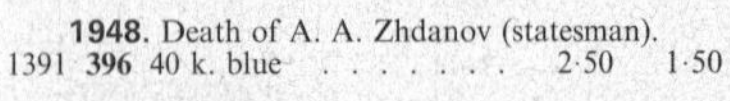

397 Sailor

398 Football

1948. Navy Day.
1392 **397** 30 k. green . . . . 1·60 1·40
1393 60 k. blue . . . . 2·75 2·00

1948. Sports.
1394 – 15 k. violet . . . . . . 1·00 15
1395 **398** 30 k. brown . . . . . . 2·00 15
1396 – 45 k. brown . . . . . . 2·00 35
1397a – 50 k. blue . . . . 3·75 35
DESIGNS—VERT: 15 k. Running; 50 k. Diving. HORIZ: 45 k. Power boat racing.

399 Tank and Drivers

1948. Tank Drivers' Day.
1398 **399** 30 k. black . . . . 2·00 1·60
1399 – 1 r. red . . . . 4·75 3·00
DESIGN: 1 r. Parade of tanks.

400 Horses and Groom

1948. Five-Year Livestock Development Plan.
1400 **400** 30 k. black . . . . 1·50 70
1401 – 60 k. green . . . . 3·75 2·10
1402 **400** 1 r. brown . . . . 5·75 5·25
DESIGN: 60 k. Dairy farming.

401 Steam and Electric Locomotives

1948. Five-Year Transport Plan.
1403 **401** 30 k. brown . . . . . . 3·00 60
1404 50 k. green . . . . 3·50 1·50
1405 – 60 k. blue . . . . 3·25 2·00
1406 – 1 r. violet . . . . 7·25 5·75
DESIGNS: 60 k. Road traffic; 1 r. Liner "Vyacheslav Molotov".

402 Iron Pipe Manufacture

1948. Five-Year Rolled Iron, Steel and Machine-building Plan.
1407 – 30 k. violet . . . . . . 1·75 90
1408 – 30 k. purple . . . . . . 1·75 90
1409 – 50 k. brown . . . . . . 2·75 1·40
1410 – 50 k. black . . . . . . 2·75 1·40
1411 – 60 k. brown . . . . . . 3·75 2·50
1412 **402** 60 k. red . . . . 3·75 2·50
1413 1 r. blue . . . . 5·75 3·25
DESIGNS—HORIZ: Nos. 1407, 1410, Foundry; No. 1408/9, Pouring molten metal; No. 1411, Group of machines.

403 Abovyan

404 Miner

1948. Death Centenary of Khachatur Abovyan (writer).
1414 **403** 40 k. purple . . . . . . 2·40 2·40
1415 50 k. green . . . . . . 3·75 3·25

1948. Five-Year Coal mining and Oil Extraction Plan.
1416 **404** 30 k. black . . . . . . 3·00 1·10
1417 60 k. brown . . . . . . 7·25 2·25
1418 – 60 k. brown . . . . . . 7·25 2·40
1419 – 1 r. green . . . . 9·00 4·25
DESIGN: Nos. 1418/19, Oil wells and tanker train.

405 Farkhadsk Power Station

406 Flying Model Aircraft

1948. Five-Year Electrification Plan.
1420 **405** 30 k. green . . . . . . 1·25 1·00
1421 – 60 k. red . . . . 4·25 3·00
1422 **405** 1 r. red . . . . 4·25 3·00
DESIGN: 60 k. Zuevsk Power Station.

1948. Government Care of School Children's Summer Vacation.
1423 **406** 30 k. green . . . . . . 3·75 1·60
1424 – 45 k. red . . . . 5·75 3·20
1425 – 45 k. violet . . . . . . 3·75 3·25
1426 – 60 k. blue . . . . 9·00 6·00
1427 – 1 r. blue . . . . 20·00 6·00
DESIGNS—VERT: No. 1424, Boy and girl saluting; 60 k. Boy trumpeter. HORIZ: No. 1425, Children marching; 1 r. Children round camp fire.

407 Children in School

408 Flag of U.S.S.R.

1948. 30th Anniv of Lenin's Young Communist League.
1428 – 20 k. purple . . . . . . 3·00 1·10
1429 – 25 k. red . . . . 2·00 1·10
1430 – 40 k. brown and red . . . 3·25 2·25
1431 **407** 50 k. green . . . . . . 6·25 3·75
1432 **408** 1 r. multicoloured . . . 10·50 4·50
1433 – 2 r. violet . . . . 22·00 17·00
DESIGNS—HORIZ: 20 k. Youth parade. VERT: 25 k. Peasant girl; 40 k. Young people and flag; 2 r. Industrial worker.

409 Interior of Theatre

410 Searchlights over Moscow

1948. 50th Anniv of Moscow Arts Theatre.
1434 **409** 50 k. blue . . . . 1·60 3·25
1435 – 1 r. purple . . . . 3·75 5·75
DESIGN: 1 r. Stanislavsky and Dantchenko.

1948. 31st Anniv of October Revolution.
1436 **410** 40 k. red . . . . 1·60 3·25
1437 1 r. green . . . . 6·00 5·75

411 Artillery Barrage

1948. Artillery Day.
1438 **411** 30 k. blue . . . . 1·60 3·25
1439 1 r. red . . . . 3·25 5·00

412 Trade Union Building (venue)

1948. 16th World Chess Championship, Moscow.
1440 **412** 30 k. blue . . . . 4·00 1·00
1441 – 40 k. violet . . . . . . 9·00 55
1442 **412** 50 k. brown . . . . . . 9·00 1·75
DESIGN—VERT: 40 k. Players badge showing chessboard and rook

413 Stasov and Building

1948. Death Centenary of Stasov (architect).
1443 – 40 k. brown . . . . . . 1·40 1·25
1444 **413** 1 r. black . . . . 3·25 3·25
DESIGN—VERT: 40 k. Portrait of Stasov.

414 Yakovlev Yak-9 Fighters and Flag

415 Statue of Ya. M. Sverdlov

1948. Air Force Day.
1445 **414** 1 r. blue . . . . 6·75 2·75

1948. 225th Anniv of Sverdlovsk City. Imperf or perf.
1446 **415** 30 k. blue 60 40
1447 – 40 k. purple . . . . . . 1·00 40
1448 **415** 1 r. green . . . . 1·75 60
DESIGN: 40 k. View of Sverdlovsk.

416 Sukhumi

417 State Emblem

1948. Views of Crimea and Caucasus.
1449 **416** 40 k. green . . . . . . 1·00 30
1450 – 40 k. violet . . . . . . 1·00 30
1451 – 40 k. mauve . . . . . . 1·00 30
1452 – 40 k. brown . . . . . . 1·00 30
1453 – 40 k. purple . . . . . . 1·00 30
1454 – 40 k. green . . . . . . 1·00 30
1455 – 40 k. blue . . . . 1·00 30
1456 – 40 k. green . . . . . . 1·00 30
DESIGNS—VERT: No. 1450, Gardens, Sochi; No. 1451, Eagle-topped monument, Pyatigorsk; No. 1452, Cliffs, Crimea. HORIZ: No. 1453, Terraced gardens, Sochi; No. 1454, Roadside garden, Sochi; No. 1455, Colonnade, Kislovodsk; No. 1456, Sea and palms, Gagry.

1949. 30th Anniv of Byelorussian Soviet Republic.
1457 **417** 40 k. red . . . . 1·60 1·60
1458 1 r. green . . . . 2·50 2·50

418 M. V. Lomonosov

419 Lenin Mausoleum

1949. Establishment of Lomonosov Museum of Academy of Sciences.
1459 **418** 40 k. brown . . . . . . 1·50 1·40
1460 50 k. green . . . . . . 2·00 1·40
1461 – 1 r. blue . . . . 4·75 2·75
DESIGN—HORIZ: 1 r. Museum.

1949. 25th Death Anniv of Lenin.
1462 **419** 40 k. brown and green . 6·00 6·00
1463 1 r. brown & dp brown . 10·50 10·50

420 Dezhnev's Ship

1949. Tercentenary of Dezhnev's Exploration of Bering Strait.
1464 – 40 k. olive . . . . 10·00 10·00
1465 **420** 1 r. black . . . . 20·00 15·00
DESIGN: 40 k. Cape Dezhnev.

421 "Women in Industry"

422 Admiral S. O. Makarov

1949. International Women's Day.
1466 **421** 20 k. violet 30 10
1467 – 25 k. blue 35 10
1468 – 40 k. red 50 10
1469 – 50 k. grey . . . . 1·10 30
1470 – 50 k. brown . . . . . . 1·10 30
1471 – 1 r. green . . . . 3·25 40
1472 – 2 r. red . . . . 4·75 1·10
DESIGNS—HORIZ: 25 k. Kindergarten; 50 k. grey, Woman teacher; 50 k. brown, Women in field; 1 r. Women sports champions. VERT: 40 k., 2 r. Woman broadcasting.

1949. Birth Centenary of Admiral S. O. Makarov (naval scientist).
1473 **422** 40 k. blue . . . . 2·00 1·00
1474 1 r. red . . . . 3·75 3·25

423 Soldier

1949. 31st Anniv of Soviet Army.
1475 **423** 40 k. red . . . . 11·50 10·00

424 Kirov Military Medical Academy

1949. 150th Anniv of Kirov Military Medical Academy.
1476 **424** 40 k. red . . . . 1·25 1·60
1477 – 50 k. blue . . . . 2·00 2·50
1478 **424** 1 r. green . . . . 4·75 5·00
DESIGN: 50 k. Professors Botkin, Pirogov and Sechenov and Kirov Academy.

425 V. R. Williams

425a Three Russians with Flag

1949. Agricultural Reform.

1479 **425** 25 k. green . . . . 4·25 4·25
1480 50 k. brown . . . . . . 5·75 5·75

1949. Labour Day.

1481 **425a** 40 k. red . . . . 1·00 80
1482 1 r. green . . . . 3·25 2·00

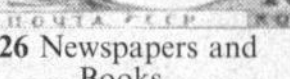

426 Newspapers and Books

427 A. S. Popov and Radio Equipment

1949. Press Day. Inscr "5 MAR 1949".

1483 **426** 40 k. red . . . . 3·25 4·75
1484 – 1 r. violet . . . . 6·75 8·25

DESIGN: 1 r. Man and boy reading newspaper.

1949. Radio Day.

1485 **427** 40 k. violet . . . . 1·90 1·90
1486 – 50 k. brown . . . . . . 3·25 3·25
1487 **427** 1 r. green . . . . 6·75 6·75

DESIGN—HORIZ: 50 k. Popov demonstrating receiver to Admiral Makarov.

428 A. S. Pushkin

429 Pushkin reading "Epistle to Decembrists"

1949. 150th Birth Anniv of Pushkin (poet).

1488 **428** 25 k. black and grey . . 1·00 75
1489 – 40 k. black and brown . . 1·90 2·10
1490 **429** 40 k. purple and red . . 3·75 3·75
1491 – 1 r. grey and brown . . . 4·50 5·25
1492 **429** 2 r. blue and brown . . . 7·50 6·75

DESIGNS—VERT: No. 1489, Pushkin portrait after Kiprensky. HORIZ: 1 r. Pushkin museum, Boldino.

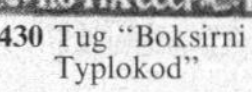

430 Tug "Boksirni Typlokod"

431 I. V. Michurin

1949. Centenary of Krasnoe Sormovo Machine-building and Ship-building Plant, Gorky.

1493 **430** 40 k. blue . . . . 6·75 5·25
1494 – 1 r. brown . . . . 9·25 9·25

DESIGN: 1 r. Tanker "Bolshaya Volga".

1949. Agricultural Reform.

1495 **431** 40 k. blue . . . . 1·50 1·40
1496 1 r. green . . . . 2·75 2·75

432 Yachting

1949. National Sports.

1497 **432** 20 k. blue . . . . 1·25 10
1498 – 25 k. green 85 15
1499 – 30 k. violet . . . . 1·50 15
1500 – 40 k. brown . . . . 1·40 25
1501 – 40 k. green . . . . 1·40 25
1502 – 50 k. grey . . . . 1·75 40
1503 – 1 r. red . . . . 4·00 85
1504 – 2 r. black . . . . 8·25 1·90

DESIGNS: 25 k. Canoeing; 30 k. Swimming; 40 k. (No. 1500), Cycling; 40 k. (No. 1501), Football; 50 k. Mountaineering; 1 r. Parachuting; 2 r. High jumping.

433 V. V. Dokuchaev

1949. Soil Research.

1505 **433** 40 k. brown . . . . . . 1·50 20
1506 1 r. green . . . . 2·50 50

434 V. I. Bazhenov

435 A. N. Radischev

1949. 150th Death Anniv of V. I. Bazhenov (architect).

1507 **434** 40 k. violet . . . . . . 1·40 30
1508 1 r. brown . . . . . . 2·00 70

1949. Birth Bicent of A. N. Radischev (writer).

1509 **435** 40 k. green . . . . . . 1·50 1·60
1510 1 r. black . . . . 2·75 2·75

436 Green Cape Sanatorium, Makhindzhauri

1949. State Sanatoria. Designs showing various buildings.

1511 **436** 40 k. green 75 15
1512 – 40 k. green 75 15
1513 – 40 k. blue 75 15
1514 – 40 k. violet 75 15
1515 – 40 k. red 75 15
1516 – 40 k. orange 75 15
1517 – 40 k. brown 75 15
1518 – 40 k. brown 75 15
1519 – 40 k. black 75 15
1520 – 40 k. black 75 15

DESIGNS—HORIZ: No. 1512, VTsSPS No. 41, Zheleznovodsk; No. 1513, Energetics, Hosta; No. 1514, VTsSPS No. 3, Kislovodsk; No. 1515, VTs SPS No. 3, Hosta; No. 1516, State Theatre, Sochi; No. 1517, Clinical, Tskhaltubo; No. 1518, Frunze, Sochi; No. 1519, VTsSPS No. 1, Kislovodsk; No. 1520, Communication, Hosta.

437 I. P. Pavlov

1949. Birth Centenary of I. P. Pavlov (scientist).

1521 **437** 40 k. brown . . . . . . 1·00 20
1522 1 r. black . . . . 2·25 85

438 Globe and Letters

1949. 75th Anniv of U.P.U. Perf or imperf.

1523 **438** 40 k. blue and brown . . 2·25 25
1524 50 k. violet and blue . . 2·25 75

439 Tree Planting Machines

440 Map of S. W. Russia

1949. Forestry and Field Conservancy.

1525 **439** 25 k. green 75 50
1526 – 40 k. violet 90 85
1527 **440** 40 k. green and black . . 90 85
1528 – 50 k. blue . . . . . . 1·40 1·40
1529 **439** 1 r. black . . . . . . 2·75 2·40
1530 – 2 r. brown . . . . . . 6·75 5·75

DESIGNS—33 × 22½ mm: 40 k. violet, Harvesters; 50 k. River scene. 33 × 19½ mm: 2 r. Old man and children.

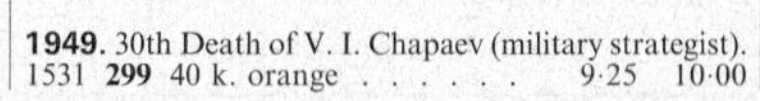

1949. 30th Death of V. I. Chapaev (military strategist).

1531 **299** 40 k. orange . . . . . . 9·25 10·00

442 I. S. Nikitin

443 Malyi Theatre, Moscow

1949. 125th Birth Anniv of Nikitin (poet).

1532 **442** 40 k. brown . . . . . . 1·10 20
1533 1 r. blue . . . . 2·00 60

1949. 125th Anniv of Malyi Theatre, Moscow.

1534 **443** 40 k. green . . . . 1·50 20
1535 50 k. orange . . . . . . 2·10 65
1536 – 1 r. brown . . . . 4·25 1·25

DESIGN: 1 r. Five portraits and theatre.

444 Crowd with Banner

1949. 32nd Anniv of October Revolution.

1537 **444** 40 k. red . . . . 2·50 2·50
1538 1 r. green . . . . 4·25 4·25

445 Sheep and Cows

446 Lenin Hydro-electric Station, Caucasus

447 Ilyushin Il–12 Airliners and Map

1949. Cattle-breeding Collective Farm.

1539 **445** 40 k. brown . . . . . . 1·50 50
1540 1 r. violet . . . . 2·40 80

1949. Air. Aerial views and map.

1541 **446** 50 k. brown on yellow . . 1·90 1·00
1542 – 60 k. brown on buff . . . 2·00 1·50
1543 – 1 r. orange on yellow . . 6·00 1·90
1544 – 1 r. brown on buff . . . 5·50 1·90
1545 – 1 r. blue on blue . . . 5·50 1·90
1546 **447** 1 r. blue, red and grey . . 10·00 5·50
1547 – 2 r. red on blue . . . . 12·00 5·50
1548 – 3 r. green on blue . . . . 23·00 13·50

DESIGNS—Ilyushin Il–12 airliner over: HORIZ: No. 1542, Farm; 1543, Sochi. VERT: 1544, Leningrad; 1545, Aleppo; 1547, Moscow; 1548, Arctic.

448 Ski Jumping

449 Diesel Train

1949. National Sports.

1549 **448** 20 k. green 80 15
1550 – 40 k. orange . . . . . . 1·40 20
1551 – 50 k. blue . . . . 2·10 45
1552 – 1 r. red . . . . 5·25 45
1553 – 2 r. violet . . . . 9·00 1·90

DESIGNS: 40 k. Girl gymnast; 50 k. Ice hockey; 1 r. Weightlifting; 2 r. Shooting wolves.

1949. Modern Railway Development.

1554 – 25 k. red . . . . 2·00 35
1555 **449** 40 k. violet . . . . . . 2·50 1·10
1556 – 50 k. brown . . . . . . 3·50 1·25
1557 **449** 1 r. green . . . . 9·00 3·25

DESIGNS: 25 k. Electric tram; 50 k. Steam train.

MINIMUM PRICE

The minimum price quoted is 10p which represents a handling charge rather than a basis for valuing common stamps. For further notes about prices, see introductory pages.

450 Arms of U.S.S.R.

451 Government Buildings, Dushanbe

1949. Constitution Day.

1558 **450** 40 k. red . . . . 7·50 5·00

1949. 20th Anniv of Republic of Tadzhikstan.

1559 – 20 k. blue 75 10
1560 – 25 k. green 70 10
1561 **451** 40 k. red . . . . 1·25 20
1562 – 50 k. violet . . . . . . 1·75 20
1563 **451** 1 r. black . . . . 3·00 75

DESIGNS: 20 k. Textile mills; 25 k. Irrigation canal; 50 k. Medical University.

452 People with Flag

453 Worker and Globe

1949. 10th Anniv of Incorporation of West Ukraine and West Byelorussia in U.S.S.R.

1564 **452** 40 k. red . . . . 9·25 9·25
1565 – 40 k. orange . . . . . . 9·25 9·25

DESIGN—VERT: No. 1565, Ukrainians and flag.

1949. Peace Propaganda.

1566 **453** 40 k. red 80 20
1567 50 k. blue . . . . 1·25 30

454 Government Buildings, Tashkent

1950. 25th Anniv of Uzbek S.S.R.

1568 – 20 k. blue 60 20
1569 – 25 k. black 60 20
1570 **454** 40 k. red . . . . 1·10 20
1571 – 40 k. violet 90 30
1572 – 1 r. green . . . . 3·00 70
1573 – 2 r. brown . . . . 5·50 1·40

DESIGNS: 20 k. Teachers' College; 25 k. Opera and Ballet House, Tashkent; 40 k. (violet) Navotz Street, Tashkent; 1 r. Map of Fergana Canal; 2 r. Lock, Fergana Canal.

455 Dam

456 Statue of Lenin

1950. 25th Anniv of Turkmen S.S.R.

1574 – 25 k. black . . . . . . 3·25 3·25
1575 **455** 40 k. brown . . . . . . 2·00 2·00
1576 – 50 k. green . . . . . . 3·75 3·75
1577 **455** 1 r. violet . . . . 6·00 6·00

DESIGNS: 25 k. Textile factory, Ashkhabad; 50 k. Carpet-making.

1950. 26th Death Anniv of Lenin.

1578 **456** 40 k. brown and grey . . 65 15
1579 – 50 k. red, brown & grn . 1·50 60
1580 – 1 r. buff, green & brown 3·25 75

DESIGNS—HORIZ: 50 k. Lenin's Office, Kremlin; 1 r. Lenin Museum.

457 Film Show

458 Voter

1950. 30th Anniv of Soviet Film Industry.

1581 **457** 25 k. brown . . . . . . 13·50 12·50

1950. Supreme Soviet Elections. Inscr "12 MAPTA 1950".

1582 **458** 40 k. green on yellow . . 4·75 4·75
1583 – 1 r. red . . . . 6·75 6·75

DESIGN: 1 r. Kremlin and flags.

459 Statue of Morozov — 460 Lenin Central Museum

1950. Unveiling of Monument to Pavlik Morozov (model Soviet youth).

1584 **459** 40 k. black and red . . . 4·00 3·25
1585 1 r. green and red . . . 6·75 5·25

1950. Moscow Museums. Buildings inscr "MOCKBA 1949".

1586 **460** 40 k. olive . . . . 1·25 25
1587 – 40 k. red . . . . 1·25 25
1588 – 40 k. turquoise . . . . . 1·25 25
1589 – 40 k. brown . . . . . . 1·25 25
1590 – 40 k. mauve . . . . . . 1·25 25
1591 – 40 k. blue (no tree) . . . 1·25 25
1592 – 40 k. brown . . . . . . 1·25 25
1593 – 40 k. blue (with tree) . . 1·25 25
1594 – 40 k. red . . . . 1·25 25

DESIGNS—HORIZ: (33½ × 23½ mm): No. 1587, Revolution Museum; No. 1588, Tretyakov Gallery; No. 1589, Timiryazev Biological Museum; No. 1591, Polytechnic Museum; No. 1593, Oriental Museum. (39½ × 26½ mm): No. 1590, Pushkin Pictorial Arts Museum. VERT: (22½ × 33½ mm); No. 1592, Historical Museum; No. 1594, Zoological Museum.

461 Hemispheres and Wireless Mast

1950. International Congress of P.T.T. and Radio Trade Unions, London.

1595 **461** 40 k. green on blue . . . 4·25 4·25
1596 50 k. blue on blue . . . 5·00 5·00

462 Three Workers — 463 A. S. Shcherbakov

1950. Labour Day.

1597 **462** 40 k. red and black . . . 3·75 3·00
1598 – 1 r. red and black . . . 5·25 5·25

DESIGN—HORIZ: 1 r. Four Russians and banner.

1950. 5th Death Anniv of Shcherbakov (statesman).

1599 **463** 40 k. black . . . . 1·60 1·40
1600 1 r. green on pink . . . 3·25 2·75

464 Marshal Suvorov — 465 Statue

1950. 150th Death Anniv of Suvorov.

1601 **464** 40 k. blue on pink . . . 3·25 2·75
1602 – 50 k. brown on pink . . 4·25 3·25
1603 – 60 k. black on blue . . . 4·25 3·25
1604 **464** 1 r. brown on blue . . . 5·25 4·25
1605 – 2 r. green . . . . 10·00 8·25

DESIGNS—VERT: 50 k. Battle (32½ × 47 mm); 60 k. Order of Suvorov and military parade (24½ × 39½ mm); 2 r. Suvorov in cloak (19½ × 33½ mm).

1950. 5th Anniv of Victory over Germany.

1606 **465** 40 k. red and brown . . 3·25 3·25
1607 – 1 r. red . . . . 6·75 3·25

DESIGN—22½ × 33 mm: 1 r. Order of Stalin.

466 Sowing on Collective Farm

1950. Agricultural Workers.

1608 – 40 k. green on blue . . . 3·25 2·00
1609 **466** 40 k. brown on buff . . 3·25 2·00
1610 1 r. blue on yellow . . . 5·00 4·25

DESIGNS: No. 1608, Collective farmers studying.

467 G. M. Dimitrov — 468 Baku Opera House

1950. 1st Death Anniv of Bulgarian Premier, Dimitrov.

1611 **467** 40 k. black on yellow . . 2·00 2·00
1612 1 r. black on red . . . . 4·75 4·75

1950. 30th Anniv of Azerbaijan S.S.R.

1613 **468** 25 k. green on yellow . . 1·40 1·40
1614 – 40 k. brown on red . . . 3·25 3·25
1615 – 1 r. black on buff . . . 5·00 5·00

DESIGNS: 40 k. Science Academy; 1 r. Stalin Avenue, Baku.

469 Lenin Street, Stalingrad

1950. Stalingrad Reconstruction.

1616 – 20 k. blue . . . . 1·25 1·25
1617 **469** 40 k. green . . . . . . 2·10 2·10
1618 – 50 k. orange . . . . . . 4·25 4·25
1619 – 1 r. black . . . . 5·00 5·00

DESIGNS—VERT: 20 k. Pobeda Cinema. HORIZ: 50 k. Gorky Theatre; 1 r. Pavlov House and Tank Memorial.

470 Kaluzhskaya Station

1950. Underground Railway Stations.

1620 **470** 40 k. green on buff . . 1·00 35
1621 A 40 k. red . . . . 1·00 35
1622 B 40 k. blue on buff . . . 1·00 35
1623 C 1 r. brown on yellow . . 3·00 1·10
1624 D 1 r. violet on blue . . . 3·00 1·10
1625 A 1 r. green on yellow . . 3·00 1·10
1626 E 1 r. black on buff . . . 3·00 1·10

DESIGNS—HORIZ: (34 × 22½ mm): A, Culture Park; B, Taganskaya; C, Kurskaya; D, Paveletskaya. (34 × 18½ mm): E, Taganskaya.

471 National Flags and Civilians

1950. Unconquerable Democracy. Flags in red, blue and yellow.

1627 **471** 40 k. black . . . . . . 1·00 15
1628 50 k. brown . . . . . . 2·10 25
1629 1 r. green . . . . 2·50 30

472 Trade Union Building — 473 Marite Melnikaite

1950. 10th Anniv of Latvian S.S.R.

1630 **472** 25 k. brown 70 85
1631 – 40 k. red . . . . 1·25 1·25
1632 – 50 k. green . . . . . . 2·10 2·10
1633 – 60 k. blue . . . . . . 2·50 2·50
1634 – 1 r. violet . . . . . . 3·75 3·75
1635 – 2 r. brown . . . . . . 6·25 6·25

DESIGNS—VERT: 40 k. Cabinet Council Offices; 50 k. Monument to Jan Rainis (poet); 2 r. Academy of Sciences. HORIZ: 60 k. Theatre, Riga; 1 r. State University, Riga.

1950. 10th Anniv of Lithuanian S.S.R.

1636 – 25 k. blue . . . . 1·00 85
1637 **473** 40 k. brown . . . . . . 2·00 1·60
1638 – 1 r. red . . . . 7·00 5·75

DESIGNS—HORIZ: 25 k. Academy of Sciences; 1 r. Cabinet Council Offices.

474 Stalingrad Square, Tallinn — 475 Signing Peace Appeal

1950. 10th Anniv of Estonian S.S.R.

1639 **474** 25 k. green 85 45
1640 – 40 k. red . . . . 1·25 1·00
1641 – 50 k. blue on yellow . . . 2·10 1·90
1642 – 1 r. brown on blue . . . 6·00 6·75

DESIGNS—HORIZ: 40 k. Government building; 50 k. Opera and Ballet Theatre, Tallin. VERT: 1 r. Victor Kingisepp (revolutionary).

1950. Peace Conference.

1643 **475** 40 k. red on buff . . . . 1·60 1·00
1644 – 40 k. black . . . . 1·60 80
1645 – 50 k. red . . . . 3·25 2·00
1646 **475** 1 r. brown on buff . . . 5·00 6·75

DESIGNS—VERT: 40 k. black, Children and teacher; 50 k. Young people with banner.

476 Bellingshausan Lazarev and Globe — 477 M. V. Frunze

1950. 130th Anniv of 1st Antarctic Expedition.

1647 **476** 40 k. red on blue . . . . 15·00 11·50
1648 – 1 r. violet on blue . . . 32·00 15·00

DESIGN—VERT: 1 r. "Mirnyi" and "Vostok" (ships) and map of Antarctica.

1950. 25th Death Anniv of Frunze (military strategist).

1649 **477** 40 k. blue on buff . . . . 4·00 3·00
1650 1 r. brown on blue . . . 9·25 7·00

478 M. I. Kalinin — 479 Picking Grapes

1950. 75th Birth Anniv of Kalinin (statesman).

1651 **478** 40 k. green . . . . 1·25 85
1652 1 r. brown . . . . 3·00 2·00
1653 5 r. violet . . . . 8·25 7·50

1950. 30th Anniv of Armenian S.S.R.

1654 **479** 20 k. blue on buff . . . . 1·40 1·40
1655 – 40 k. orange on blue . . 2·75 2·75
1656 – 1 r. black on yellow . . 6·00 6·00

DESIGNS—HORIZ: (33 × 16 mm): 40 k. Government Offices. VERT: (21½ × 33 mm): 1 r. G. M. Sundukian (dramatist).

480 Kotelnicheskaya Quay — 481 Spassky Tower, Kremlin

1950. Moscow Building Projects.

1657 **480** 1 r. brown on buff . . . 38·00 32·00
1658 – 1 r. black on buff . . . 38·00 32·00
1659 – 1 r. brown on blue . . . 38·00 32·00
1660 – 1 r. green on yellow . . . 38·00 32·00
1661 – 1 r. lilac on buff . . . 38·00 32·00
1662 – 1 r. black . . . . 38·00 32·00
1663 – 1 r. orange . . . . . . 38·00 32·00
1664 – 1 r. green on blue . . . 38·00 32·00

DESIGNS—HORIZ: No. 1659, Vosstaniya Square; No. 1660, Moscow University; No. 1662, Dorogomilovskaya Quay; No. 1664, Smolenskaya Square. VERT: No. 1658, Krasnye Vorota; No. 1661, Komsomolskaya Square; No. 1663, Zariadie.

1950. 33rd Anniv of October Revolution.

1665 **481** 1 r. red, yellow & green . 15·00 10·00

482 "Golden Autumn"

1950. 50th Death Anniv of Levitan (painter).

1666 **482** 40 k. multicoloured . . . 4·25 65
1667 – 50 k. brown . . . . . . 5·75 1·10

PORTRAIT: 50 k. Levitan seated.

483 Aivazovsky (after A. Tyranov) — 484 Newspapers "Iskra" and "Pravda"

1950. 50th Death Anniv of Aivazovsky (painter). Multicoloured centres.

1668 – 40 k. brown . . . . . . 3·75 65
1669 – 50 k. brown . . . . . . 5·25 70
1670 **483** 1 r. blue . . . . 7·75 1·90

PAINTINGS—HORIZ: 40 k. "Black Sea"; 50 k. "Ninth Wave".

1950. 50th Anniv of Newspaper "Iskra".

1671 – 40 k. red and black . . . 9·25 9·25
1672 **484** 1 r. red and black . . . 13·50 13·50

DESIGN: 40 k. Newspapers and banners.

485 Government Offices

1950. 30th Anniv of Kazakh S.S.R.

1673 **485** 40 k. black on blue . . . 4·25 2·50
1674 – 1 r. brown on yellow . . 5·00 3·25

DESIGN: 1 r. Opera House, Alma-Ata.

486 Decembrists and Senate Square, St. Petersburg

1950. 125th Anniv of Decembrist Rising.

1675 **486** 1 r. brown on yellow . . 7·25 7·00

487 Govt Offices, Tirana

1951. Friendship with Albania.

1676 **487** 40 k. green on blue . . . 17·00 13·50

488 Greeting Soviet Troops

1951. Friendship with Bulgaria.

1677 **488** 25 k. black on blue . . . 2·25 2·10
1678 – 40 k. orange on pink . . 4·50 4·50
1679 – 60 k. brown on pink . . 6·75 6·75

DESIGNS: 40 k. Lenin Square, Sofia; 60 k. Monument to Soviet fighters, Kolarovgrad.

489 Lenin at Razliv

1951. 27th Death Anniv of Lenin. Multicoloured centres.
1680 **489** 40 k. green . . . . 2·75 65
1681 – 1 r. blue . . . . 5·25 1·10
DESIGN: 1 r. Lenin talking to young Communists.

490 Horses

1951. 25th Anniv of Kirghiz S.S.R.
1682 **490** 25 k. brown on blue . . 4·00 5·00
1683 – 40 k. green on blue . . . 7·75 7·25
DESIGN—33 × 22½ mm: 40 k. Government Offices, Frunze.

490a Gathering Lemons

1951. 30th Anniv of Georgia S.S.R.
1683a – 20 k. green on yellow . 1·50 1·40
1683b **490a** 25 k. orange & purple . 2·50 2·25
1683c – 40 k. brown on blue . 4·25 3·75
1683d – 1 r. green & brown . . 10·00 6·75
DESIGNS—VERT: 20 k. Theatre, Tiflis. HORIZ: 40 k. Main thoroughfare, Tiflis; 1 r. Plucking tea.

491 University, Ulan Bator

1951. Friendship with Mongolia.
1684 **491** 25 k. violet on pink . . . 2·00 1·00
1685 – 40 k. orange on yellow . 2·75 1·25
1686 – 1 r. multicoloured . . . 7·00 4·25
DESIGNS—HORIZ: (37 × 25 mm): 40 k. State Theatre, Ulan Bator. VERT: (22 × 33 mm): 1 r. State Emblem and Mongolian Flag.

492 D. A. Furmanov

493 Soviet Soldiers Memorial, Berlin

1951. 25th Death Anniv of D. A. Furmanov (writer).
1687 **492** 40 k. brown on blue . . 1·90 1·90
1688 – 1 r. black on pink . . . 4·25 3·75
DESIGN—HORIZ: 1 r. Furmanov writing.

1951. Stockholm Peace Appeal.
1689 **493** 40 k. green and red . . . 4·25 3·25
1690 1 r. black and red . . . 9·00 8·00

494 Factories

1951. 150th Anniv of Kirov Machine-building Factory, Leningrad.
1691 **494** 40 k. brown on yellow . 6·75 5·00

495 Bolshoi State Theatre

1951. 175th Anniv of State Theatre.
1692 **495** 40 k. multicoloured . . . 4·75 45
1693 – 1 r. multicoloured . . . 7·00 1·40
DESIGN: 1 r. Medallion portraits of Glinka, Tchaikovsky, Moussorgsky, Rimsky-Korsakov, Borodin and theatre.

496 National Museum, Budapest

497 Harvesting

1951. Hungarian Peoples' Republic. Buildings in Budapest.
1694 – 25 k. green . . . . . . 1·10 1·10
1695 – 40 k. blue . . . . . . 1·50 1·40
1696 **496** 60 k. black . . . . . . 2·00 2·00
1697 – 1 r. black on pink . . . 5·25 4·50
DESIGNS—HORIZ: 25 k. Liberty Bridge; 40 k. Parliament buildings. VERT: 1 r. Liberation Monument.

1951. Agricultural Scenes.
1698 **497** 25 k. green 85 40
1699 – 40 k. green on blue . . 1·60 85
1700 – 1 r. brown on yellow . . 2·75 2·40
1701 – 2 r. green on pink . . . 4·75 4·75
DESIGNS: 40 k. Apiary; 1 r. Gathering citrus fruit; 2 r. Harvesting cotton.

498 M. I. Kalinin

499 F. E. Dzerzhinsky

1951. 5th Death Anniv of Pres. Kalinin.
1702 – 20 k. sepia and brown . 55 20
1703 **498** 40 k. brown and green . 1·75 35
1704 – 1 r. black and blue . . 3·25 1·10
DESIGNS—HORIZ: 20 k. Kalinin Museum. VERT: 1 r. Kalinin Statue.

1951. 25th Death Anniv of Dzerzhinsky (founder of Cheka).
1705 **499** 40 k. red . . . . 2·40 75
1706 – 1 r. black (portrait in uniform) . . . . . . 4·25 1·60

500 P. K. Kozlov

501 Kalinnikov

1951. Russian Scientists.
1707 **500** 40 k. orange . . . . . . 1·25 25
1708 – 40 k. orange on pink . . 1·25 25
1709 – 40 k. orange on blue . . 4·00 1·50
1710 – 40 k. brown . . . . . . 1·25 25
1711 – 40 k. brown on pink (facing left) . . . . 1·25 25
1712 – 40 k. brown on pink (facing right) . . . . 1·25 25
1713 – 40 k. grey . . . . 1·25 25
1714 – 40 k. grey on pink . . . 1·25 25
1715 – 40 k. grey on blue . . . 4·00 1·50
1716 – 40 k. green . . . . . . 1·25 25
1717 – 40 k. green on pink . . 1·25 25
1718 – 40 k. blue . . . . 1·25 25
1719 – 40 k. deep blue on pink . 1·25 25
1720 – 40 k. blue on blue . . . 1·25 25
1721 – 40 k. violet . . . . . . 1·25 25
1722 – 40 k. violet on pink . . 1·25 25
PORTRAITS: No. 1708, N. N. Miklukho-Makai; No. 1709, A. M. Butlerov; No. 1710, N. I. Lobachevsky; No. 1711, K. A. Timiryazev; No. 1712, N. S. Kurnakov; No. 1713, P. N. Yablochkov; No. 1714, A. N. Severtsov; No. 1715, K. E. Tsiolkovsky; No. 1716, A. N. Lodygin; No. 1717, A. G. Stoletov; No. 1718, P. N. Lebedev; No. 1719, A. O. Kovalesky; No. 1720, D. I. Mendeleev; No. 1721, S. P. Krasheninnikov; No. 1722, S. V. Kovalevskaya.

1951. Russian Composers.
1723 **501** 40 k. grey on pink . . . 10·00 8·25
1724 – 40 k. brown on pink . . 10·00 8·25
PORTRAIT: No. 1724, Aliabiev and bar of music.

502 Aviation Society Badge

503 V. M. Vasnetsov

1951. Aviation Developement.
1725 **502** 40 k. multicoloured . . . 1·00 15
1726 – 60 k. multicoloured . . . 2·00 20
1727 – 1 r. multicoloured . . . . 3·00 85
1728 – 2 r. multicoloured . . . . 5·75 1·50
DESIGNS—VERT: 60 k. Boys and model gliders; 1 r. Parachutists descending. HORIZ: (45 × 25 mm): 2 r. Flight of Yakovlev Yak-18U trainers.

1951. 25th Death Anniv of Vasnetsov (painter).
1729 **503** 40 k. brown and blue . . 4·00 60
1730 – 1 r. multicolour . . . . . 6·00 1·40
DESIGN (47 × 33 mm): 1 r. "Three Heroes".

504 Lenin, Stalin and Dnieperprostroi Dam

1951. 34th Anniv of October Revolution.
1731 **504** 40 k. blue and red . . . . 5·75 2·75
1732 – 1 r. brown and red . . . 7·75 5·25
DESIGN: 1 r. Lenin, Stalin and Spassky Tower.

505 Volga–Don Canal

1951. Construction of Hydro-electric Power Stations.
1733 – 20 k. multicoloured . . . 3·50 2·75
1734 **505** 30 k. multicoloured . . . 4·00 3·50
1735 – 40 k. multicoloured . . . 4·75 4·25
1736 – 60 k. multicoloured . . . 7·25 6·75
1737 – 1 r. multicoloured . . . . 11·50 10·00
DESIGNS—VERT: (32 × 47 mm): 20 k. Khakhovsky power station. HORIZ: (47 × 32 mm); 40 k. Stalingrad dam; 60 k. Excavator and map of Turkmen canal; 1 r. Kuibyshev power station.

506 Signing Peace Petition

507 M. V. Ostrogradsky

1951. 3rd U.S.S.R. Peace Conference.
1738 **506** 40 k. red and brown . . . 9·25 9·25

1951. 150th Birth Anniv of Ostrogradsky (mathematician).
1739 **507** 40 k. brown on pink . . 7·25 4·00

508 Zhizka Monument, Prague

509 Volkhovsky Hydro-electric Station and Lenin Monument

1951. Friendship with Czechoslovakia.
1740 **508** 20 k. blue on pink . . . 2·00 2·00
1741 – 25 k. red on lemon . . . 4·00 4·00
1742 – 40 k. orange on orange . 2·00 2·00
1743 – 60 k. grey . . . . 4·00 4·00
1744 – 1 r. grey . . . . 5·00 5·00
DESIGNS—VERT: 25 k. Soviet Army Monument, Ostrava; 40 k. J. Fucik; 60 k. Smetana Museum, Prague. HORIZ: 1 r. Soviet Soldiers Monument, Prague.

1951. 25th Anniv of Lenin Volkhovsky Hydro-electric Station.
1745a **509** 40 k. yellow and blue . . 85 25
1746 1 r. yellow and violet . . 2·40 35

510 Lenin when a Student

511 P. P. Semenov-Tian-Shansky

1952. 28th Death Anniv of Lenin. Multicoloured centres.
1747 **510** 40 k. green . . . . . . 2·50 1·10
1748 – 60 k. blue . . . . 2·75 1·10
1749 – 1 r. brown . . . . 2·75 1·60
DESIGNS—HORIZ: 60 k. Lenin and children; 1 r. Lenin talking to peasants.

1952. 125th Birth Anniv of Semenov-Tian-Shansky (scientist).
1750 **511** 1 r. brown on blue . . . 4·00 4·00

512 Skaters

513 V. O. Kovalevsky

1952. Winter Sports.
1751 **512** 40 k. multicoloured . . . 2·75 35
1752 – 60 k. multicoloured (Skiers) 3·25 75

1952. Birth Centenary of Kovalevsky (scientist).
1753 **513** 40 k. brown on yellow . . 5·25 3·00

514 Gogol and Character from "Taras Bulba"

1952. Death Centenary of Nikolai Gogol (writer).
1754 **514** 40 k. black on blue . . . 1·00 20
1755 – 60 k. orange and black . 1·40 30
1756 – 1 r. multicoloured . . . 2·75 1·40
DESIGNS: 60 k. Gogol and Belinsky; 1 r. Gogol and Ukrainian peasants.

515 G. K. Ordzhonikidze

516 Workers and Flag

1952. 15th Death Anniv of Ordzhonikidze (statesman).
1757 **515** 40 k. green on pink . . . 2·75 7·25
1758 1 r. black on blue . . . 4·00 7·25

1952. 15th Anniv of Stalin Constitution.
1759 **516** 40 k. red and black on cream . . . . 4·75 5·00
1760 – 40 k. red and green on green 4·75 5·00
1761 – 40 k. red and brown on blue 4·75 5·00
1762 – 40 k. red and black . . . 4·75 5·00
DESIGNS—HORIZ: No. 1760, Recreation centre; No. 1761, Old people and banners. VERT: No. 1762, Schoolgirl and Spassky Tower Kremlin.

517 Novikov-Priboy and Battleship "Orel"

518 Victor Hugo

1952. 75th Birth Anniv of Novikov-Priboy (writer).
1763 **517** 40 k. grey, yellow & grn 3·25 80

1952. 150th Birth Anniv of Victor Hugo (French writer).
1764 **518** 40 k. black, blue & brn . 1·10 30

519 Salavat Yulaev　**520** G. Ya. Sedov

1952. Birth Bicent of Yulaev (Bashkirian hero).
1765 **519** 40 k. red on pink . . . . 1·40 65

1952. 75th Birth Anniv of Sedov (Arctic explorer).
1766 **520** 40 k. brown, blue & grn . 9·25 8·00

521 Arms and Flag of Rumania　**522** Zhukovsky

1952. Friendship with Rumania.
1767 **521** 40 k. multicoloured . . . 1·40 1·40
1768 – 60 k. green on pink . . . 2·00 2·00
1769 – 1 r. blue . . . . 2·75 2·75
DESIGNS—VERT: 60 k. Soviet Soldiers' Monument, Bucharest. HORIZ: 1 r. University Square, Bucharest.

1952. Death Centenary of V. A. Zhukovsky (poet).
1770 **522** 40 k. black on blue . . . 1·00 30

523 K. P. Bryullov

1952. Death Centenary of Bryullov (artist).
1771 **523** 40 k. green on blue . . . 1·00 30

524 N. P. Ogarev　**525** G. I. Uspensky

1952. 75th Death Anniv of Ogarev (revolutionary writer).
1772 **524** 40 k. green 70 20

1952. 50th Death Anniv of Uspensky (writer).
1773 **525** 40 k. brown and blue . . 1·60 1·00

526 Admiral Nakhimov　**527** Tartu University

1952. 150th Birth Anniv of Admiral Nakhimov.
1774 **526** 40 k. multicoloured . . . 3·25 2·75

1952. 150th Anniv of Extension of Tartu University.
1775 **527** 40 k. black on salmon . . 2·75 1·60

1952. War Orders and Medals (7th series). Frame as T **282** with various centres.
1776 F 1 r. brown . . . . 11·50 11·50
1777 P 2 r. red 85 65
1778 J 3 r. violet 85 65
1779a A 5 r. lake . . . . 1·00 1·00
1780 E 10 r. red . . . . 1·00 1·00

528 Kayum Nasyri　**529** A. N. Radishchev

1952. 50th Death Anniv of Nasyri (educationist).
1781 **528** 40 k. brown on yellow . 2·75 2·50

1952. 150th Death Anniv of Radishchev (writer).
1782 **529** 40 k. black and red . . 2·40 1·00

530 Entrance to Volga–Don Canal　**531** P. A. Fedotov

1952. 35th Anniv of Russian Revolution.
1783 **530** 40 k. multicoloured . . 3·25 3·25
1784 – 1 r. yellow, red & brown 6·75 6·75
DESIGN: 1 r. Lenin, Stalin, Spassky Tower and flags.

1952. Death Centenary of Fedotov (painter).
1785 **531** 40 k. brown and lake . . 2·00 85

532 V. D. Polenov　**534** Odoevsky (after N. Bestuzhev)

533 "Moscow Courtyard" (painting)

1952. 25th Death Anniv of Polenov (painter).
1786 **532** 40 k. lake and buff . . . 1·50 85
1787 **533** 1 r. blue and grey . . . 3·75 1·60

1952. 150th Birth Anniv of A. I. Odoevsky (poet).
1788 **534** 40 k. black and red . . 1·40 30

535 Mamin-Sibiryak　**536** V. M. Bekhterev

1952. Birth Centenary of D. N. Mamin-Sibiryak (writer).
1789 **535** 40 k. green on yellow . 1·10 50

1952. 25th Death Anniv of Bekhterev (psychiatrist).
1790 **536** 40 k. black, grey & blue 1·50 65

537 Komsomolskaya Koltsevaya Station

1952. Underground Stations. Multicoloured centres.
1791 – 40 k. violet . . . . . . 1·75 55
1792 – 40 k. blue . . . . . . 1·75 55
1793 – 40 k. grey . . . . . . 1·75 55
1794 **537** 40 k. green . . . . . . 1·75 55
STATIONS: No. 1791, Byelorussia Koltsevaya; No. 1792, Botanical Gardens; No. 1793, Novoslobodskaya.

538 U.S.S.R. Arms and Flags

1952. 30th Anniv of U.S.S.R.
1795 **538** 1 r. brown, red & grn . . 4·75 3·75

539 Lenin and Flags

1953. 29th Death Anniv of Lenin.
1796 **539** 40 k. multicoloured . . . 5·00 4·25

540 Peace Prize Medal　**541** V. V. Kuibyshev

1953. Stalin Peace Prize.
1797 **540** 40 k. yellow, blue & brn . 5·00 5·00

1953. 65th Birth Anniv of Kuibyshev (statesman).
1798 **541** 40 k. black and lake . . . 1·60 1·00

542 V. V. Mayakovsky　**543** N. G. Chernyshevsky

1953. 60th Birth Anniv of Mayakovsky (poet).
1799 **542** 40 k. black and red . . 2·75 2·75

1953. 125th Birth Anniv of Chernyshevsky (writer).
1800 **543** 40 k. brown and buff . . 2·75 2·75

544 R. Volga Lighthouse

1953. Views of Volga–Don Canal. Multicoloured.
1801 40 k. Type **544** . . . . 1·50 60
1802 40 k. Lock No. 9 . . . . . 1·50 60
1803 40 k. Lock No. 13 . . . . . 1·50 60
1804 40 k. Lock No. 15 . . . . . 1·50 60
1805 40 k. Tsimlyanskaya hydro-electric station . . . . . 1·50 60
1806 1 r. "Iosif Stalin" (river vessel) 2·50 1·40

545 V. G. Korolenko　**546** Tolstoi (after N. Ge)

1953. Birth Centenary of Korolenko (writer).
1807 **545** 40 k. brown . . . . . . 1·10 20

1953. 125th Birth Anniv of Leo Tolstoi (writer).
1808 **546** 1 r. brown . . . . 6·75 5·00

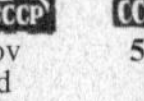

547 Lomonosov University and Students　**548** Peoples of the U.S.S.R

1953. 35th Anniv of "Komsomol" (Russian Youth Organization). Multicoloured.
1809 40 k. Type **547** . . . . 2·00 1·90
1810 1 r. Four medals and "Komsomol" badge . . . 5·00 4·75

1953. 36th Anniv of Russian Revolution. Mult.
1811 40 k. Type **548** . . . . 7·25 7·25
1812 60 k. Lenin and Stalin in Smolny Institute, 1917 . . 12·50 12·50

549 Lenin Medallion　**550** Lenin Statue

551 Peter I Monument

1953. 50th Anniv of Communist Party.
1813 **549** 40 k. multicoloured . . . 3·75 3·25

1953. Views of Leningrad as T **550/1**.
1814 **550** 40 k. black on yellow . . 1·75 1·50
1815 40 k. brown on pink . . 1·75 80
1816 – 40 k. brown on yellow . 1·60 1·50
1817 – 40 k. black on buff . . 90 85
1818 **551** 1 r. brown on blue . . . 3·25 3·00
1819 1 r. violet on yellow . . 2·50 2·10
1820 – 1 r. green on pink . . . 3·25 3·00
1821 – 1 r. brown on blue . . . 2·50 2·10
DESIGNS: As Type **550**: Nos. 1816/17, Admiralty. As Type **551**: 1820/1, Smolny Institute.

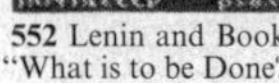

552 Lenin and Book "What is to be Done?"　**553** Pioneers and Moscow University Model

1953. 50th Anniv of 2nd Social Democratic Workers' Party Congress.
1822 **552** 1 r. brown and red . . . 7·25 6·75

1953. Peace Propaganda.
1823 **553** 40 k. black, olive and grey 4·25 4·25

554 Griboedov (after I. Kramskoi)　**555** Kremlin

1954. 125th Death Anniv of A. S. Griboedov (author).
1824 **554** 40 k. purple on buff . . 1·50 30
1825a 1 r. black on green . . 1·90 1·00

1954. General Election.
1826 **555** 40 k. grey and red . . . 2·75 2·50

556 V. P. Chkalov **557** Lenin in Smolny Institute

1954. 50th Birthday of Chkalov (aviator).
1827 **556** 1 r. brown, blue and grey . . 3·25 1·10

1954. 30th Death Anniv of Lenin. Multicoloured.
1828 40 k. Lenin (vert) . . . . . . 2·40 1·40
1829 40 k. Type **557** . . . . 2·40 1·40
1830 40 k. Cottage Museum, Ulyanovsk . . . . 2·40 1·40
1831 40 k. Lenin addressing revolutionaries . . . . . . 2·40 1·40
1832 40 k. Lenin at Kazan University 2·40 1·40
Nos. 1829/30 are 38 × 26 mm and 1831/2 48 × 35 mm.

558 Stalin **559** Supreme Soviet Buildings in Kiev and Moscow

1954. 1st Death Anniv of Stalin.
1833 **558** 40 k. brown . . . . 3·25 1·40

1954. Tercentenary of Reunion of Ukraine with Russia. Multicoloured. (a) Designs as T **559** inscr "1654–1954".
1834 40 k. Type **559** 80 40
1835 40 k. Shevchenko Memorial, Kharkhov (vert) 80 25
1836 40 k. State Opera House, Kiev 80 25
1837 40 k. Shevchenko University, Kiev 80 25
1838 40 k. Academy of Sciences, Kiev 1·50 25
1839 60 k. Bogdan Chmielnitsky Memorial, Kiev (vert) . . . 1·60 25
1840 1 r. Flags of R.S.F.S.R. and Ukrainian S.S.R. (vert) . . 3·25 55
1841 1 r. Shevchenko Monument, Kanev (vert) . . . . 2·00 85
1842 1 r. Pereyaslavskaya Rada . . 3·25 65

(b) No. 1098b optd with five lines of Cyrillic characters as inscr at top of T **559**.
1843 **h** 2 r. green . . . . 6·75 1·75

561 Running

1954. Sports. Frames in brown.
1844 **561** 40 k. black and stone . . 1·00 20
1845 – 40 k. black and blue . . 1·25 20
1846 – 40 k. brown and buff . . 1·00 20
1847 – 40 k. black and blue . . 1·00 20
1848 – 40 k. black . . . . . . 1·00 20
1849 – 1 r. grey and blue . . . . 4·00 1·50
1850 – 1 r. black and blue . . . 4·00 1·50
1851 – 1 r. brown and drab . . 4·00 1·50
DESIGNS—HORIZ: No. 1845, Yachting; No. 1846, Cycling; No. 1847, Swimming; No. 1848, Hurdling; No. 1849, Mountaineering; No. 1850, Skiing. VERT: No. 1851, Basketball.

562 Cattle **563** A. P. Chekhov

1954. Agriculture.
1852 **562** 40 k. blue, brown & cream 2·40 35
1853 – 40 k. green, brn & buff . 2·40 35
1854 – 40 k. black, blue and green 2·40 35
DESIGNS: No. 1853, Potato cultivation; No. 1854, Collective farm hydro-electric station.

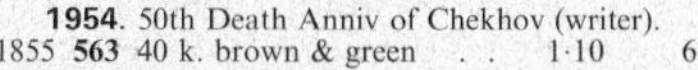

1954. 50th Death Anniv of Chekhov (writer).
1855 **563** 40 k. brown & green . . 1·10 65

564 Bredikhin, Struve, Belopolsky and Observatory **565** M. I. Glinka

1954. Rebuilding of Pulkov Observatory.
1856 **564** 40 k. black, blue & vio . 6·75 1·60

1954. 150th Birth Anniv of Glinka (composer).
1857 **565** 40 k. brown, pink & red 1·90 35
1858 – 60 k. multicoloured . . 2·10 65
DESIGN—HORIZ: (38 × 25½ mm): 60 k. "Glinka playing piano for Pushkin and Zhukovsky" (V. Artamonov).

566 Exhibition Emblem **567** N. A. Ostrovsky

1954. Agricultural Exhibition. Multicoloured.
1859 40 k. Type **566** 55 30
1860 40 k. Agricultural Pavilion . 55 30
1861 40 k. Cattle breeding Pavilion 55 30
1862 40 k. Mechanization Pavilion 55 30
1863 1 r. Exhibition Entrance . . 3·00 1·40
1864 1 r. Main Pavilion . . . . . 3·00 1·40
Nos. 1860/3 are horiz, 1860/1 being 41 × 30½ mm, 1862, 40 × 30 mm and 1863 41 × 33 mm. No. 1864 is vert 29 × 41 mm.

1954. 50th Birth Anniv of Ostrovsky (writer).
1865 **567** 40 k. multicoloured . . 1·90 40

568 Monument **569** Marx, Engels, Lenin and Stalin

1954. Centenary of Defence of Sevastopol.
1866 **568** 40 k. black, brown & grn 1·40 30
1867 – 60 k. black, brn & buff . 1·50 50
1868 – 1 r. multicoloured . . . 3·75 90
DESIGNS—HORIZ: 60 k. Defenders of Sevastopol. VERT: 1 r. Admiral Nakhimov.

1954. 37th Anniv of October Revolution.
1869 **569** 1 r. brown, red & orange 5·00 3·25

570 Kazan University

1954. 150th Anniv of Kazan University.
1870 **570** 40 k. blue on blue . . . 80 30
1871 60 k. red . . . . 2·00 55

571 Salomea Neris

1954. 50th Birth Anniv of Salomea Neris (poetess).
1872 **571** 40 k. multicoloured . . 1·00 25

572 Cultivating Vegetables **573** Stalin

1954. Agriculture. Multicoloured.
1873 40 k. Type **572** . . . . . . 1·50 30
1874 40 k. Tractor and plough . . 1·50 30
1875 40 k. Harvesting flax (49 × 25½ mm) . . . . 1·50 30
1876 60 k. Harvesting sunflowers (49 × 25½ mm) . . . . . 2·00 65

1954. 75th Birth Anniv of Stalin.
1877 **573** 40 k. purple . . . . . . 1·00 50
1878 1 r. blue . . . . 2·75 1·40

574 Rubinstein

1954. 125th Birth Anniv of Rubinstein (composer).
1879 **574** 40 k. black and purple . . 1·60 40

575 V. M. Garshin **576** Ilyushin Il-12 over Landscape

1955. Birth Centenary of Garshin (writer).
1880 **575** 40 k. black, brown & grn 1·10 60

1955. Air.
1881 – 1 r. multicoloured . . . . 1·75 60
1882 **576** 2 r. black and green . . . 3·75 75
DESIGN: 1 r. Ilyushin Il-12 over coastline.

577 K. A. Savitsky and "Construction of Railway"

1955. 50th Death Anniv of Savitsky (painter).
1883 **577** 40 k. brown . . . . . . 1·50 20

578 Clasped Hands **579** Pushkin and Mickiewicz

1955. International Conference of Postal and Municipal Workers, Vienna.
1884 **578** 50 k. multicoloured . . . 80 20

1955. 10th Anniv of Russo-Polish Friendship Agreement.
1885 **579** 40 k. multicoloured . . . 2·10 30
1886 – 40 k. black . . . . 2·10 30
1887 – 1 r. multicoloured . . . . 4·75 1·00
1888 – 1 r. multicoloured . . . . 4·75 1·00
DESIGNS: No. 1886, "Brotherhood in Arms" Monument, Warsaw (26½ × 39 mm); No. 1887, Palace of Science, Warsaw (37½ × 25½ mm); No. 1888, Copernicus and Matejko (39 × 26½ mm).

580 Lenin at Shushenskoe

1955. 85th Birth Anniv of Lenin. Multicoloured centres.
1889 **580** 60 k. red . . . . 2·00 30
1890 – 1 r. red . . . . 4·00 60
1891 – 1 r. red . . . . 4·00 60
DESIGNS: No. 1890, Lenin in secret printing house (26½ × 39 mm). As Type **580**: No. 1891, Lenin and Krupskaya at Gorky.

581 Schiller **582** Ilyushin Il-12 over Globe

1955. 150th Death Anniv of Schiller (poet).
1892 **581** 40 k. brown . . . . . . 1·10 85

1955. Air.
1893 **582** 2 r. brown . . . . 4·50 80
1894 2 r. blue . . . . 3·50 95

583 V. Mayakovsky

1955. 25th Death Anniv of Mayakovsky (poet).
1895 **583** 40 k. multicoloured . . . 1·40 30

584 Tadzhik S.S.R. Pavilion

1955. Agricultural Exhibition. Soviet Pavilion. Multicoloured designs with green frames.
1896 40 k. R.S.F.S.R. 65 30
1897 40 k. Byelorussian S.S.R. . . 65 30
1898 40 k. Type **584** 65 30
1899 40 k. Azerbaijan S.S.R. . . . 65 30
1900 40 k. Latvian S.S.R. 65 30
1901 40 k. Lithuanian S.S.R. . . . 65 30
1902 40 k. Karelo-Finnish S.S.R. . 65 30
1903 40 k. Estonian S.S.R. 65 30
1904 40 k. Armenian S.S.R. . . . 65 30
1905 40 k. Ukrainian S.S.R. . . . 65 30
1906 40 k. Georgian S.S.R. . . . 65 30
1907 40 k. Kazakh S.S.R. 65 30
1908 40 k. Turkmen S.S.R. 65 30
1909 40 k. Kirgiz S.S.R. 65 30
1910 40 k. Uzbek S.S.R. 65 30
1911 40 k. Moldavian S.S.R. . . . 65 30

585 M. V. Lomonosov and Building

1955. Bicentenary of Lomonosov University. Multicoloured.
1912 40 k. Type **585** 85 30
1913 1 r. Lomonosov University . 1·60 55

586 A. G. Venetsianov and "The Labours of Spring"

1955. 175th Birth Anniv of Venetsianov (painter). Multicoloured centre.
1914 **586** 1 r. black . . . . 2·75 55

587 A. Lyadov

1955. Birth Centenary of Lyadov (composer).
1915 **587** 40 k. multicoloured . . . 1·50 30

588 A. S. Popov

589 Lenin

590 Revolution Scene

1955. 60th Anniv of Popov's Radio Discoveries. Multicoloured centres.
1916 **588** 40 k. blue . . . . 1·50 20
1917 1 r. brown . . . . 2·75 65

1955. 38th Anniv of Russian Revolution.
1918 **589** 40 k. multicoloured . . . 2·50 1·90
1919 **590** 40 k. multicoloured . . . 1·50 1·90
1920 – 1 r. multicoloured . . . 5·00 3·00
DESIGN: As T **590**: 1 r. Lenin speaking to revolutionaries.

„Сев. полюс"
— Москва
1955 г.
(**591**)

592 Magnitogorsk

1955. Air. Opening of North Pole Scientific Stations. Nos. 1881/2 optd with T **591**.
1921 – 1 r. multicoloured . . . 8·25 5·00
1922 **576** 2 r. black and green . . . 13·50 5·00

1955. 25th Anniv of Magnitogorsk.
1923 **592** 40 k. multicoloured . . . 1·50 20

593 Mil Mi-4 Helicopter over Station

594 F. I. Shubin

1955. North Pole Scientific Stations.
1924 **593** 40 k. multicoloured . . . 3·25 30
1925 60 k. multicoloured . . . 3·50 65
1926 – 1 r. multicoloured . . . 5·50 1·00
DESIGN: 1 r. Meteorologist taking observations.

1955. 150th Death Anniv of Shubin (sculptor).
1927 **594** 40 k. multicoloured . . . 80 20
1928 1 r. multicoloured . . . 1·50 30

595 A. N. Krylov

596 Racing

1956. 10th Death Anniv of Krylov (scientist).
1929 **595** 40 k. multicoloured . . . 1·10 20

1956. International Horse Racing.
1930 **596** 40 k. sepia and brown . . 75 25
1931 60 k. blue and green . . 1·10 30
1932 – 1 r. purple and blue . . . 2·75 1·10
DESIGN—HORIZ: 1 r. Trotting.

597 Badge and Stadium

1956. 5th Spartacist Games.
1933 **597** 1 r. green and purple . . 1·50 35

598 Atomic Power Station

1956. Foundation of Atomic Power Station of Russian Academy of Sciences.
1934 **598** 25 k. multicoloured . . 1·10 15
1935 – 60 k. yellow, turq & brn 2·00 25
1936 **598** 1 r. yellow, red and blue 2·75 85
DESIGN: 60 k. Top of atomic reactor.

599 Statue of Lenin

600 Kh. Abovyan

1956. 20th Communist Party Congress.
1937 **599** 40 k. multicoloured . . 75 20
1938 1 r. multicoloured . . . 1·90 40

1956. 150th Birth Anniv of Khatchatur Abovyan (Armenian writer).
1939 **600** 40 k. black on blue . . 85 20

601 Revolutionaries

602

1956. 50th Anniv of 1905 Revolution.
1940 **601** 40 k. multicoloured . . 3·75 1·40

1941 ПАВИЛЬОН «УРАЛ»
1942 ПАВИЛЬОН СЕВЕРО-ВОСТОЧНЫХ ОБЛАСТЕЙ
1943 ПАВИЛЬОН ЦЕНТРАЛЬНЫХ ЧЕРНОЗЕМНЫХ ОБЛАСТЕЙ
1944 ПАВИЛЬОН «ЛЕНИНГРАД • СЕВЕРО-ЗАПАД»
1945 ПАВИЛЬОН МОСКОВСКОЙ, ТУЛЬСКОЙ, КАЛУЖСКОЙ, РЯЗАНСКОЙ И БРЯНСКОЙ ОБЛАСТЕЙ
1946 ПАВИЛЬОН БАШКИРСКОЙ АССР
1947 ПАВИЛЬОН ДАЛЬНЕГО ВОСТОКА
1948 ПАВИЛЬОН ТАТАРСКОЙ АССР
1949 ПАВИЛЬОН ЦЕНТРАЛЬНЫХ ОБЛАСТЕЙ
1950 ПАВИЛЬОН ЮНЫХ НАТУРАЛИСТОВ
1951 ПАВИЛЬОН СЕВЕРНОГО КАВКАЗА
1952 ПАВИЛЬОН «СИБИРЬ»
1953 ПАВИЛЬОН «ПОВОЛЖЬЕ»

Inscr at foot as shown above.

1956. Agricultural Exhibition. Multicoloured. Views of Pavilions of U.S.S.R. regions as T **602**. Inscr "BCXB".
1941 1 r. Ural . . . . 1·50 40
1942 1 r. North East . . . . . . 1·50 40
1943 1 r. Central Black Soil Region 1·50 40
1944 1 r. Leningrad . . . . . . 1·50 40
1945 1 r. Moscow-Tula-Kaluga-Ryazan-Bryansk . . . . . 1·50 40
1946 1 r. Bashkir . . . . 1·50 40
1947 1 r. Far East . . . . 1·50 40
1948 1 r. Tatar . . . . 1·50 40
1949 1 r. Central Regions . . . . 1·50 40
1950 1 r. Young Naturalists . . . 1·50 40
1951 1 r. North Caucasus . . . . 1·50 40
1952 1 r. Siberia . . . . 1·50 40
1953 1 r. Volga . . . . 1·50 40

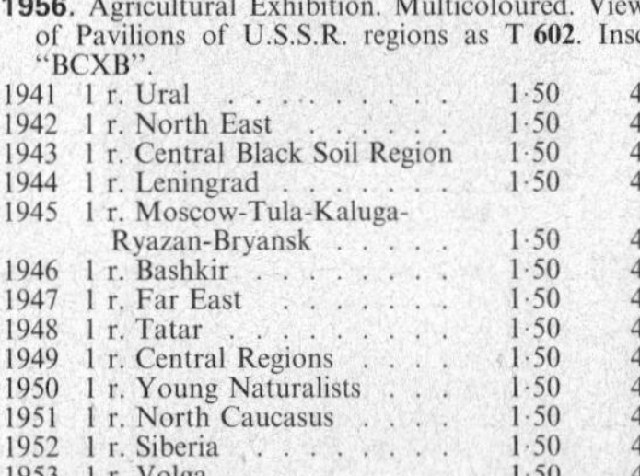

603 N. A. Kasatkin (painter)

1956. Kasatkin Commemoration.
1954 **603** 40 k. red 70 15

604 A. E. Arkhipov and Painting "On the Oka River"

1956. Arkhipov Commemoration.
1955 **604** 40 k. multicoloured . . . 1·40 20
1956 1 r. multicoloured . . . . 2·75 45

605 I. P. Kulibin

606 "Fowler" (after Perov)

1956. 220th Birth Anniv of Kulibin (inventor).
1957 **605** 40 k. multicoloured . . . 1·40 30

1956. Perov Commemoration. Inscr "1956". Multicoloured centres.
1958 – 40 k. green . . . . 1·60 25
1959 **606** 1 r. brown . . . . 3·25 85
1960 – 1 r. brown . . . . 3·25 85
DESIGNS—VERT: No. 1958, V. G. Perov. HORIZ: No. 1960, "Hunters Resting" (after Perov).

607 Lenin speaking

608 N. I. Lobachevsky

1956. 86th Birth Anniv of Lenin.
1961 **607** 40 k. multicoloured . . . 8·25 5·00

1956. Death Cent of Lobachevsky (mathematician).
1962 **608** 40 k. brown 80 15

609 Student Nurses

1956. Red Cross.
1963 **609** 40 k. red, blue & brown . 1·00 30
1964 – 40 k. red, olive & turquoise 1·00 30
DESIGN—$37\frac{1}{2} \times 25\frac{1}{2}$ mm: No. 1964, Nurse and textile factory.

610

611 I. M. Sechenov (scientist)

1956. Air. Opening of North Pole Scientific Station No. 6.
1965 **610** 1 r. multicoloured . . . . 2·50 1·40

1956. Sechenov Commemoration.
1966 **611** 40 k. multicoloured . . . 1·90 65

612 Arsenev

613 I. V. Michurin

1956. V. K. Arsenev (writer).
1967 **612** 40 k. black, violet & pink 2·00 55

1956. Birth Centenary of Michurin (naturalist). Multicoloured centres.
1968 **613** 25 k. brown 45 15
1969 – 60 k. green . . . . . . 1·10 25
1970 **613** 1 r. blue . . . . 2·00 45
DESIGN—$47\frac{1}{2} \times 26\frac{1}{2}$ mm: 60 k. Michurin and children.

614 A. K. Savrasov (painter)

615 N. K. Krupskaya (Lenin's wife)

1956. Savrasov Commemoration.
1971 **614** 1 r. brown and yellow . 1·40 50

1956. Krupskaya Commemoration.
1972 **615** 40 k. brown, black & bl . 1·60 20
For similar stamps see Nos. 2005, 2027, 2115 and 2169.

616 S. M. Kirov

617 A. A. Blok

1956. 70th Birth Anniv of Kirov (statesman).
1973 **616** 40 k. multicoloured . . . 65 15

1956. Blok (poet) Commemoration.
1974 **617** 40 k. brown, blk & olive 80 15

618 N. S. Leskov

619 Factory Building

1956. 125th Birth Anniv of Leskov (writer).
1975 **618** 40 k. multicoloured . . . 65 15
1976 1 r. multicoloured . . . 1·75 40

1956. 25th Anniv of Rostov Agricultural Machinery Works.
1977 **619** 40 k. multicoloured . . . 75 2

620 G. N. Fedotova (actress)

1956. Fedotova Commemoration.
1978 **620** 40 k. multicoloured . . . 65 20
For similar stamp see No. 2159.

621 P. M. Tretyakov and Art Gallery

1956. Centenary of Tretyakov Art Gallery.
1979 **621** 40 k. multicoloured . . . 1·75 45
1980 – 40 k. multicoloured . . . 1·75 45
DESIGN—VERT: No. 1980, "Rooks have arrived" (painting by Savrasov).

622 Relay-race

1956. Spartacist Games.
1981 **622** 10 k. red 30 10
1982 – 25 k. brown 40 10
1983 – 25 k. multicoloured . . . 40 15
1984 – 25 k. blue 40 15
1985 – 40 k. blue 65 15
1986 – 40 k. green 65 15
1987 – 40 k. brown and green . . 65 15
1988 – 40 k. deep brown, brown and green 65 15
1989 – 40 k. red, green and light green 65 15
1990 – 40 k. brown 65 15
1991 – 40 k. multicoloured . . . 65 15
1992 – 60 k. violet . . . . 1·60 25
1993 – 60 k. violet . . . . 1·60 25
1994 – 1 r. brown . . . . 2·75 1·00
DESIGNS—VERT: No. 1982, Volleyball; 1983, Swimming; 1984, Rowing; 1985, Diving; 1989, Flag and stadium; 1990, Tennis; 1991, Medal; 1993, Boxing. HORIZ: No. 1986, Cycle racing; 1987, Fencing; 1988, Football; 1992, Gymnastics; 1994, Netball.

623 Parachutist Landing **624** Construction Work

1956. 3rd World Parachute-jumping Competition.
1995 **623** 40 k. multicoloured 75 25

1956. Builders' Day.
1996a **624** 40 k. orange 65 25
1997 – 60 k. brown 80 30
1998 – 1 r. blue . . . . 2·50 50
DESIGNS: 60 k. Plant construction; 1 r. Dam construction.

625 I. E. Repin and "Volga River Boatmen"

626 "Reply of the Cossacks to Sultan Mahmoud IV"

1956. Repin (painter) Commemoration.
1999 **625** 40 k. multicoloured . . . 3·75 45
2000 **626** 1 r. multicoloured . . . 7·25 1·00

627 Robert Burns

628 Ivan Franko

1956. 160th Death Anniv of Burns (Scots poet).
2001 **627** 40 k. brown . . . . . . 7·25 5·25
2002 40 k. brown and blue . . 4·75 3·25

1956. Birth Cent of Franko (writer) (1st issue).
2003 **628** 40 k. purple 65 50
2004 1 r. blue . . . . 1·25 65
See also No. 2037.

1956. Lesya Ukrainka Commemoration. As T **615** but portrait of Ukrainka (author).
2005 40 k. black, brown & green . 65 40

629 M. Aivazov (farmer)

630 Statue of Nestor

1956. 148th Birthday of Aivazov. (a) Wrongly inscr "Muhamed" (7 characters).
2006 **629** 40 k. green . . . . . . 23·00 23·00
(b) Corrected to "Makmud" (6 characters).
2006a **629** 40 k. green . . . . . . 8·25 8·25

1956. 900th Birth Anniv of Nestor (historian).
2007 **630** 40 k. multicoloured . . 1·00 20
2008 1 r. multicoloured . . . 2·10 40

631 A. A. Ivanov **632** Feeding Poultry

1956. 150th Birth Anniv of Ivanov (painter).
2009 **631** 40 k. brown and grey . 65 20

1956. Agriculture. Multicoloured.
2010 10 k. Type **632** 35 10
2011 10 k. Harvesting 35 10
2012 25 k. Gathering maize . . . 75 20
2013 40 k. Maize field . . . . . 1·10 20
2014 40 k. Tractor station . . . . 1·10 20
2015 40 k. Cattle grazing . . . . 1·10 20
2016 40 k. "Agriculture and Industry" . . . . 1·10 20
SIZES: Nos. 2010, 2014/5, 37 × 25½ mm. Nos. 2011/3, 37 × 28 mm. No. 2016, 37 × 21 mm.

633 Mozart

634 Mirnyi Base and Supply Ship "Lena"

1956. Cultural Anniversaries.
2017 40 k. blue (Type **633**) . . . 1·90 40
2018 40 k. green (Curie) . . . . . 1·90 40
2019 40 k. lilac (Heine) . . . . . 1·90 40
2020 40 k. brown (Ibsen) . . . . 1·90 40
2021 40 k. green (Dostoevsky) . . 1·90 40
2022 40 k. brown (Franklin) . . . 1·90 40
2023 40 k. black (Shaw) . . . . . 2·00 40
2024 40 k. orange (Sessku-Toyo Oda) 1·90 40
2025 40 k. black (Rembrandt) . . 1·90 40
Nos. 2022/5 are larger 25 × 38 mm.

1956. Soviet Scientific Antarctic Expedition.
2026 **634** 40 k. turquoise, red & grey 5·50 80

1956. Julia Zhemaite Commemoration. As T **615** but portrait of Zhemaite (author).
2027 40 k. green, brown & sepia . 80 20

635 F. A. Bredikhin

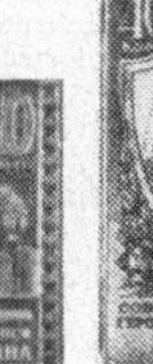
636 G. I. Kotovsky

1956. 125th Birth Anniv of Bredikhin (astronomer).
2028 **635** 40 k. multicoloured . . 5·00 1·40

1956. 75th Birth Anniv of Kotovsky (military leader).
2029 **636** 40 k. mauve . . . . . . 1·40 65

MINIMUM PRICE

The minimum price quoted is 10p which represents a handling charge rather than a basis for valuing common stamps. For further notes about prices, see introductory pages.

637 Shatura Electric Power Station

638 Marshal Suvorov

1956. 30th Anniv of Shatura Electric Power Station.
2030 **637** 40 k. multicoloured . . . 75 20

1956. 225th Birth Anniv of Marshal Suvorov.
2031 **638** 40 k. lake and orange . . 60 20
2032 1 r. brown and olive . . . 2·00 45
2033 3 r. black and brown . . 4·50 1·40

639 Kryakutni's Ascent

1956. 225th Anniv of First Balloon Flight by Kryakutni.
2034 **639** 40 k. multicoloured . . . 1·75 40

640 "Dawn at the Voskresenski Gate"

1956. 30th Death Anniv of A. M. Vasnetsov (artist).
2035 **640** 40 k. multicoloured . . . 1·40 55

641 Y. M. Shokalsky **642** Ivan Franko

1956. Birth Cent of Shokalsky (oceanographer).
2036 **641** 40 k. brown and blue . . 1·60 50

1956. Birth Centenary of Franko (writer) (2nd issue).
2037 **642** 40 k. green 55 20

643 Indian Temple and Books

644 F. G. Vokov (actor) and State Theatre

1956. Kalidasa (Indian poet) Commemoration.
2038 **643** 40 k. red 55 20

1956. Bicentenary of Leningrad State Theatre.
2039 **644** 40 k. black, red & yellow 60 20

645 Lomonosov at St. Petersburg University

1956. Russian Writers.
2040 **645** 40 k. multicoloured . . . 80 25
2041 – 40 k. multicoloured . . . 80 25
2042 – 40 k. brown and blue . . 80 25
2043 – 40 k. olive, brown & blk . 80 25
2044 – 40 k. brown and turquoise 80 25
2045 – 40 k. purple and brown . 80 25
2046 – 40 k. olive and blue . . 80 25
DESIGNS: No. 2041, Gorky and scene from "Mother" (novel); No. 2042, Pushkin and "Bronze Horseman" (statue); No. 2043, Rustavely and episode from "The Knight in the Tiger Skin" (poem); No. 2044, Tolstoy and scene from "War and Peace" (novel); No. 2045, V. G. Belinsky and titles of literary works; No. 2046, M. Y. Lermontov and Daryal Pass.
See also Nos. 2076, 2089/90, 2256, 2316/22 and 2458.

646 Vitus Bering and Routes of his Voyages

647 Mendeleev

1956. 275th Birth Anniv of Bering (explorer).
2047 **646** 40 k. multicoloured . . . 3·00 35

1957. 50th Death Anniv of Dmitri Mendeleev (chemist).
2048 **647** 40 k. brown, grey & blk 1·60 65

648 M. I. Glinka

649 Youth Festival Emblem

1957. Death Centenary of Glinka (composer). Mult.
2049a 40 k. Type **648** . . . . . 1·10 20
2050a 1 r. Scene from "Ivan Susanin" 2·10 55

1957. All Union Festival of Soviet Youth.
2051 **649** 40 k. multicoloured . . . 40 15

650 Ice Hockey Player

651 Youth Festival Emblem and Pigeon

1957. 23rd World and 35th European Ice Hockey Championships, Moscow.
2052 – 25 k. violet 90 15
2053 **650** 40 k. blue 65 15
2054 – 60 k. green . . . . . 1·00 30
DESIGNS: 25 k. Championship emblem; 60 k. Goal-keeper.

1957. 6th World Youth Festival, Moscow (1st issue). Perf or imperf.
2055 **651** 40 k. multicoloured . . . 70 15
2056 60 k. multicoloured . . . 1·10 20
See also Nos. 2084/7 and 2108/11.

652 Factory Plant

653 Sika Deer

1957. Cent of "Red Proletariat" Plant. Moscow.
2057 **652** 40 k. multicoloured . . . 1·00 25

1957. Russian Wildlife. Multicoloured.
2057a 10 k. Grey partridge . . . . 1·25 30
2058 15 k. Black grouse . . . . 1·25 15
2058a 15 k. Polar bear 70 40
2059 20 k. Type **653** 75 15
2059a 20 k. Brown hare 60 25
2059b 25 k. Tiger 75 25
2059c 25 k. Wild horse 75 25
2060 30 k. Mallard . . . . 1·50 25
2061 30 k. European bison . . . 75 20
2062 40 k. Elk . . . . 1·90 35
2063 40 k. Sable . . . . 1·90 35
2063a 40 k. Eurasian red squirrel . 80 30
2063b 40 k. Yellow-throated marten 80 30
2063c 60 k. Hazel grouse . . . . 3·25 55
2063d 1 r. Mute swan . . . . . . 4·25 1·00
Nos. 2058/a, 2059a/62, 2063a/b and 2063d are horiz.
See also Nos. 2534/6.

654 Vologda Lace-making **655** G. V. Plekhanov

1957. Regional Handicrafts. Multicoloured.

2064 40 k. Moscow wood-carving . . 1·50 25
2065 40 k. Woman engraving vase . 1·50 25
2066 40 k. Type **654** . . . . . . 1·50 25
2067 40 k. Northern bone-carving . 1·50 25
2067a 40 k. Wood-block engraving . 1·00 50
2067b 40 k. Turkmen carpet-weaving 1·00 50

1957. Birth Centenary of Plekhanov (politician).

2068 **655** 40 k. plum . . . . 1·00 20

656 A. N. Bakh **657** L. Euler

1957. Birth Centenary of Bakh (biochemist).

2069 **656** 40 k. multicoloured . . . 1·10 25

1957. 250th Birth Anniv of Euler (mathematician).

2070 **657** 40 k. black and purple 1·40 30

658 Lenin in Meditation **659** Dr. William Harvey

1957. 87th Birth Anniv of Lenin. Multicoloured.

2071 40 k. Type **658** 80 20
2072 40 k. Lenin carrying pole . . 80 20
2073 40 k. Talking with soldier and sailor 80 20

1957. 300th Death Anniv of Dr. William Harvey (discoverer of circulation of blood).

2074 **659** 40 k. brown 75 15

660 M. A. Balakirev **661** 12th-century Narrator

1957. 120th Birth Anniv of Balakirev (composer).

2075 **660** 40 k. black 75 20

1957. "The Tale of the Host of Igor".

2076 **661** 40 k. multicoloured . . . 80 20

662 Agricultural Medal **663** A. I. Herzen and N. P. Ogarev (writers)

1957. Cultivation of Virgin Soil.

2077 **662** 40 k. multicoloured . . . 1·10 25

1957. Centenary of Publication of Magazine "Kolokol".

2078 **663** 40 k. brown, blk & blue 80 25

664 Monument

250 лет
Ленинграда
(665)

1957. 250th Anniv of Leningrad. Vert designs as T **664** and stamps as Nos. 1818 and 1820 optd as T **665**.

2079 **664** 40 k. green 50 15
2080 – 40 k. violet 50 15
2081 – 40 k. brown 50 15
2082 **551** 1 r. brown on green . . 1·00 25
2083 – 1 r. green on salmon . . 1·00 25

DESIGNS: No. 2080, Nevsky Prospect, Leningrad; No. 2081, Lenin Statue.

666 Youths with Banner

1957. 6th World Youth Festival, Moscow (2nd issue). Multicoloured. Perf or imperf.

2084 10 k. Type **666** 25 10
2084a 20 k. Sculptor with statue 40 15
2085 25 k. Type **666** 80 15
2086 40 k. Dancers 85 15
2087 1 r. Festival emblem and fireworks over Moscow State University . . . . 1·10 30

667 A. M. Lyapunov **668** T. G. Shevchenko (after I. Repin) and Scene from "Katharina"

1957. Birth Centenary of Lyapunov (mathematician).

2088 **667** 40 k. brown . . . . . . 5·75 4·00

1957. 19th-Century Writers. Multicoloured.

2089 40 k. Type **668** 65 20
2090 40 k. N. G. Chernyshevsky and scene from "What is to be Done?" 65 20

669 Henry Fielding **670** Racing Cyclists

1957. 250th Birth Anniv of Fielding (novelist).

2091 **669** 40 k. multicoloured . . 45 15

1957. 10th International Cycle Race.

2092 **670** 40 k. multicoloured . . 1·00 25

671 Interior of Observatory

1957. International Geophysical Year (1st issue).

2093 **671** 40 k. brown, yellow and blue 65 40
2094 – 40 k. indigo, yellow and blue . . . . 2·00 40
2095 – 40 k. violet & lavender 1·60 1·00
2095a – 40 k. blue . . . . . . 2·00 30
2095b – 40 k. green . . . . . . 2·50 40
2095c – 40 k. yellow and blue 2·00 30

DESIGNS—As T **671**: No. 2094, Meteor in sky; 2095a, Malakhit radar scanner and balloon (meteorology); 2095b, "Zarya" (non-magnetic research schooner) (geo-magnetism); 2095c, Northern Lights and C-180 camera. 15×21 mm: No. 2095, Rocket.

See also Nos. 2371/3a.

672 Gymnast

1957. 3rd International Youth Games.

2096 **672** 20 k. brown and blue . . 20 10
2097 – 25 k. red and green . . . 25 10
2098 – 40 k. violet and red . . . 60 20
2099 – 40 k. olive, red and green 60 20
2100 – 60 k. brown and blue . . 1·10 40

DESIGNS—As Type **672**: No. 2097, Wrestlers; No. 2098, Young athletes; No. 2099, Moscow Stadium; No. 2100, Javelin thrower.

673 Football **674** Yanka Kupala

1957. Russian Successes at Olympic Games, Melbourne.

2101 – 20 k. brown, blue & blk . 30 10
2102 – 20 k. red and green . . . 30 10
2103 – 25 k. blue and orange . . 30 15
2104 **673** 40 k. multicoloured . . . 50 15
2105 – 40 k. brown and purple . 50 15
2106 – 60 k. brown and violet . 80 40

DESIGNS—VERT: No. 2101, Throwing the javelin; No. 2102, Running; No. 2103, Gymnastics; No. 2105, Boxing; No. 2106, Weightlifting.

1957. 75th Birth Anniv of Kupala (poet).

2107 **674** 40 k. brown . . . . . . 4·00 2·00

675 Moscow State University **676** Lenin Library

1957. 6th World Youth Festival (3rd issue). Moscow Views.

2108 – 40 k. black and brown . . 55 15
2109 – 40 k. black and purple . . 55 15
2110 – 1 r. black and blue . . . 1·10 30
2111 **675** 1 r. black and red . . . 1·10 30

DESIGNS—HORIZ: No. 2108, Kremlin; No. 2109, Stadium; No. 2110, Bolshoi State Theatre.

1957. Int Philatelic Exn, Moscow. Perf or imperf.

2112 **676** 40 k. turquoise 45 20

677 Dove of Peace encircling Globe **678** P. Beranger

1957. "Defence of Peace".

2113 **677** 40 k. multicoloured . . . 1·10 40
2114 1 r. multicoloured . . . . 2·50 1·25

1957. Birth Centenary of Clara Zetkin (German revolutionary). As T **615** but portrait of Zetkin.

2115 40 k. multicoloured . . . . . 1·00 20

1957. Death Centenary of Beranger (French poet).

2116 **678** 40 k. green . . . . 1·10 20

679 Krengholm Factory, Narva **680** Factory Plant and Statue of Lenin

1957. Centenary of Krengholm Textile Factory, Narva, Estonia.

2117 **679** 40 k. brown . . . . . . 1·00 20

1957. Centenary of Krasny Vyborzhetz Plant, Leningrad.

2118 **680** 40 k. blue 50 25

681 V. V. Stasov **682** Pigeon with Letter

1957. 50th Death Anniv of Stasov (art critic).

2119 **681** 40 k. brown 55 15
2120 1 r. blue . . . . 1·40 20

1957. International Correspondence Week.

2121 **682** 40 k. blue 35 20
2122 60 k. purple 85 25

683 K. E. Tsiolkovsky **684** Congress Emblem

1957. Birth Centenary of Tsiolkovsky (scientist).

2123 **683** 40 k. multicoloured . . . 6·75 1·40

1957. 4th World T.U.C., Leipzig.

2124 **684** 40 k. blue on blue . . . 45 20

685 Students **686** Workers and Emblem (Ukrane)

687 Lenin **688** Satellite encircling Globe

1957. 40th Anniv of Russian Revolution. (a) 1st issue. As T **685**. Multicoloured. Perf or imperf.

2125 10 k. Type **685** 20 10
2126 40 k. Railway worker (horiz) 50 30
2127 40 k. Portrait of Lenin on banner 30 10
2128 40 k. Lenin and workers with banners 40 25
2129 60 k. Harvester (horiz) . . 1·10 60

(b) 2nd issue. As T **686**, designs representing the Soviet Republics. Multicoloured.

2130 **686** 40 k. Ukraine 55 30
2131 – 40 k. Estonia 55 30
2132 – 40 k. Uzbekistan 55 30
2133 – 40 k. R.S.F.S.R. 75 30
2134 – 40 k. Byelorussia 55 30
2135 – 40 k. Lithuania 55 30
2136 – 40 k. Armenia 55 30
2137 – 40 k. Azerbaijan 55 30
2138 – 40 k. Georgia 55 30
2139 – 40 k. Kirghizia 55 30
2140 – 40 k. Turkmenistan . . . 55 30
2141 – 40 k. Tadzhikistan . . . 55 30
2142 – 40 k. Kazakhstan 55 30
2143 – 40 k. Latvia 55 30
2144 – 40 k. Moldavia 55 30

(c) 3rd Issue. As T **687**.

2145 **687** 40 k. blue . . . . 1·90 85
2146 – 60 k. red . . . . 1·90 80

DESIGN—HORIZ: 60 k. Lenin at desk.

1957. Launching of 1st Artifical Satellite.

2147 **688** 40 k. indigo on blue . . 3·00 85
2148 40 k. blue . . . . 3·25 1·00

689 Meteor Falling **690** Kuibyshev Power Station Turbine

1957. Sikhote-Alin Meteor.

2149 **689** 40 k. multicoloured . . . 2·40 1·10

1957. All Union Industrial Exhibition (1st issue).

2150 **690** 40 k. brown 85 20

See also Nos. 2168.

4/X-57 г. Первый в мире искусств. спутник Земли
(691)

692 Soviet War Memorial, Berlin

1957. First Artificial Satellite of the World. Optd with T **691**.
2151 **683** 40 k. multicoloured . . . 30·00 22·00

1957. Bicentenary of Academy of Arts, Moscow.
2152 – 40 k. black on salmon . . 25 10
2153 **692** 60 k. black 80 15
2154 – 1 r. black on pink . . . 1·60 30
DESIGNS—25½ × 37½ mm: 40 k. Academy and portraits of Bryullov, Repin and Surikov. 21½ × 32 mm: 1 r. Worker and Peasant Memorial, Moscow.

693 Arms of Ukraine

694 Garibaldi

1957. 40th Anniv of Ukraine S.S.R.
2155 **693** 40 k. multicoloured . . . 85 15

1957. 150th Birth Anniv of Garibaldi.
2156 **694** 40 k. purple, maroon and green 65 15

695 Edvard Grieg

696 Borovikovsky

1957. 50th Death Anniv of Grieg (composer).
2157 **695** 40 k. black on salmon . . 1·00 20

1957. Birth Bicent of Borovikovsky (painter).
2158 **696** 40 k. brown 65 15

1967. M. N. Ermolova (actress). Commemoration. As T **620** but portrait of Ermolova.
2159 40 k. brown and violet . . . 1·00 15

698 Y. Kolas

699 V. M. Kapsukas

700 G. Z. Bashindzhagian

1957. 75th Birth Anniv of Kolas (poet).
2160 **698** 40 k. black . . . . 2·40 1·50

1957. Kapsukas (Communist Party leader) Commem.
2161 **699** 40 k. brown . . . . . . 2·40 1·50

1957. Bashindzhagian (artist) Commemoration.
2162 **700** 40 k. brown . . . . . . 2·40 1·50

701 Kuibyshev Hydro-electric Station

702 Allegory of Progress

1957. 40th Anniv of Kuibyshev Hydro-electric Station.
2163 **701** 40 k. blue on flesh . . . 90 20

1957. Launching of 2nd Artificial Satellite.
2164 **702** 20 k. red and black . . . 1·00 10
2165 40 k. green and black . . 1·40 15
2166 60 k. brown and black . . 1·90 15
2167 1 r. blue and black . . 2·50 45

HAVE YOU READ THE NOTES AT THE BEGINNING OF THIS CATALOGUE?
These often provide the answers to the enquiries we receive.

703 Allegory of Industry

704 Tsi Bai-shi

1958. All Union Industrial Exn (2nd issue).
2168 **703** 60 k. red, black & lav . . 1·00 20

1958. Rosa Luxemburg Commemoration. As T **615** but portrait of Luxemburg (German revolutionary).
2169 40 k. brown and blue . . . 1·00 20

1958. Tsi Bai-shi (Chinese artist) Commem.
2170 **704** 40 k. violet 75 20

705 Linnaeus (Carl von Linne)

706 Tolstoi

1958. 250th Birth Anniv of Linnaeus.
2171 **705** 40 k. brown . . . . . . 3·25 75

1958. 75th Birth Anniv of A. N. Tolstoi (writer).
2172 **706** 40 k. bistre 65 20

707 Soldier, Sailor and Airman

708 E. Charents

1958. 40th Anniv of Red Army. Multicoloured.
2173 25 k. Battle of Narva, 1918 . 40 15
2174 40 k. Type **707** 60 20
2175 40 k. Soldier and blast-furnaceman (vert) 60 20
2176 40 k. Soldier and sailor (vert) 60 20
2177 60 k. Storming the Reichstag, 1945 . . . . 1·50 55

1958. Charents (Armenian poet) Commemoration.
2178 **708** 40 k. brown . . . . . . 2·40 2·00

709 Henry W. Longfellow

710 Blake

1958. 150th Birth Anniv of Longfellow.
2179 **709** 40 k. black . . . . . . 2·40 2·00

1958. Birth Bicentenary of William Blake (poet).
2180 **710** 40 k. black . . . . . . 2·40 2·40

711 Tchaikovsky

712 Admiral Rudnev and Cruiser "Varyag"

1958. Tchaikovsky International Music Competition, Moscow.
2181 **711** 40 k. multicoloured . . 85 30
2181 – 40 k. multicoloured . . 85 30
2183a – 1 r. purple and green . 3·25 1·00
DESIGNS—HORIZ: No. 2182, Scene from "Swan Lake" ballet. VERT: No. 2183, Pianist, violinist and inset portrait of Tchaikovsky.

1958. 45th Death Anniv of Admiral Rudnev.
2184 **712** 40 k. multicoloured . . 1·90 45

713 Gorky (writer)

714 Congress Emblem and Spassky Tower, Kremlin

1958. Gorky Commemoration.
2185 **713** 40 k. multicoloured . . . 1·00 20

1958. 13th Young Communists' League Congress, Moscow.
2186 **714** 40 k. violet on pink . . . 55 15
2187 60 k. red on flesh 80 20

715 Russian Pavilion

716 J. A. Komensky ("Comenius")

1958. Brussels Int Exhibition. Perf or imperf.
2188 **715** 10 k. multicoloured . . . 15 10
2189 40 k. multicoloured . . . 65 15

1958. Komensky Commem.
2190 **716** 40 k. green . . . . 3·25 1·40

717 Lenin

200 лет Академии художеств СССР. 1957
(718)

1958. Lenin Commemoration.
2191 **717** 40 k. blue 45 10
2192 60 k. red 55 25
2193 1 r. brown . . . . 1·50 45

1958. Bicentenary of Russian Academy of Artists. Optd with T **718**.
2194 **557** 40 k. multicoloured . . . 6·00 2·00

719 C. Goldoni

720 Lenin Prize Medal

1958. 250th Birth Anniv of C. Goldoni (Italian dramatist).
2195 **719** 40 k. brown and blue . . 1·00 15

1958. Lenin Prize Medal.
2196 **720** 40 k. red, yellow & brown 65 15

721 Karl Marx

1958. Karl Marx Commemoration.
2197 **721** 40 k. brown 65 15
2198 60 k. blue 80 25
2199 1 r. red . . . . 2·10 35

722 Federation Emblem

723 Radio Beacon, Airliner and Freighter

1958. 4th International Women's Federation Congress.
2200 **722** 40 k. blue and black . . . 45 15
2201 60 k. blue and black . . . 1·00 20

1958. Radio Day.
2202 **723** 40 k. green and red . . . 2·25 30

724 Chavchavadze

725 Flags of Communist Countries

1958. Chavchavadze (Georgian poet) Commem.
2203 **724** 40 k. black and blue . . 65 15

1958. Socialist Countries' Postal Ministers Conference, Moscow.
2204 **725** 40 k. multicoloured (A) . 17·00 6·75
2205 40 k. multicoloured (B) . 10·00 6·75
Central flag to left of inscription is in red, white and mauve. (A) has red at top and white at foot, (B) is vice versa.

726 Camp Bugler

727 Negro, European and Chinese Children

1958. "Pioneers" Day. Inscr "1958".
2206 **726** 10 k. multicoloured . . . 20 10
2207 – 25 k. multicoloured . . . 50 20
DESIGN: 25 k. Pioneer with model airplane.

1958. International Children's Day. Inscr "1958".
2208 **727** 40 k. multicoloured . . . 65 20
2209 – 40 k. multicoloured . . . 65 20
DESIGN: No. 2209, Child with toys, and atomic bomb.

728 Fooballers and Globe

729 Rimsky-Korsakov

1958. World Cup Football Championship, Sweden. Perf or imperf.
2210 **728** 40 k. multicoloured . . . 85 20
2211 60 k. multicoloured . . . 1·40 40

1958. Rimsky-Korsakov (composer) Commem.
2212 **729** 40 k. brown and blue . . 1·10 20

730 Athlete

1958. 14th World Gymnastic Championships, Moscow. Inscr "XIV". Multicoloured.
2213 40 k. Type **730** 60 15
2214 40 k. Gymnast 60 15

731 Young Construction Workers

1958. Russian Youth Day.
2215 **731** 40 k. orange and blue . 50 15
2216 60 k. orange and green . 60 20

732 Atomic Bomb, Globe, Sputniks, Atomic Symbol and "Lenin" (atomic ice-breaker)

733 Rifleman and Gun Crew

1958. International Disarmament Conf, Stockholm.
2217 **732** 60 k. black, orge & bl 3·75 65

1958. 40th Anniv of Ukrainian Communist Party.
2218 **733** 40 k. violet and red . . . 1·00 30

734 Silhouette of Moscow State University **735** Sadruddin Aini

1958. 5th Int Architects Union Congress, Moscow.
2219 **734** 40 k. blue and red . . . 1·00 15
2220 – 60 k. multicoloured . . . 1·40 25
DESIGN—VERT: 60 k. "U.I.A. Moscow 1958" in square panel of bricks and "V" in background.

1958. 80th Birth Anniv of Sadruddin Aini (Tadzhik writer).
2221 **735** 40 k. red, black & buff . 55 15

736 Third Artificial Satellite **737** Conference Emblem

1958. Launching of 3rd Artificial Satellite.
2222 **736** 40 k. red, blue & green . 1·60 50

1958. 1st World T.U. Young Workers' Conf, Prague.
2223 **737** 40 k. blue and purple . . 30 20

738 Tupolev Tu-110

1958. Civil Aviation. Perf or imperf.
2224 – 20 k. black, red & blue . 50 10
2225 – 40 k. black, red & green . 65 15
2226 – 40 k. black, red & blue . 65 15
2227 – 60 k. red, buff & blue . . 65 20
2228 **738** 60 k. black and red . . . 65 20
2229 – 1 r. black, red & orange . 1·50 30
2230 – 2 r. black, red & purple . 2·75 45
DESIGNS—Russian aircraft flying across globe: No. 2224, Ilyushin Il-14M; 2225, Tupolev Tu-104; 2226, Tupolev Tu-114; 2229, Antonov An-10; 2230, Ilyushin Il-18B. No. 2227, Global air routes.

739 L. A. Kulik (scientist)

1958. 50th Anniv of Tunguz Meteor.
2231 **739** 40 k. multicoloured . . . 1·90 40

740 Crimea Observatory **741** 15th-century Scribe

1958. 10th International Astronomical Union Congress, Moscow.
2232 **740** 40 k. turquoise & brown 1·25 30
2233 – 60 k. yellow, violet & bl . 1·60 30
2234 – 1 r. brown and blue . . 2·00 50
DESIGNS—HORIZ: 60 k. Moscow University. VERT: 1 r. Telescope of Moscow Observatory.

1958. Centenary of 1st Russian Postage Stamp.
2235 **741** 10 k. multicoloured . . . 15 10
2236 – 10 k. multicoloured . . . 15 10
2237 – 25 k. blue, black & green 30 10
2238 – 25 k. black and blue . . 30 10
2239 – 40 k. brown, pur & sep . 40 15
2240 – 40 k. lake and brown . . 40 15
2241 – 40 k. black, orange and red 40 15
2242 – 60 k. turquoise, blk & vio 1·50 25
2243 – 60 k. black, turquoise and purple . . . . . . 1·10 25
2244 – 1 r. multicoloured . . . 1·90 85
2245 – 1 r. purple, black and orange . . . . 1·90 85
DESIGNS—HORIZ: No. 2236, 16th-century courier; 2237, Ordin-Nastchokin (17th-century postal administrator) and postal sleigh coach; 2238, 18th-century mail coach; 2239, Reproduction of Lenin portrait stamp of 1947; 2240, 19th-century postal troika (three-horse sleigh); 2241, Russian Tupolev Tu-104 jet airliner; 2242, Parcel post train; 2243, V. N. Podbielsky (postal administrator, 1918-20) and postal scenes; 2244, Parcel post Tupolev Tu-104 aircraft; 2245, Globe and modern forms of mail transport.

741a Facade of Exhibition Building **742** Vladimir Gateway

1958. Stamp Cent Philatelic Exhibition, Leningrad.
2246 **741a** 40 k. brown & lt brn . 40 20

1956. 850th Anniv of Town of Vladimir. Mult.
2247 40 k. Type **742** 60 15
2248 60 k. Street scene in Vladimir 1·00 20

743 M. Chigorin **745** Red Cross Nurse and Patient

1958. 50th Death Anniv of Chigorin (chess player).
2249 **743** 40 k. green and black . 1·75 20

1958. 40th Anniv of Red Cross and Crescent Societies.
2254 **745** 40 k. multicoloured . . 85 20
2255 – 40 k. red, yellow and bistre 85 20
DESIGN: No. 2255, Convalescent home.

746 Saltykov-Shchedrin (after I. Kramskoi) and Scene from his Works **747** V. Kapnist

1958. 69th Death Anniv of Mikhail Saltykov-Shchedrin (writer).
2256 **746** 40 k. black and purple . 75 15
For similar stamps see Nos. 2316/22 and 2458.

1958. Birth Bicentenary of V. Kapnist (poet).
2257 **747** 40 k. black and blue . . 1·10 15

748 Yerevan, Armenia

1958. Republican Capitals.
2258 40 k. brown (T **748**) 55 20
2259 40 k. violet (Baku, Azerbaijan) 55 20
2260 40 k. brown (Minsk, Byelorussia) 55 20
2261 40 k. blue (Tbilisi, Georgia) 55 20
2262 40 k. green (Tallin, Estonia) 55 20
2263 40 k. green (Alma-Ata, Kazakhstan) 55 20
2264 40 k. blue (Frunze, Kirgizia) 55 20
2265 40 k. brown (Riga, Latvia) . 55 20
2266 40 k. red (Vilnius, Lithuania) 55 20
2267 40 k. bistre (Kishinev, Moldavia) 55 20
2268 40 k. violet (Moscow, R.S.F.S.R.) 55 20
2269 40 k. blue (Stalinabad, Tadzhikistan) 55 20
2270 40 k. green (Ashkhabad, Turkmenistan) 55 20
2271 40 k. mauve (Kiev, Ukraine) 55 20
2272 40 k. black (Tashkent, Uzbekistan) 55 20
See also No. 2940.

749 Open Book, Torch, Lyre and Flowers **750** Rudaki

1958. Asian-African Writers' Conference, Tashkent.
2273 **749** 40 k. orange, black and olive . . . . 1·00 15

1958. 1100th Birth Anniv of Rudaki (Tadzhik poet and musician).
2274 **750** 40 k. multicoloured . . 60 15

751 Mounted Georgian (statue)

1958. 1500th Anniv of Founding of Tblisi (Georgian capital).
2275 **751** 40 k. multicoloured . . . 1·00 20

752 Chelyabinsk Tractor Plant

1958. 25th Anniv of Industrial Plants.
2276 **752** 40 k. green and yellow . . 80 20
2277 – 40 k. blue & light blue . . 55 20
2278 – 40 k. lake & light orge . . 80 20
DESIGNS: No. 2277, Ural machine construction plant; No. 2278, Zaporozhe foundry plant.

753 Young Revolutionary **754** Marx and Lenin (bas-relief)

1958. 40th Anniv of Young Communists League. Multicoloured.
2279 10 k. Type **753** 15 10
2280 20 k. Riveters 30 10
2281 25 k. Soldier 35 15
2282 40 k. Harvester 50 15
2283 60 k. Builder 80 20
2284 1 r. Students . . . . 2·00 75

1958. 41st Anniv of October Revolution.
2285 **754** 40 k. black, yell & red . . 65 20
2286 – 1 r. multicoloured . . . . 1·10 50
DESIGN—HORIZ: 1 r. Lenin with student, peasant and miner.

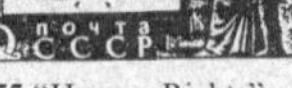

755 "Human Rights" **756** Yesenin

1958. 10th Anniv of Declaration of Human Rights.
2287 **755** 60 k. blue, black & buff . 65 15

1958. 30th Death Anniv of Sergei Yesenin (poet).
2288 **756** 40 k. multicoloured . . . 30 15

757 Kuan Han-ching **758** Ordzhonikidze

1958. Kuan Han-ching (Chinese playwright) Commemoration.
2289 **757** 40 k. black and blue . . 35 15

1958. 21st Death Anniv of G. K. Ordzhonikidze (statesman).
2290 **758** 40 k. multicoloured . . . 65 15

759 John Milton **760** Lenin's Statue, Minsk

1958. 350th Birth Anniv of John Milton (poet).
2291 **759** 40 k. brown . . . . . . 1·00 15

1958. 40th Anniv of Byelorussian Republic.
2292 **760** 40 k. brown, grey & red . 50 15

761 Fuzuli **762** Census Emblem

1958. Fuzuli (Azerbaijan poet). Commemoration.
2293 **761** 40 k. bistre & turquoise . 1·00 15

1958. All Union Census, 1959. Multicoloured.
2294 40 k. Type **762** 25 15
2295 40 k. Census official with workers family 25 15

763 Eleonora Duse **764** Rule

1958. Birth Centenary of Eleonora Duse (Italian actress).
2296 **763** 40 k. black, grey & grn . 1·00 20

1958. Death Centenary of K. F. Rule (naturalist).
2297 **764** 40 k. black and blue . . 1·10 20

765 Atomic Ice-breaker "Lenin" **766** Moon Rocket and Sputniks

1958. All-Union Industrial Exhibition. Mult.
2298 40 k. Type **765** . . . . 2·50 65
2299 60 k. "TE 3" diesel loco . . 5·50 1·50

1959. 21st Communist Party Congress, Moscow.
2300 – 40 k. multicoloured . . . 55 25
2301 – 60 k. multicoloured . . . 65 40
2302 **766** 1 r. multicoloured . . . 2·75 1·40
DESIGNS: 40 k. Lenin, Red Banner and Kremlin view; 60 k. Workers beside Lenin hydro-electric plant, Volga River.

767 E. Torricelli **768** Ice Skater

1959. 350th Birth Anniv of Torricelli (physicist).
2303 **767** 40 k. black and green . . 80 20

1959. Women's World Ice Skating Championships, Sverdlovsk.
2304 **768** 25 k. multicoloured . . . 40 10
2305 40 k. black, blue & grey 60 20

769 Charles Darwin **770** N. Gamaleya

1959. 150th Birth Anniv of Charles Darwin (naturalist).
2306 **769** 40 k. brown and blue . . 75 15

1959. Birth Centenary of Gamaleya (microbiologist).
2307 **770** 40 k. black and red . . . 1·10 50

771 Sholem Aleichem

Победа баскетбольной команды СССР. Чили 1959 г.
(772)

1959. Birth Centenary of Aleichem (Jewish writer).
2308 **771** 40 k. brown 1·00 15

1959. Russian (Unofficial) Victory in World Basketball Championships, Chile. No. 1851 optd with T **772**.
2309 – 1 r. brown and drab 8·25 5·75

1959. Birth Bicent of Robert Burns. Optd **1759 1959**.
2310 **627** 40 k. brown and blue 15·00 15·00

774 Selma Lagerlof **775** P. Cvirka

1959. Birth Centenary of Selma Lagerlof (Swedish writer).
2311 **774** 40 k. black, brown and cream 1·10 50

1959. 50th Birth Anniv of Cvirka (Lithuanian poet).
2312 **775** 40 k. black and red on yellow 45 15

776 F. Joliot-Curie (scientist) **777** Popov and Polar Rescue by "Ermak"

1959. Joliot-Curie Commemoration.
2313 **776** 40 k. black and turquoise 1·25 30

1959. Birth Centenary of A. S. Popov (radio pioneer).
2314 **777** 40 k. brown, blk & blue 1·00 30
2315 – 60 k. multicoloured 1·50 55
DESIGN: 60 k. Popov and radio tower.

1959. Writers as T **746**. Inscr "1959".
2316 40 k. grey, black and red 90 20
2317 40 k. brown, sepia & yellow 90 20
2318 40 k. brown and violet 90 20
2319 40 k. multicoloured 90 20
2320 40 k. black, olive & yellow 90 20
2321 40 k. multicoloured 1·00 20
2322 40 k. slate and violet 90 20
PORTRAITS (with scene from works): No. 2316, Anton Chekhov; 2317, Ivan Krylov (after K. Bryullov); 2318, Aleksandr Ostrovsky; 2319, Aleksandr Griboedov (after I. Kramskoi); 2320, Nikolai Gogol (after F. Moller); 2321, Sergei Aksakov (after I. Kramskoi); 2322, Aleksei Koltsov (after K. Gorbunov).

778 Saadi (Persian poet)

1959. Saadi Commemoration.
2323 **778** 40 k. black and blue 45 15

779 Orbeliani (Georgian writer) **780** Ogata Korin

1959. Orbeliani Commemoration.
2324 **779** 40 k. black and red 45 15

1959. Birth Tercentenary of Ogata Korin (Japanese artist).
2325 **780** 40 k. multicoloured 2·50 2·00

781 "Rossiya" on Odessa-Batum Service

1959. Russian Liners. Multicoloured.
2326 10 k. "Sovetsky Soyuz" on Vladivostok–Kamchatka service 30 15
2327 20 k. "Feliks Dzerzhinsky" on Odessa–Latakia service 45 15
2328 40 k. Type **781** 70 15
2329 40 k. "Kooperatsiya" on Murmansk–Tyksi service 70 15
2330 60 k. "Mikhail Kalinin" leaving Leningrad 90 15
2331 1 r. "Baltika" on Leningrad–London service 1·25 30

782 Trajectory of Moon Rocket **783** Lenin

1959. Launching of Moon Rocket. Inscr "2-1-1959".
2332 **782** 40 k. brown and pink 1·00 20
2333 – 40 k. blue & light blue 1·00 20
DESIGN: No. 2333, Preliminary route of moon rocket after launching.

1959. 89th Birth Anniv of Lenin.
2334 **783** 40 k. brown 1·00 50

784 M. Cachin **785** Youths with Banner

1959. 90th Birth Anniv of Marcel Cachin (French communist leader).
2335 **784** 60 k. brown 85 20

1959. 10th Anniv of World Peace Movement.
2336 **785** 40 k. multicoloured 55 20

786 A. von Humboldt

1959. Death Centenary of Alexander von Humboldt (German naturalist).
2337 **786** 40 k. brown and violet 1·00 15

787 Haydn **788** Mountain Climbing

1959. 150th Death Anniv of Haydn (Austrian composer).
2338 **787** 40 k. brown and blue 85 20

1959. Tourist Publicity. Multicoloured.
2339 40 k. Type **788** 65 20
2340 40 k. Map reading 65 20
2341 40 k. Cross country skiing 65 20
2342 40 k. Canoeing (horiz) 65 20

789 Exhibition Emblem and New York Coliseum **790** Statue of Repin (painter)

1959. Russian Scientific, Technological and Cultural Exhibition, New York.
2343 **789** 20 k. multicoloured 30 15
2344 40 k. multicoloured 50 15

1959. Cultural Celebrities. Inscr "1959". Statues in black.
2345 **790** 10 k. ochre 15 10
2346 – 10 k. red 15 10
2347 – 20 k. lilac 25 10
2348 – 25 k. turquoise 60 10
2349 – 60 k. green 85 10
2350 – 1 r. blue 1·25 55
STATUES: 10 k. (No. 2346), Lenin; 20 k. V. Mayakovsky (poet); 25 k. Pushkin; 60 k. Gorky; 1 r. Tchaikovsky.

791 Sturgeon **792** Louis Braille

1959. Fisheries Protection.
2350a – 20 k. black and blue 30 10
2350b – 25 k. brown and lilac 50 10
2351 **791** 40 k. black & turquoise 55 15
2351a – 40 k. purple and mauve 70 15
2352 – 60 k. black and blue 85 30
DESIGNS: 20 k. Perch; 25 k. Northern fur seals; 40 k. (No. 2351a), Salmon; 60 k. Salmon and map.

1959. 150th Birth Anniv of Braille (inventor of Braille).
2353 **792** 60 k. brown, yell & turq 65 20

793 Musa Djalil (Tatar poet) **794** Vaulting

1959. Djalil Commemoration.
2354 **793** 40 k. black and violet 65 15

1959. 2nd Russian Spartakiad. Inscr "1959".
2355 **794** 15 k. grey and purple 20 10
2356 – 25 k. grey, brown & grn 30 10
2357 – 30 k. olive and red 30 10
2358 – 60 k. grey, blue & yellow 85 15
DESIGNS—HORIZ: 25 k. Running; 60 k. Water polo. VERT: 30 k. Athletes supporting Spartakiad emblem.

795 **796** Steel Worker

1959. 2nd International T.U. Conference, Leipzig.
2359 **795** 40 k. red, blue & yellow 65 15

1959. Seven Year Plan.
2360 – 10 k. red, blue & violet 10 10
2361 – 10 k. light red, deep red and yellow 10 10
2362 – 15 k. red, yellow & brn 10 10
2363 – 15 k. brn, grn & bistre 10 10
2364 – 20 k. red, yellow & grn 15 10
2365 – 20 k. multicoloured 15 10
2366 – 30 k. red, flesh & purple 30 10
2366a – 30 k. multicoloured 30 10
2367 **796** 40 k. orange, yell & bl 35 10
2368 – 40 k. red, pink and blue 35 10
2369 – 60 k. red, blue & yellow 80 25
2370 – 60 k. red, buff and blue 80 25
DESIGNS: No. 2360, Chemist; No. 2361, Spassky Tower, hammer and sickle; No. 2362, Builder's labourer; No. 2363, Farm girl; No. 2364, Machine minder; No. 2365, Tractor driver; No. 2366, Oil technician; No. 2366a, Cloth production; No. 2368, Coal miner; No. 2369, Iron moulder; No. 2370, Power station.

797 Glaciologist **798** Novgorod

1959. International Geophysical Year (2nd issue).
2371 **797** 10 k. turquoise 60 15
2372 – 25 k. red and blue 1·25 15
2373 – 40 k. red and blue 3·50 30
2373a – 1 r. blue and yellow 2·50 75
DESIGNS: 25 k. Oceanographic survey ship 'Vityaz'; 40 k. Antarctic map, camp and emperor penguin; 1 r. Observatory and rocket.

1959. 11th Centenary of Novgorod.
2374 **798** 40 k. red, brown & blue 40 15

799 Schoolboys in Workshop **800** Exhibition Emblem

1959. Industrial Training Scheme for School-leavers. Inscr "1959".
2375 **799** 40 k. violet 30 10
2376 – 1 r. blue 1·00 30
DESIGN: 1 r. Children at night-school.

1959. All Union Exhibition.
2377 **800** 40 k. multicoloured 55 20

801 Russian and Chinese Students

1959. 10th Anniv of Chinese Peoples' Republic.
2378 **801** 20 k. multicoloured 20 15
2379 – 40 k. multicoloured 50 20
DESIGN: 40 k. Russian miner and Chinese foundryman.

802 Postwoman **803** Mahtumkuli

1959. International Correspondence Week.
2380 **802** 40 k. multicoloured 40 15
2381 60 k. multicoloured 70 20

1959. 225th Birth Anniv of Mahtumkuli (Turkestan writer).
2382 **803** 40 k. brown 65 15

804 Arms and Workers of the German Democratic Republic **805** Lunik 3's Trajectory around the Moon

1959. 10th Anniv of German Democratic Republic.
2383 **804** 40 k. multicoloured 35 10
2384 – 60 k. purple and cream 65 15
DESIGN—VERT: 60 k. Town Hall, East Berlin.

1959. Launching of "Lunik 3" Rocket.
2385 **805** 40 k. violet 1·90 20

806 Republican Arms and Emblem **807** Red Square, Moscow

1959. 30th Anniv of Tadzhikistan Republic.
2386 **806** 40 k. multicoloured 85 15

1959. 42nd Anniv of October Revolution.
2387 **807** 40 k. red 65 15

808 Capitol, Washington and Kremlin, Moscow

1959. Visit of Russian Prime Minister to U.S.A.
2388 **808** 60 k. blue and yellow 1·00 25

809 Mil Mi-1 Helicopter

1959. Military Sports.
2389 **809** 10 k. red and violet . . . 30 10
2390 – 25 k. brown and blue . . 40 10
2391 – 40 k. blue and brown . . 60 15
2392 – 60 k. bistre and blue . . 90 25
DESIGNS: 25 k. Skin diver; 40 k. Racing motor cyclist; 60 k. Parachutist.

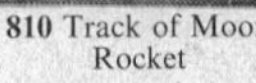

810 Track of Moon Rocket

811 Statue and Aerial View of Budapest

1959. Landing of Russian Rocket on Moon. Inscr "14.IX.1959". Multicoloured.
2393 40 k. Type **810** . . . . 1·00 20
2394 40 k. Diagram of flight trajectory . . . . 1·00 20

1959. Hungarian Republic Commem. Mult.
2395 20 k. Petofi (Hungarian poet) (horiz) 25 15
2396 40 k. Type **811** 45 20

812 Manolis Glezos (Greek Communist)

1959. Glezos Commemoration.
2397 **812** 40 k. brown and blue . . 15·00 11·50

813 A. Voskresensky (chemist)

814 River Chusovaya

1959. Voskresensky Commemoration.
2398 **813** 40 k. brown and blue . . 85 20

1959. Tourist Publicity. Inscr "1959".
2399 **814** 10 k. violet 15 10
2400 – 10 k. mauve 15 10
2401 – 25 k. blue 30 10
2402 – 25 k. red 30 10
2403 – 25 k. olive 30 10
2404 – 40 k. red 50 10
2405 – 60 k. turquoise 65 15
2406 – 1 r. green . . . . 2·25 60
2407 – 1 r. orange . . . . 1·10 60
DESIGNS: No. 2400, Riza Lake, Caucasus; No. 2401, River Lena; No. 2402, Iskanderkuly Lake; No. 2403, Coastal region; No. 2404, Lake Baikal; No. 2405, Beluha Mountains, Altay; No. 2406, Hibinsky Mountain; No. 2407, Gursuff region, Crimea.

815 "The Trumpeters of the First Horse Army" (after Grekov)

1959. 40th Anniv of Russian Cavalry.
2408 **815** 40 k. multicoloured . . . 85 20

816 A. P. Chekhov and Moscow Residence

817 M. V. Frunze

1960. Birth Centenary of Chekhov (writer).
2409 **816** 20 k. red, brown and violet 25 10
2410 – 40 k. brown, bl & sepia 75 15
DESIGN: 40 k. Chekhov and Yalta residence.

1960. 75th Birth Anniv of M. V. Frunze (military leader).
2411 **817** 40 k. brown 55 15

818 G. N. Gabrichevsky

819 Vera Komissarzhevskaya

1960. Birth Centenary of G. N. Gabrichevsky (microbiologist).
2412 **818** 40 k. brown and violet . 1·00 50

1960. 50th Death Anniv of V. F. Komissarzhevskaya (actress).
2413 **819** 40 k. brown 50 15

820 Free-skating

1960. Winter Olympic Games.
2414 – 10 k. blue and orange . . 50 10
2415 – 25 k. multicoloured . . 65 10
2416 – 40 k. orange, blue & pur 85 10
2417 **820** 60 k. violet, brown & grn 1·40 20
2418 – 1 r. blue, red and green . 2·10 35
DESIGNS: 10 k. Ice hockey; 25 k. Ice skating; 40 k. Skiing; 1 r. Ski jumping.

821 Timur Frunze (fighter pilot) and Air Battle

822 Mil Mi-4 Helicopter over Kremlin

1960. War Heroes. Multicoloured.
2419 40 k. Type **821** . . . . . 1·25 20
2420 1 r. Gen. Cherniakovksy and battle scene . . . . . . 1·10 40

1960. Air.
2421 **822** 60 k. blue . . . . 1·25 20

823 Women of Various Races

824 "Swords into Ploughshares"

1960. 50th Anniv of International Women's Day.
2422 **823** 40 k. multicoloured . . 85 20

1960. Presentation of Statue by Russia to U.N.
2423 **824** 40 k. yellow, bistre and blue 65 15

15 лет освобождения Венгрии

(**825**)

826 Lenin when a Child

1960. 15th Anniv of Liberation of Hungary. Optd with T **825**.
2424 **811** 40 k. multicoloured . . 4·25 3·25

1960. 90th Birth Anniv of Lenin. Portraits of Lenin. Multicoloured.
2425 **826** 10 k. multicoloured . . 10 10
2426 – 20 k. multicoloured . . 15 10
2427 – 30 k. multicoloured . . 25 15
2428 – 40 k. multicoloured . . 30 15
2429 – 60 k. multicoloured . . 1·40 25
2430 – 1 r. brown, blue & red . 1·40 40
DESIGNS: Lenin: 20 k. holding child; 30 k. and revolutionary scenes; 40 k. with party banners; 60 k. and industrial scenes; 1 r. with globe and rejoicing people.

827 Lunik 3 photographing Moon

828 Government House, Baku

1960. Flight of Lunik 3. Inscr "7.X.1959".
2431 **827** 40 k. yellow and blue . . 90 50
2432 – 60 k. yellow, blue & ind . 90 50
DESIGN: 60 k. Lunar map.

1960. 40th Anniv of Azerbaijan Republic.
2433 **828** 40 k. brown, bis & yell . 50 15

829 "Fraternization" (after Pokorny)

830 Furnaceman

1960. 15th Anniv of Czechoslovak Republic.
2434 **829** 40 k. black and blue . . . 30 10
2435 – 60 k. brown and yellow . 85 15
DESIGN: 60 k. Charles Bridge, Prague.

1960. Completion of First Year of Seven Year Plan.
2436 **830** 40 k. brown and red . . . 30 15

831 Popov Museum, Leningrad

1960. Radio Day.
2437 **831** 40 k. multicoloured . . . 1·00 15

832 Robert Schumann

833 Sverdlov

1960. 150th Birth Anniv of Schumann (composer).
2438 **832** 40 k. black and blue . . . 85 15

1960. 75th Birth Anniv of Ya. M. Sverdlov (statesman).
2439 **833** 40 k. sepia and brown . . 85 10

834 Magnifier and Stamp

1960. Philatelists' Day.
2440 **834** 60 k. multicoloured . . . 1·00 15

835 Petrozavodsk (Karelian Republic)

1960. Capitals of Autonomous Republic (1st issue).
2441 **835** 40 k. turquoise 85 20
2442 – 40 k. blue 85 20
2443 – 40 k. green 85 20
2444 – 40 k. purple 85 20
2445 – 40 k. red 85 20
2446 – 40 k. blue 60 20
2447 – 40 k. brown 90 20
2448 – 40 k. brown 60 20
2449 – 40 k. red 60 20
2450 – 40 k. brown 60 20
CAPITALS: Nos. 2442, Batumi (Adzharian); No. 2443, Izhevsk (Udmurt); No. 2444, Grozny (Chechen-Ingush); No. 2445, Cheboksary (Chuvash); No. 2446, Yakutsk (Yakut); No. 2447, Ordzhonikidze (North Ossetian); No. 2448, Nukus (Kara-Kalpak); No. 2449, Makhachkala (Daghestan); No. 2450, Yoshkar-Ola (Mari).
See also Nos. 2586/92 and 2703/5.

836 Children of Different Races

838 Rocket

1960. International Children's Day. Multicoloured.
2451 10 k. Type **836** 15 10
2452 20 k. Children on farm (vert) 25 15
2453 25 k. Children with snowman 40 15
2454 40 k. Children in zoo gardens 65 20

1960. 40th Anniv of Karelian Autonomous Republic. Optd **40 лет КАССР 8.VI.1960.**
2455 **835** 40 k. turquoise . . . . . 1·60 90

1960. Launching of Cosmic Rocket "Spacecraft 1" (first "Vostok" type spacecraft).
2456 **838** 40 k. red and blue . . . 1·90 60

839 I.F.A.C. Emblem

1960. 1st International Automation Control Federation Congress, Moscow.
2457 **839** 60 k. brown and yellow . 1·60 30

1960. Kosta Hetagurov Commem. As T **746**. Inscr "1960".
2458 40 k. brown and blue 85 15
DESIGN: 40 k. Portrait of Hetagurov and scene from his works.

840 Cement Works, Belgorod

1960. 1st Plant Construction of Seven Year Plan.
2459 **840** 25 k. black and blue . . 25 10
2460 – 40 k. black and red . . . 40 10
DESIGN. 40 k. Metal works, Novokrivorog.

841 Capstans and Cogwheel

1960. Industrial Mass-Production Plant.
2461 **841** 40 k. turquoise 65 10
2462 – 40 k. purple (Factory plant) 65 10

842 Vilnius (Lithuania)

1960. 20th Anniv of Soviet Baltic Republics. Multicoloured.
2463 40 k. Type **842** 45 10
2464 40 k. Riga (Latvia) 45 10
2465 40 k. Tallin (Estonia) 45 10

843 Running

Международная ярмарка в Риччоне

(**844**)

1960. Olympic Games. Inscr "1960". Multicoloured.
2466 5 k. Type **843** 15 10
2467 10 k. Wrestling 20 10
2468 15 k. Basketball 35 10
2469 20 k. Weightlifting 35 10
2470 25 k. Boxing 35 10
2471 40 k. High diving 50 15
2472 40 k. Fencing 50 15
2473 40 k. Gymnastics 50 15
2474 60 k. Canoeing 80 20
2475 1 r. Horse jumping . . . . 2·00 45

1960. 20th Anniv of Moldavian Republic. As T **842**.
2476 40 k. multicoloured 45 10
DESIGN: 40 k. Kishinev (capital).

1960. International Exhibition, Riccione. No. 2471 optd with T **844**.
2477 40 k. multicoloured . . . . . 15·00 10·00

845 "Agriculture and Industry" **846** G. H. Minkh

1960. 15th Anniv of Vietnam Democratic Republic.
2478 40 k. Type **845** 65 15
2479 60 k. Book Museum, Hanoi (vert) 85 20

1960. 125th Birth Anniv of G. H. Minkh (epidemiologist).
2480 **846** 60 k. brown and bistre . 70 15

847 "March" (after I. Levitan)

1960. Birth Centenary of I. Levitan (painter).
2481 **847** 40 k. black and olive . . 80 15

848 "Forest" (after Shishkin)

1960. 5th World Forestry Congress, Seattle.
2482 **848** 1 r. brown . . . . 2·50 75

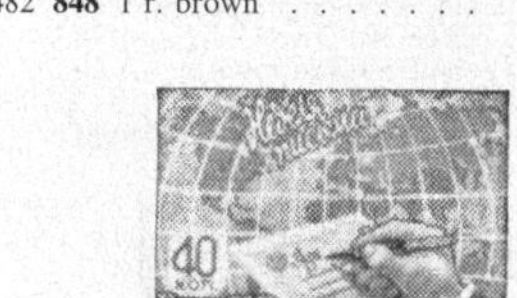

849 Addressing Letter

1960. International Correspondence Week.
2483 **849** 40 k. multicoloured . . . 40 10
2484 60 k. multicoloured . . . 70 20

850 Kremlin, Dogs "Belka" and "Strelka" and Rocket Trajectory

1960. 2nd Cosmic Rocket Flight.
2485 **850** 40 k. purple and yellow . 80 15
2486 1 r. blue and orange . . 1·90 25

851 Globes **852** People of Kazakhstan

1960. 15th Anniv of W.F.T.U.
2487 **851** 60 k. bl, drab & lilac . . 80 15

1960. 40th Anniv of Kazakh Soviet Republic.
2488 **852** 40 k. multicoloured . . . 50 10

853 "Karl Marx" **854** A. N. Voronikhin and Leningrad Cathedral

1960. River Boats. Multicoloured.
2489 25 k. Type **853** 45 10
2490 40 k. "Lenin" 65 15
2491 60 k. "Raketa" (hydro foil) . 1·10 25

1960. Birth Bicentenary of A. N. Voronikhin (architect)
2492 **854** 40 k. black and grey . . 45 10

855 Motor Coach **856** J. S. Gogebashvily

1960. Russian Motor Industry.
2493 – 25 k. black and blue . . 40 10
2494 – 40 k. blue and olive . . 55 15
2495 – 60 k. red and turquoise . 85 20
2496 **855** 1 r. multicoloured . . . 1·75 35
DESIGNS: 25 k. Lorry; 40 k. "Volga" car; 60 k. "Moskvich" car.

1960. 120th Birth Anniv of J. S. Gogebashvily (Georgian teacher).
2497 **856** 40 k. black and lake . . 45 10

857 Industrial Plant and Power Plant **858** Federation Emblem

1960. 43rd Anniv of October Revolution.
2498 **857** 40 k. multicoloured . . 55 15

1960. 15th Anniv of International Federation of Democratic Women.
2499 **858** 60 k. red and grey . . . 55 15

859 Youth of Three Races

40 лет Удмуртской АССР
4/XI 1960.
(860)

1960. 15th Anniv of World Democratic Youth Federation.
2500 **859** 60 k. multicoloured . . 80 15

1960. 40th Anniv of Udmurt Autonomous Republic. No. 2443 optd with T **860**.
2501 40 k. green . . . . 2·00 90

861 Tolstoi and his Moscow Residence **862** Government House, Yerevan

1960. 50th Death Anniv of Leo Tolstoi (writer).
2502 **861** 20 k. multicoloured . . 25 15
2503 – 40 k. brown, sepia & bl 40 15
2504 – 60 k. multicoloured . . 1·00 25
DESIGNS—HORIZ: 40 k. Tolstoi and his country estate. VERT: 60 k. Full face portrait.

1960. 40th Anniv of Armenian Republic.
2205 **862** 40 k. multicoloured . . 45 10

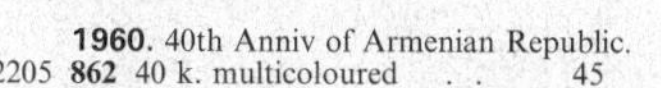

863 Students and University **864** Tulip

1960. Opening of Friendship University, Moscow.
2506 **863** 40 k. purple 45 10

1960. Russian Flowers. Multicoloured.
2507 20 k. Type **864** 30 10
2508 20 k. Autumn crocus 30 10
2509 25 k. Marsh marigold . . . 30 10
2510 40 k. Tulip 40 10
2511 40 k. Panax 40 10
2512 60 k. Hypericum 75 25
2513 60 k. Iris 75 25
2514 1 r. Wild rose . . . . . . 1·50 40

865 Engels **866** Mark Twain

1960. 140th Birth Anniv of Engels.
2515 **865** 60 k. grey . . . . 1·40 20

1960. 125th Birth Anniv of Mark Twain.
2516 **866** 40 k. bistre and orange . 3·00 1·90

867 N. Pirogov **868** Chopin

1960. 150th Birth Anniv of N. Pirogov (surgeon).
2517 **867** 40 k. brown and green . . 65 10

1960. 150th Birth Anniv of Chopin.
2518 **868** 40 k. bistre and buff . . . 1·10 20

869 North Korean Flag and Emblem **870** Lithuanian Costumes

1960. 15th Anniv of Korean Liberation.
2519 **869** 40 k. multicoloured . . . 70 15

1960. Provincial Costumes (1st issue). Inscr "1960". Multicoloured.
2520 10 k. Type **870** 35 15
2521 60 k. Uzbek costumes . . . . 1·10 25
See also Nos. 2537/45, 2796 and 2835/8.

871 A. Tseretely

1960. 120th Birth Anniv of A. Tseretely (Georgian poet).
2522 **871** 40 k. purple and lilac . . 1·00 10

Currency Revalued.

10 (old) Kopeks = 1 (new) Kopek

872 Worker **873** "Ruslan and Lyudmila"

1961. Inscr "1961".
2531 **872** 1 k. bistre 65 10
2524 – 2 k. green 25 10
2525 – 3 k. violet . . . . 1·60 10
2526 – 4 k. red 45 10
2526a – 4 k. brown . . . . . . 4·00 4·00
2527 – 6 k. red . . . . 2·00 30
2528 – 6 k. claret . . . . 1·40 10
2529 – 10 k. orange . . . . . . 1·00 10
2533 – 12 k. purple . . . . . . 1·40 10
2530 – 16 k. blue . . . . 2·75 15
DESIGNS: 2 k. Combine harvester; 3 k. Cosmic rocket; 4 k. Soviet Arms and Flag; 6 k. Spassky Tower and Kremlin; 10 k. Workers statue; 12 k. Monument and Spassky Tower; 16 k. Airliner over power station.

1961. Russian Wild Life. As T **653** but inscr "1961". Centres in natural colours. Frame colours given.
2534 1 k. sepia (Brown bear) . . . 25 15
2535 6 k. black (Eurasian beaver) . 1·00 20
2536 10 k. black (Roe deer) . . . 1·25 55
The 1 k. is vert and the rest horiz.

1961. Provincial Costumes (2nd issue). As T **870** but inscr "1961".
2537 2 k. red, brown & stone . . . 40 10
2538 2 k. multicoloured 20 10
2539 3 k. multicoloured 25 15
2540 3 k. multicoloured 30 15
2541 3 k. multicoloured 40 15
2542 4 k. multicoloured 35 15
2543 6 k. multicoloured 50 15
2544 10 k. multicoloured 75 15
2545 12 k. multicoloured . . . . 1·10 45
COSTUMES: No. 2337, Moldavia; No. 2538, Georgia; No. 2539, Ukraine; No. 2540, Byelorussia; No. 2541, Kazakhs; No. 2542, Koryaks; No. 2543, Russia; No. 2544, Armenia; No. 2545, Estonia.

1961. Scenes from Russian Fairy Tales. Mult.
2546 1 k. "Geese Swans" 45 10
2547 3 k. "The Fox, the Hare and the Cock" 55 15
2548 4 k. "The Little Humpbacked Horse" 35 15
2549 6 k. "The Muzhik and the Bear" 60 20
2550 10 k. Type **873** 95 40

874 Lenin, Map and Power Station

1961. 40th Anniv of State Electricity Plan.
2551 **874** 4 k. brown, yell & blue . 60 15
2552 10 k. black, purple and salmon . . . . 1·00 25

875 Tractor **876** N. A. Dobrolyubov

1961. Soviet Agricultural Achievements. Inscr "1961".
2553 – 3 k. mauve and blue . . 30 15
2554 **875** 4 k. black and green . . 30 10
2555 – 6 k. brown and blue . . 45 25
2556 – 10 k. purple and olive . 1·00 15
DESIGNS: 3 k. Dairy herd; 6 k. Agricultural machinery; 10 k. Fruit picking.

1961. 125th Birth Anniv of N. A. Dobrolyubov (writer).
2557 **876** 4 k. buff, black & blue . 45 15

877 N. D. Zelinsky

1961. Birth Centenary of N. D. Zelinsky (chemist).
2558 **877** 4 k. purple and mauve . 45 15

878 Georgian Republic Flag

1961. 40th Anniv of Georgian Republic.
2559 **878** 4 k. multicoloured . . . 30 10

879 Sgt. Miroshnichenko and Battle

1961. War Hero.
2560 **879** 4 k. blue & purple . . . 55 10
See also Nos. 2664/5.

880 T. G. Shevchenko and Birthplace **881** A. Rublev

1961. Death Centenary of T. G. Shevchenko (Ukrainian poet and painter).
2561 **880** 3 k. brown and violet . . 20 10
2562 – 6 k. purple and green . . 55 15
DESIGN: 6 k. Portrait of Shevchenko in old age, pen, book and candle.
See also Nos. 2956/62.

1961. 600th Birth Anniv of Rublev (painter).
2563 **881** 4 k. multicoloured . . . 60 20

882 Statue of Shevchenko (poet)
883 N. V. Sklifosovsky

1961. Cultural Celebrities.
2564 – 2 k. brown and blue . . 25 10
2565 **882** 4 k. brown and black . . 20 15
2566 – 4 k. brown and purple . . 30 15
DESIGNS: 2 k. Shchors Monument, Kiev; 4 k. (No. 2566), Kotovsky Monument, Kishinev.

1961. 125th Birth Anniv of N. Y. Sklifosovsky (surgeon).
2567 **883** 4 k. black and blue . . . 45 10

884 Robert Koch

885 Zither-player and Folk Dancers

1961. 50th Death Anniv of Robert Koch (German microbiologist).
2568 **884** 6 k. brown 70 20

1961. 50th Anniv of Russian National Choir.
2569 **885** 4 k. multicoloured . . . 45 10

886 "Popular Science"

1961. Cent of "Vokrug Sveta" (science magazine).
2570 **886** 6 k. brown, blue and deep blue 90 75

887 Venus Rocket

1961. Launching of Venus Rocket.
2571 **887** 6 k. orange and blue . . 1·00 20
2572 – 10 k. blue and yellow . . 1·75 40
DESIGN: 10 k. Capsule and flight route.

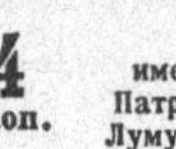
4 коп. имени Патриса Лумумбы 1961 г.
(888)

1961. Patrice Lumumba (Congolese politician) Commemoration (1st issue). Surch with T **888**.
2573 **863** 4 k. on 40 k. purple . . . 1·25 1·25
See also No. 2593.

889 African breaking Chains

1961. Africa Freedom Day. Inscr "1961".
2574 **889** 4 k. multicoloured . . . 20 10
2575 – 6 k. purple, orange & bl . . 35 20
DESIGN: 6 k. Hands clasping torch of freedom, and map.

891 Yury Gagarin

892 Lenin

1961. World's First Manned Space Flight. Inscr "12-IV-1961". Perf or imperf.
2576 **891** 3 k. blue 45 10
2577 – 6 k. blue, violet and red 55 20
2578 – 10 k. red, green and brn 1·25 60
DESIGNS—37 × 26 mm: 6 k. Rocket and Spassky Tower; 10 k. Rocket, Gagarin and Kremlin.

1961. 91st Birth Anniv of Lenin.
2579 **892** 4 k. blk, salmon and red 30 10

893 Rabindranath Tagore

894 Garibaldi

1961. Birth Centenary of Tagore (Indian writer).
2580 **893** 6 k. black, bistre & red . 40 15

1961. International Labour Exhibition, Turin.
2581 – 4 k. salmon and red . . 40 10
2582 **894** 6 k. salmon and lilac . . 55 15
DESIGN: 4 k. Statue.

895 Lenin
896 Patrice Lumumba

1961.
2583 **895** 20 k. green and brown . 1·40 1·10
2584 – 30 k. blue and brown . 2·50 2·00
2585 – 50 k. red and brown . 4·00 4·00
PORTRAITS (Lenin): 30 k. In cap; 50 k. Profile.

1961. Capitals of Autonomous Republics (2nd issue). As T **835**.
2586 4 k. deep violet 30 15
2587 4 k. blue 30 15
2588 4 k. orange 30 15
2589 4 k. black 30 15
2590 4 k. lake 55 15
2591 4 k. green 55 15
2592 4 k. deep purple 55 15
CAPITALS: No. 2586, Nalchik (Kabardino-Balkar); No. 2587, Ulan-Ude (Buryat); No. 2588, Sukhumi (Abkhazia); No. 2589, Syktyvkar (Komi); No. 2590, Nakhichevan (Nakhichevan); No. 2591, Rodina Cinema, Elista (Kalmyk); No. 2592, Ufa (Bashkir).

1961. Lumumba Commemoration (2nd issue).
2593 **896** 2 k. multicoloured . . . 15 10

897 Kindergarten

898 Chernushka and Rocket

1961. International Children's Day.
2594 **897** 2 k. blue and orange . . 15 10
2595 – 3 k. violet and ochre . . 25 10
2596 – 4 k. drab and red . . . 40 15
DESIGNS—HORIZ: 3 k. Children in Pioneer camp. VERT: 4 k. Children with toys and pets.

1961. 4th and 5th "Spacecraft" Flights.
2597 – 2 k. black, blue & violet 35 15
2598 **898** 4 k. turquoise and blue . 65 15
DESIGN—HORIZ: 2 k. Dog "Zvezdochka", rocket and Controller (inscr "25.III.1961").

899 Belinsky (after I. Astafev)

900

1961. 150th Birth Anniv of Vissarion Grigorievich Belinsky (literary critic and journalist).
2599 **899** 4 k. black and red 30 15

1961. 40th Anniv of Soviet Hydro-meteorological Service.
2600 **900** 6 k. multicoloured . . . 90 25

901 D. M. Karbyshev
902 Glider

1961. Lieut-Gen. Karbyshev (war hero).
2601 **901** 4 k. black, red & yellow . 30 10

1961. Soviet Spartakiad.
2602 **902** 4 k. red and grey 30 10
2603 – 6 k. red and grey 45 15
2604 – 10 k. red and grey 85 35
DESIGNS: 6 k. Inflatable motor boat; 10 k. Motor cyclists.

903 Sukhe Bator Monument and Govt. Buildings, Ulan Bator
904 S. I. Vavilov

1961. 40th Anniv of Revolution in Mongolia.
2605 **903** 4 k. multicoloured . . . 50 15

1961. 70th Birthday of Vavilov (scientist).
2606 **904** 4 k. brown, bistre & grn . 30 15

905 V. Pshavela

906 "Youth Activities"

1961. Birth Cent of Pshavela (Georgian poet).
2607 **905** 4 k. brown and cream . . 25 10

1961. World Youth Forum.
2608 – 2 k. brown and orange . . 20 10
2609 – 4 k. green and lilac . . . 65 10
2610 **906** 6 k. blue and ochre . . . 70 25
DESIGNS—HORIZ: 2 k. Youths pushing tank into river. VERT: 4 k. "Youths and progress".

907

908

1961. 5th Int Biochemical Congress, Moscow.
2611 **907** 6 k. multicoloured . . . 65 15

1961. Centenary of "Kalevipoeg" (Estonian Saga).
2612 **908** 4 k. yellow, turq & blk . 25 10

909 Javelin Thrower

1961. 7th Soviet Trade Union Sports.
2613 **909** 6 k. red 40 15

910 A. D. Zakharov

1961. Birth Bicentenary of Zakharov (architect).
2614 **910** buff, brown & blue . . . 40 15

911 Counter-attack

1961. War of 1941–45 (1st issue). Inscr "1961".
2615 **911** 4 k. multicoloured . . . 30 15
2616 – 4 k. multicoloured . . . 65 15
2617 – 4 k. indigo and brown . 65 15
DESIGNS: No. 2616, Sailor with bayonet; No. 2617, Soldier with tommy gun.
See also Nos. 2717 and 2851/5.

912 Union Emblem

1961. 15th Anniv of International Union of Students.
2617a **912** 6 k. violet and red . . . 35 10

913 Stamps commemorating Industry

1961. 40th Anniv of First Soviet Stamp. Centres multicoloured.
2618 **913** 2 k. ochre and brown . . 30 15
2619 – 4 k. blue and indigo . . 45 15
2620 – 6 k. green and olive . . 70 15
2621 – 10 k. buff and brown . . 1·10 45
DESIGNS (stamps commemorating): 4 k. Electrification; 8 k. Peace; 10 k. Atomic energy.

914 Titov and "Vostok 2"

1961. 2nd Manned Space Flight. Perf or imperf.
2622 – 4 k. blue and purple . . 30 10
2623 **914** 6 k. orange, grn & brn . 55 20
DESIGN: 4 k. Space pilot and globe.

915 Angara River Bridge

1961. Tercentenary of Irkutsk, Siberia.
2624 **915** 4 k. black, lilac & bistre 40 10

916 Letters and Mail Transport

1961. International Correspondence Week.
2625 **916** 4 k. black and mauve . . 55 10

917 Workers and Banners

1961. 22nd Communist Party Congress (1st issue).
2626 **917** 2 k. brown, yell & red . . 15 10
2627 – 3 k. blue and orange . . 60 15

2628 – 4 k. red, buff & purple . 25 10
2629 – 4 k. orange, blk & pur . 40 10
2630 – 4 k. sepia, brown & red . 25 15
DESIGNS: No. 2627, Moscow University and obelisk; No. 2628, Combine harvester; No. 2629, Workmen and machinery; No. 2630, Worker and slogan.
See also No. 2636.

918 Soviet Monument, Berlin

919 Adult Education

1961. 10th Anniv of International Federation of Resistance Fighters.
2631 **918** 4 k. grey and red 25 10

1961. Communist Labour Teams.
2632 – 2 k. purple & red on buff 35 15
2633 **919** 3 k. brown & red on buff 15 15
2634 – 4 k. blue & red on cream 35 25
DESIGNS: 2 k. Worker at machine; 4 k. Workers around piano.

920 Rocket and Globes

1961. Cosmic Flights. Aluminium-surfaced paper.
2635 **920** 1 r. red & black on silver 23·00 23·00

XXII съезд
КПСС
(921)

1961. 22nd Communist Party Congress (2nd issue). Optd with T **921**.
2636 **920** 1 r. red & black on silver 20·00 20·00

922 A. Imanov (Kazakh leader)

923 Liszt, Piano and Music

1961. Imanov Commemoration.
2637 **922** 4 k. sepia, brown & green 20 10

1961. 150th Birth Anniv of Liszt.
2638 **923** 4 k. brown, purple & yell 50 15

924 Flags, Rocket and Skyline

1961. 44th Anniv of October Revolution.
2639 **924** 4 k. red, purple and yell . 50 15

925 Congress Emblem

926 M. V. Lomonosov and Lomonosov University

1961. 5th W.F.T.U. Congress, Moscow. Inscr "МОСКВА 1961".
2640 **925** 2 k. red and bistre . . . 25 10
2641 – 2 k. violet and grey . . . 25 10
2642 – 4 k. brown, purple & bl . 45 10
2643 – 4 k. red, blue and violet . 45 10
2644 **925** 6 k. red, bistre & green . 40 15
2645 – 6 k. blue, purple & bistre 40 15
DESIGNS—HORIZ: Nos. 2641, 2645, Negro breaking chains. VERT: No. 2642, Hand holding hammer; No. 2643, Hands holding globe.

1961. 250th Birth Anniv of Lomonosov (scientist).
2646 **926** 4 k. brown, green & blue 30 15
2647 – 6 k. blue, buff & green . 50 20
2648 – 10 k. brown, blue & pur 1·00 40
DESIGNS—VERT: 6 k. Lomonosov at desk. HORIZ: 10 k. Lomonosov, his birthplace, and Leningrad Academy of Science.

927 Power Workers

928 Scene from "Romeo and Juliet"

1961. Young Builders of Seven Year Plan. Inscr "1961".
2649 **927** 3 k. grey, brown & red . 35 15
2650 – 4 k. brown, blue & red . 45 15
2651 – 6 k. grey, brown & red . 75 20
DESIGNS: 4 k. Welders; 6 k. Engineer with theodolite.

1961. Russian Ballet (1st issue). Inscr "1961". Multicoloured.
2652 6 k. Type **928** 45 15
2653 10 k. Scene from "Swan Lake" 80 25
See also Nos. 2666/7.

929 Hammer and Sickle

930 A. Pumpur

1961. 25th Anniv of Soviet Constitution.
2654 **929** 4 k. lake, yellow and red 30 10

1961. 120th Birth Anniv of Pumpur (Lettish poet).
2655 **930** 4 k. purple and grey . . 25 10

1961. Air. Surch **1961 r.6 kon** and bars.
2656 **822** 6 k. on 60 k. blue . . . 90 20

932 "Bulgarian Achievements"

1961. 15th Anniv of Bulgarian Republic.
2657 **932** 4 k. multicoloured . . . 25 10

933 Nansen and "Fram"

1961. Birth Centenary of Nansen (explorer).
2658 **933** 6 k. brown, blue & black 1·75 15

934 M. Dolivo-Dobrovolsky

935 A. S. Pushkin

1962. Birth Centenary of Dolivo-Dobrovolsky (electrical engineer).
2659 **934** 4 k. blue and bistre . . 25 10

1962. 125th Death Anniv of Pushkin (poet).
2660 **935** 4 k. black, red and buff 20 10

936 Soviet Woman

1962. Soviet Women.
2661 **936** 4 k. black, bistre & orge 25 10

937 People's Dancers

1962. 25th Anniv of Soviet People's Dance Ensemble.
2662 **937** 4 k. brown and red . . . 35 10

938 Skaters

1962. Ice Skating Championships, Moscow.
2663 **938** 4 k. blue and orange . . 40 10

1962. War Heroes. As T **879** but inscr "1962".
2664 4 k. brown and blue 75 15
2665 6 k. turquoise and brown . . 1·00 20
DESIGNS: 4 k. Lieut. Shalandin, tanks and Yakovlev Yak-9T fighter planes; 6 k. Capt. Gadzhiev, "K-3" submarine and sinking ship.

1962. Russian Ballet (2nd issue). As T **928** but inscr "1962".
2666 2 k. multicoloured 25 15
2667 3 k. multicoloured 35 15
DESIGNS: Scenes from—2 k. "Red Flower" (Glier); 3 k. "Paris Flame" (Prokofiev).

СОВЕТСКИЕ КОНЬКОБЕЖЦЫ–
ЧЕМПИОНЫ
МИРА
(939)

1962. Soviet Victory in Ice Skating Championships. Optd with T **939**.
2668 **938** 4 k. blue and orange . . 2·75 1·50

940 Skiing

1962. 1st People's Winter Games, Sverdlovsk.
2669 **940** 4 k. violet and red . . . 45 15
2670 – 6 k. turquoise & purple . 55 20
2671 – 10 k. red, black & blue . 95 30
DESIGN: 6 k. Ice Hockey; 10 k. Figure skating.

941 A. I. Herzen

942 Lenin on Banner

1962. 150th Birth Anniv of A. I. Herzen (writer).
2672 **941** 4 k. flesh, black & blue . 25 10

1962. 14th Leninist Young Communist League Congress. Inscr "1962".
2673 **942** 4 k. red, yellow & purple 20 10
2674 – 6 k. purple, orange & blue 25 10
DESIGN—HORIZ: 6 k. Lenin on flag.

943 Rocket and Globe

944 Tchaikovsky (after sculpture by Z. M. Vilensky)

1962. 1st Anniv of World's First Manned Space Flight. Perf or imperf.
2675 **943** 10 k. multicoloured . . . 1·10 50

1962. 2nd Int Tchaikovsky Music Competition.
2676 **944** 4 k. drab, black & blue . 40 10

945 Youth of Three Races

946 The Ulyanov (Lenin's) Family

1962. International Day of "Solidarity of Youth against Colonialism".
2677 **945** 6 k. multicoloured . . . 30 10

1962. 92nd Birth Anniv of Lenin.
2678 **946** 4 k. brown, grey and red 25 15
2679 – 10 k. purple, red & black 1·00 30
DESIGN: 10 k. Lenin.

947 "Cosmos 3"

1962. Cosmic Research.
2680 **947** 6 k. black, violet & blue 50 15

948 Charles Dickens

1962. 150th Birth Anniv of Charles Dickens.
2681 **948** 6 k. purple, turq & ol . . 50 15

949 J. J. Rousseau

950 Karl Marx Monument, Moscow

1962. 250th Birth Anniv of Rousseau.
2682 **949** 6 k. bistre, grey & purple 50 15

1962. Karl Marx Commemoration.
2683 **950** 4 k. grey and blue . . . 20 10

951 Lenin reading "Pravda"

952 Mosquito and Campaign Emblem

1962. 50th Anniv of "Pravda" Newspaper.
2684 **951** 4 k. purple, red & buff . 25 15
2685 – 4 k. multicoloured . . . 25 15
2686 – 4 k. multicoloured . . . 25 15
DESIGNS—25 × 38 mm: No. 2685, Statuary and front page of first issue of "Pravda"; No. 2686, Lenin and modern front page of "Pravda".

1962. Malaria Eradication. Perf (6 k. also imperf).
2687 **952** 4 k. black, turquoise & red 20 10
2688 6 k. black, green & red . 65 35

953 Model Rocket Construction

1962. 40th Anniv of All Union Lenin Pioneer Organization. Designs embody Pioneer badge. Multicoloured.

2689 2 k. Lenin and Pioneers giving Oath 25 10
2690 3 k. L. Golikov and V. Kotik (pioneer heroes) 25 10
2691 4 k. Type **953** 35 10
2692 4 k. Hygiene education . . . 40 20
2693 6 k. Pioneers marching . . . 70 25

954 M. Mashtotz **955** Ski Jumping

1962. 1600th Birth Anniv of Mesrop Mashtotz (author of Armenian Alphabet).

2694 **954** 4 k. brown and yellow . . 25 10

1962. F.I.S. International Ski Championships, Zakopane (Poland).

2695 **955** 2 k. red, brown & blue . 20 10
2696 – 10 k. blue, black & red . 80 35

DESIGN—VERT: 10 k. Skier.

956 I. Goncharov **957** Cycle Racing

1962. 150th Birth Anniv of I. Goncharov (writer).

2697 **956** 4 k. brown and grey . . 35 10

1962. Summer Sports Championships.

2698 **957** 2 k. black, red & brown . 40 10
2699 – 4 k. black, yellow & brn . 35 20
2700 – 10 k. black, lemon & blue 80 30
2701 – 12 k. brown, yell & blue . 95 40
2702 – 16 k. multicoloured . . . 1·25 50

DESIGN—VERT: 4 k. Volleyball; 10 k. Rowing; 16 k. Horse jumping. HORIZ: 12 k. Football (goal keeper).

1962. Capitals of Autonomous Republics. 3rd issue. As T **835**.

2703 4 k. black 50 15
2704 4 k. purple 50 15
2705 4 k. green 50 15

CAPITALS: No. 2703, Kazan (Tatar); No. 2704, Kyzyl (Tuva); No.2705, Saransk (Mordovian).

958 Lenin Library, 1862

1962. Centenary of Lenin Library.

2706 **958** 4 k. black and grey . . . 35 15
2707 – 4 k. black and grey . . . 35 15

DESIGN: No. 2707, Modern library building.

959 Fur Bourse, Leningrad and Ermine

1962. Fur Bourse Commemoration.

2708 **959** 6 k. multicoloured . . . 55 20

960 Pasteur **961** Youth and Girl with Book

1982. Centenary of Pasteur's Sterilisation Process.

2709 **960** 6 k. brown and black . . 60 15

1962. Communist Party Programme. Mult.

2710 2 k. Type **961** 15 10
2711 4 k. Workers of three races and dove 25 10

962 Hands breaking Bomb

1962. World Peace Congress, Moscow.

2712 **962** 6 k. bistre, black & blue 30 15

963 Y. Kupala and Y. Kolas

1962. Byelorussian Poets Commemoration.

2713 **963** 4 k. brown and yellow . 25 10

964 Sabir **965** Congress Emblem

1962. Birth Centenary of Sabir (Azerbaijan poet).

2714 **964** 4 k. brown, buff & blue 45 15

1962. 8th Anti-Cancer Congress, Moscow.

2715 **965** 6 k. red, black & blue . 45 15

966 N. N. Zinin **967** M. V. Nesterov (painter)

1962. 150th Birth Anniv of N. N. Zinin (chemist).

2716 **966** 4 k. brown and violet . 25 10

1962. War of 1941–45 (2nd issue). As T **911** inscr "1962".

2717 4 k. multicoloured 55 15

DESIGN: Sailor throwing petrol bomb.

1962. Russian Artists Commemoration.

2718 **967** 4 k. multicoloured . . . 30 15
2719 – 4 k. brown, pur & grey . 30 15
2720 – 4 k. black and brown . 30 15

PORTRAITS—VERT: No. 2719, I. N. Kramskoi (painter). HORIZ: No. 2220, I. D. Shadr (sculptor).

968 "Vostok-2" **969** Nikolaev and "Vostok 3"

1962. 1st Anniv of Titov's Space Flight. Perf or imperf.

2721 **968** 10 k. purple, black & bl 1·00 50
2722 10 k. orange, black & bl 1·00 50

1962. 1st "Team" Manned Space Flight. Perf or imperf.

2723 **969** 4 k. brown, red and blue 90 15
2724 – 4 k. brown, red and blue 90 15
2725 – 6 k. multicoloured . . . 1·50 20

DESIGNS: No. 2724, As Type **969** but with Popovich and "Vostok-4"; No. 2725 (47×28½ mm), Cosmonauts in flight.

970 House of Friendship

1962. People's House of Friendship, Moscow.

2726 **970** 6 k. grey and blue . . . 30 10

971 Lomonosov University and Atomic Symbols

1962. "Atoms for Peace".

2727 **971** 4 k. multicoloured . . . 35 10
2728 – 6 k. multicoloured . . . 50 20

DESIGN: 6 k. Map of Russia, Atomic symbol and "Peace" in ten languages.

972 Sazan and Bream **973** F. E. Dzerzhinsky

1962. Fish Preservation Campaign.

2729 **972** 4 k. yellow, vio & blue . 30 10
2730 – 6 k. blue, black & orge . 50 20

DESIGN: 6 k. Freshwater salmon.

1962. Birth Anniv of Feliks Dzerzhinsky (founder of Cheka).

2731 **973** 4 k. blue and green . . . 25 10

974 O. Henry

1962. Birth Cent of O. Henry (American writer).

2732 **974** 6 k. black, brown & yell . 35 10

975 Field Marshals Barclay de Tolly, Kutuzov and Bagration

1962. 150th Anniv of Patriotic War of 1812.

2733 **975** 3 k. brown 30 10
2734 – 4 k. blue 35 15
2735 – 6 k. slate 75 20
2736 – 10 k. violet 75 25

DESIGNS: 4 k. Davidov and partisans; 6 k. Battle of Borodino; 10 k. Partisans escorting French prisoners of war.

976 Vinnitsa

1962. 600th Anniv of Vinnitsa.

2737 **976** 4 k. black and bistre . . 30 10

977 Transport, "Stamp" and "Postmark" **978** Cedar

1962. International Correspondence Week.

2738 **977** 4 k. black, pur & turq . . 30 10

1962. 150th Anniv of Nikitsky Botanical Gardens. Multicoloured.

2739 3 k. Type **978** 35 10
2740 4 k. "Vostok-2" canna (plant) 55 10
2741 6 k. Strawberry tree (arbutus) 70 15
2742 10 k. "Road to the Stars" (chrysanthemum) 95 25

979 Builder **980** "Sputnik 1"

1962. "The Russian People". Multicoloured.

2743 4 k. Type **979** 30 15
2744 4 k. Textile worker 30 15
2745 4 k. Surgeon 30 15
2746 4 k. Farm girl 30 15
2747 4 k. P. T. instructor 30 15
2748 4 k. Housewife 30 15
2749 4 k. Rambler 30 15

1962. 5th Anniv of Launching of "Sputnik 1".

2750 **980** 10 k. multicoloured . . . 1·10 30

981 Akhundov **982** Harvester

1962. 150th Birth Anniv of M. F. Akhundov (poet).

2751 **981** 4 k. brown and green . . 20 10

1962. "Settlers on Virgin Lands". Multicoloured.

2752 4 k. Type **982** 50 20
2753 4 k. Surveyors, tractors and map 50 20
2754 4 k. Pioneers with flag . . . 50 20

983 N. N. Burdenko

1962. Soviet Scientists. Inscr "1962". Multicoloured.

2755 4 k. Type **983** 25 10
2756 4 k. V. P. Filatov (wearing beret) 25 10

984 Lenin Mausoleum

1962. 92nd Birth Anniv of Lenin.

2757 **984** 4 k. multicoloured . . . 25 10

985 Worker with Banner **986** "Towards the Stars"

1962. 45th Anniv of October Revolution.

2758 **985** 4 k. multicoloured . . . 20 10

1962. Space Flights Commem. Perf or imperf.

2759 **986** 6 k. black, brown & blue 65 35
2760 10 k. ultram, bis & vio . 1·00 20

ЗЕМЛЯ—МАРС
1.XI.
(987)

988 T. Moldo (Kirghiz poet)

1962. Launching of Rocket to Mars (1st issue). Optd with T **987**.

2761 **986** 10 k. blue, bistre & vio . 3·00 2·40

See also No. 2765.

1962. Poets' Anniversaries.
2762 **988** 4 k. black and red . . . 30 10
2763 – 4 k. black and blue . . . 30 10
DESIGN: No. 2763, Sayat-Nova (Armenian poet) with musical instrument.

989 Hammer and Sickle

1962. 40th Anniv of U.S.S.R.
2764 **989** 4 k. yellow, red and crimson 20 10

990 Mars Rocket in Space
(⅔-size illustration)

1962. Launching of Rocket to Mars (2nd issue).
2765 **990** 10 k. violet and red . . . 90 30

991 Chemical Industry and Statistics

1962. 22nd Communist Party Congress. "Achievements of the People". Multicoloured.
2766 4 k. Type **991** 55 20
2767 4 k. Engineering (machinery and atomic symbol) 55 20
2768 4 k. Hydro-electric power . . 55 20
2769 4 k. Agriculture (harvester) . 55 20
2770 4 k. Engineering (surveyor and welder) 55 20
2771 4 k. Communications (telephone installation) . . 55 20
2772 4 k. Heavy industry (furnace) 55 20
2773 4 k. Transport (signalman etc) 65 20
2774 4 k. Dairy farming (milkmaid, etc) 55 20
All the designs show production targets relating to 1980.

992 Chessmen

994 V. K. Blucher (military commander)

993 Four Soviet Cosmonauts
(⅓-size illustration)

1962. 30th Soviet Chess Championships, Yerevan.
2775 **992** 4 k. black and ochre . . 75 20

1962. Soviet Cosmonauts Commem. Perf or imperf.
2776 **993** 1 r. black and blue . . . 6·75 6·75

1962. V. K. Blucher Commemoration.
2777 **994** 4 k. multicoloured . . . 30 10

995 V. N. Podbelsky

996 A. Gaidar

1962. 75th Birth Anniv of V. N. Podbelsky (politician).
2778 **995** 4 k. violet and brown . . 20 10

1962. Soviet Writers.
2779 **996** 4 k. buff, black & blue . 20 10
2780 – 4 k. multicoloured . . . 20 10
DESIGN: No. 2780, A. S. Makharenko.

997 Dove and Christmas Tree

1962. New Year. Perf or imperf.
2781 **997** 4 k. multicoloured . . . 20 10

998 D. N. Pryanishnikov (agricultural chemist)

999 Rose-coloured Starlings

1962. D. N. Pryanishnikov Commemoration.
2782 **998** 4 k. multicoloured . . . 20 10

1962. Birds.
2783 **999** 3 k. black, red & green . 55 10
2784 – 4 k. black, brown & orge 70 10
2785 – 6 k. blue, black and red 85 15
2786 – 10 k. blue, black & red . 1·40 30
2787 – 16 k. red, blue & black . 2·00 50
BIRDS: 4 k. Red-breasted geese; 6 k. Snow geese; 10 k. Great white cranes; 16 k. Greater flamingoes.

1000 F.I.R. Emblem and Handclasp

1001 Badge and Yakovlev Yak-9 Fighters

1962. 4th International Federation of Resistance Heroes Congress.
2788 **1000** 4 k. violet and red . . 20 10
2789 6 k. turquoise and red . 50 15

1962. 20th Anniv of French Air Force "Normandy-Niemen" Unit.
2790 **1001** 6 k. red, green & buff . 45 15

1002 Map and Savings Book

1962. 40th Anniv of Soviet Banks.
2791 **1002** 4 k. multicoloured . . 20 10
2792 – 6 k. multicoloured . . 35 15
DESIGN: 6 k. As Type **1002** but with people and figure "53" in place of symbols and "70" within map.

1003 Fertilizer Plant, Rustavi, Georgia

1962. Heavy Industries.
2793 **1003** 4 k. black, lt blue & bl 30 15
2794 – 4 k. black, turquoise & grn 30 15
2795 – 4 k. black, blue & grey 30 15
DESIGNS: No. 2794, Construction of Bratsk hydro-electric station; No. 2795, Volzhskaya hydro-electric station, Volgograd.

1962. Provincial Costumes (3rd issue). As T **870**. Inscr "1962".
2796 3 k. red, brown and drab . . 40 15
COSTUME: 3 k. Latvia.

1004 K. S. Stanislavsky

1005 A. S. Serafimovich

1963. Russian Stage Celebrities.
2797 **1004** 4 k. green on pale grn . 30 10
2798 – 4 k. brown 30 10
2799 – 4 k. brown 30 10

PORTRAITS AND ANNIVERSARIES: No. 2797, Type **1004** (actor, birth cent); No. 2798, M. S. Shchepkin (actor, death cent); No. 2799, V. D. Durov (animal trainer and circus artiste, birth cent).

1963. Russian Writers and Poets.
2800 **1005** 4 k. brown, sepia & mve 30 10
2801 – 4 k. brown and purple . 30 10
2802 – 4 k. brown, red & buff . 30 10
2803 – 4 k. brown and green . . 30 10
2804 – 4 k. brown, sepia & mve 30 10
2805 – 4 k. multicoloured . . . 30 10
PORTRAITS AND ANNIVERSARIES: No. 2800, (birth cent); No. 2801, D. Bednii (60th birth anniv); No. 2802, G. I. Uspensky (120th birth anniv); No. 2803, N. P. Ogarev (150th birth anniv); No. 2804, V. J. Bryusov (90th birth anniv); No. 2805, F. V. Gladkov (80th birth anniv).

1006 Children in Nursery

1007 Dolls and Toys

1963. Child Welfare.
2806 **1006** 4 k. black and orange . 25 10
2807 – 4 k. purple, blue & orge 25 10
2808 – 4 k. bistre, red & green . 25 10
2809 – 4 k. purple, red & orge . 25 10
DESIGNS: No. 2807, Children with nurse; No. 2808, Young pioneers; No. 2809, Students at desk and trainee at lathe.

1963. Decorative Arts. Multicoloured.
2810 4 k. Type **1007** 25 10
2811 6 k. Pottery 35 15
2812 10 k. Books 85 20
2813 12 k. Porcelain . . . . 1·10 30

1008 Ilyushin Il-62 Airliner

1962. 40th Anniv of "Aeroflot" Airline.
2814 **1008** 10 k. black, brn & red . 80 15
2815 – 12 k. multicoloured . . 1·00 30
2816 – 16 k. red, black & blue . 1·40 90
DESIGNS: 12 k. "Aeroflot" emblem; 16 k. Tupolev Tu-124 airliner.

1009 M. N. Tukhachevsky

1010 M. A. Pavlov (scientist)

1963. 45th Anniv of Red Army and War Heroes.
2817 **1009** 4 k. green & turquoise . . 30 10
2818 – 4 k. black and brown . . 30 10
2819 – 4 k. brown and blue . . 30 10
2820 – 4 k. black and red . . . 30 10
2821 – 4 k. violet and mauve . . 30 10
DESIGNS (Army heroes and battle scenes): No. 2817, Type **1009** (70th birth anniv); No. 2818, U. M. Avetisyan; No. 2819, A. M. Matrosov; No. 2820, I. V. Panfilov; No. 2821, Ya. F. Fabricius.

1963. Academy of Sciences Members.
2822 **1010** 4 k. blue, grey & brown 25 10
2823 – 4 k. brown and green . . 25 10
2824 – 4 k. multicoloured . . . 25 10
2825 – 4 k. brown, red & blue . 25 10
2826 – 4 k. multicoloured . . . 25 10
PORTRAITS: No. 2823, I. V. Kurchatov; No. 2824, V. I. Vernadsky. LARGER (23½ × 30 mm): No. 2825, A. Krylov; No. 2826, V. Obroutchev. All commemorate birth centenaries except No. 2823 (60th anniv of birth).

1011 Games Emblem

Советские хоккеисты-чемпионы мира и Европы. Стокгольм. 1963 г.
(**1012**)

1963. 5th Soviet T.U. Winter Sports.
2827 **1011** 4 k. orge, blk & blue . . 30 10

1963. Soviet Victory in Swedish Ice Hockey Championships. No. 2670 optd with T **1012**.
2828 6 k. turquoise and purple . . 1·60 60

1013 V. Kingisepp

1014 R. M. Blauman

1963. 75th Birth Anniv of Victor Kingisepp (Estonian Communist Party Leader).
2829 **1013** 4 k. brown and blue . . 25 10

1963. Birth Centenary of Rudolf Blauman (Latvian writer).
2830 **1014** 4 k. purple and blue . . 25 10

1015 Globe and Flowers

1016 Lenin

1963. "World without Arms and Wars". Perf or imperf.
2831 **1015** 4 k. green, blue and red 25 10
2832 – 6 k. lilac, green and red 30 10
2833 – 10 k. violet, blue & red 1·00 25
DESIGNS: 6 k. Atomic emblem and pylon; 10 k. Sun and rocket.

1963. 93rd Birth Anniv of Lenin.
2834 **1016** 4 k. brown and red . . 2·50 85

1963. Provincial Costumes (4th issue). As T **870**. Inscr "1963". Multicoloured.
2835 3 k. Tadzhikistan 40 15
2836 4 k. Azerbaijan 55 15
2837 4 k. Kirgizia 55 15
2838 4 k. Turkmenistan 55 15

1017 "Luna 4" Rocket

1963. Launching of "Luna 4" Space Rocket. Perf or imperf.
2839 **1017** 6 k. red, black and blue 65 15
See also No. 3250.

1018 Woman and Lido

1963. 5th Anniv of World Health Day. Mult.
2840 2 k. Type **1018** 15 10
2841 4 k. Man and stadium . . . 25 20
2842 10 k. Child and school . . . 85 20

1019 Sputniks and Globe

1963. "Cosmonautics Day".
2843 **1019** 10 k. blue, black & pur 75 15
2844 – 10 k. purple, black & bl 75 15
2845 – 10 k. red, black & yellow 75 15
DESIGNS: No. 2844, "Vostok 1" and Moon; No. 2845, Space rocket and Sun.

1021 Cuban Horsemen with Flag

1963. Cuban-Soviet Friendship.
2846 **1021** 4 k. black, red and blue . . . 40 10
2847 – 6 k. black, blue and red . . . 50 10
2848 – 10 k. blue, red & black . . 65 20
DESIGNS: 6 k. Hands, weapon, book and flag; 10 k. Crane, hoisting tractor and flags.

1022 J. Hasek

1023 Karl Marx

1963. 40th Death Anniv of Jaroslav Hasek (writer).
2849 **1022** 4 k. black 20 10

1963. 80th Death Anniv of Karl Marx.
2850 **1023** 4 k. black and brown . . 20 10

1963. War of 1941–45 (3rd issue). As T **911** inscr "1963".
2851 4 k. multicoloured 45 15
2852 4 k. multicoloured 45 15
2853 4 k. multicoloured 45 15
2854 4 k. sepia and red 45 15
2855 6 k. olive, black and red . . 75 20
DESIGNS: No. 2851, Woman making shells (Defence of Leningrad, 1942); No. 2852, Soldier in winter kit with tommy gun (20th anniv of Battle of the Volga); No. 2853, Soldiers attacking (Liberation of Kiev, 1943); No. 2854, Tanks and map indicating Battle of Kursk, 1943; No. 2855, Tank commander and tanks.

1024 International P.O. Building

1963. Opening of Int Post Office, Moscow.
2856 **1024** 6 k. brown and blue . . 65 10

1025 Medal and Chessmen

1963. World Chess Champion, Moscow. Perf or imperf.
2857 **1025** 4 k. multicoloured . . . 65 15
2858 – 6 k. blue, mauve and ultramarine 70 20
2859 – 16 k. black, mve & pur . 1·50 50
DESIGNS: 6 k. Chessboard and pieces; 16 k. Venue and pieces.

1026 Wagner

1027 Boxers on "Glove"

1963. 150th Birth Anniv of Wagner and Verdi (composers).
2860 **1026** 4 k. black and red . . . 50 15
2861 – 4 k. purple and red . . 50 15
DESIGN: No. 2861, Verdi.

1963. 15th European Boxing Championships, Moscow. Multicoloured.
2862 4 k. Type **1027** 20 10
2863 6 k. Referee and winning boxer on "glove" 50 15

1028 Bykovsky and "Vostok 5"

Всемирный конгресс женщин.
(1029)

1963. Second "Team" Manned Space Flights (1st issue). Perf or imperf.
2864 **1028** 6 k. brown and purple . . 55 20
2865 – 6 k. red and green . . . 55 20
2866 – 10 k. red and blue . . . 1·00 30
DESIGNS: No. 2865, Tereshkova and "Vostok 6"; No. 2866, Allegory—"Man and Woman in Space".
See also Nos. 2875/7.

1963. International Women's Congress, Moscow. Optd with T **1029**.
2867 **1015** 4 k. green, blue & red . 40 25

1030 Cycling

1031 Globe, Film and Camera

1963. 3rd People's Spartakiad. Multicoloured. Perf or imperf.
2868 3 k. Type **1030** 25 10
2869 4 k. Athletics 30 10
2870 6 k. Swimming (horiz) . . . 35 15
2871 12 k. Basketball 75 30
2872 16 k. Football . . . . 1·00 40

1963. International Film Festival, Moscow.
2873 **1031** 4 k. blue, black & brown 30 10

1032 V. V. Mayakovsky

1033 Tereshkova

1963. 70th Birth Anniv of Mayakovsky (poet).
2874 **1032** 4 k. brown 25 15

1963. 2nd "Team" Manned Space Flights (2nd issue). Multicoloured.
2875 4 k. Bykovsky (horiz) . . . 30 20
2876 4 k. Tereshkova (horiz) . . 30 20
2877 10 k. Type **1033** . . . . . . 1·60 35

1034 Ice Hockey Player

1035 Lenin

1963. Russian Ice Hockey Championships.
2878 **1034** 6 k. blue and red . . . 75 20

1963. 60th Anniv of 1st Socialist Party Congress.
2879 **1035** 4 k. black and red . . 30 10

1036 Freighter and Crate

1963. Red Cross Centenary.
2880 **1036** 6 k. red and green . . 60 15
2881 – 12 k. red and blue . . 90 30
DESIGN: 12 k. Centenary emblem.

1037 Guibozo (polo)

1963. Regional Sports.
2882 – 3 k. multicoloured . . 25 10
2883 **1037** 4 k. black, red & ochre 30 10
2884 – 6 k. red, brown & yell . 55 15
2885 – 10 k. black, brn & olive 75 25
DESIGNS—HORIZ: 3 k. Lapp reindeer racing; 6 k. Buryat archery. VERT: 10 k. Armenian wrestling.

1038 Aleksandr Mozhaisky and Model Monoplane

1963. Aviation Celebrities.
2886 **1038** 6 k. black and blue . . . 50 10
2887 – 10 k. black and blue . . 75 40
2888 – 16 k. black and blue . . 1·25 35
DESIGNS: 10 k. Pyotr Nesterov and "looping the loop"; 16 k. N. E. Zhukovsky and "aerodynamics".

1039 S. S. Gulak-Artemovsky (poet) (150th birth anniv)

1040 Olga Kobilyanska (writer) (birth centenary)

1963. Celebrities.
2889 **1039** 4 k. black and red . . . 45 15
2890 – 4 k. brown and purple . . 45 15
2891 – 4 k. brown and violet . . 45 15
2892 **1040** 4 k. mauve and brown . 45 15
2893 – 4 k. mauve and green . . 45 15
DESIGNS AND ANNIVERSARIES: As Type **1039**: No. 2893, M. I. Petraskas (Lithuanian composer) and scene from one of his works (90th birth anniv). As Type **1040**: No. 2890, G. D. Eristavi (writer, death cent, 1964); No. 2891, A. S. Dargomizhsky (composer, 150th birth anniv).

1041 Antactic Map and Supply Ship "Ob"

1043 E. O. Paton

1042 Letters and Transport

1963. Arctic and Antarctic Research. Mult.
2894 3 k. Type **1041** . . . . . . 2·50 30
2895 4 k. Convoy of snow tractors and map . . . . 1·00 30
2896 6 k. Globe and aircraft at polar base . . . . 1·75 30
2897 12 k. "Sovetskaya Ukraina" (whale factory ship), whale catcher and whale . . . . . 4·00 50

1963. International Correspondence Week.
2898 **1042** 4 k. violet, orge & blk . 35 10

1963. 10th Death Anniv of Paton (engineer).
2899 **1043** 4 k. black, red & blue . 20 10

1045 D. Diderot

1046 "Peace and Progess"

1963. 250th Birth Anniv of Denis Diderot (French philosopher).
2900 **1045** 4 k. brown, blue & bistre 45 10

1963. "Peace—Brotherhood—Liberty—Labour". All black, red and lake.
2901 4 k. Type **1046** 20 15
2902 4 k. "The Plan" 20 15
2903 4 k. "Intellectual Work" . . . 20 15
2904 4 k. "People's Union" 20 15
2905 4 k. "Nation's Elite" 20 15
2906 4 k. "The Family" 20 15

HAVE YOU READ THE NOTES AT THE BEGINNING OF THIS CATALOGUE?
These often provide the answers to the enquiries we receive.

1047 Academy of Sciences, Frunze

1963. Centenary of Union of Kirgizia and Russia.
2907 **1047** 4 k. blue, yellow & red . 20 10

1049 Lenin and Congress Building

1050 Menchnikov

1963. 13th Soviet Trade Unions' Congress, Moscow.
2908 **1049** 4 k. red and black . . . 15 10
2909 – 4 k. red and black . . . 15 10
DESIGN: No. 2909, Lenin with man and woman workers.

1963. 75th Anniv of Pasteur Institute, Paris.
2910 **1050** 4 k. green and bistre . . 25 10
2911 – 6 k. violet and bistre . . 45 15
2912 – 12 k. blue and bistre . . 1·10 30
PORTRAITS: 6 k. Pasteur; 12 k. Calmette.

1051 Cruiser "Aurora" and Rockets

1052 Gur Emi Mausoleum

1963. 46th Anniv of October Revolution.
2913 **1051** 4 k. black, orge & lake 30 10
2914 4 k. black, red & lake . 50 30

1963. Ancient Samarkand Buildings. Mult.
2915 4 k. Type **1052** 40 10
2916 4 k. Shachi-Zinda Mosque . . 40 10
2917 6 k. Registan Square (55 × 28½ mm) 55 20

1053 Inscription, Globe and Kremlin

1054 Pushkin Monument, Kiev

1963. Signing of Nuclear Test-ban Treaty, Moscow.
2918 **1053** 6 k. violet and pale blue 45 15

1963.
2919 **1054** 4 k. brown 20 10

1056 Shukhov and Tower

1057 Y. M. Steklov and "Izvestia'

1963. 110th Birth Anniv of V. G. Shukhov (engineer).
2920 **1056** 4 k. black and green . . 20 10

1963. 90th Birth Anniv of Steklov (first editor of "Izvestia")
2921 **1057** 4 k. black and mauve . 20 10

1058 Buildings and Emblems of Moscow (and U.S.S.R.) and Prague (and Czechoslovakia)

1963. 20th Anniv of Soviet-Czech Friendship Treaty.
2922 **1058** 6 k. red, bistre & blue . 35 10

1059 F. A. Poletaev (soldier) and Medals

1963. Poletaev Commemoration.
2923 **1059** 4 k. multicoloured . . . 30 10

1062 J. Grimau (Spanish Communist) **1063** Rockets

1963. Grimau Commemoration.
2924 **1062** 6 k. violet, red and cream 45 10

1963. New Year (1st issue).
2925 **1063** 6 k. multicoloured . . . 50 10

1064 "Happy New Year" **1067** Topaz

1963. New Year (2nd issue).
2926 **1064** 4 k. red, blue and green 30 10
2927 6 k. red, blue and green 60 10

1963. "Precious Stones of the Urals". Multicoloured.
2928 2 k. Type **1067** 25 10
2929 4 k. Jasper 50 10
2030 6 k. Amethyst 70 15
2931 10 k. Emerald 75 25
2932 12 k. Ruby . . . . . . 1·00 45
2933 16 k. Malachite . . . . . 1·25 55

1068 Sputnik 7 **1071** Flame and Rainbow

1069 Dushanbe (formerly "Stalinabad" 1929–62), Tadzhikistan

1963. "First in Space". Gold, vermilion and grey.
2934 10 k. Type **1068** 85 30
2935 10 k. Moon landing 85 30
2936 10 k. Back of Moon 85 30
2937 10 k. Vostok 7 . . . . . . 85 30
2938 10 k. Twin flight 85 30
2939 10 k. Seagull (first woman in space) 85 30

1963. Dushanbe Commemoration.
2940 **1069** 4 k. blue 30 10

1963. 15th Anniv of Declaration of Human Rights.
2941 **1071** 6 k. multicoloured . . . 30 10

1072 F. A. Sergeev ("Artyem")

1963. 80th Birth Anniv of Sergeev (revolutionary).
2942 **1072** 4 k. brown and red . . 20 10

1073 Sun and Globe **1074** K. Donelaitis

1964. International Quiet Sun Year.
2943 – 4 k. black, orge & mve 30 10
2944 **1073** 6 k. blue, yellow & red 35 10
2945 – 10 k. violet, red & blue 40 20
DESIGNS—HORIZ: 4 k. Giant telescope and sun; 10 k. Globe and Sun.

1964. 250th Birth Anniv of K. Donelaitis (Lithuanian poet).
2946 **1074** 4 k. black and myrtle . 20 10

1075 Speed Skating

1964. Winter Olympic Games, Innsbruck.
2947 **1075** 2 k. black, mauve & bl 20 10
2948 – 4 k. black, blue & mve 35 10
2949 – 6 k. red, black & blue . 65 15
2950 – 10 k. black, mve & grn 70 25
2951 – 12 k. black, grn & mve 95 35
DESIGNS: 4 k. Skiing; 6 k. Games emblem; 10 k. Rifle shooting (biathlon); 12 k. Figure skating (pairs).
See also Nos. 2969/73.

1076 A. S. Golubkina and Statue **1077** "Agriculture"

1984. Birth Cent of A. Golubkina (sculptress).
2952 **1076** 4 k. sepia and grey . . 20 10

1964. Heavy Chemical Industries. Multicoloured.
2953 4 k. Type **1077** 50 10
2954 4 k. "Textiles" 50 10
2955 4 k. "Tyre Production" . . 50 10

150 років з дня народження. 1964 р.

(1078)

1079 Shevchenko's Statue, Kiev (M. Manizer)

1964. 150th Birth Anniv of T. G. Shevchenko (Ukrainian poet and painter). No. 2561 optd with T **1078** and designs as T **1079**.
2956 **880** 3 k. brown and violet . 1·60 1·60
2959 **1079** 4 k. green 25 10
2960 4 k. red 25 10
2961 – 6 k. blue 30 10
2962 – 6 k. brown 30 10
2957 – 10 k. violet and brown 85 30
2958 – 10 k. brown and bistre 85 30
DESIGNS: Nos. 2957/8, Portrait of Shevchenko by I. Repin; Nos. 2961/2, Self-portrait.

1080 K. S. Zaslonov

1964. War Heroes.
2963 **1080** 4 k. sepia and brown . 40 15
2964 – 4 k. purple and blue . 40 15
2965 – 4 k. blue and red . . . 40 15
2966 – 4 k. brown and blue . 40 15
PORTRAITS: No. 2964, N. A. Vilkov; No. 2965, Yu. V. Smirnov; No. 2966, V. Z. Khoruzhaya.

1081 Federov printing the first Russian book, "Apostle"

1964. 400th Anniv of First Russian Printed Book. Multicoloured.
2967 4 k. Type **1081** 20 10
2968 6 k. Federov statue, books and newspapers 30 20

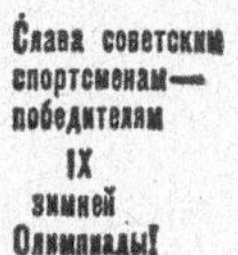

(1082) **1083** Ice Hockey Player

1964. Winter Olympic Games, Soviet Medal Winners.
(a) Nos. 2947/51 optd with T **1082** or similarly.
2969 2 k. black, mauve and blue . 20 10
2970 4 k. black, blue and mauve . 30 10
2971 6 k. red, black and blue . . . 30 15
2972 10 k. black, mauve & green . 85 25
2973 12 k. black, green & mauve . 1·00 30
(b) New designs.
2974 **1083** 3 k. red, black & turquoise 30 10
2975 – 16 k. orange and brown 1·40 80
DESIGN: 16 k. Gold medal and inscr "Triumph of Soviet Sport–11 Gold, 8 Silver, 6 Bronze medals".

1084 Militiaman and Factory Guard

1964. "Public Security".
2976 **1084** 4 k. blue, red and black 20 10

1085 Lighthouse, Odessa and Sailor

1964. 20th Anniv of Liberation of Odessa and Leningrad. Multicoloured.
2977 4 k. Type **1085** 50 10
2978 4 k. Lenin Statue, Leningrad . 25 10

1086 Sputniks **1087** N. I. Kibalchich

1964. "The Way to the Stars". Imperf or perf. (a) Cosmonautics. As T **1086**.
2979 4 k. green, black and red . . 30 10
2980 6 k. black, blue and red . . . 70 10
2981 12 k. turq, brown & black . . 1·40 30
DESIGNS: 6 k. "Mars I" space station; 12 k. Gagarin and space capsule.
(b) Rocket Construction Pioneers. As T **1087**.
2982 10 k. black, green & violet . . 1·10 45
2983 10 k. black, turquoise and red 1·10 45
2984 10 k. black, turquoise and red 1·10 45
2985 10 k. black and blue . . . . 1·00 25
DESIGNS: No. 2982, Type **1087**; No. 2983, F. A. Zander; No. 2984, K. E. Tsiolkovsky; No. 2985, Pioneers' medallion and Saransk memorial.

1088 Lenin

1964. 94th Birth Anniv of Lenin.
2986a **1088** 4 k. black, blue & mve . 3·25 3·25

1089 Shakespeare (400th Birth Anniv)

1964. Cultural Anniversaries.
2987 – 6 k. yellow, brn & sepia 60 15
2988 **1089** 10 k. brown and olive . 1·00 25
2989 – 12 k. green and brown . 1·25 35
DESIGNS AND ANNIVERSARIES: 6 k. Michelangelo (400th death anniv); 12 k. Galileo (400th birth anniv).

1090 Crop-watering Machine and Produce

1964. "Irrigation".
2990 **1090** 4 k. multicoloured . . . 20 10

1091 Gamarnik

1964. 70th Birth Anniv of Ya. B. Gamarnik (Soviet Army commander).
2991 **1091** 4 k. brown, blue & blk 20 10

1092 D. I. Gulia (Abhazian poet)

1964. Cultural Anniversaries.
2992 **1092** 4 k. black, green and light green 30 15
2993 – 4 k. black, verm & red . 30 15
2994 – 4 k. black, brn & bistre 30 15
2995 – 4 k. black, yell & brn . 30 15
2996 – 4 k. multicoloured . . . 30 15
2997 – 4 k. black, yell & brn . 30 15
DESIGNS: No. 2993, Nijazi (Uzbek writer, composer and painter); No. 2994, S. Seifullin (Kazakh poet); No. 2995, M. M. Kotsyubinsky (writer); No. 2996, S. Nazaryan (Armenian writer); No. 2997, T. Satylganov (Kirghiz poet).

1093 A. Gaidar

1964. 60th Birth Annivs of Writers A. P. Gaidar and N. A. Ostrovsky.
2998 **1093** 4 k. red and blue . . . 25 10
2999 – 4 k. green and red . . . 35 10
DESIGN: No. 2999, N. Ostrovsky and battle scene.

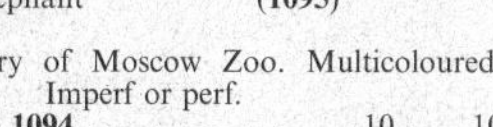

1094 Indian Elephant (1095)

1964. Centenary of Moscow Zoo. Multicoloured. Imperf or perf.
3000 1 k. Type **1094** 10 10
3001 2 k. Giant panda 15 10
3002 4 k. Polar bear 35 10
3003 6 k. Elk 45 10
3004 10 k. Eastern white pelican . 1·50 25
3005 12 k. Tiger . . . . 1·25 30
3006 16 k. Lammergeier . . . . . 3·00 50
The 2 k. and 12 k. are horiz; the 4 k. and 10 k. are "square", approx 26½ × 28 mm.

1964. 150th Anniv of Union of Azerbaijan and Russia. Surch with T **1095**.
3007 **328** 4 k. on 40 k. brown, bistre and yellow . . . . . . 2·10 1·60

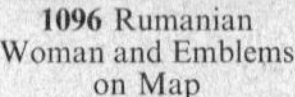
1096 Rumanian Woman and Emblems on Map

1097 Maize

1964. 20th. Anniv of Rumanian–Soviet Friendship Treaty.
3008 **1096** 6 k. multicoloured . . . 40 15

1964. Agricultural Crops. Multicoloured. Imperf or perf.
3009 2 k. Type **1097** 15 10
3010 3 k. Wheat 20 10
3011 4 k. Potatoes 30 10
3012 6 k. Peas 25 20
3013 10 k. Sugar beet 55 25
3014 12 k. Cotton 75 30
3015 16 k. Flax . . . . 1·40 40

1098 Flag and Obelisk

1099 Leningrad G.P.O

1964. 20th Anniv of Liberation of Byelorussia.
3016 **1098** 4 k. multicoloured . . . 20 10

1964. 250th Anniv of Leningrad's Postal Service.
3017 **1099** 4 k. black, bistre & red . 20 10

1100 Map of Poland and Emblems

1964. 20th Anniv of Polish People's Republic.
3018 **1100** 6 k. multicoloured . . . 35 10

1101 Horse-jumping

1102 M. Thorez (French Communist leader)

1964. Olympic Games, Tokyo. Imperf or perf.
3019 **1101** 3 k. multicoloured . . . 10 10
3020 – 4 k. red, black & yellow 15 10
3021 – 6 k. red, black and blue 25 10
3022 – 10 k. red, black & turq . 65 15
3023 – 12 k. black and grey . . 80 20
3024 – 16 k. violet, red and blue 1·40 50
DESIGNS: 4 k. Weightlifting; 6 k. Pole vaulting; 10 k. Canoeing; 12 k. Gymnastics; 16 k. Fencing.

1964. Maurice Thorez Commemoration.
3025 **1102** 4 k. black and red . . . 1·10 20

1103 Three Races

1104 Jawaharlal Nehru

1964. International Anthropologists and Ethnographers Congress, Moscow.
3026 **1103** 6 k. black and yellow . 35 10

1964. Nehru Commemoration.
3027 **1104** 4 k. brown and grey . . 35 10

1105 Globe and Banner

1106 A. V. Vishnevsky (surgeon)

1964. Centenary of "First International".
3028 **1105** 4 k. red, bistre and blue 20 10
3029 – 4 k. red, olive and black 20 10
3030 – 4 k. drab, red and lake 20 10
3031 – 4 k. red, black and blue 20 10
3032 – 4 k. multicoloured . . 20 10
DESIGNS: No. 3029, Communist Party manifesto; No. 3030, Marx and Engels; No. 3031, Chain breaker; No. 3032, Lenin.

1964. "Outstanding Soviet Physicians".
3033 **1106** 4 k. brown and pur . . 40 15
3034 – 4 k. brown, red & yellow 40 15
3035 – 4 k. brown, blue & bistre 40 15
DESIGNS: No. 3034, N. A. Semashko (public health pioneer). Both are 90th birth anniversaries. No. 3035, D. I. Ivanovsky and siphon (25 × 32 mm).

1107 Bulgarian Flag, Rose and Emblems

1108 P. Togliatti (Italian Communist leader)

1964. 20th Anniv of Bulgarian People's Republic.
3036 **1107** 6 k. red, green & drab . 30 15

1964. Togliatti Commemoration.
3037 **1108** 4 k. black and red . . 30 10

1110 Globe and Letters

1964. International Correspondence Week.
3038 **1110** 4 k. mauve, blue & brn 30 10

1111 Soviet and Yugoslav Soldiers

1112 East German Arms, Industrial Plants, Freighter "Havel" and Goods Train

1964. 20th Anniv of Liberation of Belgrade.
3039 **1111** 6 k. multicoloured . . 45 15

1964. 15th Anniv of German Democratic Republic.
3040 **1112** 6 k. multicoloured . . 45 15

1113 Woman holding Bowl of Produce (Moldavian Republic)

40 лет Советскому Таджикистану
(1115)

1964. 40th Anniv of Soviet Republic. (a) As T **1113**.
3041 **1113** 4 k. brown, green & red 20 10
3042 – 4 k. multicoloured . . 30 10
3043 – 4 k. red, purple & yell . 30 10

(b) Optd with T **1115**.
3044 **1069** 4 k. blue . . . . . . 1·10 60
DESIGNS—VERT: No. 3042, Woman holding Arms (Turkmenistan); No. 3043, Man and woman holding produce (Uzbekistan); No. 3044, commemorates the Tadzhikistan Republic.

1116 Yegorov

1964. Three-manned Space Flight. (a) Portraits in black, orange and turquoise.
3045 4 k. Type **1116** 30 10
3046 4 k. Feoktistov 30 10
3047 4 k. Komarov 30 10
These can be identified by the close proximation of the Russian names on the stamps to the English versions.

(b) Designs $73\frac{1}{2} \times 22\frac{1}{2}$ mm.
3058 6 k. purple and violet 45 15
3049 10 k. violet and blue . . . . 1·10 30
DESIGNS: 6 k. The three cosmonauts; 10 k. Space ship "Voskhod 1".

1117 Soldier and Flags

1964. 20th Anniv of Liberation of Ukraine.
3050 **1117** 4 k. multicoloured . . . 20 10

1119 Lermontov's Birthplace

1121 N. K. Krupskaya (Lenin's wife)

1120 Hammer and Sickle

1964. 150th Birth Anniv of M. Lermontov (poet).
3051 **1119** 4 k. violet 20 10
3052 – 6 k. black 30 10
3053 – 10 k. brown and flesh . 85 25
DESIGNS: 6 k. Lermontov; 10 k. Lermontov talking with Belinsky.

1964. 47th Anniv of October Revolution.
3054 **1120** 4 k. multicoloured . . . 20 10

1964. Birth Anniversaries.
3055 **1121** 4 k. multicoloured . . . 20 10
3056 – 4 k. multicoloured . . . 20 10
DESIGNS: No. 3055 (95th anniv); No. 3056, A. I. Yelizarova-Ulianova (Lenin's sister) (cent).

1122 Mongolian Woman and Lamb

1124 "Suillus luteus"

1964. 40th Anniv of Mongolian People's Republic.
3057 **1122** 4 k. multicoloured . . . 30 15

1964. Mushrooms. Multicoloured.
3058 2 k. Type **1124** 90 10
3059 4 k. "Cantharellus cibarius" . 1·50 20
3060 6 k. "Boletus edulis" . . . 2·00 30
3061 10 k. "Leccinum aurantiacum" 3·00 60
3062 12 k. "Lactarius deliciosus" . 3·75 80

1125 A. P. Dovzhenko

1126 Christmas Tree, Star and Globe

1964. 70th Birth Anniv of Dovzhenko (film producer).
3063 **1125** 4 k. blue and grey . . . 30 10

1964. New Year.
3064 **1126** 4 k. multicoloured . . . 40 15

1127 Struve

1128 S. V. Ivanov and Skiers

1964. Death Centenary of V. Ya. Struve (scientist).
3065 **1127** 4 k. brown and blue . . 60 15

1964. Birth Centenary of S. V. Ivanov (painter).
3066 **1128** 4 k. brown and black . 65 15

1129 Scene from Film

1964. 30th Anniv of Film "Chapaev".
3067 **1129** 6 k. black and green . . 35 15

1130 Test-tubes, Jar and Agricultural Scenes

1964. Chemistry for the National Economy.
3068 **1130** 4 k. purple and olive . 20 15
3069 – 6 k. black and blue . . 35 10
DESIGN: 6 k. Chemical plant.

1131 Cranberries

1132 Library

1964. Woodland Fruits. Multicoloured.
3070 1 k. Type **1131** 10 10
3071 3 k. Bilberries 15 10
3072 4 k. Rowanberries 20 10
3073 10 k. Blackberries 55 20
3074 16 k. Red bilberries 85 40

1964. 250th Anniv of Academy of Sciences Library, Leningrad.
3075 **1132** 4 k. black, green & red 20 10

1133 Congress Palace and Spassky Tower

1134 Mt Khan-Tengri

1964.
3076 **1133** 1 r. blue . . . . 7·50 1·25

1964. Mountaineering. Multicoloured.
3077 4 k. Type **1134** 20 10
3978 6 k. Mt Kazbek (horiz) . . . 40 15
3079 12 k. Mt Ushba 80 30

1136 Bowl

1964. Kremlin Treasures. Multicoloured.
3080 4 k. Helmet 70 15
3081 6 k. Quiver 90 20
3082 10 k. Coronation headgear . 1·10 35
3083 12 k. Ladle . . . . 1·25 45
3084 16 k. Type **1136** . . . . . . 1·50 80

1137 I. M. Sivko **1138** Dante

1965. War Heroes.
3085 **1137** 4 k. black and violet . . 40 15
3086 – 4 k. brown and blue . . 40 15
DESIGN: No. 3086, General I. S. Polbin.

1965. 700th Birth Anniv of Dante.
3038 **1138** 4 k. black, bistre and purple 45 10

1139 Blood Donor **1140** N. P. Kravkov

1965. Blood Donors. Multicoloured.
3088 4 k. Type **1139** 35 15
3089 4 k. Hand holding red carnation 35 15

1965. Birth Cent of N. Kravkov (pharmacologist).
3090 **1140** 4 k. multicoloured . . . 25 10

1141 Figure Skaters **1142** Alsatian

1965. European Figure Skating Championships, Moscow.
3091 **1141** 6 k. red, black & green . 40 15
See also No. 3108.

1965. World Ice Hockey Championships, Moscow. Designs similar to T **1141** but depicting ice hockey players.
3092 4 k. red, blue and bistre . . . 30 15

1965. Hunting and Service Dogs.
3093 – 1 k. black, yellow & red 15 10
3097 – 2 k. brown, blue & blk . 20 10
3098 **1142** 3 k. black, red & yellow 20 10
3099 – 4 k. black, brown & grn 30 10
3100 – 4 k. black, orange & grn 30 10
3101 – 6 k. black, brown & bl . 40 15
3102 – 6 k. black, red & blue . 40 15
3104 – 10 k. multicoloured . . 65 20
3095 – 12 k. black, brn & vio . 85 30
3096 – 16 k. multicoloured . . 1·25 35
DESIGNS—HORIZ: 1 k. Hound; 2 k. Setter; 4 k. (3099) (value in green) Fox terrier; 4 k. (3100) (value in orange) Pointer; 6 k. (3101) Borzoi; 12 k. Husky. VERT: 6 k. (3102) Sheepdog; 10 k. Collie; 16 k. Caucasion sheepdog.

1143 R. Sorge

1965. Richard Sorge (Soviet secret agent) Commem.
3103 **1143** 4 k. black and red . . . 55 15

1144 I.T.U. Emblem and Telecommunications Symbol

1965. Centenary of I.T.U.
3104 **1144** 6 k. violet and blue . . 55 15

1145 Leonov in Space

1965. Space Flight of "Voskhod 2" (1st issue). Imperf or perf.
3105 **1145** 10 k. orange, blk & bl . 1·00 30
See also Nos. 3138/9.

1965. Ice Hockey Championships. Optd **ТАМПЕРЕ 1965 г.**
3107 **1034** 6 k. blue and red . . . 1·00 40

Советские
фигуристы—
чемпионы мира
в парном катании

(**1147**)

1148 Soldier and Woman

1965. Soviet Victory in European Figure Skating Championships. Optd with T **1147**.
3108 **1141** 6 k. red, black & green 1·00 40

1965. 20th Anniversaries.
3109 **1148** 6 k. multicoloured . . 40 15
3110 – 6 k. multicoloured . . 40 15
3111 – 6 k. ochre and red . . 40 15
3112 – 6 k. multicoloured . . 40 15
3113 – 6 k. multicoloured . . 40 15
DESIGNS: No. 3109, Type **1148** (Czech Liberation); No. 3110, Statue and emblems of development (Friendship with Hungary); No. 3111, Polish and Soviet arms (Polish–Soviet Friendship Treaty); No. 3112, Viennese buildings and Russian soldier (Freeing of Vienna); No. 3113, Liberation medal, Polish flag and building reconstruction (Freeing of Warsaw).
See also Nos. 3182 and 3232.

1149 Statue Rockets and Globe **1150** Rockets and Radio-telescope

1965. National Cosmonautics Day. Nos. 3117/18 on aluminium-surfaced paper.
3114 **1149** 4 k. green, black & red 25 10
3115 – 12 k. purple, red & blue 85 40
3116 – 16 k. multicoloured . . 1·10 60
3117 **1150** 20 k. red, black and green on silver . . . . . . 6·75 5·00
3118 – 20 k. red, black and blue on silver . . . . . . 6·75 5·00
DESIGNS: 12 k. Statue and Globe; 16 k. Rockets and Globe; No. 3118, Globe, satellite and cosomonauts.

1151 Lenin

1965. Lenin's 95th Birth Anniv.
3119 **1151** 10 k. blue, black & brn 55 50

1152 Poppies **1153** Red Flag, Reichstag Building and Broken Swastika

1965. Flowers.
3120 **1152** 1 k. red, lake & green . 10 10
3121 – 3 k. yellow, brn & grn . 20 10
3122 – 4 k. lilac, black & grn 30 10
3123 – 6 k. red, deep green and green 40 10
3124 – 10 k. yellow, pur & grn 1·00 25
FLOWERS: 3 k. Marguerite; 4 k. Peony; 6 k. Carnation; 10 k. Tulips.

1965. 20th Anniv of Victory.
3125 **1153** 1 k. black, gold & red . 20 10
3126 – 2 k. red, black & gold . 25 15
3127 – 3 k. blue and gold . . 40 15
3128 – 4 k. violet and gold . . 55 15
3129 – 4 k. green and gold . . 60 15
3130 – 6 k. purple, grn & gold 1·00 20
3131 – 10 k. purple, brn & gold 1·75 25
3132 – 12 k. black, red & gold 2·00 30
3133 – 16 k. red and gold . . . 2·50 40
3134 – 20 k. black, red & gold . 3·25 75
DESIGNS: 2 k. Soviet mother holding manifesto (poster by I. Toidze); 3 k. "The Battle for Moscow" (V. Bogatkin); 4 k. (No. 3128), "Partisan Mother" (from S. Gerasimov's film); 4 k. (No. 3129), "Red Army Soldiers and Partisans" (from Yu. Neprintsev's film); 6 k. Soldiers and flag (poster by V. Ivanov); 10 k. "Mourning the Fallen Hero" (from F. Bogorodsky's film); 12 k. Soldier and worker holding bomb (poster by V. Korestsky); 16 k. Victory celebrations, Red Square, Moscow (from K. Yuon's film); 20 k. Soldier and machines of war.

1154 Marx and Lenin

1965. Marxism and Leninism.
3136 **1154** 6 k. black and red . . . 30 10
No. 3136 is similar in design to those issued by China and Hungary for the Postal Ministers' Congress, Peking, but this event is not mentioned on the stamp or in the Soviet philatelic bulletins.

1155 Bolshoi Theatre

1965. International Theatre Day.
3137 **1155** 6 k. ochre, blk & turq . 35 15

1156 Leonov **1157** Yakov Sverdlov (revolutionary)

1965. "Voskhod 2" Space Flight (2nd issue).
3138 **1156** 6 k. violet and silver . . 30 15
3139 – 6 k. purple and silver . . 30 15
DESIGN: No. 3139, Belyaev.

1965. 80th Birth Anniversaries.
3140 **1157** 4 k. black and brown . . 20 10
3141 – 4 k. black and violet . . 20 10
PORTRAIT: No. 3141, J. Akhunbabaev (statesman).

1158 Otto Grotewohl (1st death anniv) **1159** Telecommunications Satellite

1965. Annivs of Grotewohl and Thorez (Communist leaders).
3142 **1158** 4 k. black and purple . . 20 10
3143 – 6 k. brown and red . . . 40 15
DESIGN: 6 k. Maurice Thorez (65th birth anniv).

1965. International Co-operation Year. Mult.
3144 3 k. Type **1159** 20 10
3145 6 k. Star and sputnik 40 15
3146 6 k. Foundry ladle, iron works and map of India 40 15
No. 3145 signifies peaceful uses of atomic energy and No. 3146 co-operation with India.

1160 Congress Emblem, Chemical Plant and Symbols

1965. 20th International Congress of Pure and Applied Chemistry, Moscow.
3147 **1160** 4 k. red, black & blue . 25 10

1161 V. A. Serov

1965. Birth Centenary of V. A. Serov (painter).
3148 **1161** 4 k. black, brn & stone 80 20
3149 – 6 k. black and drab . . 1·50 25
DESIGN: 6 k. Full length portrait of Chaliapin (singer) by Serov.

1162 V. Ivanov and Armoured Train

1965. Famous Writers.
3150 **1162** 4 k. black and purple . 40 15
3151 – 4 k. black and violet . . 40 15
3152 – 4 k. black and blue . . 40 15
3153 – 4 k. black and grey . . 40 15
3154 – 4 k. black, red & green 40 15
3155 – 4 k. black and brown . 40 15
WRITERS AND ANNIVERSARIES: No. 3150, (70th birth anniv); No. 3151, A. Kunanbaev and military parade; No. 3152, J. Rainis (Lettish poet: 90th birth anniv); No. 3153, E. J. Vilde (Estonian author): 90th birth anniv); No. 3154, M. Ch. Abegjan (Armenian writer and critic: 90th birth anniv); No. 3155, M. L. Kropivnitsky and scene from play (Ukrainian playwright).

1163 Festival Emblem

1965. Film Festival, Moscow.
3156 **1163** 6 k. black, gold & blue 30 10

1164 Concert Arena, Tallin **1165** Hand holding "Peace Flower"

1965. 25th Anniv of Incorporation of Estonia, Lithuania and Latvia in the U.S.S.R.
3157 **1164** 4 k. multicoloured . . . 30 10
3158 – 4 k. brown and red . . 30 10
3159 – 4 k. brown, red & blue 30 10
DESIGNS—VERT: No. 3158, Lithuanian girl and Arms. HORIZ: No. 3159, Latvian Flag and Arms.

1965. Peace Issue.
3160 **1165** 6 k. yellow, blk & blue . 30 10

1167 "Potemkin" Sailors Monument, Odessa

1965. 60th Anniv of 1905 Rebellion.
3161 **1167** 4 k. blue and red . . . 20 15
3162 – 4 k. green, blk & red . 20 15
3163 – 4 k. green, blk & red . 20 15
3164 – 4 k. brown, blk & red . 20 15
DESIGNS: No. 3162, Demonstrator up lamp post; No. 3163, Defeated rebels; No. 3164, Troops at street barricade.

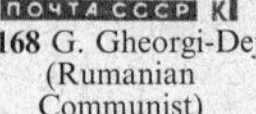

1168 G. Gheorgi-Dej (Rumanian Communist) **1169** Power Station

1965. G. Gheorgi-Dej Commemoration.
3165 **1168** 4 k. black and red . . . 25 10

1965. Industrial Progress.
3166 **1169** 1 k. multicoloured . . . 10 10
3167 – 2 k. black, orge & yell . 10 10
3168 – 3 k. vio, yell and ochre . 15 10
3169 – 4 k. deep blue, blue and red 20 10
3170 – 6 k. blue and bistre . . 30 10
3171 – 10 k. brown, yellow and orange 60 20
3172 – 12 k. turquoise and red 90 20
3173 – 16 k. purple, blue & blk 1·40 40
DESIGNS: 2 k. Steel works; 3 k. Chemical works and formula; 4 k. Machine tools production; 6 k. Building construction; 10 k. Agriculture; 12 k. Communications and transport; 16 k. Scientific research.

1170 Relay Racing **1171** Gymnastics

1965. Trade Unions Spartakiad. Multicoloured.
3174 4 k. Type **1170** 25 15
3175 4 k. Gymnastics 25 15
3176 4 k. Cycling 25 15

1965. Schoolchildren's Spartakiad.
3177 **1171** 4 k. red and blue . . . 20 10
3178 – 6 k. red, brown & turq . 35 15
DESIGN: 6 k. Cycle racing.

1172 Throwing the Javelin and Running **1173** Star, Palms and Lotus

1965. American–Soviet Athletic Meeting, Kiev.
3179 **1172** 4 k. red, brown & lilac . 15 10
3180 – 6 k. red, brown & green 25 10
3181 – 10 k. red, brown & grey 65 15
DESIGNS: 6 k. High jumping and putting the shot; 10 k. Throwing the hammer and hurdling.

1965. 20th Anniv of North Vietnamese People's Republic.
3182 **1173** 6 k. multicoloured . . . 30 15

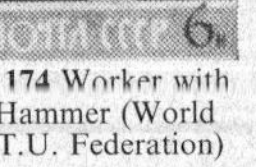

1174 Worker with Hammer (World T.U. Federation) **1176** P. K. Sternberg (astonomer: birth cent)

1965. 20th Anniv of International Organizations.
3183 **1174** 6 k. drab and plum . . 20 15
3184 – 6 k. brown, red & blue . 20 15
3185 – 6 k. lt brown & turq . . 20 15
DESIGNS: No. 3184, Torch and heads of three races (World Democratic Youth Federation); No. 3185, Woman holding dove (International Democratic Women's Federation).

1965. Scientists' Anniversaries.
3186 **1176** 4 k. brown and blue . . 60 15
3187 – 4 k. black and purple . 60 15
3188 – 4 k. black, pur & yell . 35 15
PORTRAITS: No. 3187, Ch. Valikhanov (scientific writer: death cent); No. 3188, V. A. Kistyakovsky (scientist: birth cent).

1177 "Battleship 'Potemkin'"

1965. "Soviet Cinema Art". Designs showing scenes from films. Multicoloured.
3189 4 k. Type **1177** 30 10
3190 6 k. "Young Guard" 40 15
3191 12 k. "A Soldier's Ballad" . 85 25

1178 Mounted Postman and Map

1965. History of the Russian Post Office.
3192 **1178** 1 k. green, brown & vio 20 10
3193 – 1 k. brown, ochre & grey 20 10
3194 – 2 k. brown, blue & lilac 20 10
3195 – 4 k. black, ochre & pur 45 10
3196 – 6 k. black, green & brn 65 15
3197 – 12 k. sepia, brown & bl 1·00 25
3198 – 16 k. plum, red & grey 1·25 45
DESIGNS: No. 3193, Mail coach and map; 2 k. Early steam train and medieval kogge; 4 k. Mail lorry and map; 6 k. Diesel train and various transport; 12 k. Moscow Post Office electronic facing sorting and cancelling machines; 16 k. Airports and Lenin.

1179 "Vostok" and "Mirnyi" (Antarctic exploration vessels)

1965. Polar Research Annivs.
3199 – 4 k. black, orange & bl 90 15
3200 – 4 k. black, orange & bl 90 15
3201 – 6 k. sepia and violet . . 1·00 25
3202 **1179** 10 k. black, drab & red 1·25 35
3203 – 16 k. black, vio & brn . 1·75 65
DESIGNS—HORIZ: $37\frac{1}{2} \times 25\frac{1}{2}$ mm: No. 3199, Ice breakers "Taimyr" and "Vaigach" in Arctic (50th anniv); No. 3200, Atomic ice breaker "Lenin"; No. 3201, Dikson settlement (50th anniv); No. 3203, Vostok Antarctic station. SQUARE. No. 3202, (145th anniv of Lazarev–Bellingshausen Expedition).
Nos. 3199/200 were issued together, se-tenant, forming a composite design.

1181 Agricultural Academy

1965. Centenary of Academy of Agricultural Sciences, Moscow.
3205 **1181** 4 k. violet, red & drab . 30 15

1183 N. Poussin (self-portrait) **1184** Kremlin

1965. 300th Death Anniv of Nicolas Poussin (French painter).
3207 **1183** 4 k. multicoloured . . 50 10

1965. New Year.
3208 **1184** 4 k. red, silver & black 25 10

1185 M. I. Kalinin

1966. 90th Birth Anniv of Kalinin (statesman).
3209 **1185** 4 k. lake and red 15 10

1186 Klyuchevski Volcano

1965. Soviet Volcanoes. Multicoloured.
3210 4 k. Type **1186** 40 15
3211 12 k. Karumski Volcano (vert) 1·00 30
3212 16 k. Koryaski Volcano . . . 1·10 45

1187 Oktyabrskaya Station, Moscow

1965. Soviet Metro Stations.
3213 **1187** 6 k. blue 40 15
3214 – 6 k. brown 40 15
3215 – 6 k. brown 40 15
3216 – 6 k. green 40 15
STATIONS: No. 3214, Leninksy Prospekt, Moscow; No. 3215, Moskovian Gate, Leningrad; No. 3216, Bolshevik Factory, Kiev.

1188 Common Buzzard **1189** "Red Star" (medal) and Scenes of Odessa

1965. Birds of Prey. Birds in black.
3217 **1188** 1 k. grey 40 10
3218 – 2 k. brown 55 10
3219 – 3 k. olive 65 10
3220 – 4 k. drab 75 10
3221 – 10 k. brown . . . . . 1·50 25
3222 – 12 k. blue . . . . . . 1·75 40
3223 – 14 k. blue . . . . . . 2·00 50
3224 – 16 k. purple . . . . . 2·40 60
BIRDS—VERT: 2 k. Common kestrel; 3 k. Tawny eagle; 4 k. Red kite; 10 k. Peregrine falcon; 16 k. Gyrfalcon. HORIZ: 12 k. Golden eagle; 14 k. Lammergeier.

1965. Heroic Soviet Towns. Multicoloured.
3225 10 k. Type **1189** 40 25
3226 10 k. Leningrad 40 25
3227 10 k. Kiev 40 25
3228 10 k. Moscow 40 25
3229 10 k. Brest-Litovsk 40 25
3230 10 k. Volgograd 40 25
3231 10 k. Sevastopol 40 25

1190 Flag, Map and Parliament Building, Belgrade

1965. 20th Anniv of Yugoslavia Republic.
3232 **1190** 6 k. multicoloured . . . 50 10

1191 Tupolev Tu-134

1965. Soviet Civil Aviation. Multicoloured.
3233 6 k. Type **1191** 50 10
3234 10 k. Antonov An-24 . . . . 70 15
3235 12 k. Mil Mi-10 helicopter . . 80 25
3236 16 k. Beriv Be-10 flying boat . 1·10 40
3237 20 k. Antonov An-22 Anteus . 1·75 45

1192 "The Proposal of Marriage", after P. Fedotov (150th birth anniv)

1965. Soviet Painters' Annivs.
3238 – 12 k. black and red . . 1·50 35
3239 **1192** 16 k. blue and red . . . 2·40 60
DESIGN—VERT: 12 k. "A Collective Farm Watchman" (after S. Gerasimov: 80th birth anniv).

1193 Crystallography Congress Emblem

1966. International Congresses, Moscow.
3240 **1193** 6 k. black, bl & bistre . 25 15
3241 – 6 k. black, red & blue . 25 15
3242 – 6 k. purple, grey & blk 25 15
3243 – 6 k. black and blue . . 50 15
3244 – 6 k. black, red & yellow 25 15
CONGRESS EMBLEMS: No. 3241, Microbiology; No. 3242, Poultry-raising; No. 3243, Oceanography; No. 3244, Mathematics.

1194 19th-cent Statuettes

1966. Bicentenary of Dmitrov Ceramic Works. Multicoloured.
3245 6 k. Type **1194** 30 15
3246 10 k. Modern tea set 65 25

1195 Rolland and Scene from Novel

1966. Birth Centenary of Romain Rolland (French writer) and 150th Birth Anniv of Eugene Potier (French poet).
3247 **1195** 4 k. brown and blue . . 30 15
3248 – 4 k. brn, red and black 30 15
DESIGN: No. 3248, Potier and revolutionary scene.

1196 Mongol Horseman

1966. 20th Anniv of Soviet–Mongolian Treaty.
3249 **1196** 4 k. multicoloured . . . 25 10

„ЛУНА-9" — НА ЛУНЕ!
3. 2. 1966
(1197)

1966. Landing of "Luna 9" Rocket on Moon. Optd with T **1197**.
3250 **1017** 6 k. red, black & blue . 4·25 4·25

1198 Supply Ship "Ob"

1966. 10th Anniv of Soviet Antarctic Expedition.
3251 **1198** 10 k. lake and silver . . 2·50 50
3252 – 10 k. lake, silver & blue 2·00 50
3253 – 10 k. lake, silver & blue 2·00 50
DESIGNS—TRIANGULAR: No. 3252, Snow vehicle. DIAMOND: No. 3253, Antarctic map. This stamp is partly perf across the centre.

1199 Mussa Dyalil and Scene from Poem

1966. Writers.
3254 **1199** 4 k. black and brown . 30 10
3255 – 4 k. black and green . . 30 10
3256 – 4 k. black and green . . 30 10
WRITERS: No. 3254 (Azerbaijan writer: 60th birth anniv); No. 3255, Akob Akopyan (Armenian poet: birth cent); No. 3256, Djalil Mamedkulizade (Azerbaijan writer: birth cent).

1200 Lenin (after bust by Kibalnikov)

1966. Lenin's 96th Birth Anniv
3257 **1200** 10 k. gold and green . . 1·25 65
3258 10 k. silver and red . . 80 25

1201 N. Ilin **1202** Scene from "Alive and Dead"

1966. War Heroes.
3259 **1201** 4 k. violet and red . . . 30 15
3260 – 4 k. lilac and blue . . . 30 15
3261 – 4 k. brown and green . . 30 15
PORTRAITS: No. 3260, G. P. Kravchenko; No. 3261, A. Uglovsky.

1966. Soviet Cinema Art.
3262 **1202** 4 k. black, grn & red . . 25 10
3263 – 10 k. black and blue . . 60 20
DESIGN: 10 k. Scene from "Hamlet'.

Учредительная конференция
Всесоюзного общества
филателистов. 1966

1203 Kremlin and Inscription **(1204)**

1966. 23rd Soviet Comunist Party Congress, Moscow (1st issue).
3264 **1203** 4 k. gold, red & blue . . 20 10
See also Nos. 3337/41.

1966. Philatelists All-Union Society Conference. No. 3198 optd with T **1204**.
3265 16 k. plum, red and grey . . 2·75 1·60

1205 Ice Skating

1966. 2nd People's Winter Spartakiad.
3266 **1205** 4 k. blue, red and olive 25 15
3267 – 6 k. red, lake and lilac . 35 20
3268 – 10 k. lake, red and blue 60 30
DESIGNS: Inscription emblem and 6 k. Ice hockey; 10 k. Skiing.
Nos. 3266/8 are each perf across the centre.

1206 Liner "Aleksandr Pushkin" **1207** Government Building, Frunze

1966. Soviet Transport.
3269 – 4 k. multicoloured . . 55 10
3270 – 6 k. multicoloured . . 45 10
3271 – 10 k. multicoloured . . 65 20
3272 **1206** 12 k. multicoloured . . 1·00 20
3273 – 16 k. multicoloured . . 1·00 25
DESIGNS—HORIZ: 4 k. Electric train; 6 k. Map of Lenin Volga–Baltic canal system; 16 k. Silhouette of liner on Globe. VERT: 10 k. Canal lock.
Nos. 3271/3 commemorate the inaug of Leningrad–Montreal Sea Service.

1966. 40th Anniv of Kirgizia.
3274 **1207** 4 k. red 20 10

1208 S. M. Kirov (80th Birth Anniv) **1210** A. Fersman (mineralogist)

1966. Soviet Personalities.
3275 **1208** 4 k. brown 20 10
3276 – 4 k. green 20 10
3277 – 4 k. violet 20 10
PORTRAITS: No. 3276, G. I. Ordzhonikidze (80th birth anniv); No. 3277, Ion Yakir (military commander, 70th birth anniv).

1966. Soviet Scientists. Multicoloured. Colours of name panels below.
3279 **1210** 4 k. blue 25 15
3280 – 4 k. brown 25 15
3281 – 4 k. violet 25 15
3282 – 4 k. brown and blue . . 35 15
PORTRAITS: No. 3280, D. K. Zabolotnyi (microbiologist); No. 3281, M. A. Shatelen (electrical engineer); No. 3282, O. Yu. Shmidt (arctic explorer).

„Луна-10"—XXIII съезду КПСС
(1211)

1966. Launching of "Luna 10". As No. 3284, but imperf, optd with T **1211**.
3283 **1212** 10 k. multicoloured . . 2·40 1·40

1212 Arrowheads, "Luna 9" and Orbit

1966. Cosmonautics Day. Multicoloured.
3284 10 k. Type **1212** 60 25
3285 12 k. Rocket launching and different orbit 65 30

1213 "Molniya I" in Orbit **1214** Ernst Thalmann (80th birth anniv)

1966. Launching of "Molniya I" Telecommunications Satellite.
3286 **1213** 10 k. multicoloured . . 55 20

1966. Prominent Leaders.
3287 **1214** 6 k. red 30 10
3288 – 6 k. violet 30 10
3289 – 6 k. brown 30 10
PORTRAITS: No. 3288, W. Pieck (90th birth anniv); No. 3289, Sun Yat-sen (birth cent).

1216 Spaceman and Soldier

1966. 15th Young Communist League Congress.
3290 **1216** 4 k. black and red . . . 15 10

1217 Ice Hockey Player

1966. Soviet Victory in World Ice Hockey Championships.
3291 **1217** 10 k. multicoloured . . 60 25

1218 N. I. Kuznetsov **1219** Tchaikovsky

1966. War Heroes. Guerilla Fighters.
3292 **1218** 4 k. black and green . . 20 10
3293 – 4 k. black and yellow . . 20 10
3294 – 4 k. black and blue . . . 20 10
3295 – 4 k. black and purple . . 20 10
3296 – 4 k. black and violet . . 20 10
PORTRAITS: No. 3293, I. Y. Sudmalis; No. 3294, A. A. Morozova; No. 3295, F. E. Strelets; No. 3296, T. P. Bumazhkov.

1966. 3rd International Tchaikovsky Music Competition, Moscow.
3297 – 4 k. black, red & yellow 35 10
3298 **1219** 6 k. black, red & yellow 55 10
3299 – 16 k. black, red & blue 1·10 35
DESIGNS: 4 k. Moscow State Conservatoire of Music; 16 k. Tchaikovsky's house and museum, Klin.

1220 Running

1966. Sports Events.
3300 **1220** 4 k. brown, olive & grn . 15 15
3301 – 6 k. black, bis & orge . 30 15
3302 – 12 k. black, bistre & bl . 45 25
DESIGNS: 6 k. Weightlifting; 12 k. Wrestling.

1222 Gold Medal and Chess Pieces

1966. World Chess Championship, Moscow.
3303 **1222** 6 k. multicoloured . . . 75 20

1223 Jules Rimet Cup and Football

1966. World Cup Football Championships and World Fencing Championships.
3304 **1223** 4 k. black, gold & red . 20 10
3305 – 6 k. multicoloured . . . 30 10
3306 – 12 k. multicoloured . . 60 20
3307 – 16 k. multicoloured . . 90 40
DESIGNS: 6 k. Footballers; 12 k. Fencers; 16 k. Fencer and fencing emblems.

1224 Sable, Lake Baikal and Animals (Illustration reduced. Actual size 80 × 26 mm)

1966. Barguzin Nature Reserve.
3308 **1224** 4 k. black and blue . . 50 15
3309 – 6 k. black and purple . 75 25
DESIGN: 6 k. Map of reserve, and brown bear.

1225 Lotus Plants **1226** "Venus 3" Medal, Globe and Flight Trajectory

1966. 125th Anniv of Sukhumi Botanical Gardens.
3310 **1225** 3 k. red, yellow & grn . 15 10
3311 – 6 k. bistre, brown & bl 30 10
3312 – 12 k. red, green & turq 50 30
DESIGNS: 6 k. Palms and cypresses; 12 k. Water lilies.

1966. Space Achievements.
3313 **1226** 6 k. black, silver & red . 40 15
3314 – 6 k. deep blue, blue and brown 40 15
3315 – 6 k. ochre and blue . . 40 15
3316 – 6 k. multicoloured . . . 45 15
3317 – 6 k. pink, mauve & blk 45 15
DESIGNS: No. 3314, Spacedogs, Ugolek and Veterok; No. 3315, "Luna 10"; No. 3316, "Molniya I"; No. 3317, "Luna 2's" pennant, Earth and Moon.

1227 Itkol

1966. Tourist Resorts. Multicoloured.
3318 1 k. Type **1227** 10 10
3319 4 k. Cruise ship on the Volga 30 10
3320 6 k. Archway, Leningrad . . 25 10
3321 10 k. Kislovodsk 45 20
3322 12 k. Ismail Samani Mausoleum, Bokhara . . . 1·00 15
3323 16 k. Sochi (Black Sea) . . . 1·25 30
The 6 k. is $27\frac{1}{2} \times 28$ mm.

1230 Congress Emblem

1231 Peace Dove and Japanese Crane

1966. 7th Consumers' Co-operative Societies Congress, Moscow.
3325 **1230** 4 k. yellow and brown . . 40 10

1966. Soviet-Japanese Meeting, Khabarovsk.
3326 **1231** 6 k. black and red . . . 30 15

1232 "Avtandil at a Mountain Spring", after engraving by S. Kabulazde

1966. 800th Birth Anniv of Shota Rustaveli (Georgian poet).
3327 – 3 k. black on green . . 25 10
3328 – 4 k. brown on yellow . . 30 10
3329 **1232** 6 k. black on blue . . . 40 15
DESIGNS: 3 k. Scene from poem "The Knight in the Tiger's Skin", after I. Toidze; 4 k. Rustaveli, after bas-relief by Y. Nikoladze.

1234 Arms, Moscow Skyline and Fireworks

1235 Trawler, Net and Map of Lake Baikal

1966. 49th Anniv of October Revolution.
3331 **1234** 4 k. multicoloured . . . 15 10

1966. Fish Resources of Lake Baikal. Mult.
3332 2 k. Grayling 15 10
3333 4 k. Sturgeon 20 10
3334 6 k. Type **1235** 30 10
3335 10 k. "Omul" 50 20
3336 12 k. "Sig" (salmon) 65 25
The 2, 4, 10 and 12 k. are horiz.

1236 "Agriculture and Industry"

1966. 23rd Soviet Communist Party Congress, Moscow (3rd issue).
3337 **1236** 4 k. silver and brown . . 20 10
3338 – 4 k. silver and blue . . 20 10
3339 – 4 k. silver and red . . . 20 10
3340 – 4 k. silver and red . . . 20 10
3341 – 4 k. silver and green . . 20 10
DESIGN (Map as Type **1236** with symbols of): No. 3338, "Communications and Transport"; No. 3339, "Education and Technology"; No. 3340, "Increased Productivity"; No. 3341, "Power Resources".

1237 Government Buildings, Kishinev

1966. 500th Anniv of Kishinev (Moldavian Republic).
3342 **1237** 4 k. multicoloured . . . 15 10

1238 Clouds, Rain and Decade Emblem

1239 Nikitin Monument, Map and Ships

1966. International Hydrological Decade.
3343 **1238** 6 k. multicoloured . . 30 10

1966. Nikitin's Voyage to India.
3344 **1239** 4 k. black, green & yell 20 10

1240 Scene from "Nargiz" (Muslim Magomaev)

1966. Azerbaijan Operas.
3345 **1240** 4 k. ochre and black . 35 15
3346 – 4 k. green and black . 35 15
DESIGN: No. 3346, Scene from "Kehzoglu" (Uzeir Gadzhibekov).

1241 "Luna 9" and Moon

1242 Agricultural and Chemical Symbols

1966.
3347 – 1 k. brown 10 10
3348 **1241** 2 k. violet 10 10
3349 – 3 k. purple 20 10
3350 – 4 k. red 20 10
3351 – 6 k. blue 60 10
3563 – 10 k. olive 90 35
3353 – 12 k. brown 70 10
3354 – 16 k. blue 90 15
3355 – 20 k. red, blue & drab . 1·10 50
3566 – 20 k. red . . . . 1·40 40
3356 **1242** 30 k. green . . . . . 1·75 40
3357 – 50 k. ultram, blue & grey 3·50 50
3568 – 50 k. blue . . . . . . 5·00 1·00
3358 – 1 r. brown and red . . 5·25 2·00
3569 – 1 r. brown and black . 8·25 2·00
DESIGNS—As Type **1241**: 1 k. Palace of Congresses, Kremlin; 3 k. Youth, girl and Lenin emblem; 4 k. Arms and hammer and sickle emblem; 6 k. "Communications" (Antonov An-10A Ukrainia airliner and sputnik); 10 k. Soldier and star emblem; 12 k. Furnaceman; 16 k. Girl with dove. As Type **1242**: 20 k. Workers' demonstration and flower; 50 k. "Postal communications"; 1 r. Lenin and industrial emblems.

1243 "Presenting Arms"

1245 Campaign Meeting

1966. 25th Anniv of People's Voluntary Corps.
3359 **1243** 4 k. brown and red . . 15 10

1966. "Hands off Vietnam".
3360 **1245** 6 k. multicoloured . . 20 10

1246 Servicemen

1966. 30th Anniv of Spanish Civil War.
3361 **1246** 6 k. black, red & ochre 20 10

1247 Ostankino TV Tower, "Molniya I" (satellite) and "1967"

1249 Statue, Tank and Medal

1248 Flight Diagram

1966. New Year and "50th Year of October Revolution".
3362 **1247** 4 k. multicoloured . . . 30 10

1966. Space Flight and Moon Landing of "Luna 9".
3363 **1248** 10 k. black and silver . . 55 25
3364 – 10 k. red and silver . . . 55 25
3365 – 10 k. black and silver . . 55 25
DESIGNS—SQUARE (25 × 25 mm): No. 3364, Arms of Russia and lunar pennant. HORIZ: No. 3365, "Lunar 9" on Moon's surface.

1966. 25th Anniv of Battle of Moscow.
3366 – 4 k. brown 30 10
3367 **1249** 6 k. ochre and sepia . . 30 15
3368 – 10 k. yellow & brown . . 60 20
DESIGNS—HORIZ: (60 × 28 mm): 4 k. Soviet troops advancing; 10 k. "Moscow at peace"–Kremlin, Sun and "Defence of Moscow" medal.

1250 Cervantes and Don Quixote

1966. 350th Death Anniv of Cervantes.
3369 **1250** 6 k. brown, green and deep green 30 10

1252 Bering's Ship "Sv. Pyotr" and Map of Komandor Islands

1966. Soviet Far Eastern Territories. Mult.
3370 1 k. Type **1252** 40 10
3371 2 k. Medny Island and map . 45 10
3372 4 k. Petropavlovsk Harbour, Kamchatka 65 10
3373 6 k. Geyser, Kamchatka (vert) 80 10
3374 10 k. Avatchinskaya Bay, Kamchatka . . . . 1·00 15
3375 12 k. Northern fur seals, Bering Is. . . . . 1·00 35
3376 16 k. Common guillemot colony, Kurile Islands . . . 2·75 65

1254 "The Lute Player" (Caravaggio)

1966. Art Treasures of the Hermitage Museum, Leningrad.
3377 – 4 k. black on yellow . . 20 10
3378 – 6 k. black on grey . . . 40 10
3379 – 10 k. black on lilac . . . 65 15
3380 – 12 k. black on green . . 85 20
3381 **1254** 16 k. black on buff . . . 1·10 35
DESIGNS—HORIZ: 4 k. "Golden Stag" (from Scythian battle shield (6th cent B.C.). VERT: 6 k. Persian silver jug (5th cent A.D.); 10 k. Statue of Voltaire (Houdon, 1781); 12 k. Malachite vase (Urals, 1840).

1255 Sea-water Distilling Apparatus

1967. World Fair, Montreal.
3382 **1255** 4 k. black, silver & grn 15 10
3383 – 6 k. multicoloured . . . 25 15
3384 – 10 k. multicoloured . . 45 20
DESIGNS—VERT: 6 k. "Atomic Energy" (explosion and symbol). HORIZ: 10 k. Space station "Proton 1".

1256 Lieut. B. I. Sizov

1967. War Heroes.
3386 **1256** 4 k. brown on yellow . 20 10
3387 – 4 k. brown on drab . . 20 10
DESIGN: No. 3387, Private V. V. Khodyrev.

1257 Woman's Face and Pavlov Shawl

1967. International Women's Day.
3388 **1257** 4 k. red, violet & green 20 10

1258 Cine-camera and Film "Flower"

1967. 5th International Film Festival, Moscow.
3389 **1258** 6 k. multicoloured . . . 30 10

1259 Factory Ship "Cheryashevsky"

1967. Soviet Fishing Industry. Multicoloured.
3390 6 k. Type **1259** 45 15
3391 6 k. Refrigerated trawler . . 45 15
3392 6 k. Crab canning ship . . . 45 15
3393 6 k. Trawler 45 15
3394 6 k. Seine-fishing boat, Black Sea 45 15

1260 Newspaper Cuttings, Hammer and Sickle

1261 I.S.O. Congress Emblem

1967. 50th Anniv of Newspaper "Izvestiya".
3395 **1260** 4 k. multicoloured . . . 15 10

1967. Moscow Congresses.
3396 6 k. turquoise, black & blue . 20 10
3397 6 k. red, black and blue . . 20 10
DESIGNS: No. 3396, Type **1261** (7th Congress of Int Standards Assn "I.S.O."); No. 3397, "V" emblem of 5th Int Mining Congress.

1262 I.T.Y. Emblem

1967. International Tourist Year.
3398 **1262** 4 k. blk, silver & blue . 15 10

Вена-1967
(1263)

1265 "Lenin as Schoolboy" (V. Tsigal)

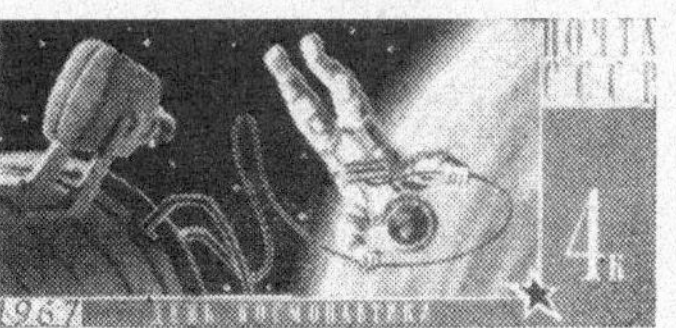

1264 A. A. Leonov in Space

1967. Victory in World Ice Hockey Championship. No. 3291 optd with T **1263**.
3399 **1217** 10 k. multicoloured . . 2·40 1·40

1967. Cosmonautics Day. Multicoloured.
3400 4 k. Type **1264** 20 10
3401 10 k. Rocket and Earth . . . 80 15
3402 16 k. "Luna 10" over Moon . 1·00 60

1967. Lenin's 97th Birth Anniv.
3403 **1265** 2 k. brown, yell & grn . 20 10
3404 – 3 k. brown and lake . . 35 10
3405 – 4 k. green, yellow and olive 45 40
3406 – 6 k. silver, black & bl . 95 40
3407 – 10 k. blue, blk & silver . 2·10 30
3408 – 10 k. black and gold . . 65 30
SCULPTURES—VERT: 3 k. Lenin's monument, Ulyanovsk; 6 k. Bust of Lenin (G. and Yu. Neroda); 10 k. (both) "Lenin as Leader" (Andreev). HORIZ: 4 k. "Lenin at Razliv" (Pinchuk).

1266 M. F. Shmyrev

1268 Marshal Biryuzov

1267 Transport crossing Ice on Lake Ladoga

1967. War Heroes.
3409 **1266** 4 k. sepia and brown . . 20 10
3410 – 4 k. brown and blue . . 20 10
3411 – 4 k. brown and violet . 20 10
DESIGNS: No. 3410, Major-General S. V. Rudnev; 3411, First Lieut. M. S. Kharchenko.

1967. Siege of Leningrad, 1941–42.
3412 **1267** 4 k. grey, red & cream . 20 10

1967. Biryuzov Commemoration.
3413 **1268** 4 k. green and yellow . 15 10

1269 Minsk Old and New

1270 Red Cross and Tulip

1967. 900th Anniv of Minsk.
3414 **1269** 4 k. green and black . 15 10

1967. Centenary of Russian Red Cross.
3415 **1270** 4 k. red and ochre . . 15 10

1271 Russian Stamps of 1918 and 1967

1967. 50th Anniv of U.S.S.R. Philatelic Exn, Moscow.
3416 **1271** 20 k. green and blue . 1·50 65

1272 Komsomolsk-on-Amur and Map

1967. 35th Anniv of Komsomolsk-on-Amur.
3418 **1272** 4 k. brown and red . . 50 10

1273 Motor Cyclist (International Motor Rally, Moscow)

1967. Sports and Pastimes. International Events.
3419 – 1 k. brown, bistre & grn 20 10
3420 – 2 k. brown 20 10
3421 – 3 k. blue 20 10
3422 – 4 k. turquoise 20 10
3423 – 6 k. purple and bistre . 30 10
3424 **1273** 10 k. purple and lilac . 75 30
DESIGNS AND EVENTS: 1 k. Draughts board and players (World Draughts Championships); 2 k. Throwing the javelin; 3 k. Running; 4 k. Long jumping (all preliminary events for Europa Cup Games); 6 k. Gymnast (World Gymnastics Championships).

1275 G. D. Gai (soldier)

1276 Games Emblem and Cup

1967. Commander G. D. Gai Commemoration.
3426 **1275** 4 k. black and red . . 35 10

1967. All Union Schoolchildren's Spartakiad.
3427 **1276** 4 k. red, black & silver 10 10

1277 Spartakiad Emblem and Cup

1967. 4th People's Spartakiad.
3428 4 k. black, red and silver . . 15 10
3429 4 k. black, red and silver . . 15 10
3430 4 k. black, red and silver . . 15 10
3431 4 k. black, red and silver . . 15 10
DESIGNS: Each with Cup. No. 3428, Type **1277**; No. 3429, Gymnastics; No. 3430, Diving; No. 3431, Cycling.

1278 V. G. Klochkov (Soviet hero)

1967. Klochkov Commemoration.
3432 **1278** 4 k. black and red . . . 15 10

1279 Crest, Flag and Capital of Moldavia

3433 АРМЯНСКАЯ ССР / ՀԱՅԿԱԿԱՆ ՍՍՀ
3434 АЗЕРБАЙДЖАНСКАЯ ССР / АЗӘРБАЈҸАН ССР
3435 БЕЛОРУССКАЯ ССР / БЕЛАРУСКАЯ ССР
3436 ЭСТОНСКАЯ ССР / EESTI NSV
3437 ГРУЗИНСКАЯ ССР / საბჭოთა სსრ
3438 КАЗАХСКАЯ ССР / ҚАЗАҚ ССР
3439 КИРГИЗСКАЯ ССР / КЫРГЫЗ ССР
3440 ЛАТВИЙСКАЯ ССР / LATVIJAS PSR
3441 ЛИТОВСКАЯ ССР / LIETUVOS TSR
3442 МОЛДАВСКАЯ ССР / РСС МОЛДОВЕНЯСКЭ
3443 РОССИЙСКАЯ СОВЕТСКАЯ ФЕДЕРАТИВНАЯ СОЦИАЛИСТИЧЕСКАЯ РЕСПУБЛИКА
3444 ТАДЖИКСКАЯ ССР / РСС ТОҶИКИСТОН
3445 ТУРКМЕНСКАЯ ССР / ТУРКМЕНИСТАН ССР
3446 УКРАИНСКАЯ ССР / УКРАЇНСЬКА РСР
3447 УЗБЕКСКАЯ ССР / ЎЗБЕКИСТОН ССР

Inscr at foot as shown above

1967. 50th Anniv of October Revolution (1st issue). Designs showing crests, flags and capitals of the Soviet Republics. Multicoloured.
3433 4 k. Armenia 15 10
3434 4 k. Azerbaijan 15 10
3435 4 k. Byelorussia 15 10
3436 4 k. Estonia 15 10
3437 4 k. Georgia 15 10
3438 4 k. Kazakhstan 15 10
3439 4 k. Kirghizia 15 10
3440 4 k. Latvia 15 10
3441 4 k. Lithuania 15 10
3442 4 k. Type **1279** 15 10
3443 4 k. Russia 15 10
3444 4 k. Tadzhikistan 15 10
3445 4 k. Turkmenistan 15 10
3446 4 k. Ukraine 15 10
3447 4 k. Uzbekistan 15 10
3448 4 k. Soviet Arms 15 10
No. 3448 is size 47 × 32 mm.
See also Nos. 3473/82.

HAVE YOU READ THE NOTES AT THE BEGINNING OF THIS CATALOGUE?
These often provide the answers to the enquiries we receive.

1280 Telecommunications Symbols

1967. "Progress of Communism".
3449 **1280** 4 k. red, purple & silver 2·50 1·40

1281 Manchurian Crane and Dove

1967. Soviet–Japanese Friendship.
3450 **1281** 16 k. brown, blk & red 1·00 35

1282 Karl Marx and Title Page

1967. Centenary of Karl Marx's "Das Kapital".
3451 **1282** 4 k. brown and red . . 25 10

1283 Arctic Fox

1285 Krasnodon Memorial

1284 Ice Skating

1967. Fur-bearing Animals.
3452 **1283** 2 k. blue, black & brn . 15 10
3453 – 4 k. blue, black & drab 20 10
3454 – 6 k. ochre, black & grn 35 10
3455 – 10 k. brown, blk & grn 50 15
3456 – 12 k. black, ochre & vio 55 25
3457 – 16 k. brown, blk & yell 70 35
3458 – 20 k. brown, black & turq 90 50
DESIGNS—VERT: 4 k. Red fox; 12 k. Stoat; 16 k. Sable. HORIZ: 6 k. Red fox; 10 k. Muskrat; 20 k. European mink.

1967. Winter Olympic Games, Grenoble (1968). Multicoloured.
3459 2 k. Type **1284** 10 10
3460 3 k. Ski jumping 15 10
3461 4 k. Games emblem (vert) . . 15 10
3462 10 k. Ice hockey 55 15
3463 12 k. Skiing 90 30

1967. 25th Anniv of Krasnodon Defence.
3464 **1285** 4 k. black, yell & pur . 15 10

1285a Map and Snow Leopard (½-size illustration)

1967. Cedar Valley Nature Reserve.
3465 **1285a** 10 k. black and bistre . 75 30

1286 Badge and Yakovlev Yak-9 Aircraft

1288 Cosmonauts in Space

1287 Militiaman and Soviet Crest

1967. 25th Anniv of French "Normandie-Niemen" Fighter Squadron.
3466 **1286** 6 k. red, blue & gold . . 35 15

1967. 50th Anniv of Soviet Militia.
3467 **1287** 4 k. red and blue . . . 20 10

1967. Space Fantasies. Multicoloured.
3468 4 k. Type **1288** 15 10
3469 6 k. Men on the Moon (horiz) 20 10
3470 10 k. Cosmic vehicle 45 15
3471 12 k. Planetary landscape (horiz) 75 20
3472 16 k. Imaginary spacecraft . 85 55

1289 Red Star and Soviet Crest

1967. 50th Anniv of October Revolution (2nd issue). "50 Heroic Years". Designs showing paintings and Soviet Arms. Multicoloured.
3473 4 k. Type **1289** 25 15
3474 4 k. "Lenin addressing Congress" (Serov—1955) . 25 15
3475 4 k. "Lenin explaining the GOELRO map" (Schmatko—1957) 25 15
3476 4 k. "The First Cavalry" (Grekov—1924) 25 15
3477 4 k. "Students" (Yoganson—1928) 25 15
3478 4 k. "People's Friendship" (Karpov—1924) 25 15
3479 4 k. "Dawn of the Five Year Plan" (construction work, Romas—1934) 35 15
3480 4 k. "Farmers' Holiday" (Gerasimov—1937) 25 15
3481 4 k. "Victory in World War II" (Korolev—1965) 25 15
3482 4 k. "Builders of Communism" (Merpert and Skripkov—1965) 25 15

1290 S. Katayama

1292 T. V. Tower, Moscow

1967. Katayama (founder of Japanese Communist Party) Commemoration.
3484 **1290** 6 k. green 15 10

1967. Opening of Ostankino T.V. Tower, Moscow.
3486 **1292** 16 k. black, sil & orge . 1·00 20

1293 Narva-Joesuu (Estonia)

1967. Baltic Health Resorts. Multicoloured.
3487 4 k. Yurmala (Latvia) 10 10
3488 6 k. Type **1293** 45 10
3489 10 k. Druskininkai (Lithuania) 55 15
3490 12 k. Zelenogradsk (Kaliningrad) (vert) 70 20
3491 16 k. Svetlogorsk (Kaliningrad) (vert) 90 25

1294 K.G.B. Emblem

1295 Moscow View

1967. 50th Anniv of State Security Commission (K.G.B.).
3492 **1294** 4 k. red, silver & blue . 15 10

1967. New Year.
3493 **1295** 4 k. brown, pink and silver 20 10

1296 Revolutionaries at Kharkov, and Monument

1967. 50th Anniv of Ukraine Republic.
3494 **1296** 4 k. multicoloured . . 15 10
3495 – 6 k. multicoloured . . 30 10
3496 – 10 k. multicoloured . . 55 15
DESIGNS: 6 k. Hammer and sickle and industrial and agricultural scenes; 10 k. Unknown Soldier's monument, Kiev, and young Ukrainians with welcoming bread and salt.

1297 Armoury, Commandant and Trinity Towers

1299 Unknown Soldier's Tomb, Kremlin

1298 Moscow Badge, Lenin's Tomb and Rockets

1967. Kremlin Buildings.
3497 **1297** 4 k. brown, pur & grn . 15 10
3498 – 6 k. brown, grn & yell . 25 10
3499 – 10 k. brown and grey . 60 15
3500 – 12 k. green, violet and cream 75 30
3501 – 16 k. brown, red and light brown 85 30
DESIGNS—HORIZ: 6 k. Cathedral of the Annunciation. VERT: 10 k. Konstantino-Yelenin, Alarm and Spassky Towers; 12 k. Ivan the Great's bell tower; 16 k. Kutafya and Trinity Towers.

1967. "50 Years of Communist Development".
3502 **1298** 4 k. lake 20 10
3503 – 4 k. brown 20 10
3504 – 4 k. green 20 10
3505 – 4 k. blue 20 10
3506 – 4 k. blue 20 10
DESIGNS—HORIZ: No. 3503, Computer-tape cogwheel and industrial scene; 3504, Ear of wheat and grain silo; 3505, Microscope, radar antennae and Moscow University. VERT: No. 3506, T.V. Tower, liner, railway bridge and jet airliner.

1967. "Unknown Soldier" Commemoration.
3507 **1299** 4 k. red 15 10

1300 "The Interrogation of Communists" (Yoganson)

1967. Paintings in the Tretyakov Gallery, Moscow. Multicoloured.
3508 3 k. Type **1300** 15 10
3509 4 k. "The Sea-shore" (Aivazovsky) 25 10
3510 4 k. "The Lace Maker" (Tropinin) (vert) 25 10
3511 6 k. "The Bakery" (Yablonskaya) 30 10
3512 6 k. "Alexander Nevsky" (part of triptych by Korin) (vert) 30 10
3513 6 k. "Boyarynya Morozova" (Surikov) 30 10
3514 10 k. "The Swan Maiden" (Vroubel) (vert) 75 20
3515 10 k. "The Arrest of a Propagandist" (Repin) . . 75 20
3516 16 k. "Moscow Suburb in February" (Nissky) . . . . 1·50 45
Nos. 3511/13 are larger 60 × 34 mm or 34 × 60 mm.

1301 Congress Emblem

1302 Lieut. S. G. Baikov

1968. 14th Soviet Trade Unions Congress, Moscow.
3517 **1301** 6 k. red and green . . . 40 10

1968. War Heroes.
3518 **1302** 4 k. black and blue . . . 20 10
3519 – 4 k. blue and green . . . 20 10
3520 – 4 k. black and red . . . 20 10
PORTRAITS: No. 3519, Lieut. P. L. Guchenko; No. 3520, A. A. Pokaltchuk.

1303 Racehorses

1304 M. Ulyanova

1968. Soviet Horse Breeding.
3521 **1303** 4 k. black, pur & blue . 25 10
3522 – 6 k. black, blue and red 35 10
3523 – 10 k. black, brn & turq . 60 15
3524 – 12 k. black, grn & brn . 65 20
3525 – 16 k. black, red & grn . 90 30
DESIGNS (each with horse's head and horses "in the field"). VERT: 6 k. Show horses; 12 k. Show jumpers. HORIZ: 10 k. Trotters; 16 k. Hunters.

1968. 90th Birth Anniv of M. I. Ulyanova (Lenin's sister).
3526 **1304** 4 k. blue and green . . . 35 10

1305 Red Star and Forces' Flags

1968. 50th Anniv of Soviet Armed Forces. Multicoloured.
3527 4 k. Type **1305** 30 15
3528 4 k. Lenin addressing recruits 30 15
3529 4 k. Recruiting poster and volunteers 30 15
3530 4 k. Red Army entering Vladivostok, 1922, and monument 30 15
3531 4 k. Dnieper Dam and statue "On Guard" 30 15
3532 4 k. "Liberators" poster and tanks in the Ukraine . . . 30 15
3533 4 k. "To the East" poster and retreating Germans fording river 30 15
3534 4 k. Stalingrad battle monument and German prisoners-of-war 30 15
3535 4 k. Victory parade, Red Square, Moscow, and monument, Treptow (Berlin) 30 15
3536 4 k. Rockets, tank, warships and Red Flag 30 15
Nos. 3527 and 3536 are vert. The rest are horiz.

HAVE YOU READ THE NOTES AT THE BEGINNING OF THIS CATALOGUE?
These often provide the answers to the enquiries we receive.

1306 Gorky (after Serov)

1307 Fireman and Appliances

1968. Birth Centenary of Maksim Gorky (writer).
3538 **1306** 4 k. brown and drab . . 15 10

1968. 50th Anniv of Soviet Fire Services.
3539 **1307** 4 k. black and red . . . 20 10

1308 Linked Satellites

1309 N. N. Popudrenko

1968. Space Link of "Cosmos" Satellites.
3540 **1308** 6 k. black, gold & pur . 20 10

1968. War Heroes.
3541 **1309** 4 k. black and green . . 20 10
3542 – 4 k. black and lilac . . 20 10
DESIGN: No. 3542, P. P. Vershigora.

1310 Protective Hand

1968. "Solidarity with Vietnam".
3543 **1310** 6 k. multicoloured . . . 15 10

1311 Leonov filming in Space

1968. Cosmonautics Day. Multicoloured.
3544 4 k. Type **1311** 25 15
3545 6 k. "Kosmos 186" and "Kosmos 188" linking in space 35 15
3546 10 k. "Venera 4" space probe 1·00 15

1312 Lenin

1968. Lenin's 98th Birth Anniv.
3547 **1312** 4 k. multicoloured . . . 85 15
3548 – 4 k. black, red & gold . 85 15
3549 – 4 k. brown, red & gold 85 15
DESIGNS: No. 3548, Lenin speaking in Red Square; No. 3549, Lenin in peaked cap speaking from lorry during parade.

1313 A. Navoi

1314 Karl Marx

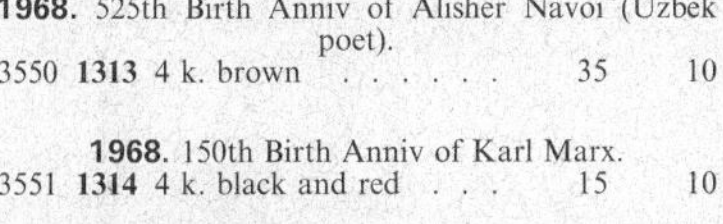

1968. 525th Birth Anniv of Alisher Navoi (Uzbek poet).
3550 **1313** 4 k. brown 35 10

1968. 150th Birth Anniv of Karl Marx.
3551 **1314** 4 k. black and red . . . 15 10

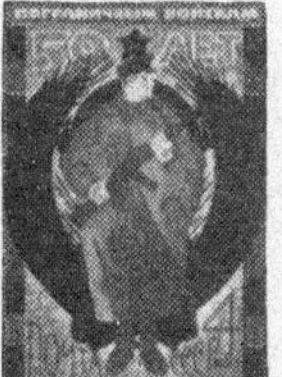
1315 Frontier Guard

1316 Gem and Congress Emblem

1968. 50th Anniv of Soviet Frontier Guards. Multicoloured.
3552 4 k. Type **1315** 15 10
3553 6 k. Jubilee badge 20 10

1968. "International Congresses and Assemblies".
3554 **1316** 6 k. deep blue, blue and green 25 15
3555 – 6 k. gold, orange & brn . 25 15
3556 – 6 k. gold, black & red . 25 15
3557 – 6 k. orange, blk & mve . 25 15
DESIGNS: No. 3554, Type **1316** (8th Enriched Minerals Congress); No. 3555, Power stations, pylon and emblem (7th World Power Conference); No. 3556, Beetle and emblem (13th Entomological Congress); No. 3557, Roses and emblem (4th Congress on Volatile Oils).

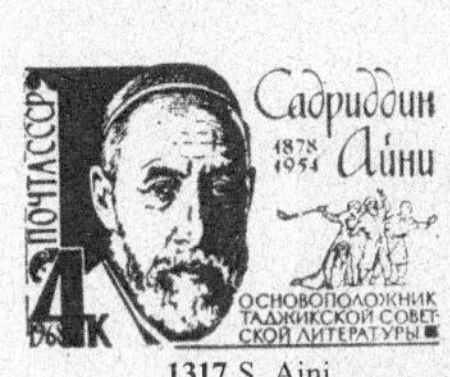
1317 S. Aini

1319 "Kiev Uprising" (after V. Boroday)

1318 Congress Emblem and Postrider

1968. 90th Birth Anniv of Sadriddin Aini (Tadzhik writer).
3570 **1317** 4 k. purple and bistre . 35 10

1968. Meeting of U.P.U. Consultative Commission, Moscow.
3571 **1318** 6 k. red and grey . . . 20 10
3572 – 6 k. red and yellow . . 30 10
DESIGN: No. 3572, Emblem and transport.

1968. 50th Anniv of Ukraine Communist Party.
3573 **1319** 4 k. red, purple & gold . 10 10

1320 Athletes and "50"

1321 Handball

1968. Young Communist League's 50th Anniv Games.
3574 **1320** 4 k. red, drab & yellow . 10 10

1968. Various Sports Events.
3575 **1321** 2 k. multicoloured . . . 15 10
3576 – 4 k. multicoloured . . . 25 10
3577 – 6 k. multicoloured . . . 30 10
3578 – 10 k. red, black & bistre 55 20
3579 – 12 k. multicoloured . . 65 25
DESIGNS AND EVENTS—VERT: Type **1321** (World Handball Games, Moscow); 6 k. Yachting (20th Baltic Regatta); 10 k. Football (70th anniv of Russian soccer). HORIZ: 4 k. Table tennis (All European Juvenile Competitions); 12 k. Underwater swimming (European Underwater Sports Championships, Alushta, Ukraine).

HAVE YOU READ THE NOTES AT THE BEGINNING OF THIS CATALOGUE?
These often provide the answers to the enquiries we receive.

1322 Girl Gymnasts

1323 Gediminas Tower, Vilnius (Vilna)

1968. Olympic Games, Mexico. Backgrounds in gold.
3580 **1322** 4 k. turquoise and blue 15 10
3581 – 6 k. violet and red . . 15 10
3582 – 10 k. green and turquoise 55 10
3583 – 12 k. brown & orange . 65 15
3584 – 16 k. blue and pink . . 85 30
DESIGNS: 6 k. Weightlifting; 10 k. Rowing; 12 k. Women's Hurdles; 16 k. Fencing match.

1968. 50th Anniv of Soviet Lithuania.
3586 **1323** 4 k. red, drab & purple 35 10

1324 Tbilisi University

1325 "Death of Laocoon and his Sons" (from sculpture by Agesandre, Polidor and Asinodor)

1968. 50th Anniv of Tbilisi University.
3587 **1324** 4 k. beige and green . . 35 10

1968. "Promote Solidarity with the Greek Democrats".
3588 **1325** 6 k. drab, purple & brn 3·75 3·75

1326 Cavalryman

1968. 50th Anniv of Leninist Young Communist League (Komsomol) (1st issue). Multicoloured.
3589 2 k. Type **1326** 10 10
3590 3 k. Young workers 10 10
3591 4 k. Army officer 10 10
3592 6 k. Construction workers . 15 10
3593 10 k. Agricultural workers . 20 20
See also No. 3654.

1327 Institute and Molecular Structure

1968. 50th Anniv of N. S. Kurnakov Institute of Chemistry.
3595 **1327** 4 k. purple, black and blue 10 10

1328 Letter

1968. Int Correspondence Week and Stamp Day.
3596 **1328** 4 k. brown, red & lake 15 10
3597 – 4 k. blue, ochre and deep blue 15 10
DESIGN: No. 3597, Russian stamps.

1329 "The 26 Baku Commissars" (statue by Makarov)

1330 T. Antikainen

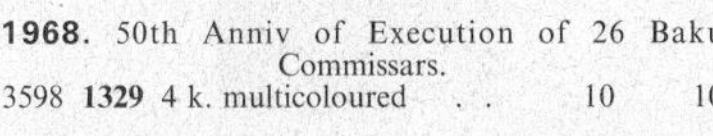

1968. 50th Anniv of Execution of 26 Baku Commissars.
3598 **1329** 4 k. multicoloured . . 10 10

1968. 70th Birthday of T. Antikainen (Finnish Communist leader).
3599 **1330** 6 k. brown and grey . 15 10

1331 Liner "Ivan Franko"

1333 P. P. Postyshev (1887–1940)

1332 Order of the October Revolution

1968. Soviet Merchant Marine.
3600 **1331** 6 k. red, dp blue & bl . 25 10

1968. 51st Anniv of October Revolution.
3601 **1332** 4 k. multicoloured . . . 10 10

1968. Soviet Personalities.
3602 **1333** 4 k. black 15 10
3603 – 4 k. black 15 10
3604 – 4 k. black 15 10
DESIGNS: No. 3603, S. G. Shaumian (1878–1918); No. 3604, A. Ikramov (1898–1938).

1334 Statuette of Warrior and Ararat Mountains

1335 I. S. Turgenev

1968. 2,750th Anniv of Yerevan (Armenian capital).
3605 **1334** 4 k. black and brown on grey 15 10
3606 – 12 k. brown & sepia on yellow 45 25
DESIGN: 12 k. Sasunsky Monument.

1968. 150th Birth Anniv of Ivan Turgenev (writer).
3607 **1335** 4 k. green 15 10

1336 American Bison and Common Zebra

1968. Fauna. Soviet Wildlife Reservations. Mult.
3608 4 k. Type **1336** 25 10
3609 4 k. Purple swamphen and lotus 45 10
3610 6 k. Great egrets (vert) . . . 60 15
3611 6 k. Ostrich and golden pheasant (vert) 60 15
3612 10 k. Eland and guanaco . . 50 25
3613 10 k. Glossy ibis and white spoonbill 80 30

1337 Building and Equipment

1968. 50th Anniv of Lenin Radio-laboratory, Gorky.
3614 **1337** 4 k. blue and ochre . . . 15 10

1338 Prospecting for Minerals

1339 Djety-Oguz Kirgizia

1968. Geology Day. Multicoloured.
3615 4 k. Type **1338** 30 10
3616 6 k. "Tracking down" metals 30 20
3617 10 k. Oil derrick 85 20

1968. Central Asian Spas. Multicoloured.
3618 4 k. Type **1339** 15 10
3619 4 k. Borovoe, Kazakhstan (horiz) 15 10
3620 6 k. Issyk-kul, Kirgizia (horiz) 25 15
3621 6 k. Borovoe, Kazakhstan . 25 15

1340 Silver Medal, "Philatec", Paris 1964

1968. Awards to Soviet Post Office at Foreign Stamp Exhibitions.
3622 4 k. black, silver and purple . 20 10
3623 6 k. black, gold and blue . . 25 10
3624 10 k. black, gold and blue . 55 15
3625 12 k. black, silver & turq . . 45 15
3626 16 k. black, gold and red . . 75 30
3627 20 k. black, gold and blue . 90 40
3628 30 k. black, gold & brown . 1·40 85
DESIGNS: 4 k. Type **1340**; 6 k. Plaque, "Debria", Berlin, 1959; 10 k. Cup and medals, Riccione, 1952, 1968; 12 k. Diploma and medal, "Thematic Biennale", Buenos Aires, 1965; 16 k. Trophies and medals, Rome, 1952, 1954; 20 k. Medals and plaques, "Wipa", Vienna, 1966; 30 k. Glass trophies, Prague, 1950, 1955, 1962.

1341 V. K. Lebedinsky

1342 Soldier with Flag

1968. Birth Centenary of Lebedinsky (physicist).
3629 **1341** 4 k. multicoloured . . . 35 10

1968. 50th Anniv of Estonian Workers' Commune.
3630 **1342** 4 k. black and red . . . 10 10

1344 Moscow Buildings and Fir Branch

1968. New Year.
3632 **1344** 4 k. multicoloured . . . 35 10

1345 G. Beregovoi (cosmonaut)

1346 Electric Train, Map and Emblem

1968. Flight of "Soyuz 3".
3633 **1345** 10 k. black, red & blue 60 10

1968. Soviet Railways.
3634 **1346** 4 k. orange and mauve 25 15
3635 – 10 k. brown and green . 65 25
DESIGN: 10 k. Track-laying train.

1347 Red Flag, Newspapers and Monument

1348 "The Reapers" (Venetsianov)

1968. 50th Anniv of Byelorussian Communist Party.
3636 **1347** 4 k. black, brown & red 15 10

1968. Paintings in State Museum, Leningrad. Mult.

3637 1 k. Type **1348** 15 10
3638 2 k. "The Last Days of Pompeii" (Bryullov) . . . 20 10
3639 3 k. "A Knight at the Crossroads" (Vaznetzov) . 25 10
3640 4 k. "Conquering a Town in Winter" (Surikov) 30 10
3641 6 k. "The Lake" (Levitan) . . 70 10
3642 10 k. "The Year 1919: Alarm" (Petrov-Vodkin) 80 15
3643 16 k. "The Defence of Sevastopol" (Deineka) . . 95 20
3644 20 k. "Homer's Bust (Korzhev) 1·10 25
3645 30 k. "The Celebration in Uritsky Square" (Kustodiev) 1·40 55
3646 50 k. "The Duel between Peresvet and Chelumbey" (Avilov) . . . . 2·10 1·10

Nos. 3638/41, 3643, 3645/6 are horiz designs, size 61 × 28 mm.

1349 House, Onega Region

1968. Soviet Architecture.

3647 **1349** 3 k. brown on buff . . 20 10
3648 – 4 k. green on yellow . . 30 10
3649 – 6 k. violet on grey . . . 60 10
3650 – 10 k. blue on green . . 85 25
3651 – 12 k. red on drab . . . 1·00 65
3652 – 16 k. black on yellow . 1·40 85

DESIGNS: 4 k. Farmhouse door, Gorky region; 6 k. Wooden church, Kishi; 10 k. Citadel, Rostov-Yaroslavl; 12 k. Entrance gate, Tsaritzino; 16 k. Master-builder Rossi's Street, Leningrad.

1968. 50th Death Anniv of N. G. Markin (1893–1918) (revolutionary). As T **1333**.

3653 4 k. black 15 10

1350 Flags and Order of October Revolution

1968. 50th Anniv of Leninist Young Communist League (Komsomol) (2nd issue).

3654 **1350** 12 k. multicoloured . . 60 15

1351 "Declaration of Republic"

1969. 50th Anniv of Byelorussian Republic. Mult.

3655 2 k. Type **1351** 10 10
3656 4 k. Partisans at war, 1941–45 10 10
3657 6 k. Reconstruction workers . 15 10

1352 Red Guard in Riga (statue)

1354 University Buildings

1969. 50th Anniv of Soviet Revolution in Latvia.

3658 **1352** 4 k. red and orange . . 10 10

1969. 150th Anniv of Leningrad University.

3660 **1354** 10 k. black and lake . . 50 10

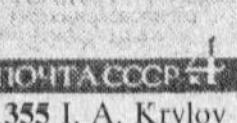

1355 I. A. Krylov

1356 N. D. Filchenkov

1969. Birth Bicent of Ivan Krylov (fabulist).

3661 **1355** 4 k. multicoloured . . . 10 10

1969. War Heroes.

3662 **1356** 4 k. brown and red . . 15 10
3663 – 4 k. brown and green . . 15 10

DESIGN: No. 3663, A. A. Kosmodemiansky.

1357 "The Wheel Turns Round Again" (sculpture, Z. Kisfaludi-Strobl)

1969. 50th Anniv of 1st Hungarian Soviet Republic.

3664 **1357** 6 k. black, red & green 15 10

1358 Crest and Symbols of Petrochemical Industry

1969. 50th Anniv of Bashkir Autonomous Soviet Socialist Republic.

3665 **1358** 4 k. multicoloured . . 15 10

1359 "Vostok 1" on Launching-pad

1969. Cosmonautics Day. Multicoloured.

3666 10 k. Type **1359** 40 15
3667 10 k. "Zond 5" in Lunar orbit (horiz) 40 15
3668 10 k. Sergei Pavlovich Korolev (space scientist) (horiz) . . 40 15

1360 Lenin University, Kazan

1969. Buildings connected with Lenin. Mult.

3670 4 k. Type **1360** 15 10
3671 4 k. Lenin Museum, Kuibyshev 15 10
3672 4 k. Lenin Museum, Pskov . 15 10
3673 4 k. Lenin Museum, Shushenskaya 15 10
3674 4 k. "Hay Hut", Razliv . . 15 10
3675 4 k. Lenin Museum, Gorky Park, Leningrad 15 10
3676 4 k. Smolny Institute, Leningrad 15 10
3677 4 k. Lenin's Office, Kremlin 15 10
3678 4 k. Library, Ulyanovsk (wrongly inscr "Lenin Museum") 15 10
3679 4 k. Lenin Museum, Ulyanovsk 15 10

1361 Telephone and Radio Set

1969. 50th Anniv of VEF Electrical Works, Riga.

3680 **1361** 10 k. brown and red . 60 15

1362 I.L.O. Emblem

1969. 50th Anniv of Int Labour Organization.

3681 **1362** 6 k. gold and red . . . 15 10

1363 Otakar Jaros **1364** P. E. Dybenko

1969. Otakar Jaros (Czech war hero) Commem.

3682 **1363** 4 k. black and blue . . . 15 10

1969. Soviet Personalities. (80th Birth Annivs).

3683 **1364** 4 k. red 15 10
3684 – 4 k. blue 15 10

DESIGN: No. 3684, S. V. Kosior (1889–1939).

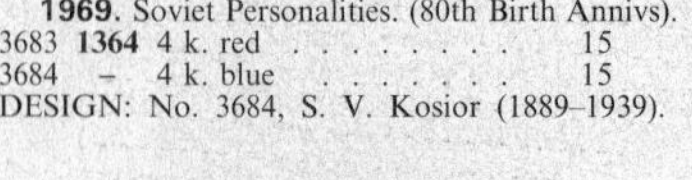

1365 Suleiman Stalsky

1969. Birth Centenary of Suleiman Stalsky (Dagestan poet).

3685 **1365** 4 k. green and brown . . 15 10

1366 "Clear Glade" Rose

1969. Academy of Sciences Botanical Gardens, Moscow. Multicoloured.

3686 2 k. Type **1366** 10 10
3687 4 k. "Slender" lily 15 10
3688 10 k. "Cattleya hybr" orchid . 35 10
3689 12 k. "Leaves Fall" dahlia . . 40 15
3690 14 k. "Ural Girl" gladiolus . 60 30

1367 Scientific Centre

1969. 50th Anniv of Ukraine Academy of Sciences, Kiev.

3691 **1367** 4 k. purple & yellow . . 15 10

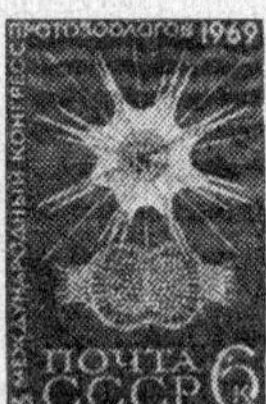

1368 Gold Medal within Film "Flower" **1369** Congress Emblem

1969. Cine and Ballet Events, Moscow. Mult.

3692 6 k. Type **1368** (6th Int Cinema Festival) 30 15
3693 6 k. Ballet dancers (1st Int Ballet Competitions) 30 15

1969. 3rd Int Protozoologists Congress, Leningrad.

3694 **1369** 6 k. multicoloured . . . 50 15

1370 Estonian Singer

1969. Centenary of Estonian Choir Festival.

3695 **1370** 4 k. red and ochre . . . 20 10

1371 Mendeleev and Formula

1969. Centenary of Mendeleev's Periodic Law of Elements.

3696 **1371** 6 k. brown and red . . 40 20

1372 Peace Banner and World Landmarks **1373** Rocket on Laser Beam, and Moon

1969. 20th Anniv of World Peace Movement.

3698 **1372** 10 k. multicoloured . . 20 15

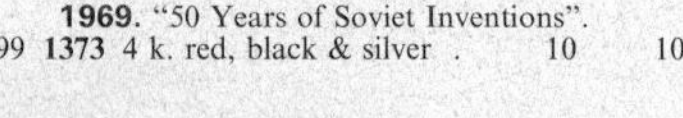

1969. "50 Years of Soviet Inventions".

3699 **1373** 4 k. red, black & silver . 10 10

1374 Kotlyarevsky (**1375**)

1969. Birth Bicentenary of Ivan Kotlyarevsky (Ukrainian writer).

3700 **1374** 4 k. black, brown & grn 10 10

1969. Soviet Ice Hockey Victory in World Championships, Stockholm. No. 2828 further optd with **1375**.

3701 6 k. turquoise and purple . . 3·25 2·00

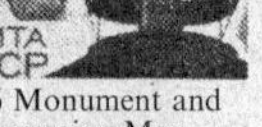

1376 Monument and Campaign Map **1377** Hands holding Torch, and Bulgarian Arms

1969. 25th Anniv of Byelorussian Liberation.

3702 **1376** 4 k. red, purple & olive 15 10

1969. 25th Anniv of Bulgarian and Polish Peoples' Republics.

3703 **1377** 6 k. multicoloured . . . 20 10
3704 – 6 k. red and ochre . . . 20 10

DESIGN: No. 3704, Polish map, flag and arms.

1378 Registan Square, Samarkand

1969. 2,500th Anniv of Samarkand. Mult.

3705 4 k. Type **1378** 15 10
3706 6 k. Intourist Hotel, Samarkand 20 15

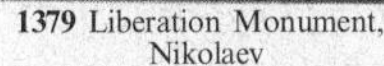

1379 Liberation Monument, Nikolaev
1380 Volleyball (European Junior Championships)

1969. 25th Anniv of Liberation of Nikolaev.
3707 1379 4 k. red, violet & black . 15 10

1969. International Sporting Events.
3708 1380 4 k. red, brown & orge . 20 10
3709 – 6 k. multicoloured . . . 30 10
DESIGN: 6 k. Canoeing (European Championships).

1381 M. Munkacsy and detail of painting, "Peasant Woman churning Butter"
1382 Miners' Statue, Donetsk

1969. 125th Birth Anniv of Mihaly Munkacsy (Hungarian painter).
3710 1381 6 k. black, orge & brn . 15 10

1969. Centenary of Donetsk.
3711 1382 4 k. mauve and grey . . 10 10

1383 "Horse-drawn Machine-guns" (M. Grekov)

1969. 50th Anniv of 1st Cavalry Army.
3712 1383 4 k. brown and red . . 25 10

1384 Ilya Repin (self-portrait)
1385 Running

1969. 125th Birth Anniv of Ilya Repin (painter). Multicoloured.
3713 4 k. "Barge-haulers on the Volga" 20 10
3714 6 k. "Unexpected" 25 15
3715 10 k. Type 1384 . . . . . . 30 15
3716 12 k. "The Refusal of Confession" 40 20
3717 16 k. "Dnieper Cossacks" . . 75 30

1969. 9th Trade Unions' Games, Moscow.
3718 1385 4 k. black, grn & red . . 10 10
3719 – 10 k. black, blue & grn . 25 10
DESIGN: 10 k. Gymnastics.

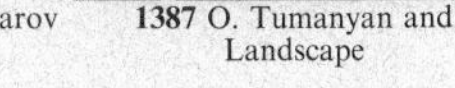
1386 V. L. Komarov
1387 O. Tumanyan and Landscape

1969. Birth Cent of V. L. Komarov (botanist).
3721 1386 4 k. brown and olive . . 15 10

1969. Birth Cent of O. Tumanyan (Armenian poet).
3722 1387 10 k. black and blue . . 50 15

1388 Turkoman Drinking-horn (2nd-cent B.C.)
1389 Mahatma Gandhi

1969. Oriental Art Treasures, State Museum of Oriental Art, Moscow. Multicoloured.
3723 4 k. Type 1388 . . . . . . 15 10
3724 6 k. Simurg vessel, Persia (13th-century) 20 10
3725 12 k. Statuette, Korea (8th-century) 35 15
3726 16 k. Bodhisatva statuette, Tibet (7th-century) 45 20
3727 20 k. Ebisu statuette, Japan (17th-century) 60 45

1969. Birth Centenary of Mahatma Gandhi.
3728 1389 6 k. brown 45 15

1390 Black Stork at Nest

1969. Belovezhaskaya Pushcha Nature Reserve. Multicoloured.
3729 4 k. Type 1390 . . . . . . 55 10
3730 6 k. Red deer and fawn . . 40 15
3731 10 k. European bison fighting 65 20
3732 12 k. Lynx and cubs 75 20
3733 16 k. Wild boar and young . 90 35
No. 3731 is larger, 76 × 24 mm.

1391 "Komitas" and Rural Scene

1969. Birth Cent of "Komitas" (S. Sogomonyan, Armenian composer).
3734 1391 6 k. black, flesh & grey 25 10

1392 Sergei Gritsevets (fighter-pilot)
1393 I. Pavlov (after portrait by A. Yar-Kravchenko)

1969. Soviet War Heroes.
3735 1392 4 k. black and green . 30 10
3736 – 4 k. brown, red & yell . 20 10
3737 – 4 k. brown and green . 20 10
DESIGNS: As Type 1392. No. 3737, Lisa Chaikina (partisan). ($35\frac{1}{2} \times 24$ mm); No. 3736, A. Cheponis, Y. Alexonis and G. Boris (Kaunas resistance fighters).

1969. 120th Birth Anniv of Ivan P. Pavlov (physiologist).
3738 1393 4 k. multicoloured . . 20 10

1394 D.D.R. Arms and Berlin Landmarks
1395 A. V. Koltsov (from portrait by A. Yar-Kravchenko)

1969. 20th Anniv of German Democratic Republic.
3739 1394 6 k. multicoloured . . 15 10

1969. 160th Birth Anniv of A. V. Koltsov (poet).
3740 1395 4 k. brown and blue . 10 10

1396 Arms of Ukraine and Memorial
1397 Kremlin, and Hammer and Sickle

1969. 25th Anniv of Ukraine Liberation.
3741 1396 4 k. red and gold . . . 15 10

1969. 52nd Anniv of October Revolution.
3742 1397 4 k. multicoloured . . . 10 10

1398 G. Shonin and V. Kubasov ("Soyuz 6")

1969. Triple Space Flights.
3744 1398 10 k. green and gold . . 55 15
3745 – 10 k. green and gold . . 55 15
3746 – 10 k. green and gold . . 55 15
DESIGNS: No. 3745, A. Filipchenko, V. Volkov and V. Gorbatko ("Soyuz 7"); No. 3746, V. Shatalov and A. Yeliseev ("Soyuz 8").

1399 Lenin when a Youth, and Emblems
1400 Corps Emblem on Red Star

1969. U.S.S.R. Youth Philatelic Exhibition to commemorate Lenin's Birth Centenary, Kiev.
3747 1399 4 k. lake and pink . . . 10 10

1969. 50th Anniv of Red Army Communications Corps.
3748 1400 4 k. red, brown & bistre 10 10

1401 "Male and Female Farmworkers" (sculptured group, V. Mukhina), and Title-page

1969. 3rd Soviet Collective Farmers' Congress, Moscow.
3749 1401 4 k. brown and gold . . 10 10

1402 "Vasilisa, the Beauty" (folk tale)

1969. Russian Fairy Tales. Multicoloured.
3750 4 k. Type 1402 . . . . 30 25
3751 10 k. "Maria Morevna" (folk tale) 75 45
3752 16 k. "The Golden Cockerel" (Pushkin) (horiz) . . . . . 1·25 60
3753 20 k. "Finist, the Fine Fellow" (folk tale) . . . . 1·50 1·10
3754 50 k. "Tale of the Tsar Saltan" (Pushkin) . . . . 2·75 2·40

1403 Venus Plaque and Radio-telescope

1969. Space Exploration.
3755 1403 4 k. red, brown & blk . 20 10
3756 – 6 k. purple, grey & blk 30 15
3757 – 10 k. multicoloured . . 55 20
DESIGNS: 6 k. Space station and capsule in orbit; 10 k. Photograph of the Earth taken by "Zond 7".

1404 Soviet and Afghan Flags
1405 Red Star and Arms

1969. 50th Anniv of U.S.S.R.–Afghanistan Diplomatic Relations.
3759 1404 6 k. red, black & green 35 10

1969. Coil Stamp.
3760 1405 4 k. red . . . . 2·00 1·60

1406 Mikoyan Gurevich MiG-3 and MiG-23 Fighters

1969. "30 Years of MiG Aircraft".
3761 1406 6 k. black, grey & red . 70 15

1407 Lenin

1969. New Year.
3762 1407 4 k. multicoloured . . . 10 10

1408 Tupolev ANT-2

1969. Development of Soviet Civil Aviation.
3763 1408 2 k. multicoloured . . . 20 10
3764 – 3 k. multicoloured . . . 25 10
3765 – 4 k. multicoloured . . . 25 10
3766 – 6 k. black, red & pur . 25 10
3767 – 10 k. multicoloured . . 55 15
3768 – 12 k. multicoloured . . 60 15
3769 – 16 k. multicoloured . . 80 20
3770 – 20 k. multicoloured . . 95 30
AIRCRAFT: 3 k. Polikarpov Po-2; 4 k. Tupolev ANT-9; 6 k. TsAGI 1-EA helicopter; 10 k. Tupolev ANT-20 "Maksim Gorky"; 12 k. Tupolev Tu-104; 16 k. Mil Mi-10 helicopter; 20 k. Ilyushin Il-62.

1409 Model Gliders

1969. Technical Sports.
3772 1409 3 k. purple 15 10
3773 – 4 k. green 15 10
3774 – 6 k. brown 25 10
DESIGNS: 4 k. Speed boat racing; 6 k. Parachuting.

1410 Rumanian Arms and Soviet Memorial, Bucharest

1411 TV Tower, Ostankino

1969. 25th Anniv of Rumanian Liberation.
3775 **1410** 6 k. red and brown . . 15 10

1969. Television Tower, Ostankino, Moscow.
3776 **1411** 10 k. multicoloured . . 20 15

1412 "Lenin" (after sculpture by N. Andreiev)

1970. Birth Centenary of V. I. Lenin (1st issue). Multicoloured.
3777 4 k. Type **1412** 15 10
3778 4 k. "Marxist Meeting, Petrograd" (A. Moravov) . 15 10
3779 4 k. "Second RSDRP Congress" (Y. Vinogradov) 15 10
3780 4 k. "First Day of Soviet Power" (F. Modorov) . . 15 10
3781 4 k. "Visiting Lenin" (F. Modorov) 15 10
3782 4 k. "Conversation with Ilyich" (A. Shirokov) 15 10
3783 4 k. "May Day 1920" (I. Brodsky) 15 10
3784 4 k. "With Lenin" (V. Serov) 15 10
3785 4 k. "Conquerors of the Cosmos" (A. Deyneka) . . 15 10
3786 4 k. "Communism Builders" (A. Korentsov, J. Merkoulov, V. Bourakov) 15 10
See also Nos. 3812/21.

1413 F. V. Sychkov and Painting "Tobogganing"

1970. Birth Centenary of F. V. Sychkov (artist).
3787 **1413** 4 k. blue and brown . . 20 10

1414 "Vostok", "Mirnyi" and Antarctic Map

1415 V. I. Peshekhonov

1970. 150th Anniv of Antarctic Expedition by Bellinghausen and Lazarev.
3788 **1414** 4 k. turquoise, mve & blue 2·00 25
3789 – 16 k. red, green & pur . 2·50 55
DESIGN: 16 k. Modern polar-station and map.

1970. Soviet War Heroes.
3790 **1415** 4 k. purple and black . 15 10
3791 – 4 k. brown and olive . . 15 10
DESIGN: No. 3791, V. B. Borshoev (1906–1945).

1416 Geographical Society Emblem

1417 "The Torch of Peace" (A. Dumpe)

1970. 125th Anniv of Russian Geographical Society.
3792 **1416** 6 k. multicoloured . . 15 10

1970. 60th Anniv of Int Women's Solidarity Day.
3793 **1417** 6 k. drab & turquoise . 35 10

1418 Ivan Bazhov (folk hero) and Crafts

1419 Lenin

1970. World Fair "Expo 70", Osaka, Japan.
3794 **1418** 4 k. black, red and grn 15 10
3795 – 6 k. silver, red & black 20 10
3796 – 10 k. multicoloured . . 25 15
DESIGNS: 6 k. U.S.S.R. Pavilion; 10 k. Boy and model toys.

1970. Lenin Birth Centenary. All-Union Philatelic Exhibition, Moscow.
3798 **1419** 4 k. black, gold & red . 10 10

1420 Friendship Tree

1970. Friendship Tree, Sochi.
3800 **1420** 10 k. multicoloured . . 30 15

1421 Ice Hockey Players

1970. World Ice Hockey Championships, Stockholm, Sweden.
3801 **1421** 6 k. green and blue . . 65 15

1422 Hammer, Sickle and Azerbaijan Emblems

1970. 50th Anniv of Soviet Republics.
3802 **1422** 4 k. red and gold . . . 15 10
3803 – 4 k. brown and silver . 15 10
3804 – 4 k. purple and gold . 15 10
DESIGNS: No. 3803, Woman and motifs of Armenia; No. 3804, Woman and emblem of Kazakh Republic.

1423 Worker and Book

1424 D. N. Medvedev

1970. U.N.E.S.C.O. "Lenin Centenary" Symposium.
3805 **1423** 6 k. ochre and lake . . 10 10

1970. War Heroes.
3806 **1424** 4 k. brown 15 10
3807 – 4 k. brown 15 10
PORTRAIT: No. 3807, K. P. Orlovsky.

(1425)

1426 Hungarian Arms and Budapest View

1970. Russian Victory in World Ice Hockey Championships, Stockholm. No. 3801 optd with T **1425**.
3808 **1421** 6 k. green and blue . . . 50 15

1970. 25th Anniv of Hungarian and Czech Liberation. Multicoloured.
3809 6 k. Type **1426** 15 10
3810 6 k. Czech Arms and Prague view 40 10

1427 Cosmonauts' Emblem

1428 Lenin, 1890

1970. Cosmonautics Day.
3811 **1427** 6 k. multicoloured . . . 10 10

1970. Birth Centenary of Lenin (2nd issue).
3812 **1428** 2 k. green 10 10
3813 – 2 k. olive 10 10
3814 – 4 k. blue 10 10
3815 – 4 k. lake 10 10
3816 – 6 k. brown 15 10
3817 – 6 k. lake 15 10
3818 – 10 k. purple 25 15
3819 – 10 k. brown 25 15
3820 – 12 k. black and silver . . 55 20
3821 – 12 k. red and gold . . . 55 20
PORTRAITS OF LENIN: No. 3813, Period, 1893–1900; No. 3814, Period, 1900–03; No. 3815, in 1916; No. 3816, in 1917; No. 3817, Period of Revolution; No. 3818, in 1918; No. 3819, in 1920; No. 3820, Sculptured head by J. Kolesnikov; No. 3821, Sculptured head by N. Andreiev.

1429 Order of Victory

1430 Komsomol Badge

1970. 25th Anniv of Victory in Second World War.
3823 **1429** 1 k. gold, grey & pur . . 10 10
3824 – 2 k. purple, brn & gold . 10 10
3825 – 3 k. red, black & gold . 10 10
3826 – 4 k. red, brown & gold . 15 10
3827 – 10 k. gold, red & purple 55 20
DESIGNS: 2 k. Eternal Flame; 3 k. Treptow Monument, Berlin; 4 k. Home Defence Order; 10 k. Hero of the Soviet Union and Hero of Socialist Labour medals.

1970. 16th Congress of Leninist Young Communist League (Komsomol).
3829 **1430** 4 k. multicoloured . . . 10 10

1431 Sculptured Head of Lenin

1970. World Youth Meeting for Lenin Birth Centenary.
3830 **1431** 6 k. red 10 10

1432 "Young Workers" and Federation Emblem

1970. 25th Anniv of World Democratic Youth Federation.
3831 **1432** 6 k. black and blue . . . 35 10

1433 Arms and Government Building, Kazan

1970. 50th Anniv of Russian Federation Autonomous Soviet Socialist Republics.
3832 **1433** 4 k. blue 15 10
3833 – 4 k. green 15 10
3834 – 4 k. red 15 10
3835 – 4 k. brown 15 10
3836 – 4 k. green 15 10
3837 – 4 k. brown 15 10
DESIGNS: Arms and Government Buildings. No. 3832, (Tatar Republic); No. 3833, Petrozavodzk (Karelian Republic); No. 3834, Cheboksary (Chuvash Republic); No. 3835, Elista (Kalmyk Republic); No. 3836, Izhevsk (Udmurt Republic); No. 3837, Ioshkar-Ola (Mari Republic).
See also Nos. 3903/7, 4052/3, 4175, 4253, 4298, 4367 and 4955.

1434 Gymnast on Bar (World Championships, Yugoslavia)

1435 "Swords into Ploughshares" (sculpture by E. Vuchetich)

1970. International Sporting Events.
3838 **1434** 10 k. red and drab . . 50 15
3839 – 16 k. brown and green . 85 50
DESIGN: 16 k. Three footballers (World Cup Championships, Mexico).

1970. 25th Anniv of United Nations.
3840 **1435** 12 k. purple and green . 50 10

1436 Cosmonauts and "Soyuz 9"

1970. Space Flight by "Soyuz 9".
3841 **1436** 10 k. black, red & purple 50 10

1437 Engels

1970. 150th Birth Anniv of Friedrich Engels.
3842 **1437** 4 k. brown and red . . 15 10

1438 Cruiser "Aurora"

1970. Soviet Warships.
3843 **1438** 3 k. pink, lilac & black 30 10
3844 – 4 k. black and yellow . 35 10

3845 – 10 k. blue and mauve . 80 15
3846 – 12 k. brown and buff . 90 20
3847 – 20 k. purple, blue & turq 1·40 40
DESIGNS: 4 k. Missile cruiser "Groznyi"; 10 k. Cruiser "Oktyabrskaya Revolyutsiya"; 12 k. Missile cruiser "Varyag"; 20 k. Nuclear submarine "Leninsky Komsomol".

1439 Soviet and Polish Workers

1440 Allegory of the Sciences

1970. 25th Anniv of Soviet-Polish Friendship Treaty.
3848 **1439** 6 k. red and blue . . . 10 10

1970. 13th Int Historical Sciences Congress, Moscow.
3849 **1440** 4 k. multicoloured . . . 10 10

1441 Mandarins

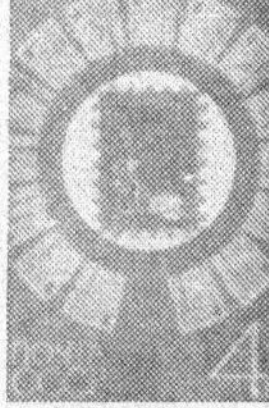
1442 Magnifying Glass, "Stamp" and Covers

1970. Fauna of Sikhote-Alin Nature Reserve. Multicoloured.
3850 4 k. Type **1441** 60 10
3851 6 k. Yellow-throated marten . 45 15
3852 10 k. Asiatic black bear (vert) 60 15
3853 16 k. Red deer 70 25
3854 20 k. Tiger . . . . 1·00 35

1970. 2nd U.S.S.R. Philatelic Society Congress, Moscow.
3855 **1442** 4 k. silver and red . . . 15 10

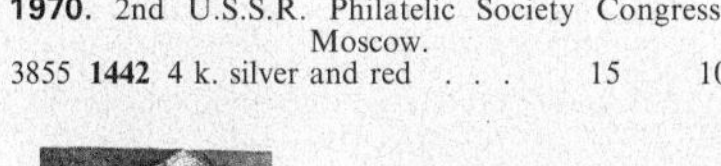

1443 V. I. Kikvidze

1444 University Building

1970. 75th Birth Anniv of V. J. Kikvidze (Civil War hero).
3856 **1443** 4 k. brown 10 10

1970. 50th Anniv of Yerevan University.
3857 **1444** 4 k. red and blue . . . 10 10

1445 Lenin Badge

1446 Library Book-plate

1970. Pioneer Organization.
3858 **1445** 1 k. gold, red and grey . 10 10
3859 – 2 k. grey and brown . . 10 10
3860 – 4 k. multicoloured . . . 10 10
DESIGNS: 2 k. "Lenin with Children" (sculpture); 4 k. Red Star, Pioneer emblem.

1970. 400th Anniv of Vilnius (Vilna) University Library (Lithuania).
3861 **1446** 4 k. black, grey & silver 10 10

1447 Woman with Bouquet

1970. 25th Anniv of International Democratic Women's Federation.
3862 **1447** 6 k. brown and blue . . 10 10

1448 Milkmaid and Cows ("Livestock")

1970. Soviet Agriculture. Multicoloured.
3863 4 k. Type **1448** 10 10
3864 4 k. Driver, tractor and harvester ("Mechanization") 10 10
3865 4 k. Lock-operator and canal ("Irrigation and Chemical Research") 10 10

1449 Lenin addressing Meeting

1970. 53rd Anniv of October Revolution.
3866 **1449** 4 k. gold and red . . . 10 10

50 лет
ленинскому плану
ГОЭЛРО • 1970
(1450)

1970. 50th Anniv of GOELRO Electrification Plan. No. 3475 optd with T **1450**.
3868 4 k. multicoloured 85 30

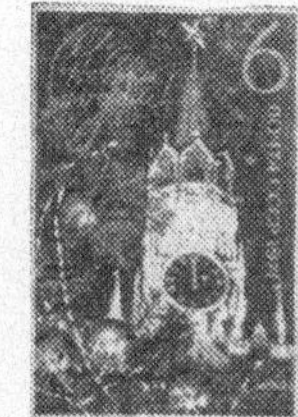
1451 Spasskу Tower, Kremlin

1452 A. A. Baikov

1970. New Year.
3869 **1451** 6 k. multicoloured . . 10 10

1970. Birth Centenary of A. A. Baikov (metallurgic scientist).
3870 **1452** 4 k. black and brown . 10 10

1453 A. D. Tsyurupa

1454 St. Basil's Cathedral, Red Square, Moscow

1970. Birth Centenary of A. D. Tsyurupa (Vice-Chairman of Soviet People's Commissars).
3871 **1453** 4 k. brown and yellow . 10 10

1970. Tourism.
3872 **1454** 4 k. multicoloured . . 15 10
3873 – 6 k. blue, indigo & brown 30 10
3874 – 10 k. brown and green 35 15
3875 – 12 k. multicoloured . . 40 15
3876 – 14 k. blue, red & brown 45 20
3877 – 16 k. multicoloured . . 60 25
DESIGNS: 6 k. Scene from "Swan Lake"; 10 k. Sika deer; 12 k. Souvenir handicrafts; 14 k. "Swords into Ploughshares" (sculpture by E. Vuchetich); 16 k. Tourist and camera.

1455 Camomile

1970. Flowers. Multicoloured.
3878 4 k. Type **1455** 15 10
3879 6 k. Dahlia 25 10
3880 10 k. Phlox 35 10
3881 12 k. Aster 40 20
3882 16 k. Clematis 60 30

1456 African Woman and Child

1457 Beethoven

1970. 10th Anniv of U.N. Declaration on Colonial Independence.
3883 **1456** 10 k. brown and blue . . 20 10

1970. Birth Bicentenary of Beethoven (composer).
3884 **1457** 10 k. purple and pink . 75 20

1458 "Luna 16" in Flight

1459 Speed Skating

1970. Flight of "Luna 16".
3885 **1458** 10 k. green 35 15
3886 – 10 k. purple 35 15
3887 – 10 k. green 35 15
DESIGNS: No. 3886, "Luna 16" on Moon's surface; No. 3887, Parachute descent.

1970. Trade Unions' Winter Games (1971).
3889 **1459** 4 k. blue, red & grey . . 15 10
3890 – 10 k. green, brn & grey . 45 15
DESIGN: 10 k. Cross-country skiing.

1460 "The Conestabile Madonna" (Raphael)

1970. Foreign Paintings in Soviet Galleries. Mult.
3891 3 k. Type **1460** 15 10
3892 4 k. "Saints Peter and Paul" (El Greco) 20 10
3893 10 k. "Perseus and Andromeda" (Rubens) (horiz) 35 15
3894 12 k. "The Return of the Prodigal Son" (Rembrandt) 35 15
3895 16 k. "Family Portrait" (Van Dyck) 80 25
3896 20 k. "The Actress Jeanne Samary" (Renoir) . . . . . 1·10 35
3897 30 k. "Woman with Fruit" (Gauguin) . . . . 1·50 85

1461 Harry Pollitt and Freighter "Jolly George"

1462 "75" Emblem

1970. 80th Birth Anniv of H. Pollitt (British Communist).
3899 **1461** 10 k. brown & purple . 35 15

1970. 75th Anniv of Int Co-operative Alliance.
3900 **1462** 12 k. red and green . . 60 10

1463 Sculptured Head of Lenin

1971. 24th Soviet Union Communist Party Congress.
3901 **1463** 4 k. red and gold . . . 10 10

1464 "50", State Emblem and Flag

1465 Genua Fortress and Cranes

1971. 50th Anniv of Georgian Soviet Republic.
3902 **1464** 4 k. multicoloured . . . 15 10

1971. 50th Anniv of Soviet Republics. Similar designs to T **1433**, but dated "1971".
3903 4 k. turquoise 15 10
3904 4 k. red 15 10
3905 4 k. red 15 10
3906 4 k. blue 15 10
3907 4 k. green 15 10
DESIGNS: No. 3903, Russian Federation Arms and Supreme Soviet building (Dagestan Republic); No. 3904, National emblem and symbols of agriculture and industry (Abkhazian Republic); No. 3905, Arms, produce and industry (Adjarian Republic); No. 3906, Arms and State building (Kabardino-Balkar Republic); No. 3907, Arms, industrial products and Government building (Komi Republic).

1971. 2500th Anniv of Feodosia (Crimean city).
3908 **1465** 10 k. multicoloured . . 50 15

1466 Palace of Culture, Kiev

1467 "Features of National Economy"

1971. 24th Ukraine Communist Party Congress, Kiev.
3909 **1466** 4 k. multicoloured . . . 10 10

1971. 50th Anniv of Soviet State Planning Organization.
3910 **1467** 6 k. red and brown . . 35 10

1468 N. Gubin, I. Chernykh and S. Kosinov (dive-bomber crew)

1971. Soviet Air Force Heroes.
3911 **1468** 4 k. brown and green . 15 10

1469 Gipsy Dance

1971. State Folk Dance Ensemble. Multicoloured.
3912 10 k. Type **1469** 40 15
3913 10 k. Russian "Summer" dance (women in circle) 40 15
3914 10 k. Ukraine "Gopak" dance (dancer leaping) 40 15
3915 10 k. Adjar "Khorumi" dance (with drummer) 40 15
3916 10 k. "On the Ice" (ballet) . . 40 15

1470 L. Ukrainka

1472 Fighting at the Barricades

1471 "Luna 17" Module on Moon

1971. Birth Centenary of Lesya Ukrainka (Ukrainian writer).
3917 **1470** 4 k. red and brown . . 10 10

1971. Soviet Moon Exploration.
3918 **1471** 10 k. brown and violet . 35 15
3919 – 12 k. brown and blue . 65 20
3920 – 12 k. brown and blue . 65 20
3921 – 16 k. brown and violet . 65 30
DESIGNS: No. 3919, Control room and radio telescope; No. 3920, Moon trench; No. 3921, "Lunokhod 1" Moon-vehicle.

1971. Centenary of Paris Commune.
3923 **1472** 6 k. black, brn & red . 10 10

1473 Hammer, Sickle and Development Emblems

1475 E. Birznieks-Upitis

1474 Gagarin Medal, Spaceships and Planets

1971. 24th Soviet Communist Party Congress, Moscow.
3924 **1473** 6 k. red, bistre & brown 10 10

1971. 10th Anniv of First Manned Space Flight (1st issue) and Cosmonautics Day.
3925 **1474** 10 k. olive, yell & brn . 35 15
3926 – 12 k. purple, bl & grey . 45 20
DESIGN: 12 k. Spaceship over Globe and economic symbols.
See also No. 3974.

1971. Birth Centenary of E. Birznieks-Upitis (Lithuanian writer).
3927 **1475** 4 k. red and green . . . 10 10

1476 Bee on Flower

1971. 23rd Int Bee-keeping Congress, Moscow.
3928 **1476** 6 k. multicoloured . . . 30 15

1478 Memorial Building

1971. Lenin Memorial Building, Ulyanovsk.
3930 **1478** 4 k. olive and red . . . 10 10

1479 Lieut-Col. N. I. Vlasov

1480 Khafiz Shirazi

1971. 26th Anniv of Victory in 2nd World War.
3931 **1479** 4 k. brown and green . 10 10

1971. 650th Birth Anniv of Khafiz Shirazi (Tadzhik writer).
3932 **1480** 4 k. multicoloured . . . 10 10

1481 "GAZ-66" Truck

1971. Soviet Motor Vehicles.
3933 **1481** 2 k. multicoloured . . 15 10
3934 – 3 k. multicoloured . . 15 10
3935 – 4 k. blue, black & lilac 20 10
3936 – 4 k. grn, purple & drab 20 10
3937 – 10 k. red, black & lilac 55 15
DESIGNS: 3 k. "BelAZ-540" tipper truck; 4 k. (3935) "Moskvitch-412" 4-door saloon; 4 k. (3936) "Zaporozhets ZAZ-968" 2-door saloon; 10 k. "Volga GAZ-24" saloon.

1482 A. A. Bogomolets

1483 Commemorative Scroll

1971. 90th Birth Anniv of A. A. Bogomolets (medical scientist).
3938 **1482** 4 k. black, pink & orge 15 10

1971. International Moscow Congresses.
3939 **1483** 6 k. brown and green . 25 15
3940 – 6 k. multicoloured . . 25 15
3941 – 6 k. multicoloured . . 25 15
DESIGNS AND EVENTS—HORIZ: No. 3939, (13th Science History Congress); No. 3940, Oil derrick and symbols (8th World Oil Congress). VERT: No. 3941, Satellite over globe (15th General Assembly of Geodesics and Geophysics Union).

1484 Sukhe Bator Statue, Ulan Bator

1971. 50th Anniv of Revolution in Mongolia.
3942 **1484** 6 k. grey, gold and red 20 10

1485 Defence Monument

1486 Treaty Emblem

1971. 30th Anniv of Defence of Liepaja.
3943 **1485** 4 k. brown, blk & grey 10 10

1971. 10th Anniv of Antarctic Treaty and 50th Anniv of Soviet Hydrometeorological Service.
3944 **1486** 6 k. deep blue, black and blue 60 30
3945 – 10 k. violet, black & red 1·00 35
DESIGN: 10 k. Hydrometeorological map.

1487 "Motherland" (sculpture by E. Vuchetich)

1488 Throwing the Discus

1971. 20th Anniv of "Federation Internationale des Resistants".
3946 **1487** 6 k. green and red . . 15 10

1971. 5th Summer Spartakiad.
3947 **1488** 3 k. blue on pink . . . 10 10
3948 – 4 k. green on flesh . . 15 10
3949 – 6 k. brown on green . 30 10
3950 – 10 k. purple on blue . 55 20
3951 – 12 k. brown on yellow . 60 20
DESIGNS: 4 k. Archery; 6 k. Horse-riding (dressage); 10 k. Basketball; 12 k. Wrestling.

1489 "Benois Madonna" (Leonardo da Vinci)

1971. Foreign Paintings in Russian Museums. Multicoloured.
3952 2 k. Type **1489** 10 10
3953 4 k. "Mary Magdalene confesses her Sins" (Titian) 15 10
3954 10 k. "The Washerwoman" (Chardin) (horiz) 35 15
3955 12 k. "Young Man with Glove" (Hals) 45 20
3956 14 k. "Tancred and Erminia" (Poussin) (horiz) 50 45
3957 16 k. "Girl Fruit-seller" (Murillo) 55 50
3958 20 k. "Child on Ball" (Picasso) 90 60

1490 Lenin Badge and Kazakh Flag

1971. 50th Anniv of Kazakh Communist Youth Assn.
3959 **1490** 4 k. brown, red & blue . 10 10

1491 Posthorn within Star

1971. International Correspondence Week.
3960 **1491** 4 k. black, blue & green 15 10

1492 A. Spendiarov (Armenian composer) (after M. Saryan)

1971. Birth Anniversaries. Multicoloured.
3961 4 k. Type **1492** (cent) 20 10
3962 4 k. Nikolai Nekrasov (after I. Kramskoi) (poet, 150th anniv) 20 10
3963 10 k. Fyodor Dostoevsky (after V. Perov) (writer, 150th anniv) 50 25

1493 Z. Paliashvili

1494 Emblem, Gorky Kremlin and Hydrofoil

1971. Birth Centenary of Z. Paliashvili (Georgian composer).
3964 **1493** 4 k. brown 20 10

1971. 750th Anniv of Gorky (formerly Nizhini-Novgorod) (1st issue).
3965 **1494** 16 k. multicoloured . . 50 20
See also No. 3974.

1495 Students and Globe

1971. 25th Anniv of Int Students Federation.
3966 **1495** 6 k. blue, red and brn . 10 10

1496 Atlantic White-sided Dolphins

1497 Star and Miners' Order

1971. Marine Fauna. Multicoloured.
3967 4 k. Type **1496** 25 10
3968 6 k. Sea otter 35 10
3969 10 k. Narwhals 45 15
3970 12 k. Walrus 60 20
3971 14 k. Ribbon seals 65 45

1971. 250th Anniv of Coal Discovery in Donetz Basin.
3972 **1497** 4 k. red, brown & black 20 10

1498 Lord Rutherford and Atomic Formula

1499 Maksim Gorky Statue and View

1971. Birth Cent of Lord Rutherford (physicist).
3973 **1498** 6 k. brown & purple . . 30 15

1971. 750th Anniv of Gorky (formerly Nizhni-Novgorod) (2nd issue).
3974 **1499** 4 k. multicoloured . . . 15 10

1500 Santa Claus in Troika

1971. New Year.
3975 **1500** 10 k. red, gold & black 25 10

1501 Workers and Marx Books ("International Socialist Solidarity") (½-size illustration)

1971. 24th Soviet Union Communist Party Congress Resolutions.
3976 **1501** 4 k. blue, ultram & red 15 10
3977 – 4 k. red, yellow & brn . 15 10
3978 – 4 k. lilac, black & red . 15 10
3979 – 4 k. bistre, brown & red 15 10
3980 – 4 k. red, green & yellow 15 10
DESIGNS: No. 3977, Farmworkers and wheatfield ("Agricultural Production"); No. 3978, Factory production line ("Increased Productivity"); No. 3979, Heavy industry ("Industrial Expansion"); No. 3980, Family in department store ("National Welfare").

1502 "Meeting" (V. Makovsky)

1503 V. V. Vorovsky

1971. Russian Paintings. Multicoloured.

3982	2 k. Type **1502**	15	10
3983	4 k. "Girl Student" (N. Yaroshenko)	20	10
3984	6 k. "Woman Miner" (N. Kasatkin)	30	10
3985	10 k. "Harvesters" (G. Myasoyedov) (horiz)	50	15
3986	16 k. "Country Road" (A. Savrasov)	70	30
3987	20 k. "Pine Forest" (I. Shishkin) (horiz)	95	40

See also Nos. 4064/70.

1971. Birth Centenary of V. V. Vorovsky (diplomat).

3989	**1503** 4 k. brown	10	10

1504 Dobrovolsky, Volkov and Patsaev

1971. "Soyuz II" Cosmonauts Commemoration.

3990	**1504** 4 k. black, purple & orge	20	10

1505 Order of the Revolution and Building Construction

1971. 54th Anniv of October Revolution.

3991	**1505** 4 k. multicoloured	10	10

1506 E. Vakhtangov (founder) and characters from "Princess Turandot"

1507 "Dzhambul Dzhabaiev" (A. Yar-Kravchenko)

1971. 50th Anniv of Vakhtangov Theatre, Moscow.

3992	**1506** 10 k. red and lake	30	15
3993	– 10 k. yellow & brown	30	15
3994	– 10 k. orange & brown	30	15

DESIGNS—HORIZ: No. 3993, B. Shchukin (actor) and scene from "The Man with the Rifle"; No. 3994, R. Simonov (director) and scene from "Cyrano de Bergerac".

1971. 125th Anniv of Dzhambul Dzhabaiev (Kazakh poet).

3995	**1507** 4 k. brown, yell & orge	10	10

1508 Pskov Kremlin

1971. Historical Buildings. Multicoloured.

3996	3 k. Type **1508**	15	10
3997	4 k. Novgorod kremlin	15	10
3998	6 k. Smolensk fortress and Liberation Monument	20	10
3999	10 k. Kolomna kremlin	35	15

1509 William Foster

1971. 90th Birth Anniv of Foster (American communist).

4001	**1509** 10 k. black and brown	17·00	17·00
4002	10 k. black and brown	60	15

No. 4001 shows the incorrect date of death "1964"; No. 4002 shows the correct date, "1961".

1510 Fadeev and Scene from "The Rout" (novel)

1971. 70th Birth Anniv of Aleksandr Fadeev (writer).

4003	**1510** 4 k. orange and blue	15	10

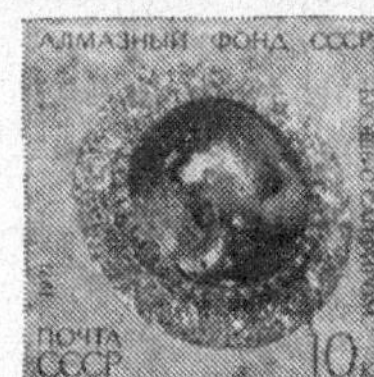
1511 Sapphire Brooch

1971. Diamonds and Jewels. Multicoloured.

4004	10 k. Type **1511**	60	15
4005	10 k. "Shah" diamond	60	15
4006	10 k. "Narcissi" diamond brooch	60	15
4007	20 k. Amethyst pendant	90	40
4008	20 k. "Rose" platinum and diamond brooch	90	40
4009	30 k. Pearl and diamond pendant	1·40	60

1512 Vanda Orchid

1514 Ice Hockey Players

1513 Peter the Great's Imperial Barge, 1723

1971. Tropical Flowers. Multicoloured.

4010	1 k. Type **1512**	20	10
4011	2 k. "Anthurium scherzerium"	20	10
4012	4 k. "Cactus epiphyllum"	30	10
4013	12 k. Amaryllis	60	20
4014	14 k. "Medinilla magnifica"	75	30

1971. History of the Russian Navy (1st series). Multicoloured.

4016	1 k. Type **1513**	15	10
4017	4 k. Galleon "Orel", 1668 (vert)	30	10
4018	10 k. Ship of the line "Poltava", 1712 (vert)	75	15
4019	12 k. Ship of the line "Ingermanland", 1715 (vert)	90	25
4020	16 k. Steam frigate "Vladimir", 1848	1·25	40

See also Nos. 4117/21, 4209/13 and 4303/6.

1971. 25th Anniv of Soviet Ice Hockey.

4021	**1514** 6 k. multicoloured	50	10

1515 Baku Oil Installations

1516 G. M. Krzhizhanovsky

1971. Baku Oil Industry.

4022	**1515** 4 k. black, red and blue	25	10

1972. Birth Centenary of G. M. Krzhizhanovsky (scientist).

4023	**1516** 4 k. brown	15	10

1517 Alexander Scriabin

1518 Red-faced Cormorant

1972. Birth Centenary of Alexander Scriabin (composer).

4024	**1517** 4 k. blue and green	30	10

1972. Sea Birds. Multicoloured.

4025	4 k. Type **1518**	60	10
4026	6 k. Ross's gull (horiz)	90	15
4027	10 k. Pair of Barnacle geese	1·10	25
4028	12 k. Pair of Spectacled eiders (horiz)	1·50	40
4029	16 k. Mediterranean gull	2·00	50

1519 Speed Skating

1520 Heart Emblem

1972. Winter Olympic Games, Sapporo, Japan. Multicoloured.

4030	4 k. Type **1519**	15	10
4031	6 k. Figure skating	20	10
4032	10 k. Ice Hockey	50	15
4033	12 k. Ski jumping	65	20
4034	16 k. Cross-country skiing	75	30

1972. World Heart Month.

4036	**1520** 4 k. red and green	15	10

1521 Fair Emblem

1522 Labour Emblems

1973. 50th Anniv of Soviet Participation in Leipzig Fair.

4037	**1521** 16 k. gold and red	85	30

1972. 15th Soviet Trade Unions Congress, Moscow.

4038	**1522** 4 k. brown, red & pink	15	10

1523 "Aloe arborescens"

1524 Alexandra Kollontai (diplomat) (birth cent)

1972. Medicinal Plants. Multicoloured.

4039	1 k. Type **1523**	10	10
4040	2 k. Yellow horned poppy	10	10
4041	4 k. Groundsel	20	10
4042	6 k. Nephrite tea	30	10
4043	10 k. Kangaroo apple	55	15

1972. Birth Anniversaries.

4044	**1524** 4 k. brown	15	10
4045	– 4 k. lake	15	10
4046	– 4 k. bistre	15	10

CELEBRITIES: No. 4045, G. Chicherin (Foreign Affairs Commissar) (birth cent); No. 4046, "Kamo" (S. A. Ter-Petrosyan—revolutionary) (90th birth anniv).

1526 "Salyut" Space-station and "Soyuz" Spacecraft

1972. Cosmonautics Day. Multicoloured.

4048	6 k. Type **1526**	30	20
4049	6 k. "Mars 2" approaching Mars	30	20
4050	16 k. Capsule, "Mars 3"	75	30

1527 Factory and Products

1972. 250th Anniv of Izhora Factory.

4051	**1527** 4 k. purple and silver	20	10

1972. 50th Anniv of Russian Federation Autonomous Soviet Socalist Republics. Designs similar to T **1433**, but dated "1972".

4052	4 k. blue	25	10
4053	4 k. mauve	25	10

DESIGNS: No. 4052, Arms, natural resources and industry (Yakut Republic); No. 4053, Arms, agriculture and industry (Checheno-Ingush Republic).

1528 L. Sobinov and scene from "Eugene Onegin"

1972. Birth Centenary of L. Sobinov (singer).

4054	**1528** 10 k. brown	50	15

1529 Symbol of Knowledge and Children reading Books

1972. International Book Year.

4055	**1529** 6 k. multicoloured	25	15

1530 P. Morosov (pioneer) and Pioneers Saluting

1972. 50th Anniv of Pioneer Organization.

4056	**1530** 1 k. multicoloured	10	10
4057	– 2 k. purple, red & grn	10	10
4058	– 3 k. blue, red & brown	15	10
4059	– 4 k. red, blue & green	15	10

DESIGNS: 2 k. Girl laboratory worker and Pioneers with book; 3 k. Pioneer Place, Chukotka, and Pioneers at work; 4 k. Pioneer parade.

1531 Pioneer Trumpeter

1972. "50th Anniv of Pioneer Organization" Youth Philatelic Exhibition, Minsk.

4061	**1531** 4 k. purple, red & yellow	15	10

1532 "World Security"

1972. European Security Conference, Brussels.

4062	**1532** 6 k. blue, turquoise & gold	75	55

1533 M. S. Ordubady

1534 G. Dimitrov

1972. Birth Centenary of M. S. Ordubady (Azerbaijan writer).
4063 **1533** 4 k. purple & orange . . 15 10

1972. Russian Paintings. As T **1502**, but dated "1972". Multicoloured.
4064 2 k. "Cossack Hetman" (I. Nikitin) 10 10
4065 4 k. "F. Volkov" (A. Lossenko) 15 10
4066 6 k. "V. Majkov" (F. Rokotov) 20 10
4067 10 k. "N. Novikov" (D. Levitsky) 35 10
4068 12 k. "G. Derzhavin" (V. Borovikovsky) 40 15
4069 16 k. "Peasants' Dinner" (M. Shibanov) (horiz) . . . 55 25
4070 20 k. "Moscow View" (F. Alexeiev) (horiz) . . . 1·10 45

1972. 90th Birth Anniv of Georgi Dimitrov (Bulgarian statesman).
4071 **1534** 6 k. brown and bistre . 20 10

1535 Congress Building and Emblem

1972. 9th Int Gerontology Congress, Kiev.
4072 **1535** 6 k. brown and blue . . 20 10

1536 Fencing

1972. Olympic Games, Munich.
4073 **1536** 4 k. purple and gold . . 15 10
4074 – 6 k. green and gold . . 20 10
4075 – 10 k. blue and gold . . 55 10
4076 – 14 k. blue and gold . . 70 20
4077 – 16 k. red and gold . . . 55 35
DESIGNS: 6 k. Gymnastics; 10 k. Canoeing; 14 k. Boxing; 16 k. Running.

1537 Amundsen, Airship N.1 "Norge" and Northern Lights

1538 Market-place, Lvov (Lemberg)

1972. Birth Centenary of Roald Amundsen (Polar explorer).
4079 **1537** 6 k. blue and brown . . 1·50 30

1972. Ukraine's Architectural Monuments. Mult.
4080 4 k. Type **1538** 15 10
4081 6 k. 17th-century house, Tchernigov (horiz) 20 15
4082 10 k. Kovnirovsky building, Kiev (horiz) 35 20
4083 16 k. Kamenetz-Podolsk Castle 50 30

1539 Indian Flag and Asokan Capital

1540 Liberation Monument, Vladivostok, and Cavalry

1972. 25th Anniv of India's Independence.
4084 **1539** 6 k. red, blue and green 20 10

1972. 50th Anniv of Liberation of Far Eastern Territories.
4085 **1540** 3 k. grey, orange & red 15 10
4086 – 4 k. grey, yellow & ochre 15 10
4087 – 6 k. grey, pink and red . 30 15
DESIGNS: 4 k. Labour Heroes Monument, Khabarovsk, and industrial scene; 6 k. Naval statue, Vladivostok, cruiser and jet fighters.

1541 Miners' Day Emblem

1972. 25th Anniv of Miners' Day.
4088 **1541** 4 k. red, black & violet 20 10

1542 "Boy with Dog" (Murillo)

1972. Paintings by Foreign Artists in Hermitage Gallery, Leningrad. Multicoloured.
4089 4 k. "Breakfast" (Velasquez) (horiz) 20 10
4090 6 k. "The Milk Seller's Family" (Le Nain) (horiz) 25 10
4091 10 k. Type **1542** 45 20
4092 10 k. "The Capricious Girl" (Watteau) 70 35
4093 20 k. "Moroccan with Horse" (Delacroix) . . . . 1·10 45

1543 "Sputnik I"

1972. 15th Anniv of "Cosmic Era". Multicoloured.
4095 6 k. Type **1543** 35 15
4096 6 k. Launch of "Vostok I" . 35 15
4097 6 k. "Lunokhod" vehicle on Moon 35 15
4098 6 k. Man in space 35 15
4099 6 k. "Mars 3" module on Mars 35 15
4100 6 k. Touch down of "Venera 7" on Venus 35 15

1544 Konstantin Mardzhanishvili

1545 Museum Emblem

1972. Birth Centenary of K. Mardzhanishvili (Georgian actor).
4101 **1544** 4 k. green 15 10

1972. Centenary of Popov Central Communications Museum.
4102 **1545** 4 k. blue, purple & grn 15 10

1546 Exhibition Labels

1972. "50th Anniv of U.S.S.R." Philatelic Exhibition.
4103 **1546** 4 k. red & black on yell 15 10

1547 Lenin

1972. 55th Anniv of October Revolution.
4104 **1547** 4 k. red and gold . . . 15 10

1548 Militia Badge and Soviet Flag

1549 Arms of U.S.S.R.

1972. 55th Anniv of Soviet Militia.
4105 **1548** 4 k. gold, red & brown . 15 10

1972. 50th Anniv of U.S.S.R.
4106 **1549** 4 k. gold, purple & red . 15 10
4107 – 4 k. gold, red & brown . 15 10
4108 – 4 k. gold, purple & green 15 10
4109 – 4 k. gold, purple & grey 15 10
4110 – 4 k. gold, purple & grey 15 10
DESIGNS: No. 4107, Lenin and banner; No. 4108, Arms and Kremlin; No. 4109, Arms and industrial scenes; No. 4110, Arms, worker and open book "U.S.S.R. Constitutions".

1550 Emblem of U.S.S.R.

1552 Savings Book

1972. U.S.S.R. Victories in Olympic Games, Munich. Multicoloured.
4112 20 k. Type **1550** . . . . . . 1·00 30
4113 30 k. Olympic medals . . . . 1·50 55

1972. "50 Years of Soviet Savings Bank".
4115 **1552** 4 k. blue and purple . . 15 10

1553 Kremlin and Snowflakes

1555 "G. Skovoroda" (P. Mesheryakov)

1554 Battleship "Pyotr Veliky"

1972. New Year.
4116 **1553** 6 k. multicoloured . . . 20 10

1972. History of the Russian Navy (2nd series). Multicoloured.
4117 2 k. Type **1554** 25 10
4118 3 k. Cruiser "Varyag" . . . 25 10
4119 4 k. Battleship "Potemkin" . 45 10
4120 6 k. Cruiser "Ochakov" . . . 55 10
4121 10 k. Minelayer "Amur" . . 1·10 25

1972. 250th Birth Anniv of Grigory S. Skovoroda.
4122 **1555** 4 k. blue 15 10

1556 "Pioneer Girl with Books" (N. A. Kasatkin)

1972. "History of Russian Painting". Mult.
4123 2 k. "Meeting of Village Party Members" (E. M. Cheptsov) (horiz) 10 10
4124 4 k. Type **1556** 15 15
4125 6 k. "Party Delegate" (G. G. Ryazhsky) 25 15
4126 10 k. "End of Winter—Midday" (K. F. Yuon) (horiz) . . . 35 20
4127 16 k. "Partisan Lunev" (N. I. Strunnikov) 55 35
4128 20 k. "Self-portrait in Fur Coat" (I. E. Grabar) . . . 75 50

1557 Child reading Safety Code

1558 Emblem of Technology

1972. Road Safety Campaign.
4130 **1557** 4 k. black, blue and red 30 10

1972. Cent of Polytechnic Museum, Moscow.
4131 **1558** 4 k. red, yellow and green 15 10

1559 "Venus 8" and Parachute

1972. Space Research.
4132 **1559** 6 k. blue, black & pur . 20 10

1560 Solidarity Emblem

1973. 15th Anniv of Asian and African People's Solidarity Organization.
4134 **1560** 10 k. blue, red & brown 25 15

1561 Town and Gediminas Tower

1562 I. V. Babushkin

1973. 650th Anniv of Vilnius (Vilna).
4135 **1561** 10 k. red, black & green 25 15

1973. Birth Cent of I. V. Babushkin (revolutionary).
4136 **1562** 4 k. black 15 10

1563 Tupolev Tu-154 and Soviet Aircraft

1973. 50th Anniv of Soviet Civil Aviation.
4137 **1563** 6 k. multicoloured . . . 40 15

1564 "30" and Admiralty Spire, Leningrad

1565 Portrait and Masks (Mayakovsky Theatre)

1973. 30th Anniv of Relief of Leningrad.
4138 **1564** 4 k. black, orange & brn 20 10

1973. 50th Anniv of Moscow Theatres.
4139 **1565** 10 k. multicoloured . . 25 10
4140 – 10 k. red and blue . . . 25 10
DESIGN: No. 4140, Commemorative panel (Mossoviet Theatre).

1566 M. Prishvin

1973. Birth Centenary of Mikhail Prishvin (writer).
4141 **1566** 4 k. multicoloured . . . 35 10

1567 Heroes' Square, Volgograd

1973. 30th Anniv of Stalingrad Victory. Detail from Heroes' Memorial.
4142 – 3 k. black, yell & orge . 20 10
4143 **1567** 4 k. yellow and black . 20 10
4144 – 10 k. multicoloured . . 40 15
4145 – 12 k. black, light red and red 60 20
DESIGNS—VERT: 3 k. Soldier and Allegory; 12 k. Hand with torch. HORIZ: 10 k. Mother mourning for child.

1568 Copernicus and Planetary Chart

1973. 500th Birth Anniv of Copernicus.
4147 **1568** 10 k. brown and blue . 55 15

1569 "Chaliapin" (K. Korovin)

1973. Birth Centenary of F. Chaliapin (opera singer).
4148 **1569** 10 k. multicoloured . . 60 15

1570 Ice Hockey Players **1571** Athletes

1973. World Ice Hockey Championships, Moscow.
4149 **1570** 10 k. brown, bl & gold . 60 15

1973. 50th Anniv of Central Red Army Sports Club.
4151 **1571** 4 k. multicoloured . . . 15 10

1572 Red Star, Tank, and Map **1573** N. E. Bauman

1973. 30th Anniv of Battle of Kursk.
4152 **1572** 4 k. black, red and grey 20 10

1973. Birth Centenary of Nikolai Bauman (revolutionary).
4153 **1573** 4 k. brown 15 10

1574 Red Cross and Red Crescent

1973. International Co-operation.
4154 **1574** 4 k. red, black & green 15 10
4155 – 6 k. light blue, red and blue 20 10
4156 – 16 k. green, red and mauve 65 25
DESIGNS AND EVENTS: 4 k. (50th anniv of Soviet Red Cross and Red Crescent Societies Union); 6 k. Mask, emblem and theatre curtain (15th Int Theatre Institution Congress); 16 k. Floral emblem (10th World Festival of Youth, Berlin).

1575 "A. N. Ostrovsky" (V. Perov) **1576** Satellites

1973. 150th Birth Anniv of Aleksandr Ostrovsky (writer).
4157 **1575** 4 k. multicoloured . . 15 10

1973. Cosmonautics Day. Multicoloured.
4158 6 k. Type **1576** 20 15
4159 6 k. "Lunokhod 2" 20 15

1577 "Guitarist" (Tropinin) **1578** Athlete and Emblems

1973. "History of Russian Painting". Mult.
4162 2 k. Type **1577** 15 10
4163 4 k. "The Young Widow" (Fedotov) 20 10
4164 6 k. "Self-portrait" (Kiprensky) 25 10
4165 10 k. "An Afternoon in Italy" (Brullov) 30 20
4166 12 k. "That's My Father's Dinner!" (boy with dog) (Venetsianov) 40 30
4167 16 k. "Lower Gallery of Albano" (A. A. Ivanov) (horiz) 55 35
4168 20 k. "Ermak conquering Siberia" (Surikov) (horiz) . 1·00 50

1973. 50th Anniv of Dynamo Sports Club.
4169 **1578** 4 k. multicoloured . . 15 10

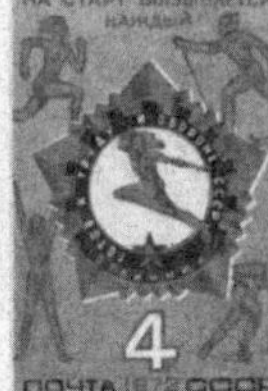

1580 Liner "Mikhail Lermontov" **1582** Sports

1581 E. T. Krenkel and Polar Scences

1973. Inauguration of Leningrad–New York Trans-Atlantic Service.
4171 **1580** 16 k. multicoloured . . 70 30

1973. 70th Birth Anniv of E. T. Krenkel (Polar explorer).
4172 **1581** 4 k. brown and blue . . 55 10

1973. "Sport for Everyone".
4173 **1582** 4 k. multicoloured . . . 15 10

1583 Girls' Choir

1973. Centenary of Latvian Singing Festival.
4174 **1583** 10 k. multicoloured . . 35 10

1973. 50th Anniv of Russian Federation Autonomous Soviet Socialist Republics. Design similar to T **1433**, but dated "1973".
4175 4 k. blue 20 10
DESIGN: No. 4175, Arms and industries of Buryat Republic.

1584 Throwing the Hammer

1973. Universiade Games, Moscow. Mult.
4176 2 k. Type **1584** 10 10
4177 3 k. Gymnastics 10 10
4178 4 k. Swimming 15 10
4179 16 k. Fencing 65 25

1586 European Bison

1973. Caucasus and Voronezh Nature Reserves. Multicoloured.
4182 1 k. Type **1586** 10 10
4183 3 k. Ibex 15 10
4184 4 k. Caucasian snowcocks . . 1·40 20
4185 6 k. Eurasian beaver with young 35 10
4186 10 k. Red deer with fawns . . 55 20

1587 Lenin, Banner and Membership Card

1973. 70th Anniv of 2nd Soviet Social Democratic Workers Party Congress.
4187 **1587** 4 k. multicoloured . . . 15 10

1588 A. R. al-Biruni **1590** "The Sculptor" (P. D. Korin)

1589 Schaumberg Palace, Bonn, and Spassky Tower, Moscow

1973. Millennium of Abu Reihan al-Biruni (astronomer and mathematician).
4188 **1588** 6 k. brown 30 15

1973. General Secretary Leonid Brezhnev's Visits to West Germany, France and U.S.A. Multicoloured.
4189 **1589** 10 k. mauve, brn & buff 30 15
4190 – 10 k. brown, ochre and yellow 30 15
4191 – 10 k. red, grey & brown 30 15
DESIGNS: No. 4190, Eiffel Tower, Paris, and Spassky Tower; No. 4191, White House, Washington, and Spassky Tower.
See also Nos. 4245 and 4257.

1973. "History of Russian Paintings". Mult.
4193 2 k. Type **1590** 15 10
4194 4 k. "Farm-workers' Supper" (A. A. Plastov) 15 10
4195 6 k. "Letter from the Battle-front" (A. Laktionov) . . 25 15
4196 10 k. "Mountain Landscape" (M. S. Saryan) 40 25
4197 16 k. "Wedding on Tomorrow's Street" (Y. Pimenov) . . . 55 35
4198 20 k. "Ice Hockey" (A. Deineka) 80 45

1591 Lenin Museum **1592** Y. Steklov

1973. Inaug of Lenin Museum, Tashkent.
4200 **1591** 4 k. multicoloured . . . 10 10

1973. Birth Centenary of Y. Steklov (statesman).
4201 **1592** 4 k. brown, red & pink 10 10

1593 "The Eternal Pen" **1594** "Oplopanax elatum"

1973. Afro-Asian Writers' Conference, Alma-Ata.
4202 **1593** 6 k. multicoloured . . . 15 10

1973. Medicinal Plants. Multicoloured.
4203 1 k. Type **1594** 20 10
4204 2 k. Ginseng 25 10
4205 4 k. Spotted orchid 30 10
4206 10 k. Arnica 35 25
4207 12 k. Lily of the valley . . . 50 35

1595 I. Nasimi

1973. 600th Birth Anniv of Imadeddin Nasimi (Azerbaijan poet).
4208 **1595** 4 k. brown 10 10

1596 Cruiser "Kirov"

1973. History of Russian Navy (3rd series). Multicoloured.
4209 3 k. Type **1596** 20 10
4210 4 k. Battleship "Oktyabrskaya Revolyutsiya" 25 10
4211 6 k. Submarine "Krasnogvardeets" 30 10
4212 10 k. Destroyer "Soobrazitelnyi" 60 25
4213 16 k. Cruiser "Krasnyi Kavkas" 1·10 35

1597 Pugachev and Battle Scene

1973. Bicentenary of Peasant War.
4214 **1597** 4 k. multicoloured . . . 15 10

1598 Red Flag encircling Globe

1973. 15th Anniv of Magazine "Problems of Peace and Socialism".
4215 **1598** 6 k. red, gold and green 15 10

1599 Leningrad Mining Institute

1973. Bicentenary of Leningrad Mining Institute.
4216 **1599** 4 k. multicoloured . . . 15 10

1600 Laurel and Hemispheres **1601** Elena Stasova

1973. World Congress of "Peaceful Forces", Moscow.
4217 **1600** 6 k. multicoloured . . . 15 10

1973. Birth Centenary of Elena Stasova (party official).
4218 **1601** 4 k. mauve 10 10

1602 Order of People's Friendship **1603** Marshal Malinovsky

1973. Foundation of Order of People's Friendship.
4219 **1602** 4 k. multicoloured 10 10

1973. 75th Birth Anniv of Marshal R. Malinovsky.
4220 **1603** 4 k. grey 15 10

1604 Workers and Red Guard **1605** D. Cantemir

1973. 250th Anniv of Sverdlovsk.
4221 **1604** 4 k. black, gold & red . 10 10

1973. 300th Birth Anniv of Dmitri Cantemir (Moldavian scientist and encyclopaedist).
4222 **1605** 4 k. red 10 10

1606 Pres. Allende of Chile

1973. Allende Commemoration.
4223 **1606** 6 k. black and brown . 30 10

1607 Kremlin **1608** N. Narimanov

1973. New Year.
4224 **1607** 6 k. multicoloured . . 15 10

1973. Birth Centenary (1970) of Nariman Narimanov (Azerbaijan politician).
4225 **1608** 4 k. green 10 10

1609 "Russobalt" Touring Car (1909)

1973. History of Soviet Motor Industry (1st series). Multicoloured.
4226 2 k. Type **1609** 15 10
4227 3 k. "AMO-F15" lorry (1924) 15 10
4228 4 k. Spartak "NAMI-1" tourer (1927) 20 10
4229 12 k. Yaroslavsky "Ya-6" bus (1929) 55 20
4230 16 k. Gorkovsky "GAZ-A" tourer (1932) 75 40
See also Nos. 4293/7, 4397/401 and 4512/16.

1610 "Game and Lobster" (Sneiders)

1973. Foreign Paintings in Soviet Galleries. Multicoloured.
4231 4 k. Type **1610** 15 10
4232 6 k. "Young Woman with Ear-rings" (Rembrandt) (vert) 20 10
4233 10 k. "Sick Woman and Physician" (Steen) (vert) . 35 15
4234 12 k. "Attributes of Art" (Chardin) 45 20
4235 14 k. "Lady in a Garden" (Monet) 50 25
4236 16 k. "Village Lovers" (Bastien-Lepage) (vert) 60 30
4237 20 k. "Girl with Fan" (Renoir) (vert) 75 40

1611 Great Sea Gate, Tallin **1612** Picasso

1973. Historical Buildings of Estonia, Latvia and Lithuania.
4239 **1611** 4 k. black, red & green 10 10
4240 – 4 k. brown, red & green 10 10
4241 – 4 k. multicoloured . . 10 10
4242 – 10 k. multicoloured . . 35 15
DESIGNS: No. 4240, Organ pipes and Dome Cathedral, Riga; No. 4241, Traku Castle, Lithuania; No. 4242, Town Hall and weather-vane, Tallin.

1973. Pablo Picasso Commemoration.
4243 **1612** 6 k. green, red & gold . 25 10

1613 Petrovsky

1973. I. G. Petrovsky (mathematician and Rector of Moscow University) Commemoration.
4244 **1613** 4 k. multicoloured . . . 15 10

1973. Brezhnev's Visit to India. As T **1589**, but showing Kremlin, Red Fort, Delhi and flags.
4245 4 k. multicoloured 10 10

1614 Soviet Soldier and Title Page **1616** Oil Workers

1615 Siege Monument and Peter the Great Statue, Leningrad

1974. 50th Anniv of "Red Star" Newspaper.
4246 **1614** 4 k. black, red & gold . 15 10

1974. 30th Anniv of Soviet Victory in Battle for Leningrad.
4247 **1615** 4 k. multicoloured . . . 25 10

1974. 10th Anniv of Tyumen Oil fields.
4248 **1616** 4 k. black, red & blue . 30 10

1617 "Comecon" Headquarters, Moscow **1618** Skaters and Stadium

1974. 25th Anniv of Council for Mutual Economic Aid.
4249 **1617** 16 k. green, red & brown 45 20

1974. European Women's Ice Skating Championships, Medeo, Alma-Ata.
4250 **1618** 6 k. red, blue & slate . . 20 10

1619 Kunstkammer Museum, Leningrad, Text and Academy **1620** L. A. Artsimovich

1974. 250th Anniv of Russian Academy of Sciences.
4251 **1619** 10 k. multicoloured . . 25 10

1974. 1st Death Anniv of Academician L. A. Artsimovich (physicist).
4252 **1620** 4 k. brown and green . . 15 10

1974. 50th Anniv of Autonomous Soviet Socialist Republics. Design similar to T **1433**, but dated "1974".
4253 4 k. brown 15 10
DESIGN: No. 4253, Arms and industries of Nakhichevan ASSR (Azerbaijan).

1621 K. D. Ushinsky **1622** M. D. Millionshchikov

1974. 150th Birth Anniv of K. D. Ushinsky (educationalist).
4254 **1621** 4 k. brown and grn . . 10 10

1974. 1st Death Anniv of M. D. Millionshchikov (scientist).
4255 **1622** 4 k. brown, pink & green 10 10

1623 Spartakiad Emblem **1624** Young Workers and Emblem

1974. 3rd Winter Spartakiad Games.
4256 **1623** 10 k. multicoloured . . 15 15

1974. General Secretary Leonid Brezhnev's Visit to Cuba. As T **1589** but showing Kremlin, Revolution Square, Havana and Flags,
4257 4 k. multicoloured 10 10

1974. Scientific and Technical Youth Work Review.
4258 **1624** 4 k. multicoloured . . . 10 10

1625 Theatre Facade **1626** Globe and Meteorological Activities

1974. Cent of Azerbaijan Drama Theatre, Baku.
4259 **1625** 6 k. brown, red & orge 15 10

1974. Cosmonautics Day.
4260 **1626** 6 k. blue, red & violet . 20 10
4261 – 10 k. brown, red & blue 35 15
4262 – 10 k. black, red & yell . 35 15
DESIGNS: No. 4261, V. G. Lazarev and O. G. Makarov, and launch of "Soyuz 12"; No. 4262, P. I. Klimuk and V. V. Lebedev, and "Soyuz 13".

1627 "Odessa by Moonlight" (Aivazovsky)

1974. Marine Paintings by Ivan Aivazovsky. Multicoloured.
4263 2 k. Type **1627** 10 10
4264 4 k. "Battle of Chesma" (vert) 15 10
4265 6 k. "St. George's Monastery" 20 10
4266 10 k. "Storm at Sea" 35 15
4267 12 k. "Rainbow" 40 20
4268 16 k. "Shipwreck" 55 30

1628 Young Communists

1974. 17th Leninist Young Communist League (Komsomol) Congress (4270) and 50th Anniv of Naming League after Lenin (4271). Multicoloured.
4270 4 k. Type **1628** 10 10
4271 4 k. "Lenin" (from sculpture by V. Tsigal) 10 10

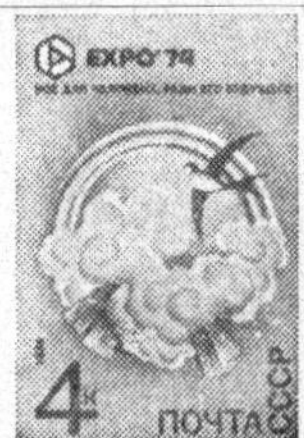

1630 Swallow ("Atmosphere") **1631** "Cobble-stone" (sculpture, I. D. Shadr)

1974. "EXPO 74" World Fair, Spokane, U.S.A. "Preserve the Environment".
4273 **1630** 4 k. black, red & lilac . 15 10
4274 – 6 k. yellow, blk & blue . 20 10
4275 – 10 k. black, vio & red . 40 15
4276 – 16 k. blue, green & blk . 55 20
4277 – 20 k. black, brn & orge 75 40
DESIGNS: 6 k. Fish and globe ("The Sea"); 10 k. Crystals ("The Earth"); 16 k. Rose bush ("Flora"); 20 k. Young red deer ("Fauna").

1974. 50th Anniv of Central Museum of the Revolution.
4279 **1631** 4 k. green, red & gold . 10 10

1632 Congress Emblem within Lucerne Grass **1634** Tchaikovsky and Competition Emblem

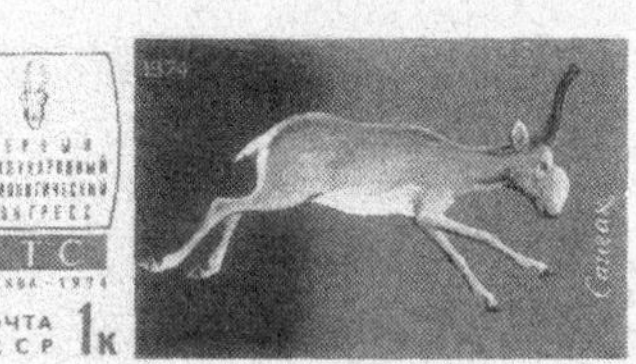

1633 Saiga

1974. 12th International Congress of Meadow Cultivation, Moscow.
4280 **1632** 4 k. red, green & dp grn 10 10

1974. 1st International Theriological Congress, Moscow. Fauna. Multicoloured.
4281 1 k. Type **1633** 10 10
4282 3 k. Asiatic wild ass 15 10
4283 4 k. Russian desman 20 10
4284 6 k. Northern fur seal 25 10
4285 10 k. Bowhead whale 60 20

1974. 5th Int Tchaikovsky Music Competition.
4286 **1634** 6 k. black, vio & grn . . 30 10

1636 Marshal F. I. Tolbukhin **1638** Runner and Emblem

1637 K. Stanislavsky, V. Nemirovich-Danchenko and Theatre Curtain

1974. 80th Birth Anniv of Marshal F. I. Tolbukhin.
4288 **1636** 4 k. green 15 10

1974. 75th Anniv of Moscow Arts Festival.
4289 **1637** 10 k. multicoloured . . 25 15

1974. 13th Soviet Schools Spartakiad, Alma Ata.
4290 **1638** 4 k. multicoloured . . . 15 10

1639 Modern Passenger Coach **1640** Shield and Monument on Battle Map

1974. Centenary of Egorov Railway Wagon Works, Leningrad.
4291 **1639** 4 k. multicoloured . . 30 10

1974. 30th Anniv of Liberation of Byelorussia.
4292 **1640** 4 k. multicoloured . . 10 10
See also No. 4301.

1974. History of Soviet Motor Industry (2nd series). As T **1609**. Multicoloured.
4293 2 k. Gorkovsky "GAZ-AA" lorry (1932) 15 10
4294 3 k. Gorkovsky "GAZ-03-30" bus (1933) 15 10
4295 4 k. Moscow Auto Works "ZIS-5" lorry (1933) 15 10
4296 14 k. Moscow Auto Works "ZIS-8" bus (1934) . . . 55 15
4297 16 k. Moscow Auto Works "ZIS-101" saloon car (1936) 65 25

1974. 50th Anniv of Soviet Republics. As T **1433**, dated "1974".
4298 4 k. red 15 10
DESIGN: 4 k. Arms and industries of North Ossetian Republic.
No. 4298 also commemorates the 200th anniv of Ossetia's merger with Russia.

1641 Liberation Monument and Skyline **1644** Admiral Isakov

1642 Warsaw Monument and Flag

1974. 800th Anniv of Poltava.
4299 **1641** 4 k. red and brown . . 10 10

1974. 30th Anniv of Polish People's Republic.
4300 **1642** 6 k. brown and red . . 15 10

1974. 30th Anniv of Liberation of Ukraine. As T **1640**, but background details and colours changed.
4301 4 k. multicoloured 15 10

1974. 80th Birth Anniv of Admiral I. S. Isakov.
4302 **1644** 4 k. blue 15 10

1645 Minesweeper

1974. History of the Russian Navy (4th series). Modern Warships. Multicoloured.
4303 3 k. Type **1645** 25 10
4304 4 k. Landing ship 25 10
4305 6 k. Helicopter carrier . . . 45 15
4306 16 k. Destroyer "Otvazhny" 1·00 25

1646 Pentathlon Sports **1647** D. Ulyanov

1974. World Modern Pentathlon Championships, Moscow.
4307 **1646** 16 k. brown, gold & blue 60 20

1974. Birth Centenary of D. Ulyanov (Lenin's brother).
4308 **1647** 4 k. green 15 10

1648 V. Menzhinsky

1650 S. M. Budennyi

1649 "Lilac" (P. P. Konchalovsky)

1974. Birth Cent of V. Menzhinsky (statesman).
4309 **1648** 4 k. maroon 10 10

1974. Soviet Paintings. Multicoloured.
4310 4 k. Type **1649** 15 10
4311 6 k. "Towards the Wind" (sailing) (E. Kalnins) . . . 20 15
4312 10 k. "Spring" (young woman) (O. Zardarjan) 40 20
4313 16 k. "Northern Harbour" (G. Nissky) 65 30
4314 20 k. "Daughter of the Soviet Kirghiz" (S. Tchnikov) (vert) 75 35

1974. Marshal S. M. Budennyi Commem.
4315 **1650** 4 k. green 15 10

1651 Page of First Russian Dictionary **1652** Soviet War Memorial, Bucharest, and Flags

1974. 400th Anniv of First Russian Primer.
4316 **1651** 4 k. red, black & gold . 10 10

1974. 30th Anniv of Rumanian Liberation.
4317 **1652** 6 k. blue, yellow & red . 15 10

1653 Vitebsk

1974. Millenary of Vitebsk.
4318 **1653** 4 k. red and green . . . 15 10

1654 Kirgizia **1655** Bulgarian Crest and Flags

1974. 50th Anniv of Soviet Republics. Flags, Agricultural and Industrial Emblems. Mult. Background colours given.
4319 **1654** 4 k. blue 15 10
4320 – 4 k. purple 15 10
4321 – 4 k. blue 15 10
4322 – 4 k. yellow 15 10
4323 – 4 k. green 15 10
DESIGNS: No. 4320, Moldavia; No. 4321, Tadzhikistan; No. 4322, Turkmenistan; No. 4323, Uzbekistan.

1974. 30th Anniv of Bulgarian Revolution.
4324 **1655** 6 k. multicoloured . . . 15 10

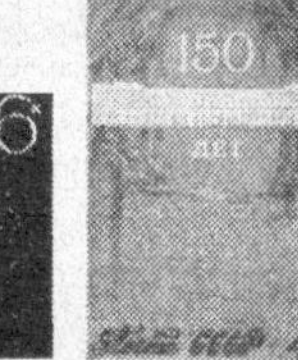
1656 G.D.R. Crest and Soviet War Memorial, Treptow, Berlin **1658** Theatre and Laurel Wreath

1974. 25th Anniv of German Democratic Republic.
4325 **1656** 6 k. multicoloured . . . 15 10

1974. 150th Anniv of Maly State Theatre, Moscow.
4327 **1658** 4 k. gold, red & black . 10 10

1659 "Guests from Overseas"

1974. Birth Centenary of Nikolai K. Rorich (painter).
4328 **1659** 6 k. multicoloured . . . 20 10

1660 Soviet Crest and U.P.U. Monument, Berne

1974. Centenary of U.P.U. Multicoloured.
4329 10 k. Type **1660** 30 15
4330 10 k. Ukraine crest, U.P.U. Emblem and U.P.U. H.Q., Berne 30 15
4331 10 k. Byelorussia crest, U.P.U. emblem and mail transport 30 15

1661 Order of Labour Glory

1974. 57th Anniv of October Revolution. Multicoloured.
4333 4 k. Type **1661** 15 10
4334 4 k. Kamaz truck (vert) . . . 15 10
4335 4 k. Hydro-electric power station, Nurek (vert) . . . 15 10

1662 Soviet "Space Stations" over Mars

1974. Soviet Space Exploration. Multicoloured.
4336 6 k. Type **1662** 20 10
4337 10 k. P. R. Popovich and Y. P. Artchunin ("Soyuz 14" cosomonauts) 30 15
4338 10 k. I. V. Sarafanov and L. S. Demin ("Soyuz 15" cosmonauts) 30 15
SIZES—VERT: No. 4337, 28×40 mm. HORIZ: No. 4338, 40×28 mm.

1663 Mongolian Crest Flag **1664** Commemorative Inscription

1974. 50th Anniv of Mongolian People's Republic.
4339 **1663** 6 k. multicoloured . . . 20 10

1974. 30th Anniv of Estonian Liberation.
4340 **1664** 4 k. multicoloured . . . 15 10

1665 Liner "Aleksandr Pushkin", Freighter and Tanker

1974. 50th Anniv of Soviet Merchant Navy.
4341 **1665** 4 k. multicoloured . . . 25 10

1666 Spassky Clock-tower, Kremlin, Moscow

1974. New Year.
4342 **1666** 4 k. multicoloured . . . 15 10

1667 "The Market Place" (Beuckelaar)

1974. Foreign Paintings in Soviet Galleries. Multicoloured.
4343 4 k. Type **1667** 15 10
4344 6 k. "Woman selling Fish" (Pieters) 25 10
4345 10 k. "A Goblet of Lemonade" (Terborsh) 35 15
4346 14 k. "Girl at Work" (Metsu) 50 20
4347 16 k. "Saying Grace" (Chardin) 55 30
4348 20 k. "The Spoilt Child" (Greuze) 80 35
Nos. 4344/8 are vert.

1668 "Ostrowskia magnifica"

1669 I. S. Nikitin

1974. Flowers. Multicoloured.
4350 1 k. Type **1668** 10 10
4351 2 k. "Paeonia intermedia" . . 10 10
4352 4 k. "Roemeria refracta" . . 20 10
4353 10 k. "Tulipia dasystemon" . 40 15
4354 12 k. "Dianthus versicolor" . 45 20

1974. 150th Birth Anniv of I. S. Nikitin (poet).
4355 **1669** 4 k. black, green & ol . 15 10

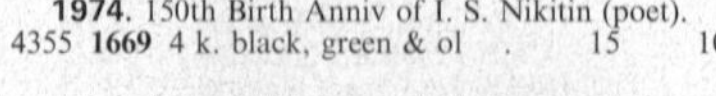

1670 Leningrad Mint Building

1974. 250th Anniv of Leningrad Mint.
4356 **1670** 6 k. multicoloured . . . 20 10

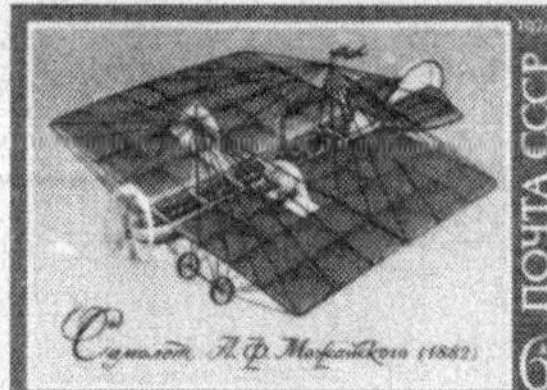

1671 Mozhaisky's Monoplane, 1884

1974. Early Russian Aircraft (1st series). Mult.
4357 6 k. Type **1671** 30 15
4358 6 k. Grizidubov No. 2 biplane, 1910 . . . . 30 15
4359 6 k. Sikorsky "Russia A", 1910 30 15
4360 6 k. Sikorsky "Russkiy Vitjaz", 1913 . . . . 30 15
4361 6 k. Grigorovich M-5 flying boat, 1914 . . . . 30 15
See also Nos. 4580/4, 4661/6 and 4791/6.

1673 Komsomol Emblem and Rotary Press ("Komsomolskaya Pravda")

1975. 50th Anniv of Children's Newspapers.
4363 **1673** 4 k. red, black & blue . 10 10
4364 – 4 k. red, black & silver 10 10
DESIGN—VERT: No. 4364, Pioneer emblem and newspaper sheet ("Pioneerskaya Pravda").

1674 Emblem and Skiers (8th Trade Unions' Games)

1975. Winter Spartakiads.
4365 **1674** 4 k. orange, black & bl 10 10
4366 – 16 k. bistre, black & bl 55 20
DESIGN—HORIZ: 16 k. Emblem, ice hockey player and skier (5th Friendly Forces Military Games).

1975. "50th Anniv of Automomous Soviet Socialist Republics. Designs similar to T **1433**, but dated "1975".
4367 4 k. green 15 10
DESIGN: No. 4367, Arms, industries and produce of Karakalpak ASSR (Uzbekistan).

1675 "David"

1975. 500th Birth Anniv of Michelangelo.
4368 **1675** 4 k. deep green & green 20 15
4369 – 6 k. brown and ochre . 25 15
4370 – 10 k. dp green & green 35 15
4371 – 14 k. brown and ochre 55 30
4372 – 20 k. dp green & green 1·00 30
4373 – 30 k. brown and ochre 1·50 65
DESIGNS: 6 k. "Crouching Boy"; 10 k. "Rebellious Slave"; 14 k. "Creation of Adam" (detail, Sistine Chapel ceiling); 20 k. Staircase of Laurentiana Library, Florence; 30 k. Christ and the Virgins (detail of "The Last Judgement", Sistine Chapel).

1676 Mozhaisky, Monoplane and Tupolev Tu-144 Jet Airliner

1975. 150th Birth Anniv of Aleksandr Mozhaisky (aircraft designer).
4375 **1676** 6 k. brown and blue . 40 10

1677 Convention Emblem

1975. Cent of International Metre Convention.
4376 **1677** 6 k. multicoloured . . 15 10

1678 Games Emblem

1975. 6th Summer Spartakiad.
4377 **1678** 6 k. multicoloured . . 15 10

1679 Towers of Charles Bridge, Prague (Czechoslovakia)

1975. 30th Anniv of Liberation. Multicoloured.
4378 6 k. Type **1679** 15 10
4379 6 k. Liberation Monument and Parliament Buildings, Budapest (Hungary) 15 10

1680 French and Soviet Flags

1681 Yury Gagarin

1975. 50th Anniv of Franco-Soviet Diplomatic Relations.
4380 **1680** 6 k. multicoloured . . . 15 10

1975. Cosmonautics Day.
4381 **1681** 6 k. red, silver and blue . 15 10
4382 – 10 k. red, black & blue . 30 15
4383 – 16 k. multicoloured . . 50 20
DESIGNS—HORIZ: 10 k. A. A. Gubarev, G. M. Grechko ("Soyuz 17") and "Salyut 4"; 16 k. A. V. Filipchenko, N. N. Rukavishnikov and "Soyuz 16".

1682 Treaty Emblem

1684 Lenin

1683 Emblem and Exhibition Hall, Sokolniki, Moscow

1975. 20th Anniv of Warsaw Treaty.
4384 **1682** 6 k. multicoloured . . . 15 10

1975. "Communication 75" International Exhibition, Moscow.
4385 **1683** 6 k. red, silver and blue . 15 10

1975. 30th Anniv of Victory in Second World War. Multicoloured.
4386 4 k. Type **1684** 15 10
4387 4 k. Eternal flame and Guard of Honour 15 10
4388 4 k. Woman in ammunition factory 15 10
4389 4 k. Partisans 15 10
4390 4 k. "Destruction of the enemy" 15 10
4391 4 k. Soviet forces 15 10

1685 "Lenin" (V. G. Tsiplakov)

1686 Victory Emblems

1975. 105th Birth Anniv of Lenin.
4393 **1685** 4 k. multicoloured . . . 15 10

1975. "Sozfilex 75" International Stamp Exhibition.
4394 **1686** 6 k. multicoloured . . . 20 10

1687 "Apollo–Soyuz" Space Link

1975. "Apollo–Soyuz" Space Project.
4396 **1687** 20 k. multicoloured . . 75 25

1975. History of Soviet Motor Industry (3rd series). As T **1609**.
4397 2 k. black, orange & blue . . 15 10
4398 3 k. black, brown & green . 15 10
4399 4 k. black, blue and green . 15 10
4400 12 k. black, buff and purple . 45 20
4401 16 k. black, green and olive . 60 25
DESIGNS: 2 k. Gorkovsky "GAZ-M1" saloon, 1936; 3 k. Yaroslavsky "YAG-6" truck, 1936; 4 k. Moscow Auto Works "ZIS-16" bus, 1938; 12 k. Moscow KIM Works "KIM-10" saloon, 1940; 16 k. Gorkovsky "GAZ-67B" field car, 1943.

1688 Irrigation Canal and Emblem

1689 Flags and Crests of Poland and Soviet Union

1975. 9th Int Irrigation Congress, Moscow.
4402 **1688** 6 k. multicoloured . . . 15 10

1975. 30th Anniv of Soviet–Polish Friendship.
4403 **1689** 6 k. multicoloured . . . 15 10

1690 A. A. Leonov in Space

1691 Ya. M. Sverdlov

1975. 10th Anniv of First Space Walk by A. A. Leonov.
4404 **1690** 6 k. multicoloured . . . 20 10

1975. 90th Birth Anniv of Ya. M. Sverdlov (statesman).
4405 **1691** 4 k. brown, buff & silver 10 10

1692 Congress Emblem

1975. 8th Int Plant Conservation Congress, Moscow.
4406 **1692** 6 k. multicoloured . . . 15 10

1693 Emblem and Flowers

1975. 12th Int Botanical Congress, Leningrad.
4407 **1693** 6 k. multicoloured . . . 60 15

1695 Festival Emblem

1975. 9th International Film Festival, Moscow.
4409 **1695** 6 k. multicoloured . . . 15 10

1696 Crews of "Apollo" and "Soyuz"

1975. "Apollo"–"Soyuz" Space Link. Mult.
4410 10 k. Type **1696** 30 10
4411 12 k. "Apollo" and "Soyuz 19" in docking procedure . . . 35 20
4412 12 k. "Apollo" and "Soyuz 19" linked together 35 20
4413 16 k. Launch of "Soyuz 19" (vert) 45 20

1697 Sturgeon

1975. Int Exposition, Okinawa. Marine Life.
4415 **1697** 3 k. bistre, black & bl . 15 10
4416 – 4 k. lilac, black & blue . 20 10
4417 – 6 k. purple, black & grn 25 10
4418 – 10 k. brown, black & bl 1·25 15
4419 – 16 k. green, blk & pur . 60 25
4420 – 20 k. blue, pur & stone . 65 30
DESIGNS: 4 k. Thomas rapa whelk; 6 k. Eel; 10 k. Long-tailed duck; 16 k. Crab; 20 k. Chrisipther.

1698 "Parade in Red Square, Moscow" (K. F. Yuon)

1975. Birth Centenaries of Soviet Painters. Multicoloured.
4422 1 k. Type **1698** 10 10
4423 2 k. "Winter Morning in Industrial Moscow" (K. P. Yuon) 10 10
4424 6 k. "Soldiers with Captured Guns" (E. E. Lansere) . . 25 10
4425 10 k. "Excavating the Metro Tunnel" (E. E. Lansere) . . 60 20
4426 16 k. "A. A. Pushkin and N. N. Pushkina at Palace Ball" (N. P. Ulyanov) (vert) 60 30
4427 20 k. "Lauriston at Kutuzov's Headquarters" (N. P. Ulyanov) 80 40

1699 Conference Emblem

1700 A. Isaakjan

1975. European Security and Co-operation Conference, Helsinki.
4428 **1699** 6 k. black, gold & blue . 15 10

1975. Birth Centenary of Avetic Isaakjan (Armenian poet).
4429 **1700** 4 k. multicoloured . . 10 10

1701 M. K. Ciurlionis

1702 J. Duclos

1975. Birth Centenary of M. K. Ciurlionis (Lithuanian composer).
4430 **1701** 4 k. gold, green & yellow 15 10

1975. Jacques Duclos (French communist leader) Commemoration.
4431 **1702** 6 k. purple and silver . 15 10

1703 Al Farabi

1704 Ruffs

1975. 1100th Birth Anniv of Al Farabi (Persian philosopher).
4432 **1703** 6 k. multicoloured . . 15 10

1975. 50th Anniv of Berezinsky and Stolby Nature Reserves. Multicoloured.
4433 1 k. Type **1704** 40 10
4434 4 k. Siberian musk deer . . 30 10
4435 6 k. Sable 30 10
4436 10 k. Capercaillie . . . . . 1·00 20
4437 16 k. Eurasian badger . . . 60 55

1705 Korean Crest with Soviet and Korean Flags

1707 S. A. Esenin

1706 Cosmonauts, "Soyuz 18" and "Salyut 4" Linked

1975. 30th Anniversaries. Multicoloured.
4438 6 k. Type **1705** (Korean liberation) 15 10
4439 6 k. Vietnamese crest, Soviet and Vietnamese flags (Vietnam Democratic Republic) 15 10

1975. Space Flight of "Soyuz 18—Salyut 4" by Cosmonauts P. Klimuk and V. Sevastyanov.
4440 **1706** 10 k. black, red & blue 25 10

1975. 80th Birth Anniv of S. A. Esenin (poet).
4441 **1707** 6 k. brown, yell & grey 15 10

1708 Standardisation Emblems

1975. 50th Anniv of Soviet Communications Standardisation Committee.
4442 **1708** 4 k. multicoloured . . 10 10

1709 Astrakhan Lamb

1710 M. P. Konchalovsky

1975. 3rd International Astrakhan Lamb Breeding Symposium, Samarkand.
4443 **1709** 6 k. black, grn & stone . 20 10

1975. Birth Centenary of M. P. Konchalovsky (therapeutist).
4444 **1710** 4 k. brown and red . . . 15 10

1711 Exhibition Emblem

1712 I.W.Y. Emblem and Rose

1975. 3rd All-Union Philatelic Exhibition, Yerevan.
4445 **1711** 4 k. red, brown & blue . 10 10

1975. International Women's Year.
4446 **1712** 6 k. red, blue & turquoise 20 10

1713 Parliament Buildings, Belgrade

1714 Title-page of 1938 Edition

1975. 30th Anniv of Yugoslav Republic.
4447 **1713** 6 k. blue, red and gold . 15 10

1975. 175th Anniv of Publication of "Tale of the Host of Igor".
4448 **1714** 4 k. red, grey and bistre 10 10

1715 M. I. Kalinin (statesman)

1975. Celebrities' Birth Centenaries.
4449 **1715** 4 k. brown 10 10
4450 – 4 k. brown 10 10
DESIGN: No. 4450, A. V. Lunacharsky (politician).

1716 Torch and Inscription

1975. 70th Anniv of Russian 1905 Revolution.
4451 **1716** 4 k. red and brown . . . 10 10

1717 Track-laying Machine and Baikal–Amur Railway

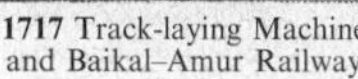

1718 "Decembrists in Senate Square" (D. N. Kardovsky) (⅔-size illustration)

1975. 58th Anniv of October Revolution. Mult.
4452 4 k. Type **1717** 35 10
4453 4 k. Rolling mill, Novolipetsk steel plant (vert) 35 10
4454 4 k. Formula and ammonia plant, Nevynomyssk chemical works (vert) 35 10

1975. 150th Anniv of Decembrist Rising.
4455 **1718** 4 k. multicoloured . . . 20 10

1975. New Year.
4456 **1719** 4 k. multicoloured . . . 10 10

1719 Star of Spasskv Tower

1720 "Village Street"

1975. 125th Birth Anniv of F. A. Vasilev (painter). Multicoloured.
4457 2 k. Type **1720** 10 10
4458 5 k. "Forest Path" 15 10
4459 6 k. "After the Thunderstorm" 20 10
4460 10 k. "Forest Marsh" (horiz) 35 15
4461 12 k. "In the Crimean Mountains" 45 20
4462 16 k. "Wet Meadow" (horiz) 60 30

1721 "Venus" Spacecraft

1975. Space Flights of "Venus 9" and "Venus 10".
4464 **1721** 10 k. multicoloured . . 30 30

1722 G. Sundukyan

1975. 150th Birth Anniv of G. Sundukyan (Armenian playwright).
4465 **1722** 4 k. multicoloured . . . 10 10

1723 Iceland Poppy

1724 A. L. Mints

1975. Flowers (1st series). Multicoloured.
4466 4 k. Type **1723** 30 10
4467 6 k. Globe flower 25 10
4468 10 k. Yellow anemone . . . 35 15
4469 12 k. Snowdrop windflower . 40 20
4470 16 k. "Eminium lehemannii" 50 30
See also Nos. 4585/9.

1975. A. L. Mints (scientist) Commemoration.
4471 **1724** 4 k. brown and gold . . 10 10

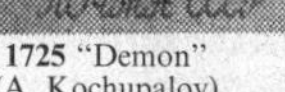

1725 "Demon" (A. Kochupalov)

1726 Pieck

1975. Miniatures from Palekh Art Museum (1st series). Multicoloured.
4472 4 k. Type **1725** 20 10
4473 6 k. "Vasilisa the Beautiful" (I. Vakurov) 30 10
4474 10 k. "The Snow Maiden" (T. Zubkova) 40 15
4475 16 k. "Summer" (K. Kukulieva) 55 25
4476 20 k. "Fisherman and Goldfish" (I. Vakurov) (horiz) . . . 90 30
See also Nos. 4561/5.

1975. Birth Centenary of Wilhelm Pieck (President of German Democratic Republic).
4477 **1726** 6 k. black 15 10

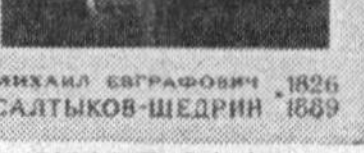

1727 M. E. Saltykov-Shchedrin **1728** Congress Emblem

1976. 150th Birth Anniv of M. Saltykov-Shchedrin (writer).
4478 **1727** 4 k. multicoloured . . . 15 10

1976. 25th Communist Party Congress, Moscow (1st issue).
4479 **1728** 4 k. gold, brown & red . 10 10
See also Nos. 4489 and 4556/60.

1729 Lenin (statue), Kiev **1730** Ice Hockey

1976. 25th Ukraine Communist Party Congress, Kiev.
4481 **1729** 4 k. black, red and blue 10 10

1976. Winter Olympic Games, Innsbruck (1st series). Multicoloured.
4482 2 k. Type **1730** 15 10
4483 4 k. Skiing 20 10
4484 6 k. Figure skating 25 10
4485 10 k. Speed skating 35 15
4486 20 k. Tobogganing 75 35

1731 Marshal C. E. Voroshilov **1732** Congress Hall and Red Banner

1976. 95th Birth Anniv of Marshal C. E. Voroshilov.
4488 **1731** 4 k. green 15 10

1976. 25th Communist Party Congress, Moscow (2nd issue).
4489 **1732** 20 k. orange, red & grn 3·75 2·50

1733 "Lenin on Red Square" (P. Vasiliev)

1976. 106th Birth Anniv of Lenin.
4490 **1733** 4 k. multicoloured . . . 15 10

1734 Atomic Symbo and Institute Emblem

1976. 20th Anniv of Joint Institute of Nuclear Research, Dubna.
4491 **1734** 6 k. multicoloured . . . 20 10

1736 Bolshoi Theatre

1976. Bicentenary of Bolshoi Theatre.
4493 **1736** 10 k. blue, brn & ochre 30 20

1737 "Back from the Fair"

1976. Birth Centenary of P. P. Konchalovsky (painter). Multicoloured.
4494 1 k. Type **1737** 10 10
4495 2 k. "The Green Glass" . . 10 10
4496 6 k. "Peaches" 20 10
4497 16 k. "Meat, Game and Vegetables by the Window" 55 30
4498 20 k. Self-portrait (vert) . . 75 35

1738 "Vostok", "Salyut" and "Soyuz" Spacecraft

1976. 15th Anniv of First Manned Space Flight by Yury Gagarin.
4499 4 k. Type **1738** 15 10
4500 6 k. "Meteor" and "Molniya" satellites 20 10
4501 10 k. Cosmonauts on board "Salyut" space-station . . 35 15
4502 12 k. "Interkosmos" satellite and "Apollo"–"Soyuz" space link 45 20

1739 I. A. Dzhavakhishvili **1740** S. Vurgun

1976. Birth Centenary of I. A. Dzhavakhishvili (scientist).
4504 **1739** 4 k. black, stone and green 10 10

1976. 70th Birth Anniv of Samed Vurgun (Azerbaijan poet).
4505 **1740** 4 k. black, brown & grn 10 10

1741 Festival Emblem **1742** F. I. P. Emblem

1976. 1st All-Union Amateur Art Festival.
4506 **1741** 4 k. multicoloured . . 10 10

1976. 50th Anniv of International Philatelic Federation.
4507 **1742** 6 k. red and blue . . . 15 10

1744 Dnepropetrovsk Crest **1745** N. N. Burdenko

1976. Bicentenary of Dnepropetrovsk.
4509 **1744** 4 k. multicoloured . . . 15 10

1976. Birth Centenary of N. N. Burdenko (neurologist).
4510 **1745** 4 k. brown and red . . . 15 10

1746 K. A. Trenev **1748** Electric Railway Train

1747 Canoeing

1976. Birth Centenary of K. A. Trenev (playwright).
4511 **1746** 4 k. multicoloured . . 10 10

1976. History of Soviet Motor Industry (4th series). As T **1609**.
4512 2 k. black, red and green . . 10 10
4513 3 k. black, orange and bistre . 15 10
4514 4 k. black, buff and blue . . 15 10
4515 12 k. black, green & brown . 45 15
4516 16 k. black, red and yellow . 65 25
DESIGNS: 2 k. Moscow Auto Works "ZIS-110" saloon, 1945; 3 k. Gorkovsky "GAZ-51" truck, 1946; 4 k. Gorkovsky "GAZ-M20 (Pobeda)" saloon, 1946; 12 k. Moscow Auto Works "ZIS-150" truck, 1947; 16 k. Moscow Auto Works "ZIS-154" bus, 1947.

1976. Olympic Games, Montreal. Multicoloured.
4517 4 k. Type **1747** 10 10
4518 6 k. Basketball (vert) . . . 20 10
4519 10 k. Graeco-Roman wrestling 25 15
4520 14 k. Discus throwing (vert) . 30 15
4521 16 k. Rifle-shooting 35 20

1976. 50th Anniv of Soviet Railway Electrification.
4523 **1748** 4 k. black, red and green 30 10

1749 L. M. Pavlichenko **1750** L. E. Rekabarren

1976. 60th Birth Anniv of L. M. Pavlichenko (war heroine).
4524 **1749** 4 k. brown, yellow and silver 15 10

1976. Birth Centenary of Luis Rekabarren (founder of Chilean Communist Party).
4525 **1750** 6 k. black, red & gold . 15 10

1751 "Fresh Partner"

1976. Russian Art. Paintings by P. A. Fedotov. Mult.
4526 2 k. Type **1751** 10 10
4527 4 k. "Fastidious Fiancee" (horiz) 15 10
4528 6 k. "Aristocrat's Breakfast" . 20 10
4529 10 k. "The Gamblers" (horiz) 35 20
4530 16 k. "The Outing" 50 30

1752 S. S. Nemetkin **1753** Soviet Armed Forces Order

1754 Marx and Lenin (sculpture, Ye. Belostotsky and E. Fridman)

1976. Birth Centenary of Sergei S. Nemetkin (chemist).
4532 **1752** 4 k. black, yellow & blue 15 10

1976. (a) As T **1753**.
4533 1 k. olive 10 10
4670 2 k. mauve 10 10
4671 3 k. red 10 10
4672 4 k. red 10 10
4673 6 k. blue 15 10
4674 10 k. green 25 10
4675 12 k. blue 25 10
4676 15 k. blue 50 35
4677 16 k. green 35 15

(b) As T **1754**.
4678 20 k. red 50 10
4679 30 k. red 70 20
4680 32 k. blue . . . . 1·60 65
4681 50 k. brown . . . . 1·40 40
4682 1 r. blue . . . . 3·00 1·00
DESIGNS: 2 k. Gold Star (military) and Hammer and Sickle (labour) decorations; 3 k. "Worker and Farmer" (sculpture); 4 k. Soviet crest; 6 k. Globe and Tupolev Tu-154 airplane (Soviet postal communications); 10 k. Soviet Reputation for Work Order; 23 k. Yuri Gagarin and rocket (space exploration); 15 k. Ostankino T.V. tower and globe; 16 k. International Lenin Prize medal (international peace and security); 30 k. Council for Mutual Economic Aid building; 32 k. Ilyushin Il-76 airplane and compass rose; 50 k. Lenin (after P. Zhukov); 1 r. Satellites orbiting globe.
The 6 and 32 k. are airmail stamps.

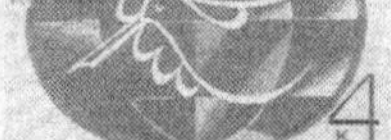

1755 Cattle Egret **1756** Peace Dove with Laurel

1976. Water Birds. Multicoloured.
4545 1 k. Type **1755** 30 15
4546 3 k. Black-throated diver . . 35 15
4547 4 k. Common coot 60 15
4548 6 k. Atlantic puffin . . . . 1·00 20
4549 10 k. Slender-billed gull . . 1·60 30

1976. 2nd Stockholm World Peace Appeal.
4550 **1756** 4 k. blue, yellow & gold 10 10

1757 Federation Emblem

1976. 25th Anniv of International Resistance Movement Federation.
4551 **1757** 6 k. black, gold & blue 15 10

1759 Soviet and Indian Flags **1761** UNESCO Emblem

1760 B. V. Volynov and V. M. Zholobov

1976. Soviet–Indian Friendship.
4553 **1759** 4 k. multicoloured . . . 10 10

1976. Space Flight of "Soyuz 21".
4554 **1760** 10 k. black, blue & brn 30 15

1976. 30th Anniv of UNESCO.
4555 **1761** 16 k. brown, bistre & bl 40 20

1762 "Industry"

1976. 25th Communist Party Congress (3rd issue).
4556 **1762** 4 k. brown, red & yell . 15 10
4557 – 4 k. green, red & orange 15 10
4558 – 4 k. violet, red & pink . 15 10
4559 – 4 k. deep red, red and grey 15 10
4560 – 4 k. violet, red & blue . 15 10
DESIGNS: No. 4557, "Agriculture"; No. 4558, "Science and Technology"; No. 4559, "Transport and Communications"; No. 4560, "International Co-operation".

1763 "The Ploughman" (I. Golikov)

1976. Minatures from Palekh Art Museum (2nd series). Multicoloured.
4561 2 k. Type **1763** 10 10
4562 4 k. "The Search" (I. Markichev) (vert) . . . 15 10
4563 12 k. "The Firebird" (A. Kotuchin) 40 20
4564 14 k. "Folk Festival" (A. Vatagin) (vert) 45 25
4565 20 k. "Victory" (I. Vakurov) (vert) 70 35

1764 Shostakovich and Part of 7th Symphony

1765 G. K. Zhukov

1976. 70th Birth Anniv of Dmitri Shostakovich (composer).
4566 **1764** 6 k. blue 30 10

1976. 80th Birth Anniversaries of Soviet Marshals.
4567 **1765** 4 k. green 15 10
4568 – 4 k. brown 15 10
DESIGN: No. 4568, K. K. Rokossovsky.

1766 "Interkosmos 14" Satellite

1767 V. I. Dal

1976. International Co-operation in Space Research.
4569 **1766** 6 k. blue, gold & black . 20 10
4570 – 10 k. violet, gold & blk . 25 10
4571 – 12 k. purple, gold & blk 35 15
4572 – 16 k. green, gold & blk . 40 15
4573 – 20 k. mauve, gold & blk 50 20
DESIGNS: 10 k. "Aryabhata" (Indian satellite); 12 k. "Apollo"–"Soyuz" space link; 16 k. "Aureole" (French satellite); 20 k. Globe and spacecraft.

1976. 175th Birth Anniv of V. I. Dal (scholar).
4574 **1767** 4 k. green 15 10

1768 Electric Power Station

1976. 59th Anniv of October Revolution. Mult.
4575 4 k. Type **1768** 15 10
4576 4 k. Balashovo fabrics factory 15 10
4577 4 k. Irrigation ditch construction 15 10

1769 Medicine Emblem

1770 M. A. Novinsky (oncologist)

1976. 50th Anniv of Petrov Institute of Cancer Research.
4578 **1769** 4 k. lilac, gold and blue 20 10

1976. Centenary of Cancer Research.
4579 **1770** 4 k. brown, blue & buff 20 10

1771 Hakkel VII Biplane, 1911

1976. Early Russian Aircraft (2nd series). Multicoloured.
4580 3 k. Type **1771** 10 10
4581 6 k. Hakkel IX monoplane, 1912 . . . . 20 10
4582 12 k. Steglau No. 2, 1912 35 15
4583 14 k. Dybovsky Dolphin, 1913 50 15
4584 16 k. Sikorsky Ilya Mourometz, 1914 . . . . 55 25
See also Nos. 4661/6 and 4791/6.

1976. Flowers (2nd series). As T **1723**. Mult.
4585 1 k. Safflower 10 10
4586 2 k. Anemone 10 10
4587 3 k. Gentian 10 10
4588 4 k. Columbine 15 10
4589 6 k. Fitillaria 20 10

1772 New Year Greeting

1976. New Year.
4590 **1772** 4 k. multicoloured . . 10 10

1773 "Parable of the Vineyard"

1976. 370th Birth Anniv of Rembrandt. Mult.
4591 4 k. Type **1773** 15 10
4592 6 k. "Danae" 20 10
4593 10 k. "David and Jonathan" (vert) 30 10
4594 14 k. "The Holy Family" (vert) 45 15
4595 20 k. "Andrian" (vert) . . . 65 25

1774 "Luna 24" and Emblem

1976. "Luna 24" Unmanned Space Flight to Moon.
4597 **1774** 10 k. brown, yell & bl . 30 15

1775 "Pailot'

1976. Russian Ice-breakers (1st series). Mult.
4598 4 k. Type **1775** 40 10
4599 6 k. "Ermak" (vert) 50 10
4600 10 k. "Fedor Litke" 70 15
4601 16 k. "Vladimir Ilich" (vert) . 95 25
4602 20 k. "Krassin" . . . . . . 1·25 45
See also Nos. 4654/60, 4843/8 and 5147.

1776 "Raduga" Experiment and Cosmonauts

1976. "Soyuz 22" Space Flight by V. F. Bykovsky and V. V. Aksenov.
4603 **1776** 10 k. green, blue & red . 30 15

1777 Olympic Torch

1976. Olympic Games, Moscow (1980).
4604 **1777** 4 k. + 2 k. black, red and blue 15 10
4605 – 10 k. + 5 k. black, blue and red 75 25
4606 – 16 k. + 6 k. black, mauve and yellow . . . . . 1·10 40
DESIGNS: 10, 16 k. Games emblem.

1778 Society Emblem and "Red Star"

1779 S. P. Korolev Memorial Medallion

1977. 50th Anniv of Red Banner Forces Voluntary Society.
4608 **1778** 4 k. multicoloured . . . 15 10

1977. 70th Birth Anniv of S. P. Korolev (scientist and rocket pioneer).
4609 **1779** 4 k. gold, black & blue . 15 10

1780 Congress Emblem

1977. World Peace Congress, Moscow.
4610 **1780** 4 k. gold, ultramarine & bl 10 10

1781 Sedov and "Sv. Foka"

1977. Birth Cent of G. Y. Sedov (polar explorer).
4611 **1781** 4 k. multicoloured . . . 1·10 20

1782 Working Class Monument, Red Flag and Newspaper Cover

1783 Ship on Globe

1977. 60th Anniv of Newspaper "Izvestiya".
4612 **1782** 4 k. black, red & silver . 10 10

1977. 24th International Navigation Congress, Leningrad.
4613 **1783** 6 k. blue, black & gold . 20 10

1784 Kremlin Palace of Congresses, Moscow

1785 L. A. Govorov

1977. 16th Soviet Trade Unions Congress.
4614 **1784** 4 k. gold, black & red . 10 10

1977. 80th Birth Anniv of Marshal L. A. Govorov.
4615 **1785** 4 k. brown 15 10

1786 Academy Emblem, Text and Building

1977. 150th Anniv of Grechko Naval Academy, Leningrad.
4616 **1786** 6 k. multicoloured . . . 15 10

1787 J. Labourbe

1788 Chess Pieces

1977. Birth Centenary of Jeanne Labourbe (French communist).
4617 **1787** 4 k. black, blue & red . 10 10

1977. 6th European Chess Team Championship, Moscow.
4618 **1788** 6 k. multicoloured . . . 50 10

1789 "Soyuz 23" and Cosmonauts

1977. "Soyuz 23" Space Flight by V. D. Zudov and V. I. Rozhdestvensky.
4619 **1789** 10 k. red, black & brn . 30 15

1790 Novikov-Priboi

1791 "Welcome" (N. M. Soloninkin)

1977. Birth Centenary of Aleksei Novikov-Priboi (writer).
4620 **1790** 4 k. black, orange & bl 10 10

1977. Folk Paintings from Fedoskino Village. Multicoloured.
4621 4 k. Type **1791** 15 10
4622 6 k. "Along the Street" (V. D. Antonov) (horiz) . 20 10
4623 10 k. "Northern Song" (J. V. Karapaev) 30 15
4624 12 k. "Fairy Tale about Tzar Sultan" (A. I. Kozlov) . . 30 15
4625 14 k. "Summer Troika" (V. A. Nalimov) (horiz) . . 40 20
4626 16 k. "Red Flower" (V. D. Lipitsky) 45 25

1792 Congress Emblem

1977. World Electronics Congress, Moscow.
4627 **1792** 6 k. red, grey and blue . 15 10

1793 "In Red Square" (K. V. Filatov)

1977. 107th Birth Anniv of Lenin.
4628 **1793** 4 k. multicoloured . . . 15 10

1794 Yury Gagarin and Spacecraft

1977. Cosmonautics Day.
4629 **1794** 6 k. blue, lilac and purple 25 15

1795 N. I. Vavilov

1796 F. E. Dzerzhinsky

1977. 90th Birth Anniv of N. I. Vavilov (biologist).
4630 **1795** 4 k. black and brown . 10 10

1977. Birth Centenary of Feliks Dzerzhinsky (founder of Cheka).
4631 **1796** 4 k. black 10 10

1797 Mountain Saxifrage

1798 V. V. Gorbatko and Yu. N. Glazkov (cosmonauts)

1977. Flowers. Multicoloured.
4632 2 k. Type **1797** 10 10
4633 3 k. Pinks 10 10
4634 4 k. "Novosieversia glacialis" 15 10
4635 6 k. "Cerastium maximum" . 20 10
4636 16 k. "Rhododendron aureum" 60 25

1977. "Soyuz 24–Salyut 5" Space Project.
4637 **1798** 10 k. black, red & blue . 50 15

1799 I. S. Konev

1800 Festival Emblem

1977. 80th Birth Anniv of Soviet Marshals.
4638 **1799** 4 k. green 15 10
4639 – 4 k. black 15 10
4640 – 4 k. brown 15 10
DESIGNS: No. 4639, V. D. Sokolovsky; No. 4640, K. A. Meretskov.

1977. 10th International Film Festival, Moscow.
4641 **1800** 6 k. gold, red and lake . 15 10

1801 Greco-Roman Wrestling

1977. Olympic Sports (1st series).
4642 **1801** 4 k. + 2 k. black, ochre and gold 15 10
4643 – 6 k. + 3 k. black, green and gold 20 10
4644 – 10 k. + 5 k. black, mauve and gold 65 20
4645 – 16 k. + 6 k. black, blue and gold 90 30
4646 – 20 k. + 10 k. black, brown and gold . . . . . . 1·25 65
DESIGNS: 6 k. Free-style wrestling; 10 k. Judo; 16 k. Boxing; 29 k. Weightlifting.
See also Nos. 4684/9, 4749/53, 4820/4, 4870/4, 4896/4900, 4962/6 and 4973/7.

1802 "Portrait of a Chambermaid"

1804 Stamps and Emblem

1977. 400th Birth Anniv of Rubens. Multicoloured.
4647 4 k. Type **1802** 15 10
4648 6 k. "The Lion Hunt" (horiz) 20 10
4649 10 k. "Stone Carriers" (horiz) 25 10
4650 12 k. "Water and Earth Alliance" 40 15
4651 20 k. "Landscape with Rainbow" (horiz) 95 35

1977. Soviet Ice-breakers (2nd series). As T **1775**. Multicoloured.
4654 4 k. "Aleksandr Sibiryakov" 25 10
4655 6 k. "Georgy Sedov" . . . 30 10
4656 10 k. "Sadko" 55 10
4657 12 k. "Dezhnev" 65 15
4658 14 k. "Sibur" 75 20
4659 16 k. "Lena" 90 30
4660 20 k. "Amguema" . . . . . 1·10 40

1977. Air. Early Soviet Aircraft (3rd series). As T **1771** but dated 1977.
4661 4 k. black, brown and blue . 15 10
4662 6 k. black, orange and green 25 10
4663 10 k. black, mauve and blue 30 10
4664 12 k. black, blue and red . . 35 15
4665 16 k. multicoloured 50 15
4666 20 k. black, green and blue . 70 20
DESIGNS: 4 k. R-IV bis biplane trainer, 1917; 6 k. Kalinin AK-1, 1924; 10 k. Tupolev ANT-3 R-3, 1925; 12 k. Tupolev ANT-4 TB-1 bomber, 1929; 16 k. Polikarpov R-5 biplane, 1929; 20 k. Shvarov Sh-2 flying boat, 1930.

1977. "60th Anniv of October Revolution" Philatelic Exhibition, Moscow.
4667 **1804** 4 k. red, blue and brown 10 10

1805 Buildings and Arms, Stavropol

1807 Yury Gargarin and "Vostok" Spacecraft

1977. Bicentenary of Stavropol.
4668 **1805** 6 k. gold, red & green . 15 10

1977. Olympic Sports (2nd series). As T **1801**.
4684 4 k. + 2 k. black, gold & red 20 10
4685 6 k. + 3 k. black, gold & blue 45 15
4686 10 k. + 5 k. black, gold & grn 70 20
4687 16 k. + 6 k. black, gold & olive 95 30
4688 20 k. + 10 k. black, gold & pur 1·40 65
DESIGNS—HORIZ: 4 k. Cycling; 10 k. Rifle shooting; 16 k. Horse-jumping; 20 k. Fencing. VERT: 6 k. Archery.

1977. 20th Anniv of Space Exploration.
4690 **1807** 10 k. red, blue & brown 30 15
4691 – 10 k. brown, blue & vio 30 15
4692 – 10 k. red, purple & grn 30 15
4693 – 20 k. green, brn & red . 55 25
4694 – 20 k. purple, red & blue 55 25
4695 – 20 k. red, blue & green 55 25
DESIGNS: No. 4691, Space walking; No. 4692, "Soyuz" spacecraft and "Salyut" space station linked; No. 4693, "Proton 4" satellite; No. 4694, "Luna Venus" and "Mars" space stations; No. 4695, "Intercosmos 10" satellite and "Apollo" and "Soyuz" spacecraft linked

1808 Carving from St. Dmitri's Cathedral, Vladimir (12th-cent)

1977. Russian Art. Multicoloured.
4697 4 k. Type **1808** 15 10
4698 6 k. Bracelet, Ryazan (12th cent). 20 15
4699 10 k. Detail of Golden Gate from Nativity Cathedral, Suzdal (13th-cent) 30 15
4700 12 k. Detail from "Arch-angel Michael" (icon) (A. Rublev) (15th-cent) 30 15
4701 16 k. Gold and marble chalice made by I. Fomin (15th-cent) 45 20
4702 20 k. St. Basil's Cathedral, Moscow (16th-cent) 55 20

1809 "Snowflake and Fir Twig"

1810 Cruiser "Aurora"

1977. New Year.
4703 **1809** 4 k. multicoloured . . . 10 10

1977. 60th Anniv of October Revolution.
4704 **1810** 4 k. multicoloured . . . 15 10
4705 – 4 k. black, red & gold . 15 10
4706 – 4 k. black, red & gold . 15 10
4707 – 4 k. multicoloured . . . 15 10
DESIGNS: No. 4705, Statue of Lenin; No. 4706, Page of "Izvestiya", book by Brezhnev and crowd; No. 4707, Kremlin spire, star and fireworks.

1811 First Clause of U.S.S.R. Constitution

1977. New Constitution.
4709 **1811** 4 k. yellow, red & brn . 10 10
4710 – 4 k. multicoloured . . . 10 10
DESIGN: No. 4710, People of the U.S.S.R. welcoming new constitution.

1813 Postwoman and Post Code

1977. Postal Communications. Multicoloured.
4713 4 k. Type **1813** 15 10
4714 4 k. Letter collection 15 10
4715 4 k. "Map-O" automatic sorting machine 15 10
4716 4 k. Mail transport 15 10
4717 4 k. Delivering the mail . . . 15 10

1814 Red Fort, Delhi and Asokan Capital

1815 Monument, Kharkov

1977. 30th Anniv of Indian Independence.
4718 **1814** 6 k. gold, purple & red . 20 10

1977. 60th Anniv of Establishment of Soviet Power in the Ukraine.
4719 **1815** 6 k. multicoloured . . . 15 10

1816 Adder

1977. Snakes and Protected Animals. Mult.
4720 1 k. Type **1816** 10 10
4721 4 k. Levantine viper 15 10
4722 6 k. Saw-scaled viper . . . 20 10
4723 10 k. Central Asian viper . . 30 15
4724 12 k. Central Asian cobra . . 30 15
4725 16 k. Polar bear and cub . . 40 25
4726 20 k. Walrus and young . . 55 25
4727 30 k. Tiger and cub 60 30

1817 Olympic Emblem and Arms of Vladimir

1977. 1980 Olympics. "Tourism around the Golden Ring" (1st issue). Multicoloured.
4728 1 r. + 50 k. Type **1817** . . . 4·50 2·75
4729 1 r. + 50 k. Vladimir Hotel . 4·50 2·75
4730 1 r. + 50 k. Arms of Suzdal 4·50 2·75
4731 1 r. + 50 k. Pozharsky monument . . . . 4·50 2·75
4732 1 r. + 50 k. Arms of Ivanovo and Frunze monument . . 4·50 2·75
4733 1 r. + 50 k. Monument to Revolutionary Fighters . . 4·50 2·75
See also Nos. 4828/31, 4850/3, 4914/17, 4928/9, 4968/9, 4981/2 and 4990/5.

1818 Combine Harvester

1819 Kremlin Palace of Congresses

1978. 50th Anniv of "Gigant" Collective Farm, Rostov.
4734 **1818** 4 k. brown, red & yellow 10 10

1978. 18th Leninist Young Communist League (Komsomol) Congress.
4735 **1819** 4 k. multicoloured . . . 10 10

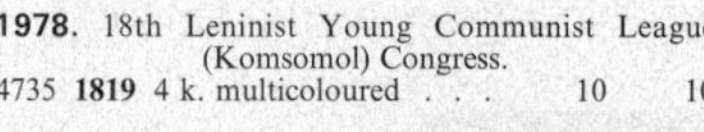

1820 Globe, Obelisk and Emblem

1978. 8th International Federation of Resistance Fighters Congress, Minsk.
4736 **1820** 6 k. red, blue & black . 15 10

1821 Red Army Detachment and Modern Sailor, Airman and Soldier

1978. 60th Anniv of Soviet Military Forces. Multicoloured.
4737 4 k. Type **1821** 15 10
4738 4 k. Defenders of Moscow monument (detail), Lenin banner and Order of Patriotic War 15 10
4739 4 k. Soviet soldier 15 10

1822 "Celebration in a Village"
(½-size illustration)

1978. Birth Centenary of Boris M. Kustodiev (artist). Multicoloured.

4740 4 k. Type **1822** 15 10
4741 6 k. "Shrovetide" 20 10
4742 10 k. "Morning" (50 × 36 mm) 30 15
4743 12 k. "Merchant's Wife drinking Tea" (50 × 36 mm) 40 15
4744 20 k. "Bolshevik" (50 × 36 mm) 55 25

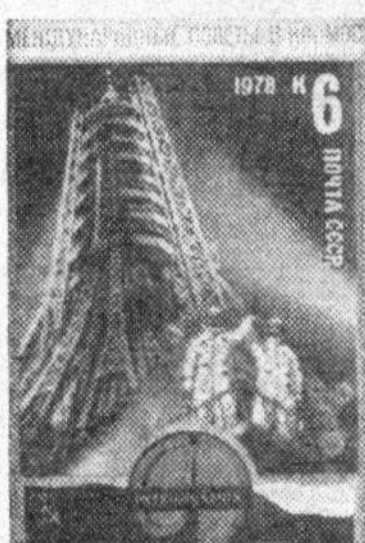
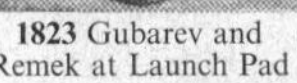
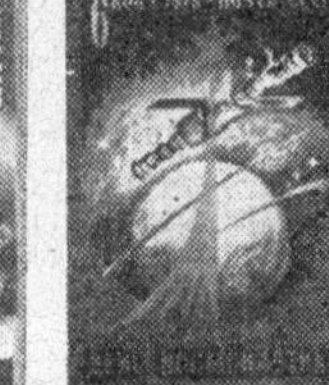
1823 Gubarev and Remek at Launch Pad
1824 "Soyuz" Capsules linked to "Salyut" Space Station

1978. Soviet–Czech Space Flight. Multicoloured.

4746 6 k. Type **1823** 15 10
4747 15 k. "Soyuz-28" docking with "Salyut-6" space station . . 35 15
4748 32 k. Splashdown . . . . . 1·00 35

1978. Olympic Sports (3rd series). As T **1801**. Multicoloured.

4749 4 k. + 2 k. Swimmer at start 15 10
4750 6 k. + 3 k. Diving (vert) . . 20 10
4751 10 k. + 5 k. Water polo . . 65 15
4752 10 k. + 6 k. Canoeist . . . . 1·00 20
4753 20 k. + 10 k. Single sculls . 1·40 70

1978. Cosmonautics Day.

4755 **1824** 6 k. gold, blue and deep blue 15 10

1825 Shield and Laurel Wreath
1826 First Russian Locomotive and Designers

1978. 9th World Congress of Trade Unions.

4756 **1825** 6 k. multicoloured . . . 15 10

1978. Russian Locomotives (1st series). Mult.

4757 1 k. Type **1826** 20 10
4758 2 k. "D series" freight train, 1845 . . . . 20 10
4759 3 k. First passenger locomotive, 1845 . . . . 20 10
4760 16 k. "Gv series" locomotive, 1863–7 . . . . 90 20
4761 20 k. "Bv series" passenger locomotive, 1863–7 . . . . 1·10 30

Nos. 4758/61 are horizontal designs.
See also Nos. 4861/5.

1828 "XI" and Laurel Branch
1830 I.M.C.O. Emblem

1829 Tulip "Bolshoi Theatre"

1978. 11th World Youth and Students Festival, Havana.

4763 **1828** 4 k. multicoloured . . 10 10

1978. Moscow Flowers. Multicoloured.

4764 1 k. Type **1829** 10 10
4765 2 k. Rose "Moscow Morning" 10 10
4766 4 k. Dahlia "Red Star" . . 10 10
4767 10 k. Gladiolus "Moscovite" 35 15
4768 12 k. Iris "To Il'ich's Anniversary" 45 15

1978. 20th Anniv of Intergovernment Maritime Consultative Organization, and World Maritime Day.

4769 **1830** 6 k. multicoloured . . 10 10

1831 "Salyut-6" Space Station performing Survey Work
1832 "Space Meteorology"

1978. "Salyut-6" Space Station. Multicoloured.

4770 15 k. Type **1831** 40 30
4771 15 k. Yu. V. Romanenko and G. M. Grechko 40 30

Nos. 4770/1 were issued in se-tenant pairs forming a composite design.

1978. Space Research. Multicoloured.

4772 10 k. Type **1832** 30 15
4773 10 k. "Soyuz" orbiting globe ("Natural resources") . . 30 15
4774 10 k. Radio waves, ground station and "Molniya" satellite ("Communication") 30 15
4775 10 k. Human figure, "Vostok" orbiting Earth ("Medicine and biology") 30 15

1833 Transporting Rocket to Launch Site

1978. Soviet–Polish Space Flight. Multicoloured.

4777 6 k. Type **1833** 15 10
4778 15 k. Crystal (Sirena experiment) 40 15
4779 32 k. Space station, map and scientific research ship "Cosmonaut Vladimir Komarov" 95 35

1834 Komsomol Awards
1835 M. V. Zakharov

1978. 60th Anniv of Leninist Young Communist League (Komsomol). Multicoloured.

4780 4 k. Type **1834** 10 10
4781 4 k. Products of agriculture and industry 20 10

1978. 80th Birth Anniv of Marshal M. V. Zakharov.

4782 **1835** 4 k. brown 15 10

1836 N. G. Chernyshevsky

1978. 150th Birth Anniv of Nikolai G. Chernyshevsky (revolutionary).

4783 **1836** 4 k. brown and yellow . 10 10

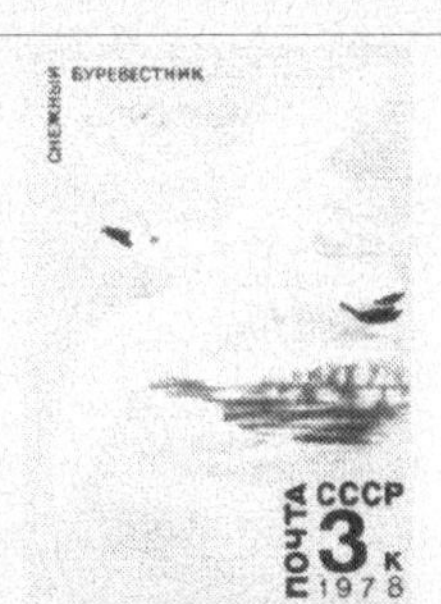
1837 Snow Petrel

1978. Antarctic Fauna. Multicoloured.

4784 1 k. Snares Island penguin (horiz) 60 15
4785 3 k. Type **1837** 75 15
4786 4 k. Emperor penguin 90 15
4787 6 k. White-blood pikes . . . 70 10
4788 10 k. Southern elephant-seal (horiz) . . . . 1·25 15

1838 Torch and Flags
1839 William Harvey

1978. Construction of Orenburg–U.S.S.R. Western Frontier Gas Pipe-line.

4789 **1838** 4 k. multicoloured . . . 10 10

1978. 400th Birth Anniv of William Harvey (discoverer of blood circulation).

4790 **1839** 6 k. green, blk & blue . 15 10

1978. Air. Early Russian Aircraft (3rd series). As T **1771**.

4791 4 k. green, brown & black . . 15 10
4792 6 k. multicoloured 20 10
4793 10 k. yellow, blue & black . . 35 15
4794 12 k. orange, blue & black . . 40 15
4795 16 k. blue, dp blue & black . 50 15
4796 20 k. multicoloured 65 20

DESIGNS: 4 k. Polikarpov Po-2 biplane, 1928; 6 k. Kalinin K-5, 1929; 10 k. Tupolev ANT-6 TB-3, 1930; 12 k. Putilov Stal-2, 1931; 16 k. Beriev Be-2 MBR-2 reconnaissance seaplane, 1932; 20 k. Polikarpov I-16, 1934.

1840 "Bathing of Red Horse"

1978. Birth Centenary of K. S. Petrov-Vodkin (painter). Multicoloured.

4797 4 k. Type **1840** 10 10
4798 6 k. "Petrograd, 1918" . . . 15 10
4799 10 k. "Commissar's Death" . 25 15
4800 12 k. "Rose Still Life" . . . 30 15
4801 16 k. "Morning Still Life" . . 40 15

1841 Assembling "Soyuz 31"

1978. Soviet-East German Space Flight. Multicoloured.

4803 6 k. Type **1841** 15 10
4804 15 k. Space photograph of Pamir mountains 35 15
4805 32 k. Undocking from space station . . . . 1·10 35

1842 "Molniya 1" Satellite, "Orbita" Ground Station and Tupolev Tu-134 Airplane

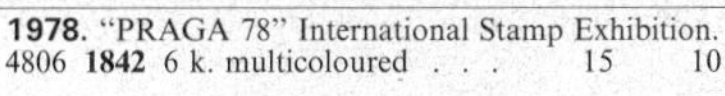
1978. "PRAGA 78" International Stamp Exhibition.

4806 **1842** 6 k. multicoloured . . . 15 10

1843 Tolstoi

1978. 150th Birth Anniv of Leo Tolstoi (novelist).

4807 **1843** 4 k. green . . . . . . 1·60 1·00

1844 Union Emblem
1845 Bronze Figure, Erebuni Fortress

1978. 14th General Assembly of International Union for the Protection of Nature and Natural Resources, Ashkhabad.

4808 **1844** 4 k. multicoloured . . 15 10

1978. Armenian Architecture. Multicoloured.

4809 4 k. Type **1845** 10 10
4810 6 k. Echmiadzin Cathedral . 15 10
4811 10 k. Khachkary (carved stones) 25 15
4812 12 k. Matenadaran building (repository of manuscripts) (horiz) 35 15
4813 16 k. Lenin Square, Yerevan (horiz) 45 20

1846 Monument (P. Kufferge)
1847 Emblem, Ostankino TV Tower and Hammer and Sickle

1978. 70th Anniv of Russian Aid to Messina Earthquake Victims.

4814 **1846** 6 k. multicoloured . . . 20 10

1978. 20th Anniv of Organization for Communications Co-operation.

4815 **1847** 4 k. multicoloured . . . 10 10

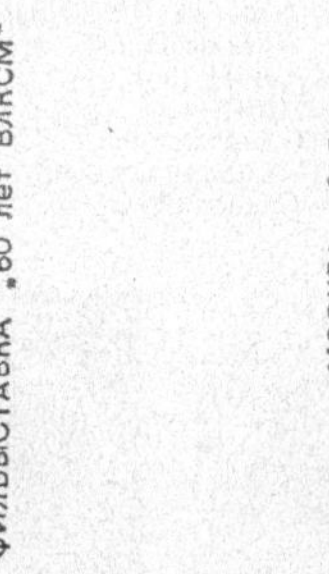

(**1848**)

1978. "60th Anniv of Komsomol" Philatelic Exhibition. Optd with T **1848**.

4816 **1834** 4 k. multicoloured . . . 1·00 50

1851 Shaumyan
1852 "Star" Class Yacht

1978. Birth Centenary of Stephan Georgievich Shaumyan (Commissar).
4819 **1851** 4 k. green 10 10

1978. Olympic Sports (4th series). Sailing Regatta, Tallin. Multicoloured.
4820 4 k. + 2 k. Type **1852** . . . 20 10
4821 6 k. + 3 k. "Soling" class yacht 30 10
4822 10 k. + 5 k. "470" class yacht 40 15
4823 16 k. + 6 k. "Finn" class yacht 60 25
4824 20 k. + 10 k. "Flying Dutchman" class yacht . . 1·10 50

1853 Industrial Structures and Flags

1854 Black Sea Ferry

1978. 61st Anniv of October Revolution.
4826 **1853** 4 k. multicoloured . . . 15 10

1978. Inauguration of Il'ichevsk–Varna, Bulgaria, Ferry Service.
4827 **1854** 6 k. multicoloured . . . 15 10

1855 Zagorsk

1978. 1980 Olympics. "Tourism around the Golden Ring" (2nd issue). Multicoloured.
4828 1 r. + 50 k. Type **1855** . . . 4·75 2·75
4829 1 r. + 50 k. Palace of Culture, Zagorsk . . . . 4·75 2·75
4830 1 r. + 50 k. Kremlin, Rostov-Veliki . . . . 4·75 2·75
4831 1 r. + 50 k. View of Rostov-Veliki . . . . 4·75 2·75

1856 Church of the Intercession on River Nerl

1978. "Masterpieces of Old Russian Culture". Multicoloured.
4832 6 k. Golden crater (horiz) . . 15 10
4833 10 k. Type **1856** 25 15
4834 12 k. "St. George and the Dragon" (15th-century icon) 30 15
4835 16 k. Tsar Cannon (horiz) . . 35 20

1857 Cup with Snake and Institute

1859 Spassky Tower, Kremlin

1858 Nestor Pechersky and "Chronicle of Past Days"

1978. 75th Anniv of Herzen Oncology Research Institute, Moscow.
4836 **1857** 4 k. gold, purple & blk 15 10

1978. History of the Russian Posts. Multicoloured.
4837 4 k. Type **1858** 10 10
4838 6 k. Birch-bark letter 15 10
4839 10 k. Messenger with trumpet 25 15
4840 12 k. Mail sledges 30 15
4841 16 k. Interior of Prikaz Post Office 35 20

1978. New Year.
4842 **1859** 4 k. multicoloured . . 10 10

1978. Soviet Ice breakers (3rd series). As T **1775**. Multicoloured.
4843 4 k. "Vasily Pronchishchev" 20 10
4844 6 k. "Kapitan Belousov" (vert) 25 10
4845 10 k. "Moskva" 30 15
4846 12 k. "Admiral Makarov" . 45 15
4847 16 k. "Lenin" atomic ice-breaker (vert) 65 20
4848 20 k. "Arktika" atomic ice-breaker 80 25

1860 V. Kovalenok and A. Ivanchenkov

1978. "140 Days in Space".
4849 **1860** 10 k. multicoloured . . 20 15

1978. 1980 Olympics "Tourism around the Golden Ring" (3rd issue). As T **1855**. Multicoloured.
4850 1 r. + 50 k. Alexander Nevsky Monument, Pereslavl-Zalessky . . . . . . 4·00 2·75
4851 1 r. + 50 k. Peter I Monument, Pereslavl-Zalessky . . . . 4·00 2·75
4852 1 r. + 50 k. Monastery of the Transfiguration, Yaroslavl 4·00 2·75
4853 1 r. + 50 k. Ferry terminal and Eternal Glory Monument, Yaroslavl . . . . 4·00 2·75

1862 Cuban Flags

1863 Government Building, Minsk

1979. 20th Anniv of Cuban Revolution.
4855 **1862** 6 k. multicoloured . . 15 10

1979. 60th Anniv of Byelorussian Soviet Socialist Republic and Communist Party.
4856 **1863** 4 k. multicoloured . . 10 10

1864 Flags and Reunion Monument

1865 Old and New University Buildings

1979. 325th Anniv of Reunion of Ukraine with Russia.
4857 **1864** 4 k. multicoloured . . 10 10

1979. 400th Anniv of Vilnius Univeristy.
4858 **1865** 4 k. black and pink . . 10 10

1866 Exhibition Hall and First Bulgarian Stamp

1979. "Philaserdica 79" International Stamp Exhibition, Sofia.
4859 **1866** 15 k. multicoloured . . 30 15

INDEX

Countries can be quickly located by referring to the index at the end of this volume.

1867 Satellites "Radio 1" and "Radio 2"

1979. Launching of "Radio" Satellites.
4860 **1867** 4 k. multicoloured . . . 35 10

1868 "A" Series Passenger Locomotive

1979. Railway Locomotives (2nd series). Mult.
4861 2 k. Type **1868** 15 10
4862 3 k. "Shch" series locomotive 15 10
4863 4 k. "L-Putilov" series locomotive 20 10
4864 6 k. "Su" series locomotive . 35 15
4865 15 k. "L" series locomotive . 1·00 35

1870 "Venera 12" over Venus

1871 Albert Einstein

1979. "Venera" Flights to Venus.
4867 **1870** 10 k. red, lilac and purple 30 10

1979. Birth Centenary of Albert Einstein (physicist).
4868 **1871** 6 k. multicoloured . . . 20 10

1872 Congress Emblem **1873** Free Exercise

1979. 21st World Veterinary Congress, Moscow.
4869 **1872** 6 k. multicoloured . . . 15 10

1979. Olympic Sports (5th series). Gymnastics.
4870 **1873** 4 k. + 2 k. brown, stone and orange 15 10
4871 – 6 k. + 3 k. blue, grey and violet 20 10
4872 – 10 k. + 5 k. red, stone and brown 30 15
4873 – 16 k. + 6 k. mauve, grey and purple 75 40
4874 – 20 k. + 10 k. red, stone and brown . . . . . 1·00 65
DESIGNS: 6 k. Parallel bars; 10 k. Horizontal bar; 16 k. Beam; 20 k. Asymmetric bars.

1874 "To Arms" (poster by R. Beren)

1875 Cosmonauts at Yury Gagarin Training Centre

1979. 60th Anniv of First Hungarian Socialist Republic.
4876 **1874** 4 k. multicoloured . . . 10 10

1979. Soviet–Bulgarian Space Flight. Multicoloured.
4877 6 k. Type **1875** 20 10
4878 32 k. Landing of cosmonauts 75 35

1876 "Intercosmos"

1979. Cosmonautics Day.
4879 **1876** 15 k. multicoloured . . 30 15

1878 Exhibition Emblem

1979. U.S.S.R. Exhibition, London.
4881 **1878** 15 k. multicoloured . . 25 15

1880 Antonov An-28

1979. Air. Soviet Aircraft. Multicoloured.
4883 2 k. Type **1880** 10 10
4884 3 k. Yakovlev Yak-42 . . . 15 10
4885 10 k. Tupolev Tu-154 . . . 35 15
4886 15 k. Ilyushin Il-76 . . . . 50 20
4887 32 k. Ilyushin Il-86 . . . . 85 35

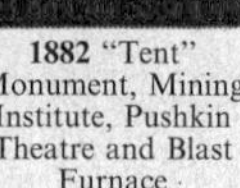
1882 "Tent" Monument, Mining Institute, Pushkin Theatre and Blast Furnace

1883 Child and Apple Blossom

1979. 50th Anniv of Magnitogorsk City.
4889 **1882** 4 k. multicoloured . . . 15 10

1979. International Year of the Child (1st issue).
4890 **1883** 4 k. multicoloured . . . 15 10
See also Nos. 4918/21.

1884 Bogorodsk Wood-carvings

1979. Folk Crafts. Multicoloured.
4891 2 k. Type **1884** 10 10
4892 3 k. Khokhloma painted dish and jars 10 10
4893 4 k. Zhostovo painted tray . 15 10
4894 6 k. Kholmogory bone-carvings 25 10
4895 15 k. Vologda lace 45 35

1885 Football

1979. Olympic Sports (6th series). Multicoloured.
4896 **1885** 4 k. + 2 k. blue, grey and orange 30 10
4897 – 6 k. + 3 k. yellow, orange and blue 40 10
4898 – 10 k. + 5 k. green, red and mauve 50 15

4899 – 16 k. + 6 k. purple, blue and green 60 25
4900 – 20 k. + 10 k. yellow, red and green . . . . . . 1·00 60
DESIGNS—VERT: 6 k. Basketball; 10 k. Volleyball. HORIZ: 16 k. Handball; 20 k. Hockey.

1886 Lenin Square Underground Station

1979. Tashkent Underground Railway.
4901 **1886** 4 k. multicoloured . . . 20 10

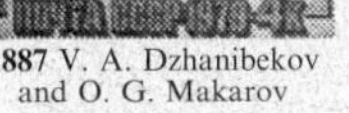
1887 V. A. Dzhanibekov and O. G. Makarov

1888 Council Building and Flags of Member Countries

1979. "Soyuz 27–Salyut 6–Soyuz 26" Orbital Complex.
4902 **1887** 4 k. multicoloured . . . 20 10

1979. 30th Anniv of Council of Mutual Economic Aid.
4903 **1888** 16 k. multicoloured . . 30 15

1889 Scene from "Battleship Potemkin"

1892 Exhibition Hall and Film Still

1979. 60th Anniv of Soviet Films (1st issue) and 11th International Film Festival, Moscow.
4904 **1889** 15 k. multicoloured . . 35 15
See also No. 4907.

1979. 60th Anniv of Soviet Films (2nd issue).
4907 **1892** 4 k. multicoloured . . . 15 10

1893 "Lilac" (K. A. Korovin)

1894 John McClean

1979. Flower Paintings. Multicoloured.
4908 1 k. "Flowers and Fruits" (I. F. Khrutsky) (horiz) 10 10
4909 2 k. "Phloxes" (I. N. Kramskoi) 15 10
4910 3 k. Type **1893** 15 10
4911 15 k. "Bluebells" (S. V. Gerasimov) 40 20
4912 32 k. "Roses" (P. P. Konchalovsky) (horiz) . . 85 40

1979. Birth Centenary of John McClean (first Soviet consul for Scotland).
4913 **1894** 4 k. black and red . . . 15 10

1979. 1980 Olympics. "Tourism around the Golden Ring" (4th issue). As T **1855**. Multicoloured.
4914 1 r. + 50 k. Narikaly Fortress, Tbilisi . . . . 4·00 2·75
4915 1 r. + 50 k. Georgian Philharmonic Society Concert Hall and "Muse" (sculpture), Tbilisi . . . . 4·00 2·75
4916 1 r. + 50 k. Chir-Dor Mosque, Samarkand . . . . . . 4·00 2·75
4917 1 r. + 50 k. People's Friendship Museum and "Courage" monument, Tashkent . . . 4·00 2·75

1895 "Friendship" (Liberda Lena)

1979. International Year of the Child (2nd issue). Children's Paintings. Multicoloured.
4918 2 k. Type **1895** 10 10
4919 3 k. "After Rain" (Akhmetshina Dania) 10 10
4920 4 k. "Dance of Friendship" (Elistratova Lilia) 15 10
4921 15 k. "On the Excursion" (Smalyuk Vika) 35 20

1896 Golden Oriole

1979. Birds. Multicoloured.
4922 2 k. Type **1896** 30 10
4923 3 k. Lesser spotted woodpecker 35 10
4924 4 k. Crested tit 40 10
4925 10 k. Barn owl 95 25
4926 15 k. European nightjar . . 1·25 45

1897 Soviet Circus Emblem

1898 Marx, Engels, Lenin and View of Berlin

1979. 60th Anniv of Soviet Circus.
4927 **1897** 4 k. multicoloured . . 20 10

1979. 1980 Olympics. "Tourism around the Golden Ring" (5th issue). As T **1855**. Multicoloured.
4928 1 r. + 50 k. Relics of Yerevan's origin . . . . 3·00 2·10
4929 1 r. + 50 k. Armenian State Opera and Ballet Theatre, Yerevan . . . . 3·00 2·10

1979. 30th Anniv of German Democratic Republic.
4930 **1898** 6 k. multicoloured . . 20 10

1899 V. A. Lyakhov, V. V. Ryumin and "Salyut 6"

1979. Lyakhov and Ryumin's 175 Days in Space. Multicoloured.
4931 15 k. Type **1899** 30 20
4932 15 k. Radio telescope mounted on "Salyut 6" 30 20
Nos. 4931/2 were issued together, se-tenant, forming a composite design.

1900 Hammer and Sickle

1901 Communications Equipment and Signal Corps Emblem

1979. 62nd Anniv of October Revolution.
4933 **1900** 4 k. multicoloured . . 15 10

1979. 60th Anniv of Signal Corps.
4934 **1901** 4 k. multicoloured . . 20 10

1902 "Katherine" (T. G. Shevchenko)

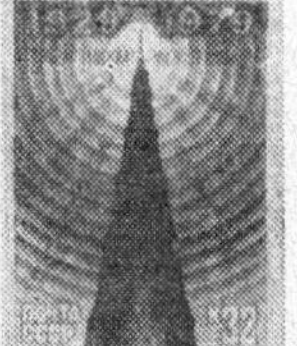
1903 Shabolovka Radio Mast, Moscow

1979. Ukrainian Paintings. Multicoloured.
4935 2 k. Type **1902** 10 10
4936 3 k. "Into Service" (K. K. Kostandi) 15 10
4937 4 k. "To Petrograd" (A. M. Lopukhov) 30 10
4938 10 k. "Return" (V. N. Kostetsky) 30 15
4939 15 k. "Working Morning" (M. G. Belsky) 40 20

1979. 50th Anniv of Radio Moscow.
4940 **1903** 32 k. multicoloured . . 1·00 30

1904 Misha (Olympic mascot)

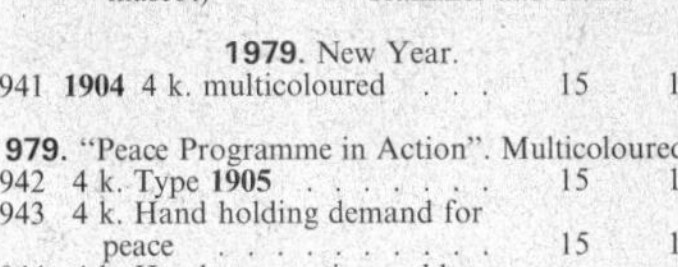
1905 "Peace" and Hammer and Sickle

1979. New Year.
4941 **1904** 4 k. multicoloured . . . 15 10

1979. "Peace Programme in Action". Multicoloured.
4942 4 k. Type **1905** 15 10
4943 4 k. Hand holding demand for peace 15 10
4944 4 k. Hands supporting emblem of peace 15 10

1906 Traffic Policeman

1909 Industrial Landscape

1907 "Vulkanolog"

1979. Road Safety. Multicoloured.
4945 3 k. Type **1906** 20 10
4946 4 k. Child playing in road . . 20 10
4947 6 k. Speeding car out of control 35 10

1979. Soviet Scientific Research Ships. Multicoloured.
4948 1 k. Type **1907** 10 10
4949 2 k. "Professor Bogorov" . . 10 10
4950 4 k. "Ernst Krenkel" 15 10
4951 6 k. "Kosmonavt Vladislav Volkov" 30 10
4952 10 k. "Kosmonavt Yury Gagarin" 60 20
4953 15 k. "Akademik Kurchatov" 85 35

1980. 50th Anniv of Mordovian ASSR of Russian Federation.
4955 **1909** 4 k. red 15 10

MINIMUM PRICE

The minimum price quoted is 10p which represents a handling charge rather than a basis for valuing common stamps. For further notes about prices, see introductory pages.

1910 Speed Skating

1912 N. I. Podvoisky

1911 Running

1980. Winter Olympic Games, Lake Placid.
4956 **1910** 4 k. blue, lt bl & orge . 15 10
4957 – 6 k. violet, blue & orge 15 10
4958 – 10 k. red, blue & gold . 40 15
4959 – 15 k. brown, bl & turq . 50 15
4960 – 20 k. turquoise, bl & red 60 25
DESIGNS—HORIZ: 6 k. Figure skating (pairs); 10 k. Ice hockey; 15 k. Downhill skiing. VERT: 20 k. Luge.

1980. Olympic Sports (7th series). Athletics. Mult.
4962 4 k. + 2 k. Type **1911** . . 20 10
4963 6 k. + 3 k. Hurdling 20 10
4964 10 k. + 5 k. Walking (vert) . 30 20
4965 16 k. + 6 k. High jumping . 70 50
4966 20 k. + 10 k. Long jumping 80 60

1980. Birth Centenary of Nikolai Ilyich Podvoisky (revolutionary).
4967 **1912** 4 k. brown 15 10

1980. 1980 Olympics. "Tourism around the Golden Ring" (6th issue). Moscow. As T **1855**. Mult.
4968 1 r. + 50 k. Kremlin . . . . 5·00 3·25
4969 1 r. + 50 k. Kalinin Prospect 5·00 3·25

1913 "Rainbow" (A. K. Savrasov)
(Illustration reduced. Actual size 74 × 38 mm)

1980. Birth Annivs of Soviet Artists. Mult.
4970 6 k. "Harvest Summer" (A. G. Venetsianov (bicent) (vert) 15 10
4971 6 k. Type **1913** (150th anniv) 15 10
4972 6 k. "Old Yerevan" (M. S. Saryan) (centenary) . . . 15 10

1980. Olympic Sports (8th series). Athletics. As T **1911**. Multicoloured.
4973 4 k. + 2 k. Pole vaulting . . 20 10
4974 6 k. + 3 k. Discus throwing 20 10
4975 10 k. + 5 k. Javelin throwing 30 35
4976 16 k. + 6 k. Hammer throwing 75 55
4977 20 k. + 10 k. Putting the shot 80 70

1915 Georg Ots

1916 Order of Lenin

1980. 60th Birth Anniv of Georg K. Ots (artist).
4980 **1915** 4 k. blue 10 10

1980. 1980 Olympics. "Tourism around the Golden Ring" (7th issue). As T **1855**. Multicoloured.
4981 1 r. + 50 k. St. Isaac's Cathedral, Leningrad . . . 5·00 3·25
4982 1 r. + 50 k. Monument to the Defenders of Leningrad . . 5·00 3·25

1980. 50th Anniv of Order of Lenin.
4983 **1916** 4 k. multicoloured . . . 10 10

1919 "Motherland" (detail of Heroes Monument, Volgograd)

1920 Government House, Arms and Flag of Azerbaijan

1980. 35th Anniv of World War II Victory. Multicoloured.

4986 4 k. Type **1919** 15 10
4987 4 k. Victory Monument, Treptow Park, Berlin . . . 15 10
4988 4 k. Victory Parade, Red Square, Moscow 15 10

1980. 60th Anniv of Azerbaijan Soviet Republic.

4989 **1920** 4 k. multicoloured . . . 10 10

1980. 1980 Olympics. "Tourism around the Golden Ring" (8th issue). As T **1855**. Multicoloured.

4990 1 r. + 50 k. Bogdan Khmelnitsky Monument and St. Sophia Monastery, Kiev 5·00 3·25
4991 1 r. + 50 k. Metro bridge over Dnieper, Kiev . . . . . . 5·00 3·25
4992 1 r. + 50 k. Sports Palace and War Memorial, Minsk . . 5·00 3·25
4993 1 r. + 50 k. House of Cinematograhy, Minsk . . 5·00 3·25
4994 1 r. + 50 k. Old City, Tallin 5·00 3·25
4995 1 r. + 50 k. Hotel Viru, Tallin 5·00 3·25

1921 Monument, Ivanovo

1922 Shield and Industrial Complexes

1980. 75th Anniv of First Soviet of Workers Deputies, Ivanovo.

4996 **1921** 4 k. multicoloured . . . 10 10

1980. 25th Anniv of Warsaw Treaty.

4997 **1922** 32 k. multicoloured . . 1·00 65

1923 Yakovlev Yak-24 Helicopter, 1953

1980. Helicopters. Multicoloured.

4998 1 k. Type **1923** 10 10
4999 2 k. Mil Mi-8, 1962 . . . . . 10 10
5000 3 k. Kamov Ka-26, 1965 . . 20 10
5001 6 k. Mil Mi-6, 1957 . . . . . 30 10
5002 15 k. Mil Mi-10K, 1965 . . . 80 20
5003 32 k. Mil Mi-V12, 1969 . . . 1·90 40

1924 Title Page of Book

1925 Medical Check-up of Cosmonauts

1980. 1500th Birth Anniv of David Anacht (Armenian philosopher).

5004 **1924** 4 k. multicoloured . . . 10 10

1980. Soviet–Hungarian Space Flight. Multicoloured.

5005 6 k. Type **1925** 15 10
5006 15 k. Crew meeting on "Salyut-6" space station 35 15
5007 32 k. Press conference . . . 95 80

1926 Red Fox

1927 Kazan

1980. Fur-bearing Animals. Multicoloured.

5008 2 k. Type **1926** 10 10
5009 4 k. Artic fox (horiz) 15 10
5010 6 k. European mink 20 10
5011 10 k. Coypu 30 15
5012 15 k. Sable (horiz) 50 50

1980. 60th Anniv of Tatar Republic.

5013 **1927** 4 k. multicoloured . . 10 10

1928 College and Emblem

1929 Ho Chi Minh

1980. 150th Anniv of Bauman Technical College, Moscow.

5014 **1928** 4 k. multicoloured . . 10 10

1980. 90th Birth Anniv of Ho Chi Minh (Vietnamese leader).

5015 **1929** 6 k. multicoloured . . 20 10

1930 Arms, Monument and Modern Buildings

1980. 40th Anniv of Soviet Socialist Republics of Lithuania, Latvia and Estonia. Multicoloured.

5016 **1930** 4 k. Lithuania 10 10
5017 – 4 k. Latvia 10 10
5018 – 4 k. Estonia 10 10

1933 Crew of "Soyuz 27" at Launching Site

1934 Avicenna

1980. Soviet–Vietnamese Space Flight. Multicoloured.

5019 6 k. Type **1933** 15 10
5020 15 k. Cosmonauts at work in space 40 20
5021 32 k. Cosmonauts returning to Earth . . . . 1·75 1·40

1980. Birth Millenary of Avicenna (Arab philosopher and physician).

5022 **1934** 4 k. multicoloured . . 10 10

1935 "Khadi-7" Gas turbine Car

1980. Racing cars designed by Kharkov Automobile and Road-building Institute. Multicoloured.

5023 2 k. Type **1935** 10 10
5024 6 k. "Khadi-10" piston engined car 20 10
5025 15 k. "Khadi-11 E" electric car 55 20
5026 32 k. "Khadi-13 E" electric car 1·00 85

1936 Arms, Flags, Government House and Industrial Complex

1980. 60th Anniv of Kazakh Soviet Socialist Republic.

5027 **1936** 4 k. multicoloured . . 15 10

1937 "Self-portrait" and "The Spring"

1980. Birth Bicentenary of Jean Ingres (French painter).

5028 **1937** 32 k. multicoloured . . 1·00 65

1938 "Morning on Kulikovo Field" (A. Bubnov)

1980. 600th Anniv of Battle of Kulikovo.

5029 **1938** 4 k. multicoloured . . . 15 10

1939 Town Hall

1940 Yuri V. Malyshev and Valdimir V. Aksenov

1980. 950th Anniv of Tartu, Estonia.

5030 **1939** 4 k. multicoloured . . . 10 10

1980. "Soyuz T-2" Space Flight.

5031 **1940** 10 k. multicoloured . . 25 15

1941 Theoretical Training

1942 Crew Training

1980. 20th Anniv of Gagarin Cosmonaut Training Centre. Multicoloured.

5032 6 k. Type **1941** 15 10
5033 15 k. Practical training . . . 35 15
5034 32 k. Physical endurance tests 95 65

1980. Soviet–Cuban Space Flight. Multicoloured.

5035 6 k. Type **1942** 15 10
5036 15 k. Physical exercise on board space complex 30 15
5037 32 k. Returned cosmonauts and space capsule 95 65

1943 "Bargaining" (Nevrev) (Reduced-size illustration. Acutal size 77 x 34 mm)

1980. 150th Birth Anniv of N. V. Nevrev and K. D. Flavitsky (painters). Multicoloured.

5038 6 k. Type **1943** 20 10
5039 6 k. "Princess Tarakanova" (Flavitsky) 20 10

1944 Vasilevsky

1945 Banner

1980. 85th Birth Anniv of Marshal A. M. Vasilevsky.

5040 **1944** 4 k. green 15 10

1980. 63rd Anniv of October Revolution.

5041 **1945** 4 k. red, gold & purple 10 10

1946 Guramishvili

1947 Ioffe

1980. 275th Birth Anniv of David Guramishvili (Georgian poet).

5042 **1946** 4 k. green, silver and black 10 10

1980. Birth Centenary of A. F. Ioffe (physicist).

5043 **1947** 4 k. brown and buff . . 15 10

1948 Siberian Cedar

1980. Trees. Multicoloured.

5044 2 k. Type **1948** 10 10
5045 4 k. Pedunculate oak 10 10
5046 6 k. Lime (vert) 10 10
5047 10 k. Sea buckthorn 25 15
5048 15 k. Ash 40 20

1950 Suvorov

1980. 250th Birth Anniv of Field Marshal A. V. Suvorov.

5050 **1950** 4 k. blue 15 10

1951 State Emblem and Republican Government House

1952 Blok (after K. Somov)

1980. 60th Anniv of Armenian Soviet Socialist Republic.

5051 **1951** 4 k. multicoloured . . . 10 10

1980. Birth Centenary of Aleksandr Aleksandrovich Blok (poet).

5052 **1952** 4 k. multicoloured . . . 10 10

1980. Soviet Scientific Research Ships (2nd series). As T **1907**. Multicoloured.

5053 2 k. "Ayu-Dag" 10 10
5054 3 k. "Valerian Uryvaev" . . 10 10
5055 4 k. "Mikhail Somov" . . . 25 10
5056 6 k. "Akademik Sergei Korolev" 25 10
5057 10 k. "Otto Schmidt" . . . 40 15
5058 15 k. "Akademik Mstislav Keldysh" 60 45

1953 Spassky Tower and Kremlin Palace of Congresses

1955 Sable in Cedar

1980. New Year.

5059 **1953** 4 k. multicoloured . . . 10 10

1980. Perf or imperf (2 r.), perf (others).

5060	–	3 k. orange	10	10
5061	–	5 k. blue	15	10
5063	**1955**	35 k. olive	1·00	35
5064	–	45 k. brown	1·40	60
5066	–	50 k. green	2·00	70
5067	–	2 r. black	5·50	2·00
5068	–	3 r. black	7·50	4·00
5068a	–	3 r. green	2·00	1·00
5069	–	5 r. blue	3·25	1·60

DESIGNS—14 × 22 mm: 3 k. State flag; 5 k. Forms of transport. 22 × 33 mm: 45 k. Spassky Tower; 50 k. Vodovzodny Tower and Grand Palace, Moscow Kremlin; 2 r. Atomic ice-breaker; 3 r. Globe, child and olive branch; 5 r. Globe and feather ("Peace").

1957 Institute Building

1980. 50th Anniv of Institute for Advanced Training of Doctors.

5075 **1957** 4 k. multicoloured . . . 15 10

1958 Lenin Monument, Leningrad, and Dneproges Hydro-electric Station

1959 Nesmeyanov

1980. 60th Anniv of GOELRO (electrification plan).

5076 **1958** 4 k. multicoloured . . . 10 10

1980. Academician A. N. Nesmeyanov (organic chemist) Commemoration.

5077 **1959** 4 k. multicoloured . . . 10 10

1960 Nagatinsky Bridge

1980. Moscow Bridges. Multicoloured.

5078 4 k. Type **1960** 15 10
5079 6 k. Luzhniki underground railway bridge 25 10
5080 15 k. Kalininsky bridge . . . 45 20

1961 Timoshenko

1962 Indian and Russian Flags with Government House, New Delhi

1980. 10th Death Anniv of Marshal S. K. Timoshenko.

5081 **1961** 4 k. purple 10 10

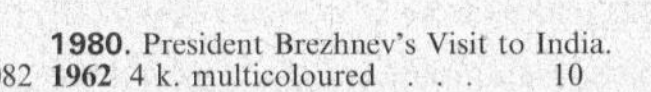

1980. President Brezhnev's Visit to India.

5082 **1962** 4 k. multicoloured . . . 10 10

1963 Antarctic Research Station

1964 Arms and Symbols of Agriculture and Industry

1981. Antarctic Exploration. Multicoloured.

5083 4 k. Type **1963** 25 10
5084 6 k. Antennae, rocket, weather balloon and tracked vehicle (Meteorological research) . 15 10
5085 15 k. Map of Soviet bases and supply ship . . . . 2·25 40

1981. 60th Anniv of Dagestan Autonomous Soviet Socialist Republic.

5086 **1964** 4 k. multicoloured . . 10 10

1965 Hockey Players and Emblem

1981. 12th World Hockey Championships, Khabarovsk.

5087 **1965** 6 k. multicoloured . . 15 10

1966 Banner and Star

1981. 26th Soviet Communist Party Congress. Multicoloured.

5088 4 k. Type **1966** 10 10
5089 20 k. Kremlin Palace of Congresses and Lenin (51 × 36 mm) . . . . . . 1·40 1·00

1967 Lenin and Congress Building

1968 Keldysh

1981. 26th Ukraine Communist Party Congress.

5090 **1967** 4 k. multicoloured . . 10 10

1981. 70th Birth Anniv of Academician Mtislav Vsevolodovich Keldysh (mathematician).

5091 **1968** 4 k. multicoloured . . 10 10

1970 Baikal–Amur Railway

1981. Construction Projects of the 10th Five Year Plan. Multicoloured.

5093 4 k. Type **1970** 20 10
5094 4 k. Urengoi gas field . . . 20 10
5095 4 k. Sayano-Shushenakaya hydro-electric dam 20 10
5096 4 k. Atommash Volga–Don atomic reactor 20 10
5097 4 k. Syktyvkar paper mill . . 20 10
5098 4 k. Giant excavator, Ekibastuz 20 10

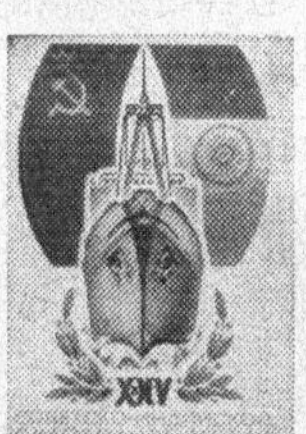

1971 Freighter and Russian and Indian Flags

1981. 25th Anniv of Soviet–Indian Shipping Line.

5099 **1971** 15 k. multicoloured . . 40 20

1972 Arms, Monument and Building

1981. 60th Anniv of Georgian Soviet Socialist Republic.

5100 **1972** 4 k. multicoloured . . . 10 10

1973 Arms and Abkhazian Scenes

1974 Institute Building

1981. 60th Anniv of Abkhazian Autonomous Soviet Socialist Republic.

5101 **1973** 4 k. multicoloured . . . 10 10

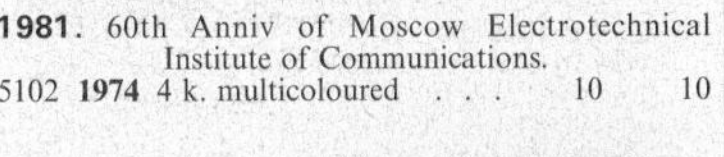

1981. 60th Anniv of Moscow Electrotechnical Institute of Communications.

5102 **1974** 4 k. multicoloured . . . 10 10

1975 Communications Equipment and Satellite

1976 L. I. Popov and V. V. Ryumin

1981. 30th All-Union Amateur Radio Exhibition.

5103 **1975** 4 k. multicoloured . . . 10 10

1981. 185 Days in Space of Cosmonauts Popov and Ryumin. Multicoloured.

5104 15 k. Type **1976** 35 20
5105 15 k. "Salyut 6" – "Soyuz" complex 35 20

1977 O. G. Makarov, L. D. Kizim and G. M. Strekalov

1961. "Soyuz T-3" Space Flight.

5106 **1977** 10 k. multicoloured . . 30 15

1978 Rocket Launch

1981. Soviet–Mongolian Space Flight. Multicoloured.

5107 6 k. Type **1978** 20 10
5108 15 k. Mongolians watching space flight on television . . 40 15
5109 32 k. Re-entry stages . . . . 1·00 65

1979 Bering

1980 Yury Gagarin and Globe

1981. 300th Birth Anniv of Vitus Bering (navigator).

5110 **1979** 4 k. blue 25 10

1981. 20th Anniv of First Manned Space Flight. Multicoloured.

5111 6 k. Type **1980** 15 10
5112 15 k. S. P. Korolev (spaceship designer) 40 15
5113 32 k. Statue of Gagarin and "Interkosmos" emblem . . 1·00 65

1981 "Salyut" Orbital Space Station

1983 Prokofiev

1981. 10th Anniv of First Manned Space Station.

5115 **1981** 32 k. multicoloured . . 1·25 65

1981. 90th Birth Anniv of S. S. Prokofiev (composer).

5117 **1983** 4 k. lilac 30 10

1984 New Hofburg Palace, Vienna

1985 Arms, Industrial Complex and Docks

1981. "WIPA 1981" International Stamp Exhibition, Vienna.

5118 **1984** 15 k. multicoloured . . 30 20

1981. 60th Anniv of Adzharskian Autonomous Soviet Socialist Republic.

5119 **1985** 4 k. multicoloured . . . 10 10

1986 N. N. Benardos

1987 Congress Emblem

1981. Centenary of Invention of Welding.

5120 **1986** 6 k. multicoloured . . . 15 10

1981. 14th Congress of International Union of Architects, Warsaw.

5121 **1987** 15 k. multicoloured . . 30 20

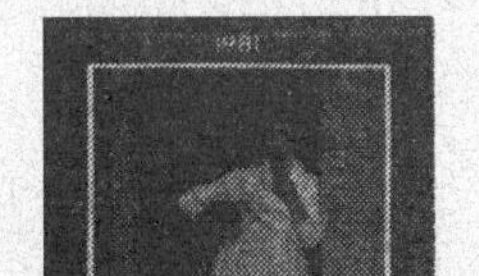

1988 "Albanian Girl in Doorway" (A. A. Ivanov)

1981. Paintings. Multicoloured.

5122 10 k. Type **1988** 30 15
5123 10 k. "Sunset over Sea at Livorno" (N. N. Ge) (horiz) 30 15
5124 10 k. "Demon" (M. A. Vrubel) (horiz) 30 15
5125 10 k. "Horseman" (F. A. Rubo) 30 15

MINIMUM PRICE

The minimum price quoted is 10p which represents a handling charge rather than a basis for valuing common stamps. For further notes about prices, see introductory pages.

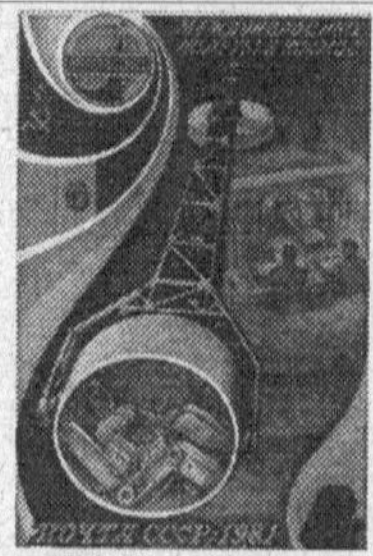

1989 Flight Simulator

1981. Soviet–Rumanian Space Flight. Multicoloured.
5126 6 k. Type **1989** 15 10
5127 15 k. "Salyut" - "Soyuz" space complex 35 20
5128 32 k. Cosmonauts greeting journalists after return . . 80 65

1990 "Primula minima"

1981. Flowers of the Carpathians. Multicoloured.
5129 4 k. Type **1990** 15 10
5130 6 k. "Carlina acaulis" 20 10
5131 10 k. "Parageum montanum" . . 35 15
5132 15 k. "Atragene alpina" . . . 50 20
5133 32 k. "Rhododendron kotschyi" 1·00 50

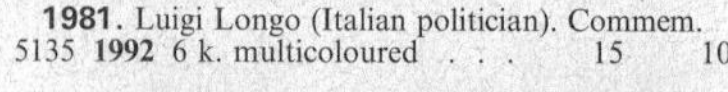

1991 Gyandzhevi 1992 Longo

1981. 840th Birth Anniv of Nizami Gyandzhevi (poet and philosopher).
5134 **1991** 4 k. brown, yell & grn . 10 10

1981. Luigi Longo (Italian politician). Commem.
5135 **1992** 6 k. multicoloured . . . 15 10

1993 Running 1994 Flag and Arms of Mongolia

1981. Sports. Multicoloured.
5136 4 k. Type **1993** 15 10
5137 6 k. Football 15 10
5138 10 k. Throwing the discus . . 25 15
5139 15 k. Boxing 40 20
5140 32 k. Swimmer on block . . 85 65

1981. 60th Anniv of Revolution in Mongolia.
5141 **1994** 6 k. multicoloured . . . 15 10

1995 Spassky Tower and Film encircling Globe 1996 "Lenin"

1981. 12th International Film Festival, Moscow.
5142 **1995** 15 k. multicoloured . . 35 15

1981. River Ships. Multicoloured.
5143 4 k. Type **1996** 20 10
5144 6 k. "Kosmonavt Gagarin" (tourist ship) 25 10
5145 15 k. "Valerian Kuibyshev" (tourist ship) 60 45
5146 32 k. "Baltysky" (tanker) . . 1·40 55

1981. Russian Ice-breakers (4th issue). As T **1775**. Multicoloured.
5147 15 k. "Malygin" 65 15

1997 Industry

1981. Resolutions of the 26th Party Congress. Multicoloured.
5148 4 k. Type **1997** 15 10
5149 4 k. Agriculture 15 10
5150 4 k. Energy 15 10
5151 4 k. Transport and communications 15 10
5152 4 k. Arts and science 15 10
5153 4 k. International co-operation 15 10

1998 Ulyanov 2000 Brushes, Palette and Gerasimov

1999 Facade of Theatre

1981. 150th Birth Anniv of I. N. Ulyanov (Lenin's father).
5154 **1998** 4 k. brown, blk & grn . 10 10

1981. 225th Anniv of Pushkin Drama Theatre, Leningrad.
5155 **1999** 6 k. multicoloured . . 15 10

1981. Birth Centenary of A. M. Gerasimov (artist).
5156 **2000** 4 k. multicoloured . . 10 10

2001 Institute Building

1981. 50th Anniv of Institute of Physical Chemistry, Academy of Sciences, Moscow.
5157 **2001** 4 k. multicoloured . . 10 10

2002 Severtzov's Tit Warbler

1981. Song Birds. Multicoloured.
5158 6 k. Type **2002** 25 10
5159 10 k. Asiatic paradise flycatcher (vert) 40 15
5160 15 k. Jankowski's bunting . 65 30
5161 20 k. Vinous-throated parrotbill (vert) 80 40
5162 32 k. Hodgson's bushchat (vert) 1·50 60

2003 Arms and Industrial Scenes

1981. 60th Anniv of Komi A.S.S.R.
5163 **2003** 4 k. multicoloured . . 30 10

2004 Orbiting Satellite and Exhibition Emblem

1981. "Svyaz 81" Communications Exhibition.
5164 **2004** 4 k. multicoloured . . 15 10

2005 Buildings, Arms and Monument 2006 Soviet Soldier (monument, Treptow Park, Berlin)

1981. 60th Anniv of Kabardino-Balkar A.S.S.R.
5165 **2005** 4 k. multicoloured . . . 10 10

1981. 25th Anniv of Soviet War Veterans Committee.
5166 **2006** 4 k. multicoloured . . . 10 10

2007 Four-masted Barque "Tovarishch"

1981. Cadet Sailing Ships. Multicoloured.
5167 4 k. Type **2007** 15 10
5168 6 k. Barquentine "Vega" . . 25 10
5169 10 k. Schooner "Kodor" (vert) 35 15
5170 15 k. Three-masted barque "Tovarishch" 50 20
5171 20 k. Four-masted barque "Kruzenshtern" 75 55
5172 32 k. Four-masted barque "Sedov" (vert) . . . . . . 1·10 85

2008 Russian and Kazakh Citizens with Flags 2009 Lavrentev

1981. 250th Anniv of Unification of Russia and Kazakhstan.
5173 **2008** 4 k. multicoloured . . . 10 10

1981. Academician Mikhail Alekseevich Lavrentev (mathematician) Commemoration.
5174 **2009** 4 k. multicoloured . . . 10 10

2010 Kremlin Palace of Congresses, Moscow, and Arch of the General Staff, Leningrad

1981. 64th Anniv of October Revolution.
5175 **2010** 4 k. multicoloured . . . 10 10

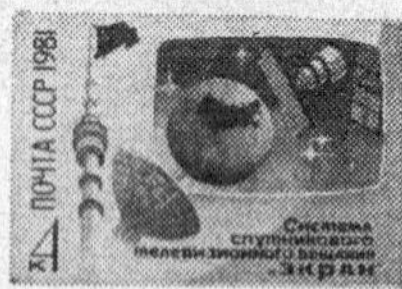

2011 Transmitter, Dish Aerial and "Ekran" Satellite

1981. "Ekran" Television Satellite.
5176 **2011** 4 k. multicoloured . . . 10 10

2012 V. V. Kovalyonok and V. P. Savinykh 2014 Merkurov

1981. "Soyuz T-4"–"Salyut 6" Space Complex. Multicoloured.
5177 10 k. Type **2012** 25 15
5178 10 k. Microscope slide, crystal and text 25 15

1981. Birth Centenary of Sergei Dmitrievich Merkurov (sculpture).
5180 **2014** 4 k. brown, grn & bis . 10 10

2015 "Autumn" (Nino A. Piromanashvili) 2016 Arms and Saviour Tower, Moscow

1981. Paintings by Georgian Artists. Multicoloured.
5181 4 k. Type **2015** 15 10
5182 6 k. "Gurian Woman" (Sh. G. Kikodze) 15 10
5183 10 k. "Travelling Companions" (U. M. Dzhaparidze) (horiz) 25 15
5184 15 k. "Shota Rustaveli" (S. S. Kobuladze) 45 25
5185 32 k. "Tea Pickers" (V. D. Gudiashvili" (horiz) . . . 90 45

1981. New Year.
5186 **2016** 4 k. multicoloured . . . 10 10

2017 Horse-drawn Sleigh (19th century)

1981. Moscow Municipal Transport.
5187 **2017** 4 k. brown and silver . 15 10
5188 – 6 k. green and silver . . 20 10
5189 – 10 k. lilac and silver . . 30 15
5190 – 15 k. black and silver . . 45 20
5191 – 20 k. brown and silver . . 60 30
5192 – 32 k. red and silver . . 90 50

DESIGNS: 6 k. Horse-drawn tram (19th century); 10 k. Horse-drawn cab (19th century); 15 k. Taxi, 1926; 20 k. British Leyland bus, 1926; 32 k. Electric tram, 1912.

2019 Modern Kiev

1982. 1500th Anniv of Kiev.
5194 **2019** 10 k. multicoloured . . 35 15

2020 S. P. Korolev 2021 Arms and Industrial Complex

1982. 75th Birth Anniv of Academician S. P. Korolev (spaceship designer).
5195 **2020** 4 k. multicoloured . . . 15 10

1982. 60th Anniv of Checheno-Ingush A.S.S.R.
5196 **2021** 4 k. multicoloured . . . 15 10

2022 Arms and Construction Sites 2023 Hikmet

1982. 60th Anniv of Yakut A.S.S.R.
5197 **2022** 4 k. multicoloured . . . 15 10

1982. 80th Birth Anniv of Nazim Hikmet (Turkish poet).
5198 **2023** 6 k. multicoloured . . . 25 10

2024 "The Oaks"

1982. 150th Birth Anniv of I. I. Shishkin (artist).
5199 **2024** 6 k. multicoloured . . . 25 10

2025 Trade Unionists and World Map

1982. 10th World Trade Unions Congress, Havana.
5200 **2025** 15 k. multicoloured . . 40 20

2026 Kremlin Palace of Congresses and Flag

2027 "Self-portrait"

1982. 17th Soviet Trade Unions Congress.
5201 **2026** 4 k. multicoloured . . . 10 10

1982. 150th Birth Anniv of Edouard Manet (artist).
5202 **2027** 32 k. multicoloured . . 80 40

2028 Show Jumping

2029 Tito

1982. Soviet Horse breeding. Multicoloured.
5203 4 k. Type **2028** 30 10
5204 6 k. Dressage 30 10
5205 15 k. Racing 60 25

1982. President Tito of Yugoslavia Commemoration.
5206 **2029** 6 k. brown and black . 15 10

2030 University, Book and Monument

1982. 350th Anniv of University of Tartu.
5207 **2030** 4 k. multicoloured . . . 10 10

2031 Heart on Globe

1982. 9th International Cardiologists Conference, Moscow.
5208 **2031** 15 k. multicoloured . . 45 20

2033 Blackberry

1982. Wild Berries. Multicoloured.
5210 4 k. Type **2033** 15 10
5211 6 k. Blueberries 20 10
5212 10 k. Cranberry 30 15
5213 15 k. Cherry 45 25
5214 32 k. Strawberry . . . . . . 1·10 55

2034 "Venera 13" and "14"

2035 "M. I. Lopukhina" (V. L. Borovikovsky)

1982. "Venera" Space Flights to Venus.
5215 **2034** 10 k. multicoloured . . 30 15

1982. Paintings. Multicoloured.
5216 6 k. Type **2035** 20 10
5217 6 k. "E. V. Davydov" (O. A. Kiprensky) 20 10
5218 6 k. "The Unequal Marriage" (V. V. Pukirev) 20 10

2036 Chukovsky

2039 Solovev-Sedoi

2037 Rocket, "Soyuz" Spaceship, Globe and Space Station

1982. Birth Cent of K. I. Chukovsky (author).
5219 **2036** 4 k. black and grey . . 15 10

1982. Cosmonautics Day.
5220 **2037** 6 k. multicoloured . . 20 10

1982. 75th Birth Anniv of V. P. Solovev-Sedoi (composer).
5222 **2039** 4 k. brown 20 10

2040 Dimitrov

2041 Masthead

1982. Birth Centenary of Georgi Dimitrov (Bulgarian statesman).
5223 **2040** 6 k. green 15 10

1982. 70th Anniv of "Pravda" (Communist Party Newspaper).
5224 **2041** 4 k. multicoloured . . 15 10

INDEX

Countries can be quickly located by referring to the index at the end of this volume.

2042 Congress Emblem and Ribbons

2043 Globe and Hands holding Seedling

1982. 19th Congress of Leninist Young Communist League (Komsomol).
5225 **2042** 4 k. multicoloured . . . 15 10

1982. 10th Anniv of U.N. Environment Programme.
5226 **2043** 6 k. multicoloured . . . 15 10

2044 Pioneers

2045 I.T.U. Emblem, Satellite and Receiving Station

1982. 60th Anniv of Pioneer Organization.
5227 **2044** 4 k. multicoloured . . . 10 10

1982. I.T.U. Delegates' Conference, Nairobi.
5228 **2045** 15 k. multicoloured . . 40 20

2046 "VL80T" Electric Locomotive

1982. Locomotives. Multicoloured.
5229 4 k. Type **2046** 20 10
5230 6 k. "TEP-75" diesel 25 10
5231 10 k. "TEM-7" diesel 50 20
5232 15 k. "VL82M" electric . . . 75 30
5233 32 k. "EP200" electric . . . . 1·75 60

2047 Players with Trophy and Football

1982. World Cup Football Championship, Spain.
5234 **2047** 20 k. lilac, yellow and brown 65 30

2048 Hooded Crane

1982. 18th International Ornithological Congress, Moscow. Multicoloured.
5235 2 k. Type **2048** 20 10
5236 4 k. Steller's sea eagle 40 15
5237 6 k. Spoon-billed sandpiper . 50 20
5238 10 k. Bar-headed goose . . . 85 25
5239 15 k. Sociable plover . . . . 1·25 35
5240 32 k. White stork . . . . . . 2·75 75

2049 Buildings and Workers with Picks

2051 U.N. Flag

2050 "The Cart"

1982. 50th Anniv of Komsomolsk-on-Amur.
5241 **2049** 4 k. multicoloured . . . 15 10

1982. Birth Centenary of M. B. Grekov (artist).
5242 **2050** 6 k. multicoloured . . . 20 10

1982. Second U.N. Conference on the Exploration and Peaceful Uses of Outer Space, Vienna.
5243 **2051** 15 k. multicoloured . . 40 20

2052 Scientific Research in Space

1982. Soviet–French Space Flight. Multicoloured.
5244 6 k. Type **2052** 15 10
5245 20 k. Rocket and trajectory . 60 30
5246 45 k. Satellites and globe . . 1·40 75

2053 "Legend of the Golden Cockerel" (P. I. Sosin)

1982. Lacquerware Paintings. Multicoloured.
5248 6 k. Type **2053** 20 10
5249 10 k. "Minin's Appeal to Count Pozharsky" (I. A. Fomichev) 30 20
5250 15 k. "Two Peasants" (A. F. Kotyagin) 45 25
5251 20 k. "The Fisherman" (N. P. Klykov) 60 35
5252 32 k. "Arrest of the Propagandists" (N. I. Shishakov) 90 55

2054 Early Telephone Moscow, Leningrad, Odessa and Riga

2055 P. Schilling (inventor)

1982. Telephone Centenary.
5253 **2054** 4 k. multicoloured . . . 15 10

1982. 150th Anniv of Electro-magnetic Telegraph in Russia.
5254 **2055** 6 k. multicoloured . . . 20 10

2056 Gymnast and Television Screen

1982. Intervision Cup Gymnastics Contest.
5255 **2056** 15 k. multicoloured . . 40 20

2057 Mastyazhart Glider

2058 Garibaldi

1982. Gliders (1st series). Multicoloured.
5256 4 k. Type **2057** 20 10
5257 6 k. Red Star, 1930 . . . . . 20 10
5258 10 k. TsAGI-2, 1934 . . . . 40 15
5259 20 k. Stakhanovets, 1939 (60 × 27 mm) 65 65
5260 32 k. GR-29, 1941 (60 × 27 mm) 1·10 1·10
See Nos. 5301/5.

1982. 175th Birth Anniv of Giuseppe Garibaldi.
5261 **2058** 6 k. multicoloured . . . 15 10

2059 Emblem

2060 F.I.D.E. Emblem, Chess Symbol for Queen and Equestrian Statue

1982. 25th Anniv of International Atomic Energy Agency.
5262 **2059** 20 k. multicoloured . . 50 30

1982. World Chess Championship Interzone Tournaments for Women (Tbilisi) and Men (Moscow). Multicoloured.
5263 6 k. Type **2060** 35 15
5264 6 k. F.I.D.E. emblem, chess symbol for King and Kremlin tower 35 15

2061 Shaposhnikov

2062 Clenched Fist

1982. Birth Cent of Marshal B. M. Shaposhnikov.
5265 **2061** 4 k. brown 15 10

1982. 70th Anniv of African National Congress.
5266 **2062** 6 k. multicoloured . . . 20 10

2063 Botkin

А. КАРПОВ — обладатель восьми „Шахматных Оскаров"
(**2065**)

1982. 150th Birth Anniv of S. P. Botkin (therapeutist).
5267 **2063** 4 k. green 15 10

1982. A. Karpov's Victory in World Chess Championship. No. 5264 optd with T **2065**.
5269 6 k. multicoloured 50 35

2066 Submarine "S-56"

1982. Soviet Naval Ships. Multicoloured.
5270 4 k. Type **2066** 20 10
5271 6 k. Minelayer "Gremyashchy" 20 10
5272 15 k. Minesweeper "Gafel" . 65 25
5273 20 k. Cruiser "Krasnyi Krim" 90 40
5274 45 k. Battleship "Sevastopol" 1·90 1·25

2067 Flag and Arms

1982. 65th Anniv of October Revolution.
5275 **2067** 4 k. multicoloured . . . 15 10

2068 House of the Soviets, Moscow

1982. 60th Anniv of U.S.S.R. Multicoloured.
5276 10 k. Type **2068** 30 20
5277 10 k. Dneiper Dam and statue 30 20
5278 10 k. Soviet war memorial and resistance poster 30 20
5279 10 k. Newspaper, worker holding peace text, and sun illuminating city 30 20
5280 10 k. Workers' Monument, Moscow, rocket, Ilyushin Il-86 jet and factories . . 30 20
5281 10 k. Soviet arms and Kremlin tower 30 20

Всесоюзная филателистическая выставка
(**2069**)

1982. All-Union Stamp Exhibition, Moscow. No. 5280 optd with T **2069**.
5282 10 k. multicoloured 40 30

2070 "Portrait of an Actor" (Domenico Fetti)

2072 Hammer and Sickle, Clock and Date

1982. Italian Paintings in the Hermitage Museum, Leningrad. Multicoloured.
5283 4 k. Type **2070** 15 10
5284 10 k. "St. Sebastian" (Pietro Perugino) 30 15
5285 20 k. "Danae" (Titian) (horiz) 60 30
5286 45 k. "Portrait of a Woman" (Correggio) . . . . 1·25 75
5287 50 k. "Portrait of a Young Man" (Capriolo) . . . . 1·40 85

1982. New Year.
5289 **2072** 4 k. multicoloured . . 10 10

2075 Kherson Lighthouse, Black Sea

2076 F. P. Tolstoi

1982. Lighthouses (1st series). Multicoloured.
5292 6 k. Type **2075** 40 15
5293 6 k. Vorontsov lighthouse, Odessa, Black Sea 40 15
5294 6 k. Temryuk lighthouse, Sea of Azov 40 15
5295 6 k. Novorossiisk lighthouse, Black Sea 40 15
5296 6 k. Dneiper harbour light . 40 15
See also Nos. 5362/6 and 5449/53.

1983. Birth Bicentenary of Fyodor Petrovich Tolstoi (artist).
5297 **2076** 4 k. multicoloured . . 15 10

2077 Masthead of "Iskra"

2078 Army Star and Flag

1983. 80th Anniv of 2nd Social Democratic Workers' Congress.
5298 **2077** 4 k. multicoloured . . 15 10

1983. 65th Anniv of U.S.S.R. Armed Forces.
5299 **2078** 4 k. multicoloured . . . 15 10

1983. Gliders (2nd series). As T **2057**. Multicoloured.
5301 2 k. A-9, 1948 . . . . 10 10
5302 4 k. KAU-12, 1957 . . . . . 15 10
5303 6 k. A-15, 1960 . . . . 20 10
5304 20 k. SA-7, 1970 . . . . . . 70 35
5305 45 k. LAK-12, 1979 . . . . . 1·50 75

2080 "The Holy Family"

2081 B. N. Petrov

1983. 500th Birth Anniv of Raphael (artist).
5306 **2080** 50 k. multicoloured . . 1·40 1·00

1983. 70th Birth Anniv of Academician B. N. Petrov (chairman of Interkosmos).
5307 **2081** 4 k. multicoloured . . . 15 10

2082 Tashkent Buildings

1983. 2000th Anniv of Tashkent.
5308 **2082** 4 k. multicoloured . . . 15 10

2083 Popov, Serebrov and Savitskaya

1983. "Soyuz T-7" – "Salyut 7" – "Soyuz T-5" Space Flight.
5309 **2083** 10 k. multicoloured . . 30 15

2085 Aleksandrov and Bars of Music

1983. Birth Centenary of A. V. Aleksandrov (composer).
5311 **2085** 4 k. multicoloured . . . 30 10

2086 "Portrait of an Old Woman"

1983. Rembrandt Paintings in Hermitage Museum, Leningrad. Multicoloured.
5312 4 k. Type **2086** 15 10
5313 10 k. "Portrait of a Learned Man" 30 15
5314 20 k. "Old Warrior" 65 30
5315 45 k. "Portrait of Mrs B. Martens Doomer" . . . 1·00 75
5316 50 k. "Sacrifice of Abraham" 1·40 1·10

2089 A. N. Berezovoi and V. V. Lebedev

1983. 211 Days in Space of Berezovoi and Lebedev. Multicoloured.
5320 10 k. Type **2089** 30 20
5321 10 k. "Salyut 7"–"Soyuz T" space complex 30 20

2090 Marx

1983. Death Centenary of Karl Marx.
5322 **2090** 4 k. multicoloured . . . 15 10

2091 Memorial, Building and Hydrofoil

1983. Rostov-on-Don.
5323 **2091** 4 k. multicoloured . . . 15 10

2092 Kirov Theatre

1983. Bicentenary of Kirov Opera and Ballet Theatre, Leningrad.
5324 **2092** 4 k. black, blue & gold 30 10

2093 Arms, Communications and Industrial Complex

1983. 60th Anniv of Buryat A.S.S.R.
5325 **2093** 4 k. multicoloured . . . 20 10

2094 Sports Vignettes

1983. 8th Summer Spartakiad.
5326 **2094** 6 k. multicoloured . . . 15 10

2095 Khachaturyan

1983. 80th Birth Anniv of Aram I. Khachaturyan (composer).
5327 **2095** 4 k. brown 30 10

2096 Tractor and Factory

1983. 50th Anniv of Lenin Tractor Factory, Chelyabinsk.

5328 **2096** 4 k. multicoloured . . . 15 10

2097 Simon Bolivar

1983. Birth Bicentenary of Simon Bolivar.

5329 **2097** 6 k. deep brown, brown and black 15 10

2098 18th-century Warship and modern Missile Cruiser

1983. Bicentenary of Sevastopol.

5330 **2098** 5 k. multicoloured . . . 40 15

2099 Snowdrops **2101** P. N. Pospelov

2100 "Vostok 6" and Tereshkova

1983. Spring Flowers. Multicoloured.

5331 4 k. Type **2099** 15 10
5332 6 k. Siberian squills 20 10
5333 10 k. "Anemone hepatica" . 35 15
5334 15 k. Cyclamen 50 25
5335 20 k. Yellow star of Bethlehem 90 45

1983. 20th Anniv of First Woman Cosmonaut Valentina V. Tereshkova's Space Flight.

5336 **2100** 10 k. multicoloured . . 30 15

1983. 85th Birth Anniv of Pyotr Nicolaievich Pospelov (scientist).

5337 **2101** 4 k. multicoloured . . . 15 10

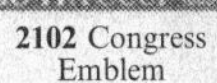

2102 Congress Emblem **2103** Film around Globe and Festival Emblem

1983. 10th European Rheumatologists' Congress, Moscow.

5338 **2102** 4 k. multicoloured . . . 20 10

1983. 13th International Film Festival, Moscow.

5339 **2103** 20 k. multicoloured . . 70 30

2104 Vakhtangov

1983. Birth Centenary of Ye. B. Vakhtangov (producer and actor).

5340 **2104** 5 k. multicoloured . . 20 10

2105 Coastal Trawlers

1983. Fishing Vessels. Multicoloured.

5341 4 k. Type **2105** 20 10
5342 6 k. Refrigerated trawler . . 25 10
5343 10 k. "Pulkovsky Meridian" (deep-sea trawler) 45 15
5344 15 k. Refrigerated freighter . . 60 25
5345 20 k. "50 let SSR" (factory ship) 1·00 50

2106 "U.S.S.R.-1" **2107** Red Salmon

1983. 50th Anniv of Stratosphere Balloon's Record Altitude Flight.

5346 **2106** 20 k. multicoloured . . 85 65

1983. Fishes. Multicoloured.

5347 4 k. Type **2107** 15 10
5348 6 k. Smarida 20 10
5349 15 k. Spotted perch 50 20
5350 20 k. Goby 65 30
5351 45 k. Starry flounder . . . . 1·40 1·00

2108 Exhibition Emblem **2110** S.W.A.P.O. Flag and Emblem

1983. "Sozphilex 83" Stamp Exhibition, Moscow.

5352 **2108** 6 k. multicoloured . . 15 10

1983. Namibia Day.

5355 **2110** 5 k. multicoloured . . 20 10

2111 Palestinian with Flag **2112** Emblem and Ostankino TV Tower, Moscow

1983. Palestinian Solidarity.

5356 **2111** 5 k. multicoloured . . . 30 10

1983. 1st European Radio-telegraphy Championship, Moscow.

5357 **2112** 6 k. multicoloured . . 20 10

2113 Council Session Emblem **2114** Mohammed al-Khorezmi

1983. 4th U.N.E.S.C.O. International Communications Development Programme Council Session, Tashkent.

5358 **2113** 10 k. blue, mauve & black 30 15

1983. 1200th Birth Anniv of Mohammed al-Khorezmi (astonomer and mathematician).

5359 **2114** 4 k. multicoloured . . . 20 10

2115 Yegorov **2116** Treaty

1983. Birth Centenary of Marshal A. I. Yegorov.

5360 **2115** 4 k. purple 15 10

1983. Bicentenary of First Russian–Georgian Friendship Treaty.

5361 **2116** 6 k. multicoloured 15 10

1983. Lighthouses (2nd series). As Type **2075**. Multicoloured.

5362 1 k. Kipu lighthouse, Baltic Sea 10 10
5363 5 k. Keri lighthouse, Gulf of Finland 25 10
5364 10 k. Stirsudden lighthouse, Gulf of Finland 40 15
5365 12 k. Takhkun lighthouse, Baltic Sea 55 30
5366 20 k. Tallin lighthouse, Gulf of Finland 75 45

2117 "Wife's Portrait with Flowers" (I. F. Khrutsky)

1983. Byelorussian Paintings. Multicoloured.

5367 4 k. Type **2117** 15 10
5368 6 k. "Early spring" (V. K. Byalynitsky-Birulya) . . . 20 10
5369 15 k. "Young Partisan" (E. A. Zaitsev) (vert) 45 20
5370 20 k. "Partisan Madonna" (M. A. Savitsky) (vert) . . 60 30
5371 45 k. "Corn Harvest" (V. K. Tsvirko) . . . . 1·40 1·00

2118 Steel Mill

1983. Centenary of Hammer and Sickle Steel Mill.

5372 **2118** 4 k. multicoloured . . . 15 10

2119 Grain Production **2120** Banner and Symbols of Economic Growth

1983. Food Programme. Multicoloured.

5373 5 k. Type **2119** 15 10
5374 5 k. Cattle breeding 15 10
5375 5 k. Fruit and vegetable production 15 10

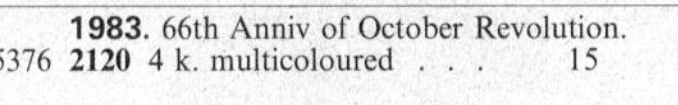

1983. 66th Anniv of October Revolution.

5376 **2120** 4 k. multicoloured . . . 15 10

2121 Ivan Fyodorov

1983. 400th Death Anniv of Ivan Fyodorov (printer) and 420th Anniv of Publication of "The Apostle" (first Russian printed book).

5377 **2121** 4 k. black 15 10

2122 Pipeline Construction

1983. Inaug of Urengoi–Uzhgorod Gas Pipeline.

5378 **2122** 5 k. multicoloured . . . 25 10

2123 Sidorenko **2124** Marchers pushing Nuclear Weapons off Globe

1983. Academician A. V. Sidorenko (geologist) Commemoration.

5379 **2123** 4 k. multicoloured . . . 20 10

1983. Nuclear Disarmament.

5380 **2124** 5 k. multicoloured . . . 20 10

2125 Makhtumkuli **2126** "Madonna and Child under Apple Tree" (Cranach the Elder)

1983. 250th Birth Anniv of Makhtumkuli (Turkmen poet).

5381 **2125** 5 k. multicoloured . . . 20 10

1983. German Paintings in the Hermitage Museum. Multicoloured.

5382 4 k. Type **2126** 15 10
5383 10 k. "Self-portrait" (Anton Raphael Mengs) 30 15
5384 20 k. "Self-portrait" (Jurgens Ovens) 60 30
5385 45 k. "On Board a Sailing Vessel" (Caspar David Friedrich) . . . . 1·25 60
5386 50 k. "Rape of the Sabine Women" (Johann Schonfeld) (horiz) . . . . 1·40 80

2127 Sukhe Bator **2128** Globe and Hand holding Baby

1983. 90th Birth Anniv of Sukhe Bator (Mongolian statesman).

5388 **2127** 5 k. multicoloured . . . 15 10

1983. International Association of Physicians against Nuclear War.

5389 **2128** 5 k. multicoloured . . . 15 10

2129 Moscow Kremlin Tower Star

1983. New Year.

5390	**2129**	5 k. multicoloured . . .	15	10

2130 Children's Music Theatre

1983. New Buildings in Moscow.

5391	**2130**	3 k. green	10	10
5392	–	4 k. blue	15	10
5393	–	6 k. brown	15	10
5394	–	20 k. green	60	30
5395	–	45 k. green	1·40	65

DESIGNS—VERT: 4 k. Hotel and Tourist Centre. HORIZ: 6 k. Russian Federation parliament building; 20 k. Hotel Izmailovo; 45 k. Novosti News and Press Agency.

2132 Cuban Flag

2133 Broadcasting Station

1984. 25th Anniv of Cuban Revolution.

5397	**2132**	5 k. multicoloured . . .	15	10

1984. 50th Anniv of Moscow Broadcasting Network.

5398	**2133**	4 k. multicoloured . . .	15	10

2134 Speed Skating

1984. Women's European Skating Championship, Alma-Ata.

5399	**2134**	5 k. multicoloured . . .	15	10

2135 "T-34" Medium Tank

1984. World War II Armoured Vehicles. Mult.

5400	10 k. Type **2135**	40	20
5401	10 k. "KV" heavy tank . . .	40	20
5402	10 k. "IS-2" heavy tank . . .	40	20
5403	10 k. "SU-100" self-propelled gun	40	20
5404	10 k. "ISU-152" heavy self-propelled gun	40	20

2136 Biathlon

1984. Winter Olympic Games, Sarajevo. Mult.

5405	5 k. Type **2136**	15	10
5406	10 k. Speed skating	35	15
5407	20 k. Ice hockey	65	30
5408	45 k. Figure skating	1·25	85

2137 Mandrill

1984. 120th Anniv of Moscow Zoo. Multicoloured.

5409	2 k. Type **2137**	10	10
5410	3 k. Blesbok	10	10
5411	4 k. Snow leopard	15	10
5412	5 k. South African crowned crane	30	10
5413	20 k. Blue and yellow macaw	70	50

2138 Yury Gagarin

1984. 50th Birth Anniv of Yury Alekseevich Gagarin (first man in Space).

5414	**2138**	15 k. blue	40	20

2140 "E. K. Vorontsova" (George Hayter)

2141 Ilyushin

1984. English Paintings in Hermitage Museum, Leningrad. Multicoloured.

5416	4 k. Type **2140**	15	10
5417	10 k. "Portrait of Mrs. Harriet Greer" (George Romney)	30	15
5418	20 k. "Approaching Storm" (George Morland) (horiz)	60	25
5419	45 k. "Portrait of an Unknown Man" (Marcus Gheeraerts, the younger)	1·25	85
5420	50 k. "Cupid untying the Robe of Venus" (Joshua Reynolds)	1·40	1·00

1984. 90th Birth Anniv of Academician S. V. Ilyushin (aircraft designer).

5422	**2141**	5 k. light brown, brown and black	15	10

2142 Bubnov

2143 Launching Site of "M-100" Meteorological Station

1984. Birth Centenary of Andrei Sergeevich Bubnov (Communist Party Leader).

5423	**2142**	5 k. light brown, brown and black	15	10

1984. Soviet–Indian Space Co-operation. Multicoloured.

5424	5 k. Type **2143**	15	10
5425	20 k. Satellite and observatory (space geodesy)	60	30
5426	45 k. Rocket, satellites and dish aerials (Soviet–Indian space flight)	1·40	65

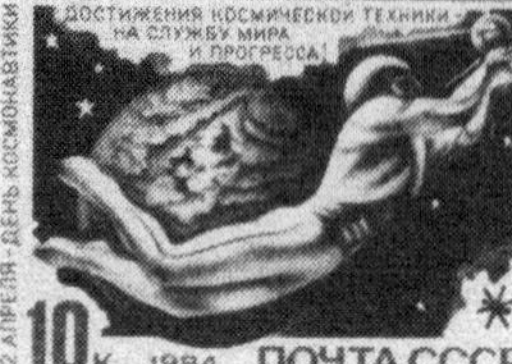

2144 Globe and Cosmonaut

1984. Cosmonautics Day.

5428	**2144**	10 k. multicoloured . .	30	15

2145 "Chelyuskin" (ice-breaker) and Route Map

1984. 50th Anniv of Murmansk–Vladivostok Voyage of "Chelyuskin". Multicoloured.

5429	6 k. Type **2145**	25	10
5430	15 k. Evacuation of sinking ship	60	25
5431	45 k. Air rescue of crew . . .	1·75	75

2148 Lotus

2149 Globe and Peace March (left)

1984. Aquatic Flowers. Multicoloured.

5434	1 k. Type **2148**	10	10
5435	2 k. Euriala	10	10
5436	3 k. Yellow water lilies (horiz)	15	10
5437	10 k. White water lilies (horiz)	35	20
5438	20 k. Marshflowers (horiz) . .	70	30

1984. Peace.

5439	**2149**	5 k. multicoloured . . .	15	10
5440	–	5 k. red, gold and black	15	10
5441	–	5 k. multicoloured . . .	15	10

DESIGNS: No. 5440, Hammer and sickle and text; No. 5441, Globe and peace march (right).

2150 Welder

2151 Communications Emblem

1984. 50th Anniv of E. O. Paton Institute of Electric Welding, Kiev.

5442	**2150**	10 k. multicoloured . .	25	15

1984. 25th Conference of Community for Mutual Economic Aid Electrical and Postal Communications Standing Committee, Cracow.

5443	**2151**	10 k. multicoloured . .	25	15

2152 Emblem and Symbols of Match Venues

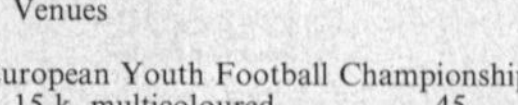

2153 Maurice Bishop

1984. European Youth Football Championship.

5444	**2152**	15 k. multicoloured . .	45	20

1984. 40th Birth Anniv of Maurice Bishop (former Prime Minister of Grenada).

5445	**2153**	5 k. brown	20	10

2154 Lenin and Museum

2155 Freighter, Monument and Aurora Borealis

1984. 60th Anniv of Lenin Central Museum, Moscow.

5446	**2154**	5 k. multicoloured . . .	15	10

1984. 400th Anniv of Archangel.

5447	**2155**	5 k. multicoloured . . .	15	10

2156 Headquarters and Spassky Tower, Moscow

2158 Liner

2157 Vladimir A. Lyakhov and Aleksandr Aleksandrov

1984. Council of Mutual Economic Aid Conferene, Moscow.

5448	**2156**	5 k. blue, red and black	15	10

1984. Lighthouses (3rd series). As T **2075**. Multicoloured.

5449	1 k. Petropavlovsk lighthouse, Kamchatka	10	10
5450	2 k. Tokarev lighthouse, Sea of Japan	10	10
5451	4 k. Basargin lighthouse, Sea of Japan	20	10
5452	5 k. Kronotsky lighthouse, Kamchatka	20	10
5443	10 k. Marekan lighthouse, Sea of Okhotsk	35	15

1984. 150 Days in Space of "Salyut 7" – "Soyuz T-9" Cosmonauts.

5454	**2157**	15 k. multicoloured . .	40	20

1984. 60th Anniv of Morflot (Soviet merchant fleet).

5455	**2158**	10 k. multicoloured . .	35	15

2159 Komsomol Badge and Banner

1984. 60th Anniv of Naming of Young Communist League (Komsomol) after Lenin.

5456	**2159**	5 k. multicoloured . . .	15	10

2160 Memorial, Minsk

1984. 40th Anniv of Byelorussian Liberation.

5457	**2160**	5 k. multicoloured . . .	15	10

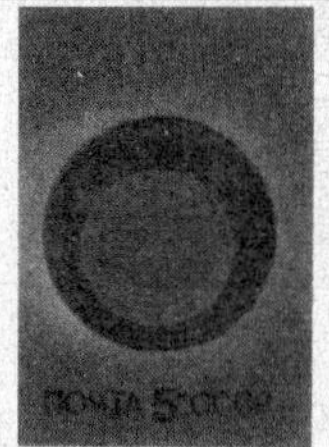

2161 Congress Emblem

2162 Polish Arms and Flag

1984. 27th International Geological Congress, Moscow.
5458 **2161** 5 k. blue, gold and deep blue 20 10

1984. 40th Anniv of Republic of Poland.
5459 **2162** 5 k. multicoloured . . . 15 10

2163 Asafev

1984. Birth Centenary of Boris Vladimirovich Asafev (composer).
5460 **2163** 5 k. green 20 10

2164 Russian and Mexican Flags and Scroll

1984. 60th Anniv of U.S.S.R.–Mexico Diplomatic Relations.
5461 **2164** 5 k. multicoloured . . . 15 10

2165 Title Page of "The Princess-Frog"

1984. Folk Tales. Illustration by I. Bilibin. Multicoloured.
5462 5 k. Type **2165** 20 15
5463 5 k. Hunter and frog in marshland 20 15
5464 5 k. Old man and hunter in forest 20 15
5465 5 k. Crowd and mute swans . 20 15
5466 5 k. Title page of "Ivan the Tsarevich, the Fire-bird and the Grey Wolf" 20 15
5467 5 k. Ivan and the fire-bird . . 20 15
5468 5 k. Grave and Ivan on horse 40 15
5469 5 k. Ivan and princess . . . 20 15
5470 5 k. Title page of "Vasilisa the Beautiful" 20 15
5471 5 k. Knight on horse 20 15
5472 5 k. Tree-man in forest . . . 40 15
5473 5 k. Vasilisa and skulls . . . 40 15

2166 Basketball

1984. "Friendship 84" Sports Meetings. Mult.
5474 1 k. Type **2166** 10 10
5475 5 k. Gymnastics (vert) . . . 15 10
5476 10 k. Weightlifting 30 10
5477 15 k. Wrestling 45 20
5478 20 k. High jumping 60 30

2167 Flag and Soviet Soldiers' Monument, Bucharest

2168 Emblem, Chess Symbol for Queen and Motherland Statue

1984. 40th Anniv of Rumania's Liberation.
5479 **2167** 5k. multicoloured . . . 15 10

1984. World Chess Championship Finals for Women (Volgograd) and Men (Moscow).
5480 **2168** 15 k. gold, red and black 70 25
5481 – 15 k. multicoloured . . 70 25
DESIGN: No. 5481, Emblem, chess symbol for king and Spassky tower, Moscow Kremlin

2169 Party House and Soviet Army Monument, Sofia, and State Emblem

2170 Arms and Flag

1984. 40th Anniv of Bulgarian Revolution.
5482 **2169** 5 k. multicoloured . . 15 10

1984. 10th Anniv of Ethiopian Revolution.
5483 **2170** 5 k. multicoloured . . 15 10

2171 Excavator

1984. 50th Anniv of Lenin Machine-building Plant, Novokramatorsk.
5484 **2171** 5 k. multicoloured . . 15 10

2172 Arms and Symbols of Industry and Agriculture

1984. 60th Anniv of Nakhichevan A.S.S.R.
5485 **2172** 5 k. multicoloured . . 15 10

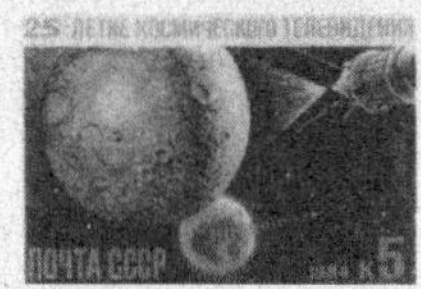

2174 "Luna 3" photographing Moon

1984. 25th Anniv of Photography in Space. Multicoloured.
5487 5 k. Type **2174** 15 10
5488 20 k. "Venera-9" and control centre 60 25
5489 45 k. "Meteor" meteorological satellite and Earth . . . . 1·40 85

2175 Arms and Flag

1984. 35th Anniv of German Democratic Republic.
5491 **2175** 5 k. multicoloured . . 15 10

2176 Arms and Motherland Statue, Kiev

1984. 40th Anniv of Liberation of the Ukraine.
5492 **2176** 5 k. multicoloured . . . 15 10

2177 Town, Arms and Countryside

1984. 60th Anniv of Moldavian Soviet Socialist Republic.
5493 **2177** 5 k. multicoloured . . . 15 10

2178 Arms, Power Station and Mountains

1984. 60th Anniv of Kirgizia Soviet Socialist Republic.
5494 **2178** 5 k. multicoloured . . . 15 10

2179 Arms and Symbols of Industry and Agriculture

2180 Flags and Spassky Tower

1984. 60th Anniv of Tadzhikistan Soviet Socialist Republic.
5495 **2179** 5 k. multicoloured . . . 15 10

1984. 67th Anniv of October Revolution.
5496 **2180** 5 k. multicoloured . . . 15 10

2181 Arms, State Building and Dam

1984. 60th Anniv of Uzbekistan Soviet Socialist Republic.
5497 **2181** 5 k. multicoloured . . . 15 10

2182 Arms, Flag and State Building

1984. 60th Anniv of Turkmenistan Soviet Socialist Republic.
5498 **2182** 5 k. multicoloured . . . 15 10

2183 Medal, Workers, Diesel Train and Map of Route

2184 Ilyushin Il-86 Airplane, Rocket, "Soyuz" - "Salyut" Complex and Museum

1984. Completion of Baikal–Amur Railway.
5499 **2183** 5 k. multicoloured . . . 30 10

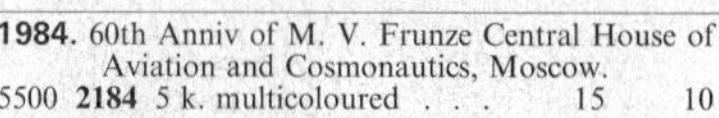

1984. 60th Anniv of M. V. Frunze Central House of Aviation and Cosmonautics, Moscow.
5500 **2184** 5 k. multicoloured . . . 15 10

2185 "Girl in Hat" (Jean-Louis Voile)

2186 Mongolian Arms and Flag

1984. French Paintings in Hermitage Museum, Leningrad. Multicoloured.
5501 4 k. Type **2185** 15 10
5502 10 k. "The Stolen Kiss" (Jean-Honore Fragonard) (horiz) 30 15
5503 20 k. "Woman at her Toilette" (Edgar Degas) 60 30
5504 45 k. "Pygmalion and Galatea" (Francois Boucher) (horiz) 1·25 60
5505 50k. "Landscape with Polyphemus" (Nicolas Poussin) (horiz) . . . . . 1·40 85

1984. 60th Anniv of Mongolian People's Republic.
5507 **2186** 5 k. multicoloured . . . 15 10

2187 Spassky Tower and Snowflakes

1984. New Year.
5508 **2187** 5 k. multicoloured . . . 15 10

2189 Horse-drawn Crew Wagon (19th century)

1984. Fire Engines (1st series). Multicoloured.
5510 3 k. Type **2189** 15 10
5511 5 k. 19th-century horse-drawn steam pump 25 10
5512 10 k. "Freze" fire engine, 1904 45 15
5513 15 k. "Lessner" fire engine, 1904 45 25
5514 20 k. "Russo-Balt" fire engine, 1913 . . . . 55 30
See also Nos. 5608/12.

2190 Space Observatory and Flight Trajectory

1984. International Venus–Halley's Comet Space Project (1st issue).
5515 **2190** 15 k. multicoloured . . 45 20
See also Nos. 5562 and 5630.

2191 Indira Gandhi

2192 Heroes of December Revolution Monument, Moscow

1984. Indira Gandhi (Indian Prime Minister) Commemoration.
5516 **2191** 5 k. lt brown & brn . . 30 10

1985. 80th Anniv of 1905 Revolution.
5517 **2192** 5 k. multicoloured . . . 15 10

2193 Jubilee Emblem 2194 Frunze

1985. 25th Anniv of Patrice Lumumba University, Moscow.
5518 **2193** 5 k. multicoloured . . . 15 10

1985. Birth Centenary of Mikhail Vasilievich Frunze (military strategist).
5519 **2194** 5 k. stone, black and blue 15 10

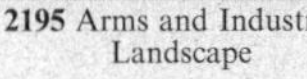
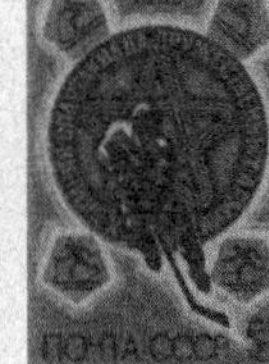

2195 Arms and Industrial Landscape **2196** Ice Hockey Player

1985. 60th Anniv of Karakalpak A.S.S.R.
5520 **2195** 5 k. multicoloured . . . 15 10

1985. 10th Friendly Armies Winter Spartakiad.
5521 **2196** 5 k. multicoloured . . . 15 10

2197 Dulcimer Player and Title Page **2198** Pioneer Badge

1985. 150th Anniv of "Kalevala" (Karelian poems collected by Elino Lonnrot).
5522 **2197** 5 k. brown, blue & blk . 20 10

1985. 60th Anniv of "Pionerskaya Pravda" (children's newspaper).
5523 **2198** 5 k. multicoloured . . . 20 10

2199 Maria Aleksandrovna Ulyanova **2200** "Young Madonna Praying" (Francisco de Zurbaran)

1985. 150th Birth Anniv of Maria Aleksandrovna Ulyanova (Lenin's mother).
5524 **2199** 5 k. black 20 10

1985. Spanish Paintings in Hermitage Museum, Leningrad. Multicoloured.
5525 4 k. Type **2200** 15 10
5526 10 k. "Still Life" (Antonio Pereda) (horiz) 30 15
5527 20 k. "The Immaculate Conception" (Bartolome Esteban Murillo) 65 30
5528 45 k. "The Grinder" (Antonio Puga) (horiz) . . . . . . 1·25 70
5529 50 k. "Count Olivares" (Diego Velazquez) . . . . 1·40 85

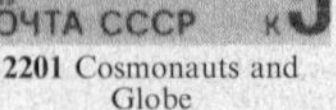

2201 Cosmonauts and Globe **2203** Hungarian Arms and Budapest

1985. "Expo 85" World's Fair, Tsukuba, Japan. Multicoloured.
5531 5 k. Type **2201** 15 10
5532 10 k. "Molniya-I" communications satellite . 30 15
5533 20 k. Energy sources of the future 65 30
5534 45 k. Futuristic city . . . . 1·40 85

1985. 40th Anniv of Hungary's Liberation.
5537 **2203** 5 k. multicoloured . . 20 10

2204 Emblem and Text **2206** Young People of Different Races

2205 Cosmonauts, "Soyuz T" Training Model and Gagarin

1985. 60th Anniv of Union of Soviet Societies of Friendship and Cultural Relations with Foreign Countries.
5538 **2204** 15 k. multicoloured . . 45 30

1985. Cosmonautics Day. 25th Anniv of Yury A. Gagarin Cosmonauts Training Centre.
5539 **2205** 15 k. multicoloured . . 45 30

1985. 12th World Youth and Students' Festival, Moscow. Multicoloured.
5540 1 k. Type **2206** 10 10
5541 3 k. Girl with festival emblem in hair 10 10
5542 5 k. Rainbow and girl . . . 15 10
5543 20 k. Youth holding camera 60 25
5544 45 k. Festival emblem . . . 1·25 85

Всесоюзная филателистческая выставка

„40 лет Великой Победы"

2207 Soviet Memorial, Berlin-Treptow (**2209**)

2208 Lenin and Paris Flat

1985. 40th Anniv of Victory in Second World War (1st issue). Multicoloured.
5545 5 k. Type **2207** 20 15
5546 5 k. Partisans 20 15
5547 5 k. Lenin, soldier and Moscow Kremlin 20 15
5548 5 k. Soldiers and military equipment 20 15
5549 5 k. Woman worker, tank, tractor and aircraft assembly 20 15
See also No. 5555.

1985. 115th Birth Anniv of Lenin. Multicoloured.
5551 5 k. Type **2208** 20 15
5552 5 k. Lenin and Lenin Museum, Tampere, Finland 20 15

1985. "Second World War Victory" Philatelic Exhibition. No. 5545 optd with T **2209**.
5554 **2207** 5 k. multicoloured . . 20 20

2210 Victory Order (½-size illustration)

1985. 40th Anniv of Victory in Second World War (2nd issue).
5555 **2210** 20 k. multicoloured . . 65 45

2211 Czechoslovakian Arms and Prague Buildings **2212** Members' Flags on Shield

1985. 40th Anniv of Czechoslovakia's Liberation.
5556 **2211** 5 k. multicoloured . . . 20 10

1985. 30th Anniv of Warsaw Pact Organization.
5557 **2212** 5 k. multicoloured . . . 20 10

2213 Sholokhov and Books **2214** Sverdlov

1985. 80th Birth Anniv of Mikhail Aleksandrovich Sholokhov (writer).
5558 **2213** 5 k. multicoloured . . . 20 15
5559 – 5 k. multicoloured . . . 20 15
5560 – 5 k. black, gold and brown 20 15
DESIGNS—As T **2213**. No. 5559, Sholokhov and books (different); 36×51 mm. No. 5560, Sholokhov.

1985. Birth Centenary of Ya. M. Sverdlov (Communist Party Leader).
5561 **2214** 5 k. brown and red . . . 20 10

1985. International Venus–Halley's Comet Space Project (2nd issue). As T **2190**. Multicoloured.
5562 15 k. "Vega" space probe and Venus 55 30

2215 Battleship "Potemkin"

1985. 80th Anniv of Mutiny on Battleship "Potemkin".
5563 **2215** 5 k. black, red and gold 20 10

2216 "VL80R" Electric Stock

1985. Locomotives and Rolling Stock.
5564 **2216** 10 k. green 45 25
5565 – 10 k. brown 45 25
5566 – 10 k. blue 45 25
5567 – 10 k. brown 45 25
5568 – 10 k. blue 45 25
5569 – 10 k. blue 45 25
5570 – 10 k. brown 45 25
5571 – 10 k. green 45 25
DESIGNS: No. 5565, Coal wagon; No. 5566, Oil tanker wagon; No. 5567, Goods wagon; No. 5568, Refrigerated wagon; No. 5569, "TEM 2" diesel locomotive; No. 5570, "Sv" passenger carriage; No. 5571, Mail van.

2217 Camp and Pioneer Badge

1985. 60th Anniv of Artek Pioneer Camp.
5572 **2217** 4 k. multicoloured . . . 20 10

2218 Leonid Kizim, Vladimir Solovyov and Oleg Atkov

1985. "237 Days in Space".
5573 **2218** 15 k. multicoloured . . 50 20

2219 Youths of different Races **2220** "Beating Swords into Ploughshares" (sculpture) and U.N. Emblem

1985. International Youth Year.
5574 **2219** 10 k. multicoloured . . 30 15

1985. 40th Anniv of U.N.O. (1st issue).
5575 **2220** 45 k. blue and gold . . 1·25 1·00
See also No. 5601.

2222 Larkspur **2224** Cecilienhof Palace and Flags

2223 V. A. Dzhanibekov, S. E. Savitskaya and I. P. Volk

1985. Plants of Siberia. Multicoloured.
5577 2 k. Type **2222** 10 10
5578 3 k. "Thermopsis lanceolata" 10 10
5579 5 k. Rose 20 10
5580 20 k. Cornflower 70 30
5581 45 k. Bergenia . . . . . . 1·40 65

1985. 1st Anniv of First Space-walk by Woman Cosmonaut.
5582 **2223** 10 k. multicoloured . . 30 15

1985. 40th Anniv of Potsdam Conference.
5583 **2224** 15 k. multicoloured . . 40 20

2225 Finland Palace **2226** Russian and N. Korean Flags and Monument

1985. 10th Anniv of European Security and Co-operation Conference, Helsinki.
5584 **2225** 20 k. multicoloured . . 75 35

1985. 40th Anniv of Liberation of Korea.
5585 **2226** 5 k. multicoloured . . . 20 10

2227 Pamir Shrew 2228 A. G. Stakhanov and Industrial Scenes

1985. Protected Animals. Multicoloured.
5586 2 k. Type **2227** 10 10
5587 3 k. Satunin's jerboa (horiz) . 10 10
5588 5 k. Desert dormouse 15 10
5589 20 k. Caracal (47 × 32 mm) . 60 30
5590 45 k. Goitred gazelle (47 × 32 mm) . . . . 1·40 65

1985. 50th Anniv of Stakhanov Movement (for high labour productivity).
5592 **2228** 5 k. yellow, red and black 15 10

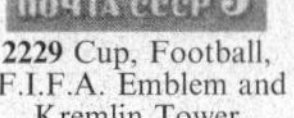

2229 Cup, Football, F.I.F.A. Emblem and Kremlin Tower 2230 Chess Pieces

1985. World Junior Football Championship, Moscow.
5593 **2229** 5 k. multicoloured . . . 20 10

1985. World Chess Championship Final between Anatoly Karpov and Gary Kasparov.
5594 **2230** 10 k. multicoloured . . 55 20

2231 Vietnam State Emblem 2232 Immortality Monument and Buildings

1985. 40th Anniv of Vietnamese Independence.
5595 **2231** 5 k. multicoloured . . . 20 10

1985. Millenary of Bryansk.
5596 **2232** 5 k. multicoloured . . . 20 10

2233 Title Page

1985. 800th Anniv of "Song of Igor's Campaigns".
5597 **2233** 10 k. multicoloured . . 35 20

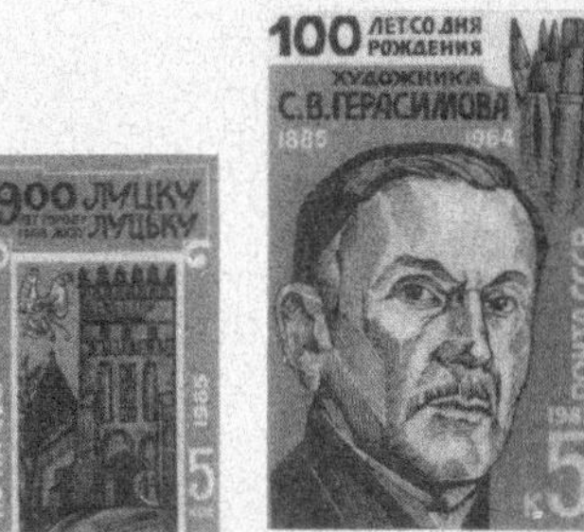

2234 Lutsk Castle 2235 Gerasimov

1985. 900th Anniv of Lutsk.
5598 **2234** 5 k. multicoloured . . . 20 10

1985. Birth Centenary of Sergei Vasilievich Gerasimov (artist).
5599 **2235** 5 k. multicoloured . . . 20 10

2236 Globe, "Aurora" and 1917 2237 Headquarters, New York, and Flag

1985. 68th Anniv of October Revolution.
5600 **2236** 5 k. multicoloured . . 20 10

1985. 40th Anniv of U.N.O. (2nd issue).
5601 **2237** 15 k. green, blue and black 45 20

2238 Krishjanis Baron

1985. 150th Birth Anniv of Krishjanis Baron (writer).
5602 **2238** 5 k. black and brown . 20 10

2239 Lenin and Worker breaking Chains

1985. 90th Anniv of Petersburg Union of Struggle for Liberating the Working Class.
5603 **2239** 5 k. multicoloured . . 20 10

2240 Telescope

1985. 10th Anniv of World's Largest Telescope.
5604 **2240** 10 k. blue 30 20

2241 Angolan Arms and Flag 2242 Yugoslav Arms, Flag and Parliament Building

1985. 10th Anniv of Independence of Angola.
5605 **2241** 5 k. multicoloured . . . 20 10

1985. 40th Anniv of Federal People's Republic of Yugoslavia.
5606 **2242** 5 k. multicoloured . . 20 10

2243 Troitsky Tower and Palace of Congresses 2244 Samantha Smith

1985. New Year.
5607 **2243** 5 k. multicoloured . . 15 10

1985. Fire Engines (2nd series). As T **2189**. Multicoloured.
5608 3 k. "AMO-F15", 1926 . . 15 10
5609 5 k. "PMZ-1", 1933 . . . 25 10
5610 10 k. "ATs-40", 1977 . . . 45 15
5611 20 k. "AL-30" with automatic ladder, 1970 . . . . . . 55 30
5612 45 k. "AA-60", 1978 . . . 1·25 85

1985. Samantha Smith (American schoolgirl peace campaigner) Commemoration.
5613 **2244** 5 k. brown, blue and red 40 10

2245 N. M. Emanuel 2246 Family and Places of Entertainment

1985. Academician N. M. Emanuel (chemist) Commemoration.
5614 **2245** 5 k. multicoloured . . . 20 10

1985. Anti-alcoholism Campaign. Multicoloured.
5615 5 k. Type **2246** 25 10
5616 5 k. Sports centre and family 25 10

2247 Emblem 2248 Banners and Kremlin Palace of Congresses

1986. International Peace Year.
5617 **2247** 20 k. blue, green & sil . 60 30

1986. 27th Soviet Communist Party Congress.
5618 **2248** 5 k. multicoloured . . . 15 10
5619 – 20 k. multicoloured . . 60 30
DESIGNS—36 × 51 mm. 20 k. Palace of Congresses, Spassky Tower and Lenin.

2249 1896 Olympics Medal 2250 Tulips

1986. 90th Anniv of First Modern Olympic Games.
5621 **2249** 15 k. multicoloured . . 45 20

1986. Plants of Russian Steppes. Multicoloured.
5622 4 k. Type **2250** 15 10
5623 5 k. Grass (horiz) 20 10
5624 10 k. Iris 35 15
5625 15 k. Violets 55 25
5626 20 k. Cornflower 70 30

2251 Voronezh and Arms 2252 Bela Kun

1986. 400th Anniv of Voronezh.
5627 **2251** 5 k. multicoloured . . . 20 10

1986. Birth Centenary of Bela Kun (Hungarian Communist Party leader).
5628 **2252** 10 k. blue 30 15

2253 Pozela 2255 "Utetheisa pulchella"

1986. 90th Birth Anniv of Karolis Pozela (founder of Lithuanian Communist Party).
5629 **2253** 5 k. grey 20 10

1986. International Venus–Halley's Comet Space Project (3rd issue). As T **2190**. Multicoloured.
5630 15 k. "Vega 1" and Halley's Comet 55 30

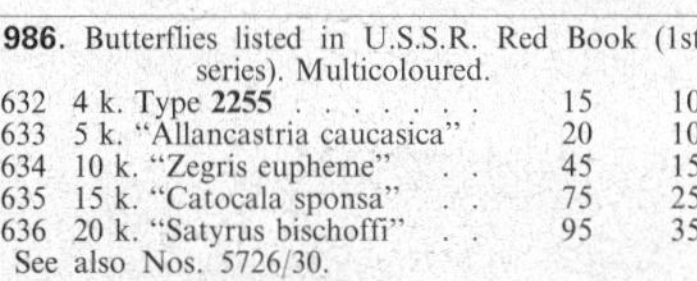

1986. Butterflies listed in U.S.S.R. Red Book (1st series). Multicoloured.
5632 4 k. Type **2255** 15 10
5633 5 k. "Allancastria caucasica" 20 10
5634 10 k. "Zegris eupheme" . . 45 15
5635 15 k. "Catocala sponsa" . . 75 25
5636 20 k. "Satyrus bischoffi" . . 95 35
See also Nos. 5726/30.

2256 Globe and Model of Space Complex 2257 Kirov

1986. "Expo '86" World's Fair, Vancouver.
5637 **2256** 20 k. multicoloured . . 60 30

1986. Birth Centenary of S. M. Kirov (Communist Party Secretary).
5638 **2257** 5 k. black 20 10

2258 Tsiolkovsky

1986. Cosmonautics Day. Multicoloured.
5639 5 k. Type **2258** 15 10
5640 10 k. Sergei Pavlovich Korolev (rocket designer) and "Vostok" rocket (vert) . . 30 15
5641 15 k. Yuri Gagarin, "Vega", sputnik and globe (25th anniv of first man in space) . . . 55 25

2259 Ice Hockey Player 2260 Thalmann

1986. World Ice Hockey Championship, Moscow.
5642 **2259** 15 k. multicoloured . . 60 20

1986. Birth Centenary of Ernst Thalmann (German politician).
5643 **2260** 10 k. brown 30 15

2261 Lenin Museum, Leipzig

1986. 116th Birth Anniv of Lenin.
5645 **2261** 5 k. multicoloured . . . 20 10
5646 – 5 k. olive, brown & blk 20 10
5647 – 5 k. multicoloured . . . 20 10
DESIGNS: No. 5646, Lenin Museum, Prague; No. 5647, Lenin Museum, Poronine, Poland.

2262 Tambov and Arms

1986. 350th Anniv of Tambov.
5648 **2262** 5 k. multicoloured . . . 20 10

2263 Dove with Olive Branch and Globe

2264 Emblem and Cyclists

1986. 25th Anniv of Soviet Peace Fund.

5649 **2263** 10 k. multicoloured . . 35 20

1986. 39th Peace Cycle Race.

5650 **2264** 10 k. multicoloured . . 45 20

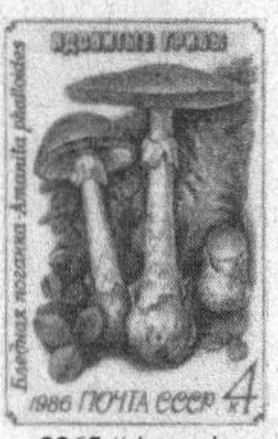

2265 "Amanita phalloides"

2266 Globe and Wildlife

1986. Fungi. Multicoloured.

5651 4 k. Type **2265** 15 10

5652 5 k. "Amanita muscaria" . . 25 10

5653 10 k. "Amanita pantherina" . 45 15

5654 15 k. "Tylopilus felleus" . . 75 25

5655 20 k. "Hypholoma fasciculare" 95 40

1986. U.N.E.S.C.O. Man and Biosphere Programme.

5656 **2266** 10 k. multicoloured . . 40 15

2267 Torch and Runner

2268 Kuibyshev

1986. 9th People's Spartakiad.

5657 **2267** 10 k. multicoloured . . 35 15

1986. 400th Anniv of Kuibyshev (formerly Samara).

5658 **2268** 5 k. multicoloured . . . 20 10

No. 5658 depicts the Lenin Museum, Eternal Glory and V. I. Chapaev monuments and Gorky State Theatre.

2269 Ostankino T.V. Tower

2270 Footballers

1986. "Communication 86" International Exhibition, Moscow.

5659 **2269** 5 k. multicoloured . . . 20 10

1986. World Cup Football Championship, Mexico. Multicoloured.

5660 5 k. Type **2270** 20 10

5661 10 k. Footballers (different) . 40 15

5662 15 k. Championship medal . 50 25

2271 "Lane in Albano" (M. I. Lebedev)

2272 Arms and City

1986. Russian Paintings in Tretyakov Gallery, Moscow. Multicoloured.

5663 4 k. Type **2271** 15 10

5664 5 k. "View of the Kremlin in foul Weather" (A. K. Savrasov) (horiz) 20 10

5665 10 k. "Sunlit Pine Trees" (I. I. Shishkin) 30 15

5666 15 k. "Journey Back" (A. E. Arkhipov) (69 × 33 mm) . 50 25

5667 45 k. "Wedding Procession in Moscow" (A. P. Ryabushkin) (69 × 33 mm) . . . . . . 1·25 40

1986. 300th Anniv of Irkutsk City Status.

5668 **2272** 5 k. multicoloured . . 20 10

2273 World Map Stadium and Runners

2274 Globe, Punched Tape and Keyboard

1986. International Goodwill Games, Moscow.

5669 **2273** 10 k. blue, brown & blk 30 15

1986. U.N.E.S.C.O. Programmes in U.S.S.R. Multicoloured.

5671 5 k. Type **2274** 20 10

5672 10 k. Landscape and geological section (geological correlation) 35 15

5673 15 k. Oceanographic research vessel, albatross and ocean (Inter-governmental Oceanographic Commission) 55 30

5674 35 k. Fluvial drainage (International Hydrological Programme) . . . . . . 1·00 60

2275 Arms and Town Buildings

1986. 400th Anniv of Tyumen, Siberia.

5675 **2275** 5 k. multicoloured . . 20 10

2276 Olof Palme

2277 Hands, Ball and Basket

1986. Olof Palme (Swedish Prime Minister) Commemoration.

5676 **2276** 10 k. blue, black & brn 35 15

1986. 10th Women's Basketball Championship.

5677 **2277** 15 k. brown, blk & red 60 25

2278 "Ural-375D"

1986. Lorries. Multicoloured.

5678 4 k. Type **2278** 15 10

5679 5 k. "GAZ-53A" 20 10

5680 10 k. "KrAZ-256B" 35 15

5681 15 k. "MAZ-515B" 55 25

5682 20 k. "ZIL-133GYa" 70 30

2279 Lenin Peak

1986. U.S.S.R. Sports Committee's International Mountaineers' Camps (1st series). Multicoloured.

5683 4 k. Type **2279** 15 10

5684 5 k. E. Korzhenevskaya Peak 20 10

5685 10 k. Belukha Peak 30 15

5686 15 k. Communism Peak . . . 55 25

5687 30 k. Elbrus Peak 95 50

See also Nos. 5732/5.

2281 Lenin Monument and Drama Theatre

2282 Ferry, Maps and Flags

1986. 250th Anniv of Chelyabinsk City.

5689 **2281** 5 k. multicoloured . . 20 10

1986. Opening of Mukran (East Germany)–Klaipeda (U.S.S.R.) Railway Ferry.

5690 **2282** 15 k. multicoloured . . 75 25

2283 Victory Monument and Buildings

2284 Lenin Monument and Moscow Kremlin

1986. 750th Anniv of Siauliai, Lithuania.

5691 **2283** 5 k. buff, brown & red . . 20 10

1986. 69th Anniv of October Revolution.

5692 **2284** 5 k. multicoloured . . . 25 35

2285 Ice-breaker "Vladivostok", Mil Mi-4 Helicopter, Satellite and Map

15.III—26.VII.1985
Дрейф во льдах Антарктики
(2286)

1986. Antarctic Drift of "Mikhail Somov" (ice-breaker). (a) As Type **2285**.

5693 5 k. blue, black and red . . . 25 10

5694 10 k. multicoloured 50 20

(b) No. 5055 optd with T **2286**.

5696 4 k. multicoloured 20 10

DESIGN: As T **2285**. 10 k. Map and "Mikhail Somov".

Nos. 5693/4 were printed together, se-tenant, forming a composite design.

2287 Class "Эu" No. EU 684–37, Slavyansk

1986. Steam Locomotive as Monuments. Mult.

5697 4 k. Type **2287** 20 10

5698 5 k. Class "FD" No. 21–3000, Novosibirsk 20 10

5699 10 k. Class "Ov" No. 5109, Volgograd 40 15

5700 20 k. Class "SO" No. 17–1613, Dnepropetrovsk 75 30

5701 30 k. Class "FDp" No. 20–578, Kiev . . . . 1·00 50

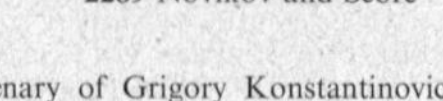

2288 G. K. Ordzhonikidze

2289 Novikov and Score

1986. Birth Centenary of Grigory Konstantinovich Ordzhonikidze (revolutionary).

5702 **2288** 5 k. grey 20 10

1986. 90th Birth Anniv of Anatoli Novikov (composer).

5703 **2289** 5 k. brown 30 10

2290 U.N. and U.N.E.S.C.O. Emblem

2291 Sun Yat-sen

1986. 40th Anniv of U.N.E.S.C.O.

5704 **2290** 10 k. silver and blue . . 40 15

1986. 120th Birth Anniv of Sun Yat-sen (first President of Chinese Republic).

5705 **2291** 5 k. black and grey . . 25 10

2292 Lomonosov

1986. 275th Birth Anniv of Mikhail Vasilievich Lomonosov (scientist).

5706 **2292** 5 k. brown 20 10

2293 Ya-1, 1927

1986. Sports Aircraft designed by Aleksandr Yakovlev. Multicoloured.

5707 4 k. Type **2293** 15 10

5708 5 k. VT-2 trainer, 1935 . . . 15 10

5709 10 k. Yak-18, 1946 . . . . . 30 15

5710 20 k. Yak-50, 1972 . . . . . 60 30

5711 30 k. Yak-55, 1981 . . . . . 95 50

2294 Spassky, Senate and Nikolsky Towers, Kremlin

2295 Computer and Terminal

1986. New Year.

5712 **2294** 5 k. multicoloured . . . 20 10

1986. Resolutions of 27th Communist Party Congress. Multicoloured.

5713 5 k. Type **2295** (scientific and technical progress) 20 10

5714 5 k. Construction engineer and building project 20 10

5715 5 k. City (welfare of people) 20 10

5716 5 k. Peace demonstration at Council for Mutual Economic Aid building (peace) . . . 20 10

5717 5 k. Spassky Tower and Kremlin Palace, Moscow Kremlin (unity of party and people) 20 10

2296 Parkhomenko

2297 Machel

1986. Birth Centenary of Aleksandr Parkhomenko (revolutionary).

5718 **2296** 5 k. black 20 10

1986. Samora Moizes Machel (President of Mozambique) Commemoration.
5719 **2297** 5 k. brown & black . . 25 10

2298 Russian State Museum (Mikhailovsky Palace)

1986. Palace Museums of Leningrad.
5720 **2298** 5 k. brown and green . 20 15
5721 – 10 k. green and blue . . 30 15
5722 – 15 k. blue and green . . 50 20
5723 – 20 k. green & brown . . 60 30
5724 – 50 k. brown and blue . 1·50 70
DESIGNS: 10 k. Hermitage Museum (Winter Palace); 15 k. Grand Palace Museum (Petrodvorets); 20 k. Catherine Palace Museum (Pushkin); 50 k. Palace Museum (Pavlovsk).

2299 Couple and Industrial Landscape
2300 "Atrophaneura alcinous"

1987. 18th Soviet Trades Union Congress, Moscow.
5725 **2299** 5 k. multicoloured . . . 20 10

1987. Butterflies listed in U.S.S.R. Red Book (2nd series). Multicoloured.
5726 4 k. Type **2300** 20 10
5727 5 k. "Papilio machaon" . . . 20 10
5728 10 k. "Papilio alexanor" . . . 35 15
5729 15 k. "Papilio maackii" . . . 60 25
5730 30 k. "Iphiclides podalirius" . 95 50

2301 Karlis Miesnieks
2302 Stasys Simkus

1987. Birth Centenary of Karlis Miesnieks (Latvian artist).
5731 **2301** 5 k. multicoloured . . . 20 10

1987. U.S.S.R. Sports Committee's International Mountaineers' Camps (2nd series). As T **2279**. Multicoloured.
5732 4 k. Chimbulak Gorge . . . 15 10
5733 10 k. Shavla Gorge 30 15
5734 20 k. Donguz-Orun and Nakra-Tau, Caucasus 70 30
5735 35 k. Kazbek, Caucasus . . . 1·00 60

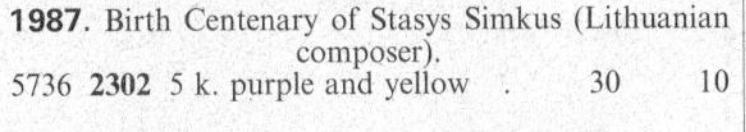

1987. Birth Centenary of Stasys Simkus (Lithuanian composer).
5736 **2302** 5 k. purple and yellow . 30 10

2303 V. I. Chapaev
2304 Lenin

1987. Birth Centenary of Vasily Ivanovich Chapaev (revolutionary).
5737 **2303** 5 k. brown 20 10

1987. 20th Leninist Young Communist League (Komsomol) Congress, Moscow.
5738 **2304** 5 k. multicoloured . . . 20 10

2305 Heino Eller
2306 Orbeli

1987. Birth Centenary of Heino Eller (Estonian composer).
5740 **2305** 5 k. lt brown & brown 30 10

1987. Birth Centenary of Academician Iosif Abgarovich Orbeli (first President of Armenian Academy of Sciences).
5741 **2306** 5 k. brown and pink . 20 10

2307 Bears in and out of Water

1987. Polar Bears. Multicoloured.
5742 5 k. Type **2307** 20 10
5743 10 k. Mother and cubs . . . 40 15
5744 20 k. Mother and cubs (different) 75 30
5745 35 k. Bears . . . . 1·00 1·00

2308 "Sputnik 1" and Globe
2309 Emblem and Headquarters, Bangkok

1987. Cosmonautics Day. Multicoloured.
5746 10 k. Type **2308** (30th anniv of launching of first artificial satellite) 35 15
5747 10 k. "Vostok-3", Vostok-4" and globe (25th anniv of first group space flight) 35 15
5748 10 k. "Mars-1" and globe (25th anniv of launching of automatic interplanetary station) 35 15

1987. 40th Anniv of U.N. Economic and Social Commission for Asia and the Pacific Ocean.
5749 **2309** 10 k. multicoloured . . 35 15

2310 "Birthday" (N. A. Sysoev)

1987. 117th Birth Anniv of Lenin. Multicoloured.
5750 5 k. Type **2310** 20 10
5751 5 k. "V. I. Lenin with Delegates to the Third Congress of the Young Communist League" (P. P. Belousov) 20 10

2311 Gymnast on Rings
2312 Cyclists and "40"

1987. European Gymnastics Championships, Moscow.
5753 **2311** 10 k. multicoloured . . 40 15

1987. 40th Peace Cycle Race.
5754 **2312** 10 k. multicoloured . . 50 15

2313 Menzbir's Marmot
2315 "Portrait of a Woman" (Lucas Cranach the Elder)

2314 "Maksim Gorky"

1987. Mammals listed in U.S.S.R. Red Book. Multicoloured.
5755 5 k. Type **2313** 20 10
5756 10 k. Ratel (horiz) 35 15
5757 15 k. Snow leopard (32 × 47 mm) 70 25

1987. River Tourist Ships. Multicoloured.
5758 5 k. Type **2314** 25 10
5759 10 k. "Aleksandr Pushkin" . 40 15
5760 30 k. "Sovetsky Soyuz" . . . 1·00 45

1987. West European Art in Hermitage Museum, Leningrad. Multicoloured.
5761 4 k. Type **2315** 15 10
5762 5 k. "St. Sebastian" (Titian) . 15 10
5763 10 k. "Justice" (drawing, Albrecht Durer) 30 15
5764 30 k. "Adoration of the Magi" (Peter Breughel the younger) (horiz) 90 45
5765 50 k. "Statue of Ceres" (Peter Paul Rubens) . . . . 1·50 1·00

2316 Car Production Line and Lenin Hydro-electric Power Station
2317 Pushkin (after T. Rait)

1987. 250th Anniv of Togliatti (formerly Stavropol).
5766 **2316** 5 k. multicoloured . . . 25 10

1987. 150th Death Anniv of Aleksandr S. Pushkin (poet).
5767 **2317** 5 k. deep brown, yellow and brown 20 10

2318 Kovpak
2319 Congress Emblem

1987. Birth Centenary of Major-General Sidor Artemevich Kovpak.
5768 **2318** 5 k. black 20 10

1987. World Women's Congress, Moscow.
5769 **2319** 10 k. multicoloured . . 30 15

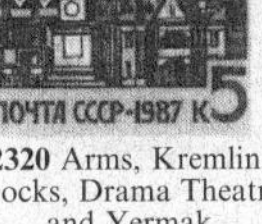

2320 Arms, Kremlin, Docks, Drama Theatre and Yermak Monument
2321 Party Flag and Mozambican

1987. 400th Anniv of Tobolsk, Siberia.
5770 **2320** 5 k. multicoloured . . . 20 10

1987. 25th Anniv of Mozambique Liberation Front (FRELIMO) (5771) and 10th Anniv of U.S.S.R.–Mozambique Friendship and Co-operation Treaty (5772). Multicoloured.
5771 5 k. Type **2321** 20 10
5772 5 k. Mozambique and U.S.S.R. flags 20 10

2322 "Scolopendrium vulgare"
2323 Moscow Kremlin and Indian Coin

1987. Ferns. Multicoloured.
5773 4 k. Type **2322** 15 10
5774 5 k. "Ceterach officinarum" . 20 10
5775 10 k. "Salvinia natans" (horiz) 35 15
5776 15 k. "Matteuccia struthiopteris" 55 25
5777 50 k. "Adiantum pedatum" . 1·50 70

1987. Indian Festival in U.S.S.R. (5778) and U.S.S.R. Festival in India (5779). Multicoloured.
5778 5 k. Type **2323** 20 15
5779 5 k. Hammer, sickle, open book, satellite and Red Fort, Delhi 20 15

2324 Rossiya Hotel (venue), Globe and Film
2325 Cosmonauts training

1987. 15th International Film Festival, Moscow.
5780 **2324** 10 k. multicoloured . . 35 15

1987. Soviet–Syrian Space Flight. Multicoloured.
5781 5 k. Type **2325** 20 10
5782 10 k. Moscow–Damascus satellite link and cosmonauts watching television screen . . 35 15
5783 15 k. Cosmonauts at Gagarin monument, Zvezdny . . . 55 25

2326 Emblem and Vienna Headquarters

1987. 30th Anniv of Int Atomic Energy Agency.
5785 **2326** 20 k. multicoloured . . 60 30

2327 14th–16th Century Messenger

1987. Russian Postal History.
5786 **2327** 4 k. black and brown . 15 10
5787 – 5 k. black and brown . 20 10
5788 – 10 k. black and brown . 35 15
5789 – 30 k. black and brown . 1·00 45
5790 – 35 k. black and brown . 1·00 50
DESIGNS: 5 k. 17th–19th century horse-drawn sledge and 17th-century postman; 10 k. 16th-century and 18th-century sailing packets; 30 k. 19th-century railway mail vans; 35 k. 1905 post car and 1926 "AMO-F-15" van.

2328 "V. I. Lenin" (P. V. Vasilev)

1987. 70th Anniv of October Revolution. Mult.
5792 5 k. Type **2328** 20 15
5793 5 k. "V. I. Lenin proclaims Soviet Power" (V. A. Serov) 20 15
5794 5 k. "Long Live the Socialist Revolution!" (V. V. Kuznetsov) 20 15
5795 5 k. "Storming the Winter Palace" (V. A. Serov) (69 × 32 mm) 20 15
5796 5 k. "On the Eve of the Storm" (portraying Lenin, Sverdlov and Podvoisky) (V. V. Pimenov) (69 × 32 mm) . . 20 15

2330 Postyshev 2331 Yuri Dolgoruky (founder) Monument

1987. Birth Centenary of Pavel Petrovich Postyshev (revolutionary).
5799 **2330** 5 k. blue 20 10

1987. 840th Anniv of Moscow.
5800 **2331** 5 k. brown, yell & orge . 20 10

2332 Ulugh Beg (astronomer and mathematician)

1987. Scientists.
5801 **2332** 5 k. multicoloured . . . 25 15
5802 – 5 k. black, green and blue 25 15
5803 – 5 k. deep brown, brown and blue 25 15
DESIGNS: No. 5801, Type **2332** (550th anniv of "New Astronomical Tables"); No. 5802, Isaac Newton (300th anniv of "Principia Mathematica"); No. 5803, Marie Curie (120th birth anniv).

Всесоюзная филателистическая выставка „70 лет Великого Октября"

(2334)

1987. "70th Anniv of October Revolution" All-Union Stamp Exhibition. No. 5795 optd with T **2334**.
5805 5 k. multicoloured 25 20

2335 "There will be Cities in the Taiga" (A. A. Yakovlev) 2336 Reed

1987. Soviet Paintings of the 1980s. Multicoloured.
5806 4 k. Type **2335** 15 10
5807 5 k. "Mother" (V. V. Shcherbakov) 15 10
5808 10 k. "My Quiet Homeland" (V. M. Sidorov) (horiz) 30 15
5809 30 k. "In Yakutsk, Land of Pyotr Alekseev" (A. N. Osipov) (horiz) 90 45
5810 35 k. "Ivan's Return" (V. I. Yerofeev) (horiz) . . . . 1·00 55

1987. Birth Centenary of John Reed (American journalist and founder of U. S. Communist Party).
5812 **2336** 10 k. brown, yell & blk . 35 15

2337 Marshak

1987. Birth Centenary of Samuil Yakovlevich Marshak (poet).
5813 **2337** 5 k. brown 20 10

2338 Chavchavadze

1987. 150th Anniv of Ilya Grigoryevich Chavchavadze (writer).
5814 **2338** 5 k. blue 20 10

2339 Indira Gandhi 2340 Vadim N. Podbelsky (revolutionary)

1987. 70th Birth Anniv of Indira Gandhi (former Indian Minister, 1966–77 and 1980–84).
5815 **2339** 5 k. brown and black . 30 10

1987. Birth Centenaries.
5816 **2340** 5 k. black 20 10
5817 – 5 k. blue 20 10
DESIGN: No. 5817, Academician Nikolai Ivanovich Vavilov (geneticist).

2341 Tokamak Thermonuclear System 2342 Bagramyan

1987. Science.
5818 **2341** 5 k. brown and grey . 20 10
5819 – 10 k. green, blue and black 35 15
5820 – 20 k. black, stone and drab 60 30
DESIGNS: 10 k. Kola borehole; 20 k. "Ratan-600" radio telescope.

1987. 90th Birth Anniv of Marshal Ivan Khristoforovich Bagramyan.
5821 **2342** 5 k. brown 20 10

2343 Moscow Kremlin 2344 Flags, Spassky Tower, Moscow, and Capitol, Washington

1987. New Year.
5822 **2343** 5 k. multicoloured . . 15 10

1987. Soviet–American Intermediate and Short-range Nuclear Weapons Treaty.
5823 **2344** 10 k. multicoloured . . 35 15

2345 Grigori Andreevich Spiridov and "Tri Svyatitelya"

1987. Russian Naval Commanders (1st series).
5824 **2345** 4 k. blue and deep blue 15 10
5825 – 5 k. purple and blue . 20 10
5826 – 10 k. purple and blue . 35 15
5827 – 25 k. blue and deep blue 85 60
5828 – 30 k. blue and deep blue 95 65
DESIGNS: 5 k. Fyodor Fyodorovich Ushakov and "Sv. Pavel"; 10 k. Dmitri Nikolaevich Senyavin and Battle of Afon; 25 k. Mikhail Petrovich Lazarev and "Azov"; 30 k. Pavel Stepanovich Nakhimov and "Imperatritsa Maria".
See also Nos. 6091/6.

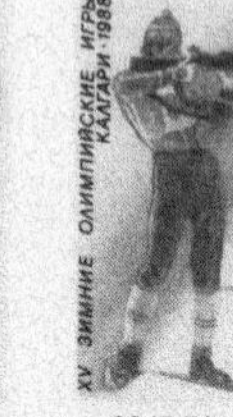

2346 Torch 2347 Biathlon

1987. 30th Anniv of Asia–Africa Solidarity Organization.
5829 **2346** 10 k. multicoloured . . 30 15

1988. Winter Olympic Games, Calgary. Mult.
5830 5 k. Type **2347** 20 10
5831 10 k. Cross-country skiing . . 35 15
5832 15 k. Slalom 45 25
5833 20 k. Figure skating (pairs) . 60 30
5834 30 k. Ski jumping 95 45

2348 1918 Stamps 2349 Emblem

1988. 70th Anniv of First Soviet Postage Stamps.
5836 **2348** 10 k. blue, brown and gold 35 15
5837 10 k. brown, blue and gold 35 15
On No. 5836 the lower stamp depicted is the 35 k. in blue, on No. 5837 the lower stamp is the 70 k. in brown.

1988. 40th Anniv of W.H.O.
5838 **2349** 35 k. gold, blue and black 1·25 55

2350 Byron

1988. Birth Bicentenary of Lord Byron (English poet).
5839 **2350** 15 k. black, green and blue 45 25

2351 Exchange Activities and National Flags 2352 Lomov-Oppokov

1988. 30th Anniv of Agreement on Cultural, Technical and Educational Exchanges with U.S.A.
5840 **2351** 20 k. multicoloured . . 60 30

1988. Birth Centenary of Georgy Ippolitovich Lomov-Oppokov (Communist party official).
5841 **2352** 5 k. black and brown . . 10 10

2353 "Little Humpbacked Horse" (dir. I. Ivanov-Vano, animated L. Milchin)

1988. Soviet Cartoon Films. Multicoloured.
5842 1 k. Type **2353** 10 10
5843 3 k. "Winnie the Pooh" (dir. F. Khitruk, animated V. Zuikov and E. Nazarov) 10 10
5844 4 k. "Gena the Crocodile" (dir. R. Kachanov, animated L. Shartsmann) 15 10
5845 5 k. "Just You Wait!" (dir. V. Kotyonochkin, animated S. Rusakov) 20 10
5846 10 k. "Hedgehog in a Mist" (dir. Yu. Norshtein, animated F. Yarbusova) 30 15

2354 Bonch-Bruevich 2355 Nurse and Emblems

1988. Birth Centenary of Mikhail Alexandrovich Bonch-Bruevich (radio engineer).
5848 **2354** 10 k. black and brown . 30 15

1988. 125th Anniv of International Red Cross and Red Crescent.
5849 **2355** 15 k. black, blue and red 45 25

2356 Skater

1988. World Speed Skating Championships, Alma-Ata.
5850 **2356** 15 k. blue, violet and black 45 25

2357 Makarenko

1988. Birth Centenary of Anton Semenovich Makarenko (educationist and writer).
5851 **2357** 10 k. green 30 15

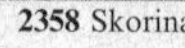

2358 Skorina 2359 Banners and Globe

1988. 500th Birth Anniv of Frantsisk Skorina (printer).
5852 **2358** 5 k. black 20 10

1988. Labour Day.
5853 **2359** 5 k. multicoloured . . . 20 10

2360 Kingisepp 2361 Track and Athlete

1988. Birth Centenary of Victor Eduardovich Kingisepp (revolutionary).
5854 **2360** 5 k. green 20 10

1988. Centenary of Russian Athletics.
5855 **2361** 15 k. multicoloured . . 45 25

2362 M. S. Shaginyan

1988. Birth Centenary of Marietta Sergeevna Shaginyan (writer).
5856 **2362** 10 k. brown 30 10

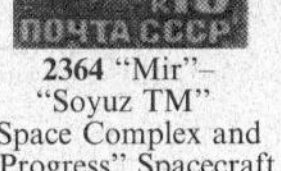

2363 Palace of Congresses, Moscow, Finlandia Hall, Helsinki, and National Flags

2364 "Mir"–"Soyuz TM" Space Complex and "Progress" Spacecraft

1988. 40th Anniv of U.S.S.R.–Finland Friendship Treaty.
5857 **2363** 15 k. multicoloured . . 45 25

1988. Cosmonautics Day.
5858 **2364** 15 k. multicoloured . . 45 25

2365 Sochi

1988. 150th Anniv of Sochi.
5859 **2365** 5 k. multicoloured . . . 20 10

2366 "Victory" (P. A. Krivonogov)

1988. V. E. Day (8 May).
5860 **2366** 5 k. multicoloured . . . 20 10

2367 Lenin Museum, Moscow

1988. 118th Birth Anniv of Lenin. Designs showing branches of Lenin Central Museum.
5861 **2367** 5 k. brown, deep brown and gold 20 10
5862 – 5 k. red, purple & gold . 20 10
5863 – 5 k. ochre, brown & gold 20 10
5864 – 5 k. yell, grn & gold . . 20 10
DESIGNS: No. 5862, Kiev; No. 5863, Leningrad; No. 5864, Krasnoyarsk.
See also Nos. 5990/2 and 6131/3.

2368 Akulov

2369 Soviet Display Emblem

1988. Birth Centenary of Ivan Alekseevich Akulov (Communist Party official).
5865 **2368** 5 k. blue 20 10

1988. "Expo 88" World's Fair, Brisbane.
5866 **2369** 20 k. multicoloured . . 60 30

2370 Marx

2373 Shvernik

2371 Soldiers and Workers

1988. 170th Birth Anniv of Karl Marx.
5867 **2370** 5 k. brown 20 10

1988. Perestroika (Reformation).
5868 **2371** 5 k. multicoloured . . 20 10
5869 – 5 k. brown, red & orange 20 10
DESIGN: No. 5869, Banner, industrial scenes and worker.

1988. Birth Centenary of Nikolai Mikhailovich Shvernik (politician).
5871 **2373** 5 k. black 20 10

2374 Russian Borzoi

1988. Hunting Dogs. Multicoloured.
5872 5 k. Type **2374** 20 10
5873 10 k. Kirgiz borzoi 30 15
5874 15 k. Russian hound 45 25
5875 20 k. Russian spaniel . . . 60 30
5876 35 k. East Siberian husky . 1·00 50

2375 Flags, Spassky Tower and Handshake

2376 Kuibyshev

1988. Soviet–American Summit, Moscow.
5877 **2375** 5 k. multicoloured . . 20 10

1988. Birth Centenary of Valerian Vladimirovich Kuibyshev (politician).
5878 **2376** 5 k. brown 20 10

2377 Flags, "Mir" Space Station and "Soyuz TM" Spacecraft

2378 Crowd and Peace Banners

1988. Soviet–Bulgarian Space Flight.
5879 **2377** 15 k. multicoloured . . 45 25

1988. "For a Nuclear-free World".
5880 **2378** 5 k. multicoloured . . 20 10

2379 Red Flag, Hammer and Sickle and Laurel Branch

2380 Flags, Skis and Globe

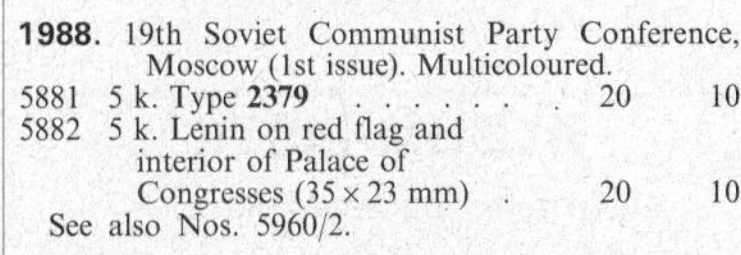

1988. 19th Soviet Communist Party Conference, Moscow (1st issue). Multicoloured.
5881 5 k. Type **2379** 20 10
5882 5 k. Lenin on red flag and interior of Palace of Congresses (35 × 23 mm) . 20 10
See also Nos. 5960/2.

1988. Soviet–Canadian Transarctic Ski Expedition.
5884 **2380** 35 k. multicoloured . . 1·00 50

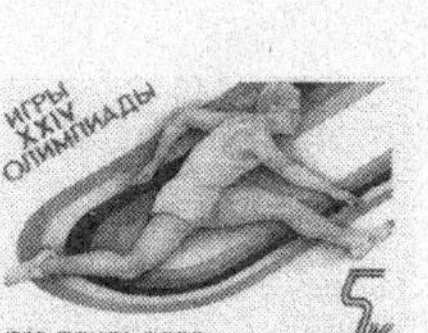

2381 Hurdling

2382 Giant Bellflower

1988. Olympic Games, Seoul. Multicoloured.
5885 5 k. Type **2381** 20 10
5886 10 k. Long jumping 30 15
5887 15 k. Basketball 45 25
5888 20 k. Gymnastics 60 30
5889 30 k. Swimming 90 45

1988. Deciduous Forest Flowers. Multicoloured.
5891 5 k. Type **2382** 20 10
5892 10 k. Spring pea (horiz) . . . 30 15
5893 15 k. Lungwort 45 25
5894 20 k. Turk's cap lily 60 30
5895 35 k. "Ficaria verna" . . . . 1·00 50

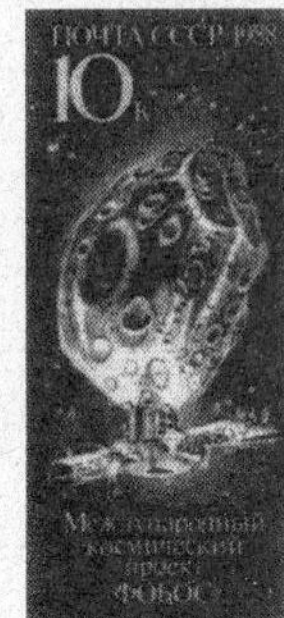

2383 Phobos and "Phobos" Space Probe

2384 Komsomol Badge

1988. Phobos (Mars Moon) International Space Project.
5896 **2383** 10 k. multicoloured . . 30 15

1988. 70th Anniv of Leninist Young Communist League (Komsomol).
5897 **2384** 5 k. multicoloured . . . 20 10

2385 Mandela

Филвыставка.
Москва

(2387)

2386 "Obeyan Serebryanyi, Light Grey Arab Stallion" (N. E. Sverchkov)

1988. 70th Birthday of Nelson Mandela (African nationalist).
5898 **2385** 10 k. multicoloured . . 30 15

1988. Paintings in Moscow Horse Breeding Museum. Multicoloured.
5899 5 k. Type **2386** 20 10
5900 10 k. "Konvoets" (Kabardin breed) (M. A. Vrubel) (vert) 35 15
5901 15 k. "Horsewoman on Orlov-Rastopchin Horse" (N. E. Sverchkov) 45 25
5902 20 k. "Letuchy, Grey Stallion of Orlov Trotter Breed" (V. A. Serov) (vert) 60 30
5903 30 k. "Sardar, an Akhaltekin Stallion" (A. B. Villevalde) 95 75

1988. Stamp Exhibition, Moscow. No. 5897 optd with T **2387**.
5904 **2384** 5 k. multicoloured . . . 20 10

MINIMUM PRICE

The minimum price quoted is 10p which represents a handling charge rather than a basis for valuing common stamps. For further notes about prices, see introductory pages.

2388 Voikov

2389 "Portrait of O. K. Lansere" (Z. E. Serebryakova)

1988. Birth Centenary of Pyotr Lazarevich Voikov (diplomat).
5905 **2388** 5 k. black 20 10

1988. Soviet Culture Fund. Multicoloured.
5906 10 k. + 5 k. Type **2389** . . . 45 25
5907 15 k. + 7 k. "Boyarynya (noblewoman) looking at Embroidery Design" (K. V. Lebedev) (horiz) 65 35
5908 30 k. + 15 k. "Talent" (N. P. Bogdanov-Belsky) . . . . 1·40 70

2390 Envelopes and U.P.U. Emblem

2391 "Mir" Space Station and "Soyuz-TM" Spacecraft

1988. International Correspondence Week.
5910 **2390** 5 k. turquoise, blue & blk 20 10

1988. Soviet–Afghan Space Flight.
5911 **2391** 15 k. green, red & blk . 45 25

2392 Emblem and Open Book

2393 Kviring

1988. 30th Anniv of "Problems of Peace and Socialism" (magazine).
5912 **2392** 10 k. multicoloured . . 30 15

1988. Birth Centenary of Emmanuil Ionovich Kviring (politician).
5913 **2393** 5 k. black 20 10

2394 "Ilya Muromets" (Russia) (R. Smirnova)

2395 "Appeal of the Leader" (detail, I. M. Toidze)

1988. Epic Poems of Soviet Union (1st series). Illustrations by artists named. Multicoloured.
5914 10 k. Type **2394** 30 15
5915 10 k. "Cossack Golota" (Ukraine) (M. Deregus) (horiz) 30 15
5916 10 k. "Musician-Magician" (Byelorussia) (N. Poplavskaya) 30 15
5917 10 k. "Koblandy Batyr" (Kazakhstan) (I. Isabaev) (horiz) 30 15
5918 10 k. "Alpamysh" (Uzbekistan) (R. Khalilov) 30 15
See also Nos. 6017/21 and 6139/43.

1988. 71st Anniv of October Revolution.
5919 **2395** 5 k. multicoloured . . . 20 10

2396 Bolotov 2397 Tupolev

1988. 250th Birth Anniv of Andrei Timofeevich Bolotov (agriculturalist).
5920 **2396** 10 k. brown 30 15

1988. Birth Centenary of Academician Andrei Nikolaevich Tupolev (aircraft designer).
5921 **2397** 10 k. blue 30 15

2398 Bear 2399 "Sibir" (atomic ice-breaker)

1988. Zoo Relief Fund. Multicoloured.
5922 10 k. + 5 k. Type **2398** . . . 45 25
5923 10 k. + 5 k. Wolf 45 25
5924 10 k. + 10 k. Fox 95 45
5925 20 k. + 10 k. Wild boar . . 95 45
5926 20 k. + 10 k. Lynx 95 45

1988. Soviet Arctic Expedition.
5927 **2399** 20 k. multicoloured . . 60 60

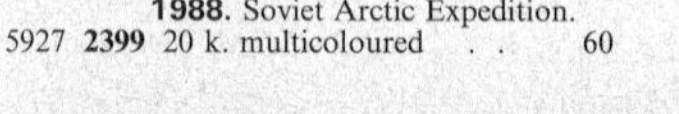

2400 Ustinov 2401 National Initials

1988. 80th Birth Anniv of Marshal Dmitri Fyodorovich Ustinov.
5928 **2400** 5 k. brown 20 10

1988. 10th Anniv of U.S.S.R.–Vietnam Friendship Treaty.
5929 **2401** 10 k. multicoloured . . 30 15

2402 Building Facade

1988. 50th Anniv of State House of Broadcasting and Sound Recording.
5930 **2402** 10 k. multicoloured . . 30 15

2403 Emblem

1988. 40th Anniv of Declaration of Human Rights.
5931 **2403** 10 k. multicoloured . . 30 15

2404 Life Guard of Preobrazhensky Regt. with Peter I's New Year Decree

1988. New Year.
5932 **2404** 5 k. multicoloured . . . 20 10

2405 Flags and Cosmonauts

1988. Soviet–French Space Flight.
5933 **2405** 15 k. multicoloured . . 45 25

2406 "Skating Rink" (Olya Krutova) 2407 Lacis

1988. Lenin Soviet Children's Fund. Children's Paintings. Multicoloured.
5934 5 k. + 2 k. Type **2406** . . . 25 15
5935 5 k. + 2 k. "Cock" (Nasta Shcheglova) 25 15
5936 5 k. + 2 k. "May is flying over the Meadows, May is flying over the Fields" (Larisa Gaidash) 25 15

1988. Birth Cent of Martins Lacis (revolutionary).
5937 **2407** 5 k. green 20 10

(2408) 2410 Post Messenger

1988. "Space Post". No. 4682 optd with T **2408**.
5938 **1** r. blue . . . . 2·75 2·75

1988.
5940 **2410** 1 k. brown 10 10
6073 – 2 k. brown 10 10
5941 – 3 k. green 10 10
6075 – 4 k. blue 10 10
6076 – 5 k. red 15 10
6077 – 7 k. blue 15 10
6078 – 10 k. brown 25 15
6079 – 12 k. purple 30 20
6080 – 13 k. violet 30 20
6081 – 15 k. blue 35 20
6082 – 20 k. brown 45 25
6083 – 25 k. green 85 30
6084 – 30 k. blue 90 35
6085 – 35 k. brown . . . . . 1·00 40
6086 – 50 k. blue . . . . . . 1·50 50
6087 – 1 r. blue . . . . . . 3·00 1·40

DESIGNS: 2 k. Old mail transport (sailing packet, steam train and mail coach); 3 k. "Aurora" (cruiser); 4 k. Spassky Tower and Lenin's Tomb, Red Square, Moscow; 5 k. State emblem and flag; 7 k. Modern mail transport (aircraft, liner, train and mail van); 10 k. "The Worker and the Collective Farmer" (statue V. I. Mukhina); 12 k. Rocket on launch pad; 13 k. Satellite; 15 k. "Orbit" dish aerial; 20 k. Symbols of art and literature; 25 k. "The Discus-thrower" (5th-century Greek statue by Miron); 30 k. Map of Antarctica and penguins; 35 k. "Mercury" (statue Giovanni da Bologna); 50 k. Great white cranes; 1 r. Universal Postal Union emblem.

2411 Great Cascade and Samson Fountain 2412 1st-cent B. C. Gold Coin of Tigran the Great

1988. Petrodvorets Fountains. Each green and grey.
5952 5 k. Type **2411** 20 10
5953 10 k. Adam fountain (D. Bonazza) 30 15
5954 15 k. Golden Mountain cascade (Niccolo Michetti and Mikhail Zemtsov) 45 25
5955 30 k. Roman fountains (Bartolomeo Rastrelli) . . 95 45
5965 50 k. Oaklet trick fountain (Rastrelli) . . . . 1·50 1·00

1988. Armenian Earthquake Relief. Armenian History. Multicoloured.
5957 20 k. + 10 k. Type **2412** . . 95 45
5958 30 k. + 15 k. Rispsime Church 1·25 65
5959 50 k. + 25 k. "Madonna and Child" (18th-century fresco, Ovnat Ovnatanyan) . . . 2·25 1·25

2413 Hammer and Sickle

1988. 19th Soviet Communist Party Conference, Moscow (2nd issue). Multicoloured.
5960 5 k. Type **2413** 20 10
5961 5 k. Hammer and sickle and building girders 20 10
5962 5 k. Hammer and sickle and wheat 20 10

2415 "Vostok" Rocket, "Lunar 1", Earth and Moon 2416 Virtanen

1989. 30th Anniv of First Russian Moon Flight.
5964 **2415** 15 k. multicoloured . . 45 25

1989. Birth Centenary of Jalmari Virtanen (poet).
5965 **2416** 5 k. brown and bistre . . 20 10

2417 Headquarters Building, Moscow

1989. 40th Anniv of Council for Mutual Economic Aid.
5966 **2417** 10 k. multicoloured . . 30 15

2418 Forest Protection 2419 18th-century Samovar

1989. Nature Conservation. Multicoloured.
5967 5 k. Type **2418** 60 20
5968 10 k. Arctic preservation . . 30 15
5969 15 k. Anti-desertification campaign 40 20

1989. Russian Samovars in State Museum, Leningrad. Multicoloured.
5970 5 k. Type **2419** 20 10
5971 10 k. 19th-century barrel samovar by Ivan Lisitsin of Tula 30 15
5972 20 k. 1830s Kabachok travelling samovar by Sokolov Brothers factory, Tula 55 30
5973 30 k. 1840s samovar by Nikolai Malikov factory, Tula . . . 85 45

2420 Mussorgsky (after Repin) and Scene from "Boris Godunov" 2421 Dybenko

1989. 150th Birth Anniv of Modest Petrovich Mussorgsky (composer).
5974 **2420** 10 k. purple and brown . 30 15

1989. Birth Centenary of Pavel Dybenko (military leader).
5975 **2421** 5 k. black 20 10

2422 Shevchenko 2423 "Lilium speciosum"

1989. 175th Birth Anniv of Taras Shevchenko (Ukrainian poet and painter).
5976 **2422** 5 k. brown, green & blk 20 10

1989. Lilies. Multicoloured.
5977 5 k. Type **2423** 20 10
5978 10 k. "African Queen" . . . 30 15
5979 15 k. "Eclat du Soir" 40 20
5980 30 k. "White Tiger" 85 45

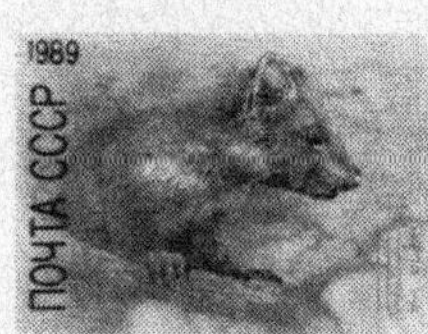
2424 Marten

1989. Zoo Relief Fund. Multicoloured.
5981 10 k. + 5 k. Type **2424** . . . 40 20
5982 10 k. + 5 k. Squirrel 40 20
5983 20 k. + 10 k. Hare 85 45
5984 20 k. + 10 k. Hedgehog . . 85 45
5985 20 k. + 10 k. Badger 85 45

2426 "Victory Banner" (P. Loginov and V. Pamfilov)

1989. Victory Day.
5987 **2426** 5 k. multicoloured . . . 20 10

2427 "Mir" Space Station

1989. Cosmonautics Day.
5988 **2427** 15 k. multicoloured . . 40 20

2428 Emblem and Flags 2430 Statue

1989. U.S.–Soviet Bering Bridge Expedition.
5989 **2428** 10 k. multicoloured . . 30 15

1989. 119th Birth Anniv of Lenin. As T **2367**. Branches of Lenin Central Museum.
5990 5 k. brown, ochre and gold . 20 10
5991 5 k. deep brown, brn & gold 20 10
5992 5 k. multicoloured 20 10

DESIGNS: No. 5990, Frunze; No. 5991, Kazan; No. 5992, Kuibyshev.

1989. 70th Anniv of First Hungarian Soviet Republic.
5994 **2430** 5 k. multicoloured . . . 20 10

2431 "Motherland Statue" **2432** Drone

1989. 400th Anniv of Volgograd (formerly Tsaritsyn).
5995 **2431** 5 k. multicoloured . . . 20 10

1989. Bees. Multicoloured.
5996 5 k. Type **2432** 20 10
5997 10 k. Bees, flowers and hive . 30 15
5998 20 k. Bee on flower 55 30
5999 35 k. Feeding queen bee . . 90 45

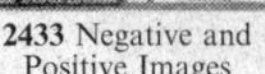

2433 Negative and Positive Images **2434** Map above Dove as Galley

1989. 150th Anniv of Photography.
6000 **2433** 5 k. multicoloured . . . 20 10

1989. "Europe—Our Common Home". Mult.
6001 5 k. Type **2434** 20 10
6002 10 k. Laying foundations of Peace 30 15
6003 15 k. White storks' nest . . . 40 20

2435 Mukhina modelling "God of Northern Wind" (after M. Nesterov) **2436** Racine

1989. Birth Centenary of Vera I. Mukhina (sculptress).
6004 **2435** 5 k. blue 20 10

1989. 150th Birth Anniv of Jean Racine (dramatist).
6005 **2436** 15 k. multicoloured . . 40 20

2437 Rabbit

1989. Lenin Soviet Children's Fund. Children's Paintings. Multicoloured.
6006 5 k. + 2 k. Type **2437** . . . 25 10
6007 5 k. + 2 k. Cat 25 10
6008 5 k. + 2 k. Nurse 25 10
See also Nos. 6162/4.

2438 Kuratov

1989. 150th Birth Anniv of Ivan Kuratov (writer).
6009 **2438** 5 k. deep brown & brown 20 10

2439 Emblem **2440** Common Shelduck

1989. 13th World Youth and Students' Festival, Pyongyang.
6010 **2439** 10 k. multicoloured . . 30 15

1989. Ducks (1st series). Multicoloured.
6011 5 k. Type **2440** 25 10
6012 15 k. Green-winged teal . . 50 20
6013 20 k. Ruddy shelduck . . . 65 30
See also Nos. 6159/61, 6264/6, 6368/70, 6420/2 6487/9 and 6555/7.

2441 "Storming of Bastille" (Gelman after Monnet)

1989. Bicentenary of French Revolution.
6014 **2441** 5 k. multicoloured . . 20 10
6015 – 15 k. blue, black & red 40 20
6016 – 20 k. blue, black & red 50 25
DESIGNS: 15 k. Jean-Paul Marat, Georges Danton and Maximilien Robespierre; 20 k. "Marseillaise" (relief by F. Rude from Arc de Triomphe).

1989. Epic Poems of Soviet Union (2nd series). Illustrations by named artists. As T **2394**. Mult.
6017 10 k. "Amirani" (Georgia) (V. Oniani) 30 15
6018 10 k. "Koroglu" (Azerbaijan) (A. Gadzhiev) 30 15
6019 10 k. "Fir, Queen of Grass Snakes" (Lithuania) (A. Makunaite) 30 15
6020 10 k. "Mioritsa" (Moldavia) (I. Bogdesko) 30 15
6021 10 k. "Lachplesis" (Lettish) (G. Wilks) 30 15

2442 Observatory **2443** Hemispheres, Roses in Envelope and Posthorn

1989. 150th Anniv of Pulkovo Observatory.
6022 **2442** 10 k. multicoloured . . 35 15

1989. International Letter Week.
6023 **2443** 5 k. multicoloured . . 20 10

2444 Lynx **2446** Buildings, Container Ship and Bicentenary Emblem

1989. 50th Anniv of Tallin Zoo.
6024 **2444** 10 k. multicoloured . . 30 15

1989. Bicentenary of Nikolaev.
6026 **2446** 5 k. multicoloured . . 20 10

2447 Nkrumah **2448** 1921 40 r. Stamp

1989. 80th Birth Anniv of Kwame Nkrumah (first Prime Minister and President of Ghana).
6027 **2447** 10 k. multicoloured . . 30 15

1989. 6th All-Union Philatelic Society Congress, Moscow.
6028 **2448** 10 k. multicoloured . . 30 15

2449 Cooper

1989. Birth Bicentenary of James Fenimore Cooper (writer) (1st issue).
6029 **2449** 15 k. multicoloured . . 40 20
See also Nos. 6055/9.

2450 V. L. Durov (trainer) and Sealions

1989. 70th Anniv of Soviet Circus. Multicoloured.
6030 1 k. Type **2450** 10 10
6031 3 k. M. N. Rumyantsev (clown "Karandash") with donkey 10 10
6032 4 k. V. I. Filatov (founder of Bear Circus) and bears on motor cycles 15 10
6033 5 k. E. T. Kio (illusionist) and act 20 10
6034 10 k. V. E. Lazarenko (clown and acrobat) and act . . . 30 15

2451 Emblem on Glove **2452** Li Dazhao

1989. International Amateur Boxing Association Championship, Moscow.
6036 **2451** 15 k. multicoloured . . 40 20

1989. Birth Centenary of Li Dazhao (co-founder of Chinese Communist Party).
6037 **2452** 5 k. brown, stone & blk 20 10

2453 Khetagurov

1989. 130th Birth Anniv of Kosta Khetagurov (Ossetian writer).
6038 **2453** 5 k. brown 20 10

2454 "October Guardsmen" (M. M. Chepik)

1989. 72nd Anniv of October Revolution.
6039 **2454** 5 k. multicoloured . . . 20 10

2455 Russian Spoons, Psaltery, Balalaika, Zhaleika and Accordion

1989. Traditional Musical Instruments (1st series). Multicoloured.
6040 10 k. Type **2455** 30 15
6041 10 k. Ukrainian bandura, trembita, drymba, svyril (pipes) and dulcimer . . . 30 15
6042 10 k. Byelorussian tambourine, bastlya (fiddle), lera and dudka (pipe) 30 15
6043 10 k. Uzbek nagors (drums), rubab, zang, karnai and gidzhak 30 15
See also Nos. 6183/6 and 6303/5.

2456 "Demonstration of First Radio Receiver, 1895" (N. A. Sysoev) **2457** National Flag and Provincial Arms

1989. 130th Birth Anniv of Aleksandr Stepanovich Popov (radio pioneer).
6044 **2456** 10 k. multicoloured . . 30 15

1989. 40th Anniv of German Democratic Republic.
6045 **2457** 5 k. multicoloured 20 10

2458 Polish National Colours forming "45" **2459** Kosior

1989. 45th Anniv of Liberation of Poland.
6046 **2458** 5 k. multicoloured . . . 20 10

1989. Birth Centenary of Stanislav Vikentievich Kosior (vice-chairman of Council of People's Commissars).
6047 **2459** 5 k. black 20 10

2460 Nehru **2461** "Village Market" (A. V. Makovsky)

1989. Birth Centenary of Jawaharlal Nehru (Indian statesman).
6048 **2460** 15 k. brown 40 20

1989. Soviet Culture Fund. Multicoloured.
6049 4 k. + 2 k. Type **2461** . . . 20 10
6050 5 k. + 2 k. "Lady in Hat" (E. L. Zelenin) 25 15
6051 10 k. + 5 k. "Portrait of the Actress Bazhenova" (A. F. Sofronova) 40 20
6052 20 k. + 10 k. "Two Women" (Hugo Shaiber) 75 65
6053 30 k. + 15 k. 19th-century teapot and plates from Popov porcelain works . . . . . 1·40 85

2462 Berzin **2463** "The Hunter"

1989. Birth Centenary of Yan Karlovich Berzin (head of Red Army Intelligence).
6054 **2462** 5 k. black 20 10

1989. Birth Bicentenary of James Fenimore Cooper (writer) (2nd issue). Illustrations of his novels. Multicoloured.
6055 20 k. Type **2463** 50 25
6056 20 k. "Last of the Mohicans" 50 25
6057 20 k. "The Pathfinder" . . . 50 25
6058 20 k. "The Pioneers" 50 25
6059 20 k. "The Prairie" 50 25
Nos. 6055/9 were printed together, se-tenant, forming a composite design.

2464 St. Basil's Cathedral and Minin and Pozharsky Statue, Moscow

2465 Dymkovo Toy

1989. Historical Monuments (1st series). Mult.

6060 15 k. Type **2464** 40 20
6061 15 k. Sts. Peter and Paul Cathedral and statue of Peter I, Leningrad 40 20
6062 15 k. St. Sophia's Cathedral and statue of Bogdan Chmielnitsky, Kiev 40 20
6063 15 k. Khodzha Ahmed Yasavi mausoleum, Turkestan . . 40 20
6064 15 k. Khazret Khyzr Mosque, Samarkand 40 20

See also Nos. 6165/72 and 6231/3.

1989. New Year.

6065 **2465** 5 k. multicoloured . . . 20 10

2466 Soviet Lunar Vehicle

2468 Acid Rain destroying Rose

1989. "Expo 89" International Stamp Exhibition, Washington D.C. Multicoloured.

6066 25 k. Type **2466** 90 65
6067 25 k. Astronaut and landing module on Moon 90 65
6068 25 k. Cosmonauts on Mars . 90 65
6069 25 k. Flag and shield on Mars 90 65

1989. Russian Naval Commanders (2nd series). As T **2345**.

6091 5 k. blue and brown 10 15
6092 10 k. blue and brown 25 15
6093 15 k. blue and deep blue . . 35 20
6094 20 k. blue and deep blue . . 45 25
6095 30 k. blue and brown 90 60
6096 35 k. blue and brown . . . . 1·10 65

DESIGNS: 5 k. V. A. Kornilov and "Pervaz Bati"; 10 k. V. I. Istomin and "Parizh"; 15 k. G. I. Nevelskoi and "Baikal"; 20 k. G. I. Butakov and iron-clad squadron; 30 k. A. A. Popov, "Pyotr Veliky" and "Vitze Admirial Popov"; 35 k. S. O. Makarov, "Intibah" (Turkish warship) and "Veliky Khyaz Konstantin".

1990. Nature Conservation. Multicoloured.

6097 10 k. Type **2468** 25 15
6098 15 k. Oil-smeared gull perching on globe 60 20
6099 20 k. Blade sawing down tree 45 25

2469 Ladya Monument and Golden Gates, Kiev (Ukraine)

2470 Flag and Hanoi Monument

1990. Republic Capitals. Multicoloured.

6100 5 k. Lenin Palace of Culture, Government House and Academy of Sciences, Alma-Ata (Kazakhstan) 15 10
6101 5 k. Library, Mollanepes Theatre and War Heroes Monument, Ashkhabad (Turkmenistan) 15 10
6102 5 k. Maiden's Tower and Divan-Khane Palace, Baku (Azerbaijan) 15 10
6103 5 k. Sadriddin Aini Theatre and Avicenna Monument, Dushanbe (Tadzhikistan) . 15 10
6104 4 k. Spendyarov Theatre and David Sasunsky Monument, Yerevan (Armenia) 15 10
6105 5 k. Satylganov Philharmonic Society building and Manas Memorial, Frunze (Kirgizia) 15 10
6106 5 k. Type **2469** 15 10
6107 5 k. Cathedral and Victory Arch, Kishinev (Moldavia) 15 10
6108 5 k. Government House and Liberation Monument, Minsk (Byelorussia) 15 10
6109 5 k. Konstantino-Yeleninsky Tower and Ivan the Great Bell Tower, Moscow (Russian Federation) 15 10
6110 5 k. Cathedral, "Three Brothers" building and Freedom Monument, Riga (Latvia) 15 10
6111 5 k. Herman the Long, Oliviste Church, Cathedral and Town hall towers and wall turret, Tallin (Estonia) 15 10
6112 5 k. Kukeldash Medrese and University, Tashkent (Uzbekistan) 15 10
6113 5 k. Metekh Temple and Vakhtang Gorgasal Monument, Tbilisi (Georgia) 15 10
6114 5 k. Gediminas Tower and St. Anne's Church, Vilnius (Lithuania) 15 10

1990. 60th Anniv of Vietnamese Communist Party.

6115 **2470** 5 k. multicoloured . . 15 10

2471 Ho Chi Minh

2472 Snowy Owl

1990. Birth Centenary of Ho Chi Minh (Vietnamese leader).

6116 **2471** 10 k. brown and black 25 15

1990. Owls. Multicoloured.

6117 10 k. Type **2472** 25 15
6118 20 k. Eagle owl (vert) . . . 45 20
6119 55 k. Long-eared owl . . . 1·10 55

2473 Sailing Ship, Posthorn and Penny Black

1990. 150th Anniv of the Penny Black.

6120 **2473** 10 k. multicoloured . . 25 15
6121 – 20 k. black and gold . . 45 25
6122 – 20 k. black and gold . . 45 25
6123 – 35 k. multicoloured . . 1·10 65
6124 – 35 k. multicoloured . . 1·10 65

DESIGNS: No. 6121, Anniversary emblem and Penny Black (lettered "TP"); No. 6122, as No. 6121 but stamp lettered "TF"; No. 6123, "Stamp World London 90" International Stamp Exhibition emblem and Penny Black (lettered "V K"); No. 6124, as No. 6123 but stamp lettered "AH".

2474 Electric Cables

1990. 125th Anniv of I.T.U.

6126 **2474** 20 k. multicoloured . . 45 25

2475 Flowers

1990. Labour Day.

6127 **2475** 5 k. multicoloured . . 15 10

2476 "Victory, 1945" (A. Lysenko)

1990. 45th Anniv of Victory in Second World War.

6128 **2476** 5 k. multicoloured . . 15 10

2477 "Mir" Space Complex and Cosmonaut

2478 Lenin

1990. Cosmonautics Day.

6129 **2477** 20 k. multicoloured . . 45 25

1990. "Leniniana '90" All-Union Stamp Exhibition.

6130 **2478** 5 k. brown 15 10

1990. 120th Birth Anniv of Lenin. Branches of Lenin Central Museum. As T **2367**.

6131 5 k. red, lake and gold . . . 15 10
6132 5 k. pink, purple and gold . . 15 10
6133 5 k. multicoloured 15 10

DESIGNS: No. 6131, Ulyanovsk; No. 6132, Baku; No. 6133, Tashkent.

2479 Scene from "Iolanta" (opera) and Tchaikovsky

1990. 150th Birth Anniv of Pyotr Ilich Tchaikovsky (composer).

6134 **2479** 15 k. black 90 60

2480 Golden Eagle

1990. Zoo Relief Fund. Multicoloured.

6135 10 k. + 5 k. Type **2480** . . . 35 20
6136 20 k. + 10 k. Saker falcon ("Falco cherrug") 90 60
6137 20 k. + 10 k. Raven ("Corvus corax") 90 60

2481 Etching by G. A. Echeistov

2482 Goalkeeper and Players

1990. 550th Anniv of "Dzhangar" (Kalmuk folk epic).

6138 **2481** 10 k. ochre, brn & blk . 25 15

1990. Epic Poems of Soviet Union (3rd series). Illustrations by named artists. As T **2394**. Mult.

6139 10 k. "Manas" (Kirgizia) (T. Gertsen) (horiz) 25 15
6140 10 k. "Gurugli" (Tadzhikistan) (I. Martynov) (horiz) . . . 25 15
6141 10 k. "David Sasunsky" (Armenia) (M. Abegyan) . 25 15
6142 10 k. "Gerogly" (Turkmenistan) (I. Klychev) 25 15
6143 10 k. "Kalevipoeg" (Estonia) (O. Kallis) 25 15

1990. World Cup Football Championship, Italy. Multicoloured.

6144 5 k. Type **2482** 15 10
6145 10 k. Players 25 15
6146 15 k. Attempted tackle . . . 35 20
6147 25 k. Referee and players . . 55 30
6148 35 k. Goalkeeper saving ball . 1·10 65

2483 Globe and Finlandia Hall, Helsinki

2484 Competitors and Target

1990. 15th Anniv of European Security and Co-operation Conference, Helsinki.

6149 **2483** 15 k. multicoloured . . 35 20

1990. 45th World Shooting Championships, Moscow.

6150 **2484** 15 k. multicoloured . . 35 20

2485 Glaciology Research

1990. Soviet–Australian Scientific Co-operation in Antarctica. Multicoloured.

6151 5 k. Type **2485** 15 10
6152 50 k. Krill (marine biology research) . . . . 1·50 1·00

2486 Emblem and Sports Pictograms

1990. Goodwill Games, Seattle.

6154 **2486** 10 k. multicoloured . . 25 15

2488 Greylag Geese

1990. Poultry. Multicoloured.

6156 5 k. Type **2488** 25 10
6157 10 k. Adlers (chickens) . . . 25 15
6158 15 k. Common turkeys . . . 35 20

2489 Mallards

1990. Ducks (2nd series). Multicoloured.

6159 5 k. Type **2489** 15 10
6160 15 k. Goldeneyes 40 20
6161 20 k. Red-crested pochards . . 50 25

1990. Lenin Soviet Children's Fund. Children's Paintings. As T **2437**. Multicoloured.

6162 5 k. + 2 k. Clown 20 10
6163 5 k. + 2 k. Ladies in crinolines 20 10
6164 5 k. + 2 k. Children with banner 20 10

1990. Historical Monuments (2nd series). As T **2464**. Multicoloured.

6165 15 k. St. Nshan's Church, Akhpat (Armenia) 35 20
6166 15 k. Shirvanshah Palace, Baku (Azerbaijan) 35 20
6167 15 k. Soroki Fortress and statue of Stefan III, Kishinev (Moldavia) 35 20
6168 15 k. Spaso-Efrosinevsky Cathedral, Polotsk (Byelorussia) 35 20
6169 15 k. St. Peter's Church and 16th-century Riga (Latvia) 35 20
6170 15 k. St. Nicholas's Church and carving of city arms, Tallin (Estonia) 35 20
6171 15 k. Mtatsminda Pantheon and statue of Nikoloz Baratashvili, Tbilisi (Georgia) 35 20
6172 15 k. Cathedral and bell tower, Vilnius (Lithuania) 35 20

2490 Sordes

1990. Prehistoric Animals. Multicoloured.

6173 1 k. Type **2490** 10 10
6174 3 k. Chalicotherium (vert) . . 10 10
6175 5 k. Indricotherium (vert) . . 15 10
6176 10 k. Saurolophus (vert) . . 25 15
6177 20 k. Thyestes 45 25

2491 "St. Basil's Cathedral and Kremlin, Moscow" (Sanjay Adhikari)

2492 Pigeon Post

1990. Indo–Soviet Friendship. Children's Paintings. Multicoloured.

6178 10 k. Type **2491** 25 10
6179 10 k. "Life in India" (Tanya Vorontsova) 25 10

1990. Letter Writing Week.

6180 **2492** 5 k. blue 15 10

2493 Traffic on Urban Roads

2495 Killer Whales

1990. Traffic Safety Week.

6181 **2493** 5 k. multicoloured . . . 15 10

1990. Traditional Musical Instruments (2nd series). As T **2455**. Multicoloured.

6183 10 k. Azerbaijani balalian, shar and caz (stringed instruments), zurna and drum 25 15
6184 10 k. Georgian bagpipes, tambourine, flute, pipes and chonguri (stringed instrument) 25 15
6185 10 k. Kazakh flute, rattle, daubra and kobyz (stringed instruments) 25 15
6186 10 k. Lithuanian bagpipes, horns and kankles 25 15

1990. Marine Mammals.

6187 25 k. Type **2495** 55 30
6188 25 k. Northern sealions . . . 55 30
6189 25 k. Sea otter 55 30
6190 25 k. Common dolphin . . . 55 30

2496 "Lenin among Delegates to Second Congress of Soviets" (S. V. Gerasimov)

2497 Ivan Bunin (1933)

1990. 73rd Anniv of October Revolution.

6191 **2496** 5 k. multicoloured . . . 15 10

1990. Nobel Prize Winners for Literature.

6192 **2497** 15 k. brown 35 20
6193 – 15 k. brown 35 20
6194 – 15 k. black 35 20

DESIGNS: No. 6193, Mikhail Sholokhov (1965); No. 6194, Boris Pasternak.

2498 "Sever-2"

1990. Research Submarines. Multicoloured.

6195 5 k. Type **2498** 15 10
6196 10 k. "Tinro-2" 25 15
6197 15 k. "Argus" 35 20
6198 25 k. "Paisis" 55 30
6199 35 k. "Mir" . . . . 1·10 65

2499 "Motherland" Statue (E. Kocher), Screen and Emblem

Филателистическая выставка „Армения-90" (2500)

Восстановление, милосердие, помощь (2501)

1990. "Armenia '90" Stamp Exhibition, Yerevan. (a) Type **2499**.

6200 **2499** 10 k. multicoloured . . 25 15

(b) Nos. 5957/9 optd with T **2500** or as T **2501**.

6201 **2500** 20 k. + 10 k. mult . . 30 35
6202 **2501** 30 k. + 15 k. mult . . 45 50
6203 50 k. + 25 k. mult . . 75 50

2502 S. A. Vaupshasov

2503 Soviet and Japanese Flags above Earth

1990. Intelligence Agents.

6204 **2502** 5 k. deep green, green and black 15 10
6205 – 5 k. deep brown, brown and black 15 10
6206 – 5 k. deep blue, blue and black 15 10
6207 – 5 k. brown, buff & blk 15 10
6208 – 5 k. brown, bistre and black 15 10

DESIGNS: No. 6205, R. I. Abel; No. 6206, Kim Philby; No. 6207, I. D. Kudrya; No. 6208, K. T. Molodyi.

1990. Soviet–Japanese Space Flight.

6209 **2503** 20 k. multicoloured . . 20 25

2504 Grandfather Frost and Toys

1990. New Year.

6210 **2504** 5 k. multicoloured . . 15 10

2505 "Unkrada"

1990. Soviet Culture Fund. Paintings by N. K. Rerikh. Multicoloured.

6211 10 k. + 5 k. Type **2505** . . 35 20
6212 20 k. + 10 k. "Pskovo-Pechorsky Monastery" . . 30 35

2507 Globe, Eiffel Tower and Flags

1990. "Charter for New Europe". Signing of European Conventional Arms Treaty, Paris.

6214 **2507** 30 k. multicoloured . . 30 35

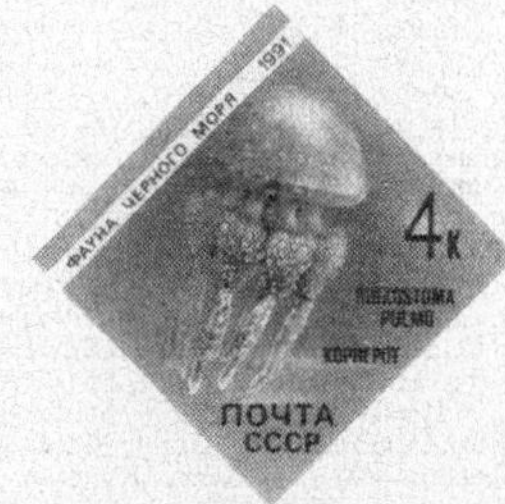

2508 Jellyfish

1991. Marine Animals. Multicoloured.

6215 4 k. Type **2508** 15 10
6216 5 k. Anemone 15 10
6217 10 k. Atlantic spiny dogfish . 25 15
6218 15 k. European anchovy . . 30 20
6219 20 k. Bottle-nosed dolphin . . 45 25

2509 Keres

1991. 75th Birth Anniv of Paul Keres (chess player).

6220 **2509** 15 k. brown 35 20

2510 Radioactive Particles killing Vegetation

1991. 5th Anniv of Chernobyl Nuclear Power Station Disaster.

6221 **2510** 15 k. multicoloured . . 35 20

2511 "Sorrento Coast with View of Capri" (Shchedrin)

1991. Birth Bicentenary of Silvestr Shchedrin and 150th Birth Anniv of Arkhip Kuindzhi (painters). Multicoloured.

6222 10 k. Type **2511** 25 15
6223 10 k. "New Rome. View of St. Angelo's Castle" (Shchedrin) 25 15
6224 10 k. "Evening in the Ukraine" (Kuindzhi) 25 15
6225 10 k. "Birch Grove" (Kuindzhi) 25 15

2512 White Stork

1991. Zoo Relief Fund.

6226 **2512** 10 k. + 5 k. mult . . . 35 30

2513 Fish and Bell Tower, Volga

1991. Environmental Protection. Multicoloured.

6227 10 k. Type **2513** 25 15
6228 15 k. Sable and Lake Baikal . 35 20
6229 20 k. Saiga and dried bed of Aral Sea 45 25

1991. Historical Monuments (3rd series). As T **2464**. Multicoloured.

6231 15 k. Minaret, Uzgen, Kirgizia 35 20
6232 15 k. Mohammed Bashar Mausoleum, Tadzhikistan . 35 20
6233 15 k. Talkhatan-baba Mosque, Turkmenistan 35 20

2515 G. Shelikhov and Kodiak, 1784

1991. 500th Anniv of Discovery of America by Columbus. Russian Settlements.

6234 **2515** 20 k. blue and black . . 45 25
6235 – 30 k. bistre, brown and black 65 35
6236 – 50 k. orange, brown and black . . . . 1·00 50

DESIGNS: 30 k. Aleksandr Baranov and Sitka, 1804; 50 k. I. Kuskov and Fort Ross, California, 1812.

2516 Satellite and Liner

2517 Yury Gagarin in Uniform

1991. 10th Anniv of United Nations Transport and Communications in Asia and the Pacific Programme.

6237 **2516** 10 k. multicoloured . . 20 10

1991. Cosmonautics Day. 30th Anniv of First Man in Space. Each brown.

6238 25 k. Type **2517** 15 25
6239 25 k. Gagarin wearing space suit 15 25
6240 25 k. Gagarin in uniform with cap 15 25
6241 25 k. Gagarin in civilian dress 15 25

2519 "May 1945" (A. and S. Tkachev)

1991. Victory Day.

6244 **2519** 5 k. multicoloured . . . 10 10

2520 "Lenin working on Book 'Materialism and Empirical Criticism' in Geneva Library" (P. Belousov)

1991. 121st Birth Anniv of Lenin.

6245 **2520** 5 k. multicoloured . . . 10 10

2521 Prokofiev

1991. Birth Centenary of Sergei Prokofiev (composer).

6246 **2521** 15 k. brown 30 15

2522 "Cypripedium calceolus"

2523 Ilya I. Mechnikov (medicine, 1908)

1991. Orchids. Multicoloured.

6247 3 k. Type **2522** 10 10
6248 5 k. "Orchis purpurea" . . . 10 10
6249 10 k. "Ophrys apifera" . . . 15 10
6250 20 k. "Calypso bulbosa" . . 15 20
6251 25 k. "Epipactis palustris" . . 15 25

1991. Nobel Prize Winners. Each black.

6252 15 k. Type **2523** 30 15
6253 15 k. Ivan P. Pavlov (medicine, 1904) 30 15
6254 15 k. A. D. Sakharov (physics, 1975) 30 15

2524 Soviet and British Flags in Space

1991. Soviet–British Space Flight.

6255 **2524** 20 k. multicoloured . . 15 20

2525 Saroyan

1991. 10th Death Anniv of William Saroyan (writer).

6256 **2525** 1 r. multicoloured . . . 65 40

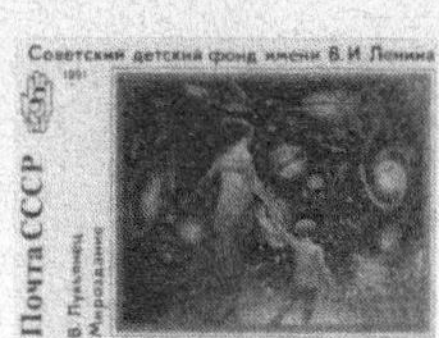

2526 "The Universe"

1991. Lenin Soviet Children's Fund. Paintings by V. Lukyanets. Multicoloured.

6257 10 k. Type **2526** 20 10
6258 10 k. "Another Planet" . . . 20 10

INDEX

Countries can be quickly located by referring to the index at the end of this volume.

2527 Miniature from "Ostromirov Gospel" (first book written in Cyrillic), 1056–57

1991. Culture of Medieval Russia. Multicoloured.
6259 10 k. Type **2527** 15 10
6260 15 k. Page from "Russian Truth" (code of laws), 11th-13th century 15 10
6261 20 k. Portrait of Sergy Radonezhsky (embroidered book cover), 1424 . . . . 15 20
6262 25 k. "The Trinity" (icon, Andrei Rublev), 1411 . . . 15 25
6263 30 k. Illustration from "Book of the Apostles", 1564 . . . . 20 30

2528 Pintails **2529** Emblem

1991. Ducks (3rd series). Multicoloured.
6264 5 k. Type **2528** 15 10
6265 15 k. Greater scaups 40 20
6266 20 k. White-headed ducks . . 50 25

1991. European Conference on Security and Co-operation Session, Moscow.
6267 **2529** 10 k. multicoloured . . . 20 10

2530 Patroness **2531** Woman in Traditional Costume

1991. Soviet Charity and Health Fund.
6268 **2530** 20 k. + 10 k. mult . . 20 30

1991. 1st Anniv of Declaration of Ukrainian Sovereignty.
6269 **2531** 30 k. multicoloured . . 20 30

2532 "Albatross" **2534** Girl with Letter

2533 "Sv. Pyotr" and Route Map

1991. Airships. Multicoloured.
6270 1 k. Type **2532** 10 10
6271 3 k. GA-42 . . . . 15 10
6272 4 k. N.1 "Norge" (horiz) . . 15 10
6273 5 k. "Pobeda" (horiz) 15 10
6274 20 k. "Graf Zeppelin" (horiz) 55 20

1991. 250th Anniv of Bering's and Chirkov's Expedition. Multicoloured.
6275 30 k. Type **2533** 60 30
6276 30 k. Sighting land 60 30

1991. Letter Writing Week.
6277 **2534** 7 k. brown 15 10

2535 Bell and Bell Towers **2536** Kayak Race and "Santa Maria"

1991. Soviet Culture Fund.
6278 **2535** 20 k. + 10 k. mult . . 20 30

1991. Olympic Games, Barcelona (1992) (1st issue). Multicoloured.
6279 10 k. Type **2536** 10 10
6280 20 k. Running and Barcelona Cathedral 15 20
6281 30 k. Football and stadium . 20 30
See also Nos. 6358/61.

2537 Rainbow, Globe and Flags **2538** Ascension Day (Armenia)

1991. Soviet–Austrian Space Flight.
6282 **2537** 20 k. multicoloured . . 15 20

1991. Folk Festivals. Multicoloured.
6283 15 k. Type **2538** 30 15
6284 15 k. Women carrying dishes of wheat (Novruz holiday, Azerbaijan) 30 15
6285 15 k. Throwing garlands in water (Ivan Kupala summer holiday, Byelorussia) . . . 30 15
6286 15 k. Stick wrestling and dancing round decorated tree (New Year, Estonia) (horiz) 30 15
6287 15 k. Masked dancers (Berikaoba spring holiday, Georgia) 30 15
6288 15 k. Riders with goat skin (Kazakhstan) (horiz) . . . 30 15
6289 15 k. Couple on horses (Kirgizia) (horiz) 30 15
6290 15 k. Couple leaping over flames (Ligo (Ivan Kupala) holiday, Latvia) (horiz) . . 30 15
6291 15 k. Family on way to church (Palm Sunday, Lithuania) (horiz) 30 15
6292 15 k. Man in beribboned hat and musicians (Plugusorul (New Year) holiday, Moldova) 30 15
6293 15 k. Sledge ride (Shrovetide, Russia) 30 15
6294 15 k. Musicians on carpet and stilt-walkers (Novruz holiday, Tadzikistan) 30 15
6295 15 k. Wrestlers (Harvest holiday, Turkmenistan) (horiz) 30 15
6296 15 k. Dancers and couple with lute and tambourine (Christmas, Ukraine) (horiz) 30 15
6297 15 k. Girls with tulips (Tulip holiday, Uzbekistan) . . . 30 15

2539 Dimitry Komar **2540** Federation Government House and Flag

1991. Defeat of Attempted Coup. Multicoloured.
6298 7 k. Type **2539** 15 10
6299 7 k. Ilya Krichevsky 15 10
6300 7 k. Vladimir Usov 15 10
Nos. 6298/6300 depict victims killed in opposing the attempted coup.

1991. Election of Boris Yeltsin as President of the Russian Federation.
6302 **2540** 7 k. blue, gold and red 15 10

1991. Traditional Musical Instruments (3rd series). As T **2455**. Multicoloured.
6303 10 k. Kirgiz flutes, komuzes and kyyak (string instruments) 20 10
6304 10 k. Latvian ganurags and stabule (wind), tambourine, duga and kokle (string instruments) 20 10
6305 10 k. Moldavian flute, bagpipes, nai (pipes), kobza and tsambal (string instruments) 20 10

2541 Decorations and Gifts **2542** Nikolai Mikhailovich Karamzin

1991. New Year.
6306 **2541** 7 k. multicoloured . . . 15 10

1991. Historians' Birth Anniversaries. Mult.
6307 10 k. Type **2542** (225th anniv) 20 10
6308 10 k. V. O. Klyuchevsky (150th anniv) 20 10
6309 10 k. S. M. Solovev (171st anniv) 20 10
6310 10 k. V. N. Tatishchev (after A. Osipov) (305th anniv) . 20 10

2543 Cross-country Skiing and Ski Jumping **2546** Golden Gate, Vladimir

1992. Winter Olympic Games, Albertville. Mult.
6311 14 k. Type **2543** 10 15
6312 1 r. Aerobatic skiing 35 35
6313 2 r. Two and four-man bobsleighs 65 65

1992.
6317 **2546** 10 k. orange 10 10
6318 – 15 k. brown 10 10
6319 – 20 k. red 10 10
6320 – 25 k. red 10 10
6321 – 30 k. black 10 10
6322 – 50 k. black 10 10
6323 – 55 k. turquoise 10 10
6324 – 60 k. green 10 10
6324a – 80 k. purple 15 10
6325 – 1 r. brown 20 10
6326 – 1 r. 50 green 30 15
6327 – 2 r. blue 40 20
6328 – 3 r. red 15 10
6328a – 4 r. brown 10 10
6329 – 5 r. brown 45 20
6329a – 6 r. blue 10 10
6330 – 10 r. blue 45 45
6330a – 15 r. brown 30 15
6331 – 25 r. red . . . . . . 1·10 1·10
6332 – 45 r. blue 80 40
6341 – 50 r. violet 15 15
6333 – 75 r. brown . . . . . 1·60 80
6334 – 100 r. green . . . . . 2·00 1·00
6334a **2546** 150 r. blue 10 10
6342 – 250 r. green 35 15
6334c – 300 r. red 10 10
6347 – 500 r. red 65 35
6334e – 750 r. green 50 25
6335 – 1000 r. grey 70 35
6335a – 1500 r. green . . . . 1·00 50
6335b – 2500 r. brown . . . . 1·75 90
6335c – 5000 r. blue . . . . . 3·50 1·75
DESIGNS: 15 k. Pskov Kremlin; 20, 50 k. St. George killing dragon; 25, 55 k. Victory Arch, Moscow; 30, 80 k. "Millenium of Russia" monument (M. Mikeshin), Novgorod; 60 k., 300 r. Minin and Pozharsky Statue, Moscow; 1, 4 r. Church, Kizki; 1 r. 50, 6 r. Statue of Peter I, St. Petersburg; 2 r. St. Basil's Cathedral, Moscow; 3 r. Tretyakov Gallery, Moscow; 5 r. Morosov House, Moscow; 10 r. St. Isaac's Cathedral, St. Petersburg; 15, 45 r. "The Horse Tamer", St. Petersburg; 25, 75 r. Yuri Dolgoruky Monument, Moscow; 50 r. Rostov Kremlin; 100 r. Moscow Kremlin; 250 r. Church, Bogulyubov; 500 r. Lomonosov University, Moscow; 750 r. National Library, Moscow; 1000 r. St. Peter and Paul Cathedral, St. Petersburg; 1500 r. Pushkin Museum, Moscow; 2500 r. Admiralty, St. Petersburg; 5000 r. Bolshoi Theatre, Moscow.

2547 "Victory" (N. N. Baskakov) **2548** Capercaillie, Oak and Pine

1992. 47th Anniv of Victory in Second World War.
6350 **2547** 5 k. multicoloured . . . 10 10

1992. Priioksko–Terrasnyi Nature Reserve.
6351 **2548** 50 k. multicoloured . . 10 10

2549 "Mir" Space Station, Flags and Cosmonauts **2551** Pinocchio

1992. Russian–German Joint Space Flight.
6352 **2549** 5 r. multicoloured . . . 40 30

1992. Characters from Children's Books (1st series). Multicoloured.
6354 25 k. Type **2551** 10 10
6355 30 k. Cipollino 10 10
6356 35 k. Dunno 10 10
6357 50 k. Karlson 10 10
See also Nos. 6391/5.

2552 Russian Cosmonaut and Space Shuttle **2553** Handball

1992. International Space Year. Multicoloured.
6358 25 r. Type **2552** 65 35
6359 25 r. American astonaut and "Mir" space station . . . 65 35
6360 25 r. "Apollo" and "Vostok" spacecraft and sputnik . . 65 35
6361 25 r. "Soyuz", "Mercury" and "Gemini" spacecraft . . . 65 35
Nos. 6344/47 were issued together, se-tenant, forming a composite design.

1992. Olympic Games, Barcelona (2nd issue).
6362 **2553** 1 r. multicoloured . . . 20 10
6363 – 2 r. red, blue & black . . 40 20
6364 – 3 r. red, green & black . 35 35
DESIGNS—HORIZ: 2 r. Fencing; 3 r. Judo.

2554 L. A. Zagoskin and Yukon River, Alaska, 1842–44

1992. Expeditions. Multicoloured.
6365 55 k. Type **2554** 10 10
6366 70 k. N. N. Miklukho-Maklai in New Guinea, 1871–74 . . . 15 10
6367 1 r. G. I. Langsdorf and route map of expedition to Brazil, 1822–28 . . . . 20 10

2555 Garganeys

1992. Ducks (4th series). Multicoloured.
6368 1 r. Type **2555** 15 10
6369 2 r. European pochards . . . 20 15
6370 3 r. Falcated teals 30 35

2556 "Taj Mahal Mausoleum in Agra"

1992. 150th Birth Anniv of Vasily Vasilevich Vereshchagin (painter).
6371 1 r. 50 Type **2556** 30 15
6372 1 r. 50 "Don't Touch, Let Me Approach!" 30 15

2557 "The Saviour" (icon, Andrei Rublev)

2558 Cathedral of the Assumption

1992.

6373 **2557** 1 r. multicoloured . . . 20 10

1992. Moscow Kremlin Cathedrals. Multicoloured.

6374	1 r. Type **2558**	20	10
6375	1 r. Cathedral of the Annunciation (15th century)	20	10
6376	1 r. Archangel Cathedral (16th century)	20	10

See also Nos. 6415/17 and 6440/2.

2559 Russian "Nutcracker" Puppets

2560 "Meeting of Joachim and Anne"

1992. Centenary of First Production of Tchaikovsky's "Nutcracker" Ballet. Multicoloured.

6377	10 r. Type **2559**	35	15
6378	10 r. German "Nutcracker" puppets	35	15
6379	25 r. Pas de deux from ballet	85	40
6380	25 r. Dance of the toys	85	40

1992. Icons. Multicoloured.

6381	10 r. Type **2560**	50	45
6382	10 r. "Madonna and Child"	50	45
6383	10 r. "Archangel Gabriel" (head)	50	45
6384	10 r. "Saint Nicolas" (½-length portrait)	50	45

2561 Clockface and Festive Symbols

2562 "Discovery of America" Monument (Z. Tsereteli)

1992. New Year.

6385 **2561** 50 k. multicoloured . . 10 10

1992. 500th Anniv of Discovery of America by Columbus.

6386 **2562** 15 r. multicoloured . . 70 70

2563 Petipa and Scene from "Paquita"

2564 Scrub 'n' Rub

1993. 175th Birth Anniv of Marius Petipa (choreographer). Multicoloured.

6387	25 r. Type **2563**	20	10
6388	25 r. "Sleeping Beauty", 1890	20	10
6389	25 r. "Swan Lake", 1895	20	10
6390	25 r. "Raimunda", 1898	20	10

1993. Characters from Children's Books (2nd series). Illustrations by Kornei Chukovsky. Mult.

6391	2 r. Type **2564**	10	10
6392	3 r. Big Cockroach	15	10
6393	10 r. The Buzzer Fly	20	10
6394	15 r. Doctor Doolittle	30	15
6395	25 r. Barmalei	55	30

Nos. 6391/5 were issued together, se-tenant, forming a composite design.

2565 Castle

2566 Part of Diorama in Belgorod Museum

1993. 700th Anniv of Vyborg.

6396 **2565** 10 r. multicoloured . . 35 25

1993. Victory Day. 50th Anniv of Battle of Kursk.

6397 **2566** 10 r. multicoloured . . 35 20

2567 African Violet

2568 "Molniya 3"

1993. Pot Plants. Multicoloured.

6398	10 r. Type **2567**	20	10
6399	15 r. "Hibiscus rosa-sinensis"	25	15
6400	25 r. "Cyclamen persicum"	55	30
6401	50 r. "Fuchsia hybrida"	1·10	55
6402	100 r. "Begonia semperflorens"	1·90	1·10

1993. Communications Satellites. Multicoloured.

6403	25 r. Type **2568**	20	10
6404	45 r. "Ekran M"	35	15
6405	50 r. "Gorizont"	85	25
6406	75 r. "Luch"	1·25	35
6407	100 r. "Ekspress"	1·60	75

2569 Snuff Box (Dmitry Kolesnikov) and Tankard

2570 Map

1993. Silverware. Multicoloured.

6409	15 r. Type **2569**	10	10
6410	25 r. Teapot	40	10
6411	45 r. Vase	75	35
6412	75 r. Tray and candlestick	1·25	55
6413	100 r. Cream jug, coffee pot and sugar basin (Aleksandr Kordes)	1·60	75

1993. Novgorod Kremlin. As T **2558**. Mult.

6415	25 r. Kukui and Knyazhaya Towers (14th–17th century)	20	10
6416	25 r. St. Sophia's Cathedral (11th century)	20	10
6417	25 r. St. Sophia belfry (15th–18th century)	20	10

1993. Inauguration of Denmark–Russia Submarine Cable and 500th Anniv of Friendship Treaty.

6419 **2570** 90 r. green & dp green 50 25

2571 Steller's Eider

1993. Ducks (5th series). Multicoloured.

6420	90 r. Type **2571**	55	25
6421	100 r. Eider	35	30
6422	250 r. King eider	90	45

2572 Ringed Seal

1993. Sea Animals. Multicoloured.

6423	50 r. Type **2572**	25	15
6424	60 r. "Paralithodes brevipes" (crab)	30	15
6425	90 r. Japanese common squid	50	25
6426	100 r. Salmon trout	50	30
6427	250 r. Fulmar	90	45

2573 Ceramic Candlestick, Skopino

2574 Banknotes and Coins

1993. Traditional Art. Multicoloured.

6428	50 r. Type **2573**	30	15
6429	50 r. Painted tray with picture "Summer Troika", Zhostovo (horiz)	30	15
6430	100 r. Painted box, lid and distaff, Gorodets	55	30
6431	100 r. Enamel icon of St. Dmitry of Solun, Rostov	55	30
6432	250 r. "The Resurrection" (lacquer miniature), Fedoskino	1·00	50

1993. 175th Anniv of Goznak (State printing works and mint).

6433 **2574** 100 r. multicoloured . . 25 35

2575 Peter I and "Goto Predestinatsiya"

1993. 300th Anniv of Russian Navy (1st issue). Mult.

6434	100 r. Type **2575**	15	10
6435	100 r. K. A. Shilder and first all-metal submarine	15	10
6436	100 r. I. A. Amosov and "Arkhimed" (frigate)	15	10
6437	100 r. I. G. Bubnov and "Bars" (submarine)	15	10
6438	100 r. B. M. Malinin and "Dekabrist" (submarine)	15	10
6439	100 r. A. I. Maslov and "Kirov" (cruiser)	15	10

See also Nos. 6502/5, 6559/62 and 6612/18.

1993. Moscow Kremlin. As T **2558**. Mult.

6440	100 r. Faceted Hall (15th century)	20	10
6441	100 r. Church of the Deposition of the Virgin's Robe (15th century)	20	10
6442	100 r. Grand Palace (17th century)	20	10

2576 Tiger

2577 Splash of Blood on Figure

1993. The Tiger. Multicoloured.

6443	50 r. Type **2576**	10	10
6444	100 r. Tiger in undergrowth	20	10
6445	250 r. Two tigers	45	25
6446	500 r. Tiger in snow	65	45

1993. Anti-AIDS Campaign.

6447 **2577** 90 r. multicoloured . . . 20 10

2578 Seasonal Decorations

1993. New Year.

6448 **2578** 25 r. multicoloured . . . 10 10

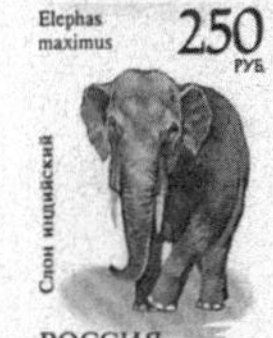

2579 Indian Elephant

1993. Animals. Multicoloured.

6449	250 r. Type **2579**	40	20
6450	250 r. Japanese white-necked crane	40	20
6451	250 r. Giant panda	40	20
6452	250 r. American bald eagle	40	20
6453	250 r. Dall's porpoise	40	20
6454	250 r. Koala	40	20
6455	250 r. Hawaiian monk seal	40	20
6456	250 r. Grey whale	40	20

2580 Rimsky-Korsakov and Scene from "Sadko"

1994. 150th Birth Anniv of Nikolai Rimsky-Korsakov (composer). Scenes from his operas. Multicoloured.

6457	250 r. Type **2580**	40	20
6458	250 r. "The Golden Cockerel"	40	20
6459	250 r. "The Tsar's Bride"	40	20
6460	250 r. "The Snow Maiden"	40	20

2581 "Epiphyllum peacockii"

2582 York Minster, Great Britain

1994. Cacti. Multicoloured.

6461	50 r. Type **2581**	10	10
6462	100 r. "Mammillaria swinglei"	20	10
6463	100 r. "Lophophora williamsii"	20	10
6464	250 r. "Opuntia basilaris"	40	20
6465	250 r. "Selenicereus grandiflorus"	40	20

1994. Churches. Multicoloured.

6466	150 r. Type **2582**	30	15
6467	150 r. Church, Athens	30	15
6468	150 r. Roskilde Cathedral, Denmark	30	15
6469	150 r. Notre Dame Cathedral, Paris	30	15
6470	150 r. St. Peter's, Vatican City	30	15
6471	150 r. Cologne Cathedral, Germany	30	15
6472	150 r. Seville Cathedral, Spain	30	15
6473	150 r. St. Basil's Cathedral, Moscow	30	15
6474	150 r. St. Patrick's Cathedral, New York	30	15

2583 "Soyuz" entering Earth's Atmosphere and "TsF-18" Centrifuge

1994. Yury Gagarin Cosmonaut Training Centre. Multicoloured.

6475	100 r. Type **2583**	10	10
6476	250 r. "Soyuz"–"Mir" space complex and "Mir" simulator	30	15
6477	500 r. Cosmonaut on space walk and hydrolaboratory	60	30

2584 Map and Rocket Launchers (Liberation of Russia)

1994. 50th Anniv of Liberation. Multicoloured.

6478	100 r. Type **2584**	20	10
6479	100 r. Map and airplanes (Ukraine)	20	10
6480	100 r. Map, tank and soldiers (Byelorussia)	20	10

2585 Red Gate, Moscow

1994. Architects' Anniversaries.
6481 **2585** 50 r. sepia, black and brown 10 15
6482 – 100 r. brown, black and flesh 15 10
6483 – 150 r. green, black and olive 20 10
6483 – 300 r. violet, black and grey 45 25

DESIGNS: 50 r. Type **2585** (D. V. Ukhtomsky, death centenary); 100 r. Academy of Sciences, St. Petersburg (Giacomo Quarenghi, 250th birth anniv); 150 r. Trinity Cathedral, St. Petersburg (V. P. Stasov, 225th birth anniv); 300 r. Church of Christ the Saviour, Moscow (K. A. Ton, birth bicentenary).

2586 "Christ and the Sinner"

1994. 150th Birth Anniv of Vasily Dmitrievich Polenev (painter). Multicoloured.
6485 150 r. Type **2586** 25 15
6486 150 r. "Golden Autumn" . . 25 15

2587 European Wigeon **2588** Games Emblem and Runners

1994. Ducks (6th series). Multicoloured.
6487 150 r. Type **2587** 20 10
6488 250 r. Tufted duck 30 15
6489 300 r. Baikal teal 50 25

1994. 3rd Goodwill Games, St. Petersburg.
6490 **2588** 100 r. multicoloured . . 15 10

2589 Pyotr Leonidovich Kapitsa **2591** Design Motifs of First Russian Stamp

2590 Olympic Flag

1994. Physics Nobel Prize Winners' Birth Anniversaries. Each sepia.
6491 150 r. Type **2589** (centenary) 30 15
6492 150 r. Pavel Alekseevich Cherenkov (90th) 30 15

1994. Centenary of International Olympic Committee.
6493 **2590** 250 r. multicoloured . . 30 15

1994. Russian Stamp Day.
6494 **2591** 125 r. multicoloured . . 20 10

2592 Snuff Box (D. Vinogradov) **2593** Centre of Asia Obelisk

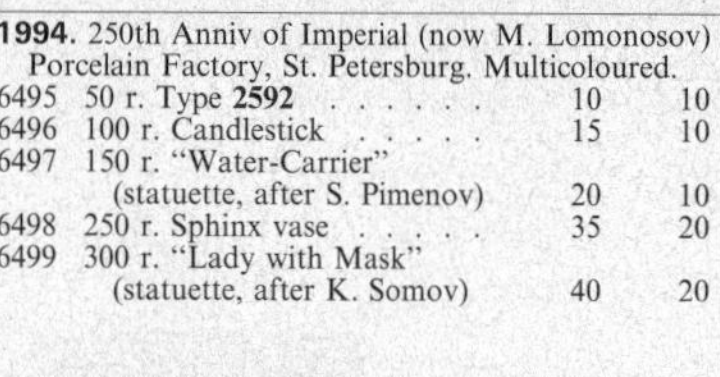

1994. 250th Anniv of Imperial (now M. Lomonosov) Porcelain Factory, St. Petersburg. Multicoloured.
6495 50 r. Type **2592** 10 10
6496 100 r. Candlestick 15 10
6497 150 r. "Water-Carrier" (statuette, after S. Pimenov) 20 10
6498 250 r. Sphinx vase 35 20
6499 300 r. "Lady with Mask" (statuette, after K. Somov) 40 20

1994. 50th Anniv of Accession of Tuva to Soviet Union.
6501 **2593** 125 r. mulitcoloured . . 15 10

2594 Vice-Admiral V. M. Golovnin (Kurile Islands, 1811)

1994. 300th Anniv (1993) of Russian Navy (2nd issue). Explorations. Multicoloured.
6502 250 r. Type **2594** 20 10
6503 250 r. Admiral I. F. Krusenshtern (first Russain round-the-world expedition, 1803–06) 20 10
6504 250 r. Admiral F. P. Vrangel (Alaska, 1829–35) 20 10
6505 250 r. Admiral F. P. Litke (Novaya Zemlya, 1821–24) 20 10

2595 Horses and Father Christmas

1994. New Year.
6506 **2595** 125 r. blue, red and black 15 10

2596 Griboedov (after Utkin)

1995. Birth Bicentenary of Aleksandr Sergeevich Griboedov (dramatist and diplomat).
6507 **2596** 250 r. brown, light brown and black 25 10

2597 "Sheherazade"

1995. 115th Birth Anniv of Mikhail Fokine (choreographer). Scenes from Ballets. Multicoloured.
6508 500 r. Type **2597** 35 20
6509 500 r. "The Fire Bird" . . . 35 20
6510 500 r. "Petrushka" 35 20

2598 Kutuzov (after J. Doe) and Sculptures from Monument, Moscow

1995. 250th Birth Anniv of Field-Marshal Mikhail Ilarionovich Kutuzov, Prince of Smolensk.
6511 **2598** 300 r. multicoloured . . 20 10

2599 English Yard, Varvarka Street **2600** Syringes and Drugs around Addict

1995. 850th Anniv (1997) of Moscow (1st issue). Multicoloured.
6512 125 r. Type **2599** 10 10
6513 250 r. House of Averky Kirillov (scribe), Bersenevskaya Embankment 15 10
6514 300 r. Volkov house, Bolshoi Kharitonevsky Lane . . . 20 10
See also Nos. 6600/2.

1995. U.N. Anti-drugs Decade.
6515 **2600** 150 r. multicoloured . . 15 10

2601 Shoreline

1995. Endangered Animals. Multicoloured.
6516 250 r. Type **2601** 20 10
6517 250 r. Ringed seal 20 10
6518 250 r. Lynx 20 10
6519 250 r. Landscape 20 10

2602 Tomb of the Unknown Soldier, Moscow

1995. 50th Anniv of End of Second World War. Multicoloured.
6520 250 r. Sir Winston Churchill, U.S. Pres. Franklin Roosevelt and Iosif Stalin (Yalta Conference) (horiz) 15 10
6521 250 r. Storm of the Reichstag, Berlin (horiz) 15 10
6522 250 r. Flags, map of Germany and German banners (Potsdam Conference) . . . 15 10
6523 250 r. Aircraft (Manchurian Operation) (horiz) 15 10
6524 250 r. Urn with victims' ashes, Auschwitz, and memorial, Sachsenhausen (liberation of concentration camps) (horiz) 15 10
6525 250 r. Type **2602** 15 10
6526 500 r. Victory Parade, Moscow 30 15

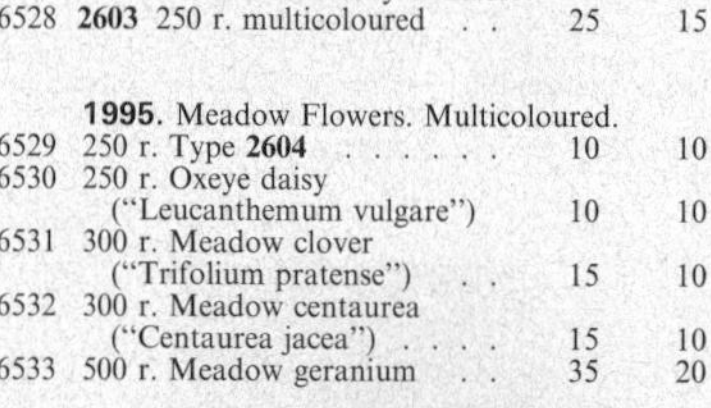
2603 Aleksandr Popov (radio pioneer) and Radio-telegraph Equipment **2604** Branchy Bell Flower ("Campanula patula")

1995. Centenary of Radio.
6528 **2603** 250 r. multicoloured . . 25 15

1995. Meadow Flowers. Multicoloured.
6529 250 r. Type **2604** 10 10
6530 250 r. Oxeye daisy ("Leucanthemum vulgare") 10 10
6531 300 r. Meadow clover ("Trifolium pratense") . . 15 10
6532 300 r. Meadow centaurea ("Centaurea jacea") 15 10
6533 500 r. Meadow geranium . . 35 20

2605 Sky Lark ("Alauda arvensis") **2606** U.S. Space Shuttle "Atlantis"

1995. Songbirds. Multicoloured.
6534 250 r. Type **2605** 15 10
6535 250 r. Song thrush ("Turdus philomelos") 15 10
6536 500 r. Goldfinch ("Carduelis carduelis") 30 15
6537 500 r. Bluethroat ("Cyanosylvia svecica") 30 15
6538 750 r. Thrush nightingale . . 45 25

1995. Russian–American Space Co-operation. Multicoloured.
6539 1500 r. Type **2606** 80 40
6540 1500 r. "Mir" space station . 80 40
6541 1500 r. "Apollo" spacecraft . 80 40
6542 1500 r. "Soyuz" spacecraft . . 80 40
Nos. 6539/42 were issued together, se-tenant, forming a composite design of the spacecraft over Earth.

2607 Cathedral of the Trinity, Jerusalem **2608** Kremlin Cathedrals

1995. Russian Orthodox Churches Abroad. Mult.
6543 300 r. Type **2607** 15 10
6544 300 r. Apostles Saints Peter and Paul Cathedral, Karlovy Vary, Czechoslovakia . . . 15 10
6545 500 r. St. Nicholas's Cathedral, Vienna 25 15
6546 500 r. St. Nicholas's Cathedral, New York 25 15
6547 750 r. St. Aleksei's Cathedral, Leipzig 40 20

1995. 900th Anniv of Ryazan.
6548 **2608** 250 r. multicoloured . . 15 10

2609 Easter Egg with Model of "Shtandart" (yacht)

1995. Faberge Exhibits in Moscow Kremlin Museum. Multicoloured.
6549 150 r. Type **2609** 10 10
6550 250 r. Goblet 15 10
6551 300 r. Cross pendant 15 10
6552 500 r. Ladle 25 15
6553 750 r. Easter egg with model of Alexander III monument . 40 20

2610 Harlequin Duck

1995. Ducks (7th series). Multicoloured.
6555 500 r. Type **2610** 25 15
6556 750 r. Baer's pochard 40 20
6557 1000 r. Goosander 60 30

2612 "The Battle of Grengam, July 27, 1720" (F. Perrault)

1995. 300th Anniv (1993) of Russian Navy (3rd issue). Paintings. Multicoloured.
6559 250 r. Type **2612** 15 10
6560 300 r. "Preparations for Attacking the Turkish Fleet in the Bay of Cesme, Night of June 26, 1770" (P. Hackert) 20 10
6561 500 r. "The Battle at the Revel Roadstead, May 2, 1790" (A. Bogolyubov) 35 20
6562 750 r. "The Kronstadt Roadstead" (I. Aivazovsky) 45 25

2613 State Flag and Arms **2614** Emblem and San Francisco Conference, 1945

1995. Constitution of the Russian Federation.
6563 **2613** 500 r. multicoloured . . 25 15

1995. 50th Anniv of U.N.O.
6564 **2614** 500 r. brown, blue and yellow 25 15

2615 White Storks in Nest

1995. Europa. Peace and Freedom. Multicoloured.
6565 1500 r. Type **2615** 80 40
6566 1500 r. Stork flying over landscape 80 40
Nos. 6565/6 were issued together, se-tenant, forming a composite design.

2616 "Christ's Nativity" (icon, Assumption Cathedral, St. Cyril's Monastery, White Sea)

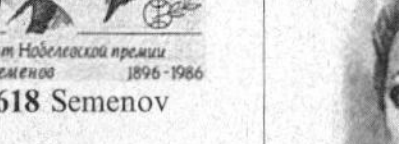
2618 Semenov

2617 Yury Dolgoruky (1090–1157), Kiev and Building of Moscow

1995. Christmas.
6567 **2616** 500 r. multicoloured . . 25 15

1995. History of Russian State. Multicoloured.
6568 1000 r. Type **2617** 55 30
6569 1000 r. Aleksandr Nevsky (1220–63), Battle of Lake Peipus and as Grand Duke of Vladimir 55 30
6570 1000 r. Mikhail Yaroslavich (1271–1318), Tver and torture by the Golden Horde . . . 55 30
6571 1000 r. Dmitry Donskoi (1350–89), Moscow Kremlin and Battle of Kulikovo 55 30
6572 1000 r. Ivan III (1440–1505), marriage to Sophia Paleologa and Battle of Ugra River . . 55 30

1996. Birth Centenary of Nikolai Semenov (Nobel Prize winner for chemistry, 1956).
6573 **2618** 750 r. brown 30 15

2619 Pansies

2620 Tabbies

1996. Flowers. Multicoloured.
6574 500 r. Type **2619** 20 10
6575 750 r. Sweet williams ("Dianthus barbatus") . . 35 20
6576 750 r. Sweet peas ("Lathyrus odoratus") 35 20
6577 1000 r. Imperial fritillary ("Fritillaria imperialis") . . 40 20
6578 1000 r. Snapdragons ("Antirhinum majus") . . 40 20

1996. Cats. Multicoloured.
6579 1000 r. Type **2620** 40 20
6580 1000 r. Russian blue 40 20
6581 1000 r. White Persian 40 20
6582 1000 r. Sealpoint Siamese . . 40 20
6583 1000 r. Siberian 40 20

2622 "Laying down of Banners" (A. Mikhailov)

1996. Victory Day.
6585 **2622** 1000 r. multicoloured . 40 20

2623 Tula

1996. 850th Anniv of Tula.
6586 **2623** 1500 r. mult. 60 30

2624 1896 Putilovsky Tram

1996. Centenary of First Russian Tramway, Nizhny Novgorod. Multicoloured.
6587 500 r. Type **2624** 20 10
6588 750 r. 1912 Sormovo tram . 35 20
6589 750 r. 1928 "X" series tram . 35 20
6590 1000 r. 1931 "KM" series tram 40 20
6591 1000 r. 1957 "LM-57" tram 40 20
6592 2500 r. 1993 "71-608K" tram 75 40

2625 Ye. Dashkova (scientist)

2626 Children walking Hand in Hand

1996. Europa. Famous Women.
6594 **2625** 1500 r. green 60 30
6595 – 1500 r. purple 60 30
DESIGN: No. 6594, S. Kovalevskaya (mathematician).

1996. 50th Anniv of U.N.I.C.E.F.
6596 **2626** 1000 r. multicoloured . . 40 20

2627 "Post Troika in Snowstorm" (P. Sokolov)

1996. Post Troikas in Paintings. Muliticoloured.
6597 1500 r. Type **2627** 60 30
6598 1500 r. "Post Troika in Summer" (P. Sokolov) . . 60 30
6599 1500 r. "Post Troika" (P. Gruzinsky) 60 30

2628 "View of Bridge over Yauza and of Shapkin House in Moscow" (J. Delabarte)

1996. 850th Anniv (1997) of Moscow (2nd issue). Paintings. Multicoloured.
6600 500 r. Type **2628** 20 10
6601 500 r. "View of Moscow from Balcony of Kremlin Palace" (detail, J. Delabarte) . . . 20 10
6602 750 r. "View of Voskresenskie and Nikolskie Gates and Kamenny Bridge" (F. Ya. Alekseev) 35 20
6603 750 r. "Moscow Yard near Volkhonka" (anon) . . . 35 20
6604 1000 r. "Varvarka Street" (anon) 40 20
6605 1000 r. "Sledge Races in Petrovsky Park" 40 20

2630 Basketball

2632 Gorsky and Scenes from "Gudula's Daughter" and "Salambo"

2631 "Yevstafy" (ship of the line), 1762

1996. Olympic Games, Atlanta, U.S.A. Multicoloured.
6607 500 r. Type **2630** 20 10
6608 1000 r. Boxing 40 20
6609 1000 r. Swimming 40 20
6610 1500 r. Gymnastics 60 30
6611 1500 r. Hurdling 60 30

1996. 300th Anniv (1993) of Russian Navy (4th issue).
(a) As T **2631**.
6612 **2631** 750 r. brown and yellow 35 20
6613 – 1000 r. deep blue, cobalt and blue 40 20
6614 – 1000 r. purple, pink and rose 40 20
6615 – 1500 r. multicoloured . . 60 30
6616 – 1500 r. black, grey and stone 60 30
DESIGNS: No. 6613, "Petropavlovsk" (battleship); 6614, "Novik" (destroyer); 6615, "Tashkent" (destroyer); 6616, "S-13" (submarine).

(b) Size 35 x 24 mm. Each blue and black.
6617 1000 r. "Principium" (galley) . 40 20
6618 1000 r. "Admiral Kuznetsov" (aircraft carrier) 40 20

1996. 125th Birth Anniv of Aleksandr Gorsky (ballet choreographer). Multicoloured.
6620 750 r. Type **2632** 35 20
6621 750 r. Scene from "La Bayadere" 35 20
6622 1500 r. Scene from "Don Quixote" 60 30
6623 1500 r. Scene from "Giselle" . 60 30

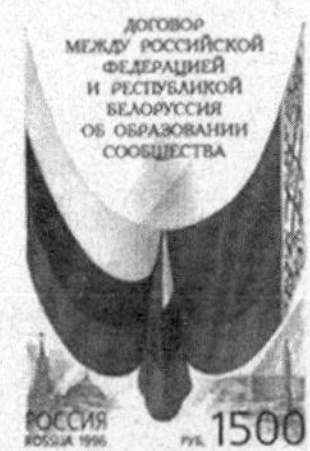
2633 National Flags

1996. Formation of Community of Sovereign Republics (union of Russian Federation and Belarus).
6624 **2633** 1500 r. multicoloured . . 60 30

2634 Chalice

1996. Objets d'Art. Multicoloured.
6625 1000 r. Type **2634** 40 20
6626 1000 r. Perfume bottles . . . 40 20
6627 1000 r. Double inkwell . . . 40 20
6628 1500 r. Coffee pot 60 30
6629 1500 r. Scent bottles 60 30

2635 Symbols of Science and Culture on Open Book

1996. 50th Anniv of U.N.E.S.C.O.
6631 **2635** 1000 r. black, gold and blue 40 20

2636 "Our Lady of Iberia" (icon), Moscow

1996. Orthodox Religion. Multicoloured.
6632 1500 r. Type **2636** 60 30
6633 1500 r. Stavrovouni Monastery, Cyprus 60 30
6634 1500 r. "St. Nicholas" (icon), Cyprus 60 30
6635 1500 r. Iberia Gate, Moscow . 60 30

EXPRESS STAMPS

E **171**

1932. Inscr "EXPRES".
E588 E **171** 5 k. sepia . . . . . . 4·00 2·25
E589 – 10 k. purple . . . . . 6·00 3·50
E590 – 80 k. green . . . . . 30·00 12·00
DESIGNS—HORIZ: 10 k. Express motor van; 80 k. Steam locomotive.

1932. Air. Airship Construction Fund. Imperf or perf.
E592 **166** 15 k. black . . . . . . 2·75 1·50

POSTAGE DUE STAMPS

Доплата 1 коп. золотом.
(D 96)

ДОПЛАТА 1 коп.
(D 99)

1924. Surch as Type **D 96**.
D401 **45** 1 k. on 35 k. blue . . . 20 30
D402 3 k. on 35 k. blue . . . 20 30
D403 5 k. on 35 k. blue . . . 20 30
D404 8 k. on 35 k. blue . . . 50 50
D405 10 k. on 35 k. blue . . . 30 60
D406 12 k. on 70 k. brown . . . 20 40
D407 14 k. on 35 k. blue . . . 20 40
D408 32 k. on 35 k. blue . . . 90 90
D409 40 k. on 35 k. blue . . . 1·00 90

1924. Surch with Type D **99.**
D421 **48** 1 k. on 100 r. yellow . . 4·50 10·00

D **104**

1925.
D464 D **104** 1 k. red 25 30
D465 2 k. violet 25 30
D466 3 k. blue 25 30
D467 7 k. yellow 35 30
D468 8 k. green 35 30
D469 10 k. blue 40 50
D470 14 k. brown 60 70

RUSSIAN POST OFFICES IN CHINA — Pt. 7

Russian Post Offices were opened in various towns in Manchuria and China from 1870 onwards.

1899. 100 kopeks = 1 rouble.
1917. 100 cents = 1 dollar (Chinese).

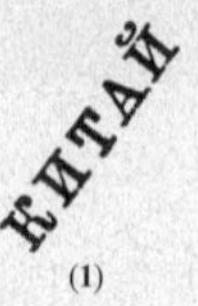

(1)

1899. Arms types (with thunderbolts) of Russia optd with T **1**.

No.	Type	Description	Unused	Used
1	**9**	1 k. orange	30	40
2		2 k. green	40	40
3		3 k. red	40	35
9	**14**	4 k. red	1·25	1·25
4	**9**	5 k. purple	50	50
5		7 k. blue	50	50
6	**14**	10 k. blue	60	50
30	**10**	14 k. red and blue	75	1·25
31		15 k. blue and brown	45	1·00
32	**14**	20 k. red and blue	40	1·25
33	**10**	25 k. violet and green	65	1·75
34		35 k. green and purple	70	1·25
35	**14**	50 k. green and purple	85	1·25
36	**10**	70 k. orange and brown	60	1·50
37	**15**	1 r. orange and brown	1·25	1·50
20	**11**	3 r. 50 grey and black	7·50	8·50
21	**20**	5 r. blue and green on grn	4·50	5·50
22	**11**	7 r. yellow and black	8·00	9·00
23	**20**	10 r. grey and red on yellow	32·00	45·00

1910. Arms types of Russia optd with T **1**.

No.	Type	Description	Unused	Used
24	**22**	1 k. orange	35	60
25		2 k. green	40	60
26		3 k. red	30	35
27	**23**	4 k. red	25	50
28	**22**	7 k. blue	35	65
29	**23**	10 k. blue	35	50

1917. Arms types of Russia surch in "cents" and "dollars" diagonally in one line.

No.	Type	Description	Unused	Used
42	**22**	1 c. on 1 k. orange	40	1·50
43		2 c. on 2 k. green	40	1·50
44		3 c. on 3 k. red	50	1·50
45	**23**	4 c. on 4 k. red	40	1·50
46	**22**	5 c. on 5 k. lilac	75	2·25
47	**23**	10 c. on 10 k. blue	50	2·25
48	**10**	14 c. on 14 k. red & blue	1·00	3·75
49		15 c. on 15 k. blue and pur	1·00	3·00
50	**14**	20 c. on 20 k. red & blue	1·25	2·75
51	**10**	25 c. on 25 k. violet & grn	1·25	3·00
52		35 c. on 35 k. green & pur	1·25	3·25
53	**14**	50 c. on 50 k. green & pur	1·10	3·00
54	**10**	70 c. on 70 k. orange & brn	1·25	4·50
55	**15**	1 d. on 1 r. orange & brown on brown	1·25	5·50
39	**10**	3 d. 50 on 3 r. 50 grey and black	7·00	12·00
40	**20**	5 d. on 5 r. blue and green	4·50	15·00
41	**11**	7 d. on 7 r. yellow & black	2·50	10·00
57	**20**	10 d. on 10 r. grey, red and yellow	20·00	45·00

1920. Arms types of Russia surch in "cents" in two lines. Perf or imperf.

No.	Type	Description	Unused	Used
65	**22**	1 c. on 1 k. orange	7·50	12·00
59		2 c. on 2 k. green	2·50	10·00
60		3 c. on 3 k. red	2·50	10·00
61	**23**	4 c. on 4 k. red	7·50	12·00
62	**22**	5 c. on 5 k. lilac	8·00	15·00
63	**23**	10 c. on 10 k. blue	30·00	45·00
64	**22**	10 c. on 10 k. on 7 k. blue	28·00	45·00

RUSSIAN POST OFFICES IN CRETE — Pt. 3

(RETHYMNON PROVINCE)

The Russian Postal Service operated from 1 May to 29 July 1899.

4 metallik = 1 grosion (Turkish piastre)

These issues were optd with circular control marks as shown on T **3/4**. Prices are for stamps with these marks, but unused examples without them are known.

1

2

1899. Imperf.

No.	Type	Description	Unused	Used
1	**1**	1 m. blue	38·00	14·00
2	**2**	1 m. green	10·00	7·50
3		2 m. red	£275	£170
4		2 m. green	10·00	7·50

3

4

1899. Without stars in oval.

No.	Type	Description	Unused	Used
5	**3**	1 m. pink	35·00	28·00
6		2 m. pink	35·00	28·00
7		1 g. pink	35·00	28·00
8		1 m. blue	35·00	28·00
9		2 m. blue	35·00	28·00
10		1 g. blue	35·00	28·00
11		1 m. green	35·00	28·00
12		2 m. green	35·00	28·00
13		1 g. green	35·00	28·00
14		1 m. red	35·00	28·00
15		2 m. red	35·00	28·00
16		1 g. red	35·00	28·00
17		1 m. orange	35·00	28·00
18		2 m. orange	35·00	28·00
19		1 g. orange	35·00	28·00
20		1 m. yellow	35·00	28·00
21		2 m. yellow	35·00	28·00
22		1 g. yellow	35·00	28·00
23		1 m. black	£550	£550
24		2 m. black	£550	£550
25		1 g. black	£475	£475

1899. Starred at each side.

No.	Type	Description	Unused	Used
26	**4**	1 m. pink	28·00	18·00
27		2 m. pink	11·00	5·50
28		1 g. pink	6·50	4·50
29		1 m. blue	16·00	9·00
30		2 m. blue	11·00	5·50
31		1 g. blue	6·50	4·50
32		1 m. green	16·00	9·00
33		2 m. green	11·00	5·50
34		1 g. green	6·50	4·50
35		1 m. red	16·00	9·00
36		2 m. red	11·00	5·50
37		1 g. red	6·50	4·50

RUSSIAN POST OFFICES IN TURKEY — Pt. 16

General issues for Russian P.O.s in the Turkish Empire and stamps specially overprinted for use at particular offices.

1863. 100 kopeks = 1 rouble.
1900. 40 paras = 1 piastre.

1 Inscription = "Dispatch under Wrapper to the East"

1863. Imperf.

No.	Type	Description	Unused	Used
2a	**1**	6 k. blue	£190	£800

2

3

1865. Imperf.

No.	Type	Description	Unused	Used
4	**2**	(10 pa.) brown and blue	£600	£400
5	**3**	(2 pi.) blue and red	£800	£450

4

5

1865. Imperf.

No.	Type	Description	Unused	Used
6	**4**	(10 pa.) red and blue	20·00	35·00
7	**5**	(2 pi.) blue and red	35·00	42·00

The values of 4/7 were 10 pa. (or 2 k.) and 2 pi. (or 20 k.).

6 Inscription = "Eastern Correspondence"

12

1868. Perf.

No.	Type	Description	Unused	Used
14	**6**	1 k. brown	8·00	4·50
11		3 k. green	22·00	13·00
16		5 k. blue	5·50	3·25
17a		10 k. red and green	4·00	3·25

See also Nos. 26/35.

1876. Surch with large figures of value.

No.	Type	Description	Unused	Used
24	**6**	7 k. on 10 k. red and green	55·00	42·00
22		8 k. on 10 k. red and green	60·00	55·00

1879.

No.	Type	Description	Unused	Used
26	**6**	1 k. black and yellow	2·25	1·25
32		1 k. orange	50	35
27		2 k. black and red	3·00	1·75
33		2 k. green	50	35
34		5 k. purple	1·25	1·00
28		7 k. red and grey	4·50	1·10
35		7 k. blue	85	35

1900. Arms types of Russia surch in "PARA" or "PIASTRES".

No.	Type	Description	Unused	Used
37	**9**	4 pa. on 1 k. orange	15	10
50	**22**	5 pa. on 1 k. orange	10	15
38	**9**	10 pa. on 2 k. green	40	25
51	**22**	10 pa. on 2 k. green	10	15
201		15 pa. on 3 k. red	20	5·00
41	**14**	20 pa. on 4 k. red	40	40
52	**23**	20 pa. on 4 k. red	10	15
42	**9**	20 pa. on 5 k. purple	40	40
181	**22**	20 pa. on 5 k. purple	10	15
43	**14**	1 pi. on 10 k. blue	20	20
53	**23**	1 pi. on 10 k. blue	10	15
182	**10**	1½ pi. on 15 k. blue & pur	15	20
183	**14**	2 pi. on 20 k. red and blue	15	20
184	**10**	2½ pi. on 25 k. violet & grn	15	20
185		3½ pi. on 35 k. green & pur	20	30
54	**14**	5 pi. on 50 k. green & lilac	50	75
55	**10**	7 pi. on 70 k. orange & brn	70	90
56	**15**	10 pi. on 1 r. orange and brown on brown	80	1·10
48	**11**	35 pi. on 3 r. 50 grey and black	6·00	6·00
202	**20**	50 pi. on 5 r. blue on green	3·25	80·00
49	**11**	70 pi. on 7 r. yellow & blk	9·00	9·00
203	**20**	100 pi. on 10 r. grey and red on yellow	14·00	£275

1909. As T **14**, **15**, and **11** of Russia, but ship and date in centre as T **12**, and surch in "paras" or "piastres".

No.	Type	Description	Unused	Used
57	**14**	5 pa. on 1 k. orange	20	30
58		10 pa. on 2 k. green	30	40
59		20 pa. on 4 k. red	60	75
60		1 pi. on 10 k. blue	60	1·10
61		5 pi. on 50 k. green & pur	1·25	2·50
62		7 pi. on 70 k. orange & brn	2·50	3·75
63	**15**	10 pi. on 1 r. orange & brn	3·75	6·50
64	**11**	35 pi. on 3 r. 50 green and purple	9·00	35·00
65		70 pi. on 7 r. pink & grn	22·00	55·00

The above stamps exist overprinted for Constantinople, Jaffa, Jerusalem, Kerassunde, Mount Athos, Salonika, Smyrna, Trebizonde, Beyrouth, Dardanelles, Mytilene and Rizeh. For full list see Part 10 (Russia) of the Stanley Gibbons Catalogue.

1913. Nos. 126/42 (Romanov types) of Russia surch.

No.	Description	Unused	Used
186	5 pa. on 1 k. orange	40	40
187	10 pa. on 3 k. green	40	40
188	15 pa. on 3 k. red	40	40
189	20 pa. on 4 k. red	40	40
190	1 pi. on 10 k. blue	40	40
191	1½ pi. on 15 k. brown	60	60
192	2 pi. on 20 k. green	70	70
193	2½ pi. on 25 k. purple	1·00	1·00
194	3½ pi. on 35 k. green & violet	2·00	2·00
195	5 pi. on 50 k. grey & brown	2·25	2·25
196	7 pi. on 70 k. brown & green	7·00	17·00
197	10 pi. on 1 r. green	8·00	17·00
198	20 pi. on 2 r. brown	3·25	5·50
199	30 pi. on 3 r. violet	4·50	£170
200	50 pi. on 5 r. brown	90·00	£475

RWANDA — Pt. 14

An independent republic established in July 1962, formerly part of Ruanda-Urundi.

100 centimes = 1 franc

1 Pres. Kayibanda and Map

1962. Independence.

No.	Type	Description	Unused	Used
1	**1**	10 c. sepia and green	10	10
2	–	40 c. sepia and purple	10	10
3	**1**	1 f. sepia and blue	70	35
4	–	1 f. 50 sepia and brown	10	10
5	**1**	3 f. 50 sepia and orange	10	10
6	–	6 f. 50 sepia and blue	15	10
7	**1**	10 f. sepia and olive	30	15
8	–	20 f. sepia and red	60	30

DESIGN: Nos. 2, 4, 6, 8, are as Type **1** but with halo around Rwanda on map in place of "R".

1963. Admission to U.N. No. 204 of Ruanda-Urundi with coloured frame obliterating old inscr (colours below), and surch **Admission a l.O.N.U. 18-9-1962 REPUBLIQUE RWANDAISE** and new value.

No.	Description	Unused	Used
9	3 f. 50 on 3 f. grey	10	10
10	6 f. 50 on 3 f. pink	1·10	90
11	10 f. on 3 f. blue	25	25
12	20 f. on 3 f. silver	40	40

1963. Flowers issue of Ruanda-Urundi (Nos. 178 etc) optd **REPUBLIQUE RWANDAISE** or surch also in various coloured panels over old inscription and values. Flowers in natural colours.

No.	Description	Unused	Used
13	25 c. orange and green	20	20
14	40 c. salmon and green	20	20
15	60 c. purple and green	20	20
16	1 f. 25 blue and green	90	90
17	1 f. 50 green and violet	90	90
18	2 f. on 1 f. 50 green and violet	1·40	1·10
19	4 f. on 1 f. 50 green and violet	1·40	1·10
20	5 f. green and purple	1·40	1·10
21	7 f. brown and green	1·40	1·10
22	10 f. olive and purple	1·75	1·50

The coloured panels are in various shades of silver except No. 19 which is in blue.

4 Ears of Wheat and Native Implements

1963. Freedom from Hunger.

No.	Type	Description	Unused	Used
23	**4**	2 f. brown and green	10	10
24		4 f. mauve and blue	10	10
25		7 f. red and grey	20	10
26		10 f. green and yellow	75	55

5 Coffee

6 Postal Services Emblem

1963. 1st Anniv of Independence.

No.	Type	Description	Unused	Used
27	**5**	10 c. brown and blue	10	10
28	–	20 c. yellow and blue	10	10
29	–	30 c. green and orange	15	15
30	**5**	40 c. brown and turquoise	10	10
31	–	1 f. yellow and purple	10	10
32	–	2 f. green and blue	80	45
33	**5**	4 f. brown and red	10	10
34	–	7 f. yellow and green	20	15
35	–	10 f. green and violet	35	30

DESIGNS: 20 c., 1, 7 f. Bananas; 30 c., 2, 10 f. Tea.

1963. 2nd Anniv of African and Malagasy Posts and Telecommunications Union. As T **56** of Mauritania, but with "AERIENNE" omitted.

No.	Description	Unused	Used
36	14 f. multicoloured	1·10	90

1963. Admission of Rwanda to U.P.U.

No.	Type	Description	Unused	Used
37	**6**	50 c. blue and pink	10	10
38		1 f. 50 brown and blue	65	45
39		3 f. purple and grey	10	10
40		20 f. green and yellow	45	20

7 Emblem

8 Child Care

1963. 15th Anniv of Declaration of Human Rights.

No.	Type	Description	Unused	Used
41	**7**	5 f. red	15	10
42		6 f. violet	50	35
43		10 f. blue	35	15

1963. Red Cross Centenary.

No.	Type	Description	Unused	Used
44	**8**	10 c. multicoloured	10	10
45	–	20 c. multicoloured	10	10
46	–	30 c. multicoloured	10	10
47	–	40 c. brown, red and violet	10	10
48	**8**	2 f. multicoloured	80	60
49	–	7 f. multicoloured	15	10
50	–	10 f. brown, red and brown	20	15
51	–	20 f. brown, red and orange	60	35

DESIGNS—HORIZ: 20 c., 7 f. Patient having blood test; 40, 20 c. Stretcher party. VERT: 30 c., 10 f. Doctor examining child.

9 Map and Hydraulic Pump

10 Boy with Crutch

1964. World Meteorological Day.
52 **9** 3 f. sepia, blue and green . . 10 10
53 7 f. sepia, blue and red . . . 35 20
54 10 f. sepia, blue and orange . 50 35

1964. Stamps of Ruanda-Urundi optd **REPUBLIQUE RWANDAISE** or surch also in black over coloured metallic panels obliterating old inscription or value.
55 10 c. on 20 c. (No. 204) 10 10
56 20 c. (No. 204) 10 10
57 30 c. on 1 f. 50 (No. 208) . . . 10 10
58 40 c. (No. 205) 10 10
59 50 c. (No. 206) 10 10
60 1 f. (No. 207) 10 10
61 2 f. (No. 209) 10 10
62 3 f. (No. 210) 10 10
63 4 f. on 3 f. 50 on 3 f. (No. 228) 20 10
64 5 f. (No. 211) 20 10
65 7 f. 50 on 6 f. 50 (No. 212) . . 45 15
66 8 f. (No. 213) . . . . 4·50 2·25
67 10 f. (No. 214) 65 20
68 20 f. (No. 229) . . . . 1·10 45
69 50 f. (No. 230) . . . . 2·10 85

1964. Gatagara Re-education Centre.
70 **10** 10 c. sepia and violet 10 10
71 – 40 c. sepia and blue 10 10
72 – 4 f. sepia and brown 10 10
73 **10** 7 f. 50 sepia and green . . . 35 15
74 – 8 f. sepia and bistre . . . 1·40 95
75 – 10 f. sepia and purple . . . 45 20
DESIGNS—HORIZ: 40 c., 8 f. Children operating sewing machines. VERT: 4, 10 f. Crippled child on crutches.

11 Running

1964. Olympic Games, Tokyo. Sportsmen in slate.
76 **11** 10 c. blue 10 10
77 – 20 c. red 10 10
78 – 30 c. turquoise 10 10
79 – 40 c. brown 10 10
80 **11** 4 f. blue 10 10
81 – 5 f. green . . . . 1·40 1·25
82 – 20 f. purple 35 35
83 – 50 f. grey . . . . 1·10 90
DESIGNS—VERT: 20 c., 5 f. Basketball; 40 c., 50 f. Football. HORIZ: 20 f. High-jumping.

12 Faculties of "Letters" and "Sciences"

13 Abraham Lincoln

1965. National University. Multicoloured.
84 10 c. Type **12** 10 10
85 20 c. Student with microscope and building ("Medicine") 10 10
86 30 c. Scales of Justice, Hand of Law ("Social Sciences" and "Normal High School") . . . 10 10
87 40 c. University buildings . . . 10 10
88 5 f. Type **12** 10 10
89 7 f. As 20 c. 15 10
90 10 f. As 30 c. . . . . 1·00 85
91 12 f. As 40 c. 30 15
The 20 c., 40 c., 7 f. and 12 f. are horiz.

1965. Death Centenary of Abraham Lincoln.
92 **13** 10 c. green and red 10 10
93 20 c. brown and blue . . . 10 10
94 30 c. violet and red . . . 10 10
95 40 c. blue and brown . . . 10 10
96 9 f. brown and purple . . . 20 15
97 40 f. purple and green . . . 1·90 70

14 Marabou Storks

15 "Telstar" Satellite

1965. Kagera National Park. Multicoloured.
98 10 c. Type **14** 40 10
99 20 c. Common zebras 10 10
100 30 c. Impalas 10 10
101 40 c. Crowned cranes, hippopotami and cattle egrets 40 10
102 1 f. African buffaloes 10 10
103 3 f. Hunting dogs 10 10
104 5 f. Yellow baboons . . . . . 4·25 1·10
105 10 f. African elephant and map 20 15
106 40 f. Reed cormorants and African darters . . . . . . 2·00 35
107 100 f. Lions . . . . 2·25 50
SIZES—As Type **14**: VERT: 30 c., 2, 5 f. HORIZ: 20, 40 c., 3, 10 f. LARGER (45×25½ mm); 40, 100 f.

1965. Centenary of I.T.U. Multicoloured.
108 10 c. Type **15** 10 10
109 40 c. "Syncom" satellite . . . 10 10
110 4 f. 50 Type **15** . . . . . . 1·40 50
111 50 f. "Syncom" satellite . . . 90 35

16 "Colotis aurigineus"

17 Cattle and I.C.Y. Emblem

1965. Rwanda Butterflies. Multicoloured.
112 10 c. "Papilio bromius" . . . 10 10
113 15 c. "Papilio hesperus" . . . 10 10
114 20 c. Type **16** 10 10
115 30 c. "Amphicallia pactolicus" 10 10
116 35 c. "Lobobunaea phaedusa" 20 10
117 40 c. "Papilio jacksoni ruandana" 10 10
118 1 f. 50 "Papilio dardanus" . . 10 10
119 3 f. "Amaurina elliotti" . . . 2·75 65
120 4 f. "Colias electo pseudohecate" 1·75 55
121 10 f. "Bunaea alcinoe" . . . 35 15
122 50 f. "Athletes gigas" . . . . 1·10 45
123 100 f. "Charaxes ansorgei R" 2·25 65
The 10, 30, 35 c., 3, 4 and 100 f. are vert.

1965. International Co-operation Year.
124 **17** 10 c. green and yellow . . 10 10
125 – 40 c. brown, blue & green 10 10
126 – 4 f. 50 green, brown & yell 1·10 50
127 – 45 f. purple and brown . . 90 40
DESIGNS: 40 c. Crater lake and giant plants; 4 f. 50, Gazelle and candelabra tree; 45 f. Mt. Ruwenzori. Each with I.C.Y. emblem.

18 Pres. Kennedy, Globe and Satellites

19 Madonna and Child

1965. 2nd Anniv of Pres. Kennedy's Death.
128 **18** 10 c. brown and green . . 10 10
129 40 c. brown and red . . . 10 10
130 50 c. brown and blue . . 10 10
131 1 f. brown and olive . . 10 10
132 8 f. brown and violet . . 1·75 1·10
133 50 f. brown and grey . . . 1·10 90

1965. Christmas.
134 **19** 10 c. green and gold . . . 10 10
135 40 c. brown and gold . . . 10 10
136 50 c. blue and gold . . . 10 10
137 4 f. black and gold . . . 70 65
138 6 f. violet and gold . . . 15 10
139 30 f. brown and gold . . . 65 45

20 Father Damien

1966. World Leprosy Day.
140 **20** 10 c. blue and brown . . . 10 10
141 – 40 c. red and blue . . . 10 10
142 **20** 4 f. 50 slate and green . . 20 15
143 – 45 f. brown and red . . . 1·75 1·25
DESIGNS: 40 c., 45 f. Dr. Schweitzer.

21 Pope Paul, Rome and New York

1966. Pope Paul's Visit to U.N. Organization.
144 **21** 10 c. blue and brown . . . 10 10
145 – 40 c. indigo and blue . . 10 10
146 **21** 4 f. 50 blue and purple . . 1·60 1·00
147 – 50 f. blue and green . . . 1·00 55
DESIGNS: 40 c., 50 f. Pope Paul, Arms and U.N. emblem.

22 "Echinops amplexicaulis" and "E. bequaertii"

1966. Flowers. Multicoloured.
148 10 c. Type **22** 10 10
149 20 c. "Haemanthus multiflorus" 10 10
150 30 c. "Helichrysum erici-rosenii" 10 10
151 40 c. "Carissa edulis" 10 10
152 1 f. "Spathodea campanulata" 10 10
153 3 f. "Habenaria praestans" . . 10 10
154 5 f. "Aloe lateritia" . . . . . 4·50 2·25
155 10 f. "Ammocharis tinneana" . 30 20
156 40 f. "Erythrina abyssinica" . 1·10 75
157 100 f. "Capparis tomentosa" . 2·75 1·40
The 20, 40 c., 1, 3, 5 and 10 f. are vert.

23 W.H.O. Building

1966. Inaug of W.H.O. Headquarters, Geneva.
159 **23** 2 f. olive 10 10
160 3 f. red 20 20
161 5 f. blue 10 10

24 Football

25 Mother and Child within Flames

1966. "Youth and Sports".
162 **24** 10 c. black, blue & green . . 10 10
163 – 20 c. black, green & red . . 10 10
164 – 30 c. black, purple & blue . 10 10
165 **24** 40 c. black, green & bistre . 10 10
166 – 9 f. black, purple & grey . . 20 10
167 – 50 f. black, blue & purple . 1·10 1·00
DESIGNS: 20 c., 9 f. Basketball; 30 c., 50 f. Volleyball.

1966. Nuclear Disarmament.
168 **25** 20 c. brown, red & mauve . 10 10
169 30 c. brown, red & green . 10 10
170 50 c. brown, red & blue . . 10 10
171 6 f. brown, red & yellow . 10 10
172 15 f. brown, red & turq . . 65 30
173 18 f. brown, red & lavender 65 40

26 Football

27 Yellow-crested Helmet Shrike and Mikeno Volcano

1966. World Cup Football Championships.
174 **26** 20 c. blue and turquoise . . 10 10
175 30 c. blue and violet . . . 10 10
176 50 c. blue and green . . . 10 10
177 6 f. blue and mauve . . . 20 10
178 12 f. blue and brown . . . 1·10 35
179 25 f. indigo and blue . . . 2·25 60

1966. Rwanda Scenery.
180 **27** 10 c. green 65 10
181 – 40 c. lake 10 10
182 – 4 f. 50 blue 50 40
183 – 55 f. purple 60 45
DESIGNS—VERT: 40 c. Nyamiranga Falls (inscr "Nyamilanga"); 55 f. Rusumo Falls (inscr "Rusumu"). HORIZ: 4 f. 50, Gahinga and Mahubura Volcanoes, and giant plants.

28 U.N.E.S.C.O. and Cultural Emblems

1966. 20th Anniv of U.N.E.S.C.O.
184 **28** 20 c. mauve and blue . . . 10 10
185 – 30 c. turquoise and black . 10 10
186 – 50 c. brown and black . . 10 10
187 – 1 f. violet and black . . . 10 10
188 **28** 5 f. green and brown . . . 10 10
189 – 10 f. brown and black . . 15 10
190 – 15 f. purple and blue . . . 55 35
191 – 50 f. blue and black . . . 65 50
DESIGNS: 30 c., 10 f. "Animal" primer; 50 c., 15 f. Atomic symbol and drill operator; 1, 50 f. Nubian monument partly submerged in the Nile.

29 "Bitis gabonica"

1967. Snakes. Multicoloured.
192 20 c. Head of mamba 10 10
193 30 c. Python 10 10
194 50 c. Type **29** 10 10
195 1 f. "Naja melanoleuca" . . . 10 10
196 3 f. Head of python 10 10
197 5 f. "Psammophis sibilans" . 20 10
198 20 f. "Dendroaspis jamesoni kaimosae" 55 35
199 70 f. "Dasypeltis scabra" . . 65 45
The 30 c., 1, 5, and 70 f. are vert.

30 Girders and Tea Flower

1967. Ntaruka Hydro-electric Project.
200 **30** 20 c. blue and purple . . . 10 10
201 – 30 c. brown and black . . 10 10
202 – 50 c. violet and brown . . 10 10
203 **30** 4 f. purple and green . . . 10 10
204 – 25 f. green and violet . . . 50 50
205 – 50 f. brown and blue . . . 1·00 1·00
DESIGNS: 30 c., 25 f. Power conductors and pyrethrum flower; 50 c., 50 f. Barrage and coffee beans.

33 "St. Martin" (Van Dyck)

1967. Paintings.
208 **33** 20 c. black, gold & violet . 10 10
209 – 40 c. black, gold & green . 10 10
210 – 60 c. black, gold and red . 10 10
211 – 80 c. black, gold and blue . 10 10
212 **33** 9 f. black, gold and brown 90 50
213 – 15 f. black, gold and red . 35 20
214 – 18 f. black, gold & bronze 35 20
215 – 26 f. black, gold and lake . 45 45
PAINTINGS—HORIZ: 40 c., 15 f. "Rebecca and Eliezer" (Murillo); 80 c., 26 f. "Job and his Friends" (attributed to Il Calabrese). VERT: 60 c., 18 f. "St. Christopher" (D. Bouts).

34 Rwanda "Round Table" Emblem and Common Zebra's Head

1967. Rwanda "Round Table" Fund for Charitable Works. Each with "Round Table" Emblem. Multicoloured.

216 20 c. Type **34** 10 10
217 40 c. African elephant's head . 10 10
218 60 c. African buffalo's head . 10 10
219 80 c. Impala's head 10 10
220 18 f. Ear of wheat 35 15
221 100 f. Palm . . . . 1·60 90

35 "Africa Place" and Dancers

1967. World Fair, Montreal.

222 **35** 20 c. blue and sepia 10 10
223 – 30 c. purple and sepia . . . 10 10
224 – 50 c. orange and sepia . . 10 10
225 – 1 f. green and sepia 10 10
226 – 3 f. violet and sepia 10 10
227 **35** 15 f. green and sepia . . . 15 15
228 – 34 f. red and sepia 50 40
229 – 40 f. turquoise and sepia . . 70 55

DESIGNS: "Africa Place" (two different views used alternately in order of value); 30 c., 3 f. Drum and handicrafts; 50 c., 40 f. Dancers leaping; 1 f., 34 f. Spears, shields and weapons.

1967. Air. 5th Anniv of U.A.M.P.T. As T **101** of Mauritania.

230 6 f. slate, brown and lake . . 20 10
231 18 f. purple and brown . . . 65 35
232 30 f. red, green and blue . . . 1·10 65

36 Common Zebra's Head and Lion's Emblem

37 Red Bishop

1967. 50th Anniv of Lions International.

233 **36** 20 c. black, blue and violet 10 10
234 80 c. black, blue and green 10 10
235 1 f. black, blue and red . . 10 10
236 8 f. black, blue and brown 20 10
237 10 f. black, blue and ultramarine 30 20
238 50 f. black, blue & green . 1·40 95

1967. Birds of Rwanda. Multicoloured.

239 20 c. Type **37** 10 10
240 40 c. Woodland kingfisher . . 10 10
241 60 c. Red-billed quelea 10 10
242 80 c. Double-toothed barbet . . 10 10
243 2 f. Pin-tailed whydah 20 10
244 3 f. Red-chested cuckoo . . . 25 10
245 18 f. Green wood hoopoe . . 1·10 20
246 25 f. Cinnamon-chested bee eater 1·50 30
247 80 f. Regal sunbird . . . . . 3·75 1·00
248 100 f. Fan-tailed whydah . . . 5·00 1·10

The 40, 80 c., 3, 25 f. and 100 f. are horiz.

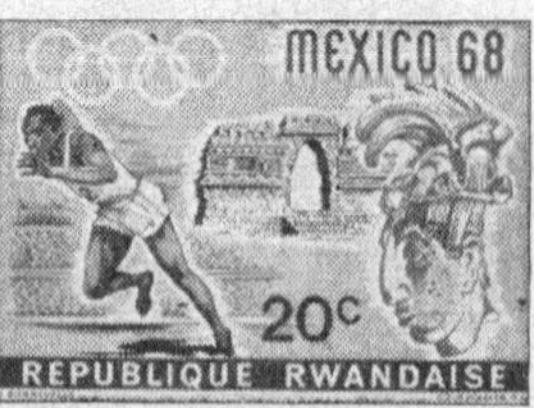

39 Running, and Mexican Antiquites

1968. Olympic Games, Mexico (1st issue). Multicoloured.

250 20 c. Type **39** 35 10
251 40 c. Hammer-throwing . . . 35 10
252 60 c. Hurdling 35 10
253 80 c. Javelin-throwing 35 10
254 8 f. Football (vert) 45 10
255 10 f. Mexican horseman and cacti (vert) 45 10
256 12 f. Hockey (vert) 55 10
257 18 f. Cathedral (vert) 70 15
258 20 f. Boxing (vert) 90 55
259 30 f. Mexico City (vert) . . . 1·10 65

The 20 c. to 80 c. include Mexican Antiquities in their designs.

41 "Diaphananthe fragrantissima"

1968. Flowers. Multicoloured.

261 20 c. Type **41** 10 10
262 40 c. "Phaeomeria speciosa" . 10 10
263 60 c. "Ravenala madagascariensis" 10 10
264 80 c. "Costus afer" 10 10
265 2 f. Banana flowers 10 10
266 3 f. Flowers and young fruit of pawpaw 10 10
267 18 f. "Clerodendron sp." . . 35 15
268 25 f. Sweet potato flowers . . 45 30
269 80 f. Baobab flower . . . . . 1·90 80
270 100 f. Passion flower . . . . 2·25 1·25

42 Horse-jumping

43 Tuareg (Algeria)

1966. Olympic Games, Mexico (2nd issue).

271 **42** 20 c. brown and orange . 10 10
272 – 40 c. brown and turquoise 10 10
273 – 60 c. brown and purple . . 10 10
274 – 80 c. brown and blue . . . 10 10
275 – 38 f. brown and red . . . 50 40
276 – 60 f. brown and green . . 1·10 65

SPORTS: 40 c. Judo; 60 c. Fencing; 80 c. High-jumping; 38 f. High-diving; 60 f. Weightlifting. Each design also represents the location of previous Olympics as at left in Type **42**.

1968. African National Costumes (1st series). Multicoloured.

277 30 c. Type **43** 10 10
278 40 c. Upper Volta 10 10
279 60 c. Senegal 10 10
280 70 c. Rwanda 10 10
281 8 f. Morocco 10 10
282 20 f. Nigeria 35 20
283 40 f. Zambia 80 35
284 50 f. Kenya . . . . 1·10 55

See also Nos. 345/52.

1968. Air. "Philexafrique" Stamp Exhibition, Abidjan (Ivory Coast, 1969) (1st issue). As T **113a** of Mauritania.

286 100 f. "Alexandre Lenoir" (J. L. David) . . . . 2·50 1·60

45 Rwanda Scene and Stamp of Ruanda-Urundi (1953)

1969. Air. "Philexafrique" Stamp Exn (2nd issue).

287 **45** 50 f. multicoloured . . . . 1·90 1·25

46 "The Musical Angels" (Van Eyck)

47 Tuareg Tribesmen

1969. "Paintings and Music". Multicoloured.

288 20 c. Type **46** (postage) . . . 10 10
289 40 c. "The Angels' Concert" (M. Grunewald) 10 10
290 60 c. "The Singing Boy" (Frans Hals) 10 10
291 80 c. "The Lute player" (G. Terborch) 10 10
292 2 f. "The Fifer" (Manet) . . . 10 10
293 6 f. "Young Girls at the Piano" (Renoir) 15 10
294 50 f. "The Music Lesson" (Fragonard) (air) . . . . . 1·40 85
295 100 f. "Angels playing their Musical Instruments" (Memling) (horiz) . . . . . 2·75 1·60

1969. African Headdresses (1st series). Multicoloured.

297 20 c. Type **47** 10 10
298 40 c. Young Ovambo woman . . 10 10
299 60 c. Ancient Guinean and Middle Congo festival headdresses 10 10
300 80 c. Guinean "Dagger" dancer 10 10
301 8 f. Nigerian Muslims 10 10
302 20 f. Luba dancer, Kabondo (Congo) 40 20
303 40 f. Senegalese and Gambian women 85 45
304 80 f. Rwanda dancer . . . . . 1·25 1·00

See also Nos. 408/15.

48 "The Moneylender and his Wife" (Quentin Metsys)

1969. 5th Anniv of African Development Bank.

305 **48** 30 f. multicoloured on silver 55 50
306 – 70 f. multicoloured on gold 1·60 1·40

DESIGN: 70 f. "The Moneylender and his Wife" (Van Reymerswaele).

50 Pyrethrum

51 Revolutionary

1969. Medicinal Plants. Multicoloured.

308 20 c. Type **50** 10 10
309 40 c. Aloes 10 10
310 60 c. Cola 10 10
311 80 c. Coca 10 10
312 3 f. Hagenia 10 10
313 75 f. Cassia . . . . 1·40 80
314 80 f. Cinchona . . . . . . 2·25 90
315 100 f. Tephrosia . . . . . . 2·50 1·10

1969. 10th Anniv of Revolution.

316 **51** 6 f. multicoloured 15 10
317 18 f. multicoloured 50 45
318 40 f. multicoloured . . . . 1·00 95

53 "Napoleon on Horseback" (David)

1969. Birth Bicent of Napoleon Bonaparte. Mult. Portraits of Napoleon. Artists name given.

320 20 c. Type **53** 10 10
321 40 c. Debret 10 10
322 60 c. Gautherot 10 10
323 80 c. Ingres 10 10
324 8 f. Pajou 20 15
325 20 f. Gros 55 40
326 40 f. Gros . . . . 1·00 55
327 80 f. David . . . . 2·25 1·25

54 "The Quarryman" (O. Bonnevalle)

1969. 50th Anniv of I.L.O. Multicoloured.

328 20 c. Type **54** 10 10
329 40 c. "Ploughing" (detail Brueghel's "Descent of Icarus") 10 10
330 60 c. "The Fisherman" (C. Meunier) 10 10
331 80 c. "Ostend Slipway" (J. van Noten) 10 10
332 8 f. "The Cook" (P. Aertsen) 20 10
333 10 f. "Vulcan's Blacksmiths" (Velazquez) 35 15
334 50 f. "Hiercheuse" (C. Meunier) 1·25 60
335 70 f. "The Miner" (P. Paulus) 1·60 80

Nos. 330, 332 and 334/5 are vert.

55 "The Derby at Epsom" (Gericault)

1970. Paintings of Horses. Multicoloured.

336 20 c. Type **55** 10 10
337 40 c. "Horses leaving the Sea" (Delacroix) 10 10
338 60 c. "Charles V at Muhlberg" (Titian) (vert) 10 10
339 80 c. "To the Races, Amateur Jockeys" (Degas) 10 10
340 8 f. "Horsemen at Rest" (Wouwermans) 20 10
341 20 f. "Officer of the Imperial Guard" (Gericault) (vert) . . 60 30
342 40 f. "Horse and Dromedary" (Bonnevalle) . . . . . . 1·50 45
343 80 f. "The Prodigal Child" (Rubens) . . . . 2·00 80

1970. African National Costumes (2nd series). As T **43**. Multicoloured.

345 20 c. Tharaka Meru woman . 10 10
346 30 c. Niger flautist 10 10
347 50 c. Tunisian water-carrier . 10 10
348 1 f. Kano ceremonial (Nigeria) 10 10
349 3 f. Mali troubador 10 10
350 5 f. Quipongo, Angola women 10 10
351 50 f. Mauritanian at prayer . 95 55
352 90 f. Sinehatiali dancers, Ivory Coast . . . . 2·00 1·00

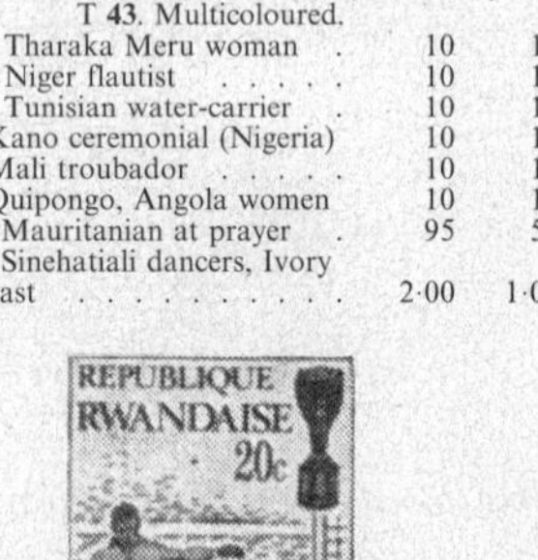

58 Footballer attacking Goal

1970. World Cup Football Championships, Mexico.

353 **58** 20 c. multicoloured 10 10
354 – 30 c. multicoloured 10 10
355 – 50 c. multicoloured 10 10
356 – 1 f. multicoloured 10 10
357 – 6 f. multicoloured 10 10
358 – 18 f. multicoloured 45 30
359 – 30 f. multicoloured 85 45
360 – 90 f. multicoloured . . . . 2·00 95

Nos. 354/60 show footballers in various positions, similar to Type **58**.

59 Flowers and Green Peafowl

1970. "EXPO 70", World Fair, Osaka, Japan. Multicoloured.

361 20 c. Type **59** . . . . 1·00 10
362 30 c. Torii gate and "Hibiscus" (Yashuda) 10 10
363 50 c. Dancer and "Musician" (Katayama) 10 10
364 1 f. Sun Tower and "Warrior" 10 10
365 3 f. House and "Seated Buddha" 10 10
366 5 f. Pagoda and "Head of Girl" (Yamakawa) 10 10
367 20 f. Greeting and "Imperial Palace" 55 35
368 70 f. Expo emblem and "Horseman" . . . . 1·60 90

60 Two Young Gorillas

1970. Gorillas of the Mountains.

369 **60** 20 c. black and green . . . 35 35
370 – 40 c. black, brown & pur . 35 35
371 – 60 c. black, blue & brown . 35 35
372 – 80 c. black, orange & brn . 35 35
373 – 1 f. black and mauve . . . 35 35
374 – 2 f. multicoloured 35 35
375 – 15 f. black and sepia . . . 70 45
376 – 100 f. black, brown & bl . 3·75 2·25

GORILLA—VERT: 40 c. Squatting; 80 c. Beating chest; 2 f. Eating banana; 100 f. With young. HORIZ: 60 c. Walking; 1 f. With family; 15 f. Heads.

61 Cinchona Bark

1970. 150th Anniv of Discovery of Quinine. Mult.

377 20 c. Type **61** 10 10
378 80 c. Pharmaceutical equipment 10 10
379 1 f. Anopheles mosquito . . . 10 10
380 3 f. Malaria patient and nurse 10 10
381 25 f. "Attack" on mosquito . 55 35
382 70 f. Pelletier and Caventou (discoverers of quinine) . . 1·50 80

62 Rocket in Flight

1970. Moon Missions. Multicoloured.

383 20 c. Type **62** 10 10
384 30 c. Separation during orbit . 10 10
385 50 c. Spaceship above the moon 10 10
386 1 f. Module and astonauts on moon 10 10
387 3 f. Take-off from the moon . 10 10
388 5 f. Return journey to earth . 15 10
389 10 f. Final separation before landing 30 15
390 80 f. Splashdown . . . . . . 2·25 1·40

63 F. D. Roosevelt and "Brasscattleya olympia alba" **65** Pope Paul VI

1970. 25th Death Anniv of F. D. Roosevelt. Portraits and Orchids.

391 **63** 20 c. brown, blue & black . 10 10
392 – 30 c. brown, red and black 10 10
393 – 50 c. brown, orge and blk . 10 10
394 – 1 f. brown, green & black . 10 10
395 – 2 f. green, brown and black 10 10
396 – 6 f. green, purple and black 20 15
397 – 30 f. green, blue and black 1·25 40
398 – 60 f. green, red and black . 2·00 70

ORCHIDS: 30 c. "Laeliocattleya callistoglossa"; 50 c. "Chondrorrhyncha chestertoni"; 1 f. "Paphiopedilum"; 2 f. "Cymbidium hybride"; 6 f. "Cattleya labiata"; 30 f. "Dendrobium nobile"; 60 f. "Laelia gouldiana".

1970. Centenary of 1st Vatican Council.

400 **65** 10 c. brown and gold . . . 10 10
401 – 20 c. green and gold . . . 10 10
402 – 30 c. lake and gold . . . 10 10
403 – 40 c. blue and gold . . . 10 10
404 – 1 f. violet and gold . . . 10 10
405 – 18 f. purple and gold . . . 50 20
406 – 20 f. orange and gold . . . 60 20
407 – 60 f. brown and gold . . . 1·60 70

POPES: 20 c. John XXIII; 30 c. Pius XII; 40 c. Pius XI; 1 f. Benedict XV; 18 f. Pius X; 20 f. Leo XIII; 60 f. Pius IX.

1971. African Headdresses (2nd series). Multicoloured. As T **47**.

408 20 c. Rendille woman 10 10
409 30 c. Chad woman 10 10
410 50 c. Bororo man (Niger) . . 10 10
411 1 f. Masai man (Kenya) . . . 10 10
412 5 f. Air girl (Niger) 10 10
413 18 f. Rwanda woman 35 20
414 25 f. Mauritania man 65 35
415 50 f. Rwanda girls . . . . . 1·50 65

68 "Beethoven" (C. Horneman) **72** "Durer" (self-portrait)

69 Horse-jumping

1971. Birth Cent (1970) of Beethoven. Portraits and funeral scene by various artists. Multicoloured.

418 20 c. Type **68** 10 10
419 30 c. K. Stieler 10 10
420 50 c. F. Schimon 10 10
421 3 f. H. Best 10 10
422 6 f. W. Fassbender 30 10
423 90 f. "Beethoven's Burial" (Stober) . . . . 2·10 2·00

1971. Olympic Games, Munich (1972) (1st issue).

424 **69** 20 c. gold and black . . . 10 10
425 – 30 c. gold and purple . . . 10 10
426 – 50 c. gold and violet . . . 10 10
427 – 1 f. gold and green 10 10
428 – 8 f. gold and red 20 10
429 – 10 f. gold and violet . . . 30 15
430 – 20 f. gold and brown . . . 50 30
431 – 60 f. gold and green . . . 1·40 65

DESIGNS: 30 c. Running (start); 50 c. Basketball; 1 f. High-jumping; 8 f. Boxing; 10 f. Pole-vaulting; 20 f. Wrestling; 60 f. Gymnastics.

See also Nos. 490/7.

1971. Air. 10th Anniv of U.A.M.P.T. As T **139a** of Mauritania. Multicoloured.

432 100 f. U.A.M.P.T. H.Q. and Rwandaise woman and child 2·10 2·00

1971. 500th Birth Anniv of Durer. Paintings. Multicoloured.

434 20 c. "Adam" 10 10
435 30 c. "Eve" 10 10
436 50 c. "Portrait of H. Holzschuher" 10 10
437 1 f. "Mourning the Dead Christ" 10 10
438 3 f. "Madonna and Child" . 10 10
439 5 f. "St. Eustace" 10 10
440 20 f. "St. Paul and St. Mark" 45 30
441 70 f. Type **72** . . . . 1·60 1·00

73 Astonauts in Moon Rover

1972. Moon Mission of "Apollo 15".

442 **73** 600 f. gold . . . . 95·00

74 Participation in Sport

1972. National Guard. Multicoloured.

443 4 f. Type **74** 10 10
444 6 f. Transport of emergency supplies 15 10
445 15 f. Helicopter transport for the sick 40 20
446 25 f. Participation in health service 65 35
447 50 f. Guard, map and emblem (vert) . . . . 1·25 1·10

75 Ice Hockey

1972. Winter Olympic Games, Sapporo, Japan. Multicoloured.

448 20 c. Type **75** 10 10
449 30 c. Speed-skating 10 10
450 50 c. Ski-jumping 10 10
451 1 f. Figure Skating 10 10
452 6 f. Cross-country skiing . . . 10 10
453 12 f. Slalom 15 15
454 20 f. Tobogganing 45 20
455 60 f. Downhill skiing . . . . . 1·40 1·10

76 Savanna Monkey and Impala

1972. Akagera National Park. Multicoloured.

456 20 c. Type **76** 10 10
457 30 c. African buffalo 10 10
458 50 c. Common zebra 10 10
459 1 f. White rhinoceros 10 10
460 2 f. Warthogs 10 10
461 6 f. Hippopotamus 15 10
462 18 f. Spotted hyenas 30 20
463 32 f. Helmet guineafowl . . . 2·50 60
464 60 f. Waterbucks . . . . . . 1·60 1·10
465 80 f. Lion and lioness . . . . 2·25 1·60

77 Family supporting Flag **78** Variable Sunbirds

1972. 10th Anniv of Referendum.

466 **77** 6 f. multicoloured 10 10
467 18 f. multicoloured 45 35
468 60 f. multicoloured . . . . 1·25 1·10

1972. Rwanda Birds. Multicoloured.

469 20 c. Common waxbills 10 10
470 30 c. Collared sunbird 10 10
471 50 c. Type **78** 15 10
472 1 f. Greater double-collared sunbird 20 10
473 4 f. Ruwenzori puff-back flycatcher 25 10
474 6 f. Red-billed fire finch . . . 30 15
475 10 f. Scarlet-chested sunbird 50 15
476 18 f. Red-headed quelea . . 1·10 35
477 60 f. Black-headed gonolek . . 4·00 1·40
478 100 f. African golden oriole . . 6·50 2·25

79 King Baudouin and Queen Fabiola with President and Mrs. Kayibanda in Rwanda

1972. "Belgica 72" Stamp Exhibition, Brussels.

479 – 18 f. multicoloured 70 70
480 – 22 f. multicoloured 90 90
481 **79** 40 f. blue, black & gold . . 1·75 1·75

DESIGNS: 18 f. Rwanda village; 22 f. View of Bruges.

Nos. 479/80 are smaller, size 39 × 36 mm.

80 Announcement of Independence

1972. 10th Anniv of Independence.

482 **80** 20 c. green and gold 10 10
483 – 30 c. purple and gold . . . 10 10
484 – 50 c. sepia and gold 10 10
485 – 6 f. blue and gold 10 10
486 – 10 f. purple and gold . . . 15 10
487 – 15 f. blue and gold 35 20
488 – 18 f. brown and gold . . . 45 30
489 – 50 f. green and gold . . . 1·10 70

DESIGNS—HORIZ: 30 c. Promotion ceremony, officers of the National Guard; 50 c. Pres. Kayibanda, wife and family; 6 f. Pres. Kayibanda casting vote in legislative elections; 10 f. Pres. and Mrs. Kayibanda at "Festival of Justice"; 15 f. President and members of National Assembly; 18 f. Investiture of Pres. Kayibanda. VERT: 50 f. President Kayibanda.

81 Horse-jumping

1972. Olympic Games, Munich (2nd issue).

490 **81** 20 c. green and gold . . . 10 10
491 – 30 c. violet and gold . . . 10 10
492 – 50 c. green and gold . . . 10 10
493 – 1 f. purple and gold . . . 10 10
494 – 6 f. black and gold 10 10
495 – 18 f. brown and gold . . . 35 30
496 – 30 f. violet and gold . . . 80 55
497 – 44 f. blue and gold . . . . 1·10 65

DESIGNS: 30 c. Hockey; 50 c. Football; 1 f. Long-jumping; 6 f. Cycling; 18 f. Yachting; 30 f. Hurdling; 44 f. Gymnastics.

82 Runners

1972. Racial Equality Year. "Working Together". Multicoloured.

498 20 c. Type **82** 10 10
499 30 c. Musicians 10 10
500 50 c. Ballet dancers 10 10
501 1 f. Medical team in operating theatre 10 10
502 6 f. Weaver and painter . . . 10 10
503 18 f. Children in class 35 20
504 24 f. Laboratory technicians . 55 35
505 50 f. U.N. emblem and hands of four races . . . . 1·00 65

84 "Phymateus brunneri"

1973. Rwanda Insects. Multicoloured.

507 20 c. Type **84** 10 10
508 30 c. "Diopsis fumipennis" (vert) 10 10
509 50 c. "Kitoko alberti" 10 10
510 1 f. "Archibracon fasciatus" (vert) 10 10
511 2 f. "Ornithacris cyanea imperialis" 10 10
512 6 f. "Clitodaca fenestralis" (vert) 15 10
513 18 f. "Senaspis oesacus" . . . 40 20
514 22 f. "Phonoctonus grandis" (vert) 55 35
515 70 f. "Loba leopardina" . . . 2·25 2·40
516 100 f. "Ceratocoris distortus" (vert) . . . . 4·00 3·10

85 "Emile Zola" (Manet) **86** Longombe

1973. International Book Year. "Readers and Writers". Paintings and portraits. Multicoloured.
518 20 c. Type **85** 10 10
519 30 c. "Rembrandt's Mother" (Rembrandt) 10 10
520 50 c. "St. Jerome removing Thorn from Lion's paw" (Colantonio) 10 10
521 1 f. "St. Peter and St. Paul" (El Greco) 10 10
522 2 f. "Virgin and Child" (Van der Weyden) 10 10
523 6 f. "St. Jerome in his Cell" (Antonella de Messina) . . 15 10
524 40 f. "St. Barbara" (Master of Flemalle) . . . . 1·00 60
525 100 f. "Don Quixote" (O. Bonnevalle) . . . . . . 2·40 1·90

1973. Musical Instruments. Multicoloured.
527 20 c. Type **86** 10 10
528 30 c. Horn 10 10
529 50 c. "Xylophone" 10 10
530 1 f. "Harp" 10 10
531 4 f. Alur horns 10 10
532 6 f. Horn, bells and drum . . 10 10
533 18 f. Drums 40 40
534 90 f. Gourds . . . . 2·00 1·40

87 "Rubens and Isabelle Brandt" (Rubens)
88 Map of Africa and Doves

1973. "IBRA" Stamp Exhibition, Munich. Famous Paintings. Multicoloured.
535 20 c. Type **87** 10 10
536 30 c. "Portrait of a Lady" (Cranach the Younger) . . . 10 10
537 50 c. "Woman peeling Turnips" (Chardin) 10 10
538 1 f. "Abduction of the Daughters of Leucippe" (Rubens) . . . 10 10
539 2 f. "Virgin and Child" (Lippi) 10 10
540 6 f. "Boys eating Fruit" (Murillo) 20 10
541 40 f. "The Sickness of Love" (Steen) 90 45
542 100 f. "Jesus divested of His Garments" (El Greco) . . . 2·25 1·40

1973. 10th Anniv of O.A.U. Multicoloured.
544 6 f. Type **88** 20 10
545 94 f. Map of Africa and hands 2·25 1·90

1973. Pan-African Drought Relief. Nos. 308/13 and 315 optd **SECHERESSE SOLIDARITE AFRICAINE** and No. 315 additionally surch.
546 **50** 20 c. multicoloured 10 10
547 – 40 c. multicoloured 10 10
548 – 60 c. multicoloured 10 10
549 – 80 c. multicoloured 10 10
550 – 3 f. multicoloured 10 10
551 – 75 f. multicoloured . . . . 1·60 1·40
552 – 100 f. + 50 f. mult . . . . 5·00 4·00

90 "Distichodus sexfasciatus"

1973. Fishes. Multicoloured.
553 20 c. Type **90** 10 10
554 30 c. "Hydrocyon forskalii" . . 10 10
555 50 c. "Synodontis angelicus" . . 10 10
556 1 f. "Tilapia nilotica" 10 10
557 2 f. "Protopterus aethiopicus" . 10 10
558 6 f. "Pareutropius mandevillei" 20 10
559 40 f. "Phenacogrammus interruptus" . . . . 1·25 90
560 150 f. "Julidochromis ornatus" 4·00 3·00

1973. 12th Anniv of U.A.M.P.T. As T **155a** of Mauritania.
562 100 f. blue, brown and mauve 3·25 3·25

1973. African Fortnight, Brussels. Nos. 408/15 optd **QUINZAINE AFRICAINE BRUXELLES 15/30 SEPT. 1973** and globe.
563 20 c. multicoloured 10 10
564 30 c. multicoloured 10 10
565 50 c. multicoloured 10 10
566 1 f. multicoloured 10 10
567 5 f. multicoloured 10 10
568 18 f. multicoloured 40 20
569 25 f. multicoloured 50 45
570 50 f. multicoloured . . . . . 1·40 85

1973. Air. Congress of French-speaking Nations, Liege. No. 432 optd **LIEGE ACCUEILLE LES PAYS DE LANGUE FRANCAISE 1973** (No. 562) or congress emblem (No. 563).
571 100 f. multicoloured . . . . 4·00 2·75
572 100 f. multicoloured . . . . 4·00 2·75

1973. 25th Anniv of Declaration of Human Rights. Nos. 443/7 optd with Human Rights emblem.
574 **74** 4 f. multicoloured 10 10
575 – 6 f. multicoloured 10 10
576 – 15 f. multicoloured 30 15
577 – 25 f. multicoloured 60 40
578 – 50 f. multicoloured . . . . 1·40 95

96 Copernicus and Astrolabe
97 Pres. Habyarimana

1973. 500th Birth Anniv of Copernicus. Mult.
580 20 c. Type **96** 10 10
581 30 c. Copernicus 10 10
582 50 c. Copernicus and heliocentric system 10 10
583 1 f. Type **96** 10 10
584 18 f. As 30 c. 65 60
585 80 f. As 50 c. . . . . 2·40 2·00

1974. "New Regime".
587 **97** 1 f. brown, black and buff 10 10
588 2 f. brown, black and blue 10 10
589 5 f. brown, black and red . 10 10
590 6 f. brown, black and blue 10 10
591 26 f. brown, black and lilac 55 45
592 60 f. brown, black & green 1·25 1·00

99 Yugoslavia v Zaire
101 "Diane de Poiters" (Fontainebleau School)

100 Marconi's Steam Yacht "Elettra"

1974. World Cup Football Championships, West Germany. Players represent specified teams. Multicoloured.
594 20 c. Type **99** 10 10
595 40 c. Netherlands v Sweden . 10 10
596 60 c. West Germany v Australia 10 10
597 80 c. Haiti v Argentina . . . 10 10
598 2 f. Brazil v Scotland 10 10
599 6 f. Bulgaria v Uruguay . . . 10 10
600 40 f. Italy v Poland 80 65
601 50 f. Chile v East Germany . 1·40 1·00

1974. Birth Centenary of Guglielmo Marconi (radio pioneer). Multicoloured.
602 20 c. Type **100** 20 10
603 30 c. Cruiser "Carlo Alberto" 20 10
604 50 c. Marconi's telegraph equipment 10 10
605 4 f. "Global Telecommunications" . . . 10 10
606 35 f. Early radio receiver . . 85 45
607 60 f. Marconi and Poldhu radio station . . . . 1·50 1·10

1974. International Stamp Exhibitions "Stockholmia" and "Internaba". Paintings from Stockholm and Basle. Multicoloured.
609 20 c. Type **101** 10 10
610 30 c. "The Flute-player" (J. Leyster) 10 10
611 50 c. "Virgin Mary and Child" (G. David) 10 10
612 1 f. "The Triumph of Venus" (F. Boucher) 10 10
613 10 f. "Harlequin Seated" (P. Picasso) 15 10
614 18 f. "Virgin and Child" (15th-century) 35 15
615 20 f. "The Beheading of St. John" (H. Fries) 45 35
616 50 f. "The Daughter of Andersdotter" (J. Hockert) 1·40 1·00

102 Monastic Messenger
105 Head of Uganda Kob

1974. Centenary of U.P.U. Multicoloured.
619 20 c. Type **102** 10 10
620 30 c. Inca messenger 10 10
621 50 c. Moroccan postman . . . 10 10
622 1 f. Indian postman 10 10
623 18 f. Polynesian postman . . . 55 40
624 80 f. Early Rwanda messenger with horn and drum . . . . 2·00 1·40

1974. 15th Anniv of Revolution. Nos. 316/18 optd **1974 15e ANNIVERSAIRE**.
625 **51** 6 f. multicoloured . . . . .
626 18 f. multicoloured . . . . .
627 40 f. multicoloured . . . . .
Set of 3 . . . . 11·00 9·50

1974. 10th Anniv of African Development Bank. Nos. 305/6 optd **1974 10e ANNIVERSAIRE**.
629 **48** 30 f. multicoloured 85 65
630 – 70 f. multicoloured . . . . 1·90 1·40

1975. Antelopes. Multicoloured.
631 20 c. Type **105** 10 10
632 30 c. Bongo with calf (horiz) . 10 10
633 50 c. Roan antelope and Sable antelope heads 10 10
634 1 f. Young sitatungas (horiz) . 10 10
635 4 f. Great kudu 10 10
636 10 f. Impala family (horiz) . . 55 10
637 34 f. Waterbuck head . . . . 1·40 70
638 100 f. Giant eland (horiz) . . . 4·00 2·50

108 Pyrethrum Daisies
111 Globe and Emblem

110 Eastern White Pelicans

1975. Agricultural Labour Year. Multicoloured.
642 20 c. Type **108** 10 10
643 30 c. Tea plant 10 10
644 50 c. Coffee berries 10 10
645 4 f. Bananas 10 10
646 10 f. Maize 20 10
647 12 f. Sorghum 35 15
648 26 f. Rice 80 45
649 47 f. Coffee cultivation . . . 1·60 90

1975. Holy Year. Nos. 400/7 optd **1975 ANNEE SAINTE**.
652 **65** 10 c. brown and gold . . . 10 10
653 – 20 c. green and gold . . . 10 10
654 – 30 c. lake and gold 10 10
655 – 40 c. blue and gold 10 10
656 – 1 f. violet and gold 10 10
657 – 18 f. purple and gold . . . 40 20
658 – 20 f. orange and gold . . . 45 20
659 – 60 f. brown and gold . . . 1·90 1·25

1975. Aquatic Birds. Multicoloured.
660 20 c. Type **110** 10 10
661 30 c. Malachite kingfisher . . 10 10
662 50 c. Goliath herons 10 10
663 1 f. Saddle-bill stork 10 10
664 4 f. African jacana 40 15
665 10 f. African darter 85 35
666 34 f. Sacred ibis . . . . . . 2·40 1·00
667 80 f. Hartlaub's duck (vert) . . 6·50 2·75

1975. World Population Year (1974). Mult.
669 20 f. Type **111** 45 30
670 26 f. Population graph 65 35
671 34 f. Symbolic doorway . . . 95 50

112 "La Toilette" (M. Cassatt)
113 "Arts"

1975. International Women's Year. Multicoloured.
672 20 c. Type **112** 10 10
673 30 c. "Mother and Child" (G. Melchers) 10 10
674 50 c. "The Milk Jug" (Vermeer) 10 10
675 1 f. "The Water-carrier" (Goya) 10 10
676 8 f. Coffee picking 20 10
677 12 f. Laboratory technician . 35 20
678 18 f. Rwandaise mother and child 55 20
679 60 f. Woman carrying water jug 1·50 1·25

1975. 10th Anniv of National University. The Faculties. Multicoloured.
681 20 c. Type **113** 10 10
682 30 c. "Medicine" 10 10
683 1 f. 50 "Jurisprudence" . . . 10 10
684 18 f. "Science" 40 20
685 26 f. "Commerce" 45 30
686 34 f. University Building, Kigali 85 55

114 Cattle at Pool, and "Impatiens stuhlmannii"

1975. Protection of Nature. Multicoloured.
688 20 c. Type **114** 10 10
689 30 c. Euphorbis "candelabra" and savannah bush 10 10
690 50 c. Bush fire and "Tapinanthus prunifolius" 10 10
691 5 f. Lake Bulera and "Nymphaea lotus" 10 10
692 8 f. Soil erosion and "Protea madiensis" 15 10
693 10 f. Protected marshland and "Melanthera brownei" . . . 20 15
694 26 f. Giant lobelias and groundsel 55 40
695 100 f. Sabyinyo volcano and "Polystachya kermesina" . 2·50 2·25

1975. Pan-African Drought Relief. Nos. 345/52 optd or surch **SECHERESSE SOLIDARITE 1975** (both words share same capital letter).
696 20 c. multicoloured 10 10
697 30 c. multicoloured 10 10
698 50 c. multicoloured 10 10
699 1 f. multicoloured 10 10
700 3 f. multicoloured 10 10
701 5 f. multicoloured 15 10
702 50 f. + 25 f. multicoloured . 1·60 1·25
703 90 f. + 25 f. multicoloured . 2·40 2·00

116 Loading Douglas DC-8F Jet Trader

1975. Year of Increased Production. Multicoloured.
704 20 c. Type **116** 10 10
705 30 c. Coffee-picking plant . . 10 10
706 50 c. Lathe operator 10 10
707 10 f. Farmer with hoe (vert) . 15 10
708 35 f. Coffee-picking (vert) . . 60 55
709 54 f. Mechanical plough . . . 1·10 95

117 African Woman with Basket on Head

1975. "Themabelga" Stamp Exhibition, Brussels. African Costumes.
710 **117** 20 c. multicoloured . . . 10 10
711 – 30 c. multicoloured . . . 10 10
712 – 50 c. multicoloured . . . 10 10
713 – 1 f. multicoloured 10 10
714 – 5 f. multicoloured 10 10
715 – 7 f. multicoloured 15 10
716 – 35 f. multicoloured . . . 70 60
717 – 51 f. multicoloured . . . 1·40 95
DESIGNS: 30 c. to 51 f. Various Rwanda costumes.

118 Dr. Schweitzer, Organ Pipes and Music Score

1976. World Leprosy Day.
719 – 20 c. lilac, brown & black 10 10
720 – 30 c. lilac, green & black . 10 10
721 **118** 50 c. lilac, brown & black 10 10

722 – 1 f. lilac, purple & black . 10 10
723 – 3 f. lilac, blue and black . 10 10
724 – 5 f. lilac, brown and black 10 10
725 **118** 10 f. lilac, blue and black . 30 10
726 – 80 f. lilac, red and black 1·90 1·40

DESIGNS: Dr. Schweitzer and: 20 c. Piano keyboard and music; 30 c. Lambarene Hospital; 1 f. Lambarene residence; 3 f. as 20 c.; 5 f. as 30 c; 80 f. as 1 f.

119 "Surrender at Yorktown"

1976. Bicentenary of American Revolution. Mult.
727 20 c. Type **119** 10 10
728 30 c. "The Sergeant-Instructor at Valley Forge" 10 10
729 50 c. "Presentation of Captured Yorktown Flags to Congress" 10 10
730 1 f. "Washington at Fort Lee" 10 10
731 18 f. "Washington boarding a British warship" 45 30
732 26 f. "Washington studying Battle plans" 55 40
733 34 f. "Washington firing a Cannon" 90 55
734 40 f. "Crossing the Delaware" 1·00 85

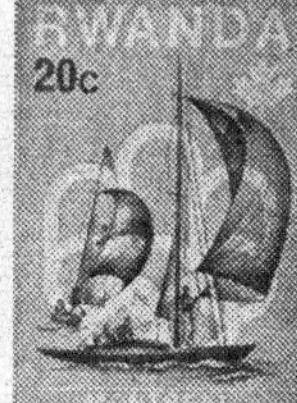

120 Sister Yohana **121** Yachting

1976. 75th Anniv of Catholic Church in Rwanda. Multicoloured.
736 20 c. Type **120** 10 10
737 30 c. Abdon Sabakati 10 10
738 50 c. Father Alphonse Brard . 10 10
739 4 f. Abbe Balthazar Gafuku . 10 10
740 10 f. Monseigneur Bigirumwami 20 10
741 25 f. Save Catholic Church (horiz) 60 45
742 60 f. Kabgayi Catholic Cathedral (horiz) . . . . 1·25 80

1976. Olympic Games, Montreal (1st issue).
743 **121** 20 c. brown and green . . 10 10
744 – 30 c. blue and green . . . 10 10
745 – 50 c. black and green . . 10 10
746 – 1 f. violet and green . . . 10 10
747 – 10 f. blue and green . . . 20 10
748 – 18 f. brown and green . . 35 30
749 – 29 f. purple and green . . 80 60
750 – 51 f. deep green & green . 1·00 80

DESIGNS: 30 c. Horse-jumping; 50 c. Long jumping; 1 f. Hockey; 10 f. Swimming; 18 f. Football; 29 f. Boxing; 51 f. Gymnastics.

See also Nos. 767/74.

122 Bell's Experimental Telephone and Manual Switchboard

1976. Telephone Centenary.
751 **122** 20 c. brown and blue . . 10 10
752 – 30 c. blue and violet . . . 10 10
753 – 50 c. brown and blue . . . 10 10
754 – 1 f. orange and blue . . . 10 10
755 – 4 f. mauve and blue . . . 10 10
756 – 8 f. green and blue . . . 15 10
757 – 26 f. red and blue . . . 70 55
758 – 60 f. lilac and blue . . . 1·40 1·00

DESIGNS: 30 c. Early telephone and man making call; 50 c. Early telephone and woman making call; 1 f. Early telephone and exchange building; 4 f. Alexander Graham Bell and "candlestick" telephone; 26 f. Dish aerial, satellite and modern hand set; 60 f. Rwanda, PTT building, operator and push-button telephones.

1976. Bicentenary of Declaration of American Independence. Nos. 727/34 optd **INDEPENDENCE DAY** and Bicentennial Emblem.
759 **119** 20 c. multicoloured . . . 10 10
760 – 30 c. multicoloured . . . 10 10
761 – 50 c. multicoloured . . . 10 10
762 – 1 f. multicoloured . . . 10 10
763 – 18 f. multicoloured . . . 35 20
764 – 26 f. multicoloured . . . 65 45
765 – 34 f. multicoloured . . . 80 55
766 – 40 f. multicoloured . . . 1·10 80

124 Football **125** "Apollo" and "Soyuz" Launches and ASTP Badge

1976. Olympic Games, Montreal (2nd issue). Multicoloured.
767 20 c. Type **124** 10 10
768 30 c. Rifle-shooting 10 10
769 50 c. Canoeing 10 10
770 1 f. Gymnastics 10 10
771 10 f. Weightlifting 15 10
772 12 f. Diving 30 20
773 26 f. Horse-riding 55 40
774 50 f. Throwing the hammer . 1·40 90

1976. "Apollo" – "Soyuz" Test Project. Mult.
776 20 c. Type **125** 10 10
777 30 c. "Soyuz" rocket 10 10
778 50 c. "Apollo" rocket 10 10
779 1 f. "Apollo" after separation 10 10
780 2 f. Approach to link-up . . 10 10
781 12 f. Spacecraft docked . . . 35 15
782 30 f. Sectional view of interiors 1·10 55
783 54 f. "Apollo" splashdown . 2·25 1·25

126 "Eulophia cucullata" **128** Hands embracing "Cultural Collaboration"

1976. Rwandaise Orchids. Multicoloured.
784 20 c. Type **126** 10 10
785 30 c. "Eulophia streptopetala" 10 10
786 50 c. "Disa stairsii" 10 10
787 1 f. "Aerangis kotschyana" . 10 10
788 10 f. "Eulophia abyssinica" . 20 10
789 12 f. "Bonatea steudneri" . . 30 15
790 26 f. "Ansellia gigantea" . . 1·10 45
791 50 f. "Eulophia angolensis" . 2·00 1·25

1977. World Leprosy Day. Nos. 719/26 optd with **JOURNEE MONDIALE 1977.**
793 – 20 c. lilac, brown & black 10 10
794 – 30 c. lilac, green & black 10 10
795 **118** 50 c. lilac, brown & black 10 10
796 – 1 f. lilac, purple & black . 10 10
797 – 3 f. lilac, blue and black . 10 10
798 – 5 f. lilac, brown & black . 20 10
799 **118** 10 f. lilac, brown & black 35 20
800 – 80 f. lilac, red and black 1·60 1·60

1977. 10th OCAM Summit Meeting, Kigali. Mult.
801 10 f. Type **128** 30 10
802 26 f. Hands embracing "Technical Collaboration" . 70 40
803 64 f. Hands embracing "Economic Collaboration" 1·25 90

1977. World Water Conference. Nos. 688/95 optd **CONFERENCE MONDIALE DE L'EAU.**
805 **114** 20 c. multicoloured . . . 10 10
806 – 30 c. multicoloured . . . 10 10
807 – 50 c. multicoloured . . . 10 10
808 – 5 f. multicoloured . . . 15 10
809 – 8 f. multicoloured . . . 20 10
810 – 10 f. multicoloured . . . 40 15
811 – 26 f. multicoloured . . . 1·40 75
812 – 100 f. multicoloured . . . 3·50 3·25

131 Roman Signal Post and African Tam-Tam

1977. World Telecommunications Day. Mult.
813 20 c. Type **131** 10 10
814 30 c. Chappe's semaphore and post-rider 10 10
815 50 c. Morse code 10 10
816 1 f. "Goliath" laying Channel cable 10 10
817 4 f. Telephone, radio and television 10 10
818 18 f. "Kingsport" and maritime communications satellite . . 65 40
819 26 f. Telecommunications satellite and aerial 50 40
820 50 f. "Mariner 2" satellite . . 1·40 90

132 "The Ascent to Calvary" (detail) **135** Long-crested Eagle

1977. 400th Birth Anniv of Peter Paul Rubens. Multicoloured.
823 20 c. Type **132** 10 10
824 30 c. "The Judgement of Paris" (horiz) 10 10
825 50 c. "Marie de Medici, Queen of France" 10 10
826 1 f. "Heads of Negroes" (horiz) 10 10
827 4 f. "St. Idelfonse Triptych" (detail) 10 10
828 8 f. "Helene Fourment with her Children" (horiz) 15 10
829 26 f. "St. Idelfonse Triptych" (different detail) 80 65
830 60 f. "Helene Fourment" . . . 2·50 1·75

1977. Air. 10th Anniv of International French Language Council. As T **236a** of Mali.
831 50 f. multicoloured . . . . . 1·60 1·10

1977. Birds of Prey. Multicoloured.
833 20 c. Type **135** 10 10
834 30 c. African harrier hawk . . 10 10
835 50 c. African fish eagle . . . 10 10
836 1 f. Hooded vulture 10 10
837 3 f. Augur buzzard 15 10
838 5 f. Black kite 25 10
839 20 f. Black-shouldered kite . . 1·25 60
840 100 f. Bateleur . . . . 5·50 3·00

1977. Dr. Wernher von Braun Commemoration. Nos. 776/83 optd with **in memoriam WERNHER VON BRAUN 1912–1977.**
841 20 c. Type **125** 10 10
842 30 c. "Soyuz" rocket 10 10
843 50 c. "Apollo" rocket 10 10
844 1 f. "Apollo" after separation . 10 10
845 2 f. Approach to link up . . . 10 10
846 12 f. Spacecraft docked . . . 40 20
847 30 f. Sectional view of interiors 1·40 50
848 54 f. "Apollo" after splashdown 2·50 1·50

138 Scout playing Whistle **139** Chimpanzees

1978. 10th Anniv of Rwanda Scout Association. Multicoloured.
851 20 c. Type **138** 10 10
852 30 c. Camp fire 10 10
853 50 c. Scouts constructing a platform 10 10
854 1 f. Two scouts 10 10
855 10 f. Scouts on look-out . . . 20 10
856 18 f. Scouts in canoe 45 35
857 26 f. Cooking at camp fire . . 80 60
858 44 f. Lord Baden-Powell . . . 1·50 1·25

1978. Apes. Multicoloured.
859 20 c. Type **139** 10 10
860 30 c. Gorilla 10 10
861 50 c. Eastern black-and-white colobus 10 10
862 3 f. Eastern needle-clawed bushbaby 10 10
863 10 f. Mona monkey 30 10
864 26 f. Potto 65 65
865 60 f. Savanna monkey . . . . 1·90 1·90
866 150 f. Olive baboon . . . . . 3·75 3·75

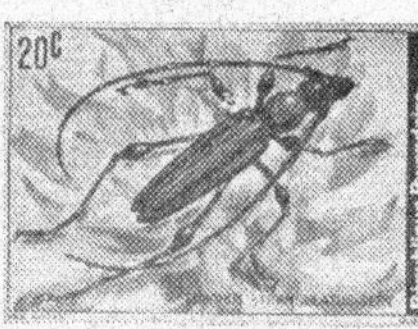

140 "Euporus strangulatus"

1978. Beetles. Multicoloured.
867 20 c. Type **140** 10 10
868 30 c. "Rhina afzelii" (vert) . . 10 10
869 50 c. "Pentalobus palini" . . 10 10
870 3 f. "Corynodes dejeani" (vert) 10 10
871 10 f. "Mecynorhina torquata" 20 10
872 15 f. "Mecocerus rhombeus" (vert) 55 10
873 20 f. "Macrotoma serripes" . 75 20
874 25 f. "Neptunides stanleyi" (vert) 90 40
875 26 f. "Petrognatha gigas" . . 90 40
876 100 f. "Eudicella gralli" (vert) 3·25 2·50

141 Poling Boat across River of Poverty

1978. National Revolutionary Development Movement. Multicoloured.
877 4 f. Type **141** 10 10
878 10 f. Poling boat to right . . 15 10
879 26 f. Type **141** 60 40
880 60 f. As 10 f. . . . . 1·10 85

142 Footballers, Cup and Flags of Netherlands and Peru

1978. World Cup Football Championship, Argentina. Multicoloured.
881 20 c. Type **142** 10 10
882 30 c. Flags of FIFA, Sweden and Spain 10 10
883 50 c. Mascot and flags of Scotland and Iran 10 10
884 2 f. Emblem and flags of West Germany and Tunisia . . . 10 10
885 3 f. Cup and flags of Italy and Hungary 10 10
886 10 f. Flags of FIFA, Brazil and Austria 20 10
887 34 f. Mascot and flags of Poland and Mexico 85 70
888 100 f. Emblem and flags of Argentina and France . . . 2·50 2·00

No. 883 shows the Union Jack.

143 Wright Brothers and Wright Flyer I, 1903

1978. Aviation History. Multicoloured.
889 20 c. Type **143** 10 10
890 30 c. Alberto Santos-Dumont and biplane "14 bis", 1906 . 10 10
891 50 c. Henri Farman and Farman Voisin No. 1 bis, 1908 . . 10 10
892 1 f. Jan Olieslagers and Bleriot XI 10 10
893 3 f. General Italo Balbo and Savoia S-17 flying boat, 1919 10 10
894 10 f. Charles Lindbergh and "Spirit of St. Louis", 1927 . 15 10
895 55 f. Hugo Junkers and Junkers Ju 52/3m, 1932 . . . . . 1·10 55
896 60 f. Igor Sikorsky and Vought-Sikorsky VS-300 helicopter prototype . . . . 1·60 85

1978. Air. "Philexafrique" Stamp Exhibition, Libreville, Gabon and Int Stamp Fair, Essen, West Germany. As T **262** of Niger. Mult.
898 30 f. Great spotted woodpecker and Oldenburg 1852 ⅓ sgr. stamp . . . . 1·90 95
899 30 f. Greater kudu and Rwanda 1967 20 c. stamp . . . . . 1·90 95

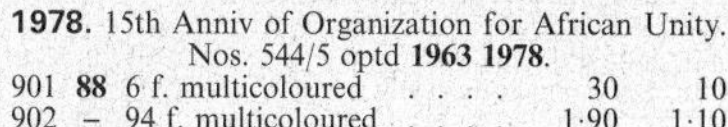

1978. 15th Anniv of Organization for African Unity. Nos. 544/5 optd **1963 1978.**
901 **88** 6 f. multicoloured 30 10
902 – 94 f. multicoloured . . . . 1·90 1·10

146 Spur-winged Goose and Mallard **147** "Papilio demodocus"

1978. Stock Rearing Year. Multicoloured.

903	20 c. Type **146**	45	10
904	30 c. Goats (horiz)	10	10
905	50 c. Chickens	10	10
906	4 f. Rabbits (horiz)	15	10
907	5 f. Pigs	15	10
908	15 f. Common turkey (horiz)	1·25	45
909	50 f. Sheep and cattle	1·25	50
910	75 f. Bull (horiz)	1·60	70

1979. Butterflies. Multicoloured.

911	20 c. Type **147**	10	10
912	30 c. "Precis octavia"	10	10
913	50 c. "Charaxes smaragdalis caerulea"	10	10
914	4 f. "Charaxes guderiana"	15	10
915	15 f. "Colotis evippe"	20	10
916	30 f. "Danaus limniace petiverana"	55	30
917	50 f. "Byblia acheloia"	1·50	55
918	150 f. "Utetheisa pulchella"	3·75	1·40

148 "Euphorbia grantii" and Women weaving

1979. "Philexafrique" Exhibition, Libreville. Mult.

919	40 f. Type **148**	1·40	85
920	60 f. Drummers and "Intelsat" satellite	2·25	1·10

149 "Polyscias fulva" **150** European Girl

1979. Trees. Multicoloured.

921	20 c. Type **149**	10	10
922	30 c. "Entandrophragma excelsum" (horiz)	10	10
923	50 c. "Ilex mitis"	10	10
924	4 f. "Kigelia africana" (horiz)	15	10
925	15 f. "Ficus thonningi"	35	10
926	20 f. "Acacia senegal" (horiz)	50	20
927	50 f. "Symphonia globulifera"	1·25	45
928	110 f. "Acacia sieberana" (horiz)	2·50	1·25

1979. International Year of the Child. Each brown, gold and stone.

929	26 f. Type **150**	65	60
930	26 f. Asian	65	60
931	26 f. Eskimo	65	60
932	26 f. Asian boy	65	60
933	26 f. African	65	60
934	26 f. South American Indian	65	60
935	26 f. Polynesian	65	60
936	26 f. European girl (different)	65	60
937	42 f. European and African (horiz)	2·00	65

151 Basket Weaving

1979. Handicrafts. Multicoloured.

939	50 c. Type **151**	10	10
940	1 f. 50 Wood-carving (vert)	10	10
941	2 f. Metal working	10	10
942	10 f. Basket work (vert)	35	10
943	20 f. Basket weaving (different)	50	20
944	26 f. Mural painting (vert)	65	55
945	40 f. Pottery	95	65
946	100 f. Smelting (vert)	2·50	1·75

153 Rowland Hill and 40 c. Ruanda Stamp of 1916

1979. Death Centenary of Sir Rowland Hill. Multicoloured.

948	20 c. Type **153**	10	10
949	30 c. 1916 Occupation stamp	10	10
950	50 c. 1918 "A.O" overprint	10	10
951	3 f. 1925 overprinted 60 c. stamp	10	10
952	10 f. 1931 50 c. African buffalo stamp	30	10
953	26 f. 1942 20 f. Common zebra stamp	65	15
954	60 f. 1953 25 f. Protea stamp	1·40	60
955	100 f. 1960 Olympic stamp	2·75	1·10

154 Strange Weaver **156** Butare Rotary Club Banner, Globe and Chicago Club Emblem of 1905

155 Armstrong's first Step on Moon

1980. Birds. Multicoloured.

956	20 c. Type **154**	10	10
957	30 c. Regal sunbird (vert)	10	10
958	50 c. White-spotted crake	10	10
959	3 f. Crowned hornbill	20	10
960	10 f. Barred owlet (vert)	50	25
961	26 f. African emerald cuckoo	1·10	60
962	60 f. Black-crowned waxbill (vert)	2·25	1·40
963	100 f. Crowned eagle (vert)	4·25	2·40

1980. 10th Anniv of "Apollo 11" Moon Landing. Multicoloured.

964	50 c. Type **155**	10	10
965	1 f. 50 Aldrin descending to Moon's surface	10	10
966	8 f. Planting the American flag	55	10
967	30 f. Placing seisometer	95	60
968	50 f. Taking samples	1·75	70
969	60 f. Setting-up experiment	2·50	90

1980. 75th Anniv of Rotary International. Mult.

971	20 c. Type **156**	10	10
972	30 c. Kigali Rotary Club banner	10	10
973	50 c. Type **156**	10	10
974	4 f. As No. 972	15	10
975	15 f. Type **156**	35	10
976	20 f. As No. 972	45	20
977	50 f. Type **156**	95	45
978	60 f. As No. 972	1·10	65

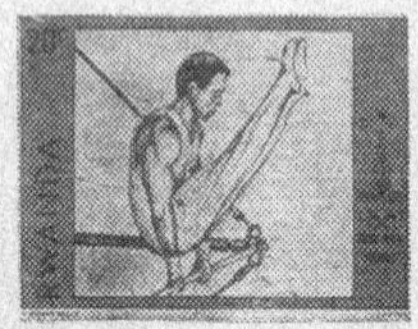
157 Gymnastics

1980. Olympic Games, Moscow.

979	**157**	20 c. yellow and black	10	10
980	–	30 c. green and black	10	10
981	–	50 c. red and black	10	10
982	–	3 f. blue and black	15	10
983	–	20 f. orange and black	45	20
984	–	26 f. purple and black	50	25
985	–	50 f. turquoise and black	1·10	45
986	–	100 f. brown and black	2·50	1·10

DESIGNS: 30 c. Basketball; 50 c. Cycling; 3 f. Boxing; 20 f. Archery; 26 f. Weightlifting; 50 f. Javelin; 100 f. Fencing.

159 "Geaster"

1980. Mushrooms. Multicoloured.

988	20 c. Type **159**	10	10
989	30 c. "Lentinus atrobrunneus"	10	10
990	50 c. "Gomphus stereoides"	10	10
991	4 f. "Cantharellus cibarius"	30	10
992	10 f. "Stilbothamnium dybowskii"	65	20
993	15 f. "Xeromphalina tenuipes"	90	20
994	70 f. "Podoscypha elegans"	3·75	80
995	100 f. "Mycena"	7·50	1·60

160 "At the Theatre" (Toulouse-Lautrec)

1980. Impressionist Paintings. Multicoloured.

996	20 c. "Still Life" (horiz) (Renoir)	10	10
997	30 c. Type **160**	10	10
998	50 c. "Seaside Garden" (Monet) (horiz)	10	10
999	4 f. "Mother and Child" (Mary Cassatt)	10	10
1000	5 f. "Starry Night" (Van Gogh) (horiz)	20	10
1001	10 f. "Three Dancers at their Toilette" (Degas)	35	10
1002	50 f. "The Card Players" (Cezanne) (horiz)	1·10	45
1003	70 f. "Tahitian Girls" (Gauguin)	1·75	65
1004	100 f. "La Grande Jatte" (Seurat) (horiz)	2·75	90

162 Revolutionary Scene

1980. 150th Anniv of Belgian Independence. Scenes of the Independence War from contemporary engravings.

1007	**162**	20 c. green and brown	10	10
1008	–	30 c. buff and brown	10	10
1009	–	50 c. blue and brown	10	10
1010	–	9 f. orange and brown	20	10
1011	–	10 f. mauve and brown	30	10
1012	–	20 f. green and brown	45	20
1013	–	70 f. pink and brown	1·50	65
1014	–	90 f. yellow and brown	1·90	1·00

163 Draining the Marshes

1980. Soil Protection and Conservation Year. Multicoloured.

1015	20 c. Type **163**	50	10
1016	30 c. Bullock in pen (mixed farming and land fertilization)	10	10
1017	1 f. 50 Land irrigation and rice	10	10
1018	8 f. Soil erosion and planting trees	20	10
1019	10 f. Terrace	30	15
1020	40 f. Crop fields	1·00	40
1021	90 f. Bean crop	2·10	85
1022	100 f. Picking tea	2·25	1·10

164 "Pavetta rwandensis"

1981. Flowers. Multicoloured.

1023	20 c. Type **164**	10	10
1024	30 c. "Cyrtorchis praetermissa"	10	10
1025	50 c. "Pavonia urens"	10	10
1026	4 f. "Cynorkis kassnerana"	10	10
1027	5 f. "Gardenia ternifolia"	15	10
1028	10 f. "Leptactina platyphylla"	20	10
1029	20 f. "Lobelia petiolata"	50	15
1030	40 f. "Tapinanthus brunneus"	90	45
1031	70 f. "Impatiens niamniamensis"	1·60	65
1032	150 f. "Dissotis rwandensis"	4·00	1·60

165 Mother and Child **166** Carol Singers

1981. SOS Children's Village. Multicoloured.

1033	20 c. Type **165**	10	10
1034	30 c. Child with pots	10	10
1035	50 c. Children drawing	10	10
1036	1 f. Girl sewing	10	10
1037	8 f. Children playing	20	10
1038	10 f. Girl knitting	20	10
1039	70 f. Children making models	1·50	70
1040	150 f. Mother and children	3·25	1·60

1981. Paintings by Norman Rockwell. Multicoloured.

1041	20 c. Type **166**	10	10
1042	30 c. People of different races	10	10
1043	50 c. Father Christmas	10	10
1044	1 f. Coachman	10	10
1045	8 f. Man at piano	15	10
1046	20 f. "Springtime"	50	20
1047	50 f. Man making donation to girl "nurse"	1·25	70
1048	70 f. Clown	1·75	1·10

167 Serval

1981. Carnivorous Animals. Multicoloured.

1049	20 c. Type **167**	10	10
1050	30 c. Black-backed jackal	10	10
1051	2 f. Servaline genet	10	10
1052	2 f. 50 Banded mongoose	10	10
1053	10 f. Zorilla	20	10
1054	15 f. Zaire clawless otter	35	10
1055	70 f. African golden cat	1·75	1·25
1056	200 f. Hunting dog (vert)	5·75	4·25

168 Drummer

1981. Telecommunications and Health. Mult.

1057	20 c. Type **168**	10	10
1058	30 c. Telephone receiver and world map	10	10
1059	2 f. Airliner and radar screen	10	10
1060	2 f. 50 Satellite and computer tape	10	10
1061	10 f. Satellite orbit and dish aerial	20	10
1062	15 f. Tanker and radar equipment	35	25
1063	70 f. Red Cross helicopter	1·90	70
1064	200 f. Satellite	4·25	2·25

169 "St. Benedict leaving His Parents"

1981. 1500th Birth Anniv of St. Benedict. Mult.

1065	20 c. Type **169**	10	10
1066	30 c. Portrait (10th century) (vert)	10	10
1067	50 c. Portrait (detail from "The Virgin of the Misericord" polyptich) (vert)	10	10
1068	4 f. "St. Benedict presenting the Rules of His Order"	10	10
1069	5 f. "St. Benedict and His Monks at their Meal"	15	10
1070	20 f. Portrait (13th century) (vert)	45	40
1071	70 f. St. Benedict at prayer (detail from "Our Lady in Glory with Sts. Gregory and Benedict")	1·75	1·40
1072	100 f. "Priest bringing the Easter Meal to St. Benedict" (Jan van Coninxlo)	2·75	1·75

170 Disabled Child painting with Mouth

1981. International Year of Disabled Persons. Multicoloured.

No.	Description	Unused	Used
1073	20 c. Type **170**	10	10
1074	30 c. Boys on crutches playing football	10	10
1075	4 f. 50 Disabled girl knitting	10	10
1076	5 f. Disabled child painting pot	15	10
1077	10 f. Boy in wheelchair using saw	20	10
1078	60 f. Child using sign language	1·25	60
1079	70 f. Child in wheelchair playing with puzzle	1·60	70
1080	100 f. Disabled child	2·00	1·10

172 Kob drinking at Pool

1981. Rural Water Supplies. Multicoloured.

No.	Description	Unused	Used
1082	20 c. Type **172**	10	10
1083	30 c. Women collecting water (vert)	10	10
1084	50 c. Constructing a pipeline	10	10
1085	10 f. Woman collecting water from pipe (vert)	20	10
1086	10 f. Man drinking	45	20
1087	70 f. Woman collecting water (vert)	1·50	70
1088	100 f. Floating pump (vert)	2·50	1·10

173 Cattle

1982. World Food Day. Multicoloured.

No.	Description	Unused	Used
1089	20 c. Type **173**	10	10
1090	30 c. Bee keeping	10	10
1091	50 c. Fish	10	10
1092	1 f. Avocado	10	10
1093	8 f. Boy eating banana	10	10
1094	20 f. Sorghum	45	15
1095	70 f. Vegetables	1·50	65
1096	100 f. Three generations and balanced diet	2·50	1·10

174 "Hibiscus berberidfolius"

1982. Flowers. Multicoloured.

No.	Description	Unused	Used
1097	20 c. Type **174**	10	10
1098	30 c. "Hypericum lanceolatum" (vert)	10	10
1099	50 c. "Canarina eminii"	10	10
1100	4 r. "Polygala ruwenzoriensis"	10	10
1101	10 f. "Kniphofia grantii" (vert)	15	10
1102	35 f. "Euphorbia candelabrum" (vert)	90	60
1103	70 f. "Disa erubescens" (vert)	1·75	80
1104	80 f. "Gloriosa simplex"	2·40	1·10

175 Pres. Habyarimana and Flags

1982. 20th Anniv of Independence. Multicoloured.

No.	Description	Unused	Used
1105	10 f. Type **175**	20	10
1106	20 f. Hands releasing doves (Peace)	35	20
1107	30 f. Clasped hands and flag (Unity)	65	35
1108	50 f. Building (Development)	1·00	50

176 Football

1982. World Cup Football Championship, Spain.

No.	Description	Unused	Used
1109 **176**	20 c. multicoloured	10	10
1110 –	30 c. multicoloured	10	10
1111 –	1 f. 50 multicoloured	10	10
1112 –	8 f. multicoloured	15	10
1113 –	10 f. multicoloured	20	10
1114 –	20 f. multicoloured	40	15
1115 –	70 f. multicoloured	1·60	65
1116 –	90 f. multicoloured	2·25	85

DESIGNS: 30 c. to 90 f. Designs show different players.

177 Microscope and Slide

1982. Centenary of Discovery of Tubercle Bacillus. Multicoloured.

No.	Description	Unused	Used
1117	10 f. Type **177**	15	10
1118	20 f. Hand with test tube and slide	40	15
1119	70 f. Lungs and slide	1·60	65
1120	100 f. Dr. Robert Koch	2·25	95

180 African Elephants

1982. 10th Anniv of United Nations Environment Programme. Multicoloured.

No.	Description	Unused	Used
1123	20 c. Type **180**	10	10
1124	30 c. Lion hunting impala	10	10
1125	50 c. Flower	10	10
1126	4 f. African buffalo	10	10
1127	5 f. Impala	10	10
1128	10 f. Flower (different)	20	10
1129	20 f. Common zebra	45	15
1130	40 f. Crowned cranes	1·50	35
1131	50 f. African fish eagle	1·75	55
1132	70 f. Woman with basket of fruit	1·60	80

181 Scout tending Injured Kob

1982. 75th Anniv of Scout Movement. Mult.

No.	Description	Unused	Used
1133	20 c. Type **181**	10	10
1134	30 c. Tents and northern doubled-collared sunbird	60	15
1135	1 r. 50 Campfire	10	10
1136	8 f. Scout	15	10
1137	10 f. Knot	20	10
1138	20 f. Tent and campfire	40	15
1139	70 f. Scout cutting stake	1·90	80
1140	90 f. Scout salute	2·40	1·00

182 Northern Double-collared Sunbird

183 Driving Cattle

1983. Nectar-sucking Birds. Multicoloured.

No.	Description	Unused	Used
1141	20 c. Type **182**	10	10
1142	30 c. Regal sunbird (horiz)	10	10
1143	50 c. Red-tufted malachite sunbird	10	10
1144	4 f. Bronze sunbird (horiz)	20	10
1145	5 f. Collared sunbird	25	10
1146	10 f. Blue-headed sunbird (horiz)	55	20
1147	20 f. Purple-breasted sunbird	1·10	50
1148	40 f. Coppery sunbird (horiz)	2·25	90
1149	50 f. Olive-bellied sunbird	2·50	1·25
1150	70 f. Red-chested sunbird (horiz)	3·50	1·75

1983. Campaign Against Soil Erosion. Mult.

No.	Description	Unused	Used
1151	20 c. Type **183**	10	10
1152	30 c. Pineapple plantation	10	10
1153	50 c. Interrupted ditches	10	10
1154	9 f. Hedged terraces	20	10
1155	10 f. Re-afforestation	20	10
1156	20 f. Anti-erosion barriers	40	15
1157	30 f. Contour planting	65	30
1158	50 f. Terraces	1·00	40
1159	60 f. River bank protection	1·40	60
1160	70 f. Alternate fallow and planted strips	1·60	80

184 Feeding Ducks

185 Young Gorillas

1983. Birth Cent of Cardinal Cardijan (founder of Young Catholic Workers Movement). Mult.

No.	Description	Unused	Used
1161	20 c. Type **184**	10	10
1162	30 c. Harvesting bananas	10	10
1163	50 c. Carrying melons	10	10
1164	10 f. Wood-carving	20	10
1165	19 f. Making shoes	35	15
1166	20 f. Children in field of millet	45	15
1167	70 f. Embroidering	1·40	60
1168	80 f. Cardinal Cardijan	1·60	65

1983. Mountain Gorillas. Multicoloured.

No.	Description	Unused	Used
1169	20 c. Type **185**	10	10
1170	30 c. Gorilla family	10	10
1171	9 f. 50 Young and adult	45	30
1172	10 f. Mother with young	45	30
1173	20 f. Heads	65	45
1174	30 f. Adult and head	90	50
1175	60 f. Adult (vert)	2·00	1·40
1176	70 f. Close-up of adult (vert)	2·40	1·50

187 "Hagenia abyssinica"

1984. Trees. Multicoloured.

No.	Description	Unused	Used
1178	20 c. Type **187**	10	10
1179	30 c. "Dracaena steudneri"	10	10
1180	50 c. "Phoenix reclinata"	10	10
1181	10 f. "Podocarpus milanjianus"	15	10
1182	19 f. "Entada abyssinica"	40	15
1183	70 f. "Parinari excelsa"	1·60	65
1184	100 f. "Newtonia buchananii"	2·00	95
1185	200 f. "Acacia gerrardi" (vert)	4·50	1·60

188 Diesel Train

189 "Le Martial", 1783

1984. World Communications Year. Multicoloured.

No.	Description	Unused	Used
1186	20 c. Type **188**	10	10
1187	30 c. Liner and radar	15	10
1188	4 f. 50 Radio and transmitter	15	10
1189	10 f. Telephone dial and cable	20	10
1190	15 f. Letters and newspaper	35	10
1191	50 f. Airliner and control tower	1·10	45
1192	70 f. Television and antenna	1·60	65
1193	100 f. Satellite and computer tape	2·50	90

1984. Bicentenary of Manned Flight. Mult.

No.	Description	Unused	Used
1194	20 c. Type **189**	10	10
1195	30 c. De Rozier and Marquis d'Arlandes flight, 1783	10	10
1196	50 c. Charles and Robert (1783) and Blanchard (1784) flights	10	10
1197	9 f. M. and Mme. Blanchard	20	10
1198	10 f. Blanchard and Jeffries, 1785	20	10
1199	50 f. Demuyter (1937) and Piccard and Kipfer (1931) flights	1·10	40
1200	80 f. Modern hot-air balloons	2·75	1·90
1201	200 f. Trans-Atlantic flight, 1978	3·50	2·50

190 Equestrian

1984. Olympic Games, Los Angeles. Multicoloured.

No.	Description	Unused	Used
1202	20 c. Type **190**	10	10
1203	30 c. Windsurfing	15	10
1204	50 c. Football	10	10
1205	9 f. Swimming	20	10
1206	10 f. Hockey	20	10
1207	40 f. Fencing	1·25	70
1208	80 f. Running	2·00	1·75
1209	200 f. Boxing	5·00	4·00

191 Mare and Foal

1984. Common Zebras and African Buffaloes. Multicoloured.

No.	Description	Unused	Used
1210	20 c. Type **191**	10	10
1211	30 c. Buffalo and calf (vert)	10	10
1212	50 c. Pair of zebras (vert)	10	10
1213	9 f. Zebras fighting	20	10
1214	10 f. Close-up of buffalo (vert)	30	10
1215	80 f. Herd of zebras	1·90	1·40
1216	100 f. Close-up of zebras (vert)	2·50	1·75
1217	200 f. Buffalo charging	4·75	3·50

193 Gorillas at Water-hole

1985. Gorillas. Multicoloured.

No.	Description	Unused	Used
1219	10 f. Type **193**	1·00	65
1220	15 f. Two gorillas in tree	1·50	70
1221	25 f. Gorilla family	2·00	1·75
1222	30 f. Three adults	2·50	2·50

194 Man feeding Fowl

1985. Food Production Year. Multicoloured.

No.	Description	Unused	Used
1224	20 c. Type **194**	10	10
1225	30 c. Men carrying pineapples	15	10
1226	50 c. Farm animals	10	10
1227	9 f. Men filling sacks with produce	20	10
1228	10 f. Agricultural instruction	30	10
1229	50 f. Sowing seeds	1·00	45
1230	80 f. Storing produce	1·60	65
1231	100 f. Working in banana plantation	2·10	80

195 Emblem

1985. 10th Anniv of National Revolutionary Redevelopment Movement.

No.	Description	Unused	Used
1232 **195**	10 f. multicoloured	20	10
1233	30 f. multicoloured	65	30
1234	70 f. multicoloured	1·60	70

196 U.N. Emblem within "40"

1985. 40th Anniv of U.N.O.

No.	Type	Description	Mint	Used
1235	196	50 f. multicoloured	1·10	90
1236		100 f. multicoloured	2·50	2·10

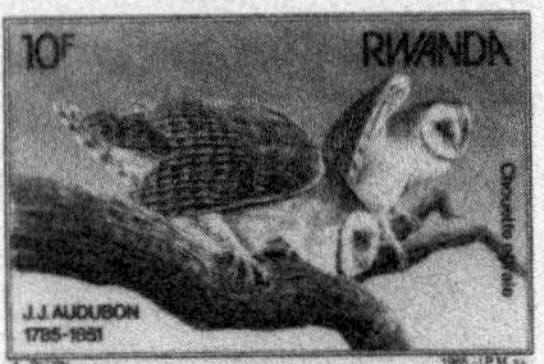

197 Barn Owls

1985. Birth Bicentenary of John J. Audubon (ornithologist). Multicoloured.

No.	Description	Mint	Used
1237	10 f. Type **197**	60	25
1238	20 f. White-faced scops owls	1·25	50
1239	40 f. Ruby-throated humming birds	2·40	1·00
1240	80 f. Eastern meadowlarks	5·75	2·25

198 "Participation, Development and Peace"

1985. International Youth Year. Multicoloured.

No.	Description	Mint	Used
1241	7 f. Type **198**	15	10
1242	9 f. Cycling	30	10
1243	44 f. Youths carrying articles on head (teamwork)	1·10	45
1244	80 f. Education	1·75	80

1985. 75th Anniv of Girl Guide Movement. Nos. 1133/40 optd **1910/1985** and guide emblem.

No.	Description	Mint	Used
1245	20 c. Type **181**	10	10
1246	30 c. Tents	30	10
1247	1 f. 50 Campfire	10	10
1248	8 f. Scout	20	10
1249	10 f. Knot	20	10
1250	20 f. Tent and campfire	45	10
1251	70 f. Scout cutting stake	1·60	65
1252	90 f. Scout salute	2·50	90

201 Container Lorry (Transport)

1986. Transport and Communications. Mult.

No.	Description	Mint	Used
1254	10 f. Type **201**	35	10
1255	30 f. Handstamping cover (posts)	80	35
1256	40 f. Kigali Earth Station (telecommunication)	1·10	45
1257	80 f. Kigali airport (aviation) (48 × 31 mm)	1·75	1·25

1986. Intensified Agriculture Year. Nos. 1152/60 optd **ANNEE 1986 INTENSIFICATION AGRICOLE** or surch also.

No.	Description	Mint	Used
1258	9 f. Hedged terraces	20	10
1259	10 f. Re-afforestation	20	10
1260	10 f. on 30c. Pineapple plantation	20	10
1261	10 f. on 50c. Interrupted ditches	20	10
1262	20 f. Anti-erosion barriers	45	20
1263	30 f. Contour planning	65	35
1264	50 f. Terraces	1·10	50
1265	60 f. River bank protection	1·40	55
1266	70 f. Alternate fallow and planted strips	1·60	70

203 Morocco v England

1986. World Cup Football Championship, Mexico. Multicoloured.

No.	Description	Mint	Used
1267	2 f. Type **203**	10	10
1268	4 f. Paraguay v Iraq	10	10
1269	5 f. Brazil v Spain	10	10
1270	10 f. Italy v Argentina	55	35
1271	40 f. Mexico v Belgium	1·60	85
1272	45 f. France v Russia	1·75	1·00

204 Roan Antelopes

1986. Akagera National Park. Multicoloured.

No.	Description	Mint	Used
1273	4 f. Type **204**	10	10
1274	7 f. Whale-headed storks	80	10
1275	9 f. Cape eland	15	10
1276	10 f. Giraffe	30	10
1277	80 f. African elephant	1·90	85
1278	90 f. Crocodile	2·25	1·00
1279	100 f. Heuglin's masked weavers	6·00	3·00
1280	100 f. Zebras and eastern white pelican	6·00	3·00

205 People of Different Races on Globe

1986. Christmas. International Peace Year. Mult.

No.	Description	Mint	Used
1281	10 f. Type **205**	35	15
1282	15 f. Dove and globe	45	15
1283	30 f. Type **205**	80	35
1284	70 f. As No. 1282	1·75	1·00

206 Mother breast-feeding Baby

1987. U.N.I.C.E.F. Child Survival Campaign. Multicoloured.

No.	Description	Mint	Used
1285	4 f. Type **206**	15	15
1286	6 f. Mother giving oral rehydration therapy to baby	20	15
1287	10 f. Nurse immunising baby	35	25
1288	70 f. Nurse weighing baby and graph	1·75	1·60

207 Couple packing Baskets with Food

1987. Food Self-sufficiency Year. Multicoloured.

No.	Description	Mint	Used
1289	5 f. Type **207**	10	10
1290	7 f. Woman and baskets of food	15	10
1291	40 f. Man with baskets of fish and fruits	1·25	45
1292	60 f. Fruits and vegetables	2·25	80

208 Pres. Habyarimana and Soldiers

1987. 25th Anniv of Independence. Multicoloured.

No.	Description	Mint	Used
1293	10 f. Type **208**	20	10
1294	40 f. President at meeting	90	45
1295	70 f. President with Pope John Paul II	2·50	85
1296	100 f. Pres. Habyarimana (vert)	2·50	1·10

209 Bananas

1987. Fruits. Multicoloured.

No.	Description	Mint	Used
1297	10 f. Type **209**	20	10
1298	40 f. Pineapples (horiz)	90	45
1299	80 f. Papaya (horiz)	2·25	90
1300	90 f. Avocados (horiz)	2·50	1·00
1301	100 f. Strawberries	2·50	1·10

210 Mother carrying cub

1987. The Leopard. Multicoloured.

No.	Description	Mint	Used
1302	50 f. Type **210**	1·40	55
1303	50 f. Leopards fighting	1·40	55
1304	50 f. Leopards with prey	1·40	55
1305	50 f. Leopard with prey in tree	1·40	55
1306	50 f. Leopard leaping from tree	1·40	55

211 Village Activities

1987. International Volunteers Day. Mult.

No.	Description	Mint	Used
1307	5 f. Type **211**	10	10
1308	12 f. Pupils in schoolroom	35	10
1309	20 f. View of village	55	30
1310	60 f. Woman tending oxen	1·75	85

213 Carpenter's Shop

1988. Rural Incomes Protection Year. Mult.

No.	Description	Mint	Used
1312	10 f. Type **213**	20	10
1313	40 f. Dairy farm	95	95
1314	60 f. Workers in field	1·50	55
1315	80 f. Selling baskets of eggs	2·10	1·50

214 Chimpanzees

1988. Primates of Nyungwe Forest. Multicoloured.

No.	Description	Mint	Used
1316	2 f. Type **214**	15	10
1317	3 f. Black and white colobus	15	10
1318	10 f. Lesser bushbabies	55	40
1319	90 f. Monkeys	3·25	2·40

215 Boxing

1988. Olympic Games, Seoul. Multicoloured.

No.	Description	Mint	Used
1320	5 f. Type **215**	10	10
1321	7 f. Relay race	15	10
1322	8 f. Table tennis	20	10
1323	10 f. Running	35	15
1324	90 f. Hurdling	2·25	1·00

216 "25" on Map of Africa

219 "Plectranthus barbatus"

218 Newspaper Fragment and Refugees in Boat

1988. 25th Anniv of Organization of African Unity. Multicoloured.

No.	Description	Mint	Used
1325	5 f. Type **216**	15	10
1326	7 f. Hands clasped across map	20	10
1327	8 f. Building on map	20	10
1328	90 f. Words forming map	2·75	2·25

1988. 125th Anniv of Red Cross Movement. Mult.

No.	Description	Mint	Used
1330	10 f. Type **218**	20	10
1331	30 f. Red Cross workers and patient	80	35
1332	40 f. Red Cross worker and elderly lady (vert)	95	40
1333	100 f. Red Cross worker and family (vert)	2·75	1·25

1989. Plants. Multicoloured.

No.	Description	Mint	Used
1334	5 f. Type **219**	10	10
1335	10 f. "Tetradenia riparia"	30	10
1336	20 f. "Hygrophila auriculata	60	20
1337	40 f. "Datura stramonium	1·25	45
1338	50 f. "Pavetta ternifolia"	1·60	60

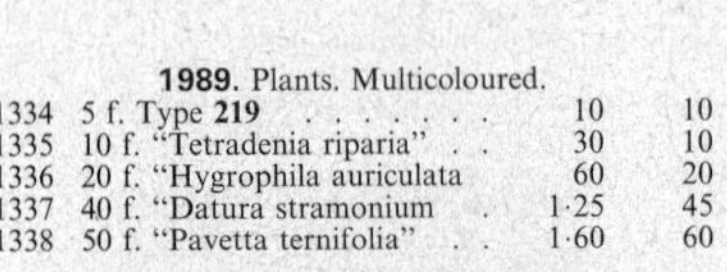

220 Emblem, Dates and Sunburst

1989. Centenary of Interparliamentary Union. Mult.

No.	Description	Mint	Used
1339	10 f. Type **220**	30	10
1340	30 f. Lake	85	65
1341	70 f. River	1·60	1·40
1342	90 f. Sun's rays	2·25	1·75

222 Throwing Clay and Finished Pots

1989. Rural Self-help Year. Multicoloured.

No.	Description	Mint	Used
1344	10 f. Type **222**	30	10
1345	70 f. Carrying baskets of produce (vert)	1·60	1·40
1346	90 f. Firing clay pots	2·50	2·00
1347	200 f. Clearing roadway	5·00	3·50

223 "Triumph of Marat" (Boilly)

1990. Bicentenary of French Revolution. Mult.

No.	Description	Mint	Used
1348	10 f. Type **223**	30	10
1349	60 f. "Rouget de Lisle singing La Marseillaise" (Pils)	1·60	1·50
1350	70 f. "Oath of the Tennis Court" (Jacques Louis David)	2·00	1·75
1351	100 f. "Trial of Louis XVI" (Joseph Court)	3·00	2·75

224 Old and New Lifestyles

1990. 30th Anniv of Revolution. Multicoloured.
1352 10 f. Type **224** 30 10
1353 60 f. Couple holding farming implements (vert) . . . . . 1·60 1·40
1354 70 f. Modernisation . . . . . 1·75 1·40
1355 100 f. Flag, map and warrior 2·50 2·50

225 Construction

1990. 25th Anniv (1989) of African Development Bank. Multicoloured.
1356 10 f. Type **225** 30 10
1357 20 f. Tea picking 55 35
1358 40 f. Road building . . . . . 1·10 95
1359 90 f. Tea pickers and modern housing . . . . 2·50 2·10

1990. World Cup Football Championship, Italy. Nos. 1267/72 optd **ITALIA 90**.
1361 **203** 2 f. multicoloured 35 35
1362 – 4 f. multicoloured 35 35
1363 – 5 f. multicoloured 40 40
1364 – 10 f. multicoloured . . . 65 65
1365 – 40 f. multicoloured . . . 2·50 2·50
1366 – 45 f. multicoloured . . . 2·75 2·75

228 Pope John Paul II

1990. Papal Visits. Multicoloured.
1367 10 f. Type **228** 75 75
1368 70 f. Pope giving blessing . . 8·25 8·25

229 Adults learning Alphabet at School

1991. International Literacy Year (1990). Mult.
1370 10 f. Type **229** 15 10
1371 20 f. Children reading at school 35 20
1372 50 f. Lowland villagers learning alphabet in field 90 80
1373 90 f. Highland villagers learning alphabet outdoors . . . . 1·40 1·10

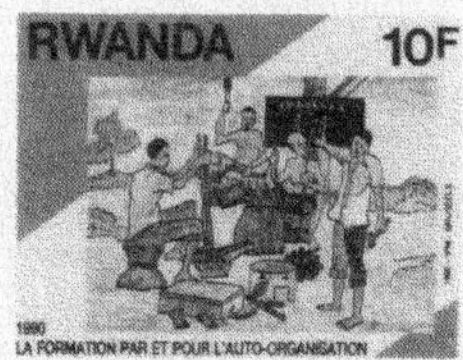

230 Tool-making

1991. Self-help Organizations. Multicoloured.
1374 10 f. Type **230** 15 10
1375 20 f. Rearing livestock 35 20
1376 50 f. Textile manufacture . . 1·40 1·10
1377 90 f. Construction . . . . . 2·00 1·50

231 Statue of Madonna

1992. Death Centenary of Cardinal Lavigerie (founder of Orders of White Fathers and Sisters).
1378 **231** 5 f. multicoloured . . . 40 35
1379 – 15 f. multicoloured . . . 1·10 90
1380 – 70 f. black and mauve . . 5·25 4·25
1381 – 110 f. black and blue . . 8·25 7·00
DESIGNS—VERT: 15 f. White sister; 110 f. Cardinal Lavigerie. HORIZ: 70 f. White Fathers in Uganda, 1908.

232 Running

1993. Olympic Games, Barcelona (1992). Multicoloured.
1382 20 f. Type **232** . . . . 2·00 1·60
1383 30 f. Swimming . . . . . . 3·25 2·75
1384 90 f. Football . . . . 9·50 8·00

RYUKYU ISLANDS Pt. 18

Group of islands between Japan and Taiwan formerly Japanese until occupied by U.S. forces in 1945. After a period of military rule they became semi-autonomous under U.S. administration. The Amami Oshima group reverted to Japan in December 1953. The remaining islands were returned to Japan on 15 May 1972. Japanese stamps are now in use.

1948. 100 sen = 1 yen.
1958. 100 cents = 1 dollar (U.S.).

1 Cycad Palm

3 Tribute Junk

1948.
1 **1** 5 s. purple . . . . 3·00 1·75
2 – 10 s. green . . . . 3·50 2·25
3 **1** 20 s. green . . . . 3·50 2·25
4 **3** 30 s. red . . . . 3·50 2·25
5 – 40 s. purple . . . . 3·00 1·75
6 **3** 50 s. blue . . . . 3·50 2·50
7 – 1 y. blue . . . . 3·50 2·50
DESIGNS: 10 s., 40 s. Easter lily; 1 y. Farmer with hoe.

6 Shi-Shi Roof Tiles

12 Dove over Map of Ryukyus

1950.
8 **6** 50 s. red 25 25
10 – 1 y. blue . . . . 2·75 1·25
11 – 2 y. purple . . . . 12·00 3·00
12 – 3 y. pink . . . . 20·00 8·00
13 – 4 y. grey . . . . 8·00 3·00
14 – 5 y. green . . . . 10·00 4·50
DESIGNS: 1 y. Shuri woman; 2 y. Former Okinawa Palace, Shuri; 3 y. Dragon's head; 4 y. Okinawa women; 5 y. Common spider and strawberry conches and radula scallop.

1950. Air.
15 **12** 8 y. blue . . . . 65·00 20·00
16 12 y. green . . . . 42·00 16·00
17 16 y. red . . . . 18·00 12·00

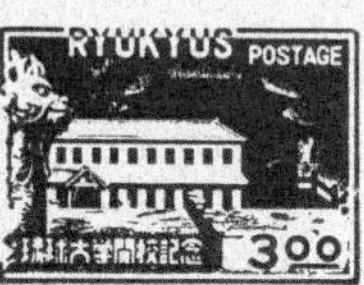

14 University and Shuri Castle

15 Pine Tree

1951. Inauguration of Ryukyu University.
19 **14** 3 y. brown . . . . 45·00 18·00

1951. Afforestation Week.
20 **15** 3 y. green . . . . 45·00 18·00

16 Flying Goddess

(**17**)

1951. Air.
21 **16** 13 y. blue . . . . 2·00 40
22 18 y. green . . . . 2·50 3·00
23 30 y. mauve . . . . 4·00 1·25
24 40 y. purple . . . . 6·00 2·25
25 50 y. orange . . . . 7·50 3·25

1952. Surch as T **17**.
27 **6** 10 y. on 50 s. red . . . . . . 10·00 5·50
29 – 100 y. on 2 y. pur (No. 11) . £2000 £850

18 Dove and Bean Seedling

19 Madanbashi Bridge

1952. Establishment of Ryukyuan Government.
30 **18** 3 y. red . . . . £100·00 20·00

1952.
31 **19** 1 y. red 25 25
32 – 2 y. green 30 25
33 – 3 y. turquoise 60 25
34 – 6 y. blue . . . . 4·00 3·25
35 – 10 y. red . . . . 1·75 50
36 – 30 y. green . . . . 4·75 2·50
37 – 50 y. purple . . . . 6·00 2·00
38 – 100 y. purple . . . . 12·00 1·50
DESIGNS: 2 y. Presence Chamber, Shuri Palace; 3 y. Shuri Gate; 6 y. Sogenji Temple Wall; 10 y. Bensaitendo Temple; 30 y. Sonohyamutake Gate; 50 y. Tamaudum Mausoleum, Shuri; 100 y. Hosho-chai Bridge.

27 Reception at Shuri Castle

28 Perry and American Fleet at Naha Harbour

29 Chofu Ota and Matrix

1953. Centenary of Commodore Perry's Visit to Okinawa.
39 **27** 3 y. purple . . . . 12·00 4·00
40 **28** 6 y. blue . . . . 2·25 2·40

1953. 3rd Press Week.
41 **29** 4 y. brown . . . . 12·00 5·00

30 Wine Flask to fit around Waist

33 Shigo Toma and Pen-nib

1954.
42 **30** 4 y. brown 50 35
43 – 15 y. red . . . . 2·25 1·75
44 – 20 y. orange . . . . 3·25 2·25
DESIGNS: 15 y. Tung Dar Bon (lacquer bowl); 20 y. Kasuri (textile pattern).

1954. 4th Press Week.
45 **33** 4 y. blue . . . . 10·00 3·50

34 Noguni Shrine and Sweet Potatoes

35 Stylized Trees

1955. 350th Anniv of Introduction of Sweet Potato Plant.
46 **34** 4 y. blue . . . . 10·00 4·00

1956. Afforestation Week.
47 **35** 4 y. green . . . . 8·00 3·00

38 Nidotekito Dance

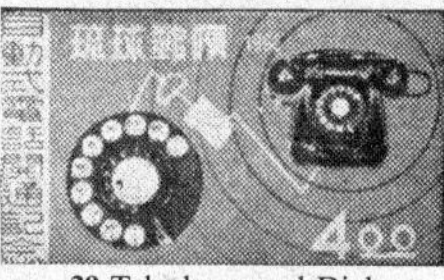

39 Telephone and Dial

1956. National Dances.
48 – 5 y. purple . . . . 1·10 60
49 – 8 y. violet . . . . 1·40 1·25
50 **38** 14 y. brown . . . . 2·25 2·25
DESIGNS: 5 y. Willow dance; 8 y. Straw-hat dance.

1956. Inauguration of Telephone Dialling System.
51 **39** 4 y. violet . . . . 12·00 8·00

34 – 6 y. blue . . . .

40 Floral Garland
41 Flying Goddess

1956. New Year.
52 40 2 y. multicoloured . . . . . 2·00 1·40

1957. Air.
53 41 15 y. green . . . . 2·00 40
54 20 y. red . . . . 4·50 3·00
55 35 y. green . . . . 10·00 4·00
56 45 y. brown . . . . 16·00 6·00
57 60 y. grey . . . . 22·00 8·50

42 "Rocket" Pencils
43 Phoenix

1957. 7th Press Week.
58 42 4 y. blue 55 55

1957. New Year.
59 43 2 y. multicoloured 40 20

44 Various Ryukyuan Postage Stamps

1958. 10th Anniv of First Postage Stamps of Ryukyu Islands.
60 44 4 y. multicoloured . . . . . 1·00 60

45 Stylized Dollar Sign over Yen Symbol

1958. With or without gum (Nos. 68/69), no gum (others).
61 45 ½ c. yellow 25 20
62 1 c. green 25 20
63 2 c. blue 25 25
64 3 c. red 20 15
65 4 c. green 60 45
66 5 c. brown . . . . 2·00 50
67 10 c. blue . . . . 3·25 50
68 25 c. blue . . . . 3·50 80
69 50 c. grey . . . . 7·00 1·00
70 $1 purple . . . . 10·00 1·25

46 Gateway of Courtesy

1958. Restoration of Shuri Gateway.
71 46 3 c. multicoloured . . . . . 1·25 50

47 Lion Dance
48 Trees

1958. New Year.
72 47 1½ c. multicoloured 30 25

1959. Afforestation Week.
73 48 3 c. multicoloured . . . . . 1·50 1·25

49 Atlas Moth
50 Hibiscus

1959. Japanese Biological Teachers' Conf, Okinawa.
74 49 3 c. multicoloured . . . . 2·00 1·25

1959. Multicoloured. (a) Inscr as in T **50**.
75 ½ c. Type **50** 30 20
76 3 c. Tropical fish . . . . . . 1·10 25
77 8 c. Zebra moon, banded bonnet and textile cone (shells) . . . 8·00 2·00
78 13 c. Leaf butterfly (value at left) 2·00 1·50
79 17 c. Jellyfish . . . . 22·00 5·50

(b) Inscr smaller and 13 c. with value at right.
87 ½ c. Type **50** 30 15
88 3 c. As No. 76 . . . . 2·00 20
89 8 c. As No. 77 . . . . 2·50 1·00
90 13 c. As No. 78 . . . . 1·75 1·00
91 17 c. As No. 79 . . . . 8·00 3·25

55 Yakazi (Ryukyuan toy)

改訂 9¢

(56)

1959. New Year.
80 55 1½ c. multicoloured 80 40

1959. Air. Surch as T **56**.
81 41 9 c. on 15 y. green . . . . 2·00 40
82 14 c. on 20 y. red . . . . . 3·50 3·00
83 19 c. on 35 y. green . . . . 5·00 4·00
84 27 c. on 45 y. brown . . . 10·00 6·00
85 35 c. on 60 y. grey . . . . 14·00 8·00

57 University Badge
60 "Munjuru"

1960. 10th Anniv of University of the Ryukyus.
86 57 3 c. multicoloured . . . . 1·25 60

1960. Air. Surch.
92 30 9 c. on 4 y. brown . . . . 5·00 60
93 – 14 c. on 5 y. pur (No. 48) . . 3·00 2·00
94 – 19 c. on 15 y. red (No. 43) . 5·00 2·75
95 38 27 c. on 14 y. brown . . . 6·00 4·25
96 – 35 c. on 20 y. orge (No. 44) 7·00 5·25

1960. Ryukyuan Dances. Mult. (a) Inscr as in T **60**.
97 1 c. Type **60** . . . . 2·00 1·00
98 2½ c. "Inohabushi" . . . . . 1·75 1·00
99 5 c. "Hatomabushi" . . . . . 1·00 1·00
100 10 c. "Hanafu" . . . . 1·50 1·00

(b) As T **60** but additionally inscr "RYUKYUS".
107 1 c. Type **60** 15 15
108 2½ c. As No. 98 . . . . 15 15
109 4 c. As No. 98 . . . . 20 15
110 5 c. As No. 99 . . . . 30 25
111 10 c. As No. 100 . . . . . . 50 15
112 20 c. "Shudun" . . . . 1·25 35
113 25 c. "Haodori" . . . . 1·25 60
114 50 c. "Nobori Kuduchi" . . . . 1·75 60
115 $ 1 "Koteibushi" . . . . . . 2·25 70

65 Start of Race

1960. 8th Kyushu Athletic Meeting.
101 – 3 c. red, green and blue . . 5·00 1·50
102 65 8 c. green and orange . . 1·75 1·00
DESIGN: 3 c. Torch and coastal scene.

66 Little Egret and Rising Sun

1960. National Census.
103 66 3 c. brown . . . . 8·00 2·00

67 Bull Fight

1960. New Year.
104 67 1½ c. brown, buff & blue . 1·00 60

68 Native Pine Tree

1961. Afforestation Week.
105 68 3 c. dp green, red & green . 1·75 90

69 Naha, Junk, Liner and City Seal

1961. 40th Anniv of Naha City.
106 69 3 c. turquoise . . . . 2·50 1·25

74 Flying Goddess
79 White Silver Temple

1961. Air.
116 74 9 c. multicoloured 50 15
117 – 14 c. multicoloured 70 60
118 – 19 c. multicoloured . . . . 1·25 75
119 – 27 c. multicoloured . . . . 1·50 75
120 – 35 c. multicoloured . . . . 2·00 75
DESIGNS: 14 c. Flying goddess playing flute; 19 c. Wind god; 27 c. Wind god (different); 35 c. Flying goddess over trees.

1961. Unification of Itoman District and Takamine, Kanegushiku and Miwa Villages.
121 79 3 c. brown . . . . 1·25 75

80 Books and Bird
81 Sunrise and Eagles

1961. 10th Anniv of Ryukyu Book Week.
122 80 3 c. multicoloured . . . . . 1·25 75

1961. New Year.
123 81 1½ c. red, black and gold . . 3·25 1·00

82 Govt Building, Steps and Trees
85 Shuri Gate and Campaign Emblem

1962. 10th Anniv of Ryukyu Government. Mult.
124 1½ c. Type **82** 60 60
125 3 c. Government building . . . 90 75

1962. Malaria Eradication. Multicoloured.
126 3 c. "Anopheles hyrcanus sinensis" (mosquito) 70 60
127 8 c. Type **85** . . . . 1·25 1·75

86 Windmill, Dolls and Horse
87 "Hibiscus lilaceus"

1962. Children's Day.
128 86 3 c. multicoloured . . . . . 2·00 1·25

1962. Ryukyu Flowers. Multicoloured.
129 ½ c. Type **87** 20 15
142 1½ c. "Etithyllum strictum" . . 30 20
130 2 c. "Ixora chinensis" 20 25
131 3 c. "Erythrina indica" . . . 50 20
132 3 c. "Caesalpinia pulcherrima" 20 20
133 8 c. "Schima mertensiana" . . 75 25
134 13 c. "Impatiens balsamina" . 1·00 50
135 15 c. "Hamaomoto" (herb) . 1·25 55
136 17 c. "Alpinia speciosa" . . . 1·00 30
No. 142 is smaller, 18¾ × 22½ mm.

95 Akaeware Bowl

1962. Philatelic Week.
137 95 3 c. multicoloured . . . . 5·00 2·25

96 Kendo (Japanese Fencing)

1962. All-Japan Kendo Meeting.
138 96 3 c. multicoloured . . . . 5·00 2·50

97 "Hare and Water" (textile design)
98 Reaching Maturity (clay relief)

1962. New Year.
139 97 1½ c. multicoloured . . . . 2·50 1·00

1963. Adults' Day.
140 98 3 c. gold, black and blue . 80 50

99 Trees and Wooded Hills
101 Okinawa Highway

1963. Afforestation Week.
141 99 3 c. multicoloured 80 50

1963. Opening of Okinawa Hightway.
143 101 3 c. multicoloured . . . . 1·00 60

102 Black Kites over Islands
103 Shioya Bridge

1963. Bird Week.
144 102 3 c. multicoloured . . . . 1·75 75

1963. Opening of Shioya Bridge, Okinawa.
145 103 3 c. multicoloured . . . . 1·00 60

104 Lacquerware Bowl
105 Convair 880 Jetliner and Shuri Gate

1963. Philatelic Week.
146 104 3 c. multicoloured . . . . 3·25 1·50

1963. Air.
147 105 5½ c. multicoloured . . . 25 20
148 – 7 c. black, red and blue . . 35 30
DESIGN: 7 c. Convair 880 jetliner over sea.

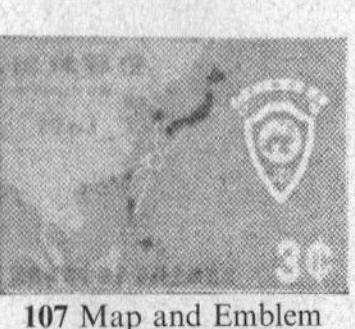
107 Map and Emblem

1963. Meeting of Junior Int Chamber, Naha.
149 107 3 c. multicoloured 60 50

108 Nakagusuku Castle Ruins

1963. Ancient Buildings Protection Week.
150 **108** 3 c. multicoloured 90 50

109 Flame

110 Bingata "dragon" (textile design)

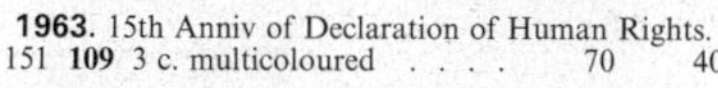
1963. 15th Anniv of Declaration of Human Rights.
151 **109** 3 c. multicoloured 70 40

1963. New Year.
152 **110** 1½ c. multicoloured 40 30

111 Carnation

112 Pineapples and Sugar-cane

1964. Mothers' Day.
153 **111** 3 c. multicoloured 60 30

1964. Agricultural Census.
154 **112** 3 c. multicoloured 45 30

113 Hand-woven Sash

114 Girl Scout and Emblem

1964. Philatelic Week.
155 **113** 3 c. brown, blue and pink 60 30

1964. 10th Anniv of Ryukyu Girl Scouts.
156 **114** 3 c. multicoloured 40 25

115 Transmitting Tower

117 Shuri Gate and Olympic Torch

1964. Inauguration of Ryukyu–Japan Microwave Link.
157 **115** 3 c. green and black . . . 1·00 85
158 – 8 c. blue and black . . . 1·40 1·00
DESIGN: 8 c. "Bowl" receiving aerial.
Both stamps have "1963" cancelled by bars and "1964" inserted in black.

1964. Passage of Olympic Torch through Okinawa.
159 **117** 3 c. multicoloured 40 30

118 "Naihanchi" (Karate stance)

121 "Miyara Dunchi" (old Ryukyuan Residence)

1964. Karate ("self-defence"). Multicoloured.
160 3 c. Type **118** 65 40
161 3 c. "Makiwara" (karate training) 60 50
162 3 c. "Kumite" exercise . . . 55 50

1964. Ancient Buildings Protection Week.
163 **121** 3 c. multicoloured 40 30

122 Bingata "snake" (textile design)

123 Boy Scouts, Badge and Shuri Gate

1964. New Year.
164 **122** 1½ c. multicoloured . . . 45 35

1965. 10th Anniv of Ryukyuan Boy Scouts.
165 **123** 3 c. multicoloured 50 40

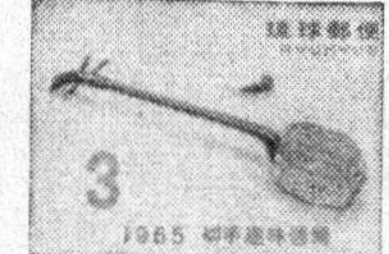
124 "Samisen" (musical instrument)

1965. Philatelic Week.
166 **124** 3 c. multicoloured 50 40

125 Stadium

1965. Completion of Onoyama Sports Ground.
167 **125** 3 c. multicoloured 30 25

126 Kin Power Station

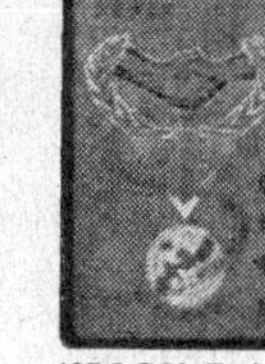
127 I.C.Y. Emblem and "Globe"

1965. Completion of Kin Power Plant.
168 **126** 3 c. multicoloured 30 25

1965. International Co-operation Year and 20th Anniv of United Nations.
169 **127** 3 c. multicoloured 30 25

128 City Hall, Naha

129 Semaruhakogame Turtle

1965. Completion of Naha City Hall.
170 **128** 3 c. multicoloured 30 25

1965. Ryukyuan Turtles. Multicoloured.
171 3 c. Type **129** 80 35
172 3 c. Taimai or hawksbill turtle 65 35
173 3 c. Yamagame or hill tortoise 65 35

132 Bingata "horse" (textile design)

133 Pryer's Woodpecker

1965. New Year.
174 **132** 1½ c. multicoloured . . . 30 25

1966. "Natural Monument" (Wildlife). Mult.
175 3 c. Type **133** 60 30
176 3 c. Sika deer 50 25
177 3 c. Dugong 50 25

136 Pacific Swallow

137 Lilies and Ruins

1966. Bird Week.
178 **136** 3 c. multicoloured 50 35

1966. Memorial Day (Battle of Okinawa).
179 **137** 3 c. multicoloured 30 25

138 University of the Ryukyus

139 Lacquer Box

1966. Transfer of University of the Ryukyus to Government Administration.
180 **138** 3 c. multicoloured 30 25

1966. Philatelic Week.
181 **139** 3 c. multicoloured 30 25

140 Ryukyuan Tiled House

141 "GRI" Museum, Shuri

1966. 20th Anniv of U.N.E.S.C.O.
182 **140** 3 c. multicoloured 30 25

1966. Completion of Government Museum, Shuri.
183 **141** 3 c. multicoloured 30 25

142 Nakasone-Tuimya Tomb

143 Bingata "ram" (textile design)

1966. Ancient Buildings Protection Week.
184 **142** 3 c. multicoloured 30 25

1966. New Year.
185 **143** 1½ c. multicoloured 30 25

144 Clown Fish

149 Tsuboya Urn

1966. Tropical Fish. Multicoloured.
186 3 c. Type **144** 50 30
187 3 c. Box fish 50 30
188 3 c. Forceps fish 50 30
189 3 c. Spotted triggerfish . . . 50 30
190 3 c. Saddleback butterfly . . . 50 30

1967. Philatelic Week.
191 **149** 3 c. multicoloured 40 25

150 Episcopal Mitre

155 Roof Tiles and Emblem

1967. Sea Shells. Multicoloured.
192 3 c. Type **150** 40 25
193 3 c. Venus comb murex ("Murex (Aranea) triremus") . . . 40 25
194 3 c. Chiragra spider conch ("Lambis (Harpago) chiragra") 60 40
195 3 c. Great green turban ("Turbo (Olearia) marmoratus") . . 60 40
196 3 c. Bubble conch ("Euprotomus bulla") 80 40

1967. International Tourist Year.
197 **155** 3 c. multicoloured 30 25

156 Mobile Clinic

1967. 15th Anniv of Anti-T.B. Association.
198 **156** 3 c. multicoloured 35 20

157 Hojo Bridge, Enkaku

1967. Ancient Buildings Protection Week.
199 **157** 3 c. multicoloured 30 25

158 Bingata "monkey" (textile design)

159 T.V. Tower and Map

1967. New Year.
200 **158** 1½ c. multicoloured . . . 30 25

1967. Opening of T.V. Broadcasting Stations in Miyako and Yaeyama.
201 **159** 3 c. multicoloured 30 25

160 Dr. Nakachi and Assistant

161 Medicine Case (after Sokei Dana)

1968. 120th Anniv of 1st Ryukyu Vaccination (by Dr. Kijin Nakachi).
202 **160** 3 c. multicoloured 30 25

1968. Philatelic Week.
203 **161** 3 c. multicoloured 50 30

162 Young Man, Book, Map and Library

1968. Library Week.
204 **162** 3 c. multicoloured 45 30

163 Postmen with Ryukyu Stamp of 1948

1968. 20th Anniv of 1st Ryukyu Islands Stamps.
205 **163** 3 c. multicoloured 40 30

164 Temple Gate

165 Old Man Dancing

1968. Restoration of Enkaku Temple Gate.
206 **164** 3 c. multicoloured 40 30

1968. Old People's Day.
207 **165** 3 c. multicoloured 40 30

166 "Mictyris longicarpus"

1968. Crabs. Multicoloured.
208 3 c. Type **166** 80 60
209 3 c. "Uca dubia" 80 60
210 3 c. "Baptozius vinosus" . . . 80 60
211 3 c. "Cardisoma carnifex" . . 80 60
212 3 c. "Ocypode ceratophthalma" 80 60

171 Saraswati Pavilion
172 Player

1968. Ancient Buildings Protection Week.
213 **171** 3 c. multicoloured 35 25

1968. 35th All-Japan East v West Men's Softball Tennis Tournament, Onoyama.
214 **172** 3 c. multicoloured 40 25

173 Bingata "cock" (textile design)
174 Boxer

1968. New Year.
215 **173** 1½ c. multicoloured 30 20

1969. 20th All-Japan Boxing Championships.
216 **174** 3 c. multicoloured 30 25

175 Inkwell Screen
176 UHF Antennae and Map

1969. Philatelic Week.
217 **175** 3 c. multicoloured 35 25

1969. Inauguration of Okinawa–Sakishima U.H.F. Radio Service.
218 **176** 3 c. multicoloured 30 25

177 Gate of Courtesy
178 "Tug of War" Festival

1969. 22nd All-Japan Formative Education Study Conference, Naha.
219 **177** 3 c. multicoloured 30 25

1969. Traditional Religious Ceremonies. Mult.
220 3 c. Type **178** 60 40
221 3 c. "Hari" canoe race 60 40
222 3 c. "Izaiho" religious ceremony 60 40
223 3 c. "Ushideiku" dance . . . 60 40
224 3 c. "Sea God" dance 60 40

1969. No. 131 surch.
225 ½ c. on 3 c. multicoloured . . 15 25

184 Nakamura-Ke

1969. Ancient Buildings Protection Week.
226 **184** 3 c. multicoloured 25 20

185 Kyuzo Toyama and Map
186 Bingata "dog and flowers" (textile design)

1969. 70th Anniv of Toyama's Ryukyu–Hawaii Emigration Project.
227 **185** 3 c. multicoloured 40 35
No. 227 has "1970" cancelled by bars and "1969" inserted in black.

1969. New Year.
228 **186** 1½ c. multicoloured . . . 20 20

187 Sake Flask

1970. Philatelic Week.
229 **187** 3 c. multicoloured 35 20

188 "Shushin-Kaneiri"
189 "Chu-nusudu"

190 "Mekarushi"
191 "Nidotichiuchi"

192 "Kokonomaki"

1970. "Kumi-Odori" Ryukyu Theatre. Multicoloured.
230 **188** 3 c. multicoloured 70 55
231 **189** 3 c. multicoloured 70 55
232 **190** 3 c. multicoloured 70 55
233 **191** 3 c. multicoloured 70 55
234 **192** 3 c. multicoloured 70 55

193 Observatory
194 Noboru Jahana (politician)

1970. Completion of Underwater Observatory, Busena-Misaki, Nago.
240 **193** 3 c. multicoloured 30 25

1970. Famous Ryukyuans.
241 **194** 3 c. purple 60 60
242 – 3 c. green 70 60
243 – 3 c. black 60 60
PORTRAITS: No. 242, Saion Gushichan Bunjaku (statesman); No. 243, Choho Giwan (Regent).

197 "Population
198 "Great Cycad of Une"

1970. Population Census.
244 **197** 3 c. multicoloured 25 25

1970. Ancient Buildings Protection Week.
245 **198** 3 c. multicoloured 40 25

199 Ryukyu Islands, Flag and Japan Diet
200 "Wild Boar" (Bingata textile design)

1970. Election of Ryukyu Representatives to the Japanese Diet.
246 **199** 3 c. multicoloured 85 60

1970. New Year.
247 **200** 1½ c. multicoloured 30 25

201 "Jibata" (hand-loom)
202 "Filature" (spinning-wheel)

203 Farm-worker wearing "Shurunnu" Coat and "Kubagasa" Hat
204 Woman using "Shiri-Ushi" (rice huller)

205 Fisherman's "Umi-Fujo" (box) and "Yutui" (bailer)

1971. Ryukyu Handicrafts.
248 **201** 3 c. multicoloured 40 30
249 **202** 3 c. multicoloured 40 30
250 **203** 3 c. multicoloured 40 30
251 **204** 3 c. multicoloured 40 30
252 **205** 3 c. multicoloured 40 30

206 "Taku" (container)
208 Restored Battlefield, Okinawa

207 Civic Emblem with Old and New City Views

1971. Philatelic Week.
253 **206** 3 c. multicoloured 35 25

1971. 50th Anniv of Naha's City Status.
254 **207** 3 c. multicoloured 30 25

1971. Government Parks. Multicoloured.
255 3 c. Type **208** 30 30
256 3 c. Haneji Inland Sea 30 30
257 4 c. Yabuchi Island 30 30

211 Deva King, Torinji Temple
212 "Rat" (Bingata textile pattern)

1971. Ancient Buildings Protection Week.
258 **211** 4 c. multicoloured 25 25

1971. New Year.
259 **212** 2 c. multicoloured 30 20

213 Student-nurse and Candle
214 Islands and Sunset

1971. 25th Anniv of Nurses' Training Scheme.
260 **213** 4 c. multicoloured 25 25

1972. Maritime Scenery. Multicoloured.
261 5 c. Type **214** 30 70
262 5 c. Coral reef (horiz) 30 70
263 5 c. Island and short-tailed albatrosses . . . . 1·00 70

217 Dove and Flags of Japan and U.S.A
218 "Yushibin" (ceremonial sake container)

1972. Ratification of Treaty for Return of Ryukyu Islands to Japan.
264 **217** 5 c. multicoloured . . . . 40 1·00

1972. Philatelic Week.
265 **218** 5 c. multicoloured . . . . 50 1·00

SPECIAL DELIVERY STAMP

E 13 Sea-horse

1951.
E18 E **13** 5 y. blue . . . . 30·00 15·00

SAAR Pt. 7

A German territory South-east of Luxembourg. Occupied by France under League of Nations control from 1920 to 1935. Following a plebiscite, Saar returned to Germany in 1935 from when German stamps were used until the French occupation in 1945, after which Nos. F1/13 of Germany followed by Nos. 203 etc of Saar were used. The territory was autonomous under French protection until it again returned to Germany at the end of 1956 following a national referendum. Issues from 1957 were authorised by the German Federal Republic pending the adoption of German currency on 6 July 1959, after which West German stamps were used.

1920–May 1921. 100 pfennig = 1 mark.
May 1921–March 1935. 100 centimes = 1 franc.
1935–47. 100 pfennig = 1 reichsmark.
1947. 100 pfennig = 1 Saarmark.
November 1947–July 1959. 100 centimes = 1 franc.
From 1959. 100 pfennig = 1 Deutsche mark.

LEAGUE OF NATIONS COMMISSION

1920. German stamps inscr "DEUTSCHES REICH" optd **Sarre** and bar.
1 **24** 2 pf. grey . . . . 75 2·25
2 2½ pf. grey . . . . 1·75 3·50
3 **10** 3 pf. brown . . . . 60 1·50
4 5 pf. green 15 25
5 **24** 7½ pf. orange 40 70
6 **10** 10 pf. red 15 25
7 **24** 15 pf. violet 15 25
8 **10** 20 pf. blue 15 25
9 25 pf. black & red on yell . 6·00 12·00
10 30 pf. black & orange on buff 10·00 20·00
11 **24** 35 pf. brown 25 45
12 **10** 40 pf. black and red . . . 30 45
13 50 pf. black & pur on cream 25 45
14 60 pf. purple 30 45
15 75 pf. black and green . . 30 45
16 80 pf. black & red on red . £200 £225
17a **12** 1 m. red . . . . 16·00 32·00

1920. Bavarian stamps optd **Sarre** or **SARRE** (Nos. 30/1) and bars.
18 **15** 5 pf. green . . . . 50 1·00
19 10 pf. red . . . . 50 1·25
20a 15 pf. red . . . . 60 1·60
21 20 pf. blue . . . . 50 1·25
22 25 pf. grey . . . . 5·00 13·00
23 30 pf. orange . . . . . . 4·50 8·50

24 15 40 pf. green 5·50 13·00
25 50 pf. brown 65 1·25
26 60 pf. green 95 3·00
27 16 1 m. brown 8·50 25·00
28 2 m. violet 50·00 £110
29 3 m. red 75·00 £850
30 – 5 m. blue (No. 192) £800 £200
31 – 10 m. green (No. 193) 90·00 £200

1920. German stamps inscr "DEUTSCHES REICH" optd **SAARGEBIET**.

32 10 5 pf. green 20 25
33 5 pf. brown 35 45
34 10 pf. red 20 25
35 10 pf. orange 25 25
36 24 15 pf. violet 20 25
37 10 20 pf. blue 20 25
38 20 pf. green 30 45
39 30 pf. black & orge on buff 25 25
40 30 pf. blue 40 65
41 40 pf. black and red 25 25
42 40 pf. red 55 60
43 50 pf. black & pur on buff 30 35
44 60 pf. purple 30 35
45 75 pf. black and green 30 35
46 12 1 m. 25 green 2·50 1·25
47 1 m. 50 brown 2·50 1·25
48 13 2 m. 50 purple 3·00 9·50
49 10 4 m. red and black 5·50 19·00

1920. No. 45 of Saar surch **20** and 102 of Germany surch **SAARGEBIET**, arms and value.

50 10 20 on 75 pf. black & green 30 1·00
51 24 5 m. on 15 pf. purple 4·50 12·00
52 10 m. on 15 pf. purple 5·50 15·00

9 Miner

11 Colliery Shafthead

12 Burbach Steelworks

1921.

53 – 5 pf. violet and green 20 25
54 9 10 pf. orange and blue 20 20
55 – 20 pf. grey and green 50 25
56 – 25 pf. blue and brown 35 25
57 – 30 pf. brown and green 30 40
58 – 40 pf. red 30 35
59 – 50 pf. black and grey 1·40 2·00
60 – 60 pf. brown and red 1·00 2·25
61 – 80 pf. blue 40 85
62 – 1 m. black and red 50 75
63 11 1 m. 25 green and brown 60 1·25
64 – 2 m. black and orange 2·25 3·25
65 – 3 m. sepia and brown 2·50 8·00
66 – 5 m. violet and yellow 5·00 17·00
67 – 10 m. brown and green 7·50 21·00
68 12 25 m. blue, black and red 25·00 55·00

DESIGNS—As Type 11. HORIZ: 5 pf. Mill above Mettlach; 20 pf. Pit head at Reden; 25 pf. River traffic, Saarbrucken; 30 pf. River Saar at Mettlach; 40 pf. Slag-heap, Volklingen; 50 pf. Signal gantry, Saarbrucken; 80 pf. "Old Bridge", Saarbrucken; 1 m. Wire-rope Railway; 2 m. Town Hall, Saarbrucken; 3 m. Pottery, Mettlach; 5 m. St. Ludwig's Church; 10 m. Chief Magistrate's and Saar Commissioner's Offices. VERT: 60 pf. Gothic Chapel, Mettlach.

See also Nos. 84/97.

1921. Nos. 55/68 surch in French currency.

70 3 c. on 20 pf. grey and green 40 20
71 5 c. on 25 pf. blue and brown 15 30
72 10 c. on 30 pf. brown & green 25 30
73 15 c. on 40 pf. red 35 25
74 20 c. on 50 pf. black and grey 70 15
75 25 c. on 60 pf. brown and red 35 25
76 30 c. on 80 pf. blue 1·00 40
77 40 f. on 1 m. black and red 1·75 40
78 50 c. on 1 m. 25 green & brown 2·75 60
79 75 c. on 2 m. black & orange 2·75 90
80 1 f. on 3 m. black and brown 2·75 1·50
81 2 f. on 5 m. violet and yellow 8·50 5·00
82 3 f. on 10 m. brown and green 10·00 19·00
83 5 f. on 25 m. blue, black & red 16·00 26·00

1922. Larger designs (except 5 f.) and value in French currency.

84 3 c. green (as No. 62) 20 35
85 5 c. black & orge (as No. 54) 20 10
86 10 c. green (as No. 61) 25 10
87 15 c. brown (as No. 62) 25 10
98 15 c. orange (as No. 62) 2·25 35
88 20 c. blue & yell (as No. 64) 1·25 15
100 25 c. red & yellow (as No. 64) 1·50 20
90 30 c. red & yell (as No. 58) 25 40
91 40 c. brown & yell (as No. 65) 50 10
92 50 c. blue & yellow (as No. 56) 75 10
101 75 c. green & yell (as No. 65) 15·00 1·75
94 1 f. brown (as No. 66) 1·00 35
95 2 f. violet (as No. 63) 3·00 2·00
96 3 f. grn & orange (as No. 60) 2·50 2·00
97 5 f. brn & chocolate (as No. 68) 17·00 42·00

14 Madonna of Blieskastel

15 Army Medical Service

1925.

102 14 45 c. purple 2·25 2·25
103 10 f. brown (31 × 36 mm) 10·00 24·00

1926. Welfare Fund.

104 15 20 c. + 20 c. green 5·50 14·00
105 – 40 c. + 40 c. brown 5·50 17·00
106 – 50 c. + 50 c. orange 5·50 14·00
107 – 1 f. 50 + 1 f. 50 blue 13·00 45·00

DESIGNS: 40 c. Hospital work (nurse and patient); 50 c. Child welfare (children at a spring); 1 f. 50, Maternity nursing service.

18 Tholey Abbey

1926.

108 – 10 c. brown 45 15
109 – 15 c. green 35 70
110 – 20 c. brown 35 15
111 18 25 c. blue 35 35
112 – 30 c. green 50 15
113 – 40 c. brown 40 15
114 18 50 c. red 40 15
114a – 60 c. orange 1·10 20
115 – 75 c. purple 40 15
116 – 80 c. orange 2·75 6·50
116a – 90 c. red 7·00 17·00
117 – 1 f. violet 2·00 20
118 – 1 f. 50 blue 5·00 20
119 – 2 f. red 5·00 25
120 – 3 f. green 12·00 75
121 – 5 f. brown 13·00 5·50

DESIGNS—VERT: 10, 30 c. Fountain, St. Johann, Saarbrucken. HORIZ: 15, 75 c. Saar Valley near Gudingen; 20, 40, 90 c. View from Saarlouis fortifications; 60, 80 c., 1 f. Colliery shafthead; 1 f. 50, 2, 3, 5 f. Burbach Steelworks.

1927. Welfare Fund. Optd **1927-28**.

122 15 20 c. + 20 c. green 9·00 14·00
123 40 c. + 40 c. brown 7·50 18·00
124 50 c. + 50 c. orange 6·50 11·00
125 1 f. 50 + 1 f. 50 blue 11·00 35·00

19 Breguet 14 Biplane over Saarbrucken

20 "The Blind Beggar" by Dyckmanns

1928. Air.

126 19 50 c. red 2·25 2·75
127 1 f. violet 3·25 3·25

1928. Christmas Charity.

128 20 40 c. (+ 40 c.) brown 7·00 22·00
129 50 c. (+ 50 c.) purple 7·00 22·00
130 1 f. (+ 1 f.) violet 7·00 22·00
131 – 1 f. 50 (+ 1 f. 50) blue 7·00 22·00
132 – 2 f. (+ 2 f.) red 8·00 24·00
133 – 3 f. (+ 3 f.) green 8·00 24·00
134 – 10 f. (+ 10 f.) brown £400 £3000

DESIGNS: 1 f. 50, 2, 3 f. "Almsgiving" by Schiestl; 10 f. "Charity" by Raphael (picture in circle).

1929. Christmas Charity. Paintings. As T **20**.

135 40 c. (+ 15 c.) green 1·50 3·25
136 50 c. (+ 20 c.) red 3·50 5·50
137 1 f. (+ 50 c.) purple 3·50 7·00
138 1 f. 50 (+ 75 c.) blue 3·50 7·00
139 2 f. (+ 1 f.) red 3·50 7·00
140 3 f. (+ 2 f.) green 5·50 16·00
141 10 f. (+ 8 f.) brown 35·00 85·00

DESIGNS: 40 c. to 1 f. "Orphaned" by H. Kaulbach; 1 f. 50, 2, 3 f. "St. Ottilia" by M. Feuerstein; 10 f. "The Little Madonna" by Ferruzzio.

1930. Nos. 114 and 116 surch.

141a 18 40 c. on 50 c. red 85 1·10
142 – 60 c. on 80 c. orange 85 1·90

1931. Christmas Charity (1930 issue). Paintings. As T **20**.

143 40 c. (+ 15 c.) brown 5·00 17·00
144 60 c. (+ 20 c.) orange 5·00 17·00
145 1 f. (+ 50 c.) red 6·50 32·00
146 1 f. 50 (+ 75 c.) blue 8·00 32·00
147 2 f. (+ 1 f.) brown 8·00 32·00
148 3 f. (+ 2 f.) green 11·00 32·00
149 10 f. (+ 10 f.) brown 65·00 £250

DESIGNS: 40, 60 c., 1 f. 50, "The Safetyman" (miner and lamp) by F. Zolnhofer; 1, 2, 3 f. "The Good Samaritan" by J. Heinemann; 10 f. "At the Window" by F. G. Waldmuller.

1931. Christmas Charity. Paintings. As T **20**.

150 40 c. (+ 15 c.) brown 10·00 25·00
151 60 c. (+ 20 c.) red 10·00 25·00
152 1 f. (+ 50 c.) purple 13·00 40·00
153 1 f. 50 (+ 75 c.) blue 15·00 40·00
154 2 f. (+ 1 f.) red 17·00 40·00
155 3 f. (+ 2 f.) green 23·00 75·00
156 5 f. (+ 5 f.) brown 55·00 £275

DESIGNS: 40 c. to 1 f. "St. Martin" by F. Boehle; 1 f. 50, 2 f. "Charity" by Ridgeway-Knight; 5 f. "The Widow's Mite" by Dubufe.

29 Airport

30 Kirkel Castle Ruins

1932. Air.

157 29 60 c. red 5·00 3·50
158 5 f. brown 35·00 90·00

1932. Christmas Charity.

159 30 40 c. (+ 15 c.) brown 7·00 22·00
160 – 60 c. (+ 20 c.) red 7·00 22·00
161 – 1 f. (+ 50 c.) purple 10·00 40·00
162 – 1 f. 50 (+ 75 c.) blue 16·00 50·00
163 – 2 f. (+ 1 f.) red 16·00 50·00
164 – 3 f. (+ 2 f.) green 40·00 £160
165 – 5 f. (+ 5 f.) brown 65·00 £275

DESIGNS—VERT: 60 c. Blieskastel Church; 1 f. Ottweiler Church; 1 f. 50, St. Michael's Church, Saarbrucken; 2 f. Cathedral and fountain, St. Wendel; 3 f. St. John's Church, Saarbrucken. HORIZ: 5 f. Kerpen Castle, Illingen.

32 Scene of the Disaster

33 "Love"

1933. Neunkirchen Explosion Disaster.

166 32 60 c. (+ 60 c.) orange 8·50 16·00
167 3 f. (+ 3 f.) green 35·00 40·00
168 5 f. (+ 5 f.) brown 35·00 60·00

1934. Christmas Charity.

169 33 40 c. (+ 15 c.) brown 4·25 13·00
170 – 60 c. (+ 20 c.) red 4·25 13·00
171 – 1 f. (+ 50 c.) mauve 6·00 16·00
172 – 1 f. 50 (+ 75 c.) blue 11·00 30·00
173 – 2 f. (+ 1 f.) red 10·00 27·00
174 – 3 f. (+ 2 f.) green 11·00 30·00
175 – 5 f. (+ 5 f.) brown 25·00 65·00

DESIGNS: 60 c. "Solicitude". 1 f. "Peace". 1 f. 50, "Consolation". 2 f. "Welfare". 3 f. "Truth". 5 f. Countess Elizabeth von Nassau.

Nos. 169/74 show statues by C. L. Pozzi in church of St. Louis, Saarbrucken.

1934. Saar Plebiscite. Optd **VOLKSABSTIMMUNG 1935**. (a) Postage. On Nos. 108/15, 116a/21 and 103.

176 – 10 c. brown 40 55
177 – 15 c. green 40 55
178 – 20 c. brown 35 35
179 18 25 c. blue 55 1·25
180 – 30 c. green 35 30
181 – 40 c. brown 35 40
182 18 50 c. red 60 1·10
183 – 60 c. orange 35 30
184 – 75 c. purple 60 1·25
185 – 90 c. red 60 1·25
186 – 1 f. violet 70 1·25
187 – 1 f. 50 blue 3·00 3·50
188 – 2 f. red 4·50 4·75
189 – 3 f. green 7·50 6·50
190 – 5 f. brown 32·00 32·00
191 14 10 f. brown 22·00 50·00

(b) Air. On Nos. 126/7 and 157/8.

192 19 50 c. red 3·50 8·00
193 29 60 c. red 2·00 2·50
194 19 1 r. violet 4·75 10·00
195 29 5 f. brown 7·50 13·00

1934. Christmas Charity. Nos. 169/75 optd **VOLKSABSTIMMUNG 1935**.

196 33 40 c. (+ 15 c.) brown 3·00 9·50
197 – 60 c. (+ 20 c.) red 3·00 9·50
198 – 1 f. (+ 50 c.) mauve 7·50 22·00
199 – 1 f. 50 (+ 75 c.) blue 7·50 22·00
200 – 2 f. (+ 1 f.) red 9·50 28·00
201 – 3 f. (+ 2 f.) green 8·00 25·00
202 – 5 f. (+ 5 f.) brown 14·00 32·00

FRENCH OCCUPATION

36 Coal-miner

37 Loop of the Saar

1947. Inscr "SAAR".

203 36 2 pf. grey 10 15
204 3 pf. orange 10 50
205 6 pf. green 10 20
206 8 pf. red 10 20
207 10 pf. mauve 10 15
208 12 pf. green 10 10
209 – 15 pf. brown 10 55
210 – 16 pf. blue 10 15
211 – 20 pf. red 10 15
212 – 24 pf. brown 10 10
213 – 25 pf. mauve 40 16·00
214 – 30 pf. green 15 45
215 – 40 pf. brown 15 45
216 – 45 pf. red 45 12·00
217 – 50 pf. violet 35 15·00
218 – 60 pf. violet 35 15·00
219 – 75 pf. blue 10 30
220 – 80 pf. orange 10 30
221 – 84 pf. brown 10 30
222 37 1 m. green 10 40

DESIGNS—As T **36**: 15 pf. to 24 pf. Steel workers; 25 pf. to 50 pf. Sugar beet harvesters; 60 pf. to 80 pf. Mettlach Abbey. As T **37**—VERT: 84 pf. Marshal Ney.

1947. As last surch in French currency.

223 36 10 c. on 2 pf. grey 10 50
224 60 c. on 3 pf. orange 10 50
225 1 f. on 10 pf. mauve 10 50
226 2 f. on 12 pf. green 10 65
227 – 3 f. on 15 pf. brown 10 50
228 – 4 f. on 16 pf. blue 15 5·00
229 – 5 f. on 20 pf. red 10 80
230 – 6 f. on 24 pf. brown 10 50
231 – 9 f. on 30 pf. green 30 6·50
232 – 10 f. on 50 pf. violet 30 10·00
233 – 14 f. on 60 pf. violet 45 6·00
234 – 20 f. on 84 pf. brown 30 8·00
235 37 50 f. on 1 m. green 1·10 12·00

42 Clasped Hands

43 Builders

44 Saar Valley

1948. Inscr "SAARPOST".

236 42 10 c. red (postage) 60 1·40
237 60 c. blue 60 1·40
238 1 f. black 25 15
239 – 2 f. red 25 10
240 – 3 f. brown 30 10
241 – 4 f. red 30 10
242 – 5 f. violet 30 15
243 – 6 f. red 65 15
244 – 9 f. blue 5·50 25
245 – 10 f. blue 2·50 20
246 – 14 f. purple 3·00 65
247 43 20 f. red 6·50 65
248 – 50 f. blue 16·00 2·50
249 44 25 f. red (air) 5·00 3·50
250 50 f. blue 2·75 1·75
251 200 f. red 24·00 28·00

DESIGNS—As Type **42**: 2, 3 f. Man's head; 4, 5 f. Woman's head; 6, 9 f. Miner's head. As Type **43**: 10 f. Blast furnace chimney; 14 f. Foundry; 50 f. Facade of Mettlach Abbey.

46 Floods in St. Johann, Sarbrucken

47 Map of Saarland

1948. Flood Disaster Relief Fund. Flood Scenes.

252 – 5 f. + 5 f. green (postage) 3·50 18·00
253 46 6 f. + 4 f. purple 3·50 18·00
254 – 12 f. + 8 f. red 3·75 24·00
255 – 18 f. + 12 f. blue 5·50 30·00
256 – 25 f. + 25 f. brown (air) 23·00 £130

DESIGNS—VERT: 18 f. Flooded street, Saarbrucken. HORIZ: 5 f. Flooded industrial area; 12 f. Landtag building, Saarbrucken; 25 f. Floods at Ensdorf, Saarlouis.

1948. 1st Anniv of Constitution.

257 47 10 f. red 1·40 2·00
258 25 f. blue 2·25 6·00

48 Hikers and Ludweiler Hostel

1949. Youth Hostels Fund.
259 **48** 8 f. + 5 f. brown . . . . . 1·75 6·00
260 – 10 f. + 7 f. green . . . . . 2·00 5·00
DESIGN: 10 f. Hikers and Weisskirchen hostel.

49 Chemical Research **50** Mare and Foal

1949. Saar University.
261 **49** 15 f. red . . . . 3·25 30

1949. Horse Day.
262 **50** 15 f. + 5 f. red . . . . . . 15·00 23·00
263 – 25 f. + 15 f. blue . . . . . 17·00 27·00
DESIGN: 25 f. Two horses in steeple-chase.

51 Symbolic of Typography **52** Labourer and Foundry

1949.
264 – 10 c. purple . . . . 20 1·40
265 – 60 c. black . . . . 30 1·40
266 – 1 f. red . . . . 1·40 10
267 – 3 f. brown . . . . 8·50 30
268 – 5 f. violet . . . . 2·00 10
269 – 6 f. green . . . . 13·00 60
270 – 8 f. green 75 35
271 **51** 10 f. orange . . . . 5·00 10
272 – 12 f. green . . . . 16·00 10
273 – 15 f. red . . . . 8·50 15
274 – 18 f. mauve . . . . 3·00 4·00
275 **52** 20 f. grey . . . . 2·00 15
276 – 25 f. blue . . . . 22·00 15
277 – 30 f. red . . . . 16·00 45
278 – 45 f. purple . . . . 5·50 35
279 – 60 f. green . . . . 5·50 1·50
280 – 100 f. brown . . . . 12·00 1·60
DESIGNS—As Type **51**: 10 c. Building trade; 60 c. Beethoven; 1 f. and 3 f. Heavy industries; 5 f. Slag heap; 6 f. and 15 f. Colliery; 8 f. Posthorn and telephone; 12 f. and 18 f. Pottery. As Type **52**—VERT: 25 f. Blast furnace worker; 60 f. Landsweiler; 100 f. Wiebelskirchen. HORIZ: 30 f. St. Arnual; 45 f. "Giant's Boot", Rentrisch.

53 Detail from "Moses Striking the Rock" (Murillo) **54** A. Kolping **55** P. Wust

1949. National Relief Fund.
281 **53** 8 f. + 2 f. blue . . . . . 7·50 23·00
282 – 12 f. + 3 f. green . . . . . 9·50 25·00
283 – 15 f. + 5 f. purple . . . . 13·00 45·00
284 – 25 f. + 10 f. blue . . . . . 18·00 80·00
285 – 50 f. + 20 f. purple . . . . 32·00 £120
DESIGNS: 12 f. "Our Lord healing the Paralytic" (Murillo); 15 f. "The Sick Child" (Metsu); 25 f. "St. Thomas of Villanueva" (Murillo); 50 f. "Madonna of Blieskastel".

1950. Honouring Adolf Kolping (miners' padre).
286 **54** 15 f. + 5 f. red . . . . . . 24·00 65·00

1950. 10th Death Anniv of Peter Wust (philosopher).
287 **55** 15 f. red . . . . 4·25 5·00

56 Mail Coach

1950. Stamp Day.
288 **56** 15 f. + 5 f. brown & red . . 55·00 90·00

57 "Food for the Hungry" **58** St. Peter

1950. Red Cross Fund.
289 **57** 25 f. + 10 f. lake & red . . 23·00 50·00

1950. Holy Year.
290 **58** 12 f. green . . . . 3·00 6·00
291 15 f. red . . . . 3·50 6·00
292 25 f. blue . . . . 6·50 14·00

59 Town Hall, Ottweiler **61**

1950. 400th Anniv of Ottweiler.
293 **59** 10 f. brown . . . . 3·00 6·50

1950. Saar's Admission to Council of Europe.
294 **61** 25 f. blue (postage) . . . 35·00 5·00
295 – 200 f. red (air) £140 £225
DESIGN: 200 f. As T **61** but with dove in flight over book.

62 St. Lutwinus enters Monastery

1950. National Relief Fund. Inscr "VOLKSHILFE".
296 **62** 8 f. + 2 f. brown . . . . 5·00 17·00
297 – 12 f. + 3 f. green . . . . 5·00 17·00
298 – 15 f. + 5 f. brown . . . . 5·50 28·00
299 – 25 f. + 10 f. blue . . . . 8·50 40·00
300 – 50 f. + 20 f. purple . . . . 12·00 60·00
DESIGNS: 12 f. Lutwinus builds Mettlach Abbey; 15 f. Lutwinus as Abbot; 25 f. Bishop Lutwinus confirming children at Rheims; 50 f. Lutwinus helping needy.

63 Orphans **65** Allegory

64 Mail-carriers, 1760

1951. Red Cross Fund.
301 **63** 25 f. + 10 f. green & red . 20·00 40·00

1951. Stamp Day.
302 **64** 15 f. purple . . . . 6·00 14·00

1951. Trade Fair.
303 **65** 15 f. green . . . . 2·00 3·75

66 Flowers and Building **67** Calvin and Luther

1951. Horticultural Show, Bexbach.
304 **66** 15 f. green . . . . 2·50 85

1951. 375th Anniv of Reformation in Saar.
305 **67** 15 f. + 5 f. brown . . . . 1·25 5·00

68 "The Good Mother" (Lepicie) **69** Mounted Postman

1951. National Relief Fund. Inscr "VOLKSHILFE 1951".
306 **68** 12 f. + 3 f. green . . . . 4·50 14·00
307 – 15 f. + 5 f. violet . . . . 4·50 14·00
308 – 18 f. + 7 f. red . . . . . 5·00 15·00
309 – 30 f. + 10 f. blue . . . . 8·00 22·00
310 – 50 f. + 20 f. brown . . . . 18·00 48·00
PAINTINGS: 18 f. "Outside the Theatre" (Kampf); 18 f. "Sisters of Charity" (Browne); 30 f. "The Good Samaritan" (Bassano); 50 f. "St. Martin and the Poor" (Van Dyck).

1952. Stamp Day.
311 **69** 30 f. + 10 f. blue . . . . 8·00 18·00

70 Athlete bearing Olympic Flame **71** Globe and Emblem

1952. 15th Olympic Games, Helsinki. Inscr "OLYMPISCHE SPIELE 1952".
312 **70** 15 f. + 5 f. green . . . . 2·50 6·00
313 – 30 f. + 5 f. blue . . . . 3·00 8·50
DESIGN: 30 f. Hand, laurels and globe.

1952. Saar Fair.
314 **71** 15 f. red . . . . 1·50 1·00

72 Red Cross and Refugees **73** G.P.O., Saarbrucken

1952. Red Cross Week.
315 **72** 15 f. red . . . . 1·50 1·00

1952. (A) Without inscr in or below design. (B) With inscr.
316 – 1 f. green (B) 15 10
317 – 2 f. violet 15 10
318 – 3 f. red 15 10
319 **73** 5 f. green (A) . . . . . . 6·00 10
320 5 f. green (B) 20 10
321 – 6 f. purple 35 10
322 – 10 f. brown 40 10
323 **73** 12 f. green (B) 40 10
324 – 15 f. brown (A) . . . . . 8·00 10
325 – 15 f. brown (B) . . . . . 5·00 10
326 – 15 f. red (B) 25 10
327 – 18 f. purple . . . . 2·75 3·25
329 – 30 f. blue 85 50
334 – 500 f. red . . . . 17·00 50·00
DESIGNS—HORIZ: 1, 15 f. (3) Colliery shafthead; 2, 10 f. Ludwigs High School, Saarbrucken; 3, 18 f. Gersweiler Bridge; 6 f. Mettlach Bridge; 30 f. University Library, Saarbrucken. VERT: 500 f. St. Ludwig's Church, Saarbrucken.

74 "Count Stroganov as a Boy" (Greuze) **75** Fair Symbol

1952. National Relief Fund. Paintings inscr "VOLKSHILFE 1952".
335 **74** 15 f. + 5 f. brown . . . . 2·75 7·00
336 – 18 f. + 7 f. red . . . . . 3·25 9·00
337 – 30 f. + 10 f. blue . . . . 4·00 11·00
PORTRAITS: 18 f. "The Holy Shepherd" (Murillo); 30 f. "Portrait of a Boy" (Kraus).

1953. Saar Fair.
338 **75** 15 f. blue . . . . 1·50 90

76 Postilions **77** Henri Dunant

1953. Stamp Day.
339 **76** 15 f. blue . . . . 2·50 10·00

1953. Red Cross Week and 125th Anniv of Birth of Dunant (founder).
340 **77** 15 f. + 5 f. brown and red . 1·50 4·25

78 "Painter's Young Son" (Rubens) **79** St. Benedict blessing St. Maurus

1953. National Relief Fund. Paintings inscr "VOLKSHILFE 1953".
341 – 15 f. + 5 f. violet . . . . 1·25 3·75
342 – 18 f. + 7 f. red . . . . . 1·40 5·00
343 **78** 30 f. + 10 f. green . . . . 2·75 7·50
DESIGNS—VERT: 15 f. "Clarice Strozzi" (Titian). HORIZ: 18 f. "Painter's Children" (Rubens).

1953. Tholey Abbey Fund.
344 **79** 30 f. + 10 f. black . . . . 1·50 5·50

80 Saar Fair **82** Red Cross and Child

81 Postal Motor Coach

1954. Saar Fair.
345 **80** 15 f. green . . . . 1·40 70

1954. Stamp Day.
346 **81** 15 f. red . . . . 2·50 9·00

1954. Red Cross Week.
347 **82** 15 f. + 5 f. brown . . . . 1·75 5·00

83 Madonna and Child (Holbein)

1954. Marian Year.
348 **83** 5 f. red . . . . 70 1·50
349 – 10 f. green . . . . 90 2·25
350 – 15 f. blue . . . . 1·40 3·25
DESIGNS: 10 f. "Sistine Madonna" (Raphael); 15 f. "Madonna and Child with Pear" (Durer).

84 "Street Urchin with a Melon" (Murillo)
85 Cyclist and Flag
86 Rotary Emblem and Industrial Plant

1954. National Relief Fund. Paintings inscr "VOLKSHILFE 1954".
351 **84** 5 f. + 3 f. red 30 75
352 – 10 f. + 5 f. green 35 95
353 – 15 f. + 7 f. violet . . . . . 40 1·10
DESIGNS: 10 f. "Maria de Medici" (A. Bronzino); 15 f. "Baron Emil von Maucler" (J. F. Dietrich).

1955. World Cross-Country Cycle Race.
354 **85** 15 f. blue, red and black . . 30 40

1955. 50th Anniv of Rotary International.
355 **86** 15 f. brown 25 40

87 Exhibitors' Flags
88 Nurse and Baby

1955. Saar Fair.
356 **87** 15 f. multicoloured 20 50

1955. Red Cross Week.
357 **88** 15 f. + 5 f. black and red . 30 65

89 Postman
91 "Mother" (Durer)

1955. Stamp Day.
358 **89** 15 f. purple . . . . 40 1·25

1955. Referendum. Optd **VOLKSBEFRAGUNG 1955**.
359 15 f. red (No. 326) 15 35
360 18 f. purple (No. 327) 15 40
361 30 f. blue (No. 329) 25 55

1955. National Relief Fund. Durer paintings inscr as in T **91**.
362 **91** 5 f. + 3 f. green 35 55
363 – 10 f. + 5 f. green . . . . 60 1·40
364 – 15 f. + 7 f. bistre . . . . 70 1·25
PAINTINGS: 10 f. "The Praying Hands"; 15 f. "The Old Man from Antwerp".

92
93 Radio Tower

1956. Saar Fair.
365 **92** 15 f. green and red 15 45

1956. Stamp Day.
366 **93** 15 f. green and turquoise . 15 45

94 Casualty Station
95

1956. Red Cross Week.
367 **94** 15 f. + 5 f. brown 20 50

1956. Olympic Games.
368 **95** 12 f. + 3 f. blue and green 15 35
369 15 f. + 5 f. brown & purple 15 35

96 Winterberg Memorial
97 "Portrait of Lucrezia Crivelli" (da Vinci)

1956. Winterberg Memorial Reconstruction Fund.
370 **96** 5 f. + 2 f. green 10 20
371 12 f. + 3 f. purple 15 30
372 15 f. + 5 f. brown 15 30

1956. National Relief Fund. Inscr as in T **97**.
373 **97** 5 f. + 3 f. blue 10 20
374 – 10 f. + 5 f. red 15 25
375 – 15 f. + 7 f. green 20 45
PAINTINGS: 10 f. "Saskia" (Rembrandt); 15 f. "Lady Playing Spinet" (Floris).

RETURN TO GERMANY

98 Arms of the Saar
99 President Heuse

1957. Return of the Saar to Germany.
376 **98** 15 f. blue and red 10 25

1957. (a) Without "F" after figure of value.
377 **99** 1 f. green 10 15
378 2 f. violet 10 15
379 3 f. brown 10 15
380 4 f. mauve 20 60
381 5 f. green 10 10
382 6 f. red 15 40
383 10 f. grey 10 30
384 12 f. orange 10 10
385 15 f. green 20 10
386 18 f. red . . . . 70 1·40
387 25 f. lilac 30 55
388 30 f. purple 35 55
389 45 f. green . . . . 1·25 2·50
390 50 f. brown . . . . 1·25 1·00
391 60 f. red . . . . 1·60 2·75
392 70 f. orange . . . . 3·00 4·50
393 80 f. green . . . . 1·10 2·50
394 90 f. grey . . . . 2·75 4·50
395 100 f. red (24 × 29½ mm) . 2·50 8·50
396 200 f. lilac (24 × 29½ mm) . 5·50 21·00

(b) With "F" after figure of value.
406 **99** 1 f. grey 10 20
407 3 f. blue 10 20
408 5 f. green 10 10
409 6 f. brown 20 60
410 10 f. violet 20 25
411 12 f. orange 20 10
412 15 f. green 35 10
413 18 f. grey . . . . 2·00 5·00
414 20 f. green . . . . 1·25 2·25
415 25 f. brown 55 45
416 30 f. mauve . . . . 1·10 45
417 35 f. brown . . . . 2·75 3·25
418 45 f. green . . . . 2·00 3·50
419 50 f. brown . . . . 1·10 1·25
420 70 f. green . . . . 4·50 5·50
421 80 f. blue . . . . 2·75 4·50
422 90 f. red . . . . 5·50 7·50
423 100 f. orange (24 × 29½ mm) 4·50 5·50
424 200 f. green (24 × 29½ mm) 10·00 22·00
425 300 f. blue (24 × 29½ mm) . 13·00 26·00

100 Iron Foundry
101 Arms of Merzig and St. Pierre Church

1957. Saar Fair.
397 **100** 15 f. red and black 10 20

1957. Centenary of Merzig.
398 **101** 15 f. blue 10 20

101a "Europa" Tree
101b Young Miner

1957. Europa.
399 **101a** 20 f. orange & yellow . . 30 70
400 35 f. violet and pink . . . 50 80

1957. Humanitarian Relief Fund.
401 **101b** 6 f. + 4 f. black & brn . 10 15
402 – 12 f. + 6 f. black & grn . 10 15
403 – 15 f. + 7 f. black & red . 15 30
404 – 30 f. + 10 f. black & blue 45 70
DESIGNS: 12 f. Miner drilling at coalface; 15 f. Miner with coal-cutting machine; 30 f. Operator at mine lift-shaft.

101c Carrier Pigeons
101d Max and Moritz (cartoon characters)

1957. International Correspondence Week.
405 **101c** 15 f. black and red . . . 10 20

1958. 150th Death Anniv of Wilhelm Busch (writer and illustrator).
426 **101d** 12 f. green and black . . 10 15
427 – 15 f. red and black . . . 10 30
DESIGN: 15 f. Wilhelm Busch.

101e "Prevent Forest Fires"
101g "The Fox who stole the Goose"

101f Diesel and First Oil Engine

1958. Forest Fires Prevention Campaign.
428 **101e** 15 f. black and red . . . 10 20

1958. Birth Centenary of Rudolf Diesel (engineer).
429 **101f** 12 f. green 15 25

1958. Berlin Students' Fund.
430 **101g** 12 f. + 6 f. red, black and green 10 20
431 – 15 f. + 7 f. brown, green and red 10 25
DESIGN: 15 f. "A Hunter from the Palatinate".

102 Saarbrucken Town Hall and Fair Emblem
103 Homburg

1958. Saar Fair.
432 **102** 15 f. purple 10 20

1958. 400th Anniv of Homburg.
433 **103** 15 f. green 10 20

103a Emblem
103b Schulze-Delitzsch

1958. 150th Anniv of German Gymnastics.
434 **103a** 12 f. black, green and grey 10 20

1958. 150th Birth of Schulze-Delitzsch (pioneer of German Co-operative Movement).
435 **103b** 12 f. green 10 20

103c "Europa"
103d Friedrich Raiffeisen (philanthropist)

1958. Europa.
436 **103c** 12 f. blue and green . . 40 70
437 – 30 f. red and blue . . . 60 90

1958. Humanitarian Relief and Welfare Funds.
438 **103d** 6 f. + 4 f. brown, light brown and chestnut 10 15
439 – 12 f. + 6 f. red, yellow and green 10 20
440 – 15 f. + 7 f. blue, green and red 20 35
441 – 30 f. + 10 f. yellow, green and blue 25 45
DESIGNS—Inscr "WOHLFAHRTSMARKE": 12 f. Dairymaid; 15 f. Vine-dresser 30 f. Farm labourer.

103e Fugger
104 Hands holding Crates

1959. 500th Birth Anniv of Jakob Fugger (merchant prince).
442 **103e** 15 f. black and red . . . 10 20

1959. Saar Fair.
443 **104** 15 f. red 10 20

105 Saarbrucken
105a Humboldt

1959. 50th Anniv of Greater Saarbrucken.
444 **105** 15 f. blue 10 20

1959. Death Centenary of Alexander von Humboldt (naturalist).
445 **105a** 15 f. blue 10 20

OFFICIAL STAMPS

1922. Nos. 84 to 94 optd **DIENSTMARKE**.
O 98 3 c. green . . . . 85 24·00
O 99 5 c. black and orange . . . 35 15
O100 10 c. green 35 15
O101 15 c. brown 35 15
O109 15 c. orange . . . . . . 2·25 30
O102 20 c. blue and yellow . . . 35 15
O111 25 c. red and yellow . . . 2·25 30
O104 30 c. red and yellow . . . 35 15
O105 40 c. brown and yellow . . 65 15
O106 50 c. blue and yellow . . . 70 15
O112 75 c. green and yellow . . 4·75 1·50
O108a 1 f. brown . . . . 8·00 1·75

1927. Nos. 108/15, 117 and 119 optd **DIENSTMARKE**.
O128 10 c. brown . . . . 1·40 1·50
O129 15 c. green . . . . 1·75 6·50
O130 20 c. brown . . . . 1·40 1·10
O131 25 c. blue . . . . 1·75 4·50
O122 30 c. green . . . . 1·75 20
O133 40 c. brown . . . . 1·25 20
O134 50 c. red . . . . 1·25 20
O135 60 c. orange 90 20
O136 75 c. purple . . . . 1·25 55
O137 1 f. violet . . . . 1·75 30
O138 2 f. red . . . . 4·00 50

O 51 Arms

1949.
O264 **O 51** 10 c. red . . . . . . 35 22·00
O265 30 c. black . . . . . . 25 22·00
O266 1 f. green 25 20
O267 2 f. red . . . . 1·40 1·25
O268 5 f. blue 45 20
O269 10 f. black 65 75
O270 12 f. mauve . . . . . . 5·50 7·00
O271 15 f. blue 65 20
O272 20 f. green . . . . . . 1·60 75
O273 30 f. mauve . . . . . . 2·00 4·00
O274 50 f. purple . . . . . . 2·00 3·25
O275 100 f. brown . . . . . . 90·00 £190

STE. MARIE DE MADAGASCAR Pt. 6

An island off the East coast of Madagascar. From 1898 used the stamps of Madagascar and Dependencies.

100 centimes = 1 franc

1894. "Tablet" key-type inscr "STE MARIE DE MADAGASCAR" in red (1, 5, 15, 25, 75 c., 1 f.) or blue (others).

1 D 1 c. black on blue 65 65
2 2 c. brown on buff 90 80
3 4 c. brown on grey . . . . . 2·75 2·25
4 5 c. green on green . . . . . 5·50 5·00
5 10 c. black on lilac . . . . . 7·75 4·75
6 15 c. blue . . . . 15·00 14·50
7 20 c. red on green . . . . . 13·50 9·50
8 25 c. black on pink . . . . . 7·50 6·75
9 30 c. brown on drab . . . . . 6·75 6·25
10 40 c. red on yellow . . . . . 8·25 6·00
11 50 c. red on pink . . . . . . 32·00 22·00
12 75 c. brown on orange . . . . 48·00 24·00
13 1 f. green . . . . 30·00 17·00

ST. PIERRE ET MIQUELON Pt. 6

A group of French islands off the S. coast of Newfoundland. The group became an Overseas Department of France on 1 July 1976. The stamps of France were used in the islands from 1 April 1978 until 3 February 1986. Separate issues for the group were reintroduced in 1986.

100 centimes = 1 franc

1885. Stamps of French Colonies surch **S P M** and value in figures only.

1 J 5 on 2 c. brown on buff . . £4250 £1600
4 5 on 4 c. brown on grey . . £275 £200
8 05 on 20 c. red on green . . 17·00 21·00
9 H 05 on 35 c. black on yell . . 85·00 60·00
5 05 on 40 c. red on yellow . . 70·00 30·00
10 05 om 75 c. red £200 £150
11 05 on 1 f. green . . . . . . 17·00 15·00
6 10 on 40 c. red on yellow . . 18·00 15·00
7 15 on 40 c. red on yellow . . 17·00 15·00
3 25 on 1 f. green £1700 £1100

The surcharge on No. 1 is always inverted.

1891. French Colonies "Commerce" type surch **15 c. S P M**.

15 J 15 c. on 30 c. brn on drab . 24·00 21·00
16 15 c. on 35 c. blk on orge . . £425 £300
17 15 c. on 40 c. red on yell . . 60·00 48·00

1891. Stamps of French Colonies "Commerce" type, optd **ST PIERRE M-on**.

23 J 1 c. black on blue . . . . . 6·75 5·00
24 2 c. brown on buff . . . . . 6·75 5·50
25 4 c. brown on grey . . . . . 7·50 5·50
26 5 c. green on green . . . . . 7·50 5·00
22 10 c. black on lilac . . . . . 11·00 11·00
28 15 c. blue on blue . . . . . . 17·00 9·75
29 20 c. red on green . . . . . 48·00 42·00
30 25 c. black on pink . . . . . 18·00 12·00
31 30 c. brown on drab . . . . 70·00 60·00
32 35 c. black on orange £300 £225
33 40 c. red on yellow . . . . . 48·00 42·00
34 75 c. red on pink . . . . . . 75·00 60·00
35 1 f. green . . . . 48·00 42·00

1891. Stamps of French Colonies, "Commerce" type, surch **ST-PIERRE M-on** and new value in figures and words (**cent.**) above and below opt.

36 J 1 c. on 5 c. green and green . 5·00 4·25
37 1 c. on 10 c. black on lilac . 6·75 5·50
38 1 c. on 25 c. black on pink . 4·50 4·25
39 2 c. on 10 c. black on lilac . 4·75 3·75
40 2 c. on 15 c. blue on blue . . 4·00 4·00
41 2 c. on 25 c. black on pink . 4·00 4·00
42 4 c. on 20 c. red on green . . 4·00 3·75
43 4 c. on 25 c. black on pink . 4·00 4·25
44 4 c. on 30 c. brn on drab . . 12·00 11·00
45 4 c. on 40 c. red on yellow . 17·00 9·75

1892. Nos. 26 and 30 surch with figure only on top of opt.

49 J 1 c. on 5 c. green on green . 6·50 3·75
46 1 on 25 c. black on pink . . 4·00 3·75
50 2 on 5 c. green on green . . 7·25 7·25
47 2 on 25 c. black on pink . . 4·00 3·75
51 4 on 5 c. green on green . . 7·25 6·50
48 4 on 25 c. black on pink . . 3·75 3·75

1892. Postage Due stamps of French Colonies optd **T ST-PIERRE M-on P**.

52 U 10 c. black . . . . 21·00 21·00
53 20 c. black . . . . 13·50 14·00
54 30 c. black . . . . 15·00 15·00
55 40 c. black . . . . 15·00 15·00
56 60 c. black . . . . 70·00 70·00
57 1 f. brown . . . . 95·00 95·00
58 2 f. brown £160 £160
59 5 f. brown £275 £275

1892. "Tablet" key-type inscr "ST PIERRE ET MIQUELON".

60 D 1 c. black and red on blue . . 50 50
61 2 c. brown & blue on buff . . 45 55
62 4 c. brown & blue on grey . . 1·00 90
63 5 c. green and red . . . . . 1·50 1·25
64 10 c. black & blue on lilac . . 3·50 2·50
74 10 c. red and blue . . . . . 2·50 95
65 15 c. blue and red . . . . . 4·75 1·90
75 15 c. grey and red . . . . . 60·00 30·00
66 20 c. red & blue on green . . 15·00 11·00
67 25 c. black & red on pink . . 5·50 1·25
76 25 c. blue and red . . . . . 8·75 6·25
68 30 c. brown & bl on drab . . 5·25 2·75
77 35 c. black & red on yell . . 3·75 3·50
69 40 c. red & blue on yellow . . 4·75 2·75
70 50 c. red and blue on pink . . 30·00 20·00
78 50 c. brown & red on blue . . 20·00 18·00
71 75 c. brown & red in orge . . 17·00 13·50
72 1 f. green and red . . . . . 14·00 8·25

17 Fisherman

18 Glaucous Gull

19 Fishing Brigantine

1909.

79 17 1 c. brown and red 20 25
80 2 c. blue and brown . . . 20 25
81 4 c. brown and violet . . . 20 30
82 5 c. olive and green . . . 30 40
109 5 c. black and blue 20 30
83 10 c. red and pink 35 40
110 10 c. olive and green . . . 30 40
111 10 c. mauve and bistre . . 30 40
84 15 c. red and purple . . . 30 40
85 20 c. purple and brown . . 70 70
86 18 25 c. blue and deep blue . . 1·50 1·00
112 25 c. green and brown . . 45 50
87 30 c. brown and orange . . 75 70
113 30 c. red and carmine . . 45 45
114 30 c. blue and red 40 35
115 30 c. green and olive . . 40 45
88 35 c. brown and green . . 45 35
89 40 c. green and brown . . 1·75 1·10
90 45 c. green and violet . . 45 45
91 50 c. green and brown . . 75 70
116 50 c. light blue and blue . 70 70
117 50 c. mauve and bistre . . 45 45
118 60 c. red and blue 45 45
119 65 c. brown and mauve . . 80 80
92 75 c. green and brown . . 70 70
120 90 c. red and scarlet . . 14·00 15·00
93 19 1 f. blue and green . . . 2·00 1·40
121 1 f. 10 red and green . . . 2·00 2·00
122 1 f. 50 blue & ultramarine 6·25 6·25
94 2 f. brown and violet . . . 2·00 1·50
123 3 f. mauve on pink . . . . 6·00 6·25
95 5 f. green and brown . . . 6·25 4·25

1912. "Tablet" issue surch in figures.

96 D 05 on 2 c. brown and blue on buff . . . . 1·40 1·40
97 05 on 4 c. brown and blue on grey 25 35
98 05 on 15 c. blue and red . 35 35
99 05 on 20 c. red and blue on green 25 35
100 05 on 25 c. black and red on pink 30 35
101 05 on 30 c. brown and blue on drab 35 45
102 05 on 35 c. black and red on yellow 70 70
103 10 on 40 c. red and blue on yellow 30 30
104 10 on 50 c. red and blue . 40 45
105 10 on 75 c. brown and red on orange . . . . . 1·10 1·25
106 10 on 1 f. green and red . 1·50 1·50

1915. Red Cross. Surch **5c** and red cross.

107 17 10 c. + 5 c. red and pink . 60 70
108 15 c. + 5 c. red & purple . 70 85

1924. Surch with new value.

124 17 25 c. on 15 c. red & purple . 30 40
125 19 25 c. on 2 f. brown & violet 30 40
126 25 c. on 5 f. green & brown 30 40
127 18 65 on 45 c. green & violet . 80 90
128 85 on 75 c. green & brown . 80 90
129 90 c. on 75 c. red and scarlet 1·25 1·50
130 19 1 f. 25 on 1 f. ultramarine and blue . . . . 1·25 1·50
131 1 f. 50 on 1 f. blue and light blue . . . . 2·00 2·00
132 3 f. on 5 f. mauve & brown 1·60 1·75
133 10 f. on 5 f. green and red 10·00 10·50
134 20 f. on 5 f. red and violet 15·00 15·00

1931. International Colonial Exhibition, Paris, key-types inscr "ST PIERRE ET MIQUELON".

135 E 40 c. green and black . . 1·75 1·75
136 F 50 c. mauve and black . . 1·75 1·60
137 G 90 c. red and black . . 1·75 1·75
138 H 1 f. 50 blue and black . . 1·75 1·75

27 Map of St. Pierre et Miquelon

28 Galantry Lighthouse

29 "Jacques Coeur" (trawler)

1932.

139 27 1 c. blue and purple 15 25
140 28 2 c. green and black 25 35
141 29 4 c. brown and red 25 40
142 5 c. brown and mauve . . . 25 40
143 28 10 c. black and purple . . . 35 45
144 15 c. mauve and blue . . . 65 65
145 27 20 c. red and black 65 70
146 25 c. green and mauve . . . 65 70
147 29 30 c. green and olive . . . 70 70
148 40 c. brown and blue . . . 70 70
149 28 45 c. green and red 70 65
150 50 c. green and brown . . . 70 70
151 29 65 c. red and brown . . . . 95 1·00
152 27 75 c. red and green 95 95
153 90 c. scarlet and red . . . 95 95
154 29 1 f. scarlet and red 70 70
155 27 1 f. 25 red and blue 95 95
156 1 f. 50 blue and deep blue . 95 1·00
157 29 1 f. 75 brown and black . . 1·25 1·25
158 2 f. green and black . . . 5·25 5·50
159 28 3 f. brown and green . . . 7·00 7·00
160 5 f. brown and red . . . . 17·00 17·00
161 29 10 f. mauve and green . . . 42·00 42·00
162 27 20 f. green and red . . . . 42·00 42·00

1934. 400th Anniv of Cartier's Discovery of Canada. Optd **JACQUES CARTIER 1534-1934**.

163 28 50 c. green and brown . . . 1·60 1·75
164 27 75 c. red and green . . . . 2·00 2·00
165 1 f. 50 blue and deep blue . 2·50 2·50
166 29 1 f. 75 brown and black . . 2·75 2·75
167 28 5 f. brown and red . . . . 19·00 19·00

32 Commerce

39 Dog Team

1937. International Exhibition, Paris.

168 32 20 c. violet . . . . 1·10 1·10
169 – 30 c. green . . . . 1·10 1·10
170 – 40 c. red . . . . 1·10 1·10
171 – 50 c. brown and blue . . . 1·00 1·10
172 – 90 c. red . . . . 1·00 1·10
173 – 1 f. 50 blue . . . . 1·00 1·10

DESIGNS—VERT: 50 c. Agriculture. HORIZ: 30 c. Sailing ships; 40 c. Women of three races; 90 c. France extends Torch of Civilisation; 1 f. 50, Diane de Poitiers.

1938. International Anti-Cancer Fund. As T **22** of Mauritania.

174 1 f. 75 + 50 c. blue . . . . 7·75 8·25

1938.

175 39 2 c. green 20 35
176 3 c. brown 20 35
177 4 c. purple 20 30
178 5 c. red 25 30
179 10 c. brown 25 30
180 15 c. purple 25 35
181 20 c. violet 25 35
182 25 c. blue . . . . 1·00 1·25
183 – 30 c. purple 25 35
184 – 35 c. green 35 45
185 – 40 c. blue 25 35
186 – 45 c. green 30 35
187 – 50 c. red 25 35
188 – 55 c. blue . . . . 1·50 1·50
189 – 60 c. violet 25 35
190 – 65 c. brown . . . . 2·25 2·50
191 – 70 c. orange 35 35
192 – 80 c. violet 60 60
193 – 90 c. blue 35 35
194 – 1 f. red . . . . 5·75 6·00
195 – 1 f. olive 35 45
196 – 1 f. 25 red . . . . 1·10 1·10
197 – 1 f. 40 brown 45 50
198 – 1 f. 50 green 40 50
199 – 1 f. 60 purple 45 45
200 – 1 f. 75 blue 85 85
201 – 2 f. purple 30 40
202 – 2 f. 25 blue 55 55
203 – 2 f. 50 orange 85 80
204 – 3 f. brown 35 45
205 – 5 f. red 33 60
206 – 10 f. blue 85 85
207 – 20 f. olive . . . . 1·10 1·10

DESIGNS: 30 to 70 c. St. Pierre harbour; 80 c. to 1 f. 75, Pointe aux Canons lighthouse (wrongly inscr "PHARE DE LA TORTUE"); 2 to 20 f. Soldiers' Cove, Langlade.

1939. New York World's Fair. As T **28** of Mauritania.

208 1 f. 25 red 80 85
209 2 f. 25 blue 80 85

1939. 150th Anniv of French Revolution. As T **29** of Mauritania.

210 45 c. + 25 c. green and black . 5·50 5·50
211 70 c. + 30 c. brown and black . 5·50 5·50
212 90 c. + 35 c. orange and black 5·50 5·50
213 1 f. 25 + 1 f. red and black . 5·50 5·50
214 2 f. 25 + 2 f. blue and black . 5·50 5·50

1941. Free French Plebiscite. Stamps of 1938 optd **Noel 1941 FRANCE LIBRE F.N.F.L.** or surch also.

215 39 10 c. brown . . . . 28·00 28·00
216 20 c. violet . . . . 28·00 28·00
217 25 c. blue . . . . 28·00 28·00
218 – 40 c. blue . . . . 28·00 28·00
219 – 45 c. green . . . . 28·00 28·00
220 – 65 c. brown . . . . 28·00 28·00
221 – 70 c. orange . . . . 28·00 28·00
222 – 80 c. violet . . . . 28·00 28·00
223 – 90 c. blue . . . . 28·00 28·00
224 – 1 f. green . . . . 28·00 28·00
225 – 1 f. 25 red . . . . 28·00 28·00
226 – 1 f. 40 brown . . . . . . 35·00 35·00
227 – 1 f. 60 purple . . . . . . 35·00 35·00
228 – 1 f. 75 blue . . . . 35·00 35·00
229 – 2 f. purple . . . . 35·00 35·00
230 – 2 f. 25 blue . . . . 35·00 35·00
231 – 2 f. 50 orange . . . . . . 35·00 35·00
232 – 3 f. brown . . . . 35·00 35·00
233 39 10 f. on 10 c. brown . . . . 60·00 60·00
234 – 20 f. on 90 c. blue . . . . 60·00 60·00

"F.N.F.L." = Forces Navales Francaises Libres (Free French Naval Forces).

1941. Various stamps overprinted **FRANCE LIBRE F. N. F. L.** or surch also. (a) Nos. 111 and 114.

245 17 10 c. mauve and bistre . . £750 £750
246 18 30 c. blue and lake £750 £750

(b) On stamps of 1932.

247 28 2 c. green and black . . . £160 £160
248 29 4 c. brown and red . . . . 35·00 35·00
249 5 c. brown and mauve . . £600 £600
250 40 c. brown and blue . . . 10·50 10·50
251 28 45 c. green and red £120 £120
252 50 c. green and brown . . 8·25 8·25
253 29 65 c. red and brown . . . 24·00 24·00
254 1 f. red and brown £250 £250
255 1 f. 75 brown and black . 8·25 8·25
256 2 f. green and black . . . 11·00 11·00
257 28 5 f. brown and red £225 £225
258 29 5 f. on 1 f. 75 brn & blk . 9·75 9·75

(c) On stamps of 1938.

259 39 2 c. green £300 £300
260 3 c. brown . . . . 90·00 90·00
261 4 c. purple . . . . 70·00 70·00
262 5 c. red £625 £625
263 10 c. brown . . . . 9·00 9·00
264 15 c. purple £1000 £1000
265 20 c. violet £140 £140
266 20 c. on 10 c. brown . . . 7·00 7·00
267 25 c. blue . . . . 9·00 9·00
268 30 c. on 10 c. brown . . . 4·75 4·75
269 – 35 c. green £525 £525
270 – 40 c. blue . . . . 11·00 11·00
271 – 45 c. green . . . . 11·00 11·00
272 – 55 c. blue £6000 £6000
273 – 60 c. violet £400 £400
274 – 60 c. on 90 c. blue . . . 5·50 5·50
275 – 65 c. brown . . . . 14·00 14·00
276 – 70 c. orange . . . . 24·00 24·00
277 – 80 c. violet £300 £300
278 – 90 c. blue . . . . 12·50 12·50
279 – 1 f. green . . . . 14·00 14·00
280 – 1 f. 25 red . . . . 11·00 11·00
281 – 1 f. 40 brown . . . . . . 9·75 9·75
282 – 1 f. 50 green £550 £550
283 – 1 f. 50 on 90 c. blue . . . 8·25 8·25
284 – 1 f. 60 purple . . . . . . 11·00 11·00
285 – 2 f. purple . . . . 42·00 42·00
286 – 2 f. 25 blue . . . . 11·00 11·00
287 – 2 f. 50 orange . . . . . . 14·00 14·00
288 7 2 f. 50 on 10 c. brown . . 11·00 11·00
289 – 3 f. brown £6500 £6500
290 – 5 f. red £1500 £1500
291 7 10 f. on 10 c. brown . . . 38·00 38·00
292 – 20 f. olive £575 £575
293 – 20 f. on 90 c. blue . . . 42·00 42·00

(d) On Nos. 208/9.

294 1 f. 25 red . . . . 8·25 8·25
295 2 f. 25 blue . . . . 7·25 8·25
296 2 f. 50 on 1 f. 25 red . . . 11·00 11·00
297 3 f. on 2 f. 25 blue . . . . 11·00 11·00

1942. Stamps of 1932 overprinted **FRANCE LIBRE F. N. F. L.** or surch also.

304 27 20 c. red and black £250 £250
305 75 c. red and green . . . . 14·00 14·00
306 1 f. 25 red and blue . . . 11·00 11·00
307 1 f. 50 blue & deep blue . £300 £300
308 10 f. on 1 f. 25 red & blue 24·00 24·00
309 20 f. on 75 c. red & green . 35·00 35·00

1942. Social Welfare Fund. Nos. 279 and 287 further surch **OEUVRES SOCIALES**, cross and premium.

320 1 f. + 50 c. green . . . . . 35·00 35·00
321 2 f. 50 + 1 f. orange . . . . 35·00 35·00

47 Fishing Schooner

1942. (a) Postage.

322 47 5 c. blue 20 30
323 10 c. pink 15 25
324 25 c. green 15 25
325 30 c. black 15 25
326 40 c. blue 15 25
327 60 c. purple 15 25
328 1 f. violet 25 35
329 1 f. 50 red 60 70
330 2 f. brown 35 45
331 2 f. 50 blue 65 70
332 4 f. orange 35 45
333 5 f. purple 35 45
334 10 f. blue 60 70
335 20 f. green . . . . 1·00 1·10

(b) Air. As T **30** of New Caledonia.
336 1 f. orange 25 35
337 1 f. 50 red 25 35
338 5 f. purple 35 45
339 10 f. black 60 70
340 25 f. blue 75 85
341 50 f. green 85 1·00
342 100 f. red 1·25 1·40

1944. Mutual Aid and Red Cross Funds. As T **31** of New Caledonia.
343 5 f. + 20 f. blue 80 1·00

1945. Eboue. As T **32** of New Caledonia.
344 2 f. black 50 60
345 25 f. green 75 85

1945. Surch.
346 **47** 50 c. on 5 c. blue 25 35
347 70 c. on 5 c. blue 25 35
348 80 c. on 5 c. blue 30 40
349 1 f. 20 on 5 c. blue 30 40
350 2 f. 40 on 25 c. green 30 40
351 3 f. on 25 c. green 45 55
352 4 f. 50 on 25 c. green 80 90
353 15 f. on 2 f. 50 blue 1·00 1·10

1946. Air. Victory. As T **34** of New Caledonia.
354 8 f. red 75 1·00

1946. Air. From Chad to the Rhine. As Nos. 300/305 of New Caledonia.
355 5 f. red 80 85
356 10 f. lilac 80 85
357 15 f. black 90 1·00
358 20 f. violet 90 1·00
359 25 f. brown 1·60 1·75
360 50 f. black 1·60 1·75

54 Soldiers' Cove, Langlade

55 Allegory of Fishing

56 Douglas DC-4 and Wrecked Fishing Schooner

1947.
361 **54** 10 c. brown (postage) 15 25
362 30 c. violet 15 25
363 40 c. purple 15 30
364 50 c. blue 15 30
365 **55** 60 c. red 25 35
366 80 c. blue 25 40
367 1 f. green 25 35
368 – 1 f. 20 green 40 45
369 – 1 f. 50 black 40 45
370 – 2 f. red 40 35
371 – 3 f. violet 85 90
372 – 3 f. 60 red 80 85
373 – 4 f. purple 75 70
374 – 5 f. yellow 80 80
375 – 6 f. blue 80 80
376 – 8 f. sepia 1·25 1·00
377 – 10 f. green 1·10 95
378 – 15 f. green 1·25 1·25
379 – 17 f. blue 2·00 1·50
380 – 20 f. red 1·25 1·25
381 – 25 f. blue 1·50 1·50
382 – 50 f. green and red (air) 3·25 2·50
383 **56** 100 f. green 4·75 3·75
384 – 200 f. blue and red 8·75 4·75
DESIGNS—As Type **55**: 1 f. 20 to 2 f. Cross and fishermen; 3 f. to 4 f. Weighing fish; 5, 6, 10 f. Trawler "Colonel Pleven"; 8, 17 f. Red fox; 15, 20, 25 f. Windswept mountain landscape. As Type **56**: 50 f. Airplane and fishing village; 200 f. Airplane and snow-bound fishing schooner.

1949. Air. 75th Anniv of U.P.U. As T **38** of New Caledonia.
395 25 f. multicoloured 7·50 8·50

1950. Colonial Welfare Fund. As T **39** of New Caledonia.
396 10 f. + 2 f. red and brown 3·00 3·50

1952. Centenary of Military Medal. As T **40** of New Caledonia.
397 8 f. blue, yellow and green 3·50 4·25

1954. Air. 10th Anniv of Liberation. As T **42** of New Caledonia.
398 15 f. red and brown 4·50 4·75

62 Refrigeration Plant

63 Codfish

64 Dog and Coastal Scene

1955.
399 **62** 30 c. blue & dp bl (postage) 25 25
400 **63** 40 c. brown and blue 15 30
401 **62** 50 c. brown, grey & black 20 35
402 **63** 1 f. brown and green 25 35
403 2 f. indigo and blue 25 35
404 **62** 3 f. purple 40 40
405 – 4 f. purple, red and lake 50 50
406 – 10 f. brown, blue & turq 75 70
407 – 20 f. multicoloured 2·00 1·50
408 – 25 f. brown, green & blue 2·75 2·25
409 **62** 40 f. turquoise 1·60 1·60
410 **64** 50 f. multicoloured (air) 24·00 15·00
411 – 100 f. black and grey 8·50 6·50
412 – 500 f. indigo and blue 35·00 19·00
DESIGNS—As Type **62/3**: 4, 10 f. Pointe aux Canons Lighthouse and fishing dinghies; 20 f. Ice hockey players; 25 f. American minks. As Type **64**: 100 f. Sud Aviation Caravelle airliner over St. Pierre and Miquelon; 500 f. Douglas DC-3 over St. Pierre port.

65 Trawler "Galantry"

67 "Picea"

1956. Economic and Social Development Fund.
413 **65** 15 f. sepia and brown 1·25 90

1958. 10th Anniv of Declaration of Human Rights. As T **48** of New Caledonia.
414 20 f. brown and blue 1·50 1·25

1959.
415 **67** 5 f. multicoloured 1·25 90

68 Flaming Torches

1959. Air. Adoption of Constitution.
416 **68** 200 f. green, lake & violet 9·50 6·50

69 "Cypripedium acaule"

1962. Flowers.
417 **69** 25 f. purple, orange and green (postage) 3·50 3·25
418 – 50 f. red and green 5·50 3·50
419 – 100 f. orange, red and green (air) 8·50 3·50
DESIGNS—VERT: 50 f. "Calopogon pulchellus". HORIZ—48 × 27 mm: 100 f. "Sarracenia purpurae".

70 Submarine "Surcouf" and Map

1962. Air. 20th Anniv of Adherence to Free French Government.
420 **70** 500 f. black, blue and red £100 70·00

1962. Air. 1st Transatlantic TV Satellite Link. As T **50** of New Caledonia.
421 50 f. brown, green and sepia 5·50 3·50

72 Eiders

73 Dr. A. Calmette

1963. Birds.
422 **72** 50 c. bistre, black & blue 1·25 65
423 – 1 f. brown, mauve & blue 1·50 80
424 – 2 f. brown, black & blue 1·60 1·10
425 – 6 f. bistre, blue & turquoise 2·75 1·60
DESIGNS: 1 f. Rock ptarmigan; 2 f. Semi-palmated plovers; 6 f. Blue-winged teal.

1963. Birth Centenary of Dr. Albert Calmette (bacteriologist).
426 **73** 30 f. brown and blue 6·00 3·50

74 Landing of Governor from "Garonne"

1963. Air. Bicentenary of Arrival of First Governor (Dangeac) in St. Pierre and Miquelon.
427 **74** 200 f. blue, green & brn 15·00 8·00

1963. Red Cross Centenary. As T **53** of New Caledonia.
428 25 f. red, grey and blue 7·00 4·00

1963. 15th Anniv of Declaration of Human Rights. As T **54** of New Caledonia.
429 20 f. orange, purple and blue 4·00 2·25

1964. "PHILATEC 1964" International Stamp Exhibition, Paris. As T **54c** of New Caledonia.
430 60 f. blue, green and purple 8·00 6·00

78 Common Rabbits

1964. Fauna.
431 **78** 3 f. choc., brown & green 1·40 1·10
432 – 4 f. sepia, blue and green 2·00 1·40
433 – 5 f. brown, sepia and blue 2·50 1·90
434 – 34 f. brown, green & blue 6·00 3·50
ANIMALS: 4 f. Red fox; 5 f. Roe deer; 34 f. Charolais bull.

79 Potez 842 Airliner and Map

1964. Air. 1st St. Pierre–New York Airmail Flight.
435 **79** 100 f. brown and blue 10·00 5·30

1965. Centenary of I.T.U. As T **56** of New Caledonia.
436 40 f. blue, brown and purple 17·00 6·50

1966. Air. Launching of First French Satellite. As Nos. 398/9 of New Caledonia.
437 25 f. brown, blue and red 5·00 3·50
438 30 f. brown, blue and red 5·00 3·50

1966. Air. Launching of Satellite "D1". As T **56e** of New Caledonia.
439 48 f. blue, green and lake 6·50 4·50

83 "Revanche" and Settlers

1966. Air. 150th Anniv of Return of Islands to France.
440 **83** 100 f. multicoloured 10·00 4·50

84 "Journal Officiel" and Old and New Printing Presses

86 Trawler and Harbour Plan

85 Map and Fishing Dinghies

1966. Air. Centenary of "Journal Officiel" Printing Works.
441 **84** 60 f. plum, lake and blue 9·00 4·00

1967. Air. Pres. De Gaulle's Visit.
442 **85** 25 f. brown, blue and red 20·00 11·00
443 – 100 f. blue, turquoise & pur 30·00 20·00
DESIGN: 100 f. Maps and cruiser "Richelieu".

1967. Opening of St. Pierre's New Harbour.
444 **86** 48 f. brown, blue and red 5·0 2·75

87 Map and Control Tower

1967. Opening of St. Pierre Airport.
445 **87** 30 f. multicoloured 2·25 1·40

88 T.V. Receiver, Aerial and Map

1967. Inauguration of Television Service.
446 **88** 40 f. red, green and olive 5·00 2·75

89 Speed Skating

91 J. D. Cassini (discoverer of group), Compasses and Chart

1968. Air. Winter Olympic Games, Grenoble. Multicoloured.
447 50 f. Type **89** 6·00 3·50
448 60 f. Ice-hockey goalkeeper 7·50 4·50

1968. 20th Anniv of W.H.O. As T **68** of New Caledonia.
449 10 f. red, yellow and blue 5·50 2·75

1968. Famous Visitors to St. Pierre and Miquelon (1st series).
450 **91** 4 f. brown, yellow and lake 2·75 2·25
451 – 6 f. multicoloured 3·50 2·50
452 – 15 f. multicoloured 4·50 3·00
453 – 25 f. multicoloured 7·00 4·50
CELEBRITIES: 6 f. Rene de Chateaubriand and warship; 15 f. Prince de Joinville, "Belle Poule" (sail frigate) and "Cassard" (survey ship); 25 f. Admiral Gauchet and flagship "Provence" (Ile aux Chiens expedition).

1968. Human Rights Year. As T **69** of New Caledonia.
454 20 f. red, blue & yellow 7·00 4·00

93 War Memorial, St. Pierre

1968. Air. 50th Anniv of Armistice.
455 **93** 500 f. multicoloured . . . 18·00 14·00

1969. Air. 1st Flight of Concorde. As T **75** of New Caledonia.
456 34 f. brown and olive . . . . 20·00 10·00

95 Mountain Stream, Langlade

1969. Tourism.
457 **95** 5 f. brn, bl & grn (postage) 3·50 2·25
458 – 15 f. brown, green & blue . 4·00 3·00
459 – 50 f. purple, olive & bl (air) 10·00 5·50
460 – 100 f. brown, indigo & bl . 18·00 11·00
DESIGNS: 15 f. River bank, Debon, Langlade; 50 f. Wild horses, Miquelon; 100 f. Gathering wood, Miquelon. The 50 f. and 100 f. are larger 48 × 27 mm.

96 Treasury

1969. Public Buildings and Monuments.
461 **96** 10 f. black, red and blue . 2·75 1·60
462 – 25 f. red, ultramarine & blue 4·50 2·75
463 – 30 f. brown, green and blue 5·00 3·50
464 – 60 f. black, red and blue . 10·00 5·50
DESIGNS: 25 f. Maritime Fisheries Scientific and Technical Institute; 30 f. Unknown Sailor's Monument; 60 f. St. Christopher's College.

97 "L'Estoile" and Granville, 1690

1969. Maritime Links with France.
465 **97** 34 f. lake, green and emerald (postage) . . . . 7·50 3·00
466 – 40 f. green, red and bistre . 10·00 5·00
467 – 48 f. multicoloured . . . . 13·50 8·00
468 – 200 f. black, lake and green (air) . . . . 30·00 11·00
DESIGNS—As Type **97**: 40 f. "La Jolie" and St. Jean de Luz, 1750; 48 f. "La Juste" and La Rochelle, 1860; 48 × 27 mm. 200 f. "L'Esperance" and St. Malo, 1600.

98 Pierre Loti, Ship and Book Titles

1969. Air. Pierre Loti (explorer and writer) Commemoration.
469 **98** 300 f. multicoloured . . . 35·00 20·00

99 Ringed Seals

1969. Marine Animals.
470 **99** 1 f. brown, purple & lake . 4·00 2·25
471 – 3 f. blue, green and red . 4·00 2·25
472 – 4 f. green, brown and red . 4·00 2·25
473 – 6 f. violet, green and red . 4·00 2·25
DESIGNS: 3 f. Sperm whales; 4 f. Long-finned pilot whale; 6 f. Common dolphins.

1969. 30th Anniv of International Labour Orangization. As T **79** of New Caledonia.
474 20 f. brown, slate and salmon 6·50 2·75

1970. New U.P.U. Headquarters Building, Berne. As T **81** of New Caledonia.
475 25 f. brown, blue and red . . 6·50 2·75
476 34 f. slate, brown and purple 10·00 5·50

102 Rocket and Japanese Women

104 "Rubus chamaemorus"

103 Rowing Fours

1970. Air. World Fair "EXPO 70", Osaka, Japan.
477 **102** 34 f. brown, lake & blue . 11·00 5·50
478 – 85 f. blue, red & orange . 20·00 11·00
DESIGN—HORIZ: 85 f. "Mountain Landscape" (Y. Taikan) and Expo "star".

1970. World Rowing Championships, St. Catherine, Canada.
479 **103** 20 f. brown, blue & lt bl . 6·00 3·50

1970. Fruit Plants.
480 **104** 3 f. green, purple & brn . 1·40 80
481 – 4 f. yellow, red and green 1·60 1·00
482 – 5 f. red, green and violet . 1·75 1·40
483 – 6 f. violet, green & purple 3·00 1·60
PLANTS: 4 f. "Fragaria vesca"; 5 f. "Rubus idaeus"; 6 f. "Vaccinium myrtillus".

105 Ewe and Lamb

1970. Livestock Breeding.
484 **105** 15 f. brown, purple & green 4·50 2·75
485 – 30 f. brown, grey and green 5·50 2·75
486 – 34 f. brown, purple & green 8·00 5·00
487 – 48 f. purple, brown & blue 8·50 4·00
DESIGNS: 30 f. Animal quarantine station; 34 f. Charolais bull; 48 f. Refrigeration plant and "Narrando" (trawler).

106 Etienne Francois, Duke of Choiseul, and Warships

1970. Air. Celebrities of St. Pierre and Miquelon.
488 **106** 25 f. brown, blue & purple 50 2·75
489 – 50 f. brown, purple & green 10·00 6·50
490 – 60 f. brown, green & purple 12·50 6·00
DESIGNS: 50 f. Jacques Cartier and "Grande Hermine"; 60 f. Sebastien Le Gonard de Sourdeval and 17th-century French galleons.

107 "St. Francis of Assisi", 1900

1971. Fisheries' Protection Vessels.
491 **107** 30 f. red, blue & turq . . 21·00 8·50
492 – 35 f. brown, green & blue 23·00 9·50
493 – 40 f. brown, blue & green 23·00 9·50
494 – 80 f. black, green & blue 27·00 18·00
DESIGNS: 35 f. "St. Jehanne", 1920; 40 f. "L'Aventure", 1950; 80 f. "Commandant Bourdais", 1970.

108 "Aconite"

1971. 30th Anniv of Allegiance to Free French Movement. British Corvettes on loan to Free French.
495 **108** 22 f. black, green & blue . 11·00 8·00
496 – 25 f. brown, turquoise & bl 11·00 8·00
497 – 50 f. black, turquoise & blue 22·00 16·00
DESIGNS: 25 f. "Alyssum"; 50 f. "Mimosa".

109 Ship's Bell

111 Haddock

1971. St. Pierre Museum. Multicoloured.
498 20 f. Type **109** . . . . 6·50 3·50
499 45 f. Navigational instruments and charts (horiz) . . . . . 10·00 4·50

1971. 1st Death Anniv of De Gaulle. As Nos. 493/4 of New Caledonia.
500 35 f. black and red . . . . . . 9·00 5·50
501 45 f. black and red . . . . . . 13·50 7·75

1972. Ocean Fish.
502 **111** 2 f. indigo, red and blue . 3·50 2·25
503 – 3 f. brown and green . . . 3·50 2·25
504 – 5 f. red and blue . . . . . 5·00 2·75
505 – 10 f. green and emerald . . 8·50 4·50
DESIGNS: 3 f. Dab; 5 f. Sea perch; 10 c. Cod.

112 De Gaulle and Servicemen

1972. Air. General De Gaulle Commemoration.
506 **112** 100 f. brown, green & pur 20·00 10·00

113 Long-tailed Ducks

116 Swimming Pool

114 Montcalm and Warships

1973. Currency Revaluation.
507 **113** 6 c. brown, purple and blue (postage) . . . . 1·10 90
508 – 10 c. black, red & blue . . 1·40 1·10
509 – 20 c. bistre, ultram & bl . 1·60 1·10
510 **113** 40 c. brown, green & vio . 2·50 1·60
511 – 70 c. black, red and green . 3·50 1·90
512 – 90 c. bistre, blue and pur . 9·00 6·00
513 **114** 1 f. 60 violet, indigo and blue (air) . . . . 5·00 2·75
514 – 2 f. purple, green & violet . 6·50 3·50
515 – 4 f. green, mauve & brn . 11·00 5·50
DESIGNS—As Type **113**: 10, 70 c. Atlantic puffins; 20, 90 c. Snowy owls. As Type **114**: HORIZ: 4 f. La Salle, map and warships. VERT: 2 f. Frontenac and various scenes.

1973. Inauguration of St. Pierre Cultural Centre.
521 **116** 60 c. brown, blue and red . 4·50 2·50
522 – 1 f. purple, orange and blue 5·50 2·75
DESIGN: 1 f. Centre building.

117 Transall C-160 in Flight

1973. Air.
523 **117** 10 f. multicoloured . . . . 35·00 20·00

118 Met Balloon and Weather Ship

120 Clasped Hands on Red Cross

119 Northern Gannet with Letter

1974. World Meteorological Day.
524 **118** 1 f. 60 blue, green & red . 9·50 5·00

1974. Centenary of Universal Postal Union.
525 **119** 70 c. ultramarine, bl & red 4·50 2·25
526 90 c. blue, red and lake . 6·00 3·50

1974. Campaign for Blood Donors.
527 **120** 1 f. 50 multicoloured . . 9·00 4·50

121 Arms and Map of Islands

1974. Air.
528 **121** 2 f. multicoloured . . . . 10·00 4·50

122 Banknotes in "Fish" Money-box

123 Copernicus and Famous Scientists

1974. Centenary of St. Pierre Savings Bank.
529 **122** 50 c. brown, blue & black 4·50 2·50

1974. Air. 500th Birth Anniv (1973) of Nicholas Copernicus (astronomer).
530 **123** 4 f. violet, red and blue . 12·00 6·00

124 St. Pierre Church and Caspian Tern, Kittiwake and Great Auk

1974. Island Churches.
531 **124** 6 c. black, brn & green . 2·75 1·10
532 – 10 c. indigo, blue & brown 2·75 1·10
533 – 20 c. multicoloured . . . 4·00 2·25
DESIGNS: 10 c. Miquelon Church and fish; 20 c. Our Lady of the Seamen Church and fishermen.

125 Red Admiral

126 Cod and St. Pierre et Miquelon Stamp of 1909

1975. Butterflies. Multicoloured.
534 1 f. Type **125** . . . . 6·00 2·25
535 1 f. 20 Orange tiger . . . . . 7·00 3·50

1975. Air. "Arphila 75" International Stamp Exhibition, Paris.
536 **126** 4 f. red, indigo and blue . 15·00 7·00

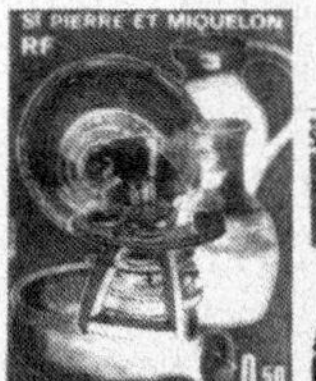

127 "Pottery" (Potter's wheel and products)
128 Pointe-Plate Lighthouse and Sea-birds

1975. Artisan Handicrafts.
537 **127** 50 c. purple, brown & grn 4·00 2·25
538 – 60 c. blue and yellow . . 4·00 2·25
DESIGN: 60 c. "Sculpture" (wood carving of Virgin and Child).

1975. Lighthouses.
539 **128** 6 c. black, violet & green 1·60 1·10
540 – 10 c. purple, green & slate 2·75 1·60
541 – 20 c. brown, indigo & blue 4·00 2·75
DESIGNS: 10 c. Galantry lighthouse, Atlantic puffin and pintail; 20 c. Cap Blanc lighthouse and blue whale.

129 Judo

1975. Air. "Pre-Olympic Year". Olympic Games, Montreal (1976).
542 **129** 1 f. 90 blue, red & violet 6·50 3·50

130 Concorde in Flight

1976. Air. Concorde's 1st Commercial Flight.
543 **130** 10 f. indigo, blue and red 22·00 11·00

1976. President Pompidou Commemoration. As T **125** of New Caledonia.
544 1 f. 10 grey and purple . . . 5·50 3·50

132 Alexander Graham Bell and Early Telephone

1976. Air. Telephone Centenary.
545 **132** 5 f. blue, orange and red 7·50 4·00

133 Washington and Lafayette

1976. Bicentenary of American Revolution.
546 **133** 1 f. multicoloured . . . . 4·50 2·75

134 Basketball

1976. Olympic Games, Montreal.
547 **134** 70 c. agate, blue & brown 3·50 2·75
548 – 2 f. 50 turquoise, grn & emerald . . . . 10·00 5·00
DESIGN—HORIZ: 2 f. 50, Swimming.

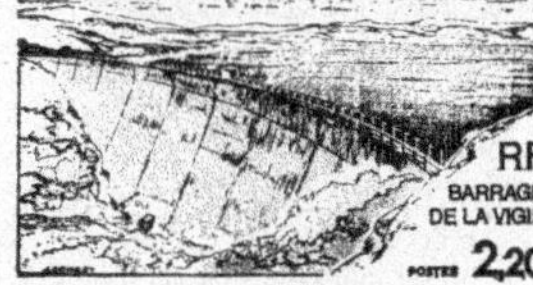

135 Vigie Dam

1976.
549 **135** 2 f. 20 brown, blue & turq 5·75 4·00

136 "Croix de Lorraine"

1976. Stern Trawlers. Multicoloured.
550 1 f. 20 Type **136** . . . . . . 5·50 3·50
551 1 f. 50 "Geolette" . . . . . 10·00 5·50

1986. Nos. 2444 etc of France optd **ST-PIERRE ET MIQUELON**.
552 **916** 5 c. green 30 30
553 10 c. red 20 20
554 20 c. green 20 20
555 30 c. red 20 20
556 40 c. brown 20 20
557 50 c. mauve 20 20
558 1 f. green 30 30
559 1 f. 80 green 55 40
560 2 f. green 65 45
561 2 f. 20 red 80 45
562 2 f. brown . . . . 1·10 90
563 3 f. 20 blue . . . . 1·25 90
564 4 f. red . . . . 1·40 1·00
565 5 f. blue . . . . 1·75 1·50
566 10 f. violet . . . . 3·50 2·25

138 Open Book

1986. 450th Anniv of Discovery of Islands by Jacques Cartier and 1st Anniv of New Constitution.
567 **138** 2 f. 20 brown, deep brown and green . . . . . . 1·40 80

139 Statue and Harbour

1986. Centenary of Statue of Liberty.
568 **139** 2 f. 50 blue and red . . . 1·50 90

141 Fish and Detection Equipment
142 "Nativity" (stained glass window, L. Balmet)

1986. Fishing.
578 **141** 1 f. red 50 35
579 1 f. 10 orange 45 35
580 1 f. 30 red 55 35
581 1 f. 40 blue 70 45
582 1 f. 40 red 55 35
583 1 f. 50 blue 65 45
584 1 f. 60 green 80 45
585 1 f. 70 green 65 45

1986. Christmas.
586 **142** 2 f. 20 multicoloured . . 1·40 80

143 Buff Cap ("Hygrophorus pratensis")

1987.
587 **143** 2 f. 50 brown and ochre . 2·00 1·00
See also Nos. 598, 609 and 645.

144 Dunan and Hospital

1987. Dr. Francois Dunan Commemoration.
588 **144** 2 f. 20 black, brown and blue 1·00 65

145 Ocean-racing Yachts

1987. Transatlantic Yacht Race (Lorient–St. Pierre et Miquelon–Lorient).
589 **145** 5 f. brown, dp blue & bl . 2·25 1·10

146 Maps

1987. Visit of President Francois Mitterand.
590 **146** 2 f. 20 multicoloured . . . 1·40 90

147 Schooner on Slipway and Share Certificate

1987. Centenary of Marine Slipway.
591 **147** 2 f. 50 brown and light brown . . . . 1·40 90

148 Hawker Siddeley H.S. 748 (St. Pierre–Montreal first flight, 1987)

1987. Air. Airplanes named "Ville de St. Pierre".
592 **148** 5 f. blue, green & turquoise 2·25 1·10
593 – 10 f. dp blue, blue & orge . 4·50 2·25
DESIGN: 10 f. Flying boat "Ville de Saint-Pierre" (first flight, 1939).

149 "La Normande" (trawler)

1987.
594 **149** 3 f. multicoloured . . . . 2·25 1·60

150 "St. Christopher carrying Christ Child" (stained glass window by L. Balmet) and Scout Emblem

1987. Christmas. 50th Anniv of Scouting.
595 **150** 2 f. 20 multicoloured . . 1·25 80

151 Horses and Ducks

1987. Natural Heritage. Le Grand Barachois. Each orange, green and brown.
596 3 f. Type **151** . . . . 1·60 1·00
597 3 f. Canada geese, gulls and seals 1·60 1·00
Nos. 596/7 were printed together, se-tenant, with intervening half stamp size label, each strip forming a composite design.

1988. Fungi. As T **143**.
598 2 f. 50 black, orange & brown 1·50 90
DESIGN: "Russula paludosa".

152 Ice Hockey Goalkeeper

1988. Winter Olympic Games, Calgary.
599 **152** 5 f. blue and red . . . . 2·00 1·40

153 Thomas and Camera

1988. Birth Centenary of Dr. Louis Thomas (photographer).
600 **153** 2 f. 20 brown, deep brown and blue 90 55

154 Airship "Hindenburg"

1988. Air. Aircraft. Each black, blue and purple.
601 5 f. Type **154** . . . . 2·25 1·10
602 10 f. Douglas DC-3 . . . . . 4·50 2·25

1988. "Philexfrance 89" International Stamp Exhibition, Paris. No. 2821 of France optd **ST-PIERRE ET MIQUELON**.
603 **1073** 2 f. 20 red, black & blue 1·50 80

156 "Nellie J. Banks" and Crates

1988. 50th Anniv of End of Prohibition and Last Liquor Smuggling Run from St. Pierre to Canada.
604 **156** 2 f. 50 ultramarine, brn & bl 1·50 90

157 "Le Marmouset" (stern trawler)

1988.
605 **157** 3 f. multicoloured . . . . 1·40 90

158 Ross Cove

1988. Natural Heritage. Each brown, deep blue and blue.
606 2 f. 20 Type **158** 80 55
607 13 f. 70 Cap Perce . . . . . . 4·50 3·25

159 Stained Glass Window 160 Judo

1988. Christmas.
608 **159** 2 f. 20 multicoloured . . . 80 55

1989. Fungi. As T **143**.
609 2 f. 50 brown and red . . . . 1·50 90
DESIGN: 2 f. 50, "Tricholoma virgatum".

1989. 25th Anniv of Judo in St. Pierre.
610 **160** 5 f. black, green & orange 1·75 1·10

161 "Liberty" (Roger Druet)

1989. Bicentenary of French Revolution and Declaration of Rights of Man. Multicoloured.
611 2 f. 20 Type **161** 90 65
612 2 f. 20 "Equality" 95 65
613 2 f. 20 "Fraternity" 95 65

162 Piper Aztec

1989. Air.
614 **162** 20 f. brown, light brown and blue . . . . 5·50 2·75

164 Fisherman in Boat

1989. Natural Heritage. Ile aux Marins. Each brown, blue and green.
616 2 f. 20 Type **164** 85 60
617 13 f. 70 Boy flying kite from boat 5·25 3·75

165 "Le Malabar" (ocean-going tug)

1989.
618 **165** 3 f. multicoloured . . . . 1·00 60

166 Georges Landry and Emblem

1989. Centenary of Islands' Bank.
619 **166** 2 f. 20 blue and brown . 80 45

167 "Christmas" (Magali Olano)

1989. Christmas.
620 **167** 2 f. 20 multicoloured . . 65 45

1990. Stamps of France optd **ST-PIERRE ET MIQUELON**.
621 **1118** 10 c. brown 10 10
622 20 c. green 10 10
623 50 c. violet 10 10
624 1 f. orange 20 10
625 2 f. green 45 25
625a 2 f. blue 45 25
626 2 f. 10 green 45 25
627 2 f. 20 green 50 30
628 2 f. 30 red 50 30
629 2 f. 40 green 55 35
630 2 f. 50 red 55 35
630a 2 f. 70 green 65 40
631 3 f. 20 blue 70 40
632 3 f. 40 blue 75 45
633 3 f. 50 green 80 50
634 3 f. 80 mauve 85 50
634a 3 f. 80 blue 90 55
635 4 f. mauve 90 55
636 4 f. 20 mauve 95 55
637 4 f. 40 blue . . . . . . 1·00 60
637a 4 f. 50 mauve . . . . . 1·10 70
638 5 f. blue . . . . 1·10 65
639 10 f. violet . . . . . . 2·25 1·40
The 2 f. 50, exists both perforated (ordinary gum) and imperforate (self-adhesive).

1990. Fungi. As T **143**.
645 2 f. 50 brown, black & orange 1·50 90
DESIGN: 2 f. 50, Hedgehog fungus ("Hydnum repandum").

168 "Pou du Ciel" and Gull

1990. Air.
646 **168** 5 f. green, blue & brown . 1·40 90

169 De Gaulle and Soldiers

1990. 50th Anniv of De Gaulle's Call to Resist.
647 **169** 2 f. 30 purple, red & blue 80 45
For design as T **169** but inscr "1890–1970", see No. 653.

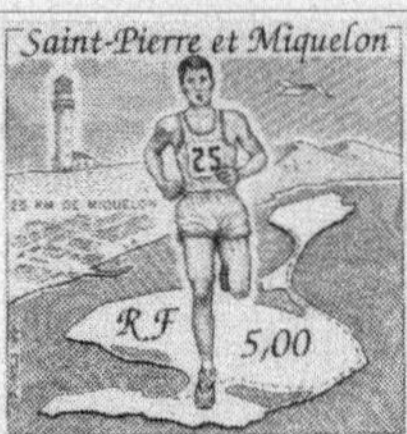
170 Runner and Map

1990. Miquelon 25 Km Race.
648 **170** 5 f. black, blue and brown 1·25 55

171 Moose, Micmac Canoe and Woman

1990.
649 **171** 2 f. 50 orange, brown & bl 80 45

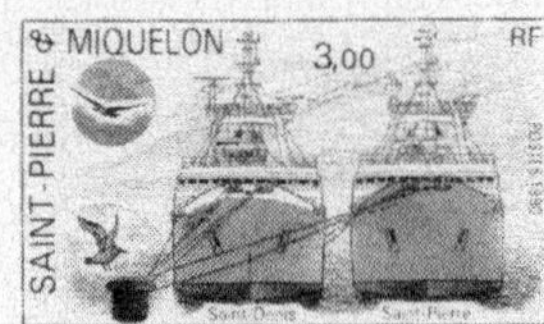
172 "Saint-Denis" and "Saint-Pierre" at Moorings

1990. Trawlers.
650 **172** 3 f. multicoloured 90 60

173 Entrance to Saint-Pierre Port

1990. St.-Pierre. Each brown, green and blue.
651 2 f. 30 Type **173** 75 45
652 14 f. 50 Interpeche fish factory 4·00 2·40
Nos. 651/2 were issued together, se-tenant, with intervening label, forming a composite design of part of St.-Pierre coastline.

1990. Birth Centenary of Charles de Gaulle (French statesman). As T **169** but inscr "1890–1970". Each purple, red and blue.
653 1 f. 70 Type **169** 55 35
654 2 f. 30 De Gaulle and trawler 70 45

174 Christmas Scene (Cindy Lechevallier)

1990. Christmas.
655 **174** 2 f. 30 multicoloured . . . 65 45

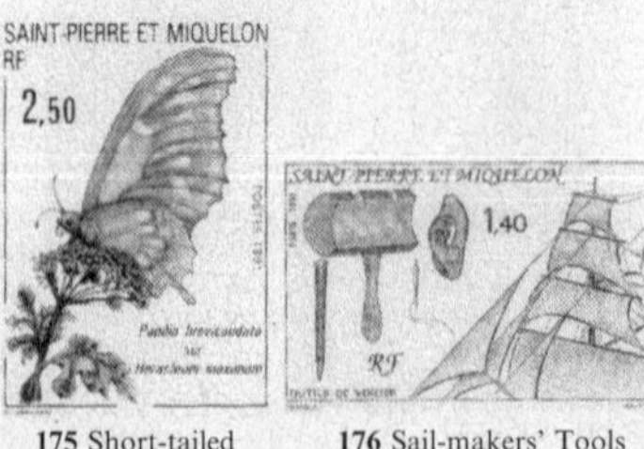
175 Short-tailed Swallowtail on "Heracleum maximum" 176 Sail-makers' Tools and Sails

1991.
656 **175** 2 f. 50 multicoloured . . . 80 45

1991.
657 **176** 1 f. 40 green and yellow . 45 20
658 1 f. 70 red and yellow . . 50 35

177 Ile aux Marins

1991. Old Views.
659 **177** 1 f. 70 blue 50 35
660 – 1 f. 70 blue 50 35
661 – 1 f. 70 blue 50 35
662 – 1 f. 70 blue 50 35
663 **177** 2 f. 50 red 70 45
664 – 2 f. 50 red 70 45
665 – 2 f. 50 red 70 45
666 – 2 f. 50 red 70 45
DESIGNS: Nos. 660, 664, Langlade; 661, 665, Miquelon; 662, 666, Saint-Pierre.

178 Piper Tomahawk

1991. Air.
667 **178** 10 f. blue, turquoise & brown 2·75 1·60

179 Musicians

1991. Centenary of Lyre Music Society.
668 **179** 2 f. 50 red, brown & orge 80 45

180 Oars

1991. St.- Pierre–Newfoundland Crossing by Rowing Boat.
669 **180** 2 f. 50 multicoloured 80 45

181 Pelota Players

1991. Basque Sports.
670 **181** 5 f. green and red . . . . 1·40 65

182 Fishermen

1991. Natural Heritage. Multicoloured.
671 2 f. 50 Type **182** 75 45
672 14 f. 50 Canada geese and shore 3·75 2·40
Nos. 671/2 were issued together, se-tenant, forming a composite design of Savoyard.

183 "Cryos" (stern trawler)

1991.
673 **183** 3 f. multicoloured 90 60

184 Free French Central Bank 100 f. Note

1991. 50th Anniv of Central Economic Co-operation Bank.
674 **184** 2 f. 50 multicoloured . . . 80 45

185 Naval Forces and Cross of Lorraine

1991. Christmas. 50th Anniv of Adherence to Free French Government.
675 **185** 2 f. 50 multicoloured . . . 80 45

186 Muselier and Harbour

1992. 110th Birth Anniv of Admiral E. Muselier (commander of 1941 Free French landing force).
676 **186** 2 f. 50 multicoloured . . . 65 35

187 Ice Skating **188** "Aeshna eremita" and "Nuphar variegatum"

1992. Winter Olympic Games, Albertville.
677 **187** 5 f. blue, ultramarine & mve 1·10 70

1992.
678 **188** 3 f. 60 multicoloured . . . 80 50

189 Boat-building Tools and Stern of Ship

1992.
679 **189** 1 f. 50 brown and blue . . 45 30
680 1 f. 80 blue and azure . . 55 40

190 Model Airplane and Remote Control

1992.
681 **190** 20 f. red, orange & brown 4·50 2·75

191 Ile aux Marins Lighthouse

1992. Lighthouses. Multicoloured.
682 2 f. 50 Type **191** 55 35
683 2 f. 50 Galantry 55 35
684 2 f. 50 Old Rouge Feu lighthouse, St. Pierre 55 35
685 2 f. 50 Pointe-Plate 55 35

192 Cones and Common Flicker

1992. Natural Heritage. Dolisie Valley, Langlade. Multicoloured.
686 2 f. 50 Type **192** 55 35
687 15 f. 10 Valley and berries . . 3·25 2·00

193 Columbus and Map on Sails

1992. 500th Anniv of Discovery of America by Columbus.
688 **193** 5 f. 10 multicoloured . . 1·10 90

194 Baron de l'Esperance, Map and Settlers

1992. 230th Anniv (1993) of Resettlement by French of Miquelon.
689 **194** 2 f. 50 brown, blue and red 55 35

195 Nativity

1992. Christmas.
690 **195** 2 f. 50 multicoloured . . 55 35

196 Birot and Free French Corvette

1993. 50th Death Anniv (1992) of Commander R. Birot.
691 **196** 2 f. 50 multicoloured . . 60 40

197 Divers and Wreck of "L'Hortense" **198** Longhorn Beetle on "Cichorium intybus"

1993. Deep Sea Diving.
692 **197** 5 f. multicoloured . . . . 1·25 75

1993.
693 **198** 3 f. 60 multicoloured . . 80 50

199 Cutting-up Cod

1993.
694 **199** 1 f. 50 multicoloured . . . 35 25
695 1 f. 80 multicoloured . . . 40 25

200 Greater Shearwater

1993. Air. Migratory Birds. Multicoloured.
696 5 f. Type **200** . . . . 1·10 70
697 10 f. American golden plover . . 2·25 1·40

201 Fleet of Ships

1993. Bicentenary of Settlement of Madeleine Islands.
698 **201** 5 f. 10 blue, green & brown 1·10 70

1993. No. 3121 of France optd **ST-PIERRE ET MIQUELON**.
699 **1118** (–) red 60 40

202 Frogfish

1993. Fishes. Multicoloured.
700 2 f. 80 Type **202** 65 40
701 2 f. 80 Fishermen and capelin . 65 40
702 2 f. 80 Skate ("Le Raie") . . . 65 40
703 2 f. 80 Halibut ("Le Fletan") . 65 40

203 Pine Cones, Otter and Left Bank

1993. Natural Heritage. Sylvain Hills. Multicoloured.
704 2 f. 80 Type **203** 65 40
705 16 f. Otter on all fours, pine cones and right bank . . . . 3·75 2·25

Nos. 704/5 were issued together, se-tenant, with intervening ¼ stamp-size label, forming a composite design of an otter pool.

204 Prefect's Residence

1993.
707 **204** 3 f. 70 blue, yellow & brn . 85 50

205 Father Christmas waving to Child

1993. Christmas.
708 **205** 2 f. 80 multicoloured . . . 65 40

206 Blaison and "Surcouf" (Free French submarine)

1994. 50th Death Anniv (1992) of Commander Louis Blaison.
709 **206** 2 f. 80 multicoloured . . 65 40

207 Player lining up Shot

1994. 1st French Overseas Territories Petanque Championship.
710 **207** 5 f. 10 multicoloured . . 1·25 75

208 "Cristalis tenax" on Dandelion

1994.
711 **208** 3 f. 70 multicoloured . . 85 50

209 Drying Cod

1994.
712 **209** 1 f. 50 black and green . . 35 20
713 1 f. 80 multicoloured . . 40 25

210 Ballot Box and Women outside Town Hall

1994. 50th Anniv of Women's Suffrage.
714 **210** 2 f. 80 multicoloured . . 70 45

211 "Saint-Pierre" (hospital ship)

1994. Centenary of Society of Sea Works.
715 **211** 2 f. 80 multicoloured . . 70 45

212 "Miquelon" (trawler)

1994. Ships. Multicoloured.
716 2 f. 80 Type **212** 70 45
717 2 f. 80 "Ile de St. Pierre" (trawler) 70 45
718 3 f. 70 "St. Georges XII" (pleasure cruiser) 95 60
719 3 f. 70 "St. Eugene IV" (pleasure cruiser) 95 60

MINIMUM PRICE

The minimum price quoted is 10p which represents a handling charge rather than a basis for valuing common stamps. For further notes about prices, see introductory pages.

213 Poolside

1994. Natural Heritage. Miranda Pool. Mult.
720 2 f. 80 Type **213** 70 45
721 16 f. Pool . . . . 4·00 2·40
Nos. 720/1 were issued together se-tenant with intervening ½ stamp-size label, forming a composite design.

214 Parochial School

1994.
722 **214** 3 f. 70 black, blue and red 95 60

215 Envelope, Magnifying Glass and Tweezers holding "Stamp"

1994. 1st European Stamp Salon, Flower Gardens, Paris.
723 **215** 3 f. 70 blue, green and yellow 95 60

216 House and Christmas Tree

1994. Christmas.
724 **216** 2 f. 80 multicoloured . . . 75 45

217 Pasteur

1995. Death Centenary of Louis Pasteur (chemist).
725 **217** 2 f. 80 multicoloured . . . 75 45

218 Sports Pictograms 219 "Dicranum scoparium" and "Cladonia cristatella"

1995. Triathlon.
726 **218** 5 f. 10 multicoloured . . . 1·40 85

1995.
727 **219** 3 f. 70 multicoloured . . . 95 60

220 Cooper at Work

1995.
728 **220** 1 f. 50 multicoloured . . 40 25
729 1 f. 80 multicoloured . . 45 30

221 Arctic Terns

1995. Air. Migratory Birds.
730 **221** 10 f. multicoloured . . . 2·50 1·50

222 Crab

1995. Crustaceans and Molluscs. Multicoloured.
731 2 f. 80 Winkle 75 45
732 2 f. 80 Type **222** 75 45
733 2 f. 80 Scallop 75 45
734 2 f. 80 Lobster 75 45

223 Geologists working at Cliff Face

1995. Geological Research. Multicoloured.
735 2 f. 80 Type **223** 75 45
736 16 f. Geological map of Langlade . . . . 4·25 2·75

224 Sister Cesarine 225 Building

1995. 150th Birth Anniv of Sister Cesarine.
737 **224** 1 f. 80 multicoloured . . 45 30

1995. Francoforum.
738 **225** 3 f. 70 grey, blue and red 95 60

226 De Gaulle and French Flag

1995. 25th Death Anniv of Charles de Gaulle (French President, 1958–69).
739 **226** 14 f. multicoloured . . . 3·75 2·25

227 Shop Window

1995. Christmas.
740 **227** 2 f. 80 multicoloured . . 75 45

228 Levasseur and Free French Corvette

1996. 50th Death Anniv (1997) of Commander Jean Levasseur.
741 **228** 2 f. 80 multicoloured . . . 70 45

229 Boxers 230 "Cladonia verticillata" and "Polytrichum juniperinum"

1996.
742 **229** 5 f. 10 multicoloured . . . 1·25 75

1996. Mosses and Lichens.
743 **230** 3 f. 70 multicoloured . . . 90 55

231 Blacksmiths at Work

1996.
744 **231** 1 f. 50 multicoloured . . . 35 25
745 1 f. 80 multicoloured . . . 45 30

232 Curlews

1996. Air. Migratory Birds.
746 **232** 15 f. multicoloured . . . . 3·75 2·25

234 The Cape

1996. Miquelon. Multicoloured.
748 3 f. Type **234** 75 45
749 15 f. 50 The village . . . . . . 3·75 2·25
Nos. 748/9 were issued together, se-tenant, with intervening ¾ stamp-size label, forming a composite design.

235 Customs House

1996. Centenary of Customs House, St. Pierre.
750 **235** 3 f. 80 blue and black . . 90 55

236 1947 Postage Due Design

1996. 50th Paris Autumn Stamp Show.
751 **236** 1 f. multicoloured 25 15

237 Crib in St. Pierre Cathedral

1996. Christmas.
752 **237** 3 f. multicoloured 75 45

238 Colmay

1997. 32nd Death Anniv of Commandant Constant Colmay.
753 **238** 3 f. multicoloured 75 45

PARCEL POST STAMPS

1901. Optd **COLIS POSTAUX**.
P79 D 10 c. black on lilac . . . . 55·00 55·00

1901. Optd **Colis Postaux**.
P80 D 10 c. red . . . . 9·00 9·00

1917. Nos. 83 and 85 optd **Colis Postaux**.
P109 **17** 10 c. red and pink . . . 1·25 1·40
P110 20 c. purple and brown . 1·25 1·10

1941. Free French Plebiscite. No. P110 optd **Noel 1941. FRANCE LIBRE F. N. F. L.**.
P303 **17** 20 c. purple and brown . £550 £550

POSTAGE DUE STAMPS

1892. Postage Due stamps of French Colonies optd **ST-PIERRE M-on**.
D60 U 5 c. black . . . . 40·00 42·00
D61 10 c. black . . . . 10·00 10·00
D62 15 c. black . . . . 10·00 10·00
D63 20 c. black . . . . 10·00 10·00
D64 30 c. black . . . . 10·00 10·00
D65 40 c. black . . . . 9·25 10·50
D66 60 c. black . . . . 42·00 42·00
D67 1 f. brown . . . . 90·00 90·00
D68 2 f. brown . . . . 90·00 90·00

1925. Postage Due type of France optd **SAINT-PIERRE-ET-MIQUELON** or surch also **centimes a percevoir** and value in figures.
D135 **D 11** 5 c. blue 25 40
D136 10 c. brown 30 50
D137 20 c. olive 40 50
D138 25 c. red 40 50
D139 30 c. red 55 60
D140 45 c. green 55 60
D141 50 c. red . . . . . . 1·10 1·25
D142 60 c. on 50 c. brown . 1·10 1·25
D143 1 f. red . . . . . . 1·25 1·50
D144 2 f. on 1 f. red . . . 1·75 2·00
D145 3 f. mauve . . . . . 5·50 5·50

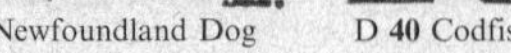
D 30 Newfoundland Dog D 40 Codfish

1932.
D163 **D 30** 5 c. black and blue . . 75 80
D164 10 c. black and green . 85 80
D165 20 c. black and red . . 1·10 1·10
D166 25 c. black and purple 1·10 1·10
D167 30 c. black & orange . 2·00 2·00
D168 45 c. black and blue . 2·25 2·25
D169 50 c. black and green . 4·00 4·25
D170 60 c. black and red . . 5·50 5·50
D171 1 f. black and brown . 14·00 14·00
D172 2 f. black and purple . 21·00 21·00
D173 3 f. black and brown . 23·00 23·00

1938.
D208 **D 40** 5 c. black 25 35
D209 10 c. purple 15 30
D210 15 c. green 25 35
D211 20 c. blue 25 35
D212 30 c. red 25 35
D213 50 c. green 30 45
D214 60 c. blue 25 45
D215 1 f. red 40 45
D216 2 f. brown . . . . . 1·40 1·60
D217 3 f. violet . . . . . 2·50 1·60

1941. Free French Plebiscite. Nos. D208/17 optd **NOEL 1941 F N F L**.
D235 **D 40** 5 c. black . . . . . . 15·00 15·00
D236 10 c. purple . . . . . 15·00 15·00
D237 15 c. green . . . . . 15·00 15·00
D238 20 c. blue . . . . . . 15·00 15·00
D239 30 c. red . . . . . . 15·00 15·00
D240 50 c. green . . . . . 28·00 28·00
D241 60 c. blue . . . . . . 65·00 65·00
D242 1 f. red . . . . 75·00 75·00
D243 2 f. brown . . . . . 80·00 80·00
D244 3 f. violet . . . . . 90·00 90·00

1941. Postage Due stamps of 1932 optd **FRANCE LIBRE F. N. F. L.** or surch also.

D298 D 30 25 c. black & purple . £190 £190
D299 30 c. black & orange . £190 £190
D300 50 c. black & green . £625 £625
D301 2 f. black & purple . . 28·00 28·00
D302 3 f. on 2 f. blk & pur . 14·00 14·00

1941. Free French Plebiscite. Nos. D208/17 optd **FRANCE LIBRE F. N. F. L.**.

D310 D 40 5 c. black . . . . . . 28·00 28·00
D311 10 c. purple . . . . . 5·50 5·50
D312 15 c. green . . . . . . 5·50 5·50
D313 20 c. blue . . . . . . 5·50 5·50
D314 30 c. red . . . . 5·50 5·50
D315 50 c. green . . . . . . 5·50 5·50
D316 60 c. blue . . . . . . 6·75 7·00
D317 1 f. red . . . . . . 14·00 14·00
D318 2 f. brown . . . . . 14·00 14·00
D319 3 f. violet £350 £350

D 57 Arms and Galleon

D 115 Newfoundland Dog and Shipwreck Scene

1947.

D385 D 57 10 c. orange 15 25
D386 30 c. blue 15 30
D387 50 c. green 25 30
D388 1 f. red 25 35
D389 2 f. green 25 35
D390 3 f. violet 55 60
D391 4 f. brown 55 60
D392 5 f. green 55 60
D393 10 f. black 70 75
D394 20 f. red 80 90

1973.

D516 D 115 2 c. black & brown . 60 60
D517 10 c. black and violet 90 90
D518 20 c. black and blue . 1·40 1·40
D519 30 c. black and red . 2·25 2·25
D520 1 f. black and blue . 5·50 5·50

1986. Nos. D2493/2502 of France optd **ST-PIERRE ET MIQUELON**.

D569 10 c. brown and black . . . 20 20
D570 20 c. black 20 20
D571 30 c. red, brown & black . . 20 20
D572 40 c. blue, brown & black . 20 20
D573 50 c. red and black 20 20
D574 1 f. black 30 30
D575 2 f. yellow and black 65 65
D576 3 f. black and red . . . . . 1·00 1·00
D577 4 f. brown and black . . . . 1·40 1·40
D578 5 f. blue, red and black . . 1·75 1·75

ST. THOMAS AND PRINCE IS.

Pt. 9; Pt. 11

Two islands in the Gulf of Guinea off the west coast of Africa. A colony and then an Overseas Province of Portugal until 1975, when it became an independent republic.

1870. 1000 reis = 1 milreis.
1913. 100 centavos = 1 escudo.
1977. 100 cents = 1 dobra.

1870. "Crown" key-type inscr "S. THOME E PRINCIPE".

17 P 5 r. black 85 75
18 10 r. orange . . . . 6·25 4·00
29 10 r. green . . . . 2·75 1·90
20 20 r. bistre . . . . 1·40 1·00
30 20 r. red . . . . 1·25 1·10
21a 25 r. red 75 50
31 25 r. lilac . . . . 1·10 75
22 40 r. blue . . . . 1·90 1·60
32 40 r. yellow . . . . 1·90 1·60
25 50 r. green . . . . 5·50 4·25
33 50 r. blue . . . . 1·40 75
26 100 r. lilac . . . . 3·25 2·50
15 200 r. orange . . . . . . 3·00 2·25
16 300 r. brown . . . . . . 3·00 2·50

1887. "Embossed" key-type inscr "S. THOME E PRINCIPE".

38 Q 5 r. black . . . . 2·25 1·50
42 10 r. green . . . . 2·25 1·50
43 20 r. red . . . . 2·40 2·00
44 25 r. mauve . . . . 2·10 1·00
45 40 r. brown . . . . 2·25 1·60
46 50 r. blue . . . . 2·25 1·25
47 100 r. brown . . . . . . 2·00 1·25
48 200 r. lilac . . . . 7·50 5·00
49 300 r. orange . . . . . . 7·50 5·00

1889. Stamps of 1887 surch. No gum.

50 Q 5 r. on 10 r. green . . . . . 11·00 8·50
51 5 r. on 20 r. red . . . . . 11·00 8·50
52 50 r. on 40 r. brown . . . . 38·00 27·00

1895. "Figures" key-type inscr "S. THOME E PRINCIPE.

60 R 5 r. yellow 50 35
61 10 r. mauve 75 60
53 15 r. brown 85 60
54 20 r. lilac 85 60
62 25 r. green 85 35
63 50 r. blue 90 40
55 75 r. pink . . . . 2·00 1·60
64 80 r. green . . . . 5·00 3·75
56 100 r. brown on buff . . . 2·00 1·50
57 150 r. red on pink . . . . 3·00 2·50
58 200 r. blue on blue . . . 3·50 2·75
59 300 r. blue on brown . . . 4·00 3·00

1898. "King Carlos" key-type inscr "S. THOME E PRINCIPE". Name and value in red (500 r.) or black (others).

66 S 2½ r. grey 15 15
67 5 r. red 15 15
68 10 r. green 25 15
69 15 r. brown . . . . 1·00 80
113 15 r. green 50 30
70 20 r. lilac 50 25
71 25 r. green 35 25
114 25 r. red 50 30
72 50 r. blue 40 30
115 50 r. brown . . . . 2·00 1·40
116 65 r. blue . . . . 4·00 2·50
73 75 r. pink . . . . 5·50 3·00
117 75 r. purple . . . . 1·00 50
74 80 r. mauve . . . . 2·10 1·90
75 100 r. blue on blue . . . . 1·25 90
118 115 r. brown on pink . . . 3·50 2·00
119 130 r. brown on yellow . . 3·50 2·00
76 150 r. brown on yellow . . 1·60 1·25
77 200 r. purple on pink . . . 2·10 1·00
78 300 r. blue on pink . . . . 2·50 2·00
120 400 r. blue on cream . . . 5·00 3·00
79 500 r. black on blue . . . 3·00 2·10
80 700 r. mauve on yellow . . 5·00 3·50

1902. Surch with new value.

121 S 50 r. on 65 r. blue . . . . 1·50 1·25
85 R 65 r. on 5 r. yellow . . . . 1·50 1·25
86 65 r. on 10 r. mauve . . . 1·50 1·25
87 65 r. on 15 r. brown . . . 1·50 1·25
81 Q 65 r. on 20 r. red . . . . . 3·00 2·00
88 R 65 r. on 20 r. lilac . . . . 1·50 1·25
83 Q 65 r. on 25 r. mauve . . . 2·00 1·60
84 65 r. on 100 r. brown . . 2·00 1·50
90 115 r. on 10 r. green . . . 2·00 1·50
92 R 115 r. on 25 r. green . . . 2·00 1·25
89 P 115 r. on 50 r. green . . . 4·50 1·50
93 R 115 r. on 150 r. red on pink 2·00 1·25
94 115 r. on 200 r. blue on bl 2·00 1·25
91 Q 115 r. on 300 r. orange . . 2·00 1·50
95 130 r. on 5 r. black . . . 2·00 1·50
98 R 130 r. on 75 r. pink . . . 1·50 1·25
99 130 r. on 100 r. brown on buff . . . . 1·50 1·25
97 Q 130 r. on 200 r. lilac . . . 2·50 1·50
100 R 130 r. on 300 r. blue on brown 1·50 1·25
108 V 400 r. on 2½ r. brown . . . 50 50
101 P 400 r. on 10 r. yellow . . . 14·00 7·50
102 Q 400 r. on 40 r. brown . . . 4·00 3·00
103 400 r. on 50 r. blue . . . 5·00 3·50
105 R 400 r. on 50 r. blue 50 50
107 400 r. on 80 r. green . . . 1·00 50

1903. Stamps of 1898 optd **PROVISORIO**.

109 S 15 r. brown 85 50
110 25 r. green 85 50
111 50 r. blue . . . . 1·10 50
112 75 r. pink . . . . 2·10 1·75

1911. Stamps of 1898 optd **REPUBLICA**.

122 S 2½ r. grey 15 15
123 5 r. orange 15 15
124 10 r. green 15 15
125 S 15 r. green 15 15
126 20 r. lilac 15 15
127 25 r. red 15 15
128 50 r. brown 15 15
129 75 r. purple 15 15
130 100 r. blue on blue 15 15
131 115 r. brown on pink . . . 60 40
132 130 r. brown on yellow . . 60 45
267 200 r. purple on pink . . . 80 50
134 400 r. blue on cream . . . 75 45
268 500 r. black on blue . . . 60 50
136 700 r. mauve on yellow . . 75 45

1912. "King Manoel" key type inscr "S. THOME E PRINCIPE" and optd **REPUBLICA**.

137 T 2½ r. lilac 10 10
138 5 r. black 10 10
139 10 r. green 10 10
140 20 r. red 50 30
141 25 r. brown 30 20
142 50 r. blue 30 20
143 75 r. brown 30 20
144 100 r. brown on green . . . 50 30
145 200 r. green on orange . . . 75 50
146 300 r. black on blue 80 50

1913. Nos. 109 and 111/2 optd **REPUBLICA**.

159 S 15 r. brown 75 60
243 50 r. blue 25 20
272 75 r. pink . . . . 3·50 2·25

1913. Stamps of 1902 optd **REPUBLICA**.

244 S 50 r. on 65 r. blue 25 20
245 Q 115 r. on 10 r. green . . . 1·00 75
246 R 115 r. on 25 r. green . . . 30 15
164 P 115 r on 50 r. green . . . 32·00 27·00
247 R 115r. on 150 r. red on pink 30 15
248 115 r. on 200 r. blue on blue 30 15
249 Q 115 r. on 300 r. orange . . 1·00 80
250 130 r. on 5 r. black . . . 2·00 1·25
251 R 130 r. on 75 r. pink . . . 30 15
252 130 r. on 100 r. brown on buff 65 55
253 Q 130 r. on 200 r. lilac . . . 70 50
254 R 130 r. on 300 r. blue on brown 50 30
197 V 400 r. on 2½ r. brown . . . 1·00 90
198 Q 400 r. on 50 r. blue . . . 25·00 22·00
200 R 400 r. on 50 r. blue . . . 1·25 1·00
202 400 r. on 80 r. green . . . 1·40 1·10

1913. Surch **REPUBLICA S. TOME E PRINCIPE** and new value on "Vasco da Gama" stamps of (a) Portuguese Colonies.

203 ¼ c. on 2½ r. green 50 40
204 ½ c. on 5 r. red 50 40
205 1 c. on 10 r. purple 50 40
206 2½ c. on 25 r. green 50 40
207 5 c. on 50 r. blue 50 40
208 7½ c. on 75 r. brown 90 80
209 10 c. on 100 r. brown 50 40
210 15 c. on 150 r. brown 60 40

(b) Macao.

211 ¼ c. on ½ c. green 70 50
212 ½ c. on 1 a. red 70 50
213 1 c. on 2 a. purple 70 50
214 2½ c. on 4 a. green 70 50
215 5 c. on 8 a. blue 80 60
216 7½ c. on 12 a. brown . . . . 1·25 1·25
217 10 c. on 16 a. brown 80 60
218 15 c. on 24 a. bistre 80 60

(c) Timor.

219 ¼ c. on ½ a green 70 50
220 ½ c. on 1 a. red 70 50
221 1 c. on 2 a. purple 70 50
222 2½ c. on 4 a. green 70 50
223 5 c. on 8 a. blue 90 70
224 7½ c. on 12 a. brown . . . . 1·25 1·10
225 10 c. on 16 a. brown 80 60
226 15 c. on 24 a. brown 80 60

1914. "Ceres" key-type inscr "S. TOME E PRINCIPE" Name and value in black.

276 U ¼ c. green 10 10
281 ½ c. black 15 15
282 1 c. green 15 15
283 1½ c. brown 15 15
284 2 c. red 15 15
285 2 c. grey 15 15
286 2½ c. violet 15 10
287 3 c. orange 15 15
288 4 c. purple 15 15
289 4½ c. grey 15 15
290 5 c. blue 15 15
291 6 c. mauve 15 15
292 7 c. blue 15 15
293 7½ c. brown 15 15
294 8 c. grey 15 15
295 10 c. brown 15 10
296 12 c. green 20 20
297 15 c. pink 20 15
298 20 c. green 20 15
299 24 c. blue 35 25
300 25 c. brown 35 25
239 30 c. brown on green . . . 75 65
301 30 c. green 25 20
240 40 c. brown on pink . . . 75 65
302 40 c. turquoise 25 20
241 50 c. orange on orange . . 1·75 1·25
303 50 c. mauve 25 20
304 60 c. blue 25 20
305 60 c. pink 75 25
306 80 c. red 75 25
242 1 e. green on blue . . . . 1·75 1·25
307 1 e. pink 90 65
308 1 e. blue 65 45
309 2 e. purple . . . . 1·00 60
310 5 e. brown . . . . 6·25 2·50
311 10 e. pink . . . . 10·00 5·00
312 20 e. green . . . . 25·00 16·00

1919. No. 109 surch **REPUBLICA** and new value.

255 S 2½ r. on 15 r. brown 35 25

1919. No. 122 surch with new value.

256 S ½ c. on 2½ r. grey . . . . . 1·60 1·40
257 1 c. on 2½ r. grey . . . . . 1·00 65
258 2½ c. on 2½ r. grey 45 30

1919. "Ceres" key-types of St. Thomas and Prince Islands surch.

259 U ½ c. on ¼ c. green 90 70
260 2 c. on ¼ c. green 90 70
261 2½ c. on ¼ c. green . . . . . 2·75 2·25

1919. "Ceres" key-type of St. Thomas and Prince Islands surch **$04 Centavos** and with old value blocked out.

262 U 4 c. on 2½ c. violet 35 30

1923. Stamps of 1913 (optd REPUBLICA) surch **DEZ CENTAVOS** and bars.

313 R 10 c. on 115 r. on 25 r. green 25 20
314 10 c. on 115 r. on 150 r. red on pink 25 20
316 10 c. on 115 r. on 200 r. blue on blue 25 20
317 10 c. on 130 r. on 75 r. pink 25 20
318 10 c. on 130 r. on 100 r. brown on buff 25 20
319 10 c. on 130 r. on 300 r. blue on brown 25 20

1925. Stamps of 1902 surch **Republica 40 C.** and bars over original surcharge.

321 V 40 c. on 400 r. on 2½ r. brn . 50 20
322 R 40 c. on 400 r. on 80 r. grn 50 20

1931. Nos. 307 and 309 surch.

323 U 70 c. on 1 e. pink 75 50
324 1 e. 40 on 2 e. purple . . . 1·10 75

1934. As T **24** of Portuguese Guinea (new "Ceres" type).

325 1 c. brown 10 10
326 5 c. brown 10 10
327 10 c. mauve 10 10
328 15 c. black 10 10
329 20 c. grey 10 10
330 30 c. green 10 10
331 40 c. red 10 10
332 45 c. turquoise 20 15
333 50 c. brown 20 15
334 60 c. green 20 15
335 70 c. brown 20 15
336 80 c. green 20 15
337 85 c. red 85 75
338 1 e. purple 35 20
339 1 e. 40 blue . . . . 1·00 60
340 2 e. mauve . . . . 1·00 75
341 5 e. green . . . . 3·25 1·50
342 10 e. brown . . . . 6·25 3·00
343 20 e. orange . . . . 22·00 11·00

1938. As T **54** and **56** of Macao, but inscr "S. TOME".

344 **54** 1 c. green (postage) 10 10
345 5 c. brown 10 10
346 10 c. red 10 10
347 15 c. purple 10 10
348 20 c. grey 10 10
349 – 30 c. purple 15 10
350 – 35 c. green 15 15
351 – 40 c. brown 15 15
352 – 50 c. mauve 15 15
353 – 60 c. black 15 15
354 – 70 c. violet 15 15
355 – 80 c. orange 15 15
356 – 1 e. red 75 20
357 – 1 e. 75 blue 65 30
358 – 2 e. red . . . . 6·25 2·75
359 – 5 e. green . . . . 5·50 2·50
360 – 10 e. blue . . . . 7·50 2·75
361 – 20 e. brown . . . . 12·50 3·50
362 **56** 10 c. red (air) . . . . . . 35·00 29·00
363 20 c. violet . . . . 15·00 10·00
364 50 c. orange 65 50
365 1 e. blue . . . . 1·00 80
366 2 e. red . . . . 1·60 1·25
367 3 e. green . . . . 2·50 1·90
368 5 e. brown . . . . 3·50 3·00
369 9 e. red . . . . 3·75 3·00
370 10 e. mauve . . . . 3·75 3·00

DESIGNS: 30 to 50 c. Mousinho de Albuquerque; 60 c. to 1 e. Dam; 1 e. 75 to 5 e. Prince Henry the Navigator; 10, 20 e. Afonso de Albuquerque.

See also Nos. 374/400.

37 Portuguese Colonial Column

41 Cola Nuts

1938. President's Colonial Tour.

371 **37** 80 c. green 75 55
372 1 e. 75 blue . . . . 3·00 1·75
373 20 e. brown . . . . 15·00 8·00

1939. As Nos. 344/70 but inscr "S. TOME e PRINCIPE".

374 **54** 1 c. green (postage) 10 10
375 5 c. brown 10 10
376 10 c. red 10 10
377 15 c. purple 10 10
378 20 c. grey 15 10
379 – 30 c. purple 15 10
380 – 35 c. green 15 10
381 – 40 c. brown 15 10
382 – 50 c. mauve 15 10
383 – 60 c. black 15 10
384 – 70 c. violet 15 10

385 – 80 c. orange 15 15
386 – 1 e. red 35 20
387 – 1 e. 75 blue 50 30
388 – 2 e. red 90 55
389 – 5 e. green . . . . 2·00 1·25
390 – 10 e. blue . . . . 5·50 1·50
391 – 20 e. brown . . . . 7·50 3·00
392 **56** 10 c. red (air) 10 10
393 20 c. violet 10 10
394 50 c. orange 10 10
395 1 e. blue 15 15
396 2 e. red 55 45
397 3 e. green 75 65
398 5 e. brown . . . . 1·40 90
399 9 e. red . . . . 2·25 1·40
400 10 e. mauve . . . . 2·25 1·40

1948. Fruits.
401 **41** 5 c. black and yellow . . . 15 10
402 – 10 c. black and orange . . . 15 20
403 – 30 c. slate and grey . . . . 1·10 80
404 – 50 c. brown and yellow . . . 1·75 95
405 – 1 e. red and pink . . . . 2·40 1·60
406 – 1 e. 75 blue and grey . . . 4·00 2·50
407 – 2 e. black and green . . . 3·25 1·60
408 – 5 e. brown and mauve . . 8·25 7·50
409 – 10 e. black and mauve . . 13·50 8·25
410 – 20 e. black and grey . . . 28·00 18·00
DESIGNS: 10 c. Bread-fruit; 30 c. Custard-apple; 50 c. Cocoa beans; 1 e. Coffee; 1 e. 75, Dendem; 2 e. Abacate; 5 e. Pineapple; 10 e. Mango; 20 e. Coconuts.

1948. Honouring the Statue of Our Lady of Fatima. As T **62** of Macao.
411 50 c. violet . . . . 3·75 3·25

1949. 75th Anniv of U.P.U. As T **34** of Portuguese Guinea.
412 3 e. 50 black . . . . 7·50 4·75

1950. Holy Year. As Nos. 425/6 of Macao.
413 2 e. 50 blue . . . . 2·00 1·10
414 4 e. orange . . . . 3·75 2·40

1951. Termination of Holy Year. As T **69** of Macao.
415 4 e. indigo and blue . . . . . 2·00 1·25

46 Doctor examining Patients
48 J. de Santarem

1952. 1st Tropical Medicine Congress, Lisbon.
416 **46** 10 c. blue and brown . . . 25 25

1952. Portuguese Navigators. Multicoloured.
417 10 c. Type **48** 10 10
418 30 c. P. Escobar 10 10
419 50 c. F. de Po 15 10
420 1 e. A. Esteves 80 10
421 2 e. L. Goncalves 50 15
422 3 e. 50 M. Fernandes 50 15

49 Cloisters of Monastery
51 Route of President's Tour

1953. Missionary Art Exhibition.
423 **49** 10 c. brown and green . . 10 10
424 50 c. brown and orange . . 50 20
425 3 e. indigo and blue . . . . 1·60 1·00

1953. Centenary of First Portuguese Postage Stamps. As T **75** of Macao.
426 50 c. multicoloured 65 60

1954. Presidential Visit.
427 **51** 15 c. multicoloured 20 15
428 5 e. multicoloured 95 70

1954. 4th Cent of Sao Paulo. As T **76** of Macao.
429 2 e. 50 multicoloured 50 20

1958. Brussels International Exhibition. As T **44** of Portuguese Guinea.
430 2 e. 50 multicoloured 60 30

1958. 6th International Congress of Tropical Medicine. As T **79** of Macao.
431 5 e. multicoloured . . . . . 2·10 1·40
DESIGN: 5 e. "Cassia occidentalis" (plant).

55 Points of Compass
56 "Religion"

1960. 500th Death Anniv of Prince Henry the Navigator.
432 **55** 10 e. multicoloured . . . 70 50

1960. 10th Anniv of African Technical Co-operation Commission.
433 **56** 1 e. 50 multicoloured . . . 45 25

1962. Sports. As T **82** of Macao. Multicoloured.
434 50 c. Fishing 10 10
435 1 e. Gymnastics 40 10
436 1 e. 50 Handball 40 15
437 2 e. Sailing 50 20
438 2 e. 50 Running 70 50
439 20 e. Skin-diving . . . . . . 1·90 1·00

1962. Malaria Eradication. Mosquito design as T **83** of Macao. Multicoloured.
440 2 e. 50 "Anopheles gambiae" . . 75 60

1963. 10th Anniv of Transportes Aereos Portugueses (airline). As T **52** of Portuguese Guinea.
441 1 e. 50 multicoloured 50 30

1964. Cent of National Overseas Bank. As T **84** of Macao, but portrait of F. de Oliveira Chamico.
442 2 e. 50 multicoloured 60 30

1965. Centenary of I.T.U. As T **85** of Macao.
443 2 e. 50 multicoloured . . . . 1·10 75

62 Infantry Officer, 1788
73 Pero Escobar and Joao de Santarem

1965. Portuguese Military Uniforms. Multicoloured.
444 20 c. Type **62** 15 10
445 35 c. Infantry sergeant, 1788 . 15 10
446 40 c. Infantry corporal, 1788 . 10 10
447 1 e. Infantryman, 1788 . . . 85 45
448 2 e. 50 Artillery officer, 1806 . 85 45
449 5 e. Light infantryman, 1811 . 1·25 1·00
450 7 e. 50 Infantry sapper, 1833 . 2·00 1·25
451 10 e. Lancers officer, 1834 . . 2·75 1·90

1966. 40th Anniv of National Revolution. As T **86** of Macao, but showing different buildings. Multicoloured.
452 4 e. Arts and Crafts School and Anti-T.B. clinic 40 30

1967. Centenary of Military Naval Association. As T **88** of Macao. Multicoloured.
453 1 e. 50 C. Rodrigues and steam corvette "Vasco da Gama" 60 30
454 2 e. 50 A. Kopke, microscope and "Glossina palpalis" (insect) . . . . 1·00 60

1967. 50th Anniv of Fatima Apparitions. As T **89** of Macao.
455 2 e. 50 multicoloured 25 15
DESIGN: 2 e. 50 Apparition appearing to children and Valinhos Monument.

1968. 500th Birth Anniv of Pedro Cabral (explorer). As T **90** of Macao. Multicoloured.
456 1 e. 50 Medal of the Jeronimos Monastery (vert) 50 30

1969. Birth Centenary of Admiral Gago Coutinho. As T **91** of Macao. Multicoloured.
457 2 e. Island route-map and monument 40 25

1969. 500th Birth Anniv of Vasco da Gama (explorer). As T **92** of Macao. Multicoloured.
458 2 e. 50 Da Gama's fleet and fireship 15 15

1969. Centenary of Overseas Administrative Reforms. As T **93** of Macao.
459 2 e. 50 multicoloured 15 15

1969. 500th Birth Anniv of King Manoel I. As T **95** of Macao. Multicoloured.
460 4 e. Manoel Gate, Guarda See 25 15

1969. 500th Anniv of Discovery of St. Thomas and Prince Islands.
461 **73** 2 e. 50 multicoloured . . . 15 15

74 President A. Tomas
76 Stamps on Coffee Plant

1970. Presidential Visit.
462 **74** 2 e. 50 multicoloured . . . 25 15

1970. Birth Centenary of Marshal Carmona. Multicoloured. As T **96** of Macao.
463 5 e. Portrait in marshal's uniform 25 15

1970. Stamp Centenary. Multicoloured.
464 1 e. Type **76** 10 10
465 1 e. 50 Head Post Office, St. Thomas (horiz) 15 10
466 2 e. 50 Se Cathedral, St. Thomas 40 15

77 "Descent from the Cross" and Caravel at St. Thomas
78 Running and Throwing the Javelin

1972. 400th Anniv of Camoens' "The Lusiads" (epic poem).
467 **77** 20 e. multicoloured . . . . 3·50 1·00

1972. Olympic Games, Munich.
468 **78** 1 e. 50 multicoloured . . . 15 15

79 Fairey IIID Seaplane "Lusitania" and Cruiser "Gladiolus" off Rock of San Pedro

1972. 50th Anniv of 1st Flight, Lisbon–Rio de Janeiro.
469 **79** 2 e. 50 multicoloured . . . 30 15

1973. Cent of World Meteorological Organization. As T **102** of Macao.
470 5 e. multicoloured 40 30

81 Flags of Portugal and St. Thomas and Prince Islands

1975. Independence.
471 **81** 3 e. multicoloured 10 10
472 10 e. multicoloured 55 20
473 20 e. multicoloured . . . . 1·00 55
474 50 e. multicoloured . . . . 2·50 1·60

82 National Flag

1975. Independence Proclamation.
475 **82** 1 e. 50 multicoloured . . . 10 10
476 4 e. multicoloured 20 15
477 7 e. 50 multicoloured . . . 45 35
478 20 e. multicoloured . . . . 1·00 60
479 50 e. multicoloured . . . . 2·75 1·60

83 Diagram and Hand

1976. National Reconstruction Fund.
480 **83** 1 e. multicoloured 10 10
481 1 e. 50 multicoloured . . . 10 10
482 2 e. multicoloured 20 10

1976. Optd **Rep. Democr. 12-7-75**.
483 **48** 10 c. Joao de Santarem . . .
484 **62** 20 c. Infantry officer, 1788
485 – 30 c. Pedro Escobar (No. 418)
486 – 35 c. Infantry sergeant, 1788
487 – 40 c. Infantry corporal, 1788
488 – 50 c. Fernao de Po (No. 419)
489 – 1 e. Alvaro Esteves (No. 420)
490 – 2 e. 50 Rebello da Silva (No. 459) . . . .
491 **73** 2 e. 50 Escobar and Santarem
492 – 3 e. 50 Martim Fernandes (No. 422) . . . .
493 – 4 e. Manoel Gate (No. 460)
494 – 5 e. W.M.O. emblem (No. 470) . . . .
495 – 7 e. 50 Infantry sapper, 1833 (No. 450) . . . . . .
496 – 10 e. Compass rose (No. 432) Set of 14 . . . . . . 4·50 3·25

85 President Pinto da Costa and National Flag

1976. 1st Anniv of Independence.
497 2 e. Type **85** 20 10
498 3 e. 50 Proclamation of Independence, 12 July 1975 20 10
499 4 e. 50 As 3 e. 50 . . . . . 45 20
500 12 e. 50 Type **85** 90 45

1977. 2nd Anniv of Independence. No. 439 optd **Rep. Democr 12-7-77.**
501 20 e. multicoloured 80 80

CHARITY TAX STAMPS

The notes under this heading in Portugal also apply here.

1925. Marquis de Pombal Commemoration. As stamps of Portugal, but additionally inscr "S. TOME E PRINCIPE".
C323 **C 73** 15 c. black and orange 20 20
C324 – 15 c. black and orange 20 20
C325 **C 75** 15 c. black and orange 20 20

1946. Fiscal stamps as in Type C **1** of Portuguese Colonies surch **Assistencia** and new value.
C401 50 c. on 1 e. green . . . . . 2·50
C402 50 c. on 4 e. red . . . . . . 5·00
C403 1 e. on 4 e. red . . . . . . 5·00
C404 1 e. on 5 e. red . . . . . . 3·50
C405 1 e. on 6 e. green . . . . . 2·50
C406 1 e. on 7 e. green . . . . . 2·50
C409 1 e. on 10 e. red . . . . . 5·00
C410 1 e. 50 on 7 e. green . . . . 3·00
C411 1 e. 50 on 8 e. green . . . . 3·50
C412 2 e. 50 on 7 e. green . . . . 2·50
C413 2 e. 50 on 9 e. green . . . . 2·50
C414 2 e. 50 on 10 e. green . . . 2·50

40 Arms

1948. Value in black.
C415 **40** 50 c. green 35 30
C416 1 e. pink 70 45
C417 1 e. green 15 10
C418 1 e. 50 brown 80 45

1965. (a) Surch **um escudo 1$00** and two heavy bars.
C452 **40** 1 e. on 5 e. yellow . . . 4·00 3·25

(b) Surch **Um escudo**.
C453 **40** 1 e. on 1 e. green 50 50

(c) As No. C 417 but inscr "UM ESCUDO" at foot, surch **1$00**.
C454 **40** 1 e. on 1 e. green 50 50

(d) Previous surch "Cinco escudos" obliterated and further surch **Um escudo 1$00.**
C455 **40** 1 e. on 5 e. yellow . . . 1·10 1·00

NEWSPAPER STAMPS

1892. Surch $2\frac{1}{2}$ **RS.** No gum.
N53 **Q** $2\frac{1}{2}$ r. on 5 r. black . . . . 19·00 14·00
N54 $2\frac{1}{2}$ r. on 10 r. green . . . . 20·00 15·00
N55 $2\frac{1}{2}$ r. on 20 r. red . . . . 21·00 13·00

1893. "Newspaper" key-type inscr "S. THOME E PRINCIPE".
N59 **V** $2\frac{1}{2}$ r. brown 40 40

1899. No. N59 optd **PROVISORIO**.
N81 **V** $2\frac{1}{2}$ r. brown . . . . . . 12·50 5·00

POSTAGE DUE STAMPS.

1904. "Due" key-type inscr "S. THOME E PRINCIPE". Name and value in black.
D121 **W** 5 r. green 20 20
D122 10 r. grey 25 25
D123 20 r. brown 25 25
D124 30 r. orange 25 25
D125 50 r. brown 45 35
D126 60 r. brown 70 55
D127 100 r. mauve . . . . . . 1·40 90
D128 130 r. blue . . . . . . 1·90 90
D129 200 r. red . . . . . . 1·90 1·40
D130 500 r. lilac . . . . . . 3·25 1·90

1911. As last optd **REPUBLICA**.
D137 **W** 5 r. green 15 15
D138 10 r. grey 15 15
D139 20 r. brown 15 15
D140 30 r. orange 15 15
D141 50 r. brown 15 15
D142 60 r. brown 30 30
D143 100 r. mauve 30 30
D144 130 r. blue 30 30
D145 200 r. red 30 30
D146 500 r. lilac 45 45

1921. "Due" key-type inscr "S. TOME E PRINCIPE". Currency changed.

D313	W	½ c. green	15	15
D314		1 c. grey	15	15
D315		2 c. brown	15	15
D316		3 c. orange	15	15
D317		5 c. brown	15	15
D318		6 c. brown	15	15
D319		10 c. mauve	15	15
D320		13 c. blue	20	20
D321		20 c. red	20	20
D322		50 c. lilac	25	25

1925. Nos. C323/5 optd **MULTA**.

D323	C 73	30 c. black and orange	20	20
D324	–	30 c. black and orange	20	20
D325	C 75	30 c. black and orange	20	20

1925. As Type D 70 of Macao, but inscr "S. TOME E PRINCIPE". Numerals in red, name in black.

D417		10 c. brown and yellow	15	15
D418		30 c. brown and blue	15	15
D419		50 c. blue and pink	15	15
D420		1 e. blue and olive	15	15
D421		2 e. green and orange	15	15
D422		5 e. brown and lilac	25	25

APPENDIX

The following stamps have either been issued in excess of postal needs or have not been available to the public in reasonable quantities at face value. Such stamps may later be given full listing if there is evidence of regular postal use.

1977.

400th Birth Anniv of Rubens. 1, 5, 10, 15, 20, 50 e.

150th Death Anniv of Beethoven. 20, 30, 50 e.

Centenary of U.P.U. Surch on Navigators and Military Uniforms issues of Portuguese administration. 1 e. on 10 c., 3 e. on 30 c., 3 e. 50 on 3 e 50, 5 e. on 50 c., 10 e. on 10 c., 15 e. on 3 e. 50, 20 e. on 30 e. on 30 c., 35 e. on 35 c., 40 e. on 40 c.

Christmas. 5, 10, 25, 50, 70 d.

60th Anniv of Russian Revolution. 15, 30, 40, 50 d.

1st Death Anniv of Mao Tse-tung. 50 d.

1978.

Nobel Peace Prizes to International Organizations. Surch on Navigators and Military Uniforms issues of Portuguese administration. 3 d. on 30 c., 5 d. on 50 c., 10 d. on 10 c., 15 d. on 3 e. 50, 20 d. on 20 c., 35 d. on 35 c.

3rd Anniv of Independence. 5 d. × 3.

3rd Anniv of Admission to United Nations. Surch on Military Uniform issue. 40 d. on 40 c.

International Stamp Exhibition, Essen. 10 d. × 5.

Centenary of U.P.U. 5 d. × 4, 15 d. × 4.

1st Anniv of New Currency. 5 d. × 5, 8 d. × 5.

World Cup Football Championship, Argentina. 3 d. × 4, 25 d. × 3.

1979.

World Cup Winners. Optd on 1978 World Cup issues. 3 d. × 4, 25 d. × 3.

Butterflies. 50 c., 10 d., 11 d. × 4.

Flowers. 1 d., 8 d. × 4, 25 d.

Telecommunications Day and 50th Anniv of C.C.I.R. 1, 11, 14, 17 d.

International Year of the Child. 1, 7, 14, 17 d.

450th Death Anniv of Durer. 50 c. × 2, 1, 7, 8, 25 d.

History of Aviation. 50 c., 1, 5, 7, 8, 17 d.

History of Navigation. 50 c., 1, 3, 5, 8, 25 d.

Birds. Postage 50 c. × 2, 1, 7, 8 d.; Air 100 d.

1980.

Fishes. Postage 50 c., 1, 5, 7, 8 d.; Air 50 d.

Balloons. 50 c., 1, 3, 7, 8, 25 d.

Airships. 50 c., 1, 3, 7, 8, 17 d.

Olympic Games. 50 c., 11 d. × 4.

Death Centenary of Sir Rowland Hill. 50 c., 1, 8, 20 d.

10th Anniv of First Manned Moon Landing. 50 c., 1, 14, 17 d.

1981.

Olympic Games, Moscow. Optd on 1977 Mao Tse-tung issue. 50 d.

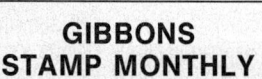

SAMOA Pt. 7

Islands in the W. Pacific administered jointly from 1889–99 by Gt. Britain, Germany and the U.S.A. (Stamps issued between 1897 and 1899 are listed in Volume 3). In 1899 the eastern islands were assigned to the U.S.A. and the western to Germany.

GERMAN COLONY

100 pfennig = 1 mark

1900. Stamps of Germany optd **Samoa**.

G1	8	3 pf. brown	7·00	10·00
G2		5 pf. green	11·00	14·00
G3	9	10 pf. red	7·00	14·00
G4		20 pf. blue	16·00	23·00
G5		25 pf. orange	40·00	85·00
G6		50 pf. brown	40·00	65·00

1901. "Yacht" key-type inscr "SAMOA".

G 7	N	3 pf. brown	70	75
G 8		5 pf. green	85	75
G 9		10 pf. red	85	75
G10		20 pf. blue	60	1·50
G11		25 pf. blk & red on yell	1·00	12·00
G12		30 pf. blk & orge on buff	1·00	12·00
G13		40 pf. black and red	1·00	13·00
G14		50 pf. blk & pur on buff	1·10	13·00
G15		80 pf. black & red on pink	2·50	32·00
G16	O	1 m. red	2·75	55·00
G17		2 m. blue	3·75	85·00
G18		3 m. black	5·50	£140
G19		5 m. red and black	£130	£475

The colony was occupied by British forces in 1914 and a League of Nations mandate given to New Zealand in 1920. For stamps issued by New Zealand administration, see volume 3.

SAN MARINO Pt. 8

An independent republic lying near the east coast of the Italian peninsula.

100 centesimi = 1 lira

1 2

1877.

1	1	2 c. green	3·50	1·60
18		2 c. blue	3·00	2·40
32		2 c. purple	2·50	1·75
2	2	5 c. yellow	38·00	5·00
33		5 c. green	1·50	80
3		10 c. blue	45·00	5·50
20		10 c. green	2·50	1·25
34		10 c. red	1·50	90
21		15 c. red	85·00	18·00
4		20 c. red	7·25	1·75
35		20 c. lilac	2·25	2·00
5		25 c. purple	55·00	6·50
36		25 c. blue	1·75	1·50
6		30 c. brown	£400	25·00
22		30 c. yellow	3·25	2·00
7		40 c. mauve	£400	25·00
23		40 c. brown	2·00	2·00
24		45 c. green	2·00	2·00
25		65 c. brown	2·00	1·75
26		1 l. red and yellow	£900	£225
37		1 l. blue	£900	£225
27		2 l. brown and buff	30·00	20·00
28		5 l. red and blue	85·00	90·00

1892. Surch **Cmi.** and figure of value.

10c	2	5 c. on 10 c. blue	35·00	6·00
12		5 c. on 30 c. brown	£275	35·00
16		10 c. on 20 c. red	17·00	1·50

1892. Surch **10 10**.

17	2	10 (c.) on 20 c. red	£150	2·50

13 Government Palace 14

15 Interior of Government Palace

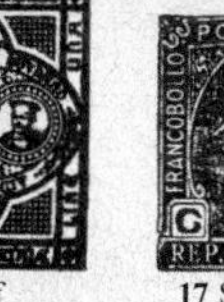

17 Statue of Liberty

1894. Opening of Government Palace and Installation of Captains-Regent.

29	13	25 c. purple and blue	1·50	70
30	14	50 c. purple and red	12·00	17·50
31	15	1 l. purple and green	10·00	2·00

1899.

38	17	2 c. brown	60	55
39		5 c. orange	1·10	85

See also Nos. 86/91.

18 19 Mt. Titano

1903.

40	18	2 c. lilac	4·25	1·10
73		2 c. brown	10	10
74	19	5 c. green	10	10
111		5 c. purple	10	10
42		10 c. pink	1·40	55
75		10 c. orange	10	10
112		10 c. green	10	10
76		15 c. green	15	15
113		15 c. purple	15	15
43		20 c. orange	48·00	11·00
77		20 c. brown	15	15
114		20 c. green	15	15
44		25 c. blue	5·50	1·25
78		25 c. grey	15	15
115		25 c. violet	15	15
45		30 c. red	2·00	2·50
79		30 c. mauve	25	25
116		30 c. orange	5·00	60
46		40 c. red	4·00	3·50
80		40 c. pink	25	25
117		40 c. brown	15	15
47		45 c. yellow	4·00	3·50
81		50 c. purple	35	35
118		50 c. grey	15	15
119		60 c. red	20	20
48		65 c. brown	4·00	3·50
82		80 c. blue	55	55
83		90 c. brown	55	55
49		1 l. green	9·00	5·50
120		1 l. blue	25	25
50		2 l. violet	£400	£100
85		2 l. red	7·50	7·50
121		2 l. green	2·00	1·75
122		5 l. blue	7·50	8·00

1905. Surch **1905 15**.

52	19	15 c. on 20 c. orange	2·75	1·75

22 23 26 Statue of Liberty

1907.

53a	22	1 c. brown	1·00	70
54	23	15 c. grey	8·00	1·75

1917. For Combatants. Surch **1917 Pro combattenti** and value.

55	18	25 c. on 2 c. lilac	1·00	90
56	19	50 c. on 2 l. violet	15·00	16·00

1918. Surch **Cent. 20 1918**.

57	23	20 c. on 15 c. grey	1·25	1·10

1918. War Casualties Fund. Inscr as in T 26.

58	26	2 c. (+ 5 c.) black & lilac	15	20
59		5 c. (+ 5 c.) black & green	15	20
60		10 c. (+ 5 c.) black & red	15	20
61		20 c. (+ 5 c.) black & orge	15	20
62		25 c. (+ 5 c.) black & blue	30	35
63		45 c. (+ 5 c.) black & brn	30	35
64	–	1 l. (+ 5 c.) black & green	6·00	6·00
65	–	2 l. (+ 5 c.) black & lilac	3·25	3·50
66	–	3 l. (+ 5 c.) black and red	3·25	3·50

DESIGN—HORIZ: 1, 2, 3 l. San Marino.

1918. Italian Victory over Austria and Premium for War Casualties Fund. Optd **3 Novembre 1918**.

67	26	20 c. (+ 5 c.) black & orge	75	70
68		25 c. (+ 5 c.) black & blue	75	70
69		45 c. (+ 5 c.) black & brn	75	70
70	–	1 l. (+ 5 c.) black & green	1·00	70
71	–	2 l. (+ 5 c.) black & lilac	4·00	3·50
72	–	3 l. (+ 5 c.) black and red	4·00	3·50

DESIGN—HORIZ: 1, 2, 3 l. As Nos. 64/66.

1922. Re-issue of T 17. Colours changed.

86	17	2 c. purple	10	10
87		5 c. green	10	10
88		10 c. brown	10	10
89		20 c. brown	15	15
90		25 c. blue	20	20
91		45 c. red	60	60

30 Arbe (Rab)

31 St. Marinus

1923. Delivery to San Marino of Italian Flag flown on Arbe, after the island returned to Yugoslavia.

92	30	50 c. green	30	30

1923. San Marino Mutual Aid Society.

93	31	30 c. brown	20	20

32 Mt. Titano

33 "Liberty"

34

1923. Red Cross Fund.

94	32	5 c. + 5 c. green	15	15
95		10 c. + 5 c. orange	15	15
96		15 c. + 5 c. green	15	15
97		25 c. + 5 c. red	30	30
98		40 c. + 5 c. purple	70	75
99		50 c. + 5 c. grey	60	15
100	33	1 l. + 5 c. blue and black	1·25	1·25

1923. San Marino Volunteers in the Great War.

101	34	1 l. brown	5·00	4·00

35 Garibaldi

36

1924. 75th Anniv of Garibaldi's Refuge in San Marino.

102	35	30 c. purple	80	70
103		50 c. brown	85	75
104		60 c. red	1·10	90
105	36	1 l. blue	1·75	1·60
106		2 l. green	2·25	1·90

1924. Red Cross stamps of 1918 surch.

107	26	30 c. on 45 c. black & brn	30	35
108	–	60 c. on 1 l. black & green	3·00	3·00
109	–	1 l. on 2 l. black and lilac	5·50	5·50
110	–	2 l. on 3 l. black and red	4·50	4·50

1926. Surch.

123	19	75 c. on 80 c. blue	40	40
124		1 l. 20 on 90 c. brown	40	40
125		1 l. 25 on 90 c. brown	1·00	1·00
126		2 l. 50 on 80 c. blue	1·60	1·60

40 Onofri

44 San Marino War Memorial

1926. Death Centenary of Antonio Onofri, "Father of the Country".

127	40	10 c. black and blue	10	10
128		20 c. black and green	55	55
129		45 c. black and violet	30	30
130		65 c. black and green	30	30
131		1 l. black and orange	1·25	1·25
132		2 l. black and mauve	1·25	1·25

1926. No. E92 surch **Lire 1,85**.

133	19	1 l. 85 on 60 c. violet	30	35

1927. Surch.

134	40	"1,25" on 1 l. black & orge	1·00	1·10
135		"2,50" on 2 l. black & mve	2·75	3·00
136		"5" on 2 l. black and mauve	19·00	20·00

1927. Unissued Express stamp (No. 115 surch **ESPRESSO 50**) surch **L. 1,75**.

137	19	1 l. 75 on 50 c. on 25 c. violet	70	75

1927. War Cenotaph Commemoration.

138	44	50 c. purple	40	50
139		1 l. 25 blue	65	70
140		10 l. violet	8·50	9·00

45 Franciscan Convent and Capuchin Church

1928. 700th Death Anniv of St. Francis of Assisi.

141	45	50 c. red	10·00	1·25
142		1 l. 25 blue	2·00	1·60
143	–	2 l. 50 brown	2·00	1·60
144	–	5 l. violet	12·00	10·00

DESIGN: 2 l. 50, 5 l. Death of St. Francis.

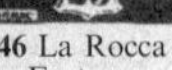

46 La Rocca Fortress **47** Government Palace **48** Statue of Liberty

1929.

145	46	5 c. blue and purple	10	10
146		10 c. mauve and blue	35	10
147		15 c. green and orange	10	10
148		20 c. red and blue	10	10
149		25 c. black and green	10	10
150		30 c. red and grey	10	10
151		50 c. green and purple	10	10
152		75 c. grey and red	10	10
153	47	1 l. green and brown	15	10
154		1 l. 25 black and blue	15	10
155		1 l. 75 orange and green	30	35
156		2 l. red and blue	25	15
157		2 l. 50 blue and red	25	15
158		3 l. blue and orange	25	15
159		3 l. 70 purple and green	25	35
160	48	5 l. green and violet	40	40
161		10 l. blue and brown	2·00	2·00
162		15 l. purple and green	25·00	20·00
163		20 l. red and blue	£170	£180

50 Mt Titano **51** G.P.O., San Marino

1931. Air.

164	50	50 c. green	1·00	1·25
165		80 c. red	1·25	1·50
166		1 l. brown	70	70
167		2 l. purple	75	75
168		2 l. 60 blue	12·00	13·00
169		3 l. grey	12·00	13·00
170		5 l. green	1·00	1·25
171		7 l. 70 brown	2·50	2·50
172		9 l. orange	2·75	2·75
173		10 l. blue	£160	£170

1932. Inauguration of New G.P.O.

174	51	20 c. green	1·40	75
175		50 c. red	3·00	1·25
176		1 l. 25 blue	90·00	35·00
177		1 l. 75 brown	40·00	24·00
178		2 l. 75 violet	13·00	9·00

52 San Marino Railway Station

1932. Opening of San Marino Electric Railway, Rimini.

179	52	20 c. green	1·25	1·25
180		50 c. red	1·50	1·50
181		1 l. 25 blue	2·50	2·25
182		5 l. brown	35·00	30·00

53 Garibaldi

1932. 50th Death Anniv of Garibaldi.

183	53	10 c. brown	45	45
184		20 c. violet	25	25
185		25 c. green	40	40
186		50 c. brown	1·25	1·25
187	–	75 c. red	1·25	1·25
188	–	1 l. 25 blue	4·00	3·00
189	–	2 l. 75 orange	8·00	10·00
190	–	5 l. green	£140	£130

DESIGN: 75 c. to 5 l. Garibaldi's arrival at San Marino.

1933. Air. "Graf Zeppelin". Surch **ZEPPELIN 1933** under airship and new value.

191	50	3 l. on 50 c. orange	55	48·00
192		5 l. on 80 c. green	26·00	48·00
193		10 l. on 1 l. blue	26·00	65·00
194		12 l. on 2 l. brown	26·00	75·00
195		15 l. on 2 l. 60 red	26·00	85·00
196		20 l. on 3 l. green	26·00	£100

1933. 20th Italian Philatelic Congress. Surch **28 MAGGIO 1933 CONVEGNO FILATELICO** and new value.

197	51	25 c. on 2 l. 75 violet	50	60
198		50 c. on 1 l. 75 brown	1·40	2·00
199		75 c. on 2 l. 75 violet	6·00	8·00
200		1 l. 25 on 1 l. 75 brown	£150	£190

1934. Philatelic Exn. Surch **12-27 APRILE 1934 MOSTRA FILATELICA** and value with wheel.

201	51	25 c. on 1 l. 25 blue	40	40
202		50 c. on 1 l. 75 brown	75	75
203	51	75 c. on 50 c. red	1·75	1·75
204		1 l. 25 on 20 c. green	13·00	15·00

1934. Surch with value and wheel.

205	51	3 l. 70 on 1 l. 25 blue	42·00	38·00
206		3 l. 70 on 2 l. 75 violet	48·00	40·00

58 Ascent to Mt Titano **59** Delfico

1935. 12th Anniv of San Marino Fascist Party.

207	58	5 c. black and brown	10	15
208		10 c. black and violet	10	15
209		20 c. black and orange	10	15
210		25 c. black and green	10	15
211		50 c. black and bistre	20	35
212		75 c. black and red	80	90
213		1 l. 25 black and blue	2·25	2·50

1935. Death Centenary of Melchiorre Delfico (historian of San Marino).

214	59	5 c. black and purple	10	15
215		7½ c. black and brown	10	15
216		10 c. black and green	10	15
217		15 c. black and red	3·25	80
218		20 c. black and orange	10	20
219		25 c. black and green	20	20
220	–	30 c. black and violet	20	20
221	–	50 c. black and green	80	80
222	–	75 c. black and red	3·00	3·00
223	–	1 l. 25 black and blue	80	80
224	–	1 l. 50 black and brown	11·00	12·00
225	–	1 l. 75 black and orange	14·00	15·00

DESIGN—25×35 mm: 30 c. to 1 l. 75, Statue of Delfico.

1936. Surch. (a) Postage.

226	40	80 c. on 45 c. black & violet	1·25	1·75
227		80 c. on 65 c. black & grn	1·25	1·75
228	45	2 l. 05 on 1 l. 25 blue	3·25	3·75
229	–	2 l. 75 on 2 l. 50 brown (No. 143)	10·00	16·00

(b) Air.

230	50	75 c. on 50 c. green	1·60	2·00
231		75 c. on 80 c. red	5·50	7·00

1941. Surch **10**.

233	19	10 c. on 15 c. purple	10	10
234		10 c. on 30 c. orange	50	40

1942. Air. Surch **Lire 10** and bars.

235	50	10 l. on 2 l. 60 blue	60·00	85·00
236		10 l. on 3 l. grey	15·00	19·00

67 Gajarda Tower, Arbe, and Flags of Italy and San Marino

1942. Restoration of Italian Flag to Arbe (Rab) annexed by Italy in 1941.

237	67	10 c. red & bistre (postage)	10	10
238		15 c. red and brown	10	10
239		20 c. grey and green	10	10
240		25 c. blue and green	10	10
241		50 c. brown and red	10	10
242		75 c. grey and red	10	10
243	–	1 l. 25 light blue and blue	10	10
244	–	1 l. 75 grey and brown	10	10
245	–	2 l. 75 blue and bistre	25	30
246	–	5 l. brown and green	2·00	3·50
247	–	25 c. grey & brown (air)	10	10
248	–	50 c. brown and green	10	10
249	–	75 c. brown and blue	10	10
250	–	1 l. brown and bistre	20	20
251	–	5 l. blue and bistre	3·00	3·50

DESIGNS—HORIZ: Nos. 243/6, Galleon in Arbe Harbour. VERT: Nos. 247/51, Granda Belfry, Arbe.

1942. Italian Philatelic Congress. Surch **GIORNATA FILATELICA RIMINI-SAN MARINO 3 AGOSTO 1942 (1641 d. F. R.) C.—30.**

252	67	30 c. on 10 c. red & bistre	10	15

1942. Surch.

253	67	30 c. on 20 c. grey & green	15	20
254	–	20 l. on 75 c. black and red (No. 222)	5·00	6·50

71 Printing Press **72** Newspapers

1943. Press Propaganda.

255	71	10 c. green	10	10
256		15 c. brown	10	10
257		20 c. brown	10	10
258		30 c. purple	10	10
259		50 c. blue	10	10
260		75 c. red	10	10
261	72	1 l. 25 blue	10	10
262		1 l. 75 violet	10	10
263		5 l. blue	30	25
264		10 l. brown	2·40	2·25

1943. Philatelic Exhibition. Optd **GIORNATA FILATELICA RIMINI – SAN MARINO 5 LUGLIO 1943 (1642 d. F. R.).**

265	71	30 c. purple	10	10
266		50 c. blue	10	10

74 Gateway **75** War Memorial

1943. Fall of Fascism. Unissued series for 20th Anniv of Fascism optd **28 LVGLIO 1943 1642 d. F.R. (the "d." is omitted on T 74)** and bars cancelling commemorative inscription.

267	74	5 c. brown (postage)	10	10
268		10 c. orange	10	10
269		20 c. blue	10	10
270		25 c. green	10	10
271		30 c. purple	10	10
272		50 c. violet	10	10
273		75 c. red	10	10
274	75	1 l. 25 blue	10	10
275		1 l. 75 orange	10	10
276		2 l. 75 brown	15	15
277		5 l. green	40	50
278		10 l. violet	60	80
279		20 l. blue	1·50	1·75
280	–	25 c. brown (air)	10	10
281	–	50 c. purple	10	10
282	–	75 c. brown	10	10
283	–	1 l. purple	10	10
284	–	2 l. blue	10	10
285	–	5 l. orange	35	35
286	–	10 l. green	50	55
287	–	20 l. black	2·25	2·25

DESIGN—Air: Nos. 280/7, Map of San Marino.

1943. Provisional Govt. Optd **GOVERNO PROVVISORIO** over ornamentation.

288	74	5 c. brown (postage)	10	10
289		10 c. orange	10	10
290		20 c. blue	10	10
291		25 c. green	10	10
292		30 c. purple	10	10
293		50 c. violet	10	10
294		75 c. red	10	10
295	75	1 l. 25 blue	10	10
296		1 l. 75 orange	15	15
297		5 l. green	35	40
298		20 l. blue	1·00	1·25
299	–	25 c. brown (air)	10	10
300	–	50 c. red	10	10
301	–	75 c. brown	10	10
302	–	1 l. purple	10	10
303	–	5 l. orange	35	45
304	–	20 l. black	1·50	1·75

78 St. Marinus

79 Mt Titano

1944.

305	78	20 l. + 10 l. brn (postage)	40	60
306	79	20 l. + 10 l. green (air)	50	60

80 Govt Palace **81** Govt Palace

1945. 50th Anniv of Government Palace.

307	80	25 l. purple (postage)	8·00	3·00
308	81	25 l. brown (air)	8·00	3·00

82 Arms of Montegiardino **83** Arms of San Marino

1945. Arms Types.

309	–	10 c. blue	10	10
310	82	20 c. red	10	10
311	–	40 c. orange	10	10
312	82	60 c. grey	10	10
313	–	80 c. green	10	10
314	–	1 l. red	10	10
315	–	1 l. 20 violet	10	10
316	–	2 l. brown	20	10
317	–	3 l. blue	20	10
317a	–	4 l. orange	20	10
318	–	5 l. brown	10	10
319	–	10 l. red and brown	2·50	1·25
319a	–	15 l. blue	2·00	1·00
320	–	20 l. red and blue	6·00	1·75
321	–	20 l. brown and blue	10·00	1·75
322	82	25 l. blue and brown	8·50	2·00
323	83	50 l. blue and green	12·00	7·50

DESIGNS (Arms of San Marino and villages in the Republic): 10 c., 1 l., 1 l. 20, 15 l. Faetano; 40 c., 5 l. San Marino; 80 c., 2, 3, 4 l. Fiorentino; 10 l. Borgomaggiore; 20 l. (2) Serravalle.

84 U.N.R.R.A. Aid for San Marino

1946. U.N.R.R.A.

324	84	100 l. red, purple and orange	6·00	5·00

85 Airplane and Mt Titano

1946. Air.

325	–	25 c. grey	20	20
326	85	75 c. red	20	20
327	–	1 l. brown	20	20
328	85	2 l. green	20	20
329		3 l. violet	20	20
330	–	5 l. blue	20	20
331	–	10 l. red	20	20
334	–	20 l. purple	1·50	1·60
332	–	35 l. red	6·00	3·50
335	–	50 l. green	12·00	5·50
333	–	100 l. brown	2·25	1·10

DESIGNS—HORIZ: 25 c., 1, 10 l. Wings over Mt Titano; 100 l. Airplane over globe. VERT: 5, 20, 35, 50 l. Four aircraft over Mt Titano.

1946. Stamp Day. Surch **L.10**.

336	83	50 l. + 10 l. blue and green	15·00	8·00

1946. National Philatelic Convention. Nos. 329/31 but colours changed and without "POSTA AEREA" surch **CONVEGNO FILATELICO 30 NOVEMBRE 1946** and premium.

336a	85	3 l. + 25 l. brown	1·00	55
336b	–	5 l. + 25 l. orange	1·00	55
336c	–	10 l. + 50 l. blue	11·00	5·50

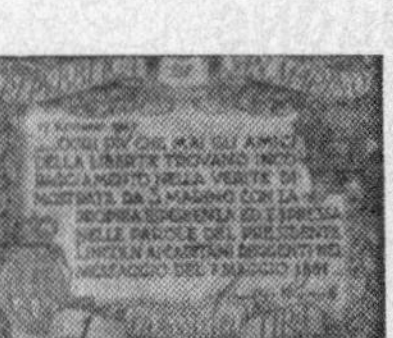

87 Quotation from F.D.R. on Liberty **88** Franklin D. Roosevelt

1947. In Memory of President Franklin D. Roosevelt.
336d **87** 1 l. brn & ochre (postage) 10 10
336e **88** 2 l. brown and blue . . . 10 10
336f – 5 l. multicoloured 10 10
336g – 15 l. multicoloured 10 10
336h **87** 50 l. brown and red . . . 45 30
336i **88** 100 l. brown and violet . . 80 50
DESIGN—HORIZ: 5 l., 15 l. Roosevelt and flags of San Marino and U.S.A.

336j – 1 l. brown and blue (air) . 10 10
336k – 2 l. brown and red 10 10
336l – 5 l. multicoloured 10 10
336m – 20 l. brown and purple . . 20 10
336n – 31 l. brown and orange . . 50 35
336o – 50 l. brown and red . . . . 1·00 65
336p – 100 l. brown and blue . . . 1·50 1·00
336q – 200 l. multicoloured . . . . 16·00 8·00
DESIGNS—HORIZ: 1, 3, 50 l. Roosevelt and eagle; 2, 20, 100 l. Roosevelt and San Marino arms. VERT: 5, 200 l. Roosevelt and flags of San Marino and U.S.A.

1947. Surch in figures.
336r **87** 3 on 1 l. brown and ochre (postage) 45 35
336s **88** 4 on 2 l. brown and blue . . 45 35
336t – 6 on 5 l. mult (No. 336f) . 45 35

336u – 3 on 1 l. brown and blue (No. 336j) (air) 45 35
336v – 4 on 2 l. brown and red (No. 336k) 45 35
336w – 6 on 5 l. mult (No. 336l) . 45 35

1947. No. 317a surch.
337 6 l. on 4 l. orange 20 10
338 21 l. on 4 l. orange 90 65

91 St. Marinus founding Republic

94 Mt Titano, Statue of Liberty and 1847 U.S.A. Stamp

95 Mt Titano and 1847 U.S.A. Stamp

1947. Reconstruction.
339 **91** 1 l. mve & grn (postage) . . 10 15
340 2 l. green and mauve . . . 10 15
341 4 l. green and brown . . . 10 15
342 10 l. blue and orange . . . 10 15
343 25 l. mauve and red 70 60
344 50 l. brown and green . . . 16·00 9·50

345 25 l. blue & orange (air) . . 2·25 1·10
346 50 l. blue and brown . . . 4·50 2·40
Nos. 343/6 are larger (24½ × 32 mm) and have two rows of ornaments forming the frame.

1947. Air. Rimini Philatelic Exhibition. No. 333 optd **Giornata Filatelica Rimini–San Marino 8 Luglio 1947.**
347 100 l. brown . . . . 1·00 70

1947. Reconstruction. Surch + and value in figures.
348 **91** 1 l. + 1 mauve and green . 10 10
349 1 l. + 2 mauve and green . 10 10
350 1 l. + 3 mauve and green . 10 10
351 1 l. + 4 mauve and green . 10 10
352 1 l. + 5 mauve and green . 10 10
353 2 l. + 1 green and mauve . 10 10
354 2 l. + 2 green and mauve . 10 10
355 2 l. + 3 green and mauve . 10 10
356 2 l. + 4 green and mauve . 10 10
357 2 l. + 5 green and mauve . 10 10
358 4 l. + 1 green and brown . 3·00 1·50
359 4 l. + 2 green and brown . 3·00 1·50

1947. Centenary of First U.S.A. Postage Stamp.
360 **94** 2 l. brown & pur (postage) 10 15
361 – 3 l. grey, red and blue . . . 10 15
362 **94** 6 l. green and blue 10 15
363 – 15 l. violet, red and blue . 35 25
364 – 35 l. brown, red and blue . 1·25 1·00
365 – 50 l. green, red and blue . . 1·40 1·00

366 **95** 100 l. brown & vio (air) . . 10·00 6·00
DESIGNS: 3, 35 l. U.S.A. stamps, 5 c. and 10 c. of 1847 and 90 c. of 1869 and flags of U.S.A. and San Marino; 15, 50 l. Similar but differently arranged.

96 Worker and San Marino Flag

1948. Workers' Issue.
367 **96** 5 l. brown 10 10
368 8 l. green 10 10
369 30 l. red 25 20
370 50 l. brown and mauve . . 1·60 75
371 100 l. blue and violet . . . 32·00 16·00
See also Nos. 506/7.

1948. Surch **L.100** between circular ornaments.
372 **59** 100 l. on 15 c. black & red 32·00 23·00

1948. Air. Surch **POSTA AEREA 200**.
373 **91** 200 l. on 25 l. mauve and red (No. 343) . . . . 18·00 16·00

99 Faetano

100 Mt Titano

1949.
374 – 1 l. blue and black . . . 10 10
375 – 2 l. red and purple . . . 10 10
376 **99** 3 l. blue and violet . . . 10 10
377 – 4 l. violet and black . . 10 10
378 – 5 l. brown and purple . . 10 10
379 **99** 6 l. black and blue . . . 55 20
380 **100** 8 l. brown & dp brown . 40 20
381 – 10 l. blue and black . . . 45 10
382 – 12 l. violet and red . . . 1·00 40
383 – 15 l. red and violet . . . 2·75 60
383a **99** 20 l. brown and blue . . 6·00 80
384 – 35 l. violet and green . . 5·50 1·50
385 – 50 l. brown and red . . . 2·75 65
385a – 55 l. green and blue . . 32·00 14·00
386 **100** 100 l. green and brown . 65·00 16·00
387 – 200 l. brown and blue . . 65·00 35·00
DESIGNS—HORIZ: 1, 5, 35 l. Guaita Tower and walls; 2, 12, 50 l. Serravalle and Mt Titano; 4, 15, 55 l. Franciscan Convent and Capuchin Church. VERT: 10, 200 l. Guaita Tower.
For similar stamps see Nos. 491/5, 522a/7a and 794/9.

1949. Stamp Day. Optd **Giornata Filatelica San Marino - Riccione 28-6-1949**.
388 **91** 1 l. mauve and green . . . 15 10
389 2 l. green and mauve . . . 15 10

104 Garibaldi

105 Garibaldi in San Marino

1949. Centenary of Garibaldi's Retreat from Rome. (a) Postage. Portraits as T **104**. (i) Size 22 × 28 mm.
390 – 1 l. red and black 10 10
391 – 2 l. blue and brown . . . 10 10
392 **104** 3 l. green and red 10 10
393 – 4 l. brown and blue . . . 10 10

(ii) Size 27 × 37 mm.
394 – 5 l. brown and mauve . . 10 10
395 – 15 l. blue and red 80 55
396 – 20 l. red and violet . . . 1·00 65
397 **104** 50 l. violet and purple . . 16·00 8·50

(b) Air. (i) Size 28 × 22 mm.
398 **105** 2 l. blue and purple . . . 10 10
399 3 l. black and green . . . 10 10
400 5 l. green and blue . . . 15 15

(ii) Size 37 × 27 mm.
401 **105** 25 l. violet and green . . 3·50 1·75
402 65 l. black and green . . 10·00 5·50
PORTRAITS—VERT: 1, 20 l. Francesco Nullo; 2, 5 l. Anita Garibaldi; 4, 15 l. Ugo Bassi.
See also Nos. 538/44.

106 Mail Coach and Mt Titano

1949. 75th Anniv of U.P.U.
403 **106** 100 l. purple & bl (postage) 8·00 5·50
404 200 l. blue (air) . . . . . 1·50 1·25
405 300 l. brown, light brown and purple . . . . . . 15·00 12·00

107 Mt Titano from Serravalle

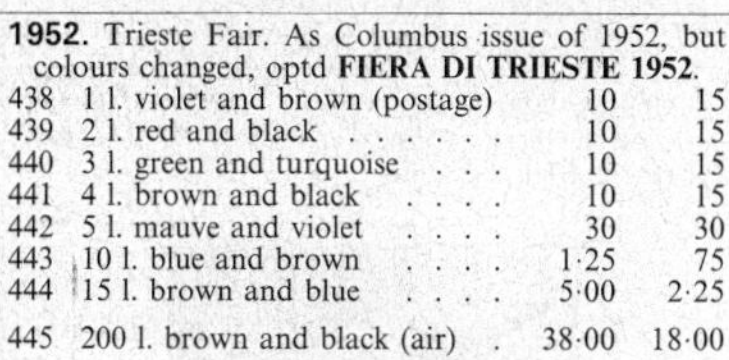
108 Second and Guaita Towers

109 Guaita Tower

1950. Air. Views.
406 **107** 2 l. green and violet . . . 10 10
407 – 3 l. brown and blue . . . 10 10
408 **108** 5 l. red and brown (22 × 28 mm) 10 10
409 – 10 l. blue and green . . . 1·10 25
410 – 15 l. violet and black . . . 1·75 40
411 – 55 l. green and blue . . . 16·00 8·00
412 **107** 100 l. black and red (37 × 27 mm) . . . . 10·00 4·00
413 **108** 250 l. brown and violet . . 50·00 12·00
414 **109** 500 l. brown and green (37 × 27 mm) . . . . . £100 60·00
415 500 l. purple, green & bl . 50·00 48·00
DESIGNS—As Type **107**: 3 l. Distant view of Domagnano; 10 l. Domagnano; 15 l. San Marino from St. Mustiola. 27 × 37 mm: 55 l. Borgo Maggiore.

1950. Air. 28th Milan Fair. As Nos. 408, 410 and 411 but in different colours, optd **XXVIII FIERA INTERNAZIONALE DI MILANO APRILE 1950**.
416 5 l. green and blue 10 10
417 15 l. black and red 70 45
418 55 l. brown and violet . . . . 3·00 2·75

111 Government Palace

113 Flag, Douglas DC-6 Airliner and Mt Titano

1951. Red Cross.
419 **111** 25 l. purple, red & brown . 6·00 3·00
420 – 75 l. brown, red & lt brown 9·00 6·00
421 – 100 l. black, red & brown . 9·00 5·00
DESIGNS—HORIZ: 75 l. Archway of Murata Nuova. VERT: 100 l. Guaita Tower.

1951. Air. Stamp Day. No. 415 surch **Giornata Filatelica San Marino–Riccione 20-8-1951 L. 300**.
422 **109** 300 l. on 500 l. purple, green and blue . . . . 38·00 28·00

1951. Air.
423 **113** 1000 l. blue and brown . . £325 £200

1951. Air. Italian Flood Relief Fund. Surch **Pro-alluvionati italiani 1951 L. 100** and bars.
424 **108** 100 l. on 250 l. brown and violet . . . . 4·75 3·00

115 "Columbus at the Council of Salamanca" (after Barabino)

1952. 500th Birth Anniv (1951) of Christopher Columbus.
425 **115** 1 l. orange & grn (postage) 15 15
426 – 2 l. brown and violet . . . 15 15
427 – 3 l. violet and brown . . . 15 15
428 – 4 l. blue and brown . . . 15 15
429 – 5 l. green and turquoise . . 30 20
430 – 10 l. brown and black . . 80 40
431 – 15 l. red and black . . . . 1·40 60
432 – 20 l. blue and green . . . 2·00 70
433 – 25 l. purple and brown . . 7·50 2·75
434 **115** 60 l. brown and violet . . 11·00 5·00
435 – 80 l. grey and black . . . 28·00 13·00
436 – 200 l. green and blue . . . 55·00 25·00

437 – 200 l. blue & black (air) . 38·00 18·00
DESIGNS—HORIZ: 2, 25 l. Columbus and fleet; 3, 10, 20 l. Landing in America; 4, 15, 80 l. Red Indians and American settlers; 5, 200 l. (No. 436) Columbus and Map of America; 200 l. (No. 437) Columbus, Statue of Liberty (New York) and skyscrapers.

1952. Trieste Fair. As Columbus issue of 1952, but colours changed, optd **FIERA DI TRIESTE 1952**.
438 1 l. violet and brown (postage) 10 15
439 2 l. red and black 10 15
440 3 l. green and turquoise . . . 10 15
441 4 l. brown and black 10 15
442 5 l. mauve and violet 30 30
443 10 l. blue and brown . . . . 1·25 75
444 15 l. brown and blue . . . . 5·00 2·25
445 200 l. brown and black (air) . 38·00 18·00

117 Rose

118 Cyclamen, Douglas DC-6 Airliner, Rose, San Marino and Riccione

1952. Air. Stamp Day and Philatelic Exhibition.
446 – 1 l. purple and violet . . 10 10
447 – 2 l. green and blue . . . 10 10
448 **117** 3 l. red and brown . . . 10 10
449 **118** 5 l. brown and purple . . 10 10
450 25 l. green and violet . . 35 35
451 200 l. multicoloured . . . 35·00 18·00
DESIGNS—As Type **117**: 1 l. Cyclamen; 2 l. San Marino and Riccione.

119 Airplane over San Marino

1952. Air. Aerial Survey of San Marino.
452 **119** 25 l. green and yellow . . 1·75 1·00
453 – 75 l. violet and brown . . 5·50 3·50
DESIGN: 75 l. Airplane over Mt Titano.

120 "The Discus Thrower"

121 Tennis

1953. Sports.
454 **120** 1 l. black & brn (postage) 10 10
455 **121** 2 l. brown and black . . 10 10
456 – 3 l. blue and black . . . 10 10
457 – 4 l. blue and green . . . 10 10
458 – 5 l. green and brown . . . 10 10
459 – 10 l. red and blue 30 30
460 – 25 l. brown and black . . 2·00 90
461 – 100 l. black and brown . . 7·00 3·00

462 – 200 l. turquoise & grn (air) 75·00 38·00
DESIGNS–As Type **120**: 3 l. Running. As Type **121**: HORIZ: 4 l. Cycling; 5 l. Football; 100 l. Roller skating; 200 l. Skiing. VERT: 10 l. Model glider flying; 25 l. Shooting.
See also No. 584.

1953. Stamp Day and Philatelic Exn. As No. 461 but colour changed, optd **GIORNATA FILATELICA S. MARINO-RICCIONE 24 AGOSTO 1953.**
463 100 l. green and turquoise . . 16·00 10·00

123 Narcissus

1953. Flowers.
464 **123** 1 l. blue, green and yellow 10 10
465 – 2 l. blue, green and yellow 10 10
466 – 3 l. blue, green and yellow 10 10
467 – 4 l. blue, green and yellow 10 10
468 – 5 l. green and red 10 10
469 – 10 l. blue, green and yellow 15 20
470 – 25 l. blue, green and pink 3·00 1·40

471 – 80 l. blue, green and red . 15·00 9·00
472 – 100 l. blue, green and pink 22·00 13·00
FLOWERS: 2 l. "Parrot" tulip; 3 l. Oleander; 4 l. Cornflower; 5 l. Carnation; 10 l. Iris; 25 l; Cyclamen; 80 l. Geranium; 100 l. Rose.

124 Douglas DC-6 Airliner over Mt. Titano and Arms

1954. Air.
473 **124** 1000 l. brown and blue . . 65·00 50·00

125 Walking **126** Statue of Liberty

1954. Sports.
474 **125** 1 l. mauve and violet . . . 10 10
475 – 2 l. violet and green . . . 10 10
476 – 3 l. chestnut and brown . 10 10
477 – 4 l. blue and turquoise . . 10 10
478 – 5 l. brown and green . . . 10 10
479 – 8 l. lilac and purple . . . 10 10
480 – 12 l. red and black 10 10
481 – 25 l. green and blue . . . 65 20
482 **125** 80 l. green and blue . . . 1·10 60
483 – 200 l. brown and lilac . . 5·00 2·50
484 – 250 l. multicoloured . . . 50·00 25·00
DESIGNS—HORIZ: 2 l. Fencing; 3 l. Boxing; 5 l. Motor-cycle racing; 8 l. Throwing the javelin; 12 l. Car racing. VERT: 4, 200, 250 l. Gymnastics; 25 l. Wrestling.
The 200 l. measures 27 × 37 mm and the 250 l. 28 × 37½ mm.

1954.
485 **126** 20 l. blue & brn (post) . . 20 10
486 60 l. green and red . . . 70 25
487 120 l. brown & blue (air) . 1·00 50

127 Hurdling **128** Yacht

1955. Air. 1st Int Exhibition of Olympic Stamps.
488 **127** 80 l. black and red . . . . 1·10 60
489 – 120 l. red and green . . . 1·60 1·10
DESIGN—HORIZ: 120 l. Relay racing.

1955. 7th International Philatelic Exhibition.
490 **128** 100 l. black and blue . . . 3·50 1·75
See also No. 518.

1955. Views as T **99**.
491 5 l. brown and blue 10 10
492 10 l. green and orange 10 10
493 15 l. red and green 10 10
494 25 l. violet and brown 15 10
495 35 l. red and lilac 30 15
DESIGNS—HORIZ: 5, 25 l. Archway of Murata Nuova. VERT: 10, 35 l. Guaita Tower; 15 l. Government Palace.
See also Nos. 519/21 and 797/9.

129 Ice Skating **130** Pointer

1955. Winter Olympic Games, Cortina D'Ampezzo.
496 **129** 1 l. brown & yell (postage) 10 10
497 – 2 l. blue and red 10 10
498 – 3 l. black and brown . . . 10 10
499 – 4 l. brown and green . . . 10 10
500 – 5 l. blue and red 10 10
501 – 10 l. blue and pink 20 15
502 – 25 l. black and red . . . . 1·00 55
503 – 50 l. brown and blue . . . 2·50 1·25
504 – 100 l. black and green . . 6·50 3·00
505 – 200 l. black & orge (air) . 30·00 14·00
DESIGNS—HORIZ: 2, 25 l. Skiing; 3, 50 l. Bobsleighing; 5, 100 l. Ice hockey; 200 l. Ski jumping. VERT: 4 l. Slalom racing; 10 l. Figure skating.

1956. Winter Relief Fund. As T **96** but additionally inscr "ASSISTENZA INVERNALE".
506 50 l. green . . . . 6·00 4·00

1956. 50th Anniv of "Arengo" (San Marino Parliament). As T **96** but additionally inscr "50° ANNIVERSARIO ARENGO 25 MARZO 1906".
507 50 l. blue . . . . 6·00 4·00

1956. Dogs. 25 l. to 100 l. have multicoloured centres.
508 **130** 1 l. brown and blue . . . 10 10
509 – 2 l. grey and red 10 10
510 – 3 l. brown and blue . . . 10 10
511 – 4 l. grey and blue 10 10
512 – 5 l. brown and red . . . 10 10
513 – 10 l. brown and blue . . 10 10
514 – 25 l. blue 35 15
515 – 60 l. red . . . . 3·00 1·25
516 – 80 l. blue . . . . 4·25 1·75
517 – 100 l. red . . . . 7·50 3·25
DOGS: 2 l. Borzoi; 3 l. Sheepdog; 4 l. Greyhound; 5 l. Boxer; 10 l. Great dane; 25 l. Irish setter; 60 l. Alsatian; 80 l. Rough collie; 100 l. Foxhound.

1956. Philatelic Exn. As T **128** but inscr "1956".
518 **128** 100 l. brown and green . 1·75 1·25

1956. Int Philatelic Congress. Designs as Nos. 491/5 but larger and new values inscr "CONGRESSO INTERNAZ. PERITI FILATELICI SAN MARINO SALSOMAGGIORE 6-8 OTTOBRE 1956".
519 20 l. brown and blue 40 20
520 80 l. red and violet . . . . . 4·00 2·50
521 100 l. green and orange . . . 1·40 1·25
SIZES—26½ × 37 mm: 20 l. Guaita Tower; 100 l. Government Palace. (36½ × 27 mm): 8 l. Archway of Murata Nuova.

1956. Air. No. 504 optd with an airplane and **POSTA AEREA**.
522 100 l. black and green . . . . 1·40 1·25

1957. Views as T **99**.
522a 1 l. green and deep green . . 10 10
523 2 l. red and green 10 10
524 3 l. brown and blue 10 10
524a 4 l. blue and brown 10 10
525 20 l. green and deep green . 15 10
525a 30 l. violet and brown . . . 55 30
526 60 l. violet and brown . . . 85 60
526a 115 l. brown and blue . . . 35 25
527 125 l. blue and black 45 30
527a 500 l. black and green . . . 60·00 40·00
DESIGNS—VERT: 2 l. Borgo Maggiore Church; 3, 30 l. Town gate, San Marino; 4, 125 l. View of San Marino from southern wall; 20, 115 l. Borgo Maggiore market place. HORIZ: 1, 60 l. View of San Marino from Hospital Avenue. 37½ × 28 mm: 500 l. Panorama of San Marino.
See also Nos. 794/6.

132 Marguerites **134** St. Marinus and Fair Entrance

1957. Flowers. Multicoloured.
528 1 l. Type **132** 10 10
529 2 l. Polyanthuses 10 10
530 3 l. Lilies 10 10
531 4 l. Orchid 10 10
532 5 l. Lillies of the valley . . . 10 10
533 10 l. Poppies 10 10
534 25 l. Pansies 10 10
535 60 l. Gladiolus 45 30
536 80 l. Wild roses 90 50
537 100 l. Anemones . . . . . . 1·50 85

1957. 150th Birth Anniv of Garibaldi. As T **104** but inscr "COMMEMORAZIONE 150° NASCITA G. GARIBALDI 1807 1957. (a) Size 22 × 28 mm.
538 – 2 l. blue and violet (as No. 391) 10 10
539 – 3 l. green and red (as No. 390) 10 10
540 **104** 5 l. drab and brown . . . 10 10
(b) Size 26½ × 37 mm.
541 – 15 l. violet and blue (as No. 395) 10 10
542 – 25 l. black and green (as No. 396) 20 20
543 – 50 l. brown and violet (as No. 394) . . . . 1·40 1·00
544 **104** 100 l. violet and brown . 1·40 1·00

1958. 36th Milan Fair.
545 **134** 15 l. yell & blue (postage) 15 10
546 – 60 l. green and red . . . 30 55
547 – 125 l. blue & brown (air) 2·25 2·00
DESIGNS—HORIZ: 60 l. Italian pavilion and giant arch. VERT: 125 l. Bristol 173 Rotocoach helicopter and airplane over fair.

MINIMUM PRICE

The minimum price quoted is 10p which represents a handling charge rather than a basis for valuing common stamps. For further notes about prices, see introductory pages.

135 Exhibition Emblem, Atomium and Mt Titano **137** Wheat

136 View of San Marino

1958. Brussels International Exhibition.
548 **135** 40 l. sepia and green . . . 10 15
549 60 l. lake and blue 20 30

1958. Air.
550 **136** 200 l. blue and brown . . 1·75 2·00
551 – 300 l. violet and red . . . 1·75 2·00
DESIGN: 300 l. Mt Titano.

1958. Fruit and Agricultural Products.
552 **137** 1 l. yellow and blue . . . 10 10
553 – 2 l. red and green 10 10
554 – 3 l. orange and blue . . . 10 10
555 – 4 l. red and green 10 10
556 – 5 l. yellow, green & blue . 10 10
557 **137** 15 l. yellow, brown & blue 10 10
558 – 25 l. multicoloured 10 10
559 – 40 l. multicoloured 35 20
560 – 80 l. multicoloured 75 40
561 – 125 l. multicoloured . . . 3·00 1·50
DESIGNS: 2, 125 l. Maize; 3, 80 l. Grapes; 4, 25 l. Peaches; 5, 40 l. Plums.

138 Naples 10 Grana stamp of 1858 and Bay of Naples

1958. Centenary of First Naples Postage Stamps.
562 **138** 25 l. brown & bl (postage) 20 20
563 125 l. brown & bistre (air) 1·40 1·00
The Naples stamps on No. 563 is the 50 gr.

139 Mediterrranean Gull **140** P. de Coubertin (founder)

1959. Air. Native Birds.
564 **139** 5 l. black and green . . . 30 10
565 – 10 l. brown, black & blue 30 10
566 – 15 l. multicoloured . . . 30 10
567 – 120 l. multicoloured . . . 1·40 35
568 – 250 l. black, yellow & grn 4·00 1·00
BIRDS: 10 l. Common kestrel; 15 l. Mallard; 120 l. Rock dove; 250 l. Barn swallow.

1959. Pre-Olympic Games Issue.
569 **140** 2 l. blk, & brn (postage) . 10 10
570 – 3 l. sepia and mauve . . . 10 10
571 – 5 l. green and blue . . . 10 10
572 – 30 l. black and violet . . . 10 10
573 – 60 l. sepia and green . . . 10 10
574 – 80 l. green and lake . . . 10 10
575 – 120 l. brown (air) . . . . 1·25 70
PORTRAITS—As Type **140**: 3 l. A. Bonacossa; 5 l. A. Brundage; 30 l. C. Montu; 60 l. J. S. Edstrom; 80 l. De Baillet-Latour. HORIZ: (36 × 21½ mm): 120 l. De Coubertin and Olympic Flame. All, except the founder, De Coubertin are executives of the Olympic Games Committee.

141 Vickers Viscount 700 Airliner over Mt Titano

1959. Air. Alitalia Inaugural Flight, Rimini–London.
576 **141** 120 l. violet . . . . 2·00 1·25

142 Abraham Lincoln and Scroll

1959. Abraham Lincoln's 150th Birth Anniv. Inscr "ABRAMO LINCOLN 1809–1959".
577 **142** 5 l. brn & sepia (postage) 10 10
578 – 10 l. green and blue . . . 10 10
579 – 15 k. grey and green . . . 10 10
580 – 70 k. violet 85 60
581 – 200 l. blue (air) . . . . . 3·00 2·50
DESIGNS—Portraits of Lincoln with: HORIZ: 10 l. Map of San Marino; 15 l. Govt Palace, San Marino; 200 l. Mt Titano. VERT: 70 l. Mt Titano.

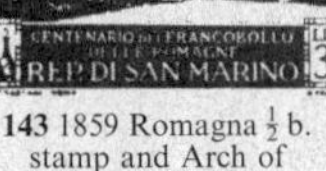

143 1859 Romagna ½ b. stamp and Arch of Augustus, Rimini **144** Portal of Messina Cathedral and ½ gr. Sicily stamp

1959. Romagna Stamp Centenary. Inscr "1859–1959".
582 **143** 30 l. brn, & sepia (postage) 10 15
583 – 120 l. green & black (air) 1·75 1·25
DESIGN: 120 l. 1989 Romagna 3 l. stamp and view of Bologna.

1959. World University Games, Turin. Inscr "UNIVERSITY TORINO 1959".
584 **120** 30 l. red 50 40

1959. Centenary of First Sicilian Postage Stamp.
585 **144** 1 l. brown & yell (postage) 10 10
586 – 2 l. red and green 10 10
587 – 3 l. slate and blue 10 10
588 – 4 l. brown and red 10 10
589 – 5 l. purple and blue . . . 10 10
590 – 25 l. multicoloured 10 10
591 – 60 l. multicoloured 10 10
592 – 200 l. multicoloured (air) . 75 65
DESIGNS—VERT: 2 l. Selinunte Temple (1 gr.); 3 l. Erice Church (2 gr.); 4 l. "Concordia" Temple, Agrigento (5 gr.); 5 l. "Castor and Pollux" Temple, Agrigento (10 gr.); 25 l. "St. John of the Hermits" Church, Palermo (20 gr.). HORIZ: 60 l. Taormina (50 gr.); 200 l. Bay of Palermo (50 gr.).

145 Golden Oriole **146** Putting the Shot

1960. Birds.
593 **145** 1 l. yellow, olive and blue 15 10
594 – 2 l. brown, red and green 15 10
595 – 3 l. red, brown and green 15 10
596 – 4 l. black, brown & green 15 10
597 – 5 l. red, brown and green 15 10
598 – 10 l. multicoloured . . . 15 10
599 – 25 l. multicoloured . . . 70 15
600 – 60 l. multicoloured . . . 2·25 70
601 – 80 l. multicoloured . . . 4·00 1·40
602 – 110 l. multicoloured . . . 4·50 1·90
DESIGNS—VERT: 2 l. Nightingale; 4 l. Hoopoe; 10 l. Goldfinch; 25 l. Common kingfisher; 80 l. Green woodpecker; 110 l. Red-breasted flycatcher. HORIZ: 3 l. Woodcock; 5 l. Red-legged partridge; 60 l. Ring-necked pheasant.

1960. Olympic Games.
603 **146** 1 l. violet & red (postage) 10 10
604 – 2 l. orange and black . . 10 10
605 – 3 l. violet and brown . . 10 10
606 – 4 l. brown and red . . . 10 10
607 – 5 l. blue and brown . . . 10 10
608 – 10 l. blue and brown . . 10 10
609 – 15 l. violet and green . . 10 10
610 – 25 l. orange and green . . 10 10
611 – 60 l. brown and green . . 10 10
612 – 110 l. red, black & green . 10 10
613 – 20 l. violet (air) 10 10
614 – 40 l. red and brown . . . 10 10
615 – 80 l. yellow and blue . . 15 10
616 – 125 l. brown and red . . 25 20
DESIGNS—VERT: 2 l. Gymnastics; 3 l. Long-distance walking; 4 l. Boxing; 10 l. Cycling; 20 l. Handball; 40 l. Breasting the tape; 60 l. Football.

HORIZ: 5 l. Fencing; 15 l. Hockey; 25 l. Rowing; 80 l. Diving; 110 l. Horse-jumping; 125 l. Rifle shooting.

147 Melvin Jones (founder) and Lions International H.Q.

1960. Lions International Commemoration.
617 – 30 l. brown and violet (postage) 10 10
618 **147** 45 l. brown and violet . . 30 30
619 – 60 l. red and blue 10 10
620 – 115 l. green and black . . 30 30
621 – 150 l. brown and violet . . 1·25 1·00
622 – 200 l. blue and green (air) 3·25 3·25
DESIGNS—VERT: 30 l. Mt Titano; 60 l. San Marino Government Palace. HORIZ: 115 l. Pres. Clarence Sturm; 150 l. Vice-Pres. Finis E. Davis; 200 l. Globe. All designs except Type **147** bear the Lions emblem.

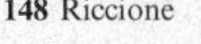

148 Riccione **149** "Youth with Basket of Fruit"

1960. 12th Riccione–San Marino Stamp Day. Centres multicoloured.
623 **148** 30 l. red (postage) 30 15
624 125 l. blue (air) . . . . . 1·25 1·10

1960. 350th Death Anniv of Caravaggio (painter).
625 **149** 200 l. multicoloured . . . 4·00 3·00

150 Hunting Roe Deer

1961. Hunting (1st issue). Historical Scenes.
626 **150** 1 l. blue and mauve . . . 10 10
627 – 2 l. red and brown 10 10
628 – 3 l. black and red 10 10
629 – 4 l. red and blue 10 10
630 – 5 l. brown and green . . . 10 10
631 – 10 l. violet and orange . . 10 10
632 – 30 l. blue and yellow . . . 10 10
633 – 60 l. brown, orange & blk 20 15
634 – 70 l. red, purple & green . 30 20
635 – 115 l. blue, purple & blk . 60 40
DESIGNS—VERT: 2 l. 16th-cent falconer; 10 l. 16th-cent falconer (mounted); 60 l. 17th-century hunter with rifle and dog. HORIZ: 3 l. 16th-cent wild boar hunt; 4 l. Duck-shooting with crossbow (16th-cent); 5 l. 16th-cent stag hunt with bow and arrow; 30 l. 17th-cent huntsman with horn and dogs; 70 l. 18th-cent hunter and beater; 115 l. Duck-shooting with bow and arrow (18th-cent).
See also Nos. 679/88.

151 Bell 47J Ranger Helicopter near Mt Titano

1961. Air.
636 **151** 1000 l. red . . . . 32·00 24·00

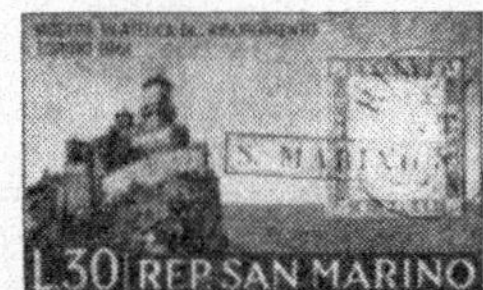

152 Guaita Tower, Mt Titano and 1858 Sardinian Stamp

1961. Centenary of Italian Independence Philatelic Exhibition, Turin.
637 **152** 30 l. multicoloured 60 40
638 70 l. multicoloured 75 55
639 200 l. multicoloured . . . 90 60

153 Mt Titano **155** King Enzo's Palace, Bologna

1961. Europe.
640 **153** 500 l. green & brown . . 5·00 5·00

1961. Bologna Stamp Exn. Inscr "BOLOGNA".
641 **155** 30 l. black and blue . . . 10 10
642 – 70 l. black and myrtle . . 15 10
643 – 100 l. black and brown . 20 15
DESIGNS: 70 l. Gateway of Merchant's Palace; 100 l. Towers of Garisenda and Asinelli, Bologna.

156 Duryea, 1892

1962. Veteran Motor Cars.
644 **156** 1 l. blue and brown . . . 10 10
645 – 2 l. orange and blue . . . 10 10
646 – 3 l. orange and black . . 10 10
647 – 4 l. red and black 10 10
648 – 5 l. orange and violet . . 10 10
649 – 10 l. orange and black . . 10 10
650 – 15 l. red and black . . . 10 10
651 – 20 l. blue and black . . . 10 10
652 – 25 l. orange and black . . 10 10
653 – 30 l. buff and black . . . 15 10
654 – 50 l. mauve and black . . 15 10
655 – 70 l. green and black . . 25 10
656 – 100 l. red, yellow & black 30 15
657 – 115 l. green, orge & blk . 35 20
658 – 150 l. yellow, orge & blk 60 40
MOTOR CARS—HORIZ: 2 l. Panhard and Levassor, 1895; 3 l. Peugeot "Vis-a-vis", 1895; 4 l. Daimler, 1899; 10 l. Decauville, 1900; 15 l. Wolseley, 1901; 20 l. Benz, 1902; 25 l. Napier, 1903; 50 l. Oldsmobile, 1904; 100 l. Isotta Fraschini, 1908; 115 l. Bianchi, 1910; 150 l. Alfa, 1910. VERT: 5 l. F.I.A.T., 1899; 30 l. White, 1903; 70 l. Renault, 1904.

157 Wright Type A Biplane **158** Roping Down

1962. Vintage Aircraft.
659 **157** 1 l. black and yellow . . 10 10
660 – 2 l. brown and green . . 10 10
661 – 3 l. brown and green . . 10 10
662 – 4 l. black and bistre . . . 10 10
663 – 5 l. red and blue 10 10
664 – 10 l. brown and green . . 10 10
665 – 30 l. bistre and blue . . . 10 10
666 – 60 l. bistre and violet . . 15 15
667 – 70 l. black and orange . . 25 15
668 – 115 l. bistre, black and grn 60 30
DESIGNS: 2 l. Archdeacon-Voisin "Boxkite" float glider; 3 l. Albert and Emile Bonnet-Labranche biplane; 4 l. Glenn Curtiss "June Bug"; 5 l. Henri Farman H.F.III biplane; 10 l. Bleriot XI, 30 l. Hubert Latham's Antoinette IV; 60 l. Alberto Santos-Dumont's biplane "14 bis"; 70 l. Alliott Verdon Roe's Triplane II; 115 l. Faccioli's airplane.

1962. Mountaineering.
669 **158** 1 l. bistre and black . . . 10 10
670 – 2 l. turquoise and black . 10 10
671 – 3 l. purple and black . . 10 10
672 – 4 l. blue and black . . . 10 10
673 – 5 l. orange and black . . 10 10
674 – 15 l. yellow and black . . 10 10
675 – 30 l. red and black . . . 10 10
676 – 40 l. blue and black . . . 10 10
677 – 85 l. green and black . . 20 20
678 – 115 l. blue and black . . 30 30
DESIGNS: 2 l. Sassolungo; 3 l. Mt Titano; 4 l. Three Lavaredo peaks; 5 l. The Matterhorn; 15 l. Skier; 30 l. Climber negotiating overhang; 40 l. Step-cutting in ice; 85 l. Aiguille du Geant; 115 l. Citadel on Mt Titano.

159 Hunter and Retriever

1962. Hunting (2nd issue). Modern scenes.
679 **159** 1 l. deep purple and green 10 10
680 – 2 l. blue and orange . . . 10 10
681 – 3 l. black and blue 10 10
682 – 4 l. sepia and brown . . . 10 10
683 – 5 l. brown and green . . . 10 10
684 – 15 l. black and green . . . 15 10
685 – 50 l. sepia and green . . . 15 10
686 – 70 l. turquoise and red . . 20 15
687 – 100 l. black and red . . . 50 50
688 – 150 l. green and lilac . . . 50 50
DESIGNS—HORIZ: 3 l. Marsh ducks (with decoys); 4 l. Roe deer; 5 l. Grey partridge; 15 l. Lapwing; 50 l. Partridge; 70 l. Marsh geese; 100 l. Wild boar. VERT: 2 l. Huntsman and hounds; 150 l. Hunter shooting pheasant.

160 Arrows encircling "Europa"

1962. Europa.
689 **160** 200 l. red and black . . . 90 1·00

161 Egyptian Merchant Ship, 2000 B.C

1963. Historical Ships.
690 **161** 1 l. blue and orange . . . 10 10
691 – 2 l. sepia and purple . . . 10 10
692 – 3 l. sepia and mauve . . . 10 10
693 – 4 l. dull purple and grey . 10 10
694 – 5 l. sepia and yellow . . . 10 10
695 – 10 l. brown and green . . 10 10
696 – 30 l. sepia and blue . . . 65 40
697 – 60 l. blue and green . . . 60 45
698 – 70 l. red and deep grey . . 75 75
699 – 115 l. brown and blue . . 1·60 1·25
DESIGNS—HORIZ: 2 l. Greek trier, 5th-cent, B.C.; 3 l. Roman trireme, 1st-cent, B.C.; 4 l. Viking longship, 10th-cent; 5 l. The "Santa Maria"; 30 l. Gallery, circa 1600; 115 l. "Duncan Dunbar" (full-rigged merchantman), 1550; VERT: 10 l. Carrack circa 1550; 60 l. "Sovereign of the Seas" (English galleon), 1637; 70 l. Danish ship of the line, circa 1750.

162 "The Fornarina" (or "The Veiled Woman") **163** Saracen Game, Arezzo

1963. Paintings by Raphael. Multicoloured.
700 30 l. Type **162** 25 35
701 70 l. Self portrait 25 15
702 100 l. Sistine Madonna (detail of woman praying) 25 20
703 200 l. "Portrait of a Young Woman" (Maddalena Strozzi) 25 35
The 200 l. is larger 27 × 44 mm.

1963. Ancient Tournaments.
704 **163** 1 l. mauve 10 10
705 – 2 l. black 10 10
706 – 3 l. black 10 10
707 – 4 l. violet 10 10
708 – 5 l. violet 10 10
709 – 10 l. green 10 10
710 – 30 l. red 10 10
711... – 60 l. blue 10 10
712 – 70 l. brown 10 10
713 – 115 l. black 20 20
TOURNAMENTS—HORIZ: 2 l. 14th-century, French cavaliers; 4 l. 15th-century, Presenting arms to an English cavalier; 30 l. Quintana game, Foligno; 70 l. 15th-century, Cavaliers (from castle mural, Malpaga). VERT: 3 l. Crossbow Championships, Gubbio; 5 l. 16th-century, Cavaliers, Florence; 10 l. Quintana game, Ascoli Piceno; 60 l. Palio (horse-race), Siena; 115 l. 13th-century, The Crusades: cavaliers' challenge.

164 Peacock **165** Corner of Government Palace, San Marino

1963. Butterflies. Multicoloured.
714 25 l. Type **164** 25 10
715 30 l. "Nessaea obrinus" . . . 25 10
716 60 l. Large tortoiseshell . . . 35 15
717 70 l. Peacock (horiz) 40 20
718 115 l. "Papilio blumei" (horiz) 60 25

1963. San Marino–Riccione Stamp Fair.
719 **165** 100 l. black and blue . . . 15 15
720 – 100 l. blue and sepia . . . 15 15
DESIGN: No. 720, Fountain, Riccione.

166 Pole Vaulting **167** "E" and Flag of San Marino

1963. Olympic Games, Tokyo (1964) (1st issue).
721 – 1 l. purple and orange . . 10 10
722 **166** 2 l. sepia and green . . . 10 10
723 – 3 l. sepia and blue 10 10
724 – 4 l. sepia and blue 10 10
725 – 5 l. sepia and red 10 10
726 – 10 l. mauve and purple . . 10 10
727 – 30 l. purple and grey . . . 10 10
728 – 60 l. sepia and yellow . . 10 10
729 – 70 l. sepia and blue . . . 10 10
730 – 115 l. sepia and green . . 15 10
SPORTS—HORIZ: 1 l. Hurdling; 3 l. Relay-racing; 4 l. High jumping (men); 5 l. Football; 10 l. High jumping (women); 60 l. Throwing the javelin; 70 l. Water polo; 115 l. Throwing the hammer. VERT: 30 l. Throwing the discus.
See also Nos. 743/52.

1963. Europa.
731 **167** 200 l. blue and brown . . 20 20

168 Tupolev Tu-104A Jetliner **169** Running

1963. Air. Contemporary Aircraft.
732 **168** 5 l. purple, brown & blue 15 10
733 – 10 l. blue and red 15 10
734 – 15 l. red, mauve & violet . 15 10
735 – 25 l. red, mauve & violet . 15 10
736 – 50 l. red and blue 15 10
737 – 75 l. orange and green . . 15 10
738 – 120 l. red and blue . . . 25 20
739 – 200 l. black and yellow . . 25 15
740 – 300 l. black and orange . . 25 20
741 – 500 l. multicoloured . . . 3·50 2·75
742 – 1000 l. multicoloured . . . 2·00 1·60
DESIGNS—HORIZ: 15 l. Douglas DC-8 jetliner; 25, 1000 l. Boeing 707 jetliner (different views); 50 l. Vickers Viscount 837 airliner; 120 l. Vickers VC-10; 200 l. Hawker Siddley Comet 4C jetliner; 300 l. Boeing 727-100 jetliner. VERT: 10 l. Boeing 707 jetliner; 75 l. Sud Aviation Caravelle jetliner; 500 l. Rolls Royce Dart 527 turboprop engine.

1964. Olympic Games, Tokyo (2nd issue).
743 **169** 1 l. brown and green . . . 10 10
744 – 2 l. brown and sepia . . . 10 10
745 – 3 l. bown and black . . . 10 10
746 – 4 l. blue and red 10 10
747 – 5 l. brown and blue . . . 10 10
748 – 15 l. purple and orange . . 10 10
749 – 30 l. blue and light blue . 10 10
750 – 70 l. brown and green . . 15 15
751 – 120 l. brown and blue . . 15 15
752 – 150 l. purple and red . . 20 20
DESIGNS—VERT: 2 l. Gymnastics; 3 l. Basketball; 120 l. Cycling; 150 l. Fencing. HORIZ: 4 l. Pistol-shooting; 5 l. Rowing; 15 l. Long jumping; 30 l. Diving; 70 l. Sprinting.

1964. "Towards Tokyo" Sports Stamp Exn, Rimini. As Nos. 749/50, but inscr "VERSO TOKIO" and colours changed.
753 30 l. blue and violet 10 10
754 70 l. brown and turquoise . . 10 10

170 Murray Blenkinsop Locomotive (1812)

1964. "Story of the Locomotive".
755 **170** 1 l. black and buff . . . 20 10
756 – 2 l. black and green . . . 20 10
757 – 3 l. black and violet . . . 20 10
758 – 4 l. black and yellow . . . 20 10
759 – 5 l. black and salmon . . 20 10
760 – 15 l. black and green . . . 20 10
761 – 20 l. black and pink . . . 20 10
762 – 50 l. black and blue . . . 20 10

763 – 90 l. black and orange . . 20 35
764 – 110 l. black and blue . . . 50 75
LOCOMOTIVES: 2 l. "Puffing Billy" (1813); 3 l. "Locomotion No. 1" (1825); 4 l. "Rocket" (1829); 5 l. "Lion" (1838); 15 l. "Bayard" (1839); 20 l. Crampton type (1849); 50 l. "Little England" (1851); 90 l. "Spitfire" (c. 1860); 110 l. "Rogers" (c. 1865).

171 Baseball Players

1964. 7th European Baseball Championships, Milan.
765 **171** 30 l. sepia and green . . . 10 10
766 – 70 l. black and red 10 15
DESIGN: 70 l. Player pitching ball.

172 "E" and Part of Globe

1964. Europa.
767 **172** 200 l. red, blue & lt blue . 25 25

173 Pres. Kennedy giving Inaugural Address
174 Cyclists at Government Palace

1964. 1st Death Anniv of John F. Kennedy (President of U.S.A.). Multicoloured.
768 70 l. Type **173** 15 15
769 130 l. Pres. Kennedy and U.S. flag (vert) 15 15

1965. Cycle Tour of Italy.
770 **174** 30 l. sepia 15 10
771 – 70 l. purple 15 10
772 – 200 l. red 15 10
DESIGNS:— Cyclists passing: 70 l. "The Rock"; 200 l. Mt Titano.

175 Brontosaurus
176 Rooks on Chessboard

1965. Prehistoric Animals.
773 **175** 1 l. purple and green . . . 20 10
774 – 2 l. black and blue 20 10
775 – 3 l. yellow and green . . . 20 10
776 – 4 l. brown and blue . . . 20 10
777 – 5 l. purple and green . . . 20 10
778 – 10 l. purple and green . . 20 10
779 – 75 l. blue and turquoise . . 40 15
780 – 100 l. purple and green . . 60 25
ANIMALS—VERT: 2 l. Brachyosaurus. HORIZ: 3 l. Pteranodon; 4 l. Elasmosaurus; 5 l. Tyrannosaurus; 10 l. Stegosaurus; 75 l. Thamatosaurus Victor; 100 l. Iguanodon; 200 l. Triceratops.

1965. Europa.
782 **176** 200 l. multicoloured . . . 35 25

177 Dante

1965. 700th Anniv of Dante's Birth.
783 **177** 40 l. sepia and blue . . . 15 10
784 – 90 l. sepia and red 15 10
785 – 130 l. sepia and brown . 15 10
786 – 140 l. sepia and blue . . 15 10
DESIGNS: 90 l. "Hell"; 130 l. "Purgatory"; 140 l. "Paradise".

178 Mt Titano and Flags

1965. Visit of Pres. Saragat of Italy.
787 **178** 115 l. multicoloured . . . 15 10

179 Trotting

1966. Equestrian Sports. Multicoloured.
788 10 l. Type **179** 20 10
789 20 l. Cross-country racing . . 20 10
790 40 l. Horse-jumping 20 10
791 70 l. Horse-racing 20 10
792 90 l. Steeple-chasing . . . 30 15
793 170 l. Polo 35 15
The 20 and 170 l. are vert.

1966. New values in previous designs.
794 5 l. brown and blue (as 522a) 10 10
795 10 l. green & black (as 524) 10 10
796 15 l. violet & brown (as 524a) 10 10
797 40 l. red and lilac (as 491) . 10 10
798 90 l. blue and black (as 492) . 10 10
799 140 l. orange & vio (as 493) . 10 10

180 "La Bella"

1966. Paintings by Titian. Multicoloured.
800 40 l. Type **180** 15 10
801 90 l. "The Three Graces" . . 15 15
802 100 l. "The Three Graces" . . 20 15
803 170 l. "Sacred and Profane Love" 25 20
The 90 and 100 l. show different details from the picture.

181 Stone Bass

1966. Sea Animals. Multicoloured.
804 1 l. Type **181** 15 10
805 2 l. Cuckoo wrasse 15 10
806 3 l. Common dolphin 15 10
807 4 l. John Dory 15 10
808 5 l. Octopus 15 10
809 10 l. Orange scorpionfish . . 15 10
810 40 l. Electric ray 15 10
811 90 l. Medusa 20 10
812 115 l. Seahorse 20 10
813 130 l. Dentex 30 10
The 5, 40, 90 and 115 l. are vert.

182 Our Lady of Europe
183 Peony

1966. Europa.
814 **182** 200 l. multicoloured . . . 30 30

1967. Flowers. Multicoloured.
815 5 l. Type **183** 10 10
816 10 l. Campanula 10 10
817 15 l. Pyrenean poppy 10 10
818 20 l. Purple deadnettle . . . 10 10
819 40 l. Hemerocallis 10 10
820 140 l. Gentian 15 10
821 170 l. Thistle 15 10
Each flower has a different background view of Mt Titano.

184 St. Marinus

185 Map of Europe

1967. Paintings by Francesco Barbieri (Guercino). Multicoloured.
822 40 l. Type **184** 10 10
823 170 l. "St. Francis" 20 15
824 190 l. "Return of the Prodigal Son" (45 × 37 mm) 20 15

1967. Europa.
825 **185** 200 l. green and orange . . 35 30

186 Caesar's Mushroom
187 Salisbury Cathedral

1967. Fungi. Multicoloured.
826 5 l. Type **186** 20 10
827 15 l. The Miller 20 10
828 20 l. Parasol mushroom . . . 20 10
829 40 l. Cep 20 10
830 50 l. "Russula paludosa" . . . 20 10
831 170 l. St. George's mushroom . 20 20

1967. Gothic Cathedrals.
832 – 20 l. violet on cream . . . 10 10
833 – 40 l. green on cream . . . 10 10
834 – 80 l. blue on cream . . . 10 10
835 **187** 90 l. sepia on cream . . . 10 10
836 – 170 l. red on cream . . . 20 15
DESIGNS: 20 l. Amiens; 40 l. Siena; 80 l. Toledo; 170 l. Cologne.

188 Cimabue Crucifix, Florence

1967. Christmas.
837 **188** 300 l. brown and violet . . 35 35

189 Arms of San Marino
190 Europa "Key"

1968. Arms of San Marino Villages. Mult.
838 2 l. Type **189** 10 10
839 3 l. Penna Rossa 10 10
840 5 l. Fiorentino 10 10
841 10 l. Montecerreto 10 10
842 25 l. Serravalle 10 10
843 35 l. Montegiardino 10 10
844 50 l. Faetano 10 10
845 90 l. Borgo Maggiore 10 10
846 180 l. Montelupo 15 10
847 500 l. State crest 35 35

1968. Europa.
848 **190** 250 l. brown 30 30

191 "The Battle of San Romano" (detail, P. Uccello)

1968. 671st Birth Anniv of Paolo Uccello (painter).
849 **191** 50 l. black on lilac 20 15
850 – 90 l. black on lilac . . . 20 15
851 – 130 l. black on lilac . . . 20 15
852 – 230 l. black on pink . . . 20 25
All stamps show details of "The Battle of San Romano". The 90 l. is vert.

192 "The Nativity" (detail, Botticelli)

1968. Christmas.
853 **192** 50 l. blue 15 10
854 90 l. red 15 10
855 180 l. sepia 15 15

193 "Peace"

1969. "The Good Government" (frescoes) by Ambrogio Lorenzetti.
856 **193** 50 l. blue 15 10
857 – 80 l. sepia 15 10
858 – 90 l. violet 15 10
859 – 180 l. red 15 15
DESIGNS—VERT: 80 l. "Justice"; 90 l. "Temperance". HORIZ: 180 l. View of Siena.

194 "Young Soldier" (Bramante)

1969. 525th Birth Anniv of Donato Bramante (architect and painter). Multicoloured.
860 50 l. Type **194** 15 15
861 90 l. "Old Soldier" (Bramante) 15 15

195 Colonnade

1969. Europa.
862 **195** 50 l. green 20 15
863 180 l. purple 20 15

196 Benched Carriage ("Char-a-banc")

1969. Horses and Carriages. Multicoloured.
864 5 l. Type **196** 15 10
865 10 l. Barouche 15 10

866 25 l. Private drag 15 10
867 40 l. Hanson cab 15 10
868 50 l. Curricle 15 10
869 90 l. Wagonette 20 15
870 180 l. Spider phaeton 20 15

197 Mt Titano

1969. Paintings by R. Viola. Multicoloured.
871 20 l. Type **197** 20 10
872 180 l. "Pier at Rimini" 20 15
873 200 l."Pier at Riccione" (horiz) 20 15

198 "Faith"

1969. Christmas. "The Theological Virtues" by Raphael.
874 **198** 20 l. violet and orange . . 10 10
875 – 180 l. violet and green . . 15 15
876 – 200 l. violet and buff . . . 15 15
DESIGNS: 180 l. "Hope"; 200 l. "Charity".

199 "Aries"

1970. Signs of the Zodiac. Multicoloured.
877 1 l. Type **199** 10 10
878 2 l. "Taurus" 10 10
879 3 l. "Gemini" 10 10
880 4 l. "Cancer" 10 10
881 5 l. "Leo" 10 10
882 10 l. "Virgo" 10 10
883 15 l. "Libra" 10 10
884 20 l. "Scorpio" 10 10
885 70 l. "Sagittarius" 10 10
886 90 l. "Capricorn" 15 10
887 100 l. "Aquarius" 20 10
888 180 l. "Pisces" 70 30

200 "Flaming Sun" 202 St. Francis' Gate

201 "The Fleet in the Bay of Naples" (Pieter Brueghel the Elder)

1970. Europa.
889 **200** 90 l. red and green 15 15
890 180 l. red and yellow 25 25

1970. 10th "Europa" Stamp Exhibition. Naples.
891 **201** 230 l. multicoloured . . . 40 35

1970. 65th Anniv of Rotary International and 10th Anniv of San Marino Rotary Club. Multicoloured.
892 180 l. Type **202** 15 15
893 220 l. "Rocco" Fort, Mt Titano 20 15

203 "Girl with Mandolin" 204 Black Pete

1970. Death Bicentenary of Giambattista Tiepolo (painter).
894 50 l. Type **203** 15 10
895 180 l. "Girl with Parrot" . . 25 15
896 220 l. "Rinaldo and Armida Surprised" 15 15
SIZES: 180 l. As Type **203**. 220 l. (57 × 37 mm).

1970. 4th Death Anniv of Walt Disney (film producer). Cartoon Characters. Multicoloured.
897 1 l. Type **204** 10 10
898 2 l. Gyro Gearloose 10 10
899 3 l. Pluto 10 10
900 4 l. Minnie Mouse 10 10
901 5 l. Donald Duck 10 10
902 10 l. Goofy 10 10
903 15 l. Scrooge McDuck . . . 10 10
904 50 l. Hewey, Dewey and Louie 40 20
905 90 l. Mickey Mouse 65 30
906 220 l. Walt Disney and scene from "The Jungle Book" (horiz) . . . . 4·00 3·00

205 "Customs House, Venice"

1971. "Save Venice" Campaign. Paintings by Canaletto. Multicoloured.
907 20 l. Type **205** 20 15
908 180 l. "Grand Canal, Balbi Palace and Rialto Bridge, Venice 40 35
909 200 l. "St. Mark's and Doge's Palace" 50 40

206 Congress Building and San Marino Flag

1971. Italian Philatelic Press Union Congress, San Marino. Multicoloured.
910 20 l. Type **206** 10 10
911 90 l. Government Palace door and emblems (vert) 10 10
912 180 l. Type **206** 15 15

207 Europa Chain 209 Day Lily

208 "Duck" Jug with "Lasa" Decoration

1971. Europa.
913 **207** 50 l. blue and yellow . . 15 15
914 90 l. orange and blue . . 15 15

1971. Etruscan Art (1st series).
915 **208** 50 l. black and orange . . 20 10
916 – 80 l. black and green . . 10 10
917 – 90 l. black and green . . 10 10
918 – 180 l. black and orange . . 15 15
DESIGNS—VERT: 80 l. Head of Hermes (bust); 90 l. Man and Wife (relief on sarcophagus). HORIZ: 180 l. Chimera (bronze).
See also Nos. 1018/21.

1971. Flowers. Multicoloured.
919 1 l. Type **209** 10 10
920 2 l. "Phlox paniculata" 10 10
921 3 l. Wild pink 10 10
922 4 l. Globe flower 10 10
923 5 l. "Centaurea dealbata" . . . 10 10
924 10 l. Peony 10 10
925 15 l. Christmas rose 10 10
926 50 l. Pasque flower 15 10
927 90 l. "Gaillardia aristata" . . . 15 15
928 220 l. "Aster dumosus" 35 30

210 "Allegory of Spring" (detail, Botticelli) 211 "Communications"

1972. "Allegory of Spring" by Sandro Botticelli. Multicoloured.
929 50 l. Type **210** 10 10
930 190 l. The Three Graces (27 × 37 mm) 20 20
931 220 l. Flora 25 25

1972. Europa.
932 **211** 50 l. multicoloured 20 15
933 90 l. multicoloured 20 15

212 "Taming the Bear"

1972. "Life of St. Marinus". 16th-century paintings from former Government Palace.
934 **212** 25 l. black and buff . . . 10 10
935 – 55 l. black and orange . . 10 10
936 – 100 l. black and blue . . . 15 10
937 – 130 l. black and yellow . . 15 15
DESIGNS: 55 l. "The Conversion of Donna Felicissima"; 100 l. "Hostile archers turned to stone"; 130 l. "Mount Titano given to St. Marinus".

213 House Sparrow 214 "Healthy Man"

1972. Birds. Multicoloured.
938 1 l. Type **213** 15 10
939 2 l. Firecrest 15 10
940 3 l. Blue tit 15 10
941 4 l. Ortulan bunting 15 10
942 5 l. Bluethroat 15 10
943 10 l. Bullfinch 15 10
944 25 l. Linnet 25 15
945 50 l. Black-eared wheatear . . 40 20
946 90 l. Sardinian warbler . . . 50 25
947 220 l. Greenfinch . . . . . 1·25 50

1972. World Heart Month. Multicoloured.
948 50 l. Type **214** 15 15
949 90 l. "Sick Man" (horiz) . . . 15 15

215 Veterans Emblem 216 Plane over Mt Titano

1972. "Veterans of Philately" Award of Italian Philatelic Federation.
950 **215** 25 l. gold and blue 10 10

1972. Air.
951 **216** 1000 l. multicoloured . . . 1·00 80

INDEX

Countries can be quickly located by referring to the index at the end of this volume.

217 Five-Cent Coin of 1864

1972. San Marino Coinage.
952 **217** 5 l. bronze, black & grey . 10 10
953 – 10 l. bronze, black & orge 10 10
954 – 15 l. silver, black & red . 10 10
955 – 20 l. silver, black & purple 10 10
956 – 25 l. silver, black & blue . 10 10
957 – 50 l. silver, black & blue . 15 10
958 – 55 l. silver, black & ochre 15 15
959 – 220 l. gold, black & green 20 20
COINS (obverse and reverse on each stamp): 10 l. 10 c. of 1935; 15 l. 1 l. of 1906; 20 l. 5 l. of 1898; 25 l. 5 l. of 1937; 50 l. 10 l. of 1932; 55 l. 20 l. of 1938; 220 l. 20 l. of 1925.

218 New York, 1673

1973. "Interpex" Stamp Exhibition and Important Cities of the World (1st series). New York.
960 **218** 200 l. brown, grey & black 35 35
961 – 300 l. blue, lilac & deep lilac 40 40
DESIGN: 300 l. New York, 1973.
See also Nos. 1032/3, 1075/6, 1144/5, 1160/1, 1197/8, 1215/16, 1230/1, 1259/60, 1271/2, 1306/7, 1331/2, 1358/9 and 1524/5.

219 Printing Press 220 "Sportsmen"

1973. Tourist Press Congress.
962 **219** 50 l. multicoloured . . . 10 10

1973. Youth Games.
963 **220** 100 l. multicoloured . . . 10 10

221 Europa "Posthorn" 222 Grapes

1973. Europa.
964 **221** 20 l. green, blue and flesh 10 10
965 180 l. mauve, red and blue 70 70

1973. Fruits. Multicoloured.
966 1 l. Type **222** 10 10
967 2 l. Mandarines 10 10
968 3 l. Apples 10 10
969 4 l. Plums 10 10
970 5 l. Strawberries 10 10
971 10 l. Pears 10 10
972 25 l. Cherries 10 10
973 50 l. Pomegranate 20 10
974 90 l. Apricots 25 20
975 200 l. Peaches 45 30

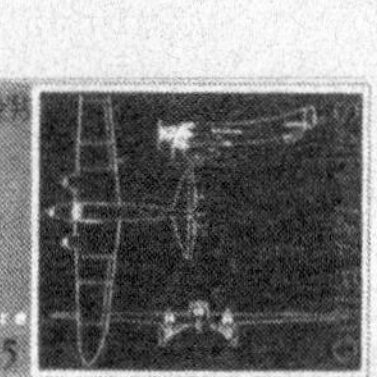

223 Couzinet 70 "Arc en Ciel" 224 Crossbowman, Serravalle Castle

1973. Aircraft.
976 **223** 25 l. blue, yellow & gold . 15 10
977 – 55 l. blue, grey and gold . 15 10
978 – 60 l. blue, pink and gold . 15 10
979 – 90 l. blue, bistre and gold 20 10
980 – 220 l. blue, orange & gold 30 15
AIRCRAFT: 55 l. Macchi Castoldi MC-72-181 seaplane; 60 l. Tupolev ANT-9; 90 l. Ryan NYP "Spirit of St. Louis" (Charles Lindburgh's plane); 220 l. Handley Page H.P.42.

1973. San Marino's Victory in Crossbow Tournament, Masa Marittima. Multicoloured.

981 5 l. Type **224** 15 10
982 10 l. Crossbowman, Pennarossa Castle 15 10
983 15 l. Drummer, Montegiardino Castle 15 10
984 20 l. Trumpeter, Fiorentino Castle 15 10
985 30 l. Crossbowman, Montecerreto Castle 15 10
986 40 l. Crossbowman, Borgo Maggiore Castle 20 10
987 50 l. Trumpeter, Guaita Castle 20 10
988 80 l. Crossbowman, Faetano Castle 25 15
989 200 l. Crossbowman, Montelupo Castle 50 20

225 "Adoration of the Magi" (detail)

226 Combat Shield (16th century)

1973. Christmas. 600th Birth Anniv of Gentile da Fabriano. Details of Gentile's altarpiece "Adoration of the Magi".

990 **225** 5 l. multicoloured 10 10
991 – 30 l. multicoloured 10 10
992 – 115 l. multicoloured . . . 10 10
993 – 250 l. multicoloured . . . 20 20

1974. Ancient Weapons from "Cesta" Museum, San Marino.

994 **226** 5 l. black brown & green 10 10
995 – 10 l. black, blue & brown 10 10
996 – 15 l. black, blue & lt blue 10 10
997 – 20 l. black, blue & brown 10 10
998 – 30 l. black, brown & blue 10 10
999 – 50 l. black, blue & pink . 10 10
1000 – 80 l. black, blue & lilac . 15 10
1001 – 250 l. black and yellow . 25 15

DESIGNS: 10 l. German armour (16th-century); 15 l. Crested morion (16th-century); 20 l. Horse head-armour (15th-16th century); 30 l. Italian morion with crest (16th-17th century); 50 l. Gauntlets and sword pommel (16th-century); 80 l. Sallet helmet (16th-century); 250 l. Sforza shield (16th-century).

227 "The Joy of Living" (Emilio Greco)

1974. Europa. Sculpture.

1002 **227** 100 l. black and brown . 20 15
1003 – 200 l. black and green . . 20 15

DESIGN: 200 l. "The Joy of Living" (complete sculpture).

228 "Sea and Mountains"

229 Arms of Sansepolcro

1974. San Marino–Riccione Stamp Fair.

1004 **228** 50 l. multicoloured . . . 15 10

1974. 9th Crossbow Tournament, San Marino. Arms. Multicoloured.

1005 15 l. Type **229** 75 75
1006 20 l. Massa Marittima . . . 75 75
1007 50 l. San Marino 75 75
1008 115 l. Gubbio 75 75
1009 300 l. Lucca 75 75

230 U.P.U. Emblem and Shadow

1974. Centenary of Universal Postal Union.

1010 **230** 50 l. multicoloured . . . 15 15
1011 90 l. multicoloured . . . 15 15

231 Glider

1974. Air. 50th Anniv of Gliding in Italy.

1012 **231** 40 l. blue, green & brown 15 10
1013 – 120 l. blue, lt blue & pur 25 15
1014 – 500 l. violet, mve & purple 45 35

DESIGNS: 120, 500 l. Gliders in "air currents" (both different).

232 Mt Titano and Verses of Hymn

233 "Madonna and Child" (4th-century painting)

1974. Death Centenary of Niccolo Tommaseo (writer).

1015 **232** 50 l. black, green & red . 15 15
1016 – 150 l. black, yellow & bl 20 15

DESIGN: 150 l. Portrait of Tommaseo.

1974. Christmas.

1017 **233** 250 l. multicoloured . . 25 30

234 "Dancing Scene", Tomb of the Leopards, Tarquinia

1975. Etruscan Art (2nd series). Tomb Paintings. Multicoloured.

1018 20 l. Type **234** 10 10
1019 30 l. "Chariot Race", Tomb of the Hill, Chiusi 10 10
1020 180 l. "Achilles and Troillus", Tomb of the Bulls, Tarquinia 30 15
1021 220 l. "Dancers", Tomb of the Triclinium, Tarquinia . . 40 25

235 "Escape Tunnel"

236 "The Blessing"

1975. 30th Anniv of Escape of 100,000 Italian Wartime Refugees to San Marino.

1022 **235** 50 l. multicoloured 15 10

1975. Europa. Details from "St. Marinus" by Guercino. Multicoloured.

1023 100 l. Type **236** 15 15
1024 200 l. "St. Marinus" 25 25

237 "The Virgin Mary"

238 "Aphrodite" (sculpture)

1975. Holy Year. Details from Frescoes by Giotto from Scrovegni Chapel, Padua. Multicoloured.

1025 10 l. Type **237** 10 10
1026 40 l. "Virgin and Child" . . 10 10
1027 50 l. "Heads of Angels" . . 10 10
1028 100 l. "Mary Magdalene" (horiz) 10 10
1029 500 l. "Heads of Saints" (horiz) 35 35

1975. 15th Europa Stamp Exhibition, Naples.

1030 **238** 50 l. black, grey & violet 15 10

239 Congress Emblem

1975. "Eurocophar" International Pharmaceutical Congress, San Marino.

1031 **239** 100 l. multicoloured . . . 15 10

240 Tokyo, 1835

1975. Important Cities of the World (2nd series). Tokyo. Multicoloured.

1032 200 l. Type **240** 30 30
1033 300 l. Tokyo, 1975 . . . . . . 40 40

241 "Woman on Balcony"

242 "Head of the Child" (detail)

1975. International Women's Year. Paintings by Gentilini. Multicoloured.

1034 50 l. Type **241** 10 10
1035 150 l. "Heads of Two Women" (horiz) 20 15
1036 230 l. "Profile of Girl" . . . 35 25

1975. Christmas. 500th Birth Anniv of Michelangelo. Painting "Doni Madonna" and details. Multicoloured.

1037 50 l. Type **242** 10 10
1038 100 l. "Head of Virgin" (detail) 15 15
1039 250 l. "Doni Madonna" . . . 25 25

243 "Modesty"

244 Capitol, Washington

1976. "The Civil Virtues". Sketches by Emilio Greco.

1039a – 5 l. black and lilac . . . 10 10
1040 **243** 10 l. black and stone . . 10 10
1041 – 20 l. black and lilac . . 10 10
1041a – 35 l. black and stone . . 10 10
1042 – 50 l. black and green . . 10 10
1043 – 70 l. black and pink . . 10 10
1044 – 90 l. black and pink . . 10 10
1045 – 100 l. black and pink . . 10 10
1046 – 120 l. black and blue . . 10 10
1047 – 150 l. black and lilac . . 10 10
1048 – 160 l. black and green . 15 15
1049 – 170 l. black and flesh . 15 15
1050 – 220 l. black and grey . . 20 15
1051 – 250 l. black and yellow . 25 20
1052 – 300 l. black and grey . . 30 20
1053 – 320 l. black and mauve . 30 20
1054 – 500 l. black and stone . 40 30
1055 – 1000 l. black and blue . 70 50
1056 – 2000 l. black & cream . 1·75 1·75

DESIGNS: 3 l. "Wisdom"; 20, 160 l. "Temperance"; 35 l. "Love"; 50, 70 l. "Fortitude"; 90, 220 l. "Prudence"; 100, 120 l. "Altruism"; 150, 170 l. "Hope"; 250 l. "Justice"; 300, 320 l. "Faith"; 500 l. "Honesty"; 1000 l. "Industry"; 2000 l. "Faithfulness".

1976. Bicentenary of American Revolution and "Interphil 1976" International Stamp Exhibition, Philadelphia. Multicoloured.

1056 70 l. Type **244** 10 10
1057 150 l. Statue of Liberty, New York 10 10
1058 180 l. Independence Hall, Philadelphia 15 15

245 Emblem and Maple Leaf

1976. Olympic Games, Montreal.

1059 **245** 150 l. black and red . . 20 20

246 Polychrome Plate (U. Bruno)

247 S.U.M.S. Emblem

1976. Europa. Handicrafts. Multicoloured.

1060 150 l. Type **246** 15 15
1061 180 l. Silver plate (A. Ruscelli) 15 15

1976. Centenary of San Marino Social Welfare Union.

1062 **247** 150 l. red, yellow & lilac 20 15

248 Children of Different Races

249 "San Marino"

1976. 30th Anniv of U.N.E.S.C.O.

1063 **248** 180 l. brown, orange & bl 15 15
1064 220 l. brown, buff & sepia 20 15

1976. "Italia '76" International Stamp Exhibition, Milan.

1065 **249** 150 l. multicoloured . . 15 15

250 "The Annunciation"

251 Mount Titano and Emblem

1976. Christmas. 400th Death Anniv of Titian. Multicoloured.

1066 150 l. Type **250** 25 25
1067 300 l. "The Nativity" 45 45

1977. "San Marino 77" International Stamp Exhibition (1st issue).

1068 **251** 80 l. red, green & olive (postage) 10 10
1069 170 l. yellow, violet & bl 15 15
1070 200 l. orange, ultram & bl 25 25
1071 200 l. ochre, green and blue (air) 25 25

See also No. 1082.

252 "San Marino" (Ghirlandaio)

253 Leonardo da Vinci's Drawing of "Helicopter"

1977. Europa. Landscapes. Multicoloured.

1072 170 l. Type **252** 25 25
1073 200 l. "San Marino" (Guercino) 25 25

1977. Centenary of Enrico Forlanini's First Vertical Flight Experiment.

1074 **253** 120 l. multicoloured . . 25 15

254 University Square, 1877

1977. Centenary of Rumanian Independence. Important Cities of the World (3rd series). Bucharest.

1075 **254** 200 l. green and blue . . 25 25
1076 – 400 l. brown and stone . . 35 35

DESIGN: 400 l. City centre, 1977.

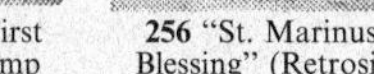

255 Design of First San Marino Stamp

256 "St. Marinus Blessing" (Retrosi)

1977. Centenary of San Marino Postage Stamps.
1077 **255** 40 l. green 10 10
1078 70 l. blue 10 10
1079 170 l. red 15 15
1080 500 l. brown 40 45
1081 1000 l. lilac 70 80

1977. "San Marino 1977" International Stamp Exhibition (2nd issue).
1082 **256** 1000 l. multicoloured . . 1·40 1·60

257 Medicinal Plants

259 Angel

258 Woman gripped by Octopus

1977. Italian Pharmacists' Union Congress.
1083 **257** 170 l. multicoloured . . . 30 20

1977. World Rheumatism Year.
1084 **258** 200 l. multicoloured . . . 30 25

1977. Christmas.
1085 **259** 170 l. black, grey & silver 25 25
1086 – 230 l. black, grey & silver 25 25
1087 – 300 l. black, grey & silver 35 35
DESIGNS: 230 l. Palm tree and olive; 300 l. The Virgin.

260 Baseball Player

261 San Francesco Gate

1978. World Baseball Championships.
1088 **260** 90 l. black, blue and ultramarine 15 15
1089 120 l. black, light green and green 20 20

1978. Europa. Architecture.
1090 **261** 170 l. blue & light blue . 20 20
1091 – 200 l. brown and stone . 25 25
DESIGN: 200 l. Ripa Gate.

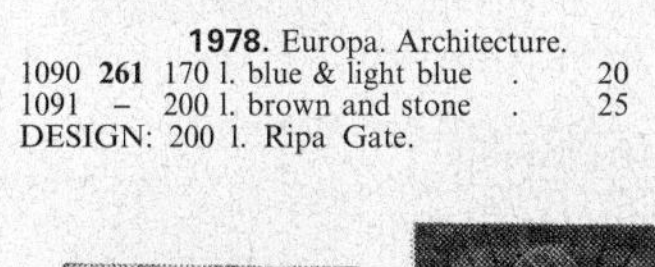

262 Feather

263 Mt Titano and Antenna

1978. World Hypertension Month.
1092 **262** 320 l. black, blue and red 40 35

1978. San Marino's Admission to the I.T.U.
1093 **263** 10 l. yellow and red . . . 10 10
1094 200 l. blue and violet . . 20 20

264 Hawk and Slender-billed Gull

1978. 30th San Marino–Riccione Stamp Fair.
1095 **264** 120 l. multicoloured . . 60 15
1096 170 l. multicoloured . . 90 25

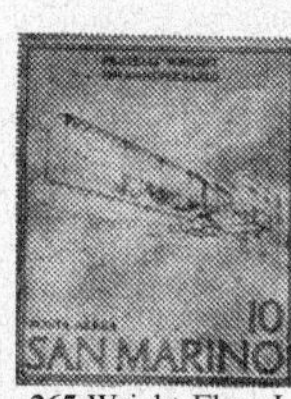

265 Wright Flyer I

266 Allegory of Human Rights

1978. Air. 75th Anniv of First Powered Flight.
1097 **265** 10 l. multicoloured . . . 20 15
1098 50 l. multicoloured . . . 30 15
1099 200 l. multicoloured . . 40 15

1978. 30th Anniv of Declaration of Human Rights.
1100 **266** 200 l. multicoloured . . 30 25

267 Holly

1978. Christmas. Multicoloured.
1101 10 l. Type **267** 10 10
1102 120 l. Star 15 10
1103 170 l. Snowflakes 20 15

268 Albert Einstein

1979. Birth Cent of Albert Einstein (physicist).
1104 **268** 120 l. brown, sepia and grey 20 15

269 Motor-coach, 1915

1979. Europa. Multicoloured.
1105 170 l. Type **269** 40 30
1106 220 l. Horse-drawn stage-coach 45 35

270 San Marino Crossbowmen Federation Emblem

271 Maigret (G. Simenon)

1979. 14th Crossbow Tournament.
1107 **270** 120 l. multicoloured . . 20 15

1979. Fictional Detectives. Multicoloured.
1108 10 l. Type **271** 10 10
1109 80 l. Perry Mason (S. Gardner) 15 10
1110 150 l. Nero Wolfe (R. Stout) 25 15
1111 170 l. Ellery Queen (F. Dannay and M. B. Lee) 30 15
1112 220 l. Sherlock Holmes (A. Conan Doyle) 50 25

272 Water Skiing

273 St. Apollonia

1979. Water Skiing Championships, Castelgandolfo.
1113 **272** 150 l. green, blue & blk . 25 15

1979. 13th International Stomatology Congress.
1114 **273** 170 l. multicoloured . . . 30 20

274 "Knowledge"

275 Horse Chestnut and Red Deer

1979. International Year of the Child. Multicoloured.
1115 20 l. Type **274** 10 10
1116 120 l. "Friendship" 15 15
1117 170 l. "Equality" 15 15
1118 220 l. "Love" 20 20
1119 350 l. "Existence" 30 30

1979. Environment Protection. Trees and Animals. Multicoloured.
1120 5 l. Type **275** 10 10
1121 10 l. Cedar of Lebanon and golden eagle 60 10
1122 35 l. Flowering dogwood and common racoon 25 10
1123 50 l. Banyan and tiger 25 10
1124 70 l. Stone pine and hoopoe . 1·25 20
1125 90 l. Larch and yellow-throated marten 20 15
1126 100 l. Tasmanian blue gum and koala 20 15
1127 120 l. Date palm and dromedary 20 15
1128 150 l. Silver maple and American beaver 20 20
1129 170 l. Baobab and African elephant 45 25

276 "Disturbing Muses"

277 St. Joseph

1979. 1st Death Anniv of Giorgio de Chirico (painter). Multicoloured.
1130 40 l. Type **276** 10 10
1131 150 l. "Ancient Horses" . . . 15 10
1132 170 l. "Self-portrait" 20 10

1979. Christmas. "The Holy Family" (fresco) by Antonio Alberti or details from it.
1133 80 l. Type **277** 10 10
1134 170 l. Infant Jesus 20 20
1135 220 l. Magus 25 25
1136 320 l. "The Holy Family" . . 30 30

278 St. Benedict of Nursia

279 Cigarette Ends

1980. 1500th Birth Anniv of Saint Benedict of Nursia (founder of Benedictine Order).
1137 **278** 170 l. multicoloured . . . 30 25

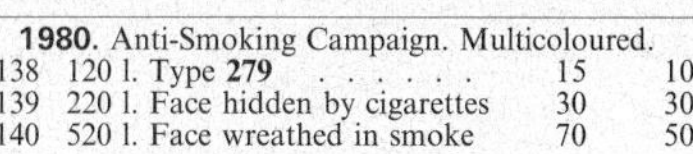

1980. Anti-Smoking Campaign. Multicoloured.
1138 120 l. Type **279** 15 10
1139 220 l. Face hidden by cigarettes 30 30
1140 520 l. Face wreathed in smoke 70 50

280 Naples

1980. "Europa" Stamp Exhibition, Naples.
1141 **280** 170 l. multicoloured . . 30 20

281 Giovanbattista Belluzzi (military architect)

1980. Europa. Multicoloured.
1142 170 l. Type **281** 20 20
1143 220 l. Antonio Orafo (silver and goldsmith) 30 30

282 London, 1850

1980. "London 1980" International Stamp Exhibition and Important Cities of the World (4th series). London.
1144 **282** 200 l. brown and green . . 30 30
1145 – 400 l. blue and lilac . . 40 40
DESIGN: 400 l. London, 1980.

283 Cycling

284 Stolz and Score of "Philatelic Waltz"

1980. Olympic Games, Moscow.
1146 **283** 70 l. black, emerald & grn 15 10
1147 – 90 l. black, orge & brn . 20 10
1148 – 170 l. black, red & mauve 20 20
1149 – 350 l. black, blue & dp bl 20 30
1150 – 450 l. black, violet & bl . 40 40
DESIGNS: 90 l. Basketball; 170 l. Running; 350 l. Gymnastics; 450 l. High jumping.

1980. Birth Centenary of Robert Stolz (composer).
1151 **284** 120 l. blue and black . . 30 15

285 Weightlifting

286 City Fortifications

1980. European Junior Weightlifting Championship.
1152 **285** 170 l. red, black & green 30 25

1980. World Tourism Conference, Manila.
1153 **286** 220 l. multicoloured . . 35 20

287 "The Annunciation" (detail)

288 St. Joseph's Eve Bonfire

1980. Christmas. Details of Paintings by Andrea del Sarto. Multicoloured.
1154 180 l. "Madonna of the Harpies" (detail) 20 20
1155 250 l. "Annunciation" (Mary) 35 35
1156 500 l. Type **287** 55 55

1981. Europa. Multicoloured.
1157 200 l. Type **288** 25 25
1158 300 l. National Day fireworks 30 30

289 Hands holding Broken Branch

1981. International Year of Disabled Persons.
1159 **289** 300 l. yellow, green and light green 30 30

290 "St. Charles' Square, 1817" (Jakob Alt)

1981. "WIPA 1981" International Stamp Exn and Important Cities of the World (5th series). Vienna. Multicoloured.
1160 200 l. Type **290** 30 30
1161 300 l. St. Charles' Square, 1981 60 60

291 Motor Cyclist **292** Girl playing Pipes

1981. San Marino Motor Cycle Grand Prix.
1162 **291** 200 l. multicoloured . . . 30 25

1981. Birth Bimillenary of Virgil (poet).
1163 **292** 300 l. grey and silver . . 35 40
1164 – 550 l. grey and silver . . 55 65
1165 – 1500 l. grey and silver . . 1·25 1·50
DESIGNS: 550 l. Soldier; 1500 l. Shepherd.

293 House **294** Judo

1981. Urban Development Scheme. Multicoloured.
1167 20 l. Type **293** 10 10
1168 80 l. Tree (provision of green belts) 15 10
1169 400 l. Gas flame (power plants) 35 35

1981. European Junior Judo Championships, San Marino.
1170 **294** 300 l. multicoloured . . . 45 35

295 "Girl with Dove" (Picasso) **296** Bread

1981. Birth Centenary of Pablo Picasso (artist). Mult.
1171 150 l. Type **295** 20 20
1172 200 l. "Homage to Picasso" (detail, Renato Guttuso) . 30 30

1981. World Food Day.
1173 **296** 300 l. multicoloured . . . 40 35

297 King presenting Gift **298** Cancellation and "San Marino 82" Emblem

1981. Christmas. 500th Birth Anniv of Benvenuto Tisi da Garofalo (artist). Details from "Adoration of the Magi and St. Bartholomew". Multicoloured.
1174 200 l. Type **297** 20 20
1175 300 l. Kneeling King 35 35
1176 600 l. Virgin and Child . . . 65 65

1982. Centenary of Postal Stationery.
1177 **298** 200 l. multicoloured . . 30 20

299 "The Cicada and the Ant" (Aesop fable)

1982. Centenary of Savings Bank.
1178 **299** 300 l. multicoloured . . 40 35

300 Assembly of Heads of Families, 1906 **301** Archimedes

1982. Europa. Multicoloured.
1179 300 l. Type **300** 40 40
1180 450 l. Napoleon at the border of San Marino, 1797 . . . . 50 50

1982. Pioneers of Science.
1181 **301** 20 l. red and black . . . 10 10
1182 – 30 l. blue and black . . 10 10
1183 – 40 l. brown and black . 10 10
1184 – 50 l. green and black . 10 10
1185 – 60 l. red and black . . . 10 10
1186 – 100 l. brown and black . 15 10
1187 – 150 l. brown and black . 15 15
1188 – 200 l. brown and black . 20 15
1189 – 250 l. red and black . . 25 25
1190 – 300 l. green and black . 30 25
1191 – 350 l. green and black . 40 35
1192 – 400 l. red and black . . 45 45
1193 – 450 l. red and black . . 45 45
1194 – 1000 l. red and black . . 1·00 1·00
1195 – 1400 l. red and black . . 1·50 1·50
1196 – 5000 l. black and blue . . 5·50 5·00
DESIGNS: 30 l. Copernicus; 40 l. Isaac Newton; 50 l. Antoine Lavoisier; 60 l. Marie Curie; 100 l. Robert Koch; 150 l. Alexander Fleming; 200 l. Thomas Edison; 250 l. Alessandro Volta; 300 l. Guglielmo Marconi; 350 l. Evangelista Torricelli; 400 l. Carl Linnaeus; 450 l. Hippocrates; 1000 l. Pythagoras; 1400 l. Leonardo da Vinci; 5000 l. Galileo.

302 "Notre Dame", 1806 (J. Hill)

1982. "Philexfrance 82" International Stamp Exhibition and Important Cities of the World (6th series). Paris.
1197 **302** 300 l. buff and black . . 30 30
1198 – 450 l. multicoloured . . 40 40
DESIGN: 450 l. Notre Dame and Ile de Cite, 1982.

303 Hands and Birds **304** Pope John Paul II

1982. 800th Birth Anniv of St. Francis of Assisi.
1199 **303** 200 l. multicoloured . . 40 25

1982. Visit of Pope John Paul II to San Marino.
1200 **304** 900 l. purple, deep green and green . . . . . . 1·00 1·00

305 Globe encircled by Flag Stamps **306** Face besplattered with Blood

1982. 5th Anniv of International Association of Stamp Philatelic Catalogue Editors (ASCAT).
1201 **305** 300 l. multicoloured . . . 35 35

1982. 15th International Congress of Amnesty International, Rimini.
1202 **306** 700 l. red and black . . . 70 70

307 "Accipe Lampadam Ardentem" (detail) **308** Refugee

1982. Christmas. Paintings by Gregorio Sciltian. Multicoloured.
1203 200 l. Type **307** 25 25
1204 300 l. "Madonna della Citta" (detail) 40 40
1205 450 l. Angel (detail, "Accipe Sal Sapientiae") 55 55

1982. "For Refugees".
1206 **308** 300 l. + 100 l. mult . . . 40 35

309 Begni Building and Quill **310** Formula One Racing Cars

1983. Centenary of Secondary School.
1207 **309** 300 l. multicoloured . . . 40 30

1983. San Marino Formula One Grand Prix.
1208 **310** 50 l. multicoloured . . . 20 15
1209 350 l. multicoloured . . . 55 40

311 Auguste Piccard and Stratosphere Balloon "F.N.R.S." **312** Amateur Radio Operator

1983. Europa. Multicoloured.
1210 400 l. Type **311** . . . . 1·00 90
1211 500 l. Piccard and bathyscaphe 1·25 1·10

1983. World Communications Year.
1212 **312** 400 l. black, blue & red . 35 35
1213 – 500 l. black, brown & red 60 50
DESIGN: 500 l. Postman on bicycle.

313 Montgolfier Balloon

1983. Bicentenary of Manned Flight.
1214 **313** 500 l. multicoloured . . . 50 50

314 "Rio de Janeiro, 1845" (Richard Bate)

1983. "Brasiliana 83" International Stamp Exhibition and Important Cities of the World (7th series). Rio de Janeiro. Multicoloured.
1215 400 l. Type **314** 40 35
1216 1400 l. Rio de Janeiro, 1983 . 2·00 1·75

315 Feeding Colt

1983. World Food Programme.
1217 **315** 500 l. multicoloured . . 65 60

316 "Madonna of the Grand Duke" **317** Demetrius Vikelas

1983. Christmas. 500th Birth Anniv of Raphael. Multicoloured.
1218 300 l. Type **316** 40 40
1219 400 l. "Madonna of the Goldfinch" (detail) 45 45
1220 500 l. "Madonna of the Chair" (detail) 60 60

1984. 90th Anniv of International Olympic Committee. I.O.C. Presidents.
1221 **317** 300 l. black and green . . 30 30
1222 – 400 l. purple and blue . . 40 40
1223 – 550 l. lilac and green . . 55 55
DESIGNS: 400 l. Lord Killanin; 550 l. Juan Samaranch.

318 Bridge

1984. Europa. 25th Anniv of C.E.P.T.
1224 **318** 400 l. yellow, vio & blk 90 90
1225 550 l. yellow, red & blk 1·00 1·00

319 Flag Waver **321** Motorcross

1984. Flag Wavers. Multicoloured.
1226 300 l. Type **319** 35 35
1227 400 l. Waver with two flags . 50 45

1984. World Motorcross Championship.
1229 **321** 450 l. multicoloured . . 60 50

322 Collins Street, 1839

1984. "Ausipex 84" International Stamp Exhibition, and Important Cities of the World (8th series). Melbourne Multicoloured.
1230 1500 l. Type **322** . . . . . . 1·60 1·60
1231 2000 l. Collins Street, 1984 . 2·75 2·75

323 Pres. Pertini and San Marino City

1984. Visit of President Sandro Pertini of Italy.
1232 **323** 1950 l. multicoloured . . 2·10 2·10

324 "Universe" **325** Angel with Book

1984. Youth Philately. Multicoloured.
1233 50 l. Type **324** 15 10
1234 100 l. Caveman and modern man framed by television ("The Evolution of Life") . 20 10
1235 150 l. Pipe smoker driving car ("The World in which we Live") 25 15
1236 200 l. Man with fig leaf and snake with apple ("Mankind") 30 20
1237 450 l. Scientist with H-bomb ("Science") 50 45
1238 550 l. Man in barrel with books and candle ("Philosophy") 65 55

1984. Christmas. Designs showing details of "Madonna of San Girolamo" by Correggio. Multicoloured.
1239 400 l. Type **325** 45 45
1240 450 l. Virgin and child . . . 55 55
1241 550 l. Attendant 65 65

326 Johann Sebastian Bach and Score **327** State Flags, Stadium and Swimming Pictogram

1985. Europa.
1242 **326** 450 l. black and brown . 80 80
1243 – 600 l. black and green . . 1·25 1·25
DESIGN: 600 l. Vincenzo Bellini and score.

1985. First Small States Games. Multicoloured.
1244 50 l. Type **327** 10 10
1245 350 l. Flags, stadium and running pictogram 35 35
1246 400 l. Flags, stadium and shooting pictogram 40 40
1247 450 l. Flags, stadium and cycling pictogram 45 45
1248 600 l. Flags, stadium and handball pictogram 65 65

328 Sunset and Birds **329** Face and Hand holding Dove

1985. Emigration.
1249 **328** 600 l. multicoloured . . . 60 60

1985. International Youth Year.
1250 **329** 400 l. yellow, blue and gold 40 40
1251 – 600 l. gold, blue and yellow 60 60
DESIGN: 600 l. Girl's face, dove and horse's head.

330 Camera and San Marino **331** Sun breaking through Clouds and Sapling

1985. 18th International Federation of Photographic Art Congress.
1252 **330** 450 l. multicoloured . . 65 60

1985. 10th Anniv of Helsinki European Security and Co-operation Conference.
1253 **331** 600 l. multicoloured . . 60 60

332 Don Abbondio and Don Rodrigo's Henchmen

1985. Birth Bicentenary of Alessandro Manzoni (writer). Scenes from "I Promessi Sposi".
1254 **332** 400 l. green 35 35
1255 – 450 l. brown 40 40
1256 – 600 l. blue 55 55
DESIGNS: 450 l. Forcing curate to bless wedding; 600 l. Plague in Milan.

333 Fish caught on Hook

1985. World Angling Championships, River Arno, Florence.
1257 **333** 600 l. multicoloured . . 60 60

334 Cat (after Pompeian mosaic)

1985. International Feline Federation Congress.
1258 **334** 600 l. multicoloured . . 70 55

335 Colosseum, 85 A.D.

1985. "Italia 85" International Stamp Exhibition, and Important Cities of the World (9th series). Rome. Multicoloured.
1259 1000 l. Type **335** 90 90
1260 1500 l. Colosseum, 1985 . . 1·60 1·60

336 Flying Angel

1985. Christmas. Multicoloured.
1261 400 l. Type **336** 55 55
1262 450 l. Madonna and Child . 60 60
1263 600 l. Angel resting 75 75

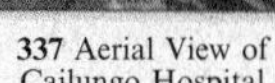

337 Aerial View of Cailungo Hospital **338** "Giotto" Space Probe

1986. 30th Anniv of Social Security Institute (450 l.) and World Health Day (650 l.). Multicoloured.
1264 450 l. Type **337** 65 60
1265 650 l. Front view of Cailungo hospital 70 65

1986. Appearance of Halley's Comet. Multicoloured.
1266 550 l. Type **338** 75 70
1267 1000 l. "Adoration of the Magi" (Giotto) . . . . 1·25 1·10

339 Player and Emblem **340** Deer

1986. World Table Tennis Championships, Rimini.
1268 **339** 450 l. blue, ultram & red . 65 65

1986. Europa. Multicoloured.
1269 550 l. Type **340** . . . . 2·50 2·00
1270 650 l. Common kestrel . . . 4·00 3·50

341 Water Tower, 1870 (lithograph, Charles Shober)

1986. "Ameripex" International Stamp Exhibition, and Important Cities of the World (10th series). Chicago. Multicoloured.
1271 2000 l. Type **341** . . . . . 2·50 2·50
1272 3000 l. Water tower, 1986 . . 3·50 3·50

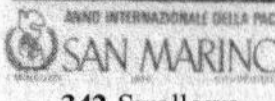

342 Swallows **344** "Apollo dancing with the Muses" (detail, Giulio Romano)

1986. International Peace Year.
1273 **342** 550 l. multicoloured . . . 75 65

1986. 25th Anniv of San Marino Choral Society.
1275 **344** 450 l. multicoloured . . . 60 60

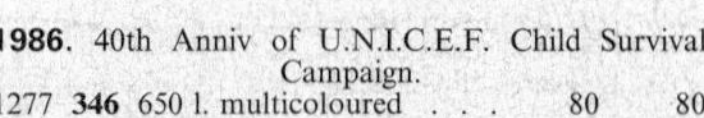

345 Boules Player **346** Boy

1986. European Boules Championships, San Marino.
1276 **345** 550 l. multicoloured . . . 70 70

1986. 40th Anniv of U.N.I.C.E.F. Child Survival Campaign.
1277 **346** 650 l. multicoloured . . . 80 80

347 "St. John the Baptist"

1986. Christmas. Triptych by Hans Memling. Multicoloured.
1278 450 l. Type **347** 75 75
1279 550 l. "Madonna and Child" 85 85
1280 650 l. "St. John the Evangelist" 90 90

348 Motor Car and Route Map (Paris–Peking Rally, 1907)

1987. Motor Rallies. Multicoloured.
1281 500 l. Type **348** 80 80
1282 600 l. Peugeot "205" (15th San Marino Rally) 85 85
1283 700 l. Motor car and crowds (60th anniv of Mille Miglia) 95 95

349 Sketch of Church **350** Modern Sculpture (Reffi Busignani)

1987. Europa. Architecture. Our Lady of Consolation Church, Borgomaggiore (Giovanni Michelucci).
1284 **349** 600 l. black and red . . 2·00 1·75
1285 – 700 l. black and yellow . 2·25 2·00
DESIGN: 700 l. Church interior.

1987. Modern Sculptures in San Marino. Designs showing works by artists named. Multicoloured.
1286 50 l. Type **350** 10 10
1287 100 l. Bini 10 10
1288 200 l. Guguianu 20 20
1289 300 l. Berti 30 30
1290 400 l. Crocetti 40 40
1291 500 l. Berti 45 45
1292 600 l. Messina 55 55
1293 1000 l. Minguzzi 90 90
1294 2200 l. Greco . . . . 2·25 2·00
1295 10000 l. Sassu . . . . 12·00 10·00

351 "Chromatic Invention" (Corrado Cagli) **352** Baroudeur Microlight, San Marino Air Club

1987. Art Biennale.
1300 – 500 l. blue, black & red . 60 60
1301 **351** 600 l. multicoloured . . 80 80
DESIGN: 500 l. "From My Brazilian Diary—Virgin Forest" (Emilio Vedova).

1987.
1302 **352** 600 l. multicoloured . . 90 90

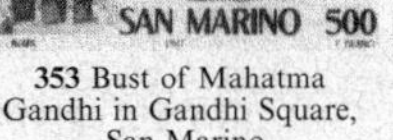

353 Bust of Mahatma Gandhi in Gandhi Square, San Marino **354** Olympic Rings and Hurdler in "Stamp"

1987. "A Society based on Non-violence".
1303 **353** 500 l. multicoloured . . 75 65

1987. "Olymphilex" Olympic Stamp Exhibition and World Light Athletics Championships, Rome.
1304 **354** 600 l. multicoloured . . 70 70

355 Sports Pictograms
357 "The Annunciation" (detail)

356 "View from Round Tower, 1836" (anon)

1987. Mediterranean Games, Syria.
1305 **355** 700 l. red, blue & black . . 80 80

1987. "Hafnia 87" International Stamp Exhibition, and Important Cities of the World (11th series). Copenhagen. Multicoloured.
1306 1200 l. Type **356** . . . . . . 1·50 1·75
1307 2200 l. View from Round Tower, 1987 . . . . 2·00 2·25

1987. Christmas. 600th Birth Anniv of Fra Giovanni of Florence (Beato Angelico). Multicoloured.
1308 600 l. Type **357** 85 85
1309 600 l. Madonna and Child (detail, Triptych of Cortona) 85 85
1310 600 l. Saint (detail, "The Annunciation") 85 85

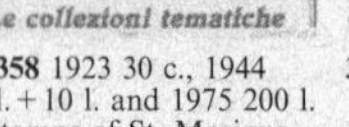

358 1923 30 c., 1944 20 l. + 10 l. and 1975 200 l. Stamps of St. Marinus
359 Maglev Monorail "Bullet" Train and Globe

1988. Thematic Collecting. Multicoloured.
1311 50 l. Type **358** 20 20
1312 150 l. Aerogramme and 1933 3 l. "Graf Zeppelin" stamp (transport) 30 30
1313 300 l. 1954 5 l. and 1981 200 l. motor cycle racing stamps and 1986 meter mark showing motor cycle (sport) 45 45
1314 350 l. 1978 200 l. human rights stamp on cover and 1982 200 l. St. Francis of Assisi stamp (art) 50 50
1315 1000 l. 1949 50 l. Garibaldi stamp, 1985 450 l. Europa stamp and 1952 1 l. Columbus stamp (famous people) . . 1·50 1·50
See also Nos. 1340/4 and 1393/7.

1988. Europa. Transport and Communications. Multicoloured.
1316 600 l. Type **359** . . . . 2·00 2·00
1317 700 l. Optical fibres and globe . 2·50 2·50

360 Carlo Malagola and Palazzo della Mercanzia
361 "La Strada"

1988. 900th Anniv of Bologna University. Mult.
1318 550 l. Type **360** 60 60
1319 650 l. Pietro Ellero and Palazzo del Podesta 75 75
1320 1300 l. Giosue Carducci and Pala dei Mercanti . . . . 1·25 1·25
1321 1700 l. Giovanni Pascoli and Atheneum . . . . 1·50 1·50

1988. Award of Celebrities of Show Business Prize to Federico Fellini (film director). Film posters. Multicoloured.
1322 300 l. Type **361** 35 35
1323 900 l. "La Dolce Vita" . . . 1·10 1·10
1324 1200 l. "Amarcord" . . . . 1·40 1·40

362 Mt Titano from Beach

1988. 40th Riccione Stamp Fair.
1325 **362** 750 l. blue, green & mauve 80 80

363 Healthy Tree with Diseased Roots

1988. Present Day Problems. International AIDS Congress, San Marino.
1326 **363** 250 l. multicoloured . . 35 35
1327 – 350 l. red and black . . 45 45
1328 – 650 l. multicoloured . . 85 85
1329 – 1000 l. multicoloured . . 1·00 1·00
DESIGNS: 350 l. "AIDS" crumbling; 650 l. Knotted cord and emblem of virus; 1000 l. Printed information.

365 "Kurhaus, Scheveningen, 1885" (anon)

1988. "Filacept" International Stamp Exhibition, and Important Cities of the World (12th series). The Hague. Multicoloured.
1331 1600 l. Type **365** . . . . . . 1·50 1·50
1332 3000 l. Kurhaus, Scheveningen, 1988 . . . . 3·00 3·00

366 "Angel with Violin"
367 Bird in Tree (Federica Sparagna)

1988. Christmas. 550th Birth Anniv of Melozzo da Forli. Multicoloured.
1333 650 l. Type **366** 75 75
1334 650 l. "Angel of the Annunciation" (20 × 37 mm) 75 75
1335 650 l. "Angel with Mandolin" 75 75

1989. "Nature is Beautiful. Nature is Useful. Nature is ...". Multicoloured.
1336 200 l. Type **367** 40 30
1337 500 l. Birds beneath tree (Giovanni Monteduro) . . 75 75
1338 650 l. Landscape (Rosa Mannarino) 90 90
Nos. 1336/8 depict the first three winning entries in a children's drawing competition.

1989. Postal History. As T **358**. Multicoloured.
1340 100 l. "San Marino 1977" Exhibition 1000 l. stamp on cover (postal tariffs) . . . 20 15
1341 200 l. 1988 350 l. stamp on cover (cancellations) 30 25
1342 400 l. Parcel receipt (parcel post) 50 45
1343 500 l. Essay by Martin Riester, 1865 . . . . 70 60
1344 1000 l. 1862 handstamp on cover (pre-stamp period) . 1·40 1·25

369 Emblem
370 Oath of the Tennis Court

1989. Sport. Multicoloured.
1345 650 l. Type **369** (30th anniv of San Marino Olympic Committee) 85 85
1346 750 l. Emblems (admission of San Marino Football Federation to UEFA and FIFA) 95 95
1347 850 l. Tennis racquet and ball (San Marino championships) 1·00 1·00
1348 1300 l. Formula 1 racing car (San Marino Grand Prix, Imola) . . . . 1·40 1·40

1989. Bicentenary of French Revolution. Mult.
1349 700 l. Type **370** . . . . 1·00 1·00
1350 1000 l. Arrest of Louis XVI . 1·50 1·50
1351 1800 l. Napoleon's army . . . 2·25 2·25

371 "Marguerite and Armand"
372 "Angel of the Annunciation"

1989. Award of Celebrities of Show Business Prize to Rudolph Nureyev (ballet dancer). Multicoloured.
1352 1200 l. Type **371** . . . . . . 1·40 1·40
1353 1500 l. "Apollo Musagete" . 1·75 1·75
1354 1700 l. Ken Russell's film "Valentino" . . . . 2·25 2·25

1989. Christmas. Details of the polyptych in Church of Servants of Mary. Multicoloured.
1355 650 l. Type **372** . . . . 1·00 1·00
1356 650 l. "Nativity" (50 × 40 mm) 1·00 1·00
1357 650 l. Mary ("Annunciation") 1·00 1·00

373 Capitol, 1850

1989. "World Stamp Expo '89" Int Stamp Exhibition, and Important Cities of the World (13th series). Washington D.C. Multicoloured.
1358 2000 l. Type **373** . . . . . 2·25 2·25
1359 2500 l. Capitol, 1989 . . . . 3·00 3·00

374 Old Post Office
375 "Martyrdom of St. Agatha" (Tiepolo) and Cardinal Alberoni leaving City

1990. Europa. Post Office Buildings. Multicoloured.
1360 700 l. Type **374** . . . . 1·00 1·00
1361 800 l. Dogana Post Office . . 1·25 1·25

1990. 250th Anniv of End of Cardinal Alberoni's Occupation of San Marino.
1362 **375** 3500 l. multicoloured . . 3·75 3·75

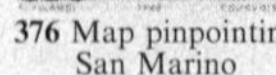

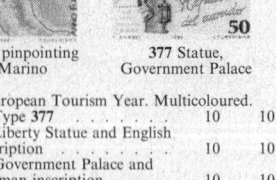

376 Map pinpointing San Marino
377 Statue, Government Palace

1990. European Tourism Year. Multicoloured.
1366 50 l. Type **377** 10 10
1367 50 l. Liberty Statue and English inscription 10 10
1368 50 l. Government Palace and German inscription 10 10
1369 50 l. Man with flag and French inscription 10 10
1363 600 l. Type **376** 80 80
1364 600 l. Aerial view showing villages 80 80
1365 600 l. First Tower 80 80
See also Nos. 1424/7.

379 Olivier in "Hamlet"
380 Mt Titano and State Flags

1990. Award of Celebrities of Show Business Prize to Laurence Olivier (actor). Multicoloured.
1374 600 l. Type **379** 90 90
1375 700 l. "Richard III" . . . . 1·10 1·10
1376 1500 l. "The Runner" . . . 2·50 2·50
Nos. 1374/6 are wrongly inscribed "Lawrence".

1990. Visit of President Francesco Cossiga of Italy.
1377 **380** 600 l. multicoloured . . 75 75

381 Pinocchio

1990. Death Centenary of Carlo Collodi (writer). Characters from "Pinocchio". Multicoloured.
1378 250 l. Type **381** 30 30
1379 400 l. Geppetto 50 50
1380 450 l. Blue fairy 55 55
1381 600 l. Cat and wolf 90 90

382 Pre-Columbian Civilizations

1990. 500th Anniv (1992) of Discovery of America by Columbus (1st issue). Multicoloured.
1382 1500 l. Type **382** . . . . . 2·25 2·25
1383 2000 l. Produce of the New World . . . . 2·50 2·50
See also Nos. 1401/2 and 1417/18.

383 Mary and Two Kings
384 Swallowtail on "Ephedra major"

1990. Christmas. Details of Cuciniello Crib. Multicoloured.
1384 750 l. Type **383** . . . . . . 1·00 1·00
1385 750 l. Baby Jesus in manger and third King . . . . 1·00 1·00
Nos. 1384/5 were issued together, se-tenant, forming a composite design.

1990. Flora and Fauna. Multicoloured.
1386 200 l. Type **384** 30 25
1387 300 l. "Apoderus coryli" (weevil) and hazelnut . . . 40 35
1388 500 l. Garden dormouse and acorns of holm oak . . . 70 60
1389 1000 l. Green lizard and "Ophrys bertolonii" (orchid) 1·50 1·50
1390 2000 l. Firecrest on black pine 3·50 3·25

385 Launch of "Ariane-4"

1991. Europa. Europe in Space. Multicoloured.
1391 750 l. Type **385** . . . . . . 3·25 3·00
1392 800 l. "E.R.S.-1." survey satellite 3·25 3·00

1991. World of Stamps. As T **358**. Multicoloured
1393 100 l. Stamp shop 20 15
1394 150 l. Stamp club 25 20
1395 200 l. Exhibition 30 25

1396 450 l. Stamp album and catalogues 60 50
1397 1500 l. Philatelic publications (25th anniv of Italian Philatelic Press Union) . . 1·75 1·75

386 Torch Bearer leaving Athens
387 Cat

1991. Olympic Games, Barcelona (1992). Mult.
1398 400 l. Type **386** 50 50
1399 600 l. Torch bearer passing through San Marino . . . 70 70
1400 2000 l. Torch bearer arriving in Barcelona . . . . 2·50 2·50

1991. 500th Anniv (1992) of Discovery of America by Columbus (2nd issue). As T **382**. Multicoloured.
1401 750 l. Navigational dividers, quadrant, hour-glass, compass and route map . . 1·25 1·25
1402 3000 l. "Santa Maria", "Nina" and "Pinta" . . . . 4·50 4·50

1991. Pets. Multicoloured.
1403 500 l. Type **387** 70 70
1404 550 l. Hamster on wheel . . 75 75
1405 750 l. Great Dane and Pomeranian . . . . 1·10 1·10
1406 1000 l. Aquarium fishes . . . 1·40 1·40
1407 1200 l. Canaries in cage . . . 1·75 1·75

388 Players, Balls and Baskets
391 Keep

389 James Clerk-Maxwell (physicist)

1991. Centenary of Basketball. Multicoloured.
1408 650 l. Type **388** . . . . 1·00 1·00
1409 750 l. James Naismith (inventor) and players . . . . 1·25 1·25

1991. 100 Years of Radio (1st issue).
1410 **389** 750 l. multicoloured . . . 90 90
Clerk-Maxwell formulated the theory of electromagnetic radiation.
See also Nos. 1431, 1452, 1479 and 1521/2.

1991. Christmas. La Rocca Fortress. Multicoloured.
1412 600 l. Type **391** (postage) . . 75 75
1413 750 l. Inland view of fortress 90 90
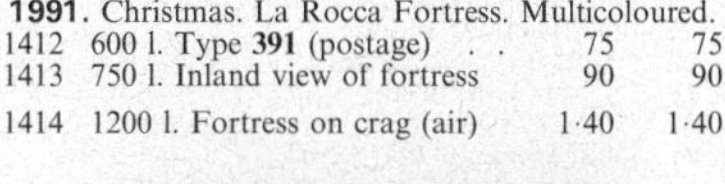
1414 1200 l. Fortress on crag (air) 1·40 1·40

392 "Bianca and Falliero" (Pesaro production)

1992. Birth Bicentenary of Gioachino Rossini (composer). Scenes from productions of his operas. Multicoloured.
1415 750 l. Type **392** 80 80
1416 1200 l. "The Barber of Seville" (La Scala Theatre, Milan) . 1·25 1·25

1992. 500th Anniv of Discovery of America by Columbus (3rd issue). As T **382**. Multicoloured.
1417 1500 l. Amerindians watching fleet . . . . 1·50 1·50
1418 2000 l. Route map of the four voyages . . . . 2·00 2·00

393 Roses
394 Courting Couple

1992. Plants. Multicoloured.
1419 50 l. Type **393** 10 10
1420 200 l. Ficus as house plant . 20 20
1421 300 l. Orchid in conservatory 30 30
1422 450 l. Cacti in pots 45 45
1423 5000 l. Pelargoniums in trough 5·00 5·00

1992. Tourism. Multicoloured. (a) As T **377**.
1424 50 l. Man with crossbow and Italian inscription 10 10
1425 50 l. Tennis player and English inscription 10 10
1426 50 l. Motor cycle rider and French inscription 10 10
1427 50 l. Ferrari racing car and German inscription . . . 10 10

(b) As T **394**.
1428 600 l. Type **394** 65 65
1429 600 l. Man in restaurant . . 65 65
1430 600 l. Woman reading on veranda 65 65

1992. 100 Years of Radio (2nd issue). As T **389**. Multicoloured.
1431 750 l. Heinrich Rudolf Hertz (physicist) 80 80
Hertz proved Clerk-Maxwell's theory.

395 Egg-shaped Globe and Caravel
397 Inedible Mushrooms

1992. Europa. 500th Anniv of Discovery of America. Multicoloured.
1432 750 l. Type **395** . . . . 1·50 1·40
1433 850 l. Caravel and island inside broken egg . . . . 1·75 1·60

1992. 3rd Titano Mycological Exhibition, Borgo Maggiore. Multicoloured.
1435 250 l. Type **397** 40 25
1436 250 l. Inedible mushrooms (different) 40 25
1437 350 l. Edible mushrooms in bowl 50 35
1438 350 l. Edible mushrooms on cloth 50 35
Stamps of the same value were issued together, se-tenant, each pair forming a composite design.

398 View and Arms of San Marino
399 "La Sacra Conversazione"

1992. Admission of San Marino to United Nations Organization. Multicoloured.
1439 1000 l. Type **398** . . . . . . 1·00 1·00
1440 1000 l. View of San Marino (different) and United Nations emblem . . . . . 1·00 1·00

1992. Christmas. 500th Death Anniv of Piero della Francesca (artist). Multicoloured.
1441 750 l. Type **399** 90 90
1442 750 l. Close-up of Madonna 90 90
1443 750 l. Close-up of shell decoration 90 90

400 Tennis Player
401 Stars

1993. Sporting Events. Multicoloured.
1444 300 l. Type **400** (Italian and San Marino Youth Games) . . 30 30
1445 400 l. Cross-country skiers (European Youth Olympic Days (winter), Aosta, Italy) 40 40
1446 550 l. Runners (European Youth Olympic Days (summer), Eindhoven, Netherlands) 50 50
1447 600 l. Fisherman (Freshwater Angling Clubs World Championship, Ostellato, Italy) 60 60
1448 700 l. Runners breasting tape (Small States Games, Malta) 70 70
1449 1300 l. Sprinters (Mediterranean Games, Rousillon, France) 1·25 1·25

1993. Europa. Contemporary Art.
1450 **401** 750 l. multicoloured . . . 90 90
1451 – 850 l. blue and orange . . 1·10 1·10
DESIGN: 850 l. Silhouette.

1993. 100 Years of Radio (3rd issue). As T **389**. Multicoloured.
1452 750 l. Edouard Branly (physicist) and his "radioconductor" 95 95
Branly developed a method of revealing Hertzian waves.

404 Scarce Swallowtail ("Iphidides podalirius") on Wild Apple
406 Carlo Goldoni

1993. Butterflies. Multicoloured.
1454 250 l. Type **404** 35 35
1455 250 l. Clouded yellow ("Colias crocea") on wild vetch . . 35 35
1456 250 l. Glanville's fritillary ("Melitaea anxia") 35 35
1457 250 l. Camberwell beauty ("Nymphalis antiopa") on white willow 35 35

1993. Death Anniversaries. Multicoloured.
1459 550 l. Type **406** (dramatist, bicentenary) 45 45
1460 650 l. Horace (Quintus Horatius Flaccus) (poet) (2000th anniv) 55 55
1461 850 l. Scene from opera "Orpheus" by Claudio Monteverdi (composer, 350th anniv) (horiz) 75 75
1462 1850 l. Guy de Maupassant (writer, centenary) (horiz) . 1·60 1·60

407 San Marino

1993. Christmas. Multicoloured.
1463 600 l. Type **407** 45 45
1464 750 l. "Adoration of the Child" (Gerrit van Honthorst) (horiz) 65 65
1465 859 l. "Adoration of the Shepherds" (Van Honthorst) 75 75

408 Long-haired Dachshund

1994. 10th International Dog Show. Multicoloured.
1466 350 l. Type **408** 30 30
1467 400 l. Afghan hound 30 30
1468 450 l. Belgian tervuren shepherd dog 35 35
1469 500 l. Boston terrier 40 40
1470 550 l. Mastiff 45 45
1471 600 l. Malamute 55 55

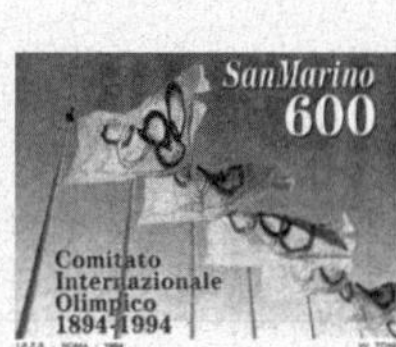
410 Gate
411 Olympic Flags

1994. Gardens. Multicoloured.
1473 100 l. Type **410** 10 10
1474 200 l. Pergola 15 15
1475 300 l. Well 25 25
1476 450 l. Gazebo 35 35
1477 1850 l. Pond . . . . 1·50 1·50

1994. Centenary of International Olympic Committee.
1478 **411** 600 l. multicoloured . . . 55 55

1994. 100 Years of Radio (4th issue). As T **389**. Multicoloured.
1479 750 l. Aleksandr Stepanovich Popov 80 80
Popov was the first to use a suspended wire as an aerial.

412 Players
413 Route Map

1994. World Cup Football Championship, U.S.A. Multicoloured.
1480 600 l. Type **412** 45 45
1481 600 l. Player kicking ball . . 45 45
1482 600 l. Player heading ball . . 45 45
1483 600 l. Players tackling . . . 45 45
1484 600 l. Goalkeeper saving goal 45 45

1994. Europa. Discoveries. Exploration of Sun by "Ulysses" Space Probe Multicoloured.
1485 750 l. Type **413** 75 75
1486 850 l. "Ulysses" approaching Sun 90 90

414 Government Palace
416 Angels playing Musical Instruments

415 St. Mark's Basilica

1994. Centenary of Government Palace. Multicoloured.
1487 150 l. Type **414** 10 10
1488 600 l. Tower and San Marino from ramparts 50 50
1489 650 l. Clock-tower 55 55
1490 1000 l. Government chamber (horiz) 90 90

1994. 900th Anniv of Dedication of St. Mark's Basilica, Venice.
1491 **415** 750 l. multicoloured . . 4·25 4·25

1994. Christmas. 500th Death Anniv of Giovanni Santi (painter). Details of "The Enthroned Madonna and Child with Saints". Multicoloured.
1493 600 l. Type **416** 50 50
1494 750 l. Madonna and child . . 60 60
1495 850 l. Angel playing harp . . 75 75

417/420 "Italy on the Road in a Sea of Flowering Greenery"

1994. Centenary of Italian Touring Club.
1496 **417** 1000 l. multicoloured . . 85 85
1497 **418** 1000 l. multicoloured . . 85 85
1498 **419** 1000 l. multicoloured . . 85 85
1499 **420** 1000 l. multicoloured . . 85 85
Nos. 1496/9 were issued together, se-tenant, forming the composite design illustrated.

421 Cyclist

422 Flora and Fauna

1995. Sporting Events. Multicoloured.
1500 100 l. Type **421** (Junior World Cycling Championships, Italy and San Marino) 10 10
1501 500 l. Volleyball (centenary) . 40 40
1502 650 l. Skater (Men's Speed-skating Championships, Baselga di Pine, Italy) . . . 55 55
1503 850 l. Sprinter (World Athletics Championships, Gothenburg, Sweden) 75 75

1995. European Nature Conservation Year. Multicoloured.
1504 600 l. Type **422** 50 50
1505 600 l. Frog, lizard and water lily 50 50
1506 600 l. Water lily, bird and ladybirds 50 50
1507 600 l. Butterfly, white-headed duckling and frog 50 50
1508 600 l. Mallard and duckling . 50 50
Nos. 1504/8 were issued together, se-tenant, forming a composite design of river life.

423 U.N. Emblem

1995. 50th Anniv of U.N.O. Multicoloured.
1509 550 l. Type **423** 45 45
1510 600 l. Rose with emblem . . 50 50
1511 650 l. Hourglass 60 60
1512 1200 l. Rainbow and emblem forming "50" . . . . . . 1·00 1·00

424 Mute Swans over Coastline

1995. Europa. Peace and Freedom. Multicoloured.
1513 750 l. Type **424** 65 65
1514 850 l. Landscape 75 75

425 Basilica and "Legend of the True Cross" (detail of fresco, Agnolo Gaddi)

1995. 700th Anniv of Santa Croce Basilica, Florence. Multicoloured.
1515 1200 l. Type **425** . . . . . . 1·00 1·00
1516 1250 l. Pazzi Chapel and "Madonna and Child with Saints" (Andrea della Robbia) . . . . 1·10 1·10

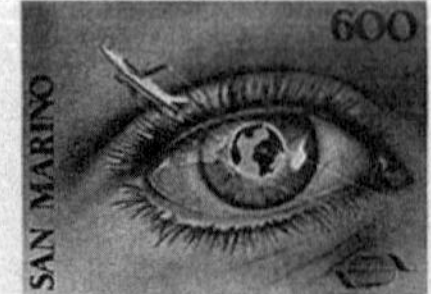

426 Eye and Airplane

1995. 20th Anniv of World Tourism Organization. Multicoloured.
1517 600 l. Type **426** 50 50
1518 750 l. Five ribbons (continents) around La Rocca fortress . 65 65
1519 850 l. Airplane and postcards circling globe 75 75
1520 1200 l. Five ribbons around globe . . . . 1·00 1·00

427 Guglielmo Marconi and Transmitter

1995. 100 Years of Radio (5th issue). Centenary of First Radio Transmission. Multicoloured.
1521 850 l. Type **427** 90 90
1522 850 l. Radio frequency dial . 90 90

429 Qianmen Complex, 1914

1995. "Beijing 1995" International Stamp and Coin Exhibition, Peking, and Important Cities of the World (14th series). Multicoloured.
1524 1500 l. Type **429** . . . . . . 1·25 1·25
1525 1500 l. Qianmen complex, 1995 1·25 1·25

430 "The Anunciation" (detail of illuminated MS)

1995. "Neri of Rimini" Art and Literature Exn.
1526 **430** 650 l. multicoloured . . 50 50

431 Reindeer pulling Sleigh

433 Throwing the Discus

432 Cheetah

1995. Christmas. Multicoloured.
1527 750 l. Type **431** 60 60
1528 750 l. Children dancing around Christmas tree 60 60
1529 750 l. Wise Men approaching stable with crib 60 60
Nos. 1527/9 were issued together, se-tenant, forming a composite design.

1995. Inauguration of San Marino Express Mail Service.
1530 **432** 6000 l. multicoloured . . 4·75 4·75

1996. Centenary of Modern Olympic Games. Multicoloured.
1531 100 l. Type **433** 10 10
1532 500 l. Wrestling 40 40
1533 650 l. Long jumping 55 55
1534 1500 l. Throwing the javelin . . 1·25 1·25
1535 2500 l. Running . . . . . . 2·10 2·10

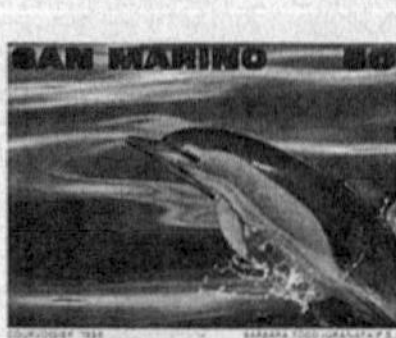

434 Dolphin swimming

1996. 3rd "Nature World" Exhibition, Rimini. Multicoloured.
1536 50 l. Type **434** 10 10
1537 100 l. Frog on leaf 10 10
1538 150 l. Penguins in snow . . . 10 10
1539 1000 l. Butterfly on flower . . 80 80
1540 3000 l. Ducks flying over water 2·40 2·40

435 Mother Theresa of Calcutta

1996. Europa. Famous Women.
1541 **435** 750 l. multicoloured . . . 60 60

436 Marco Polo and Palace in the Forbidden City

1996. 700th Anniv (1995) of Marco Polo's Return from Asia and "China '96" International Stamp Exhibition, Peking.
1542 **436** 1250 l. multicoloured . . 1·00 1·00

437 Great Wall of China

1996. 25th Anniv of San Marino–China Diplomatic Relations. Multicoloured.
1543 750 l. Type **437** 60 60
1544 750 l. Walled rampart, San Marino 60 60
Nos. 1543/4 were issued together, se-tenant, forming a composite design.

438 Traditional Weaving

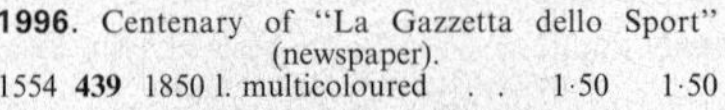

439 Front Page

1996. "Medieval Days" Traditional Festival. Multicoloured.
1546 750 l. Type **438** 60 60
1547 750 l. Potter 60 60
1548 750 l. Traditional craftswoman 60 60
1549 750 l. Playing traditional game 60 60
1550 750 l. Trumpeters (horiz) . . 60 60
1551 750 l. Flag display (horiz) . . 60 60
1552 750 l. Crossbow tournament (horiz) 60 60
1553 750 l. Dancing and playing musical instruments (horiz) 60 60

1996. Centenary of "La Gazzetta dello Sport" (newspaper).
1554 **439** 1850 l. multicoloured . . 1·50 1·50

440 Applauding Crowd

1996. 33rd "Festivalbar" Song Festival.
1555 **440** 2000 l. multicoloured . . 1·60 1·60

441 Enrico Caruso and "O Sole Mio"

1996. Italian Music. Singers and Their Songs. Multicoloured.
1556 750 l. Type **441** 60 60
1557 750 l. Armando Gill and "Come Pioveva" 60 60
1558 750 l. Ettore Petrolini and "Gastone" 60 60
1559 750 l. Vittorio de Sica and "Parlami d'Amore Mariu" . 60 60
1560 750 l. Odoardo Spadaro and "La porti un bacione a Firenze" 60 60
1561 750 l. Alberto Rabagliati and "O mia bela Madonina" . 60 60
1562 750 l. Beniamino Gigli and "Mamma" 60 60
1563 750 l. Claudio Villa and "Luna rossa" 60 60
1564 750 l. Secondo Casadei and "Romagna Mia" 60 60
1565 750 l. Renato Rascel and "Arrivederci Roma" . . . 60 60
1566 750 l. Fred Buscaglione and "Guarda che luna" 60 60
1567 750 l. Domenico Modugno and "Nel blu, dipinto di blu" . 60 60

442 Yellowstone National Park, United States

1996. 50th Anniv of U.N.E.S.C.O. World Heritage Sites. Multicoloured.
1568 450 l. Type **442** 35 35
1569 500 l. Prehistoric cave paintings, Vezere Valley, France . . 40 40
1570 650 l. San Gimignano, Italy . 50 50
1571 1450 l. Wies Pilgrimage Church, Germany . . . . 1·10 1·10

443 Hen and Chicks

1996. 50th Anniv of U.N.I.C.E.F. Multicoloured.
1572 550 l. Type **443** 45 45
1573 1000 l. Chicks in nest 80 80

444 Playing Lotto

1996. Christmas. Multicoloured.
1574 750 l. Type **444** 60 60
1575 750 l. Hanging decoration . 60 60
1576 750 l. Father Christmas on sleigh and child reading book 60 60
1577 750 l. Christmas tree 60 60
1578 750 l. Bowls of fruit and nuts 60 60
1579 750 l. Snowflakes and shooting star 60 60
1580 750 l. Children's toys 60 60
1581 750 l. Presents 60 60
1582 750 l. Hanging Father Christmas decoration . . . 60 60
1583 750 l. Nativity scene 60 60
1584 750 l. Mistletoe 60 60
1585 750 l. Stocking hanging on mantelpiece 60 60
1586 750 l. Family celebrating . . 60 60
1587 750 l. Christmas tree outside window and party 60 60
1588 750 l. Snowman outside window and party 60 60
1589 750 l. Calendar pages and bottle of champagne (New Year's celebrations) 60 60
Nos. 1574/89 were issued together, se-tenant, forming a composite design.

446/449 Championship Races

1997. World Skiing Championships, Sestriere.
1591 **446** 1000 l. multicoloured . . 80 80
1592 **447** 1000 l. multicoloured . . 80 80
1593 **448** 1000 l. multicoloured . . 80 80
1594 **449** 1000 l. multicoloured . . 80 80
Nos. 1591/4 were issued together, se-tenant, forming the composite design illustrated.

450 Acquaviva

1997. Communes. Multicoloured.
1595 100 l. Type **450** 10 10
1596 200 l. Borgomaggiore 15 15
1597 250 l. Chiesanuova 20 20
1598 400 l. Domagnano 30 30
1599 500 l. Faetano 40 40
1600 550 l. Fiorentino 45 45
1601 650 l. Montegiardino 50 50
1602 750 l. Serravalle 60 60
1603 5000 l. San Marino . . . . . 4·00 4·00

451 St. Marinus tames the Bear

1997. Europa. Tales and Legends. Multicoloured.
1604 650 l. Type **451** 50 50
1605 750 l. Felicissima begs St. Marinus to cure her son Verissimus 60 60

EXPRESS LETTER STAMPS

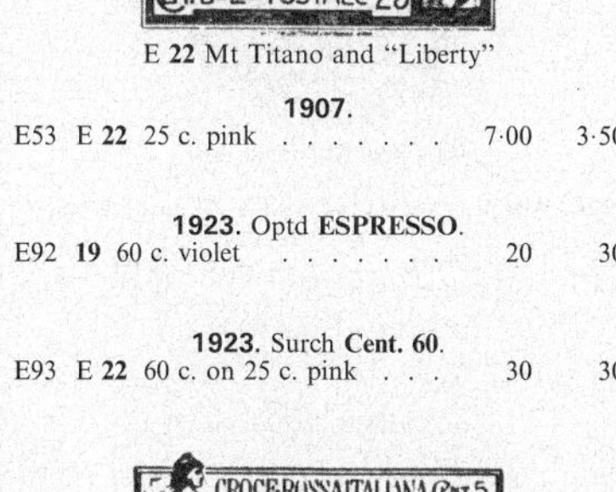

E 22 Mt Titano and "Liberty"

1907.
E53 **E 22** 25 c. pink . . . . 7·00 3·50

1923. Optd **ESPRESSO**.
E92 **19** 60 c. violet 20 30

1923. Surch **Cent. 60**.
E93 **E 22** 60 c. on 25 c. pink . . . 30 30

E 34

1923. Red Cross.
E101 **E 34** 60 c. + 5 c. red . . . 70 80

1926. No. E92 surch **Lire 1,25**.
E134 **19** 1 l. 25 on 60 c. violet . . 55 55

1927. No. E93 surch **L. 1,25** and bars over old surch.
E138 **E 22** 1 l. 25 on 60 c. on 25 c. pink 45 45

E 50 Statue of Liberty and View of San Marino

1929. As Type **E 50** but without "UNION POSTALE UNIVERSELLE" and inscr "ESPRESSO".
E164 **E 50** 1 l. 25 green 15 15

1929. Optd **UNION POSTALE UNIVERSELLE** as in Type **E 50**.
E165 **E 50** 2 l. 50 blue 55 55

E 78

1943.
E305 **E 78** 1 l. 25 green 10 10
E306 2 l. 50 orange 10 10

E 79 Mt Titano

1945.
E307 **E 79** 2 l. 50 green 10 10
E308 5 l. orange 10 10
E309 5 l. red 65 65
E310 10 l. blue . . . . . . 1·90 1·40
E419 60 l. red . . . . 6·00 4·00

E 87 Pegasus and Mt Titano

1946.
E337 **E 87** 30 l. blue . . . . . . 6·00 4·00
E420 80 l. blue . . . . . . 6·00 4·00

1947. Surch.
E339 **E 79** 15 l. on 5 l. red . . . 30 25
E340 15 l. on 10 l. blue . . 30 25
E374 **E 87** 35 l. on 30 l. blue . . 48·00 22·00
E341 60 l. on 30 l. blue . . 4·25 4·25
E545 **E 79** 75 l. on 60 l. red . . 2·25 1·75
E375 **E 87** 80 l. on 30 l. blue . . 20·00 14·00
E546 100 l. on 80 l. blue . . 2·25 1·75
E783 **E 180** 120 l. on 75 l. black and yellow 15 15
E784 135 l. on 100 l. black and orange 15 15

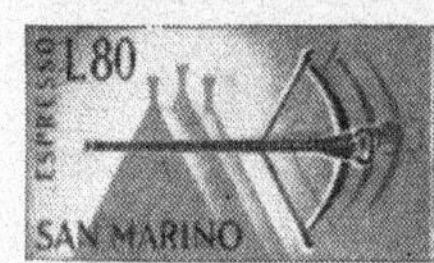

E 180 Crossbow and Three "Castles"

1966.
E800 **E 180** 75 l. black and yellow 10 10
E801 80 l. black and purple 10 10
E802 100 l. black & orange 10 10
No. E800 has crossbow in white without "shadows".

PARCEL POST STAMPS

Unused and used prices are for complete pairs.

P 46

1928.
P145 **P 46** 5 c. purple and blue . 10 10
P146 10 c. blue and light blue 10 10
P147 20 c. black and blue . 10 10
P148 25 c. red and blue . . 10 10
P149 30 c. ultramarine & blue 10 10
P150 30 c. orange and blue . 10 10
P151 60 c. red and blue . . 10 10
P152 1 l. violet and red . . 15 15
P153 2 l. green and red . . 20 20
P154 3 l. bistre and red . . 25 25
P155 4 l. grey and red . . . 30 30
P156 10 l. mauve and red . . 1·40 1·40
P157 12 l. lake and red . . 5·00 5·00
P158 15 l. green and red . . 8·00 8·00
P159 20 l. purple and red . 10·00 10·00

1945.
P309 **P 46** 5 c. purple and red . . 10 10
P310 10 c. brown and black 10 10
P311 20 c. red and green . . 10 10
P312 25 c. yellow and black 10 10
P313 30 c. mauve and red 10 10
P314 50 c. violet and black . 10 10
P315 60 c. red and black . . 10 10
P316 1 l. brown and blue . . 10 10
P317 2 l. brown and blue . . 10 10
P318 3 l. grey and brown . . 10 10
P319 4 l. green and brown 10 10
P320 10 l. grey and violet 10 10
P770 10 l. green and red . . 15 15
P321 12 l. green and blue . 2·50 1·25
P322 15 l. green and violet . 2·00 1·25
P323 20 l. violet and brown 1·60 1·25
P324 25 l. red and blue . . 32·00 20·00
P771 50 l. yellow and red . 15 15
P455 300 l. violet and red . £120 90·00
P773 300 l. violet and brown 40 40
P526 500 l. brown and red . 2·00 2·25
P775 1000 l. green and brown 75 1·00

1948. Nos. P324 and P771 surch in figures and wavy lines on each half of design.
P524 **P 46** 100 l. on 50 l. yellow and red 60 50
P375 200 l. on 25 l. red & blue £170 85·00

POSTAGE DUE STAMPS

D 18

D 82

1897.
D38 **D 18** 5 c. brown and green . 10 10
D39 10 c. brown and green . 10 10
D40 30 c. brown and green . 40 30
D41 50 c. brown and green . 1·00 75
D42 60 c. brown and green . 2·75 2·25
D43 1 l. brown and pink . . 1·75 1·10
D44 3 l. brown and pink . . 7·50 7·50
D45 5 l. brown and pink . 32·00 16·00
D46 10 l. brown and pink . . 8·50 15·00

1924.
D102 **D 18** 5 c. brown and red . . 10 10
D103 10 c. brown and red . 10 10
D104 30 c. brown and red . 15 15
D105 50 c. brown and red . 30 30
D106 60 c. brown and red . 2·00 2·00
D107 1 l. brown and green . 3·00 3·00
D108 3 l. brown and green . 10·00 10·00
D109 5 l. brown and green . 12·00 12·00
D109 5 l. brown and green . £120 £120

1925.
D111 **D 18** 5 c. brown and red . . 10 10
D113 10 c. brown and red . 10 10
D114 15 c. brown and blue . 10 10
D115 20 c. brown and blue . 20 20
D116 25 c. brown and blue . 35 35
D117 30 c. brown and blue . 15 15
D118 40 c. brown and blue . 1·75 1·40
D119 50 c. brown and blue . 25 25
D120 60 c. brown and blue . 80 70
D121 1 l. brown and orange . 2·00 50
D122 2 l. brown and orange . 80 90
D123 3 l. brown and orange . 32·00 15·00
D124 5 l. brown and orange . 8·00 2·25
D125 10 l. brown & orange . 12·00 3·75
D126 15 l. brown & orange . 60 60
D127 25 l. brown & orange . 24·00 12·00
D128 30 l. brown & orange . 3·75 5·50
D129 50 l. brown & orange . 4·75 6·00

1931. As Type **D 18** but with centre obliterated in black and new value superimposed in silver.
D164 **D 18** 15 c. on 5 c. blue . . . 10 10
D165 15 c. on 10 c. blue . . 10 10
D166 15 c. on 30 c. blue . . 10 10
D167 20 c. on 5 c. blue . . 10 10
D168 20 c. on 10 c. blue . . 10 10
D169 20 c. on 30 c. blue . . 10 10
D170 25 c. on 5 c. blue . . 65 25
D171 25 c. on 10 c. blue . . 65 25
D172 25 c. on 30 c. blue . . 5·00 2·50
D173 40 c. on 10 c. blue . . 35 10
D174 40 c. on 10 c. blue . . 50 10
D175 40 c. on 30 c. blue . . 50 10
D176 2 l. on 5 c. blue . . . 25·00 16·00
D177 2 l. on 10 c. blue . . . 42·00 26·00
D178 2 l. on 30 c. blue . . . 32·00 20·00

1936. Surch in figures and words and bars. D233/8 and D242 are brown and blue; the rest brown and orange.
D233 **D 18** 10 c. on 5 c. 25 25
D234 25 c. on 30 c. . . . . . 6·00 5·00
D236 50 c. on 5 c. . . . . . 1·60 70
D237 1 l. on 30 c. . . . . . 20·00 3·25
D238 1 l. on 40 c. . . . . . 5·00 3·00
D239 1 l. on 3 l. . . . . . 16·00 1·00
D240 1 l. on 25 l. . . . . . 45·00 6·50
D241 2 l. on 15 l. . . . . . 17·00 9·00
D242 3 l. on 20 c. . . . . . 20·00 14·00
D243 25 l. on 50 l. . . . . . 1·25 1·75

1945.
D309 **D 82** 5 c. green 10 10
D310 10 c. brown 10 10
D311 15 c. red 10 10
D312 20 c. blue 10 10
D313 25 c. violet 10 10
D314 30 c. mauve 10 10
D315 40 c. yellow 10 10
D316 50 c. grey 10 10
D317 60 c. brown 10 10
D318 1 l. orange 10 10
D319 2 l. red 15 15
D320 5 l. violet 20 20
D321 10 l. blue 25 25
D322 20 l. green . . . . . 8·50 5·00
D323 25 l. brown . . . . . 8·50 5·00
D324 50 l. brown . . . . . 8·50 5·00

SANTANDER Pt. 20

One of the states of the Granadine Confederation.

A department of Colombia from 1886, now uses Colombian stamps.

100 centavos = 1 peso

1

2

1884. Imperf.
1 **1** 1 c. blue 15 15
2 5 c. red 30 25
3 10 c. violet 50 50

1886. Imperf.
4 **2** 1 c. blue 40 40
5 5 c. red 15 15
6 10 c. lilac 20 20

1887. As T **1** but inscr "REPUBLICA DE COLOMBIA". Imperf.
7 1 c. blue 15 15
8 5 c. red 45 45
9 10 c. violet . . . . 1·50 1·50

3

4

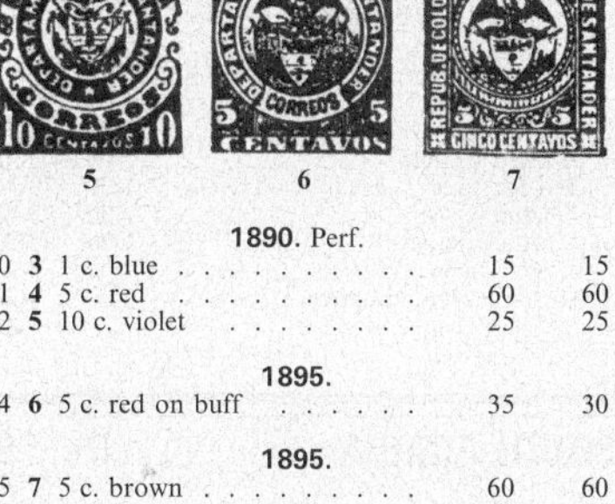

5 **6** **7**

1890. Perf.
10 **3** 1 c. blue 15 15
11 **4** 5 c. red 60 60
12 **5** 10 c. violet 25 25

1895.
14 **6** 5 c. red on buff 35 30

1895.
15 **7** 5 c. brown 60 60
16 5 c. green 60 60

8

9

10

1899.
17 **8** 1 c. black on green 20 20
18 **9** 5 c. black on red 20 20
19 **10** 10 c. blue 35 35

F 11

1903. Fiscal stamp as Type **F 11** optd **Provisional Correos de Santander**. Imperf.
21 **F 11** 50 c. red 20 20

SARDINIA Pt. 8

A former Italian kingdom, including the island of Sardinia, a large part of the mainland and parts of what is now south-east France. The Kingdom of Italy was formed by the adhesion of other Italian states to Sardinia, whose king became the first ruler of united Italy.

100 centesimi = 1 lira

1 Victor Emmanuel II **2**

1851. Imperf.

1 1 5 c. black £2750 £1600
3 20 c. blue £3000 80·00
7 40 c. pink £3000 £3000

1853. Embossed on coloured paper. Imperf.

9 1 5 c. on green £5000 £900
10 20 c. on blue £5000 80·00
11 40 c. on pink £3250 £850

1854. Embossed on white paper. Imperf.

13 1 5 c. green £24000 £425
15 20 c. blue £7500 70·00
18 40 c. red £65000 £2250

1855. Head embossed. Imperf.

28 2 5 c. green 3·00 9·50
40 10 c. bistre 3·00 5·00
39 10 c. brown 28·00 11·00
35 10 c. grey 70·00 55·00
48 20 c. blue 42·00 5·00
55 40 c. red 8·00 16·00
60 80 c. yellow 11·00 £130
61 3 l. bronze £250 £2500

For Type 2 perf, see Italy Nos. 1/4.

NEWSPAPER STAMPS

N 3

1861. Numerals embossed. Imperf.

N62 N 3 1 c. black 70 2·25
N63 2 c. black 48·00 48·00

For 2 c. stamps of similar types in yellow see Italy No. N5.

SASENO Pt. 3

An island off the W. coast of Albania, temporarily occupied by Italy.

100 centesimi = 1 lira

1923. Stamps of Italy optd **SASENO**.

1 38 10 c. red 1·00 3·75
2 15 c. grey 1·00 3·75
3 41 20 c. orange 1·00 3·75
4 39 25 c. blue 1·00 3·75
5 30 c. brown 1·00 3·75
6 50 c. mauve 1·00 3·75
7 60 c. red 2·00 4·25
8 34 1 l. brown and green 2·00 4·25

SAUDI ARABIA Pt. 19

Formerly under Turkish rule, the Hejaz became an independent kingdom in 1916 but was conquered in 1925 by the Sultan of Nejd. In 1926 the two kingdoms were combined. In 1932 the name of the state was changed to the Saudi Arabian Kingdom.

1916. 40 paras = 1 piastre.
1929. 110 guerche = 10 riyal = 1 gold sovereign.
1952. 440 guerche = 40 riyal = 1 gold sovereign.
1960. 100 halalah = 20 guerche = 1 riyal.
(1 piastre = 1 guerche.)

A. HEJAZ

5 From Stucco Work over Entrance to Cairo Railway Station

1916. As T **5** (various Arabic designs). Perf or roul.

11 5 1 pa. purple 2·00 65
12 – $\frac{1}{8}$ pi. yellow 2·25 1·00
13 – $\frac{1}{4}$ pi. green 2·25 1·10
14 – $\frac{1}{2}$ pi. red 2·40 1·50
15 – 1 pi. blue 2·40 1·50
16 – 2 pi. purple 12·00 5·25

(7 "1340 Hashemite Kingdom 1340")

1921. Optd with T **7**.

21 1 pa. purple 20·00 10·00
22 $\frac{1}{8}$ pi. yellow 30·00 15·00
23 $\frac{1}{4}$ pi. green 10·00 5·00
24 $\frac{1}{2}$ pi. red 12·00 6·00
26 1 pi. blue 10·00 5·00
28 2 pi. purple 15·00 8·00

(8) ($\frac{1}{2}$ pi.) (9) (1 pi.)

1921. No. 21 surch with T **8** or **9**.

29 5 $\frac{1}{2}$ pi. on 1 pa. purple £200 95·00
30 1 pi. on 1 pa. purple £200 95·00

(10 "1340 Hashemite Kingdom 1340")

1922. Nos. 11 to 16 optd with T **10**.

31 5 1 pa. purple 3·00 1·50
32 – $\frac{1}{8}$ pi. yellow 12·00 5·00
33 – $\frac{1}{4}$ pi. green 2·50 1·50
34 – $\frac{1}{2}$ pi. red 2·50 1·40
35 – 1 pi. blue 3·00 60
36 – 2 pi. claret 7·50 4·00

1922. No. 31 surch with T **8** or **9**.

37 5 $\frac{1}{2}$ pi. on 1 pa. purple 15·00 15·00
38 1 pi. on 1 pa. purple 4·00 25

11 Meccan Sherifian Arms

1922.

39 11 $\frac{1}{8}$ pi. brown 1·00 30
57 $\frac{1}{4}$ pi. green 6·00 2·00
41 $\frac{1}{2}$ pi. red 50 20
42 1 pi. blue 1·00 20
43 $1\frac{1}{2}$ pi. lilac 1·00 30
44 2 pi. orange 1·50 40
45 3 pi. brown 2·00 50
46 5 pi. green 4·00 1·00
58 – 10 pi. purple and mauve 6·00 5·00

DESIGN: 10 pi. As T **11** but with different corner ornaments in the centre motif.

(12) ($\frac{1}{4}$ pi.) (13) (10 pi.)

1923. Surch with T **12** or **13**.

47 11 $\frac{1}{4}$ pi. on $\frac{1}{8}$ pi. brown 24·00 5·00
49 10 pi. on 5 pi. olive 20·00 10·00

(14)

1924. Proclamation of King Hussein as Caliph. Optd with T **14**.

50 11 $\frac{1}{8}$ pi. brown 3·00 2·00
51 $\frac{1}{2}$ pi. red 2·00 1·00
52 1 pi. blue 3·00 2·00
53 $1\frac{1}{2}$ pi. lilac 3·00 2·00
54 2 pi. orange 3·00 2·00
55 3 pi. brown 3·00 2·00
56 5 pi. green 4·00 3·00

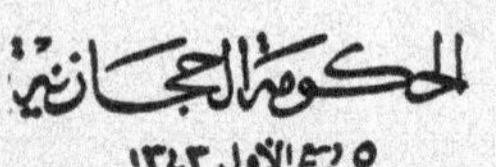

(15 "Hejaz Government. 4th October, 1924")

1924. Optd with T **15**.

66 1 pa. purple (No. 11) 15·00 6·00
77 1 pa. purple (No. 31) £120 80·00
59 $\frac{1}{8}$ pi. yellow (No. 12) 15·00 6·00
78 $\frac{1}{8}$ pi. yellow (No. 32) £1500
68 $\frac{1}{4}$ pi. green (No. 13) 19·00 9·00
79 $\frac{1}{4}$ pi. green (No. 33) 50·00 30·00
71 $\frac{1}{2}$ pi. red (No. 14) 26·00 17·00
76 $\frac{1}{2}$ pi. red (No. 24) £1800
80 $\frac{1}{2}$ pi. red (No. 34) 65·00 42·00
86 $\frac{1}{2}$ pi. red No. 41) £700
84 $\frac{1}{2}$ pi. on 1 pa. purple (No. 37) £120 50·00
73 1 pi. blue (No. 15) 30·00 20·00
81 1 pi. blue (No. 35) 85·00 55·00
85 1 pi. on 1 pa. purple (No. 38) £100 45·00
74 2 pi. purple (No. 16) 35·00 23·00
83 2 pi. purple (No. 36) £120 80·00
87 10 pi. purple and mauve (No. 58) £1300

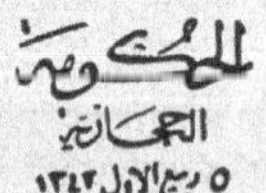

(16 "Hejaz Government, 4th October, 1924")

1924. Optd with T **16** (or smaller size).

(a) On No. 13.

90 – $\frac{1}{4}$ pi. green 45·00 12·00

(b) On Nos. 39 etc.

105 11 $\frac{1}{8}$ pi. brown 10·00 1·75
96 $\frac{1}{4}$ pi. green 15·00 5·50
116 $\frac{1}{2}$ pi. red 4·00 2·00
98 1 pi. blue 9·00 3·25
99 $1\frac{1}{2}$ pi. lilac 4·50 1·75
119 2 pi. orange 5·00 2·00
120 3 pi. brown 5·00 2·10
103 5 pi. green 7·50 1·75
104 – 10 pi. purple and mauve 15·00 6·00

(c) On Nos. 50/6.

136 11 $\frac{1}{8}$ pi. brown 30·00 6·00
137 $\frac{1}{2}$ pi. red 40·00 6·50
138 1 pi. blue 40·00 6·00
139 $1\frac{1}{2}$ pi. lilac 50·00 6·50
134 2 pi. orange 75·00 20·00
146 3 pi. brown 70·00 25·00
142 5 pi. green 28·00 6·50

For similar overprint see Nos. 172/6.

(17) (18)

1925. Stamps of 1922 surch as Type **17**.

148 11 $\frac{1}{4}$ pi. on $\frac{1}{8}$ pi. brown 70·00
149 $\frac{1}{4}$ pi. on $\frac{1}{2}$ pi. red 70·00
150 1 pi. on 2 pi. orange 70·00
151 1 pi. on 3 pi. brown 70·00
153 10 pi. on 5 pi. green £100

1925. Nos. 148/53 further surch with values in larger type as Type **18**.

154 11 $\frac{1}{4}$ pi. on $\frac{1}{4}$ pi. on $\frac{1}{8}$ pi. brown 35·00 22·00
155 $\frac{1}{4}$ pi. on $\frac{1}{4}$ pi. on $\frac{1}{2}$ pi. red 22·00 7·00
157 1 pi. on 1 pi. on 2 pi. orange 22·00 7·00
158 1 pi. on 1 pi. on 3 pi. brown 20·00 7·00
160 10 pi. on 10 pi. on 5 pi. green 12·00 4·00

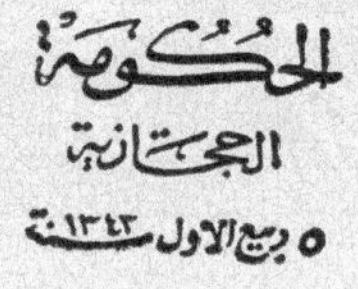

(19)

1925. Stamps of 1922 surch as T **19**.

165 11 $\frac{1}{8}$ pi. on $\frac{1}{2}$ pi. red 10·00 5·00
166 $\frac{1}{4}$ pi. on $\frac{1}{2}$ pi. red 10·00 5·00
167 1 pi. on $\frac{1}{2}$ pi. red 10·00 5·00
173c 1 pi. on $1\frac{1}{2}$ pi. lilac 10·00 6·00
174 1 pi. on 2 pi. orange 10·00 6·00
175 1 pi. on 3 pi. brown 10·00 6·00
176 10 pi. on 5 pi. green 10·00 6·00

20

(24)

1925. As T **20** (various Arabic designs) optd with T **24**.

177 $\frac{1}{8}$ pi. brown 3·00 3·00
178 $\frac{1}{4}$ pi. blue 3·00 3·00
179 $\frac{1}{2}$ pi. red 3·00 3·00
180 1 pi. green 4·50 4·50
181 $1\frac{1}{2}$ pi. orange 3·00 3·00
182 2 pi. blue 4·50 4·50
183 3 pi. green 6·00 6·00
184 5 pi. brown 6·00 6·00
185 10 pi. green and red 9·00 9·00

B. NEJDI OCCUPATION OF HEJAZ

(25) "Nejd Sultanate Post 1343"

1925. Various stamps optd with T **25**. (A.) Stamps of Turkey.

190 30 5 pa. bistre (No. 583) 17·00 11·50
191 10 pa. green (No. 503) 12·00 9·00

26

27

(B.) Hejaz Fiscal stamps.
(i) Notarial stamps.

192 26 1 pi. violet 14·00 14·00
193a 1 pi. blue 18·00 18·00

(ii) Bill stamp.

194 27 1 pi. violet 10·00 10·00

28

(iii) Railway Tax stamps.

195 28 1 pi. blue 12·00 12·00
196 2 pi. orange 16·00 16·00
197 3 pi. lilac 18·00 18·00

(C.) Hejaz Postage stamps (1922 issue).

198 11 $\frac{1}{8}$ pi. brown 15·00 15·00
198ca $\frac{1}{8}$ pi. red 18·00 18·00
199a $\frac{1}{2}$ pi. red 12·00 12·00
200 $1\frac{1}{2}$ pi. lilac 15·00 15·00
201 2 pi. orange 25·00 25·00
202 3 pi. red 15·00 15·00

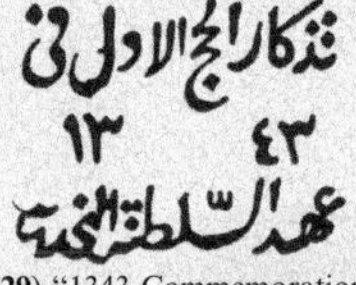

(29) "1343 Commemoration of First Pilgrimage under Sultan of Nejd"

(30) "Wednesday"

(31)

1925. Pilgrimage Commemoration. Various stamps optd with T **29** and **30** and surch as T **31**. (a) 1914 pictorial stamps of Turkey.

210 1 pi. on 10 pa. green (503) 50·00 40·00
211 5 pi. on 1 pi. blue (518) 50·00 40·00

(b) 1916 stamps of Hejaz.

212 2 pi. on 1 pa. purple 65·00 50·00
213 4 pi. on $\frac{1}{8}$ pi. yellow £225 £125

(c) Railway Tax stamp of Hejaz.

214 28 3 pi. lilac £175 60·00

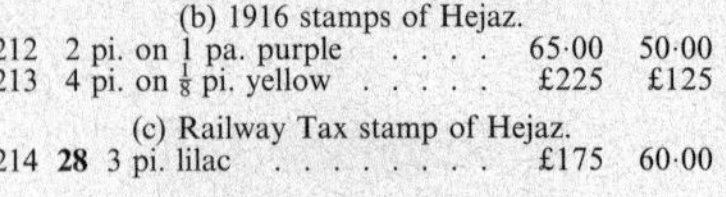

(32) "Nejd Sultanate Post"

1925. Various stamps optd with T **32**. (A.) Stamps of Turkey.

215 30 5 pa. bistre 8·00 7·00
216 – 10 pa. green (No. 503) 10·00 9·00

(B.) Hejaz Fiscal stamps.
(i) Notarial stamp.

217 26 2 pi. blue 14·00 12·00

(ii) Railway Tax Stamps.

218b 28 1 pi. blue 20·00 7·00
219 2 pi. orange 18·00 7·00
220 3 pi. lilac 15·00 10·00
221 5 pi. green 14·00 9·00

(C.) Hejaz Postage stamps.
(i) Nos. 35/6.

222 1 pi. blue 40·00 40·00
223 2 pi. purple 40·00 40·00

(ii) Stamps of 1922 (some in new colours).

224 11 $\frac{1}{8}$ pi. brown £2750
225 $\frac{1}{2}$ pi. red 7·00 4·50
226 1 pi. violet 12·00 10·00
227 $1\frac{1}{2}$ pi. pink 20·00 13·00
228 2 pi. orange 60·00 40·00
229 2 pi. purple 30·00 20·00
230 3 pi. red 15·00 12·00
231 5 pi. red 20·00 18·00

(33) (1 pi.) (34) ($1\frac{1}{2}$ pi.)

(35) (2 pi.)

1925. Stamps optd with T **32** further surch with T **33/5**.

239 11 1 pi. on $\frac{1}{2}$ pi. red 5·00 1·50
241 $1\frac{1}{2}$ pi. on $\frac{1}{2}$ pi. red 6·00 1·50
243 2 pi. on 3 pi. red 10·00 2·00

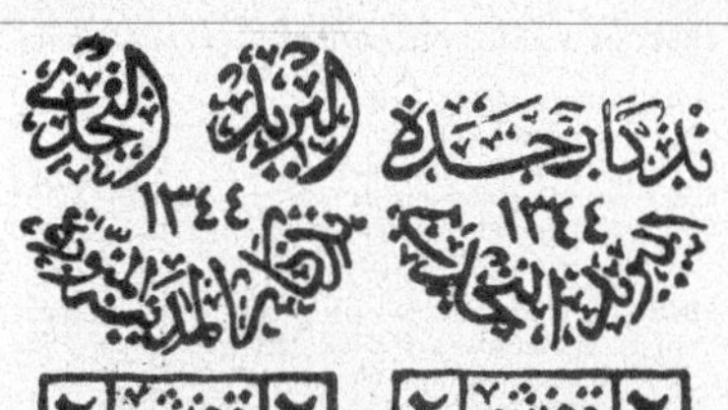
(36) "Postage of Nejd, 1344, Commemoration of Medina"
(37) "Commemoration of Jeddah, 1344, Postage of Nejd"

1925. Capture of Medina. Railway Tax stamps of Hejaz optd with T **36**.
244 **28** 1 pi. on 10 pi. mauve and violet 55·00 35·00
245 2 pi. on 50 pi. red and blue 55·00 35·00
246 3 pi. on 100 pi. brown 55·00 35·00
247 4 pi. on 500 pi. red 55·00 35·00
248 5 pi. on 1000 pi. violet and red 55·00 35·00

1925. Capture of Jeddah. Optd with T **37**.
249 **28** 1 pi. on 10 pi. mauve and violet 55·00 35·00
250 2 pi. on 50 pi. red and blue 55·00 35·00
251 3 pi. on 100 pi. brown 55·00 35·00
252 4 pi. on 500 pi. red 55·00 35·00
253 5 pi. on 1000 pi. violet and red 55·00 35·00

C. HEJAZ AND NEJD

38 **39**

1926.
254 **38** $\frac{1}{4}$ pi. violet 14·00 9·00
261 $\frac{1}{4}$ pi. orange 10·00 1·25
255 $\frac{1}{2}$ pi. grey 14·00 9·00
262 $\frac{1}{2}$ pi. green 6·00 70
256 1 pi. blue 16·00 10·00
263 1 pi. red 5·00 70
257 **39** 2 pi. green 14·00 9·00
264 2 pi. purple 5·00 70
259 3 pi. pink 20·00 13·00
265 3 pi. blue 5·00 70
266 5 pi. brown 10·00 1·25

(40) "Islamic Congress, 1 June, 1926"

1926. Pan-Islamic Congress, Cairo. Optd With T **40**.
275 **38** $\frac{1}{4}$ pi. orange 7·00 3·00
276 $\frac{1}{2}$ pi. green 7·00 3·00
277 1 pi. red 7·00 3·00
278 **39** 2 pi. purple 7·00 3·00
279 3 pi. blue 7·00 3·00
280 5 pi. brown 7·00 3·00

41 Tougra of Ibn Saud (**42** "25th Rajab 1345")

1926.
284 **41** $\frac{1}{8}$ pi. brown 5·00 35
285 $\frac{1}{4}$ pi. green 5·00 85
286 $\frac{1}{2}$ pi. red 5·00 85
287 1 pi. purple 5·00 85
288 $1\frac{1}{2}$ pi. blue 8·00 1·40
289 3 pi. green 8·00 2·75
290 5 pi. brown 13·00 3·50
291 10 pi. brown 40·00 4·00

1927. Establishment of Kingdom. Optd with T **42**.
294 **41** $\frac{1}{8}$ pi. brown 6·50 2·50
295 $\frac{1}{4}$ pi. green 6·50 2·50
296 $\frac{1}{2}$ pi. red 6·50 2·50
297 1 pi. purple 6·50 2·50
298 $1\frac{1}{2}$ pi. blue 6·50 2·50
299 3 pi. green 6·50 2·50
300 5 pi. brown 6·50 2·50
301 10 pi. brown 8·00 3·25

43 **44**

1929.
302 **43** $1\frac{3}{4}$ g. blue 13·00 1·60
303 20 g. violet 35·00 6·00
304 30 g. green 60·00 10·00

1930. 4th Anniv of King Ibn Saud's Accession.
305 **44** $\frac{1}{2}$ g. red 10·00 2·00
306 $1\frac{1}{2}$ g. violet 10·00 1·50
307 $1\frac{3}{4}$ g. blue 10·00 1·75
308 $3\frac{1}{2}$ g. green 10·00 2·50
309 5 g. purple 16·00 4·00

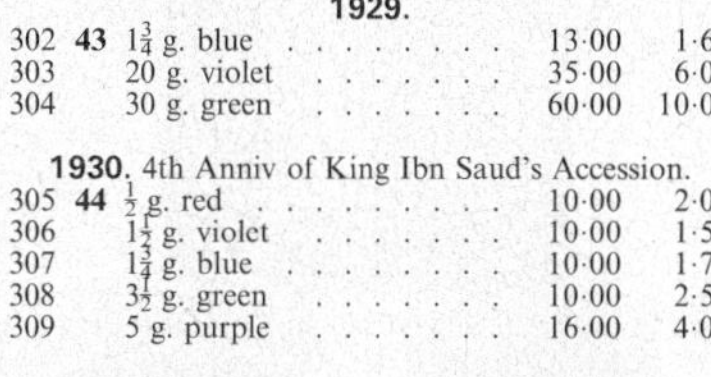

45 **46**

1931.
310 **45** $\frac{1}{8}$ g. yellow 10·00 1·60
311 $\frac{1}{4}$ g. green 10·00 1·25
312 $1\frac{3}{4}$ g. blue 32·00 1·60

1932.
313 **46** $\frac{1}{4}$ g. green 12·00 1·40
314a $\frac{1}{2}$ g. red 30·00 2·00
315 $2\frac{1}{4}$ g. blue 50·00 1·50

D. SAUDI ARABIA

47

1932. Proclamation of Emir Saud as Heir Apparent.
316 **47** $\frac{1}{4}$ g. green 4·50
317 $\frac{1}{2}$ g. red 4·50 2·00
318 $1\frac{1}{2}$ g. blue 9·00
319 3 g. green 11·50
320 $3\frac{1}{2}$ g. blue 13·50 4·00
321 5 g. yellow 38·00 20·00
322 10 g. orange 60·00
323 20 g. violet 85·00
324 30 g. violet £150
325 $\frac{1}{4}$ s. purple £120
326 $\frac{1}{2}$ s. brown £300
327 1 s. purple £600

48 **49**

1934. Charity Tax. Fund for Wounded in War with Yemen.
328 **48** $\frac{1}{2}$ g. red 80·00 4·00

1934.
329 **49** $\frac{1}{8}$ g. yellow 2·50 30
330 $\frac{1}{4}$ g. green 3·25 30
331a $\frac{1}{2}$ g. red 1·90 10
332 $\frac{7}{8}$ g. blue 3·00 40
333a 1 g. green 2·40 25
334 2 g. green 5·00 1·40
335 $2\frac{7}{8}$ g. violet 3·00 35
336b 3 g. blue 3·00 20
337 $3\frac{1}{2}$ g. blue 12·00 1·40
338a 5 g. orange 3·00 35
339b 10 g. violet 10·00 1·00
340a 20 g. purple 15·00 70
341 100 g. mauve 48·00 3·00
342a 200 g. brown 60·00 4·00

50 General Hospital, Mecca

1936. Charity. Medical Aid. Perf or roul. (a) Three palm trees.
345 **50** $\frac{1}{8}$ g. red (37×20 mm) £375 7·50
346 $\frac{1}{8}$ g. red ($30\frac{1}{2} \times 18$ mm) 30·00 70

(b) One palm tree.
348 **50** $\frac{1}{8}$ g. red ($30\frac{1}{2} \times 18$ mm) 4·00 75
351 $\frac{1}{4}$ g. red ($30\frac{1}{2} \times 18$ mm) 3·50 10

53 Egyptian Royal Yacht "Fakhr el Bihar", Radhwa

54 Map of Saudi Arabia, Flags and Emblem

1945. Meeting of King Ibn Saud and King Farouk of Egypt at Radhwa.
352 **53** $\frac{1}{2}$ g. red 5·75 1·00
353 3 g. blue 7·00 2·50
354 5 g. violet 22·00 5·00
355 10 g. purple 48·00 10·00

1946. Obligatory Tax. Return of King Ibn Saud from Egypt.
356a **54** $\frac{1}{2}$ g. mauve 9·00 70

55 Airliner

56 Arms of Saudi Arabia and Afghanistan

1949. Air.
357 **55** 1 g. green 2·50 10
358 3 g. blue 3·00 10
359 4 g. orange 3·00 10
360 10 g. violet 12·00 20
361 20 g. brown 30·00 30
362 100 g. purple 90·00 7·00

1950. Visit of King Mohamed Zahir Shah of Afghanistan.
363 **56** $\frac{1}{2}$ g. red 5·00 70
364 3 g. blue 8·50 70

57 Al-Murabba Palace, Riyadh

58 Arms of Saudi Arabia and Jordan

1950. 50th Anniv of Capture of Riyadh by King Abdulaziz Ibn Saud. Centres in purple.
365 **57** $\frac{1}{2}$ g. purple 2·75 60
366 1 g. blue 5·00 1·00
367 3 g. violet 7·50 1·40
368 5 g. orange 16·00 3·25
369 10 g. green 32·00 7·00

1951. Visit of King Talal of Jordan.
370 **58** $\frac{1}{2}$ g. red 3·75 70
371 3 g. blue 11·50 1·25

59 Arabs and Diesel Goods Train

60 Arms of Saudi Arabia and Lebanon

1952. Inaug of Dammam–Riyadh Railway.
372 **59** $\frac{1}{2}$ g. brown 7·50 2·00
373 1 g. green 10·00 2·25
374 3 g. mauve 15·00 2·00
375 10 g. red 30·00 8·50
376 20 g. blue 65·00 20·00

1953. Visit of President Chamoun of Lebanon.
377 **60** $\frac{1}{2}$ g. red 4·25 80
378 3 g. blue 9·00 2·00

61 **62** Arms of Saudi Arabia and Jordan

1953. Visit of Governor-General of Pakistan.
379 **61** $\frac{1}{2}$ g. red 5·25 80
380 3 g. blue 10·50 2·00

1953. Visit of King Hussein of Jordan.
381 **62** $\frac{1}{2}$ g. red 5·00 80
382 3 g. blue 12·00 2·00

1955. Arab Postal Union. As T **96a** of Syria but smaller, 20×34 mm. Inscr. "ROYAUME DE L'ARABIE SOUDITE" at top.
383 $\frac{1}{2}$ g. green 2·25 45
384 3 g. violet 6·50 90
385 4 g. brown 9·00 2·50

1960. Inaug of Arab League Centre, Cairo. As T **154a** of Syria, but inscr "S.A.K.".
386 2 p. green and black 1·40 15

63 Congress Building

1960. Arab Postal Union Congress, Riyadh.
387 **63** 2 p. blue 50 15
388 5 p. purple 1·25 25
389 10 p. green 3·00 40

64 Radio Mast and Globe **65** Refugee Camp

1960. Inauguration of Direct Radio Service.
390 **64** 2 p. red and black 1·60 20
391 5 p. purple and claret 2·50 25
392 10 p. indigo and blue 4·50 60

1960. World Refugee Year.
393 **65** 2 p. blue 35 15
394 8 p. violet 40 15
395 10 p. green 1·00 30

66 Gas Oil Plant

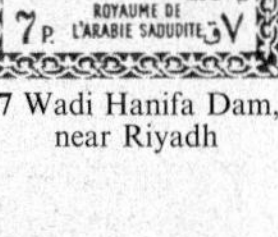
67 Wadi Hanifa Dam, near Riyadh

68 Vickers Viscount 800

(I)

(II)

1960. Cartouche of King Saud as Type I. Size $27\frac{1}{2} \times 22$ mm. (a) Postage. (i) Type **66**.
396 $\frac{1}{2}$ p. orange and red 1·10 25
397 1 p. red and blue 1·10 10
398 2 p. blue and red 1·10 10
399 3 p. green and violet 1·10 15
400 4 p. purple and green 1·10 10
401 5 p. red and purple 1·10 10
471 5 p. red and brown 7·50 35
402 6 p. lilac and brown 1·10 15
534 6 p. chocolate and brown 50·00 4·25
403 7 p. green and violet 1·10 10
404 8 p. black and green 1·50 15
405 9 p. brown and blue 2·75 15
406 10 p. red and blue 1·75 25
539 11 p. orange and green 4·00 25
540 12 p. green and brown 4·00 25
541 13 p. blue and mauve 4·00 30
542 14 p. brown and lilac 5·25 30
543 15 p. brown and mauve 6·00 40
544 16 p. red and green 8·25 40
545 17 p. brown and mauve 12·00 1·10
546 18 p. blue and black 8·00 50
547 19 p. yellow and brown 8·00 50
407 20 p. black and brown 6·00 35
549 23 p. red and orange 7·25 60
550 24 p. yellow and green 8·00 70
551 26 p. brown and purple 10·00 70
552 27 p. black and red 10·00 70
553 31 p. red and green 19·00 1·25
554 33 p. black and brown 17·00 1·25
408 50 p. green and brown 16·00 95
409 75 p. purple and red 27·00 2·75
410 100 p. brown and blue 38·00 2·00
411 200 p. green and black 65·00 5·50

(ii) Type **67**.
412 $\frac{1}{2}$ p. orange and bistre 1·00 20
413 1 p. purple and olive 1·00 10
414 2 p. brown and blue 1·00 10
415 3 p. blue and brown 1·00 15
416 4 p. chestnut and brown 1·00 10
417 5 p. purple and black 1·00 10
418 6 p. red and black 1·00 15
419 7 p. green and red 1·00 10
563 7 p. black and brown 10·00 25
420 8 p. purple and blue 1·00 20
564 8 p. brown and blue 55·00 4·25
421 9 p. red and brown 1·10 25
422 10 p. lake and green 1·10 20
567 11 p. green and red 4·75 1·75
568 12 p. blue and orange 4·75 25
569 13 p. mauve and green 4·75 30
570 14 p. green and brown 4·75 30
571 15 p. green and brown 4·75 1·75
572 16 p. lilac and red 5·50 35
573 17 p. blue and purple 5·50 1·90
574 18 p. blue and green 5·50 40
575 19 p. brown and black 8·00 45
423 20 p. green and brown 3·25 30
480 20 p. green and red 13·00 1·00
577 23 p. purple and brown 7·50 1·75
578 24 p. blue and red 7·50 50
579 26 p. yellow and green 8·00 65
580 27 p. purple and blue 8·00 65
581 31 p. blue and black 8.00 70
582 33 p. purple and green 8·00 70
424 50 p. brown and black 17·00 1·50
425 75 p. grey and brown 50·00 2·75
426 100 p. turquoise and blue 42·00 2·00
427 200 p. green and purple 70·00 5·00

(b) Air. Type **68**.
428 1 p. green and purple 45 10
429 2 p. purple and green 45 10
430 3 p. blue and red 45 10
431 4 p. purple and blue 45 10
432 5 p. red and green 45 10
433 6 p. violet and brown 90 15
484 6 p. green and orange 8.00 65
434 8 p. green and red 75 15

435 9 p. brown and violet . . . . 1·50 15
436 10 p. purple and black . . . . 3·75 35
437 15 p. brown and blue . . . . 3·75 25
438 20 p. green and brown . . . . 3·75 30
439 30 p. green and brown . . . . 10·00 90
440 50 p. blue and green . . . . 22·00 60
441 100 p. brown and grey . . . . 45·00 1·75
442 200 p. black and purple . . . . 60·00 2·50

Some values vary in size.

For similar design to Type **68** with King Saud cartouche but with different airplane, see Nos. 585/610c.

For designs with Type II cartouche, see Nos. 755 etc (1966 issue).

69 Globe, Pylon and Telegraph Pole

1960. 6th Anniv (1959) of Arab Telecommunications Union.

443 **69** 3 p. purple . . . . 1·10 15
444 6 p. black . . . . 2·40 25
445 8 p. brown . . . . 3·75 40

71 Damman Port **72** Campaign Emblem

1961. Opening of Damman Port Extension.

446 **71** 3 p. violet . . . . 1·50 25
447 6 p. blue . . . . 2·25 45
448 8 p. green . . . . 3·75 55

1962. Arab League Week. As T **76** of Libya but larger, 25×41 mm. Inscr "S.A.K.".

449 3 p. green . . . . 1·10 15
450 6 p. mauve . . . . 2·25 25
451 8 p. green . . . . 3·25 30

1962. Malaria Eradication.

452 **72** 3 p. red and blue 70 15
453 6 p. green and blue . . . . . 1·00 20
454 8 p. black and purple . . . 1·60 30

73 Koran

1963. 1st Anniv of Islamic Institute, Medina.

456 **73** 2½ p. purple and orange . . 90 15
457 7½ p. blue and green . . . 1·75 30
458 9½ p. green and black . . . 2·75 40

74 Emblem within Hands

1963. Freedom From Hunger.

459 **74** 2½ p. mauve and orange . . 1·00 15
460 7½ p. purple and pink . . . 1·10 25
461 9 p. brown and blue . . . 2·25 50

75 Boeing 707 over Airport **76** "Flame of Freedom"

1963. Opening of Dhahran Airport and Inauguration of Jet Service.

462 **75** 1 p. violet and brown . . . 1·00 20
463 3½ p. blue and green . . . 2·40 30
464 6 p. green and red . . . 4·00 40
465 7½ p. mauve and blue . . . 4·00 50
466 9½ p. red and violet . . . . 5·00 70

1964. 15th Anniv of Declaration of Human Rights.

493 **76** 3 p. blue, violet & orange . 2·75 25
494 6 p. blue, green & light blue 3·75 40
495 9 p. blue, brown and pink . 7·25 50

77 Arms and King Faisal

1964. Installation of King Faisal.

496 **77** 4 p. blue and green . . . 3·00 25

80 Boeing 720–B **81** Kaaba, Mecca

1964. Air. Type **80**. Cartouche of King Saud as Type I (illus next to T **68**).

585 1 p. green and purple . . . 60·00 2·75
586 2 p. purple and green . . . £1800 £200
587 3 p. blue and red . . . . 8·75 15
588 4 p. purple and blue . . . . 5·50 15
589 5 p. red and green £1400 £300
590 6 p. grey and brown . . . . 90·00 1·75
591 7 p. green and mauve . . . 6·00 35
592 8 p. green and red . . . . 85·00 1·60
593 9 p. brown and violet . . . 7·00 30
594 10 p. purple and black . . . 85·00 5·00
595 11 p. buff and green . . . . 75·00 16·00
596 12 p. grey and orange . . . 6·00 35
597 13 p. green and myrtle . . . 6·00 35
598 14 p. orange and blue . . . 6·00 40
599 15 p. brown and blue . . . 70·00 5·00
600 16 p. blue and black . . . 8·50 45
601 17 p. brown and ochre . . . 6·00 35
602 18 p. green and blue . . . 6·00 35
603 19 p. orange and mauve . . . 7·75 50
604 20 p. green and brown . . . £120 6·50
605 23 p. brown and green . . . £130 8·25
606 24 p. brown and blue . . . 6·50 60
607 26 p. green and red . . . 6·50 60
608 27 p. green and brown . . . 7·00 60
609 31 p. red and mauve . . . 7·50 65
610 33 p. purple and red . . . . 11·00 65
610a 50 p. blue and green . . . .
610b 100 p. brown and grey . . .
610c 200 p. brown and purple . .

For Type **80** with Type II cartouche, see Nos. 806 etc (1966 issue).

1965. Moslem League Conference, Mecca.

611 **81** 4 p. black and brown . . 3·00 25
612 6 p. black and mauve . . 4·75 35
613 10 p. black and green . . 7·00 40

82 Arms of Saudi Arabia and Tunisia

1965. Visit of President Bourguiba of Tunisia.

614 **82** 4 p. silver and mauve . . 2·50 35
615 8 p. silver and violet . . 3·25 40
616 10 p. silver and blue . . 5·00 45

83 Highway

1965. Opening of Arafat–Taif Highway.

617 **83** 2 p. black and red . . . . 1·50 20
618 4 p. black and blue . . . 2·40 35
619 6 p. black and violet . . . 3·25 45
620 8 p. black and green . . . 5·00 55

84 I.C.Y. Emblem

1965. International Co-operation Year.

621 **84** 1 p. brown and yellow . . 1·25 15
622 2 p. green and orange . . 1·25 15
623 3 p. green and blue . . 1·25 15
624 4 p. black and green . . 1·25 30
625 10 p. purple and orange . 2·50 45

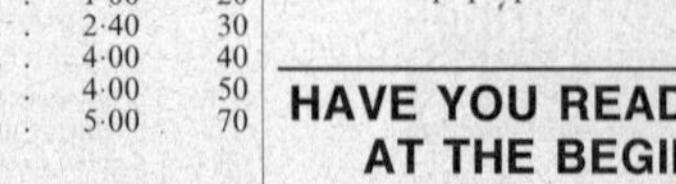

85 I.T.U. Symbol and Emblems

1965. Centenary of I.T.U.

626 **85** 3 p. black and blue . . . . 1·75 15
627 4 p. green and violet . . . 1·75 20
628 8 p. brown and green . . . 1·75 30
629 10 p. green and orange . . 1·75 35

86 Lamp and Burning Library

1966. Burning of Algiers Library in 1962.

630 **86** 1 p. red . . . . 1·25 25
631 2 p. red . . . . 1·25 25
632 3 p. purple . . . . 2·00 30
633 4 p. violet . . . . 2·75 20
634 5 p. mauve . . . . 4·75 30
635 6 p. red . . . . 8·00 45

87 A.P.U. Emblem **88** Dagger on Deir Yassin, Palestine

1966. 10th Anniv (1964) of Arab Postal Union's Permanent Office, Cairo.

636 **87** 3 p. green and purple . . . 90 15
637 4 p. green and blue . . . 90 25
638 6 p. green and purple . . . 4·00 25
639 7 p. olive and green . . . 4·00 35

1966. Deir Yassin Massacre.

640 **88** 2 p. black and green . . . . 1·25 20
641 4 p. black and brown . . . 2·75 30
642 6 p. black and blue . . . 4·50 35
643 8 p. black and orange . . . 6·00 1·10

89 Scout Badges

1966. Arab Scout Jamboree.

644 **89** 4 p. multicoloured . . . . 4·25 50
645 8 p. multicoloured . . . . 4·25 50
646 10 p. multicoloured . . . . 9·00 70

90 W.H.O. Building

1966. Inaug of W.H.O. Headquarters, Geneva.

647 **90** 4 p. multicoloured . . . . 1·00 15
648 6 p. multicoloured . . . . 1·25 35
649 10 p. multicoloured . . . . 4·00 30

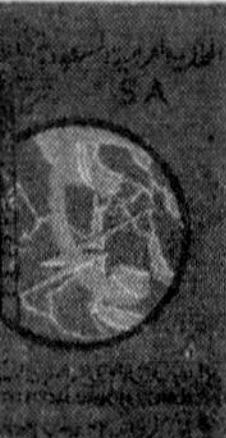

91 U.N.E.S.C.O. Emblem **92** Radio Mast, Telephone and Map

1966. 20th Anniv of U.N.E.S.C.O.

650 **91** 1 p. multicoloured . . . . 1·10 15
651 2 p. multicoloured . . . . 1·10 15
652 3 p. multicoloured . . . . 1·75 15
653 4 p. multicoloured . . . . 1·75 30
654 10 p. multicoloured . . . . 2·50 35

1966. 8th Arab Telecommunications Union Congress, Riyadh.

655 **92** 1 p. multicoloured . . . . 1·10 20
656 2 p. multicoloured . . . . 1·10 25
657 4 p. multicoloured . . . . 3·00 25
658 6 p. multicoloured . . . . 3·00 35
659 7 p. multicoloured . . . . 4·25 40

1966. As 1960 and 1964 issues, but with cartouche of King Faisal as Type II (see above No. 396).
(a) Postage. (i) Type **66**.

755 1 p. red and blue . . . . . . 8·50 85
756 2 p. blue and red . . . . . . 5·50 45
662 3 p. green and violet . . . . 12·00 50
663 4 p. purple and green . . . . 8·25 25
759 5 p. red and purple . . . . . 17·00 1·25
760 6 p. chocolate and brown . . . 23·00 1·40
666 7 p. green and lilac . . . . . 32·00 1·75
667 8 p. green and turquoise . . . 5·25 20
668 9 p. brown and blue . . . . 4·50 20
669 10 p. red and blue . . . . . 4·50 45
765 11 p. orange and green . . . 27·00 1·75
671 12 p. green and brown . . . 4·50 70
672 13 p. blue and mauve . . . . 40·00 25
673 14 p. brown and lilac . . . . 38·00 2·00
674 15 p. brown and mauve . . . 12·00 60
675 16 p. red and green . . . . 12·00 65
676 17 p. brown and mauve . . . 8·50 50
677 18 p. blue and black . . . . 13·50 1·50
678 19 p. yellow and brown . . . 16·50 1·40
679 20 p. brown and light brown 12·00 1·40
680 23 p. red and orange . . . . 27·00 1·75
681 24 p. yellow and green . . . 8·50 70
681a 26 p. brown and purple . . . £140
682 27 p. black and red . . . . 35·00 3·00
683 31 p. red and green . . . . 10·00 70
684 33 p. black and brown . . . 20·00 1·00
685 50 p. green and brown . . . £250 £130
686 100 p. brown and blue . . . £225 30·00
687 200 p. green and black . . . £275 48·00

(ii) Type **67**.

688 1 p. purple and green . . . . £120 21·00
689 2 p. brown and blue . . . . 18·00 1·50
690 3 p. blue and brown . . . . 9·00 70
691 4 p. orange and brown . . . 14·00 30
782 5 p. purple and black . . . . 25·00 1·50
783 6 p. red and black . . . . . 24·00 1·10
694 7 p. black and brown . . . . 17·00 1·60
695 8 p. brown and blue . . . . 9·00 35
696 9 p. red and brown . . . . 6·50 70
697 10 p. brown and green . . . 15·00 1·25
698 11 p. green and red . . . . 9·00 1·25
699 12 p. purple and orange . . . 6·00 1·25
700 13 p. mauve and green . . . 22·00 1·40
701 14 p. green and brown . . . 40·00 1·25
702 15 p. green and brown . . . 19·00 1·40
703 16 p. lilac and red . . . . 27·00 3·00
704 17 p. blue and purple . . . 29·00 1·75
705 18 p. blue and green . . . . 22·00 2·25
706 19 p. brown and black . . . 6·50 75
707 20 p. green and brown . . . 65·00 2·10
708 23 p. purple and brown . . . £225 12·00
708a 24 p. blue and red . . . . 45·00 5·00
709 26 p. yellow and green . . . 8·50 65
711 27 p. purple and blue . . . 7·75 65
712 33 p. purple and green . . . 38·00 2·00
713 50 p. brown and black . . . £140 30·00
714 100 p. blue and deep blue . . £250 35·00
715 200 p. green and purple . . . £250 55·00

(b) Air. Type **80**.

806 1 p. green and purple . . . . 7·00 15
807 2 p. purple and green . . . . 7·00 15
718 3 p. blue and red . . . . . 18·00 40
719 4 p. purple and blue . . . . 8·50 15
720 5 p. red and green £1400 £350
721 6 p. grey and brown . . . . 95·00 7·50
812 7 p. green and mauve . . . . 11·00 1·10
813 8 p. green and red . . . . . 32·00 4·25
724 9 p. brown and violet . . . . 5·50 45
725 10 p. brown and black . . . . 15·00 75
726 11 p. brown and green . . . . 8·50 45
727 12 p. grey and orange . . . . 50·00 3·50
728 13 p. green and myrtle . . . . 14·00 70
729 14 p. orange and blue . . . . 16·00 1·40
730 15 p. brown and blue . . . . 10·00 70
731 16 p. blue and black . . . . 16·00 2·40
732 17 p. brown and stone . . . . 13·00 1·10
733 18 p. green and blue . . . . 16·00 2·10
734 19 p. orange and mauve . . . 16·00 80
735 20 p. green and brown . . . . £150 11·00
736 23 p. brown and green . . . . 23·00 2·50
737 24 p. brown and blue . . . . 25·00 2·50
741 33 p. purple and red . . . . 10·00 45
742 50 p. blue and green £1500
743 100 p. brown and grey . . . £1500
744 200 p. black and purple . . . £1000 £150

93 Moot Emblem **94** Meteorological Apparatus

1967. 2nd Rover Moot, Mecca.

745 **93** 1 p. multicoloured . . . . 1·90 20
746 2 p. multicoloured . . . . 1·90 20
747 3 p. multicoloured . . . . 2·50 20
748 4 p. multicoloured . . . . 4·00 25
749 10 p. multicoloured . . . . 8·50 60

1967. World Meteorological Day.

750 **94** 1 p. mauve . . . . 1·10 20
751 2 p. violet . . . . 2·10 20
752 3 p. green . . . . 2·10 20
753 4 p. green . . . . 7·25 20
754 10 p. blue . . . . 9·00 60

96 Route Map and Dates

97 The Prophet's Mosque, Medina

98 Prophet's Mosque Extension

99 Ancient Wall Tomb, Madayin Saleh

100 Colonnade, Sacred Mosque, Mecca

101 Camels and Oil Derrick

102 Arab Stallion

103 Holy Ka'aba, Mecca

1968. Inauguration of Dammam–Jeddah Highway

No.	Type	Description	Unused	Used
834	96	1 p. multicoloured	1·10	15
835		2 p. multicoloured	1·10	15
836		3 p. multicoloured	2·50	15
837		4 p. multicoloured	2·75	50
838		10 p. multicoloured	8·00	70

1968. (a) Type **97**.

No.	Type	Description	Unused	Used
839	97	1 p. green and orange	3·25	25
840		2 p. green and brown	4·25	30
857		3 p. green and violet	2·50	20
945		4 p. green and brown	4·25	35
843		5 p. green and purple	8·50	75
860		6 p. green and black	12·00	90
948		10 p. green and brown	8·00	50
949		20 p. green and brown	9·50	1·25
864		50 p. green and purple	20·00	4·25
865		100 p. green and blue	15·00	3·75
866		200 p. green and red	18·00	5·00

(b) Type **98**.

No.	Type	Description	Unused	Used
952	98	1 p. green and orange	3·25	20
953		2 p. green and brown	3·25	25
954		3 p. green and black	4·75	35
868		4 p. green and red	4·50	40
851		5 p. green and red	4·25	35
852		6 p. green and blue	5·50	50
870a		8 p. green and red	21·00	1·60
871		10 p. green and brown	6·00	1·75
940		20 p. green and violet	8·50	70

(c) Type **99**.

No.	Type	Description	Unused	Used
876	99	2 p. brown and blue	18·00	3·50
878		4 p. cinnamon and brown	4·50	65
880		7 p. brown and orange	42·00	7·00
881		10 p. brown and green	10·50	1·40
883		20 p. brown and purple	10·50	1·10

(d) Type **100**.

No.	Type	Description	Unused	Used
887	100	3 p. grey and red	£300	75·00
888		4 p. grey and green	4·75	35
891		10 p. grey and purple	7·50	80

(e) Type **101**.

No.	Type	Description	Unused	Used
898	101	4 p. red and lilac	16·00	3·00
901		10 p. red and blue	11·50	2·10

(f) Type **102**.

No.	Type	Description	Unused	Used
908	102	4 p. brown and purple	4·50	60
911		10 p. brown and black	14·00	2·50
912		14 p. brown and blue	21·00	4·75
913		20 p. brown and green	9·75	1·60

(g) Type **103**.

No.	Type	Description	Unused	Used
918	103	4 p. black and green	6·25	50
920		6 p. black and purple	5·50	30
924		8 p. black and red	13·00	1·50
921		10 p. black and red	14·00	1·00

104 Saker Falcon

105 Traffic Signals

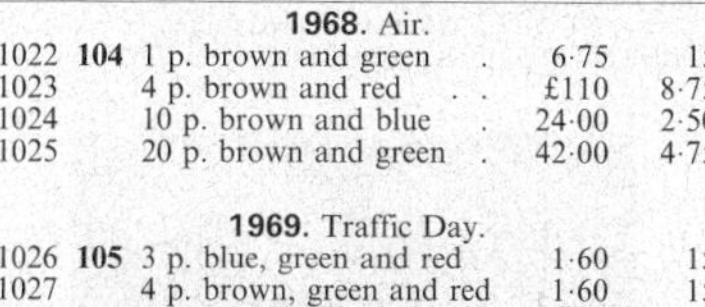

1968. Air.

No.	Type	Description	Unused	Used
1022	104	1 p. brown and green	6·75	15
1023		4 p. brown and red	£110	8·75
1024		10 p. brown and blue	24·00	2·50
1025		20 p. brown and green	42·00	4·75

1969. Traffic Day.

No.	Type	Description	Unused	Used
1026	105	3 p. blue, green and red	1·60	15
1027		4 p. brown, green and red	1·60	15
1028		10 p. purple, green & red	3·75	45

106 Scout Emblem, Camp and Flag

1969. 3rd Arab Rover Moot, Mecca.

No.	Type	Description	Unused	Used
1029	106	1 p. multicoloured	1·40	15
1030		4 p. multicoloured	4·50	30
1031		10 p. multicoloured	12·00	1·00

107 W.H.O. Emblem

1969. 20th Anniv (1968) of W.H.O.

No.	Type	Description	Unused	Used
1032	107	4 p. yellow, blue and deep blue	5·50	20

108 Conference Emblem

109 Satellite, Dish Aerial and Open Book

1970. Islamic Foreign Ministers' Conf, Jeddah.

No.	Type	Description	Unused	Used
1033	108	4 p. black and blue	2·50	25
1034		10 p. black and brown	4·00	30

1970. World Telecommunications Day.

No.	Type	Description	Unused	Used
1035	109	4 p. blue, mauve and ultramarine	3·25	35
1036		10 p. blue, mauve & grn	6·50	60

110 Steel Rolling-mill

112 Emblem and Arab Archway

1970. Inauguration (1967) of First Saudi Arabian Steel Rolling-mill.

No.	Type	Description	Unused	Used
1037	110	3 p. multicoloured	2·00	20
1038		4 p. multicoloured	3·00	20
1039		10 p. multicoloured	5·00	45

1971. 4th Arab Rover Moot, Mecca.

No.	Type	Description	Unused	Used
1049	112	10 p. multicoloured	5·00	65

113 Global Emblem

1971. World Telecommunications Day.

No.	Type	Description	Unused	Used
1050	113	4 p. black and blue	1·60	20
1051		10 p. black and lilac	3·25	35

114 University "Tower" Emblem

115 I.E.Y. Emblem

1971. 4th Anniv of Inauguration of King Abdulaziz National University.

No.	Type	Description	Unused	Used
1052	114	3 p. black and green	1·10	20
1053		4 p. black and brown	2·25	20
1054		10 p. black and blue	3·75	50

1971. International Education Year (1970).

No.	Type	Description	Unused	Used
1055	115	4 p. red and green	3·25	10

116 Arab League Emblem

117 O.P.E.C. Emblem

1971. Arab Propaganda Week.

No.	Type	Description	Unused	Used
1056	116	10 p. multicoloured	4·00	35

1971. 10th Anniv of O.P.E.C.

No.	Type	Description	Unused	Used
1057	117	4 p. blue	4·50	15

O.P.E.C. = Organization of Petroleum Exporting Countries.

118 Globe

120 Writing in Book

119 Telephone within Dial

1972. World Telecommunications Day.

No.	Type	Description	Unused	Used
1058	118	4 p. multicoloured	4·25	20

1972. Inauguration of Automatic Telephone System (1969).

No.	Type	Description	Unused	Used
1059	119	1 p. black, green and red	1·40	15
1060		4 p. black, turquoise & grn	1·40	15
1061		5 p. black, grn & mauve	2·50	20
1062		10 p. black, green & brn	5·50	45

1973. World Literacy Day (1972).

No.	Type	Description	Unused	Used
1063	120	10 p. multicoloured	6·00	30

121 Mosque, Mecca, and Moot Emblem

1973. 5th Arab Rover Moot, Mecca. Mult.

No.	Description	Unused	Used
1064	4 p. Type **121**	2·75	15
1065	6 p. Holy Ka'aba, Mecca	5·50	30
1066	10 p. Rover encampment	7·50	75

HAVE YOU READ THE NOTES AT THE BEGINNING OF THIS CATALOGUE?
These often provide the answers to the enquiries we receive.

122 Globe and Map of Palestine

1973. Universal Palestine Week.

No.	Type	Description	Unused	Used
1067	122	4 p. red, yellow and grey	2·75	15
1068		10 p. red, yellow and blue	5·00	45

123 Leaf and Emblem

1973. International Hydrological Decade.

No.	Type	Description	Unused	Used
1069	123	4 p. multicoloured	4·75	20

124 A.P.U. Emblem

1973. 25th Anniv of Founding of Arab Postal Union at Sofar Conference.

No.	Type	Description	Unused	Used
1070	124	4 p. multicoloured	3·25	20
1071		10 p. multicoloured	6·75	40

125 Balloons

126 U.P.U. Monument and Postal Emblem

1973. Universal Children's Day (1971).

No.	Type	Description	Unused	Used
1072	125	4 p. multicoloured	5·25	10

1974. Centenary of U.P.U.

No.	Type	Description	Unused	Used
1073	126	3 p. multicoloured	35·00	1·75
1074		4 p. multicoloured	35·00	3·50
1075		10 p. multicoloured	35·00	5·00

127 Handclasp and U.N.E.S.C.O. Emblem

1974. International Book Year (1972).

No.	Type	Description	Unused	Used
1076	127	4 p. multicoloured	1·75	25
1077		10 p. multicoloured	7·00	60

128 Desalination Works

1974. Inauguration of Sea-water Desalination Plant, Jeddah (1971).

No.	Type	Description	Unused	Used
1078	128	4 p. blue and orange	1·60	15
1079		6 p. lilac and green	3·25	25
1080		10 p. black and red	5·00	50

129 Interpol Emblem **130** Tower, Emblem and Hand with Letter

1974. 50th Anniv (1973) of International Criminal Police Organization (Interpol).
1081 **129** 4 p. blue and red . . . . 5·25 20
1082 10 p. blue and green . . . 11·00 60

1974. 3rd Session of Arab Postal Studies Consultative Council, Riyadh.
1083 **130** 4 p. multicoloured . . . 6·75 15

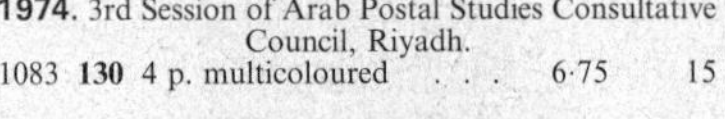

131 New Headquarters Building

1974. Inauguration (1970) of New U.P.U. Headquarters, Berne.
1084 **131** 3 p. multicoloured . . . 2·25 25
1085 4 p. multicoloured . . . 5·00 45
1086 10 p. multicoloured . . . 6·50 95

132 Armed Forces and Flame

1974. King Faisal Military Cantonment (1971).
1087 **132** 3 p. multicoloured . . . 1·40 15
1088 4 p. multicoloured . . . 3·00 25
1089 10 p. multicoloured . . . 8·50 50

133 Red Crescent "Flower" **134** Scout Emblem and Minarets

1974. 10th Anniv (1973) of Saudi Arabian Red Crescent Society.
1090 **133** 4 p. multicoloured . . . 1·40 15
1091 6 p. multicoloured . . . 3·50 35
1092 10 p. multicoloured . . . 6·75 70

1974. 6th Arab Rover Moot, Mecca.
1093 **134** 4 p. multicoloured . . . 3·25 15
1094 6 p. multicoloured . . . 6·25 25
1095 10 p. multicoloured . . . 9·50 45

135 Reading Braille

1975. Day of the Blind.
1096 **135** 4 p. multicoloured . . . 2·75 25
1097 10 p. multicoloured . . . 6·50 35

136 Anemometer and U.N. Emblem as Weather Balloon

1975. Centenary (1973) of World Meteorological Organization.
1098 **136** 4 p. multicoloured . . . 6·00 25

137 King Faisal **138** Conference Emblem

1975. King Faisal Memorial Issue.
1099 **137** 4 p. purple and green . 2·10 25
1100 16 p. green and violet . 2·75 50
1101 23 p. violet and green . 5·50 90

1975. 6th Islamic Conference of Foreign Ministers, Jeddah.
1103 **138** 10 p. black and brown . 4·00 35

139 Wheat and Sun

1975. 29th Anniv of Charity Society.
1104 **139** 4 p. multicoloured . . . 2·75 25
1105 10 p. multicoloured . . 6·00 30

140 Kaaba, Handclasp and Globe

1975. Moslem Organizations Conference, Mecca.
1106 **140** 4 p. multicoloured . . . 4·75 15
1107 10 p. multicoloured . . 9·50 45

141 Lockheed TriStar and Douglas DC-3 Aircraft

1975. 30th Anniv of National Airline "Saudia".
1108 **141** 4 p. multicoloured . . . 5·00 20
1109 10 p. multicoloured . . 9·50 35

142 Mecca and Riyadh

1975. Conference Locations.
1110 **142** 10 p. multicoloured . . . 7·25 45

143 Friday Mosque, Medina, and Juwatha Mosque, Al-Hasa

1975. Islamic Holy Places.
1111 **143** 4 p. multicoloured . . . 4·75 20
1112 10 p. multicoloured . . . 6·75 45

144 F.A.O. Emblem

1975. 10th Anniv (1973) of World Food Programme.
1113 **144** 4 p. multicoloured . . . 2·75 15
1114 10 p. multicoloured . . . 7·50 45

145 Conference Emblem

1976. Islamic Solidarity Conference of Science and Technology, Mecca.
1115 **145** 4 p. multicoloured . . . 10·00 25

146 Map and T.V. Screen

1976. 10th Anniv (1975) of Saudi Arabian Television Service.
1116 **146** 4 p. multicoloured . . . 10·00 25

147 Ear of Wheat, Atomic Symbol and Graph

1976. 2nd Five-year Plan.
1117 **147** 20 h. multicoloured . . . 2·50 25
1118 50 h. multicoloured . . . 4·25 50

148 Quba Mosque, Medina

149 Holy Kaaba, Mecca

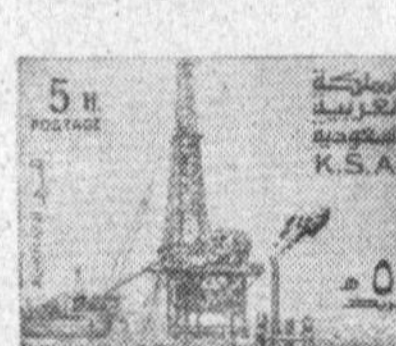

150 Oil Rig, Al-Khafji

1976. Size 36 × 26 mm. (a) Type **148**.
1122 20 h. grey and orange . . . . 1·50 10
1128 50 h. lilac and green . . . . 3·00 15

(b) Type **149**.
1137 5 h. black and lilac 10 10
1138 10 h. black and lilac 20 10
1139 15 h. black and orange . . . 30 10
1140 20 h. black and blue . . . . 3·00 10
1141 25 h. black and yellow . . . 75 10
1142 30 h. black and green . . . . 1·00 15
1143 35 h. black and brown . . . 60 10
1144 40 h. black and green . . . 4·50 20
1145 45 h. black and purple . . . 70 10
1146 50 h. black and red 75 10
1149 65 h. black and blue 95 10
1151 1 r. black and green . . . . 1·40 15
1152 2 r. black and green . . . . 5·00 25

(c) Type **150**.
1167 5 h. blue and orange . . . 10 10
1168 10 h. green and orange . . 10 10
1169 15 h. brown and orange . . 15 10
1170 20 h. green and orange . . 15 10
1171 25 h. purple and orange . . 15 10
1172 30 h. blue and orange . . . 25 10
1173 35 h. brown and orange . . 25 10
1174 40 h. purple and orange . . 25 10
1175 45 h. mauve and orange . . 30 10
1176b 50 h. pink and orange . . . 35 15
1177 55 h. green and orange . . 15·00 2·75
1179 65 h. brown and orange . . 85 25
1180 1 r. green and orange . . . 1·00 40
1181 2 r. purple and red . . . . 2·25 70

For smaller designs see Nos. 1283/1325 and 1435/7.

151 Globe and Telephones

1976. Telephone Centenary.
1191 **151** 50 h. multicoloured . . . 4·75 25

152 Emblem and Heads of State **153** Kaaba and Spinning Wheel

1976. Arab League Summit Conference.
1192 **152** 20 h. green and blue . . 4·00 20

1976. 50th Anniv of Manufacture of Kaaba Covering.
1193 **153** 20 h. multicoloured . . . 5·00 20

154 Eye and W.H.O. Emblem

1976. World Health Day. Prevention of Blindness.
1194 **154** 20 h. multicoloured . . . 8·00 20

155 Emblem

1976. Islamic Jurisprudence Conference.
1195 **155** 20 h. multicoloured . . . 5·25 15

156 Emblem **157** King Khaled

1977. 25th Anniv of Sharia Law College, Mecca.
1196 **156** 4 p. green, yellow and mauve . . . . 4·75 15

1977. 2nd Anniv of Installation of King Khaled.
(a) With incorrect dates at foot.
1197 **157** 20 h. brown and green . 10·00 30·00
1198 80 h. black and green . . 10·00 25·00
(b) With corrected dates.
1199 **157** 20 h. brown and green . 1·40 20
1200 80 h. black and green . . 2·75 40

On Nos. 1197/8 the two Arabic dates end with the same characters. On the correct version of the design, the characters differ.

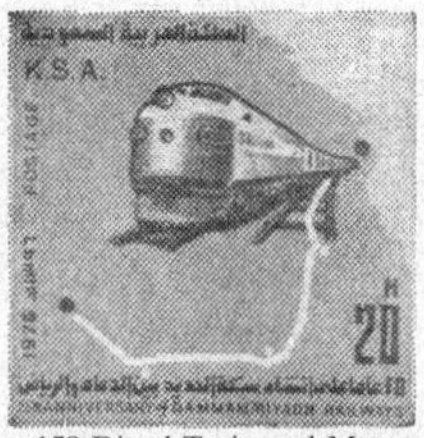

158 Diesel Train and Map

1977. 25th Anniv (1976) of Dammam–Riyadh Railway.
1201 **158** 20 h. multicoloured . . . 13·50 1·50

159/62 "The Four Imams" (½-size illustration)

1977.
1202 **159** 20 h. blue, yellow and grey 2·25 35
1203 **160** 20 h. blue, yellow and grey 2·25 35
1204 **161** 20 h. blue, yellow and grey 2·25 35
1205 **162** 20 h. blue, yellow and grey 2·25 35

Nos. 1202/5 were issued together, se-tenant, forming the composite design illustrated.

163 Moenjodaro Ruins, Pakistan

164 Map by al-Idrisi

1977. "Save Moenjodaro" Campaign.
1206 **163** 50 h. multicoloured . . . 5·25 20

1977. 1st International Arab History Symposium.
1207 **164** 20 h. multicoloured . . . 1·40 20
1208 50 h. multicoloured . . . 2·75 25

165 King Faisal Hospital, Riyadh

1977. Opening of King Faisal Hospital.
1209 **165** 20 h. multicoloured . . . 2·25 20
1210 50 h. multicoloured . . . 3·50 30

166 A.P.U. Emblem

167 Kaaba, Book and Lighthouse

1977. 25th Anniv of Arab Postal Union.
1211 **166** 20 h. multicoloured . . . 1·25 10
1212 80 h. multicoloured . . . 2·75 35

1977. 1st World Conference on Muslim Education.
1213 **167** 20 h. blue and yellow . . 3·00 10

168 Taif–Abha–Jizan Road and Route Map

1978. Opening of Taif–Abha–Jizan Road.
1214 **168** 20 h. multicoloured . . 1·60 15
1215 80 h. multicoloured . . 2·75 40

169 Mount Arafat, Pilgrims and Kaaba

1978. Pilgrimage to Mecca.
1216 **169** 20 h. multicoloured . . 1·40 15
1217 80 h. multicoloured . . 2·75 40

170 Posthorn Dhow

171 5 g. Stamp of 1930

1979. 2nd Gulf Postal Organization Conf, Dubai.
1218 **170** 20 h. multicoloured . . 1·40 15
1219 50 h. multicoloured . . 2·50 20

1979. 50th Anniv of First Commemorative Stamp Issue.
1220 **171** 20 h. multicoloured . . 1·00 15
1221 50 h. multicoloured . . 2·25 20
1222 115 h. multicoloured . . 3·50 45

172 Crown Prince Fahd

1979. Crown Prince Fahd's Birthday.
1224 **172** 20 h. multicoloured . . 1·40 15
1225 50 h. multicoloured . . 2·75 25

173 Dome of the Rock, Jerusalem

174 Golden Door of Kaaba, Mecca

1979. Soldarity with Palestinians.
1226 **173** 20 h. multicoloured . . 1·25 20

For similar design see No. 1354.

1979. Installation of New Gold Doors on Kaaba.
1227 **174** 20 h. multicoloured . . 1·25 15
1228 80 h. multicoloured . . 2·75 35

175 The Kaaba, Mecca

1979. Pilgrimage to Mecca.
1229 **175** 20 h. multicoloured . . 85 15
1230 50 h. multicoloured . . 2·00 25

176 "Birds in a Forest"

1980. International Year of the Child. Children's Paintings. Multicoloured.
1231 20 h. Type **176** . . . . 4·50 20
1232 50 h. "Paper Lanterns" . . . 7·50 35

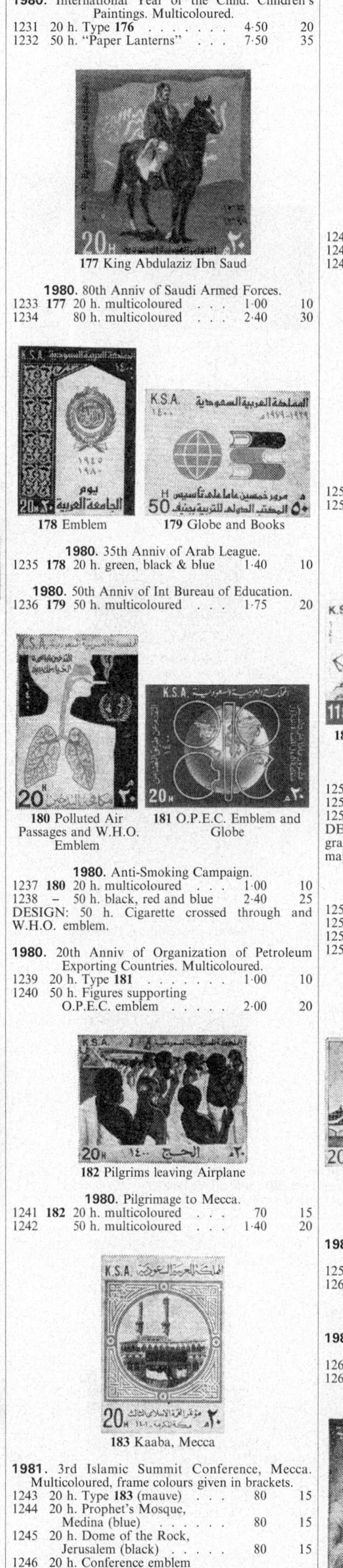

177 King Abdulaziz Ibn Saud

1980. 80th Anniv of Saudi Armed Forces.
1233 **177** 20 h. multicoloured . . . 1·00 10
1234 80 h. multicoloured . . . 2·40 30

178 Emblem

179 Globe and Books

1980. 35th Anniv of Arab League.
1235 **178** 20 h. green, black & blue 1·40 10

1980. 50th Anniv of Int Bureau of Education.
1236 **179** 50 h. multicoloured . . . 1·75 20

180 Polluted Air Passages and W.H.O. Emblem

181 O.P.E.C. Emblem and Globe

1980. Anti-Smoking Campaign.
1237 **180** 20 h. multicoloured . . . 1·00 10
1238 – 50 h. black, red and blue 2·40 25

DESIGN: 50 h. Cigarette crossed through and W.H.O. emblem.

1980. 20th Anniv of Organization of Petroleum Exporting Countries. Multicoloured.
1239 20 h. Type **181** . . . . 1·00 10
1240 50 h. Figures supporting O.P.E.C. emblem . . . . . 2·00 20

182 Pilgrims leaving Airplane

1980. Pilgrimage to Mecca.
1241 **182** 20 h. multicoloured . . . 70 15
1242 50 h. multicoloured . . . 1·40 20

183 Kaaba, Mecca

1981. 3rd Islamic Summit Conference, Mecca. Multicoloured, frame colours given in brackets.
1243 20 h. Type **183** (mauve) . . . 80 15
1244 20 h. Prophet's Mosque, Medina (blue) 80 15
1245 20 h. Dome of the Rock, Jerusalem (black) 80 15
1246 20 h. Conference emblem (35 × 35 mm) 80 15

MINIMUM PRICE

The minimum price quoted is 10p which represents a handling charge rather than a basis for valuing common stamps. For further notes about prices, see introductory pages.

184 Thour Cave, Mecca, and Quba Mosque, Medina, on Map

1981. 1400th Anniv of Hegira.
1247 **184** 20 h. multicoloured . . . 70 15
1248 50 h. multicoloured . . . 1·40 20
1249 80 h. multicoloured . . . 2·75 35

185 Royal Corporation of Jubeil and Yanbou Emblem

1981. Industry Week.
1250 **185** 20 h. brown, orge & silver 65 15
1251 80 h. brown, orge & gold 1·90 30

186 Satellite Earth Station

187 Emblem of Arab Towns Organization

1981. Telecommunications Achievements.
1252 – 20 h. gold, black & blue 25 15
1253 – 80 h. multicoloured . . . 1·90 35
1254 **186** 115 h. multicoloured . . 2·25 45

DESIGNS—As T **186**: 20 h. Modern telephone and graph. 36 × 36 mm: 80 h. Microwave antenna on map of Saudi Arabia.

1981. Arab Towns Day.
1255 **187** 20 h. multicoloured . . . 30 15
1256 65 h. multicoloured . . . 95 20
1257 80 h. multicoloured . . . 1·40 30
1258 115 h. multicoloured . . 1·90 50

188 Douglas DC-9-80 Super Eighty Jetliner

189 Flags of participating Countries and Saudi Team Emblem

1981. Inauguration of King Abdulaziz International Airport, Jeddah. Multicoloured.
1259 20 h. Type **188** 60 20
1260 80 h. Airplane over departure halls in form of tents . . . 2·25 45

1981. World Cup Football Championship Preliminary Round, Riyadh.
1261 **189** 20 h. multicoloured . . . 1·50 15
1262 80 h. multicoloured . . . 2·25 30

190 Blind Person reading Braille

191 Wheat and Cogwheel on Graph

1981. Int Year of Disabled Persons. Mult.
1263 20 h. Type **190** . . . . 1·40 15
1264 50 h. Disabled person in wheelchair weaving on loom 2·25 20

1981. 3rd Five-year Plan.
1265 **191** 20 h. multicoloured . . . 1·00 15

192 King Abdulaziz Ibn Saud and Map of Saudi Arabia

1981. 50th Anniv of Unification of Saudi Arabia.

1266 **192** 5 h. multicoloured . . . 10 10
1267 10 h. multicoloured . . . 10 10
1268 15 h. multicoloured . . . 15 10
1269 20 h. multicoloured . . . 15 15
1270 50 h. multicoloured . . . 55 25
1271 65 h. multicoloured . . . 85 25
1272 80 h. multicoloured . . . 2·10 35
1273 115 h. multicoloured . . 2·25 50

193 Pilgrims passing through Almasa'a Arcade

1981. Pilgrimage to Mecca.

1275 **193** 20 h. multicoloured . . . 1·00 15
1276 65 h. multicoloured . . . 2·25 35

194 Tractor

1981. World Food Day.

1277 **194** 20 h. multicoloured . . . 1·10 15
For similar design see No. 1343.

195 Conference Emblem

1981. 2nd Session of Gulf Co-operation Council Summit Conference, Riyadh.

1278 **195** 20 h. multicoloured . . . 60 15
1279 80 h. multicoloured . . . 2·00 30

196 University Emblem

1982. 25th Anniv of King Saud University.

1280 **196** 20 h. multicoloured . . . 60 15
1281 50 h. multicoloured . . . 1·40 20

1982. As T **149/150** but in smaller size, 25 × 20 mm.

(a) Type **149**.

1283 10 h. black and lilac 10 10
1284 15 h. black and orange . . . 10 10
1285d 20 h. black and blue 10 10
1291c 50 h. black and red 20 10
1294c 65 h. black and blue 45 15
1301c 1 r. black and green 90 15

(b) Type **150**.

1306a 5 h. blue and orange 15 10
1307c 10 h. green and orange . . . 25 10
1308c 15 h. brown and orange . . 15 10
1309c 20 h. green and orange . . . 25 15
1310 25 h. purple and orange . . 25 10
1315c 50 h. red and orange 20 15
1318c 65 h. brown and orange . . 30 15
1325c 1 r. green and orange . . . 60 25

197 Riyadh Postal Building

198 Riyadh Television Centre

1982. New Postal Buildings. Multicoloured.

1330 20 h. Type **197** 25 15
1331 65 h. Jeddah 90 20
1332 80 h. Dammam . . . . . . 1·25 30
1333 115 h. Postal mechanised sorting . . . . 1·50 45

1982. Riyadh Television Centre.

1335 **198** 20 h. multicoloured . . 95 15

199 Football and King's Cup

200 A.P.U. Emblem and Map

1982. 25th Anniv of King's Cup Football Championship.

1336 **199** 20 h. multicoloured . . 65 15
1337 65 h. multicoloured . . 1·50 25

1982. 30th Anniv of Arab Postal Union. Mult.

1338 20 h. A.P.U. Emblem and Arabic "30" 60 15
1339 65 h. Type **200** . . . . . . 1·50 25

201 Pilgrims at Muzdalefa looking for Stones to stone the Devil

1982. Pilgrimage to Mecca.

1340 **201** 20 h. multicoloured . . 60 15
1341 50 h. multicoloured . . 1·50 20

202 Saudi Arabian and World Standards Organizations Emblems

1982. World Standards Day.

1342 **202** 20 h. multicoloured . . 95 15

203 Tractor

1982. World Food Day.

1343 **203** 20 h. multicoloured . . 95 15
For similar design see No. 1277.

204 King Fahd

1983. Installation of King Fahd.

1344 **204** 20 h. multicoloured . . 20 15
1345 50 h. multicoloured . . 55 20
1346 65 h. multicoloured . . 70 30
1347 80 h. multicoloured . . 95 40
1348 115 h. multicoloured . . 1·50 50

205 Crown Prince Abdullah

1983. Installation of Crown Prince.

1349 **205** 20 h. multicoloured . . . 20 15
1350 50 h. multicoloured . . . 55 20
1351 65 h. multicoloured . . . 70 30
1352 80 h. multicoloured . . . 95 40
1353 115 h. multicoloured . . 1·50 50

206 Dome of the Rock, Jerusalem

1983. Solidarity with Palestinians.

1354 **206** 20 h. multicoloured . . . 25 15
For similar design but inscribed "K.S.A." see No. 1226.

207 Container Ship "Bar'zan"

1983. 6th Anniv of United Arab Shipping Company. Multicoloured.

1355 20 h. Type **207** 40 25
1356 65 h. "Al Drieya" (container ship) . . . . 1·25 60

208 Stoning the Devil

209 Saudi Arabia Post and U.P.U. Emblems

1983. Pilgrimage to Mecca.

1357 **208** 20 h. multicoloured . . . 25 15
1358 65 h. multicoloured . . . 60 25

1983. World Communications Year. Mult.

1359 20 h. Type **209** 20 15
1360 80 h. Saudi Arabia telephone and I.T.U. emblems 45 25

210 Terminal Building

1983. Opening of King Khaled International Airport, Riyadh. Multicoloured.

1361 20 h. Type **210** 50 20
1362 65 h. Embarkation wing of terminal . . . . 1·10 75

211 Wheat and F.A.O. Emblem

212 Al Aqsa Mosque, Jerusalem

1983. World Food Day.

1363 **211** 20 h. multicoloured . . . 25 15

1983. Solidarity with Palestinians.

1364 **212** 20 h. brown, blue & grn . 25 15

213 Riyadh

214 Shobra Palace, Taif

215 Jeddah

216 Dammam

1984. Saudi Cities. (a) Riyadh.

1365 **213** 20 h. multicoloured . . . 15 10
1366 50 h. multicoloured . . . 30 15
1370 75 h. multicoloured . . . 60 30
1371 150 h. multicoloured . . 1·40 60

(b) Taif.

1367 **214** 20 h. multicoloured . . . 15 10
1368 50 h. multicoloured . . . 55 15
1374 75 h. multicoloured . . . 50 25
1375 150 h. multicoloured . . 1·40 60

(c) Jeddah.

1377 **215** 50 h. multicoloured . . . 75 35
1378 75 h. multicoloured . . . 75 35
1379 150 h. multicoloured . . 1·25 55

(d) Dammam.

1380 **216** 50 h. multicoloured . . . 15 10
1381 75 h. multicoloured . . . 25 15
1382 150 h. multicoloured . . 50 25

223 Family and House

1984. 10th Anniv of Estate Development Fund.

1385 **223** 20 h. multicoloured . . . 25 15

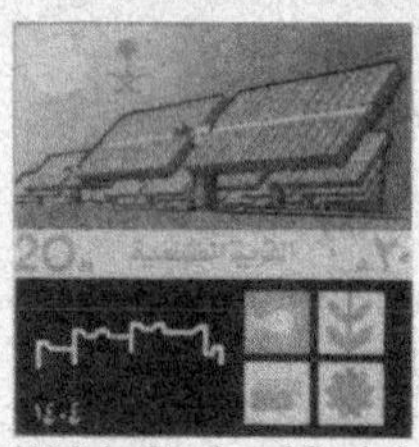
224 Solar Panels and Symbols

1984. Al-Eyenah Solar Village. Multicoloured.

1386 20 h. Type **224** 20 15
1387 80 h. Sun and solar panels . 50 20

225 Al-Kheef Mosque, Mina

1984. Pilgrimage to Mecca. Multicoloured.

1389 20 h. Type **225** 25 15
1390 65 h. Al-Kheef Mosque, Mina (different) 75 20

226 Olympic and Saudi Football Federation Emblems

227 Wheat and F.A.O. Emblem

1984. Qualification of Saudi Football Team for Olympic Games.
1391 **226** 20 h. multicoloured . . . 20 15
1392 115 h. multicoloured . . 80 30
Nos. 1391/2 have the incorrect spellings "Gamos" and "Olympied".

1984. World Food Day.
1393 **227** 20 h. green, buff and black 30 15

228 Olympic Rings and "90"

1984. 90th Anniv of Int Olympic Committee.
1394 **228** 20 h. multicoloured . . . 20 15
1395 50 h. multicoloured . . . 50 20

229 "Arabsat" and Globe

1985. Launch of "Arabsat" Satellite.
1396 **229** 20 h. multicoloured . . . 70 15

230 Emblem and Koran

1985. International Koran Reading Competition.
1397 **230** 20 h. multicoloured . . . 20 15
1398 65 h. multicoloured . . . 60 25

231 King Fahd and Jubail Industrial Complex

1985. Five Year Plan. Multicoloured.
1399 20 h. Type **231** 35 15
1400 50 h. King Fahd, T.V. tower, dish aerial and microwave tower 90 15
1401 65 h. King Fahd and agricultural landscape . . . 1·25 35
1402 80 h. King Fahd and Yanbu industrial complex . . . . 1·50 45

232 I.Y.Y. Emblem

1985. International Youth Year.
1403 **232** 20 h. multicoloured . . . 15 15
1404 80 h. multicoloured . . . 60 20

233 Map and Wheat

235 "Arabsat 2" Satellite and Launch of "Discovery" (space shuttle)

234 Loading Berth, Yanbu

1985. "Self Sufficiency in Wheat Production".
1405 **233** 20 h. multicoloured . . 35 15

1985. Abqaiq–Yanbu Oil Pipeline. Multicoloured.
1406 20 h. Type **234** 20 15
1407 65 h. Pipeline and map . . . 70 25

1985. 1st Arab Astronaut, Prince Sultan Ibn Salman Al-Saud. Multicoloured.
1408 20 h. Type **235** 20 15
1409 115 h. Space shuttle and mission emblem (51 × 26 mm) . . 95 30

236 "40" and U.N. Emblem

1985. 40th Anniv of U.N.O.
1410 **236** 20 h. light blue, blue and green 45 15

237 Highway and Map of Route

1985. Mecca–Medina Highway.
1411 **237** 20 h. multicoloured . . 20 15
1412 65 h. multicoloured . . 40 20

238 Coded Envelope and Post Emblem

1985. Post Code Publicity.
1413 **238** 20 h. multicoloured . . 20 15

239 Trophy and Football

1985. Victory in 8th (1984) Asian Football Cup Championship.
1414 **239** 20 h. multicoloured . . 20 15
1415 65 h. multicoloured . . 35 20
1416 115 h. multicoloured . . 90 35

240 Pilgrims around Kaaba

1985. Pilgrimage to Mecca.
1417 **240** 10 h. multicoloured . . 15 10
1418 15 h. multicoloured . . 20 15
1419 20 h. multicoloured . . 30 15
1420 65 h. multicoloured . . 70 30

241 Olympic Rings and Council Emblem

1985. 1st Arabian Gulf Co-operation Council Olympic Day.
1421 **241** 20 h. multicoloured . . 25 15
1422 115 h. multicoloured . . 1·10 40

242 Irrigation System

1985. World Food Day.
1423 **242** 20 h. multicoloured . . . 20 15
1424 65 h. multicoloured . . . 55 30

243 King Abdulaziz and Horsemen

1985. International Conference on King Abdulaziz.
1425 **243** 15 h. multicoloured . . . 15 15
1426 20 h. multicoloured . . . 20 15
1427 65 h. multicoloured . . . 55 30
1428 80 h. multicoloured . . . 60 45

244 Building within Roll of Printed Paper

1985. King Fahd Holy Koran Press Compound, Medina. Multicoloured.
1430 20 h. Type **244** 20 15
1431 65 h. Open book sculpture within roll of printed paper 45 25

245 O.P.E.C. Emblem and "25"

246 Doves and I.P.Y. Emblem

1985. 25th Anniv of Organization of Petroleum Exporting Countries.
1432 **245** 20 h. sepia, brown and black 20 15
1433 65 h. multicoloured . . . 45 25

1986. International Peace Year.
1434 **246** 20 h. multicoloured . . . 25 15

1986. As T **149** but size 29 × 19 mm.
1435 10 h. black and violet . . . . 2·00
1436 20 h. black and blue . . . . 6·00
1437 50 h. black and red . . . . . 10·00

247 Riyadh

248 Child in Droplet

1986. 50th Anniv of Riyadh Municipality.
1438a **247** 20 h. multicoloured . . 25 15
1439 65 h. multicoloured . . 50 25

1986. World Health Day.
1440 **248** 20 h. multicoloured . . . 20 15
1441 50 h. multicoloured . . . 45 20

249 Electricity Pylon and Flashes

1986. 10th Anniv of General Electricity Corporation.
1442 **249** 20 h. multicoloured . . . 20 15
1443 65 h. multicoloured . . . 50 25

250 Route Map of Cable

1986. Inauguration of Singapore–Marseilles Communications Cable.
1444 **250** 20 h. blue, black and green 25 15
1445 50 h. multicoloured . . . 55 20

251 Houses and Soldier

252 Holy Kaaba

1986. National Guards Housing Project, Riyadh.
1446 **251** 20 h. multicoloured . . . 25 15
1447 65 h. multicoloured . . . 80 30

1986.
1448 **252** 30 h. black and green . . 15 15
1449 40 h. black and mauve . . 20 15
1450 50 h. black and green . . 55 30
1451a 75 h. black and blue . . 55 30
1452a 150 h. black and mauve . 1·10 55

253 Mount Arafat, Pilgrims and Kaaba

1986. Pilgrimage to Mecca. Multicoloured.
1460 20 h. Type **253** . . . . 1·50 1·50
1461 20 h. Pilgrims leaving jet airliner 1·50 1·50
1462 20 h. Stoning the Devil . . . 1·50 1·50
1463 20 h. Pilgrims at Muzdalefa looking for stones to stone the Devil . . . . 1·50 1·50
1464 20 h. Pilgrims passing through Almasa'a Arcade . . . . . 1·50 1·50
1465 20 h. Kaaba, Mecca . . . . 1·50 1·50
1466 20 h. Pilgrims around Kaaba 1·50 1·50
1467 20 h. Al-Kheef Mosque, Mina 1·50 1·50

254 Refinery

255 Palm Tree and Wheat in Globe

1986. 50th Anniv of Discovery of Oil in Saudi Arabia. Multicoloured.
1468 20 h. Type **254** 20 15
1469 65 h. Oil derrick on map . . 65 20

1986. World Food Day. Multicoloured.
1470 20 h. Type **255** 20 15
1471 115 h. Corn cob and wheat in leaves of flower 70 35

256 Scroll behind Dagger and Pool of Blood

1986. 4th Anniv of Massacre of Palestinian Refugees at Sabra and Shatila Camps, Lebanon.
1472 **256** 80 h. multicoloured . . . 70 25
1473 115 h. multicoloured . . 1·10 55

257

258

259 260

261 262

263

1986. University Crests. (a) Imam Mohammed ibn Saud Islamic University, Riyadh.

1474	**257**	15 h. black and green . .	15	10
1475		20 h. black and blue	15	20
1476		50 h. black and blue . .	30	15
1477		65 h. black and blue . .	40	20
1478		75 h. black and blue . .	50	20
1479		100 h. black and pink . .	65	30
1480		150 h. black and red . .	95	50

(b) Umm al-Qura University, Mecca.

1481	**258**	50 h. black and blue . .	40	20
1482		65 h. black and blue . .	50	20
1483		75 h. black and blue . .	50	25
1484		100 h. black and pink . .	75	40
1485		150 h. black and red . .	1·10	55

(c) King Saud University, Riyadh.

1487	**259**	50 h. black and blue . .	40	20
1488		75 h. black and blue . .	50	25
1489		100 h. black and pink . .	75	40
1490		150 h. black and pink . .	1·00	50

(d) King Abulaziz University, Jeddah.

1493	**260**	50 h. black and blue . .	30	15
1494		75 h. black and blue . .	50	25
1496		150 h. black and red . .	1·00	50

(e) King Faisal University, Al-Hasa.

1499	**261**	50 h. black and blue . .	30	15
1500		75 h. black and blue . .	50	25
1502		150 h. black and red . .	1·00	35

(f) King Fahd University of Petroleum and Minerals, Dhahran.

1505	**262**	50 h. black and blue . .	30	15
1506		75 h. black and blue . .	50	25
1508		150 h. black and pink . .	95	50

(g) Islamic University, Medina.

1511	**263**	50 h. black and blue . .	35	15
1512		75 h. black and blue . .	50	25
1514		150 h. black and red . .	95	20

264 Road Bridge and Aerial View of Causeway (left)

1986. Saudi Arabia–Bahrain Causeway. Mult.

1515	20 h. Type **264**	30	20
1516	20 h. Road bridge and aerial view of causeway (right) .	30	20

265 Olympic Torch and Rings

1986. 90th Anniv of Modern Olympic Games.

1517	**265**	20 h. multicoloured . . .	20	15
1518		100 h. multicoloured . .	70	35

266 Oil Derrick and Refinery

1987. 25th Anniv of General Petroleum and Mineral Organization.

1519	**266**	50 h. multicoloured . . .	60	25
1520		100 h. multicoloured . .	1·25	45

267 Mosque and Model of Extension

1987. Restoration and Extension of Quba Mosque, Medina.

1521	**267**	50 h. multicoloured . .	70	25
1522		75 h. multicoloured . .	1·00	30

268 Drill-press Operator

1987. Technical and Vocational Training. Mult.

1523	50 h. Type **268**	75	50
1524	50 h. Lathe operator	75	50
1525	50 h. Laboratory technician	75	50
1526	50 h. Welder	75	50

Nos. 1523/6 were printed together, se-tenant, each block forming an overall design of a cogwheel.

269 Pyramid, Riyadh T.V. Tower, King Khaled International Airport and Fort

270 Dish Aerials and Satellite

1987. "Saudi Arabia—Yesterday and Today" Exhibition, Cairo.

1527	**269**	50 h. multicoloured . .	80	35
1528		75 h. multicoloured . .	1·25	90

1987. King Fahd Space Communications City, Umm al Salam, Jeddah. Multicoloured.

1529	50 h. Type **270**	75	25
1530	75 h. Dish aerials and City buildings (51 × 26 mm) . .	1·00	35

271 Map and Rifleman

273 Emblems

272 Mosque and Pilgrims

1987. Afghan Resistance to Occupation.

1531	**271**	50 h. multicoloured . .	75	25
1532		100 h. multicoloured . .	1·25	35

1987. Pilgrimage to Mecca.

1533	**272**	50 h. multicoloured . .	70	25
1534		75 h. multicoloured . .	75	45
1535		100 h. multicoloured . .	1·25	55

1987. 1st Anniv of Disabled Children's Care Home.

1536	**273**	50 h. multicoloured . .	75	25
1537		75 h. multicoloured . .	1·00	50

274 Emblems and Hands writing on Airmail Envelope

1987. World Post Day.

1538	**274**	50 h. multicoloured . .	70	25
1539		150 h. multicoloured . .	1·75	65

275 Combine Harvester within Leaf

276 Woman and Children in Hand

1987. World Food Day.

1540	**275**	50 h. multicoloured . . .	60	25
1541		75 h. multicoloured . . .	90	35

1987. 25th Anniv of First Social Welfare Society.

1542	**276**	50 h. multicoloured . . .	50	25
1543		100 h. multicoloured . .	1·00	45

277 Dome of the Rock, Jerusalem

1987.

1544	**277**	75 h. multicoloured . . .	90	30
1545		150 h. multicoloured . .	1·50	60

278 Mosque

1987. Expansion of Prophet's Mosque, Medina.

1546	**278**	50 h. multicoloured . . .	60	20
1547		75 h. multicoloured . . .	80	30
1548		150 h. multicoloured . .	1·75	55

279 Dome of the Rock, Horseman and Battle Scene

280 Emblem

1987. 800th Anniv of Battle of Hattin.

1550	**279**	75 h. multicoloured . . .	80	30
1551		150 h. multicoloured . .	1·75	55

1987. 8th Supreme Council Session of Gulf Co-operation Council, Riyadh.

1552	**280**	50 h. multicoloured . . .	60	20
1553		75 h. multicoloured . . .	1·00	30

281 Road as "3" and Ship

282 Aerial View of Stadium and Sports Pictograms

1988. 3rd International Roads Federation (Middle East Region) Meeting, Riyadh.

1554	**281**	50 h. multicoloured . . .	75	35
1555		75 h. multicoloured . . .	1·00	50

1988. Inauguration of International King Fahd Stadium, Riyadh. Multicoloured.

1556	50 h. Type **282**	80	25
1557	150 h. Side view of stadium and sports pictograms (51 × 26 mm)	1·60	65

283 Anniversary Emblem and W.H.O. Building

1988. World Health Day. 40th Anniv of W.H.O.

1588	**283**	50 h. multicoloured . . .	45	20
1589		75 h. multicoloured . . .	90	35

284 Blood Transfusion and Blood Drop

1988. Blood Donation.

1560	**284**	50 h. multicoloured . . .	45	20
1561		75 h. multicoloured . . .	90	35

285 Mosque, Holy Kaaba and King Fahd

1988. Appointment of King Fahd as Custodian of Two Holy Mosques.

1562	**285**	50 h. multicoloured . . .	40	20
1563		75 h. multicoloured . . .	60	25
1564		150 h. multicoloured . . .	1·00	50

286 Clean Air, Land and Sea

287 Palestinian Flag, Hand holding Stone and Crowd

1988. Environmental Protection.

1566	**286**	50 h. multicoloured . . .	55	20
1567		75 h. multicoloured . . .	90	30

1988. Palestinian "Intifida" Movement.

1568	**287**	75 h. multicoloured . . .	90	25
1569		150 h. multicoloured . .	1·50	50

288 Pilgrims at al-Sail al-Kabir Miqat

1988. Pilgrimage to Mecca.

1570	**288**	50 h. multicoloured . . .	55	20
1571		75 h. multicoloured . . .	90	30

289 Ear of Wheat

1988. World Food Day.

1572	**289**	50 h. multicoloured . . .	40	20
1573		75 h. multicoloured . . .	60	30

290 Mosque

1988. Expansion of Qiblatayn Mosque, Medina.

1574	**290**	50 h. multicoloured . . .	40	20
1575		75 h. multicoloured . . .	60	30

MINIMUM PRICE

The minimum price quoted is 10p which represents a handling charge rather than a basis for valuing common stamps. For further notes about prices, see introductory pages.

291 Footballer and Trophy on Globe

1989. World Youth Football Cup, Saudi Arabia.
1576 **291** 75 h. multicoloured . . . 50 20
1577 150 h. multicoloured . . 1·00 45

292 W.H.O. Emblem and Means of Communications

294 Palestinian Flag and Dome of the Rock, Jerusalem

293 Shuaibah Desalination Plant, Red Sea

1989. World Health Day.
1578 **292** 50 h. multicoloured . . . 40 20
1579 75 h. multicoloured . . . 60 30

1989. 1st Anniv of Sea Water Desalination and Electricity Power Station.
1580 **293** 50 h. multicoloured . . . 40 20
1581 75 h. multicoloured . . . 60 30

1989. "Freedom of Palestine".
1582 **294** 50 h. multicoloured . . . 35 15
1583 75 h. multicoloured . . . 55 20

295 Attan'eem Miqat, Mecca

1989. Pilgrimage to Mecca.
1584 **295** 50 h. multicoloured . . . 35 15
1585 75 h. multicoloured . . . 55 20

296 Ears of Wheat encircling Globe

297 Hands holding Trophy aloft

1989. World Food Day.
1586 **296** 75 h. multicoloured . . . 55 20
1587 150 h. multicoloured . . 95 45

1989. 3rd World Under-16 JVC Cup Soccer Championship, Scotland.
1588 **297** 75 h. multicoloured . . . 50 25
1589 150 h. multicoloured . . 95 45

298 Mosque after Expansion

1989. Expansion of Holy Mosque, Mecca.
1590 **298** 50 h. multicoloured . . . 35 15
1591 75 h. multicoloured . . . 50 25
1592 150 h. multicoloured . . 1·00 50

299 Emblem and Arabic Letters

1990. International Literacy Year.
1595 **299** 50 h. multicoloured . . 35 15
1596 75 h. multicoloured . . 50 25

300 "Aloe sheilaa"

301 "Blopharis ciliaris"

302 "Pergularia tormentosa"

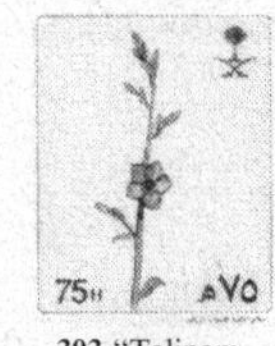

303 "Talinam cuneifolium"

304 "Echium horridum"

305 "Cleome arabica"

306 "Iris sisyrinchium"

307 "Senecio desfontaini"

308 "Cistanche phelypaea"

309 "Plumbago zeylanica"

310 "Cappario cartilaginea"

311 "Peganum harmala"

312 Acacia

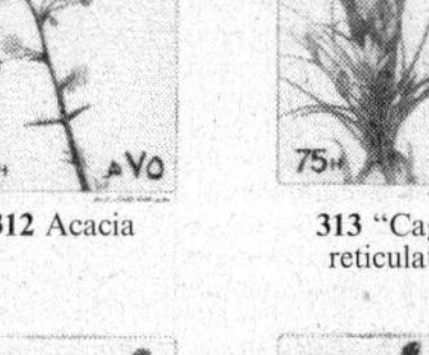

313 "Cagea reticulata"

314 "Diplotakis harra"

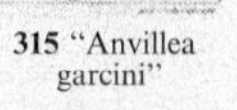

315 "Anvillea garcini"

316 "Striga asiatica"

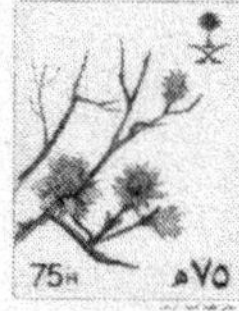

317 "Rhanterium eppaposum"

318 "Oenostachys abyssinica"

319 "Roemeria dodecandra"

320 Poppy

1990. Flowers.
1597 **300** 50 h. multicoloured . . . 25 10
1598 **301** 50 h. multicoloured . . . 25 10
1599 **302** 50 h. multicoloured . . . 25 10
1600 **303** 50 h. multicoloured . . . 25 10
1601 **304** 50 h. multicoloured . . . 25 10
1602 **305** 50 h. multicoloured . . . 25 10
1603 **306** 50 h. multicoloured . . . 25 10
1604 **307** 50 h. multicoloured . . . 25 10
1605 **308** 50 h. multicoloured . . . 25 10
1606 **309** 50 h. multicoloured . . . 25 10
1607 **310** 50 h. multicoloured . . . 25 10
1608 **311** 50 h. multicoloured . . . 25 10
1609 **312** 50 h. multicoloured . . . 25 10
1610 **313** 50 h. multicoloured . . . 25 10
1611 **314** 50 h. multicoloured . . . 25 10
1612 **315** 50 h. multicoloured . . . 25 10
1613 **316** 50 h. multicoloured . . . 25 10
1614 **317** 50 h. multicoloured . . . 25 10
1615 **318** 50 h. multicoloured . . . 25 10
1616 **319** 50 h. multicoloured . . . 25 10
1617 **320** 50 h. multicoloured . . . 25 10
1618 **300** 75 h. multicoloured . . . 40 20
1619 **301** 75 h. multicoloured . . . 40 20
1620 **302** 75 h. multicoloured . . . 40 20
1621 **303** 75 h. multicoloured . . . 40 20
1622 **304** 75 h. multicoloured . . . 40 20
1623 **305** 75 h. multicoloured . . . 40 20
1624 **306** 75 h. multicoloured . . . 40 20
1625 **307** 75 h. multicoloured . . . 40 20
1626 **308** 75 h. multicoloured . . . 40 20
1627 **309** 75 h. multicoloured . . . 40 20
1628 **310** 75 h. multicoloured . . . 40 20
1629 **311** 75 h. multicoloured . . . 40 20
1630 **312** 75 h. multicoloured . . . 40 20
1631 **313** 75 h. multicoloured . . . 40 20
1632 **314** 75 h. multicoloured . . . 40 20
1633 **315** 75 h. multicoloured . . . 40 20
1634 **316** 75 h. multicoloured . . . 40 20
1635 **317** 75 h. multicoloured . . . 40 20
1636 **318** 75 h. multicoloured . . . 40 20
1637 **319** 75 h. multicoloured . . . 40 20
1638 **320** 75 h. multicoloured . . . 40 20
1639 **300** 150 h. multicoloured . . 75 35
1640 **301** 150 h. multicoloured . . 75 35
1641 **302** 150 h. multicoloured . . 75 35
1642 **303** 150 h. multicoloured . . 75 35
1643 **304** 150 h. multicoloured . . 75 35
1644 **305** 150 h. multicoloured . . 75 35
1645 **306** 150 h. multicoloured . . 75 35
1646 **307** 150 h. multicoloured . . 75 35
1647 **308** 150 h. multicoloured . . 75 35
1648 **309** 150 h. multicoloured . . 75 35
1649 **310** 150 h. multicoloured . . 75 35
1650 **311** 150 h. multicoloured . . 75 35
1651 **312** 150 h. multicoloured . . 75 35
1652 **313** 150 h. multicoloured . . 75 35
1653 **314** 150 h. multicoloured . . 75 35
1654 **315** 150 h. multicoloured . . 75 35
1655 **316** 150 h. multicoloured . . 75 35
1656 **317** 150 h. multicoloured . . 75 35
1657 **318** 150 h. multicoloured . . 75 35
1658 **319** 150 h. multicoloured . . 75 35
1659 **320** 150 h. multicoloured . . 75 35

321 "20" within Crescent and Circle

1990. 20th Anniv of Islamic Conference Organization.
1660 **321** 75 h. multicoloured . . . 35 15
1661 150 h. multicoloured . . 90 45

322 Globe and W.H.O. Emblem

1990. World Health Day.
1662 **322** 75 h. multicoloured . . . 45 20
1663 150 h. multicoloured . . 95 45

323 White Horse

1990. 25th Anniv of Horsemanship Club. Mult.
(a) Size 38 × 29 mm.
1664 50 h. Type **323** 40 20
1665 50 h. Brown horse 40 20
1666 50 h. White horse with dark muzzle 40 20
1667 50 h. Chestnut horse 40 20
(b) Size 36 × 27 mm.
1668 50 h. As No. 1667 . . . . . 40 20
1669 75 h. As No. 1665 . . . . . 60 30
1670 100 h. Type **323** 80 40
1671 150 h. As No. 1666 . . . . 1·00 50

324 El Johfah Miqat, Rabegh

1990. Pilgrimage to Mecca.
1672 **324** 75 h. multicoloured . . . 55 25
1673 150 h. multicoloured . . 1·00 50

325 T.V. Tower and Centre

1990. 25th Anniv of Saudi Television.
1674 **325** 75 h. multicoloured . . . 55 25
1675 150 h. multicoloured . . 1·00 50

326 Ornament

1990. Islamic Heritage Year. Multicoloured.
1676 75 h. Type **326** 60 30
1677 75 h. Mosque 60 30
1678 75 h. Arabic script 60 30
1679 75 h. Decoration with stylized minarets 60 30

Nos. 1676/9 were issued together, se-tenant, each block having a composite design of a stylized rosette in the centre.

327 Boeing 747-300/400 and International Flights Route Map

1990. 45th Anniv of Saudi Airlines. Multicoloured.

1680		75 h. Type **327**	50	25
1681		75 h. Douglas DC-10 airliner and domestic flights route map	50	25
1682		150 h. Type **327**	1·00	50
1683		150 h. As No. 1681	1·00	50

328 Anniversary Emblem

1990. 30th Anniv of Organization of Petroleum Exporting Countries.

1684	**328**	75 h. multicoloured	45	20
1685		150 h. multicoloured	90	45

329 World Map

1990. World Food Day.

1686	**329**	75 h. multicoloured	45	20
1687		150 h. multicoloured	90	45

330 Industrial Site, Irrigation System and Oil Refinery

1990. 5th Five Year Plan. Multicoloured.

1688		75 h. Type **330**	45	20
1689		75 h. Radio tower, road and mine	45	20
1690		75 h. Monument, sports stadium and vocational training	45	20
1691		75 h. Television tower, environmental protection and modern building	45	20

331 Arabic Script and Decoration

332 Tidal Wave, Erupting Volcano and Earthquake-damaged House

1991. Battle of Badr, 624 A.D.

1692	**331**	75 h. green and orange	45	20
1693		150 h. dp blue, bl & grn	90	45

1991. World Health Day. Natural Disasters Relief.

1694	**332**	75 h. multicoloured	45	20
1695		150 h. multicoloured	90	45

333 Mountain Gazelle

334 Ibex

335 Arabian Oryx

336 Sand Fox

337 Bat

338 Striped Hyena

339 Sand Cat

340 Dugong

341 Arabian Leopard

1991. Animals.

1696	**333**	25 h. multicoloured	20	10
1697	**334**	25 h. multicoloured	20	10
1698	**335**	25 h. multicoloured	20	10
1699	**336**	25 h. multicoloured	20	10
1700	**337**	25 h. multicoloured	20	10
1701	**338**	25 h. multicoloured	20	10
1702	**339**	25 h. multicoloured	20	10
1703	**340**	25 h. multicoloured	20	10
1704	**341**	25 h. multicoloured	20	10
1705	**333**	50 h. multicoloured	40	20
1706	**334**	50 h. multicoloured	40	20
1707	**335**	50 h. multicoloured	40	20
1708	**336**	50 h. multicoloured	40	20
1709	**337**	50 h. multicoloured	40	20
1710	**338**	50 h. multicoloured	40	20
1711	**339**	50 h. multicoloured	40	20
1712	**340**	50 h. multicoloured	40	20
1713	**341**	50 h. multicoloured	40	20
1714	**333**	75 h. multicoloured	55	25
1715	**334**	75 h. multicoloured	55	25
1716	**335**	75 h. multicoloured	55	25
1717	**336**	75 h. multicoloured	55	25
1718	**337**	75 h. multicoloured	55	25
1719	**338**	75 h. multicoloured	55	25
1720	**339**	75 h. multicoloured	55	25
1721	**340**	75 h. multicoloured	55	25
1722	**341**	75 h. multicoloured	55	25
1723	**333**	100 h. multicoloured	70	35
1724	**334**	100 h. multicoloured	70	35
1725	**335**	100 h. multicoloured	70	35
1726	**336**	100 h. multicoloured	70	35
1727	**337**	100 h. multicoloured	70	35
1728	**338**	100 h. multicoloured	70	35
1729	**339**	100 h. multicoloured	70	35
1730	**340**	100 h. multicoloured	70	35
1731	**341**	100 h. multicoloured	70	35
1732	**333**	150 h. multicoloured	1·00	50
1733	**334**	150 h. multicoloured	1·00	50
1734	**335**	150 h. multicoloured	1·00	50
1735	**336**	150 h. multicoloured	1·00	50
1736	**337**	150 h. multicoloured	1·00	50
1737	**338**	150 h. multicoloured	1·00	50
1738	**339**	150 h. multicoloured	1·00	50
1739	**340**	150 h. multicoloured	1·00	50
1740	**341**	150 h. multicoloured	1·00	50

342 Flag and Map of Kuwait

343 Rainbow and Arrows

1991. Liberation of Kuwait.

1741	**342**	75 h. multicoloured	45	20
1742		150 h. multicoloured	90	45

1991. World Telecommunications Day.

1743	**343**	75 h. multicoloured	45	20
1744		150 h. multicoloured	90	45

344 Thee el Halifa Miqat, Medina

1991. Pilgrimmage to Mecca.

1745	**344**	75 h. multicoloured	45	20
1746		150 h. multicoloured	90	45

345 Blackboard and I.L.Y. Emblem

346 Olive Branch and F.A.O. Emblem

1991. International Literacy Year.

1747	**345**	75 h. multicoloured	45	20
1748		150 h. multicoloured	90	45

1991. World Food Day.

1749	**346**	75 h. multicoloured	45	20
1750		150 h. multicoloured	90	45

347 Child's Profile and Emblem

1991. World Children's Day.

1751	**347**	75 h. multicoloured	45	20
1752		150 h. multicoloured	90	45

348 Arabian Woodpecker

349 Arabian Bustard

350 Crested Lark

351 Turtle Dove

352 Western Reef Heron

353 Arabian Chukar

354 Hoopoe

355 Peregrine Falcon

356 Houbara Bustard

1992. Birds.

1753	**348**	25 h. multicoloured	20	10
1754	**349**	25 h. multicoloured	20	10
1755	**350**	25 h. multicoloured	20	10
1756	**351**	25 h. multicoloured	20	10
1757	**352**	25 h. multicoloured	20	10
1758	**353**	25 h. multicoloured	20	10
1759	**354**	25 h. multicoloured	20	10
1760	**355**	25 h. multicoloured	20	10
1761	**356**	25 h. multicoloured	20	10
1762	**348**	50 h. multicoloured	40	20
1763	**349**	50 h. multicoloured	40	20
1764	**350**	50 h. multicoloured	40	20
1765	**351**	50 h. multicoloured	40	20
1766	**352**	50 h. multicoloured	40	20
1767	**353**	50 h. multicoloured	40	20
1768	**354**	50 h. multicoloured	40	20
1769	**355**	50 h. multicoloured	40	20
1770	**356**	50 h. multicoloured	40	20
1771	**348**	75 h. multicoloured	55	25
1772	**349**	75 h. multicoloured	55	25
1773	**350**	75 h. multicoloured	55	25
1774	**351**	75 h. multicoloured	55	25
1775	**352**	75 h. multicoloured	55	25
1776	**353**	75 h. multicoloured	55	25
1777	**354**	75 h. multicoloured	55	25
1778	**355**	75 h. multicoloured	55	25
1779	**356**	75 h. multicoloured	55	25
1780	**348**	100 h. multicoloured	35	20
1781	**349**	100 h. multicoloured	35	20
1782	**350**	100 h. multicoloured	70	35
1783	**351**	100 h. multicoloured	70	35
1784	**352**	100 h. multicoloured	70	35
1785	**353**	100 h. multicoloured	70	35
1786	**354**	100 h. multicoloured	70	35
1787	**355**	100 h. multicoloured	70	35
1788	**356**	100 h. multicoloured	70	35
1789	**348**	150 h. multicoloured	1·00	50
1790	**349**	150 h. multicoloured	1·00	50
1791	**350**	150 h. multicoloured	1·00	50
1792	**351**	150 h. multicoloured	1·00	50
1793	**352**	150 h. multicoloured	1·00	50
1794	**353**	150 h. multicoloured	1·00	50
1795	**354**	150 h. multicoloured	1·00	50
1796	**355**	150 h. multicoloured	1·00	50
1797	**356**	150 h. multicoloured	1·00	50

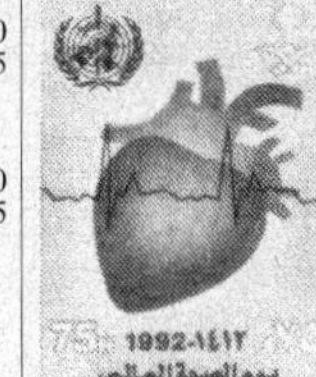
357 Heart and Cardiograph

358 Arabic Script

1992. World Health Day.

1798	**357**	75 h. multicoloured	45	20
1799		150 h. multicoloured	90	45

1992. Battle of Mt. Uhod (between Mecca and Medina, 625 A.D.) Commemoration.

1800	**358**	75 h. green and orange	45	20
1801		150 h. dp blue, bl & grn	90	45

359 Mosque, Yalamlam Miqat

1992. Pilgrimage to Mecca.

1802	**359**	75 h. multicoloured	45	20
1803		150 h. multicoloured	90	45

360 Human Pyramid inside House

1992. Population and Housing Census.

1804	**360**	75 h. multicoloured	45	20
1805		150 h. multicoloured	90	45

361 Vegetables

1992. World Food Day. Multicoloured.

1806		75 h. Type **361**	45	20
1807		150 h. Fruits	90	45

362 Decree of Regional System

363 Decree of Consultative Council

364 Decree of Essential Governing

1992. Declaration of Basic Law of Government.

1808	**362**	75 h. black, silver & grn	45	20
1809	**363**	75 h. black, silver & grn	45	20
1810	**364**	75 h. black, silver & grn	45	20
1811	**362**	150 h. multicoloured	90	45
1812	**363**	150 h. multicoloured	90	45
1813	**364**	150 h. multicoloured	90	45

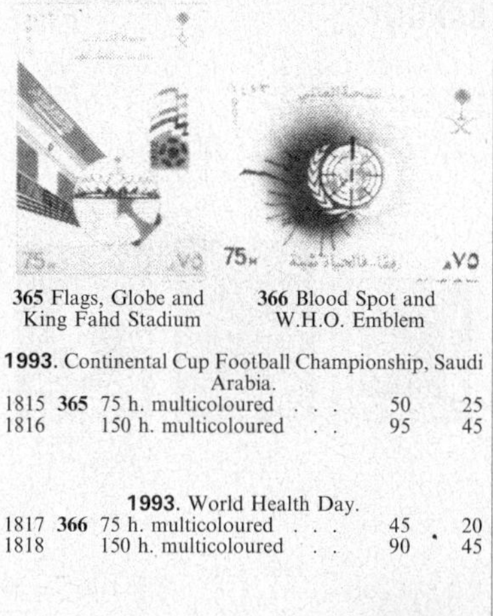

365 Flags, Globe and King Fahd Stadium

366 Blood Spot and W.H.O. Emblem

1993. Continental Cup Football Championship, Saudi Arabia.

1815 **365** 75 h. multicoloured . . . 50 25
1816 150 h. multicoloured . . 95 45

1993. World Health Day.

1817 **366** 75 h. multicoloured . . . 45 20
1818 150 h. multicoloured . . 90 45

367 Arabic Script

368 I.T.U. Emblem

1993. Battle of Khandaq (between Mecca and Medina, 627 A.D.) Commemoration.

1819 **367** 75 h. green and orange . 45 20
1820 150 h. dp blue, bl & grn . 90 45

1993. 25th Anniv of World Telecommunications Day.

1821 **368** 75 h. multicoloured . . . 45 20
1822 150 h. multicoloured . . 90 45

369 That Irq Miqat

1993. Pilgrimage to Mecca.

1823 **369** 75 h. multicoloured . . . 45 20
1824 150 h. multicoloured . . 90 45

370 Desert, Oasis, Mountains and Sea Environments

1993. World Food Day.

1825 **370** 75 h. multicoloured . . . 45 20
1826 150 h. multicoloured . . 90 45

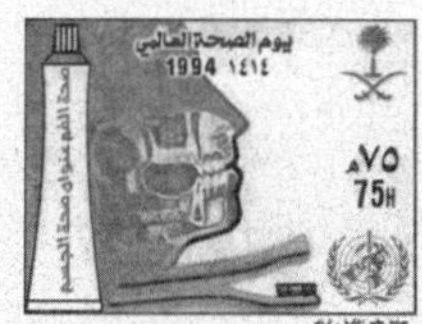

371 X-ray of Teeth and Cleaning Implements

1994. World Health Day.

1827 **371** 75 h. multicoloured . . . 45 20
1828 150 h. multicoloured . . 90 30

372 "100" and Olympic Rings

1994. Centenary of International Olympic Committee.

1829 **372** 75 h. multicoloured . . . 50 25
1830 150 h. multicoloured . . 1·00 50

373 Namirah Mosque and Tents

1994. Pilgrimage to Mecca.

1831 **373** 75 h. multicoloured . . 45 20
1832 150 h. multicoloured . . 90 45

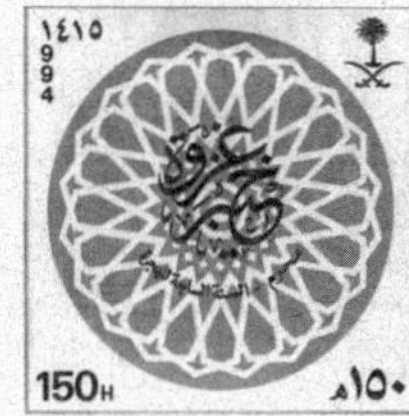

374 Arabic Script

1994. Battle of Khaibar Commemoration.

1833 **374** 75 h. green and gold . . 45 20
1834 150 h. blue, silver and green 90 45

375 Flag, International and Saudi Football Federation Emblems and Player

1994. Qualification of Saudi Arabian Team to Final Rounds of World Cup Football Championship, U.S.A. Multicoloured.

1835 75 h. Type **375** 50 25
1836 150 h. Maps of United States and Saudi Arabia and player (51 × 27 mm) . . . . . . 1·00 50

376 Council Building

1994. Establishment of Consultative Council (advisory body). Multicoloured.

1837 75 h. Type **376** 45 20
1838 150 h. Council building (closer view) 90 45

377 King Abdul Aziz Port, Dammam

378 Islam Port, Jeddah

1994. Saudi Ports. (a) Dammam.

1389a **377** 25 h. multicoloured . . 10 10
1389b 50 h. multicoloured . . 15 10
1840 75 h. multicoloured . . 45 20
1841 100 h. multicoloured . 70 35
1842 150 h. multicoloured . 90 45

(b) Jeddah.

1845 **378** 25 h. multicoloured . . 10 10
1846 50 h. multicoloured . . 15 10
1847 75 h. multicoloured . . 25 15
1848 100 h. multicoloured . . 50 25

385 Crops inside Greenhouse

1994 World Food Day. Multicoloured.

1880 75 h. Type **385** 45 20
1881 150 h. Crops on globe (36 × 37 mm) 90 45

386 U.N. Emblem

1995. 50th Anniv of U.N.O. Multicoloured.

1882 75 h. Type **386** 45 20
1883 150 h. U.N. headquarters, New York (26 × 52 mm) 90 45

387 Emblem and Map of Member Countries

1995. 50th Anniv of Arab League.

1884 **387** 75 h. yellow, mauve and green 40 20
1885 – 150 h. gold and green . . 80 40

DESIGN—36 × 27 mm: 150 h. Anniversary emblem.

388 Emblem and Family

1995. Protection of Refugees.

1886 **388** 75 h. multicoloured . . . 40 20
1887 150 h. multicoloured . . 80 40

389 Mish'ar el Haram Mosque, Muzdalefah

1995. Pilgrimage to Mecca.

1888 **389** 75 h. multicoloured . . . 40 20
1889 150 h. multicoloured . . 80 40

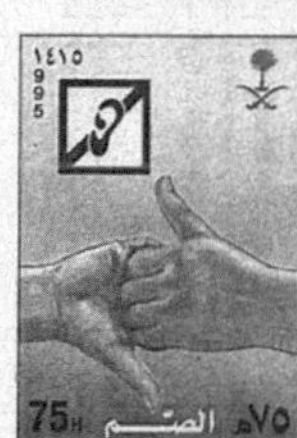

390 Hand Sign and International Symbol

391 Anniversary Emblem

1995. Deaf Week. Multicoloured.

1890 75 h. Type **390** 40 20
1891 150 h. International symbol (ear) and hand sign 80 40

1995. 50th Anniv of Saudia (national airline). Multicoloured.

1892 75 h. Type **391** 25 15
1893 150 h. Tailfins (horiz) 50 25

392 Ears of Wheat and Anniversary Emblem

1995. 50th Anniv of F.A.O. Multicoloured.

1894 75 h. Type **392** 25 15
1895 150 h. Anniversary emblem illuminating globe 50 25

393 Al-Khaif Mosque, Mecca

1996. Pilgrimage to Mecca.

1896 **393** 150 h. multicoloured . . + 50 25
1897 2 r. multicoloured . . . 65 35
1898 3 r. multicoloured . . . 1·00 50

NEWSPAPER STAMPS

NEJDI OCCUPATION OF HEJAZ

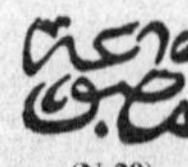
(N 29)

1925. Nos. 198 and 199a optd with Type N **29**.

No.	Type	Description	Unused	Used
N208	**11**	⅛ pi. brown	£1000	
N209		½ pi. red	£2500	

OFFICIAL STAMPS

SAUDI ARABIA

O 52

O 72

1939.

No.	Type	Description	Unused	Used
O347	O **52**	3 g. blue	3·25	1·00
O348		5 g. mauve	3·00	1·40
O349		20 g. brown	7·00	4·00
O350		50 g. turquoise	18·00	10·00
O351		100 g. olive	70·00	40·00
O352		200 g. purple	60·00	80·00

1961. Size 18½ × 22½ mm.

No.	Type	Description	Unused	Used
O449	O **72**	1 p. black	80	15
O450		2 p. green	1·25	25
O451		3 p. bistre	1·75	35
O452		4 p. blue	2·10	40
O453		5 p. red	2·75	50
O454		10 p. purple	4·50	1·50
O455		20 p. violet	7·75	3·00
O456		50 p. brown	22·00	7·50
O457		100 p. green	38·00	15·00

1964. Size 21 × 26 mm.

No.	Type	Description	Unused	Used
O497	O **72**	1 p. black	85	35
O498		2 p. green	1·75	70
O504		3 p. ochre	3·50	1·10
O505		4 p. blue	3·50	1·10
O501		5 p. red	5·50	1·00
O507		6 p. purple	6·75	1·75
O508		7 p. green	6·75	1·75
O509		8 p. red	6·75	1·75
O510		9 p. red	28·00	
O511		10 p. brown	24·00	1·75
O512		11 p. green	55·00	
O513		12 p. violet	£225	
O514		13 p. blue	8·00	2·50
O515		14 p. violet	8·00	2·50
O516		15 p. orange	60·00	1·25
O517		16 p. black	60·00	
O518		17 p. green	60·00	
O519		18 p. yellow	60·00	
O520		19 p. purple	60·00	
O520a		20 p. blue		
O521		23 p. blue	£200	
O522		24 p. green	60·00	
O523		26 p. bistre	60·00	
O524		27 p. lilac	60·00	
O525		31 p. brown	£200	
O526		33 p. green	75·00	
O527		50 p. green	£350	
O528		100 p. green	£750	

O 111

1970.

No.	Type	Description	Unused	Used
O1040	O **111**	1 p. brown	2·50	80
O1041		2 p. green	2·50	80
O1042		3 p. mauve	3·50	1·10
O1043		4 p. blue	4·00	1·75
O1044		5 p. red	4·00	1·75
O1045		6 p. orange	4·00	1·75
O1046		7 p. red	£140	
O1047		8 p. violet		
O1048		9 p. blue		
O1049		10 p. blue	6·25	2·50
O1050		11 p. green		
O1050a		12 p. brown		
O1051		20 p. blue	11·00	4·25
O1051b		23 p. brown	£300	
O1052		31 p. purple	38·00	13·50
O1053		50 p. brown		
O1054		100 p. green		

MINIMUM PRICE

The minimum price quoted is 10p which represents a handling charge rather than a basis for valuing common stamps. For further notes about prices, see introductory pages.

POSTAGE DUE STAMPS

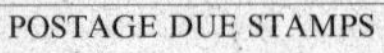

A. HEJAZ

D 7 From Old Door at El Ashra Barsbai, Shari El Ashrafuga, Cairo

(D 11)

1917.

No.	Type	Description	Unused	Used
D17	D **7**	20 pa. red	3·50	1·25
D18		1 pi. blue	3·50	1·25
D19		2 pi. purple	3·50	1·25

1921. Nos. D17/19 optd with T **7**.

No.	Type	Description	Unused	Used
D31	D **7**	20 pa. red	20·00	
D33		1 pi. blue	10·00	2·50
D34		2 pi. purple	10·00	5·00

1922. Nos. D17/19 optd with T **10**.

No.	Type	Description	Unused	Used
D39	D **7**	20 pa. red	25·00	20·00
D40		1 pi. blue	3·00	2·00
D41		2 pi. purple	4·00	2·00

1923. Optd with Type D **11**.

No.	Type	Description	Unused	Used
D47	**11**	½ pi. red	7·00	3·00
D48		1 pi. blue	9·00	10·00
D49		2 pi. orange	5·00	4·00

1924. Nos. D47/9 optd with T **14**.

No.	Type	Description	Unused	Used
D57	**11**	½ pi. red	£2500	
D58		1 pi. blue	£2500	
D59		2 pi. orange	£2500	

1925. Nos. D17/19 optd with T **15**.

No.	Type	Description	Unused	Used
D88		20 pa. red	£250	£350
D91		1 pi. blue	20·00	12·00
D92		2 pi. purple	15·00	10·00

1925. Nos. D17/19 optd with T **16**.

No.	Type	Description	Unused	Used
D93a		20 pa. red	£300	
D94		1 pi. blue	18·00	
D96		2 pi. claret	15·00	

No. D93a has the overprint inverted.

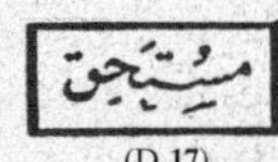
(D 17)

1925. Stamps of 1924 (optd T **16**) optd with Type D **17**.

No.	Type	Description	Unused	Used
D149	**11**	½ pi. red (No. 116)	80·00	
D150		1½ pi. lilac (No. 99)	80·00	
D151		2 pi. orange (No. 119)	£120	
D152		3 pi. brown (No. 120)	80·00	
D153		5 pi. green (No. 103)	80·00	

(D 18)

D 25

1925. Stamps of 1922 optd with Type D **18**.

No.	Type	Description	Unused	Used
D154	**11**	⅛ pi. brown	30·00	
D155		½ pi. red	30·00	
D156		1 pi. blue	30·00	
D157		1½ pi. lilac	30·00	
D158		2 pi. orange	30·00	
D160		3 pi. brown	30·00	
D161		5 pi. green	40·00	
D162	–	10 pi. purple and mauve	40·00	

1925. Nos. D154/62 optd with Type D **17**.

No.	Type	Description	Unused	Used
D163	**11**	⅛ pi. brown	15·00	4·50
D164		½ pi. red	15·00	4·50
D165		1 pi. blue	20·00	6·00
D166		1½ pi. lilac	15·00	4·50
D167		2 pi. orange	15·00	4·50
D169		3 pi. brown	15·00	4·50
D170		5 pi. green	15·00	4·50
D171	–	10 pi. purple and mauve	20·00	9·00

1925. Optd with T **24**.

No.	Type	Description	Unused	Used
D186	D **25**	½ pi. blue	6·50	
D187		1 pi. orange	6·50	
D188		2 pi. brown	6·50	
D189		3 pi. pink	6·50	

These stamps without overprint were not officially issued.

B. NEJDI OCCUPATION OF HEJAZ

1925. Nos. D47/9 of Hejaz optd with T **25**.

No.	Type	Description	Unused	Used
D203	**11**	½ pi. red	18·00	
D204c		1 pi. blue	50·00	
D205c		2 pi. orange	50·00	

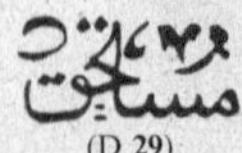
(D 29)

(D 33)

1925. Hejaz Postage Stamps of 1922 optd with Type D **29**.

No.	Type	Description	Unused	Used
D206	**11**	½ pi. red	20·00	
D207		3 pi. red	20·00	

1925. Postage stamps optd with T **32** further optd with Type D **33**.

No.	Type	Description	Unused	Used
D232	**28**	1 pi. blue	15·00	
D233		2 pi. orange	15·00	
D234	**11**	3 pi. red	12·00	
D236	**28**	5 pi. green	25·00	

1925. No. D40 of Hejaz optd with T **32**.

No.	Type	Description	Unused	Used
D238	D **7**	1 pi. blue	70·00	

C. HEJAZ AND NEJD

D 40

D 42 Tougra of Ibn Saud

1926.

No.	Type	Description	Unused	Used
D267	D **40**	½ pi. red	2·50	1·00
D270		2 pi. orange	2·50	
D272		6 pi. brown	2·50	

1926. Pan-Islamic Congress, Cairo. Optd with T **40**.

No.	Type	Description	Unused	Used
D281	D **40**	½ pi. red	5·00	3·50
D282		2 pi. orange	5·00	3·50
D283		6 pi. brown	5·00	3·50

1927.

No.	Type	Description	Unused	Used
D292	D **42**	1 pi. grey	7·50	1·00
D293		2 pi. violet	8·50	1·00

D. SAUDI ARABIA

1935. No. 331a optd **T** in a circle.

No.	Type	Description	Unused	Used
D343	**49**	½ g. red	£160	

D 52

D 72

1937.

No.	Type	Description	Unused	Used
D347	D **52**	½ g. brown	10·00	4·40
D348		1 g. blue	11·00	4·50
D349		2 g. purple	15·00	10·00

1961.

No.	Type	Description	Unused	Used
D449	D **72**	1 p. violet	4·75	3·00
D450		2 p. green	8·25	4·25
D451		4 p. red	10·50	7·50

SAXONY Pt. 7

A former kingdom in S. Germany. Stamps superseded in 1868 by those of the North German Federation.

10 pfennige = 1 neugroschen;
30 neugroschen = 1 thaler

1

2

3 Friedrich August II

1850. Imperf.

No.	Type	Description	Unused	Used
1	**1**	3 pf. red	£5000	£5000

1851. Imperf.

No.	Type	Description	Unused	Used
7	**2**	3 pf. green	£100	65·00

1851. Imperf.

No.	Type	Description	Unused	Used
10	**3**	½ ngr. black on grey	50·00	7·50
12		1 ngr. black on pink	50·00	7·00
13		2 ngr. black on blue	£225	42·00
14		3 ngr. black on yellow	£140	16·00

4 King Johann I

5

6

1855. Imperf.

No.	Type	Description	Unused	Used
16	**4**	½ ngr. black on grey	8·00	2·25
18		1 ngr. black on pink	8·00	1·50
20		2 ngr. black on blue	25·00	5·50
23		3 ngr. black on yellow	16·00	3·25
24		5 ngr. red	65·00	32·00
28		10 ngr. blue	£200	£225

1863. Perf.

No.	Type	Description	Unused	Used
31	**5**	3 pf. green	1·00	18·00
36		½ ngr. orange	60	2·25
39	**6**	1 ngr. pink	60	1·50
40		2 ngr. blue	1·75	5·00
42		3 ngr. brown	2·00	8·00
45		5 ngr. blue	10·00	32·00
46		5 ngr. purple	16·00	35·00
47		5 ngr. grey	18·00	70·00

SCHLESWIG (SLESVIG) Pt. 7

Stamps issued during the plebiscite of 1920.

100 pfennig = 1 German mark
100 ore = 1 Danish krone

1 Arms

3 View of Schleswig

1920.

No.	Type	Description	Unused	Used
1	**1**	2½ pf. grey	10	10
2		5 pf. green	10	10
3		7½ pf. brown	10	10
4		10 pf. red	10	10
5		15 pf. purple	10	10
6		20 pf. blue	10	15
7		25 pf. orange	40	1·00
8		35 pf. brown	1·25	2·50
9		40 pf. violet	40	70
10		75 pf. green	2·00	3·50
11	**3**	1 m. brown	1·25	3·00
12		2 m. blue	4·00	9·00
13		5 m. green	6·00	14·00
14		10 m. red	16·00	28·00

1920. Values in Danish currency and optd **1. ZONE**.

No.	Type	Description	Unused	Used
29	**1**	1 ore grey	10	60
30		5 ore green	10	30
31		7 ore brown	10	50
32		10 ore red	15	60
33		15 ore purple	15	60
34		20 ore blue	15	75
35		25 ore orange	40	3·50
36		35 ore brown	90	6·00
37		40 ore violet	45	2·00
38		75 ore green	50	4·00
39	**3**	1 k. brown	75	6·00
40		2 k. blue	5·50	30·00
41		5 k. green	3·50	35·00
42		10 k. red	10·00	70·00

OFFICIAL STAMPS

1920. Nos. 1/14 optd **C.I.S.** (= "Comission Interalliee Slesvig").

No.	Type	Description	Unused	Used
O15	**1**	2½ pf. grey	65·00	90·00
O16		5 pf. green	65·00	£100
O17		7½ pf. brown	65·00	90·00
O18		10 pf. red	65·00	£110
O19		15 pf. red	35·00	50·00
O20		20 pf. blue	60·00	60·00

O21 1 25 pf. orange £110 £140
O22 35 pf. brown £110 £160
O23 40 pf. violet . . . . 75·00 90·00
O24 75 pf. green £110 £250
O25 3 1 m. brown £110 £250
O26 2 m. blue £160 £275
O27 5 m. green £225 £375
O28 10 m. red £450 £550

SCHLESWIG-HOLSTEIN Pt. 7

Two former Duchies of the King of Denmark which, following a revolt, established a Provisional Government in 1848. Danish stamps were in use from 1851 in Schleswig and 1853 in Holstein.

The Duchies were invaded by Prussia and Austria in 1864 and, by the Convention of Gastein in 1865, were placed under joint sovereignty of those countries, with Holstein administered by Austria.

The Duchies were annexed by Prussia in 1867 and from 1868 used the stamps of the North German Confederation.

96 skilling = 1 Rigsbankdaler (Danish)
16 schilling = 1 mark

SCHLESWIG-HOLSTEIN

1

2

1850. Imperf.
2 1 1 s. blue £300 £4500
4 2 s. pink £500 £6000

1865. Inscr "SCHLESWIG-HOLSTEIN". Roul.
6 2 ½ s. pink . . . . 25·00 42·00
7 1¼ s. green . . . . 11·00 18·00
8 1⅓ s. mauve . . . . 38·00 £120
9 2 s. blue . . . . 40·00 £225
10 4 s. bistre . . . . 48·00 £1100

SCHLESWIG

1864. Inscr "HERZOGTH. SCHLESWIG". Roul.
24 2 ½ s. green . . . . 26·00 48·00
21 1¼ s. green . . . . 40·00 14·00
25 1¼ s. lilac . . . . 55·00 14·00
27 1⅓ s. pink . . . . 26·00 60·00
28 2 s. blue . . . . 22·00 48·00
22 4 s. red . . . . 95·00 £400
29 4 s. bistre . . . . 26·00 80·00

HOLSTEIN

6

9

10

1864. Imperf.
51 6 1¼ s. blue . . . . 35·00 45·00

1864. Roul.
59 9 1¼ s. blue . . . . 32·00 14·00

1865. Roul.
61 10 ½ s. green . . . . 55·00 90·00
62 1¼ s. mauve . . . . 32·00 15·00
63 1⅓ s. pink . . . . 55·00 38·00
64 2 s. blue . . . . 40·00 42·00
65 4 s. bistre . . . . 45·00 70·00
On the 1⅓ s. and 4 s. the word "SCHILLING" is inside the central oval.

1868. Inscr "HERZOGTH. HOLSTEIN". Roul.
66 2 1¼ s. purple . . . . 60·00 15·00
67 2 s. blue £120 £130

SENEGAL Pt. 6; Pt. 14

A French colony incorporated in French West Africa in 1944. In 1958 Senegal became an autonomous State within the French Community and in 1959 joined the Sudan to form the Mali Federation. In 1960 the Federation broke up with Mali and Senegal becoming independent republics.

100 centimes = 1 franc

1887. Stamps of French Colonies, "Commerce" type surch in figures.
1 J 5 on 20 c. red on green . . £120 £120
2 5 on 30 c. brown on drab . £190 £190
3 10 on 4 c. brown on green . 50·00 50·00
4a 10 on 20 c. red on green . . £375 £375
5 15 on 20 c. red on green . . 40·00 40·00

1892. Stamps of French Colonies, "Commerce" type, surch **SENEGAL** and new value.
6 J 75 on 15 c. blue on blue . . £350 £120
7 1 f. on 5 c. green on green . £350 £140

1892. "Tablet" key-type inscr "SENEGAL ET DEPENDANCES".
8 D 1 c. black and red on blue 50 40
9 2 c. brown & blue on buff 1·40 1·00
10 4 c. red and blue on grey . 90 90
21 5 c. green and red 85 40
12 10 c. black & blue on lilac 4·75 3·00
22 10 c. red and blue . . . . 2·25 40
13 15 c. blue and red . . . . 4·25 75
23 15 c. grey and red . . . . 2·25 80
14 20 c. red & blue on green . 4·00 4·00
15 25 c. black & red on pink . 6·00 2·25
24 25 c. blue and red . . . . 14·00 20·00
16 30 c. brown & bl on drab . 6·75 5·00
17 40 c. red & blue on yellow 13·00 12·00
18 50 c. red and blue on pink 16·00 16·00
25 50 c. brown & red on blue 27·00 27·00
19 75 c. brown & red on orge 8·50 10·00
20 1 f. green and red . . . . 10·50 10·00

1903. Surch.
26 D 5 on 40 c. red & blue on yell 8·25 8·50
27 10 on 50 c. red and blue on pink . . . . 11·50 11·50
28 10 on 75 c. brown and red on orange . . . . 11·50 11·50
29 10 on 1 f. green and red . 50·00 45·00

1906. "Faidherbe". "Palms" and "Balay" key types inscr "SENEGAL".
33 I 1 c. grey and red 70 30
34 2 c. brown and red 70 40
34a 2 c. brown and blue . . . 2·00 2·00
35 4 c. brown & red on blue . 80 25
36 5 c. green and red . . . . 1·50 35
37 10 c. pink and blue . . . 4·75 35
38 15 c. violet and red . . . 4·00 1·75
39 J 20 c. black & red on blue . 3·00 1·75
40 25 c. blue and red . . . . 1·10 75
41 30 c. brn & red on pink . 3·50 3·50
42 35 c. black & red on yell . 12·00 85
43 40 c. red & blue on blue . 5·25 5·00
44 45 c. brown & red on grn 11·00 8·75
45 50 c. violet and red . . . 5·00 4·25
46 75 c. green & red on orge 3·75 2·75
47 K 1 f. black & red on blue . 14·50 12·50
48 2 f. blue and red on pink . 22·00 17·00
49 5 f. red & blue on yellow . 40·00 35·00

1912. Surch.
58 D 05 on 15 c. grey and red . 25 40
59 05 on 20 c. red and blue on green 45 70
60 05 on 30 c. brown and blue on drab 45 70
61 10 on 40 c. red and blue on yellow 50 70
62 10 on 50 c. red and blue . 1·75 2·00
63 10 on 75 c. brown and red on orange . . . . 3·00 3·75

33 Market

1914.
64 33 1 c. violet and brown . . . 10 10
65 2 c. blue and black 10 10
66 4 c. brown and grey . . . 10 10
67 5 c. green and light green . 10 10
91 5 c. red and black 15 10
68 10 c. pink and red 20 10
92 10 c. green and light green 25 20
113 10 c. blue and purple . . . 10 10
69 15 c. purple and brown . . 10 10
70 20 c. grey and brown . . . 10 15
114 20 c. green 10 25
115 20 c. blue and grey 20 30
71 25 c. blue and ultramarine 20 15
93 25 c. black and red 10 10
72 30 c. pink and black . . . 10 10
94 30 c. carmine and red . . . 30 45
116 30 c. blue and grey 20 30
117 30 c. green and olive . . . 35 35
73 35 c. violet and orange . . 10 10
74 40 c. green and violet . . 45 10
75 45 c. brown and blue . . . 70 80
95 45 c. blue and red 15 35
118 45 c. red and carmine . . 20 20
119 45 c. red and brown . . . 1·90 2·00
76 50 c. blue and purple . . . 45 60
96 50 c. blue and ultramarine 65 95
120 50 c. green and red 15 10
121 60 c. violet on pink . . . 15 30
122 65 c. green and red 15 10
77 75 c. pink and grey 35 65
123 75 c. light blue and blue . 35 50
124 75 c. blue and pink . . . 75 75
125 90 c. carmine and red . . 70 65
78 1 f. black and violet . . . 35 65
126 1 f. blue 60 50
127 1 f. blue and black 60 50
128 1 f. 10 black and green . . 2·00 2·00
129 1 f. 25 red and green . . . 60 60
130 1 f. 50 light blue and blue 1·25 75
131 1 f. 75 green and brown . 4·75 50
79 2 f. blue and pink . . . . 1·60 1·50
97 2 f. brown and blue . . . 1·40 45
132 3 f. mauve on pink . . . . 2·50 75
80 5 f. violet and green . . . 2·00 70

1915. Surch **5c** and red cross.
89 33 10 c. + 5 c. pink and red . 60 85
90 15 c. + 5 c. purple & brown 50 90

1922. Surch.
102 33 0,01 on 15 c. purple & brn 15 40
103 0,02 on 15 c. purple & brn 15 40
104 0,04 on 15 c. purple & brn 15 35
105 0,05 on 15 c. purple & brn 15 35
106 25 c. on 5 f. violet on green 50 30
98 60 on 15 c. purple & pink 50 30
99 65 on 15 c. purple & brown 50 30
100 85 on 15 c. purple & brown 60 80
101 85 on 75 c. pink and grey . 65 80
107 90 c. on 75 c. pink & red . 35 60
108 1 f. 25 on 1 f. blue . . . 30 40
109 1 f. 50 on 1 f. lt blue & bl . 55 45
110 3 f. on 5 f. brown & purple 75 50
111 10 f. on 5 f. red and blue . 3·75 2·00
112 20 f. on 5 f. brown & mauve 4·75 4·00

1931. "Colonial Exhibition" key-types.
135 E 40 c. green and black . . . 1·40 1·40
136 F 50 c. mauve and black . . 1·40 1·40
137 G 90 c. red and black . . . 1·25 1·25
138 H 1 f. 50 blue and black . . 1·40 1·40

38 Faidherbe Bridge, Dakar

39 Senegalese Girl

1935.
139 38 1 c. blue (postage) 10 30
140 2 c. brown 10 25
141 3 c. violet 10 25
142 4 c. blue 10 50
143 5 c. orange 10 15
144 10 c. purple 10 20
145 15 c. black 10 15
146 20 c. red 10 20
147 25 c. brown 25 15
148 30 c. green 15 30
149 39 35 c. green 45 50
150 38 40 c. red 15 20
151 45 c. green 15 30
152 A 50 c. orange 10 20
153 39 55 c. brown 40 40
154 A 60 c. violet 20 25
155 65 c. violet 25 15
156 70 c. brown 45 50
157 75 c. brown 70 40
158 39 80 c. violet 65 50
159 A 90 c. red 85 95
160 39 90 c. violet 40 40
161 A 1 f. violet . . . . 6·00 1·25
162 39 1 f. red . . . . 1·25 60
163 1 f. brown 15 15
164 A 1 f. 25 brown 30 55
165 1 f. 25 red 30 55
166 1 f. 40 green 30 40
167 1 f. 50 blue 20 20
168 1 f. 60 blue 50 40
169 1 f. 75 green 35 20
170 39 1 f. 75 blue 55 60
171 A 2 f. blue 45 20
172 39 2 f. 25 blue 40 50
173 2 f. 50 black 65 85
174 A 3 f. green 30 20
175 5 f. brown 20 30
176 10 f. red 80 50
177 20 f. grey 65 50
178 B 25 c. brown (air) 20 40
179 50 c. red 40 60
180 1 f. purple 30 30
181 1 f. 25 green 20 35
182 1 f. 90 blue 40 50
183 2 f. blue 25 15
184 2 f. 90 red 35 40
185 3 f. green 30 25
186 C 3 f. 50 violet 30 20
187 B 4 f. 50 green 35 45
188 C 4 f. 75 orange 40 55
189 B 4 f. 90 brown 40 55
190 C 6 f. 50 blue 65 65
191 B 6 f. 90 orange 45 45
192 C 8 f. black . . . . 1·00 75
193 15 f. red 70 65
DESIGNS—HORIZ: A, Djourbel Mosque; B, Airplane over village; C, Airplane over camel caravan.

1937. International Exhibition, Paris. As Nos. 168/73 of St.-Pierre et Miquelon.
194 20 c. violet 40 60
195 30 c. green 40 55
196 40 c. red 35 55
197 50 c. brown 35 70
198 90 c. red 35 70
199 1 f. 50 blue . . . . 50 1·40

1938. International Anti-Cancer Fund. As T **22** of Mauritania.
201 1 f. 75 + 50 c. blue . . . . . 3·50 6·00

1939. Death Centenary of Rene Caillie (explorer). As T **27** of Mauritania.
202 90 c. orange 25 35
203 2 f. violet 35 50
204 2 f. 25 blue 35 50

1939. New York World's Fair. As T **28** of Mauritania.
205 1 f. 25 red 40 50
206 2 f. 25 blue 40 55

1939. 150th Anniv of French Revolution. As T **29** of Mauritania.
207 45 c. + 25 c. green and black (postage) . . . . 4·00 4·75
208 70 c. + 30 c. brown & black . 4·00 4·75
209 90 c. + 35 c. orange & black . 4·00 4·75
210 1 f. 25 + 1 f. red and black . 4·25 4·75
211 2 f. 25 + 2 f. blue and black . 4·25 4·75
212 4 f. 75 + 4 f. blk & orge (air) 6·75 6·75

1941. National Defence Fund. Surch **SECOURS NATIONAL** and value.
213 + 1 f. on 50 c. (No. 152) . . 2·00 2·00
214 + 2 f. on 80 c. (No. 158) . . 2·00 2·00
215 + 2 f. on 1 f. 50 (No. 167) . . 3·00 3·00
216 + 3 f. on 2 f. (No. 171) . . . 2·75 2·75

1942. Air. Colonial Child Welfare Fund. As Nos. 98g/i of Niger.
216a 1 f. 50 + 3 f. 50 green . . . 15
216b 2 f. + 6 f. brown 15
216c 3 f. + 9 f. red 15

1942. Air. "Imperial Fortnight". As No. 98j of Niger.
216d 1 f. 20 + 1 f. 80 blue and red 15

1942. Air. As T **32** of Mauritania, but inscr "SENEGAL" and similar design.
217 50 f. green and yellow . . . . 1·00 1·25
218 100 f. blue and red . . . . . 1·50 1·50
DESIGN—48 × 26 mm: 100 f. Twin-engined airliner landing.

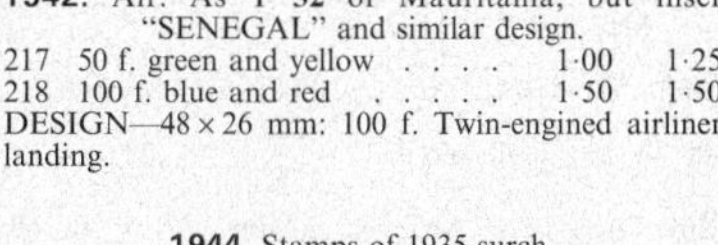

1944. Stamps of 1935 surch.
219 38 1 f. 50 on 15 c. black . . . 40 30
220 A 1 f. 50 on 65 c. violet . . . 30 40
221 38 4 f. 50 on 15 c. black . . . 40 30
222 5 f. 50 on 2 c. brown . . . 85 80
223 A 5 f. 50 on 65 c. violet . . . 40 50
224 38 10 f. on 15 c. black . . . 1·10 1·00
225 A 50 f. on 65 c. violet . . . 1·25 1·25

1944. No. 202 surch.
226 20 f. on 90 c. orange 65 75
227 50 f. on 90 c. orange . . . . 1·90 2·00

42 African Buffalo

1960. Niokolo-Koba National Park.
228 – 5 f. purple, black & green . 15 10
229 42 10 f. purple, black & green 35 15
230 – 15 f. purple, brown & sepia 40 30
231 – 20 f. brown, green & chest 50 30
232 – 25 f. brown, choc & green . 60 40
233 – 85 f. multicoloured . . . . 1·90 1·00
ANIMALS—VERT: 5 f. Roan antelope; 15 f. Warthog; 20 f. Giant eland; 85 f. Waterbuck. HORIZ: 25 f. Bushbuck.

43 African Fish Eagle

44 Mother and Child

1960. Air.
234 – 50 f. multicoloured . . . . 3·75 1·40
235 – 100 f. multicoloured . . . 6·50 1·90
236 – 200 f. multicoloured . . . 13·00 6·00
237 – 250 f. multicoloured . . . 16·00 7·25
238 43 500 f. multicoloured . . . 32·00 10·00
BIRDS—VERT: 50 f. Carmine bee-eater; 200 f. Violet turaco; 250 f. Red bishop. HORIZ: 100 f. Abyssinian roller.

1961. Independence Commemoration.
239 44 25 f. brown, blue & green . 25 20

45 Pirogue Race

1961. Sports.
240 – 50 c. brown, blue & sepia . 10 10
241 45 1 f. purple, turq & green . 10 10
242 – 2 f. sepia, bistre and blue . 10 10
243 – 30 f. purple and red . . . 70 25
244 – 45 f. black, blue & brown . 95 35
DESIGNS: 50 c. African wrestling; 2 f. Horse race; 30 f. African dancers; 45 f. Lion game.

46 Senegal Flag, U.N. Emblem and H.Q. Building

1962. 1st Anniv of Admission of Senegal to U.N.O.
245 **46** 10 f. red, ochre and green . . 15 15
246 30 f. green, ochre and red . . 30 25
247 85 f. multicoloured . . . . 1·10 55

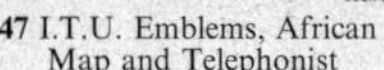

47 I.T.U. Emblems, African Map and Telephonist **48** Boxing

1962. 1st I.T.U. African Plan Sub-Committee Meeting, Dakar.
248 **47** 25 f. multicoloured 25 20

1962. Air. "Air Afrique" Airline. As T **42** of Mauritania.
249 25 f. purple, brown & myrtle . 35 20

1962. Malaria Eradication. As T **43** of Mauritania.
250 25 f. + 5 f. turquoise 40 35

1962. 1st Anniv of Union of African and Malagasy States. As T **45** of Mauritania.
251 30 f. turquoise 40 35

1963. Freedom from Hunger. As T **51** of Mauritania.
252 25 f. + 5 f. olive, brn & vio . 35 35

1963. Dakar Games. Inscr as in T **48**. Centres brown; inscr and frame colours given.
253 **48** 10 f. red and green 15 10
254 – 15 f. ochre and blue 20 15
255 – 20 f. red and blue 25 15
256 – 25 f. green and blue 30 20
257 – 30 f. red and green 70 25
258 – 85 f. blue . . . . 1·60 1·00
DESIGNS—HORIZ: 15 f. Diving; 20 f. High-jumping. VERT: 25 f. Football; 30 f. Basketball; 85 f. Running.

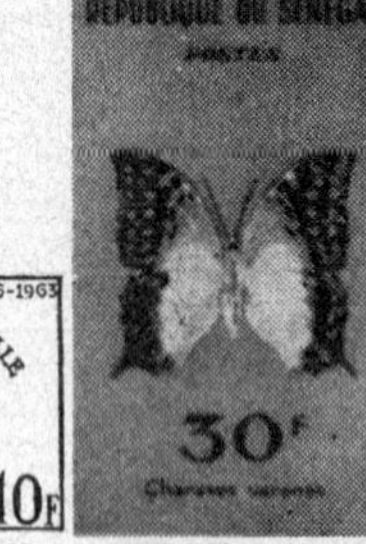

49 Main Motif of U.P.U. Monument, Berne **50** "Charaxes varanes"

1963. 2nd Anniv of Admission to U.P.U.
259 **49** 10 f. red and green 20 15
260 15 f. brown and blue . . . 20 20
261 30 f. blue and brown . . . 45 25

1963. Butterflies. Butterflies in natural colours; inscr in black; background colours given.
262 **50** 30 f. blue 90 40
263 – 45 f. orange . . . . . . 1·40 60
264 – 50 f. yellow . . . . . . 1·50 85
265 – 85 f. red . . . . 3·75 1·40
266 – 100 f. blue . . . . . . 4·50 2·10
267 – 500 f. green . . . . . . 15·00 6·75
BUTTERFLIES: 45 f. "Papilio nireus"; 10 f. "Colotis danae"; 85 f. "Epiphora bauhiniae"; 100 f. "Junonia hierta"; 500 f. "Danaus chrysippus".

1963. Air. 2nd Anniv of African and Malagasian Posts and Telecommunications Union. As T **56** of Mauritania.
268 85 f. multicoloured . . . . . 1·10 55

51 G. Berger, Owl and "Prospective" (book)

1963. 3rd Death Anniv of Prof. Gaston Berger (educationalist).
269 **51** 25 f. multicoloured 30 20

1963. Air. 1st Anniv of "Air Afrique" and "DC-8" Service Inauguration. As T **59** of Mauritania.
270 50 f. multicoloured . . . . 1·25 55

52 Globe, Scales of Justice and Flag **53** Mother and Child

1963. 15th Anniv of Declaration of Human Rights.
271 **52** 60 f. multicoloured 65 40

1963. Senegalese Red Cross.
272 **53** 25 f. multicoloured 30 25

54 Temple Gods, Abu Simbel

1964. Air. Nubian Monument Preservation Fund.
273 **54** 25 f. + 5 f. brown, green and turquoise . . . . 1·10 70

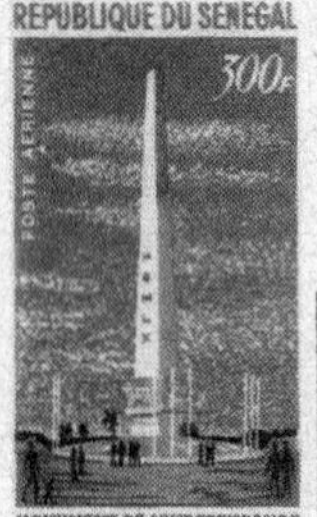

55 Independence Monument **57** Titanium Sand Dredger

56 Allegorical Figures of Twin Towns

1964. Air.
274 **55** 300 f. multicoloured . . . 3·50 1·75

1964. Air. World Twin Towns Federation Congress, Dakar.
275 **56** 150 f. brown, black & turq 2·75 1·40

1964. Senegal Industries.
276 **57** 5 f. brown, turq & lake . . 15 15
277 – 10 f. blue, brown & green . 15 10
278 – 15 f. brown, green & blue . 20 10
279 – 20 f. purple, bistre & blue 25 10
280 – 25 f. black, ochre and blue 30 10
281 – 85 f. brown, blue and red . 1·60 1·10
DESIGNS: 10 f. Titanium sorting works; 15 f. Rufisque cement works; 20 f. Loading phosphate at Pallo; 25 f. Working phosphate at Taiba; 85 f. Mineral wharf, Dakar.

58 "Supporting the Globe"

1964. Air. "Europafrique".
282 **58** 50 f. multicoloured . . . . 1·25 55

59 Basketball **60** "Syncom 2" Satellite and Rocket

1964. Air. Olympic Games, Tokyo.
283 **59** 85 f. brown and blue . . . 1·75 70
284 – 100 f. purple and green . . 2·00 90
DESIGN: 100 f. Pole-vaulting.

1964. Air. Space Telecommunications.
285 **60** 150 f. blue, brown & grn . 2·00 1·25

1964. French, African and Malagasy Co-operation. As T **68** of Mauritania.
286 100 f. brown, red and green . . 1·40 90

61 Church of Ste. Therese, Dakar **62** Pres. Kennedy

1964. Religious Buildings.
287 **61** 5 f. lake, green and blue . . 10 10
288 – 10 f. brown, black and blue 15 10
289 – 15 f. slate, brown and blue . 20 15
DESIGNS—HORIZ: 10 f. Touba Mosque. VERT: 15 f. Dakar Mosque.

1964. Air. Pres. Kennedy Commemoration.
290 **62** 100 f. brown, yellow & grn . 1·75 1·00

63 Child and Microscope

1965. Anti-Leprosy Campaign.
292 **63** 20 f. black, green & brown . 25 20
293 – 65 f. multicoloured 90 45
DESIGN: 65 f. Peycouk Village.

64 Haute Casamance

1965. Senegal Landscapes.
294 **64** 25 f. green, brown and blue (postage) 25 15
295 – 30 f. blue, green & brown . 30 15
296 – 45 f. turq, green and brown 75 30
297 – 100 f. black, green and bistre (air) . . . . 1·50 70
DESIGNS: 30 f. Sangalkam; 45 f. Senegal River forest region; 100 f. Banks of Gambia River, East Senegal (48 × 27 mm).

65 A. Seck (Director of Posts, 1873–1931) **66** Berthon-Ader Telephone

1965. Postal Services Commemoration.
298 **65** 10 f. black and brown . . . 15 15
299 – 15 f. brown and green . . . 20 15
DESIGN—HORIZ: 15 f. P.T.T. Headquarters, Dakar.

1965. I.T.U. Centenary.
300 **66** 50 f. brown, bistre & grn . 50 30
301 – 60 f. red, green and blue . 80 50
302 – 85 f. purple, red and blue 80 50
DESIGNS: 60 f. Cable-ship "Alsace"; 85 f. Picard's submarine telegraph cable relay apparatus.

67 Ploughing with Oxen

1965. Rural Development.
303 **67** 25 f. brown, violet and green 35 25
304 – 60 f. multicoloured 90 45
305 – 85 f. black, red and green . 1·25 55
DESIGNS—VERT: 50 f. Millet cultivation. HORIZ: 85 f. Rice cultivation, Casamance.

68 Goree Pirogue under Sail **69** Woman holding Child and U.N. Emblems

1965. Senegal Pirogues. Multicoloured.
306 10 f. Type **68** 20 15
307 20 f. Large pirogue at Seumbedioune 25 15
308 30 f. One-man pirogue at Fadiouth Island 65 20
309 45 f. One-man pirogue on Senegal River 95 65

1965. Air. International Co-operation Year.
310 **69** 50 f. brown, green & blue . 55 30

70 "Fruit of Cashew Tree" **71** "The Gentleman of Fashion"

1965. Fruits. Multicoloured.
311 10 f. Type **70** 15 10
312 15 f. Papaw 20 15
313 20 f. Mango 25 10
314 30 f. Groundnuts 30 15

1966. Goree Puppets.
315 **71** 1 f. blue, brown and red 10 10
316 – 2 f. orange, brown & blue 10 10
317 – 3 f. blue, brown and red 10 10
318 – 4 f. green, brown & violet 10 10
PUPPETS: 2 f. "The Lady of Fashion"; 3 f. "The Pedlar"; 4 f. "The Pounder".

72 Tom-tom Player

1966. World Festival of Negro Arts, Dakar ("Announcement").
319 **72** 30 f. brown, red & green . 30 15
See also Nos. 327/30.

73 Rocket "Diamant"

1966. Air. French Satellites.
320 **73** 50 f. red, blue & brown 70 40
321 – 50 f. black, brown & grn 70 40
322 – 90 f. blue, brown & slate 1·40 75
DESIGNS: No. 321, Satellite "A1"; No. 322, Rocket "Scout" and satellite "FR1".

74 Mackerel Tuna **76** Arms of Senegal

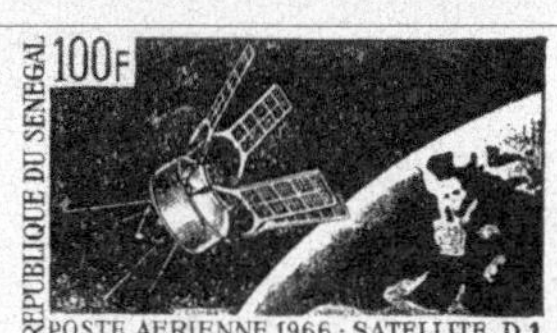

75 Satellite "D1"

1966. Senegal Fishes. Multicoloured.
323 20 f. Type **74** 25 15
324 30 f. Grouper 40 20
325 50 f. Wrasse 90 35
326 100 f. Parrot fish . . . . . . 1·75 65

1966. World Festival of Negro Arts, Dakar. As T **72**.
327 15 f. lake, orange and blue . . 15 15
328 30 f. lake, yellow and blue . . 35 20
329 75 f. black, lake and blue . . 1·25 55
330 90 f. lake, black and orange . 1·40 65
DESIGNS: 15 f. Statuette ("Sculpture"); 50 f. Musical instrument ("Music"); 75 f. Carving ("Dance"); 90 f. Ideogram.

1966. Air. Launching of Satellite "D 1".
332 **75** 100 f. blue, lake & violet . 1·50 65

1966.
333 **76** 30 f. multicoloured 25 15

1966. Air. Inauguration of DC-8F Air Services. As T **87** of Mauritania.
334 30 f. yellow, black & brown . 30 20

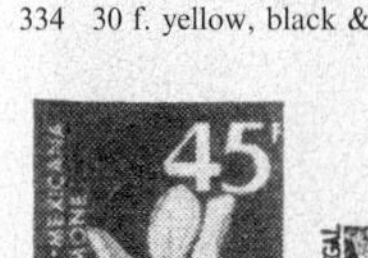

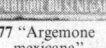

77 "Argemone mexicana" 79 Port of Ile de Goree

78 Couzinet 70 "Arc en Ciel"

1966. Flowers. Multicoloured.
335 45 f. Type **77** 45 20
336 55 f. "Dichrostachys glomerata" 50 25
337 60 f. "Haemanthus multiflorus" 60 35
338 90 f. "Adansonia digitata" . . 1·50 50

1966. Air. 30th Anniv of Disappearance of Jean Mermoz (aviator).
339 **78** 20 f. slate, purple and blue 30 20
340 – 35 f. slate, brown & green . 70 20
341 – 100 f. lake, emer & green . 1·25 45
342 – 150 f. lake, black and blue . 2·50 1·00
DESIGNS—HORIZ: 35 f. Latecoere 300 flying boat "Croix du Sud"; 100 f. Map of Mermoz's last flight across Atlantic Ocean. VERT: 150 f. Jean Mermoz.

1966. Tourism.
343 **79** 20 f. lake, blue and black . 20 15
344 – 25 f. sepia, green and red . 1·40 30
345 – 30 f. blue, red and green . 30 10
346 – 50 f. blue, green and red . 50 20
347 – 90 f. black, green and blue 1·10 45
DESIGNS: 25 f. Liner "France" at Dakar; 30 f. N'Gor Hotel and tourist cabins; 50 f. N'Gor Bay and Hotel; 90 f. Town Hall, Dakar.

80 Laying Water Mains

1967. International Hydrological Decade.
348 **80** 10 f. blue, green & brown . 15 15
349 – 20 f. brown, green & blue . 30 20
350 – 30 f. blue, orange & black . 35 20
351 – 50 f. lake, flesh and blue . 75 20
DESIGNS—HORIZ: 20 f. Cattle at trough. VERT: 30 f. Decade emblem; 50 f. Obtaining water from primitive well.

81 Terminal Building, Dakar-Yoff Airport

1967. Air.
352 **81** 200 f. indigo, blue & brown 2·50 1·00

82 Lions Emblem

1967. 50th Anniv of Lions International.
353 **82** 30 f. multicoloured 35 20

83 Blaise Diagne

1967. 95th Birth Anniv of Blaise Diagne (statesman).
354 **83** 30 f. brown, green & purple 30 20

84 Spiny Mimosa

1967. Air. Flowers. Multicoloured.
355 100 f. Type **84** . . . . 2·00 75
356 150 f. Barbary fig . . . . . . 3·00 1·75

85 "Les Demoiselles d'Avignon" (Picasso) 86 Carved Eagle and Kudu's Head

1967. Air.
357 **85** 100 f. multicoloured . . . 2·25 1·10

1967. "EXPO 67" World Fair, Montreal.
358 **86** 90 f. black and red . . . . 1·25 50
359 – 150 f. multicoloured . . . 1·75 75
DESIGN: 150 f. Maple leaf and flags.

1967. Air. 5th Anniv of U.A.M.P.T. As T **101** of Mauritania.
360 100 f. red, green and violet 90 50

87 I.T.Y. Emblem 88 Currency Tokens

1967. International Tourist Year.
361 **87** 50 f. black and blue . . . 80 35
362 – 100 f. black, green & orge 2·50 1·00
DESIGN: 100 f. Tourist photographing hippopotamus.

1967. 5th Anniv of West African Monetary Union.
363 **88** 30 f. violet, purple & grey 25 15

89 "Lyre" Stone, Kaffrine 90 Nurse feeding Baby

1967. 6th Pan-American Prehistory Congress, Dakar.
364 **89** 30 f. red, blue and green . 25 15
365 – 70 f. red, brown and blue . 65 30
DESIGN: 70 f. Ancient bowl, Bandiala.

1967. Senegalese Red Cross.
366 **90** 50 f. lake, red and green . 50 25

91 Human Rights Emblem 92 Chancellor Adenauer

1968. Human Rights Year.
367 **91** 30 f. gold and green 35 20

1968. Air. Adenauer Commemoration.
368 **92** 100 f. sepia, red & green . . 1·40 55

93 Weather Balloon, Flourishing Plants and W.M.O. Emblem 94 Parliament Building, Dakar

1968. Air. World Meteorological Day.
370 **93** 50 f. green, blue & black . . 65 40

1968. Inter-Parliamentary Union Meeting, Dakar.
371 **94** 30 f. red 30 15

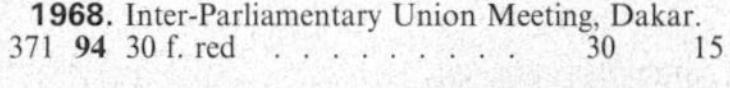

95 Spiny Lobster 96 Lesser Pied Kingfisher

1968. Marine Crustacea. Multicoloured.
372 10 f. Type **95** 15 10
373 20 f. Sea crawfish 25 15
374 35 f. Prawn 75 20
375 100 f. Gooseneck barnacle . . 2·10 65

1968. Birds. Multicoloured.
376 5 f. Type **96** (postage) 60 15
377 15 f. African jacana 90 25
378 70 f. African darter . . . . . 3·00 1·60
379 250 f. Village weaver (air) . . 7·50 2·75
380 300 f. Comb duck . . . . . . 11·50 3·75
381 500 f. Bateleur . . . . 19·00 7·00
Nos. 379/81 are $45\frac{1}{2} \times 26$ mm.

97 Ox and Syringe 98 Hurdling

1968. Campaign for Prevention of Cattle Plague.
382 **97** 30 f. red, green and blue . . 55 20

1968. Air. Olympic Games, Mexico.
383 **98** 20 f. brown, green & blue . 20 15
384 – 30 f. brown, ochre & pur . 25 15
385 – 50 f. lake, brown and blue . 75 35
386 – 75 f. bistre, brown & green . 1·25 60
DESIGNS: 30 f. Throwing the javelin; 50 f. Judo; 75 f. Basketball.

1968. Air. "Philexafrique". Stamp Exhibition, Abidjan (1st issue) (1969). As T **113a** of Mauritania. Multicoloured.
387 100 f. "Young Girl reading a Letter" (J. Raoux) . . . . . 2·25 2·00

99 Senegalese Boy 101 Faculty Building

1968. 20th Anniv of W.H.O.
388 **99** 30 f. black, red and green . 25 25
389 45 f. black, green & brown 60 20

1969. Faculty of Medicine and Pharmaceutics, and Sixth "Medical Days", Dakar.
391 **101** 30 f. blue and green . . . 30 20
392 – 50 f. green, red & brown . 35 25
DESIGN—VERT: 50 f. Emblem of "Medical Days".

1969. Air. "Philexafrique". Stamp Exn, Abidjan, Ivory Coast (2nd issue). As T **114a** of Mauritania.
393 50 f. violet, slate and green . . 1·25 1·25
DESIGN: 50 f. Modern Dakar and Senegal stamp of 1935.

102 Panet, Camels and Route-map

1969. 150th Birth Anniv of Leopold Panet, first Explorer of the Mauritanian Sahara.
394 **102** 75 f. brown and blue . . 1·50 75

103 A.I.T.Y. Emblem

1969. Air. African International Tourist Year.
395 **103** 100 f. red, green and blue 75 45

104 I.L.O. Emblem 105 Pres. Lamine Gueye

1969. 50th Anniv of I.L.O.
396 **104** 30 f. black and turquoise . 25 15
397 45 f. black and red . . . 40 20

1969. Air. President Gueye Memorial.
398 **105** 30 f. black, buff & brown 25 15
399 – 45 f. black, blue & brown 35 20
DESIGN: 45 f. Pres. Lamine Gueye (different).

106 Arms of Casamance

1969. Senegal Arms. Multicoloured.
401 15 f. Type **106** 15 10
402 20 f. Arms of Ile de Goree . . 20 15

1969. 5th Anniv of African Development Bank. As T **122a** of Mauritania.
403 30 f. brown, green and slate . 25 15
404 45 f. brown and green 35 20

108 Mahatma Gandhi **109** "Transmission of Thought" (O. Faye)

1969. Birth Centenary of Mahatma Gandhi.
405 **108** 50 f. multicoloured . . . 45 25

1969. Air. Tapestries. Multicoloured.
407 25 f. Type **109** 60 20
408 30 f. "The Blue Cock" (Mamadou Niang) 35 20
409 45 f. "The Fairy" (Papa Sidi Diop) 85 50
410 50 f. "Fari" (A. N'Diaye) . . 1·25 75
411 75 f. "Lunaris" (J. Lurcat) . . 1·25 70
SIZE—VERT: 30 f., 45 f. 37 × 49 mm. HORIZ: 50 f. 49 × 37 mm.

110 Baila Bridge

1969. Air. Europafrique.
412 **110** 100 f. multicoloured . . . 1·25 45

111 Rotary Emblem and "Sailing Ship"

1969. 30th Anniv of Dakar Rotary Club.
413 **111** 30 f. yellow, blk & blue . 35 20

1969. 10th Anniv of A.S.E.C.N.A. As T **94a** of Niger.
414 100 f. slate 90 35

113 Cape Skiring, Casamance **115** Bottle-nosed Dolphins

114 Lecrivain, Latecoere 25 Airplane and Route

1969. Tourism.
415 **113** 20 f. green, lake and blue . 20 15
416 – 30 f. lake, brown and blue 25 15
417 – 35 f. black, brown & blue 1·10 30
418 – 45 f. lake and blue . . . 75 20
DESIGNS: 30 f. Tourist camp, Niokolo-Koba; 35 f. Herd of African elephants, Niokolo-Koba Park; 45 f. Millet granaries on stilts, Fadiouth Island.

1970. Air. 40th Anniv of Disappearance of Emile Lecrivain (aviator).
419 **114** 50 f. lake, slate & green . 1·00 40

1970.
420 **115** 50 f. multicoloured . . . 1·40 60

116 R. Maran (Martinique)

1970. Air. Negro Celebrities (1st series).
421 **116** 30 f. brown, green & lake 25 15
422 – 45 f. brown, blue & pink 40 25
423 – 50 f. brown, green & yell 45 35
PORTRAITS: 45 f. M. Garvey (Jamaica); 50 f. Dr. P. Mars (Haiti).
See also Nos. 457/60.

117 Sailing Pirogue and Obelisk **118** Lenin

1970. Air. 10th Anniv of Independence.
424 **117** 500 f. multicoloured . . . 5·00 2·75

1970. Birth Centenary of Lenin.
426 **118** 30 f. brown, stone & red . 25 15

119 Bay of Naples, and Post Office, Dakar

1970. Air. 10th "Europa" Stamp Exn, Naples.
428 **119** 100 f. multicoloured . . . 1·25 55

1970. New U.P.U. Headquarters Building, Berne. As T **81** of New Caledonia.
429 30 f. plum, blue and lake . . 25 15
430 45 f. brown, lake and green . 45 20

121 Nagakawa and Mt Fuji

1970. Air. World Fair "EXPO 70", Osaka, Japan.
431 – 25 f. red, green and lake . 20 15
432 **121** 75 f. red, blue and green . 55 30
433 – 150 f. red, brown and blue 1·60 70
DESIGNS—VERT: 25 f. "Woman playing guitar" (Hokusai) and Sun tower; 150 f. "Nanboku Beauty" (Shuncho).

122 Harbour Quayside, Dakar

1970. Air. Industrial and Urban Development.
434 **122** 30 f. blue, black and red . 25 15
435 – 100 f. brown, grn & slate 1·40 45
DESIGN: 100 f. Aerial view of city centre, Dakar.

123 Beethoven, Napoleon and "Evocation of Eroica" Symphony

1970. Air. Birth Bicentenary of Beethoven.
436 **123** 50 f. brown, orange & green 45 35
437 – 100 f. red and blue . . . 1·40 75
DESIGN: 100 f. Beethoven with quillpen and scroll.

124 Heads of Four Races

1970. Air. 25th Anniv of U.N.O.
438 **124** 100 f. multicoloured . . . 1·25 55

125 Looms and Textile Works, Thies

1970. "Industrialisation".
439 **125** 30 f. red, blue and green . 30 15
440 – 45 f. blue, brown and red . 40 20
DESIGN: 45 f. Fertiliser plant, Dakar.

126 Scouts in Camp **127** Three Heads and Sun

1970. 1st African Scouting Conference, Dakar. Mult.
441 30 f. Type **126** 30 20
442 100 f. Scout badge, Lord Baden-Powell and map . . . . . . 1·40 45

1970. International Education Year.
443 **127** 25 f. brown, blue & orge . 25 15
444 – 40 f. multicoloured . . . 45 20
DESIGN: 40 f. Map of Africa on Globe, and two heads.

128 Arms of Senegal **129** De Gaulle, Map, Ears of Wheat and Cogwheel

1970.
445 **128** 30 f. multicoloured . . . 35 15
446 35 f. multicoloured . . . 35 15
446a 50 f. multicoloured . . . 35 15
446b 65 f. multicoloured . . . 35 15
803 95 f. multicoloured . . . 35 30

1970. Air. "De Gaulle the De-coloniser". Mult.
447 50 f. Type **129** . . . . 1·25 60
448 100 f. De Gaulle, and map within "sun" . . . . 2·50 1·50

130 Refugees

1971. 20th Anniv of U.N. High Commissioner for Refugees. Multicoloured.
449 40 f. Type **130** (postage) . . . 35 20
450 100 f. Building house (air) . . 80 55
No. 450 is 46 × 27 mm.

131 "Mbayang" Horse

1971. Horse-breeding Improvement Campaign. Multicoloured.
451 25 f. "Madjiguene" 25 15
452 40 f. Type **131** 65 20
453 100 f. "Pass" . . . . 1·40 85
454 125 f. "Pepe" . . . . 2·00 1·10

132 European Girl and African Boy **133** Phillis Wheatley

1971. Racial Equality Year. Multicoloured.
455 30 f. Type **132** 25 15
456 50 f. People of four races (horiz) (37 × 30 mm) 40 25

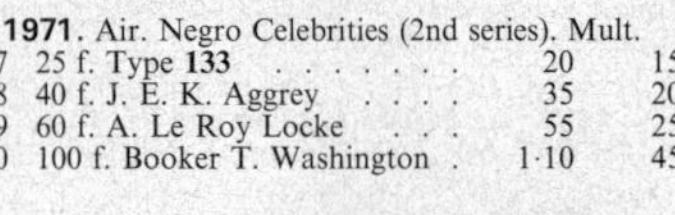

1971. Air. Negro Celebrities (2nd series). Mult.
457 25 f. Type **133** 20 15
458 40 f. J. E. K. Aggrey 35 20
459 60 f. A. Le Roy Locke . . . 55 25
460 100 f. Booker T. Washington . 1·10 45

134 "Telephones" **135** "Napoleon as First Consul" (Ingres)

1971. World Telecommunications Day.
461 **134** 30 f. brown, grn & purple 25 15
462 – 40 f. brown, red & blue . 25 20
DESIGN: 40 f. "Telecommunications" theme.

1971. Air. 150th Death Anniv of Napoleon. Mult.
463 15 f. Type **135** 30 25
464 25 f. "Napoleon in 1809" (Lefevre) 70 30
465 35 f. "Napoleon on his Death-bed" (Rouget) . . . . . . 1·00 45
466 50 f. "The Awakening to Immortality" (bronze by Rude) . . . . 1·75 80

136 Pres. Nasser **138** A. Nobel

137 Hayashida (drummer)

1971. Air. Nasser Commemoration.
467 **136** 50 f. multicoloured . . . 45 25

1971. 13th World Scout Jamboree, Asagiri, Japan. Multicoloured.
468 35 f. Type **137** 25 15
469 50 f. Japonica 40 20
470 65 f. Judo 50 25
471 75 f. Mt Fuji 60 30

1971. Air. 75th Death Anniv of Alfred Nobel (scientist and philanthropist).
472 **138** 100 f. multicoloured . . . 1·25 60

139 Persian Flag and Senegal Arms

1971. Air. 2500th Anniv of Persian Empire.
473 **139** 200 f. multicoloured . . . 2·00 1·00

140 Map and Emblem

1971. 25th Anniv of U.N.I.C.E.F. Multicoloured.
474 35 f. Type **140** 35 20
475 100 f. Nurse, children and U.N.I.C.E.F. emblem . . . 1·25 55

1971. Air. 10th Anniv of U.A.M.P.T. As T **139a** of Mauritania. Multicoloured.
476 100 f. U.A.M.P.T. H.Q., Brazzaville and arms of Senegal 80 40

142 Louis Armstrong **143** Trying for Goal

1971. Air. Louis Armstrong Commemoration.
477 **142** 150 f. brown and gold . . 2·50 1·25

1971. 6th African Basketball Championships, Dakar. Multicoloured.
478 35 f. Type **143** 30 15
479 40 f. Players reaching for ball . 35 25
480 75 f. Championships emblem . 1·00 60

144 Ice-skating

1971. Air. Winter Olympic Games, Sapporo, Japan. Multicoloured.
481 5 f. Type **144** 15 10
482 10 f. Bob-sleighing 15 10
483 125 f. Cross-country skiing . . 1·40 60

145 "Il Fonteghetto della Farina" (detail, Canaletto)

1972. Air. U.N.E.S.C.O. "Save Venice" Campaign. Multicoloured.
484 50 f. Type **145** 50 30
485 100 f. "Giudecca e S. Giorgio Maggiore" (detail, Guardi) (vert) . . . . 1·25 70

146 "Albouri and Queen Seb Fall" (scene from "The Exile of Albouri")

1972. International Theatre Day. Multicoloured.
486 35 f. Type **146** (postage) . . . 35 20
487 40 f. Scene from "The Merchant of Venice" 65 25
488 150 f. Daniel Sorano as "Shylock" ("The Merchant of Venice") (vert) (air) . . . . 2·75 1·50

147 Human Heart

1972. World Heart Month.
489 **147** 35 f. brown and blue . . 25 15
490 – 40 f. purple, grn & emer . . 30 20
DESIGN: 40 f. Doctor and patient.

148 Vegetation in Desert

1972. U.N. Environmental Conservation Conf, Stockholm. Multicoloured.
491 35 f. Type **148** (postage) . . . 35 20
492 100 f. Oil slick on shore (air) 1·25 60

149 Tartarin of Tarascon shooting Lion

1972. 75th Death Anniv of Alphonse Daudet (writer).
493 **149** 40 f. red, green & brown 45 30
494 – 100 f. brown, lt blue & bl 1·25 50
DESIGN: 100 f. Daudet and scene from "Tartarin de Tarascon".

151 Wrestling **152** Emperor Haile Selassie and Flags

1972. Olympic Games, Munich. Multicoloured.
496 15 f. Type **151** 20 15
497 20 f. Running (100 metres) . 20 15
498 100 f. Basketball . . . . . . 1·10 45
499 125 f. Judo . . . . 1·40 55

1972. Air. Emperor Haile Selassie's 80th Birthday.
501 **152** 100 f. multicoloured . . . 95 55

153 Children reading Book **154** "Senegalese Elegance"

1972. International Book Year.
502 **153** 50 f. multicoloured . . . 45 20

1972.
502a **154** 5 f. blue 10 10
502b 10 f. red 15 10
502c 15 f. orange 15 10
502d 20 f. purple 15 10
503 25 f. black 20 10
503a 30 f. brown 15 10
504 40 f. blue 30 10
504a 45 f. orange 10 10
504b 50 f. red 10 10
504c 60 f. green 35 10
504d 75 f. purple 55 35
504e 90 f. red 65 35
504f 125 f. blue 30 20
504g 145 f. orange 35 25
504h 180 f. blue 70 45
See also Nos. 1334/45.

155 Alexander Pushkin **157** "Amphicraspedum murrayanum"

1972. Pushkin (writer) Commemoration.
505 **155** 100 f. purple and pink . . 1·25 50

1972. 10th Anniv of West African Monetary Union. As T **149** of Mauritania.
506 40 f. brown, grey and blue . . 50 15

1972. Protozoe and Marine Life. Multicoloured.
507 5 f. Type **157** (postage) 10 10
508 10 f. "Pterocanium tricolpum" 15 10
509 15 f. "Ceratospyris polygona" . 15 10
510 20 f. "Cortiniscus typicus" . . 15 10
511 30 f. "Theopera cortina" . . . 15 10
512 50 f. Swordfish (air) . . . . . 1·00 50
513 65 f. Killer whale . . . . . . 1·00 65
514 75 f. Whale shark . . . . . . 1·50 80
515 125 f. Fin whale . . . . 2·25 1·25
Nos. 512/15 are size 45×27 mm.

1972. No. 353 surch **1872-1972** and value.
516 **83** 100 f. on 30 f. brown, green and chestnut . . . . . . 1·40 60

159 Melchior **160** "Sharing the Load"

1972. Christmas. Nativity Scene and Three Kings. Multicoloured.
517 10 f. Type **159** 15 15
518 15 f. Gaspard 20 15
519 40 f. Balthazar 40 20
520 60 f. Joseph 80 40
521 100 f. Mary and Baby Jesus (African representation) . . 1·50 65

1973. Europafrique.
522 **160** 65 f. black and green . . . 55 30

161 Palace of the Republic

1973. Air.
523 **161** 100 f. multicoloured . . . 1·10 60

162 Station and Aerial

1973. Inauguration of Satellite Earth Station, Gandoul.
524 **162** 40 f. multicoloured 35 20

163 Hotel Teranga

1973. Air. Opening of Hotel Teranga, Dakar.
525 **163** 100 f. multicoloured . . . 1·10 60

164 "Lions" African Emblem

1973. Air. 15th Lions International District 403 Congress, Dakar.
526 **164** 150 f. multicoloured . . . 1·50 85

165 Stages of Eclipse

1973. Eclipse of the Sun. Multicoloured.
527 35 f. Type **165** 30 15
528 65 f. Eclipse in diagramatic form 50 25
529 150 f. Eclipse and "Skylab 1" . 1·60 75

166 Symbolic Torch

1973. 10th Anniv of Organization of African Unity.
530 **166** 75 f. multicoloured . . . 55 40

1973. "Drought Relief". African Solidarity. No. 451 surch **SECHERESSE SOLIDARITE AFRICAINE** and value.
531 100 f. on 25 f. multicoloured . 1·50 75

168 "Couple with Mimosa" (Chagall)

1973. Air.
532 **168** 200 f. multicoloured . . . 3·75 2·25

169 "Riccione 1973" **171** W.H.O. Emblem and Child

1973. Air. Int Stamp Exhibition, Riccione (Italy).
533 **169** 100 f. violet, green & red . 1·25 55

1973. U.A.M.P.T. As T **155a** of Mauritania.
534 100 f. violet, green and red . . 70 35

1973. Centenary of W.M.O.
535 **171** 50 f. multicoloured . . . 35 15

172 Interpol H.Q., Paris **174** Flame Emblem and People

1973. 50th Anniv of International Criminal Police Organization (Interpol).
536 **172** 75 f. brown, blue & green 1·00 40

1973. 25th Anniv of Declaration of Human Rights. Multicoloured.
538 35 f. Type **174** 30 15
539 65 f. Emblem and drummer . 70 25

175 R. Follereau (rehabilitation pioneer) and Map

1973. Air. Cent of Discovery of Leprosy Bacillus.
540 **175** 40 f. brown, green & viol 35 15
541 – 100 f. purple, red & grn 1·25 50
DESIGN: 100 f. Dr. G. Hansen (discoverer of leprosy bacillus) and laboratory equipment.

176 "Key" Emblem
177 Amilcar Cabral and Weapons

1973. Air. World Twinned Towns Congress, Dakar. Multicoloured.

542 50 f. Type **176** 45 20
543 125 f. Arms of Dakar and meeting of citizens (horiz) . 1·25 50

1974. Amilcar Cabral (Guinea Bissau guerilla leader) Commemoration.

544 **177** 75 f. multicoloured . . . 55 40

178 Peters's Finfoot

1974. Air. Birds of Djoudj Park. Multicoloured.

545 1 f. Type **178** 10 10
546 2 f. White spoonbills 10 10
547 3 f. Crowned cranes 10 10
548 4 f. Little egret 15 10
549 250 f. Greater flamingoes (gold value) . . . . 8·00 2·10
550 250 f. Greater flamingoes (black value) . . . . 8·00 2·10

179 "Tiger attacking Wild Horse"

1974. Air. Paintings by Delacroix. Multicoloured.

551 150 f. Type **179** . . . . . . 2·00 80
552 200 f. "Tiger-hunting" . . . . 2·40 1·25

180 Athletes on Podium
182 U.P.U. Emblem, Letters and Transport

181 World Cup, Footballers and "Munich"

1974. National Youth Week. Multicoloured.

553 35 f. Type **180** 30 15
554 40 f. Dancer with mask . . . 35 20

1974. World Cup Football Championships. Footballers and locations.

555 25 f. Type **181** 15 10
556 40 f. "Hamburg" 30 15
557 65 f. "Hanover" 45 20
558 70 f. "Stuttgart" 45 25

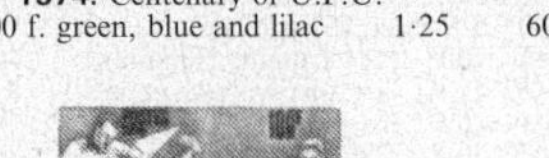

1974. Centenary of U.P.U.

559 **182** 100 f. green, blue and lilac 1·25 60

183 Archway, and Africans at Work

184 Dakar, "Gateway to Africa"

1974. 1st Dakar International Fair.

560 **183** 100 f. brown, orange & blue (postage) . . . . 1·00 35
561 **184** 350 f. silver (air) . . . . 4·00
562 1500 f. gold . . . . . . 19·00
Nos. 561/2 are embossed on foil.

1975. West Germany's Victory in World Cup Football Championships, Munich. No. 566 surch **ALLEMAGNE RFA - HOLLANDE 2-1** and value.

563 200 f. on 40 f. multicoloured . 2·00 1·25

186 Pres. Senghor and King Baudouin

1975. Visit of King Baudouin of the Belgians.

564 **186** 65 f. blue and purple . . 50 25
565 100 f. green and orange . 1·25 45

187 I.L.O. Emblem

1975. Labour Day.

566 **187** 125 f. multicoloured . . . 1·10 45

188 "Apollo" and "Soyuz" Spacecraft

1975. Air. "Apollo"–"Soyuz" Space Co-operation Project.

567 **188** 125 f. green, blue and red 1·25 60

189 Spanish "Stamp", Globe and Letters

1975. "Espana 75" (Madrid) and "Arphila 75" (Paris) International Stamp Exhibitions.

568 **189** 55 f. red, blue and green . 60 30
569 – 95 f. lt brown and brown 1·75 70
DESIGN: 95 f. Head of Apollo and "Arphila" Emblem.

190 Classroom and Tractor

1975. Technical Education.

570 **190** 85 f. brown, blue & black 75 30

191 Dr. Schweitzer

1975. Birth Centenary of Dr. Albert Schweitzer.

571 **191** 85 f. lilac and green . . . 90 55

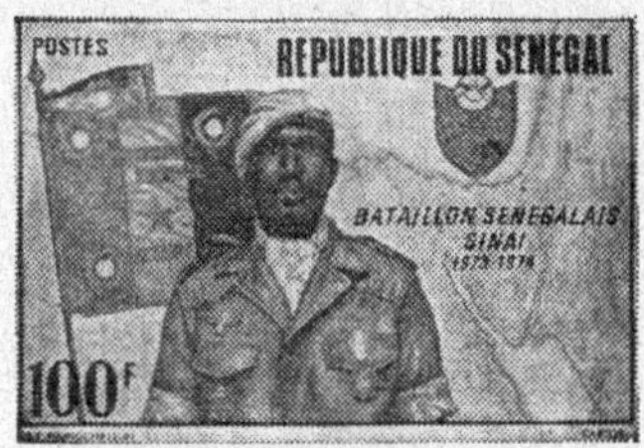

192 Soldier, Flag and Map of Sinai Desert 1973-74

1975. Senegalese Battalion with U.N.

572 **192** 100 f. multicoloured . . . 90 40

193 Stamps and Map of Italy
194 Woman pounding Maize

1975. Air. Riccione Stamp Exhibition.

573 **193** 125 f. brown, red & lilac . 1·25 75

1975. International Women's Year. Multicoloured.

574 55 f. Type **194** 35 20
575 75 f. Mother and child with woman doctor (horiz) . . . 90 25

1975. Air. "Apollo"–"Soyuz" Space Link. Optd **JONCTION 17 Juil. 1975.**

576 **188** 125 f. green, blue and red . 1·10 60

196 Stylised Caduceus

1975. French Medical Congress, Dakar.

577 **196** 50 f. multicoloured 25 15

197 "Massacre of Boston" (A. Chappel)

1975. Air. Bicentenary of American Revolution. (1st issue).

578 **197** 250 f. brown, red & blue . 2·50 1·00
579 – 500 f. red and blue . . . . 5·00 2·50
DESIGN: 500 f. Siege of Yorktown.
See also No. 593.

198 Emblem on Map of Africa

1976. International "Rights of Man" and Namibia Conferences, Dakar.

580 **198** 125 f. multicoloured . . . 60 30

199 Concorde and Flight Locations

1976. Air. Concorde's 1st Commercial Flight.

581 **199** 300 f. multicoloured . . . 4·50 2·25
See also No. 641.

200 Deep-sea Fishing

1976. "Expo", Okinawa. Multicoloured.

582 140 f. Type **200** . . . . 1·50 1·00
583 200 f. Yacht-racing . . . . . 2·00 1·25

201 Serval

1976. Basse Casamance National Park. Fauna. Mult.

584 2 f. Type **201** 10 10
585 3 f. Bar-tailed godwit (marsh bird) . . . . 1·00 30
586 4 f. Bush pig 10 10
587 5 f. African fish eagle . . . . 1·40 45
588 250 f. Sitatunga (males) . . . 2·75 1·50
589 250 f. Sitatunga (females) . . 2·75 1·50

202 Alexander Graham Bell

1976. Telephone Centenary.

590 **202** 175 f. multicoloured . . . 1·40 85

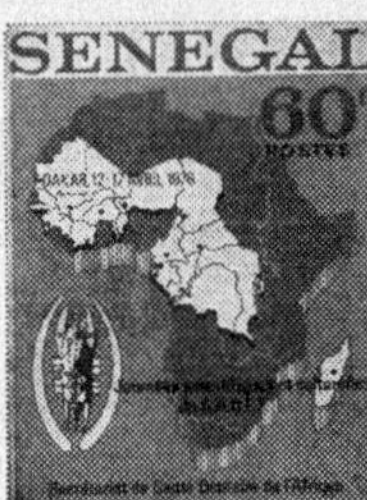

203 Map of Africa

1976. G.A.D.E.F. Scientific and Cultural Days.

591 **203** 60 f. multicoloured . . . 35 20

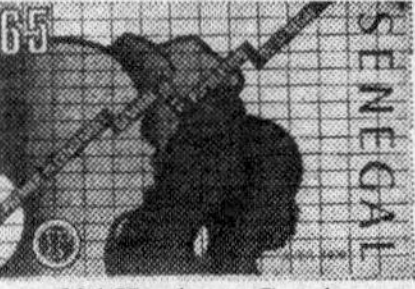

204 Heads on Graphs

1976. 1st Population Census.

592 **204** 65 f. multicoloured . . . 35 25

205 Jefferson reading Independence Declaration

1976. Bicentenary of American Revolution (2nd issue).

593 **205** 50 f. black, red and blue . 35 20

206 Plant Cultivation

1976. Operation "Sahel Vert".
594 **206** 60 f. multicoloured . . . 35 20

207 Scouts around Campfire

1976. 1st All African Scouts Jamboree, Jos, Nigeria. Multicoloured.
595 80 f. Type **207** 45 35
596 100 f. Emblem and map (vert) 90 45

208 Swimming **210** Emblem and Map

1976. Olympic Games, Montreal. Multicoloured.
597 5 f. Type **208** (postage) . . . 10 10
598 10 f. Weightlifting 10 10
599 15 f. Hurdling (horiz) 15 10
600 20 f. Horse-jumping (horiz) . 15 10
601 25 f. Steeplechasing (horiz) . 15 10
602 50 f. Wrestling (horiz) . . . 25 15
603 60 f. Hockey 30 20
604 65 f. Running 35 20
605 70 f. Gymnastics 40 25
606 100 f. Cycling (horiz) 50 30
607 400 f. Boxing (horiz) (air) . . 3·00 40
607a 500 f. Judo . . . . 3·50 1·10
608 1000 f. Basketball (41 × 41 mm) 6·50 3·50
608a 1500 f. Running (41 × 41 mm) 10·00 5·00

1976. President Senghor's 70th Birthday. Mult.
610 40 f. Type **210** 25 20
611 60 f. Star over world map . . 35 25
612 70 f. Technicians and symbol . 45 30
613 200 f. President Senghor and extended hands . . . . . . 1·60 75

211 Harvesting Tomatoes

1976. Tomato Production.
614 **211** 180 f. multicoloured . . . 1·75 1·00

212 Concorde and Route Plan

1976. Air. Dakar International Fair.
615 **212** 500 f. silver . . . . 4·50
616 1500 f. gold . . . . 18·00

213 Black Peoples' "Charter" **214** Mohammed Ali and Joe Frazier

1977. Black Peoples' Day.
617 **213** 60 f. multicoloured . . . 35 25

1977. World Boxing Championship.
618 **214** 60 f. black and blue . . . 35 15
619 – 150 f. black and green . . 1·40 50
DESIGN—HORIZ: 150 f. Mohammed Ali landing punch.

215 Dancer and Musicians

1977. 2nd World Black and African Festival of Arts and Culture, Lagos (Nigeria). Multicoloured.
620 50 f. Type **215** 25 20
621 75 f. Statuette and masks . . 70 25
622 100 f. Statuette and dancers . 90 45

216 Cog Wheels

1977. 1st Anniv of Dakar Industrial Zone.
623 **216** 70 f. brown and green . . 40 20

217 Hauling in Net **218** Burnt Tree in "Flame"

1977. Fishing. Multicoloured.
624 25 f. Type **217** (postage) . . .
625 5 f. Fishing by trawl-line (air)
626 10 f. Harpooning . . . . . .
627 15 f. Pirogue breasting wave .
628 20 f. Displaying prize catch .

1977. Fight Against Forest Fires. Multicoloured.
629 40 f. Type **218** 20 15
630 60 f. Firefighting vehicle (horiz) 40 25

219 Industrial and Pre-Industrial Communication

1977. World Telecommunications Day. Mult.
631 80 f. Type **219** 45 35
632 100 f. Printed circuit (vert) . 70 45

220 Arms of Senegal

1977. 10th Anniv of International French Language Council. Multicoloured.
633 65 f. Type **220** 35 20
634 250 f. As T **236a** of Mali . . 1·75 1·00

221 Woman rowing on River

1977. "Amphilex 1977" International Stamp Exhibition, Amsterdam. Multicoloured.
635 50 f. Type **221** 30 25
636 125 f. Senegalese woman . . 70 45

222 "Viking" and Control Centre **223** Class in Front of Blackboard

1977. Air. "Viking" Space Mission to Mars.
637 **222** 300 f. multicoloured . . . 2·00 1·25

1977. Literacy Week. Multicoloured.
638 60 f. Type **223** 35 25
639 65 f. Man with alphabet table . 35 25

224 "Mercury and Argus" (Rubens) **226** "Adoration of the Kings"

1977. Paintings. Multicoloured.
640 20 f. Type **224** 10 10
641 25 f. "Daniel and the Lions" (Rubens) 15 10
642 40 f. "The Empress" (Titian) . 20 15
643 60 f. "Flora" (Titian) 30 20
644 65 f. "Jo la belle Irlandaise" (Courbet) 35 20
645 100 f. "The Painter's Studio" (Courbet) . . . . 1·00 55

1977. Air. 1st Paris–New York Commercial Flight of Concorde. Optd **22.11.77 PARIS NEW-YORK**.
646 **199** 300 f. multicoloured . . . 4·25 2·25

1977. Christmas. Multicoloured.
647 20 f. Type **226** 10 10
648 25 f. Fanal (celebration) . . . 15 10
649 40 f. Family Christmas tree . . 20 15
650 100 f. "Three Wise Men" (horiz) 1·00 40

227 Wrestler **228** Dakar Cathedral and Parthenon, Athens

1978. Tourism. Multicoloured.
651 10 f. Type **227** 10 10
652 30 f. Soumbedioun Regatta (canoes) 20 15
653 65 f. Soumbedioun Regatta (race) (horiz) 45 25
654 100 f. Dancers (horiz) 95 50

1978. U.N.E.S.C.O. Campaign for Protection of Monuments.
655 **228** 75 f. multicoloured 35 25

229 Solar Pump

1978. Sources of Energy. Multicoloured.
656 50 f. Type **229** 25 15
657 95 f. Electricity power station . 75 30

230 Caspian and Royal Terns

1978. Saloum Delta National Park. Multicoloured.
658 5 f. Type **230** 10 10
659 10 f. Pink-backed pelicans . . 15 10
660 15 f. Grey Heron and warthog . 25 20
661 20 f. Greater flamingoes . . . 25 20
662 150 f. Grey heron and royal terns 2·10 90
663 150 f. Abyssinian ground hornbill and warthog . . . 2·10 90

231 Dome of the Rock **232** Mahatma Gandhi

1978. Palestine Freedom-Fighters.
664 **231** 60 f. multicoloured . . . 30 20

1978. Apostles of Non-Violence. Multicoloured.
665 125 f. Type **232** 85 50
666 150 f. Martin Luther King . . 90 60

233 Jenner and Vaccination of Children **234** Players, and Flags of Group 1 Countries

1978. Global Eradication of Smallpox.
668 **233** 60 f. multicoloured . . . 30 20

1978. World Cup Football Championship, Argentina. Multicoloured.
669 25 f. Type **234** 15 10
670 40 f. Players and flags of Group 2 countries 20 15
671 65 f. Players and flags of Group 3 countries 30 20
672 100 f. Players and flags of Group 4 countries 70 30

235 Symbols of Technology, Equipment and Industrialisation

1978. 3rd International Fair, Dakar.
674 **235** 110 f. multicoloured . . . 75 30

236 Wright Brothers and Wright Type A

1978. Conquest of Space. Multicoloured.
675 75 f. Type **236** (75th anniv of first powered flight) 40 20
676 100 f. Yuri Gagarin (10th death anniv of first cosmonaut) . 55 30
677 200 f. "Apollo 8" (10th anniv of first manned moon orbit) . 1·25 60

237 Henri Dunant and Children's Ward

1978. 150th Birth Anniv of Henri Dunant (founder of the Red Cross).
679 **237** 5 f. blue, black and red . 10 10
680 – 20 f. multicoloured . . . 15 10
DESIGN: 20 f. Henri Dunant and scenes of Red Cross aid.

1978. Air. "Philexafrique", Stamp Exhibition, Libreville, Gabon and International Stamp Fair, Essen, West Germany. As T **262** of Niger.
681 100 f. Capercaillie and Schleswig-Holstein 1850 1 s. stamp . . 1·50 1·25
682 100 f. Lion and Senegal 1960 200 f. Violet turaco . . . . 1·50 1·25

238 Telecommunications

1978. Post Office Achievements. Multicoloured.
683 50 f. Type **238** 25 15
684 60 f. Social welfare 30 20
685 65 f. Travelling post office . . 30 20

239 Doctor with Students

1979. 9th Medical Days, Dakar. Multicoloured.
686 50 f. Type **239** 25 15
687 100 f. Problems of pollution . 70 45

240 Agriculture

1979. Professional Pride. Multicoloured.
688 30 f. Type **240** 15 10
689 150 f. Symbols of progress . . 1·00 45

241 Open Air Class

1979. S.O.S. Children's Village. Multicoloured.
690 40 f. Type **241** 20 15
691 60 f. View of village 30 20

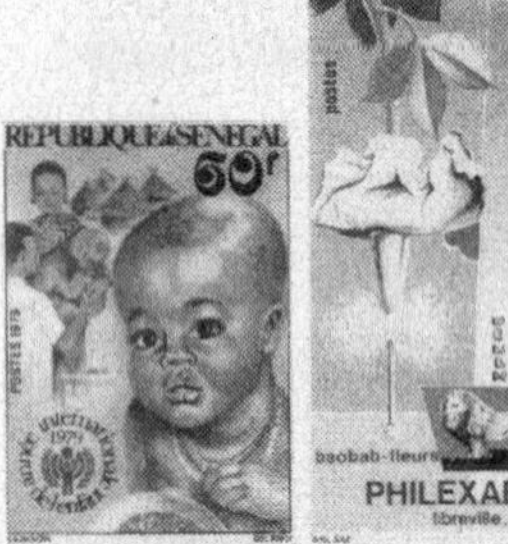

242 Young Child
243 Baobab Flower and Tree and Independence Monument

1979. International Year of the Child. Multicoloured.
692 60 f. Type **242** 30 20
693 65 f. Children with book . . . 30 20

1979. "Philexafrique" Stamp Exhibition, Libreville, Gabon. Multicoloured.
694 60 f. Type **243** 70 60
695 150 f. Drum, early telegraph apparatus and dish aerial (square, 36 × 36 mm) . . . . 1·75 1·25

244 Children ushered into Open Book

1979. 50th Anniv of International Bureau of Education.
696 **244** 250 f. multicoloured . . . 1·40 80

245 Hill and Senegal 100 f. Stamp of 1960

1979. Death Centenary of Sir Rowland Hill.
697 **245** 500 f. multicoloured . . . 3·50 2·00

246 "Black Trees" 247 Start of Race

1979. Paintings by Friedensreich Hundertwasser. Multicoloured.
698 60 f. Type **246** 75 25
699 100 f. "Head" . . . . 1·00 75
700 200 f. "Rainbow Windows" . 2·00 1·25

1980. 1st African Athletic Championships. Mult.
702 20 f. Type **247** 15 10
703 25 f. Javelin 15 10
704 50 f. Passing the relay baton . 25 10
705 100 f. Discus 45 30

248 Musicians

1980. Mudra African Arts Festival.
706 50 f. Type **248** 25 15
707 100 f. Dancers 70 25
708 200 f. Dancers and drummer . 1·25 70

249 Lions Emblem

1980. 22nd Congress of Lions' Club District 403, Dakar.
709 **249** 100 f. multicoloured . . . 45 25

250 Chimpanzees

1980. Niokolo-Koba National Park. Multicoloured.
710 40 f. Type **250** 25 10
711 60 f. African elephants . . . 35 20
712 65 f. Giant elands 60 20
713 100 f. Spotted hyenas 85 30
714 200 f. Wildlife on the savannah 1·75 70
715 200 f. Simenti Hotel . . . . 1·75 70
Nos. 714/15 were issued together, se-tenant, forming a composite deisgn.

251 Watering Sapling
252 Women with Bowls of Rice Flour and Electric Mill

1980. Tree Planting Year.
717 **251** 60 f. multicoloured . . . 45 25
718 65 f. multicoloured . . . 95 30

1980. Rural Women. Multicoloured.
719 50 f. Street market (horiz) . . 25 15
720 100 f. Type **252** 45 30
721 200 f. Drawing water (horiz) . 1·25 70

253 Wrestling

1980. Olympic Games, Moscow. Multicoloured.
722 60 f. Type **253** 30 20
723 65 f. Running 30 20
724 70 f. Games emblems 35 25
725 100 f. Judo 45 30
726 200 f. Basketball . . . . . . 1·25 70

254 Dabry, Gimie, Mermoz and Seaplane "Comte de la Vaulx"

1980. Air. 50th Anniv of First South Atlantic Airmail Flight.
728 **254** 300 f. multicoloured . . . 2·00 1·00

255 Caspian Tern, Eastern White Pelicans and Grey-headed Gulls (Pointe Kalissaye Bird Sanctuary)

1981. National Parks. Multicoloured.
729 50 f. Type **255** 80 20
730 70 f. Slender-billed gulls and gull-billed tern (Langue de Barbarie) 85 30
731 85 f. Turtle and crab (Madeline Islands) 40 25
732 150 f. White-breasted cormorant and red-billed tropic bird (Madeline Islands) . . . . . 1·75 70

256 Healthy Activities
257 Fair Visitors beneath Tree

1981. Anti-Smoking Campaign. Multicoloured.
734 75 f. Type **256** 30 30
735 80 f. Cancerous mouth with pipe 35 35

1981. 4th International Fair, Dakar.
736 **257** 80 f. multicoloured 35 35

258 Lat Dior Damel Teigne
259 "Nymphaea lotus"

1982. National Heroes. Lat Dior. Multicoloured.
737 80 f. Type **258** 35 25
738 500 f. Lat Dior on horseback . 3·00 1·25

1982. Flowers. Multicoloured.
739 50 f. Type **259** 20 20
740 75 f. "Strophanthus sarmentosus" 30 30
741 200 f. "Crinum moorei" . . . 1·25 75
742 225 f. "Cochlospermum tinctorium" . . . . 1·50 1·00

HAVE YOU READ THE NOTES AT THE BEGINNING OF THIS CATALOGUE?
These often provide the answers to the enquiries we receive.

260 "Euryphrene senegalensis" (male and female)

1982. Butterflies. Multicoloured.
743 45 f. Type **260** 60 35
744 55 f. "Hypolimnas salmacis, Precis octavia" and "Salamis cytora" 75 45
745 75 f. "Cymothoe caenis" and "Cyrestis camillus" 90 55
746 80 f. "Precis cebrene, Junonia terea" and "Salamis parhassus" . . . . 1·10 70

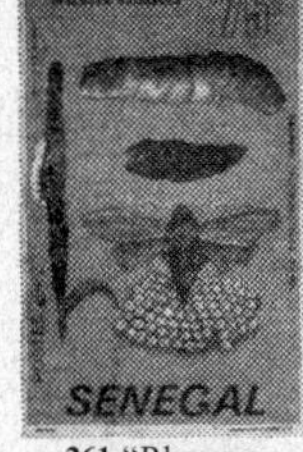

261 "Rhaguva albipunctella"
263 Black-tailed Godwit

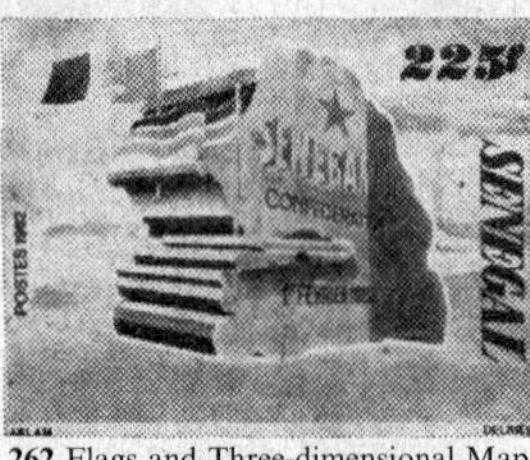

262 Flags and Three-dimensional Map of Senegambia

1982. Harmful Insects. Multicoloured.
748 75 f. Type **261** 50 45
749 80 f. "Amsacta moloneyi, Tolyposporium penicillariae" and "Sclerospore graminicola" (horiz) . . . . 1·50 45
750 100 f. "Amsacta moloneyi" . 70 60

1982. Senegambia Confederation. Multicoloured.
751 225 f. Type **262** . . . . . . 1·25 60
752 350 f. Arms of Senegal and Gambia . . . . 2·00 90

1982. Birds. Multicoloured.
753 45 f. Type **263** 45 30
754 75 f. Saddle-bill stork 95 40
755 80 f. Double-spurred francolin 1·10 45
756 500 f. Tawny eagle . . . . . 5·75 3·00

264 Footballer and Emblem
265 Flag "Stamp" and Ribbon

1982. World Cup Football Championship, Spain. Multicoloured.
757 30 f. Type **264** 15 15
758 50 f. Footballer 20 20
759 75 f. Football 30 30
760 80 f. World Cup and emblem . 35 35

1982. "Philexfrance 82" International Stamp Exhibition, Paris. Multicoloured.
762 100 f. Type **265** 40 25
763 500 f. Arms "stamp" between circling arrows . . . . . . 3·00 1·50

266 Exhibition Poster

1983. Stamp Exhibition, Dakar. Multicoloured.
764 60 f. Type **266** 25 20
765 70 f. Butterfly stamps 25 20
766 90 f. Stamps and magnifying glass 30 25
767 95 f. Exhibition hall and Dakar arms on stamp 75 30

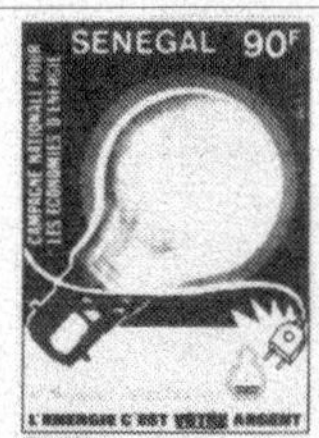

267 Light Bulb **268** Torch on Map of Africa

1983. Energy Conservation. Multicoloured.
768 90 f. Type **267** 55 30
769 95 f. Cars queueing for petrol 60 30
770 260 f. Woman cooking . . . . 1·60 85

1983. "For Namibian Independence". Multicoloured.
771 90 f. Type **268** 55 30
772 95 f. Clenched fist and broken chain on map of Africa . . 60 30
773 260 f. Woman with torch on map of Africa . . . . 1·90 85

269 Agency Building, Ziguinchor **270** Dakar Rotary Banner

1983. 20th Anniv of West African Monetary Union. Multicoloured.
774 60 f. Type **269** 25 20
775 65 f. Headquarters building, Dakar (vert) 25 25

1983. 1st Anniv of Dakar Alizes Rotary Club.
776 **270** 70 f. multicoloured . . . 50 25
777 500 f. multicoloured . . . 3·25 1·75

271 Customs Council Headquarters **272** Anniversary Emblem

1983. 30th Anniv of Customs Co-operation Council.
778 **271** 90 f. multicoloured . . . 30 30
779 300 f. multicoloured . . . 2·00 1·00

1984. 25th Anniv of Economic Commission for Africa.
780 **272** 90 f. multicoloured . . . 30 30
781 95 f. multicoloured . . . 60 30

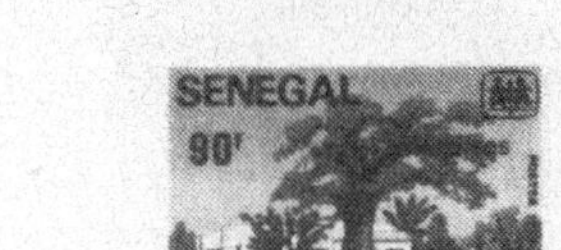

273 Village

1984. S.O.S. Children's Village. Multicoloured.
782 90 f. Type **273** 30 30
783 95 f. Foster-mother and child (vert) 65 30
784 115 f. Foster-family 80 40
785 260 f. House (vert) . . . . . 1·75 85

274 Scout Salute **275** Javelin-throwing

1984. 75th Anniv of Boy Scout Movement. Mult.
786 60 f. Type **274** 20 15
787 70 f. Scout badge 25 20
788 90 f. Scouts of different nations 35 30
789 95 f. Lord Baden-Powell (founder) 40 35

1984. Olympic Games, Los Angeles. Multicoloured.
790 90 f. Type **275** 35 30
791 95 f. Hurdling 40 35
792 165 f. Football . . . . 1·10 70

276 Basket of Food, Fishing and Farming **278** William Ponty School

1984. World Food Day. Multicoloured. Inscr "16 OCTOBRE 1983".
794 65 f. Type **276** 25 20
795 70 f. Woman cooking and child (vert) 50 20
796 225 f. Group and food . . . 1·60 85

1984. Drought Aid. No. 785 optd **Aide au Sahel 84**.
797 260 f. multicoloured . . . . 1·75 1·25

1984. World Heritage. Goree Island.
798 **278** 90 f. multicoloured . . . 35 30
799 – 95 f. black and blue . . . 40 35
800 – 250 f. multicoloured . . . 1·75 85
801 – 500 f. multicoloured . . . 3·50 2·00
DESIGN—HORIZ: 95 f. Map of Goree; 500 f. Slaves' House. VERT: 250 f. Goree Historical Museum.

279 Pump and Sprinkler **280** Globe, Envelopes and Map

1985. Irrigation Project. Multicoloured.
810 40 f. Type **279** 15 15
811 50 f. Tap and dam 15 15
812 90 f. Storage tanks and cattle 60 25
813 250 f. Women at water pump 1·75 85

1985. World Communication Year (1984).
814 **280** 90 f. multicoloured . . . 30 25
815 – 95 f. blue, green & brown 35 30
816 – 350 f. multicoloured . . . 2·25 1·10
DESIGNS: 95 f. Maps of Africa and Senegal and aerial; 350 f. Globe, dove and map of Senegal.

281 Stringed Instrument and Flute

1985. Musical Instruments. Multicoloured.
817 50 f. Type **281** 15 15
818 85 f. Drums and stringed instrument 30 25
819 125 f. Musician, stringed instruments, xylophone and drums 85 40
820 250 f. Stringed instruments . 1·60 85

282 Seaplane "Comte de la Vaulx" and Map

1985. Air. 55th Anniv of 1st Airmail Flight across South Atlantic.
821 **282** 250 f. multicoloured . . . 2·25 1·10

283 People and Broken Chain

1985. "Philexafrique" Int Stamp Exn, Lome, Togo. "Youth and Development". Mult.
822 100 f. Type **283** (political and civic education) 45 40
823 125 f. Carpenter and draughtsman (professional education) 75 45
824 150 f. Couple looking at planets (general education) 90 60
825 175 f. Farm workers (food self-sufficiency) . . . . 1·00 80

284 Laboratory and Farm Workers

1985. International Youth Year. Multicoloured.
826 40 f. Type **284** 20 15
827 50 f. Young people, forms of communication and globe . 20 15
828 90 f. Youth building "Peace" monument 40 35
829 125 f. Youth, football and globe 90 45

285 Man, Woman and Boy

1985. National Costumes. Multicoloured.
830 40 f. Type **285** 20 15
831 95 f. Man in straw hat and striped gown (vert) 40 35
832 100 f. Seated gown (vert) . . . 45 40
833 150 f. Man and woman (vert) . 90 60

286 Men bringing Boat Ashore

1986. Fishing at Kayar. Multicoloured.
834 40 f. Type **286** 20 15
835 50 f. Women waiting on shore 20 15
836 100 f. Man with large fish (vert) 70 40
837 125 f. Sorting the catch (vert) . 95 45
838 150 f. View of beach . . . . . 1·00 60

287 Perruque and Ceeli **288** Flags and Football

1986. Hairstyles. Multicoloured.
839 90 f. Type **287** 40 30
840 125 f. Ndungu, Kearly and Rasta 50 40
841 250 f. Jamono, Kura and Kooraa 150 60
842 300 f. Mbaram and Jeere . . . 1·175 70

1986. African Football Cup, Cairo. Multicoloured.
843 115 f. Type **288** 70 35
844 125 f. Footballer and map . . 75 45
845 135 f. Lion rampant with torch ascending pyramid (horiz) . 80 50
846 165 f. Lions rampant beneath flag (horiz) . . . . 1·00 65

1986. 5th Convention of District 403 of Lions International. No. 818 surch **Ve CONVENTION MULTI-DISTRICT 8-10 MAI 1988.**
847 165 f. on 85 f. Drums and stringed instrument . . . . 1·00 65

290 Doe and Calf

1986. Ndama Gazelle. Multicoloured.
848 15 f. Type **290** 10 10
849 45 f. Group of gazelle resting . 20 15
850 85 f. Gazelle among dead trees 35 30
851 125 f. Gazelle running . . . . 1·00 45

291 Immunising Child **294** Ostriches

292 Trophy, Footballers and Terracotta Offertory Vessel

1986. U.N.I.C.E.F. Child Survival Campaign. Multicoloured.
852 50 f. Type **291** 20 15
853 85 f. Child drinking from bowl 40 35

1986. World Cup Football Championship, Mexico. Multicoloured. (a) As T **292**.
854 125 f. Type **292** 50 45
855 135 f. Trophy, footballers and stucco Maya head from Palenque 80 50
856 165 f. Gold breastplate , footballers and trophy . . . 1·00 65
857 340 f. Teotihuacan porcelain mask, footballers and trophy 2·00 90

(b) Nos. 854/7 optd **ARGENTINA 3 R.F.A. 2.**
858 125 f. Type **292** 50 45
859 135 f. Trophy, footballers and stucco Maya head from Palenque 80 50
860 165 f. Gold breastplate, footballers and trophy . . . 1·00 65
861 340 f. Teotihuacan porcelain mask, footballers and trophy 2·00 90

1986. Guembeul Nature Reserve. Multicoloured
862 50 f. Type **294** . . . . 1·50 40
863 65 f. Gazelles 25 20
864 85 f. Giraffes 60 30
865 100 f. Ostrich, buffalo, gazelle and giraffe . . . . 2·25 90
866 150 f. Buffalo . . . . 1·10 60

295 Man with Puppet (Xuusmaanapaa) **296** Statue of Liberty

1986. Christmas. Customs. Multicoloured.
867 70 f. Type **295** 25 20
868 85 f. Setting up fanal (Fente) (horiz) 30 25
869 150 f. Decorating fanal (Jebele) 90 55
870 250 f. Boy praying before candle and Nativity scene (horiz) . 1·50 75

1986. Centenary of Statue of Liberty.
871 **296** 225 f. multicoloured . . . 1·50 80

297 Jellyfish and Coral

1987. Marine Fauna. Multicoloured.
872 50 f. Type **297** 20 15
873 85 f. Sea urchin and starfish . 30 25
874 100 f. Norway lobster 70 35
875 150 f. Common dolphin . . . 1·00 55
876 200 f. Octopus . . . . 2·00 1·10

298 Motor Cyclist and Lorry

299 Hands over Antelope

1987. Paris–Dakar Rally. Multicoloured.
877 115 f. Type **298** 80 40
878 125 f. Thierry Sabine, helicopter, motor cyclist, lorry and car (horiz) . . . . 1·50 60
879 135 f. Sabine and motor car (horiz) . . . . 1·00 45
880 340 f. Eiffel Tower, car and huts 2·40 1·10

1987. Endangered Fauna in Ferlo National Park. Multicoloured.
881 55 f. Type **299** 20 15
882 70 f. Ostriches . . . . 1·00 30
883 85 f. Warthog 60 25
884 90 f. Elephant 60 30

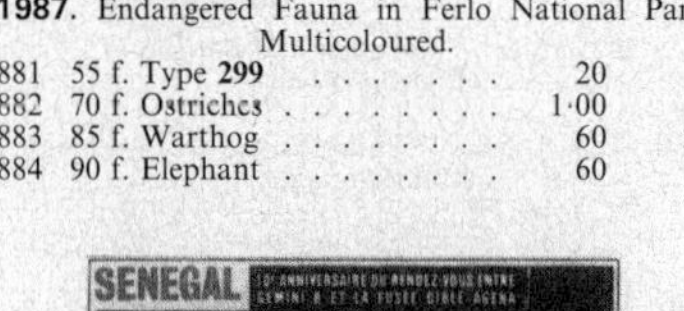
300 Spacecraft above Earth

1987. 10th Anniv of "Gemini 8" – Agena Flight.
885 **300** 320 f. multicoloured . . . 2·00 1·10

301 International Express Mail Emblem

1987. Centenary of First Senegal Stamp. Mult.
887 100 f. Type **301** 40 35
888 130 f. 1892 4 c. Senegal and Dependencies stamp 75 45
889 140 f. 1961 Senegal independence stamp 80 50
890 145 f. 1935 30 c. and 1 f. 25 Senegal stamps 85 50
891 320 f. Senegal 1887 15 c. on 20 c. stamp and cancellation . . . 2·00 1·10

302 Hand gripping Bloodied Claw above Map of South Africa

1987. Anti-Apartheid Campaign. Multicoloured.
892 130 f. Type **302** 80 45
893 140 f. Broken and bloodied chain in fist (vert) 85 50
894 145 f. Skeleton with scythe, dove and globe 85 50

303 Emblem

1987. 20th Anniv of Intelsat. Multicoloured.
895 50 f. Type **303** 20 15
896 125 f. Satellite and emblem . . 50 45
897 150 f. Emblem and globe . . . 60 55
898 200 f. Globe and satellite . . . 1·25 75

304 Emblem and Crowd

305 Yacht and Sun

1987. West African Cities Organization. Mult.
899 40 f. Type **304** 15 15
900 125 f. Emblem and clasped hands 75 45

1987. 45th Anniv of Dakar Rotary Club.
901 **305** 500 f. multicoloured . . . 3·25 1·50

306 U.N. Building, New York

307 Fr. Daniel Brottier (founder) and Angel

1987. 40th Anniv (1985) of U.N.O. Multicoloured.
902 85 f. Type **306** 60 25
903 95 f. Emblem 65 35
904 150 f. Hands of different races and emblem 90 55

1987. 50th Anniv of Cathedral of African Remembrance. Multicoloured.
905 130 f. Type **307** 85 45
906 140 f. Cathedral in 1936 and 1986 85 50

308 Hand pouring Grain into Globe

1987. World Food Day. Multicoloured.
907 130 f. Type **308** 80 45
908 140 f. Ear of wheat and F.A.O. emblem rising as sun (horiz) 85 50
909 145 f. Emblem 85 50

309 Servals

1987. Basse Casamance National Park. Mult.
910 115 f. Type **309** 70 40
911 135 f. Demidoff's galagos . . 90 45
912 150 f. Bush pig . . . . 1·00 55
913 250 f. Leopards . . . . 1·60 90
914 300 f. Little egrets . . . . . 6·50 3·00
915 300 f. Carmine bee eaters . . 6·50 3·00

310 Wrestlers

1987. Senegalese Wrestling. Multicoloured.
916 115 f. Type **310** 70 40
917 125 f. Wrestlers and musicians 70 45
918 135 f. Wrestlers (vert) 80 45
919 165 f. Referee, wrestlers and crowd (vert) . . . . 1·00 55

311 African Open-bill Stork

312 Boy dreaming of Father Christmas's Visit

1987. Djoudj National Park. Multicoloured.
920 115 f. Type **311** . . . . 1·25 65
921 125 f. Greater flamingoes (horiz) 1·40 75
922 135 f. Pink-backed pelican and greater flamingoes (horiz) . . 1·75 75
923 300 f. Pink-backed pelicans . . 3·50 1·50
924 350 f. As No. 921 . . . . . . 3·75 2·10
925 350 f. As No. 922 . . . . . . 3·75 2·10

1987. Christmas. Multicoloured.
926 145 f. Type **312** 85 50
927 150 f. Star behind Virgin gazing at Child 90 55
928 180 f. Nativity scene above people praying in church . . 1·25 65
929 200 f. Nativity scene in candle glow . . . . 1·25 75

313 Battle of Dekhele

1988. Death Centenary of Lat-Dior. Multicoloured.
930 130 f. Type **313** . . . . 1·00 45
931 160 f. Lat-Dior on his horse "Maalaw" . . . . 1·00 60

314 10th Anniv Emblem and Map

1988. Dakar International Fair.
932 **314** 125 f. multicoloured 75 45

315 Catfish

1988. Fishes. Multicoloured.
933 5 f. Type **315** 10 10
934 100 f. Angel fish 40 35
935 145 f. Common barb 90 50
936 180 f. Carp . . . . 1·40 90

316 W.M.O. Emblem and Means of Conveying Information

1988. World Meteorology Day.
937 **316** 145 f. multicoloured . . . 90 30

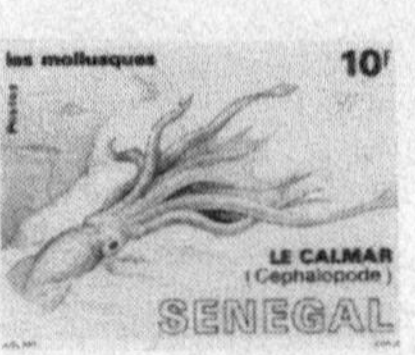
317 Motor Cyclist

1988. 10th Anniv of Paris–Dakar Rally. Mult.
938 145 f. Type **317** 90 50
939 180 f. Rally car and emblem . . 1·00 65
940 200 f. Rally cars and man . . 1·25 70
941 410 f. Thierry Sabine and motor cyclist . . . . 2·75 1·50

318 Squid

1988. Molluscs. Multicoloured.
942 10 f. Type **318** 10 10
943 20 f. Truncate donax (bivalve) 15 10
944 145 f. Giant East African snail 1·40 65
945 165 f. Banded snail . . . . . 1·75 75

319 Football, Cup and Map

1988. Africa Cup Football Championship, Rabat. Multicoloured.
946 80 f. Type **319** 30 25
947 100 f. Player's leg and ball (vert) 40 35
948 145 f. Match scene and map of Africa (vert) 90 50
949 180 f. Emblem and cup (vert) 1·25 65

320 Corps Member and Children

321 "Dictyota atomaria"

1988. 25th Anniv of American Peace Corps in Senegal.
950 **320** 190 f. multicoloured . . . 1·25 65

1988. Marine Flora. Multicoloured.
951 10 f. Type **321** 10 10
952 65 f. "Agarum gmelini" 25 20
953 145 f. "Saccorrhiza bulbosa" . 90 55
954 180 f. "Rhodymenia palmetta" 1·25 65

1988. Riccione Stamp Fair. No. 891 optd **RICCIONE 88 27-29-08-89**.
955 320 f. multicoloured . . . . . 1·75 1·25

323 Hodori (mascot) and Stadium

325 Thies Phosphate Mine

324 Thierno Saidou Nourou Tall Centre

1988. Olympic Games, Seoul. Multicoloured.
956 5 f. Type **323** 10 10
957 75 f. Athletics, swimming and football 30 25
958 300 f. Hodori, flame and sports pictograms . . . . 1·75 1·00
959 410 f. Emblem and athletics pictogram . . . . 2·40 1·40

1988.
960 **324** 125 f. multicoloured . . . 70 60

1988. Senegal Industries. Multicoloured.
961 5 f. Type **325** 10 10
962 20 f. Chemical industry . . . 10 10
963 145 f. Diourbel factory . . . 85 50
964 410 f. Mbao refinery . . . . 2·40 1·40

326 Children and Government Palace

1988. Postcards of 1900. Multicoloured.
965 20 f. Type **326** 10 10
966 145 f. Wrestlers and St. Louis Grand Mosque 85 50
967 180 f. Old Dakar railway station and young woman . . . . 1·10 65
968 200 f. Goree Governor's residence and young woman 1·25 70

327 "Packia biglobosa" **328** Mask, Rally Car and Eiffel Tower

1988. Flowers. Multicoloured.

969 20 f. Type **327** 10 10
970 60 f. "Euphorbia pulcherrima" 20 15
971 65 f. "Cyrtosperma senegalense" 25 20
972 410 f. "Bombax costatum" . . 2·60 1·40

1989. 11th Paris–Dakar Rally. Multicoloured.

973 10 f. Type **328** 10 10
974 145 f. Crash helmet and sand dunes 60 55
975 180 f. Turban and motor cyclist 1·10 70
976 220 f. Motor cyclist and Thierry Sabine . . . . 1·40 85

329 Teranga Hotel **330** Senegal Tourism Emblem

1989. Tourism (1st series). Multicoloured.

977 10 f. Type **329** 10 10
978 80 f. Thatched hut and shades on beach 30 25
979 100 f. Saly hotel 40 35
980 350 f. Dior hotel . . . . . . 2·50 1·25

1989. Tourism (2nd series). Multicoloured.

981 130 f. Type **330** 75 45
982 140 f. Rural tourism (horiz) . 85 50
983 145 f. Fishing (horiz) . . . . 1·00 55
984 180 f. Water sports (horiz) . . 1·00 70

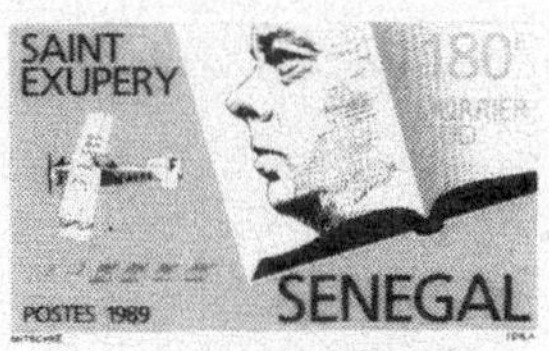

331 Saint-Exupery and Scene from "Courrier Sud"

1989. 45th Anniv of Disappearance of Antoine de Saint-Exupery (pilot and writer).

985 **331** 180 f. black, orange and grey 1·40 50
986 – 220 f. black, blue & grey . 1·75 75
987 – 410 f. multicoloured . . . 3·50 1·25

DESIGNS: 220 f. Scene from "Vol de Nuit"; 410 f. Scene from "Pilote de Guerre".

332 Presentation of Lists of Grievances by People of St. Louis

1989. Bicentenary of French Revolution. Mult.

988 180 f. Type **332** . . . . . . 1·25 1·00
989 220 f. Declaration of Rights of Man, quill pen in hand and phrygian cap (vert) . . . . 1·25 1·10
990 300 f. Revolutionaries and flag 2·00 1·50

333 Arts and Culture **335** Stamps

1989. 3rd Francophone Summit. Multicoloured.

991 5 f. Type **333** 10 10
992 30 f. Education (horiz) 15 10
993 100 f. Communication (horiz) . 40 35
994 200 f. Development (horiz) . . 1·25 75

1989. No. 960 surch.

995 555 f. on 125 f. multicoloured 2·75 1·00

1989. "Philexfrance 89" International Stamp Exhibition, Paris. Multicoloured.

996 10 f. Type **335** 10 10
997 25 f. Stamp on map of France (vert) 10 10
998 75 f. Couple viewing stamp on easel (vert) 30 25
999 145 f. Sticking stamp on envelope (vert) 60 55

336 "30" Dish Aerial and Envelope **337** Record Stacks and 1922 Postcard

1989. 30th Anniv Meeting of West African Post and Telecommunications Administrations Conference, Dakar. Multicoloured.

1000 25 f. Type **336** 10 10
1001 30 f. Telephone handset, punched tape and map on stamp 15 10
1002 180 f. Map of Africa, stamp and telephone earpiece . . . . 1·10 70
1003 220 f. Stamp, satellite, globe and map of Africa . . . . . . 1·25 85

1989. 75th Anniv (1988) of Senegal Archives. Multicoloured.

1004 15 f. Type **337** 10 10
1005 40 f. 1825 document 15 10
1006 145 f. 1825 document and archive building 85 55
1007 180 f. Bound volume . . . . 1·00 70

338 Jar with Lid **339** Nehru

1989. Pottery. Multicoloured.

1008 15 f. Type **338** 10 10
1009 30 f. Potter at work 15 10
1010 75 f. Stacked pots 30 25
1011 145 f. Woman carrying pots 85 55

1989. Birth Centenary of Jawaharlal Nehru (Indian statesman).

1012 **339** 220 f. multicoloured . . 1·25 85
1013 – 410 f. black, red & yell . . 2·50 1·40

DESIGN—HORIZ: 410 f. Nehru (different).

340 Swimming Crab

1989. Marine Life. Multicoloured.

1014 10 f. Type **340** 10 10
1015 60 f. Seahorse (vert) 25 20
1016 145 f. Barnacles 85 55
1017 220 f. Sand-hopper . . . . 1·25 85

341 Clasped Hand and People of Different Races **342** Pilgrims

1989. World Aids Day. Multicoloured.

1018 5 f. Type **341** 10 10
1019 100 f. People under umbrella 40 35
1020 145 f. Fist smashing Aids virus 85 55
1021 180 f. Hammer smashing Aids virus . . . . 1·10 70

1989. Centenary of Pilgrimage to Our Lady of Popenguine. Multicoloured.

1022 145 f. Type **342** 60 55
1023 180 f. Our Lady of Popenguine Church . . . . 1·10 70

343 White-breasted Cormorant and African Darter, Djoudj

1989. National Parks. Multicoloured.

1024 10 f. Type **343** 15 10
1025 45 f. Grey-headed gulls, Langue de Barbarie 40 25
1026 100 f. Blue-checked bee eater and long-crested eagle, Basse Casamance 75 55
1027 180 f. Western reef herons, Saloum . . . . 2·40 1·00

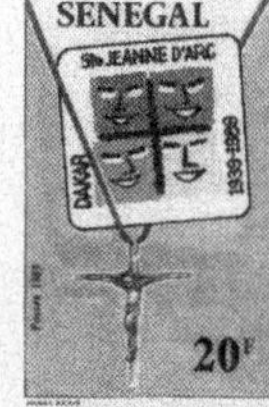

344 Boy looking at Christmas Tree **345** Crucifix and Anniversary Emblem

1989. Christmas. Multicoloured.

1028 10 f. Type **344** 10 10
1029 25 f. Teddy bear and bauble hanging from tree 10 10
1030 30 f. Animals around Baby Jesus 15 10
1031 200 f. Madonna and Child . . 1·25 75

1989. 50th Anniv of St. Joan of Arc Institute, Dakar. Multicoloured.

1032 20 f. Type **345** 10 10
1033 500 f. Emblem and Institute building . . . . 2·75 1·40

346 "Hydravion"

1989. 79th Anniv of First Flight of Henri Fabre's Seaplane. Multicoloured.

1034 125 f. Type **346** 60 55
1035 130 f. Fabre working on engine of "Hydravion" 60 55
1036 475 f. Technical drawings and Fabre (vert) . . . . 3·25 1·00

347 Basketball

1990. Olympic Games, Barcelona (1992). Mult.

1038 10 f. Type **347** 10 10
1039 130 f. High jumping 50 45
1040 180 f. Throwing the discus . . 75 70
1041 190 f. Running 80 75
1042 315 f. Lawn tennis . . . . . 1·25 1·00
1043 475 f. Show jumping . . . . 1·90 1·75

348 Rally Car

1990. 12th Paris–Dakar Rally. Multicoloured.

1045 20 f. Type **348** 10 10
1046 25 f. Motor cycle and sidecar 10 10
1047 180 f. Crowd cheering winning driver . . . . 1·10 70
1048 200 f. Thierry Sabine and car 1·10 75

349 Piazza della Signoria, Florence, and Footballer

1990. World Cup Football Championship, Italy. Multicoloured.

1049 45 f. Type **349** 20 15
1050 140 f. Piazza Navona, Rome 55 25
1051 180 f. "Virgin with St. Anne and Infant Jesus" (Leonardo da Vinci) 75 30
1052 220 f. "Giuseppe Garibaldi" (oil painting) . . . . 1·10 30
1053 300 f. "Sistine Madonna" (Raphael) . . . . 1·50 40
1054 415 f. "Virgin and Child" (Danielle da Volterra) . . 2·10 70

350 Footballer **351** Facsimile Telegraphy

1990. African Nations Cup Football Championship, Algeria. Multicoloured.

1056 20 f. Type **350** 10 10
1057 60 f. Goalkeeper 25 20
1058 100 f. Clasped hands and pennants 40 35
1059 500 f. Trophy . . . . 3·00 1·75

1990. Postal Services. Multicoloured.

1060 5 f. Type **351** 10 10
1061 15 f. Express mail service . . 10 10
1062 100 f. Postal cheques 40 35
1063 180 f. Savings 75 40

352 Hands and Umbrella protecting Children **353** Envelopes on Map

1990. Louga S.O.S. Children's Village. Multicoloured.

1064 5 f. Type **352** 10 10
1065 500 f. Children under umbrella 2·50 1·25

1990. 20th Anniv of Multinational Postal Training School, Abidjan. Multicoloured.

1066 145 f. Type **353** 60 55
1067 180 f. Man carrying wreath containing envelope . . . 75 70

354 Excursion by Pirogue, Basse-Casamance

1990. Tourism. Multicoloured.

1068 10 f. Type **354** 10 10
1069 25 f. Hotel and beach, Goree 10 10
1070 30 f. Houses on stilts, Fadiouth 15 10
1071 40 f. Rose Lake and salt drying 15 10

355 Camp

1990. Scouting. Multicoloured.

1072 30 f. Type **355** 15 10
1073 100 f. Scouts trekking alongside lake 40 35
1074 145 f. Scouts trekking through hilly landscape 60 55
1075 200 f. Scout and emblem (vert) 80 75

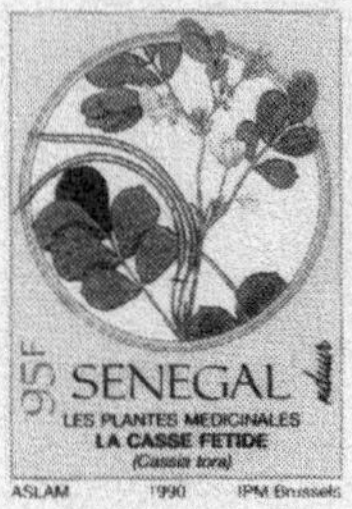

356 "Cassia tora"  **357** Angels and Tree

1990. Medicinal Plants. Multicoloured.

1076 95 f. Type **356** 40 35
1077 105 f. "Tamarind" 45 40
1078 125 f. "Cassia occidentalis" . 50 45
1079 175 f. "Leptadenia hastata" . 70 65

1990. Christmas.

1080 **357** 25 f. multicoloured . . . 10 10
1081 – 145 f. multicoloured . . 60 55
1082 – 180 f. orange, red & blk . 75 70
1083 – 200 f. multicoloured . . 80 75

DESIGNS: 145 f. Angel trumpeting stars; 180 f. Adoration of Three Kings; 200 f. Donkey and cow gazing at Child.

358 Anniversary Emblem  **359** Rally Car

1991. 125th Anniv (1988) of International Red Cross and 25th Anniv of Senegal Red Cross.

1084 **358** 180 f. multicoloured . . 70 45

1991. 13th Paris–Dakar Rally. Multicoloured.

1085 15 f. Type **359** 10 10
1086 15 f. Car and motor cycle at night 50 35
1087 180 f. Rally car (different) . . 70 45
1088 220 f. Motor cycles 90 60

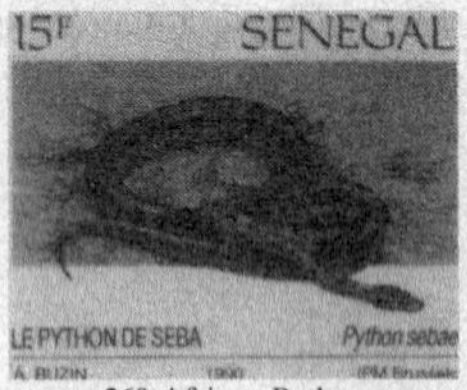

360 African Python

1991. Reptiles. Multicoloured.

1089 15 f. Type **360** 10 10
1090 60 f. Common green turtle . 25 15
1091 100 f. Nile crocodile 40 25
1092 180 f. Senegal chameleon . . 70 45

361 Sphinx, House of Slaves, Frescoes, Kirdi Houses and Mohammed's Tomb **362** Nobel

1991. "Fespaco". 12th Pan-African Cinema and Television Festival. Multicoloured.

1093 30 f. Type **361** 10 10
1094 60 f. Dogon mask, B. Dioulasso Mosque, drawing of Osiris, and camel rider 25 15
1095 100 f. Rabat, "Seated Scribe" (Egyptian statue), drum and camels 40 25
1096 180 f. Pyramids of Egypt, Djenne Mosque, Guinean mask, Moroccan architecture and Moorish door decorations 70 45

1991. 95th Death Anniv of Alfred Nobel (founder of Nobel prizes). Multicoloured. Self-adhesive.

1097 145 f. Type **362** 60 40
1098 180 f. Nobel and prize presentation (horiz) 70 45

363 Oribi

1991. National Parks. Multicoloured.

1099 5 f. Type **363** 10 10
1100 10 f. Dorcas gazelle 10 10
1101 180 f. Kob 70 45
1102 555 f. Hartebeest . . . . . 2·25 1·50

364 Cashew

1991. Trees and their Fruit. Multicoloured.

1103 90 f. Type **364** 35 25
1104 100 f. Mango 45 25
1105 125 f. Sugar-palm (vert) . . 50 35
1106 145 f. Oil palm (vert) . . . 60 45

365 Ader, Motor Car and Telephone

1991. Air. Centenary (1990) of First Heavier than Air Powered Flight. Multicoloured.

1107 145 f. Type **365** 60 40
1108 180 f. Clement Ader and his monoplane "Eole" 90 55
1109 615 f. "Eole" and Ader (vert) 3·00 2·00

366 Columbus and Haitians

1991. 500th Anniv (1992) of Discovery of America by Columbus. Multicoloured.

1111 100 f. Type **366** 40 25
1112 145 f. Arms of Castile and Leon (vert) 60 40
1113 180 f. "Santa Maria" and Columbus 70 45
1114 200 f. Vicente Yanez Pinzon and "Nina" 80 55
1115 220 f. Martin Alonzo Pinzon and "Pinta" 90 60
1116 500 f. Details of charts . . . 2·00 1·25
1117 625 f. Compass rose and Columbus with charts . . 2·50 1·75

367 Armstrong

1991. 20th Death Anniv of Louis Armstrong (musician). Multicoloured.

1118 10 f. Type **367** 10 10
1119 145 f. Armstrong singing . . 60 40
1120 180 f. Armstrong and trumpets 70 45
1121 220 f. Armstrong playing trumpet 90 65

368 Yury Gagarin and "Vostok 1"

1991. 30th Anniv of First Man in Space. Mult.

1125 15 f. Type **368** 10 10
1126 145 f. "Vostok 1" and Gagarin in spacesuit 60 40
1127 180 f. Gagarin in spacesuit and "Vostok 1" (different) . . . 70 45
1128 220 f. Globe, "Vostok 1" and Gagarin in flying kit . . . 90 60

369 Flags and Water dripping into Bowl  **370** Star and Crescents

1991. "Water, Source of Life". Senegal–Saudi Arabia Rural Water Supply Co-operation. Multicoloured.

1129 30 f. Type **369** 10 10
1130 145 f. Tap and village 60 40
1131 180 f. Tap dripping and flags 70 45
1132 220 f. Water tower and village 90 60

1991. 6th Summit Meeting of Islamic Conference Organization, Dakar. Multicoloured.

1133 15 f. Type **370** 10 10
1134 145 f. Hands 60 40
1135 180 f. Conference centre and accommodation 70 45
1136 220 f. Grand Mosque, Dakar 90 60

371 Player shooting at Basket  **372** Giving Blessing

1991. Centenary of Basketball. Multicoloured.

1137 125 f. Type **371** 50 35
1138 145 f. Player approching basket 60 40
1139 180 f. King and Queen of the Basket 70 45
1140 220 f. Lion, trophies and ball 90 60

1991. Christmas. Multicoloured.

1141 5 f. Type **372** 10 10
1142 145 f. Madonna and Child . . 60 40
1143 160 f. Angels and star 65 45
1144 220 f. Animals and Baby Jesus 90 60

373 Bust of Mozart and Score  **374** Flags on Player's Sock

1991. Death Bicentenary of Wolfgang Amadeus Mozart (composer). Multicoloured.

1145 5 f. Type **373** 10 10
1146 150 f. Mozart conducting . . 60 40
1147 180 f. Mozart at keyboard . . 70 45
1148 220 f. Mozart and score . . . 90 60

1992. 18th African Nations Cup Football Championship. Multicoloured.

1149 10 f. Type **374** 10 10
1150 145 f. Footballs forming "92" 70 45
1151 200 f. Cup and mascot . . . 95 65
1152 220 f. Players . . . . 1·10 75

1992. Papal Visit. No. 1143 surch **VISITE DU PAPE JEAN PAUL II AU SENEGAL 19-23/02/92 180F.**

1153 180 f. on 160 f. multicoloured 85 55

376 Saloum Delta

1992. National Parks. Multicoloured.

1154 10 f. Type **376** 10 10
1155 125 f. Djoudj 60 40
1156 145 f. Niokolo-Koba 70 45
1157 220 f. Basse Casamance . . . 1·10 75

377 Oil Wells, Flag and Bombs  **378** Frozen Fish

1992. Participation of Senegal Contingent in Gulf War. Multicoloured.

1158 30 f. Type **377** 15 10
1159 145 f. Senegalese officer . . 70 45
1160 180 f. Kaaba and Senegalese guard 85 55
1161 220 f. Map, dove and flag . 1·10 75

1992. Fish Products. Multicoloured.

1162 5 f. Type **378** 10 10
1163 60 f. Sandwich seller and platters of fish 30 20
1164 100 f. Woman fileting fish . . 75 40
1165 150 f. Women packing prawns 80 50

379 Niokolo Complex

1992. Tourist Sites. Multicoloured.

1166 5 f. Type **379** 10 10
1167 10 f. Basse Casamance . . . 10 10
1168 150 f. Dakar 70 45
1169 200 f. Saint-Louis 95 65

380 Teacher and Pupils carrying Saplings

1992. Reforestation by Schoolchildren. Mult.

1170 145 f. Type **380** 70 45
1171 180 f. Planting sapling . . . 85 55
1172 200 f. Planting saplings (different) 95 65
1173 220 f. Watering-in sapling (vert) 1·10 75

381 People with Cleaning Materials

1992. Manpower Services Operation, Setal. Mult.

1174 25 f. Type **381** 10 10
1175 145 f. Clearing road 70 45
1176 180 f. Sweeping streets (vert) 85 55
1177 220 f. Painting kerbstones (vert) 1·10 75

382 Education

1992. Rights of the Child. Multicoloured.

1178 20 f. Type **382** 10 10
1179 45 f. Vocational training . . 20 15
1180 165 f. Instruction 80 55
1181 180 f. Health 85 55

383 Customs Post (Free Trade)

1992. African Integration. Multicoloured.

1182 10 f. Type **383** 10 10
1183 30 f. Silhouettes (youth activities) 15 10
1184 145 f. Communications equipment 70 45
1185 220 f. Women's movements . 1·10 75

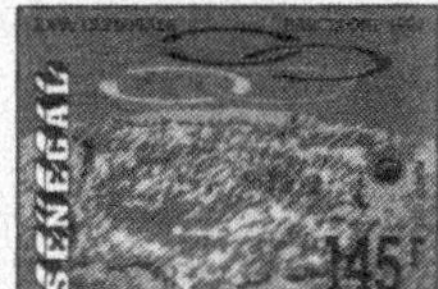

384 Rings and Map of Spain

1992. Olympic Games, Barcelona. Multicoloured.

1186	145 f. Type **384**	70	45
1187	180 f. Runner (vert)	85	55
1188	200 f. Sprinter	95	65
1189	300 f. Athlete carrying torch (vert)	1·40	95

385 Passenger Carriages

1992. "The Blue Train". Multicoloured.

1190	70 f. Type **385**	35	25
1191	145 f. Locomotives and carriages	70	45
1192	200 f. Train and track on map	95	65
1193	220 f. Railway station	1·10	75

386 Sealife around Map of Antarctic

1992. International Maritime Heritage Year.

1194	**386**	25 f. black, blue & yellow	10	10
1195	–	100 f. multicoloured	40	25
1196	–	180 f. multicoloured	85	55
1197	–	220 f. multicoloured	1·10	75

DESIGNS—VERT: 100 f. Marine life caught in sun ray; 180 f. United Nations seminar; 220 f. Fish, ship, flags and hands holding globe.

387 Coral

1992. Corals.

1198	**387**	50 f. multicoloured	25	15
1199	–	100 f. multicoloured	40	25
1200	–	145 f. mult (vert)	70	45
1201	–	220 f. multicoloured	1·10	75

DESIGNS: 100 f. to 220 f. Different corals.

388 Adenauer

389 Crab

1992. 25th Death Anniv of Konrad Adenauer (German statesman). Multicoloured.

1202	5 f. Type **388**	10	10
1203	145 f. Schaumburg Palace and flags (horiz)	70	45
1204	180 f. German flag and handshake (horiz)	85	55
1205	220 f. Map, flag and emblem of Germany (horiz)	1·10	75

1992. Crustaceans. Multicoloured.

1206	20 f. Type **389**	10	10
1207	30 f. Sea spider	15	10
1208	180 f. Crayfish	85	55
1209	200 f. King prawn	95	65

MINIMUM PRICE

The minimum price quoted is 10p which represents a handling charge rather than a basis for valuing common stamps. For further notes about prices, see introductory pages.

390 "Parkia biglobosa"

1992. Flowers and their Fruits. Multicoloured.

1210	10 f. Type **390**	10	10
1211	50 f. Desert date	25	15
1212	200 f. "Parinari macrophylla"	95	65
1213	220 f. Cactus	1·10	75

391 Rocket and Earth

1992. 30th Anniv of First American Manned Orbit of the Earth. Multicoloured.

1214	15 f. Type **391**	10	10
1215	145 f. American flag and John Glenn	35	25
1216	180 f. Rocket launch and globe	45	30
1217	200 f. Astonaut and rocket on launch-pad (vert)	45	30

392 Bakari II and Map from 14th-century Catalan Atlas

1992. Bakari II. Multicoloured.

1218	100 f. Type **392**	40	25
1219	145 f. Giant Mexican carved head and map from 15th-century atlas	75	45

393 Picture Frame and Obelisk

394 Children dancing round Decorated Globe

1992. Dakar Biennale. Multicoloured.

1220	20 f. Type **393**	10	10
1221	50 f. Mask hanging from window frame	10	10
1222	145 f. Open book	35	25
1223	220 f. Traditional string instrument	50	35

1992. Christmas. Multicoloured.

1224	15 f. Type **394**	10	10
1225	145 f. People around tree (vert)	35	25
1226	180 f. Jesus (vert)	45	30
1227	200 f. Father Christmas (vert)	45	30

1993. 15th Paris–Dakar Rally. Nos. 941 and 975 surch **Dakar le 17-01-93** and new value.

1228	145 f. on 180 f. multicoloured	35	25
1229	220 f. on 410 f. multicoloured	50	35

396 First Aid Post

1993. Accident Prevention Campaign. Mult.

1230	20 f. Type **396** (prevention, security and first aid)	10	10
1231	25 f. The Sonacos incident (reinforcement of preventative measures) (36×28 mm)	10	10
1232	145 f. Chemical accident (need for vigilance and security) (36×28 mm)	35	25
1233	200 f. Helicopter rescue (rapid and efficient intervention at air disasters)	45	30

397 Seck

398 Spotted Hyena

1993. 120th Birth Anniv of Abdoulaye Seck (Director of Posts and Telecommunications).

1234	**397**	220 f. multicoloured	50	35

1993. Wild Animals. Multicoloured.

1235	30 f. Type **398**	10	10
1236	50 f. Lioness	10	10
1237	70 f. Leopard	15	10
1238	150 f. Giraffe (vert)	35	25
1239	180 f. Stag	45	30

399 Decorated Tree, Children playing and Father Christmas

1993. Christmas. Multicoloured.

1240	5 f. Type **399**	10	10
1241	80 f. Children decorating tree and Father Christmas	20	15
1242	145 f. Children visiting Father Christmas	35	25
1243	150 f. Girl tugging Father Christmas's beard	35	25

400 U.S. Flag and Kennedy

1993. 30th Anniv of Assassination of President John F. Kennedy of the United States. Multicoloured.

1244	80 f. Type **400**	20	15
1245	555 f. Kennedy and White House	1·40	95

402 Vehicles and Tree at Sunset

1994. 16th Anniv of Paris–Dakar Rally. Multicoloured.

1250	145 f. Type **402**	35	25
1251	180 f. Boys with camel	45	30
1252	220 f. Rally cars	55	35

403 Diplodocus

1994. Prehistoric Animals. Multicoloured.

1253	100 f. Type **403**	25	15
1254	175 f. Brontosaurus	40	25
1255	215 f. Triceratops	50	35
1256	290 f. Stegosaurus	70	45
1257	300 f. Tyrannosaurus	75	50

404 Black-headed Herons

1994. Birds of Kalissaye National Park. Multicoloured.

1258	100 f. Type **404**	25	15
1259	275 f. Caspian terns	65	45
1260	290 f. Western reef herons	70	45
1261	380 f. Pink-backed pelicans (horiz)	90	60

405 Dried Eel Fat

1994. Produce of the Sea. Multicoloured.

1262	5 f. Type **405**	10	10
1263	90 f. Sifting shellfish	20	15
1264	100 f. Salted shark	25	15
1265	200 f. Drying small fry	50	35

406 "Stop Sand Extraction"

1994. Coastal Protection. Multicoloured.

1266	5 f. Type **406**	10	10
1267	75 f. Prevention of sand dunes	20	15
1268	100 f. Horizontal and vertical barrages	25	15
1269	200 f. Cleanliness of beaches	50	35

407 Water Store, Goree, and Railway Station, Rufisque

1994. Preservation of Heritage Sites. Multicoloured.

1270	100 f. Type **407**	25	15
1271	175 f. Soudan House	40	25
1272	215 f. Goree Island	50	35
1273	275 f. Pinet Laprade Fort, Sedhiou	65	45

408 Red-flowered Kapok

409 Breguet 14 Biplane over Route Map

1994. Flowers. Multicoloured.

1274	30 f. Type **408**	10	10
1275	75 f. Golden trumpet	20	15
1276	100 f. Rose periwinkle	25	15
1277	1000 f. Glory-bower	2·40	1·60

1994. 10th Toulouse–Saint-Louis Aerial Rally (1993). Multicoloured.

1278	100 f. Type **409**	25	15
1279	145 f. Henri Guillaumet and route map	35	25
1280	180 f. Jean Mermoz and route map	45	30
1281	220 f. Antoine Saint-Exupery and route map	55	35

410 Head of Elephant with Ear forming Map of Africa

1994. S.O.S. Elephant Conservation Programme. Multicoloured.

1282	30 f. Type **410**	10	10
1283	60 f. Elephant within SOS	15	10
1284	90 f. Pair of elephants with trunks forming SOS	20	15
1285	145 f. Dead elephant and tusks	35	25

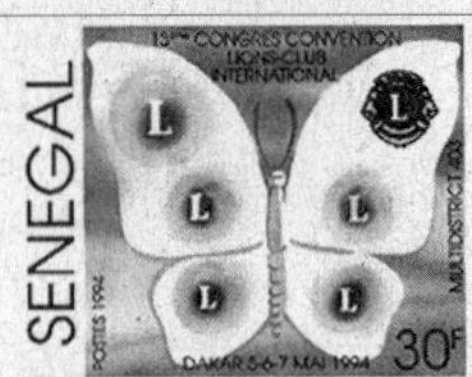

411 Emblems on Butterfly

1994. 13th Congress of District 403 of Lions Clubs International, Dakar. Multicoloured.

1286 30 f. Type **411** 10 10
1287 60 f. Emblem over butterfly . . 15 10
1288 175 f. "L"s and emblem . . . 40 25
1289 215 f. Emblem on rainbow . . 50 35

412 "Stamp" showing Children playing

1994. African Children's Day. Children's Drawings. Multicoloured.

1290 175 f. Type **412** 40 25
1291 215 f. Preparing meal outside house 50 35

413 Flags and Football

1994. World Cup Football Championship, U.S.A. Multicoloured.

1292 45 f. Type **413** 10 10
1293 175 f. World map forming part of football 40 25
1294 215 f. Player dribbling ball (horiz) 50 35
1295 665 f. Players with ball (horiz) 1·60 1·10

414 Slave House

1994. World Heritage Site. Goree.

1296 **414** 500 f. multicoloured . . 1·25 85

415 Rainbow over Globe

1994. 21st Universal Postal Union Congress and "Philakorea 1994" International Stamp Exhibition, Seoul. Multicoloured.

1297 10 f. Type **415** 10 10
1298 175 f. "Stamp" forming wing of dove 40 25
1299 260 f. "Stamp" forming sail of boat 65 45
1300 300 f. Globe, hands and airmail envelope 75 50

416 Peace Dove, People of Different Cultures and Flags

1994. International Year of the Family. Multicoloured.

1301 5 f. Type **416** 10 10
1302 175 f. People of different cultures, flags and globe . . 40 25
1303 215 f. Globe and mothers with children 50 35
1304 290 f. Globe, dove and family 70 45

417 "Murex saxatilis"

1994. Shells. Multicoloured.

1305 20 f. Type **417** 10 10
1306 45 f. "Nerita senegalensis" (vert) 10 10
1307 75 f. "Polymita picea" . . . 20 15
1308 175 f. "Scalaria pretiosa" (vert) 40 25
1309 215 f. Glory of the sea cone (vert) 50 35

418 Golden Jackal

1994. Animals. Multicoloured.

1310 60 f. Type **418** 15 10
1311 70 f. African clawless otter . 15 10
1312 100 f. Egyptian mongoose . 25 15
1313 175 f. Giant ground pangolin 40 25
1314 215 f. Nile monitor 50 35

419 Pierre de Coubertin (founder) and Anniversary Emblem

1994. Centenary of International Olympic Committee. Multicoloured.

1315 175 f. Type **419** 40 25
1316 215 f. Coubertin within wreath and anniversary emblem . 50 35
1317 275 f. Coubertin over anniversary emblem (vert) 65 45
1318 290 f. Coubertin within anniversary emblem and Olympic rings (vert) . . . 70 45

420 Africans greeting Portuguese

1994. 550th Anniv of First Portuguese Landing in Senegal.

1319 **420** 175 f. multicoloured . . 40 25

421 Father Christmas and Children with Presents

1994. Christmas. Multicoloured.

1320 175 f. Type **421** 40 25
1321 215 f. Madonna and Child and Christmas trees 50 35
1322 275 f. Adoration of the Wise Men (horiz) 65 45
1323 290 f. Madonna and Child . 70 45

422 Emblem and Ribbons 423 Sudan and Xylophone

1995. Conference of District 9100 of Rotary International. Multicoloured.

1324 260 f. Type **422** 65 45
1325 275 f. Emblem and dove in flight 65 45

1995. Centenary of Formation of French Governate-General of French West Africa. Map highlighting featured country. Multicoloured.

1326 10 f. Type **423** 10 10
1327 15 f. Dahomey and canoes . . 10 10
1328 30 f. Ivory Coast and elephant 10 10
1329 70 f. Mauritania and camel . 15 10
1330 175 f. Guinea, stringed instrument and plants . . . 40 25
1331 180 f. Upper Volta, cow and produce 45 30
1332 215 f. Niger and Cross of Agadez 50 35
1333 225 f. Senegal and lions . . . 55 35

1995. As Nos. 502a/504h but size 21 × 26 mm.

1334 **154** 5 f. orange 10 10
1335 10 f. green 10 10
1336 20 f. red 10 10
1337 25 f. green 10 10
1338 30 f. green 10 10
1339 40 f. green 10 10
1340 100 f. blue 25 15
1341 150 f. blue 35 25
1342 175 f. brown 40 25
1343 200 f. black 50 35
1344 250 f. red 60 40
1345 275 f. red 65 45

424 Communications, Map of West Africa and Energy Sources 425 Pasteur developing Rabies Vaccine

1995. 1st Economic Community of West African States Trade Fair. Multicoloured.

1346 175 f. Type **424** 40 25
1347 215 f. Members' flags, banknotes and crops (horiz) 50 35

1995. Death Centenary of Louis Pasteur (chemist). Multicoloured.

1348 275 f. Type **425** 65 45
1349 500 f. Pasteur working on pasteurisation . . . . . . 1·25 85

426 Scene from "L'Arroseur Arrose" (dir. Lumiere Brothers)

1995. Centenary of Motion Pictures. Multicoloured.

1350 100 f. Type **426** 25 15
1351 200 f. First public film screening by Lumiere brothers . . . 50 35
1352 250 f. August and Louis Lumiere watching screening of "Arrival by Train" . . . 60 40
1353 275 f. Presentation on cinematography by Antoine Lumiere, 1895 . . . . . . 65 45

427 Animal Welfare 428 People of Different Cultures

1995. 50th Anniv of F.A.O. Multicoloured.

1354 175 f. Type **427** 40 25
1355 215 f. Teaching new skills to rural communities 50 35
1356 260 f. Aquaculture 65 45
1357 275 f. Nourishment of children 65 45

1995. 50th Anniv of U.N.O.

1358 **428** 275 f. blue, violet and black 65 45
1359 – 1000 f. multicoloured . . 2·40 1·60

DESIGN: 1000 f. "ONU 50" and U.N. Headquarters, New York.

429 Figures dancing around Book

1995. 25th Anniv of Agency for Cultural and Technical Co-operation in French-speaking Countries. Multicoloured.

1360 150 f. Type **429** 35 25
1361 500 f. Panels of contestants (victory of St. Louis Military Academy in 1994 competition) . . . . 1·25 85

430 African buffalo

1995. Animals. Multicoloured.

1362 90 f. Type **430** 20 15
1363 150 f. Wart hog 35 25
1364 175 f. Bushbuck 40 25
1365 275 f. African spurred tortoise 65 45
1366 300 f. North African crested porcupine 75 50

431 Caspian Tern

1995. Endangered Birds. Terns. Multicoloured.

1367 90 f. Type **431** 20 15
1368 145 f. Gull-billed tern . . . 35 25
1369 150 f. Royal tern 35 25
1370 180 f. Common tern 45 30

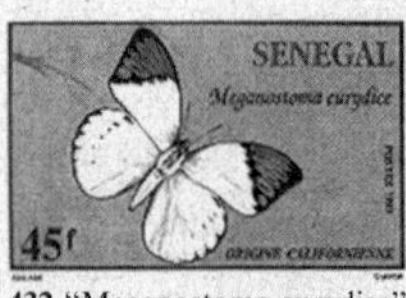

432 "Meganostoma eurydice"

1995. Butterflies. Multicoloured.

1371 45 f. Type **432** 10 10
1372 100 f. "Luehdorfia japonica" 25 15
1373 200 f. Great orange-tip . . . 50 35
1374 220 f. Small tortoiseshell . . 55 35

433 Bassari Festivals

1995. Cultural Tourism. Multicoloured.

1375 100 f. Type **433** 25 15
1376 175 f. "Baawnann" (vert) . . 40 25
1377 220 f. Pyramid-roofed houses 55 35
1378 500 f. Turu Dance . . . . . 1·25 80

OFFICIAL STAMPS

O 45 Arms of Dakar O 78 Baobab Tree

1961. Figures of value in black.

O240 **O 45** 1 f. black and blue . . 10 10
O241 2 f. blue and yellow . . 10 10
O242 5 f. lake and green . . 10 10
O243 10 f. red and blue . . 10 10
O244 25 f. blue and red . . 20 15
O245 50 f. red and grey . . 75 30
O246 85 f. purple & orange . 1·40 45
O247 100 f. red and green . 2·00 1·10

1966.

O 339 **O 78** 1 f. black & yellow . 10 10
O 340 5 f. black & orange . 10 10
O 341 10 f. black and red . 10 10
O 342 20 f. black & purple 15 10
O 342a 25 f. black & mauve 15 10
O 343 30 f. black and blue 15 10
O 344 35 f. black and blue 20 10
O 344a 40 f. black and blue 20 10
O1122 50 f. black and red . 20 15
O 345 55 f. black & green . 35 20
O 345a 60 f. black & green . 45 20
O 346 90 f. black & green . 50 35
O 347 100 f. black & brown 60 40
O1123 145 f. black & green 55 35
O1124 180 f. black & orge . 70 45

1969. No. O345 surch.
O390 O 78 60 f. on 55 f. black and green 85 10

POSTAGE DUE STAMPS

1903. Postage Due stamps of French Colonies surch.
D30 U 10 on 50 c. purple 50·00 50·00
D31 10 on 60 c. brn on buff 50·00 50·00
D32 10 on 1 f. pink on buff £250 £250

1906. "Natives" key-type.
D50 L 5 c. green and red 3·00 3·00
D51 10 c. purple and blue 4·00 3·50
D52 15 c. blue & red on blue 4·50 4·25
D53 20 c. black & red on yell 5·25 3·75
D54 30 c. red & bl on cream 6·00 5·25
D55 50 c. violet and red 6·00 5·50
D56 60 c. blk & red on buff 7·50 7·25
D57 1 f. black & red on pink 12·00 13·00

1915. "Figure" key-type.
D81 M 5 c. green 15 30
D82 10 c. red 25 20
D83 15 c. grey 25 25
D84 20 c. brown 50 40
D85 30 c. blue 75 70
D86 50 c. black 1·00 90
D87 60 c. orange 1·25 1·25
D88 1 r. violet 1·40 1·50

1927. Surch in figures.
D133 M 2 f. on 1 f. purple 2·75 2·75
D134 3 f. on 1 f. brown 2·75 2·75

D 40

1935.
D194 D 40 5 c. green 10 25
D195 10 c. orange 10 25
D196 15 c. violet 10 25
D197 20 c. olive 10 25
D198 30 c. brown 10 25
D199 50 c. purple 40 65
D200 60 c. yellow 75 80
D201 1 f. black 50 50
D202 2 f. blue 55 65
D203 3 f. red 75 95

D 43 D 77 Lion's Head

1961.
D239 D 43 1 f. orange and red 10 10
D240 2 f. blue and red 10 10
D241 5 f. brown and red 10 10
D242 20 f. green and red 25 25
D243 25 f. purple and red 5·50 5·50

1966. Head in gold and black; value in black.
D339 D 77 1 f. red 15 15
D340 2 f. brown 15 15
D341 5 f. violet 20 20
D342 10 f. blue 40 40
D343 20 f. green 50 50
D344 30 f. grey 65 65
D345 60 f. blue 65 65
D346 90 f. purple 75 75

SENEGAMBIA AND NIGER Pt. 6

A French colony later re-named Upper Senegal and Niger, and later French Sudan.

100 centimes = 1 franc

1903. "Tablet" key-type inscr "SENEGAMBIE ET NIGER" in red (1, 5, 15, 25, 75 c., 1 f.) or blue (others).
22 D 1 c. black on blue 50 1·10
23 2 c. brown on buff 1·00 1·25
24 4 c. brown on grey 1·40 2·25
25 5 c. green 3·75 2·00
26 10 c. red 3·75 2·00
27 15 c. grey 6·75 5·75
28 20 c. red on green 6·50 6·75
29 25 c. blue 9·50 9·50
30 30 c. brown on drab 8·75 9·50
31 40 c. red on yellow 14·00 14·00
32 50 c. brown on blue 25·00 28·00
33 75 c. brown on orange 30·00 32·00
34 1 f. green 38·00 40·00

SERBIA Pt. 3

A kingdom in the Balkans, S. E. Europe. Part of Yugoslavia since 1918, except during the Second World War when stamps were issued by a German sponsored Government.

100 paras = 1 dinar

2 Prince Michael (Obrenovich III) 3 Prince Milan (Obrenovich IV) 5 King Milan I

1866. Perf.
12 2 10 p. orange 70·00 90·00
15 20 p. red 12·50 18·00
14 40 p. blue 42·00 32·00

1869. Perf.
42 3 10 p. brown 4·75 4·00
45 10 p. orange 1·25 3·00
31 15 p. orange 45·00 23·00
43 20 p. blue 1·10 1·25
39 25 p. red 1·90 4·75
34 35 p. green 3·50 3·50
47 40 p. mauve 1·90 1·50
36 50 p. green 6·00 4·75

1880. Perf.
54a 5 5 p. green 25 10
55 10 p. red 50 10
56 20 p. orange 35 20
57a 25 p. blue 1·25 15
58 50 p. brown 1·00 2·10
59 1 d. violet 6·75 7·50

6 7 10
King Alexander (Obrenovich V)

1890.
60 6 5 p. green 25 10
61 10 p. red 50 10
62 15 p. mauve 50 10
63 20 p. orange 45 10
64 25 p. blue 60 20
65 50 p. brown 2·40 2·40
66 1 d. lilac 8·75 7·75

1894.
75 7 1 p. red 10 10
76 5 p. green 75 10
68 10 p. red 2·00 10
69 15 p. mauve 4·00 10
79 20 p. orange 4·50 10
80 25 p. blue 4·50 15
81a 50 p. brown 9·00 80
73 1 d. green 1·25 1·60
74 1 d. red on blue 7·50 2·50

1900. Surch.
82 7 10 p. on 20 p. red 1·00 10
84 15 p. on 1 d. red on blue 3·75 75

1901.
85a 10 5 p. green 10 10
86 10 p. red 10 10
87 15 p. mauve 10 10
88 20 p. orange 10 10
89 25 p. blue 15 10
90 50 p. yellow 20 15
91 – 1 d. brown 60 1·40
92a – 3 d. pink 6·25 8·75
93a – 5 d. violet 6·25 9·50
The 1 d. to 5 d. are larger.

12 King Alexander I (Obrenovich V) 14 Karageorge and Peter I

1903. Optd with shield.
94 12 1 p. black and red 30 60
95 5 p. black and green 25 10
96 10 p. black and red 10 10
97 15 p. black and grey 10 10
98 20 p. black and orange 15 10
99 25 p. black and blue 20 10
100 50 p. black and grey 3·00 55
101 1 d. black and green 9·50 3·00
102 3 d. black and lilac 1·90 2·25
103 5 d. black and brown 1·90 2·50

1903. Surch **1 NAPA 1**.
104 12 1 p. on 5 d. black and brown 95 2·50

1904. Coronation. Centenary of Karageorgevich Dynasty. Dated "1804 1904".
108 14 5 p. green 10 10
109 10 p. red 10 10
110 15 p. purple 10 10
111 25 p. blue 15 15
112 50 p. brown 25 25
113 – 1 d. bistre 6 75
114 – 3 d. green 1·50 3·00
115 – 5 d. violet 1·90 3·75
DESIGN: 1, 3, 5 d. Karageorge and insurgents, 1804.

16 Peter I 17 Peter I

1905.
116 16 1 p. black and grey 15 10
117 5 p. black and green 20 10
118 10 p. black and red 1·90 10
119 15 p. black and mauve 2·10 10
120 20 p. black and yellow 3·75 10
121 25 p. black and blue 5·25 10
122 30 p. black and green 2·75 10
123 50 p. black and brown 3·75 10
135 1 d. black and bistre 80 15
136 3 d. black and green 80 86
137 5 d. black and violet 3·00 2·25

1911.
146 17 1 p. black 10 10
147 2 p. violet 10 10
169 5 p. green 10 10
170 10 p. red 10 10
150 15 p. purple 70 10
171 15 p. black 10 10
151 20 p. yellow 70 10
172 20 p. brown 35 20
173 25 p. blue 10 10
153 30 p. green 20 15
173a 30 p. bronze 10 20
154 50 p. brown 30 20
174 50 p. red 10 20
155 1 d. orange 18·00 32·00
175 1 d. green 1·00 1·75
156 3 d. lake 24·00 70·00
176 3 d. yellow 95·00 £375
177 5 d. violet 2·10 17·00

19 Peter I on the Battlefield 20 Peter I and Prince Alexander

1915.
178 19 5 p. green 15 1·00
179 10 p. red 15 1·25
179a 15 p. grey 3·00
179b 20 p. brown 40
179c 25 p. blue 6·25
179d 30 p. green 3·00
179e 50 p. brown 24·00

1918.
194 20 1 p. black 10 10
195 2 p. olive 10 10
196 5 p. green 10 10
197 10 p. red 10 10
198 15 p. sepia 10 10
199 20 p. brown 10 10
208 20 p. mauve 1·40 75
200 25 p. blue 10 10
201 30 p. olive 10 10
202 50 p. mauve 10 10
220 1 d. brown 10 10
204 3 d. slate 90 75
205 5 d. brown 1·50 90

NEWSPAPER STAMPS

1 4 King Milan

1866. Imperf.
N7 1 1 p. green on red 45·00
N4 2 p. brown on lilac 60·00

1867. Perf.
N17 2 1 p. olive 9·25 £550
N18 2 p. brown 15·00 £500

1868. Imperf.
N19 2 1 p. green 15·00
N20 2 p. brown 24·00

1869. Perf.
N49 3 1 p. yellow 1·25 £275

1872. Imperf.
N51 3 1 p. yellow 5·50 11·00
N52 4 2 p. black 1·90 9·25

POSTAGE DUE STAMPS

D 8 D 21

1895.
D87 D 8 5 p. mauve 40 25
D83 10 p. blue 2·50 20
D91 20 p. brown 15 45
D85 30 p. green 15 35
D86 50 p. red 15 45

1918.
D227 D 21 5 p. red 15 15
D232 5 p. brown 20 25
D228 10 p. green 15 15
D229 20 p. brown 15 15
D230 30 p. blue 15 15
D233 30 p. grey 30 35
D231 50 p. brown 75 35

GERMAN OCCUPATION

1941. Stamps of Yugoslavia on paper with coloured network optd **SERBIEN** reading downwards.
G 1 99 25 p. black 10 75
G 2 50 p. orange 10 20
G 3 1 d. green 10 20
G 4 1 d. 50 red 10 20
G 5 2 d. red 10 20
G 6 3 d. brown 75 4·25
G 7 4 d. blue 15 55
G 8 5 d. blue 40 1·75
G 9 5 d. 50 violet 40 1·75
G10 6 d. blue 40 1·75
G11 8 d. brown 55 2·75
G12 12 d. violet 55 2·75
G13 16 d. purple 90 7·00
G14 20 d. blue 90 8·50
G15 30 d. pink 4·50 55·00

1941. Air. Stamps of Yugoslavia on paper with coloured network, optd **SERBIEN**.
G16 80 50 p. brown 3·50 19·00
G17 – 1 d. green (No. 361) 3·50 19·00
G18 – 2 d. blue (No. 362) 3·50 19·00
G19 – 2 d. 50 red (No. 363) 3·50 19·00
G20 80 5 d. violet 3·50 19·00
G21 – 10 d. red (No. 365) 3·50 19·00
G22 – 20 d. green (No. 366) 3·50 19·00
G23 – 30 d. blue (No. 367) 4·75 21·00
G24 – 40 d. green (No. 443) 8·00 £100
G25 – 50 d. blue (No. 444) 40·00 80·00

1941. Air. As last, but without network surch **SERBIEN** and value.
G26 – 1 d. on 10 d. red (No. 365) 2·00 13·50
G27 – 3 d. on 20 d. grn (No. 366) 2·00 13·50
G28 – 6 d. on 30 d. blue (No. 367) 2·00 13·50
G29 – 8 d. on 40 d. grn (No. 443) 2·50 38·00
G30 – 12 d. on 50 d. bl (No. 444) 4·75 65·00

1941. As Nos. G1/15, but with **SERBIEN** reading upwards.
G31 99 25 p. black 10 3·00
G32 50 p. orange 10 55
G33 1 d. green 15 35
G34 1 d. 50 red 15 60
G35 2 d. red 15 35
G36 3 d. brown 25 4·00
G37 4 d. blue 20 35
G38 5 d. blue 20 1·00
G39 5 d. 50 violet 40 3·00
G40 6 d. blue 50 3·00
G41 8 d. brown 70 3·00
G42 12 d. violet 90 3·00
G43 16 d. purple 90 8·50
G44 20 d. blue 90 14·00
G45 30 d. pink 5·50 48·00

4 Smederovo Fortress

6 Christ and the Virgin Mary

1941. Smederovo Explosion Relief Fund.
G46 **4** 50 p. + 1 d. brown 15 70
G47 – 1 d. + 2 d. green 15 75
G48 – 1 d. 50 + 3 d. purple 30 1·25
G49 **4** 2 d. + 4 d. blue 40 2·00
DESIGN: 1 d., 1 d. 50, Refugees.

1941. Prisoners of War Fund.
G50 **6** 50 p. + 1 d. 50 brown 20 3·00
G51 1 d. + 3 d. green 20 3·00
G52 2 d. + 6 d. red 20 3·00
G53 4 d. + 12 d. blue 20 3·00
This set also exists with an optd network, both plain and incorporating a large "E", this letter being either normal or reversed.

7

8

1942. Anti-Masonic Exn. Dated "22.X.1941".
G54 **7** 50 p. + 50 p. brown 15 35
G55 – 1 d. + 1 d. green 15 35
G56 **8** 2 d. + 2 d. red 25 75
G57 – 4 d. + 4 d. blue 25 75
DESIGNS—HORIZ: 1 d. Hand grasping snake. VERT: 4 d. Peasant demolishing masonic symbols.

9 Kalenic

11 Mother and Children

1942. Monasteries.
G58 – 50 p. violet 10 15
G59 **9** 1 d. red 10 10
G60 – 1 d. 50 brown 70 2·50
G61 – 1 d. 50 green 10 15
G62 – 2 d. purple 10 15
G63 – 3 d. blue 70 2·50
G64 – 3 d. pink 10 15
G65 – 4 d. blue 10 15
G66 – 7 d. green 10 15
G67 – 12 d. red 15 1·00
G68 – 16 d. black 45 1·50
DESIGNS—VERT: 50 p. Lazarica; 1 d. 50, Ravanica; 12 d. Gornjak; 16 d. Studenica. HORIZ: 2 d. Manasija; 3 d. Ljubostinja; 4 d. Sopocani; 7 d. Zica.

1942. As Nos. G50/53, colours changed.
G68a **6** 0.50 d. + 1.50 d. brown 50 1·40
G68b 1 d. + 3 d. green 50 1·40
G68c 2 d. + 6 d. red 50 1·40
G68d 4 d. + 12 d. blue 50 1·40

1942. Air. 1939 issue of Yugoslavia surch with airplane, "SERBIA" in cyrillic characters and new value.
G69 **99** 2 on 2 d. mauve 10 1·25
G70 4 on 4 d. blue 10 1·25
G71 10 on 12 d. violet 15 2·00
G72 14 on 20 d. blue 15 2·00
G73 20 on 30 d. pink 30 9·00

1942. War Orphans Fund.
G74 **11** 2 d. + 6 d. violet 1·00 2·50
G75 4 d. + 8 d. blue 1·00 2·50
G76 7 d. + 13 d. green 1·00 2·50
G77 20 d. + 40 d. red 1·00 2·50

12 Broken Sword

13 Post Rider

1943. War Invalids' Relief Fund.
G78 **12** 1 d. 50 + 1 d. 50 brown 40 90
G79 – 2 d. + 3 d. green 40 90
G80 – 3 d. + 5 d. mauve 60 1·60
G81 – 4 d. + 10 d. blue 90 2·50
DESIGNS—HORIZ: 2 d. Fallen standard bearer; 3 d. Wounded soldier (seated). VERT: 4 d. Nurse tending soldier.

1943. Postal Centenary. Inscr "15.X.1843-15.X.1943".
G82 **13** 3 d. red and lilac 30 1·10
G83 – 8 d. mauve and grey 30 1·10
G84 – 9 d. green and brown 75 1·00
G85 – 30 d. brown and green 30 1·10
G86 – 50 d. blue and red 30 1·10
DESIGNS: 8 d. Horse wagon; 9 d. Railway van; 30 d. Postal motor van; 50 d. Junkers Ju 52/3m mail plane.

1943. Bombing of Nish Relief Fund. Monasteries issue of 1942 on paper with network, surch **... Serbian Inscr, 20-X-1943** and value.
G87 50 p. + 2 d. violet 10 2·00
G88 1 d. + 3 d. red 10 2·00
G89 1 d. 50 + 4 d. green 10 2·00
G90 2 d. + 5 d. purple 15 2·00
G91 3 d. + 7 d. pink 15 2·00
G92 4 d. + 9 d. blue 15 2·00
G93 7 d. + 15 d. green 40 2·50
G94 12 d. + 25 d. red 40 8·00
G95 16 d. + 33 d. black 65 13·00

OFFICIAL STAMP

O 12

1943.
GO78 **O 12** 3 d. red 30 1·00

POSTAGE DUE STAMPS

D 2

D 3

D 13

1941. Unissued Postage Due stamps optd **SERBIEN**.
GD16 **D 2** 50 p. violet 35 2·75
GD17 1 d. red 35 2·75
GD18 2 d. blue 35 2·75
GD19 3 d. red 45 3·50
GD20 **D 3** 4 d. blue 75 7·50
GD21 5 d. orange 75 7·50
GD22 10 d. violet 2·00 17·00
GD23 20 d. green 6·00 70·00

1942. Types **D 2** and **D 3** without opt. Bottom inscription on white background.
GD69 **D 2** 1 d. red and green 15 1·50
GD70 2 d. blue and red 15 1·50
GD71 3 d. red and blue 20 2·50
GD72 **D 3** 4 d. blue and red 20 2·50
GD73 5 d. orange and blue 30 2·75
GD74 10 d. violet and red 35 6·50
GD75 20 d. green and red 95 16·00

1943.
GD82 **D 13** 50 p. black 15 1·00
GD83 3 d. violet 15 1·00
GD84 4 d. blue 15 1·00
GD85 5 d. green 15 1·00
GD86 6 d. orange 25 2·75
GD87 10 d. red 40 6·00
GD88 20 d. blue 1·00 13·00

SERBIAN OCCUPATION OF HUNGARY Pt. 2

BARANYA

100 filler = 1 korona

1919. Stamps of Hungary optd **1919 Baranya** or surch also. (a) "Turul" Type.
1 **7** 6 f. drab 15 15
2 50 f. red on blue 10 10
3 60 f. green on red 25 25
4 70 f. brown on green 10 10
5 80 f. violet 1·75 1·75

(b) War Charity stamp of 1915.
6 **7** 50 + 2 f. red on blue 6·00 6·00

(c) War Charity stamps of 1916.
8 **20** 10 f. (+ 2 f.) red 10 10
9 – 15 f. (+ 2 f.) violet 10 10

(d) Harvesters and Parliament Types.
10 **18** 2 f. brown 10 10
11 3 f. purple 10 10
12 5 f. green 10 10
13 6 f. blue 30 30
14 15 f. purple 10 10
15 20 f. brown 10·00 10·00
16 25 f. blue 1·40 1·40
17 35 f. brown 2·50 2·50
18 40 f. green 10·00 10·00
19 45 on 2 f. brown 20 20
20 45 on 5 f. green 10 10
21 45 on 15 f. purple 10 10
22 **19** 50 f. purple 35 35
23 **19** 75 f. blue 10 10
24 80 f. green 15 15
25 1 k. red 15 15
26 2 k. brown 15 15
27 3 k. grey and violet 15 15
28 5 k. light brown and brown 65 65
29 60 k. mauve and brown 3·00 3·00

(e) Charles and Zita stamps.
30 **27** 10 f. pink 10 10
31 20 f. brown 10 10
32 25 f. blue 55 55
33 **28** 40 f. green 6·00 6·00

(f) Stamps optd **KOZTARSASAG**. (i) Harvesters Type.
34 **18** 2 f. brown 1·50 1·50
35 45 on 2 f. brown 20 20

(ii) Zita stamp.
36 **28** 40 f. green 8·00 8·00

1919. Stamps of Hungary surch **BARANYA** and value. (a) Harvesters and Parliament Types.
42 **18** 20 on 2 f. brown 4·00 4·00
43 50 on 5 f. green 2·25 2·25
44 150 on 15 f. purple 80 80
45 **19** 200 on 75 f. blue 60 60

(b) Harvesters Type inscr "MAGYAR POSTA".
46 **18** 20 on 2 f. brown 10 10
47 30 on 6 f. blue 20 20
48 50 on 5 f. green 10 10
49 100 on 25 f. blue 10 10
50 100 on 40 f. green 10 10
51 100 on 45 f. orange 30 30
52 150 on 20 f. brown 55 55

(c) Charles stamp optd **KOZTARSASAG**.
53 **27** 150 on 15 f. purple 75 75

EXPRESS LETTER STAMPS

1919. No. E245 of Hungary surch **1919 Baranya 105**.
E37 **E 18** 105 on 2 f. green and red 55 55

1919. No. E245 of Hungary surch **BARANYA 10**.
E55 **E 18** 10 on 2 f. olive and red 10 10

NEWSPAPER STAMP

1919. No. N136 of Hungary surch **BARANYA 10**.
N54 **N 9** 10 on 2 (f). orange 10 10

POSTAGE DUE STAMPS

1919. Nos. D191 etc of Hungary optd **1919 BARANYA** or surch also.
D38 **D 9** 2 f. red and green 2·50 2·50
D39 10 f. red and green 45 45
D40 20 f. red and geen 45 45
D41 40 on 2 f. red and green 45 45

SAVINGS BANK STAMP

1919. No. B199 of Hungary surch **BARANYA 10**.
B56 **B 17** 10 on 10 f. purple 10 10

TEMESVAR

Temesvar was later occupied by Rumania which issued stamps for this area. It was then incorporated in Rumania and renamed Timosoara.

100 filler = 1 korona

1919. Stamps of Hungary surch. (a) War Charity stamp of 1916.
1 **20** 45 f. on 10 f. (+ 2 f.) red 10 10

(b) Harvesters Type.
2 **18** 10 f. on 2 f. brown 10 10
3 30 f. on 2 f. brown 10 10
4 1 k. 50 on 15 f. purple 15 15

(c) Charles stamp.
5 **27** 50 f. on 20 f. brown 10 10

POSTAGE DUE STAMPS

1919. No. D191 of Hungary surch.
D6 **D 9** 40 f. on 2 f. red & green 15 15
D7 60 f. on 2 f. red & green 15 15
D8 100 f. on 2 f. red & green 15 15

SHANGHAI Pt. 17

A seaport on the E. coast of China, which for a time had a separate postal system.

1865. 10 cash = 1 candareen; 100 candareens = 1 tael.
1890. 100 cents = 1 dollar (Chinese).

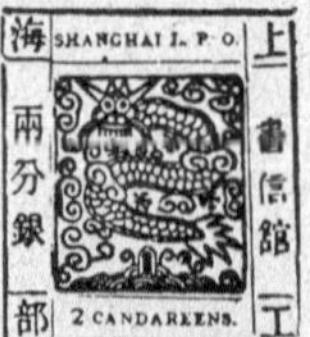

1 Dragon

1865. Value in candareens. Imperf. (a) "CANDAREEN" in singular.
28 **1** 1 ca. blue 55·00 £180
12 2 ca. black £140 £2500
29 3 ca. brown 55·00 £2500
13 4 ca. yellow £150 £2500
14 8 ca. green £100
15 16 ca. red £140

(b) "CANDAREENS" in plural.
30 **1** 2 ca. black 50·00
31 3 ca. brown 50·00 £1500
3 **1** 4 ca. yellow £140 £1800
18 6 ca. brown 85·00
20 6 ca. red £100
4 8 ca. green £150 £2500
21 12 ca. brown 90·00
22 16 ca. red 90·00

2

6

1866. Value in cents. Frames differ. Perf.
32 **2** 2 c. red 7·50 18·00
33 4 c. lilac 11·00 32·00
34 8 c. ble 15·00 32·00
35 16 c. green 22·00 48·00

1867. Value in candareens. Frames differ.
37 **6** 1 ca. brown 4·50 8·00
59 1 ca. yellow on yellow 10·00 15·00
62 1 ca. yellow 6·50 9·00
73 1 ca. red £450 £850
38 3 ca. yellow 13·00 25·00
60 3 ca. pink on pink 10·00 15·00
63 3 ca. red 35·00 45·00
39 6 ca. grey 14·00 48·00
64 6 ca. green 55·00 90·00
65 9 ca. grey 70·00 £120
40 12 ca. brown 20·00 48·00

1873. Surch with value in English and Chinese.
41 **2** 1 ca. on 2 c. red 20·00 30·00
44 1 ca. on 4 c. lilac 9·50 10·00
46 1 ca. on 8 c. blue 13·00 14·00
48 1 ca. on 16 c. green £950 £750
50 3 ca. on 2 c. red 60·00 75·00
52 3 ca. on 16 c. green £1400 £1300

1873. Surch with value in English and Chinese.
53 **6** 1 ca. on 3 ca. yellow £8250 £5750
67 1 ca. on 3 ca. red 35·00 30·00
68 1 ca. on 3 ca. pink on pink £160 £150
54 1 ca. on 6 ca. grey £225 £225
69 1 ca. on 6 ca. green 70·00 65·00
70 1 ca. on 9 ca. grey £140 £140
56 1 ca. on 12 ca. brown £190 £180
58 3 ca. on 12 ca. brown £1600 £1000

1877. Value in cash.
74 **6** 20 cash blue 3·25 3·25
75 20 cash lilac 2·75 3·00
93 20 cash green 3·00 3·25
114 20 cash grey 2·50 3·25
81 40 cash pink 5·50 7·50
94 40 cash brown 4·00 4·75
107 40 cash black 3·50 3·25
82 60 cash green 6·50 8·50
95 60 cash violet 5·50 5·50
108 60 cash red 5·50 6·50
83 80 cash blue 7·50 10·00
96 80 cash brown 4·75 2·25
109 80 cash green 5·50 5·50
84 100 cash brown 7·50 10·00
97 100 cash yellow 5·50 5·50
110 100 cash blue 7·50 8·50

1879. Surch in English and Chinese.
89 **6** 20 cash on 40 cash pink 8·00 10·00
103 20 cash on 40 cash brown 13·00 15·00
105 20 cash on 80 cash brown 7·50 7·50
111 20 cash on 80 cash green 5·50 6·00
112 20 cash on 100 cash blue 5·50 6·00
100 40 cash on 80 cash brown 4·50 7·00
101 40 cash on 100 cash yellow 5·50 6·50
90 60 cash on 80 cash blue 17·00 20·00
88 60 cash on 100 cash brown 18·00 19·00
102 60 cash on 100 cash yellow 6·50 7·50

1886. Surch **20 CASH** in English and Chinese in double-lined frame.
104 **6** 20 cash on 40 cash brown 18·00 14·00

1889. Surch **100 CASH** over **20 CASH** in English and Chinese in double-lined frame.
113 **6** 100 cash on 20 cash on 100 cash yellow 45·00 50·00

16

25

26

1890. Value in cents.
119 **16** 2 c. brown 2·25 1·50
142 2 c. green 1·50 1·50
120 5 c. pink 6·00 3·75
143 5 c. red 4·50 4·50
122 10 c. black 7·50 6·50
144 10 c. orange 13·00 16·00
123 15 c. blue 9·50 10·00
145 15 c. mauve 8·00 7·50
124 20 c. mauve 7·50 7·50
146 20 c. brown 8·50 7·50

1892. Surch **2 Cts** and in Chinese.
141 **16** 2 c. on 5 c. pink 55·00 32·00

1893. Surch in words in English and Chinese.
147 **16** ½ c. on 15 c. mauve 6·50 6·50
148 1 c. on 20 c. brown 6·50 6·50

1893. Surch $\frac{1}{2}$ **Ct** or **1 Ct.**

149 **16** $\frac{1}{2}$ c. on half of 5 c. pink . . 5·50 5·50
152 $\frac{1}{2}$ c. on half of 5 c. red . . . 5·00 5·00
155 1 c. on half of 2 c. brown . 2·00 2·00
156 1 c. on half of 2 c. green . 7·50 7·50

1893. Inscriptions in outer frame in black.

165 **25** $\frac{1}{2}$ c. orange 20 20
166 1 c. brown 20 20
187 2 c. red 25 50
188 4 c. orange on yellow . . . 1·50 2·25
161 5 c. blue 50 75
189 6 c. red on pink . . . . . 2·25 2·75
167 10 c. green . . . . 65 1·25
163 15 c. yellow . . . . 1·00 2·50
168 20 c. mauve . . . . 95 2·00

1893. Jubilee of First Settlement.

176 **26** 2 c. red and black 75 75

1893. Optd **1843 Jubilee 1893**. Inscriptions in outer frame in black.

177 **25** $\frac{1}{2}$ c. orange 20 20
178 1 c. brown 25 25
179 2 c. red 30 35
180 5 c. blue . . . . 1·75 1·75
181 10 c. green . . . . 2·25 2·75
182 15 c. yellow . . . . 3·50 3·75
183 20 c. mauve . . . . 3·50 3·75

1896. Surch in English and Chinese.

184 **25** 4 c. on 15 c. yellow . . . . 4·50 4·25
185 6 c. on 20 c. mauve . . . . 4·50 4·00

POSTAGE DUE STAMPS

1892. T **16** optd **Postage Due**.

D134 2 c. brown . . . . 2·00 1·75
D135 5 c. pink . . . . 4·50 4·50
D130 10 c. black . . . . 14·50 13·00
D138 10 c. orange . . . . 8·50 8·50
D131 15 c. blue . . . . 13·00 12·00
D139 15 c. mauve . . . . 15·00 16·00
D132 20 c. mauve . . . . 9·50 10·00
D140 20 c. brown . . . . 15·00 16·00

D 26

1893. Inscriptions in outer frame in black.

D169 D **26** $\frac{1}{2}$ c. orange 20 25
D170 1 c. brown 20 15
D171 2 c. red 20 40
D172 5 c. blue 35 65
D173 10 c. green . . . . . . 45 1·25
D174 15 c. yellow . . . . . . 50 1·75
D175 20 c. mauve . . . . . . 75 1·50

SHARJAH Pt. 19

One of the Trucial States on the Persian Gulf. Embodies the principalities of Dibbah, Khor Fakkan and Khor al-Kalba.

On 2nd December, 1971, Sharjah, together with six other Gulf Shaikdoms, formed the United Arab Emirates.

1963. 100 naye paise = 1 rupee.
1966. 100 dirhams = 1 riyal.

IMPERFORATE STAMPS. Some sets exist also imperf in limited quantities.

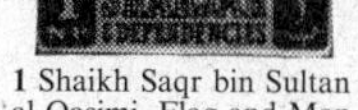

1 Shaikh Saqr bin Sultan al Qasimi, Flag and Map

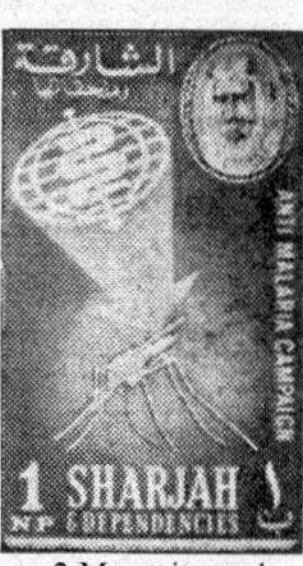

2 Mosquito and W.H.O. Emblem

1963. Multicoloured.

1 **1** 1 n.p. (postage) 10 10
2 2 n.p. 10 10
3 3 n.p. 10 10
4 4 n.p. 10 10
5 5 n.p. 10 10
6 6 n.p. 10 10
7 8 n.p. 10 10
8 10 n.p. 15 10
9 16 n.p. 30 15
10 20 n.p. 40 15
11 30 n.p. 50 20
12 40 n.p. 60 30
13 50 n.p. 75 35
14 75 n.p. . . . . 1·40 85
15 100 n.p. . . . . 1·90 1·40
16 1 r. (air) 90 50
17 2 r. . . . . 1·75 75
18 3 r. . . . . 2·00 1·25
19 **1** 4 r. . . . . 3·25 1·75
20 5 r. . . . . 4·25 2·25
21 10 r. . . . . 8·00 4·50

The air stamps are as T **1** but additionally inscr "AIRMAIL" in English and Arabic, and with a hawk in flight.

1963. Malaria Eradication.

22 **2** 1 n.p. turquoise 10 10
23 2 n.p. blue 10 10
24 3 n.p. blue 10 10
25 4 n.p. green 10 10
26 90 n.p. brown . . . . 1·90 1·25

3 "Red Crescent"

1963. Red Cross Centenary.

27 **3** 1 n.p. red and purple 10 10
28 2 n.p. red and turquoise . . 10 10
29 3 n.p. red and blue 10 10
30 4 n.p. red and green 10 10
31 5 n.p. red and brown 10 10
32 85 n.p. red and green . . . . 1·75 70

4 Campaign Emblem between Hands

1963. Freedom from Hunger.

33 **4** 1 n.p. green 10 10
34 2 n.p. brown 10 10
35 3 n.p. green 10 10
36 4 n.p. blue 10 10
37 90 n.p. red . . . . 1·75 70

1963. Surch.

38 **4** 10 n.p. on 1 n.p. green . . . 25 20
39 20 n.p. on 2 n.p. brown . . 50 40
40 30 n.p. on 3 n.p. green . . . 75 65
41 40 n.p. on 4 n.p. blue . . . 1·00 90
42 75 n.p. on 90 n.p. red . . . 2·00 1·50
43 80 n.p. on 90 n.p. red . . . 2·25 1·75
44 **2** 1 r. on 90 n.p. brown . . . 3·00 2·50

1964. Air. Pres. Kennedy Memorial Issue (1st issue). Nos. 16/21 optd **In Memoriam John F Kennedy 1917–1963** in English and Arabic, and emblems.

45 **1** 1 r. multicoloured . . . . . 1·60 1·60
46 2 r. multicoloured . . . . . 3·00 3·00
47 3 r. multicoloured . . . . . 6·00 6·00
48 4 r. multicoloured . . . . . 7·50 7·00
49 5 r. multicoloured . . . . . 12·00 11·00
50 10 r. multicoloured . . . . . 18·00 17·00

See also Nos. 98/100.

7 Orbiting Astronomical Observatory

1964. Scientific Space Research.

51 1 n.p. blue (Type **7**) 10 10
52 2 n.p. green and brown . . . 10 10
53 3 n.p. blue and black 10 10
54 4 n.p. black and bistre . . . 10 10
55 5 n.p. bistre and violet . . . 10 10
56 35 n.p. violet and blue 75 65
57 50 n.p. brown and green . . . 1·60 90

DESIGNS: 2 n.p. "Nimbus" weather satellite; 3 n.p. "Pioneer V" space probe; 4 n.p. "Explorer XIII" satellite; 5 n.p. "Explorer XII" satellite; 35 n.p. Project "Relay" satellite; 50 n.p. Orbiting solar observatory.

8 Running

1964. Olympic Games, Tokyo (1st issue).

58 1 n.p. blue, green and yellow (Type **8**) 10 10
59 2 n.p. red and turquoise . . . 10 10
60 3 n.p. brown and green 10 10
61 4 n.p. green and brown 10 10
62 20 n.p. blue and brown 50 20
63 30 n.p. bistre and pink 80 35
64 40 n.p. violet and yellow . . . . 1·00 45
65 1 r. brown and blue . . . . . 2·75 1·25

DESIGNS: 2 n.p. Throwing the discus; 3 n.p. Hurdling; 4 n.p. Putting the shot; 20 n.p. High jumping; 30 n.p. Weightlifting; 40 n.p. Throwing the javelin; 1 r. High diving.

See also Nos. 90/7.

9 Flame and World Map

1964. Air. Human Rights Day.

66 **9** 50 n.p. brown 50 25
67 1 r. violet . . . . 1·00 50
68 150 n.p. green . . . . 2·00 1·00

10 Girl Scouts Marching

1964. Sharjah Girl Scouts.

69 **10** 1 n.p. green 10 10
70 2 n.p. green 10 10
71 3 n.p. blue 10 10
72 4 n.p. violet 10 10
73 5 n.p. mauve 25 15
74 2 r. brown . . . . 3·25 2·50

11 Khor Fakkan

1964. Air. Multicoloured.

75 10 n.p. Type **11** 15 15
76 20 n.p. Bedouin camp, Beni Qatab 20 15
77 30 n.p. Dhaid oasis 30 15
78 40 n.p. Kalba Castle 55 25
79 75 n.p. Street and Wind tower, Sharjah . . . . 1·00 55
80 100 n.p. Fortress . . . . 1·75 75

12 "Mr. Gus" (oil rig) **13** Scout at Attention

1964. Air. New York World's Fair. Multicoloured.

81 20 n.p. Type **12** 30 15
82 40 n.p. Unisphere 50 25
83 1 r. New York skyline ($85\frac{1}{2} \times 44\frac{1}{2}$ mm) . . . . 1·00 50

1964. Sharjah Boy Scouts.

84 **13** 1 n.p. green 10 10
85 – 2 n.p. green 10 10
86 – 3 n.p. blue 10 10
87 **13** 4 n.p. violet 20 15
88 – 5 n.p. mauve 45 40
89 – 2 r. brown . . . . 1·60 1·10

DESIGNS—HORIZ: 2, 5 n.p. Scouts marching. VERT: 3 n.p., 2 r. Boy scout.

14 Olympic Torch

1964. Olympic Games, Tokyo (2nd issue).

90 **14** 1 n.p. green 10 10
91 2 n.p. blue 10 10
92 3 n.p. brown 10 10
93 4 n.p. turquoise 10 10
94 5 n.p. violet 10 10
95 40 n.p. blue 35 15
96 50 n.p. brown 50 25
97 2 r. brown . . . . 3·00 2·50

15 Pres. Kennedy and Statue of Liberty

1964. Air. Pres. Kennedy Commemoration (2nd issue). Inscr in gold.

98 **15** 40 n.p. blue, brown & grn . 1·40 80
99 60 n.p. brown, grn & blue . 1·40 80
100 100 n.p. green, blue & brn 1·40 80

16 Rock Dove

1965. Air. Birds. Multicoloured.

101 30 n.p. Type **16** 60 15
102 40 n.p. Red junglefowl . . . 70 25
103 75 n.p. Hoopoe . . . . 2·00 50
104 150 n.p. Type **16** . . . . . 3·00 90
105 2 r. Red junglefowl . . . . 3·50 1·25
106 3 r. Hoopoe . . . . 5·75 2·75

17 Early Telephone

1965. "Science, Transport and Communications".

107 **17** 1 n.p. black and red . . . 10 10
108 A 1 n.p. black and red . . . 10 10
109 B 2 n.p. blue and orange . . 10 10
110 C 2 n.p. blue and orange . . 10 10
111 D 3 n.p. brown and green . . 10 10
112 E 3 n.p. brown and green . . 10 10
113 F 4 n.p. violet and green . . 10 10
114 G 4 n.p. violet and green . . 10 10
115 H 5 n.p. brown and green . . 10 10
116 I 5 n.p. brown and green . . 10 10
117 J 30 n.p. indigo and blue . . 15 10
118 K 30 n.p. indigo and blue . . 15 10
119 L 40 n.p. blue and yellow . . 25 10
120 M 40 n.p. blue and yellow . . 25 10
121 N 50 n.p. brown and blue . . 60 40
122 O 50 n.p. brown and blue . . 60 40
123 P 75 n.p. brown and green . . 35 25
124 Q 75 n.p. brown and green . . 35 25
125 R 1 r. blue and yellow . . . 1·75 80
126 S 1 r. blue and yellow . . . 1·75 80

DESIGNS: A, Modern teleprinter; B, 1895 Car; C, 1964 American car; D, Early X-ray apparatus; E, T.V. X-ray machine; F, Early mail coach; G, "Telstar" satellite; H, Medieval ship; I, Nuclear-powered freighter "Savannah"; J, Early astronomers; K, Jodrell Bank radio-telescope; L, Greek messengers; M, "Relay" satellite; N, "Man's early flight" (Lilienthal biplane glider); O, Sud Aviation Caravelle jetliner; P, Persian waterwheel; Q, Hydro-electric dam; R, Old steam locomotive; S, Modern diesel train.

1965. Air. Churchill Commemoration (1st issue). Optd **In Memoriam Sir Winston Churchill 1874–1965** in English and Arabic.

127 **15** 40 n.p. multicoloured . . . 60 30
128 60 n.p. multicoloured . . . 1·00 35
129 100 n.p. multicoloured . . 1·40 40

See also Nos. 201/4.

1965. 10th Anniv (1964) of Arab Postal Union's Permanent Office. Similar design to T **43** of Kuwait.
130 5 n.p. blue and yellow 10 10
131 30 n.p. blue and red 50 25
132 65 n.p. green and orange 1·40 60

1965. Various issues of Shaikh Saqr with portrait obliterated with bars. (a) Postage. Nos. 5, 8/13.
150 **1** 5 n.p. multicoloured 10 15
151 10 n.p. multicoloured 10 15
152 16 n.p. multicoloured 20 15
153 20 n.p. multicoloured 20 15
154 30 n.p. multicoloured 25 20
155 40 n.p. multicoloured 30 15
156 50 n.p. multicoloured 35 25

(b) Air. (i) Nos. 16, 18/21.
157 **1** 1 r. multicoloured 60 30
158 3 r. multicoloured 1·90 1·25
159 4 r. multicoloured 2·25 1·50
160 5 r. multicoloured 3·00 2·25
161 10 r. multicoloured 6·00 4·75

(ii) Nos. 75/80.
144 **11** 10 n.p. multicoloured 25 20
145 – 20 n.p. multicoloured 35 20
146 – 30 n.p. multicoloured 45 20
147 – 40 n.p. multicoloured 60 20
148 – 75 n.p. multicoloured 1·10 60
149 – 100 n.p. multicoloured 1·25 70

22 Rameses II in War Chariot **23** Cable Ship "Monarch IV" and COMPAC Cable Route Map

1965. Nubian Monuments Preservation.
162 **22** 5 n.p. blue and yellow 10 10
163 10 n.p. green and brown 10 10
164 30 n.p. blue and orange 15 10
165 55 n.p. violet and blue 30 20

1965. I.T.U. Centenary. Country name in gold.
166 **23** 1 n.p. brown and blue 10 10
167 – 2 n.p. brown and blue 10 10
168 – 3 n.p. violet and green 10 10
169 – 4 n.p. brown and blue 10 10
170 **23** 5 n.p. brown and violet 10 10
171 – 50 n.p. purple and black 35 15
172 – 1 r. green and brown 65 25
173 – 120 n.p. red and green 90 30
DESIGNS: 2, 120 n.p. "Relay 1" satellite and tracking station, Goonhilly Down; 3, 50 n.p. "Telstar" satellite and Atlas-Agena rocket on launching pad; 4 n.p., 1 r. "Syncom" satellite, Post Office Tower (London) and horn paraboloid reflector aerial.

24 Running

1965. Pan-American Games, Cairo.
174 **24** 50 n.p. turquoise and lilac 20 15
175 – 50 n.p. green and brown 20 15
176 – 50 n.p. lilac and brown 20 15
177 – 50 n.p. brown and green 20 15
178 – 50 n.p. brown and turquoise 20 15
SPORTS: No. 175, Pole vaulting; No. 176, Boxing; No. 177, High jumping; No. 178, Long jumping.

25 Flags (reverse of 5 r. coin)

1966. Arabian Gulf Area Monetary Conf. Circular designs on silver foil, backed with paper inscr "Walsall Security Paper" in English and Arabic. Imperf. (a) Diameter 41 mm.
179 **25** 50 n.p. black 65 65
180 – 75 n.p. violet 65 65

(b) Diameter 52 mm.
181 **25** 1 r. purple 85 85
182 – 3 r. blue 2·10 2·10

(c) Diameter 64 mm.
183 **25** 4 r. green 3·50 3·50
184 – 5 r. orange 4·00 4·00
COINS: 75 n.p., 3 r. and 5 r. show the obverse (Pres. Kennedy).

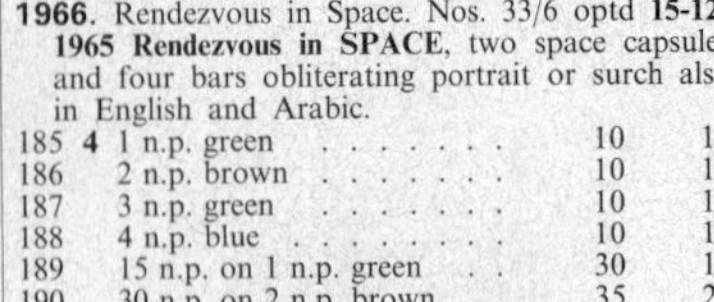

1966. Rendezvous in Space. Nos. 33/6 optd **15-12-1965 Rendezvous in SPACE**, two space capsules and four bars obliterating portrait or surch also in English and Arabic.
185 **4** 1 n.p. green 10 10
186 2 n.p. brown 10 10
187 3 n.p. green 10 10
188 4 n.p. blue 10 10
189 15 n.p. on 1 n.p. green 30 15
190 30 n.p. on 2 n.p. brown 35 20
191 50 n.p. on 3 n.p. green 65 50
192 1 r. on 4 n.p. blue 85 60

27 I.C.Y. Emblem and Prime Minister Harold Wilson

1986. International Co-operation Year.
193 **27** 80 n.p. brown and violet 50 15
194 – 80 n.p. brown and green 50 15
195 – 80 n.p. green and red 50 15
196 – 80 n.p. purple and blue 50 15
197 – 80 n.p. blue and orange 50 15
198 – 80 n.p. purple and green 50 15
199 – 80 n.p. blue and grey 50 15
200 – 80 n.p. purple and brown 50 15
DESIGNS—I.C.Y. emblem and "World Leaders": No. 194, Chancellor Erhard (West Germany); No. 195, Pres. Nasser (Egypt); No. 196, Pres. Johnson (U.S.A.); No. 197, Pope Paul VI; No. 198, Pres. De Gaulle (France); No. 199, Shaikh Isa bin Sulman al-Khalifa (Bahrain); No. 200, King Faisal (Saudi Arabia).

28 Sir Winston Churchill, Pen and Ink, and Books

1966. Churchill Commem (2nd issue). Multicoloured, printed on gold foil, backed with paper.
201 2 r. Type **28** 50 25
202 3 r. Churchill and Houses of Parliament, pen and ink 70 45
203 4 r. Churchill and St. Paul's Cathedral 1·00 60
204 5 r. Churchill and "Big Ben" (clock tower, Houses of Parliament) and Tower Bridge 1·50 70

29 Banded Butterfly-fish

1966. Fishes. Multicoloured.
206 1 n.p. Type **29** 10 10
207 2 n.p. Striped surgeon-fish 10 10
208 3 n.p. Young imperial angel-fish 10 10
209 4 n.p. False mouthbreeder 10 10
210 5 n.p. Undulate trigger-fish 10 10
211 15 n.p. Moonfish 25 10
212 20 n.p. Clown butterfly-fish 35 10
213 30 n.p. Moorish goddess 40 10
214 40 n.p. Zebra-striped angel-fish 50 10
215 50 n.p. False mouthbreeder 55 10
216 75 n.p. Undulate trigger-fish 70 20
217 1 r. Zebra-striped angel-fish 80 25
218 2 r. Moorish goddess 1·75 45
219 3 r. Clown butterfly-fish 2·50 80
220 4 r. Moonfish 2·75 95
221 5 r. Young imperial angel-fish 3·25 1·25
222 10 r. Type **29** 6·50 2·25

30 Arms of Munich and "Souvenir Sheet" **34** Pres. Kennedy

33 Greek 6th-cent Ball-player

1966. International Philatelic Federation and International Philatelic Journalists Association Congresses, Munich. Multicoloured.
223 80 n.p. Type **30** 30 15
224 120 n.p. Frauenkirche, Munich 55 25
225 2 r. Statue and Hall of Fame, Munich (81 × 41 mm) 90 40

NEW CURRENCY SURCHARGES. During the latter half of 1966 various issues appeared surcharged in dirhams and riyals. The 1966 definitives with this surcharge are listed below as there is evidence of their postal use. Nos. 102, 107/126, 135, 145, 150/61, 174/84 and 190 also exist with these surcharges.

Earlier in 1966 Nos. 98/100, 171/3, 193/4, 196, 198, 200/5 appeared surcharged in piastres and rials. As Sharjah did not adopt this currency their status is uncertain.

1966. Nos. 206/22 with currency names changed by overprinting in English and Arabic. (a) Optd "Dirham" or "Riyals".
226 **29** 1 d. on 1 n.p. multicoloured 10 10
227 – 2 d. on 2 n.p. multicoloured 10 10
228 – 3 d. on 3 n.p. multicoloured 10 10
229 – 4 d. on 4 n.p. multicoloured 10 10
230 – 5 d. on 5 n.p. multicoloured 10 10
231 – 15 d. on 15 n.p. mult 25 10
232 – 20 d. on 20 n.p. mult 35 10
233 – 30 d. on 30 n.p. mult 40 10
234 – 40 d. on 40 n.p. mult 50 10
235 – 50 d. on 50 n.p. mult 55 20
236 – 75 d. on 75 n.p. mult 75 30
237 – 1 r. on 1 r. multicoloured 85 35
238 – 2 r. on 2 r. multicoloured 1·40 75
239 – 3 r. on 3 r. multicoloured 2·00 1·50
240 – 4 r. on 4 r. multicoloured 2·50 1·75
241 – 5 r. on 5 r. multicoloured 3·25 2·00
242 **29** 10 r. on 10 r. multicoloured 5·50 3·75

(b) Optd "Dh.".
242b – 2 d. on 2 n.p. mult 10 10
242c – 3 d. on 3 n.p. mult 10 10
242f – 15 d. on 15 n.p. mult 25 10
242g – 20 d. on 20 n.p. mult 35 10
242h – 30 d. on 30 n.p. mult 40 10
242i – 40 d. on 40 n.p. mult 50 10
242j – 50 d. on 50 n.p. mult 60 30
242k – 75 d. on 75 n.p. mult 85 50

1966. World Cup Football Championship, England. Printed on coloured metal foil-surfaced paper. Multicoloured.
243 ½ r. Type **33** 85 15
244 ½ r. Tsu-chu "Kick-ball" game, China, circa 175 B.C. 85 15
245 ½ r, 14th-cent ball game 85 15
246 ½ r. Blowing up ball-bladder (17th-cent) 85 15
247 ½ r. Football game, Barnet, England, circa 1750 85 15
248 ½ r. England v. Scotland game, Kennington Oval (London), 1879 85 15
249 ½ r. Victorious England team, Wembley, 1966 (56 × 55½ mm) 85 15

1966. 3rd Death Anniv of Pres. Kennedy and Inauguration of Arlington Memorial.
251 50 d. Type **34** 35 25
252 2 r. Sharjah 50 n.p. Kennedy stamp of 1964 1·50 75
253 2 r. 50 Pres. Kennedy's grave (77 × 40 mm) 1·75 1·00

35 Shaikh Khalid bin Mohammed al Qasimi and Arms

1968. Multiocloured.
255 5 d. Type **35** (postage) 15 15
256 10 d. Flag 15 15
257 15 d. Flag and arms (vert) 20 15
258 20 d. Decorative pattern (vert) 20 15
259 35 d. Type **35** (air) 40 20
260 40 d. As 10 d. 40 15
261 60 d. As 15 d. 55 20
262 75 d. As 20 d. 70 30
363 1 r. Type **35** 85 30
264 2 r. As 10 d. 1·75 75
265 3 r. As 15 d. 2·50 1·25
266 4 r. As 20 d. 3·25 1·75
267 5 r. Type **35** 4·00 1·75
268 10 r. As 10 d. 7·50 4·50

36 Freighter at Wharf

1970. 5th Anniv of Ruler's Accession. "Progress in Sharjah".
285 **36** 5 d. deep violet and violet 10 10
286 A 5 d. deep blue and blue 10 10
287 B 5 d. brown and red 10 10
288 C 5 d. brown and green 10 10
289 D 5 d. brown and light brown 10 10
290 20 d. brown and light brown 10 10
291 **36** 35 d. deep violet and violet 15 15
292 A 35 d. deep blue and blue 15 15
293 B 35 d. brown and red 15 15
294 C 35 d. brown and green 15 15
295 D 35 d. brown and light brown 15 15
296 **36** 40 d. deep violet and violet 20 20
297 A 40 d. deep blue and blue 20 20
298 B 40 d. brown and red 20 20
299 C 40 d. brown and green 20 20
300 D 40 d. brown and light brown 20 20
301 **36** 60 d. deep violet and violet 30 30
302 A 60 d. deep blue and blue 30 30
303 B 60 d. brown and red 30 30
304 C 60 d. brown and green 30 30
305 D 60 d. brown and light brown 30 30
DESIGNS: A, Airport; B, Oil derrick; C, Modern building; D, Shaikh Khalid.

37 Turbines

1971. 6th Anniv of Ruler's Accession. "Progress in Sharjah".
306 **37** 5 d. blue, violet and green (postage)
307 A 5 d. mauve, brown and violet
308 B 5 d. multicoloured
309 C 5 d. multicoloured
310 B 35 d. multicoloured (air)
311 **37** 75 d. blue, violet and green
312 A 75 d. mauve, brown and violet
313 B 75 d. multicoloured
314 C 75 d. multicoloured
315 **37** 1 r. blue, violet and green
316 A 1 r. mauve, brown and violet
317 B 1 r. multicoloured
318 C 1 r. multicoloured
319 A 2 r. mauve, brown and violet
320 **37** 3 r. blue, violet and green
321 A 3 r. mauve, brown and violet
322 B 3 r. multicoloured
323 C 3 r. multicoloured
324 5 r. multicoloured
DESIGNS—HORIZ: A, Mosque. VERT: B, Clock fountain; C, Shaikh Khalid.

38 Shaikh Rashid of Dubai and Shaikh Khalid

1971. Air. Proclamation of United Arab Emirates. Multicoloured.
325 25 d. Type **38**
326 35 d. Shaikh Ahmed of Umm al Qiwain and Shaikh Khalid
327 65 d. United Nations and Arab League emblems
328 75 d. Shaikh Rashid of Ajman and Shaikh Khalid
329 1 r. Shaikh Mohamed of Fujeira and Shaikh Khalid
330 2 r. Shaikh Zaid of Abu Dhabi and Shaikh Khalid

197211. Various stamps surcharged. (a) 1968 Winter Olympics issue (Appendix).
331 – 35 d. on 5 d. multicoloured

(b) Nos. 255 and 262.
332 **35** 35 on 5 d. multicoloured (postage)
334 – 60 on 75 d. multicoloured

(c) 5th Anniv of Ruler's Accession (Nos. 296/300).
335 **36** 5 on 40 d. deep violet and violet
336 A 5 on 40 d. deep blue and blue
337 B 5 on 40 d. brown and red
338 C 5 on 40 d. brown and green
339 D 5 on 40 d. brown and light brown

(d) Air. Proclamation of United Arab Emirates (Nos. 325 and 328/30).

340	**38**	65 d. on 25 d. multicoloured		
341	–	65 d. on 75 d. multicoloured		
342	–	65 d. on 1 r. multicoloured		
343	–	65 d. on 2 r. multicoloured		

OFFICIAL STAMPS

1966. Optd **ON STATE SERVICE** in English and Arabic. Multicoloured.

O101	**1**	8 n.p.	15	15
O102		10 n.p.	15	15
O103		16 n.p.	30	15
O104		20 n.p.	35	15
O105		30 n.p.	50	20
O106		40 n.p.	75	30
O107		50 n.p.	1·25	60
O108		75 n.p.	2·00	1·40
O109		100 n.p.	3·25	1·75

1968. As Nos. 258 and 261 but colours changed and inscr "OFFICIAL".

O269	20 d. multicoloured		
O270	60 d. multicoloured		

For later issues see **UNITED ARAB EMIRATES**.

APPENDIX

The following stamps have either been issued in excess of postal needs or have not been available to the public in reasonable quantities at face value. Such stamps may later be given full listing if there is evidence of regular postal use.

1967.

Post Day. Japanese Paintings. 1 r. × 3.

22nd Anniv of United Nations. 10, 30, 60 d.

Olympics Preparation, Mexico 1968. Postage 1, 2, 3, 10 d; Air 30, 60 d., 2 r.

Flowers and Butterflies. Postage 1, 2, 3, 4, 5, 10, 20 d.; Air 30, 60 d., 1, 2 r.

Famous Paintings. Postage 1, 2, 3, 4, 5, 30, 40, 60, 75 d.; Air 1, 2, 3, 4, 5 r.

1968.

Winter Olympic Games, Grenoble. Postage 1, 2, 3, 4, 5 d.; Air 1, 2, 3 r.

12th World Jamboree. Postage 1, 2, 3, 4, 5, 10 d.; Air 30, 50, 60 d., 1 r. 50.

Grenoble Olympic Medal Winners. Optd on Winter Olympics, Grenoble issue. Postage 1, 2, 3, 4, 5 d.; Air 1, 2, 3 r.

Mothers' Day. Paintings. Postage 10, 20, 30, 40 d.; Air 1, 2, 3, 4 r.

American Paintings. Postage 20, 30, 40, 50, 60 d.; Air 1, 4, 5 r.

Egyptian Art. 15, 25, 35, 45, 55, 65, 75, 95 d.

Martyrs of Liberty. Air 35 d. × 4, 60 d. × 4, 1 r. × 4.

Olympic Games Mexico. 10, 20, 30 d., 2 r., 2 r. 40, 5 r.

Previous Olympic Games. Air 25, 50, 75 d., 1 r. 50, 3, 4 r.

Sportsmen and Women. Postage 20, 30, 40, 60 d., 1 r. 50, 2 r. 50; Air 25, 50 d., 1, 2 r., 3 r. 25, 4, 4 r.

Robert Kennedy Memorial. Optd on American Paintings issue. Air 4 r.

Olympic Medal Winners, Mexico. 35, 50, 60 d., 1, 2, 4 r.

1969.

Famous Men and Women. Postage 10, 20, 25, 35, 50, 60 d.; Air 1, 2, 3, 4, 5, 6 r.

"Apollo 8" Moon Mission. Postage 5 d. × 6; Air 10, 15, 20 d., 2, 3, 4 r.

"Apollo 11" Moon Mission (1st series). Postage 5 d. × 8; Air 75 d. × 8, 1 r. × 8.

Post Day. Famous Ships. Postage 5 d. × 8; Air 90 d. × 8.

"Apollo 12" Moon Mission. Optd on Famous Ships issue. 5 d. × 8.

1970.

U.N.I.C.E.F. Paintings of Children. Postage 5 d. × 9; Air 20, 25, 35, 40, 50, 60, 75 d., 1, 3 r.

Animals. Postage 3 d. × 14, 10, 10, 15, 15 d.; Air 20, 20, 35, 35 d., 1, 1, 2, 2 r.

"Expo 70" World Fair, Osaka, Japan (1st series). Japanese Paintings. Postage 3 d. × 4; Air 1 r. × 4.

"Expo 70" World Fair, Osaka, Japan (2nd series). Pavilions. Postage 2, 2, 3, 3 d.; Air 40 d. × 4.

Paintings of Napoleon. Postage 3 d. × 5; Air 20, 30, 40, 60 d., 2 r.

De Gaulle Commemoration. Postage 3 d. × 5; Air 20, 30, 40, 60 d., 2 r.

"Mercury" and "Vostok" Moon Missions. Postage 1, 2, 3, 4, 5 d.; Air 25, 40, 85 d., 1, 2 r.

"Gemini" Space Programme. Postage 1, 2, 3, 4, 5 d.; Air 25, 40, 85 d., 1, 2 r.

"Apollo", "Voskhod" and "Soyuz" Projects. Postage 1, 2, 3, 4, 5 d.; Air 25, 40, 85 d., 1, 2 r.

Events of 1970. Postage 1 d. × 5, 5 d.; Air 75 d., 1, 2, 3 r.

200th Birth Anniv of Beethoven. Postage 3 d. × 5; Air 35, 40, 60 d., 1, 2 r.

Mozart. Postage 3 d. × 5; Air 35, 40, 60 d., 1, 2 r.

The Life of Christ (1st series). Postage 1, 2, 3, 4, 5 d.; Air 25, 40, 60 d., 1, 2 r.

1971.

"Apollo 14" Moon Mission. Optd on 1969 "Apollo 11" issue. Postage 5 d. × 4; Air 75 d. × 4.

Post Day 1970. Cars. Postage 1, 2, 3, 4, 5 d.; Air 25, 50, 60 d., 2, 3 r.

Post Day (1st series). American Cars. Postage 1, 2, 3, 4, 5 d.; Air 35, 50 d., 1, 2, 3 r.

Post Day (2nd series). Trains. Postage 1, 2, 3, 4, 5 d.; Air 25, 50, 60 d., 1, 2 r.

Pres. Nasser Commemoration. Postage 5 d. × 5; Air 20, 35, 40, 60 d., 2 r.

Safe return of "Apollo 13". Optd on 1969 "Apollo 8" issue. Air 10, 15, 20 d., 2, 3, 4 r.

De Gaulle Memorial. Postage 3, 4, 5, 6, 7 d.; Air 40, 60, 75 d., 1, 2 r.

Olympics Preparation, Munich 1972. Postage 2, 3, 4, 5, 6 d.; Air. 35, 40, 60 d., 1, 2 r.

Miracles of Christ. Postage 1, 2, 3, 4, 5 d.; Air 25, 40, 60 d., 1, 2 r.

1972.

Sport. Postage 2, 3, 4, 5, 6 d.; Air 35, 40, 60 d., 1, 2 r.

The Life of Christ (2nd series). Postage 1, 2, 3, 4, 5 d.; Air 25, 40, 60 d., 1, 2 r.

Winter Olympics Preparation, Sapporo. Postage 2, 3, 4, 5, 6 d.; Air 35, 40, 60 d., 1, 2 r.

Safe Return of "Apollo 14". Optd on 1969 "Apollo 11" issue. Postage 5 d. × 4; Air 1 r. × 4.

Previous World Cup Winners. Postage 5, 10, 15, 20, 25 d.; Air 35, 75 d., 1, 2, 3 r.

Sapporo Olympic Medal Winners. Paintings. Postage 5, 10, 15, 20, 25 d.; Air 35, 75 d., 1, 2, 3 r.

Famous People, Churchill, De Gaulle and John Kennedy. Postage 5 d. × 4, 10 d. × 4, 35 d. × 4; Air 75 d. × 4, 1 r. × 4, 3 r. × 4.

Olympic Games, Munich. Postage 5, 10, 15, 20, 25 d.; Air 35, 75 d., 1, 2, 3 r.

Cats. Postage 20, 25 d.; Air 75 d., 1, 2 r.

Birds (1st series). Postage 20, 25, 75 d., Air 1, 2 r.

"Apollo 11" Moon Mission (2nd series). Postage 1, 1 r. Air 1 r. × 3.

"Apollo 16" Moon Mission. Postage 1, 1 r.; Air 1 r. × 3.

Dogs. Postage 20, 25 d.; Air 75 d., 1, 2 r.

"Apollo 17" Moon Mission. Postage 1, 1 r.; Air 1 r. × 3.

Munich Olympic Medal Winners. Air 5 r. × 20.

Horses. Postage 20, 25 d.; Air 75 d., 1, 2 r.

"Apollo 17" Astronauts. Postage 1, 1 r.; Air 1 r. × 3.

Butterflies. Postage 20, 25 d.; Air 75 d., 1, 2 r.

"Luna 9" Soviet Space Programme. Postage 1, 1 r.; Air 1 r. × 3.

Monkeys. Postage 20, 25 d.; Air 75 d., 1, 2 r.

Birds (2nd series). Air 25, 25, 35, 35, 50, 50, 65, 65 d., 1 r. × 6, 3, 3 r.

Fish. Air 25, 35, 50, 65 d., 1 r. × 5, 3 r.

Insects. Air 25, 35, 50, 65 d., 1, 3 r.

Flowers. Postage 25, 35, 50, 65 d., 1, 3 r.; Air 1 r. × 4.

Fruit. Air 1 r. × 4.

Children. Air 1 r. × 4.

Eastern Antiquities. Air 25, 35, 40, 65, 75 d., 1 r. × 4, 3 r.

Planetary Exploration. Postage 1 r. × 3; Air 1, 1 r.

13th World Jamboree. Postage 2 d. × 3, 3 d. × 3, 4 d. × 3, 5 d. × 3, 6 d. × 3; Air 35 d. × 3, 75 d. × 3, 1 r. × 3, 2 r. × 3, 3 r. × 3.

A number of issues on gold or silver foil also exist, but it is understood that these were mainly for presentation purposes, although valid for postage.

In common with the other states of the United Arab Emirates the Sharjah stamp contract was terminated on 1 August 1972, and further new issues released after that date were unauthorised.

SIBERIA — Pt. 10

Various Anti-Bolshevist governments existed in this area, culminating in Kolchak's assumption of power as "Supreme Ruler". The Kolchak Government fell in January 1920, provincial issues followed until the area was incorporated into the Soviet Union in 1922.

100 kopeks = 1 rouble

1919. Admiral Kolchak Govt. Arms types of Russia surch in figures, or in figures and words (rouble values). Imperf or perf.

5	**22**	35 on 2 k. green	25	1·25
6		50 on 3 k. red	25	1·40
3		70 on 1 k. orange	30	3·25
8	**23**	1 r. on 4 k. red	40	1·40
9	**22**	3 r. on 7 k. blue	70	3·50
10	**10**	5 r. on 14 k. red and blue	1·25	8·00

1920. Transbaikal Province. Ataman Semyonov regime. Arms types of Russia surch thus: **p. 1 p.**. Perf.

11	**23**	1 r. on 4 k. red	17·00	26·00
12	**14**	2 r. 50 on 20 k. red & blue	17·00	24·00
13	**22**	5 r. on 5 k. red	10·00	17·00
14	**10**	10 r. on 70 k. orange & brn	17·00	27·00

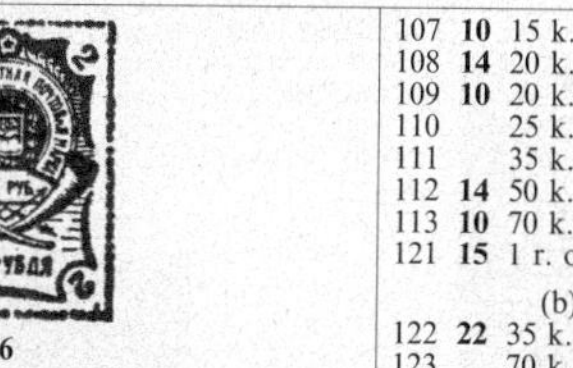

6

1920. Amur Province. Imperf.

15	**6**	2 r. red	1·60	4·50
16		3 r. green	1·60	4·50
17		5 r. blue	1·60	4·50
18		15 r. brown	1·60	4·50
19		30 r. mauve	1·60	4·50

FAR EASTERN REPUBLIC

1920. Vladivostok issue. Optd **D B P** in fancy letters or surch also. Imperf or perf (a) On Arms types of Russia.

32	**22**	1 k. orange	3·75	6·50
33		2 k. green	1·90	2·50
21		3 k. red	2·40	3·25
39	**10**	3 k. on 35 k. green & pur	4·00	5·00
22	**23**	4 k. red	2·00	4·75
40	**10**	4 k. on 70 k. orange & brn	2·50	3·50
41		7 k. on 15 k. blue & purple	1·25	1·75
23	**23**	10 k. blue	38·00	45·00
44	**11**	10 k. on 3 r. 50 green and brown	5·00	7·00
24	**10**	14 k. red and blue	6·50	15·00
25		15 k. blue and purple	4·25	6·00
25	**14**	20 k. red and blue	32·00	45·00
27	**10**	20 k. on 14 k. red & blue	3·00	4·75
28		25 k. mauve and green	4·00	8·00
29		35 k. green and purple	16·00	26·00
30	**14**	50 k. green and purple	3·25	6·50
35	**15**	1 r. orange and brown	8·00	17·00

(b) On Nos. 5 and 3 of Siberia.

37	**22**	35 k. on 2 k. green	2·75	4·00
38		70 k. on 1 k. orange	2·25	4·00

(c) On Postal Savings Bank stamps of Russia.

45	1 k. on 5 k. green on buff	5·00	7·00
46	2 k. on 10 k. brn on buff	7·00	10·00

10

11

13

1921. Chita issue. Imperf.

47	**10**	1 k. orange	50	1·10
48		3 k. red	50	60
49	**11**	4 k. brown and red	20	50
50	**10**	5 k. brown	40	70
51b		7 k. blue	40	1·00
52	**11**	10 k. red and blue	30	70
53	**10**	15 k. red	40	1·00
54	**11**	20 k. red and blue	40	1·25
55		30 k. red and green	45	1·25
56		50 k. red and black	1·00	2·00

1922. Vladivostok issue. 5th Anniv of Russian October Revolution. Optd **1917 7-XI 1922**. Imperf.

57	**13**	2 k. green	8·00	10·00
58		4 k. red	8·00	10·00
59		5 k. brown	9·00	16·00
60		10 k. blue	9·00	16·00

PRIAMUR AND MARITIME PROVINCES

Anti-Bolshevist Government.

1921. Vladivostok issue. Imperf.

61	**13**	2 k. green	40	65
62		4 k. red	40	65
63		5 k. purple	50	95
64		10 k. blue	95	1·60

(**15**)

(**16** Trans. "Priamur Territory")

Д. В.
коп. 1 коп.
ЗОЛОТОМ

(**18**)

1922. Anniv of Priamur Provisional Govt. Optd with T **15**.

89	**13**	2 k. green	13·00	17·00
90		4 k. red	13·00	17·00
91		5 k. purple	13·00	17·00
92		10 k. blue	13·00	17·00

1922. Optd or surch as T **16**.

93	**13**	1 k. on 2 k. green	1·40	3·50
94		2 k. green	1·40	3·50
95		3 k. on 4 k. red	1·40	3·50
96		4 k. red	1·40	3·50
97		5 k. purple	1·40	3·50
98		10 k. blue	1·40	3·50

1922. Optd as T **16**. Imperf or perf. (a) On Arms types of Russia.

114	**22**	1 k. orange	1·75	5·00
115		2 k. green	2·50	7·50
116		3 k. red	4·25	13·00
102	**23**	4 k. red	1·25	3·50
118	**22**	5 k. red	7·00	20·00
104		7 k. blue	13·00	28·00
105	**23**	10 k. blue	13·00	28·00
106	**10**	14 k. red and blue	30·00	60·00
107	**10**	15 k. blue and purple	2·50	6·00
108	**14**	20 k. red and blue	4·00	10·00
109	**10**	20 k. on 14 k. red & blue	38·00	80·00
110		25 k. mauve and green	11·00	24·00
111		35 k. green and purple	1·75	5·00
112	**14**	50 k. green and purple	2·25	6·00
113	**10**	70 k. orange and brown	7·00	18·00
121	**15**	1 r. orange and brown	6·00	17·00

(b) On Nos. 5 and 3 of Siberia.

122	**22**	35 k. on 2 k. green	22·00	38·00
123		70 k. on 1 k. orange	30·00	55·00

1922. Nos. 37 and 38 optd **II3K** and three bars. Imperf and perf.

125	**22**	35 k. on 2 k. green	2·00	4·00
126		70 k. on 1 k. orange	3·25	7·00

SOVIET UNION ISSUE FOR THE FAR EAST

1923. Stamps of Russia surch as T **18**. Imperf or perf.

131	**79**	1 k. on 100 r. red	35	60
128		2 k. on 70 r. purple	25	35
129	**78**	5 k. on 10 r. blue	25	50
130	**79**	10 k. on 50 r. brown	35	50

SICILY — Pt. 8

An island to the south of Italy, which, with Naples, formed the Kingdom of the Two Sicilies, until incorporated in the Kingdom of Italy.

100 grano = 1 ducato

1 King "Bomba"

1859. Imperf.

1	**1**	½ g. yellow	£200	£500
2b		1 g. olive	75·00	75·00
3		2 g. blue	50·00	48·00
4		5 g. red	£375	£250
5		10 g. blue	£350	£170
6		20 g. grey	£375	£300
7		50 g. brown	£350	£3000

SLOVAKIA — Pt. 5

Formerly part of Hungary, Slovakia joined with Bohemia and Moravia in 1918 to form Czechoslovakia. From 1939 to 1945 they were separate states.

In 1993 the federation of Czechoslovakia was dissolved and Slovakia became an independent republic.

100 haleru = 1 koruna

A. REPUBLIC OF SLOVAKIA

1939. Stamps of Czechoslovakia optd **Slovensky stat 1939**.

2	**34**	5 h. blue	55	70
3		10 h. brown	10	15
4		20 h. red	10	10
5		25 h. green	1·00	1·25
6		30 h. purple	10	10
7	**59**	40 h. blue	10	15
8	**60a**	50 h. green	10	10
9	**66**	50 h. green	10	10
10	**60a**	60 h. violet	10	10
11		60 h. blue	6·50	7·50
12	**61**	1 k. purple	10	10
13	–	1 k. 20 purple (No. 354)	20	30
14	**64**	1 k. 50 red	20	30
15	–	1 k. 60 green (No. 355a)	1·75	2·00
16	–	2 k. green (No. 356)	1·75	2·00
17	–	2 k. 50 blue (No. 357)	35	45
18	–	3 k. brown (No. 358)	40	60
19	–	3 k. 50 violet (No. 359)	18·00	20·00
20	**65**	4 k. violet	8·00	10·00
21	–	5 k. green (No. 361)	10·00	12·50
22	–	10 k. blue (No. 362)	75·00	85·00

4 Father Hlinka

7 Krivan

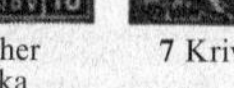

8 Chamois

9 Mgr. Tiso

10 Weaving

11 Sawyer

12 Presidential Palace, Bratislava

1939. As T **4**, but inscr "CESKO-SLOVENSKO SLOVENSKA POSTA", optd **SLOVENSKY STAT**.
23 **4** 50 h. green . . . . 1·25 50
24 1 k. red . . . . 1·00 50

1939. Perf or imperf (20, 30 h.), perf (others).
25 **4** 5 h. blue 40 40
26 10 h. green 65 55
27a 20 h. red 50 65
28 30 h. violet 65 55
29 50 h. green 65 55
33 1 k. red 65 45
34a 2 k. 50 blue 50 65
35a 3 k. sepia . . . . 1·00 75
See also No. 81.

1939.
40 – 5 h. green 15 15
41 **7** 10 h. brown 10 15
42 – 20 h. grey 10 10
43 **8** 25 h. brown 40 15
44 – 30 h. brown 20 15
45 **9** 50 h. green 40 25
46 70 h. brown 25 15
47 **10** 2 k. green . . . . 4·50 40
48 **11** 4 k. brown . . . . 1·00 60
49 – 5 k. red 90 25
50 **12** 10 k. blue 75 55
DESIGNS—As Type **7**: 5 h., Zelene Pleso; 20 h. Kvety Satier (Edelweiss); 30 h. Javorina. As Type **11**: 5 k. Woman filling ewer at spring.
For 10 to 50 h. values in larger size, see Nos. 125/9.

13 Rev. J. Murgas and Wireless Masts

1939. 10th Death Anniv of Rev. J. Murgas.
53 **13** 60 h. violet 20 15
52 1 k. 20 grey 50 15

1939. Child Welfare. As No. 45 but larger (24 × 30 mm) and inscr "+2.50 DETOM".
54 2 k. 50 + 2 k. 50 blue . . . . 2·25 2·50

14 Heinkel He 111C over Lake Csorba

15 Heinkel He 116A over Tatra Mountains

16 Eagle and Aero A-204

1939. Air.
55 **14** 30 h. violet 25 25
56 50 h. green 25 25
57 1 k. red 30 25
58 **15** 2 k. green 45 40
59 3 k. brown 90 80
60 4 k. blue . . . . 1·50 1·50
62 **16** 5 k. purple . . . . 1·00 1·40
63 10 k. grey . . . . 1·25 1·50
64 20 k. green . . . . 1·50 2·00

17 Stiavnica Castle

18 S. M. Daxner and Bishop Moyses

1941.
65 **17** 1 k. 20 purple 20 15
66 – 1 k. 50 red (Lietava) 20 15
67 – 1 k. 60 blue (Spissky Hrad) . . . 25 10
68 – 2 k. green (Bojnice) 20 10

1941. 80th Anniv of Presentation of Slovak Memorandum to Emperor Francis Joseph.
69 **18** 50 h. green . . . . 1·40 1·50
70 1 k. blue . . . . 6·00 6·00
71 2 k. black . . . . 6·00 6·00

19 Wounded Soldier and Red Cross Orderly

1941. Red Cross Fund.
72 **19** 50 h. + 50 h. green 40 45
73 1 k. + 1 k. purple 50 50
74 2 k. + 1 k. blue . . . . . 1·50 1·25

20 Mother and Child

21 Soldier with Hlinka Youth Member

1941. Child Welfare Fund.
75 **20** 50 h. + 50 h. green 75 70
76 1 k. + 1 k. brown 75 70
77 2 k. + 1 k. violet 75 70

1942. Hlinka Youth Fund.
78 **21** 70 h. + 1 k. brown 30 30
79 1 k. 30 + 1 k. blue 40 40
80 2 k. + 1 k. red . . . . . . 1·00 1·00

1942. Father Hlinka. As T **4** but inscr "SLOVENSKO" (without "POSTA").
81 1 k. 30 violet 40 15

22 Boy Stamp Collector

23 Dove and St. Stephen's

1942. Philatelic Exhibition, Bratislava.
82 – 30 h. green 90 90
83 **22** 70 h. red 90 90
84 – 80 h. violet 90 90
85 – 1 k. 30 brown 90 90
DESIGNS: 30 h., 1 k. 30, Posthorn, round various arms, above Bratislava; 80 h. Postmaster-General examining stamps.

1942. European Postal Congress.
86 **23** 70 h. green 80 75
87 1 k. 30 green 80 75
88 2 k. blue . . . . 1·75 2·00

24 Inaugural Ceremony

25 L. Stur

1942. 15th Anniv of Foundation of National Literacy Society.
89 **24** 70 h. black 15 15
90 1 k. red 15 15
91 1 k. 30 blue 15 15
92 2 k. brown 20 15
93 3 k. green 35 35
94 4 k. violet 35 35

1943.
95 **25** 80 h. green 15 10
96 – 1 k. red 20 20
97 – 1 k. 30 blue 15 10
PORTRAITS: 1 k. M. Razus; 1 k. 30, Father Hlinka.

27 National Costumes

30 Railway Tunnel

29 Infantry

1943. Winter Relief Fund.
98 **27** 50 h. + 50 h. green 30 20
99 – 70 h. + 1 k. red 30 20
100 – 80 h. + 2 k. blue 30 25
DESIGNS: 70 h. Mother and child; 80 h. Mother and two children.

1943. Fighting Forces.
106 **29** 70 h. + 2 k. red 50 70
107 – 1 k. 30 + 2 k. blue 75 85
108 – 2 k. + 2 k. green 65 65
DESIGNS—HORIZ: 2 k. Artillery. VERT: 1 k. 30, Air Force.

1943. Opening of the Strazke–Presov Railway..
109 – 70 h. purple . . . . 80 1·00
110 – 80 h. blue . . . . 1·00 1·25
111 **30** 1 k. 30 black . . . . 1·00 1·40
112 – 2 k. brown . . . . 1·25 2·00
DESIGNS—HORIZ: 70 h. Presov Church; 2 k. Railway viaduct. VERT: 80 h. Railway locomotive.

32 "The Slovak Language is our Life"

34 Prince Pribina Okolo

33 National Museum

35 Footballer

1943. Culture Fund.
113 **32** 30 h. + 1 k. brown 40 30
114 **33** 70 h. + 1 k. green 50 50
115 – 80 h. + 2 k. blue 40 30
116 – 1 k. 30 + 2 k. brown 40 30
DESIGNS—HORIZ: 80 h. Matica Slovenska College. VERT: 1 k. 30, Agricultural student.

1944. 5th Anniv of Declaration of Independence.
117 **34** 50 h. green 10 10
118 – 70 h. mauve 10 10
119 – 80 h. brown 10 10
120 – 1 k. 30 blue 15 10
121 – 2 k. blue 15 15
122 – 3 k. brown 35 25
123 – 5 k. violet 65 50
124 – 10 k. black . . . . 1·75 1·60
DESIGNS: 70 h. Prince Mojmir; 80 h. Prince Ratislav; 1 k. 30, King Svatopluk; 2 k. Prince Kocel; 3 k. Prince Mojmir II; 5 k. Prince Svatopluk II; 10 k. Prince Braslav.

1944. As 1939 issue but larger ($18\frac{1}{2} \times 22\frac{1}{2}$ mm).
125 **7** 10 h. red 15 25
126 – 20 h. blue 15 25
127 **8** 25 h. purple 15 25
128 – 30 h. purple 15 25
129 – 50 h. green 15 25
DESIGN: 50 h. Zelene Pleso (as No. 40).

1944. Sports.
130 **35** 70 h. + 70 h. green 55 65
131 – 1 k. + 1 k. violet 70 75
132 – 1 k. 30 + 1 k. 30 green . . . 70 75
133 – 2 k. + 2 k. brown . . . . . 75 1·10
DESIGNS—VERT: 1 k. Skiing; 1 k. 30, Diving. HORIZ: 2 k. Running.

36 Symbolic of "Protection"

1944. Protection Series.
134 **36** 70 h. + 4 k. blue . . . . . 80 1·10
135 1 k. 30 + 4 k. brown . . . 80 1·10
136 2 k. green 30 20
137 3 k. 80 purple 30 40

37 Children Playing

38 Mgr. Tiso

1944. Child Welfare.
138 **37** 2 k. + 4 k. blue . . . . . 3·00 3·00

1945.
139 **38** 1 k. orange 75 50
140 1 k. 50 brown 20 15
141 2 k. green 25 15
142 4 k. red 75 50
143 5 k. blue 75 50
144 10 k. purple 50 25

B. SLOVAK REPUBLIC

39 State Arms

40 Ruzomberok

1993.
145 **39** 3 k. multicoloured 20 20
146 8 k. mult (26 × 40 mm) . . 85 85

1993.
146a – 2 k. pink, black and blue . 10 10
146b – 3 k. black, blue and red . 15 10
146c – 4 k. black, green and blue 15 10
147 **40** 5 k. blue and red 25 15
147a – 6 k. blue, red and yellow . 25 15
147b – 8 k. black, blue and red . 35 20
148 – 10 k. lilac and orange . . 55 30
150 – 30 k. black, blue and red . 1·50 75
151 – 50 k. black, orange and blue 2·75 12·40
DESIGNS—VERT: 2 k. Nitra; 4 k. Nova Bana; 6 k. Arms of Senica; 10 k. Kosice; 50 k. Bratislava. HORIZ: 3 k. Banska Bystrica; 8 k. Trencin; 30 k. Suden Castle.

41 Pres. Michal Kovac

42 St. John and Charles Bridge, Prague

1993.
156 **41** 2 k. black 10 10
157 3 k. brown and mauve . . 15 10

1993. 600th Death Anniv of St. John of Nepomuk (patron saint of Bohemia).
158 **42** 8 k. multicoloured 50 25

43 Pedunculate Oak

44 Jan Levoslav Bella (composer)

1993. Trees. Multicoloured.
159 3 k. Type **43** 15 10
160 4 k. Hornbeam 20 10
161 10 k. Scots pine 55 30

1993. Anniversaries.
162 **44** 5 k. cream, brown & blue . 25 15
163 – 8 k. brown, sepia and red . 45 25
164 – 20 k. buff, blue & orange 1·00 50
DESIGNS: 5 k. Type **44** (150th birth anniv); 8 k. Alexander Dubcek (statesman) (1st death anniv); 20 k. Jan Kollar (poet and scholar) (birth bicent).

45 "Woman with Jug" (Marian Cunderlik)

1993. Europa. Contemporary Art.
165 **45** 14 k. multicoloured . . . . 1·00 1·00

46 Sun

47 Arms of Dubnica nad Vahom

1993. Anniversaries. Multicoloured.
166 2 k. Type **46** (150th anniv of Slovakian written language) 10 10
167 8 k. Sts. Cyril and Methodius (1130th anniv of arrival in Moravia) 45 25

1993.
168 **47** 1 k. silver, black and blue . 10 10

48 "The Big Pets" (Lane Smith)

1993. 14th Biennial Exhibition of Book Illustrations for Children, Bratislava.
169 **48** 5 k. multicoloured 25 15

49 Canal Lock, Gabcikovo

1993. Rhine–Main–Danube Canal.
170 **49** 10 k. multicoloured 65 35

50 Child's Face in Blood-drop

51 "Madonna and Child" (Jozef Klemens)

1993. Red Cross.
171 **50** 3 k. + 1 k. red and blue . 20 10

1993. Christmas.
172 **51** 2 k. multicoloured 10 10

53 "The Labourer's Spring" (Jozef Kostka)

1993. Art (1st series).
174 **53** 9 k. multicoloured 45 45
See also Nos. 198/9, 227/8 and 246/8.

54 Ski Jumping

55 Family

1994. Winter Olympic Games, Lillehammer, Norway.
175 **54** 2 k. black, mauve and blue 10 10

1994. International Year of the Family.
176 **55** 3 k. multicoloured 15 10

56 Antoine de Saint-Exupery (writer and pilot) (50th death)

57 Jozef Murgas (radio-telegraphy pioneer)

1994. Anniversaries.
177 **56** 8 k. red and blue 45 25
178 – 9 k. multicoloured 45 25
DESIGNS: 8 k. Janos Andras Segner (mathematician and physicist) (290th birth).

1994. Europa. Inventions.
179 **57** 28 k. multicoloured . . . 1·40 70

58 Cigarettes

59 Football Pitch as Tie

1994. World No Smoking Day.
180 **58** 3 k. multicoloured 15 10

1994. World Cup Football Championship, U.S.A.
181 **59** 2 k. multicoloured 10 10

60 Ancient Greek Runner passing Baton to Modern Athlete

1994. Centenary of International Olympic Committee.
182 **60** 3 k. multicoloured 15 10

61 Golden Eagle

63 Boat with Stamp for Sail

62 Prince Svatopluk

1994. Birds. Multicoloured.
183 4 k. Type **61** 20 10
184 5 k. Peregrine falcon 25 15
185 7 k. Eagle owl 30 15

1994. 1100th Death Anniv of Prince Svatopluk of Moravia.
186 **62** 12 k. brown, buff and black 50 50

1994. 120th Anniv of Universal Postal Union.
187 **63** 8 k. multicoloured 35 20

64 Generals Rudolf Viest and Jan Golian

1994. 50th Anniv of Slovak Uprising.
188 **64** 6 k. blue, pink and yellow 25 15
189 – 8 k. multicoloured 35 20
DESIGNS: 8 k. French volunteers and their Memorial.

66 Medal (O. Spaniel) and Faculty Emblems

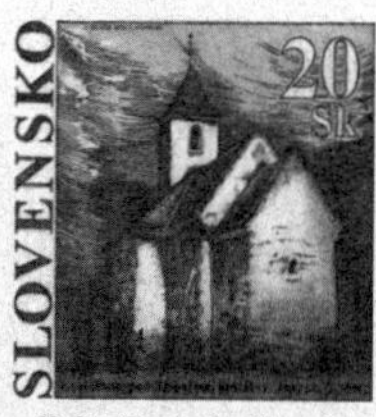

68 St. George's Church, Kostolany pod Tribecom

67 Tajar (winner of first race)

1994. 75th Anniv of Comenius University, Bratislava.
191 **66** 12 k. gold, black and red . 50 25

1994. 180th Anniv of Mojmirovce Horse Race.
192 **67** 2 k. blue and yellow 10 10

1994.
193 **68** 20 k. multicoloured 85 45

69 "Nativity" (early 19th-century glass painting)

1994. Christmas.
194 **69** 2 k. multicoloured 10 10

70 Chattam Sofer, Rabbi of Bratislava

1994. Anniversaries. Multicoloured.
195 5 k. Type **70** (165th death) . . 20 10
196 6 k. Wolfgang Kempelen (conducted study into human speech) (190th death) 25 15
197 10 k. Stefan Banic (inventor of parachute) (125th birth (1995)) 40 20

1994. Art (2nd series). As T **53**. Multicoloured.
198 7 k. "Girls" (Janko Alexy) (horiz) 30 30
199 14 k. "Bulls" (Vincent Hloznik) 60 60

71 Container Ship

1994. Ships. Multicoloured.
200 5 k. Type **71** 20 10
201 8 k. "Ryn" (cargo vessel) . . . 35 20
202 10 k. Passenger liner 40 20

72 Samuel Jurkovic (founder)

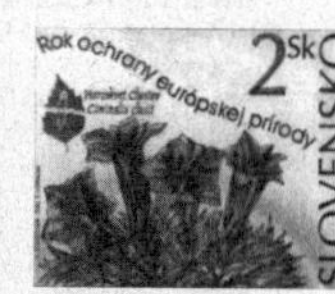

73 "Ciminalis clusii"

1995. 150th Anniv of Landlords' Association.
203 **72** 9 k. multicoloured 40 20

1995. European Nature Protection Year. Flowers. Multicoloured.
204 2 k. Type **73** 10 10
205 3 k. "Pulsatilla slavica" 15 10
206 8 k. "Onosma tornense" . . . 35 20

74 Theatre Masks

1995. 75th Anniv of Slovak National Theatre..
207 **74** 10 k. pink, black and blue 40 20

75 Ice Hockey Equipment

1995. World Cup Ice Hockey Championship Group B Qualifying Round, Bratislava.
208 **75** 5 k. yellow and blue . . . 20 10

76 Bela Bartok (composer, 50th death)

1995. Anniversaries.
209 **76** 3 k. yellow, blue and black 15 10
210 – 6 k. multicoloured 25 15
DESIGN: 6 k. Jan Bahyl (inventor, 80th death (1996)) and helicopter design.

77 Allegory of Freedom

1995. Europa. Peace and Freedom.
212 **77** 8 k. multicoloured 35 35

78 Concentration Camp Victims

1995. 50th Anniv of Liberation of Concentration Camps.
213 **78** 12 k. multicoloured 50 25

79 Scout

1995.
214 **79** 5 k. multicoloured 20 10

80 Pope John Paul II, Map and Arms

82 Banska Stiavnica

1995. Papal Visit.
215 **80** 3 k. red and pink 15 10

1995. U.N.E.S.C.O. World Heritage Sites. Multicoloured.
217 7 k. Type **82** 30 15
218 10 k. Spis Castle (horiz) . . . 45 25
219 15 k. Vlkolinec (horiz) . . . 65 35

83 Player

84 Sad Clown (Lorenzo Mattotti)

1995. Centenary of Volleyball.

220 **83** 9 k. blue, black and yellow . . . 40 20

1995. 15th Biennial Exhibition of Book Illustrations for Children, Bratislava. Multicoloured.

221 2 k. Type **84** 10 10
222 3 k. Thin and fat men with long noses (Dusan Kallay) . . . 15 10

85 Tree, Arch and Association Emblem

1995. St. Adalbert Association.

223 **85** 4 k. black, green and pink . 15 10

86 Map of Czechoslovakia, Linden Leaves and National Colours

1995. 80th Anniv of Cleveland Agreement.

224 **86** 5 k. yellow, blue and red . 20 10

87 Allegory of Celebration and Peace

1995. 50th Anniv of United Nations Organization.

225 **87** 8 k. multicoloured 35 35

88 Christmas Crib (Peter Palka)

1995. Christmas.

226 **88** 2 k. multicoloured 10 10

1995. Art (3rd series). As T **53**. Multicoloured.

227 8 k. "Hlohovec Nativity" . . 35 35
228 16 k. "Two Women" (Mikulas Galanda) 70 70

89 Jozef Ciger-Hronsky (writer)

90 Alojz Szokol, Athens, 1896

1996. Anniversaries. Multicoloured.

229 3 k. Type **89** (death centenary) 15 10
230 4 k. Jozef Ludovit Holuby (botanist, 160th birth anniv) 15 10

1996. Centenary of Modern Olympic Games.

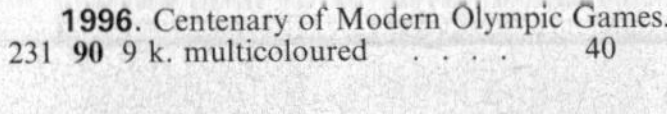

231 **90** 9 k. multicoloured 40 20

91 Dousing Woman in Water

93 Izabela Textorisova (botanist)

1996. Easter.

232 **91** 2 k. multicoloured 10 10

1996. Europa. Famous Women. Multicoloured.

234 8 k. Type **93** 30 30
235 8 k. Botanist holding thistle . 30 30

96 Cyclist

97 Page and Mountains

1996. Round Slovakia Cycle Race.

238 **96** 3 k. black, blue and red . 15 10

1996. 150th Anniv of "Slovenske Pohl'ady" ("Slovak Perspectives" (review))

239 **97** 18 k. black, red and blue . 70 35

98 European Bison

99 Popradske

1996. Mammals. Multicoloured.

240 4 k. Type **98** 15 10
241 4 k. Mouflon ("Ovis musimon") 15 10
242 4 k. Chamois ("Rupicapra rupicapra") 15 10

1996. Mountain Lakes. Multicoloured.

243 4 k. Type **99** 15 10
244 8 k. Skalnate 30 15
245 12 k. Strbsky 50 25

1996. Art (4th series). As T **53**.

246 7 k. multicoloured 30 30
247 10 k. deep blue, lilac and blue 40 40
248 14 k. multicoloured 55 55

DESIGNS: 7 k. "Queen Ntombi Twala" (Andy Warhol); 10 k. "Suppressed Laughter" (Franz Messerschmidt); 14 k. Baroque chair (Endre Nemes).

100 Horse-drawn Tram and Bratislava and Trnava Stations

101 Snow-covered Village, Kysuce

1996. Technological Monuments. Multicoloured.

249 4 k. Type **100** 15 10
250 6 k. Andrej Kvasz and his airplane 25 15

1996. Christmas.

251 **101** 2 k. multicoloured . . . 10 10

102 Unissued Stamp Design and Benka

1996. Stamp Day. 25th Death Anniv of Martin Benka (stamp designer).

252 **102** 3 k. buff and blue . . . 10 10

103 Michal Martikan

1996. Slovak Achievements at Olympic Games, Atlanta.

253 **103** 3 k. brown and stone . . 10 10

104 Bishop Stefan Moyses

105 Biathlon

1997. Birth Anniversaries of National Activists. Multicoloured.

254 3 k. Type **104** (first chairman of Matican Slovenska, bicentenary) 10 10
255 4 k. Svetozar Vajansky (writer, 150th) 15 10

1997. World Biathlon Championship, Osrblie.

256 **105** 6 k. multicoloured 25 15

106 Collecting Dew

1997. Folk Traditions.

257 **106** 3 k. multicoloured 10 10

NEWSPAPER STAMPS

1939. Nos. N364/72 of Czechoslovakia optd **1939 SLOVENSKY STAT.**

N25 2 h. brown 25 25
N26 5 h. blue 25 25
N27 7 h. red 25 25
N28 9 h. green 25 25
N29 10 h. red 25 25
N30 12 h. blue 25 25
N31 20 h. green 65 75
N32 50 h. brown . . . . 1·90 2·00
N33 1 k. green . . . . 7·00 7·50

N 7

N **29** Printer's Type

1939. Imperf.

N40 **N 7** 2 h. brown 20 15
N65 5 h. blue 20 20
N42 7 h. red 20 20
N43 9 h. green 20 20
N66 10 h. red 20 15
N45 12 h. blue 20 20
N67 15 h. purple 20 15
N68 20 h. green 40 45
N69 25 h. blue 30 45
N70 40 h. red 40 45
N71 50 h. brown 65 50
N72 1 k. green 65 50
N73 2 k. green . . . . . . 1·25 90

1943. Imperf.

N101 **N 29** 10 h. green 15 15
N102 15 h. brown 15 15
N103 20 h. blue 15 15
N104 50 h. red 20 20
N105 1 k. green 40 40
N106 2 k. blue 65 65

PERSONAL DELIVERY STAMPS

P 17

1940. Imperf.

P65 **P 17** 50 h. blue . . . . 75 1·25
P66 50 h. red . . . . 75 1·25

POSTAGE DUE STAMPS

D 13

D 24

1939.

D51 **D 13** 5 h. blue 25 40
D52 10 h. blue 25 25
D53 20 h. blue 40 20
D54 30 h. blue . . . . 1·00 65
D55 40 h. blue 50 40
D56 50 h. blue 65 75
D57 60 h. blue 75 75
D58 1 k. red . . . . 1·25 85
D59 2 k. red . . . . 7·50 6·50
D60 5 k. red . . . . 2·00 1·90
D61 10 k. red . . . . 2·50 2·40
D62 20 k. red . . . . 12·00 9·00

1942.

D 89 **D 24** 10 h. brown 10 10
D 90 20 h. brown 10 15
D 91 40 h. brown 10 15
D 92 50 h. brown 70 50
D 93 60 h. brown 15 15
D 94 80 h. brown 20 15
D 95 1 k. red 20 15
D 96 1 k. 10 red 40 45
D 97 1 k. 30 red 30 15
D 98 1 k. 60 red 40 15
D 99 2 k. red 45 15
D100 2 k. 60 red 90 75
D101 3 k. 50 red . . . . . 6·25 6·25
D102 5 k. red . . . . . . 2·25 2·00
D103 10 k. red . . . . . . 2·75 2·50

SLOVENIA Pt. 3

Formerly part of Austria, in 1918 Slovenia was combined with other areas to form Yugoslavia. Separate stamps were issued during the Second World War whilst under Italian and German Occupation.

In 1991 Slovenia seceded and became an independent state.

1941. 100 paras = 1 dinar.
1991. Tolar.

ITALIAN OCCUPATION, 1941

Co. Ci.
(1)

1941. Nos. 330/1 and 414/26 of Yugoslavia optd with Type **1**.

1 **99** 25 p. black 10 15
2 50 p. orange 10 20
3 1 d. green 10 15
4 1 d. 50 red 10 20
5 2 d. red 10 15
6 3 d. brown 10 20
7 4 d. blue 10 20
8 5 d. blue 10 20
9 5 d. 50 violet 10 20
10 6 d. blue 10 30
11 8 d. brown 10 40
12 **70** 10 d. violet 15 35
13 **99** 12 d. violet 20 30
14 **70** 15 d. olive 60·00 70·00
15 **99** 16 d. purple 20 40
16 20 d. blue 1·60 2·25
17 30 d. pink 9·00 13·50

1941. Nos. 330 and 414/26 of Yugoslavia optd **R. Commissariato Civile Territori Sloveni occupati LUBIANA**, with four lines of dots at foot.

23 **99** 25 p. black 10 20
24 50 p. orange 10 20
25 1 d. green 10 20
26 1 d. 50 red 10 15
27 2 d. red 10 15
28 3 d. brown 10 30
29 4 d. blue 10 15
30 5 d. blue 25 75
31 5 d. 50 violet 15 25
32 6 d. blue 15 25
33 8 d. brown 15 25
34 **70** 10 d. violet 45 90
35 **99** 12 d. violet 20 45
36 16 d. purple 70 90
37 20 d. blue 1·60 2·50
38 30 d. pink 15·00 22·00

1941. Nos. 446/9 of Yugoslavia optd as Nos. 23/38 but with only three lines of dots at foot.

45 50 p. + 50 p. on 5 d. violet 2·25 4·25
46 1 d. + 1 d. on 10 d. lake 2·25 4·25
47 1 d. 50 + 1 d. 50 on 20 d. grn 2·25 4·25
48 2 d. + 2 d. on 30 d. blue 2·25 4·25

1941. Nos. 360/7 and 443/4 of Yugoslavia optd as Nos. 23/38, with three or four (No. 57) lines of dots at foot.

49 50 p. brown 70 1·25
50 1 d. green 70 1·25
51 2 d. blue 85 1·25
52 2 d. 50 red 85 1·25
53 5 d. violet 1·90 2·50
54 10 d. lake 1·90 2·50
55 20 d. green 10·00 15·00
56 30 d. blue 26·00 27·00
57 40 d. green 55·00 70·00
58 50 d. blue 45·00 60·00

1941. Nos. 26 and 29 surch.

59 **99** 0 d. 50 on 1 d. 50 red 10 10
60 0 d. 50 on 1 d. 50 red £130 £225
61 1 d. on 4 d. blue 10 15

POSTAGE DUE STAMPS

1941. Postage Due stamps of Yugoslavia, Nos. D89/93 optd with Type **1**.

D18 **D 56** 50 p. violet 15 30
D19 1 d. mauve 15 30
D20 2 d. blue 15 30
D21 5 d. orange 1·50 2·00
D22 10 d. brown 1·50 2·00

Optd as Nos. 18/33, but with four lines of dots at top.

D40 **D 56** 50 p. violet 10 15
D41 1 d. mauve 10 15
D42 2 d. blue 20 55
D43 5 d. orange 9·25 12·50
D44 10 d. brown 2·25 3·00

Optd as Nos. D6/10, but with narrower lettering.

D62 **D 56** 50 p. violet 30 70
D63 1 d. mauve 40 80
D64 2 d. blue 7·00 11·00

GERMAN OCCUPATION, 1943–45

(3)

(4)

1944. Stamps of Italy optd with Types **3** or **4**. (a) On Postage stamps of 1929.

65 **4** 5 c. brown 10 90
66 **3** 10 c. brown 10 90
67 **4** 15 c. green 10 75
68 **3** 20 c. red 10 90
69 **4** 25 c. green 10 90
70 **3** 30 c. brown 10 90
71 **4** 35 c. blue 10 70
72 **3** 50 c. violet 10 1·10
73 **4** 75 c. red 10 2·10
74 **3** 1 l. violet 20 2·10
75 **4** 1 l. 25 blue 15 1·25
76 **3** 1 l. 75 orange 75 8·50
77 **4** 2 l. red 15 1·90
78 **3** 10 l. violet 3·75 24·00

Surch with new value.

79 – 2 l. 55 on 5 c. brown 25 4·50
80 **4** 5 l. on 25 c. green 30 6·00
81 20 l. on 20 c. red 3·00 30·00
82 **3** 25 l. on 2 l. red 3·75 60·00
83 **4** 50 l. on 1 l. 75 orange 6·75 £100

In No. 79 the overprint inscriptions are at each side of the eagle.

(b) On Air stamps, Nos. 270, etc.

84 **4** 25 c. green 1·00 1·50
85 **3** 50 c. brown 4·25 30·00
86 **4** 75 c. brown 1·50 9·00
87 **3** 1 l. violet 5·00 22·50
88 **4** 2 l. blue 2·50 13·00
89 **3** 5 l. green 2·50 19·00
90 **4** 10 l. red 2·25 15·00

(c) On Air Express stamp.

E91 **3** 2 l. black (No. E370) 7·50 48·00

(d) On Express Letter stamp.

E92 **3** 1 l. 25 green (No. E350) 1·40 7·50

1944. Red Cross. Express Letter stamps of Italy surch as Types **3** or **4** with a red cross and new value alongside.

102 **E 132** 1 l. 25 + 50 l. green 24·00 £300
103 2 l. 50 + 50 l. orange 24·00 £300

1944. Homeless Relief Fund. Express Letter stamps of Italy surch as Types **3** and **4**, but in circular frame, and **BREZDOMCEM DEN OBDACHLOSEN** alongside with new value between.

104 **E 132** 1 l. 25 + 50 l. green 24·00 £300
105 2 l. 50 + 50 l. orange 24·00 £300

1944. Air. Orphans' Fund. Air stamps of Italy Nos. 270, etc., surch as Types **3** and **4**, but in circular frame between **DEN WAISEN SIROTAM** and new value.

106 – 25 c. + 10 l. green 10·00 £180
107 **110** 50 c. + 10 l. brown 10·00 £180
108 – 75 c. + 20 l. brown 10·00 £180
109 – 1 l. + 20 l. violet 10·00 £180
110 **113** 2 l. + 20 l. blue 10·00 £180
111 **110** 5 l. + 20 l. green 10·00 £180

1944. Air. Winter Relief Fund. Air stamps of Italy Nos. 270, etc., surch as Types **3** and **4**, but between **ZIMSKA POMOC WINTERHILFE** and new value.

112 – 25 c. + 10 l. green 10·00 £180
113 **110** 50 c. + 10 l. brown 10·00 £180
114 – 75 c. + 20 l. brown 10·00 £180
115 – 1 l. + 20 l. violet 10·00 £180
116 **113** 2 l. + 20 l. blue 10·00 £180
117 **110** 5 l. + 20 l. green 10·00 £180

9 Railway Viaduct, Borovnice

10 Church in Novo Mesto

1945. Inscr "PROVINZ LAIBACH".

118 – 5 c. brown 20 1·50
119 – 10 c. orange 20 1·50
120 **9** 20 c. brown 50 1·50
121 – 25 c. green 20 1·50
122 **10** 50 c. violet 20 1·50
123 – 75 c. red 20 1·50
124 – 1 l. green 20 1·75
125 – 1 l. 25 blue 20 3·25
126 – 1 l. 50 green 35 3·25
127 – 2 l. blue 30 5·25
128 – 2 l. 50 brown 30 5·25
129 – 3 l. mauve 60 9·25
130 – 5 l. brown 85 9·25
131 – 10 l. green 2·10 45·00
132 – 20 l. blue 12·50 £140
133 – 30 l. red 70·00 £600

DESIGNS—VERT: 5 c. Stalagmites, Krizna Jama; 1 l. 25, Kocevje; 1 l. 50, Borovnice Falls; 3 l. Castle, Zuzemberg; 30 l. View and Tabor Church. HORIZ: 10 c. Zirknitz Lake; 25 c. Farm near Ljubljana; 75 c. View from Ribnica; 1 l. Old Castle, Ljubljana; 2 l. Castle, Kostanjevica; 2 l. 50, Castle, Turjak; 5 l. View on River Krka; 10 l. Castle, Otocec; 20 l. Farm at Dolenjskom.

POSTAGE DUE STAMPS

(D 5)

PROVINZ 30 LAIBACH
(D 6)

1944. Postage Due stamps of Italy, Nos. D395, etc., optd as Type D **5**.

D97 **D 141** 50 c. violet 15 35
D98 **D 142** 1 l. orange 60 6·25
D99 2 l. green 60 6·25

Surch as Type D **6**.

D100 **D 141** 30 c. on 50 c. violet 15 35
D101 40 c. on 5 c. brown 15 35

INDEPENDENT STATE

11 Parliament Building

SLOVENIJA 1.00 PTT 26.12.1991
12 Arms

1991. Declaration of Independence.

134 **11** 5 d. multicoloured 25 20

1991.

135 **12** 1 t. multicoloured 10 10
136 4 t. multicoloured 15 15
137 5 t. multicoloured 15 15
138 11 t. multicoloured 25 25

13 Ski Jumping

1992. Winter Olympic Games, Albertville. Multicoloured.

139 30 t. Type **13** 85 85
140 50 t. Slalom 1·40 1·40

14 Arms

15 Opera House

1992. Multicoloured, background colours given.

141 **14** 1 t. brown 10 10
142 2 t. purple 10 10
143 4 t. green 15 15
144 5 t. red 15 15
145 6 t. yellow 20 20
146 11 t. orange 25 25
147 15 t. blue 30 30
148 20 t. violet 50 50
149 50 t. green 85 85
150 100 t. grey 1·60 1·60

1992. Centenary of Ljubljana Opera House.

155 **15** 20 t. multicoloured 25 25

16 Tartini and Violins

1992. 300th Birth Anniv of Giuseppe Tartini (violinist and composer).

156 **16** 27 t. multicoloured 35 35

17 Map and Marko Anton Kappus preaching to Amerindians

HUMANOS+ ZDRUŽENI PROTI NESREČAM 3.00 SLOVENIJA
18

1992. 500th Anniv of Discovery of America by Columbus. Multicoloured.

157 27 t. Type **17** 35 35
158 47 t. Map and "Santa Maria" 60 60

1992. Obligatory Tax. Red Cross.

159 **18** 3 t. black, red and blue 10 10

19 Collapsible Chair by Niko Kralj and Map

20 Slomsek

1992. World Industrial Design Congress, Ljubljana.

160 **19** 41 t. multicoloured 55 55

1992. 130th Death Anniv of Anton Slomsek, Bishop of Maribor.

161 **20** 41 t. multicoloured 55 55

21 Wreckage

22 Rescuing Mountaineer

1992. Obligatory Tax. Solidarity Week. Perf and imperf.

162 **21** 3 t. brown, black & red 10 10

1992. 80th Anniv of Alpine Rescue Service.

164 **22** 41 t. multicoloured 55 55

23 River Jousting

24 Linden Leaf and Flowers

1992. 900th Anniv of River Jousting in Ljubljana.

165 **23** 6 t. multicoloured 10 10

1992. 1st Anniv of Independence.

166 **24** 41 t. multicoloured 55 55

25 Leon Stukelj and Medals

1992. Olympic Games, Barcelona. Multicoloured.

167 40 t. Type **25** 50 50
168 46 t. Head of Apoxymenos repeated in three Slovene colours 60 60

26 Sheepdog

1992. "Psov '92" World Dog-training Championships, Ljubljana.

169 **26** 40 t. multicoloured 50 50

27 Hand crushing Cigarettes

28 Kogoj and scene from "Black Masks" (opera)

1992. Obligatory Tax. Red Cross. Anti-smoking Week.

170 **27** 3 t. multicoloured 10 10

1992. Birth Centenary of Marij Kogoj (composer).
171 **28** 40 t. multicoloured 50 50

29 Langus (self-portrait)

1992. Birth Bicentenary of Matevz Langus (painter).
172 **29** 40 t. multicoloured 50 50

30 Nativity

1992. Christmas. Multicoloured.
173 6 t. Type **30** 10 10
174 7 t. Type **30** 10 10
175 41 t. "Madonna and Child" (stained-glass window by V. Sorli-Puc in St. Mary's Church, Bovec) (vert) . . . 55 55

31 View of Earth from Space and Satellite

1992. Birth Centenary of Herman Potocnik (space flight pioneer).
176 **31** 46 t. multicoloured 60 60

32 Illustration from "Solzice"

1993. Birth Centenary of Prezihov Voranc (writer).
177 **32** 7 t. multicoloured 10 10

33 "Underneath the Birches"

1993. 50th Death Anniv of Rihard Jakopic (painter).
178 **33** 44 t. multicoloured 45 45

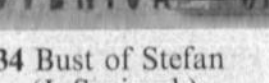

34 Bust of Stefan (J. Savinsek)
35 Honey-cake from Skofja Loka

1993. Death Centenary of Jozef Stefan (physicist).
179 **34** 51 t. multicoloured 50 50

1993. Slovene Culture.
180 **35** 1 t. brown, cinnamon and deep brown 10 10
181 – 2 t. green and lt green . . . 10 10
182 – 5 t. grey and mauve 10 10
183 – 6 t. lt green, green & yellow 10 10
186 – 7 t. red, crimson and grey . 10 10
187 – 8 t. green, dp grn & olive . 10 10
188 – 9 t. red, brown and grey . . 10 10
189 – 10 t. brown and lt brown . 10 10
190 – 11 t. green, light green and yellow 10 10
191 – 12 t. red, orange and grey . 10 10
193 – 20 t. green and grey . . . 20 20
195 – 44 t. lt blue, black & blue . 45 45
196 – 50 t. purple and mauve . . 50 50
196a – 55 t. black, grey and orange 50 50
196b – 65 t. ochre, brown and red 60 60
197 – 70 t. grey, brown and black 70 70
197a – 75 t. green, blue and lilac . 70 70
198 – 100 t. deep brown, light brown and brown . . . 1·00 1·00
198a – 300 t. chestnut and brown 3·25 3·25
198b – 400 t. red and brown . . . 4·25 4·25
DESIGNS: 2 t. Musical pipes; 5 t. Storage barn; 6 t. Shepherd's hut, Velika; 7 t. Zither; 8 t. Mill on the Mur; 9 t. Sledge; 10 t. Drum; 11 t. Hay basket; 12 t. Boy on horseback (statuette from Ribnica); 20 t. House, Prekmurju; 44 t. House, Karst; 50 t. Wind-propelled pump; 55 t. Decorated easter eggs; 65 t. Lamp; 70 t. Ski; 75 t. Wrought iron window lattice; 100 t. Cake; 300 t. Straw sculpture; 400 t. Wine press.

36 Mountains and Founder Members

1993. Centenary of Alpine Association.
199 **36** 7 t. multicoloured 10 10

37 Cop's Route up Triglav **38** Chainbreaker

1993. Birth Centenary of Joza Cop (climber and mountain rescuer).
200 **37** 44 t. multicoloured 45 45

1993. 75th Anniv of Slovenian Postal Service.
201 **38** 7 t. multicoloured 10 10

39 "St. Nicholas" (altar painting, Tintoretto)
40 "Table in Pompeii" (Marij Pregelj)

1993. 500th Anniv of College Chapter of Novo Mesto. Multicoloured.
202 7 t. Type **39** 10 10
203 44 t. Arms 45 45

1993. Europa. Contemporary Art. Multicoloured.
204 44 t. Type **40** 45 45
205 159 t. "Girl with Toy" (Gabrijel Stupica) . . . . 1·60 1·60

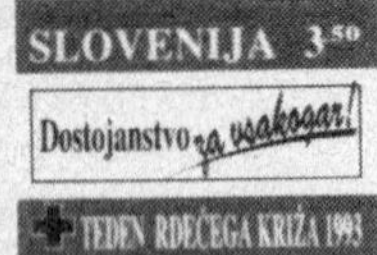

41 "Schwagerina carniolica"
42

1993. Fossils.
206 **41** 44 t. multicoloured 45 45

1993. Obligatory Tax. Red Cross.
207 **42** 3 t. 50 black, red & blue . 10 10

43 6th-century B.C. Vase
44 Red Cross Rescue Workers

1993. 1st Anniv of Admission to United Nations Organization.
208 **43** 62 t. multicoloured 65 65

1993. Obligatory Tax. Solidarity Week.
209 **44** 3 t. 50 multicoloured . . . 10 10

45 Basketball, Hurdling and Swimming

1993. Mediterranean Games, Roussillon (Languedoc).
210 **45** 36 t. multicoloured 35 35

46 "Battle of Sisak" (Janez Valvasor)

1993. 400th Anniv of Battle of Sisak.
211 **46** 49 t. multicoloured 50 50

47 "Monolistra spinosissima"

1993. Cave Fauna. Multicoloured.
212 7 t. Type **47** 10 10
213 40 t. "Aphaenopidius kamnikensis" (insect) 40 40
214 55 t. "Proteus anguinus" . . . 55 55
215 65 t. "Zospeum spelaeum" (mollusc) 65 65

48 Horse and Diagram of Movements
49 Boy smoking and Emblem

1993. European Dressage Championships, Lipica.
216 **48** 65 t. multicoloured 65 65

1993. Obligatory Tax. Red Cross. Anti-smoking Week.
217 **49** 4 t. 50 multicoloured . . . 10 10

50 Arms (death anniv of Johnann Valvasor (historian))

1993. 300th Anniversaries.
218 **50** 9 t. black, lilac and gold . . 10 10
219 – 65 t. black, stone & gold . . 65 65
DESIGN: 65 t. Arms of Academia Operosorum.

51 Christmas Crib

1993. Christmas. Multicoloured.
220 9 t. Type **51** 10 10
221 65 t. Dr. Joze Pogacnik (archbishop) 65 65

52 Illustration from "The Vagabond"
53 Hearts

1994. 150th Anniversaries. Multicoloured.
222 8 t. Type **52** (birth anniv of Josip Juncic (writer)) 10 10
223 9 t. Nightingale and bridge over river (birth anniv of Simon Gregorcic, poet) 10 10
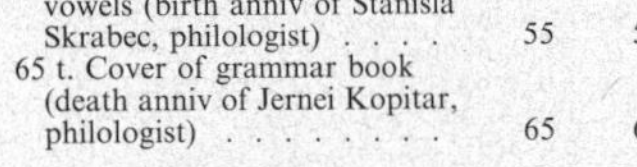
224 55 t. Book showing Slovenian vowels (birth anniv of Stanisla Skrabec, philologist) 55 55
225 65 t. Cover of grammar book (death anniv of Jernei Kopitar, philologist) 65 65

1994. Greetings Stamp.
226 **53** 9 t. multicoloured 10 10

54 Cross-country Skiing

1994. Winter Olympic Games, Lillehammer, Norway. Multicoloured.
227 9 t. Type **54** 10 10
228 65 t. Slalom skiing 70 70

55 Ski Jumping

1994. 60th Anniv of Ski Jumping Championships, Planica.
229 **55** 70 t. multicoloured 75 75

56 Town Names

1994. 850th Anniv of First Official Record of Ljubljana.
230 **56** 9 t. multicoloured 10 10

57 Janez Puhar and Camera

1994. Europa. Discoveries and Inventions. Multicoloured.
231 70 t. Type **57** (invention of glass-plate photography) 75 75
232 215 t. Moon, natural logarithm diagram and Jurij Vega (mathematician) . . . . . . 2·40 2·40

58 Balloons

1994. Obligatory Tax. Red Cross.
233 **58** 4 t. 50 multicoloured . . . 10 10

59 "Primula carniolica"

1994. Flowers. Multicoloured.
234 9 t. Type **59** 10 10
235 44 t. "Hladnikia pastinacifolia" 50 50
236 60 t. "Daphne blagayana" . . 65 65
237 70 t. "Campanula zoysii" . . 75 75

60 Red Cross Worker with Child
61 Inflating "Globe" Football

1994. Obligatory Tax. Solidarity Week.
238 **60** 4 t. 50 multicoloured . . . 10 10

1994. World Cup Football Championship, U.S.A.
239 **61** 44 t. multicoloured 50 50

62 Globes in Olympic Colours and Flags
63 Mt. Ojstrica

1994. Centenary of International Olympic Committee.
240 **62** 100 t. multicoloured . . . 1·10 1·10

1994.
241 **63** 12 t. multicoloured 15 15

64 Maks Pletersnik and University of Laibach Professors

1994. Centenary of First Slovenian–German Dictionary.
242 **64** 70 t. multicoloured 75 75

65 Roman Infantry

1994. 1600th Anniv of Battle of Frigidus.
243 **65** 60 t. red, black and grey . 65 65

66 Post Office

1994. Centenary of Maribor Post Office.
244 **66** 70 t. multicoloured 75 75

67 Locomotive kkStB 5722

1994. Centenary of Ljubljana Railway.
245 **67** 70 t. multicoloured 75 75

68 Orchestra Venue and Music

1994. Bicentenary of Ljubljana Philharmonic Society. Multicoloured.
246 12 t. Type **68** 15 15
247 70 t. Ludwig van Beethoven, Johannes Brahms, Antonin Dvorak and Joseph Haydn (composers) and Niccolo Paganini (violinist) 75 75

69 Christmas Tree, Window and Candles
70 "Madonna and Child" (statue, Loreto Basilica)

1994. Christmas and International Year of the Family.
248 **69** 12 t. multicoloured 15 15
249 – 70 t. cream, black and blue 75 75
DESIGN: 70 t. "Children with Christmas Tree" (F. Kralj) and I.Y.F. emblem.

1994. 700th Anniv of Loreto.
250 **70** 70 t. multicoloured 75 75

71 Ivan Hribar, Mihajlo Rostohar and Danilo Majaron (founders) and University

1994. 75th Anniv of Ljubljana University.
251 **71** 70 t. multicoloured 75 75

72 Postal Emblem
73 Lili Novy (writer, 110th birth)

1995.
252 **72** 13 t. multicoloured 15 15

1995. Anniversaries.
253 **73** 20 t. red, black and grey . 20 20
254 – 70 t. yellow, black and gold 70 70
255 – 70 t. multicoloured 70 70
DESIGNS—HORIZ: No. 253, Silhouettes of figures and signature of Anton Tomasz Linhart (dramatist, death bicentenary). VERT: No. 255, Detail of facade of Zadruzna Co-operative Bank, Ljubljana (110th birth anniv (1994) of Ivan Vurnik (architect)).

74 Cats and Hearts (Jure Kos)
75 Allegory

1995. Greetings Stamp.
256 **74** 20 t. multicoloured 20 20

1995. 50th Anniv of End of Second World War.
257 **75** 13 t. multicoloured 15 15

76 Skeleton and Woman

1995. Europa. Peace and Freedom. Multicoloured.
258 60 t. Type **76** (50th anniv of liberation of concentration camps) 60 60
259 70 t. Woman running free . . 70 70

77 "Karavankina schellwieni"

1995. Fossils.
260 **77** 70 t. multicoloured 70 70

78 Alpine Iris, Triglav National Park and Alpine Poppy

1995. European Nature Conservation Year.
261 **78** 70 t. multicoloured 70 70

79 Child painting Red Cross
80 First Aiders tending Casualty

1995. Obligatory Tax. Red Cross.
262 **79** 6 t. multicoloured 10 10

1995. Obligatory Tax. Solidarity Week.
263 **80** 6 t. 50 multicoloured . . . 10 10

81 Lesser Kestrel

1995. Birds. Multicoloured.
264 13 t. Type **81** 15 15
265 60 t. Common roller 60 60
266 70 t. Lesser grey shrike . . . 70 70
267 215 t. Black-headed bunting . 2·10 2·10

82 Radovljica

1995. 500th Anniv of Radovljica.
268 **82** 44 t. multicoloured 45 45

83 Steam Locomotive KRB 37 Podnart

1995. 125th Anniv of Ljubljana–Jesenice Railway.
269 **83** 70 t. black, red and yellow . 70 70

84 Mountain and Presbytery

1995. Centenary of Jakob Aljaz Presbytery, Mount Triglav.
270 **84** 100 t. blue, black and red . 1·00 1·00

85 Scouts around Campfire

1995. Scouting.
271 **85** 70 t. multicoloured 70 70

86 "Death of a Genius"

1995. Birth Centenary of France Kralz (artist). Multicoloured.
272 60 t. Type **86** 60 60
273 70 t. "Family of Horses" . . 70 70

87 Handshake, Anniversary Emblem and Different Nationalities
88 "Winter" (Marlenka Stupica)

1995. 50th Anniversaries of U.N.O. (274) and F.A.O. (275). Multicoloured.
274 70 t. Type **87** 70 70
275 70 t. Foodstuffs, anniversary emblem and different nationalities 70 70

1995. Christmas. Paintings. Multicoloured.
276 13 t. Type **88** 15 15
277 70 t. "Madonna and Child" (Leopold Layer) 70 70

89 Birds and Heart (Karmen Podgornik)

1996. Greetings Stamp.
278 **89** 13 t. multicoloured 10 10

90 Swimming

1996. The European Pond Turtle. Multicoloured.
279 13 t. Type **90** 10 10
280 50 t. On bank 45 45
281 60 t. In water 55 55
282 70 t. Pair of turtles climbing up bank 65 65

91 Ptujsko Polje

1996. Traditional Masks. Multicoloured.
283 13 t. Type **91** 10 10
284 70 t. Dravsko Polje 65 65

92 Steam Locomotive "Aussee"

1996. 150th Anniv of Slovenian Railways.
285 **92** 70 t. multicoloured 65 65

93 Fran Finzgar (writer)

1996. Birth Anniversaries. Multicoloured.
286 13 t. Type **93** (125th anniv) . . 10 10
287 100 t. Ita Rina (actress) (89th anniv) 90 90

94 Child feeding Birds and Children of different Nationalities

95 "Vase of Dahlias"

1996. 50th Anniv of U.N.I.C.E.F.
288 **94** 65 t. multicoloured 60 60

1996. 70th Death Anniv of Ivana Koblica (painter). Multicoloured.
289 65 t. "Children in the Grass" (detail) 60 60
290 75 t. Type **95** 70 70

96 Pope John Paul II

97 Anniversary Emblem

1996. Papal Visit.
291 **96** 75 t. multicoloured 070 70

1996. Obligatory Tax. 130th Anniv of Slovenian Red Cross.
293 **97** 7 t. multicoloured 10 10

98 Linked Hands

1996. Obligatory Tax. Solidarity Week.
294 **98** 7 t. multicoloured 10 10

99 Gallenberg Castle

1996. 700th Anniv of Zagorje ob Savi.
295 **99** 24 t. multicoloured 20 20

100 Cyclists

1996. World Youth Cycling Championships, Novo Mesto.
296 **100** 55 t. multicoloured . . . 50 50

101 Stars over Mountains

103 Rowing and Canoeing

1996. 5th Anniv of Independence.
297 **101** 75 t. multicoloured . . . 70 70

1996. Centenary of Modern Olympic Games and Olympic Games, Atlanta. Multicoloured.
299 75 t. Type **103** 70 70
300 100 t. Gymnastics and hurdling . 90 90

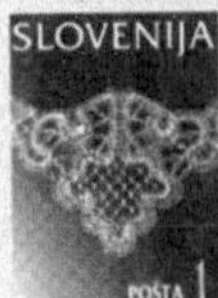

104 Corner

106 Cave

105 "Moscon Family"

1996. Traditional Lace Designs.
301 **104** 1 t. brown 10 10
302 – 1 t. brown 10 10
303 – 2 t. red 10 10
304 – 2 t. red 10 10
305 – 5 t. blue 10 10
306 – 5 t. blue 10 10
307 – 12 t. green 10 10
308 – 12 t. green 10 10
309 – 13 t. red 10 10
310 – 13 t. red 10 10
311 – 50 t. purple 45 45
312 – 50 t. purple 45 45
DESIGNS: No. 302, Corner (different); 303, Rounded collar incorporating scrolls; 304, Pointed collar with scalloped edging; 305, Flowers and leaves forming circular design; 306, Framed rose; 307, Flower; 308, Diamond with flower in centre; 309, Square enclosing diamonds containing "flowers"; 310, Square containing circular motifs; 311, Heart-shaped edging; 312, Ornate edging.

1996. 130th Death Anniv of Jozef Tominc (painter).
313 **105** 65 t. multicoloured . . . 60 60

1996. U.N.E.S.C.O. World Heritage Sites. Skocjan Cave.
314 **106** 55 t. multicoloured . . . 50 50

107 Gimbals

1996. 250th Anniv of Novo Mesto School.
315 **107** 55 t. multicoloured . . . 50 50

108 Heart

109 Post Office Building, Ljubljana, and Doves carrying Letter

1996. Centenary of Modern Cardiology.
316 **108** 12 t. red, brown and cream 10 10

1996. Centenary of Post and Telecommunications Office.
317 **109** 100 t. multicoloured . . 90 90

110 Doves carrying Letter and Stylized Letter Sorting

1996. Introduction of Automatic Letter Sorting.
318 **110** 12 t. black, red and orange 10 10

111 Children and Christmas Tree on Sledge

1996. Christmas. Multicoloured.
319 12 t. Type **111** 10 10
320 65 t. "Adoration of the Wise Men" (Stefan Subic) 60 60

SOMALIA Pt. 8; Pt. 14

A former Italian colony in East Africa on the Gulf of Aden, including Benadir (S. Somaliland), and Jubaland. Under British Administration 1943-50 (for stamps issued during this period see volume 3). Then under United Nations control with Italian Administration. Became independent on 1st July, 1960. Following a revolution in Oct. 1969, the country was designated "Somali Democratic Republic". See also Middle East Forces.

1903. 64 besa = 16 annas = 1 rupia.
1905. 100 centesimi = 1 lira.
1922. 100 besa = 1 rupia.
1926. 100 centesimi = 1 lira.
1950. 100 centesimi = 1 somalo.
1961. 100 cents = 1 Somali shilling.

ITALIAN COLONY

1 African Elephant

2 Somali Lion

1903.
1 **1** 1 b. brown . . . . 19·00 2·75
2 2 b. green . . . . 2·25 1·00
3 **2** 1 a. red . . . . 2·50 1·90
4 2 a. brown . . . . 5·00 8·50
5 2½ a. blue . . . . 2·25 3·00
6 5 a. yellow . . . . 5·00 10·00
7 10 a. lilac . . . . 5·00 10·00

1905. Surch with new value without bars at top.
10 **1** 2 c. on 1 b. brown . . . . 4·50 12·00
11 **2** 5 c. on 2 b. green . . . . 4·50 8·00
12 10 c. on 1 a. red . . . . 4·50 7·00
13 15 c. on 2 a. brown . . . . 4·50 7·00
8 15 c. on 5 a. yellow £1400 £250
13a 20 c. on 2 a. brown . . . . 7·00 3·00
14 25 c. on 2½ a. blue . . . . . 7·00 7·00
9 40 c. on 10 a. lilac £325 £125
15 50 c. on 5 a. yellow . . . . 9·50 14·00
16 1 l. on 10 a. lilac . . . . . 9·50 16·00
For stamps with bars at top, see Nos. 68, etc.

1916. Nos. 15 and 16 re-surcharged and with bars cancelling original surcharge.
17 **2** 5 c. on 50 c. on 5 a. yellow . 14·00 20·00
18 20 c. on 1 l. on 10 a. lilac . . 4·00 10·00

1916. Red Cross stamps of Italy optd **SOMALIA.**
19 **53** 10 c. + 5 c. red . . . . . . 2·00 4·00
20 **54** 15 c. + 5 c. grey . . . . . 6·00 16·00
21 20 c. + 5 c. orange . . . . 2·00 6·00
22 20 on 15 c. + 5 c. grey . . 6·00 16·00

1922. Nos. 12, etc., again surch at top.
23 **1** 3 b. on 5 c. on 2 b. green . . 5·50 13·00
24 **2** 6 b. on 10 c. on 1 a. red . . 7·00 10·00
25 9 b. on 15 c. on 2 a. brown 7·00 10·00
26 15 b. on 25 c. on 2½ a. blue 8·50 10·00
27 30 b. on 50 c. on 5 a. yellow 9·50 24·00
28 60 b. on 1 l. on 10 a. lilac . . 9·50 32·00

1922. Victory stamps of Italy surch **SOMALIA ITALIANA** and new value.
29 **62** 3 b. on 5 c. green . . . . . 50 2·00
30 6 b. on 10 c. red . . . . . 50 2·00
31 9 b. on 15 c. grey . . . . . 50 3·25
32 15 b. on 25 c. blue . . . . 50 3·25

1923. Nos. 11 to 16 re-surcharged with new values and bars (No. 33 is optd with bars only at bottom).
33 **1** bars on 2 c. on 1 b. brown . 4·25 13·00
34 2 on 2 c. on 1 b. brown . . . 4·25 13·00
35 3 on 2 c. on 1 b. brown . . . 4·25 13·00
36 **2** 5 b. on 50 c. on 5 a. yellow . 4·25 10·00
37 **1** 6 on 5 c. on 2 b. green . . . 5·50 7·50
38 **2** 18 b. on 10 c. on 1 a. red . . 5·50 7·50
39 20 b. on 15 c. on 2 a. brown 7·00 10·00
40 25 b. on 15 c. on 2 a. brown 8·00 10·00
41 30 b. on 25 c. on 2½ a. blue . 9·50 12·00
42 60 b. on 1 l. on 10 a. lilac . . 10·00 27·00
43 1 r. on 1 l. on 10 a. lilac . . 12·00 32·00

1923. Propaganda of Faith stamps of Italy surch **SOMALIA ITALIANA** and new value.
44 **66** 6 b. on 20 c. orange & grn . 1·50 6·00
45 13 b. on 30 c. orge & red . 1·50 6·00
46 20 b. on 50 c. orge & vio . 1·25 6·00
47 30 b. on 1 l. orge & blue . . 1·25 6·00

1923. Fascist March on Rome stamps of Italy surch **SOMALIA ITALIA** and new value.
48 **73** 3 b. on 10 c. green . . . . 1·75 6·00
49 13 b. on 30 c. violet . . . . 1·75 6·00
50 20 b. on 50 c. red . . . . . 1·75 6·00
51 **74** 30 b. on 1 l. blue . . . . . 1·75 6·00
52 1 r. on 2 l. brown . . . . . 1·75 6·00
53 **75** 3 l. on 5 l. black and blue . 1·75 7·50

1924. Manzoni stamps of Italy surch **SOMALIA ITALIANA** and new value.
54 **77** 6 b. on 10 c. black & purple 1·00 12·00
55 9 b. on 15 c. black & green 1·00 12·00
56 13 b. on 30 c. black . . . . 1·00 12·00
57 20 b. on 50 c. black & brn . 1·00 12·00
58 30 b. on 1 l. black & blue . 15·00 90·00
59 3 r. on 5 l. black & purple £250 £950

1925. Holy Year stamps of Italy surch **SOMALIA ITALIANA** and new value.
60 – 6 b. + 3 b. on 20 c. + 10 c. brown and green . . . . 1·00 4·25
61 **81** 13 b. + 6 b. on 30 c. + 15 c. brown and chocolate . . 1·00 4·25

62 – 15 b. + 8 b. on 50 c. + 25 c. brown and violet . . . . 1·00 4·25
63 – 18 b. + 9 b. on 60 c. + 30 c. brown and red . . . . . 1·00 4·25
64 – 30 b. + 15 b. on 1 l. + 50 c. purple and blue . . . . . 1·00 4·25
65 – 1 r. + 50 b. on 5 l. + 2 l. 50 purple and red . . . . . 1·00 4·25

1925. Royal Jubilee stamps of Italy optd **SOMALIA ITALIANA**.
66 **82** 60 c. red . . . . 15 2·75
67 1 l. blue . . . . 35 2·75
67a 1 l. 25 c. blue . . . . . . 35 8·50

1926. Nos. 10/13 and 13a/16 optd with bars at top.
68 **1** 2 c. on 1 b. brown . . . . . 9·50 25·00
69 5 c. on 2 b. green . . . . . . 7·00 20·00
70 **2** 10 c. on 1 a. pink . . . . . . 4·75 4·75
71 15 c. on 2 a. brown . . . . . 4·25 5·50
72 20 c. on 2 a. brown . . . . . 5·50 7·50
73 25 c. on 2½ a. blue . . . . . 5·50 8·50
74 50 c. on 5 a. yellow . . . . . 7·00 17·00
75 1 l. on 10 a. lilac . . . . . . 9·50 20·00

1926. St. Francis of Assisi stamps of Italy optd **SOMALIA ITALIANA** (76/8) or **Somalia** (79/80).
76 **83** 20 c. green . . . . 1·00 4·25
77 40 c. violet . . . . 1·00 4·25
78 60 c. red . . . . 1·00 4·25
79 1 l. 25 blue . . . . 1·00 4·25
80 5 l. + 2 l. 50 green . . . . 2·00 5·50

21 24

1926. Italian Colonial Institute.
81 **21** 5 c. + 5 c. brown . . . . . 20 2·25
82 10 c. + 5 c. olive . . . . . 20 2·25
83 20 c. + 5 c. green . . . . . 20 2·25
84 40 c. + 5 c. red . . . . . . 20 2·25
85 60 c. + 5 c. orange . . . . . 20 2·25
86 1 l. + 5 c. blue . . . . . . 20 2·25

1926. Italian stamps optd **SOMALIA ITALIANA**.
87 **31** 2 c. brown . . . . 1·00 2·25
88 **37** 5 c. green . . . . 1·40 2·25
89 **92** 7½ c. brown . . . . 4·75 17·00
90 **37** 10 c. pink 85 40
91 **39** 20 c. purple 90 70
92 **34** 25 c. green and light green . 35 30
92a **39** 30 c. black . . . . 4·00 6·00
93 **91** 50 c. grey and brown . . . 4·00 4·25
94 **92** 50 c. mauve . . . . 11·00 22·00
95 **39** 60 c. orange . . . . 1·10 1·25
96 **34** 75 c. red and carmine . . . 35·00 5·00
97 1 l. brown and green . . . 1·10 60
98 1 l. 25 c. blue and ultram . 3·50 1·00
99 **91** 1 l. 75 brown . . . . 18·00 7·00
100 **34** 2 l. green and orange . . . 6·00 2·50
101 2 l. 50 c. green & orange . . 7·50 3·00
102 5 l. blue and pink . . . . 17·00 12·00
103 10 l. green and pink . . . 17·00 15·00

1927. 1st National Defence issue of Italy (lira colours changed) optd **SOMALIA ITALIANA**.
104 **89** 40 c. + 20 c. black & brn . 1·00 4·25
105 – 60 c. + 30 c. brown & red . 1·00 4·25
106 – 1 l. 25 + 60 c. black & blue 1·00 4·25
107 – 5 l. + 2 l. 50 black & green 1·75 6·50

1927. Centenary of Volta Stamps of Italy (colours changed) optd **Somalia Italiana**.
108 **90** 20 c. violet . . . . 3·00 10·00
109 50 c. orange . . . . 3·00 7·00
110 1 l. 25 blue . . . . 4·00 10·00

1928. 45th Anniv of Italian–African Society.
111 **24** 20 c. + 5 c. green . . . . 75 3·50
112 30 c. + 5 c. red . . . . . 75 3·50
113 50 c. + 10 c. violet . . . . 75 3·50
114 1 l. 25 + 20 c. blue . . . . 75 3·50

1929. 2nd National Defence issue of Italy (colours changed) optd **SOMALIA ITALIANA**.
115 **89** 30 c. + 10 c. black & red . 1·40 4·75
116 – 50 c. + 20 c. grey & lilac . 1·40 4·75
117 – 1 l. 25 + 50 c. blue & brn . 1·40 6·00
118 – 5 l. + 2 l. black and green 1·40 6·00

1929. Montecassino Abbey stamps of Italy (colours changed) optd **Somalia Italiana** (10 l.) or **SOMALIA ITALIANA** (others).
119 **104** 20 c. green . . . . 1·75 4·25
120 – 25 c. red . . . . 1·75 4·25
121 – 50 c. + 10 c. red . . . . 1·75 8·50
122 – 75 c. + 15 c. brown . . . 3·25 8·50
123 **104** 1 l. 25 + 25 c. purple . . 3·25 8·50
124 – 5 l. + 1 l. blue . . . . . 3·25 8·50
125 – 10 l. + 2 l. brown . . . . 3·25 10·00

1930. Royal Wedding stamps of Italy (colours changed) optd **SOMALIA ITALIANA**.
126 **109** 20 c. green . . . . 40 1·90
127 50 c. + 10 c. red . . . . 35 2·50
128 1 l. 25 + 25 c. red . . . . 35 2·75

1930. Ferrucci stamps of Italy (colours changed) optd **SOMALIA ITALIANA**.
129 **114** 20 c. violet . . . . 50 1·60
130 – 25 c. green (No. 283) . . . 50 1·60
131 – 50 c. black (No. 284) . . . 50 1·60
132 – 1 l. 25 blue (No. 285) . . . 50 1·60
133 – 5 l. + 2 l. red (No. 286) . 1·75 2·75

1930. 3rd National Defence issue of Italy (colours changed) optd **SOMALIA ITALIANA**.
134 **89** 30 c. + 10 c. green & dp grn 5·00 15·00
135 – 50 c. + 10 c. purple & green 5·00 15·00
136 – 1 l. 25 + 30 c. brown and deep brown . . . . . . 5·00 15·00
137 – 5 l. + 1 l. 50 green & blue 12·00 42·00

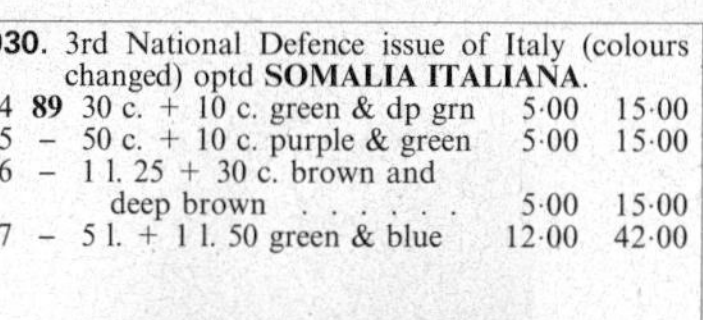

29 Irrigation Canal

1930. 25th Anniv (1929) of Colonial Agricultural Institute.
138 **29** 50 c. + 20 c. brown . . . 1·00 5·00
139 1 l. 25 + 20 c. blue . . . 1·00 5·00
140 1 l. 75 + 20 c. green . . . 1·00 5·00
141 2 l. 55 + 50 c. violet . . . 2·00 5·00
142 5 l. + 1 l. red . . . . . . 2·00 5·00

1930. Bimillenary of Virgil stamps of Italy (colours changed) optd **SOMALIA**.
143 15 c. grey . . . . 25 1·40
144 20 c. brown . . . . 25 1·40
145 25 c. green . . . . 25 1·40
146 30 c. brown . . . . 25 1·40
147 50 c. purple . . . . 25 1·40
148 75 c. red . . . . 25 1·40
149 1 l. 25 blue . . . . 25 1·40
150 5 l. + 1 l. 50 purple . . . 1·75 7·00
151 10 l. + 2 l. 50 brown . . . 1·75 7·00

1931. Stamps of Italy optd **SOMALIA ITALIANA**.
152 – 25 c. green (No. 244) . . 2·25 4·25
153 **103** 50 c. violet . . . . 5·50 1·00

1931. St. Antony of Padua stamps of Italy optd **Somalia** (75 c., 5 l.) or **SOMALIA** (others).
154 **121** 20 c. brown . . . . . . 60 2·50
155 – 25 c. green . . . . . . 60 2·50
156 – 30 c. brown . . . . . . 60 2·50
157 – 50 c. purple . . . . . . 60 1·40
158 – 75 c. grey . . . . 60 2·50
159 – 1 l. 25 blue . . . . . . 60 2·50
160 – 5 l. + 2 l. 50 brown . . . 2·00 11·00

32 Tower at Mnara-Ciromo

33 Hippopotamus

1932.
161a – 5 c. brown 15 10
162a – 7½ c. violet . . . . . . 15 1·10
163a – 10 c. black 15 10
164a – 15 c. green 15 30
165a **32** 20 c. red 15 10
166a 25 c. green 15 10
167a 30 c. brown 20 20
168a – 35 c. blue . . . . 65 1·50
169a – 50 c. violet . . . . . . 2·75 10
170 – 75 c. red 85 40
171 – 1 l. 25 blue . . . . . . 1·75 25
172 – 1 l. 75 red . . . . . . 1·25 25
173 – 2 l. red 70 35
174 – 2 l. 55 blue . . . . . . 14·00 20·00
175a – 5 l. red . . . . 5·00 1·25
176 **33** 10 l. violet . . . . . . 7·50 4·50
177 – 20 l. green . . . . . . 18·00 20·00
178 – 25 l. blue . . . . 30·00 30·00
DESIGNS—HORIZ: 5, 7½, 10, 15 c. Francesco Crispi Lighthouse, Cape Guardafui; 35, 50, 75 c. Governor's Residence, Mogadishu; 25 l. Lioness. VERT: 1 l. 25, 1 l. 75, 2 l. Termitarium (ant-hill); 2 l. 55, 5 l. Ostrich; 20 l. Lesser kudu.

1934. Honouring the Duke of the Abruzzi. Stamps of 1932 (some colours changed) optd **ONORANZE AL DUCA DEGLI ABRUZZI**.
179 10 c. brown . . . . 3·00 8·00
180 25 c. green . . . . 3·00 8·00
181 50 c. purple . . . . 2·00 8·00
182 1 l. 25 blue . . . . 2·00 8·00
183 5 l. black . . . . 3·00 8·00
184 10 l. red . . . . 2·50 8·00
185 20 l. blue . . . . 2·50 8·00
186 25 l. green . . . . 2·50 8·00
DESIGNS: As Nos. 163a to 178.

35 Woman and Child

37 King Victor Emmanuel III

36

1934. 2nd Int Colonial Exhibition, Naples.
187 **35** 5 c. green & brown (post) . 2·00 6·00
188 10 c. brown and black . . . 2·00 6·00
189 20 c. red and blue . . . . . 2·00 6·00
190 50 c. violet and brown . . . 2·00 6·00
191 60 c. brown and slate . . . 2·00 6·00
192 1 l. 25 blue and green . . . 2·00 6·00
193 – 25 c. blue & orange (air) . . 2·00 6·00
194 – 50 c. green and blue . . . . 2·00 6·00
195 – 75 c. brown and orange . . . 2·00 6·00
196 – 80 c. brown and green . . . 2·00 6·00
197 – 1 l. red and green . . . . . 2·00 6·00
198 – 2 l. blue and brown . . . . 2·00 6·00
DESIGNS: 25 c. to 75 c. Caproni Ca 101 airplane over River Juba; 80 c. to 2 l. Cheetahs watching Caproni Ca 101 airplane.

1934. Air. Rome–Mogadishu Flight.
199 **36** 25 c. + 10 c. green . . . . 2·00 5·00
200 50 c. + 10 c. brown . . . . 2·00 5·00
201 75 c. + 15 c. red . . . . . 2·00 5·00
202 80 c. + 15 c. black . . . . 2·00 5·00
203 1 l. + 20 c. brown . . . . 2·00 5·00
204 2 l. + 20 c. blue . . . . . 2·00 5·00
205 3 l. + 25 c. violet . . . . 16·00 40·00
206 5 l. + 25 c. red . . . . . 16·00 40·00
207 10 l. + 30 c. purple . . . . 16·00 40·00
208 25 l. + 2 l. green . . . . . 16·00 40·00

1934. King of Italy's Visit to Italian Somaliland.
209 **37** 5 c. + 5 c. black . . . . . 1·00 3·00
210 7½ c. + 7½ c. purple . . . . 1·00 3·00
211 15 c. + 10 c. green . . . . 1·00 3·00
212 20 c. + 10 c. red . . . . . 1·00 3·00
213 25 c. + 10 c. green . . . . 1·00 3·00
214 30 c. + 10 c. brown . . . . 1·00 3·00
215 50 c. + 10 c. violet . . . . 1·00 3·00
216 75 c. + 15 c. red . . . . . 1·00 3·00
217 1 l. 25 + 15 c. blue . . . . 1·00 3·00
218 1 l. 75 + 25 c. orange . . . 1·00 3·00
219 2 l. 75 + 25 c. blue . . . . 9·00 29·00
220 5 l. + 1 l. purple . . . . . 9·00 29·00
221 10 l. + 1 l. 80 brown . . . 9·00 29·00
222 – 25 l. + 2 l. 75 sepia & brn . 75·00 95·00
DESIGN—36×44 mm: 25 l. King Victor Emmanuel III on horseback.

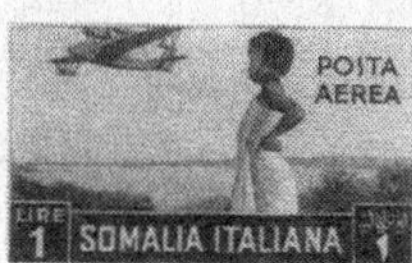

38a Native Girl and Macchi Castoldi MC-94 Flying Boat

1936. Air.
223 – 25 c. green . . . . 85 2·00
224 – 50 c. brown 20 15
225 – 60 c. orange . . . . 1·10 4·25
226 – 75 c. brown 70 90
227 **38a** 1 l. blue 15 10
228 – 1 l. 50 violet 70 35
229 – 2 l. blue . . . . 1·60 85
230 **38a** 3 l. red . . . . 5·00 2·25
231 – 5 l. green . . . . 5·00 2·75
232 – 10 l. red . . . . 6·00 9·00
DESIGNS: 25 c., 1 l. 50, Banana trees; 50 c., 2 l. Native woman in cotton plantation; 60 c., 5 l. Orchard; 75 c., 10 l. Native women harvesting.

ITALIAN TRUST TERRITORY

40 Tower at Mnara-Ciromo

41 Ostrich

42 Governor's Residence, Mogadishu

43 River Scene

1950. Air.
233 **40** 1 c. black 10 10
234 **41** 5 c. red 75 25
235 **42** 6 c. violet 15 10
236 **40** 8 c. green 15 10
237 **42** 10 c. green 10 10
238 **41** 20 c. green . . . . 1·25 20
239 **40** 35 c. red 35 20
240 **42** 55 c. blue 45 15
241 **41** 60 c. violet . . . . 1·75 35
242 **40** 65 c. brown 70 15
243 **42** 1 s. orange 85 15

1950. Air.
244 **43** 30 c. brown 30 30
245 45 c. red 30 30
246 65 c. violet 30 30
247 **43** 70 c. blue 30 30
248 90 c. brown 30 30
249 1 s. purple 45 30
250 1 s. 35 violet 70 70
251 1 s. 50 green 85 50
252 3 s. blue . . . . 7·00 2·25
253 5 s. brown . . . . 8·00 3·00
254 10 s. orange . . . . . . 9·50 2·25

44 Councillors

45 Symbol of Fair

1951. 1st Territorial Council.
255 **44** 20 c. brn & grn (postage) . 2·00 20
256 55 c. violet and brown . . 3·75 3·50
257 – 1 s. blue and violet (air) . . 2·25 70
258 – 1 s. 50 brown and green . . 3·75 2·75
DESIGN—VERT: 1 s., 1 s. 50, Flags and Savoia Marchetti S.M.95C airliner over Mogadiscio.

1952. 1st Somali Fair, Mogadiscio.
259 **45** 25 c. brn & red (postage) 1·75 1·75
260 55 c. brown and blue . . . 1·75 1·75
261 – 1 s. 20 blue & bistre (air) 2·00 2·00
DESIGN: 1 s. 20, Palm tree, Douglas DC-4 airliner and minaret.

46 Mother and Baby

47 Somali and Entrance to Fair

1953. Anti-Tuberculosis Campaign.
262 **46** 5 c. brown & vio (postage) 10 10
263 25 c. brown and red . . . 15 10
264 50 c. brown and blue . . . 70 70
265 1 s. 20 brown & grn (air) . 85 85

1953. 2nd Somali Fair, Mogadiscio.
266 **47** 25 c. green & grey (postage) 20 20
267 60 c. blue and grey 40 40
268 – 1 s. 20 red and pink (air) . . 40 40
269 – 1 s. 50 brown and buff . . 40 40
DESIGN: 1 s. 20, 1 s. 50, Palm, airplane and entrance.

48 Stamps of 1903 and Map

1953. 50th Anniv of First Stamps of Italian Somaliland. (a) Postage.
270 **48** 25 c. brown, red & lake . . 25 25
271 35 c. brown, red & green . 25 25
272 60 c. brown, red & orange 25 25

(b) Air. Aeroplane on Map.
273 **48** 60 c. brown, red & chestnut 45 45
274 1 s. brown, red & black . . 45 45

49 Airplane and Constellations

1953. Air. 75th Anniv of U.P.U.
275 **49** 1 s. 20 red and buff . . . 35 35
276 1 s. 50 brown and buff . . 40 40
277 2 s. green and blue 45 40

50 Somali Bush Country

51 Alexander Island and River Juba

1954. Leprosy Relief Convention.
278 **50** 25 c. green & blue (postage) 30 30
279 60 c. sepia and brown . . 30 30
280 **51** 1 s. 20 brn and grn (air) . 40 40

281 2 s. purple and red 55 65

52 Somali Flag 52a "Adenium somalense"

1954. Institution of Somali Flag.
282 **52** 25 c. multicoloured (post) 25 25
283 1 s. 20 multicoloured (air) 25 25

1955. Floral Designs.
290a **52a** 1 c. red, black and blue 10 10
285 – 5 c. mauve, green & blue 10 10
290c – 10 c. yellow, grn & lilac 10 10
290d – 15 c. multicoloured 20 20
290e – 25 c. yellow, grn & brn 15 10
290f – 50 c. multicoloured 30 30
288 – 60 c. red, green & black 10 15
289 – 1 s. yellow, green & pur 15 20
290 – 1 s. 20 yellow, grn & brn 20 20
FLOWERS: 5 c. Blood lily; 10 c. "Grinum scabrum"; 15 c. Baobab; 25 c. "Poinciana elata"; 50 c. Glory lily; 60 c. "Calatropis procera"; 1 s. Sea lily; 1 s. 20, "Sesamothamnus bussernus".

54 Oribi 54a Lesser Kudu

1955. Air. Antelopes. (a) As T **54**. Heads in black and orange.
291 **54** 35 c. green 30 20
292 – 45 c. violet 1·25 35
293 – 50 c. violet 30 20
294 – 75 c. red 65 25
295 – 1 s. 20 green 65 25
296 – 1 s. 50 blue 75 45
ANTELOPES: 45 c. Salt's dik-dik; 50 c. Speke's gazelle; 75 c. Gerenuk; 1 s. 20, Soemmering's gazelle; 1 s. 50, Waterbuck.

(b) As T **54a**.
296a **54a** 3 s. purple and brown 1·00 85
296b – 5 s. yellow and black 1·00 85
DESIGN: 5 s. Hunter's hartebeest.

55 Native Weaver 56 Voters and Map

1955. 3rd Somali Fair.
297 **55** 25 c. brown (postage) 25 25
298 – 30 c. green 25 25
299 – 45 c. brown & orange (air) 25 25
300 – 1 s. 20 blue and pink 35 35
DESIGNS: 30 c. Cattle fording river; 45 c. Camels around well; 1 s. 20, Native woman at well.

1956. 1st Legislative Assembly.
301 **56** 5 c. brown & grn (postage) 10 10
302 10 c. sepia and brown 10 10
303 25 c. brown and red 10 10
304 60 c. brown and blue (air) 15 15
305 1 s. 20 brown and orange 20 20

57 Somali Arms 58 Falcheiro Barrage

1957. Inauguration of National Emblem. Arms in blue and brown.
306 **57** 5 c. brown (postage) 10 10
307 25 c. red 15 15
308 60 c. violet 15 15
309 45 c. blue (air) 20 20
310 1 s. 20 green 25 25

1957. 4th Somali Fair.
311 **58** 5 c. lilac & brown (postage) 10 10
312 – 10 c. green and bistre 10 10
313 – 25 c. blue and red 15 15
314 – 60 c. brown and blue (air) 25 25
315 – 1 s. 20 black and red 25 25
DESIGNS—HORIZ: 10 c. Juba River bridge; 25 c. Silos at Margherita; 60 c. Irrigation canal. VERT: 1 s. 20, Oil well.

59 Somali Nurse with Baby 60 Track Running

1957. Tuberculosis Relief Campaign.
316 **59** 10 c. + 10 c. brown and red (postage) 15 15
317 25 c. + 10 c. brown & green 15 15
318 55 c. + 20 c. brown and blue (air) 20 20
319 1 s. 20 c. + 20 c. brown and violet 30 30

1958. Sports.
320 **60** 2 c. lilac (postage) 10 10
321 – 4 c. green (Football) 10 10
322 – 5 c. red (Discus) 10 10
323 – 6 c. black (Motor-cycling) 10 10
324 – 8 c. blue (Fencing) 10 10
325 – 10 c. orange (Archery) 10 10
326 – 25 c. green (Boxing) 10 10
327 – 60 c. brn (air) (Running) 10 10
328 – 1 s. 20 blue (Cycling) 15 15
329 – 1 s. 50 red (Basketball) 20 15
The 4, 6, 10 and 25 c. are horiz.

61 The Constitution and Assembly Building, Mogadishu 62 White Stork

1959. Opening of Constituent Assembly. Inscr "ASSEMBLEA CONSTITUENTE".
330 **61** 5 c. blue & green (postage) 10 10
331 25 c. blue and brown 10 10
332 – 1 s. 20 blue and brown (air) 25 25
333 – 1 s. 50 blue and green 25 25
DESIGNS—HORIZ: 1 s. 20, 1 s. 50, Police bugler.

1959. Somali Water Birds.
334 **62** 5 c. black, red & yellow (postage) 20 10
335 – 10 c. red, yellow & brown 20 10
336 – 15 c. black and orange 20 10
337 – 25 c. black, orange & red 20 10
338 – 1 s. 20 black, red and violet (air) 1·10 50
339 – 2 s. red and blue 1·10 50
BIRDS—VERT: 10 c. Saddle-bill stork; 15 c. Sacred ibis; 25 c. Pink-backed pelicans. HORIZ: 1 s. 20, Marabou stork; 2 s. Great egret.

63 Incense Tree 64 Institute Badge

1959. 5th Somali Fair.
340 **63** 20 c. blk & orge (postage) 10 10
341 – 60 c. black, red & orange 20 20
342 – 1 s. 20 black and red (air) 25 25
343 – 2 s. black, brown and blue 40 40
DESIGNS—VERT: 60 c. Somali child with incense-burner. HORIZ: 1 s. 20, Ancient Egyptian transport of incense; 2 s. Incense-burner and Mogadishu Harbour.

1960. Opening of University Institute of Somalia, Mogadishu.
344 **64** 5 c. red & brown (postage) 10 10
345 – 50 c. brown and blue 10 10
346 – 80 c. black and red 20 20
347 – 45 c. brown, black and green (air) 20 20
348 – 1 s. 20 blue, black & lt bl 35 35
DESIGNS—HORIZ: 45 c., 1 s. 20, Institute buildings; 50 c. Map of Africa. VERT: 80 c. Institute emblem.

65 "The Horn of Africa"

1960. World Refugee Year.
349 **65** 10 c. green, black and brown (postage) 10 10
350 – 60 c. brown, ochre & blk 10 10
351 – 80 c. green, black & pink 10 10
352 – 1 s. 50 red, blue and green (air) 1·00 40
DESIGNS—HORIZ: 60 c. Similar to Type **65**. VERT: 80 c. Palm; 1 s. 50, White stork.

REPUBLIC

1960. Optd **Somaliland Independence 26. June 1960.**
353 10 c. yellow, green & lilac (No. 290c) (postage) 12·00 12·00
354 50 c. black, orange and violet (No. 293) (air) 22·00 17·00
355 1 s. 20 blk, orge & turq (No. 295) 19·00 17·00
Nos. 353/5 were only issued in the former British protectorate, which united with Somalia when the latter became independent on 1st July, 1960.

67 Gazelle and Map of Africa 68 Olympic Flame and Somali Flag

1960. Proclamation of Independence.
356 **67** 5 c. brn, bl & lilac (post) 20 20
357 – 25 c. blue 35 35
358 – 1 s. brown, red & green (air) 40 20
359 – 1 s. 80 blue and orange 1·10 90
DESIGNS—VERT: 25 c. U.N. Flag and Headquarters Building. HORIZ: 1 s. Chamber of Deputies, Montecitorio Palace, Rome; 1 s. 80, Somali Flag.

1960. Olympic Games. Inscr "1960".
360 **68** 5 c. blue & grn (postage) 15 10
361 – 10 c. blue and yellow 15 10
362 – 45 c. blue and lilac (air) 10 15
363 – 1 s. 80 blue and red 1·10 95
DESIGNS: 10 c. Relay race; 45 c. Runner breasting tape; 1 s. 80, Runner.

69 Child drawing Giraffe 70 Girl harvesting Papaws

1960. Child Welfare. Inscr "PRO INFANZIA".
364 **69** 10 c. black, brown and green (postage) 10 10
365 – 15 c. black, lt green & red 15 15
366 – 25 c. brown, black & yell 30 30
367 – 3 s. orange, black, blue and green (air) 1·60 1·10
ANIMALS: 15 c. Common zebra; 25 c. Black rhinoceros; 3 s. Leopard.

1961. Multicoloured. Designs each show a girl harvesting.
368 5 c. Type **70** 10 10
369 10 c. Girl harvesting durra 10 10
370 20 c. Cotton 15 15
371 25 c. Sesame 15 15
372 40 c. Sugar cane 20 20
373 50 c. Bananas 35 35
374 75 c. Groundnuts (horiz) 55 55
375 80 c. Grapefruit (horiz) 1·10 1·10

71 "Amauris hyalites" 72 Shield, Bow and Arrow, Quiver and Dagger

1961. Air. Butterflies. Multicoloured.
376 60 c. Type **71** 25 15
377 90 c. "Euryphura chalcis" 30 20
378 1 s. "Papilio lormieri" 3·25 25
379 1 s. 80 "Druryia antimachus" 75 45
380 3 s. "Danaus formosa" 90 60
381 5 s. "Papilio phorcas" 3·25 90
382 10 s. "Charaxes cynthia" 6·75 2·40

1961. 6th Somali Trade Fair.
383 **72** 25 c. yellow, black and red (postage) 10 10
384 – 45 c. yellow, blk & green 20 20
385 – 1 s. yellow, blk & bl (air) 55 45
386 – 1 s. 80 brown, blk & yell 1·10 65
DESIGNS—Handicrafts—VERT: 45 c. "Tungi" wooden vase and pottery. HORIZ: 1 s. National head-dress, support and comb; 1 s. 80, Statuettes of camel and man, and balancing novelty.

73 Girl embroidering 74 Mosquito

1962. Child Welfare. Tropical Fishes. Inscr "PRO INFANZIA". Multicoloured.
387 15 c. Type **73** (postage) 15 15
388 25 c. Blue angelfish 15 15
389 40 c. Wrasse 80 80
390 2 s. 70 Red snapper (air) 2·25 1·10

1962. Malaria Eradication. Inscr "MONDO UNITO CONTRO LA MALARIA".
391 **74** 10 c. green & red (postage) 15 15
392 – 25 c. brown and mauve 30 30
393 – 1 s. brown and black (air) 55 20
394 – 1 s. 80 green and black 1·10 90
DESIGNS—VERT: 25 c. Insecticide sprayer; 1 s., 1 s. 80, Campaign emblem and mosquitoes.

75 Auxiliaries tending Casualty 76 Wooden Spoon and Fork

1963. Women's Auxiliary Forces Formation. Multicoloured.
395 5 c. Policewoman (postage) 10 10
396 10 c. Army auxiliary 20 20
397 25 c. Policewomen with patrol car 35 35
398 75 c. Type **75** 45 45
399 1 s. Policewomen marching with flag (air) 55 35
400 1 s. 80 Army auxiliaries at attention with flag 1·40 80
The 5 c., 10 c. and 25 c. are horiz.

1963. Freedom from Hunger.
401 **76** 75 c. brn & grn (postage) 45 45
402 – 1 s. multicoloured (air) 1·10 65
DESIGN: 1 s. Sower.

77 Pres. Osman and Arms 78 Open-air Theatre

1963. 3rd Anniv of Independence. Arms in blue and yellow.
403 **77** 25 c. sepia & blue (postage) 30 15
404 1 s. sepia and red (air) 65 35
405 1 s. 80 sepia and green 1·00 55

1963. 7th Somali Fair.
406 **78** 25 c. green (postage) 20 20
407 – 55 c. red 65 45
408 – 1 s. 80 blue (air) 1·40 90
DESIGNS: 55 c. African Trade Building; 1 s. 80, Government Pavilion.

HAVE YOU READ THE NOTES AT THE BEGINNING OF THIS CATALOGUE?
These often provide the answers to the enquiries we receive.

79 Credit Bank, Mogadishu

80 Running

1964. 10th Anniv of Somali Credit Bank. Multicoloured.

409 60 c. Type **79** (postage) . . . 45 20
410 1 s. Map of Somalia and globe (air) 90 45
411 1 s. 80 Bank emblem . . . . 1·40 90

1964. Olympic Games, Tokyo. Colours: sepia, brown and blue.

412 10 c. Type **80** (postage) . . . 15 15
413 25 c. High-jumping 20 20
414 90 c. Diving (air) 55 45
415 1 s. 80 Footballer . . . . . . 1·10 65

81 Douglas DC-3 Airliner

1964. Inaug of Somali Airlines.

416 **81** 5 c. blue and red (postage) 20 35
417 – 20 c. blue and orange . . . 65 35
418 – 1 s. ochre and green (air) . 1·10 55
419 – 1 s. 80 blue and black . . . 2·25 1·60

DESIGNS: 20 c. Passengers disembarking from DC-3; DC-3 in flight over: 1 s. African elephants; 1 s. 80, Mogadishu.

82 Refugees

83 I.T.U. Emblem on Map of Africa

1964. Somali Refugees Fund.

420 **82** 25 c. + 10 c. red and blue (postage) 55 20
421 – 75 c. + 20 c. purple, black and red (air) 45 45
422 – 1 s. 80 + 50 c. green, black and bistre . . . . . . 1·50 1·25

DESIGNS—HORIZ: 75 c. Ruined houses. VERT: 1 s. 80, Soldier with child refugees.

1965. I.T.U. Centenary.

423 **83** 25 c. blue & orge (postage) 45 10
424 1 s. black and green (air) . 85 55
425 1 s. 80 brown and mauve . 1·60 1·10

84 Tanning

1965. Somali Industries.

426 **84** 10 c. sepia and buff (postage) 15 15
427 – 25 c. sepia and pink 20 15
428 – 35 c. sepia and blue 35 15
429 – 1 s. 50 sepia and grn (air) . 1·10 55
430 – 2 s. sepia and mauve . . . 2·25 1·10

DESIGNS: 25 c. Meat processing and canning; 35 c. Fish processing and canning; 1 s. 50, Sugar-cutting cane and refining; 2 s. Dairying-milking and bottling.

85 Hottentot Fig and Gazelle

1965. Somali Flora and Fauna. Multicoloured.

431 20 c. Type **85** 10 10
432 60 c. African tulips and giraffes 20 10
433 1 s. White lotus and greater flamingoes 45 20
434 1 s. 30 Pervincia and ostriches 90 45
435 1 s. 80 Bignonia and common zebras . . . . 2·25 80

86 Narina Trogon

1966. Somali Birds. Multicoloured.

436 25 c. Type **86** 45 10
437 35 c. Bateleur (vert) 60 10
438 50 c. Ruppell's griffon . . . 75 25
439 1 s. 30 Common roller . . . 1·50 35
440 2 s. Vulturine guineafowl (vert) 1·75 55

87 Globe and U.N. Emblem

1966. 21st Anniv of U.N.O. Multicoloured.

441 35 c. Type **87** 35 15
442 1 s. Map of Africa and U.N. emblem 45 20
443 1 s. 50 Map of Somalia and U.N. emblem 90 45

88 Woman sitting on Crocodile

1966. Somali Art. Showing Paintings from Garesa Museum, Mogadishu. Multicoloured.

444 25 c. Type **88** 10 10
445 1 s. Woman and warrior . . 20 10
446 1 s. 50 Boy leading camel . . 45 20
447 2 s. Women pounding grain . 90 55

89 U.N.E.S.C.O. Emblem and Palm

90 Oribi

1966. 20th Anniv of U.N.E.S.C.O.

448 **89** 35 c. black, red and grey . 10 10
449 1 s. black, green & yellow 15 10
450 1 s. 80 black, blue & red . 85 45

1967. Antelopes.

451 **90** 35 c. ochre, black & blue . 10 10
452 – 60 c. brown, black & orge 15 15
453 – 1 s. bistre, black and red . 30 20
454 – 1 s. 80 ochre, black & grn 1·10 60

ANTELOPES: 60 c. Kirk's dik-dik; 1 s. Gerenuk gazelle; 1 s. 80, Soemmering's gazelle.

91 Somali Dancers

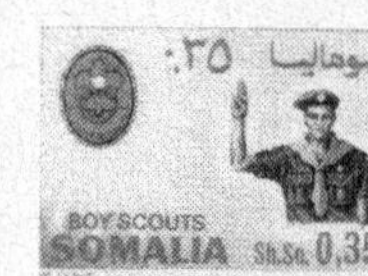

92 Badge and Scout Saluting

1967. "Popular Dances". Designs showing dancers.

455 **91** 25 c. multicoloured . . . 10 10
456 – 50 c. multicoloured . . . 10 10
457 – 1 s. 30 multicoloured . . . 35 30
458 – 2 s. multicoloured . . . . 1·10 60

1967. World Scout Jamboree. Multicoloured.

459 35 c. Type **92** 10 10
460 50 c. Scouts and flags 15 10
461 1 s. Camp scene 40 20
462 1 s. 80 Jamboree emblem . . 1·00 65

93 Pres. Schermarche and King Faisal

1967. Visit of King Faisal of Saudi Arabia.

463 **93** 50 c. black & blue (postage) 20 10
464 – 1 s. multicoloured 45 35
465 – 1 s. 80 multicoloured (air) 90 55

DESIGNS: 1 s. Somali and Saudi Arabian flags; 1 s. 80, Kaaba, Mecca and portraits as Type **93**.

94 Sweetlips

1967. Fishes. Multicoloured.

466 35 c. Type **94** 10 10
467 50 c. Butterfly fish 20 10
468 1 s. Lunar-tailed bullseye . . . 45 35
469 1 s. 80 Speckled grouper . . . 90 55

95 Inoculation

96 Somali Girl with Lemons

1968. 20th Anniv of W.H.O.

470 **95** 35 c. multicoloured 10 10
471 – 1 s. black, brown & green 20 20
472 – 1 s. 80 blac brn & orge . . 90 55

DESIGNS: 1 s. Chest examination; 1 s. 80, Heart examination.

1968. Agricultural Produce. Multicoloured.

473 5 c. Type **96** 10 10
474 10 c. Oranges 10 10
475 25 c. Coconuts 10 10
476 35 c. Papaws 15 10
477 40 c. Mangoes 15 10
478 50 c. Grapefruit 15 10
479 1 s. Bananas 55 20
480 1 s. 30 Cotton bolls 85 45

Each design includes a Somali girl.

97 Waterbuck

98 Throwing the Javelin

1968. Somali Antelopes. Multicoloured.

481 1 s. 50 Type **97** 35 20
482 1 s. 80 Speke's gazelle 45 35
483 2 s. Lesser kudu 60 35
484 5 s. Hunter's hartebeest . . . 1·40 80
485 10 s. Dibatag gazelle . . . . 4·50 1·60

1968. Olympic Games, Mexico.

486 **98** 35 c. black, brown & lemon 10 10
487 – 50 c. black, brown & red . 10 10
488 – 80 c. black, brown & pur . 20 20
489 – 1 s. 50 black, brown & grn . 1·40 65

DESIGNS: 50 c. Running; 80 c. Pole-vaulting; 1 s. 50, Basketball.

99 Great Egret

100 "Pounding Meal"

1968. Air. Birds. Multicoloured.

491 35 c. Type **99** 35 20
492 1 s. Carmine bee eater 60 20
493 1 s. 30 Yellow-bellied green pigeon . . . . 1·00 45
494 1 s. 80 Paradise whydah . . . 2·75 80

1968. Somali Art.

495 **100** 25 c. brown, black & lilac . 15 10
496 – 35 c. brown, black & red . 15 10
497 – 2 s. 80 brown, blk & grn . 20 20

DESIGNS (wood-carvings): 35 c. "Preparing food"; 2 s. 80, "Rug-making".

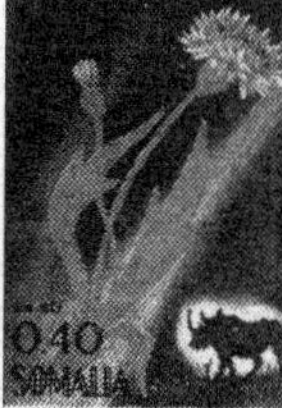

101 Cornflower

102 Workers at Anvil

1969. Flowers. Multicoloured.

498 40 c. Type **101** 10 10
499 80 c. Sunflower 20 15
500 1 s. Oleander 55 30
501 1 s. 80 Chrysanthemum . . . 1·40 85

1969. 50th Anniv of I.L.O. Multicoloured.

502 25 c. Type **102** 10 10
503 1 s. Ploughing with oxen . . . 20 20
504 1 s. 80 Drawing water for irrigation 80 45

103 Gandhi, and Hands releasing Dove

1969. Birth Centenary of Mahatma Gandhi.

505 – 35 c. purple 10 10
506 **103** 1 s. 50 orange 45 30
507 – 1 s. 80 brown . . . . . . 1·10 70

DESIGNS—VERT—(Size 25½ × 36 mm): 35 c. Mahatma Gandhi; 1 s. 80, Gandhi seated.

SOMALI DEMOCRATIC REPUBLIC

An issue for the "Apollo 11" Moon Landing was prepared in 1970, but not issued.

104 "Charaxes varanes"

105 Lenin with Children

1970. Butterflies. Multicoloured.

508 25 c. Type **104** 15 10
509 50 c. "Cethosia lamarcki" . . 40 10
510 1 s. 50 "Troides aeacus" . . . 55 45
511 2 s. "Chrysiridia ripheus" . . 1·40 55

1970. Birth Centenary of Lenin.

512 **105** 25 c. multicoloured . . . 10 10
513 – 1 s. multicoloured 20 15
514 – 1 s. 80 black, orange and brown 80 55

DESIGNS—VERT: 1 s. Lenin making speech. HORIZ: 1 s. 80, Lenin at desk.

106 Dove feeding Young

1970. 10th Anniv of Independence.

515 25 c. Type **106** 10 10
516 35 c. Dagahtur Memorial . . 10 10
517 1 s. Somali arms (vert) . . . 35 20
518 2 s. 80 Camel and star (vert) 1·10 90

107 Tractor and Produce

1970. 1st Anniv of 21st October Revolution.

519 **107** 35 c. multicoloured . . . 10 10
520 – 40 c. black and blue . . . 10 10
521 – 1 s. black and brown . . 35 20
522 – 1 s. 80 multicoloured . . 80 45

DESIGNS: 40 c. Soldier and flag; 1 s. Hand on open book; 1 s. 80, Emblems of Peace, Justice and Prosperity.

108 African within Snake's Coils

1971. Racial Equality Year.

523 **108** 1 s. 30 multicoloured . . 45 20
524 – 1 s. 80 black, red & brn . 65 45

DESIGN: 1 s. 80, Human figures, chain and barbed wire.

109 I.T.U. Emblem

1971. World Telecommunications Day.
525 **109** 25 c. black, ultram & bl . . . 10 10
526 – 2 s. 80 black, blue & grn . 1·10 65
DESIGN: 2 s. 80, Global emblem.

110 Telecommunications Map

1971. Pan-African Telecommunications Network.
527 **110** 1 s. green, black & blue . . 35 20
528 – 1 s. 50 black, grn & yell . 80 35
DESIGN: 1 s. 50, similar to Type **110** but with different network pattern.

111 White Rhinoceros

1971. Wild Animals.
529 **111** 35 c. multicoloured . . . 20 20
530 – 1 s. multicoloured 35 35
531 – 1 s. 30 black, yellow and violet 90 90
532 – 1 s. 80 multicoloured . . . 1·40 1·40
DESIGNS: 1 s. Cheetahs; 1 s. 30, Common zebras; 1 s. 80, Lion attacking dromedary.

112 Ancient Desert City

1971. East and Central African Summit Conference, Mogadishu.
533 **112** 1 s. 30 brown, blk & red . 55 55
534 – 1 s. 50 multicoloured . . . 95 95
DESIGN: 1 s. 50, Headquarters building, Mogadishu.

113 Memorial

1971. 2nd Anniv of Revolution.
535 **113** 10 c. black, cobalt & blue . 10 10
536 – 1 s. multicoloured 30 30
537 – 1 s. 35 multicoloured . . . 1·00 1·00
DESIGNS: 1 s. Agricultural workers; 1 s. 35, Building workers.

114 Inoculating Cattle

1971. Rinderpest Control Programme. Multicoloured.
538 40 c. Type **114** 55 35
539 1 s. 80 Herdsmen with cattle . 1·10 80

115 A.P.U. Emblem and Back of Airmail Envelope

1972. 10th Anniv of African Postal Union.
540 1 s. 50 A.P.U. emblem and dove with letter (postage) 80 55
541 1 s. 30 Type **115** (air) 90 65

116 Mother and Child 117 Dromedary

1972. 25th Anniv of U.N.I.C.E.F.
542 **116** 50 c. black, brown and light brown 20 10
543 – 2 s. 80 multicoloured . . 1·40 1·00
DESIGNS—HORIZ: 2 s. 80, U.N.I.C.E.F. emblem and schoolchildren.

1972. Domestic Animals.
544 **117** 5 c. multicoloured 10 10
545 – 10 c. multicoloured . . . 10 10
546 – 20 c. multicoloured . . . 10 10
547 – 40 c. black, brown & red 20 20
548 – 1 s. 70 black, green & black 1·60 1·60
DESIGNS: 10 c. Cattle on quayside; 20 c. Bull; 40 c. Black-headed sheep; 1 s. 70, Goat.

118 Child within Cupped Hands

1972. 3rd Anniv of 21st October Revolution. Multicoloured.
549 70 c. Type **118** 20 10
550 1 s. Parade of standards . . . 30 15
551 1 s. 50 Youth Camps emblem 90 55

119 Folk Dancers

1973. Folk Dances. Multicoloured.
552 5 c. Type **119** 10 10
553 40 c. Pair of dancers (vert) . 10 10
554 1 s. Team of dancers (vert) . 45 20
555 2 s. Three dancers . . . . . 1·00 55

120 Old Alphabet in Flames 121 Soldiers and Chains within O.A.U. Emblem

1973. Introduction of New Somali Script.
556 **120** 40 c. multicoloured . . . 10 10
557 – 1 s. multicoloured 20 15
558 – 2 s. black, stone & yellow 80 55
DESIGNS—HORIZ: 1 s. Alphabet in sun's rays; 2 s. Writing new script.

1974. 10th Anniv (1973) of Organization of African Unity. Multicoloured.
559 40 c. Type **121** 20 10
560 2 s. Spiral on map of Africa 90 65

122 Hurdling 123 Somali Youth and Girl

1974. Sports.
561 **122** 50 c. black, red & orange 15 10
562 – 1 s. black, grey & green . 35 20
563 – 1 s. 40 black, grey & olive 90 55
DESIGNS—HORIZ: 1 s. Running. VERT: 1 s. 40, Basketball.

1974. Guulwade Youth Movement. Multicoloured.
564 40 c. Type **123** 10 10
565 2 s. Guulwade members helping old woman . . . . 1·00 65

124 Map of League Members

1974. 30th Anniv (1975) of Arab League. Multicoloured.
566 1 s. 50 Type **124** 55 35
567 1 s. 70 Flags of Arab League countries 85 55

125 Desert Landscape

1975. 5th Anniv of 21 October Revolution. Multicoloured.
568 40 c. Type **125** 20 15
569 2 s. Somali villagers reading books (vert) 90 65

126 Doves 128

1975. Centenary of U.P.U. Multicoloured.
570 50 c. Type **126** 30 10
571 3 s. Mounted postman . . . . 2·00 1·00

1975. African Postal Union. As T **126**. Multicoloured.
572 1 s. Maps of Africa (repetitive motif) 35 20
573 1 s. 50 Dove with letter . . . . 1·00 65

1975. Traditional Costumes.
574 **128** 10 c. multicoloured 10 10
575 – 40 c. multicoloured 10 10
576 – 50 c. multicoloured 15 10
577 – 1 s. multicoloured 35 20
578 – 5 s. multicoloured . . . . 2·10 85
579 – 10 s. multicoloured . . . . 4·50 2·50
DESIGNS: 40 c. to 10 s. Various costumes.

129 Independence Square, Mogadishu 130 Hassan Statue

1976. Int Women's Year. Multicoloured.
580 50 c. Type **129** 30 10
581 2 s. 30 I.W.Y. emblem (horiz) 1·40 1·00

1976. Sayed M. A. Hassan Commemoration. Multicoloured.
582 50 c. Type **130** 15 10
583 60 c. Hassan directing warriors (vert) 20 10
584 1 s. 50 Hassan inspiring warriors (vert) 55 35
585 2 s. 30 Hassan leading attack 1·60 55

131 Nurse and Child 132 Noted Graceful Cowrie

1976. Famine Relief. Multicoloured.
586 75 c. + 25 c. Type **131** 45 45
587 80 c. + 20 c. Devastated land (horiz) 45 45
588 2 s. 40 + 10 c. Somali family with produce 80 80
589 2 s. 90 + 10 c. Relief emblem and medical officer (horiz) . . . 1·60 1·60

1976. Somali Sea Shells. Multicoloured.
590 50 c. Type **132** 30 15
591 75 c. "Charonia bardayi" . . . 30 15
592 1 s. Townsend's scallop . . . 50 25
593 2 s. Ranzani's triton . . . . . 1·25 60
594 2 s. 75 Clay cone . . . . . . 1·50 95
595 2 s. 90 Old's conch . . . . . 2·25 95

133 Benin Head and Hunters

1977. Second World Black and African Festival of Arts and Cultures, Lagos, Nigeria. Multicoloured.
597 50 c. Type **133** 20 15
598 75 c. Handicrafts 35 30
599 2 s. Dancers 85 65
600 2 s. 90 Musicians . . . . . . 1·60 1·10
The Benin Head appears on all designs.

134 Somali Flags 135 Hunting Dog

1977. 1st Anniv of Somali Socialist Revolutionary Party. Multicoloured.
601 75 c. Type **134** 20 10
602 1 s. Somali Arms (horiz) . . . 35 20
603 1 s. 50 Pres. Barre and globe (horiz) 55 35
604 2 s. Arms over rising sun . . 85 45

1977. Protected Animals. Multicoloured.
605 50 c. Type **135** 15 10
606 75 c. Lesser bushbaby 20 10
607 1 s. African ass 45 20
608 1 s. 50 Aardwolf 55 35
609 2 s. Greater kudu . . . . . . 1·10 55
610 3 s. Giraffe . . . . 2·00 90

136 Leonardo da Vinci's Drawing of Helicopter 137 Dome of the Rock

1977. 30th Anniv of I.C.A.O. Multicoloured.
612 1 s. Type **136** 35 25
613 1 s. 50 Montgolfier Brothers' balloon 45 35
614 2 s. Wright Flyer I 65 45
615 2 s. 90 Boeing 720B of Somali Airlines . . . . 1·40 65

1978. Palestine Freedom-Fighters.
617 **137** 75 c. black, green & pink 20 10
618 2 s. black, red and blue . 90 55

138 Stadium and Footballer

1978. World Cup Football Championship, Argentina. Multicoloured.
619 1 s. 50 Type **138** 45 35
620 4 s. 90 Stadium and goalkeeper 1·50 1·00
621 5 s. 50 Stadium and footballer (different) . . . . 2·00 1·40

139 "Acacia tortilis"

1978. Trees. Multicoloured.
623 40 c. Type **139** 15 10
624 50 c. "Ficus sycomorus" (vert) 30 20
625 75 c. "Terminalia catapa" (vert) 45 35
626 2 s. 90 "Adansonia digitata" 1·40 65

140 "Hibiscus rosa-sinensis"

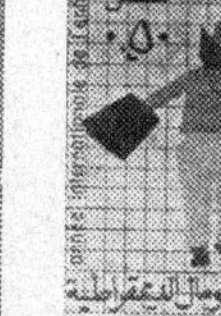
142 "Child going to School" (Ahmed Dahir Mohamed)

141 Fishing from Punt and "Siganus rivulatus"

1978. Flowers. Multicoloured.
627 50 c. Type **140** 20 10
628 1 s. "Cassia baccarinii" . . . 45 20
629 1 s. 50 "Kigelia somalensis" . 80 45
630 2 s. 30 "Dichrostachys glomerata" . . . . 1·40 65

1979. Fishing. Multicoloured.
632 75 c. Type **141** 20 10
633 80 c. Fishing from felucca and "Gaterin gaterinus" 20 15
634 2 s. 30 Fishing fleet and "Hypacanthus amia" . . . 1·00 55
635 2 s. 50 Trawler and "Scomberomorus commersoni" . . . . 1·40 85

1979. International Year of the Child. Children's Paintings. Multicoloured.
636 50 c. Type **142** 15 10
637 75 c. "Sailboat" (M. A. Mohamed) 20 15
638 1 s. 50 "House in the Country" (A. M. Ali) 45 30
639 3 s. "Bird on Blossoming Branch" (A. A. Siyad) . . . 1·10 65

143 University Students and Open-air Class

1979. 10th Anniv of Revolution. Multicoloured.
641 20 c. Type **143** 10 10
642 50 c. Housing construction . . 10 10
643 75 c. Children at play . . . 20 10
644 1 s. Health and agriculture . . 35 20
645 2 s. 40 Hydro-electric power 80 45
646 3 s. Telecommunications . . . 1·25 65

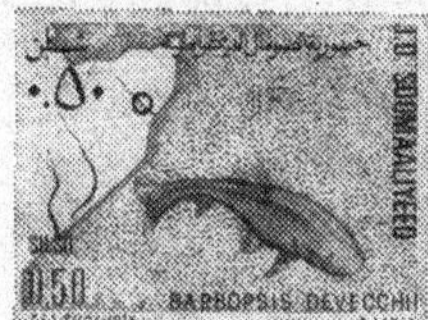
144 "Barbopsis devecchii"

1979. Fish. Multicoloured.
647 50 c. Type **144** 20 10
648 90 c. "Phreatichthys andruzzi" 50 20
649 1 s. "Uegitglanis zammaranoi" 65 35
650 2 s. 50 "Pardiglanis tarabinii" 1·10 65

145 Taleh Fortress

1980. 1st International Congress of Somali Studies.
652 **145** 2 s. 25 multicoloured . . . 85 45
653 3 s. 50 multicoloured . . . 1·10 65

146 Marka

1980. Landscapes (1st series). Multicoloured.
654 75 c. Type **146** 20 10
655 1 s. Gandershe 35 20
656 2 s. 30 Afgooye 85 35
657 3 s. 50 Mogadishu . . . . . 1·10 65
See also Nos. 673/6.

147 Pygmy Puff-back Flycatcher

148 Parabolic Antenna and Shepherd

1980. Birds. Multicoloured.
658 1 s. Type **147** 65 20
659 2 s. 25 Golden-winged grosbeak 1·60 35
660 5 s. Red-crowned bush shrike 2·75 1·10

1981. World Telecommunications Day.
662 **148** 1 s. multicoloured 40 20
663 – 3 s. blue, black and red . . 1·00 55
664 – 4 s. 60 multicoloured . . 1·40 90
DESIGNS: 3 s., 4 s. 60, Ribbons forming caduceus, I.T.U. and W.H.O. emblems.

149 F.A.O. Emblem and Stylised Wheat

150 Refugee Family

1981. World Food Day. Multicoloured.
665 75 c. Type **149** 20 15
666 3 s. 25 F.A.O. emblem on stylized field (horiz) . . . . 1·10 55
667 5 s. 50 Type **149** . . . . . . 2·00 95

1981. Refugee Aid.
668 **150** 2 s. + 50 c. multicoloured 70 45
669 6 s. 80 + 50 c. multicoloured 2·50 1·25

151 Mosques, Mecca and Medina

153 Footballer

1981. 1500th Anniv of Hejira.
671 **151** 1 s. 50 multicoloured . . 45 35
672 3 s. 80 multicoloured . . 1·50 80

1982. Landscapes (2nd series). As T **146**. Multicoloured.
673 2 s. 25 Balcad 80 45
674 4 s. Jowhar . . . . 1·40 90
675 5 s. 50 Golaleey . . . . . . 1·60 1·10
676 8 s. 30 Muqdisho . . . . . . 2·75 2·00

1982. World Cup Football Championship, Spain. Multicoloured.
677 1 s. Type **153** 35 20
678 1 s. 50 Footballer running to right 80 45
679 3 s. 25 Footballer running to left 1·60 1·00

154 I.T.U. Emblem

1982. I.T.U. Delegates' Conference, Nairobi.
681 **154** 75 c. multicoloured 20 15
682 3 s. 25 multicoloured . . . 1·10 65
683 5 s. 50 multicoloured . . . 2·00 1·10

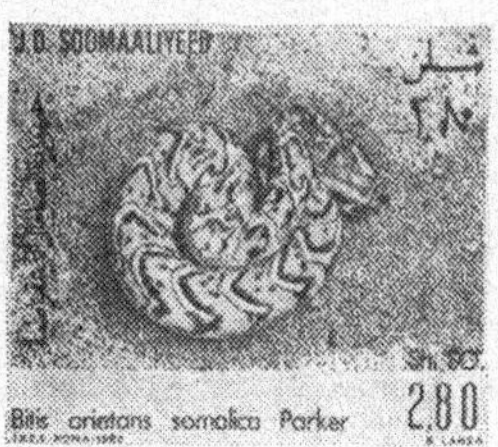
155 "Bitis arietans somalica"

1982. Snakes. Multicoloured.
684 2 s. 80 Type **155** . . . . 1·10 45
685 3 s. 20 "Psammophis punctulatus trivirgatus" . . . . 1·60 65
686 4 s. 60 "Rhamphiophis oxyrhynchis rostratus" . . . 2·25 1·10

156 Bacillus, Microscope and Dr. Robert Koch

1982. Centenary of Discovery of Tubercle Bacillus.
688 **156** 4 s. 60 + 60 c mult . . . 1·10 1·10
689 5 s. 80 + 60 c. mult . . . 1·40 1·40

157 Somali Woman

158 W.C.Y. Emblem

1982.
690 **157** 1 s. multicoloured 15 10
691 5 s. 20 multicoloured . . . 80 35
692 5 s. 80 multicoloured . . . 1·00 45
693 6 s. 40 multicoloured . . . 1·10 60
694 9 s. 40 multicoloured . . . 1·60 1·00
695 25 s. multicoloured . . . . 4·25 1·60

1983. World Communications Year.
696 **158** 5 s. 20 multicoloured . . . 45 35
697 6 s. 40 multicoloured . . . 85 40

159 View of Hamburg

1983. 2nd International Congress of Somali Studies, Hamburg. Multicoloured.
698 5 s. 20 Type **159** 85 65
699 6 s. 40 View of Hamburg (different) . . . . 1·25 1·00

160 Air Force Uniform

1983. Military Uniforms. Multicoloured.
700 3 s. 20 Type **160** 85 55
701 3 s. 20 Women's Auxiliary Corps 85 55
702 3 s. 20 Border Police 85 55
703 3 s. 20 People's Militia 85 55
704 3 s. 20 Infantry 85 55
705 3 s. 20 Custodial Corps 85 55
706 3 s. 20 Police Force 85 55
707 3 s. 20 Navy 85 55

161 Barawe

1983. Landscapes. Multicoloured.
708 2 s. 80 Type **161** 55 35
709 3 s. 20 Bur Hakaba 65 45
710 5 s. 50 Baydhabo . . . . . . 1·00 60
711 8 s. 60 Dooy Nuunaay . . . 1·60 1·10

162 "Volutocorbis rosavittoriae"

1984. Shells. Multicoloured.
712 2 s. 80 Type **162** 80 40
713 3 s. 20 Valdiva bonnet . . . . 1·25 50
714 5 s. 50 Glory of India cone 3·00 1·00

163 Running

165 Girl holding Spider Conch to Ear

164 North African Crested Porcupine

1984. Olympic Games, Los Angeles. Multicoloured.
716 1 s. 50 Type **163** 35 20
717 3 s. Throwing the discus . . . 80 45
718 8 s. High jumping . . . . . . 2·25 1·00

1984. Mammals. Multicoloured.
720 1 s. Type **164** 20 20
721 1 s. 50 White-tailed mongoose 35 20
722 2 s. Banded mongoose 55 35
723 4 s. Ratel . . . . 1·10 65

1984. 36th International Fair, Riccione.
725 **165** 5 s. 20 multicoloured . . 2·00 65
726 6 s. 40 multicoloured . . 2·75 1·10

166 Emblem within Winged Horse

1985. 40th Anniv of International Civil Aviation Organization.
727 **166** 3 s. multicoloured 65 35
728 6 s. 40 multicoloured . . 1·10 80

167 Aquila

169 Woman and Posthorn

168 Ras Kiambone

1985. Constellations. Illustrations from "The Book of Stars" by Abd al-Rahman al-Sufi. Multicoloured.

730	4 s. 30 Type **167**	55	20
731	11 s. Taurus	1·40	65
732	12 s. 50 Aries	1·60	80
733	13 s. Orion	2·00	1·10

1985. Architecture (1st series). Multicoloured.

734	2 s. Type **168**	20	20
735	6 s. 60 Hannassa	90	35
736	10 s. Mnarani	1·10	65
737	18 s. 60 Ras Kiambone (different)	2·25	1·25

See also Nos. 758/61.

1985. "Italia '85" Stamp Exhibition, Rome.

738	**169**	2 s. multicoloured	55	35
739		20 s. multicoloured	2·75	1·40

170 Persian Leaf-nosed Bat

1985. Bats. Multicoloured.

741	2 s. 50 Type **170**	55	35
742	4 s. 50 Heart-nosed false vampire bat	85	55
743	16 s. Wrinkle-lipped bat	2·25	1·40
744	18 s. Mozambique sheath-tailed bat	2·50	1·60

171 Kenyan and Somali Presidents, Solar System and Industry

1986. Trade Agreement with Kenya.

746	**171**	9 s. multicoloured	65	45
747		14 s. 50 multicoloured	1·60	65

172 Flower Arrangement

173 Seated Man holding Pottery Flask

1986. "Euroflora" International Flower Exhibition, Genoa. Multicoloured.

748	10 s. Type **172**	65	55
749	15 s. Flower arrangement (different)	1·60	1·10

1986. 3rd International Somali Studies Conference, Rome.

751	**173**	11 s. 35 multicoloured	65	45
752		20 s. multicoloured	1·60	90

174 Footballers

1986. World Cup Football Championship, Mexico. Footballing Scenes.

753	**174**	3 s. 60 multicoloured	35	20
754	–	4 s. 80 multicoloured	45	20
755	–	6 s. 80 multicoloured	90	45
756	–	22 s. 60 multicoloured	1·50	1·10

1986. Architecture (2nd series). As T **168**. Multicoloured.

758	10 s. Bulaxaar ruins	55	30
759	15 s. Saylac mosque	85	45
760	20 s. Saylac mosque (different)	1·40	65
761	31 s. Jasiiradaha Jawaay tomb	2·25	1·10

175 Rehabilitation Centre, Mogadishu

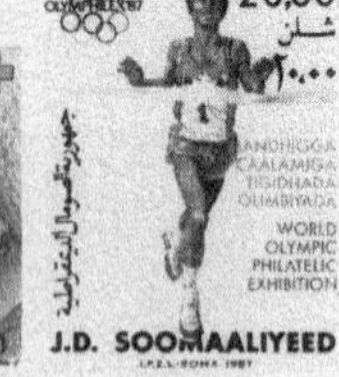

176 Runner

1987. Norwegian Red Cross in Somalia.

762	**175**	56 s. multicoloured	2·75	2·25

1987. "Olymphilex '87" Olympic Stamps Exhibition, Rome. Multicoloured.

764	20 s. Type **176**	85	55
765	40 s. Javelin thrower	2·00	1·10

177 Modern and Shanty Towns

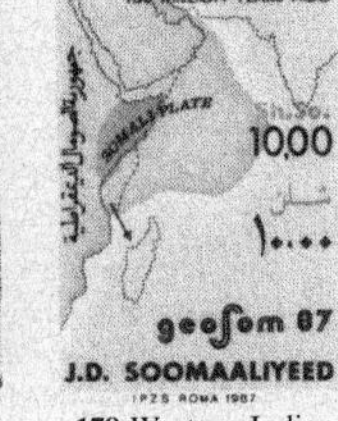

178 Western Indian Ocean 160,000,000 Years Ago

1987. International Year of Shelter for the Homeless.

767	**177**	53 s. multicoloured	1·40	65
768		72 s. multicoloured	2·00	1·10

1987. "Geosom 87" Geological Evolution of Western Indian Ocean Symposium. Multicoloured.

769	10 s. Type **178**	20	10
770	20 s. 60,000,000 years ago	55	20
771	40 s. 15,000,000 years ago	90	45
772	50 s. Today	1·60	90

179 Baby receiving Oral Vaccination (Italian inscr)

180 Somali Hare

1988. 40th Anniv of W.H.O.

774	**179**	50 s. multicoloured	45	20
775		168 s. multicoloured (English inscr)	1·75	90

1989. Animals. Multicoloured.

776	75 s. Type **180**	45	20
777	198 s. African buffalo	1·10	35
778	200 s. Hamadryas baboon (horiz)	1·25	45
779	216 s. Hippopotamus (horiz)	1·60	65

181 Water Lily and Boys playing Football

1989. 20th Anniv of 21 October Revolution. Multicoloured.

781	70 s. Type **181**	35	20
782	100 s. Boys playing on swing	45	20
783	150 s. Girls on see-saw	90	35
784	300 s. Girl skipping and boy rolling hoop	1·60	65

182 Dove and Broken Chain

183 Sun, Building and Scaffolding

1991. Liberation. (a) Type **182** (without opt).

785	**182**	150 s. multicoloured	85	35
786		300 s. multicoloured	1·60	80

(b) No. 785 additionally optd **"FREEDOM"**.

787	**182**	150 s. multicoloured	3·00	2·75

1991. Reconstruction.

788	**183**	70 s. multicoloured	35	20
789		100 s. multicoloured	55	35
790		150 s. multicoloured	80	45
791		300 s. multicoloured	1·60	65

EXPRESS LETTER STAMPS

1923. Express Letter stamps of Italy surch **Somalia Italiana** and value.

E44	**E 12**	30 b. on 60 c. red	11·00	12·00
E45	**E 13**	60 b. on 1 l. 20 blue & pink	16·00	17·00

E 17

1924.

E60	**E 17**	30 b. brown and red	8·50	6·00
E61		60 b. pink and blue	7·00	8·50

No. E61 is inscr "EXPRES".

1926. Nos. E60/1 surch.

E104	70 c. on 30 b. brown & red	5·50	6·00
E106	1 l. 25 on 30 b. brown & red	5·00	7·50
E105	2 l. 50 on 60 b. blue & pink	7·00	8·50

E 44 Grant's Gazelle

1950.

E255	**E 44**	40 c. green	1·25	60
E256		80 c. violet	1·75	1·75

E 54 "Gardenia lutea"

1955.

E291	**E 54**	50 c. yellow, grn & lilac	30	30
E292	–	1 s. red, green & blue	55	55

FLOWER: 1 s. Coral tree.

E 61 Young Gazelles

1958. Air.

E330	**E 61**	1 s. 70 red and black	85	85

OFFICIAL STAMPS

1934. Air. Rome–Mogadishu Flight. As No. 208, but colour changed, optd **SERVIZIO DI STATO** and crown.

O209	**36**	25 l. + 2 l. pink	£1400	£2750

1934. Air. As No. 193 optd **11 NOV. 1934–XIII SERVIZIO AEREO SPECIALE** and crown.

O210	25 c. blue and orange	£900	£1400

PARCEL POST STAMPS

Nos. P23 to P122 are Parcel Post stamps of Italy optd or surch on each half of stamp.

Unused prices are for complete pairs, used prices for a half stamp.

1920. Optd **SOMALIA ITALIANA.**

P23	**P 53**	5 c. brown	1·40	50
P24		10 c. blue	1·75	50
P82		20 c. black	18·00	3·75
P26		25 c. red	4·50	50
P84		50 c. orange	20·00	3·00
P28		1 l. violet	16·00	1·00
P29		2 l. green	19·00	1·50
P87		3 l. yellow	5·00	4·00
P88		4 l. grey	5·00	4·00
P89		10 l. purple	11·00	4·50
P90		12 l. brown	11·00	4·50
P91		15 l. green	11·00	4·50
P92		20 l. purple	11·00	4·50

1922. Optd **SOMALIA.**

P32	**P 53**	25 c. red	19·00	5·00
P33		50 c. orange	24·00	1·50
P34		1 l. violet	24·00	1·50
P35		2 l. green	28·00	2·00
P36		3 l. yellow	35·00	5·00
P37		4 l. grey	35·00	6·00

1923. Surch **SOMALIA ITALIANA** and value.

P44	**P 53**	3 b. on 5 c. brown	1·75	60
P45		5 b. on 5 c. brown	1·75	60
P46		10 b. on 10 c. blue	1·75	60
P47		25 b. on 25 c. red	7·00	75
P48		50 b. on 50 c. orange	12·00	1·25
P49		1 r. on 1 l. violet	17·00	1·75
P50		2 r. on 2 l. green	21·00	2·75
P51		3 r. on 3 l. yellow	24·00	4·50
P52		4 r. on 4 l. grey	26·00	7·00

1928. Optd **SOMALIA ITALIANA.**

P111	**P 92**	5 c. brown	75	80
P112		10 c. blue	1·00	80
P113		25 c. red	24·00	5·00
P114		30 c. blue	30	40

P115	P 92	50 c. orange	£10000	85·00
P116		60 c. red	30	40
P127		1 l. violet	20·00	2·00
P128		2 l. green	20·00	2·00
P119		3 l. yellow	80	80
P120		4 l. black	80	1·00
P121		10 l. mauve	£200	18·00
P122		20 l. purple	£200	18·00

P 44

1950.

P255	P 44	1 c. red	45	10
P256		3 c. violet	45	10
P257		5 c. purple	45	10
P258		10 c. orange	45	10
P259		20 c. brown	45	10
P260		50 c. green	70	20
P261		1 s. violet	3·50	50
P262		2 s. brown	4·75	80
P263		3 s. blue	5·00	1·00

POSTAGE DUE STAMPS

Nos. D17 to D199 are Postage Due stamps of Italy optd or surch.

1906. Optd **Somalia Italiana Meridionale**.

D17	D 12	5 c. mauve and orange	3·00	16·00
D18		10 c. mauve & orange	22·00	19·00
D19		20 c. mauve & orange	14·00	19·00
D20		30 c. mauve & orange	11·00	19·00
D21		40 c. mauve & orange	48·00	24·00
D22		50 c. mauve & orange	24·00	24·00
D23		60 c. mauve & orange	19·00	24·00
D24		1 l. mauve and blue	£300	80·00
D25		2 l. mauve and blue	£275	90·00
D26		5 l. mauve and blue	£275	90·00
D27		10 l. mauve and blue	65·00	£130

1909. Optd **Somalia Italiana**.

D28	D 12	5 c. mauve and orange	2·00	4·50
D29		10 c. mauve & orange	2·00	4·50
D30		20 c. mauve & orange	3·25	9·00
D31		30 c. mauve & orange	9·00	15·00
D32		40 c. mauve & orange	9·00	15·00
D33		50 c. mauve & orange	9·00	15·00
D34		60 c. mauve & orange	14·00	24·00
D35		1 l. mauve and blue	32·00	18·00
D47		2 l. mauve and blue	48·00	38·00
D48		5 l. mauve and blue	48·00	38·00
D38		10 l. mauve and blue	8·00	28·00

1923. Stamps without figures of value, surch **Somalia Italiana** and value in "besa" or "rupia" in figures and words.

D49	D 12	1 b. black and orange	75	1·75
D50		2 b. black and orange	75	1·75
D51		3 b. black and orange	75	1·75
D52		5 b. black and orange	85	1·75
D53		10 b. black and orange	85	1·75
D54		20 b. black and orange	85	1·75
D55		40 b. black and orange	85	1·75
D56		1 r. black and blue	1·25	2·50

1926. Optd **Somalia Italiana** and surch with figures only.

D76	5 c. black and orange	9·00	4·50
D77	10 c. black and orange	7·50	4·50
D78	20 c. black and orange	9·00	4·50
D79	30 c. black and orange	9·00	4·50
D80	40 c. black and orange	9·00	4·50
D81	50 c. black and orange	12·00	4·50
D82	60 c. black and orange	12·00	4·50
D83	1 l. black and blue	17·00	5·50
D84	2 l. black and blue	20·00	5·50
D85	5 l. black and blue	20·00	5·50
D86	10 l. black and blue	20·00	5·50

1934. Optd **SOMALIA ITALIANA**.

D187	D 141	5 c. brown	40	1·60
D188		10 c. blue	40	1·60
D189		20 c. red	2·50	2·50
D190		25 c. green	2·50	2·50
D191		30 c. red	5·00	5·50
D192		40 c. brown	5·00	6·00
D193		50 c. violet	6·50	1·40
D194		60 c. blue	10·00	12·00
D195	D 142	1 l. orange	13·00	3·75
D196		2 l. green	20·00	17·00
D197		5 l. violet	21·00	26·00
D198		10 l. blue	21·00	32·00
D199		20 l. red	24·00	38·00

D 44

1950.

D255	D 44	1 c. violet	20	20
D256		2 c. blue	20	20
D257		5 c. green	20	20
D258		10 c. purple	20	20
D259		40 c. violet	1·10	1·10
D260		1 s. brown	2·00	2·00

SOUTH KASAI Pt. 14

100 centimes = 1 franc

Region of Zaire around the town of Bakwanga. The area was declared autonomous in 1960, during the upheaval following independence, but returned to the control of the central government in Oct. 1962.

Various stamps of Belgian Congo were overprinted "ETAT AUTONOME DU SUD-KASAI" and some surcharged in addition with new values. These were put on sale at the Philatelic Bureau in Brussels and were also valid for use in South Kasai but no supplies were sent out.

1 Leopard's Head and "V"

2 A. D. Kalonji

1961.

1 **1** 1 f. multicoloured 10 10
2 1 f. 50 multicoloured 10 10
3 3 f. 50 multicoloured 15 15
4 8 f. multicoloured 25 25
5 10 f. multicoloured 30 30

1961.

6 **2** 6 f. 50 brown, blue and black . 20 20
7 9 f. lt brown, brown & blk . . 25 25
8 14 f. 50 brown, green & blk . . 40 40
9 20 f. multicoloured . . . . . 45 1·45

SOUTH RUSSIA Pt. 10

Stamps of various anti-Bolshevist forces and temporary governments in S. Russia after the revolution.

100 kopeks = 1 rouble

A. KUBAN TERRITORY: COSSACK GOVERNMENT

1918. Arms type of Russia surch. Imperf or perf.

8 **22** 25 k. on 1 k. orange 25 45
2 50 k. on 2 k. green 15 25
23 70 k. on 1 k. orange 30 55
10 70 k. on 5 k. red 35 60
11 1 r. on 3 k. red 20 50
13 **23** 3 r. on 4 k. red . . . . . 7·50 11·00
14 10 r. on 4 k. red . . . . . . 4·00 5·00
15 **10** 10 r. on 15 k. blue & purple 70 1·10
16 **22** 25 r. on 3 k. red . . . . . . 4·00 3·00
17 25 r. on 7 k. blue . . . . . 30·00 60·00
18 **10** 25 r. on 14 k. red and blue . 70·00 £100
19 25 r. on 25 k. mauve & grn . 35·00 65·00

1919. Postal Savings Bank stamps of Russia surch.

20 10 r. on 1 k. red on buff . . . 30·00 70·00
21 10 r. on 5 k. green on buff . . 32·00 70·00
22 10 r. on 10 k. brown on buff . . 75·00 £225

B. DON TERRITORY: COSSACK GOVERNMENT

1919. Arms type of Russia surch in figures only. Imperf or perf.

25 **22** 25 k. on 1 k. orange 20 45
29 25 k. on 2 k. green 20 40
30 25 k. on 3 k. red 25 60
31 **23** 25 k. on 4 k. red 20 45
32 **22** 50 k. on 7 k. blue . . . . . 1·75 2·75

10 T. Ermak (16th century Cossack Ataman)

13

1919. Currency stamp with arms and seven-line print on back used for postage.

33 **10** 20 k. green . . . . 16·00 £100

C. CRIMEA: REGIONAL GOVERNMENT

1919. Arms type of Russia surch **35 Коп.** Imperf.

34 **22** 35 k. on 1 k. orange 15 40

1919. Currency and postage stamp. Arms and inscription on back. Imperf.

35 **13** 50 k. brown on buff . . . . 13·00 16·00

D. SOUTH RUSSIA: GOVERNMENT OF GENERAL DENIKIN

1919. Nos. G6 and G10 of Ukraine surch in figs.

36 **G 1** 35 k. on 10 s. brown . . . . 3·75 14·00
37 **G 5** 70 k. on 50 s. red . . . . 13·00 40·00

15

16

1919. Imperf or perf.

38 **15** 5 k. yellow 10 15
39 10 k. green 10 15
40 15 k. red 10 15
41 35 k. blue 10 15
42 70 k. blue 10 15
43 **16** 1 r. red and brown 15 35
44 2 r. yellow and lilac 35 55
45 3 r. green and brown 35 60
46 5 r. violet and blue . . . . 1·00 1·50
47 7 r. pink and green . . . . 80 1·75
48 10 r. grey and red . . . . . 1·50 2·00

Higher values similar to Type **16** are bogus.

E. SOUTH RUSSIA: GOVERNMENT OF GENERAL WRANGEL

5
пять
рублей.
(17)

ЮГЪ
РОССІИ.
100
рублей.
(18)

1920. Crimea issue. Surch with T **17**. (a) On Arms types of Russia. Imperf or perf.

52 **22** 5 r. on 5 k. red . . . . . . 1·00 3·75
54 **14** 5 r. on 20 k. red and blue . 1·75 3·75

(b) On No. 41 of South Russia.

55 **15** 5 r. on 35 k. blue . . . . . 4·50 12·00

1920. Arms type of Russia surch with T **18**.

56 **22** 100 r. on 1 k. orange . . . 1·75

SOUTHERN YEMEN Pt. 19

PEOPLE'S REPUBLIC

Independent Republic comprising the areas formerly known as Aden, the Aden States and the South Arabian Federation.

From 30 November, 1970, the country was renamed The Peoples Democratic Republic of Yemen.

1000 fils = 1 dinar

1968. Stamps of South Arabian Federation optd **PEOPLE'S REPUBLIC OF SOUTHERN YEMEN** in English and Arabic.

1 **2** 5 f. blue 10 10
2 10 f. blue 10 10
3 15 f. green 10 10
4 20 f. green 10 10
5 25 f. brown 10 10
6 30 f. bistre 25 10
7 35 f. brown 20 20
8 50 f. red 35 30
9 65 f. green 40 35
10 75 f. red 55 45
11 **3** 100 f. multicoloured 80 60
12 250 f. multicoloured . . . . 1·60 1·40
13 500 f. multicoloured . . . . 3·25 2·50
14 1 d. multicoloured . . . . . 8·50 6·00

3 National Flag across Globe

1968. Independence. Multicoloured.

15 10 f. Type **3** 10 10
16 15 f. Revolutionary (vert) . . 10 10
17 50 f. Aden harbour 40 40
18 100 f. Cotton-picking . . . . 1·25 1·25

4 Girl Guides

1968. Aden Girl Guides' Movement.

19 – 10 f. brown and blue 25 25
20 – 25 f. blue and brown 35 35
21 **4** 50 f. multicoloured 65 65

DESIGNS—HORIZ: 10 f. Guides around camp-fire. VERT: 25 f. Brownies.

5 Revolutionary Soldier

1968. Revolution Day.

22 **5** 20 f. brown and blue 20 20
23 – 30 f. brown and green . . . 25 25
24 – 100 f. red and yellow . . . 85 85

DESIGNS—HORIZ: 30 f. Radfan Mountains ("where first martyr fell"). VERT: 100 f. Open book and torch ("Freedom, Socialism and Unity").

6 Sculptured Plaque "Assyrian influence")

1968. Antiquities.

25 – 5 f. yellow and green 10 10
26 – 35 f. blue and purple 35 35
27 **6** 50 f. buff and blue 75 65
28 – 65 f. green and purple . . . 95 80

DESIGNS—VERT: 5 f. King Yusdqil Far'am of Ausan (statue); 35 f. Sculptured figure ("African-inspired"). HORIZ: 65 f. Bull's head ("Moon God").

7 Martyrs' Monument, Aden

8 Albert Thomas Memorial, Geneva

1969. Martyrs' Day.

29 **7** 15 f. multicoloured 10 10
30 35 f. multicoloured 25 25
31 100 f. multicoloured 90 75

1969. 50th Anniv of I.L.O.

32 **8** 10 f. brown, black and green . 10 10
33 25 f. brown, black and mauve 40 30

9 Teacher and Class

1969. International Literacy Day.

34 **9** 35 f. multicoloured 40 30
35 100 f. multicoloured . . . . . 1·00 95

10 Mahatma Gandhi

1969. Birth Centenary of Mahatma Gandhi.

36 **10** 35 f. purple and blue . . . . 1·00 50

11 Yemeni Family

1969. Family Day.

37 **11** 25 f. multicoloured 35 25
38 75 f. multicoloured 95 70

12 U.N. Headquarters, New York

1969. United Nations Day.

39 **12** 20 f. multicoloured 20 15
40 65 f. multicoloured 70 55

13 Map and Flag

1969. 2nd Anniv of Independence. Multicoloured.

41 15 f. Type **13** 20 20
42 35 f. Type **13** 35 30
43 40 f. Bulldozers (37 × 37 mm) . 45 30
44 50 f. As No. 43 . . . . 65 45

14 Arab League Flag, Emblem and Map

1970. 25th Anniv of Arab League.

45 **14** 35 f. multicoloured 40 30

15 Lenin

16 Palestinian Guerrilla

1970. Birth Centenary of Lenin.

46 **15** 75 f. multicoloured 90 65

1970. Palestine Day. Multicoloured.

47 15 f. Type **16** 15 10
48 35 f. Guerrilla and attack on airliner 35 25
49 50 f. Guerrillas and Palestinan flag (horiz) 75 45

17 New Headquarters Building, Berne

1970. Inauguration of New U.P.U. Headquarters Building, Berne.

50 **17** 15 f. green and orange . . . 25 15
51 65 f. red and buff 55 50

18 Girl with Pitcher

1970. National Costumes. Multicoloured.

52 10 f. Type **18** 25 15
53 15 f. Woman in veil 30 25
54 20 f. Girl in burnous 45 30
55 50 f. Three Yemeni men . . . 90 45

19 Dromedary and Calf

1970. Fauna. Multicoloured.

56		15 f. Type **19**	25	20
57		25 f. Goats	45	25
58		35 f. Arabian oryx and kid	90	50
59		65 f. Socotran dwarf cows	1·50	95

20 Torch and Flags

1970. 7th Revolution Day. Multicoloured.

60		25 f. Type **20**	25	20
61		35 f. National Front Headquarters (57×27 mm)	45	40
62		50 f. Farmer and soldier (42×25 mm)	60	45

21 U.N. H.Q., New York, and Emblem

1970. 25th Anniv of United Nations.

63	**21**	10 f. orange and blue	10	10
64		65 f. mauve and blue	75	60

For later issues see **YEMEN PEOPLE'S DEMOCRATIC REPUBLIC**.

SPAIN Pt. 9

A kingdom in south-west Europe; a republic between 1873 and 1874, and from 1931 until 1939.

1850. 8½ (later 8) cuartos = 1 real.
1866. 80 cuartos = 100 centimos de escudo = 1 escudo.
1867. 1000 milesimas = 100 centimos de escudo = 80 cuartos = 1 escudo.
1872. 100 centimos = 1 peseta.

1 2 3
Queen Isabella II

1850. Imperf.

2	**1**	6 c. black	£300	11·00
3		12 c. lilac	£1700	£200
4	**2**	5 r. red	£1700	£200
5		6 r. blue	£2500	£600
6		10 r. green	£3250	£1600

1851. Imperf.

9	**3**	6 c. black	£180	2·25
10		12 c. lilac	£3000	£130
11		2 r. red	£13500	£7750
12		5 r. pink	£1700	£180
13		6 r. blue	£2750	£750
14		10 r. green	£2000	£375

4 5 7 Arms of Castile and Leon

1852. Imperf.

16	**4**	6 c. pink	£275	2·25
17		12 c. purple	£1300	£100
18		2 r. red	£11000	£3750
19		5 r. green	£1500	85·00
20		6 r. blue	£2500	£350

1853. Imperf.

22	**5**	6 c. red	£300	1·50
23		12 c. purple	£1500	85·00
24		2 r. red	£8000	£2500
25		5 r. green	£1600	85·00
26		6 r. blue	£2000	£300

1854. Imperf.

32	**7**	2 c. green	£1400	£375
33		4 c. red	£275	1·50
34		6 c. red	£225	1·10
35		1 r. blue	£2250	£250
36		2 r. red	£1100	75·00
37		5 r. green	£1100	75·00
38		6 r. blue	£1700	£225

9 12 13

1855. Imperf.

54	**9**	2 c. green	£375	28·00
55a		4 c. red	3·00	20
61		1 r. blue	14·50	16·00
57		2 r. purple	45·00	17·00

1860. Imperf.

63	**12**	2 c. green on green	£225	14·00
64		4 c. orange on green	27·00	55
65		12 c. red on buff	£225	9·25
66		19 c. brown on brown	£1900	£1000
67		1 r. blue on green	£180	8·75
68		2 r. lilac on lilac	£250	7·50

1862. Imperf.

69a	**13**	2 c. blue on yellow	25·00	7·75
70		4 c. brown on brown	1·60	40
70b		4 c. brown on white	19·00	4·75
71		12 c. blue on pink	32·00	6·50
72		19 c. red on lilac	£130	£170
72a		19 c. red on white	£190	£180
73a		1 r. brown on yellow	42·00	14·50
74		2 r. green on pink	26·00	9·25

14 15 16

1864. Imperf.

75	**14**	2 c. blue on lilac	32·00	13·50
75b		2 c. blue on white	40·00	20·00
76b		4 c. red on red	2·00	50
76c		4 c. pink on white	15·00	8·50
77a		12 c. green on pink	35·00	9·25
78		19 c. lilac on lilac	£130	£150
79		1 r. brown on green	£130	60·00
80		2 r. blue on pink	32·00	9·75
80b		2 r. blue on white	48·00	16·00

1865. Imperf.

81a	**15**	2 c. red	£200	22·00
82		12 c. pink and blue	£275	14·00
83		19 c. pink and brown	£1000	£550
84		1 r. green	£275	45·00
85		2 r. mauve	£275	23·00
85c		2 r. red	£375	45·00
85e		2 r. yellow	£350	23·00

1865. Perf.

86	**15**	2 c. red	£325	80·00
87		4 c. blue	26·00	50
88		12 c. pink and blue	£400	42·00
89		19 c. pink and brown	£2500	£1700
90		1 r. green	£1300	£375
91		2 r. lilac	£800	£170
91b		2 r. orange	£850	£200

1866. Perf.

92	**16**	2 c. pink	£180	17·00
93a		4 c. blue	29·00	55
94a		12 c. orange	£160	8·25
95		19 c. brown	£750	£300
96		10 c. de e. green	£200	18·00
97		20 c. de e. lilac	£130	14·00

1866. As T **14**, but dated 1866, and perf.

98		20 c. de e. lilac	£750	48·00

19 25 26

1867. Inscr "CORREOS DE ESPANA". Various frames.

99a	**19**	2 c. brown	£300	32·00
100		4 c. blue	17·00	65
101a		12 c. orange	£140	5·50
102		19 c. pink	£950	£275
150		19 c. brown	£1600	£350
103		10 c. de e. green	£170	16·00
104		20 c. de e. lilac	80·00	7·00

1867. Various frames.

105	**25**	5 m. green	29·00	12·00
106		10 m. brown	29·00	12·00
107	**26**	25 m. pink and blue	£170	17·00
145		25 m. blue	£180	12·00
108		50 m. brown	14·00	60
146a	**19**	50 m. purple	17·00	40
147		100 m. brown	£350	50·00
148		200 m. green	£120	8·75

1868. Various stamps optd **HABILITADO POR LA NACION.**

109	**25**	5 m. green	9·75	3·25
110		10 m. brown	8·00	3·00
111	**26**	25 m. pink and blue	21·00	7·50
151		25 m. blue	20·00	6·50
112		50 m. brown	4·00	3·25
152	**19**	50 m. purple	4·00	3·25
153		100 m. brown	45·00	15·00
154		200 m. green	15·00	5·50
113		10 c. de e. green	45·00	15·00
114		20 c. de e. lilac	15·00	5·50
115	**19**	12 c. orange	28·00	8·50
116		19 c. pink	£425	£110
156		19 c. brown	£425	£110

36 38a 38

1870.

172	**36**	1 m. brown on buff	5·75	6·50
173		2 m. black on buff	7·00	7·75
174		4 m. brown	14·00	11·50
175		10 m. red	15·00	5·75
176a		25 m. mauve	45·00	5·50
177a		50 m. blue	9·25	25
178b		100 m. brown	24·00	4·75
179		200 m. brown	24·00	4·75
180		400 m. green	£225	21·00
181		12 c. red	£190	6·00
182		19 c. green	£275	£160
183a		1 e. 600 m. lilac	£1200	£700
184		2 e. blue	£1000	£425

1872. Imperf.

185	**38a**	¼ c. blue	1·60	1·60
186	**38**	¼ c. green	95	95
187	**38a**	¼ c. green	15	10

1872. As T **25**, but currency in centavos de peseta and bottom panel inscr "COMUNICS".

192	**25**	2 c. lilac	16·00	11·50
193		5 c. green	£120	55·00

40 King Amadeo 41 42 Allegorical Figure of Peace

1872.

194	**40**	5 c. pink	17·00	5·25
195b		6 c. blue	£100	29·00
196		10 c. lilac	£250	£160
197		10 c. blue	4·75	25
199		12 c. lilac	11·50	1·50
200		20 c. lilac	95·00	55·00
201		25 c. brown	38·00	6·25
202		40 c. brown	45·00	6·25
203		50 c. green	70·00	7·00
204	**41**	1 p. lilac	70·00	35·00
205		4 p. brown	£400	£375
206		10 p. green	£1500	£1600

1873.

207	**42**	2 c. orange	11·50	5·75
208		5 c. pink	27·00	5·75
209		10 c. green	6·50	25
210		20 c. black	75·00	17·00
211		25 c. brown	26·00	5·75
212		40 c. purple	29·00	8·00
213		50 c. blue	12·00	6·00
214a		1 p. lilac	38·00	25·00
215		4 p. brown	£475	£375
216		10 p. purple	£1600	£1600

43 Allegorical Figure of Justice 44 45 King Alfonso XII

1874.

217	**43**	2 c. yellow	17·00	7·50
218a		5 c. mauve	26·00	6·50
219		10 c. blue	9·25	25
220		20 c. green	£120	38·00
221		25 c. brown	26·00	6·25
222a		40 c. mauve	£300	7·00
223		50 c. orange	90·00	7·00
224		1 p. green	65·00	26·00
225		4 p. red	£550	£350
226		10 p. black	£2000	£1600

1874.

227	**44**	10 c. brown	18·00	90

1875.

228	**45**	2 c. brown	15·00	7·50
229		5 c. lilac	50·00	8·75
230		10 c. blue	6·25	25
231		20 c. brown	£200	95·00
232		25 c. pink	42·00	5·25
233		40 c. brown	80·00	27·00
234		50 c. mauve	£130	24·00
235		1 p. black	£130	60·00
236		4 p. green	£350	£350
237		10 p. blue	£1100	£1200

46

48

49

King Alfonso XII

1876.

238	**46**	5 c. brown	8·75	2·40
239		10 c. blue	2·50	25
240		20 c. green	15·00	12·00
241		25 c. brown	5·75	3·50
242		40 c. brown	55·00	70·00
250		50 c. green	11·00	4·50
244		1 p. blue	15·00	7·00
245		4 p. purple	40·00	45·00
246		10 p. red	95·00	£100

1878.

253	**48**	2 c. mauve	26·00	8·75
254a		5 c. yellow	35·00	8·75
255		10 c. brown	5·75	30
256		20 c. black	£130	95·00
257		25 c. green	16·00	1·75
258		40 c. brown	£120	£110
259		50 c. green	65·00	7·00
260		1 p. grey	55·00	14·50
261		4 p. violet	£150	95·00
262a		10 p. blue	£275	£275

1879.

263	**49**	2 c. black	6·25	3·00
264		5 c. green	8·75	75
265		10 c. pink	8·25	25
266		20 c. brown	85·00	9·75
267		25 c. grey	10·50	25
268		40 c. brown	20·00	3·50
269b		50 c. yellow	80·00	3·50
270		1 p. red	90·00	1·50
271		4 p. grey	£500	26·00
272		10 p. bistre	£1300	£160

50 King Alfonso XII 51 52 King Alfonso XIII

1882.

273	**50**	15 c. pink	5·75	10
273b		15 c. yellow	45·00	80
274		30 c. mauve	£225	4·00
275		75 c. lilac	£225	4·00

1889.

276	**51**	2 c. green	3·50	25
289		2 c. black	21·00	4·00
277		5 c. blue	6·25	10
290		5 c. green	70·00	80
278		10 c. brown	10·50	15
291		10 c. red	£130	2·75
279		15 c. brown	2·75	15
280		20 c. green	25·00	2·75
281		25 c. blue	10·50	15
282		30 c. grey	40·00	3·00
283		40 c. brown	40·00	1·75
284		50 c. red	40·00	1·25
285		75 c. orange	£140	2·75
286		1 p. purple	30·00	25
287		4 p. red	£425	29·00
288		10 p. red	£650	65·00

For 15 c. yellow see No. O289.

1900.

292a	**52**	2 c. brown	3·75	20
293b		5 c. green	5·25	15
294		10 c. red	10·00	15
295		15 c. black	21·00	20
296		15 c. mauve	13·00	20
297		15 c. violet	7·00	20
298		20 c. black	50·00	1·75
299		25 c. blue	10·00	20
300		30 c. green	45·00	25
301		40 c. bistre	£160	3·25
302		40 c. pink	£400	3·00
303		50 c. blue	42·00	40
304		1 p. purple	38·00	40
305		4 p. purple	£300	14·50
306		10 p. orange	£300	60·00

54 Quixote setting out

1905. Tercentenary of Publication of Cervantes' "Don Quixote".

307	**54**	5 c. green	1·60	80
308	–	10 c. red	3·75	1·25
309	–	15 c. violet	3·75	1·25
310	–	25 c. blue	6·00	2·40
311	–	30 c. green	32·00	6·25
312	–	40 c. red	70·00	22·00
313	–	50 c. grey	15·00	5·00
314	–	1 p. red	£225	65·00
315	–	4 p. purple	90·00	65·00
316	–	10 p. orange	£140	£110

DESIGNS: 10 c. Quixote attacking windmill; 15 c. Meeting country girls; 25 c. Sancho Panza tossed in a blanket; 30 c. Don Quixote knighted by innkeeper; 40 c. Tilting at the flock of sheep; 50 c. On the wooden horse; 1 p. Adventure with lions; 4 p. In the bullock-cart; 10 p. The enchanted lady.

64 66 67 G.P.O., Madrid

1909.

344 **64** 2 c. brown 45 10
330 5 c. green . . . . 1·25 10
331 10 c. red . . . . 1·50 10
332 15 c. violet . . . . 7·50 10
343 15 c. yellow . . . . 3·75 10
334 20 c. green . . . . 42·00 60
335 20 c. violet . . . . 32·00 10
336 25 c. blue . . . . 3·25 10
337 30 c. green . . . . 7·50 10
338 40 c. pink . . . . 12·00 20
339a 50 c. blue . . . . 10·00 25
340 1 p. red . . . . 26·00 25
341 4 p. purple . . . . 70·00 8·75
342 10 p. orange . . . . 90·00 17·00

1920. Air. Optd **CORREO AEREO**.

353 **64** 5 c. green 90 70
354 10 c. red . . . . 1·40 95
355 25 c. blue . . . . 2·25 2·00
356 50 c. blue . . . . 9·50 5·75
357 1 p. red . . . . 30·00 24·00

1920. Imperf.

358 **66** 1 c. green 20 10

1920. U.P.U. Congress, Madrid.

361 **67** 1 c. black and green . . . 15 10
362 2 c. black and brown . . . 15 10
363 5 c. black and green . . . 80 65
364 10 c. black and red . . . 80 65
365 15 c. black and yellow . . . 1·40 95
366 20 c. black and violet . . . 1·50 95
367 25 c. black and blue . . . 2·00 2·00
368 30 c. black and green . . . 5·50 3·00
369 40 c. black and red . . . 22·00 5·25
370 50 c. black and blue . . . 25·00 15·00
371 1 p. black and pink . . . 25·00 12·50
372 4 p. black and brown . . . 80·00 60·00
373 10 p. black and orange . . . £160 £120

68 69

1922.

374 **68** 2 c. green 50 15
375 5 c. purple . . . . 3·50 10
376 5 c. red . . . . 1·50 10
377 10 c. red . . . . 1·50 80
378a 10 c. green . . . . 1·40 10
380 15 c. blue . . . . 6·50 10
382 20 c. violet . . . . 3·25 10
383a 25 c. red . . . . 3·25 10
387 30 c. brown . . . . 11·50 15
388 40 c. blue . . . . 3·75 15
389 50 c. orange . . . . 14·50 15
391 **69** 1 p. grey . . . . 14·50 15
392 4 p. red . . . . 65·00 3·25
393 10 p. brown . . . . 26·00 11·50

70 Princesses Maria Cristina and Beatriz **71** King Alfonso XIII

1926. Red Cross.

394 **70** 1 c. black . . . . 1·60 1·60
395 – 2 c. blue . . . . 1·60 1·60
396 – 5 c. purple . . . . 3·75 3·75
397 – 10 c. green . . . . 3·00 3·00
398 **70** 15 c. blue . . . . 1·25 1·25
399 – 20 c. violet . . . . 1·25 1·25
400 **71** 25 c. red 20 20
401 **70** 30 c. green . . . . 29·00 29·00
402 – 40 c. blue . . . . 18·00 18·00
403 – 50 c. red . . . . 17·00 17·00
404 – 1 p. grey . . . . 1·25 1·25
405 – 4 p. red . . . . 1·00 1·00
406 **71** 10 p. brown . . . . 1·00 1·00

DESIGNS—VERT: 2, 50 c. Queen Victoria Eugenie as nurse; 5, 40 c., 4 p. Queen Victoria Eugenie; 10, 20 c., 1 p. Prince of the Asturias.

75 CASA-built Dornier Do-J Wal Flying Boat "Plus Ultra"

76 Route Map and Gallarza and Loriga's Breguet 19A2 Biplane

1926. Air. Red Cross and Trans-Atlantic and Madrid–Manila Flights

407 **75** 5 c. violet and black . . . 1·40 1·40
408 10 c. black and blue . . . 1·75 1·75
409 **76** 15 c. blue and red . . . 25 25
410 20 c. red and green . . . 25 25
411 **75** 25 c. black and red . . . 25 25
412 **76** 30 c. brown and blue . . . 25 25
413 40 c. green and brown . . . 25 25
414 **75** 50 c. black and red . . . 25 25
415 1 p. green and black . . . 2·00 2·00
416 **76** 4 p. red and yellow . . . 75·00 75·00

1927. 25th Anniv of Coronation. Red Cross stamps of 1926 variously optd or surch **17-V 1902 17-V 1927 A XIII** or **17-V-1902 17-V-1927 ALFONSO XIII** or **17 MAYO 17 1902 1927 ALFONSO XIII** with ornaments.

(a) Postage stamps of Spain optd only.

417 **70** 1 c. black . . . . 4·25 4·25
418 – 2 c. blue . . . . 8·50 8·50
419 – 5 c. purple . . . . 2·10 2·10
420 – 10 c. green . . . . 50·00 50·00
421 **70** 15 c. blue . . . . 1·40 1·40
422 – 20 c. violet . . . . 3·00 3·00
423 **71** 25 c. red 50 50
424 **70** 30 c. green 80 80
425 – 40 c. blue 80 80
426 – 50 c. red 80 80
427 – 1 p. grey . . . . 1·40 1·40
428 – 4 p. red . . . . 8·00 8·00
429 **71** 10 p. brown . . . . 30·00 30·00

(b) Postage stamps of Spain also surch with new value.

430 – 3 c. on 2 c. blue . . . . 7·50 7·50
431 – 4 c. on 2 c. blue . . . . 7·50 7·50
432 **71** 10 c. on 25 c. red 35 35
433 25 c. on 25 c. red 35 35
434 – 55 c. on 2 c. blue 65 65
435 – 55 c. on 10 c. green . . . . 45·00 45·00
436 – 55 c. on 20 c. violet . . . . 45·00 45·00
437 **70** 75 c. on 15 c. blue 50 50
438 75 c. on 30 c. green £150 £150
439 – 80 c. on 5 c. purple . . . . 38·00 38·00
440 – 2 p. on 40 c. blue 65 65
441 – 2 p. on 1 p. grey 65 65
442 – 5 p. on 50 c. red . . . . 1·25 1·25
443 – 5 p. on 4 p. red . . . . 1·90 1·90
444 **71** 10 p. on 10 p. brown . . . . 17·00 17·00

(c) Air stamps of Spain optd only.

445 **75** 5 c. violet and black . . . 1·25 1·25
446 10 c. black and blue . . . 1·75 1·75
447 **76** 15 c. blue and red . . . 25 25
448 20 c. red and green . . . 25 25
449 **75** 25 c. black and red . . . 25 25
450 **76** 30 c. brown and blue . . . 25 25
451 40 c. green and brown . . . 25 25
452 **75** 50 c. black and red . . . 25 25
453 1 p. green and black . . . 2·25 2·25
454 **76** 4 p. red and yellow . . . 85·00 85·00

(d) Air stamps of Spain also surch with new value.

455 **75** 75 c. on 5 c. violet & black 4·00 4·00
456 75 c. on 10 c. black & blue 18·00 18·00
457 75 c. on 25 c. black & red 35·00 35·00
458 75 c. on 50 c. black & red 14·50 14·50

(e) Nos. 24/5 of Spanish Post Offices in Tangier.

460 1 p. on 10 p. violet . . . . 65·00 65·00
461 4 p. bistre . . . . 24·00 24·00

(f) Nos. 122/3 of Spanish Morocco.

462 55 c. on 4 p. bistre . . . . 13·00 13·00
463 80 c. on 10 p. violet . . . . 13·00 13·00

(g) Nos. 34 and 35 of Cape Juby.

464 5 p. on 4 p. bistre . . . . 40·00 40·00
465 10 p. on 10 p. violet . . . . 24·00 24·00

(h) Nos. 231/2 of Spanish Guinea.

466 1 p. on 10 p. violet . . . . 13·00 13·00
467 2 p. on 4 p. bistre . . . . 13·00 13·00

(i) Nos. 23/4 of Spanish Sahara.

468 80 c. on 10 p. violet . . . . 18·00 18·00
469 2 p. on 4 p. bistre . . . . 13·00 13·00

82 Pope Pius XI and King Alfonso XIII

1928. Rome Catacombs Restoration Fund.

470 **82** 2 c. black and violet . . . 25 25
471 2 c. black and purple . . . 35 35
486 2 c. red and black . . . 25 25
487 2 c. red and blue . . . 35 35
472 3 c. violet and black . . . 25 25
473 3 c. violet and blue . . . 35 35
488 3 c. blue and bistre . . . 25 25
489 3 c. blue and green . . . 35 35
474 5 c. violet and green . . . 65 65
490 5 c. red and purple . . . 65 65
475 10 c. black and green . . . 1·00 1·00
491 10 c. blue and green . . . 1·00 1·00
476 15 c. violet and green . . . 3·75 3·75
492 15 c. red and blue . . . 3·75 3·75
477 25 c. violet and red . . . 3·75 3·75
493 25 c. blue and brown . . . 3·75 3·75
478 **82** 40 c. black and blue . . . 25 25
494 40 c. red and blue . . . 25 25
479 55 c. violet and brown . . . 25 25
495 55 c. blue and brown . . . 25 25
480 80 c. black and red . . . 25 25
496 80 c. red and black . . . 25 25
481 1 p. violet and grey . . . 25 25
497 1 p. red and yellow . . . 25 25
482 2 p. black and brown . . . 5·00 5·00
498 2 p. blue and grey . . . 5·00 5·00
483 3 p. violet and pink . . . 5·00 5·00
499 3 p. red and violet . . . 5·00 5·00
484 4 p. black and purple . . . 5·00 5·00
500 4 p. red and purple . . . 5·00 5·00
485 5 p. violet and black . . . 5·00 5·00
501 5 p. blue and yellow . . . 5·00 5·00

83 A Spanish Caravel, Seville in background **84** Miniature of Exhibition Poster

1929. Seville and Barcelona Exhibitions. Inscr "EXPOSICION GENERAL (or GRAL.) ESPANOLA".

502 **83** 1 c. green 40 25
503 **84** 2 c. green 20 20
504 – 5 c. red 35 35
505 – 10 c. green 35 35
506 **83** 15 c. blue 60 60
507 **84** 20 c. violet 40 40
508 **83** 25 c. red 55 40
509 – 30 c. brown . . . . 3·25 3·25
510 – 40 c. blue . . . . 5·75 5·75
511 **84** 50 c. orange . . . . 3·25 3·25
512 – 1 p. grey . . . . 8·75 8·75
513 – 4 p. purple . . . . 18·00 18·00
514 – 10 p. brown . . . . 48·00 48·00

DESIGNS—VERT: 5, 30 c., 1 p. View of exhibition. HORIZ: 10, 40 c., 4, 10 p. Alfonso XIII and Barcelona.

87 "Spirit of St. Louis" over Coast

1929. Air. Seville and Barcelona Exhibitions.

515 **87** 5 c. brown . . . . 4·50 4·25
516 10 c. red . . . . 4·75 4·50
517 25 c. blue . . . . 5·25 5·00
518 50 c. violet . . . . 6·25 6·00
519 1 p. green . . . . 30·00 28·00
520 4 p. black . . . . 21·00 20·00

1929. Meeting of Council of League of Nations at Madrid. Optd **Sociedad de las Naciones LV reunion del Consejo Madrid.**

521 **66** 1 c. green 55 55
522 **68** 2 c. green 55 55
523 5 c. red 55 55
524 10 c. green 55 55
525 15 c. blue 55 55
526 20 c. violet 55 55
527 25 c. red 55 55
528 30 c. brown . . . . 2·10 2·10
529 40 c. blue . . . . 2·10 2·10
530 50 c. orange . . . . 2·10 2·10
531 **69** 1 p. grey . . . . 10·50 10·50
532 4 p. red . . . . 10·50 10·50
533 10 p. brown . . . . 38·00 38·00

89 Steam Locomotive **90** Stinson Junior over Congress Emblem

1930. 11th Int Railway Congress, Madrid.

534 **89** 1 c. green (postage) . . . 40 40
535 2 c. green 40 40
536 5 c. purple 40 40
537 10 c. green 40 40
538 15 c. blue 40 40
539 20 c. violet 40 40
540 25 c. red 20 20
541 30 c. brown . . . . 2·25 2·25
542 40 c. blue . . . . 1·90 1·90
543 **89** 50 c. orange . . . . 3·00 3·00
544 – 1 p. grey . . . . 3·75 3·75
545 – 4 p. red . . . . 70·00 70·00
546 – 10 p. brown £300 £300

DESIGN: 1 p. to 10 p. Steam locomotive at points.

547 **90** 5 c. brown (air) . . . . 5·50 5·50
548 10 c. red . . . . 5·50 5·50
549 25 c. blue . . . . 5·50 5·50
550 50 c. violet . . . . 14·00 14·00
551 1 p. green . . . . 27·00 27·00
552 4 p. black . . . . 27·00 27·00

91 92

Francisco Goya (after Lopez)

93 "The Naked Maja"

1930. Death Cent of Goya (painter). (a) Postage.

553 **91** 1 c. yellow 10 10
554 2 c. brown 10 10
555 **92** 2 c. green 10 10
556 **91** 5 c. mauve 10 10
557 **92** 5 c. violet 10 10
558 **91** 10 c. green 15 15
559 15 c. blue 10 10
560 20 c. purple 10 10
561 25 c. red 10 10
562 **92** 25 c. red 25 25
563 **91** 30 c. brown . . . . 4·00 4·00
564 40 c. blue . . . . 4·00 4·00
565 50 c. red . . . . 4·00 4·00
566 1 p. black . . . . 5·25 5·25
567 **93** 1 p. purple 70 70
568 4 p. black 55 55
569 10 p. brown . . . . 11·00 11·00

94 "Flight" **97** King Alfonso XIII

(b) Air. Designs show works by Goya, all with curious flying figures.

570 **94** 5 c. yellow and red 10 10
571 – 5 c. blue and green 10 10
572 – 10 c. green and turquoise . . 10 10
573 – 15 c. red and black 10 10
574 – 20 c. red and blue 10 10
575 **94** 25 c. red and purple 15 15
576 – 30 c. violet and brown . . . 35 35
577 – 40 c. blue and ultramarine . . 35 35
578 – 50 c. green and red 35 35
579 – 1 p. violet and purple . . . 35 35
580 – 4 p. black and purple . . . 2·00 2·00
581 – 4 p. blue and light blue . . 2·00 2·00
582 – 10 p. brown and sepia . . . 7·75 7·75

DESIGNS—VERT: 5, 10, 20, 40 c. Asmodeus and Cleofas; 1, 4 (581), 10 p. Woman and dwarfs in flight. HORIZ: 30, 50 c., 4 p. (580), Weird flying methods.

1930.

583 **97** 2 c. brown 10 10
584 5 c. brown 60 10
585 10 c. green . . . . 3·00 10
586 15 c. green . . . . 9·75 10
587 20 c. violet . . . . 5·50 55
588 25 c. red 60 10
589 30 c. red . . . . 12·00 1·40
590 40 c. blue . . . . 16·00 65
592 50 c. orange . . . . 16·00 1·40

MINIMUM PRICE

The minimum price quoted is 10p which represents a handling charge rather than a basis for valuing common stamps. For further notes about prices, see introductory pages.

98 The "Santa Maria" **99**

100 "Santa Maria", "Pinta" and "Nina"

101 The Departure from Palos

1930. Columbus issue.

593	**98**	1 c. brown	25	15
594		2 c. green	25	15
595	**99**	2 c. green	25	15
596	**98**	5 c. purple	25	15
597	**99**	5 c. purple	25	15
598		10 c. green	1·00	85
599	**98**	15 c. blue	1·00	85
600	**99**	20 c. violet	1·25	1·25
601	**100**	25 c. red	1·25	1·25
602	**101**	30 c. brown, blue and sepia	6·00	6·00
603	**100**	40 c. blue	5·00	5·00
604	**101**	50 c. violet, blue & purple	7·75	7·75
605	**100**	1 p. black	7·75	7·75
606	–	4 p. black and blue	8·50	8·50
607	–	10 p. brown and purple	35·00	35·00

DESIGNS—As Type **101**: 4, 10 p. Arrival in America.

103 Monastery of La Rabida

104 Martin Pinzon

106 Columbus

1930. "Columbus" Air stamps (for Europe and Africa).

608	**103**	5 c. red	15	15
609		5 c. brown	15	15
610		10 c. green	20	20
611		15 c. violet	20	20
612		20 c. blue	20	20
613	**104**	25 c. red	20	20
614	–	30 c. brown	1·60	1·60
615	**104**	40 c. blue	1·60	1·60
616	–	50 c. orange	1·60	1·60
617	**104**	1 p. violet	1·60	1·60
618	**106**	4 p. green	1·60	1·60
619		10 p. brown	9·25	9·25

DESIGNS—As Type **104**: 30, 50 c. Vincent Pinzon.

107 Monastery of La Rabida

108 Columbus

109 Columbus and the brothers Pinzon

1930. "Columbus" Air stamps (for America and Philippines).

620	**107**	5 c. red	15	15
621		10 c. green	15	15
622	**108**	25 c. red	15	15
623		50 c. grey	1·90	1·90
624		1 p. brown	1·90	1·90
625	**109**	4 p. blue	1·90	1·90
626		10 p. purple	9·00	9·00

110 Arms of Bolivia and Paraguay

113 Sidar and Douglas 0-2-M Biplane

114 Breguet 19GR "Jesus del Gran Poder" over "Santa Maria"

1930. Spanish-American Exhibition. Views of pavilions of various countries.

627	**110**	1 c. green (postage)	15	15
628	–	2 c. brown (C. America)	15	15
629	–	5 c. brown (Venezuela)	15	15
630	–	10 c. green (Colombia)	25	25
631	–	15 c. blue (Dominican Republic)	25	25
632	–	20 c. violet (Uruguay)	25	25
633	–	25 c. red (Argentina)	25	25
634	–	25 c. red (Chile)	25	25
635	–	30 c. purple (Brazil)	1·40	1·40
636	–	40 c. blue (Mexico)	80	80
637	–	40 c. blue (Cuba)	80	80
638	–	50 c. orange (Peru)	1·40	1·40
639	–	1 p. blue (U.S.A.)	2·00	2·00
640	–	4 p. purple (Portugal)	28·00	28·00
641	–	10 p. brown	1·90	1·90

The 10 p. shows King Alfonso and Queen Victoria, maps of S. America and Spain, and the Giralda, Seville. The 2, 5 c., 4, 10 p. are vert.

643	–	5 c. black (air)	60	55
644	–	10 c. green	60	55
645	–	25 c. blue	60	55
646	–	50 c. blue	1·25	1·25
647	**113**	50 c. black	1·25	1·25
648	–	1 p. red	3·00	3·00
649	–	1 p. purple	55·00	55·00
650	–	1 p. green	3·00	3·00
651	**114**	4 p. blue	5·75	5·75

DESIGNS—HORIZ: 5 c. Alberto Santos Dumont and Wright Flyer I over Rio de Janeiro; 10 c. Teodoro Fels and Douglas 0-2-M biplane; 25 c. Dagoberto Godoy and Nieuport 17 biplane; 50 c. Admiral Gago Coutinha, Sacadura Cabral and Fairey IIID seaplane; 1 p. (650) Charles Lindbergh and "Spirit of St. Louis". VERT: 1 p. (648/9) Jimenez Iglesias and Breguet 19GR "Jesus de Gran Poder".

115

121 The Fountain of the Lions

1930.

652	**115**	5 c. black	5·00	15

1931. Optd **REPUBLICA.** (a) Postage.

660	**66**	1 c. green	10	10
673	**97**	2 c. brown	10	10
662		5 c. brown	15	15
671	**115**	5 c. black	3·50	3·50
675	**97**	10 c. green	25	25
664		15 c. green	60	60
677		20 c. violet	50	35
678		25 c. red	50	35
667		30 c. red	4·50	4·50
668		40 c. blue	1·25	1·25
669		50 c. orange	1·25	1·25
670	**69**	1 p. grey	7·00	7·00

(b) Air. On Nos. 353/6.

683	**64**	5 c. green	10·00	10·00
684		10 c. red	10·00	10·00
685		25 c. blue	16·00	16·00
686		50 c. blue	28·00	28·00

1931. Optd **Republica Espanola** in two lines continuously.

687	**97**	2 c. brown	10	10
688		5 c. brown	20	10
689		10 c. green	20	10
690		15 c. green	2·75	10
691		20 c. violet	1·25	60
692		25 c. red	40	10
693		30 c. red	3·50	85
694		40 c. blue	3·50	50
695		50 c. orange	6·00	50
696	**69**	1 p. grey	42·00	75

1931. 3rd Pan-American Postal Union Congress. (a) Postage.

697	**121**	5 c. purple	10	10
698	–	10 c. green	35	35
699	–	15 c. violet	35	35
700	–	25 c. red	35	35
701	–	30 c. green	35	35
702	**121**	40 c. blue	1·00	1·00
703	–	50 c. red	1·00	1·00
704	–	1 p. black	1·90	1·90
705	–	4 p. purple	9·25	9·25
706	–	10 p. brown	30·00	30·00

DESIGNS—VERT: 10, 25, 50 c. Cordoba Cathedral. HORIZ: 15 c., 1 p. Alcantara Bridge, Toledo; 30 c. Dr. F. Garcia y Santos; 4, 10 p. Revolutionaries hoisting Republican flag, 14 April, 1931.

123 Royal Palace and San Francisco el Grande

(b) Air.

707	**123**	5 c. purple	15	15
708		10 c. green	15	15
709		25 c. red	15	15
710	–	50 c. blue	40	40
711	–	1 p. violet	65	65
712	–	4 p. black	8·25	8·50

DESIGNS—HORIZ: 50 c., 1 p. G.P.O. and Cibeles Fountain; 4 p. The Calle de Alcala.

125a Montserrat Arms

125b Airplane above Montserrat

1931. 900th Anniv of Montserrat Monastery.

713	**125a**	1 c. green (postage)	1·25	1·25
714		2 c. brown	65	65
715		5 c. brown	80	80
716		10 c. green	80	80
717	–	15 c. green	1·25	1·25
718	–	20 c. purple	2·50	2·50
719	–	25 c. purple	3·50	3·50
720	–	30 c. red	35·00	35·00
721	–	40 c. blue	20·00	20·00
722	–	50 c. orange	45·00	45·00
723	–	1 p. blue	45·00	45·00
724	–	4 p. mauve	£400	£400
725	–	10 p. brown	£325	£325

DESIGNS: 15, 50 c. Monks planning Monastery; 20, 30 c. "Black Virgin" (full length); 25 c., 1, 10 p. "Black Virgin" (profile); 40 c., 4 p. Monastery.

726	**125b**	5 c. brown (air)	50	50
727		10 c. green	2·50	2·50
728		25 c. purple	10·00	10·00
729		50 c. orange	30·00	30·00
730		1 p. blue	20·00	20·00

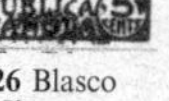

126 Blasco Ibanez

127 Pi y Margall

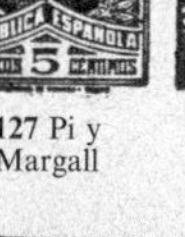

128 Joaquin Costa

129 Mariana Pineda

130 Nicolas Salmeron

131 Concepcion Arenal

132 Ruiz Zorilla

133 Pablo Iglesias

134 Ramon y Cajal

135 Azcarate

136 Jovellanos

137 Pablo Iglesias

138 Emilio Castelar

139 Pablo Iglesias

140 Velazquez

141 F. Salvoechea

142 Cuenca

1931.

738	**126**	2 c. brown	10	10
731	**127**	5 c. brown	2·75	25
740	**126**	5 c. brown	10	10
741	**128**	10 c. green	4·25	10
742	**129**	10 c. green	10	10
744	**130**	15 c. green	65	10
745	**131**	15 c. green	20	10
747		15 c. black	20	10
748	**127**	20 c. violet	25	10
749	**133**	25 c. red	16·00	10
750	**132**	25 c. red	45	10
751	**133**	30 c. red	1·90	10
752	**134**	30 c. brown	6·50	1·25
753	**135**	30 c. red	7·50	20
755	**136**	30 c. red	10	10
756	**137**	30 c. red	10	10
757	**139**	30 c. red	1·10	40
758	**138**	40 c. blue	20	10
759		40 c. red	1·10	35
760	**139**	45 c. red	10	10
761	**130**	50 c. orange	27·00	65
762		50 c. blue	1·00	55
763	**140**	50 c. blue	10	10
764	**138**	60 c. green	15	15
765	**141**	60 c. blue	75	70
766		60 c. orange	6·25	7·00
767c	**142**	1 p. black	15	10
768c	–	4 p. mauve	50	90
769c	–	10 p. brown	1·00	50

DESIGNS—As Type **142**: 4 p. Castle of Segovia; 10 p. Sun Gate, Toledo.

143

144

1933. Imperf (1 c.), perf (others).

770	**143**	1 c. green	10	10
771		2 c. brown	25	10
772	**144**	2 c. brown	10	10
773	**143**	5 c. brown	10	10
774		10 c. green	10	10

775 **143** 15 c. green 10 10
776a 20 c. violet 10 10
777a 25 c. mauve 10 10
778 30 c. red 10 10

145 Cierva C.30A Autogyro over Seville

1935.
780 **145** 2 p. blue 65 20

146 Lope De Vega's Book-plate
148 Scene from "Peribanez"

1935. 300th Death Anniv of Lope de Vega (author).
781 **146** 15 c. green . . . . 6·00 25
782 – 30 c. red . . . . 2·40 20
783 – 50 c. blue . . . . 12·00 2·00
784 **148** 1 p. black . . . . 20·00 1·40
DESIGN—As Type **146**: 30, 50 c. Lope de Vega (after Tristan).

149 Old-time Map of the Amazon

1935. Iglesias' Amazon Expedition.
785 **149** 30 c. red . . . . 2·00 65

150 M. Moya
153 Airplane over Press Association Building

151 House of Nazareth and Rotary Press

152 Pyrenean Eagle and Newspapers

1936. 40th Anniv of Madrid Press Association.
786 **150** 1 c. red (postage) 10 10
787 – 2 c. brown 10 10
788 – 5 c. brown 10 10
789 – 10 c. green 10 10
790 **150** 15 c. green 10 10
791 – 20 c. violet 15 10
792 – 25 c. mauve 15 10
793 – 30 c. red 15 10
794 **150** 40 c. orange 45 10
795 – 50 c. blue 20 10
796 – 60 c. green 50 15
797 – 1 p. black 50 15
798 **151** 2 p. blue . . . . 6·50 2·75
799 4 p. purple . . . . 6·50 4·50
800 10 p. red . . . . 16·00 11·00
PORTRAITS: 2, 20, 50 c. T. L. de Tena; 5, 25, 60 c. J. F. Rodriguez; 10, 30 c., 1 p. A. Lerroux. SIZES: 1 c. to 10 c. 22×27 mm; 15 c. to 30 c. 24×30 mm; 40 c. to 1 p. 26×31½ mm.

801 **152** 1 c. red (air) 10 10
802 **153** 2 c. brown 15 15
803 **152** 5 c. brown 10 10
804 **153** 10 c. green 15 15
805 – 15 c. blue 15 10
806 **152** 20 c. violet 15 10
807 **153** 25 c. mauve 15 15
808 – 30 c. red 10 10
809 **152** 40 c. orange 45 70
810 50 c. blue 35 70
811 **153** 60 c. green 65 70
812 – 1 p. black 65 70
813 – 2 p. blue . . . . 4·25 3·00
814 – 4 p. purple . . . . 4·75 4·25
815 – 10 p. red . . . . 13·00 9·25
DESIGNS—VERT: 15, 30, 50 c., 1 p. Cierva C.30A autogyro over House of Nazareth. HORIZ: 2, 4, 10 p. Don Quixote on wooden horse.

155 Gregorio Fernandez
156

1936. 300th Birth Anniv of Gregorio Fernandez (sculptor).
816 **155** 30 c. red . . . . 1·25 65

1939. 1st National Philatelic Exhibition, Madrid. Imperf. (a) Postage.
817 **156** 10 c. brown . . . . 38·00 38·00
818 15 c. green . . . . 38·00 38·00

(b) Air. Optd **CORREO AEREO.**
819 **156** 10 c. red £130 £130
820 15 c. blue £130 £130

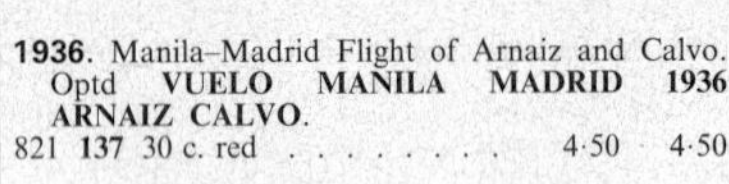
1936. Manila–Madrid Flight of Arnaiz and Calvo. Optd **VUELO MANILA MADRID 1936 ARNAIZ CALVO.**
821 **137** 30 c. red . . . . 4·50 4·50

159
160a Republican Symbol

1937. Fiscal stamp of Austrias and Leon surch.
822 **159** 25 c. on 5 c. red . . . . 10·00 8·50
823 45 c. on 5 c. red . . . . 5·50 10·00
824 60 c. on 5 c. red 40 35
825 1 p. on 5 c. red 35 30

1938. Surch **45 centimos.**
826 **143** 45 c. on 1 c. green (imperf) 4·75 4·75
827 45 c. on 1 c. grn (perf) . 30 25
830 45 c. on 2 c. brown . . . 11·50 11·00
831 **144** 45 c. on 2 c. brown . . . 10 10
832 **126** 45 c. on 2 c. brown . . . 15·00 15·00

1938.
833 **160a** 40 c. pink 10 10
834 45 c. red 10 10
835 50 c. blue 10 10
836 60 c. blue 40 30

1938. 7th Anniv of Republic. Nos. 308/9 surch **14 ABRIL 1938 VII Aniversario de la Republica** and values. (a) Postage.
837 45 c. on 15 c. violet . . . . . 12·00 11·00

(b) Air. Additionally optd **CORREO AEREO.**
838 2 p. 50 on 10 c. red . . . . . 80·00 80·00

163 Defence of Madrid

1938. Defence of Madrid Relief Fund. (a) Postage.
839 **163** 45 c. + 2 p. blue & lt bl . 50 50

(b) Air. Surch **AEREO + 5 Pts.**
841 **163** 45 c. + 2 p. + 5 p. blue and light blue £225 £225

1938. Labour Day. Surch **FIESTA DEL TRABAJO 1 MAYO 1938** and values.
843 **54** 45 c. on 15 c. violet . . . 2·75 2·75
844 1 p. on 15 c. violet . . . 4·75 4·75

167 Statue of Liberty and Flags

1938. 150th Anniv of U.S. Constitution. (a) Postage.
845 **167** 1 p. multicoloured . . . . 14·50 14·50

(b) Air. Surch **AEREO + 5 Pts.**
847 **167** 1 p. + 5 p. multicoloured £190 £190

169
172 Steelworks

1938. Red Cross. (a) Postage.
849 **169** 45 c. + 5 p. red 45 45

(b) Air. Surcharged **+ 3 Pts. Aereo.**
850 **169** 45 c. + 5 p. + 3 p. red . 8·00 7·75

1938. Air. No. 719 surch with two airplanes and **CORREO AEREO** repeated twice and value.
851 50 c. on 25 c. purple . . . . . 27·00 27·00
852 1 p. on 25 c. purple . . . . . 1·00 1·00
853 1 p. 25 on 25 c. purple . . . 1·00 1·00
854 1 p. 50 on 25 c. purple . . . 1·00 1·00
855 2 p. on 25 c. purple . . . . . 27·00 27·00

1938. Workers of Sagunto.
856 **172** 45 c. black 15 15
857 – 1 p. 25 blue 15 15
DESIGN: 1 p. 25, Blast furnace and air raid victims.

173 "Isaac Peral"

1938. Submarine Service.
857a **173** 1 p. blue . . . . 4·25 4·50
857b – 2 p. brown . . . . 8·50 9·00
857c – 4 p. orange . . . . 9·50 10·00
857d – 6 p. blue . . . . 19·00 20·00
857e – 10 p. purple . . . . 35·00 38·00
857f – 15 p. green £375 £400
DESIGNS: 2, 6 p. "Narciso Monturiol". 4, 10 p. "B-2".

174 Troops on the Alert
176a Man and Woman in Firing Position

1938. In Honour of 43rd Division. Perf or imperf.
858 **174** 25 c. green . . . . 8·00 8·00
859 – 45 c. brown . . . . 8·00 8·00
DESIGN—VERT: 45 c. Two soldiers on guard.

1938. 2nd Anniv of Defence of Madrid. Optd **SECUNDO ANIVERSARIO DE LA HEROICA DEFENSA DE MADRID 7 NOV. 1938.**
860 **163** 45 c. + 2 p. blue and light blue . . . . 2·50 2·50

1938. No. 719 surch **2'50 PTAS.** and bars and ornaments.
861 2 p. 50 on 25 c. purple 15 15

1938. In honour of the Militia.
861b **176a** 5 c. brown . . . . 2·75 2·75
861c 10 c. purple . . . . . . 2·75 2·75
861d 25 c. green . . . . 2·75 2·75
861e – 45 c. red . . . . 2·75 2·75
861f – 60 c. blue . . . . 4·75 4·75
861g – 1 p. 20 black £100 £100
861h – 2 p. orange . . . . . . 30·00 30·00
861i – 5 p. brown £170 £170
861j – 10 p. green . . . . 35·00 35·00
DESIGNS—HORIZ: 45, 60 c., 1 p. 20, Militia with machine gun. VERT: 2, 5, 10 p. Grenade-thrower.

NATIONAL STATE

The Civil War began on July 17, 1936. Until it ended on April 1, 1939, the stamps listed below were current only in areas held by the forces of General Franco.

177 Seville Cathedral
178 Xavier Castle, Navarre

1936. Junta of National Defence.
862 – 5 c. brown 55 50
863 – 15 c. green 55 35
864 **177** 25 c. red 55 35
865 **178** 30 c. red 55 35
867 – 1 p. black 65 35
DESIGNS—VERT: 5 c. Burgos Cathedral. HORIZ: 15 c. Zaragoza Cathedral; 1 p. Alcantara Bridge and Alcazar, Toledo.

179
180 Cordoba Cathedral

1936.
868 **179** 1 c. green (imperf) . . . . 4·75 4·50
869 2 c. brown 55 50
870 – 10 c. green 55 50
871 – 50 c. blue . . . . 13·00 9·25
872 **180** 60 c. green 85 70
873 – 4 p. lilac, red and yellow . 48·00 28·00
874 – 10 p. brown . . . . 48·00 28·00
DESIGNS (As T **180**)—HORIZ: 10 c. Salamanca University; 50 c. Court of Lions, Granada; 10 p. Troops disembarking at Algeciras. VERT: 4 p. National flag at Malaga.

181
182

183 "El Cid"
184 Isabella the Catholic

1937.
875 **181** 1 c. green (imperf) 10 10
876 **182** 2 c. brown 10 10
902 **183** 5 c. brown 10 10
879 10 c. green 10 10
903 10 c. red 10 10
896 15 c. green 40 10
880 **184** 15 c. black 20 10
881 20 c. violet 30 10
882 25 c. red 25 10
883 30 c. red 40 10
885 40 c. orange . . . . . . 1·75 10
886 50 c. blue . . . . 1·75 10
887 60 c. yellow 30 10
897 70 c. blue 60 10
888 1 p. blue . . . . 15·00 40
889 4 p. mauve . . . . 18·00 4·50
891 **183** 10 p. blue . . . . 26·00 12·00
See also No. 1113.

186 Santiago Cathedral
189

1937. Holy Year of Compostela.
905 – 15 c. brown . . . . 1·00 80
906 **186** 30 c. red . . . . 5·00 40
908 – 1 p. orange and blue . . 16·00 3·50
DESIGNS—VERT: 15 c. St. James of Compostela. HORIZ: 1 p. Portico de la Gloria.

1937. Anti-Tuberculosis Fund. Cross in red.
913 **189** 10 c. blue and black . . . 6·25 4·00

190 Ferdinand the Catholic

192

1938.

917	**190**	15 c. green	1·25	10
918		20 c. violet	8·00	1·60
919		25 c. red	60	10
921		30 c. red	3·75	10

1938. Air. Optd **correo aereo.**

922	**190**	50 c. blue	85	60
923		1 p. blue	2·75	60

1938. 2nd Anniv of National Uprising.

926	**192**	15 c. green and light green	4·00	3·75
927		25 c. red and pink	4·00	3·75
928		30 c. blue and light blue	2·10	2·00
929		1 p. brown and yellow	80·00	75·00

193 Isabella the Catholic

194

1938.

930	**193**	20 c. violet	55	15
931		25 c. red	5·50	50
932		30 c. red	20	10
933		40 c. mauve	20	10
934		50 c. blue	25·00	2·00
935		1 p. blue	8·00	85

1938. Anti-Tuberculosis Fund. Cross in red.

940	**194**	10 c. blue and black	4·00	1·60

195 Juan de la Cierva and Cierva C.30A Autogyro

196 General Franco

1939. Air.

1010	**195**	20 c. orange	20	15
1011		25 c. red	20	20
943		35 c. mauve	60	55
1013		50 c. brown	45	20
945		1 p. blue	65	35
1015		2 p. green	1·90	30
1016		4 p. blue	5·25	55
1017		10 p. violet	4·00	1·00

1939.

960	**196**	5 c. brown	35	10
961		10 c. red	1·60	60
962		15 c. green	40	10
1114		20 c. violet	15	10
1115		25 c. purple	15	10
950		30 c. red	25	15
1116		30 c. blue	20	10
1117		35 c. blue	35	10
951		40 c. green	30	15
966		40 c. grey	35	10
952		45 c. red	1·75	1·75
1119		45 c. blue	10	10
1120		50 c. grey	20	10
1121		60 c. orange	10	10
955		70 c. blue	40	15
956		1 Pts. black	11·00	15
974		1 PTA. black	5·25	10
975		1 PTS. grey	50·00	60
957		2 Pts. brown	16·00	1·00
1124		2 PTAS. brown	4·75	10
958		4 Pts. purple	85·00	13·00
1125		4 PTAS. red	11·00	10
959		10 Pts. brown	45·00	29·00
978		10 PTS. brown	£120	3·75
1126		10 PTAS. brown	2·10	30

For 10 c. brown imperf, see No. 981.

197 "Spain" and Wreath of Peace

1939. Homage to the Army.

980	**197**	10 c. blue	15	15

1939. Anti-Tuberculosis Fund. Imperf.

981	**196**	10 c. brown	15	15

198 Ruins of Belchite

1940. Zaragoza Cathedral Restoration Fund and 19th Centenary of Apparition of Virgin of El Pilar at Zaragoza. (a) Postage.

982	**198**	10 c. + 5 c. brown & blue	15	10
983	–	15 c. + 10 c. green & lilac	15	10
984	–	20 c. + 10 c. blue & vio	15	10
985	–	25 c. + 10 c. brown & red	15	10
986	–	40 c. + 10 c. pur & grn	15	10
987	–	45 c. + 15 c. red & blue	30	30
988	**198**	70 c. + 20 c. blk & brn	30	30
989	–	80 c. + 20 c. violet & red	35	35
990	–	1 p. + 30 c. pur & blk	35	35
991	–	1 p. 40 + 40 c. blk & violet	30·00	30·00
992	–	1 p. 50 + 50 c. pur & bl	40	40
993	–	2 p. 50 + 50 c. bl & pur	40	40
994	–	4 p. + 1 p. grey & lilac	9·75	9·75
995	–	10 p. + 4 p. brown & bl	£140	£140

DESIGNS—HORIZ: 15, 80 c. Procession of the Rosary; 20 c., 1 p. 50, El Pilar; 25 c., 1 p. Mother Rafols praying; 40 c., 2 p. 50, Sanctuary of the Virgin; 45 c., 1 p. 40, Oath of the besieged; 4 p. Miracle of Calanda; 10 p. Virgin appearing to St. James.

(b) Air.

996	25 c. + 5 c. grey & purple	25	20
997	50 c. + 5 c. violet and red	25	20
998	65 c. + 15 c. blue & violet	25	20
999	70 c. + 15 c. violet & grey	25	20
1000	90 c. + 20 c. red & brown	25	20
1001	1 p. 20 + 30 c. purple & vio	25	20
1002	1 p. 40 + 40 c. brown & bl	25	30
1003	2 p. + 50 c. violet & purple	35	35
1004	4 p. + 1 p. purple & green	8·50	8·50
1005	10 p. + 4 p. blue & brown	£190	£190

DESIGNS—VERT: 25, 70 c. Prayer during bombardment; 50 c., 1 p. 40, Caravel and Image of the Virgin; 65, 90 c. The Assumption; 1 p. 20, 2 p. Coronation of the Virgin; 4 p. "The Cave", after Goya; 10 p. Bombing of Zaragoza Cathedral.

199 Gen. Franco

200 Knight and Cross of Lorraine

1940. Anti-Tuberculosis Fund.

1006	**199**	10 c. violet & red (post)	10	10
1007		20 c. + 5 c. green & red	60	60
1008		40 c. + 10 c. blue & red	80	35
1009		10 c. pink and red (air)	75	75

1941. Anti-Tuberculosis Fund.

1018	**200**	10 c. black & red (post)	15	10
1019		20 c. + 5 c. violet & red	50	25
1020		40 c. + 10 c. grey & red	50	25
1021		10 c. blue and red (air)	25	20

201 Gen. Franco

202 St. John of the Cross

1942.

1022	**201**	40 c. brown	30	15
1023		75 c. blue	2·75	55
1024a		90 c. green	40	10
1025b		1 p. 35 violet	25	10

1942. 400th Birth Anniv of St. John of the Cross.

1026	**202**	20 c. violet	95	10
1027		40 c. orange	1·50	25
1028		75 c. blue	1·50	1·50

203 Arms and Lorraine Cross

1942. Anti-T.B. Fund. Inscr "1942–43".

1029	**203**	10 c. orange & red (post)	10	10
1030		20 c. + 5 c. brn & red	1·40	1·25
1031		40 c. + 10 c. grn & red	80	20
1032	–	10 c. orange & red (air)	70	40

DESIGN—HORIZ: No. 1032, Lorraine Cross and two doves in flight.

204 St. James of Compostela

205

1943. Holy Year. Inscr "ANO SANTO 1943".

1033	**204**	20 c. blue	20	15
1034	–	20 c. red	20	15
1035	–	20 c. lilac	20	15
1036	–	40 c. brown	50	20
1037	**205**	40 c. green	50	20
1038	–	40 c. brown	75	20
1039	–	75 c. blue	2·40	1·75
1040	–	75 c. blue	2·40	1·75
1041	–	75 c. blue	28·00	29·00

DESIGNS—VERT: Nos. 1034 and 1040. Details of pillars in Santiago Cathedral; No. 1036, St. James enthroned; No. 1038, Portal of Santiago Cathedral; No. 1039, Censer; No. 1041, Santiago Cathedral. HORIZ: No. 1035, Tomb of St. James.

206

1943. Anti-Tuberculosis Fund. Inscr "1943–1944".

1042	**206**	10 c. vio & red (postage)	30	25
1043		20 c. + 5 c. green & red	3·00	1·40
1044		40 c. + 10 c. blue & red	2·00	1·00
1045	–	10 c. violet and red (air)	85	90

DESIGN: No. 1045. Lorraine Cross and outline of bird.

207 10th-cent Tower

208 Arms of Soria

1944. Millenary of Castile. Arms designs as T **208** inscr "MILENARIO DE CASTILLA".

1046	**207**	20 c. lilac	20	20
1047	**208**	20 c. lilac	20	15
1048	–	20 c. lilac	20	20
1049	–	40 c. brown	3·75	60
1050	–	40 c. brown	3·75	60
1051	–	40 c. brown	3·00	60
1052	–	75 c. blue	3·75	3·00
1053	–	75 c. blue	3·00	3·00
1054	–	75 c. blue	4·00	3·25

DESIGNS: No. 1048, Avila (Shield at left); No. 1049, Castile (Arms in centre); No. 1050, Segovia (Shield at left); No. 1051, Burgos (Shield at right); No. 1052, Avila (Shield at left); No. 1053, Fernan Gonzalez, founder of Castile (Helmet, bow and arrows at left); No. 1054, Santander (Shield at right).

209 "Dr. Thebussem" (M. P. de Figueroa, author and postal historian)

1944. Air. Stamp Day.

1055	**209**	5 p. blue	20·00	16·00

210

211 Quevedo

1944. Anti-Tuberculosis Fund. Inscr "1944 1945". (a) Postage.

1056	**210**	10 c. orange and red	15	10
1057		20 c. + 5 c. black & red	35	25
1058		40 c. + 10 c. violet & red	65	50
1059		80 c. + 10 c. blue & red	11·50	7·75

(b) Air. Inscr "CORRESPONDENCIA AEREA".

1060	–	25 c. orange and red	5·00	3·50

DESIGN—HORIZ: No. 1060, Hospital.

1945. 300th Death Anniv of Francisco de Quevedo (author).

1061	**211**	40 c. brown	75	60

212 Conde de San Luis, Mail Vehicle of 1850 and Airplane

1945. Air. Stamp Day.

1062	**212**	10 p. green	27·00	18·00

213 Carlos de Haya Gonzalez

214 J. Garcia Morato

1945. Air. Civil War Air Aces.

1063	**213**	4 p. red	15·00	6·50
1064	**214**	10 p. purple	35·00	7·50

215 St. George and Dragon

216 Lorraine Cross and Eagle

1945. Anti-T.B. Fund.

1065	**215**	10 c. orge & red (post)	15	15
1066		20 c. + 5 c. green & red	20	15
1067		40 c. + 10 c. vio & red	40	15
1068		80 c. + 10 c. blue & red	11·00	7·75
1069	**216**	25 c. red (air)	1·60	1·10

217 E. A. de Nebrija (compiler of first Spanish Grammar)

219 Statue of Fray Bartolome de las Casas and native Indian

1946. Stamp Day and Day of the Race.

1070	**217**	50 c. red (postage)	55	15
1071	–	75 c. blue	65	40
1072	**219**	5 p. 50 green (air)	3·25	1·90

DESIGN—As Type **217**: 75 c. Salamanca University and signature of F. F. de Vitoria (founder of International Law).

220 Self-portrait of Goya

221 Woman and Child

1946. Birth Bicentenary of Goya (painter).

1073	**220**	25 c. red	15	15
1074		50 c. green	15	15
1075		75 c. blue	85	60

1946. Anti-Tuberculosis Fund. Dated "1946 1947".

1076	**221**	5 c. violet and red (postage)	15	15
1077		10 c. green and red	15	15
1078	–	25 c. orange & red (air)	35	15

DESIGN—HORIZ: 25 c. Eagle.

222 B. J. Feijoo y Montenegro

1947.

1079	**222**	50 c. green	70	45

223 Don Quixote in Library

224 Don Quixote

1947. Stamp Day and 400th Birth Anniv of Cervantes.

1080	223	50 c. brown (postage)	35	15
1081	224	75 c. blue	60	35
1082	–	5 p. 50 violet (air)	6·25	3·50

DESIGN—HORIZ: 5 p. 50, Quixote on Wooden Horse (after Gustav Dore).

226 Manuel de Falla (composer)

228 Lorraine Cross

1947. Air.

1083	226	25 p. purple	45·00	18·00
1084	–	50 p. red	£170	32·00

PORTRAIT: 50 p. Ignacio Zuloaga (painter).

1947. Anti-Tuberculosis Fund. Dated "1947 1948".

1085	228	5 c. brn & red (postage)	15	15
1086	–	10 c. blue and red	15	15
1087	–	25 c. mauve & red (air)	35	15

DESIGNS—VERT: 10 c. Deckchair in garden. HORIZ: 25 c. Santorium.

229 General Franco

230 Hernando Cortes

1948.

1088	229	5 c. brown	10	10
1088a		5 c. green	10	10
1089		15 c. green	15	10
1090		50 c. brown	15	10
1091		80 c. red	4·50	10

1948.

1092	230	35 c. black	15	10
1093	–	70 c. purple	2·75	1·75

PORTRAIT: 70 c. M. Aleman (writer).

232 Gen. Franco and Castillo de la Mota

233 Ferdinand III of Castile

1948.

1094	232	25 c. orange	10	10
1095		30 c. green	10	10
1096		35 c. green	10	10
1097		40 c. brown	75	10
1099		45 c. red	35	10
1100		50 c. purple	1·25	10
1101		70 c. violet	2·10	15
1102		75 c. blue	2·00	15
1103		1 p. red	6·25	10

1948. 700th Anniv of Institution of Castilian Navy.

1104	233	25 c. violet	35	15
1105	–	30 c. red (Admiral R. de Bonifaz)	15	15

235 Marquis of Salamanca

236 Diesel Train and Lockheed Constellation Airliner

1948. Stamp Day and Spanish Railway Cent. Inscr "F.F.C.C. ESPANOLES 1848 1948".

1106	235	50 c. brown (postage)	65	15
1107	–	5 p. green	2·75	15
1108	236	2 p. red (air)	3·25	1·50

DESIGN—HORIZ: 5 p. Garganta de Pancorbo Viaduct.

238 Aesculapius

240 Globe and Buildings

1948. Anti-Tuberculosis Fund. Dated "1948 1949".

1109	238	5 c. brn & red (postage)	15	15
1110		10 c. green and red	15	15
1111		50 c. + 10 c. brn and red	1·25	70
1112	–	25 c. blue and red (air)	45	30

DESIGN: 25 c. Lockheed Constellation airliner over sanatorium.

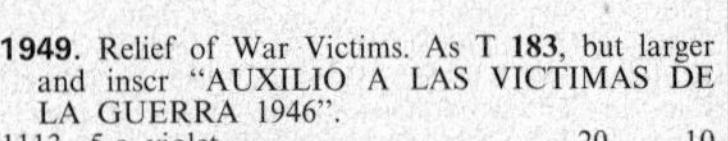

1949. Relief of War Victims. As T **183**, but larger and inscr "AUXILIO A LAS VICTIMAS DE LA GUERRA 1946".

1113		5 c. violet	20	10

1949. 75th Anniv of U.P.U.

1127	240	50 c. brown (postage)	1·00	15
1128		75 c. blue	70	35
1129		4 p. green (air)	50	20

241 Galleon

242 San Juan de Dios and Leper

1949. Anti-Tuberculosis Fund. Inscr "1949 1950".

1130	241	5 c. vio & red (postage)	15	15
1131		10 c. green and red	15	15
1132		50 c. + 10 c. brn & red	70	30
1133	–	25 c. brown and red (air)	20	15

DESIGN: 25 c. Bell.

1950. 400th Death Anniv of San Juan de Dios.

1134	242	1 p. violet	16·00	5·25

243 Calderon de la Barca (dramatist)

244 Isabella II

1950. Portraits.

1135	243	5 c. brown	10	10
1136	–	10 c. purple	10	10
1137	–	15 c. green	30	10
1138	–	20 c. violet	50	10
1139	–	2 p. blue	25·00	20
1140	–	4 p. 50 purple	1·25	1·00

PORTRAITS—VERT: 10 c. Lope de Vega (author); 15 c. Tirso de Molina (poet); 20 c. Ruiz de Alarcon (author); 2 p. Dr. Ramon y Cajal (physician); 4 p. 50, Dr. Ferran y Clua (bacteriologist).

1950. Stamp Centenary. Imperf. (a) Postage. Reproduction of T **1**.

1141	244	50 c. violet	10·50	5·25
1142		75 c. blue	10·50	5·25
1143		10 p. green	£160	£100
1144		15 p. red	£160	£100

(b) Air. Reproduction of T **2**.

1145	–	1 p. purple	10·50	5·25
1146	–	2 p. 50 brown	10·50	5·25
1147	–	20 p. blue	£160	£100
1148	–	25 p. green	£160	£100

1950. Gen. Franco's Canary Is Visit. Nos. 1100 and 1103 surch **VISITA DEL CAUDILLO A CANARIAS OCTUBRE 1950 SOBRETASA: DIEZ CTS** and No. 1083 with **Correspondencia por avion** also.

1149	232	10 c. on 50 c. purple (postage)	48·00	35·00
1150		10 c. on 1 p. red	48·00	35·00
1151	226	10 c. on 25 p. purple (air)	£500	£225

246 Candle and Conifer

247 Map

1950. Anti-T.B. Fund. Cross in red. Inscr "1950 1951".

1152	246	5 c. violet (postage)	10	10
1153		10 c. green	10	10
1154		50 c. + 10 c. brown	2·10	1·10
1155	–	25 c. blue (air)	55	25

DESIGN: 25 c. Dove and flowers.

1951. Air. 6th Conference of Spanish–American Postal Union.

1156	247	1 p. blue	6·75	2·40

248 Isabella the Catholic

248a St. Antonio Claret

1951. 5th Centenary of Birth of Isabella.

1157	248	50 c. brown	85	25
1158		75 c. blue	1·25	25
1159		90 c. purple	60	20
1160		1 p. 50 orange	14·50	6·50
1161		2 p. 80 olive	32·00	19·00

1951. Stamp Day.

1162	248a	50 c. blue	5·00	2·75

249 Children on Beach

250 Isabella the Catholic

1951. Anti-Tuberculosis Fund. Cross in red.

1163	249	5 c. red (postage)	10	10
1164		10 c. green	65	10
1165	–	25 c. brown (air)	75	15

DESIGN: 25 c. Nurse and child.

1951. Air. Stamp Day and 500th Birth Anniv of Isabella the Catholic.

1166	250	60 c. green	7·50	45
1167		90 c. yellow	95	60
1168		1 p. 30 red	10·50	5·00
1169		1 p. 90 sepia	7·50	5·50
1170		2 p. 30 blue	4·75	2·75

251 Ferdinand the Catholic

252 St. Maria Micaela

1952. 500th Birth Anniv of Ferdinand the Catholic.

1171	251	50 c. green	75	40
1172		75 c. blue	6·25	1·40
1173		90 c. purple	50	25
1174		1 p. 50 orange	14·00	7·00
1175		2 p. 80 brown	23·00	15·00

1952. 35th International Eucharistic Congress, Barcelona.

1176	252	60 c. red (postage)	15	10
1177	–	1 p. green (air)	4·00	35

DESIGN: 1 p. "The Eucharist" (Tiepolo).

252a St. Francis Xavier

254 Nurse and Baby

1952. Air. 400th Death Anniv of St. Francis Xavier.

1178	252a	2 p. blue	50·00	21·00

1952. Air. Stamp Day and 500th Anniv of Birth of Ferdinand the Catholic. As T **250** but interior scene and portrait of Ferdinand the Catholic.

1179		60 c. green	25	15
1180		90 c. orange	25	15
1181		1 p. 30 red	75	75
1182		1 p. 90 brown	3·00	2·10
1183		2 p. 30 blue	14·00	9·00

1953. Anti-Tuberculosis Fund. Cross in red.

1184	254	5 c. lake (postage)	50	10
1185		10 c. green	1·50	10
1186	–	25 c. brown (air)	5·75	5·25

DESIGN: 25 c. Girl and angel.

255 J. Sorolla (painter)

1953. Air.

1187	255	50 p. violet	£550	21·00

256 Bas-relief

257 Fray Luis de Leon

1953. Stamp Day and 700th Anniv of Salamanca University. Inscr "UNIVDAD DE SALAMANCA".

1188	256	50 c. red	45	15
1189	257	90 c. green	2·25	2·10
1190	–	2 p. brown	18·00	4·25

DESIGN—As Type **185**—HORIZ: 2 p. Salamanca University.

258 M. L. de Legazpi (founder of Manila)

259 "St. Mary Magdalene"

1953. Air. Signing of Filipino–Spanish Postal Convention.

1191	258	25 p. black	£130	33·00

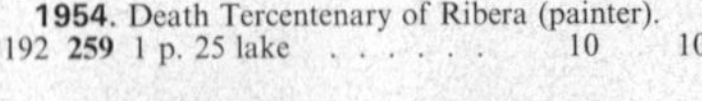

1954. Death Tercentenary of Ribera (painter).

1192	259	1 p. 25 lake	10	10

260 St. James of Compostela

261 "Purity" (after Cano)

1954. Holy Year.

1193	260	50 c. brown	50	25
1194	–	3 p. blue	50·00	3·50

DESIGN: 3 p. Santiago Cathedral.

1954. Marian Year.

1195	261	10 c. red	10	10
1196	–	15 c. green	15	10
1197	–	25 c. violet	20	10
1198	–	30 c. brown	20	10
1199	–	50 c. green	75	10
1200	–	60 c. black	15	10
1201	–	80 c. green	3·75	10
1202	–	1 p. violet	3·75	10
1203	–	2 p. brown	1·25	10
1204	–	3 p. blue	1·40	1·00

DESIGNS: 15 c. Virgin of Begona, Bilbao; 25 c. Virgin of the Abandoned, Valencia Cathedral; 30 c. The "Black Virgin" of Montserrat; 50 c. El Pilar Virgin, Zaragoza; 60 c. Covadonga Virgin; 80 c. Virgin of the Kings, Seville Cathedral; 1 p. Almudena Virgin, Madrid; 2 p. Virgin of Africa; 3 p. Guadalupe Virgin.

262 M. Menendez Pelayo (historian)

263 Gen. Franco

1954. Stamp Day.

1205	262	80 c. green	9·00	15

1955.

No.	Type	Description	Unused	Used
1206	263	10 c. red	10	10
1207		15 c. ochre	10	10
1208		20 c. green	10	10
1209		25 c. violet	10	10
1210		30 c. brown	10	10
1211		40 c. purple	10	10
1212		50 c. brown	10	10
1213		60 c. purple	10	10
1214		70 c. green	15	10
1215		80 c. turquoise	10	10
1216		1 p. orange	10	10
1217		1 p. 40 mauve	15	10
1218		1 p. 50 turquoise	10	10
1219		1 p. 80 green	15	10
1220		2 p. red	22·00	75
1221		2 p. mauve	10	10
1222		3 p. blue	10	10
1222a		4 p. red	10	10
1223		5 p. brown	15	10
1224		6 p. black	15	10
1224a		7 p. blue	10	10
1225		8 p. violet	15	10
1226		10 p. green	20	10
1226a		12 p. green	15	10
1226b		20 p. red	20	10

264 Torres Quevedo (engineer and inventor)

265 St. Ignatius of Loyola

1955. Air.

No.	Type	Description	Unused	Used
1229	–	25 p. black	29·00	75
1230	264	50 p. violet	10·50	1·90

Portrait: 25 p. Fortuny (painter)

1955. Stamp Day and 4th Centenary of Death of St. Ignatius of Loyola.

No.	Type	Description	Unused	Used
1231	265	25 c. slate	15	10
1232	–	60 c. ochre	85	50
1233	265	80 c. green	3·25	50

DESIGN—HORIZ: 60 c. St. Ignatius and Loyola Castle.

266 Lockheed L.1049 Super Constellation and Caravel

1955. Air.

No.	Type	Description	Unused	Used
1234	266	20 c. green	20	10
1235		25 c. violet	20	10
1236		50 c. brown	20	10
1237		1 p. red	25	10
1238		1 p. 10 green	25	10
1239		1 p. 40 mauve	25	10
1240		3 p. blue	30	15
1241		4 p. 80 yellow	30	15
1242		5 p. brown	1·60	20
1243		7 p. mauve	85	30
1244		10 p. green	1·10	40

267 "Telecommunications"

269 "The Holy Family" (after El Greco)

1955. Centenary of Telegraphs in Spain.

No.	Type	Description	Unused	Used
1245	267	15 c. brown	55	20
1246		80 c. green	12·00	25
1247		3 p. blue	21·00	1·00

1955. 500th Anniv of Canonization of St. Vincent Ferrer. As T **259** but portrait of the Saint (after C. Vilar).

No.	Type	Description	Unused	Used
1248		15 c. ochre	50	20

1955. Christmas.

No.	Type	Description	Unused	Used
1249	269	80 c. myrtle	6·00	65

270

272 The "Black Virgin"

271 "Ciudad de Toledo" (cargo liner)

1956. 20th Anniv of Civil War.

No.	Type	Description	Unused	Used
1250	270	15 c. brown and bistre	20	15
1251		50 c. olive and green	75	40
1252		80 c. grey and mauve	8·25	25
1253		3 p. blue and ultramarine	11·50	2·10

1956. 1st Floating Exhibition of National Products.

No.	Type	Description	Unused	Used
1254	271	3 p. blue	6·00	2·25

1956. 75th Anniv of "Black Virgin" of Montserrat.

No.	Type	Description	Unused	Used
1255	272	15 c. brown	10	10
1256	–	60 c. purple	30	20
1257	272	80 c. green	50	40

DESIGN—VERT: 60 c. Montserrat Monastery.

273 Archangel Gabriel

274 "Statistics"

1956. Stamp Day.

No.	Type	Description	Unused	Used
1258	273	80 c. green	65	40

1956. Centenary of Statistics in Spain.

No.	Type	Description	Unused	Used
1259	274	15 c. ochre	40	25
1260		80 c. green	5·25	60
1261		1 p. red	5·25	60

275 Hermitage and Monument

276 Refugee Children

1956. 20th Anniv of Gen. Franco's Assumption of Office as Head of State.

No.	Type	Description	Unused	Used
1262	275	80 c. green	5·75	30

1956. Hungarian Children's Relief.

No.	Type	Description	Unused	Used
1263	276	10 c. lake	10	10
1264		15 c. brown	15	10
1265		50 c. sepia	40	20
1266		80 c. green	5·00	25
1267		1 p. red	5·00	25
1268		3 p. blue	14·00	2·00

277 Apparition of the Sacred Heart

278 "The Great Captain"

1957. Stamp Day and Centenary Feast of the Sacred Heart.

No.	Type	Description	Unused	Used
1269	277	15 c. brown	10	10
1270		60 c. purple	25	10
1271		80 c. green	25	10

1958. 5th Birth Cent of Gonzalves de Cordoba.

No.	Type	Description	Unused	Used
1272	278	1 p. 80 green	15	10

279 Francisco Goya after Lopez

280 Exhibition Emblem

1958. Stamp Day and Goya (painter) Commem. Frames in gold.

No.	Type	Description	Unused	Used
1273	–	15 c. ochre	10	10
1274	–	40 c. purple	10	10
1275	–	50 c. green	10	10
1276	–	60 c. purple	15	10
1277	–	70 c. green	15	10
1278	279	80 c. green	20	10
1279	–	1 p. red	20	10
1280	–	1 p. 80 green	25	10
1281	–	2 p. purple	40	30
1282	–	3 p. blue	95	50

PAINTINGS—HORIZ: 15 c. "The Sunshade"; 3 p. "The Drinker". VERT: 40 c. "The Bookseller's Wife"; 50 c. "The Count of Fernan-Nunez"; 60 c. "The Crockery Vendor"; 70 c. "Dona Isabel Cobos de Porcel"; 1 p. "The Carnival Doll"; 1 p. 80, "Marianito Goya"; 2 p. "The Vintage".

For similar designs see Nos. 1301/10, 1333/42, 1391/1400, 1479/88, 1495/8, 1559/68, 1627/36, 1718/27, 1770/9, 1837/46, 1912/21, 1968/77, 2021/30, 2077/84, 2135/42 and 2204/11.

1958. Brussels International Exhibition.

No.	Type	Description	Unused	Used
1283	280	80 c. brown, red and deep brown	20	10
1284		3 p. blue, red & black	90	80

281 Emperor Charles V (after Strigell)

1958. 4th Death Cent of Emperor Charles V.

No.	Type	Description	Unused	Used
1287	281	15 c. brown and ochre	15	10
1288	–	50 c. olive and green	15	10
1289	–	70 c. green and drab	20	10
1290	–	80 c. green and brown	20	10
1291	281	1 p. red and buff	25	10
1292	–	1 p. 80 emerald & green	15	10
1293	–	2 p. purple and grey	70	60
1294	–	3 p. blue and brown	1·75	1·25

PORTRAITS of Charles V: 50 c., 1 p. 80, At Battle of Muhlberg (after Titian); 70 c., 2 p. (after Leoni); 80 c., 3 p. (after Titian).

282 Talgo Express and Escorial

1958. 17th Int Railway Congress, Madrid. Inscr "XVII CONGRESO", etc.

No.	Type	Description	Unused	Used
1295	282	15 c. ochre	15	50
1296	–	60 c. plum	20	10
1297	–	80 c. green	25	10
1298	282	1 p. orange	80	10
1299	–	2 p. purple	85	10
1300	–	3 p. blue	2·75	1·25

DESIGNS—VERT: 60 c., 2 p. Diesel train on viaduct, Despenaperros Gorge. HORIZ: 80 c., 3 p. Steam locomotive and Castillo de La Mota.

1959. Stamp Day and Velazquez Commem. Designs as T **279**. Frames in gold.

No.	Type	Description	Unused	Used
1301		15 c. sepia	15	10
1302		40 c. purple	15	10
1303		50 c. olive	15	10
1304		60 c. sepia	15	10
1305		70 c. green	15	10
1306		80 c. myrtle	15	10
1307		1 p. brown	20	10
1308		1 p. 80 green	15	10
1309		2 p. purple	45	20
1310		3 p. blue	85	45

PAINTINGS—HORIZ: 15 c. "The Drunkards". VERT: 40 c. "The Spinners" (detail); 50 c. "The Surrender of Breda"; 60 c. "Las Meninas"; 70 c. "Balthasar Don Carlos"; 80 c. Self-portrait; 1 p. "The Coronation of the Virgin"; 1 p. 80, "Aesop"; 2 p. "The Forge of Vulcan"; 3 p. "Menippus".

284 The Holy Cross of the Valley of the Fallen

1959. Completion of Monastery of the Holy Cross of the Valley of the Fallen.

No.	Type	Description	Unused	Used
1311	284	80 c. green and brown	20	10

285 Mazarin and Luis de Haro (after tapestry by Lebrun)

286 Monastery from Courtyard

1959. 300th Anniv of Treaty of the Pyrenees.

No.	Type	Description	Unused	Used
1312	285	1 p. brown and gold	20	10

1959. 50th Anniv of Entry of Franciscan Community into Guadeloupe Monastery.

No.	Type	Description	Unused	Used
1313	286	15 c. brown	10	10
1314	–	80 c. myrtle	20	10
1315	–	1 p. red	20	10

DESIGNS: 80 c. Exterior view of monastery; 1 p. Entrance doors of church.

287 "The Holy Family" (after Goya)

288 Pass with Muleta

1959. Christmas.

No.	Type	Description	Unused	Used
1316	287	1 p. brown	25	10

1960. Bullfighting.

No.	Type	Description	Unused	Used
1317	–	15 c. brown & ochre (postage)	15	10
1318	–	20 c. violet and blue	15	10
1319	–	25 c. black	15	10
1320	–	30 c. brown and bistre	15	10
1321	–	50 c. brown and violet	15	10
1322	–	70 c. green and brown	15	10
1323	288	80 c. emerald and green	15	10
1324	–	1 p. brown and red	25	10
1325	–	1 p. 40 purple and brown	15	10
1326	–	1 p. 50 green and blue	15	10
1327	–	1 p. 80 blue and green	15	10
1328	–	5 p. red and brown	65	50
1329	–	25 c. deep purple & purple (air)	15	10
1330	–	50 c. blue & turquoise	15	10
1331	–	1 p. red and vermilion	25	10
1332	–	5 p. violet and purple	65	40

DESIGNS—HORIZ: No. 1317, Fighting bull; No. 1318, Rounding-up bull; No. 1327, Placing darts from horseback; No. 1330, Pass with cape; No. 1332, Bull-ring. VERT: No. 1319, Corralling bulls at Pamplona; No. 1320, Bull entering ring; No. 1321, As No. 1330 (different pass); No. 1322, Banderillero placing darts; No. 1323/6, As Type **288** (different passes with muleta); No. 1328, Old-time bull-fighter; No. 1329, Village bull-ring; No. 1331, Dedicating the bull.

1960. Stamp Day and Murillo Commemoration. (painter). Designs as T **279**. Frames in gold.

No.	Type	Description	Unused	Used
1333		25 c. violet	15	10
1334		40 c. purple	15	10
1335		50 c. olive	15	10
1336		70 c. green	15	10
1337		80 c. turquoise	15	10
1338		1 p. brown	15	10
1339		1 p. 50 turquoise	15	10
1340		2 p. 50 red	15	10
1341		3 p. blue	1·40	65
1342		5 p. brown	40	25

PAINTINGS—VERT: 25 c. "The Good Shepherd"; 40 c. "Rebecca and Elizer"; 50 c. "The Virgin of the Rosary"; 70 c. "The Immaculate Conception"; 80 c. "Children with Shells"; 1 p. Self-portrait; 2 p. 50, "The Dice Game"; 3 p. "Children Eating"; 5 p. "Children with Coins". HORIZ: 1 p. 50, "The Holy Family with Bird".

289 "Christ of Lepanto"

290 Pelota Player

1960. Int Philatelic Congress and Exhibition, Barcelona. Inscr "CIF".

No.	Type	Description	Unused	Used
1343	289	70 c. lake & grn (postage)	1·60	1·25
1344	–	80 c. black and sage	1·60	1·25
1345	289	1 p. purple and red	1·60	1·25
1346	–	2 p. 50 slate and violet	1·60	1·25
1347	289	5 p. sepia and bistre	1·60	1·25
1348	–	10 p. sepia and ochre	1·60	1·25
1349	290	1 p. black and red (air)	4·75	2·75
1350		5 p. red and brown	4·75	2·75
1351		6 p. red and purple	4·75	2·75
1352		10 p. red and green	4·75	2·75

DESIGN—VERT: Nos. 1344, 1346, 1348, Church of the Holy Family, Barcelona.

291 St. John of Ribera **292** St. Vincent de Paul

1960. Canonization of St. John of Ribera.

No.	Type	Description	Unused	Used
1353	291	1 p. brown	15	10
1354		2 p. 50 mauve	10	10

1960. Europa. 1st Anniv of European Postal and Telecommunications Conference. As T **129a** of Luxembourg but size 38½ × 22 mm.

No.	Type	Description	Unused	Used
1355		1 p. drab and green	75	20
1356		5 p. red and brown	1·00	75

1960. 300th Death Anniv of St. Vincent de Paul.

No.	Type	Description	Unused	Used
1357	292	25 c. violet	10	10
1358		1 p. brown	15	10

293 Menendez de Aviles **294** Running

1960. 400th Anniv of Discovery and Colonization of Florida.

No.	Type	Description	Unused	Used
1359	293	25 c. blue and light blue	15	10
1360	–	70 c. green and orange	15	10
1361	–	80 c. green and stone	15	10
1362	–	1 p. brown and yellow	15	10
1363	293	2 p. red and pink	30	10
1364	–	2 p. 50 mauve & green	50	10
1365	–	3 p. blue and green	3·00	75
1366	–	5 p. brown and bistre	2·10	1·00

PORTRAITS: 70 c., 2 p. 50, Hernando de Soto; 80 c., 3 p. Ponce de Leon; 1, 5 p. Cabeza de Vaca.

1960. Sports.

No.	Type	Description	Unused	Used
1367	294	25 c. brown and blue (postage)	15	10
1368	–	40 c. orange and violet	15	10
1369	–	70 c. red and green	30	10
1370	–	80 c. red and green	25	10
1371	–	1 p. green and red	75	10
1372	294	1 p. 50 sepia & turquoise	30	10
1373	–	2 p. green and purple	1·90	10
1374	–	2 p. 50 green & mauve	30	10
1375	–	3 p. red and blue	75	30
1376	–	5 p. blue and brown	75	65
1377	–	1 p. 25 red & brown (air)	15	10
1378	–	1 p. 50 brown & violet	30	10
1379	–	6 p. red and violet	1·10	70
1380	–	10 p. red and olive	1·40	85

DESIGNS—HORIZ: 40 c., 2 p. Cycling; 70 c., 2 p. 50, Football; 1, 5 p. Hockey; 1 p. 25, 6 p. Horse-jumping. VERT: 80 c., 3 p. Gymnastics; 1 p. 50 (air), 10 p. Pelota.

295 Albeniz **296** Cloisters

1960. Birth Cent of Isaac Albeniz (composer).

No.	Type	Description	Unused	Used
1381	295	25 c. violet	10	10
1382		1 p. brown	15	10

1960. Samos Monastery.

No.	Type	Description	Unused	Used
1383	296	80 c. turquoise and green	15	10
1384	–	1 p. lake and brown	1·25	10
1385	–	5 p. sepia and bistre	1·40	90

DESIGNS—VERT: 1 p. Fountain; 5 p. Portico and facade.

297 "The Nativity" (Velazquez) **298** "The Flight to Egypt" (after Bayeu)

1960. Christmas.

No.	Type	Description	Unused	Used
1386	297	1 p. brown	30	10

1961. World Refugee Year.

No.	Type	Description	Unused	Used
1387	298	1 p. brown	20	10
1388		5 p. brown	50	30

299 L. F. Moratin (after Goya) **301** Velazquez (Prado Memorial)

1961. Birth Bicentenary of Moratin (poet and dramatist).

No.	Type	Description	Unused	Used
1389	299	1 p. red	15	10
1390		1 p. 50 turquoise	10	10

1961. Stamp Day and El Greco (painter) Commem. Designs as T **279**. Frames in gold.

No.	Type	Description	Unused	Used
1391		25 c. purple	15	10
1392		40 c. purple	15	10
1393		70 c. green	20	10
1394		80 c. turquoise	15	10
1395		1 p. purple	2·40	10
1396		1 p. 50 turquoise	15	10
1397		2 p. 50 lake	20	10
1398		3 p. blue	1·75	1·00
1399		5 p. sepia	4·00	2·25
1400		10 p. violet	50	40

PAINTINGS: 25 c. "St. Peter"; 40 c. Madonna (detail, "The Holy Family" (Madonna of the Good Milk)); 70 c. Detail of "The Agony in the Garden"; 80 c. "Man with Hand on Breast"; 1 p. Self-portrait; 1 p. 50, "The Baptism of Christ"; 2 p. 50, "The Holy Trinity"; 3 p. "Burial of the Count of Orgaz"; 5 p. "The Spoliation"; 10 p. "The Martyrdom of St. Maurice".

1961. 300th Death Anniv of Velazquez.

No.	Type	Description	Unused	Used
1401	301	80 c. green and blue	1·40	20
1402	–	1 p. brown and red	6·50	20
1403	–	2 p. 50 violet and blue	85	50
1404	–	10 p. green & lt green	9·00	1·90

PAINTINGS—VERT: 1 p. "The Duke of Olivares"; 2 p. 50, "Princess Margarita". HORIZ: Part of "The Spinners".

302 "Stamp" and "Postmark" **303** Vazquez de Mella

1961. World Stamp Day.

No.	Type	Description	Unused	Used
1409	302	25 c. black and red	15	10
1410		1 p. red and black	1·10	10
1411		10 p. green and purple	1·25	60

1961. Birth Centenary of Juan Vazquez de Mella (politician and writer).

No.	Type	Description	Unused	Used
1412	303	1 p. red	45	10
1413		2 p. 30 purple	15	15

304 Gen. Franco **305** "Portico de la Gloria" (Cathedral of Santiago de Compostela)

1961. 25th Anniv of National Uprising. Multicoloured.

No.	Type	Description	Unused	Used
1414		70 c. Angel and flag	15	10
1415		80 c. Straits of Gibraltar	15	10
1416		1 p. Knight and Alcazar, Toledo	20	10
1417		1 p. 50 Victory Arch	15	10
1418		2 p. Knight crossing River Ebro	15	10
1419		2 p. 30 Soldier, flag and troops	15	10
1420		2 p. 50 Shipbuilding	30	30
1421		3 p. Steelworks	30	30
1422		5 p. Map of Spain showing electric power stations	2·40	1·40
1423		6 p. Irrigation (woman beside dam)	1·90	1·75
1424		8 p. Mine	75	70
1425		10 p. Type **304**	65	70

The 5 p. is horiz and the rest vert.

1961. Council of Europe's Romanesque Art Exhibition. Inscr as in T **305**.

No.	Type	Description	Unused	Used
1426	305	25 c. violet and gold	15	10
1427	–	1 p. brown and gold	15	10
1428	–	2 p. purple and gold	40	10
1429	–	3 p. multicoloured	40	50

DESIGNS: 1 p. Courtyard of Dominican Monastery, Santo Domingo de Silos; 2 p. Madonna of Irache; 3 p. "Christos Pantocrator" (from Tahull Church fresco).

306 L. de Gongora (after Velazquez) **308** Burgos Cathedral

307 Doves and C.E.P.T. Emblem

1961. 400th Birth Anniv of De Gongora (poet).

No.	Type	Description	Unused	Used
1430	306	25 c. violet	10	10
1431		1 p. brown	20	10

1961. Europa.

No.	Type	Description	Unused	Used
1432	307	1 p. red	10	10
1433		5 p. brown	40	35

1961. 25th Anniv of Gen. Franco as Head of State.

No.	Type	Description	Unused	Used
1434	308	1 p. green and gold	20	10

309 S. de Belalcazar **310** Courtyard

1961. Explorers and Colonizers of America (1st series).

No.	Type	Description	Unused	Used
1435	309	25 c. violet and green	15	10
1436	–	70 c. green and buff	15	10
1437	–	80 c. green and pink	15	10
1438	–	1 p. blue and flesh	45	10
1439	309	2 p. red and blue	3·75	15
1440	–	2 p. 50 purple & mauve	90	50
1441	–	3 p. blue and grey	2·10	85
1442	–	5 p. brown and yellow	2·10	1·25

PORTRAITS: 70 c., 2 p. 50, B de Lezo; 80 c., 3 p. R. de Bastidas; 1, 5 p. N. de Chaves.

See also Nos. 1515/22, 1587/94, 1683/90, 1738/45, 1810/17, 1877/84, 1947/51, 1997/2001 and 2054/8.

1961. Escorial.

No.	Type	Description	Unused	Used
1443	–	70 c. green and turquoise	20	10
1444	310	80 c. slate and green	20	10
1445	–	1 p. red and brown	50	10
1446	–	2 p. 50 purple & violet	30	10
1447	–	5 p. sepia and ochre	1·50	85
1448	–	6 p. purple and blue	2·40	2·10

DESIGNS—VERT: 70 c. Patio of the Kings; 2 p. 50, Grand Staircase; 6 p. High Altar. HORIZ: 1 p. Monks' Garden; 5 p. View of Escorial.

311 King Alfonso XII Monument **312** Santa Maria del Naranco Church

1961. 400th Anniv of Madrid as Capital of Spain.

No.	Type	Description	Unused	Used
1449	311	25 c. purple and green	15	10
1450	–	1 p. brown and bistre	30	10
1451	–	2 p. purple and grey	30	10
1452	–	2 p. 50 violet and red	15	10
1453	–	3 p. black and blue	60	50
1454	–	5 p. blue and brown	1·40	90

DESIGNS—VERT: 1 p. King Philip II (after Pantoja); 5 p. Plaza, Madrid. HORIZ: 2 p. Town Hall, Madrid; 2 p. 50, Fountain of Cybele; 3 p. Portals of Alcala Palace.

1961. 1200th Anniv of Oviedo.

No.	Type	Description	Unused	Used
1455	312	25 c. violet and green	15	10
1456	–	1 p. brown and bistre	35	10
1457	–	2 p. sepia and purple	95	10
1458	–	2 p. 50 violet & purple	15	10
1459	–	3 p. black and blue	85	50
1460	–	5 p. brown and green	85	90

DESIGNS: 1 p. Fruela (portrait); 2 p. Cross of the Angels; 2 p. 50, Alfonso II; 3 p. Alfonso III; 5 p. Apostles of the Holy Hall, Oviedo Cathedral.

313 "The Nativity" (after Gines) **314** Cierva C.30A Autogyro

1961. Christmas.

No.	Type	Description	Unused	Used
1461	313	1 p. plum	30	10

1961. 50th Anniv of Spanish Aviation.

No.	Type	Description	Unused	Used
1462	314	1 p. violet and blue	25	15
1463	–	2 p. green and lilac	50	20
1464	–	3 p. black and green	2·25	45
1465	–	5 p. purple and slate	4·25	1·40
1466	–	10 p. brown and blue	2·00	55

DESIGNS—HORIZ: 2 p. CASA-built Dornier Do-J Wal flying boat "Plus Ultra"; 3 p. Breguet 19GR airplane "Jesus del Gran Poder" (Madrid–Manila Flight). VERT: 5 p. Avro 504K biplane hunting great bustard; 10 p. Madonna of Loreto (patron saint) and North American F-86F Sabre jet fighters.

315 Arms of Alava **316** "Ecstasy of St. Teresa" (Bernini)

1962. Arms of Provincial Capitals. Multicoloured.

No.	Type	Description	Unused	Used
1467		5 p. Type **315**	10	10
1468		5 p. Albacete	10	10
1469		5 p. Alicante	25	25
1470		5 p. Almeria	25	25
1471		5 p. Avila	25	25
1472		5 p. Badajoz	15	15
1473		5 p. Baleares	20	20
1474		5 p. Barcelona	20	20
1475		5 p. Burgos	70	50
1476		5 p. Caceres	40	35
1477		5 p. Cadiz	60	40
1478		5 p. Castellon de la Plana	3·00	2·25

See also Nos. 1542/53, 1612/23, 1692/1703 and 1756/64.

1962. Stamp Day and Zurbaran (painter) Commem. As T **279**. Frames in gold.

No.	Type	Description	Unused	Used
1479		25 c. olive	15	10
1480		40 c. purple	15	10
1481		70 c. green	15	10
1482		80 c. turquoise	15	10
1483		1 p. sepia	7·00	10
1484		1 p. 50 turquoise	65	10
1485		2 p. 50 lake	65	10
1486		3 p. blue	1·25	65
1487		5 p. brown	3·00	1·25
1488		10 p. olive	3·00	1·25

PAINTINGS—HORIZ: 25 c. "Martyr". VERT: 40 c. "Burial of St. Catalina"; 70 c. "St. Casilda"; 80 c. "Jesus crowning St. Joseph"; 1 p. Self-portrait; 1 p. 50, "St. Hieronymus"; 2 p. 50, "Madonna of the Grace"; 3 p. Detail from "Apotheosis of St. Thomas Aquinas"; 5 p. "Madonna as a Child"; 10 p. "The Immaculate Madonna".

1962. 4th Centenary of Teresian Reformation.

No.	Type	Description	Unused	Used
1489	–	25 c. violet	10	10
1490	316	1 p. brown	10	10
1491	–	3 p. blue	1·25	40

DESIGNS—As Type **316**: 25 c. St. Joseph's Monastery, Avila. (22 × 38½ mm): 3 p. "St. Teresa of Avila" (Velazquez).

317 Mercury

318 St. Benedict

1962. World Stamp Day.
1492 **317** 25 c. pink, purple & violet 15 10
1493 1 p. yellow, brown and bistre 15 10
1494 10 p. green & turquoise 1·90 90

1962. Rubens Paintings. As T **279**. Frames in gold.
1495 25 c. violet 25 10
1496 1 p. brown 3·25 10
1497 3 p. turquoise 5·00 2·40
1498 10 p. green 5·50 2·25
PAINTINGS—As Type **279**: 25 c. Ferdinand of Austria; 1 p. Self-portrait; 3 p. Philip II. (26×39 mm): 10 p. Duke of Lerma.

1962. 400th Death Anniv of Alonso Berruguete (sculptor). Sculptures by Berruguete.
1499 **318** 25 c. mauve and blue 15 10
1500 – 80 c. green and brown 20 10
1501 – 1 p. red and stone 40 10
1502 – 2 p. mauve and stone 3·25 10
1503 – 3 p. blue and mauve 1·40 1·10
1504 – 10 p. brown and pink 1·40 1·25
SCULPTURES: 80 c. "The Apostle"; 1 p. "St. Peter"; 2 p. "St. Christopher and Child Jesus"; 3 p. "Ecce Homo"; 10 p. "St. Sebastian".

319 El Cid (R. Diaz de Vivar), after statue by J. Cristobal

321 Throwing the Discus

320 Honey Bee and Honeycomb

1962. El Cid Campeador Commem. Inscr "EL CID".
1505 **319** 1 p. drab and green 15 10
1506 – 2 p. violet and sepia 1·50 10
1507 – 3 p. green and blue 4·25 2·25
1508 – 10 p. green and yellow 2·75 1·25
DESIGNS—VERT: 2 p. El Cid (equestrian statue by A. Huntington). HORIZ: 3 p. El Cid's treasure chest; 10 p. Oath-taking ceremony of Santa Gadea.

1962. Europa.
1509 **320** 1 p. red 35 10
1510 5 p. green 1·40 40

1962. 2nd Spanish-American Athletic Games, Madrid.
1511 **321** 25 c. blue and pink 15 10
1512 – 80 c. green and yellow 20 15
1513 – 1 p. brown and pink 15 10
1514 – 3 p. blue and light blue 20 30
DESIGNS: 80 c. Running; 1 p. Hurdling; 3 p. Start of sprint.

1962. Explorers and Colonizers of America (2nd series). As T **309**.
1515 25 c. mauve and grey 15 10
1516 70 c. green and pink 60 10
1517 80 c. green and yellow 45 10
1518 1 p. brown and green 90 10
1519 2 p. red and blue 3·00 25
1520 2 p. 50 violet & brown 55 35
1521 3 p. blue and pink 7·50 1·90
1522 5 p. brown and yellow 3·75 2·40
PORTRAITS: 25 c., 2 p. A. de Mendoza; 70 c., 2 p. 50, J. de Quesada; 80 c., 3 p. J. de Garay; 1 p., 5 p. P. de la Gasca.

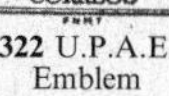

322 U.P.A.E. Emblem

323 "The Annunciation" (after Murillo)

1962. 50th Anniv of Postal Union of the Americas and Spain.
1523 **322** 1 p. brown, grn & dp grn 10 10

1962. Mysteries of the Rosary.
1524 **323** 25 c. brn & vio (postage) 15 10
1525 – 70 c. turquoise and green 15 10
1526 – 80 c. turquoise and olive 15 10
1527 – 1 p. sepia and green 4·75 60
1528 – 1 p. 50 blue and green 15 10
1529 – 2 p. sepia and violet 1·10 40
1530 – 2 p. 50 red and purple 15 10
1531 – 3 p. black and violet 15 15
1532 – 5 p. lake and brown 85 75
1533 – 8 p. black and purple 75 75
1534 – 10 p. green and myrtle 75 40
1535 – 25 c. violet and slate (air) 15 10
1536 – 1 p. olive and purple 15 15
1537 – 5 p. lake and purple 60 35
1538 – 10 p. yellow, grn & grey 1·40 90
PAINTINGS—"Joyful Mysteries": No. 1525, "Visit of Elizabeth" (Correa); No. 1526, "The Birth of Christ" (Murillo); No. 1527, "Christ shown to the Elders" (Campana); No. 1528, "Jesus lost and found in the Temple" (unknown artist). "Sorrowful Mysteries": No. 1529, "Prayer on the Mount of Olives" (Giaquinto); No. 1530, "Scourging" (Cano); No. 1531, "The Crown of Thorns" (Tiepolo); No. 1532, "Carrying the Cross" (El Greco); No. 1533, "The Crucifixion" (Murillo). "Glorious Mysteries": No. 1534, "The Resurrection" (Murillo); No. 1535, "The Ascension" (Bayeu); No. 1536, "The Sending-forth of the Holy Ghost" (El Greco); No. 1537, "The Assumption of the Virgin" (Cerezo); No. 1538, "The Coronation of the Virgin" (El Greco).

324 "The Nativity" (after Pedro de Mena)

325 Campaign Emblem and Swamp

1962. Christmas.
1539 **324** 1 p. olive 25 10

1962. Malaria Eradication.
1540 **325** 1 p. black, yellow & grn 20 10

326 Pope John and Dome of St. Peter's

327 "St. Paul" (after El Greco)

1962. Ecumenical Council. Vatican City (1st issue).
1541 **326** 1 p. slate and purple 20 10
See also Nos. 1601 and 1755.

1963. Arms of Provincial Capitals. As T **315**. Multicoloured.
1542 5 p. Ciudad Real 55 45
1543 5 p. Cordoba 4·50 1·90
1544 5 p. Coruna 55 55
1545 5 p. Cuenca 55 45
1546 5 p. Fernando Poo 1·00 1·00
1547 5 p. Gerona 15 10
1548 5 p. Gran Canaria 15 10
1549 5 p. Granada 30 35
1550 5 p. Guadalajara 55 35
1551 5 p. Guipuzcoa 15 10
1552 5 p. Huelva 15 10
1553 5 p. Huesca 15 10

1963. 1900th Anniv of Arrival of St. Paul in Spain.
1554 **327** 1 p. sepia, olive & brown 25 10

328 Poblet Monastery

329 Mail Coach

1963. Poblet Monastery.
1555 **328** 25 c. purple, sepia & grn 15 10
1556 – 1 p. orange and red 40 10
1557 – 3 p. blue and violet 1·10 30
1558 – 5 p. ochre and brown 2·10 1·60
DESIGNS—VERT: 1 p. Tomb; 5 p. Arch. HORIZ: 3 p. Aerial view of monastery.

1963. Stamp Day and Ribera (painter) Commem. As T **279**. Frames in gold.
1559 25 c. violet 15 10
1560 40 c. purple 15 10
1561 70 c. green 35 10
1562 80 c. turquoise 35 10
1563 1 p. brown 35 10
1564 1 p. 50 turquoise 35 10
1565 2 p. 50 red 2·25 10
1566 3 p. blue 3·50 70
1567 5 p. brown 11·50 2·50
1568 10 p. brown and purple 4·00 1·40
PAINTINGS: 25 c. "Archimedes"; 40 c. "Jacob's Flock"; 70 c. "Triumph of Bacchus"; 80 c. "St. Christopher"; 1 p. Self-portrait; 1 p. 50, "St. Andrew"; 2 p. 50, "St. John the Baptist"; 3 p. "St. Onofrius"; 5 p. "St. Peter"; 10 p. "The Madonna".

1963. Centenary of Paris Postal Conference.
1569 **329** 1 p. multicoloured 10 10

330 Globe

1963. World Stamp Day.
1570 **330** 25 c. multicoloured 15 10
1571 1 p. multicoloured 15 10
1572 10 p. multicoloured 1·00 65

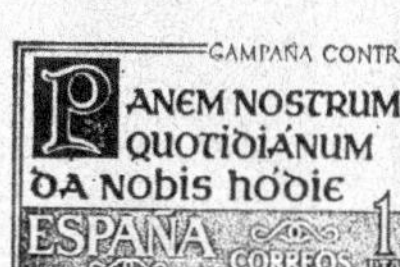

331 "Give us this day our daily bread"

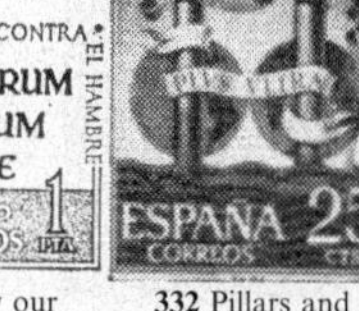

332 Pillars and Globes

1963. Freedom from Hunger.
1573 **331** 1 p. multicoloured 15 15

1963. Spanish Cultural Institutions Congress. Multicoloured.
1574 25 c. Type **332** 15 10
1575 80 c. "Santa Maria", "Pinta" and "Nina" 40 10
1576 1 p. Columbus 40 10

333 Civic Seals

334 "St. Maria of Europe"

1963. 150th Anniv of San Sebastian.
1577 **333** 25 c. blue and green 10 10
1578 – 80 c. red and purple 20 10
1579 – 1 p. green and bistre 20 10
DESIGNS: 80 c. City aflame; 1 p. View of San Sebastian, 1836.

1963. Europa.
1580 **334** 1 p. brown and bistre 15 10
1581 5 p. sepia and green 60 40

335 Arms of the Order of Mercy

336 Scenes from Parable of the Good Samaritan

1963. 75th Anniv of the Order of Mercy.
1582 **335** 25 c. red, gold & black 10 10
1583 – 80 c. sepia and green 10 10
1584 – 1 p. purple and blue 10 10
1585 – 1 p. 50 brown and blue 10 10
1586 – 3 p. black and violet 10 10
DESIGNS: 80 c. King Jaime I; 1 p. Our Lady of Mercy; 1 p. 50, St. Pedro Nolasco; 3 p. St. Raimundo de Penafort.

1963. Explorers and Colonizers of America (3rd series). As T **309**.
1587 25 c. deep blue and blue 15 10
1588 70 c. green and salmon 15 10
1589 80 c. green and cream 45 10
1590 1 p. blue and salmon 50 10
1591 2 p. red and blue 1·75 10
1592 2 p. 50 violet and flesh 1·25 10
1593 3 p. blue and pink 2·40 1·25
1594 5 p. brown and cream 3·25 2·40
PORTRAITS: 25 c., 2 p. Brother J. Serra; 70 c., 2 p. 50, Vasco Nunez de Balboa; 80 c., 3 p. J. de Galvez; 1 p., 5 p. D. Garcia de Paredes.

1963. Red Cross Centenary.
1595 **336** 1 p. violet, red and gold 10 10

337 "The Nativity" (after sculpture by Berruguete)

338 Fr. Raimundo Lulio

1963. Christmas.
1596 **337** 1 p. green 15 15

1963. Famous Spaniards (1st series).
1597 **338** 1 p. blk & vio (postage) 15 10
1598 – 1 p. 50 violet and sepia 15 10
1599 – 25 p. purple and red (air) 90 35
1600 – 50 p. black and green 1·50 50
PORTRAITS: 1 p. 50, Cardinal Belluga; 25 p. King Recaredo; 50 p. Cardinal Cisneros.
See also Nos. 1714/17.

339 Pope Paul and Dome of St. Peter's

1963. Ecumenical Council, Vatican City (2nd issue).
1601 **339** 1 p. black & turquoise 10 10

340 Alcazar de Segovia

1964. Tourist Series.
1602 – 40 c. brown, blue & grn 10 10
1603 – 50 c. sepia and blue 10 10
1604 – 70 c. blue and green 10 10
1605 – 70 c. brown and lilac 10 10
1606 – 80 c. black and blue 15 10
1607 **340** 1 p. lilac and violet 10 10
1608 – 1 p. red and purple 10 10
1609 – 1 p. black and green 10 10
1610 – 1 p. red and purple 10 10
1611 – 1 p. 50 brown, green and blue 15 10
DESIGNS—HORIZ: No. 1602, Potes; No. 1604, Crypt of St. Isidore (Leon); No. 1608, Lion Court of the Alhambra (Granada); No. 1611, Gerona. VERT: No. 1603, Leon Cathedral; No. 1605, Costa Brava; No. 1606, "Christ of the Lanterns" (Cordoba); No. 1609, Drach Caves (Majorca); No. 1610, Mosque (Cordoba).
See also Nos. 1704/13, 1786/95, 1798/1805, 1860/6, 1867/74, 1933/42, 1985/9, 1993/6, 2035/9, 2040/5, 2311/6, 2379/84, 2466/7, 2575/8, 2696/2700, 2744/8, 2858/9, 2870/1 and 2915/18.

1964. Arms of Provincial Capitals. As T **315**. Multicoloured.
1612 5 p. Ifni 15 15
1613 5 p. Jaen 15 15
1614 5 p. Leon 15 15
1615 5 p. Lerida 15 15
1616 5 p. Logrono 15 15
1617 5 p. Lugo 15 15
1618 5 p. Madrid 15 15
1619 5 p. Malaga 15 15
1620 5 p. Murcia 15 15
1621 5 p. Navarra 15 15
1622 5 p. Orense 15 15
1623 5 p. Oviedo 15 15

341 Santa Maria Monastery

1964. Monastery of Santa Maria, Huerta.
1624 – 1 p. bronze and green 15 10
1625 – 2 p. sepia, black & turq 20 10
1626 **341** 5 p. slate and violet 1·40 75
DESIGNS—VERT: 1 p. Great Hall; 2 p. Cloisters.

1964. Stamp Day and Sorolla (painter) Commem. As T **279**. Frames in gold.

1627 25 c. violet 15 10
1628 40 c. purple 15 10
1629 70 c. green 15 10
1630 80 c. turquoise 15 10
1631 1 p. brown 15 10
1632 1 p. 50 turquoise 15 10
1633 2 p. 50 mauve 15 10
1634 3 p. blue 35 40
1635 5 p. brown . . . . 1·40 1·00
1636 10 p. green 65 30

PAINTINGS—VERT: 25 c. "The Earthen Jar"; 70 c. "La Mancha Types"; 80 c. "Valencian Fisherwoman"; 1 p. Self-portrait; 5 p. "Pulling the Boat"; 10 p. "Valencian Couple on Horse". HORIZ: 40 c. "Castillan Oxherd"; 1 p. 50, "The Cattlepen"; 2 p. 50, "And people say fish is dear" (fish market); 3 p. "Children on the Beach".

342 "25 Years of Peace"

1964. 25th Anniv of End of Spanish Civil War.

1637 **342** 25 c. gold, green & blk . 15 10
1638 – 30 c. red, blue and green 15 10
1639 – 40 c. black and gold . . 15 10
1640 – 50 c. multicoloured . . . 15 10
1641 – 70 c. multicoloured . . . 15 10
1642 – 80 c. multicoloured . . . 15 10
1643 – 1 p. multicoloured . . . 20 10
1644 – 1 p. 50 olive, red & blue . 15 10
1645 – 2 p. multicoloured . . . 25 10
1646 – 2 p. 50 multicoloured . . 15 10
1647 – 3 p. multicoloured . . . 90 90
1648 – 5 p. red, green and gold . 30 30
1649 – 6 p. multicoloured . . . 45 45
1650 – 10 p. multicoloured . . . 60 60

DESIGNS—VERT: 30 c. Athletes ("Sport"); 50 c. Apartment-houses ("National Housing Plan"); 1 p. Graph and symbols ("Economic Development"); 1 p. 50, Rocks and tower ("Construction"); 2 p. 50, Wheatear and dam ("Irrigation"); 5 p. "Tree of Learning" ("Scientific Research"); 10 p. Gen. Franco. HORIZ: 40 c. T.V. screen and symbols ("Radio and T.V."); 70 c. Wheatears, tractor and landscape ("Agriculture"); 80 c. Tree and forests ("Reafforestation"); 2 p. Forms of transport ("Transport and Communications"); 3 p. Pylon and part of dial ("Electrification"); 6 p. Ancient buildings ("Tourism").

343 Spanish Pavilion at Fair

344 6 c. Stamp of 1850 and Globe

1964. New York World's Fair.

1651 **343** 1 p. green & turquoise . 20 15
1652 – 1 p. 50 brown and red . 15 15
1653 – 2 p. 50 green and blue . 15 15
1654 – 5 p. red 25 25
1655 – 50 p. blue and grey . . 85 30

DESIGNS—VERT: 1 p. 50, Bullfighting; 2 p. 50, Castillo de la Mota; 5 p. Spanish dancing; 50 p. Pelota.

1964. World Stamp Day.

1656 **344** 25 c. red and purple . . 15 10
1657 1 p. green and blue . . . 15 10
1658 10 p. orange and red . . 35 30

345 Macarena Virgin

346 Medieval Ship

1964. Canonical Coronation of Macarena Virgin.

1659 **345** 1 p. green and yellow . . 15 15

1964. Spanish Navy Commemoration.

1660 **346** 15 c. slate and purple . . 25 10
1661 – 25 c. green and orange . 25 10
1662 – 40 c. grey and blue . . 25 10
1663 – 50 c. green and slate . 25 10
1664 – 70 c. violet and blue . . 25 10
1665 – 80 c. blue and green . . 25 10
1666 – 1 p. purple and brown . 25 10
1667 – 1 p. 50 sepia and red . . 25 10
1668 – 2 p. black and green . . 75 10
1669 – 2 p. 50 red and violet . 25 10
1670 – 3 p. blue and brown . . 25 10
1671 – 5 p. blue and green . . 1·00 1·00
1672 – 6 p. violet & turquoise . 75 75
1673 – 10 p. red and orange . . 70 30

SHIPS—VERT: 25 c. Carrack; 1 p. Ship of the line "Santissima Trinidad"; 1 p. 50, Corvette "Atrevida". HORIZ: 40 c. "Santa Maria"; 50 c. Galley; 70 c. Galleon; 80 c. Xebec; 2 p. Steam frigate "Isabel II"; 2 p. 50, Frigate "Numancia"; 3 p. Destroyer "Destructor"; 5 p. Isaac Peral's submarine; 6 p. Cruiser "Baleares"; 10 p. Cadet schooner "Juan Sebastian de Elcano".

347 Europa "Flower"

348 "The Virgin of the Castle"

1964. Europa.

1674 **347** 1 p. ochre, red & green . 25 10
1675 5 p. blue, purple & grn . 90 75

1964. 700th Anniv of Reconquest of Jerez.

1676 **348** 25 c. brown and buff . . 10 10
1677 1 p. blue and grey . . . 10 10

349 Putting the Shot

350 "Adoration of the Shepherds" (after Zurbaran)

1965. Olympic Games, Tokyo and Innsbruck. Olympic rings in gold.

1678 **349** 25 c. blue and orange . 15 15
1679 – 80 c. blue and green . . 15 15
1680 – 1 p. blue & light blue . 15 15
1681 – 3 p. blue and buff . . . 20 20
1682 – 5 p. blue and violet . . 20 20

DESIGNS: 80 c. Long jumping; 1 p. Skiing (slalom); 3 p. Judo; 5 p. Throwing the discus.

1964. Explorers and Colonizers of America (4th series). As T **309**. Inscr "1964" at foot.

1683 25 c. violet and blue 15 15
1684 70 c. olive and pink 15 15
1685 80 c. green and buff 30 20
1686 1 p. violet and buff 30 15
1687 2 p. olive and blue 30 15
1688 2 p. 50 purple and turquoise 20 20
1689 3 p. blue and grey . . . . . 3·00 1·00
1690 5 p. brown and cream . . . 1·75 1·40

PORTRAITS: 25 c., 2 p. D. de Almagro; 70 c., 2 p. 50, F. de Toledo; 80 c., 3 p. T. de Mogrovejo; 1, 5 p. F. Pizarro.

1964. Christmas.

1691 **350** 1 p. brown 10 10

1965. Arms of Provincial Capitals. As T **315**. Multicoloured.

1692 5 p. Palencia 10 10
1693 5 p. Pontevedra 10 10
1694 5 p. Rio Muni 10 10
1695 5 p. Sahara 10 10
1696 5 p. Salamanca 10 10
1697 5 p. Santander 10 10
1698 5 p. Segovia 10 10
1699 5 p. Seville 10 10
1700 5 p. Soria 10 10
1701 5 p. Tarragona 10 10
1702 5 p. Tenerife 10 10
1703 5 p. Teruel 10 10

1965. Tourist Series. As T **340**.

1704 25 c. black and blue 10 10
1705 30 c. brown and turquoise . . 10 10
1706 50 c. purple and red 10 10
1707 70 c. indigo and blue 10 10
1708 80 c. purple and mauve . . . 10 10
1709 1 p. mauve, red and sepia . . 20 10
1710 2 p. 30 purple and brown . . 10 10
1711 2 p. 50 olive and blue . . . 10 10
1712 3 p. purple and purple . . . 10 10
1713 6 p. violet and slate 15 10

DESIGNS—VERT: 25 c. Columbus Monument, Barcelona; 30 c. Santa Maria Church, Burgos; 50 c. Synagogue, Toledo; 80 c. Seville Cathedral; 1 p. Cudillero Port; 2 p. 50, (No. 1710), Burgos Cathedral (interior); 3 p. Bridge at Cambados (Pontevedra); 6 p. Ceiling, Lonja (Valencia). HORIZ: 70 c. Zamora; 2 p. 50, (No. 1711), Mogrovejo (Santander).

1965. Famous Spaniards (2nd series). As T **338**.

1714 25 c. sepia and turquoise . . 15 15
1715 70 c. deep blue and blue . . 15 15
1716 2 p. 50 sepia and bronze . . 15 15
1717 5 p. bronze and green . . . 25 25

PORTRAITS: 25 c. Donoso Cortes; 70 c. King Alfonso X (the Saint); 2 p. 50, G. M. de Jovellanos; 5 p. St. Dominic de Guzman.

1965. Stamp Day and J. Romero de Torres Commem. As T **279**. Frames in gold.

1718 25 c. purple 15 15
1719 40 c. purple 15 15
1720 70 c. green 15 15
1721 80 c. turquoise 15 15
1722 1 p. brown 15 15
1723 1 p. 50 turquoise 15 15
1724 2 p. 50 mauve 15 15
1725 3 p. blue 35 30
1726 5 p. brown 35 30
1727 10 p. green 50 30

PAINTINGS (by J. Romero de Torres): 25 c. "Girl with Jar"; 40 c. "The Song"; 70 c. "The Virgin of the Lanterns"; 80 c. "Girl with Guitar"; 1 p. Self-portrait; 1 p. 50, "Poem of Cordoba"; 2 p. 50, "Marta and Maria"; 3 p. "Poem of Cordoba" (different); 5 p. "A Little Charcoal-maker"; 10 p. "Long Live the Hair!".

351 Bull and Stamps

352 I.T.U. Emblem and Symbols

1965. World Stamp Day.

1728 **351** 25 c. multicoloured . . . 15 15
1729 1 p. multicoloured . . . 15 15
1730 10 p. multicoloured . . . 40 30

1965. Centenary of I.T.U.

1731 **352** 1 p. red, black and pink . 15 15

353 Pilgrim

354 Spanish Knight and Banners

1965. Holy Year of Santiago de Compostela. Multicoloured.

1732 1 p. Type **353** 10 10
1733 2 p. Pilgrim (profile) 15 10

1965. 400th Anniv of Florida Settlement.

1734 **354** 3 p. black, red & yellow . 15 15

355 St. Benedict (after sculpture by Pereira)

356 Sports Palace, Madrid

1965. Europa.

1735 **355** 1 p. green & emerald . . 10 10
1736 5 p. violet and purple . . 40 30

1965. Int Olympic Committee Meeting, Madrid.

1737 **356** 1 p. brown, gold & grey . 10 10

1965. Explorers and Colonizers of America (5th series). As T **309**. Inscr "1965" at foot.

1738 25 c. violet and green . . . 10 10
1739 70 c. brown and pink . . . 10 10
1740 80 c. green and cream . . . 10 10
1741 1 p. violet and buff 10 10
1742 2 p. brown and blue 10 10
1743 2 p. 50 purple and turquoise . 15 15
1744 3 p. blue and grey . . . . 1·00 45
1745 5 p. brown and yellow . . . 1·00 35

PORTRAITS: 25 c., 2 p. Don Fadrique de Toledo; 70 c., 2 p. 50, Padre Jose de Anchieta; 80 c., 3 p. Francisco de Orellana; 1 p., 5 p. St. Luis Beltran.

357 Cloisters

1965. Yuste Monastery.

1746 **357** 1 p. blue and sepia . . . 10 10
1747 – 2 p. sepia and brown . . 10 10
1748 – 5 p. green and blue . . . 20 10

DESIGNS—VERT: 2 p. Charles V room. HORIZ: 5 p. Courtyard.

358 Spanish 1 r. Stamp of 1865

360 Madonna of Antipolo

359 "The Nativity" (after Mayno)

1965. Centenary of Spanish Perforated Stamps.

1749 **358** 80 c. green and bronze . 10 10
1750 – 1 p. brown and purple . 10 10
1751 – 5 p. brown and sepia . . 10 10

DESIGNS: 1 p. 1865 19 c. stamp; 5 p. 1865 2 r. stamp.

1965. Christmas.

1752 **359** 1 p. green and blue . . . 10 10

1965. 400th Anniv of Christianity in the Philippines.

1753 **360** 1 p. brown, black & buff 10 10
1754 – 3 p. blue and grey . . . 15 10

DESIGN: 3 p. Father Urdaneta.

361 Globe

362 Admiral Alvaro de Bazan

1965. 21st Ecumenical Council, Vatican City (3rd issue).

1755 **361** 1 p. multicoloured . . . 10 10

1966. Arms of Provincial Capitals. As T **315**. Multicoloured.

1756 5 p. Toledo 10 10
1757 5 p. Valencia 10 10
1758 5 p. Valladolid 10 10
1759 5 p. Vizcaya 10 10
1760 5 p. Zamora 10 10
1761 5 p. Zaragoza 10 10
1762 5 p. Ceuta 10 10
1763 5 p. Melilla 10 10
1764 10 p. Spain (26 × 38½ mm) . . 20 10

1966. Celebrities (1st series).

1765 **362** 25 c. black and blue (postage) 10 10
1766 – 2 p. violet and purple . . 10 10
1767 – 25 p. bronze & green (air) 1·25 25
1768 – 50 p. grey and blue . . 2·00 60

PORTRAITS: 2 p. Benito Daza de Valdes (doctor); 25 p. Seneca; 50 p. St. Damaso.

See also Nos. 1849/52.

363 Exhibition Emblem

364 Luno Church

1966. Graphic Arts Exn, "Graphispack", Barcelona.

1769 **363** 1 p. green, blue and red . 10 10

1966. Stamp Day and J. M. Sert Commem. Designs as T **279**. Frames in gold.

1770 25 c. violet 10 10
1771 40 c. purple 10 10
1772 70 c. green 10 10
1773 80 c. bronze 10 10
1774 1 p. brown 10 10
1775 1 p. 50 blue 10 10
1776 2 p. 50 red 10 10
1777 3 p. blue 15 10
1778 5 p. sepia 15 15
1779 10 p. green 15 10

PAINTINGS (by J. M. Sert)—VERT: 25 c. "The Magic Ball"; 70 c. "Christ Addressing the Disciples"; 80 c. "The Balloonists"; 1 p. Self-portrait; 1 p. 50, "Audacity"; 2 p. 50, "Justice"; 3 p. "Jacob's Struggle with the Angel"; 5 p. "The Five Parts of the World"; 10 p. "St. Peter and St. Paul". HORIZ: 40 c. "Memories of Toledo".

1966. 600th Anniv of Guernica. Multicoloured.

1780 80 c. Type **364** 10 10
1781 1 p. Arms of Guernica . . . 10 10
1782 3 p. "Tree of Guernica" . . 10 10

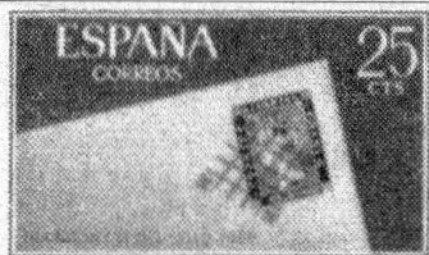

365 Postmarked 6 cuartos Stamp of 1850

1966. World Stamp Day.
1783 **365** 25 c. multicoloured . . . 10 10
1784 – 1 p. multicoloured . . . 10 10
1785 – 10 p. multicoloured . . . 20 20
DESIGNS—POSTMARKED STAMPS: 1 p. 5 r. of 1850; 10 p. 10 r. of 1850.

1966. Tourist Series. As T **340**.
1786 10 c. emerald and green . . . 10 10
1787 15 c. bistre and green . . . 10 10
1788 40 c. brown and chestnut . . 10 10
1789 50 c. purple and red 10 10
1790 80 c. purple and mauve . . . 10 10
1791 1 p. turquoise and blue . . . 10 10
1792 1 p. 50 black and blue . . . 10 10
1793 2 p. brown and blue 10 10
1794 3 p. brown and blue 10 10
1795 10 p. blue and turquoise . . 10 10
DESIGNS—VERT: 10 c. Bohi waterfalls (Lerida); 40 c. Sigena monastery (Huesca); 50 c. Santo Domingo Church (Soria); 80 c. Golden Tower (Seville); 1 p. El Teide (Canaries); 10 p. Church of St. Gregory (Valladolid). HORIZ: 15 c. Torla (Huesca); 1 p. 50, Cathedral, Guadalupe; 2 p. University, Alcala de Henares; 3 p. La Seo Cathedral (Lerida).

366 Tree and Globe

1966. World Forestry Congress.
1796 **366** 1 p. green, brown and deep brown 10 10

367 Crown and Anchor **368** Butron Castle (Vizcaya)

1966. Naval Week, Barcelona.
1797 **367** 1 p. blue and grey . . . 10 10

1966. Spanish Castles (1st series).
1798 – 10 c. sepia and blue . . . 10 10
1799 – 25 c. purple and violet . . 10 10
1800 – 40 c. green & turquoise . 10 10
1801 – 50 c. blue and indigo . . 10 10
1802 – 70 c. blue & ultramarine 10 10
1803 **368** 80 c. green and violet . . 10 20
1804 – 1 p. olive and brown . . 10 10
1805 – 3 p. purple and red . . . 10 10
CASTLES—HORIZ: 10 c. Guadamur (Toledo); 25 c. Alcazar (Segovia); 40 c. La Mota (Medina del Campo); 50 c. Olite (Navarra); 70 c. Monteagudo (Murcia); 1 p. Manzanares (Madrid). VERT: 3 p. Almansa (Albacete).

369 Don Quixote, Dulcinea and Aldonza Lorenzo

1966. 4th World Psychiatric Congress, Madrid.
1806 **369** 1 p. 50 multicoloured . . 10 10

370 "Europa and the Bull" **371** Horseman in the Sky

1966. Europa.
1807 **370** 1 p. multicoloured . . . 10 10
1808 5 p. multicoloured . . . 25 20

1966. 17th Int Astronautics Federation Congress, Madrid.
1809 **371** 1 p. 50 red, blk & blue . 10 10

1966. Explorers and Colonisers of America (6th series). As T **309**. Inscr "1966" at foot.
1810 30 c. bistre and brown . . . 10 10
1811 50 c. red and green 10 10
1812 1 p. violet and blue 10 10
1813 1 p. 20 slate and grey . . . 10 10
1814 1 p. 50 myrtle and green . . 10 10
1815 3 p. blue 10 10
1816 3 p. 50 violet and lilac . . . 20 20
1817 6 p. brown and buff 10 10
DESIGNS: 30 c. A. de Mendoza; 50 c. Title page of Dominican Fathers' "Christian Doctrine"; 1 p. J. A. Manso de Velasco; 1 p. 20, Coins of Lima Mint (1699); 1 p. 50, M. de Castro y Padilla; 3 p. Oruro Convent; 3 p. 50, M. de Amat; 6 p. Inca postal runner.

372 R. del Valle Inclan **373** Monastery Facade

1966. Spanish Writers.
1818 **372** 1 p. 50 green and black . 10 10
1819 – 3 p. violet and black . . 10 10
1820 – 6 p. blue and black . . 10 10
WRITERS: 3 p. Carlos Arniches; 6 p. J. Benavente y Martinez.
See also Nos. 1888/91.

1966. St. Mary's Carthusian Monastery, Jerez.
1821 **373** 1 p. indigo and blue . . 10 10
1822 – 2 p. lt green and green . 10 10
1823 – 5 p. plum and purple . . 15 15
DESIGNS—HORIZ: 2 p. Cloisters; 5 p. Gateway.

374 "The Nativity" (after P. Duque Cornejo) **375** Alava Costume

1966. Christmas.
1824 **374** 1 p. 50 multicoloured . 10 10

1967. Provincial Costumes. Multicoloured.
1825 6 p. Type **375** 10 10
1826 6 p. Albacete 10 10
1827 6 p. Alicante 10 10
1828 6 p. Almeria 10 10
1829 6 p. Avila 10 10
1830 6 p. Badajoz 10 10
1831 6 p. Baleares 10 10
1832 6 p. Barcelona 10 10
1833 6 p. Burgos 10 10
1834 6 p. Caceres 10 10
1835 6 p. Cadiz 10 10
1836 6 p. Castellon de la Plana . 10 10
See also Nos. 1897/1908, 1956/67, 2007/18 and 2072/6.

376 Archers

1967. Stamp Day. Cave Paintings. Multicoloured.
1837 40 c. Type **376** 10 10
1838 50 c. Boar-hunting 10 10
1839 1 p. Trees (vert) 10 10
1840 1 p. 20 Bison 10 10
1841 1 p. 50 Hands 10 10
1842 2 p. Hunter (vert) 10 10
1843 2 p. 50 Deer (vert) 10 10
1844 3 p. 50 Hunters 10 10
1845 4 p. Chamois-hunters (vert) . 10 10
1846 6 p. Deer-hunter (vert) . . . 15 10

377 Cathedral, Palma de Mallorca, and Union Emblem

1967. Interparliamentary Union Congress, Palma de Mallorca.
1847 **377** 1 p. 50 green 10 10

378 Wilhelm Rontgen (physicist)

1967. Radiology Congress, Barcelona.
1848 **378** 1 p. 50 green 10 10

1967. Celebrities (2nd series). As T **362**.
1849 1 p. 20 violet and purple . . . 10 10
1850 3 p. 50 purple 15 15
1851 4 p. sepia and brown 10 10
1852 25 p. grey and blue 20 10
PORTRAITS: 1 p. 20, Averroes (physician and philosopher); 3 p. 50, Acosta (poet); 4 p. Maimonides (physician and philosopher); 25 p. Andres Laguna (physician).

379 Cogwheels **381** Spanish 5 r. Stamp of 1850 with Numeral Postmark

380 Fair Building

1967. Europa.
1853 **379** 1 p. 50 green, brn & red . 15 10
1854 6 p. violet, blue & purple 15 15

1967. 50th Anniv of Valencia Int Samples Fair.
1855 **380** 1 p. 50 green 10 10

1967. World Stamp Day.
1856 **381** 40 c. brown, blue & blk . 10 10
1857 – 1 p. 50 lake, black and green 10 10
1858 – 6 p. blue, red and black . 10 10
DESIGNS: 1 p. 50, Spanish 12 c. stamp of 1850 with crowned "M" (Madrid) postmark; 6 p. Spanish 6 r. stamp of 1850 with "I.R." postmark.
See also Nos. 1927/8, 1980/1, 2032, 2091, 2150 and 2185.

382 Sleeping Vagrant and "Guardian Angel" **383** I.T.Y. Emblem

1967. National Day for Caritas Welfare Organization.
1859 **382** 1 p. 50 multicoloured . . 10 10

1967. Tourist Series and Int Tourist Year.
1860 – 10 c. black and blue . . . 10 10
1861 – 1 p. black and blue . . . 10 10
1862 – 1 p. 50 black and brown . 10 10
1863 – 2 p. 50 blue and turquoise 10 10
1864 **383** 3 p. 50 blue and purple . 15 15
1865 – 5 p. bronze and green . . 10 10
1866 – 6 p. purple and mauve . . 10 10
DESIGNS: 10 c. Betanzos Church (Corunna); 1 p. St. Miguel's Tower (Palencia); 1 p. 50, Castellers (acrobats); 2 p. 50, Columbus Monument (Huelva); 5 p. "Enchanted City" (Cuenca); 6 p. Church of our Lady, Sanlucar (Cadiz).

1967. Spanish Castles (2nd series). As T **368**.
1867 50 c. brown and grey 10 10
1868 1 p. violet and grey 10 10
1869 1 p. 50 green and blue . . . 10 10
1870 2 p. brown and red 10 10
1871 2 p. 50 brown and green . . 10 10
1872 5 p. blue and purple 10 10
1873 6 p. sepia and brown 10 15
1874 10 p. green and blue 15 10
CASTLES—HORIZ: 50 c. Balsareny (Barcelona); 1 p. Jarandilla (Caceres); 1 p. 50, Almodovar (Cordoba); 2 p. 50, Peniscola (Castellon); 5 p. Coca (Segovia); 6 p. Loarre (Huesca); 10 p. Belmonte (Cuenca). VERT: 2 p. Ponferrada (Leon).

384 Globe and Snow Crystal **385** Map of the Americas, Spain and the Philippines

1967. 12th Int Refrigeration Congress, Madrid.
1875 **384** 1 p. 50 blue 10 10

1967. 4th Spanish, Portuguese, American and Philippine Municipalities Congress, Barcelona.
1876 **385** 1 p. 50 violet 15 10

1967. Explorers and Colonisers of America (7th series). As T **309**. Inscr "1967" at foot.
1877 40 c. olive and orange . . . 10 10
1878 50 c. agate and grey 10 10
1879 1 p. mauve and blue 10 10
1880 1 p. 20 green and cream . . 15 10
1881 1 p. 50 green and flesh . . . 10 10
1882 3 p. violet and buff 10 10
1883 3 p. 50 blue and pink 20 20
1884 6 p. brown 20 15
DESIGNS—VERT: 40 c. J. Francisco de la Bodega y Quadra; 50 c. Map of Nutka coast; 1 p. F. A. Mourelle; 1 p. 50, E. J. Martinez; 3 p. 50, Cayetano Valdes y Florez. HORIZ: 1 p. 20, View of Nutka; 3 p. Map of Californian coast; 6 p. San Elias, Alaska.

387 Ploughing with Oxen **388** Main Portal, Veruela Monastery

1967. 2000th Anniv of Caceres. Multicoloured.
1885 1 p. 50 Statue and archway . 10 10
1886 3 p. 50 Type **387** 15 15
1887 6 p. Roman coins 10 10
Nos. 1885 and 1887 are vert.

1967. Anniversaries. Portraits as T **372**.
1888 1 p. 20 brown and black . . 10 10
1889 1 p. 50 green and black . . 10 10
1890 3 p. 50 violet and black . . 15 15
1891 6 p. blue and black 10 10
DESIGNS: 1 p. 20, P. de S. Jose Bethencourt (founder of Bethlehemite Order, 300th death anniv); 1 p. 50, Enrique Granados (composer, birth cent); 3 p. 50, Ruben Dario (poet, birth centenary); 6 p. San Ildefonso, Archbishop of Toledo (after El Greco) (1900th death anniv).

1967. Veruela Monastery.
1892 **388** 1 p. 50 blue & ultramarine 10 10
1893 – 3 p. 50 grey and green . 15 15
1894 – 6 p. purple and brown . 20 15
DESIGNS—HORIZ: 3 p. 50, Aerial view of monastery; 6 p. Cloisters.

389 "The Canonization of San Jose de Calasanz" (from painting by Goya) **390** "The Nativity" (Salzillo)

1967. Bicentenary of Canonization of San Jose de Calasanz.
1895 **389** 1 p. 50 multicoloured . . 10 10

1967. Christmas.
1896 **390** 1 p. 50 multicoloured . . 10 10

1968. Provincial Costumes. As T **375**. Multicoloured.
1897 6 p. Ciudad Real 10 10
1898 6 p. Cordoba 10 10
1899 6 p. Coruna 10 10
1900 6 p. Cuenca 10 10
1901 6 p. Fernando Poo 10 10
1902 6 p. Gerona 10 10
1903 6 p. Las Palmas (Gran Canaria) 10 10
1904 6 p. Granada 10 10
1905 6 p. Guadalajara 10 10
1906 6 p. Guipuzcoa 10 10
1907 6 p. Huelva 10 10
1908 6 p. Huesca 10 10

391 Slalom

1968. Winter Olympic Games, Grenoble. Multicoloured.
1909 1 p. 50 Type **391** 10 10
1910 3 p. 50 Bobsleighing (vert) . . . 15 15
1911 6 p. Ice hockey 15 15

1968. Stamp Day and Fortuny Commem. As T **279**. Frames in gold.
1912 40 c. purple 10 10
1913 50 c. green 10 10
1914 1 p. brown 10 10
1915 1 p. 20 violet 10 10
1916 1 p. 50 green 10 10
1917 2 p. brown 10 10
1918 2 p. 50 red 10 10
1919 3 p. 50 brown 20 15
1920 4 p. olive 10 10
1921 6 p. blue 15 15
Fortuny Paintings—HORIZ: 40 c. "The Vicarage"; 1 p. 20, "The Print Collector"; 6 p. "Queen Christina". VERT: 50 c. "Fantasia"; 1 p. "Idyll"; 1 p. 50, Self-portrait; 2 p. "Old Man Naked to the Sun"; 2 p. 50, "Typical Calabrian"; 3 p. 50, "Portrait of Lady"; 4 p. "Battle of Tetuan".

392 Beatriz Galindo

1968. Famous Spanish Women. With background scenes.
1922 **392** 1 p. 20 brown and bistre . . 10 10
1923 – 1 p. 50 blue & turquoise . 10 10
1924 – 3 p. 50 violet 15 15
1925 – 6 p. black and blue . . . 10 10
WOMEN: 1 p. 50, Agustina de Aragon; 3 p. 50, Maria Pacheco; 6 p. Rosalia de Castro.

393 Europa "Key"

1968. Europa.
1926 **393** 3 p. 50 gold, brn & blue . 10 10

1968. World Stamp Day. As T **381**, but stamps and postmarks changed. Inscr "1968".
1927 1 p. 50 black, brown & blue . 10 10
1928 3 p. 50 blue, black & green . 10 10
DESIGNS: 1 p. 50, Spanish 6 c. stamp of 1850 with Puebla (Galicia) postmark; 3 p. 50, Spanish 6 r. stamp of 1850 with Serena postmark.

394 Emperor Galba's Coin

395 Human Rights Emblem

1968. 1900th Anniv of Foundation of Leon by VIIth Roman Legion.
1929 – 1 p. brown and purple . 10 10
1930 – 1 p. 50 brown & yellow . 10 10
1931 **394** 3 p. 50 green and ochre . 20 20
DESIGNS—VERT: 1 p. Inscribed tile and town map of Leon (26 × 47 mm); 1 p. 50, Legionary with standard (statue).

1968. Human Rights Year.
1932 **395** 3 p. 50 red, green & blue . 10 10

1968. Tourist Series. As T **340**.
1933 50 c. brown 10 10
1934 1 p. 20 green 10 10
1935 1 p. 50 blue and green . . . 10 10
1936 2 p. purple 10 10
1937 3 p. 50 purple 10 10
DESIGNS—VERT: 50 c. Count Benavente's Palace, Baeza; 1 p. 50, Sepulchre, St. Vincent's Church, Avila; 3 p. 50, Main portal, Church of Santa Maria, Sanguesa (Navarra). HORIZ: 1 p. 20, View of Salamanca; 2 p. "The King's Page" (statue), Siguenza Cathedral.

1968. Spanish Castles (3rd series). As T **368**.
1938 40 c. sepia and blue 10 10
1939 1 p. 20 purple 10 10
1940 1 p. 50 black and bistre . . . 10 10
1941 2 p. 50 bronze and green . . 10 10
1942 6 p. turquoise and blue . . . 15 10
DESIGNS—HORIZ: 40 c. Escalona; 1 p. 20, Fuensaldana; 1 p. 50, Penafiel; 2 p. 50, Villas and obroso. VERT: 6 p. Frias.

396 Rifle-shooting

1968. Olympic Games, Mexico. Multicoloured.
1943 1 p0. Type **396** 10 10
1944 1 p. 50 Horse-jumping . . . 10 10
1945 3 p. 50 Cycling 15 15
1946 6 p. Yachting (vert) 20 15

1968. Explorers and Colonisers of America (8th series). As T **309** but inscr "1968" at foot.
1947 40 c. blue and light blue . . 10 10
1948 1 p. purple and blue 10 10
1949 1 p. 50 green and flesh . . . 10 10
1950 3 p. 50 blue and mauve . . 25 20
1951 6 p. brown and yellow . . . 25 20
DESIGNS—VERT: 40 c. Map of Orinoco missions; 1 p. Diego de Losada (founder of Caracas); 1 p. 50, Arms of the Losadas; 3 p. 50, Diego de Henares (builder of Caracas). HORIZ: 6 p. Old plan of Santiago de Leon de Caracas.

397 Monastery Building

398 "The Nativity" (Barocci)

1968. Santa Maria del Parral Monastery.
1952 **397** 1 p. 50 lilac and blue . . 10 10
1953 – 3 p. 50 brown & chocolate 20 20
1954 – 6 p. brown and red . . 20 10
DESIGNS—VERT: 3 p. 50, Cloisters; 6 p. "Santa Maria del Parral".

1968. Christmas.
1955 **398** 1 p. 50 multicoloured . 10 10

1969. Provincial Costumes. As T **375**. Multicoloured.
1956 6 p. Ifni 10 10
1957 6 p. Jaen 10 10
1958 6 p. Leon 10 10
1959 6 p. Lerida 10 10
1960 6 p. Logrono 10 10
1961 6 p. Lugo 10 10
1962 6 p. Madrid 10 10
1963 6 p. Malaga 10 10
1964 6 p. Murcia 10 10
1965 6 p. Navarra 10 10
1966 6 p. Orense 10 10
1967 6 p. Oviedo 10 10

1969. Stamp Day and Alonso Cano Commem. Various paintings as T **279**. Frames gold: centre colours below.
1968 40 c. red 10 10
1969 50 c. green 10 10
1970 1 p. sepia 10 10
1971 1 p. 50 green 10 10
1972 2 p. brown 10 10
1973 2 p. 50 mauve 10 10
1974 3 p. blue 10 10
1975 3 p. 50 purple 15 10
1976 4 p. purple 10 10
1977 6 p. blue 15 15
Alonso Cano paintings—VERT: 40 c. "St. Agnes"; 50 c. "St. Joseph"; 1 p. "Christ supported by an Angel"; 1 p. 50, "Alonso Cano" (Velazquez); 2 p. "The Holy Family"; 2 p. 50, "The Circumcision"; 3 p. "Jesus and the Samaritan"; 3 p. 50, "Madonna and Child"; 6 p. "The Vision of St. John the Baptist". HORIZ: 4 p. "St. John Capistrano and St. Bernardin".

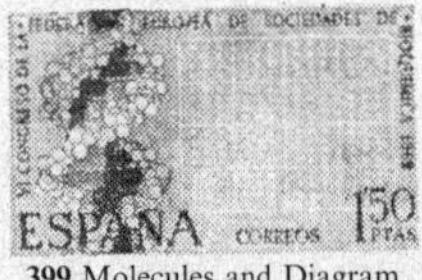

399 Molecules and Diagram

1969. 6th European Biochemical Congress.
1978 **399** 1 p. 50 multicoloured . 10 10

400 Colonnade

1969. Europa.
1979 **400** 3 p. 50 multicoloured . 20 10

1969. World Stamp Day. As T **381**.
1980 1 p. 50 black, red and green 10 10
1981 3 p. 50 green, red and blue . 10 10
DESIGNS: 1 p. 50, Spanish 6 c. stamp of 1851 with "A 3 1851" postmark; 3 p. 50, Spanish 10 r. stamp of 1851 with "CORVERA" postmark.

401 Spectrum

1969. 15th Int Spectroscopical Conf, Madrid.
1982 **401** 1 p. 50 multicoloured . . 10 10

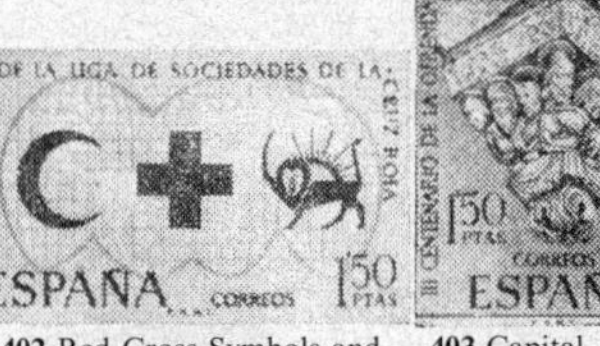

402 Red Cross Symbols and Globe
403 Capital, Lugo Cathedral

1969. 50th Anniv of League of Red Cross Societies.
1983 **402** 1 p. 50 multicoloured . . 10 10

1969. 300th Anniv of Dedication of Galicia to Jesus Christ.
1984 **403** 1 p. 50 brown, blk & grn 10 10

1969. Spanish Castles (4th series). As T **368**.
1985 1 p. purple and green . . . 10 10
1986 1 p. 50 blue and violet . . . 10 10
1987 2 p. 50 lilac and blue . . . 10 10
1988 3 p. 50 brown and green . . 20 10
1989 6 p. drab and green 10 10
CASTLES—HORIZ: 1 p. Turegano; 1 p. 50, Villalonso; 2 p. 50, Velez Blanco; 3 p. 50, Castilnovo; 6 p. Torrelobaton.

404 Franciscan Friar and Child

405 Rock of Gibraltar

1969. Bicentenary of San Diego (California).
1990 **404** 1 p. 50 multicoloured . . 10 10

1969. Aid for Spanish "ex-Gibraltar" Workers.
1991 **405** 1 p. 50 blue 10 10
1992 – 2 p. purple 10 10
DESIGN: 2 p. Aerial view of Rock.

1969. Tourist Series. As T **340**.
1993 1 p. 50 green and turquoise . 15 10
1994 3 p. turquoise and green . . 10 10
1995 3 p. 50 blue and green . . . 10 10
1996 6 p. violet and green . . . 15 10
DESIGNS—HORIZ: 1 p. 50, Alcaniz (Teruel). VERT: 3 p. Murcia Cathedral; 3 p. 50, "The Lady of Elche" (sculpture); 6 p. Church of Our Lady of the Redonda, Logrono.

1969. Explorers and Colonisers of America (9th series). Chile. As T **309**. Inscr "1969" at foot.
1997 40 c. brown on blue . . . 10 10
1998 1 p. 50 violet on flesh . . . 10 10
1999 2 p. green on mauve . . . 20 10
2000 3 p. 50 green on cream . . 35 30
2001 6 p. brown on cream . . . 25 20
DESIGNS—VERT: 40 c. Convent of Santo Dominigo, Santiago de Chile; 2 p. Ambrosio O'Higgins; 3 p. 50, Pedro de Valdivia (founder of Santiago de Chile). HORIZ: 1 p. 50, Chilean Mint; 6 p. Cal y Canto Bridge.

406 "Adoration of the Three Kings" (Maino)

407 Las Huelgas Monastery

1969. Christmas. Multicoloured.
2002 1 p. 50 Type **406** 10 10
2003 2 p. "The Nativity" (Gerona Cathedral) 10 10

1969. Las Huelgas Monastery, Burgos.
2004 **407** 1 p. 50 slate and green . . 20 10
2005 – 3 p. 50 blue 40 40
2006 – 6 p. olive and green . . 25 10
DESIGNS—HORIZ: 3 p. 50, Tombs. VERT: 6 p. Cloisters.

1970. Provincial Costumes. As T **375**. Multicoloured.
2007 6 p. Palencia 10 10
2008 6 p. Pontevedra 10 10
2009 6 p. Sahara 10 10
2010 6 p. Salamanca 10 10
2011 6 p. Santa Cruz de Tenerife . 10 10
2012 6 p. Santander 10 10
2013 6 p. Segovia 10 10
2014 6 p. Seville 10 10
2015 6 p. Soria 10 10
2016 6 p. Tarragona 10 10
2017 6 p. Teruel 10 10
2018 6 p. Toledo 10 10

408 Blessed Juan of Avila (after El Greco)

409 "St. Stephen"

1970. Spanish Celebrities.
2019 **408** 25 p. blue and lilac . . . 4·50 15
2020 – 50 p. brown and orange 1·90 25
DESIGN: 25 p. Type **408** (400th death anniv); 50 p. Cardinal Rodrigo Ximenes de Rada (after J. de Borgena) (800th birth anniv).
See also Nos. 2129/31.

1970. Stamp Day and Luis de Morales Commem. Various paintings. Multicoloured.
2021 50 c. Type **409** 10 10
2022 1 p. "The Annunciation" . . 10 10
2023 1 p. 50 "Virgin and Child with St. John" 10 10
2024 2 p. "Virgin and Child" . . . 10 10
2025 3 p. "The Presentation of the Infant Christ" 10 10
2026 3 p. 50 "St. Jerome" 10 10
2027 4 p. "St. John of Ribera" . . 15 10
2028 5 p. "Ecce Homo" 15 10
2029 6 p. "Pieta" 15 15
2030 10 p. "St. Francis of Assisi" 15 15
See also Nos. 2077/84, 2135/42, 2204/11, 2261/8, 2420/7, 2478/85, 2529/36 and 2585/90.

410 "Flaming Sun"

1970. Europa.
2031 **410** 3 p. 50 gold & ultram . 10 10

1970. World Stamp Day. As T **381** but stamp and postmark changed.
2032 2 p. red, black and green . . 15 10
DESIGN: 2 p. Spanish 12 c. stamp of 1860 with railway cachet.

411 Fair Building

412 Gen. Primo de Rivera

1970. 50th Anniv of Barcelona Fair.
2033 **411** 15 p. multicoloured . . . 20 10

1970. Birth Cent of General Primo de Rivera.
2034 **412** 2 p. green, brn & buff . 10 10

1970. Spanish Castles (5th series). As T **368**.
2035 1 p. black and blue 35 15
2036 1 p. 20 blue and turquoise . 10 10
2037 3 p. 50 brown and green . . 15 10
2038 6 p. violet and brown . . . 25 10
2039 10 p. brown & chestnut . . . 85 10
CASTLES—HORIZ: 1 p. Valencia de Don Juan; 1 p. 20, Monterrey; 3 p. 50, Mombeltran; 6 p. Sadaba; 10 p. Bellver.

1970. Tourist Series. As T **340**.
2040 50 c. lilac and blue 10 10
2041 1 p. brown and ochre . . . 10 10
2042 1 p. 50 green and blue . . . 10 10
2043 2 p. blue and deep blue . . 40 10
2044 3 p. 50 blue and violet . . . 15 10
2045 5 p. brown and blue 85 15
DESIGNS—HORIZ: 50 c. Alcazaba, Almeria; 1 p. Malaga Cathedral; 2 p. St. Francis' Convent, Orense. VERT: 1 p. 50, Our Lady of the Assumption, Lequeitio; 3 p. 50, The Lonja, Zaragoza; 5 p. The Portalon, Vitoria.

413 17th-century Tailor

1970. International Tailoring Congress.
2046 **413** 2 p. violet, red and brown 10 10

414 Diver on Map

1970. 12th European Swimming, Diving and Water-polo Championships, Barcelona.
2047 **414** 2 p. brown, blue and grn 10 10

415 Concha Espina **416** Survey Map of Southern Spain and North Africa

1970. Spanish Writers.
2048 **415** 50 c. blue, brown & buff 10 10
2049 – 1 p. violet, green & drab 10 10
2050 – 1 p. 50 green, bl & drab . 10 10
2051 – 2 p. olive, green & buff . 20 10
2052 – 2 p. 50 pur, vio & ochre . 10 10
2053 – 3 p. 50 red, brn & lilac . 10 10
WRITERS: 1 p. Guillen de Castro; 1 p. 50, J. R. Jimenez; 2 p. G. A. Becquer; 2 p. 50, Miguel de Unamuno; 3 p. 50, J. M. Gabriel y Galan.

1970. Explorers and Colonizers of America (10th series). Mexico. As T **309**.
2054 40 c. green on light green . . 10 10
2055 1 p. 50 brown on blue . . . 15 10
2056 2 p. violet on cream 50 10
2057 3 p. 50 green on light green . 15 10
2058 6 p. blue on pink 25 10
DESIGNS—VERT: 40 c. House in Queretaro; 2 p. Vasco de Quiroga; 3 p. 50, F. Juan de Zumarraga; 6 p. Morelia Cathedral. HORIZ: 1 p. 50, Cathedral, Mexico City.

1970. Centenary of Spanish Geographical and Survey Institute.
2059 **416** 2 p. multicoloured . . . 10 10

417 "The Adoration of the Shepherds" (El Greco) **418** U.N. Emblem and New York Headquarters

1970. Christmas. Multicoloured.
2060 1 p. 50 Type **417** 10 10
2061 2 p. "The Adoration of the Shepherds" (Murillo) . . . 10 10

1970. 25th Anniv of United Nations.
2062 **418** 8 p. multicoloured . . . 10 10

419 Ripoll Monastery **420** Pilgrims' Route Map

1970. Ripoll Monastery.
2063 – 2 p. purple and violet . . 50 10
2064 **419** 3 p. 50 purple & orange . 10 10
2065 – 5 p. green and slate . . 1·00 10
DESIGNS: 2 p. Entrance; 5 p. Cloisters.

1971. Holy Year of Compostela (1st issue). "St. James in Europe".
2066 **420** 50 c. brown and blue . . 10 10
2067 – 1 p. black and brown . . 25 10
2068 – 1 p. 50 purple & green . 40 15
2069 – 2 p. brown and purple . 35 10
2070 – 3 p. dp blue and blue . 45 15
2071 – 4 p. olive 70 10
DESIGNS—VERT: 1 p. Statue of St. Brigid, Vadstena (Sweden); 1 p. 50, St. Jacques' Church tower, Paris; 2 p. "St. James" (carving from altar, Pistoia, Italy). HORIZ: 3 p. St. David's Cathedral, Wales; 4 p. Carving from Ark of Charlemagne (Aachen, West Germany).
See also Nos. 2105/11 and 2121/8.

1971. Provincial Costumes. As T **375**. Mult.
2072 6 p. Valencia 15 10
2073 8 p. Valladolid 40 15
2074 8 p. Vizcaya 40 15
2075 8 p. Zamora 40 15
2076 8 p. Zaragoza 40 15

1971. Stamp Day and Ignacio Zuloaga Commem. Paintings as T **409**. Multicoloured.
2077 50 c. "My Uncle Daniel" . . 10 10
2078 1 p. "Segovia" (horiz) . . . 10 10
2079 1 p. 50 "The Duchess of Alba" 10 10
2080 2 p. "Ignacio Zuloaga" (self-portrait) 20 10
2081 3 p. "Juan Belmonte" . . . 20 10
2082 4 p. "The Countess of Noailles" 10 10
2083 5 p. "Pablo Uranga" 20 15
2084 8 p. "Boatmen's Houses, Lerma" (horiz) 20 15

421 Amadeo Vives (composer)

1971. Spanish Celebrities. Multicoloured.
2085 1 p. Type **421** 20 15
2086 2 p. St. Teresa of Avila (mystic) 20 10
2087 8 p. B. Perez Galdos (writer) 20 20
2088 15 p. R. Menendez Pidal (writer) 15 10

422 Europa Chain

1971. Europa.
2089 **422** 2 p. brown, violet & blue 50 15
2090 8 p. brown, light green and green 40 40

1971. World Stamp Day. As T **381**, but with different stamp and postmark.
2091 2 p. black, blue and green . 15 15
DESIGN: 2 p. Spanish 6 c. stamp of 1850 with "A.s." postmark.

423 Gymnast on Vaulting-horse

1971. 9th European Male Gymnastics Cup Championships, Madrid. Multicoloured.
2092 1 p. Type **423** 15 15
2093 2 p. Gymnast on bar 15 15

424 Great Bustard

1971. Spanish Fauna (1st series). Mult.
2094 1 p. Type **424** . . . . . . 1·00 10
2095 2 p. Lynx 15 15
2096 3 p. Brown bear 15 15
2097 5 p. Red-legged partridge (vert) 2·25 20
2098 8 p. Spanish ibex (vert) . . . 40 40
See also Nos. 2160/4, 2192/6, 2250/4, 2317/21, 2452/6 and 2579/83.

426 Legionaries in Battle

1971. 50th Anniv of Spanish Foreign Legion. Multicoloured.
2101 1 p. Type **426** 15 10
2102 2 p. Ceremonial parade . . . 25 15
2103 5 p. Memorial service 25 15
2104 8 p. Officer and mobile column 30 30

1971. Holy Year of Compostela (2nd issue). "En Route to Santiago". As T **420**.
2105 50 c. purple and blue 10 10
2106 6 p. blue 30 15
2107 7 p. purple and deep purple . 40 15
2108 7 p. 50 red and purple . . . 30 10
2109 8 p. purple and green 30 20
2110 9 p. violet and green 30 20
2111 10 p. brown and green . . . 55 15
DESIGNS—HORIZ: 50 c. Pilgrims' route map of northern Spain; 7 p. 50, Cloisters, Najera Monastery; 9 p. Eunate Monastery. VERT: 6 p. "Pilgrims" (sculpture, Royal Hospital, Burgos); 7 p. Gateway, St. Domingo de la Calzada Monastery; 8 p. Statue of Christ, Puente de la Reina; 10 p. Cross of Roncesvalles.

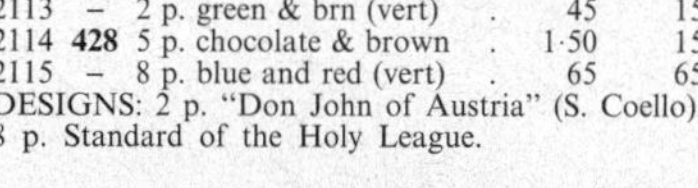
427 "Children of the World" **428** "Battle of Lepanto" (after L. Valdes)

1971. 25th Anniv of U.N.I.C.E.F.
2112 **427** 8 p. multicoloured . . . 10 10

1971. 400th Anniv of Battle of Lepanto.
2113 – 2 p. green & brn (vert) . 45 15
2114 **428** 5 p. chocolate & brown . 1·50 15
2115 – 8 p. blue and red (vert) . 65 65
DESIGNS: 2 p. "Don John of Austria" (S. Coello); 8 p. Standard of the Holy League.

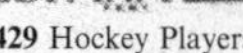

429 Hockey Players **431** "The Nativity" (detail from altar, Avia)

430 De Havilland D.H.9B over Seville

1971. World Hockey Cup Championships, Barcelona.
2116 **429** 5 p. multicoloured . . . 50 10

1971. 50th Anniv of Spanish Airmail Services. Multicoloured.
2117 2 p. Type **430** 60 10
2118 15 p. Boeing 747-100 airliner over Madrid 65 20

1971. Christmas. Multicoloured.
2119 2 p. Type **431** 10 10
2120 8 p. "The Birth" (detail from altar, Saga) 15 10

1971. Holy Year of Compostela (3rd issue). As T **420**.
2121 1 p. black and green 20 15
2122 1 p. 50 violet and purple . . . 20 20
2123 2 p. blue and green 85 15
2124 2 p. 50 violet and red 20 10
2125 3 p. purple and red 35 15
2126 3 p. 50 green and pink . . . 25 15
2127 4 p. brown and blue 25 15
2128 5 p. black and green 60 15
DESIGNS—VERT: 1 p. Santiago Cathedral; 2 p. Lugo Cathedral; 3 p. Astorga Cathedral; 4 p. San Tirso, Sahagun. HORIZ: 1 p. 50, Pilgrim approaching Santiago de Compostela; 2 p. 50, Villafranca del Bierzo; 3 p. 50, San Marcos, Leon; 5 p. San Martin, Fromista.

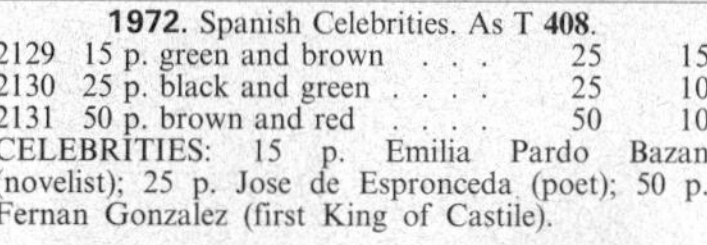
1972. Spanish Celebrities. As T **408**.
2129 15 p. green and brown . . . 25 15
2130 25 p. black and green 25 10
2131 50 p. brown and red 50 10
CELEBRITIES: 15 p. Emilia Pardo Bazan (novelist); 25 p. Jose de Espronceda (poet); 50 p. Fernan Gonzalez (first King of Castile).

432 Ski Jumping **433** Title-page of "Don Quixote" (1605)

1972. Winter Olympic Games, Sapporo, Japan. Multicoloured.
2132 2 p. Type **432** 30 10
2133 15 p. Figure skating (vert) . 15 15

1972. International Book Year.
2134 **433** 2 p. red and brown . . . 10 10

1972. Stamp Day and Solana Commem. Paintings by Solana. As T **409**. Multicoloured.
2135 1 p. "Clowns" (horiz) . . . 15 20
2136 2 p. "Solana and Family" (self-portrait) 35 15
2137 3 p. "Blind Musician" . . . 35 15
2138 4 p. "Return of the Fishermen" 70 15
2139 5 p. "Decorating Masks" . . 1·10 30
2140 7 p. "The Bibliophile" . . . 50 15
2141 10 p. "Merchant Navy Captain" 65 15
2142 15 p. "Pombo Reunion" (vert) 50 20

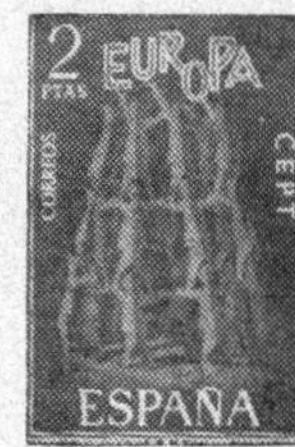

434 "Abies pinsapo" **435** "Europeans"

1972. Spanish Flora (1st series). Multicoloured.
2143 1 p. Type **434** 15 15
2144 2 p. Strawberry tree 30 15
2145 3 p. Maritime pine 35 15
2146 5 p. Holm oak 50 10
2147 8 p. "Juniperus thurifera" . . 30 25
See also Nos. 2178/82, 2278/82 and 2299/303.

1972. Europa. Multicoloured.
2148 2 p. Type **435** . . . . . . 1·60 15
2149 8 p. "Communications" . . 60 40

436 Cordoba Pre-stamp Postmark

1972. World Stamp Day.
2150 **436** 2 p. red, blk & brown . 10 10

1972. Spanish Castles (6th series). As T **368**.
2151 1 p. brown and green 40 35
2152 2 p. brown and green 75 10
2153 3 p. brown and red 75 10
2154 5 p. green and blue 75 20
2155 10 p. violet and blue . . . 2·25 20
CASTLES—VERT: 1 p. Sajazarra. HORIZ: 2 p. Santa Catalina; 3 p. Biar; 5 p. San Servando; 10 p. Pedraza.

437 Fencing

1972. Olympic Games, Munich. Multicoloured.
2156 1 p. Type **437** 15 10
2157 2 p. Weightlifting (vert) . . . 25 15
2158 5 p. Rowing (vert) 20 15
2159 8 p. Pole vaulting (vert) . . . 20 20

438 Chamois

439 Brigadier M. A. de Ustariz

1972. Spanish Fauna (2nd series). Mult.

2160		1 p. Pyrenean desman	25	10
2161		2 p. Type **438**	60	10
2162		3 p. Wolf	80	15
2163		5 p. Egyptian mongoose (horiz)	1·50	15
2164		7 p. Small-spotted genet (horiz)	1·25	15

1972. "Spain in the New World" (1st series). 450th Anniv of Puerto Rico. Multicoloured.

2165		1 p. Type **439**	15	10
2166		2 p. View of San Juan, 1870 (horiz)	20	15
2167		5 p. View of San Juan, 1625 (horiz)	50	15
2168		8 p. Map of Plaza de Bahia, 1792 (horiz)	35	35

See also Nos. 2212/5, 2271/4, 2338/41 and 2430/3.

440 Facade of Monastery

441 Grand Lyceum Theatre

1972. Monastery of St.Thomas, Avila.

2169	**440**	2 p. green and blue	80	10
2170	–	8 p. purple and brown	65	30
2171	–	15 p. blue and purple	45	15

DESIGNS—VERT: 8 p. Interior of monastery. HORIZ: 15 p. Cloisters.

1972. 125th Anniv of Grand Lyceum Theatre, Barcelona.

2172	**441**	8 p. brown and blue	25	20

442 "The Nativity"

1972. Christmas. Murals in Royal Collegiate Basilica of San Isidoro, Leon. Multicoloured.

2173		2 p. Type **442**	10	10
2174		8 p. "The Annunciation"	10	10

443 J. de Herrera and Escorial

1973. Spanish Architects (1st series).

2175	**443**	8 p. green and sepia	50	15
2176	–	10 p. blue and brown	1·60	15
2177	–	15 p. blue and green	35	15

DESIGNS: 10 p. J. de Villanueva and Prado; 15 p. V. Rodriguez and Apollo Fountain, Madrid.

See also Nos. 2295/7.

444 "Apollonias canariensis"

1973. Spanish Flora (2nd series). Canary Islands. Multicoloured.

2178		1 p. Type **444**	15	15
2179		2 p. "Myrica faya"	50	15
2180		4 p. "Phoenix canariensis"	15	15
2181		5 p. "Ilex canariensis"	50	25
2182		15 p. "Dracaena draco"	25	15

Nos. 2179/82 are vert.

445 Roman Mosaic

446 Iznajar Dam

1973. Europa.

2183	**445**	2 p. multicoloured	45	10
2184	–	8 p. blue, red and black	35	15

DESIGN—HORIZ—(37 × 26 mm): 8 p. Europa "Posthorn".

1973. World Stamp Day. As T **381**, but with different stamp and postmark.

2185		2 p. red, blue and black	10	10

DESIGN: 2 p. Spanish 6 r. stamp of 1853 with Madrid postmark.

1973. 11th Congress of Int High Dams Commission, Madrid.

2186	**446**	8 p. multicoloured	10	10

1973. Tourist Series. As T **340**.

2187		1 p. brown and green	15	15
2188		2 p. green and dark green	50	10
2189		3 p. brown and light brown	50	10
2190		5 p. violet and blue	1·40	20
2191		8 p. red and green	60	20

DESIGNS—HORIZ: 1 p. Gateway, Onate University, Guipuzcoa; 2 p. Town Square, Lugo; 5 p. Columbus' House, Las Palmas; 8 p. Windmills, La Mancha. VERT: 3 p. Llerena Square, Badajoz.

447 Black-bellied Sandgrouse

1973. Spanish Fauna (3rd series). Birds. Mult.

2192		1 p. Type **447**	60	15
2193		2 p. Black stork	1·25	15
2194		5 p. Azure-winged magpie (vert)	1·75	15
2195		7 p. Imperial eagle	2·00	15
2196		15 p. Red-crested pochard (vert)	1·25	40

448 Hermandad Standard-bearer, Castile, 1488

1973. Spanish Military Uniforms (1st series). Multicoloured.

2197		1 p. Type **448**	15	15
2198		2 p. Mounted knight, Castile, 1493 (horiz)	40	15
2199		3 p. Arquebusier, 1534	45	15
2200		7 p. Mounted arquebusier, 1560	30	15
2201		8 p. Infantry sergeant, 1567	30	20

See also Nos. 2225/7, 2255/9, 2290/4, 2322/6, 2410/14, 2441/5, 2472/6 and 2499/503.

449 Fishes in Net and Trawler

1973. World Fishing Fair and Congress, Vigo.

2202	**449**	2 p. multicoloured	10	10

450 Conference Building

1973. I.T.U. Conference, Torremolinos.

2203	**450**	8 p. multicoloured	15	10

1973. Stamp Day and Vicente Lopez Commem. Paintings. As T **409**. Multicoloured.

2204		1 p. "Ferdinand VII"	10	10
2205		2 p. Self-portrait	20	10
2206		3 p. "La Senora de Carvallo"	20	10
2207		4 p. "M. de Castelldosrrius"	15	10
2208		5 p. "Isabella II"	15	15
2209		7 p. "Goya"	15	10
2210		10 p. "Maria Amalia of Saxony"	25	10
2211		15 p. "Felix Lopez, the Organist"	20	15

451 Leon Cathedral, Nicaragua

452 Pope Gregory XI receiving St. Jerome's Petition

1973. "Spain in the New World" (2nd series). Nicaragua. Multicoloured.

2212		1 p. Type **451**	10	10
2213		2 p. Subtiava Church	25	10
2214		5 p. Colonial-style house (vert)	45	20
2215		8 p. Rio San Juan Castle	25	10

1973. 600th Anniv of Order of St. Jerome.

2216	**452**	2 p. multicoloured	10	10

453 Courtyard

454 "The Nativity" (pillar capital, Silos)

1973. Monaster of Santo Domingo de Silos, Burgos.

2217	**453**	2 p. purple and brown	40	15
2218	–	8 p. purple and blue	20	15
2219	–	15 p. blue and green	20	15

DESIGNS—HORIZ: 8 p. Cloisters. VERT: 15 p. "Three Saints" (statue).

1973. Christmas. Multicoloured.

2220		2 p. Type **454**	10	10
2221		8 p. "Adoration of the Kings" (bas-relief, Butrera) (horiz)	10	10

455 Map of Spain and the Americas

1973. 500th Anniv of Spanish Printing.

2222	**455**	1 p. blue and green	30	10
2223	–	7 p. violet and blue	15	10
2224	–	15 p. green and purple	25	15

DESIGNS—VERT: 7 p. "Teacher and pupils" (ancient woodcut); 15 p. "Los Sinodales" (manuscript).

1974. Spanish Military Uniforms (2nd series). As T **448**. Multicoloured.

2225		1 p. Mounted arquebusier, 1603	10	10
2226		2 p. Arquebusier, 1632	50	15
2227		3 p. Mounted cuirassier, 1635	65	10
2228		5 p. Mounted drummer, 1677	90	20
2229		9 p. Musketeers, "Viejos Morados" Regiment, 1694	25	20

456 14th-century Nautical Chart

457 M. Biada (construction engineer) and Early Locomotive

1974. 50th Anniv of Spanish Higher Geographical Council.

2230	**456**	2 p. multicoloured	10	10

1974. 125th Anniv of Barcelona–Mataro Railway.

2231	**457**	2 p. multicoloured	20	10

458 Stamp Collector, Album and Magnifier

459 "Woman with Offering"

1974. "ESPANA 75" Int Stamp Exhibition, Madrid.

2232	**458**	2 p. multicoloured	10	10
2233	–	5 p. blue, black & brown	35	30
2234	–	8 p. multicoloured	30	30

DESIGNS—DIAMOND (43 × 43 mm): 5 p. Exhibition emblem; 8 p. Globe and arrows.

1974. Europa. Stone Sculptures. Multicoloured.

2235		2 p. Type **459**	45	10
2236		8 p. "Woman from Baza"	20	20

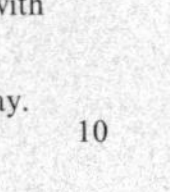

460 2 r. Stamp of 1854 with Seville Postmark

1974. World Stamp Day.

2237	**460**	2 p. multicoloured	10	10

461 Jaime Balmes (philosopher) and Monastery

462 Bramante's "Little Temple", Rome

1974. Spanish Celebrities.

2238	**461**	8 p. brown and blue	10	10
2239	–	10 p. brown and red	55	10
2240	–	15 p. blue and brown	75	15

DESIGNS: 10 p. Pedro Poveda (educationalist) and mountain village; 15 p. Jorge Juan (cosmographer and mariner) and shipyard.

1974. Centenary of Spanish Fine Arts Academy, Rome.

2241	**462**	5 p. multicoloured	15	15

463 Roman Aqueduct, Segovia

1974. Spain as a Province of the Roman Empire.

2242	**463**	1 p. black and brown	10	10
2243	–	2 p. brown and green	25	10
2244	–	3 p. brown & lt brown	10	10
2245	–	4 p. blue and green	10	10
2246	–	5 p. purple and blue	10	10
2247	–	7 p. purple and green	10	10
2248	–	8 p. green and red	10	10
2249	–	9 p. brown and purple	15	15

DESIGNS—HORIZ: 2 p. Roman Bridge, Alcantara; 3 p. Martial (poet) giving public reading; 5 p. Theatre, Merida; 7 p. Ossio, 1st Bishop of Cordoba, addressing the Synod. VERT: 4 p. Triumphal Arch, Bara; 8 p. Ruins of Curia, Talavera la Vieja; 9 p. Statue of Emperor Trajan.

464 Tortoise

1974. Spanish Fauna (4th series). Reptiles. Mult.

2250		1 p. Type **464**	15	15
2251		2 p. Chameleon	25	15
2252		5 p. Gecko	55	50
2253		7 p. Green lizard	40	20
2254		15 p. Adder	15	15

1974. Spanish Military Uniforms (3rd series). As T **448**. Multicoloured.

2255		1 p. Dismounted trooper, Hussars de la Muerte, 1705	15	10
2256		2 p. Officer, Royal Regiment of Artillery, 1710	40	15
2257		3 p. Drummer and fifer, Granada Regiment, 1734	40	15

2258 7 p. Guidon-bearer, Numancia Dragoons, 1737 . . . . . 35 15
2259 8 p. Ensign with standard, Zamora Regiment, 1739 . . 15 15

465 Swimmer making Rescue

1974. 18th World Life-saving Championships. Barcelona.
2260 **465** 2 p. multicoloured . . . 15 10

1974. Stamp Day and Eduardo Rosales. Commemoration. Various paintings as T **409**. Multicoloured.
2261 1 p. "Tobias and the Angel" 10 10
2262 2 p. Self-portrait 15 15
2263 3 p. "Testament of Isabella the Catholic" (horiz) 10 10
2264 4 p. "Nena" 15 15
2265 5 p. "Presentation of Don Juan of Austria" (horiz) 15 10
2266 7 p. "The First Steps" (horiz) 10 10
2267 10 p. "St. John the Evangelist" 25 10
2268 15 p. "St. Matthew the Evangelist" 15 15

466 Figure with Letter and Posthorns
467 Sobremonte's House, Cordoba

1974. Centenary of U.P.U. Multicoloured.
2269 2 p. Type **466** 15 10
2270 8 p. U.P.U. Monument, Berne 15 15

1974. "Spain in the New World" (3rd series). Argentina. Multicoloured.
2271 1 p. Type **467** 10 10
2272 2 p. Town Hall, Buenos Aires (1929) 35 10
2273 5 p. Ruins of St. Ignacio de Mini (vert) 30 15
2274 10 p. "The Gaucho" (M. Fierro) (vert) 25 15

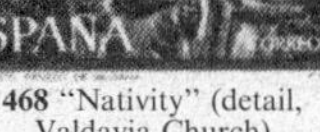

468 "Nativity" (detail, Valdavia Church)
469 "Teucrium lanigerum"

1974. Christmas. Church Fonts. Multicoloured.
2275 2 p. Type **468** 15 10
2276 3 p. "Adoration of the Kings", Valcobero Church (vert) . 10 10
2277 8 p. As No. 2276 . . . . . . 10 10

1974. Spanish Flora (3rd series). Multicoloured.
2278 1 p. Type **469** 10 10
2279 2 p. "Hypericum ericoides" 15 15
2280 4 p. "Thymus longiflorus" . 10 10
2281 5 p. "Anthyllis onobrychioides" 20 15
2282 8 p. "Helianthemum paniculatum" 15 10
The 1 p. and 8 p. are wrongly inscribed "Teucriun" and "Helianthemun" respectively.

470 Leyre Monastery
471 Spanish 6 c. and 5 p. Stamps of 1850 and 1975

1974. Leyre Monastery.
2283 **470** 2 p. grey and green . . . 40 10
2284 – 8 p. red and brown . . . 15 10
2285 – 15 p. dp green & green 30 10
DESIGNS—VERT: 8 p. Pillars and bas-relief. HORIZ: 15 p. Crypt.

1975. 125th Anniv of Spanish Postage Stamps.
2286 **471** 2 p. blue 30 30
2287 – 3 p. brown and green . 45 45
2288 – 8 p. mauve and violet . 1·10 45
2289 – 10 p. green and purple . 50 40
DESIGNS—HORIZ: 3 p. Mail coach, 1850; 8 p. Sail packet of West Indian service. VERT: 10 p. St. Mark's Chapel.

1975. Spanish Military Uniforms (4th series). As T **448**. Multicoloured.
2290 1 p. Toledo Regiment, 1750 20 10
2291 2 p. Royal Corps of Artillery, 1762 . . . . 35 15
2292 3 p. Queen's Regt of the Line, 1763 . . . . 1·50 20
2293 5 p. Vitoria Regt of Fusiliers, 1766 . . . . 45 15
2294 10 p. Dragoon of Sagunto Regt, 1775 . . . . 1·40 20

1975. Spanish Architects (2nd series). As T **443**.
2295 8 p. olive and green 15 10
2296 10 p. brown and red 40 10
2297 15 p. black and brown . . . 15 15
ARCHITECTS: 8 p. Antonio Gaudi and apartment building; 10 p. Antonio Palacios and palace; 15 p. Secundino Zuazo and block of flats.

473 Almonds

1975. Spanish Flora (4th series). Multicoloured.
2299 1 p. Type **473** 10 10
2300 2 p. Pomegranates (vert) . . 25 15
2301 3 p. Oranges (vert) 25 10
2302 4 p. Chestnuts (vert) 10 10
2303 5 p. Apples (vert) 15 15

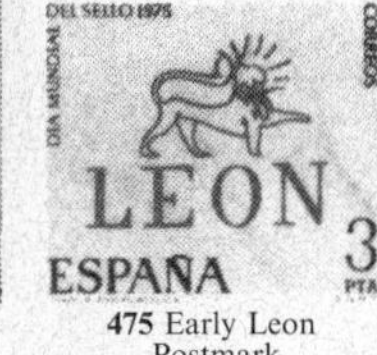

474 Woman and Pitcher, La Aranya
475 Early Leon Postmark

1975. Europa. Primitive Cave Paintings.
2304 **474** 3 p. red, brown and stone 30 10
2305 – 12 p. mauve, black & brn 35 20
DESIGN—HORIZ: 12 p. Horse, Tito Bustillo.

1975. World Stamp Day.
2306 **475** 3 p. multicoloured . . . 10 10

476 Emblem and Inscription

1975. 1st General Assembly of World Tourism Organization, Madrid.
2307 **476** 3 p. blue 10 10

477 Farm Scene

1975. 25th Anniv of "Feria del Campo".
2308 **477** 3 p. multicoloured . . . 10 10

478 Heads of Different Races

1975. International Women's Year.
2309 **478** 3 p. multicoloured . . . 10 10

479 Virgin of Cabeza Sanctuary and Forces Emblems

1975. Defence of Virgin of Cabeza Sanctuary during Civil War Commemoration.
2310 **479** 3 p. multicoloured . . . 10 10

1975. Tourist Series. As T **340**.
2311 1 p. lilac and purple 10 10
2312 2 p. deep brown and brown . 10 10
2313 3 p. black and blue 10 10
2314 4 p. mauve and orange . . . 10 10
2315 5 p. black and green 15 10
2316 7 p. indigo and blue 35 15
DESIGNS—HORIZ: 1 p. Cervantes' cell, Argamasilla de Alba; 2 p. St. Martin's Bridge, Toledo; 3 p. St. Peter's Church, Tarrasa. VERT: 4 p. Alhambra archway, Granada; 5 p. Mijas village, Malaga; 7 p. St. Mary's Chapel, Tarrasa.

480 Salamander Lizard

1975. Spanish Fauna (5th series). Reptiles and Amphibians. Multicoloured.
2317 1 p. Type **480** 10 10
2318 2 p. Triton lizard 20 10
2319 3 p. Tree-frog 20 10
2320 6 p. Toad 15 15
2321 7 p. Frog 15 15

1975. Spanish Military Uniforms (5th series). As T **448**. Multicoloured.
2322 1 p. Montesa Regt. 1788 . . . 10 10
2323 2 p. Asturias Regt of Fusiliers, 1789 . . . . 45 10
2324 3 p. Infantry of the Line, 1802 15 10
2325 4 p. Royal Corps of Artillery, 1803 . . . . 10 10
2326 7 p. Royal Engineers Regt, 1809 20 10

481 Child

1975. Child Welfare.
2327 **481** 3 p. multicoloured . . . 10 10

482 Scroll

1975. Latin Notaries' Congress, Barcelona.
2328 **482** 3 p. multicoloured . . . 10 10

483 "Blessing the Birds"

1975. Stamp Day and Millenary of Gerona Cathedral. Beatitude Miniatures. Multicoloured.
2329 1 p. Type **483** 10 10
2330 2 p. "Angel and River of Life" (vert) 15 10
2331 3 p. "Angel at Gates of Paradise" (vert) 15 10
2332 4 p. "Fox seizing Cockerel" 10 10
2333 6 p. "Daniel with the Lions" 10 10
2334 7 p. "Blessing the Multitude" (vert) 25 25
2335 10 p. "The Four Horsemen of the Apocalypse" (vert) . . 15 10
2336 12 p. "Peacock and Snake" (vert) 20 15

484 Industry Emblems

1975. Spanish Industry.
2337 **484** 3 p. violet and purple . . 10 10

485 El Cabildo, Montevideo

1975. "Spain in the New World" (4th series). 150th Anniv of Uruguayan Independence. Multicoloured.
2338 1 p. Type **485** 10 10
2339 2 p. Ox wagon 20 10
2340 3 p. Fortress, St. Teresa . . 20 10
2341 8 p. Cathedral, Montevideo (vert) 10 10

486 San Juan de la Pena Monastery
487 "Virgin and Child"

1975. San Juan de la Pena Monastery Commem.
2342 **486** 3 p. brown and green . . 25 10
2343 – 8 p. violet and mauve . . 10 10
2344 – 10 p. red and mauve . . 20 10
DESIGNS—HORIZ: 8 p. Cloisters. VERT: 10 p. Pillars.

1975. Christmas. Navarra Art. Multicoloured.
2345 3 p. Type **487** 10 10
2346 12 p. "The Flight into Egypt" (horiz) 15 10

488 King Juan Carlos I
489 Virgin of Pontevedra

1975. Proclamation of King Juan Carlos I. Multicoloured.
2347 3 p. Type **488** 10 10
2348 3 p. Queen Sophia 10 10
2349 3 p. King Juan Carlos and Queen Sophia (33 × 33 mm) 10 10
2350 12 p. As No. 2349 . . . . . 15 15

1975. Holy Year of Compostela.
2351 **489** 3 p. brown and orange . 20 10

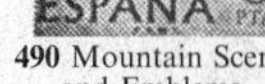

490 Mountain Scene and Emblems
491 Cosme Damian Churruca and "San Juan Nepomucendo"

1976. Centenary of Catalunya Excursion Centre.
2352 **490** 6 p. multicoloured . . . 10 10

1976. Spanish Navigators.
2353 **491** 7 p. black and brown . . 1·40 25
2354 – 12 p. violet 35 20
2355 – 50 p. brown and green . 1·00 15
NAVIGATORS—VERT: 12 p. Luis de Requesens. HORIZ: 50 p. Juan Sebastian del Cano and "Vitoria".

492 Alexander Graham Bell and Telephone Equipment

1976. Telephone Centenary.

2356	492	3 p. multicoloured	10	10

493 Crossing the Road

1976. Road Safety. Multicoloured.

2357	1 p. Type **493**	10	10
2358	3 p. Dangerous driving (vert)	30	10
2359	5 p. Wearing of seat-belts	20	10

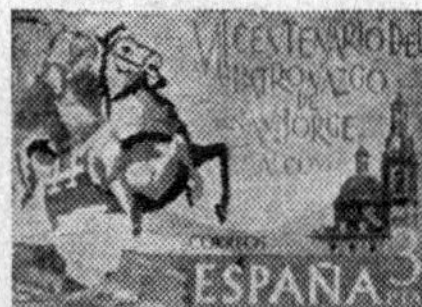

494 St. George on Horseback

1976. 700th Anniv of St. George's Guardianship of Alcoy.

2360	494	3 p. multicoloured	10	10

495 Talavera Pottery

1976. Europa. Spanish Handicrafts. Multicoloured.

2361	3 p. Type **495**	65	10
2362	12 p. Camarinas lace-making	85	25

496 Spanish 1851 6 r. Stamp with Coruna Postmark

1976. World Stamp Day.

2363	496	3 p. red, blue and black	10	10

497 Coins

1976. Bimillenary of Zaragoza. Roman Antiquities.

2364	497	3 p. brown and black	1·90	10
2365	–	7 p. blue and black	95	25
2366	–	25 p. brown and black	55	10

DESIGNS—HORIZ: 7 p. Plan of site and coin. VERT: 25 p. Mosaic.

498 Rifle, 1757

1976. Bicentenary of American Revolution.

2367	498	1 p. blue and brown	15	10
2368	–	3 p. brown and green	90	10
2369	–	5 p. green and brown	40	10
2370	–	12 p. brown and green	40	25

DESIGNS: 3 p. Bernado de Galvez and emblem; 5 p. Richmond $1 banknote of 1861; 12 p. Battle of Pensacola.

499 Customs-house, Cadiz

1976. Spanish Customs Buildings.

2371	499	1 p. brown and black	15	10
2372	–	3 p. brown and green	65	10
2373	–	7 p. purple and brown	1·10	35

BUILDINGS: 3 p. Madrid; 7 p. Barcelona.

500 Savings Jar and "Industry"

1976. Spanish Post Office. Multicoloured.

2374	1 p. Type **500**	30	10
2375	3 p. Railway mail-sorting van	55	10
2376	6 p. Mounted postman (horiz)	10	10
2377	10 p. Automatic letter sorting equipment (horiz)	20	15

501 King Juan Carlos I, Queen Sophia and Map of the Americas

1976. Royal Visit to America (1st issue).

2378	501	12 p. multicoloured	20	15

See also No. 2434.

1976. Tourist Series. As T **340**.

2379	1 p. brown and blue	10	10
2380	2 p. green and blue	65	10
2381	3 p. chocolate and brown	40	10
2382	4 p. blue and brown	20	10
2383	7 p. brown and blue	85	30
2384	12 p. purple and red	1·00	20

DESIGNS—HORIZ: 1 p. Cloisters, San Marcos, Leon; 2 p. Las Canadas, Tenerife; 4 p. Cruz de Tejeda, Las Palmas; 7 p. Gredos, Avila; 12 p. La Arruzafa, Cordoba. VERT: 3 p. Hospice of the Catholic Kings, Santiago de Compostela.

502 Rowing

1976. Olympic Games, Montreal. Multicoloured.

2385	1 p. Type **502**	10	10
2386	2 p. Boxing	30	15
2387	3 p. Wrestling (vert)	20	10
2388	12 p. Basketball (vert)	20	10

503 King Juan Carlos I

504 "Giving Blood"

1976.

2389	503	10 c. orange	10	10
2390		25 c. yellow	10	10
2391		30 c. blue	10	10
2392		50 c. purple	10	10
2393		1 p. green	10	10
2394		1 p. 50 red	10	10
2395		2 p. blue	15	10
2396		3 p. green	15	10
2397		4 p. turquoise	25	10
2398		5 p. red	15	10
2399		6 p. turquoise	10	10
2400		7 p. olive	15	10
2401		8 p. blue	15	10
2402		10 p. red	20	10
2403		12 p. brown	20	10
2403a		13 p. brown	25	10
2403b		14 p. orange	20	10
2404		15 p. violet	25	10
2405		16 p. brown	25	10
2405a		17 p. blue	30	10
2406		19 p. orange	30	10
2407		20 p. red	30	10
2408		30 p. green	40	10
2409	503	50 p. red	90	10
2409a		60 p. blue	80	10
2409b		75 p. green	1·00	10
2409c		85 p. grey	1·10	45
2409d	–	100 p. brown	1·25	10
2409e	–	200 p. green	2·50	10
2409f	–	500 p. blue	6·25	50

Nos. 2409 d/f are as Type **503**, but larger, 25 x 30 mm.

1976. Spanish Military Uniforms (6th series). As T **448**. Multicoloured.

2410	1 p. Alcantara Regiment, 1815	10	10
2411	2 p. Regiment of the line, 1821	75	10
2412	3 p. Gala Engineers, 1825	25	10
2413	7 p. Artillery Regiment, 1828	25	10
2414	25 p. Light Infantry Regiment, 1830	25	15

1976. Blood Donors Publicity.

2415	504	3 p. red and black	10	10

505 Batitales Mosaic

506 Parliament House, Madrid

1976. Bimillenary of Lugo.

2416	505	1 p. purple and black	10	10
2417	–	3 p. brown and black	20	10
2418	–	7 p. red and green	40	20

DESIGNS: 3 p. Old City Wall; 7 p. Roman coins.

1976. 63rd Inter-Parliamentary Union Congress, Madrid.

2419	506	12 p. brown and green	15	15

1976. Stamp Day and Luis Menendez Commemoration. Paintings as T **409**. Mult.

2420	1 p. "Jug, Cherries, Plums and Cheese"	10	10
2421	2 p. "Jar, Melon, Oranges and Savouries"	10	10
2422	3 p. "Barrel, Pears and Melon"	10	10
2423	4 p. "Pigeons, Basket and Bowl"	10	10
2424	6 p. "Fish and Oranges" (horiz)	10	10
2425	7 p. "Melon and Bread" (horiz)	25	25
2426	10 p. "Jug, Plums and Bread" (horiz)	25	10
2427	12 p. "Pomegranates, Apples and Grapes" (horiz)	25	20

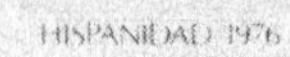

507 "The Nativity"

508 Nicoya Church

1976. Christmas. Statuettes. Multicoloured.

2428	3 p. Type **507**	65	10
2429	12 p. St. Christopher carrying Holy Child (vert)	1·50	45

1976. "Spain in the New World" (5th series). Costa Rica. Multicoloured.

2430	1 p. Type **508**	10	10
2431	2 p. Juan Vazquez de Coronado	20	15
2432	3 p. Orosi Mission (horiz)	15	10
2433	12 p. Tomas de Acosta	25	15

1976. Royal Visit to America (2nd issue). As T **501**. Multicoloured.

2434	12 p. "Santa Maria" and South America	50	15

510 San Pedro de Alcantara Monastery

1976. Monastery of San Pedro de Alcantara.

2435	510	3 p. brown and purple	25	10
2436	–	7 p. purple and blue	15	20
2437	–	20 p. chocolate. and brown	25	10

DESIGNS—VERT: 7 p. High Altar; 20 p. San Pedro de Alcantara.

511 Hand releasing Doves

1976. Civil War Invalids' Assoc Commemoration.

2438	511	3 p. multicoloured	10	10

512 Pablo Casals and Cello

1976. Birth Centenaries.

2439	512	3 p. black and blue	10	10
2440	–	5 p. green and red	10	10

DESIGN: 5 p. Manuel de Falla and "Fire Dance".

1977. Spanish Military Uniforms (7th series). Vert designs as T **448**. Multicoloured.

2441	1 p. Calatrava Regiment of Lancers, 1844	10	10
2442	2 p. Engineers' Regiment, 1850	30	10
2443	3 p. Light Infantry Regiment, 1861	15	10
2444	4 p. Infantry of the Line, 1861	10	10
2445	20 p. Horse Artillery, 1862	20	15

513 King James I and Arms of Aragon

1977. 700th Death Anniv of King James I.

2446	513	4 p. brown and violet	10	10

514 Jacinto Verdaguer (poet)

516 Salmon

515 King Charles III

1977. Spanish Celebrities.

2447	514	5 p. red and purple	25	10
2448	–	7 p. green and brown	15	15
2449	–	12 p. green and blue	20	15
2450	–	50 p. brown and green	50	10

DESIGNS: 7 p. Miguel Servet (theologian and physician); 12 p. Pablo Sarasate (violinist); 50 p. Francisco Tarrega (guitarist).

1977. Bicentenary of Economic Society of the Friends of the Land.

2451	515	4 p. brown and green	10	10

1977. Spanish Fauna (6th series). Freshwater Fishes. Multicoloured.

2452	1 p. Type **516**	10	10
2453	2 p. Brown trout (horiz)	10	10
2454	3 p. Eel (horiz)	10	10
2455	4 p. Carp (horiz)	10	10
2456	6 p. Barbel (horiz)	10	10

517 Skiing

1977. World Ski Championships, Granada.

2457	517	5 p. multicoloured	10	10

518 La Cuadra, 1902

1977. Vintage Cars. Multicoloured.
2458 2 p. Type **518** 10 10
2459 4 p. Hispano Suiza, 1916 . . 10 10
2460 5 p. Elizade, 1915 . . . . . 10 10
2461 7 p. Abadal, 1914 . . . . . 15 15

519 Donana

1977. Europa. Landscapes, National Parks. Multicoloured.
2462 3 p. Type **519** 15 10
2463 12 p. Ordesa 20 15

520 Plaza Mayor, Madrid and Stamps

1977. 50th Anniv of Philatelic Bourse on Plaza Mayor, Madrid.
2464 **520** 3 p. green, red and vio . 10 10

521 Enrique de Osso (founder)

1977. Centenary of Society of St. Theresa of Jesus.
2465 **521** 8 p. multicoloured . . . 10 10

1977. Tourist Series. As T **340**.
2466 1 p. brown and orange . . . 10 10
2467 2 p. grey and brown 10 10
2468 3 p. purple and blue 10 10
2469 4 p. green and blue 10 10
2470 7 p. grey and brown 10 10
2471 12 p. brown and violet . . . 15 10
DESIGNS—HORIZ: 1 p. Toledo Gate, Ciudad Real; 2 p. Roman Aqueduct, Almunecar; 7 p. Ampudia Castle, Palencia; 12 p. Bisagra Gate, Toledo. VERT: 3 p. Jaen Cathedral; 4 p. Bridge and Gate, Ronda Gorge, Malaga.

1977. Spanish Military Uniforms (8th series). As T **448**. Multicoloured.
2472 1 p. Administration officer, 1875 . . . . 10 10
2473 2 p. Lancer, 1883 . . . . . . 10 10
2474 3 p. General Staff commander, 1884 . . . . 15 10
2475 7 p. Trumpeter, Divisional Artillery, 1887 . . . . . . 15 15
2476 25 p. Medical Corps officer, 1895 . . . . 25 10

522 San Marino de la Cogalla (carving) and Early Castilian Manuscript

1977. Millenary of Castilian Language.
2477 **522** 5 p. brown, grn & pur . 10 10

1977. Stamp Day and F. Madrazo (painter) Commemoration. Portraits. As T **409**. Mult.
2478 1 p. "The Youth of Florez" . . 10 10
2479 2 p. "Duke of San Miguel" . 10 10
2480 3 p. "C. Coronado" 10 10
2481 4 p. "Campoamor" 10 10
2482 6 p. "Marquesa de Montelo" . 10 10
2483 7 p. "Rivadeneyra" 10 10
2484 10 p. "Countess of Vilches" . 10 15
2485 15 p. "Gomez de Avellaneda" . 15 10

523 West Indies Sailing Packet and Map of Mail Routes to America

1977. Bicentenary of Mail to the Indies, and "Espamer 77" Stamp Exhibition, Barcelona.
2486 **523** 15 p. green and brown . 70 50

524 St. Francis's Church

1977. Spanish–Guatemalan Relations. Guatemala City Buildings. Multicoloured.
2487 1 p. Type **524** 10 10
2488 3 p. High-rise flats 10 10
2489 7 p. Government Palace . . 10 10
2490 12 p. Monument, Columbus Square 15 10

525 Monastery Building

1977. St. Peter's Monastery, Cardena Commem.
2491 **525** 3 p. grey and blue . . . 10 10
2492 – 7 p. red and brown . . 10 10
2493 – 20 p. grey and green . . 25 10
DESIGNS: 7 p. Cloisters; 20 p. El Cid (effigy).

526 Adoration of the Kings

1977. Christmas. Miniatures from Manuscript "Romanico de Huesca". Multicoloured.
2494 5 p. Type **526** 10 10
2495 12 p. Flight into Egypt (vert) 15 10

527 Rohrbach Ro.VII Roland, 1927, and Douglas DC-10

1977. 50th Anniv of IBERIA (State Airline).
2496 **527** 12 p. multicoloured . . . 60 10

528 Crown Prince Felipe **529** Judo

1977. Felipe de Borbon, Prince of Asturias.
2497 **528** 5 p. multicoloured . . . 10 10

1977. 10th World Judo Championships.
2498 **529** 3 p. black, red and brown 10 10

1977. Spanish Military Uniforms (9th series). Multicoloured. Vert designs as T **448**.
2499 1 p. Standard bearer, Royal Infantry Regiment, 1908 . 10 10
2500 2 p. Lieutenant-colonel, Pavia Hussars', 1909 . . . . . . 10 10
2501 3 p. Lieutenant, Horse Artillery, 1912 . . . . 10 10
2502 5 p. Engineers' Captain, 1921 10 10
2503 12 p. Captain-General of the Armed Forces, 1925 . . . 15 10

530 Hilarion Eslava (composer) **531** "The Deposition of Christ" (detail Juan de Juni)

1977. Spanish Celebrities.
2504 **530** 5 p. black and purple . . 10 10
2505 – 8 p. black and green . . . 15 10
2506 – 25 p. black and green . . 25 10
2507 – 50 p. purple and brown . 50 10
DESIGNS: 8 p. Jose Clara (sculptor); 25 p. Pio Baroja (writer); 50 p. Antonio Machado (writer).

1978. Anniversaries of Artists.
2508 **531** 3 p. multicoloured . . . 10 10
2509 – 3 p. multicoloured . . . 10 10
2510 – 3 p. mauve and violet . . 10 10
2511 – 5 p. multicoloured . . . 10 10
2512 – 5 p. multicoloured . . . 10 10
2513 – 5 p. brown and black . . 10 10
2514 – 8 p. multicoloured . . . 10 10
2515 – 8 p. multicoloured . . . 10 10
2516 – 8 p. pink and green . . . 10 10
DESIGNS—As T **531**. No. 2510, Portrait of Juan de Juni (sculptor, 400th death anniv); No. 2511, Detail of "Rape of the Sabines" (Rubens); No. 2513, Artist's palette and Ruben's signature; No. 2514, Detail of "Bacchanal" (Titian); No. 2516, Artist's palette and Titian's initial. 46 × 25 mm: No. 2509, Different detail of "Deposition of Christ" and sculptor's tools; No. 2512, Different detail of "Rape of the Sabines" and portrait of Rubens (400th birth anniv); No. 2515, Different detail of "Bacchanal" and portrait of Titian (500th birth anniv).

532 Edelweiss in the Pyrenees

1978. Protection of the Environment. Mult.
2517 3 p. Type **532** 10 10
2518 5 p. Fish and red-breasted merganser 35 10
2519 7 p. Forest (fire prevention) 10 10
2520 12 p. Tanker, oil rig and industrial complex (protection of the sea) . . . 25 10
2521 20 p. Audouin's gull and Mediterranean monk seal (vert) 55 25

533 Palace of Charles V, Granada

1978. Europa.
2522 **533** 5 p. green & light green 10 10
2523 – 12 p. red and green . . . 15 10
DESIGN: 12 p. Exchange building, Seville.

534 Council Emblem and Map of Spain

1978. Membership of the Council of Europe.
2524 **534** 12 p. multicoloured . . . 15 10

535 Columbus Hermitage

1978. 500th Anniv of Las Palmas. Gran Canaria. Multicoloured.
2525 3 p. 16th-century plan of city (horiz) 10 10
2526 5 p. Type **535** 10 10
2527 12 p. View of Las Palmas (16th century) (horiz) 15 10

536 Post Box, Stamp, U.P.U. Emblem and Postal Transport

1978. World Stamp Day.
2528 **536** 5 p. green & dp green 30 10

1978. Stamp Day and Picasso Commemoration. As T **409**. Multicoloured.
2529 3 p. "Portrait of Senora Canals" 10 10
2530 5 p. Self-portrait 10 10
2531 8 p. "Portrait of Jaime Sabartes" 10 10
2532 10 p. "The End of the Number" 10 10
2533 12 p. "Science and Charity" (horiz) 15 10
2534 15 p. "Las Meninas" (horiz) 15 10
2535 20 p. "The Pigeons" 20 10
2536 25 p. "The Painter and Model" (horiz) 25 10

537 Jose de San Martin

1978. Latin-American Heroes.
2537 **537** 7 p. brown and red . . . 10 10
2538 – 12 p. violet and red . . . 15 20
DESIGNS: 12 p. Simon Bolivar.

538 Flight into Egypt

1978. Christmas. Capitals from Santa Maria de Nieva. Multicoloured.
2539 5 p. Type **538** 10 10
2540 12 p. The Annunciation . . 15 10

539 Aztec Calendar **540** Philip V

1978. Royal Visits to Mexico, Peru and Argentina. Multicoloured.
2541 5 p. Type **539** 10 10
2542 5 p. Macchu Piccu, Peru . . 10 10
2543 5 p. Pre-Columbian pots, Argentina 10 10

1978. Spanish Kings and Queens of the House of Bourbon.
2544 **540** 5 p. red and blue 10 10
2545 – 5 p. deep green and green 10 10
2546 – 8 p. lake and blue . . . 10 10
2547 – 10 p. black and green . . 10 10
2548 – 12 p. lake and brown . . 15 10
2549 – 15 p. blue and green . . 15 10
2550 – 20 p. blue and olive . . 25 10
2551 – 25 p. violet and blue . . 30 15
2552 – 50 p. brown and red . . 55 20
2553 – 100 p. violet and blue . . 1·10 35
DESIGNS: 5 p. (No. 2545), Luis I; 8 p. Ferdinand VI; 10 p. Charles III; 12 p. Charles IV; 15 p. Ferdinand VII; 20 p. Isabel II; 25 p. Alfonso XII; 50 p. Alfonso XIII; 100 p. Juan Carlos I.

541 Miniatures from Bible

1978. Millenary of Consecration of Third Basilica of Santa Maria, Ripoll.
2554 **541** 5 p. multicoloured . . . 10 10

542 Flag, First Lines of Constitution and Cortes Building

1978. New Constitution.

2555 **542** 5 p. multicoloured . . . 10 10

543 Car and Oil Drop

544 St. Jean Baptiste de la Salle (founder)

1979. Energy Conservation. Multicoloured.

2556 5 p. Type **543** 10 10
2557 8 p. Insulated house and thermometer 10 10
2558 10 p. Hand removing electric plug 10 10

1979. Centenary of Brothers of the Christian Schools in Spain.

2559 **544** 5 p. brown, blue & mauve 10 10

545 Jorge Manrique (poet)

546 Running and Jumping

1979. Spanish Celebrities.

2560 **545** 5 p. brown and green . . 10 10
2561 – 8 p. blue and red 10 10
2562 – 10 p. violet and brown . . 10 10
2563 – 20 p. green and bistre . . 20 10

DESIGNS: 8 p. Fernan Caballero (novelist); 10 p. Francisco Villaespesa (poet); 20 p. Gregorio Maranon (writer).

1979. Sport for All.

2564 **546** 5 p. red, green & black . 10 10
2565 – 8 p. blue, ochre & black . 10 10
2566 – 10 p. brown, blue & black 10 10

DESIGNS: 8 p. Football, running, skipping and cycling; 10 p. Running.

547 School Library (child's drawing)

548 Cabinet Messenger and Postilion, 1761

1979. International Year of the Child.

2567 **547** 5 p. multicoloured . . . 10 10

1979. Europa.

2568 **548** 5 p. deep brown and brown on yellow 10 10
2569 – 12 p. green and brown on yellow 15 10

DESIGN—HORIZ: 12 p. Manuel de Ysasi (postal reformer).

549 Wave Pattern and Television Screen

1979. World Telecommunications Day. Mult.

2570 5 p. Type **549** 10 10
2571 8 p. Satellite and receiving aerial (horiz) 10 10

550 First Bulgarian Stamp and Exhibition Hall

1979. "Philaserdica 79" Stamp Exhibition, Sofia.

2572 **550** 12 p. multicoloured . . 15 10

551 Tank, "Roger de Lauria" (destroyer) and Hawker Siddeley Matador Jet Fighter

1979. Armed Forces Day.

2573 **551** 5 p. multicoloured . . . 60 10

552 King receiving Messenger

1979. Stamp Day.

2574 **552** 5 p. multicoloured . . . 10 10

1979. Tourist Series. As T **340**.

2575 5 p. lilac and blue 10 10
2576 8 p. brown and blue 10 10
2577 10 p. green and myrtle . . . 10 10
2578 20 p. sepia and brown . . . 20 10

DESIGNS—VERT: 5 p. Daroca Gate, Zaragoza; 8 p. Gerona Cathedral; 10 p. Interior of Carthusian Monastery Church, Granada; 20 p. Portal of Marques de Dos Aguas Palace, Valencia.

553 Turkey Sponge

1979. Spanish Fauna (7th series). Invertebrates. Multicoloured.

2579 5 p. Type **553** 10 10
2580 7 p. Crayfish 10 10
2581 8 p. Scorpion 10 10
2582 20 p. Starfish 20 10
2583 25 p. Sea anemone 25 10

554 Antonio Gutierrez

555 Cathedral and Statue of Virgin and Child, Zaragoza

1979. Defence of Tenerife, 1797.

2584 **554** 5 p. multicoloured . . . 30 10

1979. Stamp Day and J. de Juanes (painter) Commemoration. Religious Paintings as T **409**. Multicoloured.

2585 8 p. "Immaculate Conception" 10 10
2586 10 p. "Holy Family" 10 10
2587 15 p. "Ecce Homo" 15 10
2588 20 p. "St. Stephen in the Synagogue" 20 15
2589 25 p. "The Last Supper" (horiz) 25 10
2590 50 p. "Adoration of the Mystic Lamb" (horiz) 55 15

1979. 8th Mariological Congress, Zaragoza.

2591 **555** 5 p. multicoloured . . . 10 10

556 St. Bartholomew's College, Bogota

1979. Latin-American Architecture.

2592 **556** 7 p. green, blue & brown 10 10
2593 – 12 p. indigo, purple & brn 15 10

DESIGN: 12 p. University of San Marcos, Lima.

557 Hands and Governor's Palace, Barcelona

1979. Catalonian Autonomy.

2594 **557** 8 p. multicoloured . . . 10 10

558 Autonomy Statute

559 Prince of Asturias and Hospital

1979. Basque Autonomy.

2595 **558** 8 p. multicoloured . . . 10 10

1979. Centenary of Hospital of the Child Jesus, Madrid.

2596 **559** 5 p. multicoloured . . . 10 10

560 Barcelona Tax Stamp, 1929

1979. 50th Anniv of Barcelona Exhibition Tax Stamps.

2597 **560** 5 p. multicoloured . . . 10 10

561 The Nativity

1979. Christmas. Capitals from San Pedro el Viejo, Huesca. Multicoloured.

2598 8 p. Type **561** 10 10
2599 19 p. Flight into Egypt . . . 20 10

562 Charles I

1979. Spanish Kings of the House of Hapsburg.

2600 **562** 15 p. green and blue . . . 20 10
2601 – 20 p. blue and mauve . . 30 10
2602 – 25 p. violet and brown . . 40 10
2603 – 50 p. brown and green . . 65 15
2604 – 100 p. mauve & brown . 1·10 30

DESIGNS: 20 p. Philip II; 25 p. Philip III; 50 p. Philip IV; 100 p. Charles II.

563 Olive Plantation and Harvester

1979. International Olive Oil Year.

2605 **563** 8 p. multicoloured . . . 15 10

564 Electric Train

1980. Public Transport.

2606 **564** 3 p. lake and brown . . . 10 10
2607 – 4 p. blue and brown . . . 10 10
2608 – 5 p. green and brown . . 10 10

DESIGNS: 4 p. Motorbus; 5 p. Underground train.

565 Steel Products

1980. Spanish Exports (1st series). Multicoloured.

2609 5 p. Type **565** 10 10
2610 8 p. Tankers 10 10
2611 13 p. Footwear 20 10
2612 19 p. Industrial machinery . 25 10
2613 25 p. Factory buildings, bridge and symbols of technology 30 15

See also Nos. 2653/5.

566 Federico Garcia Lorca

1980. Europa. Writers.

2614 **566** 8 p. violet and green . . 10 10
2615 – 19 p. brown and green . 20 10

DESIGN: 19 p. J. Ortega y Gasset.

567 Footballers

1980. World Cup Football Championship, Spain (1982) (1st issue). Multicoloured.

2616 8 p. Type **567** 10 10
2617 19 p. Football and flags . . 20 10

See also Nos. 2640/1, 2668/9 and 2683/4.

568 Armed Forces

1980. Armed Forces Day.

2618 **568** 8 p. multicoloured . . . 50 10

569 Bourbon Arms, Ministry of Finance, Madrid

1980. Public Finances under the Bourbons.

2619 **569** 8 p. dp brown & brown . 10 10

570 Helen Keller

1980. Birth Centenary of Helen Keller.

2620 **570** 19 p. red and green . . . 20 10

571 Postal Courier (14th century)

1980. Stamp Day.

2621 **571** 8 p. brown, stone & red . 10 10

572 King Alfonso XIII and Count of Maceda at Exhibition

573 Altar of the Virgin, La Palma Cathedral

1980. 50th Anniv of First National Stamp Exhibition.

2622 **572** 8 p. multicoloured . . . 10 10

1980. 300th Anniv of Appearance of the Holy Virgin at La Palma.

2623 **573** 8 p. brown and black . . 10 10

574 Ramon Perez de Ayala

1980. Birth Centenary of Ramon Perez de Ayala (writer).

2624 **574** 100 p. green and brown . 1·10 20

576 Juan de Garay and Founding of Buenos Aires (after Moreno Carbonero)

1980. 400th Anniv of Buenos Aires.

2626 **576** 19 p. blue, green & red . 20 10

578 Palace of Congresses, Madrid

579 "Nativity" (mural from Church of Santa Maria de Cuina, Oza de los Rios)

1980. European Security and Co-operation Conference, Madrid.

2628 **578** 22 p. multicoloured . . . 25 10

1980. Christmas. Multicoloured.

2629 10 p. Type **579** 10 10

2630 22 p. "Adoration of the Kings" (doorway of Church of St. Nicholas of Cines, Oza de los Rios) (horiz) 25 10

580 Pedro Vives and Farman H.F.III Biplane

1980. Aviation Pioneers. Multicoloured.

2631 5 p. Type **580** 15 10

2632 10 p. Benito Loygorri and Farman H.F.20 type biplane 15 10

2633 15 p. Alfonso de Orleans and Caudron G-3 . . . . . . 30 10

2634 22 p. Alfredo Kindelan and biplane 35 15

581 Games Emblem and Skier

1981. Winter University Games.

2635 **581** 30 p. multicoloured . . . 35 15

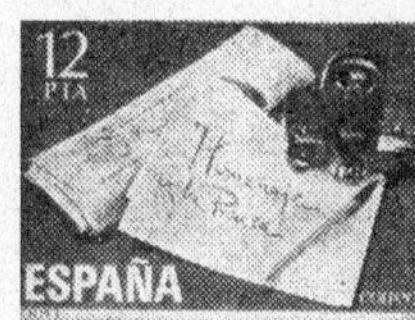

582 "Homage to Picasso" (Joan Miro)

1981. Birth Centenary of Pablo Picasso (artist).

2636 **582** 100 p. multicoloured . . 1·10 15

583 Newspaper, Camera, Notepaper and Pen

1981. The Press.

2637 **583** 12 p. multicoloured . . 15 10

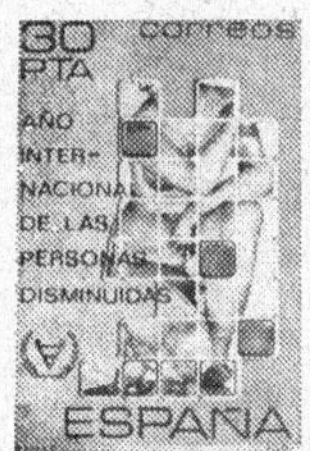

584 Map of Galicia, Arms and National Anthem

1981. Galician Autonomy.

2638 **584** 12 p. multicoloured . . 15 10

585 Mosaic forming Human Figure

586 Heading Ball

1981. International Year of Disabled Persons.

2639 **585** 30 p. multicoloured . . 30 10

1981. World Cup Football Championship (1982) (2nd issue). Multicoloured.

2640 12 p. Type **586** 15 10

2641 30 p. Kicking ball (horiz) . . 35 10

587 La Jota (folk dance)

588 King Juan Carlos reviewing Army

1981. Europa.

2642 **587** 12 p. black and brown . 15 10

2643 – 30 p. dp lilac and lilac . 35 10

DESIGN: 30 p. Procession of the Virgin of Rocio.

1981. Armed Forces Day.

2644 **588** 12 p. multicoloured . . 15 10

589 Gabriel Miro (writer)

590 Messenger (14th-century woodcut)

1981. Spanish Celebrities.

2645 **589** 6 p. violet and green . . 10 10

2646 – 12 p. brown and violet . 15 10

2647 – 30 p. green and brown . . 30 10

DESIGNS: 12 p. Francisco de Quevedo (writer); 30 p. St. Benedict.

1981. Stamp Day.

2648 **590** 12 p. pink, brown & grn . 15 10

591 Map of the Balearic Islands (from Atlas of Diego Homem, 1563)

1981. Spanish Islands. Multicoloured.

2649 7 p. Type **591** 15 10

2650 12 p. Map of the Canary Islands (from map of Mateo Prunes, 1563) 20 10

592 Alfonso XII, Juan Carlos and Arms

1981. Century of Public Prosecutor's Office.

2651 **592** 50 p. brown, green & bl . 60 10

593 King Sancho VI of Navarre with Foundation Charter

1981. 800th Anniv of Vitoria.

2652 **593** 12 p. multicoloured . . . 15 10

594 Citrus Fruit

1981. Spanish Exports (2nd series). Multicoloured.

2653 6 p. Type **594** 10 10

2654 12 p. Wine 15 10

2655 30 p. CASA C-212 Aviocar airplane, car and lorry . . . 45 10

595 Foodstuffs

1981. World Food Day.

2656 **595** 30 p. multicoloured . . . 30 10

597 Congress Palace, Buenos Aires

598 "Adoration of the Kings" (from Cervera de Pisuerga)

1981. "Espamer 81" International Stamp Exhibition, Buenos Aires.

2658 **597** 12 p. red and blue 15 10

1981. Christmas. Multicoloured.

2659 12 p. Type **598** 15 10

2660 30 p. "Nativity" (from Paredes de Nava) 30 10

599 Plaza de Espana, Seville

1981. Air.

2661 **599** 13 p. green and blue . . 25 10

2662 – 20 p. blue and brown . . 35 10

DESIGN: 20 p. Rande Bridge, Ria de Vigo.

600 Telegraph Operator

1981. Postal and Telecommunications Museum, Madrid.

2663 **600** 7 p. green and brown . . 15 15

2664 – 12 p. brown and violet . 20 15

DESIGN: 12 p. Post wagon.

601 Royal Mint, Seville

602 Iparraguirre

1981. Financial Administration by the Bourbons in Spain and the Indies.

2666 **601** 12 p. brown and grey . . 15 10

1981. Death Centenary of Jose Maria Iparraguirre.

2667 **602** 12 p. blue and black . . 15 10

603 Publicity Poster by Joan Miro

604 Andres Bello (author and philosopher) (birth bicent)

1982. World Cup Football Championship, Spain (3rd issue). Multicoloured.

2668 14 p. Type **603** 15 10

2669 33 p. World Cup trophy and championship emblem . . 40 15

1982. Anniversaries (1981).

2670 **604** 30 p. deep green and green 30 10

2671 – 30 p. green and blue . . 30 10

2672 – 50 p. violet and black . . 50 10

DESIGNS: No. 2671, J. R. Jimenez (author, birth centenary); No. 2672, P. Calderon (playwright, 300th death anniv).

605 St. James of Compostela (Codex illustration)

606 Manuel Fernandez Caballero

1982. Holy Year of Compostela.

2673 **605** 14 p. multicoloured . . . 15 10

1982. Masters of Operetta (1st series). As T **606** (2674, 2676, 2678) or T **625** (others). Multicoloured.

2674 3 p. Type **606** 10 10

2675 3 p. Scene from "Gigantes y Cabezudos" (horiz) 10 10

2676 6 p. Amadeo Vives Roig . . 10 10

2677 6 p. Scene from "Maruxa" (horiz) 10 10

2678 8 p. Tomas Breton y Hernandez 10 10

2679 8 p. Scene from "La Verbena de la Paloma" (horiz) 10 10

See also Nos. 2713/8 and 2772/7.

607 Arms, Seals and Signatures (Unification of Spain, 1479)

1982. Europa. Multicoloured.

2680 14 p. Type **607** 15 10

2681 33 p. Symbolic ship, Columbus map of "La Spanola" and signature (Discovery of America) 40 10

608 Swords, Arms and Flag

609 Tackling

1982. Armed Forces Day and Centenary of General Military Academy.

2682 **608** 14 p. multicoloured . . . 15 10

1982. World Cup Football Championship, Spain (4th issue). Multicoloured.

2683 14 p. Type **609** 15 15

2684 33 p. Goal 35 35

610 "St. Andrew and St. Francis"

612 "Transplants"

611 Map of Tenerife and Letter

1982. Air. Paintings by El Greco. Multicoloured.

2686 13 p. Type **610** 15 10

2687 20 p. "St. Thomas" 20 10

1982. Stamp Day.

2688 **611** 14 p. multicoloured . . . 20 10

1982. Organ Transplants.

2689 **612** 14 p. multicoloured . . . 15 10

613 White Storks and Modern Locomotive

1982. 23rd International Railway Congress, Malaga. Multicoloured.

2690 9 p. Type **613** 15 10

2691 14 p. Locomotive "Antigua" (37 × 26 mm) 50 10

2692 33 p. Locomotive "Montana" (wrongly inscr "Santa Fe") (37 × 26 mm) 60 10

614 La Fortaleza, San Juan

1982. "Espamer 82" Stamp Exhibition, San Juan, Puerto Rico.

2693 **614** 33 p. blue and lilac . . . 35 10

615 St. Theresa of Avila (sculpture by Gregorio Hernandez)

1982. 400th Death Anniv of St. Theresa of Avila.

2694 **615** 33 p. brown, blue and green 35 15

616 Pope John Paul II

1982. Papal Visit.

2695 **616** 14 p. blue and brown . 25 10

1982. Tourist Series. As T **340**.

2696 4 p. blue and grey 10 10

2697 6 p. grey and blue 10 10

2698 9 p. lilac and blue 10 10

2699 14 p. lilac and blue 20 10

2700 33 p. brown and red 40 10

DESIGNS—VERT: 4 p. Arab water-wheel, Alcantarilla; 9 p. Dying Christ, Seville; 14 p. St. Martin's Tower, Teruel; 33 p. St. Andrew's Gate, Villalpando. HORIZ: 6 p. Bank of Spain, Madrid.

617 "Adoration of The Kings" (sculpture, Covarrubias Collegiate Church)

618 "The Prophet"

1982. Christmas. Multicoloured.

2701 14 p. Type **617** 15 10

2702 33 p. "The Flight into Egypt" (painting) 40 10

1982. Birth Centenary of Pablo Gargallo (sculptor).

2703 **618** 14 p. green and blue . . 15 10

619 St. John Bosco (founder) and Children

1982. Centenary of Salesian Schools in Spain.

2704 **619** 14 p. multicoloured . . 15 10

620 Arms of Spain

1983.

2705 **620** 14 p. multicoloured . . . 15 10

621 Sunrise over Andalusia

1983. Andalusian Autonomy.

2706 **621** 14 p. multicoloured . . . 20 10

622 Arms of Cantabria, Mountains and Monuments

1983. Cantabrian Autonomy.

2707 **622** 14 p. multicoloured . . . 20 10

623 National Police

624 Cycling

1983. State Security Forces. Multicoloured.

2708 9 p. Type **623** 10 10

2709 14 p. Civil Guard 15 10

2710 33 p. Superior Police Corps 40 15

1983. Air. Sports. Multicoloured.

2711 13 p. Type **624** 15 10

2712 20 p. Bowling (horiz) 20 10

625 Scene from "La Parranda"

1983. Masters of Operetta (2nd series). As T **625** (2714, 2716, 2718) or T **606** (others). Multicoloured.

2713 4 p. Francisco Alonso (vert) 10 10

2714 4 p. Type **625** 10 10

2715 6 p. Jacinto Guerrero (vert) 10 10

2716 6 p. Scene from "La Rosa del Azafran" 10 10

2717 9 p. Jesus Guridi (vert) . . . 15 10

2718 9 p. Scene from "El Caserio" 15 10

626 Cervantes and Scene from "Don Quixote"

1983. Europa.

2719 **626** 16 p. red and green . . . 20 10

2720 – 38 p. sepia and brown . . 40 15

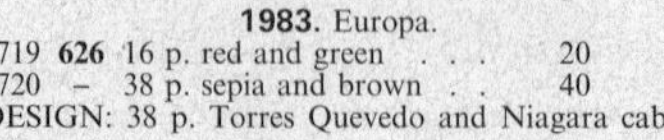

DESIGN: 38 p. Torres Quevedo and Niagara cable-car.

627 Francisco Salzillo (artist)

628 W.C.Y. Emblem

1983. Spanish Celebrities.

2721 **627** 16 p. purple and green . 20 10

2722 – 38 p. blue and brown . . 45 15

2723 – 50 p. blue and brown . . 60 10

2724 – 100 p. brown and violet . 1·10 20

DESIGNS: 38 p. Antonio Soler (composer); 50 p. Joaquin Turina (composer); 100 p. St. Isidro Labrador (patron saint of Madrid).

1983. World Communications Year.

2725 **628** 38 p. multicoloured . . . 45 10

629 Leaves

1983. Riojan Autonomy.

2726 **629** 16 p. multicoloured . . . 25 10

630 Army Monument, Burgos

1983. Armed Forces Day.

2727 **630** 16 p. multicoloured . . . 20 10

631 Burgos Setter

1983. Spanish Dogs.

2728 **631** 10 p. blue, brown & red 15 10

2729 – 16 p. multicoloured . . . 25 10

2730 – 26 p. multicoloured . . . 35 25

2731 – 38 p. multicoloured . . . 45 10

DESIGNS: 16 p. Spanish mastiff; 26 p. Ibiza spaniel; 38 p. Navarrese basset.

632 Juan-Jose and Fausto Elhuyar y de Suvisa

1983. Anniversaries. Multicoloured.

2732 16 p. Type **632** (bicentenary of discovery of wolfram) . . 20 10

2733 38 p. Scout camp (75th anniv of Boy Scout Movement) . . 40 10

2734 50 p. University of Zaragoza (400th anniv) 60 10

633 Arms of Murcia

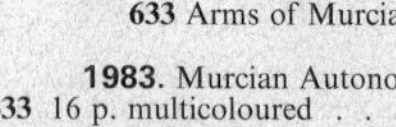

1983. Murcian Autonomy.

2735 **633** 16 p. multicoloured . . . 20 10

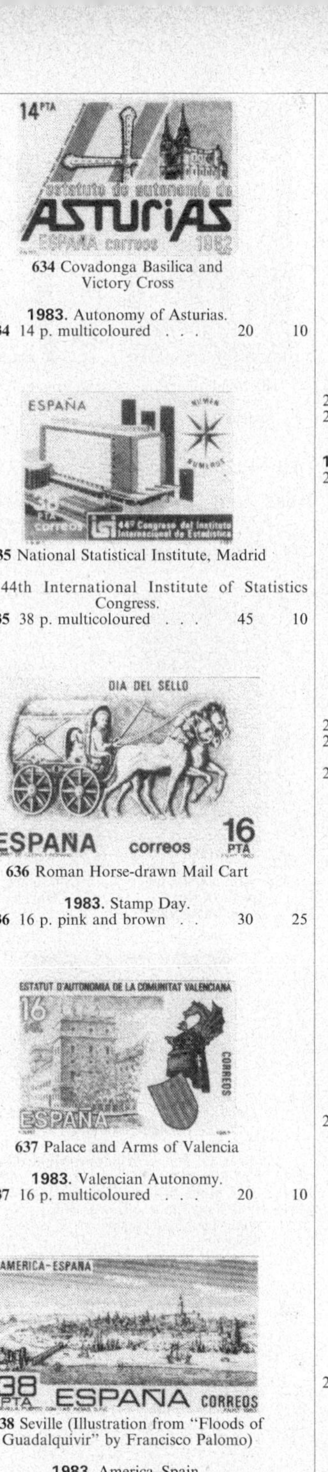

634 Covadonga Basilica and Victory Cross

1983. Autonomy of Asturias.
2736 **634** 14 p. multicoloured . . . 20 10

635 National Statistical Institute, Madrid

1983. 44th International Institute of Statistics Congress.
2737 **635** 38 p. multicoloured . . . 45 10

636 Roman Horse-drawn Mail Cart

1983. Stamp Day.
2738 **636** 16 p. pink and brown . . 30 25

637 Palace and Arms of Valencia

1983. Valencian Autonomy.
2739 **637** 16 p. multicoloured . . . 20 10

638 Seville (Illustration from "Floods of Guadalquivir" by Francisco Palomo)

1983. America–Spain.
2740 **638** 38 p. violet and blue . . 40 15

639 "Biblical King" (Leon Cathedral)

1983. Stained Glass Windows. Multicoloured.
2741 10 p. Type **639** 10 10
2742 16 p. "Epiphany" and Gerona Cathedral 20 10
2743 38 p. "St. James" and Santiago de Compostela Hospital . . 50 10

1983. Tourist Series. As T **340**.
2744 3 p. blue and green 10 10
2745 6 p. indigo 10 10
2746 16 p. violet and red 20 10
2747 38 p. red and brown 40 20
2748 50 p. red and brown 50 10
DESIGNS: 3 p. Church and tower, Llivia, Gerona; 6 p. Santa Maria del Mar, Barcelona; 16 p. Ceuta Cathedral; 38 p. Bridge gateway, Melilla; 50 p. Charity Hospital, Seville.

640 "Nativity" (altarpiece, Tortosa)
641 Indalecio Prieto

1983. Christmas. Multicoloured.
2749 16 p. Type **640** 20 10
2750 38 p. "Adoration of the Kings" (altarpiece, Vich) 40 20

1983. Birth Centenary of Indalecio Prieto (politician).
2751 **641** 16 p. brown and black . 20 10

642 Worker falling from Scaffolding

1984. Safety at Work. Multicoloured.
2752 7 p. Type **642** 10 10
2753 10 p. Burning factory and extinguisher 10 10
2754 16 p. Electric plug and wiring, cutters, gloved hands and warning sign 20 10

643 Tree

1984. Extremaduran Autonomy.
2755 **643** 16 p. multicoloured . . 20 10

644 Burgos Cathedral and Coat of Arms

1984. 1500th Anniv of Burgos City.
2756 **644** 16 p. brown and blue . 20 10

645 Carnival Dancer, Santa Cruz, Tenerife

1984. Festivals. Multicoloured.
2757 16 p. Type **645** 20 10
2758 16 p. Carnival figure and fireworks, Valencia . . . 20 10

646 "Man" (Leonardo da Vinci)

1984. Man and Biosphere.
2759 **646** 38 p. multicoloured . . 40 20

647 Map and Flag of Aragon and "Justice"

1984. Aragon Autonomy.
2760 **647** 16 p. multicoloured . . 20 10

649 F.I.P. Emblem

1984. 53rd International Philatelic Federation Congress, Madrid.
2762 **649** 38 p. red and violet . . . 40 15

650 Bridge

1984. Europa.
2763 **650** 16 p. red 20 10
2764 38 p. blue 40 20

651 Monument to the Alcantara Cazadores Regiment, Valladolid (Mariano Benlliure)

1984. Armed Forces Day.
2765 **651** 17 p. multicoloured . . . 20 10

652 Arms of Canary Islands

1984. Autonomy of Canary Islands.
2766 **652** 16 p. multicoloured 20 10

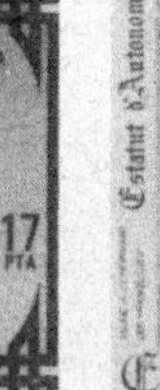

653 Arms of Castilla-La Mancha
655 "James III confirming Grants"

654 King Alfonso X, the Wise, of Castile and Leon (700th death anniv)

1984. Autonomy of Castilla–La Mancha.
2767 **653** 17 p. multicoloured . . . 20 10

1984. Anniversaries.
2768 **654** 16 p. red, blue & black 20 10
2769 – 38 p. blue, red & black 40 20
DESIGN: 38 p. Ignacio Barraquer (opthalmologist, birth centenary).

1984. Autonomy of Balearic Islands.
2770 **655** 17 p. multicoloured . . . 20 10

656 Running before Bulls

1984. Pamplona Festival, San Fermin.
2771 **656** 17 p. multicoloured . . . 20 10

1984. Masters of Operetta (3rd series). Horiz designs as T **625** (2772, 2775/6) or vert designs as T **606** (others). Multicoloured.
2772 6 p. Scene from "El Nino Judio" 10 10
2773 6 p. Pablo Luna 10 10
2774 7 p. Ruperto Chapi 10 10
2775 7 p. Scene from "La Revoltosa" 10 10
2776 10 p. Scene from "La Reina Mora" 15 10
2777 10 p. Jose Serrano 15 10

657 Bronze of Swimmer ready to Dive

1984. Olympic Games, Los Angeles. Mult.
2778 1 p. Roman quadriga (horiz) 10 10
2779 2 p. Type **657** 10 10
2780 5 p. Bronze of two wrestlers (horiz) 10 10
2781 8 p. "The Discus-thrower" (statue, Miron) 15 10

658 Arms and Map of Navarra

1984. Autonomy of Navarra.
2782 **658** 17 p. multicoloured . . . 20 10

659 Cyclist
660 Arms (Levante Building Salamanca University)

1984. International Cycling Championship, Barcelona.
2783 **659** 17 p. multicoloured . . . 20 10

1984. Autonomy of Castilla y Leon.
2784 **660** 17 p. multicoloured . . . 20 10

661 Women gathering Grapes

1984. Vintage Festival, Jerez.
2785 **661** 17 p. multicoloured . . . 25 10

662 Egeria on Donkey and Map of Middle East

1984. 1600th Anniv of Nun Egeria's Visit to Middle East.
2786 **662** 40 p. multicoloured . . . 40 20

663 Arab Courier

1984. Stamp Day.
2787 **663** 17 p. multicoloured . . . 25 10

664 Father Junipero Serra **665** "Adoration of the Kings" (Miguel Moguer) (Campos altarpiece)

1984. Death Bicentenary of Father Junipero Serra (missionary).
2788 **664** 40 p. red and blue . . . 40 20

1984. Christmas. Multicoloured.
2789 17 p. "Nativity" (15th-century retable) (horiz) 20 10
2790 40 p. Type **665** 40 20

666 Arms, Buildings and Trees

1984. Autonomy of Madrid.
2791 **666** 17 p. multicoloured . . . 25 10

667 Flags and Andean Condor

1985. 15th Anniv (1984) of Andes Pact.
2792 **667** 17 p. multicoloured . . . 45 10

668 "Virgin of Louvain" (attr Jan Gossaert) **669** College Porch and Tympanum

1985. "Europalia 85 Espana" Festival.
2793 **668** 40 p. multicoloured . . . 45 20

1985. 500th Anniv of Santa Cruz College, Valladolid University.
2794 **669** 17 p. yellow, brn & red 20 10

670 Flames and "Olymphilex '85"

1985. "Olymphilex 85" International Olympic Stamps Exhibition, Lausanne.
2795 **670** 40 p. red, yellow & black 40 15

671 Havana Cathedral

1985. "Espamer '85" International Stamp Exhibition, Havana, Cuba.
2796 **671** 40 p. blue and purple . 40 20

672 Couple in Traditional Dress on Horseback

1985. April Fair, Seville.
2797 **672** 17 p. multicoloured . . 25 10

673 Heads as Holder for Flames

1985. International Youth Year.
2798 **673** 17 p. green, black and red 20 10

674 Moors and Christians fighting

1985. Festival of Moors and Christians, Alcoy.
2799 **674** 17 p. multicoloured . . 25 10

675 Don Antonio de Cabezon (organist)

1985. Europa.
2800 **675** 18 p. red, black and blue on yellow 25 10
2801 – 45 p. red, black and green on yellow 60 25
DESIGN: 45 p. Musicians of National Youth Orchestra.

676 Capitania General Headquarters, La Coruna

1985. Armed Forces Day.
2802 **676** 18 p. multicoloured . . 25 10

677 Carlos III's Arms, 1785 Decree and "Santissima Trinidad" (ship of the line)

1985. Bicentenary of National Flag. Mult.
2803 18 p. Type **677** 25 10
2804 18 p. State arms, 1978 constitution and lion (detail from House of Deputies) . 20 10

678 Sunflower and Bird

1985. World Environment Day.
2805 **678** 17 p. multicoloured . . 25 10

679 Monstrance in Decorated Street **680** King Juan Carlos I

1985. Corpus Christi Festival, Toledo.
2806 **679** 18 p. multicoloured . . . 45 10

1985.
2807 **680** 10 c. blue 10 10
2808 50 c. green 10 10
2809 1 p. blue 10 10
2810 2 p. green 10 10
2811 3 p. brown 10 10
2812 4 p. bistre 10 10
2813 5 p. purple 10 10
2814 6 p. brown 10 10
2815 7 p. violet 15 10
2816 7 p. green 10 10
2817 8 p. grey 10 10
2818 10 p. red 10 10
2819 12 p. red 10 10
2820 13 p. blue 15 10
2821 15 p. green 15 10
2822 17 p. orange 20 10
2823 18 p. green 20 10
2824 19 p. brown 20 10
2825 20 p. mauve 20 10
2825a 25 p. green 25 10
2825b 27 p. mauve 30 10
2826 30 p. blue 25 10
2827 45 p. green 50 10
2828 50 p. blue 55 10
2828a 55 p. brown 55 10
2829 60 p. red 65 10
2830 75 p. mauve 80 10

681 Planetary System

1985. Inauguration of Astrophysical Observatories, Canary Islands.
2831 **681** 45 p. multicoloured . . . 50 20

682 Ataulfo Argenta (conductor)

1985. European Music Year. Multicoloured.
2832 12 p. Type **682** 15 10
2833 17 p. Tomas Luis de Victoria (composer) 20 10
2834 45 p. Fernando Sor (guitarist and composer) 50 20

683 Bernal Diaz del Castillo (conquistador)

1985. Celebrities.
2835 **683** 7 p. red, black and green on yellow 10 10
2836 – 12 p. red, black and blue on yellow 15 10
2837 – 17 p. green, red and black on yellow 20 10
2838 – 45 p. green, black and brown on yellow . . . 50 20
DESIGNS: 12 p. Esteban Terradas (mathematician); 17 p. Vicente Aleixandre (poet); 45 p. Leon Felipe Camino (poet).

684 Canoeist

1985. "Descent down the Sella" Canoe Festival, Asturias.
2839 **684** 17 p. multicoloured . . . 40 10

685 Monk returning with Rotulet to Savigni Abbey, 1122 **686** Ribbon Exercise

1985. Stamp Day.
2840 **685** 17 p. multicoloured . . . 25 10

1985. 12th World Rhythmic Gymnastics Championship, Valladolid. Multicoloured.
2841 17 p. Type **686** 20 10
2842 45 p. Hoop exercise 45 10

688 "Virgin and Child" (Escalas Chapel, Seville Cathedral) **690** Subalpine Warbler

689 "Nativity" (detail of altarpiece by Ramon de Mur)

1985. Stained Glass Windows. Multicoloured.
2844 7 p. Type **688** 10 10
2845 12 p. Monk (Toledo Cathedral) 15 10
2846 17 p. King Enrique II of Castile and Leon (Alcazar of Segovia) 20 10

1985. Christmas. Multicoloured.
2847 17 p. Type **689** 20 10
2848 45 p. "Adoration of the Magi" (embroidered frontal, after Jaume Huguet) 50 10

1985. Birds. Multicoloured.
2849 6 p. Type **690** 35 10
2850 7 p. Rock thrush 45 10
2851 12 p. Spotless starling . . . 80 20
2852 17 p. Bearded reedling . . . 1·25 35

691 Count of Penaflorida

1985. Death Bicentenary of Count of Penaflorida (founder of Economic Society of Friends of the Land).
2853 **691** 17 p. blue 20 10

692 Royal Palace, Madrid

1986. Admission of Spain and Portugal to European Economic Community. Multicoloured.
2854 7 p. Type **692** 10 10
2855 17 p. Map and flags of member countries 15 10
2856 30 p. Hall of Columns, Royal Palace 30 15
2857 45 p. Flags of Portugal and Spain uniting with flags of other members 55 25

1986. Tourist Series. As T **340**.
2858 12 p. black and red 15 10
2859 35 p. brown and blue 40 15
DESIGNS: 12 p. Lupiana Monastery, Guadalajara; 35 p. Balcony of Europe, Nerja.

693 Merino

1986. Second World Conference on Merinos.
2860 **693** 45 p. multicoloured . . . 50 15

694 "Revellers" (detail, F. Hohenleiter)

1986. Cadiz Carnival.
2861 **694** 17 p. multicoloured . . . 25 10

695 Helmets and Flower

1986. International Peace Year.
2862 **695** 45 p. multicoloured . . . 45 20

696 Organ Pipes

1986. Religious Music Week, Cuenca.
2863 **696** 17 p. multicoloured . . . 25 10

697 "Swearing in of Regent, Queen Maria Cristina" (detail, Joaquin Sorolla y Bastida)

1986. Centenary of Chambers of Commerce, Industry and Navigation.
2864 **697** 17 p. black and green . . 20 10

698 Man with Suitcase

1986. Emigration.
2865 **698** 45 p. multicoloured . . . 45 20

699 Boy and Birds

1986. Europa. Multicoloured.
2866 17 p. Type **699** 20 10
2867 45 p. Woman watering young tree 35 20

700 Our Lady of the Dew

1986. Our Lady of the Dew Festival, Rocio, near Almonte.
2868 **700** 17 p. multicoloured . . 25 10

701 Capitania General Building, Tenerife

1986. Armed Forces Day.
2869 **701** 17 p. multicoloured . . 20 10

1986. Tourist Series. As T **340**. Multicoloured.
2870 12 p. black and blue 20 10
2871 35 p. brown and blue . . . 45 10
DESIGNS: 12 p. Ciudad Rodrigo Cathedral, Salamanca; 35 p. Calella lighthouse, Barcelona.

702 Hands and Ball

1986. 10th World Basketball Championship.
2872 **702** 45 p. multicoloured . . 50 15

703 Francisco Loscos (botanist)

704 Apostles awaiting Angels carrying Virgin's Soul

1986. Celebrities.
2873 **703** 7 p. green and black . . 10 10
2874 – 11 p. red and black . . 15 10
2875 – 17 p. brown and black . 20 10
2876 – 45 p. purple, orange and black 45 20
DESIGNS: 11 p. Salvador Espriu (writer); 17 p. Azorin (Jose Martinez Ruiz) (writer); 45 p. Juan Gris (artist).

1986. Elche Mystery Play.
2877 **704** 17 p. multicoloured . . 20 10

705 Swimmer

1986. 5th World Swimming, Water Polo, Leap and Synchronous Swimming Championships.
2878 **705** 45 p. multicoloured . . 45 20

706 Pelota Player

1986. 10th World Pelota Championship.
2879 **706** 17 p. multicoloured . . 20 10

707 King's Messenger with Letter summoning Nobleman to Court

1986. Stamp Day.
2880 **707** 17 p. multicoloured . . 20 10

709 Aristotle

1986. 500th Anniv (1992) of Discovery of America by Columbus (1st issue). Designs showing historic figures and prophecies of discovery of New World.
2882 **709** 7 p. black and mauve . . 10 10
2883 – 12 p. black and lilac . . . 15 10
2884 – 17 p. black and yellow . . 20 10
2885 – 30 p. black and mauve . 30 10
2886 – 35 p. black and green . . 35 10
2887 – 45 p. black and orange . 45 10
DESIGNS: 12 p. Seneca and quote from "Medea"; 17 p. St. Isidoro of Seville and quote from "Etymologies"; 30 p. Cardinal Pierre d'Ailly and quote from "Imago Mundi"; 35 p. Mayan and quote from "Chilam Balam" books; 45 p. Conquistador and quote from "Chilam Balam" books.
See also Nos. 2932/7, 2983/8, 3035/40, 3079/82, 3126/9, 3175/6 and 3190.

710 Gaspar de Portola

711 "Holy Family" (detail, Diego de Siloe)

1986. Death Bicentenary of Gaspar de Portola (first Governor of California).
2888 **710** 22 p. blue, red & black . 25 10

1986. Christmas. Wood Carvings. Multicoloured.
2889 19 p. Type **711** 20 10
2890 48 p. "Nativity" (detail, Toledo Cathedral altarpiece, Felipe de Borgona) (horiz) 50 10

712 Abd-er Rahman II and Cordoba Mosque

1986. Hispanic Islamic Culture.
2891 **712** 7 p. brown and red . . . 10 10
2892 – 12 p. brown and red . . . 15 10
2893 – 17 p. blue and black . . . 20 10
2894 – 45 p. green and black . . 45 10
DESIGNS: 12 p. Ibn Hazm (writer) and burning book; 17 p. Al-Zarqali (astronomer) and azophea (astrolabe); 45 p. King Alfonso VII of Castile and Leon and scholars of Toledo School of Translators.

713 "The Good Curate"

1986. Birth Centenary of Alfonso Castelao (artist and writer).
2895 **713** 32 p. multicoloured . . . 35 10

714 Chateau de la Muette (headquarters)

1987. 25th Anniv of Organization for Economic Co-operation and Development.
2896 **714** 48 p. multicoloured . . . 60 10

715 Abstract Shapes

1987. "Expo 92" World's Fair, Seville (1st issue). Multicoloured.
2897 19 p. Type **715** 30 10
2898 48 p. Moon surface, Earth and symbol 90 10
See also Nos. 2941/2, 2951/2, 3004/7, 3052/5, 3094/7, 3143 and 3148/71.

716 Francisco de Vitoria

1987. 500th Birth Anniv of Francisco de Vitoria (jurist).
2899 **716** 48 p. brown 60 10

717 18th-century Warship and Standard Bearer

718 University

1987. 450th Anniv of Marine Corps.
2900 **717** 19 p. multicoloured . . . 40 10

1987. Centenary of Deusto University.
2901 **718** 19 p. red, green and black 20 10

719 Breastfeeding Baby

1987. U.N.I.C.E.F. Child Survival Campaign.
2902 **719** 19 p. brown and deep brown 25 10

720 Crowd

721 15th-century Pharmacy Jar, Manises

1987. 175th Anniv of Constitution of Cadiz. Multicoloured.
2903 25 p. Type **720** 25 20
2904 25 p. Crowd and herald on steps 25 20
2905 25 p. Dignitaries on dais . . 25 20
2906 25 p. Crown and Constitution 25 20
Nos. 2903/6 were printed together, se-tenant, the first three stamps forming a composite design showing "The Promulgation of the Constitution of 1812" by Salvador Viniegra.

1987. Ceramics. Multicoloured.
2907 7 p. Type **721** 10 10
2908 14 p. 20th-century glazed figure, Sargadelos 15 10
2909 19 p. 18th-century vase, Buen Retiro 20 10
2910 32 p. 20th-century pot, Salvatierra de los Barros . . 35 20
2911 40 p. 18th-century jar, Talavera 40 20
2912 48 p. 18-19th century jug, Granada 50 20

722 "Procession at Dawn, Zamora" (Gallego Marquina)

723 Bilbao Bank, Madrid (Saenz de Oiza)

1987. Holy Week Festivals. Multicoloured.
2913 19 p. Type **722** 20 10
2914 48 p. Gate of Pardon, Seville Cathedral and "Passion" (statue by Martinez Montanes) 60 10

1987. Tourist Series. As T **340**.
2915 14 p. green and blue 15 10
2916 19 p. deep green and green . 20 10
2917 40 p. brown 40 10
2918 48 p. black 50 10
DESIGNS—HORIZ: 14 p. Ifach Rock, Calpe, Alicante; 19 p. Ruins of Church of Santa Maria d'Ozo, Pontevedra; 40 p. Palace of Sonanes, Villacarriedo, Santander. VERT: 48 p. 11th-century monastery of Sant Joan de les Abadesses, Gerona.

1987. Europa. Architecture.
2919 **723** 19 p. multicoloured . . . 20 10
2920 – 48 p. brown, bistre & grn 50 10
DESIGN—HORIZ: 14 p. National Museum of Roman Art, Merida (Rafael Moneo).

724 Horse's Head and Harnessed Pair

1987. Jerez Horse Fair.
2921 **724** 19 p. multicoloured . . . 20 10

725 Carande

1987. Birth Centenary of Ramon Carande (historian and Honorary Postman).
2922 **725** 40 p. black and brown . 40 10

726 Numbers on Pen Nib

1987. Postal Coding.
2923 **726** 19 p. multicoloured . . . 20 10

727 Arms and School

1987. 75th Anniv of Eibar Armoury School.
2924 **727** 20 p. multicoloured . . . 20 10

728 Batllo House Chimneys (Antonio Gaudi)

1987. Nomination of Barcelona as 1992 Olympic Games Host City. Multicoloured.
2925 32 p. Type **728** 35 10
2926 65 p. Athletes 75 15

729 Festival Poster (Fabri)

1987. 25th Pyrenees Folklore Festival, Jaca.
2927 **729** 50 p. multicoloured . . . 50 10

730 Monturiol (after Marti Alsina) and Diagrams of Submarine "Ictineo"

1987. Death Cent of Narcis Monturiol (scientist).
2928 **730** 20 p. black and brown . 30 10

731 Detail from Jaime II of Majorca's Law appointing Couriers

1987. Stamp Day.
2929 **731** 20 p. multicoloured . . 20 10

734 Amerigo Vespucci

1987. 500th Anniv (1992) of Discovery of America by Columbus (2nd issue). Explorers. Multicoloured.
2932 14 p. Type **734** 15 10
2933 20 p. King Ferdinand and Queen Isabella the Catholic and arms on ships 20 10
2934 32 p. Juan Perez and departing ships 35 10
2935 40 p. Juan de la Cosa and ships 40 10
2936 50 p. Map, ship and Christopher Columbus . . 50 10
2937 65 p. Native on shore, approaching ships and Martin Alonzo and Vincente Yanez Pinzon 70 10

735 Star and Baubles **736** Macho (self-sculpture)

1987. Christmas. Multicoloured.
2938 20 p. Type **735** 25 10
2939 50 p. Zambomba and tambourine 50 10

1987. Birth Centenary of Victorio Macho (sculptor).
2940 **736** 50 p. brown and black . 50 10

1987. "Expo '92" World's Fair, Seville (2nd issue). As Nos. 2897/8 but values changed. Multicoloured.
2941 20 p. Type **715** 25 10
2942 50 p. As No. 2898 . . . . . 50 10

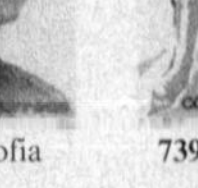

737 Queen Sofia **739** Speed Skating

738 Campoamor

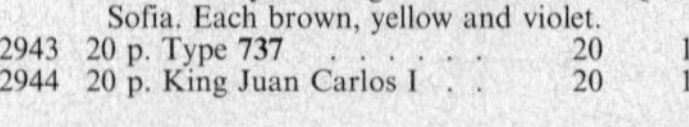

1988. 50th Birthdays of King Juan Carlos I and Queen Sofia. Each brown, yellow and violet.
2943 20 p. Type **737** 20 10
2944 20 p. King Juan Carlos I . . 20 10

1988. Birth Centenary of Clara Campoamor (politician and women's suffrage campaigner).
2945 **738** 20 p. multicoloured . . . 20 10

1988. Winter Olympic Games, Calgary.
2946 **739** 45 p. multicoloured . . . 45 10

740 "Christ tied to the Pillar" (statue) and Valladolid Cathedral **742** Globe and Stylized Roads

741 Ingredients for and Dish of Paella

1988. Holy Week Festivals. Multicoloured.
2947 20 p. Type **740** 20 10
2948 50 p. Float depicting Christ carrying the Cross, Malaga 50 10

1988. Tourist Series. Multicoloured.
2949 18 p. Type **741** 25 20
2950 45 p. Covadonga National Park (70th anniv of National Parks) 75 10

1988. "Expo '92" World's Fair, Seville (3rd issue).
2951 8 p. Type **742** 10 10
2952 45 p. Compass rose and globe (horiz) 45 10

743 18th-Century Valencian Chalice **744** Francis of Taxis (organiser of European postal service, 1505)

1988. Glassware. Multicoloured.
2953 20 p. Type **743** 20 10
2954 20 p. 18th-century pitcher, Cadalso de los Vidrios, Madrid 20 10
2955 20 p. 18th-century crystal sweet jar, La Granja de San Ildefonso 20 10
2956 20 p. 18th-century Andalusian two-handled jug, Castril . . 20 10
2957 20 p. 17th-century Catalan four-spouted jug 20 10
2958 20 p. 20th-century bottle, Balearic Islands 20 10

1988. Stamp Day.
2959 **744** 20 p. violet and brown . 20 10

745 Pablo Iglesias (first President)

1988. Centenary of General Workers' Union.
2960 **745** 20 p. multicoloured . . . 20 10

746 "La Junta" (1st Cuban railway locomotive), 1837

1988. Europa. Transport and Communications.
2961 **746** 20 p. red and black . . . 20 10
2962 – 50 p. green and black . . 50 10
DESIGN: 50 p. Light telegraph, Philippines, 1818.

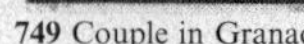

747 Monnet **749** Couple in Granada

748 Emblem

1988. Birth Cent of Jean Monnet (statesman).
2963 **747** 45 p. blue 45 10

1988. Centenary of 1888 Universal Exhibition, Barcelona.
2964 **748** 50 p. multicoloured . . . 50 10

1988. International Festival of Music and Dance, Granada.
2965 **749** 50 p. multicoloured . . . 50 10

750 Bull

1988. "Expo 88" World's Fair, Brisbane.
2966 **750** 50 p. multicoloured . . . 55 10

751 "Virgin of Hope"

1988. Coronation of "Virgin of Hope", Malaga.
2967 **751** 20 p. multicoloured . . . 20 10

753 Orreo (agricultural store), Cantabria

1988. Tourist Series.
2969 **753** 18 p. green, brown & bl . 20 10
2970 – 45 p. black, brn & ochre 55 10
DESIGN: 45 p. Dulzaina (wind instrument), Castilla y Leon.

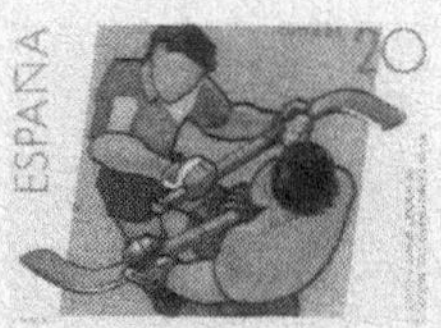

754 Players

1988. 28th World Roller Skate Hockey C'ship, La Coruna.
2971 **754** 20 p. multicoloured . . . 20 10

755 Congress Emblem **756** "Olympic" Class Yacht

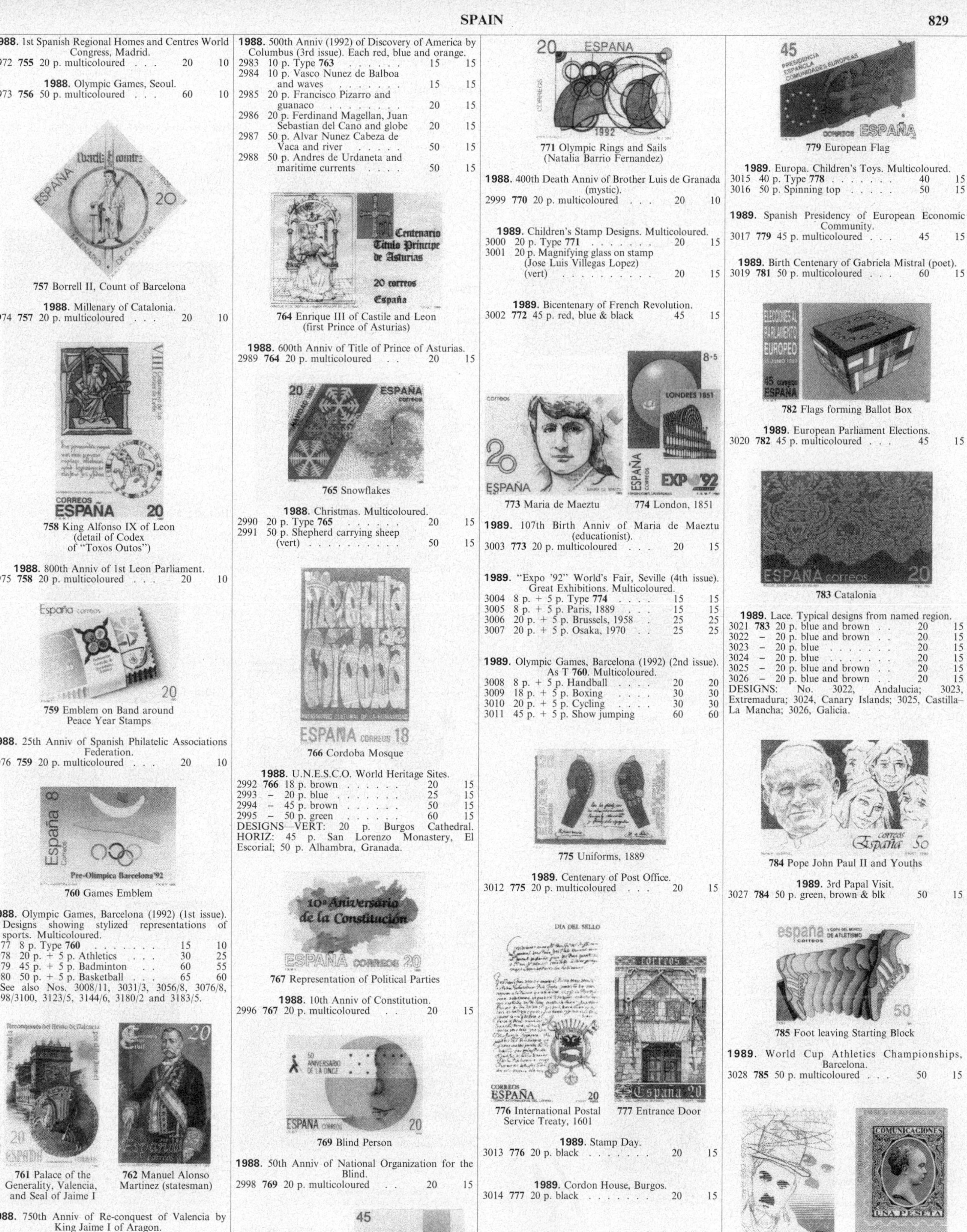

1988. 1st Spanish Regional Homes and Centres World Congress, Madrid.
2972 **755** 20 p. multicoloured . . . 20 10

1988. Olympic Games, Seoul.
2973 **756** 50 p. multicoloured . . . 60 10

757 Borrell II, Count of Barcelona

1988. Millenary of Catalonia.
2974 **757** 20 p. multicoloured . . . 20 10

758 King Alfonso IX of Leon (detail of Codex of "Toxos Outos")

1988. 800th Anniv of 1st Leon Parliament.
2975 **758** 20 p. multicoloured . . . 20 10

759 Emblem on Band around Peace Year Stamps

1988. 25th Anniv of Spanish Philatelic Associations Federation.
2976 **759** 20 p. multicoloured . . . 20 10

760 Games Emblem

1988. Olympic Games, Barcelona (1992) (1st issue). Designs showing stylized representations of sports. Multicoloured.
2977 8 p. Type **760** 15 10
2978 20 p. + 5 p. Athletics . . . 30 25
2979 45 p. + 5 p. Badminton . . 60 55
2980 50 p. + 5 p. Basketball . . . 65 60
See also Nos. 3008/11, 3031/3, 3056/8, 3076/8, 3098/3100, 3123/5, 3144/6, 3180/2 and 3183/5.

761 Palace of the Generality, Valencia, and Seal of Jaime I

762 Manuel Alonso Martinez (statesman)

1988. 750th Anniv of Re-conquest of Valencia by King Jaime I of Aragon.
2981 **761** 20 p. multicoloured . . . 25 15

1988. Centenary of Civil Code.
2982 **762** 20 p. multicoloured . . . 20 10

763 Hernan Cortes and Quetzalcoatl Serpent

1988. 500th Anniv (1992) of Discovery of America by Columbus (3rd issue). Each red, blue and orange.
2983 10 p. Type **763** 15 15
2984 10 p. Vasco Nunez de Balboa and waves 15 15
2985 20 p. Francisco Pizarro and guanaco 20 15
2986 20 p. Ferdinand Magellan, Juan Sebastian del Cano and globe 20 15
2987 50 p. Alvar Nunez Cabeza de Vaca and river 50 15
2988 50 p. Andres de Urdaneta and maritime currents 50 15

764 Enrique III of Castile and Leon (first Prince of Asturias)

1988. 600th Anniv of Title of Prince of Asturias.
2989 **764** 20 p. multicoloured . . 20 15

765 Snowflakes

1988. Christmas. Multicoloured.
2990 20 p. Type **765** 20 15
2991 50 p. Shepherd carrying sheep (vert) 50 15

766 Cordoba Mosque

1988. U.N.E.S.C.O. World Heritage Sites.
2992 **766** 18 p. brown 20 15
2993 – 20 p. blue 25 15
2994 – 45 p. brown 50 15
2995 – 50 p. green 60 15
DESIGNS—VERT: 20 p. Burgos Cathedral. HORIZ: 45 p. San Lorenzo Monastery, El Escorial; 50 p. Alhambra, Granada.

767 Representation of Political Parties

1988. 10th Anniv of Constitution.
2996 **767** 20 p. multicoloured . . 20 15

769 Blind Person

1988. 50th Anniv of National Organization for the Blind.
2998 **769** 20 p. multicoloured . . 20 15

770 Luis de Granada

772 Abstract

771 Olympic Rings and Sails (Natalia Barrio Fernandez)

1988. 400th Death Anniv of Brother Luis de Granada (mystic).
2999 **770** 20 p. multicoloured . . . 20 10

1989. Children's Stamp Designs. Multicoloured.
3000 20 p. Type **771** 20 15
3001 20 p. Magnifying glass on stamp (Jose Luis Villegas Lopez) (vert) 20 15

1989. Bicentenary of French Revolution.
3002 **772** 45 p. red, blue & black 45 15

773 Maria de Maeztu

774 London, 1851

1989. 107th Birth Anniv of Maria de Maeztu (educationist).
3003 **773** 20 p. multicoloured . . . 20 15

1989. "Expo '92" World's Fair, Seville (4th issue). Great Exhibitions. Multicoloured.
3004 8 p. + 5 p. Type **774** 15 15
3005 8 p. + 5 p. Paris, 1889 . . . 15 15
3006 20 p. + 5 p. Brussels, 1958 . . 25 25
3007 20 p. + 5 p. Osaka, 1970 . . 25 25

1989. Olympic Games, Barcelona (1992) (2nd issue). As T **760**. Multicoloured.
3008 8 p. + 5 p. Handball 20 20
3009 18 p. + 5 p. Boxing 30 30
3010 20 p. + 5 p. Cycling 30 30
3011 45 p. + 5 p. Show jumping 60 60

775 Uniforms, 1889

1989. Centenary of Post Office.
3012 **775** 20 p. multicoloured . . . 20 15

776 International Postal Service Treaty, 1601

777 Entrance Door

1989. Stamp Day.
3013 **776** 20 p. black 20 15

1989. Cordon House, Burgos.
3014 **777** 20 p. black 20 15

778 Skittles

781 Manuscript and Portrait

779 European Flag

1989. Europa. Children's Toys. Multicoloured.
3015 40 p. Type **778** 40 15
3016 50 p. Spinning top 50 15

1989. Spanish Presidency of European Economic Community.
3017 **779** 45 p. multicoloured . . . 45 15

1989. Birth Centenary of Gabriela Mistral (poet).
3019 **781** 50 p. multicoloured . . . 60 15

782 Flags forming Ballot Box

1989. European Parliament Elections.
3020 **782** 45 p. multicoloured . . . 45 15

783 Catalonia

1989. Lace. Typical designs from named region.
3021 **783** 20 p. blue and brown . . 20 15
3022 – 20 p. blue and brown . . 20 15
3023 – 20 p. blue 20 15
3024 – 20 p. blue 20 15
3025 – 20 p. blue and brown . . 20 15
3026 – 20 p. blue and brown . . 20 15
DESIGNS: No. 3022, Andalucia; 3023, Extremadura; 3024, Canary Islands; 3025, Castilla–La Mancha; 3026, Galicia.

784 Pope John Paul II and Youths

1989. 3rd Papal Visit.
3027 **784** 50 p. green, brown & blk 50 15

785 Foot leaving Starting Block

1989. World Cup Athletics Championships, Barcelona.
3028 **785** 50 p. multicoloured . . . 50 15

786 Chaplin

787 1 p. Stamp

1989. Birth Centenary of Charlie Chaplin (actor).
3029 **786** 50 p. multicoloured . . . 50 15

1989. Centenary of First King Alfonso XIII Stamps.
3030 **787** 50 p. brown, grey & red 50 15

1989. Olympic Games, Barcelona (1992) (3rd issue). As T **760**.
3031 18 p. + 5 p. Fencing 60 60
3032 20 p. + 5 p. Football . . . 60 60
3033 45 p. + 5 p. Gymnastics . . 1·25 1·25

788 Fr. Andres Manjon (founder)

1989. Centenary of Ave Maria Schools.
3034 **788** 20 p. multicoloured . . . 20 15

789 Maize

1989. 500th Anniv (1992) of Discovery of America by Columbus (4th issue). Multicoloured.
3035 8 p. + 5 p. Type **789** 15 15
3036 8 p. + 5 p. Cacao nut . . . 15 15
3037 20 p. + 5 p. Tomato 25 25
3038 20 p. + 5 p. Horse 25 25
3039 50 p. + 5 p. Potato 60 60
3040 50 p. + 5 p. Turkey 60 60

790 Inca irrigating Corn (from "New Chronicle" by Waman Puma)
791 "Navidad 89"

1989. America. Pre-Columbian Life.
3041 **790** 50 p. multicoloured . . . 50 15

1989. Christmas. Multicoloured.
3042 20 p. Type **791** 20 15
3043 45 p. Girl with Christmas present (horiz) 45 15

792 Altamira Caves

1989. World Heritage Sites. Multicoloured.
3044 20 p. Type **792** 20 15
3045 20 p. Segovia Aqueduct . . . 20 15
3046 20 p. Santiago de Compostela 20 15
3047 20 p. Guell Park and Palace and Mila House 20 15

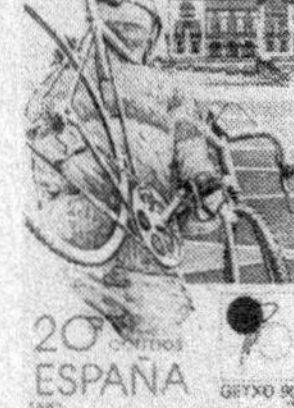

794 Olympic Rings, Compass Rose, Church of Holy Family, Barcelona, and Seville
795 Getxo City Hall and Competitor

1990. Children's Stamp Design.
3049 **794** 20 p. multicoloured . . . 20 15

1990. World Cyclo-cross Championship, Getxo.
3050 **795** 20 p. multicoloured . . . 20 15

796 Victoria Kent
797 Curro (mascot) flying over Path of Discoveries

1990. 3rd Death Anniv of Victoria Kent (prison reformer).
3051 **796** 20 p. lilac 20 15

1990. "Expo '92" World's Fair, Seville (5th issue). Multicoloured.
3052 8 p. + 5 p. Type **797** . . . 15 15
3053 20 p. + 5 p. Curro and Exhibition building . . . 25 25
3054 45 p. + 5 p. Curro and view of Project Cartuja '93 . . . . 55 55
3055 50 p. + 5 p. Curro crossing bridge in Project Cartuja '93 65 65

1990. Olympic Games, Barcelona (1992) (4th issue). As T **760**. Multicoloured.
3056 18 p. + 5 p. Weightlifting . 25 25
3057 20 p. + 5 p. Hockey 25 25
3058 45 p. + 5 p. Judo 50 50

798 Rafael Alvarez Sereix (Honorary Postman)

1990. Stamp Day.
3059 **798** 20 p. flesh, brown & grn 20 15

799 Vitoria Post Office

1990. Europa. Post Office Buildings.
3060 20 p. Type **799** 20 15
3061 50 p. Malaga Post Office (vert) 50 15

800 "Hispasat" Communications Satellite

1990. 125th Anniv of I.T.U.
3062 **800** 8 p. multicoloured . . . 15 15

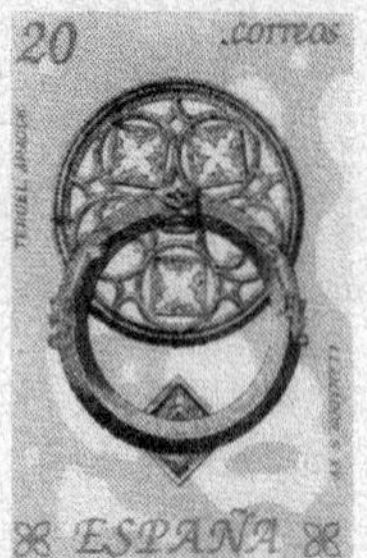

801 Door Knocker, Aragon

1990. Wrought Ironwork. Each black, grey and red.
3063 20 p. Type **801** 20 15
3064 20 p. Door knocker, Andalucia 20 15
3065 20 p. Pistol, Catalonia . . . 20 15
3066 20 p. Door knocker, Castilla-La Mancha 20 15
3067 20 p. Mirror with lock, Galicia 20 15
3068 20 p. Basque fireback . . . 20 15

803 "Charity" (Lopez Alonso)
805 Poster

1990. Anniversaries.
3070 **803** 8 p. multicoloured . . . 15 15
3071 – 20 p. multicoloured . . 25 15
3072 – 45 p. orange and brown 60 15
3073 – 50 p. red and blue . . . 65 15
DESIGNS—VERT: 8 p. Type **803** (bicent of arrival in Spain of Daughters of Charity); 50 p. Page of book (500th anniv of publication of "Tirant lo Blanch" by Joanot Martorell and Marti Joan de Galba). HORIZ: 20 p. Score of "Leilah" and Jose Padilla (composer, birth centenary (1989)); 45 p. Palace of Kings of Navarre (900th anniv of grant of privileges to Estella).

1990. 17th International Historical Sciences Congress, Madrid.
3075 **805** 50 p. multicoloured . . . 50 15

1990. Olympic Games, Barcelona (1992) (5th issue). As T **760**. Multicoloured.
3076 8 p. + 5 p. Wrestling 20 20
3077 18 p. + 5 p. Swimming . . . 35 35
3078 20 p. + 5 p. Baseball 45 45

806 Caravel and Compass Rose

1990. 500th Anniv of Discovery of America by Columbus (5th issue). Multicoloured.
3079 8 p. + 5 p. Type **806** 25 15
3080 8 p. + 5 p. Caravels 25 15
3081 20 p. + 5 p. Caravel 45 25
3082 20 p. + 5 p. Galleons 45 25

807 Puerto Rican Todys
808 Sun

1990. America. The Natural World.
3083 **807** 50 p. multicoloured . . . 70 15

1990. Christmas. Details of "Cosmic Poem" by Jose Antonio Sistiaga. Multicoloured.
3084 25 p. Type **808** 25 15
3085 45 p. Moon (horiz) 45 15

810 Tourism Logo (Joan Miro)
811 Church of St. Miguel de Lillo, Oviedo

1990. European Tourism Year.
3087 **810** 45 p. multicoloured . . . 45 15

1990. World Heritage Sites. Multicoloured.
3088 20 p. Type **811** 25 15
3089 20 p. St. Peter's Tower, Teruel 25 15
3090 20 p. Bujaco Tower, Caceres (horiz) 25 15
3091 20 p. St. Vincent's Church, Avila (horiz) 25 15

812 Conductor and Orchestra
813 Maria Moliner

1990. Spanish National Orchestra.
3092 **812** 25 p. green, turq & blk . 25 15

1991. 10th Death Anniv of Maria Moliner (philologist).
3093 **813** 25 p. multicoloured . . . 25 10

814 La Cartuja (Santa Maria de las Cuevas Monastery)

1991. "Expo 92" World's Fair, Seville (6th issue). Views of Seville. Multicoloured.
3094 15 p. + 5 p. Type **814** . . . 25 25
3095 25 p. + 5 p. The Auditorium 35 35
3096 45 p. + 5 p. La Cartuja bridge 60 60
3097 55 p. + 5 p. La Barqueta bridge 70 70

1991. Olympic Games, Barcelona (1992) (6th series). As T **760**.
3098 15 p. + 5 p. grey, black and red 25 25
3099 25 p. + 5 p. multicoloured . 35 35
3100 45 p. + 5 p. multicoloured . 60 60
DESIGNS: 15 p. Modern pentathlon; 25 p. Canoeing; 45 p. Rowing.

815 Olympic Rings and Yachts
817 Juan de Tassis y Peralta (Chief Courier to Kings Philip III and IV)

1991. Children's Stamp Design.
3101 **815** 25 p. multicoloured . . . 30 10

1991. Stamp Day.
3103 **817** 25 p. black 30 10

819 Dish Aerials, INTA-NASA Earth Station, Robledo de Chavela

1991. Europa. Europe in Space. Multicoloured.
3105 25 p. Type **819** 30 10
3106 45 p. "Olympus I" telecommunications satellite 50 10

820 Brother Luis Ponce de Leon (translator and poet, 400th death anniv)
822 Choir (after mural mosaic, Palau de la Musica)

821 Apollo Fountain

1991. Anniversaries.
3107 – 15 p. multicoloured . . 15 10
3108 **820** 15 p. orange, red & blk 15 10
3109 – 25 p. multicoloured . . 30 10
3110 – 25 p. multicoloured . . 30 10
DESIGNS—HORIZ: No. 3107, Table and chair (400th death anniv of St. John of the Cross). VERT: No. 3109, Banner and cap (500th birth anniv of St. Ignatius de Loyola (founder of Society of Jesus)); 3110, Abd-er Rahman III, Emir of Cordoba (1100th birth anniv).

1991. Madrid. European City of Culture (1st issue). Multicoloured.
3111 15 p. + 5 p. Type **821** . . . 25 25
3112 25 p. + 5 p. "Don Alvaro de Bazan" (statue, Mariano Benlliure) 35 35
3113 45 p. + 5 p. Bank of Spain 60 60
3114 55 p. + 5 p. Cloisters, St. Isidro Institute 70 70
See also Nos. 3195/8.

1991. Centenary of Orfeo Catala (Barcelona choral group).
3115 **822** 25 p. multicoloured . . . 30 10

823 Basque Drug Cupboard

824 Hands holding Net

1991. Furniture. Multicoloured.

3116 25 p. Type **823** 30 10
3117 25 p. Kitchen dresser, Castilla y Leon 30 10
3118 25 p. Chair, Murcia 30 10
3119 25 p. Cradle, Andalucia . . . 30 10
3120 25 p. Travelling chest, Castilla-La Mancha 30 10
3121 25 p. Bridal chest, Catalonia 30 10

1991. World Fishing Exhibition, Vigo.

3122 **824** 55 p. multicoloured . . . 65 15

1991. Olympic Games, Barcelona (1992) (7th series). As T **760**. Multicoloured.

3123 15 p. + 5 p. Tennis 35 35
3124 25 p. + 5 p. Table tennis . . 50 50
3125 55 p. + 5 p. Shooting . . . 1·00 1·00

825 Garcilaso de la Vega (Spanish-Inca poet)

1991. 500th Anniv of Discovery of America by Columbus (6th issue). Multicoloured.

3126 15 p. + 5 p. Type **825** . . . 45 45
3127 25 p. + 5 p. Pope Alexander VI 65 65
3128 45 p. + 5 p. Luis de Santangel (banker) . . . . 1·10 1·10
3129 55 p. + 5 p. Brother Toribio Motolinia (missionary) . . 1·40 1·40

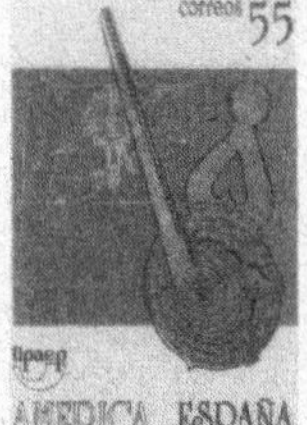

826 Nocturlabe

827 "Nativity" (from "New Chronicle" by Guaman Poma de Ayala)

1991. America. Voyages of Discovery.

3130 **826** 55 p. brown and purple . 65 15

1991. Christmas.

3131 **827** 25 p. buff and brown . . 30 10
3132 – 45 p. multicoloured . . . 50 10

DESIGN: 45 p. "Nativity" (16th-century Russian icon).

829 Alcantara Gate, Toledo

830 Gen. Carlos Ibanez de Ibero (cartographer)

1991. World Heritage Sites.

3134 **829** 25 p. agate and brown . 30 10
3135 – 25 p. black and brown . . 40 10
3136 – 25 p. brown and blue . . 30 10
3137 – 25 p. violet and green . . 30 10

DESIGNS—VERT: No. 3135, Casa de las Conchas, Salamanca. HORIZ: No. 3136, Seville Cathedral; 3137, Aeonio (flower) and Garajonay National Park, Gomera.

1991. Anniversaries and Events. Multicoloured.

3138 25 p. Type **830** (death centenary) 30 10
3139 55 p. "Las Palmas" (Antarctic survey ship) (signing of Antarctic Treaty protocol of Madrid declaring the Antarctic a nature reserve) 95 40

831 Margarita Xirgu

1992. 23rd Death Anniv of Margarita Xirgu (actress).

3140 **831** 25 p. brown and red . . 30 10

832 "Expo 92, Seville"

1992. Children's Stamp Design.

3141 **832** 25 p. multicoloured . . 30 10

833 Pedro Rodriguez, Count of Campomanes (administrator and postal consultant)

1992. Stamp Day.

3142 **833** 27 p. multicoloured . . 35 10

834 Spanish Pavilion

1992. "Expo '92" World's Fair, Seville (7th issue).

3143 **834** 27 p. grey, black & brown 30 10

1992. Olympic Games, Barcelona (8th issue). As T **760**. Multicoloured.

3144 15 p. + 5 p. Archery . . . 30 30
3145 25 p. + 5 p. Sailing . . . 40 40
3146 55 p. + 5 p. Volleyball . . 85 85

836 Cable-cars

1992. "Expo '92" World's Fair, Seville (8th issue). Multicoloured.

3148 17 p. Exhibition World Trade Centre 25 10
3149 17 p. Type **836** 25 10
3150 17 p. Fourth Avenue 25 10
3151 17 p. Barqueta entrance . . 25 10
3152 17 p. Nature pavilion . . . 25 10
3153 17 p. Bioclimatic sphere . . 25 10
3154 17 p. Alamillo bridge . . . 25 10
3155 17 p. Press centre 25 10
3156 17 p. Pavilion of the 15th century 25 10
3157 17 p. Expo harbour 25 10
3158 17 p. Tourist train 25 10
3159 17 p. One-day entrance ticket showing bridge 25 10
3160 27 p. Santa Maria de las Cuevas Carthusian monastery . . 40 10
3161 27 p. Palisade 40 10
3162 27 p. Monorail 40 10
3163 27 p. Avenue of Europe . . 40 10
3164 27 p. Pavilion of Discovery . 40 10
3165 27 p. Auditorium 40 10
3166 27 p. First Avenue 40 10
3167 27 p. Square of the Future . 40 10
3168 27 p. Italica entrance 40 10
3169 27 p. Last avenue 40 10
3170 27 p. Theatre 40 10
3171 27 p. Curro (official mascot) 40 10

837 Wheelchair Sports

1992. Paralympic (Physically Handicapped) Games, Barcelona.

3173 **837** 27 p. multicoloured . . 30 10

839 "Preparation before leaving Palos" (R. Espejo)

841 "Water and the Environment"

1992. Europa. 500th Anniv of Discovery of America by Columbus (7th issue).

3175 **839** 17 p. multicoloured . . . 20 10
3176 – 45 p. grey and brown . . 50 15

DESIGN: 45 p. Map of the Americas, Columbus's fleet and Monastery of Santa Maria de La Rabida.

1992. World Environment Day.

3178 **841** 27 p. blue and yellow . . 30 10

842 "Albertville", Olympic Rings and "Barcelona"

1992. Winter Olympic Games, Albertville, and Summer Games, Barcelona.

3179 **842** 45 p. multicoloured . . . 50 10

843 Victorious Athlete

1992. Olympic Games, Barcelona (9th issue). Multicoloured.

3180 17 p. + 5 p. Type **843** . . . 25 25
3181 17 p. + 5 p. Cobi (official mascot) 25 25
3182 17 p. + 5 p. Olympic torch (horiz) 25 25

844 Olympic Stadium

845 Cobi holding Magnifying Glass and Stamp Album

1992. Olympic Games, Barcelona (10th issue). Multicoloured.

3183 27 p. + 5 p. Type **844** . . . 35 35
3184 27 p. + 5 p. San Jordi sports arena 35 35
3185 27 p. + 5 p. I.N.E.F. sports university 35 35

1992. "Olymphilex 92" International Stamp Exhibition, Barcelona. Multicoloured.

3186 17 p. + 5 p. Type **845** . . . 25 25
3187 17 p. + 5 p. Church of the Holy Family, Barcelona, and exhibition emblem 25 25

846 Athletes

1992. Paralympic (Mentally Handicapped) Games, Madrid.

3188 **846** 27 p. blue and red 30 10

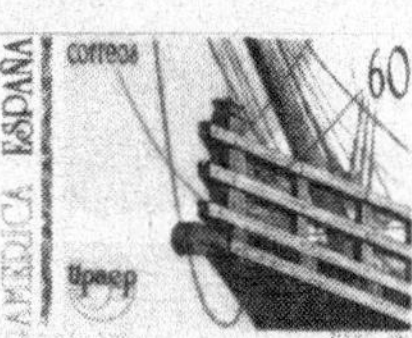

848 Quarterdeck of "Santa Maria"

1992. America. 500th Anniv of Discovery of America by Columbus (8th issue).

3190 **848** 60 p. brown, cinnamon and ochre 70 20

849 Luis Vives (philosopher)

850 Helmet of Mercury and European Community Emblem

1992. Anniversaries. Multicoloured.

3191 17 p. Type **849** (500th birth anniv) 20 10
3192 27 p. Pamplona Choir (centenary) (horiz) 30 10

1992. European Single Market.

3193 **850** 45 p. blue and yellow . . 50 10

851 "Nativity" (Obdulia Acevedo)

852 Municipal Museum

1992. Christmas.

3194 **851** 27 p. multicoloured . . . 30 10

1992. Madrid, European City of Culture (2nd issue). Multicoloured.

3195 17 p. + 5 p. Type **852** . . . 25 25
3196 17 p. + 5 p. Queen Sofia Art Museum 25 25
3197 17 p. + 5 p. Prado Museum 25 25
3198 17 p. + 5 p. Royal Theatre 25 25

854 Bird, Sun, Leaves and Silhouettes

855 Maria Zambrano

1993. Public Services. Protection of the Environment.

3200 **854** 28 p. blue and green . . 30 10

1993. 2nd Death Anniv of Maria Zambrano (writer).

3201 **855** 45 p. multicoloured . . . 50 10

856 Figures and Blue Cross

857 Segovia

1993. Public Services. Health and Sanitation.

3202 **856** 65 p. blue and green . . 75 25

1993. Birth Centenary of Andres Segovia (guitarist).

3203 **857** 65 p. black and brown . 75 25

858 Post-box, Cadiz, 1908

1993. Stamp Day.

3204 **858** 28 p. multicoloured . . . 30 10

859 Parasol Mushroom ("Lepiota procera")

861 Road Safety

1993. Fungi (1st series). Multicoloured.
3205 17 p. Type **859** 20 10
3206 17 p. Caesar's mushroom ("Amanita caesarea") . . . 20 10
3207 28 p. "Lactarius sanguifluus" 30 10
3208 28 p. The charcoal burner ("Russula cyanoxantha") 30 10
See also Nos. 3256/9 and 3312/13.

1993. Public Services.
3210 **861** 17 p. green and red . . . 40 10

863 "Fusees"

1993. Europa. Contemporary Art. Paintings by Joan Miro.
3212 **863** 45 p. black and blue . . 50 10
3213 – 65 p. multicoloured . . . 75 25
DESIGN—VERT: 65 p. "La Bague d'Aurore".

864 "Translation of Body from Palestine to Galicia" (detail of altarpiece, Santiago de Compostela Cathedral)

1993. St. James's Holy Year (1st issue). Mult.
3214 17 p. Type **864** 20 10
3215 28 p. "Discovery of St. James's tomb by Bishop Teodomiro" (miniature from "Tumbo A" (codex)) 30 10
3216 45 p. "St. James" (illuminated initial letter from Bull issued by Pope Alexander III declaring Holy Years of St. James) 50 10
See also No. 3218.

865 Letters, Map and Satellite

1993. World Telecommunications Day.
3217 **865** 28 p. multicoloured . . . 30 10

866 Bagpipe Player (Isaac Diaz Pardo)

867 King Juan Carlos I

1993. St. James's Holy Year (2nd issue).
3218 **866** 28 p. multicoloured . . . 30 10

1993.
3220 **867** 1 p. blue and gold . . . 10 10
3222 10 p. red and gold . . . 10 10
3224 17 p. orange and gold . . 15 10
3225 18 p. turquoise and gold 20 10
3226 19 p. brown and gold . 20 10
3229 28 p. brown and gold . 30 10
3230 29 p. green and gold . 30 10
3231 30 p. blue and gold . . 30 10
3234 45 p. green and gold . . 45 10
3235 55 p. brown and gold . 55 10
3236 60 p. red and gold . . . 60 10
3237 65 p. orange and gold . 65 10

868 "Water and the Environment"

869 Count of Barcelona (after Ricardo Macarrion)

1993. World Environment Day.
3240 **868** 28 p. multicoloured . . 30 10

1993. Juan de Borbon, Count of Barcelona (King Juan Carlos's father) Commemoration.
3241 **869** 28 p. multicoloured . . 30 10

870 Locomotive

1993. Centenary of Igualada–Martorell Railway.
3242 **870** 45 p. green and black . 50 10

871 "The Mint" (lithograph, Pic de Leopold, 1866)

1993. Cent of National Coin and Stamp Mint.
3243 **871** 65 p. blue 75 25

872 Alejandro Malaspina (navigator)

873 "Road to Santiago"

1993. Explorers. Multicoloured.
3244 45 p. Type **872** 50 10
3245 65 p. Jose Celestino Mutis (naturalist) (vert) 75 25

1993. Children's Stamp Design.
3246 **873** 45 p. multicoloured . . 60 15

874 Black Stork

1993. America. Endangered Animals.
3247 **874** 65 p. black and orange 75 25
3248 – 65 p. black and red . . 75 25
DESIGN: No. 3248, Lammergeier.

875 Old and Young Hands

1993. European Year of Senior Citizens and Solidarity between Generations.
3249 **875** 45 p. multicoloured . . 50 10

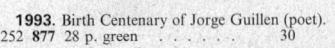

876 Star and Three Wise Men

877 Guillen

1993. Christmas. Multicoloured.
3250 17 p. Type **876** 20 10
3251 28 p. Holy Family (vert) . . 30 10

1993. Birth Centenary of Jorge Guillen (poet).
3252 **877** 28 p. green 30 10

878 Santa Maria de Poblet Monastery, Tarragona

1993. World Heritage Sites.
3253 **878** 50 p. brown, blue & grn 60 15

879 Luis Bunuel and Camera

1994. Spanish Cinema (1st series). Multicoloured.
3254 29 p. Type **879** 35 10
3255 55 p. Segundo de Chomon and scene from "Goblin House" 65 15
See also Nos. 3308/9.

1994. Fungi (2nd series). As T **859**. Multicoloured.
3256 18 p. Cep ("Boletus edulis") . 20 10
3257 18 p. Satan's mushroom ("Boletus satanas") 20 10
3258 29 p. Death cap ("Amanita phalloides") 35 10
3259 29 p. Saffron milk cap ("Lactarius deliciosus") . . 35 10

880 Cinnabar

1994. Minerals (1st series).
3260 **880** 29 p. multicoloured . . . 35 10
3261 – 29 p. multicoloured . . . 35 10
3262 – 29 p. multicoloured . . . 35 10
3263 – 29 p. black and blue . . . 35 10
DESIGNS: 3261, Blende (inscr "Esfalerita"); 3262, Pyrites; 3263, Galena.
See also Nos. 3314/16 and 3366/7.

881 Barristers' Mailbox, Barcelona

1994. Stamp Day.
3264 **881** 29 p. brown and cinnamon 35 10

882 Worker (detail of sculpture), I.L.O. Building, Geneva.

1994. 75th Anniv of I.L.O., Geneva.
3265 **882** 65 p. multicoloured . . . 75 25

883

1994. 90th Birth Anniv of Salvador Dali (painter). Multicoloured.
3266 18 p. Type **883** 20 10
3267 18 p. "Portrait of Gala" (horiz) 20 10
3268 29 p. "Port Alguer" 35 10
3269 29 p. "The Great Masturbator" (horiz) 35 10
3270 55 p. "The Bread Basket" . . 65 10
3271 55 p. "Soft Self-portrait" . . 65 10
3272 65 p. "Galatea of the Spheres" 75 10
3273 65 p. "The Enigma without End" (horiz) 75 10

884 Pla

1994. 13th Death Anniv of Josep Pla (writer).
3274 **884** 65 p. green and red . . . 75 15

885 "Martyrdom of St. Andrew" (Peter Paul Rubens)

886 "Foundation of Santa Cruz de Tenerife" (Gonzalez Mendez)

1994. 400th Anniv of Carlos de Amberes Foundation (philanthropic organization).
3275 **885** 55 p. multicoloured . . . 65 10

1994. Anniversaries. Multicoloured.
3276 18 p. Type **886** (500th anniv of city) 20 10
3277 29 p. Sancho IV's Foundation Charter at Alcala, 1293 (700th anniv of Complutense University, Madrid) (horiz) 35 10

887 Severo Ochoa (biochemist)

1994. Europa. Discoveries. Multicoloured.
3278 55 p. Type **887** (research into DNA) 65 15
3279 65 p. Miguel Catalan (spectrochemist) (research into atomic structures) . . 75 15

888 "Family of Pascual Duarte"

889 Sancho I Ramirez

1994. Spanish Literature. Works of Camilo Jose Cela. Multicoloured.
3280 18 p. Type **888** 20 10
3281 29 p. Walker and horse rider ("Journey to Alcarria") . . 35 10

1994. 900th Death Anniv of King Sancho I Ramirez of Aragon (3282) and 500th Anniv of Treaty of Tordesillas (defining Portuguese and Spanish spheres of influence) (others).
3282 **889** 18 p. red, yellow and blue 20 10
3283 – 29 p. multicoloured . . 35 10
3284 – 55 p. green, orange and brown 65 10
DESIGNS—HORIZ: 29 p. Compass rose and arms of Tordesillas; 55 p. Treaty House, Tordesillas.

891 "Giralda" (yacht)

893 Knight of Swords (14th-century Catalan deck)

892 Forum Caryatid and Tablet bearing Roman Name of Merida

1994. Ships sailed by Count of Barcelona. Multicoloured.

3286 16 p. Type **891** 20 10
3287 29 p. "Saltillo" (schooner) . . 35 10

1994. World Heritage Site. Merida.

3288 **892** 55 p. brn, cinnamon & red 55 10

1994. Playing Card Museum, Vitoria. Multicoloured.

3289 18 p. Type **893** 20 10
3290 29 p. Jack of Clubs (Catalan Tarot deck, 1900) 35 10
3291 55 p. King of Cups (Spanish deck by Juan Barbot, 1750) 65 10
3292 65 p. "Mars", Jack of Diamonds (English deck by Stopforth, 1828) 75 15

894 Globe and Douglas DC-8

1994. America. Postal Transport.

3293 **894** 65 p. multicoloured . . . 75 15

895 Civil Guard (150th anniv)

1994. Public Services.

3294 – 18 p. red and blue . . . 20 10
3295 **895** 29 p. multicoloured . . . 35 10
DESIGN: As T **854**—18 p. Underground train (75th anniv of Madrid Metro).

896 Map of Member Countries

1994. 40th Anniv of Western European Union.

3296 **896** 55 p. multicoloured . . . 65 10

897 Running

1994. Centenary of International Olympic Committee. Spanish Olympic Gold Medal Sports. Mult.

3297 29 p. Type **897** 35 10
3298 29 p. Cycling 35 10
3299 29 p. Skiing 35 10
3300 29 p. Football 35 10
3301 29 p. Show jumping 35 10
3302 29 p. Hockey 35 10
3303 29 p. Judo 35 10
3304 29 p. Swimming 35 10
3305 29 p. Archery 35 10
3306 29 p. Yachting 35 10
See also Nos. 3332/45 and 3373/81.

898 "Adoration of the Kings" (detail of Ripoll altarpiece, Esteve Bover)

1994. Christmas.

3307 **898** 29 p. multicoloured . . . 35 10

899 "Belle Epoque" (dir. Fernando Trueba)

1995. Spanish Cinema (2nd series). Film posters. Multicoloured.

3308 30 p. Type **899** 30 10
3309 60 p. "Volver a Empezar" (dir. Jose Luis Garci) 60 10

900 Logrono

1995. 900th Anniv of Logrono Law Code.

3310 **900** 30 p. multicoloured . . 30 10

902 Shaggy Ink Cap

1995. Fungi (3rd series). Multicoloured.

3312 19 p. Type **902** 20 10
3313 30 p. "Dermocybe cinnamomea" 30 10

1995. Minerals (2nd series). As T **880**. Multicoloured.

3314 30 p. Aragonite 30 10
3315 30 p. Advanced Mining Engineering Technical School and Mining Museum, Madrid 30 10
3316 30 p. Dolomite 30 10

903 19th-century Lion's Head Letter Box

1995. Stamp Day.

3317 **903** 30 p. brown and green . 30 10

904 Goicoechea and Modern Train

1995. Birth Centenary of Alejandro Goicoechea (inventor of TALGO articulated train).

3318 **904** 30 p. multicoloured . . 30 10
3319 – 60 p. blue and brown . 60 10
DESIGN: 60 p. Goicoechea and early TALGO train.

905 Globe as Tree on Hand

907 Angel (from illuminated manuscript)

1995. European Nature Conservation Year.

3320 **905** 60 p. multicoloured . . 60 10

1995. 900th Anniv of Monastery of Liebana. Multicoloured.

3322 30 p. Type **907** 30 10
3323 60 p. Liebana landscape . . 60 10

908 Miguel Hernandez and part of "El Nino Yuntero"

1995. Literature.

3324 **908** 19 p. multicoloured . . . 20 10
3325 – 30 p. blue, green and black 30 10
DESIGN—VERT: 30 p. Juan Valera and scene from "Juanita la Larga".

909 Marti

1995. Death Centenary of Jose Marti (Cuban poet).

3326 **909** 60 p. multicoloured . . . 60 10

910 Captain Trueno

1995. Comic Strip Characters. Multicoloured.

3327 30 p. Type **910** 30 10
3328 60 p. Carpanta (vert) 60 10

911 Chain and Laurel Twig

1995. Europa. Peace and Freedom.

3329 **911** 60 p. multicoloured . . . 60 10

912 Lumiere Brothers

1995. Centenary of Motion Pictures.

3330 **912** 19 p. brown 20 10

913 Typewriter, Pen and Camera

1995. Centenary of Madrid Press Association.

3331 **913** 30 p. multicoloured . . . 30 10

1995. Spanish Olympic Silver Medal Sports. As T **897**. Multicoloured.

3332 30 p. Type **897** 30 10
3333 30 p. Basketball 30 10
3334 30 p. Boxing 30 10
3335 30 p. As No. 3300 . . . . . 30 10
3336 30 p. Gymnastics 30 10
3337 30 p. As No. 3301 . . . . . 30 10
3338 30 p. As No. 3302 . . . . . 30 10
3339 30 p. Canoeing 30 10
3340 30 p. Polo 30 10
3341 30 p. Rowing 30 10
3342 30 p. Tennis 30 10
3343 30 p. Shooting 30 10
3344 30 p. As No. 3306 . . . . . 30 10
3345 30 p. Water polo 30 10

914 King Juan Carlos I at National Assembly, 1986

1995. Anniversaries. Multicoloured.

3346 60 p. Type **914** (50th anniv of U.N.O.) 60 10
3347 60 p. Anniversary emblem, globes and wheat ears (50th anniv of F.A.O.) (vert) . . 60 10
3348 60 p. Emblem and coloured bands (20th anniv of World Tourism Organization) . . 60 10

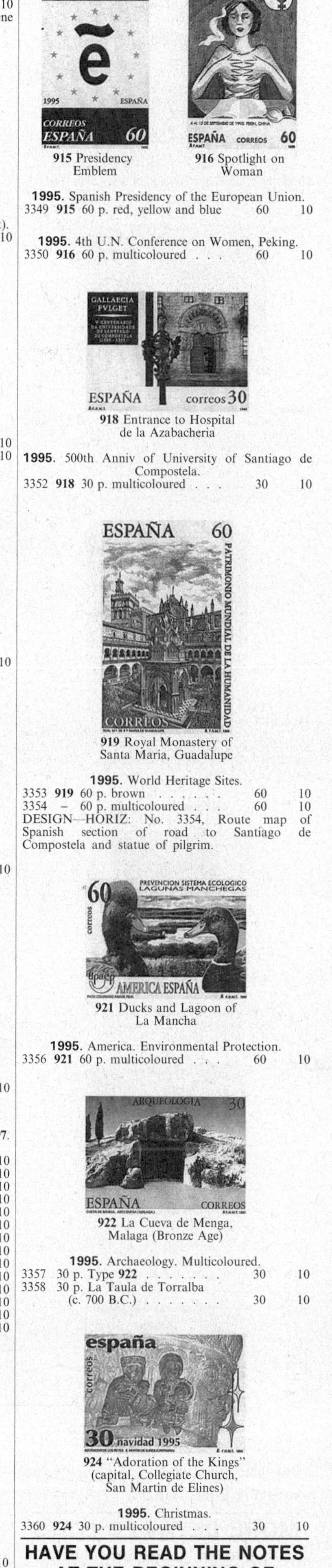

915 Presidency Emblem

916 Spotlight on Woman

1995. Spanish Presidency of the European Union.

3349 **915** 60 p. red, yellow and blue 60 10

1995. 4th U.N. Conference on Women, Peking.

3350 **916** 60 p. multicoloured . . . 60 10

918 Entrance to Hospital de la Azabacheria

1995. 500th Anniv of University of Santiago de Compostela.

3352 **918** 30 p. multicoloured . . . 30 10

919 Royal Monastery of Santa Maria, Guadalupe

1995. World Heritage Sites.

3353 **919** 60 p. brown 60 10
3354 – 60 p. multicoloured . . . 60 10
DESIGN—HORIZ: No. 3354, Route map of Spanish section of road to Santiago de Compostela and statue of pilgrim.

921 Ducks and Lagoon of La Mancha

1995. America. Environmental Protection.

3356 **921** 60 p. multicoloured . . . 60 10

922 La Cueva de Menga, Malaga (Bronze Age)

1995. Archaeology. Multicoloured.

3357 30 p. Type **922** 30 10
3358 30 p. La Taula de Torralba (c. 700 B.C.) 30 10

924 "Adoration of the Kings" (capital, Collegiate Church, San Martin de Elines)

1995. Christmas.

3360 **924** 30 p. multicoloured . . . 30 10

HAVE YOU READ THE NOTES AT THE BEGINNING OF THIS CATALOGUE?

These often provide the answers to the enquiries we receive.

925 King Juan Carlos

1995. 20th Anniv of Accession of King Juan Carlos I.
3361 **925** 1000 p. violet . . . . . . 10·00 6·00

926 Plaza de Armas Railway Station, Seville (venue)

1995. "Espamer" Spanish–Latin American and "Aviation and Space" Stamp Exhibitions, Seville. Multicoloured.
3362 60 p. Type **926** 60 10
3363 60 p. Dr. Lorenzo Galindez de Carvajal (Master Courier of the Indies and Terra Firma of the Ocean Sea, 1514) . . . 60 10

927 "Leaving Mass at Pilar de Zaragoza" (first Spanish film, 1896)

1996. Centenary of Motion Pictures.
3364 **927** 30 p. brown, mauve and black 30 10
3365 – 60 p. multicoloured . . . 65 10
DESIGN: 60 p. "Bienvenido, Mister Marshall!" (poster).

928 Miner's Lamp

1996. Minerals (3rd series). Multicoloured.
3366 30 p. Type **928** 30 10
3367 60 p. Amber fluorite 60 10

929 Jose Mathe Aragua (General Director) and Telegraph Tower

1996. Stamp Day. 150th Anniv of Madrid–Irun Telegraph Signal Line.
3368 **929** 60 p. green and red . . 60 10

930 Columbus (statue), "B" and Arch of Triumph

1996. 10th Anniv (1995) of Start of Barcelona Urbanisation Programme.
3369 **930** 30 p. multicoloured . . . 30 10

MORE DETAILED LISTS

are given in the Stanley Gibbons Catalogues referred to in the country headings. For lists of current volumes see introduction

931 Brown Bear with Cubs

935 Carmen Amaya (flamenco dancer)

933 Scales

1996. Endangered Species.
3370 **931** 30 p. multicoloured . . 30 10

1996. 400th Anniv of Madrid Bar Assocation.
3372 **933** 19 p. multicoloured . . 20 10

1996. Spanish Olympic Bronze Medal Sports. As T **897**. Multicoloured. Dated "1996".
3373 30 p. Type **897** 30 10
3374 30 p. As No. 3334 . . . . . 30 10
3375 30 p. As No. 3299 . . . . . 30 10
3376 30 p. As No. 3302 . . . . . 30 10
3377 30 p. As No. 3304 . . . . . 30 10
3378 30 p. As No. 3339 . . . . . 30 10
3379 30 p. As No. 3342 . . . . . 30 10
3380 30 p. As No. 3343 . . . . . 30 10
3381 30 p. As No. 3306 . . . . . 30 10

1996. Europa. Famous Women.
3383 **935** 60 p. multicoloured . . 60 10

936 El Jabato (Victor Mora and Francisco Darnis)

937 "General Don Antonio Ricardos"

1996. Comic Strip Characters. Multicoloured.
3384 19 p. Type **936** 20 10
3385 30 p. Reporter Tribulete (Guillermo Cifre) (horiz) . 30 10

1996. 250th Birth Anniv of Francisco de Goya (artist). Multicoloured.
3386 19 p. Type **937** 20 10
3387 30 p. "The Milkmaid of Bordeaux" 30 10
3388 60 p. "Boys with Mastiffs" (horiz) 60 10
3389 130 p. "3rd of May 1808 in Madrid" (horiz) . . . . . 1·25 50

938 Magnifying Glass and Stamp Album

1996. 50th Anniv of Philatelic Service.
3390 **938** 30 p. multicoloured . . 30 10

939 Jose Monge Cruz (Camaron de la Isla)

1996. Flamenco Artistes.
3391 **939** 19 p. multicoloured . . 20 10
3392 – 30 p. purple and red . . 30 10
DESIGN—HORIZ: 30 p. Lola Flores.

940 Lanuza Market, Zaragoza (Felix Navarro Perez)

1996. 19th International Architects Congress, Barcelona. Metallic Buildings.
3393 **940** 30 p. multicoloured . . . 30 10

941 Gerardo Diego and Pen (poet, birth centenary)

1996. Anniversaries.
3394 **941** 19 p. violet and red . . 20 10
3395 – 30 p. multicoloured . . . 30 10
3396 – 60 p. black, red and blue 60 10
DESIGNS—HORIZ: 30 p. Joaquin Costa and birthplace (politician and historian, 150th birth anniv). VERT: 60 p. The five senses (50th anniv of U.N.I.C.E.F.).

942 Naveta (tomb) des Tudons, Minorca

1996. Archaeology. Multicoloured.
3397 30 p. Type **942** 30 10
3398 30 p. Cabezo de Alcala de Azila, Teruel 30 10

944 Salamancan Costumes

945 Albaicin Quarter, Granada

1996. America. Traditional Costumes.
3400 **944** 60 p. multicoloured . . . 60 10

1996. World Heritage Sites.
3401 **945** 19 p. blue 20 10
3402 – 30 p. purple 30 10
3403 – 60 p. blue 60 10
DESIGNS—HORIZ: 30 p. Tiberiades Square and statue of Maimonides (centre of Cordova). VERT: 60 p. Deer, Donana National Park.

946 Oviedo Cathedral, Leopoldo Alas and Quotation from "La Regenta"

1996. Literature.
3404 **946** 30 p. blue and purple . . 30 10
3405 60 p. blue and purple . . 60 10
DESIGN—HORIZ: 60 p. Scene from "Don Juan Tenorio" by Jose Zorrilla.

EXPRESS LETTER STAMPS

E 53 Pegasus and Arms

1905.
E308 **E 53** 20 c. red . . . . 30·00 75

E 77 Spanish Royal Family

1926. Red Cross.
E417 **E 77** 20 c. purple and deep purple . . . . 6·50 6·50

1927. 25th Anniv of Coronation. No. E417 optd **17-V-1902 17-V-1927 ALFONSO XIII.**
E459 **E 77** 20 c. purple and deep purple . . . . 5·50 5·50

E 88 Gazelle

E 89

1929. Seville and Barcelona Exhibitions.
E521 **E 88** 20 c. brown . . . . . 13·00 13·00

1929.
E522 **E 89** 20 c. red . . . . 13·50 2·75

1929. Optd **Sociedad de las Naciones LV reunion del Consejo Madrid.**
E534 **E 89** 20 c. red . . . . 12·50 12·50

1930. Optd **URGENCIA**.
E535 **E 89** 20 c. red . . . . 9·75 80

E 91 Electric Locomotive

1930. 11th Int Railway Congress, Madrid.
E553 **E 91** 20 c. red . . . . 75·00 85·00

1930. "Goya" types optd **URGENTE**.
E570 **91** 20 c. mauve (postage) . . . 20 20
E583 20 c. brown and blue (air) 20 20

1930. "Columbus" type optd **URGENTE**.
E608 **99** 20 c. purple . . . . 2·00 2·00

E 113 Seville Exhibition

1930. Spanish–American Exhibition.
E643 **E 113** 20 c. orange 35 35

1931. Optd **REPUBLICA.**
E660 **E 89** 20 c. red (No. E535) . . 3·25 3·25
E672 20 c. red (No. E522) . . 4·25 4·25

1931. Optd **Republica Espanola** in two lines continuously.
E697 **E 89** 29 c. red (No. E522) . . 6·00 2·00

E 126

E 145

1931. 900th Anniv of Montserrat Monastery.
E731 **E 126** 20 c. red . . . . 19·00 19·00

1934.
E779 **E 145** 20 c. red 10 10

E 152 Newspaper Boy E 185 Pegasus

1936. 40th Anniv of Madrid Press Assoc.

E801	E 152	20 c. red	30	30

1937.

E906	E 185	20 c. brown	1·00	35

E 198 Pegasus

1939.

E1022	E 198	25 c. red	15	15

E 199

1940. 19th Centenary of Apparition of Virgin of El Pilar at Zaragoza.

E1006	E 199	25 c. + 5 c. red & buff	30	30

E 270 "Speed" E 271 Centaur

1956.

E1250	E 270	2 p. red	10	10
E1251		3 p. red	10	10
E1252	E 271	4 p. mauve & black	10	10
E1253	E 270	5 p. red	10	10
E1254	E 271	6 p. 50 red & violet	10	10

E 425 Roman Chariot

1971.

E2099	E 425	10 p. grn, blk & red	10	10
E2100	–	15 p. blue, blk & red	15	10

DESIGN—VERT: 15 p. Letter encircling globe.

E 862 Communications

1993. Public Services.

E3211	E 862	180 p. red & yellow	2·00	80

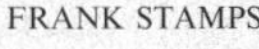

FRANK STAMPS

F 36

F 50

1869. For use on "Cartilla Postal de Espana" (book) by Senor Castell.

F172	F 36	(–) Blue	55·00	45·00

1881. For use on book by A. F. Duro.

F273	F 50	(–) Black on buff	40·00	16·00

F 163

1938. For use by Agencia Filatelica Oficial, Barcelona.

F839	F 163	(–) Blue	—	2·40
F840		(–) Lilac	—	2·40
F841		(–) Green	—	2·40
F842		(–) Brown	—	2·40
F843		(–) Black	—	2·40

OFFICIAL STAMPS

O 9

O 10

1854. Imperf.

O46	O 9	½ onza black on orange	2·00	2·25
O47		1 onza black on pink	2·50	3·00
O48		4 onza black on green	7·00	8·75
O49		1 libra black on blue	48·00	55·00

The face values of Nos. O46/53 are expressed in onzas (ounces) and libra (pound) which refer to the maximum weight for which each value could prepay postage.

1855. Imperf.

O50	O 10	½ onza black on yellow	2·00	2·25
O55		1 onza black on pink	2·00	3·25
O52		4 onza black on green	7·00	8·75
O53		1 libra black on blue	15·00	17·00

O 52

1895. For use by Members of Chamber of Deputies.

O289	51	15 c. yellow	7·00	2·75
O290	O 52	(–) Pink	5·00	1·75
O291		(–) Blue	17·00	5·75

O 66 National Library

O 67 Cervantes (from painting by J. de Jauregui)

O 68 Statue of Cervantes by A. Sola

1916. Death Tercent of Cervantes. (a) For use by Members of the Chamber of Deputies.

O353	–	(–) black and violet	80	80
O354	O 66	(–) black and green	80	80
O355	O 67	(–) black and violet	80	80
O356	O 68	(–) black and red	80	80

(b) For use by Members of the Senate.

O357	–	(–) black and green	80	80
O358	O 66	(–) black and red	80	80
O359	O 67	(–) black and brown	80	80
O360	O 68	(–) black and brown	80	80

DESIGN—As Type O 66: Chamber of Deputies.

1931. 3rd Pan-American Postal Union Congress. T 121 etc optd **Oficial**.

O707	5 c. purple	20	20
O708	10 c. green	20	20
O709	15 c. violet	20	20
O710	25 c. red	20	20
O711	30 c. green	20	20
O712	40 c. blue	45	45
O713	50 c. orange	45	45
O714	1 p. grey	45	45
O715	4 p. mauve	9·25	9·25
O716	10 p. brown	22·00	22·00

Air. T 123 etc optd **OFICIAL**.

O717	5 c. brown	15	15
O718	10 c. green	15	15
O719	25 c. red	15	15
O720	50 c. blue	15	15
O721	1 p. lilac	15	15
O722	4 p. grey	3·50	3·50

WAR TAX STAMPS

W 42

W 48

W 49

1874. The 5 c. perf or imperf.

W217	W 42	5 c. de p. black	8·00	85
W218		10 c. de p. blue	9·75	1·60

1875. As Type **W 42**, but large figures in bottom corners.

W228a	5 c. de p. green	5·00	55
W229	10 c. de p. mauve	10·50	2·75

1876. 2nd Carlist War (1873–76) and Cuban War (1868–78).

W253	W 48	5 c. de p. green	3·50	55
W254		10 c. de p. blue	3·50	55
W255		25 c. de p. black	26·00	9·75
W256		1 p. lilac	£325	70·00
W257		5 p. pink	£500	£200

1877. Cuban War (1868–78).

W258	W 49	15 c. de p. purple	17·00	55
W259		50 c. de p. yellow	£475	65·00

W 52

W 53

W 163

1897. Cuban War of Independence (1895–98). Inscr "1897–1898" (15 c.) or "1897 A 1898" (others).

W289	W 52	5 c. green	2·75	1·75
W290		10 c. green	2·75	1·75
W291		15 c. green	£350	£170
W292		20 c. green	6·25	2·75

1898. Cuban War of Independence (1895–98) and Spanish-American War (1898). Inscr "1898–99".

W293	W 52	5 c. black	2·25	1·75
W294		10 c. black	2·25	1·75
W295		15 c. black	42·00	8·75
W296		20 c. black	3·25	3·00

1898. Cuban War of Independence (1895–98) and Spanish-American War (1898).

W297	W 53	5 c. black	7·00	55

1938.

W839	W 163	10 c. red	30	30
W840		20 c. blue	30	30
W841		60 c. pink	1·75	2·50
W842		1 p. blue	85	85
W843		2 p. green	90	90
W844		10 p. blue	2·50	4·00

Nos. W842/3 have coloured figures of value on white backgrounds.

SPANISH GUINEA Pt. 9

A Spanish colony consisting of the islands of Fernando Poo, Annobon and the Corisco Islands off the west coast of Africa and Rio Muni on the mainland. In 1959 it was divided into the two Spanish Overseas Provinces of Fernando Poo and Rio Muni.

100 centimos = 1 peseta

1902. "Curly Head" key-type inscr "GUINEA ESPANOLA 1902".

1	Z	5 c. green	9·00	3·00
2		10 c. grey	9·00	3·00
3		25 c. red	65·00	29·00
4		50 c. brown	65·00	27·00
5		75 c. lilac	65·00	27·00
6		1 p. red	£100	27·00
7		2 p. green	£120	£140
8		5 p. red	£190	£140

1903. Fiscal stamps inscr "POSESIONES ESPANOLAS DE AFRICA OCCIDENTAL", surch **HABILITADO PARA CORREOS 10 cen de peseta**.

9	10 c. on 25 c. black	£350	£150
10	10 c. on 50 c. orange	90·00	27·00
11	10 c. on 1 p. 25 pink	£600	£275
12	10 c. on 2 p. red	£650	£400
13a	10 c. on 2 p. 50 brown	£950	£600
14a	10 c. on 5 p. black	£1000	£350
15	10 c. on 10 p. brown	£850	£350
16	10 c. on 5 p. lilac	£650	£350
17	10 c. on 25 p. blue	£650	£350
18	10 c. on 50 p. brown	£850	£500
19	10 c. on 70 p. violet	£950	£500
20	10 c. on 100 p. green	£1300	£600

1903. "Curly Head" key-type inscr "GUINEA CONTIAL-ESPANOLA PARA 1903".

21	Z	¼ c. black	90	70
22		½ c. green	90	70
23		1 c. purple	90	65
24		2 c. green	90	65
25		3 c. brown	90	65
26		4 c. red	90	65
27		5 c. black	90	65
28		10 c. brown	1·50	70
29		15 c. blue	5·50	5·50
30		25 c. orange	5·50	5·50
31		50 c. red	9·75	12·00
32		75 c. lilac	14·00	12·00
33		1 p. green	22·00	18·00
34		2 p. green	22·00	18·00
35		3 p. red	60·00	25·00
36		4 p. blue	70·00	42·00
37		5 p. purple	£130	65·00
38		10 p. red	£225	85·00

1905. "Curly Head" key-type inscr as above but dated "1905".

39	Z	1 c. black	15	10
40		2 c. green	15	10
41		3 c. red	15	10
42		4 c. green	15	10
43		5 c. brown	15	10
44		10 c. red	90	60
45		15 c. brown	3·00	1·90
46		25 c. brown	3·00	1·90
47		50 c. blue	6·50	4·25
48		75 c. orange	7·00	4·25
49		1 p. red	7·00	4·25
50		2 p. lilac	16·00	9·25
51		3 p. green	42·00	19·00
52		4 p. green	42·00	27·00
53		5 p. red	70·00	30·00
54		10 p. blue	£120	90·00

1905. No. 19/34 of Elobey optd **CONTINENTAL GUINEA CORREOS ASSOBLA**.

55	Z	1 c. pink	5·50	2·40
56		2 c. purple	5·50	2·40
57		3 c. black	5·50	2·40
58		4 c. red	5·50	2·40
59		5 c. green	5·50	2·40
60		10 c. green	11·00	7·00
61		15 c. lilac	20·00	10·00
62		25 c. red	20·00	10·00
63		50 c. orange	27·00	12·50
64		75 c. blue	32·00	14·50
65		1 p. brown	60·00	28·00
66		2 p. brown	85·00	20·00
67		3 p. red	£120	42·00
68		4 p. brown	£450	£150
69		5 p. green	£450	£150
70		10 p. red	£1900	£800

1907. As T **3** of Rio de Oro, but inscr "GUINEA CONTIAL ESPANOLA".

71	1 c. green	45	15
72	2 c. blue	45	15
73	3 c. lilac	45	15
74	4 c. green	45	15
75	5 c. red	45	15
76	10 c. bistre	2·75	1·10
77	15 c. brown	2·00	70
78	25 c. blue	2·00	70
79	50 c. brown	2·00	70
80	75 c. green	2·00	70
81	1 p. orange	3·50	1·25
82	2 p. brown	6·50	5·50
83	3 p. black	6·50	5·50
84	4 p. red	8·25	5·50
85	5 p. green	8·50	8·00
86	10 p. purple	13·00	10·00

1908. Surch **HABILITADO PARA** and value in figures and **CTMS**.

87	3	05 c. on 1 c. green	4·00	2·50
88		05 c. on 2 c. blue	4·00	2·50
89		05 c. on 3 c. lilac	4·00	2·50
90		05 c. on 4 c. green	4·00	2·50
91		05 c. on 10 c. bistre	4·00	2·50
92		15 c. on 10 c. bistre	18·00	10·50

1909. Fiscal stamps inscr "TERRITORIOS ESPANOLES DEL AFRICA OCCIDENTAL", surch **HABILITADO PARA CORREOS 10 cen de peseta.**

No.	T	Description	Unused	Used
93		10 c. on 50 c. green	80·00	55·00
94		10 c. on 1 p. 25 violet	£225	65·00
95		10 c. on 2 p. brown	£600	£400
96		10 c. on 5 p. mauve	£600	£400
97		10 c. on 25 p. brown	£800	£550
98		10 c. on 50 p. red	£2750	£1500
99		10 c. on 75 p. pink	£2750	£1500
100		10 c. on 100 p. orange	£2750	£1500

1909. As T **7** of Rio de Oro but inscr "TERRITORIOS ESPANOLES DEL GOLFO DE GUINEA".

No.	T	Description	Unused	Used
101		1 c. brown	10	10
102		2 c. red	10	10
103		5 c. green	85	10
104		10 c. red	25	10
105		15 c. brown	25	10
106		20 c. mauve	45	25
107		25 c. blue	45	25
108		30 c. brown	50	10
109		40 c. red	30	10
110		50 c. lilac	30	10
111		1 p. green	9·25	4·75
112		4 p. orange	2·25	3·00
113		10 p. orange	2·25	3·00

1911. Nos. 101/13 optd **GUINEA 1911.**

No.	T	Description	Unused	Used
114		1 c. brown	25	25
115		2 c. red	25	25
116		5 c. green	1·00	30
117		10 c. red	65	40
118		15 c. brown	1·00	75
119		20 c. mauve	1·25	1·10
120		25 c. blue	1·60	2·10
121		30 c. brown	2·25	2·75
122		40 c. red	2·40	3·00
123		50 c. lilac	4·00	4·50
124		1 p. green	35·00	12·00
125		4 p. orange	37·00	11·50
126		10 p. orange	22·00	23·00

1912. As T **11** of Rio de Oro, but inscr "TERRS. ESPANOLES DEL GOLFO DE GUINEA".

No.	T	Description	Unused	Used
127		1 c. black	10	10
128		2 c. brown	10	10
129		5 c. green	10	10
130		10 c. red	20	10
131		15 c. red	20	10
132		20 c. red	35	10
133		25 c. blue	20	10
134		30 c. red	2·25	1·40
135		40 c. red	1·50	75
136		50 c. orange	1·10	30
137		1 p. lilac	1·50	90
138		4 p. mauve	3·25	1·90
139		10 p. green	7·00	7·00

1914. As T **12** of Rio de Oro but inscr as 1912 issue.

No.	T	Description	Unused	Used
140		1 c. violet	15	10
141		2 c. red	15	15
142		5 c. green	15	10
143		10 c. red	15	15
144		15 c. purple	15	15
145		20 c. brown	50	35
146		25 c. blue	20	20
147		30 c. brown	90	35
148		40 c. green	90	35
149		50 c. red	40	25
150		1 p. orange	1·00	1·40
151		4 p. red	3·75	3·00
152		10 p. brown	4·75	5·50

1917. Nos. 127/39 optd **1917.**

No.	T	Description	Unused	Used
153		1 c. black	70·00	45·00
154		2 c. brown	70·00	45·00
155		5 c. green	25	15
156		10 c. orange	25	15
157		15 c. purple	25	15
158		20 c. red	25	15
159		25 c. blue	10	15
160		30 c. red	25	20
161		40 c. pink	40	25
162		50 c. orange	20	15
163		1 p. brown	40	25
164		4 p. violet	5·50	3·25
165		10 p. green	5·50	3·25

1918. Stamps of 1912 surch **HTADO-1917.** and value in figures and words.

No.	T	Description	Unused	Used
166	11	5 c. on 40 c. pink	25·00	8·50
167		10 c. on 4 p. violet	25·00	8·50
168		15 c. on 20 c. red	45·00	15·00
169		25 c. on 10 p. green	45·00	15·00

12 — 13 — 14 Nipa House

1919.

No.	T	Description	Unused	Used
170	12	1 c. violet	70	30
171		2 c. red	70	30
172		5 c. red	70	30
173		10 c. purple	1·10	30
174		15 c. brown	1·10	30
175		20 c. blue	2·10	65
176		25 c. green	1·10	65
177		30 c. orange	1·10	65
178		40 c. orange	3·00	65
179		50 c. red	3·00	65
180		1 p. green	3·00	2·00
181		4 p. red	6·00	7·25
182		10 p. brown	11·00	14·00

1920. As T **15** of Rio de Oro, but inscr as T **12**.

No.	T	Description	Unused	Used
183		1 c. brown	15	15
184		2 c. red	15	15
185		5 c. green	15	15
186		10 c. red	15	15
187		15 c. orange	15	15
188		20 c. yellow	15	15
189		25 c. blue	40	25
190		30 c. green	24·00	15·00
191		40 c. brown	35	25
192		50 c. purple	1·10	25
193		1 p. brown	1·10	35
194		4 p. red	3·50	3·75
195		10 p. violet	5·00	7·50

1922.

No.	T	Description	Unused	Used
196	13	1 c. brown	40	20
197		2 c. red	40	20
198		5 c. green	40	20
199		10 c. red	2·75	90
200		15 c. orange	40	20
201		20 c. mauve	1·90	80
202		25 c. blue	3·00	90
203		30 c. violet	2·75	1·10
204		40 c. blue	2·10	45
205		50 c. red	2·10	45
206		1 p. green	2·10	45
207		4 p. brown	8·50	10·00
208		10 p. yellow	17·00	19·00

1925.

No.	T	Description	Unused	Used
209	14	5 c. blue and brown	20	10
210		10 c. blue and green	20	20
211		15 c. black and red	20	15
212		20 c. black and violet	20	20
213		25 c. black and red	45	20
214		30 c. black and orange	45	20
215		40 c. black and blue	45	20
216		50 c. black and red	45	20
217		60 c. black and brown	50	20
218		1 p. black and violet	1·75	20
219		4 p. black and blue	4·50	1·90
220		10 p. black and green	9·00	4·50

1926. Red Cross stamps of Spain optd **GUINEA ESPANOLA.**

No.	T	Description	Unused	Used
221	–	5 c. brown	8·00	8·00
222	–	10 c. green	8·00	8·00
223	70	15 c. violet	1·75	1·75
224	–	20 c. purple	1·75	1·75
225	71	25 c. red	1·75	1·75
226	70	30 c. green	1·75	1·75
227	–	40 c. blue	35	35
228	–	50 c. red	35	35
229	71	60 c. green	35	35
230	–	1 p. red	35	35
231	–	4 p. bistre	1·50	1·50
232	71	10 p. violet	5·50	5·50

1929. Seville and Barcelona Exhibition stamps of Spain (1929) optd **GUINEA.**

No.	T	Description	Unused	Used
233		5 c. red	25	25
234		10 c. green	25	25
235		15 c. blue	25	25
236		20 c. violet	25	25
237		25 c. red	25	25
238		30 c. brown	25	25
239		40 c. blue	40	40
240		50 c. orange	40	40
241		1 p. grey	7·50	7·50
242		4 p. red	16·00	16·00
243		10 p. brown	30·00	30·00

17 Porter — 24 — 26 Gen. Franco

1931.

No.	T	Description	Unused	Used
244	17	1 c. green	10	10
245		2 c. brown	10	10
246		5 c. black	10	10
318		5 c. grey	1·90	10
247		10 c. green	10	10
248		15 c. black	15	10
290		15 c. green	2·75	10
249		20 c. lilac	15	10
250	–	25 c. red	15	10
251	–	30 c. red	20	10
252	–	40 c. blue	65	45
320	–	40 c. green	70	10
253	–	50 c. orange	1·50	1·00
292	–	50 c. blue	6·00	50
254	–	80 c. blue	2·75	1·60
255	–	1 p. black	4·50	3·75
256	–	4 p. mauve	30·00	17·00
257	–	5 p. brown	12·50	12·50

DESIGNS: 25 c. to 50 c. Native drummers; 80 c. to 5 p. King Alfonso XIII and Queen Victoria.

1931. Optd **REPUBLICA ESPANOLA** horiz.

No.	T	Description	Unused	Used
258	17	1 c. green	10	10
259		2 c. brown	10	10
260		5 c. grey	10	10
261		10 c. green	15	10
262		15 c. blue	15	10
263		20 c. violet	15	10
264	–	25 c. red	15	10
265	–	30 c. red	15	20
266	–	40 c. blue	1·40	40
267	–	50 c. orange	9·00	5·25
268	–	80 c. blue	2·75	1·50
269	–	1 p. black	9·50	3·25
270	–	4 p. red	16·00	10·00
271	–	5 p. brown	16·00	10·00

1933. Optd **Republica Espanola.**

No.	T	Description	Unused	Used
272	17	1 c. green	10	10
273		2 c. brown	10	10
274		5 c. grey	15	10
275		10 c. green	15	10
276		15 c. blue	15	10
277		20 c. violet	40	10
278	–	25 c. red	35	20
279	–	30 c. red	35	20
280	–	40 c. blue	2·75	60
281	–	50 c. orange	9·75	3·25
282	–	80 c. blue	4·75	2·75
283	–	1 p. black	10·00	2·75
284	–	4 p. red	32·00	13·00
285	–	5 p. brown	38·00	13·00

1937. Surch **HABILITADO 30 Cts.**

No.	T	Description	Unused	Used
293	–	30 c. on 40 c. (No. 252)	3·25	1·90
294	–	30 c. on 40 c. (No. 266)	13·00	3·00
295	–	30 c. on 40 c. (No. 280)	50·00	15·00

1939. Stamps of Spain, 1937, optd **Territorios Espanoles del Golfo de Guinea** in script type.

No.	T	Description	Unused	Used
296	183	10 c. green	1·40	40
297	184	15 c. black	1·40	40
298		20 c. violet	3·25	1·40
299		25 c. red	3·25	1·40

1939. Surch **Habilitado 40 cts.**

No.	T	Description	Unused	Used
300	–	40 c. on 80 c. (No. 268)	10·50	6·50
301	–	40 c. on 80 c. (No. 282)	10·50	3·75

1940. Fiscal stamps as T **24** inscr "ESPECIAL MOVIL", "TIMBRE MOVIL" or "IMPUESTO SOBRE CONTRATOS" and surch or optd **Habilitado Correos.**

No.	T	Description	Unused	Used
302		5 c. red	4·00	1·25
304		5 c. on 35 c. green	5·00	1·60
307		10 c. on 75 c. brown	6·00	2·10
308		15 c. on 1 p. 50 violet	5·00	2·00
305		25 c. on 60 c. brown	5·00	2·00
306		50 c. on 75 c. brown	6·00	2·10
310		1 p. bistre	75·00	30·00
303		1 p. on 15 c. green	19·00	6·00
316		1 p. on 17 p. red	38·00	12·00
315		1 p. on 40 p. green	10·00	3·50

1940.

No.	T	Description	Unused	Used
311	26	5 c. brown	2·75	70
312		40 c. blue	3·50	70
314		50 c. green	4·75	70

1941. Air. Fiscal stamp as T **24** inscr "IMPUESTO SOBRE CONTRATOS" surch **Habilitado para Correo Aereo Intercolonial Una Peseta** and bar.

No.	T	Description	Unused	Used
317a		1 p. on 17 p. red	28·00	7·00

1942. No. 249 surch **Habilitado 3 Pesetas.**

No.	T	Description	Unused	Used
321	17	3 p. on 20 c. violet	11·00	1·40

1942. Stamps of Spain, 1939, optd **Golfo de Guinea.**

No.	T	Description	Unused	Used
322	196	1 PTA. black	35	15
323		4 PTAS. pink	7·50	65

1942. Air. Air stamp of Spain optd **Golfo de Guinea.**

No.	T	Description	Unused	Used
324	195	1 p. blue	1·50	20

1943. Stamp of Spain, 1939, optd **Territorios espanoles del Golfo de Guinea.**

No.	T	Description	Unused	Used
325	196	2 PTAS. brown	95	15

1948. Air. Ministerial Visit. No. 323 optd **CORREO AEREO Viaje Ministerial 10-19 Enero 1948.**

No.	T	Description	Unused	Used
326	196	4 PTAS. pink	10·00	2·75

1949. Nos. 322 and 325 surch **Habilitado para** and value in words.

No.	T	Description	Unused	Used
327	196	5 c. on 1 PTA. black	20	10
328		15 c. on 2 PTAS. brown	20	10

33 Natives in Pirogue

1949. 75th Anniv of U.P.U.

No.	T	Description	Unused	Used
329	33	4 p. violet	1·75	65

34 Count Argalejo and San Carlos Bay

1949. Air. Colonial Stamp Day.

No.	T	Description	Unused	Used
330	34	5 p. green	1·75	65

35 San Carlos Bay — 36 Manuel Iradier y Bulfy

1949.

No.	T	Description	Unused	Used
331	35	2 c. brown	20	10
332	–	5 c. violet	20	10
333	–	10 c. blue	20	10
334	–	15 c. green	20	10
335	35	25 c. brown	20	10
336	–	30 c. yellow	20	10
337	–	40 c. green	20	10
338	–	45 c. purple	20	10
339	35	50 c. orange	20	10
340	–	75 c. blue	20	10
341	–	90 c. green	20	10
342	–	1 p. black	1·50	20
343	35	1 p. 35 violet	5·50	1·10
344	–	2 p. brown	15·00	2·50
345	–	5 p. mauve	20·00	8·00
346	35	10 p. brown	80·00	30·00

DESIGNS: 5, 30, 75 c., 2 p. Benito River rapids; 10, 40, 90 c., 5 p. Coast scene and Clarence Peak, Fernando Poo; 15, 45, 1 p. Niepan, Benito River.

1950. Air. Colonial Stamp Day.

No.	T	Description	Unused	Used
347	36	5 p. brown	2·75	65

37 Hands and Natives — 38 Mt. Mioco

1951. Native Welfare.

No.	T	Description	Unused	Used
348	37	50 c. + 10 c. blue	20	15
349		1 p. + 25 c. green	11·00	3·75
350		6 p. 50 + 1 p. 65 orange	2·75	1·75

1951. Air.

No.	T	Description	Unused	Used
351	–	25 c. yellow	20	20
352	38	50 c. mauve	20	20
353	–	1 p. green	20	20
354	–	2 p. blue	35	20
355	38	3 p. 25 violet	1·00	20
356	–	5 p. sepia	6·00	3·00
357	–	10 p. red	24·00	7·00

DESIGNS: 25 c., 2, 10 p. Benito Rapids; 1, 5 p. Santa Isabel Bay.

1951. Air. 500th Birth Anniv of Isabella the Catholic. As T **9a** of Spanish Sahara.

No.	T	Description	Unused	Used
358		5 p. blue	19·00	4·00

39 Leopard — 40 Native and Map

1951. Colonial Stamp Day.

No.	T	Description	Unused	Used
359	39	5 c. + 5 c. brown	10	10
360		10 c. + 5 c. orange	10	10
361		60 c. + 15 c. olive	20	15

1951. International West African Conference.

No.	T	Description	Unused	Used
362	40	50 c. orange	20	10
363		5 p. blue	7·00	90

41 Native Man — 42 "Crinum giganteum"

1952.

No.	T	Description	Unused	Used
364	41	5 c. brown	10	10
365		50 c. olive	10	10
366		5 p. violet	2·10	10

1952. Native Welfare Fund.

No.	T	Description	Unused	Used
367	42	5 c. + 5 c. brown	10	10
368		50 c. + 10 c. black	10	10
369		2 p. + 30 c. blue	1·25	60

43 Ferdinand the Catholic

44 Brown-cheeked Hornbills

1952. Air. 500th Birth Anniv of Ferdinand the Catholic.

370	43	5 p. brown	25·00	5·00

1952. Colonial Stamp Day.

371	44	5 c. + 5 c. brown	55	20
372		10 c. + 5 c. purple	65	35
373		60 c. + 15 c. green	1·00	60

45 Native Musician

46 Native Woman and Dove

1953. Native Welfare Fund. Inscr "PRO INDIGENAS 1953".

374	45	5 c. + 5 c. lake	10	10
375	–	10 c. + 5 c. purple	10	10
376	45	15 c. olive	10	10
377	–	60 c. brown	10	10

DESIGN: 10, 60 c. Musician facing right.

1953.

378	46	5 c. orange	10	10
379		10 c. purple	10	10
380		60 c. brown	10	10
381	–	1 p. lilac	80	10
382	–	1 p. 90 green	2·10	20

DESIGN: 1, 1 p. 90, Native drummer.

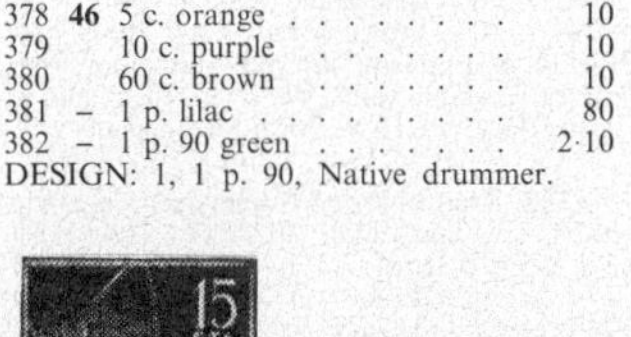

47 "Tragocephala nobilis" (longhorn beetle)

48 Hunting with Bow and Arrow

1953. Colonial Stamp Day. Inscr "DIA DEL SELLO COLONIAL 1953".

383	47	5 c. + 5 c. blue	15	10
384	–	10 c. + 5 c. purple	25	10
385	47	15 c. green	35	15
386	–	60 c. brown	35	15

DESIGN: 10, 60 c. African giant swallowtail (butterfly).

1954. Native Welfare Fund. Inscr "PRO-INDIGENAS 1954".

387	48	5 c. + 5 c. lake	10	10
388	–	10 c. + 5 c. lilac	10	10
389	48	15 c. green	10	10
390	–	60 c. brown	20	10

DESIGN: 10, 60 c. Native hunting elephant with spear.

49 Turtle

1954. Colonial Stamp Day. Inscr "DIA DEL SELLO COLONIAL 1954".

391	49	5 c. + 5 c. red	10	10
392	–	10 c. + 5 c. purple	10	10
393	49	15 c. green	10	10
394	–	60 c. brown	20	10

DESIGN: 10, 60 c. "Leptocharias smithi" (fish).

50 M. Iradier y Bulfy

51 Native Priest

1955. Birth Centenary of Iradier (explorer).

395	50	60 c. brown	15	10
396		1 p. violet	2·75	25

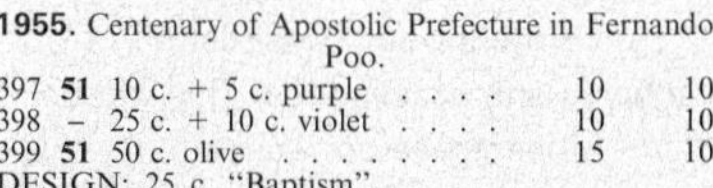

1955. Centenary of Apostolic Prefecture in Fernando Poo.

397	51	10 c. + 5 c. purple	10	10
398	–	25 c. + 10 c. violet	10	10
399	51	50 c. olive	15	10

DESIGN: 25 c. "Baptism".

52 Footballers

53 El Pardo Palace, Madrid

1955. Air.

400	52	25 c. grey	10	10
401		50 c. olive	10	10
402		1 p. 50 brown	85	10
403		4 p. red	2·75	25
404		10 p. green	1·60	25

1955. Treaty of Pardo, 1778.

405	53	5 c. brown	10	10
406		15 c. red	10	10
407		80 c. green	10	10

54 Moustached Monkeys

55 "Orquidea"

1955. Colonial Stamp Day. Inscr "DIA DEL SELLO COLONIAL 1955".

408	54	5 c. + 5 c. lake & brown	10	15
409	–	15 c. + 5 c. sepia & lake	10	15
410	54	70 c. blue and slate	15	10

DESIGN—HORIZ: 15 c. Talapoin and young.

1956. Native Welfare Fund. Inscr "PRO INDIGENAS 1956".

411	55	5 c. + 5 c. olive	10	10
412	–	15 c. + 5 c. ochre	10	10
413	55	20 c. turquoise	10	10
414	–	50 c. brown	10	10

DESIGN: 15, 50 c. "Strophantus kombe".

56 Arms of Santa Isabel

57 Grey Parrot

1956. Colonial Stamp Day. Inscr "DIA DEL SELLO 1956".

415	56	5 c. + 5 c. brown	10	10
416	–	15 c. + 5 c. violet	10	10
417	56	70 c. green	10	10

DESIGN—HORIZ: 15 c. Arms of Bata and natives.

1957. Native Welfare Fund. Inscr "PRO INDIGENAS 1957".

418	57	5 c. + 5 c. purple	15	10
419	–	15 c. + 5 c. ochre	25	10
420	57	70 c. green	55	25

DESIGN—HORIZ: 15 c. Grey parrot in flight.

58 "Flight"

1957. Air. 30th Anniv of Spain–Fernando Poo Flight by "Atlantida" Seaplane Squadron.

421	58	25 p. sepia and bistre	8·00	85

59 African Elephant and Calf

1957. Colonial Stamp Day.

422	59	10 c. + 5 c. mauve	10	10
423	–	15 c. + 5 c. brown	10	10
424	59	20 c. turquoise	10	10
425	–	70 c. green	15	10

DESIGN—VERT: 15, 70 c. African elephant trumpeting.

60 Doves and Arms of Valencia and Santa Isabel

1958. "Aid for Valencia".

426	60	10 c. + 5 c. brown	10	10
427		15 c. + 10 c. ochre	10	10
428		50 c. + 10 c. brown	10	10

61 Boxing

1958. Sports.

429	61	5 c. brown	10	10
430	–	10 c. brown	10	10
431	–	15 c. brown	10	10
432	–	80 c. green	10	10
433	61	1 p. red	10	10
434	–	2 p. purple	20	10
435	–	2 p. 30 lilac	35	10
436	–	3 p. blue	35	10

DESIGNS—VERT: 10 c., 2 p. Basketball; 80 c., 3 p. Running. HORIZ: 15 c., 2 p. 30, Long jumping.

62 Missionary holding Cross

63 African Monarchs

1958. Native Welfare Fund. Inscr "1883 PRO-INDIGENAS 1958".

437	62	10 c. + 5 c. brown	10	10
438	–	15 c. + 5 c. ochre	10	10
439	62	20 c. turquoise	10	10
440	–	70 c. green	10	10

DESIGN: 15, 70 c. The Crucifixion.

1958. Colonial Stamp Day. Inscr "1958".

441	63	10 c. + 5 c. red	10	10
442	–	25 c. + 10 c. violet	30	10
443	–	50 c. + 10 c. olive	35	15

DESIGNS: 25, 50 c. Different views of butterflies on plants.

64 Digitalis

65 Boy on "Penny-farthing" Cycle

1959. Child Welfare Fund. Floral designs as T **64**. Inscr "PRO-INFANCIA 1959".

444	64	10 c. + 5 c. lake	10	10
445	–	15 c. + 5 c. ochre	10	10
446	–	20 c. myrtle	10	10
447	64	70 c. green	10	10

DESIGN: 15, 20 c. Castor bean.

1959. Colonial Stamp Day. Inscr "1959".

448	65	10 c. + 5 c. lake	10	10
449	–	20 c. + 5 c. myrtle	10	10
450	–	50 c. + 20 c. olive	10	10

DESIGNS: 20 c. Racing cyclists; 50 c. Winning cyclist.

EXPRESS LETTER STAMP

E 38 Fernando Poo

1951.

E358	E 38	25 c. red	20	15

SPANISH MOROCCO Pt. 9

100 centimos = 1 peseta

I. SPANISH POST OFFICES IN MOROCCO.

Nos. 2/150, except Nos. 93/8 and 124/37 are all stamps of Spain overprinted.

1903. Optd **CORREO ESPANOL MARRUECOS.**

2	38a	¼ c. green	15	10

1903. Optd **CORREO ESPANOL MARRUECOS.**

3	52	2 c. brown	1·00	1·00
4		5 c. green	1·10	55
5		10 c. red	1·50	20
6		15 c. violet	2·00	60
7		20 c. black	7·25	2·75
8		25 c. blue	65	60
9		30 c. green	4·50	2·75
10		40 c. pink	8·00	4·50
11		50 c. blue	4·50	4·25
12		1 p. purple	9·50	6·50
13		4 p. purple	24·00	11·00
14		10 p. orange	24·00	27·00

1908. Stamps of Spain handstamped **TETUAN.**

15	38a	¼ c. green	12·50	5·25
16	52	2 c. brown	50·00	19·00
17		5 c. green	65·00	30·00
18		10 c. red	65·00	32·00
19		15 c. violet	65·00	32·00
20		20 c. black	£225	£170
21		25 c. blue	£100	55·00
22		30 c. green	£250	£100
23		40 c. bistre	£325	£170

1908. Nos. 2/5 and 7/8 handstamped **TETUAN.**

24	38a	¼ c. green	20·00	13·00
25	52	2 c. brown	£170	95·00
26		5 c. green	£160	50·00
27		10 c. red	£160	50·00
28		20 c. grey	£375	£170
29		25 c. blue	£140	48·00

1909. Optd **CORREO ESPANOL MARRUECOS.**

30	64	2 c. brown	45	15
31		5 c. green	2·40	55
32		10 c. red	3·00	15
33		15 c. violet	7·00	30
34		20 c. green	17·00	70
35		25 c. blue	£110	
36		30 c. green	5·50	30
37		40 c. pink	5·50	30
38		50 c. blue	9·50	9·00
39		1 p. lake	21·00	18·00
40		4 p. purple	£110	
41		10 p. orange	£110	

After the appearance of Nos. 42/54 for the Spanish Protectorate in 1914, the use of Nos. 30/41 was restricted to Tangier.

II. SPANISH PROTECTORATE (excluding Tangier).

1914. Optd **MARRUECOS.**

42	38a	¼ c. green	10	10
43	64	2 c. brown	10	10
44		5 c. green	25	20
45		10 c. red	25	20
46		15 c. violet	1·00	80
47		20 c. green	1·90	1·40
48		25 c. blue	1·90	1·10
49		30 c. green	3·75	1·90
50		40 c. pink	8·75	2·75
51		50 c. blue	4·50	1·90
52		1 p. red	4·50	2·75
53		4 p. purple	22·00	19·00
54		10 p. orange	32·00	25·00

1915. Optd **PROTECTORADO ESPANOL EN MARRUECOS.**

55	38a	¼ c. green	10	10
56	64	2 c. brown	15	15
57		5 c. green	45	15
58		10 c. red	35	15
59		15 c. violet	50	15
60		20 c. green	1·25	25
61		25 c. blue	1·25	25
62		30 c. green	1·40	35
63		40 c. pink	2·40	35
64		50 c. blue	4·00	25
65		1 p. red	4·00	35
66		4 p. purple	28·00	18·00
67		10 p. orange	40·00	21·00

1916. Optd **ZONA DE PROTECTORADO ESPANOL EN MARRUECOS.**

68	38a	¼ c. green	25	10
69	66	1 c. green	1·25	15
70	64	2 c. brown	1·10	25
71		5 c. green	4·50	25
72		10 c. red	6·00	25
73		15 c. orange	6·25	25
74		20 c. violet	8·50	15
75		25 c. blue	18·00	3·00
76		30 c. green	24·00	20·00
77		40 c. red	22·00	60
78		50 c. blue	11·50	30
79		1 p. red	26·00	2·25
80		4 p. purple	40·00	29·00
81		10 p. orange	90·00	65·00

1920. Optd **PROTECTORADO ESPANOL EN MARRUECOS** perf through centre and each half surch in figures and words.

82	64	10 c. + 10 c. on 20 c. green	3·25	1·60
83		15 c. + 15 c. on 30 c. green	8·00	6·00

1920. No. E68 perf through centre, and each half surch **10 centimos.**

84	E 53	10 c. + 10 c. on 20 c. red	9·50	6·00

1920. Fiscal stamps showing figure of Justice, bisected and surch **CORREOS** and value.

93		5 c. on 5 p. blue	7·00	1·40
94		5 c. on 10 p. green	15	10
95		10 c. on 25 p. green	15	10
96		10 c. on 50 p. grey	30	20
97		15 c. on 100 p. red	30	20
98		15 c. on 500 p. red	9·25	4·75

1923. Optd **ZONA DE PROTECTORADO ESPANOL EN MARRUECOS**.

No.	Type	Description	Unused	Used
101	68	2 c. green	65	10
102		5 c. purple	65	10
103		10 c. green	2·50	10
105		15 c. blue	2·50	10
106		20 c. violet	5·50	10
107		25 c. red	11·00	1·25
108		40 c. blue	11·50	4·00
109		50 c. orange	29·00	7·00
110	69	1 p. grey	45·00	4·00

1926. Red Cross stamps optd **ZONA PROTECTORADO ESPAÑOL**.

No.	Type	Description	Unused	Used
111	70	1 c. orange	6·50	6·50
112	–	2 c. red	9·50	9·50
113	–	5 c. brown	3·25	3·25
114	–	10 c. green	3·25	3·25
115	70	15 c. violet	60	60
116	–	20 c. purple	60	60
117	71	25 c. red	60	60
118	70	30 c. green	60	60
119	–	40 c. blue	15	15
120	–	50 c. red	15	15
121	–	1 p. red	15	15
122	–	4 p. bistre	60	60
123	71	10 p. violet	2·40	2·40

11 Mosque of Alcazarquivir

12 Moorish Gateway, Larache

1928.

No.	Type	Description	Unused	Used
124	11	1 c. red	10	10
126		2 c. violet	25	20
127		3 c. blue	10	10
128		10 c. green	10	10
129		15 c. brown	30	10
130	12	20 c. olive	30	10
131		25 c. red	30	10
132		30 c. brown	1·10	10
133		40 c. blue	1·50	10
134		50 c. purple	3·00	10
135	–	1 p. green	4·50	25
136	–	2 p. 50 purple	14·50	6·00
137	–	4 p. blue	8·00	1·50

DESIGNS—HORIZ: 1 p. Well at Alhucemas; 2 p. 50, Xauen; 4 p. Tetuan.

1929. Seville–Barcelona Exhibition stamps, Nos. 502/14 optd **PROTECTORADO MARRUECOS**.

No.	Description	Unused	Used
138	1 c. blue	20	20
139	2 c. green	20	20
140	5 c. red	20	20
141	10 c. green	20	20
142	15 c. blue	20	20
143	20 c. violet	20	20
144	25 c. red	20	20
145	30 c. brown	55	55
146	40 c. blue	55	55
147	50 c. orange	55	55
148	1 p. grey	4·75	4·75
149	4 p. red	11·00	11·00
150	10 p. brown	23·00	23·00

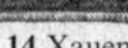

14 Xauen

15 Market-place, Larache

1933.

No.	Type	Description	Unused	Used
151	14	1 c. red	10	10
152	–	2 c. green	10	10
153	–	5 c. mauve	10	10
154	–	10 c. green	25	25
155	–	15 c. yellow	1·40	30
156	14	20 c. green	55	30
157	–	25 c. red	14·50	40
165	–	25 c. violet	80	10
158	–	30 c. lake	4·25	30
166	–	30 c. red	12·00	20
159	15	40 c. blue	9·50	30
167		40 c. red	6·25	30
160	–	50 c. red	28·00	7·50
168	–	50 c. blue	6·25	30
169	–	60 c. green	6·25	30
161	–	1 p. grey	10·00	30
170	–	2 p. lake	32·00	8·50
162	–	2 p. 50 brown	18·00	7·50
163	–	4 p. green	18·00	7·50
164	–	5 p. black	24·00	7·50

DESIGNS—HORIZ: 2 c., 1 p. Xauen; 5 c., 2 p. 50, Arcila; 25 c. (No. 157), 5 p. Sultan and bodyguard; 30 c. (No. 166), 50 c. (No. 168), 2 p. Forest at Ketama. VERT: 10 c., 30 c. (No. 158), Tetuan; 15 c., 4 p. Alcazarquivir; 25 c. (No. 165), 40 c. (No. 167), Wayside scene at Arcila.

See also Nos. 177/83 and 213/6.

1936. Air. No. 157 surch with new value and **18-7-36**.

No.	Description	Unused	Used
171	25 c. + 2 p. on 25 c. red	25·00	5·75

1936. Surch.

No.	Type	Description	Unused	Used
172	–	1 c. on 4 p. blue (137)	25	15
173	–	2 c. on 2 p. 50 pur (136)	25	15
174	12	5 c. on 25 c. red (131)	15	15
175	–	10 c. on 1 p. green (135)	7·25	3·50
176	E 12	15 c. on 20 c. black	6·00	1·90

1937. Pictorials as T **14/15**.

No.	Description	Unused	Used
177	1 c. green	10	10
178	2 c. mauve	10	10
179	5 c. orange	15	10
180	15 c. violet	15	10
181	30 c. red	40	20
182	1 p. blue	4·25	30
183	10 p. brown	50·00	24·00

DESIGNS—VERT: 1, 15 c. Caliph and Viziers; 30 c. Tetuan; 1 p. Arcila; 10 p. Caliph on horseback. HORIZ: 2 c. Bokoia; 5 c. Alcazarquivir.

18 Legionaries

19 General Franco

1937. 1st Anniv of Civil War.

No.	Type	Description	Unused	Used
184	–	1 c. blue	10	10
185	18	2 c. brown	10	10
186	–	5 c. mauve	10	10
187	–	10 c. green	10	10
188	–	15 c. blue	10	10
189	–	20 c. purple	10	10
190	–	25 c. mauve	10	10
191	–	30 c. red	10	10
192	–	40 c. orange	10	10
193	–	50 c. blue	10	10
194	–	60 c. green	10	10
195	–	1 p. violet	10	10
196	–	2 p. blue	8·00	7·50
197	–	2 p. 50 black	8·00	7·50
198	–	4 p. brown	8·00	7·50
199	–	10 p. black	8·00	7·50

DESIGNS—VERT: 1 c. Sentry; 5 c. Trooper; 10 c. Volunteers; 15 c. Colour bearer; 20 c. Desert halt; 25 c. Ifni mounted riflemen; 30 c. Trumpeters; 40 c. Cape Juby Camel Corps; 50 c. Infantryman; 60 c., 1, 2, 4 p. Sherifian Guards; 2 p. 50, Cavalryman. HORIZ: 10 p. "Road to Victory".

1937. Obligatory Tax. Disabled Soldiers in N. Africa.

No.	Type	Description	Unused	Used
200	19	10 c. brown	70	20
201		10 c. blue	70	20

20 Yellow-billed Stork over Mosque

22 Soldier on Horseback

1938. Air.

No.	Type	Description	Unused	Used
203	–	5 c. brown	10	10
204	20	10 c. green	45	10
205	–	25 c. red	10	10
206	–	40 c. blue	2·00	70
207	–	50 c. mauve	10	10
208	–	75 c. blue	10	10
209	–	1 p. brown	10	10
210	–	1 p. 50 violet	2·75	40
211	–	2 p. red	40	10
212	–	3 p. black	1·40	30

DESIGNS—VERT: 5 c. Mosque de Baja, Tetuan; 25 c. Straits of Gibraltar; 40 c. Desert natives; 1 p. Mounted postman; 1 p. 50, Farmers; 2 p. Sunset; 3 p. Shadow of airplane over city. HORIZ: 50 c. Airplane over Tetuan; 75 c. Airplane over Larache.

1939. Pictorials as T **14**.

No.	Description	Unused	Used
213	5 c. orange	15	10
214	10 c. green	15	10
215	15 c. brown	35	10
216	20 c. blue	35	10

DESIGNS: 5 c. "Carta de Espana'; 10 c. "Carta de Marruecos"; 15 c. Larache; 20 c. Tetuan.

1940. Pictorials as T **14**, inscr "ZONA" on back.

No.	Description	Unused	Used
217	1 c. brown	10	10
218	2 c. olive	10	10
219	5 c. blue	15	15
220	10 c. lilac	15	15
221	15 c. green	15	15
222	20 c. violet	15	15
223	25 c. sepia	15	15
224	30 c. green	15	15
225	40 c. green	15	15
226	45 c. orange	1·25	15
227	50 c. brown	50	15
228	70 c. blue	50	15
229	1 p. brown and blue	1·60	15
230	2 p. 50 green and brown	9·50	3·50
231	5 p. sepia and purple	1·60	20
232	10 p. brown and olive	17·00	6·50

DESIGNS—VERT: 1 c. Postman; 2 c. Pillar-box; 5 c. Winter landscape; 10 c. Alcazar street; 15 c. Castle wall, Xauen; 20 c. Palace sentry, Tetuan; 25 c. Caliph on horseback; 30 c. Market-place, Larache; 40 c. Gateway, Tetuan; 45 c. Gateway, Xauen; 50 c. Street, Alcazarquivir; 70 c. Post Office; 1 p. Spanish War veterans.

1940. 4th Anniv of Civil War. Nos. 184/99 optd **17-VII-940 40 ANIVERSARIO**.

No.	Description	Unused	Used
233	1 c. blue	50	50
234	2 c. brown	50	50
235	5 c. mauve	50	50
236	10 c. green	50	50
237	15 c. blue	50	50
238	20 c. purple	50	50
239	25 c. mauve	50	50
240	30 c. red	50	50
241	40 c. orange	80	80
242	50 c. blue	80	80
243	60 c. green	80	80
244	1 p. violet	80	80
245	2 p. blue	32·00	32·00
246	2 p. 50 black	32·00	32·00
247	4 p. brown	32·00	32·00
248	10 p. black	32·00	32·00

1941. Obligatory Tax for Disabled Soldiers.

No.	Type	Description	Unused	Used
249	22	10 c. green	4·00	25
250		10 c. pink	4·00	25
251		10 c. red	4·00	25
252		10 c. blue	2·00	10

23 Larache

25 General Franco

1941.

No.	Type	Description	Unused	Used
253	23	5 c. brown & deep brown	10	10
263	–	5 c. blue	10	10
254	–	10 c. deep red and red	15	10
255	–	15 c. yellow and green	15	10
256	–	20 c. blue and deep blue	35	10
264	–	40 c. brown	15·00	20
257	–	40 c. red and purple	95	10

DESIGNS: 5 c. blue, 10 c. Alcazarquivir; 15, 40 c. brown, Larache market; 20 c. Moorish house; 40 c. purple, Gateway, Tangier.

1942. Air. New designs as T **14**, optd **Z**.

No.	Description	Unused	Used
258	5 c. blue	20	15
259	10 c. brown	20	15
260	15 c. green	20	15
261	90 c. red	20	15
262	5 p. black	80	40

DESIGNS—VERT: 5 c. Atlas mountains; 10 c. Mosque at Tangier; 15 c. Velez fortress; 90 c. Sanjurjo harbour; 5 p. Straits of Gibraltar.

1943. Obligatory Tax for Disabled Soldiers.

No.	Type	Description	Unused	Used
265	25	10 c. grey	8·00	15
266		10 c. blue	8·00	15
267		10 c. brown	8·00	15
268		10 c. violet	8·00	15
283		10 c. brown and mauve	8·00	15
284		10 c. green and orange	8·00	15
295		10 c. brown and blue	8·00	15
296		10 c. lilac and grey	8·00	15

26 Homeward Bound

1944. Agricultural Scenes.

No.	Type	Description	Unused	Used
269	–	1 c. blue and brown	30	10
270	–	2 c. green	10	10
271	26	5 c. black and brown	10	10
272	–	10 c. orange and blue	10	10
273	–	15 c. green	10	10
274	–	20 c. black and red	10	10
275	–	25 c. brown and blue	15	10
276	–	30 c. blue and green	1·25	25
277	–	40 c. purple and brown	10	10
278	26	50 c. brown and blue	35	10
279	–	75 c. blue and green	40	10
280	–	1 p. brown and blue	40	10
281	–	2 p. 50 blue and black	5·50	2·25
282	–	10 p. black and orange	9·25	5·25

DESIGNS—HORIZ; 1, 30 c. Ploughing; 2, 40 c. Harvesting; 10, 75 c. Threshing; 15 c., 1 p. Vegetable garden; 20 c., 2 p. 50, Gathering oranges; 25 c., 10 p. Shepherd and flock.

27 Dyers

28 Sanatorium

1946. Craftsmen.

No.	Type	Description	Unused	Used
285	–	1 c. brown and purple	10	10
286	27	2 c. violet and green	10	10
287	–	10 c. blue and orange	10	10
288	27	15 c. green and blue	10	10
289	–	25 c. blue and green	10	10
290	–	40 c. brown and blue	10	10
291	27	45 c. red and black	40	10
292	27	1 p. blue and green	45	10
293	–	2 p. 50 green and orange	1·25	40
294	–	10 p. grey and blue	2·50	1·90

DESIGNS: 1, 10, 25 c. Potters; 40 c. Blacksmiths; 1 p. Cobblers; 2 p. 50, Weavers; 10 p. Metal workers.

1946. Anti-T.B. Fund.

No.	Type	Description	Unused	Used
297	–	10 c. green and red	10	10
298	28	25 c. brown and red	10	10
299	–	25 c. + 5 c. violet & red	10	10
300	–	50 c. + 10 c. blue & red	20	15
301	–	90 c. + 10 c. brown & red	50	35

DESIGNS: 10 c. Emblem and arabesque ornamentation; 25 c. + 5 c. Mountain roadway; 50 c. + 10 c. Fountain; 90 c. + 10 c. Wayfarers.

29 Sanatorium

30 Steam Goods Train

1947. Anti-T.B. Fund.

No.	Type	Description	Unused	Used
302	–	10 c. blue and red	10	10
303	29	25 c. brn and red	10	10
304	–	25 c. + 5 c. lilac and red	10	10
305	–	50 c. + 10 c. blue & red	20	20
306	–	90 c. + 10 c. brown & red	50	50

DESIGNS: 10 c. Emblem, mosque and palm tree; 25 c. + 5 c. Hospital ward; 50 c. + 10 c. Nurse and children; 90 c. + 10 c. Arab swordsman.

1948. Transport and Commerce.

No.	Type	Description	Unused	Used
307	30	2 c. brown and violet	10	10
308	–	5 c. violet and red	10	10
309	–	15 c. green and blue	10	10
310	–	25 c. green and black	10	10
311	–	35 c. black and blue	10	10
312	–	50 c. violet and orange	10	10
313	–	70 c. blue and green	10	10
314	–	90 c. green and red	10	10
315	–	1 p. violet and blue	35	30
316	30	2 p. 50 green and purple	7·50	7·50
317	–	10 p. blue and black	2·25	1·10

DESIGNS: 5, 35 c. Road transport; 15, 70 c. Urban market; 25, 90 c. Rural market; 50 c., 1 p. Camel caravan; 10 p. "Arango" (freighter) at quay.

31 Emblem

32 Herald

1948. Anti-T.B. Fund.

No.	Type	Description	Unused	Used
318	31	10 c. green and red	10	10
319	–	25 c. green and red	1·25	60
320	32	50 c. + 10 c. purple & red	15	10
321	–	90 c. + 10 c. black & red	80	40
322	–	2 p. 50 + 50 c. brn & red	6·50	3·00
323	–	5 p. + 1 p. violet & red	10·00	5·50

DESIGNS: 25 c. Airplane over sanatorium; 90 c. Arab swordsman; 2 p. 50, Natives sitting in the sun; 5 p. Airplane over Ben Karrich.

33 Market Day

34 Caliph on Horseback

1949. Air.

No.	Type	Description	Unused	Used
324	–	5 c. green and purple	10	10
325	33	10 c. mauve and black	10	10
326	–	30 c. grey and blue	10	10
327	–	1 p. 75 blue and black	10	10
328	33	3 p. black and blue	20	10
329	–	4 p. red and black	40	25
330	–	6 p. 50 brown and green	1·10	25
331	–	8 p. blue and mauve	2·00	45

DESIGNS—VERT: 5 c., 1 p. 75, Straits of Gibraltar; 30 c., 4 p. Kebira Fortress; 6 p. 50, Arrival of mail plane; 8 p. Galloping horseman.

1949. Caliph's Wedding Celebrations.

No.	Type	Description	Unused	Used
332	34	50 c. + 10 c. red (postage)	20	20
333	–	1 p. + 10 c. black (air)	70	30

DESIGN: 1 p. Wedding crowds in palace grounds.

35 Emblem

36 Postman, 1890

1949. Anti-T.B. Fund.
334 **35** 5 c. green and red 10 10
335 – 10 c. blue and red 10 10
336 – 25 c. black and red 50 20
337 – 50 c. + 10 c. brown & red 25 10
338 – 90 c. + 10 c. green & red . 70 20
DESIGNS: 10 c. Road to recovery; 25 c. Palm tree and tower; 50 c. Flag and followers; 90 c. Moorish horseman.

1950. 75th Anniv of U.P.U.
339 **36** 5 c. blue and brown 10 10
340 – 10 c. black and blue . . . 10 10
341 – 15 c. green and black . . . 10 10
342 – 35 c. black and violet . . . 10 10
343 – 45 c. mauve and red . . . 15 15
344 **36** 50 c. black and green . . . 10 10
345 – 75 c. blue and deep blue . . 10 10
346 **36** 90 c. red and black 10 10
347 – 1 p. green and purple . . . 10 10
348 – 1 p. 50 blue and red . . . 40 10
349 – 5 p. purple and black . . . 70 15
350 – 10 p. blue and violet . . . 14·00 12·00
DESIGNS: 10, 45 c., 1 p. Mounted postman; 15 c., 1 p. 50, Mail coach; 35, 75 c., 5 p. Mail van; 10 p. Steam mail train.

37 Morabito

38 Hunting

1950. Anti-T.B. Fund.
351 – 5 c. black and red 10 10
352 – 10 c. green and red 10 10
353 – 25 c. blue and red 55 30
354 – 50 c. + 10 c. brown & red 20 10
355 **37** 90 c. + 10 c. green & red . 1·50 65
DESIGNS: 5 c. Arab horseman; 10 c. Fort; 25 c. Sanatorium; 50 c. Crowd at Fountain of Life.

1950.
356 **38** 5 c. mauve and brown . . 10 10
357 – 10 c. grey and red 10 10
358 **38** 50 c. sepia and green . . . 10 10
359 – 1 p. red and violet 35 10
360 – 5 p. violet and red 55 10
361 – 10 p. red and green . . . . 2·00 50
DESIGNS: 10 c., 1 p. Hunters and hounds; 5 p. Fishermen; 10 p. Carabo (fishing boat).

39 Emblem

40 Mounted Riflemen

1951. Anti-T.B. Fund.
362 **39** 5 c. green and red 10 10
363 – 10 c. blue and red 10 10
364 – 25 c. black and red 60 35
365 – 50 c. + 10 c. brown & red 10 10
366 – 90 c. + 10 c. blue and red 25 15
367 – 1 p. + 5 p. blue and red . 8·00 3·50
368 – 1 p. 10 + 25 c. sepia & red 2·75 1·75
DESIGNS: 10 c. Natives and children; 25 c. Airplane over Nubes; 50 c. Moorish horsemen; 90 c. Riverside fortress; 1 p. Brig "Hernan Cortes"; 1 p. 10, Airplane over caravan.

1952.
369 **40** 5 c. brown and blue 10 10
370 – 10 c. mauve and sepia . . . 10 10
371 – 15 c. green and black . . . 10 10
372 – 20 c. purple and green . . . 10 10
373 – 25 c. blue and red 10 10
374 – 35 c. orange and olive . . . 10 10
375 – 45 c. red 10 10
376 – 50 c. green and red 10 10
377 – 75 c. blue and purple . . . 10 10
378 – 90 c. purple and blue . . . 10 10
379 – 1 p. brown and blue . . . 10 10
380 – 5 p. blue and red . . . . 1·25 30
381 – 10 p. black and green . . . 1·90 40
DESIGNS—HORIZ: 10 c. Grooms leading horses; 15 c. Parade of horsemen; 20 c. Peasants; 25 c. Monastic procession; 35 c. Native band; 45 c. Tribesmen; 50 c. Natives overlooking roof tops; 75 c. Inside a tea house; 90 c. Wedding procession; 1 p. Pilgrims on horseback; 5 p. Storyteller and audience; 10 p. Natives talking.

41 Road to Tetuan

1952. Air. Tetuan Postal Museum Fund.
382 **41** 2 p. blue and black . . . 10 10
383 – 4 p. red and black 30 10
384 – 8 p. green and black . . . 40 25
385 – 16 p. brown and black . . 2·00 80
DESIGNS: 4 p. Moors watching airplane; 8 p. Horseman and airplane; 16 p. Shadow of airplane over Tetuan.

42 Natives at Prayer

43 Sidi Saidi

1952. Anti-T.B. Fund. Frame in red.
386 **42** 5 c. green 10 10
387 – 10 c. brown 10 10
388 – 25 c. blue 30 20
389 – 50 c. + 10 c. black . . . 10 10
390 – 60 c. + 25 c. green . . . 60 35
391 – 90 c. + 10 c. purple . . . 55 30
392 – 1 p. 10 + 25 c. violet . . 1·60 75
393 – 5 p. + 2 p. black . . . . 4·00 2·00
DESIGNS: 10 c. Beggars outside doorway; 25 c. Airplane over cactus; 50 c. Natives on horseback; 60 c. Airplane over palms; 90 c. Hilltop fortress; 1 p. 10, Airplane over agaves; 5 p. Mounted warrior.

1953. Air.
394 – 35 c. red and blue 15 10
395 **43** 60 c. green and lake . . . 15 10
396 – 1 p. 10 black and blue . . 25 10
397 – 4 p. 50 brown and lake . . 85 20
DESIGNS: 35 c. Carabo (fishing boat); 1 p. 10, Le Yunta (ploughing); 4 p. 50, Fortress, Xauen.

1953. Air. No. 208 surch **50**.
398 50 c. on 75 c. blue 30 10

1953. Anti-T.B. Fund. As T **32** but inscr "PRO TUBERCULOSOS 1953". Frame in red.
400 5 c. green 10 10
401 10 c. purple 10 10
402 25 c. green 70 40
403 50 c. + 10 c. violet 10 10
404 60 c. + 25 c. brown . . . . 1·40 80
405 90 c. + 10 c. black 45 25
406 1 p. 10 + 25 c. brown . . . 2·50 1·25
407 5 p. + 2 p. blue . . . . . 8·75 5·00
DESIGNS: 5 c. Herald; 10 c. Moorish horseman; 25 c. Airplane over Ben Karrich; 50 c. Mounted warrior; 60 c. Airplane over sanatorium; 90 c. Moorish horseman; 1 p. 10, Airplane over sea; 5 p. Arab swordsman.

46

47 Water-carrier

1953.
408 **46** 5 c. red 10 10
409 10 c. green 10 10

1953. 25th Anniv of 1st Pictorial Stamps of Spanish Morocco.
410 – 25 c. purple and green . . 10 10
411 **47** 50 c. green and red 10 10
412 – 90 c. orange and blue . . 10 10
413 – 1 p. green and brown . . 10 10
414 – 1 p. 25 mauve and green . 10 10
415 – 2 p. blue and purple . . . 25 15
416 **47** 2 p. 50 orange and grey . . 55 20
417 – 4 p. 50 green and mauve . 3·25 45
418 – 10 p. black and green . . 3·75 90
DESIGNS—VERT: 35 c., 1 p. 25, Mountain women; 90 c., 2 p. Mountain tribesmen; 1, 4 p. 50, Veiled Moorish women; 10 p. Arab dignitary.

1954. Anti-T.B. Fund. As T **32**, but inscr "PRO TUBERCULOSOS 1954". Frame in red.
419 5 c. turquoise 10 10
420 5 c. + 5 c. purple 70 30
421 10 c. sepia 10 10
422 25 c. blue 15 15
423 50 c. + 10 c. green 60 30
424 5 p. + 2 p. black . . . . . 7·50 3·75
DESIGNS: 5 c. Convent; 5 c. + 5 c. White stork on a tower; 10 c. Moroccan family; 25 c. Airplane over Spanish coast; 50 c. Father and child; 5 p. Chapel.

48 Saida Gate

49 Celebrations

1955. Frames in black.
425 – 15 c. green 10 10
426 **48** 25 c. purple 10 10
427 – 80 c. blue 10 10
428 **48** 1 p. mauve 20 10
429 – 15 p. turquoise . . . . . 2·40 85
DESIGNS: 15 c., 80 c. Queen's Gate; 15 p. Ceuta Gate.

1955. 30th Anniv of Caliph's Accession.
430 **49** 15 c. olive and brown . . . 10 10
431 – 25 c. lake and purple . . . 10 10
432 – 30 c. green and sepia . . . 10 10
433 **49** 70 c. green and myrtle . . . 10 10
434 – 80 c. brown and olive . . . 10 10
435 – 1 p. brown and blue . . . 10 10
436 **49** 1 p. 80 violet and black . . 20 10
437 – 3 p. grey and blue 20 10
438 – 5 p. brown and myrtle . . . 1·10 35
439 – 15 p. green and brown . . . 2·50 1·25
DESIGNS: 25 c., 80 c., 3 p. Caliph's portrait; 30 c., 1, 5 p. Procession; 15 p. Coat of Arms.

EXPRESS LETTER STAMPS

Express Letter Stamps of Spain overprinted.

1914. Optd **MARRUECOS**.
E55 E **53** 20 c. red . . . . 3·75 1·90

1915. Optd **PROTECTORADO ESPANOL EN MARRUECOS**.
E68 E **53** 20 c. red . . . . 3·25 1·40

1923. Optd **ZONA DE PROTECTORADO ESPANOL EN MARRUECOS**.
E111 E **53** 20 c. red . . . . 9·50 8·25

1926. Red Cross. Optd **ZONA PROTECTORADO ESPANOL**.
E124 E **77** 20 c. black and blue . . 2·50 2·50

E 12 Moorish Courier

E 16

1928.
E138 E **12** 20 c. black . . . . . . 3·00 2·75

1935.
E171 E **16** 20 c. red . . . . 1·40 30

E 19 Moorish Courier

E 21

1937. 1st Anniv of Civil War.
E200 E **19** 20 c. red 10 10

1940.
E233 E **21** 25 c. red 30 20

1940. No. E200 optd as Nos. 233/48 and surch also.
E249 E **19** 25 c. on 20 c. red . . . 10·00 10·00

E 37 Air Mail 1935

E 41 Moorish Courier

1950. 75th Anniv of U.P.U.
E351 E **37** 25 c. black and red . . 19·00 18·00

1952.
E382 E **41** 25 c. red 10 10

E 48 Moorish Courier

E 49 Tangier Gate

1953. 25th Anniv of First Pictorial Stamps of Spanish Morocco.
E419 E **48** 25 c. mauve and blue . 20 15

1955.
E430 E **49** 2 p. violet and black . 15 10

For later issues see **MOROCCO**.

SPANISH POST OFFICES IN TANGIER Pt. 9

See note below No. 41 of Spanish P.O.s in Morocco, concerning the exclusive use of Nos. 30/41 in Tangier after 1914.

Postage stamps of Spain overprinted.

1921. Optd **CORREO ESPANOL MARRUECOS**.
1 **66** 1 c. green 15 10
2 **64** 2 c. brown £300
3 15 c. yellow . . . . 1·10 10
4 20 c. violet . . . . 1·90 10

1939. Optd as 1921.
5 **68** 2 c. green . . . . 3·75 15
6 5 c. purple . . . . 3·75 15
7 5 c. red . . . . 3·75 15
8a 10 c. green . . . . 4·25 15
10 20 c. violet . . . . 7·50 90
11 50 c. orange . . . . . . 32·00 6·50
12 **69** 10 p. brown . . . . 4·25 4·25

1926. Red Cross stamps optd **CORREO ESPANOL TANGER**.
13 **70** 1 c. orange . . . . 6·25 6·25
14 – 2 c. red . . . . 6·25 6·25
15 – 5 c. grey . . . . 3·00 3·00
16 – 10 c. green . . . . 3·00 3·00
17 **70** 15 c. violet . . . . 1·25 1·25
18 – 20 c. purple . . . . 1·25 1·25
19 **71** 25 c. red . . . . 1·25 1·25
20 **70** 30 c. olive . . . . 1·25 1·25
21 – 40 c. blue 25 25
22 – 50 c. brown 25 25
23 – 1 p. red 55 55
24 – 4 p. brown 55 55
25 **71** 10 p. lilac . . . . 3·00 3·00

1929. Seville–Barcelona Exhibition stamps, Nos. 504/14 optd **TANGER**.
27 5 c. red 25 25
28 10 c. green 25 25
29 15 c. blue 25 25
30 20 c. violet 25 25
31 25 c. red 25 25
32 30 c. brown 25 25
33 40 c. blue 70 70
34 50 c. orange 70 70
35 1 p. grey . . . . 7·00 7·00
36 4 p. red . . . . 19·00 19·00
37 10 p. brown . . . . 28·00 28·00

1930. Optd as 1921.
38 **97** 10 c. green . . . . 2·40 30
39 15 c. turquoise . . . . . . £110 1·25
40 20 c. violet . . . . 2·50 50
41 30 c. red . . . . 2·75 1·25
42 40 c. blue . . . . 10·00 6·50

1933. Optd **MARRUECOS**.
43 **143** 1 c. green (imperf) 15 15
44 2 c. brown 15 15
45 **127** 5 c. brown 15 15
46 **128** 10 c. green 15 15
47 **130** 15 c. blue 15 15
48 **127** 20 c. violet 15 15
49 **132** 25 c. red 15 15
50 **133** 30 c. red . . . . 45·00 5·50
51 **138** 40 c. blue 25 15
52 **130** 50 c. orange 60 15
53 **138** 60 c. green 60 15
54 **142** 1 p. black 60 25
55 – 4 p. mauve . . . . 1·60 2·40
56 – 10 p. brown . . . . 2·40 5·50

1937. Optd **TANGER**.
58 **143** 1 c. green (imperf) 30 15
59 2 c. brown 30 15
60 **127** 5 c. brown 30 15
61 **128** 10 c. green 30 15
62 **130** 15 c. blue 40 15
63 **127** 20 c. violet 40 40
64 **132** 25 c. red 40 40
65 **136** 30 c. red 40 15
66 **138** 40 c. blue . . . . 1·10 50
67 **130** 50 c. orange . . . . . . 3·25 50
68 **142** 1 p. black . . . . 6·00 3·00
69 – 4 p. mauve (No. 768c) . . £160
70 – 10 p. brown (No. 769c) . . £200

1938. Optd **Correo Espanol Tanger.**
71 **143** 5 c. brown 1·60 90
72 10 c. green 1·60 90
73 15 c. green 1·60 90
74 20 c. violet 1·60 60
75 25 c. mauve 1·60 60
76 30 c. red 6·50 3·00
77 **160a** 40 c. red 3·25 1·40
78 45 c. red 1·10 40
79 50 c. blue 1·10 40
80 60 c. blue 3·25 1·40
81 **145** 2 p. blue 20·00 8·00
82 – 4 p. mauve (No. 768c) 20·00 8·00

1938. Air. Optd **Correo Aereo TANGER.**
83 **143** 25 c. mauve 85 45
84 **160a** 50 c. blue 85 45

1938. Air. Optd **CORREO AEREO TANGER.**
86 **142** 1 p. black 85 45
85 **145** 2 p. blue 6·50 2·50
87 – 4 p. mauve (No. 768c) 6·50 2·50
88 – 10 p. brown (No. 769c) 48·00 30·00

1939. Optd Tanger.
89 **143** 5 c. brown 60 40
90 10 c. green 60 40
91 15 c. green 60 40
92 20 c. violet 60 40
93 25 c. mauve 60 40
94 30 c. red 60 40
95 **160a** 40 c. red 60 40
96 45 c. red 60 40
97 50 c. blue 1·60 1·00
98 60 c. blue 80 40
99 **142** 1 p. black 1·10 60
100 **145** 2 p. blue 21·00 12·50
101 – 4 p. mauve (No. 768c) 21·00 12·50
102 – 10 p. brown (No. 769c) 21·00 12·50

1939. Air. Optd **Via Aerea Tanger.**
103 **143** 5 c. brown 85 80
104 10 c. green 85 80
105 15 c. green 80 65
106 20 c. violet 80 65
107 25 c. mauve 80 65
108 30 c. red 1·40 95
109 **160a** 40 c. red 38·00
110 45 c. red 40 40
111 50 c. blue 80·00
112 60 c. blue 80·00 16·00
113 **142** 1 p. black 25·00
114 – 4 p. mauve (No. 768c) 40·00 24·00
115 – 10 p. brown (No. 769c) £110

1939. Air. Express Letter stamp optd **Via Aerea Tanger.**
116 E **145** 20 c. red 2·75 1·40

1939. Various fiscal types inscr "DERECHOS CONSULARES ESPANOLES" optd **Correo Tanger.**
117 50 c. pink 17·00 17·00
118 1 p. pink 4·25 4·25
119 2 p. pink 4·25 4·25
120 5 p. red and green 4·75 4·25
121 10 p. red and violet 20·00 20·00

1939. Air. Various fiscal types inscr "DERECHOS CONSULARES ESPANOLES" optd **Correo Aereo Tanger.**
122 1 p. blue 48·00 48·00
123 2 p. blue 48·00 48·00
124 5 p. blue 80·00 80·00
125 10 p. blue 6·00 6·00

15 Moroccan Woman **16** Douglas DC-3

1948.
126 – 1 c. green 10 10
127 – 2 c. orange 10 10
128 – 5 c. purple 10 10
129 – 10 c. blue 10 10
130 – 20 c. sepia 10 10
131 – 25 c. green 10 10
132 – 30 c. grey 25 10
133 – 45 c. red 25 10
134 **15** 50 c. red 25 10
135 – 75 c. blue 50 10
136 – 90 c. green 40 10
137 – 1 p. 35 red 1·75 30
138 **15** 2 p. violet 3·25 30
139 – 10 p. green 3·75 60
DESIGNS: 1, 2 c. Woman's head facing right; 5, 25 c. Palm tree; 10, 20 c. Woman's head facing left; 30 c., 1 p. 35, Old map of Tangier; 45 c., 10 p. Street scene; 75, 90 c. Head of Moor.

1949. Air.
140 – 20 c. brown 50 10
141 **16** 25 c. red 50 10
142 – 35 c. green 50 10
143 – 1 p. violet 1·50 10
144 **16** 2 p. green 2·50 30
145 – 10 p. purple 3·50 1·10
DESIGNS: 20 c., 1 p. Lockheed Constellation and map; 35 c., 10 p. Boeing 377 Stratocruiser in clouds.

EXPRESS LETTER STAMPS

Express Letter Stamps of Spain overprinted.

1926. Red Cross. Optd **CORREO ESPANOL TANGER.**
E26 E **77** 20 c. black and blue 3·00 3·00

1933. No. E17 optd **MARRUECOS.**
E57 E **145** 20 c. red 1·10 35

E **17** Courier

1949.
E146 E **17** 25 c. red 55 30

SPANISH SAHARA Pt. 9

Former Spanish territory on the north-west coast of Africa, previously called Rio de Oro. Later divided between Morocco and Mauritania.

100 centimos = 1 peseta

1 Tuareg and Camel

1924.
1 **1** 5 c. green 1·50 40
2 10 c. green 1·50 40
3 15 c. blue 1·50 40
4 20 c. violet 1·50 65
5 25 c. red 1·50 65
6 30 c. brown 1·50 65
7 40 c. blue 1·50 65
8 50 c. orange 1·50 65
9 60 c. purple 1·50 65
10 1 p. red 7·50 3·50
11 4 p. brown 38·00 17·00
12 10 p. purple 85·00 50·00

1926. Red Cross stamps of Spain optd **SAHARA ESPANOL.**
13 – 5 c. grey 7·00 7·00
14 – 10 c. green 7·00 7·00
15 **70** 15 c. violet 2·25 2·25
16 – 20 c. purple 2·25 2·25
17 **71** 25 c. red 2·25 2·25
18 **70** 30 c. olive 2·25 2·25
19 – 40 c. blue 15 15
20 – 50 c. brown 15 15
21 **71** 60 c. green 15 15
22 – 1 p. red 15 15
23 – 4 p. brown 1·90 1·90
24 **71** 10 p. lilac 5·00 5·00

1929. Seville and Barcelona Exn stamps of Spain. Nos. 504/14, optd **SAHARA.**
25 5 c. red 15 15
26 10 c. green 15 15
27 15 c. blue 15 15
28 20 c. violet 15 15
29 25 c. red 15 15
30 30 c. brown 15 15
31 40 c. blue 40 40
32 50 c. orange 40 40
33 1 p. grey 2·40 2·40
34 4 p. red 18·00 18·00
35 10 p. brown 35·00 35·00

1931. Optd **Republica Espanola.**
36 **1** 5 c. green 45 40
37 10 c. green 45 40
38 15 c. blue 45 40
39 20 c. violet 45 40
40 25 c. red 55 40
41 30 c. brown 55 40
42 40 c. blue 2·75 60
43 50 c. orange 2·75 1·40
44 60 c. purple 2·75 1·40
45 1 p. red 2·75 1·40
46 4 p. brown 26·00 14·00
47 10 p. purple 50·00 28·00

1941. Stamps of Spain optd **SAHARA ESPANOL.**
47a **181** 1 c. green 1·40 1·40
47b **182** 2 c. brown 1·40 1·40
48 **183** 5 c. brown 40 40
49 10 c. red 1·40 1·40
50 15 c. green 40 40
51 **196** 20 c. violet 40 40
52 25 c. red 95 80
53 30 c. blue 95 95
54 40 c. green 40 40
55 50 c. blue 5·00 1·25
56 70 c. blue 3·50 1·90
57 1 PTA. black 16·00 2·50
58 2 PTAS. brown 90·00 60·00
59 4 PTAS. red £200 £140
60 10 PTS. brown £650 £225

6 Dorcas Gazelles **7** Ostriches

1943.
61 **6** 1 c. mauve & brown (postage) 10 10
62 – 2 c. blue and green 10 10
63 – 5 c. blue and red 10 10
64 **6** 15 c. green and myrtle 10 10
65 – 20 c. brown and mauve 10 10
66 **6** 40 c. mauve and purple 10 10
67 – 45 c. red and purple 15 15
68 – 75 c. blue and indigo 15 15
69 **6** 1 p. brown and red 65 65
70 – 3 p. green and violet 1·25 1·25
71 – 10 p. black and sepia 21·00 18·00
DESIGNS—VERT: 2, 20, 45 c., 3 p. Camel caravan; 5, 75 c., 10 p. Camel troops.

72 **7** 5 c. brown and red (air) 1·00 30
73 – 25 c. olive and green 20 15
74 **7** 50 c. turquoise and blue 2·00 40
75 – 1 p. blue and mauve 50 25
76 **7** 1 p. 40 blue and green 2·75 45
77 – 2 p. brown and purple 85 85
78 **7** 5 p. mauve and brown 5·50 2·50
79 – 6 p. green and blue 18·00 16·00
DESIGN: 25 c., 1, 2, 6 p. Airplane and camels.

8 Boy carrying Lamb **9** Diego de Herrera

1950. Child Welfare.
80 **8** 50 c. + 10 c. brown 20 15
81 1 p. + 25 c. red 9·75 5·25
82 6 p. 50 + 1 p. 65 green 5·25 1·60

1950. Air. Colonial Stamp Day.
83 **9** 5 p. violet 2·75 1·00

9a Woman and Dove **9b** General Franco

1951. Air. 500th Birth Anniv of Isabella the Catholic.
84 **9a** 5 p. green 21·00 6·50

1951. Visit of General Franco.
85 **9b** 50 c. orange 10 10
86 1 p. brown 25 20
87 5 p. turquoise 30·00 11·00

10 Dromedary and Calf **11** Native Woman

1951. Colonial Stamp Day.
88 **10** 5 c. + 5 c. brown 10 10
89 10 c. + 5 c. orange 10 10
90 60 c. + 15 c. olive 30 10

1952. Child Welfare Fund.
91 **11** 5 c. + 5 c. brown 10 10
92 50 c. + 10 c. black 10 10
93 2 p. + 30 c. blue 1·40 95

12 Morion, Sword and Banner **13** Head of Ostritch

1952. Air. 500th Birth Anniv of Ferdinand the Catholic.
94 **12** 5 p. brown 25·00 6·50

1952. Colonial Stamp Day.
95 **13** 5 c. + 5 c. brown 15 10
96 10 c. + 5 c. red 30 15
97 60 c. + 15 c. green 45 25

14 "Geography" **15** Woman Musician

1953. 75th Anniv of Royal Geographical Society.
98 **14** 5 c. red 10 10
99 35 c. green 10 10
100 60 c. brown 20 10

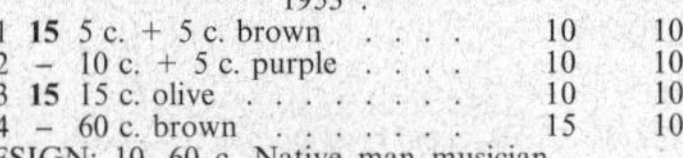

1953. Child Welfare Fund. Inscr "PRO INFANCIA 1953".
101 **15** 5 c. + 5 c. brown 10 10
102 – 10 c. + 5 c. purple 10 10
103 **15** 15 c. olive 10 10
104 – 60 c. brown 15 10
DESIGN: 10, 60 c. Native man musician.

16

1953. Colonial Stamp Day. Inscr "DIA DEL SELLO COLONIAL 1953".
105 **16** 5 c. + 5 c. violet 10 10
106 – 10 c. + 5 c. green 10 10
107 **16** 15 c. olive 10 10
108 – 60 c. orange 15 10
DESIGN—HORIZ: 10, 60 c. Two fishes.

17 Hurdlers

1954. Child Welfare Fund. Inscr "PRO INFANCIA 1954".
109 **17** 5 c. + 5 c. brown 10 10
110 – 10 c. + 5 c. violet 10 10
111 **17** 15 c. green 10 10
112 – 60 c. brown 10 10
DESIGN—VERT: 10, 60 c. Native runner.

18 Flying Fish

1954. Colonial Stamp Day. Inscr "DIA DEL SELLO COLONIAL 1954".
113 **18** 5 c. + 5 c. red 10 10
114 – 10 c. + 5 c. purple 10 10
115 **18** 15 c. green 10 10
116 – 60 c. brown 10 10
DESIGN—HORIZ: 10, 60 c. "Sparus auratus" (fish).

19 E. Bonelli

1955. Birth Centenary of Bonelli (explorer).
117 **19** 10 c. + 5 c. purple 10 10
118 – 25 c. + 10 c. violet 10 10
119 **19** 50 c. olive 15 15
DESIGN: 25 c. Bonelli and felucca.

20 Scimitar Oryx **21** "Antirrhinum ramosissimum"

1955. Colonial Stamp Day. Inscr "DIA DEL SELLO COLONIAL 1955".
120 **20** 5 c. + 5 c. brown 10 10
121 – 15 c. + 5 c. bistre 10 10
122 **20** 70 c. green 15 10
DESIGN: 15 c. Scimitar oryx's head.

1956. Child Welfare Fund. Inscr "PRO-INFANCIA 1956".
123 **21** 5 c. + 5 c. olive 10 10
124 – 15 c. + 5 c. ochre 10 10
125 **21** 20 c. turquoise 10 10
126 – 50 c. brown 10 10
DESIGN: 15, 50 c. "Sesuvium portulacastrum" (wrongly inscr "Sesiviun").

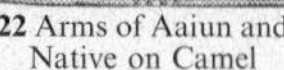

22 Arms of Aaiun and Native on Camel **23** Dromedaries

1956. Colonial Stamp Day. Inscr "DIA DEL SELLO 1956".
127 **22** 5 c. + 5 c. black & violet . 10 10
128 – 15 c. + 5 c. green & ochre 10 10
129 **22** 70 c. brown and green . . 10 10
DESIGN—VERT: 15 c. Arms of Villa Cisneros and native chief.

1957. Animals.
130 **23** 5 c. violet 10 10
131 – 15 c. ochre 50 10
132 – 50 c. brown 10 10
133 **23** 70 c. green 70 10
134 – 80 c. turquoise . . . . . . 2·50 20
135 – 1 p. 80 mauve 70 20
DESIGNS: 15, 80 c. Ostrich; 50 c., 1 p. 80, Dorcas gazelle.

24 Golden Eagle **25** Head of Striped Hyena

1957. Child Welfare Fund. Inscr "PRO-INFANCIA 1957".
136 **24** 5 c. + 5 c. brown 20 15
137 – 15 c. + 5 c. bistre 35 25
138 **24** 70 c. green 55 35
DESIGN: 15 c. Tawny eagle in flight.

1957. Colonial Stamp Day. Inscr "DIA DEL SELLO 1957".
139 **25** 10 c. + 5 c. purple 10 10
140 – 15 c. + 5 c. ochre 10 10
141 **25** 20 c. green 10 10
142 – 70 c. myrtle 15 10
DESIGN: 15, 70 c. Striped hyena.

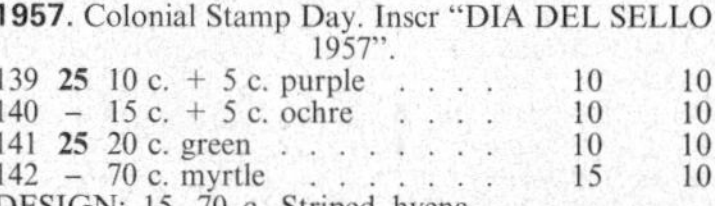

26 White Stork and Arms of Valencia and Aaiun **27** Cervantes

1958. Aid for Valencia.
143 **26** 10 c. + 5 c. brown 15 10
144 15 c. + 10 c. ochre 20 15
145 50 c. + 10 c. brown . . . 55 25

1958. Child Welfare Fund. Inscr "1958".
146 **27** 10 c. + 5 c. brown & chest 10 10
147 – 15 c. + 5 c. myrtle & orge 10 10
148 – 20 c. green and brown . . 10 10
149 **27** 50 c. green and yellow . . 10 10
DESIGNS—VERT: 15 c. Don Quixote and Sancho Panza on horseback. HORIZ: 20 c. Don Quixote and the lion.

28 Hoopoe Lark **29** Lope de Vega (author)

1958. Colonial Stamp Day. Inscr "1958".
150 **28** 10 c. + 5 c. red 15 10
151 – 25 c. + 10 c. violet . . . 35 20
152 – 50 c. + 10 c. olive 60 35
DESIGNS—HORIZ: 25 c. Hoopoe lark feeding young. VERT: 50 c. Fulvous babbler.

1959. Child Welfare Fund. Inscr "PRO INFANCIA 1959".
153 **29** 10 c. + 5 c. olive & brown 10 10
154 – 15 c. + 5 c. brown & bis . 10 10
155 – 20 c. sepia and green . . . 10 10
156 **29** 70 c. myrtle and green . . 10 10
DESIGNS—Characters from the comedy "The Star of Seville": 15 c. Spanish lady; 20 c. Caballero.

30 Grey Heron **31** Sahara Postman

1959. Birds.
157 **30** 25 c. violet 10 10
158 – 50 c. green 10 10
159 – 75 c. sepia 15 10
160 **30** 1 p. red 20 10
161 – 1 p. 50 green 30 10
162 – 2 p. purple . . . . 2·00 10
163 **30** 3 p. blue . . . . 2·00 10
164 – 5 p. brown . . . . 3·75 10
165 – 10 p. olive . . . . 11·50 6·50
DESIGNS: 50 c., 1 p. 50, 5 p. European sparrow hawk; 75 c., 2, 10 p. Herring gull.

1959. Colonial Stamp Day. Inscr "1959".
166 **31** 10 c. + 5 c. brown & red . 10 10
167 – 20 c. + 5 c. brown & grn 10 10
168 – 50 c. + 20 c. slate & olive 10 10
DESIGNS: 20 c. Postman tendering letters; 50 c. Camel postman.

32 F. de Quevedo (writer) **33** Leopard

1960. Child Welfare Fund. Inscr "PRO-INFANCIA 1960".
169 **32** 10 c. + 5 c. purple 10 10
170 – 15 c. + 5 c. bistre 10 10
171 – 35 c. green 10 10
172 **32** 80 c. turquoise 10 10
DESIGNS—VERT: (representing Quevedo's works): 15 c. Winged wheel and hour-glass; 25 c. Man in plumed hat wearing cloak and sword.

1960. Stamp Day. Inscr "1960".
173 **33** 10 c. + 5 c. mauve . . . 10 10
174 – 20 c. + 5 c. myrtle . . . 10 10
175 – 30 c. + 10 c. brown . . . 50 20
176 – 50 c. + 20 c. brown . . . 25 10
DESIGNS: 20 c. Fennec fox; 30 c. Golden eagle defying leopard; 50 c. Red fox.

34 Houbara Bustard **35** Cameleer and Airplane

1961.
177 **34** 25 c. violet 10 10
178 – 50 c. brown 15 10
179 **34** 75 c. dull purple 20 10
180 – 1 p. red 30 10
181 **34** 1 p. 50 green 40 10
182 – 2 p. mauve . . . . 1·60 10
183 **34** 3 p. blue . . . . 1·90 45
184 – 5 p. brown . . . . 2·50 60
185 **34** 10 p. olive . . . . 6·25 2·40
DESIGN: 50 c., 1, 2, 5 p. Rock doves.

1961. Air.
186 **35** 25 p. sepia . . . . 3·25 85

36 Dorcas Gazelle **37**

1961. Child Welfare. Inscr "PRO-INFANCIA 1961".
187 **36** 10 c. + 5 c. red 10 10
188 – 25 c. + 10 c. violet 10 10
189 **36** 80 c. + 20 c. green 10 10
DESIGN: 25 c. One dorcas gazelle.

1961. 25th Anniv of Gen. Franco as Head of State.
190 – 25 c. grey 10 10
191 **37** 50 c. olive 10 10
192 – 70 c. green 10 10
193 **37** 1 p. orange 10 10
DESIGNS—VERT: 25 c. Map; 70 c. Aaiun Chapel.

38 A. Fernandez de Lugo **39** "Neurada procumbres linn"

1961. Stamp Day. Inscr "DIA DEL SELLO 1961".
194 **38** 10 c. + 5 c. salmon 10 10
195 – 25 c. + 10 c. plum 10 10
196 **38** 30 c. + 10 c. brown 10 10
197 – 1 p. + 10 c. orange 10 10
PORTRAIT: 25 c., 1 p. D. de Herrera.

1962. Flowers.
198 **39** 25 c. violet 10 10
199 – 50 c. sepia 10 10
200 – 70 c. green 10 10
201 **39** 1 p. orange 10 10
202 – 1 p. 50 turquoise 30 10
203 – 2 p. purple . . . . 1·10 10
204 **39** 3 p. blue . . . . 1·90 30
205 – 10 p. olive . . . . 4·00 1·40
FLOWERS: 50 c., 1 p. 50, 10 p. "Anabasis articulata moq"; 70 c., 2 p. "Euphorbia resinifera".

40 Two Barred Fishes **42** Seville Cathedral

41 Goats

1962. Child Welfare.
206 **40** 25 c. violet 10 10
207 – 50 c. green 10 10
208 **40** 1 p. brown 15 10
DESIGN—HORIZ: 50 c. Two fishes.

1962. Stamp Day.
209 **41** 15 c. green 10 10
210 – 35 c. purple 10 10
211 **41** 1 p. brown 15 10
DESIGN: 35 c. Sheep.

1963. Seville Flood Relief.
212 **42** 50 c. olive 15 10
213 1 p. brown 10 10

43 Cameleer and Camel **44** Dove in Hands

1963. Child Welfare. Inscr "PRO-INFANCIA 1963".
214 – 25 c. violet 10 10
215 **43** 50 c. grey 10 10
216 – 1 p. red 15 10
DESIGN: 25 c., 1 p. Three camels.

1963. "For Barcelona".
217 **44** 50 c. turquoise 10 10
218 1 p. brown 10 10

45 Fish ("Zeus faber")

1964. Stamp Day. Inscr "DIA DEL SELLO 1963".
219 **45** 25 c. violet 15 10
220 – 50 c. olive 20 10
221 **45** 1 p. brown 30 10
FISH—VERT: 50 c. "Cossus pulchra".

46 Striped Hawk Moth **47** Mounted Dromedary and Microphone

1964. Child Welfare.
222 **46** 25 c. violet 10 10
223 – 50 c. olive 20 10
224 **46** 1 p. red 40 15
DESIGN—VERT: 50 c. Goat moths.

1964.
225 **47** 25 c. purple 10 10
226 – 50 c. olive 10 10
227 – 70 c. green 10 10
228 **47** 1 p. purple 10 10
229 – 1 p. 50 turquoise 10 10
230 – 2 p. turquoise 15 10
231 – 3 p. blue 20 15
232 – 10 p. lake . . . . 1·40 65
DESIGNS: 50 c., 1 p. 50, 3 p. Flute-player; 70 c., 2, 10 p. Women drummer.

48 Barbary Ground Squirrel

1964. Stamp Day.
233 – 50 c. olive 10 10
234 **48** 1 p. lake 10 10
235 – 1 p. 50 green 10 10
DESIGN—VERT: 50 c., 1 p. 50, Eurasian red squirrel eating.

49 Doctor tending Patient, and Hospital

1965. 25th Anniv of End of Spanish Civil War.
236 – 50 c. olive 10 10
237 **49** 1 p. red 10 10
238 – 1 p. 50 blue 10 10
DESIGNS—VERT: 50 c. Saharan woman; 1 p. 50, Desert installation and cameleer.

50 "Anthia sexmaculata" (ground beetle) **51** Handball

1965. Child Welfare. Insects.
239 **50** 50 c. blue 10 10
240 – 1 p. green 10 10
241 **50** 1 p. 50 brown 15 10
242 – 3 p. blue . . . . 1·25 60
INSECTS—VERT: 1, 3 p. "Blepharopsis mendica" (praying mantis).

1965. Stamp Day.
243 **51** 50 c. red 10 10
244 – 1 p. purple 10 10
245 **51** 1 p. 50 blue 10 10
DESIGN: 1 p. Arms of Spanish Sahara.

52 Bows of "Rio de Oro"

1966. Child Welfare.

246	52	50 c. olive	10	10
247		1 p. brown	10	10
248	–	1 p. 50 green	15	10

DESIGN: 1 p. 50, Freighter "Fuerta Ventura".

53 "Parathunnus obesus" (fish)

54 Fig

1966. Stamp Day.

249	53	10 c. blue and yellow	10	10
250	–	40 c. grey and salmon	10	10
251	53	1 p. 50 brown and green	10	10
252	–	4 p. purple and green	15	10

DESIGN—VERT: 40 c., 4 p. "Mola mola" (fish).

1967. Child Welfare.

253	54	10 c. yellow and blue	10	10
254	–	40 c. purple and green	10	10
255	54	1 p. 50 yellow and green	10	10
256	–	4 p. orange and blue	15	10

DESIGN: 40 c., 4 p. Lupin.

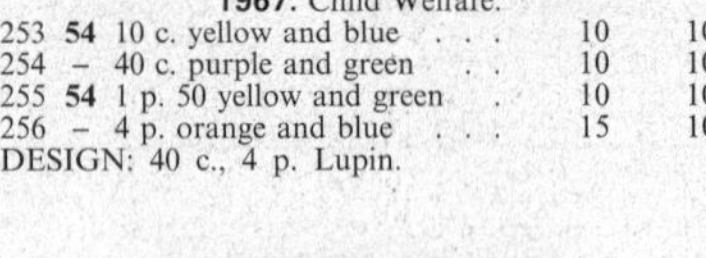

55 Quay, Aaiun

1967. Inauguration of Sahara Ports.

257	55	1 p. 50 brown and blue	10	10
258	–	4 p. ochre and blue	20	10

DESIGN: 4 p. Port of Villa Cisneros.

56 Ruddy Shelduck

56a Scorpio (scorpion)

1968. Stamp Day.

259	56	1 p. brown and green	35	10
260	–	1 p. 50 mauve and black	50	20
261	–	3 p. 50 lake and brown	65	40

DESIGNS—VERT: 1 p. 50, Greater flamingo. HORIZ: 3 p. 50, Rufous bushchat.

1968. Child Welfare. Signs of the Zodiac.

262	56a	1 p. mauve on yellow	10	10
263	–	1 p. 50 brown on pink	10	10
264	–	2 p. 50 violet on yellow	15	15

DESIGNS: 1 p. 50, Capricorn (goat); 2 p. 50, Virgo (virgin).

57 Dove, and Stamp within Posthorn

58 Head of Dorcas Gazelle

1968. Stamp Day.

265	57	1 p. blue and purple	10	10
266	–	1 p. 50 green & light green	10	10
267	–	2 p. 50 blue and orange	15	10

DESIGNS: 1 p. 50, Postal handstamp, stamps and letter; 2 p. 50, Saharan postman.

1969. Child Welfare.

268	58	1 p. brown and black	10	10
269	–	1 p. 50 brown and black	15	10
270	–	2 p. 50 brown and black	20	10
271	–	6 p. brown and black	30	10

DESIGNS: 1 p. 50, Dorcas gazelle tending young; 2 p. 50, Dorcas gazelle and camel; 6 p. Dorcas gazelle leaping.

59 Woman beating Drum

61 Dorcas Gazelle and Arms of El Aaiun

60 "Grammodes boisdeffrei" (moth)

1960. Stamp Day.

272	59	50 c. brown and bistre	15	10
273	–	1 p. 50 turquoise & green	15	10
274	–	2 p. blue and brown	15	30
275	–	25 p. brown and green	80	25

DESIGNS—VERT: 1 p. 50, Man playing flute. HORIZ: 2 p. Drum and mounted cameleer; 25 p. Flute.

1970. Child Welfare. As T **58**.

276	50 c. ochre and blue	10	10
277	2 p. brown and blue	15	10
278	2 p. 50 ochre and blue	20	10
279	6 p. ochre and blue	30	10

DESIGNS: 50 c. Fennec fox; 2 p. Fennec fox walking; 2 p. 50, Head of fennec fox; 6 p. Fennec fox family.

1970. Stamp Day. Butterflies. Multicoloured.

280	50 c. Type **60**	10	10
281	1 p. Type **60**	10	10
282	2 p. African monarch	25	10
283	5 p. As 2 p.	60	15
284	8 p. Spurge hawk moth	90	20

1971. Child Welfare.

285	61	1 p. multicoloured	10	10
286	–	2 p. green and olive	10	10
287	–	5 p. blue, brown and grey	15	10
288	–	25 p. green, grey & blue	70	15

DESIGNS—VERT: 25 p. Smara Mosque. HORIZ: 2 p. Tourist inn, Aaiun; 5 p. Assembly House, Aaiun.

63 Trumpeter Finch

1971. Stamp Day. Multicoloured.

290	1 p. 50 Type **63**	50	15
291	2 p. Type **63**	75	20
292	5 p. Cream-coloured courser	1·00	25
293	24 p. Lanner falcon	3·00	60

64 Seated Woman

65 Tuareg Woman

1972. Saharan Nomads.

294	64	1 p. black, pink and blue	10	10
295	–	1 p. 50 slate, lilac & brown	10	10
296	–	2 p. black, flesh & green	10	10
297	64	5 p. purple, olive & green	10	10
298	–	8 p. violet, green & black	20	10
299	–	10 p. green, grey & black	30	10
300	–	12 p. multicoloured	35	20
301	–	15 p. multicoloured	40	30
302	–	24 p. multicoloured	90	50

DESIGNS: 1 p. 50, 2 p. Squatting nomad; 8, 10 p. Head of nomad; 12 p. Woman with bangles; 15 p. Nomad with rifle; 24 p. Woman displaying trinkets.

1972. Child Welfare. Multicoloured.

303	8 p. Type **65**	20	10
304	12 p. Tuareg elder	30	15

66 Mother and Child

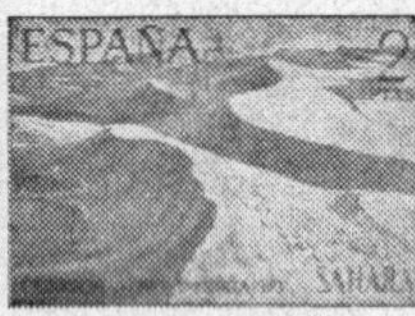

67 Sahara Desert

1972. Stamp Day. Multicoloured.

305	4 p. Type **66**	15	10
306	15 p. Nomad	40	15

1973. Child Welfare. Multicoloured.

307	2 p. Type **67**	10	10
308	7 p. City Gate, El Aaiun	15	10

68 Villa Cisneros

1973. Stamp Day. Multicoloured.

309	2 p. Type **68**	10	10
310	7 p. Tuareg (vert)	15	10

69 U.P.U. Monument, Berne

70 Archway, Smara Mosque

1974. Centenary of Universal Postal Union.

311	69	15 p. multicoloured	35	15

1974. Child Welfare. Multicoloured.

312	1 p. Type **70**	10	10
313	2 p. Villa Cisneros Mosque	15	10

71 Eagle Owl

1974. Stamp Day. Multicoloured.

314	2 p. Type **71**	90	20
315	5 p. Lappet-faced vulture	1·60	40

72 "Espana" Emblem and Spanish Sahara Stamp

74 Tuareg Elder

73 Desert Conference

1975. "Espana 75" International Stamp Exhibition, Madrid.

316	72	8 p. yellow, blue & black	15	10

1975. Child Welfare. Multicoloured.

317	1 p. 50 Type **73**	10	10
318	3 p. Desert oasis	10	10

1975.

319	74	3 p. purple, green & blk	10	10

EXPRESS LETTER STAMP

1943. Design as No. 63 inscr "URGENTE".

E80	25 c. red and myrtle	65	65

E 62 Despatch-rider

1971.

E289	E 62	10 p. brown and red	35	20

SPANISH WEST AFRICA Pt. 9

100 centimos = 1 peseta

Issues for use in Ifni and Spanish Sahara.

1 Native

2 Isabella the Catholic

1949. 75th Anniv of U.P.U.

1	1	4 p. green	1·75	85

1949. Air. Colonial Stamp Day.

2	2	5 p. brown	1·50	85

3 Tents

1950.

3	3	2 c. brown	10	10
4	–	5 c. violet	10	10
5	–	10 c. blue	10	10
6	–	15 c. black	15	10
7	3	25 c. brown	15	10
8	–	30 c. yellow	10	10
9	–	40 c. olive	10	10
10	–	45 c. red	10	10
11	3	50 c. orange	10	10
12	–	75 c. blue	15	15
13	–	90 c. green	10	10
14	–	1 p. grey	10	10
15	3	1 p. 35 violet	55	40
16	–	2 p. sepia	1·00	85
17	–	5 p. mauve	10·00	3·00
18	3	10 p. brown	20·00	13·00

DESIGNS: 5, 30, 75 c., 2 p. Palm trees, Lake Tinzgarrentz; 10, 40, 90 c., 5 p. Camels and irrigation; 15, 45 c., 1 p. Camel transport.

8 Camel Train

1951. Air.

19	–	25 c. yellow	30	10
20	8	50 c. mauve	15	10
21	–	1 p. green	35	10
22	–	2 p. blue	65	10
23	8	3 p. 25 violet	1·25	45
24	–	5 p. sepia	11·00	1·50
25	–	10 p. red	23·00	18·00

DESIGNS: 25 c., 2, 10 p. Desert camp; 1, 5 p. Four camels.

EXPRESS LETTER STAMP

E 10 Port Tilimenzo

1951.

E26	E 10	25 c. red	1·25	35

SUDAN Pt. 14

A territory in Africa, extending S. from Egypt towards the equator, jointly administered by Gt. Britain and Egypt until 1954 when the territory was granted a large measure of self-government. Became independent 1 Jan. 1956 (for issues before this date see volume 3).

1956. 1000 milliemes = 100 piastres = £1 Sudanese.
1993. Dinar.

52 "Independent Sudan"

1956. Independence Commemoration.
143 **52** 15 m. orange and purple 15 10
144 3 p. orange and blue 35 15
145 5 p. orange and green 50 35

53 Globe on Rhinoceros (Badge of Sudan) — 54 Sudanese Soldier and Farmer

1958. Arab Postal Congress, Khartoum.
146 **53** 15 m. orange and purple 20 10
147 3 p. orange and blue 35 15
148 5 p. orange and green 50 35

1959. 1st Anniv of Army Revolution.
149 **54** 15 m. yellow, blue & brown 15 10
150 3 p. multicoloured 50 20
151 55 m. multicoloured 65 40

1960. Inauguration of Arab League Centre, Cairo. As T **154a** of Syria.
152 15 m. black and green 15 10

55 Refugees — 56 Football

1960. World Refugee Year.
153 **55** 15 m. blue, black & brown 15 15
154 55 m. red, black and sepia 55 45

1960. Olympic Games, Rome.
155 **56** 15 m. multicoloured 20 10
156 3 p. multicoloured 45 25
157 55 m. multicoloured 65 35

57 Forest — 58 King Ta'rhaqa

1960. 5th World Forestry Congress, Seattle.
158 **57** 15 m. green, brown & red 15 10
159 3 p. green, brown and deep green 35 20
160 55 m. multicoloured 60 35

1961. Sudanese Nubian Monuments Preservation Campaign.
161 **58** 15 m. brown and green 20 10
162 3 p. violet and orange 35 20
163 55 m. brown and blue 60 35

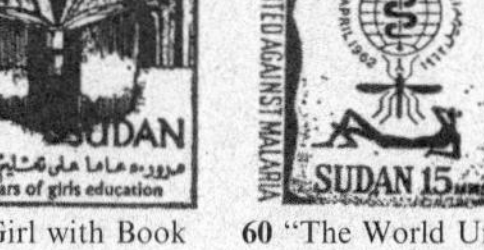

59 Girl with Book — 60 "The World United against Malaria"

1961. "50 Years of Girls' Education in the Sudan".
164 **59** 15 m. mauve, purple & bl 15 10
165 3 p. blue, orange & black 40 20
166 55 m. brown, green & blk 55 40

1962. Malaria Eradication.
167 **60** 15 m. violet, blue & black 15 10
168 55 m. green, emerald & blk 50 35

1962. Arab League Week. As T **76** of Libya but larger, 24×41 mm.
169 15 m. orange 15 10
170 55 m. turquoise 45 35

62 Republican Palace — 63 Nile Felucca

64 Camel Postman — 65 Campaign Emblem and "Millet" Cobs

1962.
185 **62** 5 m. blue 10 10
186 – 10 m. purple and blue 10 10
187 – 15 m. purple, orge & bis 10 10
188 **62** 2 p. purple 10 10
189 – 3 p. brown and green 20 10
190 – 35 m. brn, dp brn & grn 55 10
191 – 4 p. mauve, red & blue 55 10
192 – 55 m. black and green 55 20
193 – 6 p. brown and blue 65 20
194 – 8 p. green 65 20
195 **63** 10 p. brown, bistre & bl 80 35
196 – 20 p. green and bronze 1·40 55
194a – 25 p. brown and green 10 10
197 – 50 p. green, blue & blk 3·50 1·25
469 **64** £S1 brown and green 7·25 4·25
198 – £S5 green and brown 45 25
199 **63** £S10 orange and green 90 40
DESIGNS: As Type **62**—HORIZ: 15 m. "Tabbaque" (food cover); 55 m., 6, 25 p. Cattle; 8 p. Date palms. VERT: 10 m., 3 p. Cotton picking; 35 m., 4 p. Wild game. As Type **63**—HORIZ: 20 p., £S5 Bohein Temple; 50 p. Sennar Dam.

1963. Freedom from Hunger.
226 **65** 15 m. green and brown 15 15
227 55 m. violet, lilac & blue 55 35

66 Centenary Emblem and Medallions — 67 "Knight"

1963. Centenary of Red Cross.
228 **66** 15 m. multicoloured 35 15
229 55 m. multicoloured 65 35

1964. Nubian Monuments Preservation. Frescoes from Faras Church, Nubia. Multicoloured.
230 15 m. Type **67** 20 15
231 30 m. "Saint" (horiz) 35 20
232 55 m. "Angel" 85 55

68 Sudan Map — 69 Chainbreakers and Mrs. E. Roosevelt

1964. New York World's Fair. Multicoloured.
233 15 m. Khashm el Girba Dam 10 10
234 3 p. Sudan Pavilion 20 15
235 55 m. Type **68** 50 30
Nos. 233/4 are horiz.

1964. 80th Birth Anniv of Mrs. Eleanor Roosevelt (Human Rights pioneer).
236 **69** 15 m. blue and black 10 10
237 3 p. violet and black 30 15
238 55 m. brown and black 45 30

70 Postal Union Emblem — 71 I.T.U. Symbol and Emblems

1964. 10th Anniv of Arab Postal Unions' Permanent Bureau.
239 **70** 15 m. black, gold and red 10 10
240 3 p. black, gold and green 30 15
241 55 m. black, gold and violet 45 30

1965. Centenary of I.T.U.
242 **71** 15 m. brown and gold 10 10
243 3 p. black and gold 30 15
244 55 m. green and gold 45 30

72 Gurashi (martyr) and Demonstrators

1965. 1st Anniv of 21 October Revolution.
245 **72** 15 m. black and brown 10 10
246 3 p. black and red 20 15
247 55 m. black and grey 45 30

73 I.C.Y. Emblem — 74 El Siddig El Mahdi

1965. International Co-operation Year.
248 **73** 15 m. lilac and black 10 10
249 3 p. green and black 20 15
250 55 m. red and black 45 30

1966. 5th Death Anniv of Imam El Siddig El Mahdi.
251 **74** 15 m. violet and blue 35 15
252 3 p. brown and orange 50 35
253 55 m. brown and grey 1·10 60

75 M. Zaroug (politician)

1966. Mubarak Zaroug Commemoration.
254 **75** 15 m. olive and pink 35 15
255 3 p. green and light green 50 35
256 55 m. brown and chestnut 1·10 55

76 W.H.O. Building — 77 Crests of Upper Nile, Blue Nile and Kassala Provinces

1966. Inaug of W.H.O. Headquarters, Geneva.
257 **76** 15 m. blue 10 10
258 3 p. purple 20 15
259 55 m. brown 45 30

1967. "The Month of the South".
260 **77** 15 m. multicoloured 10 10
261 – 3 p. multicoloured 20 10
262 – 55 m. multicoloured 80 40
DESIGNS (Crests of): 3 p. Equatoria, Kordofan and Khartoum Provinces; 55 m. Bahr El Gazal, Darfur and Northern Provinces.

78 Giraffe and Tourist Emblem — 79 Handclasp Emblem

1967. International Tourist Year.
263 **78** 15 m. multicoloured 20 10
264 3 p. multicoloured 45 25
265 55 m. multicoloured 70 25

1967. Arab Summit Conference, Khartoum.
266 **79** 15 m. multicoloured 10 10
267 3 p. green and orange 20 10
268 55 m. violet and yellow 45 20

80 P.L.O. Shoulder Flash

1967. Palestine Liberation Organization.
269 **80** 15 m. multicoloured 10 10
270 3 p. multicoloured 20 10
271 55 m. multicoloured 45 20

81 Mohamed Nur El Din

1968. Nur El Din (politician) Commemoration.
272 **81** 15 m. green and blue 35 15
273 3 p. bistre and blue 50 30
274 55 m. ultramarine & blue 1·10 50

82 Abdullahi El Fadil El Mahdi

1968. Abdullahi El Fadil El Mahdi (Ansar leader) Commemoration.
275 **82** 15 m. violet and blue 35 15
276 3 p. green and blue 50 30
277 55 m. green and orange 1·10 50

83 Ahmed Yousif Hashim

1968. 10th Death Anniv of Ahmed Yousif Hashim (journalist).
278 **83** 15 m. brown and green 35 10
279 3 p. brown and blue 50 10
280 55 m. violet and blue 1·10 30

84 Mohamed Ahmed El Mardi

1968. Mohamed Ahmed El Mardi (politician) Commemoration.
281 **84** 15 m. ultramarine and blue 35 15
282 3 p. orange, blue and pink 50 35
283 55 m. brown and blue 1·10 55

85 Douglas DC-3 Airliner

1968. 20th Anniv of Sudan Airways. Mult.

284 15 m. Type **85** 10 10
285 2 p. De Havilland Dove 20 10
286 3 p. Fokker Friendship 40 20
287 55 m. Hawker Siddeley Comet 4C 65 45

87 Anniversary and Bank Emblems

1969. 5th Anniv of African Development Bank.

288 **87** 2 p. black and gold 15 10
289 4 p. red and gold 30 15
290 65 m. green and gold 45 20

88 I.L.O. Emblem

1969. 50th Anniv of Int Labour Organization.

291 **88** 2 p. black, red and blue 15 10
292 4 p. black, blue & yellow 30 15
293 65 m. black, mauve & grn 45 20

89 "Solidarity of the People"

1970. 1st Anniv of May 25th Revolution (1st issue).

294 **89** 2 p. multicoloured
295 4 p. multicoloured
296 65 m. multicoloured
Set of 3 25·00

Nos. 294/6 were withdrawn on day of issue (25 May) as being unsatisfactory. They were later replaced by Nos. 297/9 and the 1st issue may be easily distinguished by the figures of value which appear on the extreme left of the design.

90 "Solidarity of the People"

1970. 1st Anniv of May 25th Revolution (2nd issue).

297 **90** 2 p. brown, green and red 15 10
298 4 p. blue, green and red 35 15
299 65 m. green, blue and red 50 25

91 Map of Egypt, Libya and Sudan

92 I.E.Y. Emblem

1971. 1st Anniv of Tripoli Charter.

300 **91** 2 p. green, black and red 20 10

1971. International Education Year.

301 **92** 2 p. multicoloured 15 10
302 4 p. multicoloured 30 10
303 65 m. multicoloured 45 20

93 Laurel and Bayonets on Star

94 Emblems of Arab League and Sudan Republic

1971. 2nd Anniv of 25th May Revolution.

304 **93** 2 p. black, green & yell 15 10
305 4 p. black, green and blue 35 15
306 10½ p. black, green & grey 60 35

1972. 25th Anniv of Arab League.

307 **94** 2 p. black, yellow & green 15 10
308 4 p. multicoloured 35 15
309 10½ p. multicoloured 70 35

95 U.N. Emblem and Text

96 Cogwheel Emblem

1972. 25th Anniv of United Nations.

310 **95** 2 p. green, orange & red 15 10
311 4 p. blue, orange & red 35 15
312 10½ p. black, orge & red 70 40

1972. World Standards Day (14.10.71).

313 **96** 2 p. multicoloured 15 10
314 4 p. multicoloured 40 20
315 10½ p. multicoloured 85 55

97 Sudanese Arms and Pres. Nemery

1972. Presidential Elections.

316 **97** 2 p. multicoloured 15 10
317 4 p. multicoloured 35 15
318 10½ p. multicoloured 70 40

98 Arms and Emblem

1972. Socialist Union's Founding Congress (January, 1972).

319 **98** 2 p. black, yellow & blue 10 10
320 4 p. mauve, yellow & black 20 15
321 10½ p. black, yellow & grn 65 25

99 Airmail Envelope and A.P.U. Emblem

1972. 10th Anniv of African Postal Union (1971).

322 **99** 2 p. multicoloured 10 10
323 4 p. multicoloured 20 15
324 10½ p. multicoloured 80 30

100 Provincial Emblems

101 Emperor Haile Selassie of Ethiopia

1973. National Unity.

325 **100** 2 p. multicoloured 10 10
326 – 4 p. brown and black 20 10
327 – 10½ p. green, orange & sil 80 35

DESIGNS—HORIZ: 4 p. Revolutionary Council. VERT: 10½ p. Entwined trees.

1973. 80th Birthday of Emperor Haile Selassie.

328 **101** 2 p. multicoloured 20 15
329 4 p. multicoloured 50 20
330 10½ p. multicoloured 1·10 45

102 President Nasser

104 Scout Emblem

103 Ancient Gateway

1973. 3rd Death Anniv of Pres. Nasser.

331 **102** 2 p. black 10 10
332 4 p. black and green 20 10
333 10½ p. black and violet 65 35

1973. 10th Anniv of World Food Programme.

334 **103** 2 p. multicoloured 10 10
335 4 p. multicoloured 20 10
336 10½ p. multicoloured 80 45

1973. World Scout Conference, Nairobi and Addis Ababa.

337 **104** 2 p. multicoloured 30 10
338 4 p. multicoloured 45 20
339 10½ p. multicoloured 95 55

105 Interpol Emblem

1974. 50th Anniv of International Criminal Police Organization (Interpol).

340 **105** 2 p. multicoloured 10 10
341 4 p. multicoloured 30 15
342 10½ p. multicoloured 70 35

106 K.S.M. Building, Khartoum University

107 African Postal Union Emblem

1974. 50th Anniv of Faculty of Medicine, Khartoum University.

343 **106** 2 p. multicoloured 15 10
344 4 p. green, brown & red 35 10
345 10½ p. red, brown & grn 70 45

1974. Centenary of Universal Postal Union. Multicoloured.

346 2 p. Type **107** 10 10
347 4 p. Arab Postal Union emblem 20 15
348 10½ p. Universal Postal Union emblem 80 35

108 A. A. Latif and A. F. Elmaz (revolution leaders)

1975. 50th Anniv of 1924 Revolution.

349 **108** 2½ p. green and blue 10 10
350 4 p. red and blue 20 10
351 10½ p. brown and blue 80 35

109 Bank and Commemorative Emblems

1975. 10th Anniv of African Development Bank.

352 **109** 2½ p. multicoloured 10 10
353 4 p. multicoloured 20 10
354 10½ p. multicoloured 80 35

110 Earth Station and Camel Postman

1976. Inauguration of Satellite Earth Station.

355 **110** 2½ p. multicoloured 15 10
356 4 p. multicoloured 30 15
357 10½ p. multicoloured 65 35

111 Woman, Flag and IWY Emblem

1976. International Women's Year.

358 **111** 2½ p. multicoloured 10 10
359 4 p. multicoloured 30 15
360 10½ p. multicoloured 70 35

112 Arms of Sudan and "Gold Medal"

113 "Unity"

1976. Olympic Games, Montreal.

361 **112** 2½ p. multicoloured 40 10
362 4 p. multicoloured 45 20
363 10½ p. multicoloured 1·10 55

1977. 5th Anniv of National Unity.

364 **113** 2½ p. red, black and blue 10 10
365 4 p. red, black and green 20 15
366 10½ p. red, black & brown 65 30

114 Archbishop Capucci

1977. Archbishop Capucci's Imprisonment. Commemoration.

367 **114** 2½ p. black 45 10
368 4 p. black and green 65 20
369 10½ p. black and red 1·10 45

115 Fair Emblem and Flags

1978. International Fair, Khartoum.

370 **115** 3 p. multicoloured 20 10
371 4 p. multicoloured 35 15
372 10½ p. multicoloured 55 25

117 Commemorative and A.P.U. Emblems

1978. Silver Jubilee of Arab Postal Union.

373 **117** 3 p. black, silver & red 15 10
374 4 p. black, silver & green 30 10
375 10½ p. black, silver & blue 65 35

118 Jinnah and Sudanese Flag

1978. Birth Cent of Mohammed Ali Jinnah (first Governor-General of Pakistan).

376	118	3 p. multicoloured	20	10
377		4 p. multicoloured	35	15
378		10½ p. multicoloured	55	25

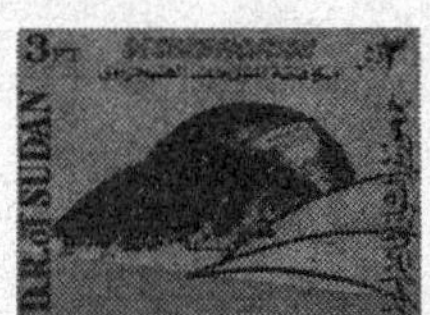

119 Desert Scene

1978. U.N. Conference on Desertification.

379	119	3 p. black, yellow & green	20	10
380		4 p. black, pink & green	35	15
381		10½ p. black, brown & grn	85	45

120 Lion God Apedemek and O.A.U. Emblem — 121 Sudanese Flag

1978. 15th African Summit Conference, Khartoum.

382	120	3 p. black, yellow & purple	15	10
383		4 p. black, yellow & blue	30	15
384		10½ p. black, yellow & grn	55	30

1979. 10th Anniv of May Revolution.

385	121	3½ p. multicoloured	15	10
386		6 p. multicoloured	35	15
387		13 p. multicoloured	60	30

122 I.B.E. and U.N.E.S.C.O. Emblems — 123 I.Y.C. Emblem and Hands carrying Child

1980. 50th Anniv of International Bureau of Education (1979).

388	122	4½ p. black and orange	20	15
389		8 p. black and green	45	25
390		15½ p. black and blue	90	40

1980. International Year of the Child (1979).

391	123	4½ p. multicoloured	20	15
392		8 p. multicoloured	40	25
393		15½ p. multicoloured	70	40

124 National Flag, Arms and Sudanese Warrior

1982. 25th Anniv of Independence.

396	124	60 m. multicoloured	20	10
397		120 m. multicoloured	45	20
398		250 m. multicoloured	90	45

125 Hands reaching for F.A.O. Emblem on Map of Sudan

1983. World Food Day.

399	125	60 m. blue, green & blk	20	10
400	–	120 m. green, black & red	45	20
401	–	250 m. green, black & red	90	45

DESIGNS: 120 m. F.A.O. emblem, crops and cattle; 250 m. Emblem, crops and cattle on map of Sudan.

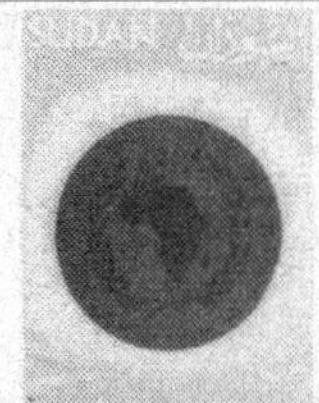

126 Commission Emblem — 127 Warrior on Horseback

1984. 25th Anniv of Economic Commission for Africa.

402	126	10 p. lilac and silver	20	15
403		25 p. blue and silver	55	35
404		40 p. green and silver	1·00	60

1984. Centenary of Shaykan Battle, Kordofan.

405	127	10 p. multicoloured	20	15
406		25 p. multicoloured	55	35
407		40 p. multicoloured	90	50

128 Sudan Olympic Committee Emblem — 129 Emblem and Flags

1984. First Olympic Week.

408	128	10 p. multicoloured	20	15
409		25 p. multicoloured	60	30
410		40 p. multicoloured	1·10	55

1984. 2nd Anniv of Sudan–Egypt Co-operation Treaty.

411	129	10 p. multicoloured	20	15
412		25 p. multicoloured	55	35
413		40 p. multicoloured	90	50

130 Institute Emblem — 131 Map and Broken Chain

1985. 50th Anniv of Bakht Erruda Teacher Training Institute, Eddueim Town.

414	130	10 p. multicoloured	20	15
415		25 p. multicoloured	55	35
416		40 p. multicoloured	90	50

1986. 1st Anniv of 6th April Rising.

417	131	5 p. black, green & brn	10	10
418		25 p. black, green & bl	55	30
419		40 p. black, green & brn	90	45

132 Fishermen hauling in Nets

1988. World Food Day (1986).

420	132	25 p. black, silver and brown	30	15
421	–	30 p. green and black	35	15
422	–	50 p. multicoloured	55	35
423	–	75 p. black, deep blue and blue	80	45
424	–	300 p. blue, black and silver	3·00	1·40

DESIGNS—VERT: 30 p. Two fishes. HORIZ: 50 p. Plant and globe; 75 p. Outline of fish and waves; 300 p. Shoal of fish.

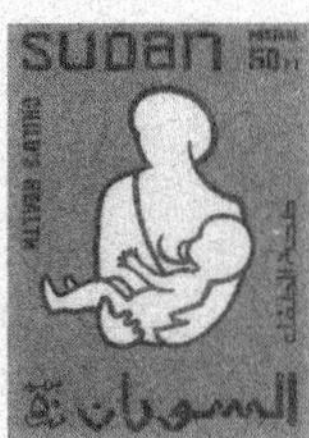

133 Mother breastfeeding Baby — 134 Emblem

1988. Child Health Campaign.

426	133	50 p. black and mauve	55	20
427	–	75 p. multicoloured	85	35
428	–	100 p. multicoloured	1·10	45
429	–	150 p. multicoloured	1·60	65

DESIGNS—HORIZ: No. 427, Mother spoon-feeding child; 428, Child being given oral vaccination; 429, Children on scales.

1988. 30th Anniv of Sudan Red Crescent.

431	134	40 p. black, yellow & red	40	30
432	–	100 p. black, red & green	90	60
433	–	150 p. black, red & blue	1·25	80

DESIGNS: 100 p. Candle; 150 p. Figure with crescent on head.

135 Anniversary Emblem

1988. 75th Anniv of Bank of Khartoum. Mult.

434	40 p. Type **135**	40	20
435	100 p. Bubbles and medal	90	45
436	150 p. Inscription and emblem	1·25	65

136 Plough — 137 Emblem

1988. World Food Day. The Small Farmer. Multicoloured.

437	40 p. Type **136**	40	20
438	100 p. Farmer ploughing	90	45
439	150 p. Farmer drawing water from river	1·25	65

1989. "Freedom of Palestine".

440	137	100 p. multicoloured	50	20
441		150 p. multicoloured	80	35
442		200 p. multicoloured	95	55

138 Crowd of Youths — 139 Emblem

1989. Palestinian "Intifada" Movement.

443	138	100 p. multicoloured	50	20
444		150 p. multicoloured	80	35
445		200 p. multicoloured	95	55

1989. 25th Anniv of African Development Bank.

446	139	100 p. green, blk & silver	50	20
447		150 p. blue, black & silver	80	35
448		200 p. purple, blk & silver	95	55

140 Map — 141 Leopard

1990. 34th Anniv of Independence.

449	140	50 p. blue and yellow	20	10
450		100 p. brown and yellow	50	20
451		150 p. mauve and yellow	80	35
452		200 p. mauve and yellow	1·00	55

1990. Mammals. Multicoloured.

453	25 p. Type **141**	15	10
454	50 p. African elephant	35	20
455	75 p. Giraffe (vert)	45	35
456	100 p. White rhinoceros	60	45
457	125 p. Addax (vert)	65	55

142 Pied ("Zande") Hornbill — 146 Flag

143 Mardoum Dance

1990. Birds. Multicoloured.

458	25 p. Type **142**	25	10
459	50 p. Marabou stork	60	20
460	75 p. Crested ("Buff-crested") bustard	85	35
461	100 p. Saddle-bill stork	1·10	50
462	150 p. Waldrapp ("Bald-headed Ibis")	1·50	60

1990. Traditional Dances. Multicoloured.

463	25 p. Type **143**	15	10
464	50 p. Zandi dance (vert)	35	20
465	75 p. Kambala dance (vert)	45	35
466	100 p. Nubian dance (vert)	60	45
467	125 p. Sword dance	65	55

1990. No. 195 surch with new value in Arabic.

468	63	£S1 on 10 p. brn, bis & bl	10	10

1991. 1st Anniv of "National Salvation Revolution".

470	146	150 p. multicoloured	10	10
471		200 p. multicoloured	15	10
472		250 p. multicoloured	20	10
473		£S5 multicoloured	40	25
474		£S10 multicoloured	75	65

147 Whale-headed Stork ("Shoebill") — 148 Camel Postman

1991. (a) As T **147**. Multicoloured.

475	25 p. Type **147**	10	10
476	50 p. Sunflower	10	10
477	75 p. Collecting gum arabic	10	10
478	100 p. Cotton	10	10
479	125 p. South African crowned crane	10	10
480	150 p. Kenana Sugar Co Ltd (29½ × 25 mm)	10	10
481	175 p. Secretary bird (24 × 30½ mm)	15	10
482	£S2 Atbara Cement Factory (29½ × 25 mm)	15	10
483	250 p. King Taharka (statue) (26 × 37 mm)	20	10
484	£S3 Republican Palace (26 × 37 mm)	25	15
485	£S4 Hug (scent container) (24 × 30½ mm)	30	20
486	£S5 Gabanah (coffee pot) (24 × 30½ mm)	40	30

(b) As T **148**. Multicoloured.

487	£S8 Devil firefish (horiz)	60	50
488	£S10 Goat, ox and camel (horiz)	75	65
489	£S15 Nubian ibex	1·25	1·00
490	£S20 Type **148**	1·50	1·10

150 Campaign Emblem — (151)

1991. Pan-African Campaign against Rinderpest.

507	150	£S1 black and green	10	10
508		£S2 violet and green	15	10
509		£S5 orange and green	40	30

1993. Various stamps handstamped as T **151**.

510	–	1 d. on 100 p. multicoloured (No. 478)	10	10
511	–	2 d. on £S2 multicoloured (No. 482)	20	10
512	147	2½ d. on 25 p. multicoloured (No. 475)	25	15
513	–	3 d. on £S3 multicoloured (No. 484)	30	20
514	–	4 d. on £S4 multicoloured (No. 485)	40	25

152 Emblem — 153 Arabic Script and Hearts

1993. 500th Anniv of Fung Sultanate and Abdalab Islamic Shaikhdom. Multicoloured.

515		£S4 Type **152**	40	25
516		£S5 Arabic script on bottle	50	30
517		750 p. Arabic script in cartouche and helmet (horiz)	80	50

Nos. 515/17 were sold at 4, 5 and 7½ dinar respectively.

1993. International Human Rights Day.

518	**153**	£S4 multicoloured	40	25
519	–	£S5 multicoloured	50	30
520	–	750 p. black, green and red	80	50

DESIGNS—HORIZ: £S5 Rainbow breaking through chains. VERT: 750 p. Rose and Arabic script.

Nos. 518/20 were sold at 4, 5 and 7½ dinar respectively.

154 Feeding Young **155** Olympic Flag

1994. The Wild Ass. Multicoloured.

521		4 d. Type **154**	15	10
522		8 d. Adult	35	20
523		10 d. Adult galloping	40	25
524		15 d. Head of adult	60	35

1994. Centenary of International Olympic Committee.

525	**155**	5 d. multicoloured	20	10
526		7 d. multicoloured	30	20
527		15 d. multicoloured	60	35

156 Anniversary Emblem (157)

1994. 50th Anniv of I.C.A.O.

528	**156**	5 d. purple, yellow & blk	20	10
529		7 d. brown, yellow & blk	30	20
530		15 d. blue, yellow & black	60	35

1995. Various stamps handstamped as T **157**.

531		2½ d. on 25 p. green and brown (No. 194a)	10	10
532		15 d. on 150 p. multicoloured (No. 480)	45	25
533		20 d. on 75 p. multicoloured (No. 477)	60	35

158 Goalkeeper **159** Map and Emblem

1995. World Cup Football Championship, U.S.A. (1994). Multicoloured.

534		4 d. Type **158**	10	10
535		5 d. Type **158**	15	10
536		7 d. Player in green shirt	15	10
537		8 d. As No. 533 but red shirt	20	10
538		10 d. Player heading ball	25	15
539		15 d. Brazilian player	40	25
540		20 d. German player	50	30
541		25 d. American player	60	35
542		35 d. As No. 537	85	50

1995. 50th Anniv of Arab League.

544	**159**	15 d. green and black	25	15
545		25 d. blue and black	40	25
546		30 d. violet and black	45	25

160 Emblem

1996. Common Market for Eastern and Southern Africa.

547	**160**	15 d. multicoloured	15	10
548		25 d. multicoloured	25	15
549		30 d. multicoloured	35	20

OFFICIAL STAMPS

ح.س.

(O 65 "S.G.")

1962. Nos. 171/84 optd with Type O **65** (larger on 10 p. to £S10).

O185	**62**	5 m. blue	10	10
O186	–	10 m. purple and blue	10	10
O187	–	15 m. pur, orge & bis	10	10
O188	**62**	2 p. violet	10	10
O189	–	3 p. brown and green	45	10
O190	–	35 m. brown, deep brown and green	55	20
O191	–	4 p. purple, red & bl	65	20
O192	–	55 m. brown & green	90	20
O193	–	6 p. brown and blue	90	35
O194	–	8 p. green	1·10	55
O222	**63**	10 p. brown, blk & bl	1·10	55
O223	–	20 p. green and olive	2·75	90
O223a	–	25 p. brown and green	10	10
O224	–	50 p. green, bl & blk	4·50	2·00
O198	**64**	£S1 brown and green	9·00	4·50
O226	–	£S5 green and brown	65	40
O227	**63**	£S10 orange and blue	1·40	85

1991. Nos. 475/90 optd similarly to Type O **65**.

O491		25 p. multicoloured	10	10
O492		50 p. multicoloured	10	10
O493		75 p. multicoloured	10	10
O494		100 p. multicoloured	15	10
O495		125 p. multicoloured	15	10
O496		150 p. multicoloured	20	10
O497		175 p. multicoloured	25	15
O498		£S2 multicoloured	25	15
O499		250 p. multicoloured	35	20
O500		£S3 multicoloured	40	25
O501		£S4 multicoloured	55	35
O502		£S5 multicoloured	65	40
O503		£S8 multicoloured	1·10	65
O504		£S10 multicoloured	1·40	85
O505		£S15 multicoloured	2·00	1·25
O506		£S20 multicoloured	2·75	1·75

SURINAM Pt. 4; Pt. 20

A Netherlands colony on the north-east coast of South America. In December 1954 Surinam became an autonomous state within the Kingdom of the Netherlands.

Became an independent state in November 1975.

100 cents = 1 gulden

1 King William III

3

1873. No gum.

32	**1**	1 c. grey	2·50	2·50
33		2 c. yellow	1·40	1·40
14		2½ c. red	1·40	1·40
15		3 c. green	20·00	16·00
16		5 c. lilac	16·00	5·25
17		10 c. bistre	3·50	2·00
34		12½ c. blue	16·00	7·25
18		15 c. grey	21·00	7·25
19		20 c. green	35·00	29·00
20		25 c. blue	80·00	9·00
22		30 c. brown	35·00	32·00
23		40 c. brown	32·00	29·00
12		50 c. brown	29·00	18·00
35		1 g. grey and brown	50·00	50·00
13		2½ g. brown and green	70·00	65·00

The gulden values are larger.

1890.

44	**3**	1 c. grey	1·75	1·00
45		2 c. brown	2·50	2·10
46		2½ c. red	2·10	1·75
47		3 c. green	5·00	3·25
48		5 c. blue	22·00	1·00

1892. Surch **2½ CENT.**

53	**1**	2½ c. on 50 c. brown	£275	10·00

5

6 Queen Wilhelmina

1892. No gum.

56	**5**	2½ c. black and yellow	1·40	90

1892.

63	**6**	10 c. bistre	35·00	2·75
64		12½ c. mauve	40·00	5·25
65		15 c. grey	3·25	2·50
66		20 c. green	3·50	2·50
67		25 c. blue	9·00	4·50
68		30 c. brown	4·50	3·50

1898. Surch **10 CENT.**

69	**1**	10 c. on 12½ c. blue	25·00	3·50
70		10 c. on 15 c. grey	60·00	50·00
71		10 c. on 20 c. green	3·00	2·75
72		10 c. on 25 c. blue	4·50	4·50
74		10 c. on 30 c. brown	4·50	4·50

1900. Stamps of Netherlands surch **SURINAME** and value.

77	**13**	50 c. on 50 c. red & green	22·00	6·25
78	**11**	1 g. on 1 g. green	20·00	11·00
79		2½ g. on 2½ g. lilac	16·00	10·00

1900. Surch.

83	**1**	25 c. on 40 c. brown	2·50	2·50
84		25 c. on 50 c. brown	2·50	1·75
86		50 c. on 1 g. grey & brown	30·00	27·00
82		50 c. on 2½ g. brown & green	£130	£140

11 (shaded background) 12

13

1902.

87	**11**	½ c. lilac	90	75
88		1 c. green	1·75	1·00
89		2 c. brown	10·00	3·50
90		2½ c. green	4·50	40
91		3 c. yellow	7·25	4·00
92		5 c. red	7·25	40
93		7½ c. grey	15·00	6·75
94	**12**	10 c. slate	10·00	70
95		12½ c. blue	3·50	15
96		15 c. brown	27·00	9·00
97		20 c. green	25·00	4·50
98		22½ c. green and brown	20·00	10·50
99		25 c. violet	16·00	1·00
100		30 c. brown	40·00	12·50
101		50 c. brown	30·00	7·75

1907.

102	**13**	1 g. purple	50·00	14·50
103		2½ g. slate	50·00	50·00

14

17

1909. Roul or perf. No gum.

104	**14**	5 c. red	10·00	8·00

1911. Surch with crown and value.

106	**3**	½ c. on 1 c. grey	1·40	70
107		½ c. on 2 c. brown	9·00	7·50
108	**6**	15 c. on 25 c. blue	65·00	50·00
109		20 c. on 30 c. brown	10·00	7·25
110	–	30 c. on 2½ g. on 2½ g. purple (No. 79)	£110	£100

1912. No gum.

113	**17**	½ c. lilac	90	90
114		2½ c. green	90	90
115		5 c. red	7·50	7·50
116		12½ c. blue	9·00	9·00

18 (unshaded background)

19

20

21

1913. With or without gum.

117	**18**	½ c. lilac	20	25
118		1 c. green	20	15
119		1½ c. blue	20	15
120		2 c. brown	1·40	1·10
121		2½ c. green	90	10
122		3 c. yellow	75	40
123		3 c. green	2·50	2·25
125		4 c. blue	7·50	4·25
126		5 c. pink	1·40	10
127		5 c. green	1·75	75
128		5 c. violet	1·40	10
129		6 c. buff	2·50	2·25
130		6 c. red	2·00	30
131		7½ c. brown	1·00	15
132		7½ c. red	1·25	30
133		7½ c. yellow	8·00	8·00
134		10 c. lilac	4·50	4·50
135		10 c. red	3·75	55
136	**19**	10 c. red	1·25	45
137		12½ c. blue	1·50	40
138		12½ c. red	1·75	2·00
139		15 c. green	45	45
140		15 c. blue	6·50	4·00
142		20 c. blue	2·25	1·75
143		20 c. green	3·00	2·75
144		22½ c. orange	2·50	2·25
145		25 c. mauve	3·50	30
146		30 c. grey	4·25	90
147		32½ c. violet and orange	13·50	17·00
148		35 c. blue and orange	4·50	12·50
149	**20**	50 c. green	4·00	70
150		1 g. brown	5·25	55
151		1½ g. purple	30·00	30·00
152a		2½ g. pink	25·00	23·00

1923. Queen's Silver Jubilee.

169a	**21**	5 c. green	90	55
170		10 c. red	1·40	1·25
171		20 c. blue	3·00	2·40
172a		50 c. orange	16·00	19·00
173		1 g. purple	23·00	12·00
174		2 g. 50 grey	60·00	£190
175		5 g. brown	80·00	£225

1925. Surch.

176	**18**	3 c. on 5 c. green	70	80
177	**19**	10 c. on 12½ c. red	1·60	1·50
180		12½ c. on 22½ c. orange	21·00	24·00
178		15 c. on 12½ c. blue	1·25	1·10
179		15 c. on 20 c. blue	1·10	1·00

1926. Postage Due stamps surch **Frankeerzegel 12½ CENT SURINAME.** (a) In three lines with bars.

181	D **6**	12½ c. on 40 c. mauve and black	2·50	2·50

(b) In four lines without bars.

182	D **6**	12½ c. on 40 c. lilac	23·00	23·00

28

29

1927.
183 **28** 10 c. red 70 30
184 12½ c. orange 1·40 1·50
185 15 c. blue 1·60 45
186 20 c. blue 1·60 70
187 21 c. brown 15·00 14·50
188 22½ c. brown 7·25 9·00
189 25 c. purple 2·50 55
190 30 c. green 2·50 90
191 35 c. sepia 2·75 3·00

1927. Green Cross Fund. Various designs incorporating green cross.
192 **29** 2 c. + 2 c. green & slate 1·00 1·00
193 – 5 c. + 3 c. green & purple 1·00 1·00
194 – 10 c. + 3 c. green & red 1·50 1·50

1927. Unissued Marine Insurance stamps (as Type M **22** of Netherlands but inscr "SURINAME") surch **FRANKEER ZEGEL** and value.
195 3 c. on 15 c. green 15 20
196 10 c. on 60 c. red 20 25
197 12½ c. on 75 c. brown 25 15
198 15 c. on 1 g. 50 blue 1·90 1·90
199 25 c. on 2 g. 25 brown 4·50 4·25
200 30 c. on 4½ g. black 10·00 8·50
201 50 c. on 7½ g. red 4·50 4·25

32 Indigenous Disease **33** The Good Smaritan

1928. Governor Van Heemstrastichting Medical Foundation Fund.
202 **32** 1½ c. + 1½ c. blue 4·00 4·00
203 2 c. + 2 c. green 4·00 4·00
204 5 c. + 3 c. violet 4·00 4·00
205 7½ c. + 2½ c. red 4·00 4·00

1929. Green Cross Fund.
206 **33** 1½ c. + 1½ c. green 5·75 5·75
207 2 c. + 2 c. red 5·75 5·75
208 5 c. + 3 c. blue 5·75 5·75
209 6 c. + 4 c. black 5·75 5·75

1930. No. 132 surch **6**.
210 **18** 6 c. on 7½ c. red 1·60 95

35 Mercury and Posthorn **37** Mother and Child

1930. Air.
276 **35** 10 c. red 2·00 80
212 15 c. blue 3·25 55
213 20 c. green 10 20
214 40 c. red 20 30
215 60 c. purple 40 35
216 1 g. black 1·25 1·40
217 1½ g. brown 1·40 1·50
281 2½ g. yellow 12·50 11·00
282 5 g. green £250 £275
283 10 g. bistre 29·00 42·00

1931. Air. "Dornier 10" Flight. Optd **Vlucht Do. X. 1931**.
218 **35** 10 c. red 18·00 15·00
219 15 c. blue 18·00 15·00
220 20 c. green 18·00 15·00
221 40 c. red 27·00 22·00
222 60 c. purple 60·00 50·00
223 1 g. black 70·00 60·00
224 1½ g. brown 70·00 65·00

1931. Child Welfare.
225 **37** 1½ c. + 1½ c. black 4·00 4·00
226 2 c. + 2 c. red 4·00 4·00
227 5 c. + 3 c. blue 4·00 4·00
228 6 c. + 4 c. green 4·00 4·00

37a William I (after Key) **38** "Supplication"

1933. 400th Birth Anniv of William I of Orange.
229 **37a** 6 c. red 5·25 1·40

1935. Bicent of Moravian Mission in Surinam.
230 **38** 1 c. + ½ c. brown 2·25 1·75
231 2 c. + 1 c. blue 2·40 1·75
232 – 3 c. + 1½ c. green 2·50 2·50
233 – 4 c. + 2 c. orange 2·50 2·50
234 – 5 c. + 2½ c. black 2·50 2·75
235 **38** 10 c. + 5 c. red 2·50 2·75
DESIGN: 3, 4, 5 c. Cross and clasped hands.

39 "Johannes van Walbeeck" (galleon) **40** Queen Wilhelmina

1936.
236 **39** ½ c. brown 20 25
237 1 c. green 30 10
238 1½ c. blue 45 35
239 2 c. brown 55 25
240 2½ c. green 10 15
241 3 c. blue 50 35
242 4 c. orange 55 65
243 5 c. grey 55 20
244 6 c. red 2·25 1·60
245 7½ c. purple 10 10
246 **40** 10 c. red 65 10
247 12½ c. green 2·75 1·00
248 15 c. blue 1·00 55
249 20 c. orange 1·75 50
250 21 c. black 2·50 2·50
251 25 c. red 2·00 85
252 30 c. purple 3·00 70
253 35 c. bistre 3·50 3·25
254 50 c. green 3·50 1·40
255 1 g. blue 6·50 2·00
256 1 g. 50 brown 18·00 14·50
257 2 g. 50 red 11·00 7·50
Nos. 254/7 are larger 22 × 33 mm.

41 "Infant Support"

1936. Child Welfare.
258 **41** 2 c. + 1 c. green 2·10 2·10
259 3 c. + 1½ c. blue 2·10 2·10
260 5 c. + 2½ c. black 2·75 2·75
261 10 c. + 5 c. red 2·75 2·75

42 "Emancipation" **42a** Surinam Girl

1938. 75th Anniv of Liberation of Slaves in Surinam and Paramaribo Girls' School Funds.
262 **42** 2½ c. + 2 c. green 1·60 1·40
263 **42a** 3 c. + 2 c. black 1·60 1·40
264 5 c. + 3 c. brown 1·75 1·60
265 7½ c. + 5 c. blue 1·75 1·60

1938. 40th Anniv of Coronation. As T **87** of Netherlands.
266 2 c. violet 35 25
267 7½ c. red 80 75
268 15 c. blue 2·25 2·00

44 Creole **44d** Dutch Royal Family

1940. Social Welfare Fund.
269 **44** 2½ c. + 2 c. green 1·60 1·75
270 – 3 c. + 2 c. red 1·60 1·75
271 – 5 c. + 3 c. blue 1·60 1·75
272 – 7½ c. + 5 c. red 1·60 1·75
DESIGNS: 3 c. Javanese woman; 5 c. Hindu woman; 7½ c. Indian woman.

1941. Prince Bernhard and "Spitfire" Funds. As T **69** of Netherlands Indies.
273 7½ c. + 7½ c. blue and orange 2·75 2·75
274 15 c. + 15 c. blue and red 3·00 3·00
275 1 g. + 1 g. blue and grey 23·00 20·00

1941. As T **94** of Netherlands.
342 12½ c. blue 25 20
284 15 c. blue 18·00 6·25

1942. Red Cross. Surch with red cross and new values.
289 **39** 2 c. + 2 c. brown (post) 1·75 1·75
291 2½ c. + 2 c. green 1·75 1·75
292 7½ c. + 5 c. purple 1·75 1·75
293 **35** 10 c. + 5 c. red (air) 4·25 4·25

1943. Birth of Princess Margriet.
294 **44d** 2½ c. orange 20 40
295 7½ c. red 20 15
296 15 c. black 2·00 1·50
297 40 c. blue 2·50 2·00

1945. Surch.
298 **39** ½ c. on 1 c. green 10 20
299 1½ c. on 7½ c. purple 10 20
300 2½ c. on 7½ c. purple 1·75 2·25
301 **40** 2½ c. on 10 c. red 85 20
302 5 c. on 10 c. red 60 45
303 7½ c. on 10 c. red 65 45

1945. Air. Surch.
304 **35** 22½ c. on 60 c. purple 35 60
305 1 g. on 2½ g. yellow 13·00 13·00
306 5 g. on 10 g. bistre 18·00 19·00

1945. National Welfare Fund. Surch **CENT/ VOOR HET/ NATIONAAL/ STEUNFONDS** and premium.
307 **49** 7½ c. + 5 c. orange 7·00 8·00
308 **50** 15 c. + 10 c. brown 2·50 2·10
309 20 c. + 15 c. green 2·50 2·10
310 22½ c. + 20 c. grey 2·50 2·10
311 40 c. + 35 c. red 2·50 2·10
312 60 c. + 50 c. violet 2·50 2·10

49 Sugar-cane Train

50 Queen Wilhelmina **51** **53** Star

1945.
313 – 1 c. red 50 50
314 – 1½ c. red 1·00 1·00
315 – 2 c. violet 45 35
316 – 2½ c. brown 45 35
317 – 3 c. green 1·00 50
318 – 4 c. brown 95 55
319 – 5 c. blue 1·75 45
320 – 6 c. olive 1·90 1·25
321 **49** 7½ c. orange 2·75 75
322 **50** 10 c. blue 1·25 10
323 15 c. brown 1·50 20
324 20 c. green 2·50 15
325 22½ c. grey 3·00 70
326 25 c. red 8·00 3·25
327 30 c. olive 8·00 40
328 35 c. blue 13·50 6·00
329 40 c. red 8·00 25
330 50 c. red 8·00 20
331 60 c. violet 8·00 65
332 **51** 1 g. brown 10·00 25
333 1 g. 50 lilac 9·00 60
334 2 g. 50 brown 16·00 70
335 5 g. red 35·00 10·00
336 10 g. orange 60·00 15·00
DESIGNS—As Type **49**: 1 c. Bauxite mine, Moengo; 1½ c. Natives in canoes; 2 c. Native and stream; 2½ c. Road in Coronie; 3 c. River Surinam near Berg en Dal; 4 c. Government Square, Paramaribo; 5 c. Mining gold; 6 c. Street in Paramaribo.

1946. Air. Anti-tuberculosis Fund. Surch **LUCHT POST** and premium.
340 **50** 10 c. + 40 c. blue 1·00 1·00
341 15 c. + 60 c. brown 1·00 1·00

1947. Anti-Leprosy Fund.
343 **53** 7½ c. + 12½ c. orge (post) 2·50 2·25
344 12½ c. + 37½ c. blue 2·50 2·25
345 22½ c. + 27½ c. grey (air) 2·50 2·25
346 27½ c. + 47½ c. green 2·50 2·25

1948. Types of Netherlands inscr "SURINAME". (a) Numeral type as T **118**.
347 1 c. red 10 10
348 1½ c. purple 10 20
349 2 c. violet 25 10
350 2½ c. green 1·25 15
351 3 c. green 15 10
352 4 c. brown 20 15
353 5 c. blue 1·25 10
354 7½ c. orange 2·75 1·10

(b) Portrait of Queen Wilhelmina as T **119**.
355 5 c. blue 35 15
356 6 c. green 90 65
357 7½ c. red 25 20
358 10 c. blue 55 10
359 12½ c. blue 1·00 90
360 15 c. brown 1·40 30
361 17½ c. purple 1·60 1·25
362 20 c. green 1·25 15
363 22½ c. blue 1·25 65
364 25 c. red 1·25 25
365 27½ c. red 1·25 20
366 30 c. green 1·60 15
367 37½ c. brown 2·50 1·75
368 40 c. purple 1·75 25
369 50 c. orange 1·90 25
370 60 c. violet 2·00 35
371 70 c. black 2·25 50

1948. Queen Wilhelmina's Golden Jubilee. As T **125** of Netherlands.
372 7½ c. orange 65 60
373 12½ c. blue 65 60

1948. Accession of Queen Juliana. As T **126** of Netherlands.
374 7½ c. orange 2·75 2·75
375 12½ c. blue 2·75 2·75

55 Women of Netherlands and Surinam **56** Marie Curie

1949. Air. 1st K.L.M. Flight on Paramaribo–Amsterdam Service.
376 **55** 27½ c. brown 5·75 2·75

1949. 75th Anniv of U.P.U. As T **50** of Netherlands Antilles.
377 7½ c. red 5·25 2·50
378 27½ c. blue 5·25 2·00

1950. Cancer Research Fund.
379 **56** 7½ c. + 7½ c. violet 14·50 7·50
380 – 7½ c. + 22½ c. green 14·50 7·50
381 – 27½ c. + 12½ c. blue 14·50 7·50
382 **56** 27½ c. + 97½ c. brown 14·50 7·50
PORTRAIT: Nos. 380/1, Wilhelm Rontgen.

1950 Surch **1 Cent** and bars.
383 **49** 1 c. on 7½ c. orange 1·00 1·60

1951. Portrait of Queen Juliana as T **129/30** of Netherlands.
395 **129** 10 c. blue 35 10
396 15 c. brown 95 25
397 20 c. turquoise 2·25 10
398 25 c. red 1·50 35
399 27½ c. lake 1·40 15
400 30 c. green 1·40 30
401 35 c. olive 1·60 1·00
402 40 c. mauve 1·75 35
403 50 c. orange 2·25 35
404 **130** 1 g. brown 24·00 30

1953. Netherlands Flood Relief Fund. Nos. 374/5 surch **STORMRAMP NEDERLAND 1953** and premium.
405 12½ c. + 7½ c. on 7½ c. orange 2·50 2·50
406 20 c. + 10 c. on 12½ c. blue 2·50 2·50

60 Fisherman **61** Surinam Stadium

1953.
407 – 2 c. brown 10 10
408 **60** 2½ c. green 25 20
409 – 5 c. grey 25 10
410 – 6 c. blue 1·50 1·10
411 – 7½ c. violet 15 10
412 – 10 c. red 20 10
413 – 12½ c. blue 1·60 1·25
414 – 15 c. red 2·00 30
415 – 17½ c. brown 3·00 1·75
416 – 20 c. green 45 10
417 – 25 c. green 2·25 70
DESIGNS—HORIZ: 2 c. Native shooting fish; 10 c. Woman gathering fruit. VERT: 5 c. Bauxite mine; 6 c. Log raft; 7½ c. Ploughing with buffalo; 12½ c. "Kwie kwie" fish; 15 c. Blue and yellow macaw; 17½ c. Nine-banded armadillo; 20 c. Poling pirogue; 25 c. Iguana.

1953. Sports Week.
419 **61** 10 c. + 5 c. red 10·00 7·25
420 15 c. + 7½ c. brown 10·00 7·25
421 30 c. + 15 c. green 10·00 7·25

62 Posthorn and Globe **63** Native Children and Youth Centre

1954. Air. 25th Anniv of Surinam Airlines.
422 **62** 15 c. blue 1·10 1·00

1954. Child Welfare Fund.
423 **63** 7½ c. + 3 c. purple 5·50 4·50
424 10 c. + 5 c. green 5·50 4·50
425 15 c. + 7½ c. brown 5·50 4·50
426 30 c. + 15 c. blue 5·50 4·50

1954. Ratification of Statute for the Kingdom. As T **158** of Netherlands.
427 7½ c. purple 50 60

64 Doves of Peace **65** Gathering Bananas

1955. 10th Anniv of Liberation of Netherlands and War Victims Relief Fund.

428 **64** 7½ c. + 3½ c. red . . . . . 2·50 2·50
429 15 c. + 8 c. blue . . . . . 2·50 2·50

1955. 4th Caribbean Tourist Assn Meeting.

430 **65** 2 c. green . . . . 1·40 1·10
431 – 7½ c. yellow . . . . 2·50 1·75
432 – 10 c. brown . . . . 2·50 1·75
433 – 15 c. blue . . . . 2·50 1·75
DESIGNS: 7½ c. Pounding rice; 10 c. Preparing cassava; 15 c. Fishing.

66 Caduceus and Globe

67 Queen Juliana and Prince Bernhard

1955. Surinam Fair.

434 **66** 5 c. blue 35 25

1955. Royal Visit.

435 **67** 7½ c. + 2½ c. olive 50 50

68 Flags and Caribbean Map

69 Facade of 19th-century Theatre

1956. 10th Anniv of Caribbean Commission.

447 **68** 10 c. blue and red 25 25

1958. 120th Anniv of "Thalia" Amateur Dramatic Society.

448 **69** 7½ c. + 3 c. blue & black 40 45
449 – 10 c. + 5 c. purple & blk 40 45
450 – 15 c. + 7½ c. green & blk 40 45
451 – 20 c. + 10 c. orange & blk 40 45
DESIGNS: 10 c. Early 20th-century theatre; 15 c. Modern theatre; 20 c. Performance on stage.

1959. No. 399 surch **8 C**.

452 8 c. on 27½ c. red 15 15

71 Queen Juliana

72 Symbolic Plants

1959.

453 **71** 1 g. purple . . . . 1·40 10
454 1 g. 50 brown . . . . . . 2·25 45
455 2 g. 50 red . . . . 3·00 25
456 5 g. blue . . . . 6·00 25

1959. 5th Anniv of Ratification of Statute for the Kingdom.

457 **72** 20 c. multicoloured . . . . 2·50 1·50

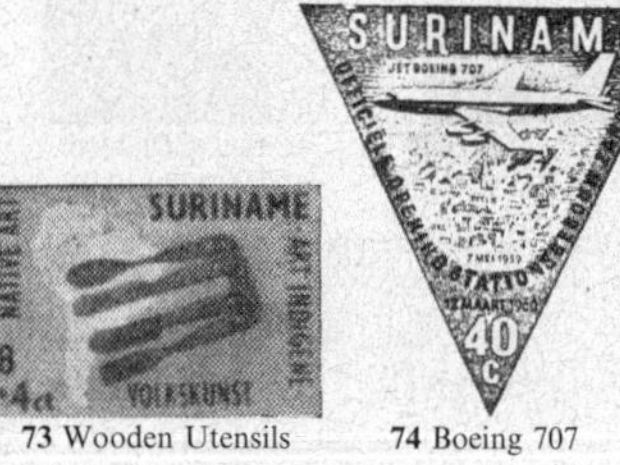

73 Wooden Utensils

74 Boeing 707

1960. Surinam Handicrafts.

458 **73** 8 c. + 4 c. multicoloured . 80 80
459 – 10 c. + 5 c. red, blue and brown 80 80
460 – 15 c. + 7 c. grn, brn & red 80 80
461 – 20 c. + 10 c. multicoloured 80 80
DESIGNS: 10 c. Indian chief's headgear; 15 c. Clay pottery; 20 c. Wooden stool.

1960. Opening of Zanderij Airport Building.

462 – 8 c. blue . . . . 1·25 1·25
463 – 10 c. green . . . . 1·75 1·50
464 – 15 c. red . . . . 1·75 1·50
465 – 20 c. lilac . . . . 1·90 1·75
466 **74** 40 c. brown . . . . 2·75 2·75
DESIGNS: 8 c. Charles Lindbergh's seaplane, 1929; 10 c. Fokker "De Snip", 1934; 15 c. Cessna 170A, 1954; 20 c. Lockheed Super Constellation 1957.

75 "Uprooted Tree"

76 Surinam Flag

1960. World Refugee Year.

467 **75** 8 c. + 4 c. green & brown 15 20
468 10 c. + 5 c. green & blue . 15 20

1960. Freedom Day. Multicoloured.

469 10 c. Type **76** 40 40
470 15 c. Coat-of-arms (30 × 26 mm) 40 40

77 Putting the Shot

78 Bananas

1960. Olympic Games, Rome.

471 **77** 8 c. + 4 c. brown, black and grey 60 60
472 – 10 c. + 5 c. brown, black and orange 75 75
473 – 15 c. + 7 c. brown, black and violet 80 80
474 – 20 c. + 10 c. brown, black and blue 80 80
475 – 40 c. + 20 c. brown, black and green 80 80
DESIGNS: 10 c. Basketball; 15 c. Running; 20 c. Swimming; 40 c. Football.

1961. Local Produce.

476 **78** 1 c. yellow, black & green 10 10
477 – 2 c. green, black & yellow 10 10
478 – 3 c. brown, black & choc 10 10
479 – 4 c. yellow, black and blue 10 10
480 – 5 c. red, black and brown . 10 10
481 – 6 c. yellow, black & grn . 10 10
482 – 8 c. yellow, black and blue 10 10
DESIGNS: 2 c. Citrus fruit; 3 c. Cocoa; 4 c. Sugar-cane; 5 c. Coffee; 6 c. Coconuts; 8 c. Rice.

79 Treasury

80 Commander Shepard, Rocket and Globe

1961. Surinam Buildings. Multicoloured.

483 10 c. Type **79** 15 10
484 15 c. Court of Justice 20 10
485 20 c. Concordia Masonic Lodge 25 15
486 25 c. Neve Shalom Synagogue 65 30
487 30 c. Lock Gate, Nieuw Amsterdam . . . . 1·40 1·25
488 35 c. Government Building . 1·40 1·40
489 40 c. Governor's House . . . 65 50
490 50 c. Legislative Assembly . . 70 25
491 60 c. Old Dutch Reform Church 80 75
492 70 c. Fort Zeelandia (1790) . 1·00 1·00
The 10, 15, 20 and 30 c. are vert and the rest horiz.

1961. Air. "Man in Space". Multicoloured.

493 15 c. Globe and astronaut in capsule 70 75
494 20 c. Type **80** 70 75

81 Girl Scout saluting

82 Dag Hammarskjold

1961. Caribbean Girl Scout Jamborette. Mult.

495 8 c. + 2 c. Semaphoring (horiz) 45 35
496 10 c. + 3 c. Type **81** 45 35
497 15 c. + 4 c. Brownies around a "toadstool" (horiz) 45 35
498 20 c. + 5 c. Campfire sing-song 45 45
499 25 c. + 6 c. Lighting fire (horiz) 45 45

1962. Dag Hammarskjold Memorial Issue.

500 **82** 10 c. black and blue . . . 10 15
501 20 c. black and violet . . . 15 20

1962. Royal Silver Wedding. As T **187** of Netherlands.

502 20 c. green 30 25

83 "Hibiscus rosa sinensis"

84 Campaign Emblem

1962. Red Cross Fund. Flowers in natural colours. Background colours given.

503 **83** 8 c. + 4 c. olive 30 30
504 – 10 c. + 5 c. blue 30 30
505 – 15 c. + 6 c. brown 30 30
506 – 20 c. + 10 c. violet 30 30
507 – 25 c. + 12 c. turquoise . . 30 30
FLOWERS: 10 c. "Caesalpinia pulcherrima"; 15 c. "Heliconia psittacorum"; 20 c. "Lochnera rosea"; 25 c. "Ixora macrothyrsa".

1962. Malaria Eradication.

508 **84** 8 c. red 15 15
509 10 c. blue 15 20

85 Stoelmans Guesthouse

1962. Opening of New Hotels. Multicoloured.

510 10 c. Type **85** 30 30
511 15 c. Torarica Hotel 30 30

86 Sisters' Residence

87 Wildfowl

1962. Nunnery and Hospital of the Deaconesses. Multicoloured.

512 10 c. Type **86** 30 30
513 20 c. Hospital building 30 30

1962. Animal Protection Fund.

514 **87** 2 c. + 1 c. red and blue . . 10 10
515 – 8 c. + 2 c. red and black . 20 20
516 – 10 c. + 3 c. black & green 20 20
517 – 15 c. + 4 c. black and red 25 25
ANIMALS: 8 c. Dog; 10 c. Donkey; 15 c. Horse.

88 Emblem in Hands

1963. Freedom from Hunger.

518 **88** 10 c. red 15 15
519 – 20 c. blue 15 15
DESIGN—VERT: 20 c. Tilling the land.

89 "Freedom"

1963. Centenary of Abolition of Slavery in Dutch West Indies.

520 **89** 10 c. black and red 15 15
521 20 c. black and green . . . 15 15

90 Indian Girl

91 North American X-15

1963. Child Welfare Fund.

522 **90** 8 c. + 3 c. green 10 10
523 – 10 c. + 4 c. brown 10 10
524 – 15 c. + 10 c. blue 25 25
525 – 20 c. + 10 c. red 25 25
526 – 40 c. + 20 c. purple . . . 35 35
PORTRAITS OF CHILDREN: 10 c. Bush negro; 15 c. Hindustani; 20 c. Indonesian; 40 c. Chinese.

1963. 150th Anniv of Kingdom of the Netherlands. As T **199** of Netherlands but smaller, size 26 × 26 mm.

528 10 c. black, bistre and blue . . 10 10

1964. Aeronautical and Astronomical Foundation, Surinam.

529 3 c. + 2 c. sepia and lake . . 15 15
530 8 c. + 4 c. sepia, indigo & bl 20 20
531 10 c. + 5 c. sepia and green . 20 20
532 15 c. + 7 c. sepia and brown 20 20
533 20 c. + 10 c. sepia & violet . 25 25
DESIGNS: 3, 15 c. Type **91**; 8 c. Foundation flag; 10, 20 c. Agena B-Ranger rocket.

92 "Camp Fire"

93 Skipping

1964. Scout Jamborette, Paramaribo, and 40th Anniv of Surinam Boy Scouts Association.

534 **92** 3 c. + 1 c. light yellow, yellow and bistre 15 15
535 8 c. + 4 c. brown, blue and deep blue 15 15
536 10 c. + 5 c. brown, red and deep red 15 15
537 20 c. + 10 c. brown, green and blue 20 20

1964. Child Welfare.

538 **93** 8 c. + 3 c. blue 10 10
539 – 10 c. + 4 c. red 10 10
540 – 15 c. + 9 c. green 10 10
541 – 20 c. + 10 c. purple . . . 15 15
DESIGNS: 10 c. Children swinging; 15 c. Child on scooter; 20 c. Child with hoop.

94 Crown and Wreath

95 Expectant Mother ("Prenatal Care")

1964. 10th Anniv of Statute of the Kingdom.

543 **94** 25 c. multicoloured 20 20

1965. 50th Anniv of "Het Groene Kruis" (The Green Cross).

544 **95** 4 c. + 2 c. green 15 15
545 – 10 c. + 5 c. brown & green 15 15
546 – 15 c. + 7 c. blue & green 15 15
547 – 25 c. + 12 c. violet & grn 20 20
DESIGNS: 10 c. Mother and baby ("Infant care"); 15 c. Young girl ("Child care"); 25 c. Old man ("Care in old age").

96 Abraham Lincoln

97 I.C.Y. Emblem

1965. Death Centenary of Abraham Lincoln.

548 **96** 25 c. purple and bistre . . 10 10

1965. International Co-operation Year.

549 **97** 10 c. orange and blue . . . 10 10
550 15 c. red and blue 10 10

98 Surinam Waterworks

99 Bauxite Mine, Moengo

1965. Air. Size 25 × 18 mm.

551 **98** 10 c. green 10 10
552 – 15 c. ochre 15 10
553 – 20 c. green 20 10
554 – 25 c. indigo 25 10
555 – 30 c. turquoise 25 15
556 – 35 c. red 35 20
557 – 40 c. orange 35 15
558 – 45 c. red 40 45
559 – 50 c. red 45 15
560 **98** 55 c. green 45 25
561 – 65 c. yellow 50 35
562 – 75 c. blue 55 35
DESIGNS: 15, 65 c. Brewery; 20 c. River scene; 25, 75 c. Timber yard; 30 c. Bauxite mine; 35, 50 c. Poelepantje Bridge; 40 c. Shipping; 45 c. Jetty.

For same designs but size 22 × 18 mm, see Nos. 843a/h.

1965. Opening of Brokopondo Power Station.
563 **99** 10 c. ochre 25 25
564 – 15 c. green 10 10
565 – 20 c. blue 10 10
566 – 25 c. red 15 15
DESIGNS: 15 c. Alum-earth works, Paranam; 20 c. Power station and dam, Afobaka; 25 c. Aluminium smeltery, Paranam.

100 Girl with Leopard

101 Red-breasted Blackbird

1965. Child Welfare.
567 **100** 4 c. + 4 c. black, turquoise and green 15 15
568 – 10 c. + 5 c. black, brown and light brown 15 15
569 – 15 c. + 7 c. black, orange and red 15 15
570 – 25 c. + 10 c. black, blue and cobalt 15 15
DESIGNS: 10 c. Boy with monkey; 15 c. Girl with tortoise; 25 c. Boy with rabbit.

1966. Intergovernmental Committee for European Migration (I.C.E.M.) Fund. As T **215** of Netherlands.
572 10 c. + 5 c. green & black 10 10
573 25 c. + 10 c. red and black 15 15

1966. Birds. Multicoloured.
575 1 c. Type **101** 10 10
576 2 c. Great kiskadee 15 10
577 3 c. Silver-beaked tanager 25 10
578 4 c. Ruddy ground dove 35 15
579 5 c. Blue-grey tanager 45 15
580 6 c. Straight-billed hermit 50 20
581 8 c. Turquoise tanager 70 25
582 10 c. Pale-breasted thrush 85 30

102 Hospital Building

103 Father P. Donders

1966. Opening of Central Hospital, Paramaribo. Multicoloured.
583 10 c. Type **102** 10 10
584 15 c. Different view 10 10

1966. Centenary of Redemptorists Mission.
585 **103** 4 c. black and brown 10 10
586 – 10 c. black, brown & red 10 10
587 – 15 c. black and ochre 10 10
588 – 25 c. black and lilac 15 15
DESIGNS: 10 c. Batavia Church, Coppename; 15 c. Mgr. J. B. Swinkels; 25 c. Paramaribo Cathedral.

104 Mary Magdalene and Disciples

105 "Century Tree"

1966. Easter Charity.
589 **104** 10 c. + 5 c. black, red and gold 15 15
590 15 c. + 8 c. black, violet and blue 15 15
591 20 c. + 10 c. black, yellow and blue 15 15
592 25 c. + 12 c. black, green and gold 20 20
593 30 c. + 15 c. black, blue and gold 20 20
On Nos. 590/3 the emblems at bottom left differ for each value. These represent various welfare organizations.

1966. Centenary of Surinam Parliament.
594 **105** 25 c. black, green & red 10 10
595 30 c. black, red & green 10 10

106 TV Mast, Eye and Globe

107 Boys with Bamboo Gun

1966. Inauguration of Surinam Television Service.
596 **106** 25 c. red and blue 10 10
597 30 c. red and brown 10 10

1966. Child Welfare. Multicoloured.
598 10 c. + 5 c. Type **107** 10 10
599 15 c. + 8 c. Boy pouring liquid on another 15 15
600 20 c. + 10 c. Children rejoicing 10 10
601 25 c. + 12 c. Children on merry-go-round 15 15
602 30 c. + 15 c. Children decorating room 20 20
The designs symbolise New Year's Eve, the End of Lent, Liberation Day, Queen's Birthday and Christmas respectively.

108 Mining Bauxite, 1916

109 "The Good Samaritan"

1966. 50th Anniv of Surinam Bauxite Industry.
604 **108** 20 c. black, orange & yell 25 10
605 – 25 c. black, orange & blue 25 10
DESIGN: 25 c. Modern bauxite plant.

1967. Easter Charity. Printed in black, background colours given.
606 **109** 10 c. + 5 c. yellow 10 10
607 – 15 c. + 8 c. blue 15 15
608 – 20 c. + 10 c. ochre 15 15
609 – 25 c. + 12 c. pink 20 20
610 – 30 c. + 15 c. green 20 20
DESIGNS: 15 to 30 c. Various episodes illustrating the parable of "The Good Samaritan".

110 Central Bank

1967. 10th Anniv of Surinam Central Bank.
611 **110** 10 c. black and yellow 10 10
612 – 25 c. black and lilac 10 10
DESIGN: 25 c. Aerial view of Central Bank.

111 Amelia Earhart and Lockheed 10E Electra Airplane

112 Siva Nataraja and Ballerina's Foot

1967. 30th Anniv of Visit of Amelia Earhart to Surinam.
613 **111** 20 c. red and yellow 15 10
614 25 c. green and yellow 15 10

1967. 20th Anniv of Surinam Cultural Centre. Multicoloured.
615 10 c. Type **112** 10 10
616 25 c. "Bashi-Lele" mask and violin scroll 10 10

113 Fort Zeelandia, Paramaribo (c. 1670)

114 Stilt-walking

1967. 300th Anniv of Treaty of Breda. Multicoloured.
617 10 c. Type **113** 15 15
618 20 c. Nieuw Amsterdam (c. 1660) 20 20
619 25 c. Breda Castle (c. 1667) 20 20

1967. Child Welfare. Multicoloured.
620 10 c. + 5 c. Type **114** 10 10
621 15 c. + 8 c. Playing marbles 20 20
622 20 c. + 10 c. Playing dibs 20 20
623 25 c. + 12 c. Kite-flying 20 20
624 30 c. + 15 c. "Cooking" game 25 25

115 "Cross of Ashes"

116 W.H.O. Emblem

1968. Easter Charity.
626 10 c. + 5 c. grey and violet 10 10
627 15 c. + 8 c. green and red 15 15
628 20 c. + 10 c. green & yellow 20 20
629 25 c. + 12 c. black and grey 20 20
630 30 c. + 15 c. brown & yellow 20 20
DESIGNS: 10 c. Type **115** (Ash Wednesday); 15 c. Palm branches (Palm Sunday); 20 c. Cup and wafer (Maundy Thursday); 25 c. Cross (Good Friday); 30 c. Symbol of Christ (Easter).

1968. 20th Anniv of W.H.O.
631 **116** 10 c. blue and purple 10 10
632 25 c. violet and blue 20 20

117 Chandelier, Reformed Church

119 Map of Joden Savanne

118 Missionary Shop, 1768

1968. 300th Anniv of Reformed Church, Paramaribo.
633 **117** 10 c. blue 10 10
634 – 25 c. green 15 15
DESIGN: 25 c. No. 633 reversed; chandelier on left.

1968. Bicentenary of Evangelist Brothers' Missionary Store, G. Kersten and Co.
635 **118** 10 c. black and yellow 10 10
636 – 25 c. black and blue 15 15
637 – 30 c. black and mauve 15 15
DESIGNS: 25 c. Paramaribo Church and Kersten's store, 1868; 30 c. Kersten's modern store, Paramaribo.

1968. Restoration of Joden Savanne Synagogue. Multicoloured.
638 20 c. Type **119** 40 40
639 25 c. Synagogue, 1685 40 40
640 30 c. Gravestone at Joden Savanne, dated 1733 50 50

120 Playing Hopscotch

121 Western Hemisphere illuminated by Full Moon

1968. Child Welfare.
641 **120** 10 c. + 5 c. black & brn 10 10
642 – 15 c. + 8 c. black & blue 15 15
643 – 20 c. + 10 c. black & pink 15 15
644 – 25 c. + 12 c. black & grn 25 25
645 – 30 c. + 15 c. blk & lilac 30 30
DESIGNS: 15 c. Forming "pyramids"; 20 c. Playing ball; 25 c. Handicrafts; 30 c. Tug-of-war.

1969. Easter Charity.
647 **121** 10 c. + 5 c. blue & lt blue 25 25
648 15 c. + 8 c. grey & yellow 25 25
649 20 c. + 10 c. turq & green 30 30
650 25 c. + 12 c. brown & buff 30 30
651 30 c. + 15 c. violet & grey 30 30

122 Cayman

123 Mahatma Gandhi

1969. Opening of Surinam Zoo, Paramaribo. Multicoloured.
652 10 c. Type **122** 45 35
653 20 c. Common squirrel-monkey (vert) 45 35
654 25 c. Nine-banded armadillo 45 35

1969. Birth Centenary of Mahatma Gandhi.
655 **123** 25 c. black and red 40 25

124 I.L.O. Emblem

125 Pillow Fight

1969. 50th Anniv of Int Labour Organization.
656 **124** 10 c. green and black 15 15
657 25 c. red and black 20 20

1969. Child Welfare.
658 10 c. + 5 c. purple and blue 10 10
659 15 c. + 8 c. brown & yellow 25 25
660 20 c. + 10 c. blue and grey 20 20
661 25 c. + 12 c. blue and pink 25 25
662 30 c. + 15 c. brown & green 25 25
DESIGNS: 10 c. Type **125**; 15 c. Eating contest; 20 c. Pole-climbing; 25 c. Sack-race; 30 c. Obstacle-race.

1969. 15th Anniv of Statute for the Kingdom. As T **240** of Netherlands.
664 25 c. multicoloured 25 25

127 "Flower"

128 "1950–1970"

1970. Easter Charity. "Wonderful Nature". Multicoloured.
665 10 c. + 5 c. Type **127** 55 55
666 15 c. + 8 c. "Butterfly" 55 55
667 20 c. + 10 c. "Bird" 55 55
668 25 c. + 12 c. "Sun" 55 55
669 30 c. + 15 c. "Star" 55 55

1970. 20th Anniv of Secondary Education in Surinam.
670 **128** 10 c. yellow, green & brown 10 10
671 25 c. yellow, blue & green 15 15

129 New U.P.U. Headquarters Building

130 U.N. "Diamond"

1970. New U.P.U. Headquarters Building.
672 **129** 10 c. violet, blue & turq 15 15
673 – 25 c. black and red 20 20
DESIGN: 25 c. Aerial view of H.Q. Building.

1970. 25th Anniv of United Nations.
674 **130** 10 c. multicoloured 15 15
675 25 c. multicoloured 20 20

131 Aircraft over Paramaribo Town Plan

132 Football Pitch (ball in centre)

1970. "40 years of Inland Airmail Flights".
676 **131** 10 c. grey, ultram & bl 25 25
677 – 20 c. grey, red & yellow 25 25
678 – 25 c. grey, red and pink 25 25
DESIGNS: As Type **131**, but showing different background maps—20 c. Totness; 25 c. Nieuw-Nickerie.

1970. 50th Anniv of Surinam Football Association.
679 **132** 4 c. brown, yellow & black 10 10
680 – 10 c. brown, olive & black 20 20
681 – 15 c. brown, green & black 20 20
682 – 25 c. brown, green & black 30 30
DESIGNS: As Type **132**, but with ball: 10 c. in "corner"; 15 c. at side ("throw-in"); 25 c. at top ("goal").

133 Beethoven (1786) **134** Grey Heron

1970. Child Welfare. Birth Bicentenary of Beethoven (composer).

683 **133** 10 c. + 5 c. yellow, drab and green . . . 45 45
684 – 15 c. + 8 c. yellow, drab and red . . . 45 45
685 – 20 c. + 10 c. yellow, drab and blue . . . 45 45
686 – 25 c. + 12 c. yellow, drab and orange . . . 45 45
687 – 30 c. + 15 c. yellow, drab and violet . . . 45 45

DESIGNS: Beethoven 15 c. 1804; 20 c. 1812; 25 c. 1814; 30 c. 1827.

1971. 25th Anniv of Netherlands–Surinam–Netherlands Antilles Air Service. Multicoloured.

689 15 c. Type **134** . . . 75 50
690 20 c. Greater flamingo . . . 95 55
691 25 c. Scarlet macaw . . . 1·10 55

135 Donkey and Palm **136** Morse Key

1971. Easter. The Bible Story. Multicoloured.

692 10 c. + 5 c. Type **135** . . . 55 55
693 15 c. + 8 c. Cockerel . . . 60 60
694 20 c. + 10 c. Lamb . . . 60 60
695 25 c. + 12 c. Crown of Thorns . . . 60 60
696 30 c. + 15 c. Sun ("The Resurrection") . . . 60 60

1971. World Telecommunications Day. Mult.

697 15 c. Type **136** . . . 45 45
698 20 c. Telephones . . . 50 50
699 25 c. Lunar module and telescope . . . 60 60

EVENTS: 15 c. First national telegraph, Washington—Baltimore, 1843; 20 c. First international telephone communication, England—Sweden, 1926; 25 c. First interplanetary television communication, Earth—Moon, 1969.

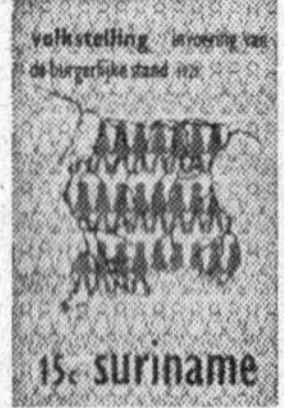

137 Prince Bernhard **138** Population Map

1971. Prince Bernhard's 60th Birthday.

700 **137** 25 c. multicoloured . . . 30 25

1971. 50th Anniv of 1st Census and Introduction of Civil Registration.

701 **138** 15 c. blue, black & red . . . 15 15
702 30 c. red, black & blue . . . 25 25

DESIGN: 30 c. "Individual" representing civil registration.

139 William Mogge's Map of Surinam

1971. 300th Anniv of First Surinam Map.

703 **139** 30 c. brown on yellow . . . 65 45

140 Leap-frog **141** Plan of Albina

1971. Child Welfare. Details from Brueghel's "Children's Games". Multicoloured.

704 10 c. + 5 c. Type **140** . . . 65 65
705 15 c. + 8 c. Strewing flowers . . . 65 65
706 20 c. + 10 c. Rolling hoop . . . 65 65
707 25 c. + 12 c. Playing ball . . . 70 70
708 30 c. + 15 c. Stilt-walking . . . 70 70

1971. 125th Anniv of Albina Settlement.

710 **141** 15 c. black on blue . . . 30 30
711 – 20 c. black on green . . . 30 30
712 – 25 c. black on yellow . . . 30 30

DESIGNS—HORIZ: 20 c. Albina and River Marowijne. VERT: 25 c. August Kappler (naturalist and founder).

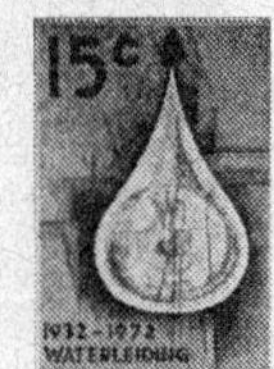

142 Drop of Water **143** Easter Candle

1972. 40th Anniv of Surinam Waterworks.

713 **142** 15 c. black and violet . . . 25 25
714 – 30 c. black and blue . . . 30 30

DESIGN: 30 c. Water tap.

1972. Easter Charity. Multicoloured.

715 10 c. + 5 c. Type **143** . . . 50 50
716 15 c. + 8 c. "Christ teaching the Apostles" . . . 50 50
717 20 c. + 10 c. Hands holding cup ("Christ in Gethsemane") . . . 50 50
718 25 c. + 12 c. Fishes in net ("Miracle of the Fishes") . . . 50 50
719 30 c. + 15 c. Pieces of silver ("Judas's Betrayal") . . . 50 50

144 "Eucyane bicolor" **145** Air-letter Motif

1972. Moths and Butterflies. Multicoloured.

720 15 c. Type **144** . . . 30 15
721 20 c. Gold drop . . . 30 15
722 25 c. Orange swallowtail . . . 40 20
723 30 c. White tailed page . . . 40 10
724 35 c. "Stalachtis calliope" . . . 60 35
725 40 c. "Stalachtis phlegia" . . . 60 25
726 45 c. Malachite . . . 60 10
727 50 c. Spear-winged cattle heart . . . 75 10
728 55 c. Red anartia . . . 90 50
729 60 c. Five continent butterfly . . . 1·00 80
730 65 c. Doris . . . 1·00 50
731 70 c. "Nessaea obrinus" . . . 1·10 75
732 75 c. Cracker . . . 1·00 45

1972. 50th Anniv of 1st Airmail in Surinam.

733 **145** 15 c. red and blue . . . 20 20
734 30 c. blue and red . . . 25 25

146 Doll and Toys (kindergarten) **147** Giant Tree

1972. Child Welfare. Multicoloured.

735 10 c. + 5 c. Type **146** . . . 50 45
736 15 c. + 8 c. Clock and abacus (primary education) . . . 50 45
737 20 c. + 10 c. Blocks (primary education) . . . 50 45
738 25 c. + 12 c. Molecule complex (secondary education) . . . 55 50
739 30 c. + 15 c. Wrench and blue-print (technical education) . . . 55 50

1972. 25th Anniv of Surinam Forestry Commission.

741 **147** 15 c. brown and yellow . . . 25 25
742 – 20 c. brown, black & blue . . . 30 30
743 – 30 c. chocolate, brn & grn . . . 40 40

DESIGNS: 20 c. Aerial transport of logs; 30 c. Planting tree.

148 "The Storm on the Lake" **149** Hindu Peasant Woman

1973. Easter Charity. Jesus's Life and Death. Multicoloured.

744 10 c. + 5 c. Type **148** . . . 50 50
745 15 c. + 8 c. "Washing the Disciples' Feet" . . . 50 50
746 20 c. + 10 c. "Jesus taken to Execution" . . . 50 50
747 25 c. + 12 c. The Cross . . . 50 50
748 30 c. + 15 c. "The Men of Emmaus" . . . 50 50

1973. Centenary of Arrival of Indian Immigrants in Surinam.

749 **149** 15 c. violet and yellow . . . 25 20
750 – 25 c. red and grey . . . 25 20
751 – 30 c. orange and blue . . . 35 30

DESIGNS: 25 c. J. F. A. Cateau van Rosevelt, Head of Department of Immigration, holding map; 30 c. Symbols of immigration.

150 Queen Juliana

1973. Silver Jubilee of Queen Juliana's Reign.

752 **150** 30 c. black, orange & sil . . . 50 50

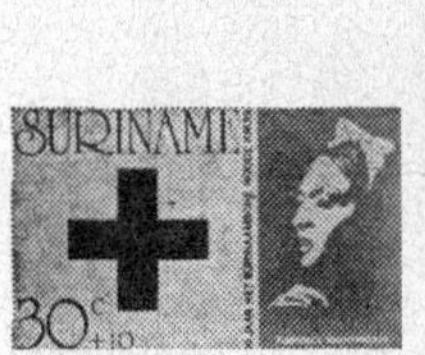

151 Florence Nightingale and Red Cross **152** Interpol Emblem

1973. 30th Anniv of Surinam Red Cross.

753 **151** 30 c. + 10 c. multicoloured . . . 70 70

1973. 50th Anniv of International Criminal Police Organization (Interpol). Multicoloured.

754 15 c. Type **152** . . . 40 25
755 30 c. Emblem within passport stamp . . . 40 30

153 Flower **154** Carrier-pigeons

1973. Child Welfare.

756 **153** 10 c. + 5 c. multicoloured . . . 30 30
757 – 15 c. + 8 c. green, brown and emerald . . . 45 45
758 – 20 c. + 10 c. violet, blue and green . . . 35 35
759 – 25 c. + 12 c. multicoloured . . . 55 55
760 – 30 c. + 15 c. multicoloured . . . 55 55

DESIGNS: 15 c. Tree; 20 c. Dog; 25 c. House; 30 c. Doll.

1973. Stamp Centenary.

762 **154** 15 c. green and blue . . . 15 15
763 – 25 c. multicoloured . . . 25 25
764 – 30 c. multicoloured . . . 60 60

DESIGNS: 25 c. Postman; 30 c. Map and postal routes.

155 "Quassia amara" **156** Nurse and Blood Transfusion Equipment

1974. Easter Charity Flowers. Multicoloured.

765 10 c. + 5 c. Type **155** . . . 45 45
766 15 c. + 8 c. "Passiflora quadrangularis" . . . 45 45
767 20 c. + 10 c. "Combretum rotundifolium" . . . 45 45
768 25 c. + 12 c. "Cassia alata" . . . 50 50
769 30 c. + 15 c. "Asclepias curassavica" . . . 50 50

1974. 75th Anniv of Surinam Medical School. Multicoloured.

770 15 c. Type **156** . . . 20 15
771 30 c. Microscope slide and oscilloscope scanner . . . 30 20

157 Aerial Crop-spraying **158** Commemorative Text superimposed on Early Newspaper

1974. 25th Anniv of Mechanised Agriculture. Multicoloured.

772 15 c. Type **157** . . . 20 15
773 30 c. Fertiliser plant . . . 25 20

1974. Bicentenary of Surinam's "Weekly Wednesday" Newspaper.

774 **158** 15 c. multicoloured . . . 20 15
775 30 c. multicoloured . . . 25 20

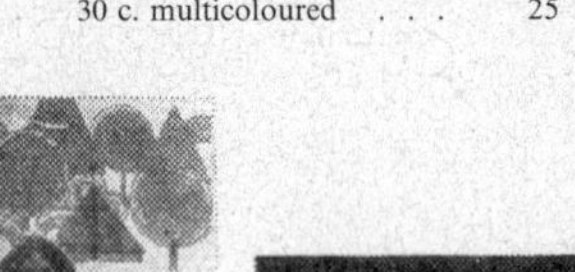

159 Scout and Tent **160** G.P.O., Paramaribo

1974. "50 Years of Scouting in Surinam". Multicoloured.

776 10 c. + 5 c. Type **159** . . . 35 35
777 15 c. + 8 c. Jamboree emblem . . . 35 35
778 20 c. + 10 c. Scouts and badge . . . 40 40

1974. Centenary of Universal Postal Union.

779 **160** 15 c. black and brown . . . 20 20
780 – 30 c. black and blue . . . 25 25

DESIGN: 30 c. G.P.O., Paramaribo (different view).

161 Girl with Fruit

1974. Child Welfare.

781 **161** 10 c. + 5 c. green, emerald and pink . . . 25 25
782 – 15 c. + 8 c. brown, mauve and green . . . 35 35
783 – 20 c. + 10 c. yellow, orange and mauve . . . 35 35
784 – 25 c. + 12 c. brown, lilac and yellow . . . 55 55
785 – 30 c. + 15 c. cobalt, blue and lilac . . . 65 65

DESIGNS: 15 c. Birds and nest; 20 c. Mother and Child with flower; 25 c. Young boy in cornfield; 30 c. Children at play.

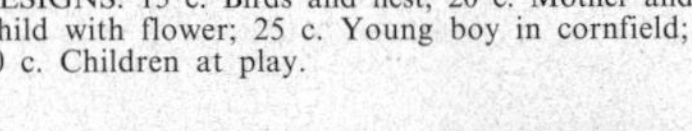

162 Panning for Gold **163** "I am the Good Shepherd"

1975. Centenary of Prospecting Concession Policy.

787 **162** 15 c. brown and bistre . . . 25 20
788 – 30 c. purple and red . . . 30 25

DESIGN: 30 c. Claws of modern excavator.

1975. Easter Charity.

789 **163** 15 c. + 5 c. yellow and green . . . 45 40
790 – 20 c. + 10 c. yellow and blue . . . 60 60
791 – 30 c. + 15 c. yellow and red . . . 70 65
792 – 35 c. + 20 c. blue and violet . . . 70 65

DESIGNS—Quotations from the New Testament. 20 c. "I do not know the man"; 30 c. "He is not here; He has been raised again"; 35 c. "Because you have seen Me you have found faith. Happy are they who never saw Me and yet have found faith".

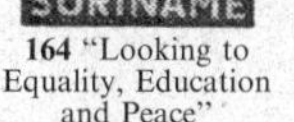

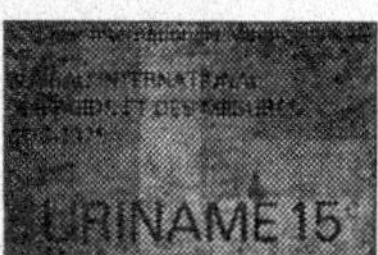

164 "Looking to Equality, Education and Peace" **165** "Weights and Measures"

1975. International Women's Year.
793 **164** 15 c. + 5 c. blue & green . . 60 55
794 30 c. + 15 c. vio & mauve . . 60 55

1975. Centenary of Metre Convention.
795 **165** 15 c. multicoloured . . . 30 30
796 25 c. multicoloured . . . 30 30
796a 30 c. multicoloured . . . 40 30

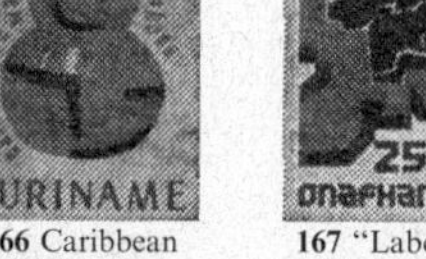

166 Caribbean Water Jug **167** "Labour and Technology"

1975. Child Welfare. Multicoloured.
797 15 c. + 5 c. Type **166** 55 55
798 20 c. + 10 c. Indian arrowhead 85 75
799 30 c. + 15 c. "Maluana" (protection against evil spirits) 85 85
800 35 c. + 20 c. Indian arrowhead (different) . . . . 2·40 2·25

1975. Independence. "Nation in Development". Multicoloured.
802 25 c. Type **167** 20 20
803 50 c. Open book ("Education and Art") 50 50
804 75 c. Hands with ball ("Physical Training") 70 70

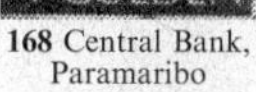

168 Central Bank, Paramaribo **169** "Oncidium lanceanum"

1975.
805 **168** 1 g. black, mve and pur . 90 25
806 1½ g. black, orge & brn . . 1·50 25
807 2½ g. black, red and brn . 2·75 35
808 5 g. black, emer & grn . . 5·50 55
809 10 g. black, bl & dp bl . . 11·00 1·10

1976. Surinam Orchids. Multicoloured.
809 1 c. Type **169** 10 10
810 2 c. "Epidendrum stenopetalum" 10 10
811 3 c. "Brassia lanceana" . . . 10 10
812 4 c. "Epidendrum ibaguense" 10 10
813 5 c. "Epidendrum fragans" . . 10 10

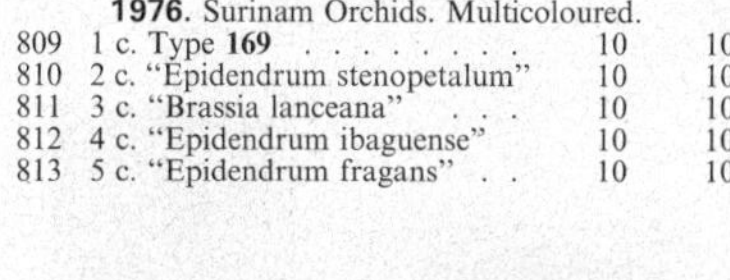

170 Surinam Flag **171** "Feeding the Hungry"

1976. Multicoloured.
814 25 c. Type **170** 30 30
815 35 c. Surinam arms 35 35

1976. Easter. Paintings in Alkmaar Church. Multicoloured.
816 20 c. + 10 c. Type **171** . . . 30 30
817 25 c. + 15 c. "Visiting the Sick" 35 35
818 30 c. + 15 c. "Clothing the Naked" 40 40
819 35 c. + 15 c. "Burying the Dead" 45 55
820 50 c. + 25 c. "Refreshing the Thirsty" 70 80

172 "Pomacanthus semicirculatus"

1976. Fishes. Multicoloured.
822 1 c. Type **172** (postage) . . . 10 10
823 2 c. "Adioryx diadema" . . . 10 10
824 3 c. "Pogonoculius zebra" . . 10 10
825 4 c. "Balistes vetula" 10 10
826 5 c. "Myripristis jacobus" 10 10
827 35 c. "Chaetodon unimaculatus" (air) 40 35
828 60 c. "Centropyge loriculus" 70 60
829 95 c. "Chaetodon collare" . . 1·00 90

173 Early Telephone and Switchboard

1976. Telephone Centenary.
830 20 c. Type **173** 25 20
831 35 c. Globe, satellite and modern telephone 40 35

174 "Anansi Tori" (A. Baag)

1976. Paintings by Surinam Artists. Mult.
832 20 c. Type **174** 25 20
833 30 c. "Surinam Now" (R. Chang) 35 30
834 35 c. "Lamentation" (N. Hatterman) (vert) 45 40
835 50 c. "Chess-players" (Q. Jan Telting) 60 55

175 "Join or Die" (Franklin's "Divided Snake" poster of 1754)

1976. Bicentenary of American Revolution.
836 **175** 20 c. black, grn & cream 25 20
837 60 c. black, red and cream 75 75

176 Pekinese **177** "Ionopsis utricularioides"

1976. Child Welfare. Pet Dogs.
838 20 c. + 10 c. Type **176** . . . 40 40
839 25 c. + 10 c. Alsatian . . . 45 45
840 30 c. + 10 c. Dachshund . . 55 55
841 35 c. + 15 c. Surinam breed . 60 60
842 50 c. + 25 c. Mongrel . . . 85 85

1976. As Nos. 551/7 and new values but size 22 × 18 mm.
843a – 5 c. brown 10 10
843b **98** 10 c. green 15 10
843c – 20 c. green 25 15
843d – 25 c. blue 25 15
843e – 30 c. green 30 15
843f – 35 c. red 35 20
843g – 40 c. orange 50 25
843h – 60 c. red 75 35
NEW VALUES: 5 c. Brewery; 60 c. Jetty.

1977. Surinam Orchids. Multicoloured.
844 20 c. Type **177** 30 25
845 30 c. "Rodiguezia secunda" . . 45 40
846 35 c. "Oncidium pusillum" . . 50 45
847 55 c. "Sobralia sessilis" . . . 75 65
848 60 c. "Octomeria surinamensis" 80 70

178 Javanese Costume **179** Triptych, left panel (Jan Mostaert)

1977. Surinam Costumes (1st series). Mult.
849 10 c. Type **178** 15 10
850 15 c. Forest Negro 20 15
851 35 c. Chinese 40 35
852 60 c. Creole 75 65
853 75 c. Aborigine Indian 95 85
854 1 g. Hindustani . . . . . . 1·25 1·25
DESIGNS: 15 c. to 1 g. Various women's festival costumes.
See also Nos. 906/11.

1977. Easter. Multicoloured.
855 20 c. + 10 c. Type **179** . . . 25 30
856 25 c. + 15 c. Right panel . . 35 40
857 30 c. + 15 c. Right panel . . . 40 45
858 35 c. + 15 c. Centre panel (30 × 38 mm.) 50 55
859 50 c. + 25 c. Left panel . . . 70 80
The 20 c. and 25 c. show the triptych closed, the 30 c. and 50 c. show designs on the reverse of the doors, and the 35 c. shows the centre panel.

180 Green Honeycreeper

1977. Air. Birds. Multicoloured.
860 20 c. Red-breasted blackbird . 60 35
861 25 c. Type **180** 70 40
862 30 c. Paradise tanager 75 45
863 40 c. Spot-tailed nightjar . . 90 55
864 45 c. Yellow-backed tanager 95 60
865 50 c. White-tailed goldenthroat 1·00 70
866 55 c. Grey-breasted sabrewing 1·10 75
867 60 c. Caica parrot (vert) . . . 1·10 80
868 65 c. Cuvier's toucan (vert) . 1·25 90
869 70 c. Crimson-hooded manakin (vert) . . . . 1·40 95
870 75 c. Hawk-headed parrot (vert) 1·50 1·00
871 80 c. Spangled cotinga (vert) 1·75 1·10
872 85 c. Black-tailed trogon (vert) 1·90 1·25
872a 90 c. Orange-winged amazon (vert) . . . . 1·75 1·10
873 95 c. Black-banded owl (vert) 2·00 1·40

181 "Liopropoma carmabi"

1977. Fishes. Multicoloured.
875 1 c. Type **181** (postage) . . . 10 10
876 2 c. "Holacanthus ciliaris" . . 10 10
877 3 c. "Opistognathus aurifrons" 10 10
878 4 c. "Anisotremus virginicus" . 10 10
879 5 c. "Gramma loreto" 10 10
880 60 c. "Chaetodon striatus" (air) 75 65
881 90 c. "Bodianus pulchellus" . . 1·10 95
882 120 c. "Centropyge argi" . . . 1·50 1·40

182 Edison's Phonograph, 1877

1977. Centenary of Sound Reproduction. Mult.
883 20 c. Type **182** 25 20
883a 60 c. Modern gramophone turntable 75 75

183 Paddle Steamer "Curacao" **185** Dog

1977. 150th Anniv of Regular Passenger Steam Service with Netherlands.
884 **183** 5 c. blue and light blue . 15 10
885 – 15 c. red and orange . . . 30 15
886 – 30 c. black and ochre . . 40 35
887 – 35 c. black and olive . . . 50 40
888 – 60 c. black and lilac . . . 80 70
889 – 95 c. green & light green . 1·50 1·50
DESIGNS: 15 c. Hellevoetsluis port; 30 c. Chart of steamer route from Hellevoetsluis to Paramaribo; 35 c. Log of "Curacao"; 60 c. Chart of Paramaribo and 1852 postmark; 95 c. Passenger liner "Stuyvesant".

1977. Surch.
890 – 1 c. on 25 c. mult (No. 722) 10 10
891 **144** 4 c. on 15 c. multicoloured 10 10
892 – 4 c. on 30 c. mult (No. 723) 10 10
893 – 5 c. on 40 c. mult (No. 725) 10 10
894 – 10 c. on 75 c. mult (No. 732) 15 15
The word "LUCHTPOST" ("AIR-MAIL") on the original stamp is obliterated by bars.

1977. Child Welfare. Multicoloured.
895 20 c. + 10 c. Type **185** . . . 30 35
896 25 c. + 15 c. Monkey 40 45
897 30 c. + 15 c. Rabbit 45 50
898 35 c. + 15 c. Cat 50 55
899 50 c. + 25 c. Parrot 75 80

186 "Passiflora quadrangularis" **187** Javanese Costumes

1978. Flowers. Multicoloured.
901 20 c. Type **186** 25 20
902 30 c. "Centropogon surinamensis" 35 30
903 55 c. "Gloxinia perennis" . . 65 55
904 60 c. "Hydrocleys nymphoides" 70 60
905 75 c. "Clusia grandiflora" . . 85 75

1978. Surinam Costumes (2nd series). Mult.
906 10 c. Type **187** 15 10
907 20 c. Forest Negro 25 20
908 35 c. Chinese 40 35
909 60 c. Creole 75 60
910 75 c. Aborigine Indian 85 75
911 1 g. Hindustani . . . . . . 1·25 1·25

188 Cross and Halo **189** Municipal Church, 1783

1978. Easter Charity.
912 **188** 20 c. + 10 c. mult . . . 30 35
913 – 25 c. + 15 c. brown, yellow and red 45 50
914 – 30 c. + 15 c. brown, red and yellow 50 55
915 – 35 c. + 15 c. brown, violet and red 55 60
916 – 60 c. + 30 c. brown, yellow and green . . . . . . 1·00 1·10
DESIGNS: 25 c. Serpent and cross; 30 c. Blood and lamb; 35 c. Passover dish and chalice; 60 c. Eclipse and crucifix.

1978. Bicentenary of Church of Evangelistic Brothers Community.
917 **189** 10 c. brown, black & blue 10 10
918 – 20 c. black and grey . . . 20 20
919 – 55 c. black and purple . . 55 55
920 – 60 c. black and orange . . 70 70
DESIGNS: 20 c. Brother Johannes King, 1830–1899; 55 c. Modern Municipal Church; 60 c. Brother Johannes Raillard, 1939–1954.

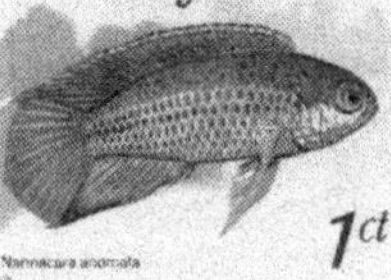

190 "Nannacara anomala" **192** Coconuts

1978. Tropical Fish. Multicoloured.
921 1 c. Type **190** (postage) . . . 10 10
922 2 c. "Leporinus fasciatus" . . 10 10
923 3 c. "Pristella riddlei" . . . 10 10
924 4 c. "Nannostomus beckfordi" 10 10
925 5 c. "Rivulus agilae" 10 10
926 60 c. "Astyanax species" (air) 75 65
927 90 c. "Corydoras wotroi" . . 1·25 1·10
928 120 c. "Gasteropelecus sternicla" 1·50 1·40

1978. Fruits. Multicoloured.
930 5 c. Type **192** 10 10
931 10 c. Citrus 10 10
932 15 c. Papaya 15 15
933a 20 c. Bananas 15 15
934 25 c. Sour-sop 25 25
934b 30 c. Cacao 25 25
935 35 c. Water melons 35 35

193 Children's Heads and Kittens

194 Daedalus and Icarus

1978. Child Welfare.
936 **193** 20 c. + 10 c. multicoloured 25 30
937 – 25 c. + 15 c. multicoloured 35 40
938 – 30 c. + 15 c. multicoloured 40 45
939 – 35 c. + 15 c. multicoloured 40 45
940 – 60 c. + 30 c. multicoloured 80 90
DESIGNS: 25 c. to 60 c. Different designs showing kittens at play.

1978. 75th Anniv of First Powered Flight. Multicoloured.
942 20 c. Type **194** 25 20
943 60 c. Wright Flyer I (horiz) . . 60 50
944 95 c. Douglas DC-8-63 (horiz) 85 70
945 125 c. Concorde (horiz) . . . 1·25 1·25

195 Black Curassow

196 "Rodriguezia candida"

1979. Air.
946 **195** 5 g. purple . . . . 8·00 6·00

1979. Orchids. Multicoloured.
947 10 c. Type **196** 15 10
948 20 c. "Stanhopea grandiflora" 25 20
949 35 c. "Scuticaria steelei" . . . 40 35
950 60 c. "Bollea violacea" . . . 65 60

197 Javanese Dance

198 Church, Chalice and Cross

1979. Dancing Costumes. Multicoloured.
951 5 c. Type **197** 10 10
952 10 c. Forest Negro 10 10
953 15 c. Chinese 20 15
954 20 c. Creole 20 20
955 25 c. Aborigine Indian 25 20
956 25 c. Hindustani 35 35

1979. Easter Charity.
957 **198** 20 c. + 10 c. multicoloured 25 30
958 – 30 c. + 15 c. multicoloured 35 40
959 – 35 c. + 15 c. multicoloured 40 45
960 – 40 c. + 20 c. multicoloured 45 50
961 – 60 c. + 30 c. multicoloured 70 80
DESIGNS: 30 c. to 60 c. Different churches.

199 "Equetus pulchellus"

1979. Fishes. Multicoloured.
962 1 c. Type **199** (postage) . . . 10 10
963 2 c. "Apogon binotatus" . . . 10 10
964 3 c. "Anisotremus virginicus" . . 10 10
965 5 c. "Bodianus rufus" 10 10
966 35 c. "Microspathodon chrysurus" 35 35
967 60 c. "Cantherinus macrocerus" (air) 65 65
968 90 c. "Holocentrus rufus" . . 95 95
969 120 c. "Holacanthus tricolor" 1·25 1·25

200 Javanese Wooden Head

1979. Art Objects. Multicoloured.
970 20 c. Type **200** 20 20
971 35 c. American Indian hair ornament 30 30
972 60 c. Javanese horse's head . 55 55

201 S.O.S. Children's Village and Emblem

202 Sir Rowland Hill

1979. International Year of the Child. Multicoloured.
973 20 c. Type **201** 20 15
974 60 c. Different view of Village, and emblem 55 55

1979. Death Centenary of Sir Rowland Hill.
975 **202** 1 g. green and yellow . . 1·00 1·00

203 Bird, Running Youth and Blood Transfusion Bottle

204 Javanese

1979. Child Welfare.
976 **203** 20 c. + 10 c. blk, vio & red 25 30
977 30 c. + 15 c. black, red and violet 40 45
978 35 c. + 15 c. multicoloured 45 50
979 40 c. + 20 c. multicoloured 50 55
980 60 c. + 30 c. multicoloured 70 80

1980. Children's Costumes. Multicoloured.
982 10 c. Type **204** 10 10
983 15 c. Forest Negro 15 15
984 25 c. Chinese 25 20
985 60 c. Creole 55 55
986 90 c. Indian 80 80
987 1 g. Hindustani 85 85

205 Handshake and Rotary Emblem

206 Church Interior

1980. 75th Anniv of Rotary International. Each blue and yellow.
988 20 c. Type **205** 20 20
989 60 c. Globe and Rotary emblem 50 50

1980. Easter Charity. Various Easter symbols.
990 **206** 20 c. + 10 c. multicoloured 25 30
991 – 30 c. + 15 c. multicoloured 40 45
992 – 40 c. + 20 c. multicoloured 50 55
993 – 50 c. + 25 c. multicoloured 60 70
994 – 60 c. + 30 c. multicoloured 70 80

207 Mail Coach

208 Weightlifting

1980. "London 1980" International Stamp Exhibition.
995 **207** 50 c. yellow, black & blue 40 40
996 – 1 g. yellow, black & purple 80 80
997 – 2 g. pink, black & turq . 1·60 1·60
DESIGNS: 1 g. Sir Rowland Hill; 2 g. People posting letters.

1980. Olympic Games, Moscow.
999 **208** 20 c. multicoloured . . . 20 20
1000 – 30 c. multicoloured . . . 25 25
1001 – 50 c. green, yellow & red 40 40
1002 – 75 c. multicoloured . . . 60 60
1003 – 150 c. multicoloured . . . 1·25 1·25
DESIGNS: 30 c. Diving; 50 c. Gymnastics; 75 c. Basketball; 150 c. Running.

209 "Osteoglossum bicirrhosum"

210 Anansi disguised as Spider

1980. Tropical Fishes. Multicoloured.
1005 10 c. Type **209** (postage) . . . 10 10
1006 15 c. "Colossoma species" . . 15 15
1007 25 c. "Hemigrammus pulcher" 25 20
1008 30 c. "Petitella georgiae" . . 30 25
1009 45 c. "Copeina guttata" . . . 45 40
1010 60 c. "Symhysodon discus" (air) 60 55
1011 75 c. "Aequidens curviceps" . 70 65
1012 90 c. "Catoprion mento" . . 80 75

1980. Child Welfare. "The Story of Anansi and his Creditors".
1013 **210** 20 c. + 10 c. bistre and yellow 30 35
1014 – 25 c. + 15 c. yellow, brown and orange 35 40
1015 – 30 c. + 15 c. brown, red and orange 40 45
1016 – 35 c. + 15 c. green, light green & yellow 45 50
1017 – 60 c. + 30 c. multicoloured 80 90
DESIGNS: (Anansi in various disguises) 25 c. Bear; 30 c. Cockerel; 35 c. Hunter; 60 c. Beetle.

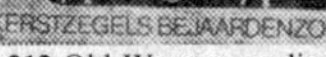

212 Old Woman reading

213 "Passiflora laurifolia"

1980. Welfare of the Aged. Multicoloured.
1020 25 c. + 10 c. Type **212** . . . 30 35
1021 50 c. + 15 c. Old man tending flowers 50 60
1022 75 c. + 20 c. Grandfather and grandchildren 80 90

1981. Flower Drawings by Maria Sibylle Merian. Multicoloured.
1023 20 c. Type **213** 20 20
1024 30 c. "Aphelandra pectinata" 30 25
1025 60 c. "Caesalpinia pulcherrima" 55 55
1026 75 c. "Hibiscus mutabilis" . . 70 70
1027 1 g. 25 "Hippeastrum puniceum" . . . . 1·25 1·25

214 Justice and Text "Renewal of the Governmental and Political Order"

215 Christ with Jug

1981. The Four Renewals.
1028 – 30 c. yellow, brown and deep yellow 25 25
1029 – 60 c. orange, brn & red . 50 50
1030 – 75 c. green, deep green and olive 60 60
1031 **214** 1 g. deep yellow, green and yellow 80 80
DESIGNS: 30 c. "Renewal of the Economic Order"; 60 c. "Renewal of the Educational Order"; 75 c. "Renewal of the Social Order".

1981. Easter Charity. Multicoloured.
1033 20 c. + 10 c. Type **215** . . . 25 30
1034 30 c. + 15 c. Christ and pointing hand 40 45
1035 50 c. + 25 c. Christ and Roman soldier 60 65
1036 60 c. + 30 c. Christ wearing crown of thorns 70 80
1037 75 c. + 35 c. Christ and Mary 80 90

218 "Phyllomedusa hypochondrialis"

1981. Frogs. Multicoloured.
1040 40 c. Type **218** (postage) . . 40 35
1041 50 c. "Leptodactylus pentadactylus" 45 40
1042 60 c. "Hyla boans" 55 50
1043 75 c. "Phyllomedusa burmeisteri" (vert) (air) . . 70 65
1044 1 g. "Dendrobates tinctorius" (vert) 90 85
1045 1 g. 25 "Bufo guttatus" (vert) 1·25 1·25

219 Deaf Child

1981. International Year of Disabled Persons.
1046 **219** 50 c. yellow and green . 40 40
1047 – 100 c. yellow and green . 80 80
1048 – 150 c. yellow and red . . 1·25 1·25
DESIGNS: 100 c. Child reading braille; 150 c. Woman in wheelchair.

220 Planter's House on the Parakreek River

221 Indian Girl

1981. Illustrations to "Journey to Surinam" by P. I. Benoit. Multicoloured.
1049 20 c. Type **220** 20 20
1050 30 c. Sarameca Street, Paramaribo 25 25
1051 75 c. Negro hamlet, Paramaribo 60 60
1052 1 g. Fish market, Paramaribo 80 80
1053 1 g. 25 Blaauwe Berg Cascade 1·00 1·00

1981. Child Welfare. Multicoloured.
1055 20 c. + 10 c. Type **221** . . . 25 30
1056 30 c. + 15 c. Negro girl . . 40 45
1057 50 c. + 25 c. Hindustani girl 60 70
1058 60 c. + 30 c. Javanese girl . 70 80
1059 75 c. + 35 c. Chinese girl . . 80 90

222 Satellites orbiting Earth

1982. Peaceful Uses of Outer Space. Mult.
1061 35 c. Type **222** 35 30
1062 65 c. Space shuttle 60 55
1063 1 g. U.S.–Russian space link 85 85

223 "Caretta caretta"

224 Pattern from Stained Glass Window

1982. Turtles. Multicoloured.
1064 5 c. Type **223** (postage) . . . 10 10
1065 10 c. "Chelonia mydas" . . 10 10
1066 20 c. "Dermochelys coriacea" 20 20
1067 25 c. "Eretmochelys imbricata" 25 25
1068 35 c. "Lepidochelys olivacea" 30 30
1069 65 c. "Platemys platycephala" (air) 60 60
1070 75 c. "Phrynops gibba" . . . 75 75
1071 125 c. "Rihnoclemys punctularia" . . . . 1·10 1·10

1982. Easter. Stained-glass windows, Church of Saints Peter and Paul, Paramaribo.
1072 **224** 20 c. + 10 c. multicoloured 25 30
1073 – 35 c. + 15 c. multicoloured 40 45
1074 – 50 c. + 25 c. multicoloured 60 70
1075 – 65 c. + 30 c. multicoloured 75 85
1076 – 75 c. + 35 c. multicoloured 80 90
DESIGNS: 35 c. to 75 c. Different patterns.

225 Lions Emblem **226** Father Donders with the Sick

1982. 25th Anniv of Surinam Lions Club.
1077 **225** 35 c. multicoloured . . . 30 30
1078 70 c. multicoloured . . . 60 60

1982. Beatification of Father Peter Donders.
1079 **226** 35 c. multicoloured . . . 30 30
1080 – 65 c. silver, black and red 50 50
DESIGN: 65 c. Portrait, birthplace, Tilburg, and map of South America.

227 Stamp Designer **228** Dr. Robert Koch

1982. "Philexfrance 82" International Stamp Exhibition, Paris. Multicoloured.
1082 50 c. Type **227** 40 40
1083 100 c. Stamp printing 80 80
1084 150 c. Stamp collector . . . 1·25 1·25

1982. Cent of Discovery of Tubercle Bacillus.
1086 **228** 35 c. yellow and green . . 35 30
1087 – 65 c. orange and brown . 60 55
1088 – 150 c. light blue, blue and red . . . . 1·50 1·50
DESIGNS: 65 c. Dr. Koch and microscope; 150 c. Dr. Koch and Bacillus.

229 Sugar Mill **230** Cleaning Tools and Flag

1982. Cent of Marienburg Sugar Company.
1089 **229** 35 c. yellow, green and black 30 30
1090 – 65 c. orange and brown 50 50
1091 – 100 c. light blue, blue and black . . . . 1·10 1·10
1092 – 150 c. lilac and purple . . 1·25 1·25
DESIGNS: 65 c. Workers in cane fields; 100 c. Sugar cane railway; 150 c. Mill machinery.

1982. Child Welfare. "Keep Surinam Tidy" (children's paintings). Multicoloured.
1093 20 c. + 10 c. Type **230** . . . 25 30
1094 35 c. + 15 c. Man with barrow 40 45
1095 50 c. + 25 c. Litter bin and cleaning tools 60 70
1096 65 c. + 30 c. Spraying weeds 75 85
1097 75 c. + 35 c. Litter bin . . . 85 95

231 Municipal Church, Paramaribo

1982. 250th Anniv of Moravian Church Mission in the Caribbean.
1099 **231** 35 c. multicoloured . . . 30 30
1100 – 65 c. light blue, black and blue 50 50
1101 – 150 c. multicoloured . . 1·25 1·25
DESIGNS—HORIZ: 65 c. Aerial view of St. Thomas Monastery. VERT: 150 c. Johann Leonhardt Dober (missionary).

232 "Erythrina fusca"

1983. Flower Paintings by Maria Sibylle Merian. Multicoloured.
1102 1 c. Type **232** 10 10
1103 2 c. "Ipomoea acuminata" . 10 10
1104 3 c. "Heliconia psittacorum" 10 10
1105 5 c. "Ipomoea" 10 10
1106 10 c. "Herba non denominata" 10 10
1107 15 c. "Anacardium occidentale" 15 15
1108 20 c. "Inga edulis" (vert) . . 20 15
1109 25 c. "Abelmoschus moschatus" (vert) 25 20
1110 30 c. "Argemone mexicana" (vert) 30 25
1111 35 c. "Costus arabicus" (vert) 35 30
1112 45 c. "Muellera frutescens" (vert) 45 45
1113 65 c. "Punica granatum" (vert) 60 60

233 Scout Anniversary Emblem **234** Dove of Peace

1983. Year of the Scout.
1114 **233** 40 c. mauve, vio & grn . 45 40
1115 – 65 c. lt grey, bl & grey . 70 60
1116 – 70 c. multicoloured . . 80 70
1117 – 80 c. blue, lt grn & grn . 85 80
DESIGNS: 65 c. Lord Baden-Powell; 70 c. Tent and campfire; 80 c. Axe in tree trunk.

1983. Easter. Multicoloured.
1118 10 c. + 5 c. Type **234** . . . 15 15
1119 15 c. + 5 c. Bread 20 25
1120 25 c. + 10 c. Fish 30 35
1121 50 c. + 25 c. Eye 60 70
1122 65 c. + 30 c. Chalice . . . 75 85

235 Drawing by Raphael

1983. 500th Birth Anniv of Raphael.
1123 **235** 5 c. multicoloured . . . 10 10
1124 – 10 c. multicoloured . . 10 10
1125 – 40 c. multicoloured . . 35 35
1126 – 65 c. multicoloured . . 60 60
1127 – 70 c. multicoloured . . 65 65
1128 – 80 c. multicoloured . . 70 70
DESIGNS: Drawings by Raphael.

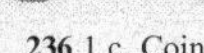

236 1 c. Coin **237** "25" on Map of Surinam

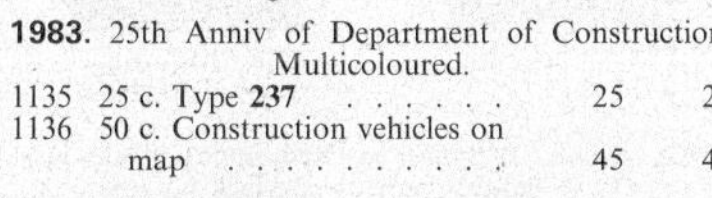

1983. Coins and Banknotes. Multicoloured.
1129 5 c. Type **236** 10 10
1130 10 c. 5 c. coin 10 10
1131 40 c. 10 c. coin 45 40
1132 65 c. 25 c. coin 65 65
1133 70 c. 1 g. note 70 70
1134 80 c. 2½ g. note . . . . . . 1·50 90

1983. 25th Anniv of Department of Construction. Multicoloured.
1135 25 c. Type **237** 25 25
1136 50 c. Construction vehicles on map 45 45

238 "Papilio anchisiades" **239** Montgolfier Balloon "Le Martial", 1783

1983. Butterfly Paintings by Maria Sibylle Merian. Multicoloured.
1137 1 c. Type **238** 10 10
1138 2 c. "Urania leilus" 10 10
1139 3 c. "Morpho deidamia" . . 10 10
1140 5 c. "Thysania agrippina" . . 10 10
1141 10 c. "Morpho sp." 20 10
1142 15 c. "Philaethria dido" . . 30 20
1143 20 c. "Morpho menelaus" (horiz) 40 25
1144 25 c. "Protoparce rustica" (horiz) 50 30
1145 30 c. "Rothschildia aurota" (horiz) 60 40
1146 35 c. "Phoebis sennae" (horiz) 80 50
1147 45 c. "Papilio androgeos" (horiz) 90 70
1148 65 c. "Dupo vitis" (horiz) . 1·40 1·00

1983. Bicentenary. of Manned Flight. Mult.
1149 5 c. Type **239** 10 10
1150 10 c. Montgolfier balloon (1st manned free flight by D'Arlandes and Pilatre de Rozier, 1783) 10 10
1151 40 c. Charles's hydrogen balloon, 1783 . . . . . . 40 40
1152 65 c. Balloon "Armand Barbes", 1870 65 65
1153 70 c. Balloon "Double Eagle II" (transatlantic flight, 1978) 70 70
1154 80 c. Hot-air balloons at International Balloon Festival, Albuquerque, U.S.A. 75 75

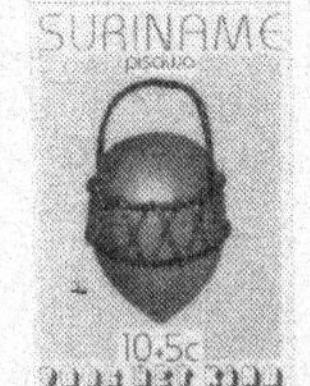

240 Calabash Pitcher **241** Martin Luther

1983. Child Welfare. Caribbean Artifacts. Multicoloured.
1155 10 c. + 5 c. Type **240** 15 15
1156 15 c. + 5 c. Umari (headdress) 15 20
1157 25 c. + 10 c. Maraka (medicine man's rattle) 20 35
1158 50 c. + 25 c. Manari (sieve) 60 70
1159 65 c. + 30 c. Pasuwa/pakara (basket) 70 80

1983. 500th Birth Anniv of Martin Luther (Protestant reformer).
1161 **241** 25 c. yellow, brown and black 20 20
1162 – 50 c. pink, purple & blk . 40 40
DESIGN: 50 c. Selling of indulgences.

242 "Catasetum discolor" **243** Atlantic Turkey Wing

1983. Orchids. Multicoloured.
1163 5 c. Type **242** 10 10
1164 10 c. "Menadenium labiosum" 10 10
1165 40 c. "Comparettia falcata" 45 40
1166 50 c. "Rodriguezia decora" 70 60
1167 70 c. "Oncidium papilio" . . 80 70
1168 75 c. "Epidendrum porpax" 85 75

1984. Sea Shells. Multicoloured.
1169 40 c. Type **243** 45 45
1170 65 c. American prickly cockle 80 80
1171 70 c. Sunrise tellin 80 80
1172 80 c. Knorr's worm shell . . 95 95

244 Cross and Flower **245** Sikorsky S-40 Flying Boat

1984. Easter. Multicoloured.
1173 10 c. + 5 c. Type **244** 15 15
1174 15 c. + 5 c. Cross and gate of cemetery 15 20
1175 25 c. + 10 c. Candle flames . 30 35
1176 50 c. + 25 c. Cross and crown of thorns 60 70
1177 65 c. + 30 c. Lamp 70 80

1984. 40th Anniv of I.C.A.O. Multicoloured.
1178 35 c. Type **245** 40 40
1179 65 c. Surinam Airways De Havilland Twin Otter 200/300 85 85

246 Running **247** Emblem of 8th Caribbean Scout Jamboree

1984. Olympic Games, Los Angeles. Multicoloured.
1180 2 c. Type **246** 10 10
1181 3 c. Javelin, discus and long jump 10 10
1182 5 c. Massage 10 10
1183 10 c. Rubbing with ointment 10 10
1184 15 c. Wrestling 15 15
1185 20 c. Boxing 20 20
1186 30 c. Horse-racing 30 30
1187 35 c. Chariot-racing 35 35
1188 45 c. Temple of Olympia . . 40 40
1189 50 c. Entrance to Stadium, Olympia 45 45
1190 65 c. Stadium, Olympia . . . 60 60
1191 75 c. Zeus 70 70

1984. 60th Anniv of Scouting in Surinam. Multicoloured.
1193 30 c. + 10 c. Type **247** . . . 40 40
1194 35 c. + 10 c. Scout saluting 50 50
1195 50 c. + 10 c. Scout camp . . 65 65
1196 90 c. + 10 c. Campfire and map 95 95

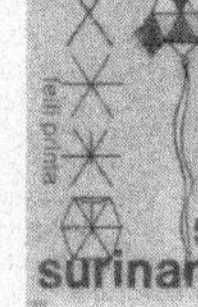

248 Ball entering Basket **249** Red Square, Moscow

1984. International Military Sports Council Basketball Championship. Multicoloured.
1197 50 c. Type **248** 50 45
1198 90 c. Ball leaving basket . . 85 75

1984. World Chess Championship, Moscow.
1199 **249** 10 c. brown 10 10
1200 – 15 c. green & light green 15 15
1201 – 30 c. lt brown and brown 30 30
1202 – 50 c. brown and purple . 50 50
1203 – 75 c. brown & lt brown . 80 80
1204 – 90 c. green and blue . . 90 90
DESIGNS: 15 c. Knight, king and pawn on board; 30 c. Gary Kasparov; 50 c. Start of game and clock; 75 c. Anatoly Karpov; 90 c. Position during Andersen–Kizeritski game.

250 Children collecting Milk from Cow **251** Kite

1984. World Food Day. Multicoloured.
1206 50 c. Type **250** 50 45
1207 90 c. Platter of food 85 75

1984. Child Welfare. Multicoloured.
1208 5 c. + 5 c. Type **251** 10 10
1209 10 c. + 5 c. Kites 15 15
1210 30 c. + 10 c. Pingi-pingi-kasi (game) 40 40
1211 50 c. + 25 c. Cricket 85 85
1212 90 c. + 30 c. Peroen, peroen (game) . . . . 1·10 1·10

252 Leaf Cactus

1985. Cacti. Multicoloured.
1215 5 c. Type **252** 10 10
1216 10 c. Melocactus 10 10
1217 30 c. Pillar cactus 25 25
1218 50 c. Fig cactus 45 45
1219 75 c. Night queen 70 70
1220 90 c. Segment cactus 80 80

253 "Peace" and Star **254** Crosses

1985. 5th Anniv of Revolution. Multicoloured.

1221 5 c. Type **253** 10 10
1222 30 c. "Unity in labour" and manual workers 20 20
1223 50 c. "5 years of Steadfastness" and flower 40 40
1224 75 c. "Progress" and wheat as flower 60 60
1225 90 c. "Unity", flower and dove 70 70

1985. Easter. Multicoloured.

1227 5 c. + 5 c. Type **254** 10 10
1228 10 c. + 5 c. Crosses (different) 10 10
1229 30 c. + 15 c. Sun's rays illuminating crosses 30 30
1230 50 c. + 25 c. Crosses (different) 55 65
1231 90 c. + 30 c. Crosses and leaves (Resurrection) 75 85

255 Emblem

256 U.N. Emblem and State Arms

1985. 75th Anniv of Chamber of Commerce and Industry.

1232 **255** 50 c. yellow, green & red 40 40
1233 – 90 c. green, blue & yell . 70 70
DESIGN: 90 c. Chamber of Commerce building.

1985. 40th Anniv of U.N.O.

1234 **256** 50 c. multicoloured . . . 40 40
1235 90 c. multicoloured . . . 70 70

257 Sugar-cane Train (detail of 1945 stamp)

1985. Railway Locomotives.

1236 **257** 5 c. orange and blue . . 10 10
1237 – 5 c. green, red & blue . . 10 10
1238 – 10 c. multicoloured . . . 15 10
1239 – 10 c. multicoloured . . . 15 10
1240 – 20 c. multicoloured . . . 30 20
1241 – 20 c. multicoloured . . . 30 20
1242 – 30 c. multicoloured . . . 55 30
1243 – 30 c. multicoloured . . . 55 30
1244 – 50 c. multicoloured . . . 95 55
1245 – 50 c. multicoloured . . . 95 55
1246 – 75 c. multicoloured . . . 1·25 80
1247 – 75 c. multicoloured . . . 1·25 80
DESIGNS: No. 1237, Monaco 3 f. Postage due train stamp; 1238, Steam locomotive "Dam"; 1239, Modern electric locomotive and carriage unit; 1240, Steam locomotive "3737"; 1241, Electric locomotive "NS-IC III"; 1242, Stephenson's "Rocket"; 1243, French "TGV" (high speed) locomotive; 1244, Stephenson's "Der Adler"; 1245, French double-decker "UB2N"; 1246, American locomotive "The General"; 1247, Japanese "Shinkansen" train.

258 Purple Gallinule

259 German Letterbox, 1900

1985. Birds. Multicoloured.

1248 1 g. Type **258** . . . . 1·25 1·00
1249 1 g. 50 Rufescent tiger heron 1·60 1·40
1250 2 g. 50 Scarlet ibis . . . . . 3·00 2·50
1251 5 g. Guianan cock of the rock 3·75 3·00
1252 10 g. Harpy eagle . . . . . . 8·00 7·00

1985. Old Letterboxes. Multicoloured.

1254 15 c. Type **259** 15 15
1255 30 c. French letterbox, 1900 20 20
1256 50 c. English pillar box, 1932 35 35
1257 90 c. Dutch letterbox, 1850 55 55

260 Emblem on Map

261 Studying

1985. 25th Anniv of Evangelical Brotherhood in Surinam.

1258 **260** 30 c. + 10 c. multicoloured 30 30
1259 – 50 c. + 10 c. red, yellow and brown 45 45
1260 – 90 c. + 20 c. yellow, brown and red 75 75
DESIGNS: 50 c. Different population groups around cross and clasped hands emblem; 90 c. List of work undertaken by Brotherhood.

1985. Child Welfare. Multicoloured.

1261 5 c. + 5 c. Type **261** 10 10
1262 10 c. + 5 c. Writing alphabet on board 15 15
1263 30 c. + 10 c. Writing . . . 30 30
1264 50 c. + 25 c. Reading . . . 55 55
1265 90 c. + 30 c. Thinking . . . 80 80

1985. Victory of Kasparov in World Chess Championship. No. 1201 optd **КАСПАРОВ Wereldkampioen 9 nov. 1985.**

1267 30 c. light brown and brown 30 20

263 Agriculture

264 "Epidendrum ciliare"

1985. 10th Anniv of Independence.

1268 **263** 50 c. yellow and green . 40 40
1269 – 90 c. orange and brown 70 70
DESIGN: 90 c. Industry.

1986. Orchids. Multicoloured.

1271 5 c. Type **264** 35 35
1272 15 c. "Cycnoches chlorochilon" 1·10 1·10
1273 30 c. "Epidendrum anceps" 1·75 1·75
1274 50 c. "Epidendrum vespa" . 3·25 3·25

265 Bayeux Tapestry (detail)

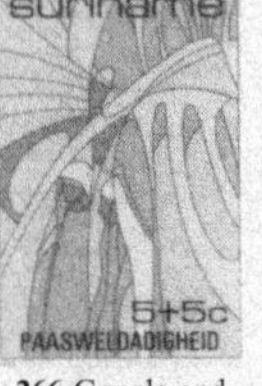

266 Couple and Palm Leaves

1986. Appearance of Halley's Comet. Multicoloured.

1275 50 c. Type **265** 35 35
1276 110 c. Comet 75 75

1986. Easter.

1277 **266** 5 c. + 5 c. multicoloured 10 10
1278 10 c. + 5 c. multicoloured 15 15
1279 30 c. + 15 c. multicoloured 30 30
1280 50 c. + 25 c. multicoloured 55 55
1281 90 c. + 30 c. multicoloured 80 80

1986. Nos. 1244/5 surch.

1282 15 c. on 50 c. multicoloured 45 15
1283 15 c. on 50 c. multicoloured 45 20

268 Cathedral

270 National Forestry Emblem

1986. Centenary of St. Peter and St. Paul's Cathedral, Paramaribo.

1284 **268** 30 c. + 10 c. brown and ochre 30 30
1285 – 50 c. + 10 c. brown and red 50 50
1286 – 110 c. + 30 c. deep brown and brown . . . . . 1·10 1·10
DESIGNS: 50 c. Relief of St. Peter and St. Paul; 110 c. Font.

1986. 150th Anniv of Finance Building. No. 1133 surch **30 c 150 jaar FINANCIENGE BOUW.**

1287 30 c. on 70 . multicoloured . 30 30

1986. Centenary of Foresters' Court Charity. Multicoloured.

1288 50 c. + 20 c. Type **270** . . . 60 60
1289 110 c. + 30 c. First Court building . . . . 1·25 1·25

271 Emblem

1986. 50th Anniv of Surinam Shipping Line. Multicoloured.

1290 50 c. Type **271** 40 40
1291 110 c. Container ship "Saramacca" . . . . 2·00 1·10

1986. No. 862 surch **15ct.**

1292 15 c. on 30 c. multicoloured . 70 25

273 Children playing Hopscotch

1986. Child Welfare. Multicoloured.

1293 5 c. + 5 c. Type **273** 10 10
1294 10 c. + 5 c. Ballet class . . . 15 15
1295 30 c. + 10 c. Children boarding library bus 35 35
1296 50 c. + 25 c. Boys at display of craftwork 65 65
1297 110 c. + 30 c. Children in class 1·10 1·10

274 Red Howler

1987. Monkeys. Multicoloured.

1299 35 c. Type **274** 30 30
1300 60 c. Night monkey 55 55
1301 110 c. Common squirrel-monkey 85 85
1302 120 c. Red uakari 90 90

275 Emblem

1987. Centenary of Esperanto (invented language). Multicoloured.

1303 60 c. Type **275** 55 55
1304 110 c. Dove holding "Esperanto" banner across world map 85 85
1305 120 c. L. L. Zamenhof (inventor) 90 90

1987. Various stamps surch.

1306 – 10 c. on 85 c. multicoloured (No. 872) 70 20
1307 – 10 c. on 95 c. multicoloured (No. 873) 70 20
1308 **168** 50 c. on 1½ g. black, orange and brown 45 45
1309 60 c. on 2½ g. black, red and brown 55 55

277 "Crucifixion"

278 Mushroom (Brownie emblem)

1987. Easter. Etchings by Rembrandt. Each light mauve, mauve and black.

1310 5 c. + 5 c. Type **277** 10 10
1311 10 c. + 5 c. "Christ on the Cross" 15 15
1312 35 c. + 15 c. "Descent from the Cross" 35 35
1313 60 c. + 30 c. "Christ carried to His Tomb" 65 65
1314 110 c. + 50 c. "Entombment of Christ" . . . . 1·10 1·10

1987. 40th Anniv of Surinam Girl Guides.

1315 **278** 15 c. + 10 c. mult . . . 20 20
1316 – 60 c. + 10 c. mult . . . 50 50
1317 – 110 c. + 10 c. mult . . . 80 80
1318 – 120 c. + 10 c. green, black and yellow 90 90
DESIGNS: 60 c. Cloverleaf and star (Guide emblem); 110 c. Campfire (Rangers emblem) on Guide trefoil; 120 c. Ivy leaves (Captain's emblem).

279 Football

280 Commission Emblem

1987. 10th Pan-American Games, Indianapolis.

1319 **279** 90 c. blue, green and brown 80 80
1320 – 110 c. blue, light blue and brown 90 90
1321 – 150 c. blue, mauve and brown . . . . 1·25 1·25
DESIGNS: 110 c. Swimming; 150 c. Basketball.

1987. 40th Anniv of Forestry Commission. Multicoloured.

1322 90 c. Type **280** 80 80
1323 120 c. Loading tree trunks for export 95 95
1324 150 c. Green-winged macaw in forest . . . . 2·50 1·25

282 Boy and Tents

283 Banana

1987. International Year of Shelter for the Homeless (90, 120 c.) and Centenary of Salvation Army in the Caribbean Territory (150 c.). Multicoloured.

1331 90 c. Type **282** 70 70
1332 120 c. Shanty town and man 85 85
1333 150 c. William and Catherine Booth and emblem . . . . 1·10 1·10

1987. Fruits. Multicoloured.

1334 10 c. Type **283** 10 10
1335 15 c. Cacao bean 15 15
1336 20 c. Pineapple 15 15
1337 25 c. Papaya 20 20
1338 35 c. China orange 30 30

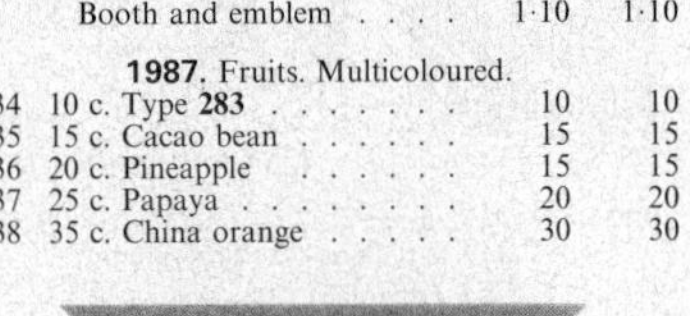

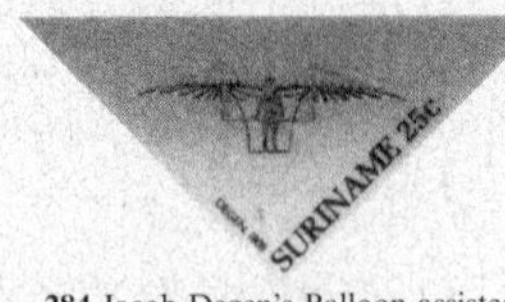

284 Jacob Degen's Balloon-assisted "Ornithopter", 1808

1987. Aircraft. Multicoloured.

1339 25 c. Type **284** 20 20
1340 25 c. Microlight airplane . . 20 20
1341 35 c. Ellehammer II, 1906 . . 30 30
1342 35 c. Concorde 30 30
1343 60 c. Fokker F.VII (inscr "F.7"), 1924 . . . . . . 50 50
1344 60 c. Fokker F28 Friendship 50 50
1345 90 c. Fokker monoplane "Haarlem Spin", 1910 . . 75 75
1346 90 c. Douglas DC-10 . . . . 75 75
1347 110 c. Lockheed 9 Orion, 1932 80 80
1348 110 c. Boeing 747 . . . . . . 80 80
1349 120 c. 1967 Amelia Earhart 25 c. stamp 95 95
1350 120 c. 1978 Douglas DC-8-63 95 c. stamp 95 95

285 Herring-bone Design

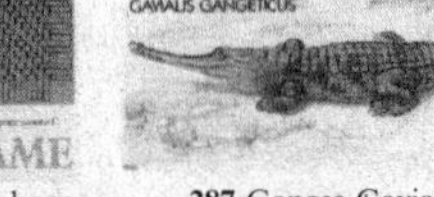

287 Ganges Gavial

1987. Child Welfare. Indian Weaving.

1351 **285** 50 c. + 25 c. grn & blk 65 65
1352 – 60 c. + 30 c. orange and black 70 70
1353 – 110 c. + 50 c. red & blk 1·25 1·25
DESIGNS: 60 c. Tortoise-back design; 110 c. Concentric diamonds design.

1987. Nos. 869 and 805 surch.

1356 – 25 c. on 70 c. mult . . . 75 40
1357 **168** 35 c. on 1 g. black, mauve and purple 60 60

1988. Reptiles. Multicoloured.

1358 50 c. Type **287** 40 40
1359 60 c. Nile crocodile 50 50
1360 90 c. Black cayman 70 70
1361 110 c. Mississippi alligator . . 80 80

288 Javanese Costumes

290 Cross and Chalice

1988. Wedding Costumes. Multicoloured.

1362 35 c. Type **288** 30 30
1363 60 c. Bushman 50 50
1364 80 c. Chinese 65 65
1365 110 c. Creole 80 80
1366 120 c. Amerindian 85 85
1367 130 c. Hindustan 90 90

1988. Various stamps surch.
1368 – 60 c. on 75 c. mult (No. 1246) . . . . 1·40 1·00
1369 – 60 c. on 75 c. mult (No. 1247) . . . . 1·40 1·00
1370 **168** 125 c. on 10 g. black, blue and deep blue . . . . 1·75 1·75

1988. Easter.
1371 **290** 50 c. + 25 c. mult . . . 65 65
1372 60 c. + 30 c. mult . . . 75 75
1373 110 c. + 50 c. mult . . . 1·40 1·40

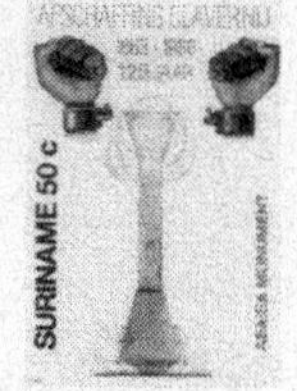
291 Relay **292** Abaisa Monument

1988. Olympic Games, Seoul. Multicoloured.
1374 90 c. Type **291** 80 80
1375 110 c. Football 90 90
1376 120 c. Pole vaulting . . . . . 1·00 1·00
1377 250 c. Tennis . . . . 2·00 2·00

1988. 125th Anniv of Abolition of Slavery. Multicoloured.
1379 50 c. Type **292** 50 50
1380 110 c. Kwakoe monument . . 90 90
1381 120 c. Anton de Kom's house 1·10 1·10

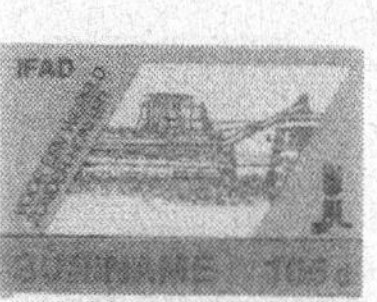

293 Combine Harvester **294** Egypt 1906 4 m. Stamp

1988. 10th Anniv of International Agricultural Development Fund. "For a World without Hunger". Multicoloured.
1382 105 c. Type **293** 90 90
1383 110 c. Fishing 95 95
1384 125 c. Cultivation . . . . . 1·25 1·25

1988. "Filacept" International Stamp Exhibition, The Hague.
1385 **294** 120 c. red, black & orge . 1·00 1·00
1386 – 150 c. green, blk & bl . . 1·25 1·25
1387 – 250 c. red, black & deep red 2·25 2·25
DESIGNS: No. 1386, Netherlands 1952 10 c. Stamp Centenary stamp; No. 1387, Surinam 1949 7½ c. U.P.U. stamp.

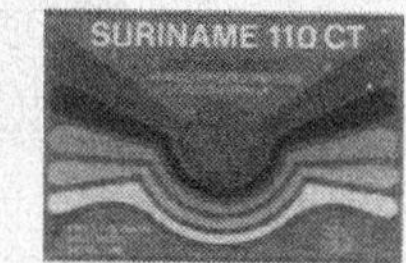
295 Anniversary Emblem **296** Symbolic Representation of Butterfly Stroke

1988. 125th Anniv of Red Cross. Multicoloured.
1389 60 c. + 30 c. Type **295** . . . 85 85
1390 120 c. + 60 c. Anniversary emblem and red cross in blood drop . . . . 1·60 1·60

1988. Anthony Nesty, Seoul Olympic Gold Medal Winner for 100 m Butterfly.
1391 **296** 110 c. multicoloured . . 95 95

297 "Man and Animal"

1988. 25th Anniv of Child Welfare Stamps. Multicoloured.
1392 50 c. + 25 c. Type **297** . . . 70 70
1393 60 c. + 30 c. "The Child in Nature" 85 85
1394 110 c. + 50 c. Children helping each other ("Stop Drugs") 1·50 1·50

1988. Nos. 1238/9 and 1244/5 surch.
1396 2 c. on 10 c. mult (No. 1238) 10 10
1397 2 c. on 10 c. mult (No. 1239) 10 10
1398 3 c. on 50 c. mult (No. 1244) 10 10
1399 3 c. on 50 c. mult (No. 1245) 10 10

299 Otter on Rock **300** "The Passion" (left wing)

1989. Otters. Multicoloured.
1400 10 c. Type **299** 10 10
1401 20 c. Two otters 20 10
1402 25 c. Two otters (different) . 25 25
1403 30 c. Otter with fish 30 30
1404 185 c. Two otters (vert) (air) 1·60 1·60

1989. Easter. Altarpiece by Tamas of Koloszvar. Multicoloured.
1405 60 c. + 30 c. Type **300** . . . 85 85
1406 105 c. + 50 c. "Crucifixion" (centre panel) (28 × 36 mm) 1·50 1·50
1407 110 c. + 55 c. "Resurrection" (right wing) . . . . . . 1·50 1·50

301 Mercedes Touring Car, 1930

1989. Motor Cars. Multicoloured.
1408 25 c. Type **301** 15 15
1409 25 c. Mercedes Benz "300 E", 1985 . . . . 15 15
1410 60 c. Daimler, 1897 . . . . 40 40
1411 60 c. Jaguar "Sovereign", 1986 40 40
1412 90 c. Renault "Voiturette", 1898 60 60
1413 90 c. Renault "25 TX", 1989 60 60
1414 105 c. Volvo "Jacob", 1927 70 70
1415 105 c. Volvo "440", 1989 . . 70 70
1416 110 c. Left-half of 1961 1 f. Monaco stamp 75 75
1417 110 c. Right-half of 1961 1 f. Monaco stamp 75 75
1418 120 c. Toyota "AA", 1936 . . 80 80
1419 120 c. Toyota "Corolla" sedan, 1988 . . . . 80 80

303 Joseph Nicephore Niepce (pioneer) **304** Jade Statuette

1989. 150th Anniv of Photography. Mult.
1421 60 c. Type **303** 40 40
1422 110 c. First camera using daguerreotype process . . 75 75
1423 120 c. Louis Jacques Mande Daguerre (inventor of daguerreotype process) . . 80 80

1989. America. Pre Columbian Artifacts. Multicoloured.
1424 60 c. Type **304** 40 40
1425 110 c. Statuette of pregnant woman 75 75

305 1976 25 c. Surinam Stamp **306** "Children Helping Each Other" (Gianna Karg)

1989. "World Stamp Expo '89" International Stamp Exhibition, Washington, D.C. Multicoloured.
1426 110 c. Type **305** 75 75
1427 150 c. 1950 3 c. U.S.A. White House stamp . . . . . . 1·00 1·00
1428 250 c. 1976 60 c. Surinam "Divided Snake" stamp . . 1·75 1·75

1989. Child Welfare. Children's Paintings. Multicoloured.
1430 60 c. + 30 c. Type **306** . . . 60 60
1431 105 c. + 50 c. "Child and Nature" (Tamara Busropan) 1·00 1·00
1432 110 c. + 55 c. "In the School Bus" (Cindy Kross) . . . 1·10 1·10

307 Local Emblem **308** Temple

1990. International Literacy Year. Multicoloured.
1434 60 c. Type **307** 40 40
1435 110 c. I.L.Y. emblem 75 75
1436 120 c. Emblems and boy reading 80 80

1990. 60th Anniv of Arya Dewaker Temple.
1437 **308** 60 c. brown, red & black 40 40
1438 110 c. violet and black . . 75 75
1439 200 c. green and black . . 1·40 1·40

309 Mary and Baby Jesus **310** Surinam 1930 10 c. Air Stamp

1990. Easter. Multicoloured.
1440 60 c. + 30 c. Type **309** . . . 55 55
1441 105 c. + 50 c. Jesus teaching 90 90
1442 110 c. + 55 c. Jesus's body taken from cross . . . . . 1·00 1·00

1990. "Stamp World London 90" International Stamp Exhibition, London, and 150th Anniv of the Penny Black. Multicoloured.
1443 110 c. Type **310** 65 65
1444 200 c. Penny Black . . . . . 1·25 1·25
1445 250 c. G.B. 1929 2½d. Postal Union Congress stamp . . 1·50 1·50

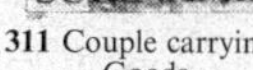

311 Couple carrying Goods **313** Swamp

312 Pomegranate

1990. Centenary of Javanese Immigration. Mult.
1447 60 c. Type **311** 35 35
1448 110 c. Woman 65 65
1449 120 c. Man 70 70

1990. Flowers. Paintings by Maria Sibylle Merian. Multicoloured.
1450 25 c. Type **312** 15 15
1451 25 c. Passion flower 15 15
1452 35 c. "Hippeastrum puniceum" 20 20
1453 35 c. Sweet potato 20 20
1454 60 c. Rose of Sharon 35 35
1455 60 c. Jasmine 35 35
1456 105 c. Blushing hibiscus . . . 60 60
1457 105 c. "Musa serapionis" . . 60 60
1458 110 c. Frangipani 65 65
1459 110 c. "Hibiscus diversifolius" 65 65
1460 120 c. Annatt ("Bixa orellana") 70 70
1461 120 c. Dwarf poinciana ("Caesalpinia pulcherima") 70 70

1990. America. Natural World.
1462 **313** 60 c. multicoloured . . . 35 35
1463 110 c. multicoloured . . . 65 65

314 Anniversary Emblem **315** Fish and Flag as Map

1990. Centenary of Organization of American States.
1464 **314** 100 c. multicoloured . . . 65 65

1990. 15th Anniv of Independence. Multicoloured.
1465 10 c. Type **315** 10 10
1466 60 c. Passion flower and flag as map 35 35
1467 110 c. Dove and flag as map 65 65

316 Painting by Janneke Fleskens

1990. Child Welfare. The Child in Nature. Paintings by children named. Multicoloured.
1468 60 c. + 30 c. Type **316** . . . 55 55
1469 105 c. + 50 c. Tahlita Zuiverloon 90 90
1470 110 c. + 55 c. Samuel Jensen 1·00 1·00

317 Green Aracari

1991. Birds. Multicoloured.
1472 10 c. Type **317** 10 10
1473 15 g. Blue and yellow macaw 9·75 9·75
1542 25 g. Barn owl . . . . 19·00 19·00

318 Christ carrying Cross **319** Shipping Company Store

1991. Easter. Multicoloured.
1474 60 c. + 30 c. Type **318** . . . 60 60
1475 105 c. + 50 c. Christ wearing crown of thorns . . . . . 1·00 1·00
1476 110 c. + 55 c. Woman cradling Christ's body . . . . . . 1·10 1·10

1991. Buildings.
1478 **319** 35 c. black, blue & lt bl . 20 20
1479 – 60 c. black, green and emerald 40 40
1480 – 75 c. blk, yell & lemon . 50 50
1481 – 105 c. black, orange and light orange 70 70
1482 – 110 c. black, pink & red 70 70
1483 – 200 c. black, deep mauve and mauve . . . . . 1·25 1·25
DESIGNS: 60 c. Upper class house; 75 c. House converted into Labour Inspection offices; 105 c. Plantation supervisor's house; 110 c. Ministry of Labour building; 200 c. Houses.

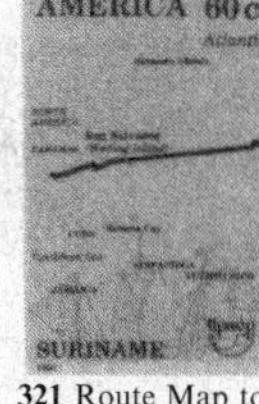
320 Puma **321** Route Map to Bahamas via San Salvador

1991. The Puma. Multicoloured.
1484 10 c. Type **320** (postage) . . 10 10
1485 20 c. Stalking 15 15
1486 25 c. Stretching 15 15
1487 30 c. Licking nose 20 20
1488 125 c. Lying down (horiz) (air) 80 80
1489 500 c. Leaping (horiz) . . . 3·25 3·25

1991. America. Voyages of Discovery. Each red, blue and black.
1490 60 c. Type **321** 65 65
1491 110 c. Route map from Canary Islands . . . . 1·00 1·00
Nos. 1490/1 were printed together, se-tenant, forming a composite design.

322 Green Tree Boa ("Corallus caninus")

1991. Snakes. Multicoloured.
1492 25 c. Type **322** 15 15
1493 25 c. Garden tree boa ("Corallus enydris") . . . 15 15
1494 35 c. Boa constrictor 20 20
1495 35 c. Bushmaster ("Lachesis muta") 20 20
1496 60 c. South American rattlesnake ("Crotalus durissus") 40 40
1497 60 c. Surinam coral snake ("Micrurus surinamensis") 40 40
1498 75 c. Mussurana ("Clelia cloelia") 50 50

1499 75 c. Anaconda ("Eunectes murinus") 50 50
1500 110 c. Rainbow boa ("Epicrutes cenchris") 70 70
1501 110 c. Sipo ("Chrironius carinatus") 70 70
1502 200 c. Black and yellow rat snake ("Spilotes pullatus") 1·25 1·25
1503 200 c. Vine snake ("Oxybelis argenteus") . . . . 1·25 1·25

323 Child in Wheelchair
324 "Cycnoches haagii"

1991. Child Welfare. Multicoloured.
1504 60 c. + 30 c. Type **323** . . . 60 60
1505 105 c. + 50 c. Trees and girl 1·10 1·00
1506 110 c. + 55 c. Girls playing in yard . . . . 1·10 1·10

1992. Orchids. Multicoloured.
1508 50 c. Type **324** 30 30
1509 60 c. "Lycaste cristata" . . . 40 40
1510 75 c. "Galeandra dives" (horiz) 50 50
1511 125 c. "Vanilla mexicana" . . 80 80
1512 150 c. "Cyrtopodium glutiniferum" . . . . . . 1·00 1·00
1513 250 c. "Gongora quinquenervis" . . . . . . 1·60 1·60

325 Crucifixion
327 Basketball

1992. Easter. Multicoloured.
1514 60 c. + 30 c. Type **325** . . . 70 70
1515 105 c. + 50 c. Women taking away Christ's body . . . . 1·10 1·10
1516 110 c. + 55 c. The Resurrection 1·25 1·25

1992. Olympic Games, Barcelona. Multicoloured.
1518 35 c. Type **327** 25 25
1519 60 c. Volleyball 45 45
1520 75 c. Sprinting 55 55
1521 125 c. Football 95 95
1522 150 c. Cycling . . . . 1·10 1·10
1523 250 c. Swimming . . . . 1·90 1·90

328 Emblems

1992. 50th Anniv of Young Women's Christian Association.
1525 **328** 60 c. multicoloured . . . 45 45
1526 250 c. multicoloured . . 1·90 1·90

1992. Nos. 1236/7 surch **1 c.**
1527 1 c. on 5 c. orange and blue . 10 10
1528 1 c. on 5 c. green, red & blue 10 10

330 Nau

331 Matzeliger and Shoe-lasting Machine

1992. 500th Anniv of Expulsion of Jews from Spain.
1529 **330** 250 c. multicoloured . . 2·25 2·25

1992. 140th Birth Anniv of Jan E Matzeliger (inventor).
1530 **331** 60 c. multicoloured . . . 45 45
1531 250 c. multicoloured . . 1·90 1·90

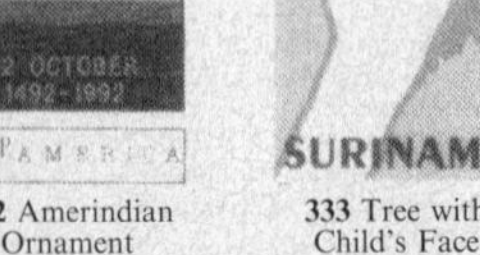
332 Amerindian Ornament

333 Tree with Child's Face

1992. America. 500th Anniv of Discovery of America by Columbus.
1532 **332** 60 c. multicoloured . . 45 45
1533 250 c. multicoloured . . 1·90 1·90

1992. Child Welfare. Multicoloured.
1534 60 c. + 30 c. Type **333** . . . 70 70
1535 105 c. + 50 c. Tree with child's face beside flower . . . . 1·10 1·10
1536 110 c. + 55 c. Children hanging from tree . . . . 1·25 1·25

334 Star and Holly
336 "Costus arabicus"

1992. Christmas. Multicoloured.
1538 10 c. Type **334** 10 10
1539 60 c. Candle 45 45
1540 250 c. Parcels . . . . 1·90 1·90
1541 400 c. Crown . . . . 3·00 3·00

1993. Air. No. 865 surch **35 ct.**
1543 35 c. on 50 c. multicoloured 25 25

1993. Medicinal Plants. Multicoloured.
1544 50 c. Type **336** 40 40
1545 75 c. "Quassia amara" . . . 55 55
1546 125 c. "Combretum rotundifolium" (horiz) . . 95 95
1547 500 c. "Bixa orellana" (horiz) 3·75 3·75

337 Christ and Cross
339 90 r. "Bull's Eye" Stamp

338 Long-horned Beetle ("Macrodontia cervicornis")

1993. Easter. Multicoloured.
1548 60 c. + 30 c. Type **337** . . . 70 70
1549 110 c. + 50 c. Crucifixion . 1·25 1·25
1550 125 c. + 60 c. Resurrection 1·40 1·40

1993. Insects. Multicoloured.
1551 25 c. Type **338** 20 20
1552 25 c. Locust 20 20
1553 35 c. Weevil ("Curculionidae") 25 25
1554 35 c. Grasshopper ("Acrididae") 25 25
1555 50 c. Goliath beetle ("Euchroma gigantea") 40 40
1556 50 c. Bush cricket ("Tettigonidae") 40 40
1557 100 c. "Tettigonidae" 75 75
1558 100 c. Scarab beetle ("Phanaeus festivus") 75 75
1559 175 c. Cricket ("Grylllidae") 1·25 1·25
1560 175 c. Dung beetle ("Phanaeus lancifer") . . . . 1·25 1·25
1561 220 c. "Tettigonidae" (different) 1·60 1·60
1562 220 c. Longhorn beetle ("Batus barbicornis") . . . . . . 1·60 1·60

1993. 150th Anniv of First Brazilian Stamps and "Brasiliana 93" International Stamp Exhibition, Rio de Janeiro.
1563 **339** 50 c. black and violet . 40 40
1564 – 250 c. black and blue . . 1·90 1·90
1565 – 500 c. black and green . 3·75 3·75
DESIGNS: 250 c. 60 r. "Bull's eye" stamp; 500 c. 30 r. "Bull's eye" stamp.

340 Dwarf Cayman

341 Afro-Caribbean Angel

1993. America. Endangered Animals.
1567 **340** 50 c. multicoloured . . . 40 40
1568 100 c. multicoloured . . . 75 75

1993. Christmas. Multicoloured.
1569 25 c. Type **341** 20 20
1570 45 c. Asian angel 35 35
1571 50 c. Oriental angel 40 40
1572 150 c. Amerindian angel . . . 1·10 1·10

342 Hopscotch
344 Sambura

1993. Child Welfare. Children's Games.
1573 **342** 25 g. + 10 g. brown & grn 25 25
1574 – 35 g. + 10 g. brown & bl . 35 35
1575 – 50 g. + 25 g. brown & grn 55 55
1576 – 75 g. + 25 g. brown & bl . 75 75
DESIGNS: 35 g. Hopscotch (different); 50 g. Djoel (variant of hopscotch); 75 g. Djoel (different).

1993. Nos. 1252 and 1473 surch **f 5.-.**
1578 5 g. on 10 g. multicoloured . 3·75 3·75
1579 5 g. on 15 g. multicoloured . 3·75 3·75

1994. Traditional Drums. Multicoloured.
1580 25 g. Type **344** 20 20
1581 50 g. Apinti 40 40
1582 75 g. Terbangan 60 60
1583 100 g. Dhol 80 80

345 Roseate Spoonbill

1994.
1584 **345** 1300 g. multicoloured . . 10·00 10·00

1994. Air. No value expressed. Nos. 864 and 866/7 optd **Port Paye.**
1585 (–) on 45 c. multicoloured . . 35 35
1586 (–) on 55 c. multicoloured . . 45 45
1587 (–) on 60 c. multicoloured . . 55 55

347 Smoking Chimneys
348 Goalkeeper's Gloves and Ball

1994. Environmental Protection. Multicoloured.
1588 50 g. Type **347** 40 40
1589 350 g. Dead fish in polluted sea 2·60 2·60

1994. World Cup Football Championship, U.S.A. Multicoloured.
1590 100 g. Type **348** 30 30
1591 250 g. Boot on ball 80 80
1592 300 g. Goal net on ball . . . 95 95

349 Anniversary Emblem

1994. Centenary of International Olympic Committee.
1594 **349** 250 g. multicoloured . . 80 80

350 "Dulcedo sp."

1994. Butterflies. Multicoloured.
1595 25 g. Type **350** 10 10
1596 25 g. "Ithomia sp." 10 10
1597 30 g. "Danaus sp." (brown wings) 10 10
1598 30 g. "Danaus sp." (black and gold wings) 10 10
1599 45 g. "Bithijs sp." 15 15
1600 45 g. "Echenais sp." 15 15
1601 75 g. White peacock ("Anartia jatrophae") 25 25
1602 75 g. Caribbean buckeye ("Junonia evarete") . . . 25 25
1603 250 g. Small postman ("Heliconius erato") . . . 80 80
1604 250 g. "Heliconius sp." . . . 80 80
1605 300 g. "Parides sp." 95 95
1606 300 g. "Eurytides sp." . . . 95 95

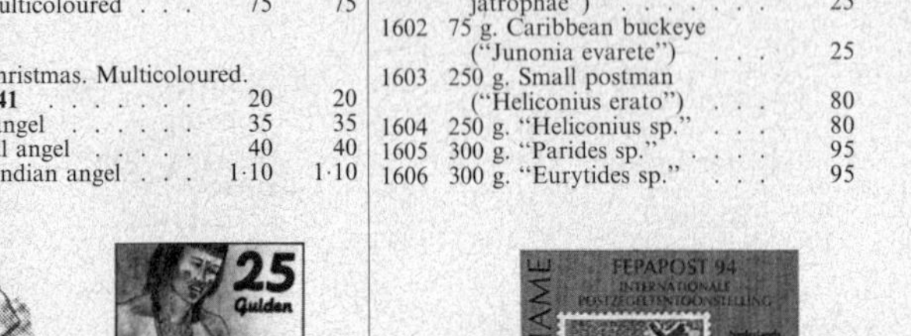

351 Netherlands 1943 Stamp Day Issue

1994. "Fepapost 94" European Stamp Exhibition, The Hague. Multicoloured.
1607 250 g. Type **351** 80 80
1608 300 g. Surinam 1936 1 c. stamp 95 95

352 Canoe and Airplane

1994. America. Postal Transport. Multicoloured.
1610 50 g. Type **352** 15 15
1611 400 g. Donkey-cart and motor van . . . . 1·25 1·25

353 Mother reading to Children

354 Hands and Globes

1994. Christmas. Multicoloured. (a) Value indicated by letter "A".
1612 An Angel hovering over pine forest 25 25

(b) With face value.
1613 250 g. Type **353** 80 80
1614 625 g. Woman praying . . . 2·00 2·00

1995. Centenary of Volleyball. Multicoloured.
1616 375 g. Type **354** . . . . . . 1·25 1·25
1617 650 g. Balls . . . . 2·10 2·10

355 "Stachytarpheta jamaicense"

1995. Medicinal Plants. Multicoloured.
1619 30 g. Type **355** 10 10
1620 30 g. "Ruellia tuberosa" . . . 10 10
1621 50 g. Sweet basil ("Ocimum sanctum") 15 15
1622 50 g. "Peperomia pellucida" . 15 15
1623 75 g. "Phyllanthus amarus" . 25 25
1624 75 g. "Portulaca oleracea" . 25 25
1625 250 g. "Wulffia baccata" . . 80 80
1626 250 g. Sesame ("Sesamum indicum") 80 80
1627 500 g. Blood flower ("Asclepias curassavica") . . . . . . 1·60 1·60
1628 500 g. "Heliotropium indicum" 1·60 1·60
1629 600 g. "Wedelia tribolata" . . 1·90 1·90
1630 600 g. "Lantana camara" . . 1·90 1·90

356 Jaguarundi

357 Emblem, Dove and "50"

1995. Big Cats. Multicoloured.
1631 25 g. Type **356** (postage) . . 10 10
1632 30 g. Head of jaguarundi . . 10 10
1633 50 g. Tiger cat 15 15
1634 100 g. Head of tiger cat . . . 30 30
1635 1000 g. Tree ocelot (air) . . 3·25 3·25
1636 1200 g. Head of tree ocelot . 3·75 3·75

1995. 50th Anniv of U.N.O. Multicoloured.
1637 135 g. Type **357** 45 45
1638 740 g. As T **357** but dove flying towards right . . . . . . 2·40 2·40

358 Emblem

1995. Centenary of Surinam Police Force.
1639 **358** 875 g. multicoloured . . 2·75 2·75

359 Emblem and Creed

1995. 25th Anniv of Nilom Junior Chamber.
1640 **359** 700 g. orange, blue and deep blue . . . . . . 2·25 2·25

360 Toucan

1995. Birds. Multicoloured.
1641 1780 g. Type **360** . . . . . . 5·75 5·75
1642 2225 g. Hummingbird . . . . 7·00 7·00
1643 2995 g. Hoatzin . . . . . . 9·50 9·50
See also Nos. 1679/81.

361 Waterfall **362** Shepherds and Star of Bethlehem

1995. America. Environmental Protection. Multicoloured.
1644 135 g. Forest floor 45 45
1645 1500 g. Type **361** . . . . . . 4·75 4·75

1995. Christmas. Multicoloured.
1646 70 g. Type **362** 20 20
1647 135 g. Joseph with Mary on donkey 45 45
1648 295 g. Three wise men bearing gifts 95 95
1649 1000 g. Wise men adoring child Jesus (horiz) . . . . 3·25 3·25

363 Jester and Bird **365** Hawk-headed Parrot

364 "Cyrtopodium cristatum"

1995. Paintings by Corneille. Multicoloured.
1651 135 g. Type **363** 45 45
1652 615 g. Jester and cat . . . . 1·90 1·90

1996. Flowers. Multicoloured.
1653 10 g. Type **364** 10 10
1654 10 g. "Epidendrum cristatum" 10 10
1655 75 g. "Cochleanthes guianensis" 25 25
1656 75 g. "Otostylis lepida" . . . 25 25
1657 135 g. "Catasetum longifolium" 40 40
1658 135 g. "Rudolfiella aurantiaca" 40 40
1659 250 g. "Encyclia granitica" . . 75 75
1660 250 g. "Maxillaria splendens" 75 75
1661 300 g. "Brassia caudata" . . 90 90
1662 300 g. "Catasetum macrocarpum" 90 90
1663 750 g. "Maxillaria rufescens" 2·25 2·25
1664 750 g. "Vanilla grandiflora" . 2·25 2·25

1996.
1665 **365** 2000 g. multicoloured . 6·00 6·00

366 Traditional Huts **367** Radio Apparatus

1996. Eco-tourism. Multicoloured.
1666 70 g. Type **366** 20 20
1667 70 g. Butterfly on leaf . . . 20 20
1668 135 g. Men in traditional costumes 40 40
1669 135 g. Woman hand-spinning 40 40

1996. Centenary of Guglielmo Marconi's Patented Wireless Telegraph. Multicoloured.
1670 135 g. Type **367** 40 40
1671 615 g. Marconi and world map (horiz) . . . . 1·90 1·90

368 Basketball **370** Women

1996. Olympic Games, Atlanta. Multicoloured.
1672 70 g. Type **368** 20 20
1673 135 g. Running 40 40
1674 195 g. Badminton 60 60
1675 200 g. Swimming 60 60
1676 900 g. Cycling . . . . 2·75 2·75
1677 1000 g. Hurdling . . . . . 3·00 3·00

1996. Birds. As T **360**. Multicoloured.
1679 75 g. Green kingfisher . . . 25 25
1680 160 g. Falcon 50 50
1681 1765 g. Red-legged honey-creeper . . . . 5·25 5·25

1996. America. Traditional Costumes. Multicoloured.
1682 135 g. Type **370** 40 40
1683 990 g. Young women . . . 3·00 3·00
Nos. 1682/3 were issued together, se-tenant, forming a composite design.

371 Mother praying over Child in Crib **372** Brown Dog and Injured Boy

1996. Christmas. Multicoloured.
1684 10 g. Type **371** 10 10
1685 70 g. Mother kneeling beside child 20 20
1686 135 g. Mother with backpack kneeling beside "eye" on mouth/cushion 40 40
1687 285 g. Mother playing with child on floor 85 85
1688 750 g. Mother and child rocking on floor . . . . 2·25 2·25

1996. Child Welfare. Paintings by Jan Telting. Multicoloured.
1690 135 g. Type **372** 40 40
1691 865 g. White dog and injured boy . . . . 2·75 2·75

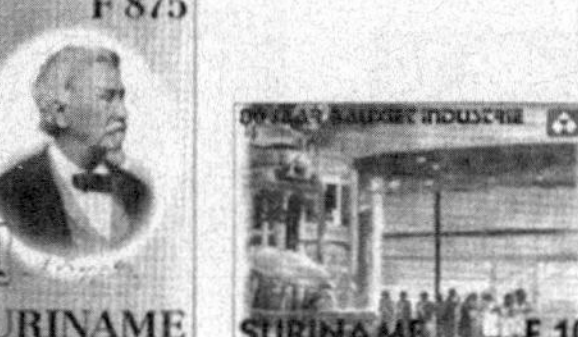

373 August Kappier (founder) **374** Inauguration of Alumium Smelter, Paranam, 1965

1996. 150th Anniv of Town of Albina.
1692 **373** 875 g. multicoloured . 2·75 2·75

1996. 80th Anniv of Bauxite Industry. Paintings by Michel Pawiroredjo. Multicoloured.
1693 10 g. Type **374** 10 10
1694 70 g. Drilling blasting holes, Moengo, 1947 . . . . . . 20 20
1695 130 g. Labourers' huts, Moengo, 1919 . . . . . . 40 40
1696 150 g. Loading "Tarpon" with alumina, Paranam, 1995 . 45 45
1697 160 g. Construction of dam and power station, 1960 . . . . 50 50
1698 730 g. "Moengo" (schooner), 1922 . . . . 2·25 2·25

POSTAGE DUE STAMPS

D 2 D 6

1885.
D36 **D 2** 2½ c. mauve and black . . 2·00 2·00
D37 5 c. mauve and black . . 6·25 6·25
D38 10 c. mauve and black . £100 70·00
D39 20 c. mauve and black . 6·25 6·25
D40 25 c. mauve and black . 9·00 9·00
D41 30 c. mauve and black . 2·50 2·50
D42 40 c. mauve and black . 4·00 4·00
D43 50 c. mauve and black . 2·25 2·25

1892.
D57 **D 6** 2½ c. mauve and black . . 20 20
D58 5 c. mauve and black . 80 65
D59 10 c. mauve and black . 15·00 11·50
D60 20 c. mauve and black . 1·75 1·10
D61 25 c. mauve and black . 7·00 5·75
D62 40 c. mauve and black . 2·00 2·40

1911.
D111 **D 2** 10 c. on 30 c. mauve and black . . . . 80·00 80·00
D112 10 c. on 50 c. mauve and black £100 £100

1913.
D153 **D 6** ½ c. lilac 10 10
D154 1 c. lilac 10 15
D155 2 c. lilac 15 20
D156 2½ c. lilac 15 10
D157 5 c. lilac 10 10
D158 10 c. lilac 15 10
D159 12 c. lilac 20 20
D160 12½ c. lilac 20 10
D161 15 c. lilac 25 25
D162 20 c. lilac 60 25
D163 25 c. lilac 25 10
D164 30 c. lilac 20 35
D165 40 c. lilac . . . . 9·75 9·50
D166 50 c. lilac 75 65
D167 75 c. lilac 90 90
D168 1 g. lilac . . . . 1·10 90

D 52 D 68

1945.
D337 **D 52** 1 c. purple 30 35
D338 5 c. purple . . . . . . 3·25 1·40
D339 25 c. purple . . . . . 8·00 20

1950. As Type **D 121** of Netherlands.
D384 1 c. purple . . . . 1·60 1·75
D385 2 c. purple . . . . 2·75 1·75
D386 2½ c. purple . . . . 2·75 1·75
D387 5 c. purple . . . . 3·25 30
D388 10 c. purple . . . . 2·25 30
D389 15 c. purple . . . . 6·75 2·10
D390 20 c. purple . . . . 1·75 2·75
D391 25 c. purple . . . . 21·00 20
D392 50 c. purple . . . . 27·00 1·40
D393 75 c. purple . . . . 40·00 30·00
D394 1 g. purple . . . . 29·00 6·00

1956.
D436 **D 68** 1 c. purple 10 10
D437 2 c. purple 35 20
D438 2½ c. purple 35 30
D439 5 c. purple 25 25
D440 10 c. purple 35 30
D441 15 c. purple 60 45
D442 20 c. purple 60 50
D443 25 c. purple 65 20
D444 50 c. purple . . . . . . 1·60 35
D445 75 c. purple . . . . . . 2·25 1·00
D446 1 g. purple . . . . . . 2·75 10

1987. Various stamps optd **TE BETALEN**.
D1325 65 c. mult (No. 868) . . . 1·75 50
D1326 65 c. mult (No. 1132) . . . 50 50
D1327 80 c. mult (No. 1134) . . . 1·75 60
D1328 90 c. mult (No. 872a) . . . 1·75 70
D1329 95 c. mult (No. 873) . . . . 2·00 75
D1330 1 g. mult (No. 1248) . . . 2·00 75

MINIMUM PRICE

The minimum price quoted is 10p which represents a handling charge rather than a basis for valuing common stamps. For further notes about prices, see introductory pages.

SWEDEN Pt. 11

A kingdom of N. Europe, united to Norway till 1905.

1855. 48 skilling banco = 1 riksdaler.
1858. 100 ore = 1 riksdaler.
1875. 100 ore = 1 krona.

1 2 3

1855.
1 **1** 3 s. green £5000 £2500
2 4 s. blue . . . . £1000 42·00
3 6 s. grey £6500 £700
4 8 s. orange £3500 £3500
5 24 s. red £5000 £1250

1858.
6b **1** 5 ore green . . . . £120 13·00
7a 9 ore purple £275 £150
8a 12 ore blue . . . . £130 1·40
9 24 ore orange . . . . . . £300 19·00
10 30 ore brown . . . . . . £275 19·00
11b 50 ore red . . . . £375 65·00

1862.
12c **2** 3 ore brown . . . . . . 75·00 9·50
13 **3** 17 ore purple £450 £950
14 17 ore grey £700 £600
15b 20 ore red . . . . £160 13·00

4 5 6 King Oscar II

1872.
29 **4** 2 ore orange . . . . . . 1·50 3·00
30 3 ore brown . . . . . . 7·75 11·00
31 4 ore grey . . . . 19·00 60
32 5 ore green . . . . . . 40·00 30
33a 6 ore mauve . . . . . . 17·00 30·00
20 6 ore green . . . . . . £650 35·00
34 **6** 10 ore pink . . . . . . 55·00 10
21 **4** 12 ore blue . . . . . . 19·00 25
35 20 ore red . . . . 70·00 30
23a 24 ore yellow . . . . . 32·00 13·50
36 30 ore brown £110 55
37a 50 ore red . . . . £100 2·40
26 **5** 1 r. blue and bistre . . . £600 42·00
38 1 k. blue and bistre . . . 50·00 1·40
On No. 26 the value is expressed as one riksdaler; on No. 38 the value is one krona.

1889. Surch **10 10 T10 ORE** and Arms.
39 **4** 10 ore on 12 ore blue . . . 1·60 2·50
40 10 ore on 24 ore yellow . . . 7·25 20·00

9 10 Oscar II 11

1891.
41 **9** 1 ore blue and brown . . . 1·00 20
42a 2 ore yellow and blue . . . 3·00 10
43 3 ore orange and brown . . 55 80
44 4 ore blue and red . . . . 4·75 10
45c **10** 5 ore green . . . . 1·75 10
46 8 ore purple . . . . . . 1·90 60
47 10 ore red . . . . 4·00 10
48 15 ore brown . . . . . . 14·50 10
49 20 ore blue . . . . 17·00 10
56 25 ore orange . . . . . . 19·00 2·50
51a 30 ore brown . . . . . . 32·00 10
53 50 ore grey . . . . 50·00 20
54 **11** 1 k. grey and red £110 80

13 G.P.O., Stockholm

14

15 Gustav V

1903. Opening of new Post Office.
57 **13** 5 k. blue . . . . £150 19·00

1910.
65 **14** 1 ore black 10 10
66 2 ore orange 10 10
67 3 ore brown 10 10
68 4 ore mauve 10 10
69 **15** 5 ore green . . . . 1·10 10
70 7 ore green 15 10
71 8 ore purple 15 10

72 15 10 ore red 1·60 10
73 12 ore purple 15 10
74 15 ore brown 4·00 10
75 20 ore blue 5·25 10
76 25 ore orange 20 10
77 27 ore blue 40 70
78 30 ore brown 10·50 10
79 35 ore violet 9·50 10
80 40 ore green 15·00 10
81 50 ore grey 38·00 10
82 55 ore blue £1000 £3500
83 65 ore green 65 1·50
84 80 ore black £1000 £3500
85 90 ore green 70 40
86 1 k. black on yellow 60·00 20
64 5 k. purple on yellow 2·50 2·00

1916. Clothing Fund for Mobilized Reservists ("Landstorm"). (a) Postage stamps surch **FRIMARKE LANDSTORMEN** and value in figures and words round Arms.

86a 4 5 + 5 on 2 ore orange 3·50 4·25
86b 5 + 5 on 3 ore brown 3·50 4·25
86c 5 + 5 on 4 ore grey 3·50 4·25
86d 5 + 5 on 5 ore green 3·50 4·25
86e 5 + 5 on 6 ore mauve 3·50 4·25
86f 10 + 10 on 12 ore blue 3·50 4·25
86g 10 + 10 on 20 ore red 3·50 4·25
86h 10 + 10 on 24 ore yellow 3·50 4·25
86i 10 + 10 on 30 ore brown 3·50 4·25
86j 10 + 10 on 50 ore red 3·50 4·25

(b) Postage Due stamps surch **FRIMARKE SVERIGE** in frame round Arms, **LANDSTORMEN** and value in figures and words.

86k D 6 5 + 5 on 1 ore black 11·00 7·00
86l 5 + 5 on 3 ore red 3·00 4·00
86m 5 + 5 on 5 ore brown 3·00 4·00
86n 5 + 10 on 6 ore orange 3·00 4·75
86o 5 + 15 on 12 ore red 26·00 19·00
86p 10 + 20 on 20 ore blue 8·75 15·00
86q 10 + 40 on 24 ore mauve 35·00 65·00
86r 10 + 20 on 30 ore green 3·00 4·25
86s 10 + 40 on 50 ore brown 13·00 23·00
86t 10 + 90 on 1 k. blue and brown £100 £275

(c) No. 57 surch **FRIMARKE ORE 10 ORE FRIMARKE LANDSTORMEN KR. 4, 90** and Arms.

86u 13 10 ore + 4 k. 90 on 5 k. blue £110 £225

1917. Surch in figures only.

87 15 7 on 10 ore red 20 10
88 12 on 25 ore orange 1·40 25
89 12 on 65 ore green 70 95
90 27 on 55 ore blue 45 1·00
91 27 on 65 ore green 1·10 2·50
92 27 on 80 ore black 60 1·25
93 1.98 k. on 5 k. pur on yellow 1·25 3·50
94 2.12 k. on 5 k. pur on yellow 1·25 3·50

1918. Landstorm Fund. Charity stamps of 1916 surch.

94a 4 7 + 3 on 5 ore on 2 ore 6·00 6·00
94b 7 + 3 on 5 ore on 3 ore 1·75 1·00
94c 7 + 3 on 5 ore on 4 ore 1·75 1·00
94d 7 + 3 on 5 ore on 5 ore 1·75 1·00
94e 7 + 3 on 5 ore on 6 ore 1·75 1·00
94f 12 + 8 on 10 ore on 12 ore 1·75 1·00
94g 12 + 8 on 10 ore on 20 ore 1·75 1·00
94h 12 + 8 on 10 ore on 24 ore 1·75 1·00
94i 12 + 8 on 10 ore on 30 ore 1·75 1·00
94j 12 + 8 on 10 ore on 50 ore 1·75 1·00

19 Arms **20** Lion (after sculpture by B. Foucquet)

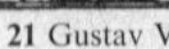

21 Gustav V **22** Emblem of Swedish Post

1920.

95 19 3 ore red 10 20
96 20 5 ore green 60 30
97a 5 ore brown 80 2·25
98 10 ore green 1·50 40
99 10 ore violet 2·75 10
102a 21 10 ore red 7·25 3·50
103 15 ore purple 15 20
104a 20 ore blue 17·00 3·75
100 20 25 ore orange 7·00 25
101 30 ore brown 20 25
105 22 35 ore yellow 26·00 20
106 40 ore green 24·00 35
107 45 ore brown 1·00 40
108 60 ore purple 12·00 20
109 70 ore brown 45 1·75
110 80 ore green 30 20
111 85 ore green 2·00 30
112 90 ore blue 38·00 10
113 1 k. orange 4·75 10
114 110 ore blue 40 10
115 115 ore brown 5·50 20
116 120 ore black 45·00 45
117 120 ore mauve 9·50 50
118 140 ore black 75 15
119 145 ore green 5·75 70

23 Gustavus II Adolphus **24** Gustav V (after portrait by E. Osterman) **25** Gustavus Vasa

1920. Tercentenary of Swedish Post between Stockholm and Hamburg.

120 23 20 ore blue 1·25 10

1920. Air. Official stamps surch **LUFTPOST** and value.

120a O 17 10 on 3 ore brown 1·50 4·50
120b 20 on 2 ore yellow 2·50 7·00
120c 50 on 4 ore lilac 11·00 13·50

1921.

121 24 15 ore violet 11·00 10
122 15 ore red 11·00 15
123 15 ore brown 3·00 10
124 20 ore violet 30 10
125 20 ore red 15·00 20
126 20 ore orange 30 15
128 25 ore red 50 1·00
129 25 ore blue 10·50 10
131 25 ore orange 22·00 10
133 30 ore brown 15·00 10
134 30 ore blue 4·75 35
135 35 ore purple 13·00 10
136 40 ore blue 40 35
137 40 ore green 28·00 50
138 45 ore brown 3·00 30
139a 50 ore black 1·25 15
140 85 ore green 10·50 1·00
141 115 ore brown 7·25 85
142 145 ore green 5·50 1·00

1921. 400th Anniv of Liberation of Sweden.

143 25 20 ore violet 7·75 16·00
144 110 ore blue 38·00 3·75
145 140 ore black 20·00 3·75

26 Old City, Stockholm **27** Gustav V

1924. 8th Congress of U.P.U. Perf.

146 26 5 ore brown 1·10 1·75
147 10 ore green 1·10 1·75
148 15 ore violet 1·25 1·10
149 20 ore red 9·00 9·00
150 25 ore orange 10·50 13·00
151 30 ore blue 10·00 13·00
152 35 ore black 13·50 16·00
153 40 ore green 17·00 19·00
154 45 ore brown 22·00 22·00
155 50 ore grey 22·00 22·00
156 60 ore purple 35·00 35·00
157 80 ore green 28·00 28·00
158 27 1 k. green 45·00 65·00
159 2 k. red £130 £190
160 5 k. blue £225 £350

28 Post Rider and Friedrichsafen FF-49 Seaplane **29** Carrier-pigeon

1924. 50th Anniv of U.P.U. Perf.

161 28 5 ore brown 1·75 2·25
162 10 ore green 1·75 3·50
163 15 ore violet 1·75 1·75
164 20 ore red 15·00 21·00
165 25 ore orange 15·00 21·00
166 30 ore blue 15·00 23·00
167 35 ore black 19·00 38·00
168 40 ore green 20·00 21·00
169 45 ore brown 26·00 24·00
170 50 ore grey 32·00 42·00
171 60 ore purple 35·00 50·00
172 80 ore green 30·00 23·00
173 29 1 k. green 60·00 75·00
174 2 k. red £175 65·00
175 5 k. blue £250 £175

29a King Gustav V **29c** Night Flight by Junkers F-13 (with skis) over Stockholm

1928. 70th Birthday of King Gustav V and Cancer Research Fund.

175a 29a 5 (+ 5) ore green 1·75 4·25
175b 10 (+ 5) ore violet 1·75 4·25
175c 15 (+ 5) ore red 1·75 2·50
175d 20 (+ 5) ore orange 3·00 1·75
175e 25 (+ 5) ore blue 3·00 2·50

1930. Air.

175f 29c 10 ore blue 15 40
175g 50 ore violet 40 1·00

30 Royal Palace, Stockholm **31** Death of Gustavus Adolphus at Lutzen

1931.

176 30 5 k. green 75·00 8·75

1932. Death Tercentenary of Gustavus Adolphus.

177 31 10 ore violet 1·75 10
178 15 ore red 1·75 10
179 25 ore blue 4·25 55
180 90 ore green 17·00 1·50

32 Allegory of Thrift **33** Stockholm Cathedral

1933. 50th Anniv of Swedish Postal Savings Bank.

181 32 5 ore green 1·60 55

1935. 500th Anniv of First Swedish Parliament. Stockholm Buildings.

182 – 5 ore green 1·00 10
183 – 10 ore violet 4·00 10
184 33 15 ore red 1·60 10
185 – 25 ore blue 4·25 45
186 – 35 ore purple 8·75 1·60
187 – 60 ore purple 11·00 1·40

DESIGNS: 5 ore Old City Hall; 10 ore Exchange; 25 ore House of the Nobility; 35 ore Houses of Parliament; 60 ore Arms of Engelbrekt and representatives of the Four Estates.

35 A. Oxenstierna (after D. Dumonstier) **38** Junkers W.34 over Scandinavia

1936. Tercentenary of Swedish Post.

188 35 5 ore green 1·25 10
189 – 10 ore violet 1·25 10
190 – 15 ore red 1·75 10
191 – 20 ore blue 8·00 2·50
192 – 25 ore blue 6·00 40
193 – 30 ore brown 11·00 2·10
194 – 35 ore mauve 3·75 85
195 – 40 ore green 7·50 2·00
196 – 45 ore green 5·50 1·10
197 – 50 ore grey 14·50 1·75
198 – 60 ore purple 28·00 50
199 – 1 k. blue 8·00 5·00

DESIGNS: 10 ore Early courier; 15 ore Post rider; 20 ore Sailing packet "Hiorten"; 25 ore Paddle-steamer "Constitutionen"; 30 ore Mail coach; 35 ore Arms; 40 ore Steam train; 45 ore A. W. Roos (Postmaster General 1867–89); 50 ore Motor bus and trailer; 60 ore Liner "Gripsholm"; 1 k. Junkers Ju 52/3m seaplane.

For similar designs, but dated "1972" at foot, see Nos. 700/4.

1936. Inauguration of Bromma Aerodrome.

200 38 50 ore blue 5·50 6·50

39 E. Swedenborg (after P. Krafft) **40** Governor Printz and Red Indian

1938. 250th Birth Anniv of Swedenborg.

201 39 10 ore violet 1·40 10
202 100 ore green 6·00 90

1938. 300th Anniv of Founding of New Sweden, U.S.A.

203 40 5 ore green 85 10
204 – 15 ore brown 1·25 10
205 – 20 ore red 2·50 50
206 – 30 ore blue 7·00 65
207 – 60 ore purple 9·50 20

DESIGNS: 15 ore Emigrant ships "Calmare Nyckel" and "Fagel Grip"; 20 ore Swedish landing in America; 30 ore First Swedish church, Wilmington; 60 ore Queen Christina (after S. Bourdon).

41 King Gustav V **42** **43** Small Arms of Sweden

1938. 80th Birthday of King Gustav V.

208 41 5 ore green 85 10
209 15 ore brown 85 10
210 30 ore blue 19·00 55

1939.

234b 42 5 ore green 10 10
299 5 ore orange 15 10
235b 10 ore violet 10 10
300 10 ore green 15 10
236b 15 ore brown 10 10
237 20 ore red 10 10
238 25 ore orange 1·75 10
301 25 ore violet 1·00 10
239 30 ore blue 30 10
240 35 ore purple 60 10
241 40 ore green 60 10
242 45 ore brown 60 10
243 50 ore grey 4·75 10
301a 43 50 ore grey 3·50 10
302 55 ore brown 1·00 10
221 60 ore red 2·50 10
302a 65 ore green 55 10
302b 70 ore blue 3·50 60
302c 75 ore brown 2·50 50
303 80 ore green 60 10
222 85 ore green 50 10
303a 85 ore brown 5·25 1·00
223 90 ore blue 65 10
224 1 k. orange 65 10
303b 1 k. 05 blue 1·40 25
304 1 k. 10 violet 5·50 10
225 1 k. 15 brown 45 10
226 1 k. 20 purple 2·50 10
304a 1 k. 20 blue 3·50 2·50
305 1 k. 40 green 65 10
227 1 k. 45 green 3·00 50
305a 1 k. 50 purple 1·25 1·00
305b 1 k. 50 brown 65 20
305c 1 k. 70 red 1·25 10
306 1 k. 75 blue 9·50 5·25
306a 1 k. 80 blue 1·60 40
306b 1 k. 85 blue 3·00 70
306c 2 k. purple 80 10
306ca 2 k. mauve 55 10
306d 2 k. 10 blue 7·00 10
306e 2 k. 15 green 3·50 25
306f 2 k. 30 brown 6·50 10
306g 2 k. 50 green 65 10
306h 2 k. 55 red 2·50 1·50
306i 2 k. 80 red 90 10
306j 2 k. 85 orange 3·00 3·50
306k 3 k. blue 1·25 10

44 P. H. Ling (after J. G. Sandberg) **45** Carl von Linne (Linnaeus) (after A. Roslin) **47** Carl Michael Bellman

1939. Death Centenary of P. H. Ling (creator of "Swedish Drill").

228 44 5 ore green 10 10
229 25 ore brown 1·25 10

1939. Bicent of Swedish Academy of Sciences.

230a – 10 ore violet 3·00 40
231 45 15 ore brown 20 10
232 – 30 ore blue 16·00 25
233 45 50 ore grey 16·00 55

PORTRAIT: 10 ore, 30 ore J. J. Berzelius (after O. J. Sodermark).

1940. Birth Bicent of C. M. Bellman (poet).

244 47 5 ore green 10 10
245 35 ore red 55 20

48 Johan Tobias Sergel (self-portrait bust) **49** Reformers presenting Bible to Gustavus Vasa

1940. Birth Bicent of Sergel (sculptor).

246 48 15 ore brown 4·75 10
247 50 ore grey 23·00 60

1941. 400th Anniv of First Authorized Version of Bible in Swedish.

248 49 15 ore brown 20 10
249 90 ore blue 28·00 60

50 Hasjo Belfry **50a** Royal Palace, Stockholm

1941. 50th Anniv of Foundation of Skansen Open-air Museum.
250 **50** 10 ore violet . . . . 3·25 10
251 60 ore purple . . . . 14·00 30

1941.
252 **50a** 5 k. blue . . . . 1·40 10

51 A. Hazelius
52 St. Bridget (from altar painting, Vasteras Cathedral) 

1941. Artur Hazelius (founder of Skansen Museum).
253 **51** 5 ore green 10 10
254 1 k. orange . . . . 10·50 2·10

1941. 550th Anniv of Canonization of St. Bridget (Foundress of Brigittine Order of Our Saviour).
255 **52** 15 ore brown 10 10
256 120 ore purple . . . . . . 40·00 7·00

53 Mute Swans
54 King Gustavus III (after A. Roslin) 

1942.
257a **53** 20 k. blue . . . . 3·50 40

1942. 150th Anniv of National Museum, Stockholm.
258 **54** 20 ore red 70 10
259 – 40 ore green . . . . 23·00 75
PORTRAIT: 40 ore Carl Gustaf Tessin (architect and chancery president) (after Gustav Lundberg).

55 Count Rudenschold and Nils Mansson
56 Carl Wilhelm Scheele 

1942. Centenary of Institution of National Elementary Education.
260 **55** 10 ore red 30 30
261 90 ore blue . . . . 3·75 4·75

1942. Birth Bicent of C. W. Scheele (chemist).
262 **56** 5 ore green 10 10
263 60 ore red . . . . 11·00 25

57 King Gustav V
58 Rifle Assn Badge 

1943. 85th Birthday of King Gustav V.
264 **57** 20 ore red 80 10
265 30 ore blue . . . . 1·10 2·00
266 60 ore purple . . . . 1·75 2·25

1943. 50th Anniv of National Voluntary Rifle Association.
267 **58** 10 ore purple 10 10
268 90 ore blue . . . . 5·50 25

59 O. Montelius (after E. Stenberg)
60 First Swedish Navigators' Chart 

1943. Birth Centenary of Oscar Montelius (archaeologist).
269 **59** 5 ore green 10 10
270 120 ore purple . . . . 8·50 1·75

1944. Tercent of First Swedish Marine Chart.
271 **60** 5 ore green 20 10
272 60 ore red . . . . 7·25 30

61 "Smalands Lejon" (ship of the line)

1944. Swedish Fleet (Tercentenary of Battle of Femern).
273 **61** 10 ore violet 20 10
274 – 20 ore red 40 10
275 – 30 ore blue 55 60
276 – 40 ore green 70 55
277 – 90 ore grey . . . . 10·50 1·40
DESIGNS—27 × 22½ mm: 30 ore "Kung Karl" (ship of the line); 40 ore Stern of "Amphion" (royal yacht); 90 ore "Gustav V" (cruiser). 18½ × 20½ mm: 20 ore Admiral C. Fleming (after L. Pasch).
See also Nos. 517/22.

62 Red Cross
63 Press Symbols 

1945. 80th Anniv of Swedish Red Cross and Birthday of Prince Carl.
278 **62** 20 ore red 40 10

1945. Tercentenary of Swedish Press.
279 **63** 5 ore green 10 10
280 60 ore red . . . . 5·25 20

64 Viktor Rydberg (after A. Edelfelt)
65 Oak Tree, Savings Banks' Symbol 

1945. 50th Death Anniv of Viktor Rydberg (author).
281 **64** 20 ore red 20 10
282 90 ore blue . . . . 5·50 25

1945. 125th Anniv of Swedish Savings Banks.
283 **65** 10 ore violet 10 10
284 40 ore green . . . . 1·10 65

66 Cathedral Model
67 Lund Cathedral 

1946. 800th Anniv of Lund Cathedral.
285 **66** 15 ore brown 60 10
286 **67** 20 ore red 20 10
287 **66** 90 ore blue . . . . 6·00 50

68 Mare and Foal
69 Tegner (after bust by J. N. Bystrom) 
70 A. Nobel 

1946. Centenary of Swedish Agricultural Show.
288 **68** 5 ore green 15 10
289 60 ore red . . . . 6·50 20

1946. Death Centenary of Esaias Tegner (poet).
290 **69** 10 ore violet 10 10
291 40 ore green . . . . 1·00 25

1946. 50th Death Anniv of Alfred Nobel (scientist and creator of Nobel Foundation).
292 **70** 20 ore red 65 10
293 30 ore blue . . . . 1·40 45

71 E. G. Geijer (after J. G. Sandberg)
72 King Gustav V 
73 Ploughman and Skyscraper 

1947. Death Centenary of Erik Gustav Geijer (historian, philosopher, poet and composer).
294 **71** 5 ore green 10 10
295 90 ore blue . . . . 2·75 10

1947. Forty Years Reign of King Gustav V.
296 **72** 10 ore violet 10 10
297 20 ore red 25 10
298 60 ore purple 90 95

1948. Centenary of Swedish Pioneers in U.S.A.
307 **73** 15 ore brown 15 10
308 30 ore blue 40 25
309 1 k. orange . . . . 1·00 60

73a King Gustav V
74 J. A. Strindberg (after R. Bergh) 
75 Gymnasts 

1948. King Gustav V's 90th Birthday, and Youth Fund.
309a **73a** 10 ore + 10 ore green . . 30 35
309b 20 ore + 10 ore red . . 30 50
309c 30 ore + 10 ore blue . . 30 40

1949. Birth Centenary of Strindberg (dramatist).
310 **74** 20 ore red 20 10
311 30 ore blue 50 50
312 80 ore green . . . . 2·10 35

1949. 2nd Lingiad, Stockholm.
313 **75** 5 ore blue 10 10
314 15 ore brown 35 50

76 Globe and Hand Writing
77 

1949. 75th Anniv of U.P.U.
315 **76** 10 ore green 10 10
316 20 ore red 10 10
317 **77** 30 ore blue 25 25

78 King Gustav VI Adolf
79 Christopher Polhem (after G. E. Schroder) 
80 

1951. (a) Coloured lettering and figures.
318 **78** 10 ore green 15 10
318b 10 ore brown 10 10
319 15 ore brown 20 10
388 15 ore red 15 10
320 20 ore red 20 10
391 20 ore black 20 10
322a 25 ore black 40 10
323 25 ore red 80 10
324a 25 ore blue 15 10
392 25 ore brown 45 10
393 30 ore blue 30 10
326 30 ore brown 40 20
326a 30 ore red . . . . 8·75 10
327 40 ore blue 55 10
328 40 ore green 55 10

(b) White lettering and figures.
429 **78** 15 ore red 10 10
430 20 ore black 25 10
431a 25 ore brown 10 10
432a 30 ore blue 45 10
433 30 ore violet 35 10
433b 30 ore red 50 60
434 35 ore violet 50 10
435a 35 ore blue 20 10
436 35 ore black 50 10
437 40 ore green 70 10
438a 40 ore blue 20 10
439a 45 ore orange 50 10
439b 45 ore blue 60 10
440 50 ore green 70 10
440a 50 ore green 40 10
440c 55 ore red 40 10
441 60 ore red 70 50
441a 65 ore blue . . . . 1·00 10
441c 70 ore mauve 60 10
441d 85 ore purple . . . . 1·00 20

1951. Death Bicentenary of Polhem (engineer).
329a **79** 25 ore black 20 20
330 45 ore brown 30 20

1951.
383 **80** 5 ore red 10 10
386 10 ore blue 10 10
387a 10 ore brown 10 10
389 15 ore green 10 10
390a 15 ore brown 30 35

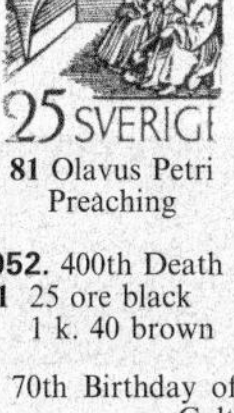

81 Olavus Petri Preaching
81a King Gustav VI Adolf 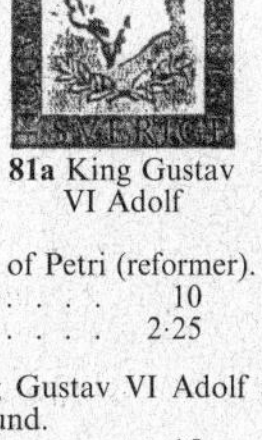

1952. 400th Death Anniv of Petri (reformer).
332 **81** 25 ore black 10 10
333 1 k. 40 brown . . . . 2·25 45

1952. 70th Birthday of King Gustav VI Adolf and Culture Fund.
333a **81a** 10 ore + 10 ore green . . 15 20
333ba 25 ore + 10 ore red . . 15 25
333c 40 ore + 10 ore blue . . 25 35

82 Ski Jumping
83 Stockholm, 1650

1953. 50th Anniv of Swedish Athletic Assn.
334 **82** 10 ore green 30 10
335 – 15 ore brown 70 40
336 – 40 ore blue . . . . 1·00 1·40
337 – 1 k. 40 mauve . . . . . . 2·75 70
DESIGNS—HORIZ: 1 k. 40, Wrestling. VERT: 15 ore (335) Ice hockey; 40 ore Slingball.

1953. 700th Anniv of Stockholm.
338 **83** 25 ore blue 20 10
339 – 1 k. 70 red . . . . 2·10 55
DESIGN: 1 k. 70, Seal of Stockholm, 1296 (obverse and reverse).

84 "Radio"
85 Skier

1953. Cent of Telecommunications in Sweden.
340 – 25 ore blue ("Telephones") 20 10
341 **84** 40 ore green . . . . 1·00 1·10
342 – 60 ore red ("Telegraphs") 2·00 2·25

1954. World Skiing Championships.
343 **85** 20 ore grey 30 30
344 – 1 k. blue (Woman skier) . 7·25 80

86 Anna Maria Lenngren (after medallion, J. T. Sergel)
87 Rock-carvings 
88 

1954. Birth Bicentenary of Anna Maria Lenngren (poetess).
345 **86** 20 ore grey 20 10
346 65 ore brown . . . . 4·25 1·75

1954.
347 **87** 50 ore grey 30 10
348 55 ore red . . . . 1·10 10
349 60 ore red 40 10
350 65 ore green . . . . 1·40 10
351 70 ore orange 50 10
352 75 ore brown . . . . 1·60 10
353 80 ore green 60 10
355 90 ore blue 75 10
356 95 ore violet . . . . 3·00 2·75

1955. Centenary of First Swedish Postage Stamps.
362 **88** 25 ore blue 10 10
363 40 ore green 80 25

89 Swedish Flag
91 P. D. A. Atterbom (after Fogelberg)

1955. National Flag Day.
364 **89** 10 ore yellow, blue & grn . 10 10
365 15 ore yellow, blue & red . 15 10

1955. Cent of First Swedish Postage Stamps and "Stockholmia" Philatelic Exn. As T **1** but with two rules through bottom panel.
366 **1** 3 ore green . . . . 2·00 4·75
367 4 ore blue . . . . 2·00 4·75
368 6 ore grey . . . . 2·00 4·75
369 8 ore yellow . . . . 2·00 4·75
370 24 ore orange . . . . 2·00 4·75
Nos. 366/70 were sold only at the Exhibition in single sets, at 2 k. 45 ore (45 ore face + 2 k. entrance fee).

1955. Death Centenary of Atterbom (poet).
371 **91** 20 ore blue 20 10
372 1 k. 40 brown . . . . 3·00 55

92 Greek Horseman, (from Parthenon frieze)
93 Railway Construction

1956. 16th Olympic Games Equestrian Competitions, Stockholm.
373 **92** 20 ore red 10 10
374 25 ore blue 25 10
375 40 ore green . . . . 1·50 1·25

1956. Northern Countries' Day. As T **101a** of Norway.
376 25 ore red 75 10
377 40 ore blue . . . . 2·25 40

1956. Centenary of Swedish Railways.
378 **93** 10 ore green 55 15
379 – 25 ore blue 40 15
380 – 40 ore orange . . . . . . 3·00 2·50
DESIGNS: 25 ore First Swedish steam locomotive, "Fryckstad"; 40 ore Arsta Bridge, Stockholm.

94 Trawler in Distress and Lifeboat

1957. 50th Anniv of Swedish Life Saving Service.
381a **94** 30 ore blue . . . . 3·00 1·10
382 1 k. 40 red . . . . 4·00 90

95 Galleon and "Gripsholm II"
96 Bell 47G Helicopter with Floats

1958. Postal Services Commemoration.
395 **95** 15 ore red 20 10
396 **96** 30 ore blue 15 10
397 **95** 40 ore green . . . . 4·25 2·10
398 **96** 1 k. 40 brown . . . . . . 4·50 75

97 Footballer
98 Bessemer Tilting-furnace

1958. World Cup Football Championship.
399 **97** 15 ore red 10 10
400 20 ore green 20 10
401 1 k. 20 blue . . . . 1·10 65

1958. Centenary of Swedish Steel Industry.
402 **98** 30 ore blue 20 10
403 170 ore brown . . . . . . 2·50 65

99 Selma Lagerlof (after bust by G. Malmquist)
100 Overhead Power Lines

1958. Birth Centenary of Selma Lagerlof (writer).
404 **99** 20 ore red 10 10
405 30 ore blue 15 10
406 80 ore green 50 60

1959. 50th Anniv of Swedish State Power Board.
407 **100** 30 ore blue 25 10
408 – 90 ore red . . . . 3·00 1·75
DESIGN—HORIZ: 90 oe Dam sluice-gates.

101 Henri Dunant (founder)
102 Heidenstam

1959. Red Cross Centenary.
409 **101** 30 ore + 10 ore red 40 50

1959. Birth Centenary of Verner von Heidenstam (poet).
410 **102** 15 ore red 50 10
411 1 k. black . . . . 2·75 60

103 Forest Trees

104 S. Arrhenius

1959. Centenary of Crown Lands and Forests Administration.
412 **103** 30 ore green 70 10
413 – 1 k. 40 red . . . . 3·75 50
DESIGN: 1 k. 40, Forester felling tree.

1959. Birth Centenary of Arrhenius (chemist).
414 **104** 15 ore brown 20 10
415 1 k. 70 blue . . . . . . 2·75 30

105 Anders Zorn (self-portrait)
106 "Uprooted Tree"

1960. Birth Cent of Zorn (painter and etcher).
416 **105** 30 ore grey 20 10
417 80 ore brown . . . . . . 2·40 90

1960. World Refugee Year.
418 **106** 20 ore brown 10 10
419 – 40 ore violet 20 20
DESIGN—VERT: 40 ore Refugees.

107 Target-shooting
108 G. Froding

1960. Centenary of Voluntary Shooting Organization.
420 **107** 15 ore red 20 10
421 – 90 ore blue . . . . 1·90 90
DESIGN: 90 ore Organization members marching, 1860.

1960. Birth Centenary of Gustav Froding (poet).
422 **108** 30 ore brown 20 10
423 1 k. 40 green . . . . . . 2·00 25

1960. Europa. As T **113a** of Norway.
424 40 ore blue 10 10
425 1 k. red 25 25

109 H. Branting
111 "Coronation of Gustav III" (after Pilo)

1960. Birth Centenary of Hjalmar Branting (statesman).
426 **109** 15 ore red 10 10
427 1 k. 70 blue . . . . 2·25 30

1961. 10th Anniv of Scandinavian Airlines System. As T **113b** of Norway.
428 40 ore blue 20 10

1961. 250th Birth Anniv of Carl Gustav Pilo (painter).
442 **111** 30 ore brown 20 10
443 1 k. 40 blue . . . . 2·40 65

112 J. Alstromer (after bust by P. H. l'Archeveque)
113 Printing Works and Library

1961. Death Bicentenary of Jonas Alstromer (industrial reformer).
444 **112** 15 ore purple 15 10
445 90 ore blue . . . . 1·10 1·00

1961. Tercentenary of Royal Library Regulation.
446 **113** 20 ore red 10 10
447 1 k. blue . . . . 5·50 60

114 Motif on Runic Stone at Oland
115 Nobel Prize Winners of 1901

1961.
448 **114** 10 k. purple . . . . . . 12·00 30

1961. Nobel Prize Winners.
449 **115** 20 ore red 15 10
450 40 ore blue 25 10
451 50 ore green 25 10
See also Nos. 458/9, 471/2, 477/8, 488/9, 523/4, 546/7 and 573/4.

116 Postman's Footprints
117 Code, Voting Instrument and Mallet

1962. Cent of Swedish Local Mail Delivery Service.
452 **116** 30 ore violet 10 10
453 1 k. 70 red . . . . 2·40 30

1962. Centenary of Municipal Laws.
454 **117** 30 ore blue 20 10
455 2 k. red . . . . 3·00 30

118 St. George and Dragon, Storkyrkan ("Great Church"), Stockholm
119 Ice Hockey Player

118a King Gustav VI Adolf and Cultural Themes

1962. Swedish Monuments (1st series).
456 **118** 20 ore purple 15 10
457 – 50 ore green 40 10
DESIGN—HORIZ: 50 ore Skokloster Castle.
See also Nos. 469/70 and 479/80.

1962. King Gustav's 80th Birthday and Swedish Culture Fund.
457b **118a** 20 ore + 10 ore brown . 15 20
457c 35 ore + 10 ore blue . . 15 20

1962. Nobel Prize Winners. As T **115** but inscr "NOBELPRIS 1902".
458 25 ore red 25 10
459 50 ore blue 35 10
PORTRAITS—Nobel Prize Winners of 1902: 25 ore Theodor Mommsen (literature) and Sir Ronald Ross (medicine); 50 ore Emil Hermann Fischer (chemistry) and Pieter Zeeman and Hendrik Lorentz (physics).

1963. World Ice Hockey Championships.
460 **119** 25 ore 10 10
461 1 k. 70 blue . . . . 2·25 30

120 Hands reaching for Wheat
121 Engineering and Industrial Symbols

1963. Freedom from Hunger.
462 **120** 35 ore mauve 10 10
463 50 ore violet 20 15

1963. "Engineering and Industry".
464 **121** 50 ore black 20 10
465 1 k. 05 orange . . . . . . 2·10 1·75

122 Dr. G. F. Du Rietz (after D. K. Ehrenstrahl)

123 Linne's Hammarby (country house)

1963. 300th Anniv of Swedish Board of Health.
466 **122** 25 ore brown 25 10
467 35 ore blue 25 10
468 2 k. red . . . . 2·75 45

1963. Swedish Monuments (2nd series).
469 **123** 20 ore red 15 10
470 50 ore green 20 10

1963. Nobel Prize Winners. As T **115** but inscr "NOBELPRIS 1903".
471 25 ore green 50 35
472 50 ore brown 60 15
PORTRAITS—Nobel Prize winners of 1903: 25 ore Svante Arrhenius (chemistry), Niels Ryberg Finsen (medicine) and Bjornstjerne Bjornson (literature); 50 ore Antoine Henri Becquerel and Pierre and Marie Curie (physics).

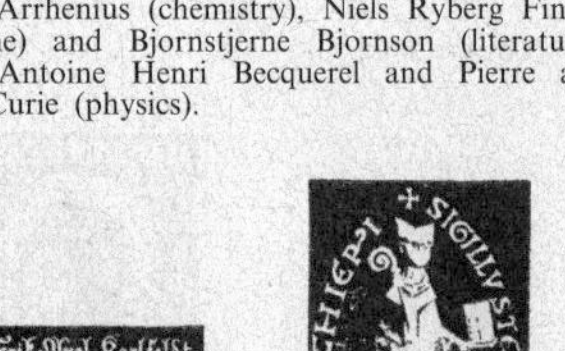

124 Motif from Poem "Elie Himmelsfard"
125 Seal of Archbishop Stefan

1964. Birth Centenary of E. A. Karlfeldt (poet).
473 **124** 35 ore blue 50 10
474 1 k. 05 red . . . . 3·00 2·50

1964. 800th Anniv of Archbishopric of Uppsala.
475 **125** 40 ore green 10 10
476a 60 ore brown 20 20

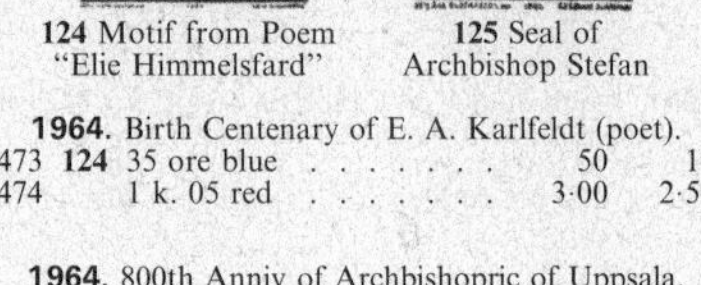

1964. Nobel Prize Winners. As T **115** but inscr "NOBELPRIS 1904".
477 30 ore blue 30 25
478 40 ore red 55 10
PORTRAITS– Nobel Prize winners of 1904: 30 ore Jose Echegaray y Eizaguirre and Frederic Mistral (literature) and J. W. Strutt (Lord Rayleigh) (physics); 40 ore Sir William Ramsay (chemistry) and Ivan Petrovich Pavlov (medicine).

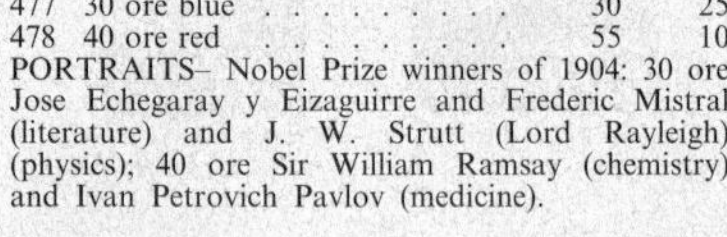

126 Visby Town Wall
127 Posthorns
128 Telecommunications

1965. Swedish Monuments (3rd series).
479 **126** 30 ore mauve 10 10
480 2 k. blue . . . . 3·25 10

1965.
481 **127** 20 ore blue and yellow . . 10 10

1965. Centenary of I.T.U.
482 **128** 60 ore violet 25 10
483 1 k. 40 blue . . . . 1·60 70

129 Prince Eugen (after D. Tagtstrom)
130 F. Bremer (after O. J. Sodermark)

1965. Birth Centenary of Prince Eugen (painter).
484 **129** 40 ore black 10 10
485 1 k. brown . . . . 1·60 15

1965. Death Centenary of Fredrika Bremer (novelist).
486 **130** 25 ore violet 10 10
487 3 k. green . . . . 4·00 30

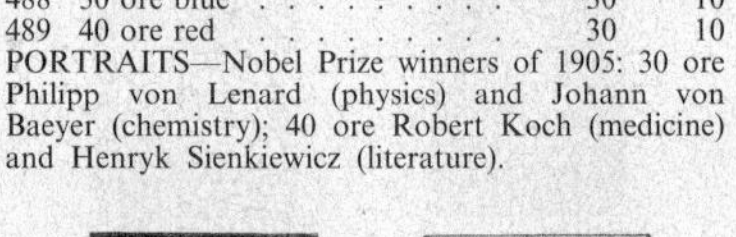

1965. Nobel Prize Winners. As T **115** but inscr "NOBELPRIS 1905".
488 30 ore blue 30 10
489 40 ore red 30 10
PORTRAITS—Nobel Prize winners of 1905: 30 ore Philipp von Lenard (physics) and Johann von Baeyer (chemistry); 40 ore Robert Koch (medicine) and Henryk Sienkiewicz (literature).

131 N. Soderblom

132 Skating

1966. Birth Centenary of Nathan Soderblom, Archbishop of Uppsala.
490 **131** 60 ore brown 20 10
491 80 ore green 50 10

1966. World Men's Speed Skating Championships, Gothenburg.
492 **132** 5 ore red 10 10
493 25 ore green 15 15
494 40 ore blue 20 30

133 Entrance Hall, National Museum   134 Ale's Stones, Ship Grave, Kaseberga

1966. Centenary of Opening of National Museum Building.

495 **133** 30 ore violet 10 10
496 2 k. 30 green 85 70

1966.

498 – 35 ore brown and blue . . 10 10
499 **134** 3 k. 50 grey 80 10
500 – 3 k. 70 violet . . . . . . 1·00 10
501 – 4 k. 50 red . . . . . . 1·00 10
502 – 7 k. red and blue . . . . 1·75 30

DESIGNS—HORIZ: 35 ore Fjeld (mountains); 7 k. Gripsholm Castle. VERT: 3 k. 70, Lion Fortress, Gothenburg; 4 k. 50, Uppsala Cathedral (interior).

135 Louis de Geer (advocate of reform)

1966. Cent of Representative Assembly Reform.

510 **135** 40 ore blue 30 10
511 3 k. red . . . . 3·00 40

136 Theatre Stage   137 Almqvist (after C. P. Mazer)

1966. Bicentenary of Drottningholm Theatre.

512 **136** 5 ore red on pink 10 10
513 25 ore bistre on pink . . . 10 10
514 40 ore purple on pink . . 25 40

1966. Death Centenary of Carl Almqvist (writer).

515 **137** 25 ore mauve 20 10
516 1 k. green . . . . 1·60 20

1966. National Cancer Fund. Swedish Ships. Designs as T **61**, but with imprint "1966" at foot.

517 10 ore red 15 20
518 15 ore red 15 20
519 20 ore green 15 20
520 25 ore blue 15 15
521 30 ore red 15 20
522 40 ore red 15 20

SHIPS—HORIZ: 10 ore "Smalands Lejon"; 15 ore "Calmare Nyckel" and "Fagel Grip"; 20 ore "Hiorten"; 25 ore "Constitutionen"; 30 ore "Kung Karl"; 40 ore Stern of "Amphion".

1966. Nobel Prize Winners. As T **115** but inscr "NOBELPRIS 1906".

523 30 ore red 30 10
524 40 ore green 20 10

PORTRAITS—Nobel Prize winners of 1906: 30 ore Sir Joseph John Thomson (physics) and Giosue Carducci (literature); 40 ore Henri Moissan (chemistry) and Camillo Golgi and Santiago Ramon y Cajal (medicine).

138 Handball   139 "E.F.T.A."

1967. World Handball Championships.

525 **138** 45 ore blue 10 10
526 2 k. 70 mauve . . . . . . 1·90 80

1967. European Free Trade Assn ("E.F.T.A.").

527 **139** 70 ore orange 30 10

140 Table Tennis Player   141 Axeman and Beast

1967. World Table Tennis Championships, Stockholm.

528 **140** 35 ore mauve 10 10
529 90 ore blue 70 35

1967. Iron Age Helmet Decorations, Oland.

530 **141** 10 ore blue and brown . . 10 10
531 – 15 ore brown and blue . . 20 15
532 – 30 ore mauve and brown . 20 15
533 – 35 ore brown and mauve . 20 15

DESIGNS: 15 ore Man between two bears; 30 ore "Lion man" putting enemy to flight; 35 ore Two warriors.

142 "Solidarity"   144 18th-century Post-rider

143 "Keep to the Right"

1967. Finnish Settlers in Sweden.

534 **142** 10 ore multicoloured . . 10 10
535 35 ore multicoloured . . 10 10

1967. Adoption of Changed Rule of the Road.

536 **143** 35 ore black, yellow & bl 10 10
537 45 ore black, yellow & grn 10 10

1967.

538 **144** 5 ore black and red . . 10 10
539 – 10 ore black and blue . . 15 10
539b – 20 ore black on flesh . . 10 10
540 – 30 ore red and blue . . 10 10
541 – 40 ore blue, green & blk 20 10
541b – 45 ore black and blue . . 10 10
542 – 90 ore brown and blue . . 20 10
543 – 1 k. green 30 10

DESIGNS—As T **144**. VERT: 10 ore "Svent Skepp" (warship); 20 ore "St. Stephen" (ceiling painting, Dadesjo Church, Smaland); 30 ore Angelica plant on coast. HORIZ: 40 ore Haverud Aqueduct, Dalsland Canal. $27\frac{1}{2}\times22\frac{1}{2}$ mm: 45 ore Floating logs; 90 ore Elk; 1 k. Dancing cranes.

145 King Gustav VI Adolf   146 Berwald, Violin and Music

1967. 85th Birthday of King Gustav VI Adolf.

544 **145** 45 ore blue 10 10
545 70 ore green 15 10

1967. Nobel Prize Winners. As T **115**, but inscr "NOBELPRIS 1907".

546 35 ore red 60 30
547 45 ore blue 35 10

PORTRAITS—Nobel Prize winners of 1907: 35 ore Eduard Buchner (chemistry) and Albert Abraham Michelson (physics); 45 ore Charles Louis Alphonse Laveran (medicine) and Rudyard Kipling (literature).

1968. Death Centenary of Franz Berwald (composer).

548 **146** 35 ore black and red . . 25 10
549 2 k. black, blue & yellow 1·90 45

147 Bank Seal   148 Butterfly Orchids

1968. 300th Anniv of Bank of Sweden.

550 **147** 45 ore blue 10 10
551 70 ore black on orange . 15 10

1968. Wild Flowers.

552 **148** 45 ore green 70 30
553 – 45 ore green 70 30
554 – 45 ore red and green . . 70 30
555 – 45 ore green 70 30
556 – 45 ore green 70 30

DESIGNS: No. 553, Wood anemone; 554, Wild rose; 555, Wild cherry; 556, Lily of the valley.

149 University Seal

1968. 300th Anniv of Lund University.

557 **149** 10 ore blue 10 10
558 35 ore red 20 20

150 Ecumenical Emblem   151 "The Universe"

1968. 4th General Assembly of World Council of Churches, Uppsala.

559 **150** 70 ore purple 30 30
560 90 ore blue 80 10

1968. Centenary of the People's College.

561 **151** 45 ore red 10 10
562 2 k. blue . . . . 2·25 25

152 "Orienteer" crossing Forest   153 "The Tug of War" (wood-carving by Axel Petersson)

1968. World "Orienteering" Championships, Linkoping.

563 **152** 40 ore red and violet . . . 20 10
564 2 k. 80 violet and green . . 1·90 1·60

1968. Birth Centenary of Axel Petersson ("Doderhultarn").

565 **153** 5 ore green 10 10
566 25 ore brown 65 95
567 45 ore brown and sepia . . 10 10

154 Red Fox   155 "The Worker" (A. Amelin)

1968. Bruno Liljefors' Fauna Sketches. Perf.

568 – 30 ore blue 50 55
569 – 30 ore black 50 55
570 **154** 30 ore brown 50 55
571 – 30 ore brown 50 55
572 – 30 ore blue 50 55

DESIGNS: No. 568, Arctic hare; 569, Great black-backed gull; 571, Golden eagle and carrion crows; 572, Stoat.

1968. Nobel Prize Winners. As T **115**, but inscr "NOBELPRIS 1908".

573 35 ore red 35 20
574 45 ore green 30 10

PORTRAITS—Nobel Prize winners of 1908: 35 ore Ilya Mechnikov and Paul Ehrlich (medicine) and Lord Rutherford (chemistry); 45 ore Gabriel Lippman (physics) and Rudolf Eucken (literature).

1969. 50th Anniv of Northern Countries Union. As T **161a** of Norway.

575 45 ore brown 20 10
576 70 ore blue 50 40

1969. 50th Anniv of I.L.O.

577 **155** 55 ore red 10 10
578 70 ore blue 50 25

156 Colonnade   157 A. Engstrom with Eagle Owl (self-portrait)

1969. Europa.

579 **156** 70 ore multicoloured . . . 65 10
580 1 k. multicoloured 95 10

1969. Birth Centenary of Albert Engstrom (painter and writer).

581 **157** 35 ore black 25 10
582 55 ore blue 35 10

159 Tjorn Bridges   160 Helmeted Figure (carving)

1969. Tjorn Bridges.

584 **159** 15 ore blue on blue . . . 90 40
585 – 30 ore green and black on blue 90 40
586 – 55 ore black and blue on blue 90 40

DESIGNS—As T **159**: 30 ore Tjorn Bridges (different). 41 × 19 mm: 55 ore Tjorn Bridges (different).

1969. Warship "Wasa" Commemoration.

587 **160** 55 ore red 20 15
588 – 55 ore brown 20 15
589 – 55 ore blue 40 30
590 – 55 ore brown 20 15
591 – 55 ore red 20 15
592 – 55 ore blue 40 30

DESIGNS—As T **160**: No. 588, Crowned lion's head (carving); 590, Lion's head (carving); 591, Carved support. 46 × 28 mm: No. 589, Ship's coat-of-arms; 592, Ship of the line "Wasa", 1628.

161 H. Soderberg (writer)   163 "The Adventures of Nils" by S. Lagerlof (illus by J. Bauer)

162 Lighthouses and Lightship "Cyklop"

1969. Birth Centenaries of Hjalmar Soderberg and Bo Bergman.

593 **161** 45 ore brown on cream . . 20 10
594 – 55 ore green on green . . 20 10

DESIGN—HORIZ: 55 ore Bo Bergman (poet).

1969. 300th Anniv of Swedish Lighthouse Service.

595 **162** 30 ore black, red and grey 40 15
596 55 ore black, orge & blue 40 10

1969. Swedish Fairy Tales. Perf.

597 – 35 ore brown, red & orge 1·40 1·25
598 **163** 35 ore brown . . . . . . 1·40 1·25
599 – 35 ore brown, red & orge 1·40 1·25
600 – 35 ore brown . . . . . . 1·40 1·25
601 – 35 ore red and orange . . 1·40 1·25

DESIGNS: No. 597, "Pelle's New Suit" written and illus by Elsa Beskow; 599, "Pippi Longstocking" by A. Lindgren (illus by I. Vang Nyman); 600, "Vill-Vallareman, the Shepherd" (from "With Pucks and Elves" illus by J. Bauer); 601, "The Cat's Journey" written and illus by I. Arosenius.

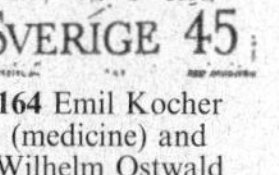

164 Emil Kocher (medicine) and Wilhelm Ostwald (chemistry)   165 Weathervane, Soderala Church

1969. Nobel Prize Winners.

602 **164** 45 ore green 70 30
603 – 55 ore black on flesh . . 50 10
604 – 70 ore black 50 40

DESIGNS—Prize winners of 1909: 55 ore Selma Lagerlof (literature); 70 ore Guglielmo Marconi and Ferdinand Braun (physics).

1970. Swedish Forgings.

605 **165** 5 ore green and brown . . 35 15
606 – 10 green and brown . . . 35 15
607 – 30 ore black and green . . 35 15
608 – 55 ore brown and green . . 35 15

DESIGNS—As T **165**: 10 ore As Type **165**, but design and country name/figures of value in reverse order; 30 ore Memorial Cross, Eksharad Churchyard. 24 × 44 mm: 55 ore 14th-century door, Bjorksta Church.

166 Seal of King Magnus Ladulas   167 River Ljungan

1970.

609 **166** 2 k. 55 blue on cream . . 80 35
610a – 3 k. blue on cream . . . 50 10
611a – 5 k. green on cream . . 1·00 10

DESIGNS: 3 k. Seal of Duke Erik Magnusson; 5 k. Great Seal of Erik IX.

1970. Nature Conservation Year.

612 **167** 55 ore multicoloured . . 30 10
613 70 ore multicoloured . . 50 35

168 View of Kiruna

1970. Sweden within the Arctic Circle.

614 **168** 45 ore brown 45 60
615 – 45 ore blue 45 60
616 – 45 ore green 45 60
617 – 45 ore brown 45 60
618 – 45 ore blue 45 60
DESIGNS: No. 615, Winter landscape and skiers; 616, Lake and Lapp hut, Stora National Park; 617, Reindeer herd; 618, Rocket-launching.

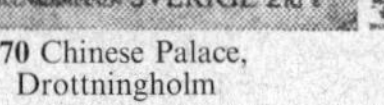
170 Chinese Palace, Drottningholm — **171** Lumber Trucks

1970. Historic Buildings.

619 – 55 ore green 20 10
620 **170** 2 k. multicoloured . . . . 1·25 10
DESIGN—21 × 27½ mm: 55 ore Glimmingehus (15th-century Castle).

1970. Swedish Trade and Industry.

621 **171** 70 ore brown and blue . . 2·50 2·75
622 – 70 ore blue, brn & pur . . 4·25 3·75
623 – 70 ore purple and blue . . 4·25 3·75
624 – 70 ore blue and purple . . 5·50 3·75
625 – 70 ore blue and purple . . 5·50 3·75
626 – 70 ore brown & purple . . 2·50 2·75
627a – 1 k. black on cream . . . 30 10
DESIGNS—As Type **171**: No. 623, Ship's propeller; 624, Dam and electric locomotive; 626, Technician and machinery. 44 × 20 mm: No. 622, Loading freighter at quayside; 625, Mine and electric ore train. 26 × 20 mm: No. 627a, Miners at coal face.

173 Three Hearts

1970. 25th Anniv of United Nations.

628 **173** 55 ore red, yellow & black . . 15 10
629 – 70 ore green, yellow & blk . . 25 10
DESIGN: 70 ore Three four-leaved clovers.

174 Blackbird — **175** Paul Heyse (literature)

1970. Christmas. Birds. Multicoloured.

630 30 ore Type **174** 90 60
631 30 ore Great tit 90 60
632 30 ore Bullfinch 90 60
633 30 ore Greenfinch 90 60
634 30 ore Blue tit 90 60

1970. Nobel Prize Winners.

635 **175** 45 ore violet 70 25
636 – 55 ore blue 40 10
637 – 70 ore black 70 50
PORTRAITS—Prize winners of 1910: 55 ore Otto Wallach (chemistry) and Johannes van der Waals (physics); 70 ore Albrecht Kossel (medicine).

176 Ferry "Storskar" and Royal Palace, Stockholm — **178** Kerstin Hesselgren (suffragette)

1971.

638 **176** 80 ore black and blue . . 30 10
639 – 4 k. black 90 10
639a – 6 k. blue 90 10
DESIGN: 4 k. 16th-century "Blood Money" coins; 6 k. Gustav Vasa's dollar.

1971. 50th Anniv of Swedish Women's Suffrage.

640 **178** 45 ore violet on green . . 20 10
641 1 k. brown on yellow . . 45 10

179 Arctic Terns — **180** "The Prodigal Son" (painting, Sodra Rada Church)

1971. Nordic Help for Refugees Campaign.

642 **179** 40 ore red 35 25
643 55 ore blue 70 10

1971.

644 **180** 15 ore green on green . . 10 10
645 – 25 ore blue and brown . 10 10
646 – 25 ore blue and brown . 10 10
DESIGNS—HORIZ (Panels from Grodinge Tapestry, Swedish Natural History Museum): No. 645, Griffin; No. 646, Lion.

182 Container Port, Gothenburg

1971.

647 **182** 55 ore violet and blue . . 25 30
648 – 60 ore brown on cream . . 15 10
649 – 75 ore green on green . . 25 10
DESIGNS—28 × 23 mm: 60 ore Timber-sledge; 75 ore Windmills, Oland.

184 Musical Score — **186** "The Three Wise Men"

185 "The Mail Coach" (E. Schwab)

1971. Bicent of Swedish Royal Academy of Music.

650 **184** 55 ore purple 20 10
651 85 ore green 30 20

1971.

652 **185** 1 k. 20 multicoloured . . 35 10

1971. Gotland Stone-masons Art.

653 **186** 5 ore violet and brown . 50 30
654 – 10 ore violet and green . 50 30
655 – 55 ore green and brown . 60 20
656 – 65 ore brown and violet . 30 10
DESIGNS—As T **186**: 10 ore "Adam and Eve". 40 × 21 mm: 55 ore "Winged Knight" and "Samson and the Lion"; 65 ore "The Flight into Egypt".

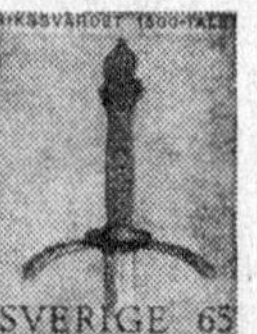

187 Child beside Lorry Wheel — **188** State Sword of Gustavus Vasa, ca. 1500

1971. Road Safety.

657 **187** 35 ore black and red . . 20 20
658 65 ore blue and red . . . 35 10

1971. Swedish Crown Regalia. Multicoloured.

659 65 ore Type **188** 40 40
660 65 ore Erik XIV's sceptre, 1561 40 40
661 65 ore Erik XIV's crown, 1561 40 40
662 65 ore Erik XIV's orb, 1561 . 40 40
663 65 ore Karl IX's anointing horn, 1606 . . . . 40 40

189 Santa Claus and Gifts — **190** "Nils Holgersson on Goose" (from "The Wonderful Adventures of Nils" by Selma Lagerlof)

1971. Christmas. Traditional Prints.

664 **189** 35 ore red . . . . 1·10 90
665 – 35 ore blue . . . . 1·10 90
666 – 35 ore purple . . . . . . 1·10 90
667 – 35 ore blue . . . . 1·10 90
668 – 35 ore green . . . . 1·10 90
DESIGNS: No. 665, Market scene; 666, Musical evening; 667, Skating; 668, Arriving for Christmas service.

1971.

669 **190** 65 ore blue on cream . . . 20 10

191 Maurice Maeterlinck (literature) — **192** Fencing

1971. Nobel Prize Winners.

670 **191** 55 ore orange 40 20
671 – 65 ore green 40 10
672 – 85 ore red 40 40
DESIGNS—Prize winners of 1911: 65 ore Allvar Gullstrand (medicine) and Wilhelm Wien (physics); 85 ore Marie Curie (chemistry).

1972. Sportswomen. Perf.

673 **192** 55 ore purple 60 60
674 – 55 ore blue 60 60
675 – 55 ore green 60 60
676 – 55 ore purple 60 60
677 – 55 ore blue 60 60
DESIGNS: No. 674, Diving; 675, Gymnastics; 676, Tennis; 677, Figure-skating.

193 L. J. Hierta (newspaper editor, statue by C. Eriksson) — **195** Roe Deer

1972. Anniversaries of Swedish Cultural Celebrities.

678 **193** 35 ore multicoloured . . . 15 10
679 – 50 ore violet 20 10
680 – 65 ore blue 40 10
681 – 85 ore multicoloured . . . 40 20
DESIGNS AND ANNIVERSARIES—VERT: 35 ore (death cent); 85 ore G. Stiernhielm (poet 300th death anniv) (portrait by D. K. Ehrenstrahl). HORIZ: 50 ore F. M. Franzen (poet and hymn-writer, birth bicent) (after K. Hultstrom); 65 ore Hugo Alfven (composer, birth cent) (granite bust by C. Milles).

1972.

682 **195** 95 ore brown on cream . . 20 10

196 Glass-blowing

1972. Swedish Glass Industry.

683 **196** 65 ore black 85 40
684 – 65 ore blue 85 40
685 – 65 ore red 85 40
686 – 65 ore black 85 40
687 – 65 ore blue 85 40
DESIGNS: No. 684, Glass-blowing (close-up); 685, Shaping glass; 686, Handling glass vase; 687, Bevelling glass vase.

197 Horses, Borgholm Castle (after N. Kreuger)

1972. Tourism in South-east Sweden.

688 **197** 55 ore brown on cream . . 45 45
689 – 55 ore blue on cream . . . 45 45
690 – 55 ore brown on cream . . 45 45
691 – 55 ore green on cream . . 45 45
692 – 55 ore blue on cream . . . 45 45
DESIGNS: No. 689, Oland Bridge and sailing barque "Meta"; 690, Kalmar Castle; 691, Salmon-fishing, Morrumsan; 692, Cadet schooner "Falken", Karlskrona Naval Base.

198 Conference Emblem and Motto, "Only One Earth"

1972. U.N. Environment Conservation Conference, Stockholm.

693 **198** 65 ore blue and red on cream 20 10
694 – 85 ore mult on cream . . 50 30
DESIGN—28 × 45 mm: 85 ore "Spring" (wooden relief by B. Hjorth).

199 Junkers F-13 — **201** Early Courier

200 Reindeer and Sledge (woodcut from "Lapponia")

1972. Swedish Mailplanes.

695 **199** 5 ore lilac 10 10
696 – 15 ore blue 40 10
697 – 25 ore blue 40 10
698 – 75 ore green 30 10
DESIGNS—45 × 19 mm: 15 ore Junkers Ju 52/3m; 25 ore Friedrichshafen FF-49 seaplane; 75 ore Douglas DC-3.

1972. Centenary of "Lapponia" (book by J. Schefferus).

669 **200** 1 k. 40 red and blue . . 35 10

1972. "Stockholmia 74" Stamp Exhibition (1st issue) and Birth Centenary of Olle Hjortzberg (stamp designer).

700 **201** 10 ore red 30 40
701 – 15 ore green 30 40
702 – 40 ore blue 60 60
703 – 50 ore brown 30 40
704 – 60 ore blue 40 40
DESIGNS: 15 ore Post-rider; 40 ore Steam train; 50 ore Motor bus and trailer; 60 ore Liner "Gripsholm".
See also Nos. 779/82.

202 Figurehead of Royal Yacht "Amphion" (Per Ljung) — **203** Christmas Candles (J. Wikstrom)

1972. Swedish 18th-century Art.

705 – 75 ore green 25 20
706 – 75 ore brown 25 20
707 **202** 75 ore red 25 20
708 – 75 ore red 25 20
709 – 75 ore black, brn & red . . 25 20
710 – 75 ore black, blue & purple 25 20
DESIGNS—59 × 24 mm: No. 705, "Stockholm" (F. Martin); 706, "The Forge" (P. Hillestrom). As T **202**: No. 708, "Quadriga" (Sergel). 28 × 37 mm: No. 709, "Lady with a Veil" (A. Roslin); 710, "Sophia Magdalena" (C. G. Pilo).

1972. Christmas. Multicoloured.

711 45 ore Type **203** 25 10
712 45 ore Father Christmas (E. Flygh) 25 10
713 75 ore Carol singers (S. Hagg) (40 × 23 mm) 40 10

204 King Gustav VI Adolf — **205** King Gustav with Book

1972.

714 **204** 75 ore blue 20 10
715 1 k. red 35 10

1972. King Gustav VI Adolf's 90th Birthday.

716 **205** 75 ore blue . . . . 1·10 2·25
717 – 75 ore green . . . . 1·10 2·25
718 – 75 ore red . . . . 1·10 2·25
719 – 75 ore blue . . . . 1·10 2·25
720 – 75 ore green . . . . 1·10 2·25
DESIGNS: No. 717, Chinese objets d'art; 718, Opening Parliament; 719, Greek objets d'art; 720, King Gustav tending flowers.

206 Alexis Carrel (medicine)

207 "Tintomara" Stage Set (B-R. Hedwall)

1972. Nobel Prize Winners of 1912.

721 – 60 ore brown 45 20
722 **206** 65 ore blue 50 25
723 – 75 ore violet 75 10
724 – 1 k. brown 75 15

DESIGNS—HORIZ: 60 ore Paul Sabatier and Victor Grignard (chemistry). VERT: 75 ore Nils Gustav Dalen (physics); 1 k. Gerhart Hauptmann (literature).

1973. Bicentenary of Swedish Royal Theatre.

725 **207** 75 ore green 30 10
726 – 1 k. purple 30 15

DESIGN—41 × 23 mm: 1 k. "Orpheus" (P. Hillestrom).

208 Modern Mail Coach, Vietas

210 Horse (bas relief)

209 Vasa Ski Race

1973.

727 – 60 ore black on yellow . . 20 20
728 **208** 70 ore orange, blue & grn 25 10

DESIGN: 60 ore Mail bus, 1923.

1973. Tourism in Dalecarlia.

729 **209** 65 ore green 30 25
730 – 65 ore green 30 25
731 – 65 ore black 30 25
732 – 65 ore green 30 25
733 – 65 ore red 30 25

DESIGNS: No. 730, "Going to the Church in Mora" (A. Zorn); 731, Church stables in Rattvik; 732, "The Great Pit"; 733, "Mid-summer Dance" (B. Nordenberg).

1973. Gottland's Picture Stones.

734 **210** 5 ore purple 10 10
735 – 10 blue 10 10

DESIGN: 10 ore Viking longship (bas relief).

211 "Row of Willows" (P. Persson)

1973. Swedish Landscapes.

736 **211** 40 ore brown 10 10
737 – 50 ore black and brown . . 10 10
738 – 55 ore green on cream . . 20 10

DESIGNS—20 × 28 mm: 50 ore "View of Trosa" (R. Ljunggren). 27 × 23 mm: 55 ore "Spring Birches" (O. Bergman).

212 Lumberman

213 Observer reading Thermometer

1973. 75th Anniv of Swedish Confederation of Trade Unions.

739 **212** 75 ore red 20 10
740 1 k. 40 blue 30 10

1973. Centenary of I.M.O./W.M.O. and Swedish Meteorological Organizations.

741 **213** 65 ore green 60 30
742 – 65 ore blue and black . . . 60 30

DESIGN: No. 742, U.S. satellite weather picture.

214 Nordic House, Reykjavik

1973. Nordic Countries' Postal Co-operation.

743 **214** 75 ore multicoloured . . 30 10
744 1 k. multicoloured . . . 40 10

215 C. P. Thunberg, Japanese Flora and Scene

1973. Swedish Explorers.

745 **215** 1 k. brown, green & blue 90 1·00
746 – 1 k. multicoloured . . . 90 1·00
747 – 1 k. brown, green & blue 90 1·00
748 – 1 k. multicoloured . . . 90 1·00
749 – 1 k. multicoloured . . . 90 1·00

DESIGNS: No. 746, Anders Sparrman and Tahiti; 747, Adolf Erik Nordenskiold and the "Vega"; 748, Salomon Andree and wreckage of balloon "Ornen"; 749, Sven Hedin and camels.

216 Team of Oxen

217 Grey Seal

1973. Centenary of Nordic Museum.

750 **216** 75 ore black . . . . . . 1·10 30
751 – 75 ore brown . . . . . . 1·10 30
752 – 75 ore black . . . . . . 1·10 30
753 – 75 ore purple . . . . . . 1·10 30
754 – 75 ore brown . . . . . . 1·10 30

DESIGNS: No. 751, Braking flax; 752, Potato-planting; 753, Baking bread; 754, Spring sowing.

1973. "Save Our Animals".

755 **217** 10 ore green 10 10
756 – 20 ore violet 40 10
757 – 25 ore blue 20 10
758 – 55 ore blue 30 10
759 – 65 ore violet 30 10
760 – 75 ore green 60 15

DESIGNS: 20 ore Peregrine falcon; 25 ore Lynx; 55 ore European otter; 65 ore Wolf; 75 ore White-tailed sea eagle.

218 King Gustav VI Adolf

220 "Goosegirl" (E. Josephson)

219 "Country Dance" (J. Nilsson)

1973. King Gustav VI Adolf Memorial Issue.

761 **218** 75 ore blue 20 10
762 1 k. purple 30 10

1973. Christmas. Peasant Paintings. Mult.

763 45 ore Type **219** 40 10
764 45 ore "The Three Wise Men" (A. Clemetson) 40 10
765 75 ore "Gourd Plant" (B. A. Hansson) (23 × 28 mm) . . 1·10 10
766 75 ore "The Rider" (K. E. Jonsson) (23 × 28 mm) . . 1·10 10

1973. Ernst Josephson Commemoration.

767 **220** 10 k. multicoloured . . . 1·75 10

221 A. Werner (chemistry) and H. Kamerlingh-Onnes (physics)

1973. Nobel Prize Winners. Inscr "NOBELPRIS 1913".

768 **221** 75 ore violet 40 10
769 – 1 k. brown 50 10
770 – 1 k. 40 green 60 10

DESIGNS—Prize winners of 1913. VERT: 1 k. Charles Robert Richet (medicine); 1 k. 40, Rabindranath Tagore (literature).

222 Ski Jumping

1974. "Winter Sports on Skis".

771 **222** 65 ore green 40 40
772 – 65 ore blue 40 40
773 – 65 ore green 40 40
774 – 65 ore red 40 40
775 – 65 ore blue 40 40

DESIGNS: No 772, Cross-country (man); 773, Relay-racing; 774, Downhill-racing; 775, Cross-country (woman).

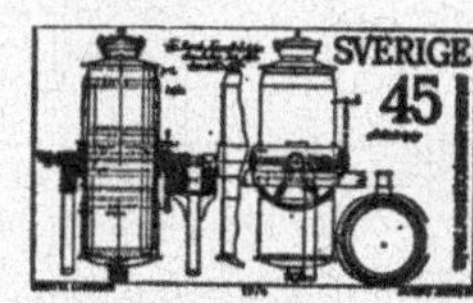

223 Ekman's Sulphite Pulping Machine

1974. Swedish Anniversaries.

776 **223** 45 ore brown on grey . . 15 10
777 – 60 ore green 20 10
778 – 75 ore red 25 10

DESIGNS AND EVENTS: 45 ore Type **223** (centenary of first sulphite pulp plant, Bergvik); 60 ore Hans Jarta and part of Government Act (birth bicent); 75 ore Samuel Owen and engineers (birth bicent).

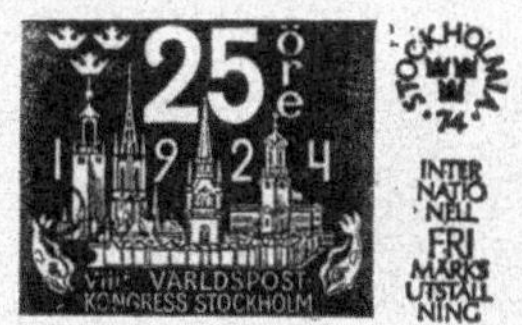

224 U.P.U. Congress Stamp of 1924

1974. "Stockholmia '74" Stamp Exn (2nd issue).

779 **224** 20 ore green 15 20
780 25 ore blue 15 20
781 30 ore brown 15 20
782 35 ore red 15 20

225 Great Falls

226 "Figure in a Storm" (B. Marklund)

1974.

784 **225** 35 ore black and blue . . 15 10
785 – 75 ore brown 20 10

DESIGN—HORIZ: 75 ore Ystad (town).

1974. Europa. Sculptures.

786 **226** 75 ore purple 90 10
787 – 1 k. green . . . . 1·00 10

DESIGN: 1 k. Picasso statue (from "Les Dames de Mougins"), Kristinehamn.

227 King Carl XVI Gustav

228 Central Post Office, Stockholm

1974.

788 **227** 75 ore green 30 10
789 90 ore blue 40 10
790 1 k. purple 30 10
791 1 k. 10 red 20 10
792 1 k. 30 green 20 10
793 1 k. 40 blue 30 15
794 1 k. 50 mauve 30 10
795 1 k. 70 orange 40 10
796 2 k. brown 40 10

1974. Centenary of Universal Postal Union.

800 **228** 75 ore purple 70 25
801 – 75 ore purple 70 25
802 – 1 k. green 35 10

DESIGNS—As Type **228**: No. 801, Interior of Central Post Office, Stockholm. 40 × 24 mm: No. 802, Rural postman.

229 Regatta

1974. Tourism on Sweden's West Coast.

803 **229** 65 ore red 50 30
804 – 65 ore blue 50 30
805 – 65 ore green 50 30
806 – 65 ore green 50 30
807 – 65 ore brown 50 30

DESIGNS: No. 804, Vinga Lighthouse; 805, Varberg Fortress; 806, Seine fishing; 807, Mollosund.

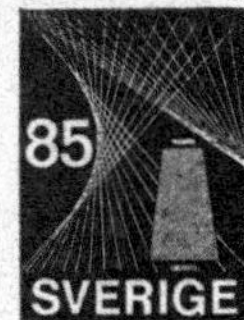

230 "Mr. Simmons" (A. Fridell)

231 Thread and Spool

1974. Centenary of Publicists' Club (Swedish press, radio and television association).

808 **230** 45 ore black 15 15
809 1 k. 40 purple 35 10

1974. Swedish Textile and Clothing Industry.

810 **231** 85 ore violet 25 25
811 – 85 ore black and orange . 25 25

DESIGN: No. 811, Stylised sewing-machine.

232 Deer

1974. Christmas. Mosaic Embroideries of Mythical Creatures. Each blue, red and green (45 ore) or multicoloured (75 ore).

812 45 ore Type **232** 70 70
813 45 ore Griffin 70 70
814 45 ore Lion 70 70
815 45 ore Griffin 70 70
816 45 ore Unicorn 70 70
817 45 ore Horse 70 70
818 45 ore Lion 70 70
819 45 ore Griffin 70 70
820 45 ore Lion 70 70
821 45 ore Lion-like creature . . 70 70
822 75 ore Deer-like creature . . 20 10

No. 813 is facing right and has inscr at top, No. 815 faces left with similar inscr and No. 819 has inscr at bottom.

No. 814 has the inscr at top, No. 818 has it at the foot of the design, the lion having blue claws, No. 820 has similar inscr, but white claws.

233 Tanker "Bill"

1974. Swedish Shipping. Each blue.

823 1 k. Type **233** 70 60
824 1 k. "Snow Storm" (liner) . . 70 60
825 1 k. "Tor" and "Atle" (ice-breakers) 70 60
826 1 k. "Skanes" (train ferry) . . 70 60
827 1 k. Tugs "Bill", "Bull" and "Starkodder" 70 60

234 Max von Laue (physics)

235 Sven Jerring (first announcer), Children and Microphone

1974. Nobel Prize Winners of 1914.

828 **234** 65 ore red 35 20
829 – 70 ore green 35 20
830 – 1 k. blue 65 15

DESIGNS:—70 ore Theodore William Richards (chemistry); 1 k. Richard Barany (medicine).

1974. 50th Anniv of Swedish Broadcasting Corporation.

831 **235** 75 ore blue and brown . . 70 20
832 – 75 ore blue and brown . . 70 20

DESIGN: No. 832, Television camera at Parliamentary debate.

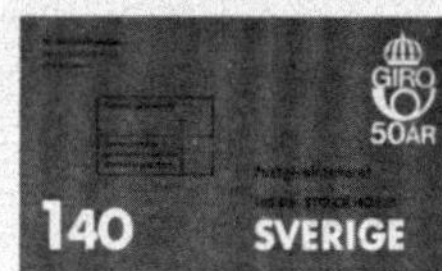

236 Giro Envelope

1975. 50th Anniv of Swedish Postal Giro Office.

833 **236** 1 k. 40 black and brown . 30 10

237 Male and Female Engineers

238 Bronze Helmet Decoration, Vendel

1975. International Women's Year.
834 **237** 75 ore green 20 10
835 – 1 k. purple 35 10
DESIGN—VERT: 1 k. Jenny Lind (singer) (portrait by O. J. Sodermark).

1975. Archaeological Discoveries.
836 **238** 10 ore red 10 10
837 – 15 ore green 10 10
838 – 20 ore violet 10 10
839 – 25 ore yellow 10 10
840 – 55 ore brown 10 10
DESIGNS: 15 ore Iron sword hilt and chapel, Vendel; 20 ore Iron shield buckle, Vendel; 25 ore Embossed gold plates (Gold Men), Eketorp Fortress, Oland; 55 ore Iron helmet, Vendel.

239 "New Year's Eve at Skansen (Eric Hallstrom)

1975. Europa. Paintings. Multicoloured.
841 90 ore Type **239** 25 10
842 1 k. 10 "Inferno" (August Strindberg) (vert) 30 10

240 Metric Tape-measure (centenary of Metre Convention)

241 Western European Hedgehog

1975. Anniversaries.
843 **240** 55 ore blue 15 10
844 – 70 ore sepia and brown . 15 10
845 – 75 ore violet 15 10
DESIGNS AND EVENTS—44×27 mm: 70 ore Peter Hernqvist (founder) and title-page of his book "Comprehensive Thesis on Glanders in Horses" (bicent of Swedish Veterinary Service). 24×31 mm: 75 ore "Folke Filbyter" (birth centenary of Carl Milles (sculptor)).

1975.
846 **241** 55 ore black 20 10
847 – 75 ore red 20 10
848 – 1 k. 70 blue 40 10
849 – 2 k. purple 50 10
850 – 7 k. green 90 10
DESIGNS—HORIZ: 75 ore Key-fiddler; 1 k. 70, Capercaillie ("cock of the woods"). VERT: 2 k. Rok stone (ancient inscribed rock), Ostergotland; 7 k. Ballet dancers (from "Romeo and Juliet").

242 Village Buildings, Skelleftea

1975. European Architectural Heritage Year.
851 **242** 75 ore black 20 20
852 – 75 ore red 20 20
853 – 75 ore black 20 20
854 – 75 ore red 20 20
855 – 75 ore blue 20 20
DESIGNS: No. 852, Engelsberg iron-works, Vastmanland; 853, Gunpowder tower, Visby, Gotland; 854, Iron-mine, Falun; 855, Rommehed military barracks, Dalecarlia.

243 Fire Brigade

1975. "Watch, Guard and Help". Public Services.
856 **243** 90 ore red 55 20
857 – 90 ore blue 55 20
858 – 90 ore red 55 20
859 – 90 ore blue 55 20
860 – 90 ore green 55 20
DESIGNS: No. 857, Customs service; 858, Police service; 859, Ambulance and hospital service; 860, Shipwreck of "Merkur" (Sea rescue service).

244 "Fryckstad"

1975. Swedish Steam Locomotives.
861 **244** 5 ore green 10 10
862 – 5 ore blue 10 10
863 – 90 ore green 80 15
DESIGNS—As Type **244**: No. 862, "Gotland". 49×22 mm: 90 ore "Prince August".

245 Canoeing

246 "Madonna" (sculpture), Vikiau church, Gotland

1975. Scouting. Multicoloured.
864 90 ore Type **245** 80 20
865 90 ore Camping 80 20

1975. Christmas. Religious Art.
866 **246** 55 ore multicoloured . . . 20 10
867 – 55 ore multicoloured . . 20 10
868 – 55 ore multicoloured . . 20 10
869 – 90 ore brown 30 10
870 – 90 ore red 60 10
871 – 90 ore blue 60 10
DESIGNS—VERT: No. 867, "Birth of Christ" (embossed copper), Broddetorp church, Vastergotland; 868, "The Sun" (embossed copper), Broddetorp church, Vastergotland; 869, "Mourning Mary" (sculpture), Oja church, Gotland. HORIZ: Nos. 870, 871, "Jesse at Foot of Christ's genealogical tree" (retable), Lofta church, Smaland.

247 W. H. and W. L. Bragg (physics)

248 Bronze Coiled Snake Brooch, Vendel

1975. Nobel Prize Winners of 1915.
872 **247** 75 ore purple 20 20
873 – 90 ore blue 30 10
874 – 1 k. 10 green 30 20
DESIGNS: 90 ore Richard Willstatter (chemistry); 1 k. 10, Romain Rolland (literature).

1976.
875 **248** 15 ore bistre 10 10
876 – 20 ore green 10 10
877 – 30 ore purple 10 10
878 – 85 ore blue 30 10
879 – 90 ore blue 20 10
880 – 1 k. purple 20 10
881 – 1 k. 90 green 40 10
882 – 9 k. deep green and green 1·50 15
DESIGNS—21×19 mm: 20 ore Pilgrim badge. 28×21 mm: 30 ore Drinking horn; 85 ore Common guillemot and razorbills. 28×23 mm: 1 k. 90, "Cave of the Winds" (sculpture) (Eric Grate). 21×28 mm: 90 ore Chimney sweep; 1 k. Bobbin lace-making; 9 k. "Girl's Head" (wood-carving) (Bror Hjorth).

249 Early and Modern Telephones

250 Wheat and Cornflower Seed

1976. Telephone Centenary.
883 **249** 1 k. 30 mauve 30 15
884 3 k. 40 red 80 15

1976. Swedish Seed-testing Centenary.
885 **250** 65 ore brown 20 20
886 – 65 ore green and brown . . 20 20
DESIGN: No. 886, Viable and non-viable plants.

251 Lapp Spoon

253 Ship's Wheel and Cross

252 "View from Ringkallen" (H. Osslund)

1976. Europa. Handicrafts.
887 **251** 1 k. black, pink and blue 35 10
888 – 1 k. 30 multicoloured . . 35 10
DESIGN: 1 k. 30, Tile stove (from aquarell by C. Slania).

1976. Tourism. Angermanland.
889 **252** 85 ore green 20 20
890 – 85 ore blue 20 20
891 – 85 ore brown 20 20
892 – 85 ore blue 20 20
893 – 85 ore red 20 20
DESIGNS: No. 890, Tug towing timber; 891, Hay-drying racks; 892, Granvagsnipan; 893, Seine-net fishing.

1976. Centenary of Swedish Seamen's Church.
894 **253** 85 ore blue 25 10

254 Torgny Segerstedt and "Goteborg Handels- och Sjofartstidning"

1976. Birth Centenary of Torgny Segerstedt (newspaper editor).
895 **254** 1 k. 90 black and brown . 40 10

255 King Carl XVI Gustav and Queen Silvia

257 Hands and Cogwheels

256 John Ericsson (marine propeller)

1976. Royal Wedding.
896 **255** 1 k. red 20 10
897 1 k. 30 green 30 10

1976. Swedish Technological Pioneers. Mult.
898 1 k. 30 Type **256** 55 55
899 1 k. 30 Helge Palmcrantz (hay maker) 55 55
900 1 k. 30 Lars Magnus Ericsson (telephone improvements) . . 55 55
901 1 k. 30 Sven Wingquist (ball bearing) 55 55
902 1 k. 30 Gustaf de Laval (milk separator and reaction turbine) 55 55

1976. Industrial Safety.
903 **257** 85 ore orange and violet . 25 10
904 1 k. green and brown . . . 25 10

258 Verner von Heidenstam

259 "Archangel Michael Destroying Lucifer" (Flemish prayer book)

1976. Literature Nobel Prize Winner of 1916.
905 **258** 1 k. green 30 10
906 1 k. 30 blue 40 20

1976. Christmas. Mediaeval Book Illustrations. Multicoloured.
907 65 ore Type **259** 20 10
908 65 ore "St. Nicholas awakening Children from Dead" (Flemish prayer book) 20 10
909 1 k. "Mary visiting Elizabeth" (Austrian prayer book) . . . 30 10
910 1 k. "Prayer to the Virgin" (Austrian prayer book) . . . 30 10
Nos. 909/10 are vertical, 26×44 mm.

1977. Nordic Countries Co-operation in Nature Conservation and Environment Protection. As T **222** of Norway.
911 1 k. multicoloured 30 10
912 1 k. 30 multicoloured 20 20

261 Tawny Owl

262 "Politeness"

1977.
913 **261** 45 ore green 40 20
914 – 70 ore blue 20 10
915 – 1 k. 40 brown 30 15
916 – 2 k. 10 brown 35 10
DESIGNS—23×29 mm: 70 ore Norwegian cast-iron stove decoration. 41×21 mm: 1 k. 40, Gotland ponies. 28×22 mm: 2 k. 10, Tailor.

1977. Birth Centenary of Oskar Andersson (cartoonist).
917 **262** 75 ore black 15 10
918 3 k. 80 red 70 20

263 Skating

1977. Keep-fit Activities.
919 **263** 95 ore blue 20 30
920 – 95 ore green 20 30
921 – 95 ore red 20 30
922 – 95 ore green 20 30
923 – 95 ore blue 20 30
DESIGNS: No. 920, Swimming; 921, Cycling; 922, Jogging; 923, Badminton.

264 Gustavianum Building

1977. 500th Anniv of Uppsala University.
924 **264** 1 k. 10 black, yellow & bl 30 10

265 Winter Forest Scene

1977. Europa. Landscapes. Multicoloured.
925 1 k. 10 Type **265** 30 10
926 1 k. 40 Rapadalen valley, Sarek 40 30

266 Calle Schewen at Breakfast

267 Blackberries

1977. Tourism. Roslagen. Poem "Calle Schewen Waltz" by E. Taube.
927 **266** 95 ore green 20 30
928 – 95 ore violet 50 30
929 – 95 ore black and red . . . 20 30
930 – 95 ore blue 20 30
931 – 95 ore red 20 30
DESIGNS: No. 928, Black-headed gull; 929, Calle Schewen dancing; 930, Fishing; 931, Sunset.

1977. Wild Berries. Multicoloured.
932 75 ore Type **267** 20 20
933 75 ore Cowberries 20 20
934 75 ore Cloudberries 20 20
935 75 ore Bilberries 20 20
936 75 ore Strawberries 20 20

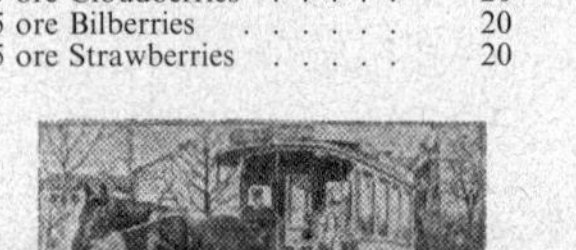

268 Horse-drawn Tram

1977. Public Transport.
937 **268** 1 k. 10 green 60 40
938 – 1 k. 10 blue 60 40
939 – 1 k. 10 blue 60 40
940 – 1 k. 10 blue 60 40
941 – 1 k. 10 green 60 40
DESIGN: No. 938, Electric tram; 939, Ferry "Djurgarden 6"; 940, Articulated bus; 941, Underground train.

269 H. Pontoppidan and K. A. Gjellerup (literature)

270 Erecting Sheaf for Birds

1977. Nobel Prize Winners of 1917.
942 **269** 1 k. 10 brown 30 10
943 – 1 k. 40 green 40 20
DESIGN: 1 k. 40, Charles Glover Barkla (physics).

1977. Christmas. Seasonal Customs.
944 **270** 75 ore violet 20 10
945 – 75 ore orange 20 10
946 – 75 ore green 20 10
947 – 1 k. 10 green 30 10
948 – 1 k. 10 red 30 10
949 – 1 k. 10 blue 30 10
DESIGNS: No. 945, Making gingersnaps; 946, Bringing in the Christmas tree; 947, Preparing the traditional fish dish; 948, Making straw goats for the pantomime; 949, Candle-making.

271 Brown Bear **272** Orebro Castle

1978.
950 **271** 1 k. 15 brown 40 10
951 – 2 k. 50 blue 40 10
DESIGN: 2 k. 50, "Space without Affiliation" (sculpture by Arne Jones).

1978. Europa.
952 **272** 1 k. 30 green 40 10
953 – 1 k. 70 red 50 25
DESIGN—VERT: 1 k. 70, Doorway, Orebro Castle.

273 Pentecostal Meeting

1978. Independent Christian Associations.
954 **273** 90 ore purple 30 30
955 – 90 black 30 30
956 – 90 ore violet 30 30
957 – 90 ore green 30 30
958 – 90 ore purple 30 30
DESIGNS: No. 955, Minister with children (Swedish Missionary Society); 956, Communion Service, Ethiopia (Evangelical National Missionary Society); 957, Baptism (Baptist Society); 958, Salvation Army band.

274 Brosarp Hills

1978. Travels of Carl Linne (botanist).
959 **274** 1 k. 30 black 50 30
960 – 1 k. 30 blue . . . . . . 1·25 30
961 – 1 k. 30 purple 50 30
962 – 1 k. 30 red 50 30
963 – 1 k. 30 blue 50 30
964 – 1 k. 30 purple 50 30
DESIGNS—58 × 23 mm: No. 960, Avocets. 27 × 23 mm: No. 961, Grindstone production (after J. W. Wallander); 962, "Linnaea borealis". 27 × 36 mm: No. 963, Red limestone cliff; 964, Linnaeus wearing Lapp dress and Dutch doctor's hat, and carrying Lapp drum (H. Kingsbury).

275 Glider over Alleberg Plateau

1978. Tourism. Vastergotland.
965 **275** 1 k. 15 green 40 30
966 – 1 k. 15 red 40 30
967 – 1 k. 15 blue 40 30
968 – 1 k. 15 grey 40 30
969 – 1 k. 15 black and purple . 40 30
DESIGNS: No. 966, Common cranes; 967, Fortress on Lacko Island Skara; 968, Rock tomb, Luttra; 969, "Traders of South Vastergotland" (sculpture, N. Sjogren).

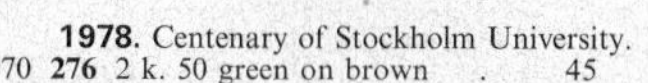
276 Diploma and Laurel Wreath

1978. Centenary of Stockholm University.
970 **276** 2 k. 50 green on brown . 45 10

277 "The Homecoming" (Carl Kylberg)

1978. Paintings by Swedish Artists. Multicoloured.
971 90 ore Type **277** 30 10
972 1 k. 15 "Standing Model seen from Behind" (Karl Isakson) 30 10
973 4 k. 50 "Self-portrait with a Floral Wreath" (Ivar Arosenius) 80 20

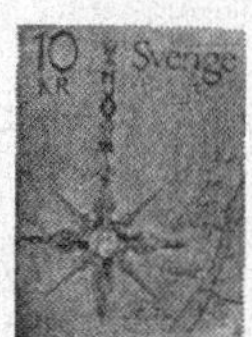
278 Northern Arrow

280 "Russula decolorans"

279 Coronation Carriage, 1699

1978.
974 **278** 10 k. mauve . . . . . . 1·75 10

1978.
975 **279** 1 k. 70 red on buff . . . 40 30

1978. Edible Mushrooms. Multicoloured. Perf.
976 1 k. 15 Type **280** 50 40
977 1 k. 15 Common puff-ball ("Lycoperdon perlatum") 50 40
978 1 k. 15 Parasol mushroom ("Macrolepiota procera") 50 40
979 1 k. 15 Chanterelle ("Cantharellus cibarius") 50 40
980 1 k. 15 Cep ("Boletus edulis") 50 40
981 1 k. 15 Cauliflower clavaria ("Ramaria botrytis") . . . 50 40

281 Dalecarlian Horse

282 Fritz Haber (chemistry)

1978. Christmas. Old Toys.
982 **281** 90 ore multicoloured . . 30 10
983 – 90 ore multicoloured . . 30 10
984 – 90 ore green and red . . 30 10
985 – 1 k. 30 multicoloured . . 30 10
986 – 1 k. 30 multicoloured . . 30 10
987 – 1 k. 30, blue 30 10
DESIGNS—VERT: No. 983, Swedish Court doll; 984, Meccano; 987, Teddy bear. HORIZ: No. 985, Tops; 986, Equipage with water barrel (metal toy).

1978. Nobel Prize Winners of 1918.
988 **282** 1 k. 30 brown 40 10
989 – 1 k. 70 black 50 30
DESIGN: 1 k. 70, Max Planck (physics).

283 Bandy Players fighting for Ball

1979. Bandy.
990 **283** 1 k. 05 blue 20 10
991 2 k. 50 orange 50 10

284 Child in Gas-mask

285 Wall Hanging

1979. International Year of the Child.
992 **284** 1 k. 70 blue 30 20

1979.
993 **285** 4 k. blue and red 80 10

286 Carrier Pigeon and Hand with Quill

287 Sledge-boat

1979. Rebate Stamp.
994 **286** (1 k.) yellow, black & blue . 30 10
No. 994 was only issued in booklets of 20 sold at 20 k. in exchange for tokens distributed to all households in Sweden. Valid for inland postage only, they represented a rebate of 30 ore on the normal rate of 1 k. 30.

1979. Europa.
995 **287** 1 k. 30 black and green . . 40 10
996 – 1 k. 70 black and brown . 45 30
DESIGN: 1 k. 70, Hand using telegraph key.

288 Felling Tree

1979. Farming.
997 **288** 1 k. 30 black, red & grn . 35 15
998 – 1 k. 30 green and black . 35 15
999 – 1 k. 30 green and black . 35 15
1000 – 1 k. 30 brown and green . 35 15
1001 – 1 k. 30 red, black & grn . 35 15
DESIGNS: No. 998, Sowing; No. 999, Cows; No. 1000, Harvesting; No. 1001, Ploughing.

289 Tourist Launch "Juno"

1979. Tourism. Gota Canal.
1002 **289** 1 k. 15 violet 45 45
1003 – 1 k. 15 green 45 45
1004 – 1 k. 15 purple 45 45
1005 – 1 k. 15 red 45 45
1006 – 1 k. 15 violet 45 45
1007 – 1 k. 15 green 45 45
DESIGNS—As T **289**: No. 1003, Borenshult lock. $27 \times 23\frac{1}{2}$ mm: No. 1004, Hajstorp roller bridge; 1005, Opening lock gates. $27 \times 36\frac{1}{2}$ mm: No. 1006, Motor barge "Wilhelm Tham" in lock; 1007, Kayak in lock.

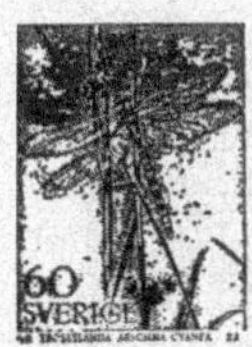

290 "Aeshna cyanea" (dragonfly)

291 Workers leaving Sawmills

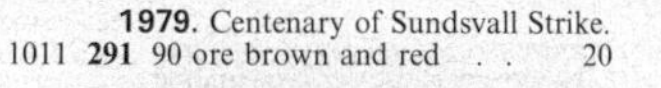

1979. Wildlife.
1008 **290** 60 ore violet 40 10
1009 – 65 ore green 50 10
1010 – 80 ore green 50 10
DESIGNS—41 × 21 mm: 65 ore Pike. 27 × 22 mm: 80 ore Green spotted toad.

1979. Centenary of Sundsvall Strike.
1011 **291** 90 ore brown and red . . 20 10

292 Banner

293 J. J. Berzelius

1979. Centenary of Swedish Temperance Movement.
1012 **292** 1 k. 30 multicoloured . . 30 10

1979. Birth Bicentenaries of J. J. Berzelius (chemist) and J. O. Wallin (poet and hymn-writer).
1013 **293** 1 k. 70 brown and green . 30 20
1014 – 4 k. 50 blue 80 30
DESIGN: 4 k. 50, J. O. Wallin and hymn numbers.

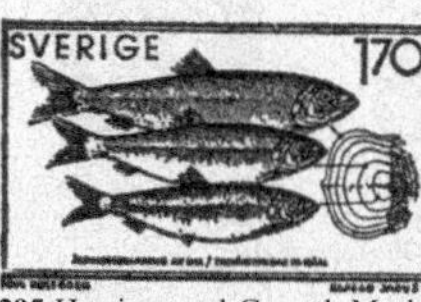

295 Herrings and Growth Marks

296 Ljusdal Costume

1979. Marine Research.
1016 **295** 1 k. 70 green and blue . 50 40
1017 – 1 k. 70 brown 50 40
1018 – 1 k. 70 green and blue . 50 40
1019 – 1 k. 70 brown 50 40
1020 – 1 k. 70 green and blue . 50 40
DESIGNS: No. 1017, Acoustic survey of sea-bed; 1018, Plankton bloom; 1019, Echo-sounding chart of Baltic Sea, October 1978; 1020, Fishery research ship "Argos".

1979. Peasant Costumes and Jewellery.
1021 **296** 90 ore multicoloured . . 20 20
1022 – 90 ore multicoloured . . 20 20
1023 – 90 ore blue 20 10
1024 – 1 k. 30 multicoloured . . 30 20
1025 – 1 k. 30 multicoloured . . 30 20
1026 – 1 k. 30 red 30 10
DESIGNS: As T **296**: No. 1022, Osteraker costume. 21 × 27 mm: No. 1023, Brooch from Jamtland; 1026, Brooch from Smaland. 23 × 40 mm: No. 1024, Goinge church dress; 1025, Mora church dress.

297 Jules Bordet (chemistry)

298 Wind Power

1979. Nobel Prize Winners of 1919.
1027 **297** 1 k. 30 mauve 30 10
1028 – 1 k. 70 blue 40 40
1029 – 2 k. 50 green 70 20
DESIGNS: 1 k. 70, Johannes Stark (physics); 2 k. 50, Carl Spitteler (literature).

1980. Renewable Energy Sources.
1030 **298** 1 k. 15 blue 30 40
1031 – 1 k. 15 buff and green . . 30 40
1032 – 1 k. 15 orange 30 40
1033 – 1 k. 15 green 30 40
1034 – 1 k. 15 green and blue . . 30 40
DESIGNS: No. 1031, Biological energy; No. 1032, Solar energy; No. 1033, Geothermal energy; No. 1034, Wave energy.

299 King Carl XVI Gustav and Crown Princess Victoria

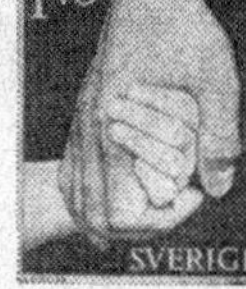

300 Child's Hand in Adult's

1980. New Order of Succession to Throne.
1035 **299** 1 k. 30 blue 20 10
1036 1 k. 70 red 30 20

1980. Care.
1037 **300** 1 k. 40 brown 25 10
1038 – 1 k. 60 green 25 10
DESIGN: 1 k. 60, Aged hand clasping stick.

301 Squirrel

302 Elise Ottesen-Jensen (pioneer of birth control)

1980. Rebate Stamp.
1039 **301** (1 k.) yellow, blue & blk 30 10
No. 1039 was only issued in booklets of 20 sold at 20 k. on production of tokens distributed to all households in Sweden.

1980. Europa.
1040 **302** 1 k. 30 green 40 10
1041 – 1 k. 70 red 40 30
DESIGN: 1 k. 70, Joe Hill (member of workers' movement).

303 Tybling Farm, Tyby

1980. Tourism. Halsingland.
1042 **303** 1 k. 15 red 30 30
1043 – 1 k. 15 blue and purple . 30 30
1044 – 1 k. 15 green 30 30
1045 – 1 k. 15 purple 30 30
1046 – 1 k. 15 blue 30 30
DESIGNS: No. 1043, Old iron works, Iggesund; No. 1044, Blaxas ridge, Forsa; No. 1045, Banga farm, Alfta; No. 1046, Sunds Canal, Hudiksvall.

304 Chair from Scania (1831) **305** Motif from film "Diagonal Symphony"

1980. Nordic Countries' Postal Co-operation.
1047 **304** 1 k. 50 green 30 10
1048 – 2 k. brown 40 10
DESIGN: 2 k. Cradle from North Bothnia (19th century).

1980. Birth Bicentenary of Viking Eggeling (film-maker).
1049 **305** 3 k. blue 60 10

307 Bamse **308** "Necken" (Ernst Josephson)

1980. Christmas. Swedish Comic Strips.
1051 **307** 1 k. 15 blue and red . . 25 10
1052 – 1 k. 15 multicoloured . . 25 10
1053 – 1 k. 50 black 30 10
1054 – 1 k. 50 multicoloured . . 30 10
DESIGNS—As T **307** but VERT: No. 1052, Karlsson; 1053, Adamson. 40 × 23 mm: No. 1054, Kronblom.

1980.
1055 **308** 8 k. brown, black & blue 1·25 15

309 Knut Hamsun (literature) **310** Angel blowing Horn

1980. Nobel Prize Winners of 1920.
1056 **309** 1 k. 40 blue 30 20
1057 – 1 k. 40 red 30 20
1058 – 2 k. green 40 25
1059 – 2 k. brown 40 25
DESIGNS: No. 1057, August Krogh (medicine); 1058, Charles-Edouard Guillaume (physics); 1059, Walther Nernst (chemistry).

1980. Christmas.
1060 **310** 1 k. 25 brown and blue . 30 10

311 Ernst Wigforss **312** Thor catching Midgard Serpent

1981. Birth Centenary of Ernst Wigforss (politician).
1061 **311** 5 k. red 90 20

1981. Norse Mythology.
1062 **312** 10 ore black 10 10
1063 – 15 ore red 10 10
1064 – 50 ore red 10 10
1065 – 75 ore green 20 10
1066 – 1 k. black 20 10
DESIGNS: 15 ore Heimdall blowing horn; 50 ore Freya riding boar; 75 ore Freya in carriage drawn by cats; 1 k. Odin on eight-footed steed.

313 Gyrfalcon **314** Troll

1981.
1067 **313** 50 k. brown, black & blue 7·50 80

1981. Europa.
1068 **314** 1 k. 50 blue and red . . 50 10
1069 – 2 k. red and green . . . 60 20
DESIGN: 2 k. The Lady of the Woods.

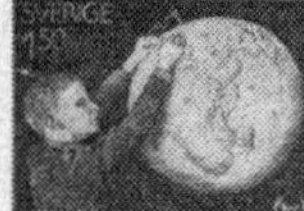

315 Blind Boy feeling Globe **316** Arms of Bohuslan

1981. International Year of Disabled Persons.
1070 **315** 1 k. 50 green 30 10
1071 3 k. 50 violet 70 20

1981. Rebate stamps. Arms of Swedish Provinces (1st series). Multicoloured.
1072 1 k. 40 Ostergotland 45 10
1073 1 k. 40 Jamtland 45 10
1074 1 k. 40 Dalarna 45 10
1075 1 k. 40 Type **316** 45 10
See also Nos. 1112/15, 1153/6, 1189/92, 1246/9 and 1302/5.

317 King Carl XVI Gustav **318** Boat from Bohuslan

1981.
1076 **317** 1 k. 65 green 30 10
1077 – 1 k. 75 blue 40 10
1077a **317** 1 k. 80 blue 30 10
1077b 1 k. 90 red 30 10
1078 2 k. 40 purple 50 10
1078a – 2 k. 40 green 50 10
1078b **317** 2 k. 70 purple 50 10
1078c – 3 k. 20 red 60 15
DESIGN: 1 k. 75, 2 k. 40 (1078a), 3 k. 20, Queen Silvia.

1981. Provincial Sailing Boats.
1079 **318** 1 k. 65 blue 50 20
1080 – 1 k. 65 blue 50 20
1081 – 1 k. 65 blue 50 20
1082 – 1 k. 65 blue 50 20
1083 – 1 k. 65 blue 50 20
1084 – 1 k. 65 blue 50 20
DESIGNS: No. 1080, Boat from Blekinge; No. 1081, Boat from Norrbotten; No. 1082, Boat from Halsingland; No. 1083, Boat from Gotland; No. 1084, Boat from West Skane.

319 "Night and Day" **320** Par Lagerkvist riding Railway Trolley with Father (illustration from "Guest of Reality")

1981.
1085 **319** 1 k. 65 violet 30 10

1981.
1086 **320** 1 k. 50 green 30 10

321 Electric Locomotive

1981. "Sweden in the World".
1087 **321** 2 k. 40 red 65 40
1088 – 2 k. 40 red 65 40
1089 – 2 k. 40 purple 65 40
1090 – 2 k. 40 violet 65 40
1091 – 2 k. 40 blue 65 40
1092 – 2 k. 40 blue 65 40
DESIGNS—As T **321**: No. 1088, Scania trucks with rock drilling equipment; 1089, Birgit Nilsson (opera singer) and Sixten Ehrling (conductor); 1090, North Sea gas rig. 19 × 23 mm: No. 1091, Bjorn Borg (tennis player); 1092, Ingemar Stenmark (skier).

322 Baker's Sign **324** Wooden Bird

1981. Business Mail.
1093 **322** 2 k. 30 brown 55 10
1094 – 2 k. 30 brown 55 10
DESIGN: No. 1094, Pewterer's sign.

1981. Christmas.
1096 **324** 1 k. 40 red 30 10
1097 – 1 k. 40 green 30 10
DESIGN: No. 1097, Wooden bird (different).

325 Albert Einstein (physics)

1981. Nobel Prize Winners of 1921.
1098 **325** 1 k. 35 red 40 10
1099 – 1 k. 65 green 40 10
1100 – 2 k. 70 blue 60 20
DESIGNS: 1 k. 65, Anatole France (literature); 2 k. 70, Frederick Soddy (chemistry).

326 Knight on Horseback **327** Impossible Triangle

1982. Birth Centenary of John Bauer (illustrator of fairy tales).
1101 **326** 1 k. 65 blue, yellow & lilac 30 30
1102 – 1 k. 65 multicoloured . . 30 30
1103 – 1 k. 65 black & yellow . . 30 30
1104 – 1 k. 65 yellow and lilac . 30 30
DESIGNS: No. 1102, "What a wretched pale creature, said the Troll Woman"; No. 1103, "The Princess beside the Forest Lake"; No. 1104, "Now it is already twilight Night".

1982.
1105 **327** 25 ore brown 10 10
1106 – 50 ore brown 10 10
1107 – 75 ore blue 20 10
1108 – 1 k. 35 blue 30 10
1109 – 5 k. purple 85 10
DESIGNS: 50 ore, 75 ore, Impossible figures (different); 1 k. 35, Newspaper distributor; 5 k. "Graziella wonders if she could be a Model" (etching, Carl Larsson).

328 Villages before and after Land Reform

1982. Europa.
1110 **328** 1 k. 65 green and black . 1·25 10
1111 – 2 k. 40 green 75 60
DESIGN—26 × 22 mm: 2 k. 40, Anders Celsius.

1982. Rebate Stamps. Arms of Swedish Provinces (2nd series). As T **316**. Multicoloured.
1112 1 k. 40 Dalsland 45 10
1113 1 k. 40 Oland 45 10
1114 1 k. 40 Vastmanland 45 10
1115 1 k. 40 Halsingland 45 10

329 Elin Wagner **330** Burgher House

1982. Birth Centenary of Elin Wagner (novelist).
1116 **329** 1 k. 35 brown on grey . . 30 10

1982. Centenary of Museum of Cultural History, Lund.
1117 **330** 1 k. 65 brown 25 10
1118 – 2 k. 70 brown 45 20
DESIGN: 2 k. 70, Embroidered lace.

331 Lateral Mark

1982. New International Buoyage System.
1119 **331** 1 k. 65 blue and green . . 50 20
1120 – 1 k. 65 green and blue . . 50 20
1121 – 1 k. 65 deep blue and blue 50 20
1122 – 1 k. 65 blue and green . . 50 20
1123 – 1 k. 65 deep blue and blue 50 20
DESIGNS: No. 1120, Cardinal mark and Sweden–Finland ferry "Sally"; 1121, Racing yachts and special mark; 1122, Safe-water mark; 1123, Pilot boat, isolated danger mark and lighthouse.

332 Scene from "The Emigrants" (film)

1982. Living Together.
1124 **332** 1 k. 65 green 50 20
1125 – 1 k. 65 purple 50 20
1126 – 1 k. 65 blue 50 20
1127 – 1 k. 65 red 50 20
DESIGNS: No. 1125, Vietnamese boat people in factory; No. 1126, Immigrants examining local election literature; No. 1127, Three girls arm-in-arm.

334 Angel

1982. Christmas. Medieval Glass Paintings from Lye Church. Multicoloured.
1129 1 k. 40 Type **334** 30 30
1130 1 k. 40 "The Child in the Temple" 30 30
1131 1 k. 40 "Adoration of the Magi" 30 30
1132 1 k. 40 "Tidings to the Shepherds" 30 30
1133 1 k. 40 "The Birth of Christ" 30 30

335 Quantum Mechanics (Niels Bohr, 1922)

1982. Nobel Prize Winners for Physics.
1134 **335** 2 k. 40 blue 80 60
1135 – 2 k. 40 red 80 60
1136 – 2 k. 40 green 80 60
1137 – 2 k. 40 lilac 80 60
1138 – 2 k. 40 red 80 60
DESIGNS: No. 1135, Fuse distribution (Erwin Schrodinger, 1933); No. 1136, Wave pattern (Louis de Broglie, 1929); No. 1137, Electrons (Paul Dirac, 1933); No. 1138, Atomic model (Werner Heisenberg, 1932).

336 Horse Chestnut **337** Ferlin (statue by K. Bejemark)

1983. Fruits.
1139 **336** 5 ore brown 10 10
1140 – 10 ore green 10 10
1141 – 15 ore red 10 10
1142 – 20 ore blue 10 10
DESIGNS: 10 ore Norway maple; 15 ore Dog rose; 20 ore Blackthorn.

1983. 85th Birth Anniv of Nils Ferlin (poet).
1143 **337** 6 k. green 85 20

339 Lead Type

1983. Centenary of Swedish Peace Movement.
1144 **338** 1 k. 35 blue 30 25

338 Peace March **340** Family Cycling in Countryside

1983. 500th Anniv of Printing in Sweden.
1145 **339** 1 k. 65 black and brown on stone 40 20
1146 – 1 k. 65 black, green and red on stone 40 20
1147 – 1 k. 65 brown and black on stone 40 20

1148 **339** 1 k. 65 black and brown on stone 40 20
1149 – 1 k. 65 brown, green and black on stone 40 20
DESIGNS: No. 1146, Ox plough (illustration from "Dialogus creaturarum" by Johan Snell, 1483); No. 1147, Title page of Karl XII's Bible, 1703; No. 1148, 18th-century alphabet books; No. 1149, Laser photocomposition.

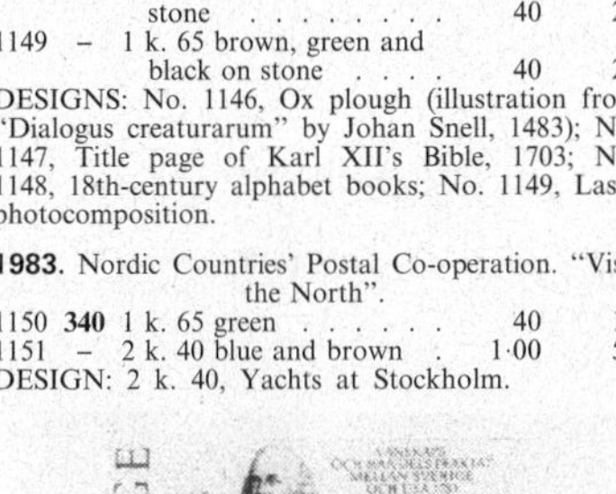

1983. Nordic Countries' Postal Co-operation. "Visit the North".
1150 **340** 1 k. 65 green 40 10
1151 – 2 k. 40 blue and brown . 1·00 55
DESIGN: 2 k. 40, Yachts at Stockholm.

341 Benjamin Franklin and Great Seal of Sweden

1983. Bicentenary of Sweden–U.S.A. Treaty of Amity and Commerce.
1152 **341** 2 k. 70 blue, brown & blk 50 30

1983. Rebate Stamps. Arms of Swedish Provinces (3rd series). As T **316**. Multicoloured.
1153 1 k. 60 Vastergotland 40 10
1154 1 k. 60 Medelpad 40 10
1155 1 k. 60 Gotland 40 10
1156 1 k. 60 Gastrikland 40 10

342 Costume Sketch by Fernand Leger for "Creation du Monde"   **343** Essay for Unissued Stamp, 1885

1983. Europa.
1157 1 k. 65 chocolate & brown . 95 10
1158 2 k. 70 blue . . . . 1·00 1·00
DESIGNS: 1 k. 65, Type **342** (Swedish Ballet); 2 k. 70, J. P. Johansson's adjustable spanner.

1983. "Stockholmia 86" International Exhibition (1st issue). Oscar II stamp designs by Max Mirowsky.
1159 **343** 1 k. blue 50 50
1160 – 2 k. red 45 45
1161 – 3 k. blue 55 55
1162 – 4 k. green 75 75
DESIGNS: 2 k. Issued stamp of 1885; 3 k. Essay for unissued stamp, 1891; 4 k. Issued stamp of 1891.
See also Nos. 1199/1202, 1252/5, 1285/8 and 1310/13.

344 Greater Karlso   **345** Freshwater Snail

1983.
1163 **344** 1 k. 60 blue 30 10
1164 **345** 1 k. 80 green 35 10
1165 – 2 k. 10 green 40 10
DESIGN—22 × 27 mm: 2 k. 10, Arctic fox.

346 Bergman   **347** Helgeandsholmen, 1580 (after Franz Hogenberg) and Riksdag

1983. Birth Centenary of Hjalmar Bergman (novelist and dramatist).
1166 **346** 1 k. 80 blue 35 10
1167 – 1 k. 80 multicoloured . . 35 10
DESIGN: No. 1167, Jac the Clown (novel character).

1983. Return of Riksdag (Parliament) to Helgeandsholmen Island, Stockholm.
1168 **347** 2 k. 70 purple & blue . . 45 35

MINIMUM PRICE

The minimum price quoted is 10p which represents a handling charge rather than a basis for valuing common stamps. For further notes about prices, see introductory pages.

348 Red Cross   **350** Dancing round the Christmas Tree

1983. Swedish Red Cross.
1169 **348** 1 k. 50 red 30 10

1983. Christmas. Early Christmas Cards. Multicoloured.
1171 1 k. 60 Type **350** 40 10
1172 1 k. 60 Straw goats 40 10
1173 1 k. 60 The Christmas table 40 10
1174 1 k. 60 Carrying Christmas presents on pole 40 10

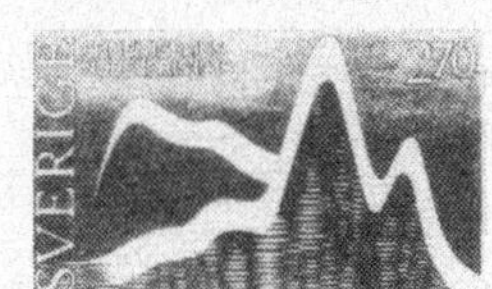

351 Electrophoresis (Arne Tiselius, 1948)

1983. Nobel Prize Winners for Chemistry.
1175 **351** 2 k. 70 black 60 50
1176 – 2 k. 70 violet 60 50
1177 – 2 k. 70 mauve 60 50
1178 – 2 k. 70 violet 60 50
1179 – 2 k. 70 black 60 50
DESIGNS: No. 1176, Radioactive isotopes (George de Hevesy, 1943); 1177, Electrolytic dissociation (Svante Arrhenius, 1903); 1178, Colloids (Theodor Svedberg, 1926); 1179, Fermentation of sugar (Hans von Euler-Chelpin, 1929).

352 Three Crowns (detail from Postal Savings Receipt)

1984. Centenary of Postal Savings.
1180 **352** 100 ore orange 20 15
1181 – 1 k. 60 violet 30 15
1182 – 1 k. 80 mauve 40 10
DESIGNS: 1 k. 60, 1 k. 80, Postal Savings badge.

353 Bridge

1984. Europa. 25th Anniv of European Post and Telecommunications Conference.
1183 **353** 1 k. 80 red 50 10
1184 2 k. 70 blue . . . . . . 1·50 1·00

354 Norway Lemming   **355** Paraffin Stove (F. W. Lindqvist)

1984. Swedish Mountain World.
1185 **354** 1 k. 90 brown 40 10
1186 – 1 k. 90 blue 40 10
1187 – 2 k. green 45 10
1188 – 2 k. 25 black 55 25
DESIGNS: No. 1186, Musk ox; 1187, Garden angelica; 1188, Tolpagorni mountain.

1984. Rebate Stamps. Arms of Swedish Provinces (4th series). As T **316**. Multicoloured.
1189 1 k. 60 Sodermanland . . . 40 10
1190 1 k. 60 Blekinge 40 10
1191 1 k. 60 Vasterbotten . . . 40 10
1192 1 k. 60 Skane 40 10

1984. "Made in Sweden". Centenary of Patent Office. Patented Swedish Inventions.
1193 **355** 2 k. 70 red 60 50
1194 – 2 k. 70 lilac 60 50
1195 – 2 k. 70 green 60 50
1196 – 2 k. 70 green 60 50
1197 – 2 k. 70 lilac 60 50
1198 – 2 k. 70 blue 60 50
DESIGNS: No. 1194, "ASEA IRB 6" industrial robot for arc welding; 1195, Vacuum cleaner (Axel Wennergren); 1196, "AQ 200" inboard/outboard engine; 1197, Integrated circuit; 1198, Tetrahedron container.

356 King Erik XIV (after S. van der Meulen) and Letter to Queen Elizabeth I of England   **358** Genetic Symbols forming "100"

357 Jonkoping

1984. "Stockholmia 86" International Stamp Exhibition (2nd issue).
1199 **356** 1 k. brown, blue and ultramarine 50 50
1200 – 2 k. multicoloured . . . 45 45
1201 – 3 k. multicoloured . . . 55 55
1202 – 4 k. multicoloured . . . 75 75
DESIGNS: 2 k. Erik Dahlbergh (architect) (after J. H. Stromer) and letter to Sten Bielke (Paymaster General), 1674; 3 k. Feather letter, 1843; 4 k. Harriet Bosse and letter from her husband, August Strindberg, 1905.

1984. Old Towns. 17th-century views by M. Karl (1207) or Erik Dahlberg (others).
1203 **357** 1 k. 90 blue 40 30
1204 – 1 k. 90 brown 40 30
1205 – 1 k. 90 blue 50 30
1206 – 1 k. 90 brown 40 30
1207 – 1 k. 90 blue 40 30
1208 – 1 k. 90 brown 40 30
DESIGNS: No. 1204, Karlstad; 1205, Gavle; 1206, Sigtuna; 1207, Norrkoping; 1208. Vadstena.

1984. Centenary of Fredrika Bremer Association (for promotion of male/female equal rights).
1209 **358** 1 k. 50 purple 30 10
1210 6 k. 50 red . . . . 1·10 25

359 "Viking" in Orbit   **361** Hawfinch

1984. Launch of Swedish "Viking" Satellite.
1211 **359** 1 k. 90 ultramarine, blue and deep blue 40 10
1212 – 3 k. 20 green, yellow and black 85 50
DESIGN: 3 k. 20, Dish aerial and rocket pad at Esrange space station.

1984. Christmas. Birds. Multicoloured.
1214 1 k. 60 Type **361** 70 40
1215 1 k. 60 Bohemian waxwing . 70 40
1216 1 k. 60 Great-spotted woodpecker 70 40
1217 1 k. 60 European nuthatch . . 70 40

362 Inner Ear (Georg von Bekesy, 1961)

1984. Nobel Prize Winners for Medicine.
1218 **362** 2 k. 70 blue, black and red 80 70
1219 – 2 k. 70 blue and black . . 80 70
1220 – 2 k. 70 red, black and blue 80 70
1221 – 2 k. 70 blue and black . . 80 70
1222 – 2 k. 70 red, black and blue 80 70
DESIGNS: No. 1219, Nerve cell activation (John Eccles, Alan Hodgkin and Andrew Huxley, 1963); 1220, Nerve cell signals (Bernard Katz, Ulf von Euler and Julius Axelrod, 1970); 1221, Functions of the brain (Roger Sperry, 1981); 1222, Eye (David Hubel and Torsten Wiesel, 1981).

363 Post Office Emblem   **364** King Carl XVI Gustav

1985.
1223 **363** 1 k. 60 blue 30 10
1224 1 k. 70 violet 40 10
1326 1 k. 80 purple 35 10
1225 2 k. 50 yellow 45 10
1226 2 k. 80 green 60 10
1327 3 k. 20 brown 50 10
1227 4 k. red 70 10
1328 6 k. turquoise . . . . . 1·10 10

1985.
1228 **364** 2 k. black 35 10
1229 2 k. 10 blue 50 10
1230 2 k. 20 blue 35 10
1230a 2 k. 30 green 45 10
1230b 2 k. 50 purple 45 10
1231 2 k. 70 brown 45 10
1232 2 k. 90 green 55 10
1233 3 k. 10 brown 55 10
1234 – 3 k. 20 blue 85 85
1235 **364** 3 k. 30 purple 60 25
1236 – 3 k. 40 red 70 10
1237 – 3 k. 60 green 60 10
1238 – 3 k. 90 blue 70 35
1239 – 4 k. 60 orange 85 45
DESIGNS: 3 k. 20 and 3 k. 40 to 4 k. 60, Queen Silvia.

365 Hazel Dormouse   **366** Jan-Ove Waldner

1985. Nature.
1240 **365** 2 k. brown and black . . 45 15
1241 – 2 k. orange and black . 45 15
1242 – 2 k. 20 red 60 20
1243 – 3 k. 50 red and green . . 80 20
DESIGNS: No. 1241, Char; 1242, Black vanilla orchid; 1243, White water-lily.

1985. World Table Tennis Championships, Gothenburg.
1244 **366** 2 k. 70 blue 70 30
1245 – 3 k. 20 mauve 80 45
DESIGN: 3 k. 20, Cai Zhenhua (Chinese player).

1985. Rebate Stamps. Arms of Swedish Provinces (5th series). As T **316**. Multicoloured.
1246 1 k. 80 Narke 40 10
1247 1 k. 80 Angermanland . . . 40 10
1248 1 k. 80 Varmland 40 10
1249 1 k. 80 Smaland 40 10

367 Clavichord

1985. Europa. Music Year.
1250 **367** 2 k. purple on buff . . . 1·50 10
1251 – 2 k. 70 brown on buff . . 90 55
DESIGN—28 × 24 mm: 2 k. 70, Keyed fiddle.

368 "View of Slussen" (Sigrid Hjerten)   **369** Syl Hostel, 1920

1985. "Stockholmia 86" International Stamp Exhibition (3rd issue). Multicoloured.
1252 2 k. Type **368** 40 40
1253 2 k. "Skeppsholmen, Winter" (Gosta Adrian-Nilsson) . . 40 40
1254 3 k. "A Summer's Night by Riddarholmen Canal" (Hilding Linnqvist) 55 55
1255 4 k. "Klara Church Tower" (Otte Skold) 70 70

1985. Centenary of Swedish Touring Club.
1256 **369** 2 k. blue and black . . . 50 15
1257 – 2 k. black and blue . . . 60 15
DESIGN—58 × 24 mm: No. 1257, "Af Chapman" (youth hostel in Stockholm).

370 Canute and Helsingborg   **371** Nilsson's Music Shop Sign

1985. 900th Anniv of Saint Canute's Deed of Gift to Lund.

1258 – 2 k. blue and black . . . 40 10
1259 **370** 2 k. red and black . . . 40 10

DESIGN: No. 1258, Canute and Lund Cathedral.

1985. Trade Signs.

1260 **371** 10 ore blue 10 10
1261 – 20 ore brown 10 10
1262 – 20 ore brown 10 10
1263 – 50 ore blue 15 10
1264 – 2 k. green 50 10

DESIGNS: No. 1261, Erik Johansson's furrier's sign; 1262, O. L. Sjowals's coppersmith's sign; 1263, Bodecker's hatter's sign; 1264, Berggren's shoemaker's sign.

372 "Otryades" (Johan Tobias Sergel)

1985. 250th Anniv of Royal Academy of Fine Arts.

1265 **372** 2 k. blue 35 10
1266 – 7 k. brown . . . . 1·25 30

DESIGN—20 × 28 mm: 7 k. "Baron Carl Fredrik Adelcrantz" (former Academy president) (Alexander Roslin).

373 Fox and Geese **374** Birger Sjoberg (writer)

1985. Board Games.

1267 **373** 50 ore blue 10 10
1268 – 60 ore green 15 10
1269 – 70 ore yellow 15 10
1270 – 80 ore red 25 10
1271 – 90 ore mauve 25 10
1272 – 3 k. purple . . . . 1·10 20

DESIGNS—As T **373**: 60 ore Dominoes; 70 ore Ludo; 80 ore Chinese checkers; 90 ore Backgammon. 23 × 28 mm: 3 k. Chess.

1985. Birth Centenaries.

1273 – 1 k. 60 red and black . . 40 10
1274 **374** 4 k. green 85 25

DESIGN—40 × 24 mm: 1 k. 60, Per Albin Hansson (politician).

376 "Annunciation" **377** American Deep South Scene (William Faulkner, 1949)

1985. Christmas. Medieval Church Frescoes by Albertus Pictor.

1276 **376** 1 k. 80 blue, brown and red 35 20
1277 – 1 k. 80 brown, blue and red 35 20
1278 – 1 k. 80 brown, blue and red 35 20
1279 – 1 k. 80 blue, brown and red 35 20

DESIGNS: No. 1277, "Birth of Christ"; 1278, "Adoration of the Magi"; 1279, "Mary as the Apocalyptic Virgin".

1985. Nobel Prize Winners for Literature.

1280 **377** 2 k. 70 green 70 60
1281 – 2 k. 70 brown, blue and green 70 60
1282 – 2 k. 70 green and brown 70 60
1283 – 2 k. 70 green and blue 1·50 60
1284 – 2 k. 70 brown and blue . 70 60

DESIGNS: No. 1281, Icelandic scene (Halldor Kiljan Laxness, 1955); 1282, Guatemalan scene (Miguel Angel Asturias, 1967); 1283, Japanese scene (Yasunari Kawabata, 1968); 1284, Australian scene (Patrick White, 1973).

378 1879 "20 TRETIO" Error **379** Eiders

1986. "Stockholmia 86" International Stamp Exhibition (4th issue).

1285 **378** 2 k. orange, pur & grn . 70 60
1286 – 2 k. multicoloured . . . 70 60
1287 – 3 k. purple, blue and green 80 70
1288 – 4 k. multicoloured . . . 80 80

DESIGNS: No. 1286, Sven Ewert (engraver); 1287, Magnifying glass and United States 1938 Scandinavian Settlement 3 c. stamp; 1288, Boy soaking stamps.

1986. Water Birds.

1289 **379** 2 k. 10 blue and brown . 1·25 45
1290 – 2 k. 10 brown . . . . . 1·25 45
1291 – 2 k. 30 blue . . . . . . 1·25 55

DESIGNS: No. 1290, Whimbrel; 1291, Black-throated diver.

380 Swedish Academy Emblem **381** Jubilee Emblem

1986. Bicentenaries of Swedish Academy and Royal Swedish Academy of Letters, History and Antiquities.

1292 **380** 1 k. 70 green and red on grey 50 30
1293 – 1 k. 70 blue and purple on grey 50 30

DESIGN: No. 1293, Royal Swedish Academy Emblem.

1986. 350th Anniv of Post Office.

1294 **381** 2 k. 10 blue and yellow . 45 10

382 Palme **383** Carl Gustav Birdwatching

1986. Olof Palme (Prime Minister) Commemoration.

1295 **382** 2 k. 10 purple 50 40
1296 2 k. 90 black 75 70

1986. 40th Birthday of King Carl XVI Gustav.

1297 **383** 2 k. 10 black and green . 45 15
1298 – 2 k. 10 gold, mauve and blue 45 15
1299 – 2 k. 10 dp blue & blue . 45 15
1300 – 2 k. 10 gold, blue and deep blue 45 15
1301 – 2 k. 10 black & mauve . 45 15

DESIGNS: Nos. 1298, 1300, Crowned cypher; 1299, King presenting Nobel Prize for Literature to Czeslaw Milosz; 1301, King and family during summer holiday at Solliden Palace.

1986. Rebate Stamps. Arms of Swedish Provinces (6th series). As T **316**. Multicoloured.

1302 1 k. 90 Harjedalen 55 10
1303 1 k. 90 Uppland 55 10
1304 1 k. 90 Halland 55 10
1305 1 k. 90 Lappland 55 10

384 Uppsala **385** Forest and Car Fumes

1986. Nordic Countries' Postal Co-operation. Twinned Towns.

1306 **384** 2 k. 10 green, chestnut and brown 65 10
1307 – 2 k. 90 green, red & brn 85 40

DESIGN: 2 k. 90, Eskilstuna.

1986. Europa. Each black, green and red.

1308 2 k. 10 Type **385** . . . . . 1·25 10
1309 2 k. 90 Forest and industrial pollution 75 60

386 Tomteboda Sorting Office (20th-century) **388** Olive branch sweeping away Weapons

1986. "Stockholmia 86" International Stamp Exhibition (5th issue). Multicoloured.

1310 2 k. 10 19th-century mail carriage . . . . 3·00 3·00
1311 2 k. 10 Type **386** . . . . . 3·00 3·00
1312 2 k. 90 17th-century farmhand postal messenger . . . . . 3·00 3·00
1313 2 k. 90 18th-century post office 3·00 3·00

1986. International Peace Year (1315) and 25th Anniv of Amnesty International (1316).

1315 **388** 3 k. 40 green and black . . 80 80
1316 – 3 k. 40 red and black . . 80 80

DESIGN: No. 1316, Emblem above broken manacles.

389 Bertha von Suttner (founder of Austrian Society of Peace Lovers, 1905)

1986. Nobel Prize Winners for Peace.

1317 **389** 2 k. 90 black, red & blue 75 60
1318 – 2 k. 90 black and red . . 75 60
1319 – 2 k. 90 black, brown and blue 75 60
1320 – 2 k. 90 brown and black . 75 60
1321 – 2 k. 90 red, black & blue 75 60

DESIGNS: No. 1318, Carl von Ossietzky (anti-Nazi fighter and concentration camp victim, 1935); 1319, Albert Luthuli (South African anti-apartheid leader, 1960); 1320, Martin Luther King (American civil rights leader, 1964); 1321, Mother Teresa (worker amongst poor of Calcutta, 1979).

390 Mail Van **391** Clouded Apollo

1986. Christmas. Designs showing a village at Christmas. Multicoloured.

1322 1 k. 90 Type **390** 45 15
1323 1 k. 90 Postman on cycle delivering mail 45 15
1324 1 k. 90 Children and sledge loaded with parcels 45 15
1325 1 k. 90 Christmas tree, man carrying parcel and child posting letter 45 15

Nos. 1322/5 were printed together, se-tenant, forming a composite design.

1987. Threatened Species of Meadows and Pastures.

1331 **391** 2 k. 10 black, green and purple 50 10
1332 – 2 k. 10 black, green and purple 50 10
1333 – 2 k. 50 brown 60 20
1334 – 4 k. 20 green and yellow . 1·00 20

DESIGNS: 2 k. 10 (1332), Field gentian; 2 k. 50, Leather beetle; 4 k. 20, Arnica.

392 SAAB-Fairchild SF-340 **393** Boys flying over Rooftops ("Karlsson")

1987. Swedish Aircraft.

1335 **392** 25 k. purple . . . . 4·75 25

1987. Rebate Stamps. Characters from Children's Books by Astrid Lindgren. Multicoloured.

1336 1 k. 90 Type **393** 45 15
1337 1 k. 90 Girl holding doll ("Bullerby Children") . . . 45 15
1338 1 k. 90 Girls dancing ("Madicken") 45 15
1339 1 k. 90 Boys on horse ("Mio, Min Mio") 45 15
1340 1 k. Boy doing handstand ("Nils Karlsson-Pyssling") 45 15
1341 1 k. 90 Emil picking cherries ("Emil") 45 15
1342 1 k. 90 "Ronja the Robber's Daughter" 45 15
1343 1 k. 90 "Pippi Longstocking" 45 15
1344 1 k. 90 Dragon ("Brothers Lionheart") 45 15
1345 1 k. 90 "Lotta" 45 15

394 Hans Brask, Bishop of Linkoping (sculpture, Karl-Olav Bjork) **395** Stockholm City Library (Gunnar Asplund)

1987. Town Anniversaries. Each brown, blue and black.

1346 2 k. 10 Type **394** (700th anniv) 55 20
1347 2 k. 10 Nykoping Castle (800th anniv) 55 20

1987. Europa. Architecture.

1348 **395** 2 k. 10 brown & blue . . 1·00 10
1349 3 k. 10 brown & green . 70 70
1350 – 3 k. 10 purple & green . 70 70

DESIGN: No. 1350, Marcus Church (Sigurd Lewerentz).

396 "King Gustavus Vasa" (anon) **398** Clowns

397 Raoul Wallenberg (rescuer of Hungarian Jews) and Prisoners

1987. 450th Anniv of Gripsholm Castle.

1351 **396** 2 k. 10 multicoloured . . 45 15
1352 – 2 k. 10 multicoloured . . 45 15
1353 – 2 k. 10 multicoloured . . 45 15
1354 – 2 k. 10 brown, black and blue 45 15

DESIGNS: No. 1352, "Blue Tiger" (David Klocker Ehrenstrahl); 1353, "Hedvig Charlotta Nordenflycht" (after Johan Henrik Scheffel); 1354, "Gripsholm Castle" (lithograph, Carl Johan Billmark).

1987. "In the Service of Humanity".

1355 **397** 3 k. 10 blue 70 60
1356 – 3 k. 10 green 70 60
1357 – 3 k. 10 brown 70 60

DESIGNS: No. 1356, Dag Hammarskjold (U.N. Secretary-General, 1953–1961); 1357, Folke Bernadotte (leader of "white bus" relief action to rescue prisoners, 1945).

1987. Stamp Day. Bicentenary of Circus in Sweden. Multicoloured.

1358 2 k. 10 Type **398** 80 60
1359 2 k. 10 Reino riding one-wheel cycle on wire 80 60
1360 2 k. 10 Acrobat on horseback 80 60

399 "Victoria cruziana" at Bergian Garden, Stockholm University **400** Porridge left for the Grey Christmas Elf

1987. Bicentenary of Swedish Botanical Gardens.

1361 **399** 2 k. 10 green, deep green and blue 50 25
1362 – 2 k. 10 green & brown . 50 25
1363 – 2 k. 10 deep green, green and blue 50 25
1364 – 2 k. 10 yellow, brown and green 50 25

DESIGNS: No. 1362, Uppsala University Baroque Garden plan and Carl Harleman (architect); 1363, Rock garden, Gothenburg Botanical Garden; 1364, "Liriodendron tulipifera", Lund Botanical Garden.

1987. Christmas. Folk Customs. Multicoloured.

1365 2 k. Type **400** 35 15
1366 2 k. Staffan ride (watering horses in North-running spring on Boxing Day) . . 35 15
1367 2 k. Christmas Day sledge race home from church 35 15
1368 2 k. Bullfinches on corn sheaf 35 15

401 Pulsars (Antony Hewish, 1974)

1987. Nobel Prize Winners for Physics.
1369 **401** 2 k. 90 blue 70 60
1370 – 2 k. 90 black 70 60
1371 – 2 k. 90 blue 70 60
1372 – 2 k. 90 blue 70 60
1373 – 2 k. 90 black 70 60
DESIGNS: No. 1370, Formula of maximum white dwarf star mass (S. Chandrasekhar, 1983); 1371, Heavy atom nuclei construction (William Fowler, 1983); 1372, Temperature of cosmic background radiation (A. Penzias and R. Wilson, 1978); 1373, Radio telescopes receiving radio waves from galaxy (Martin Ryle, 1974).

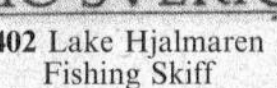

402 Lake Hjalmaren Fishing Skiff
404 White-tailed Sea Eagle

403 Bishop Hill and Erik Jansson (founder)

1988. Inland Boats. Each purple on buff.
1374 3 k. 10 Type **402** 60 30
1375 3 k. 10 Lake Vattern market boat 60 30
1376 3 k. 10 River Byske logging boat 60 30
1377 3 k. 10 Lake Asnen rowing boat 60 30
1378 3 k. 10 Lake Vanern ice boat 60 30
1379 3 k. 10 Lake Lockne church longboat 60 30

1988. 350th Anniv of New Sweden (settlement in America).
1380 – 3 k. 60 multicoloured . . 85 70
1381 **403** 3 k. 60 multicoloured . . 85 70
1382 – 3 k. 60 brown 85 70
1383 – 3 k. 60 blue and brown . . 85 70
1384 – 3 k. 60 blue, yellow and red 85 70
1385 – 3 k. 60 black, blue and red 85 70
DESIGNS—As T **403**: No. 1380, Map, settlers, Indians, "Calmare Nyckel" and "Fagel Grip". 27×23 mm: No. 1382, Carl Sandburg (American poet) and Jenny Lind (Swedish soprano); 1383, Charles Lindbergh (aviator) and Ryan NYP Special "Spirit of St. Louis". 27×37 mm: No. 1384, Alan Bean (astronaut) on Moon with Hasselblad camera; 1385, Ice hockey.

1988. Coastal Wildlife.
1386 **404** 2 k. 20 brown and red . 65 15
1387 – 2 k. 20 brown and blue . 40 15
1388 – 4 k. black, brown and green 80 40
DESIGNS: No. 1387, Grey seal; 1388, Eel.

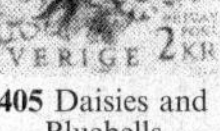

405 Daisies and Bluebells
406 Detail of "Creation" Stained Glass Window (Bo Beskow), Skara Cathedral

1988. Rebate stamps. Midsummer Festival. Multicoloured.
1389 2 k. Type **405** 40 15
1390 2 k. Garlanded longboat . . 40 15
1391 2 k. Children making garlands 40 15
1392 2 k. Raising the maypole . . 40 15
1393 2 k. Fiddlers 40 15
1394 2 k. "Norrskar" (tourist launch) 40 15
1395 2 k. Couples dancing 40 15
1396 2 k. Accordianist 40 15
1397 2 k. Archipelago with decorated landing stage 40 15
1398 2 k. Bouquet of seven wild flowers 40 15

1988. Anniversaries.
1399 **406** 2 k. 20 multicoloured . . 50 15
1400 – 4 k. 40 red on brown . . 90 40
1401 – 8 k. red, green & black . 1·50 40
DESIGNS: 2 k. 20, Type **406** (millenary of Skara). 23×41 mm: 4 k. 40, "Falun Copper Mine" (Pehr Hillestrom) (700th anniv of Stora Kopparberg (mining company)); 8 k. Scene from play "The Queen's Diamond Ornament" (bicentenary of Royal Dramatic Theatre, Stockholm).

407 "Self-portrait" (Nils Dardel)
408 "X2" High-speed Train

1968. Swedish Artists in Paris. Multicoloured.
1402 2 k. 20 Type **407** 40 40
1403 2 k. 20 "Autumn, Gubbhuset" (Vera Nilsson) (40×43 mm) 40 40
1404 2 k. 20 "Self-Portrait" (Isaac Grunewald) 40 40
1405 2 k. 20 "Visit to an Eccentric Lady" (Nils Dardel) . . . 40 40
1406 2 k. 20 "Soap Bubbles" (Vera Nilsson) (40×43 mm) . . 40 40
1407 2 k. 20 "The Singing Tree" (Isaac Grunewald) 40 40

1988. Europa. Transport and Communications.
1408 **408** 2 k. 20 blue, orange and brown . . . . 1·10 10
1409 3 k. 10 blue, black and purple 60 60
1410 – 3 k. 10 black and purple 60 60
DESIGN: No. 1410, Narrow-gauge steam locomotive.

409 Common Swift
410 Andersson

1988.
1411 **409** 20 k. purple and mauve 3·75 80

1988. Birth Centenary of Dan Andersson (poet). Each violet, green and blue.
1412 2 k. 20 Type **410** 40 10
1413 2 k. 20 Lake, Finnmarken (58×24 mm) 40 10

411 Players
412 Angel and Shepherds

1988. Swedish Football. Multicoloured.
1414 2 k. 20 Type **411** 50 50
1415 2 k. 20 Three players . . . 50 50
1416 2 k. 20 Women players . . . 50 50

1988. Christmas. Multicoloured.
1417 2 k. Type **412** 35 15
1418 2 k. Horse and angel 35 15
1419 2 k. Birds singing in trees . . 35 15
1420 2 k. Three wise men 35 15
1421 2 k. Holy Family 35 15
1422 2 k. Shepherds and sheep . . 35 15
Nos. 1417/22 were printed together, se-tenant, forming a composite design.

413 Archaeologist, Carbon 14 Dating Graph and Tutankhamun
414 Nidingen 1946 Concrete and 1832 Twin Lighthouses

1988. Nobel Prize Winners for Chemistry. Mult.
1423 3 k. 10 Type **413** (Willard Frank Libby, 1960) 55 55
1424 3 k. 10 Plastics molecules (Karl Ziegler and Giulio Natta, 1963) 55 55
1425 3 k. 10 Electron microscope (Aaron Klug, 1982) . . . 55 55
1426 3 k. 10 Landscape and symbols (Ilya Prigogine, 1977) . . 55 55

1989. Lighthouses.
1427 **414** 1 k. 90 green, brown and black 35 10
1428 – 2 k. 70 blue, red and deep blue 50 25
1429 – 3 k. 80 brown, deep blue and blue 70 35
1430 – 3 k. 90 black, red & brn . 70 45
DESIGNS: 2 k. 70, Soderarm stone lighthouse; 3 k. 80, Sydostbrotten caisson lighthouse; 3 k. 90, Sandhammaren iron lighthouse.

415 Wolverine

1989. Animals in Threatened Habitats.
1431 **415** 2 k. 30 brown, orange and green 45 20
1432 – 2 k. 30 brown, green and orange 60 20
1433 – 2 k. 40 brown, chocolate and red 60 20
1434 – 2 k. 60 agate, brown and orange 70 25
1435 – 3 k. 30 deep green, green and brown 60 35
1436 – 4 k. 60 black, green and orange . . . . 1·00 50
DESIGNS: 2 k. 30 (1432), Ural owl: 2 k. 40, Lesser spotted woodpecker; 2 k. 60, Dunlin; 3 k. 30, Common tree frog; 4 k. 60, Red-breasted flycatcher.

416 Globe Arena

1989. Opening of Globe Arena, Stockholm. Mult.
1437 2 k. 30 Type **416** 45 15
1438 2 k. 30 Ice hockey 45 15
1439 2 k. 30 Gymnastics 45 15
1440 2 k. 30 Pop concert 45 15

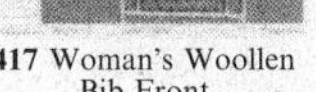

417 Woman's Woollen Bib Front
418 Sailing

1989. Nordic Countries' Postal Co-operation. Traditional Lapp Costumes.
1441 2 k. 30 Type **417** 45 15
1442 3 k. 30 Man's belt pouch . . 60 50

1989. Rebate stamps. Summer Activities. Mult.
1443 2 k. 10 Type **418** 50 15
1444 2 k. 10 Beach ball 50 15
1445 2 k. 10 Cycling 50 15
1446 2 k. 10 Canoeing 50 15
1447 2 k. 10 Fishing 50 15
1448 2 k. 10 Camping 50 15
1449 2 k. 10 Croquet 50 15
1450 2 k. 10 Badminton 50 15
1451 2 k. 10 Gardening 50 15
1452 2 k. 10 Sand castle, bucket and spade 50 15

419 "Protest March" (Nils Kreuger)
420 Playing with Boats

1989. Centenary of Swedish Labour Movement.
1453 **419** 2 k. 30 black and red . . 45 15

1989. Europa. Children's Games and Toys.
1454 **420** 2 k. 30 brown 70 15
1455 3 k. 30 mauve 60 60
1456 – 3 k. 30 green 60 60
DESIGN: No. 1456, Girl riding kick-sled.

421 Lounger (Varnamo)
422 Researcher in Greenland and Temperature Curve

1989. Industries of Smaland Towns. Each mauve, orange and red.
1457 2 k. 30 Type **421** 45 45
1458 2 k. 30 Tools for self-assembly furniture (Almhult) 45 45
1459 2 k. 30 Sewing machine and embroidery (Huskvarna) 45 45
1460 2 k. 30 Blowing glass (Afors) 45 45
1461 2 k. 30 Coathanger hook and clothes-peg spring (Gnosjo) 45 45
1462 2 k. 30 Match (Jonkoping) . 45 45

1989. 250th Anniv of Swedish Academy of Sciences. Polar Research. Multicoloured.
1463 3 k. 30 Type **422** 75 75
1464 3 k. 30 Abisko Natural Science Station, Lapland (40×43 mm) 75 75
1465 3 k. 30 "Oden" (ice research ship) and researchers . . . 75 75
1466 3 k. 30 Otto Nordenskiold 1901–03 expedition's "Antarctic" and Emperor penguin with chick . . . . 1·00 75
1467 3 k. 30 1988 Antarctic expedition's vehicles and Hughes Model 500 helicopter (40×43 mm) 75 75
1468 3 k. 30 Geodimeter and McCormick's skua . . . . 1·00 75

423 Eagle Owl

1989.
1469 **423** 30 k. brown, blk & mve . 6·50 2·25

424 Arctic Rhododendron
425 Jamthund

1989. National Parks (1st series).
1470 **424** 2 k. 40 mauve, grn & bl . 45 10
1471 – 2 k. 40 mauve & green . 45 10
1472 – 4 k. 30 red, black & blue 1·10 40
DESIGNS: No. 1471, Calypso ("Calypso bulbosa"); 1472, Black guillemots at Bla Jungfrun.
See also Nos. 1486/90.

1989. Centenary of Swedish Kennel Club. Mult.
1473 2 k. 40 Type **425** 60 60
1474 2 k. 40 Hamilton foxhound . 60 60
1475 2 k. 40 Vastgota sheep dog . 60 60

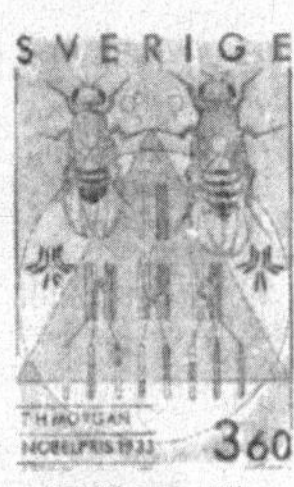

426 Decorated Tree
427 Vinegar Flies (T. H. Morgan, 1933)

1989. Christmas. Multicoloured.
1476 2 k. 10 Type **426** 35 15
1477 2 k. 10 Candelabra and food 35 15
1478 2 k. 10 Star, poinsettia and tureen 35 15
1479 2 k. 10 Decorated tree and straw goat 35 15
1480 2 k. 10 Girl watching television 35 15
1481 2 k. 10 Family with present . 35 15
Nos. 1476/81 were issued together, se-tenant, forming a composite design.

1989. Nobel Prize Winners for Medicine.

1482 **427** 3 k. 60 brown, yell & bl . 75 45
1483 – 3 k. 60 yellow, bl & red . 60 45
1484 – 3 k. 60 multicoloured . . 60 45
1485 – 3 k. 60 multicoloured . . 60 45

DESIGNS: No. 1483 X-ray diffractogram and D.N.A. molecule (Francis Crick, James Watson and Maurice Wilkins, 1962); 1484, D.N.A. molecule cut by restriction enzyme (W. Arber, D. Nathans and H. O. Smith, 1978); 1485, Maize kernels (Barbara McClintock, 1983).

428 Angso

429 Lumberjack

1990. National Parks (2nd series).

1486 **428** 2 k. 50 blue, green & red 60 20
1487 – 2 k. 50 red, green & blue 45 15
1488 – 3 k. 70 blue, brown & grn 1·00 35
1489 – 4 k. 10 blue, green & brn 70 45
1490 – 4 k. 80 green, brown & bl 85 50

DESIGNS: No. 1487, Pieljekaise; 1488, Muddus; 1489, Padjelanta; 1490, Sanfjallet.

1990. Centenary of Industrial Safety Inspectorate.

1491 **429** 2 k. 50 blue and brown . 45 15

430 Postal Museum, Stockholm

431 Carved Bone Head and Cast Dragon Head

1990. Europa. Post Office Buildings.

1492 **430** 2 k. 50 brown, orge & bl 60 10
1493 – 3 k. 80 blue, yellow and brown 70 50
1494 – 3 k. 80 brown, blue and yellow 70 50

DESIGNS: No. 1493, Sollebrunn Post Office; 1494, Vasteras Post Office.

1990. Vikings. Multicoloured.

1495 2 k. 50 Type **431** 45 25
1496 2 k. 50 Returning Viking longships (34 × 29 mm) . . 60 25
1497 2 k. 50 Wooden houses (34 x 29 mm) 45 25
1498 2 k. 50 Bronze figurine of God of Fertility and silver cross 45 25
1499 2 k. 50 Crosier and gold embroidered deer 45 25
1500 2 k. 50 Vikings in roundship (34 × 29 mm) 60 25
1501 2 k. 50 Viking disembarking (34 × 29 mm) 60 25
1502 2 k. 50 Viking swords 45 25

Nos. 1496/7 and 1500/1 form a composite design.

432 Worker collecting Pollen

433 Prow of "Wasa" and Museum

1990. Rebate stamps. Honey Bees. Multicoloured.

1503 2 k. 30 Type **432** 45 25
1504 2 k. 30 Worker on bilberry . 45 25
1505 2 k. 30 Worker flying back to hive 45 25
1506 2 k. 30 Beehive 45 25
1507 2 k. 30 Bees building honeycombs 45 25
1508 2 k. 30 Drone 45 25
1509 2 k. 30 Queen 45 25
1510 2 k. 30 Swarm on branch . . 45 25
1511 2 k. 30 Beekeeper collecting frame 45 25
1512 2 k. 30 Pot of honey 45 25

1990. Opening of New "Wasa" (17th-century ship of the line) Museum.

1513 **433** 2 k. 50 black and red . . 55 10
1514 – 4 k. 60 blue and red . . 95 50

DESIGNS: 4 k. 60, Stern of "Wasa" and museum.

434 Endurance Event

1990. World Equestrian Games, Stockholm. Mult.

1515 3 k. 80 Type **434** 70 50
1516 3 k. 80 Mark Todd on Carisma jumping wall (3-day event) 70 50
1517 3 k. 80 John Whitaker on Next Milton jumping fence (show jumping) 70 50
1518 3 k. 80 Louise Nathorst (dressage) 70 50
1519 3 k. 80 Team vaulting . . . 70 50
1520 3 k. 80 Pahlsson brothers driving four-in-hand . . . 70 50

435 Papermaking, 1600

436 "Dearest Brothers, Sisters and Friends"

1990. Centenary of Swedish Pulp and Paper Industry. Multicoloured.

1521 2 k. 50 Type **435** 45 15
1522 2 k. 50 Crown watermark . 45 15
1523 2 k. 50 Foreign newspapers using Swedish newsprint . 45 15
1524 2 k. 50 Rolls of paper . . . 45 15

1990. 250th Birth Anniv of Carl Michael Bellman (poet) (1525/7) and Birth Centenary of Evert Taube (poet) (1528/30). Designs showing illustrations of their poems.

1525 **436** 2 k. 50 brown and black 45 25
1526 – 2 k. 50 multicoloured . 45 25
1527 – 2 k. 50 black, bl and red 45 25
1528 – 2 k. 50 multicoloured . 45 25
1529 – 2 k. 50 multicoloured . 45 25
1530 – 2 k. 50 multicoloured . 45 25

DESIGNS—As Type **436**: No. 1527, "Fredman in the Gutter"; 1528, "Happy Baker of San Remo"; 1530, "Violava". 40 × 43 mm: 1526, "Proud City"; 1529, "At Sea".

437 Oved Castle

1990.

1531 **437** 40 k. brown, blk & red . 5·50 50

438 Moa Martinson

439 Box Camera with Bellows

1990. Birth Centenary of Moa Martinson (novelist).

1532 **438** 2 k. 50 black and red . . 45 15
1533 – 2 k. 50 black and violet 45 15

DESIGN: No. 1533, Fredrika and Sofi bathing (from "Women and Apple Trees").

1990. 150 Years of Photography. Multicoloured.

1534 2 k. 50 Type **439** 60 60
1535 2 k. 50 August Strindberg (self-photograph) 60 60
1536 2 k. 50 Modern 35 mm camera 60 60

440 Cumulus Clouds

441 Christmas Cactus

1990. Clouds.

1537 **440** 4 k. 50 multicoloured . 75 20
1538 – 4 k. 70 black and blue . 1·00 50
1539 – 4 k. 90 blue, grn & brn 85 50
1540 – 5 k. 20 blue & ultram . 90 30

DESIGNS: 4 k. 70, Cumulonimbus; 4 k. 90, Cirus uncinus; 5 k. 20, Altocumulus lenticularis.

1990. Christmas. Flowers. Multicoloured.

1541 2 k. 30 Type **441** 45 15
1542 2 k. 30 Christmas rose . . . 45 15
1543 2 k. 30 Azalea 45 15
1544 2 k. 30 Amaryllis 45 15
1545 2 k. 30 Hyacinth 45 15
1546 2 k. 30 Poinsettia 45 15

INDEX

Countries can be quickly located by referring to the index at the end of this volume.

442 Par Lagerkvist (1951)

1990. Nobel Prize Winners for Literature.

1547 **442** 3 k. 80 blue 70 70
1548 – 3 k. 80 red 70 70
1549 – 3 k. 80 green 70 70
1550 – 3 k. 80 violet 70 70

DESIGNS: No. 1548, Ernest Hemingway (1954); 1549, Albert Camus (1957); 1550, Boris Pasternak (1958).

443 European Catfish

444 "Carta Marina", 1572 (Olaus Magnus)

1991. Freshwater Fishes.

1551 **443** 2 k. 50 black, grn & brn . 45 10
1552 – 2 k. 50 black, grn & brn . 45 10
1553 – 5 k. black, blue & brown 85 10
1554 – 5 k. 40 black, vio & red . 95 50
1555 – 5 k. 50 brown and green . 95 10
1556 – 5 k. 60 black, bl & orge . 1·00 50

DESIGNS: No. 1552, European catfish (different); 1553, Siberian spiny loach; 1554, Gudgeon; 1555, Bearded stone leach; 1556, Verkhovka.

Nos. 1551/2 form a composite design of two catfish.

1991. Maps. Multicoloured.

1557 5 k. Type **444** 85 85
1558 5 k. Sweden, Denmark and Norway, 1662 (A. Bureus and J. Blaeu) (40 × 43 mm) . . 85 85
1559 5 k. Star globe, 1759 (Anders Akerman) 85 85
1560 5 k. Relief map of Areskutan, 1938 . . . . 85 85
1561 5 k. Stockholm old town, 1989 (40 × 43 mm) 85 85
1562 5 k. Bed-rock map of Areskutan, 1984 . . . . . 85 85

445 Queen Silvia

447 Seglora Church

446 Drottningholm Palace (after Erik Dahlbergh)

1991.

1564 – 2 k. 80 blue 50 10
1565 – 2 k. 90 green 50 10
1566 – 3 k. 20 violet 55 10
1568 **445** 5 k. purple 85 10
1569 6 k. red . . . . 1·00 10
1570 6 k. 50 violet . . . . . . 1·10 25

DESIGN: 2 k. 80 to 3 k. 20, King Carl XVI Gustav.

1991. 10th Anniv of Royal Residence at Drottningholm Palace.

1576 **446** 25 k. brown, black & grn 3·50 85

1991. Rebate stamps. Centenary of Skansen Park, Stockholm. Multicoloured.

1577 2 k. 40 Type **447** 55 20
1578 2 k. 40 Celebration of Swedish Flag and National Days at Skansen 50 20
1579 2 k. 40 Wedding at Skansen . 55 20
1580 2 k. 40 Animals, Skansen Zoo 55 20

448 Park Entrance

449 Polar Bears

1991. Centenary of Public Amusement Parks. Each blue. Imperf.

1581 2 k. 50 Type **448** 45 15
1582 2 k. 50 Dancers and violinist 45 15

1991. Nordic Countries' Postal Co-operation. Tourism. Animals in Kolmarden Zoo.

1583 **449** 2 k. 50 black, brn & bl . 45 15
1584 – 4 k. red and purple . . . 70 35

DESIGN: 4 k. Dolphins and trainer.

450 "Hermes" Rocket

451 Magda Julin (figure skating, Antwerp, 1920)

1991. Europa. Europe in Space. Multicoloured.

1585 4 k. Type **450** 70 70
1586 4 k. "Freja" Northern Lights research satellite 70 70
1587 4 k. "Tele-X" television satellite 70 70

1991. Olympic Games Gold Medallists (1st issue). Multicoloured.

1588 2 k. 50 Type **451** 45 25
1589 2 k. 50 Toini Gustafsson (cross-country skiing, Grenoble, 1968) 45 25
1590 2 k. 50 Agneta Andersson and Anna Olsson (canoeing, Los Angeles, 1984) 45 25
1591 2 k. 50 Ulrika Knape (high diving, Munich, 1972) . . 45 25

See also Nos. 1619/22 and 1635/8.

452 Spetal Mine, Norberg (after Carl David af Uhr)

1991. Bergslagen Iron Industry. Multicoloured.

1592 2 k. 50 Type **452** 45 25
1593 2 k. 50 Walloon smithy, Forsmark Mill (after J. Wilhem Wallender) 45 25
1594 2 k. 50 Forge (27 × 24 mm) 45 25
1595 2 k. 50 Foundry (after Johann Ahlback) (27 × 24 mm) . . 45 25
1596 2 k. 50 Dannemora Mine (after Elias Martin) (27 × 37 mm) 45 25
1597 2 k. 50 Pershyttan Mill (27 × 37 mm) 45 25

453 Stromsholm Castle

1991.

1598 **453** 10 k. green and black . . 1·75 25

454 Lena Philipsson

455 Close-up of Gustav III

1991. Rock and Pop Music. Multicoloured.

1599 2 k. 50 Type **454** 45 25
1600 2 k. 50 Roxette (duo) 45 25
1601 2 k. 50 Jerry Williams . . . 45 25

1991. 70th Birthday of Czeslaw Slania (engraver). Designs showing "Coronation of King Gustav III" by Carl Gustav Pilo.

1602 **455** 10 k. blue . . . . 2·50 2·50
1603 – 10 k. violet . . . . . . 2·50 2·50
1604 – 10 k. black . . . . . . 2·50 2·50

DESIGNS—As T **455**: No. 1603, Close-up of lowering of crown onto King's head. 76 × 44 mm: 1604, Complete picture.

456 "Mans and Mari from Spring to Winter" (Kaj Beckman)
457 Henri Dunant (founder of Red Cross), 1901

1991. Christmas. Illustrations from children's books. Multicoloured.

1605 2 k. 30 Type **456** 45 10
1606 2 k. 30 Family dancing round Christmas tree ("Peter and Lottas's Christmas", Elsa Beskow) 45 10
1607 2 k. 30 Dressed cat by Christmas tree ("Pettersson gets a Christmas Visit", Sven Nordqvist) 45 10
1608 2 k. 30 Girl by bed ("Little Anna's Christmas Present", Lasse Sandberg) 45 10

1991. Nobel Prize Winners for Peace.

1609 **457** 4 k. red 95 75
1610 – 4 k. green 95 75
1611 – 4 k. blue 95 75
1612 – 4 k. lilac 95 75

DESIGNS: No. 1610, Albert Schweitzer (medical missionary), 1953; 1611, Alva Myrdal (disarmament negotiator), 1982; 1612, Andrei Sakharov (human rights activist), 1975.

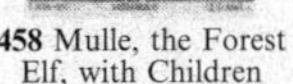

458 Mulle, the Forest Elf, with Children
459 Roe Buck

1992. Centenary of Outdoor Life Association.

1613 **458** 2 k. 30 brown, red & grn 45 10

1992. Wildlife.

1614 **459** 2 k. 80 brown, agate & grn 50 10
1615 – 2 k. 80 agate, brn & grn 50 10
1617 – 6 k. brown and agate . . 1·00 50
1618 – 7 k. brown and green . . 1·25 60

DESIGNS—As T **459**: No. 1615, Roe deer with fawn. 20 × 28 mm: No. 1617, Eurasian red squirrel; 1618, Elk.

1992. Olympic Games Gold medallists (2nd issue). As T **451**. Multicoloured.

1619 2 k. 80 Gunde Svan (cross-country skiing, Sarajevo, 1984, and Calgary, 1988) . 50 35
1620 2 k. 80 Thomas Wassberg (cross-country skiing, Lake Placid, 1980, and Sarajevo, 1984) 50 35
1621 2 k. 80 Tomas Gustafson (speed skating, Sarajevo, 1984, and Calgary, 1988) 50 35
1622 2 k. 80 Ingemar Stenmark (slalom, Lake Placid, 1980) 50 35

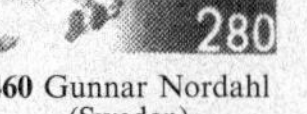

460 Gunnar Nordahl (Sweden)
461 1855 3 s. Green

1992. European Football Championship, Sweden. Each blue and green.

1623 2 k. 80 Type **460** 50 15
1624 2 k. 80 Lothar Matthaus (Germany) and Tomas Brolin (Sweden) 50 15

1992. Stamp Year.

1625 **461** 2 k. 80 green, yell & blk . 1·75 1·75
1626 – 4 k. 50 green, yell & blk . 1·75 1·75
1627 – 5 k. 50 yellow, grey & blk 85 60

DESIGN: 5 k. 50, 1857 3 s. yellow error.

462 "Sprengtporten" (frigate), 1785
463 Rabbit (Emma Westerberg)

1992. Europa. 500th Anniv of Discovery of America by Columbus. Multicoloured.

1628 4 k. 50 Type **462** 90 75
1629 4 k. 50 "Superb" (brig), 1855 90 75
1630 4 k. 50 "Big T" (yacht) (competitor in Discovery Race) 90 75

1992. Rebate stamps. Centenary of "Kamratposten" (children's magazine). Multicoloured.

1631 2 k. 50 Type **463** 45 15
1632 2 k. 50 Horses (Helena Johansson) 45 15
1633 2 k. 50 Kitten (Sabina Ostermark) 45 15
1634 2 k. 50 Elephant (Hanna Bengtsson) 45 15

1992. Olympic Games Gold Medallists (3rd series). As T **451**. Multicoloured.

1635 5 k. 50 Gunnar Larsson (swimming, Munich, 1972) 95 90
1636 5 k. 50 Bernt Johansson (cycling, Montreal, 1976) 95 90
1637 5 k. 50 Anders Garderud (steeplechase, Montreal, 1976) 95 90
1638 5 k. 50 Gert Fredriksson (canoeing, London, 1948) 95 90

464 Karlberg Castle

1992.

1639 **464** 20 k. black, green & blue 3·00 85

465 Hand holding Flower
466 Gustaf Dalen's Sun Valve and First Automated Lighthouse, Gasfeten

1992. Greetings stamps. Multicoloured.

1640 2 k. 80 Type **465** 50 25
1641 2 k. 80 Wedge of cheese ("Lyckans ost") 50 25
1642 2 k. 80 New-born baby ("Lev val!") 50 25
1643 2 k. 80 Writing with feather "Gratulerar" 50 25

1992. Centenary of Patent and Registration Office.

1644 **466** 2 k. 80 black and blue . 50 15

467 Riksdag (Parliament), Helgeandsholmen Island

1992. 88th Interparliamentary Union Conference, Stockholm.

1645 **467** 2 k. 80 violet on buff . . 50 15

468 "Kitchen Maid" (Rembrandt)
469 Plateosaurus

1992. Bicentenary of National Museum of Fine Arts. Multicoloured.

1646 5 k. 50 Type **468** 95 95
1647 5 k. 50 "Triumph of Venus" (Francois Boucher) (40 x 44 mm) 95 95
1648 5 k. 50 "Portrait of a Girl" (Albrecht Durer) 95 95
1649 5 k. 50 Rorstrand vase decorated by Erik Wahlberg 95 95
1650 5 k. 50 "Seine Motif" (Carl Fredrik Hill) (40 × 44 mm) 95 95
1651 5 k. 50 "Sergel in his Studio" (Carl Larsson) 95 95

1992. Prehistoric Animals. Mult.

1652 2 k. 80 Type **469** 60 50
1653 2 k. 80 Crocodile ("Thoracosaurus scanicus") 60 50
1654 2 k. 80 Woolly-haired rhino ("Coelodonta antiquitatis") 60 50
1655 2 k. 80 Mammoth ("Mammuthus primigenius") 60 50

470 Volvo "PV831", 1950
471 Osprey ("Pandion haliaetus")

1992. Swedish Cars.

1656 **470** 4 k. blue 70 35
1657 – 4 k. green and blue . . . 70 35

DESIGN: No. 1657 Saab "92", 1950.

1992. Birds of the Baltic.

1658 **471** 4 k. 50 black and blue . . 75 75
1659 – 4 k. 50 brown, blk & bl . 75 75
1660 – 4 k. 50 deep brown, brown and blue 75 75
1661 – 4 k. 50 black, brn & bl . 75 75

DESIGNS: No. 1659, Black-tailed godwit ("Limosa limosa"); 1660, Goosander ("Mergus merganser"); 1661, Common shelducks ("Tadorna tadorna").

472 "Meeting of Joachim and Anna"
473 Walcott

1992. Christmas. Icons. Multicoloured.

1662 2 k. 30 Type **472** 45 15
1663 2 k. 30 "Madonna and Child" 45 15
1664 2 k. 30 "Archangel Gabriel" (head) 45 15
1665 2 k. 30 "Saint Nicholas" (½-length portrait) 45 15

1992. Award of Nobel Literature Prize to Derek Walcott.

1666 **473** 5 k. 50 purple, bl & brn . 95 70
1667 – 5 k. 50 purple, brn & bl . 95 70

DESIGN: No. 1667, Palm trees, ocean and text.

474 Brown Bear Cubs

1993. Wildlife.

1668 **474** 2 k. 90 brown & black . . 50 15
1669 – 2 k. 90 brown & black . . 50 15
1671 – 3 k. multicoloured . . . 50 35
1672 – 5 k. 80 blk, grey & brn . 1·00 25
1673 – 12 k. brown, blue & red . 2·10 70

DESIGNS—As T **474**: No. 1669, Brown bear. 27 × 21 mm: No. 1671, Polecat; 1672, Wolf. 21 × 27 mm: No. 1673, Lynx.

475 "Big Bird" Glider (World Gliding Championships, Borlange)
476 Gooseberries

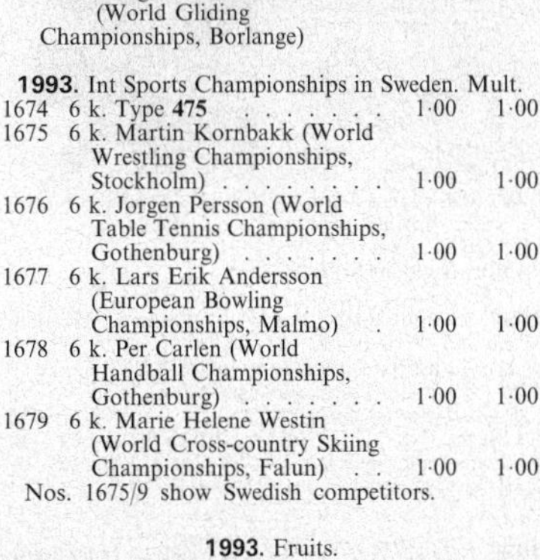

1993. Int Sports Championships in Sweden. Mult.

1674 6 k. Type **475** . . . . 1·00 1·00
1675 6 k. Martin Kornbakk (World Wrestling Championships, Stockholm) . . . . 1·00 1·00
1676 6 k. Jorgen Persson (World Table Tennis Championships, Gothenburg) . . . . 1·00 1·00
1677 6 k. Lars Erik Andersson (European Bowling Championships, Malmo) . 1·00 1·00
1678 6 k. Per Carlen (World Handball Championships, Gothenburg) . . . . 1·00 1·00
1679 6 k. Marie Helene Westin (World Cross-country Skiing Championships, Falun) . . 1·00 1·00

Nos. 1675/9 show Swedish competitors.

1993. Fruits.

1680 **476** 2 k. 40 green 40 15
1681 – 2 k. 40 green 40 15
1682 – 2 k. 40 red 40 15

DESIGNS: No. 1681, Pears; 1682, Cherries.

477 The Creation (relief, Uppsala Cathedral)
478 "Poseidon" (Carl Milles)

1993. 400th Anniv of Uppsala Convocation.

1683 **477** 2 k. 90 violet and buff . 85 15
1684 – 2 k. 90 red and buff . . 85 15

DESIGN: No. 1684, Uppsala Cathedral before fire of 1702.

1993. Nordic Countries' Postal Co-operation. Tourism. Tourist Attractions in Gothenburg.

1685 **478** 3 k. 50 green, yell & bl 60 35
1686 – 3 k. 50 indigo, yellow and blue 60 35

DESIGN: No. 1686, Liseberg Loop (fairground ride).

479 Ox-eye Daisies
480 "Oguasark" (Olle Baertling)

1993. Rebate stamps. Flowers. Multicoloured.

1687 2 k. 60 Type **479** 45 15
1688 2 k. 60 Poppies 45 15
1689 2 k. 60 Buttercups 45 15
1690 2 k. 60 Harebells 45 15

1993. Europa. Contemporary Art. Multicoloured.

1691 5 k. Type **480** 85 85
1692 5 k. "Ade-Ledic-Nander II" (Oyvind Fahlstrom) (horiz) 85 85
1693 5 k. "The Cubist Chair" (Otto Carlsund) 85 85

481 Swallowtail ("Papilio machaon")

1993. Butterflies. Multicoloured.

1694 6 k. Type **481** . . . . 1·00 70
1695 6 k. Camberwell beauty ("Nymphalis antiopa") . . 1·00 70
1696 6 k. Moorland clouded yellow ("Colias palaeno") . . . . 1·00 70
1697 6 k. Scarce fritillary ("Euphydryas maturna") 1·00 70

482 Fireworks ("Hurray")
483 Red-breasted Merganser ("Mergus serrator")

1993. Greetings Stamps. Multicoloured.

1698 2 k. 90 Type **482** 50 15
1699 2 k. 90 "Hor av Dig" ("Get in touch") 50 15
1700 2 k. 90 "Tycker om Dig" ("I like you") 50 15
1701 2 k. 90 "Lycka Till" ("Good luck") 50 15

1993. Sea Birds. Multicoloured.

1702 5 k. Type **483** 85 50
1703 5 k. Velvet scoter ("Melanitta fusca") 85 50
1704 5 k. Tufted duck ("Aythya fuligula") 85 50
1705 5 k. Eider ("Somateria mollissima") 85 50

484 Surveyor, 1643 (cover of Johan Mansson's nautical book)

485 King Carl Gustav

1993. 350th Anniv of Hydrographic Service.
1706 **484** 2 k. 90 brown, blue & blk . . 50 15
1707 – 2 k. 90 brown, blue & blk . . 50 15
DESIGN: No. 1707, Survey ship "Nils Stromcrona", 1993.

1993. 20th Anniv of Accession of King Carl XVI Gustav and Queen Silvia's 50th Birthday.
1708 8 k. Type **485** . . . . 2·10 2·10
1709 10 k. King Carl Gustav wearing medals . . . . 2·10 2·10
1710 10 k. Queen Silvia . . . . . 2·10 2·10
1711 12 k. Family group and Stockholm and Drottningholm Palaces (75 × 44 mm) . . . . 2·10 2·10

486 Plaited Heart

487 Stockholm City Hall

1993. Christmas.
1712 **486** 2 k. 40 green 40 10
1713 – 2 k. 40 red 40 10
DESIGN: No. 1713, Straw goat.

1993. Award of Nobel Literature Prize to Toni Morrison.
1714 **487** 6 k. red and blue . . . . 1·00 60
1715 – 6 k. brown and red . . . 1·00 60
DESIGN: No. 1715, Toni Morrison.

488 Victoria Plums

489 North Sweden Horse's Head

1994. Fruits.
1716 **488** 2 k. 80 multicoloured . . 50 15
1717 – 2 k. 80 multicoloured . . 50 15
1718 – 2 k. 80 lt green & green . . 50 15
DESIGNS: No. 1717, Opal plums; 1718, "James Grieve" apples.

1994. Domestic Animals.
1719 **489** 3 k. 20 brown, agate and red 55 15
1720 – 3 k. 20 brown, agate and red 55 15
1721 – 3 k. 20 black, brn & bl . . 55 15
1722 – 6 k. 40 black and green . 55 15
DESIGNS—VERT: No. 1720, North Sweden horses in harness. HORIZ: 1721, Gotland sheep; 1722, Mountain cow.

490 Mother Svea and European Union Emblem

491 Siamese

1994. Single European Market.
1723 **490** 5 k. blue 85 50

1994. Cats. Multicoloured.
1724 4 k. 50 Type **491** 75 75
1725 4 k. 50 Persian 75 75
1726 4 k. 50 European 75 75
1727 4 k. 50 Abyssinian 75 75

492 Illustration from "Le Roman de la Rose"

1994. Franco–Swedish Cultural Relations. Multicoloured.
1728 5 k. Type **492** 85 85
1729 5 k. Swedish and French flags . 85 85
1730 5 k. Sketch by De la Vallee of Knight's House (40 × 43 mm) 85 85
1731 5 k. "Household Chores" (Pehr Hillestrom) 85 85
1732 5 k. "Banquet for Gustav III at the Trianon, 1784" (Niclas Lafrensen the younger) (40 × 43 mm) 85 85
1733 5 k. "Carl XIV Johan" (Francois Gerard) 85 85

493 Martin Dahlin during Match

1994. World Cup Football Championship, U.S.A.
1734 **493** 3 k. 20 blue and red . . 55 15

494 Wild Rose ("Rosa dumalis")

495 Lunar Module "Eagle" and Astronauts

1994. Roses. Multicoloured.
1735 3 k. 20 Type **494** 55 15
1736 3 k. 20 "Rosa alba maxima" . 55 15
1737 3 k. 20 "Tuscany Superb" . 55 15
1738 3 k. 20 "Peace" 55 15
1739 3 k. 20 "Four Seasons" . . 55 15

1994. 25th Anniv of First Manned Moon Landing.
1740 **495** 6 k. 50 orange, blk & blue 1·10 65

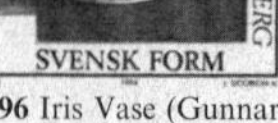

496 Iris Vase (Gunnar Wennerberg), 1897

497 Cat ("Love and Kisses")

1994. 150th Annivs of Stockholm College of Arts, Crafts and Design and of Swedish Society of Crafts and Design. Multicoloured.
1741 6 k. 50 Type **496** . . . . . 1·10 1·10
1742 6 k. 50 Wallpaper (Uno Ahren) and Chair (Carl Malmsten), 1917 . . . . 1·10 1·10
1743 6 k. 50 Aralia cloth, 1920, and cabinet, 1940 (Josef Frank) 1·10 1·10
1744 6 k. 50 Crystal bowl engraved with fireworks design (Edward Hald), 1921 . . . 1·10 1·10
1745 6 k. 50 Silver water jug, 1941, and sketch of coffee pot, 1970s (Wiwen Nilsson) . . 1·10 1·10
1746 6 k. 50 Linen towel (Astrid Sampe), plate (Stig Lindberg) and cutlery (Sigurd Persson), 1955 . . . . 1·10 1·10

1994. Greetings booklet stamps. Multicoloured.
1747 3 k. 20 Type **497** 55 15
1748 3 k. 20 Snail ("You've got time") 55 15
1749 3 k. 20 Frog ("You're lovely just as you are") 55 15
1750 3 k. 20 Dog ("Hi there!") . 55 15

498 Musicians (sketch, Johan Silvius) and Opening Bars of "Drottningholm Music"

499 [illegible] (javelin)

1994. 300th Birth Anniv of Johan Helmich Roman (composer) (1751) and Inauguration of Gothenburg Opera House (1752).
1751 **498** 3 k. 20 brown and blue . 55 15
1752 – 3 k. 20 multicoloured . 55 15
DESIGN: No. 1752, Opera House (designed Jan Izikowitz) and opening bars of opera "Aniara" by Karl Birger (inaugural programme).

1994. Sweden–Finland Athletics Meeting, Stockholm. Multicoloured.
1753 4 k. 50 Type **499** 75 65
1754 4 k. 50 Patrik Sjoberg (high jump) 75 65

500 Erland Nordenskiold (South America)

501 Caspian Tern

1994. Europa. Discoveries. Swedish Explorers. Multicoloured.
1755 5 k. 50 Type **500** 90 90
1756 5 k. 50 Eric von Rosen (Africa) 90 90
1757 5 k. 50 Sten Bergman (Asia and Australasia) 90 90

1994. Endangered Birds. Multicoloured.
1758 5 k. 50 Type **501** 90 85
1759 5 k. 50 White-tailed sea eagle 90 85
1760 5 k. 50 White-backed woodpecker 90 85
1761 5 k. 50 Lesser white-fronted goose 90 85

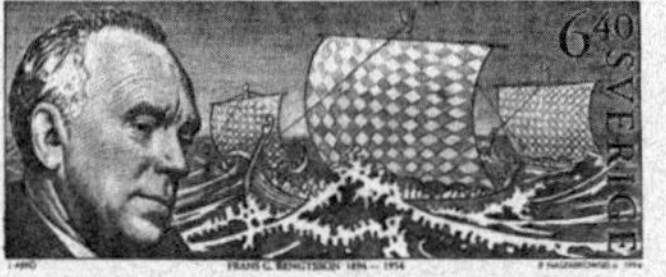

502 Bengtsson and Illustration from "The Longships" (novel)

1994. Birth Centenary of Frans Bengtsson (writer).
1762 **502** 6 k. 40 violet, red and black 1·10 65

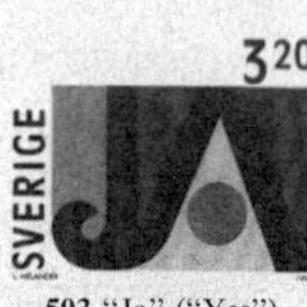

503 "Ja" ("Yes")

504 "The Annunciation"

1994. European Union Membership Referendum (1st issue). Multicoloured.
1763 3 k. 20 Type **503** 55 15
1764 3 k. 20 "Nej" ("No") 55 15
See also Nos. 1791/2.

1994. Christmas. Details from Askeby altarpiece. Multicoloured.
1765 2 k. 80 Type **504** 50 15
1766 2 k. 80 "Flight into Egypt" . 50 15

505 Erik Axel Karlfeldt (1931)

506 King Carl XVI Gustav

1994. Swedish Winners of the Nobel Literature Prize.
1767 **505** 4 k. 50 brown, dp bl & bl 75 25
1768 – 5 k. 50 deep brn, bl & brn 90 50
1769 – 6 k. 50 brn, dp grn & grn 1·10 65
DESIGNS: 5 k. 50, Eyvind Johnson (1974); 6 k. 50, Harry Martinsson (1974).

1995.
1772 **506** 3 k. 70 red 70 20
1773 3 k. 85 black 75 45
1775 – 6 k. green . . . . 1·10 65
1776 – 7 k. 50 purple . . . . . 1·40 80
DESIGN: 6 k., 7 k. 50, Queen Silvia.

507 Swedish Dwarf Cock

508 Strawberries

1995. Domestic Animals.
1785 **507** 3 k. 10 brown, chocolate and red 60 20
1786 – 3 k. 70 chestnut, brown and red 70 20
1787 – 3 k. 70 chestnut, brown and red 70 20
DESIGNS—VERT: No. 1786, Red poll cow; 1787, Goat.

1995. Berries.
1788 **508** 3 k. 35 red, green and black on cream 65 20
1789 – 3 k. 35 black, green and purple on cream . . . 65 20
1790 – 3 k. 35 red, green and black on cream 65 20
DESIGNS: No. 1789, Blackberries; 1790, Raspberries.

1995. European Union Membership Referendum (2nd issue). Designs as Nos. 1763/4 but colours and values changed. Multicoloured.
1791 3 k. 70 Type **503** 70 20
1792 3 k. 70 "Nej" ("No") . . . 70 20

509 Cottage with Allotment

1995. Traditional Houses. Multicoloured.
1793 3 k. 70 Type **509** 70 20
1794 3 k. 70 Soldier's smallholding 70 20
1795 3 k. 70 17th-century farmhouse, Skane 70 10
1796 3 k. 70 19th-century farmhouse, Jamtland 70 20
1797 3 k. 70 18th-century manor house 70 20

510 Jesus, Walt Whitman and Socrates

511 Scanian Geese

1995. Europa. Peace and Freedom. "Love, Peace and Labour" (wooden relief, Bror Hjorth). Multicoloured.
1798 5 k. Type **510** 95 85
1799 5 k. Lumumba, Albert Schweitzer and people of different races 95 85
1800 6 k. Type **510** . . . . 1·10 90
1801 6 k. As No. 1799 . . . . . . 1·10 90

1995. Domestic Animals.
1802 **511** 7 k. 40 deep brown, brown and green . . . . . . 1·40 80
1803 – 7 k. 50 brown, green and blue . . . . 1·40 80
DESIGN: 7 k. 50, Yellow duck.

512 Members' Flags forming "EU"

1995. Admission of Sweden to European Union.
1804 **512** 6 k. multicoloured . . . 1·10 65

513 Ice Hockey

1995. World Ice Hockey Championship, Stockholm and Gavle (1805) and World Athletics Championships, Gothenburg (1806). Mult.
1805 3 k. 70 Type **513** 70 20
1806 3 k. 70 Erica Johansson (1992 junior long jump champion) (27½ x 28 mm) 70 20

514 Rock Speedwell

515 "Wilhelm Tham" (tourist launch) on Gota Canal

1995. Mountain Flowers. Multicoloured.
1807 3 k. 70 Type **514** 70 20
1808 3 k. 70 Cloudberry (white flowers) 70 20
1809 3 k. 70 Mountain heath (pink flowers) and black bearberry 70 20
1810 3 k. 70 Alpine arnica (yellow flowers) and crowberry . . 70 20

1995. Nordic Countries' Postal Co-operation. Tourism.
1811 **515** 5 k. green 95 55
1812 – 5 k. violet 95 55
DESIGN: No. 1812, Moored yacht, Lake Vattern.

516 English Horse-drawn Tram, Gothenburg

1995. Trams.
1813 **516** 7 k. 50 red . . . . 1·40 1·25
1814 – 7 k. 50 purple . . . . . 1·40 1·25
1815 – 7 k. 50 green . . . . . 1·40 1·25
1816 – 7 k. 50 lilac . . . . . . 1·40 1·25
1817 – 7 k. 50 blue . . . . . . 1·40 1·25
DESIGNS: No. 1814, Electric tram, Norrkoping; 1815, Commuter tram, Helsingborg; 1816, Narrow gauge tram, Kiruna; 1817, Mustang tram, Stockholm.

517 "Non-Violence" (sculpture, Carl Frederik Reutersward) (U.N. Building, New York)

1995. 50th Anniv of U.N.O.
1818 **517** 3 k. 70 deep blue and blue 70 20

518 "The Ball is Yours!" (Mikael Angesjo) 519 Maria Akraka

1995. Greetings stamps. Winning Entries in Children's Drawing Competition. Multicoloured.
1819 3 k. 70 Type **518** 70 20
1820 3 k. 70 Happy man saying "Hello" (Erica Sandstrom) 70 20
1821 3 k. 70 Teddy bear saying "I miss you" (Linda Nordenhem) 70 20
1822 3 k. 70 Shy mussel saying "Hello" (Christoffer Stenbom) 70 20

1995. World Athletics Championships, Gothenburg.
1823 **519** 7 k. 50 multicoloured . . 1·40 80

520 "Soldier Bom" (1948)

1995. Centenary of Motion Pictures. Scenes from Swedish Films. Multicoloured.
1824 6 k. Type **520** . . . . 1·10 65
1825 6 k. "Sir Arne's Treasure" (1919) . . . . 1·10 65
1826 6 k. "Wild Strawberries" (1957) 1·10 65
1827 6 k. "House of Angels" (1992) 1·10 65
1828 6 k. "One Summer of Happiness" (1951) . . . . 1·10 65
1829 6 k. "The Apple War" (1971) 1·10 65

521 Nilsson 522 Bronze Figures (Bronze Age)

1995. Birth Centenary of Fritiof Nilsson (writer).
1830 **521** 3 k. 70 blue and red . . 70 20

1995. Ancient Treasures from Museum of National Antiquities, Stockholm. Multicoloured.
1831 3 k. 70 Type **522** 70 20
1832 3 k. 70 Gold collar (400–550 A.D.) 70 20
1833 3 k. 70 Pendant (400–550 A.D.) 70 20
1834 3 k. 70 Bronze drum (Bronze Age) 70 20

523 Uraniborg (Palace Observatory) 524 Santa Candlestick, Varmland

1995. 450th Birth Anniv of Tycho Brahe (astronomer). Multicoloured.
1835 5 k. Type **523** 95 55
1836 6 k. Instrument for measuring positions in space . . . . 1·10 65

1995. Christmas. Candlesticks. Multicoloured.
1837 3 k. 35 Type **524** 65 20
1838 3 k. 35 Apple candlestick, Smaland 65 20
1839 3 k. 35 Wrought iron candlestick, Dalarna . . . 65 20
1840 3 k. 35 Three-armed candlestick, Bergslagen 65 20

525 Nobel and Testament

1995. Centenary of Nobel Prize Trust Fund. Multicoloured.
1841 6 k. Type **525** . . . . 1·10 65
1842 6 k. Nobel's home in Paris . 1·10 65
1843 6 k. Laboratory, Bjorkborn Manor, Karlskoga . . . . 1·10 65
1844 6 k. Medal and award ceremony for Wilhelm Rontgen, 1901 1·10 65

526 Rose Hips and Juniper 527 West European Hedgehog

1996. Winter Berries. Multicoloured.
1845 3 k. 50 Type **526** 70 20
1846 3 k. 50 Cowberries and sloes 70 20
1847 3 k. 50 Holly 70 20
1848 7 k. 50 Rowan . . . . . . 1·40 80

1996. Wildlife.
1849 **527** 1 k. sepia, brown and green 20 10
1850 – 3 k. 20 multicoloured . 60 20
1851 – 3 k. 85 multicoloured . 75 25
1854 – 3 k. 85 green, olive and black 75 25
1852 – 7 k. 70 brown, deep brown and chocolate . . . . 1·50 90
DESIGNS—VERT: No. 1850, Eurasian beaver. HORIZ: No. 1851, Stoat; 1852, Red fox; 1854, European otter.

528 Postal Sorters and Modern Mail Carriage

1996. Discontinuation of Mail Sorting on Trains.
1855 **528** 6 k. black, blue and red 1·10 65

529 Post Office and Railway Station, Halsingland

1996. Traditional Houses (2nd series). Multicoloured.
1856 3 k. 85 Type **529** 75 25
1857 3 k. 85 Motala Assembly Hall, Ostergotland 75 25
1858 3 k. 85 Parish storehouse, Smaland (27 × 23 mm) . 75 25
1859 3 k. 85 Octagonal log barn, Vasterbotten (27 × 23 mm) 75 25
1860 3 k. 85 Sheep shelter, Gotland (27 × 36 mm) 75 25
1861 3 k. 85 Old Town Hall, Lidkoping (27 × 36 mm) 75 25

530 In Tyresta National Park 531 Karin Kock (politician)

1996. 50th Birthday of King Carl XVI Gustaf. Multicoloured.
1862 10 k. Type **530** . . . . 1·90 1·10
1863 10 k. In Bernadotte Gallery with painting of King Karl XIV Johan . . . . 1·90 1·10
1864 10 k. With King Albert of Belgium . . . . 1·90 1·10
1865 20 k. With royal family (76 × 43 mm) . . . . 3·75 2·25

1996. Europa. Famous Women.
1866 **531** 6 k. brown and red . . . 1·10 65
1867 – 6 k. blue and red . . . . 1·10 65
DESIGN: No. 1867, Astrid Lindgren (children's writer).

532 "West Coast" (Sven X:et Erixson)

1996. Summer Paintings. Multicoloured.
1868 3 k. 85 Type **532** 75 25
1869 3 k. 85 "Summer's Night" (Roland Svensson) 75 25
1870 3 k. 85 "The Gentlefolk" (Eric Hallstrom) 75 25
1871 3 k. 85 "Summer Flowers" (Thage Nordholm) 75 25
1872 3 k. 85 "Women and Children at Seaside" (Ragnar Sandberg) 75 25

533 Annika Sorenstam 534 Theatre Masks

1996. Golf.
1873 **533** 3 k. 50 green on cream . 65 20

1996. Greetings Stamps.
1874 **534** 3 k. 85 multicoloured . . 75 25
1875 – 3 k. 85 blue, yellow and black 75 25
1876 – 3 k. 85 violet, yellow and black 75 25
1877 – 3 k. 85 red, black and pink 75 25
DESIGNS: No. 1875, Hearts forming four-leaved clover ("Be Happy!"); 1876, Heart within posthorn; 1877, Girl and hearts ("Do you remember me?").

535 Cep 536 Grass Slopes, Haga Park

1996. Fungi. Multicoloured.
1878 3 k. 85 Type **535** 75 25
1879 5 k. "Russula integra" . . . 95 55
1880 5 k. Chanterelle ("Cantherellus cibarius") 95 55
1881 5 k. Death trumpets ("Craterellus cornucopioides") 95 55
1882 5 k. Shaggy ink caps ("Coprinus comatus") 95 55

1996. The Ecopark, Stockholm. Multicoloured.
1883 7 k. 50 Type **536** . . . . . . 1·40 80
1884 7 k. 50 Copper tents, Haga Park . . . . 1·40 80
1885 7 k. 50 Rosendal Palace . . . 1·40 80
1886 7 k. 50 Herons, Isbladskarret Swamp . . . . 1·40 80

537 1930s Errand Boy 538 Baroque Chair (Endre Nemes)

1996. Four Decades of Youth. Multicoloured.
1887 3 k. 85 Type **537** 75 25
1888 3 k. 85 1960s flowerchild . . 75 25
1889 3 k. 85 1940s zoot-suiter . . 75 25
1890 3 k. 85 1950s biker 75 25

1996. Art.
1891 **538** 6 k. multicoloured . . . 1·10 65

539 "The Annunciation"

1996. Christmas. Illustrations from 15th-century Book of Hours. Multicoloured.
1892 3 k. 50 Type **539** 65 20
1893 3 k. 50 "Nativity" 65 20
1894 3 k. 50 "Adoration of the Wise Men" 65 20

540 Sune Bergstrom (1982)

1996. Swedish Winners of the Nobel Physiology and Medicine Prize.
1895 **540** 5 k. black, blue and green 95 55
1896 – 5 k. black and green . . 95 55
1897 – 5 k. black, blue and green 95 55
1898 – 5 k. blue, green and black 95 55
DESIGNS: No. 1896, Bengt Samuelsson (1982); 1897, Hugo Theorell (1955); 1898, Ragnar Granit (1967).

541 Wolverine 543 Roses forming Heart

542 Queen Margareta, Coronation Document and Erik of Pommern

1997. Wildlife.
1899 **541** 3 k. 20 black, green and blue 60 20
1900 – 3 k. 50 black, green and red 65 20
1901 – 7 k. 70 black, red and green . . . . 1·50 90
DESIGNS—HORIZ: 3 k. 50, Snowy owl. VERT: 7 k. 70, White stork.

1997. 600th Anniv of Kalmar Union (of Sweden, Denmark and Norway).
1902 **542** 3 k. 85 blue 75 25

1997. Greetings Stamps.
1903 **543** 3 k. 85 multicoloured (red roses) 75 25
1904 3 k. 85 multicoloured (pink roses) 75 25

544 Dalby

1997. Churches. Multicoloured.
1905 3 k. 85 Type **544** 75 25
1906 3 k. 85 Vendel 75 25
1907 3 k. 85 Hagby (27 × 23 mm) . 75 25
1908 3 k. 85 Overtornea (27 × 23 mm) 75 25
1909 3 k. 85 Varnhem (27 × 37 mm) 75 25
1910 3 k. 85 Ostra Amtervik (27 × 23 mm) 75 25

OFFICIAL STAMPS

O 6 O 17

1874.
O27 **O 6** 2 ore orange . . . . . 1·10 1·50
O28 3 ore bistre . . . . . . 1·10 2·00
O29b 4 ore grey . . . . . . 1·25 25
O30b 5 ore green . . . . . . 1·25 15
O31 6 ore lilac . . . . . . 15·00 20·00
O32 6 ore grey . . . . . . £275 75·00
O33b 10 ore red . . . . . . 1·50 10
O34 12 ore blue . . . . . . 30·00 9·50

O35	**O 6**	20 ore red	£110	1·00
O36		20 ore blue	2·75	10
O37		24 ore yellow	38·00	8·50
O38b		30 ore brown	12·00	30
O39		50 ore red	80·00	9·00
O40		50 ore grey	9·00	1·10
O41c		1 k. blue and bistre	5·00	90

1889. Surch **TJENSTE FRIMARKE**, two crowns, and **TIO 10 ORE** on scroll.

O42	**O 6**	10 ore on 12 ore blue	7·50	10·00
O43		10 ore on 24 ore yellow	10·00	13·00

1910.

O 87	**O 17**	1 ore black	15	10
O101		2 ore yellow	20	10
O102		3 ore brown	30	35
O103		4 ore lilac	20	10
O104		5 ore green	20	10
O105		7 ore green	40	45
O 91		8 ore purple	40	45
O107		10 ore red	20	10
O108		12 ore red	20	10
O109		15 ore brown	20	10
O110		20 ore blue	20	10
O111		25 ore orange	80	30
O112		30 ore brown	35	25
O113		35 ore violet	70	30
O114		50 ore grey	1·50	90
O 98		1 k. black on yellow	6·50	4·75
O 99		5 k. purple on yellow	9·00	2·50

POSTAGE DUE STAMPS

D 6

1874.

D27	**D 6**	1 ore black	1·10	2·00
D28a		3 ore red	2·50	3·75
D29a		5 ore brown	1·25	2·10
D30a		6 ore yellow	1·75	2·40
D31		12 ore red	3·50	2·50
D32		20 ore blue	2·50	2·25
D33a		24 ore lilac	13·00	16·00
D34		24 ore grey	24·00	30·00
D35		30 ore green	2·50	2·25
D36		50 ore brown	4·25	3·00
D37		1 k. blue and bistre	19·00	12·00

SWITZERLAND Pt. 8

A federal republic in central Europe between France, Germany and Italy.

100 rappen = 1 franken
100 centimes = 1 franc
100 centesimi = 1 franco

These are expressions of the same currency in three languages.

For the issues under the Cantonal Administrations of Basel, Geneva and Zurich, see Stanley Gibbons' Part 8 (Italy and Switzerland) Catalogue.

1

6

1850. Imperf. (a) Inscr "ORTS-POST".

1	**1**	$2\frac{1}{2}$ r. black and red	£1500	£1000

(b) Inscr "POSTE LOCALE".

3	**1**	$2\frac{1}{2}$ r. black and red	£1200	£900

1850. As T 1 but inscr "RAYON I", "II" or "III". Imperf.

6	**1**	5 r. red, black and blue (I)	£900	£300
13		5 r. red and blue (I)	£350	90·00
10		10 r. red, black and yell (II)	£500	75·00
23		15 rp. red (III)	£1000	80·00
21		15 cts. red (III)	£8000	£600

1854. Imperf.

46	**6**	2 r. grey	£150	£300
47a		5 r. brown	£100	8·00
48		10 r. blue	£100	6·50
49a		15 r. pink	£190	30·00
50		20 r. orange	£225	40·00
51		40 r. green	£225	42·00
38		1 f. lilac	£700	£500

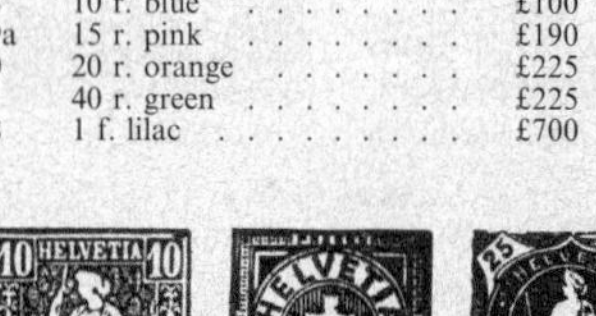

7 9 10

1862. Perf.

52	**7**	2 c. grey	55·00	2·00
61		2 c. brown	1·00	25
61a		2 c. bistre	1·50	75
53		3 c. black	5·00	75·00
54		5 c. brown	1·60	10
55		10 c. blue	£225	10
62		10 c. pink	1·60	10
63		15 c. yellow	2·00	24·00
56a		20 c. orange	1·00	1·00
64		25 c. green	1·00	1·50
57		30 c. red	£700	18·00
65a		30 c. blue	£225	4·00
58		40 c. green	£700	35·00
66		40 c. grey	1·00	80·00
67		50 c. purple	35·00	24·00
59		60 c. bronze	£600	£100
60a		1 f. gold	12·00	75·00

1882.

126B	**9**	2 c. brown	80	15
127cB		3 c. brown	1·50	1·50
128d		5 c. purple	11·00	10
196		5 c. green	3·00	10
130e		10 c. red	1·75	10
131e		12 c. blue	3·50	10
132		15 c. yellow	£110	10·00
133b		15 c. violet	25·00	70

1882.

214	**10**	20 c. orange	1·75	1·75
146cB		25 c. green	7·50	40
207		25 c. blue	4·00	50
202		30 c. brown	3·00	1·25
209		40 c. grey	20·00	6·50
150B		50 c. blue	38·00	4·00
218		50 c. green	4·00	6·00
152cb		1 f. purple	35·00	2·00
219		1 f. red	15·00	3·00
154B		3 f. brown	£100	16·00

11

1900. 25th Anniv of U.P.U.

191	**11**	5 c. green	2·00	50
189		10 c. red	8·00	50
190		25 c. blue	15·00	10·00

15 Tell's Son **16** **17**

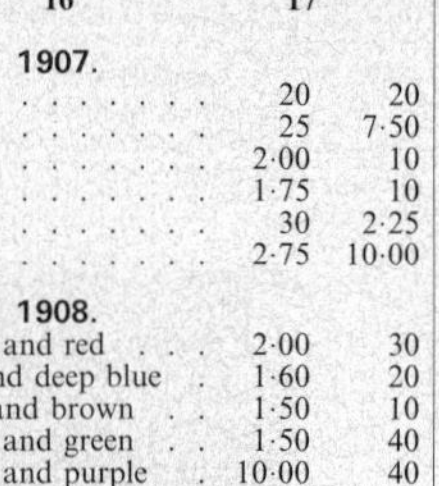

1907.

225	**15**	2 c. yellow	20	20
226		3 c. brown	25	7·50
227		5 c. green	2·00	10
228	**16**	10 c. red	1·75	10
229		12 c. brown	30	2·25
230		15 c. mauve	2·75	10·00

1908.

232	**17**	20 c. yellow and red	2·00	30
233		25 c. blue and deep blue	1·60	20
234		30 c. green and brown	1·50	10
235		35 c. yellow and green	1·50	40
236		40 c. yellow and purple	10·00	40
238		40 c. blue	1·75	10
239		40 c. green	22·00	10
240a		50 c. green & deep green	6·50	30
241		60 c. brown	8·50	10
242		70 c. yellow and brown	55·00	8·00
243		70 c. buff and violet	15·00	60
244		80 c. buff and grey	9·50	20
245		1 f. green and purple	6·50	15
246		3 f. yellow and bistre	£175	1·00

18 Cord in front of Shaft

19

1908.

247	**18**	2 c. bistre	25	70
248		3 c. violet	15	10·00
249		5 c. green	2·00	10
250	**19**	10 c. red	60	10
251		12 c. brown	75	10
252		15 c. mauve	23·00	45

20a Cord behind Shaft **21** William Tell

1910.

260	**20a**	2 c. brown	10	10
261		$2\frac{1}{2}$ c. purple	10	80
262		$2\frac{1}{2}$ c. bistre on buff	40	1·25
254		3 c. violet	10	10
255		3 c. brown	10	10
256		3 c. blue on buff	2·00	4·50
263		5 c. green	55	10
264		5 c. orange on buff	10	10
265		5 c. grey on buff	10	10
266		5 c. purple on buff	10	10
267		5 c. green on buff	30	10
258		$7\frac{1}{2}$ c. grey	1·00	10
259		$7\frac{1}{2}$ c. green on buff	30	1·75

1914.

279	**21**	10 c. red on buff	45	10
280		10 c. green on buff	10	10
282		10 c. violet on buff	1·00	10
283		12 c. brown on buff	35	4·00
284		13 c. green on buff	1·40	20
285		15 c. purple on buff	7·50	10
286		15 c. red on buff	3·25	1·75
287		20 c. purple on buff	1·50	10
289		20 c. red on buff	35	10
291		25 c. red on buff	1·00	35
292		25 c. brown on buff	3·25	75
293		30 c. blue on buff	8·00	10

22 The Mythen

1914. Mountain Views.

294	**22**	3 f. green	£650	4·00
295		3 f. red	80·00	35
296	–	5 f. blue	30·00	1·25
297	–	10 f. mauve	90·00	1·25
337	–	10 f. green	£225	20·00

DESIGNS: 5 f. The Rutli; 10 f. The Jungfrau and girl holding shield.

1915. Surch.

298	**20a**	1 c. on 2 c. brown	10	30
307		$2\frac{1}{2}$ c. on 3 c. brown	10	25
308		3 c. on $2\frac{1}{2}$ c. bistre on buff	10	1·50
309		5 c. on 2 c. brown	10	2·50
310		5 c. on $7\frac{1}{2}$ c. grey	10	10
312		5 c. on $7\frac{1}{2}$ c. grn on buff	15	6·00
313	**21**	10 c. on 13 c. green on buff	15	1·60
299	**19**	13 c. on 12 c. brown	10	7·50
300	**21**	13 c. on 12 c. brn on buff	20	70
314a		20 c. on 15 c. purple on buff	60	1·25
315	**17**	20 c. on 25 c. blue and deep blue	15	25
301		80 c. on 70 c. yell & brn	24·00	12·00

1919. Air. Optd with wings and propeller.

302	**17**	30 c. green and brown	£100	£1100
303		50 c. green & deep green	30·00	95·00

31

32

33

1919. Peace Celebrations.

304	**31**	$7\frac{1}{2}$ c. green and black	65	1·50
305	**32**	10 c. yellow and red	1·00	6·00
306	**33**	15 c. yellow and violet	1·75	1·50

35 Monoplane

36 Pilot

37

38 Biplane

39 Icarus

40

1923. Air.

316	**35**	15 c. green and red	2·75	5·50
317a		20 c. green and dp green	30	15
318		25 c. grey and blue	7·00	15·00
319	**36**	35 c. cinnamon and brown	10·00	42·00
320a	**37**	35 c. brown and ochre	5·00	40·00
321	**36**	40 c. lilac and violet	13·00	48·00
322a	**37**	40 c. blue and green	30·00	40·00
323	**38**	45 c. red and blue	1·50	7·00
324a		50 c. grey and red	1·25	1·00
325a	**39**	65 c. blue and deep blue	1·00	5·00
326		75 c. orange and purple	12·00	60·00
327a		1 f. lilac and purple	1·00	2·50
328a	**40**	2 f. chestnut, sepia and brown	8·00	5·50

41

42 Seat of First U.P.U. Congress

1924.

329 **41** 90 c. red, deep green and green 14·00 20
330 1 f. 20 red, lake and pink 6·00 45
331 1 f. 50 red, blue and turquoise 22·00 60
332 2 f. red, black and grey 45·00 2·25

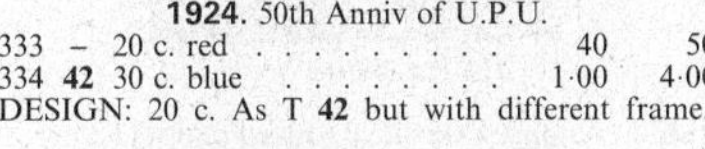

1924. 50th Anniv of U.P.U.

333 – 20 c. red 40 50
334 **42** 30 c. blue 1·00 4·00
DESIGN: 20 c. As T **42** but with different frame.

43 The Mythen

1931.

335 **43** 3 f. brown 50·00 1·60

44 Symbol of Peace

45 "After the Darkness, Light"

46 Peace and the Air Post

1932. International Disarmament Conference.

338 **44** 5 c. green (postage) 10 10
339 10 c. orange 20 10
340 20 c. mauve 30 10
341 30 c. blue 3·00 40
342 60 c. brown 15·00 2·00
343 **45** 1 f. grey and blue 17·00 4·00

344 **46** 15 c. light green and green (air) 30 1·25
345 20 c. pink and red 65 2·00
346 90 c. light blue and blue 6·00 22·00

47 Louis Favre (engineer)

48 Staubbach Falls

1932. 50th Anniv of St. Gotthard Railway.

347 **47** 10 c. brown 10 10
348 – 20 c. red 25 20
349 – 30 c. blue 40 1·40
DESIGNS: 20 c. Alfred Escher (President of Railway); 30 c. Emil Welti (founder).

1934. Landscapes.

350 **48** 3 c. green 25 1·50
351 – 5 c. green 25 10
352 – 10 c. mauve 50 10
353 – 15 c. orange 55 80
354 – 20 c. red 80 10
355 – 25 c. brown 6·00 5·00
356 – 30 c. blue 30·00 40
DESIGNS: 5 c. Mt. Pilatus; 10 c. Chillon Castle and Dents du Midi; 15 c. Grimsel Pass; 20 c. Landwasser Viaduct, Filisur (St. Gotthard Railway); 25 c. Viamala Gorge; 30 c. Rhine Falls near Schaffhausen.

1935. Air. Surch.

358 **35** 10 on 15 c. green and red 5·00 30·00
359 **46** 10 on 15 c. light green and green 40 40
360 10 on 20 c. pink and red 40 1·60
381 **39** 10 on 65 c. blue & dp blue 20 30
361 **46** 30 on 90 c. lt blue & blue 2·50 12·00
362 40 on 20 c. pink and red 3·00 12·00
363 40 on 90 c. lt blue & blue 3·00 12·00

51 Freiburg Cowherd

52 Staubbach Falls

1936. National Defence Fund.

364 **51** 10 c. + 5 c. violet 35 50
365 20 c. + 10 c. red 70 3·00
366 30 c. + 10 c. blue 3·00 14·00

1936. As T **48** but redrawn with figure of value lower down. Various landscapes.

368 **52** 3 c. green 10 10
369 – 5 c. green 10 10
489 – 5 c. brown 20 10
370d – 10 c. purple 35 10
372 – 10 c. brown 10 10
490 – 10 c. green 30 10
373 – 15 c. orange 40 15
374d – 20 c. red (Railway) 7·00 10
375 – 20 c. red (Lake) 15 10
491 – 20 c. brown 60 10
376 – 25 c. brown 60 30
492 – 25 c. red 1·50 1·25
377 – 30 c. blue 1·00 10
378 – 35 c. green 1·00 70
379 – 40 c. grey 7·00 10
494 – 40 c. blue 21·00 40
DESIGNS: 5 c Mt. Pilatus; 10 c. Chillon Castle and Dents du Midi; 15 c. Grimsel Pass; 20 c. (374d) Landwasser Viaduct, Filisur; 20 c. (Nos. 375, 491) Lake Lugano and Mt. San Salvatore; 25 c. (No. 376) Viamala Gorge; 25 c. (No. 492) National Park; 30 c. Rhine Falls; 35 c. Mt. Neufalkenstein and Klus; 40 c. Mt. Santis and Lake Seealp.

53 Mobile P.O.

1937. For Mobile P.O. Mail.

380 **53** 10 c. yellow and black 30 10

55 International Labour Bureau

1938.

382 **55** 20 c. red and buff 20 10
383 – 30 c. blue and light blue 30 10
384 – 60 c. brown and buff 1·75 1·00
385 – 1 f. black and buff 6·50 9·00
DESIGNS: 30c. Palace of League of Nations; 60 c. Inner courtyard of Palace of League of Nations; 1 f. International Labour Bureau (different)..

1938. Air. Special Flights. Surch **1938 "PRO AERO" 75 75** and bars.

386 **38** 75 c. on 50 c. green & red † 5·00

60 William Tell's Chapel

1938. National Fete. Fund for Swiss Subjects Abroad.

387 **60** 10 c. + 10 c. violet & yellow 40 35

61 First Act of Federal Parliament

1938.

388A **61** 3 f. brown on blue 12·00 3·00
388c 3 f. brown on buff 6·00 10
389A – 5 f. blue on blue 8·00 2·00
389c – 5 f. blue on buff 6·00 10
390A – 10 f. green on blue 40·00 24·00
390c – 10 f. green on buff 8·00 35
DESIGNS: 5 f. "The Assembly at Stans"; 10 f. Polling booth.

62 Symbolical of Swiss Culture

64 Crossbow and Floral Branch

1939. National Exhibition, Zurich. Inscr in French (F.), German (G.) or Italian (I.).

			F.		G.		I.	
391	–	10 c. vio	25	10	20	10	25	10
392	**62**	20 c. red	50	10	35	10	1·75	10
393	–	30 c. blue & buff	2·00	3·00	2·00	1·00	2·00	5·00

DESIGNS: 10 c. Group symbolic of Swiss Industry and Agriculture; 30 c. Piz Rosegg and Tschirva Glacier.

1939. National Exhibition, Zurich. Inscr in French (F.), German (G.) or Italian (I.).

			F.		G.		I.	
394a	**64**	5 c. green	70	1·50	70	1·25	70	1·50
395a/b		10 c. brn	75	1·25	55	80	85	1·50
396a		20 c. red	1·50	1·25	1·25	1·00	1·40	2·25
397		30 c. blue	3·50	6·00	3·00	5·50	3·00	6·50

65 Laupen Castle

1939. National Fete. Fund for Destitute Mothers.

398 **65** 10 c. + 10 c. brown, grey and red 30 25

66 Geneva

1939. 75th Anniv of Geneva (Red Cross) Convention.

399 **66** 20 c. red and buff 30 10
400 30 c. blue, grey and red 45 90

67 "Les Rangiers"

68 "William Tell" (Ferdinand Hodler)

1940. National Fete and Red Cross Fund. Memorial designs inscr "FETE NATIONALE 1940" in German (5 c., 20 c.), Italian (10 c.) and French (30 c.).

401 – 5 c. + 5 c. black & green 30 90
402 – 10 c. + 5 c. black & orange 30 25
403 – 20 c. + 5 c. black & red 2·00 75
404 **67** 30 c. + 10 c. black & blue 1·60 5·00
DESIGNS—Battle Memorials: 5 c. Sempach; 10 c. Giornico; 20 c. Calven.

1941. Historical designs.

405 – 50 c. blue on green 4·00 10
406 **68** 60 c. brown on cinnamon 6·00 10
407 – 70 c. purple on mauve 2·00 50
408 – 80 c. black on grey 70 10
408a – 80 c. black on mauve 75 20
409 – 90 c. red on pink 70 10
409a – 90 c. red on buff 1·00 30
410 – 1 f. green on green 70 10
411 – 1 f. 20 purple on grey 70 10
411a – 1 f. 20 purple on lilac 1·00 25
412 – 1 f. 50 blue on buff 1·00 10
413 – 2 f. red on pink 1·50 10
413a – 2 f. red on cream 2·00 25
DESIGNS—(Works of art): 50 c. "Oath of Union" (James Vibert); 70 c. "Kneeling Warrior" (Ferdinand Hodler); 80 c. "Dying Ensign" (Hodler); 90 c. "Standard Bearer" (Niklaus Deutsch). Portraits: 1 f. Col. Louis Pfyffer; 1 f. 20, George Jenatsch; 1 f. 50, Lt. Gen. Francois de Reynold; 2 f. Col. Joachim Forrer.

69 Ploughing

1941. Agricultural Development Plan.

414 **69** 10 c. brown and buff 15 15

70 The Jungfrau

71 Chemin Creux near Kussnacht

1941. Air. Landscapes.

415 **70** 30 c. blue on orange 1·00 10
415a – 30 c. grey on orange 7·50 10·00
416 – 40 c. grey on orange 1·00 10
416a – 40 c. blue on orange 42·00 1·75
417 – 50 c. green on orange 1·25 10
418 – 60 c. brown on orange 1·75 10
419 – 70 c. violet on orange 1·25 30
420 – 1 f. green on buff 2·50 35
421 – 2 f. red on buff 6·50 1·50
422 – 5 f. blue on buff 25·00 7·50
DESIGNS: 40 f. Valais; 50 c. Lac Leman; 60 c. Alpstein; 70 c. Ticino; 1 f. Lake Lucerne; 2 f. Engadin; 5 f. Churfirsten.

1941. Air. Special (Buochs–Payerne) Flights. No. 420 with "PRO AERO 28.V.1941" added.

423 – 1 f. green on buff 5·50 20·00

1941. National Fete and 650th Anniv of Swiss Confederation.

424 – 10 c. + 10 c. bl, red & yell 25 45
425 **71** 20 c. + 10 c. scarlet, red and buff 25 40
DESIGN: 10 c. Relief Map of Lake Lucerne with Arms of Uri, Schwyz and Unterwalden.

72 Arms of Berne, Masons laying Cornerstone and Knight

1941. 750th Anniv of Berne.

426 **72** 10 c. multicoloured 10 30

73 "To survive collect salvage"

1942. Salvage Campaign. Inscr in French (F.), German (G.) or Italian (I.).

			F.		G.		I.	
427	**73**	10 c. brn	50	15	10	10	7·00	2·00

INSCRIPTIONS: (G.) Zum Durchhalten/Alstoffe sammeln"; (I.) "PER RESISTERE/ RACCOGLIETE/LA ROBA VECCHIA".

74 View of Old Geneva

75 Soldiers' Memorial at Forch, near Zurich

1942. National Fete, National Relief Fund and Bimillenary of Geneva.

428 **74** 10 c. + 10 c. black, yellow and red 30 40
429 **75** 20 c. + 10 c. red & yellow 30 45

76

1943. Cent of Swiss Cantonal Postage Stamp.

430 **76** 10 c. (4 + 6) black 10 10

77 Intragna (Ticino)

78 Apollo of Olympia

1943. National Fete and Youth's Vocational Training Fund.

431 **77** 10 c. + 10 c. black, buff and red 30 45
432 – 20 c. + 10 c. red and buff 35 65
DESIGN: 20 c. Federal Palace, Berne.

1943. Air. Special Flights. 30th Anniv of First Flight across Alps by Oscar Bider. No. 432 optd **PRO AERO 13.VII.1943** and value.

433 – 1 f. red and buff 1·25 9·00

1944. Olympic Games Jubilee.

434	**78**	10 c. black and orange	15	50
435		20 c. black and red	35	50
436		30 c. black and blue	70	7·50

79 Heiden

1944. National Fete and Red Cross Fund.

437	**79**	5 c. + 5 c. grn, buff & red	35	1·60
438	–	10 c. + 10 c. grey, buff and red	35	35
439	–	20 c. + 10 c. red and buff	35	55
440	–	30 c. + 10 c. blue, buff and red	2·00	13·00

DESIGNS: 10 c. St. Jacques on the R. Birs; 20 c. Castle Ruins, Mesocco; 30 c. Basel.

80 Haefeli DH-3 Biplane

81 Symbolical of Faith, Hope and Charity

1944. Air. 25th Anniv of National Air Post.

441	**80**	10 c. brown and green	15	10
442	–	20 c. red and stone	20	10
443	–	30 c. ultramarine and blue	40	45
444	–	1 f. 50 agate, brown and red	6·50	16·00

AIRCRAFT: 20 c. Fokker F.VIIb/3m; 30 c. Lockheed 9B Orion; 1 f. 50, Douglas DC-3.

1945. War Relief Fund.

445	**81**	10 c. + 10 c. green, black and grey	30	40
446		20 c. + 60 c. red, black and grey	75	4·50

82 Trans "Peace to men of good will"

83 Olive Branch

1945. Peace. Inscr "PAX".

447	**82**	5 c. green and grey	10	15
448		10 c. brown and grey	25	10
449		20 c. red and grey	40	10
450		30 c. blue and grey	90	2·25
451		40 c. orange and grey	3·00	9·00
452	**83**	50 c. red and buff	4·00	15·00
453	–	60 c. grey and light grey	3·75	5·00
454	–	80 c. green and buff	9·00	70·00
455	–	1 f. blue and buff	11·00	75·00
456	–	2 f. brown and buff	40·00	£120
457	–	3 f. green on buff	50·00	50·00
458	–	5 f. brown on buff	£140	£250
459	–	10 f. violet on buff	£180	£100

DESIGNS—As Type **83**: 60 c. Keys; 80 c. Horn of plenty; 1 f. Dove; 2 f. Spade and flowers in ploughed field. 38 × 21 mm: 3 f. Crocuses; 5 f. Clasped hands; 10 f. Aged couple.

1945. Red Cross. As T **82**, but red cross and "5 + 10" in centre of stamp.

460		5 c. + 10 c. green	45	50

85 Silk Weaving

1945. National Fete.

461	**85**	5 c. + 5 c. green and red	75	1·50
462	–	10 c. + 10 c. brown, grey and red	60	40
463	–	20 c. + 10 c. red and buff	75	40
464	–	30 c. + 10 c. blue, grey and red	8·00	20·00

DESIGNS: 10, 20 c. Jura and Emmental farmhouses; 30 c. Timbered house.

86 J. H. Pestalozzi

87 Zoglig Instructional Glider

1946. Birth Bicentenary of J. H. Pestalozzi (educational reformer).

465	**86**	10 c. purple	10	10

1946. Air. Special (Lausanne, Lucerne, Locarno) Flights.

466	**87**	1 f. 50 red and grey	22·00	28·00

88 Cheese-making

89 Chalet in Appenzell

1946. National Fete and Fund for Swiss Citizens Abroad.

467	**88**	5 c. + 5 c. green and red	60	1·75
468	–	10 c. + 10 c. brown, buff and red	40	50
469	**89**	20 c. + 10 c. red and buff	50	50
470	–	30 c. + 10 c. blue, grey and red	5·00	7·50

DESIGNS: 10 c. Chalet in Vaud; 30 c. Chalet in Engadine.

90 Douglas DC-4 Airliner, Statue of Liberty and St. Peter's Cathedral, Geneva

1947. Air. 1st Geneva–New York "Swissair" Flight.

472	**90**	2 f. 50 dp blue, blue & red	12·00	20·00

92 Rorschach Station

1947. National Fete. Professional Education of Invalids and Anti-Cancer Funds. Inscr "I VIII 1947". Arms in red.

473	–	5 c. + 5 c. green	50	1·75
474	**92**	10 c. + 10 c. black & buff	50	60
475	–	20 c. + 10 c. red and buff	60	60
476	–	30 c. + 10 c. blue & grey	5·00	8·00

DESIGNS: 5 c. Platelayers; 20 c. Luen-Castiel station; 30 c. Fluelen station.

93 "Limmat", First Swiss Steam Locomotive

1947. Centenary of Swiss Federal Railways.

477	**93**	5 c. green, yellow & black	30	35
478	–	10 c. black and brown	40	30
479	–	20 c. red, buff and lake	40	30
480	–	30 c. blue, grey & light blue	2·00	2·00

DESIGNS: 10 c. Steam freight locomotive; 20 c. Electric train crossing Melide causeway; 30 c. Railway bridge.

95 Sun of St. Moritz

96 Ice Hockey

1948. 5th Winter Olympic Games.

481	**95**	5 c. + 5 c. brn, yell & grn	50	1·25
482	–	10 c. + 10 c. blue, light blue and brown	65	1·25
483	**96**	20 c. + 10 c. yellow, black and purple	75	1·50
484	–	30 c. + 10 c. black, light blue and blue	2·25	5·50

DESIGN: 10 c. Snow crystals; 30 c. Ski-runner.

97 Johann Rudolf Wettstein

1948. Tercentenary of Treaty of Westphalia and Centenaries of the Neuchatel Revolution and Swiss Federation.

485	**97**	5 c. green and deep green	10	20
486	–	10 c. black and grey	15	10
487	–	20 c. red and pink	20	10
488	–	30 c. blue, grey and brown	60	75

DESIGNS: 10 c. Neuchatel Castle; 20 c. Symbol of Helvetia; 30 c. Symbol of Federal State.

99 Frontier Guard

1948. National Fete and Anti-Tuberculosis Fund. Coat of arms in red.

495	**99**	5 c. + 5 c. green	50	75
496	–	10 c. + 10 c. slate & grey	40	50
497	–	20 c. + 10 c. red and buff	50	60
498	–	30 c. + 10 c. blue & grey	3·00	5·75

DESIGNS: 10 c., 20 c., 30 c. Typical houses in Fribourg, Valais and Ticino respectively.

101 Glider

1949. Air. Special (La Chaux-de-Fonds–St. Gallen–Lugano) Flights.

499	**101**	1 f. 50 purple & yellow	18·00	32·00

102 Posthorn

1949. Centenary of Federal Post.

500	**102**	5 c. yellow, pink & grey	10	20
501	–	20 c. yellow, violet & grey	40	10
502	–	30 c. yellow, brn & grey	70	5·50

DESIGNS: 20 c. Mail coach drawn by five horses; 30 c. Postal motor coach and trailer.

103 Main Motif of U.P.U. Monument, Berne

1949. 75th Anniv of U.P.U.

503	**103**	10 c. green	15	10
504	–	25 c. purple	70	7·00
505	–	40 c. blue	90	1·50

DESIGNS: 25 c. Globe and ribbon; 40 c. Globe and pigeons.

104 Postman

1949. National Fete and Youth Fund. T **104** and designs as T **89**, but dated "I. VIII. 1949". Arms in red.

506	**104**	5 c. + 5 c. purple	40	1·00
507	–	10 c. + 10 c. grn & buff	30	50
508	–	20 c. + 10 c. brn & buff	40	50
509	–	40 c. + 10 c. blue & lt bl	4·00	8·00

DESIGNS—Typical houses in: 10 c. Basel; 20 c. Lucerne; 40 c. Prattigau.

106 High tension Pylons

107 Sitter Viaducts near St. Gall

1949. Landscapes.

510	**106**	3 c. black	4·00	3·50
511	**107**	5 c. orange	30	10
512	–	10 c. green	25	10
513	–	15 c. turquoise	30	10
514a	–	20 c. purple	40	10
515	–	25 c. red	50	10
516	–	30 c. green	60	10
517	–	35 c. brown	85	30
518	–	40 c. blue	3·00	10
519	–	50 c. grey	2·50	10
520	–	60 c. green	7·00	10
521	–	70 c. violet	2·25	25

DESIGNS: 10 c. Mountain cog railway, Rochers de Naye; 15 c. Rotary snowplough; 20 c. Grimsel Reservoir; 25 c. Lake Lugano and Melide railway causeway; 30 c. Verbois hydro-electric power station; 35 c. Alpine road (Val d'Anniviers); 40 c. Rhine harbour, Basel; 50 c. Suspension railway, Santis; 60 c. Railway viaduct, Landswasser; 70 c. Survey mark, Finsteraarhorn.

110 First Federal Postage Stamps

111 Putting the Weight

1950. National Fete, Red Cross Fund and Cent of First Federal Postage Stamps. T **110** and designs, as T **111**, inscr "I. VIII. 1950". Coat of arms in red.

522	**110**	5 c. + 5 c. black	40	55
523	**111**	10 c. + 10 c. grn & grey	1·10	50
524	–	20 c. + 10 c. grn & grey	1·25	65
525	–	30 c. + 10 c. mve & grey	6·50	15·00
526	–	40 c. + 10 c. blue & grey	7·00	8·50

DESIGNS: 20 c. Wrestling; 30 c. Sprinting; 40 c. Rifle-shooting.

112 Arms of Zurich

113 Valaisan Polka

1951. National Fete, Mothers' Fund and 600th Anniv of Zurich. Coat of arms in red.

527	**112**	5 c. + 5 c. black	50	50
528	**113**	10 c. + 10 c. grn & grey	1·25	50
529	–	20 c. + 10 c. grn & grey	1·25	45
530	–	30 c. + 10 c. mve & grey	7·00	12·00
531	–	40 c. + 10 c. blue & grey	6·50	9·00

DESIGNS—As Type **113**: 20 c. Flag-swinging; 30 c. "Hornussen" (game); 40 c. Blowing alphorn.

114 "Telegraph"

1952. Centenary of Swiss Telecommunications.

532	**114**	5 c. orange and yellow	40	25
533	–	10 c. green and pink	50	10
534	–	20 c. mauve and lilac	65	10
535	–	40 c. blue and light blue	3·00	2·75

DESIGNS: 10 c. "Telephone"; 20 c. "Radio"; 40 c. "Television".

115 Arms of Glarus and Zug

116 River Doubs

1952. Pro Patria. Cultural Funds and 600th Anniv of Glarus and Zug joining Confederation.

536	**115**	5 c. + 5 c. red and black	50	60
537	**116**	10 c. + 10 c. green and cream	60	40
538	–	20 c. + 10 c. pur & pink	60	40
539	–	30 c. + 10 c. brn & buff	4·00	6·00
540	–	40 c. + 10 c. bl & lt bl	4·00	5·75

DESIGNS—As T **116**: 20 c. St. Gotthard Lake; 30 c. River Moesa; 40 c. Marjelen Lake.

1953. Pro Patria. Emigrants' Fund and 600th Anniv of Berne joining Confederation.

541		5 c. + 5 c. red and black	50	70
542		10 c. + 10 c. green & cream	40	40
543		20 c. + 10 c. purple and pink	50	40
544		30 c. + 10 c. brown and buff	4·00	7·00
545		40 c. + 10 c. blue & light blue	4·00	6·00

DESIGNS—As T **115**: 5 c. Arms of Berne (inscr "BERN 1353"). As T **116** (inscr "PRO PATRIA 1953"): 10 c. Rapids, R. Reuss; 20 c. Lake Sihl; 30 c. Aqueduct, Bisse; 40 c. Lac Leman.

119 Zurich Airport

1953. Inauguration of Zurich Airport.
546 **119** 40 c. blue, grey and red . 4·75 7·00

120 Alpine Postal Coach and Winter Landscape

1953. For Mobile P.O. Mail.
547 **120** 10 c. yellow, green and emerald 20 10
548 – 20 c. yellow, red and scarlet 20 10
DESIGN: 10 c. Alpine postal coach and summer landscape.

121 Ear of Wheat and Flower 122 Rhine Map and Steering Wheel

1954. Publicity Issue.
549 **121** 10 c. multicoloured 40 10
550 – 20 c. multicoloured . . . 80 10
551 **122** 25 c. green, blue and red . 1·00 2·50
552 – 40 c. blue, yellow & black 2·00 1·50
DESIGNS—HORIZ: 10 c. Type **121** (Agricultural Exhibition, Lucerne); 20 c. Winged spoon (Cooking Exhibition, Berne); 40 c. Football and world map (World Football Championship). VERT: 25 c. Type **122** (50th anniv of navigation of River Rhine).

123 Opening Bars of "Swiss Hymn"

1954. Pro Patria. Youth Fund and Death Centenary of Father Zwyssig (composer of "Swiss Hymn").
553 **123** 5 c. + 5 c. green 40 75
554 – 10 c. + 10 c. grn & turq 60 40
555 – 20 c. + 10 c. purple and cream 60 40
556 – 30 c. + 10 c. brn & buff 3·25 7·00
557 – 40 c. + 10 c. deep blue and blue . . . . 3·50 5·50
DESIGNS: 10 c. Lake Neuchatel; 20 c. Maggia River; 30 c. Taubenloch Gorge Waterfall; Schuss River; 40 c. Lake Sils.

124 Lausanne Cathedral 125 Alphorn Blower

1955. Publicity Issue. Inscr "1955".
558 **124** 5 c. multicoloured . . . 40 10
559 – 10 c. multicoloured . . . 40 10
560 **125** 20 c. brown and red . . . 1·00 10
561 – 40 c. pink, black and blue 3·00 1·25
DESIGNS—HORIZ: 5 c. Type **124** (National Philatelic Exhibition, Lausanne); 10 c. Vaud girl's hat (Vevey Winegrowers' Festival); 40 c. Car steering-wheel (25th International Motor Show, Geneva). VERT: 20 c. Type **125** (Alpine Herdsman and Costume Festival, Interlaken).

126 Federal Institute of Technology, Zurich

1955. Pro Patria. Mountain Population Fund and Centenary of Federal Institute of Technology.
562 **126** 5 c. + 5 c. grey 60 60
563 – 10 c. + 10 c. green and cream 60 40
564 – 20 c. + 10 c. red & pink 60 40
565 – 30 c. + 10 c. brn & buff 3·75 6·00
566 – 40 c. + 10 c. blue and light blue . . . . 3·75 5·50
DESIGNS: 10 c. Grandfey railway viaduct, River Saane; 20 c. Lake Aegeri; 30 c. Lake Grappelensee; 40 c. Lake Bienne.

127 "Road Safety" 128 Fokker F.VIIb/3m and Douglas DC-6 Aircraft

1956. Publicity Issue. Inscr "1956".
567 – 5 c. yellow, black and green 20 25
568 – 10 c. black, green and red 40 10
569 **127** 20 c. multicoloured . . . 70 10
570 **128** 40 c. blue and red . . . . 2·50 80
DESIGNS—HORIZ: 5 c. First postal motor coach (50th anniv of postal motor coach service); 10 c. Electric train emerging from Simplon Tunnel and Stockalper Palace (50th anniv of opening of Simplon Tunnel).
The 40 c. commemorates 25th anniv of Swissair.

129 Rose, Scissors and Tape-measure 130 Printing Machine's Inking Rollers

1956. Pro Patria. Swiss Women's Fund. T **129** and design as T **116** but inscr "PRO PATRIA 1956".
571 **129** 5 c. + 5 c. green 40 75
572 – 10 c. + 10 c. emerald and green 40 40
573 – 20 c. + 10 c. pur & pink 50 50
574 – 30 c. + 10 c. brown and light brown . . . . 3·00 6·00
575 – 40 c. + 10 c. blue and light blue . . . . 3·00 5·00
DESIGNS: 10 c. R. Rhone at St. Maurice; 20 c. Katzensee; 30 c. R. Rhine at Trin; 40 c. Walensee.

1957. Publicity Issue. Inscr "1957".
576 **130** 5 c. multicoloured 15 10
577 – 10 c. brown, grn & turq . 1·75 10
578 – 20 c. grey and red . . . 30 10
579 – 40 c. multicoloured . . . 1·25 80
DESIGNS: 10 c. Electric train crossing bridge (75th anniv of St. Gotthard Railway); 20 c. Civil Defence shield and coat of arms ("Civil Defence"); 40 c. Munatius Plancus, Basel and Rhine (2000th anniv of Basel).
The 5 c. commemorates "Graphic 57" International Exhibition, Lausanne.

131 Shields of Switzerland and the Red Cross 132 "Charity"

1957. Pro Patria. Swiss Red Cross and National Cancer League Funds. Cross in red.
580 **131** 5 c. + 5 c. red and grey 30 60
581 **132** 10 c. + 10 c. pur & grn 40 20
582 20 c. + 10 c. grey & red 40 20
583 30 c. + 10 c. blue & brn 3·25 5·00
584 40 c. + 10 c. brown & bl 3·75 3·75

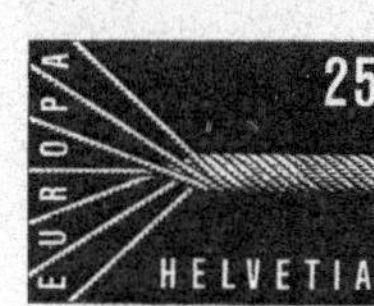

133 Symbol of Unity

1957. Europa.
585 **133** 25 c. red 70 10
586 40 c. blue . . . . 2·25 10

134 Nyon Castle (2000th anniv of Nyon)

1958. Publicity Issue. Inscr "1958".
587 **134** 5 c. violet, buff and green . 20 10
588 – 10 c. myrtle, red and green 20 10
589 – 20 c. red, lilac and vermilion 40 10
590 – 40 c. multicoloured 1·25 75
DESIGNS: 10 c. Woman's head with ribbons (Saffa Exhibition, Zurich); 20 c. Crossbow (25th anniv as symbol of Swiss manufacture); 40 c. Salvation Army bonnet (75th anniv of Salvation Army in Switzerland).

135 "Needy Mother" 136 Fluorite

1958. Pro Patria. For Needy Mothers. T **135** and designs showing minerals, rocks and fossils as T **136**. Inscr "PRO PATRIA 1958".
591 5 c. + 5 c. purple 20 50
592 10 c. + 10 c. yell, grn & blk 30 30
593 20 c. + 10 c. bistre, red & blk 40 30
594 30 c. + 10 c. purple, brn & blk 2·50 4·00
595 40 c. + 10 c. blue, ultram & blk 2·50 3·50
DESIGNS: 20 c. "Lytoceras fimbriatus" ammonite; 30 c. Garnet; 40 c. Rock crystal.

137 Atomic Symbol

1958. 2nd U.N. Atomic Conference, Geneva.
596 **137** 40 c. red, blue and cream . 35 30

138 Modern Transport 139 "Swiss Citizens Abroad"

1959. Publicity Issue. Inscr "1959".
597 5 c. multicoloured 25 10
598 10 c. yellow, grey and green 25 10
599 20 c. multicoloured 55 10
600 50 c. blue, violet & light blue 90 75
DESIGNS: 5 c. Type **138** (opening of "The Swiss House of Transport and Communications"); 10 c. Lictor's fasces of the Coat of Arms of St. Gall and posthorn (NABAG—National Philatelic Exhibition, St. Gall); 20 c. Owl, hare and fish (Protection of Animals); 50 c. J. Calvin, Th. de Beze and University building (4th centenary of University of Geneva).

1959. Pro Patria. For Swiss Citizens Abroad. T **139** and other designs showing minerals, rocks and fossils as T **136**, and inscr "PRO PATRIA 1959".
601 5 c. + 5 c. red and grey . . . 25 50
602 10 c. + 10 c. multicoloured . . 30 35
603 20 c. + 10 c. multicoloured . . 35 35
604 30 c. + 10 c. vio, brn & blk . 2·00 2·75
605 40 c. + 10 c. blue, turquoise and black . . . . 2·00 2·25
DESIGNS: 10 c. Agate; 20 c. Tourmaline; 30 c. Amethyst; 40 c. Fossilized giant salamander.

140 "Europa"

142 "Campaign against Cancer"

1959. Europa.
606 **140** 30 c. red 40 10
607 50 c. blue 40 10

1959. European P.T.T. Conference, Montreux. Optd **REUNION DES PTT D'EUROPE 1959**.
608 **140** 30 c. red . . . . 7·50 7·00
609 50 c. blue . . . . 7·50 7·00

1960. Publicity Issue. Inscr "1460–1960" (20 c.) or "1960" (50 c., 75 c.).
610 10 c. red, light green & green . 45 10
611 20 c. multicoloured 60 10
612 50 c. yellow, ultramarine & blue 75 90
613 75 c. red, black and blue . . . 2·50 2·75
DESIGNS: 10 c. Type **142** (50th anniv of Swiss National League for Cancer Control); 20 c. Charter and sceptre (500th anniv of Basel University); 50 c. "Uprooted tree" (World Refugee Year); 75 c. Douglas DC-8 jetliner ("Swissair enters the jet age").

143 15th-century Schwyz Cantonal Messenger 143a Lausanne Cathedral

1960. Postal History and "Architectural Monuments" (1st series).
614 – 5 c. blue 10 10
615 **143** 10 c. green 10 10
616 – 15 c. red 15 10
617 – 20 c. mauve 20 10
618 **143a** 25 c. green 25 10
619p – 30 c. red 25 10
620 – 35 c. red 50 45
621p – 40 c. purple 35 10
622 – 50 c. blue 50 10
623 – 60 c. red 60 10
624 – 70 c. orange 70 40
625 – 75 c. blue . . . . . . 1·00 25
626p – 80 c. purple 80 15
627p – 90 c. green 80 10
628 – 1 f. orange . . . . . 1·00 10
629 – 1 f. 20 red . . . . . 1·10 10
632 – 1 f. 30 brown on lilac . 1·25 10
630 – 1 f. 50 green . . . . 1·40 25
633 – 1 f. 70 purple on lilac . 1·50 15
631 – 2 f. blue . . . . . . 6·00 65
634 – 2 f. 20 green on green . 2·00 40
635 – 2 f. 80 orange on orge . 2·75 25
DESIGNS—HORIZ: 5 c. 17th-century Fribourg Cantonal messenger; 15 c. 17th-century mule-driver; 20 c. 19th-century mounted postman; 1 f. Fribourg Town Hall; 1 f. 20, Basel Gate, Solothurn; 1 f. 50, Ital Reding's house, Schwyz; 1 f. 70, 2 f., 2 f. 20 Abbey Church, Einsiedeln. VERT: 30 c. Grossmunster, Zurich; 35 c., 1 f. 30, Woodcutters Guildhall, Bienne; 40 c. St. Peter's Cathedral, Geneva; 50 c. Spalentor (gate), Basel; 60 c. Clock Tower, Berne; 70 c. Collegiate Church of St. Peter and St. Stephen, Bellinzona; 75 c. Kapellbrucke (bridge) and Wasserturm, Lucerne; 80 c. St. Gall Cathedral; 90 c. Munot Fort, Schaffhausen; 2 f. 80, as 70 c. but redrawn without bell-tower.
See also Nos. 698/713 and 1276.

144 Symbols of Occupational Trades 144a Conference Emblem

1960. Pro Patria. For Swiss Youth. T **144** and other designs showing minerals, rocks and fossils as T **136** and inscr "PRO PATRIA 1960".
636 – 5 c. + 5 c. multicoloured 60 75
637 – 10 c. + 10 c. pink, green and black 60 25
638 – 20 c. + 10 c. yellow, purple and black 60 25
639 – 30 c. + 10 c. blue, brown and black . . . . . . 3·75 3·75
640 **144** 50 c. + 10 c. gold & blue 3·75 2·75
DESIGNS: 5 c. Smoky quartz; 10 c. Orthoclase (feldspar); 20 c. Devil's toenail (fossil shell); 30 c. Azurite; 50 c. Type **144** ("50 Years of National Day Collection").

1960. Europa.
642 **144a** 30 c. red 40 10
643 50 c. blue 40 10

145 "Aid for Development"

1961. Publicity Issue.
644 **145** 5 c. red, blue and grey . . 25 10
645 – 10 c. yellow and blue . . 25 10
646 – 20 c. multicoloured . . . 70 10
647 – 50 c. red, green and blue . 1·10 90
DESIGNS: 5 c. Type **145** ("Aid to countries in process of development"); 10 c. Circular emblem ("Hyspa" Exhibition of 20th-century Hygiene, Gymnastics and Sport, Berne); 20 c. Hockey stick (World and European Ice Hockey Championships, Geneva and Lausanne); 50 c. Map of Switzerland with telephone centres as wiring diagram (inauguration of Swiss fully automatic telephone service).

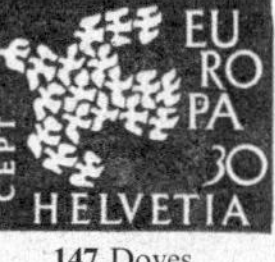

146 "Cultural Works of Eternity" 147 Doves

1961. Pro Patria. For Swiss Cultural Works. T **146** and other designs showing minerals, rocks and fossils as T **136** and inscr "PRO PATRIA 1961".
648 5 c. + 5 c. blue 20 40
649 10 c. + 10 c. purple, green and black 40 30
650 20 c. + 10 c. red, blue and black 50 30
651 30 c. + 10 c. blue, orange and black . . . . 1·50 3·00
652 50 c. + 10 c. bistre, blue and black . . . . 1·75 3·00
DESIGNS: 10 c. Fluorite; 20 c. Petrified fish; 30 c. Lazulite; 50 c. Fossilised fern.

1961. Europa.

653	**147**	30 c. red	40	10
654		50 c. blue	50	10

148 St. Matthew

149 W.H.O. Emblem and Mosquito

1961. Wood Carvings from St. Oswald's Church, Zug.

655	**148**	3 f. red	3·00	10
656	–	5 f. blue	4·50	10
657	–	10 f. brown	7·50	15
658	–	20 f. red	12·00	1·75

DESIGNS: 5 f. St. Mark; 10 f. St. Luke; 20 f. St. John.

1962. Publicity Issue.

659	–	5 c. multicoloured	70	10
660	–	10 c. bistre, purple and green	40	10
661	–	20 c. multicoloured	1·00	10
662	**149**	50 c. green, mauve and blue	90	80

DESIGNS: 5 c. Electric train (introduction of Trans-Europe Express); 10 c. Oarsman (World Rowing Championship, Lucerne); 20 c. Jungfraujoch and Monch (50th anniv of Jungfraujoch Railway Station); 50 c. Type **149** (malaria eradication).

150 Rousseau

151 Obwalden Silver Half-taler

1962. Pro Patria. For Swiss Old People's Homes and Cultural Works.

663	**150**	5 c. + 5 c. blue	20	15
664	**151**	10 c. + 10 c. blue, black and green	25	20
665	–	20 c. + 10 c. yellow, black and red	30	20
666	–	30 c. + 10 c. green, blue and red	90	1·60
667	–	50 c. + 10 c. violet, black and blue	90	1·60

COINS—As Type **151**: 20 c. Schwyz gold ducat; 30 c. Uri batzen; 50 c. Nidwalden batzen.

152 Europa "Tree"

1962. Europa.

668	**152**	30 c. orange, yellow & brn	40	25
669		50 c. blue, green & brown	90	40

153 Campaign Emblem (Freedom from Hunger)

1963. Publicity Issue.

670	–	5 c. brown, red and blue	80	25
671	–	10 c. red, grey and green	40	10
672	–	20 c. lake, red and grey	1·50	10
673	**153**	30 c. yellow, brown & grn	1·50	1·50
674	–	50 c. red, silver and blue	75	60
675	–	50 c. multicoloured	75	60

DESIGNS: No. 670, Boy scout (50th anniv of Swiss Boy Scout League); No. 671, Badge (Swiss Alpine Club cent); No. 672, Luegelkinn Viaduct (50th anniv of Lotschberg Railway); No. 674, Jubilee Emblem (Red Cross cent); No. 675, Hotel des Postes, Paris, 1863 (Paris Postal Conference).

154 Dr. Anna Heer (nursing pioneer)

155 Roll of Bandage

1963. Pro Patria. For Swiss Medical and Refugee Aid. T **154** and other designs as T **155** showing Red Cross activities. Inscr "PRO PATRIA 1963".

676	5 c. + 5 c. blue	20	25
677	10 c. + 10 c. red, grey and green	20	20
678	20 c. + 10 c. multicoloured	35	20
679	30 c. + 10 c. multicoloured	1·25	1·40
680	50 c. + 10 c. red, indigo & bl	1·50	1·25

DESIGNS: 20 c. Gift parcel; 30 c. Blood plasma; 50 c. Red Cross brassard.

156 Glider and Jet Aircraft

1963. Air 25th Anniv of Swiss "Pro Aero" Foundation. Berne–Locarno or Langenbruck–Berne (helicopter feeder) Special Flights.

681	**156**	2 f. multicoloured	5·50	4·00

157 "Co-operation"

158 Exhibition Emblem

1963. Europa.

682	**157**	50 c. brown and blue	60	25

1963. Swiss National Exhibition, Lausanne.

683	**158**	10 c. green and olive	20	10
684		20 c. red and brown	30	10
685	–	50 c. blue, grey and red	40	35
686	–	75 c. violet, grey and red	60	50

DESIGNS: 50 c. "Outlook" (emblem on globe and smaller globe); 75 c. "Insight" (emblem on large globe).

159 Great St. Bernard Tunnel

1964. Publicity Issue.

687	5 c. blue, red and green	20	10
688	10 c. green and blue	25	10
689	20 c. multicoloured	40	10
690	50 c. multicoloured	80	70

DESIGNS: 5 c. Type **159** (Opening of Great St. Bernard Road Tunnel); 10 c. Ancient "god of the waters" (Protection of water supplies); 20 c. Swiss soldiers of 1864 and 1964 (Centenary of Swiss Association of Non-commissioned Officers); 50 c. Standards of Geneva and Swiss Confederation (150th anniv of arrival of Swiss in Geneva).

160 J. G. Bodmer (inventor)

161 Europa "Flower"

1964. Pro Patria. For Swiss Mountain Aid and Cultural Funds. T **160** and vert designs of Swiss coins as T **151**. Inscr "PRO PATRIA 1964".

691	5 c. + 5 c. blue	10	10
692	10 c. + 10 c. drab, blk & grn	20	15
693	20 c. + 10 c. blue, blk & mve	25	20
694	30 c. + 10 c. blue, blk & orge	75	80
695	50 c. + 10 c. yellow, brn & blue	80	80

COINS: 10 c. Zurich copper; 20 c. Basel "doppeldicken"; 30 c. Geneva silver thaler; 50 c. Berne half gold florin.

1964. Europa.

696	**161**	20 c. red	35	10
697		50 c. blue	65	15

1964. "Architectural monuments" (2nd series). As T **143a**.

698	5 c. mauve	10	10
699	10 c. blue	10	10
700	15 c. brown	15	10
701	20 c. green	15	10
702	30 c. red	25	10
703	50 c. blue	40	10
704	70 c. brown	60	10
705	1 f. green	85	10
706	1 f. 20 red	1·00	10
707	1 f. 30 blue	1·50	50
708	1 f. 50 green	1·25	10
709	1 f. 70 red	1·50	75
710	2 f. orange	1·75	15
711	2 f. 20 green	2·75	50
712	2 f. 50 green	2·25	25
713	3 f. 50 purple	3·00	25

DESIGNS—HORIZ: 5 c. Lenzburg Castle; 10 c. Freuler Mansion, Nafels; 15 c. Mauritius Church, Appenzell; 20 c. Planta House, Samedan; 30 c. Town Square, Gais; 50 c. Neuchatel Castle and Collegiate Church. VERT: 70 c. Lussy "Hochhus", Wolfenschiessen; 1 f. Riva San Vitale Church; 1 f. 20, Payerne Abbey Church; 1 f. 30, St. Pierre-de Clages Church; 1 f. 50, Gateway, Porrentruy; 1 f. 70, Frauenfeld Castle; 2 f. Castle Seedorf (Uri); 2 f. 20, Thomas Tower and Arch, Liestal; 2 f. 50, St. Oswald's Church, Zug; 3 f. 50, Benedictine Abbey, Engelberg.

162 Swiss 5 r. Stamp of 1854 with "Lozenge" Cancellation

1965. Publicity Issue.

714	–	5 c. black, red and blue	10	10
715	**162**	10 c. brown, blue & green	10	10
716	–	20 c. multicoloured	20	10
717	–	50 c. red, black and blue	40	35

DESIGNS, etc: 5 c. Nurse and patient ("Nursing"); 10 c. Type **162** ("NABRA 1965" National Stamp Exhibition, Berne); 20 c. WAC Officer (25th anniv of Women's Army Corps); 50 c. World telecommunications map (centenary of I.T.U.).

163 Father T. Florentini

164 Fish-tailed Goose ("Evil")

1965. Pro Patria. For Swiss Abroad and Art Research. Inscr "PRO PATRIA 1965".

719	**163**	5 c. + 5 c. blue	10	10
720	**164**	10 c. + 10 c. multicoloured	10	10
721	–	20 c. + 10 c. multicoloured	15	10
722	–	30 c. + 10 c. brown & blue	30	35
723	–	50 c. + 10 c. blue & brown	50	40

DESIGNS—As Type **164**: (Ceiling paintings in St. Martin's Church, Zillis (Grisons): 20 c. One of the magi journeying to Herod; 30 c. Fishermen; 50 c. The Temptation of Christ.

165 Swiss Emblem and Arms of Cantons

1965. 150th Anniv of Entry of Valais, Neuchatel and Geneva into Confederation.

724	**165**	20 c. multicoloured	25	10

166 Matterhorn

167 Europa "Sprig"

1965. Mobile P.O. Issue.

725	**166**	10 c. multicoloured	20	10
726		30 c. multicoloured	50	50

The 30 c. is inscr "CERVIN".

1965. Europa.

727	**167**	50 c. green and blue	45	20

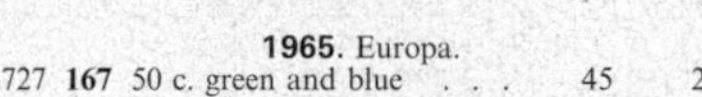

168 I.T.U. Emblem and Satellites

1965. I.T.U. Centenary Congress, Montreux. Multicoloured.

728	10 c. Type **168**	10	10
729	30 c. Symbols of world telecommunications	35	25

169 Figure Skating

1965. World Figure Skating Championships. Davos.

730	**169**	5 c. multicoloured	10	10

170 Common Kingfisher

171 H. Federer (author)

1966. Publicity Issue. Multicoloured.

731	10 c. Type **170**	25	10
732	20 c. Mercury's helmet and laurel twig	15	10
733	50 c. Phase in nuclear fission and flags	40	35

PUBLICITY EVENTS: 10 c. Preservation of natural beauty; 20 c. 50th Swiss Industrial Fair, Basel (MUBA); 50 c. International Institute for Nuclear Research (CERN).

1966. Pro Patria. For Aid to Mothers. Inscr "PRO PATRIA 1966".

734	**171**	5 c. + 5 c. blue	10	10
735	–	10 c. + 10 c. multicoloured	10	10
736	–	20 c. + 10 c. multicoloured	20	10
737	–	30 c. + 10 c. multicoloured	30	30
738	–	50 c. + 10 c. multicoloured	50	45

DESIGNS—As Type **164**: ("The Flight to Egypt" from ceiling paintings in St. Martin's Church, Zillis (Grisons)) 10 c. Joseph's dream; 20 c. Joseph on his way; 30 c. Virgin and Child; 50 c. Angel pointing the way.

172 Society Emblem

173 Europa "Ship"

1966. 50th Anniv of New Helvetic Society for Swiss Abroad.

739	**172**	20 c. red and blue	15	10

1966. Europa.

740	**173**	20 c. red	20	10
741		50 c. blue	45	15

174 Finsteraarhorn

1966. "Swiss Alps".

742	**174**	10 c. multicoloured	10	10

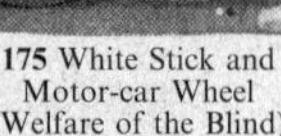

175 White Stick and Motor-car Wheel (Welfare of the Blind)

176 C.E.P.T. Emblem and Cogwheels

1967. Publicity Issue.

743	**175**	10 c. multicoloured	15	10
744	–	20 c. multicoloured	20	10

DESIGN: 20 c. Flags of European Free Trade Area countries (abolition of E.F.T.A. tariffs).

1967. Europa.

745	**176**	30 c. blue	25	10

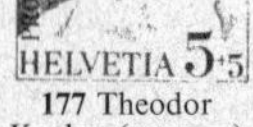

177 Theodor Kocher (surgeon)

178 Cogwheel and Swiss Emblem

1967. Pro Patria. For National Day Collection. Inscr "PRO PATRIA 1967".

746	**177**	5 c. + 5 c. blue	10	10
747	–	10 c. + 10 c. multicoloured	10	10
748	–	20 c. + 10 c. multicoloured	20	10
749	–	30 c. + 10 c. multicoloured	30	30
750	–	50 c. + 10 c. multicoloured	50	50

DESIGNS—As Type **164**: (Ceiling paintings in St. Martin's Church, Zillis (Grisons): 10 c. Annunciation to the Shepherds; 20 c. Christ and the woman of Samaria; 30 c. Adoration of the Magi; 50 c. Joseph seated on throne.

1967. Publicity Issue. Multicoloured.
751 10 c. Type **178** 10 10
752 20 c. Hour-glass and Sun . . . 15 10
753 30 c. San Bernadino highway . 25 10
754 50 c. "OCTI" emblem 40 35
PUBLICITY EVENTS: 10 c. 50th anniv of Swiss Week; 20 c. 50th anniv of Aged People Foundation; 30 c. Opening of San Bernardino road tunnel; 50 c. 75th anniv of Central Office for International Railway Transport (OCTI).

179 "Mountains" and Swiss Emblem

1968. Publicity Issue.
755 10 c. multicoloured 10 10
756 20 c. yellow, brown and blue . 20 10
757 30 c. blue, ochre and brown . 35 10
758 50 c. red, turquoise and blue . 45 35
DESIGNS AND EVENTS: 10 c. T **179** (50th anniv of Swiss Women's Alpine Club); 20 c. Europa "key" (Europa); 30 c. Staunton rook and chessboard (18th Chess Olympiad, Lugano); 50 c. Dispatch "satellites" and aircraft tail-fin (inauguration of new Geneva Air Terminal).

180 "Maius" **181** Protective helmet

1968. Pro Patria. For National Day Collection. Inscr "PRO PATRIA 1968".
759 **180** 10 c. + 10 c. multicoloured 10 10
760 – 20 c. + 10 c. multicoloured 20 10
761 – 30 c. + 10 c. multicoloured 30 15
762 – 50 c. + 20 c. multicoloured 50 50
DESIGNS (Stained-glass panels in the rose window, Lausanne Cathedral): 20 c. "Leo"; 30 c. "Libra"; 50 c. "Pisces" (symbols of the months and signs of the zodiac).

1968. Publicity Issue. Multicoloured.
763 10 c. Type **181** 10 10
764 20 c. Geneva and Zurich stamps of 1843 . . . . 30 10
765 30 c. Part of Swiss map . . . 25 10
766 50 c. "Six Stars" (countries) and anchor 45 35
PUBLICITY EVENTS: 10 c. 50th anniv of Swiss Accident Insurance Company; 20 c. 125th anniv of Swiss stamps; 30 c. 25th anniv of Swiss Territorial Planning Society; 50 c. Centenary of Rhine Navigation Act.

182 Guide Camp and Emblem

1969. Publicity Issue. Multicoloured.
767 10 c. Type **182** 25 10
768 20 c. Pegasus constellation . . 40 10
769 30 c. Emblem of Comptoir Suisse 25 10
770 50 c. Emblem of Gymnaestrade 40 40
771 2 f. Haefeli DH-3 biplane and Douglas DC-8 jetliner . . . 1·75 1·40
EVENTS: 10 c. 50th anniv of Swiss Girl Guides' Federation; 20 c. Opening of first Swiss Planetarium, Lucerne; 30 c. 50th anniv of Comptoir Suisse, Lausanne; 50 c. 5th Gymnaestrada, Basel; 2 f. 50th anniv of Swiss Airmail Services.

183 Colonnade **184** "St. Francis of Assisi preaching to the Birds" (Abbey-church, Konigsfelden)

1969. Europa.
772 **183** 30 c. multicoloured . . . 25 10
773 50 c. multicoloured . . . 45 35

1969. Pro Patria. For National Day Collection. Stained-glass Windows. Multicoloured.
774 10 c. + 10 c. Type **184** . . . 10 15
775 20 c. + 10 c. "The People of Israel drinking" (Berne Cathedral) 20 15
776 30 c. + 10 c. "St. Christopher" (Laufelfingen Church, Basle) 30 20
777 50 c. + 20 c. "Madonna and Child" (St. Jacob's Chapel, Grapplang, Flums) 50 50

185 Kreuzberge **186** Huldrych Zwingli (Protestant reformer)

1969. Publicity and "Swiss Alps" Issues. Multicoloured.
778 20 c. Type **185** 25 10
779 30 c. Children crossing road 25 10
780 50 c. Hammersmith 45 35
EVENTS: 30 c. Road Safety campaign for children; 50 c. 50th anniv of I.L.O.

1969. Swiss Celebrities.
781 **186** 10 c. violet 15 10
782 – 20 c. green 20 10
783 – 30 c. red 30 10
784 – 50 c. blue 50 50
785 – 80 c. brown 75 60
CELEBRITIES: 20 c. General Henri Guisan; 30 c. Francesco Borromini (architect); 50 c. Othmar Schoeck (composer); 80 c. Germaine de Stael (writer).

187 Telex Tape **188** "Flaming Sun"

1970. Publicity Issue. Multicoloured.
786 20 c. Type **187** 20 10
787 30 c. Fireman saving child . . 40 10
788 30 c. "Chained wing" emblem 25 10
789 50 c. U.N. emblem 30 45
790 80 c. New U.P.U. Headquarters 80 70
EVENTS: 20 c. 75th anniv of Swiss Telegraphic Agency; 30 c. (No. 787), Centenary of Swiss Firemen's Assn; 30 c. (No. 788), 50th anniv of "Pro Infirmis" Foundation; 50 c. 25th anniv of U.N. Organization; 80 c. Inauguration of new U.P.U. headquarters, Berne.

1970. Europa.
791 **188** 30 c. red 30 10
792 50 c. blue 50 30

1970. Pro Patria. For National Day Collection. Glass paintings by contemporary artists. As T **184** but inscr "1970". Multicoloured.
793 10 c. + 10 c. "Sailor" (G. Casty) 15 15
794 20 c. + 10 c. Architectonic composition (Celestino Piatti) 20 20
795 30 c. + 10 c. "Bull" symbol of Marduk, from "The Four Elements" (Hans Stocker) 30 15
796 50 c. + 20 c. "Man and Woman" (Max Hunziker and Karl Ganz) 50 55

189 Footballer (75th Anniv of Swiss Football Association) **190** Numeral

1970. Publicity and "Swiss Alps" (30 c.) Issue. Multicoloured.
797 10 c. Type **189** 30 10
798 20 c. Census form and pencil (Federal Census) 20 10
799 30 c. Piz Palu, Grisons 30 10
800 50 c. Conservation Year Emblem (Nature Conservation Year) 45 40

1970. Coil Stamps.
801 **190** 10 c. red 10 10
802 20 c. green 20 10
803 50 c. blue 40 25

191 Female Gymnasts ("Youth and Sport") **193** Europa Chain

1971. Publicity Issue.
804 **191** 10 c. multicoloured . . . 20 20
805 – 10 c. multicoloured . . . 20 20
806 – 20 c. multicoloured . . . 20 10
807 – 30 c. multicoloured . . . 25 10
808 – 50 c. brown and blue . . 45 35
809 – 80 c. multicoloured . . . 75 60
DESIGNS AND EVENTS: 10 c. (No. 805), Male athletes ("Youth and Sport" constitutional amendment); 20 c. Stylized rose (child welfare); 30 c. "Rayon II" stamp of 1850 and basilisk ("NABA" Philatelic Exhibition, Basel); 50 c. "Co-operation" symbol (aid for technical development); 80 c. "Intelsat 4" (I.T.U. Space Conference).

1971. Europa.
811 **193** 30 c. yellow and mauve . . 30 10
812 50 c. yellow and blue . . . 50 25

1971. Pro Patria. For National Day Collection. Contemporary Glass Paintings. As T **184**.
813 10 c. + 10 c. "Religious Abstract", (J. F. Comment) . 20 15
814 20 c. + 10 c. "Cockerel", (J. Prahin) 30 20
815 30 c. + 10 c. "Fox", (K. Volk) 40 20
816 50 c. + 20 c. "Christ's Passion" (B. Schorderet) 65 55

194 "Telecommunications Services" (50th anniv of Radio-Suisse) **195** Alexandre Yersin (bacteriologist)

1971. Publicity and "Swiss Alps" (30 c.).
817 – 30 c. purple, grey & mve . 30 10
818 **194** 40 c. multicoloured 40 35
DESIGN: 30 c. Les Diablerets, Vaud.

1971. Famous Physicians.
819 **195** 10 c. green 10 10
820 – 20 c. green 20 10
821 – 30 c. red 30 10
822 – 40 c. blue 60 60
823 – 80 c. purple 80 70
PHYSICIANS: 20 c. Auguste Forel (psychiatrist); 30 c. Jules Gonin (opthalmologist); 40 c. Robert Koch (German bacteriologist); 80 c. Frederick Banting (Canadian physiologist).

196 Warning Triangle and Wrench (75th Annivs of Motoring Organisations)

1972. Publicity Issue.
824 **196** 10 c. multicoloured 15 10
825 – 20 c. multicoloured 30 10
826 – 30 c. orge, red & carmine . 30 10
827 – 40 c. violet, green & blue . 50 35
DESIGNS AND EVENTS: 20 c. Signal-box switch-table (125th anniv of Swiss Railways); 30 c. Stylized radio waves and girl's face (50th anniv of Swiss Broadcasting); 40 c. Symbolic tree (50th "Swiss Citizens Abroad" Congress).

197 Swissair Boeing 747-100 Jetliner **198** "Communications"

1972. Air. Pro Aero Foundation and 50th Annivs of North Atlantic and Int Airmail Services.
828 **197** 2 f. + 1 f. multicoloured . 2·50 2·25

1972. Europa.
829 **198** 30 c. multicoloured 30 10
830 40 c. multicoloured 45 20

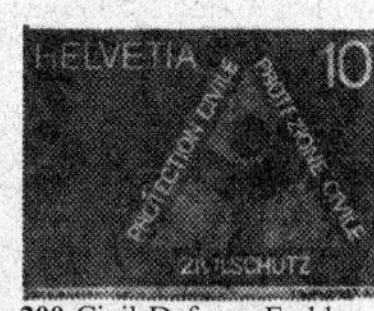

199 Late Stone Age Harpoon Heads **200** Civil Defence Emblem

1972. Pro Patria. For National Day Collection. Archaeological Discoveries (1st series). Mult.
831 10 c. + 10 c. Type **199** 25 20
832 20 c. + 10 c. Bronze water-vessel, c. 570 B.C. 35 20
833 30 c. + 10 c. Gold bust of Marcus Aurelius, 2nd cent A.D. 45 25
834 40 c. + 20 c. Alemannic disc. 7th-cent A.D. . . . . 1·00 90
See also Nos. 869/72, 887/90 and 901/4.

1972. Publicity and "Swiss Alps" (20 c.) Issue. Mult.
835 10 c. Type **200** 10 10
836 20 c. Spannorter 30 10
837 30 c. Sud Aviation Alouette III rescue helicopter 35 10
838 40 c. The "Four Elements" (53 × 31 mm) 50 40
SUBJECTS: 10 c. Swiss Civil Defence; 20 c. Tourism; 30 c. Swiss Air Rescue Service; 40 c. Protection of the environment.

201 Alberto Giacometti (painter) **202** Dish Aerial

1972. Swiss Celebrities.
839 **201** 10 c. black and buff . . . 10 10
840 – 20 c. black and bistre . . 15 10
841 – 30 c. black and pink . . . 25 10
842 – 40 c. black and blue . . . 50 45
843 – 80 c. black and purple . . 75 75
PORTRAITS: 20 c. Charles Ramuz (novelist); 30 c. Le Corbusier (architect); 40 c. Albert Einstein (physicist); 80 c. Arthur Honegger (composer).

1973. Publicity Issue. Multicoloured.
844 15 c. Type **202** 25 15
845 30 c. Quill pen 25 10
846 40 c. Interpol emblem 45 35
EVENTS: 15 c. Construction of Satellite Earth Station, Leuk-Brentjong; 30 c. Centenary of Swiss Association of Commercial Employees; 40 c. 50th anniv of International Criminal Police Organisation (Interpol).

203 Sottoceneri **204** Toggenburg Inn Sign

1973.
847 **203** 5 c. blue and stone . . . 15 10
848 – 10 c. green and purple . . 15 10
849 – 15 c. blue and orange . . 15 10
850 – 25 c. violet and green . . 20 10
851 – 30 c. violet and red . . . 25 10
852 – 35 c. violet and orange . 35 20
853 – 40 c. grey and blue . . . 40 10
854 – 50 c. green and orange . . 50 10
855 – 60 c. brown and grey . . 60 10
856 – 70 c. green and purple . . 70 10
857 – 80 c. red and green . . . 80 10
858 – 1 f. purple 95 10
859 – 1 f. 10 blue . . . . . . 1·00 10
860 – 1 f. 20 red . . . . 1·10 1·00
861 **204** 1 f. 30 orange . . . . . 1·40 20
862 – 1 f. 50 green . . . . . . 1·40 10
863 – 1 f. 70 grey . . . . . . 1·60 25
864 – 1 f. 80 red . . . . 1·75 15
865 – 2 f. blue . . . . 2·00 10
866 – 2 f. 50 brown . . . . . . 2·50 25
866a – 3 f. red . . . . 3·00 30
866b – 3 f. 50 green . . . . . . 3·00 55
DESIGNS—VERT: 10 c. Grisons; 15 c. Central Switzerland; 25 c. Jura; 30 c. Simmental; 35 c. Houses, Central Switzerland; 40 c. Vaud; 50 c. Valais; 60 c. Engadine; 70 c. Sopraceneri; 80 c. Eastern Switzerland. HORIZ: 1 f. Rose window, Lausanne Cathedral; 1 f. 10, Gallus portal, Basel Cathedral; 1 f. 20, Romanesque capital, St.-Jean-Baptiste Church, Grandson; 1 f. 50, Medallion, St. Georgen Monastery, Stein am Rhein; 1 f. 70, Roman Capital, St.-Jean-Baptiste Church, Grandson; 1 f. 80, Gargoyle, Berne Cathedral; 2 f. Oriel, Schaffhausen; 2 f. 50, Weathercock, St. Ursus Cathedral, Solothurn; 3 f. Font, St. Maurice Church, Saanen; 3 f. 50, Astronomical clock, Berne.

205 Europa "Posthorn"

1973. Europa.
867 **205** 25 c. yellow and red . . . 25 20
868 40 c. yellow and blue . . 40 25

1973. Pro Patria. For National Day Collection. Archaeological Discoveries (2nd series). As T **199**, but horiz. Multicoloured.
869 15 c. + 5 c. Rauraric jar . . 20 20
870 30 c. + 10 c. Head of a Gaul (bronze) 35 20
871 40 c. + 20 c. Almannic "Fish" brooches 70 65
872 60 c. + 20 c. Gold bowl . . . 90 95

206 Horological Emblem

1973. Publicity Issue. Multicoloured.

873 15 c. Type **206** 20 10
874 30 c. Skiing emblem 30 10
875 40 c. Face of child 45 30

SUBJECTS: 15 c. Inaug (1974) of Int Horological Museum, Neuchatel; 30 c. World Alpine Skiing Championships, St. Moritz (1974); 40 c. "Terre des Hommes" (Child-care organisation).

207 Global Hostels **209** "Continuity" (Max Bill)

1974. Publicity Issue. Multicoloured.

876 15 c. Type **207** 20 10
877 30 c. Gymnast and hurdlers 35 10
878 40 c. Pistol and target 60 40

SUBJECTS: 15 c. "50 Years of Swiss Youth Hostels"; 30 c. Centenary of Swiss Workmen's Gymnastics and Sports Assn (S.A.T.U.S.); 40 c. World Shooting Championships, 1974.

1974. Europa. Swiss Sculptures.

880 **209** 30 c. black and red 30 10
881 – 40 c. brown, blue & black 45 35

DESIGN: 40 c. "Amazone" (Carl Burckhardt).

210 Eugene Borel (first Director of International Bureau, U.P.U.) **211** View of Berne

1974. Centenary of U.P.U.

882 **210** 30 c. black and pink 25 10
883 – 40 c. black and grey 40 35
884 – 80 c. black and green 75 70

DESIGNS: 40 c. Heinrich von Stephan (founder of U.P.U.); 80 c. Montgomery Blair (U.S. Postmaster-General and initiator of 1863 Paris Postal Conference.

1974. 17th U.P.U. Congress, Lausanne. Mult.

885 30 c. Type **211** 30 25
886 30 c. View of Lausanne 30 25

1974. Pro Patria. For National Day Collection. Archaeological Discoveries (3rd series). As T **199** but horiz. Multicoloured.

887 15 c. + 5 c. Glass bowl 25 20
888 30 c. + 10 c. Bull's head (bronze) 40 15
889 40 c. + 20 c. Gold brooch 75 65
890 60 c. + 20 c. "Bird" vessel (clay) 1·00 95

212 "Oath of Allegiance" (sculpture) (W. Witschi)

1974. Publicity Issue.

891 **212** 15 c. deep green, green and lilac 15 10
892 – 30 c. multicoloured 25 10
893 – 30 c. multicoloured 25 10

EVENTS AND COMMEMORATIONS: No. 891, Centenary of Federal Constitution; No. 892, Foundation emblem (Aid for Swiss Sport Foundation); No. 893, Posthorn and "postal transit" arrow (125th anniv of Federal Posts).

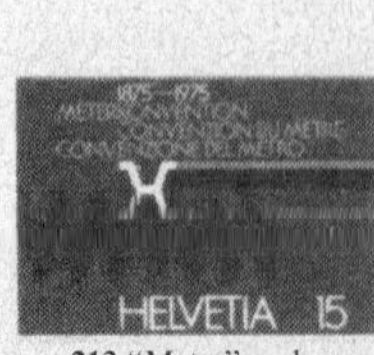

213 "Metre" and Krypton Line **214** "The Monch" (F. Hodler)

1975. Publicity Issue.

894 **213** 15 c. orange, blue & grn 30 10
895 – 30 c. brown, purple & yell 30 10
896 – 60 c. red, black and blue 60 45
897 – 90 c. multicoloured 1·10 70

DESIGNS AND EVENTS: 15 c. Centenary of International Metre Convention; 30 c. Heads of women (International Women's Year); 60 c. Red Cross flag and barbed-wire (Conference on Humanitarian International Law, Geneva); 90 c. Astra airship "Ville de Lucerne", 1910 ("Aviation and Space Travel" Exhibition, Transport and Communications Museum, Lucerne).

1975. Europa. Paintings. Multicoloured.

898 30 c. Type **214** 30 10
899 50 c. "Still Life with Guitar" (R. Auberjonois) 50 40
900 60 c. "L'effeuilleuse" (M. Barraud) 60 50

1975. Pro Patria. Archaeological Discoveries. (4th series). As T **199**. Multicoloured.

901 15 c. + 10 c. Gold brooch, Oron-le-Chatel 30 25
902 30 c. + 20 c. Bronze head of Bacchus, Avenches 50 30
903 50 c. + 20 c. Bronze daggers, Bois-de-Vaux, Lausanne 85 75
904 60 c. + 25 c. Glass decanter, Maralto 1·00 80

215 "Eliminate Obstacles!"

1975. Publicity Issue.

905 **215** 15 c. black, green & lilac 15 10
906 – 30 c. black, rosine and red 25 10
907 – 50 c. brown and bistre 50 45
908 – 60 c. multicoloured 60 45

DESIGNS: 30 c. Organization emblem (Inter-confessional Pastoral Care by Telephone Organization); 50 c. European Architectural Heritage Year emblem; 60 c. Beat Fischer von Reichenbach (founder) (300th anniv of Fischer postal service).

216 Forest Scene (Federal Forest Laws Cent) **217** Floral Embroidery

1976. Publicity Issue.

919 **216** 20 c. multicoloured 15 10
910 – 40 c. multicoloured 30 10
911 – 40 c. black, orange & pur 30 10
912 – 80 c. black and blue 75 60

DESIGNS: No. 910, Fruit and vegetables (campaign to promote nutriments as opposed to alcohol); No. 911, African child (fight against leprosy); No. 912, Early and modern telephones (telephone centenary).

1976. Europa. Handicrafts.

913 **217** 40 c. yellow, brn & pink 35 10
914 – 80 c. blue, red and stone 70 55

DESIGN: 80 c. Decorated pocket watch.

218 Kyburg Castle, Zurich **219** Roe Deer Fawn, Barn Swallow and Frog (World Fed. for Protection of Animals)

1976. Pro Patria. Swiss Castles (1st series). Multicoloured.

915 20 c. + 10 c. Type **218** 40 30
916 40 c. + 20 c. Grandson, Vaud 70 30
917 40 c. + 20 c. Murten, Fribourg 70 30
918 80 c. + 40 c. Bellinzona, Ticino 2·00 1·75

See also Nos. 932/5, 955/8 and 977/80.

1976. Publicity Issue.

919 **219** 20 c. black, brown & grn 50 10
920 – 40 c. black, yellow & red 30 10
921 – 40 c. multicoloured 50 10
922 – 80 c. red, violet and blue 80 70

DESIGNS: No. 920, "Sun" and inscription ("Save Energy" campaign); No. 921, St. Gotthard mountains (Swiss Alps); No. 922, Skater (World Speed Skating Championships, Davos).

220 Oskar Bider and Bleriot XI **221** Blue Cross (society for care of alcoholics, cent)

1977. Swiss Aviation Pioneers.

923 **220** 40 c. black, mauve & red 45 10
924 – 80 c. black, pur and blue 1·10 80
925 – 100 c. black, grn & bistre 1·00 70
926 – 150 c. black, brn & grn 1·75 1·00

DESIGNS: 80 c. Eduard Spelterini and balloon basket; 100 c. Armand Dufaux and Dufaux IV biplane; 150 c. Walter Mittelholzer and Dornier Do-B Merkur seaplane "Switzerland".

1977. Publicity Issues.

927 **221** 20 c. blue and brown 15 10
928 – 40 c. multicoloured 35 10
929 – 80 c. multicoloured 80 75

DESIGNS: 40 c. Festival emblem (Vevey vintage festival); 80 c. Balloons carrying letters ("Juphilex 1977" youth stamp exhibition, Berne).

222 St. Ursanne

1977. Europa. Landscapes. Multicoloured.

930 40 c. Type **222** 35 10
931 80 c. Sils-Baselgia 65 55

1977. Pro Patria. Swiss Castles (2nd series). As T **218**. Multicoloured.

932 20 c. + 10 c. Aigle, Vaud 30 25
933 40 c. + 20 c. Pratteln, Basel-Landschaft 50 15
934 70 c. + 30 c. Sargans, St. Gallen 1·10 1·25
935 80 c. + 40 c. Hallwil, Aargau 1·50 1·25

223 Factory Worker

1977. Publicity Issue. Multicoloured.

936 20 c. Type **223** 15 10
937 40 c. Ionic capital 35 10
938 80 c. Association emblem and butterfly 75 75

EVENTS: 20 c. Centenary of Federal Factories Act; 40 c. Protection of cultural monuments; 80 c. Swiss Footpaths Association.

224 Sternsingen, Bergun **225** Mailcoach Route Plate, Vaud Canton

1977. Regional Folk Customs.

939 **224** 5 c. green 10 10
940 – 10 c. red 10 10
941 – 20 c. orange 15 10
941b – 25 c. brown 40 15
941c – 30 c. green 35 10
942 – 35 c. green 35 10
943 – 40 c. purple 35 10
943c – 45 c. blue 50 35
944 – 50 c. red 45 10
944b – 60 c. brown 70 40
945 – 70 c. lilac 70 15
946 – 80 c. blue 85 20
947 – 90 c. brown 1·00 25

DESIGNS: 10 c. Sechselauten, Zurich; 20 c. Silvesterklause, Herisau; 25 c. Chesstete, Solothurn; 30 c. Rollelibutzen, Alstatten; 35 c. Gansabhauet, Sursee; 40 c. Escalade, Geneva; 45 c. Klausjagen, Kussnacht; 50 c. Archetringele, Laupen; 60 c. Schnabelgeissen, Ottenbach; 70 c. Processioni storiche, Mendrisio; 80 c. Vogel Gryff, Basel; 90 c. Roitschaggata, Lotschental.

1978. Publicity Issue. Multicoloured.

948 20 c. Type **225** 15 10
949 40 c. View of Lucerne 40 10
950 70 c. Title page of book "Melusine" 65 50
951 80 c. Stylised camera and lens 75 70

EVENTS: 20 c. "Lemanex '78" National Stamp Exhibition; 40 c. 800th anniv of Lucerne; 70 c. 500th anniv of Printing at Geneva; 80 c. 2nd International Triennial Exhibition of Photography, Fribourg.

227 Stockalper Palace, Brig **228** Abbe Joseph Bovet (composer)

1978. Europa.

953 **227** 40 c. multicoloured 35 15
954 – 80 c. blue, brown & black 75 60

DESIGN: 80 c. Old Diet Hall, Berne.

1978. Pro Patria. Swiss Castles (3rd series). As T **218**.

955 20 c. + 10 c. Hagenwil, Thurgau 30 25
956 40 c. + 20 c. Burgdorf, Berne 60 20
957 70 c. + 30 c. Tarasp, Graubunden 1·10 1·25
958 80 c. + 40 c. Chillon, Vaud 1·50 1·25

1978. Celebrities.

959 **228** 20 c. green 20 10
960 – 40 c. purple 40 10
961 – 70 c. grey 65 50
962 – 80 c. blue 80 50

DESIGNS: 40 c. Henri Dunant (founder of Red Cross); 70 c. Carl Gustav Jung (psychiatrist); 80 c. Auguste Piccard (physicist).

229 Worker wearing Goggles

1978. Safety at Work. Multicoloured.

963 40 c. Type **229** 40 15
964 40 c. Worker wearing respirator 40 15
965 40 c. Worker wearing safety helmet 40 15

230 Arms of Switzerland and Jura

1978. Creation of Canton of Jura.

966 **230** 40 c. red, black & stone 40 10

231 Rainer Maria Rilke (writer) **232** Othmar H. Ammann and Verrazano Narrows Bridge

1979. Celebrities.

967 **231** 20 c. green 20 10
968 – 40 c. red 40 10
969 – 70 c. brown 70 50
970 – 80 c. blue 80 50

DESIGNS: 40 c. Paul Klee (artist); 70 c. Herman Hesse (novelist and poet); 80 c. Thomas Mann (novelist).

1979. Publicity Issue. Multicoloured.

971 20 c. Type **232** 20 10
972 40 c. Target and marker 40 10
973 70 c. Hot-air balloon "Esperanto" 75 60
974 80 c. Aircraft tail fins 85 70

SUBJECTS: 20 c. Birth centenary of O. H. Ammann (engineer); 40 c. 50th Federal Riflemen's Festival, Lucerne; 70 c. World Esperanto Congress, Lucerne; 80 c. Basel-Mulhouse Airport.

233 Old Letter Box, Basel **234** Gold Stater

1979. Europa.

975 **233** 40 c. multicoloured 40 15
976 – 80 c. blue, lt blue & stone 85 70

DESIGN: 80 c. Alpine relay station on the Jungfraujoch.

1979. Pro Patria. Swiss Castles (4th series). As T **218**. Multicoloured.

977 20 c. + 10 c. Oron, Vaud 30 30
978 40 c. + 20 c. Spiez, Berne 50 20
979 70 c. + 30 c. Porrentruy, Jura 1·00 1·00
980 80 c. + 40 c. Rapperswil, St. Gallen 1·40 1·40

1979. Publicity Issue. Multicoloured.

981 20 c. Type **234** 20 15
982 40 c. Child on dove (horiz) 40 15
983 70 c. Morse key and satellite (horiz) 70 60
984 80 c. "Ariane" rocket 80 70

EVENTS: 20 c. Centenary of Swiss Numismatic Society; 40 c. International Year of the Child; 70 c. 50th anniv of Swiss Radio Amateurs; 80 c. European Space Agency.

MINIMUM PRICE

The minimum price quoted is 10p which represents a handling charge rather than a basis for valuing common stamps. For further notes about prices, see introductory pages.

235 Tree in Blossom **236** Johann Konrad Kern (politician)

1980. Publicity Issue. Multicoloured.
985 20 c. Type **235** 20 10
986 40 c. Carved milk vessel . . . 40 10
987 70 c. Winterthur Town Hall . 70 50
988 80 c. Pic-Pic motor car 85 65
SUBJECTS: 20 c. Horticultural and Landscape Gardening Exhibition, Basel; 40 c. 50th anniv of Arts and Crafts Centre; 70 c. Centenary of Society for Swiss Art History; 80 c. 50th International Motor Show, Geneva.

1980. Europa.
989 **236** 40 c. flesh, black & pink . 40 10
990 – 80 c. flesh, black & blue . 80 60
DESIGN: 80 c. Gustav Adolf Hasler (communications pioneer).

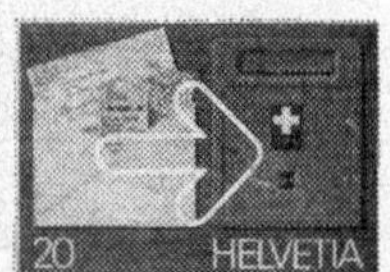

237 Mason and Carpenter **238** Girocheque and Letter Box

1980. Pro Patria. Trade and Craft Signs. Mult.
991 20 c. + 10 c. Type **237** . . . 30 30
992 40 c. + 20 c. Barber 50 20
993 70 c. + 30 c. Hatter . . . . . 1·00 1·10
994 80 c. + 40 c. Baker . . . . . 1·25 1·25

1980. Swiss P.T.T. Services.
995 **238** 20 c. multicoloured . . . 20 15
996 – 40 c. multicoloured . . . 40 15
997 – 70 c. brown, blk & lilac . 70 60
998 – 80 c. multicoloured . . . 1·00 80
DESIGNS: 40 c. Postbus; 70 c. Transfer roller (50th anniv of P.T.T. postage stamp printing office); 80 c. Flowers and telephone (centenary of telephone in Switzerland).

239 Weather Chart

1980. Publicity Issue. Multicoloured.
999 20 c. Type **239** 20 10
1000 40 c. Figures and cross . . . 40 10
1001 80 c. Motorway sign . . . . 1·10 90
SUBJECTS: 20 c. Centenary of Swiss Meteorological Office; 40 c. Centenary of Swiss Trades Union Federation; 80 c. Opening of St. Gotthard road tunnel.

240 Granary from Kiesen

1981. Publicity Issue. Multicoloured.
1002 20 c. Type **240** 20 10
1003 40 c. Disabled figures 40 10
1004 70 c. "The Parish Clerk" (Albert Anker) (vert) 70 70
1005 80 c. Theodolite and rod . . 75 55
1006 110 c. Tail of DC9-81 . . . . 1·10 85
SUBJECTS: 20 c. Ballenberg Open-air Museum; 40 c. International Year of Disabled Persons; 70 c. 150th birth anniv of Albert Anker (artist); 80 c. 16th International Federation of Surveyors Congress, Montreux; 110 c. 50th anniv of Swissair.

241 Figure leaping from Earth **242** Dancing Couple

1981. 50th Anniv of Swissair.
1007 **241** 2 f. + 1 f. lilac, violet and yellow . . . . 2·25 2·00

1981. Europa. Multicoloured.
1008 40 c. Type **242** 35 10
1009 80 c. Stone putter 90 70

243 Aarburg Post Office Sign, 1685 **244** Seal of Fribourg

1981. Pro Patria. Postal Signs. Multicoloured.
1010 20 c. + 10 c. Type **243** . . . 30 30
1011 40 c. + 20 c. Mail coach sign of Fribourg Cantonal Post . . . 50 20
1012 70 c. + 30 c. Gordola Post office sign (Ticino Cantonal Post) 90 95
1013 80 c. + 40 c. Splugen post office sign . . . . 1·10 1·10

1981. 500th Anniv of Covenant of Stans.
1014 **244** 40 c. red, black & brown 35 15
1015 – 40 c. green, black & purple 35 15
1016 – 80 c. brown, black & bl 85 60
DESIGNS: 40 c. (No. 1015) Seal of Solothurn; 80 c. Old Town Hall, Stans.

245 Voltage Regulator from Jungfrau Railway's Power Station

1981. Publicity Issue. Multicoloured.
1017 20 c. Type **245** 20 10
1018 40 c. Crossbow quality seal . 40 10
1019 70 c. Group of youths . . . 70 60
1020 1 f. 10 Mosaic . . . . 1·00 85
SUBJECTS: 20 c. Opening of Technorama of Switzerland, Winterthur (museum of science and technology); 40 c. 50th anniv of Organization for Promotion of Swiss Products and Services; 70 c. 50th anniv of Swiss Association of Youth Organizations; 1 f. 10, Restoration of St. Peter's Cathedral, Geneva.

246 "C 4/5" Class Steam Locomotive

1982. Centenary of St. Gotthard Railway.
1021 **246** 40 c. black and purple . 50 20
1022 – 40 c. multicoloured . . 50 20
DESIGN: No. 1022, "Re 6/6" class electric locomotive.

247 Hoteliers Association Emblem

1982. Publicity Issue. Multicoloured.
1023 20 c. Type **247** 20 10
1024 40 c. Flag formed by four Fs 40 10
1025 70 c. Gas flame encircling emblem 70 50
1026 80 c. Lynx and scientific instruments 90 50
1027 110 c. Retort . . . . 1·10 75
SUBJECTS: 20 c. Centenary of Swiss Hoteliers Association; 40 c. 150th anniv of Swiss Gymnastics Association; 70 c. 50th anniv of International Gas Union; 80 c. 150th anniv of Natural History Museum, Berne; 110 c. Centenary of Swiss Society of Chemical Industries.

248 "Swearing Oath of Eternal Fealty, Rutli Meadow" (detail of mural, Heinrich Danioth)

1982. Europa. Multicoloured.
1028 40 c. Type **248** 60 10
1029 80 c. Treaty of 1291 founding Swiss Confederation . . . 1·00 75

249 "The Sun", Willisau **250** "Aquarius" and Old Berne

1982. Pro Patria. Inn Signs (1st series). Multicoloured.
1030 20 c. + 10 c. Type **249** . . . 40 30
1031 40 c. + 20 c. "On the Wave", St. Saphorin 60 20
1032 70 c. + 30 c. "The Three Kings", Rheinfelden . . . 1·00 1·00
1033 80 c. + 40 c. "The Crown", Winterhur . . . . 1·25 1·00
See also Nos. 1056/9.

1982. Signs of the Zodiac and Landscapes.
1034 **250** 1 f. multicoloured . . . 1·00 10
1035 – 1 f. 10 brown, bl & vio . 1·00 10
1036 – 1 f. 20 green, bl & brn . 1·25 10
1036a – 1 f. 40 multicoloured . . 1·40 1·00
1037 – 1 f. 50 blue, azure and orange . . . . 1·50 15
1038 – 1 f. 60 multicoloured . . 1·75 90
1039 – 1 f. 70 cobalt, brown and blue . . . . 1·75 10
1040 – 1 f. 80 brown, green and deep green . . . . . . 1·75 70
1041 – 2 f. cobalt, brown & blue 2·25 1·75
1042 – 2 f. cobalt, brown & blue 1·75 20
1042a – 2 f. 50, red, green and deep green . . . . 2·40 50
1043 – 3 f. red, green & black 2·75 15
1044 – 4 f. green, violet & pur . 3·75 45
1045 – 4 f. 50 ochre, blue and brown . . . . 4·25 60
DESIGNS: 1 f. 10, "Pisces" and Nax near Sion; 1 f. 20, "Aries" and the Graustock, Obwalden; 1 f. 40, "Gemini" and Bischofszell; 1 f. 50, "Taurus" and Basel Cathedral; 1 f. 60, "Gémini" and Schonengrund; 1 f. 70, "Cancer" and Wetterhorn; 1 f. 80, "Leo" and Areuse Gorge; 2 f. (1041), "Virgo" and Aletsch Glacier; 2 f. (1042), "Virgo" and Schwarzsee above Zermatt; 2 f. 50, "Libra" and Fechy; 3 f. "Scorpio" and Corippo; 4 f. "Sagittarius" and Glarus; 4 f. 50, "Capricorn" and Schuls.

251 Articulated Tram

1982. Publicity Issue. Multicoloured.
1046 20 c. Type **251** 50 15
1047 40 c. Salvation Army singer and guitarist 40 10
1048 70 c. Dressage rider 75 55
1049 80 c. Emblem 80 50
SUBJECTS: 20 c. Centenary of Zurich trams; 40 c. Centenary of Salvation Army in Switzerland; 70 c. World Dressage Championship, Lausanne; 80 c. 14th International Water Supply Association Congress, Zurich.

252 Perch **253** Jost Burgi's Celestial Globe, 1594

1983. Publicity Issue. Multicoloured.
1050 20 c. Type **252** 50 10
1051 40 c. University of Zurich . . 40 10
1052 70 c. Teleprinter tape forming "JP" 70 50
1053 80 c. Micrometer and cycloidal computer drawing 80 50
EVENTS: 20 c. Centenary of Swiss Fishing and Pisciculture Federation; 40 c. 150th anniv of University of Zurich; 70 c. Centenary of Swiss Journalists' Federation; 80 c. Centenary of Swiss Machine Manufacturers' Association.

1983. Europa.
1054 **253** 40 c. orange, pink and brown 40 10
1055 – 80 c. green, blue & blk . 85 60
DESIGN: 80 c. Niklaus Riggenbach's rack and pinion railway, 1871.

1983. Pro Patria. Inn Sings (2nd series). As T **249**. Multicoloured.
1056 20 c. + 10 c. "The Lion", Heimiswil 30 30
1057 40 c. + 20 c. "The Cross", Sachseln 60 20
1058 70 c. + 30 c. "The Jug", Lenzburg Castle . . . . 1·00 95
1059 80 c. + 40 c. "The Cavalier", St. George . . . . 1·25 1·00

254 Seal, 1832–48 **255** Gallo-Roman Capital, Martigny

1983. 150th Anniv of Basel-Land Canton.
1060 **254** 40 c. multicoloured . . . 35 10

1983. Publicity Issue.
1061 **255** 20 c. orange and black . 25 10
1062 – 40 c. multicoloured . . . 45 10
1063 – 70 c. multicoloured . . . 75 60
1064 – 80 c. multicoloured . . 1·00 60
DESIGNS: 20 c. Type **255** (Bimillenary of Octodurus/Martigny); 40 c. Bernese shepherd-dog and Schwyz hunting dog (Centenary of Swiss Kennel Club); 70 c. Cyclists (Centenary of Swiss Cyclists and Motor Cyclists Federation); 80 c. Carrier pigeon and world map (World Communications Year).

256 Pre-stamp Cover, 1839 **257** Bridge

1984. Publicity Issue. Multicoloured.
1065 25 c. Type **256** 40 10
1066 50 c. Collegiate Church clock and buildings 40 10
1067 80 c. Olympic rings and Lausanne 90 50
SUBJECTS: 25 c. National Stamp Exhibition, Zurich; 50 c. 1100th anniv of Saint-Imier; 80 c. Permanent headquarters of International Olympic Committee at Lausanne.

1984. Europa. 25th Anniv of European Posts and Telecommunications Conference.
1068 **257** 50 c. purple, red and crimson 40 10
1069 80 c. ultramarine, blue and deep blue 75 55

258 Hexagonal Stove from Rosenburg Mansion, Stans **260** Burning Match

1984. Pro Patria. Tiled Stoves. Multicoloured.
1070 35 c. + 15 c. Type **258** . . . 50 30
1071 50 c. + 20 c. Winterthur stove (by Hans Heinrich Pfau) Freuler Palace, Nafels . . 70 20
1072 70 c. + 30 c. Box-stove (by Rudolf Stern) from Plaisance, Riaz . . . . 90 1·00
1073 80 c. + 40 c. Frame-modelled stove (by Leonard Racle) . 1·25 1·10

1984. Fire Prevention.
1075 **260** 50 c. multicoloured . . . 40 10

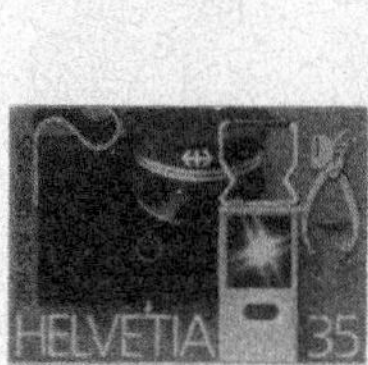

261 Railway Conductor's Equipment **262** Ernest Ansermet (orchestral conductor)

1985. Publicity Issue. Multicoloured.
1076 35 c. Type **261** (cent of Train Staff Association) 40 15
1077 50 c. Stone with Latin inscription (2000 years of Rhaeto-Romanic culture) 50 10
1078 70 c. Rescue of man (cent of International Lake Geneva Rescue Society) 70 60
1079 80 c. Grande Dixence dam (International Large Dams Congress, Lausanne) . . . 80 60

1985. Europa. Music Year. Multicoloured.
1080 50 c. Type **262** 50 10
1081 80 c. Frank Martin (composer) 85 60

263 Music Box, 1895

1985. Pro Patria. Musical Instruments. Mult.
1082 25 c. + 10 c. Type **263** . . . 35 35
1083 35 c. + 15 c. 18th - century box rattle 50 50
1084 50 c. + 20 c. Emmental necked zither (by Peter Zaugg), 1828 65 20
1085 70 c. + 30 c. Drum, 1571 . . 1·00 1·00
1086 80 c. + 40 c. 20th - century diatonic accordion . . . . 1·25 1·00

264 Baker

1985. Publicity Issue. Multicoloured.
1087 50 c. Type **264** (centenary of Swiss Master Bakers' and Confectioners' Federation) 50 10
1088 70 c. Cross on abstract background (50th anniv of Swiss Radio International) 70 60
1089 80 c. Geometric pattern and emblem (Postal, Telegraph and Telephone International World Congress, Interlaken) 80 70

265 Intertwined Ropes

1986. Publicity Issue.
1090 **265** 35 c. multicoloured . . . 35 15
1091 – 50 c. deep brown, brown and red 50 10
1092 – 80 c. orange, green and black 80 60
1093 – 90 c. multicoloured . . . 90 60
1094 – 1 f. 10 multicoloured . . 1·10 95
DESIGNS: 35 c. Type **265** (50th anniv of Swiss Workers' Relief Organization); 50 c. Battle site on 1698 map (600th anniv of Battle of Sempach); 80 c. Statuette of Mercury (2000th anniv of Roman Chur); 90 c. Gallic head (2000th anniv of Vindonissa); 1 f. 10, Roman coin of Augustus (2000th anniv of Zurich).

266 Sportsmen **267** Woman's Head

1986. Pro Sport.
1095 **266** 50 c. + 20 c. multicoloured 80 50

1986. Europa. Multicoloured.
1096 50 c. Type **267** 50 10
1097 90 c. Man's head . . . . 1·00 75

268 "Bridge in the Sun" (Giovanni Giacometti) **269** Franz Mail Van

1986. Pro Patria. Paintings. Multicoloured.
1098 35 c. + 15 c. Type **268** . . . 60 40
1099 50 c. + 20 c. "The Violet Hat" (Cuno Amiet) 80 20
1100 80 c. + 40 c. "After the Funeral" (Max Buri) . . . 1·25 1·25
1101 90 c. + 40 c. "Still Life" (Felix Vallotton) . . . . 1·40 1·25

1986. The Post Past and Present.
1102 **269** 5 c. yellow, purple & red 10 10
1103 – 10 c. deep green, green and orange 10 10
1104 – 20 c. orange, brown & bl 25 15
1105 – 25 c. deep blue, blue and yellow 35 10
1106 – 30 c. grey, black & yell 25 15
1107 – 35 c. lake, red and yellow 40 25
1108 – 45 c. blue, black & brn . 40 20
1109 – 50 c. violet, green & pur 45 10
1110 – 60 c. orange, yell & brn 55 20
1111 – 75 c. grn, dp grn & red . 70 45
1112 – 80 c. indigo, blue & brn 1·00 25
1113 – 90 c. olive, brown & green 1·10 50
DESIGNS: 10 c. Mechanized parcel sorting; 20 c. Mule post; 25 c. Letter cancelling machine; 30 c. Stagecoach; 35 c. Post Office counter clerk; 45 c. Paddle-steamer "Stadt Luzern", 1830s; 50 c. Postman; 60 c. Loading mail bags onto airplane; 75 c. 17th-century mounted courier; 80 c. Town postman, 1900s; 90 c. Interior of railway mail sorting carriage.

270 Stylized Doves (International Peace Year)

1986. Publicity Issue. Multicoloured.
1115 35 c. Type **270** 35 20
1116 50 c. Sun behind snow-covered tree (50th anniv of Swiss Winter Relief Fund) . . . 45 10
1117 80 c. Symbols of literature and art (cent of Berne Convention for protection of literary and artistic copyright) 85 70
1118 90 c. Red Cross, Red Crescent and symbols of aggression (25th Int Red Cross Conference meeting, Geneva) 95 70

271 Mobile Post Office

1987. Publicity Issue. Multicoloured.
1119 35 c. Type **271** (50th anniv of mobile post offices) . . . 45 20
1120 50 c. Lecturers of the seven faculties (450th anniv of Lausanne University) . . 45 10
1121 80 c. Profile, maple leaf and logarithmic spiral (150th anniv of Swiss Engineers' and Architects' Association) . 90 80
1122 90 c. Boeing 747-300/400 jetliner and electric train (Geneva Airport rail link) 1·25 80
1123 1 f. 10 Symbolic figure and water (2000th anniv of Baden thermal springs) . . . . . 1·25 1·25

272 "Scarabaeus" (Bernhard Luginbuhl)

1987. Europa. Sculpture. Multicoloured.
1124 50 c. Type **272** 50 10
1125 90 c. "Carnival Fountain", Basel (Jean Tinguely) . . 1·00 85

273 Wall Cabinet, 1764

1987. Pro Patria. Rustic Furniture. Multicoloured.
1126 35 c. + 15 c. Type **273** . . . 70 50
1127 50 c. + 20 c. 16th-century chest 85 70
1128 80 c. + 40 c. Cradle, 1782 . 1·25 1·40
1129 90 c. + 40 c. Wardrobe, 1698 1·25 1·50

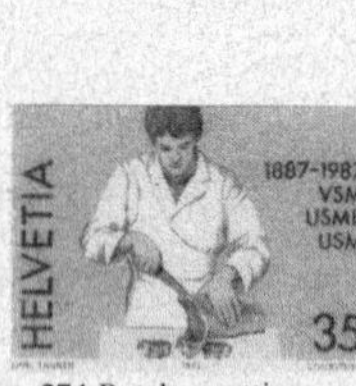

274 Butcher cutting Chops **275** Zug Clock Tower

1987. Publicity Issue. Multicoloured.
1130 35 c. Type **274** (centenary of Swiss Master Butchers' Federation) 40 25
1131 50 c. Profiles on stamps (50th anniv of Stamp Day) . . . 60 10
1132 90 c. Cheesemaker breaking up curds (centenary of Swiss Dairying Association) . . 1·00 90

1987. Bicentenary of Tourism. Multicoloured.
1133 50 c. Type **275** 55 10
1134 80 c. St. Charles's church, Negrentino, Prugiasco/Blenio valley 85 80
1135 90 c. Witches Tower, Sion . 95 80
1136 1 f. 40 Jorgenberg Castle, Waltensburg/Vuorz, Surselva 1·50 1·40

1987. Flood Victims Relief Fund. No. 1109 surch **7.9.87 + 50** and clasped hands.
1138 50 c. + 50 c. vio, grn & pur 1·25 90

277 Society Emblem

1988. Publicity Issue. Multicoloured.
1139 25 c. Type **277** (cent of Swiss Women's Benevolent Society) 35 20
1140 35 c. Brushing woman's hair (centenary of Swiss Master Hairdressers' Association) 40 25
1141 50 c. St. Fridolin banner and detail of Aegidius Tschudy's manuscript (600th anniv of Battle of Naefels) 50 10
1142 80 c. Map and farming country seen from Beromunster radio tower (European Campaign for Rural Areas) 80 80
1143 90 c. Girl playing shawm (50th anniv of Lucerne Int Music Festival) . . . . 1·00 90

278 Junkers Ju 52/3m "Auntie Ju" flying past Matterhorn **279** Rudolf von Neuenburg

1988. 50th Anniv of Pro Aero Foundation.
1144 **278** 140 c. + 60 c. mult . . . 2·75 2·75

1988. Pro Patria. Minnesingers. Multicoloured.
1145 35 c. + 15 c. Type **279** . . . 65 50
1146 50 c. + 20 c. Rudolf von Rotenburg 85 25
1147 80 c. + 40 c. Johannes Hadlaub 1·40 1·40
1148 90 c. + 40 c. Hardegger . . . 1·60 1·40

280 Arrows on Map of Europe **281** Snap Link

1988. Europa. Transport and Communications.
1149 **280** 50 c. bistre, emerald and green 50 10
1150 – 90 c. lilac, green and vio 1·00 80
DESIGN: 90 c. Computer circuit on map of Europe.

1988. Publicity Issue. Multicoloured.
1151 35 c. Type **281** (50th anniv of Swiss Accident Prevention Office) 40 25
1152 50 c. Drilling letters (cent of Swiss Metalworkers' and Watchmakers' Association) 50 10
1153 80 c. Triangulation pyramid, theodolite and map (150th anniv of Swiss Federal Office of Topography) 90 80
1154 90 c. International Red Cross Museum, Geneva (inauguration) . . . . . . 1·00 90

282 "Meta" (Jean Tinguely)

1988. Modern Art.
1155 **282** 90 c. multicoloured . . . 4·75 4·00

283 Army Postman

1989. Publicity Issue. Multicoloured.
1156 25 c. Type **283** (centenary of Swiss Army postal service) 40 20
1157 35 c. Fontaine du Sauvage and Porte au Loup, Delemont (700th anniv of granting of town charter) 40 30
1158 50 c. Eye and composite wheel (cent of Public Transport Association) 50 10
1159 80 c. Diesel train on viaduct (centenary of Rhaetian railway) . . . . 1·10 80
1160 90 c. St. Bernard dog and hospice (2000th anniv of Great St. Bernard Pass) . . 1·00 80

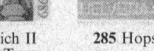

284 King Friedrich II presenting Berne Town Charter (Bendicht Tschachtlan Chronicle) **285** Hopscotch

1989. Pro Patria. Medieval Chronicles. Mult.
1161 35 c. + 15 c. Type **284** . . . 60 50
1162 50 c. + 20 c. Adrian von Bubenberg watching troops entering Murten (Diebold Schilling's Berne Chronicle) 80 20
1163 80 c. + 40 c. Messenger presenting missive to Council of Zurich (Gerold Edlibach Chronicle) . . . . 1·40 1·40
1164 90 c. + 40 c. Schilling presenting Chronicle to Council of Lucerne (Diebold Schilling's Lucerne Chronicle) 1·50 1·40

1989. Europa. Children's Games. Multicoloured.
1165 50 c. Type **285** 50 15
1166 90 c. Blind-man's buff . . . 1·00 85

286 Bricklayer **287** Testing Device

1989. Occupations.
1168 **286** 2 f. 75 purple, blk & yell 2·50 50
1169 – 2 f. 80 yellow, brn & bl 2·50 50
1170 – 3 f. blue, dp brn & brn 2·50 50
1171 – 3 f. 60 orge, brn & pur 3·25 70
1173 – 3 f. 75 deep green, green and light green . . . 3·50 75
1173a – 4 f. multicoloured . . . 3·50 75
1174 – 5 f. ultram, stone & bl . 4·25 85
1175 – 5 f. 50 grey, red and mauve 5·00 1·00
DESIGNS: 2 f. 80, Cook; 3 f. Carpenter; 3 f. 60, Pharmacist; 3 f. 75, Fisherman; 4 f. Vine grower; 5 f. Cheesemaker; 5 f. 50, Dressmaker.

1989. Publicity Issue. Multicoloured.
1181 35 c. Type **287** (cent of Swiss Electrotechnical Association) 40 20
1182 50 c. Family on butterfly (50th anniv of Swiss Travel Fund) 55 10
1183 80 c. "Wisdom" and "Science" (bronze statues) (centenary of Fribourg University) . . . 90 75
1184 90 c. Audio tape (1st anniv of National Sound Archives) 1·00 85
1185 1 f. 40 Bands of colour forming bridge (centenary of Inter-parliamentary Union) . . 1·60 1·50

288 Exercises

1989. Pro Sport.
1186 **288** 50 c. + 20 c. multicoloured 85 75

289 1882 5 c. and 50 c. Stamps and Emblem **290** Cats

1990. Publicity Issue. Multicoloured.
1187 25 c. Type **289** (centenary of Union of Swiss Philatelic Societies) 30 20
1188 35 c. Locomotive and control car (inauguration of Zurich Rapid Transit System) . . 80 30
1189 50 c. Mountain farmer (50th anniv of Assistance for Mountain Communities) . 55 10
1190 90 c. Ice hockey players (A-series World Ice Hockey Championships, Berne and Fribourg) 95 90

1990. Animals. Multicoloured.
1192 10 c. Cow 15 10
1193 50 c. Type **290** 50 10
1194 70 c. Rabbit 70 25
1195 80 c. Barn owls . . . . . . 1·25 45
1196 100 c. Horse and foal . . . 85 30
1197 110 c. Geese 95 30
1198 120 c. Dog . . . . 1·00 35
1199 140 c. Sheep . . . . 1·25 40
1200 150 c. Goats . . . . 1·25 45
1201 160 c. Turkey . . . . 1·60 50
1202 170 c. Donkey . . . . 1·50 50
1203 200 c. Chickens . . . . . . 1·75 55

291 Flyswats and Starch Sprinklers Seller

292 Lucerne Post Office

1990 Pro Patria. Street Criers. Engravings by David Herrliberger. Multicoloured.
1205 35 c. + 15 c. Type **291** . . . 65 50
1206 50 c. + 20 c. Clock seller . . 80 20
1207 80 c. + 40 c. Knife grinder . 1·25 1·40
1208 90 c. + 40 c. Couple selling pinewood sticks . . . . . 1·40 1·50

1990. Europa. Post Office Buildings. Mult.
1209 50 c. Type **292** 50 15
1210 90 c. Geneva Post Office . . 85 75

293 Conrad Ferdinand Meyer (writer)

294 Anniversary Emblem and Crosses

1990. Celebrities.
1211 **293** 35 c. black and green . . 50 25
1212 – 50 c. black and blue . . 50 15
1213 – 80 c. black and yellow . 90 75
1214 – 90 c. black and pink . . 1·10 80
DESIGNS: 50 c. Angelika Kauffmann (painter); 80 c. Blaise Cendrars (writer); 90 c. Frank Buchser (painter).

1990. 700th Anniv (1991) of Swiss Confederation (1st issue).
1215 50 c. Type **294** 50 15
1216 90 c. Emblem and crosses (different) . . . . 1·25 85
See also Nos. 1219/22 and 1224.

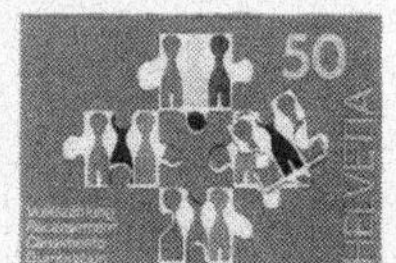
296 Figures on Jigsaw Pieces

1990. Population Census.
1218 **296** 50 c. multicoloured . . . 50 15

297 "700 JAHRE"

298 Alps and City Skyline

1991. 700th Anniv of Swiss Confederation (2nd issue). Multicoloured.
1219 50 c. Type **297** 45 15
1220 50 c. "700 ONNS" 45 15
1221 50 c. "700 ANS" 45 15
1222 50 c. "700 ANNI" 45 15
Nos. 1219/22 were issued together, se-tenant. forming a composite design of the Swiss cross in the centre.

1991. 800th Anniv of Berne.
1223 **298** 80 c. multicoloured . . . 80 40

299 Federal Palace, Berne, and Capitol, Washington

1991. 700th Anniv of Swiss Confederation (3rd issue). Swiss Emigration to U.S.A.
1224 **299** 160 c. multicoloured . . 1·75 80

300 Jettison of "Ariane" Rocket Friction Protection Jacket

301 Abstract

1991. Europa. Europe in Space. Multicoloured.
1225 50 c. Type **300** 50 15
1226 90 c. Orbit of Halley's Comet, "Giotto" space probe and its trajectory 90 75

1991. Pro Patria. Modern Art. Multicoloured.
1227 50 c. + 20 c. Type **301** . . . 75 20
1228 70 c. + 30 c. Artist's monogram 1·00 1·00
1229 80 c. + 40 c. "Labyrinth" . 1·25 1·25
1230 90 c. + 40 c. "Man and Beast" 1·40 1·50

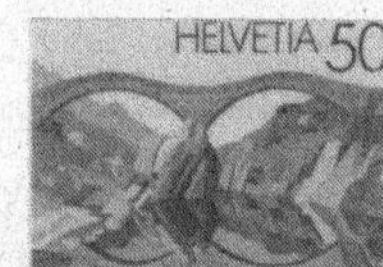
302 Stone Bridge, Lavertezzo

1991. Bridges. Multicoloured.
1231 50 c. Type **302** 50 15
1232 70 c. Wooden Neubrugg, Bremgarten 70 75
1233 80 c. Koblenz–Felsenau iron truss railway bridge . . . 80 75
1234 90 c. Ganter concrete bridge, Simplon Pass 90 80

303 P.T.T. Employees

304 Lake Moesola

1991. Centenary of Swiss Postal, Telephone and Telegraph Officials' Union.
1235 **303** 80 c. multicoloured . . 80 40

1991. Mountain Lakes.
1236 **304** 50 c. multicoloured . . 50 15
1237 – 80 c. brown, red & pur 80 15
DESIGN: 80 c. Fishing boat moored at jetty on Melchsee.
See also No. 1257.

305 Mouth of River Rhine and Caspian Tern

306 Map of Americas and "Santa Maria"

1992. Publicity Issue. Multicoloured.
1238 50 c. Type **305** (centenary of Treaty for International Regulation of the Rhine) 60 25
1239 80 c. Family (50th anniv of Pro Familia) 80 40
1240 90 c. Chemical formula and model of difluorobutane molecule (centenary of International Chemical Nomenclature Conference, Geneva) 80 70

1992. Europa. 500th Anniv of Discovery of America by Columbus. Multicoloured.
1241 50 c. Type **306** 50 15
1242 90 c. Route map of first voyage and sketch for statue of Columbus (Vincenzo Vela) 90 70

307 Skier

308 1780s Earthenware Plate, Heimberg

1992. Sierre Int Comics Festival. Mult.
1243 50 c. Type **307** 45 15
1244 80 c. Mouse-artist drawing strip 75 40
1245 90 c. Love-struck man holding bunch of stamp-flowers behind back 80 70

1992. Pro Patria. Folk Art. Multicoloured.
1246 50 c. + 20 c. Type **308** . . . 70 20
1247 70 c. + 30 c. Paper cut-out by Johann Jakob Hauswirth 1·00 90
1248 80 c. + 40 c. Maplewood cream spoon, Gruyeres . . . . . 1·40 1·10
1249 90 c. + 40 c. Carnation from 1780 embroidered saddle cloth, Grisons . . . . . . 1·50 1·25

309 Flags and Alps

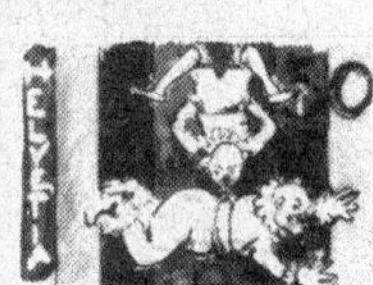
310 Clowns on Trapeze

1992. Alpine Protection Convention.
1250 **309** 90 c. multicoloured . . . 90 70

1992. The Circus. Multicoloured.
1251 50 c. Type **310** 50 15
1252 70 c. Sealion with Auguste the clown 70 60
1253 80 c. Chalky the clown and elephant 80 40
1254 90 c. Harlequin and horse . . 90 70

311 Sport Pictograms

1992. Pro Sport.
1255 **311** 50 c. + 20 c. black & bl 65 65

312 Train and Map

313 "A" (first class) Mail

1992. Centenary (1993) of Central Office for International Rail Carriage.
1256 **312** 90 c. multicoloured . . . 85 70

1993.
1257 – 60 c. dp blue, yellow & bl 55 15
1258 **313** 80 c. red, orange and scarlet 75 40
DESIGN: 60 c. Lake Tanay.

314 Zurich and Geneva 1843 Stamps

315 Paracelsus (after Augustin Hirschvogel) (500th birth anniv)

1993. 150th Anniv of Swiss Postage Stamps. Multicoloured.
1259 60 c. Type **314** 50 20
1260 80 c. Postal cancellation (stamps for postage) 70 40
1261 100 c. Magnifying glass (stamp collecting) 85 75

1993. Publicity Issue.
1262 **315** 60 c. brown, grey & blue . 50 20
1263 – 80 c. multicoloured . . . 70 40
1264 – 180 c. multicoloured . . . 1·60 1·40
DESIGNS—VERT: 80 c. Discus thrower (from Greek vase) (inauguration of Olympic Museum, Lausanne). HORIZ: 180 c. Worker's head (cent of International Metalworkers' Federation).

316 "Hohentwiel" (lake steamer) and Flags

317 Interior of Media House, Villeurbanne, France

1993. Lake Constance European Region.
1265 **316** 60 c. multicoloured . . . 50 20

1993. Europa. Contemporary Architecture.
1266 **317** 60 c. ultram, black & blue 50 20
1267 – 80 c. red, black and grey . 70 40
DESIGN: 80 c. House, Breganzona, Ticino.

318 Appenzell Dairyman's Earring

1993. Pro Patria. Folk Art. Multicoloured.
1268 60 c. + 30 c. Type **318** . . . 80 40
1269 60 c. + 30 c. Fluhli enamelled glass bottle, 1738 . . . . . 80 40
1270 80 c. + 40 c. Driving cows to summer pasture (detail of mural, Sylvestre Pidoux) . 1·00 1·00
1271 100 c. + 40 c. Straw hat ornaments . . . . 1·25 1·25

319 "Work No. 095" (Emma Kunz)

320 Kapell Bridge and Water Tower, Lucerne

1993. Paintings by Swiss Women Artists. Mult.
1272 60 c. Type **319** 50 20
1273 80 c. "Great Singer Lilas Goergens" (Aloise) (33 × 33 mm) 70 40
1274 100 c. "Under the Rain Cloud" (Meret Oppenheim) (33 × 33 mm) 85 75
1275 120 c. "Four Spaces with Horizontal Bands" (Sophi Taeuber-Arp) (33 × 33 mm) 1·00 90

1993. Kapell Bridge Restoration Fund.
1276 **320** 80 c. + 20 c. carmine and red . . . . 2·00 2·00

321 Hieroglyphic, Cuneiform and Roman Scripts

1994. "Books and the Press" Exhibition, Geneva. Multicoloured.
1277 60 c. Type **321** 50 15
1278 80 c. Gothic letterpress script 70 40
1279 100 c. Modern electronic fonts 85 75

322 Athletes

1994. Publicity Issue. Multicoloured.,
1280 60 c. Type **322** (50th Anniv of National Sports School, Magglingen) 50 20
1281 80 c. Jakob Bernoulli (mathematician) (after Nicolas Bernoulli) and formula and diagram of the law of large numbers (Int Mathematicians' Congress, Zurich) 70 40
1282 100 c. Heads, Unisource emblem, globe and flags (collaboration of Swiss, Dutch and Swedish telecommunications companies) 85 75
1283 180 c. Radar image, airliner and globe (50th anniv of I.C.A.O.) 1·75 1·60

323 Footballers

324 "Trieste" (bathyscaphe)

1994. World Cup Football Championship, U.S.A., and Cent (1995) of Swiss Football Association.
1284 **323** 80 c. multicoloured . . . 70 40

1994. Europa. Discoveries and Inventions. Vehicles used by Auguste Piccard in Stratospheric and Deep-sea Explorations. Multicoloured.
1285 60 c. Type **324** 50 20
1286 100 c. "F.N.R.S." (stratosphere balloon) 85 75

325 Neuchatel Weight-driven Clock (Jacques Matthey-Jonais)

326 Symbolic Condom

1994. Pro Patria. Folk Art. Multicoloured.
1287 60 c. + 30 c. Type **325** . . . 80 40
1288 60 c. + 30 c. Embroidered pomegranate on linen . . . 80 40
1289 80 c. + 40 c. Mould for Krafli pastry . . . . 1·00 1·00
1290 100 c. + 40 c. Paper-bird cradle mobile . . . . 1·25 1·25

1994. Anti-AIDS Campaign.
1291 **326** 60 c. multicoloured . . . 50 20

327 Simenon and his Home, Echandens Castle, Lausanne

1994. 5th Death Anniv of Georges Simenon (novelist).
1292 **327** 100 c. multicoloured . . 85 75

Schweizer Elektrizität Electricité Suisse Elettricità Svizzera 1895–1995 Helvetia 60

328 "Swiss Electricity"

1995. Publicity Issue.
1293 **328** 60 c. multicoloured . . . 50 20
1294 – 60 c. blue and black . . . 70 40
1295 – 80 c. multicoloured . . . 70 40
1296 – 180 c. multicoloured . . 1·60 1·60
DESIGNS—HORIZ: No. 1293, Type **328** (centenary of Swiss Association of Electricity Producers and Distributors); 1295, "(sda ats)" (centenary of Swiss News Agency); 1296, "ONU UNO" (50th anniv of U.N.O.). VERT: No. 1294, Wrestlers (centenary of Swiss Wrestling Association and National Wrestling and Alpine Herdsmen's Festival, Chur).

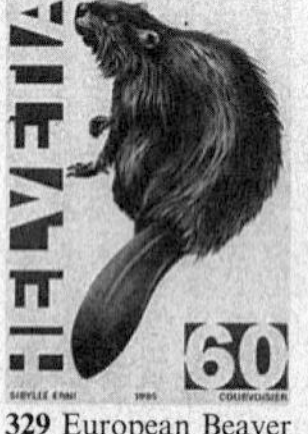

329 European Beaver

330 Cream Pail, 1776

1995. Endangered Animals. Multicoloured.
1297 60 c. Type **329** 50 20
1298 80 c. Map butterfly 70 40
1299 100 c. Green tree frog 85 75
1300 120 c. Little owl . . . . . . 1·40 1·25

1995. Pro Patria. Folk Art. Multicoloured.
1301 60 c. + 30 c. Type **330** 80 40
1302 60 c. + 30 c. Neuchatel straw hat 80 40
1303 80 c. + 40 c. Detail of chest lock, 1580 . . . . 1·00 1·00
1304 100 c. + 40 c. Langnau ceramic sugar bowl . . . . 1·25 1·25

331 Couple and Dove

1995. Europa. Peace and Freedom.
1305 **331** 60 c. blue and cobalt . . 50 20
1306 – 100 c. brown and ochre . . 85 75
DESIGN: 100 c. Europa with Zeus as bull.

333 Coloured Ribbons woven through River

1995. Switzerland–Liechtenstein Co-operation.
1308 **333** 60 c. multicoloured . . 65 40
No. 1308 was valid for use in both Switzerland and Liechtenstein (see No. 1106 of Liechtenstein).

334 "The Vocation of Andre Carrel" (1925)

1995. Centenary of Motion Pictures. Multicoloured.
1309 60 c. Type **334** 50 20
1310 80 c. "Anna Goldin - The Last Witch" 70 40
1311 150 c. "Pipilotti's Mistakes - Absolution" . . . . 1·25 1·10

335 Ear, Eye and Mouth

336 "A" (first class) Mail

1995. "Telecom 95" International Telecommunications Exhibition, Geneva.
1312 **335** 180 c. multicoloured . . 1·60 1·40

1995.
1313 **336** 90 c. blue, red and yellow 80 50

337 Emblem

1996. Publicity Issue. Multicoloured.
1314 70 c. Type **337** (centenary of Touring Club of Switzerland) 60 25
1315 70 c. Heart (50th anniv of charity organizations) . . 60 25
1316 90 c. Brass band (30th Federal Music Festival, Interlaken) 80 50
1317 90 c. Young girls (centenary of Pro Filia (girls' aid society)) 80 50
1318 180 c. Jean Piaget (child psychologist, birth centenary) 1·60 1·60

338 Coloured Ribbons and "Bern 96" Gymnastic Festival Emblem

339 Corinna Bille (writer)

1996. Pro Sport.
1319 **338** 70 c. + 30 c. mult . . 85 45

1996. Europa. Famous Women. Multicoloured.
1320 70 c. Type **339** 60 25
1321 110 c. Iris von Roten-Meyer (feminist writer) 95 85

340 Magdalena Chapel, Wolfenschiessen, and Cross

341 Olympic Rings

1996. Pro Patria. Heritage. Multicoloured.
1322 70 c.+35 c. Type **340** . . . 60 30
1323 70 c.+35 c. Underground sawmill and workshop, Col-des-Roches 60 30
1324 90 c.+40 c. Baroque baths, Pfafers . . . . 1·10 1·10
1325 110 c.+50 c. Roman road and milestone, Great St. Bernhard . . . . 1·40 1·40

1996. Centenary of Modern Olympic Games.
1326 **341** 180 c. multicoloured . . 1·60 1·40

342 Representation of 1995 "A" Mail Stamp

343 Musical Movement and Mechanical Ring (Isaac-Daniel Piguet)

1996. Guinness World Record for Largest "Living" Postage Stamp represented by Human Beings (arrangement of people to represent stamp design).
1327 **342** 90 c. multicoloured . . . 80 50

1996. Bicentenary of Antoine Favre-Salomon's Invention of the Metal Teeth System for Music Boxes. Multicoloured.
1328 70 c. Type **343** 60 25
1329 90 c. "Basso-piccolo mandolin" cylinder music box (Eduard Jaccard) 90 50
1330 110 c. Station automaton (Paillard & Co) 95 85
1331 180 c. Kalliope disc music box 1·60 1·40

344 Pattern

345 "The Golden Cow" (Daniel Ammann)

1996. Greetings Stamps. Multicoloured. Self-adhesive.
1332 90 c. Type **344** 80 50
1333 90 c. Mottled pattern 80 50
1334 90 c. Coil pattern 80 50
1335 90 c. Flower and leaf pattern 80 50

1996. Winning Entries in Stamp Design Competition.
1336 **345** 70 c. gold and blue . . . 60 25
1337 – 90 c. multicoloured . . . 80 50
1338 – 110 c. multicoloured . . 95 85
1339 – 180 c. brown, black and blue . . . . . . 1·60 1·40
DESIGNS: 90 c. "Wake with a Smile" (Max Sprick); 110 c. "Leaves" (Elena Emma-Pugliese); 180 c. "Dove" (Rene Conscience).

FRANK STAMPS

Issued to charity hospitals for free transmission of their mails.

F 21

F 49 Deaconess

1911. With control figures at top.
F268 F **21** 2 c. red and green . . 10 15
F269 3 c. red and green . . 2·00 25
F270 5 c. red and green . . 60 10
F271 10 c. red and green . . 1·00 10
F272 15 c. red and green . . 15·00 3·00
F273 20 c. red and green . . 2·75 40

1935. With or withour control figures.
F358A F **49** 5 c. green . . . . . 2·00 20
F359A – 10 c. violet . . . . . 2·00 10
F360A – 20 c. red . . . . . . 2·50 25
DESIGNS: 10 c. Sister of the Ingenbohl Order; 20 c. Henri Dunant (founder of Red Cross).

OFFICIAL STAMPS

1918. Optd **Industrielle Kriegs-wirtschaft**.
O308 **20a** 3 c. brown . . . . . . 3·00 20·00
O300 5 c. green . . . . 10·00 25·00
O310 7½ c. grey . . . . 3·00 18·00
O303 **21** 10 c. red on buff . . . 13·00 30·00
O304 15 c. purple on buff . . 11·00 32·00
O313 **17** 20 c. yellow and red . . 7·50 40·00
O314 25 c. blue and dp blue . 7·50 40·00
O315 30 c. green and brown . 12·00 70·00

1938. Optd with Geneva Cross.
O381 **52** 3 c. green 15 20
O382 – 5 c. green (No. 369) . . 15 20
O383 – 10 c. purple (No. 370) . 1·00 40
O384 – 15 c. orange (No. 373) . 35 1·25
O385 – 20 c. red (No. 375) . . . 50 30
O386 – 25 c. brown (No. 376) . . 55 1·00
O387 – 30 c. blue (No. 377) . . 75 75
O388 – 35 c. green (No. 378) . . 70 1·00
O389 – 40 c. grey (No. 379) . . 70 50
O390 **17** 50 c. green and dp green 80 1·00
O391 60 c. brown . . . . . . 1·25 1·50
O392 70 c. buff and violet . . 75 3·00
O393 80 c. buff and grey . . . 1·25 2·00
O395 **41** 90 c. red, dp green & grn 1·60 2·50
O394 **17** 1 f. green and purple . . 1·50 2·25
O396 **41** 1 f. 20 red, lake and pink 1·75 3·00
O397 1 f. 50 red, blue & turquoise 2·25 4·50
O398 – 2 f. red, black and grey . 2·40 5·00

1942. Optd **Officiel**. (a) Landscape designs of 1936.
O427 **52** 3 c. green . . . . 30 1·25
O428 – 5 c. green 30 15
O430 – 10 c. brown 25 30
O431 – 15 c. orange . . . . . . 60 1·25
O432 – 20 c. red (Lake) 60 20
O433 – 25 c. brown . . . . . . 60 1·75
O434 – 30 c. blue . . . . 1·75 60
O435 – 35 c. green . . . . . . 1·75 2·00
O436 – 40 c. grey . . . . 1·10 45

(b) Historical designs of 1941.
O437 – 50 c. blue on green . . . 4·50 3·25
O438 **68** 60 c. brown on brown . 4·75 7·25
O439 – 70 c. purple on mauve . 5·00 6·00
O440 – 80 c. black on grey . . . 1·25 1·10
O441 – 90 c. red on pink . . . . 1·50 1·00
O442 – 1 f. green on green . . . 1·75 1·50
O443 – 1 f. 20 purple on grey . . 1·90 1·75
O444 – 1 f. 50 blue on buff . . 2·25 2·75
O445 – 2 f. red on pink . . . . 3·00 3·00

1950. Landscape designs of 1949 optd **Officiel**.
O522 **107** 5 c. orange 70 60
O523 – 10 c. green . . . . . . 1·25 60
O524 – 15 c. turquoise . . . . 11·00 11·00
O525 – 20 c. purple . . . . . . 2·00 35
O526 – 25 c. red . . . . 5·00 6·00
O527 – 30 c. green . . . . . . 3·00 2·00
O528 – 35 c. brown . . . . . . 5·00 9·00
O529 – 40 c. blue . . . . 5·00 2·50
O530 – 50 c. grey . . . . 6·00 6·00
O531 – 60 c. green . . . . . . 8·50 4·00
O532 – 70 c. violet . . . . . . 22·00 16·00

For Swiss stamps overprinted for the use of officials of the League of Nations, International Labour Office and other special U.N. Agencies having their headquarters at Geneva, see sub-section INTERNATIONAL ORGANIZATIONS SITUATED IN SWITZERLAND.

POSTAGE DUE STAMPS

D 10

D 21

D 41

1878.
D89 D **10** 1 c. blue . . . . . . 1·25 75
D90 2 c. blue . . . . . . 1·25 75
D91 3 c. blue . . . . . . 9·00 10·00
D92 5 c. blue . . . . . . 12·00 5·00
D100A 10 c. blue . . . . . £130 5·00
D101A 20 c. blue . . . . . £150 3·00
D102A 50 c. blue . . . . . £300 9·50
D96 100 c. blue . . . . . £400 10·00
D97 500 c. blue . . . . . £350 15·00
The 1 c. has a rayed background behind the figure of value.

1883. Numerals in red.

D268	D 10	1 c. green	15	35
D181C		3 c. green	2·75	2·75
D269B		5 c. green	50	60
D270A		10 c. green	1·00	1·00
D271B		20 c. green	3·50	3·50
D204B		50 c. green	11·00	1·90
D205B		100 c. green	12·00	1·50
D187		500 c. green	95·00	11·00

The above were issued in a wide range of shades from pale turquoise to olive between 1883 and 1910. A detailed list of these appears in the Stanley Gibbons Part 8 (Italy and Switzerland) Catalogue.

1910.

D274	D 21	1 c. green and red	10	10
D275		3 c. green and red	10	10
D276		5 c. green and red	10	10
D277		10 c. green and red	5·00	10
D278		15 c. green and red	50	75
D279		20 c. green and red	11·00	10
D280		25 c. green and red	80	30
D281		30 c. green and red	65	30
D282		50 c. green and red	90	45

1916. Surch.

D299	D 21	5 on 3 c. red & green	10	20
D300		10 on 1 c. red & green	20	6·50
D301		10 on 3 c. red & green	20	1·00
D302		20 on 50 c. red & green	80	1·00

1924.

D329	D 41	5 c. red and green	60	10
D330		10 c. red and green	1·90	10
D331		15 c. red and green	1·75	40
D332A		20 c. red and green	3·00	80
D333		25 c. red and green	1·75	35
D334		30 c. red and green	2·00	40
D335		40 c. red and green	3·00	40
D336		50 c. red and green	3·00	50

1937. Surch.

D380	D 41	5 on 15 c. red & green	75	3·25
D381		10 on 30 c. red & green	75	1·00
D382		20 on 50 c. red & green	1·25	4·00
D383		40 on 50 c. red & green	2·00	10·00

D 54

1938.

D384	D 54	5 c. red	35	10
D385		10 c. red	65	10
D386		15 c. red	75	1·60
D387		20 c. red	85	10
D388		25 c. red	1·00	1·50
D389		30 c. red	1·25	75
D390		40 c. red	1·50	20
D391		50 c. red	2·00	1·75

"PRO JUVENTUTE" CHARITY STAMPS

PREMIUMS. All "Pro Juventute" stamps are sold at an additional premium which goes to Benevolent Societies. Until 1937 these premiums were not shown on the stamps, but were as follows: 2 c. for all 3 c. franking values; 5 c. for all 5, 7½, 10, 15 and 20 c. values and 10 c. for all 30 and 40 c. values.

From 1937, when the premium first appeared on the designs, we show it in the catalogue listing.

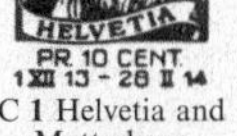

C 1 Helvetia and Matterhorn

C 2 Appenzell

1913. Children's Fund.

J1	C 1	5 c. green	2·75	3·75

1915. Children's Fund.

J1a	C 2	5 c. green on buff	2·75	4·75
J2	–	10 c. red on buff	85·00	60·00

DESIGN: 10 c. Girl from Lucerne.

C 4 Berne

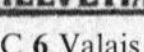

C 6 Valais

C 9 Uri

1916. Children's Fund.

J3	–	3 c. violet on buff	5·00	23·00
J4	C 4	5 c. green on buff	11·00	5·00
J5	–	10 c. red on buff	35·00	45·00

DESIGNS: 3, 10 c. Girls of Freiburg and Vaud.

1917. Children's Fund.

J6	C 6	3 c. violet on buff	4·00	27·00
J7	–	5 c. green on buff	7·00	3·50
J8	–	10 c. red on buff	18·00	16·00

DESIGNS: 5 c. Man of Unterwalden; 10 c. Girl of Ticino.

1918. Children's Fund. Dated "1918".

J 9	C 9	10 c. red, yellow and black on buff	6·50	10·00
J10	–	15 c. multicoloured on buff	9·00	6·00

ARMS: 15 c. Geneva.

1919. Children's Fund. As Type C 9 but dated "1919". Cream paper.

J11		7½ c. red, grey and black	2·50	10·00
J12		10 c. green, red and black	2·50	10·00
J13		15 c. red, violet and black	4·00	4·50

ARMS: 7½ c. Nidwalden; 10 c. Vaud; 15 c. Obwalden.

1920. Children's Fund. As Type C 9 but dated "1920". Cream paper.

J14		7½ c. red, grey and black	2·75	10·00
J15		10 c. blue, red and black	4·25	10·00
J16		15 c. red, blue, violet & blk	2·75	3·50

ARMS: 7½ c. Schwyz; 10 c. Zurich; 15 c. Ticino.

1921. Children's Fund. As Type C 9 but dated "1921". Cream paper.

J17		10 c. red, black and green	20	2·00
J18		20 c. multicoloured	2·00	2·50
J19		40 c. red and blue	8·00	30·00

ARMS: 10 c. Valais; 20 c. Berne; 40 c. Switzerland.

1922. Children's Fund. As Type C 9 but dated "1922". Cream paper.

J20		5 c. orange, blue and black	50	3·75
J21		10 c. green and black	50	1·25
J22		20 c. violet, blue and black	75	1·25
J23		40 c. blue, red and black	7·50	40·00

ARMS: 5 c. Zug; 10 c. Freiburg; 20 c. Lucerne; 40 c. Switzerland.

1923. Children's Fund. As Type C 9 but dated "1923". Cream paper.

J24		5 c. orange and black	25	3·00
J25		10 c. multicoloured	25	1·25
J26		20 c. multicoloured	25	1·25
J27		40 c. blue, red and black	6·75	30·00

ARMS: 5 c. Basel; 10 c. Glarus; 20 c. Neuchatel; 40 c. Switzerland.

1924. Children's Fund. As Type C 9 but dated "1924". Cream paper.

J28		5 c. black and lilac	10	1·00
J29		10 c. red, green and black	15	70
J30		20 c. black, yellow and red	30	70
J31		30 c. red, blue and black	1·40	8·00

ARMS: 5 c. Appenzell; 10 c. Solothurn; 20 c. Schaffhausen; 30 c. Switzerland.

1925. Children's Fund. As Type C 9 but dated "1925". Cream paper.

J32		5 c. green, black and violet	15	80
J33		10 c. black and green	15	70
J34		20 c. multicoloured	20	70
J35		30 c. red, blue and black	90	7·50

ARMS: 5 c. St. Gall; 10 c. Appenzell-Ausser-Rhoden; 20 c. Graubunden; 30 c. Switzerland.

1926. Children's Fund. As Type C 9 but dated "1926". Cream paper.

J36		5 c. multicoloured	20	80
J37		10 c. green, black and red	20	70
J38		20 c. red, black and blue	30	70
J39		30 c. blue, red and black	1·10	7·50

ARMS: 5 c. Thurgau; 10 c. Basel; 20 c. Aargau; 30 c. Switzerland and Lion of Lucerne.

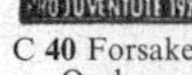

C 40 Forsaken Orphan

C 42 J. H. Pestalozzi

C 43 J. H. Pestalozzi

1927. Children's Fund. Dated "1927".

J40	C 40	5 c. pur & yell on grey	15	1·00
J41	–	10 c. grn & pink on grn	15	25
J42	C 42	20 c. red	20	25
J43	C 43	30 c. blue and black	1·00	4·50

DESIGN—As Type C 40: 40 c. Orphan at Pestalozzi School.

C 44 Lausanne

C 47 J. H. Dunant

1928. Children's Fund. Dated "1928".

J44	C 44	5 c. red, purple and black on buff	15	75
J45	–	10 c. red, green and black on buff	15	45
J46	–	20 c. black, yellow and red on buff	15	30
J47	C 47	30 c. blue and red	1·25	4·00

DESIGNS—As Type C 44: 10 c. Arms of Winterthur; 20 c. Arms of St. Gall.

C 48 Mt. San Salvatore, Lake Lugano

1929. Children's Fund. Dated "1929".

J48	C 48	5 c. red and violet	15	60
J49	–	10 c. blue and brown	15	25
J50	–	20 c. blue and red	20	25
J51	–	30 c. blue	1·25	7·00

DESIGNS: 10 c. Mt. Titlis, Lake Engstlen; 20 c. Mt. Lyskamm from Riffelberg; 30 c. Nicholas de Flue.

C 50 Freiburg

C 51 A. Bitzius—"Jeremias Gotthelf"

1930. Children's Fund. Dated "1930".

J52	C 50	5 c. blue, black and green on buff	15	70
J53	–	10 c. multicoloured on buff	15	40
J54	–	20 c. multicoloured on buff	20	40
J55	C 51	30 c. blue	1·25	4·25

ARMS—As Type C 51: 10 c. Altdorf; 20 c. Schaffhausen.

C 52 St. Moritz and Silvaplana Lakes

1931. Children's Fund. Dated "1931".

J56	C 52	5 c. green	40	90
J57	–	10 c. violet	35	35
J58	–	20 c. red	50	40
J59	–	30 c. blue	3·75	10·00

DESIGNS: 10 c. The Wetterhorn; 20 c. Lac Leman; 30 c. Alexandre Vinet.

C 54 Flag swinging

C 56 Vaud

C 59 A. von Haller

1932. Children's Fund. Dated "1932".

J60	C 54	5 c. red and green	50	1·00
J61	–	10 c. orange	60	1·00
J62	–	20 c. red	60	1·00
J63	–	30 c. blue	2·00	4·75

DESIGNS: 10 c. Putting the weight; 20 c. Wrestlers; 30 c. Eugen Huber.

1933. Children's Fund. Dated "1933".

J64	C 56	5 c. green and buff	40	80
J65	–	10 c. violet and buff	40	40
J66	–	20 c. scarlet and buff	55	40
J67	–	30 c. blue	2·50	4·75

DESIGNS: 10 c. Swiss girl from Berne; 20 c. Swiss girl from Ticino; 30 c. Father Gregoire Girard.

1934. Children's Fund. Dated "1934".

J68	–	5 c. green and buff	40	90
J69	–	10 c. violet and buff	50	35
J70	–	20 c. red and buff	50	35
J71	C 59	30 c. blue	2·40	5·00

SWISS GIRL DESIGNS—As Type C 56: 5 c. Appenzell; 10 c. Valais; 20 c. Graubunden.

C 61 Stefano Franscini

C 62 H. G. Nageli

1935. Children's Fund. Dated "1935".

J72	–	5 c. green and buff	25	1·00
J73	–	10 c. violet and buff	40	40
J74	–	20 c. red and buff	40	60
J75	C 61	30 c. blue	2·25	5·50

SWISS GIRL DESIGNS—As Type C 56: 5 c. Basel; 10 c. Lucerne; and 20 c. Geneva.

1936. Children's Fund.

J76	C 62	5 c. green	30	35
J77	–	10 c. purple and buff	30	40
J78	–	20 c. red and buff	35	75
J79	–	30 c. blue and buff	3·25	14·00

SWISS GIRL DESIGNS—As Type C 56: 10 c. Neuchatel; 20 c. Schwyz; and 30 c. Zurich.

C 64 Gen. Henri Dufour

C 66 "Youth"

1937. Children's Fund.

J80	C 64	5 c. + 5 c. green	10	15
J81	–	10 c. + 5 c. purple	10	15
J82	C 66	20 c. + 5 c. red, buff and silver	40	30
J83	–	30 c. + 10 c. blue, buff and silver	1·25	3·00

DESIGNS: 10 c. Nicholas de Flue; 30 c. as Type C 66, but girl's head facing other way.

C 67 Salomon Gessner

C 69 Gen. Herzog

1938. Children's Fund. Dated "1938".

J84	C 67	5 c. + 5 c. green	15	20
J85	–	10 c. + 5 c. vio & buff	15	20
J86	–	20 c. + 5 c. red & buff	25	20
J87	–	30 c. + 10 c. blue & buff	1·50	3·00

SWISS GIRL DESIGNS – As Type C 56: 10 c. St. Gall; 20 c. Uri; 30 c. Aargau.

1939. Children's Fund.

J88	C 69	5 c. + 5 c. green	15	20
J89	–	10 c. + 5 c. vio and buff	20	20
J90	–	20 c. + 5 c. red & buff	35	30
J91	–	30 c. + 10 c. blue & buff	1·75	4·25

SWISS GIRL DESIGNS—As Type C 56: 10 c. Freiburg; 20 c. Nidwalden; 30 c. Basel.

C 71 Gottfried Keller

C 73 Johann Kasper Lavater

1940. Children's Fund. Dated "1940".

J92	C 71	5 c. + 5 c. green	10	20
J93	–	10 c. + 5 c. brn & buff	20	15
J94	–	20 c. + 5 c. red and buff	30	20
J95	–	30 c. + 10 c. blue & buff	1·50	6·00

SWISS GIRL DESIGNS—As Type C 56: 10 c. Thurgau; 20 c. Solothurn; 30 c. Zug.

1941. Children's Fund. Bicentenary of Birth of Lavater (philosopher) and of Death of Richard (clockmaker). Dated "1941".

J96	C 73	5 c. + 5 c. green	15	15
J97	–	10 c. + 5 c. brn & buff	25	20
J98	–	20 c. + 5 c. red & buff	30	25
J99	–	30 c. + 10 c. blue	1·25	4·00

DESIGNS—As Type C 56: 10 c., 20 c. Girls in national costumes of Schaffhausen and Obwalden. As Type C 73: 30 c. Daniel Jean Richard.

C 74 Niklaus Riggenbach (rack railway pioneer)

C 75 Emanuel von Fellenberg

C 76 Silver Thistle

1942. Children's Fund. Dated "1942".

J100	C 74	5 c. + 5 c. green	20	30
J101	–	10 c. + 5 c. brn & buff	25	25
J102	–	20 c. + 5 c. red & buff	30	25
J103	–	30 c. + 10 c. blue	1·50	4·00

DESIGNS: 10 c. and 20 c. Girls in national costumes of Appenzell Ausser-Rhoden and Glarus; 30 c. Conrad Escher von der Linth (statesman).

1943. Death Centenary of Philip Emanuel von Fellenberg (economist).

J104	C 75	5 c. + 5 c. green	15	20
J105	C 76	10 c. + 5 c. green, buff and grey	25	15
J106	–	20 c. + 5 c. red, yellow and pink	30	15
J107	–	30 c. + 10 c. blue, light blue and black	1·40	7·00

FLOWERS: As Type C 76: 20 c. "Ladies slipper"; 30 c. Gentian.

C 77 Numa Droz

C 78 Ludwig Forrer

1944. Birth Centenary of Droz (statesman).

J108 C 77 5 c. + 5 c. green . . . 20 15
J109 – 10 c. + 5 c. olive, yellow and green 20 15
J110 – 20 c. + 5 c. red, yellow and grey 30 15
J111 – 30 c. + 10 c. blue, grey and blue . . . . . . 1·00 6·50

DESIGNS: 10 c. Edelweiss; 20 c. Martagon lily; 30 c. "Aquilegia alpina".

1945. Children's Fund. Centenary of Births of Ludwig Forrer (statesman) and Susanna Orelli (social reformer). Dated "1945".

J112 C 78 5 c. + 5 c. green . . . 30 25
J113 – 20 c. + 10 c. brown . . 30 15
J114 – 20 c. + 10 c. red, pink and yellow 60 15
J115 – 30 c. + 10 c. blue, mauve and grey . . . . . . 2·50 6·00

DESIGNS: 10 c. Susanna Orelli; 20 c. Alpine dog rose; 30 c. Spring crocus.

C 79 Rudolf Toepffer

C 80 Jacob Burckhardt (historian)

1946. Death Centenary of Rudolf Toepffer (author and painter). Type C 79 and floral designs inscr "PRO JUVENTUTE 1946".

J116 C 79 5 c. + 5 c. green . . . 25 15
J117 – 10 c. + 10 c. green, grey and orange 30 15
J118 – 20 c. + 10 c. red, grey and yellow 40 15
J119 – 30 c. + 10 c. blue, grey and mauve . . . . . . 2·75 5·75

DESIGNS – As Type C 76: 10 c. Narcissus; 20 c. Houseleek; 30 c. Blue thistle.

1947. Children's Fund. Type C 80 and floral designs inscr "PRO JUVENTUTE 1947".

J120 C 80 5 c. + 5 c. green . . . 15 15
J121 – 10 c. + 10 c. black, yellow and grey 25 15
J122 – 20 c. + 10 c. brown, orange and grey . . . 35 15
J123 – 30 c. + 10 c. blue, pink and grey . . . . . . 2·00 4·25

DESIGNS – As Type C 76: 10 c. Alpine primrose; 20 c. Orange lily; 30 c. Cyclamen.

C 81 Gen. U. Wille

C 82 Nicholas Wengi

1948. Children's Fund. Type C 81 and floral designs as Type C 76. Dated "1948".

J124 C 81 5 c. + 5 c. purple . . . 25 10
J125 – 10 c. + 10 c. green, yellow and grey 40 15
J126 – 20 c. + 10 c. brown, red and buff 50 15
J127 – 40 c. + 10 c. blue, yellow and grey . . . . . . 2·50 4·50

FLOWERS: 10 c. Yellow foxglove; 20 c. Rust-leaved Alpine rose; 40 c. Lily of Paradise.

1949. Children's Fund. Type C 82 and floral designs inscr "PRO JUVENTUTRE 1949".

J128 C 82 5 c. + 5 c. red 20 10
J129 – 10 c. + 10 c. green, grey and yellow 30 15
J130 – 20 c. + 10 c. brown, blue and buff . . . . . . [illegible] 15
J131 – 40 c. blue, mauve and yellow . . . . 2·75 5·00

DESIGNS – As Type C 76: 10 c. "Pulsatilla alpina"; 20 c. Alpine clematis; 40 c. Superb pink.

C 83 General Theophil Sprecher von Bernegg

C 84 Red Admiral Butterfly

1950. Children's Fund. Inscr "PRO JUVENTUTE 1950".

J132 C 83 5 c. + 5 c. brown . . 20 15
J133 C 84 10 c. + 10 c. mult . . 50 20
J134 – 20 c. + 10 c. black, blue and orange 55 20
J135 – 30 c. + 10 c. brown, grey and mauve . . . . . 5·00 12·00
J136 – 40 c. + 10 c. yellow, brown and blue . . 4·25 9·50

DESIGNS: 20 c. Clifden's nonpareil (moth); 30 c. Honey bee; 40 c. Moorland clouded yellow (butterfly).

C 85 Johanna Spyri (authoress)

C 86 "Portrait of a Boy" (Anker)

1951. Children's Fund. Type C 85 and various insects as Type C 84. Inscr "PRO JUVENTUTE 1951".

J137 C 85 5 c. + 5 c. purple . . 20 10
J138 – 10 c. + 10 c. bl & grn 40 20
J139 – 20 c. + 10 c. black, cream and mauve 50 20
J140 – 30 c. + 10 c. black, orange and green . . . . . 4·00 8·00
J141 – 40 c. + 10 c. brown, red and blue . . . . . . 4·00 7·50

INSECTS: 10 c. Banded agrion (dragonfly); 20 c. Scarce swallowtail (butterfly); 30 c. Orange-tip (butterfly); 40 c. Viennese emperor moth.

1952. Children's Fund. Type C 86 and insects as Type C 84. Inscr "PRO JUVENTUTE 1952".

J142 C 86 5 c. + 5 c. red 20 15
J143 – 10 c. + 10 c. orange, black and green 35 15
J144 – 20 c. + 10 c. cream, black and mauve 45 15
J145 – 30 c. + 10 c. blue, black and brown . . . . . 3·50 6·50
J146 – 40 c. + 10 c. buff, brown and blue . . . . . 3·50 6·50

INSECTS: 10 c. Seven-spotted ladybird; 20 c. Marbled white (butterfly); 30 c. Chalk-hill blue (butterfly); 40 c. Oak eggar moth.

1953. Children's Fund. Portraits as Type C 86 and insects as Type C 84. Inscr "PRO JUVENTUTE 1953".

J147 5 c. + 5 c. red 20 10
J148 10 c. + 10 c. pink, brown and green 35 15
J149 20 c. + 10 c. black, buff and mauve 45 15
J150 30 c. + 10 c. blk, red & grn 3·50 7·50
J151 40 c. + 10 c. blue . . . . . 4·25 5·50

DESIGNS: 5 c. "Portrait of a girl" (Anker); 10 c. Black arches moth; 20 c. Camberwell beauty (butterfly); 30 c. "Purpureus kaehleri" (longhorn beetle); 40 c. F. Hodler (self-portrait).

1954. Children's Fund. Portrait as Type C 85 and insects as Type C 84. Inscr "PRO JUVENTUTE 1954".

J152 5 c. + 5 c. brown 20 10
J153 10 c. + 10 c. multicoloured 40 15
J154 20 c. + 10 c. multicoloured 55 35
J155 30 c. + 10 c. multicoloured 4·00 6·00
J156 40 c. + 10 c. multicoloured 4·00 6·50

DESIGNS: 5 c. Jeremias Gotthelf (novelist) (after Albert Bitzius); 10 c. Garden tiger moth; 20 c. Buff-tailed bumble bee; 30 c. "Ascalaphus libelluloides" (owl-fly); 40 c. Swallowtail (butterfly).

1955. Children's Fund. Portrait as Type C 85 and insects as Type C 84. Inscr "PRO JUVENTUTE 1955".

J157 5 c. + 5 c. purple 20 15
J158 10 c. + 10 c. multicoloured 40 20
J159 20 c. + 10 c. multicoloured 45 20
J160 30 c. + 10 c. multicoloured 4·00 4·50
J161 40 c. + 10 c. black red & bl 4·00 4·50

DESIGNS: 5 c. C. Pictet-de-Rochemont; 10 c. Peacock (butterfly); 20 c. Great horntail; 30 c. Yellow tiger moth; 40 c. Apollo (butterfly).

1956. Children's Fund. Portrait as Type C 85 and insects as Type C 84. Inscr "PRO JUVENTUTE 1956".

J162 5 c. + 5 c. purple 20 10
J163 10 c. + 10 c. deep green, red and green 40 15
J164 20 c. + 10 c. multicoloured 50 20
J165 30 c. + 10 c. blue, indigo and yellow . . . . 2·40 4·25
J166 40 c. + 10 c. yell, brn & bl 2·50 4·50

DESIGNS: 5 c. Carlo Maderno (architect); 10 c. Common burnet (moth); 20 c. Lesser purple emperor (butterfly); 30 c. Blue ground beetle; 40 c. Large white (butterfly).

1957. Children's Fund. Portrait as Type C 85 and insects as Type C 84. Inscr "PRO JUVENTUTE 1957".

J167 5 c. + 5 c. purple 30 10
J168 10 c. + 10 c. multicoloured 40 15
J169 20 c. + 10 c. yellow, brown and mauve 45 15
J170 30 c. + 10 c. emerald, green and purple . . . . 2·40 4·00
J171 40 c. + 10 c. multicoloured 2·50 3·00

DESIGNS: 5 c. L. Euler (mathematician); 10 c. Clouded yellow (butterfly); 20 c. Magpie moth; 30 c. Rose chafer (beetle); 40 c. Rosy underwing (moth).

C 92 Albrecht von Haller (naturalist)

C 93 Pansy

1958. Children's Fund. Type C 92 and flowers as Type C 93. Inscr "PRO JUVENTUTE 1958".

J172 C 92 5 c. + 5 c. purple . . . 15 10
J173 C 93 10 c. + 10 c. yellow, brown and green . . 40 10
J174 – 20 c. + 10 c. mult . . . 50 20
J175 – 30 c. + 10 c. mult . . . 2·00 2·75
J176 – 40 c. + 10 c. mult . . . 2·00 2·50

FLOWERS: 20 c. Chinese aster; 30 c. Morning Glory; 40 c. Christmas rose.

1959. Children's Fund. Portrait as Type C 92 and flowers as Type C 93. Inscr "PRO JUVENTUTE 1959".

J177 5 c. + 5 c. purple 15 10
J178 10 c. + 10 c. multicoloured 30 15
J179 20 c. + 10 c. red, green and purple 40 15
J180 30 c. + 10 c. multicoloured 2·00 3·00
J181 50 c. + 10 c. multicoloured 2·00 2·75

DESIGNS: 5 c. Karl Hilty (lawyer); 10 c. Marsh marigold; 20 c. Poppy; 30 c. Nasturtium; 50 c. Sweet pea.

1960. Children's Fund. Portrait as Type C 92 and flowers as Type C 93. Inscr "PRO JUVENTUTE 1960".

J182 5 c. + 5 c. blue 20 10
J183 10 c. + 10 c. yellow, drab and green 30 10
J184 20 c. + 10 c. green, brown and mauve 40 20
J185 30 c. + 10 c. green, blue and brown . . . . 3·00 3·50
J186 50 c. + 10 c. yell, grn & bl 3·00 3·00

DESIGNS: 5 c. Alexandre Calame (painter); 10 c. Dandelion; 20 c. Phlox; 30 c. Larkspur; 50 c. Thorn apple.

1961. Children's Fund. Portrait as Type C 92 and flowers as Type C 93. Inscr "PRO JUVENTUTE 1961".

J187 5 c. + 5 c. blue 15 10
J188 10 c. + 10 c. multicoloured . 20 10
J189 20 c. + 10 c. multicoloured . 25 15
J190 30 c. + 10 c. multicoloured . 1·50 2·25
J191 50 c. + 10 c. multicoloured . 1·75 2·25

DESIGNS: 5 c. J. Furrer (first President of Swiss Confederation); 10 c. Sunflower; 20 c. Lily-of-the-Valley; 30 c. Iris; 50 c. Silverweed.

C 97 "Child's World"

C 98 Mother and Child

1962. Children's Fund. 50th Anniv of Pro Juventute Foundation. Inscr "1912–1962".

J192 – 5 c. + 5 c. multicoloured 15 10
J193 C 97 10 c. + 10 c. red & green 25 10
J194 C 98 20 c. + 10 c. mult . . . 50 20
J195 – 30 c. + 10 c. red, mauve and yellow . . . . . 1·25 2·25
J196 – 50 c. + 10 c. yellow, brown and blue . . . 1·50 2·25

DESIGNS—As Type C 97: 5 c. Apple blossom; 30 c. "Child's World" (child in meadow); 50 c. Forsythia.

1963. Children's Fund. Portrait as Type C 86 and flowers as Type C 93. Inscr "PRO JUVENTUTE 1963".

J197 5 c. + 5 c. blue 10 35
J198 10 c. + 10 c. multicoloured 30 2·25
J199a 20 c. + 10 c. red, green and carmine 90 50
J200 30 c. + 10 c. multicoloured 1·50 1·50
J201 50 c. + 10 c. purple, green and blue . . . . 1·50 1·50

DESIGNS: 5 c. "Portrait of a Boy" (Anker); 10 c. Oxeye daisy; 20 c. Geranium; 30 c. Cornflower; 50 c. Carnation.

1964. Children's Fund. Portrait as Type C 86 and flowers as Type C 93. Inscr "PRO JUVENTUTE 1964".

J202 5 c. + 5 c. blue 10 10
J203 10 c. + 10 c. orange, yellow and green 15 10
J204 20 c. + 10 c. red, green and carmine 20 10
J205 30 c. + 10 c. purple, green and brown 50 50
J206 50 c. + 10 c. multicoloured 65 60

DESIGNS: 5 c. "Portrait of a Girl" (Anker); 10 c. Daffodil; 20 c. Rose; 30 c. Red clover; 50 c. White water-lily.

C 101 Western European Hedgehogs

C 102 Roe Deer

1965. Children's Fund. Animals. Inscr "PRO JUVENTUTE 1965".

J207 C 101 5 c. + 5 c. ochre, brown and red 10 10
J208 – 10 c. + 10 c. mult . . . 10 10
J209 – 20 c. + 10 c. blue, brown and chestnut . . . 30 10
J210 – 30 c. + 10 c. blue, black and yellow 35 40
J211 – 50 c. + 10 c. black brown and blue . . 50 50

ANIMALS: 10 c. Alpine marmots; 20 c. Red deer; 30 c. Eurasian badgers; 50 c. Arctic hares.

1966. Children's Fund. Animals. As Type C 101 but inscr "PRO JUVENTUTE 1966". Multicoloured.

J212 5 c. + 5 c. Stoat 10 10
J213 10 c. + 10 c. Eurasian red squirrel 10 10
J214 20 c. + 10 c. Red fox . . . 30 10
J215 30 c. + 10 c. Brown hare . . 35 40
J216 50 c. + 10 c. Chamois . . . 50 50

1967. Children's Fund. Animals. Inscr "PRO JUVENTUTE 1967". Multicoloured.

J217 10 c. + 10 c. Type C 102 . . 15 10
J218 20 c. + 10 c. Pine marten . . 20 10
J219 30 c. + 10 c. Ibex 30 10
J220 50 c. + 10 c. European otter 50 50

1968. Children's Fund. Birds. As Type C 102 but inscr "1968". Multicoloured.

J221 10 c. + 10 c. Capercaillie . . 30 10
J222 20 c. + 10 c. Bullfinch . . . 40 10
J223 30 c. + 10 c. Woodchat shrike 60 15
J224 50 c. + 20 c. Firecrest . . . 90 60

1969. Children's Fund. Birds. As Type C 102. Inscr "1969". Multicoloured.

J225 10 c. + 10 c. Goldfinch . . 30 10
J226 20 c. + 10 c. Golden oriole 40 15
J227 30 c. + 10 c. Wallcreeper . . 50 15
J228 50 c. + 20 c. Jay 75 70

1970. Children's Fund. Birds. As Type C 102. Inscr "1970". Multicoloured.

J229 10 c. + 10 c. Blue tits . . . 20 15
J230 20 c. + 10 c. Hoopoe . . . 30 10
J231 30 c. + 10 c. Great spotted woodpecker 40 15
J232 50 c. + 20 c. Great crested grebes 90 95

1971. Children's Fund. Birds. As Type C 102. Inscr "1971". Multicoloured.

J233 10 c. + 10 c. Redstarts . . . 30 20
J234 20 c. + 10 c. Bluethroats . . 50 10
J235 30 c. + 10 c. Peregrine falcon 70 20
J236 40 c. + 20 c. Mallards . . . 1·60 1·10

C 104 "McGredy's Sunset" Rose

C 105 Chestnut

1972. Children's Fund. Roses. Multicoloured.

J237 10 c. + 10 c. Type C 104 . . 25 15
J238 20 c. + 10 c. "Miracle" . . 35 15
J239 30 c. + 10 c. "Papa Meilland" 60 15
J240 40 c. + 20 c. "Madame Dimitriu" . . . . 1·00 1·00

See also Nos. J258/61 and J279/82.

1973. Children's Fund. "Fruits of the Forest". Multicoloured.

J241 15 c. + 5 c. Type C 105 . . 15 10
J242 30 c. + 10 c. Cherries . . 30 10
J243 40 c. + 20 c. Blackberries . 70 65
J244 60 c. + 20 c. Bilberries . . 90 95

See also Nos. J245/8, J250/3 and J254/7.

1974. Children's Fund. "Fruits of the Forest". Poisonous Plants. As Type C 105. Inscr "1974". Multicoloured.

J245 15 c. + 10 c. Daphne . . . 20 10
J246 30 c. + 20 c. Belladonna . . 40 10
J247 50 c. + 20 c. Laburnum . . 75 75
J248 60 c. + 25 c. Mistletoe . . . 90 75

1975. Children's Fund. As Type C 105. Inscr "1975". Multicoloured.

J249 10 c. + 5 c. "Post-Brent" (postman's hamper) . . . 10 10
J250 15 c. + 10 c. Hepatica . . . 20 15
J251 30 c. + 20 c. Rowan 35 10
J252 50 c. + 20 c. Yellow deadnettle 75 75
J253 60 c. + 25 c. Sycamore . . . 80 75

1976. Children's Fund. "Fruits of the Forest". As Type C 105. Inscr "1976". Multicoloured.

J254 20 c. + 10 c. Barberry . . . 25 15
J255 40 c. + 20 c. Black elder . . 40 15
J256 40 c. + 20 c. Lime 40 15
J257 80 c. + 40 c. Lungwort . . . 1·25 1·10

1977. Children's Fund. Roses. As Type C **104**. Inscr "1977". Multicoloured.

J258	20 c. + 10 c. "Rosa foetida bicolor"	25	10
J259	40 c. + 20 c. "Parfum de l'Hay"	45	10
J260	70 c. + 30 c. "R. foetida persiana"	1·00	1·00
J261	80 c. + 40 c. "R. centifolia muscosa"	1·10	1·10

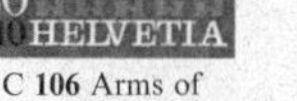

C **106** Arms of Aarburg

C **107** Letter Balance

1978. Children's Fund. Arms of the Communes (1st series). Multicoloured.

J262	20 c. + 10 c. Type C **106**	25	10
J263	40 c. + 20 c. Gruyeres	45	10
J264	70 c. + 30 c. Castasegna	1·00	1·00
J265	80 c. + 40 c. Wangen	1·00	1·10

See also Nos. J266/9, J270/3 and J274/7.

1979. Children's Fund. Arms of the Communes (2nd series). As Type C **106**. Multicoloured.

J266	20 c. + 10 c. Cadro	20	15
J267	40 c. + 20 c. Rute	40	10
J268	70 c. + 30 c. Schwamendingen	90	95
J269	80 c. + 40 c. Perroy	1·00	95

1980. Children's Fund. Arms of the Communes (3rd series). As Type C **106**. Multicoloured.

J270	20 c. + 10 c. Cortaillod	25	20
J271	40 c. + 20 c. Sierre	50	10
J272	70 c. + 30 c. Scuol	85	1·00
J273	80 c. + 40 c. Wolfenschiessen	1·00	1·00

1981. Children's Fund. Arms of the Communes (4th series). As Type C **106**. Multicoloured.

J274	20 c. + 10 c. Uffikon	30	20
J275	40 c. + 20 c. Torre	50	10
J276	70 c. + 30 c. Benken	85	1·00
J277	80 c. + 40 c. Preverenges	1·00	1·00

1982. Children's Fund. Type C **107** and roses as Type C **104**. Multicoloured.

J278	10 c. + 10 c. Type C **107**	20	20
J279	20 c. + 10 c. "La Belle Portugaise"	25	15
J280	40 c. + 20 c. "Hugh Dickson"	50	15
J281	70 c. + 30 c. "Mermaid"	90	90
J282	80 c. + 40 c. "Madame Caroline"	1·00	90

C **108** Kitchen Stove, c. 1850

C **109** Heidi and Goat (Johanna Spyri)

1983. Children's Fund. Toys. Multicoloured.

J283	20 c. + 10 c. Type C **108**	30	20
J284	40 c. + 20 c. Rocking horse, 1826	55	15
J285	70 c. + 30 c. Doll, c. 1870	1·00	95
J286	80 c. + 40 c. Steam locomotive, c. 1900	1·25	1·00

1984. Children's Fund. Characters from Children's Books. Multicoloured.

J287	35 c. + 15 c. Type C **109**	50	35
J288	50 c. + 20 c. Pinocchio and kite (Carlo Collodi)	75	10
J289	70 c. + 30 c. Pippi Longstocking (Astrid Lindgren)	1·00	1·00
J290	80 c. + 40 c. Max and Moritz on roof (Wilhelm Busch)	1·25	1·25

1985. Children's Fund. Characters from Children's Books. As Type C **109**. Multicoloured.

J291	35 c. + 15 c. Hansel, Gretel and Witch	50	35
J292	50 c. + 20 c. Snow White and the Seven Dwarfs	75	15
J293	80 c. + 40 c. Red Riding Hood and Wolf	1·00	1·00
J294	90 c. + 40 c. Cinderella and Prince Charming	1·25	1·25

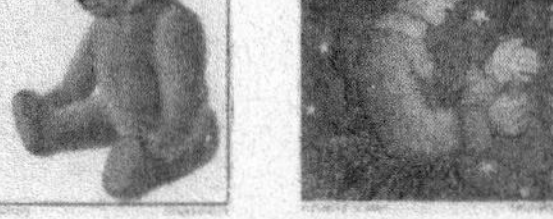

C **110** Teddy Bear

C **111** Girl carrying Pine Branch and Candle

1986. Children's Fund. Toys. Multicoloured.

J295	35 c. + 15 c. Type C **110**	50	45
J296	50 c. + 20 c. Spinning top	65	70
J297	80 c. + 40 c. Steamroller	1·50	1·40
J298	90 c. + 40 c. Doll	1·60	1·50

1987. Children's Fund. Child Development. Pre-school Age. Multicoloured.

J299	25 c. + 10 c. Type C **111**	40	30
J300	35 c. + 15 c. Mother breast-feeding baby	60	55
J301	50 c. + 20 c. Toddler playing with bricks	90	15
J302	80 c. + 40 c. Children playing in sand	1·50	1·40
J303	90 c. + 40 c. Father with child on his shoulders	1·50	1·50

C **112** Learning to Read

C **113** Community Work

1988. Children's Fund. Child Development. School Age. Multicoloured.

J304	35 c. + 15 c. Type C **112**	60	50
J305	50 c. + 20 c. Playing triangle	80	15
J306	80 c. + 40 c. Learning arithmetic	1·40	1·40
J307	90 c. + 40 c. Drawing	1·50	1·40

1989. Children's Fund. Child Development. Adolescence. Multicoloured.

J308	35 c. + 15 c. Type C **113**	60	50
J309	50 c. + 20 c. Young couple (friendship)	80	15
J310	80 c. + 40 c. Boy at computer screen (vocational training)	1·40	1·40
J311	90 c. + 40 c. Girl in laboratory (higher education and research)	1·50	1·50

C **114** Building Model Ship (hobbies)

C **115** Ramsons

1990. Child Development. Leisure Activities. Multicoloured.

J312	35 c. + 15 c. Type C **114**	60	50
J313	50 c. + 20 c. Youth group	80	15
J314	80 c. + 40 c. Sport	1·40	1·40
J315	90 c. + 40 c. Music	1·50	1·50

1991. Woodland Flowers. Multicoloured.

J316	50 c. + 25 c. Type C **115**	75	15
J317	70 c. + 30 c. Wood cranesbill	1·00	1·00
J318	80 c. + 40 c. Nettle-leaved bellflower	1·25	1·25
J319	90 c. + 40 c. Few-leaved hawkweed	1·50	1·50

C **116** Melchior (wood puppet)

1992. Christmas (J320) and Trees (others). Multicoloured.

J320	50 c. + 25 c. Type C **116**	70	15
J321	50 c. + 25 c. Beech	70	15
J322	70 c. + 30 c. Norway maple	90	90
J323	80 c. + 40 c. Pedunculate oak	1·10	1·10
J324	90 c. + 40 c. Norway spruce	1·25	1·25

Nos. J321/4 show silhouette of tree and close-up of its leaves and fruit.

C **117** Christmas Wreath

C **118** Candles

1993. Christmas (J325) and Woodland Plants (others). Multicoloured.

J325	60 c. + 30 c. Type C **117**	50	25
J326	60 c. + 30 c. Male fern	50	25
J327	80 c. + 40 c. Guelder rose	1·00	1·00
J328	100 c. + 50 c. "Mnium punctatum"	1·25	1·25

1994. Christmas (J329) and Fungi (others). Multicoloured.

J329	60 c. + 30 c. Type C **118**	65	35
J330	60 c. + 30 c. Wood blewit	1·00	50
J331	80 c. + 40 c. Red boletus	1·25	1·25
J332	100 c. + 50 c. Shaggy pholiota	1·60	1·60

C **119** "The Annunciation" Detail of (Bartolome Murillo)

1995. Christmas (J333) and Wildlife (others). Multicoloured.

J333	60 c. + 30 c. Type C **119**	80	40
J334	60 c. + 30 c. River trout	80	40
J335	80 c. + 40 c. Grey wagtail	1·00	1·00
J336	100 c. + 50 c. Spotted salamander	1·25	1·25

C **120** Shooting Star and Constellations

1996. Christmas (J337) and Wildlife (others). Multicoloured.

J337	70 c. + 35 c. Type C **120**	90	45
J338	70 c. + 35 c. Graylings (fish)	90	45
J339	90 c. + 45 c. Crayfish	1·25	1·25
J340	110 c. + 55 c. European otter	1·40	1·40

INTERNATIONAL ORGANIZATIONS SITUATED IN SWITZERLAND

The stamps listed under this heading were issued by the Swiss Post Office primarily for the use of officials of the Organizations named, situated in Geneva.

These stamps could not be legitimately obtained unused before February 1944.

A. LEAGUE OF NATIONS.

1922. Optd **SOCIETE DES NATIONS**.

LN 1	**20a**	2½ c. bistre on buff	—	30
LN 2		3 c. blue on buff	—	6·00
LN 3		5 c. orange on buff	—	4·25
LN 4		5 c. grey on buff	—	2·00
LN 5		5 c. purple on buff	—	1·60
LN 5a		5 c. green on buff	—	10·00
LN 6		7½ c. green on buff	—	30
LN 7	**21**	10 c. green on buff	—	30
LN 8		10 c. violet on buff	—	2·00
LN 9		15 c. red on buff	—	80
LN10		20 c. purple on buff	—	6·00
LN11		20 c. red on buff	—	1·75
LN13		25 c. red on buff	—	70
LN14		25 c. brown on buff	—	12·00
LN15	**17**	30 c. green and brown	—	10·00
LN16	**21**	30 c. blue on buff	—	6·00
LN17	**17**	35 c. yellow and green	—	6·00
LN18		40 c. blue	—	1·00
LN19		40 c. green and mauve	—	10·00
LN20a		50 c. green & dp grn	80	1·50
LN21		60 c. brown	20·00	1·00
LN22a		70 c. buff and violet	1·00	2·00
LN23a		80 c. buff and grey	2·50	1·75
LN24a	**41**	90 c. red, deep green and green	—	4·00
LN25a	**17**	1 f. green and purple	—	4·25
LN26b	**41**	1 f. 20 red, lake & pink	2·00	3·50
LN27a		1 f. 50 red, blue and turquoise	2·00	4·00
LN28a		2 f. red, black and grey	2·50	4·00
LN29	**22**	3 f. red	—	24·00
LN29a	**43**	3 f. brown	—	£180
LN30	–	5 f. blue (No. 296)	—	45·00
LN32	–	10 f. mauve (No. 297)	—	£120
LN33	–	10 f. green (No. 337)	—	£110

1932. International Disarmament Conference. Optd **SOCIETE DES NATIONS**.

LN34	**44**	5 c. green	—	14·00
LN35		10 c. orange	—	1·00
LN36		20 c. mauve	—	1·00
LN37		30 c. blue	—	35·00
LN38		60 c. brown	—	10·00
LN39	**45**	1 f. grey and blue	—	10·00

1934. Landscape designs of 1934 optd **SOCIETE DES NATIONS**.

LN40	**48**	3 c. green	—	20
LN41	–	5 c. green	—	25
LN42	–	15 c. orange	—	75
LN43	–	25 c. brown	—	12·00
LN44	–	30 c. blue	—	1·10

1937. Landscape designs of 1936 optd **SOCIETE DES NATIONS**.

LN45	**52**	3 c. green	10	10
LN46	–	5 c. green	20	15
LN47c	–	10 c. purple	—	80
LN49	–	10 c. brown	55	60
LN50	–	15 c. orange	40	30
LN51	–	20 c. red (railway)	—	1·25
LN51c	–	20 c. red (lake)	60	1·00
LN52	–	25 c. brown	60	75
LN53	–	30 c. blue	60	70
LN54	–	35 c. green	60	75
LN55	–	40 c. grey	75	90

1938. Nos. 382/5 optd **SOCIETE DES NATIONS**.

LN56	**55**	20 c. red and buff	—	2·00
LN57	–	30 c. blue and light blue	—	3·00
LN58	–	60 c. brown and buff	—	5·00
LN59	–	1 f. black and buff	—	6·00

1938. Nos. 382/5 optd **SERVICE DE LA SOCIETE DES NATIONS** in circle.

LN60	**55**	20 c. red and buff	—	2·00
LN61	–	30 c. blue and light blue	—	3·50
LN62	–	60 c. brown and buff	—	6·00
LN63	–	1 f. black and buff	—	10·00

1939. Nos. 388c/90c optd **SOCIETE DES NATIONS**.

LN64	**61**	3 f. brown on buff	3·00	7·00
LN65	–	5 f. blue on buff	4·50	10·00
LN66	–	10 f. green on buff	9·50	24·00

1944. Optd **COURRIER DE LA SOCIETE DES NATIONS**. (a) Landscape designs of 1936.

LN67	**52**	3 c. green	15	20
LN68	–	5 c. green	15	20
LN69	–	10 c. brown	30	40
LN70	–	15 c. orange	25	30
LN71	–	20 c. red (lake)	40	45
LN72	–	25 c. brown	60	60
LN73	–	30 c. blue	70	70
LN74	–	35 c. green	75	75
LN75	–	40 c. grey	75	90

(b) Historical designs of 1941.

LN76	–	50 c. blue on green	1·00	1·50
LN77	**68**	60 c. brown on brown	1·40	1·75
LN78	–	70 c. purple on mauve	1·40	2·00
LN79	–	80 c. black on grey	1·25	1·60
LN80	–	90 c. red on pink	1·25	1·60
LN81	–	1 f. green on green	1·50	2·00
LN82	–	1 f. 20 purple on grey	1·60	2·40
LN83	–	1 f. 50 blue on buff	2·00	2·75
LN84	–	2 f. red on pink	3·00	3·25

(c) Parliament designs of 1938.
LN85 **61** 3 f. brown on buff . . . 5·00 7·00
LN86 – 5 f. blue on buff . . . 6·50 10·00
LN87 – 10 f. green on buff . . . 12·00 22·00

B. INTERNATIONAL LABOUR OFFICE

Optd **S.d.N. Bureau International du Travail** (Nos. LB1/47).

1923.
LB 1 **20a** 2½ c. bistre on buff . . — 20
LB 2 3 c. blue on buff . . . — 90
LB 3 5 c. orange on buff . . — 30
LB 4 5 c. purple on buff . . — 20
LB 5 7½ c. green on buff . . — 25
LB 6 **21** 10 c. green on buff . . — 20
LB 8 15 c. red on buff . . . — 90
LB 9 20 c. purple on buff . . — 12·00
LB10 20 c. red on buff . . . — 4·00
LB11 25 c. red on buff . . . — 80
LB12 25 c. brown on buff . . — 2·25
LB13 **17** 30 c. green and brown — 50·00
LB14 **21** 30 c. blue on buff . . . — 1·50
LB15 **17** 35 c. yellow and green — 9·00
LB16 40 c. blue . . . . . — 90
LB17 40 c. green and mauve — 14·00
LB18a 50 c. green & dp grn . 1·50 1·60
LB19 60 c. brown . . . . . 1·25 1·75
LB20a 70 c. buff and violet . 1·50 2·50
LB21 80 c. buff and grey . 8·50 1·50
LB22 **41** 90 c. red, green and deep green . . . . . . — 3·25
LB23 **17** 1 f. green and purple . — 2·00
LB24b **38** 1 f. 20 red, lake & pink 10·00 3·00
LB25a 1 f. 50 red, blue and turquoise . . . . . 2·25 2·50
LB26a 2 f. red, black and grey 2·75 4·50
LB27 **22** 3 f. red . . . . . . — 23·00
LB27a **43** 3 f. brown . . . . . . — £160
LB28 – 5 f. blue (No. 296) . . — 30·00
LB30 – 10 f. mauve (No. 297) . — £120
LB31 – 10 f. green (No. 337) . — £110

1932. International Disarmament Conference.
LB32 **44** 5 c. green . . . . . . — 90
LB33 10 c. orange . . . . . — 60
LB34 20 c. mauve . . . . . — 1·10
LB35 30 c. blue . . . . . . — 7·00
LB36 60 c. brown . . . . . — 7·50
LB37 **45** 1 f. grey and blue . . . — 7·50

1937. Landscape design of 1934.
LB38 **48** 3 c. green . . . . . . — 4·25

1937. Landscape designs of 1936.
LB39 **52** 3 c. green 20 15
LB40 – 5 c. green 20 15
LB41 – 10 c. purple . . . . . — 90
LB41e – 10 c. brown 45 60
LB42 – 15 c. orange 40 30
LB43 – 20 c. red (railway) . . . — 70
LB43c – 20 c. red (lake) . . . . 45 1·00
LB44 – 25 c. brown 50 60
LB45 – 30 c. blue 55 70
LB46 – 35 c. green . . . . . 55 1·00
LB47 – 40 c. grey . . . . . . 80 1·10

1938. Nos. 382/5 optd **S.d.N. Bureau International du Travail**.
LB48 **55** 20 c. red and buff . . . — 1·50
LB49 – 30 c. blue and light blue — 2·75
LB50 – 60 c. brown and buff . . — 6·00
LB51 – 1 f. black and buff . . . — 6·50

1938. Nos. 382/5 optd **SERVICE DU BUREAU INTERNATIONAL DU TRAVAIL** in circle.
LB52 **55** 20 c. red and buff . . . — 4·50
LB53 – 30 c. blue and light blue — 3·50
LB54 – 60 c. brown and buff . . — 6·50
LB55 – 1 f. black and buff . . . — 6·50

1939. Nos. 388c/90c optd **S.d.N. Bureau International du Travail**.
LB56 **61** 3 f. brown on buff . . . 4·50 8·00
LB57 – 5 f. blue on buff . . . 5·50 11·00
LB58 – 10 f. green on buff . . . 9·50 24·00

1944. Optd **COURRIER DU BUREAU INTERNATIONAL DU TRAVAIL.** (a) Landscape designs of 1936.
LB59 **52** 3 c. green 20 20
LB60 – 5 c. green 20 20
LB61 – 10 c. brown 30 30
LB62 – 15 c. orange 45 45
LB63 – 20 c. red (lake) 70 70
LB64 – 25 c. brown 80 80
LB65 – 30 c. blue . . . . . . 1·10 1·10
LB66 – 35 c. green . . . . . 1·25 1·25
LB67 – 40 c. grey . . . . . . 1·50 1·50

(b) Historical designs of 1941.
LB68 – 50 c. blue on green . . . 2·50 4·50
LB69 **68** 60 c. brown on brown 2·50 4·50
LB70 – 70 c. purple on mauve . 2·50 4·00
LB71 – 80 c. black on grey . . . 80 1·25
LB72 – 90 c. red on pink . . . . 80 1·25
LB73 – 1 f. green on green . . . 90 1·25
LB74 – 1 f. 20 purple on grey . . 1·25 1·40
LB75 – 1 f. 50 blue on buff . . 1·40 1·50
LB76 – 2 f. red on pink . . . . 2·25 2·25

(c) Parliament designs of 1938.
LB77 **61** 3 f. brown on buff . . . 5·00 6·00
LB78 – 5 f. blue on buff . . . 6·50 8·00
LB79 – 10 f. green on buff . . . 12·50 14·00

1950. Landscape designs of 1949 optd **BUREAU INTERNATIONAL DU TRAVAIL**.
LB80 **107** 5 c. orange . . . . . 4·75 4·00
LB81 – 10 c. green . . . . . 4·75 5·00
LB82 – 15 c. turquoise . . . . 6·50 5·00
LB83 – 20 c. purple . . . . . 6·50 5·00
LB84 – 25 c. red . . . . . . 7·00 6·00
LB85 – 30 c. green . . . . . 7·00 7·00
LB86 – 35 c. brown . . . . . 7·00 7·00
LB87 – 40 c. blue . . . . . 7·00 5·50
LB88 – 50 c. grey . . . . . 9·50 7·50
LB89 – 60 c. green . . . . . 10·00 8·50
LB90 – 70 c. violet . . . . . 14·50 14·00

LB 4 Miners (bas-relief)

1952. Inscr as in Type LB 4.
LB91 LB 4 5 c. purple 10 10
LB92 10 c. green 10 10
LB94 – 20 c. red 15 15
LB95 – 30 c. orange 20 20
LB96 LB 4 40 c. blue . . . . . 1·75 1·75
LB97 50 c. blue 30 30
LB98 – 60 c. brown 40 35
LB99 – 2 f. purple . . . . . 1·25 75
DESIGN—HORIZ: 20, 30, 60 c., 2 f. Globe, flywheel and factory chimney.

1969. Pope Paul's Visit to Geneva. No. LB95 optd **Visite du Pape Paul VI Geneve 10 juin 1969**.
LB100 30 c. orange 15 15

LB 6 New Headquarters Building

1974. Inauguration of New I.L.O. Headquarters, Geneva.
LB101 LB 6 80 c. multicoloured . 50 50

LB 7 Man at Lathe

1975.
LB102 LB 7 30 c. brown 30 30
LB103 – 60 c. blue 45 45
LB104 – 90 c. brown, red and green 80 80
LB105 – 100 c. green 80 80
LB106 – 120 c. ochre and brn 1·00 1·00
DESIGNS: 60 c. Woman at drilling machine; 90 c. Welder and laboratory assistant; 100 c. Surveyor with theodolite; 120 c. Apprentice and instructor with slide rule.

LB 8 Keys

1994. 75th Anniv of I.L.O.
LB107 LB 8 180 c. multicoloured 1·60 1·60

C. INTERNATIONAL EDUCATION OFFICE

1944. Optd **COURRIER DU BUREAU INTERNATIONAL D'EDUCATION.** (a) Landscape designs of 1936.
LE1 **52** 3 c. green 20 50
LE2 – 5 c. green . . . . . . 50 1·40
LE3 – 10 c. brown . . . . . 55 1·40
LE4 – 15 c. orange . . . . . 50 1·40
LE5 – 20 c. red (lake) . . . . 50 1·40
LE6 – 25 c. brown . . . . . 30 1·40
LE7 – 30 c. blue . . . . . . 1·75 2·50
LE8 – 35 c. green . . . . . 75 2·00
LE9 – 40 c. grey . . . . . . 90 2·25

(b) Historical designs of 1941.
LE10 – 50 c. blue on green . . . 4·50 9·00
LE11 **68** 60 c. brown on brown 4·50 9·00
LE12 – 70 c. purple on mauve . 4·50 9·00
LE13 – 80 c. black on grey . . . 60 1·40
LE14 – 90 c. red on pink . . . . 70 1·75
LE15 – 1 f. green on green . . . 80 2·00
LE16 – 1 f. 20 purple on grey . . 1·10 2·50
LE17 – 1 f. 50 blue on buff . . 1·40 3·00
LE18 – 2 f. red on pink . . . . 1·75 4·00

(c) Parliament designs of 1938.
LE19 **61** 3 f. brown on buff . . . 7·00 15·00
LE20 – 5 f. blue on buff . . . 9·50 25·00
LE21 – 10 f. green on buff . . . 14·00 35·00

1946. Optd **BIE**.
LE22 **86** 10 c. purple 15 15

Optd **BUREAU INTERNATIONAL D'EDUCATION** (Nos. LE23/39).

1948. Landscape designs of 1936.
LE23 5 c. brown . . . . 2·50 2·75
LE24 10 c. green . . . . 2·50 2·75
LE25 20 c. brown . . . . 2·50 2·75
LE26 25 c. red . . . . 2·50 2·75
LE27 30 c. blue . . . . 2·50 2·75
LE28 40 c. blue . . . . 2·50 2·75

1950. Landscape designs of 1949.
LE29 **107** 5 c. orange 60 60
LE30 – 10 c. green 80 80
LE31 – 15 c. turquoise 90 90
LE32 – 20 c. purple . . . . . 3·50 3·50
LE33 – 25 c. red . . . . . . 9·00 8·00
LE34 – 30 c. green . . . . . 9·00 8·00
LE35 – 35 c. brown . . . . . 5·50 7·00
LE36 – 40 c. blue . . . . . 5·50 7·00
LE37 – 50 c. grey . . . . . 6·00 7·50
LE38 – 60 c. green . . . . . 7·50 8·50
LE39 – 70 c. violet . . . . . 9·00 10·00

LE 3 Globe on Books

1958. Inscr as in Type LE 3.
LE40 LE 3 5 c. purple 10 10
LE41 10 c. green 10 10
LE43 – 20 c. red 15 15
LE44 – 30 c. orange 25 25
LE45 LE 3 40 c. blue . . . . . 2·25 2·25
LE46 50 c. blue 35 35
LE47 – 60 c. brown 50 50
LE48 – 2 f. purple . . . . . 1·25 1·25
DESIGN—VERT: 20, 30, 60 c., 2 f. Pestalozzi Monument, Yverdon.

D. WORLD HEALTH ORGANIZATION

1948. Optd **ORGANISATION MONDIALE DE LA SANTE**. (a) Landscape designs of 1936.
LH1 5 c. brown (No. 489) . . . . 3·50 2·00
LH2 10 c. green (No. 490) . . . . 3·50 4·00
LH3 20 c. brown (No. 491) . . . . 3·50 4·50
LH4 25 c. red (No. 492) . . . . 3·50 5·50
LH5 40 c. blue (No. 494) . . . . 3·50 4·00

(b) Landscape designs of 1949.
LH 6 **107** 5 c. orange 45 30
LH 7 – 10 c. green 90 80
LH 8 – 15 c. turquoise . . . . 1·25 1·50
LH 9 – 20 c. purple . . . . . 4·00 3·25
LH10 – 25 c. red . . . . . . 4·50 3·75
LH11 – 30 c. green . . . . . 2·00 2·00
LH12 – 35 c. brown . . . . . 2·75 4·00
LH13 – 40 c. blue . . . . . 2·75 1·50
LH14 – 50 c. grey . . . . . 3·00 3·75
LH15 – 60 c. green . . . . . 3·75 3·50
LH16 – 70 c. violet . . . . . 4·50 3·75

(c) Historical designs of 1941 (Nos. 408/13).
LH17 80 c. black on grey . . . . 3·50 3·00
LH18 90 c. red on pink . . . . 7·00 5·50
LH19 1 f. green on green . . . . 3·50 3·00
LH20 1 f. 20 purple on grey . . . 8·00 9·00
LH21 1 f. 50 blue on buff . . . . 18·00 10·00
LH22 2 f. red on pink . . . . . 6·00 4·00

(d) Parliament designs of 1938.
LH23 **61** 3 f. brown on buff . . . 38·00 32·00
LH24 – 5 f. blue on buff . . . 15·00 8·00
LH25 – 10 f. green on buff . . . 75·00 80·00

LH 2 Staff of Aesculapius

1957.
LH26 LH 2 5 c. purple 10 10
LH27 10 c. green 10 10
LH29 20 c. red 15 15
LH30 30 c. orange 25 25
LH31 40 c. blue . . . . . . 2·25 2·25
LH32 50 c. blue 35 30
LH33 60 c. brown 45 45
LH34 2 f. purple . . . . . . 1·25 1·10

1962. Malaria Eradication. Optd **ERADICATION DU PALUDISME**.
LH35 LH 2 50 c. blue 25 35

LH 4 Staff of Aesculapius

1975.
LH36 LH 4 30 c. green, purple and pink 25 30
LH37 60 c. yellow, blue and light blue 45 45
LH38 90 c. yellow, violet and light violet 75 60
LH39 100 c. blue, brown and orange 85 75
LH40 140 c. green, turquoise and red . . . . . 1·25 1·25

LH 5 Staff of Aesculapius

1995.
LH41 LH 5 180 c. yellow, brown and red . . . . 1·60 1·60

E. INTERNATIONAL REFUGEES ORGANIZATION

Optd **ORGANISATION INTERNATIONALE POUR LES REFUGIES**.

1950. (a) Landscape designs of 1949.
LR1 **107** 5 c. orange . . . . . 16·00 10·00
LR2 – 10 c. green . . . . . 16·00 10·00
LR3 – 20 c. purple . . . . . 16·00 10·00
LR4 – 25 c. red . . . . . . 16·00 10·00
LR5 – 40 c. blue . . . . . 16·00 10·00

(b) Historical designs of 1941 (Nos. 408/13).
LR6 80 c. black on grey . . . . . 16·00 10·00
LR7 1 f. green on green . . . . . 16·00 10·00
LR8 2 f. red on pink . . . . . . 16·00 10·00

F. WORLD METEOROLOGICAL ORGANIZATION

LM 1 "The Elements" LM 2 W.M.O. Emblem

1956. Inscr as in Type LM 1.
LM1 LM 1 5 c. purple 10 10
LM2 10 c. green 10 10
LM4 – 20 c. red 20 20
LM5 – 30 c. orange 25 25
LM6 LM 1 40 c. blue . . . . . 2·00 2·00
LM7 50 c. blue 35 30
LM8 – 60 c. brown 45 45
LM9 – 2 f. purple . . . . . 1·25 1·25
DESIGN: 20, 30, 60 c., 2 f. Weathervane.

1973. Centenary of World Meteorological Organization.
LM10 LM 2 30 c. red 25 25
LM11 – 40 c. blue 30 30
LM12 – 80 c. violet and gold . 60 60
LM13 – 1 f. brown 80 80
DESIGN: 80 c. Emblem and "OM1 OMM 1873 1973".

G. UNIVERSAL POSTAL UNION

LP 1 U.P.U. Monument, Berne LP 2 "Letter Post"

1957. Inscr as in Type LP 1.
LP1 LP 1 5 c. purple 10 10
LP2 – 10 c. green 10 10
LP4 – 20 c. red 20 20
LP5 – 30 c. orange 25 25
LP6 LP 1 40 c. blue . . . . . 2·00 2·00
LP7 50 c. blue 35 35
LP8 60 c. brown . . . . . [illegible] [illegible]
LP9 LP 1 2 f. purple . . . . . 1·25 1·25
DESIGN: 10, 20, 30, 60 c. Pegasus (sculpture).

1976.
LP10 LP 2 40 c. purple, blue and claret 35 35
LP11 – 80 c. multicoloured . . 70 70
LP12 – 90 c. multicoloured . . 80 80
LP13 – 100 c. multicoloured . 85 85
LP14 – 120 c. multicoloured . 1·00 1·00
LP15 – 140 c. grey, blue and red 1·25 1·25
DESIGNS: 80 c. "Parcel Post"; 90 c. "Financial Services"; 100 c. Technical co-operation; 120 c. Carrier pigeon, international reply coupon and postal money order; 140 c. Express Mail Service.
The 120 and 140 c. are additionally inscribed "TIMBRE DE SERVICE".

LP **3** Computer, Mail Sacks and Globe

1995.

LP16	LP **3**	180 c. multicoloured	1·60	1·60

H. UNITED NATIONS

1950. Optd **NATIONS UNIES OFFICE EUROPEEN.** (a) Landscape designs of 1949.

LU 1	**107**	5 c. orange	45	90
LU 2	–	10 c. green	45	90
LU 3	–	15 c. turquoise	90	1·40
LU 4	–	20 c. purple	1·40	1·75
LU 5	–	25 c. red	2·75	4·00
LU 6	–	30 c. green	2·75	4·00
LU 7	–	35 c. brown	2·75	8·00
LU 8	–	40 c. blue	4·00	3·75
LU 9	–	50 c. grey	4·75	6·50
LU10	–	60 c. green	5·00	8·50
LU11	–	70 c. violet	6·00	8·00

(b) Historical designs of 1941 (Nos. 408/13).

LU12	80 c. black on grey	10·00	10·00
LU13	90 c. red on pink	10·00	10·00
LU14	1 f. green on green	10·00	10·00
LU15	1 f. 20 purple on grey	12·50	12·50
LU16	1 f. 50 blue on buff	12·50	14·00
LU17	2 f. red on pink	12·50	11·00

(c) Parliament designs of 1938.

LU18	**61**	3 f. brown on buff	£120	£120
LU19	–	5 f. blue on buff	£120	£120
LU20	–	10 f. green on buff	£150	£150

LU 2

LU 4

1955. 10th Anniv of U.N.O.

LU21	LU **2**	40 c. blue and yellow	3·25	4·50

1955. Nos. LU22/3 and LU27/8 are as Type LU **2** but without dates.

LU22	–	5 c. purple	10	10
LU23	–	10 c. green	10	10
LU25	LU **4**	20 c. red	20	20
LU26		30 c. orange	25	25
LU27	–	40 c. blue	4·50	4·00
LU28	–	50 c. blue	35	35
LU29	LU **4**	60 c. brown	35	35
LU30		2 f. purple	1·25	1·00

1960. World Refugee Year. Nos. LU25 and LU28 optd **ANNEE MONDIALE DU REFUGIE 1959 1960.**

LU31	20 c. red	15	15
LU32	50 c. blue	25	25

LU **6** Palace of Nations, Geneva

1960. 15th Anniv of U.N.O.

LU33	LU **6**	5 f. blue	3·50	3·50

LU 7

LU **8** UNCSAT Emblem

1962. Opening of U.N. Philatelic Museum, Geneva.

LU34	LU **7**	10 c. green and red	10	10
LU35	–	30 c. red and blue	20	25
LU36	LU **7**	50 c. blue and red	30	30
LU37	–	60 c. brown and grn	35	40

DESIGN—HORIZ: 30, 60 c. As Type LU **4** but inscr "ONU MUSEE PHILATELIQUE".

1963. U.N. Scientific and Technological Conference, Geneva.

LU38	LU **8**	50 c. red and blue	30	30
LU39	–	2 f. green and purple	80	1·00

DESIGN—HORIZ: 2 f. As Type LU **4**, but with emblem.

From 1969 stamps for the Geneva Headquarters were issued by the United Nations (q.v.).

I. INTERNATIONAL TELECOMMUNICATION UNION

LT **1** Transmitting Aerial

LT **2** New H.Q. Building

1958. Inscr as in Type LT **1**.

LT1	LT **1**	5 c. purple	10	10
LT2		10 c. green	10	10
LT4	–	20 c. red	20	20
LT5	–	30 c. orange	25	25
LT6	LT **1**	40 c. blue	1·75	2·00
LT7		50 c. blue	35	35
LT8	–	60 c. brown	45	45
LT9	–	2 f. purple	1·25	1·25

DESIGN: 20, 30, 60 c., 2 f. Receiving aerials.

1973. Inauguration of New I.T.U. Headquarters, Geneva.

LT10	LT **2**	80 c. black and blue	55	55

LT **3** Boeing 747 Jetliner and Ocean Liner

1976. World Telecommunications Network.

LT11	–	40 c. blue and red	35	35
LT12	LT **3**	90 c. violet, bl & yell	75	75
LT13	–	1 f. red, green & yell	80	80

DESIGNS: 40 c. "Sound waves"; 1 f. Face and microphone in television screen.

LT **4** Optical Fibre Cables

1988.

LT14	LT **4**	1 f. 40 multicoloured	1·75	1·75

LT **5** Emblem emitting Radio Signals

1994. 100 Years of Radio.

LT15	LT **5**	1 f. 80 multicoloured	1·60	1·60

J. WORLD INTELLECTUAL PROPERTY ORGANIZATION

LV **1** WIPO Seal

1989. Multicoloured.

LV1	40 c. Type LV **1**	35	35
LV2	50 c. Face and symbolic representation of intellect	45	45
LV3	80 c. WIPO building, Geneva	70	70
LV4	100 c. Hand pressing buttons, retort and cogwheel (industrial property)	1·00	1·00
LV5	120 c. Head, ballet dancer, cello and book (copyright)	1·25	1·25

SYRIA Pt. 19

A country at the E. end of the Mediterranean Sea, formerly Turkish territory. Occupied by the Allies in 1918 and administered under French Military Occupation. An Arab kingdom was set up in the Aleppo and Damascus area during 1919, but the Emir Faisal came into conflict with the French and was defeated in July 1920. In April 1920, the Mandate was offered to France, becoming effective in September 1923. Separate governments were established for the Territories of Damascus, Aleppo, the Alaouites (including Latakia), Great Lebanon and the Jebel Druze. Syria became a republic in 1934, and the Mandate ended with full Independence in 1942.

In 1958 the United Arab Republic was formed which comprised Egypt and Syria but separate stamps were issued for each territory as they employed different currencies. In 1961 Syria left the U.A.R. and the Syrian Arab Republic was established.

1919. 40 paras = 10 milliemes = 1 piastre.
1920. 100 centimes (or centiemes) = 1 piastre; 100 piastres = 1 Syrian Pound.

A. FRENCH MILITARY OCCUPATION.

1919. Stamps of France surch **T. E. O.** and value in "MILLIEMES" or "PIASTRES".

1 **11** 1 m. on 1 c. grey £160 £160
2 2 m. on 2 c. purple £400 £475
3 3 m. on 3 c. orange £170 £170
4 **15** 4 m. on 15 c.green . . . . 40·00 40·00
5 **18** 5 m. on 5 c. green . . . . . 20·00 20·00
6 1 p. on 10 c. red . . . . . . 28·00 28·00
7 2 p. on 25 c. blue . . . . . 17·00 17·00
8 **13** 5 p. on 40 c. red and blue . 24·00 24·00
9 9 p. on 50 c. brown and lilac 45·00 45·00
10 10 p. on 1 f. red and yellow 75·00 75·00

1919. Nos. 9/13a and 19/23 of French Post Offices in the Turkish Empire ("Blanc", "Mouchon" and "Merson" key-types inscr "LEVANT") optd **T. E. O.** or surch in "MILLIEMES" also.

11 A 1 m. on 1 c. grey 80 80
12 2 m. on 2 c. purple 80 80
13 3 m. on 3 c. red . . . . . . 1·40 1·40
14 B 4 m. on 15 c. red . . . . . 45 1·10
15 A 5 m. on 5 c. green . . . . . 45 1·10
16 B 1 p. on 25 c. blue . . . . . 1·00 1·00
17 C 2 p. on 50 c. brown and lilac 1·60 1·60
18 4 p. on 1 f. red and green . 2·00 1·75
19 8 p. on 2 f. lilac and buff . . 5·00 4·75
20 20 p. on 5 f. blue & buff . . £325 £225

1920. Stamps of France surch **O. M. F. Syrie** and value in "MILLIEMES" or "PIASTRES".

25 **11** 1 m. on 1 c. grey . . . . . 50 1·00
26 2 m. on 2 c.purple . . . . 1·00 1·50
27 **18** 3 m. on 5 c. green . . . . . 65 1·25
28 5 m. on 10 c. red . . . . . 50 1·10
29 **13** 20 p. on 5 f. blue and buff . 75·00 75·00

1920. Stamps of France surch **O. M. F. Syrie** and value. (a) Value in "CENTIMES" or "PIASTRES".

31 **11** 25 c. on 1 c. grey . . . . . 1·25 1·25
32 50 c. on 2 c. purple . . . . 1·25 1·25
33 75 c. on 3 c. orange . . . . 1·25 1·25
35 **18** 1 p. on 5 c. green . . . . . 1·10 25
36 2 p. on 10 c. red . . . . . 70 1·10
37 2 p. on 25 c. blue 70 25
38 3 p. on 25 c. blue . . . . . 1·25 1·10
39 **15** 5 p. on 15 c. green . . . . . 1·25 1·25
40 **13** 10 p. on 40 c. red and blue . 1·50 1·50
41 25 p. on 50 c. brown and lilac 1·90 1·90
42 50 p. on 1 f. red and yellow 24·00 24·00
44 100 p. on 5 f. blue and buf . 45·00 45·00

(b) Value in "CENTIEMES".

45 **11** 25 c. on 1 c. grey 50 60
46 50 c. on 2 c. purple 25 25
47 75 c. on 3 c. orange . . . . 18·00 18·00

1920. Air. Nos. 35 and 39/40 optd **POSTE PAR AVION** in frame.

57 **18** 1 p. on 5 c. green . . . . . £170 40·00
58 **15** 5 p. on 15 c. green . . . . . £300 60·00
59 **13** 10 p. on 40 c. red and blue £400 90·00

1921. Issued at Damascus. Nos. K88/95 of Arab Kingdom surch **O. M. F. Syrie** and value in "CENTIEMES" or "PIASTRES".

60 **K 3** 25 c. on $\frac{1}{10}$ m. brown . . . 2·50 2·00
61 50 c. on $\frac{1}{10}$ p. green . . . 2·50 2·00
62 1 p. on $\frac{3}{10}$ p. yellow . . . 3·00 2·50
63 **K 4** 1 p. on 5 m. red . . . . 3·50 2·50
64a 2 p. on 5 m. red . . . . 5·00 4·25
65 **K 3** 3 p. on 1 p. blue . . . . 7·50 5·50
66 5 p. on 2 p. green . . . . 8·00 6·00
67 10 p. on 5 p. purple . . . 12·00 9·00
68 25 p. on 10 p. grey . . . . 13·00 10·00

1921. Stamps of France surch **O. M. F. Syrie** and value in "CENTIEMES" or "PIASTRES" (in two lines).

69 **18** 25 c. on 5 c. green 90 70
70 50 c. on 10 c. red 60 20
71 **15** 75 c. on 15 c. green 90 70
72 **18** 1 p. on 20 c. red . . . . . 1·00 15
73 **13** 2 p. on 40 c. red and blue . 1·00 80
74 3 p. on 60 c. violet & blue . 1·25 35
75 5 p. on 1 f. red and yellow . 2·00 1·75
76 10 p. on 2 f. orange & green 3·00 3·00
77 25 p. on 5 f. blue and buff . £160 £150

See also Nos. 81/5.

1921. Air. Nos. 72 and 75/6 optd **POSTE PAR AVION** in frame.

78 **18** 1 p. on 20 c. red . . . . . . 85·00 40·00
79 **13** 5 p. on 1 f. red and yellow . £400 £300
80 10 p. on 2 f. orange & grn . £400 £300

1921. Stamps of France surch **O.M.F. Syrie** and value in "PIASTRES" in one line.

81 **13** 2 p. on 40 c. red and blue . . 90 25
82 3 p. on 60 c. violet & blue . 1·00 35
83 5 p. on 1 f. red and yellow . 5·50 4·00
84 10 p. on 2 f. orange & grn . 10·00 9·00
85 25 p. on 5 f. blue & buff . . 9·00 8·75

1921. Air. Nos. 72 and 75/6 optd **AVION**.

86 **18** 1 p. on 20 c. red . . . . . 50·00 42·00
87 **13** 5 p. on 1 f. red and yellow . £140 80·00
88 10 p. on 2 f. orange & grn . £180 65·00

1922. Air. Stamps of France surch **Poste par Avion O. M. F. Syrie** and value.

89 **13** 2 p. on 40 c. red and blue . 17·00 20·00
90 3 p. on 60 c. violet & blue . 20·00 20·00
91 5 p. on 1 f. red and yellow . 20·00 20·00
92 10 p. on 2 f. orange & grn . 20·00 20·00

1922. Stamps of France surch **O. M. F. Syrie** and value in "CENTIEMES" or "PIASTRES".

93 **11** 10 c. on 2 c. purple . . . 80 1·00
94 **18** 10 c. on 5 c. orange . . . 60 90
95 25 c. on 5 c. orange . . . 1·10 35
96 50 c. on 10 c. green . . . 1·25 35
96a 1,25 p. on 25 c. blue . . . 1·40 50
96b 1,50 p. on 30 c. orange . . 1·10 65
96c **13** 2,50 p. on 50 c. brn & lilac 90 75
96d **15** 2,50 p. on 50 c. blue . . . 1·50 55

B. ARAB KINGDOM.

Prior to the issues listed below, the Kingdom used stamps of Turkey variously overprinted. These are listed in Part 19 (Middle East) of the Stanley Gibbons Catalogue.

K 3 K 4

1920. As Type **K 3** and Type **K 4**.

K88 **K 3** $\frac{1}{10}$ m. brown (22 × 17 mm) 10 10
K89 $\frac{1}{10}$ p. green (27 × 21 mm) 45 30
K90 $\frac{3}{10}$ p. yellow (27 × 21 mm) 20 20
K91 **K 4** 5 m. red 20 20
K92 **K 3** 1 p. blue (27 × 21 mm) 20 10
K93 2 p. green (27 × 21 mm) 1·90 60
K94 5 p. purple (32 × 35 mm) 2·50 1·25
K95 10 p. grey (32 × 35 mm) 2·50 1·90

For 1 p. black as Type **K 3**, see Postage Due No. KD96.

1920. Independence Commemoration Optd with Arabic inscription.

K98 **K 4** 5 m. red £350 £200

C. FRENCH MANDATED TERRITORY.

Issues for Lebanon and Syria.

Nos. 97/174 are all stamps of France surch.

1923. (a) Surch **Syrie Grand Liban** in two lines and value.

97 **11** 10 c. on 2 c. purple . . . 30 50
98 **18** 25 c. on 5 c. orange . . . 65 70
99 50 c. on 10 c. green . . . 65 35
100 **15** 75 c. on 15 c. green . . . 90 95
101 **18** 1 p. on 20 c. brown . . . 80 45
102 1,25 p. on 25 c. blue . . . 90 95
103 1,50 p. on 30 c. orange . . 90 85
104 1,50 p. on 30 c. red . . . 75 1·10
105 **15** 2,50 p. on 50 c. blue . . . 35 55

(b) Surch **Syrie-Grand Liban** in one line and value.

106 **13** 2 p. on 40 c. red and blue . 90 50
107 3 p. on 60 c. violet & blue 1·25 1·40
108 5 p. on 1 f. red and yellow 1·90 1·90
109 10 p. on 2 f. orange & grn 6·00 6·25
110 25 p. on 5 f. blue & buff . 23·00 24·00

(c) "Pasteur" issue surch **Syrie Grand Liban** in two lines and value.

111 **30** 50 c. on 10 c. green . . . 1·00 1·25
112 1,50 p. on 30 c. red . . . 1·25 1·25
113 2,50 p. on 50 c. blue . . . 90 1·25

1923. Air. Surch **Post par Avion Syrie-Grand Liban** and value.

114 **13** 2 p. on 40 c. red and blue 28·00 26·00
115 3 p. on 60 c. violet & blue 28·00 28·00
116 5 p. on 1 f. red & yellow . 28·00 22·00
117 10 p. on 2 f. orange and green 30·00 28·00

Issues for Syria only.

1924. Surch **SYRIE** and value in two lines. (a) Stamps of 1900–20.

118 **11** 10 c. on 2 c. purple . . . 70 80
119 **18** 25 c. on 5 c. orange . . . 65 70
120 50 c. on 10 c. green . . . 70 60
121 **15** 75 c. on 15 c. green . . . 90 85
122 **18** 1 p. on 20 c. brown . . . 90 35
123 1,25 p. on 25 c. blue . . . 1·00 90
124 1,50 p. on 30 c. orange . . 1·00 1·10
125 1,50 p. on 30 c. red . . . 1·00 1·10
127 **13** 2 p. on 40 c. red and blue 90 50
126 **15** 2,50 p. on 50 c. blue . . . 90 45
128 **13** 3 p. on 60 c. violet & blue 1·25 90
129 5 p. on 1 f. red and yellow 2·25 2·25
130 10 p. on 2 f. orange & grn 2·25 2·25
131 25 p. on 5 f. blue & yellow 4·00 4·00

(b) "Pasteur" issue.

132 **30** 50 c. on 10 c. green . . . 75 90
133 1,50 p. on 30 c. red . . . 1·00 1·10
134 2,50 p. on 50 c. blue . . . 75 90

1924. Air. Surch **Poste par Avion Syrie** and value.

135 **13** 2 p. on 40 c. red and blue 2·00 2·25
136 3 p. on 60 c. violet & blue 2·00 2·25
137 5 p. on 1 f. red and yellow 2·25 2·25
138 10 p. on 2 f. orange & grn 2·25 2·25

1924. Olympic Games issue (Nos. 401/4) surch **SYRIE** and value.

139 **31** 50 c. on 10 c. green and light green . . . . 38·00 38·00
140 – 1,25 p. on 25 c. carmine and red . . . . 38·00 38·00
141 – 1,50 p. on 30 c. red & blk 38·00 38·00
142 – 2,50 p. on 50 c. ultramarine and blue . . . . . . 38·00 38·00

1924. Surch **Syrie** and value in French and Arabic. (a) Issues of 1900–20.

143 **11** 0, p. 10 on 2 c. red . . . . 50 1·00
144 **18** 0, p. 25 on 5 c. orange . . . 50 95
145 0, p. 50 on 10 c. green . . . 55 1·25
146 **15** 0, p. 75 on 15 c. green . . . 70 1·10
147 **18** 1 p. on 20 c. brown . . . . 1·00 35
148 1, p. 25 on 25 c. blue . . . 1·00 1·25
149 1 p. 50 on 30 c. red (no comma) . . . . 1·10 1·25
150 1, p. 50 on 30 c. orange . . 2·25 2·25
151 2 p. on 35 c. violet . . . . 1·10 1·40
152 **13** 2 p. on 40 c. red and blue . 1·10 90
153 2 p. on 45 c. green & blue . 3·50 3·75
154 3 p. on 60 c. violet & blue . 1·50 1·60
155 **15** 3 p. on 60 c. violet . . . . 1·25 1·75
156 4 p. on 85 c. red . . . . . 70 1·40
157 **13** 5 p. on 1 f. red and yellow . 1·25 1·75
158 10 p. on 2 f. orange & grn . 2·00 2·25
159 25 p. on 5 f. blue & buff . . 2·25 2·25

(b) "Pasteur" issue.

160 **30** 0, p. 50 on 10 c. green . . . 1·10 35
161 0 p. 75 on 15 c. green . . . 1·40 1·50
162 1, p. 50 on 30 c. red . . . . 1·25 1·50
163 2 p. on 45 c. red . . . . . 1·10 1·25
164 2 p. 50 on 50 c. blue . . . 1·25 1·10
165 4 p. on 75 c. blue . . . . . 1·10 1·75

(c) Olympic Games Issue (Nos. 401/4).

166 **31** 0, p. 50 on 10 c. green and light green . . . . 38·00 38·00
167 – 1 p. 25 on 25 c. carmine and red . . . . 38·00 38·00
168 – 1 p. 50 on 30 c. red & blk . 38·00 38·00
169 – 2 p. 50 on 50 c. ultramarine and blue . . . . 38·00 38·00

(d) Ronsard stamp.

170 **35** 4 p. on 75 c. blue on blue . 75 1·50

1924. Air. Surch **Syrie Avion** and new value in French and Arabic.

171 **13** 2 p. on 40 c. red and blue . 4·25 4·50
172 3 p. on 60 c. violet & blue . 4·00 4·75
173 5 p. on 1 f. red and yellow . 3·25 4·75
174 10 p. on 2 f. orange & grn . 4·25 4·75

16 Hama

17 Merkab **18** Damascus

1925. Views.

175 **16** 0 p. 10 violet 15 35
176 **17** 0 p. 25 black 50 90
177 – 0 p. 50 green 55 25
178 – 0 p. 75 red . . . . 25 1·10
179 **18** 1 p. purple 55 15
180 – 1 p. 25 green . . . . . . 1·50 1·60
181 – 1 p. 50 pink 60 15
182 – 2 p. brown . . . . 1·25 20
183 – 2 p. 50 blue . . . . . . 1·10 60
184 – 3 p. brown . . . . 1·10 15
185 – 5 p. violet 80 15
186 – 10 p. purple . . . . . . 3·50 25
187 – 25 p. blue . . . . 3·75 2·25

DESIGNS—As Type **17**: 0 p. 50, Alexandretta; 0 p. 75, Hama; 1 p. 25, Latakia; 1 p. 50, Damascus; 2, 25 p. Palmyra (different views); 2 p. 50, Kalat Yamoun; 3 p. Bridge of Daphne; 5, 10 p. Aleppo (different views).

1925. Air. Nos. 182 and 184/6 optd **AVION** in French and Arabic.

188 2 p. brown . . . . 1·50 2·25
189 3 p. brown . . . . 1·75 2·25
190 5 p. violet . . . . 1·60 2·25
191 10 p. purple . . . . 1·75 2·25

1926. Air. Nos. 182 and 184/6 optd with Bleriot XI airplane.

192 2 p. brown . . . . 1·60 1·60
193 3 p. brown . . . . 1·25 1·75
194 5 p. violet . . . . 1·90 2·00
195 10 p. purple . . . . 1·90 2·00

1926. War Refugees Fund. Nos. 176 etc and 192/5 surch **Secours aux Refugies Afft** and value in French and Arabic.

196 **17** 0 p. 25 on 0 p. 25 black (postage) . . . . 1·90 2·50
197 – 0 p. 25 on 0 p. 50 green . . 2·25 2·50
198 – 0 p. 25 on 0 p. 75 red . . . 1·25 2·50
199 **18** 0 p. 50 on 1 p. purple . . . 2·25 2·50
200 – 0 p. 50 on 1 p. 25 green . . 2·50 2·50
201 – 0 p. 50 on 1 p. 50 pink . . 1·75 2·50
202 – 0 p. 75 on 2 p. brown . . 2·50 2·50
203 – 0 p. 75 on 2 p. 50 blue . . 2·50 2·50
204 – 1 p. on 3 p. brown . . . 2·50 2·50
205 – 1 p. on 5 p. violet . . . 2·50 2·50
206 – 2 p. on 10 p. purple . . . 1·90 2·50
207 – 5 p. on 25 p. blue . . . 2·50 2·50
208 – 1 p. on 2 p. brown (air) . . 2·25 2·75
209 – 2 p. on 3 p. brown . . . 2·00 2·75
210 – 3 p. on 5 p. violet . . . 2·00 2·75
211 – 5 p. on 10 p. purple . . . 2·00 2·75

1926. No. 175 etc surch with new value in English and Arabic.

221 05 on 0 p. 10 violet . . . . . 40 1·00
222 1 p. on 3 p. brown . . . . . 1·60 30
223 2 p. on 1 p. 25 green . . . . 1·10 20
212 3 p. 50 on 0 p. 75 red . . . . 1·00 1·25
224 4 p. on 0 p. 25 black . . . . 1·00 15
215 4 p. 50 on 0 p. 75 red 75 25
216 6 p. on 2 p. 50 blue . . . . . 1·00 70
217 7 p. 50 on 2 p. 50 blue . . . 1·50 60
218 12 p. on 1 p. 25 green . . . . 1·50 95
219 15 p. on 25 p. blue . . . . . 1·50 30
220 20 p. on 1 p. 25 green . . . . 2·50 1·60

1929. Air. Nos. 177 etc, optd with Bleriot XI airplane or surch also in English and Arabic.

225 0 p. 50 green . . . . 85 1·40
226 1 p. purple . . . . 1·25 1·25
227 2 p. on 1 p. 25 green . . . . 2·25 1·60
228 15 p. on 25 p. blue . . . . . 3·25 2·50
229 25 p. blue . . . . 4·00 3·75

1929. Damascus Industrial Exn. Nos. 177 etc and various air stamps optd **EXPOSITION INDUSTRIELLE DAMAS 1929** in French and Arabic.

230 0 p. 50 green (postage) . . . 2·25 2·75
231 1 p. purple . . . . 2·25 2·75
232 1 p. 50 pink . . . . 2·25 2·75
233 3 p. brown . . . . 2·75 2·75
234 5 p. violet . . . . 2·75 2·75
235 10 p. purple . . . . 2·75 2·75
236 25 p. blue . . . . 2·75 2·75
237 0 p. 50 green (No. 225) (air) . 2·25 2·50
238 1 p. purple (No. 226) . . . . 2·25 2·50
239 2 p. brown (No. 192) . . . . 2·25 2·50
240 3 p. brown (No. 193) . . . . 2·25 2·50
241 5 p. violet (No. 194) . . . . 2·25 2·50
242 10 p. purple (No. 195) . . . . 2·25 2·50
243 25 p. blue (No. 229) . . . . 2·25 2·50

26 Hama

27 Damascus

1930. Views.

244 **26** 0 p. 10 mauve 70 60
244b 0 p. 10 purple 15 70
245 – 0 p. 20 blue 45 80
245a – 0 p. 20 red 80 75
246 – 0 p. 25 green 70 80
246a – 0 p. 25 violet 70 90
247 – 0 p. 50 violet 40 15
247a – 0 p. 75 red 70 60
248 – 1 p. green 80 15
248a – 1 p. brown 90 15
249 – 1 p. 50 brown . . . . . . 4·25 3·00
249a – 1 p. 50 green . . . . . . 3·00 2·75
250 – 2 p. violet 80 15
251 – 3 p. green 90 70
252 **27** 4 p. orange 50 15
253 – 4 p. 50 red . . . . 1·10 50
254 – 6 p. black 50 75
255 – 7 p. 50 blue 90 40
256 – 10 p. brown . . . . . . 1·25 25
257 – 15 p. green . . . . . . 1·50 55
258 – 25 p. purple . . . . . . 2·00 1·10
259 – 50 p. brown . . . . . . 30·00 25·00
260 – 100 p. red . . . . 75·00 40·00

DESIGNS—As Type **26**: 0 p. 20, Aleppo; 0 p. 25, Hama (different). As Type **27**: 0 p. 50, Alexandretta; 0 p. 75, 4 p. 50, Homs; 1 p., 7 p. 50, Aleppo (different); 1 p. 50., 100 p. Damascus (different); 2, 10 p. Antioch; 3 p. Bosra; 5 p. Sednaya; 15 p. Hama; 25 p. St. Simeon; 50 p. Palmyra.

28 River Euphrates

1931. Air. Views with Potez 29-4 biplane.

261 – 0 p. 50 yellow (Homs) . . 70 1·00
261a – 0 p. 50 brown (Homs) . . 95 1·25
262 – 1 p. brown (Damascus) . 90 1·00
263 **28** 2 p. blue . . . . 2·00 2·25
264 – 3 p. green (Palmyra) . . . 1·40 1·00
265 – 5 p. purple (Deir-el-Zor) . 90 1·00
266 – 10 p. blue (Damascus) . . 90 1·00
267 – 15 p. red (Aleppo citadel) 1·50 1·25
268 – 25 p. orange (Hama) . . 2·00 2·00
269 – 50 p. black (Zebdani) . . 2·00 2·00
270 – 100 p. mauve (Telebisse) 2·50 2·75

D. REPUBLIC UNDER FRENCH MANDATE.

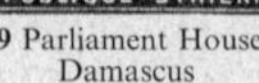

29 Parliament House, Damascus

30 Aboulula el Maari

31 Farman F.190 Airplane over Bloudan

1934. Establishment of Republic.
271 **29** 0 p. 10 green (postage) 1·50 1·60
272 0 p. 20 black 1·25 1·50
273 0 p. 25 red 1·50 1·60
274 0 p. 50 blue 1·25 1·50
275 0 p. 75 purple 1·50 1·60
276 **30** 1 p. red 3·25 3·25
277 1 p. 50 green 5·00 4·75
278 2 p. brown 5·00 4·75
279 3 p. blue 20·00 5·00
280 4 p. violet 5·00 4·25
281 4 p. 50 red 5·00 4·25
282 5 p. blue 5·00 4·50
283 6 p. brown 5·00 4·50
284 7 p. 50 blue 5·00 4·00
285 – 10 p. brown 8·25 8·00
286 – 15 p. blue 11·00 7·75
287 – 25 p. red 16·00 16·00
288 – 50 p. brown 30·00 30·00
289 – 100 p. red 32·00 30·00
DESIGNS—As Type **30**: Nos. 285/7, President Mohammed Ali Bey el-Abed; Nos. 288/9, Sultan Saladin.
290 **31** 0 p. 50 brown (air) 2·00 2·25
291 1 p. green 2·00 2·00
292 2 p. blue 2·25 2·00
293 3 p. red 2·25 2·25
294 5 p. purple 2·25 2·25
295 10 p. violet 21·00 24·00
296 15 p. brown 21·00 21·00
297 25 p. blue 26·00 28·00
298 50 p. black 32·00 35·00
299 100 p. brown 60·00 60·00

1936. Damascus Fair. Optd **1936 FOIRE DE DAMAS** in Arabic and French. (a) Postage stamps of 1930.
300 – 0 p. 50 violet 2·00 2·25
301 – 1 p. brown 2·00 2·25
302 – 2 p. violet 2·00 2·25
303 – 3 p. green 2·00 2·25
304 **27** 4 p. orange 2·50 2·25
305 – 4 p. 50 red 2·50 2·25
306 – 6 p. green 2·50 2·25
307 – 7 p. blue 2·50 2·50
308 – 10 p. brown 3·00 3·25
(b) Air stamps of 1931.
309 – 0 p. 50 brown 2·50 3·75
310 – 1 p. brown 2·50 3·75
311 **28** 2 p. blue 2·50 3·75
312 – 3 p. green 2·50 3·75
313 – 5 p. purple 3·25 3·75

33 Exhibition Pavilion

1937. Air. Paris International Exhibition.
314 **33** ½ p. green 1·60 1·75
315 1 p. green 1·60 2·50
316 2 p. brown 1·60 1·75
317 3 p. red 1·60 2·50
318 5 p. orange 1·90 2·75
319 10 p. green 3·00 4·50
320 15 p. blue 3·75 5·50
321 25 p. violet 3·75 5·50

34 Savoia Marchetti S-73 over Aleppo

1937. Air.
322 **34** ½ p. violet 30 40
323 – 1 p. black 30 90
324 **34** 2 p. green 30 1·00
325 – 3 p. blue 35 1·25
326 **34** 5 p. mauve 90 1·10
327 – 10 p. brown 65 1·10
328 **34** 15 p. brown 1·75 2·25
329 – 25 p. blue 3·00 5·00
DESIGN: 1, 3, 10, 25 p. Potez 62 airplane over Damascus.

1938. Stamps of 1930 surch in English and Arabic.
330 0 p. 25 on 0 p. 75 red 15 70
331 0 p. 50 on 1 p. 50 green 15 65
332 2 p. on 7 p. 50 blue 55 55
333 2 p. 50 on 4 p. orange 65 25
334 5 p. on 7 p. 50 blue 1·25 55
335 10 p. on 50 p. brown 1·10 75
336 10 p. on 100 p. red 1·10 80

MINIMUM PRICE

The minimum price quoted is 10p which represents a handling charge rather than a basis for valuing common stamps. For further notes about prices, see introductory pages.

38 CAMS 53H Flying Boat, Maurice Nogues and Flight Route

1938. Air. 10th Anniv of 1st Air Service Flight between France and Syria.
337 **38** 10 p. green 1·50 2·75

39 Pres. Atasi 41 Palmyra

1938. Unissued stamp surch **12.50** and in Arabic figures.
338 **39** 12 p. 50 on 10 p. blue 1·00 45

1938.
339 **39** 10 p. blue 1·10 50
339a 20 p. brown 1·00 50

1940.
340 **41** 5 p. pink 1·00 40

42 Damascus Museum 45 Deir-el-Zor Bridge

1940.
341 **42** 0 p. 10 red (postage) 15 50
342 0 p. 20 blue 10 15
343 0 p. 25 brown 10 50
344 0 p. 50 blue 10 15
345 – 1 p. blue 20 20
346 – 1 p. 50 brown 50 75
347 – 2 p. 50 green 15 60
348 – 5 p. violet 35 20
349 – 7 p. 50 red 55 60
350 – 50 p. purple 1·60 1·75
DESIGNS—As Type **45**: 1 p., 1 p. 50, 2 p. 50, Hotel de Bloudan; 5 p., 7 p. 50, 50 p. Kasr-el-Heir Fortress.
351 **45** 0 p. 25 black (air) 15 50
352 0 p. 50 blue 15 45
353 1 p. blue 20 1·00
354 2 p. brown 20 1·00
355 5 p. green 55 1·10
356 10 p. red 60 1·00
357 50 p. violet 2·25 2·50

E. SYRIAN REPUBLIC.

46 President Taj Addin el-Husni 47

1942. National Independence. Inscr "PROCLAMATION/DE L'INDEPENDENCE/27 Septembre 1941".
358 **46** 0 p. 50 green (postage) 3·25 3·25
359 1 p. 50 brown 3·25 3·25
360 6 p. red 3·25 3·25
361 15 p. blue 3·25 3·25
362 – 10 p. blue (air) 2·50 2·50
363 – 50 p. purple 2·50 2·50
DESIGN: 10, 50 p. As Type **46**, but President bareheaded and airplane inset.

1942. (a) Postage. Portrait in oval frame.
364 **47** 6 p. purple and pink 1·90 1·90
365 15 p. blue and light blue 1·90 1·90
(b) Air. Portrait in rectangular frame.
366 10 p. green and emerald 3·75 3·75

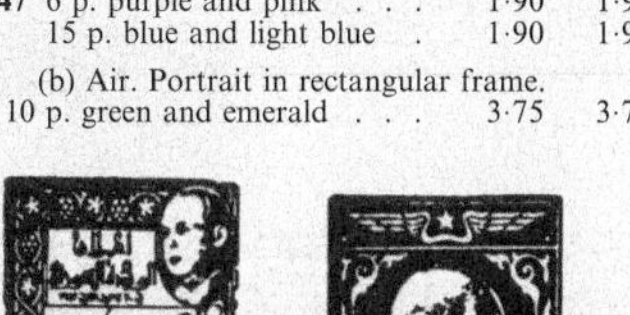

48 Syria and late President's portrait 49 Pres. Shukri Bey al-Quwatli

1943. Union of Latakia and Jebel Druze with Syria. (a) President bare-headed.
367 **48** 1 p. green (postage) 1·90 1·90
368 4 p. brown 1·90 1·90
369 8 p. violet 1·90 1·90
370 10 p. orange 1·90 1·90
371 20 p. blue 1·90 1·90
(b) President wearing turban.
372 2 p. brown (air) 1·90 1·90
373 10 p. purple 1·90 1·90
374 20 p. blue 1·90 1·90
375 50 p. pink 1·90 1·90

1943. Death of President Taj Addin-el-Husni. Nos. 367/75 optd with narrow black border.
376 **48** 1 p. green (postage) 1·90 1·90
377 4 p. brown 1·90 1·90
378 8 p. violet 1·90 1·90
379 10 p. orange 1·90 1·90
380 20 p. blue 1·90 1·90
381 – 2 p. brown (air) 1·90 1·90
382 – 10 p. purple 1·90 1·90
383 – 20 p. blue 1·90 1·90
384 – 50 p. pink 1·90 1·90

1944. Air.
385 **49** 200 p. purple 7·00 7·00
386 500 p. blue 12·00 12·00

(**50** Trans. "First Congress of Arab Lawyers, Damascus") (**51** Trans. "Aboulula-el-Maari. Commemoration of Millenary, 363–1363")

1944. Air. 1st Arab Lawyers' Congress. Optd with T **50**.
387 – 10 p. brown (No. 327) 2·25 2·25
388 – 15 p. red (No. 267) 2·25 2·20
389 – 25 p. orange (No. 268) 2·25 2·25
390 – 100 p. mauve (No. 270) 6·50 6·50
391 **49** 200 p. purple 9·50 9·50

1945. Millenary of Aboulula-el-Maari (Arab poet and philosopher). Optd with T **51**.
392 – 2 p. 50 green (No. 347) (postage) 2·50 2·50
393 – 7 p. 50 red (No. 349) 2·50 2·50
394 – 15 p. red (No. 267) (air) 2·25 2·25
395 – 25 p. orange (No. 268) 2·25 2·25
396 **49** 500 p. blue 19·00 19·00

52 Pres. Shukri Bey al-Quwatli 53 Pres. Shukri Bey al-Quwatli

1945. Resumption of Constitutional Govt.
397 **52** 4 p. violet (postage) 30 30
398 6 p. blue 30 30
399 10 p. red 30 30
400 15 p. brown 55 55
401 20 p. green 60 60
402 40 p. orange 1·10 1·10
403 **53** 5 p. green (air) 35 40
404 10 p. red 40 40
405 15 p. orange 40 40
406 25 p. blue 75 40
407 50 p. violet 1·25 55
408 100 p. brown 2·75 95
409 200 p. red 6·75 3·25

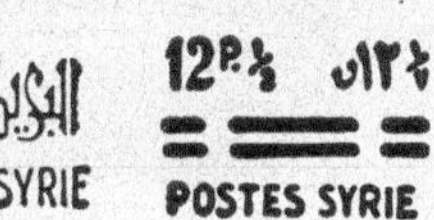

(**54**) (**55**)

1945. Fiscal stamps inscr "TIMBRE FISCAL", optd with T **54** (No. 411 surch also).
410 25 p. brown 3·25 3·25
411 50 p. on 75 p. brown 3·75 3·75
412 75 p. brown 5·50 5·50
413 100 p. green 6·25 6·25
(b) Surch as T **55**.
414 12½ p. on 15 p. green 1·75 1·75
415 25 p. on 25 s. purple 2·10 2·10
(c) Optd or surch (416) with T **54** and with additional Arabic inscription at top.
416 50 p. on 75 p. brown 1·40 1·40
417 50 p. mauve 1·75 1·75
418 100 p. green 2·40 2·40

(**56**) 57 Ear of Wheat

58 Pres. Shukri Bey al-Quwatli 60 Arab Horse

1946. Fiscal stamp optd with T **56**.
419 200 p. blue 18·00 10·00

1946.
420 **57** 0 p. 50 orange (postage) 15 10
421 1 p. violet 25 10
422 2 p. 50 grey 30 15
423 5 p. green 40 20
424 **58** 7 p. 50 brown 15 10
425 10 p. blue 15 10
426 12 p. 50 violet 50 15
427 – 15 p. red 20 20
428 – 20 p. violet 40 25
429 – 25 p. blue 60 25
430 **60** 50 p. brown 3·25 60
431 100 p. green 7·50 1·75
432a 200 p. purple 60·00 5·50
DESIGN—As Type **58**: 15, 20, 25 p. Pres. Shukri Bey al-Quwatli bareheaded.
433 – 3 p. red (air) 80 25
434 – 5 p. green 80 25
435 – 6 p. orange 80 25
436 – 10 p. grey 30 10
437 – 15 p. red 30 10
438 – 25 p. blue 45 20
439 – 50 p. violet 65 25
440 – 100 p. blue 2·10 55
441 – 200 p. brown 4·00 1·10
442 – 300 p. brown 12·00 2·50
443 – 500 p. green 13·00 4·50
DESIGNS—HORIZ: 3, 5, 6 p. Flock of sheep; 10, 15, 25 p. Kattineh dam; 50, 100, 200 p. Temple ruins, Kanaouat; 300, 500 p. Sultan Ibrahim Mosque.

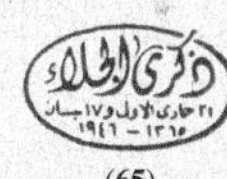
(**65**)

1946. Evacuation of Foreign Troops from Syria. Optd with T **65**.
444 **58** 10 p. blue (postage) 55 55
445 12 p. 50 violet 75 75
446 **60** 50 p. brown 2·25 2·25
447 – 25 p. blue (No. 438) (air) 1·50 1·10

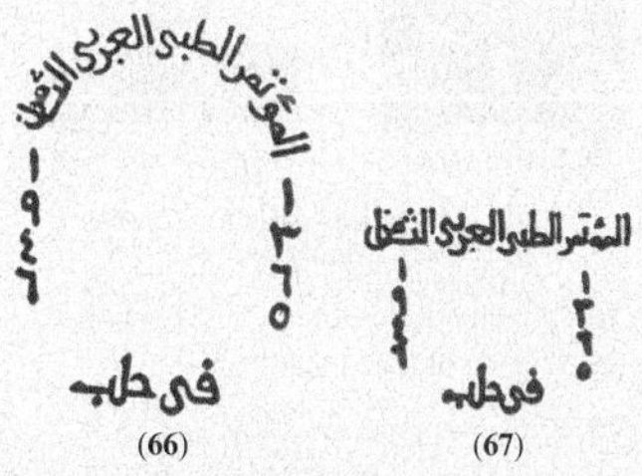
(**66**) (**67**)

1946. 8th Arab Medical Congress, Aleppo. (a) Postage. Optd with T **66**.
448 25 p. blue (No. 429) 1·60 1·40
(b) Air. Optd with T **67**.
449 25 p. blue (No. 438) 1·60 90
450 50 p. violet (No. 439) 2·50 1·25
451 100 p. blue (No. 440) 5·00 2·25

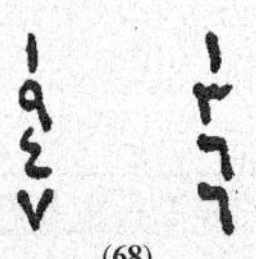
(**68**)

1947. 1st Anniv of Evacuation of Allied Forces. Nos. 444/447 optd as T **68** (= "1947 1366").
452 **58** 10 p. blue (postage) 50 15
453 12 p. 50 violet 75 20
454 **60** 50 p. brown 2·25 65
455 – 25 p. blue (air) 1·90 1·10

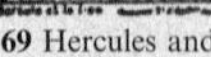

69 Hercules and Lion 70 Mosaic of the Mosque of the Omayades

1947. 1st Arab Archaeological Congress, Damascus.
456 **69** 12 p. 50 green (postage) . . 80 65
457 **70** 25 p. blue . . . . 1·75 95
458 – 12 p. 50 violet (air) . . . . 1·25 65
459 – 50 p. brown . . . . 4·50 1·90
DESIGNS—As T **70**: 12 p. 50, Window at Kasr El-Heir El-Gharbi; 50 p. King Hazael's throne.

71 Courtyard of Azem Palace 72 Congress Symbol

1947. 3rd Arab Engineers' Congress, Damascus. Inscr "3e CONGRES DES INGENIEURS ARABES 1947".
460 **71** 12 p. 50 purple (postage) . 60 50
461 – 25 p. blue . . . . 1·40 75
462 – 12 p. 50 green (air) 95 50
463 **72** 50 p. violet . . . . 3·50 1·75
DESIGNS—HORIZ: No. 461, Telephone Exchange Building; No. 462, Fortress at Kasr El-Heir El-Charqui.

73 Parliament Building 74 Pres. Shukri Bey al-Quwatli

1948. Re-election of Pres. Shukri Bey al-Quwatli.
464 **73** 12 p. 50 brown and grey (postage) 50 20
465 **74** 25 p. mauve . . . . 1·00 45
466 **73** 12 p. 50 blue and violet (air) 50 20
467 **74** 50 p. purple and green . . 2·50 90

75 Syrian Arms 76 Soldier and Flag

1948. Compulsory Military Service.
468 **75** 12 p. 50 brown and grey (postage) 50 25
469 **76** 25 p. multicoloured . . . . 1·00 40
470 **75** 12 p. 50 blue and light blue (air) 65 25
471 **76** 50 p. green, red and black . 3·25 75

1948. Surch. (a) Postage.
472 – 0 p. 50 on 0 p. 75 red (No. 247a) 20 10
472ab **60** 2 p. 50 on 200 p. purple . 40 10
472b 10 p. on 100 p. green . . 45 20
473 25 p. on 200 p. purple . . 3·25 45

(b) Air.
474 – 2 p. 50 on 3 p. (No. 433) 10 10
475 – 2 p. 50 on 6 p. (No. 435) 10 10
475a – 2 p. 50 on 100 p. (No. 440) 10 10
476 – 25 p. on 200 p. (No. 441) 60 20
477 – 50 p. on 300 p. (No. 442) 15·00 75
478 – 50 p. on 500 p. (No. 443) 15·00 75

78 Palmyra 79 President Husni el-Zaim and Lockheed Super Constellation over Damascus

1949. 75th Anniv of U.P.U.
479 – 12 p. 50 violet (postage) . 1·90 1·90
480 **78** 25 p. blue . . . . 3·25 3·25
481 – 12 p. 50 purple (air) . . . 6·25 6·25
482 **79** 50 p. black . . . . 18·00 12·50
DESIGNS—HORIZ: No. 479, Ain-el-Arous; No. 481, Globe and mountains.

80 President Husni el-Zaim 81 Pres. Husni el-Zaim and Map

1949. Revolution of 30 March, 1949.
483 **80** 25 p. blue (postage) . . . 85 45
484 50 p. brown (air) . . . . 3·50 2·10

1949. Presidential Election.
485 **81** 25 p. brn & blue (postage) 2·75 1·90
486 50 p. green and pink (air) . 3·50 1·90

82 Tel-Chehab 83 Damascus

1949.
487 **82** 5 p. grey 15 15
488 7 p. 50 brown 25 15
524 7 p. 50 green 40 15
489 **83** 12 p. 50 purple 50 20
490 25 p. blue . . . . 1·00 45

84 Syrian Arms 85 G.P.O., Damascus

1950.
491 **84** 0 p. 50 brown 10 10
492 2 p. 50 pink 15 10
493 – 10 p. violet 35 20
494 – 12 p. 50 green 65 40
495 **85** 25 p. blue . . . . 1·25 25
496 50 p. black . . . . 4·00 60
DESIGN—HORIZ: 10, 12 p. 50, Abous–Damascus road.

86 Port of Latakia

1950. Air.
497 **86** 2 p. 50 violet 45 10
526 10 p. blue 50 10
499 15 p. brown . . . . 3·00 25
500 25 p. blue . . . . 6·25 40

87 Parliament Building

88 Book and Torch

1951. New Constitution, 1950.
501 **87** 12 p. 50 black (postage) . . 30 20
502 25 p. blue 65 40
503 **88** 12 p. 50 red (air) 35 15
504 50 p. purple . . . . 1·25 70

89 Hama

1952.
505 **89** 0 p. 50 brown (postage) . . 10 10
506 2 p. 50 blue 20 10
507 5 p. green 20 10
508 10 p. red 25 10
509 – 12 p. 50 black 65 10
510 – 15 p. purple . . . . 4·00 25
511 – 25 p. blue . . . . 1·90 35
512 – 100 p. brown . . . . . . 7·50 1·90
513 – 2 p. 50 red (air) 15 10
514 – 5 p. green 35 10
515 – 15 p. violet 50 15
516 – 25 p. blue 65 30
517 – 100 p. purple . . . . . . 4·50 85
DESIGNS—Postage: 12 p. 50 to 100 p. Palace of Justice, Damascus. Air: 2 p. 50 to 15 p. Palmyra; 25, 100 p. Citadel, Aleppo.

1952. Air. United Nations Social Welfare Seminar, Damascus. Optd **U. N. S. W. S. Damascus 8-20 Dec. 1952** and curved line of Arabic.
518 **86** 10 p. blue . . . . 1·90 95
519 – 15 p. violet (No. 515) . . . 1·90 95
520 – 25 p. blue (No. 516) . . . . 3·25 1·60
521 – 50 p. violet (No. 439) . . . 8·25 2·25

91 Qalaat el Hasn Fortress 92 "Labour"

93 "Family" 94 "Communications"

1953.
522 **91** 0 p. 50 red (postage) . . . 15 10
523 – 2 p. 50 brown 20 10
525 **91** 12 p. 50 blue . . . . 1·75 15
527 – 50 p. brown (air) . . . . . 1·60 25
DESIGNS: 2 p. 50, Qalaat el Han fortress (different); 50 p. G.P.O., Aleppo.

1954.
528 **92** 1 p. green (postage) 10 10
529 2½ p. red 10 10
530 5 p. blue 10 10
531 **93** 7½ p. red 20 10
532 10 p. black 25 10
533 12½ p. violet 40 10
534 – 20 p. purple 60 20
535 – 25 p. violet . . . . 1·40 40
536 – 50 p. green . . . . 3·50 75
537 **94** 5 p. violet (air) 20 10
538 10 p. brown 25 10
539 15 p. green 25 10
540 – 30 p. brown 65 20
541 – 35 p. blue 95 20
542 – 40 p. orange . . . . 1·25 40
543 – 50 p. purple . . . . 1·60 50
544 – 70 p. violet . . . . 2·75 65
DESIGNS—As Type **93**. Postage: 20 to 50 p. "Industry". Air: 30 to 70 p. Syrian University.

95 96a

1954. Air. Damascus Fair. Inscr as in T **95**.
545 **95** 40 p. mauve 95 45
546 – 50 p. green . . . . 1·25 50
DESIGN—VERT: 50 p. Mosque and Syrian flag.

1954. Cotton Festival, Aleppo. Optd **FESTIVAL du COTON. Alep. oct. 1954** and Arab inscription.
547 **93** 10 p. black (postage) . . . 90 40
548 – 25 p. violet (No. 535) . . . 1·00 50
549 – 50 p. brown (No. 527) (air) 95 65
550 – 100 p. purple (No. 517) . . 2·25 1·60

1955. Arab Postal Union.
551 **96a** 12½ p. green (postage) . . 50 15
552 25 p. violet 90 25
553 5 p. brown (air) 30 15

97 98

1955. Air. Middle East Rotary Congress.
554 **97** 35 p. red 75 40
555 65 p. green . . . . 1·90 75

1955. Air. 50th Anniv of Rotary International.
556 **98** 25 p. violet 50 25
557 75 p. blue . . . . 2·25 95

99 "Facing the Future" 100 Mother and Child

1955. Air. 9th Anniv of Evacuation of Foreign Troops from Syria.
558 **99** 40 p. mauve 65 40
559 – 60 p. blue . . . . 2·00 60
DESIGN: 60 p. Tank and infantry attack.
See also Nos. 847/9.

1955. Mothers' Day.
560 **100** 25 p. red (postage) . . . 45 25
561 35 p. violet (air) 95 45
562 40 p. black . . . . 1·60 60

101 Lockheed Super Constellation Airliner, Flag and Crowd 102 Syrian Pavilion

1955. Air. Emigrants' Congress.
563 **101** 5 p. mauve 50 20
564 – 15 p. blue 65 30
DESIGN: 15 p. Lockheed Super Constellation over globe.

1955. Air. International Fair, Damascus.
565 **102** 25 p. + 5 p. black . . . 50 50
566 – 35 p. + 5 p. blue . . . 70 70
567 – 40 p. + 10 p. purple . . 90 90
568 – 70 p. + 10 p. green . . . 1·40 1·40
DESIGNS: 35, 40 p. "Industry and Agriculture"; 70 p. Exhibition pavilions and flags.

103 Mother and Baby 104 U.N. Emblem and Torch

1955. Air. International Children's Day.
569 **103** 25 p. blue 65 35
570 50 p. purple . . . . . . 1·25 50

1955. 10th Anniv of U.N.O.
571 **104** 7½ p. red (postage) 50 25
572 12½ p. green 85 35
573 – 15 p. blue (air) 65 30
574 – 35 p. brown . . . . . . 1·25 50
DESIGN: 15, 35 p. Globe, dove and Scales of Justice.

مؤتمر البريد العربي
القاهرة ١٩٥٥/٣/١٥

105 Saracen Gate, Aleppo Citadel (106)

1955. Installation of Aleppo Water Supply from River Euphrates.
575 **105** 7 p. 50 violet (postage) . . 25 10
576 12 p. 50 red 35 15
577 30 p. blue (air) . . . . . 2·25 90

1955. 2nd Arab Postal Union Congress, Cairo. Nos. 551/3 optd with T **106**.
578 12½ p. green (postage) 40 25
579 25 p. violet . . . . 1·25 50
580 5 p. brown (air) 50 15

ذكرى زيارة عاهل الاردن
نيسان ١٩٥٦

(107) 108 Monument

1956. Visit of King Hussein of Jordan. Nos. 551/3 optd with T **107**.
581 12½ p. green (postage) 50 40
582 25 p. violet 90 75
583 5 p. brown (air) 50 20

1956. Air. 10th Anniv of Evacuation of Foreign Troops from Syria.
584 **108** 35 p. sepia 65 45
585 – 65 p. red 95 65
586 – 75 p. grey . . . . 1·90 95
DESIGNS: 65 p. Winged female figure; 75 p. Pres. Shukri Bey al-Quwatli.

109 Pres. Shukri Bey al-Quwatli 110 Cotton

1956. Air.
587 **109** 100 p. black . . . . 1·25 95
588 200 p. violet . . . . 2·50 1·25
589 300 p. red . . . . 3·75 3·00
590 500 p. green . . . . 7·75 5·00

1956. Aleppo Cotton Festival.
591 **110** 2½ p. green 50 25

1956. Air. Nos. 565/8 with premiums obliterated by bars.
592 **102** 25 p. black 50 25
593 – 35 p. blue 65 40
594 – 40 p. purple . . . . 1·25 50
595 – 70 p. green . . . . 1·50 1·10

111 Gate of Kasr al-Heir, Palmyra 112 Clay Alphabetical Tablet

1956. Air. 3rd International Fair, Damascus.
596 **111** 15 p. brown 40 40
597 – 20 p. blue 50 50
598 – 30 p. green . . . . 1·10 1·10
599 – 35 p. blue 90 90
600 – 50 p. purple 90 90
DESIGNS: 20 p. Cotton mill; 30 p. Tractor; 35 p. Phoenician galley and cogwheels; 50 p. Textiles, carpets and pottery.

1956. Air. International Campaign for Museums.
601 **112** 20 p. black 90 50
602 – 30 p. red . . . . 1·00 50
603 – 50 p. brown . . . . 1·90 1·00
DESIGNS—VERT: 30 p. Syrian legionary's helmet. HORIZ: 50 p. Lintel of Belshamine Temple, Palmyra.

1956. 11th Anniv of U.N.O. Nos. 571/4 optd **11eme ANNIVERSAIRE de L'ONU** in French and Arabic.
604 **104** 7½ p. red (postage) 55 30
605 – 12½ p. green 70 45
606 – 15 p. blue (air) . . . . . . 1·25 50
607 – 35 p. brown . . . . 2·50 1·10

114 Oaks and Mosque

1956. Air. Afforestation Day.
608 **114** 10 p. brown 40 20
609 40 p. green 90 50

115 Azem Palace, Damascus

1957.
610 **115** 12½ p. purple 25 10
611 15 p. black 40 10

116 "Resistance"

1957. Syrian Defence Force.
612 **116** 5 p. mauve 20 10
613 20 p. green 50 25

1957. Evacuation of Port Said. Optd **22.12.56 EVACUATION PORT SAID** in French and Arabic.
614 **116** 5 p. mauve 25 10
615 20 p. green 65 40

118 Mother and Child 119 "Sword of Liberty"

1957. Air. Mothers' Day.
616 – 40 p. blue 65 45
617 **118** 60 p. red . . . . 1·25 80
DESIGN: 40 p. Mother fondling child.

1957. Air. 11th Anniv of Evacuation of Foreign Troops from Syria.
618 **119** 10 p. brown 10 10
619 – 15 p. green 25 10
620 – 25 p. violet 50 15
621 – 35 p. mauve 65 35
622 **119** 40 p. black . . . . 1·00 55
DESIGNS: 15, 35 p. Map and woman holding torch; 25 p. Pres. Shukri Bey al-Quwatli.

120 Freighter "Latakia" and Fair Emblem 121 "Cotton"

1957. Air. 4th Damascus Fair.
623 **120** 25 p. mauve 50 40
624 – 30 p. brown 50 40
625 – 35 p. blue 90 50
626 – 40 p. green . . . . 1·10 65
627 **120** 70 p. green . . . . 1·40 65
DESIGNS—VERT: 30, 40 p. Girls harvesting and cotton picking. HORIZ: 35 p. Interior of processing plant.

1957. Aleppo Cotton Festival.
628 **121** 12½ p. blk & grn (postage) 50 25
629 17½ p. black & orge (air) . 60 40
630 40 p. black and blue . . 1·25 50

122 Children at Work and Play 123 Letter and Post-box

1957. International Children's Day.
631 **122** 12½ p. green (postage) . . 65 25
632 17½ blue (air) . . . . . . 1·25 50
633 20 p. brown . . . . 1·25 50

1957. International Correspondence Week.
634 **123** 5 p. mauve (postage) . . . 50 25
635 – 5 p. green (air) 50 15
DESIGN: 5 p. (air) Family writing letters.

اسبوع التحصين
١-٧ تشرين الثاني ١٩٥٧

(124) 125 Scales of Justice, Map and Damascus Silhouette

1957. National Defence Week. Optd with T **124**.
636 **116** 5 p. mauve 15 10
637 20 p. green 50 25

1957. 3rd Arab Lawyers Union Congress, Damascus.
638 **125** 12½ p. green (postage) . . 40 20
639 17½ p. red (air) 40 25
640 40 p. black 90 50

126 Glider

1957. Air. Gliding Festival.
641 **126** 25 p. brown 80 35
642 35 p. green . . . . 1·25 40
643 40 p. blue . . . . 2·75 60

127 Torch and Map 128 Khaled Ibn el-Walid Mosque, Homs

1957. Afro-Asian Jurists' Congress, Damascus.
644 **127** 20 p. brown (postage) . . 65 25
645 30 p. green (air) 50 30
646 50 p. violet 75 40

1957.
647 **128** 2½ p. brown 20 15

UNITED ARAB REPUBLIC

129 Telecommunications Building 129a Union of Egypt and Syria

1958. Five Year Plan.
648 **129** 25 p. blue (postage) . . . 40 25
649 10 p. green (air) 25 10
650 – 15 p. brown 30 20
DESIGN—VERT: 15 p. Telephone, radio tower and telegraph pole.

1958. Birth of United Arab Republic.
651 **129a** 12½ p. green and yellow (postage) 35 20
652 17½ p. brown & blue (air) 50 30

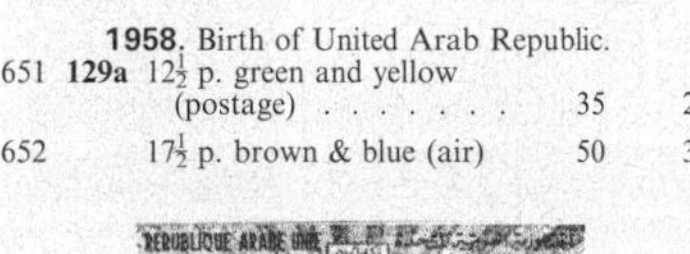

130 "Eternal Flame"

1958. 12th Anniv of Evacuation of Foreign Troops from Syria.
653 **130** 5 p. violet & yellow (postage) 50 25
654 15 p. red and green . . . 90 40
655 – 35 p. black and red (air) . 95 45
656 – 45 p. brown and blue . . 1·60 60
DESIGN: 35, 45 p. Broken chain, dove and olive branch.

131 Scout fixing Tent-peg

1958. Air. 3rd Pan-Arab Scout Jamboree.
657 **131** 35 p. brown . . . . . . 2·25 2·25
658 40 p. blue . . . . 2·75 2·75

132 Mosque, Chimneys and Cogwheel 133 Bronze Rattle

1958. Air. 5th Int Fair, Damascus. Inscr "1.9.58".
659 – 25 p. red 80 60
660 – 30 p. green . . . . 1·25 90
661 **132** 45 p. violet . . . . 1·40 1·00
DESIGNS—HORIZ: 25 p. View of Fair. VERT: 30 p. Minaret, vase and emblem.

1958. Ancient Syrian Art.
662 **133** 10 p. green 10 10
663 – 15 p. brown 15 10
664 – 20 p. purple 15 15
665 – 30 p. brown 25 15
666 – 40 p. grey 45 20
667 – 60 p. green 65 25
668 – 75 p. blue . . . . 1·25 40
669 – 100 p. purple . . . . . . 1·50 65
670 – 150 p. purple . . . . . . 3·25 90
DESIGNS: 15 p. Goddess of Spring; 20 p. "Lamgi Mari" (statue); 30 p. Mithras fighting bull; 40 p. Aspasia; 60 p. Minerva; 75 p. Ancient gourd; 100 p. Enamelled vase; 150 p. Mosaic from Omayyad Mosque, Damascus.

1958. International Children's Day. Optd **R A U** and Arabic inscription.
670a **122** 12½ p. green (postage) . . 60·00 50·00
670b 17½ p. blue (air) . . . . 35·00 35·00
670c 20 p. brown . . . . . . 35·00 35·00

134 Cotton and Textiles 134a Hand holding Torch, and Iraqi Flag

1958. Air. Aleppo Cotton Festival.
671 **134** 25 p. yellow and brown . 55 50
672 35 p. red and brown . . . 95 60

1958. Republic of Iraq Commemoration.
673 **134a** 12½ p. red 25 15

135 Light Airplane and Children with Model Airplane 137 U.N. Emblem and Charter

136 Damascus

1958. Air. Gliding Festival.
674 **135** 7½ p. green 90 50
675 12½ p. green . . . . 3·00 1·75

1958. 4th N.E. Regional Conference, Damascus.
676 **136** 12½ p. green (postage) . . 40 20
677 17½ p. violet (air) 35 20

1958. Air. 10th Anniv of Declaration of Human Rights.
678 **137** 25 p. purple 35 25
679 35 p. grey 45 30
680 40 p. brown 65 40

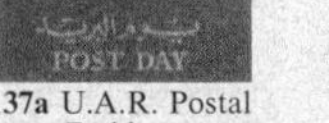

137a U.A.R. Postal Emblem **137b**

1959. Post Day and Postal Employees' Social Fund.
681 **137a** 20 p. + 10 p. red, black and green 60 60

1959. 1st Anniv of United Arab Republic.
682 **137b** 12½ p. red, black and green 25 15

138 Secondary School, Damascus

1959.
683 **138** 12½ p. green 25 10

138a "Telecommunications"

1959. Air. Arab Telecommunications Union Commemoration.
684 **138a** 40 p. black and green . . 75 50

1959. No. 684 optd **2nd CONFERANCE DAMASCUS 1-3-1959** in English and Arabic.
685 **138a** 40 p. black and green . . 50 25

139a U.A.R. and Yemeni Flags

1959. 1st Anniv of Proclamation of United Arab States (U.A.R. and Yemen).
686 **139a** 12½ p. red and green . . 25 15

140 Mother with Children **142**

1959. Arab Mothers' Day.
687 **140** 15 p. red 30 20
688 25 p. green 45 30

1959. Surch **U.A.R 2½p** and also in Arabic.
689 **92** 2½ p. on 1 p. green 20 10

1959. Air. 13th Anniv of Evacuation of Foreign Troops from Syria.
690 **142** 15 p. green and yellow . 25 10
691 – 35 p. red and grey . . . 50 30
DESIGN: 35 p. Broken chain and flame.

143 **144** "Emigration"

1959. Patterns as T **143**.
692 **143** 2½ p. violet 10 10
693 – 5 p. brown 10 10
694 – 7½ p. blue 10 10
695 – 10 p. green 20 10
DESIGNS: 5 to 10 p. Different styles of ornamental scrollwork.

1959. Air. Emigrants' Congress.
696 **144** 80 p. black, red & green . 1·10 65

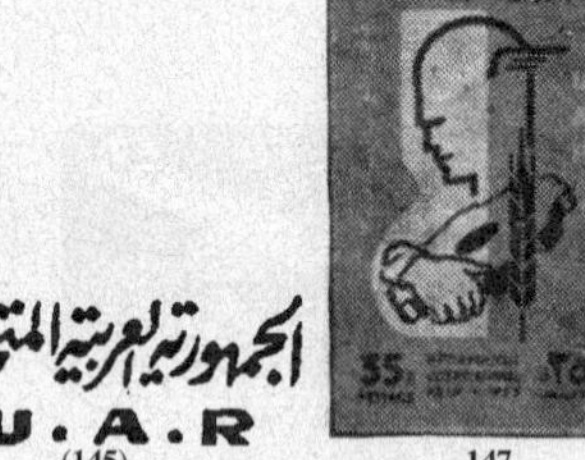

(**145**) **147**

146 Oil Refinery

1959. Optd as T **145**.
697 **115** 15 p. black (postage) . . 30 15
698 – 50 p. green (No. 536) . . 75 55
690 – 5 p. green (No. 635) (air) 15 15
700 – 50 p. purple (No. 543) . . 60 30
701 – 70 p. violet (No. 544) . . 95 40

1959. Air. Inauguration of Oil Refinery.
702 **146** 50 p. red, black and blue 1·40 65

1959. 6th Damascus Fair.
703 **147** 35 p. green, vio & grey . 60 25

148 **149** Child and Factory

1959. Air. Aleppo Cotton Festival.
704 **148** 45 p. blue 65 25
705 50 p. purple 65 40

1959. Air. Children's Day.
706 **149** 25 p. red, blue and lilac . 40 15

150 Boys' College, Damascus **150a** "Shield against Aggression"

1959.
707 **150** 25 p. blue 45 20
708 – 35 p. brown 65 25
DESIGN: 35 p. Girls' College, Damascus.

1959. Army Day.
709 **150a** 50 p. brown 75 40

151 Ears of Corn, Cotton, Cogwheel and Factories **152** Mosque and Oaks

1959. Industrial and Agricultural Production Fair, Aleppo.
710 **151** 35 p. brown, blue & grey . 60 25

1959. Tree Day.
711 **152** 12½ p. brown and green . . 30 20

153 A. R. Kawakbi **153a**

1960. 50th Death Anniv of A. R. Kawakbi (writer).
712 **153** 15 p. green 25 10

1960. 2nd Anniv of U.A.R.
713 **153a** 12½ p. green and red . . . 25 10

154 Diesel Train

1960. Latakia–Aleppo Railway Project.
714 **154** 12½ p. brown, black & bl . 1·50 65

154a Arab League Centre, Cairo

1960. Inaug of Arab League Centre, Cairo.
715 **154a** 12½ p. black and green . . 25 15

1960. Mothers' Day. Optd **ARAB MOTHERS DAY 1960** in English and Arabic.
716 **140** 15 p. red 30 15
717 25 p. green 40 25

155a Mother, Child and Map of Palestine

1960. World Refugee Year.
718 **155a** 12½ p red 35 15
719 50 p. green 65 40

156 Government Building and Inscription

1960. 14th Anniv of Evacuation of Foreign Troops from Syria.
720 **156** 12½ p. multicoloured . . . 35 10

157 Hittin School

1960.
721 **157** 17½ p. lilac 40 10

1960. Industrial and Agricultural Production Fair, Aleppo. Optd **1960** and in Arabic.
722 **151** 35 p. brown, blue & grey 40 25

159 Mobile Crane and Compasses (**160**)

1960. Air. 7th International Damascus Fair.
723 **159** 50 p. black, bistre & red . 60 35

1960. Air. Aleppo Cotton Festival. Optd with T **160**.
724 **148** 45 p. blue 65 25
725 50 p. purple 65 40

161 **162** Basketball

1960. Children's Day.
726 **161** 35 p. brown and green . . 60 30

1960. Air. Olympic Games.
727 **162** 15 p. brown, black & bl . 40 20
728 – 20 p. brown, black & bl . 50 20
729 – 25 p. multicoloured . . . 50 20
730 – 40 p. violet, pink & black 95 50
DESIGNS: 20 p. Swimming; 25 p. Fencing (Arab-style); 40 p. Horse-jumping.

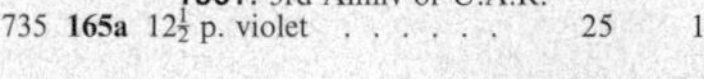

(**163**) **164** "UN" and Globe

1960. Tree Day. Optd with T **163**.
731 **152** 12½ p. brown and green . 40 15

1960. Air. 15th Anniv of U.N.O.
732 **164** 35 p. red, green & blue . 50 25
733 50 p. blue, brown & red . 65 40

165 Hanano **165a** State Emblem

1961. Air. 25th Death Anniv (1960) of Ibrahim Hanano (patriot).
734 **165** 50 p. green and brown . . 60 35

1961. 3rd Anniv of U.A.R.
735 **165a** 12½ p. violet 25 15

166 St. Simeon's Monastery **167** Raising the Flag

1961.
736 **166** 12½ p. blue (postage) . . . 25 15
746 – 200 p. blue (air) . . . . . 2·50 1·50
DESIGN—VERT: 200 p. Entrance to St. Simeon's Monastery.

1961. Air. 15th Anniv of Evacuation of Foreign Troops from Syria.
737 **167** 40 p. green 60 30

168 Eye and Hand "reading" Braille
169 Palestinian and Map 

1961. Air. U.N. Campaign for Welfare of Blind.
738 **168** 40 p. + 10 p. black & grn 65 50

1961. Air. Palestine Day.
739 **169** 50 p. blue and black . . . 75 40

170 Cogwheel and Corn
171 Abou Tammam (796–846) 

1961. Industrial and Agricultural Production Fair, Aleppo.
740 **170** 12½ p. multicoloured . . . 30 20

1961. Air. Abou Tammam (writer) Commem.
741 **171** 50 p. brown 65 30

172 Damascus University, Discus-thrower and Lyre
173 Open Window on World 

1961 Air. 5th Universities Youth Festival.
742 **172** 15 p. black and red . . . 30 10
743 35 p. violet and green . . 95 30

1961 Air. 8th International Damascus Fair.
744 **173** 17½ p. violet and green . . 25 15
745 – 50 p. violet and black . . 55 30
DESIGN: 50 p. U.A.R. Pavilion.

SYRIAN ARAB REPUBLIC

175 Assembly Chamber 
176 The Noria, Hama

177 Arch of Triumph, Latakia
178 Arab League Emblem and Headquarters, Cairo 

1961. Establishment of Syrian Arab Republic.
747 **175** 15 p. red 25 10
748 35 p. green 65 25

1961.
749 **176** 2½ p. red (postage) . . . 10 10
750 5 p. blue 10 10
751 – 7½ p. green 25 10
752 – 10 p. orange 40 10
753 **177** 12½ p. brown 60 10
754 – 12½ p. green 45 10
755 – 15 p. blue 50 10
756 – 17½ p. brown 60 10
757 – 22½ p. turquoise 65 10
758 **177** 25 p. brown 85 10
759 – 45 p. yellow (air) 50 30
760 – 50 p. red 65 40
761 – 85 p. purple . . . . . . 1·10 50
762 – 100 p. purple . . . . . . 1·40 55
763 – 200 p. green . . . . . . 2·50 1·00
764 – 300 p. blue . . . . . . 3·25 1·10
764a – 500 p. purple . . . . . 5·00 2·50
764b – 1000 p. black . . . . . 11·00 4·50
DESIGNS: 7½, 10 p. Khaled ibn-el-Walid Mosque, Homs; 12½ p. (No. 754), 15, 17½, 22½, 45, 50 p. "The Beauty of Palmyra" (statue); 85, 100 p. Archway and columns, Palmyra; 200 to 1000 p. King Zahir Bibar's tomb.
See also Nos. 799/800.

1962. Air. Arab League Week.
765 **178** 17½ p. turquoise and green 20 10
766 22½ p. violet and blue . . 35 20
767 50 p. brown and orange . . 75 30

179 Campaign Emblem
180 Prancing Horse 

1962. Air. Malaria Eradication.
768 **179** 12½ p. violet, brown & blue 25 15
769 50 p. green, brown & yell 70 40

1962. Air. 16th Anniv of Evacuation of Foreign Troops from Syria.
770 **180** 45 p. orange and violet . . 50 25
771 – 55 p. violet and blue . . 75 35
DESIGN: 55 p. Military commander.

181 Qalb Lozah Church
182 Martyrs' Memorial, Swaida 

1962.
772 **181** 17½ p. green 35 10
773 35 p. green 50 25

1962. Syrian Revolution Commemoration.
774 **182** 12½ p. brown and drab . 20 10
775 35 p. green and turquoise 50 20

183 Jupiter Temple Gate
184 Globe, Monument and Handclasp 

1962.
776 **183** 2½ p. turquoise 10 10
777 5 p. brown 20 10
778 7½ p. brown 35 10
779 10 p. purple 20 10

1962. Air. 9th Int Fair, Damascus.
780 **184** 17½ p. brown and purple . 20 10
781 22½ p. mauve and red . . 25 10
782 – 40 p. purple and brown . 40 20
783 – 45 p. blue and green . . 65 30
DESIGN: 40, 45 p. Fair entrance.

185 Festival Emblem
186 Pres. Kudsi 

1962. Air. Aleppo Cotton Festival.
784 **185** 12½ p. multicoloured . . . 25 10
785 50 p. multicoloured . . . 65 40
See also Nos. 820/1.

1962. Presidential Elections.
786 **186** 12½ p. brown and blue (postage) 30 10
787 50 p. blue and buff (air) . 65 30

187 Zenobia
188 Saadallah el-Jabiri 

1962. Air.
788 **187** 45 p. violet 55 20
789 50 p. red 70 25
790 85 p. green 80 40
791 100 p. purple . . . . . 1·75 60
See also Nos. 801/4.

1962. Air. 15th Death Anniv of Saadallah el-Jabiri (revolutionary).
792 **188** 50 p. blue 50 30

189 Moharde Woman
190 Ears of Wheat, Hand and Globe 

1962. Air. Women in Regional Costumes. Multicoloured.
793 40 p. Marje Sultan 40 15
794 45 p. Kalamoun 50 25
795 50 p. Type **189** 65 30
796 55 p. Jabal al-Arab 75 35
797 60 p. Afrine 80 35
798 65 p. Hauran . . . . 1·00 45

1963. As previous designs but size 20×26 mm.
799 – 2½ p. violet 15 10
800 – 5 p. purple 15 10
801 **187** 7½ p. grey 35 10
802 10 p. brown 65 10
803 12½ p. blue 95 10
804 15 p. brown . . . . . . 1·60 15
DESIGN: Nos. 799/800, "The Beauty of Palmyra" (statue).

1963. Freedom from Hunger.
805 **190** 12½ p. blk & bl (postage) . 20 10
806 – 50 p. black and red (air) . 50 25
DESIGN: 50 p. Bird feeding young in nest.

191 Faris el-Khouri (politician)
192 S.A.R. Emblem 

1963. Air. 17th Anniv of Evacuation of Foreign Troops from Syria.
807 **191** 17½ p. brown 30 15
808 **192** 22½ p. green and black . . 30 15

193 Eagle
194 Ala el-Ma'ari (bust) 

1963. Air. Baathist Revolution Commemoration.
809 **193** 12½ p. green 10 10
810 50 p. mauve 55 35

1963. Air. 990th Birth Anniv of Ala el-Ma'ari (poet).
811 **194** 50 p. violet 50 35

195 Copper Water Jug
196 Central Bank 

1963. Air. 10th International Fair, Damascus.
812 **195** 37½ p. multicoloured . . . 55 25
813 50 p. multicoloured . . . 70 40

1963. Damascus Buildings.
814 – 17½ p. violet . . . . . . 1·00 25
815 – 22½ p. violet 35 20
816 **196** 25 p. brown 25 15
817 – 35 p. purple 40 20
BUILDINGS: 17½ p. Hejaz Railway Station; 22½ p. Mouassat Hospital; 35 p. Post Office, Al-Jalaa.

197 "Red Crescent" and Centenary Emblem
198 Child with Ball 

1963. Air. Red Cross Centenary. Crescent in red.
818 **197** 15 p. black and blue . . . 25 20
819 – 50 p. black and green . . 65 40
DESIGN: 50 p. "Red Crescent", globe and centenary emblem.

1963. Aleppo Cotton Festival. As T **185** but inscr "POSTAGE" and "1963" in place of "AIRMAIL" and "1962".
820 **185** 17½ p. multicoloured . . . 25 10
821 22½ p. multicoloured . . . 45 15

1963. Children's Day.
822 **198** 12½ p. green and deep green 20 10
823 22½ p. green and red . . . 35 10

199 Firas el-Hamadani
200 Flame on Head 

1963. Air. Death Millenary of Abou Firas el-Hamadani (poet).
824 **199** 50 p. brown and bistre . . 50 40

1963. Air. 15th Anniv of Declaration of Human Rights. Flame in red.
825 **200** 17½ p. black and grey . . 20 10
826 22½ p. black and green . . 25 15
827 50 p. black and violet . . 60 25

201 Emblem and Flag

1964. Air. 1st Anniv of 8th March Baathist Revolution. Emblem and flag in red, black and green; inscr in black.
828 **201** 15 p. green 10 10
829 17½ p. pink 20 10
830 22½ p. grey 40 15

202 Ugharit Princess
203 Chahba, Thalassa, Mosaic 

1964.
831 **202** 2½ p. grey (postage) . . . 10 10
832 5 p. brown 10 10
833 7½ p. purple 10 10
834 10 p. green 10 10
835 12½ p. violet 10 10
836 17½ p. blue 20 10
837 20 p. red 50 10
838 25 p. orange 80 15

839 **203** 27½ p. red (air) 25 10

840 45 p. brown 45 15

841 50 p. green 60 15

842 55 p. green 65 25

843 60 p. blue 75 30

204 Kaaba, Mecca, and Mosque, Damascus

1964. Air. 1st Arab Moslem Wakf Ministers' Conference.

844 **204** 12½ p. black and blue . . 10 10

845 22½ p. black and purple . 25 15

846 50 p. black and green . . 65 25

1964. Air. 18th Anniv of Evacuation of Foreign Troops from Syria. As T **99** but larger, 38½×26 mm. Inscr "1964".

847 **99** 20 p. blue 15 10

848 25 p. purple 30 15

849 60 p. green 55 25

205 Abou al Zahrawi **206** Bronze Chimes

1964. Air. 4th Arab Dental and Oral Surgery Congress, Damascus.

850 **205** 60 p. brown 65 40

1964. Air. 11th International Fair, Damascus.

851 **206** 20 p. multicoloured . . . 50 10

852 – 25 p. multicoloured . . . 55 20

DESIGN: 25 p. Fair emblem.

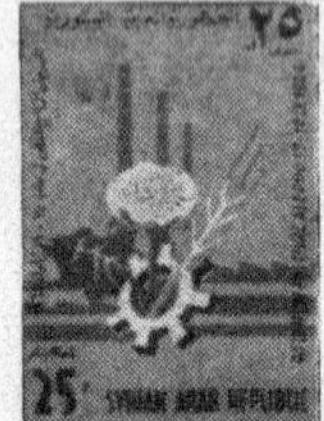

207 Cotton Plant and Symbols **(208)**

1964. Air. Aleppo Cotton Festival. No. 854 is optd with T **208**.

853 **207** 25 p. multicoloured . . . 25 10

854 25 p. multicoloured . . . 40 25

209 Aero Club Emblem

1964. Air. 10th Anniv of Syrian Aero Club.

855 **209** 12½ p. black and green . . 20 10

856 17½ p. black and red . . . 30 15

857 20 p. black and blue . . . 65 20

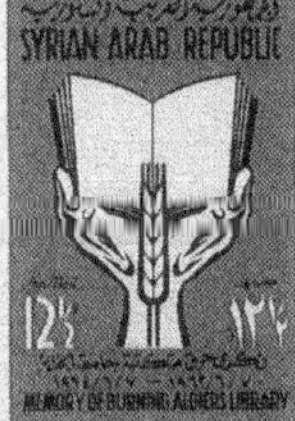

210 A.P.U. Emblem **211** Book within Hands

1964. Air. 10th Anniv of Arab Postal Union's Permanent Office, Cario.

858 **210** 12½ p. black and orange . . 15 10

859 20 p. black and green . . 20 10

860 25 p. black and mauve . . 25 15

1964. Air. Burning of Algiers Library.

861 **211** 12½ p. black and green . . 10 10

862 17½ p. black and red . . . 20 10

863 20 p. black and blue . . . 25 15

212 Tennis

1965. Air. Olympic Games, Tokyo. Multicoloured.

864 12½ p. Type **212** 15 10

865 17½ p. Wrestling 30 20

866 20 p. Weightlifting 45 20

213 Flag, Map and Revolutionaries

1965. 2nd Anniv of Baathist Revolution of March 8th 1963.

867 **213** 12½ p. multicoloured . . 10 10

868 17½ p. multicoloured . . 20 10

869 20 p. multicoloured . . . 25 10

214 Rameses II in War Chariot, Abu Simbel

1965. Air. Nubian Monuments Preservation.

870 **214** 22½ p. black, blue & green 30 20

871 – 50 p. black, green & blue 65 30

DESIGN: 50 p. Heads of Rameses II.

215 Weather Instruments and Map

1965. World Meteorological Day.

872 **215** 12½ p. black and purple . 10 10

873 27½ p. black and blue . . 40 15

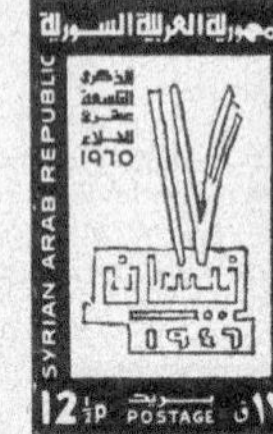

216 Al-Radi **217** Evacuation Symbol

1965. Air. 950th Death Anniv of Al-Sharif al-Radi (writer).

874 **216** 50 p. black 65 40

1965. 19th Anniv of Evacuation of Foreign Troops from Syria.

875 **217** 12½ p. green and blue . . 10 10

876 27½ p. lilac and red . . . 25 15

218 Hippocrates and Avicenna

1965. Air. "Medical Days of the Near and Middle East".

877 **218** 60 p. black and green . . 75 50

219 Dagger on Deir Yassin, Palestine **220** I.T.U. Emblem and Symbols

1965. Air. Deir Yassin Massacre on 9 April 1948.

878 **219** 12½ p. multicoloured . . . 20 10

879 60 p. multicoloured . . . 50 30

1965. Air. Centenary of I.T.U.

880 **220** 12½ p. multicoloured . . . 25 10

881 27½ p. multicoloured . . . 40 15

882 60 p. multicoloured . . . 70 45

221 Arab Family, Flags and Map **222** Hands holding Hoe and Pick

1965. Palestine Week.

883 **221** 12½ p. + 5 p. multicoloured 25 20

884 25 p. + 5 p. multicoloured 25 25

1965. Peasants' Union.

885 **222** 2½ p. green 10 10

886 12½ p. violet 10 10

887 15 p. purple 10 10

The above stamps are inscr "RERUBLIC" for "REPUBLIC".

223 Welcoming Emigrant **224** Fair Entrance

1965. Air. "Welcome Arab Emigrants".

888 **223** 25 p. multicoloured . . . 25 10

889 100 p. multicoloured . . . 90 40

1965. Air. 12th Int Fair, Damascus. Multicoloured.

890 12½ p. Type **224** 10 10

891 27½ p. Globe and compasses . 25 10

892 60 p. Syrian brassware . . . 65 30

226 Cotton Boll and Shuttles

1965. Air. Aleppo Industrial and Agricultural Production Fair. Optd **INDUSTRIAL & AGRICULTURAL PRODUCTION FAIR-ALEPPO 1965** in English and Arabic.

893 **226** 25 p. multicoloured . . . 40 10

1965. Air. Aleppo Cotton Festival.

894 **226** 25 p. multicoloured . . . 40 10

227 I.C.Y. Emblem and View of Damascus

1965. Air. International Co-operation Year.

895 **227** 25 p. multicoloured . . . 40 15

228 Arabs, Torch and Map **229** Industrial Workers

1965. National Revolution Council.

896 **228** 12½ p. multicoloured . . . 10 10

897 25 p. multicoloured . . . 25 10

1966. Labour Unions.

898 **229** 12½ p. blue 10 10

899 15 p. red 10 10

900 20 p. lilac 20 10

901 25 p. brown 25 15

230 Radio Aerial, Globe and Flag **231** Dove-shaped Hand holding Flower

1966. Air. Arab Information Ministers' Conf, Damascus.

902 **230** 25 p. multicoloured . . . 20 10

903 60 p. multicoloured . . . 50 25

1966. Air. 3rd Anniv of March 8th Baathist Revolution. Multicoloured.

904 12½ p. Type **231** 10 10

905 17½ p. Revolutionaries (horiz) 25 10

906 50 p. Type **231** 90 25

232 Colossi, Abu Simbel **233** Roman Lamp

1966. Air. Nubian Monuments Preservation Week.

907 **232** 25 p. blue 30 10

908 60 p. grey 65 25

1966.

909 **233** 2½ p. green 10 10

910 5 p. purple 20 10

911 – 7½ p. brown 10 10

912 – 10 p. violet 15 10

DESIGN: 7½, 10 p. 12th-century Islamic vessel.

234 U.N. Emblem and Headquarters

1966. Air. 20th Anniv of U.N.O.

913 **234** 25 p. black and grey . . . 15 10

914 50 p. black and green . . 50 25

236 "Evacuation" (abstract)

1966. 20th Anniv of Evacuation of Foreign Troops from Syria.

916 **236** 12½ p. multicoloured . . . 10 10

917 27½ p. multicoloured . . . 25 15

237 Workers marching across Globe

1966. Air. Labour Day.

918 **237** 60 p. multicoloured 50 25

238 W.H.O. Building **239** Traffic Signals and Map on Hand

1966. Air. Inauguration of W.H.O. Headquarters, Geneva.
919 **238** 60 p. black, blue & yellow 50 25

1966. Air. Traffic Day.
920 **239** 25 p. multicoloured . . . 35 10

240 Astarte and Tyche (wrongly inscr "ASTRATE") **241** Fair Emblem

1966. Air.
921 **240** 50 p. brown 50 25
922 60 p. grey 75 40

1966. Air. 13th International Fair, Damascus.
923 **241** 12½ p. multicoloured . . . 10 10
924 60 p. multicoloured . . . 55 35

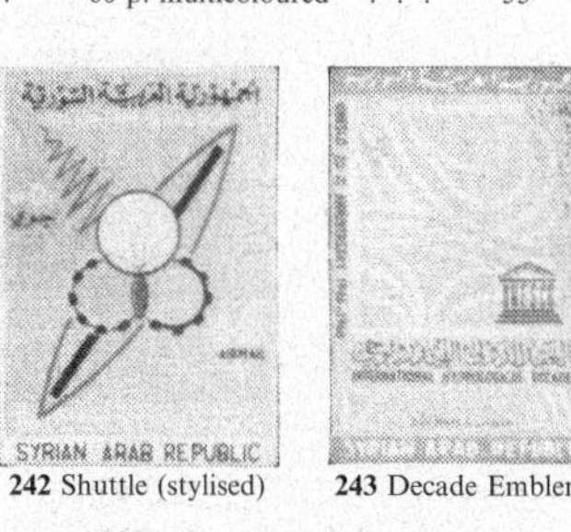

242 Shuttle (stylised) **243** Decade Emblem

1966. Air. Aleppo Cotton Festival.
925 **242** 50 p. black, red and grey . 50 25

1966. Air. International Hydrological Decade.
926 **243** 12½ p. black, orange & grn 15 10
927 60 p. black, orange & blue 65 35

244 Emir Abd-el-Kader **245** U.N.R.W.A. Emblem

1966. Air. Return of Emir Abd-el-Kader's Remains to Algiers.
928 **244** 12½ p. black and green . . 30 10
929 50 p. brown and green . . 45 30

1966. Air. 21st Anniv of U.N. Day and Refugee Week.
930 **245** 12½ p. + 2½ p. black and blue 10 10
931 50 p. + 5 p. black and green 45 45

246 Handclasp and Map **247** Doves and Oil Pipelines

1967. Air. Solidarity Congress, Damascus.
932 **246** 20 p. multicoloured . . . 20 10
933 25 p. multicoloured . . . 25 15

1967. Air. 4th Anniv of Baathist Revolution of 8 March 1963.
934 **247** 17½ p. multicoloured . . . 25 10
935 25 p. multicoloured . . . 30 20
936 27½ p. multicoloured . . . 45 20

248 Soldier and Citizens with Banner **249** Workers' Monument, Damascus

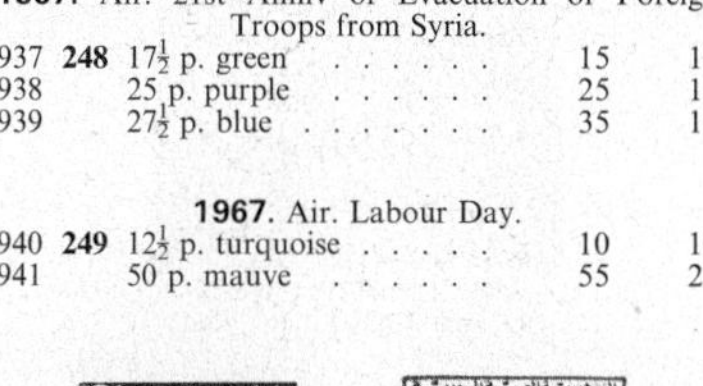

1967. Air. 21st Anniv of Evacuation of Foreign Troops from Syria.
937 **248** 17½ p. green 15 10
938 25 p. purple 25 15
939 27½ p. blue 35 15

1967. Air. Labour Day.
940 **249** 12½ p. turquoise 10 10
941 50 p. mauve 55 25

250 Core Bust **251** "African Woman" (vase)

252 Head of a Young Man from Amrith **253** Flags and Fair Entrance

1967.
942 **250** 2½ p. green (postage) . . 10 10
943 5 p. red 10 10
944 10 p. blue 10 10
945 12½ p. brown 10 10
946 **251** 15 p. purple 10 10
947 20 p. blue 15 10
948 25 p. green 25 10
949 27½ p. blue 35 10
950 **252** 45 p. red (air) 40 20
951 50 p. mauve 55 20
952 60 p. blue 60 40
953 – 100 p. green 80 50
954 – 500 p. red . . . . . . 3·75 2·50
DESIGN—VERT: 100, 500 p. Bust of Princess (2nd-century bronze).

1967. Air. 14th International Damascus Fair.
955 **253** 12½ p. multicoloured . . 10 10
956 60 p. multicoloured . . . 55 30

254 Statue of Ur-Nina and Tourist Emblem **255** Cotton Boll and Cogwheel

1967. Air. International Tourist Year.
957 **254** 12½ p. purple, black & bl 10 10
958 25 p. red, black and blue 15 10
959 27½ p. blue, black & lt bl 40 20

1967. Air. Aleppo Cotton Festival.
961 **255** 12½ p. black, brown and yellow 10 10
962 60 p. black, brown and yellow 65 25

1967. Air. Industrial and Agricultural Production Fair, Aleppo. Optd **INDUSTRIAL AND AGRICULTURAL PRODUCTION FAIR ALEPPO 1967** in English and Arabic.
963 **255** 12½ p. black, brown & yell 10 10
964 60 p. black, brown & yell 65 25

257 Ibn el-Naphis (scientist) **258** Acclaiming Human Rights

1967. Air. Sciences Week.
965 **257** 12½ p. red and green . . . 10 10
966 27½ p. mauve and blue . . 40 10

1968. Air. Human Rights Year.
967 **258** 12½ p. black, turquoise and blue 10 10
968 60 p. black, red and pink 55 35

259 Learning to Read **260** "The Arab Revolutionary" (Damascus statue)

1968. Air. Literacy Campaign.
970 **259** 12½ p. multicoloured . . . 10 10
971 – 17½ p. multicoloured . . . 10 10
972 **259** 25 p. multicoloured . . . 25 10
973 – 45 p. multicoloured . . . 45 25
DESIGN: 17½, 45 p. Flaming torch and open book.

1968. 5th Anniv of March 8th Baathist Revolution.
974 **260** 12½ p. brown, yell & blk 10 10
975 25 p. mauve, pink & blk 30 10
976 27½ p. green, light green and black 30 15

261 Map of North Africa and Arabia **263** Hands holding Spanner, Rifle and Torch

262 Euphrates Dam

1968. 21st Anniv of Baath Arab Socialist Party.
977 **261** 12½ p. multicoloured . . . 10 10
978 60 p. multicoloured . . . 50 25

1968. Air. Euphrates Dam Project.
979 **262** 12½ p. multicoloured . . . 20 10
980 17½ p. multicoloured . . . 20 15
981 25 p. multicoloured . . . 45 20

1968. "Mobilisation Efforts".
982 **263** 12½ p. multicoloured . . . 10 10
983 17½ p. multicoloured . . . 15 10
984 25 p. multicoloured . . . 25 10

264 Railway Track and Sun **266** Torch, Map and Laurel

265 Oil Pipeline Map

1968. 22nd Anniv of Evacuation of Foreign Troops from Syria.
985 **264** 12½ p. multicoloured . . . 50 50
986 27½ p. multicoloured . . . 1·50 1·50

1968. Syrian Oil Exploration.
987 **265** 12½ p. blue, green and light green 25 10
988 17½ p. blue, brown & pink 50 20

1968. Palestine Day.
989 **266** 12½ p. multicoloured . . . 15 10
990 25 p. multicoloured . . . 20 15
991 27½ p. multicoloured . . . 35 15

267 Refugee Family

1968. Red Crescent Refugees Fund.
992 **267** 12½ p. + 2½ p. black, purple and blue 35 35
993 27½ p. + 7½ p. black, red and violet 35 35

268 Avenzoar (physician) and W.H.O. Emblem **269** Ear of Corn, Cogwheel and Saracen Gate, Aleppo Citadel

1968. Air. 20th Anniv of W.H.O.
994 **268** 12½ p. multicoloured . . . 10 10
995 – 25 p. multicoloured . . . 25 10
996 – 60 p. multicoloured . . . 65 25
DESIGNS—As Type **268**, but with different portraits of Arab physicians: 25 p. Razi; 60 p. Jabir.

1968. Industrial and Agricultural Production Fair, Aleppo.
997 **269** 12½ p. multicoloured . . . 10 10
998 27½ p. multicoloured . . . 20 10

270 Emblems of Fair, Agriculture and Industry **271** Gathering Cotton

1968. 15th International Damascus Fair.
999 **270** 12½ p. black, grn & brn . 10 10
1000 – 27½ p. multicoloured . . 25 10
1001 **270** 60 p. black, orge & blue 45 30
DESIGN—HORIZ: 27½ p. Flag, hand with torch and emblems.

1968. Aleppo Cotton Festival.
1002 **271** 12½ p. multicoloured . . 10 10
1003 27½ p. multicoloured . . 25 10

272 Monastery of St. Simeon the Stylite **273** Oil Derrick

1968. Air. Ancient Monuments (1st series).
1004 **272** 15 p. multicoloured 10 10
1005 – 17½ p. deep brown, brown and chocolate 15 15
1006 – 22½ p. multicoloured . . 20 20
1007 – 45 p. multicoloured . . . 40 20
1008 – 50 p. brown, sepia and blue 45 30
DESIGNS—VERT: 17½ p. El Tekkieh Mosque, Damascus; 22½ p. Temple columns, Palmyra. HORIZ: 45 p. Chapel of St. Paul, Bab Kisan; 50 p. Amphitheatre, Bosra.
See also Nos. 1026/30.

1968.
1009 **273** 2½ p. green and blue . . 10 10
1010 5 p. blue and green . . . 10 10
1011 7½ p. blue and green . . 10 10
1012 10 p. green and yellow . 15 10
1013 12½ p. red and yellow . . 15 10
1014 15 p. brown and bistre . 20 10
1015 27½ p. brown & orange . 30 10

274 Al-Jahez (scientist)

275 Throwing the Hammer

1968. 9th Science Week.

1016 274 12½ p. black and green . . 10 10
1017 27½ p. black and grey . . 40 20

1968. Air. Olympic Games, Mexico.

1018 275 12½ p. black, mauve and green 10 10
1019 – 25 p. black, red & green . 25 10
1020 – 27½ p. black, grey and green 30 10
1021 – 60 p. multicoloured . . . 45 25

DESIGNS: 25 p. Throwing the discus; 27½ p. Running; 60 p. Basketball.

276 Aerial View of Airport

1969. Air. Construction of Damascus Int Airport.

1023 276 12½ p. green, blue & yell . 15 10
1024 17½ p. violet, red and green 30 10
1025 60 p. black, mauve and yellow 95 30

277 Baal-Shamin Temple, Palmyra

1969. Air. Ancient Monuments (2nd series). Multicoloured.

1026 25 p. Type 277 . . . . . . 15 10
1027 45 p. Omayyad Mosque, Damascus (vert) 25 10
1028 50 p. Amphitheatre, Palmyra 30 15
1029 60 p. Khaled ibn el-Walid Mosque, Homs (vert) . . . 45 20
1030 100 p. St. Simeon's Column, Jebel Samaan 75 40

278 "Sun" and Clenched Fists in Broken Handcuffs

279 "Sun of Freedom"

1969. 6th Anniv of March 8th Baathist Revolution.

1031 278 12½ p. multicoloured . . 10 10
1032 25 p. multicoloured . . . 25 10
1033 27½ p. multicoloured . . 30 10

1969. 5th Youth Festival, Homs.

1034 279 12½ p. red, yellow and blue 10 10
1035 25 p. red, yellow and green 20 10

280 Symbols of Progress

281 "Workers", Cogwheel and I.L.O. Emblem

1969. 23rd Anniv of Evacuation of Foreign Troops from Syria.

1036 280 12½ p. multicoloured . . 10 10
1037 27½ p. multicoloured . . 20 10

1969. Air. 50th Anniv of I.L.O.

1038 281 12½ p. multicoloured . . 10 10
1039 27½ p. multicoloured . . 30 10

282 Russian Dancers

283 "Fortune" (statue)

1969. Air. 16th Int Damascus Fair. Mult.

1041 12½ p. Type 282 . . . . . . 20 10
1042 27½ p. Ballet dancers 35 15
1043 45 p. Lebanese dancers . . . 40 25
1044 55 p. Egyptian dancers . . . 45 25
1045 60 p. Bulgarian dancers . . 60 30

1969. Air. 9th International Archaeological Congress, Damascus. Multicoloured.

1046 17½ p. Type 283 . . . . . . 25 10
1047 25 p. "Lady from Palmyra" (statue) 30 10
1048 60 p. "Motherhood" (statue) 60 25

284 Children dancing

285 Mahatma Gandhi

1969. Air. Children's Day.

1049 284 12½ p. green, blue and turquoise 15 10
1050 25 p. violet, blue & red . 20 10
1051 27½ p. grey, dp blue & blue 25 10

1969. Birth Centenary of Mahatma Gandhi.

1052 285 12½ p. brown and buff . . 15 10
1053 27½ p. green and yellow . 25 15

286 Cotton

287 "Arab World" (6th Arab Science Congress)

1969. Aleppo Cotton Festival.

1054 286 12½ p. multicoloured . . 10 10
1055 17½ p. multicoloured . . 10 10
1056 25 p. multicoloured . . 25 15

1969. 10th Science Week.

1057 287 12½ p. blue and green . . 10 10
1058 – 25 p. violet and pink . . 20 15
1059 – 27½ p. brown and green . 25 20

DESIGNS: 25 p. Arab Academy (50th anniv); 27½ p. Damascus University (50th anniv of Faculty of Medicine).

288 Cockerel

1969. Air. Damascus Agricultural Museum. Multicoloured.

1060 12½ p. Type 288 . . . . . . 20 10
1061 17½ p. Cow 25 15
1062 20 p. Maize 35 15
1063 50 p. Olives 50 25

289 Rising Sun, Hand and Book

1970. 7th Anniv of March 8th Baathist Revolution.

1064 289 17½ p. black, brn & blue 10 10
1065 25 p. black, blue & red . 20 10
1066 27½ p. black, brn & grn . 25 15

290 Map of Arab World, League Emblem and Flag

1970. Silver Jubilee of Arab League.

1067 290 12½ p. multicoloured . . . 10 10
1068 25 p. multicoloured . . . 20 10
1069 27½ p. multicoloured . . . 25 15

291 Dish Aerial and Hand on Book

1970. Air. World Meteorological Day.

1070 291 25 p. black, yellow & grn 30 10
1071 60 p. black, yellow & blue 60 35

292 Lenin

1970. Air. Birth Centenary of Lenin.

1072 292 15 p. brown and red . . . 10 10
1073 60 p. green and red . . . 45 30

293 Battle of Hattin

1970. 24th Anniv of Evacuation of Foreign Troops from Syria.

1074 293 15 p. brown and cream . 15 10
1075 35 p. violet and cream . . 40 20

294 Emblem of Workers' Syndicate

1970. Air. Labour Day.

1076 294 15 p. brown and green . . 10 10
1077 60 p. brown and orange . 55 30

295 Young Syrians and Map

1970. Revolution's Youth Union, 1st Youth Week.

1078 295 15 p. green and brown . . 10 10
1079 25 p. brown and ochre . . 20 15

This issue is inscr "YOUTH'S FIRST WEAK" in error.

296 Refugee Family

1970. World Arab Refugee Week.

1080 296 15 p. multicoloured . . . 10 10
1081 25 p. multicoloured . . . 25 10
1082 35 p. multicoloured . . . 25 10

297 Dish Aerial and Open Book

1970. Air. World Telecommunications Day.

1083 297 15 p. black and lilac . . 10 10
1084 60 p. black and blue . . 60 35

298 New U.P.U. Headquarters Building

1970. Air. New U.P.U. Headquarters Building.

1085 298 15 p. multicoloured . . . 10 10
1086 60 p. multicoloured . . . 55 30

299 "Industry" and Graph

300 Khaled ibn el-Walid

1970.

1087 299 2½ p. red and brown (postage) 10 10
1088 5 p. blue and orange . . 10 10
1089 7½ p. grey and purple . . 10 10
1090 10 p. brown and light brown 10 10
1091 12½ p. red and blue . . . 10 10
1092 15 p. mauve and green . 15 10
1093 20 p. brown and blue . . 15 10
1094 22½ p. green and brown . 20 10
1095 25 p. blue and grey . . . 20 10
1096 27½ p. brown and green . 25 10
1097 35 p. green and red . . 35 20
1098 300 45 p. mauve (air) 40 20
1099 50 p. green 45 25
1100 60 p. brown 60 35
1101 100 p. blue 85 35
1102 200 p. green . . . . . . 1·60 85
1103 300 p. violet . . . . . . 2·75 1·60
1104 500 p. grey . . . . . . 3·75 3·00

301 Medieval Warriors

1970. Air. Folk Tales and Legends.

1105 301 5 p. multicoloured . . . 10 10
1106 – 10 p. multicoloured . . . 10 10
1107 – 15 p. multicoloured . . . 15 15
1108 – 20 p. multicoloured . . . 20 15
1109 – 60 p. multicoloured . . . 70 35

Nos. 1106/9 show horsemen similar to Type 301.

302 Cotton

1970. Aleppo Agricultural and Industrial Fair. Multicoloured.

1110 5 p. Type 302 . . . . . . 10 10
1111 10 p. Tomatoes 10 10
1112 15 p. Tobacco 15 15
1113 20 p. Sugar beet 20 15
1114 35 p. Wheat 45 25

303 Mosque in Flames

1970. Air. 1st Anniv of Burning of Al-Aqsa Mosque, Jerusalem.
1115 **303** 15 p. multicoloured . . . 15 10
1116 60 p. multicoloured . . . 60 35

304 Wood-carving

1970. Air. 17th Damascus Int Fair. Mult.
1117 15 p. Type **304** 10 10
1118 20 p. Jewellery 20 10
1119 25 p. Glass-making 20 15
1120 30 p. Copper-engraving . . . 45 20
1121 60 p. Shell-work 95 40

305 Scout, Encampment and Badge

1970. Pan-Arab Scout Jamboree, Damascus.
1122 **305** 15 p. green 35 20

306 Olive Tree and Emblem **307** I.E.Y. Emblem

1970. World Year of Olive-oil Production.
1123 **306** 15 p. multicoloured . . . 20 10
1124 25 p. multicoloured . . . 40 15

1970. Air. International Education Year.
1125 **307** 15 p. brown, green & blk 10 10
1126 60 p. brown, blue & blk . 55 30

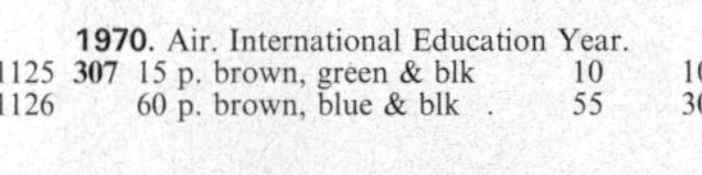

308 U.N. Emblems

1970. Air. 25th Anniv of U.N.O.
1127 **308** 15 p. multicoloured . . . 10 10
1128 60 p. multicoloured . . . 55 30

309 Protective Shield **310** Girl holding Garland

1971. 8th Anniv of March 8th Baathist Revolution.
1129 **309** 15 p. blue, yellow & grn . 10 10
1130 22½ p. green, yellow & brn 15 10
1131 27½ p. brown, yellow & bl 25 15

1971. Air. 25th Anniv of Evacuation of Foreign Troops from Syria.
1132 **310** 15 p. multicoloured . . . 10 10
1133 60 p. multicoloured . . . 55 35

311 Globe and World Races

1971. Air. Racial Equality Year.
1134 **311** 15 p. multicoloured . . . 10 10
1135 60 p. multicoloured . . . 50 25

312 Soldier, Worker and Labour Emblems

1971. Labour Day.
1136 **312** 15 p. purple, blue & yell 10 10
1137 25 p. deep blue, blue and yellow 25 10

313 Hailing Traffic

1971. World Traffic Day.
1138 **313** 15 p. red, blue & black . 10 10
1139 – 25 p. multicoloured . . 20 15
1140 **313** 45 p. red, yellow & blk . 45 30
DESIGN—VERT: 25 p. Traffic signs and signal lights.

314 Cotton, Cogwheel and Factories

1971. Aleppo Agricultural and Industrial Fair.
1141 **314** 15 p. black, blue & grn . 10 10
1142 30 p. black, scarlet and red 25 20

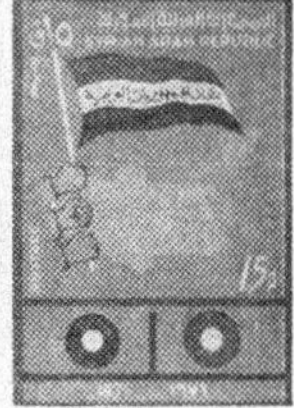
315 A.P.U. Emblem **317** Flag and Federation Map

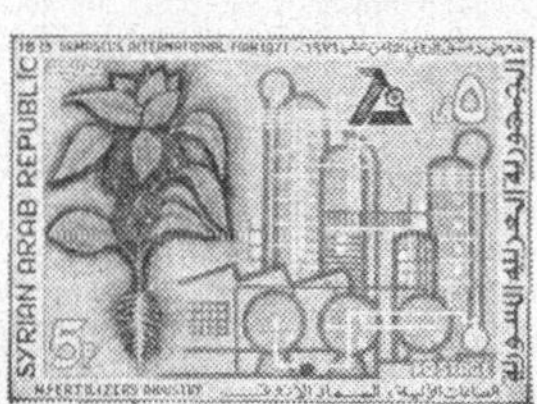
316 Peppers and Fertiliser Plant

1971. 25th Anniv of Sofar Conference and Founding of Arab Postal Union.
1143 **315** 15 p. multicoloured . . 10 10
1144 20 p. multicoloured . . 20 10

1971. 18th Damascus International Fair. Industries. Multicoloured.
1145 5 p. Type **316** 10 10
1146 15 p. TV set and telephone ("Electronics") 10 10
1147 35 p. Oil lamp and dish ("Glassware") 40 15
1148 50 p. Part of carpet ("Carpets") 55 25

1971. Arab Federation Referendum.
1149 **317** 15 p. green, black & red 20 10

318 Pres. Hafez al-Assad and People's Council Chamber

1971. Air. People's Council and Presidential Election.
1150 **318** 15 p. multicoloured . . 10 10
1151 65 p. multicoloured . . 70 25

319 Pres. Nasser **320** "Telstar" and Dish Aerial

1971. Air. 1st Death Anniv of Pres. Nasser of Egypt.
1152 **319** 15 p. brown and green . . 10 10
1153 20 p. brown and grey . . 25 10

1971. 25th Anniv of U.N.E.S.C.O.
1154 **320** 15 pp. multicoloured . . 10 10
1155 50 p. multicoloured . . . 50 30

321 Flaming Torch **322** Quill-pen and Open Book

1971. "Movement of 16 November 1970".
1156 **321** 15 p. multicoloured . . . 10 10
1157 20 p. multicoloured . . . 20 15

1971. 8th Writers' Congress.
1158 **322** 15 p. brown, orange and green 20 10

323 Children with Ball **324** Book Year Emblem

1971. 25th Anniv of U.N.I.C.E.F.
1159 **323** 15 p. red, blue and deep blue 10 10
1160 25 p. brown, green & bl . 25 15

1972. International Book Year.
1161 **324** 15 p. violet, blue & brown 10 10
1162 20 p. green, light green and brown 25 10

325 Emblems of Reconstruction **326** Baath Party Emblem

1972. 9th Anniv of March 8th Baathist Revolution.
1163 **325** 15 p. violet and green . . 10 10
1164 20 p. red and bistre . . . 15 10

1972. 25th Anniv of Baath Party.
1165 **326** 15 p. multicoloured . . . 10 10
1166 20 p. multicoloured . . . 15 10

327 Eagle, Factory Chimneys and Rifles **328** Flowers and Broken Chain

1972. 1st Anniv of Arab Republics Federation.
1167 **327** 15 p. gold, black & red . 25 10

1972. 26th Anniv of Evacuation of Foreign Troops from Syria.
1168 **328** 15 p. grey and red 10 10
1169 50 p. grey and green . . . 50 30

329 Hand with Spanner **331** Environment Emblem

330 Telecommunications Emblem

1972. Labour Day.
1170 **329** 15 p. multicoloured . . . 10 10
1171 50 p. multicoloured . . . 50 30

1972. Air. World Telecommunications Day.
1172 **330** 15 p. multicoloured . . . 10 10
1173 50 p. multicoloured . . . 60 25

1972. United Nations Environmental Conservation Conference, Stockholm.
1174 **331** 15 p. blue, azure & pink 10 10
1175 50 p. purple, orge & yell 60 30

332 Discus, Football and Swimming

1972. Olympic Games, Munich.
1176 **332** 15 p. violet, black & bis . 10 10
1177 – 60 p. orange, black & bl 50 40
DESIGN: 60 p. Running, gymnastics and fencing.

334 Dove and Factory **335** President Hafez al-Assad

1972. Aleppo Agricultural and Industrial Fair.
1179 **334** 15 p. multicoloured . . . 10 10
1180 20 p. multicoloured . . . 15 10

1972. Air.
1181 **335** 100 p. green . . . . . . 1·00 45
1182 500 p. brown . . . . . 4·50 1·90

336 Women's Dance

1972. 19th Damascus International Fair. Mult.
1183 15 p. Type **336** 15 10
1184 20 p. Tambourine dance . . 20 15
1185 50 p. Men's drum dance . . 65 35

337 Airline Emblem **338** Emblem of Revolution

1972. Air. 25th Anniv of "Syrianair" Airline.
1186 **337** 15 p. blue, light blue and black 25 10
1187 50 p. blue, grey & black 70 25

1973. 10th Anniv of March 8th Baathist Revolution.
1188 **338** 15 p. green, red & black 10 10
1189 20 p. orange, red & blk . 15 10
1190 25 p. blue, red & black 25 10

339 Human Heart **340** Emblems of Agriculture and Industry

1973. 25th Anniv of W.H.O.

1191 **339** 15 p. blue, purple & grey . . . 20 10
1192 20 p. blue, purple & brn . . . 50 25

1973. 27th Anniv of Evacuation of Foreign Troops from Syria.

1193 **340** 15 p. multicoloured . . . 10 10
1194 20 p. multicoloured . . . 15 10

341 Globe and Workers

1973. Labour Day.

1195 **341** 15 p. black, purple and stone . . . 15 10
1196 50 p. black, blue & buff . . . 45 25

342 Family and Emblems
343 Three Heads

1973. 10th Anniv of World Food Programme.

1197 **342** 15 p. red and green . . . 10 10
1198 50 p. blue and lilac . . . 40 25

1973.

1199 **343** $2\frac{1}{2}$ p. green . . . 10 10
1200 5 p. orange . . . 10 10
1201 – $7\frac{1}{2}$ p. brown . . . 10 10
1202 – 10 p. red . . . 10 10
1203 **343** 15 p. blue . . . 10 10
1204 – 25 p. blue . . . 15 10
1205 – 35 p. blue . . . 25 15
1206 – 55 p. green . . . 35 15
1207 – 70 p. purple . . . 50 25

DESIGNS—HORIZ: $7\frac{1}{2}$, 10, 55 p. As Type **343**, but with one head above the other two. VERT: 25, 35, 70 p. Similar to Type **343**, but with heads in vertical arrangement.

344 Stock

1973. Int Flower Show, Damascus. Mult.

1208 5 p. Type **344** . . . 15 10
1209 10 p. Gardenia . . . 15 10
1210 15 p. Jasmine . . . 20 10
1211 20 p. Rose . . . 30 10
1212 25 p. Narcissus . . . 35 10

345 Cogs and Flowers

1973. Aleppo Agricultural and Industrial Fair.

1213 **345** 15 p. multicoloured . . . 20 10

346 Euphrates Dam

1973. Euphrates Dam Project. Diversion of the River.

1214 **346** 15 p. multicoloured . . . 25 10
1215 50 p. multicoloured . . . 45 25

MINIMUM PRICE

The minimum price quoted is 10p which represents a handling charge rather than a basis for valuing common stamps. For further notes about prices, see introductory pages.

347 Deir Ezzor Costume
348 Anniversary Emblem

1973. 20th Damascus International Fair. Costumes. Multicoloured.

1216 5 p. Type **347** . . . 15 10
1217 10 p. Hassake . . . 15 10
1218 20 p. As Sahel . . . 20 10
1219 25 p. Zakie . . . 30 10
1220 50 p. Sarakeb . . . 40 25

1973. 25th Anniv of Declaration of Human Rights.

1221 **348** 15 p. black, red & green . . . 10 10
1222 50 p. black, red & blue . . . 40 15

349 Citadel of Ja'abar

1973. "Save the Euphrates Monuments" Campaign. Multicoloured.

1223 10 p. Type **349** . . . 10 10
1224 15 p. Meskeneh Minaret (vert) . . . 15 10
1225 25 p. Psyche, Anab al-Safinah (vert) . . . 20 10

350 W.M.O. Emblem

1973. Centenary of W.M.O.

1226 **350** 70 p. multicoloured . . . 50 25

351 Ancient City of Maalula

1973. Arab Emigrants' Congress, Buenos Aires.

1227 **351** 15 p. black and blue . . . 10 10
1228 – 50 p. black and brown . . . 35 15

DESIGN: 50 p. Ruins of Afamia.

352 Soldier and Workers
353 Copernicus

1973. 3rd Anniv of November 16th Revolution.

1229 **352** 15 p. blue and bistre . . . 10 10
1230 25 p. violet and red . . . 15 10

1973. 14th Science Week.

1231 **353** 15 p. black and gold . . . 10 10
1232 – 25 p. black and gold . . . 20 10

DESIGN: 25 p. Al-Biruni.

354 National Symbols

355 U.P.U. Monument, Berne

1973. 11th Anniv of March 8th Baathist Revolution.

1233 **354** 10 p. blue and green . . . 10 10
1234 25 p. blue and green . . . 10 10

1974. Centenary of U.P.U. Multicoloured.

1235 15 p. Type **355** . . . 10 10
1236 20 p. Emblem on airmail letter (horiz) . . . 15 10
1237 70 p. Type **355** . . . 50 30

356 Postal Institute

1974. Inauguration of Higher Arab Postal Institute, Damascus.

1238 **356** 15 p. multicoloured . . . 20 10

357 Sun and Monument
358 Machine Fitter

1974. 28th Anniv of Evacuation of Foreign Troops from Syria.

1239 **357** 15 p. multicoloured . . . 10 10
1240 20 p. multicoloured . . . 10 10

1974. Labour Day.

1241 **358** 15 p. multicoloured . . . 10 10
1242 50 p. multicoloured . . . 35 20

359 Abul Fida (historian)
360 Diamond and Part of Cogwheel

1974. Famous Arabs.

1243 **359** 100 p. green . . . 65 40
1244 – 100 p. brown . . . 1·40 75

DESIGN: 200 p. Al-Farabi (philosopher and encyclopedist).

1974. 21st Damascus International Fair. Mult.

1245 15 p. Type **360** . . . 10 10
1246 25 p. "Sun" within cogwheel . . . 20 10

361 Figs
362 Flowers within Drop of Blood

1974. Aleppo Agricultural and Industrial Fair. Fruits. Multicoloured.

1247 5 p. Type **361** . . . 15 10
1248 15 p. Grapes . . . 15 10
1249 20 p. Pomegranates . . . 15 10
1250 25 p. Cherries . . . 20 15
1251 35 p. Rose-hips . . . 35 20

1974. 1st Anniv of October Liberation War. Multicoloured.

1252 15 p. Type **362** . . . 25 10
1253 20 p. Flower and stars . . . 40 10

363 Knight and Rook

364 Symbolic Figure, Globe and Emblem

1974. 50th Anniv of International Chess Federation.

1254 **363** 15 p. blue, lt blue & blk . . . 65 15
1255 – 50 p. multicoloured . . . 2·10 1·25

DESIGN: 50 p. Knight on chessboard.

1974. World Population Year.

1256 **364** 50 p. multicoloured . . . 35 20

365 Ishtup-ilum
366 Oil Rig and Crowd

1974. Statuettes.

1257 **365** 20 p. green . . . 15 10
1258 – 55 p. brown . . . 30 15
1259 – 70 p. blue . . . 55 25

DESIGNS: 55 p. Woman with vase; 70 p. Ur-nina.

1975. 12th Anniv of Baathist Revolution of 8 March 1963.

1260 **366** 15 p. multicoloured . . . 20 10

367 Savings Emblem and Family ("Savings Certificates")
368 Dove Emblem

1975. Savings Campaign.

1261 **367** 15 p. black, orge & grn . . . 10 10
1262 – 20 p. brown, black & orge . . . 20 10

DESIGN: 20 p. Family with savings box and letter ("Postal Savings Bank").

1975. 29th Anniv of Evacuation of Foreign Troops from Syria.

1263 **368** 15 p. multicoloured . . . 10 10
1264 25 p. multicoloured . . . 15 10

369 Worker supporting Cog
370 Camomile

1975. Labour Day.

1265 **369** 15 p. multicoloured . . . 10 10
1266 25 p. multicoloured . . . 15 10

1975. Int Flower Show, Damascus. Mult.

1267 5 p. Type **370** . . . 15 10
1268 10 p. Chincherinchi . . . 15 10
1269 15 p. Carnations . . . 20 10
1270 20 p. Poppy . . . 25 10
1271 25 p. Honeysuckle . . . 45 15

371 "Destruction and Reconstruction"

1975. Reoccupation of Qneitra.

1272 **371** 50 p. multicoloured . . . 40 20

372 Apples
373 Arabesque Pattern

1975. Aleppo Agricultural and Industrial Fair. Fruits. Multicoloured.

1273 5 p. Type **372** . . . 15 10
1274 10 p. Quinces . . . 15 10
1275 15 p. Apricots . . . 20 10
1276 20 p. Grapes . . . 25 10
1277 25 p. Figs . . . 40 15

1975. 22nd International Damascus Fair.
1278 **373** 15 p. multicoloured . . . 10 10
1279 35 p. multicoloured . . . 35 15

374 Pres. Hafez al-Assad

1975. 5th Anniv of "Movement of 16 November 1970".
1280 **374** 15 p. multicoloured . . . 10 10
1281 50 p. multicoloured . . . 30 20

375 Symbolic Woman 376 Bronze "Horse" Lamp

1976. International Women's Year. Multicoloured.
1282 10 p. Type **375** 10 10
1283 15 p. "Motherhood" 10 10
1284 25 p. "Education" 15 10
1285 50 p. "Science" 35 25

1976.
1286 – 5 p. green 10 10
1287 **376** 10 p. green 10 10
1288 – 10 p. blue 10 10
1289 – 15 p. brown 20 10
1290 **376** 20 p. red 10 10
1291 25 p. blue 15 10
1292 – 30 p. brown 20 10
1293 – 35 p. green 20 10
1294 – 40 p. orange 25 10
1295 – 50 p. blue 40 20
1296 – 55 p. mauve 40 10
1297 – 60 p. violet 45 15
1298 – 70 p. red 45 15
1299 – 75 p. orange 50 30
1300 – 80 p. green 60 20
1301 – 100 p. mauve 65 25
1302 – 200 p. blue . . . . . . 1·40 50
1303 – 300 p. mauve . . . . . . 2·10 85
1304 – 500 p. grey . . . . . . 3·50 2·40
1305 – 1000 p. green . . . . . . 6·25 3·75
DESIGNS—VERT: 5 p. Wall-painting showing figure of a man; 10 p. (No. 1288) Flying goddess with wreath; 30, 35, 40 p. Man's head inkstand; 50, 55, 60 p. Statue of Nike; 70, 75, 80 p. Statue of Hera; 100 p. Imdugub-Mari (bird goddess); 200 p. Arab astrolabe; 500 p. Palmyrean coin of Valabathus; 1000 p. Abraxas stone. HORIZ: 15 p. Wall-painting showing figures; 300 p. Herodian coin from Palmyra.

377 National Theatre, Damascus

1976. 13th Anniv of March 8th Baathist Revolution.
1306 **377** 25 p. green, blk & silver . 15 10
1307 35 p. green, blk & silver . 20 15

378 Nurse and Emblem 380 Eagle and Stars

379 Syrian 5 m. Stamp of 1920

1976. 8th Arab Red Crescent Societies' Conference, Damascus.
1308 **378** 25 p. blue, black & red . 20 10
1309 100 p. violet, blk & red . 65 50

1976. Arab Post Day.
1310 **379** 25 p. multicoloured . . . 25 10
1311 35 p. multicoloured . . . 40 20

1976. 30th Anniv of Evacuation of Foreign Troops from Syria.
1312 **380** 25 p. multicoloured . . 20 10
1313 35 p. multicoloured . . 25 15

381 Hand gripping Spanner 382 Cotton Boll

1976. Labour Day.
1314 **381** 25 p. blue and black . . 20 10
1315 – 60 p. multicoloured . . 45 30
DESIGN: 60 p. Hand supporting globe.

1976. Aleppo Agricultural and Industrial Fair.
1316 **382** 25 p. multicoloured . . 30 10
1317 35 p. multicoloured . . 25 15

383 Tulips

1976. Int Flower Show, Damascus. Mult.
1318 5 p. Type **383** 15 10
1319 15 p. Yellow daisies 15 10
1320 20 p. Turk's-cap lilies . . . 20 10
1321 25 p. Irises 40 10
1322 35 p. Honeysuckle 50 25

384 Pottery

1976. Air. 23rd International Damascus Fair. Handicraft Industries. Multicoloured.
1323 10 p. Type **384** 15 10
1324 25 p. Rug-making 25 10
1325 30 p. Metalware 25 10
1326 35 p. Wickerware 40 10
1327 100 p. Wood-carving 95 65

385 People supporting Olive Branch

1976. Non-aligned Countries Summit Conference, Colombo. Multicoloured.
1328 40 p. Type **385** 25 20
1329 60 p. Symbolic arrow penetrating "grey curtain" 40 25

386 Football 387 Construction Emblems

1976. 5th Pan-Arab Games. Multicoloured.
1330 5 p. Type **386** 10 10
1331 10 p. Swimming 15 10
1332 25 p. Running 20 10
1333 35 p. Basketball 35 20
1334 50 p. Throwing the javelin . 50 25

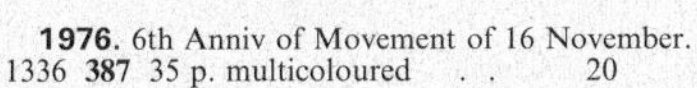

1976. 6th Anniv of Movement of 16 November.
1336 **387** 35 p. multicoloured . . 20 10

388 "The Fox and the Crow" 389 Muhammad Kurd-Ali (philosopher)

1976. Fairy Tales. Multicoloured.
1337 10 p. Type **388** 15 10
1338 15 p. "The Hare and the Tortoise" (horiz) 15 10
1339 20 p. "Little Red Riding Hood" 15 10
1340 25 p. "The Wolf and the Goats" (horiz) 20 10
1341 35 p. "The Wolf and the Lamb" 30 15

1976. Birth Centenary of Muhammad Kurd-Ali.
1342 **389** 25 p. multicoloured . . . 20 10

390 Boeing 747SP

1977. Civil Aviation Day.
1343 **390** 35 p. multicoloured . . . 75 20

391 Woman hoisting Flag 392 A.P.U. Emblem

1977. 14th Anniv of 8th March Baathist Revolution.
1344 **391** 35 p. multicoloured . . . 40 20

1977. 25th Anniv of Arab Postal Union.
1345 **392** 35 p. multicoloured . . . 25 10

393 Mounted Horseman

1977. 31st Anniv of Evacuation of Foreign Troops from Syria.
1346 **393** 100 p. multicoloured . . 75 50

394 Industrial Scene and Tools

1977. Labour Day.
1347 **394** 60 p. multicoloured . . . 40 25

395 I.C.A.O. Emblem, Boeing 747SP and Globe

1977. 30th Anniv of I.C.A.O.
1348 **395** 100 p. multicoloured . . 1·00 75

396 Lemon 397 Mallows

1977. International Agricultural Fair, Aleppo. Multicoloured.
1349 10 p. Type **396** 15 10
1350 20 p. Lime 15 10
1351 25 p. Grapefruit 20 10
1352 35 p. Oranges 45 20
1353 60 p. Tangerines 50 20

1977. International Flower Show. Multicoloured.
1354 10 p. Type **397** 15 10
1355 20 p. Cockscomb 15 10
1356 25 p. Convolvulus 20 10
1357 35 p. Balsam 40 15
1358 60 p. Lilac 50 30

398 Young Pioneers and Emblem

1977. Al Baath Pioneers Organization.
1359 **398** 35 p. multicoloured . . . 35 20

399 Arabesque Pattern and Coffee Pot 400 Globe and Measures

1977. 24th International Damascus Fair.
1360 **399** 25 p. red, blue & black . 15 10
1361 60 p. brown, grn & blk . 40 25

1977. World Standards Day.
1362 **400** 15 p. multicoloured . . . 20 10

401 Microscope, Book and Lyre

1977. 30th Anniv of U.N.E.S.C.O.
1363 **401** 25 p. multicoloured . . . 25 10

402 Shield, Surgeon and Crab 403 Archbishop Capucci and Map of Palestine

1977. Fighting Cancer Week.
1364 **402** 100 p. multicoloured . . 65 30

1977. 3rd Anniv of Archbishop Capucci's Arrest.
1365 **403** 60 p. multicoloured . . . 40 20

404 Blind Man, Eye and Globe 405 Dome of the Rock, Jerusalem

1977. World Blind Week.
1366 **404** 55 p. multicoloured . . . 25 15
1367 70 p. multicoloured . . . 40 20

1977. Palestinian Welfare.
1368 **405** 5 p. multicoloured . . . 15 10
1369 10 p. multicoloured . . . 25 10

406 Pres. Hafez al-Assad and Government Palace, Damascus

408 Arrow and Blood Circulation

407 Goldfinch

1977. 7th Anniv of Movement of 16 November.
1370 **406** 50 p. multicoloured . . . 25 10

1978. Birds. Multicoloured.
1371 10 p. Type **407** . . . . 1·60 90
1372 20 p. Peregrine falcon . . . . 1·90 1·25
1373 25 p. Rock dove . . . . . . 1·90 1·25
1374 35 p. Hoopoe . . . . 3·50 1·50
1375 60 p. Chukar partridge . . . 4·25 2·00

1978. World Health Day. "Fighting Blood Pressure".
1376 **408** 100 p. multicoloured . . 60 30

409 Factory, Moon and Stars

410 Geometric Design

1978. 32nd Anniv of Evacuation of Foreign Troops from Syria.
1377 **409** 35 p. green, orge & blk . 20 10

1978. 14th Arab Engineering Conference, Damascus.
1378 **410** 25 p. green and black . . 25 10

411 Map of Arab Countries, Flag, Eye and Police

412 Trout

1978. 6th Arab Conference of Police Commanders.
1379 **411** 35 p. multicoloured . . . 30 10

1978. Fishes. Multicoloured.
1380 10 p. Type **412** 25 15
1381 20 p. Sea-bream 30 15
1382 25 p. Grouper 30 15
1383 35 p. Goatfish 35 25
1384 60 p. Catfish 45 35

413 President Assad

1978. Air. Re-election of President Hafez al-Assad.
1385 **413** 25 p. multicoloured . . . 25 15
1386 35 p. multicoloured . . . 35 15
1387 60 p. multicoloured . . . 45 15

414 "Lobivia sp."

415 President Hafez al-Assad

1978. International Flower Show, Damascus. Mult.
1389 25 p. Type **414** 15 10
1390 30 p. "Mamillaria sp." . . . 25 15
1391 35 p. "Opuntia sp." 25 15
1392 50 p. "Chamaecereus sp." . 40 20
1393 60 p. "Mamillaria sp." (different) 40 20

1978. 8th Anniv of Movement of November 16.
1394 **415** 60 p. multicoloured . . 30 15

416 Euphrates Dam

1978. Inauguration of Euphrates Dam.
1395 **416** 60 p. multicoloured . . 50 25

417 Fair Emblem

418 Averroes (philosopher)

1979. 25th International Damascus Fair.
1396 **417** 25 p. multicoloured . . 20 10
1397 35 p. black, violet and silver 20 10

1979. Averroes Commemoration.
1399 **418** 100 p. multicoloured . . 1·00 40

419 Standing Figures within Globe

420 Pyramid and Flower

1979. International Year to Combat Racism.
1400 **419** 35 p. multicoloured . . 25 10

1979. 16th Anniv of Baathist 8th March Revolution.
1401 **420** 100 p. multicoloured . . 70 25

421 Hands supporting Globe

422 Helmet of Homs

1979. 30th Anniv of Declaration of Human Rights.
1402 **421** 60 p. multicoloured . . 35 15

1979. Exhibits from National Museum, Damascus.
1403 – 5 p. red 10 10
1404 – 10 p. green 15 10
1405 – 15 p. mauve 25 10
1406 **422** 20 p. green 10 10
1407 – 25 p. red 20 10
1408 – 35 p. brown 20 10
1409 – 75 p. blue 50 20
1410 – 160 p. green 90 40
1411 – 500 p. brown . . . . . 3·25 1·25
DESIGNS—VERT: 5, 160 p. Umayyad window; 10 p. Figurine; 15 p. Rakka horseman (Abbcid ceramic); 25 p. Head of Clipeata (Cleopatra); 35 p. Seated statue of Ishtar (Astarte). HORIZ: 75 p. Abdul Malik gold coin; 500 p. Umar B. Abdul Aziz gold coin.

423 Geometric Design and Flame

424 Ibn Assaker

1979. 33rd Anniv of Evacuation of Foreign Troops from Syria.
1416 **423** 35 p. multicoloured . . . 20 10

1979. 900th Anniv of Ibn Assaker (historian and biographer).
1417 **424** 75 p. brown, blue & grn . 40 20

425 Tooth, Emblem and Mosque

426 Welder working on Power Pylon

1979. International Middle East Dental Congress.
1418 **425** 35 p. multicoloured . . . 40 10

1979. Labour Day.
1419 **426** 50 p. multicoloured . . . 25 10
1420 75 p. multicoloured . . . 35 20

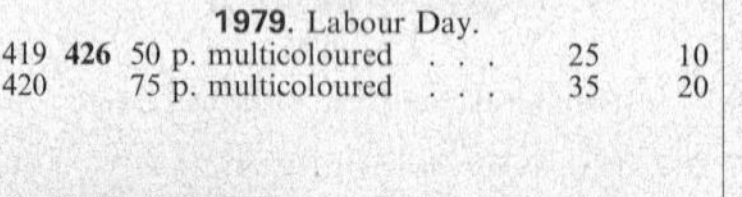

427 Girl holding Emblem with Flowers

428 Wright Type A

1979. International Year of the Child. Multicoloured.
1421 10 p. Type **427** 10 10
1422 15 p. Boy and globe 20 10

1979. 75th Anniv of First Powered Flight. Multicoloured.
1423 50 p. Type **428** 35 10
1424 75 p. Bleriot's plane crossing English Channel 50 30
1425 100 p. Lindbergh's "Spirit of St. Louis" 70 45

429 Power Station

430 Flags and Pavilion

1979.
1426 **429** 5 p. blue 10 10
1427 10 p. mauve 10 10
1428 15 p. green 10 10

1979. 26th International Damascus Fair. Mult.
1429 60 p. Type **430** 35 15
1430 75 p. Lamp post and flags . . . 40 20

431 Running

1979. 8th Mediterranean Games, Split. Mult.
1431 25 p. Type **431** 10 10
1432 35 p. Swimmer on starting-block 20 10
1433 50 p. Football 25 15

432 President Assad with Symbols of Agriculture and Industry

1979. 9th Anniv of Movement of 16 November.
1434 **432** 100 p. multicoloured . . 75 20

433 Swllowtail

434 Astrolabe

1979. Butterflies. Multicoloured.
1435 20 p. Type **433** 35 10
1436 25 p. Peacock 40 15
1437 30 p. White admiral 50 20
1438 35 p. Blue morpho 65 25
1439 50 p. Apollo 85 40

1979. International Flower Show, Damascus. Designs similar to T **414** showing various roses.
1440 5 p. multicoloured 10 10
1441 10 p. multicoloured 15 10
1442 15 p. multicoloured 15 10
1443 50 p. multicoloured 30 15
1444 75 p. multicoloured 45 25
1445 100 p. multicoloured 75 35

1980. 2nd International Symposium on History of Arab Science.
1446 **434** 50 p. violet 25 10
1447 100 p. brown 55 25
1448 1000 p. green . . . . . 5·50 2·25

435 "8" over Buildings

436 Smoker

1980. 17th Anniv of Baathist Revolution of 8 March 1963.
1449 **435** 40 p. multicoloured . . . 25 10

1980. World Health Day. Anti-smoking Campaign.
1450 **436** 60 p. brown, grn & blk . 50 25
1451 – 100 p. multicoloured . . 80 30
DESIGN: 100 p. Skull and cigarette.

437 Monument

1980. 34th Anniv of Evacuation of Foreign Troops from Syria.
1452 **437** 40 p. multicoloured . . . 20 10
1453 60 p. multicoloured . . . 25 15

438 Wrestling

1980. Olympic Games, Moscow. Multicoloured.
1454 15 p. Type **438** 20 10
1455 25 p. Fencing 25 10
1456 35 p. Weightlifting 30 10
1457 50 p. Judo 35 10
1458 75 p. Boxing 50 20

439 "Savings"

1980. Savings Certificates.
1460 **439** 25 p. violet, red & blue . . 20 10

440 "Aladdin and the Magic Lamp"

1980. Popular Stories. Multicoloured.
1461 15 p. "Sinbad the Sailor" . . 15 10
1462 20 p. "Shahrazad and Shahrayar" 20 10
1463 35 p. "Ali Baba and the Forty Thieves" 30 10
1464 50 p. "Hassan the Clever" . . 45 10
1465 100 p. Type **440** 65 30

441 Kaaba and Mosque, Mecca

1980. 1400th Anniv of Hegira.
1466 **441** 35 p. multicoloured . . . 35 20

442 Daffodils

443 "Industry"

1980. International Flower Show, Damascus. Multicoloured.
1467 20 p. Type **442** 20 10
1468 30 p. Dahlias 25 10
1469 40 p. Bergamot 30 10
1470 60 p. Globe flowers 50 15
1471 100 p. Cornflowers 75 25

1980. 10th Anniv of Movement of 16 November.
1472 **443** 100 p. multicoloured . . 65 25

444 Construction Worker

445 Children encircling Globe

1980. Labour Day.
1473 **444** 35 p. multicoloured . . . 35 15

1980. International Children's Day.
1474 **445** 25 p. green, black & yell 25 10

446 Steam-powered Passenger Wagon, 1830

447 Mother's Arms around Child

1980. Cars. Multicoloured.
1475 25 p. Type **446** 20 15
1476 35 p. Benz, 1899 . . . . . . 40 15
1477 40 p. Rolls-Royce, 1903 . . . 40 15
1478 50 p. Mercedes, 1906 . . . . 50 20
1479 60 p. Austin, 1915 . . . . . 65 20

1980. Mothers' Day. Multicoloured.
1480 40 p. Type **447** 35 10
1481 100 p. Faces of mother and child 70 25

448 Fair Emblem

1980. 27th International Damascus Fair. Mult.
1482 50 p. Type **448** 40 15
1483 100 p. As T **448** but with different motif on right . . 75 25

449 Armed Forces

1980. Army Day.
1484 **449** 50 p. multicoloured . . 1·00 30

450 Arabesque Pattern

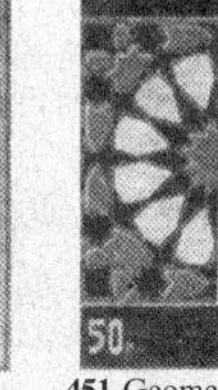

451 Geometric Design, Laurel and Hand holding Torch

1981. 18th Anniv of Baathist Revolution of 8 March 1963.
1485 **450** 50p. multicoloured . . . 35 15

1981. 35th Anniv of Evacuation of Foreign Troops from Syria.
1486 **451** 50 p. multicoloured . . 40 15

452 Mosque and Script

1981. History of Arab-Islamic Civilization World Conference, Damascus.
1487 **452** 100 p. green, deep green and black 70 35

453 Marching Workers and Emblem

454 Human Figure and House on Graph

1981. May Day.
1488 **453** 100 p. multicoloured . . 65 25

1981. Housing and Population Census.
1489 **454** 50 p. multicoloured . . 40 15

455 Family and Savings Emblem

456 Dove and Map on Globe

1981. Savings Certificates.
1490 **455** 50 p. black and brown . 40 15

1981. International Syrian and Palestinian Solidarity Conference, Damascus.
1491 **456** 160 p. multicoloured . . 1·90 65

457 Avicenna

459 Festival Emblem

458 Glass Lamp

1981. Birth Millenary of Avicenna (philosopher and physician).
1492 **457** 100 p. multicoloured . . 75 35

1981. Damascus Museum Exhibits.
1493 **458** 50 p. red 35 15
1494 – 180 p. multicoloured . . 1·60 50
1495 – 180 p. multicoloured . . 1·60 50
DESIGNS: No. 1494, "Grand Mosque, Damascus" (painting); No. 1495, Hunting scene (tapestry).

1981. Youth Festival.
1496 **459** 60 p. multicoloured . . . 45 15

460 Decorative Pattern

461 Palestinians and Dome of the Rock

1981. 28th International Damascus Fair.
1497 **460** 50 p. mauve, blue & grn . 35 15
1498 – 160 p. brown, yell & lilac 95 45
DESIGN: 160 p. Globe encircled by wheat and cogwheel.

1981. Palestinian Solidarity.
1499 **461** 100 p. multicoloured . . 80 30

462 F.A.O. Emblem

463 Tobacco Flowers

1981. World Food Day.
1500 **462** 180 p. blue, green and black 1·40 55

1981. International Flower Show, Damascus. Multicoloured.
1501 25 p. Type **463** 25 10
1502 40 p. Mimosa 35 20
1503 50 p. Ixias 40 20
1504 60 p. Passion flower 65 25
1505 100 p. Dendrobium . . . . . 1·10 50

464 Hands releasing Dove and Horseman

1981. 1300th Anniv of Bulgarian State.
1506 **464** 380 p. multicoloured . . 2·25 95

465 Classroom

1981. International Children's Day.
1507 **465** 180 p. black, red & green 1·50 65

467 President Assad and Diesel Train

468 Symbols of Development

1981. 11th Anniv of Movement of 16 November.
1509 **467** 60 p. blue, black and brown 1·50 35

1982. 19th Anniv of Baathist Revolution of 8 March 1963.
1510 **468** 50 p. grey, red and black 45 15

469 Robert Koch and Microscope

1982. Cent of Discovery of Tubercle Bacillus.
1511 **469** 180 p. blue, brown and black . . . . 1·50 65

470 Pattern and Hand holding Rifle

471 Disabled People and Emblem

1982. 36th Anniv of Evacuation of Foreign Troops from Syria.
1512 **470** 70 p. red and blue . . . 50 25

1982 International Year of Disabled Persons (1981).
1513 **471** 90 p. black, blue and yellow 80 30

472 A.P.U. Emblem

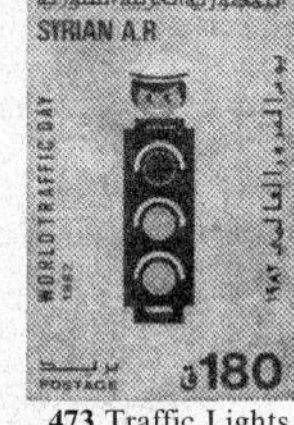

473 Traffic Lights

1982. 30th Anniv of Arab Postal Union.
1514 **472** 60 p. red, green and yellow 50 20

1982. World Traffic Day.
1515 **473** 180 p. black, red and blue 1·50 65

474 Geometric Pattern

1982. World Telecommunications Day.
1516 **474** 180 p. light yellow, brown and yellow . . . . . . 1·25 65

475 Oil Rig, Factory Chimneys and Hand holding Torch

476 Mother and Children

1982. Labour Day.
1517 **475** 180 p. red, blue and light blue . . . . 1·25 65

1982. Mothers' Day.
1518 **476** 40 p. green 30 10
1519 75 p. brown 50 25

477 Olives

478 Pres. Assad

1982.
1520 **477** 50 p. green 40 25
1521 60 p. grey 40 25
1522 – 100 p. mauve 65 30
1523 **478** 150 p. blue . . . . 1·00 50
1524 – 180 p. red . . . . 1·25 65
DESIGN: 100, 180 p. Harbour.

479 Footballer

1982. World Cup Football Championship, Spain. Multicoloured.
1525 40 p. Type **479** 35 25
1526 60 p. Two footballers 50 25
1527 100 p. Two footballers (different) 75 40

480 Policeman

481 Government Building

1982. Police Day.
1529 **480** 50 p. black, red and green 45 20

1982.
1530 **481** 30 p. brown 20 10
1531 – 70 p. green 45 25
1532 – 200 p. red . . . . 1·40 70
DESIGNS—HORIZ: 200 p. Ruins. VERT: 70 p. Arched wall.

482 Communications Emblem and Map

1982. Arab Telecommunication Day.
1533 **482** 50 p. blue, ultramarine and red 45 20

483 Scout pitching Tent

1982. 75th Anniv of Boy Scout Movement.
1534 **483** 160 p. green . . . . 1·40 65

484 Dish Aerial and World Map

1982. I.T.U. Delegates' Conference, Nairobi.
1535 **484** 180 p. blue, ultramarine and red . . . . 1·60 75

485 President Assad

1982. 12th Anniv of Movement of 16 November.
1536 **485** 50 p. blue and grey . . 40 20

486 Water-wheel, Hama

487 Dragonfly

1982.
1537 **486** 5 p. brown 10 10
1538 10 p. violet 10 10
1539 20 p. red 20 10
1540 50 p. turquoise 50 20

1982. Insects. Multicoloured.
1541 5 p. Type **487** 25 25
1542 10 p. Stag beetle 30 30
1543 20 p. Seven-spotted ladybird 50 50
1544 40 p. Desert locust 90 90
1545 50 p. Honey bee . . . . . . 1·00 1·00

488 Honeysuckle

489 Satellites within Dove

1982. Int Flower Show, Damascus. Mult.
1546 50 p. Type **488** 50 25
1547 60 p. Geranium 65 40

1982. U.N. Conference on Exploration and Peaceful Uses of Outer Space, Vienna.
1548 **489** 50 p. multicoloured . . 50 20

490 Dove on Gun

1982. International Palestine Day.
1549 **490** 50 p. multicoloured . . 75 30

491 Damascus International Airport

1983. 20th Anniv of Baathist Revolution of 8 March.
1550 **491** 60 p. multicoloured . . 1·25 50

492 Communications Emblems

1983. World Communications Year.
1551 **492** 180 p. multicoloured . . 1·50 70

493 Figurine

1983.
1552 **493** 380 p. brown and green 3·25 1·25

494 Pharmacist

1983. Arab Pharmacists' Day.
1553 **494** 100 p. multicoloured . . 1·00 40

495 Liberation Monument, Qneitra

496 Wave within Ship's Wheel

1983. 9th Anniv of Liberation of Qneitra.
1554 **495** 50 p. green 95 40
1555 – 100 p. brown . . . . . . 1·90 40
DESIGN: 100 p. Ruined buildings.

1983. 25th Anniv of I.M.O.
1556 **496** 180 p. multicoloured . . 1·75 65

497 Flame on Map

1983. Namibia Day.
1557 **497** 180 p. blue, mauve and black . . . . 1·25 65

498 I.S.O. Emblem and Factory

499 Gateway, Bosra

1983. World Standards Day.
1558 **498** 50 p. multicoloured . . . 45 25
1559 – 100 p. violet, green & blk 1·00 55
DESIGN: 100 p. I.S.O. emblem and measuring equipment.

1983. 10th Anniv of World Heritage Agreement.
1560 **499** 60 p. brown 55 25

500 Flowers

501 Farmland

1983. Int Flower Show, Damascus. Mult.
1561 50 p. Type **500** 55 25
1562 60 p. Hibiscus 65 40

1983. World Food Day.
1563 **501** 180 p. green, cream and deep green . . . . . . 1·60 75

502 Factory

503 Statuette

1983.
1564 **502** 50 p. green 50 10

1984. International Deir Ez-Zor History and Archaeology Symposium.
1565 **503** 225 p. brown . . . . . . 2·25 95

504 Aleppo

505 Alassad Library

1984. International Symposium for the Conservation of Aleppo.
1566 **504** 245 p. multicoloured . . 2·25 95

1984. 21st Anniv of Baathist Revolution of 8 March.
1567 **505** 60 p. multicoloured . . . 60 30

506 Bodies and mourning Woman with Child

1984. Sabra and Shatila (refugee camps in Lebanon) Massacres.
1568 **506** 225 p. multicoloured . . 1·90 80

507 Mother and Child

509 Swimming

508 Dam, Emblem and Pioneers

1984. Mothers' Day.
1569 **507** 245 p. brown & green . 2·25 95

1984. 9th Regional Festival of Al Baath Pioneers. Multicoloured.
1570 50 p. Type **508** 50 25
1571 60 p. Pioneers, ruins and emblems 65 30

1984. Olympic Games, Los Angeles. Multicoloured.
1572 30 p. Type **509** 35 10
1573 50 p. Wrestling 50 20
1574 60 p. Running 55 25
1575 70 p. Boxing 65 30
1576 90 p. Football 90 40

510 Flowers

511 Pres. Assad and Text

1984. Int Flower Show, Damascus. Mult.
1578 245 p. Type **510** . . . . . . 2·50 1·25
1579 285 p. Flowers (different) . . 2·75 1·60

1984. 4th Revolutionary Youth Union Congress.
1580 **511** 50 p. brown, deep brown and green 45 25
1581 – 60 p. multicoloured . . . 50 35
DESIGN—37 x 25 mm: 60 p. Pres. Assad and saluting youth.

512 Emblem and Administration Building, Damascus

1984. Arab Postal Union Day.
1582 **512** 60 p. multicoloured . . . 50 30

513 Globe, Dish Aerial and Telephone
514 Arabesque Pattern

1984. World Telecommunications Day.
1583 **513** 245 p. multicoloured . . 2·25 1·00

1984. 31st International Damascus Fair. Mult.
1584 45 p. Type **514** 40 20
1585 100 p. Ornate gold decoration 1·25 45

515 Stylized Aircraft and Emblem

1984. 40th Anniv of I.C.A.O.
1586 **515** 45 p. blue and deep blue 40 20
1587 – 245 p. blue, ultramarine and deep blue . . . . . . 1·90 95
DESIGN: 245 p. Emblem and stylized building.

516 Text, Flag and Pres. Assad

1984. 14th Anniv of Movement of 16 Nov.
1588 **516** 65 p. orange, black and brown 65 35

517 Palmyra Roman Arch and Colonnades

1984. International Tourism Day.
1589 **517** 100 p. brown, black and blue 90 45

518 Wooded Landscape

1985. Woodland Conservation.
1590 **518** 45 p. multicoloured . . . 60 25

519 University and Students

1985. 26th Anniv (1984) of Aleppo University.
1591 **519** 45 p. black, blue and brown 45 25

520 Oil Lamp

1985. 26th Anniv (1984) of Supreme Council of Science.
1592 **520** 65 p. green, red and black 65 40

521 Soldier holding Flag

1985. Army Day.
1593 **521** 65 p. brown and bistre . 65 40

522 Pres. Assad

1985. Re-election of President Assad
1594 **522** 200 p. multicoloured . . 1·90 1·25
1595 300 p. multicoloured . . 2·50 1·50
1596 500 p. multicoloured . . 4·50 2·25

523 Flag and Party Emblem
524 Torch and "22"

1985. 8th Baath Arab Socialist Party Congress.
1598 **523** 50 p. multicoloured . . 55 20

1985. 22nd Anniv of Baathist Revolution of 8 March 1963.
1599 **524** 60 p. multicoloured . . 60 25

525 Tractor and Cow

1985. Aleppo Industrial and Agricultural Fair (1984). Multicoloured.
1600 65 p. Type **525** 65 25
1601 150 p. Fort and carrots (vert) 1·75 50

526 Liberation Movement, Qneitra

1985. 10th Anniv (1984) of Liberation of Qneitra.
1602 **526** 70 p. multicoloured . . 1·25 40

527 Parliament Building

1985. 10th Anniv of Arab Parliamentary Union.
1603 **527** 245 p. multicoloured . . 2·50 1·25

528 U.P.U. Emblem and Pigeon with Letter
529 A.P.U. Emblem

1985. World Post Day.
1604 **528** 285 p. multicoloured . . 3·25 95

1985. 12th Arab Postal Union Conference, Damascus.
1605 **529** 60 p. multicoloured . . . 55 20

530 Medal

1985. Labour Day.
1606 **530** 60 p. multicoloured . . . 55 20

531 Old and New Locomotives

1985. 2nd Scientific Symposium.
1607 **531** 60 p. blue . . . . 1·25 45

532 Emblem and Child with empty Bowl

1985. U.N. Child Survival Campaign.
1608 **532** 60 p. black, green & pink 55 20

533 Pres. Assad and Road

1985. 15th Anniv of Movement of 16 Nov.
1609 **533** 60 p. multicoloured . . . 55 20

534 Emblem and "40"
535 Lily-flowered Tulip

1985. 40th Anniv of U.N.O.
1610 **534** 245 p. multicoloured . . 1·90 75

1986. Int Flower Show, Damascus (1985). Mult.
1611 30 p. Type **535** 30 15
1612 60 p. Tulip 70 25

536 Flask

1986. 32nd International Damascus Fair (1985).
1613 **536** 60 p. multicoloured . . . 55 20

INDEX

Countries can be quickly located by referring to the index at the end of this volume.

537 Abd-er-Rahman I
538 Pres. Hafez al-Assad

1986. 1200th Anniv of Abd-er-Rahman I ad Dakhel, Emir of Cordoba.
1614 **537** 60 p. brown, cinnamon and light brown 60 20

1988.
1615 **538** 10 p. red 10 10
1616 30 p. blue 20 10
1616a 50 p. lilac 10 10
1617 100 p. blue 65 20
1618 150 p. brown 75 40
1619 175 p. violet 95 40
1620 200 p. brown . . . . . 1·25 45
1621 300 p. mauve . . . . . 1·90 75
1622 500 p. orange . . . . . 3·50 1·25
1623 550 p. pink . . . . . 3·00 1·50
1624 600 p. green . . . . . 3·75 1·75
1625 1000 p. mauve . . . . 7·00 2·75
1626 2000 p. green . . . . . 14·00 5·75
For similar design but with full-face portrait, see Nos. 1774/80.

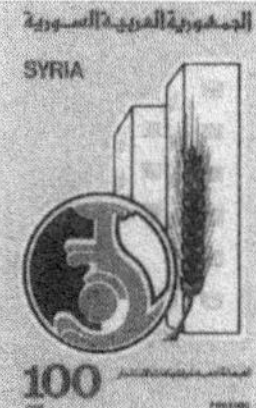

539 Tooth and Map
540 Tower Blocks, Ear of Wheat and Kangaroo

1986. 19th Arab Dentists' Union Congress, Damascus.
1627 **539** 110 p. multicoloured . . 1·25 50

1986. 15th Anniv of Syrian Investment Certificates.
1628 **540** 100 p. multicoloured . . 90 25

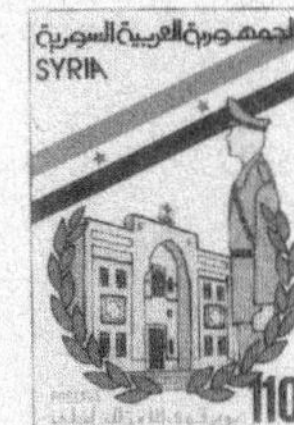

541 Traffic Policewoman, Globe and Traffic Lights
542 Policeman and Building in Laurel Wreath

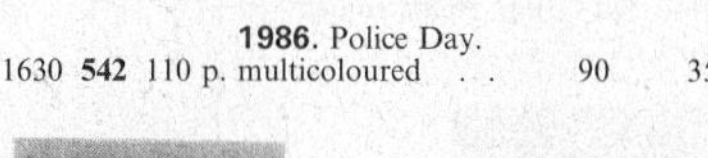

1986. World Traffic Day.
1629 **541** 330 p. multicoloured . . 3·00 1·25

1986. Police Day.
1630 **542** 110 p. multicoloured . . 90 35

543 Industrial Symbols and Hand Holding Spanner
544 Building

1986. Labour Day.
1631 **543** 330 p. red, black & blue 2·40 1·00

1986. 12th Anniv of Liberation of Qneitra.
1632 **544** 110 p. multicoloured . . 85 35

545 Pictogram and Ball
546 Mother and Children

1986. World Cup Football Championship, Mexico.
1633 **545** 330 p. multicoloured . . 2·25 90
1634 370 p. multicoloured . . 2·75 1·00

1986. Mothers' Day.
1636 **546** 100 p. multicoloured . . 80 30

547 Pres. Assad and Train

1986. 23rd Anniv of Baathist Revolution of 8 March 1963.
1637 **547** 110 p. multicoloured . . 1·50 80

548 A.P.U. Emblem, Post Office and Box
549 Fists, Map and Globe

1986. Arab Post Day.
1638 **548** 110 p. multicoloured . . 80 30

1986. International Palestine Day.
1639 **549** 110 p. multicoloured . . 80 30

550 Tulips

1986. Int Flower Show, Damascus. Mult.
1640 10 p. Type **550** 15 10
1641 50 p. Mauve flowers 45 15
1642 100 p. Yellow flowers 95 30
1643 110 p. Pink flowers . . . . . 1·10 50
1644 330 p. Yellow flowers (different) 2·75 1·40

551 Pres. Assad and Tishreen Palace

1986. 16th Anniv of Movement of 16 Nov.
1645 **551** 110 p. multicoloured . . 75 30

552 Rocket and Flags
553 Jug and Star

1986. 1st Anniv of Announcement of Syrian–Soviet Space Flight.
1646 **552** 330 p. multicoloured . . 2·50 1·25

1986. 33rd International Damascus Fair.
1647 **553** 110 p. multicoloured . . 85 35
1648 – 330 p. black, green and brown . . . . 2·40 95
DESIGN: 330 p. Coffee pot.

554 Girls and National Flag

1987. International Children's Art Exhibition.
1649 **554** 330 p. multicoloured . . 1·90 75

555 U.P.U. Emblem and Airmail Envelope
556 Children in Balloon over Town

1987. World Post Day.
1650 **555** 330 p. multicoloured . . 1·90 75

1987. International Children's Day.
1651 **556** 330 p. multicoloured . . 1·90 75

557 Citadel, Aleppo

1987. International Tourism Day.
1652 330 p. Type **557** . . . . . . 1·90 75
1653 370 p. Water-wheel, Hama . 2·25 85

558 Industrial Symbols

1987. 24th Anniv of Baathist Revolution of 8 March 1963.
1654 **558** 100 p. multicoloured . . 65 25

559 Doves flying from Globe
560 Party Emblem

1987. International Peace Year.
1655 **559** 370 p. multicoloured . . 2·25 85

1987. 40th Anniv of Baath Arab Socialist Party.
1656 **560** 100 p. multicoloured . . 65 25

561 Stars

1987. 41st Anniv of Evacuation of Foreign Troops from Syria.
1657 **561** 100 p. multicoloured . . 65 25

562 Draughtsman

1987. 6th Arab Ministers of Culture Conference.
1658 **562** 330 p. blue, green & blk 2·50 1·00

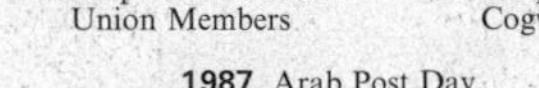

563 Map of Arab Postal Union Members
564 Couple within Cogwheel

1987. Arab Post Day.
1659 **563** 110 p. multicoloured . . 65 25

1987. Labour Day.
1660 **564** 330 p. multicoloured . . 1·90 75

565 Statue

566 Pres. Assad with Children and Nurse

1987. 13th Anniv of Liberation of Qneitra.
1661 **565** 100 p. multicoloured . . 60 30

1987. Child Vaccination Campaign.
1662 **566** 100 p. multicoloured . . 65 35
1663 330 p. multicoloured . . 2·25 95

567 Dome of the Rock, Battle Scene and Saladin

1987. 800th Anniv of Battle of Hattin.
1664 **567** 110 p. multicoloured . . 75 35

568 Rocket Launch and National Flags

1987. Syrian–Soviet Space Flight. Multicoloured.
1665 330 p. Type **568** . . . . . . 2·00 1·00
1666 330 p. Spacecraft docking with "Mir" space station (37 × 25 mm) . . . . 2·00 1·00
1667 330 p. Space capsule re-entering Earth's atmosphere and group of cosmonauts (25 × 37 mm) . . . . 2·00 1·00

569 Flags, Cosmonauts and Pres. Assad

1987. President's Space Conversation with Lt-Col. Mohammed Faris (Syrian cosmonaut).
1669 **569** 500 p. multicoloured . . 3·50 1·60

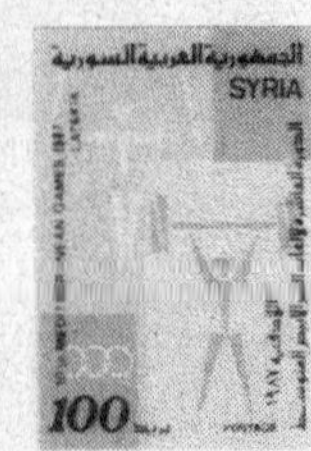
570 Stylized Flowers
571 Sports Pictograms

1987. 34th International Damascus Fair.
1670 **570** 330 p. multicoloured . . 2·00 1·00

1987. 10th Mediterranean Games, Latakia.
1671 **571** 100 p. purple & black . . 65 35
1672 – 110 p. multicoloured . . 85 40
1673 – 330 p. multicoloured . . 2·40 1·50
1674 – 370 p. multicoloured . . 2·50 1·25
DESIGNS—As Type **571** but HORIZ: 110 p. Swimming bird and emblem. 52 × 23 mm—330 p. Phoenician galley (Games emblem); 370 p. Flags forming "SYRIA".

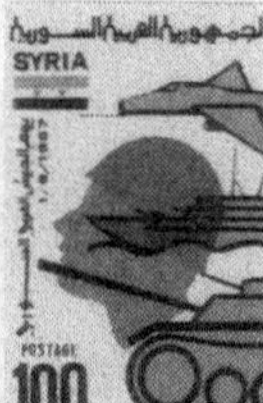

572 Soldier, Mikoyan Gurevich MiG-21D Fighter, Ship and Tank
573 Trees, Sun and Birds

1987. Army Day.
1676 **572** 100 p. multicoloured . . 1·00 40

1987. Tree Day.
1677 **573** 330 p. multicoloured . . 1·90 1·10

574 Poppies
576 Barbed Wire around Map of Israel

575 Pres. Assad acknowledging Applause

1987. International Flower Show, Damascus.
1678 330 p. Type **574** . . . . . . 2·25 90
1679 370 p. Mauve flower . . . . 2·50 1·00

1987. 17th Anniv of Corrective Movement of 16 November.
1680 **575** 150 p. multicoloured . . 1·00 45

1987. International Palestine Day.
1681 **576** 500 p. multicoloured . . 3·25 1·50

577 U.P.U. and U.N. Emblems

1988. World Post Day.
1682 **577** 500 p. multicoloured . . 3·50 1·75

578 Bosra Amphitheatre

1988. International Tourism Day. Multicoloured.
1683 500 p. Type **578** . . . . . . 3·25 1·40
1684 500 p. Palmyra ruins . . . . 3·25 1·40

579 Children as Cosmonauts

1988. International Children's Day.
1685 **579** 500 p. multicoloured . . 3·25 1·40

580 Hand holding Torch
581 Woman cradling Baby, Children and Adults

1988. 25th Anniv of Baathist Revolution of 8 March 1963.
1686 **580** 150 p. multicoloured . . 85 45

1988. Mothers' Day.
1688 **581** 500 p. multicoloured . . 3·25 1·40

582 Arms, Cogwheel, Laurel Branch and Book

583 Dove, Airmail Envelope and Map

1988. 42nd Anniv of Evacuation of Foreign Troops from Syria.
1689 **582** 150 p. multicoloured . . 85 45

1988. Arab Post Day.
1690 **583** 150 p. multicoloured . . 85 45

584 Spanner, Chimney, Cogwheel and Scroll

585 Modern Buildings

1988. Labour Day.
1691 **584** 550 p. multicoloured . . 3·00 1·50

1988. Arab Engineers' Union.
1692 **585** 150 p. multicoloured . . 85 45

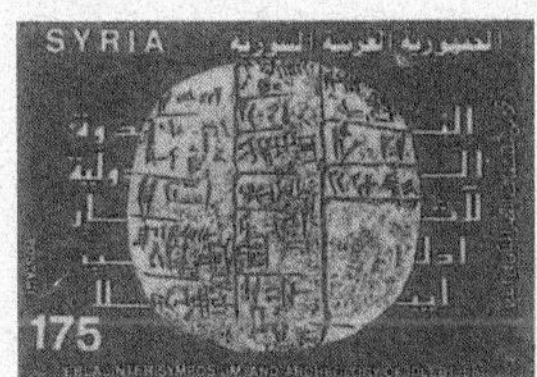

586 Lily

1988. Int Flower Show, Damascus. Mult.
1693 550 p. Type **586** . . . . . . 3·25 1·60
1694 600 p. Carnations . . . . . 3·75 1·90

587 Clay Tablet

1988. Int Symposium on Archaeology of Ebla.
1695 **587** 175 p. black and brown . 1·00 50
1696 – 550 p. brown, blue & blk 3·25 1·60
1697 – 600 p. multicoloured . . 3·50 1·75
DESIGNS: 550 p. King making offering (carving from stone votive basin); 600 p. Golden statue of goddess Ishtar.

588 Old City

589 Emblem

1988. Preservation of Sana'a, Yemen.
1698 **588** 550 p. multicoloured . . 3·50 1·60

1988. Children's Day.
1699 **589** 600 p. black, green and emerald . . . . 3·50 1·75

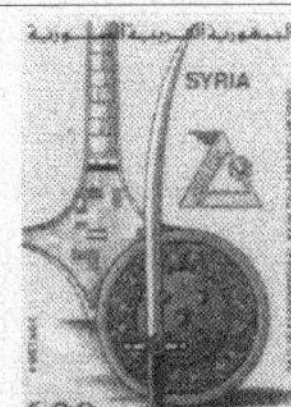

590 Sword, Shield and Emblems

591 Emblem and People

1988. 35th International Damascus Fair.
1700 **590** 600 p. multicoloured . . 3·50 1·75

1988. 40th Anniv of W.H.O.
1701 **591** 600 p. multicoloured . . 3·50 1·75

592 Emblems and Map

1988. 50th Anniv of Arab Scout Movement.
1702 **592** 150 p. mutlicoloured . . 1·25 50

593 Cycling

1988. Olympic Games, Seoul. Multicoloured.
1703 550 p. Type **593** . . . . . . 3·75 1·50
1704 600 p. Football . . . . . . 3·75 1·75

594 Old Houses and Modern Flats

1988. Housing. Multicoloured.
1706 150 p. Type **594** (Arab Housing Day) . . . . 1·25 65
1707 175 p. House and makeshift shelter (International Year of Shelter for the Homeless (1987)) . . . . 1·25 50
1708 550 p. Types of housing (World Housing Day) . . . . . . 3·00 1·50
1709 600 p. As No. 1707 but inscr for International Day for Housing the Homeless . . 3·25 1·75

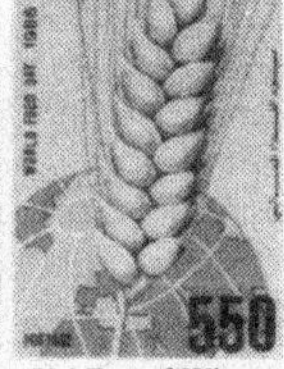

595 Euphrates Bridge, Deir el Zor

596 Ear of Wheat and Globe

1988. International Tourism Day. Multicoloured.
1710 550 p. Type **595** . . . . . . 3·00 1·50
1711 600 p. Tetrapylon of Latakia 3·25 1·75
No. 1711 is erroneously inscribed "INTEPNATIONAL".

1988. World Food Day.
1712 **596** 550 p. multicoloured . . 3·25 1·40

597 Al-Assad University Hospital

1988. 18th Anniv of Corrective Movement of 16 November 1970.
1713 **597** 150 p. multicoloured . . 90 45

598 Tree and Flowers

599 Dove with Envelope over Globe

1988. Tree Day.
1714 **598** 600 p. multicoloured . . 3·50 1·60

1988. World Post Day.
1715 **599** 600 p. multicoloured . . 3·25 1·60

600 Emblem and Doctor within Stethoscope

602 Pres. Assad and Women

601 Symbols of Agriculture and Industry

1989. 10th Anniv of Arab Board for Medical Specializations.
1716 **600** 175 p. multicoloured . . 1·00 45

1989. 26th Anniv of Baathist Revolution of 8 March 1963.
1717 **601** 150 p. multicoloured . . 40 20

1989. 5th General Congress of Union of Women.
1718 **602** 150 p. multicoloured . . 40 20

603 Candle and Books

1989. Arab Teachers' Day.
1719 **603** 175 p. multicoloured . . 45 20

604 Nehru

605 Mother and Children

1989. Birth Centenary of Jarwaharlal Nehru (Indian statesman).
1720 **604** 550 p. brown & lt brown 1·40 65

1989. Mothers' Day.
1721 **605** 550 p. multicoloured . . 1·25 60

606 Goldfinch

1989. Birds. Multicoloured.
1722 600 p. Type **606** . . . . . . 1·50 85
1723 600 p. European bee eater . . 1·50 85
1724 600 p. Turtle dove . . . . . . 1·50 85

607 State Arms on Map

608 Workers

1989. 43rd Anniv of Evacuation of Foreign Troops from Syria.
1725 **607** 150 p. multicoloured . . 40 20

1989. Labour Day.
1726 **608** 850 p. green and black . 1·90 85

609 Snapdragons

610 Girl and Envelope

1989. Int Flower Show, Damascus. Mult.
1727 150 p. Type **609** 40 25
1728 150 p. "Canaria" 40 25
1729 450 p. Cornflowers . . . . . 1·25 65
1730 850 p. "Clematis sackmani" . 1·90 1·00
1731 900 p. "Gesneriaceae" . . . 1·90 1·00

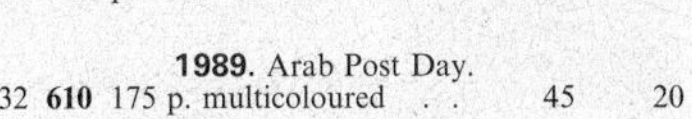

1989. Arab Post Day.
1732 **610** 175 p. multicoloured . . 45 20

611 Emblem and Map

612 Painted Lady

1989. 13th Arab Teachers' Union General Congress.
1733 **611** 175 p. multicoloured . . 45 20

1989. Butterflies. Multicoloured.
1734 550 p. Type **612** . . . . . . 1·25 85
1735 550 p. Clouded yellow . . . 1·25 85
1736 550 p. Large (inscr "small") white . . . . 1·25 85

613 Symbols of International Co-operation

1989. World Telecommunications Day.
1737 **613** 550 p. multicoloured . . 1·25 65

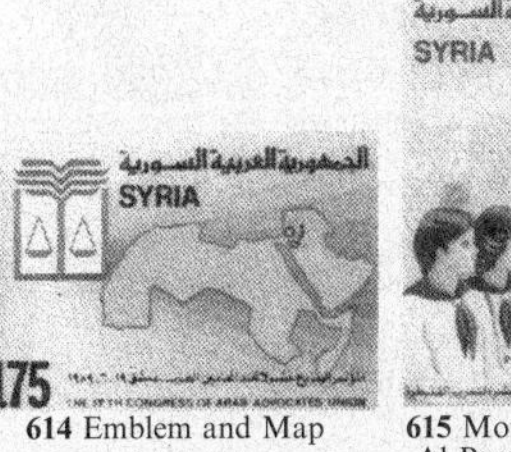

614 Emblem and Map

615 Monument and Al-Baath Pioneers

1989. 17th Arab Lawyers' Union Congress.
1738 **614** 175 p. multicoloured . . 45 20

1989. 15th Anniv of Liberation of Qneitra.
1739 **615** 450 p. multicoloured . . 1·25 50

616 Globe and Envelopes

1989. World Post Day.
1740 **616** 550 p. multicoloured . . 1·25 65

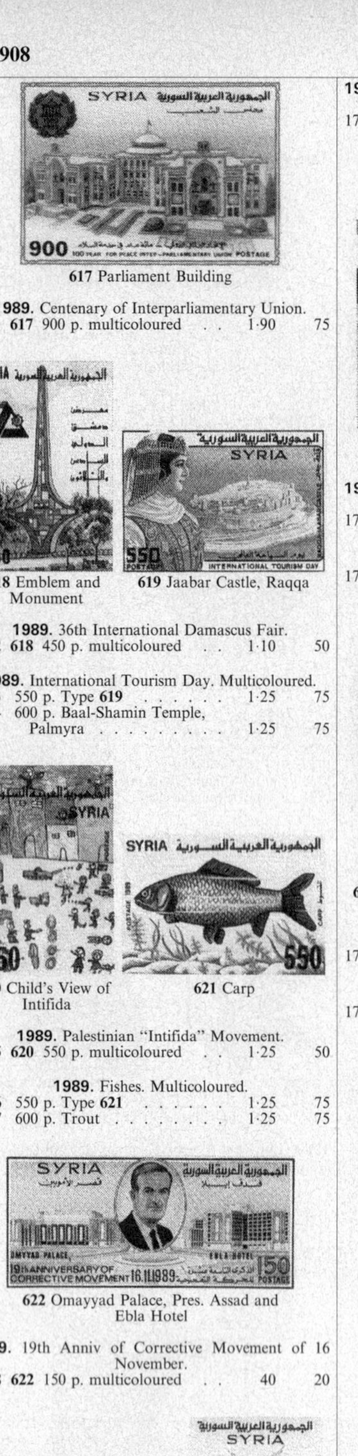

617 Parliament Building

1989. Centenary of Interparliamentary Union.
1741 **617** 900 p. multicoloured . . 1·90 75

618 Emblem and Monument 619 Jaabar Castle, Raqqa

1989. 36th International Damascus Fair.
1742 **618** 450 p. multicoloured . . 1·10 50

1989. International Tourism Day. Multicoloured.
1743 550 p. Type **619** . . . . . . 1·25 75
1744 600 p. Baal-Shamin Temple, Palmyra . . . . 1·25 75

620 Child's View of Intifida 621 Carp

1989. Palestinian "Intifida" Movement.
1745 **620** 550 p. multicoloured . . 1·25 50

1989. Fishes. Multicoloured.
1746 550 p. Type **621** . . . . . . 1·25 75
1747 600 p. Trout . . . . 1·25 75

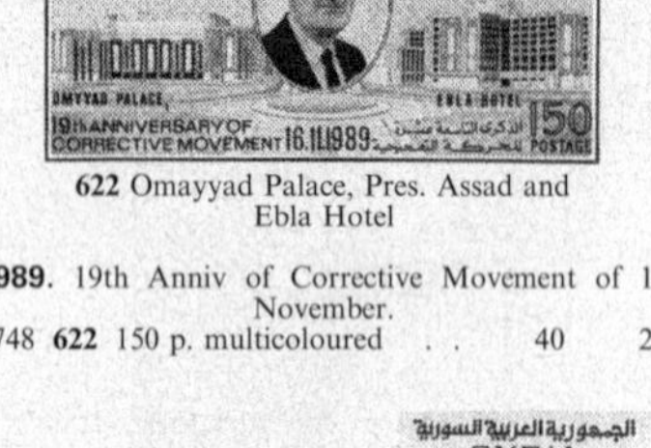

622 Omayyad Palace, Pres. Assad and Ebla Hotel

1989. 19th Anniv of Corrective Movement of 16 November.
1748 **622** 150 p. multicoloured . . 40 20

623 Children of Different Races taking Food from Large Bowl 624 Dove, Globe and Children of Different Races

1990. World Food Day (1989).
1749 **623** 850 p. multicoloured . . 1·90 1·00

1990. International Children's Day.
1750 **624** 850 p. multicoloured . . 1·90 90

625 Flag, Emblem and Ear of Wheat 626 Tree-lined Road

1990. 5th Revolutionary Youth Union Congress.
1751 **625** 150 p. multicoloured . . 40 20

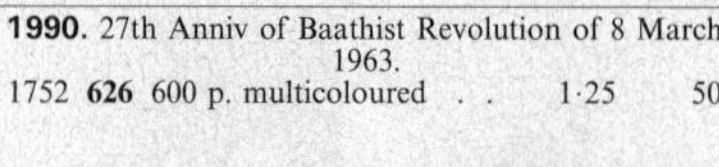

1990. 27th Anniv of Baathist Revolution of 8 March 1963.
1752 **626** 600 p. multicoloured . . 1·25 50

627 Flag and Arab Fighters 628 Woman carrying Child

1990. 44th Anniv of Evacuation of Foreign Troops from Syria.
1753 **627** 175 p. multicoloured . . 40 20

1990. Mothers' Day.
1754 **628** 550 p. multicoloured . . 1·25 50

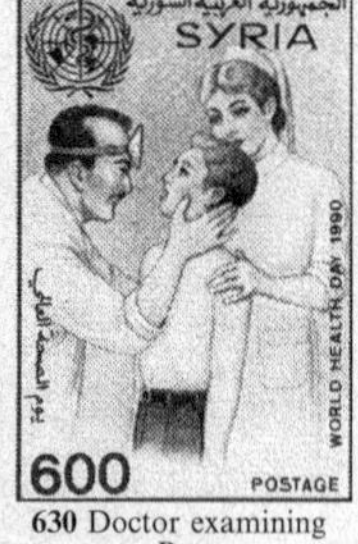

629 Globe and Couple 630 Doctor examining Boy

1990. Labour Day.
1755 **629** 550 p. multicoloured . . 1·25 60

1990. World Health Day.
1756 **630** 600 p. multicoloured . . 1·25 65

631 Lilies 633 Flag, Tree and City

632 Goalkeeper saving Goal

1990. Int Flower Show, Damascus. Mult.
1757 600 p. Type **631** . . . . . . 1·25 75
1758 600 p. Cyclamen . . . . . . 1·25 75
1759 600 p. Marigolds . . . . . 1·25 75
1760 600 p. "Viburnum opulus" . . 1·25 75
1761 600 p. Swan river daisies . . 1·25 75

1990. World Cup Football Championship, Italy. Multicoloured.
1762 550 p. Type **632** . . . . . . 1·25 65
1763 550 p. Players marking opponent . . . . 1·25 90
1764 600 p. Map of Italy and ball (vert) . . . . 1·25 1·00

1990. 16th Anniv of Liberation of Qneitra.
1766 **633** 550 p. multicoloured . . 1·25 50

634 Man and Book 635 Weather Map

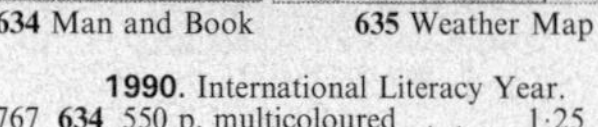

1990. International Literacy Year.
1767 **634** 550 p. multicoloured . . 1·25 50

1990. World Meteorology Day.
1768 **635** 450 p. multicoloured . . 1·00 50

636 Emblem 637 Old and Modern Methods of Ploughing

1990. 37th International Damascus Fair.
1769 **636** 550 p. multicoloured . . 1·25 50

1990. United Nations Conference on Least Developed Countries.
1770 **637** 600 p. multicoloured . . 1·40 65

638 Boy watering Young Tree 639 Children with Bread and Water in Wheat Field

1990. Tree Day.
1771 **638** 550 p. multicoloured . . 1·25 65

1990. World Food Day.
1772 **639** 850 p. multicoloured . . 1·90 75

640 Al-Maqdisi and Map 641 Pres. Hafez al-Assad

1990. Death Millenary of Al-Maqdisi (geographer).
1773 **640** 550 p. multicoloured . . 1·25 65

1990. (a) As T **538** but with full-face portrait.
1774 50 p. lilac 10 10
1775 70 p. grey 15 10
1776 100 p. blue 20 10
1777 150 p. brown 25 10
1778 300 p. mauve 50 25
1779 350 p. grey 60 30
1780 400 p. red 65 30

(b) Type **641**.
1781 175 p. multicoloured 30 20
1782 300 p. multicoloured 55 20
1783 550 p. multicoloured 95 25
1784 600 p. multicoloured . . . . 1·25 45

(c) Horiz design with portrait as T **641** within decorative frame.
1786 1000 p. multicoloured . . . . 1·90 65
1787 1500 p. multicoloured . . . . 2·75 95
1788 2000 p. multicoloured . . . . 3·75 1·25
1789 2500 p. multicoloured . . . . 4·75 1·60

643 Control Tower, Douglas DC-9-80 Super Eighty Airliner and Emblem

1990. Arab Civil Aviation Day.
1796 **643** 175 p. multicoloured . . 45 25

644 Emblem, Open Book, Cogwheel and Ear of Wheat 645 U.P.U. Emblem and Girl posting Letter

1990. 40th Anniv of United Nations Development Programme.
1797 **644** 550 p. multicoloured . . 1·25 65

1990. World Post Day.
1798 **645** 550 p. multicoloured . . 1·25 65

646 Leapfrog 647 Emblem, Flames and Open Book

1990. World Children's Day.
1799 **646** 550 p. multicoloured . . 1·25 65

1990. Arab–Spanish Cultural Symposium.
1800 **647** 550 p. multicoloured . . 1·40 75

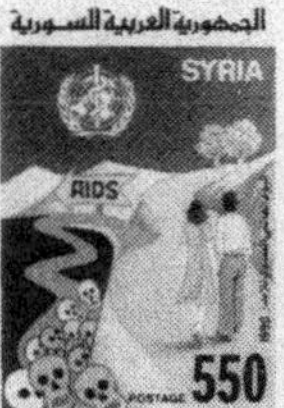

648 Paths to and away from Aids 649 Modern Roads and Buildings

1990. World AIDS Day.
1801 **648** 550 p. multicoloured . . 1·40 75

1991. 28th Anniv of Baathist Revolution of 8 March 1963.
1802 **649** 150 p. multicoloured . . 40 20

650 Lesser Purple Emperor 651 Golden Orioles

1991. Butterflies. Multicoloured.
1803 550 p. Type **650** (inscr "Change Ful Great Mars") . . . . 1·40 75
1804 550 p. Small tortoiseshell . . 1·40 75
1805 550 p. Swallowtail . . . . . 1·40 75

1991. Birds. Multicoloured.
1806 600 p. Type **651** . . . . . . 1·50 75
1807 600 p. House sparrows . . . 1·50 75
1808 600 p. Common ("European") roller . . . . 1·50 75

652 Three Generations 653 Statue

1991. Mothers' Day.
1809 **652** 550 p. multicoloured . . 1·40 65

1991. 45th Anniv of Evacuation of Foreign Troops from Syria.
1810 **653** 150 p. multicoloured . . 40 20

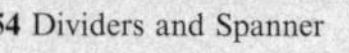

654 Dividers and Spanner 655 Daffodils

1991. Labour Day.
1811 **654** 550 p. multicoloured . . 1·40 65

1991. International Flower Show, Damascus. Mult.
1812 550 p. Type **655** . . . . . . 1·40 65
1813 600 p. Bee balm . . . . . . 1·60 65

656 City and Ruins

1991. 17th Anniv of Liberation of Qneitra.
1814 **656** 550 p. multicoloured . . 1·40 65

657 Running **658** Hall

1991. 11th Mediterranean Games, Athens. Mult.
1815 550 p. Type **657** . . . . . . 1·40 65
1816 550 p. Football . . . . 1·40 65
1817 600 p. Show jumping . . . . 1·50 65

1991. 38th International Damascus Fair.
1819 **658** 550 p. multicoloured . . 1·40 65

659 Courtyard, Azem Palace, Damascus **660** People encircling Block of Flats

1991. International Tourism Day. Multicoloured.
1820 450 p. Type **659** . . . . . . 1·10 50
1821 550 p. Castle, Arwad Island . 1·40 65

1991. Housing Day.
1822 **660** 175 p. multicoloured . . 45 25

661 Roller Skating **662** Rhazes treating Patient

1991. International Children's Day.
1823 **661** 600 p. multicoloured . . 1·50 65

1991. Science Week.
1824 **662** 550 p. multicoloured . . 1·40 65

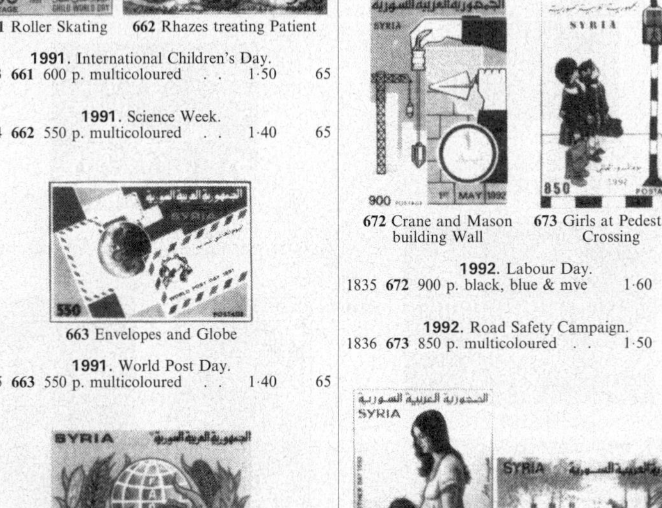

663 Envelopes and Globe

1991. World Post Day.
1825 **663** 550 p. multicoloured . . 1·40 65

664 Globe, Produce and Livestock

1991. World Food Day.
1826 **664** 550 p. multicoloured . . 1·40 65

665 Tomb of Unknown Soldier, Damascus

1991.
1827 **665** 600 p. multicoloured . . 1·50 65

667 Polluted and Clean Environments **668** Transmission Mast, Globe and Satellite

1991. Environmental Protection.
1830 **667** 175 p. multicoloured . . 50 30

1991. International Telecommunications Fair.
1831 **668** 600 p. multicoloured . . 1·50 65

669 Leaf and Port

1992. 29th Anniv of Baathist Revolution of 8 March.
1832 **669** 600 p. multicoloured . . 1·10 55

671 Chimneys, Gun-barrel, Ear of Wheat, Dove and Flag

1992. 45th Anniv of Baath Arab Socialist Party.
1834 **671** 850 p. multicoloured . . 1·50 75

672 Crane and Mason building Wall **673** Girls at Pedestrian Crossing

1992. Labour Day.
1835 **672** 900 p. black, blue & mve 1·60 80

1992. Road Safety Campaign.
1836 **673** 850 p. multicoloured . . 1·50 75

674 Girl listening to Mother's Stomach **675** Memorial

1992. Mothers' Day.
1837 **674** 900 p. multicoloured . . 1·60 80

1992. 46th Anniv of Evacuation of Foreign Troops from Syria.
1838 **675** 900 p. multicoloured . . 1·60 80

676 Flax **677** Football

1992. International Flower Show, Damascus. Multicoloured.
1839 300 p. Type **676** 50 25
1840 800 p. "Yucca filamentosa" (vert) . . . . 1·40 70
1841 900 p. "Zinnia elegans" (vert) 1·60 80

1992. Olympic Games, Barcelona. Multicoloured.
1842 150 p. Type **677** 25 15
1843 150 p. Running 25 15
1844 450 p. Swimming 75 35
1845 750 p. Wrestling . . . . . . 1·25 60

678 Smoker standing in Ashtray **679** Pendant

1992. Anti-smoking Campaign.
1847 **678** 750 p. multicoloured . . 1·25 60

1992. 39th International Damascus Fair.
1848 **679** 900 p. multicoloured . . 1·50 75

680 Football

1992. 7th Pan-Arab Games, Damascus. Mult.
1849 750 p. Type **680** . . . . . . 1·25 60
1850 850 p. Gymnastics . . . . . 1·50 75
1851 900 p. Pole vaulting . . . . . 1·60 80

681 Envelopes, Dove and Globe **682** Boy blowing Dandelion Clock

1992. World Post Day.
1852 **681** 600 p. multicoloured . . 1·10 55

1992. International Children's Day.
1853 **682** 850 p. multicoloured . . 1·50 75

683 Sebtt el-Mardini (astronomer) **684** Table Tennis

1992.
1854 **683** 850 p. multicoloured . . 1·50 75

1992. Paralympic Games for Mentally Handicapped, Madrid.
1855 **684** 850 p. multicoloured . . 1·50 75

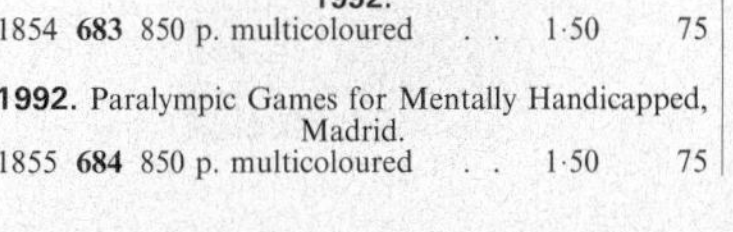

685 People's Square, Damascus **686** Tree

1992. 22nd Anniv of Corrective Movement of 16 November.
1856 **685** 450 p. multicoloured . . 80 40

1992. Tree Day.
1857 **686** 600 p. multicoloured . . 1·10 55

687 Statue of Pres. Assad, Damascus

1993. 30th Anniv of Baathist Revolution of 8th March 1963.
1858 **687** 1100 p. multicoloured . . 1·10 55

688 Common Blue **689** Family

1993. Butterflies. Multicoloured.
1859 1000 p. Type **688** 90 45
1860 1500 p. Silver-washed fritillary 1·25 60
1861 2500 p. Blue argus . . . . . 2·10 1·00

1993. Mothers' Day.
1862 **689** 1100 p. multicoloured . . 1·10 55

690 Saladin Monument, Damascus

1993. 47th Anniv of Evacuation of Foreign Troops from Syria.
1863 **690** 1100 p. multicoloured . . 1·10 55

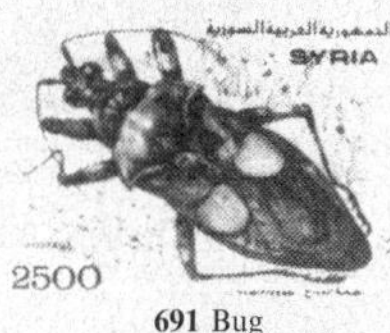

691 Bug

1993.
1864 **691** 2500 p. multicoloured . . 2·10 1·00

692 Tractor in Field of Crops

1993. 25th Anniv of Arab Agrarian Union.
1865 **692** 1150 p. multicoloured . . 1·10 55

693 Oil Workers

1993. Labour Day.
1866 **693** 1100 p. multicoloured . . 1·10 55

694 Eye and Eye-chart

1993. 2nd Pan-Arab Ophthalmology International Council Congress.
1867 **694** 1100 p. multicoloured . . 1·10 55

695 Landscapes and Eye 696 "Alcea setosa"

1993. 25th Anniv of National Ophthalmological Association.
1868 **695** 1150 p. multicoloured . . 1·10 55

1993. 21st Int Flower Show, Damascus. Mult.
1869 1000 p. Type **696** 95 45
1870 1100 p. Primulas . . . . . . 1·10 55
1871 1150 p. Gesnerias . . . . . . 1·10 55

697 Prism Tomb

1993. International Tourism Day.
1872 **697** 1000 p. multicoloured . . 1·10 55

698 Hand posting Letter and Globe

1993. World Post Day.
1873 **698** 1000 p. multicoloured . . 1·10 55

699 Boys playing Football 700 Ibn al-Bittar (chemist)

1993. International Children's Day.
1874 **699** 1150 p. multicoloured . . 1·10 55

1993. Science Week.
1875 **700** 1150 p. multicoloured . . 1·10 55

702 White Horse

1993. Arab Horses. Multicoloured.
1877 1000 p. Type **702** 95 45
1878 1000 p. Horse with white feet 95 45
1879 1500 p. Black horse . . . . . . 1·25 60
1880 1500 p. White horse with brown mane . . . . 1·25 60

703 Orchard in Blossom

1993. Tree Day.
1881 **703** 1100 p. multicoloured . . 1·10 55

704 Flags outside Venue

1993. 40th International Damascus Fair.
1882 **704** 1100 p. multicoloured . 1·10 55

705 Basel al-Assad

1994. Basel al-Assad (President's son) Commem.
1883 **705** 2500 p. multicoloured . 2·25 1·10

706 Oranges

1994. 31st Anniv of Baathist Revolution of 8th March 1963. Multicoloured.
1884 1500 p. Type **706** . . . . . 1·25 60
1885 1500 p. Mandarins . . . . . 1·25 60
1886 1500 p. Lemons . . . . . . 1·25 60

707 Flags, Flame, Laurel and Dates

1994. 48th Anniv of Evacuation of Foreign Troops from Syria.
1887 **707** 1800 p. multicoloured . 1·50 75

708 Mechanical Digger loading Truck

1994. Labour Day.
1888 **708** 1700 p. multicoloured . 1·50 75

709 Mother and Child at Different Ages

1994. Mothers' Day.
1889 **709** 1800 p. multicoloured . 1·50 75

710 Emblem, "50" and "75"

1994. 75th Anniv of I.L.O. and 50th Anniv of Philadelphia Declaration (social charter).
1890 **710** 1700 p. multicoloured . 1·25 60

711 Match Scene

1994. World Cup Football Championship, U.S.A. Multicoloured.
1891 1700 p. Type **711** . . . . . . 1·25 60
1892 1700 p. Match scene (different) 1·25 60

712 Olympic Flag, Greek Temple and "100"

1994. Centenary of International Olympic Committee.
1894 **712** 1700 p. multicoloured . . 1·10 55

713 Flags, Lanterns and Fountain 714 Camomile

1994. 41st International Damascus Fair.
1895 **713** 1800 p. multicoloured . . 1·25 60

1994. Int Flower Show, Damascus. Mult.
1896 1800 p. Type **714** . . . . . . 1·25 60
1897 1800 p. Gloxinia . . . . . . 1·25 60
1898 1800 p. Mimosa . . . . . . 1·25 60

715 Apollo

1994. Butterflies. Multicoloured.
1899 1700 p. Type **715** . . . . . . 1·10 55
1900 1700 p. Purple emperor (value at right) . . . . 1·10 55
1901 1700 p. Birdwing (value at left) 1·10 55

716 Symbols and Map

1994. 4th Population Census.
1902 **716** 1000 p. multicoloured . . 65 30

717 Al-Kinsi (philosopher)

1994. Science Week.
1903 **717** £S10 multicoloured . . . 70 35

719 Airport

1994. 50th Anniv of I.C.A.O.
1905 **719** £S17 multicoloured . . . 1·10 55

720 Al-Marjeh Square 721 Child with Tennis Racquet

1994.
1906 **720** £S50 mauve . . . . . . 3·25 1·60

1994. International Children's Day.
1907 **721** £S10 multicoloured . . . 70 35

722 Girl watching Birds with Envelopes 723 Palmyra Roman Arch

1994. World Post Day.
1908 **722** £S10 multicoloured . . . 70 35

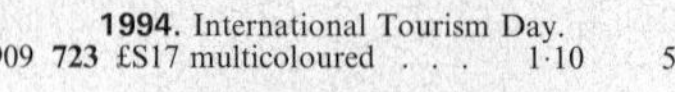
1994. International Tourism Day.
1909 **723** £S17 multicoloured . . . 1·10 55

724 Modern Building

1995. 32nd Anniv of Baathist Revolution of 8 March 1963.
1910 **724** £S18 multicoloured . . . 85 40

725 League Emblem and Map 726 Water Pump

1995. 50th Anniv of Arab League.
1911 **725** £S17 multicoloured . . . 80 40

1995. World Water Day.
1912 **726** £S17 multicoloured . . . 80 40

727 Woman sheltering Figures

1995. Mothers' Day.
1913 **727** £S17 multicoloured . . . 80 40

728 Hand holding Tree 729 Family

1995. Tree Day.
1914 **728** 1800 p. multicoloured . . 85 40

1995. International Year of the Family (1994).
1915 **729** 1700 p. multicoloured . . 80 40

730 Statue and Flag

731 Honey Bees on Flowers

1995. 49th Anniv of Evacuation of Foreign Troops from Syria.
1916 **730** £S17 multicoloured . . . 80 40

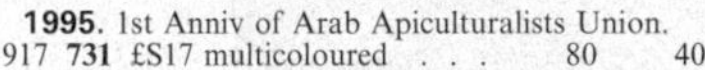

1995. 1st Anniv of Arab Apiculturalists Union.
1917 **731** £S17 multicoloured . . . 80 40

732 Pres. Assad

733 Welder

1995.
1920 **732** £S10 purple 30 15
1921 £S17 lilac 55 25
1922 £S18 green 55 25
1923 £S100 blue . . . . 3·00 1·50
1924 £S500 yellow . . . . . . 5·50 2·25

1995. Labour Day.
1925 **733** £S10 multicoloured . . . 70 35

734 Anniversary Emblem

1995. 50th Anniv of F.A.O.
1926 **734** £S15 multicoloured . . . 75 35

735 Desert Festival

1995. Tourism Day.
1927 **735** £S18 multicoloured . . . 85 40

736 Astilbe

737 Anniversary Emblem on U.N. Headquarters

1995. 23rd Int Flower Show, Damascus. Mult.
1928 £S10 Type **736** 70 35
1929 £S10 Evening primrose . . . 70 35
1930 £S10 Campanula (blue carpet) 70 35

1995. 50th Anniv of U.N.O.
1931 **737** £S18 multicoloured . . . 85 40

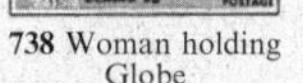

738 Woman holding Globe

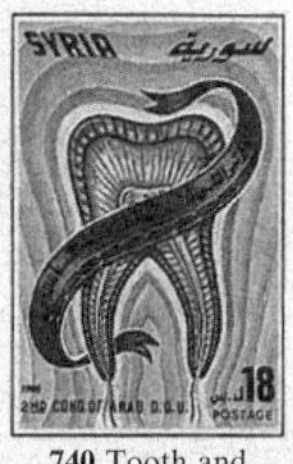

740 Tooth and Ribbon

739 Fair Entrance

1995. 4th World Conference on Women, Peking.
1932 **738** £S18 multicoloured . . 85 40

1995. 42nd International Damascus Fair.
1933 **739** £S15 multicoloured . . 75 35

1995. 2nd Congress of Arab Dentists' Association.
1934 **740** £S18 multicoloured . . 85 40

741 Writing Letters and Air Mail Colours around Globe

1995. World Post Day.
1935 **741** £S15 multicoloured . . 75 35

742 Children playing on Beach

1995. World Children's Day.
1936 **742** £S18 multicoloured . . 85 40

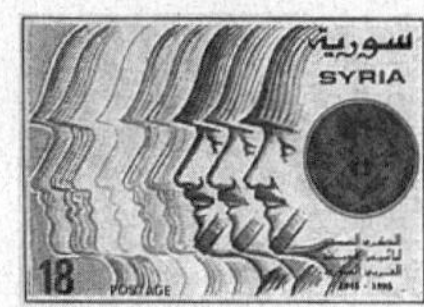

743 Soldiers

1995. 50th Anniv of Syrian Army.
1937 **743** £S18 multicoloured . . 85 40

744 Ahmed ben Maged

1995. 500th Death Anniv of Ahmed ben Maged (cartographer).
1938 **744** £S18 multicoloured . . 85 40

745 Pres. Assad

1995. 25th Anniv of Corrective Movement of 16 November 1970.
1939 **745** £S10 multicoloured . . 70 35

746 Mother and Chicks

1995. Birds. Multicoloured.
1941 £S18 Type **746** 55 25
1942 £S18 Robin in snow 55 25
1943 £S18 Bird on post 55 25

747 Pasteur and Laboratory

1995. Death Centenary of Louis Pasteur (chemist).
1944 **747** £S18 multicoloured . . . 55 25

748 Olive Tree

749 Pumping Station, Kudairan

1996. Tree Day.
1945 **748** £S17 multicoloured . . . 50 25

1996. 33rd Anniv of Baathist Revolution of 8 March 1963.
1946 **749** £S25 multicoloured . . . 75 35

750 Woman and Horsemen

1996. 50th Anniv of Evacuation of Foreign Troops from Syria.
1947 **750** £S10 multicoloured . . . 30 15
1948 £S25 multicoloured . . . 75 35

751 Woman and Baby

1996. Mothers' Day.
1950 **751** £S10 multicoloured . . . 30 15

752 Textile Factory Workers

1996. Labour Day.
1951 **752** £S15 multicoloured . . . 45 20

753 Memorial

1996. 22nd Anniv of Liberation of Qneitra.
1952 **753** £S10 multicoloured . . . 30 15

754 Map, Palestinian Flag and Arabic Script

1996. 50th Anniv of "Al-Baath" (newspaper).
1953 **754** £S18 multicoloured . . . 55 25

755 "Mammilaria erythosperma"

1996. 24th International Flower Show, Damascus. Cacti. Multicoloured.
1954 £S18 Type **755** 55 25
1955 £S18 "Notocactus graessnerii" 55 25

756 Wrestling

1996. Olympic Games, Atlanta, U.S.A. Multicoloured.
1956 £S17 Type **756** 50 25
1957 £S17 Swimming 50 25
1958 £S17 Running 50 25

757 Guglielmo Marconi and Transmitter

1996. Centenary (1995) of First Radio Transmissions.
1960 **757** £S17 multicoloured . . 50 25

758 Family protected from burning "AIDS"

759 Fair Emblem, Pattern and Globe

1996. World AIDS Day.
1961 **758** £S17 multicoloured . . 50 25

1996. 43rd International Damascus Fair.
1962 **759** £S17 multicoloured . . 50 25

760 Computer, Emblem and Globe

1996. 5th Anniv of National Information Centre.
1963 **760** £S18 multicoloured . . 55 25

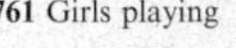

761 Girls playing

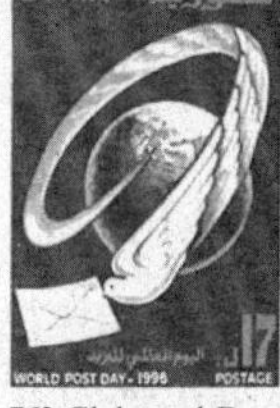

762 Globe and Dove with Letter

1996. World Children's Day.
1964 **761** £S10 multicoloured . . 30 15

1996. World Post Day.
1965 **762** £S17 multicoloured . . 50 25

763 Sons of Musa ibn Shaker

1996. Science Week.
1966 **763** £S10 multicoloured . . 30 15

764 Pres. Assad

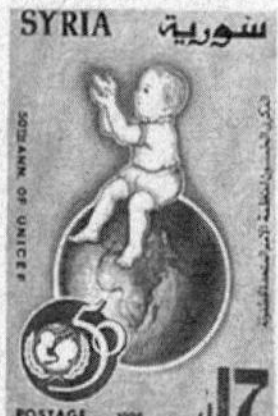

765 Child sitting on Globe

1996. 26th Anniv of Corrective Movement of 16 November 1970.
1967 **764** £S10 multicoloured . . 30 15

1996. 50th Anniv of U.N.I.C.E.F.
1969 **765** £S17 multicoloured . . 50 25

OBLIGATORY TAX STAMPS

T 57

T 58

T 59

T 60

T 61

1945. Syrian Army Fund. Revenue Stamps surch or optd.
T419 T **57** 5 p. on 25 p. on 40 p. pink 65·00 3·00
T420 – 5 p. on 25 p. on 40 p. pink 90·00 7·50
T421 T **58** 5 p. on 25 p. on 40 p. pink 65·00 1·50
T422 T **59** 5 p. blue £100 90
T423 T **60** 5 p. blue . . . . . . 65·00 1·10
T424 – 5 p. blue . . . . . . 80·00 30
T425 T **61** 5 p. blue . . . . . . 80·00 1·00
T426 – 5 p. blue . . . . . . £100 2·00

No. T420 is as Type **57** but with additional overprint as top line of Type **61**.

No. T424 has top line of overprint as Type **59** and other lines as Type **60**.

No. T426 has top line overprinted as Type **61** and other lines as Type **60**.

POSTAGE DUE STAMPS

A. FRENCH MILITARY OCCUPATION

1920. "Mouchon" and "Merson" key-types of French Post Offices in the Turkish Empire (inscr "LEVANT") surch **O. M. F. Syrie Ch. taxe** and value.
D48 B 1 p. on 10 c. red £170 £170
D49 2 p. on 20 c. brown . . . £170 £170
D50 3 p. on 30 c. lilac . . . £170 £170
D51 C 4 p. on 40 c. red & blue . £170 £170

1920. Postage Due stamps of France surch **O. M. F. Syrie** and value.
D60 D **11** 50 c. on 10 c. brown . . 75 1·25
D52 1 p. on 10 c. brown . . 1·50 1·90
D61 1 p. on 20 c. green . . 75 1·25
D53 2 p. on 20 c. green . . 1·50 1·90
D62 2 p. on 30 c. red . . . 2·25 2·25
D54 3 p. on 30 c. red . . . 1·50 1·90
D63 3 p. on 50 c. purple . . 2·50 2·75
D55 4 p. on 50 c. purple . . 3·75 4·50
D64 5 p. on 1 f. purple on yellow . . . . . . 5·00 5·75

1921. Issued at Damascus. No. KD96 of Arab Kingdom surch **O. M. F. Syrie Chiffre Taxe** and value.
D69 K **3** 50 c. on 1 p. black . . . 3·00 3·00
D70 1 p. on 1 p. black . . . 2·25 2·25

1921. Issued at Damascus. No. 64a/5 of Syria optd **TAXE**.
D89 K **4** 2 p. on 5 m. red . . . . 4·25 4·25
D90 K **3** 3 p. on 1 p. blue . . . . 9·00 8·50

B. ARAB KINGDOM

1920. As No. K92 but colour changed.
KD96 K **3** 1 p. black . . . . . . 1·25 1·25

C. FRENCH MANDATED TERRITORY

1923. Postage Due stamps of France surch **Syrie Grand Liban** and value.
D118 D **11** 50 c. on 10 c. brown . 1·10 1·25
D119 1 p. on 20 c. green . . 1·60 1·60
D120 2 p. on 30 c. red . . . 1·50 1·50
D121 3 p. on 50 c. purple . 1·50 1·60
D122 5 p. on 1 f. purple on yellow . . . . . . 2·75 3·00

1924. Postage Due stamps of France surch **SYRIE** and value.
D139 D **11** 50 c. on 10 c. brown . 95 95
D140 1 p. on 20 c. green . . 1·00 1·00
D141 2 p. on 30 c. red . . . 1·25 1·25
D142 3 p. on 50 c. purple . 90 1·25
D143 5 p. on 1 f. purple on yellow . . . . . . 1·50 1·60

1924. Postage Due stamps of France surch **Syrie** and value and also in Arabic.
D175 D **11** 0 p. 50 on 10 c. brown 40 1·25
D176 1 p. on 20 c. olive . . 85 1·25
D177 2 p. on 30 c. red . . . 1·25 1·25
D178 3 p. on 50 c. purple . 1·25 1·40
D179 5 p. on 1 f. red on yellow 1·60 1·60

D 20 Hama

1925.
D192 D **20** 0 p. 50 brown on yell 25 35
D193 – 1 p. purple on pink . 15 45
D194 – 2 p. black on blue . . 50 1·10
D195 – 3 p. black on red . . 1·00 1·50
D196 – 5 p. black on green . 85 95
D197 – 8 p. black on blue . 3·50 3·75
D198 – 15 p. black on pink . 6·25 6·50

DESIGNS—VERT: 1 p. Antioch. HORIZ: 2 p. Tarsus; 3 p. Banias; 5 p. Castle; 8 p. Ornamental design; 15 p. Lion.

E. SYRIAN REPUBLIC

D 221

1965.
D883 D **221** $2\frac{1}{2}$ p. blue 10 10
D884 5 p. brown 10 10
D885 10 p. green 15 10
D886 $17\frac{1}{2}$ p. red 40 40
D887 25 p. blue 55 55

TAHITI Pt. 6

The largest of the Society Islands in the S. Pacific Ocean. Later renamed Oceanic Settlements.

100 centimes = 1 franc

1882. Stamps of French Colonies. "Peace and Commerce" type, surch **25 c.**
1 H 25 c. on 35 c. black on orange £170 £160
3a 25 c. on 40 c. red on yellow £2500 £3000

1884. Stamps of French Colonies, "Commerce" (perf) and "Peace and Commerce" (imperf) types, surch **TAHITI** and value.
4 J 5 c. on 20 c. red on green . . £120 £190
5 10 c. on 20 c. red on green £160 £150
2 H 25 c. on 35 c. black on orge £3000 £3000
6 25 c. on 1 f. green £375 £300

1893. Stamps of French Colonies, "Commerce" type, optd **TAHITI**.
7 J 1 c. black on blue £425 £375
8 2 c. brown on buff £2000 £1500
9 4 c. brown on grey £700 £550
10 5 c. green on green . . . . . 20·00 20·00
11 10 c. black on lilac . . . . . 20·00 20·00
12 15 c. blue . . . . 20·00 20·00
13 20 c. red on green . . . . . 27·00 27·00
14 25 c. brown £4250 £4250
15 25 c. black on pink . . . . . 20·00 20·00
16 35 c. black on orange £1400 £1200
17 75 c. red on pink . . . . . . 35·00 35·00
18 1 f. green . . . . 38·00 38·00

1893. Stamps of French Colonies, "Commerce" type, optd **1893 TAHITI**.
32 J 1 c. black on blue £425 £400
33 2 c. brown on buff £2250 £1700
34 4 c. brown on grey £1000 £800
35 5 c. green on green £575 £500
36 10 c. black on lilac £190 £190
37 15 c. blue . . . . 20·00 20·00
38 20 c. red on green . . . . . 20·00 20·00
39 25 c. brown £17000 £15000
40 25 c. black on pink . . . . . 20·00 20·00
41 35 c. black on orange £1400 £1200
42 75 c. red on pink . . . . . . 20·00 20·00
43 1 f. green . . . . 20·00 20·00

1903. Stamps of Oceanic Settlements, "Tablet" key-type, surch **TAHITI 10 centimes**.
57 D 10 c. on 15 c. blue and red . 4·00 4·00
58 10 c. on 25 c. black and red on pink . . . . 4·00 4·00
59 10 c. on 40 c. red and blue on yellow . . . . 4·75 4·75

1915. Stamps of Oceanic Settlements, "Tablet" key-type, optd **TAHITI** and red cross.
60 D 15 c. blue and red £110 £110
61 15 c. grey and red . . . . . 13·50 13·50

POSTAGE DUE STAMPS

1893. Postage Due stamps of French Colonies optd **TAHITI**.
D19 U 1 c. black £250 £250
D20 2 c. black £250 £250
D21 3 c. black £300 £300
D22 4 c. black £300 £300
D23 5 c. black £300 £300
D24 10 c. black £300 £300
D25 15 c. black £300 £300
D26 20 c. black £250 £250
D27 30 c. black £300 £300
D28 40 c. black £300 £300
D29 60 c. black £300 £300
D30 1 f. brown £575 £575
D31 2 f. brown $575 £575

1893. Postage Due stamps of French Colonies optd **1893 TAHITI**.
D44 U 1 c. black £1500 £1500
D45 2 c. black £400 £400
D46 3 c. black £400 £400
D47 4 c. black £400 £400
D48 5 c. black £400 £400
D49 10 c. black £400 £400
D50 15 c. black £400 £400
D51 20 c. black £250 £250
D52 30 c. black £400 £400
D53 40 c. black £400 £400
D54 60 c. black £400 £400
D55 1 f. brown £400 £400
D56 2 f. brown £400 £400

For later issues see **OCEANIC SETTLEMENTS**.

TAJIKISTAN Pt. 10

Formerly a constituent republic of the Soviet Union, Tajikistan became independent in 1991.

1992. 100 kopeks = 1 (Russian) rouble.
1995. 100 tangas = 1 (Tajik) rouble.

1 Hunter (gold relief)

2 Sheikh Muslihiddin Mosque

1992.
1 **1** 50 k. multicoloured . . . . . 2·90 2·90

1992.
2 **2** 50 k. multicoloured . . . . . 2·90 2·90

3 Traditional Musical Instruments

1992.
3 **3** 35 k. multicoloured 55 55

4 Argali

1992.
4 **4** 30 k. multicoloured 55 55

3.00
Точикистон
5.00
1992
(5)

1992
Тадж.
(7)

1992. No. 2 surch as T **5**.
5 **2** 5 r. on 50 k. multicoloured . . 1·60 1·60
6 25 r. on 50 k. multicoloured . 2·75 2·75

1992. No. 3 surch.
7 **3** 15 r. on 35 k. multicoloured . 2·75 2·75
8 50 r. on 35 k. multicoloured . 2·75 2·75

1993. No. 5940 of Russia surch as T **7**.
9 **2410** 3 r. on 1 k. brown . . . . 4·75 4·75
10 100 r. on 1 k. brown . . . 4·75 4·75

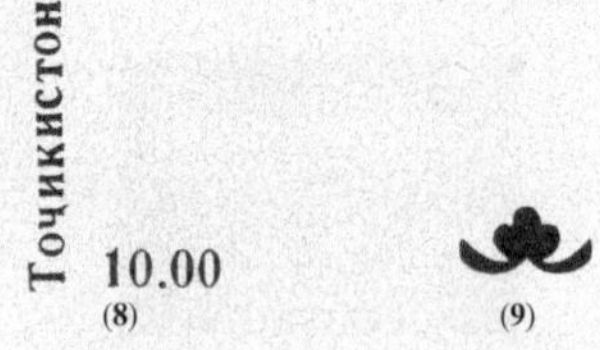

(8) (9)

1993. No. 6073 of Russia surch as T **8**.
11 10 r. on 2 k. brown 70 70
12 15 r. on 2 k. brown 70 70

On No. 12 the surcharge is in smaller letters.

1993. No. 1 surch with T **9**.
13 **1** 60 r. on 50 k. multicoloured . 1·25 1·25

10 Mountain Landscape

1993. Multicoloured.
16 1 r. Statue of Abuabdullokhi Rudaki, Dushanbe (vert) . . 10 10
17 5 r. Type **10** 25 25
18 15 r. Mausoleum of Sadriddin Aini (poet), Dushanbe (vert) 75 75
19 20 r. State flag and map . . . 95 95
20 25 r. Gissar Fort . . . . . . 1·00 1·00
21 50 r. Aini Opera and Ballet House, Dushanbe . . . . 2·25 2·25
22 100 r. State flag and map (different) . . . . 4·25 4·25

11 Brown Bear

1993. Mammals. Multicoloured.
23 3 r. Type **11** 15 15
24 10 r. Red deer 20 20
25 15 r. Markhor 35 35
26 25 r. Porcupine 45 45
27 100 r. Snow leopard . . . . . 2·25 2·25

12 Geb and Talkhand in Battle

1993. Millenary of "Book of Kings" by Abu-I Kasim Mansur, Firdausi (poet). Multicoloured.

No.	Description	Unused	Used
28	5 r. Type **12**	60	60
29	20 r. Rustam and Sukhrov in combat	2·00	2·00
30	30 r. Eagle Simurg brings Zola to his father Som (vert)	3·00	3·00

14 Ceiling Decoration

15 Arms

1993.

No.	Type	Description	Unused	Used
33	**14**	1 r. 50 multicoloured	1·00	1·00

1994.

No.	Type	Description	Unused	Used
34	**15**	10 r. multicoloured	10	10
35		15 r. multicoloured	10	10
36		35 r. multicoloured	10	10
37		50 r. multicoloured	15	15
38		100 r. multicoloured	25	25
39		160 r. multicoloured	30	30
40		500 r. mult (23 x 37 mm)	1·00	1·00
41		1000 r. mult (23 x 37 mm)	2·00	2·00

16 Hamadony

18 Post Office

1994. 680th Birth Anniv of Ali Hamadony (Persian mystic).

No.	Type	Description	Unused	Used
42	**16**	1000 r. multicoloured (inscr in Latin alphabet)	2·00	2·00
43		1000 r. multicoloured (inscr in Cyrillic)	2·00	2·00

1994. Historic Monuments. Multicoloured.

No.	Description	Unused	Used
45	10 r. Statue of Firdausi (vert)	10	10
46	35 r. Type **18**	10	10
47	100 r. Theatre	30	30
48	160 r. Ulum Academy	35	35
49	160 r. "Safar" building	35	35

19 Tyrannosaurus

1994. Prehistoric Animals. Multicoloured.

No.	Description	Unused	Used
50	500 r. Type **19**	75	75
51	500 r. Stegosaurus	75	75
52	500 r. Anatosaurus	75	75
53	500 r. Parasaurolophus	75	75
54	500 r. Triceratops	75	75
55	500 r. Diatryma	75	75
56	500 r. Tyrannosaurus (different)	75	75
57	500 r. Spinosaurus	75	75

1995. No. 33 surch **1995** and value.

No.	Type	Description	Unused	Used
58	**14**	100 r. on 1 r. 50 mult	10	10
59		600 r. on 1 r. 50 mult	45	45
60		1000 r. on 1 r. 50 mult	75	75
61		5000 r. on 1 r. 50 mult	2·00	2·00

21 Gecko ("Alsophylax loricatus")

1995. Lizards. Multicoloured.

No.	Description	Unused	Used
62	500 r. Type **21**	65	65
63	500 r. Sunwatcher ("Phrynocephalus helioscopus")	65	65
64	500 r. Toad-headed agama ("Phrynocephalus mystaceus")	65	65
65	500 r. Toad agama ("Phrynocephalus sogdianus")	65	65
66	500 r. Plate-tailed gecko ("Teratoscincus scineus")	65	65
67	500 r. Transcaspian desert monitor ("Varanus griseus")	65	65

22 National Flag

25 State Arms

1995. Membership of International Organizations. Multicoloured.

No.	Description	Unused	Used
69	1000 r. Type **22** (Organization for Security and Co-operation in Europe)	1·25	1·25
70	1000 r. National flag and New York Headquarters (United Nations) (horiz)	1·25	1·25
71	1000 r. Emblem and national flag (Universal Postal Union)	1·25	1·25

1995. "Beijing '95" International Stamp Exhibition, China (73) and "Singapore '95" International Stamp Exhibition (74). Nos. 64 and 67 optd with relevant exhibition emblem.

No.	Description	Unused	Used
73	500 r. multicoloured	65	65
74	500 r. multicoloured	65	65

1995.

No.	Type	Description	Unused	Used
75	**25**	1 r. multicoloured	10	10
76		2 r. multicoloured	10	10
77		5 r. multicoloured	10	10
78		12 r. multicoloured	10	10
79		40 r. multicoloured	10	10

26 Bar-headed Goose ("Anser indicus")

1996. Birds. Multicoloured.

No.	Description	Unused	Used
80	200 r. Type **26**	40	40
81	200 r. Indian black-headed gull ("Larus brunnicephalus")	40	40
82	200 r. Bustard ("Otis undulata")	40	40
83	200 r. Daurian partridge ("Perdix dauricae")	40	40
84	200 r. Tibetan sandgrouse ("Syrrhaptes tibetana")	40	40
85	200 r. Tibetan snowcock ("Tetraogallus tibetanus")	40	40

27 New York Headquarters

1996. 50th Anniv of U.N.O.

No.	Type	Description	Unused	Used
87	**27**	100 r. multicoloured	40	40

29 Pallas's Cat

1996. Wild Cats. Multicoloured. (a) With World Wildlife Fund emblem. Pallas's Cat.

No.	Description	Unused	Used
90	100 r. Type **29**	65	65
91	100 r. Close-up	65	65
92	150 r. Head	90	90
93	150 r. Sitting	90	90

(b) Without W.W.F. emblem.

No.	Description	Unused	Used
95	200 r. Jungle cat ("Felis chaus")	1·40	1·40
96	200 r. Lynx ("Felis lynx")	1·40	1·40

30 Diving

31 Kamol Khujandi

1996. Olympic Games, Atlanta, U.S.A. Mult.

No.	Description	Unused	Used
97	200 r. Type **30**	1·25	1·25
98	200 r. Football	1·25	1·25
99	200 r. Throwing the hammer	1·25	1·25
100	200 r. Judo	1·25	1·25
101	200 r. Baron Pierre de Coubertin (founder of modern Games)	1·25	1·25

1996. Kamol Khujandi (writer) Commemoration.

No.	Type	Description	Unused	Used
102	**31**	500 r. multicoloured (inscr in English)	2·50	2·50
103		500 r. multicoloured (inscr in Tajik)	2·50	2·50

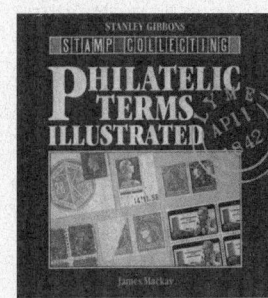

TCHONGKING (CHUNGKING) Pt. 17

An Indo-Chinese Post Office was opened at Chungking in February 1902 and operated until it closed in December 1922.

1903. 100 centimes = 1 franc.
1919. 100 cents = 1 piastre.

Stamps of Indo-China surch.

1903. "Tablet" key-type surch with value in Chinese and **TCHONGKING**.

1 D 1 c. black and red on blue . 1·60 1·60
2 2 c. brown and blue on buff 1·60 1·60
3 4 c. brown and blue on grey 1·60 1·60
4 5 c. green and red 1·60 1·60
5 10 c. red and blue 1·60 1·60
6 15 c. grey and red 1·50 1·50
7 20 c. red and blue on green 1·60 1·60
8 25 c. blue and red 24·00 24·00
9 25 c. black and red on pink 3·25 3·25
10 30 c. brown and blue on drab 5·50 5·25
11 40 c. red and blue on yellow 25·00 25·00
12 50 c. red and blue on pink . £120 £120
13 50 c. brown and red on blue 75·00 75·00
14 75 c. brown and red on orange 24·00 24·00
15 1 f. green and red 30·00 30·00
16 5 f. mauve and blue on lilac 55·00 55·00

1906. Surch with value in Chinese and **Tch'ong K'ing**.

17 8 1 c. green 95 95
18 2 c. purple on yellow 95 95
19 4 c. mauve on blue 95 95
20 5 c. green 95 95
21 10 c. pink 95 95
22 15 c. brown on blue 3·25 3·25
23 20 c. red on green 95 95
24 25 c. blue 2·00 2·00
25 30 c. brown on cream 1·50 1·50
26 35 c. black on yellow 1·50 1·50
27 40 c. black on grey 3·25 3·25
28 50 c. brown on cream 3·25 3·25
29 D 75 c. brown and red on orange 20·00 20·00
30 8 1 f. green 13·50 13·50
31 2 f. brown on yellow 13·50 13·50
32 D 5 f. mauve and blue on lilac 60·00 60·00
33 8 10 f. red on green 75·00 75·00

1908. Native types surch with value in Chinese and **TCHONGKING**.

34 10 1 c. black and brown 15 25
35 2 c. black and brown 30 35
36 4 c. black and blue 35 40
37 5 c. black and green 55 55
38 10 c. black and red 65 75
39 15 c. black and violet 90 90
40 11 20 c. black and violet 1·50 1·50
41 25 c. black and blue 1·50 1·50
42 30 c. black and brown 1·60 1·60
43 35 c. black and green 3·00 3·00
44 40 c. black and brown 7·25 7·25
45 50 c. black and red 4·75 4·75
46 12 75 c. black and orange 4·75 4·75
47 – 1 f. black and red 6·00 6·25
48 – 2 f. black and green 50·00 50·00
49 – 5 f. black and blue 17·00 17·00
50 – 10 f. black and violet £150 £150

1919. As last, but surch in addition in figures and words.

51 10 ⅖ c. on 1 c. black & brown . 45 45
52 ⅘ c. on 2 c. black & brown . 50 55
53 1⅗ c. on 4 c. black and blue . 65 65
54 2 c. on 5 c. black & green . 50 45
55 4 c. on 10 c. black and red . 50 45
56 6 c. on 15 c. black & violet . 50 45
57 11 8 c. on 20 c. black & violet . 50 45
58 10 c. on 25 c. black & blue . 70 60
59 12 c. on 30 c. blk & brown . 90 60
60 14 c. on 35 c. black & green 90 55
61 16 c. on 40 c. black & brown 1·00 90
62 20 c. on 50 c. black & red . 5·00 5·00
63 12 30 c. on 75 c. black & orge . 1·10 1·00
64 – 40 c. on 1 f. black and red 1·60 1·00
65 – 80 c. on 2 f. black & green . 2·75 2·25
66 – 2 p. on 5 f. black & blue . 3·75 3·25
67 – 4 p. on 10 f. black & violet . 5·75 4·00

TETE Pt. 9

Formerly using the stamps of Mozambique, this district of Mozambique was permitted to issue its own stamps from 1913 until 1920 when Mozambique stamps were again used.

100 centavos = 1 escudo

1913. Surch **REPUBLICA TETE** and new value on "Vasco da Gama" issues of (a) Portugese Colonies.

1 ¼ c. on 2½ r. green 40 35
2 ½ c. on 5 r. red 40 35
3 1 c. on 10 r. purple 40 35
4 2½ c. on 25 r. green 40 35
5 5 c. on 50 r. blue 40 35
6 7½ c. on 75 r. brown 75 55
7 10 c. on 100 r. brown 45 40
8 15 c. on 150 r. brown 45 40

(b) Macao.

9 ¼ c. on ½ a. green 40 35
10 ½ c. on 1 a. red 40 35
11 1 c. on 2 a. purple 40 35
12 2½ c. on 4 a. green 40 35
13 5 c. on 8 a. blue 40 35
14 7½ c. on 12 a. brown 75 60
15 10 c. on 16 a. brown 45 40
16 15 c. on 24 a. brown 45 40

(c) Timor.

17 ¼ c. on ½ c. green 40 35
18 ½ c. on 1 a. red 40 35
19 1 c. on 2 a. purple 40 35
20 2½ c. on 4 a. green 40 35
21 5 c. on 8 a. blue 40 35
22 7½ c. on 12 a. brown 75 60
23 10 c. on 16 a. brown 45 40
24 15 c. on 24 a. brown 45 40

1914. "Ceres" key-type inscr "TETE".

25 U ¼ c. green 35 25
26 ½ c. black 35 25
27 1 c. green 35 20
28 1½ c. brown 35 20
29 2 c. red 35 25
30 2½ c. violet 35 20
31 5 c. blue 35 25
32 7½ c. brown 50 50
33 8 c. grey 50 50
34 10 c. red 60 60
35 15 c. purple 75 60
36 20 c. green 75 60
37 30 c. brown on green 75 60
38 40 c. brown on pink 90 65
39 50 c. orange on orange 90 85
40 1 e. green on blue 1·25 1·00

THAILAND Pt. 21

An independent kingdom in S.E. Asia, previously known as Siam.

1883. 32 solot = 16 atts = 8 peinung (sio) = 4 songpy (sik) = 2 fuang = 1 salung; 4 salungs = 1 tical.
1909. 100 satangs = 1 tical.
1912. 100 satangs = 1 baht.

1 King Chulalongkorn 2

3 King Chulalongkorn 9

1883.

1 1 1 solot (⅛ a.) blue 4·25 5·75
2 1 att red 7·00 8·50
3 1 sio (2 a.) red 17·00 21·00
4 2 1 sik (4 a.) yellow 7·00 8·50
5 3 1 salung (16 a.) orange 25·00 28·00

1885. Surch. (a) **1 TICAL**.

6 1 1 t. on 1 solot blue £1800 £950

(b) **1 Tical**.

7 1 1 t. on 1 solot blue £275 £200

1887.

11 9 1 a. green 1·25 85
12 2 a. green and red 1·25 85
13 3 a. green and blue 2·00 1·00
14 4 a. green and brown 5·75 2·75
15 8 a. green and yellow 4·25 2·00
16 12 a. purple and red 11·50 1·25
17 24 a. purple and blue 14·50 1·40
18 64 a. purple and brown 55·00 14·50

อัฐ (11) ๑ อัฐ 1 (12)

1889. Surch with T **11**.

19 1 1 a. on 1 sio red 5·75 5·75

1889. (a) Surch as T **12**.

20 9 1 a. on 2 a. green and red 1·40 1·40
24 1 a. on 3 a. green and blue 4·25 3·50
26 2 a. on 3 a. green and blue 15·00 15·00

(b) No. 24 further surch as T 12.

28 9 2 a. on 1 a. on 3 a. green & blue £1000 £700

1 Att.

ราคา๔อัฐ (23) ราคา ๑ อัฐ (42)

1892. Surch with T **23**.

32 9 4 a. on 24 a. purple and blue 22·00 22·00

1892. No. 32 further surch with English value in **atts**.

33 9 4 a. on 24 a. purple and blue 4·25 3·00

1892. Surch as T **42**.

63 9 1 Att. on 12 a. purple and red 5·75 1·75
54 1 Att. on 12 a. purple and red £110 £110
37 1 Att. on 64 a. purple and brown 2·10 2·10
46 1 Att. on 64 a. purple & brown 85 85
44 2 a. on 64 a. purple & brown 85 85
58 3 a. on 12 a. purple and red 4·25 1·75
60 4 a. on 12 a. purple and red 4·25 1·40
50 10 a. on 24 a. purple & blue 2·25 85

49 50 53 Wat Cheng "Temple of Light"

1899.

67 49 1 a. green 85 45
68 2 a. green 1·10 45
69 2 a. red and blue 1·40 55
70 3 a. red and blue 3·25 1·10
71 3 a. green 8·50 5·50
72 4 a. red 1·40 55
73 4 a. brown and pink 4·50 1·10
74 6 a. red 12·50 7·00
75 8 a. green and orange 2·75 60
76 10 a. blue 4·25 1·40
77 12 a. purple and red 17·00 1·40
78 14 a. blue 11·50 8·50
79 24 a. purple and blue 85·00 5·50
80 28 a. brown and blue 13·00 10·00
81 64 a. purple and brown 28·00 3·00

1899.

82 50 1 a. green £150 75·00
83 2 a. green and red £200 £120
84 3 a. red and blue £250 £160
85 4 a. black and green £2250 £550
86 10 a. pink and green £2500 £750

1905. Surch in English and Siamese.

90 49 1 a. on 14 a. blue 4·25 3·25
91 2 a. on 28 a. brown & blue 4·75 3·75

1905.

92 53 1 a. green and yellow 70 30
93 2 a. grey and violet 1·25 55
94 2 a. green 4·25 2·10
95 3 a. green 1·90 90
96 3 a. grey and violet 6·75 2·75
97 4 a. red and brown 2·00 60
98 4 a. red 3·50 60
99 5 a. red 4·00 1·40
100 8 a. bistre and black 3·50 55
101 9 a. blue 12·50 4·50
102 12 a. blue 9·50 1·60
103 18 a. brown 35·00 8·75
104 24 a. brown 16·00 3·00
105 1 t. bistre and blue 27·00 4·25

54

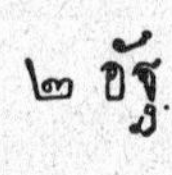

2 Atts.

(57)

1907. Fiscal stamps surch **Siam. Postage** and new value.

106 54 10 t. green £450 70·00
107 20 t. green £4250 £200
108 40 t. green £3500 £450

1907. Surch **1 att.** and thin line.

109 9 1 a. on 24 a. purple & blue . 85 55

1908. Surch in English and Siamese as T **57**.

110 9 2 a. on 24 a. purple & blue 85 55
111 53 4 a. on 5 a. red 5·00 2·25
112 49 9 a. on 10 a. blue 5·75 3·00

1908. 40th Anniv of Reign of King Chulalongkorn. Optd **Jubilee 1868–1908** in English and Siamese.

113 53 1 a. green and yellow 85 60
114 3 a. green 1·40 1·25
115 4 a. on 5 a. (No. 111) 2·00 1·75
116 8 a. bistre and black 13·00 13·00
117 18 a. brown 18·00 12·50

61 Statue of King Chulalongkorn, Bangkok 64 King Chulalongkorn

1908.

118 61 1 t. violet and green 22·00 1·40
119 2 t. orange and purple 45·00 5·75
120 3 t. blue and green 55·00 8·75
121 5 t. green and lilac 80·00 17·00
122 10 t. red and green £950 60·00
123 20 t. brown and grey £190 50·00
124 40 t. brown and blue £325 £140

1909. Surch in satangs in English and Siamese.

125 53 2 s. on 1 a. green & yellow 55 30
127a 2 s. on 2 a. green 60 30
164 2 s. on 2 a. grey & violet . 1·40 1·25
129 3 s. on 3 a. green 1·40 1·40
130 3 s. on 3 a. grey & violet . 1·25 30
131 6 s. on 4 a. red and brown 35·00 32·00
132a 6 s. on 4 a. red 1·25 55
134 6 s. on 5 a. red 1·40 1·40
138 49 6 s. on 6 a. red 1·10 1·10
135 53 12 s. on 8 a. bistre & black 2·25 30
136 14 s. on 9 a. blue 3·00 85
137 14 s. on 12 a. blue 11·50 11·50
139 9 14 s. on 12 a. purple & red 42·00 42·00
140 49 14 s. on 14 a. blue 10·00 10·50

1910.

141 64 2 s. green and orange 60 30
142 3 s. green 90 30
143 6 s. red 1·40 30
144 12 s. brown and black 3·00 60
145 14 s. blue 8·75 85
146 28 s. brown 20·00 4·00

65 King Vajiravudh 66

1912.

166 65 2 s. brown 45 15
167 3 s. green 70 30
168 5 s. red 60 15
149 6 s. red 1·60 30
169 10 s. brown and black 85 20
150 12 s. brown and black 2·40 35
151 14 s. blue 3·75 45
170 15 s. blue 1·75 45
152 28 s. brown 12·00 3·75
153 66 1 b. brown and blue 11·50 75
154 2 b. brown and red 17·00 1·40
155 3 b. black and green 23·00 2·40
156 5 b. black and violet 30·00 2·25
157 10 b. purple and green £160 38·00
158 20 b. brown and blue £275 35·00

1914. Surch in **Satang** in English and Siamese.

165 64 2 s. on 14 s. blue 85 45
159 65 2 s. on 14 s. blue 60 15
160 5 s. on 6 s. red 1·25 15
161 10 s. on 12 s. brown & blk 1·10 30
162 15 s. on 28 s. brown 2·40 45

1918. Red Cross Fund. Optd with small cross in circle.

177 65 2 s. (+ 3 s.) brown 60 60
178 3 s. (+ 2 s.) green 60 60
179 5 s. (+ 5 s.) red 1·25 90
180 10 s. (+ 5 s.) brown and black 3·00 1·75
181 15 s. (+ 5 s.) blue 3·25 1·75
182 66 1 b. (+ 25 s.) brown & blue 14·00 8·00
183 2 b.(+ 30 s.) brown and red 22·00 12·00
184 3 b. (+ 35 s.) black and green 30·00 20·00
185 5 b. (+ 40 s.) black and violet 90·00 42·00
186 10 b.(+ 1 b.) purple & green £275 £110
187 20 b. (+ 1 b.) brown & grn £1400 £800

1918. Optd **VICTORY** in English and Siamese.

188 65 2 s. brown 55 50
189 3 s. green 75 50
190 5 s. red 1·25 1·10
191 10 s. brown and black 1·40 1·25
192 15 s. blue 2·50 2·00
193 66 1 b. brown and blue 18·00 15·00
194 2 b. brown and red 35·00 30·00
195 3 b. black and green 80·00 45·00
196 5 b. black and violet £180 £150

1919. Surch in English and Siamese with figures only.

197 65 5 s. on 6 s. red 75 15
198 10 s. on 12 s. brown & black 1·75 15

(72a) (72b)

1920. Scouts' Fund. Various stamps handstamped. (a) With Type **72a**.

199 65 2 s. (+3 s.) brown 25·00 25·00
200 3 s. (+2 s.) green 25·00 25·00
201 5 s. on 6 s. (+5 s.) red (No. 160) 35·00 35·00
202 10 s. on 12 s. (+5 s.) brown and black (No. 161) 35·00 35·00
203 15 s. (+5 s.) blue 70·00 70·00
204 53 1 t. (+25 s.) bistre & blue £275 £275

(b) With Type **72b**.

205	**65**	2 s. (+3 s.) brown	10·00	10·00
206		3 s. (+2 s.) green	10·00	10·00
207	**73**	5 s. (+5 s.) red on pink	75·00	75·00
208	**65**	10 s. on 12 s. (+5 s.) brown and black (No. 161)	15·00	15·00
209		15 s. (+5 s.) blue	15·00	15·00
210	**53**	1 t. (+25 s.) bistre & blue	£250	£250

These stamps were sold in aid of the "Wild Tiger" Scouts organization at the premium stated.

73

บำรุงเสือป่า

SCOUT'S FUND

(**73a**)

1920.

211	**73**	2 s. brown on yellow	75	15
212		3 s. green on green	1·00	25
213		3 s. brown	1·00	15
214		5 s. red on pink	1·25	15
215		5 s. green	12·00	1·60
216		5 s. violet on mauve	2·50	25
217		10 s. brown and black	2·50	15
218		15 s. blue on blue	3·75	20
219		15 s. red	20·00	2·25
220		25 s. brown	10·00	1·25
221		25 s. blue	16·00	45
222		50 s. black and brown	24·00	75

1920. Scouts' Fund. Optd with T **73a**.

223	**73**	2 s. (+ 3 s.) brown on yellow	7·00	7·00
224		3 s. (+ 3 s.) green on green	7·00	7·00
225		5 s. (+ 5 s.) red on pink	7·00	7·00
226		10 s. (+ 5 s.) brown and black	7·00	7·00
227		15 s. (+ 5 s.) blue on blue	14·00	14·00
228		25 s. (+ 25 s.) brown	38·00	38·00
229		50 s. (+ 30 s.) black & brn	£180	£180

74 "Garuda" Bird　**75** Coronation Stone

1925. Air.

230	**74**	2 s. brown on yellow	60	15
231		3 s. brown	60	15
239		5 s. green	60	15
240		10 s. orange and black	60	15
234		15 s. red	2·50	50
242		25 s. blue	1·25	75
243		50 s. black and brown	1·25	75
237		1 b. brown and blue	23·00	6·50

1926.

244	**75**	1 t. green and lilac	7·50	1·25
245		2 t. red and carmine	18·00	3·75
246		3 t. blue and green	38·00	16·00
247		5 t. green and violet	38·00	12·00
248		10 t. brown and red	£100	15·00
249		10 t. brown and blue	£100	48·00

1928. Surch in English and Siamese.

250	**73**	5 s. on 15 s. red	2·50	1·25
251	**65**	10 s. on 28 s. brown	7·50	1·00

76 King Prajadhipok **77**

1928.

252	**76**	2 s. brown	50	15
253		3 s. green	50	25
254		5 s. violet	50	15
255		10 s. red	50	15
256		15 s. blue	55	25
257		25 s. orange and black	2·50	50
258		50 s. black and orange	1·25	75
259		80 s. black and blue	2·50	50
260	**77**	1 b. black and blue	3·75	75
261		2 b. brown and red	5·00	1·50
262		3 b. black and green	7·50	2·00
263		5 b. brown and violet	12·00	3·00
264		10 b. purple and green	25·00	5·00
265		20 b. brown and green	50·00	10·00
266		40 b. brown and green	90·00	38·00

1930. Surch in English and Siamese.

267	**64**	10 s. on 12 s. brown & blk	2·50	50
268		25 s. on 28 s. brown	12·00	75

79 Kings Prajadhipok and Chao Phya Chakri　**81** Chao Phya Chakri (Rama I)

80 Kings Prajadhipok and Chao Phya Chakri

1932. 150th Anniv of Chakri Dynasty and of Bangkok as Capital and Opening of Memorial Bridge over Menam.

269	**79**	2 s. red	1·00	15
270		3 s. green	1·50	25
271		5 s. violet	1·00	15
272	**80**	10 s. black and red	1·50	15
273		15 s. black and blue	5·00	50
274		25 s. black and mauve	7·50	75
275		50 s. black and purple	32·00	1·90
276	**81**	1 b. blue	50·00	8·50

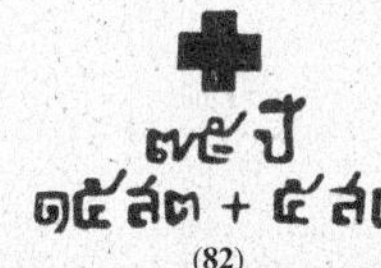

(**82**)

1939. Red Cross Fund. 75th Anniv of Membership of the International Red Cross. Surch as T **82**.

277	**66**	5 + 5 s. on 1 b. (153)	8·50	8·50
278		10 + 5 s. on 2 b. (154)	20·00	20·00
279		15 + 5 s. on 3 b. (155)	16·00	16·00

83 National Assembly Hall　**84** Chakri Palace and "Garuda" Bird

1939. 7th Anniv of Constitution and National Day (1st issue).

280	**83**	2 s. brown	2·50	35
281		3 s. green	5·00	1·25
282		5 s. purple	2·50	15
283		10 s. red	7·50	15
284		15 s. blue	20·00	65

1940. National Day (2nd issue).

285	**84**	2 s. brown	1·25	35
286		3 s. green	3·75	1·25
287		5 s. purple	2·50	15
288		10 s. red	12·00	15
289		15 s. blue	25·00	65

85 King Ananda Mahidol　**86** Ploughing Rice Field

87 Ban Pa'im Palace, Ayuthia　**88** Monument of Democracy, Bangkok

1941.

290	**85**	2 s. brown	50	15
291		3 s. green	75	25
292		5 s. violet	50	15
293		10 s. red	75	15
294	**86**	15 s. grey and blue	75	25
295		25 s. orange and grey	75	25
296		50 s. grey and orange	1·00	25
297	**87**	1 b. grey and blue	2·75	65
298		2 b. grey and red	5·00	1·25
299		3 b. grey and green	13·00	4·00
300		5 b. red and black	32·00	12·00
301		10 b. yellow and green	48·00	30·00

1942. Air. With or without gum.

302	**88**	2 s. brown	1·25	1·00
303		3 s. green	20·00	22·00
304		5 s. purple	1·25	50
305		10 s. red	12·00	75
306		15 s. blue	2·75	1·40

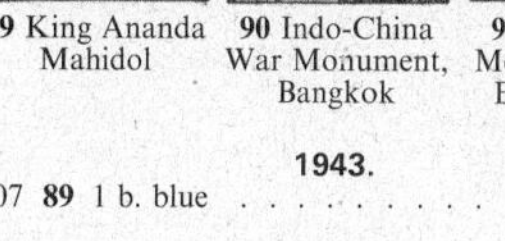

89 King Ananda Mahidol　**90** Indo-China War Monument, Bangkok　**91** Bangkaen Monument and Ears of Rice

1943.

307	**89**	1 b. blue	10·00	1·00

1943.

310	**90**	3 s. green	1·25	75

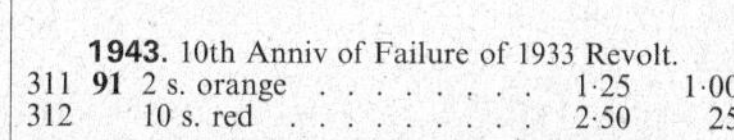

1943. 10th Anniv of Failure of 1933 Revolt.

311	**91**	2 s. orange	1·25	1·00
312		10 s. red	2·50	25

92 King Bhumibol **93**

1947.

313	**92**	5 s. violet	50	15
314		10 s. red	75	15
315		20 s. brown	50	15
316		50 s. green	75	15
317		1 b. blue and violet	5·00	15
318		2 b. green and blue	13·00	90
319		3 b. black and red	20·00	2·00
320		5 b. red and green	45·00	3·00
321		10 b. violet and brown	£180	1·00
322		20 b. purple and black	£225	3·75

The baht values are larger, size 21½×27 mm.

1947. Coming of Age of King Bhumibol. With gum (10, 50 s.) or without gum (others).

323	**93**	5 s. orange	1·00	1·00
324		10 s. brown	38·00	40·00
325		10 s. green	1·00	1·00
326		20 s. blue	3·00	1·00
327		50 s. green	7·50	2·00

94 King and Palace　**95** King Bhumibol

1950. King's Coronation.

328	**94**	5 s. purple	25	15
329		10 s. red	50	15
330		15 s. violet	1·75	1·75
331		20 s. brown	50	15
332		80 s. green	5·50	2·50
333		1 b. blue	2·00	15
334		2 b. yellow	8·00	1·00
335		3 b. grey	35·00	6·00

1951.

336	**95**	5 s. purple	25	10
337		10 s. green	25	10
338		15 s. brown	75	15
339		20 s. brown	75	10
340		25 s. red	25	10
341		50 s. green	75	10
342		1 b. blue	1·00	15
343		1 b. 15 blue	25	15
344		1 b. 25 red	3·75	25
345		2 b. green	4·50	25
346		3 b. grey	7·50	40
347		5 b. red and blue	30·00	50
348		10 b. violet and brown	£180	90
349		20 b. green and black	£160	9·00

96 U.N. Emblem　**97** "Garuda" Bird

1951. United Nations Day.

350	**96**	25 s. blue	2·50	2·50

1952. Air.

351	**97**	1 b. purple	1·25	25
352		2 b. blue	7·50	1·50
353		3 b. grey	10·00	75

1952. United Nations Day. Optd **1952**.

354	**96**	25 s. blue	1·50	1·50

1952. 20th Anniv of Constitution. Surch with Vase emblem and **+20** in English and Siamese.

355	**76**	80 s. + 20 s. black & blue	12·00	11·00

99 Dancer over Cross　**103** Processional Elephant

1953. 60th Anniv of Thai Red Cross Society. Cross in red, figures in blue and red.

356	**99**	25 s. + 25 s. cream & green	3·75	3·75
357		50 s. + 50 s. cream & pink	13·00	13·00
358		1 b. + 1 b. cream & blue	15·00	15·00

1953. United Nations Day. Optd **1953**.

359	**96**	25 s. blue	1·00	1·00

1954. United Nations Day. Optd **1954** vert.

360	**96**	25 s. blue	2·50	2·50

1955. Optd **THAILAND** in English and Siamese.

361	**76**	5 s. violet	3·75	5·00
362		10 s. red	3·75	5·00

1955. Surch.

363	**92**	5 s. on 20 s. brown	1·00	35
364		10 s. on 20 s. brown	1·50	35

1955. 400th Birth Anniv of King Naresuan.

365	**103**	25 s. red	75	15
366		80 s. purple	13·00	4·00
367		1 b. 25 green	30·00	75
368		2 b. blue	7·00	1·10
369		3 b. brown	26·00	60

1955. Red Cross Fair. Optd **24 98**.

370	**99**	25 s. + 25 s. multicoloured	13·00	13·00
371		50 s. + 50 s. multicoloured	75·00	75·00
372		1 b. + 1 b. red, cream & blue	£100	£100

105 Tao Suranari　**106** Equestrian Statue

1955. Tao Suranari Commemoration.

373	**105**	10 s. lilac	75	25
374		25 s. green	50	15
375		1 b. brown	24·00	1·60

1955. King Taksin Commemoration.

376	**106**	5 s. blue	75	25
377		25 s. green	5·50	10
378		1 b. 25 red	21·00	1·75

1955. U.N. Day. Optd **1955** vert.

379	**96**	25 s. blue	2·50	2·50

107 Don Chedi Pagoda　**108** Dharmachakra and Sambar

1956.

380	**107**	10 s. green	1·25	1·10
381		50 s. brown	13·00	1·00
382		75 s. violet	3·75	75
383		1 b. 50 brown	13·00	75

1956. U.N. Day. Optd **1956** vert.

384	**96**	25 s. blue	1·25	1·25

1957. 2500th Anniv of Buddhist Era.

385	**108**	5 s. brown	50	15
386		10 s. purple	50	15
387		15 s. green	1·25	1·00
388	–	20 s. orange	1·25	1·00
389	–	25 s. brown	25	10
390	–	50 s. mauve	1·00	30
391	–	1 b. brown	1·50	40
392	–	1 b. 25 blue	20·00	2·75
393	–	2 b. purple	3·75	50

DESIGNS: 20 s. to 50 s. Hand of Peace and Dharmachakra; 1 b. to 2 b. Nakon Phatom pagoda.

110 U.N. Emblem and Laurel Sprays　**111** Gateway to Grand Palace

1957. United Nations Day.
394 110 25 s. green 60 25
395 25 s. brown (1958) 60 25
400 25 s. blue (1959) 75 25

1959. 1st South-East Asia Peninsula Games.
396 111 10 s. orange 25 15
397 – 25 s. red 40 15
398 – 1 b. 25 green 1·90 1·00
399 – 2 b. blue 2·00 50
DESIGNS: 25 s. Royal parasols; 1 b. 25, Bowman; 2 b. Wat Arun (temple) and prow of royal barge.

112 Pagoda **113** Wat Arun Temple

1960. World Refugee Year.
401 112 50 s. brown 25 10
402 2 b. green 75 40

1960. Leprosy Relief Campaign.
403 113 50 s. red 25 10
404 2 b. blue 1·75 45

114 Indian Elephant **115** S.E.A.T.O. Emblem

1960. 5th World Forestry Congress, Seattle.
405 114 25 s. green 50 15

1960. S.E.A.T.O. Day.
406 115 50 s. brown 60 15

116 Siamese Child **117** Letter-writing

1960. Children's Day.
407 116 50 s. mauve 25 10
408 1 b. brown 1·75 45

1960. International Correspondence Week.
409 117 50 s. mauve 35 10
410 2 b. blue 2·10 55

118 U.N. Emblem and Globe **119** King Bhumibol

1960. U.N. Day.
411 118 50 s. violet 50 15
446 50 s. red (1961) 35 15
467 50 s. red (1962) 35 15

1961.
422 119 5 s. purple 15 10
423 10 s. green 15 10
424 15 s. brown 25 10
425 20 s. brown 15 10
426 25 s. red 25 10
427 50 s. green 25 10
428 80 s. orange 1·25 65
429 1 b. brown and blue 90 15
430 1 b. 25 green and red 2·50 50
431 1 b. 50 green and violet 80 15
432 2 b. violet and red 1·10 10
433 3 b. blue and brown 2·75 25
434 4 b. black and bistre 3·00 1·00
435 5 b. green and blue 9·00 30
436 10 b. black and red 45·00 40
437 20 b. blue and green 40·00 2·00
438 25 b. blue and green 15·00 1·25
439 40 b. black and yellow 32·00 3·00

120 Children in Garden

1961. Children's Day.
440 120 10 s. blue 50 15
441 2 b. violet 1·50 50

121 Pen, Letters and Globe **122** Thai Scout Badge and Saluting Hand

1961. International Correspondence Week.
442 – 25 s. myrtle 25 15
443 – 50 s. purple 15 10
444 121 1 b. red 80 35
445 2 b. blue 90 40
DESIGN: 25 s., 50 s. Pen, and world map on envelope.

1961. 50th Anniv of Thai Scout Movement.
447 122 50 s. red 25 15
448 – 1 b. green 50 40
449 – 2 b. blue 75 50
DESIGNS—VERT: 1 b. Scout camp and scout saluting flag; 2 b. King Vajiravudh in uniform, and scout, cub and guide marching.

123 Campaign Emblem and Temple **124** Bangkok

1962. Malaria Eradication.
450 123 5 s. brown 15 10
451 10 s. brown 15 10
452 20 s. blue 15 10
453 50 s. red 15 10
454 – 1 b. green 75 15
455 – 1 b. 50 purple 1·75 50
456 – 2 b. blue 1·00 25
457 – 3 b. violet 3·25 1·75
DESIGN: 1 b. to 3 b. Hanuman fighting mosquitoes.

1962. "Century 21" Exhibition, Seattle.
458 124 50 s. purple 50 15
459 2 b. blue 3·25 50

125 Thai Child with Doll **126** Correspondence Symbols **127** Exhibition Emblem

1962. Children's Day.
460 125 25 s. green 40 15
461 50 s. brown 50 10
462 2 b. mauve 3·75 55

1962. International Correspondence Week.
463 126 25 s. violet 25 15
464 50 s. red 25 10
465 – 1 b. bistre 2·00 30
466 – 2 b. green 3·75 50
DESIGN: 1, 2 b. Quill pen.

1962. Students' Exhibition, Bangkok.
468 127 50 s. bistre 60 15

128 Harvesting

1963. Freedom from Hunger.
469 128 20 s. green 60 25
470 50 s. brown 50 15

129 "Temple Guardian" **130** Centenary Emblem

1963. 1st Anniv of Asian-Oceanic Postal Union.
471 129 50 s. green and brown 50 10

1963. Red Cross Centenary.
472 130 50 s. + 10 s. red & grey 20 15
473 – 50 s. + 10 s. red & grey 20 15
DESIGN: No. 473, As Type **130**, but with positions of emblem and inscriptions reversed.

131 G.P.O. Bangkok and (inset) old P.O.

1963. 80th Anniv of Post and Telegraph Department.
474 131 50 s. green, orange and violet 75 15
475 3 b. brown, green and red 3·00 1·10

132 King Bhumibol **133** Children with Dolls

1963.
476 132 5 s. mauve 10 10
477 10 s. green 10 10
478 15 s. brown 10 10
479 20 s. brown 10 10
480 25 s. red 10 10
481 50 s. green 15 10
482 75 s. lilac 25 10
483 80 s. orange 75 30
484 1 b. brown and blue 75 15
485 1 b. 25 bistre and brown 3·75 75
486 1 b. 50 green and violet 75 15
487 2 b. violet and red 60 10
488 3 b. blue and brown 1·25 20
489 4 b. black and bistre 1·50 25
490 5 b. green and blue 5·50 25
491 10 b. black and red 10·00 55
492 20 b. blue and green 85·00 3·25
493 25 b. blue and green 7·75 50
494 40 b. black and yellow 70·00 3·75

1963. Children's Day.
505 133 50 s. red 25 10
506 2 b. blue 3·50 45

134 "Garuda" Bird with Scroll in Beak

1963. International Correspondence Week.
507 134 50 s. purple & turquoise 50 15
508 1 b. purple and green 2·00 40
509 – 2 b. blue and brown 20·00 50
510 – 3 b. green and brown 7·50 2·00
DESIGN: 2 b., 3 b. Thai women writing letters.

135 U.N. Emblem **137** Mother and Child

136 King Bhumibol

1963. U.N. Day.
511 135 50 s. blue 35 10

1963. King Bhumibol's 36th Birthday.
512 136 1 b. 50 indigo, yellow & bl 1·25 25
513 5 b. blue, yellow & mauve 10·00 1·50

1964. 17th Anniv of U.N.I.C.E.F.
514 137 50 s. blue 25 10
515 2 b. green 2·25 35

138 "Hand" of Flags, Pigeon and Globe

1964. International Correspondence Week.
516 138 50 s. mauve and green 25 10
517 – 1 b. brown and green 2·25 30
518 – 2 b. violet and yellow 7·50 35
519 – 3 b. brown and blue 2·50 1·25
DESIGNS: 1 b. Thai girls and map; 2 b. Map, pen and pencil; 3 b. Hand with quill pen, and globe.

139 Globe and U.N. Emblem **140** King Bhumibol and Queen Sirikit

1964. United Nations Day.
520 139 50 s. grey 75 10

1965. 15th Royal Wedding Anniv.
521 140 2 b. multicoloured 3·75 25
522 5 b. multicoloured 9·00 1·50

141 I.T.U. Emblem and Symbols

1965. I.T.U. Centenary.
523 141 1 b. green 2·50 35

142 Goddess, Letters and Globes

1965. International Correspondence Week. Mult.
524 50 s. Type **142** 25 10
525 1 b. Type **142** 2·25 30
526 2 b. Handclasp, letters and world map 8·00 40
527 3 b. As 2 b. 12·00 1·75

143 Grand Palace, Bangkok **145** U.P.U. Monument, Berne, and Map of Thailand

1965. International Co-operation Year and 20th Anniv of United Nations.
528 143 50 s. lt blue, yellow & bl 1·00 10

1965. 80th Anniv of Thailand's Admission to Universal Postal Union.
529 145 20 s. blue and mauve 25 10
530 50 s. black and blue 50 15
531 1 b. brown and blue 3·00 30
532 3 b. green and brown 8·00 1·50

146 Child and Lotus

1965. Children's Day.
533 146 50 s. brown and black 35 10
534 – 1 b. green and black 1·50 15
DESIGN: 1 b. Child mounting stairs.

147 Cycling

1966. Publicity for 5th Asian Games, Bangkok.
535 20 s. red (Type **147**) 25 10
536 25 s. violet (Tennis) 50 15
537 50 s. red (Running) 25 10
538 1 b. blue (Weightlifting) 1·50 25
539 1 b. 25 black (Boxing) 2·50 1·50
540 2 b. blue (Swimming) 5·00 25
541 3 b. brown (Basketball) 11·00 2·40
542 5 b. purple (Football) 32·00 8·00
See also Nos. 553/6.

148 Emblem and Fair Buildings **149** "Reading and Writing"

1966. 1st International Trade Fair, Bangkok.

543 **148** 50 s. purple 75 25
544 1 b. brown 1·25 50

1966. International Correspondence Week.

545 – 50 s. red 25 10
546 – 1 b. brown 1·00 20
547 **149** 2 b. violet 7·50 25
548 3 b. green 2·50 1·50

DESIGN: 50 s., 1 b. "Map" envelope representing the five continents and pen.

150 U.N. Emblem **151** Pra Buddha Bata (monastery)

1966. United Nations Day.

549 **150** 50 s. blue 50 10

1966. 20th Anniv of U.N.E.S.C.O.

550 **151** 50 s. green and black 35 10

152 "Goddess of Rice"

1966. International Rice Year.

551 **152** 50 s. blue and green 1·25 25
552 3 b. red and purple 7·50 2·25

153 Thai Boxing

1966. 5th Asian Games, Bangkok. Each black, red and brown.

553 50 s. Type **153** 50 15
554 1 b. Takraw (ball game) 2·00 90
555 2 b. "Kite fighting" 16·00 1·50
556 3 b. "Cudgel play" 12·50 6·50

154 "Channa striatus"

1967. Fishes. Multicoloured.

557 1 b. Type **154** 2·50 75
558 2 b. "Rastrelliger brachysomus" 17·00 1·25
559 3 b. "Puntius gonionotus" 7·50 3·00
560 5 b. "Betta splendens" 10·00 3·75

The 2 and 3 b. are size 45×26 mm.

155 Djarmachakra and Globe

1967. Establishment of Buddhist World Fellowship Headquarters in Thailand.

561 **155** 2 b. black and yellow 2·50 50

156 Great Indian Hornbill **157** "Vandopsis parishii"

1967. Birds. Multicoloured.

562 20 s. Type **156** 50 25
563 25 s. Hill ("inscr "Talking") myna 75 50
564 50 s. White-rumped shama 1·25 15
565 1 b. Siamese ("Diard's") fireback pheasant 2·50 75
566 1 b. 50 Spotted dove (inscr "Spotted-necked") 2·50 85
567 2 b. Sarus crane 15·00 1·25
568 3 b. White-breasted kingfisher 7·50 3·75
569 5 b. Asian open-bill stork 16·00 5·00

1967. Thai Orchids. Multicoloured.

570 20 s. Type **157** 50 25
571 50 s. "Ascocentrum curvifolium" 75 15
572 80 s. "Rhynchostylis retusa" 1·25 85
573 1 b. "Rhynchostylis gigantea 2·50 75
574 1 b. 50 "Dendrobium alconeri" 2·50 75
575 2 b. "Paphiopedilum callosum" 12·50 1·00
576 3 b. "Dendrobium formosum" 7·50 3·75
577 5 b. "Dendrobium primulinum" 14·50 5·00

158 Thai House

1967. Thai Architecture.

578 **158** 50 s. violet and blue 80 25
579 – 1 b. 50 chestnut & brown 1·75 1·00
580 – 2 b. blue and turquoise 11·00 1·25
581 – 3 b. brown and yellow 7·75 5·00

BUILDINGS: 1 b. 50, Pagodas; 2 b. Temple bell-tower; 3 b. Temple.

159 "Sri Suphanahong" (royal barge) and Palace

1967. International Tourist Year.

582 **159** 2 b. brown and blue 3·00 50

160 Dove, Globe, People and Letters

1967. International Correspondence Week.

583 **160** 50 s. multicoloured 25 10
584 1 b. multicoloured 1·00 30
585 – 2 b. black and green 3·75 40
586 – 3 b. black and brown 5·00 1·75

DESIGNS: 2, 3 b. Handclasp, globe and doves.

161 U.N. Emblem

1967. U.N. Day.

587 **161** 50 s. multicoloured 35 10

162 National Flag

1967. 50th Anniv of Thai National Flag.

588 **162** 50 s. red, blue & turquoise 35 10
589 2 b. red, blue and green 3·50 90

163 Elephant carrying Teak Log

1968. Export Promotion.

590 **163** 2 b. brown and red 2·50 25

See also Nos. 630, 655 and 673.

164 Satellite and Thai Tracking Station

1968. "Satellite Communications".

591 **164** 50 s. multicoloured 25 10
592 3 b. multicoloured 1·75 80

165 "Goddess of the Earth"

1968. International Hydrological Decade.

593 **165** 50 s. multicoloured 40 10

166 Snakeskin Gourami

1968. Thai Fishes. Multicoloured.

594 10 s. Type **166** 25 10
595 20 s. Red-tailed black shark 25 15
596 25 s. Barb 50 15
597 50 s. Giant catfish 75 15
598 80 s. Thai catfish 1·25 1·00
599 1 b. 25 Goby 3·75 2·00
600 1 b. 50 Thai carp 11·50 1·50
601 4 b. Knife fish 28·00 8·75

167 Blue Peacock

1968. Thai Butterflies. Multicoloured.

602 50 s. Type **167** 70 15
603 1 b. Golden birdwing 3·75 60
604 3 b. Great mormon 12·00 3·00
605 4 b. "Papilio palinurus" 19·00 6·50

168 Queen Sirikit

1968. Queen Sirikit's "Third Cycle" Anniversary. Designs showing Queen Sirikit in different Thai costumes.

606 **168** 50 s. multicoloured 15 10
607 – 2 b. multicoloured 1·25 45
608 – 3 b. multicoloured 2·75 1·40
609 – 5 b. multicoloured 6·50 1·40

169 W.H.O. Emblem and Medical Equipment

1968. 20th Anniv of W.H.O.

610 **169** 50 s. black and green 40 10

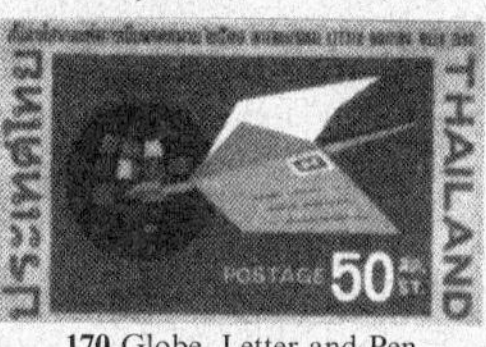

170 Globe, Letter and Pen

1968. International Correspondence Week. Mult.

611 50 s. Type **170** 25 10
612 1 b. Globe on pen nib 80 20
613 2 b. Type **170** 1·50 30
614 3 b. Globe on pen nib 4·00 1·40

171 U.N. Emblem and Flags **173** King Rama II

172 Human Rights Emblem and Sculpture

1968. United Nations Day.

615 **171** 50 s. multicoloured 40 10

1968. 20th Anniv of Human Rights Year.

616 **172** 50 s. violet, red and green 50 10

1968. Birth Bicentenary of King Rama II.

617 **173** 50 s. yellow and brown 25 10

174 National Assembly Building

1969. First Election Day under New Constitution.

618 **174** 50 s. multicoloured 25 10
619 2 b. multicoloured 1·75 45

175 I.L.O. Emblem within Cogwheels

1969. 50th Anniv of I.L.O.

620 **175** 50 s. blue, black & violet 25 10

176 Ramwong Dance

1969. Thai Classical Dances. Multicoloured.

621 50 s. Type **176** 25 10
622 1 b. Candle dance 80 30
623 2 b. Krathop Mai dance 1·60 25
624 3 b. Nohra dance 2·75 1·60

177 "Letters by Post"

1969. International Correspondence Week. Mult.

625 50 s. Type **177** 15 10
626 1 b. Type **177** 40 20
627 2 b. Writing and posting a letter 1·00 30
628 3 b. As 2 b. 1·60 80

178 Globe in Hand

1969. United Nations Day.

629 **178** 50 s. multicoloured 25 10

179 Tin Mine

1969. Export Promotion and 2nd Technical Conf of the International Tin Council, Bangkok.
630 **179** 2 b. blue, brown and light blue . . . . 2·00 25

180 Loy Krathong Festival

1969. Thai Ceremonies and Festivals. Multicoloured.
631 50 s. Type **180** 15 10
632 1 b. Marriage ceremony . . . 65 20
633 2 b. Khwan ceremony 80 25
634 5 b. Songkran festival . . . . 2·40 90

181 Breguet 14 Mail Plane

1969. 50th Anniv of Thai Airmail Services.
635 **181** 1 b. brown, green & blue . 65 15

182 "Phra Rama"

1969. Nang Yai Shadow Theatre. Multicoloured.
636 50 s. Type **182** 25 10
637 2 b. "Ramasura" . . . . . . 2·00 20
638 3 b. "Mekhala" . . . . . . 1·60 75
639 5 b. "Ongkhot" . . . . . . 2·75 75

183 "Improvement of Productivity"

1969. Productivity Year.
640 **183** 50 s. multicoloured . . . 25 10

184 Thai Temples within I.C.W. Emblem

1970. 19th Triennial Conference of International Council of Women, Bangkok.
641 **184** 50 s. black and blue . . . 40 10

185 Dish Aerials

1970. 3rd Anniv of Thai Satellite Communications.
642 **185** 50 s. multicoloured . . . 25 10

MINIMUM PRICE

The minimum price quoted is 10p which represents a handling charge rather than a basis for valuing common stamps. For further notes about prices, see introductory pages.

186 Households and Data

1970. 7th Population Census.
643 **186** 1 b. multicoloured . . . 25 10

187 New Headquarters Building

1970. Inauguration of New U.P.U. Headquarters Building, Berne.
644 **187** 50 s. black, green & blue 25 10

188 Khun Ram Kamhang as Teacher

1970. International Education Year.
645 **188** 50 s. multicoloured . . . 25 10

189 Swimming Stadium

1970. 6th Asian Games, Bangkok.
646 **189** 50 s. lilac, red & yellow . 25 15
647 – 1 b. 50 green, red & blue 55 20
648 – 3 b. black, red & bronze . 1·25 30
649 – 5 b. blue, red and green . 1·40 80
STADIUMS: 1 b. 50, Velodrome; 3 b. Subhajalasaya Stadium; 5 b. Kittikachorn Indoor Stadium.
See also No. 660.

190 Boy and Girl writing Letter

1970. International Correspondence Week. Mult.
650 50 s. Type **190** 15 10
651 1 b. Woman writing letter . . 55 20
652 2 b. Women reading letters . 1·25 30
653 3 b. Man reading letter . . . 1·40 80
See also Nos. 683/6.

191 U.N. Emblem and Royal Palace, Bangkok

194 King Bhumibol lighting Flame

193 The Heroes of Bangrachan

1970. 25th Anniv of United Nations.
654 **191** 50 s. multicoloured . . . 55 10

1970. Export Promotion. As T **163**.
655 2 b. brn, red and green . . . 1·25 20
DESIGN: 2 b. Rubber plantation.

1970. Heroes and Heroines of Thai History.
656 **193** 50 s. violet and red 25 10
657 – 1 b. purple and violet . . . 65 30
658 – 2 b. brown and mauve . . 1·25 50
659 – 3 b. green and blue . . . . 1·10 65
DESIGNS: 1 b. Heroines Thao Thepkrasatri and Thao Srisunthorn on ramparts; 2 b. Queen Suriyothai riding elephant; 3 b. Phraya Phichaidaphak and battle scene.

1970. Inaug of 6th Asian Games, Bangkok.
660 **194** 1 b. multicoloured 25 10

195 Woman playing So Sam Sai

1970. Classical Thai Musical Instruments. Mult
661 50 s. Type **195** 25 10
662 2 b. Khlui phiang-o (flute) . . 80 20
663 3 b. Krachappi (guitar) . . . . 1·60 40
664 5 b. Thon rammana (drums) 2·75 80

196 Chocolate-pointed Siamese

1971. Siamese Cats. Multicoloured.
665 50 s. Type **196** 15 10
666 1 b. Blue-pointed cat 90 35
667 2 b. Seal-pointed cat . . . . . 1·60 30
668 3 b. Pure white cat and kittens 2·75 1·40

197 Pagoda, Nakhon Si Thammarat

1971. Buddhist Holy Places in Thailand. Pagodas.
669 **197** 50 s. black, brown & mauve 25 10
670 – 1 b. brown, violet & grn . 50 20
671 – 3 b. sepia, brown & orange 1·40 30
672 – 4 b. brown, sepia & blue . 1·90 1·60
DESIGNS: 1 b. Nakhon Phanom; 3 b. Nakhon Pathom; 4 b. Chiang Mai.

1971. Export Promotion. As T **163**.
673 2 b. multicoloured . . . . . . 1·00 20
DESIGN: 2 b. Corncob and field.

199 Buddha's Birthplace, Lumbini, Nepal

1971. 20th Anniv of World Fellowship of Buddhists.
674 **199** 50 s. black and blue . . . 15 10
675 – 1 b. black and green . . . 55 20
676 – 2 b. black and brown . . . 1·25 25
677 – 3 b. black and red . . . . 1·10 80
DESIGNS: 1 b. "Place of Enlightenment", Buddha Gaya, Bihar; 2 b. "Place of First Sermon", Sarnath, Banaras; 3 b. "Place of Final Passing Away", Kusinara.

200 King Bhumibol and Thai People

201 Floating Market, Wat Sai

1971. 25th Anniv of Coronation.
678 **200** 50 s. multicoloured 20 10

1971. Visit ASEAN Year.
679 **201** 4 b. multicoloured . . . . 1·40 30
ASEAN = Association of South East Asian Nations.

202 King and Queen in Scout Uniform

1971. 60th Anniv of Thai Boy Scout Movement.
680 **202** 50 c. black, red & yellow . 25 10

1971. "THAILANDAPEX 71" National Stamp Exhibition, Bangkok. Optd 4–8 AUGUST 1971 **THAILANDPEX'71** in English and Thai and map within "perforations", covering four stamps.
681 **119** 80 s. orange . . . . . . 2·00 2·00
682 **132** 80 s. orange . . . . . . 2·00 2·00
Prices are for blocks of four stamps showing the entire overprint.

1971. International Correspondence Week. As T **190**. Multicoloured.
683 50 s. Two girls writing a letter 15 10
684 1 b. Two girls reading letters 40 20
685 2 b. Women with letter on veranda . . . . 1·10 25
686 3 b. Man handing letter to woman . . . . 1·60 60

205 Marble Temple, Bangkok

1971. United Nations Day.
687 **205** 50 s. multicoloured . . . 25 10

206 Raising Ducks

1971. Rural Life. Multicoloured.
688 50 s. Type **206** 15 10
689 1 b. Growing tobacco seedlings 40 30
690 2 b. Cooping fish 80 20
691 3 b. Cleaning rice-seed . . . . 1·40 65

207 Mother and Child

1971. 25th Anniv of U.N.I.C.E.F.
692 **207** 50 s. multicoloured . . . 25 10

208 Costumes from Chiang Saen Period (17th-century)

1972. Historical Costumes. Multicoloured.
693 50 s. Type **208** 15 10
694 1 b. Sukhothai period (13th-14th centuries) 40 20
695 1 b. 50 Ayudhya period (14th-17th centuries) 80 25
696 2 b. Bangkok period (18th-19th centuries) . . . . 1·90 50

209 Globe and A.O.P.U. Emblem

1972. 10th Anniv of Asian–Oceanic Postal Union.
697 **209** 75 s. blue 25 10

210 King Bhumibol

1972.

698	**210**	10 s. green	10	10
699		20 s. blue	15	10
700		25 s. red	15	10
701		50 s. green	20	10
702		75 s. lilac	15	10
703		1 b. 25 pink and green	55	15
704		2 b. violet and red	25	10
705		2 b. 75 turquoise and purple	55	10
706		3 b. blue and brown	2·10	15
707		4 b. red and blue	80	15
708		5 b. brown and violet	80	10
709		6 b. violet and green	2·10	20
710		10 b. black and red	90	15
711		20 b. green and orange	3·00	75
898d		40 b. violet and brown	2·75	65
712a		50 b. green and purple	20·00	1·75
713		100 b. blue and orange	40·00	4·00

211 Two Women, Iko Tribe

1972. Hill Tribes of Thailand. Multicoloured.

714	50 s. Type **211**	15	10
715	2 b. Musician and children, Musoe tribe	90	20
716	4 b. Woman embroidering, Yao tribe	4·25	2·40
717	5 b. Woman with chickens, Maeo tribe	5·50	60

212 Ruby

1972. Precious Stones.

718	**212**	75 s. multicoloured	25	10
719	–	2 b. multicoloured	3·75	35
720	–	4 b. black and green	5·25	2·50
721	–	6 b. brown, black and red	11·00	2·00

DESIGNS: 2 b. Yellow sapphire; 4 b. Zircon; 6 b. Star sapphire.

213 Prince Vajiralongkorn

214 Thai Ruan-ton Costume

1972. Prince Vajiralongkorn's 20th Birthday.

722	**213**	75 s. multicoloured	25	10

1972. Thai Women's National Costumes. Mult.

723	75 s. Type **214**	15	10
724	2 b. Thai Chitrlada	65	20
725	4 b. Thai Chakri	1·90	1·25
726	5 b. Thai Borompimarn	2·75	55

215 Rambutan

1972. Thai Fruits. Multicoloured.

728	75 s. Type **215**	15	10
729	1 b. Mangosteen	90	30
730	3 b. Durian	2·00	75
731	5 b. Mango	7·50	1·40

216 Princess-Mother with Old People

1972. Princess-Mother Sisangwan's 72nd Birthday.

732	**216**	75 s. green and orange	25	10

217 Lod Cave, Phangnga

1972. International Correspondence Week. Mult.

733	75 s. Type **217**	15	10
734	1 b. 25 Kang Kracharn Reservoir, Phetchaburi	40	20
735	2 b. 75 Erawan Waterfall, Kanchanaburi	3·25	15
736	3 b. Nok-kaw Mountain, Loei	2·10	90

218 Globe on U.N. Emblem

220 Crown Prince Vajiralongkorn

219 Watphrajetubon Vimolmanklaram Rajvaramahaviharn (ancient university)

1972. 25th Anniv of E.C.A.F.E.

737	**218**	75 s. multicoloured	25	10

1972. International Book Year.

738	**219**	75 s. multicoloured	25	10

1972. Investiture of Crown Prince.

739	**220**	2 b. multicoloured	50	15

221 Servicemen and Flag

1973. 25th Anniv of Veterans' Day.

740	**221**	75 s. multicoloured	25	10

1973. Red Cross Fair (1972). Nos. 472/3 surch **75+25 2515 1972**.

741	**130**	75 s. + 25 s. on 50 s. + 10 s.	50	50
742	–	75 s. + 25 s. on 50 s. + 10 s.	50	50

223 Emblem, Bank and Coin-box

1973. 60th Anniv of Government Savings Bank.

743	**223**	75 s. multicoloured	25	10

224 "Celestial Being" and Emblem

1973. 25th Anniv of W.H.O.

744	**224**	75 s. multicoloured	25	10

225 "Nymphaea pubescens"

1973. Lotus Flowers. Multicoloured.

745	75 s. Type **225**	25	10
746	1 b. 50 "Nymphaea pubescens" (different)	50	30
747	2 b. "Nelumbo nucifera"	1·75	25
748	4 b. "Nelumbo nucifera" (different)	4·75	1·25

227 King Bhumibol

1973.

749	**227**	5 s. purple	15	10
1031		20 s. blue	15	10
1031a		25 s. red	15	10
1032		50 s. green	50	10
1032a		75 s. violet	15	10
753		5 b. brown and violet	2·25	50
754		6 b. violet and green	1·40	50
755		10 b. brown and red	4·00	75
755a		20 b. green and orange	55·00	5·50

228 Silverware

1973. Thai Handicrafts. Multicoloured.

756	75 s. Type **228**	25	10
757	2 b. 75 Lacquerware	1·00	20
758	4 b. Pottery	3·25	1·50
759	5 b. Paper umbrellas	3·00	50

229 King Janaka's Procession

1973. "Ramayana" Mural, Temple of Emerald Buddha, Bangkok. Multicoloured.

760	25 s. Type **229**	25	15
761	75 s. Contest for Sita's hand	15	10
762	1 b. 50 Monkey prince toppling portico	1·50	1·00
763	2 b. Monkey king breaking umbrella	2·75	90
764	2 b. 75 Maleenarj as Court chief	1·25	20
765	3 b. Sprinkling holy water	5·50	1·40
766	5 b. Tapansura fighting Rama	6·75	3·00
767	6 b. Bharata on march	2·25	1·10

230 "Postal Services"

1973. 90th Anniv of Thai Post and Telegraph Department. Multicoloured.

768	75 s. Type **230**	30	10
769	2 b. "Telecommunication Services"	90	40

231 1 Solot Stamp of 1883

1973. "THAIPEX 73" National Stamp Exn.

770	**231**	75 s. blue and red	25	10
771	–	1 b. 25 red and blue	1·00	30
772	–	1 b. 50 purple and green	1·25	50
773	–	2 b. green and orange	1·25	70

DESIGNS: 1 b. 25, 6 s. stamp of 1912; 1 b. 50, 5 s. stamp of 1928; 2 b. 3 s. stamp of 1941.

232 Interpol Emblem

1973. 50th Anniv of International Criminal Police Organization (Interpol).

775	**232**	75 s. multicoloured	25	10

233 "Lilid Pralaw"

1973. Int Correspondence Week. Characters from Thai Literature. Multicoloured.

776	75 s. Type **233**	15	10
777	1 b. 50 "Khun Chang Khun Phan"	65	30
778	2 b. "Sang Thong"	1·25	55
779	5 b. "Pha Apai Manee"	3·25	90

234 Wat Suan Dok Temple, Chiangmai

1973. United Nations Day.

781	**234**	75 s. multicoloured	25	10

235 Schomburgk's Deer

1973. Protected Wild Animals. Multicoloured.

782	20 s. Type **235**	25	10
783	25 s. Kouprey	25	10
784	75 r. Common gorals	50	10
785	1 b. 25 Water buffaloes	50	25
786	1 b. 50 Javan rhinoceros	2·75	1·50
787	2 b. Thamin	5·50	1·60
788	2 b. 75 Sumatran rhinoceros	2·75	40
789	4 b. Mainland serows	4·25	3·75

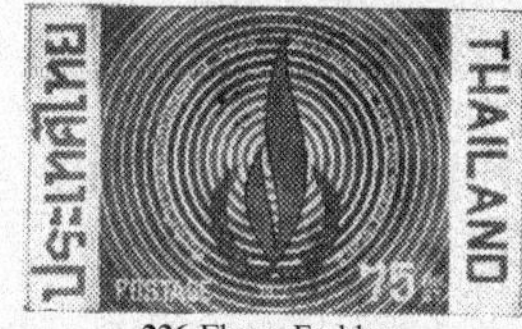
236 Flame Emblem

1973. 25th Anniv of Declaration of Human Rights.

790	**236**	75 s. multicoloured	50	10

238 Children within Flowers

241 "Pha la Phiang Lai"

240 Statue of Krom Luang Songkia Nakarin

1973. Children's Day.

791	**238**	75 s. multicoloured	40	10

1974. Red Cross Fair. Nos. 472/3 surch **75+25 1973** in English and Thai.

792	**130**	75 s.+25 s. on 50 s.+10 s.	30	30
793	–	75 s.+25 s. on 50 s.+10 s.	30	30

1974. 84th Anniv of Siriraj Hospital.

794	**240**	75 s. multicoloured	25	10

1974. Thai Classical Dance. Multicoloured.

795 75 s. Type **241** 25 10
796 2 b. 75 "Phra Lak Phlaeng Rit" 1·00 20
797 4 b. "Chin Sao Sai" . . . . . 2·50 1·40
798 5 b. "Charot Phra Sumen" . . 2·50 50

242 World's Largest Teak, Amphur Nam-Pad

1974. 15th Anniv of Arbor Day.

799 **242** 75 s. multicoloured . . . 25 10

243 "Increasing Population"

1974. World Population Year.

800 **243** 75 s. multicoloured . . . 25 10

244 Royal Chariot

1974. Centenary of National Museum. Mult.

801 75 s. Type **244** 15 10
802 2 b. Ban Chiang painted pottery vase 50 30
803 2 b. 75 Avalokitesavara Bodhisattva statue . . . . . 1·10 25
804 3 b. King Mongkut Rama IV . . 1·60 50

Nos. 802/4 have the face values incorrectly shown as "BATH".

245 "Cassia fistula"

1974. International Correspondence Week. Tropical Plants. Multicoloured.

805 75 s. Type **245** 15 10
806 2 b. 75 "Butea superba" . . . 65 20
807 3 b. "Jasminum sambac" . . . 1·75 25
808 4 b. "Lagerstroemia speciosa" 1·40 1·10

246 "UPU 100"

1974. Centenary of U.P.U.

810 **246** 75 s. multicoloured . . . 25 10

247 Wat Suthat Thepvararam

1974. United Nations Day.

811 **247** 75 s. multicoloured . . . 25 10

248 Elephant Round-up

1974. Tourism.

812 **248** 4 b. multicoloured . . . . 1·50 75

249 "Vanda coerulea"

1974. Thai Orchids (1st series). Multicoloured.

813 75 s. Type **249** 15 10
814 2 b. 75 "Dendrobium aggregatum" 65 20
815 3 b. "Dendrobium scabrilingue" 1·75 40
816 4 b. "Aerides falcata" var "houlletiana" . . . . . . 1·25 90

See also Nos. 847/50.

250 Boy riding Toy Horse

1974. Children's Day.

818 **250** 75 c. multicoloured . . . 40 10

252 Democracy Monument

1975. Democratic Institutions Campaign. Mult.

819 75 s. Type **252** 15 10
820 2 b. "Rights and Liberties" . 65 25
821 2 b. 75 "Freedom to choose work" . . . . 1·00 20
822 5 b. Top of monument and text 1·75 65

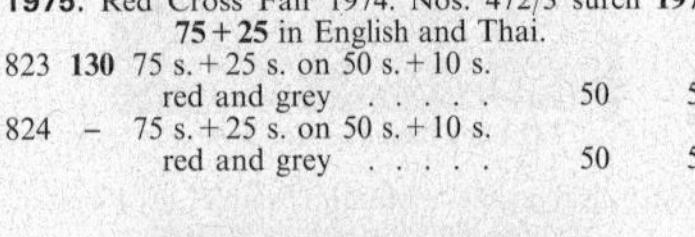

1975. Red Cross Fair 1974. Nos. 472/3 surch **1974 75+25** in English and Thai.

823 **130** 75 s.+25 s. on 50 s.+10 s. red and grey 50 50
824 – 75 s.+25 s. on 50 s.+10 s. red and grey 50 50

254 Marbled Cat

1975. Protected Wild Animals (1st series). Mult.

825 20 s. Type **254** 25 15
826 75 s. Gaur 50 10
827 2 b. 75 Indian elephant . . . 3·75 55
828 3 b. Clouded leopard . . . . 2·50 1·25

See Nos. 913/16.

255 White-eyed River Martin

1975. Thailand Birds. Multicoloured.

829 75 s. Type **255** 35 15
830 2 b. Asiatic paradise fly catcher 1·50 75
831 2 b. 75 Long-tailed broadbill 1·75 45
832 5 b. Sultan tit . . . . 3·50 1·40

256 King Bhumibol and Queen Sirikit

1975. Silver Wedding of King Bhumibol and Queen Sirikit. Multicoloured.

833 75 s. Type **256** 25 10
834 3 b. As Type **256**, but different background 50 20

257 "Roundhouse Kick"

1975. Thai Boxing. Multicoloured.

835 75 s. Type **257** 25 15
836 2 b. 75 "Reverse elbow" . . . 1·00 25
837 3 b. "Flying knee" . . . . . . 1·75 90
838 5 b. "Ritual homage" . . . . 5·25 1·40

258 Toskanth

1975. Thai Culture. Masks. Multicoloured.

839 75 s. Type **258** 15 10
840 2 b. Kumbhakarn . . . . . . 1·50 20
841 3 b. Rama . . . . 2·00 55
842 4 b. Hanuman . . . . 5·75 2·40

259 "Thaipex 75" Emblem

1975. "Thaipex 75" National Stamp Exhibition, Bangkok. Multicoloured.

843 75 s. Type **259** 25 10
844 2 b. 75 Stamp designer 75 20
845 4 b. Stamp printing works . . 1·40 90
846 5 b. "Stamp collecting" . . . . 1·50 40

1975. Thai Orchids (2nd series). As T **249**. Multicoloured.

847 75 s. "Dendrobium cruentum" 25 10
848 2 b. "Dendrobium parishii" . . 80 30
849 2 b. 75 "Vanda teres" . . . . 1·10 25
850 5 b. "Vanda denisoniana" . . 2·75 80

260 Green Mussel

1975. Sea Shells. Multicoloured.

852 75 s. Type **260** 75 50
853 1 b. Great green turban . . . 50 15
854 2 b. 75 "Oliva mustelina" . . . 2·75 25
855 5 b. Money cowrie . . . . . . 6·75 2·40

261 Yachting

1975. 8th South-East Asian Peninsula Games, Bangkok (1st issue).

856 **261** 75 s. black and blue . . . 15 10
857 – 1 b. 25 black and mauve 40 20
858 – 1 b. 50 black and red . . . 1·10 65
859 – 2 b. black and green . . . 1·60 65

DESIGNS: 1 b. 25, Badminton; 1 b. 50, Volleyball; 2 b. Rifle and pistol shooting.

See also Nos. 878/81.

262 Pataya Beach

1975. International Correspondence Week. Mult.

861 75 s. Type **262** 25 10
862 2 b. Samila Beach 80 30
863 3 b. Prachuap Bay . . . . . . 1·50 25
864 5 b. Laem Singha Bay . . . . 2·25 90

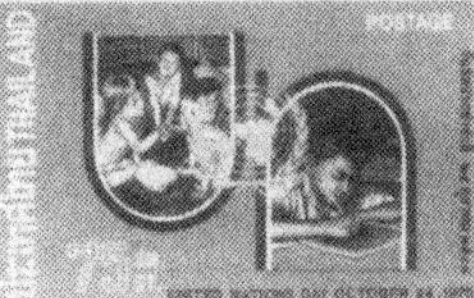

263 Children within Letters "U N"

1975. United Nations Day.

865 **263** 75 s. multicoloured . . . 25 10

264 Early Telegraphs

1975. Centenary of Telegraph Service. Mult.

866 75 s. Type **264** 40 25
867 2 b. 75 Teleprinter and dish aerial 75 25

265 "Sukhrip Khrong Muang"

1975. Thai Ceremonial Barges. Multicoloured.

868 75 s. Type **265** 25 10
869 1 b. Royal barge "Anekchat Phuchong" . . . . 1·00 40
870 2 b. Royal barge "Anantanakarat" . . . . . 1·50 50
871 2 b. 75 "Krabi Ran Ron Rap" 1·75 50
872 3 b. "Asura Wayuphak" . . . 2·75 80
873 4 b. "Asura Paksi" . . . . . 2·10 1·50
874 5 b. Royal barge "Sri Suphanahong" . . . . . . 5·50 4·00
875 6 b. "Phali Rang Thawip" . . 3·50 2·00

266 King's Cipher and Thai Crown

1975. King Bhumibol's 48th Birthday. Multicoloured.

876 75 s. Type **266** 15 10
877 5 b. King Bhumibol in uniform 90 30

267 Putting the Shot

1975. 8th South-East Asian Peninsula Games, Bangkok (2nd issue).

878 **267** 1 b. black and orange . . 25 10
879 – 2 b. black and green . . . 75 50
880 – 3 b. black and yellow . . 90 35
881 – 4 b. black and violet . . . 1·25 65

DESIGNS: 2 b. Table tennis; 3 b. Cycling; 4 b. Relay-running.

268 I.W.Y. Emblem on Globe

1975. International Women's Year.

883 **268** 75 s. blue, orange & black 25 10

269 Children writing

1976. Children's Day.
884 **269** 75 s. multicoloured . . . 25 10

270 "Macrobrachium rosenbergii"

1976. Thai Lobsters and Shrimps. Multicoloured.
885 75 s. Type **270** 25 10
886 2 b. "Penaeus merguiensis" . . 2·25 55
887 2 b. 75 "Panulirus ornatus" . . 2·00 25
888 5 b. "Penaeus monodon" . . 5·00 1·60

1976. Red Cross Fair 1975. Nos. 472/3 surch **75+25 2518 1975.**
889 **130** 75 s.+25 s. on 50 s.+10 s. red and grey 25 25
890 – 75 s.+25 s. on 50 s.+10 s. red and grey 25 25

271 Golden-backed Three-toed Woodpecker

272 Ben Chiang Pot

1976. Thailand Birds. Multicoloured.
891 1 b. Type **271** 35 20
892 1 b. 50 Greater green-billed malcoha 60 40
893 3 b. Long-billed scimitar babbler 4·75 1·60
894 4 b. Green magpie . . . . . . 1·90 80

1976. Ben Chiang Pottery.
895 **272** 1 b. multicoloured 25 10
896 – 2 b. miltcoloured . . . . 3·00 30
897 – 3 b. multicoloured . . . . 1·75 25
898 – 4 b. multicoloured . . . . 2·25 1·60
DESIGNS: 2 b. to 4 b. Various items of pottery.

273 Postman of 1883

275 "Drug Addictions"

274 Kinnari

1976. Postmen's Uniforms. Multicoloured.
899 1 b. Type **273** 25 10
900 3 b. Postman of 1935 . . . . 1·00 20
901 4 b. Postman of 1950 . . . . 1·75 1·25
902 5 b. Postman of 1974 . . . . 3·25 50

1976. Int Correspondence Week. Deities. Mult.
903 1 b. Type **274** . . . . 2·50 65
904 2 b. Suphan-Mat-Cha 25 15
905 4 b. Garuda 75 25
906 5 b. Naga . . . . 1·00 20

1976. United Nations Day.
907 **275** 1 b. multicoloured 25 10

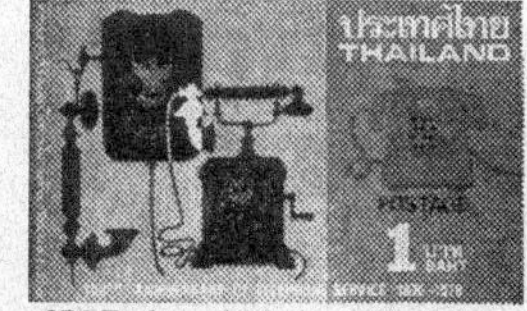

276 Early and Modern Telephones

1976. Telephone Centenary.
908 **276** 1 b. multicoloured 25 10

277 Sivalaya

1976. Thai Royal Halls. Multicoloured.
909 1 b. Type **277** 15 10
910 2 b. Cakri . . . . 3·75 30
911 4 b. Mahisra . . . . 1·75 1·00
912 5 b. Dusit . . . . 2·00 65

1976. Protected Wild Animals (2nd series). As T **254**. Multicoloured.
913 1 b. Bangteng . . . . 1·25 50
914 2 b. Malayan tapir . . . . . 1·75 75
915 4 b. Sambar 65 25
916 5 b. Hog-deer 90 25

278 "From Child to Adult"

1977. Children's Day.
917 **278** 1 b. multicoloured . . . 25 10

279 Alsthom Electric Locomotive

1977. 80th Anniv of Thai State Railway. Multicoloured.
918 1 b. Type **279** 50 10
919 2 b. Davenport electric locomotive . . . . 2·25 30
920 4 b. Pacific steam locomotive 5·75 2·50
921 5 b. George Egestoff's steam locomotive . . . . 9·50 2·10

280 University Building

1977. 60th Anniv of Chulalongkorn University.
922 **280** 1 b. multicoloured . . . 40 10

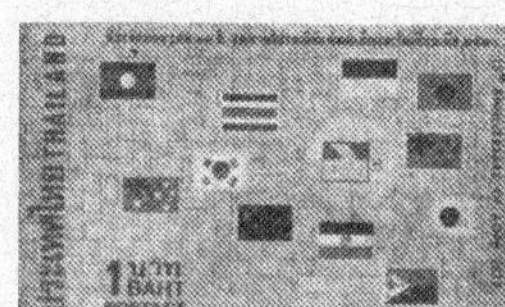

281 Flags of A.O.P.U. Countries

1977. 15th Anniv of Asian-Oceanic Postal Union.
923 **281** 1 b. multicoloured . . . 40 10

282 Crippled Ex-Serviceman

1977. Sai-Jai-Thai Foundation Day.
924 **282** 5 b. multicoloured . . . 75 15

1977. Red Cross Fair. Nos. 472/3 surch **75+25 2520–1977.**
925 **130** 75 s.+25 s. on 50 s. +10 s. red and grey 25 25
926 – 75 s.+25 s. on 50 s.+10 s. red and grey 25 25

284 Phra Aphai Mani and Phisua Samut

1977. Puppet Shows. Multicoloured.
927 2 b. Type **284** 25 10
928 3 b. Rusi and Sutsakhon . . . 1·00 20
929 4 b. Nang Vali and Usren . . . 50 25
930 5 b. Phra Aphai Mani and Nang Laweng's portrait 75 40

285 Drum Dance

1977. Thai Folk Dances. Multicoloured.
931 2 b. Type **285** 25 10
932 3 b. Dance of Dip-nets . . . . 1·00 15
933 4 b. Harvesting dance 40 20
934 5 b. Kan dance 65 25

286 1 b. Stamp of 1972

1977. "THAIPEX 77" National Stamp Exhibition.
935 **286** 75 s. multicoloured 40 10

287 "Pla Bu Thong"

1977. International Correspondence Week, Scenes from Thai Literature. Multicoloured.
936 75 s. Type **287** 50 10
937 2 b. "Krai Thong" 75 40
938 5 b. "Nang Kaew Na Ma" . . 1·25 25
939 6 b. "Pra Rot Mali . . . . . 1·25 30

288 U.N. Building, Bangkok

1977. United Nations Day.
940 **288** 75 s. multicoloured 50 10

289 King Bhumibol in Scout Uniform, and Camp Fire

1977. 9th National Scout Jamboree.
941 **289** 75 s. multicoloured 75 10

290 Map of A.S.E.A.N. Countries

1977. 10th Anniv of Association of South East Asian Nations.
942 **290** 5 b. multicoloured . . . . 1·00 20

291 Elbow and Wrist Joints

1977. World Rheumatism Year.
943 **291** 75 s. multicoloured . . . 40 10

292 Children with Thai Flag

1978. Children's Day.
944 **292** 75 s. multicoloured . . . 50 10

293 "Dendrobium heterocarpum"

1978. 9th World Orchid Conference. Mult.
945 75 s. Type **293** 50 25
946 1 b. "Dendrobium pulchellum" 75 25
947 1 b. 50 "Doritis pulcherrima var buyssoniana" . . . . 1·25 75
948 2 b. "Dendrobium hercoglossum" 25 15
949 2 b. 75 "Aerides odorata" . . 2·50 10
950 3 b. "Trichoglottis fasciata" . . 25 10
951 5 b. "Dendrobium wardianum" 40 20
952 6 b. "Dendrobium senile" . . 40 35

294 Agricultural Scenes and Rice Production Graph

1978. Agricultural Census.
953 **294** 75 s. multicoloured . . . 20 10

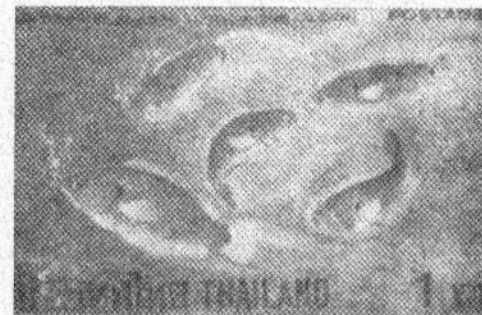

295 Blood Donation and Red Cross

1978. Red Cross.
954 **295** 2 b. 75 + 25 s. multicoloured 75 75

296 "Anabas testudineus"

1978. Fishes. Multicoloured.
955 1 b. Type **296** . . . . 1·25 65
956 2 b. "Datnioides microlepis" 15 10
957 3 b. "Kryptopterus apogon" 40 15
958 4 b. "Probarbus jullieni" . . . 50 30

297 "Birth of Prince Siddhartha"

1978. "Buddha's Story" Mural; Puthi Savan Hall, National Museum. Multicoloured.
959 2 b. Type **297** 50 15
960 3 b. "Prince Siddhartha cuts his hair" . . . . 1·00 25
961 5 b. "Buddha descends from Tavatimsa Heaven" . . . . 4·00 90
962 6 b. "Buddha enters Nirvana" 2·00 1·00

298 Bhumibol Dam

1978. Dams. Multicoloured.

963 75 s. Type **298** 50 10
964 2 b. Sirikit Dam 50 15
965 2 b. 75 Vajiralongkorn Dam 1·25 20
966 6 b. Ubolratana Dam . . . . 1·50 1·25

299 "Idea lynceus"

1978. Butterflies.

967 **299** 2 b. black, violet and red . 50 15
968 – 3 b. multicoloured 75 15
969 – 5 b. multicoloured . . . . 2·75 15
970 – 6 b. multicoloured . . . . 1·50 1·00

DESIGNS: 3 b. Eastern courtier; 5 b. "Charaxes durnfordi"; 6 b. "Cethosia penthesilea".

300 Phra Chedi Chai Mongkhon, Ayutthaya **301** Mother and Children

1978. International Correspondence Week. Mult.

971 75 s. Type **300** 25 10
972 2 b. Phra That Hariphunchai, Lamphun 40 15
973 2 b. 75 Phra Borom That Chaiya, Surat Thani . . . . 1·50 20
974 5 b. Phra That Choeng Chum, Sakon Nakhon 90 65

1978. United Nations Day.

975 **301** 75 s. multicoloured . . . 25 10

302 Basketball, Hockey and Boxing

1978. 8th Asian Games, Bangkok. Multicoloured.

976 25 s. Silhouettes of boxers, footballer & pole-vaulter . . 15 10
977 2 b. Silhouettes of Javelin-thrower, weightlifter and runner 25 15
978 3 b. Football, shuttlecock, yacht and table-tennis bat and ball 65 20
979 5 b. Type **302** . . . . 1·50 75

303 World Map and Different Races holding Hands

1978. International Anti-Apartheid Year.

980 **303** 75 s. multicoloured . . . 25 10

304 Children and S.O.S. Village, Tambol Bangpu

1979. International Year of the Child. Mult.

981 75 s. Children painting Thai flag (horiz) 75 20
982 75 s. Type **304** 25 10

305 "Matuta lunaris"

1979. Crabs. Multicoloured.

983 2 b. Type **305** 40 15
984 2 b. 75 "Matuta planipes" . . 1·75 15
985 3 b. "Portunus pelagicus" . . 65 15
986 5 b. "Scylla serrata" . . . . 1·75 75

306 Eye and Blind People **307** Sugar Apples

1979. Red Cross.

987 **306** 75 s. + 25 s. multicoloured 40 30

1979. Fruits. Multicoloured.

988 1 b. Type **307** 75 15
989 2 b. Pineapple 50 15
990 5 b. Bananas . . . . 1·50 65
991 6 b. Longans . . . . 1·00 90

308 Planting Sapling

1979. 20th Arbor Day.

992 **308** 75 s. multicoloured . . . 25 10

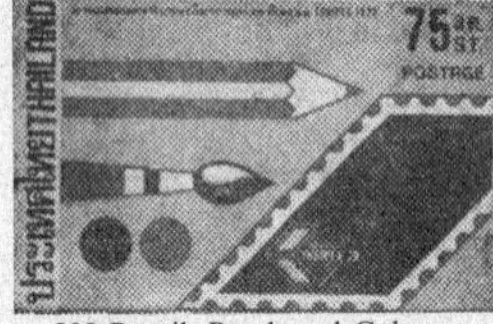

309 Pencil, Brush and Colours

1979. "Thaipex '79" National Stamp Exhibition, Bangkok. Multicoloured.

993 75 s. Type **309** 15 10
994 2 b. Envelopes 25 15
995 2 b. 75 Stamp stockbook . . 50 15
996 5 b. Tweezers, stamps and magnifying glass . . . . . 1·60 70

310 Baisi Pak Cham **311** U.N.O. Emblem, Farmer, Cattle and Wheat

1979. International Correspondence Week. Traditional Flower Arrangements. Mult.

997 75 s. Kruai upatcha (used at Buddhist ordination ceremony) 15 10
998 2 b. Type **310** (used at Braminical ceremonies) . . 25 15
999 2 b. 75 Krathong dokmai (for paying respects to elders or superiors) 50 15
1000 5 b. Phum dokmai (altar decoration) . . . . 1·60 70

1979. United Nations Day.

1001 **311** 75 s. multicoloured . . . 25 10

312 "Makutrajakumarn" (frigate)

1979. Ships of the Royal Thai Navy. Mult.

1002 2 b. Type **312** 40 15
1003 3 b. "Tapi" (frigate) 40 15
1004 5 b. "Prabparapak" (missile craft) . . . . 2·50 75
1005 6 b. T 91 (patrol boat) . . . 3·00 1·00

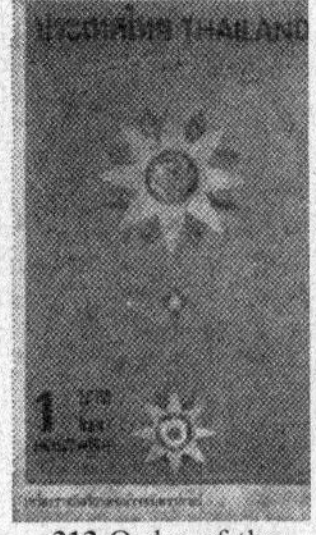

313 Order of the Rajamitrabhorn **314** Transplanting Rice

1979. Royal Orders and Decorations. Mult.

1006 1 b. Type **313** 50 25
1007 1 b. Rajamitrabhorn ribbon 50 25
1008 2 b. Order of the Royal House of Chakri 50 15
1009 2 b. Royal House of Chakri ribbon 50 15
1010 5 b. Order of the Nine Gems 1·00 40
1011 5 b. Nine Gems ribbon . . . 1·00 40
1012 6 b. Knight Grand Cross of the Order of Chula Chom Klao 1·25 50
1013 6 b. Chula Chom Klao ribbon 1·25 50

1980. Children's Day. Multicoloured.

1014 75 s. Type **314** 40 15
1015 75 s. Harvesting rice 40 15

315 Family House and Map of Thailand **316** Golden-fronted Leafbird

1980. Population and Housing Census.

1016 **315** 75 s. multicoloured . . . 20 10

1980. 9th Conference of Int Commission for Bird Preservation (Asian Section), Chiang Mai. Mult.

1017 75 s. Type **316** 25 20
1018 2 b. Chinese yellow tit 45 25
1019 3 b. Chestnut-tailed minla . . 1·10 35
1020 5 b. Scarlet minivet . . . . . 1·75 1·10

317 Extracting Snake Venom

1980. Red Cross.

1021 **317** 75 s. + 25 s. mult 40 30

318 Smokers and Diagram of Lungs

1980. World Health Day. Anti-smoking Campaign.

1022 **318** 75 s. multicoloured . . . 20 10

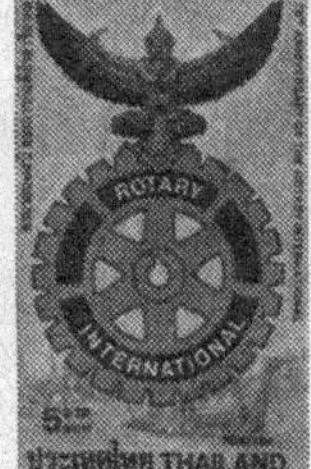

319 Garuda and Rotary Emblem

1980. 75th Anniv of Rotary International.

1023 **319** 5 b. multicoloured . . . 75 20

320 Sai Yok Falls, Kanchanaburi

1980. Waterfalls. Multicoloured.

1024 1 b. Type **320** 15 10
1025 2 b. Punyaban Falls, Ranong 25 15
1026 5 b. Heo Suwat Falls, Nakhon Ratchasima . . . . 1·00 45
1027 6 b. Siriphum Falls, Chiang Mai 90 65

321 Family and Reverse of F.A.O. Medal

1980. Queen Sirikit's "Fourth Cycle" Anniv (48th Birthday). Multicoloured.

1028 75 s. Queen Sirikit (vert) . . 15 10
1029 5 b. Type **321** 75 25
1030 5 b. Thai family and obverse of F.A.O. medal 75 25

322 Khao Phanomrung Temple, Buri Ram

1980. Int Correspondence Week. Temples. Mult.

1033 75 s. Type **322** 15 10
1034 2 b. Prang Ku Temple, Chaiyaphum 25 15
1035 2 b. 75 Phimai Temple, Nakhon Ratchasima 40 15
1036 5 b. Srikhoraphum Temple, Surin . . . . 1·00 55

323 Princess Mother **324** Golden Mount Temple, Bangkok

1980. The Princess Mother's 80th Birthday.

1037 **323** 75 s. multicoloured . . . 20 10

1980. United Nations Day.

1038 **324** 75 s. multicoloured . . . 20 10

325 King Bhumibol **326** "King Rama VII signing Constitutional Document"

1980.

1039	325	25 s. red	50	10
1179		50 s. green	1·25	10
1040		75 s. violet	15	10
1041		1 b. blue	10	10
1040a		1 b. 25 green	15	10
1180a		1 b. 50 orange	1·00	85
1041a		2 b. purple and red	3·00	15
1235b		2 b. brown	25	10
1042a		3 b. blue and brown	15	10
1042b		4 b. brown and blue	25	10
1043a		5 b. brown and lilac	25	10
1044a		6 b. lilac and green	25	10
1044b		6 b. 50 olive & green	50	15
1044c		7 b. dp brown & brn	50	10
1044d		7 b. 50 blue and red	40	20
1044e		8 b. green and brown	40	15
1045		8 b. 50 brown & green	50	20
1045a		9 b. brown and blue	45	15
1046		9 b. 50 green & olive	50	20
1047		10 b. green and red	50	10
1048		20 b. green & orange	1·00	20
1049		50 b. green and lilac	3·50	40
1050		100 b. blue & orange	5·00	90

1980. Monument to King Prajadhipok (Rama VII).

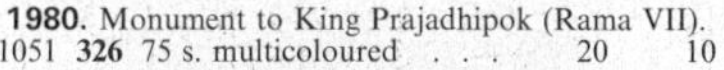

1051 **326** 75 s. multicoloured . . . 20 10

327 Bowl

1980. Bencharong Ware. Multicoloured.

1052	2 b. Type **327**	40	15
1053	2 b. 75 Covered bowls	40	15
1054	3 b. Jar	75	25
1055	5 b. Stem-plates	75	50

328 King Vajiravudh 329 "Youth in Electronics Age" (Veth Maichun)

1981. Birth Centenary of King Vajiravudh.
1056 **328** 75 s. multicoloured . . . 20 10

1981. Children's Day.
1057 **329** 75 s. multicoloured . . . 30 10

330 Mosque, Pattani Province

1981. 1400th Anniv of Hegira.
1058 **330** 5 b. multicoloured . . . 1·25 40

331 Palm Leaf Fish Mobile

1981. Int Handicraft Exhibition. Mult.

1059	75 s. Type **331**	15	10
1060	75 s. Carved teakwood elephant	15	10
1061	2 b. 75 Basketwork	50	30
1062	2 b. 75 Thai folk dolls	50	30

332 Scout aiding Cripple 334 Ongkhot

333 Red Cross Volunteer aiding Refugee

1981. Int Year of Disabled Persons. Mult.

1063	75 s. Type **332**	15	10
1064	5 b. Disabled person cutting gem-stones	65	20

1981. Red Cross.
1065 **333** 75 s. + 25 s. green and red 75 75

1981. Khon (Thai classical dance) Masks. Mult.

1066	75 s. Type **334**	15	10
1067	2 b. Maiyarab	25	15
1068	3 b. Sukrip	65	20
1069	5 b. Indrajit	75	50

336 8 a. Stamp, 1899

1981. "Thaipex '81" National Stamp Exn. Mult.

1070	75 s. Type **336**	15	10
1071	75 s. 28 s. stamp, 1910	15	10
1072	2 b. 75 50 s. stamp, 1919	50	25
1073	2 b. 75 3 s. stamp, 1932	50	25

337 Luang Praditphairo 338 Mai Hok-Hian

1981. Birth Centenary of Luang Praditphairo (musician).
1074 **337** 1 b. 25 multicoloured . 25 10

1981. International Correspondence Week. Dwarf Trees. Multicoloured.

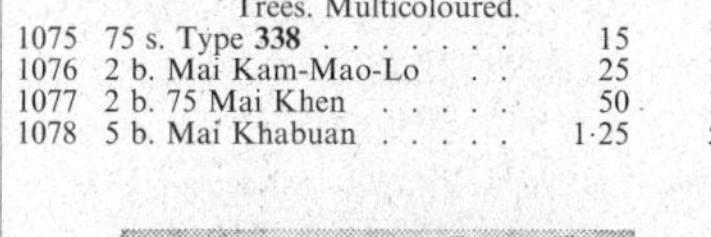

1075	75 s. Type **338**	15	10
1076	2 b. Mai Kam-Mao-Lo	25	15
1077	2 b. 75 Mai Khen	50	15
1078	5 b. Mai Khabuan	1·25	55

339 Food Produce

1981. World Food Day.
1079 **339** 75 s. multicoloured . . . 25 10

340 Samran Mukhamat Pavilion, Bangkok

1981. United Nations Day.
1080 **340** 1 b. 25 multicoloured . 25 10

341 Expressway at Klongtoey

1981. Inaug of First Thai Expressway. Mult.

1081	1 b. Type **341**	15	10
1082	5 b. Expressway interchange	1·00	30

342 King Cobra

1981. Snakes. Multicoloured.

1083	75 s. Type **342**	15	10
1084	2 b. Banded krait	50	30
1085	2 b. 75 Thai cobra	50	15
1086	5 b. Malayan pit viper	1·25	50

343 Girl carrying Child 344 Scouts reaching for Peace

1982. Children's Day.
1087 **343** 1 b. 25 multicoloured . . 25 10

1982. 75th Anniv of Boy Scout Movement.
1088 **344** 1 b. 25 multicoloured . . 25 10

345 King Buddha Yod-Fa (Rama I)

1982. Bicentenary of Chakri Dynasty and of Bangkok. Multicoloured.

1089	1 b. Type **345**	15	10
1090	1 b. 25 Aerial view of Bangkok	15	10
1091	2 b. King Buddha Lert La Naphalai (Rama II)	25	10
1092	3 b. King Nang Klao (Rama III)	75	15
1093	4 b. King Mongkut (Rama IV)	50	15
1094	5 b. King Chulalongkorn (Rama V)	1·00	25
1095	6 b. King Vajiravudh (Rama VI)	1·00	30
1096	7 b. King Prajadhipok (Rama VII)	1·25	50
1097	8 b. King Ananda Mahidol (Rama VIII)	65	25
1098	9 b. King Bhumipol Adulyadej (Rama IX)	65	30

346 Dr. Robert Koch and Cross of Lorraine

1982. Cent of Discovery of Tubercle Bacillus.
1100 **346** 1 b. 25 multicoloured . . 20 10

347 "Quisqualis indica"

1982. Flowers. Multicoloured.

1101	1 b. 25 Type **347**	15	10
1102	1 b. 50 "Murraya paniculata"	25	15
1103	6 b. 50 "Mesua ferrea"	75	40
1104	7 b. "Desmos chinensis"	65	30

348 Wat Bowon Sathan Sutthawat

1982. "Bangkok 1983" International Stamp Exhibition (1st issue). Multicoloured.

1105	1 b. 25 Type **348**	15	10
1106	4 b. 25 Wat Phra Chetuphon Wimon Mangkhalaram	40	20
1107	6 b. 50 Wat Mahathat Yuwarat Rangsarit	65	40
1108	7 b. Wat Phra Sri Rattana Satsadaram	90	25

See also Nos. 1133/4 and 1142/5.

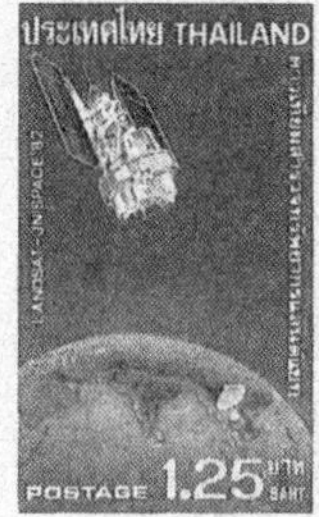

349 "Landsat" Satellite 350 Prince Purachatra

1982. 2nd U.N. Conference on the Exploration and Peaceful Uses of Outer Space, Vienna.
1110 **349** 1 b. 25 multicoloured . . 20 10

1982. Birth Centenary of Prince Purachatra.
1111 **350** 1 b. 25 multicoloured . . 20 10

351 Covered Jar

1982. International Correspondence Week. Sangalok Pottery. Multicoloured.

1112	1 b. 25 Type **351**	15	10
1113	3 b. Small jar	65	15
1114	4 b. 25 Celadon plate	50	30
1115	7 b. Plate with fish design	75	50

352 Loha Prasat, Bangkok

1982. United Nations Day.
1116 **352** 1 b. 25 multicoloured . . 20 10

353 Chap and Ching

1982. Thai Musical Instruments. Multicoloured.

1117	50 s. Type **353**	10	10
1118	1 b. Pi nok and pi nai (pipes)	30	10
1119	1 b. 25 Klong that and taphon (drums)	15	10
1120	1 b. 50 Khong mong (gong) and krap (wooden sticks)	15	15
1121	6 b. Khong wong yai (glockenspiel)	2·00	65
1122	7 b. Khong wong lek (glockenspiel)	90	25
1123	8 b. Ranat ek (xylophone)	75	40
1124	9 b. Ranat thum (xylophone)	75	40

354 Pileated Gibbon 355 Emblem and Flags of Member Countries

1982. National Wild Animal Preservation Day. Monkeys. Multicoloured.

1125 1 b. 25 Type **354** 15 10
1126 3 b. Pigtail macaque 90 20
1127 5 b. Slow loris 50 40
1128 7 b. Silvered leaf monkey . . 75 40

1982. 15th Anniv of Association of South-East Asian Nations.

1129 **355** 6 b. 50 multicoloured . . 75 25

356 Child sweeping

1983. Children's Day.

1130 **356** 1 b. 25 multicoloured . . 20 10

357 Postcodes

1983. 1st Anniv of Postcodes. Multicoloured.

1131 1 b. 25 Type **357** 25 10
1132 1 b. 25 Postcoded envelope 25 10

358 Old General Post Office

1983. "Bangkok 1983" International Stamp Exhibition (2nd issue).

1133 **358** 7 b. multicoloured . . . 75 20
1134 10 b. multicoloured . . . 1·25 30

359 Junks

1983. 25th Anniv of International Maritime Organization.

1136 **359** 1 b. 25 multicoloured . . 20 10

360 Civil Servant's Shoulder Strap

362 Prince Sithiporn Kridakara

361 Giving and receiving Aid and Red Cross

1983. Civil Servants' Day.

1137 **360** 1 b. 25 multicoloured . . 20 10

1983. Red Cross.

1138 **361** 1 b. 25+25 s. multicoloured 50 50

1983. Birth Centenary of Prince Sithiporn Kridakara (agriculturalist).

1139 **362** 1 b. 25 multicoloured . . 20 10

363 Satellite, Map and Dish Aeria

1983. Domestic Satellite Communications System.

1140 **363** 2 b. multicoloured . . . 25 10

364 Prince Bhanurangsi

366 Cable Map of A.S.E.A.N. Countries and Cable Ship

365 Post Box Clearance

1983. Prince Bhanurangsi (founder of Thai postal service) Commemoration.

1141 **364** 1 b. 25 multicoloured . 25 10

1983. "Bangkok 1983" International Stamp Exhibition (3rd issue). Multicoloured.

1142 1 b. 25 Type **365** 15 10
1143 7 b. 50 Post office counter . 75 30
1144 8 b. 50 Mail transportation 1·00 65
1145 9 b. 50 Mail delivery 50 25

1983. Inauguration of Malaysia–Singapore–Thailand Submarine Cable. Multicoloured.

1147 1 b. 25 Type **366** 40 15
1148 7 b. Map of new cable . . . 65 30

367 Flower Coral

1983. Int Correspondence Week. Corals. Mult.

1149 2 b. Type **367** 25 15
1150 3 b. Lesser valley coral . . . 75 15
1151 4 b. Mushroom coral . . . 25 25
1152 7 b. Common lettuce coral . 1·00 50

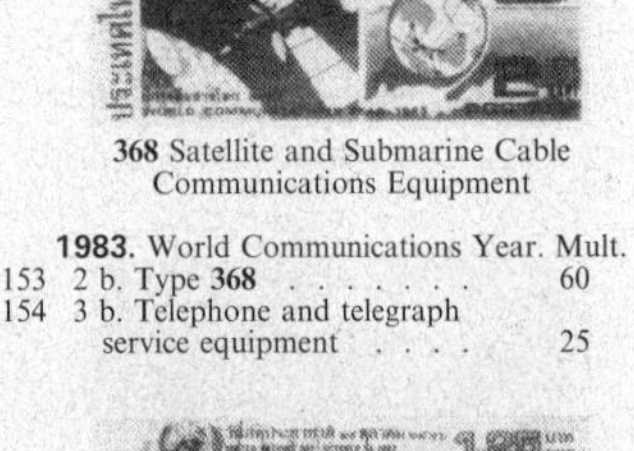

368 Satellite and Submarine Cable Communications Equipment

1983. World Communications Year. Mult.

1153 2 b. Type **368** 60 15
1154 3 b. Telephone and telegraph service equipment 25 15

369 Fishing for Skipjack

1983. United Nations Day.

1155 **369** 1 b. 25 multicoloured . 25 10

370 Buddha (sculpture)

1983. 700th Anniv of Thai Alphabet.

1156 **370** 3 b. multicoloured . . . 50 15
1157 – 7 b. black and brown . . 75 25
1158 – 8 b. multicoloured . . . 40 25
1159 – 9 b. multicoloured . . . 40 25

DESIGNS—HORIZ: 3 b. Sangkhalok pottery; 7 b. Thai characters. VERT: 9 b. Mahathat Temple.

371 Prince Mahidol of Songkhla

1983. 60th Anniv of Co-operation between Siriraj Hospital and Rockefeller Foundation.

1160 **371** 9 b. 50 multicoloured . . 75 50

372 Lotus Blossoms within Heads

1984. Children's Day.

1161 **372** 1 b. 25 multicoloured . . 20 10

373 Running

1984. 17th National Games, Phitsanulok Province. Multicoloured.

1162 1 b. 25 Type **373** 30 10
1163 3 b. Football 25 15

374 Skeletal Joints, Globe and Emblem

1984. 5th South East Asia and Pacific Area League against Rheumatism Congress.

1164 **374** 1 b. 25 multicoloured . . 20 10

375 Statue of King Naresuan and Modern Armed Forces

376 Royal Institute Emblem in Door Arch

1984. Armed Forces Day.

1165 **375** 1 b. 25 multicoloured . . 30 10

1984. 50th Anniv of Royal Institute.

1166 **376** 1 b. 25 multicoloured . . 20 10

1984. Red Cross. No. 954 surch **3.25 + 0.25** in English and Thai.

1167 **295** 3 b. 25+25 s. on 2 b. 75+25 s. mult . . 1·00 60

378 King and Queen examining Land Development Project

1984. Royal Initiated Projects. Multicoloured.

1168 1 b. 25 Type **378** 25 10
1169 1 b. 25 Improving barren area 25 10
1170 1 b. 25 Dam, terrace farming and rain-making aircraft . 25 10
1171 1 b. 25 Crops, fish and farm animals 25 10
1172 1 b. 25 King and Queen of Thailand 25 10

379 Dome Building and University Emblem

1984. 50th Anniv of Thammasat University.

1173 **379** 1 b. 25 multicoloured . . 20 10

381 A.B.U. Emblem and Map

1984. 20th Anniv of Asia-Pacific Broadcasting Union.

1174 **381** 4 b. multicoloured . . . 50 20

382 Chiang Saen Style Buddha

384 "Alocasia indica var. metallica"

1984. Thai Sculptures of Buddhas. Multicoloured

1175 1 b. 25 Type **382** 15 10
1176 7 b. Sukhothai style 75 30
1177 8 b. 50 Thong style 40 40
1178 9 b. 50 Ayutthaya style . . . 40 40

1984. International Correspondence Week. Medicinal Plants. Multicoloured.

1181 1 b. 50 Type **384** 15 10
1182 2 b. "Aloe barbadensis" . . 20 10
1183 4 b. "Gynura pseudo-china" 35 15
1184 10 b. "Rhoeo spathacea" . . 1·25 70

385 Princess Mother

386 Threshing Rice

1984. 84th Birthday of Princess Mother.

1185 **385** 1 b. 50 multicoloured . . 15 10

1984. United Nations Day.

1186 **386** 1 b. 50 multicoloured . . 15 10

387 Bhutan Glory

1984. Butterflies. Multicoloured.
1187 2 b. Type **387** 40 20
1188 3 b. "Stichophthalma louisa" 60 25
1189 5 b. Clipper . . . . 1·00 55
1190 7 b. "Stichophthalma godfreyi" 1·25 65

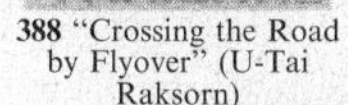
388 "Crossing the Road by Flyover" (U-Tai Raksorn)

390 Monument to Tao-Thep-Krasattri and Tao-Sri-Sundhorn

389 Bangkok Mail Centre

1985. Children's Day. Multicoloured.
1191 1 b. 50 Type **388** 15 10
1192 1 b. 50 "Crossing the Road by Flyover" (Sravudh Charoennawee) (horiz) . . 15 10

1985. Inauguration of Bangkok Mail-sorting Centre.
1193 **389** 1 b. 50 multicoloured . . 25 10

1985. Heroines of Phuket. Bicentennial Ceremony.
1194 **390** 2 b. multicoloured . . . 20 10

1985. Red Cross. No. 987 surch **2+.25 BAHT.**
1195 **306** 2 b.+25 s. on 75 s.+25 s. multicoloured 75 75

392 Bank Headquarters, Bangkok, and King Vajiravudh (Rama VI)

1985. 72nd Anniv of Government Savings Bank.
1196 **392** 1 b. 50 multicoloured . . 15 10

393 Satellite over Thai Buildings

1985. 20th Anniv of International Telecommunications Satellite Organization.
1197 **393** 2 b. multicoloured . . . 25 10

394 Douglas DC-6 and DC-8 and Loi-Krathong Festival

1985. 25th Anniv of Thai Airways. Mult.
1198 2 b. Type **394** 15 10
1199 7 b. 50 Douglas DC-10-30 and Thai classical dancing . . . 1·00 55
1200 8 b. 50 Airbus Industrie A-300 and Thai buildings . . . . 1·10 80
1201 9 b. 50 Boeing 747-200 and world landmarks . . . . . 1·10 80

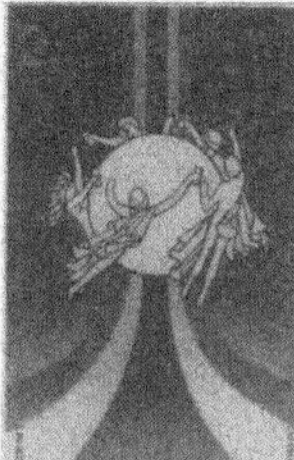
395 U.P.U.Emblem

397 Aisvarya Pavilion

396 Pigeon

1985. Centenary of Membership of U.P.U. and I.T.U. Multicoloured.
1202 2 b. Type **395** 15 10
1203 10 b. I.T.U. Emblem 55 20

1985. National Communications Day.
1204 **396** 2 b. blue, red & ultram . 20 10

1985. "Thaipex '85" Stamp Exhibition. Multicoloured.
1205 2 b. Type **397** 15 10
1206 3 b. Varopas Piman Pavilion (horiz) 25 15
1207 7 b. Vehas Camrun Pavilion (horiz) 50 20
1208 10 b. Vitoon Tassana Tower 60 50

398 King Mongkut, Eclipsed Sun and Telescope

1985. National Science Day.
1210 **398** 2 b. multicoloured . . . 20 10

399 Department Seals, 1885 and 1985

1985. Centenary of Royal Thai Survey Department.
1211 **399** 2 b. multicoloured . . . 20 10

400 Boxing

1985. 13th South-East Asia Games, Bangkok (1st issue). Multicoloured.
1212 2 b. Type **400** 20 10
1213 2 b. Putting the shot 20 10
1214 2 b. Badminton 20 10
1215 2 b. Throwing the javelin . . 20 10
1216 2 b. Weightlifting 20 10
See also Nos. 1229/32.

401 Golden Trumpet

402 Mothers and Children at Clinic

1985. International Correspondence Week. Climbing Plants. Multicoloured.
1218 2 b. Type **401** 25 15
1219 3 b. "Jasminum auriculatum" 35 15
1220 7 b. Passion flower 50 25
1221 10 b. Coral-vine 60 35

1985. United Nations Day.
1222 **402** 2 b. multicoloured . . . 20 10

403 Prince Dhani Nivat

404 Prince of Jainad

1985. Birth Centenary of Prince Dhani Nivat, Kromamun Bidyalabh Bridhyakorn.
1223 **403** 2 b. multicoloured . . . 15 10

1985. Birth Centenary of Rangsit, Prince of Jainad (Minister of Health).
1224 **404** 1 b. 50 multicoloured . . 15 10

405 Emblem and Buildings

1985. 5th Asian–Pacific Postal Union Congress.
1225 **405** 2 b. multicoloured . . . 15 10
1226 – 10 b. multicoloured . . . 55 25
DESIGN: 10 b. As Type **405** but different buildings.

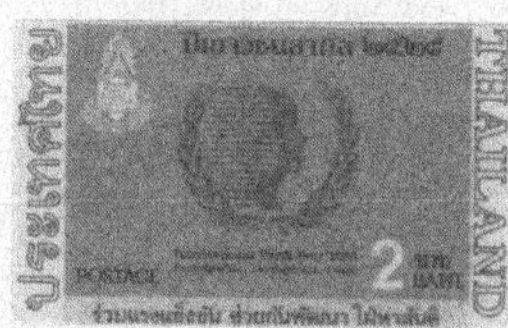
406 Emblem

1985. International Youth Year.
1227 **406** 2 b. multicoloured . . . 25 10

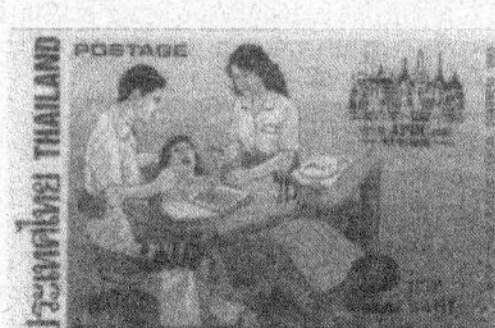
407 Dentist and Nurse tending Patient

1085. 12th Asian–Pacific Dental Congress.
1228 **407** 2 b. multicoloured . . . 20 10

408 Volleyball

409 Chevalier de Chaumont presenting Message from Louis XIV to King Narai the Great, 1685

1985. 12th South-East Asia Games, Bangkok (2nd issue). Multicoloured.
1229 1 b. Type **408** 20 15
1230 2 b. Sepak-takraw (kick-ball) 20 10
1231 3 b. Gymnastics 25 15
1232 4 b. Bowls 25 20

1985. 300th Anniv of Franco–Thai Relations. Multicoloured.
1234 2 b. Type **409** 15 10
1235 8 b. 50 Siamese emissaries carrying reply from King Narai to Louis XIV (horiz) 50 40

410 Emblem

1986. 3rd Anniv of International and Inauguration of Domestic Express Mail Services.
1236 **410** 2 b. multicoloured . . . 15 10

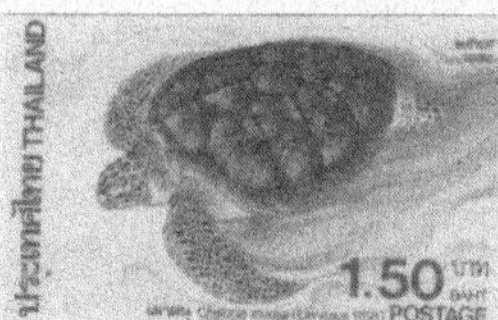
411 Green Turtle

1986. Turtles. Multicoloured.
1237 1 b. 50 Type **411** 15 10
1238 3 b. Hawksbill turtle 35 10
1239 5 b. Leatherback turtle . . . 1·00 20
1240 10 b. Olive turtle 75 25

412 "Family picking Lotus" (Areeya Makarabhundhu)

414 Statue of Sunthon Phu (Sukij Laidej), Amphoe Klaeng

1986. Children's Day.
1241 **412** 2 b. multicoloured . . . 20 10

1986. Red Cross. No. 1021 surch. **1986 2+.25 BAHT** in English and Thai.
1242 **317** 2 b.+25 s. on 75 s.+25 s. multicoloured 75 75

1986. Birth Bicentenary of Sunthon Phu (poet).
1243 **414** 2 b. multicoloured . . . 20 10

415 Watermelon

1986. Fruit. Multicoloured.
1244 2 b. Type **415** 50 15
1245 2 b. Malay apple ("Eugenia malaccensis") 50 15
1246 6 b. Pomelo ("Citrus maxima") 50 15
1247 6 b. Papaya ("Carica papaya") 50 15

416 Trees on Grid and Water Line

1986. National Tree Year.
1248 **416** 2 b. multicoloured . . . 15 10

417 Pigeon flying from Man's Head to Transmission Masts

1986. National Communications Day.
1249 **417** 2 b. multicoloured . . . 15 10

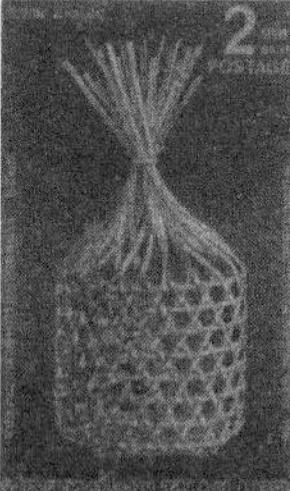
418 Chalom

1986. International Correspondence Week. Bamboo Baskets. Multicoloured.

1250 2 b. Type **418** 15 10
1251 2 b. Krabung 15 10
1252 6 b. Kratib 35 15
1253 6 b. Kaleb 35 15

1986. No. 1031 surch **1 BAHT**.

1254 **227** 1 b. on 20 s. blue 20 10

420 Emblem and War Scenes

1986. International Peace Year.

1255 **420** 2 b. light blue, blue & red 20 10

421 Industrial and Agricultural Scenes within Emblem

1986. Productivity Year.

1256 **421** 2 b. multicoloured . . . 20 10

422 Scouts saluting and Scout helping Blind Man across Road

1986. 75th Anniv of Thai Scouting. Mult.

1257 2 b. + 50 s. Type **422** . . . 15 15
1258 2 b. + 50 s. Scouting activities 15 15
1259 2 b. + 50 s. King and Queen making presentations to scouts 15 15
1260 2 b. + 50 s. 15th Asia–Pacific Scout Conference, Thailand 15 15

423 Vanda "Varavuth"

1986. 6th ASEAN Orchid Congress, Thailand. Multicoloured.

1261 2 b. Type **423** 20 10
1262 3 b. Ascocenda "Emma" . . 20 15
1263 4 b. Dendrobium "Sri-Siam" (horiz) 35 30
1264 5 b. Dendrobium "Ekapol Panda" (horiz) 35 25

424 Chinese Mushroom

1986. Edible Fungi. Multicoloured.

1266 2 b. Type **424** 50 15
1267 2 b. Oyster fungus ("Pleurotus ostreatus") 50 15
1268 6 b. Ear mushroom ("Auricularia polytricha") . 1·75 55
1269 6 b. Abalone mushroom "Pleurotus cystidiosus" . . 1·75 55

425 Labeo

1986. 60th Anniv of Fisheries Department. Multicoloured.

1270 2 b. Type **425** 15 10
1271 2 b. Featherback ("Notopterus blanci") 15 10
1272 7 b. Malayan bony-tongue ("Scleropages formosus") . 35 15
1273 7 b. "Pangasianodon gigas" 35 15

426 Children in Playground

1987. Children's Day. Multicoloured.

1274 2 b. Type **426** 20 10
1275 2 b. Children in and around swimming pool 20 10

Nos. 1274/5 were printed together, se-tenant, forming a composite design showing "Our School" by Lawan Maneenetr.

427 Northrop F-5 Tiger II and General Dynamics Fighting Falcon Fighters and Pilot

1987. 72nd Anniv of Royal Thai Air Force.

1276 **427** 2 b. multicoloured . . . 25 10

428 King Rama III and Temples

1987. Birth Bicentenary of King Rama III.

1277 **428** 2 b. multicoloured . . . 20 10

429 Communications and Transport Systems

1987. 75th Anniv of Ministry of Communications.

1278 **429** 2 b. multicoloured . . . 25 10

1987. Red Cross. No. 1065 surch **2 + 0.50 BAHT**.

1279 **333** 2 b. + 50 s. on 75 s. + 25 s. green and red 75 75

431 Tree-lined Street

1987. National Tree Year.

1280 **431** 2 b. multicoloured . . . 15 10

432 Gold Peacock

1987. "Thaipex'87" National Stamp Exhibition. Handicrafts. Multicoloured.

1281 2 b. Type **432** 15 10
1282 2 b. Gold hand-mirrors . . 15 10
1283 6 b. Gold lustre water urn and finger bowls with trays (horiz) 30 15
1284 6 b. Gold swan vase (horiz) . 30 15

433 Flying Bird and Animal Horn (Somsak Junthavorn)

1987. National Communications Day.

1286 **433** 2 b. multicoloured . . . 15 10

434 King Rama IX at Presentation Ceremony, King Rama V and Emblem

1987. Centenary of Chulachomklao Royal Military Academy, Khao Cha-Ngok.

1287 **434** 2 b. multicoloured . . . 15 10

435 Spiral Ropes leading to Member Countries' Flags

1987. 20th Anniv of Association of South-East Asian Nations.

1288 **435** 2 b. multicoloured . . . 10 10
1289 3 b. multicoloured . . . 20 10
1290 4 b. multicoloured . . . 30 15
1291 5 b. multicoloured . . . 50 20

436 People and Open Book

437 Flower-offering Ceremony, Saraburi

1987. International Literacy Day.

1292 **436** 2 b. multicoloured . . . 10 10

1987. Visit Thailand Year.

1293 2 b. Type **437** 15 10
1294 3 b. Duan Sib Festival (honouring ancestors), Nakhon Si Thammarat . . 20 10
1295 5 b. Bang Fai (rain) Festival, Yasothon 30 20
1296 7 b. Loi Krathong, Sukhothai 55 20

438 Ministry Building

1987. 72nd Anniv of Auditor General's Office.

1297 **438** 2 b. multicoloured . . . 15 10

439 Temple of Dawn, "Sri Suphanahong" (royal barge) and Mt Fuji within "100"

1987. Centenary of Japan–Thailand Friendship Treaty.

1298 **439** 2 b. multicoloured . . . 15 10

440 Tasselled Garland

1987. International Correspondence Week. Ceremonial Floral Garlands. Multicoloured.

1299 2 b. Floral tassle 15 10
1300 3 b. Type **440** 25 10
1301 5 b. Wrist garland 30 20
1302 7 b. Double-ended garland . 35 25

1987. No. 1180a surch **2 BAHT**.

1303 **325** 2 b. on 1 b. 50 orange . 15 10

442 Thai Pavilion

1987. Inauguration of Social Education and Cultural Centre.

1304 **442** 2 b. multicoloured . . . 15 10

443 King Bhumibol Adulyadej as a Boy

1987. King Bhumibol Adulyadej's 60th Birthday. Multicoloured (except 1320).

1305 2 b. Type **443** 15 10
1306 2 b. Wedding photograph of King Bhumibol Adulyadej and Queen Sirikit, 1950 . . 15 10
1307 2 b. King on throne during Accession ceremony at Paisan Hall, 1950 . . . . 15 10
1308 2 b. King as monk on alms round 15 10
1309 2 b. Elderly woman greeting King 15 10
1310 2 b. King demonstrating to hill tribes how to take medicine 15 10
1311 2 b. King and Queen presenting gift bag to wounded serviceman 15 10
1312 2 b. King examining new system for small farms 15 10
1314 2 b. Princess Mother Somdej Phra Sri Nakarindra Boromrajjonnani 15 10
1315 2 b. Crown Prince Maha Vajiralongkorn 15 10
1316 2 b. Princess Maha Chakri Sirindhorn 15 10
1317 2 b. Princess Chulabhorn . . 15 10
1318 2 b. King Bhumibol Adulyadej and Queen Sirikit 15 10
1319 2 b. King and family (48 × 33 mm) 15 10
1320 100 b. gold and blue (King Bhumibol Adulyadej) (48 × 33 mm) . . . . 38·00 38·00

444 "Teacher's Day" (Nutchaliya Suddhiprasit)

445 Prince Kromamun Bridhyalongkorn (founder)

1988. Children's Day.

1321 **444** 2 b. multicoloured . . . 15 10

1988. 72nd Anniv of Thai Co-operatives.

1322 **445** 2 b. multicoloured . . . 15 10

446 Society Building

1988. 84th Anniv of Siam Society (for promotion of arts and sciences).
1323 **446** 2 b. multicoloured . . . 15 10

447 Phra Phai Luang Monastery

1988. Sukhothai Historical Park. Multicoloured.
1324 2 b. Type **447** 15 10
1325 3 b. Traphang Thonglang Monastery 20 10
1326 4 b. Maha That Monastery . 30 15
1327 6 b. Thewalai Maha Kaset . 45 25

1988. No. 1040a surch **1 BAHT**.
1557 **325** 1 b. on 1 b. 25 green . . 10 10

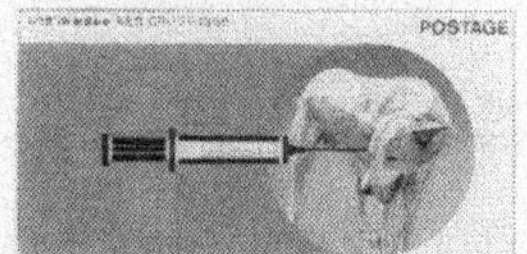
449 Syringe between Red Cross and Dog

1988. Red Cross Anti-rabies Campaign.
1329 **449** 2 b. multicoloured . . . 15 10

450 King Rama V (founder) **452** Hand holding Coloured Ribbons

451 Crested Fireback Pheasant

1988. Centenary of Siriraj Hospital.
1330 **450** 5 b. multicoloured . . . 50 15

1988. Pheasants. Multicoloured.
1331 2 b. Type **451** 30 15
1332 3 b. Kalij pheasant 35 20
1333 6 b. Silver pheasant 60 30
1334 7 b. Mrs. Hume's pheasant . 70 35

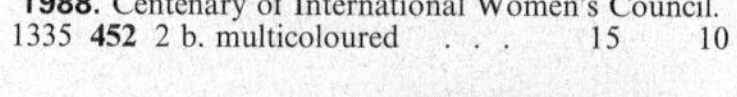
1988. Centenary of International Women's Council.
1335 **452** 2 b. multicoloured . . . 15 10

453 King Rama IX in King's Own Bodyguard Uniform **454** King Rama IX in Full Robes

1988.
1631 **453** 25 s. brown 10 10
1336 50 s. green 10 10
1337 1 b. blue 10 10
1753 2 b. red 10 10
1339 3 b. blue and brown . . 15 10
1340 4 b. red and blue 20 10
1341 5 b. brown and lilac . . 25 10
1342 6 b. purple and green . . 30 10
1343 7 b. deep brown & brown 35 15
1344 8 b. green and brown . . 40 20
1345 **453** 9 b. brown and blue . . 45 15
1346 10 b. green and red . . 50 15
1348 20 b. green and orange . 1·00 40
1350 25 b. blue and green . . 1·25 50
1352 50 b. green and lilac . . 2·50 70
1354 100 b. blue and orange . 5·00 3·75

1988. 42nd Anniv of Accession to Throne of King Rama IX. Multicoloured. (a) T **454**.
1356 2 b. Type **454** 15 10

(b) Royal Regalia. Size 33 × 48 mm (1357) or 48 × 33 mm (others).
1357 2 b. Great Crown of Victory 15 10
1358 2 b. Sword of Victory and scabbard (horiz) 15 10
1359 2 b. Sceptre (horiz) 15 10
1360 2 b. Royal Fan and Fly Whisk (horiz) 15 10
1361 2 b. Slippers (horiz) 15 10

(c) Thrones.
1362 2 b. Atthathit Uthumphon Ratchaat throne (octagonal base) 15 10
1363 2 b. Phatthrabit throne (rectangular base) 15 10
1364 2 b. Phuttan Kanchanasinghat throne (gold throne on angular steps) 15 10
1365 2 b. Butsabokmala Mahachakkraphatphiman throne (ship shape) . . . 15 10
1366 2 b. Throne inlaid with mother-of-pearl (blue throne on angular steps) 15 10
1367 2 b. Peony design niello throne (circular steps) 15 10

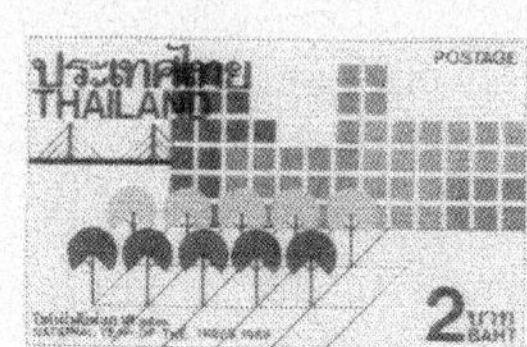
455 Bridge, Building and Trees

1988. National Tree Year.
1369 **455** 2 b. multicoloured . . . 15 10

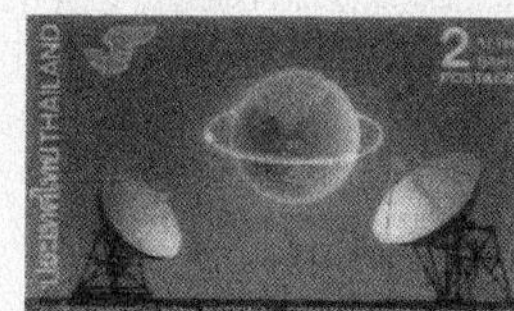
456 Globe and Dish Aerials

1988. National Communications Day.
1370 **456** 2 b. multicoloured . . . 15 10

458 Grasshopper

1988. International Correspondence Week. Woven Coconut-leaf Folk Toys. Multicoloured.
1371 2 b. Type **458** 15 10
1372 2 b. Carp 15 10
1373 6 b. Bird 30 15
1374 6 b. Takro 30 15

459 Flats and Construction Workers

1988. Housing Development.
1375 **459** 2 b. multicoloured . . . 15 10

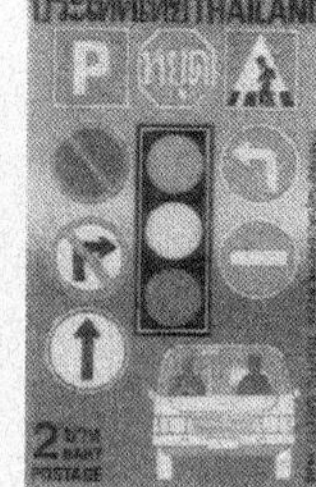
460 King Rama V in Full Uniform **461** Road Signs

1988. 120th Anniv of King's Own Bodyguard.
1376 **460** 2 b. multicoloured . . . 20 10

1988. Road Safety Campaign.
1377 **461** 2 b. multicoloured . . . 15 10

462 "Crotalaria sessiliflora" **464** Knight Grand Commander of Honourable Order of Rama

463 Buddha's Birthplace

1988. New Year. Multicoloured.
1378 1 b. Type **462** 10 10
1379 1 b. "Uvaria grandiflora" . . 10 10
1380 1 b. "Reinwardtia trigyna" . 10 10
1381 1 b. "Impatiens griffithii" . . 10 10

1988. Buddha Monthon Celebrations. Mult.
1382 2 b. Type **463** 15 10
1383 3 b. Buddha's place of enlightenment 15 10
1384 4 b. Site of Buddha's first sermon 20 15
1385 5 b. Buddha's Place of Nirvana 30 15
1386 6 b. Statue of Buddha (vert) . 35 20

1988. Insignia of Orders. Multicoloured.
1387 2 b. Type **464** 15 10
1388 2 b. Close-up of badge . . . 15 10
1389 3 b. Knight Grand Cordon (Special Class) of Most Exalted Order of the White Elephant 20 15
1390 3 b. Close-up of badge . . . 20 15
1391 5 b. Knight Grand Cordon of Most Noble Order of Crown of Thailand 25 15
1392 5 b. Close-up of badge . . . 25 15
1393 7 b. Close-up of Rarana Varabhorn Order of Merit . 35 20
1394 7 b. Badge on chain of office 35 20

Stamps of the same value were issued together, se-tenant, each pair forming a composite design.

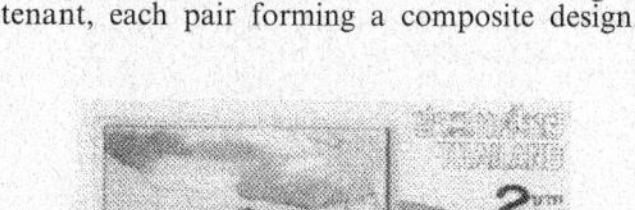
465 "Floating Market" (Thongbai Siyam)

1989. National Children's Day. Plasticine Paintings by Blind People. Multicoloured.
1395 2 b. Type **465** 20 10
1396 2 b. "Flying Birds" (Kwanchai Kerd-Daeng) 20 10
1397 2 b. "Little Mermaid" (Chalermpol Jiengmai) . . 20 10
1398 2 b. "Golden Fish" (Natetip Korsantirak) 20 10

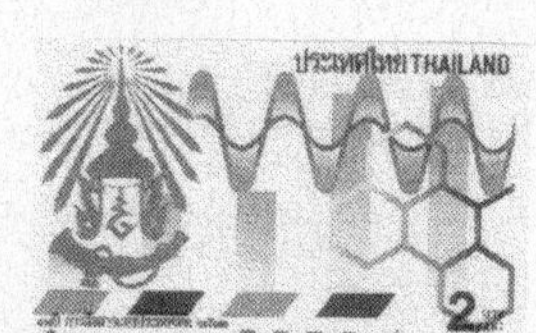
466 Emblem and Symbols of Communication

1989. 12th Anniv of Thai Communications Authority.
1399 **466** 2 b. multicoloured . . . 15 10

467 Statue of Kings Rama V and VI and Auditorium

1989. 72nd Anniv of Chulalongkorn University.
1400 **467** 2 b. multicoloured . . . 5 10

468 Red Cross Worker **469** Phra Kaeo Monastery

1989. 96th Anniv of Thai Red Cross (1401) and 125th Anniv of Int Red Cross (1402). Mult.
1401 2 b. Type **468** 15 10
1402 10 b. Red Cross and pillar . 50 30

1989. Phra Nakhon Khiri Historical Park. Multicoloured.
1403 2 b. Type **469** 15 10
1404 3 b. Chatchawan Wiangchai Observatory 25 15
1405 5 b. Phra That Chom Phet stupa 35 25
1406 6 b. Wetchayan Wichian Phrasat Throne Hall . . . 50 35

470 Lottery Office Building and Profit Recipients

1989. 50th Anniv of Government Lottery Office.
1407 **470** 2 b. multicoloured . . . 15 10

471 Campaign Emblem and Figures **472** Gold Nielloware Figures

1989. International Anti-drugs Day.
1408 **471** 2 b. multicoloured . . . 15 10

1989. National Arts and Crafts Year. Mult.
1409 2 b. Type **472** 15 10
1410 2 b. Ceramics 15 10
1411 6 b. Ornament inlaid with gemstones (horiz) 30 15
1412 6 b. Triangular cushion (horiz) 30 15

473 Thailand Cone

1989. Shells. Multicoloured.
1413 2 b. Type **473** 15 10
1414 3 b. Thorny oyster 25 15
1415 6 b. Great spotted cowrie . . 35 20
1416 10 b. Chambered nautilus . . 75 60

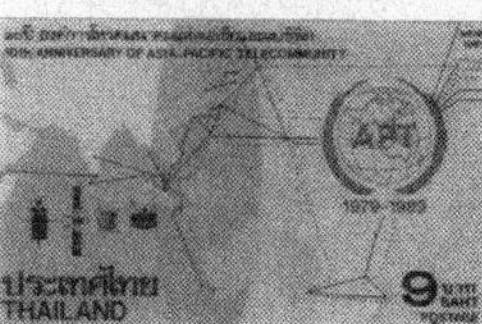
474 Satellites, Submarine Cable Network and Emblem

1989. 10th Anniv of Asia–Pacific Telecommunity.
1417 **474** 9 b. multicoloured . . . 45 20

475 Phya Anuman Rajadhon

1989. Birth Centenary (1988) of Phya Anuman Rajadhon (writer).

1418 **475** 2 b. multicoloured . . . 15 10

476 Emblem and School

1989. Centenary of Post and Telecommunications School.

1419 **476** 2 b. multicoloured . . . 15 10

477 Communications Symbols **478** Post Box

1989. National Communications Day.

1420 **477** 2 b. multicoloured . . . 20 10

1989. "Thaipex '89" National Stamp Exhibition. Post Boxes. Multicoloured.

1421 2 b. Type **478** 15 10
1422 3 b. Provincial box 20 10
1423 4 b. City box 25 15
1424 5 b. Imported English box . . 30 15
1425 6 b. West German box sent as gift on introduction of Thai Postal Service 30 15

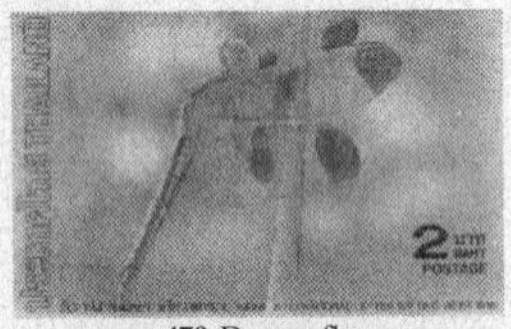

479 Dragonfly

1989. Int Correspondence Week. Mult.

1426 2 b. Type **479** 20 10
1427 5 b. Dragonfly (different) . . 30 15
1428 6 b. Dragonfly (different) . . 45 20
1429 10 b. Damselfly 60 40

480 Means of Transport and Communications

1989. Asia–Pacific Transport and Communications Decade.

1431 **480** 2 b. multicoloured . . . 20 10

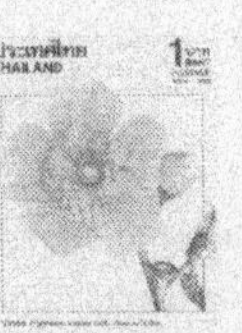
481 Figure and "Thoughts" **482** "Hypericum uralum"

1989. Centenary of Mental Health Care.

1432 **481** 2 b. multicoloured . . . 15 10

1989. New Year. Flowers. Multicoloured.

1433 1 b. Type **482** 10 10
1434 1 b. "Uraria rufescens" . . . 10 10
1435 1 b. "Manglietia garrettii" . 10 10
1436 1 b. "Aeschynanthus macranthus" 10 10

483 "Catacanthus incarnatus" (shieldbug)

1989. Beetles. Multicoloured.

1438 2 b. Type **483** 20 10
1439 3 b. "Aristobia approximator" 25 10
1440 6 b. "Chrysochroa chinensis" 60 20
1441 10 b. "Enoplotrupes sharpi" 60 50

484 Medallists on Rostrum

1989. Sports Welfare Fund. Multicoloured.

1442 2 b.+1 b. Type **484** 15 15
1443 2 b.+1 b. Nurse attending fallen cyclist 15 15
1444 2 b.+1 b. Boxing 15 15
1445 2 b.+1 b. Football 15 15

485 Official, Family and Graph

1990. Population and Housing Census.

1446 **485** 2 b. multicoloured . . . 15 10

486 Skipping (Phethai Setharangsi)

1990. National Children's Day. Multicoloured.

1447 2 b. Type **486** 15 10
1448 2 b. Various sports activities (Chalermpol Wongpim) (vert) 15 10

487 Skull splitting Heart **488** Tiap

1990. Red Cross. Anti-AIDS Campaign.

1449 **487** 2 b. blue, red & black . 15 10

1990. Heritage Conservation Day. Mother-of-Pearl Inlaid Containers. Multicoloured.

1450 2 b. Type **488** 15 10
1451 2 b. Phan waenfa 15 10
1452 8 b. Lung (horiz) 40 25
1453 8 b. Chiat klom (horiz) . . . 40 25

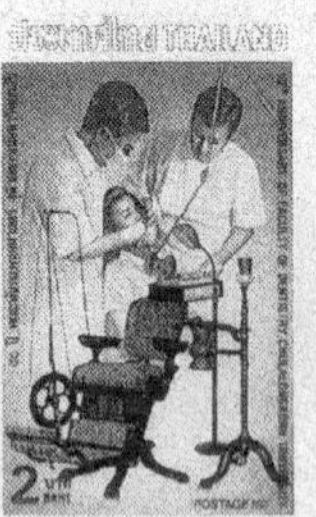

489 Dental Students and Old Chair **490** Tin

1990. 50th Anniv of Chulalongkorn University Dentistry Faculty.

1454 **489** 2 b. multicoloured . . . 15 10

1990. Minerals. Multicoloured.

1460 2 b. Type **490** 15 10
1461 3 b. Zinc 15 10
1462 5 b. Lead 25 15
1463 6 b. Fluorite 30 20

491 Pigeon

1990. National Communications Day.

1465 **491** 2 b. blue, violet & purple 15 10

492 Pigeons and Envelopes

1990. 20th Anniv of Asian–Pacific Postal Training Centre, Bangkok.

1466 **492** 2 b. green, blue & black . 15 10
1467 8 b. blue, green & black . 40 30

493 Jaipur Foot Project

1990. 60th Anniv of Rotary International in Thailand. Multicoloured.

1468 2 b. Type **493** 15 10
1469 3 b. Child anti-polio vaccination campaign 15 10
1470 6 b. Literacy campaign . . . 30 15
1471 8 b. King Chulalongkorn and his engraved cypher (Thai Museum, Nordkapp, Norway 60 30

494 Account and Staff at Computer Terminals

1990. Centenary of Comptroller-General's Department.

1472 **494** 2 b. multicoloured . . . 15 10

495 Flowers in Dish (Cho Muang)

1990. Int Correspondence Week. Mult.

1473 2 b. Type **495** 15 10
1474 3 b. Flowers on tray (Cha Mongkut) 20 15
1475 5 b. Sweetmeats on tray with leaf design (Sane Chan) . . 25 20
1476 6 b. Fruit in bowl (Luk Chup) 35 25

496 Princess Mother with Flower **497** "Cyrtandromoea grandiflora"

1990. 90th Birthday of Princess Mother.

1478 **496** 2 b. multicoloured . . . 20 10

1990. New Year. Flowers. Multicoloured.

1479 1 b. Type **497** 15 10
1480 1 b. "Rhododendron arboreum sp. delavayi" 15 10
1481 1 b. "Merremia vitifolia" . . 15 10
1482 1 b. "Afgekia mahidolae" . . 15 10

498 Wiman Mek Royal Hall

1990. Dusit Palace. Multicoloured.

1484 2 b. Type **498** 15 10
1485 3 b. Ratcharit Rungrot Royal House 15 10
1486 4 b. Aphisek Dusit Royal Hall 20 15
1487 5 b. Amphon Sathan Palace . 25 15
1488 6 b. Udon Phak Royal Hall . 30 20
1489 8 b. Anantasamakhom Throne Hall 40 30

499 Phrachetuphon Wimolmangkalaram Temple and Supreme Patriarch

1990. Birth Bicentenary of Supreme Patriarch Somdet Phra Maha Samanachao Kromphra Paramanuchitchinorot (formerly Prince Wasukri).

1490 **499** 2 b. multicoloured . . . 15 10

500 Judo

1990. Sports Welfare Fund. Multicoloured.

1491 2 b.+1 b. Type **500** 20 20
1492 2 b.+1 b. Archery 20 20
1493 2 b.+1 b. High jumping . . 20 20
1494 2 b.+1 b. Windsurfing . . . 20 20

501 Aspects of Petroleum Industry

1990. 12th Anniv of Thai Petroleum Authority.

1495 **501** 2 b. multicoloured . . . 15 10

502 Mae Klong Railway Locomotive No. 6

1990. Steam Locomotives. Multicoloured.

1496 2 b. Type **502** 15 10
1497 3 b. "Sung Noen" locomotive No. 32 . . . . 25 15
1498 5 b. "C 56" locomotive No. 715 40 30
1499 6 b. "Mikado" locomotive No. 953 . . . . 40 30

503 Luk Khang (tops)

1991. Children's Day. Games. Multicoloured.

1501 2 b. Type **503** 15 10
1502 3 b. Pid Ta Ti Mo (blindfolded child smashing vase) . . . 15 10
1503 5 b. Doen Kala (walking on stones) 25 20
1504 6 b. Phong Phang (blind man's bluff) 30 20

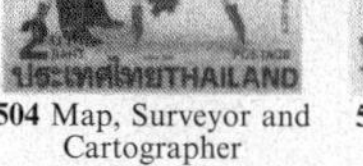
504 Map, Surveyor and Cartographer

505 Princess (patron) wearing Red Cross Uniform

1991. Land Deeds Project.
1505 **504** 2 b. multicoloured . . . 15 10

1991. Red Cross. Princess Maha Chaki Sirindhorn's "Third Cycle" (36th) Birthday.
1506 **505** 2 b. multicoloured . . . 15 10

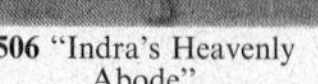
506 "Indra's Heavenly Abode"

507 Goddess riding Goat

1991. Heritage Conservation Day. Floral Hanging Decorations. Multicoloured.
1508 2 b. Type **506** 15 10
1509 3 b. "Celestial Couch" . . . 15 10
1510 4 b. "Crystal Ladder" . . . 20 15
1511 5 b. "Crocodile" 25 20

1991. Songkran (New Year) Day. Year of the Goat.
1513 **507** 2 b. multicoloured . . . 1·25 35

508 Prince Narisranuvattivongs

1991. 44th Death Anniv of Prince Narisranuvattivongs.
1515 **508** 2 b. brown, deep brown and yellow 15 10

509 Pink Lotus (Sutthiporn Wiset)

511 Yok

510 World Map, Communication Systems and Healthy Tree

1991. Runners-up in International Correspondence Week Competition. Multicoloured.
1516 2 b. Type **509** 10 10
1517 3 b. Pink lotuses (Mathayom Suksa group, Khonkaen-vityayon School) 15 10
1518 5 b. White lotus (Rattanaporn Sukhasem) (horiz) 25 20
1519 6 b. Red lotuses (Phanupongs Sayasombat and Kanokwan Cholaphum) (horiz) 30 20

1991. National Communications Day. "Communications and Preservation of the Environment".
1520 **510** 2 b. multicoloured . . . 10 10

1991. "Thaipex '91" National Stamp Exhibition. Textile Patterns. Multicoloured.
1521 2 b. Type **511** 10 10
1522 4 b. Mudmee 20 10
1523 6 b. Khit 30 15
1524 8 b. Chok 40 30

512 Workers and Productivity Arrow

1991. International Productivity Congress.
1526 **512** 2 b. multicoloured . . . 15 10

513 "Co-operation of Women around the World"

1991. 26th Int Council of Women Triennial.
1527 **513** 2 b. multicoloured . . . 15 10

514 Black

1991. International Correspondence Week. Japanese Bantams. Multicoloured.
1528 2 b. Type **514** 10 10
1529 3 b. Black-tailed buff . . . 20 10
1530 6 b. Buff 30 15
1531 8 b. White 40 30

515 Silver Coin of King Rama IV and Wat Phra Sri Rattana Satsadaram

1991. World Bank and International Monetary Fund Annual Meetings. Multicoloured.
1533 2 b. Type **515** 10 10
1534 4 b. Pod Duang money, Wat Mahathat Sukhothai and Wat Aroonrachawararam . . . 20 10
1535 8 b. Chieng and Hoi money and Wat Phrathat Doi Suthep 40 25
1536 10 b. Funan, Dvaravati and Srivijaya money, Phra Pathom Chedi and Phra Borommathat Chaiya . . 50 35

516 1908 1 t. Stamp

518 "Dillenia obovata"

517 Adult and Calves

1991. "Bangkok 1993" International Stamp Exhibition (1st series). Stamps from the 1908 King Chulalongkorn Issue. Multicoloured.
1538 2 b. Type **516** 10 10
1539 3 b. 2 t. stamp 15 10
1540 4 b. 3 t. stamp 20 15
1541 5 b. 5 t. stamp 25 15
1542 6 b. 10 t. stamp 30 15
1543 7 b. 20 t. stamp 35 20
1544 8 b. 40 t. stamp 40 25
See also Nos. 1618/22, 1666/9 and 1700/3.

1991. The Indian Elephant. Multicoloured.
1546 2 b. Type **517** 10 10
1547 4 b. Elephants pulling log . . 20 15
1548 6 b. Adult male resting . . . 30 15
1549 8 b. Adults bathing 40 25

1991. New Year. Flowers. Multicoloured.
1551 1 b. Type **518** 10 10
1552 1 b. "Melastoma sanguineum" 10 10
1553 1 b. "Commelina diffusa" . . 10 10
1554 1 b. "Plumbago indica" . . . 10 10

520 Jogging

522 Prince Mahidol

521 Large Indian Civet

1991. Sports Welfare Fund. Multicoloured.
1558 2 b.+1 b. Type **520** 15 15
1559 2 b.+1 b. Cycling 15 15
1560 2 b.+1 b. Skipping 15 15
1561 2 b.+1 b. Swimming 15 15

1991. Mammals. Multicoloured.
1562 2 b. Type **521** 10 10
1563 3 b. Banded linsang 15 10
1564 6 b. Asiatic golden cat 30 15
1565 8 b. Black giant squirrel . . . 40 30

1992. Birth Centenary (1991) of Prince Mahidol of Songkla (pioneer of modern medicine in Thailand).
1567 **522** 2 b. brown, gold & yellow 15 10

523 Archaeologists and Dinosaur Skeletons

1992. Centenary of Department of Mineral Resources. Multicoloured.
1568 2 b. Type **523** 10 10
1569 2 b. Mining excavation . . . 10 10
1570 2 b. Extracting natural gas and oil 10 10
1571 2 b. Digging artesian wells . . 10 10

524 Drawing by Nachadong Bunprasoet

1992. Children's Day. "World under the Sea". Children's Drawings. Multicoloured.
1572 2 b. Type **524** 15 10
1573 3 b. Fishes and seaweed (Varaporn Phadkhan) . . . 15 10
1574 5 b. Mermaid (Phannipha Ngoenkon) (vert) 35 20

525 Battle Scene (mural, Chan Chittrakon)

1992. 400th Anniv of Duel between King Naresuan the Great of Thailand and Phra Maha Upparacha of Burma.
1575 **525** 2 b. multicoloured . . . 15 10

526 "Paphiopedilum bellatulum"

1992. 4th Asia–Pacific Orchid Conf. Mult.
1576 2 b. Type **526** 10 10
1577 2 b. "Paphiopedilum exul" . 10 10
1578 3 b. "Paphiopedilum godefroyae" 15 10
1579 3 b. "Paphiopedilum concolor" 15 10
1580 6 b. "Paphiopedilum niveum" 30 15
1581 6 b. "Paphiopedilum villosum" 30 15
1582 10 b. "Paphiopedilum parishii" 50 35
1583 10 b. "Paphiopedilum sukhahulii" 50 35

527 Sugar Cane

528 Prince Rabi Badhanasakdi (founder of School of Law)

1992. 21st International Sugar Cane Technologists Society Congress.
1585 **527** 2 b. multicoloured . . . 15 10

1992. Centenary of Ministry of Justice. Legal Reformers. Multicoloured.
1586 3 b. Type **528** 15 10
1587 5 b. King Rama V (reformer of Courts system) 25 15

529 "Innocent" (Kamolporn Tapsuang)

1992. Red Cross.
1588 **529** 2 b. multicoloured . . . 15 10

530 Container Ships and Lorry

531 Prince Damrong Rajanubharb (first Minister)

1992. 80th Anniv of Ministry of Transport and Communications. Multicoloured.
1589 2 b. Type **530** 10 10
1590 3 b. Train and bus 15 10
1591 5 b. Boeing 747-200 airliner and control tower 25 15
1592 6 b. Lorry, satellites and aerials 30 20

1992. Cent of Ministry of the Interior. Mult.
1593 2 b. Type **531** 10 10
1594 2 b. Polling station 10 10
1595 2 b. Emergency services and army 10 10
1596 2 b. Child fetching water . . 10 10

532 Royal Ceremony of First Ploughing

1992. Centenary of Ministry of Agriculture and Co-operatives.
1597 **532** 2 b. multicoloured . . . 10 10
1598 3 b. multicoloured . . . 15 10
1599 4 b. multicoloured . . . 20 15
1600 5 b. multicoloured . . . 25 20

533 Ministry

1992. Centenary of Ministry of Education.
1601 **533** 2 b. multicoloured . . . 10 10

534 Western Region

1992. Thai Heritage Conservation Day. Traditional Carts. Multicoloured.
1602 2 b. Type **534** 10 10
1603 3 b. Northern region 15 10
1604 5 b. North-eastern region . . 25 15
1605 10 b. Eastern region 50 35

535 Demon riding Monkey **536** American Brahman and Livestock

1992. Songkran (New Year) Day. Year of the Monkey.
1607 **535** 2 b. multicoloured . . . 10 10

1992. 50th Anniv of Department of Livestock Development.
1609 **536** 2 b. multicoloured . . . 10 10

537 Birth of Buddha (mural, Wat Angkaeo, Bangkok) **538** Weather Balloon, Dish Aerial, Satellite and Map

1992. Wisakhabucha Day. Multicoloured.
1610 2 b. Type **537** 10 10
1611 3 b. "Enlightenment of Buddha" (illustration by Phraya Thewaphinimmit from biography) 20 15
1612 5 b. Death of Buddha (mural, Wat Kanmatuyaram, Bangkok) 25 20

1992. 50th Anniv of Meteorological Department.
1613 **538** 2 b. multicoloured . . . 10 10

539 Bua Tong Field, Mae Hong Son Province **540** 1887 64 a. stamp

1992. Association of South-East Asian Nations Tourism Year. Multicoloured.
1614 2 b. Type **539** 10 10
1615 3 b. Klong Larn Waterfall, Kamphaeng Phet Province 15 10
1616 4 b. Coral, Chumphon Province 20 15
1617 5 b. Khao Ta-Poo, Phangnga Province 30 20

1992. "Bangkok 1993" International Stamp Exhibition (2nd series). Multicoloured.
1618 2 b. Type **540** 10 10
1619 3 b. 1916 20 b. stamp . . . 15 10
1620 5 b. 1928 40 b. stamp . . . 25 15
1621 7 b. 1943 1 b. stamp . . . 35 20
1622 8 b. 1947 20 b. stamp . . . 40 25

541 Prince Chudadhuj Dharadilok **543** Culture and Sports

542 "Communications"

1992. Birth Centenary of Prince Chudadhuj Dharadilok of Bejraburna.
1624 **541** 2 b. multicoloured . . . 10 10

1992. National Communications Day.
1625 **542** 2 b. multicoloured . . . 10 10

1992. 25th Anniv of Association of South-East Asian Nations. Multicoloured.
1626 2 b. Type **543** 10 10
1627 3 b. Tourist sites 15 10
1628 5 b. Transport and communications 35 15
1629 7 b. Agriculture 35 20

544 Sirikit Medical Centre

1992. Inauguration of Sirikit Medical Centre.
1630 **544** 2 b. multicoloured . . . 10 10

545 Wedding Ceremony

546 Queen Sirikit and Cipher

1992. 60th Birthday of Queen Sirikit. (a) As T **545**. Multicoloured.
1635 2 b. Type **545** 10 10
1636 2 b. Royal couple seated at Coronation ceremony . . 10 10
1637 2 b. Anointment as Queen . 10 10
1638 2 b. Seated on chair 10 10
1639 2 b. Visiting hospital patient 10 10
1640 2 b. Talking to subjects . . 10 10

(b) Royal Regalia. Enamelled gold objects. As T **546**. Multicoloured.
1642 2 b. Bowls on footed tray (betel and areca nut set) 10 10
1643 2 b. Kettle 10 10
1644 2 b. Water holder within bowl 10 10
1645 2 b. Box on footed tray (betel and areca nut set) 10 10
1646 2 b. Vase 10 10

(c) Type **546**.
1647 100 b. blue and gold . . . . 5·00 5·00

547 Prince Wan Waithayakon **548** Bhirasri

1992. Birth Centenary (1991) of Prince Wan Waithayakon, Krommun Naradhip Bongsprabandh (diplomat).
1648 **547** 2 b. multicoloured . . . 10 10

1992. Birth Centenary of Silpa Bhirasri (sculptor).
1649 **548** 2 b. multicoloured . . . 10 10

549 "Catalaphyllia jardinei"

1992. Int Correspondence Week. Corals. Mult.
1650 2 b. Type **549** 10 10
1651 3 b. "Porites lutea" 15 10
1652 6 b. "Tubastraea coccinea" . 30 20
1653 8 b. "Favia pallida" 40 30

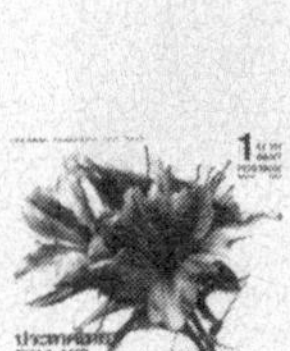

550 "Rhododendron simsii" **551** Figures of Man and Woman

1992. New Year. Flowers. Multicoloured.
1655 1 b. Type **550** 10 10
1656 1 b. "Cynoglossum lanceolatum" 10 10
1657 1 b. "Tithonia diversifolia" . 10 10
1658 1 b. "Agapetes parishii" . . . 10 10

1992. 1st Asian–Pacific Allergy and Immunology Congress, Bangkok.
1660 **551** 2 b. multicoloured . . . 10 10

552 Anantasamakhom Throne Hall, National Assembly Building and King Prajadhipok's Monument

1992. 60th Anniv of National Assembly.
1661 **552** 2 b. multicoloured . . . 10 10

553 Bank's Emblem and Bang Khun Phrom Palace (old headquarters)

1992. 50th Anniv of Bank of Thailand.
1662 **553** 2 b. multicoloured . . . 10 10

554 "River and Life" (Prathinthip Mensin)

1993. Children's Day. Drawings. Mult.
1663 2 b. Type **554** 15 10
1664 2 b. "Lovely Wild Animals and Beautiful Forest" (Pratsani Thammaprasert) 15 10
1665 2 b. "Communications in the Next Decade" (Natchaliya Sutiprasit) 15 10

555 Kendi, Water Dropper and Bottle

1993. "Bangkok 1993" International Stamp Exn (3rd series). Traditional Pottery. Multicoloured.
1666 3 b. Type **555** 15 10
1667 6 b. Vase and bottles 30 20
1668 7 b. Bowls 35 20
1669 8 b. Jars 40 25

556 Anniversary Emblem

1993. Centenary of Thai Teacher Training Institute.
1671 **556** 2 b. multicoloured . . . 10 10

557 Agricultural Produce

1993. 50th Anniv of Kasetsart University.
1672 **557** 2 b. multicoloured . . . 10 10

558 Buddha preaching (mural, Wat Kanmatuyaram, Bangkok) **559** Queen Sri Bajarindra (first royal patron)

1993. Maghapuja Day.
1673 **558** 2 b. multicoloured . . . 10 10

1993. Centenary of Thai Red Cross.
1674 **559** 2 b. multicoloured . . . 10 10

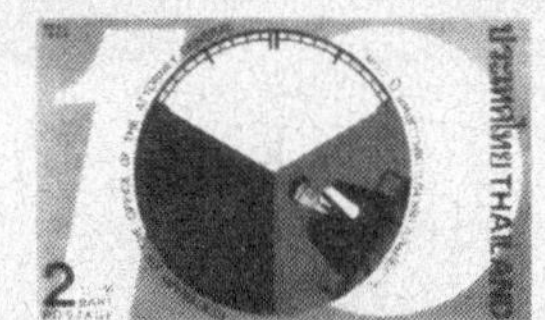

560 Clock, Emblem and Attorney General

1993. Centenary of Attorney General's Office.
1675 **560** 2 b. multicoloured . . . 15 10

561 Wat Chedi Chet Thaeo

1993. Thai Heritage Conservation Day. Si Satchanalai Historical Park, Sukhothai Province. Mult.
1676 3 b. Type **561** 15 10
1677 4 b. Wat Chang Lom 20 15
1678 6 b. Wat Phra Si Rattanamahathat 30 20
1679 7 b. Wat Suan Kaeo Utthayan Noi 40 20

562 Demon riding Cock

1993. Songkran (New Year) Day. Year of the Cock.
1681 **562** 2 b. multicoloured 10 10

563 "Marasmius sp."

1993. Fungi. Multicoloured.
1683 2 b. Type **563** 15 10
1684 4 b. "Coprinus sp." 30 20
1685 6 b. "Mycena sp." 45 25
1686 8 b. "Cyathus sp." 65 30

564 "Communications in the Next Decade"

1993. National Communications Day.
1688 **564** 2 b. multicoloured 10 10

565 Emblem, Morse Key and Satellite

1993. 110th Anniv of Post and Telegraph Department.
1689 **565** 2 b. multicoloured 10 10

566 Monument, Park and Reservoir

1993. Unveiling of Queen Suriyothai's Monument.
1690 **566** 2 b. multicoloured 10 10

567 Fawn Ridgeback

1993. International Correspondence Week. The Thai Ridgeback. Multicoloured.
1691 2 b. Type **567** 10 10
1692 3 b. Black 15 10
1693 5 b. Tan 25 15
1694 10 b. Grey 50 30

568 Tangerine

569 Bencharong Cosmetic Jar

1993. Fruits. Multicoloured.
1696 2 b. Type **568** 10 10
1697 3 b. Bananas 15 10
1698 6 b. Star gooseberry 30 15
1699 8 b. Marian plum 40 25

1993. "Bangkok 1993" International Stamp Exhibition (4th issue). Multicoloured.
1700 3 b. Type **569** 15 10
1701 5 b. Bencharong round cosmetic jar 25 15
1702 6 b. Lai Nam Thong tall cosmetic jar 30 20
1703 7 b. Lai Nam Thong cosmetic jar 35 20

570 Emblem and Oil Rigs

1993. 5th Association of South East Asian Nations Council on Petroleum Conference and Exhibition.
1706 **570** 2 b. multicoloured 10 10

571 King Prajadhipok 572 "Ipomea cairica"

1993. Birth Centenary of King Prajadhipok (Rama VII).
1707 **571** 2 b. brown and gold 15 10

1993. New Year. Flowers. Multicoloured.
1708 1 b. Type **572** 10 10
1709 1 b. "Decaschistia parviflora" 10 10
1710 1 b. "Hibiscus tiliaceus" 10 10
1711 1 b. "Passiflora foetida" 10 10

1993. No. 1031a surch **1 BAHT**.
1713 **227** 1 b. on 25 s. red 10 10

574 "Thaicom-1" Satellite, "Ariane 4" Rocket and Map of Thailand

1993. Launch of "Thaicom-1" (1st Thai communications satellite).
1714 **574** 2 b. multicoloured 10 10

575 "Play Land" (Piyathida Chapirom)

1994. Children's Day.
1715 **575** 2 b. multicoloured 10 10

576 Hospital Administrative Building

1994. Red Cross. 80th Anniv of Chulalongkorn Hospital.
1716 **576** 2 b. multicoloured 10 10

577 Emblem and Book

1994. 60th Anniv of Royal Institute.
1717 **577** 2 b. multicoloured 10 10

578 Wat Ratchaburana

1994. Thai Heritage Conservation Day. Phra Nakhon Si Ayutthaya Historical Park. Multicoloured.
1718 2 b. Type **578** 10 10
1719 3 b. Wat Maha That 15 10
1720 6 b. Wat Maheyong 30 20
1721 9 b. Wat Phra Si Sanphet 45 30

579 Friendship Bridge

1994. Inauguration of Friendship Bridge (between Thailand and Laos).
1723 **579** 9 b. multicoloured 45 30

580 Demon riding Dog

1994. Songkran (New Year) Day. Year of the Dog.
1724 **580** 2 b. multicoloured 10 10

582 Football

1994. Centenary of Int Olympic Committee. Mult.
1727 2 b. Type **582** 10 10
1728 3 b. Running 15 10
1729 5 b. Swimming 25 15
1730 6 b. Weightlifting 30 20
1731 9 b. Boxing 45 30

583 Dome Building

1994. 60th Anniv of Thammasat University.
1732 **583** 2 b. multicoloured 10 10

584 "Buddha giving First Sermon" (mural from Wat Thong Thammachat)

1994. Asalhapuja Day.
1733 **584** 2 b. multicoloured 10 10

585 Communications orbiting Thailand

1994. National Communications Day.
1734 **585** 2 b. multicoloured 10 10

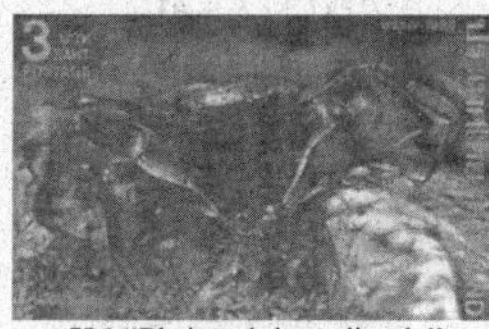
586 "Phricotelphusa limula"

1994. Crabs. Multicoloured.
1735 3 b. Type **586** 15 10
1736 5 b. "Thaipotamon chulabhorn" 25 15
1737 6 b. "Phricotelphusa sirindhorn" 30 20
1738 10 b. "Thaiphusa sirikit" 50 30

587 Gold Niello Betel Nut Set

1994. International Correspondence Week. Betel Nut Sets.
1740 2 b. Type **587** 10 10
1741 6 b. Gold-plated silver niello set 30 20
1742 8 b. Silver niello set 40 25
1743 9 b. Gold niello set 45 25

588 Emblem and Workers

1994. 75th Anniv of I.L.O.
1745 **588** 2 b. multicoloured 10 10

589 "Eriocaulon odoratum"

1994. New Year. Flowers. Multicoloured.
1746 1 b. Type **589** 10 10
1747 1 b. "Utricularia bifida" 10 10
1748 1 b. "Utricularia delphinioides" 10 10
1749 1 b. "Utricularia minutissima" 10 10

590 Making Garland

1994. 60th Anniv of Suan Dusit Teachers' College.
1751 **590** 2 b. multicoloured 10 10

591 Chakri Mahaprasart Throne Hall and Kings Chulalongkorn and Bhumibol

1994. 120th Anniv of Council of State.
1754 **591** 2 b. stone, blue and green 10 10

592 Emblem and Airplane

1994. 50th Anniv of I.C.A.O.
1755 **592** 2 b. multicoloured . . . 10 10

593 Dvaravati Grinding Stone (7–11th century)

1994. 80th Anniv of Pharmacy in Thailand.
1756 2 b. Type **593** 10 10
1757 6 b. Lopburi grinding stone (11–13th century) 30 20
1758 9 b. Bangkok period grinding stone (18–20th century) . . 45 30

594 Water Polo

1994. 18th South-East Asian Games, Chiang Mai. Multicoloured.
1759 2 b. + 1 b. Type **594** 15 10
1760 2 b. + 1 b. Tennis 15 10
1761 2 b. + 1 b. Hurdling 15 10
1762 2 b. + 1 b. Gymnastics . . . 15 10

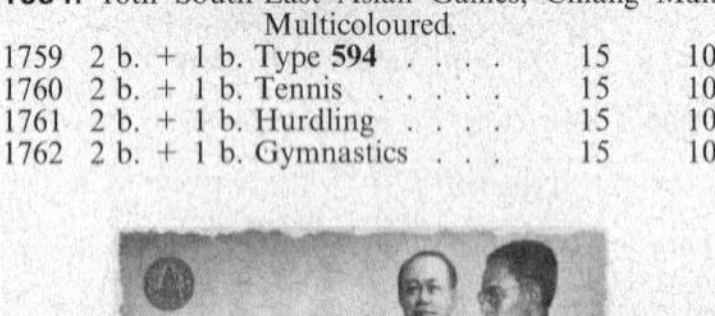

595 First Bar Building and Kings Vajiravudh and Bhumibol

1995. 80th Anniv of the Bar.
1764 **595** 2 b. multicoloured . . . 10 10

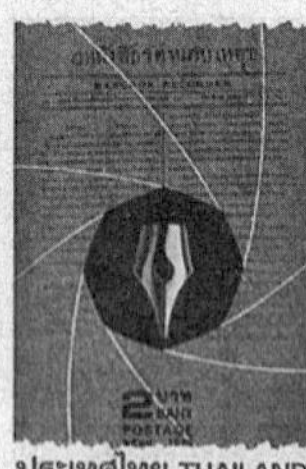

596 "Kites decorate the Summer Sky" (Kontorn Taechoran)

597 Front Page of First Edition and Pen Nib in Camera Shutter

1995. Children's Day. Multicoloured.
1765 2 b. Type **596** 10 10
1766 2 b. "Trees and Streams" (Yuvadee Samutpong) (horiz) 10 10
1767 2 b. "Youths and Religion" (Yutdanai Polyium) (horiz) 10 10

1995. 150th Anniv of "Bangkok Recorder" (newspaper).
1768 **597** 2 b. multicoloured . . . 10 10

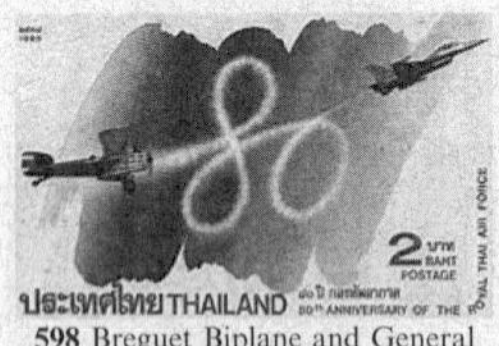

598 Breguet Biplane and General Dynamics Fighting Falcon Jet Fighter

1995. 80th Anniv of Royal Thai Airforce.
1769 **598** 2 b. multicoloured . . . 10 10

599 "Wetchapha"

1995. Red Cross. 40th Anniv of "Wetchapha" (floating clinic).
1770 **599** 2 b. multicoloured . . . 10 10

600 Naga Bridge

1995. Thai Heritage Conservation Day. Phimai Historical Park. Multicoloured.
1771 3 b. Type **600** 15 10
1772 5 b. Brahmin Hall 25 15
1773 6 b. Gateway in inner wall . 30 20
1774 9 b. Main pagoda 45 30

601 Administration Hall

1995. 108th Anniv of Ministry of Defence.
1776 **601** 2 b. multicoloured . . . 10 10

602 Woman riding Boar

1995. Songkran (New Year) Day.
1777 **602** 2 b. multicoloured . . . 10 10

603 King Rama V and Saranrom Palace

1995. 120th Anniv of Ministry of Foreign Affairs.
1779 **603** 2 b. multicoloured . . . 10 10

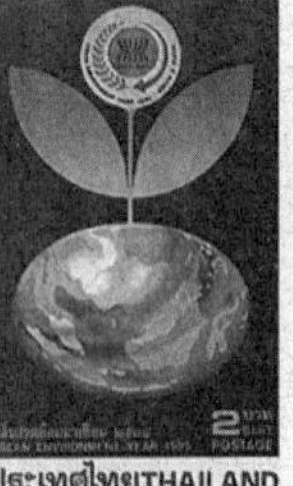

604 Emerald Buddha

605 Emblem forming Flower and Globe

1995. Visakhapuja Day. Statues of Buddha. Multicoloured.
1780 2 b. Type **604** 10 10
1781 6 b. Phra Phuttha Chinnarat 30 20
1782 8 b. Phra Phuttha Sihing . . 40 25
1783 9 b. Phra Sukhothai Traimit 45 30

1995. Association of South East Asian Nations Environment Year.
1785 **605** 2 b. multicoloured . . . 10 10

606 Emblem

1995. Thailand Information Technology Year.
1786 **606** 2 b. multicoloured . . . 10 10

607 Asian Elephants and Young

1995. 20th Anniv of Thailand–China Diplomatic Relations. Multicoloured.
1787 2 b. Type **607** 10 10
1788 2 b. Asian elephants at river (face value at left) 10 10
Nos. 1787/8 were issued together, se-tenant, forming a composite design.

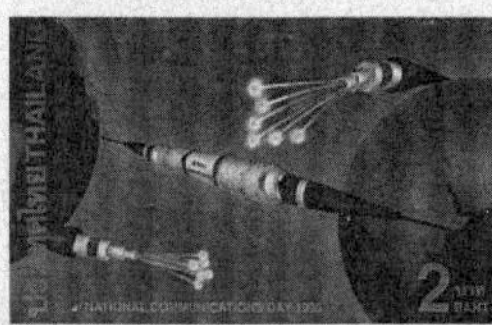

608 Optical Fibre Cables

1995. National Communications Day.
1790 **608** 2 b. multicoloured . . . 10 10

609 Khoa Manee

610 Headquarters

1995. "Thaipex'95" National Stamp Exhibition. Cats. Multicoloured.
1791 3 b. Type **609** 15 10
1792 6 b. Korat 30 20
1793 7 b. Sealpoint Siamese 35 20
1794 9 b. Burmese 45 30

1995. 80th Anniv of Revenue Department.
1796 **610** 2 b. multicoloured . . . 10 10

611 Money and Industry

1995. 120th Anniv of National Auditing.
1797 **611** 2 b. multicoloured . . . 10 10

612 Khong

1995. International Correspondence Week. Wicker Aquatic Animal Baskets.
1798 2 b. Type **612** 10 10
1799 2 b. Krachangklom (round basket) 10 10
1800 9 b. Sum (open-ended basket) 45 30
1801 9 b. Ichu (jar) 45 30

613 Foodstuffs and Anniversary Emblem

1995. 50th Anniv of F.A.O.
1803 **613** 2 b. multicoloured . . . 10 10

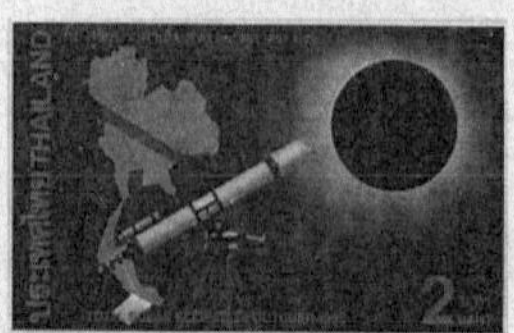

614 Telescope and Eclipse

1995. Total Solar Eclipse.
1804 **614** 2 b. multicoloured . . . 10 10

615 U.N. Building, Thailand

1995. 50th Anniv of U.N.O.
1805 **615** 2 b. multicoloured . . . 10 10

616 Tower

617 "Adenium obesum"

1995. "WORLDTECH'95" International Agricultural and Industrial Exhibition, Suranaree. Multicoloured.
1806 2 b. Type **616** 10 10
1807 5 b. Agriculture 25 15
1808 6 b. Modern technology (horiz) 30 15
1809 9 b. Reservoirs and coastline (horiz) 45 30

1996. New Year. Flowers. Multicoloured.
1810 2 b. Type **617** 10 10
1811 2 b. "Bauhinia acuminata" . . 10 10
1812 2 b. "Cananga odorata" . . 10 10
1813 2 b. "Thunbergia erecta" . . 10 10

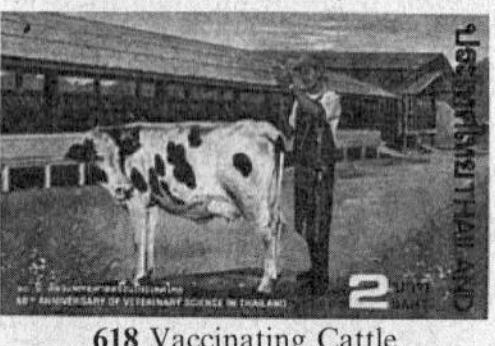

618 Vaccinating Cattle

1995. 60th Anniv of Veterinary Science in Thailand.
1815 **618** 2 b. multicoloured . . . 10 10

619 Fencing

620 Queen Somdej Phra Sri Patcharin (founder)

1995. 18th South-East Asian Games, Chiang Mai. Multicoloured.
1816 2 b. + 1 b. Type **619** 15 10
1817 2 b. + 1 b. Snooker 15 10
1818 2 b. + 1 b. Diving 15 10
1819 2 b. + 1 b. Pole vaulting . . . 15 10
Nos. 1815/18 were issued together, se-tenant, forming a composite design.

1996. Centenary of Siriraj School of Nursing and Midwifery.
1821 **620** 2 b. multicoloured . . . 10 10

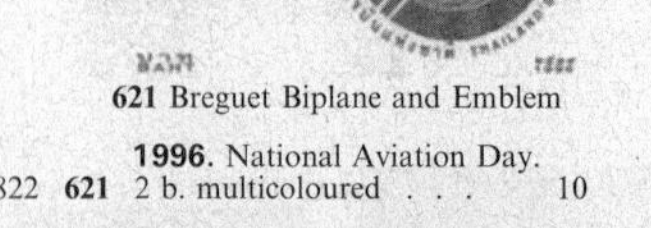

621 Breguet Biplane and Emblem

1996. National Aviation Day.
1822 **621** 2 b. multicoloured . . . 10 10

622 "Visakhapuja Day" (Malinee Sanaewong)

1996. Children's Day. Children's Drawings. Multicoloured.
1823 2 b. Type **622** 10 10
1824 2 b. "Maghapuja Day" (Thirapon Deephlub) (tree in centre) (vert) 10 10
1825 2 b. "Asalhapuja Day" (Voraphat Pankian) (tree at left) (vert) 10 10

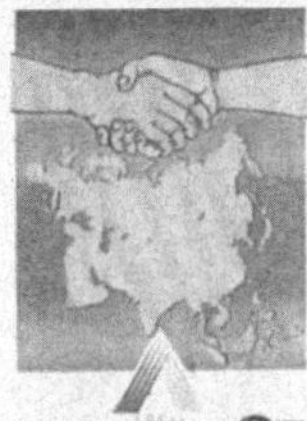

623 Handshake and Map of Asia and Europe

1996. Asia–Europe Summit Meeting, Thailand.

1826 **623** 2 b. multicoloured . . . 10 10

624 Temiyajataka

1996. Maghapuja Day. Multicoloured.

1827 2 b. Type **624** 10 10
1828 6 b. Mahajanakajataka . . . 30 15
1829 8 b. Suvannasamjataka . . . 40 25
1830 9 b. Nemijataka 45 30

625 Princess Mother and Golden Crematorium

1996. Princess Mother's Cremation.

1832 **625** 2 b. multicoloured . . . 10 10

626 Wat Phra Kaeo

1996. Thai Heritage Conservation Day. Kamphaeng Phet Historical Park. Multicoloured.

1833 2 b. Type **626** 10 10
1834 3 b. Wat Phra Non 15 10
1835 6 b. Wat Chang Rop 30 15
1836 9 b. Wat Pgra Si Iriyabot . . 45 30

627 Buddhist Pagoda, Wat Chiang Man

1996. 700th Anniv of Chiang Mai. Multicoloured.

1838 2 b. Type **627** 10 10
1839 6 b. Angel sculpture, Wat Chet Yot's Pagoda 30 15
1840 8 b. Insignia of Wat Phan Tao monastery 40 25
1841 9 b. Sattaphanta 45 30

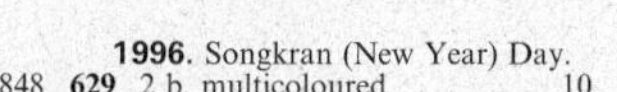
628 Rufous-necked Hornbills **629** Angel riding Rat

1996. 2nd International Asian Hornbill Workshop. Multicoloured.

1843 3 b. Type **628** 15 10
1844 3 b. Long-crested ("White-crowned") hornbill 15 10
1845 9 b. Plain-pouched hornbill . . 45 30
1846 9 b. Rhinoceros hornbill . . 45 30

1996. Songkran (New Year) Day.

1848 **629** 2 b. multicoloured . . . 10 10

630 Royal Ablutions Ceremony

631 King Bhumibol

1996. 50th Anniv of King Bhumibol's Accession to Throne as Rama IX. Multicoloured. (a) Coronation Ceremony. Multicoloured.

1851 3 b. Type **630** 15 10
1852 3 b. Pouring of the Libation 15 10
1853 3 b. Grand Audience 15 10
1854 3 b. Royal Progress by land 15 10
1855 3 b. Making speech from balcony 15 10

(b) Royal Regalia. As T **630.**

1857 3 b. Betal and areca-nut set . 15 10
1858 3 b. Water urn 15 10
1859 3 b. Gold-enamelled cuspidor and golden spittoon (horiz) 15 10

(c) National Development. As T **630** but horiz.

1861 3 b. Cultivation of vetiver grass (prevention of soil erosion) 15 10
1862 3 b. Chai Pattana aerator (improvement of water quality) 15 10
1863 3 b. Airplane (rain-making project) 15 10
1864 3 b. Dam (water resources development) 15 10
1865 3 b. Sapling (Golden Jubilee Reforestation Campaign) . 15 10

(d) Type **631.**

1867 100 b. multicoloured . . . . 5·00 3·25

632 Baron Pierre de Coubertin (founder) and Grave **633** King Bhumibol using Short-wave Radio

1996. Centenary of Modern Olympic Games. Multicoloured.

1868 2 b. Type **632** 10 10
1869 3 b. Lighting Olympic flame at Olympia, Greece 15 10
1870 5 b. First modern Games and Olympic flag 25 15
1871 9 b. Athlete and medal from 1896 Games 45 30

1996. National Communications Day.

1872 **633** 2 b. multicoloured . . 10 10

634 Tropical Rain Forest

1996. Centenary of Royal Forest Department. Multicoloured.

1873 3 b. Type **634** 15 10
1874 6 b. Evergreen mountain forest 30 15
1875 7 b. Swamp forest 35 20
1876 9 b. Mangrove forest 45 30

635 "Ramayana"

1996. International Correspondence Week. Thai Novels. Multicoloured.

1878 3 b. Type **635** 15 10
1879 3 b. Inao and Budsaba in cave ("Inao") 15 10
1880 9 b. Lunhap being shown round forest ("Ngao Pa") 45 30
1881 9 b. The cursing of Nang Mathanal ("Mathanapatha") 45 30

636 Youth Activities

1996. Asia Regional Conference of Rotary International, Thailand.

1883 **636** 2 b. multicoloured . . . 10 10

OFFICIAL STAMPS

O 133 (Trans "For Government Service Statistical Research")

1963.

O495 **O 133** 10 s. red and pink . . 10 10
O496 20 s. red and green . . 15 10
O500 20 s. green 25 20
O497 25 s. red and blue . . 25 25
O501 25 s. blue 25 25
O502 50 s. red 60 75
O498 1 b. red and grey . . 75 1·10
O503 1 b. grey 45 45
O499 2 b. red and bronze . 1·25 1·10
O504 2 b. bistre . . . . . . 1·40 1·60

The above were used compulsorily by Government Departments between 1st October 1963 and 31st January 1964, to determine the amount of mail sent out by the different departments for the purpose of charging them in the future. They were postmarked in the usual way.

THESSALY Pt. 16

Special stamps issued during the Turkish occupation in the Graeco-Turkish War of 1898.

40 paras = 1 piastre

20

1898.

M162	**20**	10 pa. green	2·75	2·75
M163		20 pa. red	2·75	2·75
M164		1 pi. blue	2·75	2·75
M165		2 pi. orange	2·75	2·75
M166		5 pi. violet	2·75	2·75

THRACE Pt. 3

A portion of Greece to the N. of the Aegean Sea for which stamps were issued by the Allies in 1919 and by the Greek Government in 1920. Now uses Greek stamps.

1919. 100 stotinki = 1 leva.
1920. 100 lepta = 1 drachma.

1920. Stamps of Bulgaria optd **THRACE INTERALLIEE** in two lines.

28	**49**	1 s. black	10	15
29		2 s. grey	10	15
30	**50**	5 s. green	10	15
31		10 s. red	10	15
32		15 s. violet	15	15
33	–	25 s. black & blue (No. 165)	10	15
34	–	1 l. brown (No. 168)	65	1·00
35	–	2 l. brown (No. 191)	1·25	1·50
36	–	3 l. red (No. 192)	1·75	2·50

1920. Stamps of Bulgaria optd **THRACE INTERALLIEE** in one line.

40	**49**	1 s. black	30	45
41		2 s. grey	30	45
42	**50**	5 s. green	20	15
43		10 s. red	20	15
44		15 s. violet	35	35
45	–	25 s. black & blue (No. 165)	35	35

1920. Stamps of Bulgaria optd **THRACE Interalliee** in two lines vertically.

46	**50**	5 s. green	10	10
47		10 s. red	10	10
48		15 s. violet	10	10
49		50 s. brown	25	25

1920. Stamps of Bulgaria optd **THRACE OCCIDENTALE.**

50	**50**	5 s. green	10	10
51		10 s. red	10	10
52		15 s. violet	10	10
53		25 s. blue	10	10
54		30 s. brown (imperf)	15	15
55		50 s. brown	10	10

Διοίκησις
Δυτικῆς
Θράκης
(8)

1920. 1911 stamps of Greece optd with T **8**.

69	**29**	1 l. green	20	20
70	**30**	2 l. red	20	20
71	**29**	3 l. red	20	20
72	**31**	5 l. green	20	20
73	**29**	10 l. red	20	20
74	**30**	15 l. blue	20	20
75		25 l. blue	45	45
76	**31**	30 l. red	14·00	14·00
77	**30**	40 l. blue	90	90
78	**31**	50 l. purple	1·00	1·00
79	**32**	1 d. blue	5·50	5·50
80		2 d. red	12·00	12·00
65		3 d. red	32·00	32·00
66		5 d. blue	11·00	11·00
67		10 d. blue	7·00	7·00
68	–	25 d. blue (No. 212)	26·00	26·00

The opt on the 25 d. is in capital letters.

1920. 1916 stamps of Greece, with opt Greece T 38 optd with T **8**.

81	**29**	1 l. green (No. 269)	20	20
82	**30**	2 l. red	20	20
83	**29**	10 l. red	25	25
84	**30**	20 l. purple	55	55
85	**31**	30 l. red	70	70
86	**32**	2 d. red	14·00	14·00
87		3 d. red	4·50	4·50
88		5 d. blue	17·00	17·00
89		10 d. blue	12·00	12·00

Διοίκησις
Θράκης
(10)

Ὑπάτη Ἁρμοστεία
Θράκης
5 Λεπτὰ 5
(11)

1920. Issue for E. Thrace. 1911 stamps of Greece optd with T **10**.

93	**29**	1 l. green	20	20
94	**30**	2 l. red	20	20
95	**29**	3 l. red	20	20
96	**31**	5 l. green	20	20
97	**29**	10 l. red	55	55
98	**30**	20 l. lilac	55	55
99		25 l. blue	80	80
100		40 l. blue	1·50	1·50
101	**31**	50 l. purple	1·75	1·75
102	**32**	1 d. blue	5·50	5·50
103		2 d. red	13·00	13·00
92	–	25 d. blue (No. 212)	40·00	40·00

1920. 1916 stamps of Greece with opt T **38** of Greece, optd with T **10**.

104	**30**	2 l. red (No. 270)	25	25
105	**31**	5 l. green	1·40	1·40
106	**30**	20 l. purple	50	50
107	**31**	30 l. red	50	50
108	**32**	3 d. red	5·00	5·00
109		5 d. blue	9·50	9·50
110		10 d. blue	19·00	19·00

1920. Occupation of Adrianople. Stamps of Turkey surch as T **11**.

111	**72**	1 l. on 5 pa. orange	45	60
112	–	5 l. on 3 pi. blue (No. 965)	45	55
113	–	20 l. on 1 pi. grn (No. 964)	60	60
114	**69**	25 l. on 5 pi. on 2 pa. blue	70	70
115	**78**	50 l. on 5 pi. black & grn	2·25	2·25
116	**74**	1 d. on 20 pa. red	1·75	1·75
117	**30**	2 d. on 10 pa. on 2 pa. olive	2·25	2·25
118	**85**	3 d. on 1 pi. blue	6·00	6·00
119	**31**	5 d. on 20 pa. red	7·50	7·50

POSTAGE DUE STAMPS

1919. Postage Due stamps of Bulgaria optd **THRACE INTERALLIEE.** Perf.

D37	**D 37**	5 s. green	15	15
D38		10 s. violet	25	25
D39		50 s. blue	40	50

1920. Postage Due stamps of Bulgaria optd **THRACE OCCIDENTALE.** Imperf or perf (10 s.).

D56	**D 37**	5 s. green	10	10
D57		10 s. violet	60	60
D58		20 s. orange	10	10
D59		50 s. blue	30	30

THURN AND TAXIS Pt. 7

The Counts of Thurn and Taxis had a postal monopoly in parts of Germany and issued special stamps.

N. District. 30 silbergroschen = 1 thaler.
S. District. 60 kreuzer = 1 gulden.

NORTHERN DISTRICT

1

1852. Imperf.

1	**1**	¼ sgr. black on brown	£130	32·00
2		⅓ sgr. black on pink	50·00	£250
3		½ sgr. black on green	£200	17·00
5		1 sgr. black on blue	£350	50·00
8		2 sgr. black on pink	£325	15·00
10		3 sgr. black on yellow	£300	9·00

1859. Imperf.

12	**1**	¼ sgr. red	30·00	42·00
20		⅓ sgr. black	12·00	38·00
21		⅓ sgr. green	15·00	£300
13		½ sgr. green	£150	55·00
23		½ sgr. orange	48·00	26·00
14		1 sgr. blue	£150	17·00
25		1 sgr. pink	30·00	13·00
15		2 sgr. pink	80·00	42·00
27		2 sgr. blue	22·00	60·00
17		3 sgr. red	80·00	60·00
29		3 sgr. brown	10·00	27·00
18		5 sgr. mauve	1·00	£275
19		10 sgr. orange	1·00	£550

1865. Rouletted.

31	**1**	¼ sgr. black	8·50	£550
32		⅓ sgr. green	10·00	£300
33		½ sgr. yellow	20·00	32·00
34		1 sgr. pink	22·00	16·00
35		2 sgr. blue	1·25	65·00
36		3 sgr. brown	1·75	28·00

SOUTHERN DISTRICT

3

1852. Imperf.

51	**3**	1 k. black on green	85·00	9·50
53		3 k. black on blue	£375	22·00
57		6 k. black on pink	£400	16·00
58		9 k. black on yellow	£325	8·50

1859. Imperf.

60	**3**	1 k. green	12·00	6·00
62		3 k. blue	£300	12·00
68		3 k. pink	27·00	10·00
63		6 k. pink	£300	38·00
70		6 k. blue	5·00	18·00
65		9 k. yellow	£300	50·00
73		9 k. brown	5·00	18·00
66		15 k. purple	1·00	£150
67		30 k. orange	1·00	£425

1865. Roul.

74	**3**	1 k. green	11·00	12·00
81		3 k. pink	1·00	17·00
76		6 k. blue	1·25	20·00
77		9 k. brown	1·25	23·00

TIBET Pt. 17

Former independent state in the Himalayas, now part of China.

A. CHINESE POST OFFICES

12 pies = 1 anna;
16 annas = 1 Indian rupee

分貳
One Anna

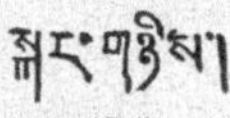

(C 1)

1911. Stamps of China of 1898 surch as Type **C 1**.

C 1	**32**	3 p. on 1 c. buff	2·25	6·00
C 2		½ a. on 2 c. green	3·25	6·50
C 3		1 a. on 4 c. red	3·50	6·50
C 4		2 a. on 7 c. lake	3·50	8·00
C 5		2½ a. on 10 c. blue	3·50	8·00
C 6	**33**	3 a. on 16 c. olive	10·00	12·00
C 7		4 a. on 20 c. red	8·50	12·00
C 8		6 a. on 30 c. red	14·00	18·00
C 9		12 a. on 50 c. green	25·00	30·00
C10	**34**	1 r. on $1 red and salmon	£150	£150
C11		2 r. on $2 red and yellow	£500	£500

These stamps were used in Post Offices set up by the Chinese army sent to Tibet in 1910. Following a revolt by the Tibetans these troops were withdrawn during 1912.

B. INDEPENDENT STATE

6⅔ trangka = 1 sang

1 (⅙ t.)

⅓ t. ½ t. ⅔ t. 1 t. 1 s.

1912. Imperf.

1	**1**	⅙ t. green	10·00	15·00
2		⅓ t. blue	14·00	15·00
3		½ t. purple	15·00	15·00
4		⅔ t. red	19·00	18·00
5		1 t. red	22·00	40·00
6		1 s. green	45·00	45·00

2 (4 t.)

1914. Imperf.

7b	**2**	4 t. blue	£225	£225
8b		8 t. red	£140	£140

In the 8 t. the rays from the circles in the corners of the stamp point outwards towards the corner.

3 (1 t.) Tibetan Lion ½ t. ⅔ t. 2 t. 4 t.

1933. Perf or Imperf.

9a	**3**	½ t. yellow to orange	8·50	15·00
10b		⅔ t. blue	10·00	12·00
11a		1 t. red	8·00	8·50
11b		1 t. orange	8·00	9·00
12a		2 t. red	9·00	8·00
12c		2 t. orange	9·50	9·00
13d		4 t. green	8·50	5·50

TIERRA DEL FUEGO Pt. 20

An island at the extreme S. of S. America. Stamp issued for use on correspondence to the mainland. Currency is expressed in centigrammes of gold dust.

1 Gold-digger's Pick and Hammer

1891.

1	**1**	10 c. red	12·00	

TIMOR Pt. 9

The eastern part of Timor in the Indonesian Archipelago. Administered as part of Macao until 1896, then as a separate Portuguese Overseas Province until 1975.

Following a civil war and the intervention of Indonesian forces the territory was incorporated into Indonesia on 17th July, 1976.

1885. 1000 reis = 1 milreis.
1894 100 avos = 1 pataca.
1960. 100 centavos = 1 escudo.

1885. "Crown" key-type inscr "MACAU" optd **TIMOR.**

1	**P**	5 r. black	70	60
12		10 r. green	1·50	1·25
3		20 r. red	3·25	1·75
4		25 r. lilac	60	30
5		40 r. yellow	1·25	1·00
6		50 r. blue	70	50
7		80 r. grey	1·75	1·10
8		100 r. purple	70	60
19		200 r. orange	1·75	1·40
20		300 r. brown	1·75	1·40

1887. "Embossed" key-type inscr "CORREIO DE TIMOR".

21	**Q**	5 r. black	1·10	70
22		10 r. green	1·25	1·10
23		20 r. red	2·00	1·10
24		25 r. mauve	2·10	1·25
25		40 r. brown	4·25	1·75
26		50 r. blue	4·25	1·75
27		80 r. grey	5·75	2·00
28		100 r. brown	5·75	2·40
29		200 r. lilac	10·00	5·00
30		300 r. orange	12·00	6·00

1892. "Embossed" key-type inscr "PROVINCIA DE MACAU" surch **TIMOR 30 30.** No gum.

32	**Q**	30 on 300 r. orange	2·75	1·60

1894. "Figures" key-type inscr "TIMOR".

33	**R**	5 r. orange	85	50
34		10 r. mauve	85	60
35		15 r. brown	1·00	60
36		20 r. lilac	1·00	60
37		25 r. green	1·10	60
38		50 r. blue	1·75	1·25
39		75 r. pink	2·10	1·90
40		80 r. green	2·10	1·90
41		100 r. brown on buff	2·00	1·90
42		150 r. red on pink	6·75	3·75
43		200 r. blue on blue	6·75	3·75
44		300 r. blue on brown	8·50	4·25

1894. Nos. 21/30 surch **PROVISORIO** and value in European and Chinese. No gum.

46	**Q**	1 a. on 5 r. black	85	50
47		2 a. on 10 r. green	1·00	85
48		3 a. on 20 r. red	1·25	85
49		4 a. on 25 r. purple	1·25	85
50		6 a. on 40 r. brown	1·75	85
51		8 a. on 50 r. blue	2·75	1·75
52		13 a. on 80 r. grey	4·00	4·00
53		16 a. on 100 r. brown	4·00	4·00
54		31 a. on 200 r. lilac	13·50	7·50
55		47 a. on 300 r. orange	15·00	11·00

1895. No. 32 further surch **5 avos PROVISORIO** and Chinese characters with bars over the original surch.

56	**Q**	5 a. on 30 on 300 r. orange	2·75	2·00

1898. 400th Anniv of Vasco da Gama's Discovery of Route to India. As T **40, 43** and **44** of Portugal, but inscr "TIMOR" and value in local currency.

58	½ a. green	90	60
59	1 a. red	90	60
60	2 a. purple	85	60
61	4 a. green	85	60
62	8 a. blue	1·25	1·00
63	12 a. brown	1·75	1·10
64	16 a. brown	1·75	1·50
65	24 a. brown	2·10	1·50

1898. "King Carlos" key-type inscr "TIMOR". Name and value in red (78 a.) or black (others). With or without gum.

68	**S**	½ a. grey	25	25
69		1 a. red	25	25
70		2 a. green	25	25
71		2½ a. brown	25	25
72		3 a. lilac	70	25
112		3 a. green	85	70
73		4 a. green	70	25
113		5 a. red	85	70
114		6 a. brown	85	70
74		8 a. blue	70	25

115 S 9 a. brown 85 70
75 10 a. blue 70 25
116 10 a. brown 85 70
76 12 a. pink 70 25
117 12 a. blue 4·25 3·75
118 13 a. mauve 1·25 85
119 15 a. lilac 2·00 1·75
78 16 a. blue on blue 1·90 1·75
79 20 a. brown on yellow 1·90 1·75
120 22 a. brown on pink 2·00 1·75
80 24 a. brown on buff 1·90 1·75
81 31 a. purple on pink 1·90 1·75
121 31 a. brown on cream 2·00 1·75
82 47 a. blue on pink 3·25 2·75
122 47 a. purple on pink 2·00 1·75
83 78 a. black on blue 4·25 3·75
123 78 a. blue on yellow 4·75 3·75

1899. Nos. 78 and 81 surch **PROVISORIO** and value in figures and bars.
84 S 10 on 16 a. blue on blue 1·25 1·10
85 20 on 31 a. purple on pink 1·25 1·10

1902. Surch.
88 R 5 a. on 5 r. orange 65 45
86 Q 5 a. on 25 r. mauve 1·00 60
89 R 5 a. on 25 r. green 65 40
90 5 a. on 50 r. blue 70 60
87 Q 5 a. on 200 r. lilac 1·60 1·00
95 V 6 a. on 2½ r. brown 40 30
92 Q 6 a. on 10 r. green 55·00 42·00
94 R 6 a. on 20 r. lilac 70 65
93 Q 6 a. on 300 r. orange 1·50 1·10
100 R 9 a. on 15 r. brown 70 55
98 Q 9 a. on 40 r. brown 1·75 1·75
101 R 9 a. on 75 r. pink 70 55
99 Q 9 a. on 100 r. brown 1·25 1·25
124 S 10 a. on 12 a. blue 1·25 1·10
104 R 15 a. on 10 r. mauve 1·00 85
102 Q 15 a. on 20 r. red 1·75 1·25
103 15 a. on 50 r. blue 50·00 42·00
105 R 15 a. on 100 r. brn on buff 1·00 85
106 15 a. on 300 r. bl on brn 1·00 85
107 Q 22 a. on 80 r. grey 3·25 2·75
108 R 22 a. on 80 r. green 1·75 1·50
109 22 a. on 200 r. blue on bl 1·75 1·50

1902. Nos. 72 and 76 optd **PROVISORIO**.
110 S 3 a. lilac 1·00 70
111 12 a. pink 2·75 2·00

1911. Nos. 68, etc, optd **REPUBLICA**.
125 S ½ a. grey 15 15
126 1 a. red 15 15
127 2 a. green 15 15
128 3 a. green 15 15
129 5 a. red 30 15
130 6 a. brown 30 15
131 9 a. brown 30 15
132 10 a. brown 70 55
133 13 a. purple 70 55
134 15 a. lilac 70 55
135 22 a. brown on pink 70 55
136 31 a. brown on cream 70 60
163 31 a. purple on pink 1·25 1·10
137 47 a. purple on pink 1·10 1·00
165 47 a. blue on pink 1·90 1·75
167 78 a. blue on yelow 1·75 1·40
168 78 a. black on blue 2·25 2·00

1911. No. 112 and provisional stamps of 1902 optd **Republica**.
139 S 3 a. green 1·40 1·25
140 R 5 a. on 5 r. orange 60 30
141 5 a. on 25 r. green 60 30
142 5 a. on 50 r. blue 1·75 1·25
144 V 6 a. on 2½ r. brown 1·40 80
146 R 6 a. on 20 r. lilac 55 60
147 9 a. on 15 r. brown 85 60
148 S 10 a. on 12 a. blue 85 60
149 R 15 a. on 100 r. brown on buff 90 60
150 22 a. on 80 r. green 1·75 1·25
151 22 a. on 200 r. blue on bl 1·75 1·25

1913. Provisional stamps of 1902 optd **REPUBLICA**.
192 S 3 a. lilac (No. 110) 30 20
194 R 5 a. on 5 r. orange 30 20
195 5 a. on 25 r. green 30 20
196 5 a. on 50 r. blue 30 20
200 V 6 a. on 2½ r. brown 30 20
201 R 6 a. on 20 r. lilac 30 20
202 9 a. on 15 r. brown 30 20
203 9 a. on 75 r. pink 30 20
193 S 10 a. on 10 a. blue 30 20
204 R 15 a. on 10 r. mauve 30 20
205 15 a. on 100 r. brown on buff 40 20
206 15 a. on 300 r. bl on brn 40 20
207 22 a. on 80 r. green 1·00 70
208 22 a. on 200 r. blue on bl 1·60 1·10

1913. Vasco da Gama stamps of Timor optd **REPUBLICA** or surch also.
169 ½ a. green 40 30
170 1 a. red 40 30
171 2 a. purple 40 30
172 4 a. green 40 30
173 8 a. blue 70 40
174 10 a. on 12 a. brown 90 85
175 16 a. brown 70 60
176 24 a. brown 1·00 85

1914. "Ceres" key-type inscr "TIMOR". Name and value in black.
211 U ½ a. green 30 25
212 1 a. black 30 25
213 1½ a. green 60 55
214 2 a. green 30 25
180 3 a. brown 40 30
181 4 a. red 40 30
182 6 a. violet 60 30
216 7 a. green 90 80
217 7½ a. blue 90 80
218 9 a. blue 1·00 80
183 10 a. blue 60 30
219 11 a. grey 1·25 80
184 12 a. brown 70 45
221 15 a. mauve 2·50 2·10
185 16 a. grey 85 60
222 18 a. blue 3·00 2·10
223 19 a. green 3·00 2·10
186 20 a. red 6·50 2·25
224 U 36 a. turquoise 3·00 2·10
187 40 a. purple 3·75 2·00
225 54 a. brown 3·00 2·10
188 58 a. brown on green 3·75 2·10
226 72 a. red 6·00 4·00
189 76 a. brown on pink 3·75 3·25
190 1 p. orange on orange 6·00 5·00
191 3 p. green on blue 13·50 10·00
227 5 p. red 25·00 12·50

1920. No. 196 surch ½ **Avo P. P. n°. 68 19-3-1920** and bars.
229 R ½ a. on 5 a. on 50 r. blue 2·00 1·75

1932. Nos. 226 and 221 surch with new value and bars.
230 U 6 a. on 72 a. red 70 60
231 12 a. on 15 a. mauve 70 60

1935. As T **40** of Portuguese India ("Portugal" and San Gabriel), but inscr "TIMOR".
232 **40** ½ a. brown 15 15
233 1 a. brown 15 15
234 2 a. green 15 15
235 3 a. mauve 35 15
236 4 a. black 35 15
237 5 a. grey 35 25
238 6 a. brown 35 25
239 7 a. red 35 25
240 8 a. turquoise 60 25
241 10 a. red 60 25
242 12 a. blue 60 25
243 14 a. green 60 25
244 15 a. purple 60 25
245 20 a. orange 60 25
246 30 a. green 60 25
247 40 a. violet 1·75 50
248 50 a. brown 1·75 50
249 1 p. blue 3·25 2·50
250 2 p. brown 9·00 4·25
251 3 p. green 13·50 5·00
252 5 p. mauve 22·00 9·25

1938. As T **54** and **56** of Macao. Name and value in black.
253 **54** 1 a. green (postage) 25 25
254 2 a. brown 25 25
255 3 a. violet 25 25
256 4 a. green 25 25
257 – 5 a. red 25 25
258 – 6 a. grey 25 25
259 – 8 a. purple 25 25
260 – 10 a. mauve 25 25
261 – 12 a. red 25 25
262 – 15 a. orange 30 30
263 – 20 a. blue 30 30
264 – 40 a. black 40 30
265 – 50 a. brown 1·00 60
266 – 1 p. red 3·00 2·00
267 – 2 p. olive 6·75 2·00
268 – 3 p. blue 8·25 4·75
269 – 5 p. brown 20·00 8·75
270 **56** 1 a. red (air) 30 30
271 2 a. violet 30 30
272 3 a. orange 30 30
273 5 a. blue 40 30
274 10 a. red 50 40
275 20 a. green 1·10 70
276 50 a. brown 2·10 2·00
277 70 a. red 2·75 2·10
278 1 p. mauve 5·75 3·75
DESIGNS—POSTAGE: 5 a. to 8 a. Mousinho de Albuquerque; 10 a. to 15 a. Prince Henry the Navigator; 20 a. to 50 a. Dam; 1 p. to 5 p. Afonso de Albuquerque.

1946. Stamps as above but inscr "MOCAMBIQUE" surch **TIMOR** and new value.
279 **54** 1 a. on 15 c. purple (post) 2·40 1·60
280 – 4 a. on 35 c. green 2·40 1·60
281 – 8 a. on 50 c. mauve 2·40 1·60
282 – 10 a. on 70 c. violet 2·40 1·60
283 – 12 a. on 1 e. red 2·40 1·60
284 – 20 a. on 1 e. 75 blue 2·40 1·60
285 **56** 8 a. on 50 c. orange (air) 2·40 1·60
286 12 a. on 1 e. blue 2·40 1·60
287 40 a. on 3 e. green 2·40 1·60
288 50 a. on 5 e. brown 2·40 1·60
289 1 p. on 10 e. mauve 2·40 1·60

1947. Nos. 253/64 and 270/78 optd **LIBERTACAO**.
290 **22** 1 a. green (postage) 6·25 2·10
291 2 a. brown 14·00 7·50
292 3 a. violet 5·75 2·25
293 4 a. green 5·75 2·25
294 – 5 a. red 2·25 90
295 – 8 a. purple 60 20
296 – 10 a. mauve 2·25 1·00
297 – 12 a. red 2·25 1·00
298 – 15 a. orange 2·25 1·00
299 – 20 a. blue 32·00 18·00
300 – 40 a. black 7·50 4·75
301 **27** 1 a. red (air) 9·25 3·00
302 2 a. violet 9·25 3·00
303 3 a. orange 9·25 3·00
304 5 a. blue 9·25 3·00
305 10 a. red 2·25 90
306 20 a. green 2·25 90
307 50 a. brown 3·00 90
308 70 a. red 9·25 2·50
309 1 p. mauve 4·00 55

30 Girl with Gong **31** Pottery-making

1948.
310 – 1 a. brown and turquoise 50 25
311 **30** 3 a. brown and grey 90 50
312 – 4 a. green and mauve 1·10 1·00
313 – 8 a. grey and red 70 25
314 – 10 a. green and brown 70 25
315 – 20 a. ultramarine and blue 70 30
316 – 1 p. blue and orange 12·50 3·00
317 – 3 p. brown and violet 13·50 6·75
DESIGNS: 1 a. Native woman; 4 a. Girl with baskets; 8 a. Chief of Aleixo de Ainaro; 10 a. Timor chief; 20 a. Warrior and horse; 1, 3 p. Tribal chieftains.

1948. Honouring the Statue of Our Lady of Fatima. As T **62** of Macao.
318 8 a. grey 4·00 4·00

1949. 75th Anniv of U.P.U. As T **64** of Macao.
319 16 a. brown 9·25 5·75

1950.
320 **31** 20 a. blue 45 30
321 – 50 a. brown (Young girl) 1·25 60

1950. Holy Year. As Nos. 425/6 of Macao.
322 40 a. green 90 70
323 70 a. brown 1·75 1·00

32 "Belamcanda chinensis" **34** Statue of The Virgin

1950.
324 **32** 1 a. red, green and grey 30 20
325 – 3 a. yellow, green & brown 1·75 1·10
326 – 10 a. pink, green and blue 1·75 1·25
327 – 16 a. multicoloured 3·75 1·75
328 – 20 a. yellow, green and turquoise 1·75 1·10
329 – 30 a. yellow, green & blue 1·75 1·10
330 – 70 a. multicoloured 2·25 1·40
331 – 1 p. red, yellow and green 4·00 3·25
332 – 2 p. green, yellow and red 6·25 5·25
333 – 5 p. pink, green and black 11·50 8·50
FLOWERS: 3 a. "Caesalpinia pulcherrima"; 10 a. "Calotropis gigantea"; 16 a. "Delonix regia"; 20 a. "Plumeria rubra"; 30 a. "Allamanda cathartica"; 70 a. "Haemanthus multiflorus"; 1 p. "Bauhinia"; 2 p. "Eurycles amboiniensis"; 5 p. "Crinum longiflorum".

1951. Termination of Holy Year. As T **69** of Macao.
334 86 a. blue and turquoise 1·25 1·10

1952. 1st Tropical Medicine Congress, Lisbon. As T **46** of St. Thomas and Prince Islands.
335 10 a. brown and green 70 60
DESIGN: Nurse weighing baby.

1952. 400th Death Anniv of St. Francis Xavier. Designs as No. 452/4 of Macao.
336 1 a. black and grey 15 10
337 16 a. brown and buff 55 40
338 1 p. red and grey 2·10 1·25

1953. Missionary Art Exhibition.
339 **34** 3 a. brown and light brown 10 10
340 16 a. brown and stone 40 30
341 50 a. blue and brown 1·25 1·10

1954. Portuguese Stamp Cent. As T **75** of Macao.
342 10 a. multicoloured 70 60

1954. 400th Anniv of Sao Paulo. As T **76** of Macao.
343 16 a. multicoloured 70 40

35 Map of Timor **38** Elephant Jar

1956.
344 **35** 1 a. multicoloured 10 10
345 3 a. multicoloured 10 10
346 8 a. multicoloured 20 10
347 24 a. multicoloured 20 10
348 32 a. multicoloured 30 10
349 40 a. multicoloured 60 25
350 1 p. multicoloured 1·40 40
351 3 p. multicoloured 4·25 2·10

1958. 6th Int Congress of Tropical Medicine. As T **79** of Macao.
352 32 a. multicoloured 2·10 1·75
DESIGN: 32 a. "Calophyllum inophyllum" (plant).

1958. Brussels Int Exn. As T **78** of Macao.
353 40 a. multicoloured 40 30

1960. New currency. Nos. 344/51 surch thus: **$05** and bars.
354 **35** 5 c. on 1 a. multicoloured 10 10
355 10 c. on 3 a. multicoloured 10 10
356 20 c. on 8 a. multicoloured 10 10
357 30 c. on 24 a. multicoloured 10 10
358 50 c. on 32 s. multicoloured 10 10
359 1 e. on 40 a. multicoloured 15 10
360 2 e. on 40 a. multicoloured 20 15
361 5 e. on 1 p. multicoloured 45 30
362 10 e. on 3 p. multicoloured 1·75 90
363 15 e. on 3 p. multicoloured 1·75 1·10

1960. 500th Death Anniv of Prince Henry the Navigator. As T **55** of St. Thomas and Prince Islands. Multicoloured.
364 4 e. 50 Prince Henry's motto (horiz) 40 25

1962. Timor Art. Multicoloured.
365 5 c. Type **38** 10 10
366 10 c. House on stilts 10 10
367 20 c. Idol 25 10
368 30 c. Rosary 25 25
369 50 c. Model of outrigger canoe (horiz) 25 25
370 1 e. Casket 40 30
371 2 e. 50 Archer 30 30
372 4 e. Elephant 60 30
373 5 e. Native climbing palm tree 70 30
374 10 e. Statuette of woman 90 30
375 20 e. Model of cockfight (horiz) 2·75 90
376 50 e. House, bird and cat 6·75 2·10

1962. Sports. As T **82** of Macao. Multicoloured.
377 50 c. Game shooting 10 10
378 1 e. Horse-riding 50 15
379 1 e. 50 Swimming 25 10
380 2 e. Athletes 25 15
381 2 e. 50 Football 35 25
382 15 e. Big-game hunting 1·25 80

1962. Malaria Eradication. Mosquito design as T **83** of Macao. Multicoloured.
383 2 e. 50 "Anopheles sundaicus" 40 30

1964. Centenary of National Overseas Bank. As T **84** of Macao but portrait of M. P. Chagas.
384 2 e. 50 multicoloured 50 30

1965. I.T.U. Centenary. As T **85** of Macao.
385 1 e. 50 multicoloured 70 40

1966. 40th Anniv of National Revolution. As T **86** of Macao but showing different buildings. Mult.
386 4 e. 50 Dr. V. Machado's College and Health Centre, Dili 60 35

1967. Centenary of Military Naval Assn. As T **88** of Macao. Multicoloured.
387 10 c. Gago Coutinho and gunboat "Patria" 15 15
388 4 e. 50 Sacadura Cabral and Fairey IIID seaplane "Lusitania" 1·00 40

39 Sepoy Officer, 1792 **40** Pictorial Map of 1834, and Arms

1967. Portuguese Military Uniforms. Mult.
389 35 c. Type **39** 15 15
390 1 e. Infantry officer, 1815 95 25
391 1 e. 50 Infantryman 1879 15 15
392 2 e. Infantryman, 1890 15 15
393 2 e. 50 Infantry officer, 1903 25 15
394 3 e. Sapper, 1918 35 25
395 4 e. 50 Commando, 1964 70 25
396 10 e. Parachutist, 1964 95 60

1967. 50th Anniv of Fatima Apparitions. As T **89** of Macao.
397 3 e. Virgin of the Pilgrims 25 10

1968. 500th Birth Anniv of Pedro Cabral (explorer). As T **90** of Macao. Multicoloured.
398 4 e. 50 Lopo Homen-Reineis' map, 1519 (horiz) 70 30

1969. Birth Centenary of Admiral Gago Coutinho. As T **91** of Macao. Multicoloured.
399 4 e. 50 Frigate "Almirante Gago Coutinho" (horiz) 1·75 70

1969. Bicentenary of Dili (capital of Timor).
400 **40** 1 e. multicoloured 25 15

1969. 500th Anniv of Vasco da Gama (explorer). As T **92** of Macao. Multicoloured.
401 5 e. Convert Medallion 25 20

1969. Centenary of Overseas Administrative Reforms. As T **93** of Macao.
402 5 e. multicolured 25 15

1969. 500th Birth Anniv of King Manoel I. As T **95** of Macao. Multicoloured.
403 4 e. Emblem of Manoel I in Jeronimos Monastery 20 15

41 Map, Sir Ross Smith, and Arms of Britain, Timor and Australia

1969. 50th Anniv of 1st England–Australia Flight.
404 **41** 2 e. multicoloured 35 25

1970. Birth Centenary of Marshal Carmona. As T **96** of Macao.
414 1 e. Portrait in civilian dress 15 15

1972. 400th Anniv of Camoens' "The Lusiads" (epic poem). As T **77** of St. Thomas and Prince Islands. Multicoloured.
415 1 e. Missionaries, natives and galleon 15 15

1972. Olympic Games, Munich. As T **78** of St. Thomas and Prince Islands. Multicoloured.
416 4 e. 50 Football 40 25

1972. 50th Anniv of 1st Flight from Lisbon to Rio de Janeiro. As T **79** of St. Thomas and Prince Islands. Multicoloured.
417 1 e. Aviators Gago Coutinho and Sacadura Cabral in Fairey IIID seaplane 30 25

1973. W.M.O. Centenary. As T **102** of Macao.
418 20 e. multicoloured 1·10 90

CHARITY TAX STAMPS

The notes under this heading in Portugal also apply here.

1919. No. 211 surch **2 AVOS TAXA DA GUERRA**. With or without gum.
C228 U 2 a. on ½ a. green 2·25 1·10

1919. No. 196 surch **2 TAXA DE GUERRA** and bars.
C230 R 2 on 5 a. on 50 r. blue 28·00 16·00

1925. Marquis de Pombal Commem. As Nos. 666/8 of Portugal, but inscr "TIMOR".
C231 C **73** 2 a. red 20 20
C232 – 2 a. red 20 20
C233 C **75** 2 a. red 20 20

1934. Educational Tax. Fiscal stamps as Type C **1** of Portuguese Colonies, with values in black, optd **Instrucao D. L. n.° 7 de 3-2-1934** or surch also. With or without gum.
C234 2 a. green 1·75 1·00
C235 5 a. green 2·75 1·25
C236 7 a. on ½ a. pink 2·75 1·75

1936. Fiscal stamps as Type C **1** of Portuguese Colonies, with value in black, optd **Assistencia D. L. n.° 72**. With or without gum.
C253 10 a. pink 1·75 1·25
C254 10 a. green 1·25 1·00

C 29

C 42 Woman and Star

1948. No gum.
C310 C **29** 10 a. blue 1·25 1·10
C311 20 a. green 2·00 1·25
The 20 a. has a different emblem.

1960. Similar design. New currency. No gum.
C364 70 c. blue 1·00 1·00
C400 1 e. 30 green 1·10 1·10

1969.
C405 C **42** 30 c. blue and light blue 10 10
C406 50 c. purple & orange 10 10
C407 1 e. brown & yellow 10 10

1970. Nos. C364 and C400 surch **D. L. no. 776** and value.
C408 30 c. on 70 c. blue 2·75 2·75
C409 30 c. on 1 e. 30 green 2·75 2·75
C410 50 c. on 70 c. blue 4·00 4·00
C411 50 c. on 1 e. 30 green 2·75 2·75
C412 1 e. on 70 c. blue 4·00 4·00
C413 1 e. on 1 e. 30 green 2·75 2·75

NEWSPAPER STAMPS

1892. "Embossed" key-type inscr "PROVINCIA DE MACAU" surch **JORNAES TIMOR 2½ 2½**. No gum.
N31 Q 2½ on 20 r. red 1·00 60
N32 2½ on 40 r. brown 1·00 60
N33 2½ on 80 r. grey 1·00 60

1893. "Newspaper" key-type inscr "TIMOR".
N36 V 2½ r. brown 50 30

1894. No. N36 surch **½ avo PROVISORIO** and Chinese Characters.
N58 V ½ a. on 2½ r. brown 30 30

POSTAGE DUE STAMPS

1904. "Due" key-type inscr "TIMOR". Name and value in black. With or without gum (1, 2 a.), no gum (others).
D124 W 1 a. green 30 30
D125 2 a. grey 30 30
D126 5 a. brown 90 75
D127 6 a. orange 90 75
D128 10 a. brown 90 75
D129 15 a. brown 1·50 1·10
D130 24 a. blue 3·00 2·50
D131 40 a. red 3·00 2·50
D132 50 a. orange 4·00 3·00
D133 1 p. lilac 7·00 5·25

1911. "Due" key-type of Timor optd **REPUBLICA**.
D139 W 1 a. green 25 25
D140 2 a. grey 25 25
D141 5 a. brown 25 25
D142 6 a. orange 30 30
D143 10 a. brown 60 40
D144 15 a. brown 85 50
D145 24 a. blue 1·10 90
D146 40 a. red 1·40 1·10
D147 50 a. orange 1·40 1·10
D178 1 p. lilac 3·75 2·50

1925. Marquis de Pombal tax stamps. As Nos. C231/3 of Timor, optd **MULTA**.
D231 C **73** 4 a. red 20 20
D232 – 4 a. red 20 20
D233 C **75** 4 a. red 20 20

1952. As Type D **70** of Macao, but inscr "TIMOR PORTUGUES". Numerals in red; name in black.
D336 1 a. sepia and brown 10 10
D337 3 a. brown and orange 10 10
D338 5 a. green and turquoise 10 10
D339 10 a. green and light green 15 15
D340 30 a. violet & light violet 20 15
D341 1 p. red and orange 55 30

TOGO Pt. 7; Pt. 6; Pt. 14

A territory in W. Africa, formerly a German Colony. Divided between France and Gt. Britain in 1919, the British portion being attached to the Gold Coast for administration and using the stamps of that country. In 1956 the French portion became an autonomous republic within the French Union. Full independence was achieved in April 1960.

GERMAN ISSUES

100 pfenning = 1 mark

1897. Stamps of Germany optd **TOGO**.
G1a **8** 3 pf. brown 3·75 6·50
G2 5 pf. green 3·50 2·25
G3 **9** 10 pf. red 3·50 2·25
G4 20 pf. blue 4·50 12·00
G5 25 pf. orange 32·00 60·00
G6 50 pf. brown 32·00 60·00

1900. "Yacht" key-types inscr "TOGO".
G 7 N 3 pf. brown 65 75
G21 5 pf. green 1·00 2·00
G 9 10 pf. red 35·00 55
G10 20 pf. blue 85 1·25
G11 25 pf. black & red on yell 85 10·00
G12 30 pf. blk & orge on buff 1·25 10·00
G13 40 pf. black and red 85 10·00
G14 50 pf. black and purple on buff 1·25 8·50
G15 80 pf. black & red on pink 2·00 22·00
G16 O 1 m. red 2·50 48·00
G17 2 m. blue 4·00 80·00
G18 3 m. black 6·00 £150
G19 5 m. red and black £100 £500

FRENCH OCCUPATION

1914. Stamps of German Colonies, "Yacht" key-type, optd **Togo Occupation franco-anglaise** or surch also.
1 N 05 on 3 pf. brown 35·00 35·00
9 5 pf. green £750 £325
2 10 on 5 pf. green 14·00 12·50
10 10 pf. red £875 £350
3 20 pf. blue 35·00 35·00
4 25 pf. black & red on yell 38·00 35·00
5 30 pf. blk & orge on orge 65·00 60·00
6 40 pf. black and red £450 £400
15 50 pf. black & pur on buff £7500 £6500
7 80 pf. black & red on pink £450 £400
16 O 1 m. red — £14000
17 2 m. blue — £14000
18 3 m. black — £14000
19 5 m. red and black

1916. Stamps of Dahomey optd **TOGO Occupation franco-anglaise**.
20 **6** 1 c. black and violet 15 30
21 2 c. pink and brown 20 25
22 4 c. brown and black 20 25
23 5 c. green and light green 40 45
24 10 c. pink and orange 30 30
25 15 c. purple and red 60 60
26 20 c. brown and grey 45 45
27 25 c. blue and ultramarine 45 45
28 30 c. violet and brown 45 70
29 35 c. black and brown 60 90
30 40 c. orange and black 55 80
31 45 c. blue and grey 45 65
32 50 c. brown and chocolate 45 60
33 75 c. violet and blue 3·25 4·00
34 1 f. black and green 4·50 5·00
35 2 f. brown and yellow 6·00 6·75
36 5 f. blue and violet 7·25 5·50

FRENCH MANDATE

1921. Stamps of Dahomey optd **TOGO**.
37 **6** 1 c. green and grey 10 30
38 2 c. orange and blue 10 20
39 4 c. orange and green 20 30
40 5 c. black and red 20 30
41 10 c. green and turquoise 20 30
42 15 c. red and brown 40 60
43 20 c. orange and green 55 60
44 25 c. orange and grey 35 35
45 30 c. red and carmine 40 60
46 35 c. green and purple 55 75
47 40 c. grey and green 90 1·25
48 45 c. grey and purple 90 1·25
49 50 c. blue 45 50
50 75 c. blue and brown 95 1·25
51 1 f. blue and grey 1·10 1·25
52 2 f. red and green 3·25 3·50
53 5 f. black and yellow 4·75 4·75

1922. Stamps of 1921 (No. 57 colour changed) surch.
54 **6** 25 c. on 15 c. red and brown 20 25
55 25 c. on 2 f. red and green 25 40
56 25 c. on 5 f. black & orange 25 40
57 60 on 75 c. violet on pink 55 75
58 65 on 45 c. grey and purple 80 1·00
59 85 on 75 c. blue and brown 95 1·25

5 Coconut Palms

1924.
60 **5** 1 c. black and yellow 10 15
61 2 c. black and red 10 20
62 4 c. black and blue 10 25
63 5 c. black and orange 10 10
64 10 c. black and mauve 10 10
65 15 c. black and green 10 10
66 – 20 c. black and grey 10 10
67 – 25 c. black & green on yellow 10 10
68 – 30 c. black and green 30 30
69 – 30 c. green and olive 10 10
70 – 35 c. black and brown 20 35
71 – 35 c. green and turquoise 35 45
72 – 40 c. black and red 15 50
73 – 45 c. black and red 10 15
74 – 50 c. black & orange on blue 20 25
75 – 55 c. red and blue 10 10
76 – 60 c. black & purple on pink 30 55
77 – 60 c. red 10 30
78 – 65 c. brown and lilac 25 45
79 – 75 c. black and blue 20 35
80 – 80 c. lilac and blue 35 35
81 – 85 c. brown and orarnge 60 75
82 – 90 c. pink and red 50 65
83 – 1 f. black & purple on blue 60 80
84 – 1 f. blue 45 60
85 – 1 f. green and lilac 25 25
86 – 1 f. orange and red 1·40 1·40
87 – 1 f. 10 brown and mauve 3·00 2·00
88 – 1 f. 25 red and mauve 65 70
89 – 1 f. 50 blue 25 35
90 – 1 f. 75 pink and brown 4·75 1·40
91 – 1 f. 75 blue and ultramarine 60 70
92 – 2 f. grey and black on blue 65 65
93 – 3 f. red and green 80 80
94 – 5 f. black & orange on blue 1·00 1·10
95 – 10 f. pink and brown 1·10 1·25
96 – 20 f. black & red on yellow 1·25 1·40
DESIGNS: 20 c. to 90 c. Cocoa trees; 1 f. to 20 f. Palm trees.

1926. No. 84 surch.
98 1 f. 25 on 1 f. blue 25 25

1931. "Colonial Exhibition" key-types inscr "TOGO".
99 E 40 c. green and black 3·00 3·50
100 F 50 c. mauve and black 3·00 3·25
101 G 90 c. red and black 3·00 3·50
102 H 1 f. 50 blue and black 3·25 3·25

1937. International Exhibition, Paris. As Nos. 168/73 of St.-Pierre et Miquelon.
103 20 c. violet 1·00 1·25
104 30 c. green 1·00 1·40
105 40 c. red 95 1·25
106 50 c. brown 95 1·40
107 90 c. red 95 1·25
108 1 f. 50 blue 95 1·25

1938. International Anti-Cancer Fund. As T **22** of Mauritania.
109 1 f. 75 + 50 c. blue 10·50 13·50

1939. Centenary of Death of R. Caillie. As T **27** of Mauritania.
110 90 c. orange 45 60
111 2 f. violet 45 55
112 2 f. 25 blue 45 50

1939. New York World's Fair. As T **28** of Mauritania.
113 1 f. 25 red 45 60
114 2 f. 25 blue 50 60

1939. 150th Anniv of French Revolution. As T **29** of Mauritania.
115 45 c. + 25 c. green and black 4·00 4·75
116 70 c. + 30 c. brown & black 4·00 4·75
117 90 c. + 35 c. orange & black 4·00 4·75
118 1 f. 25 + 1 f. red and black 4·00 4·75
119 2 f. 25 + 2 f. blue and black 4·00 4·75

1940. Air. As T **30** of Mauritania.
120 1 f. 90 blue 15 30
121 2 f. 90 red 15 30
122 4 f. 30 green 25 40
123 4 f. 90 olive 35 50
124 6 f. 90 orange 60 70

8 Pounding Meal

9 Riverside Village

10 Hunting

11 Young Girl

1940.
125 **8** 2 c. violet 10 30
126 3 c. green 10 30
127 4 c. black 10 25
128 5 c. red 10 25
129 10 c. blue 10 25
130 15 c. brown 10 30
131 **9** 20 c. plum 10 25
132 25 c. blue 10 20
133 30 c. black 15 20
134 40 c. red 20 30
135 45 c. green 10 30
136 50 c. brown 20 40
137 60 c. violet 25 30
138 **10** 70 c. black 40 55
139 90 c. violet 65 85
140 1 f. green 25 45
141 1 f. 25 red 60 85
142 1 f. 40 brown 30 55
143 1 f. 60 orange 40 55
144 2 f. blue 40 65
145 **11** 2 f. 25 blue 70 90
146 2 f. 50 red 65 75
147 3 f. violet 50 75
148 5 f. red 60 60
149 10 f. violet 80 95
150 20 f. black 1·50 10

1941. National Defence Fund. Surch **SECOURS NATIONAL** and value.
151 + 1 f. on 50 c. (No. 136) 2·00 2·00
152 + 2 f. on 80 c. (No. 80) 2·75 3·00
153 + 2 f. on 1 f. 50 (No. 89) 2·75 3·00
154 + 3 f. on 2 f. (No. 144) 3·00 3·00

1942. Air. As T **32** of Mauritania.
154a 50 f. violet and yellow 70 80

1944. Nos. 75 and 82 surch **1 f. 50**.
155 1 f. 50 on 55 c. red and blue 45 60
156 1 f. 50 on 90 c. pink and red 45 60

1944. No. 139 surch in figures and ornament.
157 **10** 3 f. 50 on 90 c. violet 45 60
158 4 f. on 90 c. violet 45 60
159 5 f. on 90 c. violet 70 90
160 5 f. 50 on 90 c. violet 90 1·10
161 10 f. on 90 c. violet 90 1·10
162 20 f. on 90 c. violet 1·40 1·60

18 Oil Extraction Process

19 Archer

20 Postal Runner and Lockheed Constellation

1947.
163 **18** 10 c. red (postage) 15 25
164 30 c. blue 15 30
165 50 c. green 15 30
166 **19** 60 c. pink 15 30
167 1 f. brown 20 20
168 1 f. 20 green 20 40
169 – 1 f. 50 orange 35 60
170 – 2 f. bistre 35 35
171 – 2 f. 50 black 80 1·00
172 – 3 f. blue 40 65
173 – 3 f. 60 red 60 75
174 – 4 f. blue 40 45
175 – 5 f. brown 1·00 60
176 – 6 f. blue 1·00 1·25
177 – 10 f. red 1·25 40
178 – 15 f. green 1·40 50
179 – 20 f. green 1·25 70
180 – 25 f. pink 1·40 60

181 – 40 f. blue (air) 4·00 2·50
182 – 50 f. mauve and violet 1·90 1·10
183 – 100 f. brown and green 3·00 2·00
184 **20** 200 f. pink 5·00 4·00
DESIGNS—As Type **18**: VERT: 1 f. 50, to 2 f. 50, Women hand-spinning cotton. HORIZ: 3 f. to 4 f. Drummer and village; 5 f. to 10 f. Red-fronted gazelles; 15 f. to 25 f. Trees and village. As Type **20**: 40 f. African elephants and Sud Ouest SO.95 Corse II airplane; 50 f. Airplane; 100 f. Lockheed Constellation.

1949. Air. 75th Anniv of U.P.U. As T **38** of New Caledonia.
185 25 f. multicoloured 3·25 4·00

1950. Colonial Welfare Fund. As T **39** of New Caledonia.
186 10 f. +2 f. blue and indigo 2·00 2·25

1952. Centenary of Military Medal. As T **40** of New Caledonia.
187 15 f. brown, yellow & green 3·00 3·25

1954. Air. 10th Anniv of Liberation. As T **42** of New Caledonia.
188 15 f. violet and blue 2·50 2·75

22 Gathering Palm Nuts **23** Roadway through Forest

1954.
189 **22** 8 f. purple, lake and violet (postage) 70 60
190 15 f. brown, grey & blue 95 40
191 **23** 500 f. blue & green (air) 35·00 28·00

AUTONOMOUS REPUBLIC

24 Goliath Beetle **25** Rural School

1955. Nature Protection.
192 **24** 8 f. black and green 1·90 1·10

1956 Economic and Social Fund Development Fund.
193 **25** 15 f. brown and chestnut 3·00 1·40

26 Togolese Woman and Flag

1957. New National Flag.
194 **26** 15 f. brown, red & turquoise 60 30

27 Togolese Woman and "Liberty" releasing Dove

1957. Air. 1st Anniv of Autonomous Republic.
195 **27** 25 f. sepia, red and blue 55 45

28 Konkomba Helmet **29** Kob

30 Torch and Flags

1957. Inscr "REPUBLIQUE AUTONOME DU TOGO".
196 **28** 30 c. lilac and red (postage) 10 25
197 50 c. indigo and blue 10 25
198 1 f. lilac and purple 10 25
199 2 f. brown and green 10 25
200 3 f. black and green 15 25
201 **29** 4 f. black and blue 55 30
202 5 f. purple and grey 55 30
203 6 f. grey and red 70 35
204 8 f. violet and grey 70 35
205 10 f. brown and green 70 35
206 – 15 f. multicoloured 45 30
207 – 20 f. multicoloured 50 30
208 – 25 f. multicoloured 70 35
209 – 40 f. multicoloured 1·10 50
210 **30** 50 f. multicoloured (air) 1·10 50
211 100 f. multicoloured 2·00 1·10
212 200 f. multicoloured 3·75 1·90
213 – 500 f. indigo, green & blue 32·00 12·00
DESIGNS—HORIZ: 15 f. to 40 f. Teak forest; 48 × 27 mm: 500 f. Great egret.
See also Nos. 217/35.

31 "Human Rights" **32** "Bombax"

1958. 10th Anniv of Human Rights Declaration.
214 **31** 20 f. red and green 65 35

1959. Tropical Flora.
215 **32** 5 f. multicoloured 40 30
216 – 20 f. yellow, green & blk 75 35
DESIGN—HORIZ: 20 f. "Tectona".

1959. As Nos. 196/213 but colours changed and inscr "REPUBLIQUE DU TOGO".
217 **28** 30 c. blue & black (post) 10 25
218 50 c. green and green 20 25
219 1 f. purple and green 20 10
220 2 f. brown and green 20 10
221 3 f. violet and purple 20 25
222 **29** 4 f. violet and purple 45 30
223 5 f. brown and green 45 30
224 6 f. blue and ultramarine 45 40
225 8 f. bistre and green 45 35
226 10 f. brown and violet 45 30
227 – 15 f. multicoloured 50 30
228 – 20 f. multicoloured 60 50
229 – 25 f. multicoloured 80 45
230 – 40 f. multicoloured 1·00 45
231 – 25 f. brown, green and blue (air) 45 30
232 **30** 50 f. multicoloured 90 45
233 100 f. multicoloured 1·90 85
235 – 500 f. sepia, green & purple 4·25 1·75
DESIGN—VERT: 25 f. (No. 231) Togo flag and shadow of airliner over Africa.

32a Patient on Stretcher **33** "The Five Continents"

1959. Red Cross Commemoration.
236 **32a** 20 f. +5 f. red, orange and slate 80 80
237 – 30 f. +5 f. red, brown and blue 80 80
238 – 50 f. +10 f. red, brown and green 80 80
DESIGNS: 30 f. Mother feeding child; 50 f. Nurse superintending blood transfusion.

1959. United Nations Day.
239 **33** 15 f. blue and brown 30 30
240 20 f. blue and violet 35 30
241 25 f. blue and brown 45 35
242 40 f. blue and green 55 45
243 60 f. blue and red 75 50

34 Skiing **35** "Uprooted Tree"

1960. Olympic Games, California and Rome.
244 **34** 30 c. turquoise, red & green 15 25
245 – 50 c. purple, red and black 35 30
246 – 1 f. green, red and black 35 30
247 – 10 f. brown, blue & indigo 40 10
248 – 15 f. purple and green 45 40
249 – 20 f. chocolate, green & brn 55 40
250 – 25 f. brown, red & orange 85 45
DESIGNS—HORIZ: 50 c. Ice hockey; 1 f. Tobogganing; 10 f. Cycling; 25 f. Running. VERT: 125 f. Throwing the discus; 20 f. Boxing.

1960. World Refugee Year.
251 **35** 25 f. +5 f. green, brown and blue 55 75
252 – 45 f. +5 f. olive, black and blue 75 75
DESIGN: 45 f. As Type **35** but "TOGO" at foot.

INDEPENDENT REPUBLIC

36 Prime Minister S. Olympio and Flag **37** Benin Hotel

1960. Independence Commemoration. (a) Postage. Centres mult; backgrounds cream; inscription and frame colours given.
253 **36** 30 c. sepia 10 10
254 50 c. brown 10 10
255 1 f. purple 10 10
256 10 f. blue 15 10
257 20 f. red 40 15
258 25 f. green 50 20

(b) Air.
259 **37** 100 f. red, yellow & green 1·60 50
260 200 f. multicoloured 2·75 90
261 – 500 f. brown and green 11·00 2·75
DESIGN—As Type **37**: VERT: 500 f. Palm-nut vulture and map of Togo.

38 Union Jack and Flags

1960. Four-Power "Summit" Conf, Paris. Flags and inscr in red and blue.
262 **38** 50 c. buff 10 10
263 – 1 f. turquoise 10 10
264 – 20 f. grey 35 20
265 – 25 f. blue 40 20
DESIGNS—As Type **38** but flags of: 1 f. Soviet Union; 20 f. France; 25 f. U.S.A. The Conference did not take place.

39 Togo Flag **40** South African Crowned Cranes

1961. Admission of Togo into U.N.O. Flag in red, yellow and green.
266 **39** 30 c. red 10 10
267 50 c. brown 10 10
268 1 f. blue 10 10
269 10 f. purple 20 10
270 25 f. black 40 15
271 30 f. violet 45 20

1961.
272 **40** 1 f. multicoloured 50 10
273 10 f. multicoloured 70 15
274 25 f. multicoloured 1·10 40
275 30 f. multicoloured 1·25 50

41 Augustino de Souza (statesman) **42** Daniel Beard (founder of American Boy Scout Movement) and Scout Badge

1961. 1st Anniv of Independence.
276 **41** 50 c. black, red and yellow 10 10
277 1 f. black, brown and green 10 10
278 10 f. black, violet and blue 20 15
279 25 f. black, green & salmon 40 10
280 30 f. black, blue and mauve 50 20

1961. Boy Scout Movement Commemoration.
281 **42** 50 c. lake, green and red 10 10
282 – 1 f. violet and red 10 10
283 – 10 f. black and brown 20 10
284 – 25 f. multicoloured 55 15
285 – 30 f. red, brown & green 65 20
286 – 100 f. mauve and blue 1·60 60
DESIGNS—HORIZ: 1 f. Lord Baden Powell; 10 f. Daniel Mensah ("Rover" Scout Chief); 100 f. Scout salute. VERT: 25 f. Chief Daniel Wilson (Togolese Scout); 30 f. Campfire on triangular emblem.

43 Jet Airliner and Motor Launch **44** U.N.I.C.E.F. Emblem

1961. U.N. Economic Commission on Africa. Multicoloured.
287 20 f. Type **43** 30 15
288 25 f. Electric train and gantry 70 15
289 30 f. Excavator and pylons 65 30
290 85 f. Microscope and atomic symbol 1·25 50
The designs are superimposed on a map of Africa spread over the four stamps when the 30 and 85 f. are mounted below the 20 and 25 f.

1961. 15th Anniv of U.N.I.C.E.F.
291 **44** 1 f. blue, green and black 10 10
292 – 10 f. multicoloured 15 10
293 – 20 f. multicoloured 20 10
294 – 25 f. multicoloured 45 20
295 – 30 f. multicoloured 80 20
296 – 85 f. multicoloured 1·25 60
DESIGNS: 10 f. to 85 f. Children dancing round the globe. The six stamps, arranged in the following order, form a composite picture: Upper row, 1, 25 and 20 f. Lower row, 10, 85 and 30 f.

45 Alan Shepard **47** Togolese Girl

1962. Space Flights Commemoration.
297 **45** 50 c. green 10 10
298 – 1 f. mauve 15 10
299 **45** 25 f. blue 35 20
300 – 30 f. violet 50 30
DESIGN: 1, 30 f. As Type **45** but portrait of Yuri Gagarin.

1962. Col. Glenn's Space Flight. Surch **100 F COL. JOHN H. GLENN U S A VOL ORBITAL 20 FEVRIER 1962.**
301 **45** 100 f. on 50 c. green 2·00 2·00

1962. 2nd Anniv of Independence.
303 – 50 c. multicoloured 10 10
304 **47** 1 f. green and pink 10 10
305 – 5 f. multicoloured 20 15
306 **47** 20 f. violet and yellow 30 15
307 – 25 f. multicoloured 35 15
308 **47** 30 f. red and yellow 35 15
DESIGN: 50 c., 5, 25 f. Independence Monument.

48 Arrows piercing Mosquito

1962. Malaria Eradication.
309 **48** 10 f. multicoloured 30 10
310 25 f. multicoloured 45 20
311 30 f. multicoloured 50 35
312 85 f. multicoloured 1·00 55

49 Presidents Kennedy and Olympio, and Capitol, Washington

1962. Visit of President Olympio to U.S.A.
313 **49** 50 c. slate and ochre . . . 10 10
314 1 f. slate and blue 10 10
315 2 f. slate and red 10 10
316 5 f. slate and mauve . . . 10 10
317 25 f. slate and lilac 40 15
318 100 f. slate and green . . . 1·60 70

50 Stamps of 1897 and Mail-coach

1963 65th Anniv of Togolese Postal Services.
319 **50** 30 c. multicoloured (post) . 10 10
320 – 50 c. multicoloured 10 10
321 – 1 f. multicoloured 10 10
322 – 10 f. multicoloured 45 15
323 – 25 f. multicoloured 60 20
324 – 30 f. multicoloured 85 40
325 – 100 f. multicoloured (air) . 2·25 80
DESIGNS (Togo stamps of): 50 c. 1900 and German imperial yacht "Hohenzollern"; 1 f. 1915 and steam mail train; 10 f. 1924 and motor-cycle mail carrier; 25 f. 1940 and mail-van; 30 f. 1947 and Douglas DC-3 airplane; 100 f. 1960 and Boeing 707 airplane.

51 Hands reaching for F.A.O. Emblem

1963. Freedom from Hunger.
326 **51** 50 c. multicoloured 10 10
327 1 f. multicoloured 10 10
328 25 f. multicoloured 60 20
329 30 f. multicoloured 85 30

52 Lome Port and Togolese Flag **53** Centenary Emblem

1963. 3rd Anniv of Independence. Flag in red, yellow and green.
330 **52** 50 c. black and brown . . 10 10
331 1 f. black and red 15 10
332 25 f. black and blue 35 20
333 50 f. black and ochre . . . 70 35

1963. Red Cross Centenary. Flag red, yellow and green; cross red.
334 **53** 25 f. blue and black 85 30
335 30 f. green and black . . . 1·10 40

54 Broken Shackles and Abraham Lincoln **55** Flame and U.N. Emblem

1963. Cent of American Slaves' Emancipation. Centre in grey and green.
336 **54** 50 c. black & brown (post) 10 10
337 1 f. black and blue 10 10
338 25 f. black and red 45 15
339 100 f. black & orange (air) 1·40 60

1963. 15th Anniv of Declaration of Human Rights. Flame in red.
340 **55** 50 c. blue & ultramarine . 10 10
341 1 f. green and black 15 10
342 25 f. lilac and blue 40 15
343 85 f. gold and blue . . . . 1·10 60

56 Hibiscus **58** Temple and Isis

1964. Multicoloured.
344 50 c. "Odontoglossum grande" (orchid) (postage) 10 10
345 1 f. Type **56** 10 10
346 2 f. "Papilio dardanus" (butterfly) 35 10
347 3 f. "Morpho aega" (butterfly) 55 10
348 4 f. "Pandinus imperator" (scorpion) 40 10
349 5 f. Tortoise 20 15
350 6 f. Strelitzia (flower) 55 15
351 8 f. Python 45 15
352 10 f. "Bunaea alcinde" (butterfly) 85 15
353 15 f. Chameleon . . . . . . 1·25 15
354 20 f. Common octopus . . . 1·50 20
355 25 f. "Zeus faber" (fish) . . . 1·25 20
356 30 f. "Pomacanthus arcuatus" (fish) . . . . 1·50 35
357 40 f. Pygmy hippopotamus . . 2·00 35
358 45 f. African palm civet . . . 3·25 60
359 60 f. Bohar reedbuck . . . . 4·50 90
360 85 f. Olive baboon . . . . . 5·50 1·00
361 50 f. Black-bellied seedcracker (air) . . . . 4·75 90
362 100 f. Black and white mannikin 7·50 1·60
363 200 f. Red-faced lovebird . . 16·00 3·25
364 250 f. Grey parrot . . . . . 38·00 7·50
365 500 f. Yellow-breasted barbet 50·00 12·00

1964. President Kennedy Memorial Issue. Optd **En Memoire de JOHN F. KENNEDY 1917-1963**. Centre in grey and green.
366 **54** 50 c. blk & brn (postage) . 15 10
367 1 f. black and blue 15 10
368 25 f. black and red 50 20
369 100 f. black & orge (air) . 1·60 80

1964. Nubian Monuments Preservation.
370 **58** 20 f. multicoloured 30 10
371 – 25 f. mauve and black . . 35 20
372 – 30 f. olive, black & yellow 50 30
DESIGNS: 25 f. Head of Rameses II, Abu Simbel; 30 f. Temple of Philae.

59 Phosphate Mine, Kpeme

1964. 4th Anniv of Independence.
373 **59** 5 f. ochre, bistre & brown 10 10
374 – 25 f. lake, brown & violet . 35 15
375 – 60 f. yellow, olive & green 60 35
376 – 85 f. blue, slate & violet . 1·25 50
DESIGNS: 25 f. Mine installations; 60 f. Phosphate train; 85 f. Loading phosphate onto "Panama Maru" bulk carrier.

60 Togolese breaking Chain **61** Pres. Grunitzky and "Papilio memnon"

1964. 1st Anniv of African Heads of State Conf, Addis Ababa.
377 **60** 5 f. sepia & orge (postage) 15 10
378 25 f. sepia and green . . . 35 15
379 85 f. sepia and red 95 45
380 100 f. sepia & turq (air) . 1·25 65

1964. "National Union and Reconciliation".
381 **61** 1 f. violet and mauve . . . 20 10
382 – 5 f. sepia and ochre . . . 10 10
383 – 25 f. violet and blue . . . 45 15
384 **61** 45 f. purple and red . . . 1·75 50
385 – 85 f. bronze and green . . 1·90 60
DESIGNS—President and: 5 f. Dove; 25, 85 f. Flowers.

62 Football

1964. Olympic Games, Tokyo.
386 **62** 1 f. green (postage) . . . 10 10
387 – 5 f. blue (Running) 15 15
388 – 25 f. red (Throwing the discus) 50 15
389 **62** 45 f. turquoise 80 40
390 – 100 f. brown (Tennis) (air) 1·50 55

1964. French, African and Malagasy Co-operation. As T **68** of Mauritania.
391 25 f. brown, bistre and purple . 40 20

63 Charles's Hydrogen Balloon, Giffard's Steam-powered Dirigible Airship and Airship LZ-5

1964. Inaug of "Air Togo" (National Airline).
392 **63** 5 f. multicoloured (postage) 10 10
393 10 f. blue, lake and green . 30 10
394 – 25 f. ultramarine, orge & bl 50 15
395 – 45 f. mauve, green & blue . 1·10 35
396 – 100 f. multicoloured (air) . 1·90 80
DESIGNS: 25, 45 f. Farman H.F. III biplane, Lilienthal biplane glider and Boeing 707; 100 f. Boeing 707 and Togolese flag.

64 Sun, Globe and Satellites "Ogo" and "Mariner"

1964. International Quiet Sun Years. Sun yellow.
397 **64** 10 f. blue and red 15 10
398 – 15 f. blue, brown & mauve . 20 10
399 – 20 f. green and violet . . . 30 10
400 – 25 f. purple, green & blue . 35 15
401 **64** 45 f. blue and green 70 35
402 – 50 f. green and red 80 40
SATELLITES: 15, 25 f. "Tiros", "Telstar" and orbiting solar observatory; 20, 50 f. "Nimbus", "Syncom" and "Relay".

65 Pres. Grunitzky and the Mount of the Beatitudes Church

1965. Israel–Togo Friendship. Inscr "AMITIE ISRAEL–TOGO 1964".
403 – 5 f. purple 10 10
404 **65** 20 f. blue and purple . . . 20 10
405 – 25 f. turquoise and red . . 35 15
406 – 45 f. olive, bistre & purple . 70 35
407 – 85 f. turquoise and purple . 1·10 50
DESIGNS—VERT: 5 f. Togolese stamps being printed on Israel press. HORIZ: 25, 85 f. Arms of Israel and Togo; 45 f. As Type **65** but showing old synagogue, Capernaum.

66 "Syncom 3", Dish Aerial and I.T.U. Emblem

1965. I.T.U. Centenary.
408 **66** 10 f. turquoise and green . 15 10
409 20 f. olive and black 35 15
410 25 f. blue and ultramarine . 40 15
411 45 f. rose and red 70 35
412 50 f. green and black . . . 90 45

67 Abraham Lincoln **68** Throwing the Discus

1965. Death Centenary of Lincoln.
413 **67** 1 f. purple (postage) 10 10
414 5 f. greeen 10 10
415 20 f. brown 35 10
416 25 f. blue 45 20
417 100 f. olive (air) . . . . . 1·60 70

1965. 1st African Games, Brazzaville. Flags in red, yellow and green.
418 **68** 5 f. purple (postage) . . . 10 10
419 – 10 f. blue 15 10
420 – 15 f. brown 35 10
421 – 25 f. purple 90 20
422 – 100 f. green (air) . . . . 1·50 65
SPORTS: 10 f. Throwing the javelin; 15 f. Handball; 25 f. Running; 100 f. Football.

69 Sir Winston Churchill

1965. Churchill Commemoration.
423 **69** 5 f. green (postage) 10 10
424 – 10 f. violet and blue . . . 15 10
425 **69** 20 f. brown 40 15
426 – 45 f. blue 65 35
427 **69** 85 f. red (air) . . . . . . 1·50 65
DESIGNS—HORIZ: 10, 45 f. Stalin, Roosevelt and Churchill at Teheran Conference, 1943.

70 Unisphere

1965. New York World's Fair.
428 **70** 5 f. plum and blue 15 10
429 – 10 f. sepia and green . . . 20 10
430 **70** 25 f. myrtle and brown . . 35 20
431 – 50 f. myrtle and violet . . 65 40
432 **70** 85 f. brown and red . . . 1·10 50
DESIGNS: 10 f. Native dancers and drummer; 50 f. Michelangelo's "Pieta".

71 "Laying Bricks of Peace"

1965. International Co-operation Year.
433 **71** 5 f. multicoloured 10 10
434 15 f. multicoloured 15 15
435 – 25 f. multicoloured 30 15
436 – 40 f. multicoloured 60 30
437 – 85 f. multicoloured . . . . 1·00 50
DESIGNS. 25, 40 f. Hands suppporting globe; 85 f. I.C.Y. emblem.

72 Leonov with Camera

1965. Astronauts in Space.
438 **72** 25 f. mauve and blue . . . 50 20
439 – 50 f. brown and green . . . 90 40
DESIGN: 50 f. White with rocket-gun.

73 "ONU" and Doves

1966. 20th Anniv of U.N.O.
440 **73** 5 f. brown, yellow and blue (postage) 10 10
441 – 10 f. blue, turquoise and orange 20 10
442 – 20 f. orange, green and light green 35 15
443 – 25 f. blue, turquoise & yell 45 20
444 – 100 f. ochre, blue and light blue (air) . . . . 1·60 55
DESIGNS: 10 f. U.N. Headquarters and emblem; 20 f. "ONU" and orchids; 25 f. U.N. Headquarters and Adlai Stevenson; 100 f. "ONU", fruit and ears of wheat.

74 Pope Paul, Boeing 707 and U.N. Emblem

1966. Pope Paul's Visit to U.N. Organization. Multicoloured.
445 5 f. Type **74** (postage) 10 10
446 15 f. Pope before microphones at U.N. (vert) 20 10
477 20 f. Pope and U.N. Headquarters 35 15
448 30 f. As 15 f. 45 20
449 45 f. Pope before microphones at U.N., and map (air) 80 30
450 90 f. Type **74** . . . . 1·60 80

75 W.H.O. Building and Roses

1966. Inaug of W.H.O Headquarters, Geneva. Multicoloured designs showing W.H.O. Building and flower as given.
451 5 f. Type **75** (postage) 20 10
452 10 f. Alstroemerias 35 10
453 15 f. Asters 45 20
454 20 f. Freesias 55 35
455 30 f. Geraniums 65 35
456 50 f. Asters (air) 95 35
457 50 f. Type **75** . . . . 1·50 55

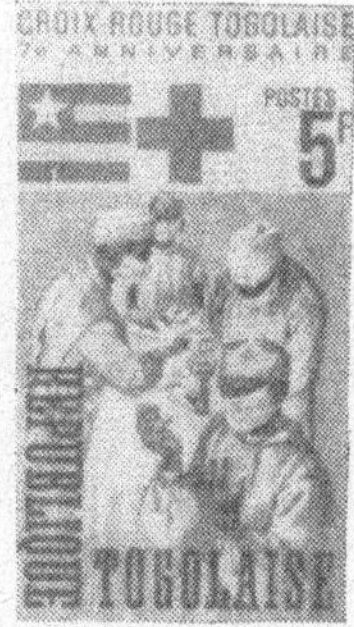

76 Surgical Operation

1966. 7th Anniv of Togolese Red Cross. Mult.
459 5 f. Type **76** (postage) 10 10
460 10 f. Blood transfusion 15 10
461 15 f. Type **76** 30 15
462 30 f. Blood transfusion 40 15
463 45 f. African man and woman 70 45
464 100 f. J. H. Dunant (air) . . . 1·75 90

1966. Space Achievements. Nos. 438/9 optd as below or surch also.
465 50 f. (**ENVOLEE SURVEYOR 1**) 85 40
466 50 f. (**ENVOLEE GEMINI 9**) 85 40
467 100 f. on 25 f. (**ENVOLEE LUNA 9**) . . . . 1·60 70
468 100 f. on 25 f. (**ENVOLEE VENUS 3**) . . . . 1·60 70

78 Wood-carving

79 Togolese Man

1966. Togolese Arts and Crafts.
469 **78** 5 f. brn, yell & bl (postage) 10 10
470 – 10 f. brown, salmon & grn 15 10
471 – 15 f. brown, yellow & red . 30 15
472 – 30 f. brown, bistre & violet 55 20
473 – 60 f. brown, salmon and blue (air) . . . . 1·40 60
474 **78** 90 f. brown, yellow & red . 1·40 60
DESIGNS: 10, 60 f. Basket-making; 15 f. Weaving; 30 f. Pottery.

1966. Air. Inauguration of Douglas DC-8F Air Services. As T **87** of Mauritania.
475 30 f. black, green & yellow . 65 25

1966. Togolese Costumes and Dances. Multicoloured.
476 5 f. Type **79** (postage) 10 10
477 10 f. Togolese woman 10 10
478 20 f. Female dancer 40 10
479 25 f. Male dancer 50 15
480 30 f. Dancer in horned helmet 65 20
481 45 f. Drummer . . . . 1·00 50
482 50 f. Female dancer (air) . . 85 45
483 60 f. Dancer in horned helmet 1·40 60

80 Footballers and Jules Rimet Cup

1966. World Cup Football Championships, England. Showing football scenes and Jules Rimet Cup.
484 **80** 5 f. mult (postage) 10 10
485 – 10 f. multicoloured 20 10
486 – 20 f. multicoloured 40 10
487 – 25 f. multicoloured 40 15
488 – 30 f. multicoloured 55 20
489 – 45 f. multicoloured 85 40
490 – 50 f. multicoloured (air) . 85 30
491 – 60 f. multicoloured . . . . 1·25 40

81 African Mouthbreeder

1967. Fishes. Multicoloured designs showing fishes with fishing craft in the background.
493 5 f. Type **81** (postage) 20 10
494 10 f. Golden cavally 35 10
495 15 f. Six banded distichodus . 40 10
496 25 f. Spotted cichlid 60 20
497 30 f. Type **81** 80 35
498 45 f. As 10 f. (air) . . . . . 1·25 45
499 90 f. As 15 f. . . . . 1·75 65

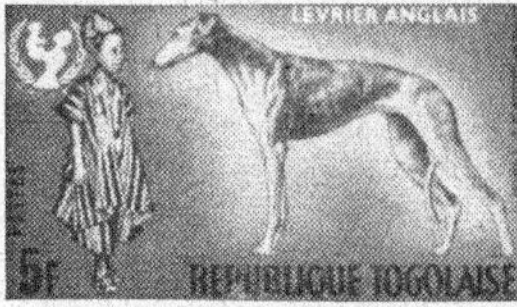

82 African Boy and Greyhound

1967. 20th Anniv (1966) of U.N.I.C.E.F.
500 **82** 5 f. multicoloured (postage) 20 10
501 – 10 f. brown, grn, & lt grn . 30 15
502 **82** 15 f. blk, brown & mauve 45 20
503 – 20 f. black, ultram & blue 60 30
504 **82** 30 f. black, blue & olive 95 35
505 – 45 f. bronze, brown and yellow (air) . . . . . . 1·00 40
506 **82** 90 c.. black, bronze & bl . 1·50 55
DESIGNS: 10 f. Boy and Irish setter; 20 f. Girl and doberman; 45 f. Girl and miniature poodle.

83 Launching "Diamant" Rocket

1967. French Space Achievements. Multicoloured.
508 5 f. Type **83** (postage) 10 10
509 10 f. Satellite "A-1" (horiz) . . 20 10
510 15 f. Satellite "FR-1" 30 10
511 20 f. Satellite "D-1" (horiz) . . 40 15
512 25 f. 25 f. As 10 f. 50 30
513 40 f. As 20 f. 70 35
514 50 f. Type **83** (air) 95 40
515 90 f. As 15 f. . . . . 1·50 55

84 Bach and Organ

1967. 20th Anniv (1966) of U.N.E.S.C.O.
517 **84** 5 f. mult (postage) 10 10
518 – 10 f. multicoloured 20 10
519 – 15 f. multicoloured 45 20
520 – 20 f. multicoloured 55 20
521 – 30 f. multicoloured 90 45
522 **84** 45 f. multicoloured (air) . . 1·10 40
523 – 90 f. multicoloured . . . . 1·60 55
DESIGNS: 10, 90 f. Beethoven, violin and clarinet; 15, 30 f. Duke Ellington, saxophone, trumpet and drums; 20 f. Debussy, grand piano and harp.

85 British Pavilion and Lilies

1967. World Fair, Montreal. Multicoloured.
525 5 f. Type **85** (postage) 15 10
526 10 f. French Pavilion and roses 20 10
527 30 f. "Africa Place" and strelitzia 55 15
528 45 f. As 10 f. (air) 85 35
529 60 f. Type **85** 95 45
530 90 f. As 30 f. . . . . 1·50 60
531 105 f. U.S. Pavilion and daisies 1·60 65

86 "Peace"

1967. Air. Disarmament. Designs showing sections of the "Peace" mural by J. Zanetti at the U.N. Headquarters Building Conference Room.
533 **86** 5 f. multicoloured . . . 15 10
534 A 15 f. multicoloured . . . 20 10
535 B 30 f. multicoloured . . . 40 10
536 **86** 45 f. multicoloured . . . 70 35
537 A 60 f. multicoloured . . . 1·25 45
538 B 90 f. multicoloured . . . 1·60 55

MINIMUM PRICE

The minimum price quoted is 10p which represents a handling charge rather than a basis for valuing common stamps. For further notes about prices, see introductory pages.

87 Lions Emblem with Supporters

1967. 50th Anniv of Lions International Mult.
540 10 f. Type **87** 20 10
541 20 f. Flowers and Lions emblem 35 15
542 30 f. Type **87** 45 20
543 45 f. As 20 f. . . . . 1·25 45

88 Bohar Reedbuck

1967. Wildlife.
544 **88** 5 f. brown & pur (postage) 10 10
545 – 10 f. blue, red and yellow . 1·25 40
546 – 15 f. black, lilac & green . 45 15
547 – 20 f. blue, sepia & yellow . 1·75 50
548 – 25 f. brown, yellow & olive 85 35
549 – 30 f. blue, violet & yellow . 2·25 70
550 – 45 f. brown & blue (air) . . 90 35
551 – 60 f. black, brown and green 1·25 50
DESIGNS: 10, 20, 30 f. Montagu's harriers (birds of prey); 15 f. Common zebra; 25 f. Leopard; 45 f. Lion; 60 f. African elephants.

1967. Air. 5th Anniv of U.A.M.P.T. As T **101** of Mauritania.
552 100 f. brown, blue and green . 1·60 1·10

89 Stamp Auction and Togo Stamps—1 m. (German) of 1900 and 100 f. Conference of 1964

1967. 70th Anniv of 1st Togolese Stamps. Mult.
553 5 f. Type **89** (postage) 15 10
554 10 f. Exhibition and 1d. (British) of 1915 and 50 f. I.T.U. of 1965 . . . . 15 10
555 15 f. Stamp shop and 50 c. (French) of 1924 . . . . . 40 10
556 20 f. Stamp-packet vending machine and 5 f. U.N. of 1965 40 10
557 30 f. As 15 f. 60 30
558 45 f. As 10 f. 85 40
559 90 f. Type **89** (air) . . . . . . 1·50 60
560 105 f. Father and son with album and 1 f. Kennedy of 1964 . 1·75 80

1967. 5th Anniv of West African Monetary Union. As T **103** of Mauritania.
562 30 f. blue and green 55 30

90 Long Jumping

1967. Olympic Games. Mexico and Grenoble (1968). Multicoloured.
563 5 f. Type **90** (postage) 10 10
564 15 f. Ski-jumping 20 10
565 30 f. Relay runners 55 20
566 45 f. Bob-sleighing 90 35
567 60 f. As 30 f. (air) . . . . . . 1·10 40
568 90 f. Type **90** . . . . 1·00 55

1967. National Day (29 Sept). Nos. 525/31 optd **JOURNEE NATIONALE DU TOGO 29 SEPTEMBRE 1967.**
570 5 f. multicoloured (postage) . 35 20
571 10 f. multicoloured 35 20
572 30 f. multicoloured . . . . . 1·00 40
573 45 f. multicoloured (air) . . . 40 20
574 60 f. multicoloured 80 35
575 90 f. multicoloured . . . . . 1·25 45
576 105 f. multicoloured . . . . . 1·40 65

92 "The Gleaners" (Millet) and Benin Phosphate Mine

1968. Paintings and Local Industries.

577 **92** 10 f. multicoloured 10 10
578 – 20 f. multicoloured 30 10
579 **92** 30 f. multicoloured 45 15
580 – 45 f. multicoloured 70 20
581 **92** 60 f. multicoloured 95 45
582 – 90 f. multicoloured 1·40 70

DESIGN: 20, 45, 90 f. "The Weaver at the Loom" (Van Gogh) and textile plant, Dadia.

93 Brewing Beer

1968. Benin Brewery. Multicoloured.

583 20 f. Type **93** 35 10
584 30 f. "Drinking at a Bar" (detail from painting by Manet) 60 30
585 45 f. Bottling-washing machine and bottle of Benin beer 70 40

The 30 f. is a vert design.

94 Decade Emblem and Sunflowers

96 Dr. Adenauer and Europa "Key"

95 Viking Longship and Portuguese Galleon

1968. International Hydrological Decade.

586 **94** 30 f. mult (postage) 60 30
587 60 f. multicoloured (air) 85 40

1968. Inaug of Lome Port. Multicoloured.

588 5 f. Type **95** (postage) 15 10
589 10 f. Paddle-steamer "Clermont" and Liner "Athlone Castle" 20 10
590 20 f. Quayside, Lome Port 60 20
591 30 f. Type **95** 85 35
592 45 f. As 10 f. (air) 95 35
593 90 f. Nuclear-powered freighter "Savannah" 1·60 55

1968. Adenauer (German statesman) Commem.

595 **96** 90 f. multicoloured 1·60 80

97 "Dr. Turp's Anatomy Lesson" (Rembrandt)

1968. 20th Anniv of World Health Organization. Paintings. Multicoloured.

596 15 f. "Expulsion from the Garden of Eden" (Michelangelo) (postage) 30 10
597 20 f. Type **97** 40 15
598 30 f. "Johann Deyman's Anatomy Lesson" (Rembrandt) 55 20
599 45 f. "Christ healing the sick" (Raphael) 85 35
600 60 f. As 30 f. (air) 85 40
601 90 f. As 45 f 1·10 55

98 Wrestling

1968. Olympic Games, Mexico. Multicoloured.

603 15 f. Type **98** (postage) 20 15
604 20 f. Boxing 45 15
606 45 f. Running 80 35
607 60 f. Type **98** (air) 90 40
608 90 f. As 45 f. 1·25 55

99 "Try Your Luck" **100** Scout and Tent

1968. 2nd Anniv of National Lottery. Mult.

610 30 f. Type **99** 55 25
611 45 f. Lottery ticket, horse-shoe and cloverleaf 80 30

1968. Air. "Philexafrique" Stamp Exn, Abidjan (Ivory Coast 1969) (1st issue). As T **113a** of Mauritania. Multicoloured.

612 100 f. "The Letter" (J. A. Franquelin) 2·75 1·90

1968. Togolese Scouts. Multicoloured.

613 5 f. Type **100** (postage) 10 10
614 10 f. Scoutmaster with cubs 30 10
615 20 f. Giving first aid 40 15
616 30 f. Scout game 50 20
617 45 f. As 10 f. 65 35
618 60 f. As 20 f. (air) 90 45
619 90 f. As 30 f. 1·25 65

The 10, 20, 45 and 60 f. are horiz.

101 "The Adoration of the Shepherds" (Giorgione)

1968. Christmas. Paintings. Multicoloured.

621 15 f. Type **101** (postage) 35 10
622 20 f. "The Adoration of the Kings" (Brueghel) 45 10
623 30 f. "The Adoration" (Botticelli) 55 15
624 45 f. "The Adoration" (Durer) 90 35
625 60 f. As 20 f. (air) 1·00 40
626 90 f. As 45 f. 1·50 55

102 Martin Luther King **104** Module landing on Moon

103 Football

1969. Human Rights Year.

628 **102** 15 f. grn & brn (postage) 20 10
629 – 20 f. violet & turquoise 35 15
630 **102** 30 f. blue and red 55 20
631 – 45 f. red and olive 1·10 45
632 – 60 f. blue & purple (air) 90 45
633 **102** 90 f. brown and green 1·25 55

PORTRAITS: 20 f. Prof. Rene Cassin (Nobel Peace Prize-winner); 45 f. Pope John XXIII; 60 f. Robert E. Kennedy.

1969. Air. "Philexafrique" Stamp Exn, Abidjan, Ivory Coast (2nd issue). As T **114a** of Mauritania.

635 50 f. red, brown and green 80 80

DESIGN: 50 f. Aledjo Rock and stamp of 1900.

1969. Inaug of Sports Stadium, Lome.

636 **103** 10 f. brown, red and green (postage) 10 10
637 – 15 f. brown, blue and orange 30 10
638 – 20 f. brown, green and yellow 40 15
639 – 30 f. brown, blue and green 50 20
640 – 45 f. brown, violet and orange 65 30
641 – 60 f. brown, red and blue (air) 90 35
642 – 90 f. brown, mauve and blue 1·25 55

DESIGNS: 15 f. Handball; 20 f. Volleyball; 30 f. Basketball; 45 f. Tennis; 60 f. Boxing; 90 f. Cycling.

1969. 1st Man on the Moon. Multicoloured.

644 1 f. Type **104** (postage) 10 10
645 20 f. Astronaut and module on Moon 20 10
646 30 f. As Type **104** 40 15
647 45 f. As 20 f. 65 35
648 60 f. Astronaut exploring lunar surface (air) 85 40
649 100 f. Astronaut gathering Moon rock 1·40 70

105 "The Last Supper" (Tintoretto)

1969. Religious Paintings. Multicoloured.

651 5 f. Type **105** (postage) 15 10
652 10 f. "Christ's Vision at Emmaus" (Velazquez) 30 10
653 20 f. "Pentecost" (El Greco) 50 20
654 30 f. "The Annunciation" (Botticelli) 70 20
655 45 f. As 10 f. 1·10 45
656 90 f. As 20 f. (air) 1·90 65

1969. Eisenhower Commem. Nos. 628/33 optd with Eisenhower's silhouette and **EN MEMOIRE DWIGHT D. EISENHOWER 1890-1968**.

658 **102** 15 f. grn & brn (postage) 25 15
659 – 20 f. violet and turquoise 45 15
660 **102** 30 f. blue and red 55 20
661 – 45 f. red and olive 95 30
662 – 60 f. blue & purple (air) 90 45
663 **102** 90 f. brown and green 1·25 65

107 Bank in Hand and Emblem

1969. 5th Anniv of African Development Bank. Multicoloured.

665 30 f. Type **107** (postage) 85 20
666 45 f. Diesel locomotive in hand, and emblem 1·10 35
667 100 f. Farmer and cattle in hand, and emblem (air) 1·25 55

108 Dunant and Red Cross Workers

1969. 50th Anniv of League of Red Cross Societies. Multicoloured.

668 15 f. Type **108** (postage) 35 10
669 20 f. Pasteur and help for flood victims 40 10
670 30 f. Fleming and flood control 75 20
671 45 f. Rontgen and Red Cross post 95 30
672 60 f. As 45 f. (air) 90 45
673 90 f. Type **108** 1·25 65

109 Weeding Corn

1969. Young Pioneers Agricultural Organization. Multicoloured.

675 1 f. Type **109** (postage) 10 10
676 2 f. Glidji Agricultural Centre 10 10
677 3 f. Founding meeting 10 10
678 4 f. Glidji class 15 10
679 5 f. Student "pyramid" 15 10
680 7 f. Students threshing 15 10
681 8 f. Gardening instruction 15 10
682 10 f. Co-op village 15 10
683 15 f. Students gardening 30 15
684 20 f. Cattle-breeding 35 15
685 25 f. Poultry-farming 45 15
686 30 f. Independence parade 45 20
687 40 f. Boys on high-wire 65 35
688 45 f. Tractor and trailer 80 35
689 50 f. Co-op village 85 35
690 60 f. Tractor-driving tuition 90 45
691 90 f. Harvesting manioc (air) 1·10 45
692 100 f. Gardening instruction 1·40 55
693 200 f. Thinning-out corn 2·25 1·10
694 250 f. Drummers marching 4·25 1·50
695 500 f. Young pioneers marching 9·50 3·00

111 Books and Map **113** George Washington

1969. 12th Anniv of International African Library Development Association.

700 **111** 30 f. multicoloured 45 30

1969. Christmas. No. 644/5 and 647/9 optd **JOYEUX NOEL**.

701 1 f. Type **104** (postage) 35 20
702 20 f. Astronaut and module on Moon 1·10 45
703 45 f. As 20 f. 1·50 1·00
704 60 f. Astronaut exploring lunar surface (air) 1·90 65
705 100 f. Astronaut gathering Moon rock 3·00 1·00

1969. "Leaders of World Peace". Multicoloured.

707 15 f. Type **113** (postage) 30 10
708 20 f. Albert Luthule 35 10
709 30 f. Mahatma Gandhi 55 15
710 45 f. Simon Boliver 90 20
711 60 f. Friedrich Ebert (air) 90 35
712 90 f. As 30 f. 1·25 50

114 "Ploughing" (Klodt)

1970. 50th Anniv of I.L.O. Paintings. Multicoloured.

713 5 f. Type **114** (postage) 10 10
714 10 f. "Gardening" (Pissarro) 20 10
715 20 f. "Harvesting Fruit" (Rivera) 35 10
716 30 f. "Seeds of Spring" (Van Gogh) 80 35
717 45 f. "Workers of the Fields" (Rivera) 80 35
718 60 f. As 30 f. (air) 1·00 35
719 90 f. As 45 f. 1·50 50

115 Model Coiffures

1970. Togolese Hair-styles. Multicoloured.

721 5 f. Type **115** (postage) 15 10
722 10 f. As T **115**, but different styles 35 10
723 20 f. Fefe style 50 15
724 30 f. Danmlongbedji style . . 1·25 20

725 45 f. Blom style (air) 90 30
726 90 f. Aklui and Danmlongbedji styles . . . . 1·60 65

Nos. 723/5 are vert.

116 Togo Stamp and Independence Monument, Lome

1970. 10th Anniv of Independence. Multicoloured.

727 20 f. Type **116** (postage) . . . 45 15
728 30 f. Pres. Eyademe and Palace 65 20
729 50 f. Map, dove and monument (vert) . . . . 1·10 35

730 60 f. Togo stamp and monument (air) 80 30

117 New U.P.U. Headquarters Building

1970. New U.P.U. Headquarters Building.

731 **117** 30 f. violet and orange (postage) . . . . 1·00 35
732 50 f. red and blue (air) . . 80 35

118 Italy and Uruguay

1970. World Cup Football Championships, Mexico. Multicoloured.

733 5 f. Type **118** (postage) 10 10
734 10 f. England and Brazil . . . 20 10
735 15 f. Russia and Mexico . . . 35 10
736 20 f. Germany and Morocco . 45 10
737 30 f. Rumania and Czechoslovakia 85 20

738 50 f. Sweden and Israel (air) . 55 30
739 60 f. Bulgaria and Peru . . . 65 35
740 90 f. Belgium and El Salvador 1·25 50

119 Lenin

1970. Birth Centenary of Lenin. Multicoloured.

742 30 f. Type **119** (postage) . . . 1·00 45

743 50 f. "Peasant messengers with Lenin" (Serov) (air) . . . . 1·10 35

120 British Pavilion

1970. "Expo 70", Osaka, Japan. Multicoloured.

744 2 f. Pennants, Sanyo Pavilion (57×36 mm) 15 10
745 20 f. Type **120** 20 10
746 30 f. French Pavilion 45 15
747 50 f. Soviet Pavilion 85 30
748 60 f. Japanese Pavilion . . . . 1·10 45

121 Armstrong, Collins and Aldrin

1970. "Apollo" Moon Flights. Multicoloured.

750 1 f. Type **121** (postage) . . . 10 10
751 2 f. U.S. flag and moon-rock 10 10
752 20 f. Astronaut and module on Moon 35 10
753 30 f. Conrad, Gordon and Bean 65 20
754 50 f. As 2 f. . . . . 1·00 35

755 200 f. Lovell, Haise and Swigert ("Apollo 13") (air) . . . . 2·50 1·40

1970. Safe Return of "Apollo 13". As Nos. 750/5, but additionally inscr "FELICITATIONS BON RETOUR APOLLO XIII".

757 **121** 1 f. multicoloured (postage) 10 10
758 – 2 f. multicoloured 10 10
759 – 20 f. multicoloured . . . 35 10
760 – 30 f. multicoloured . . . 65 20
761 – 50 f. multicoloured . . . 1·00 35

762 – 200 f. multicoloured (air) 2·50 1·60

123 "Euchloron megaera"

1970. Butterflies and Moths. Multicoloured.

764 1 f. Type **123** (postage) . . . 15 10
765 2 f. "Cymothoe sangaris" . . 30 10
766 30 f. "Danaus chrysippus" . . 1·50 35
767 50 f. "Morpho sp." . . . . . 2·75 65

768 60 f. Type **123** (air) . . . . . 3·00 70
769 90 f. "Pseudacraea boisiduvali" 4·25 95

124 Painting by Velasquez (I.L.O.)

1970. 25th Anniv of U.N.O. Multicoloured.

770 1 f. Type **124** (postage) . . . 10 10
771 15 f. Painting by Delacroix (F.A.O.) 10 10
772 20 f. Painting by Holbein (U.N.E.S.C.O.) 20 15
773 30 f. Painting of U.N. H.Q., New York 60 15
774 50 f. Painting by Renoir (U.N.I.C.E.F.) 90 35

775 60 f. Painting by Van Gogh (U.P.U.) (air) . . . . . . 1·00 35
776 90 f. Painting by Carpaccio (W.H.O./O.M.S.) . . . . . 1·50 50

125 "The Nativity" (Botticelli)

1970. Christmas. "Nativity" Paintings by Old Masters. Multicoloured.

778 15 f. Type **125** (postage) . . . 15 10
779 20 f. Veronese 15 10
780 30 f. El Greco 55 15
781 50 f. Fra Angelico 90 30

782 60 f. Botticelli (different) (air) 1·00 30
783 90 f. Tiepolo . . . . 1·50 45

1971. De Gaulle Commemoration (1st issue). Nos. 708/9, 711/12 optd **EN MEMOIRE Charles De Gaulle 1890-1970** or surch in addition.

785 30 f. multicoloured (postage) . 1·10 35
786 30 f. on 90 f. multicoloured . 1·10 35
787 150 f. on 20 f. multicoloured . 6·75 1·75

788 200 f. on 60 f. mult (air) . . . 5·25 2·50

127 De Gaulle and Churchill

1971. De Gaulle Commemoration (2nd issue).

789 **127** 20 f. blue & blk (postage) . 55 15
790 – 30 f. red and black 65 20
791 – 40 f. green and black . . . 1·00 40
792 – 50 f. brown and black . . 1·25 50

793 – 60 f. violet & blk (air) . . 2·25 55
794 – 90 f. blue and black . . . 3·25 80

DESIGNS. 30 f. De Gaulle with Eisenhower; 40 f. With Pres. Kennedy; 50 f. With Adenauer; 60 f. With Pope Paul VI; 90 f. General De Gaulle.

128 Shepard and Moon Exploration

1971 Moon Mission of "Apollo 14". Mult.

796 1 f. Type **128** (postage) 10 10
797 10 f. Mitchell and rock-gathering 15 10
798 30 f. Roosa and module approaching Moon 50 15
799 40 f. Launch from Moon . . . 90 30

800 50 f. "Apollo 14" emblem (air) 60 20
801 100 f. As 40 f. . . . . 1·25 40
802 200 f. As 50 f. . . . . 2·10 80

129 "The Resurrection" (after Raphael)

1971. Easter. Paintings of "The Resurrection" by various artists. Multicoloured.

804 1 f. Type **129** (postage) 15 10
805 30 f. Master of Trebon 55 15
806 40 f. Type **129** 95 30

807 50 f. M. Grunewald (air) . . . 80 30
808 60 f. As 30 f. . . . . 1·00 40
809 90 f. El Greco . . . . 1·50 55

130 Cocoa Tree and Pods

1971. International Cocoa Day. Multicoloured.

811 30 f. Type **130** (postage) . . . 55 15
812 40 f. Sorting beans 85 20
813 50 f. Drying beans . . . . . 1·10 35

814 60 f. Agricultural Ministry, Lome (air) 60 30
815 90 f. Type **130** . . . . 1·10 50
816 100 f. As 40 f. . . . . 1·25 60

131 Sud Aviation Caravelle over Control Tower

132 Napoleon

1971. 10th Anniv of A.S.E.C.N.A. (Aerial Navigation Security Agency).

817 **131** 30 f. multicoloured (postage) 90 35
818 100 f. multicoloured (air) . 1·50 65

1971. 150th Death Anniv of Napoleon. Embossed on gold foil.

819 **132** 1000 f. gold . . . . 22·00

133 Great Market, Lome

1971. Tourism. Multicoloured.

821 20 f. Type **133** (postage) . . . 35 10
822 30 f. Wooden sculpture and protea 55 15
823 40 f. Aledjo Gorge and olive baboon 80 20

824 50 f. Vale Castle and red-fronted gazelle (air) 65 20
825 60 f. Lake Togo and alligator 90 30
826 100 f. Furnace, Tokpli, and hippopotamus . . . . . . 1·25 40

134 Gbatchoume Image

1971. Togolese Religions. Multicoloured.

827 20 f. Type **134** (postage) . . . 35 15
828 30 f. High priest, Temple of Atta Sakuma 50 20
829 40 f. "Holy Stone" ceremony . 85 30

830 50 f. Moslem worshippers, Lome Mosque (air) 55 20
831 60 f. Protestants 70 30
832 90 f. Catholic ceremony, Djogbegan Monastery . . . 95 40

1971. Memorial Issue for "Soyuz 11" Astronauts. Nos. 799/802 optd **EN MEMOIRE DOBROVOLSKY - VOLKOV - PATSAYEV SOYUZ 11** or surch also.

834 40 f. multicoloured (postage) . 1·00 35

835 90 f. on 50 f. multicoloured (air) 90 35
836 100 f. multicoloured . . . . . 1·10 40
837 200 f. multicoloured . . . . . 2·00 65

136 Speed-skating

1971. Winter Games, Sapporo, Japan (1972). Multicoloured.

839 1 f. Type **136** (postage) . . . 10 10
840 10 f. Slalom skiing 10 10
841 20 f. Figure-skating 35 10
842 30 f. Bob-sleighing 55 20
843 50 f. Ice-hockey . . . . . . 1·10 35

844 200 f. Ski-jumping (air) . . . 2·25 95

1971. Air. 10th Anniv of African and Malagasy Posts and Telecommunications Union. As T **139a** of Mauritania. Multicoloured.

846 100 f. U.A.M.P.T. H.Q. and Adjogobo dancers . . . . . 1·10 55

137 Togolese Child and Mask

1971. Air. "Children of the World". Embossed on gold foil.
847 **137** 1500 f. gold . . . . 15·00

138 Wooden Crocodile

1971. 25th Anniv of U.N.I.C.E.F. Mult.
848 20 f. Type **138** (postage) . . . 20 10
849 30 f. Toy "Bambi" and butterfly 45 15
850 50 f. Toy monkey 80 30
851 50 f. Wooden elephant on wheels 1·00 30
852 60 f. Toy turtle (air) 55 20
853 90 f. Toy parrot 85 35

139 "Virgin and Child" (Botticelli)

1971. Christmas. "Virgin and Child" Paintings by Old Masters. Multicoloured.
855 10 f. Type **139** (postage) . . . 10 10
856 30 f. (Maitre de la Vie de Marie) 65 20
857 40 f. (Durer) . . . . 1·10 35
858 50 f. (Veronese) . . . . . . 1·40 45
859 60 f. (Giorgione) (air) . . . . 1·00 35
860 100 f. (Raphael) . . . . 1·75 55

140 St. Mark's Basilica, Venice

1972. U.N.E.S.C.O. "Save Venice" Campaign. Multicoloured.
862 30 f. Type **140** (postage) . . . 90 30
863 40 f. Rialto Bridge . . . . . . 1·25 40
864 100 f. Doge's Palace (air) . . . 1·40 65

141 "The Crucifixion" (unknown artist)

1972. Easter. Religious Paintings. Multicoloured.
866 25 f. Type **141** (postage) . . . 45 15
867 30 f. "The Deposition" (Botticelli) 70 15
868 40 f. Type **141** 90 30
869 50 f. "The Resurrection" (Thomas de Coloswar) (air) 85 20
870 100 f. "The Ascension" (Mantegna) . . . . 1·60 40

142 Heart Emblem and Blacksmith

145 Woman preparing Cassava

143 Hotel de la Paix, Lome

1972. World Heart Month. Multicoloured.
872 30 f. Type **142** (postage) . . . 45 15
873 40 f. Typist 55 20
874 60 f. Javelin-thrower 85 35
875 100 f. Type **142** (air) . . . . 1·25 45

1972. O.C.A.M. Summit Conference, Lome. Embossed on gold foil.
877 **143** 1000 f., gold, red & green 10·00

1972. Pres. Nixon's Visit to China. Nos. 823/4 optd **VISITE DU PRESIDENT NIXON EN CHINE FEVRIER 1972.** and additionally surch (No. 879).
878 300 f. on 40 f. mult (postage) 4·00 1·90
879 50 f. multicoloured (air) . . . 1·00 35

1972. Cassava Industries. Multicoloured.
880 25 f. Collecting cassava (horiz) (postage) 45 15
881 40 f. Type **145** 65 20
882 60 f. Cassava truck and factory (horiz) (air) 90 20
883 80 f. Mother with Benin tapioca cake . . . . 1·25 45

146 Video-telephone

148 Basketball

1972. World Telecommunications Day. Multicoloured.
884 40 f. Type **146** (postage) . . . 1·00 35
885 100 f. "Intelsat 4" and map of Africa (air) . . . . 1·50 45

1972. Air. Pres. Nixon's Visit to Russia. No. 743, surch **VISITE DU PRESIDENT NIXON EN RUSSIE MAI 1972**, and value.
886 300 f. on 50 f. multicoloured . 5·00 2·75

1972. Olympic Games, Munich. Multicoloured.
887 30 f. Type **148** (postage) . . . 50 15
888 40 f. Running 65 20
889 50 f. Throwing the discus . . 90 30
890 90 f. Gymnastics (air) 65 35
891 200 f. Type **148** . . . . 1·75 80

149 Pin-tailed Whydah

150 Paul Harris (founder)

1973. Exotic Birds. Multicoloured.
893 25 f. Type **149** (postage) . . . 70 25
894 30 f. Broad-tailed paradise whydah . . . . 1·00 35
895 40 f. Yellow-mantled whydah 1·40 55
896 60 f. Long-tailed whydah . . 2·75 90
897 90 f. Rose-ringed parakeet (air) 3·50 1·25

1972. Rotary International. Multicoloured.
899 40 f. Type **150** (postage) . . . 40 20
900 50 f. Rotary and Togo flags . 50 30
901 60 f. Rotary emblem, map and laurel (air) 65 20
902 90 f. As 50 f. 90 35
903 100 f. Type **150** . . . . 1·25 45

151 "Mona Lisa" (L. da Vinci)

1972. Famous Paintings. Multicoloured.
905 25 f. Type **151** (postage) . . . 95 30
906 40 f. "Virgin and Child" (Bellini) 1·10 30
907 60 f. "Mystical Marriage of St. Catherine" (Master P.N.'s assistant) (air) 80 30
908 80 f. "Self-portrait" (L. da Vinci) 1·10 35
909 100 f. "St. Marie and Angels" (Botticelli) . . . . 1·40 50

1972. 10th Anniv of West African Monetary Union. As T **149** of Mauritania.
911 40 f. brown, grey and red . . . 55 40

152 Party H.Q. of R.P.T. and Presidents Pompidou and Eyadama

1972. Visit of President Pompidou to Togo. Multicoloured.
912 40 f. Type **152** (postage) . . . 1·10 45
913 100 f. Party H.Q. rear view and portraits as T **152** (air) . . . 1·75 55

153 Goethe

1972. Air. 140th Death Anniv of Goethe (poet).
914 **153** 100 f. multicoloured . . . 1·50 65

154 "The Annunciation" (unknown artist)

1972. Christmas. Religious Paintings. Multicoloured.
915 25 f. Type **154** (postage) . . . 35 20
916 30 f. "The Nativity" (Master Theodor of Prague) 55 20
917 40 f. Type **154** 80 20
918 60 f. As 30 f. (air) 80 20
919 80 f. "The Adoration of the Magi" (unknown artist) . . 1·00 30
920 100 f. "The Flight into Egypt" (Giotto) . . . . 1·25 45

155 R. Follerau and Allegory

1973. "World Day of the Leper". (a) Postage. 20th Anniv of Follereau Foundation.
922 **155** 40 f. violet and green . . 1·60 55

(b) Air. Cent of Hansen's Bacillus Discovery.
923 – 100 f. blue and red . . . . 2·50 85
DESIGN: 100 f. Dr. Hansen, microscope and bacillus slide.

156 W.H.O. Emblem **157** The Crucifixion

1973. 25th Anniv of W.H.O.
924 **156** 30 f. multicoloured . . . 45 15
925 40 f. multicoloured . . . 55 20

1973. Easter. Multicoloured.
926 25 f. Type **157** (postage) . . . 35 15
927 30 f. The Deposition 55 20
928 40 f. The Resurrection 80 20
929 90 f. "Christ in Majesty" (air) 1·25 45

158 Astronauts Cernan, Evans and Schmitt

1973. "Apollo 17" Moon Flight. Multicoloured.
931 30 f. Type **158** (postage) . . . 80 15
932 40 f. Moon rover . . . . . . 1·00 30
933 100 f. Discovery of "orange" rock (air) . . . . 1·10 40
934 200 f. Pres. Kennedy and lift-off 2·25 85

159 Erecting Tent

160 Heliocentric System

1873. Int Scout Congress. Nairobi/Addis Ababa. Multicoloured.
936 10 f. Type **159** (postage) . . . 20 10
937 20 f. Cooking meal (horiz) . . 45 10
938 30 f. Rope-climbing 65 15
939 40 f. Type **159** 85 20
940 100 f. Canoeing (horiz) (air) . 1·25 40
941 200 f. As 20 f. . . . . 2·50 85

1973. 500th Birth Anniv of Copernicus. Multicoloured.
943 10 f. Type **160** (postage) . . . 15 10
944 20 f. Copernicus 30 10
945 30 f. "Astronomy" and "Astronautics" 65 15
946 40 f. Astrolabe 85 20
947 90 f. Type **160** (air) . . . . . 1·25 35
948 100 f. As 20 f. . . . . 1·40 45

161 Ambulance Team

1973. Togolese Red Cross. Multicoloured.
950 40 f. Type **161** (postage) . . . 90 35
951 100 f. Dove of peace, sun and map (air) . . . . 1·90 65

1973. "Drought Relief". African Solidarity. No. 766 surch **SECHERESSE SOLIDARITE AFRICAINE** and value.
952 100 f. on 30 f. multicoloured . 1·25 85

163 Classroom

1973. Literacy Campaign. Multicoloured.
953 30 f. Type **163** (postage) . . . 35 15
954 40 f. African reading book (vert) 85 30
955 90 f. Classroom (different) (air) 85 45

1973. African and Malagasy Posts and Telecommunications Union. As T **155a** of Mauritania.
956 100 f. red, yellow and purple . 1·10 65

164 Interpol Emblem and H.Q. Paris
165 W.M.O. Emblem in Weather-vane

1973. 50th Anniv of Interpol.
957 **164** 30 f. green, brown & yell . 45 15
958 40 f. blue, mauve & grn . . . 65 20

1973. Centenary of W.M.O.
959 **165** 40 f. grn, brn & yell (post) 90 35
960 200 f. brn, vio & blue (air) 1·90 85

166 Togo Stamp and Diesel Locomotives

1973. 75th Anniv of Togolese Postal Services. Multicoloured.
961 25 f. Type **166** (postage) . . . 50 15
962 30 f. Togo stamp and mail coaches 60 20
963 90 f. Togo stamps and mail boats 1·60 45
964 100 f. Togo stamps and mail-planes (air) . . . . 1·90 65

167 Kennedy and A. Schaerf
168 Flame Emblem and "People"

1973. 10th Death Anniv of Pres. Kennedy.
966 **167** 20 f. violet and black on blue (postage) 35 10
967 – 30 f. brown and black on brown 50 20
968 – 40 f. green & blk on grn . 85 30
969 – 90 f. purple and black on mauve (air) . . . . . . 1·60 45
970 – 100 f. blue & black on bl . 1·60 45
971 – 200 f. brown & blk on brn 2·75 80

DESIGNS: 30 f. Kennedy and Harold Macmillan; 40 f. Kennedy and Konrad Adenauer; 90 f. Kennedy and Charles de Gaulle; 100 f. Kennedy and Nikita Kruschev; 200 f. Kennedy and "Apollo" spacecraft.

1973. Air. 25th Anniv of Declaration of Human Rights.
973 **168** 250 f. multicoloured . . . 2·75 1·40

169 "Virgin and Child" (anon)
173 "Girl Before Mirror" (Picasso)

171 Footballers

1973. Christmas. Multicoloured.
974 25 f. Type **169** (postage) . . . 50 15
975 30 f. "Adoration of the Magi" (Vivarini) 60 20
976 90 f. "Virgin and Child" (S. di Pietro) (air) . . . . 1·00 35
977 100 f. "Adoration of the Magi" (anon) . . . . 1·40 40

1974. Lome District Rotary International Convention. Nos. 899, 901 and 903 optd **PREMIERE CONVENTION 210eme DISTRICT FEVRIER 1974 LOME.**
979 **150** 40 f. mult (postage) . . . 55 35
980 – 60 f. multicoloured (air) . 45 20
981 **150** 100 f. multicoloured . . . 90 35

1974. World Cup Football Championships, Munich.
982 **171** 20 f. mult (postage) . . . 35 15
983 – 30 f. multicoloured . . . 45 15
984 – 40 f. multicoloured . . . 55 20
985 – 90 f. multicoloured (air) . 90 35
986 – 100 f. multicoloured . . . 1·00 40
987 – 200 f. multicoloured . . . 2·00 70

DESIGNS: Nos. 983/7, similar designs to Type **171**, showing footballers in action.

1974. 10th Anniv of World Food Programme. Nos. 880/1 optd **10e ANNIVERSAIRE DU P. A. M.** or surch also.
989 **145** 40 f. multicoloured . . . 55 35
990 – 100 f. on 25 f. multicoloured 1·25 80

1974. Picasso Commemoration. Multicoloured.
991 20 f. Type **173** (postage) . . . 55 20
992 30 f. "The Turkish Shawl" . 80 35
993 40 f. "Mandoline and Guitar" 1·10 35
994 90 f. "The Muse" (air) . . . 1·00 35
995 100 f. "Les Demoiselles d'Avignon" . . . . 1·25 40
996 200 f. "Sitting Nude" . . . . 2·50 85

174 Kpeme Village
175 Togolese Postman

1974. Coastal Scenes. Multicoloured.
998 30 f. Type **174** (postage) . . 45 20
999 40 f. Tropicana tourist village 65 40
1000 90 f. Fisherman on Lake Togo (air) . . . . 1·00 35
1001 100 f. Mouth of Aneche River 1·25 40

1974. Centenary of U.P.U. Multicoloured.
1003 30 f. Type **175** (postage) . . 40 20
1004 40 f. Postman with cleft carrying-stick 50 30
1005 50 f. Type **175** (air) 60 30
1006 100 f. As 40 f. . . . . 1·25 45

1974. 15th Anniv of Council of Accord. As T **158** of Dahomey.
1007 40 f. multicoloured 50 30

177 Hauling-in Net
178 Earth Station and Probe

1974. Lagoon Fishing. Multicoloured.
1008 30 f. Type **177** (postage) . . 45 20
1009 40 f. Throwing net 65 30
1010 90 f. Fishes in net (air) . . . 1·00 30
1011 100 f. Fishing with lines . . 1·25 35
1012 200 f. Fishing with basket (vert) 2·75 70

1974. U.S. "Jupiter" Space Mission. Mult.
1014 30 f. Type **178** (postage) . . 35 15
1015 40 f. Probe transmitting to Earth (horiz) 45 20
1016 100 f. Blast-off (air) 95 40
1017 200 f. Jupiter probe (horiz) . 1·75 70

1974. "Internaba 1974" Stamp Exhibition Basel. Nos. 884/5 optd **INTERNABA 1974 · CENTENARIUM U P U** and emblem.
1019 **146** 40 f. mult (postage) . . 3·50 1·00
1020 – 100 f. mult (air) . . . . 4·25 1·40

180 "Tympanotomus radula"
181 Groom with Horses

1974. Sea Shells. Multicoloured.
1021 10 f. Type **180** (postage) . . . 25 20
1022 20 f. Giant tun 35 20
1023 30 f. Trader cone 55 20
1024 40 f. Great ribbed cockle . . 85 20
1025 90 f. Ponsonbyi's volute . . . 1·40 40
1026 100 f. Iredale's bonnet . . . . 1·90 40

1974. Horse-racing. Multicoloured.
1028 30 f. Type **181** (postage) . . . 45 20
1029 40 f. Exercising horses 65 30
1030 90 f. Steeple-chaser taking fence (air) . . . . 1·00 35
1031 100 f. Horses racing . . . . . 1·50 45

1974. Air. West Germany's Victory in World Cup Football Championships, Munich. Nos. 890/1 optd **COUPE DU MONDE DE FOOTBALL MUNICH 1974 VAINQUERS REPUBLIQUE FEDERALE ALLEMAGNE.**
1033 – 90 f. multicoloured . . . 90 35
1034 **148** 200 f. multicoloured . . . 1·75 80

183 Leopard

1974. Wild Animals. Multicoloured.
1036 20 f. Type **183** (postage) . . . 35 15
1037 30 f. Giraffes 45 20
1038 40 f. Two African elephants . 65 35
1039 90 f. Lion and lioness (air) . . 1·00 45
1040 100 f. Black rhinoceros and calf 1·50 45

184 Herd of Cows

1974. Pastoral Economy. Multicoloured.
1042 30 f. Type **184** (postage) . . . 45 20
1043 40 f. Milking 65 30
1044 90 f. Cattle at water-hole (air) 85 45
1045 100 f. Village cattle-pen . . . 1·10 55

185 Churchill and Frigate H.M.S."Loch Fada"

1974. Birth Centenary of Sir Winston Churchill. Multicoloured.
1047 30 f. Type **185** (postage) . . . 50 15
1048 40 f. Churchill and Supermarine Spitfires 60 20
1049 100 f. Type **185** (air) . . . . 1·40 35
1050 200 f. As 40 f. . . . . 2·25 80

1975. Opening of Hotel de la Paix, Lome. Optd **Inauguration de l'hotel Paix 9-1-75.**
1051a **143** 1000 f. gold, red and green 9·50

186 "Strelitzia reginae"
188 Radio Station, Kamina

1975. Flowers of Togo. Multicoloured.
1052 25 f. Type **186** (postage) . . . 35 15
1053 30 f. "Strophanthus sarmentosus" 45 15
1054 40 f. "Chlamydocarya macrocarpa" (horiz) 55 20
1055 60 f. "Clerodendrum scandens" (horiz) 90 35
1056 100 f. "Clerodendrum thosonae" (horiz) (air) . . . 1·40 45
1057 200 f. "Gloriosa superba" (horiz) . . . . 2·50 65

1975. 70th Anniv of Rotary International. Optd **70e ANNIVERSAIRE 23 FEVRIER 1975.**
1059 **150** 40 f. mult (postage) . . . 30 25
1060 – 90 f. multicoloured (No. 902) (air) 85 35
1061 **150** 100 f. multicoloured . . 1·00 40

1975. Tourism. Multicoloured.
1062 25 f. Type **188** 20 10
1063 30 f. Benedictine Monastery, Zogbegan 35 20
1064 40 f. Causeway, Atchinedji . 45 30
1065 60 f. Ayome Waterfalls . . . 80 40

189 "Jesus Mocked" (El Greco)

1975. Easter. Multicoloured.
1066 25 f. Type **189** (postage) . . . 20 10
1067 30 f. "The Crucifixion" (Master Janoslen) 35 10
1068 40 f. "The Descent from the Cross" (Bellini) 55 20
1069 90 f. "Pieta" (anon) 95 40
1070 100 f. "Christ rising from the Grave" (Master MS) (air) . 1·10 35
1071 200 f. "The Holy Trinity" (detail) (Durer) . . . . . 1·90 80

190 Stilt-walking

1975. 15th Anniv of Independence. Mult.
1073 25 f. Type **190** (postage) . . 30 10
1074 30 f. Dancers 35 15
1075 50 f. Independence parade (vert) (air) 40 15
1076 60 f. Dancer 60 35

191 Hunting Bush Hare with Club

1975. Hunting. Multicoloured.
1078 30 f. Type **191** (postage) . . 45 20
1079 40 f. Hunting Eurasian beavers with bow 55 35
1080 90 f. Hunting red deer with snare (air) . . . . 1·25 45
1081 100 f. Hunting wild boar with gun . . . . 1·40 55

192 Pounding Palm Nuts

1975. Palm-oil Production. Multicoloured.
1082 30 f. Type **192** (postage) . . 35 15
1083 40 f. Extracting palm-oil (vert) 40 20
1084 85 f. Selling palm-oil (vert) (air) 80 45
1085 100 f. Oil-processing plant, Aloknegbe 90 55

193 "Apollo" and "Soyuz" in Docking Procedure

1975. "Apollo–Soyuz" Space Link. Mult.
1087 30 f. Type **193** (postage) . . 45 15
1088 50 f. "Soyuz" spacecraft (vert) (air) 40 15
1089 60 f. Slaton, Brand and Stafford ("Apollo" astronauts) . . 55 20
1090 90 f. Leonov and Kubasov ("Soyuz" cosmonauts) . . 70 30
1091 100 f. U.S., Soviet flags and "Apollo" and "Soyuz" linked 1·10 50
1092 200 f. Emblem and globe . . 2·25 65

194 "African Women"

1975. International Women's Year.
1094 **194** 30 f. multicoloured . . . 40 15
1095 40 f. multicoloured . . . 45 20

195 Dr. Schweitzer, and Children drinking Milk

1975. Birth Centenary of Dr. Albert Schweitzer. Multicoloured.
1096 40 f. Type **195** (postage) . . . 55 30
1097 80 f. Schweitzer playing organ (vert) (air) 90 30
1098 90 f. Schweitzer feeding Eastern white pelican (vert) . . . . 1·10 35
1099 100 f. Schweitzer and Lambarene Hospital . . . 1·25 35

196 "Merchant writing Letter" (V. Carpaccio) **199** "Virgin and Child" (Mantegna)

1975. International Letter-writing Week. Multicoloured.
1101 40 f. Type **196** (postage) . . . 55 30
1102 80 f. "Erasmus writing Letter" (Holbein) (air) 90 35

1975. 30th Anniv of United Nations. Nos. 851/3 optd **30eme Anniversaire des Nations-Unies**.
1103 50 f. multicoloured (postage) 55 30
1104 60 f. multicoloured (air) . . . 50 20
1105 90 f. multicoloured 60 30

1975. Air. World Scout Jamboree, Norway. Nos. 940/1 optd **14eme JAMBOREE MONDIAL DES ECLAIREURS**.
1107 100 f. multicoloured 95 45
1108 200 f. multicoloured . . . . 1·75 80

1975. Christmas. "Virgin and Child" paintings by artists named. Multicoloured.
1110 20 f. Type **199** (postage) . . . 30 20
1111 30 f. El Greco 40 20
1112 40 f. Barend van Orley . . . 45 20
1113 90 f. Federigo Barocci (air) . 80 30
1114 100 f. Bellini 90 35
1115 200 f. Correggio . . . . . . 1·60 55

200 Crashed Airplane

1975. Pres. Eyadema's Escape in Air Crash at Sarakawa.
1117 **200** 50 f. multicoloured . . . 7·25 5·00
1118 60 f. multicoloured . . . 7·25 5·00

200a Pole Vault

1976. Olympic Games. Montreal. Multicoloured.
1118a 1000 f. Type **200a** . . . . . 10·00
1118b 1000 f. Diving . . . . . . 10·00
1118c 1000 f. Running . . . . . 10·00
1118d 1000 f. Show-jumping . . . 10·00
1118e 1000 f. Cycling . . . . . . 10·00

201 "Frigates forcing the Hudson Passage"

1976. Bicentenary of American Revolution. Mult.
1119 35 f. Type **201** (postage) . . 40 20
1120 50 f. "George Washington" (G. Stuart) (vert) 55 30
1121 60 f. "Surrender of Burgoyne" (Trumbull) (air) 65 20
1122 70 f. "Surrender at Trenton" (Trumbull) (vert) 85 30
1123 100 f. "Signing of Declaration of Independence" (Trumbull) 90 35
1124 200 f. "Washington crossing the Delaware" (E. Leutze) . . 1·75 60

202 Cable-laying Ship **203** Blind Man and Mosquito

1976. Telephone Centenary. Multicoloured.
1126 25 f. Type **202** (postage) . . 20 15
1127 30 f. Automatic telephone and tape-recording equipment . 40 30
1128 70 f. Edison and communications equipment (air) . 55 30
1129 105 f. Alexander Graham Bell, early and modern telephones 85 40

1976. World Health Day. Multicoloured.
1131 50 f. Type **203** (postage) . . 65 30
1132 60 f. Eye examination (air) . 55 20

204 A.C.P. and C.E.E. Emblems **205** Exhibition Hall

1976. 1st Anniv of A.C.P./C.E.E. Treaty (between Togo and European Common Market). Multicoloured.
1133 10 f. Type **204** (postage) . . 15 10
1134 50 f. Map of Africa, Europe and Asia 40 30
1135 60 f. Type **204** (air) 45 20
1136 70 f. As 50 f. 55 30

1976. Anniversaries. Multicoloured.
1136a 5 f. Type **205** (postage) . . 10 10
1136b 10 f. Electricity pylon and flags 15 10
1137 50 f. Type **205** 50 30
1138 60 f. As 10 f. (air) 50 30

The 5 f. and 50 f. commemorate the 10th anniv of the Marine Exhibition and the 10 f. and 60 f. the 1st anniv of the Ghana–Togo–Dahomey Electricity Link.

1976. Air. "Interphil '76" International Stamp Exhibition, Philadelphia. Nos. 1121/4 optd **INTERPHIL MAI 29 - JUIN 6 1976**.
1139 60 f. multicoloured 40 15
1140 70 f. multicoloured 60 20
1141 10 f. multicoloured 90 30
1142 200 f. multicoloured . . . . 1·40 55

207 Running

1976. Olympic Games, Montreal. Multicoloured.
1144 25 f. Type **207** (postage) . . 20 10
1145 30 f. Canoeing 35 15
1146 50 f. High-jumping 45 20
1147 70 f. Sailing (air) 55 20
1148 105 f. Motorcycling 85 35
1149 200 f. Fencing . . . . 1·60 55

208 "Titan 3" and "Viking" Emblem

1976. "Viking" Space Mission. Multicoloured.
1151 30 f. Type **208** (postage) . . . 15 10
1152 50 f. "Viking" en route between Earth and Mars 40 20
1153 60 f. "Viking landing on Mars" (air) 55 20
1154 70 f. Nodus Gordii, Mars . . 65 20
1155 100 f. "Viking" over Mare Tyrrhenum 85 40
1156 200 f. "Viking" landing on Mars (different) . . . . . . 1·50 55

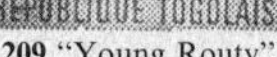

209 "Young Routy" **212** Quaid-i-Azam

211 "Adoration of the Shepherds" (Pontormo)

1976. 75th Death Anniv of Toulouse-Lautrec (painter). Multicoloured.
1158 10 f. Type **209** (postage) . . . 15 10
1159 20 f. "Helene Vary" 40 15
1160 35 f. "Louis Pascal" 65 15
1161 60 f. "Carmen" (air) 80 20
1162 70 f. "Maurice at the Somme" 90 30
1163 200 f. "Messalina" . . . . . 2·25 60

1976. International Children's Day. Nos. 950/1 optd **Journee Internationale de l'Enfance**.
1165 **161** 40 f. mult (postage) . . . 45 15
1166 – 100 f. multicoloured (air) 80 45

1976. Christmas. Nativity scenes by artists named. Multicoloured.
1167 25 f. Type **211** (postage) . . . 35 15
1168 30 f. Crivelli 45 15
1169 50 f. Pontormo 80 20
1170 70 f. Lotto (air) 65 20
1171 105 f. Pontormo (different) . 1·90 35
1172 200 f. Lotto (different) . . . 1·60 55

1976. Birth Centenary of Mohammad Ali Jinnah, "Quaid-i-Azam".
1174 **212** 50 f. multicoloured . . . 55 30

1977. Gold Medal Winners, Montreal Olympic Games. Nos. 1146/7 and 1149 optd **CHAMPIONS OLYMPIQUES** with events and countries.
1175 50 f. multicoloured (postage) . 50 20
1176 70 f. multicoloured (air) . . . 60 35
1177 200 f. multicoloured . . . . . 1·40 80

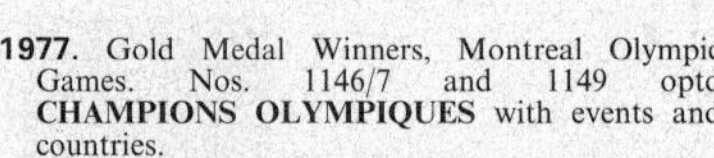

OPTD: 50 f. **SAUT EN HAUTEUR POLOGNE**; 70 f. **YACHTING - FLYING DUTCHMAN REPUBLIQUE FEDERALE ALLEMAGNE**; 200 f. **ESCRIME-FLEURET PAR EQUIPES REPUBLIQUE FEDERALE ALLEMAGNE**.

214 Queen Elizabeth II

1977. Silver Jubilee of Queen Elizabeth II.
1179 **214** 1000 f. multicoloured . . 7·75

215 Phosphate Complex, Kpeme

1977. 10th Anniv of Eyadema Regime. Multicoloured.
1181 50 f. Type **215** (postage) . . 55 20
1182 60 f. Parliament Building, Lome (air) 55 30
1183 100 f. Crowd greeting Pres. Eyadema 80 40

216 Gongophone

1977. Musical Instruments. Multicoloured.
1185 5 f. Type **216** (postage) . . . 15 10
1186 10 f. Tamtam (vert) 20 10
1187 25 f. Dondon 55 15
1188 60 f. Atopani (air) 65 20
1189 80 f. One-string fiddle (vert) . 1·00 30
1190 105 f. African flutes (vert) . 1·40 35

217 Victor Hugo and Guernsey Scene

1977. 175th Birth Anniv of Victor Hugo (writer). Multicoloured.
1192 50 f. Victor Hugo as a young man, and residence (postage) 55 15
1193 60 f. Type **217** (air) 60 30

218 Beethoven and Birthplace, Bonn

1977. 150th Death Anniv of Ludwig van Beethoven. Multicoloured.
1195 30 f. Type **218** (postage) . . 55 15
1196 50 f. Beethoven's bust and Heiligenstadt residence . . 65 20
1197 100 f. Young Beethoven and grand piano (air) . . . . . 1·10 35
1198 200 f. Beethoven on death-bed and Trinity Church, Vienna 1·90 65

219 Benz, 1894

1977. Early Motor Cars. Multicoloured.
1200 35 f. Type **219** (postage) . . 65 20
1201 50 f. De Dion Bouton, 1903 . 1·00 30
1202 60 f. Cannstatt-Daimler, 1899 (air) 80 20
1203 70 f. Sunbeam, 1904 . . . . 90 20
1204 100 f. Renault, 1908 . . . . 1·10 35
1205 200 f. Rolls-Royce, 1909 . . 1·90 65

220 Lindbergh, Ground Crew and "Spirit of St. Louis"

1977. 50th Anniv of Lindbergh's Transatlantic Flight. Multicoloured.
1207 25 f. Type **220** (postage) . . 35 15
1208 50 f. Lindbergh before take-off 65 20
1209 60 f. Lindbergh with son (air) 50 15
1210 85 f. Lindbergh's home, Kent (England) 80 20
1211 90 f. "Spirit of St. Louis" over Atlantic 80 30
1212 100 f. Concorde over New York City . . . . 1·25 50

1977. 10th Anniv of International French Language Council. Nos. 1192/3 optd **10eme ANNIVERSAIRE DU CONSEIL INTERNATIONAL DE LA LANGUE FRANCAISE.**

1214 **217** 50 f. mult (postage) . . . 60 40
1215 60 f. multicoloured (air) . 55 35

222 Nile Crocodile

1977. Endangered Wildlife. Multicoloured.

1216 5 f. African crocodile (postage) 15 15
1217 15 f. Type **222** 40 20
1218 60 f. Western black-and-white colobus (air) 80 15
1219 90 f. Chimpanzee (vert) . . . 90 20
1220 100 f. Leopard . . . . 1·10 30
1221 200 f. African manatee . . . 1·90 55

223 Agricultural School, Tove

1977. Agricultural Development. Multicoloured.

1223 50 f. Type **223** (postage) . . . 50 20
1224 60 f. Corn silo (air) 55 15
1225 100 f. Hoeing and planting . 70 30
1226 200 f. Tractor . . . . 1·50 55

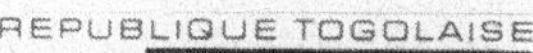

224 "Landscape at Sunset" (Rubens)

1977. 400th Birth Anniv of Rubens. Multicoloured.

1228 15 f. Type **224** (postage) . . . 35 10
1229 35 f. "Exchange of the Princesses at Hendaye" . . 80 15
1230 60 f. "Four Negro Heads" (air) 85 15
1231 100 f. "Anne of Austria" . . 1·10 40

225 Shuttle after Landing

1977. Space Shuttle. Multicoloured.

1233 20 f. Type **225** (postage) . . . 20 10
1234 30 f. Launching 35 15
1235 50 f. Ejecting propellant tanks 55 15
1236 90 f. Retrieving a satellite (air) 70 20
1237 100 f. Ejecting repaired satellite 85 30
1238 200 f. Shuttle landing . . . . 1·50 60

226 Lafayette at 19 (after Le Mire)

227 Lenin and Cruiser "Aurora"

1977. Bicentenary of Lafayette's Arrival in America.

1240 **226** 25 f. brown, yellow and purple (postage) . . . 30 10
1241 – 50 f. red, violet & pink . 55 15
1242 – 60 f. turquoise, green and deep green (air) . . . 50 15
1243 – 105 f. blue, light blue and purple 90 35

DESIGNS—HORIZ: 50 f. Lafayette at Montpelier; 60 f. Lafayette's arrival in New York; 105 f. Lafayette with Washington at Valley Forge.

1977. 60th Anniv of Russian Revolution.

1245 **227** 50 f. multicoloured . . . 80 30

228 "Madonna and Child" (Lotto)

229 Edward Jenner

1977. Christmas. "Madonna and Child" by artists named. Multicoloured.

1246 20 f. Type **228** (postage) . . 20 15
1247 30 f. Crivelli 35 15
1248 50 f. C. Tura 55 15
1249 90 f. Crivelli (different) (air) 65 30
1250 100 f. Bellini 90 35
1251 200 f. Crivelli (different) . . 1·50 55

1978. World Eradication of Smallpox.

1253 **229** 5 f. ochre, black and lilac (postage) 10 10
1254 – 20 f. multicoloured 20 10
1255 **229** 50 f. ochre, black and green (air) 35 15
1256 – 60 f. multicoloured 40 15

DESIGN—HORIZ: 20, 60 f. Patients queuing for vaccination.

230 Wright Brothers

1978. 75th Anniv of 1st Flight by Wright Brothers. Multicoloured.

1258 35 f. Type **230** (postage) . . 45 20
1259 50 f. Wilbur Wright flying Glider No. III 85 35
1260 60 f. Orville Wright Flight of 7 min 31 sec (air) . . . . 1·00 40
1261 70 f. Wreckage of Wright Type A . . . . 1·10 40
1262 200 f. Wright Brothers' cycle workshop, Dearborn, Michigan . . . . 1·40 55
1263 300 f. Wright Flyer I (1st motorised flight). . . . . 2·00 85

231 "Apollo 8" (10th anniv of first mission)

232 St. John

1978. Anniversaries and Events. Multicoloured.

1265 1000 f. Type **231** . . . . . 8·25
1266 1000 f. High-jumping (Olympic Games, 1980) . . . . . . 8·25
1267 1000 f. Westminster Abbey (25th anniv of Queen Elizabeth II's Coronation) 8·25
1268 1000 f. "Duke of Wellington" (150th death anniv of Goya) 8·25
1269 1000 f. Footballers and Cup (World Cup Football Championship) . . . . . 8·25

1978. The Evangelists. Multicoloured.

1271 5 f. Type **232** 10 10
1272 10 f. St. Luke 10 10
1273 25 f. St. Mark 20 10
1274 30 f. St. Mathew 30 10

233 Fishing Harbour

1978. Autonomous Port of Lome. Multicoloured.

1276 25 f. Type **233** (postage) . . 45 15
1277 60 f. Industrial port (air) . . 55 20
1278 100 f. Merchant port 80 30
1279 200 f. General view . . . . 1·25 55

234 "Venera 1" Probe

235 Goalkeeper catching Ball

1978. Space Mission–Venus. Multicoloured.

1281 20 f. Type **234** (postage) . . . 15 10
1282 30 f. "Pioneer" (horiz) . . . 20 15
1283 50 f. Soviet fuel base and antenna 40 15
1284 90 f. "Venera" blast jets (horiz) (air) 40 20
1285 100 f. "Venera" antennae . . 55 30
1286 200 f. "Pioneer" in orbit . . . 1·00 55

1978. World Cup Football Championship, Argentina. Multicoloured.

1288 30 f. Type **235** (postage) . . . 30 10
1289 50 f. Two players with ball . 40 15
1290 60 f. Heading the ball (air) . . 50 15
1291 80 f. High kick 60 20
1292 200 f. Chest stop . . . . . . 1·25 55
1293 300 f. Player with ball . . . . 2·00 85

236 Thomas Edison (inventor)

237 "Celerifere" 1818

1878. Centenary of Invention of the Phonograph. Multicoloured.

1295 30 f. Type **236** (postage) . . . 20 10
1296 50 f. Couple dancing to H.M.V. "Victor", phonograph 1905 45 15
1297 60 f. Edison's original phonograph (horiz) (air) . . 40 15
1298 80 f. Berliner's first phonograph, 1888 . . . . 50 20
1299 200 f. Berliner's improved phonograph, 1894 (horiz) . 1·25 55
1300 300 f. "His Master's Voice" phonograph, c. 1900 (horiz) 2·00 85

1978. Early Bicycles. Multicoloured.

1302 25 f. Type **237** (postage) . . . 35 15
1303 50 f. First bicycle side-car (vert) 65 20
1304 60 f. Bantam bicycle (vert) (air) 55 15
1305 85 f. Military folding bicycle 65 20
1306 90 f. "La Draisienne" (vert) . 90 35
1307 100 f. Penny-farthing (vert) 95 40

238 Dunant's Birthplace, Geneva

240 Eiffel Tower

239 "Threshing" (Raoul Dufy)

1978. 150th Birth Anniv of Henri Dunant (founder of Red Cross).

1309 **238** 5 f. blue & red (postage) . 10 10
1310 – 10 f. brown and red . . . 15 10
1311 – 25 f. greeen and red . . . 30 10
1312 – 60 f. purple and red (air) . 55 20

DESIGNS: 10 f. Dunant at 35; 25 f. Tending battle casualties, 1864; 60 f. Red Cross pavilions, Paris Exhibition, 1867.

1978. Air. "Philexafrique" Stamp Exhibition, Libreville (Gabon), and Int Stamp Fair, Essen, West Germany. As T **262** of Niger. Mult.

1314 100 f. Jay and Thurn and Taxis ¼ sgr. stamp of 1854 . . . 1·90 1·40
1315 100 f. Warthog and Togo 50 f. stamp, 1964 . . . . 1·90 1·40

1978. Artists' Anniversaries. Multicoloured.

1316 25 f. Type **239** (25th death anniv) (postage) 40 15
1317 50 f. "Horsemen on the Seashore" (Gauguin 75th death anniv) 70 15
1318 60 f. "Langlois Bridge" (Van Gogh 125th birth anniv) (air) 50 15
1319 70 f. "Sabbath of the Witches" (Goya 150th death anniv) 60 20
1320 90 f. "Christ Among the Doctors" (Durer 450th death anniv) 60 20
1321 200 f. "View of Arco" (Durer) 1·40 55

1978. Centenary of Paris U.P.U. Congress. Multicoloured.

1323 50 f. Type **240** (postage) . . 80 20
1324 60 f. Full-rigged ship "Slieve Roe" (air) 65 25
1325 105 f. Congress medallion . . 70 30
1326 200 f. 1870s locomotive . . . 1·40 55

241 "Madonna and Child" (Antonello)

242 H.M.S. "Endeavour" and Route round New Zealand

1978. Christmas. Paintings of the Virgin and Child by artists shown below. Multicoloured.

1328 20 f. Type **241** (postage) . . 20 15
1329 30 f. Crivelli 35 15
1330 50 f. Tura 55 15
1331 90 f. Crivelli (different) (air) . 65 30
1332 100 f. Tura (different) . . . 90 30
1333 200 f. Crivelli (different) . . 1·50 55

1979. Death Bicentenary of Captain James Cook. Multicoloured.

1335 25 f. Type **242** (postage) . . 50 15
1336 50 f. Careening H.M.S "Endeavour" (horiz) . . . 80 35
1337 60 f. "Freelove" at Whitby (horiz) (air) 75 35
1338 70 f. Antarctic voyage of H.M.S. "Resolution" (horiz) 1·25 45
1339 90 f. Capt. Cook . . . . . . 1·25 45
1340 200 f. Sail plan of H.M.S. "Endeavour" . . . . . . 2·50 1·10

243 Christ entering Jerusalem

1979. Easter. Multicoloured.

1342 30 f. Type **243** (postage) . . 20 10
1343 40 f. The Last Supper (horiz) 30 15
1344 50 f. Descent from the Cross (horiz) 40 15
1345 60 f. Resurrection (air) . . . 45 15
1346 100 f. Ascension 65 30
1347 200 f. Jesus appearing to Mary Magdalene . . . . 1·25 55

244 Statuette of Drummer

1979. Air. "Philexafrique 2" Stamp Exhibition, Libreville. Multicoloured.

1349 60 f. Type **244** . . . . 1·10 55
1350 100 f. Hands with letter . . . 1·60 1·10

245 Einstein Observatory, Potsdam

1979. Birth Centenary of Albert Einstein (physicist).

1351 245 35 f. red, yellow and black (postage) 20 10
1352 – 50 f. green, mve & blk . 35 10
1353 – 60 f. multicoloured (air) . 40 10
1354 – 85 f. lilac, brown & blk . 60 15
1355 – 100 f. multicoloured . . 65 20
1356 – 200 f. green, brn & blk . 1·40 40

DESIGNS—HORIZ: 50 f. Einstein and J. R. Macdonald in Berlin, 1931; 60 f. Sight and actuality diagram. VERT: 85 f. Einstein playing violin; 100 f. Atomic symbol and relativity formula; 200 f. Albert Einstein.

246 Children with Flag 247 Planting Sapling

1979. International Year of the Child. Multicoloured.

1358 5 f. Type **246** 10 10
1359 10 f. Mother with children . 10 10
1360 15 f. Children's Village symbol on map of Africa (horiz) . 15 10
1361 20 f. Woman taking children to Children's Village (horiz) . 15 10
1362 25 f. Children sitting round Fan palm 30 10
1363 30 f. Map of Togo showing Children's Villages 35 10

1979. Tree Day.

1365 247 50 f. green and violet (postage) 50 15
1366 – 60 f. brown and grn (air) 55 20

DESIGN: 60 f. Watering sapling.

248 Sir Rowland Hill 249 Stephenson's "Rocket", 1829

1979. Death Centenary of Sir Rowland Hill. Multicoloured.

1367 20 f. Type **248** (postage) . . . 15 10
1368 30 f. French mail sorting office in the reign of Louis XV (horiz) 20 10
1369 50 f. Parisian postbox, 1850 . 40 15
1370 90 f. Bellman collecting letters, 1820 (air) 60 20
1371 100 f. "Centre-cycles" used for mail delivery, 1880 (horiz) . 65 20
1372 200 f. Post Office railway carriage, 1848 (horiz) . . . 1·25 40

1979. Railway Locomotives. Multicoloured.

1374 35 f. Type **249** (postage) . . . 35 10
1375 50 f. William Norris' "Austria", 1843 . . . . 45 15
1376 60 f. "The General", 1862 (air) 55 15
1377 85 f. Stephenson locomotive, 1843 . . . . 75 35
1378 100 f. De Witt Clinton train, 1831 . . . . 85 35
1379 200 f. D. Joy's "Jenny Lind" 1·75 55

Nos. 1375/9 are horizontal.

250 Skiing 251 Native praying

1979. Olympic Games, Lake Placid and Moscow. Multicoloured.

1381 20 f. Type **250** (postage) . . 15 10
1382 30 f. Yachting 20 15
1383 50 f. Throwing the discus . . 40 10
1384 90 f. Ski-jumping (air) . . . 65 20
1385 100 f. Canoeing 70 20
1386 200 f. Gymnastics (ring exercise) 1·40 40

1979. Togo Religions.

1388 251 30 f. brown, green and yellow (postage) . . . 20 10
1389 – 50 f. blue, brown & red 35 10
1390 – 60 f. purple, blue and buff (air) 45 15
1391 – 70 f. lilac, orange & grn 50 20

DESIGNS—HORIZ: 50 f. Catholic priests; 60 f. Muslims at prayer; 70 f. Protestant preachers.

252 Astronaut on Moon 253 Dish Aerial

1979. 10th Anniv of First Moon Landing. Multicoloured.

1393 35 f. Type **252** (postage) . . 30 10
1394 50 f. Capsule orbiting Moon 40 10
1395 60 f. Armstrong descending to Moon 45 10
1396 70 f. Astronaut and flag (air) 50 15
1397 200 f. Astronaut performing experiment . . . . 1·25 35
1398 300 f. Module leaving Moon 2·00 50

1979. 3rd World Telecommunications Exposition, Geneva.

1400 – 50 f. light brown, brown and green (postage) . 35 10
1401 253 60 f. green, blue and deep blue (air) 50 20

DESIGN—HORIZ: 50 f. Television screen.

254 Pres. Eyadema

1979. Air. 10th Anniv of R.P.T. Multicoloured.

1402 1000 f. Pres. Eyadema and Party badge . . . . 6·75
1403 1000 f. Type **254** . . . . . . 6·75

255 Holy Family 256 Rotary Emblem

1979. Christmas. Multicoloured.

1404 20 f. Type **255** (postage) . . 15 10
1405 30 f. Madonna and Child and angels playing musical instruments 20 10
1406 50 f. Adoration of the shepherds 40 10
1407 90 f. Adoration of the Magi (air) 55 20
1408 100 f. Mother presenting Child 70 20
1409 200 f. The Flight into Egypt 1·50 40

1980. 75th Anniv of Rotary International. Multicoloured.

1411 25 f. Type **256** postage) . . . 15 10
1412 30 f. Anniversary emblem . . 30 10
1413 40 f. Paul Harris (founder) . . 35 10
1414 90 f. Figure exercising and sun (health) (air) 65 20
1415 100 f. Fish and grain (food) . 70 20
1416 200 f. Family group (humanity) 1·40 40

257 Shooting (Biathlon)

1980. Winter Olympic Games, Lake Placid. Multicoloured.

1418 50 f. Type **257** (postage) . . . 50 10
1419 60 f. Downhill skiing 40 10
1420 100 f. Speed skating (air) . . 70 20
1421 200 f. Cross-country skiing . 1·40 40

258 Swimming

1980. Olympic Games, Moscow. Multicoloured.

1423 20 f. Type **258** (postage) . . . 15 10
1424 30 f. Gymnastics 20 10
1425 50 f. Running 40 10
1426 100 f. Fencing (air) 65 20
1427 200 f. Pole vaulting . . . . . 1·25 45
1428 300 f. Hurdles . . . . 2·00 55

259 Truck going to Market

1980. Market Scenes. Multicoloured.

1430 1 f. Grinding savo (postage) . 10 10
1431 2 f. Women preparing meat . 10 10
1432 3 f. Type **259** 10 10
1433 4 f. Unloading produce . . . 10 10
1434 5 f. Sugar-cane seller 10 10
1435 6 f. Barber doing child's hair . 10 10
1436 7 f. Vegetable seller 10 10
1437 7 f. Mangoes (vert) 10 10
1438 9 f. Grain seller 10 10
1439 10 f. Fish seller 10 10
1440 15 f. Clay pot seller 10 10
1441 20 f. Straw baskets 15 10
1442 25 f. Lemon and onion seller (vert) 15 10
1443 30 f. Straw baskets (different) 20 10
1444 40 f. Shore market 30 15
1445 45 f. Selling cooked food . . 35 15
1446 50 f. Women carrying produce (vert) 35 15
1447 60 f. Selling oil 45 15
1448 90 f. Linen seller (air) 55 15
1449 100 f. Bananas 65 20
1450 200 f. Pottery . . . . 1·25 45
1451 250 f. Setting-up stalls . . . . 1·60 55
1452 500 f. Vegetable seller (different) 3·00 1·10
1453 1000 f. Drink seller . . . . . 6·00 2·25

260 Concorde and Map of Africa

1980. 20th Anniv of African Air Safety Organization.

1458 260 50 f. mult (postage) . . . 55 20
1459 60 f. multicoloured (air) . 55 25

261 "Christ with Angels" (Mantegna) 263 Radio Waves

1980. Easter. Multicoloured.

1460 30 f. Type **261** (postage) . . 30 15
1461 40 f. "Christ with Disciples" (Crivelli) 40 15
1462 50 f. "Christ borne by His Followers" (Pontormo) . . 45 15
1463 60 f. "The Deposition" (Lotto) (air) 50 10
1464 100 f. "The Crucifixion" (El Greco) 70 20
1465 200 f. "Christ with Angels" (Crivelli) . . . . 1·40 45

1980. "London 1980" International Stamp Exhibition. No. 1267 optd **Londres 1980.**

1467 1000 f. Westminster Abbey . 7·25

1980. World Telecommunciations Day.

1469 – 50 f. violet and green (postage) 45 10
1470 263 60 f. pink, brown and blue (air) 50 15

DESIGN—HORIZ: 50 f. Satellite.

264 Red Cross and Globe 265 Jules Verne

1980. Togo Red Cross. Multicoloured.

1471 50 f. Type **264** (postage) . . 55 10
1472 60 f. Nurses and patient (air) 45 15

1980. 75th Death Anniv of Jules Verne (writer). Multicoloured.

1473 30 f. Type **265** (postage) . . 30 10
1474 50 f. "20,000 Leagues under the Sea" 40 10
1475 60 f. "From the Earth to the Moon" (air) 40 15
1476 80 f. "Around the World in Eighty Days" 55 20
1477 100 f. "From the Earth to the Moon" (different) . . . . 1·40 60
1478 200 f. "20,000 Leagues under the Sea" (different) . . . . 1·75 60

266 "Baroness James de Rothschild"

1980. Birth Bicentenary of Jean Ingres (painter). Multicoloured.

1480 25 f. Type **266** (postage) . . 35 10
1481 30 f. "Napoleon I on the Imperial Throne" 55 10
1482 40 f. "Don Pedro of Toledo putting down the Sword of Henry IV" 50 10
1483 90 f. "Jupiter and Thetis" (air) 65 20
1484 100 f. "The Countess of Hassonville" 85 20
1485 200 f. "Tu Marcellus Eris" . . 1·50 35

267 Minnie holding Mirror for Leopard

1980. Walt Disney Characters and Wildlife.

No.	Description		
1487	1 f. Type **267**	10	10
1488	2 f. Goofy cleaning hippo's teeth	10	10
1489	3 f. Donald clinging to crocodile	10	10
1490	4 f. Donald hanging over cliff edge from rhino's horn	10	10
1491	5 f. Goofy riding a water buffalo	10	10
1492	10 f. Monkey photographing Mickey	10	10
1493	100 f. Doctor Mickey examining giraffe	80	20
1494	300 f. Elephant showering Goofy	1·60	40

1980. 50th Anniv of Pluto. As T **267**.

No.	Description		
1496	200 f. Pluto in party mood	1·60	40

268 Wreath

1980. Famous Men of the Decade.

No.	Description		
1498 **268**	25 f. orange and green (postage)	15	10
1499 –	40 f. dp green & green	65	20
1500 –	90 f. dp blue & bl (air)	60	20
1501 –	100 f. lilac and pink	1·10	20

DESIGNS: 40 f. Mao Tse Tung; 90 f. Pres. Allende; 100 f. Pope Paul VI; 200 f. Pres. Kenyatta.

269 Tourist Hotel Emblem

270 Human Rights Emblem and Map of Australia

1980. World Tourism Conference, Manila. Multicoloured.

No.	Description		
1504	50 f. Type **269**	35	10
1505	150 f. Conference emblem	1·00	35

1980. 30th Anniv of Human Rights Convention.

No.	Description		
1506 **270**	30 f. violet, purple and black (postage)	30	10
1507 –	50 f. green, light green and black	40	10
1508 –	60 f. deep blue, blue and black (air)	40	15
1509 –	150 f. brown, orge & blk	1·00	35

DESIGNS: 50 f. Map of Eurasia; 60 f. Map of the Americas; 250 f. Map of Africa.

271 Emblem

1980. Air. General Conclave of French-speaking Countries of the American Order of Rosicrucians, Lome.

No.	Description		
1511 **271**	60 f. multicoloured	50	15

272 Church at Melk, Austria

1980. Christmas. Multicoloured.

No.	Description		
1512	20 f. Type **272** (postage)	15	10
1513	30 f. Tarragona Cathedral, Spain	20	10
1514	50 f. Church of St. John the Baptist, Florence	35	10
1515	100 f. Cologne Cathedral (air)	65	20
1516	150 f. Notre-Dame, Paris	1·00	30
1517	200 f. Canterbury Cathedral	1·40	35

1980. 5th Anniv of African Posts and Telecommunications Union. As T **292** of Niger.

No.	Description		
1519	100 f. multicoloured	65	40

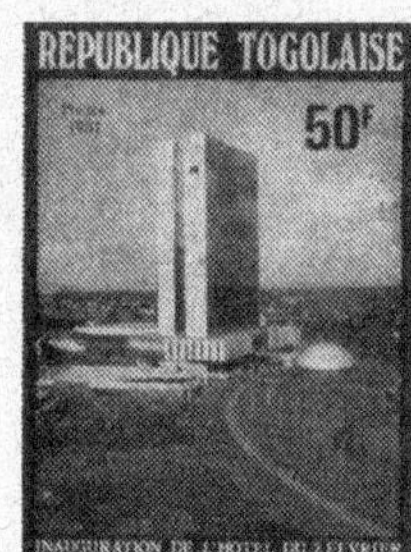

273 "February 2nd" Hotel

1981. Inauguration of "February 2nd" Hotel.

No.	Description		
1520 **273**	50 f. mult (postage)	45	15
1521	60 f. multicoloured (air)	45	15

274 "Rembrandt's Father"

1981. Easter. Rembrandt Paintings. Multicoloured.

No.	Description		
1522	30 f. Type **274** (postage)	30	10
1523	40 f. "Self-portrait"	35	10
1524	50 f. "Rembrandt's Father as an Old Man"	40	10
1525	60 f. "Rider on Horseback"	50	15
1526	100 f. "Rembrandt's Mother" (air)	70	20
1527	200 f. "Man in a Ruff"	1·50	45

275 Grey-necked Bald Crow

1981. Birds. Multicoloured.

No.	Description		
1529	30 f. Type **275** (postage)	55	25
1530	40 f. Splendid sunbird	70	25
1531	60 f. Violet starling	90	40
1532	90 f. Red-collard whydah	1·40	55
1533	50 f. Violet-backed sunbird (air)	90	40
1534	100 f. Red bishop	1·60	85

276 Dish Aerial

1981. 6th African Postal Union Council Meeting. Multicoloured.

No.	Description		
1536	70 f. Type **276**	50	15
1537	90 f. Telecommunications control room	60	20
1538	105 f. Map of Togo and Africa (vert)	70	30

277 Blind Man with Guide Dog

1981. International Year of Disabled People. Multicoloured.

No.	Description		
1539	70 f. Type **277** (postage)	85	30
1540	90 f. One-legged carpenter (air)	60	15
1541	200 f. Wheelchair basket-ball	1·60	55

278 "Woman with Hat"

1981. Birth Centenary of Pablo Picasso. Mult.

No.	Description		
1543	25 f. Type **278** (postage)	35	10
1544	50 f. "She-goat"	45	10
1545	60 f. "Violin"	55	15
1546	90 f. "Violin and Bottle on Table" (air)	80	20
1547	100 f. "Baboon with Young"	90	30
1548	200 f. "Mandolin and Clarinet"	1·90	55

279 Aachen Cathedral, West Germany

1981. World Heritage Convention. Multicoloured.

No.	Description		
1550	30 f. Type **279** (postage)	20	10
1551	40 f. Yellowstone National Park, U.S.A.	30	10
1552	50 f. Nahanni National Park, Canada	35	10
1553	60 f. Cruciform rock churches, Lalibela, Ethiopia	40	15
1554	100 f. Old city centre, Cracow, Poland (air)	65	20
1555	200 f. Goree Island, Senegal	1·25	35

280 "Vostok I" (20th anniv of first Manned Space Flight)

1981. Space Anniversaries. Multicoloured.

No.	Description		
1557	25 f. Type **280** (postage)	15	10
1558	50 f. "Freedom 7", first American in space (20th anniv)	35	10
1559	60 f. "Lunar Orbiter I" (15th anniv)	40	15
1560	90 f. "Soyuz 10" (10th anniv) (air)	60	15
1561	100 f. Astronauts on Moon ("Apollo XIV", 10th anniv)	65	20

281 "Adoration of the Magi"

282 Association Emblem and Togo Flag

1981. Christmas. Paintings by Rubens. Multicoloured.

No.	Description		
1563	20 f. Type **281** (postage)	15	10
1564	30 f. "Adoration of the Shepherds"	20	10
1565	50 f. "Coronation of St. Catherine"	40	10
1566	100 f. "Adoration of the Magi" (different) (air)	60	20
1567	200 f. "Madonna and Child"	1·40	45
1568	300 f. "The Madonna giving the Robe to St. Idefonse"	2·25	65

1981. West African Rice Development Association.

No.	Description		
1570 **282**	70 f. mult (postage)	60	20
1571	105 f. multicoloured (air)	65	30

283 Peace Dove and National Flag

1982. 15th Anniv of National Liberation. Mult.

No.	Description		
1572	70 f. Type **283** (postage)	55	20
1573	90 f. Pres. Eyadema and citizens (vert)	60	20
1574	105 f. Pres. Eyadema and citizens holding hands (vert) (air)	65	35
1575	130 f. Hotel complex	90	45

284 Scouts

1982. 75th Anniv of Boy Scout Movement. Multicoloured.

No.	Description		
1576	70 f. Type **284** (postage)	50	15
1577	90 f. Signalling (air)	65	20
1578	120 f. Constructing a tower	85	30
1579	130 f. Scouts with canoe	90	50
1580	135 f. Scouts and tent	95	35

285 Moses and the Burning Bush

286 Togo and Italy Olympic Stamps

1982. Easter. The Ten Commandments. Multicoloured.

No.	Description		
1582	10 f. Type **285** (postage)	10	10
1583	25 f. Jephtha's daughter	15	10
1584	30 f. St. Vincent Ferrer preaching in Verona	20	10
1585	45 f. The denouncing of Noah	30	10
1586	50 f. Cain and Abel	35	10
1587	70 f. Potiphar's wife	50	20
1588	90 f. Isaac blessing Jacob	60	35
1589	105 f. Susannah and the elders (air)	65	30
1590	120 f. Bathsheba	85	35

1982. Air. "Romolymphil" Stamp Exhibition.
1592 **286** 105 f. multicoloured . . 70 30

287 First Stamps of France and Togo

1982. Air. "Philexfrance '82" International Stamp Exhibition.
1593 **287** 90 f. multicoloured . . . 65 40

288 Goalkeeper

1982. World Cup Football Championship, Spain. Multicoloured.
1594 25 f. Type **288** (postage) . . . 15 10
1595 45 f. Tackle 35 10
1596 105 f. Heading ball (air) . . . 65 20
1597 200 f. Fighting for possession 1·25 45
1598 300 f. Dribble . . . . 2·00 55

289 "Papilio dardanus"

1982. Butterflies. Multicoloured.
1600 15 f. Type **289** (postage) . . 20 10
1601 20 f. "Belenois calypso" . . . 35 10
1602 25 f. "Palla decius" 40 10
1603 90 f. "Euxanthe eurinome" (air) 1·40 90
1604 105 f. "Mylothris rhodope" . 1·60 1·00

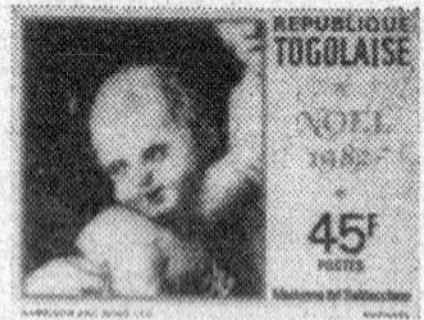

290 Infant Jesus

1982. Christmas. Details of Raphael's "Madonna del Baldacchino". Multicoloured.
1606 45 f. Type **290** 40 10
1607 70 f. Madonna 55 15
1608 105 f. Angel 70 20
1609 130 f. Angel (different) . . . 1·00 30
1610 150 f. Putti . . . . 1·10 35

291 Building, Sokode

1983. Visit of President Mitterrand of France. Multicoloured.
1612 35 f. Type **291** (postage) . . . 20 10
1613 45 f. Children of different races and world map 35 15
1614 70 f. French and Togolese soldiers (vert) 55 20
1615 90 f. President Mitterrand (air) (vert) 70 30
1616 105 f. Presidents Mitterrand and Eyadema shaking hands (vert) 80 35
1617 130 f. Presidents Mitterrand and Eyadema and crowds . . . 1·00 40

1983. World Cup Football Championship Results. Nos. 1594/8 optd **VAINQUER COUPE DU MONDE FOOTBALL 82 "ITALIE"**. Multicoloured.
1618 25 f. Type **288** (postage) . . . 15 10
1619 45 f. Tackle 35 15
1620 105 f. Heading ball (air) . . . 65 35
1621 200 f. Fighting for possession 1·25 55
1622 300 f. Dribble . . . . 2·00 80

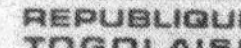

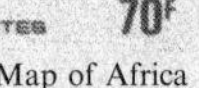

293 Map of Africa showing W.A.M.U. Members
294 Drummer

1983. 20th Anniv of West African Monetary Union. Multicoloured.
1624 70 f. Type **293** 50 15
1625 90 f. West African coin . . . 60 20

1983. World Communications Year. Multicoloured.
1626 70 f. Type **294** (postage) . . 55 15
1627 90 f. Modern post office and telecommunications system (air) 65 20

295 Boxing

1983. Air. Pre-Olympic Year. Multicoloured.
1628 70 f. Type **295** 50 15
1629 90 f. Hurdles 60 20
1630 105 f. Pole vault 65 20
1631 130 f. Sprinting . . . . . . 1·00 30

296 Kondona Dance

1983. Traditional Dances. Multicoloured.
1633 70 f. Type **296** (postage) . . 60 20
1634 90 f. Kondona dance (different) (air) 80 20
1635 105 f. Toubole dance 90 20
1636 130 f. Adjogbo dance . . . 1·10 20

297 Painting by Bellini

1983. Easter. Multicoloured.
1637 35 f. Type **297** (postage) . . 30 10
1638 70 f. Raphael (vert) 50 15
1639 90 f. Carracci (air) 65 20

298 Catholic Church, Kante

1983. Christmas. Multicoloured.
1641 70 f. Type **298** (postage) . . 50 15
1642 90 f. Altar, Dapaong Cathedral (air) 60 20
1643 105 f. Protestant church, Dapaong 70 20

299 Wrecked Airplane

1984. 10th Anniv of Sarakawa Assassination Attempt. Multicoloured.
1645 70 f. Type **299** (postage) . . . 50 25
1646 90 f. Wrecked airplane (different) 60 30
1647 120 f. Memorial Hall (air) . . 85 40
1648 270 f. Statue of President Eyadema (vert) . . . . . . 1·90 70

300 Picking Coffee Beans

1984. World Food Programme Day. Multicoloured.
1649 35 f. Type **300** 20 10
1650 70 f. Harvesting cocoa pods . 50 15
1651 90 f. Planting rice 65 20

301 Flags, Agriculture and Symbols of Unity Growth

1984. 25th Anniv of Council of Unity.
1653 **301** 70 f. multicoloured . . . 50 15
1654 90 f. multicoloured . . . 60 20

1984. Air. 19th Universal Postal Union Congress, Hamburg. Nos 1451/2 optd **19E CONGRES UPU HAMBOURG 1984**.
1655 250 f. multicoloured . . . . . 1·60 85
1656 500 f. multicoloured . . . . . 3·25 1·60

303 Tim Thorpe (gold, pentathlon and decathlon, 1912)
304 Thief on right-hand Cross

1984. Air. Olympic Games Medal Winners (1st series). Multicoloured.
1657 500 f. Type **303** . . . . 4·50 85
1658 500 f. Mathias Behr (silver, fencing, 1984) . . . . 4·50 85
1659 500 f. Fredy Schmidtke (gold, cycling, 1984) . . . . 4·50 85
1660 500 f. Dietmar Mogenburg (gold, high jumping, 1984) . 4·50 85
1661 500 f. Sabine Everts (bronze, heptathlon, 1984) . . . . . 4·50 85
1662 500 f. Jesse Owens (gold, 200 metres, 1936) . . . . 4·50 85
1663 500 f. Bob Beamon (gold, long jumping, 1968) . . . . 4·50 85
1664 500 f. Muhammad Ali (gold, boxing, 1960) . . . . . . 22·00 85
See also Nos. 1825/32.

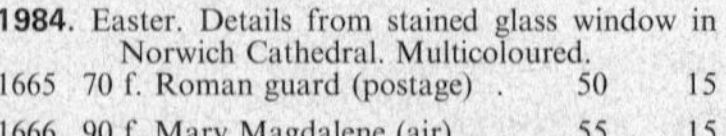
1984. Easter. Details from stained glass window in Norwich Cathedral. Multicoloured.
1665 70 f. Roman guard (postage) . 50 15
1666 90 f. Mary Magdalene (air) . 55 15
1667 120 f. The Apostles comforting Mary 80 20
1668 270 f. Type **304** . . . . 1·60 45
1669 300 f. Thief on left-hand Cross 2·00 55

305 Baguida (site of Protectorate Treaty signature, 1884)

1984. Centenary of Proclamation of German Protectorate. Multicoloured.
1671 35 f. Type **305** 20 20
1672 35 f. Degbenou School, 1893 (horiz) 20 20
1673 35 f. Degbenou Catholic Mission, 1893 (horiz) . . . 20 20
1674 35 f. Kara suspension bridge, 1911 (horiz) 20 20
1675 35 f. Adjido state school (horiz) 20 20
1676 35 f. Administration post, Sansane Mango, 1908 (horiz) 20 20
1677 35 f. Sokode cotton market, 1910 (horiz) 20 20
1678 45 f. Main street, Lome, 1895, and 5 m. "Yacht" stamp (horiz) 35 35
1679 45 f. Governor's Palace, Lome, 1905 (horiz) 35 35
1680 45 f. Drilling police squad, 1905 (horiz) 35 35
1681 45 f. Guillaume fountain, Atakpame, 1906 . . . . . 35 35
1682 45 f. Constructing Lome–Atakpame railway (horiz) . 35 35
1683 45 f. Rue de Commerce, Lome, and 10 pf. "Yacht" stamp (horiz) 35 35
1684 70 f. 20 pf. and 2 m. "Yacht" stamps, 1900 (horiz) . . . 50 45
1685 70 f. Lome wharf, 1903 (horiz) 50 45
1686 90 f. Farming, Sansane Mango, 1908 (horiz) 60 55
1687 90 f. Chancellor Otto von Bismark 60 55
1688 90 f. Emperor Wilhelm II . . 60 55
1689 90 f. Commissioner J. von Puttkamer, 1891–93 . . . 60 55
1690 90 f. Consul-General G. Nachtigal, 1884 . . . . 60 55
1691 90 f. Governor A. Koehler, 1895–1902 . . . . 60 55
1692 90 f. Governor W. Horn, 1902–1905 . . . . 60 55
1693 90 f. Governor J. G. von Zech, 1905–10 . . . . 60 55
1694 90 f. Governor E. Bruckner, 1911–12 . . . . 60 55
1695 90 f. Governor A. F. von Mecklenberg, 1912–14 . . 60 55
1696 90 f. Governor H. G. von Doering, 1914 . . . . 60 55
1697 120 f. Signing of Protectorate Treaty, 1885 (horiz) . . . 90 85
1698 120 f. Postmen, 1885 . . . . 90 85
1699 150 f. Children dancing around maps and flags . . . . . . 1·10 95
1700 270 f. German gunboat "Mowe", 1884 (horiz) . . 2·00 1·75
1701 270 f. German sail corvette "Sophie", 1884 . . . . . 2·00 1·75
1702 270 f. Steam train from Aneho railway, 1905 (horiz) . . . 2·00 1·75
1703 270 f. "Mallet" train from Kpalime, railway, 1907 (horiz) . . . . 2·00 1·75
1704 270 f. Flags and Presidents of Togo and Germany (horiz) 2·25 1·90

306 High Jumping

1984. Air. Olympic Games, Los Angeles. Mult.
1705 70 f. Type **306** 45 25
1706 90 f. Cycling 55 20
1707 120 f. Football 80 30
1708 250 f. Boxing (horiz) . . . . 1·60 50
1709 400 f. Running (horiz) . . . 2·75 80

307 Donald with Presents and Chip

1984. 50th Anniv of Donald Duck (cartoon character). Multicoloured.
1711 1 f. Type **307** (postage) . . . 10 10
1712 2 f. Donald and Chip'n'Dale 10 10
1713 3 f. Huey, Chip and Dale blowing up balloons . . . 10 10
1714 5 f. Donald and Chip holding birthday cake 10 10
1715 10 f. Daisy kissing Donald . 30 10
1716 15 f. Goofy giving Donald his present 40 10
1717 105 f. Huey, Dewey and Louie decorating cake (air) . . . 85 15
1718 500 f. Huey, Dewey, Louie and Donald with birthday cake 4·50 95
1719 1000 f. Huey, Duey and Louie startling Donald . . . . . 7·50 1·60

308 West African Manatee

1984. Endangered Wildlife. Multicoloured.
1722 45 f. Type **308** (postage) . . . 85 15
1723 70 f. Manatee (close up) . . 1·10 20
1724 90 f. Manatees in water (air) . 1·40 35
1725 105 f. Manatee with cub . . 1·40 35

309 Flame and Eleanor Roosevelt

1984. Birth Cent of Eleanor Roosevelt. Mult.
1727 70 f. Type **309** (postage) . . . 55 15
1728 90 f. Eleanor Roosevelt and Statue of Liberty (air) . . . 65 15

310 Lockheed Constellation, 1944

1984. 40th Anniv of International Civil Aviation Organization. Multicoloured.
1729 70 f. Type **310** (postage) . . . 55 30
1730 105 f. Boeing 707, 1954 (air) 60 40
1731 200 f. Douglas DC-8-61, 1966 1·25 80
1732 500 f. Concorde, 1966 . . . . 3·25 1·75

311 Bristol "400", 1947

1984. Classic Cars. Multicoloured.
1734 1 f. Type **311** (postage) . . . 10 10
1735 2 f. Frazer Nash "Standard", 1925 . . . . 10 10
1736 3 f. Healey "Silverstone", 1950 10 10
1737 4 f. Kissell "Gold Bug Speedstar", 1925 . . . . . 10 10
1738 50 f. La Salle 5 litre, 1927 . . 80 15
1739 90 f. Minerva 30 h.p., 1921 (air) 70 15
1740 500 f. Morgan "Plus 4", 1950 4·25 95
1741 1000 f. Napier 40/50 T75 Six", 1921 . . . . 7·75 2·25

313 "Connestabile Madonna"

1984. Christmas. Paintings by Raphael. Multicoloured.
1744 70 f. Type **313** (postage) . . 55 15
1745 290 f. "The Cowper Madonna" (air) . . . . 1·90 65
1746 300 f. "The Alba Madonna" 2·00 65
1747 500 f. "Madonna of the Curtain" . . . . 3·25 1·10

314 "Decapotable" Locomotive, Madeira

1984. Railway Locomotives. Multicoloured.
1749 1 f. Type **314** (postage) . . . 10 10
1750 2 f. British-made locomotive, Egyptian railway 10 10
1751 3 f. "Garratt" locomotive, Algerian railway 10 10
1752 4 f. Diesel train, Congo-Ocean railway 10 10
1753 50 f. Italian-made locomotive, Libyan railway 65 15
1754 90 f. No. "49" Northern railway locomotive (air) 55 15
1755 105 f. "Mallet" locomotive, Togo railway 65 20
1756 500 f. Steam locomotive, Rhodesian railway . . . . 3·75 70
1757 1000 f. Beyer-Garratt steam locomotive, East African railway . . . . 7·25 2·25

315 Map of Americas and Flags **316** St. Paul

1984. 3rd E.E.C.–African States Convention, Lome. Multicoloured.
1759 100 f. Type **315** 80 20
1760 130 f. Map of Europe and Africa and flags . . . . . 1·10 30
1761 270 f. Map of Asia and Australasia and flags . . . 2·00 60

Nos. 1759/61 were printed in se-tenant strips of three, forming a composite design showing map of the world.

1984. The Twelve Apostles. Multicoloured.
1763 1 f. Type **316** (postage) . . . 10 10
1764 2 f. Saint Thomas 10 10
1765 3 f. Saint Matthew 10 10
1766 4 f. Saint James, the Less . . 10 10
1767 5 f. Saint Simon, the Zealot 10 10
1768 70 f. Saint Thaddeus 85 15
1769 90 f. Saint Bartholomew (air) 55 15
1770 105 f. Saint Philip 65 15
1771 200 f. Saint John . . . . . 1·25 35
1772 270 f. Saint James, son of Zebedee . . . . 1·60 45
1773 400 f. Saint Andrew . . . . 2·50 80
1774 500 f. Saint Peter . . . . . 3·25 90

317 Allez France

1985. Racehorses. Multicoloured.
1776 1 f. Type **317** (postage) . . . 10 10
1777 2 f. Arkle (vert) 10 10
1778 3 f. Tingle Creek (vert) . . . 10 10
1779 4 f. Interco 10 10
1780 50 f. Dawn Run 95 15
1781 90 f. Seattle Slew (vert) (air) . 85 20
1782 500 f. Nijinsky . . . . 4·75 90
1783 1000 f. Politician . . . . . . 7·75 2·25

318 Map, Globe and Doves

1985. Air. Peace and Human Rights. Multicoloured.
1785 230 f. Type **318** . . . . . . 1·50 55
1786 270 f. Palm tree by shore and emblem . . . . 1·75 55
1787 500 f. Mining and emblem . . 3·25 1·10
1788 1000 f. Human Rights monument . . . . 6·75 2·50

319 "Christ and the Fisherman"

1985. Easter. Paintings by Raphael. Multicoloured.
1789 70 f. "Christ and the Apostles" (postage) 55 15
1790 90 f. Type **319** 60 20
1791 135 f. "Christ making Benediction" (vert) (air) . . 1·00 20
1792 150 f. "The Entombment" (vert) 1·10 30
1793 250 f. "The Resurrection" (vert) 1·75 50

320 Profiles and Emblem

1985. 15th Anniv of Cultural and Technical Co-operation Agency.
1795 **320** 70 f. multicoloured . . . 50 20
1796 90 f. multicoloured . . . 60 30

321 Adifo Dance

1985. Air. Traditional Dances. Multicoloured.
1797 120 f. Type **321** 80 30
1798 125 f. Whip dance 90 35
1799 290 f. Idjombi dance . . . . 1·90 65
1800 500 f. Moba dance . . . . . 3·25 95

322 Kabye Man **324** Muricate Turrid

323 Woman carrying Basket on Head and Workers on Map

1985. Tribal Markings. Multicoloured.
1801 25 f. Type **322** (postage) . . . 15 10
1802 70 f. Mollah woman 50 20
1803 90 f. Moba man (air) 60 20
1804 105 f. Kabye woman 80 20
1805 270 f. Peda woman . . . . . 1·90 65

1985. "Philexafrique" Stamp Exhibition, Lome. "Youth and Development". Multicoloured.
1806 200 f. Type **323** . . . . . . 1·60 90
1807 200 f. Man ploughing field with oxen . . . . 1·60 90

1985. Sea Shells. Multicoloured.
1808 70 f. Type **324** (postage) . . 95 20
1809 90 f. Desjardin's marginalla (air) . . . . 1·00 25
1810 120 f. Nifat turrid . . . . . 1·25 25
1811 135 f. Rat cowrie . . . . . 1·50 25
1812 270 f. Garter cone . . . . . 3·00 60

1985. "Expo '85" World's Fair, Tsukuba, Japan. Nos. 1738 and 1741 optd **EXPOSITION MONDIALE 1985 TSUKUBA, JAPON.**
1814 50 f. La Salle 5 litre, 1927 (postage) 85 20
1815 1000 f. Napier "40/50 T75 Six", 1921 (air) . . . . 9·50 2·75

326 Pope giving Blessing **327** Brown Pelican

1985. Air. Visit of Pope John Paul II. Multicoloured.
1817 90 f. Pope and children . . . 85 20
1818 130 f. Type **326** . . . . . . 1·10 35
1819 500 f. Pres. Eyadema greeting Pope . . . . 4·25 2·25

1985. Birth Bicentenary of John J. Audubon (ornithologist). Multicoloured.
1820 120 f. Type **327** (postage) . . 1·50 1·00
1821 270 f. Golden eagle . . . . 3·75 2·25
1822 90 f. Bonaparte's gulls (air) . 1·40 75
1823 135 f. Great-tailed grackle . 1·90 1·10
1824 500 f. Red-headed woodpecker 7·75 4·75

1985. Air. Olympic Games Medal Winners (2nd series). Nos. 1657/64 optd.
1826 500 f. **"ITALIE MEDAILLE D'OR"** . . . . 4·00 85
1827 500 f. **"PHILIPPE BOISSE/ FRANCE/MEDAILLE D'OR"** . . . . 4·00 85
1828 500 f. **"ROLF GOLZ/R.F.A./ MEDAILLE D'ARGENT"** 4·00 85
1829 500 f. **"PATRIK SJOBERG/ SUEDE/MEDAILLE D'ARGENT"** . . . . . . 4·00 85
1830 500 f. **"GLYNIS NUNN/ AUSTRALIE/MEDAILLE D'OR"** . . . . 4·00 85
1831 500 f. **"KIRK BAPTISTE/ ETATS UNIS/MEDAILLE D'ARGENT"** . . . . . . 4·00 85
1832 500 f. **"CARL LEWIS/ETATS UNIS/MEDAILLE D'OR"** 4·00 85
1833 500 f. **"KEVIN BARRY/NLE ZELANDE/MEDAILLE D'ARGENT"** . . . . . . 4·00 85

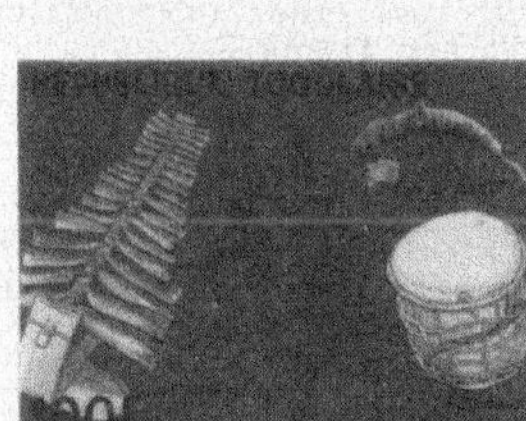

330 Gongophone, Kante Horn and Drum

1985. Air. "Philexafrique" Stamp Exhibition, Lome (2nd issue). Musical Instruments. Multicoloured.
1835 100 f. Type **330** . . . . . . 1·40 65
1836 100 f. Twin drums, Bassar horn and castanets . . . . . . 1·40 65

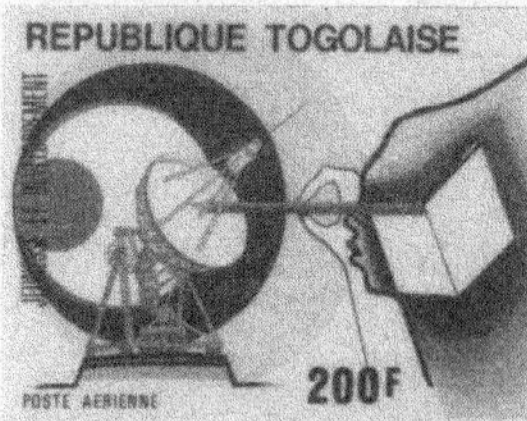

331 Open Book, Profile, Hand holding Pencil and Dish Aerial

1985. Air. "Philexafrique" Stamp Exhibition, Lome (3rd issue). "Youth and Development". Mult.
1837 200 f. Type **331** . . . . . . 1·90 1·10
1838 200 f. Profiles, factory, cogwheel and maize . . . . 1·90 1·10

332 Dove, Sun and U.N. Emblem

1985. 40th Anniv of U.N.O. Multicoloured.

1839 90 f. Type **332** (postage) . . . 60 20
1840 115 f. Hands reaching up to Emblem . . . 90 20
1841 150 f. Building new bridge on river Kara (air) . . . 1·10 35
1842 250 f. Preparing experimental field of millet at Atalote, Keran . . . 1·60 50
1843 500 f. Pres. Eyadema, U.N. Secretary-General, U.N. and national flags . . . 3·25 85

333 "Madonna of the Rose Garden" (Sandro Botticelli)

335 "The Resurrection" (Andrea Mantegna)

1985. Christmas. Multicoloured.

1844 90 f. Type **333** (postage) . . . 65 20
1845 115 f. "Madonna and Child" (11th-century Byzantine painting) (air) . . . 90 20
1846 150 f. "Rest during the flight into Egypt" (Gerard David) . . . 1·00 30
1847 160 f. "African Madonna" (16th-century statue) . . . 1·10 30
1848 250 f. "African Madonna" (statue, 1900) . . . 2·00 45

1985. Various stamps optd. (a) Nos. 1739/40 optd **10e ANNIVERSAIRE DE APOLLO-SOYUZ**.

1850 90 f. Minerva 30 h.p., 1921 . . 85 30
1851 500 f. Morgan "Plus 4", 1950 . . 4·75 1·40

(b) Nos. 1752, 1755 and 1757 optd **80e ANNIVERSAIRE du/ROTARY INTERNATIONAL**.

1853 4 f. Train, Congo-Ocean railway . . 85 20
1854 105 f. "Mallet" locomotive, Togo railways . . . 65 30
1855 1000 f. Beyer-Garratt steam locomotive, East African railway . . . 8·25 2·75

(c) 150th Anniv of German Railways. Nos. 1753/4 and 1756 optd **"150e ANNIVERSAIRE/DE CHEMIN FER 'LUDWIG'"**

1857 50 f. Italian-made locomotive, Libyan railway . . . 85 20
1858 90 f. No. "49" Northern railway locomotive . . . 85 30
1859 500 f. Locomotive, Rhodesian railway . . . 4·75 1·40

(d) Nos. 1773/4 optd **"75e ANNIVERSAIRE DE LA/MORT DE HENRI DUNANT/ FONDATEUR DE LA/CROIX ROUGE"**.

1861 400 f. Saint Andrew . . . 3·25 1·10
1862 500 f. Saint Peter . . . 4·00 1·40

(e) Nos. 1780 and 1783 optd **"75e ANNIVERSAIRE/ DU SCOUTISME FEMININ"**.

1864 50 f. Dawn Run . . . 85 20
1865 1000 f. Politician . . . 8·25 2·25

1986. Easter. Multicoloured.

1867 25 f. Type **335** (postage) . . . 20 10
1868 70 f. "Calvary" (Paul Veronese) . . 55 15
1869 90 f. "The Last Supper" (Jacopo Robusti Tintoretto) (horiz) (air) . . . 65 30
1870 200 f. "Christ in the Tomb" (Berruguette) (horiz) . . . 1·50 55

336 "Suisie" Space Probe and Kohoutek's Comet

1986. Appearance of Halley's Comet (1st issue). Multicoloured.

1872 70 f. Type **336** (postage) . . 55 15
1873 90 f. "Vega I" space probe and people pointing at comet (air) . . 55 20
1874 150 f. Comet and observation equipment . . . 90 30
1875 200 f. "Giotto" space probe and comet over town . . . 1·25 40

See also Nos. 1917/20.

337 New York, Statue and Eiffel Tower

338 Cashew Nut

1986. Air. Centenary of Statue of Liberty. Multicoloured.

1877 70 f. Type **337** . . . 50 15
1878 90 f. Statue, Arc de Triomphe and Brooklyn Bridge . . . 60 20
1879 500 f. Statue, Pantheon and Empire State Building . . 3·25 1·10

1986. Fruit. Multicoloured.

1880 70 f. Type **338** (postage) . . 55 15
1881 90 f. Pineapple . . . 80 20
1882 120 f. Avocado (air) . . . 90 20
1883 135 f. Papaw . . . 1·10 20
1884 290 f. Mango (vert) . . . 2·25 65

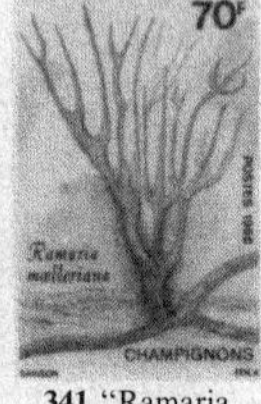

339 Footballers

341 "Ramaria moelleriana"

1986. World Cup Football Championship, Mexico.

1885 **339** 70 f. mult (postage) . . 55 15
1886 – 90 f. mult (air) . . . 55 30
1887 – 130 f. multicoloured . . 85 35
1888 – 300 f. multicoloured . . 1·90 70

DESIGNS: 90 f. to 300 f. Various footballing scenes.

1986. Air. "Ameripex '86" International Stamp Exhibition, Chicago. Nos. 1718/19 optd **AMERIPEX 86**.

1890 500 f. Huey, Dewey, Louie and Donald with birthday cake . . 4·50 1·10
1891 1000 f. Huey, Dewey and Louie startling Donald . . . 8·25 2·25

1986. Fungi. Multicoloured.

1893 70 f. Type **341** . . . 1·00 50
1894 90 f. "Hygrocybe firma" . . 1·25 70
1895 150 f. "Kalchbrennera corallocephala" . . . 2·25 1·25
1896 200 f. "Cookeina tricholoma" . . 3·25 1·75

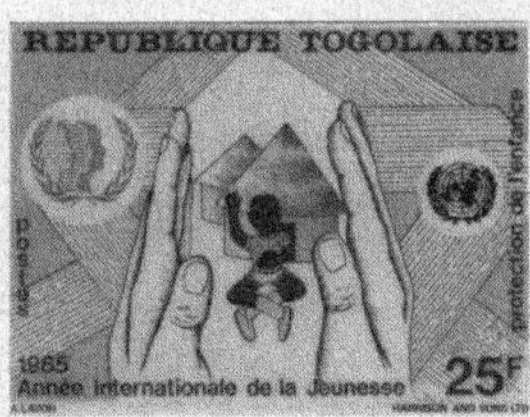

342 Hand framing Huts and Child

1986. International Youth Year (1985). Mult.

1897 25 f. Type **342** . . . 30 15
1898 90 f. Children feeding birds . 1·10 40

343 Wrestlers

344 Miss Sarah Ferguson

1986. Evala Wrestling Contest.

1899 **343** 15 f. mult (postage) . . . 15 10
1900 – 20 f. multicoloured . . . 30 10
1901 – 70 f. multicoloured . . . 65 15
1902 – 90 f. multicoloured (air) . . 40 35

DESIGNS: 20 to 90 f. Wrestling scenes.

1986. Wedding of Prince Andrew. Multicoloured.

1903 10 f. Type **344** (postage) . . . 55 10
1904 1000 f. Prince Andrew (air) . 6·75 2·25

1986. World Cup Winners. Nos. 1886/9 optd.

1906 70 f. **DEMI-FINALE/ ARGENTINE 2/BELGIQUE 0** (postage) . . . 55 35
1907 90 f. **DEMI-FINALE/ ALLEMAGNE/DE L'OUEST 2/FRANCE 0** (air) . 55 20
1908 130 f. **3 eme et 4 eme PLACE/ FRANCE 4/BELGIQUE 2** . 85 35
1909 300 f. **FINALE/ARGENTINE 3/ALLEMAGNE/DE L'OUEST 2** . . . 1·90 80

346 Fazao Hotel

1986. Hotels. Multicoloured.

1910 70 f. Type **346** (postage) . . . 55 15
1911 90 f. Sarakawa Hotel (air) . . 65 30
1912 120 f. The Lake Hotel . . . 90 40

347 Spur-winged Geese

1986. Keran National Park. Multicoloured.

1913 70 f. Type **347** (postage) . . . 1·50 45
1914 90 f. Antelope (air) . . . 65 30
1915 100 f. African elephant . . . 80 35
1916 130 f. Kob . . . 1·00 45

1986. Appearance of Halley's Comet (2nd issue). Nos. 1872/5 optd as T **213a** of Maldive Islands.

1917 **336** 70 f. mult (postage) . . . 1·25 35
1918 – 90 f. multicoloured (air) . . 1·00 30
1919 – 150 f. multicoloured . . . 1·50 40
1920 – 200 f. multicoloured . . . 1·90 70

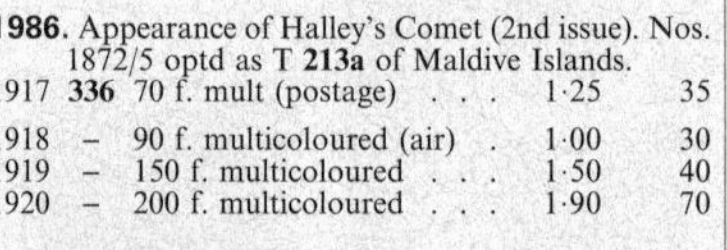

349 "The Annunciation"

350 Rainbow and Douglas DC-10

1986. Christmas. Multicoloured.

1922 45 f. Type **349** (postage) . . . 45 15
1923 120 f. "Nativity" (air) . . . 90 35
1924 130 f. "Adoration of the Magi" 1·10 45
1925 200 f. "Flight into Egypt" . . 1·50 65

1986. Air. 25th Anniv of Air Afrique.

1927 **350** 90 f. multicoloured . . . 75 45

351 Pres. Eyadema and Phosphate Mine

1987. 20th Anniv of National Liberation. Multicoloured.

1928 35 f. Type **351** (postage) . . . 20 10
1929 50 f. Anie sugar refinery . . . 35 15
1930 70 f. Nangbeto Dam . . . 50 20
1931 90 f. February 2 Hotel and Posts and Telecommunications building, Lome . . . 60 20
1932 100 f. Post and Telecommunications building, Kara (air) . . . 55 15
1933 120 f. Peace monument . . . 80 30
1934 130 f. Baby being vaccinated . 90 35

352 "The Last Supper"

1987. Easter. Paintings from Nadoba Church, Keran. Multicoloured.

1936 90 f. Type **352** (postage) . . 65 30
1937 130 f. "Christ on the Cross" (air) . . . 90 30
1938 300 f. "The Resurrection" . 2·00 65

353 Adenauer speaking in the Bundestag

1987. Air. 20th Death Anniv of Konrad Adenauer (German Chancellor). Multicoloured.

1940 120 f. Type **353** . . . 85 30
1941 500 f. Adenauer with John F. Kennedy . . . 3·25 1·10

354 Player falling with Ball

1987. World Rugby Football Cup. Multicoloured.

1943 70 f. Type **354** (postage) . . 80 30
1944 130 f. Player running with ball (air) . . . 1·25 35
1945 300 f. Scrum . . . 2·75 1·25

355 "Adenium obesum"

1987. Flowers. Multicoloured.

1947 70 f. Type **355** (postage) . . 60 20
1948 90 f. "Amorphophallus abyssinicus" (vert) (air) . . 65 30
1949 100 f. "Ipomoea mauritiana" . 80 30
1950 120 f. "Salacia togoica" (vert) . 90 35

356 Wilhelm I Coin and Victory Statue

1987. Air. 750th Anniv of Berlin. Multicoloured.

1951 90 f. Type **356** . . . 65 30
1952 150 f. Friedrich III coin and Brandenburg Gate . . . 1·00 35
1953 300 f. Wilhelm II coin and Place de la Republique . . . 2·00 65

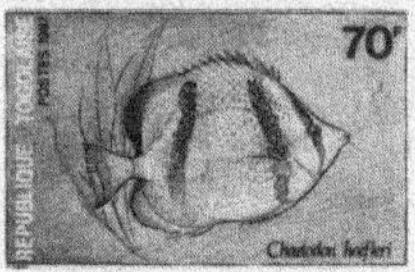

357 "Chaetodon hoefleri"

1987. Fishes. Multicoloured.

1955 70 f. Type **357** . . . 55 20
1956 90 f. "Tetraodon lineatus" . 65 25
1957 120 f. "Chaetodipterus goreensis" . . . 85 35
1958 130 f. "Labeo parvus" . . 1·00 35

358 Long Jumping

1987. Olympic Games, Seoul (1988). Mult.
1959 70 f. Type **358** (postage) . . . 60 20
1960 90 f. Relay race (air) 60 20
1961 200 f. Cycling . . . . 1·25 45
1962 250 f. Javelin throwing . . . 1·60 55

1987. Endangered Wildlife. As Nos. 1722/5 but values changed and size 37×24 mm.
1964 60 f. Type **308** (postage) . . . 80 20
1965 75 f. Manatee (close up) . . 90 35
1966 80 f. Manatees in water . . . 1·10 35
1967 100 f. Manatee with cub (air) 1·40 40

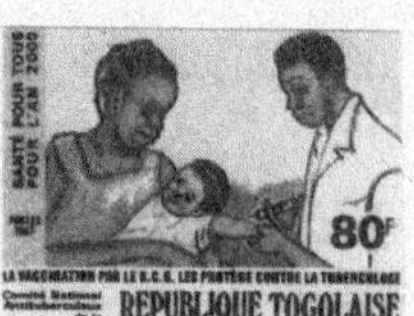

359 Doctor vaccinating Child

1987. "Health for All by Year 2000". Anti-tuberculosis Campaign. Multicoloured.
1968 80 f. Type **359** (postage) . . . 55 30
1969 90 f. Family under umbrella (vert) (air) 60 30
1970 115 f. Faculty of Medicine building, Lome University . 80 35

360 "Spring or the Earthly Paradise"

1987. Christmas. Multicoloured.
1971 40 f. Type **360** (postage) . . . 35 10
1972 45 f. "The Creation of Adam" (Michelangelo) 35 10
1973 105 f. "Presentation in the Temple" (vert) (air) 65 20
1974 270 f. "The Original Sin" (vert) 1·75 65

361 Men ploughing and Women collecting Water

1988. 10th Anniv of Agricultural Development Fund.
1976 **361** 90 f. multicoloured . . . 65 20

363 "The Dance"

1988. 15th Death Anniv of Pablo Picasso (painter). Multicoloured.
1978 45 f. Type **363** (postage) . . . 45 10
1979 160 f. "Portrait of a Young Girl" . . . . 1·50 35
1980 300 f. "Gueridon" (air) . . . 2·75 85

364 Cement

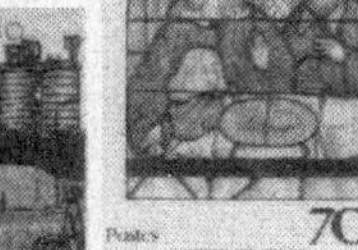

365 "Jesus and the Disciples at Emmaus"

1988. Industries. Multicoloured.
1982 125 f. Type **364** 85 30
1983 165 f. Brewery . . . . 1·10 40
1984 195 f. Phosphates . . . . . . 1·25 45
1985 200 f. Plastics . . . . 1·25 45
1986 300 f. Milling (vert) . . . . . 2·10 65

1988. Easter. Stained Glass Windows. Mult.
1987 70 f. Type **365** (postage) . . 60 15
1988 90 f. "Mary at the Foot of the Cross" 80 20
1989 120 f. "Crucifixion" (air) . . 85 30
1990 200 f. "St. Thomas and Resurrected Jesus" . . . . 1·40 45

366 Paris Crowd welcoming Kennedy, 1961

367 Watchi Chief

1988. 25th Death Anniv of John F. Kennedy (U.S. President). Multicoloured.
1992 125 f. Type **366** . . . . . . 1·00 20
1993 155 f. Kennedy at Paris Town Hall (vert) . . . . 1·10 20
1994 165 f. Kennedy and De Gaulle at Elysee Palace (vert) . . 1·25 40
1995 180 f. John and Jacqueline Kennedy at Orly Airport . . 1·40 75

1988. Traditional Tribal Costumes. Multicoloured.
1997 80 f. Type **367** 55 20
1998 125 f. Watchi woman . . . 85 20
1999 165 f. Kotokoli man . . . . 1·10 35
2000 175 f. Ewe man . . . . . . 1·10 35

368 Basketball

369 People with Candles

1988. Olympic Games, Seoul. Multicoloured.
2002 70 f. Type **368** (postage) . . 50 15
2003 90 f. Tennis 60 20
2004 120 f. Archery (air) 85 30
2005 200 f. Throwing the discus . 1·40 45

1988. 40th Anniv of W.H.O. Multicoloured.
2007 80 f. Type **369** 55 15
2008 125 f. Maps, emblem and "40" 85 20

370 Plaited Style

1988. Hairstyles. Multicoloured.
2009 80 f. Type **370** 55 20
2010 125 f. Knotted style 85 20
2011 170 f. Plaited style with bow 1·00 40
2112 180 f. Style with plaits all over head (vert) . . . . . . 1·25 40

371 Collecting Water (B. Gossner)

372 "Adoration of the Magi" (Pieter Brueghel the Elder)

1988. "Philtogo" National Stamp Exhibition. Designs depicting winning entries of a schools drawing competition. Multicoloured.
2014 10 f. Type **371** 10 10
2015 35 f. Villagers working on farm (K. Ekoue-Kouvahey) . . 20 10
2016 70 f. Family (A. Abbey) . . 65 15
2017 90 f. Village women preparing food (T. D. Lawson) . . . 85 30
2018 120 f. Fishermen and boats on shore (A. Tazzar) . . . . 1·10 35

1988. Christmas. Multicoloured.
2019 80 f. Type **372** (postage) . . 55 20
2020 150 f. "The Virgin, The Infant Jesus, Saints Jerome and Dominic" (Fra. Filippo Lippi) (air) . . . . 1·00 20
2021 175 f. "The Madonna, The Infant Jesus, St. Joseph and the Infant St. John the Baptist" (Federico Barocci) 1·25 35
2022 195 f. "The Virgin and Child" (Gentile Bellini) . . . . . . 1·40 45

373 Wreckage of Airplane

1989. 15th Anniv of Sarakawa Assassination Attempt. Multicoloured.
2024 10 f. Type **373** 10 10
2025 80 f. Tail section (vert) . . . 55 25
2026 125 f. Soldiers and wreckage . 85 50

374 Anniversary Emblem

1989. 20th Anniv of Benin Electricity Community.
2027 **374** 80 f. multicoloured . . . 60 20
2028 125 f. multicoloured . . . 95 20

375 Boxing

1989. Prince Emanuel of Liechtenstein Foundation. Multicoloured.
2029 80 f. Type **375** 55 20
2030 125 f. Long jumping 55 30
2031 165 f. Running . . . . 1·10 40

376 Table Tennis

1989. Olympic Games, Barcelona (1992). Mult.
2032 80 f. Type **376** (postage) . . . 65 20
2033 125 f. Running (horiz) 90 20
2034 165 f. Putting the shot . . . . 1·00 35
2035 175 f. Basketball . . . . 1·25 35
2036 380 f. High jumping (horiz) (air) 2·50 55
2037 425 f. Boxing (horiz) . . . . 3·00 55

377 Footballers and St. Janvier's Cathedral, Naples

1989. World Cup Football Championship, Italy. Multicoloured.
2039 80 f. Type **377** (postage) . . . 55 20
2040 125 f. Milan Cathedral . . . 85 20
2041 165 f. Bevilacqua Palace, Verona . . . . 1·10 35
2042 175 f. Baptistry, Florence . . 1·10 35
2043 380 f. Madama Palace, Turin (air) . . . . 2·75 55
2044 425 f. St. Laurent's Cathedral, Genoa . . . . 2·75 55

378 Bundestag

1989. 40th Anniv of Federal Republic of Germany. Multicoloured.
2046 90 f. Type **378** 65 20
2047 125 f. Konrad Adenauer (Chancellor, 1949–63) and Theodor Heuss (President, 1949–59) (vert) 95 30
2048 180 f. West German flag and emblem . . . . 1·25 40

379 Tractor, Map and Woman at Water-pump

1989. 30th Anniv of Council of Unity.
2049 **379** 75 f. multicoloured . . . 55 20

380 Boys learning First Aid

1989. 125th Anniv of International Red Cross. Multicoloured.
2050 90 f. Type **380** 50 20
2051 125 f. Founding meeting . . 85 35

381 Storming the Bastille

383 People with Banners and Pres. Eyadema

382 Jacques Necker (statesman) and The Three Orders

1989. Bicentenary of French Revolution (1st issue). Multicoloured.
2052 90 f. Type **381** 65 20
2053 125 f. Oath of the Tennis Court (horiz) . . . . 1·00 35
2054 180 f. Abolition of Privileges (horiz) . . . . 1·40 45
See also Nos. 2056/9.

1989. Bicentenary of French Revolution (2nd issue). Multicoloured.
2056 90 f. Type **382** (postage) . . 65 20
2057 190 f. Guy le Chapelier and abolition of seigneurial rights 1·50 45
2058 425 f. Talleyrand-Perigord (statesman) and La Fayette's oath . . . . 2·75 55
2059 480 f. Paul Barras (revolutionary) and overthrow of Robespierre . 3·25 55

1989. 20th Anniv of Kpalime Appeal. Mult.
2061 90 f. Type **383** 60 20
2062 125 f. Pres. Eyadema addressing gathering 90 35

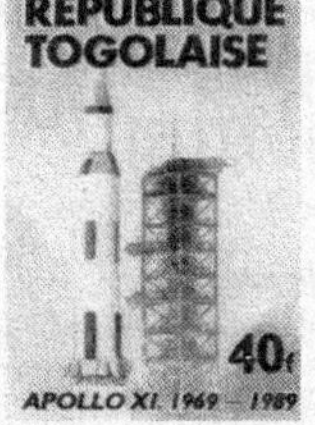

384 "Apollo II" Launch

386 Emblem

385 Figures on Map (dated "DEC.89")

1989. 20th Anniv of First Manned Landing on Moon. Multicoloured.

2063	40 f. Type **384**		30	10
2064	90 f. Space capsule in orbit		55	20
2065	150 f. Landing capsule		1·10	35
2066	250 f. Splashdown		1·60	45

1989. 4th Lome Convention (on relations between European Community and African, Caribbean and Pacific countries). Multicoloured.

2068	100 f. Type **385**		80	30
2069	100 f. As T **385** but dated "15 DEC.89"		80	30

1990. 10th Anniv of Pan-African Postal Union.

2070	**386**	125 f. gold, blue & brown	90	30

387 Party Headquarters, Kara

1990. 20th Anniv (1989) of Rally of Togolese People Party. Multicoloured.

2071	45 f. Type **387**		35	15
2072	90 f. Pres. Eyadema and anniversary emblem		60	20

388 "Myrina silenus" and Scout

389 "Danaus chrysippus"

1990. Scouts, Butterflies and Fungi. Mult.

2073	80 f. Type **388** (postage)		65	15
2074	90 f. "Phlebobus silvaticus" (fungus)		65	15
2075	125 f. "Volvariella esculenta" (fungus)		90	20
2076	165 f. "Hypolycaena antifaunus" (butterfly)		1·10	35
2077	380 f. "Termitomyces striatus" (fungus) (air)		3·00	55
2078	425 f. "Axiocerces harpax" (butterfly)		3·00	55

1990. Butterflies. Multicoloured.

2080	5 f. Type **389**		10	10
2081	10 f. "Morpho aega"		10	10
2082	15 f. "Papilio demodocus"		10	10
2083	90 f. "Papilio dardanus"		60	35

390 Emblem **391** Nile Monitor

1990. 9th Convention of Lions Club Internationals District 403, Lome.

2085	**390**	90 f. multicoloured	60	35
2086		125 f. multicoloured	85	55
2087		165 f. multicoloured	1·10	80

1990. Reptiles. Multicoloured.

2088	1 f. Type **391**		10	10
2089	25 f. Puff adder		15	10
2090	60 f. Black-lipped cobra		45	15
2091	90 f. African rock python		65	20

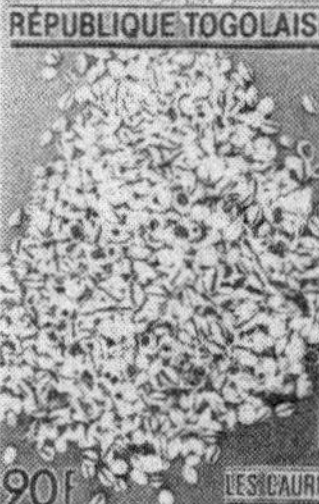

392 Pile of Cowrie Shells **393** Maps, Cogwheel and Arrows

1990. Money Cowrie Shells. Multicoloured.

2092	90 f. Type **392**		75	20
2093	125 f. Cowrie and bead ornament		1·25	25
2094	180 f. Headdress with cowries and animal horns		1·60	55

1990. United States–Togo Friendship. Mult.

2095	125 f. Type **393**		90	35
2096	180 f. Presidents Bush and Eyadema shaking hands (horiz)		1·25	35

394 Cinkasse Post Office

1990. Stamp Day.

2098	**394**	90 f. multicoloured	60	35

395 Addressing Crowd, Brazzaville, 1944

1990. 20th Death Anniv of Charles de Gaulle (statesman).

2099	**395**	125 f. multicoloured	85	45

396 Thatched Houses

1990. Traditional Housing. Multicoloured.

2100	90 f. Type **396**		60	35
2101	125 f. Village		85	45
2102	190 f. Tamberma house		1·25	65

397 Airport, Airliners and Airline Emblems

1990. New Lome Airport.

2103	**397**	90 f. multicoloured	60	35

398 Woman carrying Basket on Head (Sikou Dapau)

1990.

2104	**398**	90 f. multicoloured	60	35

399 Chimpanzee, Missahoue Kloto

1991. Forests. Multicoloured.

2105	90 f. Type **399**		60	35
2106	170 f. Jardine's parrot, Aledjo Forest		1·40	65
2107	185 f. Grey parrot, Chateau Vial Kloto Forest		1·50	65

400 Dancers

1992. Spirit Dances.

2108	**400**	90 f. multicoloured	60	35
2109	–	125 f. multicoloured	85	55
2110	–	190 f. multicoloured	1·25	80

DESIGNS: 125, 190 f. Various dances.

401 Royal Python hatching

1992. The Royal Python. Multicoloured.

2111	90 f. Type **401**		60	35
2112	125 f. Hatchlings emerging from shells		85	35
2113	190 f. Hatchlings and empty shells		1·25	65
2114	300 f. Close-up of hatchling and empty shell		1·90	90

402 Emblem

403 Postal Sorter

1994. 120th Anniv of U.P.U.

2115	**402**	180 f. multicoloured	45	20

1994. World Post Day.

2117	**403**	90 f. multicoloured	20	10
2118		120 f. multicoloured	30	10

404 Footballers

1994. World Cup Football Championship, U.S.A.

2119	**404**	5 f. multicoloured	10	10
2120	–	10 f. multicoloured	10	10
2121	–	25 f. multicoloured	10	10
2122	–	60 f. multicoloured	15	10
2123	–	90 f. multicoloured	20	10
2124	–	100 f. multicoloured	25	10
2125	–	200 f. multicoloured	50	20
2126	–	1000 f. multicoloured	2·40	95

DESIGNS: 10 f. to 1000 f. Various footballing scenes.

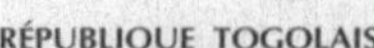

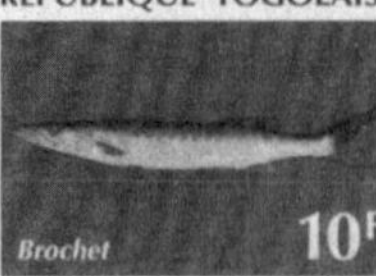

405 Pike

1995. Fishes. Multicoloured.

2128	10 f. Type **405**		10	10
2129	90 f. Green snapper		20	10
2130	180 f. Carps		45	20

406 "The Resurrection" (detail) (Andrea Mantegna) **407** Hill

1995. Easter. Multicoloured.

2131	90 f. Type **406**		20	10
2132	180 f. "Calvary" (Paolo Veronese)		45	20
2133	190 f. "The Last Supper" (Jacopo Tintoretto) (horiz)		45	20

1995. Birth Bicentenary of Sir Rowland Hill (instigator of postage stamp).

2134	**407**	125 f. multicoloured	30	10

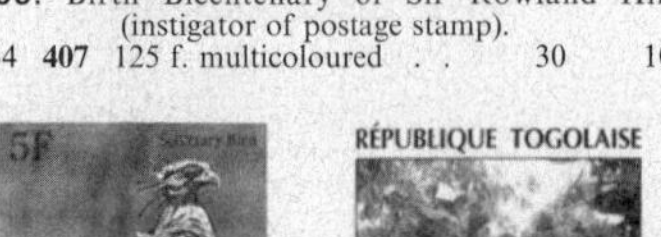

408 Secretary Bird

409 Madagascan Belvache

1995. Birds. Multicoloured.

2135	5 f. Type **408**		10	10
2136	10 f. Paradise flycatcher		10	10
2137	25 f. African spoonbill (horiz)		10	10
2138	60 f. Cordon bleu (horiz)		15	10
2139	90 f. Orange-breasted sunbird		20	10
2140	100 f. Yellow-billed hornbill		25	10
2141	180 f. Barn owl (horiz)		45	20
2142	200 f. Hoopoe feeding chick (horiz)		50	20
2143	300 f. Red-crowned ("Fire-crowned") bishop		75	30
2144	1000 f. Red-throated bee eater		2·40	95

1995. Plants. Multicoloured.

2146	15 f. Type **409**		10	10
2147	90 f. Marigolds		20	10
2148	125 f. Agave (horiz)		30	10

410 Anniversary Emblem **411** Globe and Doves

1995. 50th Anniv of U.N.O (1st issue).

2149	**410**	180 f. multicoloured	45	20

See also Nos. 2150/2.

1995. 50th Anniversaries. Multicoloured. (a) U.N.O. (2nd issue).

2150	25 f. Type **411**		10	10
2151	90 f. Doves and Headquarters building, New York		20	10
2152	400 f. Globe and doves (different)		95	40

Nos. 2150/2 were issued together, se-tenant, forming a composite design.

(b) Food and Agriculture Organization.

2154	45 f. Cattle		10	10
2155	125 f. Cow		30	10
2156	125 f. Mother and child collecting water (horiz)		30	10
2157	200 f. Herdsmen		50	20

Nos. 2154/5 and 2157 were issued together, se-tenant, forming a composite design.

412 Montecassino, Italy

1995. 50th Anniv of End of Second World War (1st issue). Victory in Europe. Multicoloured.

2159	45 f. Type **412**		10	10
2160	90 f. Warsaw in ruins		20	10
2161	125 f. Russian tanks in Berlin		30	10
2162	200 f. German fighter planes		50	20
2163	200 f. American cruiser in north Atlantic		50	20
2164	200 f. Capture of Ludendorf Bridge		50	20
2165	200 f. Russian "Katyusha" rockets		50	20
2166	500 f. United Nations flag		1·25	50

See also Nos. 2191/6.

413 National Flag and Scout Badge

414 Manfred Eigen (Chemistry, 1967)

1995. 18th World Scout Jamboree, Dronten, Netherlands. Multicoloured.

2168	90 f. Type **413**	20	10
2169	190 f. Saluting scout and camp	45	20
2170	300 f. Lord Baden-Powell (founder of Boy Scout Movement)	75	30

1995. Centenary of Nobel Prize Trust Fund. Multicoloured.

2172	200 f. Type **414**	50	20
2173	200 f. Donald J. Cram (Chemistry, 1987	50	20
2174	200 f. Paul J. Flory (Chemistry, 1974)	50	20
2175	200 f. Johann Deisenhofer (Chemistry, 1988)	50	20
2176	200 f. Percy Williams Bridgman (Physics, 1946)	50	20
2177	200 f. Otto Stern (Physics, 1943)	50	20
2178	200 f. Arne Tiselius (Chemistry, 1948)	50	20
2179	200 f. J. Georg Bednorz (Physics, 1987)	50	20
2180	200 f. Albert Claude (Medicine, 1974)	50	20
2181	200 f. Elihu Root (Peace, 1912)	50	20
2182	200 f. Alfred Fried (Peace, 1911)	50	20
2183	200 f. Henri Moissan (Chemistry, 1906)	50	20
2184	200 f. Charles Barkla (Physics, 1917)	50	20
2185	200 f. Rudolf Eucken (Literature, 1908)	50	20
2186	200 f. Carl von Ossietzky (Peace, 1935)	50	20
2187	200 f. Sir Edward Appleton (Physics, 1947)	50	20
2188	200 f. Camillo Golgi (Medicine, 1906)	50	20
2189	200 f. Wilhelm Rontgen (Physics, 1901)	50	20

415 Admiral Isoroko Yamamoto

1995. 50th Anniv of End of Second World War (2nd issue). Victory in the Pacific. Japanese commanders. Multicoloured.

2191	200 f. Type **415**	50	20
2192	200 f. General Hideki Tojo (Minister of War, 1940–41 and Premier, 1941–44)	50	20
2193	200 f. Vice-admiral Shigeru Fukudome	50	20
2194	200 f. Admiral Shigetaro Shimada	50	20
2195	200 f. Rear-admiral Chuichi Nagumo	50	20
2196	200 f. General Shizu Ichi Tanaka	50	20

416 Drawing

417 Original and Current Emblems

1995. 95th Birthday of Queen Elizabeth the Queen Mother. Multicoloured.

2198	250 f. Type **416**	60	25
2199	250 f. Carrying umbrella	60	25
2200	250 f. Seated at writing table (face value white)	60	25
2201	250 f. As young woman	60	25
2202	250 f. As No. 2200 but face value black	60	25
2203	250 f. Cutting cake	60	25
2204	250 f. Waving from car	60	25

1995. 90th Anniv of Rotary International.

2206	**417**	1000 f. multicoloured	2·40	95

418 Woman buying Stamps

1995. World Post Day. Multicoloured.

2208	220 f. Type **418**	55	20
2209	315 f. Clerk arranging stamps on page	75	30
2210	335 f. Sorting office	80	30

419 Nativity

1995. Christmas. Paintings. Multicoloured.

2211	90 f. Type **419**	20	10
2212	325 f. Adoration of the Wise Men	80	30
2213	340 f. Adoration of the shepherds (horiz)	80	30

POSTAGE DUE STAMPS

1921. Postage Due stamps of Dahomy, "figure" key-type, optd **TOGO**.

D54	M	5 c. green	40	70
D55		10 c. red	40	70
D56		15 c. grey	65	70
D57		20 c. brown	1·50	2·00
D58		30 c. blue	1·50	2·00
D59		50 c. black	1·10	1·40
D60		60 c. orange	1·40	1·60
D61		1 f. violet	2·75	3·25

D 8 Cotton Growing

1925. Centres and inscr in black.

D 97	D 8	2 c. blue	10	30
D 98		4 c. red	10	30
D 99		5 c. greeen	10	30
D100		10 c. red	20	45
D101		15 c. yellow	20	45
D102		20 c. mauve	30	55
D103		25 c. grey	40	65
D104		30 c. yellow on blue	25	40
D105		50 c. brown	35	60
D106		60 c. green	45	70
D107		1 f. violet	50	80

1927. Surch.

D108	D 8	2 f. on 1 f. mauve and red	2·75	2·25
D109		3 f. on 1 f. blue and brown	2·50	3·25

D 12 Native Mask

D 21

D 31 Kon-komba Helmet

1940.

D151	D 12	5 c. black	10	30
D152		10 c. green	15	25
D153		15 c. red	10	30
D154		20 c. blue	20	45
D155		30 c. brown	20	45
D156		50 c. olive	1·00	1·40
D157		60 c. violet	25	45
D158		1 f. blue	55	80
D159		2 f. red	30	60
D160		3 f. violet	60	85

1947.

D185	D 21	10 c. blue	10	30
D186		30 c. red	10	30
D187		50 c. green	10	30
D188		1 f. brown	10	30
D189		2 f. red	20	40
D190		3 f. black	25	45
D191		4 f. blue	40	55
D192		5 f. brown	50	65
D193		10 f. orange	50	80
D194		20 f. blue	70	90

1957.

D214	D 31	1 f. violet	10	25
D215		2 f. orange	10	25
D216		3 f. grey	15	30
D217		4 f. red	15	30
D218		5 f. blue	15	30
D219		10 f. green	35	45
D220		20 f. purple	50	55

1959. As Nos. D214/20 but colours changed and inscr "REPUBLIQUE DU TOGO".

D244	D 31	1 f. brown	10	25
D245		2 f. turquoise	10	25
D246		3 f. orange	10	25
D247		4 f. blue	15	30
D248		5 f. purple	15	30
D249		10 f. violet	25	45
D250		20 f. black	55	60

D 57 "Cardium costatum"

D 110 Tomatoes

1964. Sea Shells. Multicoloured.

D366	1 f. Butterfly cone	10	10
D367	2 f. Ermine marginella	10	10
D368	3 f. Rat cowrie	10	10
D369	4 f. Bubonian conch	20	20
D370	5 f. Type D **57**	50	50
D371	10 f. "Cancellaria cancellata"	60	60
D372	15 f. African Neptue volute	1·75	1·75
D373	20 f. "Tympanotomus radula"	1·90	1·90

1969. Young Pioneers Agricultural Organization. Multicoloured.

D696	5 f. Type D **110**	10	10
D697	10 f. Corn on the cob	30	30
D698	19 f. Red pepper	40	40
D699	20 f. Peanuts	55	55

1980. As T **259**. Multicoloured.

D1454	5 f. Women examining produce (vert)	10	10
D1455	10 f. Market stall	10	10
D1456	25 f. Poultry seller	15	10
D1457	50 f. Carvings and ornaments	35	15

APPENDIX

The following stamps have either been issued in excess of postal needs or have not been available to the public in reasonable quantities at face value. Such stamps may later be given full listing if there is evidence of regular postal use.

All embossed on gold foil.

1989.

Prince Emanuel of Liechtenstein Foundation. Air. 1500 f. × 2

Bicentenary of French Revolution (2nd issue). Air. 1500 f.

Scouts, Butterflies, and Fungi. Air. 1500 f.

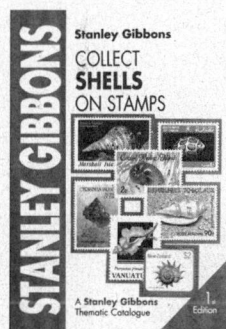

TOLIMA Pt. 20

One of the states of the Granadine Confederation.

A department of Colombia from 1886, now uses Colombian stamps.

100 centavos = 1 peso

1 2 3

1870. On white or coloured paper. Imperf.

No.	Type	Description	Unused	Used
6	1	5 c. black	25·00	20·00
13		10 c. black	30·00	18·00

1871. Various frames. Imperf.

No.	Type	Description	Unused	Used
14	2	5 c. brown	75	75
15	3	10 c. blue	2·00	2·00
16		50 c. green	3·00	3·00
17		1 p. red	6·00	6·00

6 7 8

9 10 11

1879. Imperf.

No.	Type	Description	Unused	Used
18a	6	5 c. brown	20	20
19	7	10 c. blue	25	25
20a	8	50 c. green	25	30
21a	9	1 p. red	90	1·00

1883. Imperf.

No.	Type	Description	Unused	Used
22	6	5 c. orange	20	20
23	7	10 c. red	35	35
24	10	20 c. violet	50	50

1884. Imperf.

No.	Type	Description	Unused	Used
25	11	1 c. grey	10	10
26		2 c. red	10	10
27		2½ c. orange	10	10
28		5 c. brown	10	10
29a		10 c. blue	15	15
30		20 c. yellow	30	30
31		25 c. black	15	15
32		50 c. green	20	20
33		1 p. red	25	25
34		2 p. violet	40	35
35		5 p. orange	25	25
36		10 p. red	60	60

12 16

1886. Condor's wings touch Arms. Perf.

No.	Type	Description	Unused	Used
37	12	5 c. brown	50	50
38		10 c. blue	1·75	1·75
39		50 c. green	60	60
40		1 p. red	1·25	1·25

1886. Condor's wings do not touch Arms. Perf or imperf.

No.	Type	Description	Unused	Used
45	16	1 c. grey	2·50	2·50
46		2 c. red	3·25	3·25
47		2½ c. pink	12·00	12·00
48		5 c. brown	4·50	4·50
49		10 c. blue	6·00	6·00
50		20 c. yellow	3·25	3·25
51		25 c. black	3·00	3·00
52		50 c. green	1·40	1·10
53		1 p. red	2·25	2·25
54		2 p. violet	4·00	4·00
55		5 p. orange	7·50	7·50
56		10 p. red	3·50	3·50

20

21

1888. Perf.

No.	Type	Description	Unused	Used
67	20	1 c. blue on red	15	15
68		2 c. green on green	15	15
69		5 c. red	10	10
70		10 c. green	20	25
71		20 c. blue on yellow	30	30
65		50 c. blue	45	45
72		1 p. brown	75	75

1903. Imperf or perf.

No.	Type	Description	Unused	Used
85	21	4 c. black on green	10	10
78		10 c. green	10	10
87		20 c. orange	20	20
88		50 c. black on red	15	15
81		1 p. brown	10	10
82		2 p. grey	10	10
91		5 p. red	10	10
92		10 p. black on blue	15	15
92a		10 p. black on green	15	15

TRANSCAUCASIAN FEDERATION Pt. 10

A Federation of Armenia, Azerbaijan and Georgia, which was absorbed into the U.S.S.R. in 1923.

100 kopeks = 1 rouble

1 Mt Ararat and Oilfield

2 Mts Ararat and Elbruz and Oil-derricks

1923.

No.	Type	Description	Unused	Used
1	1	40,000 r. purple	1·50	3·00
2		75,000 r. green	1·50	3·00
3		100,000 r. grey	1·00	1·50
4		150,000 r. red	70	90
5	2	200,000 r. green	1·00	50
6		300,000 r. blue	70	1·40
7		350,000 r. brown	70	1·40
8		500,000 r. red	1·25	2·50

1923. Surch **700000 RYb.**

No.	Type	Description	Unused	Used
9	1	700,000 r. on 40,000 r. purple	1·50	3·00
10		700,000 r. on 75,000 r. green	1·50	3·00

1923. Values in gold kopeks.

No.	Type	Description	Unused	Used
11	2	1 k. orange	70	1·25
12		2 k. green	70	1·25
13		3 k. red	70	1·25
14		4 k. brown	70	1·00
15	1	5 k. purple	70	1·25
16		9 k. blue	70	1·25
17		18 k. grey	70	1·25

TRIESTE Pt. 8

The Free Territory of Trieste situated on the Adriatic Coast between the frontiers of Italy and Yugoslavia. In 1954 when the Territory was divided between Italy and Yugoslavia, the overprinted issues were superseded by the ordinary issues of these countries in their respective zones.

For stamps of Italy surcharged **1.V.1945. TRIESTE TRST**, five-pointed star and value, see Venezia Giulia Nos. 20/32.

ZONE A
ALLIED MILITARY GOVERNMENT

100 centesimi = 1 lira

Stamps of Italy variously overprinted **A.M.G. F.T.T.** or **AMG-FTT** (Allied Military Government — Free Territory of Trieste) except where otherwise stated.

1947. Postage stamps of 1945, Nos. 647, etc.

No.	Type	Description	Unused	Used
1		25 c. blue	15	10
2		50 c. violet	15	10
3		1 l. green	15	10
4		2 l. brown	15	10
5		3 l. red	15	10
6		4 l. red	15	10
7		5 l. blue	15	10
8		6 l. violet	15	10
9		8 l. green	1·10	75
10		10 l. grey	20	10
11		10 l. red	4·00	10
12		15 l. blue	25	10
13		20 l. violet	1·25	10
14		25 l. green	2·00	1·00
15		30 l. blue	75·00	1·25
16		50 l. purple	2·25	75
17		100 l. red (No. 669)	10·00	3·75

1947. Air stamps of 1945, Nos. 670, etc.

No.	Type	Description	Unused	Used
18		1 l. grey	20	25
19		2 l. blue	20	30
20		5 l. green	1·00	1·00
21		10 l. red	1·00	1·00
22		25 l. brown	2·00	1·25
23		50 l. violet	10·00	1·25
24		100 l. green	30·00	1·40
25		300 l. mauve	7·50	9·00
26		500 l. blue	9·50	12·00
27		1000 l. brown	80·00	90·00

1947. Air. 50th Anniv of Radio (Nos. 688/93).

No.	Type	Description	Unused	Used
59		6 l. violet	80	85
60		10 l. red	80	85
61		20 l. orange	3·50	1·00
62		25 l. blue	80	90
63		35 l. blue	80	90
64		50 l. purple	3·50	90

1948. Cent of 1848 Revolution (Nos. 706, etc.).

No.	Type	Description	Unused	Used
65		3 l. brown	15	10
66		4 l. purple	15	10
67		5 l. blue	20	10
68		6 l. green	25	15
69		8 l. brown	20	15
70		10 l. red	25	10
71		12 l. green	40	85
72		15 l. black	8·00	4·50
73		20 l. red	10·00	4·50
74		30 l. blue	1·50	1·10
75		50 l. violet	7·00	9·00
76		100 l. blue	13·00	24·00

1948. Trieste Philatelic Congress stamps of 1945 optd **A.M.G. F.T.T. 1948 TRIESTE** and posthorn.

No.	Type	Description	Unused	Used
77		8 l. green (postage)	10	15
78		10 l. red	10	15
79		30 l. blue	1·50	1·50
80		10 l. red (air)	25	20
81		25 l. brown	60	50
82		50 l. violet	60	50

1948. Rebuilding of Bassano Bridge.

No.	Type	Description	Unused	Used
84	209	15 l. green	1·00	75

1948. Donizetti.

No.	Type	Description	Unused	Used
85	210	15 l. brown	3·50	1·00

1949. 25th Biennial Art Exhibition, Venice.

No.	Type	Description	Unused	Used
86	212	5 l. red and flesh	70	75
87	–	15 l. green and cream	7·00	7·00
88	–	20 l. brown and buff	4·00	75
89	–	50 l. blue and yellow	10·00	5·00

1949. 27th Milan Fair.

No.	Type	Description	Unused	Used
90	211	20 l. brown	5·00	1·00

1949. 75th Anniv of U.P.U.

No.	Type	Description	Unused	Used
91	213	50 l. blue	2·50	2·50

1949. Centenary of Roman Republic.

No.	Type	Description	Unused	Used
92	214	100 l. brown	30·00	38·00

1949. 1st Trieste Free Election.

No.	Type	Description	Unused	Used
93	218	20 l. red	2·50	1·25

1949. European Recovery Plan.

No.	Type	Description	Unused	Used
94	215	5 l. green	6·00	3·75
95		15 l. violet	6·00	7·50
96		20 l. brown	6·00	7·00

1949. 2nd World Health Congress, Rome.

No.	Type	Description	Unused	Used
97	219	20 l. violet	10·00	2·75

1949. Giuseppe Mazzini.

No.	Type	Description	Unused	Used
98	216	20 l. black	5·00	1·75

1949. Bicentenary of Vittorio Alfieri.

No.	Type	Description	Unused	Used
99	217	20 l. brown	5·00	1·75

1949. 400th Anniv of Palladio's Basilica at Vicenza.

No.	Type	Description	Unused	Used
100	220	20 l. violet	10·00	7·50

1949. 500th Birth Anniv of Lorenzo de Medici.

No.	Type	Description	Unused	Used
101	221	20 l. blue	4·50	1·50

1949. 13th Bari Fair.

No.	Type	Description	Unused	Used
102	222	20 l. red	5·00	1·75

1949. (a) Postage.

No.	Type	Description	Unused	Used
103	195	1 l. green	10	10
104	–	2 l. brown (No. 656)	10	10
105	–	3 l. red (No. 657)	10	10
106	193	5 l. blue	10	10
107	195	6 l. violet	10	10
108	–	8 l. green (No. 661)	6·00	3·00
109	193	10 l. red	10	10
110	195	15 l. blue	1·00	10
111	–	20 l. purple (No. 665)	50	10
112	196	25 l. green	12·00	1·10
113		50 l. purple	17·00	70
114	197	100 l. red	40·00	3·00

(b) Air.

No.	Type	Description	Unused	Used
115	198	10 l. red	10	10
116	–	25 l. brown (No. 676)	30	30
117	198	50 l. violet	20	20
118	–	100 l. green (No. 911)	65	20
119	–	300 l. mauve (No. 912)	6·00	6·00
120	–	500 l. blue (No. 913)	7·00	7·50
121	–	1000 l. purple (No. 914)	12·00	12·00

1949. 150th Anniv of Volta's Discovery of the Electric Cell.

No.	Type	Description	Unused	Used
135	223	20 l. red	2·00	1·75
136	224	50 l. blue	8·00	7·00

1949. Rebuilding of Holy Trinity Bridge, Florence.

No.	Type	Description	Unused	Used
137	225	20 l. green	2·00	1·25

1949. Death Bimillenary of Catullus (poet).

No.	Type	Description	Unused	Used
138	226	20 l. blue	2·25	1·25

1949. Birth Bicentenary of Domenico Cimarosa (composer).

No.	Type	Description	Unused	Used
153	227	20 l. violet	2·00	1·25

1950. 28th Milan Fair.

No.	Type	Description	Unused	Used
154	228	20 l. brown	2·00	1·00

1950. 32nd Int Automobile Exn, Turin.

No.	Type	Description	Unused	Used
155	229	20 l. violet	1·25	80

1950. 5th General U.N.E.S.C.O. Conference.

No.	Type	Description	Unused	Used
156	–	20 l. green	2·00	70
157	230	55 l. blue	7·00	6·50

1950. Holy Year.

No.	Type	Description	Unused	Used
158	231	20 l. violet	2·00	70
159		55 l. blue	6·00	6·50

1950. Honouring Gaudenzio Ferrari (painter).

No.	Type	Description	Unused	Used
160	232	20 l. green	2·00	1·25

1950. International Radio Conference.

No.	Type	Description	Unused	Used
161	233	20 l. violet	5·00	3·25
162		55 l. blue	12·00	15·00

1950. Death Bicentenary of Ludovico Murator (historian).

No.	Type	Description	Unused	Used
163	234	20 l. brown	2·50	1·25

1950. 900th Death Anniv of D'Arezzo.

No.	Type	Description	Unused	Used
164	235	20 l. green	2·25	1·40

1950. 14th Levant Fair, Bari.

No.	Type	Description	Unused	Used
165	236	20 l. brown	1·60	1·25

1950. 2nd Trieste Fair. Optd **AMG FTT Fiera di Trieste 1950.**

No.	Type	Description	Unused	Used
166	195	15 l. blue	1·00	1·10
167	–	20 l. purple (No. 665)	1·00	40

1950. Wool Industry Pioneers.

No.	Type	Description	Unused	Used
168	237	20 l. blue	60	70

1950. European Tobacco Conf (Nos. 755/7).

No.	Type	Description	Unused	Used
169		5 l. green and mauve	40	80
170		20 l. green and brown	1·50	80
171		55 l. brown and blue	10·00	12·00

1950. Bicentenary of Fine Arts Academy.

No.	Type	Description	Unused	Used
172	239	20 l. red and deep brown	1·75	90

1950. Birth Centenary of Augusto Righi.

No.	Type	Description	Unused	Used
173	240	20 l. black and buff	2·00	90

1950. Provincial Occupations (Nos. 760/78).

No.	Type	Description	Unused	Used
176		50 c. blue	10	15
177		1 l. violet	10	10
178		2 l. brown	10	10
179		5 l. black	10	10
180		6 l. brown	10	10
181		10 l. green	10	10
182		12 l. green	40	30
183		15 l. blue	75	10
184		20 l. violet	45	10
185		25 l. brown	1·00	10
186		30 l. purple	30	20
187		35 l. red	1·00	75
188		40 l. brown	70	30
189		50 l. violet	15	10
190		55 l. blue	15	30
191		60 l. red	3·00	1·50
192		65 l. green	15	30
193		100 l. brown	2·00	10
194		200 l. brown	1·25	2·25

1951. Centenary of 1st Tuscan Stamp.

No.	Type	Description	Unused	Used
195	249	20 l. red and purple	2·00	1·25
196		55 l. blue & ultramarine	20·00	20·00

1951. 33rd International Motor Show, Turin.

No.	Type	Description	Unused	Used
197	243	20 l. green	1·40	1·25

1951. Consecration of Hall of Peace, Rome.

No.	Type	Description	Unused	Used
198	244	20 l. violet	1·25	1·00

1951. 29th Milan Fair.

No.	Type	Description	Unused	Used
199	245	20 l. brown	2·00	1·50
200	246	55 l. blue	1·50	1·75

1951. 10th International Textiles Exn, Turin.

No.	Type	Description	Unused	Used
201	247	20 l. violet	1·10	1·10

1951. 500th Birth Anniv of Columbus.

No.	Type	Description	Unused	Used
202	248	20 l. green	2·00	2·00

1951. International Gymnastic Festival, Florence.

No.	Type	Description	Unused	Used
203	249	5 l. red and brown	3·25	6·00
204		10 l. red and green	3·25	6·00
205		15 l. red and blue	3·25	6·00

1951. Restoration of Montecassino Abbey.

No.	Type	Description	Unused	Used
206	250	20 l. violet	60	50
207	–	55 l. blue (No. 791)	1·25	1·40

1951. 3rd Trieste Fair, Optd **AMG-FTT FIERA di TRIESTE 1951** and shield.

No.	Type	Description	Unused	Used
208		6 l. brown (No. 764)	35	40
209		20 l. violet (No. 768)	50	30
210		55 l. blue (No. 774)	65	65

1951. 500th Birth Anniv of Perugino.

No.	Type	Description	Unused	Used
211	251	20 l. brown and sepia	55	50

1951. Triennial Art Exhibition, Milan.

No.	Type	Description	Unused	Used
212	252	20 l. black and green	70	65
213	–	55 l. pink and blue (No. 794)	1·40	1·60

1951. World Cycling Championship.

No.	Type	Description	Unused	Used
214	253	25 l. black	2·00	50

1951. 15th Levant Fair, Bari.

No.	Type	Description	Unused	Used
215	254	25 l. blue	70	55

1951. Birth Centenary of F. P. Michetti.

No.	Type	Description	Unused	Used
216	255	25 l. brown	65	50

1951. Sardinian Stamp Centenary.

No.	Type	Description	Unused	Used
217	256	10 l. black and brown	40	50
218	–	25 l. green and red (799)	50	30
219	–	60 l. red and blue (800)	70	75

1951. 3rd Industrial and Commercial Census.

No.	Type	Description	Unused	Used
220	257	10 l. green	45	60

1951. 9th National Census.

No.	Type	Description	Unused	Used
221	258	25 l. black	50	40

1951. Forestry Festival.

No.	Type	Description	Unused	Used
222	260	10 l. green and olive	60	75
223		25 l. green (No. 807)	60	60

1951. Verdi.

No.	Type	Description	Unused	Used
224	–	10 l. green & purple (803)	75	75
225	259	25 l. sepia and brown	60	50
226	–	60 l. blue & green (805)	85	85

1952. Bellini.
227 **261** 25 l. black 65 40

1952. Caserta Palace.
228 **262** 25 l. bistre and green . . . 50 35

1952. 1st International Sports Stamps Exn, Rome.
229 **263** 25 l. brown and black . . 40 30

1952. 30th Milan Fair.
230 **264** 60 l. blue . . . . 1·00 1·40

1952. Leonardo da Vinci.
231 **265** 25 l. orange 20 20
232 – 60 l. blue (813) 55 85
233 **265** 80 l. red . . . . 1·25 35

1952. Overseas Fair, Naples.
234 **268** 25 l. blue 45 30

1952. Modena and Parma Stamp Centenaries.
235 **267** 25 l. black and brown . . 50 40
236 60 l. indigo and blue . . . 60 80

1952. Art Exhibition, Venice.
237 **269** 25 l. black and cream . . 50 40

1952. 30th Padua Fair.
238 **270** 25 l. red and blue 35 25

1952. 4th Trieste Fair.
239 **271** 25 l. grn, red and brown . 45 30

1952. 16th Levant Fair, Bari.
240 **272** 25 l. green 40 25

1952. Savonarola.
241 **273** 25 l. violet 40 25

1952. 1st Private Aeronautics Conf, Rome.
242 **274** 60 l. blue & ultramarine . 1·25 1·60

1952. Alpine Troops National Exhibition.
243 **275** 25 l. black 50 25

1952. Armed Forces Day.
244 **276** 10 l. green 10 10
245 **277** 25 l. brown and light brown 35 15
246 – 60 l. black and blue (827) . 45 50

1952. Mission to Ethiopia.
247 **278** 25 l. deep brown & brown 50 30

1952. Birth Centenary of Gemito (sculptor).
248 **279** 25 l. brown 40 25

1952. Birth Centenary of Mancini (painter).
249 **280** 25 l. green 40 25

1952. Centenary of Martyrdom of Belfiore.
250 **281** 25 l. blue and black . . . 40 25

1953. Antonello Exhibition, Messina.
251 **282** 25 l. red 35 25

1953. 20th "Mille Miglia" Car Race.
252 **283** 25 l. violet 60 40

1953. Labour Orders of Merit.
253 **284** 25 l. violet 50 25

1953. 300th Birth Anniv. of Corelli.
254 **285** 25 l. brown 60 30

1953. Coin type.
255 **286** 5 l. grey 10 10
256 10 l. red 10 10
257 12 l. green 10 10
258 13 l. purple 10 10
259 20 l. brown 15 10
260 25 l. violet 15 10
261 35 l. red 35 35
262 60 l. blue 35 35
263 80 l. brown 40 40

1953. 7th Death Centenary of St. Clare.
264 **287** 25 l. red and brown . . . 75 40

1953. 5th Trieste Fair. Optd **V FIERA DI TRIESTE AMG FTT 1953.**
265 10 l. green (No. 765) 20 35
266 25 l. orange (No. 769) 25 20
267 60 l. red (No. 775) 40 50

1953. Mountains Festival.
272 **288** 25 l. green 50 25

1953. International Agricultural Exn, Rome.
273 **289** 25 l. brown 30 20
274 60 l. blue 40 40

1953. 4th Anniv of Atlantic Pact.
275 **290** 25 l. turquoise and orange 45 35
276 60 l. blue and mauve . . . 1·60 1·75

1953. 5th Birth Centenary of Signorelli.
277 **291** 25 l. green and brown . . 50 40

1953. 6th Int Microbiological Congress, Rome.
278 **292** 25 l. brown and black . . 50 30

1953. Tourist series (Nos. 855/60).
279 10 l. brown and sepia 15 15
280 12 l. black and blue 15 20
281 20 l. brown and orange . . . 15 15
282 25 l. green and blue 15 10
283 35 l. brown and buff 25 30
284 60 l. blue and green 30 35

1954. 25th Anniv of Lateran Treaty.
285 **294** 25 l. sepia anad brown . . 30 20
286 60 l. blue and light blue . 45 50

1954. Introduction of Television in Italy.
287 **295** 25 l. violet 30 20
288 60 l. green 50 55

1954. Encouragement to Taxpayers.
289 **296** 25 l. violet 40 25

1954. Milan–Turin Helicopter Mail Flight.
290 **297** 25 l. green 35 25

1954. 10th Anniv of Resistance Movement.
291 **298** 25 l. black and brown . . 60 40

1954. 6th Trieste Fair. Nos. 282 and 284 of Trieste additionally optd **FIERA DI TRIESTE 1954.**
292 – 25 l. green and blue . . . 40 20
293 **293** 60 l. blue and green . . . 40 40

1954. Birth Centenary of Catalani.
294 **299** 25 l. green 50 25

1954. 7th Birth Centenary of Marco Polo.
295 **300** 25 l. brown 35 35
296 60 l. green 50 60

1954. 60th Anniv of Italian Touring Club.
297 **301** 25 l. green and red . . . 50 55

1954. International Police Congress, Rome.
298 **302** 25 l. red 30 15
299 60 l. blue 35 30

CONCESSIONAL LETTER POST

1947. Optd **A.M.G. F.T.T.** in two lines.
CL44 – 1 l. brown (No. CL649) 20 10
CL45 CL **201** 8 l. red . . . . . . 3·00 40
CL46 CL **220** 15 l. violet . . . . 14·00 2·50

1949. Optd **AMG-FTT.**
CL122 CL **220** 15 l. violet 80 15
CL123 20 l. violet . . . . 2·00 15

CONCESSIONAL PARCEL POST

1953.
CP268 CP **288** 40 l. orange . . . 3·00 50
CP269 50 l. blue . . . . 3·00 50
CP270 75 l. brown . . . 3·00 1·00
CP271 110 l. pink . . . . 3·00 1·00
Unused prices are for the complete stamp, used prices for the left half of the stamp.

EXPRESS LETTER STAMPS

1947. Express Letter stamps optd **A.M.G. F.T.T.** in two lines.
E28 – 15 l. red (No. E681) . . 20 20
E29 **200** 25 l. orange . . . . . 12·00 3·00
E30 30 l. violet 40 40
E31 – 60 l. red (No. E685) . . 7·00 5·50

1948. Centenary of 1848 Revolution. Express Letter stamp optd **A.M.G.-F.T.T.**
E83 E **209** 35 l. violet . . . . . . 3·00 4·00

1950. Express Letter stamps optd **AMG-FTT** in one line.
E174 E **209** 50 l. purple 95 60
E175 – 60 l. red (No. E685) . 95 60

PARCEL POST STAMPS
Unused prices are for complete stamps, used prices for a half-stamp.

1947. Parcel Post stamps optd **A.M.G. F.T.T.** in two lines on each half of stamp.
P32 P **201** 1 l. brown 25 10
P33 2 l. blue 40 10
P34 3 l. orange 40 10
P35 4 l. grey 45 10
P36 5 l. purple . . . . . . 1·25 15
P37 10 l. violet . . . . . . 2·50 10
P38 20 l. purple . . . . . . 3·75 10
P39 50 l. red . . . . 5·00 10
P40 100 l. blue . . . . . . 6·50 10
P41 200 l. green . . . . . £200 3·50
P42 300 l. purple . . . . . £100 1·50
P43 500 l. brown . . . . . 50·00 90

1949. Parcel Post stamps optd **AMG-FTT** in one line on each half of stamp.
P139 P **201** 1 l. brown 55 15
P140 2 l. blue 15 10
P141 3 l. orange 15 10
P142 4 l. grey 15 10
P143 5 l. purple 15 10
P144 10 l. violet 25 10
P145 20 l. purple 30 10
P146 30 l. purple 30 10
P147 50 l. red 80 10
P148 100 l. blue . . . . . 2·00 15
P149 200 l. green . . . . . 14·00 40
P150 300 l. purple . . . . 48·00 40
P151 500 l. brown . . . . 26·00 60
P152 P **928** 1000 l. blue . . . . £130 4·25

POSTAGE DUE STAMPS

1947. Postage Due stamps optd **A.M.G. F.T.T.** in two lines.
D44 D **192** 1 l. orange 10 10
D48 D **201** 1 l. orange 15 30
D49 2 l. green 15 10
D50 3 l. red 45 65
D51 4 l. brown . . . . . . 3·75 4·25
D45 D **192** 5 l. violet . . . . . . 1·50 10
D52 D **201** 5 l. violet . . . . . . 40·00 6·00
D53 6 l. blue . . . . . . 10·00 10·00
D54 8 l. mauve . . . . . . 20·00 20·00
D46 D **192** 10 l. blue . . . . . . 6·00 35
D55 D **201** 10 l. blue . . . . . . 40·00 3·00
D56 12 l. brown . . . . . 8·00 10·00
D47 D **192** 20 l. red . . . . 7·00 35
D57 D **201** 20 l. purple . . . . . 7·00 1·50
D58 50 l. green . . . . . 1·25 25

1949. Postage Due stamps optd **AMG-FTT** in one line.
D122 D **201** 1 l. orange 15 10
D123 2 l. green 15 10
D124 3 l. red 15 10
D125 5 l. violet 40 10
D126 6 l. blue 20 10
D127 8 l. mauve 20 10
D128 10 l. blue 20 10
D129 12 l. brown 50 15
D130 20 l. purple . . . . . 1·25 10
D131 25 l. red . . . . . . 1·25 1·50
D132 50 l. green . . . . . 1·50 10
D133 100 l. orange . . . . 3·00 20
D134 500 l. purple & blue . . 30·00 11·00

ZONE B

YUGOSLAV MILITARY GOVERNMENT

1948. 100 centesimi = 1 lira.
1949. 100 paras = 1 dinar.

Apart from the definitive issues illustrated below the following are stamps of Yugoslavia (sometimes in new colours), variously overprinted **STT VUJA** or **VUJA-STT** or (Nos. B65 onwards) **STT VUJNA** unless otherwise stated.

B 1  B 2

1948. Labour Day.
B1 B **1** 100 l. red and stone (A) . . 2·00 1·50
B2 100 l. red and stone (B) . . 2·00 1·50
B3 100 l. red and stone (C) . . 2·00 1·50
Inscr in Slovene (A) "I. MAJ 1948 V STO"; Italian (B) "I. MAGGIO 1948 NEL TLT"; or Croat (C) "I. SVIBANJ 1948 U STT".

1948. Red Cross. No. 545 optd and surch.
B3a **131** 2 l. on 50 p. brown & red 12·00 10·00

1948. Air. Economic Exhibition, Capodistria.
B4 B **2** 25 l. grey 75 55
B5 50 l. orange 75 55

B 3 Clasped Hands, Hammer and Sickle

B 4 Fishermen and Flying Boat

B 5 Man with Donkey

B 6 Mediterranean Gull over Chimneys

1949. Labour Day.
B6 B **3** 10 l. green 50 60

1949. Air.
B7 B **4** 1 l. turquoise 15 20
B8 B **5** 2 l. brown 15 20
B9 B **4** 5 l. blue 15 20
B10 B **5** 10 l. violet . . . . 1·00 1·00
B11 B **4** 25 l. brown . . . . 1·50 1·40
B12 B **5** 50 l. green . . . . 1·25 1·00
B13 B **6** 100 l. brown . . . . . . 4·00 3·00

1949. Partisans issue.
B14 **119** 50 p. grey 15 10
B15 1 d. green 15 10
B16 **120** 2 d. red 15 10
B17 – 3 d. red (No. 508) . . . 30 10
B18 **120** 4 d. blue 30 10
B19 – 5 d. blue (No. 511) . . . 30 10
B20 – 9 d. mauve (No. 514) . . 40 30
B21 – 12 d. blue (No. 515) . . . 2·00 1·50
B22 **119** 16 d. blue . . . . 2·00 1·00
B23 – 20 d. red (No. 517) . . . 3·00 1·50

1949. 75th Anniv of U.P.U.
B24 – 5 d. blue (No. 612) . . . 9·00 9·00
B25 **158** 12 d. brown . . . . 9·00 9·00

1949. Air. Optd **DIN** or surch also.
B26 B **4** 1 d. turquoise 15 10
B27 B **5** 2 d. brown 15 10
B28 B **4** 5 d. blue 20 10
B29 B **5** 10 d. violet 40 25
B30 B **4** 15 d. on 25 l. brown . . . 6·50 5·00
B31 B **5** 20 d. on 50 l. green . . . 1·50 1·00
B32 B **6** 30 d. on 100 l. purple . . 2·25 1·00

1950. Centenary of Yugoslav Railways.
B33 **116** 2 d. green . . . . 1·50 1·00
B34 – 3 d. red (No. 632) . . . 2·25 1·40
B35 – 5 d. blue (No. 633) . . . 3·75 2·50
B36 – 10 d. orange (No. 633a) . 7·50 5·00

B 10 Girl on Donkey

B 11 Workers

1950.
B37 B **10** 50 p. grey 10 10
B38 – 1 d. red (Cockerel) . . 10 10
B38a – 1 d. brown (Cockerel) . 15 10
B39 – 2 d. blue (Geese) . . . 10 10
B40 – 3 d. brown (Bees) . . . 20 10
B40a – 3 d. red (Bees) 20 10
B41 – 5 d. green (Oxen) . . . 35 10
B42 – 10 d. brown (Turkey) . . 50 10
B43 – 15 d. violet (Kids) . . 3·50 3·00
B44 – 20 d. green (Silkworms) 1·60 80

1950. May Day.
B45 B **11** 3 d. violet 55 50
B46 10 d. red 80 60

1950. Red Cross.
B47 **160** 50 p. brown and red . . 1·00 75

B 12 Worker

B 13 P. P. Vergerio Jr.

1951. May Day.
B48 B **12** 3 d. red 70 45
B49 10 d. green 90 85

1951. Red Cross.
B49a **191** 0 d. 50 blue and red . . 10·00 8·00

1951. Festival of Italian Culture.
B50 B **13** 5 d. blue 80 70
B51 10 d. purple 80 70
B52 20 d. brown 80 70

1951. Cultural Anniversaries.
B53 **189** 10 d. orange 90 50
B54 – 12 d. black (As No. 699) 90 50

B 14a Koper Square

B 15 Cyclists

1952. Air. 75th Anniv of U.P.U.
B54a B **14a** 5 d. brown . . . . . 11·00 9·50
B54b – 15 d. blue . . . . . . 11·00 9·50
B54c – 25 d. green . . . . . . 11·50 9·50
DESIGNS—VERT: 15 d. Lighthouse, Piran. HORIZ: 25 d. Hotel, Portoroz.

1952. Physical Culture Propaganda.
B55 B **15** 5 d. brown 15 10
B56 – 10 d. green 20 10
B57 – 15 d. red 20 10
B58 – 28 d. blue 50 25
B59 – 50 d. red . . . . 1·00 30
B60 – 100 d. blue . . . . . . 4·25 3·00
DESIGNS: 10 d. Footballers; 15 d. Rowing four; 28 d. Yachting; 50 d. Netball players; 100 d. Diver.

1952. Marshal Tito's 60th Birthday. As Nos. 727/9 of Yugoslavia additionally inscr "STT VUJA".
B61 **196** 15 d. brown . . . . . . 1·10 70
B62 **197** 28 d. red . . . . 1·25 80
B63 – 50 d. green (No. 729) . . 1·40 1·00

1952. Children's Week.
B64 **198** 15 d. pink 75 30

1952. 15th Olympic Games, Helsinki. As Nos. 731/6.
B65 **199** 5 d. brown on flesh . . . 30 10
B66 – 10 d. green on cream . . 30 10
B67 – 15 d. violet on mauve . . 30 10
B68 – 28 d. brown on buff . . 1·00 35
B69 – 50 d. brown on yellow . 6·00 3·50
B70 – 100 d. blue on pink . . . 24·00 15·00

1952. Navy Day (Nos. 737/9).
B71 – 15 d. purple . . . . . . 1·50 1·50
B72 **200** 28 d. brown . . . . . . 1·50 1·50
B73 – 50 d. black . . . . . . 2·00 1·50

1952. Red Cross.
B74 **201** 50 p. red, grey & black . 40 35

1952. 6th Yugoslav Communist Party Congress.
B75 **202** 15 d. brown 60 50
B76 15 d. turquoise 60 50
B77 15 d. brown 60 50
B78 15 d. blue 60 50

B 17 Starfish

1952. Philatelic Exhibition, Koper.
B78a B 17 15 d. brown 2·00 2·40

1953. 10th Death Anniv of Tesla (inventor).
B79 203 15 d. red 25 20
B80 30 d. blue 1·10 90

1953. Pictorials of 1950.
B81 1 d. grey (No. 705) 3·25 3·00
B86 2 d. red (No. 718) 10 10
B82 3 d. red (No. 655) 20 10
B87 5 d. orange (No. 719) 10 10
B83 10 d. green (No. 721) 20 10
B88 15 d. red (No. 723) 20 10
B84 30 d. blue (No. 712) 40 15
B85 50 d. turquoise (No. 714) 2·75 2·50

1953. United Nations (Nos. 747/9).
B89 204 15 d. green 10 10
B90 – 30 d. blue 20 10
B91 – 50 d. red 70 35

1953. Adriatic Car Rally. As Nos. 750/3.
B92 205 15 d. brown and yellow 25 10
B93 – 30 d. green and emerald 25 10
B94 – 50 d. mauve and orange 25 10
B95 – 70 d. deep blue and blue 85 50

1953. Marshal Tito.
B96 206 50 d. green 2·00 1·10

1953. 38th Esperanto Congress, Zagreb.
B97 207 15 d. green and turquoise (postage) 1·25 1·25
B98 300 d. green and violet (air) £250 £275

1953. 10th Anniv of Liberation of Istria and Slovene Coast.
B99 209 15 d. blue 1·90 1·25

1953. Death Centenary of Radicevic (poet).
B100 210 15 d. black 1·25 75

1953. Red Cross.
B101 211 2 d. red and bistre 40 40

1953. 10th Anniv of 1st Republican Legislative Assembly. As Nos. 762/4.
B102 212 15 d. violet 75 60
B103 – 30 d. red 75 60
B104 – 50 d. green 75 60

1954. Air. As Nos. 675 etc.
B108 1 d. lilac 15 10
B109 2 d. green 15 10
B110 3 d. purple 15 10
B111 5 d. brown 15 10
B112 10 d. turquoise 15 10
B113 20 d. brown 25 10
B114 30 d. blue 25 15
B115 50 d. black 50 20
B116 100 d. red 1·40 90
B117 200 d. violet 3·25 1·40
B118 500 d. orange 14·00 12·50

1954. Animals. As Nos. 765/76.
B119 2 d. grey, buff and red 30 20
B120 5 d. slate, buff and grey 30 20
B121 10 d. brown and green 30 20
B122 15 d. brown and blue 35 30
B123 17 d. sepia and brown 40 30
B124 25 d. yellow, blue and brown 45 30
B125 30 d. brown and violet 60 30
B126 35 d. black and purple 70 50
B127 50 d. brown and green 1·00 90
B128 65 d. black and brown 3·00 2·50
B129 70 d. brown and blue 6·00 4·00
B130 100 d. black and blue 22·00 15·00

1954. Serbian Insurrection. As Nos. 778/81.
B131 – 15 d. multicoloured 60 30
B132 214 30 d. multicoloured 60 30
B133 – 50 d. multicoloured 60 30
B134 – 70 d. multicoloured 1·25 75

POSTAGE DUE STAMPS

1948. Red Cross. No. D546 surch **VUJA STT** and new value.
BD4 131 2 l. on 50 p. green & red £180 £150

1949. On 1946 issue.
BD26 D 126 50 p. orange 30 30
BD27 1 d. orange 30 30
BD74 1 d. brown 10 10
BD28 2 d. blue 45 30
BD75 2 d. green 10 10
BD29 3 d. green 30 20
BD30 5 d. violet 60 50
BD76 5 d. blue 15 10
BD77 10 d. red 10 10
BD78 20 d. violet 20 10
BD79 30 d. orange 20 15
BD80 50 d. blue 35 20
BD81 100 d. purple 4·00 4·00
Nos. BD26/30 optd **STT VUJA** and the rest **STT VUJNA**.

1950. Red Cross. No. D617 optd **VUJA STT**.
BD48 160 50 p. purple and red 1·25 1·00

BD 12 Fish

1950.
BD49 – 50 p. brown 30 15
BD50 – 1 d. green 55 45
BD51 BD 12 2 d. blue 1·25 70
BD52 3 d. blue 1·25 70
BD53 5 d. purple 3·00 1·50
DESIGN: 50 p., 1 d. Two fishes.

1951. Red Cross. No. D703 optd **STT VUJA**.
BD54 191 0 d. 50 green and red £150 £125

The following are optd **STT VUJNA**.

1952. Red Cross. No. D741.
BD82 D 202 50 p. red and grey 50 50

1953. Red Cross. As No. D762.
BD102 211 2 d. red and purple 50 50

TRIPOLITANIA Pt. 8

One of the provinces into which the Italian colony of Libya was divided.

100 centesimi = 1 lira

Stamps optd **Tripoli di Barberia** formerly listed here will be found under Italian P.O.s in the Levant Nos. 171/81.

Nos. 1/138, except where otherwise described, are Italian stamps, sometimes in new colours, overprinted **TRIPOLITANIA**.

1923. Propagation of the Faith.
1 66 20 c. orange and green 2·00 6·00
2 30 c. orange and red 2·00 6·00
3 50 c. orange and violet 2·00 6·00
4 1 l. orange and blue 2·00 6·00

1923. Fascist March on Rome.
5 73 10 c. green 1·40 6·00
6 30 c. violet 1·40 6·00
7 50 c. red 1·40 6·00
8 74 1 l. blue 1·40 6·00
9 2 l. brown 1·40 6·00
10 75 5 l. black and blue 1·40 7·50

1924. Manzoni.
11 77 10 c. black and purple 75 12·00
12 – 15 c. black and green 75 12·00
13 – 30 c. black 75 12·00
14 – 50 c. black and brown 75 12·00
15 – 1 l. black and blue 18·00 90·00
16 – 5 l. black and purple £250 £1000

1925. Holy Year.
17 – 20 c. + 10 c. brown & grn 1·00 4·25
18 81 30 c. + 15 c. brown & choc 1·00 4·25
19 – 50 c. + 25 c. brown & vio 1·00 4·25
20 – 60 c. + 30 c. brown & red 1·00 4·25
21 – 1 l. + 50 c. purple & blue 1·00 4·25
22 – 5 l. + 2 l. 50 purple & red 1·00 4·25

1925. Royal Jubilee.
23 82 60 c. red 25 2·75
24 1 l. blue 30 2·75
24c 1 l. 25 blue 60 9·00

1926. St. Francis of Assisi.
25 83 20 c. green 1·00 4·25
26 – 40 c. violet 1·00 4·25
27 – 60 c. red 1·00 4·25
28 – 1 l. 25 blue 1·00 4·25
29 – 5 l. + 2 l. 50 green 2·00 5·50

1926. As Colonial Propaganda stamps of Somalia, T 21, but inscr "TRIPOLITANIA".
30 5 c. + 5 c. brown 20 2·25
31 10 c. + 5 c. green 20 2·25
32 20 c. + 5 c. green 20 2·25
33 40 c. + 5 c. red 20 2·25
34 60 c. + 5 c. orange 20 2·25
35 1 l. + 5 c. blue 20 2·25

6 Port of Tripoli

9 Palm Tree

1927. 1st Tripoli Trade Fair.
36 6 20 c. + 05 c. black & purple 2·00 3·00
37 25 c. + 05 c. black & green 2·00 3·00
38 – 40 c. + 10 c. black & brown 2·00 3·00
39 – 60 c. + 10 c. black & brown 2·00 3·00
40 – 75 c. + 20 c. black and red 2·00 3·00
41 – 1 l. 25 + 20 c. black & blue 7·50 9·50
DESIGNS: 40, 60 c. Arch of Marcus Aurelius; 75 c., 1 l. 25, View of Tripoli.

1927. 1st National Defence issue.
42 88 40 + 20 c. black & brown 1·00 4·25
43 60 + 30 c. brown and red 1·00 4·25
44 1 l. 25 + 60 c. black & blue 1·00 4·25
45 5 l. + 2 l. 50 black & green 1·50 6·50

1927. Death Centenary of Volta.
46 91 20 c. violet 3·00 10·00
47 50 c. orange 3·00 7·00
48 1 l. 25 blue 4·00 10·00

1928. 2nd Tripoli Trade Fair.
49 – 30 c. + 20 c. brown & purple 1·60 4·25
50 9 50 c. + 20 c. brown & green 1·60 4·25
51 – 1 l. 25 + 20 c. brown & red 1·60 4·25
52 – 1 l. 75 + 20 c. brown & blue 1·60 4·25
53 – 2 l. 55 + 50 c. sepia & brown 2·25 6·00
54 – 5 l. + 1 l. brown and violet 3·00 9·00
DESIGNS: As T 9: 30 c. Tripoli; 1 l. 25, Camel riders. 38 × 22½ mm: 1 l. 75, Arab citadel; 2 l. 55, Tripoli; 5 l. Desert outpost.

1928. 45th Anniv of Italian-African Society. As T 25 of Somalia.
55 20 c. + 5 c. green 75 3·50
56 30 c. + 5 c. red 75 3·50
57 50 c. + 10 c. violet 75 3·50
58 1 l. 25 + 20 c. blue 75 3·50

1929. 2nd National Defence issue.
59 89 30 c. + 10 c. black and red 1·40 4·75
60 – 50 c. + 20 c. grey 1·40 4·75
61 – 1 l. 25 + 50 c. blue & brown 1·75 6·00
62 – 5 l. + 2 l. black and olive 1·75 6·00

1929. 3rd Tripoli Trade Fair. Inscr "1929".
63 30 c. + 20 c. black and purple 5·00 12·00
64 50 c. + 20 c. black and green 5·00 12·00
65 1 l. 25 + 20 c. black and red 5·00 12·00
66 1 l. 75 + 20 c. black and blue 5·00 12·00
67 2 l. 55 + 50 c. black & brown 5·00 12·00
68 5 l. + 1 l. black and violet 90·00 £170
DESIGNS: As T 9: 30 c., 1 l. 25, Different trees; 50 c. Dorcas gazelle. 38 × 22½ mm: 1 l. 75, Goats; 2 l. 55, Camel caravan; 5 l. Trees.

1929. Abbey of Montecassino.
69 104 20 c. green 1·75 4·25
70 – 25 c. red 1·75 4·25
71 – 50 c. + 10 c. red 1·75 8·50
72 – 75 c. + 15 c. brown 1·75 8·50
73 104 1 l. 25 + 25 c. purple 3·25 8·50
74 – 5 l. + 1 l. blue 3·25 8·50
75 – 10 l. + 2 l. brown 3·25 10·00

1930. 4th Tripoli Trade Fair. Inscr "1930".
76 30 c. brown 1·40 4·75
77 50 c. violet 1·40 4·75
78 1 l. 25 blue 1·40 4·75
79 1 l. 75 + 20 c. red 1·40 7·00
80 2 l. 55 + 45 c. green 8·00 12·00
81 5 l. + 1 l. orange 8·00 15·00
82 10 l. + 2 l. purple 8·00 17·00
DESIGNS—As T 9: 30 c. Gathering bananas; 50 c. Tobacco plant; 1 l. 25, Venus of Cyrene. 38 × 22½ mm: 5 l. Motor and camel transport; 10 l. Rome pavilion, at exhibition entrance.

1930. Marriage of Prince Humbert and Princess Marie Jose.
83 109 20 c. green 45 1·90
84 50 c. + 10 c. red 45 2·50
85 1 l. 25 + 25 c. red 45 2·75

1930. Ferrucci.
86 114 20 c. violet (postage) 50 1·60
87 – 25 c. green (No. 283) 50 1·60
88 – 50 c. black (as No. 284) 50 1·60
89 – 1 l. 25 blue (No. 285) 50 1·60
90 – 5 l. + 2 l. red (as No. 286) 1·75 2·75
91 117 50 c. purple (air) 80 2·25
92 1 l. blue 80 2·25
93 5 l. + 2 l. red 4·50 10·00

1930. 3rd National Defence issue.
94 89 30 c. + 10 c. green and deep green 5·00 15·00
95 – 50 c. + 10 c. violet and green 5·00 15·00
96 – 1 l. 25 + 30 c. brown and deep brown 5·00 15·00
97 – 5 l. + 1 l. 50 green and blue 14·00 42·00

17 Roman Arch

18 Columns of Leptis

19

1930. 25th Anniv (1929) of Italian Colonial Agricultural Institute.
98 17 50 c. + 20 c. brown 1·00 5·00
99 1 l. 25 + 20 c. blue 1·00 5·00
100 1 l. 75 + 20 c. green 1·00 5·00
101 2 l. 55 + 50 c. violet 1·75 5·00
102 5 l. + 1 l. red 1·75 5·00

1930. Virgil.
103 – 15 c. grey (postage) 40 1·40
104 – 20 c. brown 40 1·40
105 – 25 c. green 40 1·10
106 – 30 c. brown 40 1·40
107 – 50 c. purple 40 1·10
108 – 75 c. red 40 1·40
109 – 1 l. 25 blue 40 1·40
110 – 5 l. + 1 l. 50 purple 2·00 7·00
111 – 10 l. + 2 l. 50 brown 2·00 7·00
112 119 50 c. green (air) 1·00 2·25
113 1 l. red 1·00 2·25
114 7 l. 70 + 1 l. 30 brown 2·75 10·00
115 9 l. + 2 l. blue 2·75 10·00

1931. Air.
116 18 50 c. red 20 10
117 60 c. red 1·60 6·00
117a 75 c. blue 1·60 6·00
118 80 c. purple 3·00 6·50
119 19 1 l. blue 45 10
120 1 l. 20 brown 6·50 10·00
121 1 l. 50 red 3·00 6·00
122 5 l. green 7·00 7·00

20 Statue of Youth

22 Savoia Marchetti S-55A Flying Boat over Ruins

1931. 5th Tripoli Trade Fair.
123 20 10 c. black (postage) 2·00 5·00
124 – 25 c. green 2·00 5·00
125 – 50 c. violet 2·00 5·00
126 – 1 l. 25 blue 2·00 5·00
127 – 1 l. 75 + 25 c. red 2·40 7·00
128 – 2 l. 75 + 45 c. orange 2·40 10·00
129 – 5 l. + 1 l. purple 8·00 17·00
130 – 10 l. + 2 l. brown 30·00 45·00
131 – 50 c. blue (air) 2·00 5·00
DESIGNS—As Type 20: 25 c. Arab musician; 50 c. (postage) View of Zeughet; 1 l. 25, Snake charmer; 1 l. 75, House and windmill; 2 l. 75, Libyan "Zaptie"; 5 l. Arab horseman. As Type E 21: 10 l. Exhibition Pavilion; 50 c. (air) Airplane over desert.

1931. St. Antony of Padua.
132 121 20 c. brown 55 2·50
133 – 25 c. green 55 2·50
134 – 30 c. black 55 2·50
135 – 50 c. purple 55 1·40
136 – 75 c. grey 55 2·50
137 – 1 l. 25 blue 55 2·50
138 – 5 l. + 2 l. 50 brown 2·00 11·00

1931. Air. 25th Anniv (1929) of Italian Colonial Agricultural Institute.
139 22 50 c. blue 1·50 6·00
140 80 c. violet 1·50 6·00
141 1 l. black 1·50 6·00
142 2 l. green 3·00 7·00
143 5 l. + 2 l. red 5·00 15·00

23 Paw-paw Tree

24 Arch of Marcus Aurelius

1932. 6th Tripoli Trade Fair. Inscr "1932".
144 23 10 c. brown (postage) 3·00 6·00
145 – 20 c. brown 3·00 6·00
146 – 25 c. green 3·00 6·00
147 – 30 c. green 3·00 6·00
148 – 50 c. violet 3·00 6·00
149 – 75 c. red 4·00 10·00
150 – 1 l. 25 blue 4·00 10·00
151 – 1 l. 75 + 25 c. brown 18·00 32·00
152 – 5 l. + 1 l. blue 20·00 45·00
153 – 10 l. + 2 l. purple 50·00 90·00
154 – 50 c. blue (air) 5·50 12·00
155 – 1 l. brown 5·50 12·00
156 – 2 l. + 1 l. black 16·00 45·00
157 – 5 l. + 2 l. red 50·00 90·00
DESIGNS—POSTAGE. VERT: 10 c. to 50 c. Various trees; 75 c. Roman mausoleum at Ghirza; 10 l. Dorcas gazelle. HORIZ: 1 l. 25, Mogadiscio aerodrome; 1 l. 75, Lioness; 5 l. Arab and camel. AIR. HORIZ: 50 c., 1 l. Marina Fiat MF.5 flying boat over Bedouin camp; 2, 5 l. Marina Fiat MF.5 flying boat over Tripoli.

1933. 7th Tripoli Trade Fair. Inscr "1933".
158 – 10 c. purple (postage) 24·00 15·00
159 – 25 c. green 12·00 11·00
160 – 30 c. brown 12·00 15·00
161 24 50 c. violet 12·00 9·00
162 – 1 l. 25 blue 22·00 38·00
163 – 5 l. + 1 l. brown 35·00 85·00
164 – 10 l. + 2 l. 50 red 35·00 85·00

165 **24** 50 c. green (air) 6·00 12·00
166 – 75 c. red 6·00 12·00
167 – 1 l. blue 6·00 12·00
168 – 2 l. + 50 c. violet 12·00 24·00
169 – 5 l. + 1 l. brown 15·00 32·00
170 – 10 l. + 2 l. 50 black 15·00 32·00
DESIGNS—POSTAGE. VERT: 10 c. Ostrich; 25 c. Incense plant; 1 l. 25, Golden eagle; 10 l. Tripoli and Fascist emblem. HORIZ: 30 c. Arab drummer; 5 l. Leopard. AIR. HORIZ: 50 c., 2 l. Seaplane over Tripoli; 75 c., 10 l. Caproni Ca 101 airplane over Tagiura; 1, 5 l. Seaplane leaving Tripoli.

25 Mercury

1933. Airship "Graf Zeppelin".
171 **25** 3 l. brown 5·00 35·00
172 – 5 l. violet 5·00 35·00
173 – 10 l. green 5·00 55·00
174 **25** 12 l. blue 5·00 85·00
175 – 15 l. red 5·00 70·00
176 – 20 l. black 5·00 95·00
DESIGNS: 5, 15 l. "Graf Zeppelin" and Arch of Marcus Aurelius; 10, 20 l. "Graf Zeppelin" and allegory of "dawn".

26 "Flight"

1933. Air. Balbo Transatlantic Mass Formation Flight.
177 **26** 19 l. 75 brown and black 10·00 £225
178 44 l. 75 green and blue 10·00 £225

1934. Air. Rome–Buenos Aires Flight. Optd with Savoia Marchetti S-71 airplane and **1934 XII PRIMO VOLO DIRETTO ROMA = BUENOS-AYRES TRIMOTORE LOMBARDI-MAZZOTTI**, or surch also in Italian.
179 **19** 2 l. on 5 l. brown 1·50 27·00
180 3 l. on 5 l. green 1·50 27·00
181 5 l. brown 1·50 27·00
182 10 l. on 5 l. red 1·50 27·00

27 Water Carriers

1934. 8th Tripoli Trade Fair.
183 **27** 10 c. brown (postage) 2·00 5·00
184 – 20 c. red 2·00 5·00
185 – 25 c. green 2·00 5·00
186 – 30 c. brown 2·00 5·00
187 – 50 c. violet 2·00 5·00
188 – 75 c. red 2·00 5·00
189 – 1 l. 25 blue 24·00 38·00
DESIGNS—VERT: 20 c. Arab; 25 c. Minaret; 50 c. Statue of Emperor Claudius. HORIZ: 30 c., 1 l. 25, Moslem shrine; 75 c. Ruins of Ghadames.

190 50 c. blue (air) 4·50 12·00
191 75 c. red 4·50 12·00
192 5 l. + 1 l. green 38·00 95·00
193 10 l. + 2 l. purple 38·00 95·00
194 25 l. + 3 l. brown 42·00 95·00
DESIGNS—HORIZ: 50 c., 5 l. Marina Fiat MF.5 flying boat off Tripoli; 75 c., 10 l. Airplane over mosque. VERT: 25 l. Caproni Ca 101 airplane and camel.
See also Nos. E195/6.

1934. Air. Oasis Flight. As Nos. 190/4 optd **CIRCUITO DELLE OASI TRIPOLI MAGGIO 1934-XII.**
197 50 c. red 4·50 10·00
198 75 c. bistre 4·50 10·00
199 5 l. + 1 l. brown 4·50 10·00
200 10 l. + 2 l. blue £140 £200
201 25 l. + 3 l. violet £140 £200
See also Nos. E202/3.

29 Village

1934. 2nd International Colonial Exn, Naples.
204 **29** 5 c. brown & green (postage) 1·75 7·50
205 10 c. black and brown 1·75 7·50
206 20 c. blue and red 1·75 7·50
207 50 c. brown and violet 1·75 7·50
208 60 c. blue and brown 1·75 7·50
209 1 l. 25 green and blue 1·75 7·50

210 **29** 25 c. orange & blue (air) 1·75 7·50
211 – 50 c. blue and green 1·75 7·50
212 – 75 c. orange and brown 1·75 7·50
213 – 80 c. green and brown 1·75 7·50
214 – 1 l. green and red 1·75 7·50
215 – 2 l. brown and blue 1·75 7·50
DESIGNS: 25 c. to 75 c. Shadow of airplane over desert; 80 c. to 2 l. Arab camel corps and Caproni Ca 101 airplane.

30

1934. Air. Rome–Mogadiscio Flight.
216 **30** 25 c. + 10 c. green 1·75 5·00
217 50 c. + 10 c. brown 1·75 5·00
218 75 c. + 15 c. red 1·75 5·00
219 80 c. + 15 c. black 1·75 5·00
220 1 l. + 20 c. brown 1·75 5·00
221 2 l. + 20 c. blue 1·75 5·00
222 3 l. + 25 c. violet 14·00 40·00
223 5 l. + 25 c. orange 14·00 40·00
224 10 l. + 30 c. purple 14·00 40·00
225 25 l. + 2 l. green 14·00 40·00

32 Camel Transport

1935. 9th Tripoli Exhibition.
226 – 10 c. + 10 c. brown (post) 50 2·50
227 – 20 c. + 10 c. red 50 2·50
228 – 50 c. + 10 c. violet 50 2·50
229 – 75 c. + 15 c. red 50 2·50
230 – 1 l. 25 + 25 c. blue 50 2·50
231 – 2 l. + 50 c. green 50 2·50

232 – 25 c. + 10 c. green (air) 70 3·00
233 **32** 50 c. + 10 c. blue 70 3·00
234 – 1 l. + 25 c. blue 70 3·00
235 – 2 l. + 30 c. red 70 3·50
236 – 3 l. + 1 l. 50 brown 70 3·75
237 – 10 l. + 5 l. purple 6·00 15·00
DESIGNS—POSTAGE. VERT: 10, 20 c. Pomegranate tree; 50 c., 2 l. Arab flautist; 75 c., 1 l. 25, Arab in burnous. AIR. VERT: 25 c., 3 l. Watch-tower. HORIZ: 1 l., 10 l. Arab girl and Caproni Ca 101 airplane.

For issue inscr "XII FIERA CAMPIONARIA TRIPOLI" and dated "1938", see Libya Nos. 88/95.

CONCESSIONAL LETTER POST

1931. Optd **TRIPOLITANIA.**
CL123 CL **109** 10 c. brown 4·00 5·00

EXPRESS LETTER STAMPS

Express stamps optd **TRIPOLI DI BARBERIA** formerly listed here will be found under Italian P.O.s in the Levant Nos. E6/7.

1927. 1st Tripoli Exhibition. Inscr "EXPRES".
E42 1 l. 25 + 30 c. black & vio 8·00 8·00
E43 2 l. 50 + 1 l. black & yellow 8·00 8·00
DESIGN—As T **6**: 1 l. 25, 2 l. 50, Camels and palm trees.

E 21 War Memorial

1931. 5th Tripoli Trade Fair.
E132 **E 21** 1 l. 25 + 20 c. red 4·50 10·00

1934. Air. 8th Tripoli Trade Fair.
E195 2 l. 25 black 14·00 38·00
E196 4 l. 50 + 1 l. blue 14·00 38·00
DESIGN—As T **27**: Nos. E195/6, Caproni Ca 101 airplane over Bedouins in desert.

1934. Air. Oasis Flight. As Nos. E195/6 optd **CIRCUITO DELLE OASI TRIPOLI MAGGIO 1934-XII.**
E202 2 l. 25 red 4·50 10·00
E203 4 l. 50 + 1 l. red 4·50 10·00

OFFICIAL STAMPS

1934. No. 225 (colour changed) optd **SERVIZIO DI STATO** and Crown.
O226 **30** 25 l. + 2 l. red £1300 £2750

From 1943 to 1951 Tripolitania was under British administration; stamps issued during this period are listed in Volume 3. From 1952 it was part of independent Libya.

INDEX

Countries can be quickly located by referring to the index at the end of this volume.

TUNISIA Pt. 6; Pt. 14

Formerly a French Protectorate in N. Africa, Tunisia became an independent kingdom in 1956 and a republic in 1957.

1888. 100 centimes = 1 franc.
1959. 1000 milliemes = 1 dinar.

1

2

1888. Arms on plain background.
1 **1** 1 c. black on blue 2·75 1·75
2 2 c. brown on buff 2·75 1·75
3 5 c. green on green 18·00 9·25
4 15 c. blue on blue 45·00 16·00
5 25 c. black on pink 80·00 50·00
6 40 c. red on yellow 75·00 50·00
7 75 c. pink on pink 80·00 55·00
8 5 f. mauve on lilac £400 £275

1888. Arms on shaded background.
9 **2** 1 c. black on blue 1·25 50
10 2 c. brown on buff 1·25 30
22 5 c. green 6·25 75
12 10 c. black on lilac 6·25 75
23 10 c. red 5·00 75
14 15 c. blue 40·00 50
24 15 c. grey 10·50 1·00
15 20 c. red on green 15·00 1·00
16 25 c. black on pink 17·00 1·25
25 25 c. blue 10·50 1·25
26 35 c. brown 40·00 1·25
17 40 c. red on yellow 13·50 1·25
18 75 c. pink on pink £180 75·00
19 75 c. violet on yellow 20·00 6·75
20 1 f. green 28·00 6·75
27 2 f. lilac £150 £120
21 5 f. mauve on lilac £160 65·00

1902. Surch **25** and bars.
28 **2** 25 on 15 c. blue 2·75 2·50

4 Mosque at Kairouan

6 Ruins of Hadrian's Aqueduct

5 Agriculture

7 Carthaginian Galley

1906.
30 **4** 1 c. black on yellow 10 10
31 2 c. brown 10 10
32 3 c. red 10 30
33 5 c. green on green 10 10
34 **5** 10 c. red 10 10
35 15 c. violet 75 15
36 20 c. brown 15 10
37 25 c. blue 1·00 35
38 **6** 35 c. brown and green 8·00 1·00
39 40 c. red and brown 4·00 25
40 75 c. red and purple 55 50
41 **7** 1 f. brown and red 65 35
42 2 f. green and brown 4·50 1·25
43 5 f. blue and violet 10·00 4·50
See also Nos. 72/8, 105 and 107/13.

1908. Surch.
44 **2** 10 on 15 c. grey 1·25 1·25
45 35 on 1 f. green 2·25 2·25
46 40 on 2 f. lilac 5·25 5·25
47 75 on 5 f. mauve on lilac 4·25 4·25

1911. Surch in figures and bar.
48 **5** 10 on 15 c. violet 1·60 60
60 15 c. on 10 c. red 75 10
79 20 c. on 15 c. violet 85 15

1915. Red Cross Fund. Optd with red cross.
49 **5** 15 c. violet 85 60

1916. Red Cross Fund. Optd with red cross and bars.
50 **4** 5 c. green on green 1·25 1·25

1916. Prisoners-of-War Fund. Surch with red cross and **10 c.**
51 **5** 10 c. on 15 c. brown on blue 85 85
52 10 c. on 20 c. brown on yell 1·00 1·00
53 10 c. on 25 c. blue on green 3·00 3·00
54 **6** 10 c. on 35 c. violet & green 6·25 6·25
55 10 c. on 40 c. black & brown 3·00 3·00
56 10 c. on 75 c. green and red 7·50 7·50
57 **7** 10 c. on 1 f. green and red 3·00 3·00
58 10 c. on 2 f. blue and brown 75·00 75·00
59 10 c. on 5 f. red and violet £100 £100

1918. Prisoners-of-War Fund. Surch **15c** and red cross.
61 **5** 15 c. on 20 c. black on grn 1·50 1·50
62 15 c. on 25 c. blue 1·60 1·60
63 **6** 15 c. on 35 c. red and olive 1·75 1·75
64 15 c. on 40 c. blue & brown 4·25 4·25
65 15 c. on 75 c. black and red 6·25 6·25
66 **7** 15 c. on 1 f. violet and red 18·00 18·00
67 15 c. on 2 f. red and brown 65·00 65·00
68 15 c. on 5 f. black and violet £120 £120

1919. Air. Optd **Poste Aerienne** and wings or surch **30 c.** and bars also.
69 **6** 30 c. on 35 c. brown & green 1·10 85
70 30 c. blue and olive 35 40

1920. New values and colours changed.
72 **4** 5 c. orange 10 20
73 **5** 10 c. green 25 30
74 25 c. violet 25 10
75 **6** 30 c. violet and purple 70 30
76 **5** 30 c. red 35 40
77 50 c. blue 30 25
78 **6** 60 c. violet and green 30 25

18 Ruin at Dougga

1922.
80 **18** 10 c. green 10 20
81 30 c. red 85 90
82 50 c. blue 25 40
See also Nos. 104 and 106.

1923. War Wounded Fund. Surch **AFFt**, medal and new value.
83 **4** 0 c. on 1 c. blue 60 45
84 0 c. on 2 c. brown 60 45
85 1 c. on 3 c. green 60 45
86 2 c. on 5 c. mauve 60 45
87 **18** 3 c. on 10 c. mauve on bl 60 45
88 **5** 5 c. on 15 c. green 60 45
89 5 c. on 20 c. blue on red 1·25 1·25
90 5 c. on 25 c. mauve on blue 1·25 1·25
91 **18** 5 c. on 30 c. orange 1·50 1·50
92 **6** 5 c. on 35 c. mauve & blue 1·60 1·50
93 5 c. on 40 c. brown & blue 1·60 1·50
94 **18** 10 c. on 50 c. black on blue 2·25 2·25
95 **6** 10 c. on 60 c. blue & brown 2·25 2·25
96 10 c. on 75 c. green & mve 4·00 4·00
97 **7** 25 c. on 1 f. mauve & lake 4·00 4·00
98 25 c. on 2 f. red and blue 14·00 14·00
99 25 c. on 5 f. brown & green 55·00 55·00

1923. Surch.
100 **4** 10 on 5 c. green on green 30 25
101 **5** 20 on 15 c. violet 85 55
102 30 on 20 c. brown 15 25
103 50 on 25 c. blue 85 10

1923. New values and colours.
104 **18** 10 c. pink 15 25
105 **5** 15 c. brown on orange 10 20
106 **18** 30 c. mauve 35 20
107 **5** 40 c. black on pink 1·00 45
108 40 c. green 10 15
109 **6** 60 c. carmine and red 30 30
110 75 c. scarlet and red 20 25
111 **7** 1 f. light blue and blue 25 25
112 2 f. red & green on pink 35 45
113 5 f. green and lilac 55 75

1925. Parcel Post stamps surch **PROTECTION DE L'ENFANCE POSTES** and value in figures.
114 **P 8** 1 c. on 5 c. red and brown on rose 50 40
115 2 c. on 10 c. blue and brown on yellow 50 40
116 3 c. on 20 c. red and purple on mauve 85 55
117 5 c. on 25 c. red and green on green 85 70
118 5 c. on 40 c. green and red on yellow 85 70
119 10 c. on 50 c. green and violet on mauve 2·00 2·00
120 10 c. on 75 c. brown and green on green 1·25 1·25
121 25 c. on 1 f. green and blue on blue 1·25 1·40
122 25 c. on 2 f. purple and red on rose 7·50 7·50
123 25 c. on 5 f. brown and red on green 35·00 35·00

21 Arab Woman

22 Grand Mosque, Tunis

23 Mosque, Place Halfaouine, Tunis

24 Amphitheatre, El Djem

1926.
124 **21** 1 c. red 10 15
125 2 c. green 10 15
126 3 c. blue 10 20
127 5 c. green 10 10
128 10 c. mauve 10 15

No.	Type	Description	Unused	Used
129	22	15 c. lilac	20	15
130		20 c. red	10	10
131		25 c. green	10	20
131a		25 c. mauve	15	15
132		30 c. mauve	15	15
133		30 c. green	15	20
134		40 c. brown	15	15
134a		45 c. green	50	60
135	23	50 c. black	10	10
135a		50 c. blue	45	10
135b		50 c. green	15	20
135c		60 c. red	15	30
135d		65 c. blue	35	20
135e		70 c. red	15	30
136		75 c. red	30	25
136a		75 c. mauve	30	10
137		80 c. blue	30	30
137a		80 c. brown	45	65
138		90 c. red	15	10
138a		90 c. blue	7·50	7·50
139		1 f. purple	25	10
139a		1 f. red	10	10
140	24	1 f. 05 pink and blue	25	25
141		1 f. 25 blue & light blue	50	65
141a		1 f. 25 red	1·00	1·00
141b		1 f. 30 violet and blue	55	65
141c		1 f. 40 purple	55	60
142		1 f. 50 blue & light blue	40	15
142a		1 f. 50 orange and red	50	65
143		2 f. brown and red	40	20
143a		2 f. red	50	15
143b		2 f. 25 blue	65	80
143c		2 f. 50 green	50	55
144		3 f. orange and blue	60	20
144a		3 f. violet	15	15
145		5 f. green & red on green	2·50	45
145a		5 f. brown	1·00	1·40
146		10 f. grey & red on blue	7·50	1·75
146a		10 f. pink	65	75
146b		20 f. red & mve on pink	1·75	90

For similar designs see Nos. 172/91, 220/31 and 257/286.

1927. Surch **1f 50**.

No.	Type	Description	Unused	Used
147	24	1 f. 50 on 1 f. 25 blue and ultramarine	30	20

1927. Air. Optd **Poste Aerienne** and airplane or surch in figures and bars also.

No.	Type	Description	Unused	Used
148	7	1 f. light blue and blue	40	50
152	24	1 f. 30 mauve and orange	1·50	1·90
169		1 f. 50 on 1 f. 30 mauve and orange	1·25	75
170		1 f. 50 on 1 f. 80 red and green	1·75	75
171		1 f. 50 on 2 f. 55 brown and mauve	4·00	1·50
149	6	1 f. 75 on 75 c. scarlet and red	40	70
150	7	1 f. 75 on 5 f. green and lilac	1·50	1·90
153	24	1 f. 80 red and green	2·00	2·00
151	7	2 f. red and green on pink	1·60	1·50
154	24	2 f. 55 brown and mauve	1·00	1·00

26 First Tunis–Chad Motor Service

1928. Child Welfare.

No.	Type	Description	Unused	Used
155	26	40 c. + 40 c. brown	1·00	80
156		50 c. + 50 c. purple	1·00	1·00
157		75 c. + 75 c. blue	1·10	1·10
158		1 f. + 1 f. red	1·10	1·10
159		1 f. 50 + 1 f. 50 blue	1·00	80
160		2 f. + 2 f. green	1·25	1·10
161		5 f. + 5 f. brown	1·60	1·60

1928. Surch.

No.	Type	Description	Unused	Used
162	4	3 c. on 5 c. orange	10	30
163	5	10 c. on 15 c. brn on orge	15	20
164	18	25 c. on 30 c. mauve	15	20
165	23	40 c. on 80 c. blue	15	30
166	22	50 c. on 40 c. brown	4·25	50
167	23	50 c. on 75 c. red	25	40

1929. Precancelled **AFFRANCHts POSTES** and surch **10**.

No.	Type	Description	Unused	Used
168	22	10 on 30 c. mauve	1·60	90

28  29  30

31

1931.

No.	Type	Description	Unused	Used
172	28	1 c. blue	10	25
173		2 c. brown	10	30
174		3 c. black	15	40
175		5 c. green	10	25
176		10 c. red	10	30
177	29	15 c. purple	35	30
178		20 c. brown	10	15
179		25 c. red	10	15
180		30 c. green	20	25
181		40 c. orange	10	15
182	30	50 c. blue	20	10
183		75 c. yellow	85	85
184		90 c. red	60	45
185		1 f. olive	60	50
186	31	1 f. 50 blue	60	50
187		2 f. brown	65	50
188		3 f. green	8·00	8·00
189		5 f. red	19·00	17·00
190		10 f. black	32·00	28·00
191		20 f. brown	50·00	40·00

1937. Surch.

No.	Type	Description	Unused	Used
191a	23	25 c. on 65 c. blue	10	10
192		0.65 on 50 c. blue	50	10
193		65 on 50 c. blue	75	10
193b		1 FR on 90 c. blue	45	15
193c	24	1 F. on 1 f. 25 red	20	30
193d		1 F. on 1 f. 40 purple	20	30
193e		1 F. on 2 f. 25 blue	20	30
194		1 f. 75 on 1 f. 50 blue and light blue	4·25	1·25

1938. 50th Anniv of Tunisian Postal Service. Surch **1888 1938** and value.

No.	Type	Description	Unused	Used
196	28	1 c. + 1 c. blue	1·60	1·60
197		2 c. + 2 c. brown	1·60	1·60
198		3 c. + 3 c. black	1·60	1·60
199		5 c. + 5 c. green	1·60	1·60
200		10 c. + 10 c. red	1·60	1·60
201	29	15 c. + 15 c. purple	1·60	1·60
202		20 c. + 20 c. brown	1·60	1·60
203		25 c. + 25 c. red	1·60	1·60
204		30 c. + 30 c. green	1·60	1·60
205		40 c. + 40 c. orange	1·60	1·60
206	30	50 c. + 50 c. blue	1·60	1·60
207		75 c. + 75 c. yellow	1·60	1·60
208		90 c. + 90 c. red	1·60	1·60
209		1 f. + 1 f. olive	1·60	1·60
210	31	1 f. 50 + 1 f. blue	1·60	1·60
211		2 f. + 1 f. 50 brown	3·00	3·00
212		3 f. + 2 f. green	3·00	3·00
213		5 f. + 3 f. red	16·00	16·00
214		10 f. + 5 f. black	32·00	32·00
215		20 f. + 10 f. brown	55·00	55·00

1941. National Relief. Surch **SECOURS NATIONAL 1941** and value.

No.	Type	Description	Unused	Used
216	22	1 f. on 45 c. green	2·00	2·00
217	24	1 f. 30 on 1 f. 25 red	2·00	2·00
218		1 f. 50 on 1 f. 40 purple	2·00	2·00
219		2 f. on 2 f. 25 blue	2·00	2·00

1941. As stamps of 1926 but without monogram "RF".

No.	Type	Description	Unused	Used
220	22	30 c. red	55	65
221	23	1 f. 20 grey	15	30
222		1 f. 50 brown	25	20
223	24	2 f. 40 pink and red	30	45
224		2 f. 50 light blue and blue	30	40
225		3 f. violet	45	55
226		4 f. blue and black	25	25
227		4 f. 50 brown and green	30	45
228		5 f. black	30	25
229		10 f. violet and purple	30	25
230		15 f. red	3·25	2·75
231		20 f. red and lilac	1·75	85

41a "Victory"  42 Allied Soldiers

1943.

No.	Type	Description	Unused	Used
232	41a	1 f. 50 red	15	30

1943. Charity. Tunisian Liberation.

No.	Type	Description	Unused	Used
233	42	1 f. 50 + 8 f. 50 red	25	30

43 Mosque and Olive Trees  44 Sidi Mahrez Mosque

45 Ramparts of Sfax

1944.

No.	Type	Description	Unused	Used
234	43	30 c. yellow	25	25
235		40 c. brown	25	30
236		60 c. orange	25	35
237		70 c. red	25	35
238		80 c. green	35	40
239		90 c. violet	25	30
240		1 f. red	25	30
241		1 f. 50 blue	20	30
242		2 f. 40 red	35	45
243	43	2 f. 50 brown	25	35
244		3 f. violet	25	25
245		4 f. blue	30	25
246		4 f. 50 green	40	35
247		5 f. grey	35	25
248		6 f. brown	40	25
249		10 f. lake	45	35
250		15 f. brown	50	40
251		20 f. lilac	45	45

Nos. 234/41 are smaller $15\frac{1}{2} \times 19$ mm.

1944. Forces Welfare Fund. Surch + **48 frcs pour nos Combattants**.

No.	Type	Description	Unused	Used
252	43	2 f. + 48 f. red ($21\frac{1}{4} \times 26\frac{1}{2}$ mm)	85	80

1945. Forces Welfare Fund. Surch **POUR NOS COMBATTANTS** and value.

No.	Type	Description	Unused	Used
253	44	1 f. 50 + 8 f. 50 brown	50	75
254	45	3 f. + 12 f. green	60	80
255	–	4 f. + 21 f. brown	75	75
256	–	10 f. + 40 f. red	75	75

DESIGNS—HORIZ: 4 f. Camel patrol at Fort Saint; 10 f. Mosque at Sidi-bou-Said.

1945. New values and colours.

No.	Type	Description	Unused	Used
257	23	10 c. brown	10	25
258		30 c. olive	10	25
259		40 c. red	15	25
260		50 c. turquoise	10	15
261		60 c. blue	15	15
262		80 c. green	15	15
263		1 f. 20 brown	15	30
264		1 f. 50 lilac	10	15
265		2 f. green	10	15
267	24	2 f. 40 red	30	50
268	23	2 f. 50 brown	25	20
269	24	3 f. brown	10	10
270	23	3 f. red	15	15
271	24	4 f. blue	40	50
272	23	4 f. violet	40	25
273	24	4 f. violet	50	45
273a	23	4 f. orange	25	30
274		4 f. 50 blue	25	20
275	24	5 f. green	20	20
275a	23	5 f. blue	35	40
275b		5 f. green	30	10
276	24	6 f. blue	10	25
277		6 f. red	50	50
278	23	6 f. red	15	15
279	24	10 f. orange	20	40
280		10 f. blue	25	20
281		15 f. mauve	20	20
281a	23	15 f. red	35	30
282	24	20 f. green	20	20
283		25 f. violet	40	45
284		25 f. orange	1·00	95
285		50 f. red	1·10	50
286		100 f. red	1·25	65

1945. Anti-Tuberculosis Fund. Type of France optd **TUNISIE**.

No.	Type	Description	Unused	Used
287	222	2 f. + 1 f. orange	30	35

1945. Postal Employees' War Victims' Fund. Type of France optd **TUNISIE**.

No.	Type	Description	Unused	Used
288	223	4 f. + 6 f. brown	30	45

1945. Stamp Day. Type of France (Louis XI) optd **TUNISIE**.

No.	Type	Description	Unused	Used
289	228	2 f. + 3 f. green	30	45

1945. War Veterans' Fund. Surch **ANCIENS COMBATTANTS R F** and value.

No.	Type	Description	Unused	Used
290	21	4 f. + 6 f. on 10 c. blue	30	45
291	23	10 f. + 30 f. on 80 c. green	30	45

49 Legionary

1946. Welfare Fund for French Troops in Indo-China.

No.	Type	Description	Unused	Used
292	49	20 f. + 30 f. black, red and green	1·25	1·25

1946. Red Cross Fund. Surch with cross **1946** and new values.

No.	Type	Description	Unused	Used
293	23	80 c. + 50 c. green	85	85
294		1 f. 50 + 1 f. 50 lilac	85	85
295		2 f. + 2 f. green	85	85
296	24	2 f. 40 + 2 f. red	85	75
297		4 f. + 4 f. blue	85	75

1946. Stamp Day. La Varane Type of France optd **TUNISIE**.

No.	Type	Description	Unused	Used
298	241	3 f. + 2 f. blue	60	65

1947. Stamp Day. Louvois Type of France optd **TUNISIE**.

No.	Type	Description	Unused	Used
299	253	4 f. 50 + 5 f. 50 brown	85	70

1947. Naval Charities. Type of France surch **TUNISIE** and new value.

No.	Type	Description	Unused	Used
300	234	10 + 15 on 2 f. + 3 f. blue	85	70

1947. Welfare Fund. Surch **SOLIDARITE 1947 + 40 F.**

No.	Type	Description	Unused	Used
301	24	10 f. + 40 f. black	85	70

53 Arabesque Ornamentation from Great Mosque at Kairouan

54 Neptune

1947.

No.	Type	Description	Unused	Used
302	53	3 f. green and turquoise	75	60
303		4 f. red and purple	35	50
304	54	5 f. black and green	85	65
305	53	6 f. red and brown	10	10
306	54	10 f. black and brown	25	20
306a	53	10 f. violet	25	10
306b		12 f. brown	55	30
306c		12 f. orange and brown	70	20
306d		15 f. red and brown	65	50
307	54	18 f. blue and green	1·10	55
307a		25 f. turquoise and blue	1·25	75
307b	53	30 f. blue and deep blue	7·50	75

55 Feeding a Fledgling  57 Triumphal Arch, Sbeitla

1947. Infant Welfare Fund.

No.	Type	Description	Unused	Used
308	55	4 f. 50 + 5 f. 50 green	75	75
309		6 f. + 9 f. blue	75	75
310		8 f. + 17 f. red	1·00	1·00
311		10 f. + 40 f. violet	1·00	1·00

1948. Stamp Day. Type of France (Arago) optd **TUNISIE**.

No.	Type	Description	Unused	Used
312	253	6 f. + 4 f. red	1·00	90

1948. Anti-Tuberculosis Fund. Surch **AIDEZ LES TUBERCULEUX + 10f**.

No.	Type	Description	Unused	Used
313	53	4 f. + 10 f. orange & green	40	65

1948. Army Welfare Fund.

No.	Type	Description	Unused	Used
315	57	10 f. + 40 f. green & bistre	1·00	85
316		18 f. + 42 f. dp blue & bl	1·00	85

1949. Stamp Day. Type of France (Choiseul), optd **TUNISIE**.

No.	Type	Description	Unused	Used
317	278	15 f. + 5 f. black	90	1·25

58 Child in Cot

1949. Child Welfare Fund.

No.	Type	Description	Unused	Used
318	58	25 f. + 50 f. green	1·75	1·75

59 Oued Mellegue Barrage

1949. Tunisian Development.

No.	Type	Description	Unused	Used
319	59	15 f. black	2·50	65

60 Bird from Antique Mosaic  61 Globe, Mounted Postman and Sud Est Languedoc Airliner

1949. Air.

No.	Type	Description	Unused	Used
320	60	100 f. brown and green	3·00	75
321		200 f. black & blue (A)	5·00	1·75
322		200 f. black & blue (B)	5·00	2·00

In A the Arabic inscription is in two lines and in B it is in one line.

1949. 75th Anniv of U.P.U.

323	**61**	5 f. green on bl (postage)	1·25	1·10
324		15 f. brown on blue	1·25	1·10
325		15 f. blue on blue (air)	1·75	1·75

1949. Free French Association Fund. Surch Lorraine Cross and **FFL + 15F.**

326	**54**	10 f. + 15 f. red and blue	1·00	95

1950. Stamp Day. Type of France (Postman) optd **TUNISIE.**

327	**292**	12 f. + 3 f. green	1·50	1·50

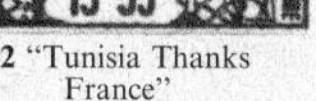

62 "Tunisia Thanks France" **63** Old Soldier

1950. Franco-Tunisian Relief Fund.

328	**62**	15 f. + 35 f. red	1·25	1·10
329		25 f. + 45 f. blue	1·25	1·10

1950. Veterans' Relief Fund.

330	**63**	25 f. + 25 f. blue	1·60	1·40

64 Horse (bas-relief) **65** Hermes of Berbera

1950. (a) Size $21\frac{1}{2} \times 17\frac{1}{2}$ mm.

331	**64**	10 c. blue	15	30
332		50 c. brown	10	30
333		1 f. violet	15	30
334		2 f. grey	20	20
335		3 f. brown	30	35
336		4 f. orange	25	30
337		5 f. green	20	10
338		8 f. blue	30	30
340		12 f. red	75	20
341		15 f. red	30	25
342		15 f. blue	40	10

(b) Size $22\frac{1}{2} \times 18\frac{3}{4}$ mm.

343	**64**	15 f. red	60	50
344		15 f. blue	60	55
345		30 f. blue	1·40	65

1950.

346	**65**	15 f. red	50	50
347		25 f. blue	50	35
348		50 f. green	1·75	35

1951. Stamp Day. Type of France (Sorting Van), but colour changed optd **TUNISIE.**

349	**300**	12 f. + 3 f. grey	2·25	2·50

66 Sleeping Child

1951. Child Welfare Fund.

350	**66**	30 f. + 15 f. blue	1·75	1·90

67 Gammarth National Cemetery **68** Panel from Great Mosque at Kairouan

1951. War Orphans' Fund.

351	**67**	30 f. + 10 f. blue	1·40	1·40

1952. Stamp Day. Type of France (Mail Coach), optd **TUNISIE.**

352	**319**	12 f. + 3 f. violet	80	80

1952. Army Welfare Fund. Inscr "OEUVRES SOCIALES DE L'ARMEE".

353	–	15 f. + 1 f. indigo and blue (postage)	70	60
354	**68**	50 f. + 10 f. green and black (air)	2·50	2·50

DESIGN: 15 f. Ornamental stucco, Bardo Palace.

69 Schoolboys clasping Hands **70** Charles Nicolle

1952. Holiday Camp Fund.

355	**69**	30 f. + 10 f. green	1·10	1·10

1952. Golden Jubilee of Tunisian Medical Sciences Society.

356	**70**	15 f. brown	1·10	80
357		30 f. blue	1·10	80

1952. Centenary of Military Medal. Type of France surch **Tunisie + 5F.**

358	**327**	15 f. + 5 f. green	75	1·25

1953. Stamp Day. Type of France (Count D'Argenson), optd **TUNISIE.**

359	**334**	12 f. + 3 f. red	1·25	1·25

71 Tower and Flags **72** Tozeur Mosque

1953. 1st International Fair, Tunis.

360	**71**	8 f. brown & deep brown	60	70
361		12 f. green and emerald	60	70
362		15 f. indigo and blue	60	70
363		18 f. deep violet & violet	60	70
364		30 f. red and carmine	65	70

1953. Air.

365	–	100 f. blue, turq & green	3·50	80
366	–	200 f. sepia, purple & brn	4·75	1·40
367	–	500 f. brown and blue	23·00	11·00
368	**72**	1000 f. green	40·00	22·00

DESIGNS: 100, 200 f. Monastir; 500 f. View of Korbous.

For similar stamps but without "R F" see Nos. 423/6.

1954. Stamp Day. Type of France (Lavallette), optd **TUNISIE.**

369	**346**	12 f. + 3 f. blue	1·00	80

73 Courtyard, Sousse **74** Sidi Bou Maklouf Mosque, Le Kef

1954.

370	**73**	50 c. green	10	30
371		1 f. red	10	20
372	–	2 f. purple	25	30
373	–	4 f. turquoise	30	35
374	–	5 f. violet	20	20
375	–	8 f. brown	30	30
376	–	10 f. green	30	35
377	–	12 f. brown	25	15
378	–	15 f. blue (18 × 22 mm)	1·50	20
386	–	15 f. blue ($17 \times 21\frac{1}{2}$ mm)	35	10
379	**74**	18 f. brown	1·25	70
380	–	20 f. blue	55	25
381	–	25 f. blue	70	30
382	–	30 f. purple	55	40
383	–	40 f. green	1·00	50
384	–	50 f. lilac	1·75	30
385	–	75 f. red	4·25	1·75

DESIGNS—As Type **73**: 2, 4 f. Takrouna ramparts; 5, 8 f. Dwellings and Mosque, Tatahouine; 10, 12 f. Cave dwellings, Matmata; 15 f. Street, Sidi-bou-said. As Type **74**: 20, 25 f. Genoese Fort, Tabarka; 30, 40 f. Bab-el-Khadra Gate, Tunis; 50, 75 f. Four-storey dwellings, Medenine.

For similar stamps but without "R F" see Nos. 406/22.

76 Bey of Tunisia **76a** Paris Balloon Post, 1870

1954.

387	**76**	8 f. deep blue and blue	45	55
388		12 f. indigo and blue	45	55
389		15 f. red and carmine	45	55
390		18 f. deep brown & brown	45	55
391		30 f. deep green & green	1·25	1·10

1955. Stamp Day.

392	**76a**	12 f. + 3 f. brown	90	90

77

1955. 50th Anniv of "L'Essor" (Tunisian Amateur Dramatic Society).

393	**77**	15 f. blue, red and orange	45	50

78 Tunisian Buildings and Rotary Emblem **79** Bey of Tunisia

1955. 50th Anniv of Rotary International.

394	**78**	12 f. deep brown & brown	45	55
395		15 f. brown and grey	45	55
396		18 f. lilac and violet	45	55
397		25 f. deep blue and blue	45	55
398		30 f. indigo and blue	1·25	1·10

1955.

399	**79**	15 f. blue	40	10

80 "Embroidery" **81** Bey of Tunisia

80a Francis of Taxis

1955. 3rd International Fair, Tunis.

400	**80**	5 f. lake	50	60
401		12 f. blue	50	60
402	–	15 f. green	55	65
403	–	18 f. red	60	65
404	–	20 f. violet	70	80
405	–	30 f. purple	70	80

DESIGNS: 15, 18 f. "Pottery"; 20, 30 f. "Jasmin sellers".

1956. Nos. 365/6 and 368/86 re-engraved without "R F".

406	50 c. green (postage)	10	30
407	1 f. red	10	10
408	2 f. purple	15	20
409	4 f. blue	15	20
410	5 f. violet	15	15
411	8 f. brown	15	30
412	10 f. green	15	10
413	12 f. brown	15	30
414	15 f. blue (18 × 22 mm)	1·25	40
415	15 f. blue ($17 \times 21\frac{1}{2}$ mm)	15	15
416	18 f. brown	25	30
417	20 f. blue	30	15
418	25 f. blue	25	10
419	30 f. purple	1·25	25
420	40 f. green	1·10	25
421	50 f. lilac	1·10	25
422	75 f. red	2·00	1·25
423	100 f. blue, turquoise and green (air)	1·90	85
424	200 f. sepia, purple & brown	3·75	1·40
425	500 f. brown and blue	7·50	4·25
426	1000 f. green	14·00	8·75

1956. Stamp Day.

427	**80a**	12 f. + 3 f. green	85	70

INDEPENDENT KINGDOM

1956. Autonomous Government.

428	**81**	5 f. blue	35	35
429	–	12 f. purple	35	35
430	**81**	15 f. red	35	35
431	–	18 f. grey	45	35
432	**81**	20 f. green	45	35
433	–	30 f. brown	90	40

DESIGN: 12, 18, 30 f. Tunisian girl releasing dove.

82 Farhat Hached **83** Market Scene

1956. Labour Day.

434	**82**	15 f. lake	30	30
435		30 f. blue	35	35

1956. Tunisian Products.

436	–	12 f. violet, purple & mauve	60	20
437	–	15 f. green, brown & bl	60	20
438	–	18 f. blue	90	35
439	–	20 f. brown	90	35
440	**83**	25 f. brown	1·25	55
441		30 f. blue	1·40	55

DESIGNS—VERT: 12 f. Bunch of grapes; 15 f. Sprig of olives; 18 f. Harvesting; 20 f. Man with basket containing wedding offering.

84 Pres. Habib Bourguiba **85** Pres. Bourguiba and Agricultural Workers

1957. 1st Anniv of Independence.

442	**84**	5 f. blue	20	20
443	**85**	12 f. pink	20	20
444	**84**	20 f. blue	30	20
445	**85**	25 f. green	35	20
446	**84**	30 f. brown	40	30
447	**85**	50 f. red	80	50

86 Dove and Handclasp

1957. 5th Int Confederation of Free Trade Unions Congress.

448	**86**	18 f. purple	35	35
449	–	20 f. red	40	40
450	**86**	25 f. green	40	40
451	–	30 f. blue	45	45

DESIGN—VERT: 20, 30 f. Handclasp and Labour Exchange.

INDEPENDENT REPUBLIC

نصف شهر الجيش ١٩٥٧

+

10f (87)

1957. Tunisian Army Fortnight. No. 417 optd with T **87.**

452	20 f. + 10 f. blue	55	55

88 Tunisian Soldiers and Flag

1957. Proclamation of Republic.

453	**88**	20 f. red	16·00	16·00
454		25 f. violet	16·00	16·00
455		30 f. brown	16·00	16·00

1957. 5th Int Fair, Tunis. As No. 404 but additionally inscr "5e FOIRE INTERNATIONALE" and Arabic inscriptions at sides, surch + **10 F.**

456	20 f. + 10 f. violet	45	45

90 Pres Bourguiba on Ile de la Galite **91** Tunisian Emblems and Map

1958. 6th Anniv of Exile of Pres. Bourguiba.
457 **90** 20 f. blue and brown 55 35
458 25 f. blue and violet 55 35

1958. 2nd Anniv of Independence.
459 **91** 20 f. green and brown 35 15
460 – 25 f. brown and blue 35 15
461 – 30 f. brown, deep brown & red 45 20
DESIGNS: 25 f. Mother and child; 30 f. Clenched fist holding Tunisian flag.
For 20 f. brown and blue see No. 464.

92 Andreas Vesalius (scientist) and A. ibn Khaldoun
93 Planting Olives

1958. Brussels International Exhibition.
462 **92** 30 f. green and bistre 45 20

1958. Labour Day.
463 **93** 20 f. multicoloured 45 45

1958. 3rd Anniv of Return of Pres. Bourguiba. As T **91** but with inscr altered.
464 **91** 20 f. brown and blue 40 20

94
95 Pres. Bourguiba

1958. 1st Anniv of Proclamation of Tunisian Republic.
465 **94** 5 f. purple and bistre 45 20
466 10 f. dp green & lt green 45 20
467 15 f. brown and orange 45 20
468 20 f. violet, olive & yellow 45 20
469 25 f. purple 45 20

1958. Pres. Bourguiba's 55th Birthday.
470 **95** 20 f. purple and violet 35 20

96 Fishermen with Catch
97 U.N.E.S.C.O. Headquarters, Paris

1958. 6th International Fair.
471 **96** 25 f. purple, red & green 55 35

1958. Inaug of U.N.E.S.C.O. Building.
472 **97** 25 f. myrtle 60 35

98 "Shedding the Veil"
99 Hand holding Plant

1959. Emancipation of Tunisian Women.
473 **98** 20 m turquoise 45 30

1959. 25th Anniv of Neo-Destour (Nationalist Party) and Victory Congress.
474 **99** 5 m. red, brown & purple 30 10
475 – 10 m. multicoloured 35 15
476 – 20 m. blue 40 20
477 – 30 m. blue, turq & brown 65 40
DESIGNS—VERT: 10 m. Tunisians with flaming torch and flag on shield; 20 m. Pres. Bourguiba in exile at Borj le Boeuf, 1954. HORIZ: 30 m. Pres. Bourguiba and Borj le Boeuf, 1934.

100 "Tunisia"

1959. 3rd Anniv of Independence.
478 **100** 50 m. multicoloured 65 35

101 Tunisian Horseman
102 "Freedom"

1959. Designs as T **101**.
479 ½ m. brown, green & emerald 70 15
480 1 m. bistre and blue 10 10
481 2 m. brown, yellow & blue 15 10
482 3 m. myrtle 10 10
483 4 m. brown 30 15
484 5 m. myrtle 20 10
485 6 m. violet 20 15
486 8 m. purple 65 30
487 10 m. red, green and bistre 20 10
487a 12 m. violet and bistre 65 20
488 15 m. blue 60 10
489 16 m. green 30 20
490 20 m. turquoise 1·00 30
491 20 m. purple, olive & myrtle 2·25 30
492 25 m. blue, brown & turq 30 20
493 30 m. brown, green & turq 45 10
494 40 m. green 1·60 20
495 45 m. green 70 30
496 50 m. multicoloured 90 20
497 60 m. brown and green 1·25 35
498 70 m. multicoloured 1·40 50
499 75 m. brown 1·25 55
500 90 m. brown, green & blue 1·60 55
501 95 m. multicoloured 1·90 1·00
502 100 m. multicoloured 2·00 90
503 200 m. red, bistre and blue 5·00 2·50
504 ½ d. brown 16·00 6·75
505 1 d. ochre and green 25·00 13·50
DESIGNS—VERT: ½ m. Ain Draham; 2 m. Camel-driver; 3 m. Saddler's shop; 5 m. Type **101**; 6 m. Weavers; 8 m. Gafsa; 10 m. Woman holding pomegranates; 12 m. Turner; 20 m. (No. 491), Gabes; 40 m. Kairouan; 70 m. Carpet weaver; 75 m. Nabeul vase; 95 m. Olive-gatherer; ½ d. Sbeitla. HORIZ: 1 m. Kairouan environs; 4 m. Medenine; 15 m. Monastir; 16 m. Tunis; 20 m. (No. 490), Room in Arab house, Sidi-Bou-Said; 25 m. Sfax; 30 m. Aqueduct, Medjerda Valley; 45 m. Bizerta; 50 m. Djerba; 60 m. Le Jerid; 90 m. Le Kef; 100 m. Sidi-bou-Said highway; 200 m. Old port of Sfax; 1 d. Beja ploughman.

1959. Africa Freedom Day.
506 **102** 40 m. brown and blue 50 35

103 Postman
104 Clenched Hands

1959. Stamp Day.
507 **103** 20 m. + 5 m. brown & orge 45 45

1959. U.N. Day.
508 **104** 80 m. brown, blue & pur 65 45

105
106 Dancer and Coin

1959. Red Crescent Day.
509 **105** 10 m. + 5 m. multicoloured 35 35

1959. 1st Anniv of Tunisian Central Bank.
510 **106** 50 m. black and blue 50 50

107 "Uprooted Tree"
108 Camel Rider telephoning

1960. World Refugee Year. Inscr "ANNEE MONDIALE DES REFUGIES 1959–1960".
511 **107** 20 m. blue 40 20
512 – 40 m. black and purple 50 35
DESIGN—HORIZ: 40 m. Doves.

1960. Stamp Day.
513 **108** 60 m. + 5 m. orange, blue and olive 80 80

109 Pres. Bourguiba signing Promulgation
110 Fair Emblems

1960. Promulgation of Constitution.
514 **109** 20 m. red, brown & green 40 35

1960. 5th Sousse National Fair.
515 **110** 100 m. black and green 65 45

111 President Bourguiba
112 Jamboree Emblems

1960.
516 **111** 20 m. black 20 10
517 30 m. black, red and blue 35 10
518 40 m. black, red & green 45 20

1960. 4th Arab Scout Jamboree, Tunis.
519 **112** 10 m. turquoise 35 35
520 – 25 m. purple, red & green 40 35
521 – 30 m. lake, violet & green 60 35
522 – 40 m. black, blue and red 65 40
523 – 60 m. violet, pur & sepia 1·25 55
DESIGNS: 25 m. Saluting hand with scouts as fingers; 30 m. Camp bugler; 40 m. Scout peacock badge; 60 m. Scout by camp fire.

113 Cyclist in Stadium
114

1960. Olympic Games.
524 **113** 5 m. brown and olive 30 25
525 – 10 m. purple, green & bl 35 30
526 – 15 m. carmine and red 35 30
527 – 25 m. slate and blue 45 40
528 – 50 m. blue and green 85 65
DESIGNS: 10 m. Flowers composed of Olympic rings; 15 m. Girl with racquet; 25 m. Runner; 50 m. Handball player.

1960. 5th World Forestry Congress, Seattle.
529 **114** 8 m. lake, green and blue 35 15
530 – 15 m. green 40 20
531 – 25 m. red, green & violet 65 30
532 – 50 m. turquoise, brn & grn 1·10 50
DESIGNS: 15 m. Removing bark from tree; 25 m. Tree within leaf; 50 m. Diamond pattern featuring palm.

115 U.N. Emblem and People's Arms
116 Dove of Peace

1960. U.N. Day.
533 **115** 40 m. blue, red and black 65 45

1961. 5th Anniv of Independence.
534 **116** 20 m. blue, bistre & pur 30 20
535 30 m. brown, violet & blue 35 20
536 40 m. ultram, bl & grn 55 40
537 – 75 m. blue, mauve & olive 80 45
DESIGN: 75 m. Globe and Arms of Tunisia.

117 Tunisian Animals and Map of Africa
118 Stamps and Magnifier

1961. Africa Day and 3rd Anniv of Accra Conference. Inscr "JOURNEE DE L'AFRIQUE 15.4.1961".
538 **117** 40 m. green, brown and bistre 35 20
539 – 60 m. black, brn & turq 40 30
540 – 100 m. violet, emerald and grey 70 45
541 – 200 m. brown & orange 1·40 1·00
DESIGNS (all showing outline of Africa): 50 m. Profiles of Negress and Arab woman; 100 m. Masks and "Africa Day" in Arabic; 200 m. Clasped hands.

1961. Stamp Day. Inscr "JOURNEE DU TIMBRE 1961". Multicoloured.
542 12 m. + 4 m. Kerkennah dancer and costume of stamps 45 45
543 15 m. + 5 m. Mobile postal delivery 60 60
544 20 m. + 6 m. Type **118** 65 65
545 50 m. + 5 m. Postman in shirt depicting stamps 80 80
The 12 m. and 20 m. are vert and the rest horiz.

119 "Celebration"
120 Dag Hammarskjoeld

1961. National Day.
546 **119** 25 m. brown, red & violet 45 15
547 – 50 m. brown, choc & grn 45 20
548 – 95 m. mauve, brown & bl 65 40
DESIGNS: 50 m. Family celebrating in street; 95 m. Girl astride crescent moon.

1961. U.N. Day.
549 **120** 40 m. blue 60 35

121 Arms of Tunisia
122 Mosquito in Web

1962. 10th Anniv of Independence Campaign. Arms in red, yellow, blue and black.
550 **121** 1 m. yellow and black 10 10
551 2 m. pink and black 15 15
552 3 m. blue and black 15 15
553 6 m. grey and black 20 20

1962. Malaria Eradication. Inscr "LE MONDE UNI CONTRE LE PALUDISME".
554 **122** 20 m. brown 45 30
555 – 30 m. brown, grn & choc 45 30
556 – 40 m. red, green & brown 80 35
DESIGNS—VERT: 30 m. "Horseman" attacking mosquito; 40 m. Hands destroying mosquito.

123 African

1962. Africa Day. Inscr "JOURNEE DE L'AFRIQUE 1962".
557 **123** 50 m. brown and buff 55 35
558 – 10 m. multicoloured 80 45
DESIGN: 100 m. Symbolic figure clasping "Africa".

124 Dancer

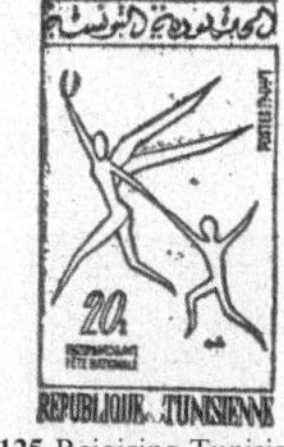
125 Rejoicing Tunisians

1962. May Day. Inscr "FETE DU TRAVAIL 1962".
559 **124** 40 m. multicoloured . . . 40 20
560 – 60 m. brown 45 30
DESIGN: 60 m. Worker with pneumatic drill.

1962. National Day.
561 **125** 20 m. black and salmon . 50 35

126 Gabes Costume

127 U.N. Emblem and Tunisian Flag

1962. Republic Festival. Regional Costumes. Multicoloured.
562 5 m. Type **126** 55 20
563 10 m. Mahdia 65 35
564 15 m. Kairouan 90 45
565 20 m. Hammamet . . . . . . 1·10 55
566 25 m. Djerba . . . . 1·25 55
567 30 m. As 10 m. . . . . . . 1·25 65
568 40 m. As 20 m. . . . . . . 1·40 65
569 50 m. Type **126** . . . . . . 1·40 85
570 55 m. Ksar Hellal . . . . . . 2·50 1·00
571 60 m. Tunis . . . . 3·00 1·40

1962. U.N. Day.
572 **127** 20 m. red, black & grey . 35 30
573 – 30 m. multicoloured . . . 40 30
574 – 40 m. blue, black & brown 65 35
DESIGNS—HORIZ: 30 m. "Plant" with three leaves and globe. VERT: 40 m. Globe and dove.

128 A. Q. Chabbi (poet)

129 Pres. Bourguiba

1962. Aboul Qasim Chabbi Commemoration.
575 **128** 15 m. violet 35 20

1962.
576 **129** 20 m. blue 15 15
577 30 m. red 15 10
578 40 m. green 20 15

130 Hached Telephone Exchange

131 Runners

1962. Modernisation of Telephone System.
579 **130** 5 m. multicoloured . . . 30 20
580 – 10 m. multicoloured . . . 35 20
581 – 15 m. multicoloured . . . 50 35
582 – 50 m. flesh, brown & blk . 80 50
583 – 100 m. blue, purple & blk 2·00 90
584 – 200 m. multicoloured . . 2·75 1·40
DESIGNS: 10 m. Carthage Telephone Exchange; 15 m. Aerial equipment; 50 m. Telephone switch-board operators; 100 m. Telephone equipment as human figure; 200 m. Belvedere Telephone Exchange.

1963. 13th International Military Sports Council Cross-country Championships.
585 **131** 30 m. brown, green & blk 60 45

MINIMUM PRICE

The minimum price quoted is 10p which represents a handling charge rather than a basis for valuing common stamps. For further notes about prices, see introductory pages.

132 Dove with Wheatear and Globe

133 Centenary Emblem

1963. Freedom from Hunger.
586 **132** 20 m. blue and brown . . 30 20
587 – 40 m. purple and brown . 40 20
DESIGN: 40 m. Child taking nourishment.

1963. Red Cross Centenary.
588 **133** 20 m. red, grey & brown 45 20

1963. U.N. Day. Nos. 542/5 optd **1963 O.N.U.** in English and Arabic.
589 12 m. +4 m. multicoloured . 30 30
590 15 m. +5 m. multicoloured . 35 35
591 20 m. +6 m. multicoloured . 40 40
592 50 m. +5 m. multicoloured . 65 65

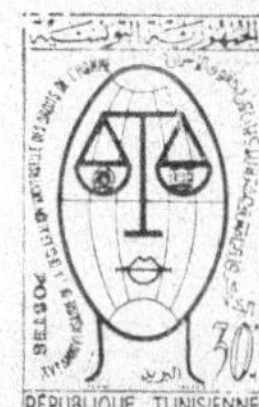
135 "Miss World"

136 "Out of Reach"

1963. 15th Anniv of Declaration of Human Rights.
593 **135** 30 m. brown and green . 45 30

1964. Nubian Monuments Preservation.
594 **136** 50 m. ochre, brown & blue 45 30

137 "Unsettled Forecast"

138 Mohamed Ali (trade union leader)

1964. World Meteorological Day.
595 **137** 40 m. mauve, bl & brn . . 45 20

1964. 70th Birth Anniv of Mohamed Ali.
596 **138** 50 m. purple 45 35

139 Africa within Flower

140 Pres. Bourguiba

1964. 1st Anniv of Addis Ababa Conference of the Organization of African Unity.
597 **139** 60 m. multicoloured . . . 50 30

1964. National Day.
598 **140** 20 m. blue 15 10
599 30 m. brown 20 10

141 "Bizerte" ("ship")

142 Fulvous Babbler

1964. Neo-Destour Congress, Bizerta.
600 **141** 50 m. green and black . . 40 30

1965. Air. Tunisian Birds. Multicoloured.
601 25 m. Type **142** . . . . . . 1·90 50
602 55 m. Great grey strike . . . 2·75 75
603 55 m. Cream-coloured courser 3·00 95
604 100 m. Chaffinch . . . . . . 3·50 1·10
605 150 m. Greater flamingoes . . 6·25 2·40
606 200 m. Barbary partridge . . 9·75 2·75
607 300 m. Common roller . . . 15·00 5·25
608 500 m. Houbara bustard . . 19·00 6·25
SIZES—As Type **142**: 55 m. (both). Others, 23 × 32½ mm.

143 Early Telegraphist and Aerial Mast

144 Carthaginian Coin

1965. I.T.U. Centenary.
609 **143** 55 m. blue and black . . . 50 30

1965. Festival of Popular Arts, Carthage.
610 **144** 5 m. purple and green . . 15 10
611 10 m. purple and yellow . 30 20
612 75 m. purple and blue . . 65 20

145 Girl reading Book

146 Joined Hooks

1965. Opening of Students' Home, Tunis.
613 **145** 25 m. blue, black and red . 30 20
614 40 m. black, blue and red . 40 20
615 50 m. red, black and blue . 45 30

1965. International Co-operation Year.
617 **146** 40 m. blue, purple & blk . 45 25

147 Women bathing

149 Independence

148 Pres. Bourguiba and Hands

1966. Mineral Springs. Inscr "EAUX MINERALES".
618 **147** 10 m. red, ochre & grey . 30 20
619 – 20 m. multicoloured . . . 40 30
620 – 30 m. red, blue & yellow . 45 35
621 – 100 m. olive, yellow & bl . 1·10 55
DESIGNS: 20 m. Man pouring water; 30 m. Woman pouring water; 100 m. Mountain and fronds of tree.

1966. 10th Anniv of Independence.
622 **148** 5 m. lilac and blue . . . 15 10
623 10 m. green and blue . . 20 15
624 **149** 25 m. multicoloured . . . 20 15
625 – 40 m. multicoloured . . . 55 20
626 – 60 m. multicoloured . . . 80 35
DESIGNS—As Type **149**—HORIZ: 40 m. "Development". VERT: 60 m. "Promotion of Culture" ("man" draped in books, palette, musical instruments, etc.).

150 Sectional Map of Africa

152 "Athletics"

151 U.N.E.S.C.O. Emblem of the Muses

1966. 2nd U.N. African Regional Cartographic Conference, Tunisia.
627 **150** 15 m. multicoloured . . . 30 20
628 35 m. multicoloured . . . 35 20
629 40 m. multicoloured . . . 50 35

1966. 20th Anniv of U.N.E.S.C.O.
631 **151** 100 m. brown and black . . 85 35

1967. Publicity for Mediterranean Games (September, 1967).
632 **152** 20 m. brown, blue & red . 20 15
633 30 m. black and blue . . 40 30

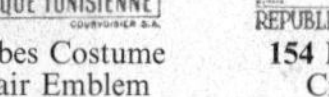
153 Gabes Costume and Fair Emblem

154 Emblems of Civilisation

1967. "Expo 67" World Fair, Montreal. T **154** and earlier designs redrawn as T **153**.
634 – 50 m. mult (As No. 566) . 35 15
635 **153** 75 m. multicoloured . . . 50 30
636 **154** 100 m. green, blk & turq . 80 30
637 110 m. red, sepia & blue . 95 40
638 – 155 m. mult (As No. 605) 1·75 45

155 Tunisian Pavilion, Pres. Bourguiba and Map

1967. "National Day at World Fair, Montreal".
639 **155** 65 m. purple and red . . 40 35
640 – 105 m. brown, red & blue 50 35
641 – 120 m. blue 60 40
642 – 200 m. black, red & pur . 1·25 50
DESIGNS: 105 m. As Type **155**, but with profile bust of Pres. Bourguiba. Tunisian pavilion (different view) with: 120 m. Silhouette and 200 m. Bust of Pres. Bourguiba.

156 "Tunisia" holding Clover

158 Bas-relief from Statue of Apollo

157 Tennis Club

1967. 10th Anniv of Republic. Multicoloured.
643 25 m. Type **156** 20 15
644 40 m. Woman releasing doves (vert) 35 15

1967. Mediterranean Games, Tunis.
645 **157** 5 m. red and green . . . 20 20
646 – 10 m. multicoloured . . . 20 15
647 – 15 m. black 35 20
648 – 35 m. turq, pur & blk . . 45 20
649 – 75 m. green, violet & red . 80 40
DESIGNS—VERT: 10 m. "Spring Triumphs" (squared panel). HORIZ: 15 m. Olympic swimming pool; 35 m. Sports Palace; 75 m. Olympic stadium.

1967. Tunisian History. Punic period.
650 **158** 15 m. red, black & green . 30 20
651 – 20 m. flesh, red & blue . 35 20
652 – 25 m. brown and olive . . 45 20
653 – 30 m. red and grey . . . 45 20
654 – 40 m. lemon, yell & pur . 50 20
655 – 60 m. multicoloured . . . 75 30
DESIGNS: 20 m. Sea horseman (Kerkouane medallion); 25 m. Hannibal (bronze bust); 30 m. "The Sacrifice" (votive stele); 40 m. Hamilcar (coin); 60 m. Glass funeral pendant mask.

159 "Human Rights"

160 "Electronic Man"

1968. Human Rights Year.

656 **159** 25 m. red 40 35
657 60 m. blue 45 20

1968. Electronics in Postal Service.

658 **160** 25 m. blue, brown & pur . 35 30
659 40 m. black, brown & grn 35 30
660 60 m. purple, slate & blue 45 35

161 "Doctor and Patient" **162** Arabian Jasmine

1968. 20th Anniv of W.H.O.

661 **161** 25 m. green & turquoise . 40 35
662 60 m. red and lake 45 35

1968. Tunisian Flowers. Multicoloured.

663 5 m. Flax 20 15
664 6 m. Indian shot 20 15
665 10 m. Pomegranate 30 15
666 12 m. Type **162** 30 15
667 15 m. Raponticum 35 15
668 20 m. Geranium 40 20
669 25 m. Madonna lily 40 30
670 40 m. Almond 60 30
671 50 m. Capers 80 45
672 60 m. Ariana rose . . . . . . 1·25 70
673 100 m. Jasmine . . . . 1·90 1·10

163 Globe on "Sunflower" **164** Flautist

1968. Red Crescent Day.

674 **163** 15 m. red, green & blue . 35 30
675 – 25 m. red and purple . . . 40 30
DESIGN: 25 m. Red crescent on wings of dove.

1968. Stamp Day.

676 **164** 20 m. multicoloured . . . 35 20
677 50 m. multicoloured . . . 40 35

165 Golden Jackal **166** Worker

1968. Fauna. Multicoloured.

678 5 m. Type **165** 20 15
679 8 m. North African crested porcupine 30 20
680 10 m. Dromedary 40 20
681 15 m. Dorcas gazelle 75 20
682 20 m. Fennec fox . . . . . . 1·25 45
683 25 m. Algerian hedgehog . . . 1·50 55
684 40 m. Horse . . . . 1·90 80
685 60 m. Wild boar . . . . 2·50 1·25

1969. 50th Anniv of I.L.O. Multicoloured.

686 25 m. Type **166** 35 30
687 60 m. Youth and girl holding "May 1" banner 50 35

167 Musicians and Veiled Dancers **168** Tunisian Arms

1969. Stamp Day.

688 **167** 100 m. multicoloured . . 70 35

1969.

689 **168** 15 m. multicoloured . . . 20 20
690 25 m. multicoloured . . . 30 20
691 40 m. multicoloured . . . 35 20
692 60 m. multicoloured . . . 40 20

169 "Industrial Development" **170** Lute

1969. 5th Anniv of African Development Bank.

693 **169** 60 m. multicoloured 40 30

1970. Musical Instruments. Multicoloured.

694 25 m. Type **170** 45 35
695 50 m. Zither 55 35
696 70 m. Rehab 80 35
697 90 m. Naghrat (drums) . . . 1·00 35
Nos. 695 and 697 are horiz, size 33 × 22 mm.

171 Nurse, Caduceus and Flags **172** New U.P.U. Headquarters Building

1970. 6th North-African Maghreb Medical Seminar, Tunis.

698 **171** 25 m. multicoloured . . . 35 20

1970. New U.P.U. Headquarters Building, Berne.

699 **172** 25 m. brown and red . . 40 20

173 Mounted Postman

1970. Stamp Day. Multicoloured.

700 25 m. Type **173** 20 20
701 35 m. "Postmen of yesterday and today" (23 × 38 mm) . . . 35 20

174 U.N. Emblem, "N" and Dove forming "O.N.U." **175** "The Flower-seller"

1970. 25th Anniv of United Nations.

702 **174** 40 m. multicoloured . . . 40 20

1970. "Tunisian Life" (1st series). Multicoloured.

703 20 m. Type **175** 20 15
704 25 m. "The husband's third day of marriage" 30 20
705 35 m. "The Perfumer" . . . 45 35
706 40 m. "The Fish-seller" . . . 50 35
707 85 m. "The Coffee-house keeper" 80 35
See also Nos. 715/18, 757/62 and 819/23.

176 Lenin **177** Dish Aerial and Flags

1970. Birth Centenary of Lenin.

709 **176** 60 m. lake . . . . 1·25 35

1971. Maghreban Posts and Telecommunciations Co-ordination.

710 **177** 25 m. multicoloured . . . 40 35

178 U.N. Building and Symbol **179** Globe and Satellites

1971. Racial Equality Year.

711 **178** 80 m. multicoloured . . . 45 30

1971. World Telecommunications Day.

712 **179** 70 m. multicoloured . . . 40 20

180 Moon, Earth and Satellites

1971. "Conquest of Space".

713 **180** 15 m. black and blue . . . 35 20
714 – 90 m. black and red . . . 60 30
DESIGN: 90 m. Space allegory.

181 "The Pottery Dealer" **182** Pres. Bourguiba

1971. "Tunisian Life" (2nd series). Multicoloured.

715 25 m. Type **181** 35 20
716 30 m. "The Esparto dealer" . . 35 20
717 40 m. "The Poulterer" 45 20
718 50 m. "The Dyer" 55 30

1971. 8th P.S.D. Destourian Socialist Party Congress, Tunis. Multicoloured.

720 25 m. Type **182** 20 20
721 30 m. Bourguiba in bed, 1938 (horiz) 20 20
722 50 m. Bourguiba acclaimed . . 35 30
723 80 m. Bourguiba—"Builder of the Nation" (horiz) 45 30
SIZES: 30 m., 80 m. 13½ × 14; 50 m. As Type **182**.

183 Shah Mohammed Riza Pahlavi and Achaemenidian Effigy **184** Pimento

1971. 2500th Anniv of Persian Empire. Mult.

724 25 m. Type **183** 30 20
725 50 m. "King Bahram-Gur hunting" (14th-century) . . 35 20
726 100 m. "Coronation of Louhrasap" (Persian 11th-century miniature) 60 30

1971. "Flowers, Fruits and Folklore". Mult.

728 1 m. Type **184** 10 10
729 2 m. Mint 20 15
730 5 m. Pear 35 20
731 25 m. Laurel rose 40 30
732 60 m. Quince 80 20
733 100 m. Grapefruit . . . . . 1·50 35
Each design includes a scene from Tunisian folklore.

185 "The Musicians of Kerkena" **186** Telephone

1971. Stamp Day.

735 **185** 50 m. multicoloured . . . 40 20

1971. Pan-African Telecommunications Network.

736 **186** 95 m. multicoloured . . . 50 45

187 U.N.I.C.E.F. Emblem **189** Olive-tree Emblem

188 Rialto Bridge, Venice

1971. 25th Anniv of U.N.I.C.E.F.

737 **187** 110 m. multicoloured . . . 50 35

1971. U.N.E.S.C.O. "Save Venice" Campaign. Multicoloured.

738 25 m. Gondolier (vert) 35 20
739 30 m. De Medici and Palace (vert) 40 20
740 50 m. Prow of gondola (vert) . 45 35
741 80 m. Type **188** 80 35

1972. World Olive-oil Year.

742 **189** 60 m. multicoloured . . . 40 20

190 Tunisian reading Book **191** Heart Emblem

1972. International Book Year.

743 **190** 90 m. multicoloured . . . 50 40

1972. World Health Day. Multicoloured.

744 25 m. Type **191** 35 20
745 60 m. Heart within "hour-glass" 55 35

192 "Old Age" **193** "Only One Earth"

1972. Tunisian Red Crescent.

746 **192** 10 m. + 10 m. violet & red 35 30
747 – 75 m. + 10 m. brown & red 50 35
DESIGN: 75 m. Mother and Child ("Child Care").

1972. U.N. Environmental Conservation Conf, Stockholm.

748 **193** 60 m. green and brown . 50 20

194 Hurdling **195** Chessboard

1972. Olympic Games, Munich.

749 – 5 m. multicoloured . . . 10 10
750 **194** 15 m. multicoloured . . . 15 10
751 – 20 m. black, green & gold 15 10
752 – 25 m. multicoloured . . . 15 15
753 – 60 m. multicoloured . . . 35 20
754 – 80 m. multicoloured . . . 45 30
DESIGNS—VERT: 5 m. Handball; 20 m. Athletes saluting. HORIZ: 25 m. Football; 60 m. Swimming; 80 m. Running.

1972. 20th Chess Olympiad, Skopje, Yugoslavia.

756 **195** 60 m. multicoloured . . . 1·25 55

196 "The Fisherman"

1972. "Tunisian Life" (3rd series). Multicoloured.

757		5 m. Type **196**	20	15
758		10 m. "The Basket-maker" . .	20	15
759		25 m. "The Musician"	30	15
760		50 m. "The Berber Bride" . .	55	20
761		60 m. "The Flower-seller" . .	80	20
762		80 m. "The Mystic"	1·10	40

197 New P.T.T. H.Q., Tunis

1972. Stamp Day.

764	**197**	25 m. multicoloured . . .	30	20

198 Dome of the Rock, Jerusalem

1973. Dome of the Rock Commemoration.

765	**198**	25 m. multicoloured . . .	40	30

199 Globe and Beribboned Pen

1973. 9th Writers' Congress and 11th Poetry Festival. Multicoloured.

766		25 m. Type **199**	20	20
767		60 m. Lyre emblem	35	20

200 Heads of Family

201 Figures "10" and Bird feeding Young

1973. Family Planning. Multicoloured.

768		20 m. Type **200**	20	20
769		25 m. Family profiles and bird	35	30

1973. 10th Anniv of World Food Programme. Multicoloured.

770		25 m. Type **201**	60	20
771		60 m. Symbolic "10"	60	20

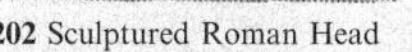

202 Sculptured Roman Head

203 Red Crescent Nurse

1973. U.N.E.S.C.O. "Save Carthage" Campaign. Multicoloured.

772		5 m. Type **202**	30	20
773		25 m. Carthagian mosaics . .	45	35
774		30 m. "Cycle of mosaics" . .	45	35
775		40 m. "Goodwill" stele (vert)	60	35
776		60 m. Preacher's hand (from Korba statue)	70	35
777		75 m. "Malga" (17th-century potsherd) (vert)	85	40

1973. Tunisian Red Crescent.

779	**203**	25 m. + 10 m. multicoloured	45	35
780	–	60 m. + 10 m. red & grey	65	35

DESIGN—HORIZ: 60 m. Arms of blood donors.

204 "World Telecommunications"

205 Smiling Youth

1973. 5th World Telecommunications Day. Multicoloured.

781		60 m. Type **204**	35	20
782		75 m. "The Universe"	40	20

1973. 1st Pan-African Festival of Youth. Multicoloured.

783		25 m. Festival Map	35	30
784		40 m. Type **205**	40	30

206 Scout Badge

1973. International Scouting.

785	**206**	25 m. multicoloured . . .	35	30

207 "Rover" in Car

1973. 2nd Pan-Arab Rover Rally.

786	**207**	60 m. multicoloured . . .	40	35

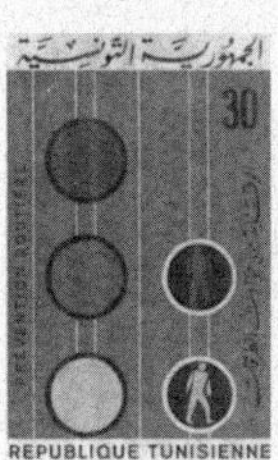

208 Traffic Lights

209 Winged Camel

1973. Road Safety. Multicoloured.

787		25 m. Motorway junction (horiz)	35	30
788		30 m. Type **208**	40	30

1973. Stamp Day. Multicoloured.

789		10 m. Peacock ("collectors pride") (horiz)	35	20
790		65 m. Type **209**	40	35

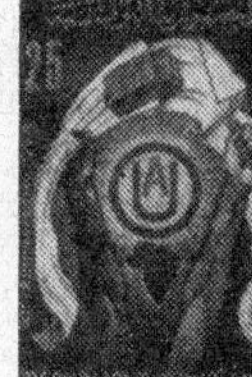

210 Copernicus

211 O.A.U. Emblems within Arms

1973. 500th Birth Anniv of Copernicus.

791	**210**	60 m. multicoloured . . .	1·25	35

1973. 10th Anniv of Organization of African Unity.

792	**211**	25 m. multicoloured . . .	40	20

212 Interpol Emblem and Handclasp

213 Flower Offering

1973. 50th Anniv of International Criminal Police Organization (Interpol).

793	**212**	65 m. multicoloured . . .	45	35

1973. 25th Anniv of Declaration of Human Rights.

794	**213**	60 m. multicoloured . . .	55	35

214 W.M.O. H.Q., Geneva

1973. W.M.O. Centenary Multicoloured.

795		25 m. Type **214**	40	20
796		60 m. Earth and emblems . .	45	30

215 President Bourguiba, 1934

216 Scientist using Microscope

1974. 40th Anniv of Neo-Destour Party.

797	**215**	15 m. purple, red & black .	20	20
798	–	25 m. brown, orge & blk	20	20
799	–	60 m. blue, red and black	30	20
800	–	75 m. brown, mve & blk	35	20
801	–	100 m. green, orge & blk	45	35

DESIGNS: Nos. 798/801, Various portraits of Pres. Bourguiba (founder), similar to Type **215**.

1974. 6th Africn Micro-Palaeontologica Conference, Tunis.

803	**216**	60 m. multicoloured . . .	1·40	60

217 "Blood Donation"

218 Telephonist holding Globe

1974. Tunisian Red Crescent. Multicoloured.

804		25 m. + 10 m. Type **217** . . .	35	35
805		75 m. + 10 m. "Blood Transfusion"	45	45

1974. Inauguration of International Automatic Telephone Service. Multicoloured.

806		15 m. Type **218**	20	20
807		60 m. Telephone dial	45	35

219 Population Emblems

1974. World Population Year.

808	**219**	110 m. multicoloured . . .	55	35

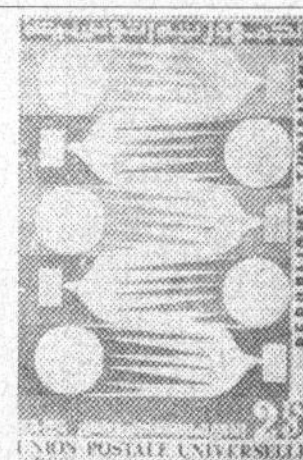

220 Pres. Bourguiba and Emblem

222 "Carrier-pigeons"

221 Aircraft crossing Globe

1974. Destourian Socialist Party Congress.

809	**220**	25 m. blue, turq & blk . .	20	20
810	–	60 m. red, yellow & black	30	25
811	–	200 m. purple, grn & blk .	90	50

DESIGNS—HORIZ: 60 m. Pres. Bourguiba and sunflower; 200 m. Pres. Bourguiba and sunflower.

1974. 25th Anniv of Tunisian Aviation.

813	**221**	60 m. multicoloured . . .	45	35

1974. Centenary of U.P.U. Multicoloured.

814		25 m. Type **222**	35	25
815		60 m. Handclasp	45	30

223 Bardo Palace as "Ballot Box"

224 Postman with Parcels on Head

1974. Legislative and Presidential Elections.

816	**223**	25 m. blue, green & blk .	35	30
817	–	100 m. black and orange .	50	35

DESIGN: 100 m. Pres. Bourguiba on poll card.

1974. Stamp Day.

818	**224**	75 m. multicoloured . . .	45	20

225 "The Water-carrier"

226 Stylised Bird

1975. "Scenes from Tunisian Life" (4th series). Multicoloured.

819		5 m. Type **225**	15	15
820		15 m. "The Scent Sprinkler" .	20	20
821		25 m. "The Washer-women" .	20	20
822		60 m. "The Potter"	35	20
823		110 m. "The Fruit-seller" . .	85	50

1975. 13th Arab Engineers' Union Conference, Tunis. Multicoloured.

825		25 m. Skyscraper and scaffolding (vert)	20	20
826		65 m. Type **226**	75	30

227 Gold Coffee-pot and Tray

1975. Handicrafts. Multicoloured.

827		10 m. Type **227**	20	20
828		15 m. Horseman and saddlery (embroidery)	20	20
829		25 m. Still life (painting) . . .	30	20
830		30 m. Bird-cage (fine-crafts) (vert)	35	20
831		40 m. Silver head-dress (jewellery) (vert)	35	20
832		60 m. Textile patterns	55	30

228 Man and Scales **229** "Telecommunications"

1975. Tunisian Red Crescent Campaign against Malnutrition.
833 **228** 50 m. + 10 m. mult . . . 40 35

1975. 7th World Telecommunications Day.
834 **229** 50 m. multicoloured . . . 30 20

230 Allegory of Victory **231** Tunisian Woman

1975. 20th Anniv of "Victory" (Return of Bourguiba). Multicoloured.
835 25 m. Type **230** 20 20
836 65 m. Return of President Bourguiba (horiz) 35 20

1975. International Women's Year.
837 **231** 110 m. multicoloured . . 55 30

232 Children on Road Crossing

1975. Road Safety Campaign.
838 **232** 25 m. multicolured 20 20

233 Djerba

1975. "Tunisia, Yesterday and Today" (1st series). Multicoloured.
839 10 m. Type **233** 20 20
840 15 m. Tunis 20 20
841 20 m. Monastir 20 20
842 65 m. Sousse 45 30
843 500 m. Tozeur . . . . 3·75 35
844 1 d. Kairouan . . . . 6·25 2·50
See also Nos. 864/7.

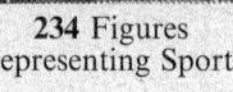
234 Figures representing Sport **235** Bouquet of Flowers

1975. 7th Mediterranean Games, Algiers. Multicoloured.
845 25 m. Type **234** 20 20
846 50 m. "Ship of sport" (horiz) . 35 20

1975. Stamp Day.
847 **235** 100 m. multicoloured . . 45 20

236 College Building

1975. Centenary of Sadiki College.
848 **236** 25 m. multicoloured . . . 30 20

237 "Duck" **238** Early and Modern Telephones

1976. Tunisian Mosaics. Multicoloured.
849 5 m. Type **237** 30 20
850 10 m. Fish 30 20
851 25 m. Lioness (40 × 27 mm) . 55 45
852 60 m. Gorgon (40 × 27 mm) . 60 45
853 75 m. Circus spectators (27 × 40 mm) 65 45
854 100 m. Virgil (27 × 40 mm) . 1·25 45

1976. Telephone Centenary.
856 **238** 150 m. multicoloured . . 55 30

239 Figures "20" and Banners **240** Blind Man with Stick

1976. 20th Anniv of Independence. Mult.
857 40 m. Type **239** 20 20
858 100 m. Figures "20" and flag emblem 40 20
859 150 m. Floral allegory of "Tunisia" 60 30

1976. World Health Day.
861 **240** 100 m. black and red . . 45 20

241 Blood Donation **242** "Urban Development"

1976. Tunisian Red Crescent.
862 **241** 40 m. + 10 m. mult . . . 40 30

1976. "Habitat" Human Settlements Conference, Vancouver.
863 **242** 40 m. multicoloured . . . 30 20

243 Henna Tradition

1976. "Tunisia, Yesterday and Today" (2nd series). Multicoloured.
864 10 m. Type **243** 20 20
865 50 m. Diving for sponges . . 35 20
866 65 m. Weaving 35 20
867 110 m. Pottery 50 35

244 "Spirit of 1776" (Willard)

1976. Bicentenary of American Revolution.
868 **244** 200 m. multicoloured . . 1·40 65

245 Running **246** Girl reading Book

1976. Olympic Games, Montreal. Multicoloured.
870 50 m. Type **245** 20 20
871 75 m. Olympic flags and rings . 35 20
872 120 m. Olympic "dove" . . . 55 30

1976. Literature for Children.
873 **246** 100 m. multicoloured . . . 45 20

247 Bird and Faces Emblem **248** Mausoleum, Tunis

1976. 15th Anniv of 1st Non-aligned Countries' Conference, Belgrade.
874 **247** 150 m. multicoloured . . . 60 20

1976. Cultural Heritage. Multicoloured.
875 85 m. Type **248** 35 20
876 100 m. Great Mosque, Kairouan 40 20
877 150 m. Ribat, Monastery, Monastir 60 20
878 200 m. Barber's Mosque, Kairouan 90 35

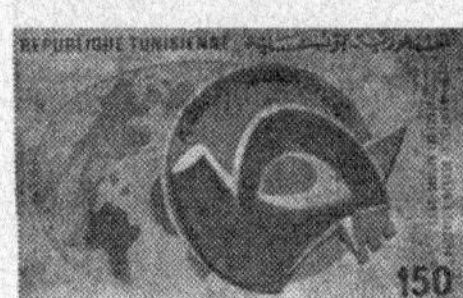
249 Emblem and Globe

1976. 25th Anniv of U.N. Postal Administration.
879 **249** 150 m. multicoloured . . . 65 30

250 Red Crescent on Litter

1977. Tunisian Red Crescent.
880 **250** 50 m. + 10 m. mult . . . 40 35

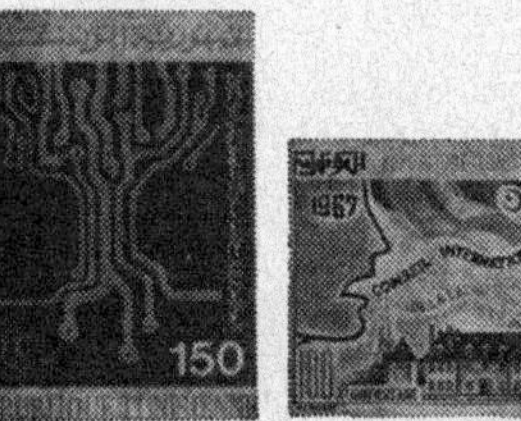
251 Circuit Diagram **252** "Dialogue"

1977. World Telecommunications Day.
881 **251** 150 m. multicoloured . . . 65 40

1977. 10th Anniv of International French Language Council.
882 **252** 100 m. multicoloured . . . 80 35

253 Footballers **254** Gold Coin

1977. 1st World Junior Football Tournament.
883 **253** 150 m. multicoloured . . . 90 45

1977. Cultural Patrimony. Multicoloured.
884 10 m. Type **254** 10 10
885 15 m. 13th-century stele . . . 15 15
886 20 m. 17th-century illuminated manuscript 20 15
887 30 m. Glass painting 35 20
888 40 m. Ceramic pot decor . . . 40 20
889 50 m. Gate, Sidi-Bou-Said . . 45 20

255 "The Young Republic" **257** Globe and Cogwheels

256 A.P.U. Emblem within Postmark

1977. 20th Anniv of Republic. Multicoloured.
890 40 m. Type **255** 35 20
891 100 m. "The Confident Republic" 40 20
892 150 m. "The Determined Republic" 65 30

1977. 25th Anniv of Arab Postal Union.
894 **256** 40 m. multicoloured . . . 20 20

1977. World Rheumatism Year.
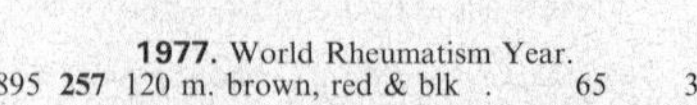
895 **257** 120 m. brown, red & blk . 65 35

258 Harvester and Rural Cameos

1977. Rural Development.
896 **258** 40 m. multicoloured . . . 35 20

259 Factory Workers **260** Pres. Bourguiba and Flaming Torch within "9"

1978. Employment Priority Plan. Multicoloured.
897 20 m. Forms of transport and driver (horiz) 20 15
898 40 m. Tractor driver and farm workers (horiz) 20 20
899 100 m. Type **259** 45 30

1978. 40th Anniv of April 9th Revolution.
900 **260** 40 m. green, brn & olive . 20 20
901 – 60 m. red, brown, & blk . 20 20
DESIGN: 60 m. President Bourguiba within figure "9".

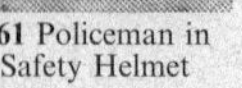

261 Policeman in Safety Helmet **262** "Blood Donors"

1978. 6th African Regional Interpol Conference.
902 **261** 150 m. multicoloured . . 80 35

1978. Tunisian Red Crescent.
903 **262** 50 m. + 10 m. mult . . . 45 30

263 Goalkeeper catching World Cup Emblem
264 Hammer and Chisel chipping away Apartheid

1978. World Cup Football Championship, Argentina. Multicoloured.
904 40 m. Type **263** 30 20
905 150 m. Footballer, map and flags 85 35

1978. International Anti-Apartheid Year. Mult.
906 50 m. Type **264** 20 20
907 100 m. Black and white doves 45 30

265 Flora, Fauna and Polluting Factory
266 Crane removing Smallpox from Globe

1978. Protection of Nature and the Environment. Multicoloured.
908 10 m. Type **265** 15 15
909 50 m. "Pollution of the oceans" 40 20
910 120 m. "Making the deserts green" 95 20

1978. Global Eradication of Smallpox.
911 **266** 150 m. multicoloured . . 65 35

267 Zlass Horseman
268 Lenin Banner

1978. Calligraphy, Art and Traditions. Multicoloured.
912 5 m. Type **267** 10 10
913 60 m. Djerba wedding 30 15
914 75 m. Women potters from the Mogods 40 15
915 100 m. Dove over cupolas of Marabout Sidi Mahrez . . . 45 20
916 500 m. Opening of the ploughing season, Jenduba . . . . . . 3·25 1·00
917 1 d. Man on swing between palm trees (Spring Festival, Tozeur) 5·50 2·25

1978. 60th Anniv of Russian Revolution.
918 **268** 150 m. multicoloured . . 1·10 45

269 Farhat Hached
270 Family Group

1978. Farhat Hached (Trade Union leader). Commemoration.
919 **269** 50 m. multicoloured . . . 35 10

1978. 10th Anniv of Tunisian Family Planning Association.
920 **270** 50 m. multicoloured . . . 40 20

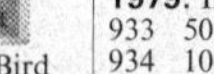
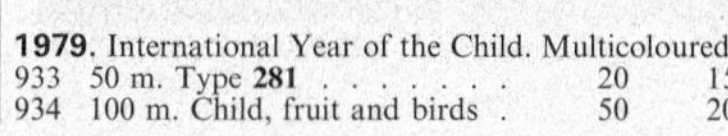

271 "The Sun"
273 Hand holding Bird

272 Boeing 747 and Flags

1978. Solar Energy.
921 **271** 100 m. multicoloured . . 60 20

1978. 20th Anniv of Tunisian Civil Aeronautics and Meteorology.
922 **272** 50 m. multicoloured . . . 30 20

1979. Tunisian Red Crescent.
923 **273** 50 m. + 10 m. mult . . 40 30

274 Pres. Bourguiba
275 Sun, Yacht and Golfer

1979. 20th Anniv of Constitution.
924 **274** 50 m. brown, yell & blk . 20 20

1979. Inauguration of El Kantaoui Port.
925 **275** 150 m. multicoloured . . 65 30

276 Korbous
277 Bow-net Making

1979. Tunisian Landscapes. Multicoloured.
926 50 m. Type **276** 15 10
927 100 m. Mides 35 15

1979. Crafts. Multicoloured.
928 10 m. Type **277** 15 10
929 50 m. Bee-keeping 35 10

278 Pres. Bourguiba and "10"
279 Dish Aerial and Satellite

1979. 10th Congress of Socialist Destourian Party.
930 **278** 50 m. multicoloured . . . 30 10

1979. 3rd World Telecommunications Exhibition, Geneva.
931 **279** 150 m. multicoloured . . 65 35

280 World Map, Koran and Symbols of Arab Achievements
281 Children crossing Road

1979. The Arabs.
932 **280** 50 m. multicoloured . . . 20 15

1979. International Year of the Child. Multicoloured.
933 50 m. Type **281** 20 15
934 100 m. Child, fruit and birds . 50 20

282 Dove and Olive Tree
283 Symbolic Figure

1979. 2nd World Olive-oil Year.
935 **282** 150 m. multicoloured . . . 80 35

1979. 20th Anniv of Central Bank of Tunisia.
936 **283** 50 m. multicolourd 20 20

284 Children and Jujube Tree

1979. Animals and Plants. Multicoloured.
937 20 m. Type **284** 20 10
938 30 m. Common peafowl . . . 50 15
939 70 m. Goat 65 20
940 85 m. Girl and date palm . . . 70 20

285 Coded Letter

1980. Introduction of Postal Coding.
941 **285** 50 m. multicoloured . . . 30 20

286 Smoker

1980. World Health Day. Anti-smoking Campaign.
942 **286** 150 m. multicoloured . . . 65 30

287 Red Crescent and Globe forming an Eye
288 President Bourguiba, Flower and Open Book

1980. Tunisian Red Crescent.
943 **287** 50 m. + 10 m. mult . . . 40 30

1980. 25th Anniv of Victory and Return of President Bourguiba. Multicoloured.
944 50 m. Type **288** 20 20
945 100 m. Pres. Bourguiba, dove and mosque 85 35

289 Gymnast as Butterfly
290 Tools

1980. Turin Gymnastic Games.
946 **289** 100 m. multicoloured . . . 45 20

1980. Handicrafts. Multicoloured.
947 30 m. Type **290** 30 20
948 75 m. Woman embroidering . 40 20

291 Ibn Khaldoun (philosopher)
292 Avicenna

1980. Ibn Khaldoun Commemoration.
949 **291** 50 m. multicoloured . . . 20 20

1980. Birth Millenary of Avicenna (philosopher).
950 **292** 100 m. sepia and brown . 65 35

293 Al-Biruni and Scientific Diagram

1980. The Arabs' Contribution to Science.
951 **293** 50 m. multicoloured . . . 35 20

294 Yachts at Sidi Bou Said

1980. Sidi Bou Said.
952 **294** 100 m. multicoloured . . 65 35

295 "Tourists"

1980. World Tourism Conference, Manila.
953 **295** 150 m. multicoloured . . 55 20

296 "Wedding at Djerba"

1980. Yahia (painter) Commemoration.
954 **296** 50 m. multicoloured . . . 40 30

297 Aircraft over Tozeur
298 "Eye"

1980. Opening of Tozeur International Airport.
955 **297** 85 m. multicoloured . . . 35 20

1980. 7th Afro-Asian Congress on Ophthalmology.
956 **298** 100 m. multicoloured . . 55 35

299 Spider's Web

1980. 1400th Anniv of Hegira. Multicoloured.
957 50 m. Type **299** 20 20
958 80 m. Minarets 35 20

300 Face as Camera **301** "Ophrys scolopax scolopax"

1980. Carthage Cinematographic Days.

959 **300** 100 m. multicoloured . . . 45 30

1980. Flora and Fauna. Multicoloured.

960 20 m. Type **301** 20 20
961 25 m. "Cyclamen europaeum" . . 20 20
962 50 m. Mouflon 20 20
963 100 m. Golden eagle . . . . . 1·10 30

302 Kairouan Mosque

1980. Conservation of Kairouan.

964 **302** 85 m. multicoloured . . . 35 20

303 H. von Stephan **304** Hands holding Bottle containing Blood Drop

1981. 150th Birth Anniv of Heinrich von Stephan (founder of U.P.U.).

965 **303** 150 m. multicoloured . . 65 35

1981. 20th Anniv of Tunisian Blood Donors Association.

966 **304** 75 m. multicoloured . . . 65 45

305 Flags and Pres. Bourguiba

1981. 25th Anniv of Independence. Multicoloured.

967 50 m. Type **305** 20 20
968 60 m. Stork and ribbons forming "25" 35 20
969 85 m. Stylized birds 55 35
970 120 m. Victory riding a winged horse 55 35

306 Flower and Pres. Bourguiba

1981. Special Congress of Destourian Socialist Party. Multicoloured.

972 50 m. Type **306** 20 15
973 75 m. Arrows forming flower . . 35 20

307 Mosque, Mahdia and Galley

1981. Tourism. Multicoloured.

974 50 m. Type **307** 20 20
975 85 m. Djerid bride passing Great Mosque of Tozeur (vert) . . 35 30
976 100 m. Needle rocks, Tabarka 45 30

308 Stylized Peacock hatching Egg

1981. Red Crescent.

977 **308** 50 m. + 10 m. mult . . 35 35

309 I.T.U. and W.H.O. Emblems and Ribbons forming Caduceus **310** Flowers and Youths

1981. World Telecommunications Day.

978 **309** 150 m. multicoloured . . 60 30

1981. Youth Festival.

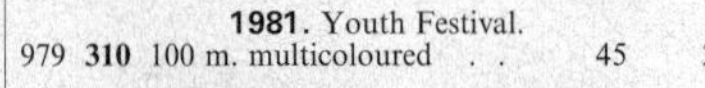

979 **310** 100 m. multicoloured . . 45 20

311 Kemal Ataturk **312** Skifa Khala, Mahdia

1981. Birth Centenary of Kemal Ataturk.

980 **311** 150 m. multicoloured . . 65 35

1981. Tunisian Monuments.

981 **312** 150 m. multicoloured . . 65 35

313 Cheikh Mohamed Tahar ben Achour and Minaret

1981. Cheikh Mohamed Tahar ben Achour (scholar and teacher) Commemoration.

982 **313** 200 m. multicoloured . . 1·00 45

314 Rejoicing Woman **315** Tree with Broken Branch

1981. 25th Anniv of Personal Status Code. Multicoloured.

983 50 m. Type **314** 20 20
984 100 m. Dove and head of woman 40 30

1981. International Year of Disabled People.

985 **315** 250 m. multicoloured . . 1·00 65

316 Stylized Figure and Ka'aba, Mecca **317** Food Sources

1981. Pilgrimage to Mecca.

986 **316** 50 m. multicoloured . . . 30 20

1981. World Food Day.

987 **317** 200 m. multicoloured . . . 90 50

318 Dome of the Rock

1981. Palestinian Welfare.

988 **318** 50 m. + 5 m. mult 35 20
989 150 m. + 5 m. mult . . . 60 35
990 200 m. + 5 m. mult . . . 90 50

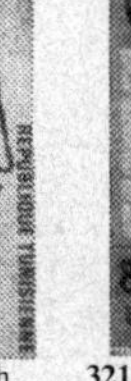

319 Mnaguech (earring) **321** Chemist (detail from 13th-century manuscript)

320 Ship passing under Bridge

1981. Jewellery. Multicoloured.

991 150 m. Type **319** 60 30
992 180 m. Mahfdha (pendant) (horiz) 70 35
993 200 m. Essalta (hairnet) . . . 90 40

1981. Bizerta Drawbridge.

994 **320** 230 m. multicoloured . . . 80 40

1982. Arab Pharmacists' Union.

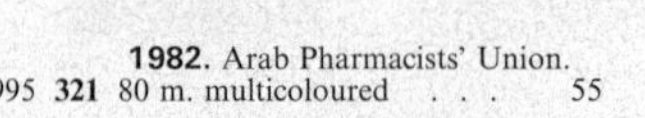

995 **321** 80 m. multicoloured . . . 55 35

322 Ring of People around Red Crescent

1982. Red Crescent.

996 **322** 80 m. + 10 m. mult . . . 40 30

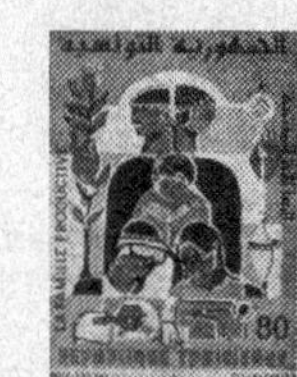

323 "Ocean Research" **324** "Productive Family"

1982. International Symposium "Ocean Venture", Tunis.

997 **323** 150 m. multicoloured . . . 80 45

1982. The Productive Family.

998 **324** 80 m. multicoloured . . . 35 20

325 Pres. Bourguiba and Woman's Head **326** Scout within "50"

1982. 25th Anniv of Republic.

999 **325** 80 m. blue and black . . 30 20
1000 – 100 m. multicoloured . . 40 30
1001 – 200 m. multicoloured . . 65 35

DESIGNS: 100 m. President and woman with "XXV" headband; 200 m. President and woman with "25" in hair.

1982. 75th Anniv of Scout Movement and 50th Anniv of Tunisian Scout Movement. Multicoloured.

1003 80 m. Type **326** 35 20
1004 200 m. Scout camp (vert) . . . 65 20

327 "Pseudophillipsia azzouzi" **328** Tunisian Woman

1982. Fossils. Multicoloured.

1005 80 m. Type **327** 45 35
1006 200 m. "Mediterraneotrigonia cherahilensis" . . . . . . 1·40 65
1007 280 m. "Numidiopleura enigmatica" (horiz) . . . . 1·10 80
1008 300 m. "Micreschara tunisiensis" . . . . 2·00 1·40
1009 500 m. "Mantelliceras pervinquieri" . . . . . . 3·75 2·00
1010 1000 m. "Elephas africanavus" (horiz) . . . . 6·25 3·00

1982. 30th Anniv of Arab Postal Union.

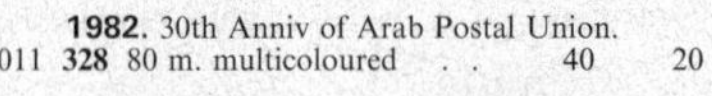

1011 **328** 80 m. multicoloured . . 40 20

329 I.T.U. Emblem **330** Tunisian Buildings and Congress Centre

1982. I.T.U. Delegates' Conference, Nairobi.

1012 **329** 200 m. multicoloured . . 65 45

1982. "Tunisia Land of Congresses".

1013 **330** 200 m. multicoloured . . 65 30

331 "Feeding the World" **332** Tahar Haddad

1982. World Food Day.

1014 **331** 200 m. multicoloured . . 65 30

1982. Tahar Haddad (social reformer) Commemoration.

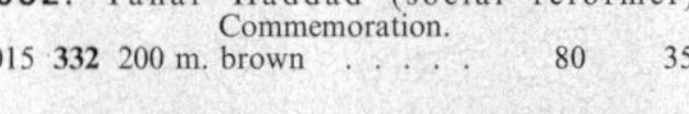

1015 **332** 200 m. brown 80 35

333 Microscope **334** Figure dancing in Rain

1982. Cent of Discovery of Tubercle Bacillus.

1016 **333** 100 m. multicoloured . . 55 30

1982. Stories and Songs from Tunisia. Multicoloured.

1017 20 m. Type **334** 15 15
1018 30 m. Woman with broom . . 15 15
1019 70 m. Boy and fisherman . . 20 15
1020 80 m. Chicken (horiz) . . . 30 20
1021 100 m. Woman admiring herself in mirror (horiz) 40 20
1022 120 m. Two girls 45 30

335 Clasped Hands and Palestine Flag

1982. Palestinian Solidarity Day.
1023 **335** 80 m. multicoloured . . 30 20

336 Farhat Hached   337 Bourguiba Sidi Saad Dam

1982. 30th Death Anniv of Farhat Hached.
1024 **336** 80 m. red 35 20

1982. Inauguration of Bourguiba Sidi Saad Dam.
1025 **337** 80 m. multicoloured . . 45 20

338 Environment Emblem on Blackboard   339 Giving Blood

1982. Opening of Environment Training Work School.
1026 **338** 80 m. multicoloured . . 35 15

1983. Red Crescent.
1027 **339** 80 m. + 10 m. mult . . 50 30

340 "Communications"

1983. World Communications Year.
1028 **340** 200 m. multicoloured . . 55 30

341 Dove and Map of Africa   342 Customs Officer, Globes and Suitcases

1983. 20th Anniv of Organization of African Unity.
1029 **341** 230 m. blue & dp blue . 65 40

1983. 20th Anniv of Customs Co-operation Council.
1030 **342** 100 m. multicoloured . . 35 20

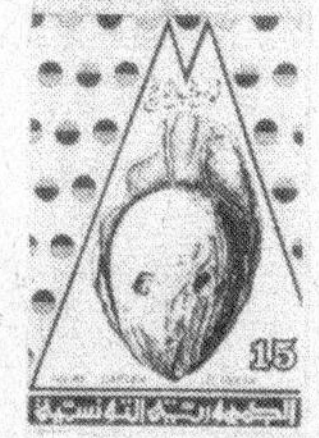

343 Aly Ben Ayed   344 Carved Face, El Mekta

1983. Aly Ben Ayed (actor) Commemoration.
1031 **343** 80 m. red, black and deep red 30 30

1983. Pre-historic Artefacts. Multicoloured.
1032 15 m. Type **344** 20 20
1033 20 m. Neolithic necklace, Kef el Agab (horiz) 30 20
1034 30 m. Neolithic grindstone, Redeyef (horiz) 30 20
1035 40 m. Animal petroglyph, Gafsa 35 20
1036 80 m. Dolmen, Mactar (horiz) 40 30
1037 100 m. Bi-face flint, El Mekta 55 30

345 Dove, Barbed Wire and Dome of the Rock

1983. Palestinian Welfare.
1038 **345** 80 m. + 5 m. mult . . . 40 40

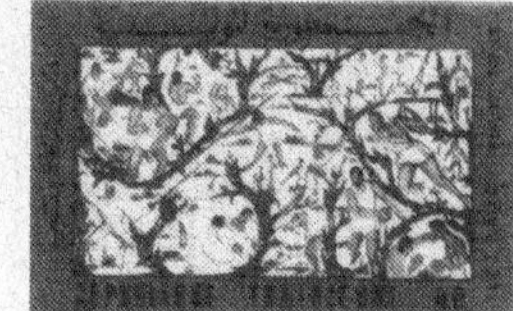

346 Sporting Activities

1983. Sport for All.
1039 **346** 40 m. multicoloured . . 15 10

347 Tunisian with Flag and French Freighter   348 Fishing Boats and Fish

1983. 20th Anniv of Evacuation of Foreign Troops.
1040 **347** 80 m. multicoloured . . 30 20

1983. World Fishing Day.
1041 **348** 200 m. multicoloured . . 1·00 25

349 "The Weaver" (Hedi Khayachi)

1983. Hedi Khayachi (painter) Commem.
1042 **349** 80 m. multicoloured . . 45 35

350 Saluting the Flag   351 Air Hostess and Airliner

1983. Salute to the Flag.
1043 **350** 100 m. multicoloured . . 35 20

1983. 25th Anniv of Tunisian Civil Aviation and Meteorology.
1044 **351** 150 m. multicoloured . . 55 20

352 Pres. Bourguiba and Archway   353 Map of Africa

1984. 50th Anniv of Neo-Destour Party. Multicoloured.
1045 40 m. Type **352** 15 10
1046 70 m. Bourguiba and torch . 20 10
1047 80 m. Bourguiba and flag . . 30 15
1048 150 m. Bourguiba and wall . 50 30
1049 200 m. Bourguiba and dove (horiz) 60 35
1050 230 m. Pres. Bourguiba (horiz) 70 45

1984. 4th School of Molecular Biology.
1052 **353** 100 m. multicoloured . . 55 30

354 First Aid

1984. Red Crescent.
1053 **354** 80 m. + 10 m. mult . . . 40 30

355 Ibn el Jazzar   356 "Co-operation"

1984. Ibn el Jazzar (doctor) Commem.
1054 **355** 80 m. multicoloured . . . 40 30

1984. Economic Co-operation among Developing Countries.
1055 **356** 230 m. multicoloured . . 80 35

357 Witch, Maiden and Coquette

1984. Stories and Songs from Tunisia. Multicoloured.
1056 20 m. Type **357** 10 10
1057 80 m. Puppet, hands and mouse 30 20
1058 100 m. Boy and horse (vert) . 35 15

358 Family facing the Future

1984. 20th Anniv of Tunisian Education and Family Organization.
1059 **358** 80 m. multicoloured . . . 30 20

359 Medina, Tunis   360 Aboul Qasim Chabbi

1984. National Heritage Protection.
1060 **359** 100 m. multicoloured . . 35 30

1984. 50th Death Anniv of Aboul Qasim Chabbi (poet).
1061 **360** 100 m. sepia, light brown and brown 35 20

361 Emblem, Stylised Bird and Airplane

1984. 40th Anniv of International Civil Aviation Organization.
1062 **361** 200 m. multicoloured . . 65 20

362 Band and Singers

1984. Sahara Festival.
1063 **362** 20 m. multicoloured . . 45 20

363 Telephonist, Satellite and Dish Aerial

1984. 20th Anniv of "Intelsat" Communication Satellite.
1064 **363** 100 m. multicoloured . . 35 15

364 "Mediterranean Countryside"

1984. Jilani Abdulwahelb (artist) Commem.
1065 **364** 100 m. multicoloured . . 55 35

365 Profile and Exterior of House   366 Crescents and Stars within Circle

1985. "Expo 85" World's Fair, Tsukuba.
1066 **365** 200 m. multicoloured . . 65 35

1985. Red Crescent.
1067 **366** 100 m. + 10 m. mult . . 35 30

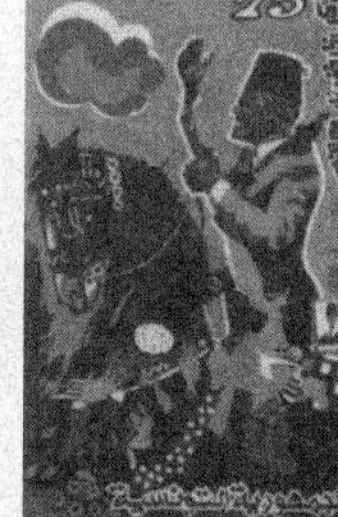

367 Hands reaching from Sea and Flames   368 Pres. Bourguiba on Horseback

1985. 3rd Civil Protection Week.
1068 **367** 100 m. multicoloured . . 30 15

1985. 30th Anniv of Independence. Mult.
1069 75 m. Type **368** 20 10
1070 100 m. Pres. Bourguiba in boat and crowd on quay (horiz) 30 10
1071 200 m. Pres. Bourguiba in sombrero 55 20
1072 230 m. Pres. Bourguiba waving to crowd from balcony (horiz) 60 20

369 Pres. Bourguiba and Ancient Sculpture

1985. Tunisian Day at "Expo '85" World's Fair, Tsukuba.
1074 **369** 250 m. multicoloured . . 80 30

370 Images within Film

372 Heart as Dove and I.Y.Y. Emblem

371 Dark Clouds, Sun and Flowers

1985. International Amateur Film Festival, Kelibia.
1075 **370** 250 m. multicoloured . . 1·50 1·10

1985. Stories and Songs from Tunisia. Multicoloured.
1076 25 m. Type **371** 10 10
1077 50 m. Man's profile and hand holding women 15 10
1078 100 m. Man and cooking pot over fire 35 15

1985. International Youth Year.
1079 **372** 250 m. multicoloured . . 80 30

373 "The Perfumiers Hall"

1985. Painting by Hedi Larnaout.
1080 **373** 100 m. multicoloured . . 45 20

374 Matmata Wedding Dress

375 Stylized People and U.N. Emblem

1985. Wedding Dresses (1st series). Mult.
1081 20 m. Type **374** 10 10
1082 50 m. Moknine dress 15 10
1083 100 m. Tunis dress 35 15
See also Nos. 1099/1101.

1985. 40th Anniv of U.N.O.
1084 **375** 250 m. multicoloured . . 80 30

376 Harvest (Makthar stele)

1985. Food Self-sufficiency.
1085 **376** 100 m. multicoloured . . 35 20

377 Emblem illuminating Globe and Flags

378 Aziza Othmana

1985. 40th Anniv of Arab League.
1086 **377** 100 m. multicoloured . . 30 15

1985. Aziza Othmana (founder of hospitals) Commemoration.
1087 **378** 100 m. brown, green and red 45 20

379 Surveying Instruments and Books forming Face

380 Dove and Pres. Bourguiba

1985. Centenary of Land Law.
1088 **379** 100 m. multicoloured . . 30 10

1986. 30th Anniv of Independence.
1089 **380** 100 m. multicoloured . . 30 10
1090 – 120 m. black, blue and deep blue 35 15
1091 – 280 m. blue, violet and black 80 35
1092 – 300 m. multicoloured . . 85 40
DESIGNS—HORIZ: 120 m. Rocket; 280 m. Horse and rider. VERT: 300 m. Balloons.

381 Hulusi Behcet (dermatologist)

382 Map and Red Crescent

1986. 3rd Mediterranean Rheumatology Days, Tunis, and Ninth International Society of Geographical Ophthalmology Congress, Monastir. Multicoloured.
1094 300 m. Type **381** . . . . . . 1·25 35
1095 380 m. Behcet and sun and eye emblems . . . . 1·60 45

1986. World Red Crescent and Red Cross Day.
1096 **382** 120 m. + 10 m. mult . 40 30

383 Pres. Bourguiba, Symbols and "12"

1986. 12th Destourian Socialist Party Congress, Tunis. Multicoloured.
1097 120 m. Type **383** 30 10
1098 300 m. Flaming torch, Pres. Bourguiba and "12" . . . 85 30

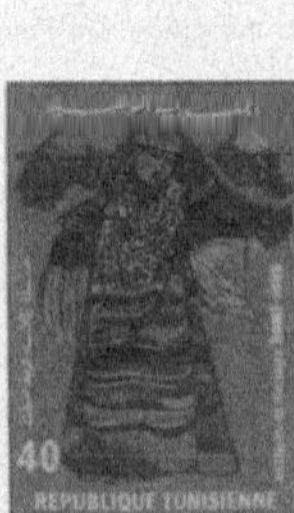

384 Homt Souk Dress

385 Hassen Husni Abdulwaheb

1986. Wedding Dresses (2nd series). Mult.
1099 40 m. Type **384** 10 10
1100 280 m. Mahdia dress 80 30
1101 300 m. Nabeul dress 90 35

1986. Hassen Husni Abdulwaheb (historian) Commemoration.
1102 **385** 160 m. red 55 20

386 Reconstructed View of Carthage

1986. 2800th Anniv of Foundation of Carthage.
1103 **386** 2 d. purple . . . . 6·75 2·50

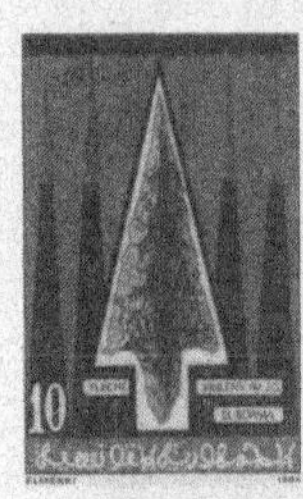

387 Arrow Head, El Borma, 3000 B.C.

388 "Bedouins"

1986. Prehistoric Artefacts. Multicoloured.
1104 10 m. Type **387** 20 20
1105 20 m. Tomb, Sejnane, 1000 B.C. 20 20
1106 50 m. Bas-relief, Zaghouan, 1000 B.C. (horiz) 35 20
1107 120 m. Neolithic vase, Kesra (horiz) 55 20
1108 160 m. Painting of Phoenician ship, Kef el Blida, 800 B.C. (horiz) 65 20
1109 250 m. 7th-century decorated pottery, Sejnane . . . . . 1·40 35

1986. Painting by Ammar Farhat.
1110 **388** 250 m. multicoloured . . 1·25 35

389 Doves and Globe

1986. International Peace Year.
1111 **389** 300 m. multicoloured . . 85 35

390 Emblem

391 Computer Terminal

1986. 40th Anniv of F.A.O.
1112 **390** 280 m. multicoloured . . 80 30

1986. Introduction of Computers into Education.
1113 **391** 2 d. multicoloured . . . 6·75 2·50

392 Mother and Child

393 Mountain Gazelle (Chambi National Park)

1986. Child Survival.
1114 **392** 120 m. multicoloured . . 35 10

1986. National Parks. Multicoloured.
1115 60 m. Type **393** 15 10
1116 120 m. Addax (Bou Hedma National Park) 30 10
1117 350 m. Monk seal (Zembra and Zembretta National Park) . 85 30
1118 380 m. Greylag goose (Ichkeul National Park) . . . . . . 2·00 80

394 Pres. Bourguiba and Arms

1987. Centenary of Monastir Municipality.
1119 **394** 120 m. multicoloured . . 35 15

395 Radiation and Red Crescent Symbols in Face

1987. Radiation Protection and Red Crescent.
1120 **395** 150 m. + 10 m. mult . . 55 45

396 Samuel Morse (inventor) and Morse Key

1987. 150th Anniv of Morse Telegrarph.
1121 **396** 500 m. multicoloured . . 1·40 55

397 Pres. Bourguiba and Woman's Head

1987. 30th Anniv of Republic. Designs each show Pres. Bourguiba and a different woman's head.
1122 **397** 150 m. mauve, brown and yellow 35 25
1123 – 250 m. brown, red and yellow 55 25
1124 – 350 m. blue, brown and green 80 20
1125 – 500 m. multicoloured . . 1·10 35

398 Hand injecting Baby in Globe and Dove holding Syringe

399 "The Road"

1987. Universal Vaccination for Everyone by 1990. 40th Anniv of United Nations Children's Fund.
1127 **398** 250 m. multicoloured . . 65 45

1987. 25th Death Anniv of Azouz Ben Rais (painter).
1128 **399** 250 m. multicoloured . . 90 45

400 Couple's Faces in House

1987. Arab Housing Day.
1129 **400** 150 m. multicoloured . . 40 30

401 Dove carrying Parcel

402 Ibn Mandhour

1987. 30th Anniv of Consultative Postal Studies Council. Multicoloured.
1130 150 m. Type **401** 35 10
1131 350 m. Postman and electronically sorted letters 80 30

1987. 675th Death Anniv of Ibn Mandhour (lexicographer).
1132 **402** 250 m. purple 80 45

403 Bunches of Grapes **404** Player with Ball

1987. International Vine Year.
1133 **403** 250 m. multicoloured . . 80 35

1987. 6th African Nations Volleyball Championship, Tunis.
1134 **404** 350 m. multicoloured . . 1·10 45

405 Players and Ball **406** Tunis Institute and Adrien Loir (first director)

1987. African Basketball Championships.
1135 **405** 350 m. multicoloured . . 1·40 45

1987. Centenary of Pasteur Institute, Paris.
1136 **406** 250 m. green, brown and black 80 35

407 Midoun **408** Narcissi

1987. Costumes. Multicoloured.
1137 20 m. Type **407** 10 10
1138 30 m. Tozeur 10 10
1139 150 m. Sfax 40 15

1987. Flowers. Multicoloured.
1140 30 m. Type **408** 10 10
1141 150 m. Gladioli 40 15
1142 400 m. Iris . . . . 1·00 35
1143 500 m. Tulips . . . . 1·50 55

409 Hand holding Scales of Justice

1988. Declaration of 7 November, 1987. Multicoloured.
1144 150 m. Type **409** (Justice for all) 35 20
1145 200 m. Girl with party badges as flowers in hair (Multi-party system) (vert) 45 20
1146 350 m. Girl in cornfield wearing coat of arms (International co-operation and friendship) 80 35
1147 370 m. Maghreb states emblem (vert) 90 35

410 Couple

1988. Youth and Change. Multicoloured.
1149 75 m. Type **410** 20 15
1150 150 m. Young people 35 15

411 Crowd with Banners

1988. 50th Anniv of Martyrs' Day.
1151 **411** 150 m. orange & brown 35 15
1152 – 500 m. multicoloured . . 1·40 40
DESIGN: 500 m. Martyrs monument.

412 Roses and Banners

1988. 125th Anniv of Red Cross.
1153 **412** 150 m. + 10 m. mult . 45 35

413 Hand saving drowning Country

1988. 1st Democratic Constitutional Assembly Congress.
1154 **413** 150 m. multicoloured . . 35 15

414 Sportsmen

1988. Olympic Games, Seoul. Multicoloured.
1155 150 m. Type **414** 40 20
1156 430 m. Sportsman (different) 1·00 45

415 Beit Hussein Sari and Eye **416** "7" and Flowers

1988. Restoration of Sana'a, Yemen.
1157 **415** 200 m. multicoloured . . 45 20

1988. 1st Anniv of Presidency of Zine el Abidine.
1158 **416** 150 m. multicoloured . . 35 15

417 "Amilcar Beach, 1942"

1988. 70th Birth Anniv of Amara Debbeche (painter).
1159 **417** 100 m. multicoloured . . 35 20

418 Boeing 747 and Globe forming "40" **419** Man holding Book

1988. 40th Anniv of Tunis Air.
1160 **418** 500 m. multicoloured . . 1·50 70

1988. 40th Anniv of Declaration of Human Rights.
1161 **419** 370 m. black 85 45

420 Tweezers and Magnifying Glasses forming "100"

1988. Cent of First Tunisian Postage Stamps.
1162 **420** 150 m. multicoloured . . 55 30

421 18th-century Door, Rue du Tresor **422** Ali Douagi

1988. Tunis Doorways and Fountains. Mult.
1163 50 m. Type **421** 10 10
1164 70 m. 19th-century door, Rue el Mbazaa 15 10
1165 100 m. 15th-16th century door, Rue des Fabricants de Tamis 20 10
1166 150 m. 19th-century door, Rue Bach Hamba 30 15
1167 370 m. 16th-17th century door, Rue el Ariane 70 30
1168 400 m. Fountain, Manouba, 1793 . . . . 80 35

1989. 40th Death Anniv of Ali Douagi (writer).
1169 **422** 1 d. blue . . . . 2·50 65

423 Stretcher Bearers **424** Crippled Person and Healthy Girl

1989. Red Crescent.
1170 **423** 150 m. + 10 m. mult . . 40 30

1989. National Day for Disabled People.
1171 **424** 150 m. multicoloured . . 45 20

425 Children using Computer and Microscope

1989. Knowledge Day.
1172 **425** 180 m. multicoloured . . 40 20

426 Clasped Hands

1989. 20th Anniv of Tunisian Family Planning Association.
1173 **426** 150 m. multicoloured . . 35 15

427 Family

1989. Family Welfare.
1174 **427** 150 m. multicoloured . . 35 15

428 Tortoise

1989. Endangered Animals. Multicoloured.
1175 250 m. Type **428** 65 35
1176 350 m. Oryx . . . . 1·00 45

429 Flags and Emblem **430** Beyram

1989. Tunis International Fair (1990). Mult.
1177 150 m. Type **429** 35 15
1178 370 m. Fair Pavilion 80 35

1989. Death Centenary of Mohamed Beyram (writer).
1179 **430** 150 m. purple and black 35 15

431 Actors wearing Comedy Masks **432** Monument, Tunis

1989. Carthage Theatre Festival.
1180 **431** 300 m. multicoloured . . 65 35

1989. 2nd Anniv of Declaration of 7 November, 1987.
1181 **432** 150 m. multicoloured . . 35 20

433 Nehru **434** Members' Flags

1989. Birth Centenary of Jawaharlal Nehru (Indian statesman).
1182 **433** 300 m. brown 65 35

1990. Maghreb Union Presidential Summit.
1183 **434** 200 m. multicoloured . . 45 30

435 Museum and Sculptures

1990. Centenary of Bardo Museum.
1184 **435** 300 m. multicoloured . . 80 45

436 Ceramic Tiles, Vases and Crockery

1990. Arts and Crafts. Multicoloured.
1185 75 m. Type **436** 15 10
1186 100 m. Copper pots and grinder 20 15

437 Ram and Ewes

1990. Ram Museum. Multicoloured.
1187 400 m. Type **437** 90 35
1188 450 m. Ram's head . . . . . 1·25 45

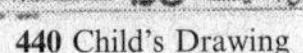

438 Houses within Crescent 440 Child's Drawing

439 Olympic Rings and Athlete

1990. Red Crescent.
1190 **438** 150 m. + 10 m. mult . . 35 20

1990. Tunisian Olympic Movement.
1191 **439** 150 m. multicoloured . . 35 15

1990. The Child and the Environment.
1192 **440** 150 m. multicoloured . . 35 15

441 Sbiba Horseman 442 Dougga

1990. Costumes. Multicoloured.
1193 150 m. Type **441** 45 35
1194 500 m. Bou Omrane man . . 1·40 65

1990. Tourism.
1195 **442** 300 m. multicoloured . . 65 35

443 Adults learning to Read and Write

1990. International Literacy Year.
1196 **443** 120 m. multicoloured . . 30 15

444 Figures, Tree and Fishes in Water 445 Fireworks and Date

1990. Water.
1197 **444** 150 m. multicoloured . . 45 30

1990. 3rd Anniv of Declaration of 7 November, 1987. Multicoloured.
1198 150 m. Type **445** 35 15
1199 150 m. Clock tower 35 15

HAVE YOU READ THE NOTES AT THE BEGINNING OF THIS CATALOGUE?
These often provide the answers to the enquiries we receive.

446 Kheireddine et Tounsi 447 Red Deer

1990. Death Centenary of Kheireddine et Tounsi (political reformer).
1200 **446** 150 m. green 45 20

1990. Flora and Fauna. Multicoloured.
1201 150 m. Type **447** 35 15
1202 200 m. Thistle 45 15
1203 300 m. Water buffalo . . . 65 20
1204 600 m. Orchid . . . . 1·40 55

448 Members' Flags forming Stars 449 Montazah Tabarka

1991. 2nd Anniv of Maghreb Union.
1205 **448** 180 m. multicoloured . . 45 20

1991. Tourism.
1206 **449** 450 m. multicoloured . . 1·00 45

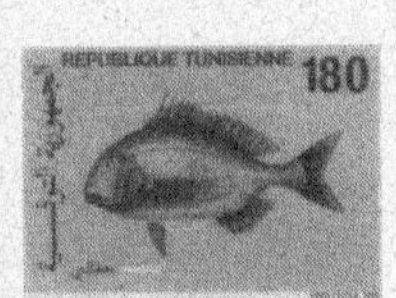

450 Doves and Emblem 451 Sea Bream

1991. Red Crescent. Help for War Victims.
1207 **450** 180 m. + 10 m. mult . 45 35

1991. Fishes. Multicoloured.
1208 180 m. Type **451** 45 20
1209 350 m. Red mullet 85 35
1210 450 m. Mackerel . . . . . . 1·10 45
1211 550 m. Gunner bream . . . 1·40 65

452 Vase of Flowers (Taieb Khlif)

1991. Children's Rights.
1212 **452** 450 m. multicoloured . . 1·25 35

453 "Plein-Sud" (anon.)

1991.
1213 **453** 400 m. multicoloured . . 90 35

454 Bracelets and Ring 455 Date and Profile of Woman

1991. Jewellery. Multicoloured.
1214 120 m. Type **454** 30 15
1215 180 m. Headdress and necklace (vert) 40 15
1216 220 m. Headdress, earrings and collar (vert) 45 20
1217 730 m. Key ring (vert) . . . . 2·25 80

1991. 4th Anniv of Declaration of 7 November, 1987.
1218 **455** 180 m. multicoloured . . 45 20

456 Sorting Office

1991. Tunis-Carthage Sorting Office.
1219 **456** 80 m. blue, red & green . 20 10

457 Dove and Globe 458 Bayram Ettounsi

1991. World Human Rights Day.
1220 **457** 450 m. blue . . . . 1·25 35

1991. 31st Death Anniv of Bayram Ettounsi.
1221 **458** 200 m. blue 45 15

459 Emblem on Microchip 460 G.P.O

1992. "Expo '92" World's Fair, Seville.
1222 **459** 180 m. multicoloured . . 45 20

1992. Centenary of General Post Office, Tunis.
1223 **460** 180 m. brown 45 20
1224 – 450 m. brown . . . . . . 1·25 35
DESIGN—VERT: 450 m. Different view of G.P.O.

461 "When the Subconscious Awakes" (Moncef ben Amor)

1992.
1225 **461** 500 m. multicoloured . . 1·40 45

462 Running 463 European Bee Eater

1992. Olympic Games, Barcelona. Multicoloured.
1226 180 m. Type **462** 65 30
1227 450 m. Judo (vert) . . . . . 1·60 55

1992. Birds. Multicoloured.
1228 100 m. Type **463** 45 15
1229 180 m. Goldfinch 65 35
1230 200 m. Serin 85 35
1231 500 m. Greenfinch . . . . . 2·00 85

464 President and Children 465 Women and Open Book

1992. United Nations Convention on Rights of the Child.
1233 **464** 180 m. multicoloured . . 45 30

1992. African Regional Human Rights Conference, Tunis.
1234 **465** 480 m. multicoloured . . 1·50 65

466 Ribbon forming "7" 467 "Acacia tortilis"

1992. 5th Anniv of Declaration of 7 November, 1987. Multicoloured.
1235 180 m. Type **466** 45 20
1236 730 m. President with people and doves . . . . 2·10 90

1992. National Tree Day.
1237 **467** 180 m. multicoloured . . 45 30

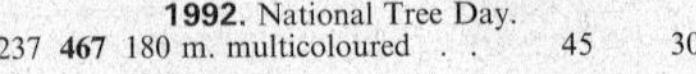

468 Stylized Figure and Emblems

1992. International Nutrition Conference, Rome.
1238 **468** 450 m. multicoloured . . 1·50 55

469 Chemesse 470 "Billy Goat between Two Bushes" (El Jem)

1992. Traditional Costumes. Multicoloured.
1239 100 m. Type **469** 30 20
1240 350 m. Hanifites 85 45

1992. Mosaics. Multicoloured.
1241 100 m. Type **470** 30 15
1242 180 m. "Wild Duck" (El Jem) 75 35
1243 350 m. "Racehorse" (Sidi Abdallah) . . . . 1·25 45
1244 450 m. "Gazelle in the Grass" (El Jem) . . . . 1·40 70

471 Wolf

1992. Flora and Fauna. Multicoloured.
1245 20 m. Type **471** 10 10
1246 60 m. "Hoya carnosa" (plant) (vert) 10 10

472 Line Graph on World Map

1993. United Nations World Conference on Human Rights, Vienna.
1247 **472** 450 m. multicoloured . . 1·40 60

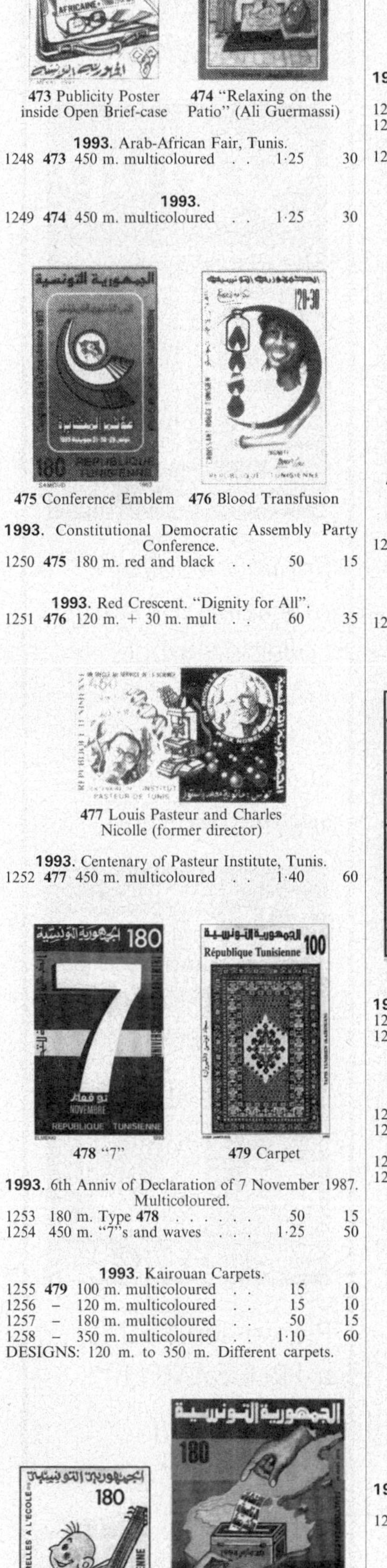

473 Publicity Poster inside Open Brief-case
474 "Relaxing on the Patio" (Ali Guermassi)

1993. Arab-African Fair, Tunis.
1248 **473** 450 m. multicoloured . . 1·25 30

1993.
1249 **474** 450 m. multicoloured . . 1·25 30

475 Conference Emblem
476 Blood Transfusion

1993. Constitutional Democratic Assembly Party Conference.
1250 **475** 180 m. red and black . . 50 15

1993. Red Crescent. "Dignity for All".
1251 **476** 120 m. + 30 m. mult . . 60 35

477 Louis Pasteur and Charles Nicolle (former director)

1993. Centenary of Pasteur Institute, Tunis.
1252 **477** 450 m. multicoloured . . 1·40 60

478 "7"
479 Carpet

1993. 6th Anniv of Declaration of 7 November 1987. Multicoloured.
1253 180 m. Type **478** 50 15
1254 450 m. "7"s and waves . . . 1·25 50

1993. Kairouan Carpets.
1255 **479** 100 m. multicoloured . . 15 10
1256 – 120 m. multicoloured . . 15 10
1257 – 180 m. multicoloured . . 50 15
1258 – 350 m. multicoloured . . 1·10 60
DESIGNS: 120 m. to 350 m. Different carpets.

480 Boy with Guitar (Donia Haik)
481 Ballot Box, Hands and Map

1993. School Cultural Activities. Children's drawings. Multicoloured.
1259 180 m. Type **480** 50 15
1260 180 m. Painting and reading (Anissa Chatbouri) (horiz) . 50 15

1994. Presidential and Legislative Elections.
1261 **481** 180 m. multicoloured . . 50 15

482 Players, Trophy and Mascot

1994. African Nations Cup Football Championship. Multicoloured.
1262 180 m. Type **482** 50 15
1263 350 m. Trophy, goalkeeper making save and mascot . 1·00 25
1264 450 m. Map of Africa, Olympic Rings, player, trophy and mascot . . . . 1·25 60

483 Workers, "75" and Emblem
484 Family within House

1994. 75th Anniv of I.L.O.
1265 **483** 350 m. multicoloured . . 1·10 25

1994. International Year of the Family.
1266 **484** 180 m. multicoloured . . 50 15

485 President Ben Ali

486 Blackthorn

1994. Re-election of President Zine el Abidine Ben Ali.
1267 **485** 180 m. multicoloured . . 50 15
1268 350 m. multicoloured . . 1·00 75

1994. Plants. Multicoloured.
1270 50 m. Type **486** 10 10
1271 100 m. "Xeranthemum inapertum" 15 10
1272 200 m. "Orchis simia" . . . 60 15
1273 1 d. "Scilla peruviana" . . . 2·75 1·50

487 Dove and Emblem

1994. 30th Organization of African Unity Summit Meeting, Tunis.
1274 **487** 480 m. multicoloured . . 1·40 60

488 Torch with Map as Flame and Centenary Emblem

1994. Centenary of International Olympic Committee.
1275 **488** 450 m. multicoloured . . 1·50 60

489 Pencil and Postal and Tourism Motifs

1994. "Philakorea 1994" International Stamp Exhibition, Seoul.
1276 **489** 450 m. multicoloured . . 1·50 60

490 Clouded Yellow

1994. Butterflies. Multicoloured.
1277 100 m. Type **490** 15 10
1278 180 m. Red admiral 50 15
1279 300 m. Scarce swallowtail (vert) 75 20
1280 350 m. African monarch . . . 1·00 50
1281 450 m. Painted lady (vert) . . 1·25 60
1282 500 m. Swallowtail (vert) . . 1·50 60

491 President Ben Ali and Anniversary Emblem

492 Boxers and Globe

1994. 7th Anniv of Declaration of 7th November 1987. Multicoloured.
1283 350 m. Type **491** . . . . . . 1·00 25
1284 730 m. "7", fireworks and state crest (vert) . . . . 1·90 50

1994. 41st Military Boxing Championships, Tunis.
1285 **492** 450 m. multicoloured . . 1·40 60

493 Tailfins
494 Greylag Geese

1994. 50th Anniv of I.C.A.O.
1286 **493** 450 m. multicoloured . . 1·00 30

1994. Wildlife. Multicoloured.
1287 180 m. Type **494** 25 15
1288 350 m. Tufted duck and European pochard (horiz) . 75 25
1289 500 m. Water buffaloes . . . 1·10 60
1290 1000 m. European otters (horiz) . . . . 2·10 1·25

495 "Composition" (Ridha Bettaieb)

1994.
1291 **495** 500 m. multicoloured . . 1·10 35

496 "50", Map and Emblem

497 Oil Lamp

1995. 50th Anniv of League of Arab States.
1292 **496** 180 m. multicoloured . 25 15

1995. Glassware. Multicoloured.
1293 450 m. Type **497** 60 30
1294 730 m. Oil lamp with handle 95 50

498 Chebbi

1995. 60th Death Anniv (1994) of Aboulkacem Chebbi (poet).
1295 **498** 180 m. multicoloured . 25 15

499 Earring

1995. 4th World Conference on Women, Peking.
1296 **499** 180 m. multicoloured . 25 15

500 Farming

1995. 50th Anniv of F.A.O.
1297 **500** 350 m. multicoloured . 45 25

501 U.N. Workers and Anniversary Emblem over World Map

1995. 50th Anniv of U.N.O.
1298 **501** 350 m. multicoloured . 45 25

502 Crops

1995. Anti-desertification Campaign.
1299 **502** 180 m. multicoloured . 25 15

503 President Ben Ali visiting Village

504 Hannibal (Carthaginian general)

1995. 8th Anniv of Declaration of 7th November 1987. Multicoloured.
1300 180 m. Type **503** 25 15
1301 350 m. President Ben Ali meeting children 45 25

1995.
1302 **504** 180 m. purple 25 15

505 Human Rights Award

1995. World Human Rights Day.

1304	**505**	350 m. multicoloured	45	25

506 Bird carrying Olive Branch and People crossing Road

1995. Safety of Pedestrians.

1305	**506**	350 m. multicoloured	45	25

507 "Ophrys lapethica"

508 Modern and Traditional Work

1995. Flora and Fauna. Multicoloured.

1306	50 m. Type **507**	10	10
1307	180 m. Dorcas gazelle	25	15
1308	300 m. "Scupellaria cypria"	40	20
1309	350 m. Houbara bustard	45	25

1996. 50th Anniv of Tunisian General Workers' Union.

1310	**508**	440 m. multicoloured	55	30

509 Man's Jebba, Khamri

510 "March 20 1996 1956"

1996. National Traditional Costume Day. Mult.

1311	170 m. Type **509**	20	10
1312	200 m. Woman's embroidered kaftan, Hammamet	25	15

1996. 40th Anniv of Independence. Multicoloured.

1313	200 m. Type **510**	25	15
1314	390 m. "20", "40", dove and rainbow	50	25

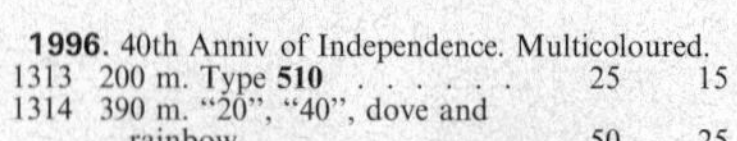

511 "Hannana" (Noureddine Khayachi)

1996.

1315	**511**	810 m. multicoloured	1·00	50

512 Seven-spotted Ladybirds

1996. Insects. Multicoloured.

1316	200 m. Type **512**	25	15
1317	810 m. Honey bee	1·00	50

513 Mascot

514 Magnifying Glass on "Stamp"

1996. World Environment Day.

1318	**513**	390 m. multicoloured	50	25

1996. "Capex'96" International Stamp Exhibition, Toronto, Canada.

1319	**514**	200 m. multicoloured	25	15

515 Flags over Stadium

516 Woman's Hands holding Dove

1996. Centenary of Olympic Games and Olympic Games, Atlanta. Multicoloured.

1320	20 m. Type **515**	10	10
1321	200 m. Runner, fireworks and "100" (vert)	25	15
1322	390 m. Mosaic of ancient Greek wrestlers	50	25

1996. 40th Anniv of Code of Personal Status.

1323	**516**	200 m. multicoloured	25	15

517 Ramparts of Sousse

518 Hammer breaking Chain on Anvil

1996. Ancient Buildings. Multicoloured.

1324	20 m. Type **517**	10	10
1325	200 m. Numide de Dougga mausoleum (vert)	25	15
1326	390 m. Arch of Trajan, Makthar	50	25

1996. International Year against Poverty.

1327	**518**	390 m. multicoloured	50	25

519 Candles on "7" and Map

1996. 9th Anniv of Declaration of 7th November 1987. Multicoloured.

1328	200 m. Type **519**	25	15
1329	390 m. Girl with doves	50	25

520 Camels outside Traditional Dwellings

1996. National Saharan Tourism Day. Multicoloured.

1330	200 m. Type **520**	25	15
1331	200 m. Traditional pattern	25	15

Nos. 1330/1 were issued together, se-tenant, forming a composite design.

PARCEL POST STAMPS

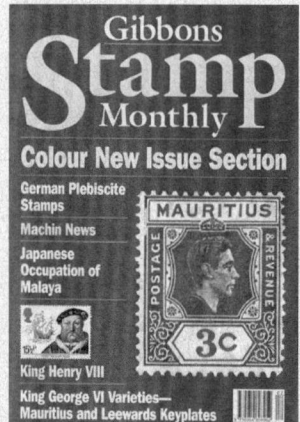

P 8 Mail Carrier

P 25 Date Gathering

1906.

P44	**P 8**	5 c. purple and green	20	15
P45		10 c. pink and red	75	20
P46		20 c. red and brown	1·00	20
P47		25 c. brown and blue	1·60	20
P48		40 c. red and grey	2·50	25
P49		50 c. violet and brown	1·75	15
P50		75 c. blue and brown	3·00	20
P51		1 f. red and brown	1·75	10
P52		2 f. blue and red	5·50	25
P53		5 f. brown and violet	15·00	55

1926.

P147	**P 25**	5 c. blue and brown	15	20
P148		10 c. mauve and red	20	20
P149		20 c. black and green	25	20
P150		25 c. black & brown	30	25
P151		40 c. green and red	1·50	70
P152		50 c. black and violet	1·50	75
P153		60 c. red and brown	1·50	70
P154		75 c. green and lilac	1·50	65
P155		80 c. brown and red	1·50	40
P156		1 f. pink and blue	1·50	35
P157		2 f. red and mauve	3·00	30
P158		4 f. black and red	3·50	25
P159		5 f. violet and brown	5·00	30
P160		10 f. green and red on green	9·25	50
P161		20 f. violet and green on pink	18·00	1·50

POSTAGE DUE STAMPS

D 3

D 20 Carthaginian Statue

D 86 Agricultural Produce

1901.

D28	**D 3**	1 c. black	15	15
D29		2 c. orange	35	15
D30		5 c. blue	35	10
D31		10 c. brown	50	10
D32		20 c. green	2·75	60
D33		30 c. red	1·50	40
D34		50 c. lake	1·25	45
D35		1 f. olive	1·00	45
D36		2 f. red on green	3·00	1·25
D37		5 f. black on yellow	45·00	32·00

1914. Surch **2 FRANCS**.

D49	**D 3**	2 f. on 5 f. black on yell	1·00	80

1923.

D100	**D 20**	1 c. black	10	35
D101		2 c. black on yellow	10	40
D102		5 c. purple	10	40
D103		10 c. blue	20	25
D104		20 c. orange on yellow	20	20
D105		30 c. brown	35	20
D106		50 c. red	40	30
D107		60 c. mauve	40	35
D108		80 c. brown	25	30
D109		90 c. red	40	40
D110		1 f. green	15	20
D111		2 f. green	75	25
D112		3 f. violet on pink	20	30
D113		5 f. violet	60	45

1945.

D287	**D 20**	10 c. green	10	30
D288		50 c. violet	10	30
D289		2 f. pink	15	20
D290		4 f. blue	25	45
D291		10 f. mauve	25	45
D292		20 f. brown	60	55
D293		30 f. blue	80	70

Nos. D293 is inscribed "TIMBRE TAXE".

1957.

D448	**D 86**	1 f. green	20	20
D449		2 f. brown	20	20
D450		3 f. green	40	40
D451		4 f. blue	45	45
D452		5 f. mauve	45	45
D453		10 f. red	45	45
D454		20 f. sepia	1·75	1·75
D455		30 f. blue	1·90	1·90

1960. Inscr "REPUBLIQUE TUNISIENNE" and new currency.

D534	**D 86**	1 m. green	10	10
D535		2 m. brown	10	10
D536		3 m. green	15	15
D537		4 m. blue	15	15
D538		5 m. violet	20	20
D539		10 m. red	40	40
D540		20 m. brown	60	60
D541		30 m. blue	70	70
D542		40 m. brown	15	15
D543		100 m. green	40	30

TURKEY Pt. 16

Formerly an empire, this country is now a republic, the greater part of its territory lying in Asia Minor.

1863. 40 paras = 1 piastre or grush.
1942. 100 paras = 1 kurus.
1947. 100 kurus = 1 lira.

For designs as Types **1, 2, 9, 15, 21, 23, 25, 28** and **30** but in black or brown, see Postage Due stamps.

1 2

1863. Imperf.

1 **1** 20 pa. black on yellow 60·00 25·00
2 1 pi. black on purple 75·00 27·00
3 2 pi. black on blue 85·00 38·00
4 5 pi. black on red 95·00 55·00

1865. Perf.

11 **2** 10 pa. green 2·75 8·50
64 10 pa. mauve 15 40
35a 10 pa. brown 40·00 2·25
12 20 pa. yellow 90 1·50
65 20 pa. green 15 40
94 20 pa. grey 55 85
13 1 pi. lilac 1·75 2·00
66 1 pi. yellow 20 25
14 2 pi. blue 1·00 1·25
95 2 pi. red to brown 25 25
15 5 pi. red 50 2·25
46 5 pi. blue 20 95
39c 5 pi. grey 7·50 12·00
16 25 pi. orange 95·00 £130
48 25 pi. red 6·00 20·00

1876. Surch with value in figures and **Pres**.

77 **2** ¼ pre. on 10 pa. mauve 1·00 1·00
78 ½ pre. on 20 pa. green 2·25 2·25
79 1¼ pre. on 50 pa. red 20 2·50
80 2 pre. on 2 pi. brown 8·00 2·25
81 5 pre. on 5 pi. blue 1·00 10·00

9 15

1876.

89 **9** 5 pa. black and yellow 20 20
96 5 pa. lilac 35·00 38·00
109 5 pa. black 15 55
113 5 pa. green and yellow 15 15
82 10 pa. black and mauve 25 30
90 10 pa. black and green 20 20
97 10 pa. green 20 10
83 20 pa. purple and green 24·00 2·25
91 20 pa. black and pink 1·00 15
103 20 pa. pink 15 10
84 50 pa. blue and yellow 40 60
92 1 pi. black and grey (A) 1·50 15
93 1 pi. black and blue (B) 25·00 1·00
99 1 pi. blue 15 10
85 2 pi. black and flesh 20 35
126a 2 pi. yellow 20 20
110 2 pi. orange and blue 15 15
114 2 pi. mauve and grey 25 25
86 5 pi. pink and blue 75 1·50
115 5 pi. brown 75 2·50
111 5 pi. green 65 2·00
87 25 pi. purple and mauve 6·00 18·00
107 25 pi. black 65·00 £110
112 25 pi. brown 9·00 15·00
116 25 pi. red and yellow 9·00 22·00

1892. Various frames.

141 **15** 10 pa. green 15 10
142a 20 pa. red 25 10
143 1 pi. blue 4·50 10
144 2 pi. brown 40 15
145 5 pi. purple 1·50 2·00

1897. Surch **5 5 Cinq Paras**.

160 **15** 5 pa. on 10 pa. green 35 10

21 22 23

1901. For Internal Mail.

167 **21** 5 pa. violet 15 10
168 10 pa. green 15 10
169 20 pa. red 15 10
170 1 pi. blue 15 10
171 2 pi. orange 40 10
203 5 pi. mauve 1·00 20
173 25 pi. brown 3·75 1·50
174 50 pi. brown 6·50 2·00

1901. For Foreign Mail.

175 **22** 5 pa. brown 25 15
176 10 pa. green 15 10
177 20 pa. mauve 15 10
178 1 pi. blue 40 10
179 2 pi. blue 60 20
180 5 pi. brown 1·75 85
181 25 pi. green 13·00 8·00
182 50 pi. yellow 40·00 25·00

1905.

212 **23** 5 pa. brown 10 10
213 10 pa. green 10 10
214 20 pa. pink 10 10
215 1 pi. blue 15 10
216 2 pi. blue 25 10
217 2½ pi. purple 45 15
218 5 pi. brown 75 25
219 10 pi. orange 1·10 30
220 25 pi. green 2·75 1·75
221 50 pi. purple 12·00 4·75

ب

(24)

Type **24** is the Turkish letter "B" which stands for Behie = discount.

1906. Optd with T **24**.

230 **23** 10 pa. green 20 10
231 20 pa. pink 20 10
232 1 pi. blue 40 10
233 2 pi. blue 3·00 2·50

25 27 28

1908.

234 **25** 5 pa. brown 10 10
235 10 pa. green 20 10
236 20 pa. red 6·00 10
237 1 pi. blue 1·50 10
238 2 pi. black 1·75 15
239 2½ pi. brown 70 15
240 5 pi. purple 2·75 15
241 10 pi. red 8·00 1·75
242 25 pi. green 3·00 2·25
243 50 pi. brown 8·00 5·50

1908. Optd as T **24** but smaller.

252 **25** 10 pa. green 85 30
253 20 pa. red 1·25 40
254 1 pi. blue 1·90 70
255 2 pi. black 4·00 1·75

1908. Granting of Constitution.

256 **27** 5 pa. brown 20 15
257 10 pa. green 20 15
258 20 pa. red 45 25
259 1 pi. blue 50 25
260 2 pi. black 6·50 3·00

1909.

271 **28** 2 pa. green 10 10
261 5 pa. brown 10 10
262 10 pa. green 10 10
263 20 pa. red 15 10
264 1 pi. blue 25 10
265 2 pi. black 25 10
266 2½ pi. brown 8·50 6·00
267 5 pi. purple 1·75 20
268 10 pi. red 3·00 40
269 25 pi. green 55·00 25·00
270 50 pi. brown 22·00 22·00

1909. Optd as T **24** but smaller.

289 **28** 10 pa. green 35 10
290 20 pa. red 20 10
291 1 pi. blue 45 20
292 2 pi. black 6·00 3·25

1910. No. 261 surch **2** and Turkish inscr.

296 **28** 2 pa. on 5 pa. brown 10 10

30 G.P.O., Constantinople 31 Mosque of Selim

1913.

333 **30** 2 pa. green 10 10
334 5 pa. bistre 10 10
335 10 pa. green 10 10
336 20 pa. pink 10 10
337 1 pi. blue 10 10
338 2 pi. grey 15 10
339 5 pi. purple 35 15
340 10 pi. red 1·25 55
341 25 pi. green 4·25 2·00
342 50 pi. brown 13·00 14·00

1913. Optd as T **24** but smaller.

343 **30** 10 pa. green 15 10
344 20 pa. pink 15 10
345 1 pi. blue 40 10
346 2 pi. grey 2·50 1·00

1913. Recapture of Adrianople.

353 **31** 10 pa. green 35 20
963 20 pa. red 15 10
355 40 pa. blue 85 55

For Type **31** surcharged, see Postage Due stamps.

32 Obelisk of Theodosius 34 Leander's Tower

1914.

499 **32** 2 pa. purple 10 20
500 – 4 pa. brown 10 25
501 **34** 5 pa. purple 10 10
961 5 pa. brown 10 15
502 – 6 pa. blue 15 30
503 – 10 pa. green 15 10
504 – 20 pa. red 40 10
518 – 1 pi. blue 30 10
964 – 1 pi. green 1·75 25
506 – 1½ pi. grey and red 40 35
507 – 1¾ pi. brown and grey 25 10
508 – 2 pi. black and green 1·00 30
509 – 2½ pi. green and orange 50 15
965 – 3 pi. blue 20 20
510 – 5 pi. lilac 2·75 40
966 – 5 pi. grey 6·50 50
511 – 10 pi. brown 3·75 50
967 – 10 pi. lilac 2·25 25
512 – 25 pi. green 24·00 2·75
968 – 25 pi. purple 60 1·25
513 – 50 pi. pink 3·50 2·25
969 – 50 pi. brown 75 2·50
514 – 100 pi. blue 22·00 18·00
515 – 200 pi. black and green £225 £150

DESIGNS—VERT: 4 pa. Column of Constantine; 6 pa. Seven Towers Castle, Yedikule. HORIZ: 10 pa. Lighthouse-Garden, Constantinople; 20 pa. Castle of Europe; 1 pi. Mosque of Sultan Ahmed; 1½ pi. Monument to Martyrs of Liberty; 1¾, 3 pi. Fountains of Suleiman; 2 pi. Cruiser "Hamidiye"; 2½, 5 (966) pi. Candilli, Bosphorus; 5 pi. (510) Former Ministry of War; 10 pi. Sweet Waters of Europe; 25 pi. Suleiman Mosque; 50 pi. Bosphorus at Rumeli Hisar; 100 pi. Sultan Ahmed's Fountain; 200 pi. Sultan Mohamed V.

SIZES—As Type **32**: 4, 6 pa; 31½ × 20 mm: 10 pa. to 1 pi; 26 × 21 mm: 1½ pi. to 2½ pi; 38 × 24 mm: 5 pi. to 50 pi; 40 × 25½ mm: 100, 200 pi.

1914. Stamps of 1914 optd with small star.

516 10 pa. green 20 20
517 20 pa. red 2·25 40
518 1 pi. blue 45 15
519 1¾ pi. brown and grey 35 30
520 2 pi. black and green 12·00 1·00

(49)

1914. 7th Anniv of Constitution No. 506 surch with T **49**.

521 1 pi. on 1½ pi. grey and red 75 75

(50)

1914. Abrogation of the Capitulations. Nos. 501/11 optd with T **50**.

524 5 pa. purple 25 25
526 10 pa. green 35 30
527 20 pa. red 75 35
528 1 pi. blue 1·25 70
530 2 pi. black and green 3·00 75
532 5 pi. lilac 9·00 2·40
533 10 pi. brown 20·00 14·00

(51)

1915. Nos. 514/15 surch as T **51**.

534 10 pi. on 100 pi. blue 18·00 7·50
535 25 pi. on 200 pi. black & grn 10·00 5·00

(53) ("1331" = 1915)

1915. Various issues optd with T **53**.

I. On postage stamps. (a) 1892 and 1897 issues.

536 **15** 5 pa. on 10 pa. green 15 10
537 10 pa. green 15 10
538 2 pi. brown 20 10
539 5 pi. purple 1·50 25

(b) 1901 issues (i) For Internal mail.

540 **21** 5 pa. violet 10 10
541 10 pa. green 20 10
542 20 pa. red 20 10
543 1 pi. blue 40 10
544 2 pi. orange 1·50 20
545 5 pi. mauve 40 15
546 25 pi. brown 2·75 2·00

(ii) For Foreign mail.

547 **22** 5 pa. brown 10 10
548 1 pi. blue 40 15
549 2 pi. blue 40 10
550 5 pi. brown 2·50 60
551 25 pi. green 14·00 6·00

(c) 1905 and 1906 issues.

552 **23** 5 pa. buff 10 10
553b 10 pa. green 25 10
561 10 pa. green (230) 20 10
554a 20 pa. pink 25 10
555a 1 pi. blue 60 10
556b 2 pi. grey 80 10
562 2 pi. grey (233) 75 20
557 2½ pi. purple 50 10
558a 5 pi. brown 75 10
559 10 pi. orange 3·00 60
560 25 pi. green 10·00 2·50

(d) 1908 issues.

563 **25** 5 pa. brown 40·00 30·00
564 2 pi. black 35·00 15·00
569a 2 pi. black (255) 3·25 80
565 2½ pi. brown 60 20
566a 5 pi. purple 22·00 10·00
567 10 pi. red 3·25 1·50
568 25 pi. green 8·00 2·25

(e) 1909 issues.

570 **28** 5 pa. brown 10 10
572 20 pa. red 20 10
579 20 pa. red (290) 15 10
573 1 pi. blue 40 10
581 1 pi. blue (291) 50 15
574 2 pi. black 40 10
582 2 pi. black (292) 45 15
575 2½ pi. brown 20·00 8·50
576 5 pi. purple 40 10
577 10 pi. red 2·25 20
578 25 pi. green £325 £300

(f) 1913 issues.

583 **30** 5 pa. bistre 10 10
584 10 pa. green 10 10
591 10 pa. green (343) 25 15
585 20 pa. pink 10 10
592 20 pa. pink (344) 40 10
586 1 pi. blue 20 10
593 1 pi. blue (345) 50 15
587 2 pi. grey 75 25
594 2 pi. grey (346) 3·00 85
588 5 pi. purple 1·00 60
589 10 pi. red 3·25 60
590 25 pi. green 12·00 4·50

II. On printed matter stamps (for use as postage stamps). (a) 1894 issue.

595 **15** 10 pa. green 25 10
596 2 pi. brown 1·25 30

(b) 1901 issues.

597 **21** 5 pa. violet 25 10
600 **22** 10 pa. green 20 10
598 **21** 20 pa. red 75 20
599 5 pi. mauve 6·00 1·10

(c) 1905 issues.

601b **23** 5 pa. buff 25 10
602 2 pi. grey 2·75 1·25
603 5 pi. brown 2·25 50

(d) 1908 issues.

604 **25** 2 pi. black £250 £160
605a 5 pi. purple 30·00 10·00

(e) 1909 issues.

606 **28** 5 pa. brown 20 10
608 5 pi. purple 30·00 10·00

(54) (56)

1915. Various issues optd with T **54** (star varies).

I. On postage stamps. (a) 1892 issue, also surch with T **56**.

630 **15** 10 pa. on 20 pa. red 15 10

(b) 1901 issues.

631 **21** 1 pi. blue 20 10
632a 5 pi. mauve 1·50 30

(c) 1905 and 1906 issues, Nos. 633 and 636 also surch with T **56**.

609a **23** 10 pa. green 10 10
611b 10 pa. green (230) 4·75 1·75
633 10 pa. on 20 pa. pink 25 10
636 10 pa. on 20 pa. pink (231) 20 10
634 1 pi. blue 30 10
637 1 pi. blue (232) 25 10
610 10 pi. orange 2·25 40

(d) 1908 issues.

612 **25** 10 pa. green 20 10
614a 10 pa. green (252) 35·00 22·00
638 20 pa. red
640a 20 pa. red (253) 25 15
641 1 pi. blue (254) 1·10 10
613 5 pi. purple 8·00 2·25
639 10 pi. red 60·00 40·00

(e) 1909 issues.

616 **28** 10 pa. green 20 10
620 10 pa. green (289) 15 10
643 20 pa. red 15 10
647 20 pa. red (290) 20 10
645 1 pi. blue 15 10
649 1 pi. blue (291) 25 10
619 5 pi. purple 2·00 40
646 10 pi. red 22·00 20·00

(f) 1913 issues.

623 **30** 10 pa. green 20 10
625 10 pa. green (343) 20 10
650 20 pa. pink 15 10
653 20 pa. pink (344) 15 10
624 1 pi. blue 25 10
652 10 pi. red . . . . 5·50 2·75

(g) 1916 Postal Jubilee issue.

654 **60** 10 pa. red 15 10
655 20 pa. blue 20 10
656 1 pi. black and violet . . . 15 10
657 5 pi. black and brown . . . 60 15

II. On printed matter stamps (for use as postage stamps). (a) 1894 issue, also surch with T **56**.

658 **15** 10 pa. on 20 pa. red . . . 15 10

(b) 1901 issue.

659 **22** 5 pi. brown . . . . . . 2·00 60

(c) 1908 issue.

626 **25** 10 pa. green . . . . . . 35·00 22·00
627 5 pi. purple . . . . . . 40·00 22·00

(d) 1909 issue.

629 **28** 10 pa. green 15 10

(57) (58) (59)
("1332" = 1916)

1916. Various issues optd with T **57**, some also surch in piastres as T **58**.

I. On postage stamps. (a) 1892 and 1897 issues.

660 **15** 5 pa. on 10 pa. green (160) 15 10
661 10 pa. green 30 10
662 20 pa. red 15 10
663 1 pi. blue . . . . 12·00 12·00
664 2 pi. brown . . . . . . 1·25 65
665 5 pi. purple . . . . . . 12·00 12·00

(b) 1901 issues. (i) Internal mail.

666 **21** 5 pa. violet . . . . . . 11·00 10·00
667 10 pa. green 50 35
668 20 pa. red 20 10
669 1 pi. blue 25 10
670 2 pi. orange 60 20
671a 10 pi. on 25 pi. brown . . 2·50 95
672 10 pi. on 50 pi. brown . . 3·25 1·25
673a 25 pi. brown . . . . . . 2·50 1·00
674 50 pi. brown . . . . . . 4·50 65

(ii) Foreign mail.

675 **22** 5 pa. brown 10 10
676 10 pa. green 60 25
677 20 pa. mauve 15 10
678 1 pi. blue 30 10
679 2 pi. blue . . . . 1·75 95
680 5 pi. on 25 pi. green . . 15·00 14·00
681 10 pi. on 25 pi. green . . 15·00 14·00
682 25 pi. green . . . . . . 16·00 14·00

(c) 1905 and 1906 issues.

683 **23** 5 pa. buff 15 15
692a 10 pa. green (230) 35 15
684 20 pa. pink 25 10
693 20 pa. pink (231) 35 15
685a 1 pi. blue 40 10
694a 1 pi. blue (232) 60 15
686a 2 pi. grey . . . . 1·25 40
687 $2\frac{1}{2}$ pi. purple . . . . . . 1·50 60
688 10 pi. on 25 pi. green . . 3·50 1·75
689 10 pi. on 50 pi. purple . . 3·75 1·50
690 25 pi. green . . . . . . 3·50 1·00
691 50 pi. purple . . . . . . 5·00 1·25

(d) 1908 issues.

701 **25** 2 pi. black (255) . . . . 14·00 12·00
695 $2\frac{1}{2}$ pi. brown . . . . . . 12·00 11·00
696 10 pi. on 25 pi. green . . 5·50 3·25
697a 10 pi. on 50 pi. brown . . 14·00 14·00
698 25 pi. on 50 pi. brown . . 14·00 14·00
699 25 pi. green . . . . . . 3·50 3·25
700 50 pi. brown . . . . . . 15·00 15·00

(e) 1908 Constitution issue.

702 **27** 5 pa. brown . . . . . . 15·00 15·00

(f) 1909 issues.

703 **28** 5 pa. brown 15 10
704 10 pa. green . . . . . . 13·00 13·00
705 20 pa. red . . . . 14·00 13·00
707 1 pi. blue 85 15
711 1 pi. blue (291) . . . . 12·00 12·00
708 2 pi. black . . . . 1·10 45
712 2 pi. black (292) . . . . 12·00 12·00
709 $2\frac{1}{2}$ pi. brown . . . . . . 12·00 12·00
710 5 pi. purple . . . . . . 13·00 12·00

(g) 1913 issues.

713 **30** 5 pa. bistre 15 10
714 20 pa. pink 45 20
715 1 pi. blue 45 10
720 1 pi. blue (345) 60 10
716 2 pi. grey . . . . 1·10 40
717 10 pi. on 50 pi. brown . . 4·00 1·90
718 25 pi. green . . . . . . 4·00 75
719 50 pi. brown . . . . . . 4·25 1·75

(h) 1913 Adrianople issue.

721 **31** 10 pa. green 15 10
722 20 pa. red 60 20
723 40 pa. blue 75 40

(i) 1914 Constitution issue with further surch.

724 60 pa. on 1 pi. on $1\frac{1}{2}$ pi. grey and red . . . . 1·00 25

(j) 1916 Postal Jubilee issues.

725 **60** 5 pi. black and brown . . . 50 10

II. On printed matter stamps (for use as postage stamps). (a) 1894 issues.

726 **15** 5 pa. on 10 pa. green . . . 15 10
727 10 pa. green 35 15
728 20 pa. red 20 15
729 5 pi. purple . . . . . . 15·00 15·00

(b) 1901 issues. (i) Internal mail.

730 **21** 5 pa. violet . . . . . . 14·00 14·00
731 10 pa. green . . . . . . 14·00 14·00
732 20 pa. red 40 15
733 1 pi. blue 40 15
734 2 pi. orange 60 15

(ii) Foreign mail.

735 **22** 5 pa. brown 15 10
736 10 pa. green 25 10
737 20 pa. mauve 20 10
738 1 pi. blue 35 15

(c) 1905 issue.

739 **23** 5 pa. buff 15 10
740 10 pa. green . . . . . . 14·00 12·00
741 20 pa. pink . . . . 14·00 12·00
742a 1 pi. blue 60 15

(d) 1908 issue.

743a **25** 5 pa. brown . . . . . . 15·00 14·00

(e) 1909 issue.

744 **28** 5 pa. brown . . . . . . 15·00 14·00

III. On 1913 Adrianople postage due issues (for use as postage stamps).

745 **31** 10 on 2 pa. on 10 pa. green 18·00 12·00
746 20 on 5 pa. on 20 pa. red . 18·00 12·00
747 40 on 10 pa. on 40 pa. blue 18·00 12·00

1916. Occupation of Sinai Peninsula. Optd with T **59**.

749 **21** 5 pa. violet 45 25
750 10 pa. green 60 25
751 **28** 20 pa. red 75 45
752 1 pi. blue . . . . 1·00 45
753 **30** 5 pi. purple . . . . . . 10·00 3·75

60 Old G.P.O., Constantinople
(61)

1916. Jubilee of Constantinople City Post.

754 **60** 5 pa. green 10 10
755 10 pa. red 10 10
756 20 pa. blue 20 10
757 1 pi. black and violet . . . 30 10
758 5 pi. black and brown . . . 7·00 85

1916. National Fete. Optd with T **61**.

759 **15** 10 pa. green . . . . . . 85 1·00
760b **23** 20 pa. red 90 55
761a 1 pi. blue . . . . 1·25 60
762b 2 pi. grey . . . . 2·50 55
763 $2\frac{1}{2}$ pi. purple . . . . . . 3·25 55

62 Dolmabahce Palace

63 Sentry **64** Sultan Mohamed V

1916.

764 **62** 10 pi. violet . . . . . . 2·75 50
765 10 pi. green on grey . . . 1·50 35
766 10 pi. brown . . . . . . 3·25 25
767 **63** 25 pi. red on buff 40 30
768 **64** 50 pi. red . . . . 1·75 70
769 50 pi. green on yellow . . 4·00 3·00
770 50 pi. blue 35 35

65 Off to the Front (66)

1917. Charity.

771 **65** 10 pa. purple 10 10

1917. Various issues optd with T **66** or surch in addition.

A. On postage stamp issue of 1865.

782 **2** 10 pa. mauve . . . . . . 10·00 10·00
772a 20 pa. yellow . . . . . . 10·00 10·00
783 20 pa. green . . . . . . 10·00 10·00
785 20 pa. grey . . . . 10·00 10·00
773b 1 pi. lilac . . . . 10·00 10·00
784 1 pi. yellow . . . . . . 10·00 10·00
774 **2** 2 pi. blue . . . . 10·00 10·00
780 2 pi. red to brown . . . . 10·00 10·00
775 5 pi. red . . . . 10·00 10·00
778 5 pi. blue . . . . 10·00 10·00
779 25 pi. red . . . . 10·00 10·00

B. On surcharged postage stamp issue of 1876.

787 **2** $\frac{1}{4}$ pre. on 10 pa. mauve . . . 10·00 10·00
788 $\frac{1}{2}$ pre. on 20 pa. green . . . 10·00 10·00
789 $1\frac{1}{4}$ pre. on 50 pa. red . . . 10·00 10·00

C. On postage stamp issue of 1876.

790 **9** 5 pa. black and yellow . . . 10·00 10·00
791 5 pa. black 40 50
792 10 pa. black and green . . . 10·00 10·00
793 10 pa. green . . . . . . 10·00 10·00
794 50 pa. black and yellow . . . 10·00 10·00
795 2 pi. black and flesh . . . 10·00 10·00
796 2 pi. ochre . . . . 10·00 10·00
797 2 pi. orange and blue . . . 1·10 1·50
798 5 pi. brown . . . . 10·00 10·00
799 5 pi. green . . . . 10·00 10·00
801 25 pi. purple and mauve . . 10·00 10·00
802 25 pi. brown . . . . . . 10·00 10·00

D. On postage stamp issue of 1892.

803 **15** 20 pa. purple 50 50
804 2 pi. brown . . . . 1·25 1·25

E. On postage stamp issue of 1901.

805 **21** 5 pa. violet . . . . . . 10·00 10·00
806 10 pa. green . . . . . . 1·00 1·00
807 20 pa. red 25 20
808 1 pi. blue 25 25
809 2 pi. orange 75 75
810 5 pi. mauve . . . . . . 10·00 10·00
811 10 pi. on 50 pi. brown . . 10·00 10·00
812 25 pi. brown . . . . . . 2·00 1·00

F. On postage stamp issue of 1901.

813 **22** 5 pa. brown 75 75
814 20 pa. mauve 30 30
815 1 pi. blue . . . . 1·00 1·00
816 2 pi. blue . . . . 2·00 2·00
817 5 pi. brown . . . . . . 10·00 10·00
818 10 pi. on 50 pi. yellow . . 28·00 28·00
819 25 pi. green . . . . . . 15·00 15·00

G. On postage stamp issues of 1905 and 1906.

820 **23** 5 pa. buff 10 10
821 10 pa. green . . . . . . 11·00 11·00
830 10 pa. green (No. 230) . . 15 15
822 20 pa. pink 15 10
831 20 pa. pink (No. 231) . . 25 15
823 1 pi. blue 15 10
832 1 pi. blue (No. 232) . . . 60 25
824 2 pi. grey . . . . 1·00 50
833 2 pi. grey (No. 233) . . . 10·00 10·00
825 $2\frac{1}{2}$ pi. purple . . . . . . 1·25 65
826 5 pi. brown . . . . . . 10·00 10·00
827 10 pi. orange . . . . . . 12·00 10·00
828 10 pi. on 50 pi. purple . . 10·00 10·00
829 25 pi. green . . . . . . 12·00 10·00

H. On postage stamp issues of 1908.

834a **25** 5 pa. brown . . . . . . 1·00 1·00
835 10 pa. green . . . . . . 2·00 15
840 10 pa. green (No. 252) . . 10·00 10·00
841 1 pi. blue (No. 254) . . . 10·00 10·00
836 2 pi. black . . . . 4·50 5·50
842 2 pi. black (No. 255) . . . 4·00 3·25
837a $2\frac{1}{2}$ pi. brown . . . . . . 6·50 6·50
838 10 pi. on 50 pi. brown . . 10·00 10·00
839 25 pi. green . . . . . . 10·00 10·00

I. On Constitution issue of 1908.

843 **27** 5 pa. brown 40 40

J. On postage stamp issues of 1909.

844 **28** 5 pa. brown 25 25
846 10 pa. green 20 20
854 10 pa. green (No. 289) . . 25·00 25·00
847 20 pa. red 25 25
849 1 pi. blue 25 25
856 1 pi. blue (No. 291) . . . 50 50
850 2 pi. black . . . . 1·00 75
857 2 pi. black (No. 292) . . . 5·50 5·50
851 $2\frac{1}{2}$ pi. brown . . . . . . 10·00 10·00
852a 5 pi. purple . . . . . . 10·00 10·00
853 10 pi. red . . . . 10·00 10·00

K. On postage stamp issues of 1913.

858 **30** 5 pa. bistre 30 30
859 10 pa. green . . . . . . 10·00 10·00
865 10 pa. green (No. 343) . . . 40 40
860 20 pa. pink 30 30
861 1 pi. blue 30 30
866 1 pi. blue (No. 345) . . . 1·00 1·00
862 2 pi. grey 75 75
867 2 pi. grey (No. 346) . . . 10·00 10·00
863 5 pi. purple . . . . . . 10·00 10·00
864 10 pi. red . . . . 10·00 10·00

L. On Adrianople Commem stamps of 1913.

868 **31** 10 pa. green 50 50
869 40 pa. blue 65 65

M. On Constitution Commem of 1914 with additional surch in Turkish.

870 60 pa. on 1 pi. on $1\frac{1}{2}$ pi. grey and red (No. 521) . . . . 1·00 1·00

N. On postage stamp issues of 1916.

871 **63** 25 pi. red on buff 75 75
872 **64** 50 pi. red . . . . 6·50 3·25
873 50 pi. green on yellow . . . 5·50 3·50
874 50 pi. blue . . . . 7·50 5·50

O. On stamps of Eastern Roumelia of 1881 (T **9** of Turkey, but inscr "ROUMELIE ORIENTALE" at left).

876 5 pa. lilac . . . . 11·00 11·00
877 10 pa. green . . . . . . 11·00 11·00
875 20 pa. black and red . . . . 11·00 11·00
878 20 pa. red . . . . 11·00 11·00

P. On printed matter stamps of 1893 optd with Type N **16**.

879 **15** 20 pa. red (No. N 156a) . . 1·00 1·00
880 1 pi. blue (No. N 157) . . . 20 20

Q. On printed matter stamps of 1901 optd with Type N **23**.

881 **21** 5 pa. violet (No. N183) . . 50 50
882 10 pa. green (No. N184) . . 6·00 5·50
883 20 pa. red (No. N185) . . . 50 25
884 1 pi. blue (No. N186) . . . 60 50
885 **21** 2 pi. orange (No. N187) . . 60 50
886 5 pi. mauve (No. N188) . . 10·00 10·00

R On printed matter stamps of 1901 optd with Type N **23**.

887 **22** 5 pa. brown (No. N189) . . 75 75
888 10 pa. green (No. N190) . . 75 75
889 20 pa. mauve (No. N191) . . 75 75
890 2 pi. blue (No. N193) . . . 10·00 10·00

S. On printed matter stamps of 1905 optd with Type N **23**.

891d **23** 5 pa. brown (No. N222) . . 15 15
892 10 pa. green (No. N223) . . 60 60
893 20 pa. pink (No. N224) . . 15 10
894 1 pi. blue (No. N225) . . 25 25
895 2 pi. grey (No. N226) . . 10·00 10·00
896 5 pi. brown (No. N227) . . 10·00 10·00

T. On printed matter stamp of 1908 optd with Type N **27**.

897 **25** 5 pa. brown (No. N244) . . 10·00 10·00

U. On postage due stamps of 1865.

898 D **4** 20 pa. brown . . . . . . 10·00 10·00
899 1 pi. brown . . . . . . 10·00 10·00
900 2 pi. brown . . . . . . 10·00 10·00
901 5 pi. brown . . . . . . 10·00 10·00
902 25 pi. brown . . . . . . 10·00 10·00

V. On postage due stamps of 1888.

904 **9** 1 pi. black (D118) . . . . . 10·00 10·00
905 2 pi. black (D119) . . . . . 10·00 10·00

W. On postage due stamps of 1892.

906 **15** 20 pa. black (D146) . . . 50 50
907 1 pi. black (D148) 50 50
908 2 pi. black (D149) 50 25

X. On Adrianople commemoration issue of 1913 (postage due stamps surch in Arabic further surch).

909 **31** 10 on 2 pa. on 10 pa. green (D356) 10 10
910 20 on 5 pa. on 20 pa. red (D357) 15 15
911 40 on 10 pa. on 40 pa. blue (D358) 30 30
912 40 on 20 pa. on 40 pa. blue (D359) 45 35

The overprints on printed matter and postage due stamps were used for ordinary postage.

67 In the Trenches **69** Howitzer at Sedd el Bahr

1917. Surch variously in Turkish.

913 **67** 5 pa. on 1 pi. red 10 10
915 **65** 10 pa. on 20 pa. red . . . 20 10
914 **69** 5 pi. on 2 pa. blue . . . 2·25 40

72 Mosque at Ortakoy **73** Lighthouse, Achir Kapu

74 Martyrs' Column **77** Seraglio Point

75 Map of Gallipoli **76**

1917.

916 **69** 2 pa. violet 10 20
917 **72** 5 pa. orange 10 15
918 **73** 10 pa. green 10 10
919 **74** 20 pa. red 10 10
920 **75** 1 pi. blue 25 10
921 **76** 50 pa. blue 10 45
921a **77** 2 pi. blue and brown . . . [illegible] [illegible]
922 – 5 pi. brown and blue . . 7·00 1·10

DESIGNS—As T **77**. 5 pi. Pyramids.

1918. Surch **5 Piastres 5** and in Turkish.

923 **69** 5 pi. on 2 pa. blue 65 20

1918. No. 913 with additional surch.

924 **67** 2 pa. on 5 pa. on 1 pi. red 10 25

(81) **84** Wells at Beersheba

85 Sentry at Beersheba

87 Turkish Column in Sinai

1918. Armistice. Optd. as T **81**.

925	**84**	20 pa. purple	15	40
926	**75**	1 pi. blue	1·75	2·75
927	**85**	1 pi. blue	50·00	50·00
937	**D 51**	1 pi. blue (No. D518)	50·00	60·00
928	**76**	50 pa. blue	20	60
929	**77**	2 pi. blue and brown	20	75
930	–	2½ pi. green and orange (No. 509)	50·00	50·00
931	–	5 pi. brown and blue (No. 922)	20	85
932	**62**	10 pi. green on grey	2·25	4·50
933	**63**	25 pi. red on buff	2·25	4·50
934	**87**	25 pi. blue	50·00	50·00
935	–	50 pi. pink (No. 513)	50·00	50·00
936	**64**	50 pi. green on yellow	2·25	4·50

1918. Stamp of 1909 optd with Sultan's toughra and surch in Turkish.

938	**28**	5 pa. on 2 pa. green	10	40

86 Dome of the Rock, Jerusalem

١٩١٩ ١٣٣٥

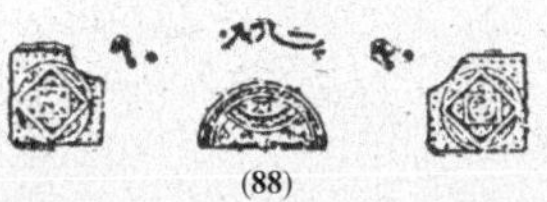
(88)

1919. Accession of Sultan Mohamed VI. Optd with date as in T **88** and ornaments or inscription.

939	**84**	20 pa. purple	35	2·25
940	**85**	1 pi. blue	1·00	3·50
941	**86**	60 pa. on 10 pa. green	1·00	4·50
942	**87**	25 pi. blue	10·00	15·00

The illustrations Type **85** (optd with date and inscription at foot) and **86** (surch with T **88**) illustrate Nos. 940/1. Nos. 939 and 942 are overprinted with the date and the central motif only at bottom of Type **88**.

(89)

(91)

(90)

1919. 1st Anniv of Sultan's Accession. Optd or surch as T **89**, **90** or **91**.

943	**69**	2 pa. violet	40	75
944	**72**	5 pa. orange	10	45
945	**28**	5 pa. on 2 pa. green	10	25
946	**30**	10 pa. on 2 pa. green	10	30
960a	**D 49**	10 pa. on 5 pa. brown	7·50	8·50
947	**73**	10 pa. green	45	65
948	**74**	20 pa. red	15	45
960b	**D 50**	20 pa. red	7·50	8·50
949	**75**	1 pi. blue	10	40
960c	**D 51**	1 pi. blue	7·50	8·50
950	**76**	60 pa. on 50 pa. blue	75	1·50
951	**77**	60 pa. on 2 pi. blue and brown	15	1·00
952		2 pi. blue and brown	45	1·00
960d	**D 52**	2 pi. blue	7·50	8·50
952a	–	2½ pi. green and orange (No. 509)	8·00	10·00
953	–	5 pi. brown and blue (No. 922)	15	1·00
954	**62**	10 pi. brown	1·00	2·25
955	**84**	10 pi. on 20 pa. purple	1·00	2·50
956	**63**	25 pi. red and buff	1·00	2·50
957	**85**	35 pi. on 1 pi. blue	2·50	3·50
958	**64**	50 pi. green on yellow	4·50	7·00
958a		50 pi. red	8·50	10·00
959	**86**	100 pi. on 60 pa. on 10 pa. green	5·50	7·50
960	**87**	250 pi. on 25 pi. blue	7·50	8·50

Types **84** and **87** illustrate Nos. 955 and 960.

1921. Surch in figures and words and in Turkish characters.

970	**65**	30 pa. on 10 pa. purple	15	10
971	–	60 pa. on 10 pa. green (No. 503)	15	10
972	**67**	4½ pi. on 1 pi. red	1·00	75
973	–	7½ on 3 pi. blue (No. 965)	2·25	55

Numerous fiscal and other stamps were surcharged or overprinted by the Turkish Nationalist Government at Angora during 1921, but as they are not often met with by general collectors we omit them. A full listing will be found in Part 16 (Central Asia) of the Stanley Gibbons catalogue.

Nos. A79/90 and A119/24 were the only definitive issue of the Angora Government at this period.

A **24** National Pact

A **25** Parliament House, Sivas

1921.

A79	A **24**	10 pa. purple	20	10
A80	–	20 pa. green	25	10
A81	–	1 pi. blue	40	10
A82	–	2 pi. purple	85	10
A83	–	5 pi. blue	90	10
A84	–	10 pi. brown	3·00	10
A85	–	25 pi. red	4·25	10
A86	A **25**	50 pi. blue (A)	1·25	65
A87		50 pi. blue (B)	1·25	75
A88	–	100 pi. violet	30·00	1·00
A89	–	200 pi. violet	70·00	12·00
A90	–	500 pi. green	40·00	8·00

DESIGNS—HORIZ: 20 pa. Izmir Harbour; 1 pi. Mosque, Adrianople; 10 pi. Legendary grey wolf, Boz Kurt; 25 pi. Castle Adana; 200 pi. Map of Anatolia. VERT: 2 pi. Mosque, Konya; 5 pi. Soldier taking oath; 100 pi. Mosque, Ourfa; 500 pi. Declaration of faith from Koran.

Type (B) of the 50 pi. as illustrated. In Type (A) the inscription at the top is similar to that of Type A **30** and the figures in the value tablets are above instead of below the Turkish inscription.

A **30** First Parliament House, Angora

1922.

A119	A **30**	5 pa. mauve	20	10
A120		10 pa. green	25	10
A121		20 pa. red	35	20
A122		1 pi. orange	2·25	50
A123		2 pi. brown	9·50	1·25
A124		3 pi. red	1·00	90

اقتصاد قونفره سى

١٧ شباط ٣٣٩

(94a)

1923. Izmir (Smyrna) Economic Congress. Nos. 918 and A80/4 optd with T **94a**.

973b	**73**	10 pa. green	1·75	1·25
973c	–	20 pa. green	1·75	1·25
973d	–	1 pi. blue	2·50	1·25
973e	–	2 pi. purple	3·75	3·25
973f	–	5 pi. blue	4·00	2·75
973g	–	10 pi. brown	7·50	6·00

95

96 Kemal Ataturk and Sakarya Bridge

1923.

974	**95**	10 pa. grey	25	10
975		20 pa. yellow	30	10
976		1 pi. mauve	30	10
977		1½ pi. green	35	10
978		2 pi. green	80	10
979		3 pi. brown	45	10
980		3¾ pi. brown	85	25
1001		4½ pi. red	50	10
1002		5 pi. violet	1·50	10
1003		7½ pi. blue	90	10
1004		10 pi. grey	3·25	25
1012a		10 pi. blue	28·00	15
986	**95**	11¼ pi. pink	1·10	35
1006		15 pi. brown	3·25	25
988		18¾ pi. green	1·75	60
989		22½ pi. orange	2·75	80
990		25 pi. brown	7·50	25
991		50 pi. grey	25·00	55
992		100 pi. purple	32·00	70
993		500 pi. green	£160	40·00

1924. Treaty of Lausanne.

1013	**96**	1½ pi. green	55	25
1014		3 pi. violet	60	25
1015		4½ pi. pink	1·00	95
1016		5 pi. brown	1·50	25
1017		7½ pi. blue	80	55
1018		50 pi. orange	13·00	7·50
1019		100 pi. purple	30·00	15·00
1020		200 pi. olive	40·00	27·00

97 Legendary Blacksmith and Grey Wolf, Boz Kurt

98 Gorge and R Sakarya

99 Fortress af Ankara

100 Kemal Ataturk

1926.

1021	**97**	10 pa. grey	10	10
1022		20 pa. orange	15	10
1023		1 gr. red	15	10
1024	**98**	2 gr. green	50	10
1025		2½ gr. black	50	10
1026		3 gr. red	60	10
1027	**99**	5 gr. violet	1·10	10
1028		6 gr. red	60	10
1029		10 gr. blue	1·60	10
1030		15 gr. orange	2·00	10
1031	**100**	25 gr. black and green	4·50	10
1032		50 gr. black and red	5·50	10
1033		100 gr. black and olive	12·00	55
1034		200 gr. black and brown	30·00	1·25

١٩٢٧

(**101** "1927 Izmir Exhibition")

(**102** "Izmir, 9 Sept, 1928")

1927. Izmir (Smyrna) Exhibition. Optd with T **101**.

1035	**97**	1 gr. red	20	10
1036	**98**	2 gr. green	1·60	40
1037		2½ gr. black	1·60	40
1038		3 gr. red	2·25	75
1039	**99**	5 gr. violet	85	35
1040		6 gr. red	35	15
1041		10 gr. blue	2·25	85
1042		15 gr. orange	2·40	85
1043	**100**	25 gr. black and green	6·50	3·25
1044		50 gr. black and red	11·00	6·00
1045		100 gr. black and olive	25·00	25·00

1928. 2nd Izmir Exhibition. T **97/9** optd with T **102** and T **100** optd **928** and 2 lines of Turkish.

1053	**97**	10 pa. grey	15	10
1054		20 pa. orange	15	10
1055		1 gr. red	20	10
1056	**98**	2 gr. green	1·10	30
1057		2½ gr. black	1·10	40
1058		3 gr. red	1·10	75
1059	**99**	5 gr. violet	1·90	1·00
1060		6 gr. red	65	10
1061		10 gr. blue	1·90	65
1062		15 gr. orange	2·10	50
1063	**100**	25 gr. black and green	6·00	2·25
1064		50 gr. black and red	11·00	5·00
1065		100 gr. black and olive	25·00	12·00
1066		200 gr. black and brown	35·00	18·00

1929. Surch with value in "Paradir" or "Kurustur".

1067	**97**	20 par. on 1 gr. red	40	10
1068	**99**	2½ kur. on 5 gr. violet	55	10
1069		6 kur. on 10 gr. blue	7·50	10

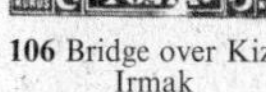
106 Bridge over Kizil-Irmak

107 Gorge and R. Sakarya

1929. T **106/7** and 1926 stamps but inscr "TURKIYE CUMHURIYETI".

1076	**97**	10 pa. green	10	10
1077	**106**	20 pa. violet	25	10
1078		1 k. green	50	10
1079	**97**	1½ k. green	15	10
1070	**106**	2 k. black	1·00	10
1080		2 k. violet	2·00	10
1081		2½ k. green	25	10
1072		3 k. purple	1·60	10
1082		3 k. red	2·75	10
1083	**97**	4 k. red	2·50	10
1084	**99**	5 k. purple	3·25	10
1085	**97**	6 k. blue	3·25	10
1086	**107**	7½ k. red	65	10
1088	**99**	12½ k. blue	45	10
1089		15 k. orange	55	10
1090	**107**	17½ k. black	65	50
1091	**99**	20 k. brown	20·00	25
1092	**107**	25 k. brown	1·75	15
1093	**99**	30 k. brown	1·75	15
1094	**107**	40 k. purple	2·00	15
1075	**100**	50 k. black and red	21·00	60

109 **112** **113**
Kemal Ataturk

1930.

1095	**109**	50 k. black and red	1·90	10
1096		100 k. black and olive	3·25	30
1097		200 k. black and green	2·25	50
1098		500 k. black and brown	12·00	2·25

1930. Opening of the Ankara–Sivas Railway. Surch **Sivas D.Y. 30 ag. 930** and value.

1099	**97**	10 pa. on 10 pa. green	10	10
1100	**106**	10 pa. on 20 pa. violet	15	10
1101		20 pa. on 1 k. green	15	10
1102	**97**	1 k. on 1½ k. green	20	15
1103	**106**	1½ k. on 2 k. violet	35	30
1104		2 k. on 2½ k. green	50	40
1105		2½ k. on 3 k. red	55	50
1106	**97**	3 k. on 4 k. red	70	40
1107	**99**	4 k. on 5 k. purple	1·40	1·25
1108	**97**	5 k. on 6 k. blue	1·90	1·75
1109	**107**	6 k. on 7½ k. red	70	65
1110	**99**	7½ k. on 12½ k. blue	95	85
1111		12½ k. on 15 k. orange	2·10	1·00
1112	**107**	15 k. on 17½ k. black	2·75	2·50
1113	**99**	17½ k. on 20 k. brown	2·75	2·00
1114	**107**	20 k. on 25 k. brown	2·75	2·50
1115	**99**	25 k. on 30 k. brown	2·75	2·50
1116	**107**	30 k. on 40 k. purple	3·75	3·00
1117	**109**	40 k. on 50 k. black and red	4·75	2·50
1118		50 k. on 100 k. black and green	27·00	8·00
1119		100 k. on 200 k. black and green	32·00	12·00
1120		250 k. on 500 k. black and brown	32·00	10·00

1931. Surch **1 Kurus**.

1121	**97**	1 k. on 1½ k. green	1·25	10

1931.

1122	**112**	10 pa. green	10	10
1444		10 pa. brown	10	10
1444a		10 pa. red	10	10
1123		10 pa. orange	10	10
1445		20 pa. green	10	10
1453b		20 pa. yellow	10	10
1123a		30 pa. violet	10	10
1124	**113**	1 k. green	10	10
1453c		1 k. orange	10	10
1124a	**112**	1½ k. lilac	15	10
1125	**113**	2 k. violet	15	10
1125a		2 k. green	25	10
1447		2 k. mauve	25	10
1447a		2 k. yellow	60	10
1453d		2 k. pink	10	10
1126	**112**	2½ k. green	25	10
1126a	**113**	3 k. brown	20	10
1448		3 k. orange	45	10
1448a		3 k. blue	40	10
1127		4 k. black	1·75	10
1453f		4 k. green	20	10
1128		5 k. red	45	10
1128a		5 k. black	1·00	10
1453g		5 k. blue	20	10
1449a		5 k. purple	2·75	10
1129		6 k. blue	2·00	10
1129a		6 k. red	15	10
1130	**112**	7½ k. red	20	10
1130a	**113**	8 k. blue	40	10
1453h		8 k. violet	10	10
1131	**112**	10 k. black	2·25	10
1131a		10 k. blue	4·00	10
1450		10 k. brown	1·25	10
1453i		10 k. green	10	10
1132		12 k. brown	30	10
1453j		12 k. red	15	10
1133		12½ k. blue	35	10
1134		15 k. yellow	40	10
1451		15 k. violet	1·60	10
1453k		15 k. red	20	10
1135		20 k. green	40	10
1452		20 k. blue	10·00	10
1453la		20 k. purple	2·10	10
1136		25 k. blue	55	10
1137		30 k. purple	85	10
1453		30 k. pink	10·00	10
1453m		30 k. green	80	10
1138		100 k. brown	60	10
1139		200 k. violet	1·25	10
1453a		200 k. brown	4·50	45
1140		250 k. brown	4·50	10

114 Tree with Roots in Six Balkan Capitals

115 "Rebirth of Turkey"

1931. 2nd Balkan Conference.
1141 114 2½ k. green 10 10
1142 4 k. red 15 10
1143 6 k. blue 15 10
1144 7½ k. red 20 10
1145 12 k. orange 20 10
1146 12½ k. blue 35 10
1147 30 k. violet 60 10
1148 50 k. brown 1·00 10
1149 100 k. purple 2·25 25

1933. 10th Anniv of Turkish Republic.
1150 115 1½ k. green 45 10
1151 2 k. bistre 45 10
1152 – 3 k. red 45 10
1153 – 6 k. blue 45 10
1154 115 12½ k. blue 1·10 75
1155 25 k. brown 2·75 2·75
1156 – 50 k. brown 4·50 2·75
DESIGNS—HORIZ: 3, 6, 50 k. Wheat, cogwheels, factory, "X" and Kemal Ataturk.

1934. Air. Optd **1934** and airplane or surch also.
1157 107 7½ k. lake 40 25
1158 99 12½ k. on 15 k. orange 40 20
1159 107 20 k. on 25 k. brown 70 35
1160 25 k. brown 90 55
1161 40 k. purple 1·50 70

1934. Izmir International Fair. Optd **Izmir 9 Eylul 934 Sergisi** or surch also.
1162 97 10 pa. green 25 10
1163 1 k. on 1½ k. green 35 10
1164 107 2 k. on 25 k. brown 2·50 80
1165 5 k. on 7½ k. red 3·50 80
1166 6 k. on 17½ k. black 2·00 50
1167 99 12½ k. blue 4·50 1·00
1168 15 k. on 20 k. brown 42·00 20·00
1169 107 20 k. on 25 k. brown 32·00 32·00
1170 109 50 k. on 100 k. black and green 30·00 17·00

119 Alliance Badge

120 Mrs. C. Chapman Catt

1935. 12th Congress of the International Women's Alliance, Istanbul.
1171 119 20 pa. + 20 pa. bistre 35 25
1172 – 1 k. + 1 k. red 40 25
1173 – 2 k. + 2 k. blue 40 25
1174 – 2½ k. + 2½ k. green 40 30
1175 – 4 k. + 4 k. blue 65 55
1176 – 5 k. + 5 k. purple 90 75
1177 – 7½ k. + 7½ k. red 1·60 1·50
1178 120 10 k. + 10 k. orange 2·75 2·00
1179 – 12½ k. + 12½ k. blue 4·00 4·00
1180 – 15 k. + 15 k. violet 4·00 3·00
1181 – 20 k. + 20 k. red 8·00 6·00
1182 – 25 k. + 25 k. green 14·00 14·00
1183 – 30 k. + 30 k. blue 40·00 25·00
1184 – 50 k. + 50 k. green 85·00 65·00
1185 – 100 k. + 100 k. red 48·00 40·00
DESIGNS: 1 k. Woman teacher; 2 k. Woman farmer; 2½ k. Typist; 4 k. Woman pilot and policewoman; 5 k. Women voters; 7½ k. Yildiz Palace, Istanbul; 12½ k. Jane Addams; 15 k. Grazia Deledda; 20 k. Selma Lagerlof; 25 k. Bertha von Suttner; 30 k. Sigrid Undset; 50 k. Mme. Curie-Sklodowska; 100 k. Kemal Ataturk.

1936. Remilitarization of Dardanelles. Surch **BOGAZLAR MUKAVELESININ IMZASI 20/7/1936** and value in figures.
1186 107 4 k. on 17½ k. black 1·25 65
1187 5 k. on 25 k. brown 1·25 65
1188 100 6 k. on 50 k. black and red 75 20
1189 109 10 k. on 100 k. black and olive 1·00 20
1190 20 k. on 200 k. black and green 2·25 25
1191 50 k. on 500 k. black and brown 7·50 1·50

122 Stag

124 Arms of Turkey, Greece, Rumania and Yugoslavia

1937. 2nd Turkish Historical Congress.
1192 122 3 k. violet 60 25
1193 – 6 k. blue 65 25
1194 122 7½ k. red 1·25 60
1195 – 12½ k. blue 2·00 85
DESIGN: 6, 12½ k. Bust of Ataturk.

1937. Balkan Entente.
1196 124 8 k. red 4·50 1·25
1197 12½ k. blue 9·50 1·75

1938. Air. Surch **1937** with airplane above and value.
1198 107 4½ k. on 7½ k. lake 2·00 1·25
1199 99 9 k. on 15 k. orange 12·00 12·00
1200 107 35 k. on 40 k. purple 3·25 9·75

127 Fig Tree

129 Railway Bridge

1938. Izmir International Fair.
1201 – 10 pa. brown 20 10
1202 – 30 pa. violet 20 10
1203 127 2½ k. green 30 15
1204 – 3 k. orange 20 10
1205 – 5 k. green 45 25
1206 – 6 k. brown 1·75 60
1207 – 7½ k. red 1·10 40
1208 – 8 k. red 75 45
1209 – 12 k. purple 65 45
1210 – 12½ k. blue 2·50 2·00
DESIGNS—HORIZ: 10 pa. An Izmir boulevard; 30 pa. Izmir Fair; 6 k. Woman gathering grapes. VERT: 3 k. Clock Tower, Hukunet Square; 5 k. Olive branch; 7½ k. Woman gathering grapes; 8 k. Izmir Harbour; 12 k. Equestrian statue of Ataturk; 12½ k. Ataturk.

1938. 15th Anniv of Proclamation of Turkish Republic.
1211 – 2½ k. green 15 10
1212 – 3 k. red 15 10
1213 – 6 k. bistre 25 15
1214 129 7½ k. red 2·25 60
1215 – 8 k. purple 60 70
1216 – 12½ k. blue 60 1·00
DESIGNS—HORIZ: 2½ k. Military display; 3 k. Aerial view of Kayseri; 8 k. Scout buglers. VERT: 6 k. Ataturk driving a tractor; 12½ k. Ataturk.

130 Kemal Ataturk teaching Alphabet

1938. 10th Anniv of Introduction of Latin Alphabet into Turkey.
1217 130 2½ k. green 25 15
1218 3 k. orange 20 20
1219 6 k. purple 25 20
1220 7½ k. red 45 40
1221 8 k. red 1·25 1·10
1222 12½ k. blue 75 75

1938. Death of Kemal Ataturk. Mourning Issue. Optd **21-11-1938** and bar.
1223 113 3 k. brown 20 10
1224 5 k. red 20 10
1225 6 k. blue 35 30
1226 112 7½ k. red 25 10
1227 113 8 k. blue 50 40
1228 112 12½ k. blue 1·10 1·10

133 Presidents Inonu and Roosevelt and Map of North America

1939. 150th Anniv of U.S. Constitution.
1229 – 2½ k. green, red & blue 15 15
1230 133 3 k. brown and blue 15 15
1231 – 6 k. violet, red & blue 15 15
1232 – 7½ k. red and blue 20 10
1233 133 8 k. purple and blue 35 35
1234 – 12½ k. ultram & blue 1·25 75
DESIGNS—VERT: 2½, 6 k. Turkish and U.S. flags. HORIZ: 7½, 12½ k. Ataturk and George Washington.

1939. Cession of Hatay to Turkey. Surch **Hatayin Anavatana Kavusmasi 23/7/1939** and new values.
1235 107 3 k. on 25 k. brown 80 25
1236 109 6 k. on 200 k. black and green 10 20
1237 107 7½ k. on 25 k. brown 2·00 30
1238 109 12 k. on 100 k. (1096) 25 25
1239 12½ k. on 200 k. (1097) 40 40
1240 17½ k. on 500 k. (1098) 45 60

135 Railway Bridge

136 Kemal Ataturk

1939. Opening of Ankara–Erzurum Railway.
1241 135 3 k. red 3·25 4·00
1242 – 6 k. brown 6·00 8·50
1243 – 7½ k. red 6·75 9·50
1244 – 12½ k. blue 8·75 11·00
DESIGNS—VERT: 6 k. Locomotive. HORIZ: 7½ k. Railway and mountain gorge; 12½ k. Tunnel entrance at Atma-Bogazi.

1939. 1st Death Anniv of Kemal Ataturk.
1245 – 2½ k. green 15 10
1246 – 3 k. blue 20 15
1247 – 5 k. brown 25 15
1248 136 6 k. brown 20 20
1249 – 7½ k. red 35 40
1250 – 8 k. olive 25 30
1251 – 12½ k. blue 45 20
1252 – 17½ k. brown 1·25 95
DESIGN: 2½ k. Ataturk's residence; 3 k. to 17½ k. Portraits of Kemal Ataturk as Type **136**.

1940. Balkan Entente. As T **103** of Yugoslavia, but with the torch and Arms of Turkey, Greece, Rumania and Yugoslavia rearranged.
1253 8 k. blue 1·25 40
1254 10 k. blue 1·50 25

137 Namik Kemal

139 Map and Census Figures

1940. Birth Centenary of Namik Kemal (poet).
1255 137 6 k. brown 25 15
1256 8 k. olive 45 45
1257 12 k. red 60 45
1258 12½ k. blue 1·50 1·00

1940. Izmir International Fair. Surch **IZMIR ENTERNASYONAL FUARI 1940** and value.
1259 109 6 k. on 200 k. black and green 30 25
1260 10 k. on 200 k. black and green 30 25
1261 12 k. on 500 k. black and brown 35 35

1940. National Census.
1262 139 10 pa. green 15 10
1263 3 k. orange 20 15
1264 6 k. red 35 30
1265 10 k. blue 90 60

140 Hurdling

1940. 11th Balkan Games.
1266 – 3 k. olive 75 65
1267 – 6 k. red 1·75 1·50
1268 140 8 k. brown 1·25 45
1269 – 10 k. blue 1·75 2·00
DESIGNS—VERT: 3 k. Running; 6 k. Pole vaulting; 10 k. Throwing the discus.

141 Postmen of 1840 and 1940

1940. Centenary of First Adhesive Postage Stamps.
1270 – 3 k. green 20 10
1271 141 6 k. red 40 30
1272 – 10 k. blue 1·50 65
1273 – 12 k. brown 1·00 60
DESIGNS—HORIZ: 3 k. Mail carriers on horseback. VERT: 10 k. Early paddle-steamer and modern mail launch; 12 k. G.P.O., Istanbul.

142 Exhibition Building

1941. Izmir International Fair.
1274 – 30 pa. green 20 10
1275 142 3 k. grey 10 10
1276 – 6 k. red 25 10
1277 – 10 k. blue 20 15
1278 – 12 k. purple 35 20
1279 – 17½ k. brown 65 50
DESIGNS—HORIZ: 30 pa. Freighter "Etrusk" in Izmir harbour; 6, 17½ k. Exhibition pavilions; 12 k. Girl in field. VERT: 10 k. Equestrian statue.

143 Barbarossa's Corsair Fleet

144 Barbarossa

1941. 400th Death Anniv of Barbarossa (Khair-ed-Din).
1280 – 20 pa. violet 10 10
1281 143 3 k. blue 20 10
1282 6 k. red 35 20
1283 10 k. blue 45 25
1284 12 k. brown 1·00 30
1285 144 17½ k. multicoloured 1·10 60
DESIGN—24 × 37 mm: 20 pa. Barbarossa's tomb.

1941. Air. Surch with airplane and new value.
1286 107 4½ k. on 25 k. brown 75 1·40
1287 109 9 k. on 200 k. blk & grn 6·00 5·00
1288 35 k. on 500 k. black and brown 3·50 3·25

146 President Inonu 147

1942.
1289 146 0.25 k. bistre 10 10
1290 0.50 k. green 10 10
1291 1 k. grey 10 10
1292 1½ k. mauve 10 10
1293 2 k. green 10 10
1294 4 k. brown 10 10
1295 4½ k. black 10 10
1296 5 k. blue 10 10
1297 6 k. red 10 10
1298 6¾ k. blue 45 10
1299 9 k. violet 45 10
1300 10 k. blue 15 10
1301 13½ k. purple 15 10
1302 16 k. green 20 10
1303 17½ k. red 20 10
1304 20 k. purple 35 10
1305 27½ k. orange 25 10
1306 37 k. brown 20 10
1307 50 k. violet 40 10
1308 100 k. brown 2·50 85
1309 147 200 k. brown 8·50 15

148 Ankara

150 Pres. Inonu

149 Tile-decorating

1943. Inscr "TURKIYE POSTALARI" between two crescents and stars.
1310 **148** 0.25 k. yellow 10 10
1311 – 0.50 k. green 25 10
1312 – 1 k. olive 10 10
1313 – 1½ k. violet 10 10
1314 – 2 k. green 20 10
1315 – 4 k. red 85 15
1316 – 4½ k. black 2·50 30
1317 **149** 5 k. blue 45 15
1318 – 6 k. red 20 10
1319 – 6¾ k. blue 15 10
1320 – 10 k. blue 20 10
1321 – 13½ k. mauve 25 10
1322 – 16 k. green 1·10 15
1323 – 17½ k. brown 45 10
1324 – 20 k. brown 45 10
1325 – 27½ k. orange 1·25 10
1326 – 27 k. brown 40 10
1327 – 50 k. purple 3·25 20
1328 – 100 k. olive 4·50 20
1329 **150** 200 k. brown 6·50 15
DESIGNS—VERT: 0.50 k. Mohair goats; 2 k. Oranges; 4 k. Merino sheep; 4½ k. Steam train entering tunnel; 6 k. Statue of Kemal Ataturk, Ankara; 6¾, 10 k. Full face portrait of Pres. Inonu; 17½ k. Republic Monument, Istanbul; 20 k. National Defence Monument, Ankara; 27½ k. P.O., Istanbul; 37 k. Monument at Afyon; 100 k. Ataturk and Inonu. HORIZ: 1 k. Antioch; 1½ k. Ankara Reservoir; 13½ k. National Assembly building; 16 k. View of Arnavutkoy; 50 k. People's House, Ankara.

152 Fair Entrance

1943. Izmir International Fair.
1330 – 4½ k. grey 20 10
1331 **152** 6 k. red 20 10
1332 – 6¾ k. blue 20 10
1333 **152** 10 k. blue 20 10
1334 – 13½ k. brown 50 20
1335 – 27½ k. grey 55 30
DESIGNS—VERT: 4½, 13½ k. Girl eating grapes. HORIZ: 6¾, 27½ k. Fair Pavilion.

153 Marching Athletes
154 Soldier guarding Flag

1943. 20th Anniv of Republic.
1336 **153** 4½ k. olive 40 25
1337 **154** 6 k. red 10 10
1338 – 6¾ k. blue 60 60
1339 – 10 k. blue 20 10
1340 – 13½ k. olive 25 15
1341 – 27½ k. brown 35 25
DESIGNS—HORIZ: 6¾ k. Bridge; 10 k. Hospital; 13½ k. Ankara. VERT: 27½ k. President Inonu.

155 Filling Census Form
157 Pres. Inonu

1945. National Census.
1342 **155** 4½ k. olive 45 20
1343 9 k. violet 45 20
1344 10 k. blue 45 20
1345 18 k. red 95 40

1945. Surch **4½ KURUS**.
1346 4½ k. on 6¾ k. blue (No. 1319) 20 10

1946.
1347 **157** 0.25 k. red 10 10
1348 1 k. green 10 10
1349 1½ k. purple 15 10
1350 9 k. violet 35 10
1351 10 k. blue 35 10
1352 50 k. brown 3·00 15

158 U.S.S. "Missouri"
159 Sower

1946. Visit of U.S. Battleship "Missouri" to Istanbul.
1353 **158** 9 k. violet 35 10
1354 10 k. blue 50 15
1355 27½ k. grey 1·10 35

1946. Agrarian Reform.
1356 **159** 9 k. violet 10 10
1357 10 k. blue 10 10
1358 18 k. olive 20 15
1359 27½ k. orange 40 35

160 Dove of Peace
161 Monument at Afyon

1947. Izmir International Fair.
1360 **160** 15 k. purple and violet 10 10
1361 20 k. blue and deep blue 10 10
1362 30 k. brown and black 15 10
1363 1 l. olive and green 75 25

1947. 25th Anniv of Battle of Dumlupinar.
1364 **161** 10 k. brown and lt brn 10 10
1365 – 15 k. violet and grey 10 10
1366 – 20 k. blue and grey 15 10
1367 **161** 30 k. green and grey 20 10
1368 – 60 k. green and bistre 35 15
1369 – 1 l. green and grey 90 40
DESIGN: 15, 60 k. Ismet Inonu; 20 k., 1 l. Kemal Ataturk.

163 Istanbul, Grapes and Ribbon

1947. International Vintners' Congress.
1370 **163** 15 k. purple 10 10
1371 20 k. blue 10 10
1372 60 k. brown 20 15

164 Steam Express Train
165 Pres. Inonu

1947. International Railway Congress, Istanbul.
1373 **164** 15 k. purple 80 40
1374 20 k. blue 1·50 85
1375 60 k. olive 1·60 1·75

1948.
1376 **165** 0.25 k. red 10 10
1377 1 k. black 10 10
1378 2 k. purple 10 10
1379 3 k. orange 10 10
1380 4 k. green 10 10
1381 5 k. blue 10 10
1382 10 k. brown 15 10
1383 12 k. red 15 10
1384 15 k. violet 15 10
1385 20 k. blue 30 10
1386 30 k. brown 40 15
1387 60 k. black 65 15
1388 1 l. olive 3·75 20
1389 2 l. brown 12·50 45
1390 5 l. purple 6·25 6·25
The lira values are larger.

167 Signing the Treaty
168 Statue of Kemal Ataturk

1948. 25th Anniv of Treaty of Lausanne.
1391 **167** 15 k. purple 10 10
1392 – 20 k. blue 15 20
1393 – 40 k. green 30 20
1394 **167** 1 l. brown 40 40
DESIGN: 20, 40 k. Lausanne Palace.

1948. 25th Anniv of Proclamation of Republic.
1395 **168** 15 k. violet 10 10
1396 20 k. blue 15 10
1397 40 k. green 20 10
1398 1 l. brown 60 30

170 Douglas DC-6 over Izmir

1949. Air.
1399 **170** 5 k. violet and lilac 25 10
1400 – 20 k. brown and lilac 20 10
1401 – 30 k. green and grey 25 10
1402 **170** 40 k. blue and light blue 85 15
1403 – 50 k. brown and mauve 75 25
1404 – 1 l. green and blue 2·25 60
AIRCRAFT: 20, 50 k. Vickers Viking 1B; 30 k., 1l. Light monoplane.

172 Wrestlers

1949. 5th European Wrestling Championships. Designs depicting wrestling holds and inscr as in T **172**.
1405 – 15 k. mauve (vert) 40 25
1406 – 20 k. blue (vert) 1·00 40
1407 **172** 30 k. brown 40 25
1408 – 60 k. green (horiz) 75 75

173 Galley

1949. Navy Day.
1409 **173** 5 k. violet 25 10
1410 – 10 k. brown 60 10
1411 – 15 k. red 65 10
1412 – 20 k. blue 70 20
1413 – 30 k. slate 1·25 40
1414 – 40 k. olive 75 60
DESIGNS—HORIZ: 15 k. Cruiser "Hamidiye"; 20 k. Submarine "Sakarya"; 30 k. Battlecruiser "Yavuz". VERT: 10 k. Ship of the line "Mahmudiye"; 40 k. Statue of Barbarossa.

175 Exhibition Building

1949. Istanbul Fair.
1415 **175** 15 k. brown 15 10
1416 20 k. blue 15 10
1417 30 k. olive 35 20

176 U.P.U. Monument, Berne

1949. 75th Anniv of U.P.U.
1418 – 15 k. violet 10 10
1419 – 20 k. blue 15 10
1420 **176** 30 k. red 15 10
1421 40 k. green 40 15
DESIGN: 15, 20 k. as Type **176** but vert.

177 Sud Est Languedoc over Bogazia

1950. Air.
1422 **177** 2 l. 50 green and blue 10·00 7·50

178 Youth, Istanbul and Ankara
180 Voting

1950. 2nd World Youth Union Meeting.
1423 **178** 15 k. violet 15 10
1424 20 k. blue 25 15

1950. General Election.
1425 **180** 15 k. brown 10 10
1426 20 k. blue 15 10
1427 – 30 k. blue and green 25 10
DESIGNS—HORIZ: 30 k. Kemal Ataturk and map of Turkey.

181 Hazel Nut
182 Map and Statistics

1950. Izmir Fair.
1428 **181** 8 k. green and yellow 20 10
1429 – 12 k. mauve 25 10
1430 – 15 k. brown 35 10
1431 – 20 k. blue and light blue 45 20
1432 – 30 k. brown 55 20
DESIGN: 12 k. Acorns; 15 k. Cotton; 20 k. Fair symbol; 30 k. Tobacco.

1950. National Census.
1433 **182** 15 k. brown 20 10
1434 20 k. blue 20 10

183 Hezarfen Celebi's "Bird Flight" and Tower
184 Farabi (philosopher)

1950. Air. International Civil Aviation Congress, Istanbul.
1435 **183** 20 k. blue and green 50 10
1436 – 40 k. blue and brown 75 15
1437 – 60 k. blue and violet 1·75 75
DESIGNS—VERT: 40 k. Biplane over Taurus Mountains. HORIZ: 60 k. Douglas DC-3 airplane over Istanbul.

1950. 1000th Death Anniv of Farabi.
1438 **184** 15 k. multicoloured 25 20
1439 20 k. multicoloured 50 20
1440 60 k. multicoloured 1·00 35
1441 1 l. multicoloured 1·50 75

185 Mithat Pasha and Deposit Bank

1950. 3rd Co-operative Congress, Istanbul.
1442 **185** 15 k. violet 30 10
1443 – 20 k. blue 35 15
DESIGN: 20 k. Agricultural Bank.

1951. Air. Industrial Congress, Ankara. Nos. 1399, 1401 and 1403 optd **SANAYI KONGRESI 9-NISAN-1951**.
1454 **170** 5 k. violet and lilac 50 80
1455 – 30 k. green and grey 50 20
1456 – 50 k. brown and mauve 1·25 30

187 "Iskendrun" (liner)

1951. 25th Anniv of Coastal Trading Rights.

No.	Type	Description	Unused	Used
1457	–	15 k. blue	55	15
1458	**187**	20 k. blue	85	15
1459	–	30 k. grey	65	20
1460	–	1 l. green	75	60

DESIGNS—HORIZ: 15 k. Tug "Hora" and liner "Providence"; 30 k. Diver and launch. VERT: 1 l. Lighthouse.

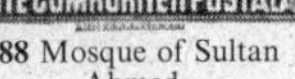

188 Mosque of Sultan Ahmed — 189 Count Carton de Wiart

1951. 40th Interparliamentary Conference, Istanbul.

No.	Type	Description	Unused	Used
1461	**188**	15 k. green	20	10
1462	–	20 k. blue	20	10
1463	**189**	30 k. brown	40	10
1464	–	60 k. purple	1·60	70

DESIGNS—As Type **188**: 20 k. Dolmabahce Palace; 60 k. Rumeli Tower.

190 F.A.O. Emblem and Silo — 191 A. H. Tarhan

1952. U.N. Economic Conf, Ankara. Inscr "Ankara 1951".

No.	Type	Description	Unused	Used
1465	**190**	15 k. green	30	20
1466	–	20 k. violet	30	20
1467	–	30 k. blue	40	20
1468	–	60 k. red	45	40

DESIGNS: 20 k. Int Bank emblem and hydro-electric station; 30 k. U.N. emblem and New York headquarters; 60 k. Ankara University.

1952. Birth Centenary of Tarhan (writer).

No.	Type	Description	Unused	Used
1469	**191**	15 k. purple	10	10
1470		20 k. blue	10	10
1471		30 k. brown	25	15
1472		60 k. green	60	40

192 Bergama — 193 Kemal Ataturk

1952. Views. Imperf or perf.

No.	Type	Description	Unused	Used
1473	**192**	1 k. orange	10	10
1474	–	2 k. green	10	10
1475	–	3 k. brown	10	10
1476	–	4 k. green	10	10
1477	–	5 k. brown	10	10
1478	**193**	10 k. brown	15	10
1479		12 k. red	20	10
1480		15 k. violet (medallion)	25	10
1481		20 k. blue (medallion)	35	10
1482	–	30 k. green	40	10
1483	–	40 k. blue	65	10
1484	–	50 k. green	40	10
1485	–	75 k. black	75	10
1486	–	1 l. violet	40	10
1487	–	2 l. blue	1·25	10
1488	–	5 l. brown	12·50	4·00

DESIGNS—VERT: 2 k. Ruins at Milas; 3 k. Karatay Gate, Konya; 4 k. Trees on Kozak Plateau; 5 k. Urgup; 30 k. Emirsultan Mosque, Bursa; 40 k. Yenicami (New Mosque), Istanbul. HORIZ: 50 k. Waterfall, Tarsus; 75 k. Rocks at Urgup; 1 l. Dolmabahce Palace, Istanbul; 2 l. Pavilion, Istanbul; 5 l. Interior of Istanbul Museum.

1952. Surch **0.50 Kurus**.

No.	Type	Description	Unused	Used
1489	**192**	0.50 k. on 1 k. orange	20	10

MINIMUM PRICE

The minimum price quoted is 10p which represents a handling charge rather than a basis for valuing common stamps. For further notes about prices, see introductory pages.

196 Congress Building — 197 Turkish Sentry

1952. 8th Int Mechanics Congress, Istanbul.

No.	Type	Description	Unused	Used
1490	**196**	15 k. violet	35	15
1491		20 k. blue	35	15
1492		60 k. brown	40	25

1952. Turkish Participation in Korean War.

No.	Type	Description	Unused	Used
1493	**197**	15 k. slate	25	15
1494	–	20 k. blue	20	15
1495	–	30 k. brown	25	25
1496	–	60 k. red and green	80	40

DESIGNS: 20 k. Turkish soldier and flag; 30 k. Soldier and Korean child reading comic paper; 60 k. Soldiers planting Turkish flag.

198 Doves, Hand and Red Crescent — 199 Bas-relief on Monument

1952. 75th Anniv of Red Crescent Society.

No.	Type	Description	Unused	Used
1497	**198**	15 k. red and green	50	30
1498	–	20 k. red and blue	75	50

DESIGN: 20 k. Red Crescent flag.

1952. 75th Anniv of Battle of Erzurum.

No.	Type	Description	Unused	Used
1499	**199**	15 k. violet	20	15
1500	–	20 k. blue	20	15
1501	–	40 k. grey	55	25

DESIGNS—HORIZ: 20 k. Azizye Monument, Erzurum; 40 k. View of Erzurum.

200 Pigeon carrying Newspaper — 202 Sultan Mohammed II (after Gentile Bellini)

201 Rumeli Fort

1952.

No.	Type	Description	Unused	Used
1502	**200**	0.50 k. green	10	10
1503		0.50 k. violet	10	10
1503a		0.50 k. orange	10	10
1503b		0.50 k. brown	10	10

1953. 500th Anniv of Fall of Constantinople.

No.	Type	Description	Unused	Used
1504	**201**	5 k. blue & ultramarine	50	10
1505	–	8 k. grey	55	10
1506	–	10 k. blue	20	10
1507	–	12 k. purple	50	10
1508	–	15 k. brown	50	10
1509	–	20 k. red	55	15
1510	–	30 k. green	80	15
1511	–	40 k. violet	1·90	25
1512	–	60 k. brown	80	35
1513	–	1 l. green	2·50	60
1514	–	2 l. multicoloured	3·75	1·10
1515	**202**	2½ l. lt brown, yell & brn	5·00	1·90

DESIGNS—As Type **201**: HORIZ: 8 k. Turkish army at Edirne; 10 k. Horsemen and fleet; 12 k. Landing of Turkish Army; 15 k. Topkapi ramparts; 40 k. Sultan Mohammed II and Patriarch Yenadios; 60 k. 15th-century map of Constantinople; 1 l. Mausoleum of Mohammed II. VERT: 20 k. Turkish army entering Constantinople; 30 k. Sultan Mohammed II Mosque. As Type **202**: 2 l. Sultan Mohammed II (after miniature by Sinan).

203 Odeon Theatre, Ephesus

1953. Views of Ephesus. Inscr "EFES". Multicoloured centres.

No.	Type	Description	Unused	Used
1516	**203**	12 k. green	15	10
1517	–	15 k. violet	15	10
1518	–	20 k. slate	25	10
1519	–	40 k. turquoise	40	25
1520	–	60 k. blue	30	25
1521	–	1 l. red	1·25	60

DESIGNS: 15 k. St. John's Church and Acropolis; 20 k. Statue of Blessed Virgin, Panaya Kapulu; 40 k. Council Church ruins; 60 k. Grotto of the Seven Sleepers; 1 l. House of the Blessed Virgin, Panaya Kapulu.

204 Pres. Bayar, Mithat Pasha, Dr. Delitsch and Ankara Bank

1953. 5th International Public Credit Congress.

No.	Type	Description	Unused	Used
1522	**204**	15 k. brown	15	10
1523	–	20 k. turquoise	25	15

DESIGN: 20 k. Pres. Bayar, Mithat Pasha and Ankara University.

205 Berdan Barrage

1953. 30th Anniv of Republic.

No.	Type	Description	Unused	Used
1524	–	10 k. bistre	10	10
1525	**205**	15 k. slate	10	10
1526	–	20 k. red	10	10
1527	–	30 k. olive	3·50	1·75
1528	–	35 k. blue	20	10
1529	–	55 k. lilac	25	15

DESIGNS—HORIZ: 10 k. Combine-harvester; 20 k. Soldiers on parade; 30 k. Diesel-engined train; 35 k. Yesilkoy airport. VERT: 55 k. Kemal Ataturk.

206 Kemal Ataturk and Mausoleum

1953. Transfer of Ashes of Kemal Ataturk to Mausoleum.

No.	Type	Description	Unused	Used
1530	**206**	15 k. black	20	10
1531		20 k. purple	25	15

207 Map of World and Compass

1954. 5th Anniv of N.A.T.O.

No.	Type	Description	Unused	Used
1532	**207**	15 k. brown	25	25
1533	–	20 k. blue	25	25
1534	–	40 k. green	3·25	2·00

DESIGNS: 20 k. Globe and stars; 40 k. Allegory of growth of N.A.T.O.

208 "Industry, Agriculture and Construction" — 209 Flying Exercise

1954. 5th Anniv of Council of Europe.

No.	Type	Description	Unused	Used
1535	**208**	10 k. brown	2·00	1·00
1536	–	15 k. green	75	25
1537	–	20 k. blue	75	25
1538	**208**	30 k. violet	4·50	2·50

DESIGN: 15, 20 k. Flag and figure of "Peace and Justice".

1954. 47th Conference of Int Aeronautical Federation. Inscr "20.IX.1954".

No.	Type	Description	Unused	Used
1539	**209**	20 k. black	20	10
1540	–	35 k. lilac	35	15
1541	–	45 k. blue	85	20

DESIGNS: 35 k. Baron Delagrange and glider; 45 k. Ataturk and formation of De Havilland Tiger Moth biplanes.

210 Z. Gokalp — 211 Yesilkoy Airport

1954. 30th Death Anniv of Gokalp (sociologist).

No.	Type	Description	Unused	Used
1542	**210**	15 k. violet	10	10
1543		20 k. green	20	10
1544		30 k. red	35	15

1954. Air.

No.	Type	Description	Unused	Used
1545	**211**	5 k. blue and brown	15	10
1546	–	20 k. blue and brown	25	10
1547	–	35 k. blue and green	25	10
1548	**211**	40 k. blue and red	35	10
1549	–	45 k. blue and violet	55	20
1550	–	55 k. blue and black	1·25	25

DESIGNS: 20, 45 k. Frontal view of Yesilkoy Airport; 35, 55 k. Ankara Airport.

212 Kemal Ataturk — 213 Relief Map of the Dardanelles

1955.

No.	Type	Description	Unused	Used
1551	**212**	15 k. red	10	10
1552		20 k. blue	15	10
1553		40 k. slate	20	10
1554		50 k. green	30	10
1555		75 k. brown	65	10

1955. 40th Anniv of Battle of Canakkale (Dardanelles).

No.	Type	Description	Unused	Used
1556	**213**	15 k. green	10	10
1557	–	20 k. brown	15	10
1558	–	30 k. blue	50	20
1559	–	60 k. drab	60	35

DESIGNS—VERT: 20 k. Gunner Seyid loading gun; 60 k. Ataturk in uniform. HORIZ: 30 k. Minelayer "Nusret".

214 "Reconstruction" — 215 Lillies

1955. Town Planning Congress.

No.	Type	Description	Unused	Used
1560	**214**	15 k. grey	15	10
1561		20 k. blue	20	10
1562		50 k. brown	25	15
1563		1 l. violet	60	25

1955. Spring Flower Festival. Inscr "ISTANBUL 1955".

No.	Type	Description	Unused	Used
1564	–	10 k. red and green	30	10
1565	–	15 k. yellow and green	25	10
1566	–	20 k. red and green	35	10
1567	**215**	50 k. green and yellow	1·00	35

FLOWERS: 10 k. Carnations; 15 k. Tulips; 20 k. Roses.

216 First-aid Centre

1955. 18th Congress of International Documentation Office of Military Medicine.

No.	Type	Description	Unused	Used
1568	**216**	20 k. red and grey	20	10
1569	–	30 k. green and lt green	20	15

DESIGN: 30 k. Gulhane Military Hospital, Ankara.

217 Footballers

1955. Int Military Football Championships.

No.	Type	Description	Unused	Used
1570	**217**	15 k. blue	20	15
1571	–	20 k. red	30	10
1572	–	1 l. green	75	45

DESIGNS—VERT: 20 k. Footballers' badge. HORIZ: 1 l. Championship plaque.

218 Police Monument, Ankara

1955. International Police Commission Meeting, Istanbul.
1573 218 15 k. green and turquoise 20 10
1574 – 20 k. violet and lilac 25 10
1575 – 30 k. black and grey 35 15
1576 – 45 k. brown and lt brn 45 25
DESIGNS: 20 k. Dolmabahce Palace, Istanbul; 30 k. Police College, Ankara; 45 k. Police Martyrs' Monument, Istanbul.

219 Radio Mast 220 Istanbul University

1955. Cent of Telecommunications in Turkey.
1577 – 15 k. olive 20 10
1578 219 20 k. red 20 10
1579 – 45 k. brown 25 10
1580 219 60 k. blue 35 15
DESIGNS—HORIZ: 15, 45 k. Telegraph table and pole.

1955. 10th Meeting of Governors of Int Reconstruction and Development Bank and Int Monetary Fund.
1581 – 15 k. orange 20 10
1582 220 20 k. red 20 10
1583 – 60 k. purple 25 15
1584 – 1 l. blue 30 25
DESIGNS: 15 k. Faculty of Letters, Istanbul; 60 k. Hilton Hotel; 1 l. Kiz Kulesi.

221 Ruins, Istanbul 222

1955. 10th International Congress of Byzantine Research.
1585 221 15 k. green and blue 25 10
1586 – 20 k. red and orange 20 10
1587 – 30 k. brown and pink 30 10
1588 – 75 k. blue and lilac 45 25
DESIGNS—VERT: 20 k. Obelisk and Sultan Ahmed Mosque; 75 k. Map of Istanbul in 1422. HORIZ: 30 k. Church of St. Sophia.

1955. 10th International Road Planning Congress.
1589 – 20 k. mauve 20 10
1590 222 30 k. green 25 15
1591 – 55 k. blue 1·00 40
DESIGNS: 20 k. Congress emblem; 55 k. Bridges.

223 Population Pictograph

1955. National Census.
1592 223 15 k. grey and red 25 10
1593 20 k. lilac and red 20 10
1594 30 k. blue and red 20 10
1595 60 k. green and red 40 10

224 Santa Claus Church, Demre 225 Kemal Ataturk

1955. Tourism.
1596 – 18 k. green and blue 25 10
1597 – 20 k. brown and blue 25 10
1598 – 30 k. brown and green 30 10
1599 – 45 k. green and brown 70 25
1600 – 50 k. brown and green 35 20
1601 224 65 k. black and red 40 15
DESIGNS—VERT: 18 k. Waterfall near Antalya; 45 k. Theatre doorway ruins, Side; 50 k. Countryside, Antalya. HORIZ: 20 k. Alanya; 30 k. Amphitheatre, Aspendos.

1955.
1602 225 0.50 k. pink 10 10
1603 1 k. yellow 10 10
1604 2 k. blue 10 10
1605 3 k. red 10 10
1606 5 k. brown 10 10
1606a 6 k. green 25 10
1607 10 k. green 10 10
1607a 18 k. purple 25 10
1608 20 k. blue 10 10
1609 25 k. olive 25 10
1610 30 k. violet 25 10
1611 40 k. brown 25 10
1612 75 k. slate 1·00 15

226 Mausoleum of Hudavent Hatum 227 Zubeyde

1956. 25th Anniv of Turkish Historical Association.
1613 226 40 k. deep blue & blue 20 10

1956. Mothers' Day.
1614 227 20 k. brn & buff (perf) 10 10
1615 20 k. olive and green (imperf) 50 30

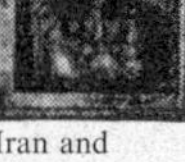

228 Shah of Iran and Queen Soraya 229 Kemal Ataturk

1956. Visit of Shah of Iran to Turkey.
1616 228 100 k. green and light green (perf) 60 10
1617 100 k. red and green (imperf) 3·00 2·25

1956.
1618 229 ½ k. green 10 10
1619 1 k. orange 10 10
1620 3 k. green 10 10
1621 5 k. violet 10 10
1622 6 k. mauve 10 10
1623 10 k. purple 10 10
1624 12 k. brown 10 10
1625 15 k. blue 10 10
1626 18 k. pink 10 10
1627 20 k. brown 10 10
1628 25 k. green 15 10
1629 30 k. slate 15 10
1630 40 k. olive 15 10
1631 50 k. orange 20 10
1632 60 k. blue 25 10
1633 70 k. turquoise 60 15
1634 75 k. brown 50 10
See also Nos. 1659/78.

230 Erenkoy Sanatorium 231

1956. Turkish Post Office Health Service.
1635 230 50 k. turquoise & pink 35 10

1956. 25th Izmir International Fair.
1636 231 45 k. green (postage) 10 10
1637 25 k. brown (air) 15 10

232 Serpent in Bottle 233 Medical Clinic, Kayseri

1956. International Anti-Alcoholism Congress.
1638 232 25 k. multicoloured 25 10

1956. 750th Anniv of Medical Clinic, Kayseri.
1639 233 60 k. violet & yellow 20 10

234 Sariyar Barrage 235 Wrestling

1956. Inaug of Sariyar Dam.
1640 234 20 k. red 15 10
1641 20 k. blue 15 10

1956. Olympic Games. Inscr as in T 235.
1642 235 40 k. sepia on green 40 20
1643 – 65 k. red on grey 50 20
DESIGN: 65 k. Another wrestling match.

236 Mehmet Akif Ersoy 237 Vase of Troy

1956. 20th Death Anniv of Ersoy (poet).
1644 236 20 k. brown and green 15 10
1645 20 k. red and grey 15 10
1646 20 k. violet and pink 15 10
Each stamp is inscribed with a different line of verse from the Turkish National Anthem composed by Ersoy.

1956. Troy Commemoration. Inscr "TRUVA (TROIA)".
1647 – 15 k. green 75 25
1648 237 20 k. purple 50 25
1649 – 30 k. brown 90 75
DESIGNS—HORIZ: 15 k. Troy Amphitheatre; 30 k. Trojan Horse.

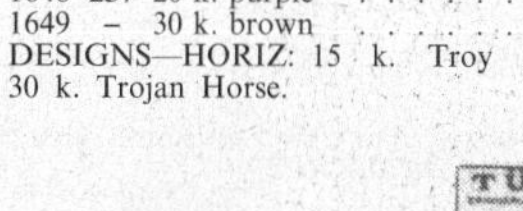

238 Mobile X-ray Unit 239 Pres. Heuss

1957. T.B. Relief Campaign.
1650 238 25 k. red and drab 15 10

1957. Visit of President of West Germany.
1651 239 40 k. brown and yellow (postage) 25 10
1652 40 k. purple and pink (air) 20 10

240 View of Bergama

1957. Bergama Fair.
1653 240 30 k. brown 15 10
1654 – 40 k. green 10 10
DESIGN: 40 k. Folk-dancing.

241

1957. Turkish-American Friendship.
1655 241 25 k. violet 20 10
1656 40 k. blue 25 15

242 Osman Hamdi Bey (founder) 243 Kemal Ataturk

1957. 75th Anniv of Fine Arts Academy, Istanbul.
1657 242 20 k. drab, buff & black 20 10
1658 – 30 k. grey, grn & lt grn 25 10
DESIGN—HORIZ: 30 k. Hittite relic of Alacahoyuk; Inscr "GUZEL SANATLAR AKADEMISI 75. YIL".

1957.
1659 243 ½ k. brown 10 10
1660 1 k. blue 10 10
1661 2 k. violet 10 10
1662 3 k. orange 10 10
1663 5 k. green 10 10
1664 6 k. green 10 10
1665 10 k. violet 10 10
1666 12 k. green 10 10
1667 15 k. green 10 10
1668 18 k. mauve 10 10
1669 20 k. sepia 10 10
1670 25 k. brown 10 10
1671 30 k. blue 15 10
1672 40 k. slate 15 10
1673 50 k. yellow 20 10
1674 60 k. black 25 10
1675 70 k. purple 25 10
1676 75 k. olive 35 10
1677 – 100 k. red 40 15
1678 – 250 k. olive 15 10
Nos. 1677/8 are larger 21 × 29 mm.

244 Mohammed Zahir Shah 245 Amasya Medical Centre

1957. Visit of Mohammed Zahir Shah of Afghanistan.
1679 244 45 k. red and orange (postage) 15 10
1680 25 k. deep green and green (air) 15 10

1957. 11th Congress of World Medical Association.
1681 245 25 k. red and yellow 10 10
1682 – 65 k. blue and yellow 30 15
DESIGN—HORIZ: 65 k. Sultan Mohammed School, 1557.

246 Sultan Mohammed II Mosque

1957. 400th Anniv of the Suleiman Mosque, Istanbul.
1683 246 20 k. green 10 10
1684 – 1 l. brown 35 15
DESIGN—VERT: 1 l. Mimar Koca Sinan (architect).

1957. 2nd Philatelic Exhibition, Istanbul. Surch **50 Kurus ISTANBUL Filatelik II. Sergisi 1957.**
1685 50 k. on 2 l. bl (No. 1487) 25 10

248 Forestry Map of Turkey

1957. Centenary of Forestry Teaching.
1686 248 20 k. green and brown 15 10
1687 – 25 k. green and blue 20 10
DESIGN—VERT: 25 k. Planting fir-tree.

249 Fuzuli (poet) 250 Franklin

1957. Fuzuli Year.

No.	Type	Description	Unused	Used
1688	249	50 k. multicoloured	25	10

1957. 250th Birth Anniv of Benjamin Franklin.

No.	Type	Description	Unused	Used
1689	250	65 k. purple	25	10
1690		65 k. blue	25	10

251 Mevlana's Tomb, Konya

252 Adana

1957. 750th Birth Anniv of Mevlana (poet).

No.	Type	Description	Unused	Used
1691	251	50 k. violet, blue & green	20	15
1692	–	100 k. dp blue and blue	40	25

DESIGN—HORIZ: 100 k. Konya Museum.

1958. Turkish Towns. As T **252**. (a) 26×21 mm.

No.	Type	Description	Unused	Used
1693		5 k. brown (Adana)	10	10
1694		5 k. mauve (Adapazari)	10	10
1695		5 k. red (Adiyaman)	10	10
1696		5 k. brown (Afyon)	10	10
1697		5 k. green (Amasya)	10	10
1698		5 k. blue (Ankara)	10	10
1699		5 k. green (Antakya)	10	10
1700		5 k. green (Antalya)	10	10
1701		5 k. lilac (Artvin)	10	10
1702		5 k. orange (Aydin)	10	10
1703		5 k. violet (Balikesir)	10	10
1704		5 k. green (Bilecik)	10	10
1705		5 k. purple (Bingol)	10	10
1706		5 k. blue (Bitlis)	10	10
1707		5 k. purple (Bolu)	10	10
1708		5 k. brown (Burdur)	10	10
1709		5 k. green (Bursa)	10	10
1710		5 k. blue (Canakkale)	10	10
1711		5 k. violet (Cankiri)	10	10
1712		5 k. blue (Corum)	10	10
1713		5 k. blue (Denizli)	10	10
1714		5 k. orange (Diyrbakir)	10	10
1715		5 k. violet (Edirne)	10	10
1716		5 k. green (Elazig)	10	10
1717		5 k. blue (Erzincan)	10	10
1718		5 k. orange (Erzurum)	10	10
1719		5 k. green (Eskisehur)	10	10
1720		5 k. green (Gaziantep)	10	10
1721		5 k. blue (Giresun)	10	10
1722		5 k. blue (Gumusane)	10	10
1723		5 k. purple (Hakkari)	10	10
1724		5 k. mauve (Isparta)	10	10
1725		5 k. blue (Istanbul)	10	10
1726		5 k. blue (Izmir)	10	10
1727		5 k. blue (Izmit)	10	10
1728		5 k. violet (Karakose)	10	10
1729		5 k. green (Kars)	10	10
1730		5 k. mauve (Kastamonu)	10	10
1731		5 k. green (Kayseri)	10	10
1732		5 k. brown (Kirklareli)	10	10
1733		5 k. orange (Kirsehir)	10	10
1734		5 k. blue (Konya)	10	10
1735		5 k. violet (Kutahya)	10	10
1736		5 k. brown (Malatya)	10	10
1737		5 k. green (Manisa)	10	10
1738		5 k. purple (Maras)	10	10
1739		5 k. red (Mardin)	10	10
1740		5 k. green (Mersin)	10	10
1741		5 k. green (Mugla)	10	10
1742		5 k. green (Mus)	10	10
1743		5 k. green (Nevsehir)	10	10
1744		5 k. red (Nigde)	10	10
1745		5 k. blue (Ordu)	10	10
1746		5 k. violet (Rize)	10	10
1747		5 k. purple (Samsun)	10	10
1748		5 k. brown (Siirt)	10	10
1749		5 k. blue(Sinop)	10	10
1750		5 k. green (Sivas)	10	10
1751		5 k. blue (Tekirdag)	10	10
1752		5 k. red (Tokat)	10	10
1753		5 k. blue (Trabzon)	10	10
1754		5 k. orange (Tunceli)	10	10
1755		5 k. brown (Urfa)	10	10
1756		5 k. green (Usak)	10	10
1757		5 k. red (Van)	10	10
1758		5 k. mauve (Yozgat)	10	10
1759		5 k. blue (Zonguldak)	10	10

(b) 32½×22 mm.

No.	Type	Description	Unused	Used
1760		20 k. brown (Adana)	20	20
1761		20 k. mauve (Adapazari)	20	20
1762		20 k. red (Adiyaman)	20	20
1763		20 k. brown (Afyon)	20	20
1764		20 k. green (Amasya)	20	20
1765		20 k. blue (Ankara)	20	20
1766		20 k. blue (Antakya)	20	20
1767		20 k. green (Antalya)	20	20
1768		20 k. blue (Artvin)	20	20
1769		20 k. orange (Aydin)	20	20
1770		20 k. purple (Balikesir)	20	20
1771		20 k. green (Bilecik)	20	20
1772		20 k. grey (Bingol)	20	20
1773		20 k. violet (Bitlis)	20	20
1774		20 k. purple (Bolu)	20	20
1775		20 k. brown (Burdur)	20	20
1776		20 k. green (Bursa)	20	20
1777		20 k. blue (Canakkale)	20	20
1778		20 k. purple (Cankiri)	20	20
1779		20 k. grey (Corum)	20	20
1780		20 k. blue (Denizli)	20	20
1781		20 k. red (Diyrbakir)	20	20
1782		20 k. grey (Edirne)	20	20
1783		20 k. green (Elazig)	20	20
1784		20 k. blue (Erzincan)	20	20
1785		20 k. orange (Erzurum)	20	20
1786		20 k. green (Eskisehur)	20	20
1787		20 k. green (Gaziantep)	20	20
1788		20 k. blue (Giresun)	20	20
1789		20 k. blue (Gumusane)	20	20
1790		20 k. purple (Hakkari)	20	20
1791		20 k. mauve (Isparta)	20	20
1792		20 k. blue (Istanbul)	20	20
1793		20 k. blue (Izmir)	20	20
1794		20 k. green (Izmit)	20	20
1795		20 k. violet (Karakose)	20	20
1796		20 k. green (Kars)	20	20
1797		20 k. mauve (Kastamonu)	20	20
1798		20 k. green (Kayseri)	20	20
1799		20 k. brown (Kirklareli)	20	20
1800		20 k. brown (Kirsehir)	20	20
1801		20 k. blue (Konya)	20	20
1802		20 k. violet (Kutahya)	20	20
1803		20 k. brown (Malatya)	20	20
1804		20 k. green (Manisa)	20	20
1805		20 k. purple (Maras)	20	20
1806		20 k. red (Mardin)	20	20
1807		20 k. green (Mersin)	20	20
1808		20 k. green (Mugla)	20	20
1809		20 k. green (Mus)	20	20
1810		20 k. green (Nevsehir)	20	20
1811		20 k. red (Nigde)	20	20
1812		20 k. blue (Ordu)	20	20
1813		20 k. violet (Rize)	20	20
1814		20 k. purple (Samsun)	20	20
1815		20 k. brown (Siirt)	20	20
1816		20 k. blue (Sinop)	20	20
1817		20 k. green (Sivas)	20	20
1818		20 k. blue (Tekirdag)	20	20
1819		20 k. red (Tokat)	20	20
1820		20 k. blue (Trabzon)	20	20
1821		20 k. red (Tunceli)	20	20
1822		20 k. brown (Urfa)	20	20
1823		20 k. grey (Usak)	20	20
1824		20 k. red (Van)	20	20
1825		20 k. red (Yozgat)	20	20
1826		20 k. blue (Zonguldak)	20	20

253

254 Hierapolis at Pamukkale

1958. 75th Anniv of the Institute of Economics and Commerce, Ankara.

No.	Type	Description	Unused	Used
1827	253	20 k. orange, bl & bis	10	10
1828		25 k. blue, orge & bis	10	10

1958. Pamukkale Tourist Publicity. Inscr "PAMUKKALE".

No.	Type	Description	Unused	Used
1829	254	20 k. brown	10	10
1830	–	25 k. blue	15	10

DESIGN—HORIZ: 25 k. Travertins (rocks) near Denizli.

255 Katib Celebi

256 Letters

1958. 300th Death Anniv of Katib Celebi (author).

No.	Type	Description	Unused	Used
1831	255	50 k. + 10 k. black	20	15

1958. International Correspondence Week.

No.	Type	Description	Unused	Used
1832	256	20 k. orange and black	10	10

257 Symbol of Industry

258 Symbol of "Europa"

1958. Industrial Fair, Istanbul.

No.	Type	Description	Unused	Used
1833	257	40 k. black and blue	15	10

1958. Europa.

No.	Type	Description	Unused	Used
1834	258	25 k. lilac and violet	20	10
1835		40 k. blue & ultramarine	30	10

259 Bulldozer

260 Flame of Remembrance

1958. 35th Anniv of Republic.

No.	Type	Description	Unused	Used
1836	259	15 k. + 5 k. orange	10	10
1837	–	20 k. + 5 k. brown	10	10
1838	–	25 k. + 5 k. green	30	10

DESIGNS—VERT: 20 k. Portrait of Kemal Ataturk. HORIZ: 25 k. Army tanks and Republic F-84G Thunderjets

1958. 20th Death Anniv of Kemal Ataturk.

No.	Type	Description	Unused	Used
1839	260	25 k. red	10	10
1840	–	75 k. green	20	15

DESIGN: 75 k. Sword, sprig and bust of Kemal Ataturk.

261

262 Blackboard

1959. 25th Anniv of Faculty of Agriculture, Ankara University.

No.	Type	Description	Unused	Used
1841	261	25 k. yellow and violet	10	10

1959. 75th Anniv of Boys' High School, Istanbul.

No.	Type	Description	Unused	Used
1842	262	75 k. black and yellow	25	15

263 Eagle

1959. Air. Birds.

No.	Type	Description	Unused	Used
1843	–	40 k. purple and mauve	35	10
1844	–	65 k. myrtle & turquoise	35	15
1845	–	85 k. blue and black	50	20
1846	263	105 k. bistre and yellow	60	20
1847	–	125 k. lilac and violet	1·00	25
1848	–	155 k. green & yellow	1·10	30
1849	–	195 k. blue and black	1·25	45
1850	–	245 k. brown & orange	1·75	80

BIRDS (in flight)—HORIZ: 40 k. Barn swallows; 65 k. Cranes; 85 k. Gulls. VERT: 125 k. House martin; 155 k. Demoiselle crane; 195 k. Gulls; 245 k. Turtle dove.

264 Theatre, Ankara

1959. Centenary of Turkish Theatre.

No.	Type	Description	Unused	Used
1851	264	20 k. brown and green	10	10
1852	–	25 k. green and orange	10	10

DESIGN: 25 k. Portrait of Sinasi and masks.

265 "Karadeniz" (liner)

267 Northern Hemisphere and Stars

1959.

No.	Type	Description	Unused	Used
1853	–	1 k. blue	10	10
1854	265	5 k. blue	20	10
1855	–	10 k. blue	10	10
1856	–	15 k. brown	20	10
1857	–	20 k. green	10	10
1858	–	25 k. lilac	15	10
1859a	–	30 k. purple	20	10
1860	–	40 k. blue	20	10
1861	–	45 k. violet	20	10
1862	–	55 k. brown	25	10
1863	–	60 k. green	35	10
1864	–	75 k. olive	2·75	10
1865	–	90 k. blue	2·75	10
1866	–	100 k. grey	1·90	10
1867	–	120 k. purple	2·00	10
1868	–	150 k. orange	1·25	20
1869	–	200 k. green	1·90	25
1870	–	250 k. brown	1·90	45
1871	–	500 k. blue	2·50	60

DESIGNS—HORIZ: 1 k. Vickers Viscount 700 airliner; 10 k. Grain silo; 15 k. Steel works; 20 k. Euphrates Bridge; 25 k. Zonguldak Harbour; 30 k. Oil refinery; 40 k. Rumeli Hisari Fortress; 45 k. Sugar factory; 55 k. Coal mine; 150 k. Combine-harvester. VERT: 60 k. Telegraph pole; 75 k. Railway; 90 k. Crane loading ships; 100 k. Cement factory; 120 k. Coast road; 200 k. Electric transformer; 250, 500 k. Portrait of Ataturk.

1959. Postage Due Stamps surch **20=20** for ordinary postage.

No.	Type	Description	Unused	Used
1872	D 121	20 k. on 20 pa. brown	10	10
1873		20 k. on 2 k. violet	10	10
1874		20 k. on 3 k. violet	10	10
1875		20 k. on 5 k. green	10	10
1876		20 k. on 12 k. red	10	10

1959. 10th Anniv of N.A.T.O.

No.	Type	Description	Unused	Used
1877	267	105 k. red	10	10
1878		195 k. green	10	10

268 Amphitheatre, Aspendos

270 Basketball Players

1959. Aspendos Festival.

No.	Type	Description	Unused	Used
1879	268	20 k. violet and bistre	10	10
1880		20 k. brown and green	10	10

1959. 10th Anniv of Council of Europe. Surch **X. YIL** in circle of stars, **105 AVRUPA KONSEYI**.

No.	Type	Description	Unused	Used
1881	259	105 k. on 15 k. + 5 k. orange	15	15

1959. 11th European and Mediterranean Basketball Championships, Istanbul.

No.	Type	Description	Unused	Used
1882	270	25 k. red and blue	25	10

271 Marine Symbols

272 Goreme

1959. 50th Anniv of Turkish Merchant Marine College.

No.	Type	Description	Unused	Used
1883	271	30 k. multicoloured	10	10
1884	–	40 k. multicoloured	15	10

DESIGN: 40 k. As 30 k. but sea-horse in place of anchor symbol.

1959. Tourist Publicity.

No.	Type	Description	Unused	Used
1885	272	105 k. + 10 k. orange and violet	25	25

273 Mounted Warrior

1959. 888th Anniv of Battle of Malazgirt.

No.	Type	Description	Unused	Used
1886	273	2½ l. purple and blue	50	15

274 Istanbul

1959. 15th International T.B. Conf, Istanbul.

No.	Type	Description	Unused	Used
1887	274	105 k. + 10 k. blue and red	35	20

275 Ornamental Pattern

276 Kemal Ataturk

1959. 1st International Congress of Turkish Arts.

No.	Type	Description	Unused	Used
1888	275	30 k. red and black	10	10
1889	–	40 k. blue, blk & ochre	15	10
1890	–	75 k. blue, yellow & red	30	10

DESIGNS—HORIZ: 40 k. Sultan Mohammed II Mosque in silhouette. VERT: 75 k. Circular ornament.

1959.

No.	Type	Description	Unused	Used
1891	276	500 k. blue	1·00	25

277 Faculty Building

278 Crossed Sabres

1959. Centenary of Turkish Political Science Faculty.
1892 **277** 40 k. brown and green . 15 10
1893 40 k. blue and brown . . 15 10
1894 – 1 l. ochre and violet . . . 25 10
DESIGN—VERT: 1 l. "S.B.F." emblem of Faculty.

1960. 125th Anniv of Territorial War College.
1895 **278** 30 k. red and yellow . . 10 10
1896 – 40 k. yellow, brown & red 20 10
DESIGN: 40 k. Bayonet in bowl of fire.

279 "Uprooted Tree" and Globe

1960. World Refugee Year.
1897 **279** 90 k. black & turquoise . 10 10
1898 – 105 k. black and yellow . 10 10
DESIGN: 105 k. "Uprooted Tree" and houses representing refugee camp.

280 Mental Home, Manisa **281** Carnations

1960. Manisa Fair. Inscr "MANISA MESIR BAYRAMI".
1899 **280** 40 k. + 5 k. violet & mve 15 10
1900 40 k. + 5 k. green & blue 15 10
1901 – 90 k. + 5 k. purple & mve 25 10
1902 – 105 k. + 10 k. mult . . 25 10
DESIGNS—VERT: 90 k. Sultan Mosque, Manisa; $30\frac{1}{2} \times 42\frac{1}{2}$ mm: 105 k. Merkez Muslihittin Efendi (portrait).

1960. Spring Flowers Festival, Istanbul. Inscr "1960". Flowers in natural colours. Colours of inscriptions and backgrounds given.
1903 **281** 30 k. red and yellow . . 20 15
1904 – 40 k. green and grey . . 25 20
1905 – 75 k. red and blue . . . 50 25
1906 – 105 k. green and pink . . 70 25
FLOWERS: 40 k. Jasmine; 75 k. Rose; 105 k. Tulips.

282 Map of Cyprus

1960. Proclamation of Cyprus Republic. Inscr "KIBRIS CUMHURIYETI".
1907 **282** 40 k. mauve and blue . . 25 10
1908 – 105 k. yellow, blue & grn 45 20
DESIGN: 40 k. Town Centre, Nicosia.

283 Globe

1960. 16th Women's Int Council Meeting.
1909 **283** 30 k. yellow and lilac . . 10 10
1910 – 75 k. drab and blue . . . 25 10
DESIGN: 75 k. Women, "W.I.C." emblem and nest.

283a Football **285** "Population"

1960. Olympic Games.
1911 30 k. green (Type **283a**) . . . 25 20
1912 30 k. black (Basketball) . . . 25 20
1913 30 k. blue (Wrestling) . . . 25 20
1914 30 k. purple (Hurdling) . . . 25 20
1915 30 k. brown (Show jumping) 25 20

1960. Europa. As T **129a** of Luxembourg but size $32\frac{1}{2} \times 22\frac{1}{2}$ mm.
1916 75 k. turquoise and green . . 25 25
1917 105 k. light and deep blue . . 40 25

1960. National Census.
1918 – 30 k. + 5 k. red and blue 20 10
1919 **285** 50 k. + 5 k. blue and turq 20 10
DESIGN—HORIZ: 30 k. Graph showing outlines of human faces.

286 "Justice" **287** Agah Efendi and Front Page of Newspaper "Turcamani Ahval"

1960. Trial of Ex-Government Officials.
1920 – 40 k. bistre and violet . 15 10
1921 – 105 k. red and green . . 15 10
1922 **286** 195 k. red and green . . 20 10
DESIGNS—HORIZ: 40 k. Badge of Turkish Army; 105 k. Trial scene.

1960. Turkish Press Centenary.
1923 **287** 40 k. purple and blue . 15 10
1924 60 k. purple and ochre . 20 10

288 U.N. Headquarters and Emblem

1960. 15th Anniv of U.N.O.
1925 – 90 k. ultramarine and blue 20 10
1926 **288** 105 k. brown and green 25 10
DESIGN—VERT: 90 k. U.N. emblem, "XV" and hand holding torch.

289 Revolutionaries

1960. Revolution of 27th May, 1960.
1927 **289** 10 k. grey and black . . 10 10
1928 – 30 k. violet 10 10
1929 – 40 k. red and black . . 10 10
1930 – 105 k. multicoloured . . 25 25
DESIGNS—HORIZ: 30 k. Kemal Ataturk and hand with torch; 105 k. Soldiers and wounded youth. VERT: 40 k. Prancing horse breaking chain.

290 Faculty Building

1960. 25th Anniv of History and Geography Faculty.
1931 **290** 30 k. black and green . 10 10
1932 – 40 k. black and buff . . 15 10
1933 – 60 k. olive, buff & green 20 10
DESIGNS—HORIZ: 40 k. Sun disc, cuneiform writing and map of Turkey. VERT: 60 k. Ataturk's statue.

291 "Communications and Transport" **292**

1961. 9th Central Treaty Organization Ministers' Meeting, Ankara.
1934 **291** 30 k. black and violet . 30 15
1935 – 40 k. black and green . 60 20
1936 – 75 k. black and blue . . 25 10
DESIGNS: 40 k. Road and rail construction, telephone and telegraph; 75 k. Parliament building, Ankara.

1961. 1st Anniv of 27th May Revolution.
1937 **292** 30 k. multicoloured . . 10 10
1938 – 40 k. green, cream & blk 15 10
1939 – 60 k. red, green and deep green 25 10
DESIGNS—HORIZ: 40 k. Boz Kurt and warriors. VERT: 60 k. "Progress".

293 North American F100 Jet and Rocket

1961. 50th Anniv of Turkish Air Force.
1940 – 38 k. orange, lake & blk . 20 10
1941 **293** 40 k. violet and red . . . 20 10
1942 – 75 k. buff, grey & black . 50 15
DESIGNS—HORIZ: 30 k. Rockets. VERT: 75 k. Ataturk, eagle and North American Super Sabre jets.

294 Old Observatory

1961. 50th Anniv of Kandilli Observatory, Istanbul.
1943 10 k. + 5 k. turq & green . . 10 10
1944 30 k. + 5 k. voilet & black . 20 10
1945 40 k. + 5 k. brown & sepia . 20 10
1946 75 k. + 5 k. olive and green . 40 15
DESIGNS—HORIZ: 10 k. Type **294**; 30 k. Observatory emblem; 75 k. Observatory building. VERT: 40 k. F. Gokmen.

295 Kemal Ataturk **295a**

1961.
1947 **295a** 1 k. brown 10 10
1948 5 k. blue 20 10
1949 **295** 10 k. mauve 25 10
1950 **295a** 10 k. sepia 50 10
1951 30 k. green . . . . . 1·40 10
1952 10 l. vio (22 × 32 mm) . 3·75 15

296 Doves

1961. Europa.
1960 **296** 30 k. blue 20 20
1961 40 k. grey 20 20
1962 75 k. red 50 50

297 Tulip and Cogwheel **298** "The Constitution"

1961. Centenary of Professional and Technical Schools.
1963 **297** 30 k. pink, silver and slate 10 10
1964 – 75 k. red, black & blue . 20 10
DESIGN—HORIZ: 75 k. Inscr "100 Yili 1861–1961" and tulip and cogwheel emblem.

1961. Opening of Turkish Parliament.
1965 **298** 30 k. black, bistre & red . 10 10
1966 75 k. black, grn & bl . . 25 10

299 Insecticide-sprayers ("Malaria Eradication") **300** N.A.T.O. and Anniversary Emblem

1961. 15th Anniv of U.N.I.C.E.F.
1967 **299** 10 k. + 5 k. turquoise . . 10 10
1968 – 30 k. + 5 k. violet . . . 20 10
1969 – 75 k. + 5 k. brown . . . 25 10
DESIGNS—HORIZ: 30 k. Mother and child ("Child Welfare"). VERT: 75 k. Mother giving pasteurized milk to children ("Education on Nourishment")

1962. 10th Anniv of Turkish Admission to N.A.T.O.
1970 – 75 k. black, silver & blue 30 10
1971 **300** 105 k. black, silver & red 40 15
DESIGN—VERT: 75 k. Peace dove over N.A.T.O. and Anniv emblems.

301 Mosquito on Map of Turkey **302** "Strelitzia reginae"

1962. Malaria Eradication.
1972 **301** 30 k. + 5 k. brown . . . 15 10
1973 75 k. + 5 k. mve & blk . 25 10

1962. Flowers. Multicoloured.
1974 30 k. + 10 k. "Poinsettia pulcherrima" 35 15
1975 40 k. + 10 k. Type **302** . . . 40 20
1976 75 k. + 10 k. "Nymphea alba" 75 25

303 Scouts in Camp **304** Soldier (Victory Monument, Ankara)

1962. 50th Anniv of Turkish Scout Movement.
1977 **303** 30 k. red, black & green 25 10
1978 – 60 k. red, black & lilac . 35 10
1979 – 105 k. red, black & brn . 35 10
DESIGNS: 60 k. Two scouts with flag; 105 k. Wolf Cub and Brownie.

1962. 40th Anniv of Battle of Dumlupinar.
1980 **304** 30 k. green 15 10
1981 – 40 k. brown and black . 20 10
1982 – 75 k. grey 35 10
DESIGNS—HORIZ: 40 k. Ox-cart carrying ammunition. (Victory Monument, Ankara). VERT: 75 k. Kemal Ataturk.

305 Europa "Tree" **306** Shrine of the Virgin Mary

1962. Europa.
1983 **305** 75 k. sepia and green . . 30 20
1984 105 k. sepia and red . . 35 30
1985 195 k. sepia and blue . . 45 35

1962. Tourist Issue. Multicoloured.
1986 30 k. Type **306** 20 10
1987 40 k. Interior 25 15
1988 75 k. Exterior 30 10
1989 105 k. Statue of the Virgin . 25 15
DESIGNS: The 40 and 75 k. show horiz views of the Virgin Mary's house at Ephesus.

307 Turkish 20 pa. Stamp of 1863 **308** Julian's Column, Ankara

1963. Stamp Centenary.
1990 **307** 10 k. black, yell & brn . 10 10
1991 – 30 k. black, pink & vio . 20 10
1992 – 40 k. black, blue & turq 20 10
1993 – 75 k. black, pink & brn . 35 15
DESIGNS—Turkish stamps of 1863: 30 k. (1 pi.); 40 k. (2 pi.); 75 k. (5 pi.).

1963.
1994 **308** 1 k. green and olive . . 10 10
1995 1 k. violet 10 10
1996 – 5 k. sepia and brown . . 10 10
1997 – 10 k. mauve and green . 15 10
1998 – 30 k. black and violet . . 50 10
1999 – 50 k. green, brn & yell . 35 10
2000 – 60 k. grey 85 10
2001 – 100 k. brown 65 10
2002 – 150 k. green . . . . . 3·75 25
DESIGNS—HORIZ: 5 k. Ethnographic Museum; 10 k. Citadel; 30 k. Educational Establishment, Gazi; 50 k. Ataturk's Mausoleum; 60 k. Presidential Palace, Ankara; 100 k. Ataturk's house; 150 k. National Museum, Ankara.

309 "Clinging to the World" 310 Wheat and Census Graph

1963. Freedom from Hunger.
2010 **309** 30 k. deep blue and blue . . . 10 10
2011 – 40 k. dp brown & brown . . . 15 15
2012 – 75 k. dp green & green . . . 25 20
DESIGNS: 40 k. Sowers; 75 k. Emblem and Globe within hands.

1963. Agricultural Census. Unissued stamps with "KASIM 1960" obliterated with bars. Inscr "UMUMI ZIRAAT SAYIMI".
2013 **310** 40 k. + 5 k. multicoloured . . . 20 20
2014 – 60 k. + 5 k. multicoloured . . . 25 25
DESIGN—HORIZ: 60 k. Wheat and chart.

311 Atomic Symbol on Map 312 Ucserefili Mosque

1963. 1st Anniv of Opening of Turkish Nuclear Research Centre.
2015 **311** 50 k. brown & dp brown . . . 20 10
2016 – 60 k. multicoloured . . . 25 15
2017 – 100 k. blue & ultram . . . 35 25
DESIGNS: 60 k. Various symbols; 100 k. Emblem of Turkish Atomic Energy Commission.

1963. 600th Anniv of Conquest of Edirne.
2018 **312** 10 k. green, ultramarine and blue . . . 10 10
2019 – 30 k. blue and red . . . 15 10
2020 – 60 k. multicoloured . . . 20 10
2021 – 100 k. multicoloured . . . 30 20
DESIGNS—HORIZ: 30 k. Meric Bridge; 60 k. Kum Kasri (building). VERT: 100 k. Sultan Amurat I.

313 Soldier and Sun

1963. 600th Anniv of Turkish Army.
2022 **313** 50 k. black, red & blue . . . 20 10
2023 100 k. black, red & bistre . . . 35 25

314 Globe and Emblems 315 Mithat Pasha (founder)

1963. Red Cross Centenary. Multicoloured.
2024 50 k. + 10 k. Type **314** . . . 25 25
2025 60 k. + 10 k. "Flowers" emblem (vert) . . . 35 30
2026 100 k. + 10 k. Three emblems on flags . . . 45 40

1963. Centenary of Turkish Agricultural Bank.
2027 – 30 k. brown, green and yellow . . . 10 10
2028 – 50 k. blue and lilac . . . 20 10
2029 **315** 60 k. green and black . . . 25 20
DESIGNS—HORIZ: 30 k. Ploughing and irrigation; 50 k. Agricultural Bank, Ankara.

316 Exhibition Hall, Istanbul, and 5 pi. stamp of 1863

1963. "Istanbul '63" International Stamp Exn.
2030 **316** 10 k. salmon, black and yellow . . . 10 10
2031 – 50 k. green, red and black . . . 15 10
2032 – 60 k. sepia, black & blue . . . 20 10
2033 – 100 k. violet and purple . . . 40 30
2034 – 130 k. brown, orge & yell . . . 60 40
DESIGNS: 50 k. Sultan Ahmed's Mosque, Obelisk and 3 pi. on 2 pa. Nationalist Government (Angora) stamp of 1920; 60 k. Istanbul skyline and 10 pi. (Angora) stamp of 1922; 100 k. Rumeli Fort and 6 k. stamp of 1929/30; 130 k. Ankara Fort and 12½ k. air stamp of 1934.

317 "Co-operation"

1963. Europa.
2035 **317** 50 k. orange, blk & red . . . 25 10
2036 130 k. blue, black & grn . . . 45 25

318 Ataturk and Old Parliament House 319 Kemal Ataturk

1963. 40th Anniv of Turkish Republic. Multicoloured.
2037 30 k. Type **318** . . . 20 10
2038 50 k. Ataturk and flag . . . 25 15
2039 60 k. Ataturk and new Parliament House . . . 35 20

1963. 25th Death Anniv of Kemal Ataturk.
2040 **319** 50 k. multicoloured . . . 20 15
2041 60 k. multicoloured . . . 30 20

320 R.S. Dag (painter) 321 N.A.T.O. Emblem and "XV"

1964. Cultural Celebrities.
2042 – 1 k. black and red . . . 10 10
2043 – 5 k. black and green . . . 10 10
2044 **320** 10 k. black and brown . . . 10 10
2045 – 50 k. black and blue . . . 20 10
2046 – 60 k. black and grey . . . 55 15
2047 – 100 k. ultram & blue . . . 65 10
2048 – 130 k. black and green . . . 2·10 20
PORTRAITS: 1 k. H. R. Gurpinar (romanticist, birth centenary); 5 k. J. H. Izmirli (savant, 20th death anniv); 10 k. Type **320** (20th death anniv); 50 k. R. Z. M. Ekrem (writer, 50th death anniv); 60 k. A. M. Pasa (commander, 125th birth anniv); 100 k. A. Rasim (writer, birth centenary); 130 k. S. Zeki (mathematician, birth centenary).

1964. 15th Anniv of N.A.T.O.
2049 **321** 50 k. red, violet & turq . . . 25 10
2050 – 130 k. black and red . . . 50 15
DESIGN: 130 k. N.A.T.O. emblem and laurel sprig.

322 "Europa" holding Torch

1964. 15th Anniv of Council of Europe.
2051 **322** 50 k. blue, brown & yell . . . 35 10
2052 – 130 k. orange, ultramarine and blue . . . 50 25
DESIGN: 130 k. Torch and circlet of stars.

323 Haga Mosque, Istanbul 324 Kars Castle

1964. Tourist Issue.
2053 **323** 50 k. green and olive . . . 25 15
2054 – 50 k. red and purple . . . 25 15
2055 – 50 k. violet and blue . . . 25 15
2056 – 60 k. green, black & pur . . . 35 20
2057 – 60 k. brown and sepia . . . 35 20
DESIGNS—HORIZ: No. 2054 Temple of Zeus, Silifke; 2055 Amasra. VERT: No. 2056 Mersin; 2057 Augustus' Temple, Ankara.

1964. 900th Anniv of Conquest of Kars.
2058 **324** 50 k. black and lilac . . . 20 15
2059 – 130 k. multicoloured . . . 45 25
DESIGN: 130 k. Alpaslan warrior.

325 Europa "Flower" 326 Grazing Cattle

1964. Europa.
2060 **325** 50 k. blue, grey & orge . . . 25 20
2061 130 k. purple, green & bl . . . 35 25

1964. Animal Protection Fund. Multicoloured.
2062 10 k. + 5 k. Type **326** . . . 10 10
2063 30 k. + 5 k. Horned sheep . . . 20 10
2064 50 k. + 5 k. Horses . . . 30 10
2065 60 k. + 5 k. Three horned sheep . . . 40 10
2066 100 k. + 5 k. Dairy cows . . . 60 25
The 30 k. and 60 k. are vert.

327 Running 328 Mustafa Resit

1964. Olympic Games, Tokyo.
2067 **327** 10 k. + 5 k. black, red and brown . . . 15 10
2068 – 50 k. + 5 k. black, red and olive . . . 25 10
2069 – 60 k. + 5 k. black, red and blue . . . 25 10
2070 – 100 k. + 5 k. black, red and violet . . . 50 25
DESIGNS—VERT: 50 k. Torch-bearer; 60 k. Wrestling; 100 k. Throwing the discus.

1964. 125th Anniv of Reformation Decrees. Multicoloured.
2071 50 k. Mustafa Resit and the pashas (horiz 48 × 32 mm) . . . 25 10
2072 60 k. Type **328** . . . 25 10
2073 100 k. As 50 k. . . . 40 15

329 Kemal Ataturk 330 Glider

1964.
2074 **329** 1 k. green . . . 10 10
2075 5 k. blue . . . 10 10
2076 10 k. blue . . . 20 10
2077 25 k. green . . . 50 10
2078 30 k. purple . . . 55 10
2079 50 k. brown . . . 1·00 10
2080 150 k. orange . . . 2·50 10

1965. 40th Anniv of Turkish Civil Aviation League. Multicoloured.
2081 60 k. Parachutist . . . 25 10
2082 90 k. Type **330** . . . 35 10
2083 130 k. Ataturk and squadron of aircraft . . . 80 10
The 60 k. and 130 k. are vert.

331 CENTO Emblem

1965. Completion of CENTO Telecommunications Projects. Multicoloured.
2084 30 k. Type **331** . . . 10 10
2085 50 k. Aerial mast (vert) . . . 15 10
2086 75 k. Hand pressing button (inaugural ceremony) . . . 25 10

332 Monument and Soldiers

1965. 50th Anniv of Battle of the Dardanelles. Multicoloured.
2087 50 k. + 10 k. Wreath and map . . . 20 20
2088 90 k. + 10 k. Type **332** . . . 25 20
2089 130 k. + 10 k. Dardanelles Monument and flag (vert) . . . 15 35

333 Beach at Ordu

1965. Tourism. Multicoloured.
2090 30 k. Type **333** . . . 20 15
2091 50 k. Manavgat Falls . . . 25 10
2092 60 k. Istanbul . . . 25 10
2093 100 k. Urfa . . . 40 20
2094 130 k. Alanya . . . 45 25

334 I.T.U. Emblem and Symbols

1965. I.T.U. Centenary.
2095 **334** 50 k. multicoloured . . . 25 20
2096 130 k. multicoloured . . . 30 30

335 I.C.Y. Emblem

1965. International Co-operation Year.
2097 **335** 100 k. red, green and salmon . . . 35 10
2098 130 k. violet, green and grey . . . 50 25

336 "Co-operation" 337 R. N. Guntekin

1965. 1st Anniv of Regional Development Co-operation Pact. Multicoloured.
2099 50 k. Type **336** . . . 25 10
2100 75 k. Globe and flags of Turkey, Iran and Pakistan . . . 30 15

1965. Cultural Celebrities.
2101 **337** 1 k. black and red . . . 10 10
2102 – 5 k. black and blue . . . 10 10
2103 – 10 k. black and ochre . . . 15 10
2104 – 25 k. black and brown . . . 30 10
2105 – 30 k. black and grey . . . 30 10
2106 – 50 k. black and yellow . . . 65 10
2107 – 60 k. black and purple . . . 40 10
2108 – 150 k. black and green . . . 75 10
2109 – 220 k. black and brown . . . 55 35
PORTRAITS: 5 k. Dr. B. O Akalin; 10 k. T. Fikret; 25 k. T. Cemil; 30 k. Ahmet Vefik Pasa; 50 k. O. Seyfettin; 60 k. K. Mimaroglu; 150 k. H. Z. Usakligil; 220 k. Y. K. Beyatli.

338 Kemal Ataturk and Signature 339 Tobacco Plant

1965.
2110 **338** 1 k. black and mauve . . . 10 10
2111 5 k. black and green . . . 15 10
2112 10 k. black and blue . . . 15 10
2113 50 k. black and gold . . . 15 10
2114 150 k. black and silver . . . 50 10
See also Nos. 2170/4.

1965. 2nd International Tobacco Congress. Mult.
2115 30 k. + 5 k. Type **339** . . . 25 20
2116 50 k. + 5 k. Leander's Tower and tobacco leaves (horiz) . . . 25 20
2117 100 k. + 5 k. Tobacco leaf . . . 20 40

340 Europa "Sprig" **341** Civilians supporting Map

1965. Europa.

2118	**340**	50 k. green, blue & grey	50	35
2119		130 k. grn, blk & ochre	60	40

1965. National Census. Inscr "GENEL NUFUS SAYIMI".

2120	**341**	10 k. multicoloured	10	10
2121	–	50 k. light green, green and black	20	10
2122	–	100 k. black, bl & orge	25	15

DESIGNS—HORIZ: 50 k. Year "1965". VERT: 100 k. Human eye and figure.

342 Ankara Castle and Airliner

1965. "Ankara '65" National Stamp Exn. Inscr "I. MILLI PUL SERGISI".

2123	**342**	10 k. red, yellow & violet	10	10
2124	–	30 k. multicoloured	15	10
2125	–	50 k. blue, red & olive	20	10
2126	–	100 k. multicoloured	40	15

DESIGNS: 30 k. Archer; 50 k. Horseman; 100 k. Three thematic "stamps" and medal.

343 Training-ship "Savarona" **344** Halide E. Adivar

1965. Turkish Naval Society Congress.

2128	**343**	50 k. brown and blue	35	20
2129	–	60 k. indigo and blue	45	20
2130	–	100 k. brown and blue	65	30
2131	–	130 k. purple and blue	1·10	60
2132	–	220 k. black and blue	1·90	90

DESIGNS: 60 k. Submarine "Piri Reis"; 100 k. Destroyer "Alpaslan"; 130 k. Destroyer "Gelibolu"; 220 k. Destroyer "Gemlik".

1966. Cultural Celebrities.

2133	–	25 k. brown and grey	50	10
2134	–	30 k. brown and mauve	25	10
2135	**344**	50 k. black and blue	25	10
2136	–	60 k. brown and green	60	10
2137	–	130 k. black and blue	1·50	15

PORTRAITS: 25 k. H. S. Arel; 30 k. K. Akdik; 60 k. Abdurrahman Seref; 130 k. Naima.

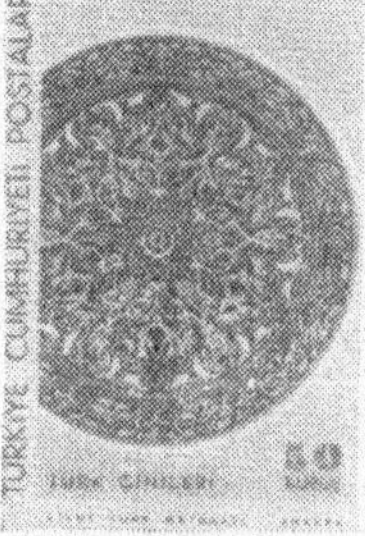

345 Roof Panel, Green Mausoleum, Burs **346** Volleyball

1966. Turkish Faience. Multicoloured.

2138	50 k. Type **345**	35	20
2139	60 k. "Spring Flowers", Sultan Mausoleum, Istanbul	1·10	75
2140	130 k. 16th-cent tile, Iznik	75	40

1966. Int Military Volleyball Championships.

2141	**346**	50 k. multicoloured	35	20

347 Bodrum **348** Golden Pitcher

1966. Tourism. Multicoloured.

2142	10 k. Type **347**	10	10
2143	30 k. Kusadasi	55	40
2144	50 k. Anadoluhisari	15	10
2145	90 k. Marmaris	30	20
2146	100 k. Izmir	35	25

The 50 k. and 100 k. are horiz.

1966. Ancient Works of Art. Multicoloured.

2147	30 k. + 5 k. Ivory eagle and rabbit	10	20
2148	50 k. + 5 k. Deity in basalt	10	25
2149	60 k. + 5 k. Bronze bull	15	10
2150	90 k. + 5 k. Type **348**	20	15

The 30 k. is horiz.

349 View of Dam

1966. Inaug of Keban Dam. Multicoloured.

2151	50 k. Type **349**	15	10
2152	60 k. Keban valley and bridge	20	10

350 King Faisal

1966. Visit of King of Saudi Arabia.

2153	**350**	100 k. deep red and red	15	30

351 "Stamp" and "Postmark"

1966. "Balkanfila" Stamp Exhibition, Istanbul. Multicoloured.

2154	50 k. Type **351**	15	10
2155	60 k. Stamp "flower"	20	15
2156	75 k. "Stamps" in form of display frames	25	20

353 Sultan Suleiman on Horseback **354** Europa "Ship"

1966. 400th Death Anniv of Sultan Suleiman. Multicoloured.

2158	60 k. Type **353**	25	20
2159	90 k. Mausoleum, Istanbul	55	25
2160	130 k. Sultan Suleiman (profile)	1·25	65

1966. Europa.

2161	**354**	50 k. ultram, bl & blk	75	25
2162		130 k. purple, lilac & blk	75	55

355 Grand Hotel Ephesus, Izmir

1966. 33rd International Fairs Union Congress, Izmir. Multicoloured.

2163	50 k. + 5 k. Type **355**	20	10
2164	60 k. + 5 k. Konak Square, Izmir (vert)	25	15
2165	130 k. + 5 k. Izmir Fair	35	20

356 "Education, Science and Culture"

1966. 20th Anniv of U.N.E.S.C.O.

2166	**356**	130 k. chestnut, yellow and brown	20	20

357 University of Technology **358** Ataturk (equestrian statue)

1966. 10th Anniv of Middle East University of Technology. Multicoloured.

2167	50 k. Type **357**	15	10
2168	100 k. Atomic symbol	25	10
2169	130 k. Symbols of the sciences	35	15

1966. As Nos. 2110/14.

2170	**338**	25 k. black and green	15	10
2171		30 k. black and pink	15	10
2172		50 k. black and violet	50	10
2173		90 k. black and brown	75	10
2174		100 k. black and drab	80	10

1966. Greetings Card Stamp.

2175	**358**	10 k. black and yellow	15	10

See also Nos. 2218/9, 2257/8, 2303 and 2418.

359 De Havilland Dragon Rapide **360** A. Mithat (author)

1967. Air. Aircraft.

2176	**359**	10 k. black and pink	25	10
2177	–	60 k. red, black & grn	25	10
2178	–	130 k. red, black & blue	65	20
2179	–	220 k. red, sepia and ochre	1·10	35
2180	–	270 k. red, blue and salmon	1·75	50

DESIGNS: 60 k. Fokker F27 Friendship; 130 k. Douglas DC-9-30; 220 k. Douglas DC-3; 270 k. Vickers Viscount 700.

1967. Cultural Celebrities.

2181	**360**	1 k. black and green	10	10
2182	–	5 k. black and ochre	10	10
2183	–	50 k. black and violet	40	10
2184	–	100 k. black and yellow	90	10
2185	–	150 k. black and yellow	1·40	10

PORTRAITS: 5 k. T. Reis (naval commander); 50 k. S. Mehmet (statesman); 100 k. Nedim (philosopher); 150 k. O. Hamdi (painter).

361 Karogoz and Hacivat (puppets)

1967. International Tourist Year. Multicoloured.

2186	50 k. Type **361**	40	10
2187	60 k. Sword and shield game	50	15
2188	90 k. Military Band	55	40
2189	100 k. Karagoz (puppet) (vert)	95	45

362 "Vaccination" **363** Fallow Deer

1967. 250th Anniv of 1st Smallpox Vaccination, Edirne.

2190	**362**	100 k. multicoloured	40	15

1967. Game Animals. Multicoloured.

2191	50 k. Type **363**	45	10
2192	60 k. Wild goat	50	20
2193	100 k. Brown bear	75	25
2194	130 k. Wild boar	1·00	35

364 Emblem and Footballers **365** Cogwheels

1967. 20th Int Junior Football Tournament. Mult.

2195	50 k. Type **364**	25	15
2196	130 k. Footballers and emblem	40	35

1967. Europa.

2197	**365**	100 k. + 10 k. mult	40	15
2198		130 k. + 10 k. mult	65	25

366 Kemal Ataturk **367** Road Junction on Map

1967.

2199	**366**	10 k. black and green	45	10
2200		50 k. black and pink	45	10

1967. Opening of "E 5" Motorway. Mult.

2201	60 k. + 5 k. Type **367**	20	10
2202	130 k. + 5 k. Motorway map and emblem (vert)	40	15

368 Sivas Hospital

1967. 750th Anniv of Sivas Hospital.

2203	**368**	50 k. multicoloured	25	10

369 Selim Tarcan and Olympic Rings

1967. 1st Turkish Olympic Competitions, Istanbul. Multicoloured.

2204	50 k. Type **369**	35	25
2205	60 k. Pierre de Coubertin and Olympic Rings	35	25

370 St. John's Church, Ephesus **371** Common Kestrel

1967. Pope Paul VI's Visit to Virgin Mary's House, Ephesus. Multicoloured.

2206	130 k. Interior of Virgin Mary's House, Ephesus	35	15
2207	220 k. Type **370**	60	20

1967. Air. Birds.

2208	**371**	10 k. brown and salmon	1·10	15
2209	–	60 k. brown and yellow	65	15
2210	–	130 k. purple and blue	1·25	30
2211	–	220 k. sepia and green	1·60	45
2212	–	270 k. brown and lilac	2·00	55

DESIGNS: 60 k. Imperial eagle; 130 k. Pallid harrier; 220 k. European sparrow hawk; 270 k. Common buzzard.

372 Exhibition Emblem

1967. International Ceramics Exn, Istanbul.

2213	**372**	50 k. multicoloured	30	15

373 Emblem and Istanbul Skyline **374** "Stamps" and Map

1967. Congress of International Large Dams Commission, Istanbul.

2214	**373**	130 k. blue and drab	30	20

1967. "Izmir '67" Stamp Exhibition. Mult.

2215	50 k. Type **374**	20	12
2216	60 k. "Stamps" and grapes	25	20

1967. Greetings Card Stamps. As T **358**.

2218	10 k. black and green	25	10
2219	10 k. black and red	25	10

DESIGNS: Equestrian statues of Ataturk at: No. 2218 Samsun; No. 2219 Izmir.

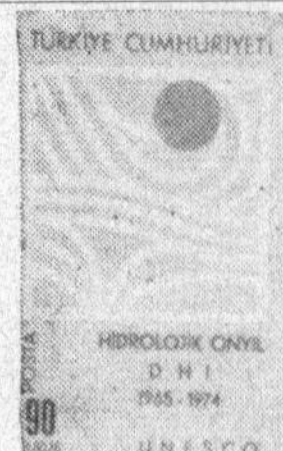

375 Decade Emblem **376** Girl with Angora Cat

1967. International Hydrological Decade.

2220 **375** 90 k. yellow, blk & grn . . 25 10
2221 130 k. yellow, blk & lilac 25 15

1967. 125th Anniv of Turkish Veterinary Medical Service. Multicoloured.

2222 50 k. Type **376** 15 10
2223 60 k. Horse 20 10

377 Human Rights Emblem **378** Kemal Ataturk

1968. Human Rights Year.

2224 **377** 50 k. multicoloured . . . 10 10
2225 130 k. multicoloured . . 15 10

1968.

2226 **378** 1 k. blue and light blue . 10 10
2227 5 k. green and lt green . 25 10
2228 50 k. brown and yellow . 90 10
2229 200 k. brown and pink . 1·90 15

379 "The Investiture"

1968. Turkish Book Miniatures. Multicoloured.

2230 50 k. Type **379** 25 20
2231 60 k. "Suleiman the Magnificent receiving an ambassador" (vert) 35 20
2232 90 k. "The Sultan's Archery Practice" 45 30
2233 100 k. "The Musicians" . . . 65 35

380 Scales of Justice

1968. Turkish Courts Centenary. Multicoloured. (a) Supreme Court.

2234 50 k. Type **380** 20 15
2235 60 k. Ahmet Cevdet Pasha (president) and scroll . . 25 20

(b) Court of Appeal.

2236 50 k. Book 20 15
2237 60 k. Mithat Pasha (first president) and scroll . . . 25 20

381 W.H.O. Emblem **382** Europa "Key"

1968. 20th Anniv of W.H.O.

2238 **381** 130 k. + 10 k. yellow, black and blue 55 30

1968. Europa.

2239 **382** 100 k. yellow, red & blue 50 25
2240 130 k. yellow, red & grn . 75 40

383 Etem Pasha and Dr. Marko

1968. Turkish Red Crescent Fund. Multicoloured.

2241 50 k. + 10 k. Type **383** . . 35 20
2242 60 k. + 10 k. Omer Pasha and Dr. Abdullah 40 35
2243 100 k. + 10 k. Kemal Ataturk and Dr. Refik Saydam in front of Red Crescent Headquarters (vert) . . . 50 40

384 "Kismet" **385** "Protection against Usury" (after Koseoglu)

1968. Sadun Boro's World Voyage in Ketch "Kismet".

2244 **384** 50 k. multicoloured . . 45 15

1968. Centenary of Pawnbroking Office, Istanbul.

2245 **385** 50 k. multicoloured . . 30 20

386 Battle of Sakarya and Obverse of Medal

1968. Independence Medal. Multicoloured.

2246 50 k. Type **386** 20 20
2247 130 k. National Anthem and reverse of medal 45 30

387 Old and New Emblems within "100"

1968. Centenary of Galatasaray High School. Multicoloured.

2248 50 k. Type **387** 20 20
2249 60 k. Gulbaba offering flowers to Bayazet II 30 20
2250 100 k. Kemal Ataturk and School Building 45 35

388 President De Gaulle **389** Kemal Ataturk

1968. President De Gaulle's Visit to Turkey.

2251 **388** 130 k. multicoloured . . 25 25

1968. 30th Death Anniv of Kemal Ataturk.

2252 **389** 30 k. black and yellow . 15 10
2253 – 50 k. black and green . 15 10
2254 – 60 k. black and turq . . 50 20
2255 – 100 k. black, green and bistre 40 20
2256 – 250 k. multicoloured . . 95 40

DESIGNS: 50 k. Ataturk's Cenotaph; 60 k. Ataturk at railway carriage window. ($32\frac{1}{2} \times 43$ mm): 100 k. Ataturk's portrait and "address to youth"; 250 k. Ataturk in military uniform.

1968. Greetings Card Stamps. As T **358** but dated "1968".

2257 10 k. black and mauve . . . 10 10
2258 10 k. black and blue 10 10

DESIGNS: Equestrian statues of Ataturk at: No. 2257 Antakya; No. 2258 Zonguldak.

390 Ince Minara Mosque, Konya **391** Dove and N.A.T.O. Emblem

1968. Historic Buildings.

2259 **390** 1 k. sepia and brown . . 10 10
2260 – 10 k. maroon and purple 15 10
2261 – 50 k. green and grey . . . 25 10
2262 – 100 k. green & lt green . 1·00 10
2263 – 200 k. blue & light blue . 50 10

DESIGNS: 10 k. Doner Kumbet (tomb), Kayseri; 50 k. Karatay University, Konya; 100 k. Ortakoy Mosque, Istanbul; 200 k. Ulu Mosque, Divrigi.

1969. 20th Anniv of N.A.T.O.

2264 **391** 50 k. + 10 k. black, blue and green 10 15
2265 – 130 k. + 10 k. gold, blue and deep blue 20 15

DESIGN: 130 k. Stars around globe and N.A.T.O. emblem.

392 "Education"

1969. Turkish Economy.

2266 **392** 1 k. black and red 10 10
2267 1 k. black and green . . . 10 10
2268 1 k. black and violet . . 10 10
2269 1 k. black and brown . . 10 10
2270 1 k. black and grey . . . 10 10
2271 – 50 k. brown and ochre . 40 10
2272 – 90 k. black and olive . . 50 10
2273 – 100 k. red and black . . 65 10
2274 – 180 k. violet and orange . 1·75 10

DESIGNS: 50 k. Farm workers and tractor ("Agriculture"); 90 k. Ladle, factory and cogwheel ("Industry"); 100 k. Road sign and graph ("Highways"); 180 k. Derricks ("Oil Industry").

393 I.L.O Emblem

1969. 50th Anniv of I.L.O.

2275 **393** 130 k. red and black . . 25 10

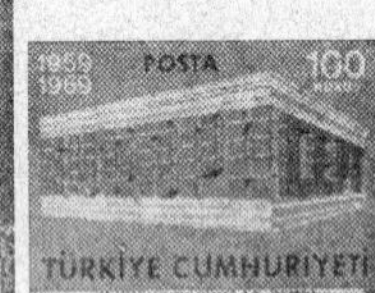

394 "Hafsa Sultan" (unknown artist) **395** Colonnade

1969. Hafsa Sultan (medical pioneer) Commem.

2276 **394** 60 k. multicoloured . . . 30 10

1969. Europa.

2277 **395** 100 k. multicoloured . . 15 25
2278 130 k. multicoloured . . 25 15

396 Kemal Ataturk in 1919 **397** Symbolic Map of Istanbul

1969. 50th Anniv of Kemal Ataturk's Landing at Samsun. Multicoloured.

2279 50 k. Type **396** 20 15
2280 60 k. Cargo liner "Bandirma" (horiz) 50 15

1969. 22nd Int Chambers of Commerce Congress, Istanbul.

2281 **397** 130 k. multicoloured . . 20 10

398 "Suleiman the Great holding Audience" (16th-cent Turkish miniature) **399** Kemal Ataturk in Civilian Dress

1969. 5th Anniv of Regional Co-operation for Development. Multicoloured.

2282 50 k. Type **398** 30 15
2283 80 k. "Kneeling Servant" (17th-cent Persian) 45 20
2284 130 k. "Lady on Balcony" (18th-cent Mogul–Pakistan) 65 40

1969. 50th Anniv of Erzurum Congress.

2285 **399** 50 k. black and violet . . 20 15
2286 – 60 k. black and green . . 20 15

DESIGN—HORIZ: 60 k. Ataturk's statue, Erzurum.

401 Red Cross Societies' Emblems

1969. 21st International Red Cross Conf, Istanbul.

2291 **401** 100 k. + 10 k. red, blue and ultramarine 35 20
2292 – 130 k. + 10 k. mult . . 40 20

DESIGN: 130 k. Conference emblem and silhouette of Istanbul.

402 Congress Hall

1969. 50th Anniv of Sivas Congress.

2293 **402** 50 k. purple, blk and red 20 15
2294 – 60 k. olive, black & yell . 25 15

DESIGN: 60 k. Congress delegates.

403 Halay Scarf Dance

1969. Turkish Folk-dances. Multicoloured.

2295 30 k. Bar dancers 15 15
2296 50 k. Caydacira "candle" dance 30 20
2297 60 k. Type **403** 35 25
2298 100 k. Kilic-Kalkan sword dance 60 25
2299 130 k. Zeybek dance (vert) . 65 50

404 Bleriot XI "Prince Celaladdin"

1969. 55th Anniv of First Turkish Airmail Service.

2300 **404** 60 k. deep blue & blue . 40 10
2301 – 75 k. black and bistre . . 25 15

DESIGN: 75 k. 1914 First Flight cover.

405 "Kutadgu Bilig"

1969. 900th Anniv of "Kutadgu Bilig" (political manual) Compilation.

2302 **405** 130 k. brown, gold and bistre 25 10

1969. Greetings Card Stamp. As T **358**.

2303 10 k. brown and green . . . 10 10

DESIGN: 10 k. Equestrian statue of Ataturk at Bursa.

406 "Ataturk's Arrival" (S. Tuna)

1969. 50th Anniv of Kemal Ataturk's Arrival in Ankara. Multicoloured.

2304 50 k. Type **406** 30 10
2305 60 k. Ataturk's motorcade . . 30 15

407 "Erosion Control"

1970. Nature Conservation Year. Multicoloured.

2306 50 k. + 10 k. Type **407** . . . 25 20
2307 60 k. + 10 k. "Protection of Flora" 10 25
2308 130 k. + 10 k. "Protection of Wildlife" 45 35

408 Bosphorus Bridge (model)
(Illustration reduced. Actual size 79 × 30½ mm)

1970. Commencement of Work on Bosphorus Bridge. Multicoloured.

2309 60 k. Type **408** 25 15
2310 130 k. Symbolic bridge linking Europe and Asia 45 25

409 Ataturk and Signature

410 Education Year Emblem

1970.

2311 **409** 1 k. brown and red . . . 10 10
2312 50 k. green and olive . . 25 10

1970. International Education Year.

2313 **410** 130 k. blue, purple & mve 25 10

411 Turkish Pavilion Emblem

413 Opening Ceremony

(412 Kemal Ataturk)

1970. World Fair "Expo '70", Osaka, Japan. Multicoloured.

2314 50 k. Type **411** 15 10
2315 100 k. Turkish pavilion and Expo emblem 30 10

1970.

2316 **412** 5 k. black and silver . . 10 10
2317 30 k. black and bistre . . 25 10
2318 50 k. black and pink . . 35 10
2319 75 k. black and lilac . . 55 10
2320 100 k. black and blue . . 60 10

1970. 50th Anniv of Turkish National Assembly. Multicoloured.

2321 50 k. Type **413** 15 10
2322 60 k. First Assembly in session 20 10

414 Emblem of Cartography Directorate

1970. "75 Years of Turkish Cartography". Multicoloured.

2323 50 k. Type **414** 10 10
2324 60 k. Dornier Do-28 airplane and contour map 35 10
2325 100 k. Survey equipment . . 20 10
2326 130 k. Lt.-Gen. Mehmet Sevki Pasha and relief map of Turkey 25 10

Nos. 2324 and 2326 are larger, size 48 × 33 mm.

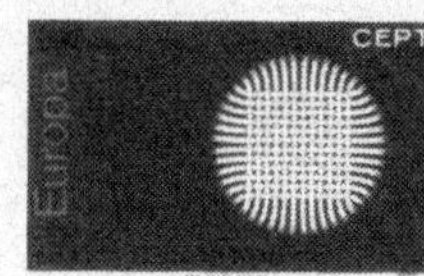
415 "Flaming Sun"

1970. Europa.

2327 **415** 100 k. red, orange & blk 45 10
2328 130 k. green, orge & blk 75 25

416 New U.P.U. Headquarters Building

1970. New U.P.U. Headquarters Building, Berne.

2329 **416** 60 k. black, blue & lt bl . 15 10
2330 130 k. black, green and light green 25 10

417 "Roe-deer" (Seker Ahmet Pasha)

418 "Turkish Folklore"

1970. Turkish Paintings. Multicoloured.

2331 250 k. Type **417** 80 50
2332 250 k. "Lady with Mimosa" (Osman Hamdi) 45 20

See also Nos. 2349/50, 2364/5, 2396/7, 2416/17 and 2443/4.

1970. "Ankara 70" National Stamp Exhibition. Multicoloured.

2333 10 k. "Tree" of stamps and open album (vert) 10 10
2334 50 k. Type **418** 25 10
2335 60 k. Ataturk statue and "stamps" 30 15

419 Fethiye (Turkey)

1970. 6th Anniv of Regional Co-operation for Development. Multicoloured.

2337 60 k. Type **419** 20 10
2338 80 k. Seeyo-Se-Pol Bridge, Isfahan (Iran) 25 10
2339 130 k. Saiful Malook Lake (Pakistan) 35 10

No. 2338 is larger 41 × 26 mm.

420 Tomb of Haci Bektas Veli

421 Symbolic "Fencer" and Globe

1970. 700th Death Anniv of Haci Bektas Veli (mystic). Multicoloured.

2340 30 k. Type **420** 10 10
2341 100 k. Sultan Balim's tomb (vert) 35 10
2342 180 k. Haci Bektas Veli (vert) 40 15

No. 2342 is larger, size 32 × 49 mm.

1970. World Fencing Championships.

2343 **421** 90 k. + 10 k. black, blue and light blue 25 10
2344 – 130 k. + 10 k. orange, green, black and blue . 30 10

DESIGN: 130 k. Modern fencer, folk-dancer and globe.

422 I.S.O. Emblem 423 U.N. Emblem within Windmill

1970. 8th Int Standardisation Organisation General Assembly, Ankara.

2345 **422** 110 k. red, gold & black . 25 10
2346 150 k. blue, gold & black 30 15

1970. 25th Anniv of United Nations. Mult.

2347 100 k. Type **423** 30 10
2348 220 k. World's people supporting U.N. (vert) . . 40 15

1970. Turkish Paintings. As T **417**. Mult.

2349 250 k. "Fevzi Cakmak" (Avni Lifij) (vert) 60 25
2350 250 k. "Fishing-boats" (Nazmi Ziya) (75 × 33 mm) 70 25

424 Turkish Troops Advancing

1971. 50th Anniv of First Battle of Inonu.

2351 **424** 100 k. multicoloured . . 30 20

See also No. 2368.

425 Kemal Ataturk

429 Hands enclosing "Four Races"

428 "Turkish Village" (A.Sekur)

1971.

2352 **425** 5 k. blue and grey 15 10
2353 25 k. red and grey 40 10
2354 – 25 k. brown and pink . . 15 10
2355 **425** 100 k. violet and grey . . 75 10
2356 – 100 k. green and flesh . . 60 10
2357 – 250 k. blue and drab . . 1·25 10
2358 **425** 400 k. green and bistre . 1·75 10

DESIGNS: Nos. 2354, 2356 and 2357, Portraits similar to Type **425** but larger, 21 × 26 mm, and with face value at bottom right.

1971. Turkish Paintings. Multicoloured.

2364 250 k. Type **428** 65 25
2365 250 k. "Yildiz Palace Garden" (A. R. Bicakcilar) 65 25

See also Nos. 2396/7, 2416/17 and 2443/4.

1971. Racial Equality Year.

2366 **429** 100 k. multicoloured . . 20 10
2367 250 k. multicoloured . . 25 10

1971. 50th Anniv of Second Battle of Inonu. Design similar to T **424**. Multicoloured.

2368 100 k. Turkish machine-gunners 40 10

430 Europa Chain

431 Pres. C. Gursel

1971. Europa.

2369 **430** 100 k. violet, yell & blue 55 25
2370 150 k. green, red & orge 65 40

1971. 11th Anniv of May 27th 1960 Revolution.

2371 **431** 100 k. multicoloured . . 30 10

432 Lockhead Super Starfighter

433 "Care of Children"

1971. Air. "60 Years of Turkish Aviation". Multicoloured.

2372 110 k. Type **432** 60 10
2373 200 k. Victory Monument, Afyon and aircraft 85 10
2374 250 k. Air Force emblem and jet fighters (horiz) 95 10
2375 325 k. Lockheed Super Starfighters and pilot . . . 1·50 10
2376 400 k. Bleriot XI airplane of 1911 (horiz) . . . . 1·25 10
2377 475 k. Hezarfen Celebi's "bird flight" from Galata Tower (horiz) . . . . 2·00 15

1971. 50th Anniv of Children's Protection Society.

2378 **433** 50 k. + 10 k. red, pur & blk 20 10
2379 – 100 k. + 15 k. mult . . 25 15
2380 – 110 k. + 15 k. mult . . 35 15

DESIGNS—VERT: 100 k. Child standing on protective hand. HORIZ: 110 k. Mother and child.

434 Selimiye Mosque, Edirne

1971. 7th Anniv of Regional Co-operation for Development Pact. Mosques. Multicoloured.

2381 100 k. Type **434** 20 15
2382 150 k. Chalharbagh Mosque School (Iran) 25 15
2383 200 k. Badshahi Mosque (Pakistan) (horiz) 25 25

435 Alpaslan (Seljuk leader) and Cavalry

1971. 900th Anniv of Battle of Malazgirt.

2384 **435** 100 k. multicoloured . . 25 15
2385 – 250 k. red, yellow & blk 55 25

DESIGN: 250 k. Seljuk mounted archer.

436 Officer and Troop Column

1971. 50th Anniv of Battle of Sakarya.

2386 **436** 100 k. multicoloured . . 40 10

437 Diesel Train and Map (Turkey–Iran route)

1971. International Rail Links.
2387 – 100 k. multicoloured . . 1·75 20
2388 – 110 k. violet and blue . . 1·60 20
2389 **437** 250 k. multicoloured . . 75 45
DESIGNS: 100 k. Diesel train crossing bridge (Turkey–Bulgaria route); 110 k. Train ferry "Orhan Atliman", Lake Van (Turkey–Iran route).

438 Football

1971. Mediterranean Games, Izmir.
2390 **438** 100 k. black, violet & bl . 25 10
2391 – 200 k. multicoloured . . 30 15
DESIGN—VERT: 200 k. "Athlete and stadium".

439 Tomb of Cyrus the Great

1971. 2500th Anniv of Persian Empire.
2393 **439** 25 k. multicoloured . . . 15 10
2394 – 100 k. multicoloured . . 30 15
2395 – 150 k. brown and drab . 50 15
DESIGNS—VERT: 100 k. Persian mosaic of woman. HORIZ: 150 k. Kemal Ataturk and Riza Shah Pahlavi.

1971. Turkish Paintings. As T **428**. Mult.
2396 250 k. "Sultan Mohammed I and Entourage" 45 25
2397 250 k. "Cinili Kosk Palace" . 45 25

441 U.N.I.C.E.F. Emblem

442 Yunus Emre

1971. 25th Anniv of U.N.I.C.E.F.
2404 **441** 100 k. + 10 k. mult . . 30 15
2405 250 k. + 15 k. mult . . 30 25

1971. 650th Death Anniv of Yunus Emre (folk-poet).
2406 **442** 100 k. multicoloured . . 30 20

443 First Turkish Map of the World (1072) and Book Year Emblem

1972. International Book Year.
2407 **443** 100 k. multicoloured . . 30 15

444 Doves and N.A.T.O. Emblem

445 Human Heart

1972. 20th Anniv of Turkey's Membership of N.A.T.O.
2408 **444** 100 k. black, grey & grn . 65 20
2409 250 k. black, grey & blue 75 45

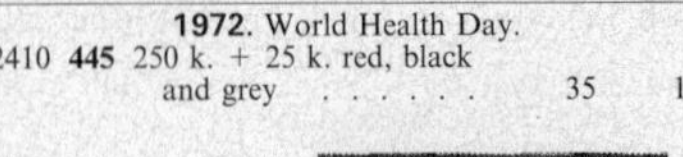

1972. World Health Day.
2410 **445** 250 k. + 25 k. red, black and grey 35 15

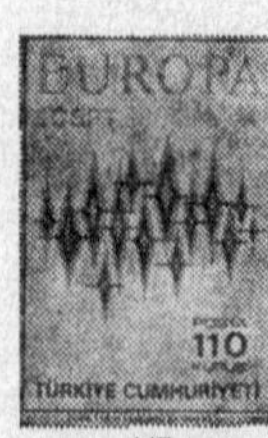

447 "Communications"

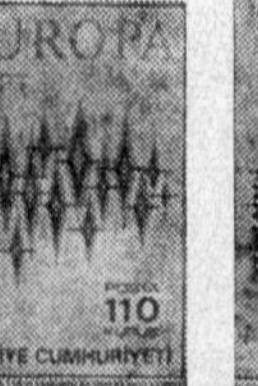

448 "Fisherman" (G. Dareli)

1972. Europa.
2414 **447** 110 k. multicoloured . . 60 30
2415 250 k. multicoloured . . 1·00 45

1972. Turkish Paintings. As T **428**. Multicoloured.
2416 250 k. "Gebze" (Osman Hamdi) 45 25
2417 250 k. "Forest" (S. A. Pasa) 45 25

1972. As T **358**.
2418 25 k. black and brown . . . 10 10
DESIGN: 25 k. Equestrian statue of Ataturk at Ankara.

1972. Regional Co-operation for Development. Multicoloured.
2419 100 k. Type **448** 40 20
2420 125 k. "Will and Power" (Chughtai) 40 20
2421 150 k. "Iranian Woman" (Behzad) 65 35

449 Olympic Rings

1972. Olympic Games, Munich.
2422 **449** 100 k. + 15 k. mult . . 30 20
2423 – 110 k. + 25 k. mult . . 15 20
2424 – 250 k. + 25 k. mult . . 20 40
DESIGNS: 110 k. "Athletes"; 250 k. "Stadium".

450 Ataturk at Observation Post

1972. 50th Anniv of Turkish War of Liberation. Multicoloured. (a) The Great Offensive.
2425 100 k. Type **450** 30 15
2426 110 k. Artillery 40 20

(b) Commander-in-Chief's Offensive.
2427 100 k. Hand-to-hand fighting 30 15

(c) Entry into Izmir.
2428 100 k. Commanders in open car 30 15

451 "Diagnosis and Cure"

452 Kemal Ataturk

1972. Fight against Cancer.
2429 **451** 100 k. red, black & blue 25 10

1972. Various sizes.
2430 **452** 5 k. lt blue on blue . . 10 10
2430a 25 k. orange on orange 10 10
2431 100 k. lake on buff . . 60 10
2431a 100 k. lt grey on grey 10 10
2431b 100 k. olive on green . 20 10
2432 110 k. blue on blue . . 50 10
2432a 125 k. green and grey . 65 10
2433 150 k. brown on buff . 60 10
2433a 150 k. green on green . 10 10
2434 175 k. purple on yellow 80 10
2434a 200 k. red on buff . . 60 10
2434b 200 k. brown on buff . . 20 10
2435 250 k. lilac on pink . . 55 10
2435a 400 k. turquoise on blue 25 10
2436 500 k. violet on pink . 1·10 10
2437 500 k. blue on blue . . 40 10
2438 10 l. mauve on pink . . 1·00 10

INDEX

Countries can be quickly located by referring to the index at the end of this volume.

453 U.I.C Emblem

454 University Emblem

1972. 50th Anniv of International Railway Union.
2439 **453** 100 k. brn, buff and grn . 60 15

1973. Bicent of Technical University, Istanbul.
2440 **454** 100 k. + 25 k. mult . . . 30 15

455 Europa "Posthorn"

456 Helmet and Sword

1973. Europa.
2441 **455** 110 k. multicoloured . . 65 20
2442 250 k. multicoloured . . 1·00 35

1973. Turkish Painters. As T **428**. Multicoloured.
2443 250 k. "Old Almshouses, Istanbul" (Ahmet Ziya Akbulut) (horiz) 65 30
2444 250 k. "Flowers in Vase" (Suleyman Seyyit) (vert) . . 65 30

1973. Land Forces' Day.
2445 **456** 90 k. green, brn & grey . 15 10
2446 – 100 k. green, brown and light green 20 15
DESIGN: 100 k. As Type **456**, but wreath enclosing design.

457 Carved Head, Tomb of Antiochus I (Turkey)

458 Peace Dove and "50"

1973. Regional Co-operation for Development. Multicoloured.
2447 100 k. Type **457** 20 10
2448 150 k. Statue, Lut excavations (Iran) 30 15
2449 200 k. Street in Moenjodaro (Pakistan) 40 20

1973. 50th Anniv of Lausanne Peace Treaty.
2450 **458** 100 k. + 25 k. mult . . . 25 10

459 Minelayer "Nusret II"

460 "Al-Biruni" (from 16th-century miniature)

1973. Bicentenary of Turkish Navy. Mult.
2451 5 k. Type **459** 10 10
2452 25 k. Destroyer "Istanbul" . 15 10
2453 100 k. Motor torpedo-boat "Simsek" 30 25
2454 250 k. Cadet brig "Nurud-i-Futuh" (48 × 32 mm) . . . 2·25 45

1973. Millenary of Abu Reihan al Biruni.
2455 **460** 250 k. multicoloured . . 30 10

461 "Equal Opportunity"

463 "Balkanfila" Emblem

1973. Centenary of Darussafaka High School.
2456 **461** 100 k. multicoloured . . 25 10

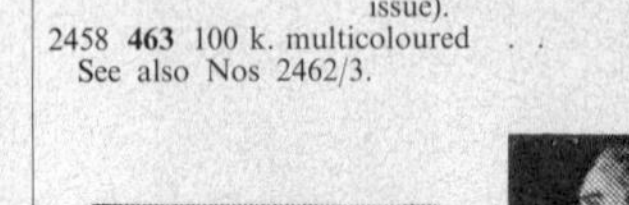

1973. "Balkanfila IV" Stamp Exhibition, Izmir (1st issue).
2458 **463** 100 k. multicoloured . . 25 10
See also Nos 2462/3.

464 Sivas Sheepdog

465 Kemal Ataturk

1973. Animals.
2459 **464** 25 k. blue, yellow & blk 10 10
2460 – 100 k. yellow, black & bl 60 10
DESIGN: 100 k. Angora cat.

1973. 35th Death Anniv of Kemal Ataturk.
2461 **465** 100 k. brown and drab . 25 10

466 Bosphorus and "Stamps"

467 "Flower" Emblem

1973. "Balkanfila IV" Stamp Exhibition (2nd issue). Multicoloured.
2462 110 k. Type **466** 20 10
2463 250 k. "Balkanfila" in decorative script 35 15

1973. 50th Anniv of Republic.
2464 **467** 100 k. red, violet and blue 15 10
2465 – 250 k. multicoloured . . 25 10
2466 – 475 k. yellow and blue . 35 15
DESIGNS: 250 k. "Hands" supporting "50"; 475 k. Cogwheels and ears of corn.

468 Bosphorus Bridge

469 Bosphorus Bridge and U.N.I.C.E.F. Emblem

1973. Opening of Bosphorus Bridge, Istanbul. Multicoloured.
2468 100 k. Type **468** 25 10
2469 150 k. View of Bosphorus and bridge 35 15

1973. U.N.I.C.E.F. Ceremony. Children of Europe and Asia linked by Bosphorus Bridge.
2470 **469** 200 k. multicoloured . . 40 10

470 Mevlana Celaleddin

471 Cotton

1973. 700th Death Anniv of Mevlana Celaleddin (poet and mystic).
2471 – 100 k. green, blue & blk 20 10
2472 **470** 250 k. multicoloured . . 35 10
DESIGN: 100 k. Tomb and dancing dervishes.

1973. Export Products.
2473 **471** 75 k. grey, blue & black 10 10
2474 – 90 k. bistre, blue & blk . 15 10
2475 – 100 k. black, blue & grn 20 10
2476 – 250 k. multicoloured . . 1·25 15
2477 – 325 k. yellow, blue & blk 95 10
2478 – 475 k. black, blue & brn 60 10
DESIGNS: 90 k. Grapes; 100 k. Figs; 250 k. Citrus fruits; 325 k. Tobacco; 475 k. Hazelnuts.

472 Fokker Fellowship

473 President Inonu

1973. Air. Multicoloured.
2479 110 k. Type **472** 55 10
2480 250 k. Douglas DC-10 . . . 85 10

1973. President Inonu's Death.
2481 **473** brown and buff 20 10

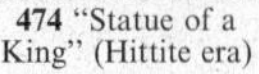

474 "Statue of a King" (Hittite era) **475** Doctor and Patient

1974. Europa. Sculptures. Multicoloured.
2482 110 k. Type **474** 75 30
2483 250 k. "Statuette of a Child" (c. 2000 B.C.) . . . . 1·10 55

1974. 75th Anniv of Sisli Paediatrics Hospital.
2484 **475** 110 k. black, grey & blue 20 10

476 Silver and Gold Idol **477** Population Year Emblem

1974. Archaeological Treasures. Multicoloured.
2485 125 k. Type **476** 20 10
2486 175 k. Painted jar (horiz) . . 20 10
2487 200 k. Bulls (statuettes) (horiz) 35 10
2488 250 k. Jug 45 25

1974. World Population Year.
2489 **477** 250 k. + 25 k. mult . . 40 15

479 Turkish Carpet

1974. Regional Co-operation for Development. Multicoloured.
2496 100 k. Type **479** 40 10
2497 150 k. Iranian carpet 50 15
2498 200 k. Pakistani carpet . . . 75 10

480 Dove and Map of Cyprus

1974. Turkish Intervention in Cyprus.
2499 **480** 250 k. multicoloured . . 20 10

481 "Getting to Grips" **482** Dove with Letter

1974. World Free-style Wrestling Championships, Ankara. Multicoloured.
2500 90 k. Type **481** 25 10
2501 100 k. "Throw" (vert) . . . 30 10
2502 250 k. "Lock" 40 20

1974. Centenary of Universal Postal Union.
2503 **482** 110 k. gold, dp blue & bl 20 10
2504 – 200 k. brown and green . 35 15
2505 – 250 k. multicoloured . . 40 15
DESIGNS: 200 k. Dove; 250 k. Arrows encircling globe.

483 Open Book (Law Reform)

1974. Works and Reforms of Ataturk (1st series).
2506 **483** 50 k. black and blue . . 10 10
2507 – 150 k. multicoloured . . 20 10
2508 – 400 k. multicoloured . . 25 10
DESIGNS—VERT: 150 k. "Tree" ("National Economy"); 400 k. Students facing sun ("Reform of Education").
See also Nos. 2543/5, 2566/8, 2597/9, 2639/41 and 2670/2.

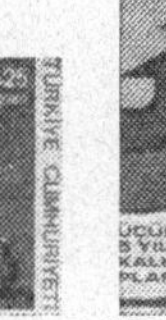

484 Marconi **485** Arrows (3rd Five Year Development Programme)

1974. Birth Centenary of Marconi (radio pioneer).
2509 **484** 250 k. + 25 k. black, brown and red 40 30

1974. "Turkish Development".
2510 **485** 25 k. black and brown . 15 10
2511 – 100 k. grey and brown . 35 10
DESIGNS—HORIZ: 100 k. Map of Turkey within cogwheel (industrialisation).

486 Volleyball **487** Dr. Albert Schweitzer

1974. Ball Games.
2512 **486** 125 k. black and blue . 25 10
2513 – 175 k. black and orange 30 10
2514 – 250 k. black and green . 40 10
DESIGNS: 175 k. Basketball; 250 k. Football.

1975. Birth Centenary of Dr. Albert Schweitzer.
2515 **487** 250 k. + 50 k. mult . . 25 25

488 Automatic Telex Network

1975. Posts and Telecommunications.
2516 **488** 5 k. black and yellow . 10 10
2517 – 50 k. green and orange . 15 10
2518 – 100 k. black and blue . 20 10
DESIGNS: 50 k. Postal cheques; 100 k. Radio link.

489 "Going to the Classroom" (I. Sivga) **490** Karacaoglan Monument (H. Gezer), Mut

1975. Children's Drawings. Multicoloured.
2519 25 k. Type **489** 10 10
2520 50 k. "View from a Village" (H. Dogru) 10 10
2521 100 k. "Folklore" (B. Aktan) 20 10

1975. Karacaoglan (musician) Commem.
2522 **490** 110 k. mauve, grn & brn 15 10

491 "Orange-gathering in Hatay" (C. Tollu)

1975. Europa. Paintings. Multicoloured.
2523 110 k. Type **491** 55 10
2524 250 k. "The Yoruks" (T. Zaim) 90 40

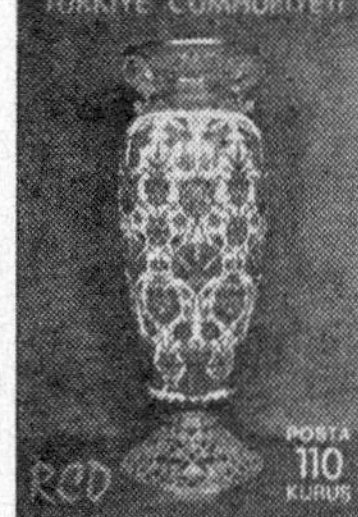

492 Turkish Porcelain Vase **493** Namibia located on Map of Africa

1975. Regional Co-operation for Development. Traditional Crafts. Multicoloured.
2525 110 k. Type **492** 35 15
2526 200 k. Ceramic plate (Iran) (horiz) 55 25
2527 250 k. Camel-skin vase (Pakistan) 75 35

1975. Namibia Day.
2528 **493** 250 k. + 50 k. mult . . . 35 15

494 Horon Folk-dancers

1975. Turkish Folk Dances. Multicoloured.
2529 100 k. Type **494** 25 10
2530 125 k. Kasik 25 10
2531 175 k. Bengi 35 10
2532 250 k. Kasap 45 15
2533 325 k. Kafkas (vert) 65 15

495 "Oguz Khan slaying Dragon" **497** Turbot

1975. Tales of Dede Korkut. Multicoloured.
2534 90 k. Type **495** 20 10
2535 175 k. Tale of Duha Koca Oglu Deli Dumrul Hikayesi (horiz) 25 10
2536 200 k. "Pillaging the Home of Salur Kazan" 30 10

1975. Fishes. Multicoloured.
2538 75 k. Type **497** 25 10
2539 90 k. Common carp 40 10
2540 175 k. Trout 50 10
2541 250 k. Red mullet . . . . . 1·50 15
2542 475 k. Red bream . . . . . . 1·75 15

498 Two Women and Symbol (Women's Participation in Public Life)

1975. Works and Reforms of Ataturk (2nd series).
2543 **498** 100 k. red, black & stone 15 10
2544 – 110 k. multicoloured . . 15 10
2545 – 250 k. multicoloured . . 25 10
DESIGNS—VERT: 110 k. Symbol and inscription (Nationalisation of Insurance Companies). HORIZ: 250 k. Arrows (Orientation of the Fine Arts).

499 Z. Gokalp **500** Ceramic Plate

1976. Birth Cent of Ziya Gokalp (philosopher).
2546 **499** 200 k. + 25 k. mult . . 25 10

1976. Europa. Multicoloured.
2547 200 k. Type **500** 55 25
2548 400 k. Dessert jug . . . . . 1·25 45

501 Silhouette of Istanbul

1976. 7th Islamic Conference, Istanbul.
2549 **501** 500 k. multicoloured . . 45 10

502 "Lunch in Field" (S. Yucel)

1976. "Samsun '76" Youth Stamp Exn. Mult.
2550 50 k. Type **502** 10 10
2551 200 k. "Boats on the Bosphorus" (E. Kosemen) (vert) 20 10
2552 400 k. "Winter View" (R. Cetinkaya) 35 10

503 Sultan Marshes

1976. European Wetlands Conservation Year. Turkish Landscapes. Multicoloured.
2553 150 k. Type **503** . . . . . 2·00 50
2554 200 k. Lake Manyas 40 10
2555 250 k. Lake Borabey 60 10
2556 400 k. Manavgat waterfalls . . 60 15

504 "Hodja with Liver" **505** Games Emblem and Flame

1976. Nasreddin Hodja (humourist) Commem. "The Liver and the Kite". Multicoloured.
2557 150 k. Type **504** 20 10
2558 250 k. "Friend offers recipe" 25 10
2559 600 k. "Kite takes liver, leaving recipe" 30 15

1976. Olympic Games, Montreal.
2560 **505** 100 k. red and blue . . . 25 10
2561 – 400 k. multicoloured . . 35 10
2562 – 600 k. multicoloured . . 25 15
DESIGNS—HORIZ: 400 k. "Athlete" as "76". VERT: 600 k. Games emblem.

506 Kemal Ataturk (Turkey)

1976. Regional Co-operation for Development. Heads of State. Multicoloured.
2563 100 k. Type **506** 25 10
2564 200 k. Riza Shah Pahlavi (Iran) 25 10
2565 250 k. Mohammed Ali Jinnah (Pakistan) 35 15

507 Peace Dove and Sword (Army Reform) **508** White Spoonbill

1976. Works and Reforms of Ataturk (3rd series).
2566 **507** 100 k. black and red . . 10 10
2567 – 200 k. multicoloured . . 20 10
2568 – 400 k. multicoloured . . 40 25
DESIGNS: 200 k. Words, books and listeners (Ataturk's speeches); 400 k. Peace doves and globe ("Peace throughout the World").

1976. Turkish Birds. Multicoloured.
2569 100 k. + 25 k. Type **508** . . 50 25
2570 150 k. + 25 k. Common roller 60 40
2571 200 k. + 25 k. Greater flamingo 85 50
2572 400 k. + 25 k. Waldrapp (horiz) 1·90 75

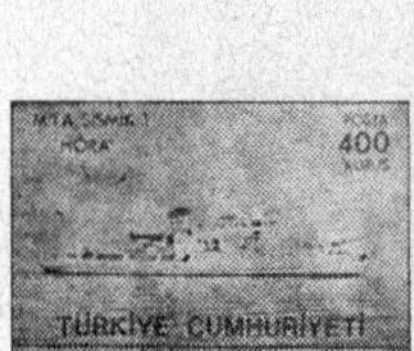

509 "Hora" (oil exploration ship) **510** Musical Symbols

1977.
2573 **509** 400 k. multicoloured . . 85 25

1977. 150th Anniv of Presidential Symphony Orchestra.
2574 **510** 200 k. multicoloured . . 25 10

511 Kemal Ataturk in "100"

1977. Centenary of Parliament.
2575 **511** 200 k. black and red . . 15 10
2576 – 400 k. black and brown . 25 10
DESIGN: 400 k. Hand placing ballot-paper in box.

512 Pamukkale

1977. Europa. Landscapes. Multicoloured.
2577 200 k. Type **512** 50 20
2578 400 k. Zelve . . . . 1·00 40

513 Edict of Karamanoglu Mehmet Bey and "Ongun" Bird

1977. 700th Anniv of Official Turkish Language.
2579 **513** 200 k. + 25 k. black and green 20 10

514 Head-shaped Vase, Turkey

1977. Regional Co-operation for Development. Pottery. Multicoloured.
2580 100 k. Type **514** 25 10
2581 255 k. Earthenware pot (Iran) 45 10
2582 675 k. Model bullock cart (Pakistan) . . . . 1·10 10

515 Stylized Sailing Yacht **522** "Globe" and Emblem

1977. European Finn Class Sailing Championships.
2584 **515** 150 k. black, blue and light blue 25 10
2585 – 200 k. blue and deep blue 45 15
2586 – 250 k. black and blue . 65 20
DESIGNS—HORIZ: 200 k. VERT: 250 k. Both showing stylized sailing yachts.

1977. Surch **10 KURUS**.
2592 **409** 10 k. on 1 k. brn & red . 15 10

1977. 10th World Energy Conference.
2593 **522** 100 k. + 25 k. black, brown and pink 15 10
2594 – 600 k. + 50 k. red, black and blue 30 25
DESIGN: 600 k. Similar design showing a "globe" and emblem.

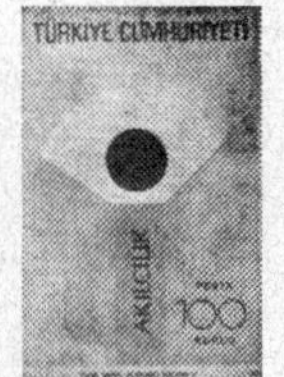

523 Kemal Ataturk **524** "Head and Book" (Rationalism)

1977. Size 20½ × 22½ mm.
2595 **523** 200 k. blue on light blue 25 10
2596 250 k. turq on blue . . 30 10
See also Nos. 2619/25.

1977. Works and Reform of Ataturk (4th series). Multicoloured.
2597 100 k. Type **524** 10 10
2598 200 k. Words by Ataturk (National Sovereignty) . . 15 10
2599 400 k. Symbol (Leadership for Liberation of Nations) . . 25 10

525 Allama Muhammad Iqbal **526** Overturned Car

1977. Birth Centenary of Allama Muhammad Iqbal (Pakistani poet).
2600 **525** 400 k. multicoloured . . 25 10

1977. Road Safety.
2601 **526** 50 k. black, blue & red . 10 10
2602 – 150 k. black, grey & red 15 10
2603 – 250 k. black, brn & red . 20 10
2604 – 500 k. black, grey & red 40 10
2605 – 800 k. deep green, green and red 65 10
2606 – 10 l. green, red & blk . 75 10
DESIGNS—VERT: 150 k. Arrow crossing white lines and pool of blood; 500 k. "Children crossing" sign; 800 k. "No overtaking" sign; 10 l. Footprints in road and on pedestrian crossing. HORIZ: 250 k. Tractor pulling trailer loaded with people.

527 Lighted Match and Trees **531** Riza Shah Pahlavi of Iran

530 Ishakpasa Palace, Dogubeyazit

1977. Forest Conservation.
2607 **527** 50 k. black, red & grn . . 15 10
2608 – 250 k. black, grn & grey . 25 10
DESIGN: 250 k. "Tree germination".
See also No. 2699.

1978. Europa. Multicoloured.
2616 2½ l. Type **530** 45 10
2617 5 l. Anamur Castle 85 25

1978. Birth Centenary of Riza Shah Pahlavi of Iran.
2618 **531** 5 l. multicoloured 30 10

1978. As Type **523** but larger, 19 × 25 mm.
2619 10 k. brown 10 10
2620 50 k. grey 10 10
2621 1 l. red 10 10
2622 2½ l. lilac 10 10
2623 5 l. blue 20 10
2624 25 l. blue and light blue . . . 85 10
2625 50 l. orange & light orange . . 1·50 10

532 Athletics

1978. "Gymnasiade '78" World School Games.
2626 **532** 1 l. + 50 k. deep green and green 10 10
2627 – 2½ l. + 50 k. blue & orge 25 10
2628 – 5 l. + 50 k. blue & pink . 30 15
2629 – 8 l. + 50 k. blue & green 50 20
DESIGNS: 2½ l. Gymnastics; 5 l. Table tennis; 8 l. Swimming.

533 Salmon Rose

1978. Regional Co-operation for Development. Multicoloured.
2630 2½ l. Type **533** 15 10
2631 3½ l. Pink roses 25 10
2632 8 l. Red roses 40 10

534 Anti-Apartheid Year Emblem **535** View of Ankara

1978. International Anti-Apartheid Year.
2633 **534** 10 l. multicoloured . . . 45 10

1978. Turkish–Libyan Friendship. Multicoloured.
2634 2½ l. Type **535** 25 10
2635 5 l. View of Tripoli 35 10

536 Ribbon and Chain **538** Independence Medal

1978. 25th Anniv of European Convention on Human Rights.
2636 **536** 2½ l. + 50 k. blue, green and black 35 20
2637 – 5 l. + 50 k. red, blue and black 40 30
DESIGN: 5 l. Ribbon and flower.

1978. Works and Reforms of Ataturk (5th series).
2639 **538** 2½ l. multicoloured . . . 10 10
2640 – 3½ l. red and black . . . 15 10
2641 – 5 l. multicoloured . . . 30 10
DESIGNS—HORIZ: 3½ l. Talking heads (Language Reform). VERT: 5 l. "ABC" in Arabic and Roman scripts (Adoption of Latin alphabet).

539 Bosphorus Waterside Residence of Koprulu Huseyin Pasa, Istanbul (1699)

1978. Traditional Turkish Houses. Multicoloured.
2642 1 l. Type **539** 10 10
2643 2½ l. Residence of Saatci Ali Efendi, Izmit, 1774 . . . . 20 10
2644 3½ l. House of Bey, Kula (vert) 30 10
2645 5 l. House of Bahaeddin Aga, Milas (vert) 35 10
2646 8 l. House of Safranbolu . . 45 15

541 Children with Globe as Balloon **542** Mail Transport

1979. International Year of the Child.
2649 – 2½ l. + 50 k. black, gold and red 10 10
2650 **541** 5 l. + 50 k. multicoloured 30 15
2651 – 8 l. + 50 k. multicoloured 50 25
DESIGNS: 2½ l. Children embracing beneath hearts; 8 l. Adult and child balancing globe.

1979. Europa.
2652 **542** 2½ l. black, green and blue 35 10
2653 – 5 l. orange and black . . 15 10
2654 – 7½ l. black and blue . . . 25 10
DESIGNS: 5 l. Telex keyboard, morse key and telegraph poles; 7½ l. Telephone dial and dish aerial.

543 Kemal Ataturk **544** "Turkish Harvest" (Namik Ismail)

1979.
2655 **543** 50 k. green 10 10
2656 1 l. green and lt green . 10 10
2657 2½ l. lilac 15 10
2657a 2½ l. blue 10 10
2748 2½ l. orange 15 10
2658 5 l. blue and lt blue . . 15 10
2659 7½ l. brown 40 10
2659a 7½ l. red 30 10
2660 10 l. mauve 50 10
2661a 10 l. mauve (22 × 22 mm) 40 10
2661 20 l. grey 40 10

1979. Regional Co-operation for Development. Paintings. Multicoloured.
2662 5 l. Type **544** 20 10
2663 7½ l. "Iranian Goldsmith" (Kamal el Molk) 25 10
2664 10 l. "Pakistan Village Scene" (Ustad Baksh) 35 20

545 Colemanite **546** Highway forming Figure 8

1979. 10th World Mining Congress. Mult.
2665 5 l. Type **545** 15 10
2666 7½ l. Chromite 20 10
2667 10 l. Antimonite 25 10
2668 15 l. Sulphur 35 10

1979. 8th European Communications Ministers' Symposium.
2669 **546** 5 l. multicoloured . . . 30 25

547 "Confidence in Youth" **548** Poppy ("Papaver somniferum")

1979. Works and Reforms of Ataturk (6th series).
2670 **547** 2½ l. multicoloured . . . 15 10
2671 – 3½ l. multicoloured . . . 20 10
2672 – 5 l. black and orange . . 25 10
DESIGNS—HORIZ: 3½ l. "Secularism". VERT: 5 l. "National Oath".

1979. Flowers (1st series). Multicoloured.
2673 5 l. Type **548** 25 10
2674 7½ l. Oleander ("Nerium oleander") 30 10

2675 10 l. Late spider orchid ("Ophrys holosericea") . . 25 20
2676 15 l. Mandrake ("Mandragora autumnalis") 60 10
See also Nos. 2705/8.

549 Ibrahim Muteferrika (first printer) and Presses

1979. 250th Anniv of Turkish Printing.
2678 **549** 10 l. multicoloured . . . 35 15

550 Black Partridge

551 Olives, Leaves and Globe in Oil-drop

1979. Wildlife Conservation. Multicoloured.
2679 5 l. + 1 l. Type **550** 65 20
2680 5 l. + 1 l. Great bustard . . 65 20
2681 5 l. + 1 l. Demoiselle crane . 65 20
2682 5 l. + 1 l. Goitred gazelle . . 55 15
2683 5 l. + 1 l. Mouflon 55 15
Nos. 2679/83 were issued together, se-tenant, forming a composite design.

1979. 2nd World Olive-Oil Year.
2684 **551** 5 l. multicoloured 20 10
2685 – 10 l. yellow and green . . 35 10
DESIGN: 10 l. Globe in oil drop.

553 Uskudarli Hoca Ali Riza (artist)

1980. Europa. Multicoloured.
2692 7½ l. Type **553** 20 10
2693 10 l. Ali Sami Boyar (artist) . 35 10
2694 20 l. Dr. Hulusi Behcet (skin specialist) 60 20

554 Flowers and Trees

555 Lighted Match and Trees

1980. Environmental Protection. Multicoloured.
2695 2½ l. + 1 l. Type **554** 10 10
2696 7½ l. + 1 l. Sun and water . . 15 10
2697 15 l. + 1 l. Factory polluting atmosphere 25 15
2698 20 l. + 1 l. Flower surrounded by oil 35 25

1980. Forest Conservation.
2699 **555** 50 k. green, red & brn . 10 10
See also No. 2607.

556 Seismological Graph

557 Games Emblem and Pictograms

1980. 7th World Conference on Earthquake Engineering.
2700 – 7½ l. brown, blue & orge . 15 10
2701 **556** 20 l. black, orge & blue . 40 20
DESIGN: 7½ l. Pictorial representation of earthquake within globe.

1980. 1st Islamic Games, Izmir. Multicoloured.
2702 7½ l. Type **557** 15 10
2703 20 l. As No. 2702 but with different sports around emblem 40 20

558 Ornamental Window

559 "Bracon hebetor" and Larva of Dark Arches Moth

1980. 1400th Anniv of Hegira.
2704 **558** 20 l. multicoloured . . . 40 15

1980. Flowers (2nd series). As T **548**. Mult.
2705 2½ l. Manisa tulip ("Tulipa hayatii") 10 10
2706 7½ l. Ephesian bellflower ("Campanula ephesia") . 15 10
2707 15 l. Crocus ("Crocus ancyrensis") 25 15
2708 20 l. Anatolian orchid ("Orchis anatolica") 45 25

1980. Useful Insects (1st series). Multicoloured.
2709 2½ l. + 1 l. "Rodolia cardinalis" (ladybird) and cottony cushion scale 25 15
2710 7½ l. + 1 l. Type **559** 25 20
2711 15 l. + 1 l. Caterpillar-hunter and larva of gypsy moth . 35 25
2712 20 l. + 1 l. "Deraeocoris rutilus" (leaf bug) 40 30
See also Nos. 2763/6.

560 Kemal Ataturk

561 Ibn Sina Teaching

1980.
2713 **560** 7½ l. brown and pink . 20 10
2714 10 l. brown & lt brown 10 10
2719a 15 l. blue 20 10
2715 20 l. violet and mauve . 25 10
2719b 20 l. orange 25 10
2716 30 l. grey and lt grey . 30 10
2717 50 l. red and yellow . . 60 10
2719c 65 l. green 75 10
2718 75 l. green and lt green 1·10 10
2719d 90 l. mauve . . . . . 1·25 10
2719 100 l. blue and lt blue . 1·40 10

1980. Birth Millenary of Ibn Sina (Avicenna) (philosopher and physician). Multicoloured.
2720 7½ l. Type **561** 25 10
2721 20 l. Ibn Sina (vert) 45 15

562 Ataturk and Figures "100"

563 Disabled Person in Wheelchair

1981. "Balkanfila VIII" Stamp Exhibition, Ankara.
2722 **562** 10 l. red and black . . . 25 10

1981. International Year of Disabled Persons.
2723 **563** 10 l. + 2½ l. multicoloured 25 20
2724 20 l. + 2½ l. multicoloured 35 30

564 Sultan Mohammed the Conqueror

565 Gaziantep

1981. 500th Death Anniv of Mohammed the Conqueror.
2725 **564** 10 l. multicoloured . . . 20 10
2726 20 l. multicoloured . . . 35 20

1981. Folk Dances and Europa (35, 70 l.). Multicoloured.
2727 ½ l. Type **565** 15 10
2728 10 l. Balikesir 15 10
2729 15 l. Kahramanmaras . . . 25 10
2730 35 l. Antalya 60 30
2731 70 l. Burdur . . . . 1·25 55

566 Ataturk in 1919 (S.G. 2279)

568 Carpet

1981. Birth Centenary of Kemal Ataturk. Previous stamps showing Ataturk. Multicoloured.
2732 **566** 2½ l. multicoloured . . . 10 10
2733 – 7½ l. black and brown . . 10 10
2734 – 10 l. multicoloured . . . 15 10
2735 – 20 l. blue, red and black . 25 15
2736 – 25 l. black, red & orange 30 20
2737 – 35 l. multicoloured . . . 45 30
DESIGNS: 7½ l. Ataturk in civilian dress (S.G. No. 2285); 10 l. Ataturk and old Parliament House (S.G. No. 2037); 20 l. Ataturk teaching Latin alphabet (S.G. No. 1222); 25 l. Remilitarization of Dardanelles surcharged stamp (S.G. No. 1188); 35 l. Ataturk in evening dress (from miniature sheet).

1981. Various stamps surch **10 LIRA**.
2739 – 10 l. on 60 k. red, black and green (No. 2177) . . . 25 10
2740 **452** 10 l. on 110 k. blue on blue 25 10
2741 10 l. on 400 k. turquoise on blue 25 10
2742 – 10 l. on 800 k. green, turq & red (No. 2605) 25 10

1981. 2nd International Congress of Turkish Folklore. Multicoloured.
2743 7½ l. Type **568** 15 10
2744 10 l. Embroidery 15 10
2745 15 l. Drum and "zurna" . . . 25 15
2746 20 l. Embroidered napkin . . 40 15
2747 30 l. Rug 50 20

570 Ataturk Centenary and E.P.S. Emblem

1981. 5th European Physical Society General Congress.
2750 **570** 10 l. multicoloured . . . 30 10
2751 30 l. multicoloured . . . 45 20

571 F.A.O. Emblem

1981. World Food Day.
2752 **571** 10 l. multicoloured . . . 20 10
2753 30 l. multicoloured . . . 50 20

572 Olive Branch and Constitution on Map of Turkey

1981. Inauguration of Constituent Assembly.
2754 **572** 10 l. multicoloured . . . 25 10
2755 30 l. multicoloured . . . 45 30

574 Kemal Ataturk

575 Green Tiger Beetle

1981.
2762 **574** 2½ l. red on grey 15 10

1981. Useful Insects (2nd series). Multicoloured.
2763 10 l. + 2½ l. Type **575** 30 20
2764 20 l. + 2½ l. "Syrphus vitripennis" (hover fly) . . 45 35
2765 30 l. + 2½ l. "Ascalaphus macaronius" (owl-fly) . . . 60 45
2766 40 l. + 2½ l. "Empusa fasciata" 75 55

MINIMUM PRICE
The minimum price quoted is 10p which represents a handling charge rather than a basis for valuing common stamps. For further notes about prices, see introductory pages.

576 Students and Silhouette of Ataturk

577 Sun

578 Kemal Ataturk

1981. Literacy Campaign.
2767 **576** 2½ l. orange and blue . . 15 10

1982. Energy Conservation.
2768 **577** 10 l. yellow, blue & green 25 10

1982.
2769 **578** 1 l. green 10 10
2770 – 2½ l. lilac 10 10
2771 – 5 l. blue 20 10
2772 – 10 l. red 30 10
2773 – 35 l. brown 65 10
DESIGNS: 2½ to 35 l. Different portraits of Ataturk.

579 "Magnolias"

580 Dr. Tevfik Saglam

1982. Birth Centenary of Ibrahim Calli (painter). Multicoloured.
2774 10 l. Type **579** 20 10
2775 20 l. "Fishermen" (horiz) . . 40 10
2776 30 l. "Sewing Woman" . . . 60 10

1982. Centenary of Discovery of Tubercle Bacillus. Multicoloured.
2777 10 l. + 2½ l. Type **580** . . . 30 15
2778 30 l. + 2½ l. Dr. Robert Koch 60 35

582 Kul Tigin Monument

584 Demirkazik

583 Tanker and Emblem

1982. 1250th Anniv of Kul Tigin Monument. Multicoloured.
2780 10 l. Type **582** 15 10
2781 30 l. Head of Kul Tigin . . . 35 15

1982. Inauguration of Pendik Shipyard.
2782 **583** 30 l. multicoloured . . . 35 15

1982. Anatolian Mountains. Multicoloured.
2783 7½ l. Agri Dagi 15 10
2784 10 l. Buzul Dagi (horiz) . . . 20 10
2785 15 l. Type **584** 25 10
2786 20 l. Erciyes (horiz) 40 10
2787 30 l. Kackar Dagi 55 10
2788 35 l. Uludag (horiz) 75 10

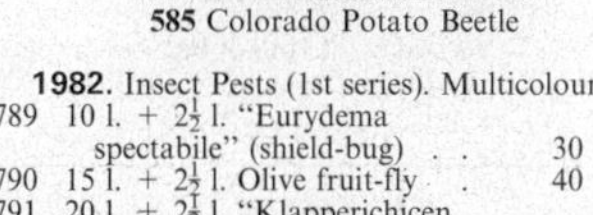
585 Colorado Potato Beetle

1982. Insect Pests (1st series). Multicoloured.
2789 10 l. + 2½ l. "Eurydema spectabile" (shield-bug) . . 30 25
2790 15 l. + 2½ l. Olive fruit-fly . 40 30
2791 20 l. + 2½ l. "Klapperichicen viridissima" (cicada) . . . 45 40
2792 20 l. + 2½ l. Type **585** . . . 60 50
2793 35 l. + 2½ l. "Rhynchites auratus" (weevil) 70 55
See also Nos. 2830/4.

586 Open Book and Figures

587 Drum

1982. Centenary of Beyazit State Library.
2794 **586** 30 l. multicoloured . . . 35 10

1982. Musical Instruments. Multicoloured.
2796 $7\frac{1}{2}$ l. Type **587** 20 10
2797 10 l. Lute ("Baglama") . . . 25 10
2798 15 l. Horn ("Zurna") (horiz) 30 10
2799 20 l. Stringed instrument ("Kemence") (horiz) . . . 45 15
2800 30 l. Flute ("Mey") 85 20

588 Temple of Artemis, Sart

1982. Ancient Cities.
2801 **588** 30 l. multicoloured . . . 35 10

589 Family on Map

1983. Family Planning and Mother and Child Health. Multicoloured.
2802 10 l. Type **589** 20 10
2803 35 l. Mother and child . . . 25 10

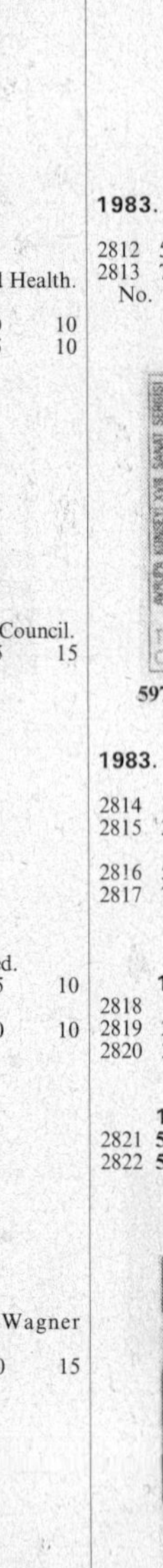

590 Council Emblem

1983. 30th Anniv of Customs Co-operation Council.
2804 **590** 45 l. multicoloured . . . 65 15

591 People, Ballot Box and Constitution

1983. 1982 Constitution. Multicoloured.
2805 10 l. Type **591** 15 10
2806 30 l. Constitution, scales and olive branch 30 10

592 Richard Wagner

1983. Death Centenary of Richard Wagner (composer).
2807 **592** 30 l. + 5 l. mult 30 15

593 Hamdi Bey

1983. 38th Death Anniv of Hamdi Bey (telegraphist).
2808 **593** 35 l. multicoloured . . . 35 10

INDEX

Countries can be quickly located by referring to the index at the end of this volume.

594 Piri Reis (geographer) and Map

1983. Europa. Multicoloured.
2809 50 l. Type **594** 90 15
2810 100 l. Ulugh Bey (Central Asian ruler) and observatory . . 2·10 55

595 Olive Branch and Athletes

1983. Youth Week.
2811 **595** 15 l. multicoloured . . . 20 10

596 Junkers Ju 52/3m and Boeing 727

1983. 50th Anniv of Turkish State Airline. Multicoloured.
2812 50 l. Type **596** . . . . . . 1·00 15
2813 70 l. Airport at night . . . . 1·00 15
No. 2812 is wrongly inscribed "F-13".

597 Hellenic Statue of Eros

598 Oludeniz

1983. 18th Council of Europe Art Exhibition, Istanbul. Multicoloured.
2814 15 l. Type **597** 30 10
2815 35 l. Hittite carving of two-headed duck (horiz) . . . 45 10
2816 50 l. Ottoman zinc flask and jug 75 15
2817 70 l. Busts of Marcus Aurelius and his wife Faustina (horiz) 85 15

1983. Coastal Protection. Multicoloured.
2818 10 l. Type **598** 15 10
2819 25 l. Olimpos 50 10
2820 35 l. Kekova 65 15

1983. Nos. 2655 and 2699 surch **5 LIRA**.
2821 **543** 5 l. on 50 k. green . . . 25 10
2822 **555** 5 l. on 50 k. green, red and brown 25 10

600 Dove carrying Letter

601 Kemal Ataturk

1983. World Communications Year. Mult.
2823 15 l. Type **600** 35 10
2824 50 l. Telephone pole and telephone wires (horiz) . . 45 10
2825 70 l. Telephone dial and letter within ornamental design . 50 15

1983.
2826 **601** 15 l. blue and lt blue . . 15 10
2827 50 l. blue and green . . 55 10
2828 100 l. blue and orange . 1·25 10

602 Topkapi Serail, Istanbul

1983. Aga Khan Award for Architecture.
2829 **602** 50 l. yellow, blk & grn . . 65 10

1983. Insect Pests (2nd series). As T **585**. Multicoloured.
2830 15 l. + 5 l. Sun pest 25 35
2831 25 l. + 5 l. "Phyllobius nigrofasciatus" (weevil) . . 45 45
2832 35 l. + 5 l. "Cercopsis intermedia" (froghopper) . 55 55
2833 50 l. + 10 l. Striped bug . . 80 80
2834 75 l. + 10 l. "Capnodis miliaris" . . . . 1·00 1·00

604 Map and Flag of Turkey

1983. 60th Anniv of Republic.
2836 **604** 15 l. multicoloured . . . 25 10
2837 50 l. multicoloured . . . 55 15

605 Temple of Aphrodite, Aphrodisias

1983. Ancient Cities.
2838 **605** 50 l. multicoloured . . . 50 10

607 St. Sophia's from Sultan Ahmed Mosque, Istanbul

608 Police Badge and Ribbon protecting Citizens

1984. U.N.E.S.C.O. International Campaign for Istanbul and Goreme. Multicoloured.
2850 25 l. Type **607** 25 10
2851 35 l. Rock dwellings and chapels, Goreme 40 10
2852 50 l. Suleymaniye district, Istanbul 60 10

1984. Turkish Police Organization.
2853 **608** 15 l. multicoloured . . . 20 10

609 Bridge

610 Kaftan (16th-century)

1984. Europa. 25th Anniv of C.E.P.T.
2854 **609** 50 l. multicoloured . . . 75 15
2855 100 l. multicoloured . . . 1·50 25

1984. Topkapi Museum (1st series). Mult.
2856 20 l. + 5 l. Type **610** 40 15
2857 70 l. + 15 l. Ceremonial ewer 75 15
2858 90 l. + 20 l. Gold inlaid and jewelled swords . . . . . . 1·00 15
2859 100 l. + 25 l. Kaaba lock . . 1·10 20
See also Nos. 2892/5, 2925/8 and 2967/70.

611 Mete Khan and Flag of Great Hun Empire

1984. Turkic States (1st series). Multicoloured.
2860 10 l. Type **611** 20 10
2861 20 l. Panu and flag of Western Hun Empire 40 10
2862 50 l. Attila and flag of European Hun Empire . . . . 1·00 15
2863 70 l. Aksunvar and flag of Ak Hun Empire . . . . . . 1·50 25
See also Nos. 2896/9, 2930/3 and 2971/4.

612 Peace Dove

1984. 10th Anniv of Turkish Forces in Cyprus.
2864 **612** 70 l. multicoloured . . . 60 10

613 Olympic Colours

614 Marsh Mallow

1984. Olympic Games, Los Angeles. Mult.
2865 20 l. + 5 l. Type **613** 25 10
2866 70 l. + 15 l. Medallion of wrestler (vert) 80 15
2867 100 l. + 20 l. Stylised athlete 1·25 25

1984. Wild Flowers. Multicoloured.
2868 5 l. "Narcissus tazetta" . . 10 10
2868a 10 l. Type **614** 15 10
2869 20 l. Common poppy . . . 15 10
2870 70 l. "Cyclamen pseudoibericum" 80 10
2870a 100 l. False chamomile . . 60 10
2871 200 l. Snowdrops . . . . . 1·10 15
2872 300 l. "Tulipa sintenesii" . 1·90 15

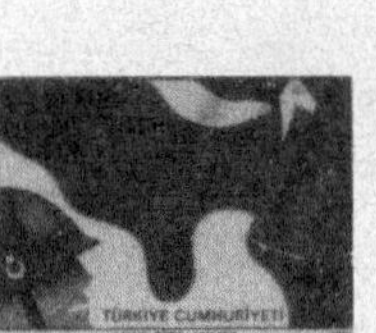

615 Soldier and Flag

616 Liquidamber

1984. Armed Forces Day.
2873 **615** 20 l. multicoloured . . . 15 10
2874 – 50 l. multicoloured . . . 40 10
2875 – 70 l. red, blue and black 65 15
2876 – 90 l. multicoloured . . . 75 15
DESIGNS: 50 l. Olive branch as sword hilt; 70 l. Emblem, soldier and flag; 90 l. Soldier, olive branch and map.

1984. Forest Resources. Multicoloured.
2877 10 l. Type **616** 25 10
2878 20 l. Oriental spruce 35 10
2879 70 l. Oriental beech 85 10
2880 90 l. Cedar of Lebanon . . . 1·00 15

617 Pres. Inonu

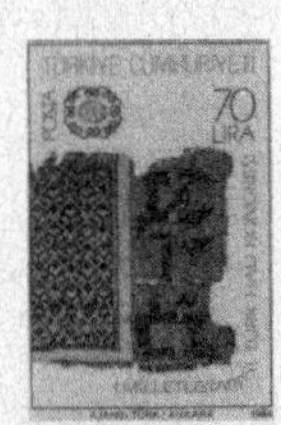

618 Detail of 13th-century Seljukian Carpet

1984. Birth Centenary of Ismet Inonu (Prime Minister 1923–37 and 1962–65; President 1938–50).

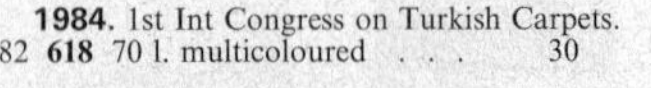

2881 **617** 20 l. multicoloured . . . 50 10

1984. 1st Int Congress on Turkish Carpets.
2882 **618** 70 l. multicoloured . . . 30 10

619 Great Mosque and University, Harran

1984. Ancient Cities.
2883 **619** 70 l. multicoloured . . . 90 10

620 Women and Ballot Box

1984. 50th Anniv of Turkish Women's Suffrage.
2884 **620** 20 l. multicoloured . . . 25 10

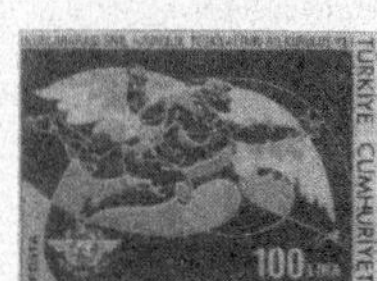

621 "Icarus" (Hans Herni)

1984. 40th Anniv of I.C.A.O.
2885 **621** 100 l. multicoloured . . . 1·00 15

623 Glider and Parachutist

1985. 60th Anniv of Turkish Aviation League. Multicoloured.
2887 10 l. Type **623** 45 15
2888 20 l. Cameron Viva 77 hot-air balloon (vert) 55 15

624 Globe and Satellite

625 Score and Ulvi Cemal Erkin (composer)

1985. 20th Anniv of International Telecommunications Satellite Organization.
2889 **624** 100 l. multicoloured . . . 65 15

1985. Europa. Music Year. Multicoloured.
2890 100 l. Type **625** . . . . 1·00 15
2891 200 l. Score and Mithat Fenmen (composer and pianist) . . 1·50 25

1985. Topkapi Museum (2nd series). As T **610**. Multicoloured.
2892 10 l. + 5 l. Plate decorated with peacock 15 10
2893 20 l. + 10 l. Jug and cup . . 25 15
2894 100 l. + 15 l. Porcelain ewer and bowl . . . . 1·25 25
2895 120 l. + 20 l. Chinese porcelain plate . . . . 1·40 30

1985. Turkic States (2nd series). As T **611**. Multicoloured.
2896 10 l. Bilge Kagan and flag of Gokturk Empire 10 10
2897 20 l. Bayan Kagan and flag of Avar Empire 20 10
2898 70 l. Hazar Kagan and flag of Hazar Empire . . . . . . 1·25 15
2899 100 l. Kutlug Kul Bilge Kagan and flag of Uygur Empire . 1·60 15

626 Louis Pasteur working in Laboratory

627 I.Y.Y. Emblem within Globe and Profiles

1985. Centenary of Discovery of Anti-rabies Vaccine.
2900 **626** 100 l. + 15 l. mult . . . 75 15

1985. International Youth Year. Multicoloured.
2901 100 l. Type **627** 50 10
2902 120 l. Globe and I.Y.Y. Emblem 85 10

628 Postman and Couple Dancing

629 Aynalikavak Palace

1985. Introduction of Post Codes.
2903 **628** 10 l. black, yellow & brn 10 10
2904 20 l. black, yellow & red 15 10
2905 20 l. black, yellow & grn 15 10
2906 20 l. black, yellow & bl . 15 10
2907 70 l. blue, yellow & pur 45 10
2908 100 l. black, yellow and grey 65 10

1985. National Palaces Symposium. Multicoloured.
2909 20 l. Type **629** 15 10
2910 100 l. Beylerbeyi Palace . . 60 15

630 U.N. Emblem, Headquarters and Flags in "40"

1985. 40th Anniv of U.N.O.
2911 **630** 100 l. multicoloured . . 60 20

631 Alanya

632 Satellite and Infra-red Picture of Earth's Surface

1985. Ancient Cities.
2912 **631** 100 l. multicoloured . . 60 15

1985. 60th Anniv of Meteorological Institute.
2913 **632** 100 l. multicoloured . . 85 15

633 Emblem

634 Kemal Ataturk

1985. Centenary of Isik Lyceum, Istanbul.
2914 **633** 20 l. gold, blue & red . 25 10

1985.
2915 **634** 10 l. blue and cobalt . . 10 10
2916 20 l. brown and lilac . . 15 10
2917 100 l. purple and lilac . 55 10

635 Girl and Flower

1986. International 23rd April Children's Festival, Ankara. Multicoloured.
2918 20 l. Type **635** 10 10
2919 100 l. Family 35 10
2920 120 l. Balloon seller 55 10

636 Boy drawing in Smoke from Chimney

637 Trophy

1986. Europa. Multicoloured.
2921 100 l. Type **636** 55 10
2922 200 l. Plaster on dead half of leaf (vert) . . . . 1·25 50

1986. Ataturk International Peace Prize. Multicoloured.
2923 20 l. Type **637** 10 10
2924 100 l. Front view of trophy . 35 10

1986. Topkapi Museum (3rd series). As T **610**. Multicoloured.
2925 20 l. + 5 l. Censer 15 10
2926 100 l. + 10 l. Jade and jewelled tankard 60 15
2927 120 l. + 15 l. Dagger and sheath 1·00 25
2928 200 l. + 30 l. Willow buckler 1·25 30

638 "Abdulhamit"

639 Wrestlers oiling Themselves

1986. Centenary of Turkish Submarine Fleet.
2929 **638** 20 l. multicoloured . . . 15 10

1986. Turkic States (3rd series). As T **611**. Multicoloured.
2930 10 l. Bilge Kul Kadir Khan and flag of Kara Khanids Empire 15 10
2931 20 l. Alp Tekin and flag of Ghaznavids Empire 25 10
2932 100 l. Seljuk and flag of Great Seljuk Empire . . . . . . 1·00 10
2933 120 l. Muhammed Harezmsah and flag of Harezmsah State 1·90 10

1986. Kirkpinar Wrestling. Multicoloured.
2934 10 l. Type **639** 10 10
2935 20 l. Opening ceremony . . . 15 10
2936 100 l. Wrestlers . . . . 1·25 15

640 Chateau de la Muette, Paris (headquarters)

1986. 25th Anniv of Organization for Economic Co-operation and Development.
2937 **640** 100 l. multicoloured . . . 55 10

641 Benz "Einspur" Tricar, 1886

1986. Centenary of Motor Car. Multicoloured.
2938 10 l. Type **641** 15 10
2939 20 l. Rolls-Royce "Silver Ghost", 1906 . . . . 35 10
2940 100 l. Mercedes touring car, 1928 . . . . 1·25 15
2941 200 l. Impression of speeding car . . . . 1·90 20

642 "Arrangement with Tulips" (Feyhaman Duran)

643 Celal Bayar

1986. Artists' Birth Centenaries. Multicoloured.
2942 100 l. Type **642** 35 10
2943 120 l. "Landscape with Fountain" (Huseyin Avni Lifij) (horiz) 55 15

1986. Celal Bayar (Prime Minister 1937–39; President 1950–60) Commemoration.
2944 **643** 20 l. brown, gold and mauve 10 10
2945 – 100 l. green, gold and mauve 45 10
DESIGN: 100 l. Profile of Celal Bayar.

645 Kubad-Abad

1986. Ancient Cities.
2950 **645** 100 l. multicoloured . . 45 10

646 N.A.T.O. Emblem and Dove with Olive Branch

1986. 32nd N.A.T.O. Assembly, Istanbul.
2951 **646** 100 l. + 20 l. mult . . . 95 15

647 Ersoy and National Flag

648 Driver wearing Seat Belt

1986. 50th Death Anniv of Mehmet Akif Ersoy (composer of national anthem).
2952 **647** 20 l. multicoloured . . . 25 10

1987. Road Safety.
2953 **648** 10 l. violet, red & blue . 15 10
2954 – 20 l. red, blue & brown . 25 10
2955 – 150 l. brown, red & grn . 85 10
DESIGNS: 20 l. Smashed drinking glass and road; 150 l. Broken speed limit sign and road.

649 Spurge Hawk Moth

1987. Moths and Butterflies. Multicoloured.
2956 10 l. Type **649** 15 10
2957 20 l. Red admiral 20 15
2958 100 l. Jersey tiger moth . . . 55 15
2959 120 l. Clouded yellow . . . 65 20

650 Modern Housing and Emblem

651 Casting

1987. International Year of Shelter for the Homeless.
2960 **650** 200 l. multicoloured . . 75 10

1987. 50th Anniv of Turkish Iron and Steel Works. Multicoloured.
2961 50 l. Type **651** 15 10
2962 200 l. Karabuk Works . . . 65 10

652 Map of Turkey and Grand National Assembly Building, Ankara

1987. "Sovereignty belongs to the People".
2963 **652** 50 l. multicoloured . . . 15 10

653 Turkish History Institution, Ankara (Turgut Cansever and Ertur Yener)

1987. Europa. Architecture. Multicoloured.

2964 50 l. Type **653** 15 10
2965 200 l. Social Insurance Institution, Zeyrek (Sedad Hakki Eldem) . . . . . . 1·00 10

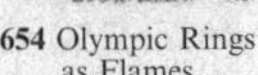

654 Olympic Rings as Flames **655** Men

1987. 92nd Session of International Olympic Committee, Istanbul.

2966 **654** 200 l. multicoloured . . . 75 10

1987. Topkapi Museum (4th series). As T **610**. Multicoloured.

2967 20 l. + 5 l. Crystals and jewelled ewer 20 10
2968 50 l. + 10 l. Emerald, gold and diamond ceiling pendant (horiz) 30 10
2969 200 l. + 15 l. Sherbet jug . . 85 15
2970 250 l. + 30 l. Crystal, gold and jewelled writing drawer (horiz) . . . . 1·10 20

1987. Turkic States (4th series). As T **611**. Multicoloured.

2971 10 l. Batu Khan and flag of Golden Horde State . . . 15 10
2972 20 l. Timur (Tamerlane) and flag of Great Timur Empire 20 10
2973 50 l. Babur Shah and flag of Mughal Empire 65 10
2974 200 l. Osman Bey and flag of Ottoman Empire . . . . . 2·75 10

1987. Paintings from Mehmet Siyah Kalem's "Album of the Conqueror". Multicoloured.

2975 10 l. Type **655** 10 10
2976 20 l. Donkey rider and attendants (horiz) 10 10
2977 50 l. Man whipping fallen horse (horiz) 45 10
2978 200 l. Demon . . . . 1·25 10

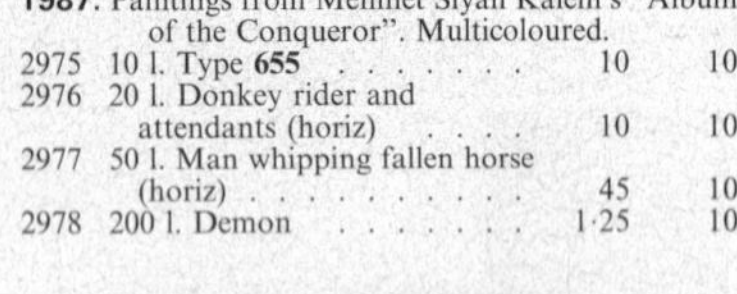

656 Cancer Cells and Pipette holding Drug

1987. 15th International Chemotherapy Congress, Istanbul.

2979 **656** 200 l. + 25 l. mult . . . 75 20

657 Ihlamur Pavilion

1987. Royal Pavilions (1st series). Multicoloured.

2980 50 l. Type **657** 15 10
2981 200 l. Kucuksu Pavilion . . . 60 10

See also Nos. 3019/20.

658 Suleiman receiving Barbarossa (miniature)

1987. Suleiman the Magnificent. Multicoloured.

2982 30 l. Suleiman 10 10
2983 50 l. Suleiman's tougra (horiz) 15 10
2984 200 l. Type **658** . . . . . . 1·25 10
2985 270 l. Sculpture of Suleiman from U.S. House of Representatives and inscribed scroll . . . . 1·50 10

660 Sinan and Selimiye Mosque, Edirne **661** Means of Transport

1988. 400th Death Anniv of Mimar Sinan (architect). Multicoloured.

2987 50 l. Type **660** 15 10
2988 200 l. Suleiman Mosque . . 55 10

1988. Europa. Transport and Communications. Multicoloured.

2989 200 l. Type **661** 30 10
2990 600 l. Electric impulses forming globe between telephone and computer terminal (horiz) 85 15

662 Syringes between Healthy and Sick Children

1988. Health. Multicoloured.

2991 50 l. Type **662** 10 10
2992 200 l. Capsules forming cross on bottle (vert) 20 10
2993 300 l. Heart in cogwheel and heart-shaped worker . . . 35 10
2994 600 l. Organs for transplant on open hands (vert) 60 10

663 American Standard Steam Locomotive, 1850s

1988. Locomotives. Each agate, light brown and brown.

2995 50 l. Type **663** 15 10
2996 100 l. Steam locomotive, 1913 35 10
2997 200 l. Henschel Krupp steam locomotive, 1926 . . . . 50 20
2998 300 l. Toshiba "E 43001" electric locomotive, 1987 . 70 25
2999 600 l. MTE-Tulomsas diesel-electric locomotive, 1984 . 1·75 25

664 Articulated Lorry

1988. 21st International Road Transport Union World Congress, Istanbul.

3000 **664** 200 l. + 25 l. mult . . . 25 15

665 Scales and Map

1988. 120th Anniv of Court of Cassation (appeal court).

3001 **665** 50 l. multicoloured . . . 10 10

666 Fatih Sultan Mohamed Bridge, Bosphorus

1988. Completion of Bridges. Multicoloured.

3002 200 l. Type **666** 60 10
3003 300 l. Seto Great road and rail Bridge, Japan 85 10

667 Telephone Dial and Wires over Villages

1988. Completion of Telephone Network to Every Village.

3004 **667** 100 l. multicoloured . . . 15 10

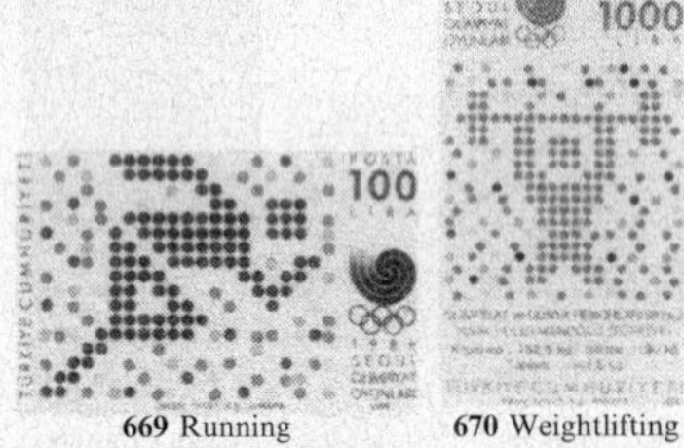

669 Running **670** Weightlifting

1988. Olympic Games, Seoul. Multicoloured.

3005 100 l. Type **669** 15 10
3006 200 l. Archery 20 10
3007 400 l. Weightlifting 30 10
3008 600 l. Football (vert) 85 15

1988. Naim Suleymanoglu, Olympic and World Heavyweight Record Holder for Weightlifting.

3009 **670** 1000 l. multicoloured . . 1·50 15

671 Lush Scene in Hands surrounded by Barren Earth **672** General Dynamics F-16 Fighters and Cogwheel

1988. European Campaign for Rural Areas. Multicoloured.

3010 100 l. + 25 l. Type **671** . . . 15 10
3011 400 l. + 50 l. Rural scene in eye 60 15

1988. Turkish Aerospace Industries. Mult.

3012 50 l. Type **672** 10 10
3013 200 l. Birds forming jet fighter (horiz) 40 10

673 "Gonepteryx cleopatra"

1988. Butterflies. Multicoloured.

3014 100 l. Type **673** (wrongly inscr "G. rhamni") 10 10
3015 200 l. Hermit 25 15
3016 400 l. Eastern festoon 75 20
3017 600 l. Camberwell beauty . . 1·25 35

1988. Royal Pavilions (2nd series). As T **657**. Multicoloured.

3019 100 l. Kasr-i Humayun Imperial Lodge, Maslak 15 10
3020 400 l. Sale Pavilion, Yildiz . . 75 10

675 Large-leaved Lime

1988. Medicinal Plants. Multicoloured.

3022 150 l. Type **675** 20 10
3023 300 l. Common mallow . . . 35 10
3024 600 l. Henbane 55 10
3025 900 l. Deadly nightshade . . 95 15

676 Seated Goddess with Child (clay statuette)

1989. Archaeology (1st series). Multicoloured.

3026 150 l. Type **676** 10 10
3027 300 l. Lead figurine of god and goddess 25 10
3028 600 l. Clay human-shaped vase 1·00 10
3029 1000 l. Hittite ivory figurine of mountain god . . . . . . 1·50 15

See also Nos. 3062/5, 3104/7 and 3134/7.

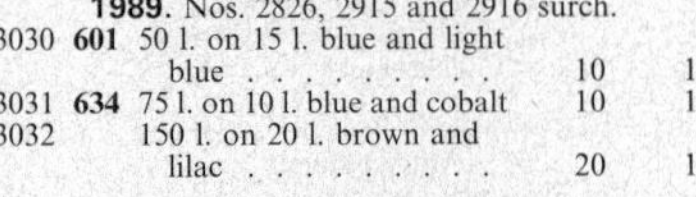

1989. Nos. 2826, 2915 and 2916 surch.

3030 **601** 50 l. on 15 l. blue and light blue 10 10
3031 **634** 75 l. on 10 l. blue and cobalt 10 10
3032 150 l. on 20 l. brown and lilac 20 10

678 Dove and Emblem

1989. 40th Anniv of N.A.T.O.

3033 **678** 600 l. ultram, blue & red 35 10

679 Silkworm Moth Larva on Leaf **680** Leap-frog

1989. Silk Industry. Multicoloured.

3034 150 l. + 50 l. Type **679** . . . 15 15
3035 600 l. + 100 l. Silkworm moth cocoon and lengths of cloth 50 50

1989. Europa. Children's Games. Multicoloured.

3036 600 l. Type **680** 75 10
3037 1000 l. Children going under arch formed by other children ("Open the Door, Head Bezirgan") . . . . 1·25 10

681 Arrow and Anniversary Emblem

1989. 40th Anniv of Council of Europe.

3038 **681** 600 l. + 100 l. mult . . 50 20

683 Paddle-steamer "Sahilbent" **684** Birds

1989. Steamers. Multicoloured.

3045 150 l. Type **683** 40 15
3046 300 l. "Ragbet" (paddle-steamer) 50 15
3047 600 l. "Tari" (freighter) . . . 1·10 20
3048 1000 l. "Guzelhisar" (ferry) . 1·75 25

1989. Bicentenary of French Revolution.

3049 **684** 600 l. multicoloured . . 75 10

685 Kemal Ataturk

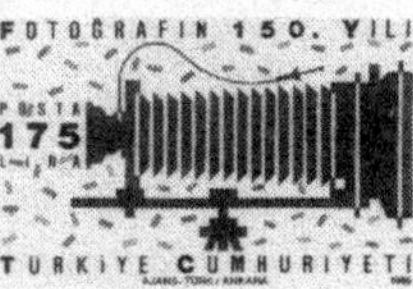
687 Camera

1989.
3050 **685** 2000 l. blue and grey . . 1·00 15
3051 5000 l. brown and grey . 1·50 25
See also Nos. 3093/4, 3144 and 3199/3200.

1989. No. 2916 surch **LIRA 500**.
3052 **634** 500 l. on 20 l. brown and lilac 30 10

1989. 150th Anniv of Photography. Mult.
3053 175 l. Type **687** 10 10
3054 700 l. Coloured lens shutter . 35 10

688 "Manzara" (Hikmet Onat)

689 Nehru

1989. State Exhibition of Paintings and Sculpture. Multicoloured.
3055 200 l. Type **688** 10 10
3056 700 l. "Sari Saz" (Bedri Rahmi Eyuboglu) 35 10
3057 1000 l. "Kadin" (sculpture, Zuhtu Muridoglu) 55 10

1989. Birth Centenary of Jawaharlal Nehru (Indian statesman).
3058 **689** 700 l. multicoloured . . . 45 10

690 Loggerhead Turtle

691 Turkish Memorial

1989. Sea Turtles. Multicoloured.
3059 700 l. Type **690** 55 10
3060 1000 l. Common green turtle 75 20

1990. Archaeology (2nd series). As T **676**. Multicoloured.
3062 100 l. Ivory statuette of goddess (vert) 10 10
3063 200 l. Clay ram's head and antelope's head twin ceremonial vessel 10 10
3064 500 l. Gold goddess pendant (vert) 25 10
3065 700 l. Ivory statuette of lion . 55 10

1990. 75th Anniv of Gallipoli Campaign.
3066 **691** 1000 l. multicoloured . . 55 10

692 Turkish Garden (left half)

1990. International Garden and Greenery Exposition, Osaka. Multicoloured.
3067 1000 l. Type **692** 55 10
3068 1000 l. Right half of garden . 55 10
Nos. 3067/8 were issued together, se-tenant, forming a composite design.

1990. Various stamps surch.
3069 – 50 l. on 5 l. mult (No. 2868) 10 10
3070 **648** 100 l. on 10 l. red, violet and blue 35 10
3071 150 l. on 10 l. red, violet and blue 35 10
3072 – 200 l. on 70 l. mult (No. 2870) 70 10
3073 – 300 l. on 20 l. red, blue and brown (No. 2954) . . . 60 10
3074 – 300 l. on 70 l. mult (No. 2870) 60 10
3075 – 1500 l. on 20 l. mult (No. 2869) . . . . 2·10 10

694 "70" and Ataturk

695 Antalya

1990. 70th Anniv of Establishment of Nationalist Provisional Government.
3076 **694** 300 l. multicoloured . . 15 10

1990. European Tourism Year. Multicoloured.
3077 300 l. + 50 l. Type **695** . . 15 10
3078 1000 l. + 100 l. Istanbul . . 55 20

696 Ankara Post Office

697 Map and Dove as Open Book

1990. Europa. Post Office Buildings. Mult.
3079 700 l. Type **696** 30 10
3080 1000 l. Istanbul Post Office (horiz) 55 10

1990. European Supreme Courts' Conference, Ankara.
3081 **697** 1000 l. blue, dp bl & red 55 10

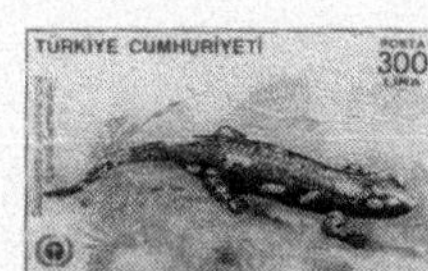
698 Fire Salamander

1990. World Environment Day. Multicoloured.
3082 300 l. Type **698** 15 10
3083 500 l. Banded newt 25 10
3084 1000 l. Fire-bellied toads . . 55 10
3085 1500 l. Common tree frog (vert) 65 10

699 "Ertugrul" (frigate) and Turkish and Japanese Women

701 Smoker's Body shattering

1990. Centenary of First Turkish Envoy to Japan.
3086 **699** 1000 l. multicoloured . . 75 15

1990. Anti-addiction Campaign. Multicoloured.
3087 300 l. on 50 l. Type **701** . . 15 10
3088 1000 l. on 100 l. Addict injecting drug into skeletal arm (horiz) 55 20

702 "Self-portrait"

703 Emblem, Pen, Open Book and Globe

1990. Death Centenary of Vincent van Gogh (painter). Multicoloured.
3089 300 l. Type **702** 15 10
3090 700 l. "Boats in Saintes Maries" (horiz) 60 10
3091 1000 l. "Sunflowers" 85 10
3092 1500 l. "Road with Cypress" 1·25 10

1990. As T **685** but inscription redrawn and dated "1990".
3093 **685** 500 l. green and grey . . 25 10
3094 1000 l. mauve and grey . 50 10

1990. International Literacy Year.
3095 **703** 300 l. multicoloured . . . 15 10

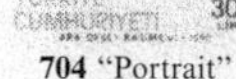
704 "Portrait" (Nurullah Berk)

705 Tatar Courier and Modern Postal Transport

1990. State Exhibition of Painting and Sculpture. Multicoloured.
3096 300 l. Type **704** 15 10
3097 700 l. "Derya Kuzulari" (Cevat Dereli) 30 10
3098 1000 l. "Artist's Mother" (bust) (Nijad Sirel) 50 10

1990. 150th Anniv of Ministry of Posts and Telecommunications. Multicoloured.
3099 200 l. Type **705** 10 10
3100 250 l. Computer terminal and Morse key 10 10
3101 400 l. Manual and digital telephone exchanges 20 10
3102 1500 l. Telegraph wires, dish aerial and satellite 60 10

1991. Archaeology (3rd series). As T **676**. Multicoloured.
3104 300 l. Clay figurine of woman (vert) 10 10
3105 500 l. Bronze sistrum (vert) . 20 10
3106 1000 l. Clay kettle on stand (vert) 40 10
3107 1500 l. Clay ceremonial vessel (vert) 85 10

707 Lake Abant

708 Satellite and Map of Europe

1991. Lakes. Multicoloured.
3110 250 l. Type **707** 10 10
3111 500 l. Lake Egirdir 15 10
3112 1500 l. Lake Van 50 10

1991. Europa. Europe in Space. Multicoloured.
3113 1000 l. Type **708** 40 10
3114 1500 l. Satellite and map of Europe (different) 50 10

709 Graph on Globe

1991. National Statistics Day.
3115 **709** 500 l. multicoloured . . . 15 10

710 Cable Ship, Map, Cable and Telephone Handset

711 Emblem

1991. Eastern Mediterranean Fibre Optic Cable System (EMOS-1).
3116 **710** 500 l. multicoloured . . . 20 10

1991. European Transport Ministers' Conference, Antalya.
3117 **711** 500 l. multicoloured . . . 15 10

MINIMUM PRICE

The minimum price quoted is 10p which represents a handling charge rather than a basis for valuing common stamps. For further notes about prices, see introductory pages.

712 Emre

713 Harpsichord, Score and Mozart

1991. "Yunus Emre (13th-century poet) Year of Love". Multicoloured.
3118 500 l. + 100 l. Type **712** . . 15 10
3119 1500 l. + 100 l. Globe, and Emre as tree 45 20

1991. Death Bicentenary of Wolfgang Amadeus Mozart (composer).
3120 **713** 1500 l. + 100 l. mult . . 45 20

714 "Abdulcanbaz" (Turhan Selcuk)

715 13th-century Seljukian Wall Plaque

1991. Caricature. Multicoloured.
3121 500 l. "Amcabey" (Cemal Nadir Guler) (horiz) 30 10
3122 1000 l. Type **714** 30 10

1991. Turkish Ceramics. Multicoloured.
3123 500 l. Type **715** 15 10
3124 1500 l. Late 16th-century Ottoman wall plaque . . . 45 10

716 Emblem

717 Dam, Water and Sun

1991. Turkish Grand National Assembly's Protection of Human Rights International Symposium, Ankara.
3125 **716** 500 l. multicoloured . . 15 10

1991. South-eastern Anatolia Project (hydro-electric power and irrigation development).
3126 **717** 500 l. multicoloured . . 15 10

718 Keloglan and Genie with Tra of Food

719 Sand Boa

1991. "Keloglan" (fairy tale). Multicoloured.
3127 500 l. Type **718** 10 10
3128 1000 l. Keloglan and dinner guests 25 10
3129 1500 l. Keloglan ploughing . 60 10

1991. World Environment Day. Snakes. Mult.
3130 250 l. Type **719** 10 10
3131 500 l. Four-lined snake . . . 10 10
3132 1000 l. Ottoman viper . . . 25 10
3133 1500 l. Caucasus viper . . . 35 10

1992. Archaeology (4th series). As T **676**. Multicoloured.
3134 300 l. Clay statuette of Mother Goddess (vert) 10 10
3135 500 l. Bronze statuette (vert) 10 10
3136 1000 l. Hittite clay vase (vert) 20 10
3137 1500 l. Urartian lion (vert) . 25 10

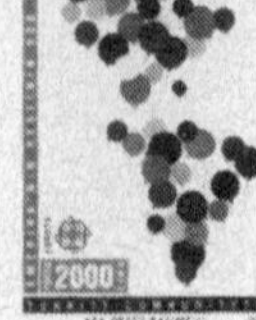

721 Emblem and People **722** Balloons

1992. 30th Anniv of Supreme Court.
3140 **721** 500 l. + 100 l. mult . . 10 10

1992. Europa. 500th Anniv of Discovery of America by Columbus.
3141 – 1500 l. blue and red . . . 20 10
3142 **722** 2000 l. multicoloured . . 30 10
DESIGN—HORIZ: 1500 l. Stylised caravel.

723 Immigrant Ship **724** Kemal Ataturk

1992. 500th Anniv of Jewish Immigration.
3143 **723** 1500 l. multicoloured . . 20 10

1992.
3144 – 250 l. orange, ochre and gold 10 10
3145 **724** 10000 l. bl, grey & gold . 2·25 15
DESIGN: 250 l. Portrait of Ataturk as in Type **685**.

725 Court Emblem **726** Congress Emblem

1992. 130th Anniv of Court of Accounts.
3146 **725** 500 l. multicoloured . . . 10 10

1992. 3rd Turkish Economy Congress, Izmir.
3147 **726** 1500 l. multicoloured . . 20 10

727 Lapwing **728** Ears of Grain, Cogwheel and Hands

1992. World Environment Day. Birds. Mult.
3148 500 l. Type **727** 10 10
3149 1000 l. Golden oriole 15 10
3150 1500 l. Common shelduck . . 20 10
3151 2000 l. White-breasted kingfisher (vert) 30 10

1992. Black Sea Economic Co-operation Conference, Istanbul.
3152 **728** 1500 l. multicoloured . . 20 10

729 Doves forming Olympic Flame **730** Soldiers and Old Woman

1992. Olympic Games, Barcelona. Multicoloured.
3153 500 l. Type **729** 10 10
3154 1000 l. Boxing 15 10
3155 1500 l. Weightlifting 20 10
3156 2000 l. Wrestling 30 10

1992. Legend of Anatolia. Multicoloured.
3157 500 l. Type **730** 10 10
3158 1000 l. Old woman filling trough with buttermilk . . 15 10
3159 1500 l. Soldiers drinking from trough 20 10

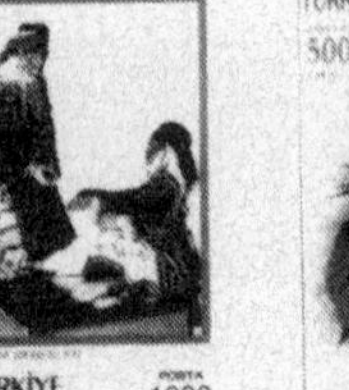

731 Bride and Mother-in-law Dolls from Merkez Kapikaya **732** Cherries

1992. Traditional Crafts. Multicoloured.
3160 500 l. Knitted flowers from Icel-Namrun (horiz) 10 10
3161 1000 l. Type **731** 15 10
3162 3000 l. Woven saddlebag from Hakkari (horiz) 40 10

1992. Fruit (1st series). Multicoloured.
3163 500 l. Type **732** 10 10
3164 1000 l. Apricots 15 10
3165 3000 l. Grapes 40 10
3166 5000 l. Apples 70 10
See also Nos. 3176/9.

734 Mountaineering **735** Sait Faik Abasiyanik

1992. 26th Anniv of Turkish Mountaineering Federation (3169) and 80th Anniv of Turkish Scout Movement (3170). Multicoloured.
3169 1000 l. + 200 l. Type **734** . 15 10
3170 3000 l. + 200 l. Scouts watering sapling (horiz) 45 20

1992. Anniversaries. No value expressed.
3171 **735** (T) blue, indigo and red 10 10
3172 – (T) blue, orange & violet 10 10
3173 – (M) blue, green & orange 15 10
3174 – (M) blue, red and indigo 15 10
3175 – (M) blue, red and green 15 10
DESIGNS: No. 3171, Type **935** (writer, 86th birth anniv); 3172, Fikret Mualla Saygi (painter, 25th death anniv); 3173, Muhsin Ertugrul (actor and producer, birth centenary); 3174, Cevat Sakir Kabaagaeli (writer, 19th death anniv); 3175, Asik Veysel Satiroglu (poet, 98th birth anniv).
Nos. 3171/2 were intended for greeting cards and Nos. 3173/5 for inland letters.

1993. Fruit (2nd series). As T **732**. Multicoloured.
3176 500 l. Bananas 10 10
3177 1000 l. Oranges 10 10
3178 3000 l. Pears 45 10
3179 5000 l. Pomegranates . . . 75 10

736 Sculpture (Hadi Bara) **737** Terraces

1993. Europa. Contemporary Art. Multicoloured.
3180 1000 l. Type **736** 10 10
3181 3000 l. Carved figure (Zuhtu Muridoglu) 15 10

1993. Campaign for the Preservation of Pamukkale. Multicoloured.
3182 1000 l. + 200 l. Type **737** . . 10 10
3183 3000 l. + 500 l. Close-up of terrace 15 10

738 Buildings and Emblem **739** Rize

1993. Economic Co-operation Organization Conference, Istanbul.
3184 **738** 2500 l. ultramarine, blue and gold 10 10

1993. Traditional Houses (1st series). Multicoloured.
3185 1000 l. Type **739** 10 10
3186 2500 l. Rize (different) (horiz) 10 10
3187 3000 l. Trabzon 40 10
3188 5000 l. Black Sea houses (horiz) 50 10
See also Nos. 3222/5, 3256/9 and 3283/6.

740 Mausoleum

1993. 900th Birth Anniv of Hoca Ahmet Yesevi (philosopher).
3189 **740** 3000 l. gold, blue & lt bl . 15 10

741 Haci Arif Bey

1993. Death Anniversaries. No value expressed. Each brown and red.
3190 (T) Type **741** (composer, 109th) 10 10
3191 (T) Neyzen Tevfik Kolayli (singer, 40th) 10 10
3192 (M) Orhan Veli Kanik (poet, 43rd) 10 10
3193 (M) Cahit Sitki Taranci (poet, 27th) 10 10
3194 (M) Munir Nurettin Seluk (composer, 12th) 10 10
Nos. 3190/1 were intended for greetings cards and Nos. 3192/4 for inland letters.

742 Emblem

1993. Istanbul's Bid to host Summer Olympic Games in Year 2000.
3195 **742** 2500 l. multicoloured . . 35 10

1993. As T **685** but inscription redrawn and dated "1993".
3199 **685** 5000 l. violet and gold . . 75 10
3200 20000 l. mauve & gold . . 3·00 10

744 Amphora on Sea-bed

1993. Mediterranean Treaty. Multicoloured.
3201 1000 l. Type **744** 10 10
3202 3000 l. Dolphin 45 10

745 Emblem

1993. U.N. Natural Disaster Relief Day.
3203 **745** 3000 l. + 500 l. mult . . 15 10

746 Prayer Mat **747** Laurel Wreath, Torch and Silhouette of Kemal Ataturk

1993. Handicrafts. Multicoloured.
3204 1000 l. Type **746** 10 10
3205 2500 l. Silver earrings 10 10
3206 5000 l. Crocheted purse . . . 20 10

1993. 70th Anniv of Republic.
3207 **747** 1000 l. multicoloured . . 10 10

748 Man in Gas Mask and Fire

1993. Civil Defence.
3208 **748** 1000 l. multicoloured . . 10 10

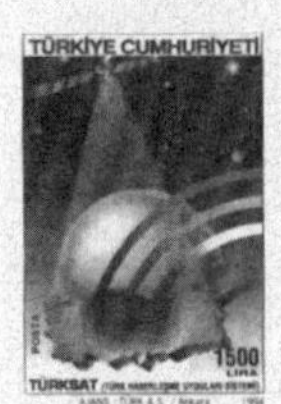
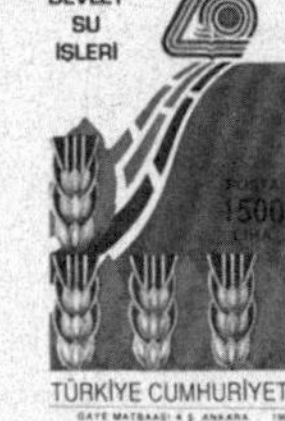

749 Satellite, Globe and Map **750** Ears of Corn

1994. "Turksat" Communications Satellite. Multicoloured.
3209 1500 l. Type **749** 10 10
3210 5000 l. Satellite and map showing satellite's "footprint" 20 10

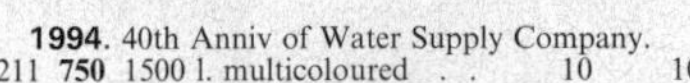

1994. 40th Anniv of Water Supply Company.
3211 **750** 1500 l. multicoloured . . 10 10

751 Ezogelin Corbasi

1994. Traditional Dishes. Multicoloured.
3212 1000 l. Type **751** 10 10
3213 1500 l. Karisik dolma . . . 10 10
3214 3500 l. Shish kebabs 10 10
3215 5000 l. Baklava 15 10

752 Marie Curie

1994. Europa. Discoveries. Multicoloured.
3216 1500 l. Type **752** (discoverer of radium) 10 10
3217 5000 l. Albert Einstein and equation (formulator of Theory of Relativity) (horiz) 15 10

754 Faselis, Antalya

1994. Environment Day. Multicoloured.
3220 6000 l. Type **754** 15 10
3221 8500 l. Gocek, Mugla (vert) . 25 10

755 Bursa

1994. Traditional Houses (2nd series). Multicoloured.
3222 2500 l. Type **755** 10 10
3223 3500 l. Uskudar 10 10
3224 6000 l. Anadolu Hisari . . . 15 10
3225 8500 l. Edirne 25 10

756 Trekking in Mountains **757** Centenary Emblem over City

1994. Tourism. Multicoloured.
3226 5000 l. Type **756** 15 10
3227 10000 l. White-water rafting (horiz) 30 10

1994. Centenary of International Olympic Committee.
3228 **757** 12500 l. + 500 l. mult . 65 15

758 "2001"

1994. Seven Year Plan.
3229 **758** 2500 l. multicoloured . . 10 10

759 Kusak Design **760** Kemal Ataturk

1994. Embroidery. Multicoloured.
3230 7500 l. Type **759** 20 10
3231 12500 l. Paalik design (horiz) 65 10

1994.
3232 **760** 50000 l. violet, mve & red 1·50 20

761 Common Morel **762** "Platanus orientalis"

1994. Fungi. Multicoloured.
3233 2500 l. Type **761** 10 10
3234 5000 l. "Agaricus bernardii" . 25 10
3235 7500 l. Saffron milk cap . . . 35 10
3236 12500 l. Parasol mushroom . 1·10 10

1994. Trees. Multicoloured.
3237 7500 l. + 500 l. Type **762** . . . 25 10
3238 12500 l. + 1000 l. "Cupressus sempervirens" (vert) . . . 65 15

763 Silver Jug **765** Starry Sky

1994. Traditional Crafts. Multicoloured.
3239 2500 l. Type **763** 10 10
3240 5000 l. Silver censer 15 10
3241 7500 l. Necklace (horiz) . . . 20 10
3242 12500 l. Gold brooch (half horse and half fish) (horiz) . . . 65 10

1995. Centenary of Motion Pictures.
3245 **765** 15000 l. blue and red . . 30 10

766 Women

1995. Nevruz Festival.
3246 **766** 3500 l. multicoloured . . 10 10

767 "Ballad of Manas" (Kirghiz epic, millenary)

1995. Anniversaries.
3247 **767** 3500 l. + 500 l. brown, yellow and red 10 10
3248 – 3500 l. + 500 l. mult . . 10 10
DESIGN—VERT: No. 3248, Abay Kunanbay and books (Kazakh philosopher and politician, 150th birth anniv).

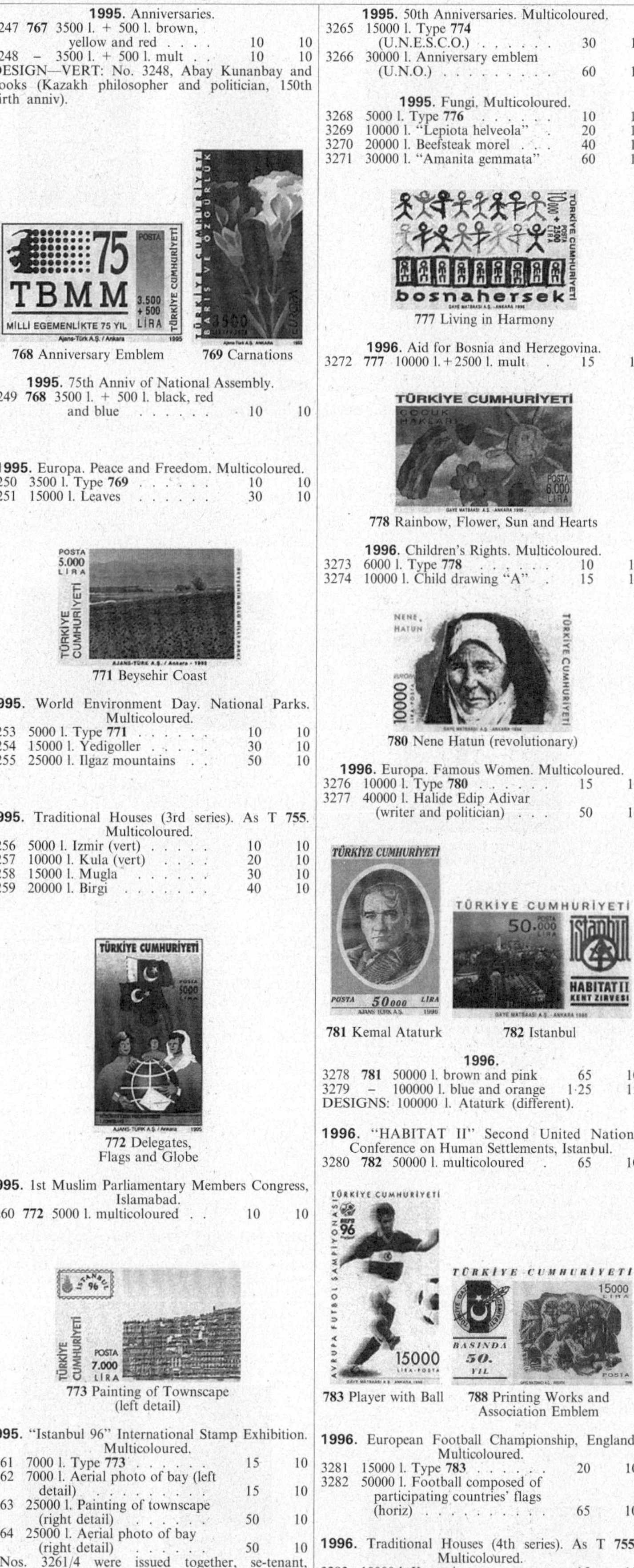

768 Anniversary Emblem **769** Carnations

1995. 75th Anniv of National Assembly.
3249 **768** 3500 l. + 500 l. black, red and blue 10 10

1995. Europa. Peace and Freedom. Multicoloured.
3250 3500 l. Type **769** 10 10
3251 15000 l. Leaves 30 10

771 Beyshir Coast

1995. World Environment Day. National Parks. Multicoloured.
3253 5000 l. Type **771** 10 10
3254 15000 l. Yedigoller 30 10
3255 25000 l. Ilgaz mountains . . 50 10

1995. Traditional Houses (3rd series). As T **755**. Multicoloured.
3256 5000 l. Izmir (vert) 10 10
3257 10000 l. Kula (vert) 20 10
3258 15000 l. Mugla 30 10
3259 20000 l. Birgi 40 10

772 Delegates, Flags and Globe

1995. 1st Muslim Parliamentary Members Congress, Islamabad.
3260 **772** 5000 l. multicoloured . . 10 10

773 Painting of Townscape (left detail)

1995. "Istanbul 96" International Stamp Exhibition. Multicoloured.
3261 7000 l. Type **773** 15 10
3262 7000 l. Aerial photo of bay (left detail) 15 10
3263 25000 l. Painting of townscape (right detail) 50 10
3264 25000 l. Aerial photo of bay (right detail) 50 10
Nos. 3261/4 were issued together, se-tenant, forming two composite designs.

774 Spirit embracing Earth **776** Death Cap

1995. 50th Anniversaries. Multicoloured.
3265 15000 l. Type **774** (U.N.E.S.C.O.) 30 10
3266 30000 l. Anniversary emblem (U.N.O.) 60 10

1995. Fungi. Multicoloured.
3268 5000 l. Type **776** 10 10
3269 10000 l. "Lepiota helveola" . . 20 10
3270 20000 l. Beefsteak morel . . . 40 10
3271 30000 l. "Amanita gemmata" 60 10

777 Living in Harmony

1996. Aid for Bosnia and Herzegovina.
3272 **777** 10000 l. + 2500 l. mult . 15 10

778 Rainbow, Flower, Sun and Hearts

1996. Children's Rights. Multicoloured.
3273 6000 l. Type **778** 10 10
3274 10000 l. Child drawing "A" . 15 10

780 Nene Hatun (revolutionary)

1996. Europa. Famous Women. Multicoloured.
3276 10000 l. Type **780** 15 10
3277 40000 l. Halide Edip Adivar (writer and politician) . . . 50 10

781 Kemal Ataturk **782** Istanbul

1996.
3278 **781** 50000 l. brown and pink 65 10
3279 – 100000 l. blue and orange 1·25 15
DESIGNS: 100000 l. Ataturk (different).

1996. "HABITAT II" Second United Nations Conference on Human Settlements, Istanbul.
3280 **782** 50000 l. multicoloured . 65 10

783 Player with Ball **788** Printing Works and Association Emblem

1996. European Football Championship, England. Multicoloured.
3281 15000 l. Type **783** 20 10
3282 50000 l. Football composed of participating countries' flags (horiz) 65 10

1996. Traditional Houses (4th series). As T **755**. Multicoloured.
3283 10000 l. Kayseri 15 10
3284 15000 l. Konya 20 10
3285 25000 l. Ankara (vert) . . . 35 10
3286 50000 l. Konya (vert) 65 10

1996. Various stamps surch. (a) Postcard Rate. Surch **T** and emblem.
3292 – T (10000 l.) on 250 l. orange, brown and gold (No. 3144) 15 10
3293 **685** T (10000 l.) on 2000 l. blue and grey 15 10
(b) Domestic Letter Rate. Nos. 3099 and 3101/2 surch **M.**
3294 **705.** M (15000 l.) on 200 l. multicoloured 20 10
3295 – M (15000 l.) on 400 l. multicoloured 20 10
3296 – M (15000 l.) on 1500 l. multicoloured 20 10

1996. 50th Anniv of Journalists' Association.
3297 **788** 15000 l. multicoloured . 20 10

790 Cogwheels on Sphere and Globe

1996. Year of Small and Medium Businesses.
3299 **790** 15000 l. multicoloured . 20 10

791 Emblem

1996. 50th Anniv of Ankara University.
3300 **791** 15000 l. + 2500 l. mult 25 10

792 Amasya Bayezit Public Library

1996. Historical Buildings. Multicoloured.
3301 10000 l. Type **792** (500th anniv) 15 10
3302 15000 l. Divrigi Mosque and Hospital 20 10

OBLIGATORY TAX STAMPS

T 101 Nurse bandaging Patient
T 102 Biplane

1926. Red Crescent.
T1035 – 1 g. red, yellow & blk . . 20 10
T1036 T 101 2½ g. multicoloured . 25 10
T1037 – 5 g. multicoloured . 35 15
T1038 – 10 g. multicoloured . 70 45
DESIGNS—VERT: 1 g. Red crescent and decorative archway; 5 g. Refugees. HORIZ: 10 g. Stretcher bearers.

1926. Aviation Fund.
T1039 T 102 20 pa. brown & grn . 65 15
T1040 1 g. green & stone . 65 15
T1041 5 g. violet & green . 1·50 25
T1042 5 g. red and green . . 19·00 2·10
The 5 g. stamps are 40 × 29 mm.

T 103 Biplane over Ankara

۲۰ پاره

(T 104)

1927. Aviation Fund.
T1043 T 102 20 pa. red and green 10 10
T1044 1 g. green and ochre 10 10
T1045 T 103 2 g. brown & green . 50 40
T1046 2½ g. red and green . 2·50 2·00
T1047 5 g. blue and buff . . 35 35
T1048 10 g. blue and pink . 3·00 2·00
T1049 15 g. green & yellow 2·25 2·50
T1050 20 g. brown & ochre 3·00 2·00
T1051 50 g. blue & lt blue . 5·50 4·00
T1052 100 g. red and blue . 35·00 23·00
The 20 pa. and 1 g. are 25 × 15 mm.

1927. Red Crescent No. T1035 and charity labels surch with Type T 104 or similar types.
T1053 20 pa. on 1 g. red, yellow and black 75 25
T1054 20 pa. on 1 g. brown . . . 2·00 45
T1055 20 pa. on 2½ g. lilac 80 50
DESIGNS: 26 × 21 mm. No. T1054 Hospital ship. No. T1055 Nurse tending patient.
No. T1053 has an extra line of Turkish characters in the surcharge.

T 105 Red Crescent on Map of Turkey
T 106 Cherubs holding Star

1928. Red Crescent. Various frames. Crescent in red.
T1067 T 105 ½ pi. brown 10 10
T1068 1 pi. purple 10 10
T1069 2½ pi. orange 10 10
T1070 5 pi. brown 10 10
T1071 10 pi. green 40 30
T1072 20 pi. blue 85 30
T1073 50 pi. purple . . . . 2·25 1·60
See also Nos. T1171/4 and T1198/1212.

1928. Child Welfare.
T1074 T 106 1 g. olive and red . . 10 10
T1075 2½ g. brown and red . 20 10
T1076 5 g. green and red . . 25 20
T1077 25 g. black and red . 2·00 1·10
See also Nos. T1160/1 and T1165/6.

1930. Aviation Fund. Nos. T1039, T1043, T1045 and T1049 surch.
T1099 T 102 Bir (1) k. on 20 pa. brown & green . . 32·00 22·00
T1100 Bir (1) k. on 20 pa. red and green 10 10
T1101 T 103 Yuz (100) pa. on 2 g. brown & green . . 10 15
T1102 T 102 5 k. on 20 pa. red and green 15 15
T1103 Bes (5) k. on 20 pa. red and green 90 15
T1104 T 103 On (10) k. on 2 g. brown and green . . 35 25
T1105 Elli (50) k. on 2 g. brown and green . . 3·25 1·25
T1106 Bir (1) l. on 2 g. brown and green . . . 7·50 2·00
T1107 Bes (5) l. on 15 g. green and yellow £180 £120

T 114 Biplane over Ankara
T 118 Biplane

1931. Aviation Fund.
T1141 T 114 20 pa. black 30 10
See also Nos. T1154/6.

1932. Child Welfare. No. T1074 surch.
T1150 T 106 20 pa. on 1 g. olive and red 30 10
T1153 3 k. on 1 g. olive and red 70 10

1932. Aviation Fund. As Type T 114 but larger, 22 × 30 mm, and with sky shaded.
T1154 1 k. purple 10 10
T1155 5 k. red 45 20
T1156 10 k. green 80 25

1932. Red Crescent. Nos. T1067, T1069 and T1071 surch.
T1157 T 105 1 k. on 2½ pi. orange 25 15
T1158 5 k. on ½ pi. brown . 50 20
T1159 5 k. on 10 pi. green 60 30

1933. Child Welfare. As Type T 106 but inscr "IZMIR HIMAYEI ETFAL CEMIYETI"
T1160 1 k. violet and red 30 10
T1161 5 k. brown and red 75 35

1933. Aviation Fund.
T1162 T 118 On (10) pa. green . 30 10
T1163 Bir (1) k. red . . . 50 15
T1164 Bes (5) k. lilac . . . 60 40

1934. Child Welfare. As Type T 106 but inscr "Turkiye Himayeietfal Cemiyeti".
T1165 20 pa. purple and red . . . 20 10
T1166 15 k. green and red . . . . 1·25 45

T 119 Red Crescent and Map of Turkey

1934. Inscr "TURKIYE HILALIAHMER CEMIYETI" (different frame on 5 k.).
T1171 T 119 ½ k. blue and red . . 10 10
T1172 1 k. brown and red . 10 10
T1173 2½ k. brown and red 10 10
T1174 5 k. green and red . 40 30
See also Nos. T1198/1212.

1936. Child Welfare. Nos. T1074/5 and T1165 optd **P.Y.S.** or surch also.
T1186 T 106 20 pa. purple & red 75 25
T1187 1 g. olive and red 55 15
T1188 3 k. on 2½ g. brn & red 75 35

1937. Red Crescent. As Types T 105 and T 119 but inscr "TURKIYE KIZILAY CEMIYETI". Various frames.
T1204 ½ k. blue and red 10 10
T1199 1 k. mauve and red 10 10
T1200 2½ k. orange and red . . . 10 10
T1201 5 k. green and red 25 10
T1209 5 k. brown and red 60 15
T1202 10 k. green and red 75 25
T1203 20 k. black and red . . . . 1·25 60
T1211 50 k. purple and red . . . 3·75 75
T1212 1 l. blue and red . . . . 12·00 2·25

1938. Child Welfare. No. T1075 surch. (a) Value in figures and words above **P. Y. S.**
T1213 T 106 20 pa. on 2½ g. brown and red 45 20
T1214 1 k. on 2½ g. brown and red 45 20

(b) **P. Y. S.** above value in figures and words.
T1215 T 106 20 pa. on 2½ g. brown and red 55 30
T1216 1 k. on 2½ g. brown and red 55 25

(c) **1 kurus**
T1217 T 106 1 k. on 2½ g. brown and red 65 20

T 138 Laughing Child
T 139 Nurse and Baby

1940. Child Welfare. Star in red.
T1259 T 138 20 pa. green 10 10
T1260 1 k. lilac 10 10
T1261 T 139 1 k. blue 10 10
T1262 2½ k. mauve 10 10
T1263 T 138 3 k. black 10 10
T1264 T 139 5 k. lilac 15 10
T1265 10 k. green 60 20
T1266 T 138 15 k. blue 30 15
T1267 T 139 25 k. olive . . . . 1·25 40
T1268 50 k. olive . . . . 2·75 70

T 145 Soldier and Map of Turkey
T 151 Child eating

1941. National Defence.
T1289 T 145 1 k. violet 25 10
T1290 2 k. blue . . . . . . 1·50 10
T1291 3 k. brown . . . . . 1·50 20
T1292 4 k. mauve . . . . . 1·25 10
T1293 5 k. pink . . . . . 5·50 40
T1294 10 k. blue . . . . . 10·00 60

1943. Child Welfare. Inscr "SEFKAT PULLARI 1943".
T1330 T 151 0.50 k. violet and red 10 10
T1331 0.50 k. green and red 10 10
T1332 – 1 k. blue and red . . 10 10
T1333 – 3 k. red and orange . 25 10
T1334 – 15 k. black, buff and red 40 20
T1335 – 100 k. blue and red . 1·25 60
DESIGNS—VERT: 1 k. Nurse with baby; 15 k. Baby and emblem; 100 k. President Inonu and child. HORIZ: 3 k. Nurse and child.

T 152 Child Welfare Emblem
T 155 Pres. Inonu and Victim

1943. Child Welfare. Star in red.
T1337 T 152 20 pa. blue 10 10
T1338 – 1 k. green 10 10
T1339 – 3 k. brown 10 10
T1340 – 5 k. orange 85 20
T1341 – 5 k. brown 20 15
T1342 – 10 k. red 25 15
T1343 – 15 k. lilac 45 15
T1344 – 25 k. violet 95 15
T1345 – 50 k. blue . . . . . 1·60 20
T1346 – 100 k. green . . . . 3·00 40
DESIGNS—VERT: 1 k. Hospital; 3 k. Nurse and children; 5 k. Baby in cot; 10 k. Nurse bathing baby; 15 k. Nurse helping child to drink; 50 k. Child. HORIZ: 25 k. Baby with bottle; 100 k. Hospital.

1944. Red Crescent. Inscr "TURKIYE KIZILAY CEMIYETI".
T1347 – 20 pa. brown, flesh, red and blue 15 10
T1348 T 155 1 k. olive, yellow, green and red 15 10
T1349 – 2½ k. blue and red . . 25 10
T1350 – 5 k. blue and red . . 70 10
T1351 – 10 k. blue, green and red 80 25
T1352 – 50 k. green, black and red . . . . 2·25 60
T1353 – 1 l. yellow, black and red . . . . 4·50 85
DESIGNS—VERT: 20 pa. Nurse tending dreaming patient; 5 k. Soldier and nurse; 10 k. Feeding victims; 50 k. Wounded soldiers on raft; 1 l. Nurse within red crescent. HORIZ: 2½ k. Stretcher bearers and hospital ship.

T 156 Nurse helping Child to Drink
T 159 Nurse tucking Baby in Cot

1945. Child Welfare. Star in red.
T1354 – 1 k. lilac 10 10
T1355 – 2½ k. blue 20 15
T1356 T 156 5 k. green 20 25
T1357 – 10 k. brown . . . . 1·75 25
T1358 – 250 k. black . . . . 12·50 2·75
T1359 – 500 k. violet . . . . 30·00 2·50
DESIGNS—VERT (21 × 20 mm): 1 k. Nurse carrying baby; 2½ k. Nurse holding child; 10 k. Child sucking thumb. HORIZ (28 × 22 mm): 250, 500 k. Emblem.

1946. 25th Anniv of Child Welfare Organization.
T1360 T 159 20 pa. brown & red . 10 10
T1361 – 1 k. blue and red . . 10 10
T1362 – 2½ k. red 35 10
T1363 – 5 k. brown and red . 60 35
T1364 – 15 k. purple & red . 75 35
T1365 – 25 k. green and red . 1·25 30
T1366 – 50 k. green and red . 1·75 40
T1367 – 150 k. brown and red 2·50 60
DESIGNS: 1 k. Mother and baby; 2½ k. Nurse holding child above head; 5 k. Doctor examining baby; 15 k. Nurse feeding baby; 25 k. Nurse bathing baby; 50 k. Nurse weighing baby; 150 k. Nurse, and child in cot.

T 160 Pres. Inonu and Victim
T 169 Nurse and Children playing

1946. Red Crescent. As Nos. T1347/8, T1350 and T1353 and new design inscr "TURKIYE KIZILAY DERNEGI".
T1369 – 20 pa. yellow, grey, blue and red 10 10
T1532 – 20 pa. brown, yellow, violet and red . . 10 10
T1370 T 155 1 k. multicoloured . 2·00 10
T1371 T 160 1 k. brown, blue and red 20 10
T1533 – 1 k. grn, blk & red . 10 10
T1372 – 5 k. blue and red . . 40 10
T1373 – 20 k. red, bl & pur . 1·00 60
T1374 – 1 l. blk, yell & red . 2·50 2·50
T1375 – 250 k. black, green and red . . . . 5·00 75
T1376 – 5 l. black, pink and red 10·00 1·00
T1377 – 10 l. blue and red . 20·00 10·00
DESIGNS—VERT: 20 pa. As No. T1347; 1 k. (T1533), As No. T1352; 5 k. As No. T1350; 1 l. As No. T1353; 5 l. Nurse tending patient; 10 l. Soldier, red crescent and figure symbolising Victory. HORIZ: 20 k. Ankara Hospital; 250 k. Nurse helping injured soldier.

1948. Child Welfare. Star in red.
T1399 T 169 20 pa. blue 10 10
T1400 – 20 pa. mauve 10 10
T1401 – 1 k. green 10 10
T1402 – 3 k. purple 25 25
T1403 – 15 k. grey . . . . . 1·90 50
T1404 – 30 k. orange . . . . 1·90 1·00
T1405 – 150 k. green . . . . 3·25 1·75
T1406 – 300 k. red . . . . . 8·25 3·75
DESIGNS—VERT: 20 pa. (No. 1400) Nurse and children walking; 1 k. Nurse feeding two children; 3 k. Nurse with three children; 15 k. Parents and two children; 150 k. Nurse holding baby; 300 k. Heads of nurse and child. HORIZ: 30 k. Father handing baby to nurse.

T 177 Ruins and Tent
T 179 "Grief"

1949. Red Crescent.
T1422 T 177 5 k. black, red & pur 25 10
T1423 10 k. purple, red and flesh 25 10

1950. Red Crescent. Crescent in red.
T1425 T 179 ½ k. blue . . . . . . 1·00 25
T1426 1 k. blue 10 10
T1427 2 k. mauve 15 10
T1428 2½ k. orange 15 10
T1429 3 k. green 15 10
T1430 4 k. drab 25 20
T1431 5 k. blue 50 10
T1432 10 k. pink . . . . . 1·75 15
T1433 25 k. brown . . . . 2·00 35
T1434 – 50 k. blue . . . . . 3·25 60
T1435 – 100 k. green . . . . 5·00 75
DESIGN: 50, 100 k. Plant with broken stem.

1952. (a) Red Crescent. Nos. T1427 and T1429/30 surch.
T1489 T 179 20 pa. on 2 k. mauve and red 55 10
T1490 20 pa. on 3 k. green and red 25 10
T1491 20 pa. on 4 k. drab and red 25 10

(b) Child Welfare. Nos. T1355, T1362 and T1339 surch.
T1492 – 1 k. on 2½ k. blue and red 50 10
T1493 – 1 k. on 2½ k. red 75 10
T1494 – 1 k. on 3 k. brown and red 20 10

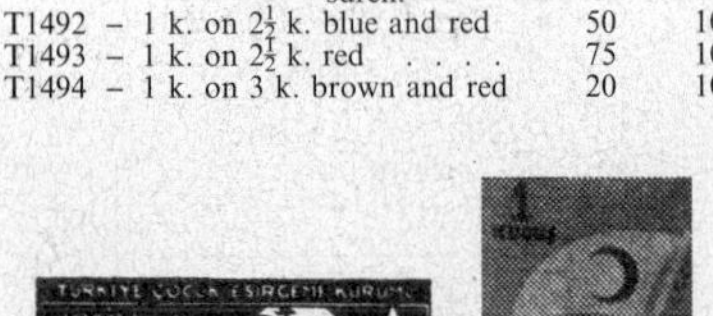

T 208 Nurse and Baby
T 211 Globe and Flag

1954. Child Welfare. Inscr "SEFKAT PULLARI 1954".

T1534 – 20 pa. yellow & orge 10 10
T1535 – 20 pa. green and red 10 10
T1536 T 208 1 k. blue and red 10 10

DESIGN: Nos. 1534/5, Nurse with two children.
See also Nos. T1569 and T1573/4.

1954. Red Crescent.

T1545 T 211 1 k. multicoloured 10 10
T1546 – 5 k. red, grey and green 10 10
T1547 – 10 k. grey, green and red 15 10

DESIGNS: 5 k. Nurse with wings on cloud; 10 k. Arm and hand.
See also Nos. T1652, T1656/8, T1838 and T1840/3.

T 212 Florence Nightingale

T 215 Children Kissing

1954. Red Crescent. Centenary of Florence Nightingale's Arrival at Scutari.

T1551 T 212 20 k. green, brown and red 10 20
T1552 – 30 k. brown, black and red 15 25
T1553 – 50 k. stone, black and red 15 10

DESIGNS: 30 k. Florence Nightingale (three-quarter face); 50 k. Selimiye Barracks.

1955. Child Welfare. Inscr "SEFKAT PULLARI 1955". Star in red.

T1564 T 215 20 pa. blue 10 10
T1565 20 pa. brown 10 10
T1566 1 k. purple 10 10
T1567 3 k. bistre 10 10
T1568 5 k. orange 10 10
T1569 T 208 10 k. green 1·10 1·00
T1570 – 15 k. blue 10 10
T1571 – 25 k. lake 40 25
T1572 – 50 k. green 45 25
T1573 T 208 2½ l. brown £120 38·00
T1574 10 l. violet £190 65·00

DESIGN: 15 to 50 k. Nurse carrying baby.

1955. Red Crescent. Nos. T1373 and T1435 surch.

T1575 20 pa. on 20 k. red, blue and purple 10 10
T1576 20 pa. on 100 k. green and red 20 10

T 219 Nurse

T 227 Woman and Children

1955. Red Crescent. Congress of International Council of Nurses.

T1578 T 219 10 k. brown, red and black 25 25
T1579 – 15 k. green, red and black 25 25
T1580 – 100 k. blue and red 1·10 75

DESIGNS—HORIZ: 15 k. Nurses marching. VERT: 100 k. Emblem, Red Cross and Red Crescent flags and nurses.

1956. Child Welfare. Star in red.

T1614 T 227 20 pa. salmon 10 10
T1615 20 pa. olive 10 10
T1616 1 k. blue 15 10
T1617 1 k. violet 15 10
T1618 3 k. brown 1·00 35
T1619 – 10 k. red 1·90 1·25
T1620 – 25 k. green 3·25 1·25
T1621 – 50 k. blue 5·00 1·90
T1622 – 2½ l. lilac 10·00 4·25
T1623 – 5 l. brown 17·00 7·50
T1624 – 10 l. green 38·00 19·00

DESIGNS: 10 k. to 50 k. Flag and building; 2½ l. to 10 l. Mother and baby.

1956. Red Crescent. No. T1545 surch.

T1625 T 211 20 pa. on 1 k. mult 15 10
T1626 2.5 k. on 1 k. mult 10 10

1956. Child Welfare. Nos. 1399/1406 optd **IV. DUNYA Cocuk Gunu 1 Ekim 1956**. Nos. 1644/6 surch, also.

T1639 T 169 20 pa. red and blue 7·50 7·50
T1640 – 20 pa. mauve & red 7·50 7·50
T1641 – 1 k. green and red 7·50 7·50
T1642 – 3 k. purple and red 7·50 7·50
T1643 – 15 k. grey and red 7·50 7·50
T1644 – 25 k. on 30 k. orange and red 7·50 7·50
T1645 – 100 k. on 150 k. green and red 7·50 7·50
T1646 – 250 k. on 300 k. deep red and red 7·50 7·50

1957. Red Crescent. As No. T1373 but inscr "TURKIYE KIZILAY CEMIYETI", new design and as Nos. T1545/6. Crescent in red.

T1651 – ½ k. drab & brown 10 10
T1652 T 211 1 k. black, bis & grn 10 10
T1653 – 2½ k. green & dp grn 10 10
T1655 – 20 k. red, brown and blue 1·10 15
T1656 T 211 25 k. grey, black and green 1·00 45
T1657 50 k. blue and green 1·40 50
T1658 100 k. violet, black and green 2·00 40

DESIGNS—VERT: ½, 2½ k. Flower being watered. HORIZ: 20 k. Ankara hospital.

T 239 Two Babies

T 246 Nurse and Child

1957. Child Welfare.

T1659 T 239 20 pa. green and red 10 10
T1660 20 pa. pink and red 10 10
T1661 1 k. blue and red 10 10
T1662 3 k. orange and red 75 15
T1683 T 246 100 k. brown & red 35 25
T1684 150 k. green and red 35 25
T1685 250 k. violet and red 35 25

T 254 Florence Nightingale

T 255 Child's Head and Butterfly

1958. Florence Nightingale Foundation. Crescent in red.

T1829 T 254 1 l. green 25 25
T1830 1½ l. grey 25 10
T1831 2½ l. blue 25 10

1958. Child Welfare. Butterflies. Multicoloured.

T1832 20 k. Type T 255 25 15
T1833 25 k. Brimstone 25 15
T1834 50 k. Little tiger blue (horiz) 30 25
T1835 75 k. Green-veined white (horiz) 85 70
T1836 150 k. Peacock 2·00 1·50

1958. Red Crescent. As Nos. T1651/3, T1546 and T1656/8 but colours changed. Crescent in red.

T1837 – ½ k. lilac 15 10
T1838 T 211 1 k. black, brown and green 15 10
T1839 – 2½ k. grey and red 25 10
T1840 – 5 k. red, brown and green 35 10
T1841 T 211 25 k. black, green and brown 1·25 20
T1842 50 k. purple, black and green 1·50 25
T1843 100 k. drab, black and green 2·00 35

OFFICIAL STAMPS

O 160

O 241

O 284

1947.

O1360 O 160 10 pa. brown 10 10
O1361 1 k. green 10 10
O1362 2 k. purple 15 10
O1363 3 k. orange 15 10
O1364 5 k. turquoise 11·00 10
O1365 10 k. brown 3·75 10
O1366 15 k. violet 80 10
O1367 20 k. blue 85 10
O1368 30 k. olive 90 10
O1369 50 k. blue 90 10
O1370 1 l. green 1·25 10
O1371 2 l. red 3·00 10

1951. Postage stamps optd **RESMI** between bars with star and crescent above.

O1458 165 0.25 k. red 10 10
O1454 5 k. blue 20 10
O1461 10 k. brown 20 10
O1462 15 k. violet 40 10
O1456 20 k. blue 50 10
O1469 30 k. brown 35 10
O1470 60 k. black 1·90 10

1955. Postage stamps optd **RESMI** between wavy bars with star and crescent above or surch also.

O1568 165 0.25 k. red 10 10
O1587 ½ k. on 1 k. black 10 10
O1569 1 k. black 10 10
O1570 2 k. purple 10 10
O1593 165 2 k. on 4 k. green 10 10
O1571 3 k. orange 10 10
O1594 3 k. on 4 k. green 10 10
O1572 4 k. green 10 10
O1573 5 k. on 15 k. violet 10 10
O1581 5 k. blue 35 10
O1595 10 k. on 12 k. red 10 10
O1574 10 k. on 15 k. violet 10 10
O1575 15 k. violet 10 10
O1576 20 k. blue 15 10
O1585 30 k. brown 60 10
O1577 40 k. on 1 l. olive 25 10
O1590 75 k. on 1 l. olive 35 10
O1578 75 k. on 2 l. brown 35 15
O1579 75 k. on 5 l. purple 5·75 6·25

1957.

O1655 O 241 5 k. blue 10 10
O1843 5 k. red 10 10
O1656 10 k. brown 10 10
O1844 10 k. olive 10 10
O1657 15 k. violet 10 10
O1845 15 k. red 10 10
O1658 20 k. red 10 10
O1846 20 k. violet 10 10
O1659 30 k. olive 10 10
O1660 40 k. purple 15 10
O1847 40 k. blue 10 10
O1661 50 k. grey 15 10
O1662 60 k. green 20 10
O1848 60 k. orange 30 10
O1663 75 k. orange 30 10
O1849 75 k. grey 30 10
O1664 100 k. green 35 10
O1850 100 k. violet 35 10
O1665 200 k. lake 70 25
O1851 200 k. brown 85 15

1960.

O1916 O 284 1 k. orange 10 10
O1917 5 k. red 10 10
O1918 10 k. green 60 10
O1919 30 k. brown 10 10
O1920 60 k. green 20 10
O1921 1 l. purple 40 10
O1922 1½ l. blue 25 10
O1923 2½ l. violet 35 10
O1924 5 l. blue 3·25 20

O 303

O 320

1962.

O1977 O 303 1 k. brown 10 10
O1978 5 k. green 10 10
O1979 10 k. brown 10 10
O1980 15 k. blue 10 10
O1981 25 k. red 10 10
O1982 30 k. blue 15 10

1963. Surch.

O2003 O 303 50 k. on 30 k. blue 25 10
O2004 O 284 100 k. on 60 k. green 20 10

1963.

O2042 O 320 1 k. green 10 10
O2043 5 k. brown 10 10
O2044 10 k. green 10 10
O2045 50 k. red 15 10
O2046 100 k. blue 30 10

O 329

O 344

1964.

O2074 O 329 1 k. grey 10 10
O2075 5 k. blue 15 10
O2076 10 k. yellow 15 10
O2077 30 k. red 40 10
O2078 50 k. green 40 10
O2079 60 k. brown 85 10
O2080 80 k. turquoise 2·25 10
O2081 130 k. blue 1·75 10
O2082 200 k. purple 3·00 10

1965.

O2133 O 344 1 k. green 10 10
O2134 10 k. blue 10 10
O2135 50 k. orange 20 10

O 358 Usak Carpet

O 372 Doves Emblem

O 383

1966. Turkish Carpets.

O2175 O 358 1 k. orange 10 10
O2176 – 50 k. green 10 10
O2177 – 100 k. red 30 10
O2178 – 150 k. blue 40 10
O2179 – 200 k. bistre 40 10
O2180 – 500 k. lilac 1·00 10

DESIGNS (Carpets of): 50 k. Bergama; 100 k. Ladik; 150 k. Selcuk; 200 k. Nomad; 500 k. Anatolia.

1967.

O2213 O 372 1 k. blue & lt blue 10 10
O2214 50 k. blue & orange 15 10
O2215 100 k. blue & mauve 25 10

1968.

O2241 O 383 50 k. brown & green 10 10
O2242 150 k. black & orge 25 10
O2243 500 k. brown & blue 30 10

O 400

O 427

O 440

1969.

O2287 O 400 1 k. red and green 10 10
O2288 10 k. blue & green 10 10
O2289 50 k. brown & green 10 10
O2290 100 k. mauve & grn 35 10

1971.

O2359 O 427 5 k. blue & brown 10 10
O2360 10 k. red and blue 10 10
O2361 30 k. violet & orge 15 10
O2362 50 k. brown & blue 20 10
O2363 75 k. green & buff 35 10

1971. Face-value and border colour given first.

O2398 O 440 5 k. blue and grey 10 10
O2399 25 k. green & brown 10 10
O2400 100 k. brown & grn 25 10
O2401 200 k. brn & ochre 20 10
O2402 250 k. purple & vio 25 10
O2403 500 k. blue & light blue 65 10

O 446

O 462

O 478 Trellis Motif

1972.

O2411 O 446 5 k. blue & brown 10 10
O2412 100 k. green & brn 25 10
O2413 200 k. red & brown 40 20

1973.

O2457 O 462 100 k. blue & cream 20 10

1974.

O2490 O 478 10 k. brown on pink 10 10
O2491 25 k. purple on blue 10 10
O2492 50 k. red on mauve 10 10
O2493 150 k. brown on grn 20 10
O2494 250 k. red on pink 30 10
O2495 500 k. brown on yell 65 10

O 496

O 528

O 529

1975.

O2537 O 496 100 k. red and blue 15 10

1977. Surch.

O2587 O 320 5 k. on 1 k. green 10 10
O2588 O 329 5 k. on 1 k. grey 10 10
O2589 O 344 5 k. on 1 k. green 10 10
O2590 O 358 5 k. on 1 k. orange 10 10
O2591 O 372 5 k. on 1 k. blue and light blue 10 10

1977.

O2609 O 528 250 k. green & blue 25 10

1978.

O2610 O 529 50 k. pink and red 10 10
O2611 2½ l. buff and brown 10 10
O2612 4½ l. lilac and green 15 10
O2613 5 l. blue and violet 20 10
O2614 10 l. light green and green 65 10
O2615 25 l. yellow and red 1·25 10

O 540

O 552

O 573

1979.

O2647 O 540 50 k. deep orange and orange 10 10
O2648 2½ l. blue & lt blue 15 10

1979.

O2686 O 552 50 k. violet & pink 10 10
O2687 1 l. red and green 10 10
O2688 2½ l. mauve and light mauve 10 10

O2689 O **552** 5 l. purple & blue . 15 10
O2690 7½ l. blue and lilac . 20 10
O2691 10 l. blue and buff . 25 10
O2692 35 l. purple & silver . 45 10
O2693 50 l. blue and pink . 65 10

1981.
O2756 O **573** 5 l. red and yellow . 50 10
O2757 10 l. red and pink . 60 10
O2758 35 l. mauve & grey . 75 10
O2759 50 l. blue and pink . 1·25 10
O2760 75 l. emerald & green 1·75 10
O2761 100 l. blue & lt blue 2·50 10

O 606 O 644 O 720

1983.
O2839 O **606** 5 l. blue & yellow . 10 10
O2840 15 l. blue & yellow . 15 10
O2841 20 l. blue and grey . 15 10
O2842 50 l. blue and lt blue 40 10
O2843 65 l. blue & mauve . 70 10
O2844 70 l. blue and pink . 25 10
O2845 90 l. blue & brown . 95 10
O2846 90 l. blue & lt blue . 45 10
O2847 100 l. blue & green . 60 10
O2848 125 l. blue & green . 1·00 10
O2849 230 l. blue & orange 1·10 10

1986.
O2946 O **644** 5 l. blue and yellow . 10 10
O2947 10 l. blue and pink . 10 10
O2948 20 l. blue and grey . 10 10
O2949 50 l. blue & lt blue . 15 10
O2950 100 l. blue & green . 40 10
O2951 300 l. blue and lilac . 65 10

1989. Various stamps surch.
O3039 O **644** 500 l. on 10 l. blue and pink 25 10
O3040 O **606** 500 l. on 15 l. blue and yellow 25 10
O3041 O **644** 500 l. on 20 l. blue and grey 25 10
O3042 O **606** 1000 l. on 70 l. blue and pink 50 10
O3043 1000 l. on 90 l. blue and brown 50 10
O3044 1250 l. on 230 l. blue and orange . . . 85 10

1991. Nos. O2843 and O2846 surch.
O3108 O **606** 100 l. on 65 l. blue and mauve 10 10
O3109 250 l. on 90 l. blue and light blue 10 10

1992.
O3138 O **720** 3000 l. deep brown and brown 45 15
O3139 5000 l. grn & lt grn . 1·00 25

O 733 O 743 O 753

1992.
O3167 O **733** 1000 l. blue & green 15 10
O3168 10000 l. green & blue 1·40 45

1993.
O3196 O **743** 1000 l. green & brn . 10 10
O3197 1500 l. green & brn . 10 10
O3198 5000 l. brn & green . 20 10

1994.
O3218 O **753** 2500 l. dp mve & mve 10 10
O3219 25000 l. brn & stone 1·25 25

O 764 O 770 O 775

1995.
O3243 O **764** 3500 l. violet and light violet 10 10
O3244 17500 l. green and light green 35 10

1995.
O3252 O **770** 50000 l. green and olive 1·00 35

1995.
O3267 O **775** 5000 l. red and orange 10 10

O 785

1996.
O3288 O **785** 15000 l. red and blue 20 10
O3289 – 20000 l. violet and green 25 10
O3290 – 50000 l. green and violet 65 20
O3291 – 100000 l. blue and red 1·25 40
DESIGNS: 20000 l. Hearts forming pattern; 50000 l. Leaves forming pattern; 100000 l. Ornate scroll pattern.

POSTAGE DUE STAMPS

D 2 D 4

1863. Imperf.
D 7 D **2** 20 pa. black on brown . 55·00 22·00
D 8 1 pi. black on brown . . 66·00 24·00
D 9 2 pi. black on brown . . £225 65·00
D10 5 pi. black on brown . . £100 55·00

1865.
D18 D **4** 20 pa. brown . . . . . 15 1·00
D19 1 pi. brown 15 90
D74 2 pi. brown . . . . . . 30 1·00
D70 5 pi. brown . . . . . . 25 2·50
D76 25 pi. brown . . . . . 5·00 12·00

1888. As T **9**.
D117 **9** 20 pa. black . . . . . . 1·50 45
D118 1 pi. black 25 75
D119 2 pi. black . . . . 25 1·00

1892. As T **15**.
D146 **15** 20 pa. black . . . . . . 1·50 45
D147 20 pa. black on red . . 20 50
D148 1 pi. black . . . . 2·75 95
D149 2 pi. black . . . . 1·25 60

1901. As T **21**.
D195 **21** 10 pa. black on red . . 55 30
D196 20 pa. black on red . . 60 50
D197 1 pi. black on red . . . 50 45
D198 2 pi. black on red . . . 75 45

1905. As T **23**.
D228 **23** 1 pi. black on red . . . 85 75
D229 2 pi. black on red . . . 1·75 1·75

1908. As T **25**.
D250 **25** 1 pi. black on red . . . 15·00 1·50
D251 2 pi. black on red . . . 2·00 4·75

1909. As T **28**.
D288 **28** 1 pi. black on red . . . 2·50 7·50
D287 2 pi. black on red . . . 18·00 20·00

1913. As T **30**.
D347 **30** 2 pa. black on red . . . 10 40
D348 5 pa. black on red . . . 10 40
D349 10 pa. black on red . . . 10 40
D350 20 pa. black on red . . . 10 40
D351 1 pi. black on red . . . 85 75
D352 2 pi. black on red . . . 1·75 3·25

1913. Adrianople Issue surch.
D356 **31** 2 pa. on 10 pa. green . . 30 15
D357 5 pa. on 20 pa. red . . . 40 30
D358 10 pa. on 40 pa. blue . . 1·25 60
D359 20 pa. on 40 pa. blue . . 3·50 1·75

D 49 D 50

D 51 D 52

1914.
D516 D **49** 5 pa. brown . . . . . 40 1·25
D517 D **50** 20 pa. red . . . . . . 40 1·00
D518 D **51** 1 pi. blue . . . . 75 1·25
D519 D **52** 2 pi. blue . . . . 1·50 1·75

AD 26 D **101** Bridge over Kizil Irmak

1921.
AD91 AD **26** 20 pa. green 20 45
AD92 1 pi. green 30 50
AD93 2 pi. brown . . . . . 1·10 1·10
AD94 3 pi. red . . . . . . 1·75 2·25
AD95 5 pi. blue . . . . . . 2·25 2·75

1926.
D1035 D **101** 20 pa. orange . . . 35 20
D1036 1 gr. red . . . . . . 1·00 25
D1037 2 gr. green . . . . . 1·10 45
D1038 3 gr. purple . . . . . 1·60 50
D1039 5 gr. violet . . . . . 3·75 1·45

D 121

1936.
D1186 D **121** 20 pa. brown 10 10
D1187 2 k. blue 10 10
D1188 3 k. violet 10 10
D1189 5 k. green 10 10
D1190 12 k. red 10 10

PRINTED MATTER STAMPS

1879. Optd **IMPRIMES** in scroll.
N88 **9** 10 pa. black and mauve . . . 65·00 45·00

(N 14)

1891. Stamps of 1876 optd with Type N **14**.
N132 **9** 10 pa. green . . . . 4·75 2·50
N134 20 pa. pink . . . . 6·50 2·00
N136 1 pi. blue . . . . 28·00 10·00
N138 2 pi. yellow . . . . £170 35·00
N139 5 pi. brown £225 £130

1892. Stamps of 1892 optd with Type N **14**.
N150 **15** 10 pa. green . . . . . . 35·00 5·00
N151 20 pa. red . . . . 60·00 24·00
N152 1 pi. blue . . . . 15·00 8·00
N153 2 pi. brown . . . . 24·00 12·00
N154 5 pi. purple £350 £350

(N 16) (N 23) (N 27)

1894. Stamps of 1892 optd with Type N **16**.
N161 **15** 5 pa. on 10 pa. grn (160) 40 20
N155 10 pa. green 20 15
N156a 20 pa. red 20 15
N157 1 pi. blue 20 15
N158 2 pi. brown . . . . 4·50 1·50
N159 5 pi. purple . . . . . . 25·00 7·50

1901. Stamps of 1901 optd with Type N **23**.
N183 **21** 5 pa. violet 25 15
N184 10 pa. green . . . . . . 2·75 50
N185 20 pa. red 15 10
N186 1 pi. blue . . . . 1·50 20
N187 2 pi. orange . . . . . . 7·50 1·10
N188 5 pi. mauve . . . . . . 15·00 6·50

1901. Stamps of 1901 optd with Type N **23**.
N189 **22** 5 pa. brown 20 20
N190 10 pa. green 65 35
N191 20 pa. mauve . . . . . . 2·40 1·40
N192 1 pi. blue . . . . 3·75 1·90
N193 2 pi. blue . . . . 20·00 9·00
N194 5 pi. brown . . . . . . 30·00 16·00

1905. Stamps of 1905 optd with Type N **23**.
N222 **23** 5 pa. brown 20 10
N223 10 pa. green . . . . . . 2·75 80
N224 20 pa. pink 40 10
N225 1 pi. blue 40 10
N226 2 pi. blue . . . . 9·00 3·00
N227 5 pi. brown . . . . . . 15·00 5·00

1908. Stamps of 1908 optd with Type N **27**.
N244 **25** 5 pa. brown . . . . . . 2·00 15
N245 10 pa. green . . . . . . 2·00 25
N246 20 pa. red . . . . 2·10 55
N247 1 pi. blue . . . . 5·50 75
N248 2 pi. black . . . . 14·00 2·25
N249 5 pi. purple . . . . . . 22·00 4·00

1909. Stamps of 1909 optd with Type N **27**.
N276 **28** 5 pa. brown 45 15
N277 10 pa. green 70 15
N278 20 pa. red . . . . 5·50 75
N279 1 pi. blue . . . . 12·00 2·25
N280 2 pi. black . . . . 25·00 12·00
N281 5 pi. purple . . . . . . 28·00 12·00

1911. New value of 1909 issue.
N332 **28** 2 pa. olive 10 10

1920. No. 500 surch.
N961 – 5 on 4 pa. brown 10 45

INDEX

Countries can be quickly located by referring to the index at the end of this volume.

TURKMENISTAN Pt. 10

Formerly a constituent republic of the Soviet Union, Turkmenistan became independent on 27 October, 1991.

1992. 100 kopeks = 1 rouble.
1994. 100 tenge = 1 manat.

1 19th-century Gold and Jewelled Bib **2** Asiatic Wild Ass

1992. Treasure in National Museum.
1 **1** 50 k. multicoloured . . . . . 1·25 1·25
See also No. 4.

1992. Animals of Central Asia. Multicoloured.
2 20 k. Type **2** 15 15
3 40 k. Cobra (vert) 35 35

3 President Saparmyrat Niyazov and Reverse of National Flag

1992. History and Culture.
4 10 r. Type **1** 75 75
5 10 r. Girl in traditional dress and Kopet-Daga Mountains . . . 75 75
6 10 r. Mollanepes Drama Theatre, Ashkhabad 75 75
7 10 r. Akhaltekin horseman (vert) 75 75
8 15 r. Arms (vert) . . . . 1·10 1·10
9 25 r. Type **3** . . . . 1·50 1·50
For similar design to Type **3** but with flag reversed, see No. 12.

4 Traditional Musical Instruments

1992.
11 **4** 35 k. multicoloured 60 60

5 National Flag and President Saparmyrat Niyazov

1992. 1st Anniv of Independence.
12 **5** 25 r. multicoloured . . . . . 1·50 1·50
For similar design but with flag reversed, see No 9.

6 Carpet

1992.
13 **6** 1 r. multicoloured 35 35

1992. Nos. 7/8 optd with horse's head.
14 10 r. multicoloured 25 25
15 15 r. multicoloured 60 60

8 Weightlifting

1993. Olympic Games, Barcelona. Multicoloured.

(a) As T **8**.

16	1 r. Type **8**	10	10
17	3 r. Show jumping	40	40
18	5 r. Wrestling	60	60
19	10 r. Canoeing	1·40	1·40
20	15 r. National Olympic emblem	2·25	2·25

(b) Nos. 16/20 surch.

21	10 r. on 3 r. Show jumping	45	45
22	15 r. on 5 r. Wrestling	70	70
23	15 r. on 10 r. Canoeing	70	70
24	25 r. on 1 r. Type **8**	1·10	1·10
25	50 r. on 15 r. National Olympic emblem	2·25	2·25

10 Presidents William Clinton and Niyazov

1993. Visit of President Saparmyrat Niyazov to United States of America. Type **10** with different dates. Multicoloured.

27	**10**	100 r. Dated "21.03.93"	90	90
28		100 r. Dated "22.03.93"	90	90
29		100 r. Dated "23.03.93"	90	90
30		100 r. Dated "24.03.93"	90	90
31		100 r. Dated "25.03.93"	90	90

11 Seal on Ice

1993. The Caspian Seal. Multicoloured.

32	15 r. Type **11**	10	10
33	25 r. Seal on sandy beach	10	10
34	50 r. Seal on pebble beach	15	15
35	100 r. Adult with young	35	35
36	150 r. Seal swimming	50	50
37	500 r. Seal on sandy beach (different)	1·75	1·75

Nos. 33 and 37 were issued together, se-tenant, forming a composite design.

12 Sulphur Spring, Cheleken

1994. 115th Anniv of Nobel Partnership to Exploit Black Sea Oil. Multicoloured.

38	1 m. Type **12**	40	40
39	1 m. 50 "Turkmen" (oil tanker)	60	60
40	2 m. Drilling in Cheleken	75	75
41	3 m. Nobel brothers and Petr Bilderling (partners) (vert)	1·25	1·25

13 Repetek Institute

1994. Repetek Nature Reserve. Multicoloured.

43	3 m. Type **13**	25	35
44	5 m. Dromedaries in Repetek Desert	80	80
45	5 m. Saw-scaled viper	80	80
46	10 m. Transcaspian desert monitor	1·60	1·60
47	20 m. Tortoise	3·25	3·25

14 Emblem

1994. Centenary of International Olympic Committee.

49	**14**	11 m. 25 multicoloured	1·75	1·75

TUSCANY Pt. 8

Formerly an independent duchy in C. Italy, now part of Italy.

1851. 60 quattrini = 20 soldi = 12 crazie = 1 Tuscan lira.
1859. 1 Tuscan lira = 1 Italian lira.

1 Arms of Tuscany

5 Arms of Savoy

1851. Imperf.

No.	Type	Description	Unused	Used
1	**1**	1 q. black on blue	£4000	£900
2		1 q. black on grey	£3000	£900
24		1 q. black	£400	£500
4		1 s. orange on blue	£6000	£1200
5		1 s. orange on grey	£5000	£1200
25		1 s. buff	£15000	£2750
6		2 s. red on blue	£20000	£4000
7		1 c. red on blue	£3000	£100
9		1 c. red on grey	£2000	25·00
26		1 c. red	£3000	£130
10		2 c. blue on blue	£3000	70·00
11		2 c. blue on grey	£1200	24·00
28		2 c. blue	£800	24·00
13		4 c. green on blue	£3500	£140
14		4 c. green on grey	£2250	40·00
30		4 c. green	£2750	65·00
16		6 c. blue on blue	£3500	£100
17		6 c. blue on grey	£2500	40·00
31		6 c. blue	£3000	50·00
20		9 c. purple on blue	£650	£175
22		9 c. purple on grey	£6000	70·00
33		9 c. brown	£10000	£3000
23		60 c. red on blue	£35000	£12000

1860. Imperf.

No.	Type	Description	Unused	Used
36	**5**	1 c. purple	£700	£375
40		5 c. green	£3000	90·00
43		10 c. brown	£500	12·00
45		20 c. blue	£2500	50·00
48		40 c. red	£3500	£100
50		80 c. red	£10000	£500
51		3 l. buff	£110000	£48000

NEWSPAPER STAMP TAX

N 3

1854.

No.	Type	Description	Unused	Used
N1	**N 3**	2 s. black	13·00	

TUVA Pt. 10

A province lying between the Sajan and Tannu Ola range. Formerly known as North Mongolia and Tannu, Tuva was incorporated into the U.S.S.R. on 11th October 1944.

PRICES. The prices quoted in the used column are for stamps cancelled to order where these occur. Postally used copies are worth considerably more.

1926. 100 kopeks = 1 rouble.
1934. 100 kopeks = 1 tugrik.
1936. 100 kopeks = 1 aksha.

1 Wheel of Eternity

1926.

No.	Type	Description	Unused	Used
1	**1**	1 k. red	1·00	1·10
2		2 k. blue	1·00	1·10
3		5 k. orange	1·10	1·10
4		8 k. green	1·25	1·25
5		10 k. violet	1·25	1·25
6		30 k. brown	1·50	1·25
7		50 k. black	1·50	1·25
8		1 r. turquoise	2·25	2·25
9		3 r. red	4·00	4·50
10		5 r. blue	7·00	6·00

The rouble values are larger $22\frac{1}{2} \times 30$ mm.

1927. Surch **TOUVA POSTAGE** and value.

No.	Type	Description	Unused	Used
11	**1**	8 k. on 50 k. black	4·75	5·50
12		14 k. on 1 r. turquoise	5·00	5·50
13		18 k. on 3 r. red	7·50	9·00
14		28 k. on 5 r. blue	8·00	9·50

4 Tuvan Woman

5 Map of Tuva

6 Mongolian Sheep and Tents

7 Fording a River

8 Reindeer
($\frac{2}{3}$-size illustration)

1927.

No.	Type	Description	Unused	Used
15	**4**	1 k. brown, red and black	40	35
16	–	2 k. brown, green & violet	80	45
17	–	3 k. green, yellow & black	1·25	50
18	–	4 k. brown and blue	45	35
19	–	5 k. blue, black and orange	45	35
20	**5**	8 k. sepia, blue and red	55	55
21	–	10 k. red, black and green	3·50	75
22	–	14 k. orange and blue	6·50	3·25
23	**6**	18 k. brown and blue	7·00	3·50
24	–	28 k. sepia and green	4·50	2·25
25	**7**	40 k. green and red	3·25	2·00
26	–	50 k. brown, black and green	2·50	1·75
27	–	70 k. bistre and red	4·00	2·75
28	**8**	1 r. violet and brown	7·50	5·50

DESIGNS—As Type **4**: 2 k. Red deer; 3 k. Common goral; 4 k. Mongolian tent; 5 k. Tuvan man. As Type **5**: 10 k. Archers; 14 k. Camel caravan. As Type **6**: 28 k. Landscape. As Type **7**: 50 k. Girl carpet-weaver; 70 k. Horseman.

1932. Stamps of 1927 surch **TbBA POSTA** and value (10 k. optd only).

No.	Type	Description	Unused	Used
29	**7**	1 k. on 40 k. green and red	4·75	6·50
30	–	2 k. on 50 k. brown, black and green	5·00	5·50
31	–	3 k. on 70 k. bistre and red	5·50	5·50
32	**5**	5 k. on 8 k. sep, blue & red	5·50	5·50
33	–	10 k. red, black and green	6·00	7·50
34	–	15 k. on 14 k. orange & blue	6·50	7·00

1932. Stamps of 1927 surch.

No.	Type	Description	Unused	Used
35	**5**	10 k. on 8 k. brown	£120	
36	–	15 k. on 14 k. orange & blue	£120	
37	**6**	35 k. on 18 k. brown & blue	48·00	60·00
38	–	35 k. on 28 k. sepia and green	55·00	70·00

1933. Fiscal stamps (20 × 39 mm) surch **Posta** and value. (a) Numerals $6\frac{3}{4}$ mm tall.

No.	Type	Description	Unused	Used
39		15 k. on 6 k. yellow	55·00	70·00
40		35 k. on 15 k. brown	£190	£275

(b) Numerals $5\frac{1}{4}$ mm tall.

No.	Type	Description	Unused	Used
41		15 k. on 6 k. yellow	70·00	90·00
42		35 k. on 15 k. brown	£225	£350

12 Mounted Hunter

13 Interior of Tent

14 Yak

1934. Perf or imperf.

No.	Type	Description	Unused	Used
43	**12**	1 k. orange	75	40
44	–	2 k. green	90	75
45	**13**	3 k. red	90	75
46	–	4 k. purple	1·50	1·50
47	**14**	5 k. blue	1·50	1·50
48	–	10 k. brown	1·50	1·50
49	–	15 k. lake	1·50	1·50
50	–	20 k. black	2·25	2·00

DESIGNS—As Type **12**: 2 k. Hunter. As Type **13**: 4 k. Tractor. As Type **14**: 10 k. Camel caravan; 15 k. Lassoing reindeer; 20 k. Corsac fox-hunting.

15 Yaks

16 Capercaillie

1934 Air.

No.	Type	Description	Unused	Used
51	**15**	1 k. red	85	75
52	–	5 k. green	85	75
53	**16**	10 k. brown	2·75	2·25
54	–	15 k. red	1·60	75
55	–	25 k. purple	1·60	75
56	**15**	50 k. green	1·60	75
57	–	75 k. red	1·60	75
58	**15**	1 t. blue	1·60	1·25
59	–	2 t. blue (55 × 28 mm)	2·10	2·25

DESIGNS (embodying monoplane) As Type **15**: 5, 15 k. Camels. As Type **16**: 25 k. Argali; 75 k. Ox-cart; 2 t. Roe deer.

The 2 t. also comes larger, 61 × 31 mm.

1935. No. 49 surch.

No.	Type	Description	Unused	Used
60		20 k. on 15 k. lake	85·00	

18 Map of Tuva

19 Rocky Outcrop

1935. Landscapes.

No.	Type	Description	Unused	Used
61	**18**	1 k. orange	75	75
62	–	3 k. green	75	75
63	–	5 k. red	90	75
64	–	10 k. violet	90	75
65	**19**	15 k. green	90	95
66	–	25 k. blue	90	95
67	–	50 k. sepia	90	1·00

DESIGNS—As Type **18**: 3, 5, 10 k. Views of River Yenisei. As Type **19**: 25 k. Bei-kem rapids; 50 k. Mounted hunter.

20 Eurasian Badger

21 Corsac Fox

22 Elk

1935. Animals.

No.	Type	Description	Unused	Used
68	**20**	1 k. orange	90	85
69	–	3 k. green	90	85
70	–	5 k. mauve	90	90
71	**21**	10 k. red	90	90
72	–	25 k. red	1·00	1·00
73	–	50 k. blue	1·00	1·00
74	**22**	1 t. violet	1·00	1·00
75	–	2 t. blue	1·00	1·00
76	–	3 t. brown	1·10	1·10
77	–	5 t. blue	1·25	1·25

DESIGNS—As Type **20**—VERT: 3 k. Eurasian red squirrel. HORIZ: 5 k. Sable. As Type **21**: 25 k. European Otter; 50 k. Lynx. LARGER (61 × 31 mm): 2 t. Yak; 3 k. Bactrian camel. As Type **22**: 5 t. Brown bear.

See also No. 115.

23 Arms of Republic

24 Wrestlers

25 Herdsman

26 Sports Meeting

27 Partisans

1936. 15th Anniv of Independence. (a) Postage.

No.	Type	Description	Unused	Used
78	**23**	1 k. green	1·10	55
79	–	2 k. sepia	1·10	55
80	–	3 k. blue	1·25	60
81	**24**	4 k. red	1·50	60
82	–	5 k. purple	2·50	50
83	**24**	6 k. green	2·50	50
84	–	8 k. purple	2·25	55
85	–	10 k. red	2·50	50
86	–	12 k. agate	3·25	75
87	–	15 k. green	3·50	55
88	–	20 k. blue	3·50	75
89	**25**	25 k. red	3·00	55
90	–	30 k. purple	6·00	1·00
91	**25**	35 k. red	2·50	55
92	–	40 k. sepia	2·50	55
93	–	50 k. blue	2·50	55
94	**26**	70 k. plum	3·50	1·10
95	–	80 k. green	3·00	1·10
96	**27**	1 a. red	3·00	1·10
97		2 a. red	3·00	1·10
98	–	3 a. blue	3·25	1·10
99	–	5 a. agate	3·25	1·40

DESIGNS—As Type **23**: 2 k. President Gyrmittazi; 3 k. Camel and driver. As Type **24**: 5, 8 k. Archers; 10, 15 k. Fishermen; 12, 20 k. Brown bear hunt. As Type **25**: 30 k. Bactrian camel and steam train; 40, 50 k. Horse-racing. As Type **26**: 8 k., 5 a. 1921 war scene; 3 a. Confiscation of cattle.

See also Nos. 116 and 118/19.

28 Yak Transport

29 Horseman and Airship

30 Seaplane over Waves

(b) Air.

No.	Type	Description	Unused	Used
100	**28**	5 k. blue and flesh	2·25	75
101	–	10 k. purple and brown	2·50	80
102	**28**	15 k. agate and grey	2·50	80
103	**29**	25 k. purple and cream	3·50	90
104	–	50 k. red and cream	3·00	1·10
105	**29**	75 k. green and yellow	3·00	1·10
106	**30**	1 a. green and turquoise	3·00	1·25
107		2 a. red and cream	3·50	1·25
108		3 a. sepia and flesh	3·50	2·00

DESIGNS—As Type **28**: 10 k. Horse-drawn reaper. As Type **29**: 50 k. Feast of the women.

See also No. 117.

1938. Various stamps surch with large numerals and old values obliterated.

109	5 k. on 2 a. red (No. 97)
110	5 k. on 2 a. red and cream (No. 107)
111	10 k. on 1 t. blue (No. 58)
112	20 k. on 50 k. sepia (No. 67)
113	30 k. on 2 a. red and cream (No. 107)
114	30 k. on 3 a. sepia & flesh (No. 108)

See also Nos. 120/1.

1938. Previous types with designs modified and colours changed.

No.	Description	Unused
115	5 k. green (No. 70)	85·00
116	10 k. blue (No. 85)	90·00
117	15 k. brown (No. 102)	85·00
118	20 k. red (No. 88)	£225
119	30 k. purple (as No. 95)	£100

In Nos. 116/19 the dates have been removed and in No. 117 "AIR MAIL" also.

1939. Nos. 58 and 67 surch with small thick numerals and old values obliterated.

120	1 k. on 1 t. blue
121	20 k. on 50 k. sepia

See also Nos. 122/3.

1940. Various stamps surch.

122	10 k. on 1 t. blue (No. 58)
123	20 k. on 50 k. sepia (No. 67)
124	20 k. on 50 k. blue (No. 73)
125	20 k. on 50 k. blue (No. 93)
126	20 k. on 50 k. red on cream (No. 104)
127	20 k. on 75 k. green and yellow (No. 105)
128	20 k. on 80 k. green (No. 95)

1942. Nos. 98/9 surch.

129	25 k. on 3 a. blue
130	25 k. on 5 a. agate

34 Tuvan Woman

1942. 21st Anniv of Independence. Imperf.

No.	Type	Description	Unused
131	**34**	25 k. blue	£225
132	–	25 k. blue	£225
133	–	25 k. blue	£225

DESIGNS: No. 132 Agricultural Exhibition building; No. 133 Government building.

35 Coat of Arms

36 Government Building

1943. 22nd Anniv of Independence. With or without gum.

No.	Type	Description	Unused
134	**35**	25 k. blue	20·00
135		25 k. black	30·00
136		25 k. green	60·00
137	**36**	50 k. green	60·00

UBANGI-SHARI Pt. 6

Formerly part of the French Congo. Ubangi-Shari became a separate colony in 1904 (although stamps of the French Congo continued to be used until 1915). From 1915 to 1922 it shared a postal administration with Chad.

From 1936 to 1958 Ubangi-Shari was part of French Equatorial Africa. In December 1958 it became the autonomous state of the Central African Republic.

100 centimes = 1 franc

A. UBANGI-SHARI-CHAD

1915. Stamps of Middle Congo optd **OUBANGUI-CHARI-TCHAD**.

No.	Type	Description	Unused	Used
1	**1**	1 c. green and brown	25	40
2		2 c. violet and brown	20	45
3		4 c. blue and brown	40	65
4		5 c. green and blue	30	50
19		5 c. yellow and blue	65	70
5		10 c. red and blue	70	80
20		10 c. green and turquoise	55	65
5a		15 c. purple and pink	1·40	1·40
6		20 c. brown and blue	2·25	2·50
7	**2**	25 c. blue and green	75	85
21		25 c. green and black	55	60
8		30 c. red and green	65	70
22		30 c. red	55	65
9		35 c. brown and blue	3·75	4·50
10		40 c. green and brown	3·75	5·50
11		45 c. violet and orange	3·50	5·50
12		50 c. green and orange	4·25	6·75
23		50 c. blue and green	55	70
13		75 c. brown and blue	9·00	11·00
14	**3**	1 f. green and violet	9·75	11·00
15		2 f. violet and green	10·00	11·00
16		5 f. blue and pink	35·00	38·00

1916. No. 5 surch **5c** and cross.

No.	Description	Unused	Used
18	10 c. + 5 c. red and blue	55	80

B. UBANGI-SHARI

1922. Stamps of Middle Congo, new colours, optd **OUBANGUI-CHARI**.

No.	Type	Description	Unused	Used
24	**1**	1 c. violet and green	35	55
25		2 c. green and pink	50	65
26		4 c. brown and purple	60	80
27		5 c. blue and pink	75	95
28		10 c. green and turquoise	1·40	1·40
29		15 c. pink and blue	1·50	1·90
30		20 c. brown and pink	4·00	5·75
31	**2**	25 c. violet and pink	3·00	5·00
32		30 c. red	2·00	3·00
33		35 c. violet and green	3·75	5·50
34		40 c. blue and mauve	3·25	5·00
35		45 c. brown and mauve	3·25	5·00
36		50 c. blue and light blue	2·00	3·00
37		60 on 75 c. violet on pink	2·50	3·25
38		75 c. brown and pink	3·50	5·75
39	**3**	1 f. green and blue	4·25	5·75
40		2 f. green and pink	5·25	8·00
41		5 f. green and brown	12·50	16·00

1924. Stamps of 1922 and similar stamps additionally overprinted **AFRIQUE EQUATORIALE FRANCAISE**.

No.	Type	Description	Unused	Used
42	**1**	1 c. violet and green	10	45
43		2 c. green and pink	10	45
44		4 c. brown and chocolate	10	45
44c		4 c. brown	1·10	1·10
45		5 c. blue and pink	15	45
46		10 c. green and turquoise	40	55
47		10 c. red and blue	30	45
48		15 c. pink and blue	45	75
49		20 c. brown and pink	40	65
50	**2**	25 c. violet and pink	45	30
51		30 c. red	35	45
52		30 c. brown and pink	45	45
53		30 c. olive and green	75	90
54		35 c. violet and green	20	45
55		40 c. blue and mauve	50	60
56		45 c. brown and mauve	55	70
57		50 c. blue and light blue	55	55
58		50 c. grey and blue	1·00	80
59		60 on 75 c. violet on pink	50	55
60		65 c. brown and blue	1·75	1·90
61		75 c. brown and pink	75	80
62		75 c. blue and light blue	50	60
63		75 c. purple and brown	1·60	1·90
64		90 c. pink and red	4·25	5·75
65a	**3**	1 f. green and blue	50	60
66		1 f. 10 brown and blue	2·00	2·25
67		1 f. 25 mauve and green	4·25	5·25
68		1 f. 50 ultramarine & blue	5·75	6·75
69		1 f. 75 brown and orange	7·50	7·50
70		2 f. green and pink	80	80
71		3 f. mauve on pink	5·25	5·50
72		5 f. green and brown	3·50	3·50

1925. As last but new colours and surch.

No.	Type	Description	Unused	Used
73	**3**	65 on 1 f. violet and brown	50	1·40
74		85 on 1 f. violet and brown	1·00	1·40
75	**2**	90 on 75 c. pink and red	95	1·40
76	**3**	1 f. 25 on 1 f. blue & ultram	70	80
77		1 f. 50 on 1 f. ultram & blue	1·00	85
78		3 f. on 5 f. brown and red	1·90	2·25
79		10 f. on 5 f. red and mauve	12·00	16·00
80		20 f. on 5 f. mauve and grey	20·00	23·00

1931. "International Colonial Exhibition" key-types inscr "OUBANGUI-CHARI".

No.	Type	Description	Unused	Used
103	E	40 c. green	3·00	4·50
104	F	50 c. mauve	3·00	3·75
105	G	90 c. red	3·00	4·50
106	H	1 f. 50 blue	3·50	3·75

POSTAGE DUE STAMPS

1928. Postage Due type of France optd **OUBANGUI-CHARI A. E. F.**

No.	Type	Description	Unused	Used
D81	D **11**	5 c. blue	85	1·90
D82		10 c. brown	1·00	1·90
D83		20 c. olive	1·40	1·90
D84		25 c. red	1·40	1·90
D85		30 c. red	1·40	1·90
D86		45 c. green	1·40	1·90
D87		50 c. purple	1·60	2·25
D88		60 c. brown on cream	1·90	2·75
D89		1 f. red on cream	2·25	3·50
D90		2 f. red	2·50	4·50
D91		3 f. violet	2·50	4·50

D **12** Mobaye D **13** E. Gentil

1930.

No.	Type	Description	Unused	Used
D 92	D **12**	5 c. olive and blue	40	80
D 93		10 c. brown and red	50	1·10
D 94		20 c. brown and green	80	1·40
D 95		25 c. brown and blue	1·10	1·40
D 96		30 c. green and brown	1·60	2·25
D 97		45 c. olive and green	2·50	3·50
D 98		50 c. brown and mauve	4·25	6·25
D 99		60 c. black and violet	5·00	6·75
D100	D **13**	1 f. black and brown	1·75	2·50
D101		2 f. brown and mauve	2·00	4·00
D102		3 f. brown and red	2·50	6·00

UKRAINE Pt. 10

A district of S.W. Russia, which issued stamps during its temporary independence after the Russian Revolution. In 1923 it became a constituent republic of the U.S.S.R.

In 1991 it became an independent republic.

1918. 100 shagiv = 1 grivna or hriven;
2 grivni or hriven = 1 rouble;
100 kopeks = 1 rouble.
1992 (Nov). Karbovanets (coupon currency).
1996. 100 kopiykas = 1 hyrvna.

(6)

(8)

1918. Arms types of Russia optd with Trident device in various types according to the district. Imperf or perf.

No.	Type	Description	Unused	Used
L 51	**22**	1 k. orange	10	10
L 52		2 k. green	10	10
L 53		3 k. red	10	10
L 54	**23**	4 k. red	10	10
L 55	**22**	5 k. red	10	10
L138		7 k. blue	10	10
L 57	**23**	10 k. blue	10	10
L 58	**22**	10 k. on 7 k. blue	15	10
L159	**9**	14 k. red and blue	15	20
L 60		15 k. blue and purple	10	10
L 61	**14**	20 k. red and blue	10	10
L 62	**9**	20 k. on 14 k. red & blue	10	10
L145		25 k. mauve and green	10	25
L 64		35 k. green and purple	10	10
L 65	**14**	50 k. green and purple	10	10
L 66	**9**	70 k. orange and brown	10	10
L 47	**15**	1 r. orange and brown	15	15
L 72	**11**	3 r. 50 grey and black	10·00	16·00
L212		3 r. 50 green and brown	20	20
L 49	**20**	5 r. blue and green	40	60
L 73	**11**	7 r. yellow and black	7·00	10·00
L 14		7 r. pink and green	90	2·00
L 36	**20**	10 r. grey, red and yellow	5·50	6·50

1 Trident (from Arms of Grand Duke Vladimir the Great)

2 Peasant

3 Ceres

4 Trident

5

1918. Without inscription on back. Imperf.

No.	Type	Description	Unused	Used
1	**1**	10 s. brown on buff	20	50
2	**2**	20 s. brown	20	50
3	**3**	30 s. blue	20	50
4	**4**	40 s. green	20	50
5	**5**	50 s. red	20	50

1918. With trident and four lines of inscription on back.

No.	Type	Description	Unused	Used
6	**1**	10 s. brown	2·50	5·00
7	**2**	20 s. brown	2·50	5·00
8	**3**	30 s. blue	2·50	5·00
9	**4**	40 d. green	2·50	5·00
10	**5**	50 s. red	2·50	5·00

6a Trident

6b Parliament Building

Stamps of the above and similar designs were prepared for use but never used.

7 Spectre of Famine

8 T. G. Shevchenko (Ukrainian poet)

1923. Charity.

12 7 10+10 k. blue and black . . 1·00 2·25
13 8 20+20 k. brown & orange . 1·00 2·25
14 – 90+30 k. black and bistre . . 2·00 4·50
15 – 150+50 k. red and black . . 4·00 6·00

DESIGNS—VERT: 90 k. "Death" and peasant; 150 k. "Ukraine" (woman) distributing bread.

11 Cossack Chief with Musician and Standard Bearer

12 Ukrainian Emigrant Couple

1992. 500th Anniv (1990) of Ukraine Cossacks.

20 11 15 k. multicoloured 40 40

1992. Centenary (1991) of Ukrainian Emigration to Canada.

21 12 15 k. multicoloured 40 40

13 Mykola Lysenko and Score from "Taras Bulba"

1992. 150th Birth Anniv of Mykola Lysenko (composer).

22 13 1 r. brown, red and bistre . 1·10 1·10

14 Mykola Kostamarov, Quill, Pen and Scroll

15 Ceres

1992. 175th Birth Anniv of Mykola Kostamarov (historian).

23 14 20 k. brown and light brown 35 35

1992.

24 15 50 k. blue 10 10
25 70 k. brown 10 10
26 1 r. green 10 20
27 2 r. violet 15 15
28 5 r. blue 30 30
29 10 r. red 40 40
30 20 r. green 80 80
31 50 r. brown . . . . 2·00 2·00

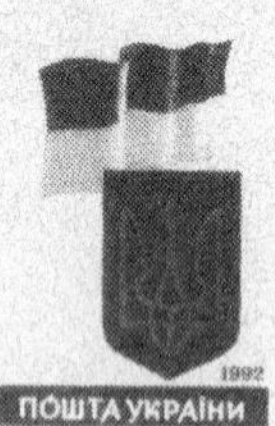

16 Gymnastics

17 Ukraine Flag and Trident Symbol

1992. Olympic Games, Barcelona. Multicoloured.

32 3 r. Type 16 . . . . 25 25
33 4 r. Pole vaulting 45 45
34 5 r. Type 16 . . . . 50 50

1992. 1st Anniv of Regained Independence.

35 17 2 r. multicoloured 35 35

18 Three Cranes on Globe

1992. World Congress of Ukrainians, Kiev.

36 18 2 r. multicoloured 35 35

20 U.P.U. Symbol and Hand writing

1992. Correspondence Week.

38 20 5 r. multicoloured 50 50

21 Congress Emblem

1992. World Congress of Ukrainian Jurists, Kiev.

39 21 15 r. multicoloured . . . . 1·25 1·25

22 Embroidery

1992. Ukraine Folk Art.

40 22 0.50 k. black and orange . 10 10

23 Arms of Austria and Ukraine with Traditional Costumes of Galicia and Bukovina

1992. Ukrainians in Austria.

41 23 5 k. multicoloured . . . . 1·25 1·25

24 Laying Foundation Stone, 1632

1992. 360th Anniv of Mogilyanska's Academy, Kiev.

42 24 1 k. 50 black, blue & brown 35 35

26 Lvov Arms

27 Cardinal Slipij

1993. Regional Arms.

44 26 3 k. blue, dp blue & gold . 95 95
45 – 5 k. lake, gold and red . . 1·25 1·25

DESIGN: 5 k. Kiev.

1993. Birth Centenary (1992) of Cardinal Joseph Slipij.

68 27 15 k. multicoloured . . . . 1·75 1·75

28 Hansa Brandenburg C-I

1993. 75th Anniv of First Vienna–Cracow–Lvov–Kiev Flight.

69 28 35 k. black, blue & mauve . 65 65
70 – 50 k. multicoloured 80 80

DESIGN: 50 k. Airbus Industrie A300.

29 Candles and Traditional Foods

1993. Easter.

71 29 15 k. multicoloured . . . . 1·25 1·25

30 "Country Wedding in Lower Austria" (Ferdinand Georg Waldmuller)

31 Cross and Figures

1993. 45th Anniv of Declaration of Human Rights.

72 30 5 k. multicoloured . . . . . 1·25 1·25

1993. 60th Anniv of Famine Deaths.

73 31 75 k. brown 80 80

32 1918 10 sh. Stamp

1993. Stamp Day. 75th Anniv of First Ukrainian Postage Stamps.

74 32 100 k. blue and brown . . . 1·00 1·00

33 Kiev

34 Mowing

1993. 50th Anniv of Liberation of Kiev.

75 33 75 k. multicoloured 90 90

1993. Agricultural Scenes.

76 34 50 k. green 10 10
77 – 100 k. blue 15 15
78 – 150 k. red 25 25
79 – 200 k. orange 30 30
80 – 300 k. purple 55 55
81 – 500 k. brown 85 85

DESIGNS: 100 k. Laden bullock carts; 150, 300 k. Shepherd and flock; 200, 500 k. Women cutting corn.

35 Madonna and Child

36 Agapit

1994. Ukrainian Health Fund.

82 35 150 k. + 20 k. black, gold and red . . . . 1·40 1·40

1994. Agapit (medieval doctor).

83 36 200 k. black and red . . . . 1·75 1·75

37 Dog's-tooth Violet ("Erythronium denscanis")

38 Laden Bullock Carts

1994. Red Book of Ukraine. Multicoloured.

84 200 k. Type 37 . . . . 70 70
85 200 k. Lady's slipper ("Cypripedium calceolus") . 70 70

1994. Agricultural Scenes. Value expressed by Cyrillic letter.

86 – A (5000 k.) red 60 60
87 38 V (10000 k.) blue . . . . . 1·25 1·25

DESIGN: A, Shepherd and flock.

The Cyrillic "V" on No. 87 resembles a "B".

39 Harvesting Wheat

40 Mowing

1994. Agricultural Scenes. Value expressed by Cyrillic letter.

88 39 B (100 k.) brown 10 10
89 40 G (250 k.) green 25 25

42 Kiev University

1994. 160th Anniv of Kiev University.

91 42 10000 k. multicoloured . . 75 75

43 Map and Airplanes (Liberation of Ukraine)

1994. 50th Anniv of Liberation. Multicoloured.

93 500 k. Map and rocket launchers (Russia) 25 25
94 500 k. Type 43 . . . . 25 25
95 500 k. Map, tank and soldiers (Byelorussia) 25 25

44 Ploughing

45 Fishing

1994. Agricultural Scenes. Value expressed by Cyrillic letter.

96 44 D (100 k.) mauve 10 10
97 45 Zh (5300 k.) blue 70 70

46 Bee-Keeping

47 Potter at Wheel

1994. Agricultural Scenes. Value expressed by Cyrillic letter.

98 46 Ye (1800 k.) brown . . . . 2·00 2·00
99 47 E (17000 k.) red . . . . . . 4·25 4·25

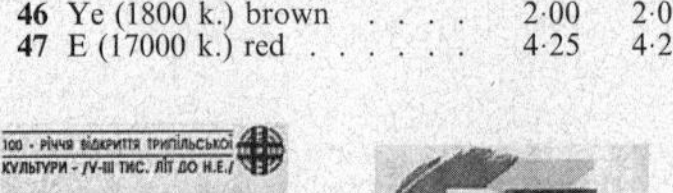

48 Ceramics and Map

49 Reader and Arms

1994. 100th Anniv of Excavation of Tripillia.

100 48 4000 k. multicoloured . . 55 55

1994. 500th Anniv of First Book printed in Ukrainian Language.

101 49 4000 k. multicoloured . . 55 55

INDEX

Countries can be quickly located by referring to the index at the end of this volume.

50 Repin and Study of Soldier

1994. 150th Birth Anniv of Ilya Repin (painter).
102 **50** 4000 k. multicoloured . . 55 55

51 Sofievka Park and Statue

1994. 200th Anniv of Sofievka Nature Park, Uman.
103 **51** 5000 k. multicoloured . . 60 60

52 Uzgorod Castle

1995. 1100th Anniv of Uzgorod.
104 **52** 5000 k. multicoloured . . 60 60

53 Ivan Franko (writer)

54 Peregrine Falcon

1995. Personalities. Multicoloured.
105 3000 k. Type **53** 40 40
106 3000 k. Ivan Pulyui (physicist) (vert) 40 40
107 3000 k. Lesya Ukrainka (writer) 40 40

1995. Red Book of Ukraine. Birds. Multicoloured.
108 5000 k. Type **54** 50 50
109 10000 k. Common crane . . . 1·50 1·50

55 Rilsky

56 Doves, St. Peter's Church, Kiev, and National Colours

1995. Birth Centenary of Maksim Rilsky (writer).
110 **55** 50000 k. multicoloured . . 2·40 2·40

1995. 50th Anniv of End of Second World War.
111 **56** 100000 k. multicoloured . 4·75 4·75

57 Figures around Globe on Map of Ukraine

1995. Artek International Children's Holiday Camps.
112 **57** 5000 k. multicoloured . . 45 45

58 Ivan Kotlyarevsky and Scene from "Eneida" (poem)

1995. Writers. Multicoloured.
113 1000 k. Type **58** 20 20
114 3000 k. Taras Shevchenko and cover of "Kobzar" 60 60

59 Siege of Theodosia

1995. 17th-century Hetmans. Petro Konashevich-Sagaidachny.
115 **59** 30000 k. multicoloured . 80 80

60 Lugansk

1995. Regional Arms.
116 **60** 10000 k. multicoloured . 20 20

61 "Stamp" and National Museum

1995. National Stamp Exhibition, Lvov.
117 **61** 50000 k. + 5000 k. mult . 1·25 1·25

62 Chmelnitsky Church (Subotiv) and Battle Scene

1995. 17th-century Hetmans. Bogdan Chmelnitsky.
118 **62** 40000 k. multicoloured . . 65 65

63 Nikolaus Hospital Church, Kiev

1995. 17th-century Hetmans. Ivan Mazepa.
119 **63** 30000 k. multicoloured . . 75 75

64 Part of Rainbow and Stork

65 Girl carrying Water Pails

1995. European Nature Conservation Year.
120 **64** 50000 k. multicoloured . . 75 75

1995. Regional Arms. As T **60**.
121 10000 k. multicoloured . . . 20 20
DESIGN: 10000 k. Chernigov.

1995. International Children's Day.
122 **65** 50000 k. multicoloured . . 75 75

66 Anniversary Emblem

67 Grushevsky

1995. 50th Anniv of U.N.O.
123 **66** 50000 k. blue, violet and black . . . . 1·50 1·50

1995. 60th Death Anniv (1994) of Mikhailo Grushevsky (first President).
124 **67** 50000 k. multicoloured . . 1·50 1·50

68 Karpenko-Kary

69 Shafarik

1995. 150th Birth Anniv of Ivan Karpenko-Kary (dramatist).
125 **68** 50000 k. multicoloured . . 75 75

1995. Birth Bicentenary of Pavel Shafarik (historian and philologist).
126 **69** 30000 k. green 75 75

70 Trolleybus

71 Train

72 Bus

1995. Transport. Value expressed by Cyrillic letter.
127 **70** I (1000 k.) blue 10 10
128 **71** K (2000 k.) green 15 15
129 **72** Z (3000 k.) pink 20 20

74 Research Aids

75 Krimsky

1996. 150th Anniv of Observatory, Taras Shevchenko University, Kiev. Multicoloured.
131 20000 k. Type **74** 35 35
132 30000 k. Telescope 40 40
133 50000 k. Sun over observatory buildings 75 75

1996. 125th Birth Anniv of A. Krimsky (writer).
134 **75** 20000 k. brown and ochre . 30 30

76 Kozlovsky

77 Animals

1996. 3rd Death Anniv of Ivan Kozlovsky (tenor).
135 **76** 20000 k. multicoloured . . 30 30

1996. Centenary of Kharkov Zoo.
136 **77** 20000 k. olive, green and blue 35 35

78 Dovshenko and Birthplace

1996. Birth Centenary of Aleksandr Dovshenko (film producer and set designer).
137 **78** 4000 k. multicoloured . . . 15 15

79 Lighted Candle within Tower

80 Vasil Fedorovich, Volodimir Levkovich and Levko Platonovich Simirenko

1996. 10th Anniv of Chernobyl Nuclear Disaster.
138 **79** 20000 k. multicoloured . . 35 35

1996. Simirenko Family.
139 **80** 20000 k. multicoloured . . 35 35
Vasil was a sugar refiner; Volodimir and Levko fruit breeders and researchers.

81 Stefanik

1996. 60th Death Anniv of Vasil Stefanik (writer and politician).
140 **81** 20000 k. multicoloured . . 35 35

82 Miklukho-Maklai

1996. 150th Birth Anniv of Mikola Mikolaiovich Miklukho-Maklai (explorer and philologist).
141 **82** 40000 k. multicoloured . . 20 20

83 Wrestling

1996. Olympic Games, Atlanta, U.S.A. Multicoloured.
142 20000 k. Type **83** 30 30
143 40000 k. Handball 65 65

84 "100" and Ancient Greek Athletes

85 Trident Emblem and "V" in National Colours

1996. Centenary of Modern Olympic Games.
145 **84** 40000 k. bistre, turquoise and blue 60 60

1996. 5th Anniv of Independence.
146 **85** 20000 k. multicoloured . . 35 35

86 "Sich-1"

87 Class "OD" Steam Locomotive

1996. 1st Ukrainian Satellite.
147 **86** 20000 k. multicoloured . . 35 35

1996. Railway Locomotives. Multicoloured.
148 20000 k. Type **87** 30 30
149 40000 k. Class "2TE-116" diesel locomotive 65 65

88 Antonov 89 Piddubny

1996. 90th Birth Anniv of O. K. Antonov (aircraft designer). Multicoloured.
150 20000 k. Type **88** 30 30
151 20000 k. Antonov An-2 biplane 30 30
152 40000 k. Antonov An-124 airliner 65 65
153 40000 k. Antonov An-225 piggybacking airplane . . . 65 65

1996. 125th Birth Anniv of Ivan Piddubny (boxing champion).
154 **89** 40 k. multicoloured 65 65

90 Academician Vernadsky Antarctic Station 91 Eidelwiess

1996. 1st Ukrainian Antarctic Expedition.
155 **90** 20 k. multicoloured 35 35

1996. Protected Flowers. Multicoloured.
156 20 k. Type **91** 30 30
157 40 k. "Narcissus anqustifolius" 65 65

92 Emblem 93 Kosenko

1996. 50th Anniv of U.N.E.S.C.O.
158 **92** 20 k. multicoloured 35 35

1996. Birth Centenary of W. S. Kosenko (composer).
159 **93** 20 k. multicoloured 35 35

94 St. Sophia Cathedral, Kiev

1996. Churches. Multicoloured.
160 20 k. Type **94** 35 35
161 20 k. Illinska Church, Subotov 35 35
162 20 k. St. George's Church, Drogobych 35 35
163 20 k. Trinity Cathedral, Novomoskovsk 35 35

95 Mogil

1996. 400th Birth Anniv of Petro Mogil (Metropolitan of Kiev).
164 **95** 20 k. black and brown . . 35 35

96 Emblem and Rainbow

1996. 50th Anniv of U.N.I.C.E.F.
165 **96** 20 k. multicoloured 35 35

UMM AL QIWAIN Pt. 19

One of the Trucial States in the Persian Gulf. In July 1971 formed the United Arab Emirates with five other Gulf Shaikdoms.

1964. 100 naye paise = 1 rupee.
1967. 100 dirhams = 1 riyal.

1 Shaikh Ahmed bin Rashid al Moalla and Mountain Gazelles

1964. Multicoloured. (a) Size as T **1**.
1 1 n.p. Type **1** 15 15
2 2 n.p. Snake 15 15
3 3 n.p. Striped hyena 15 15
4 4 n.p. Fish 15 15
5 5 n.p. Fish (different) 15 15
6 10 n.p. Fish (different) 15 15
7 15 n.p. Palace 15 15
8 20 n.p. Town buildings 15 15
9 30 n.p. Tower 20 15

(b) Size 42½ × 27 mm.
10 40 n.p. Type **1** 25 20
11 50 n.p. Snake 40 25
12 50 n.p. Striped hyena 55 30
13 1 r. Fish 70 40
14 1 r. 50 Fish (different) 90 50
15 2 r. Fish (different) . . . . 1·40 95

(c) Size 53½ × 33½ mm.
16 3 r. Palace . . . . 2·50 1·50
17 5 r. Town buildings . . . . 4·00 2·25
18 10 r. Tower . . . . 6·50 4·25

2 Discus Thrower and Stadium

1964. Olympic Games, Tokyo. Multicoloured.
19 50 n.p. Type **2** 20 15
20 1 r. Main stadium 35 30
21 1 r. 50 Swimming pool 55 40
22 2 r. Main stadium 70 55
23 3 r. Komazawa gymnasium . . 1·10 95
24 4 r. Stadium entrance . . . . 1·90 1·40
25 5 r. Type **2** . . . . 2·40 1·90

3 Cortege leaving White House

1965. Pres. Kennedy Commem. Each black and gold on coloured paper as given below.
26 **3** 10 n.p. blue 15 15
27 – 15 n.p. stone 15 15
28 – 50 n.p. stone 20 15
29 – 1 r. pink 40 30
30 – 2 r. stone 75 60
31 – 3 r. lilac . . . . 1·25 95
32 – 5 r. blue . . . . 2·25 1·90
33 – 7 r. 50 buff . . . . . . 3·25 2·25
DESIGNS—As T **3** (Funeral scenes): 15 n.p. Coffin-bearers; 50 n.p. Hearse; 1 r. Presidents Eisenhower and Truman; 2 r. Foreign dignitaries. 33 × 51 mm: 3 r. Mrs. Kennedy and family at grave; 5 r. Last salute; 7 r. 50, Pres. Kennedy.

1965. Air. Designs similar to Nos. 1/9 but inscr "AIR MAIL". Multicoloured. (a) Size 43 × 26½ mm.
34 15 n.p. Type **1** 15 15
35 25 n.p. Snake 15 15
36 35 n.p. Striped hyena 25 15
37 50 n.p. Fish 30 20
38 75 n.p. Fish (different) 55 30
39 1 r. Fish (different) 65 40

(b) Size 53 × 34 mm.
40 2 r. Palace . . . . 1·75 65
41 3 r. Town buildings . . . . 2·25 95
42 5 r. Tower . . . . 3·25 1·60

MINIMUM PRICE

The minimum price quoted is 10p which represents a handling charge rather than a basis for valuing common stamps. For further notes about prices, see introductory pages.

4 Tribute to Ruler (reverse of 10 n.p. piece)

1965. Arabian Gulf Area Monetary Conf. Circular designs on silver foil, backed with paper inscr overall "Walsall Security Paper" in English and Arabic. Imperf. (a) Diameter 43 mm.
43 **4** 10 n.p. purple and black . . . 15 15
44 – 25 n.p. blue and green 15 15

(b) Diameter 55½ mm.
45 **4** 1 r. red and violet 40 40
46 – 2 r. green and orange 45 45

(c) Diameter 64 mm.
47 **4** 3 r. blue and mauve . . . . . 1·00 1·00
48 – 5 r. purple and blue . . . . . 1·75 1·75
SILVER PIECES: Nos. 44, 46, 48 each show the obverse side (Shaikh Ahmed).

5 "Penny Black" and Egyptian 5 p. Stamp of 1866

1966. Centenary Stamp Exhibition, Cairo.
49 **5** 3 n.p. multicoloured 10 10
50 – 5 n.p. multicoloured 10 10
51 – 7 n.p. multicoloured 15 15
52 – 10 n.p. multicoloured 15 15
53 – 15 n.p. multicoloured 15 15
54 – 25 n.p. multicoloured 15 15
55 – 50 n.p. multicoloured 35 20
56 – 75 n.p. multicoloured 45 20
57 – 1 r. multicoloured 65 25
58 – 2 r. multicoloured . . . . . 1·10 55
DESIGNS: As Type **5** with Egyptian 5 p. stamp: 7 n.p. Brazil 30 r. "Bull's-eye" of 1843; 15 n.p. Mauritius "Post Office" One Penny of 1847; 50 n.p. Belgium 10 c. "Epaulettes" of 1849; 1 r. New South Wales One Penny and Victoria One Penny of 1850. As Type **5**, but with Egyptian "Pyramid and Star" watermark of 1866: 5 n.p. Basel 2½ r. "Dove" of 1845, Geneva 5 c. + 5 c. "Double Eagle" and Zurich 4 r. "Numeral" of 1843; 10 n.p. U.S. St. Louis "Bears" 5 c., Baltimore 5 c. and New York 5 c. "Postmasters" stamps of 1845; 25 n.p. France 20 c. "Ceres" of 1849; 75 n.p. Bavaria 1 k. of 1850; 2 r. Spain 6 c. of 1850.

6 Sir Winston Churchill with Lord Alanbrooke and Field Marshal Montgomery

1966. Churchill Commemoration. Multicoloured designs each including Churchill.
59 3 n.p. Type **6** 10 10
60 4 n.p. With Roosevelt and Stalin at Yalta 10 10
61 5 n.p. In garden at No. 10 Downing Street, London . . 10 10
62 10 n.p. With Eisenhower . . . 15 15
63 15 n.p. With Lady Churchill in car 15 15
64 50 n.p. Painting in Morocco . . 25 15
65 75 n.p. Walking — on holiday . 40 15
66 1 r. Funeral cortege 65 20
67 3 r. Lying-in-state, Westminster Hall . . . . 1·60 60
68 5 r. Churchill giving "Victory" sign . . . . 2·40 1·10

7 Communications Satellite

1966. Centenary (1965) of I.T.U. Communications Satellites. Multicoloured.
70 5 n.p. Type **7** 15 15
71 10 n.p. "Tiros" 20 15
72 25 n.p. "Telstar" 20 15
73 50 n.p. "Ariel" 50 15
74 75 n.p. "Ranger" 65 15
75 1 r. "Alouette" 95 25
76 2 r. "Vanguard 1" . . . . . . 1·75 40
77 3 r. "Explorer 10" . . . . . . 2·50 50
78 5 r. "Early Bird" . . . . 4·75 90

NEW CURRENCY SURCHARGES. In 1967 various issues appeared surcharged in dirhams and riyals. The 1964 definitives, 1965 air stamps and officials with this surcharge are listed as there is evidence of their postal use. Nos. 19/33 and 49/68 also exist with these surcharges.

1967. Various issues with currency names changed by overprinting. (i) Nos. 1/18 (1964 Definitives).
80 1 d. on 1 n.p. 10 10
81 2 d. on 2 n.p. 10 10
82 3 d. on 3 n.p. 10 10
83 4 d. on 4 n.p. 10 10
84 5 d. on 5 n.p. 15 10
85 10 d. on 10 n.p. 15 10
86 15 d. on 15 n.p. . . . . 2·50 1·00
87 20 d. on 20 n.p. . . . . 2·50 1·00
88 30 d. on 30 n.p. . . . . 2·50 1·00
89 40 d. on 40 n.p. 45 15
90 50 d. on 50 n.p. 55 25
91 70 d. on 70 n.p. 70 30
92 1 r. on 1 r. 85 35
93 1 r. 50 on 1 r. 50 . . . . . . 1·40 60
94 2 r. on 2 r. . . . . 1·75 70
95 3 r. on 3 r. . . . . 6·50 2·50
96 5 r. on 5 r. . . . . 8·50 3·75
97 10 r. on 10 r. . . . . 13·00 6·00

(ii) Nos. 34/42 (Airmails).
98 15 d. on 15 n.p. 15 10
99 25 d. on 25 n.p. 20 10
100 35 d. on 35 n.p. 25 20
101 50 d. on 50 n.p. 50 25
102 75 d. on 75 n.p. 60 35
103 1 r. on 1 r. 75 45
104 2 r. on 2 r. . . . . 2·50 90
105 3 r. on 3 r. . . . . 2·50 1·25
106 5 r. on 5 r. . . . . 3·50 2·50

9 Box Fish

1967. Fish of the Arabian Gulf. Multicoloured. (a) Postage. (i) Size 46 × 21 mm.
116 1 d. Type **9** 10 10
117 2 d. Parrot fish 10 10
118 3 d. Sweet lips 10 10
119 4 d. Butterfly fish 10 10
120 5 d. Soldier fish 15 10
121 10 d. Damsel fish 15 10
122 15 d. Picasso triggerfish . . . 15 10
123 20 d. Striped triggerfish . . . 25 10
124 30 d. Israeli puffer 35 10

(ii) Size 56 × 26 mm.
125 40 d. Type **9** 40 10
126 50 d. As 2 d. 50 15
127 70 d. As 3 d. 70 15
128 1 r. As 4 d. 80 15
129 1 r. 50 As 5 d. . . . . 1·25 25
130 2 r. As 10 d. . . . . 1·40 35
131 3 r. As 15 d. (No. 122) . . . . 2·00 45
132 5 r. As 20 d. . . . . 3·25 75
133 10 r. As 30 d. . . . . 5·00 1·50

(b) Air. Size 70 × 35 mm.
134 15 d. Type **9** 15 10
135 25 d. As 2 d. 25 10
136 35 d. As 3 d. 35 10
137 50 d. As 4 d. 50 15
138 75 d. As 5 d. 70 15
139 1 r. As 10 d. 80 15
140 2 r. As 15 d. (No. 122) . . . . 1·40 35
141 3 r. As 20 d. . . . . 2·00 45
142 5 r. As 30 d. . . . . 3·25 75

OFFICIAL STAMPS

1965. Designs similar to Nos. 1/9, additionally inscr "ON STATE'S SERVICE". Multicoloured. (a) Postage. Size 42½ × 27 mm.
O49 25 n.p. Type **1** 15 15
O50 40 n.p. Snake 20 15
O51 50 n.p. Striped hyena 25 15
O52 75 n.p. Fish 55 20
O53 1 r. Fish (different) . . . . . 1·25 40

(b) Air. (i) Size 42½ × 27 mm.
O54 75 n.p. Fish (different) . . . 50 20

(ii) Size 53 × 34 mm.
O55 2 r. Palace . . . . 1·40 40
O56 3 r. Town buildings . . . . 2·10 75
O57 5 r. Tower . . . . 3·75 1·25

1967. Nos. O49/57 with currency names changed by overprinting.
O107 25 d. on 25 n.p.(postage) . . 30 15
O108 40 d. on 40 n.p. 35 15
O109 50 d. on 50 n.p. 45 25
O110 75 d. on 75 n.p. 60 35
O111 1 r. on 1 r. 80 45
O112 75 d. on 75 d. (air) 60 35
O113 2 r. on 2 r. . . . . 2·00 90
O114 3 r. on 3 r. . . . . 2·50 1·40
O115 5 r. on 5 r. . . . . 3·75 2·40

For later issues see **UNITED ARAB EMIRATES**.

APPENDIX

The following stamps have either been issued in excess of postal needs or have not been available to the public in reasonable quantities at face value. Such stamps may later be given full listing if there is evidence of regular postal use.

1967.

Self-portraits of Famous Painters. Postage 10, 15, 25, 50, 75 d., 1, 1 r. 50; Air 1 r. 25, 2, 2 r. 50, 3, 5 r.

Dogs. Postage 15, 25, 50, 75 d., 1 r.; Air 1 r. 25, 2 r. 50, 4 r.

"Expo 67" World Fair, Montreal. Famous Paintings. 25, 50, 75 d., 1, 1 r. 50, 2, 3 r.

1968.

Falcons. Postage 15, 25, 50, 75 d., 1 r.; Air 1 r. 50, 3, 5 r.

Winter Olympic Games, Grenoble. Postage 10, 25, 75 d., 1 r.; Air 1 r. 50, 2, 3, 5 r.

Famous Paintings. Postage 25, 50, 75 d., 1, 1 r. 50, 2 r. 50; Air 1, 2, 3, 4, 5 r.

Olympic Games, Mexico (1st issue). Optd on (a) 1964 Tokyo Olympic Games Issue. Postage 1 r. 50, 2, 4, 5 r. (b) 1968 Winter Olympic Games issue. Air 1 r. 50, 2, 5 r.

Robert Kennedy Memorial. Optd on 1965 Pres. Kennedy issue. Postage 3, 5, 7 r. 50.

Olympic Games, Mexico (2nd issue). Postage 10, 25, 50 d., 1, 2 r.; Air 2 r. 50, 3, 4, 5 r.

Still Life Paintings. Postage 25, 50 d., 1, 1 r. 50, 2 r.; Air 1 r. 25, 2 r. 50, 3, 3 r. 50, 5 r.

Mexico Olympic Medal Winners. Optd on Olympic Games, Mexico issue. Postage 10, 25, 50 d., 1, 2 r.; Air 2 r. 50, 3, 4, 5 r.

Aviation History. Aircraft. Postage 25, 50 d., 1, 1 r. 50, 2 r.; Air 1 r. 25, 2 r. 50, 3, 5 r.

1969.

"Apollo 8" Moon Orbit. Optd on 1968 Aviation History issue. Postage 25, 50 d., 1, 1 r. 50, 2 r.; Air 1 r. 25, 2 r. 50, 3, 5 r.

Horses (1st series). Postage 25, 50, 75 d., 1, 2 r.; Air 1 r. 50, 2 r. 50, 4, 5 r.

Olympic Games, Munich, 1972 (1st issue). Optd on 1968 Olympic Games, Mexico issue. Postage 10, 25, 50 d., 1, 2 r.; Air 2 r. 50, 3, 4, 5 r.

Winter Olympic Games, Sapporo 1972 (1st issue). Optd on 1968 Winter Olympics Grenoble issue. Postage 10, 25, 75 d., 1 r.; Air 1 r. 50, 2, 3, 5 r.

Veteran and Vintage Cars. Postage 15 d. × 8, 25 d. × 8, 50 d. × 8, 75 d. × 8; Air 1 r. × 8, 2 r. × 8.

Famous Films. Postage 10, 15, 25, 50, 75 d., 1 r.; Air 1 r. 50, 2 r. 50, 3, 4, 5 r.

"Apollo 12" Moon Landing. 10, 20, 30, 50, 75 d., 1 r.

1970.

"Apollo 13" Astronauts. 10, 30, 50 d.

"Expo 70" World Fair, Osaka, Japan. 5, 10, 20, 40 d., 1, 1 r. 25.

150th Anniv of British Landing on Trucial Coast. Uniforms. 10, 20, 30, 50, 75 d., 1 r.

1971.

Animals. Postage 10, 15, 20, 25 d.; Air 5 r.

Winter Olympic Games, Saporro, 1972 (2nd issue). Postage 5, 10, 15, 20, 25 d.; Air 50, 75 d., 1, 3, 5 r.

Olympic Games, Munich, 1972 (2nd issue). Postage 5, 10, 15, 20, 25 d.; Air 50, 75 d., 1, 3, 5 r.

1972.

Durer's Religious Paintings. Postage 5, 10, 15, 20, 25 d.; Air 3 r.

Horses (2nd series). Postage 10, 15, 20, 25 d.; Air 50 d., 3 r.

Locomotives (plastic surfaced). Postage 5, 10, 20, 40, 50 d.; Air 6 r.

Winter Olympic Games, Sapporo, 1972 (3rd issue) (plastic surfaced). Postage 5, 10, 20, 40, 50 d.; Air 6 r.

Easter, Religious Paintings. Postage 5, 10, 20, 50 d.; Air 1, 3 r.

Kennedy Brothers Memorial. Postage 5, 10, 15, 20 d.; Air 1, 3 r.

Winston Churchill Memorial. Postage 5, 10, 15, 20 d.; Air 3 r.

Arab Rulers. Postage 5 d. × 6, 10 d. × 6, 15 d. × 6, 20 d. × 6; Air 3 r. × 6.

13th World Jamboree, 1971 (plastic surfaced). Postage 5, 10, 20, 40, 50 d.; Air 6 r.

Fish. Postage 5, 10, 20, 40, 50 d.; Air 6 r.

International Airlines. Postage 5, 10, 15, 20, 25 d.; Air 50 d.

"Apollo 15" Moon Mission. Postage 5, 10, 15, 20, 25 d.; Air 50, 75 d., 1, 3, 5 r.

Olympic Games, Munich, 1972 (3rd issue) (plastic surfaced). Postage 5, 10, 20, 40, 50 d.; Air 6 r.

2500th Anniv of Founding of Persian Empire. Postage 10, 20, 30, 40, 50, 60 d.; Air 1 r.

Portraits of Charles de Gaulle. 5, 10, 15, 20, 25 d.

Paintings of Napoleon. Postage 5, 10, 15, 20, 25 d.; Air 5 r.

Butterflies. Postage 5, 10, 15, 20, 25 d.; Air 3 r.

Penguins. Postage 5, 10, 15, 20 d.; Air 50 d., 4 r.

Cars. Postage 5, 10, 15, 20, 25 d.; Air 3 r.

Masks (1st series). Postage 5, 10, 15, 20, 25 d.; Air 50 d., 1, 3 r.

Dogs and Cats. Postage 5, 5, 10, 10, 15, 15, 20, 20, 25, 25 d.; Air 5, 5 r.

Roses. Postage 10, 15, 20, 25 d.; Air 50 d., 5 r.

Marine Fauna. Postage 5, 10, 15, 20, 25, 50 d.; Air 1, 3 r.

Masks (2nd series). Postage 5, 10, 15, 20, 25 d.; Air 50 d., 1, 3 r.

Navigators. Postage 5, 10, 15, 20, 25, 50 d.; Air 1, 3 r.

Exotic Birds (1st series). Horiz and vert designs. Air 1 r. × 16.

Exotic Birds (2nd series). Horiz designs. Air 1 r. × 16.

In common with the other states of the United Arab Emirates the Umm al Qiwain stamp contract was terminated on 1 August 1972 and any further new issues released after that date were unauthorised.

UNITED ARAB EMIRATES Pt. 19

Following the withdrawal of British forces from the Gulf and the ending of the Anglo-Trucial States treaties six of the states, Abu Dhabi, Ajman, Dubai, Fujeira, Sharjah and Umm al Qiwain, formed an independent union on 2nd December 1971. The seventh state, Ras al Khaima, joined during February 1972. Each emirate continued to use its own stamps, pending the introduction of a unified currency. A Union Postal administration came into being on 1st August 1972 and the first stamps appeared on 1st January 1973.

For Abu Dhabi stamps optd U.A.E., etc, see under that heading).

100 fils = 1 dirham

1 U.A.E. Flag and Map of Gulf

1973. Multicoloured. (a) Size 42 × 25 mm.

1 **1** 5 f. Type **1** . . . 10 10
2 10 f. Type **1** . . . 10 10
3 15 f. Eagle emblem . . . 20 15
4 35 f. As 15 f. . . . 35 35

(b) Size 46 × 30 mm.

5 65 f. Almaqta Bridge, Abu Dhabi 70 70
6 75 f. Khor Fakkan, Sharjah . 85 85
7 1 d. Clock Tower, Dubai . . . 1·10 1·10
8 1¼ d. Buthnah Fort, Fujeira . . 1·75 2·50
9 2 d. Alfalaj Fort, Umm al Qiwain 21·00 5·25
10 3 d. Khor Khwair, Ras al Khaima 5·00 5·00
11 5 d. Ruler's Palace, Ajman . . 5·50 5·50
12 10 d. President Shaikh Zaid . 11·00 11·00

2 Youth and Girl within Shield

1973. National Youth Festival. Multicoloured.

13 10 f. Type **2** . . . 2·40 15
14 1 d. 25 Allegory of Youth . . 5·75 4·25

3 Traffic Lights and Road Sign

1973. Traffic Week. Multicoloured.

15 35 f. Type **3** . . . 1·75 95
16 75 f. Pedestrian-crossing (horiz) 3·25 1·75
17 1 d. 25 Traffic policeman . . . 5·75 2·75

4 "Three Races of the World"

1973. 25th Anniv of Declaration of Human Rights.

18 **4** 35 f. black, yellow and blue . 95 40
19 65 f. black, yellow and red . . 2·50 85
20 1¼ d. black, yellow & green . 4·00 1·60

5 U.P.U. Emblem

1974. Centenary of Universal Postal Union.

21 **5** 25 f. multicoloured . . . 1·00 35
22 60 f. multicoloured . . . 1·75 85
23 1¼ d. multicoloured . . . 3·25 1·40

6 Medical Equipment (Health Service)

1974. Third National Day.

24 **6** 10 f. red, brown and lilac . . 65 10
25 – 35 f. gold, green and blue . 1·25 50
26 – 65 f. brown, sepia and blue . 1·75 95
27 – 1¼ d. multicoloured . . . 3·75 2·40

DESIGNS—49 × 30 mm: 35 f. Children reading (Education); 65 f. Tools and buildings (Construction); 1¼ d. U.A.E. flag with emblems of U.N. and Arab League.

7 Arab Couple with Candle and Book

1974. International Literacy Day.

28 **7** 35 f. multicoloured . . . 1·25 20
29 – 65 f. black, blue and brown . 1·50 60
30 – 1 d. 25 black, blue & brown . 3·25 1·40

DESIGN—VERT: 65 f., 1 f. 25, Arab couple with book.

8 Oil De-gassing Installation

1975. 9th Arab Oil Conference. Multicoloured.

31 25 f. Type **8** . . . 60 25
32 50 f. "Al Ittiad" (offshore oil drilling platform) . . . 1·75 45
33 100 f. Underwater storage tank 2·50 1·10
34 125 f. Marine oil production platform . . . 3·00 1·75

9 Station and Dish Aerial

1975. Inauguration of Jabal Ali Satellite Earth Station. Multicoloured.

36 15 f. Type **9** . . . 70 25
37 35 f. Satellite beaming information to Earth . . . 1·75 40
38 65 f. As 35 f. . . . 2·75 55
39 2 d. Type **9** . . . 5·75 3·00

10 "Snapshots" within Eagle Emblem

11 Symbols of Learning

1975. Fourth National Day. Multicoloured.

40 10 f. Type **10** . . . 35 15
41 35 f. Shaikh Mohamed bin Hamad al Sharqi of Fujeira . 1·00 45
42 60 f. Shaikh Rashid bin Humaid al Naimi of Ajman . . . 1·50 60
43 80 f. Shaikh Ahmed bin Rashid al Moalla of Umm al Qiwain . 2·25 1·00
44 90 f. Shaikh Sultan bin Mohammed al Qasimi of Sharjah . . . 2·50 1·50
45 1 d. Shaikh Saqr bin Mohammed al Qasimi of Ras al Khaima . 2·50 1·50
46 1 d. 40 Shaikh Rashid bin Said of Dubai . . . 3·75 2·75
47 5 d. Shaikh Zaid bin Sultan al Nahayyan of Abu Dhabi, President of U.A.E. . . . 14·00 10·00

1976. Arab Literacy Day. Multicoloured.

48 15 f. Type **11** . . . 40 10
49 50 f. Arabs seeking enlightenment 75 55
50 3 d. As 50 f. . . . 4·50 3·25

1976. No. 6 surch **50** in English and Arabic.

50a 50 f. on 75 f. multicoloured . 13·00 8·00

12 Man and Road Signs

13 Headphones

1976. Traffic Week. Multicoloured.

51 15 f. Type **12** . . . 40 40
52 80 f. Example of dangerous driving and road signals (horiz) 2·00 2·00
53 140 f. Children on road crossing (horiz) . . . 3·50 3·50

1976. International Telecommunications Day.

54 **13** 50 f. multicoloured . . . 65 25
55 80 f. multicoloured . . . 1·40 50
56 2 d. multicoloured . . . 4·00 1·75

14 U.A.E. Crest

15 President Shaikh Zaid

1976.

57 **14** 5 f. red . . . 10 30
58 10 f. brown . . . 15 20
59 15 f. pink . . . 20 20
60 35 f. brown . . . 35 10
61 50 f. violet . . . 55 15
62 60 f. bistre . . . 70 15
63 80 f. green . . . 80 25
64 90 f. blue . . . 85 65
65 1 d. blue . . . 1·25 75
66 140 f. green . . . 1·50 95
67 250 f. violet . . . 1·75 1·10
68 2 d. grey . . . 2·25 1·50
69 5 d. blue . . . 5·75 3·75
70 10 d. mauve . . . 11·50 7·75

1976. Fifth National Day.

71 **15** 15 f. multicoloured . . . 1·00 20
72 140 f. multicoloured . . . 4·00 2·00

MINIMUM PRICE

The minimum price quoted is 10p which represents a handling charge rather than a basis for valuing common stamps. For further notes about prices, see introductory pages.

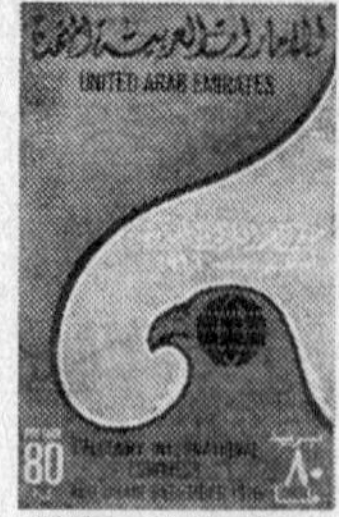

16 Falcon's Head and Gulf **17** Mohammed Ali Jinnah (Quaid-i-Azam)

1976. International Falconry Congress, Abu Dhabi.

73 **16** 80 f. multicoloured . . . . 1·75 70
74 2 d. multicoloured . . . . . 4·25 2·00

1976. Birth Centenary of Mohammed Ali Jinnah (founder of Pakistan).

75 **17** 50 f. multicoloured . . . . 2·50 80
76 80 f. multicoloured . . . . 3·50 1·60

19 A.P.U. Emblem **20** U.A.E. Crest

1977. 25th Anniv of Arab Postal Union.

78 **19** 50 f. multicoloured . . . . 2·00 80
79 80 f. multicoloured . . . . 3·00 1·50

1977.

80 **20** 5 f. red and black 15 35
81 10 f. brown and black . . . 20 25
82 15 f. pink and black 30 25
83 35 f. brown and black . . . 60 15
84 50 f. mauve and black . . . 85 20
85 60 f. bistre and black . . . 1·50 40
86 80 f. green and black . . . 1·50 30
87 90 f. blue and black . . . . 1·60 15
88 1 d. blue and black . . . . 2·25 35
89 1 d. 40 green and black . . 3·00 75
90 1 d. 50 violet and black . . 3·50 95
91 2 d. grey and black . . . . 4·25 1·25
92 5 d. blue and black . . . 10·00 4·00
93 10 d. purple and black . . . 18·00 8·00

21 Arab Scholar and Emblems

1977. International Literacy Day.

94 **21** 50 f. multicoloured . . . . 1·50 50
95 3 d. multicoloured . . . . . 6·00 4·00

22 Armoured Cars

1977. Sixth National Day. Multicoloured.

96 15 f. Type **22** . . . .
97 50 f. Anti-aircraft missiles . . . .
98 150 f. Soldiers marching
Set of 3 £400

Nos. 96/8 were withdrawn from sale on day of issue as the date in Arabic was wrongly inscribed backwards.

23 Posthorn Dhow **24** Koran on Map of World

1979. Second Gulf Postal Organization Conf, Dubai.

99 **23** 50 f. multicoloured 50 30
100 5 d. multicoloured . . . . 4·00 3·25

1980. The Arabs.

101 **24** 50 f. multicoloured 50 30
102 1 d. 40 multicoloured . . . 1·25 90
103 3 d. multicoloured . . . . 2·75 2·00

25 Dassault Mirage III Jet Fighters and Sud Aviation Alouette III Helicopter

1980. Ninth National Day.

104 **25** 15 f. multicoloured 30 15
105 50 f. multicoloured 90 30
106 80 f. multicoloured . . . . 1·25 90
107 150 f. multicoloured . . . 2·50 1·90

26 Family on Graph **27** Mosque and Kaaba, Mecca

1980. Population Census.

109 **26** 15 f. blue and pink 30 15
110 – 80 f. brown and grey . . . 1·25 50
111 – 90 f. brown and buff . . . 1·40 75
112 **26** 2 d. blue and cobalt . . . 4·25 3·50

DESIGN: 80, 90 f. Figure standing in doorway.

1980. 1400th Anniv of Hejira.

113 **27** 15 f. multicoloured 30 15
114 80 f. multicoloured 90 50
115 90 f. multicoloured . . . . 1·10 65
116 140 f. multicoloured . . . 2·75 1·75

28 Figures supporting O.P.E.C. Emblem **29** Policeman helping Child across Road

1980. 20th Anniv of Organization of Petroleum Exporting Countries. Multicoloured.

118 50 f. Type **28** 60 35
119 80 f. Type **28** . . . . 1·00 55
120 90 f. O.P.E.C. emblem and globe 1·25 70
121 140 f. As No. 120 . . . . . . 2·25 1·75

1981. Traffic Week. Multicoloured.

123 15 f. Type **29** 30 15
124 50 f. Policeman and traffic signs (21 × 31 mm) 60 35
125 80 f. Type **29** 90 50
126 5 d. As No. 124 . . . . . . 3·75 3·25

30 Symbols of Industry

1981. Tenth National Day.

127 **30** 25 f. blue and black . . . 30 15
128 – 150 f. multicoloured . . . 1·60 1·10
129 – 2 d. red, green and black . 2·75 1·90

DESIGNS: 150 f. Soldiers; 2 r. Flag and U.N. and U.A.E emblems.

31 Helping the Disabled (pictogram) and I.Y.D.P. Emblem **32** U.A.E. Crest

1981. Int Year of Disabled Persons. Mult.

130 25 f. Type **31** 45 15
131 45 f. Disabled person in wheelchair (pictogram) (vert) 80 35
132 150 f. As No. 131 . . . . . . 1·75 1·50
133 2 d. Type **31** . . . . 2·75 2·25

1982. Multicoloured. Background colour given.

(a) Size 17 × 21 mm.

134 **32** 5 f. pink 10 10
135 10 f. green 10 10
136 15 f. violet 10 10
137 25 f. brown 15 10
138 35 f. brown 20 15
139 50 f. blue 30 25
140 75 f. yellow 50 40
141 100 f. grey 65 50
142 110 f. green 65 50
143 125 f. mauve 80 60
144 150 f. blue . . . . 1·00 80
145 175 f. blue . . . . 1·25 75

(b) Size 23 × 27 mm.

146 **32** 2 d. green . . . . 1·40 1·25
147 250 f. pink . . . . 1·50 1·40
148 3 d. blue . . . . 1·90 1·75
149 5 d. yellow . . . . 2·50 2·25
150 10 d. brown . . . . 5·00 5·00
151 20 d. silver . . . . 8·00 8·00
151c 50 d. purple . . . . 20·00 18·00

33 Flags of Competing Countries and Emblem

1982. 6th Arab Gulf Football Championships. Multicoloured.

152 25 f. Type **33** 50 20
153 75 f. American bald eagle holding ball over stadium (vert) . . . 1·25 65
154 125 f. Footballers (vert) . . . 1·60 1·10
155 3 d. As No. 153 . . . . 3·50 3·00

34 Figure breaking Gun

1982. 2nd U.N. Disarmament Conference.

156 **34** 25 f. multicoloured 30 15
157 75 f. multicoloured 95 65
158 125 f. multicoloured . . . . 1·60 1·25
159 150 f. multicoloured . . . . 1·90 1·40

35 National Emblems

1982. 11th National Day. Multicoloured.

160 25 f. Type **35** 35 15
161 75 f. Dove and flag (vert) . . . 1·00 60
162 125 f. As 75 f. . . . . 1·75 95
163 150 f. Type **35** . . . . 1·90 1·40

36 Arab writing **37** W.C.Y. Emblem

1983. Arab Literacy Day.

164 – 25 f. multicoloured . . . . 10·00
165 **36** 35 f. brown, violet & black . 30 30
166 – 75 f. yellow, black & mauve 13·00
167 **36** 3 d. brown, yellow & black 2·00 2·00

DESIGN: 25, 75 f. Koran and lamp.

1983. World Communications Year.

168 **37** 25 f. multicoloured 50 15
169 150 f. multicoloured . . . . 1·25 1·10
170 2 d. multicoloured . . . . 1·90 1·50
171 3 d. multicoloured . . . . 3·00 2·75

38 Satellite Orbit within "20"

1984. 20th Anniv of International Telecommunications Satellite Consortium.

172 **38** 2 d. blue, purple & dp blue 2·50 2·00
173 2½ d. blue, purple & green . 3·50 3·00

39 Shaikh Hamad bin Mohamed al Sharqi and Buthnah Fort, Fujeira

1984. 13th National Day. Multicoloured.

174 1 d. Type **39** . . . . 1·25 95
175 1 d. Shaikh Rashid bin Ahmed al Moalla and Alfalaj Fort, Umm al Qiwain . . . . 1·25 95
176 1 d. Shaikh Humaid bin Rashid al Naimi and Palace, Ajman 1·25 95
177 1 d. Shaikh Saqr bin Mohammed al-Qasimi and harbour, Ras al Khaima . . . . 1·25 95
178 1 d. Shaikh Zaid bin Sultan al Nahayyan and refinery, Abu Dhabi . . . . 1·25 95
179 1 d. Shaikh Sultan bin Mohammed al Qasimi, oil well and mosque, Sharjah . . . 1·25 95
180 1 d. Shaikh Rashid bin Said and building, Dubai . . . . . . 1·25 95

40 Pictograms of Refuse Collection **41** Globe and Knights

1985. Tidy Week.

181 **40** 5 d. orange and black . . 4·75 4·75

1985. World Junior Chess Championship, Sharjah.

182 **41** 2 d. multicoloured . . . . 2·75 1·75
183 250 f. multicoloured . . . 3·75 2·50

42 Map and Hand holding Flag **43** Stylised People and Map

1985. 14th National Day.

184 **42** 50 f. multicoloured 40 20
185 3 d. multicoloured . . . . 3·00 1·75

1985. Population Census.

186 **43** 50 f. multicoloured 40 20
187 1 d. multicoloured 90 45
188 3 d. multicoloured . . . . 2·75 1·60

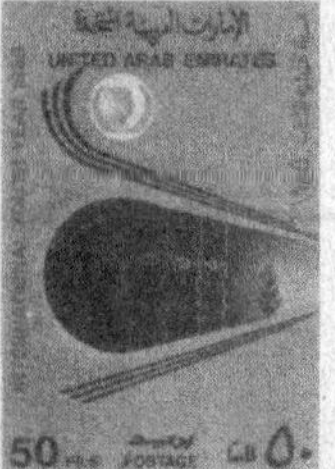

44 Profiles looking at Sapling **45** Emblem

1985. International Youth Year. Multicoloured.

189 50 f. Type **44** 30 20
190 175 f. Open book, flame and people between hemispheres (horiz) . . . . 1·25 90
191 2 d. Youth carrying globe on back . . . . 1·50 1·00

1986. Arabic Woman and Family Day.
192 **45** 1 d. multicoloured 75 45
193 3 d. multicoloured . . . . 2·00 1·50

46 Globe, Map and Posthorn **47** Sakar Falcon

1986. 1st Anniv of General Postal Authority. Multicoloured.
194 50 f. Type **46** 40 20
195 1 d. Banner around globe (vert) 85 50
196 2 d. As No. 195 . . . . . . 1·60 1·40
197 250 f. Type **46** . . . . 1·90 1·75

1986.
198 **47** 50 f. gold, blue and green . 50 50
199 75 f. gold, blue and mauve 75 75
200 125 f. gold, blue and grey . 1·25 1·25

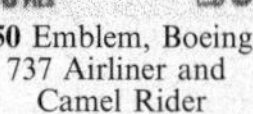
48 Container Ship in Dock **49** Dawn, Satellite, Emblem and Dish Aerials

1986. 10th Anniv of United Arab Shipping Company. Multicoloured.
201 2 d. Type **48** . . . . 1·75 1·25
202 3 d. Container ship at sea (vert) 2·50 1·75

1986. 10th Anniv of Emirates Telecommunications Corporation.
203 250 f. Type **49** . . . . 2·10 1·50
204 3 d. As Type **49** but with sun behind emblem . . . . . . 2·50 1·90

50 Emblem, Boeing 737 Airliner and Camel Rider **51** Emblem and Member States' Crests

1986. 1st Anniv of Emirates Airlines. Multicoloured.
205 50 f. Type **50** 50 40
206 175 f. Boeing 737, emblem and national colours . . . . . . 2·75 2·10

1986. 7th Supreme Council Session of Gulf Co-operation Council, Abu Dhabi.
207 50 f. Type **51** 50 30
208 1 d. 75 Emblem beneath tree . 1·75 1·50
209 3 d. As No. 208 . . . . 2·75 2·75
The face value of No. 208 is wrongly shown as "1.75 FILS".

52 Dubai Trade Centre

1986. 27th Chess Olympiad, Dubai. Mult.
210 50 f. Type **52** 70 50
211 2 d. Chess players (miniature from King Alfonso X's "Book of Chess, Dice and Tablings") (horiz) . . . . 3·00 2·50
212 250 f. Chess players (miniature) (different) (horiz) . . . . . 3·50 3·00

53 Dhow, Oil Rig, Tower Block and Sun's Rays

1986. 15th National Day. Multicoloured.
214 50 f. Type **53** 45 20
215 1 d. Type **53** 90 50
216 175 f. Flag and hands holding Arabic "15" (vert) . . . . 1·75 1·40
217 2 d. As No. 216 . . . . . . 2·25 2·00

54 Emblem

1986. Arab Police Day.
218 **54** 50 f. multicoloured 70 50
219 1 d. multicoloured . . . . 1·40 1·10

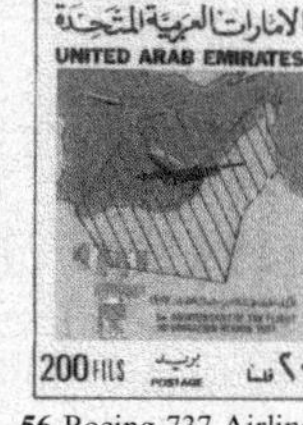
55 Emblem on Landscape **56** Boeing 737 Airliner and Map

1987. Municipalities and Environment Week.
220 **55** 50 f. multicoloured 45 35
221 1 d. multicoloured 90 75

1987. 1st Anniv of United Arab Emirates Flight Information Region.
222 **56** 200 f. multicoloured . . . 2·00 2·00
223 250 f. multicoloured . . . 2·50 2·50

57 Flower in Droplet **58** University Emblem

1987. "Save Energy". Multicoloured.
224 50 f. Type **57** 50 50
225 2 d. Globe as sun over oil derrick 5·00 5·00

1987. 10th Anniv of U.A.E. University.
226 **58** 1 d. multicoloured 80 80
227 3 d. multicoloured . . . . 2·25 2·25

59 Oil Rig

1987. 25th Anniv of First Crude Oil Shipment from Abu Dhabi.
228 **59** 50 f. multicoloured 50 45
229 – 1 d. light blue, black and blue 90 85
230 – 175 f. grey, black and blue 1·60 1·50
231 – 2 d. multicoloured . . . . 2·00 2·00
DESIGNS—VERT: 1 d. Aerial view of drilling platform; 175 f. Rig workers with drill head. HORIZ: 2 d. Oil tanker at sea.

60 Trees and Dates in Arched Window **61** Graph and Woman holding Baby

1987. Arab Palm Tree and Dates Day. Multicoloured.
232 50 f. Type **60** 45 45
233 1 d. Trees and fruit 85 85

1987. U.N.I.C.E.F Child Survival Campaign.
234 **61** 50 f. multicoloured 35 35
235 – 1 d. blue, black and pink . 65 65
236 – 175 f. black, green & emer . 1·10 1·10
237 – 2 d. multicoloured . . . . 1·50 1·50
DESIGNS—VERT: 1 d. Vaccinating baby; 175 f. Oral rehydration therapy. HORIZ: 2 d. Mother breastfeeding.

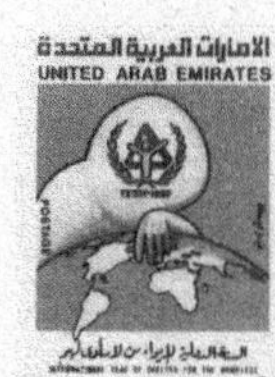
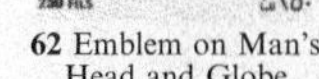
62 Emblem on Man's Head and Globe **63** Salim bin Ali al-Owais

1987. International Year of Shelter for the Homeless.
238 **62** 2 d. multicoloured . . . . 1·60 1·60
239 250 f. multicoloured . . . . 1·90 1·90

1987. Birth Centenary of Salim bin Ali al-Owais (poet).
240 **63** 1 d. multicoloured . . . . 1·10 1·10
241 2 d. multicoloured . . . . 2·40 2·40

64 Lockheed TriStar 500 and Terminal Building

1987. 6th Anniv of Abu Dhabi Int Airport. Mult.
242 50 f. Type **64** 50 50
243 50 f. Reception area 50 50
244 100 f. Lockheed TriStar 500 over air traffic control centre . . 1·25 1·25
245 100 f. Lockheed TriStar 500 and Boeing 737 at gangways . . 1·25 1·25

65 Writing in Sand, Black-lip Pearl Oyster and Pearls

1988. National Arts Festival.
246 **65** 50 f. multicoloured 50 50
247 250 f. multicoloured . . . . 1·75 1·75

66 Fisherman on Shore (Layla Mohammed Khalfan)

1988. Children's Paintings. Multicoloured.
248 50 f. Type **66** 45 30
249 1 d. Woman and flowers (Zeinab Nasir Mohammed) (vert) . . 80 65
250 1 d. 75 Flowers with girls' faces (Fatma Ali Abdullah) (vert) . 1·40 1·10
251 2 d. Teddy bear, cat and girls playing (Saaly Mohammed Jowda) . . . . 1·50 1·25

67 Masked Youth **68** Emblem and Urban and Desert Scenes

1988. Palestinian "Intifida" Movement.
252 **67** 2 d. multicoloured . . . . 1·40 1·40
253 250 f. multicoloured . . . . 1·75 1·75

1988. National Banking Anniversaries. Mult.
254 50 f. Type **68** (20th anniv of National Bank of Abu Dhabi) 1·00 1·00
255 50 f. Emblem (25th anniv of National Bank of Dubai Ltd) 1·00 1·00

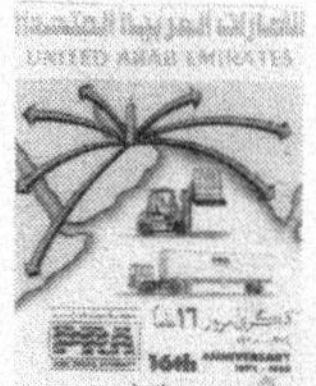
69 Map, Fork-lift Truck and Container Lorry **70** Swimming

1988. 16th Anniv of Port Rashid. Multicoloured.
256 50 f. Type **69** 35 35
257 1 d. Container ship and view of port 70 70
258 175 f. Ro-ro ferry and small boats at anchorages . . . . 1·25 1·25
259 2 d. Container ship at dockside 1·60 1·60

1988. Olympic Games, Seoul. Multicoloured.
260 2 d. Type **70** . . . . 1·50 1·50
261 250 f. Cycling . . . . 1·75 1·75

71 Vase

1988. 1st Anniv of Ras al Khaimah National Museum. Multicoloured.
262 50 f. Type **71** 30 30
263 3 d. Gold ornament (horiz) . 1·60 1·60

72 Emblem

1988. 18th Arab Scouts Conference, Abu Dhabi.
264 **72** 1 d. multicoloured 55 55

73 Dahlia

1989. 10th Tree Day. Multicoloured.
265 50 f. Ghaf tree 30 30
266 100 f. Palm tree 60 60
267 250 f. Type **73** . . . . 1·40 1·40

74 Airport

1989. 10th Anniv of Sharjah International Airport.
268 **74** 50 f. multicoloured 40 40
269 100 f. multicoloured . . . 90 90

75 Short S.23 Flying Boat **76** Newspaper

1989. 80th Anniv of Gulf Postal Services. Multicoloured.
270 50 f. Type **75** 35 35
271 3 d. "Bombala" (freighter) . . 1·60 1·60

1989. 20th Anniv of "Al-Ittihad" (newspaper). Multicoloured.

272 50 f. Type **76** 30 30
273 1 d. Newspaper offices 60 60

77 Emblem and Map

1989. 5th Anniv of Gulf Investment Corporation.

274 **77** 50 f. multicoloured 25 25
275 2 d. multicoloured . . . . 1·00 1·00

78 Offering Leaf to Child

1989. International Volunteer Day. U.A.E. Red Crescent Society. Multicoloured.

276 2 d. Type **78** . . . . 1·00 1·00
277 250 f. Crippled child in open hands (vert) . . . . 1·40 1·40

79 Bank Emblem and Buildings

80 Compass and Dhow

1989. 20th Anniv of Commercial Bank of Dubai. Multicoloured.

278 50 f. Type **79** 30 30
279 1 d. Bank building 60 60

1989. Bin Majid (15th-century navigator) Heritage Revival. Multicoloured.

280 1 d. Type **80** 50 50
281 3 d. Dhow (vert) . . . . 1·50 1·50

81 Festival Sites

82 Saker Falcon

1990. 3rd National Arts Festival, Al-Ain.

282 **81** 50 f. multicoloured 30 30
283 1 d. multicoloured 60 60

1990. Multicoloured, background colour given.

(a) Size 18 × 23 mm.

284 **82** 5 f. blue 10 10
285 20 f. mauve 10 10
286 25 f. pink 15 15
287 50 f. brown 25 25
288 100 f. bistre 45 45
289 150 f. green 70 70
290 175 f. green 80 80

(b) Size 21 × 26 mm.

291 **82** 2 d. lilac 90 90
292 250 f. blue . . . . 1·10 1·10
293 3 d. pink . . . . 1·40 1·40
294 5 d. orange . . . . 2·25 2·25
295 10 d. yellow . . . . 4·50 4·50
296 20 d. green . . . . 9·00 9·00
297 50 d. green . . . . 22·00 22·00

83 Children and Leaves

84 Leaning Tower of Pisa, Flag and U.A.E. Mascot

1990. Children's Culture Festival.

301 **83** 50 f. multicoloured 30 30
302 250 f. multicoloured . . . 1·40 1·40

1990. World Cup Football Championship, Italy. Multicoloured.

303 50 f. Type **84** 30 30
304 1 d. Desert, flag and mascot (vert) 55 55
305 2 d. Mascot on ball (vert) . . 1·10 1·10
306 250 f. Flags around mascot . 1·40 1·40

85 Projects and Buildings

1990. 25th Anniv of Dubai Chamber of Commerce and Industry. Multicoloured.

308 **85** 50 f. multicoloured 30 30
309 1 d. multicoloured 60 60

86 Weeping Eyes and Child on Globe

87 Periwinkle ("Catharanthus roseus")

1990. Child Survival Programme. Multicoloured.

310 175 f. Type **86** 90 90
311 2 d. Emaciated child and newspapers . . . . 1·00 1·00

1990. Flowers. Multicoloured.

312 50 f. "Centavrea pseudo sinaica" 30 30
313 50 f. Ushar bush ("Calotropis procera") 30 30
314 50 f. "Argyrolobeum roseum" 30 30
315 50 f. "Lamranthus roseus" . 30 30
316 50 f. "Hibiscus rosa sinensis" 30 30
317 50 f. "Nerium oleander" . . 30 30
318 50 f. Type **87** 30 30
319 50 f. "Bougainvillaea glabra" (wrongly inscr "Bogainvillea") 30 30

88 O.P.E.C. Emblem and Flame

89 Industrial Pollution and Dead Animals

1990. 30th Anniv of Organization of Petroleum Exporting Countries. Multicoloured.

321 50 f. Emblem, flames, hands and oil rigs 30 30
322 1 d. Type **88** 55 55
323 175 f. Emblem and droplet . 1·00 1·00

1990. "Our Planet Our Health". Multicoloured.

324 50 f. Type **89** 25 25
325 3 d. Industrial and vehicle pollution covering globe . . 1·50 1·50

90 Grand Mosque, Abu Dhabi

91 U.A.E. Crest and Graph

1990. Mosques. Multicoloured.

326 1 d. Type **90** 55 55
327 2 d. Al-Jumeirah Mosque, Dubai (vert) . . . . 1·00 1·00

1990. 10th Anniv of Central Bank. Mult.

328 50 f. Type **91** 25 25
329 175 f. Banknotes and building (horiz) 90 90

92 Tree

93 Globes and Buildings

1990. International Conference on High-salinity Tolerant Plants, Al-Ain. Multicoloured.

330 50 f. Type **92** 25 25
331 250 f. Trees along shoreline . . 1·40 1·40

1991. Abu Dhabi International Fair.

332 **93** 50 f. multicoloured 30 30
333 2 d. multicoloured . . . . 1·25 1·25

94 Emblem

1991. World Telecommunications Day. "Telecommunications and Safety of Human Life".

334 **94** 2 d. multicoloured . . . . 1·10 1·10
335 3 d. multicoloured . . . . 1·50 1·50

95 Shaikh Saqr Mosque, Ras al Khaimah

1991. Mosques. Multicoloured.

336 1 d. Type **95** 55 55
337 2 d. King Faisal Mosque, Sharjah . . . . 1·10 1·10

See also Nos. 371/2 and 411/2.

96 "Native Games" (Robba Mohamed Sofian)

1991. Children's Paintings. Multicoloured.

338 50 f. Type **96** 30 30
339 1 d. "National Day" (Yasmin Mohamed al-Rahim) 60 60
340 175 f. "Blind Man's Buff" (Amal Ibrahim Mohamed) . . . . 1·00 1·00
341 250 f. "Native Dance" (Amina Ali Hassan) . . . . 1·40 1·40

97 Yellow-marked Butterfly Fish

1991. Fishes. Multicoloured.

342 50 f. Type **97** 30 30
343 50 f. Red snapper 30 30
344 50 f. Golden trevally 30 30
345 50 f. Two-banded porgy . . . 30 30
346 1 d. Black bream 55 55
347 1 d. Three-banded grunt . . . 55 55
348 1 d. Greasy grouper 55 55
349 1 d. Rabbit fish 55 55

98 Shaikh Rashid and Abu Dhabi Airport

99 Fire Fighting

1991. 1st Death Anniv of Shaikh Rashid bin Said al-Maktoum (ruler of Dubai). Multicoloured.

351 50 f. Type **98** 30 30
352 1 d. Shaikh Rashid and modern and old buildings (horiz) . . 55 55
353 175 f. Shaikh Rashid and seafront hotels 95 95
354 2 d. Jebel Ali container port, Shaikh Rashid and dish aerial (horiz) . . . . 1·10 1·10

1991. Civil Defence Day.

355 **99** 50 f. multicoloured 30 30
356 1 d. multicoloured 60 60

100 Panavia Tornado F Mk 3 Jet Fighter over Dubai Airport

101 Flags and Emblem

1991. Int Aerospace Exhibition, Dubai. Mult.

357 175 f. Type **100** 90 90
358 2 d. View of under-side of Panavia Tornado over Dubai airport . . . . 1·00 1·00

1991. 10th Anniv of Gulf Co-operation Council.

359 **101** 50 f. multicoloured . . . 25 25
360 3 d. multicoloured . . . . 1·50 1·50

102 Shaikh Zaid bin Sultan al Nahayyan of Abu Dhabi (President of U.A.E.)

1991. 20th National Day. Multicoloured.

361 75 f. Type **102** 45 45
362 75 f. Shaikh Humaid bin Rashid al Naimi of Ajman and fort (to right of stamp) with cannon 45 45
363 75 f. Shaikh Maktoum bin Rashid al-Maktoum of Dubai and fort (to left of stamp) with cannon 45 45
364 75 f. Shaikh Hamad bin Mohamed al Sharqi of Fujeira and fort on hillock 45 45
365 75 f. Shaikh Saqr bin Mohamed al-Qasimi of Ras al Khaima and fort (tower and tree in foreground) 45 45
366 75 f. Shaikh Sultan bin Mohamed al Qasimi of Sharjah and fort (to left of stamp with Arabs in doorway) 45 45
367 75 f. Shaikh Rashid bin Ahmed al Moalla of Umm al Qiwain and fort (to right of stamp with trees growing over walls) . . 45 45

103 Derrick

104 Fort Jahili, Al Ain

1992. 20th Anniv of Abu Dhabi National Oil Company.

369 **103** 175 f. multicoloured . . . 90 90
370 250 f. multicoloured . . . 1·25 1·25

1992. Mosques. As T **95**. Multicoloured.

371 50 f. Shaikh Rashid bin Humaid al Naimi Mosque, Ajman . 30 30
372 1 d. Shaikh Ahmed bin Rashid al Moalla Mosque, Umm al Qiwain 60 60

1992. "Expo '92" World's Fair, Seville.

373 **104** 2 d. multicoloured . . . . 1·10 1·10
374 250 f. multicoloured . . . 15·00 15·00

105 Emblem and Family

1992. Deaf Child Week. Multicoloured.
375 1 d. Type **105** 60 60
376 3 d. Hearing aid in ear . . . . 1·50 1·50

106 Aerial View of Port

1992. 20th Anniv of Zayed Sea Port, Abu Dhabi. Multicoloured.
377 50 f. Type **106** 30 30
378 1 d. Cranes on dockside . . . 60 60
379 175 f. Loading container ship . 90 90
380 2 d. Map showing routes from port . . . . 1·10 1·10

107 Yachting **108** Football Match (Najla Saif Mohamed Harib)

1992. Olympic Games, Barcelona. Multicoloured.
381 50 f. Type **107** 30 30
382 1 d. Running 60 60
383 175 f. Swimming 90 90
384 250 f. Cycling . . . . 1·25 1·25

1992. Children's Paintings. Multicoloured.
386 50 f. Type **108** 30 30
387 1 d. Children in park (Anoud Adnan Ali Mohamed) . . . 60 60
388 2 d. Family at playground (Ahlam Ibrahim Ahmed) . . 1·10 1·10
389 250 f. Children playing amongst trees (Dallal Ali Salih) . . . 1·25 1·25

109 Bank Building **110** Tambourah

1992. 15th Anniv of Emirates Bank International.
390 **109** 50 f. multicoloured . . . 30 30
391 – 175 f. gold, brown & red . 90 90
DESIGN—33 × 40 mm: 175 f. Bank emblem.

1992. Musical Instruments. Multicoloured.
392 50 f. Type **110** 30 30
393 50 f. Oud (stringed instrument) 30 30
394 50 f. Rababah (stringed instrument with bow) . . . 30 30
395 1 d. Mizmar (wind instrument) and shindo (drum) (horiz) . 60 60
396 1 d. Marwas and duff (hand-held drums) (horiz) 60 60
397 1 d. Tabel (drum) and hibban (bagpipe) (horiz) 60 60

111 Emblem

1992. 13th Supreme Council Session of Gulf Co-operation Council, Abu Dhabi.
399 **111** 50 f. multicoloured . . . 30 30
400 2 d. multicoloured . . . 1·10 1·10

112 Camel Race

1992. The Dromedary. Multicoloured.
401 50 f. Type **112** 30 30
402 1 d. Camel riders and mother with young (vert) 55 55
403 175 f. Camels at well and mother with young 90 90
404 2 d. Camels (vert) . . . . . 1·10 1·10

113 Golf **114** Club Building

1993. Tourism. Multicoloured.
405 50 f. Type **113** 30 30
406 1 d. Fishing (vert) 55 55
407 2 d. Sailing . . . . 1·10 1·10
408 250 f. Sight-seeing by car . . 1·40 1·40

1993. Dubai Creek Golf and Yacht Club. Mult.
409 2 d. Type **114** . . . . 1·10 1·10
410 250 f. Club building and sea shore . . . . 1·40 1·40

1993. Mosques. As T **95**. Multicoloured.
411 50 f. Thabit bin Khalid Mosque, Fujeira 30 30
412 1 d. Sharq al Morabbah Mosque, Al-Ain 55 55

115 National Crest and Sports

1993. National Youth Festival. Multicoloured.
413 50 f. Type **115** 30 30
414 3 d. National crest and sciences 1·60 1·60

116 Textile Cone

1993. Sea Shells. Multicoloured.
415 25 f. Type **116** 15 10
416 50 f. Atlantic pearl oyster . . 25 25
417 100 f. Woodcock murex . . . 50 50
418 150 f. "Natica pulicaris" . . 75 75
419 175 f. Giant spider conch . . 90 90
420 200 f. "Cardita bicolor" . . . 1·00 1·00
421 250 f. Gray's cowrie . . . . 1·25 1·25
422 300 f. "Cymatium trilineatum" 1·50 1·50

117 Addict within Capsule

1993. Anti-drugs Campaign. Multicoloured.
423 50 f. Type **117** 30 30
424 1 d. Family on skull, globe and drugs (vert) 60 60

118 Commercial Buildings **119** Aerial View of Port

1993. 25th Anniv of Abu Dhabi National Bank. Multicoloured.
425 50 f. Type **118** 30 30
426 1 d. Bank emblem 60 60
427 175 f. Bank building and emblem 1·10 1·10
428 2 d. Commercial buildings within shield . . . . 1·25 1·25

1993. Dubai Ports Authority. Multicoloured.
429 50 f. Type **119** 30 30
430 1 d. Cranes loading containers 60 60
431 2 d. Aerial view of port (different) . . . . 1·10 1·10
432 250 f. Arrowed routes on globe 1·50 1·50

120 Soldiers on Parade (Mouza Musabah al-Mazroui)

1993. National Day. Children's Paintings. Multicoloured.
433 50 f. Type **120** 30 30
434 1 d. Woman and children (Shreen Naeem Hassan Radwan) (vert) 60 60
435 175 f. Flag and dhow (Samiha Mohamad Sultan) . . . . . 1·25 1·25
436 2 d. Decorations and fireworks (Omer Abdulla Rabia Thani) 1·25 1·25

121 Hili Tomb

1993. Archaeological Finds from Al-Ain. Multicoloured.
437 50 f. Type **121** 30 30
438 1 d. Hili decorative tile 60 60
439 175 f. Qattarah figure . . . . 1·00 1·00
440 250 f. Hili bowl . . . . 1·50 1·50

122 Horse rearing

1994. Arab Horses. Multicoloured.
441 50 f. Type **122** 30 30
442 1 d. Grey (horiz) 60 60
443 175 f. Bay with white blaze . . 1·00 1·00
444 250 f. Piebald (horiz) . . . . . 1·50 1·50

123 Children with Flags and Balloons

1994. 10th Children's Festival, Sharjah. Children's Paintings. Multicoloured.
445 50 f. Type **123** 30 30
446 1 d. Children in forest 60 60
447 175 f. Children with balloons and child painting . . . . 1·00 1·00
448 2 d. Children in garden . . . . 1·10 1·10

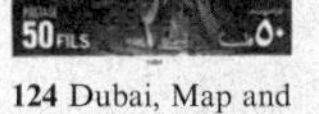

124 Dubai, Map and Emblems **125** Holy Kaaba and Globe

1994. 10th Arab Towns Organization Congress, Dubai. Multicoloured.
449 50 f. Type **124** 25 25
450 1 d. Different view of Dubai, map and emblems (horiz) . . 55 55

1994. Pilgrimage to Mecca. Multicoloured.
451 50 f. Type **125** 25 25
452 2 d. Crowds around Holy Kaaba 1·10 1·10

126 Homes (Arab Housing Day) **127** Covered Vessel

1994. Anniversaries and Events. Multicoloured.
453 1 d. Type **126** 55 55
454 1 d. Children playing and couple (International Year of the Family) (horiz) 55 55
455 1 d. National Olympic Committee emblem, rings and sports (cent of Int Olympic Committee) (horiz) 55 55
456 1 d. Paper, pen-nib and dove (10th anniv of Emirates Writers' Association) . . . 55 55

1994. Archaeological Finds from Al-Qusais, Dubai. Multicoloured.
457 50 f. Type **127** 25 25
458 1 d. Jug (horiz) 55 55
459 175 f. Jug (different) (horiz) . 95 95
460 250 f. Bowl (horiz) . . . . . 1·25 1·25

128 Arabian Leopard

1994. Environmental Protection. The Cat Family. Multicoloured.
461 50 f. Type **128** 30 30
462 1 d. Gordon's wildcat 60 60
463 2 d. Caracal . . . . 1·25 1·25
464 250 f. Sandcat . . . . 1·75 1·75

129 Little Green Bee Eaters

1994. Birds. Multicoloured.
465 50 f. Type **129** 30 30
466 175 f. White-collared kingfishers 1·00 1·00
467 2 d. Crab plovers . . . . . 1·25 1·25
468 250 f. Indian rollers . . . . . 1·75 1·75

130 Championship Emblem **131** Horse's Head

1994. 12th Arab Gulf Football Championship, Abu Dhabi. Multicoloured.
470 50 f. Type **130** 25 25
471 3 d. Match scene (horiz) . . . 1·60 1·60

1995. Archaeological Finds from Mulaiha, Sharjah. Multicoloured.
472 50 f. Type **131** 25 25
473 175 f. Coin 95 95
474 2 d. Ancient writing on leather 1·10 1·10
475 250 f. Stone tablet (horiz) . . 1·25 1·25

132 Al-Naashat

1995. National Dances. Multicoloured.
476 50 f. Type **132** 25 25
477 175 f. Al-Ayaalah 95 95
478 2 d. Al-Shahhoh . . . . . . 1·10 1·10

133 Helicopters **134** Arab League

1995. International Defence Exhibition and Conference, Abu Dhabi. Multicoloured.
479 50 f. Type **133** 25 25
480 1 d. Exhibition emblem 50 50
481 175 f. Missile corvettes (horiz) . 90 90
482 2 d. Artillery (horiz) . . . . . 1·00 1·00

1995. 50th Anniversaries. Anniversary Emblems. Multicoloured.

483 1 d. Type **134** 50 50
484 2 d. F.A.O. . . . . 1·00 1·00
485 250 f. U.N.O. . . . . 1·25 1·25

135 Symbols of Postal Services

1995. 10th Anniv of General Postal Authority.

486 **135** 50 f. multicoloured 20 20

136 Exhibition Emblem

1995. 1st Gulf Co-operation Council Stamp Exhibition, Abu Dhabi.

487 **136** 50 f. multicoloured 20 20

137 Rolling Hoop

138 Lesser Kestrel

1995. National Games. Multicoloured.

488 50 f. Type **137** 20 20
489 175 f. Swinging 65 65
490 2 d. Sticks in stone square game 75 75
491 250 f. Stone game 95 95

1995. Birds. Multicoloured.

492 50 f. Type **138** 20 20
493 175 f. Socotra cormorant . . . 75 75
494 2 d. Cream-coloured courser . 90 90
495 250 f. Hoopoe . . . . 1·10 1·10

139 Figures and Tower Block

1995. Population and Housing Census. Mult.

496 50 f. Type **139** 15 15
497 250 f. City and stylized family 85 85

140 "Folklore Show" (Ibtisam Mussa)

1995. National Day. Children's Paintings. Multicoloured.

498 50 f. Type **140** 15 15
499 175 f. "Children dancing" (Shimaa Mohamed Abdullah Khoury) 60 60
500 2 d. "Children holding balloons" (Khoula Ibrahim) 70 70
501 250 f. "Car festival" (Fatima Jumaa) 85 85

141 Dugongs

1996. Environmental Protection. Sea Mammals. Multicoloured.

502 50 f. Type **141** 15 15
503 2 d. Common dolphins . . . 70 70
504 3 d. Humpback whales . . . 1·00 1·00

142 Competitor

143 Earthenware Urn (Bathna-Fujaira)

1996. Hobie Cat 16 World Championships. Mult.

506 50 f. Type **142** 15 15
507 3 d. Yacht and building . . . 1·00 1·00

1996. Archaeological Finds. Multicoloured.

508 50 f. Type **143** 15 15
509 175 f. Earthenware pot with handles (Bidya-Fujaira) . . 60 60
510 250 f. Bronze bangle (Qidfa-Fujaira) 85 85
511 3 d. Bronze ring (Dibba-Fujaira) (horiz) . . . . 1·00 1·00

144 Shooting

1996. Olympic Games, Atlanta. Multicoloured.

512 50 f. Type **144** 15 15
513 1 d. Cycling (vert) 35 35
514 250 f. Running (vert) 85 85
515 350 f. Swimming . . . . . . 1·25 1·25

145 Emblem

146 Emblem, Landmarks and Players

1996. 21st Anniv of Women's Union. Multicoloured.

516 50 f. Type **145** 15 15
517 3 d. Woman's hands and emblem (horiz) . . . . 1·00 1·00

1996. 11th Asian Football Cup Championship. Multicoloured.

518 1 d. Type **146** 35 35
519 250 f. Player with ball 85 85

147 "Drug" Snake crushing weeping Globe

1996. Anti-drugs Campaign. Multicoloured.

520 50 f. Type **147** 15 15
521 3 d. Healthy man and drug-wrecked skull . . . . . . 1·00 1·00

148 Shaikh Said and House

1996. Centenary of Shaikh Said al Maktoum House (museum). Multicoloured.

522 50 f. Type **148** 15 15
523 250 f. Shaikh Said and close-up view of House 85 85
524 350 f. House at sunset . . . . 1·25 1·25

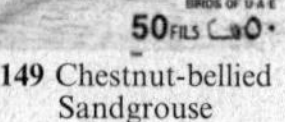

149 Chestnut-bellied Sandgrouse

150 Head forming Waterfall (Abdullah Muhammed Abdullah al-Sharhan)

1996. Birds. Multicoloured.

525 50 f. Type **149** 15 15
526 150 f. Striated scops owl . . . 50 50
527 250 f. Grey hypocolius 85 85
528 3 d. White-throated robin . . 1·00 1·00
529 350 f. Sooty falcon . . . . . . 1·25 1·25

1996. Children's Paintings. Multicoloured.

530 50 f. Type **150** 15 15
531 1 d. Dhows (Hamda Muhammed Abdullah) (horiz) 35 35
532 250 f. Flowers (Hind Muhammed bin Dhahi) 85 85
533 350 f. Girl and tent (Lin Atta Yaghi) . . . . 1·25 1·25

151 Emirates Rulers

1996. 25th National Day. Multicoloured.

534 50 f. Type **151** 15 15
535 1 d. Emirates crest and flag . . 35 35
536 150 f. Type **151** 50 50
537 3 d. As No. 535 . . . . 1·00 1·00

UNITED NATIONS Pt. 22; Pt. 8; Pt. 2

A. NEW YORK HEADQUARTERS

For use on mail posted at the Post Office at U.N. Headquarters, New York.

NOTE: Similar designs, but in different colours and values in Swiss Francs (F.S.) are issues of the Geneva office. Those with face values in Austrian Schillings are issues of the Vienna office. These are listed after the New York issues.

100 cents = 1 dollar

1 "Peoples of the World"

3 U.N. Emblem

1951.

1 **1** 1 c. mauve 10 10
2 – $1\frac{1}{2}$ c. green 10 10
3 **3** 2 c. violet 10 10
4 – 3 c. blue and purple 10 10
5 – 5 c. blue 15 10
6 **1** 10 c. brown 15 10
7 – 15 c. blue and violet 20 15
8 – 20 c. brown 50 30
9 – 25 c. blue and black 45 30
10 – 50 c. blue . . . . 5·00 1·75
11 **3** $1 red . . . . 2·00 85

DESIGNS—VERT: $1\frac{1}{2}$, 50 c. U.N. Headquarters, New York; 5 c. Clasped hands. HORIZ: 3, 15, 25 c. U.N. flag; 20 c. Hemispheres and U.N. emblem.

A **7** Seagull and Airplane

1951. Air.

A12 A **7** 6 c. red 15 15
A7 10 c. green 15 15
A14 – 15 c. blue 25 15
A15 – 25 c. black 90 40

DESIGN: 15, 25 c. Swallows and U.N. emblem.

7 Veterans' War Memorial Building, San Francisco

1952. 7th Anniv of Signing of U.N. Charter.

12 **7** 5 c. blue 25 15

8 "Flame of Freedom"

1952. Human Rights Day.

13 **8** 3 c. green 15 15
14 5 c. blue 40 15

9 Homeless Family

1953. Protection for Refugees.

15 **9** 3 c. brown 15 15
16 5 c. blue 70 30

10 "Universal Postal Union"

1953. Universal Postal Union.

17 **10** 3 c. sepia 20 15
18 5 c. blue 90 25

11 Gearwheels and U.N. Emblem

12 "Flame of Freedom"

1953. Technical Assistance for Underdeveloped Areas.

19 **11** 3 c. grey 15 15
20 5 c. green 75 30

1953. Human Rights Day.

21 **12** 3 c. blue 20 15
22 5 c. red . . . . 1·40 25

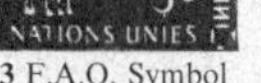

13 F.A.O. Symbol

14 U.N. Emblem and Anvil

1954. Food and Agriculture Organization.

23 **13** 3 c. yellow and green . . . 40 15
24 8 c. yellow and blue 85 40

NOTE. In the following issues the majority of the values unillustrated have the commemorative inscription or initials in another language.

1954. International Labour Organization.

25 **14** 3 c. brown 20 15
26 8 c. mauve . . . . 1·50 40

15 U.N. European Office, Geneva

16 Mother and Child

1954. United Nations Day.

27 **15** 3 c. violet . . . . 2·75 60
28 8 c. red 25 15

1954. Human Rights Day.

29 **16** 3 c. orange . . . . 6·50 1·25
30 8 c. green 25 15

17 "Flight"

1955. International Civil Aviation Organization.

31 **17** 3 c. blue . . . . 2·50 40
32 8 c. red 80 60

18 U.N.E.S.C.O. Symbol

1955. U.N. Educational, Scientific and Cultural Organization.

33 **18** 3 c. mauve 40 15
34 8 c. blue 15 15

19 U.N. Charter

20 "Flame of Freedom"

1955. 10th Anniv of U.N.

35 **19** 3 c. red . . . . 2·50 35
36 4 c. green 20 10
37 8 c. black 20 15

1955. Human Rights Day.

39 **20** 3 c. blue 15 15
40 8 c. green 50 20

21 "Telecommunication"

22 Staff of Aesculapius

1956. International Telecommunication Union.

41 **21** 3 c. blue 40 15
42 8 c. red . . . . 1·10 40

1956. World Health Organization.

43 **22** 3 c. blue 15 15
44 8 c. brown 85 45

23 General Assembly

1956. United Nations Day.

45 **23** 3 c. slate 10 10
46 8 c. olive 15 15

24 "Flame of Freedom"

25 Weather Balloon

1956. Human Rights Day.

47 **24** 3 c. purple 10 10
48 8 c. blue 15 10

1957. World Meteorological Organization.

49 **25** 3 c. blue 10 10
50 8 c. red 20 10

26 U.N.E.F. Badge

A 26 "Flight"

1957. United Nations Emergency Force.

51 **26** 3 c. blue 10 10
52 8 c. red 15 10

1957. Air.

A51 **A 26** 4 c. brown 10 10
A52 5 c. red 10 10
A53 – 7 c. blue 20 15

DESIGNS—HORIZ: 7 c. U.N. flag and Douglas DC-8-60 airplane.

On the 5 c. value inscriptions are redrawn larger than those on Type A **26**.

27 U.N. Emblem over Globe

28 "Flames of Freedom"

1957. U.N. Security Council.

55 **27** 3 c. brown 10 10
56 8 c. green 15 10

1957. Human Rights Day.

57 **28** 3 c. brown 10 10
58 8 c. black 10 10

29 Atomic Symbol

30 Central Hall, Westminster (site of first General Assembly)

1958. International Atomic Energy Agency.

59 **29** 3 c. olive 10 10
60 8 c. blue 15 10

1958. U.N. General Assembly Buildings.

61 **30** 3 c. blue 10 10
62 8 c. purple 10 10

See also Nos. 69/70, 77/8 and 123/4.

31 U.N. Seal

32 Cogwheels

1958.

63 **31** 4 c. orange 10 10
64 8 c. blue 15 10

1958. Economic and Social Council.

65 **32** 4 c. turquoise 10 10
66 8 c. red 15 10

33 Hands holding Globe

1958. Human Rights Day.

67 **33** 4 c. green 10 10
68 8 c. brown 15 10

34 New York City Building, Flushing Meadows (1946–50)

35 Emblems of U.N. Industry and Agriculture

1959. U.N. General Assembly Buildings.

69 **34** 4 c. mauve 10 10
70 8 c. turquoise 15 10

1959. U.N. Economic Commission for Europe.

71 **35** 4 c. blue 10 10
72 8 c. red 20 15

36 "The Age of Bronze" (Rodin)

37 "Protection for Refugees"

1959. U.N. Trusteeship Council.

73 **36** 4 c. red 10 10
74 8 c. green 15 10

1959. World Refugee Year.

75 **37** 4 c. red and bistre 10 10
76 8 c. blue and bistre 10 10

38 Palais de Chaillot, Paris (1948, 1951)

1960. U.N. General Assembly Buildings.

77 **38** 4 c. blue and purple 10 10
78 8 c. brown and green 10 10

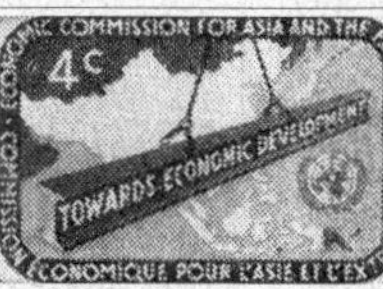

39 Steel Girder and Map

1960. U.N. Economic Commission for Asia and the Far East ("ECAFE").

79 **39** 4 c. purple, buff and turq . . 10 10
80 8 c. green, pink and blue . . 15 15

40 Tree and Emblems

41 U.N. Headquarters and Emblem

1960. 5th World Forestry Congress, Seattle.

81 **40** 4 c. multicoloured 10 10
82 8 c. multicoloured 20 15

1960. 15th Anniv of U.N.

83 **41** 4 c. blue 10 10
84 8 c. black 20 10

42 Double Block and Hook

43 Scales of Justice

1960. International Bank for Reconstruction and Development ("World Bank").

86 **42** 4 c. multicoloured 10 10
87 8 c. multicoloured 20 10

1961. International Court of Justice.

88 **43** 4 c. black, brown & yellow . 10 10
89 8 c. black, green & yellow . 20 15

44 I.M.F. Emblem

1961. International Monetary Fund.

90 **44** 4 c. blue 10 10
91 7 c. brown and yellow . . . 20 15

45 "Peace"

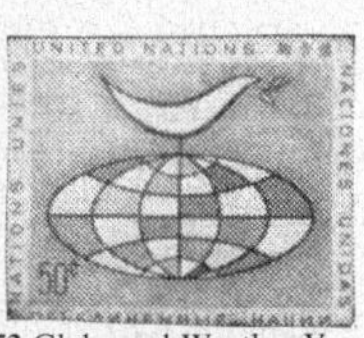

53 Globe and Weather Vane

52 Flags

1961.

92 **45** 1 c. multicoloured 10 10
93 – 2 c. multicoloured 10 10
94 – 3 c. multicoloured 10 10
95 – 5 c. red 15 10
96 – 7 c. brown, black & blue . 15 10
97 – 10 c. black, green & blue . 15 10
98 – 11 c. gold, light blue and blue 15 10
99 **52** 30 c. multicoloured 35 15
100 **53** 50 c. multicoloured 75 25

DESIGNS—HORIZ: 32 × 23 mm: 2 c. Map of the World; 10 c. Three figures on globe ("Races United"). $30\frac{1}{2} \times 23\frac{1}{2}$ mm: 3 c. U.N. Flag. $36\frac{1}{2} \times 23\frac{1}{2}$ mm: 5 c. Hands supporting "UN" and globe. $37\frac{1}{2} \times 22\frac{1}{2}$ mm: 11 c. U.N. emblem across globe. VERT—21 × 26 mm: 7 c. U.N. emblem as flowering plant.

For 1 c. in same design, but smaller, see No. 146 and for 5 c. multicoloured see No. 165.

54 Cogwheel and Map of S. America **55** Africa Hall, Addis Ababa

1961. Economic Commission for Latin America.
101 **54** 4 c. red, olive and blue . . 15 10
102 11 c. purple, red and green 25 15

1961. Economic Commission for Africa.
103 **55** 4 c. multicoloured 10 10
104 11 c. multicoloured 20 15

56 Bird feeding Young **57** "Housing and Community Facilities"

1961. 15th Anniv of U.N.I.C.E.F.
105 **56** 3 c. multicoloured 10 10
106 4 c. multicoloured 10 10
107 13 c. multicoloured 20 15

1962. U.N. Housing and Related Community Facilities Programme.
108 **57** 4 c. multicoloured 10 10
109 7 c. multicoloured 15 10

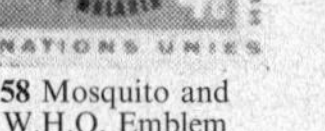

58 Mosquito and W.H.O. Emblem **59** U.N. Flag at Half-mast

1962. Malaria Eradication.
110 **58** 4 c. multicoloured 10 10
111 11 c. multicoloured 15 10

1962. Dag Hammarskjold (U.N. Secretary-General, 1953–61) Memorial Issue.
112 **59** 5 c. indigo, blue and black . 10 10
113 15 c. blue, grey and black . 40 15

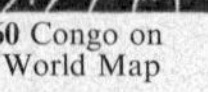

60 Congo on World Map **61** "Peace in Space"

1962. U.N. Congo Operation.
114 **60** 4 c. multicoloured 15 10
115 11 c. multicoloured 30 15

1962. U.N. Committee on Peaceful Uses of Outer Space.
116 **61** 4 c. blue 10 10
117 11 c. mauve 15 10

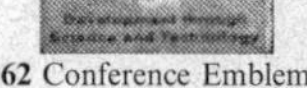

62 Conference Emblem **63** Wheat

1963. Science and Technology Conf, Geneva.
118 **62** 5 c. multicoloured 10 10
119 11 c. multicoloured 20 15

1963. Freedom from Hunger.
120 **63** 5 c. yellow, green & orange 15 10
121 11 c. yellow, red & orange . 20 15

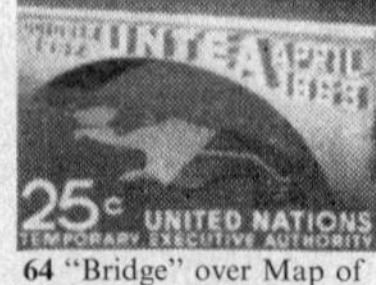

A **65** "Flight" **64** "Bridge" over Map of West New Guinea

1963. Air. Multicoloured.
A122 6 c. "Space" 10 10
A123 8 c. Type **A65** 15 10
A124 13 c. "Bird" 20 15
A125 15 c. "Birds in Flight" . . 25 15
A126 25 c. Douglas DC-8 and airmail envelope 50 20
SIZES—HORIZ: 6 c. As Type **A 65**: 13, 25 c. $30\frac{1}{2}\times23$ mm. VERT: 15 c. $23\times30\frac{1}{2}$ mm.

1963. United Nations Temporary Executive Authority (UNTEA) in West New Guinea.
122 **64** 25 c. green, blue & drab . 40 15

65 General Assembly Building and Flags **66** "Flame of Freedom"

1963. U.N. General Assembly Buildings.
123 **65** 5 c. multicoloured 10 10
124 11 c. multicoloured . . . 20 15

1963. 15th Anniv of Declaration of Human Rights.
125 **66** 5 c. multicoloured 10 10
126 11 c. multicoloured . . . 20 15

67 Ships at Sea

1964. Inter-Governmental Maritime Consultative Organization (I.M.C.O.).
127 **67** 5 c. multicoloured 15 10
128 11 c. multicoloured . . . 35 30

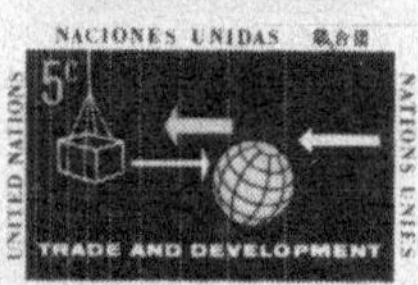

68 "Trade and Development"

1964. U.N. Trade and Development Conf, Geneva.
129 **68** 5 c. yellow, black & red . 10 10
130 11 c. yellow, black & bistre 20 15

69 Opium Poppy and Reaching Hands **70** Atomic Explosion and Padlock

1964. Narcotics Control.
131 **69** 5 c. red and black 15 10
132 11 c. green and black . . . 40 20

1964. Cessation of Nuclear Testing.
133 **70** 5 c. sepia and brown . . . 10 10

71 "Teaching" **72** Key, Globe and "Graph"

1964. "Education for Progress".
134 **71** 4 c. multicoloured 10 10
135 5 c. multicoloured 10 10
136 11 c. multicoloured . . . 15 15

1965. U.N. Special Fund.
137 **72** 5 c. multicoloured 10 10
138 11 c. multicoloured . . . 20 15

73 Cyprus "Leaves" and U.N. Emblem **74** "From Semaphore to Satellite"

1965. Peace-keeping Force in Cyprus.
139 **73** 5 c. olive, black & orange . 10 10
140 11 c. green, black & lt grn . 20 15

1965. I.T.U. Centenary.
141 **74** 5 c. multicoloured 10 10
142 11 c. multicoloured 25 20

75 I.C.Y. Emblem **76** "Peace"

1965. 20th Anniv of United Nations and International Co-operation Year.
143 **75** 5 c. blue 15 10
144 15 c. mauve 30 20

1965.
146 **76** 1 c. multicoloured 10 10
147 – 15 c. multicoloured 20 10
148 – 20 c. multicoloured 25 15
149 – 25 c. ultramarine and blue . 40 15
150 – $1 blue and turquoise . . . 1·25 60
DESIGNS—$24\frac{1}{2}\times30$ mm: 15 c. Opening words, U.N. Charter. 22×32 mm: 20 c. U.N. emblem and Headquarters. 24×24 mm: 25 c. U.N. emblem. 33×23 mm: $1 U.N. emblem encircled.

81 "Expanding Population" **82** Globe and Flags

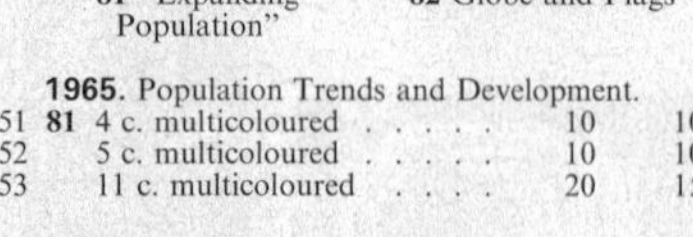

1965. Population Trends and Development.
151 **81** 4 c. multicoloured 10 10
152 5 c. multicoloured 10 10
153 11 c. multicoloured 20 15

1966. World Federation of United Nations Assns. (W.F.U.N.A.).
154 **82** 5 c. multicoloured 10 10
155 15 c. multicoloured 20 20

83 W.H.O. Building

1966. Inaug of W.H.O. Headquarters, Geneva.
156 **83** 5 c. multicoloured 10 10
157 11 c. multicoloured 20 20

84 Coffee

1966. International Coffee Agreement of 1962.
158 **84** 5 c. multicoloured 10 10
159 11 c. multicoloured 20 15

85 Military Observer **86** Children in Closed Rail Wagon

1966. U.N. Military Observers.
160 **85** 15 c. multicoloured 25 20

1966. 20th Anniv of U.N.I.C.E.F. Multicoloured.
161 4 c. Type **86** 10 10
162 5 c. Children in locomotive and tender 15 10
163 11 c. Children in open rail wagon 30 20

89 U.N. Headquarters and World Map **91** "UN" and Emblem

1967.
164 **89** $1\frac{1}{2}$ c. multicoloured 10 10
165 – 5 c. multicoloured 15 10
166 – 6 c. multicoloured 15 10
167 **91** 13 c. blue, gold & black . . 30 20
DESIGNS—HORIZ: 5 c. As No. 95, 23×34 mm: 6 c. Aerial view of U.N. Headquarters.

92 "Progress through Development" **93** U.N. Emblem and Fireworks

1967. U.N. Development Programme.
168 **92** 5 c. multicoloured 10 10
169 11 c. multicoloured 20 15

1967. New Independent Nations Commem.
170 **93** 5 c. multicoloured 10 10
171 11 c. multicoloured 20 15

94 "Peace" **99** Baggage Labels

1967. "Expo 67", World Fair, Montreal.
172 **94** 4 c. brown and red 10 10
173 – 5 c. brown and blue . . . 10 10
174 – 8 c. multicoloured 15 10
175 – 10 c. brown and green . . 20 15
176 – 15 c. chestnut and brown . 30 30
DESIGNS—VERT: 5 c. "Justice"; 10 c. "Fraternity"; 15 c. "Truth". HORIZ ($32\times23\frac{1}{2}$ mm): 8 c. Facade of U.N. Pavilion.

The above stamps are expressed in Canadian currency and were valid for postage only from the U.N. Pavilion at the World Fair.

1967. International Tourist Year.
177 **99** 5 c. multicoloured 15 10
178 15 c. multicoloured 35 20

100 "Towards Disarmament" **101** "The Kiss of Peace" (part of Chagall's stained glass window)

1967. Disarmament Campaign.
179 **100** 6 c. multicoloured 10 10
180 13 c. multicoloured . . . 25 15

1967. United Nations Art (1st issue). Chagall's Memorial Window in U.N. Secretariat Building.
181 **101** 6 c. multicoloured 10 10
[illegible] and 251/2.

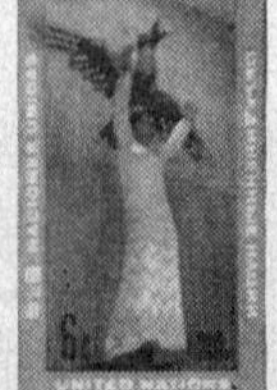

103 Globe and Diagram of U.N. Organs **104** Starcke's Statue

1968. U.N. Secretariat.

183 **103** 6 c. multicoloured 10 10
184 13 c. multicoloured . . . 20 15

1968. United Nations Art (2nd issue). Henrik Starcke's Statue in U.N. Trusteeship Council Chamber.

185 **104** 6 c. multicoloured 15 10
186 75 c. multicoloured . . . 1·00 70

105 Industrial Skyline

1968. U.N. Industrial Development Organization (U.N.I.D.O.).

187 **105** 6 c. multicoloured 10 10
188 13 c. multicoloured . . . 20 15

A **106** "Winged Envelopes"

A **107** Aircraft and U.N. Emblem

1968. Air.

A189 A **106** 10 c. multicoloured . 25 15
A190 A **107** 20 c. multicoloured . 30 25

106 Radar Scanner

1968. World Weather Watch.

189 **106** 6 c. multicoloured 15 10
190 20 c. multicoloured . . . 40 30

107 Human Rights Emblem

108 Textbooks

1968. Human Rights Year.

191 **107** 6 c. gold, ultramarine & bl 15 10
192 13 c. gold, red and pink . 20 15

1969. United Nations Institute for Training and Research (U.N.I.T.A.R.).

193 **108** 6 c. multicoloured 10 10
194 13 c. multicoloured . . . 20 15

In the 13 c. the name and value panel is at foot of stamp.

109 U.N. Building, Santiago

1969. U.N. Building, Santiago, Chile.

195 **109** 6 c. blue, lt blue & green . 10 10
196 15 c. purple, red & buff . 25 20

110 "Peace Through International Law"

111 "Labour and Development"

1969. 20th Anniv of Session of U.N. Int Law Commission.

197 **110** 6 c. multicoloured 10 10
198 13 c. multicoloured . . . 20 15

1969. 50th Anniv of I.L.O.

199 **111** 6 c. multicoloured 10 10
200 20 c. multicoloured . . . 30 20

112 "Ostrich"

114 Peace Bell

1969. United Nations Art (3rd issue). 3rd-century A.D. Tunisian Mosaic, Delegates' North Lounge. Multicoloured.

201 6 c. Type **112** 10 10
202 13 c. "Ring-necked Pheasant" 20 15

1970. United Nations Art (4th issue). Japanese Peace Bell.

203 **114** 6 c. multicoloured 10 10
204 25 c. multicoloured . . . 35 30

115 River, Power Lines and Map

1970. Lower Mekong Basin Development Project.

205 **115** 6 c. multicoloured 10 10
206 13 c. multicoloured . . . 20 15

116 "Fight Cancer"

1970. 10th Int Cancer Congress, Houston, Texas.

207 **116** 6 c. black and blue . . . 10 10
208 13 c. black and olive . . 35 15

117 Laurel Branch

120 Scales and Olive-branch

1970. 25th Anniv of United Nations.

209 **117** 6 c. multicoloured 15 15
210 13 c. multicoloured . . . 20 20
211 – 25 c. gold, lt blue & blue 40 40

DESIGN—VERT: 25 c. U.N. emblem.
On No. 210 the inscription is in French.

1970. "Peace, Justice and Progress" (Aims of the United Nations).

213 **120** 6 c. multicoloured 10 10
214 13 c. multicoloured . . . 20 15

121 U.N. Emblem on Sea-bed

122 "Refugees" (sculpture, Kaare Nygaard)

1971. Peaceful Uses of the Sea-bed.

215 **121** 6 c. multicoloured 15 10

1971. U.N. Work with Refugees.

216 **122** 6 c. black, yellow & brown 10 10
217 13 c. black, turq & blue . 20 15

123 Wheatsheaf on Globe

124 New U.P.U. H.Q. Building

1971. World Food Programme.

218 **123** 13 c. multicoloured . . . 30 20

1971. Opening of New U.P.U. Headquarters Building, Berne.

219 **124** 20 c. multicoloured . . . 30 25

125 Four-leafed Clover

127 U.N. H.Q., New York

1971. Racial Equality Year. Multicoloured.

220 8 c. Type **125** 15 10
221 13 c. Linked globes (horiz) . . 15 15

1971. Multicoloured.

222 8 c. Type **127** 15 10
223 60 c. U.N. emblem and flags . 60 45
224 95 c. "Letter changing Hands" 1·00 45

130 "Maia" (Picasso)

131 "X" over Atomic Explosion

1971. U.N. International Schools.

225 **130** 8 c. multicoloured 15 10
226 21 c. multicoloured 35 30

1972. Non-proliferation of Nuclear Weapons.

227 **131** 8 c. blue, black and pink . 30 15

132 "Proportions of Man" (Leonardo da Vinci)

A **134** Birds in Flight

1972. World Health Day.

228 **132** 15 c. multicoloured 30 15

1972. Air.

A229 – 9 c. multicoloured . . 15 10
A230 A **134** 11 c. multicoloured . . 15 10
A231 – 17 c. orange, yellow and red 25 15
A232 – 21 c. multicoloured . . 30 20

DESIGNS—23×31 mm: 9 c. "Contemporary Flight". 38×23 mm: 17 c. Clouds. 33×23 mm: 21 c. "U.N." jetstream.

137 Environmental Emblem

138 Europe "Flower"

1972. U.N. Environmental Conservation Conf, Stockholm.

233 **137** 8 c. multicoloured 15 10
234 15 c. multicoloured 25 20

1972. Economic Commission for Europe (E.C.E.).

235 **138** 21 c. multicoloured 35 30

139 "World United" (detail, Sert mural, Geneva)

140 Laurel and Broken Sword

1972. United Nations Art (5th issue).

236 **139** 8 c. brown, gold & lt brn 15 10
237 15 c. brown, gold & green . 40 25

1973. Disarmament Decade.

238 **140** 8 c. multicoloured 15 10
239 15 c. multicoloured 25 20

141 Skull on Poppy

142 Emblems within Honeycomb

1973. "Stop Drug Abuse" Campaign.

240 **141** 8 c. multicoloured 25 15
241 15 c. multicoloured . . . 45 25

1973. U.N. Volunteers Programme.

242 **142** 8 c. multicoloured 15 10
243 21 c. multicoloured . . . 35 30

143 Namibia on Map of Africa

1973. U.N. Resolution on Namibia (South West Africa).

244 **143** 8 c. multicoloured 15 10
245 15 c. multicoloured . . . 35 30

144 Human Rights Flame

1973. 25th Anniv of Declaration of Human Rights.

246 **144** 8 c. multicoloured 20 10
247 21 c. multicoloured . . . 35 20

145 H.Q. Building

1973. Inauguration of New I.L.O. Headquarters Building, Geneva.

248 **145** 10 c. multicoloured . . . 20 10
249 21 c. multicoloured . . . 35 30

146 Globe within Posthorn

1974. Centenary of U.P.U.

250 **148** 10 c. multicoloured . . . 15 10

147 "Children's Choir" (mural detail, C. Portinari)

148 Peace Dove

1974. United Nations Art (6th issue). Brazilian Peace Mural, Delegates' Lobby.

251 **147** 10 c. multicoloured . . . 15 15
252 18 c. multicoloured . . . 25 25

1974.

253 **148** 2 c. blue and ultramarine 10 10
254 – 10 c. multicoloured . . . 15 10
255 – 18 c. multicoloured . . . 25 15

DESIGNS—VERT: 10 c. U.N. Headquarters, New York; 18 c. Globe over U.N. emblem and flags.

A **151** Globe and Jet Aircraft

154 Young Children with Globe

1974. Air. Multicoloured.
A256 13 c. Type A **151** 20 15
A257 18 c. "Channels of Communication" (38 × 23 mm) 25 15
A258 26 c. Dove in flight and U.N. Headquarters 35 30

1974. World Population Year.
259 **154** 10 c. multicoloured 20 10
260 18 c. multicoloured 35 30

155 Ship and Fish **156** Satellite, Globe and Symbols

1974. U.N. Conference on "Law of the Sea".
261 **155** 10 c. multicoloured 25 15
262 26 c. multicoloured 60 35

1975. Peaceful Uses of Outer Space.
263 **156** 10 c. multicoloured 20 10
264 26 c. multicoloured 45 40

157 "Sex Equality" **158** "The Hope of Mankind"

1975. International Women's Year.
265 **157** 10 c. multicoloured 15 10
266 18 c. multicoloured 30 25

1975. 30th Anniv of U.N.O.
267 **158** 10 c. multicoloured 15 10
268 26 c. multicoloured 35 30

160 Cupped Hand **161** Wild Rose and Barbed Wire

1975. "Namibia—United Nations Direct Responsibility".
270 **160** 10 c. multicoloured 20 10
271 18 c. multicoloured 25 25

1975. U.N. Peace-keeping Operations.
272 **161** 13 c. blue 20 15
273 26 c. mauve 40 35

162 "Bird of Peace" **166** Linked Ribbons

1976. Multicoloured.
274 3 c. Type **162** 10 10
275 4 c. "Gathering of Peoples" (39 × 23 mm) 10 10
276 30 c. U.N. flag (23 × 39 mm) 50 30
277 50 c. "Universal Peace" (Dove and rainbow) (23 × 39 mm) 95 50

1976. World Federation of U.N. Associations.
278 **166** 13 c. multicoloured 15 10
279 26 c. multicoloured 40 35

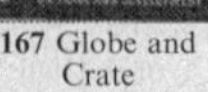

167 Globe and Crate **168** Houses bordering Globe

1976. U.N. Conf on Trade and Development.
280 **167** 13 c. multicoloured 25 15
281 31 c. multicoloured 50 45

1976. U.N. Conf on Human Settlements.
282 **168** 13 c. multicoloured 25 15
283 25 c. multicoloured 50 45

169 Magnifying Glass and Emblem **170** Stylised Ear of Wheat

1976. 25th Anniv of U.N. Postal Administration.
284 **169** 13 c. multicoloured 40 15
285 31 c. multicoloured 2·75 1·10

1976. World Food Council.
286 **170** 13 c. multicoloured 30 25

171 U.N. Emblem **173** Rain Drops and Funnel

172 W.I.P.O. Headquarters Building

1976.
287 **171** 9 c. multicoloured 20 10

1977. World Intellectual Property Organization Headquarters.
288 **172** 13 c. multicoloured 25 15
289 31 c. multicoloured 45 35

1977. United Nations Water Conference.
290 **173** 13 c. multicoloured 25 15
291 25 c. multicoloured 45 35

174 Severed Fuse **175** Winged Airmail Letter

1977. Security Council.
292 **174** 13 c. multicoloured 15 15
293 31 c. multicoloured 35 35

1977. Air. Multicoloured.
A294 25 c. Type **175** 35 30
A295 31 c. Globe and airplane (horiz) 40 40

177 "Combat Racism" **178** Atomic Symbol and Produce

1977. Campaign Against Racial Discrimination.
296 **177** 13 c. black and yellow 25 15
297 25 c. black and red 40 30

1977. Peaceful Uses of Atomic Energy.
298 **178** 13 c. multicoloured 25 15
299 18 c. multicoloured 35 25

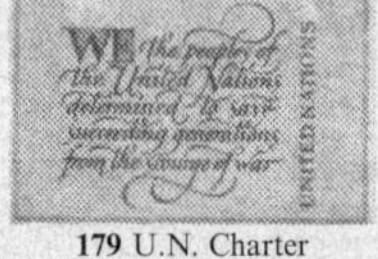

179 U.N. Charter

1978. Multicoloured.
300 1 c. Type **179** 10 10
301 25 c. Knotted flags 30 20
302 $1 Multi-racial group 1·40 80

182 Smallpox Bacilli

1978. Global Eradication of Smallpox.
303 **182** 13 c. black and red 30 15
304 31 c. black and blue 65 45

183 Broken Manacle **184** Clouds within Ribbon

1978. "Namibia: Liberation, Justice, Co-operation".
305 **183** 13 c. multicoloured 25 15
306 18 c. multicoloured 35 30

1978. International Civil Aviation Organization—Safety in the Air.
307 **184** 13 c. multicoloured 25 15
308 25 c. multicoloured 40 35

185 General Assembly

1978. General Assembly.
309 **185** 13 c. multicoloured 20 15
310 18 c. multicoloured 30 30

186 Hemispheres within Cogwheels **187** Hand holding Olive Branch

1978. Technical Co-operation among Developing Countries.
311 **186** 13 c. multicoloured 25 15
312 31 c. multicoloured 50 40

1979. Multicoloured.
313 5 c. Type **187** 10 10
314 14 c. Multiple "tree" 20 10
315 15 c. Globe and peace dove 25 15
316 20 c. Doves crossing globe 30 15

191 Fire and Flood

1979. U.N. Disaster Relief Co-ordinator.
317 **191** 15 c. multicoloured 25 20
318 20 c. multicoloured 35 25

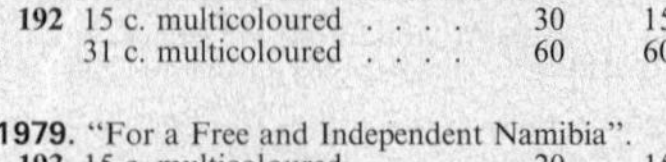

192 Child's Drawing **193** Olive Branch and Map of Namibia

1979. International Year of the Child.
319 **192** 15 c. multicoloured 30 15
320 31 c. multicoloured 60 60

1979. "For a Free and Independent Namibia".
321 **193** 15 c. multicoloured 20 15
322 31 c. multicoloured 50 40

194 Sword and Scales of Justice **195** Graph

1979. International Court of Justice.
323 **194** 15 c. olive, green & black 20 15
324 20 c. blue, lt blue & black 30 30

1980. New International Economic Order. Multicoloured.
325 15 c. Type **195** 25 15
326 31 c. Key 50 50

197 Doves

1980. U.N. Decade for Women.
327 **197** 15 c. multicoloured 30 20
328 20 c. multicoloured 35 30

198 Helmet

1980. Peace-keeping Operations.
329 **198** 15 c. blue and black 30 20
330 – 31 c. multicoloured 55 45
DESIGN: 31 c. "Peace-keeping".

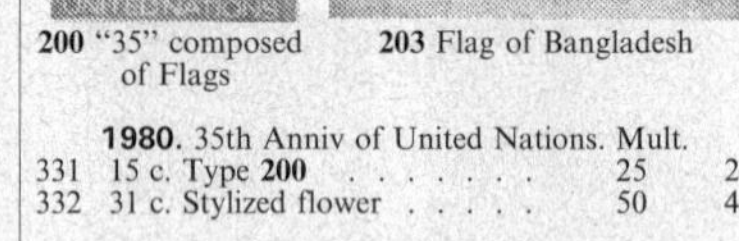

200 "35" composed of Flags **203** Flag of Bangladesh

1980. 35th Anniv of United Nations. Mult.
331 15 c. Type **200** 25 20
332 31 c. Stylized flower 50 45

1980. Flags of Member Nations (1st series). Multicoloured.
334 15 c. Type **203** 30 30
335 15 c. Guinea 30 30
336 15 c. Mali 30 30
337 15 c. Surinam 30 30
338 15 c. Cameroun 30 30
339 15 c. Hungary 30 30
340 15 c. Madagascar 30 30
341 15 c. Rwanda 30 30
342 15 c. El Salvador 30 30
343 15 c. France 30 30
344 15 c. Venezuela 30 30
345 15 c. Yugoslavia 30 30
346 15 c. Fiji 30 30
347 15 c. Luxembourg 30 30
348 15 c. Turkey 30 30
349 15 c. Vietnam 30 30
See also Nos. 359/74, 383/98, 408/23, 434/9, 458/74, 486/501, 508/23, 537/52, 563/78 and 710/17.

204 Various Emblems forming Bunch of Flowers

1980. Economic and Social Council. Mult.
350 15 c. Type **204** 30 20
351 20 c. Economic and social emblems 40 30

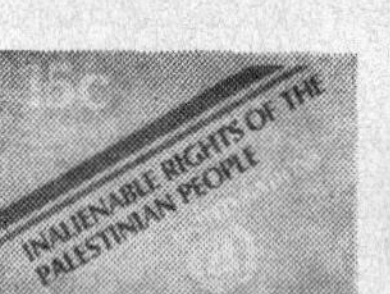

206 Text and U.N. Emblem **207** Jigsaw

1981. Inalienable Rights of the Palestinian People.
352 **206** 15 c. multicoloured 30 20

1981. International Year of Disabled Persons.
353 **207** 20 c. multicoloured 35 30
354 – 35 c. black and orange 55 30
DESIGN: 35 c. Disabled person.

209 "Sebastocrator Kaloyan and his Wife Desislava" (13th-cent Bulgarian fresco)

210 Sun and Sea

1981. Art.
355 **209** 20 c. multicoloured 35 35
356 31 c. multicoloured 55 60

1981. New and Renewable Sources of Energy.
357 **210** 20 c. multicoloured 30 30
358 – 40 c. gold and blue 65 70
DESIGN: 40 c. U.N. energy conference emblem.

1981. Flags of Member Nations (2nd series). As T **203**. Multicoloured.
359 20 c. Djibouti 30 30
360 20 c. Sri Lanka 30 30
361 20 c. Bolivia 30 30
362 20 c. Equatorial Guinea 30 30
363 20 c. Malta 30 30
364 20 c. Czechoslovakia 30 30
365 20 c. Thailand 30 30
366 20 c. Trinidad and Tobago 30 30
367 20 c. Ukrainian S.S.R. 30 30
368 20 c. Kuwait 30 30
369 20 c. Sudan 30 30
370 20 c. Egypt 30 30
371 20 c. United States 30 30
372 20 c. Singapore 30 30
373 20 c. Panama 30 30
374 20 c. Costa Rica 30 30

212 Grafted Plant

214 "Respect for Human Rights"

1981. 10th Anniv of U.N. Volunteers Programme. Multicoloured.
375 18 c. Type **212** 30 25
376 28 c. "10" enclosing symbols of services 45 50

1982. Multicoloured.
377 17 c. Type **214** 25 10
378 28 c. "Granting of Independence to Colonial Countries and Peoples" 40 20
379 40 c. "Second Disarmament Decade" 60 30

217 Hand holding Seedling

219 Olive Branch and U.N. Emblem

1982. Human Environment. Multicoloured.
380 20 c. Type **217** 30 30
381 40 c. Symbols of the environment 65 70

1982. Second United Nations Conference on Exploration and Peaceful Uses of Outer Space.
382 **219** 20 c. ultramarine, blue and green 45 30

1982. Flags of Member Nations (3rd series). As T **203**. Multicoloured.
383 20 c. Austria 30 30
384 20 c. Malaysia 30 30
385 20 c. Seychelles 30 30
386 20 c. Ireland 30 30
387 20 c. Mozambique 30 30
388 20 c. Albania 30 30
389 20 c. Dominica 30 30
390 20 c. Solomon Islands 30 30
391 20 c. Philippines 30 30
392 20 c. Swaziland 30 30
393 20 c. Nicaragua 30 30
394 20 c. Burma 30 30
395 20 c. Cape Verde 30 30
396 20 c. Guyana 30 30
397 20 c. Belgium 30 30
398 20 c. Nigeria 30 30

220 Tree (flora)

222 Interlocking Arrows

1982. Conservation and Protection of Nature. Multicoloured.
399 20 c. Type **220** 30 30
400 28 c. Butterfly (insects) 50 60

1983. World Communications Year. Mult.
401 20 c. Type **222** 50 35
402 40 c. Cable network 90 75

224 Ship and Buoy

226 Giving Food

1983. Safety at Sea: International Maritime Organization. Multicoloured.
403 20 c. Type **224** 60 35
404 37 c. Stylized liner 1·00 90

1983. World Food Programme.
405 **226** 20 c. red 55 35

227 Coins and Cogwheels

229 "Window Right"

1983. Trade and Development. Multicoloured.
406 20 c. Type **227** 50 35
407 28 c. Emblems of trade 75 55

1983. Flags of Member Nations (4th series). As T **203**. Multicoloured.
408 20 c. United Kingdom 35 30
409 20 c. Barbados 35 30
410 20 c. Nepal 35 30
411 20 c. Israel 35 30
412 20 c. Malawi 35 30
413 20 c. Byelorussian S.S.R. 35 30
414 20 c. Jamaica 35 30
415 20 c. Kenya 35 30
416 20 c. China 35 30
417 20 c. Peru 35 30
418 20 c. Bulgaria 35 30
419 20 c. Canada 35 30
420 20 c. Somalia 35 30
421 20 c. Senegal 35 30
422 20 c. Brazil 35 30
423 20 c. Sweden 35 30

1983. 35th Anniv of Declaration of Human Rights. Multicoloured.
424 20 c. Type **229** 40 25
425 40 c. "Treaty with Nature" 1·00 70

231 World Population

1984. International Conference on Population, Mexico.
426 **231** 20 c. multicoloured 50 20
427 40 c. multicoloured 1·10 65

232 Fertilizing Crops

1984. World Food Day. Multicoloured.
428 20 c. Type **232** 40 20
429 40 c. Planting rice 85 45

234 Grand Canyon, U.S.A

236 Mother with Baby

1984. World Heritage—U.N. Educational, Scientific and Cultural Organization. Multicoloured.
430 20 c. Type **234** 40 20
431 50 c. Polonnaruwa, Sri Lanka 1·25 65

1984. Future for Refugees.
432 **236** 20 c. brown and black 40 20
433 – 50 c. black and blue 1·00 70
DESIGN: 50 c. Mother with child.

1984. Flags of Member Nations (5th series). As T **203**. Multicoloured.
434 20 c. Burundi 50 40
435 20 c. Pakistan 50 40
436 20 c. Benin 50 40
437 20 c. Italy 50 40
438 20 c. Poland 50 40
439 20 c. Papua New Guinea 50 40
440 20 c. Uruguay 50 40
441 20 c. Chile 50 40
442 20 c. Paraguay 50 40
443 20 c. Bhutan 50 40
444 20 c. Central African Republic 50 40
445 20 c. Australia 50 40
446 20 c. Tanzania 50 40
447 20 c. United Arab Emirates 50 40
448 20 c. Ecuador 50 40
449 20 c. Bahamas 50 40

238 Emblem and Figures linking Arms

239 Turin Centre Emblem

1984. International Youth Year.
450 **238** 20 c. multicoloured 50 15
451 35 c. multicoloured 90 40

1985. 20th Anniv of Turin Centre of International Labour Organization.
452 **239** 23 c. blue 60 35

240 Farming and Mediums of Communication

1985. 10th Anniv of United Nations University, Tokyo.
453 **240** 50 c. multicoloured 1·25 75

241 People of Various Nations

1985. Multicoloured.
454 22 c. Type **241** 30 15
455 $3 Paintbrush and emblem 4·50 2·75

243 "Snow Scene" (Andrew Wyeth)

1985. 40th Anniv of U.N.O. Multicoloured.
456 22 c. Type **243** 45 20
457 45 c. "Harvest Scene" (Andrew Wyeth) 95 65

1985. Flags of Member Nations (6th series). As T **203**. Multicoloured.
459 22 c. Grenada 50 40
460 22 c. Federal Republic of Germany 50 40
461 22 c. Saudi Arabia 50 40
462 22 c. Mexico 50 40
463 22 c. Liberia 50 40
464 22 c. Mauritius 50 40
465 22 c. Chad 50 40
466 22 c. Dominican Republic 50 40
467 22 c. Oman 50 40
468 22 c. Ghana 50 40
469 22 c. Sierra Leone 50 40

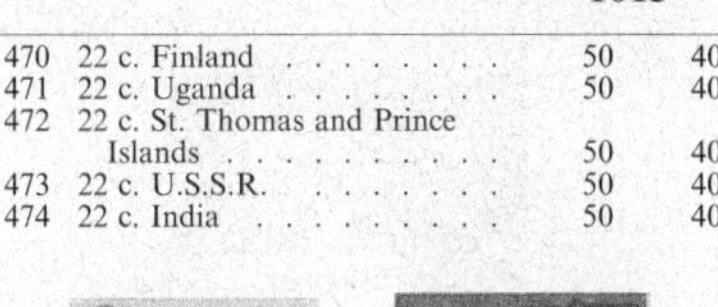

470 22 c. Finland 50 40
471 22 c. Uganda 50 40
472 22 c. St. Thomas and Prince Islands 50 40
473 22 c. U.S.S.R. 50 40
474 22 c. India 50 40

246 Woman feeding Child

248 "Africa in Crisis"

1985. U.N.I.C.E.F. Child Survival Campaign. Multicoloured.
475 32 c. Type **246** 45 25
476 33 c. Mother breast-feeding child 85 55

1986. Africa in Crisis.
477 **248** 22 c. multicoloured 45 25

249 Dam

1986. Development Programme. Water Resources. Multicoloured.
478 22 c. Type **249** 1·00 70
479 22 c. Working in the fields 1·00 70
480 22 c. Girls at waterhole 1·00 70
481 22 c. Women at well 1·00 70
Nos. 478/81 were printed together, se-tenant, forming a composite design.

253 Magnifying Glass and Stamp

1986. Philately: the International Hobby.
482 **253** 22 c. lilac and blue 50 20
483 – 44 c. brown and green 90 55
DESIGN: 44 c. Engraver.

255 Peace Doves

1986. International Peace Year.
484 **255** 22 c. multicoloured 60 20
485 – 33 c. multicoloured 80 50
DESIGN: 33 c. Words for "Peace" around U.N. emblem.

1986. Flags of Member Nations (7th series). As T **203**. Multicoloured.
486 22 c. New Zealand 45 35
487 22 c. Laos 45 35
488 22 c. Burkina Faso 45 35
489 22 c. Gambia 45 35
490 22 c. Maldives 45 35
491 22 c. Ethiopia 45 35
492 22 c. Jordan 45 35
493 22 c. Zambia 45 35
494 22 c. Iceland 45 35
495 22 c. Antigua and Barbuda 45 35
496 22 c. Angola 45 35
497 22 c. Botswana 45 35
498 22 c. Rumania 45 35
499 22 c. Togo 45 35
500 22 c. Mauritania 45 35
501 22 c. Colombia 45 35

258 Trygve Lie (after Harald Dal)

259 Men with Surveying Equipment and Blueprints

1987. 9th Death Anniv of Trygve Lie (first U.N. Secretary-General).
503 **258** 22 c. multicoloured 45 20

1987. International Year of Shelter for the Homeless.
504 **259** 22 c. deep brown, brown and black 40 20
505 – 44 c. multicoloured 85 65
DESIGN: 44 c. Cutting bamboo.

261 Construction Workers

1987. Anti-Drugs Campaign. Multicoloured.

506	22 c. Type **261**	45	20
507	33 c. University graduates	80	55

1987. Flags of Member Nations (8th series). As T **203**. Multicoloured.

508	22 c. Comoros	40	30
509	22 c. People's Democratic Republic of Yemen	40	30
510	22 c. Mongolia	40	30
511	22 c. Vanuatu	40	30
512	22 c. Japan	40	30
513	22 c. Gabon	40	30
514	22 c. Zimbabwe	40	30
515	22 c. Iraq	40	30
516	22 c. Argentina	40	30
517	22 c. Congo	40	30
518	22 c. Niger	40	30
519	22 c. St. Lucia	40	30
520	22 c. Bahrain	40	30
521	22 c. Haiti	40	30
522	22 c. Afghanistan	40	30
523	22 c. Greece	40	30

263 Family and U.N. Building, New York **265** Measles

1987. United Nations Day. Multicoloured.

524	22 c. Type **263**	35	15
525	39 c. Dancers	75	65

1987. "Immunize Every Child". Multicoloured.

526	22 c. Type **265**	40	15
527	44 c. Tetanus	85	75

267 Wheat as U.N. Emblem

1988. "For a Better World".

528	**267** 3 c. yellow, brown and black	15	10

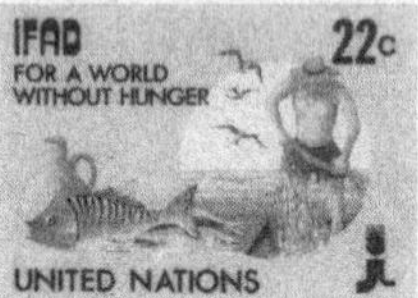

268 Fisherman

1988. International Fund for Agricultural Development "For a World Without Hunger" Campaign. Multicoloured.

529	2 c. Type **268**	40	15
530	33 c. Farmers ploughing with oxen	55	50

270 Tropical Rain Forest Canopy **272** Teacher at Blackboard

1988. "Survival of the Forests". Multicoloured.

531	25 c. Type **270**	1·75	70
532	44 c. Tropical rain forest floor	4·00	2·10

Nos. 531/2 were printed together, se-tenant, forming a composite design.

1988. International Volunteer Day. Mult.

533	25 c. Type **272**	30	15
534	50 c. Teaching basketry (horiz)	70	65

274 Cycling **276** Flame

1988. "Health in Sports". Multicoloured.

535	25 c. Type **274**	45	20
536	38 c. Marathon (horiz)	65	55

1988. Flags of Member Nations (9th series). As T **203**. Multicoloured.

537	25 c. Spain	40	30
538	25 c. St. Vincent and Grenadines	40	30
539	25 c. Ivory Coast	40	30
540	25 c. Lebanon	40	30
541	25 c. Yemen	40	30
542	25 c. Cuba	40	30
543	25 c. Denmark	40	30
544	25 c. Libya	40	30
545	25 c. Qatar	40	30
546	25 c. Zaire	40	30
547	25 c. Norway	40	30
548	25 c. German Democratic Republic	40	30
549	25 c. Iran	40	30
550	25 c. Tunisia	40	30
551	25 c. Samoa	40	30
552	25 c. Belize	40	30

1989. 40th Anniv of Declaration of Human Rights.

553	**276** 25 c. multicoloured	40	25

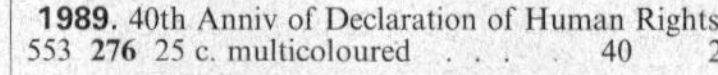

278 Electricity Production **280** "Blue Helmet" Soldier

1989. World Bank. Multicoloured.

555	25 c. Type **278**	40	15
556	45 c. Planting rice	70	50

1989. Award of Nobel Peace Prize to United Nations Peace-keeping Forces.

557	**280** 25 c. multicoloured	40	15

281 U.N. Headquarters, New York

1989.

558	**281** 45 c. multicoloured	70	40

282 Satellite Image of Storm over Chesapeake Bay Area **284** Band

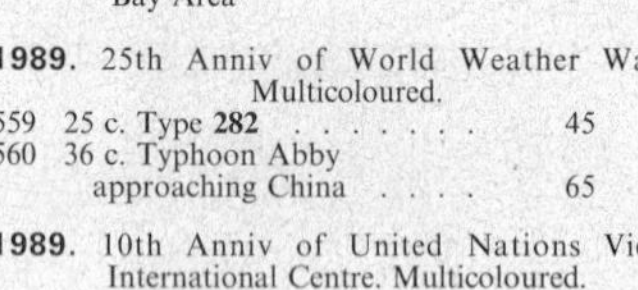

1989. 25th Anniv of World Weather Watch. Multicoloured.

559	25 c. Type **282**	45	20
560	36 c. Typhoon Abby approaching China	65	40

1989. 10th Anniv of United Nations Vienna International Centre. Multicoloured.

561	25 c. Type **284**	45	15
562	90 c. Mountain and butterfly as tree	1·40	1·10

1989. Flags of Member Nations (10th series). As T **203**. Multicoloured.

563	25 c. Indonesia	35	30
564	25 c. Lesotho	35	30
565	25 c. Guatemala	35	30
566	25 c. Netherlands	35	30
567	25 c. Algeria	35	30
568	25 c. Brunei	35	30
569	25 c. St. Kitts and Nevis	35	30
570	25 c. United Nations	35	30
571	25 c. Honduras	35	30
572	25 c. Kampuchea	35	30
573	25 c. Guinea-Bissau	35	30
574	25 c. Cyprus	35	30
575	25 c. South Africa	35	30
576	25 c. Portugal	35	30
577	25 c. Morocco	35	30
578	25 c. Syria	35	30

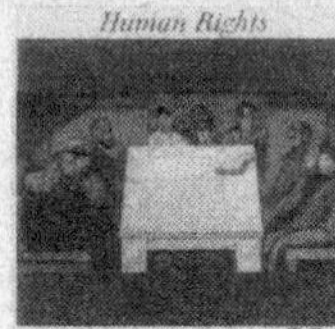

286 "Table of Universal Brotherhood" (Jose Clemente Orozco) (Article 1)

1989. Declaration of Human Rights (1st series). Multicoloured.

579	25 c. Type **286**	40	15
580	45 c. "Composition II" (V. Kandinsky) (Article 2)	70	40

See also Nos. 592/3, 609/10, 626/7 and 637/8.

288 Port Activities

1990. International Trade Centre.

581	**288** 25 c. multicoloured	60	20

289 "AIDS" **291** Madagascar Periwinkle

1990. Anti-AIDS Campaign. Multicoloured.

582	25 c. Type **289**	50	20
583	40 c. Group at risk	1·00	45

1990. Medicinal Plants. Multicoloured.

584	25 c. Type **291**	45	15
585	90 c. American ginseng	1·40	1·10

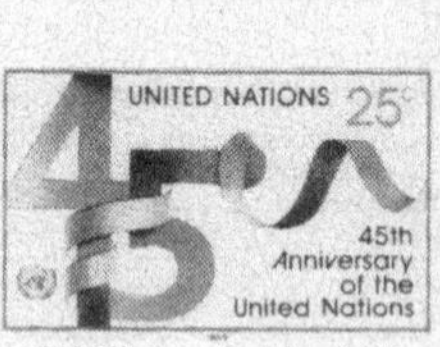

293 Ribbons forming "45" **296** Youth waylaying Elderly Man

1990. 45th Anniv of U.N.O. Multicoloured.

586	25 c. Type **293**	50	20
587	45 c. "45" and U.N. Emblem	1·40	80

1990. Crime Prevention. Multicoloured.

590	25 c. Type **296**	70	25
591	36 c. Burglars leaving burning building	1·40	80

1990. Universal Declaration of Human Rights (2nd series). As T **286**. Multicoloured.

592	25 c. Sarcophagus of Plotinus (detail) (Article 7)	35	20
593	45 c. "Combined Chambers of High Court of Appeal" (Charles Paul Renouard), from "The Dreyfus Case" (Article 8)	60	35

300/303 Alpine Lake and Wildlife

1991. Economic Commission for Europe. "For a Better Environment".

594	**300** 30 c. multicoloured	60	35
595	**301** 30 c. multicoloured	60	35
596	**302** 30 c. multicoloured	60	35
597	**303** 30 c. multicoloured	60	35

Nos. 594/7 were printed together, se-tenant, forming the composite design illustrated.

304 Desert **306** U.N. Building

1991. 1st Anniv of Namibian Independence. Multicoloured.

598	30 c. Type **304**	45	20
599	50 c. Open grassland	75	45

1991.

600	**306** $2 blue	2·50	1·50

307 Children around Globe (Nicole Delia Legnani)

1991. 30th Anniv (1989) of U.N. Declaration on the Rights of the Child and 1990 World Summit on Children, New York. Children's Drawings. Multicoloured.

601	30 c. Type **307**	40	20
602	70 c. Dove, rainbow and houses (Alissa Duffy)	95	55

309 Bubbles of Toxin approaching City

1991. Banning of Chemical Weapons. Mult.

603	30 c. Type **309**	40	20
604	90 c. Hand pushing back barrels of toxins	95	55

311 U.N. Flag

1991. Multicoloured.

605	30 c. Type **311**	40	15
606	50 c. "The Golden Rule" (mosaic, Norman Rockwell) (vert)	65	35

313 1951 1 c. Stamp

1991. 40th Anniv of United Nations Postal Administration.

607	**313** 30 c. red on cream	40	20
608	– 40 c. purple on cream	55	30

DESIGN: 40 c. 1951 2 c. stamp.

1991. Declaration of Human Rights (3rd series). As T **286**. Multicoloured.

609	30 c. "The Last of England" (Ford Maddox Brown) (Article 13)	40	20
610	50 c. "The Emigration to the East" (Tito Salas) (Article 14)	65	35

317 Uluru National Park, Australia **319/20** Sea Life (½-size illustration)

1992. 20th Anniv of U.N.E.S.C.O. World Heritage Convention. Multicoloured.
611 30 c. Type **317** 40 20
612 50 c. Great Wall of China . . 65 25

1992. "Clean Oceans".
613 **319** 29 c. multicoloured . . . 40 15
614 **320** 29 c. multicoloured . . . 40 15
Nos. 613/14 were issued together, se-tenant, forming the composite design illustrated.

321/324 Planet Earth

1992. 2nd U.N. Conference on Environment and Development, Rio de Janeiro.
615 **321** 29 c. multicoloured . . . 40 15
616 **322** 29 c. multicoloured . . . 40 15
617 **323** 29 c. multicoloured . . . 40 15
618 **324** 29 c. multicoloured . . . 40 15
Nos. 615/18 were issued together, se-tenant, forming the composite design illustrated.

325/326 "Mission Planet Earth" (⅔-size illustration)

1992. International Space Year. Roul.
619 **325** 29 c. multicoloured . . . 40 20
620 **326** 29 c. multicoloured . . . 40 20
Nos. 619/20 were issued together, se-tenant, forming the composite design illustrated.

327 Winged Man with V.D.U.

1992. Commission on Science and Technology for Development. Multicoloured.
621 29 c. Type **327** 40 15
622 50 c. Man sitting in crocodile's mouth 65 35

329 Aerial View of Building

1992. United Nations University, Tokyo. Mult.
623 4 c. Type **329** 10 10
624 40 c. Front elevation of building 55 30

331 U.N. Headquarters, New York
334 Family Life

1992.
625 **331** 29 c. multicoloured . . . 40 15

1992. Universal Declaration of Human Rights (4th series). As T **286**. Multicoloured.
626 29 c. "Lady writing a letter with her Maid" (Johannes Vermeer) (Article 19) 40 15
627 50 c. "The Meeting"(Ester Almqvist) (Article 20) . . . 65 35

1993. "Ageing: Dignity and Participation". 10th Anniv (1992) of International Plan of Action on Ageing. Multicoloured.
628 29 c. Type **334** 40 15
629 52 c. Health and nutrition . . 70 40

336 Queensland Hairy-nosed Wombat

1993. Endangered Species (1st series). Multicoloured.
630 29 c. Type **336** 40 15
631 29 c. Whooping crane ("Grus americana") 40 15
632 29 c. Giant clams ("Tridacnidae") 40 15
633 29 c. Sable antelope ("Hippotragus niger") . . . 40 15
See also Nos. 649/52, 667/70 and 694/7.

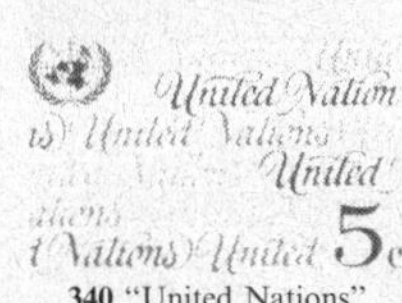

340 "United Nations"

1993.
634 **340** 5 c. multicoloured 10 10

341 Personal Environment

1993. 45th Anniv of W.H.O. Multicoloured.
635 29 c. Type **341** 40 15
636 50 c. Family environment . . 65 35

1993. Declaration of Human Rights (5th series). As T **286**. Multicoloured.
637 29 c. "Shocking Corn" (Thomas Hart Benton) (Article 25) . 40 15
638 35 c. "The Library" (Jacob Lawrence) (Article 26) . . 45 25

345/348 Peace

1993. International Peace Day. Roul.
639 **345** 29 c. multicoloured . . . 40 15
640 **346** 29 c. multicoloured . . . 40 15
641 **347** 29 c. multicoloured . . . 40 15
642 **348** 29 c. multicoloured . . . 40 15
Nos. 639/42 were issued together, se-tenant, forming the composite design illustrated.

349 Chameleon

1993. The Environment—Climate. Mult.
643 29 c. Type **349** 40 15
644 29 c. Storm 40 15
645 29 c. Antelopes fleeing from flood 40 15
646 29 c. Lesser bird of paradise . 40 15
Nos. 643/6 were issued together, se-tenant, forming a composite design.

353 Equality across Generations

1994. Int Year of the Family. Mult.
647 29 c. Type **353** 35 10
648 45 c. Poor family 55 30

1994. Endangered Species (2nd series). As T **336**. Multicoloured.
649 29 c. Chimpanzees ("Pan troglodytes") 35 10
650 29 c. St. Lucia amazon ("Amazona versicolor") . . 35 10
651 29 c. American crocodile ("Crocodylus acutus") . . . 35 10
652 29 c. Addra gazelles ("Gazelle dama") 35 10

359 "Dove of Peace" (mosaic)

362 Refugee crossing Bridge of Hands

1994.
653 **359** 10 c. multicoloured 10 10
654 – 19 c. multicoloured 25 10
655 – $1 brown . . . . 1·25 75
DESIGNS: 19 c. "Sleeping Child" (stained-glass window after drawing by Stanislaw Wyspianski); $1 "Mourning Owl" (Vanessa Isitt).

1994. United Nations High Commissioner for Refugees.
656 **362** 50 c. multicoloured 60 35

363/366 Shattered Globe and "Warning" (⅔-size illustration)

1994. International Decade for Natural Disaster Reduction.
657 **363** 29 c. multicoloured 35 10
658 **364** 29 c. multicoloured 35 10
659 **365** 29 c. multicoloured 35 10
660 **366** 29 c. multicoloured 35 10
Nos. 657/60 were issued together, se-tenant, forming the composite design illustrated.

367 Children playing (health and family planning)

1994. International Population and Development Conference, Cairo. Multicoloured.
661 29 c. Type **367** 35 10
662 52 c. Family unit (demographic changes) 65 35

369 Map and Looped Ribbon

371 Anniversary Emblem

1994. 30th Anniv of United Nations Conference on Trade and Development. Multicoloured.
663 29 c. Type **369** 35 10
664 50 c. Map and coiled ribbon . 60 35

1995. 50th Anniv of U.N.O. (1st issue).
665 **371** 32 c. multicoloured 40 15
See also Nos. 673/4 and 679/90.

372 "Social Summit 1995"

1995. World Summit for Social Development, Copenhagen.
666 **372** 50 c. multicoloured . . . 65 35

1995. Endangered Species (3rd series). As T **336**. Multicoloured.
667 32 c. Giant armadillo ("Priodontes maximus") . 40 15
668 32 c. American bald eagle ("Haliaeetus leucocephalus") 40 15
669 32 c. Fijian banded iguana ("Brachylophus fasciatus") 40 15
670 32 c. Giant panda ("Ailuropoda melanoleuca") 40 15

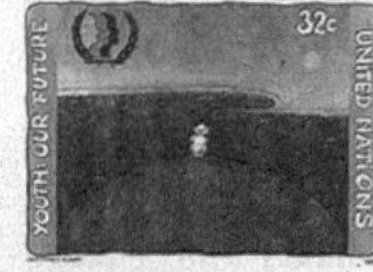

377 Man looking out to Sea

1995. "Youth: Our Future". 10th Anniv of International Youth Year. Multicoloured.
671 32 c. Type **377** 40 15
672 55 c. Family cycling 70 40

379 Signing U.N. Charter

1995. 50th Anniv of U.N.O. (2nd issue).
673 **379** 32 c. black 40 15
674 – 50 c. purple 65 35
DESIGN: 50 c. Opera House, San Francisco (venue for signing of Charter).

382 Mother and Child

1995. 4th World Conference on Women, Peking.
676 32 c. Type **382** 40 15
677 40 c. Harpist and cranes . . . 50 30

384 U.N. Headquarters, New York

1995.
678 **384** 20 c. multicoloured 25 15

385/387 (½-size illustration)

388/390 (½-size illustration)

391/393
(½-size illustration)

394/396
(½-size illustration)

1995. 50th Anniv of U.N.O. (3rd issue).

679 **385** 32 c. multicoloured . . . 40 15
680 **386** 32 c. multicoloured . . . 40 15
681 **387** 32 c. multicoloured . . . 40 15
682 **388** 32 c. multicoloured . . . 40 15
683 **389** 32 c. multicoloured . . . 40 15
684 **390** 32 c. multicoloured . . . 40 15
685 **391** 32 c. multicoloured . . . 40 15
686 **392** 32 c. multicoloured . . . 40 15
687 **393** 32 c. multicoloured . . . 40 15
688 **394** 32 c. multicoloured . . . 40 15
689 **395** 32 c. multicoloured . . . 40 15
690 **396** 32 c. multicoloured . . . 40 15

Nos. 679/81 and 682/4 form the left and right halves respectively of a composite design, and Nos. 685/7 and 688/90 another composite design.

397 Rainbow and Faces within "Sun"

398 Mural

1996. 50th Anniv of World Federation of United Nations Associations.

691 **397** 32 c. multicoloured . . . 40 15

1996. Murals by Fernand Leger in General Assembly, U.N. Headquarters. Multicoloured.

692 32 c. Type **398** 40 15
693 60 c. Mural (different) 80 45

1996. Endangered Species (4th series). As T **336**. Multicoloured.

694 32 c. "Masdevallia veitchiana" 40 15
695 32 c. Saguaro ("Carnegiea gigantea") 40 15
696 32 c. West Australian pitcher plant ("Cephalotus follicularis") 40 15
697 32 c. "Encephalartos horridus" 40 15

404 Deer under Tree

1996. "Habitat II" Second United Nations Conference on Human Settlements, Istanbul, Turkey. Multicoloured.

698 32 c. Type **404** 40 15
699 32 c. City and countryside . . 40 15
700 32 c. Walking in city 40 15
701 32 c. City and village 40 15
702 32 c. Village and parrot . . . 40 15

Nos. 698/702 were issued together, se-tenant, forming a composite design.

INDEX

Countries can be quickly located by referring to the index at the end of this volume.

409 Basketball

1996. Sport and the Environment. Multicoloured.

703 32 c. Type **409** 40 15
704 50 c. Volleyball 60 35

412 Two Birds

1996. "A Plea for Peace". Winners of China Youth Design Competition. Multicoloured.

706 32 c. Type **412** 40 15
707 60 c. Peace dove 75 45

414 "Yeh-Shen" (Chinese tale)

416 Cherry Tree

1996. 50th Anniv of U.N.I.C.E.F. Children's Stories.

708 32 c. Type **414** 40 15
709 60 c. "The Ugly Duckling" (Hans Christian Andersen) 75 45

1997. Flags of Member Nations (11th series). As T **203**. Multicoloured.

710 32 c. Armenia 40 15
711 32 c. Georgia 40 15
712 32 c. Kazakhstan 40 15
713 32 c. Republic of Korea . . . 40 15
714 32 c. Latvia 40 15
715 32 c. Liechtenstein 40 15
716 32 c. Namibia 40 15
717 32 c. Tajikistan 40 15

1997. Multicoloured.

718 8 c. Type **416** 10 10
719 55 c. Rose "Peace" (horiz) . . 70 40

B. GENEVA HEADQUARTERS

For use on mail posted at the United Nations Geneva Headquarters. Before 1969 the Swiss PTT issued stamps for use at the Palais des Nations; these are listed at the end of Switzerland.

100 centimes = 1 Swiss franc

NOTE: References to numbers and types in this section. other than to those with a "G" prefix are to the United Nations (New York Office) listing. Designs adapted for the Geneva issue are inscribed in French and have face values in francs.

G **4** Palais des Nations, Geneva

G **5** Palais des Nations, Geneva

1969. Existing United Nations (New York) designs adapted with new colours and values in Swiss francs (F.S.). 30 and 40 c. new designs. Multicoloured unless otherwise stated.

G 1 – 5 c. (As No. 164) . . . 10 10
G 2 – 10 c. (As No. 94) . . . 10 10
G 3 – 20 c. (As No. 97) . . . 10 10
G 4 **G 4** 30 c. multicoloured . . 15 10
G 5 **G 5** 40 c. multicoloured . . 25 15
G 6 – 50 c. (As No. 147, but scroll inscr in French) 30 20
G 7 – 60 c. gold, red and brown (As No. 98) 35 25
G 8 – 70 c. red, gold and black (As No. 167) 40 30
G 9 – 75 c. (As No. A125) . . 50 30
G10 – 80 c. (As No. 148) . . . 50 40
G11 **52** 90 c. (Inscr in French) . . 70 50
G12 – 1 f. deep green and green (As No. 149) 75 50
G13 **53** 2 f. multicoloured . . . 1·25 1·25
G14 **104** 3 f. multicoloured . . . 2·00 2·00
G15 **3** 10 f. blue . . . . 7·00 6·00

1971. Peaceful Uses of the Sea-bed.

G16 **121** 30 c. multicoloured . . . 30 30

1971. United Nations Work with Refugees.

G17 **122** 50 c. black, orge & red . 80 80

1971. World Food Programme.

G18 **123** 50 c. multicoloured . . . 75 75

1971. Opening of new Universal Postal Union Headquarters Building, Berne.

G19 **124** 75 c. multicoloured . . . 1·00 1·00

1971. Racial Equality Year. Designs as Nos. 220/1, with background colours changed.

G20 30 c. Type **125** 40 40
G21 50 c. Linked globes (horiz) . . 40 40

1971. U.N. International Schools.

G22 **130** 1 f. 10 multicoloured . . 1·00 1·00

1972. Non-proliferation of Nuclear Weapons.

G23 **131** 40 c. multicoloured . . . 90 90

1972. World Health Day.

G24 **132** 80 c. multicoloured . . . 1·00 1·00

1972. United Nations Environmental Conservation Conference, Stockholm.

G25 **137** 40 c. multicoloured . . . 50 50
G26 80 c. multicoloured . . . 90 90

1972. Economic Commission for Europe (ECE).

G27 **138** 1 f. 10 multicoloured . . 1·50 1·50

1972. United Nations Art.

G28 **139** 40 c. multicoloured . . . 50 50
G29 80 c. multicoloured . . . 1·00 1·00

1973. Disarmament Decade.

G30 **140** 60 c. multicoloured . . . 45 45
G31 1 f. 10 multicoloured . . 90 90

1973. "No Drugs" Campaign.

G32 **141** 60 c. multicoloured . . . 1·00 1·00

1973. U.N. Volunteers Programme.

G33 **142** 80 c. multicoloured . . . 75 75

1973. "Namibia" (South West Africa).

G34 **143** 60 c. multicoloured . . . 60 60

1973. 25th Anniv of Declaration of Human Rights.

G35 **144** 40 c. multicoloured . . . 35 35
G36 80 c. multicoloured . . . 75 75

1973. Inauguration of New I.L.O. Headquarters, Geneva.

G37 **145** 60 c. multicoloured . . . 40 40
G38 80 c. multicoloured . . . 70 70

1973. Centenary of Universal Postal Union.

G39 **146** 30 c. multicoloured . . . 25 25
G40 60 c. multicoloured . . . 55 55

1974. Brazilian Peace Mural.

G41 **147** 60 c. multicoloured . . . 50 50
G42 1 f. multicoloured . . . 70 70

1974. World Population Year.

G43 **154** 60 c. multicoloured . . . 50 50
G44 80 c. multicoloured . . . 60 60

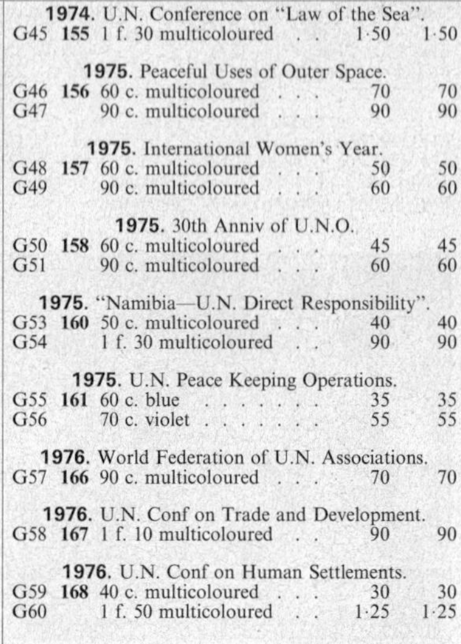

1974. U.N. Conference on "Law of the Sea".

G45 **155** 1 f. 30 multicoloured . . 1·50 1·50

1975. Peaceful Uses of Outer Space.

G46 **156** 60 c. multicoloured . . . 70 70
G47 90 c. multicoloured . . . 90 90

1975. International Women's Year.

G48 **157** 60 c. multicoloured . . . 50 50
G49 90 c. multicoloured . . . 60 60

1975. 30th Anniv of U.N.O.

G50 **158** 60 c. multicoloured . . . 45 45
G51 90 c. multicoloured . . . 60 60

1975. "Namibia—U.N. Direct Responsibility".

G53 **160** 50 c. multicoloured . . . 40 40
G54 1 f. 30 multicoloured . . 90 90

1975. U.N. Peace Keeping Operations.

G55 **161** 60 c. blue 35 35
G56 70 c. violet 55 55

1976. World Federation of U.N. Associations.

G57 **166** 90 c. multicoloured . . . 70 70

1976. U.N. Conf on Trade and Development.

G58 **167** 1 f. 10 multicoloured . . 90 90

1976. U.N. Conf on Human Settlements.

G59 **168** 40 c. multicoloured . . . 30 30
G60 1 f. 50 multicoloured . . 1·25 1·25

G **46** U.N. Emblem within Posthorn

G **49** Rain Drop and Globe

1976. 25th Anniv of U.N. Postal Administration.

G61 G **46** 80 c. multicoloured . . 2·00 2·00
G62 1 f. 10 multicoloured . . 2·00 2·00

1976. World Food Council Publicity.

G63 **170** 70 c. multicoloured . . . 75 75

1977. World Intellectual Property Organization Publicity.

G64 **172** 80 c. multicoloured . . . 70 70

1977. U.N. Water Conference.

G65 G **49** 80 c. multicoloured . . 50 50
G66 1 f. 10 multicoloured . 1·10 1·10

G **50** Protective Hands

1977. Security Council Commemoration.

G67 G **50** 80 c. multicoloured . . 50 50
G68 1 f. 10 multicoloured . . 90 90

G **51** "Intertwining of Races"

1977. "Combat Racism".

G69 G **51** 40 c. multicoloured . . 35 35
G70 1 f. 10 multicoloured . . 90 90

G **52** Atoms and Laurel Leaf

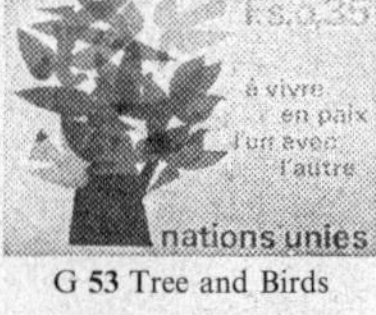
G **53** Tree and Birds

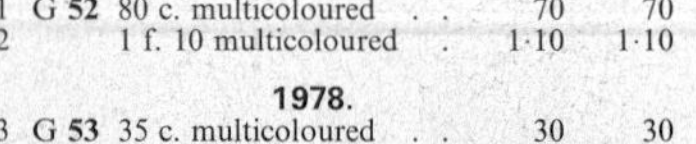

1977. "Peaceful Uses for Atomic Energy".

G71 G **52** 80 c. multicoloured . . 70 70
G72 1 f. 10 multicoloured . . 1·10 1·10

1978.

G73 G **53** 35 c. multicoloured . . . 30 30

G **54** Smallpox Bacilli and Globe

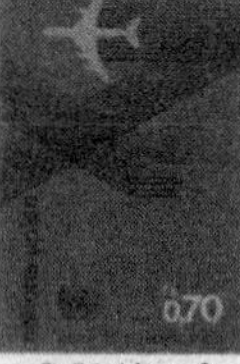
G **56** Aircraft Flightpaths

1978. Global Eradication of Smallpox.
G74 G **54** 80 c. multicoloured . . 70 70
G75 1 f. 10 multicoloured . . 90 90

1978. "Namibia: Liberation, Justice, Co-operation".
G76 **183** 80 c. multicoloured . . . 65 65

1978. International Civil Aviation Organization—Safety in the Air.
G77 G **56** 70 c. multicoloured . . 50 50
G78 80 c. multicoloured . . 70 70

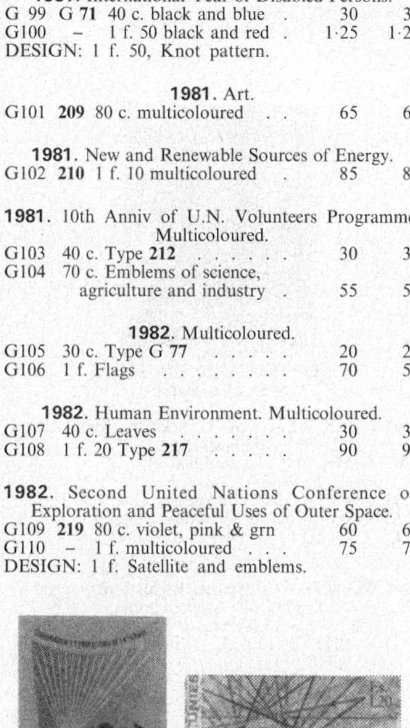

G **57** Globe, Flags and General Assembly Interior

1978. General Assembly.
G79 G **57** 70 c. multicoloured . . 50 50
G80 1 f. 10 multicoloured . . 90 90

1978. Technical Co-operation among Developing Countries.
G81 **186** 80 c. multicoloured . . . 60 60

G **59** "Disaster"

1979. United Nations Disaster Relief Co-ordinator.
G82 G **59** 80 c. multicoloured . . 65 65
G83 1 f. 50 multicoloured . 1·25 1·25

G **60** Children and Rainbow

G **62** Int Court of Justice and Scales

1979. International Year of the Child.
G84 G **60** 80 c. multicoloured . . 1·00 1·00
G85 1 f. 10 multicoloured . . 1·00 1·00

1979. "For a Free and Independent Namibia".
G86 **193** 1 f. 10 multicoloured . . 1·00 1·00

1979. International Court of Justice.
G87 G **62** 80 c. multicoloured . . 50 50
G88 1 f. 10 multicoloured . . 95 95

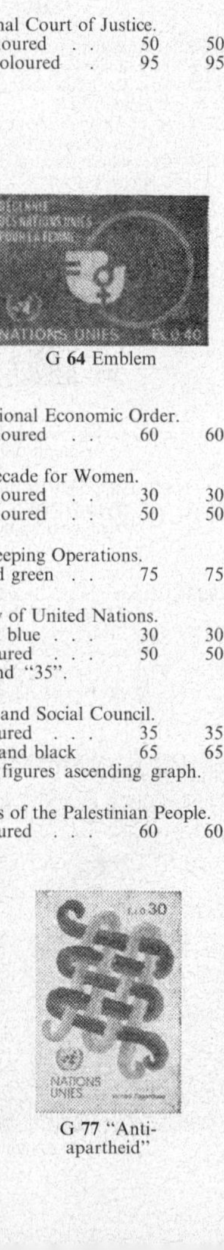

G **63** Key symbolizing Unity of Action

G **64** Emblem

1980. New International Economic Order.
G89 G **63** 80 c. multicoloured . . 60 60

1980. U.N. Decade for Women.
G90 G **64** 40 c. multicoloured . . 30 30
G91 70 c. multicoloured . . 50 50

1980. Peace Keeping Operations.
G92 **198** 1 f. 10 blue and green . . 75 75

1980. 35th Anniv of United Nations.
G93 – 40 c. black and blue . . . 30 30
G94 **200** 70 c. multicoloured . . . 50 50
DESIGN: 40 c. Dove and "35".

1980. Economic and Social Council.
G96 **204** 40 c. multicoloured . . . 35 35
G97 – 70 c. blue, red and black 65 65
DESIGN: 70 c. Human figures ascending graph.

1981. Inalienable Rights of the Palestinian People.
G98 **206** 80 c. multicoloured . . . 60 60

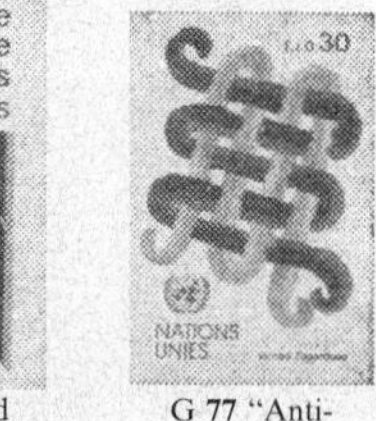

G **71** Disabled Person

G **77** "Anti-apartheid"

1981. International Year of Disabled Persons.
G 99 G **71** 40 c. black and blue . 30 30
G100 – 1 f. 50 black and red . 1·25 1·25
DESIGN: 1 f. 50, Knot pattern.

1981. Art.
G101 **209** 80 c. multicoloured . . 65 65

1981. New and Renewable Sources of Energy.
G102 **210** 1 f. 10 multicoloured . 85 85

1981. 10th Anniv of U.N. Volunteers Programme. Multicoloured.
G103 40 c. Type **212** 30 30
G104 70 c. Emblems of science, agriculture and industry . 55 55

1982. Multicoloured.
G105 30 c. Type G **77** 20 20
G106 1 f. Flags 70 50

1982. Human Environment. Multicoloured.
G107 40 c. Leaves 30 30
G108 1 f. 20 Type **217** 90 90

1982. Second United Nations Conference on Exploration and Peaceful Uses of Outer Space.
G109 **219** 80 c. violet, pink & grn 60 60
G110 – 1 f. multicoloured . . . 75 75
DESIGN: 1 f. Satellite and emblems.

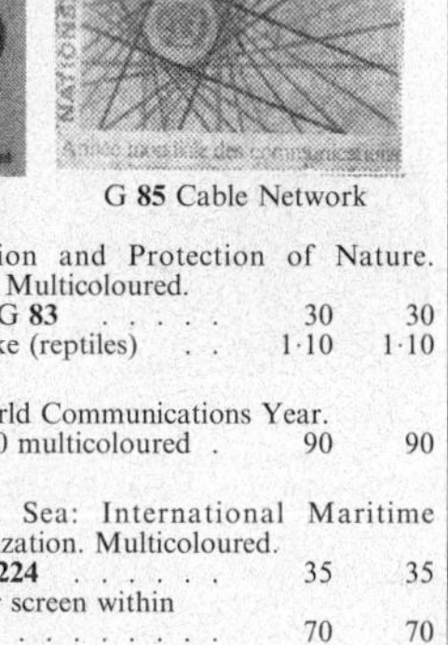

G **83** Bird

G **85** Cable Network

1982. Conservation and Protection of Nature. Multicoloured.
G111 40 c. Type G **83** 30 30
G112 1 f. 50 Snake (reptiles) . . 1·10 1·10

1983. World Communications Year.
G113 G **85** 1 f. 20 multicoloured . 90 90

1983. Safety at Sea: International Maritime Organization. Multicoloured.
G114 40 c. Type **224** 35 35
G115 80 c. Radar screen within lifebelt 70 70

1983. World Food Programme.
G116 **226** 1 f. 50 blue . . . . . . 1·25 1·25

1983. Trade and Development. Multicoloured.
G117 80 c. Type **227** 65 65
G118 1 f. 10 Exports 90 90

G **91** "Homo Humus Humanitas"

G **93** World Housing

1983. 35th Anniv of Universal Declaration of Human Rights. Multicoloured.
G119 40 c. Type G **91** 30 30
G120 1 f. 20 "Droit de Creer" . . 90 90

1984. International Conference on Population, Mexico City.
G121 G **93** 1 f. 20 multicoloured . 1·00 1·00

G **94** Fishing

1984. World Food Day. Multicoloured.
G122 50 c. Type G **94** 40 40
G123 80 c. Planting saplings . . . 65 65

G **96** Fort St. Angelo, Malta (wrongly inscr "Valetta")

1984. World Heritage—U.N.E.S.C.O. Mult.
G124 50 c. Type G **96** 40 40
G125 70 c. Los Glaciares, Argentina 60 60

G **98** Man and Woman

G **100** Heads

1984. Future for Refugees.
G126 G **98** 35 c. black and green . 25 25
G127 – 1 f. 50 black & brown . 1·10 1·10
DESIGN: 1 f. 50, Head of woman.

1984. International Youth Year.
G128 G **100** 1 f. 20 multicoloured . 90 90

1985. 20th Anniv of Turin Centre of I.L.O.
G129 **239** 80 c. red 60 60
G130 V **43** 1 f. 20 green 90 90

G **103** Ploughing and Group of People

1985. 10th Anniv of U.N. University, Tokyo.
G131 G **103** 50 c. multicoloured . 35 35
G132 80 c. multicoloured . 55 55

G **104** Postman

G **108** Children

1985.
G133 G **104** 20 c. multicoloured . 20 20
G134 – 1 f. 20 blue and black 1·10 1·10
DESIGN: 1 f. 20, Doves.

1985. 40th Anniv of United Nations Organization. Multicoloured.
G135 50 c. Type **243** 60 60
G136 70 c. "Harvest Scene" (Andrew Wyeth) 70 70

1985. U.N.I.C.E.F. Child Survival Campaign. Multicoloured.
G138 50 c. Type G **108** 40 40
G139 1 f. 20 Child drinking . . . 1·10 1·10

G **110** Children raising Empty Bowls to weeping Mother

G **111** Herring Gulls

1986. Africa in Crisis.
G140 G **110** 1 f. 40 multicoloured . 1·50 1·50

1986.
G141 G **111** 5 c. multicoloured . . 30 30

G **112** Tents in Clearing

1986. Development Programme. Timber Production. Multicoloured.
G142 35 c. Type G **112** 85 85
G143 35 c. Felling tree 85 85
G144 35 c. Logs on lorries 85 85
G145 35 c. Girls with sapling . . . 85 85
Nos. G142/5 were printed together, se-tenant, forming a composite design.

1986. Philately: International Hobby.
G146 **253** 50 c. green and red . . . 50 50
G147 – 80 c. black and orange . 90 90
DESIGN: 80 c. United Nations stamps.

G **118** Ribbon forming Dove

1986. International Peace Year. Multicoloured.
G148 45 c. Type G **118** 50 50
G149 1 f. 40 "Paix" and olive branch . . . . 1·40 1·40

1987. 9th Death Anniv of Trygve Lie (first U.N. Secretary-General).
G151 **258** 1 f. 40 multicoloured . 1·25 1·25

G **122** Abstract

G **124** Mixing Cement and Carrying Bricks

1987. Multicoloured.
G152 90 c. Type G **122** 65 65
G153 1 f. 40 Armillary Sphere, Geneva Centre (30 × 30 mm) 95 95

1987. International Year of Shelter for the Homeless.
G154 G **124** 50 c. green and black 70 70
G155 – 90 c. blue, turquoise and black . . . . . . 1·00 1·00
DESIGN: 90 c. Fitting windows and painting.

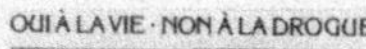

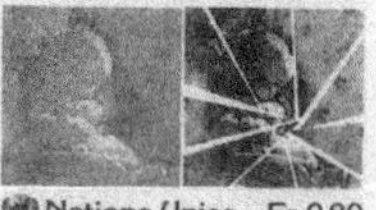

G **126** Mother and Baby

1987. Anti-Drugs Campaign. Multicoloured.
G156 80 c. Type G **126** . . . . 1·00 1·00
G157 1 f. 20 Workers in paddy field 1·25 1·25

G **128** People in Boat and Palais des Nations, Geneva

G **130** Whooping Cough

1987. United Nations Day. Multicoloured.
G158 35 c. Type G **128** 50 50
G159 50 c. Dancers 75 75

1987. "Immunize Every Child". Multicoloured.
G160 90 c. Type G **130** . . . . 1·00 1·00
G161 1 f. 70 Tuberculosis . . . . 1·50 1·50

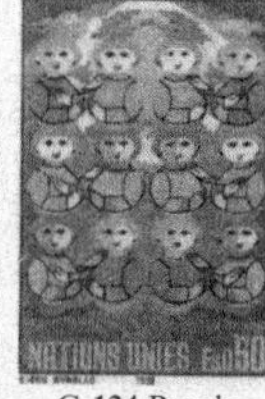

G **132** Goatherd

G **134** People

1988. International Fund for Agricultural Development "For a World Without Hunger" Campaign. Multicoloured.
G162 35 c. Type G **132** 50 50
G163 1 f. 40 Women and baskets of fruit . . . . 1·25 1·25

1988.
G164 G **134** 50 c. multicoloured . 40 40

G **135** Mountains and Pine Forest

G **137** Instruction in Fruit Growing

1988. "Survival of the Forests". Multicoloured.
G165 50 c. Type G **135** 4·00 4·00
G166 1 f. 10 Pine forest and lake shore 4·00 4·00
Nos. G165/6 were printed together, se-tenant, forming a composite design.

1988. International Volunteer Day. Mult.
G167 80 c. Type G **137** 70 70
G168 90 c. Teaching animal husbandary (horiz) 80 80

G **139** Football G **142** Communications

1988. "Health in Sports". Multicoloured.
G169 50 f. Type G **139** 45 45
G170 1 f. 40 Swimming 1·25 1·25

1988. 40th Anniv of Declaration of Human Rights.
G171 **276** 90 c. multicoloured 80 80

1989. World Bank. Multicoloured.
G173 80 c. Type G **142** 70 70
G174 1 f. 40 Industry 1·25 1·25

1989. Award of Nobel Peace Prize to United Nations Peace-keeping Forces.
G175 **280** 90 c. multicoloured 80 80

G **145** Cold Arctic Air over Europe G **147** Tree and Birds

1989. 25th Anniv of World Weather Watch.
G176 90 c. Type G **145** 80 80
G177 1 f. 10 Surface temperatures of Kattegat 95 95

1989. 10th Anniv of United Nations Vienna International Centre.
G178 50 c. Type G **147** 75 75
G179 2 f. Woman and flower 2·00 2·00

G **149** "Young Mother sewing" (Mary Cassatt) (Article 3)

1989. Universal Declaration of Human Rights (1st series). Multicoloured.
G180 35 f. Type G **149** 25 25
G181 80 f. "Runaway Slave" (Albert Mangones) (Article 4) 60 60
See also Nos. G193/4, G209/10, G224/5 and G234/5.

1990. International Trade Centre.
G182 **288** 1 f. 50 multicoloured 1·25 1·25

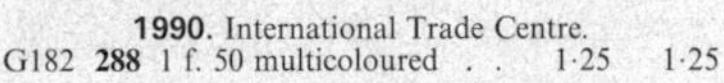

G **152** Palais des Nations G **155** Frangipani

1990.
G183 G **152** 5 f. multicoloured 3·75 3·75

1990. Anti-AIDS Campaign. Multicoloured.
G184 50 c. Type **289** 45 45
G185 80 c. "Man" (Leonardo da Vinci) 70 70

1990. Medicinal Plants. Multicoloured.
G186 90 c. Type G **155** 70 70
G187 1 f. 40 "Cinchona officinalis" 1·10 1·10

G **157** Projects forming "45"

1990. 45th Anniv of U.N.O. Multicoloured.
G188 90 c. Type G **157** 70 70
G189 1 f. 10 Dove and "45" 85 85

G **159** Men making Deal over Painting

1990. Crime Prevention. Multicoloured.
G191 50 c. Type G **159** 55 55
G192 2 f. Man spilling waste from cart 2·00 2·00

1990. Universal Declaration of Human Rights (2nd series). As Type G **149**.
G193 35 c. multicoloured 30 30
G194 90 c. black and flesh 75 75
DESIGNS: 35 c. "Prison Courtyard" (Vincent van Gogh) (Article 9); 90 c. "Katho's Son Redeems the Evil Doer from Execution" (Albrecht Durer) (Article 10).

G **163/166** Lake

1991. Economic Commission for Europe. "For a Better Environment".
G195 G **163** 90 c. multicoloured 2·00 2·00
G196 G **164** 90 c. multicoloured 2·00 2·00
G197 G **165** 90 c. multicoloured 2·00 2·00
G198 G **166** 90 c. multicoloured 2·00 2·00
Nos. G195/8 were issued together, se-tenant, forming the composite design illustrated.

G **167** Mountains G **169** Papers and Ballot Box

1991. 1st Anniv of Namibian Independence. Multicoloured.
G199 70 c. Type G **167** 65 65
G200 90 c. Baobab 80 80

1991. Multicoloured.
G201 80 c. Type G **169** 75 75
G202 1 f. 50 U.N. emblem 1·40 1·40

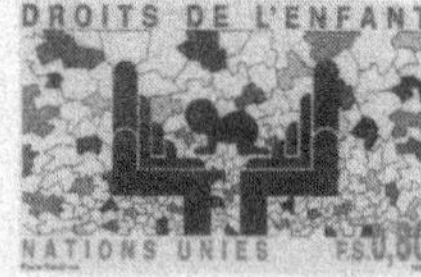

G **171** Baby in Open Hands (Ryuta Nakajima)

1991. 30th Anniv (1989) of U.N. Declaration of the Rights of the Child and 1990 World Summit on Children, New York. Children's Drawings. Multicoloured.
G203 80 c. Type G **171** 75 75
G204 1 f. 10 Children playing amongst flowers (David Popper) 1·00 1·00

G **173** Bubble of Toxin, City and Drums

1991. Banning of Chemical Weapons. Mult.
G205 80 c. Type G **173** 75 75
G206 1 f. 40 Hand pushing back gas mask 1·25 1·25

G **175** U.N. (New York) 1951 15 c. Stamp

1991. 40th Anniv of United Nations Postal Administration.
G207 G **175** 50 c. blue and lilac on cream 45 45
G208 – 1 f. 60 bl on cream 1·50 1·50
DESIGN: 1 f. 60, U.N. (New York) 1951 50 c. stamp.

1991. Declaration of Human Rights (3rd series). As Type G **149**. Multicoloured.
G209 50 c. "Early Morning in Ro, 1925" (Paul Klee) (Article 15) 45 45
G210 90 c. "The Marriage of Arnolfini" (Jan van Eyck) (Article 16) 80 80

G **179** Sagarmatha National Park, Nepal G **181** U.N. Headquarters, New York

1992. 20th Anniv of U.N.E.S.C.O. World Heritage Convention. Multicoloured.
G211 50 c. Type G **179** 45 45
G212 1 f. 10 Stonehenge, United Kingdom 1·00 1·00

1992.
G213 G **181** 3 f. multicoloured 2·75 2·75

G **182/183** Sea Life (½-size illustration)

1992. "Clean Oceans".
G214 G **182** 80 c. multicoloured 1·00 1·00
G215 G **183** 80 c. multicoloured 1·00 1·00
Nos. G214/15 were issued together, se-tenant, forming the composite design illustrated.

G **184/187** Planet Earth

1992. 2nd U.N. Conference on Environment and Development, Rio de Janeiro.
G216 G **184** 75 c. multicoloured 70 70
G217 G **185** 75 c. multicoloured 70 70
G218 G **186** 75 c. multicoloured 70 70
G219 G **187** 75 c. multicoloured 70 70
Nos. G216/19 were issued together, se-tenant, forming the composite design illustrated.

G **188/189** "Mission Planet Earth" (⅔-size illustration)

1992. International Space Year. Roul.
G220 G **188** 1 f. 10 multicoloured 1·00 1·00
G221 G **189** 1 f. 10 multicoloured 1·00 1·00
Nos. G220/1 were issued together, se-tenant, forming the composite design illustrated.

G **190** Women in Science and Technology G **194** Voluntary Work

1992. Commission on Science and Technology for Development. Multicoloured.
G222 90 c. Type G **190** 80 80
G223 1 f. 60 Graduate using V.D.U. 1·50 1·50

1992. Universal Declaration of Human Rights (4th series). As Type G **149**. Multicoloured.
G224 50 c. "The Oath of the Tennis Court" (Jacques Louis David) (Article 21) 45 45
G225 90 c. "Rocking Chair I" (Henry Moore) (Article 22) 80 80

1993. "Ageing: Dignity and Participation". 10th Anniv (1992) of International Plan of Action on Ageing. Multicoloured.
G226 50 c. Type G **194** 45 45
G227 1 f. 60 Security of employment 1·50 1·50

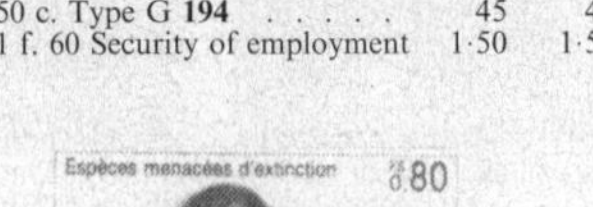

G **196** Gorilla

1993. Endangered Species (1st series.) Multicoloured.
G228 80 c. Type G **196** 1·00 1·00
G229 80 c. Peregrine falcon ("Falco peregrinus") 1·00 1·00
G230 80 c. Amazon manatee ("Tricheous inunguis") 1·00 1·00
G231 80 c. Snow leopard ("Panthera uncia") 1·00 1·00
See also Nos. G246/9, G264/7 and G290/3.

G **200** Neighbourhood and Community Environment

1993. 45th Anniv of W.H.O. Multicoloured.
G232 60 c. Type G **200** 55 55
G233 1 f. Urban environment 90 90

1993. Declaration of Human Rights (5th series). As Type G **149**. Multicoloured.
G234 50 c. "Three Musicians" (Pablo Picasso) (Article 27) 45 45
G235 90 c. "Voice of Space" (Rene Magritte) (Article 28) 80 80

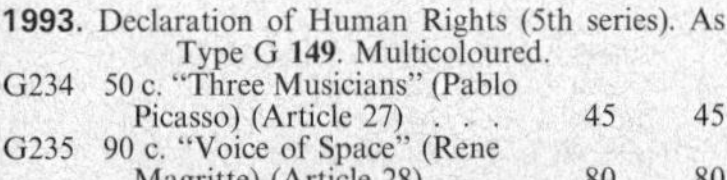

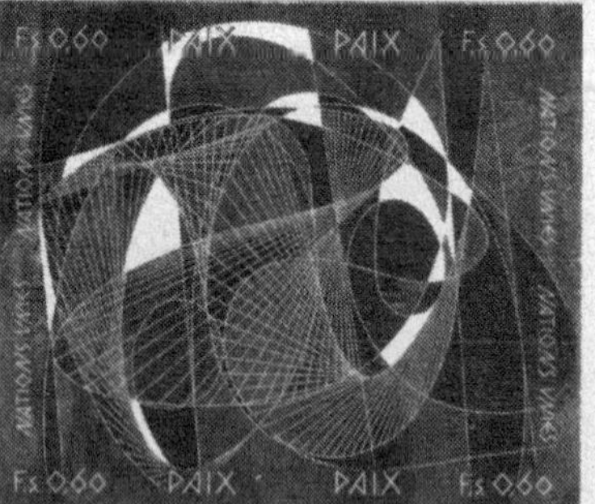

G **204/207** Peace

1993. International Peace Day. Roul.
G236 G **204** 60 c. multicoloured . 55 55
G237 G **205** 60 c. multicoloured . 55 55
G238 G **206** 60 c. multicoloured . 55 55
G239 G **207** 60 c. multicoloured . 55 55
Nos. G236/9 were issued together, se-tenant, forming the composite design illustrated.

G **208** Polar Bears

1993. The Environment—Climate. Multicoloured.
G240 1 f. 10 Type G **208** . . . . 1·50 1·50
G241 1 f. 10 Whale in melting ice . 1·50 1·50
G242 1 f. 10 Elephant seal . . . . 1·50 1·50
G243 1 f. 10 Adelie penguins . . . 1·50 1·50
Nos. G240/3 were issued together, se-tenant, forming a composite design.

G **212** Father calling Child G **218** Hand delivering Refugee to New Country

1994. Int Year of the Family. Mult.
G244 80 c. Type G **212** 70 70
G245 1 f. Three generations . . . 85 85

1994. Endangered Species (2nd series). As Type G **196**. Multicoloured.
G246 80 c. Mexican prairie dogs ("Cynomys mexicanus") . 1·10 1·10
G247 80 c. Jabiru ("Jabiru mycteria") . . . . 1·10 1·10
G248 80 c. Blue whale ("Balaenoptera musculus") 1·10 1·10
G249 80 c. Golden lion tamarin ("Leontopithecus rosalia") 1·10 1·10

1994. U.N. High Commissioner for Refugees.
G250 G **218** 1 f. 20 multicoloured 1·00 1·00

G **219/222** Shattered Globe and "Evaluation" (⅔-size illustration)

1994. International Decade for Natural Disaster Reduction.
G251 G **219** 60 c. multicoloured . 70 70
G252 G **220** 60 c. multicoloured . 70 70
G253 G **221** 60 c. multicoloured . 70 70
G254 G **222** 60 c. multicoloured . 70 70
Nos. G251/4 were issued together, se-tenant, forming the composite design illustrated.

G **223** Mobilization of Resources in Developing Countries

1994. International Population and Development Conference, Cairo. Multicoloured.
G255 60 c. Type G **223** 50 50
G256 80 c. Internal migration of population 70 70

G **225** Palais des Nations

1994. Multicoloured.
G257 60 c. Type G **225** 50 50
G258 80 c. "Creation of the World" (detail of tapestry, Oili Maki) 70 70
G259 1 f. 80 Palais des Nations . 1·50 1·50

G **228** Map and Linked Ribbons

1994. 30th Anniv of United Nations Conference on Trade and Development.
G260 80 c. Type G **228** 70 70
G261 1 f. Map and ribbons . . . 85 85

1995. 50th Anniv of U.N.O. (1st issue).
G262 **371** 80 c. multicoloured . . 70 70
See also Nos. G270/1 and G275/86.

G **231** "Social Summit 1995"

1995. World Summit for Social Development, Copenhagen.
G263 G **231** 1 f. multicoloured . . 85 85

1995. Endangered Species (3rd series). As Type G **196**. Multicoloured.
G264 80 c. Crowned lemur ("Lemur coronatus") 90 90
G265 80 c. Giant scops owl ("Otus gurneyi") 90 90
G266 80 c. Painted frog ("Atelopus varius zeteki") 90 90
G267 80 c. American wood bison ("Bison bison athabascae") 90 90

G **236** Field in Summer

1995. "Youth: Our Future". 10th Anniv of International Youth Year. Multicoloured.
G268 80 c. Type G **236** 70 70
G269 1 f. Field in winter 85 85

1995. 50th Anniv of U.N.O. (2nd issue).
G270 **379** 60 c. purple 50 50
G271 – 1 f. 80 green . . . . . 1·50 1·50
DESIGN: 1 f. 80, Veteran's Memorial Hall and Opera House, San Francisco (venue for signing of Charter).

G **240** Woman and Cranes G **254** Catching Fish

1995. 4th World Conference on Women, Peking. Multicoloured.
G273 60 c. Type G **240** 50 50
G274 1 f. Women worshipping (30 × 49 mm) 85 85

1995. 50th Anniv of U.N.O. (3rd issue).
G275 **385** 30 c. multicoloured . . 25 25
G276 **386** 30 c. multicoloured . . 25 25
G277 **387** 30 c. multicoloured . . 25 25
G278 **388** 30 c. multicoloured . . 25 25
G279 **389** 30 c. multicoloured . . 25 25
G280 **390** 30 c. multicoloured . . 25 25
G281 **391** 30 c. multicoloured . . 25 25
G282 **392** 30 c. multicoloured . . 25 25
G283 **393** 30 c. multicoloured . . 25 25
G284 **394** 30 c. multicoloured . . 25 25
G285 **395** 30 c. multicoloured . . 25 25
G286 **396** 30 c. multicoloured . . 25 25
Nos. G275/80 and G281/6 respectively were issued together, se-tenant, forming two composite designs.

1996. 50th Anniv of World Federation of United Nations Associations.
G287 G **254** 80 c. multicoloured . 70 70

G **255** "Galloping Horse treading on a Flying Swallow" (Chinese bronze sculpture, Han Dynasty)

1996. Multicoloured.
G288 40 c. Type G **255** 35 35
G289 70 c. Palais des Nations, Geneva 60 60

1996. Endangered Species (4th series). As Type G **196**. Multicoloured.
G290 80 c. "Paphiopedilum delenatii" 70 70
G291 80 c. "Pachypodium baronii" 70 70
G292 80 c. Yellow amaryllis ("Sternbergia lutea") . . . 70 70
G293 80 c. Cobra plant ("Darlingtonia californica") 70 70

G **261** Family on Verandah of House

1996. "Habitat II" Second United Nations Conference on Human Settlements, Istanbul, Turkey. Multicoloured.
G294 70 c. Type G **261** 60 60
G295 70 c. Women in traditional dress in gardens 60 60
G296 70 c. Produce seller and city . 60 60
G297 70 c. Boys playing on riverside 60 60
G298 70 c. Elderly couple reading newspaper 60 60
Nos. G294/8 were issued together, se-tenant, forming a composite design.

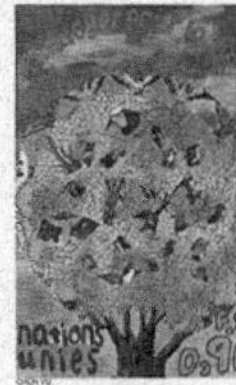

G **266** Cycling G **268** Birds in Treetop

1996. Sport and the Environment. Centenary of Modern Olympic Games. Multicoloured.
G299 70 c. Type G **266** 60 60
G300 1 f. 10 Running (horiz) . . . 95 95

1996. "A Plea for Peace". Winning Entries in China Youth Design Competition. Multicoloured.
G302 90 c. Type G **268** 80 80
G303 1 f. 10 Flowers growing from bomb 95 95

G **270** "The Sun and the Moon" (South American legend)

1996. 50th Anniv of U.N.I.E.C.F. Multicoloured.
G304 70 c. Type G **270** 60 60
G305 1 f. 80 "Ananse" (African spider tale) . . . . 1·50 1·50

G **272** U.N. Flag

1997.
G306 10 c. Type G **272** 10 10
G307 1 f. 10 "Building Palais des Nations" (detail of fresco, Massimo Campigli) 95 95

C. VIENNA HEADQUARTERS.

For use on mail posted at the United Nations Vienna International Centre and by the International Atomic Energy Agency.

100 groschen = 1 schilling

NOTE. Reference to numbers and types in this section, other than those with a "V" prefix, are to the United Nations (New York or Geneva) Headquarters listing. Designs adapted for the Vienna issues are inscribed in Austrian and have face values in schillings.

V **4** Donaupark Complex

1979. Some designs adapted from issues of New York or Geneva Headquarters. Multicoloured.
V1 50 g. Type G **53** 10 10
V2 1 s. As No. 94 . . . . 10 10
V3 2 s. 50 Type **162** 30 30
V3a 3 s. "...for a better world" . . 35 35
V4 4 s. Type V **4** 45 45
V5 5 s. Type A **134** 55 55
V6 6 s. Aerial view of Donaupark (vert) 65 65
V7 10 s. As Type **52**, but without frame . . . . 1·10 1·10

1980. New International Economic Order.
V8 **195** 4 s. multicoloured . . . . 1·00 90

V **9** Dove and World Map

1980. U.N. Decade for Women.
V 9 V **9** 4 s. multicoloured . . . 40 30
V10 6 s. multicoloured . . . 85 65

V **10** "Peace-keeping" V **11** Dove and "35"

1980. Peace-keeping Operations.
V11 V **10** 6 s. multicoloured . . . 65 65

1980. 35th Anniv of U.N.O.
V12 V **11** 4 s. black and red . . . 35 30
V13 – 6 s. multicoloured . . . 75 70
DESIGN: 6 s. Stylized flower.

V **13** Economic and Social Emblems

1980. Economic and Social Council. Multicoloured.
V15 V **13** 4 s. multicoloured . . . 45 40
V16 – 6 s. green, red & black . . 65 55
DESIGN: 6 s. Figures ascending graph.

1981. Inalienable Rights of the Palestinian People.
V17 **206** 4 s. multicoloured . . . 65 50

1981. International Year of Disabled Persons.
V18 **207** 4 s. multicoloured . . . 45 35
V19 – 6 s. orange and black . . 65 55
DESIGN: 6 s. Knot pattern.

1981. Art.
V20 **209** 6 s. multicoloured . . . 60 60

V **19** U.N. Energy Conference Emblem

1981. New and Renewable Sources of Energy.
V21 V **19** 7 s. 50 gold and mauve 70 70

V **20** Symbols of Services

1981. 10th Anniv of U.N. Volunteers Programme. Multicoloured.
V22 5 s. Type V **20** 45 40
V23 7 s. Emblems of science, agriculture and industry . . 65 60

V **22** Symbols of the Environment V **24** Satellite and Emblems

1982. Human Environment. Multicoloured.
V24 5 s. Type V **22** 45 45
V25 7 s. Leaves 65 65

1982. Second United Nations Conference on Exploration and Peaceful Uses of Outer Space.
V26 V **24** 5 s. multicoloured . . . 70 60

V **25** Fish V **28** Radar Screen within Lifebelt

1982. Conservation and Protection of Nature. Multicoloured.
V27 5 s. Type V **25** 60 60
V28 7 s. Elephant (mammals) . . 1·00 80

1983. World Communications Year.
V29 **222** 4 s. multicoloured 60 50

1983. Safety at Sea: International Maritime Organization. Multicoloured.
V30 4 s. Type V **28** 50 50
V31 6 s. Stylized liner 75 75

1983. World Food Programme.
V32 **226** 5 s. green 60 50
V33 7 s. brown 65 60

V **31** Exports V **33** "Die Zweite Haut"

1983. Trade and Development. Multicoloured.
V34 5 s. Type V **31** 50 40
V35 8 s. 50 Emblems of trade . . 90 85

1983. 35th Anniv of Declaration of Human Rights. Multicoloured.
V36 5 s. Type V **33** 50 40
V37 7 s. "Recht auf Traume" . . 75 60

V **35** World Agriculture

1984. International Conference on Population, Mexico City.
V38 V **35** 7 s. multicoloured . . . 95 95

V **36** Irrigation

1984. World Food Day. Multicoloured.
V39 4 s. 50 Type V **36** 45 45
V40 6 s. Combine harvesters . . . 65 65

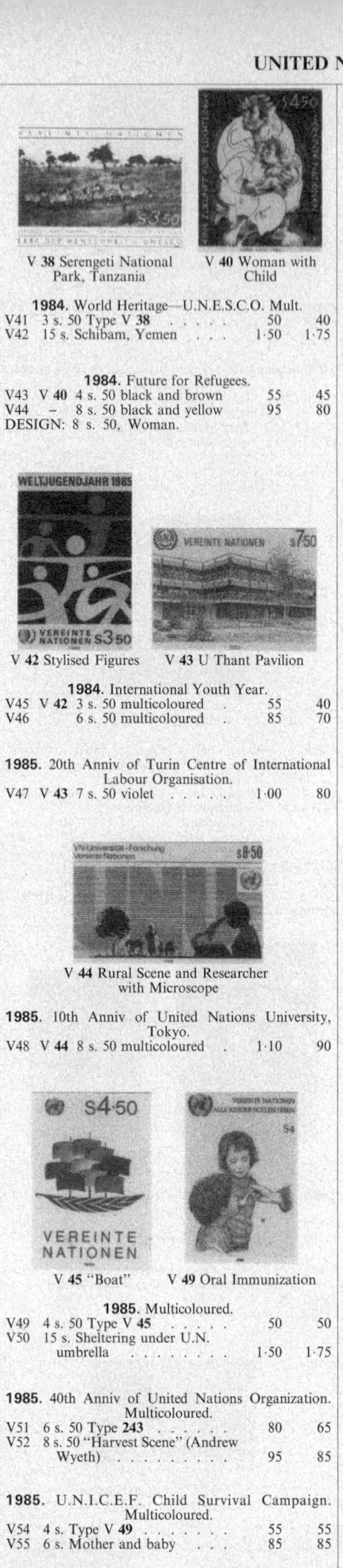

V **38** Serengeti National Park, Tanzania V **40** Woman with Child

1984. World Heritage—U.N.E.S.C.O. Mult.
V41 3 s. 50 Type V **38** 50 40
V42 15 s. Schibam, Yemen . . . 1·50 1·75

1984. Future for Refugees.
V43 V **40** 4 s. 50 black and brown 55 45
V44 – 8 s. 50 black and yellow 95 80
DESIGN: 8 s. 50, Woman.

V **42** Stylised Figures V **43** U Thant Pavilion

1984. International Youth Year.
V45 V **42** 3 s. 50 multicoloured . . 55 40
V46 6 s. 50 multicoloured . 85 70

1985. 20th Anniv of Turin Centre of International Labour Organisation.
V47 V **43** 7 s. 50 violet . . . . . 1·00 80

V **44** Rural Scene and Researcher with Microscope

1985. 10th Anniv of United Nations University, Tokyo.
V48 V **44** 8 s. 50 multicoloured . 1·10 90

V **45** "Boat" V **49** Oral Immunization

1985. Multicoloured.
V49 4 s. 50 Type V **45** 50 50
V50 15 s. Sheltering under U.N. umbrella . . . . 1·50 1·75

1985. 40th Anniv of United Nations Organization. Multicoloured.
V51 6 s. 50 Type **243** 80 65
V52 8 s. 50 "Harvest Scene" (Andrew Wyeth) 95 85

1985. U.N.I.C.E.F. Child Survival Campaign. Multicoloured.
V54 4 s. Type V **49** 55 55
V55 6 s. Mother and baby . . . 85 85

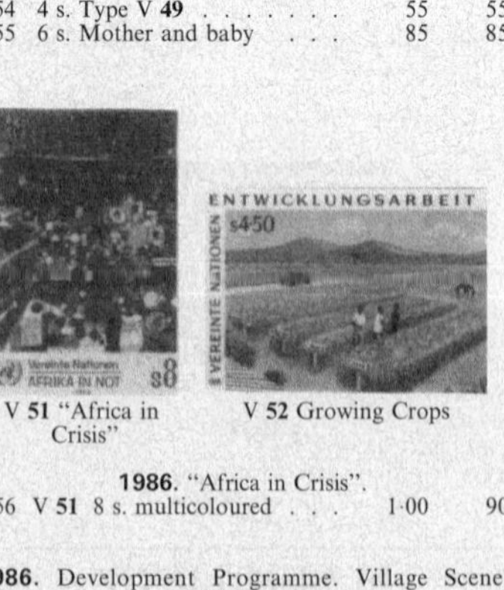

V **51** "Africa in Crisis" V **52** Growing Crops

1986. "Africa in Crisis".
V56 V **51** 8 s. multicoloured . . . 1·00 90

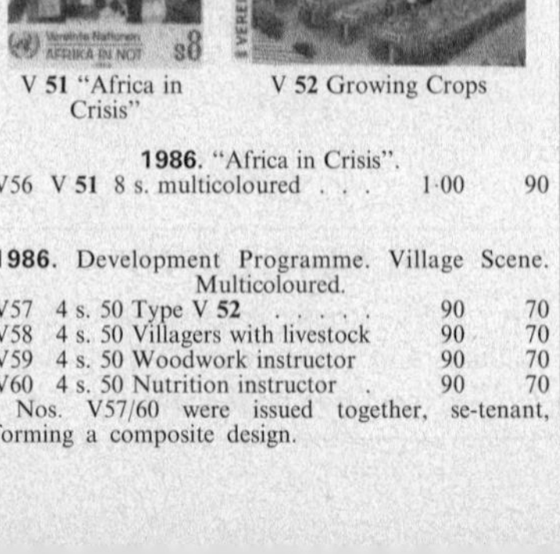

1986. Development Programme. Village Scene. Multicoloured.
V57 4 s. 50 Type V **52** 90 70
V58 4 s. 50 Villagers with livestock 90 70
V59 4 s. 50 Woodwork instructor 90 70
V60 4 s. 50 Nutrition instructor . 90 70
Nos. V57/60 were issued together, se-tenant, forming a composite design.

V **56** United Nations Stamps

1986. Philately: An International Hobby.
V61 V **56** 3 s. 50 blue and brown . 50 40
V62 – 6 s. 50 blue and red . . 75 70
DESIGN: 6 s. 50, Engraver.

V **58** Olive Branch and Rainbow

1986. International Peace Year. Multicoloured.
V63 5 s. Type V **58** 65 55
V64 6 s. Doves on U.N. emblem . 75 65

1986. 9th Death Anniv of Trygve Lie (first U.N. Secretary-General).
V66 **259** 8 s. multicoloured . . . . 1·00 90

V **62** Family looking at New Houses

1987. International Year of Shelter for the Homeless.
V67 V **62** 4 s. orange, black and yellow 65 50
V68 – 9 s. 50 orange and black 1·40 1·10
DESIGN: 9 s. 50, Family entering door of new house.

V **64** Footballers

1987. Anti-drugs Campaign. Multicoloured.
V69 5 s. Type V **64** 75 60
V70 8 s. Family . . . . 1·25 90

V **66** U.N. Centre, Vienna

1987. Multicoloured.
V71 2 s. Type V **66** 25 25
V72 17 s. Wreath of olive leaves and doves around globe . . . . 1·90 1·90

V **68** Dancers and Vienna Headquarters V **70** Poliomyelitis

1987. United Nations Day. Multicoloured.
V73 5 s. Type V **68** 70 60
V74 6 s. Dancers 80 70

1987. "Immunize Every Child". Multicoloured.
V75 4 s. Type V **70** 65 50
V76 9 s. 50 Diphtheria . . . . . . 1·25 1·10

V **72** Woman planting

1987. International Fund for Agricultural Development "For a World without Hunger" Campaign. Multicoloured.
V77 4 s. Type V **72** 55 55
V78 6 s. Women and foodstuffs . 70 70

V **74** Hills and Forest in Autumn V **76** Testing Blood Pressure

1988. "Survival of the Forests". Multicoloured.
V79 4 s. Type V **74** . . . . 1·75 1·00
V80 5 s. Forest in autumn . . . . 2·25 1·00
Nos. V79/80 were issued together, se-tenant, forming a composite design.

1988. International Volunteer Day. Multicoloured.
V81 6 s. Type V **76** 80 70
V82 7 s. 50 Building houses (horiz) 95 80

V **78** Skiing V **81** Transport

1988. "Health in Sports". Multicoloured.
V83 6 s. Type V **78** 75 70
V84 8 s. Tennis (horiz) . . . . . 1·00 90

1988. 40th Anniv of Declaration of Human Rights.
V85 **276** 5 s. multicoloured 65 60

1989. World Bank. Multicoloured.
V87 5 s. 50 Type V **81** 75 65
V88 8 s. Health and education . . 1·00 80

1989. Award of Nobel Peace Prize to United Nations Peace-keeping Forces.
V89 **280** 6 s. multicoloured . . . 75 65

V **84** Depression over Italy V **86** Man in Winter Clothes

1989. 25th Anniv of World Weather Watch.
V90 4 s. Type V **84** 60 40
V91 9 s. 50 Short-range rainfall forecast for Tokyo . . . . 1·25 90

1989. 10th Anniv of United Nations Vienna International Centre. Multicoloured.
V92 5 s. Type V **86** 55 45
V93 7 s. 50 Abstract 85 70

V **88** "Prisoners" (Kathe Kollwitz) (Article 5)

1989. Universal Declaration of Human Rights (1st series).
V94 V **88** 4 s. black 40 35
V95 – 6 s. multicoloured . . . 70 65
DESIGN: 6 s. "Jurisprudence" (Raphael) (Article 6).
See also Nos. V107/8, V122/3, V138/9 and V149/150.

1990. International Trade Centre.
V96 **287** 12 s. multicoloured . . . 1·75 1·75

V **91** "Earth" (painting by Kurt Regschek in I.A.E.A. Building)

1990.

V97 V **91** 1 s. 50 multicoloured . . 20 15

1990. Anti-AIDS Campaign. Multicoloured.

V98 5 s. Type **289** 75 45
V99 11 s. Attacking infected blood 1·50 1·00

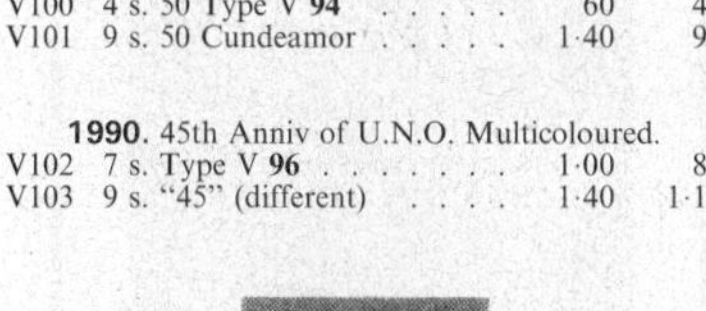

V **94** Annatto V **96** "45"

1990. Medicinal Plants. Multicoloured.

V100 4 s. 50 Type V **94** 60 40
V101 9 s. 50 Cundeamor . . . . . 1·40 90

1990. 45th Anniv of U.N.O. Multicoloured.

V102 7 s. Type V **96** . . . . 1·00 80
V103 9 s. "45" (different) . . . . 1·40 1·10

V **98** Men fighting

1990. Crime Prevention. Multicoloured.

V105 6 s. Type V **98** 85 70
V106 8 s. Masked man damaging painting . . . . 1·10 90

1990. Universal Declaration of Human Rights (2nd series). As Type V **88**. Multicoloured.

V107 4 s. 50 "Before the Judge" (Sandor Bihari) (Article 11) 60 50
V108 7 s. "Young Man greeted by Woman writing Poem" (Suzuki Harunobu) (Article 12) 80 65

V **102/105** Mediterranean Coastline and Wildlife

1991. Economic Commission for Europe. "For a Better Environment".

V109 V **102** 5 s. multicoloured . . 95 60
V110 V **103** 5 s. multicoloured . . 95 60
V111 V **104** 5 s. multicoloured . . 95 60
V112 V **105** 5 s. multicoloured . . 95 60

Nos. V109/12 were issued together, se-tenant, forming the composite design illustrated.

V **106** Scrubland V **108** Different Races

1991. 1st Anniv of Namibian Independence. Multicoloured.

V113 6 s. Type V **106** 70 60
V114 9 s. 50 Sand dune . . . . . 1·10 90

1991.

V115 V **108** 20 s. multicoloured . 2·25 1·90

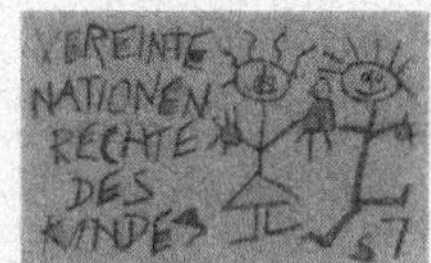

V **109** Boy and Girl (Anna Harmer)

1991. 30th Anniv (1989) of U.N. Declaration of the Rights of the Child and 1990 World Summit on Children, New York. Children's Drawings. Multicoloured.

V116 7 s. Type V **109** 80 65
V117 9 s. Child's world (Emiko Takegawa) . . . . 1·00 80

V **111** City, Bubbles of Toxin and Gas Mask

1991. Banning of Chemical Weapons. Mult.

V118 5 s. Type V **111** 55 45
V119 10 s. Hand pushing back cloud of toxin sprayed from airplane . . . . 1·10 90

V **113** U.N. (New York) 1951 20 c. Stamp

1991. 40th Anniv of United Nations Postal Administration.

V120 V **113** 5 s. brown on cream 55 45
V121 – 8 s. blue on cream . 90 75

DESIGN: 8 s. U.N. (New York) 1951 5 c. stamp.

1991. Declaration of Human Rights (3rd series). As Type V **88**. Multicoloured.

V122 4 s. 50 Ancient Mexican pottery (Article 17) 50 40
V123 7 s. "Windows, 1912" (Robert Delaunay) (Article 18) . . 80 65

V **117** Iguacu National Park, Brazil V **119/120** Sea Life (½-size illustration)

1992. 20th Anniv of U.N.E.S.C.O. World Heritage Convention. Multicoloured.

V124 5 s. Type V **117** 55 45
V125 9 s. Abu Simbel, Egypt . . 1·00 80

1992. "Clean Oceans".

V126 V **119** 7 s. multicoloured . . 80 65
V127 V **120** 7 s. multicoloured . . 80 65

Nos. V126/7 were issued together, se-tenant, forming the composite design illustrated.

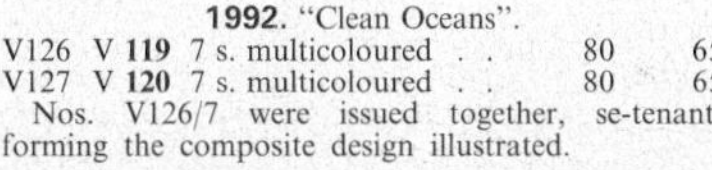

V **121/124** Planet Earth

1992. 2nd U.N. Conference on Environment and Development, Rio de Janeiro.

V128 V **121** 5 s. 50 multicoloured 60 50
V129 V **122** 5 s. 50 multicoloured 60 50
V130 V **123** 5 s. 50 multicoloured 60 50
V131 V **124** 5 s. 50 multicoloured 60 50

Nos. V128/131 were issued together, se-tenant, forming the composite design illustrated.

V **125/126** "Mission Planet Earth" (⅔-size illustration)

1992. International Space Year. Roul.

V132 V **125** 10 s. multicoloured . . 1·10 90
V133 V **126** 10 s. multicoloured . . 1·10 90

Nos. V132/3 were printed together, se-tenant, forming the composite design illustrated.

V **127** Woman with Book emerging from V.D.U. V **129** Woman's Profile, Birds, Butterfly and Rose

1992. Commission on Science and Technology for Development. Multicoloured.

V134 5 s. 50 Type V **127** 60 50
V135 7 s. Flowers growing from thumb 80 65

1992. Multicoloured.

V136 5 s. 50 Type V **129** 60 50
V137 7 s. Vienna International Centre (horiz) 80 65

1992. Universal Declaration of Human Rights (4th series). As Type V **88**. Multicoloured.

V138 6 s. "The Builders" (Fernand Leger) (Article 23) 70 60
V139 10 s. "Sunday Afternoon on the Island of La Grande Jatte" (Georges Seurat) (Article 24) 1·10 90

V **133** Housing and Environment V **135** Grevy's Zebra

1993. "Ageing: Dignity and Participation". 10th Anniv (1992) of International Plan of Action on Ageing. Multicoloured.

V140 5 s. 50 Type V **133** 60 50
V141 7 s. Education 80 65

1993. Endangered Species (1st series). Multicoloured.

V142 7 s. Type V **135** 80 65
V143 7 s. Humboldt penguin ("Spheniscus humboldti") . 80 65
V144 7 s. Desert monitor ("Varanus griseus") 80 65
V145 7 s. Wolf ("Canis lupus") . . 80 65

See also Nos. V161/4, V179/82 and V205/8.

V **139** Globe, Doves and U.N. Emblem V **140** Regional and National Environment

1993.

V146 V **139** 13 s. multicoloured . . 1·50 1·25

1993. 45th Anniv of W.H.O. Multicoloured.

V147 6 s. Type V **140** 70 60
V148 10 s. Continental and global environment . . . . 1·10 90

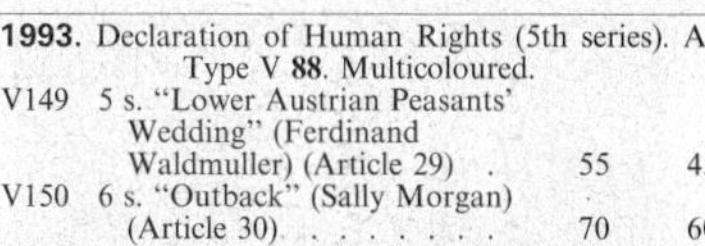

1993. Declaration of Human Rights (5th series). As Type V **88**. Multicoloured.

V149 5 s. "Lower Austrian Peasants' Wedding" (Ferdinand Waldmuller) (Article 29) . 55 45
V150 6 s. "Outback" (Sally Morgan) (Article 30) 70 60

V **144/147** Peace

1993. International Peace Day. Roul.

V151 V **144** 5 s. 50 multicoloured 60 50
V152 V **145** 5 s. 50 multicoloured 60 50
V153 V **146** 5 s. 50 multicoloured 60 50
V154 V **147** 5 s. 50 multicoloured 60 50

Nos. V151/4 were issued together, se-tenant, forming the composite design illustrated.

V **148** Monkeys

1993. The Environment—Climate. Multicoloured.

V155 7 s. Type V **148** 80 65
V156 7 s. Eastern bluebird and factory chimneys 80 65
V157 7 s. Volcano, smokestacks and tree stumps 80 65
V158 7 s. Great horned owl in desert 80 65

Nos. V155/8 were issued together, se-tenant, forming a composite design.

V **152** Family holding Hands

1994. International Year of the Family. Mult.

V159 5 s. 50 Type V **152** 70 60
V160 8 s. Family at work . . . . . 1·00 80

1994. Endangered Species (2nd series). As Type V **135**. Multicoloured.

V161 7 s. Ocelot ("Felis pardalis") 90 75
V162 7 s. White-crested white eye ("Zosterups albogularis") 90 75
V163 7 s. Mediterranean monk seals ("Monachus monachus") . 90 75
V164 7 s. Indian elephant ("Elephas maximus") 90 75

V **158** Tree and Doves V **161** Hands ready to help Refugees

1994. Multicoloured.

V165 50 g. Type V **158** 10 10
V166 4 s. Herring gulls 50 40
V167 30 s. Globe and dove . . . 3·75 3·00

1994. United Nations High Commissioner for Refugees.

V168 V **161** 12 s. multicoloured . 1·50 1·25

V **162/165** Shattered Globe and "Preparation" (⅔-size illustration)

1994. International Decade for Natural Disaster Reduction.
V169 V **162** 6 s. multicoloured . . 75 60
V170 V **163** 6 s. multicoloured . . 75 60
V171 V **164** 6 s. multicoloured . . 75 60
V172 V **165** 6 s. multicoloured . . 75 60
Nos. V169/72 were issued together, se-tenant, forming the composite design illustrated.

V **166** Enhancing Role of Women

1994. International Population and Development Conference, Cairo. Multicoloured.
V173 5 s. 50 Type V **166** 70 60
V174 7 s. Relationship of population and environment 90 75

V **168** Map and Crossed Ribbons

1994. 30th Anniv of United Nations Conference on Trade and Development. Multicoloured.
V175 6 s. Type V **168** 75 60
V176 7 s. Map and ribbons forming star 90 75

1995. 50th Anniv of U.N.O. (1st issue).
V177 **371** 7 s. multicoloured . . . 90 75
See also Nos. V185/6 and V190/201.

V **171** "Social Summit 1995"

1995. World Summit for Social Development, Copenhagen.
V178 V **171** 14 s. multicoloured . . 1·75 1·40

1995. Endangered Species (3rd series). As Type V **135**. Multicoloured.
V179 7 s. Black rhinoceros ("Diceros bicornis") 90 75
V180 7 s. Golden conure ("Aratinga guarouba") 90 75
V181 7 s. Variegated langur ("Pygathrix nemaeus") . . 90 75
V182 7 s. Arabian oryx ("Oryx leucoryx") 90 75

V **176** Village in Winter

1995. "Youth: Our Future". 10th Anniv of International Youth Year. Multicoloured.
V183 6 s. Type V **176** 75 60
V184 7 s. Wheat stacks in field . . 90 75

1995. 50th Anniv of U.N.O. (2nd issue).
V185 **379** 7 s. green 90 75
V186 – 10 s. black . . . . 1·25 1·00
DESIGN: 10 s. Opera House, San Francisco (venue for signing of U.N. Charter).

V **180** Women in Jungle
V **194** Jester holding Dove

1995. 4th World Conference on Women, Peking. Multicoloured.
V188 5 s. 50 Type V **180** 70 60
V189 6 s. Woman reading book . 75 60

1995. 50th Anniv of U.N.O. (3rd issue).
V190 **385** 3 s. multicoloured . . . 40 35
V191 **386** 3 s. multicoloured . . . 40 35
V192 **387** 3 s. multicoloured . . . 40 35
V193 **388** 3 s. multicoloured . . . 40 35
V194 **389** 3 s. multicoloured . . . 40 35
V195 **390** 3 s. multicoloured . . . 40 35
V196 **391** 3 s. multicoloured . . . 40 35
V197 **392** 3 s. multicoloured . . . 40 35
V198 **393** 3 s. multicoloured . . . 40 35
V199 **394** 3 s. multicoloured . . . 40 35
V200 **395** 3 s. multicoloured . . . 40 35
V201 **396** 3 s. multicoloured . . . 40 35
Nos. V190/5 and V196/201 respectively were issued together, se-tenant, forming two composite designs.

1996. 50th Anniv of World Federation of United Nations Associations. Multicoloured.
V202 V **194** 7 s. multicoloured . . 90 75

V **195** U.N. Flag
V **201** Family with Agricultural Products

1996. Multicoloured.
V203 1 s. Type V **195** 15 10
V204 10 s. Abstract painting (Karl Korab) . . . . 1·25 1·00

1996. Endangered Species (4th series). As Type V **135**. Multicoloured.
V205 7 s. Venus slipper orchid ("Cypripedium calceolus") 80 65
V206 7 s. "Aztekium ritteri" . . . 80 65
V207 7 s. "Euphorbia cremersii" . 80 65
V208 7 s. "Dracula bella" 80 65

1996. "Habitat II" Second U.N. Conf on Human Settlements, Istanbul, Turkey. Mult.
V209 6 s. Type V **201** 70 60
V210 6 s. Women with sacks of grain 70 60
V211 6 s. Woman and city 70 60
V212 6 s. Ploughing with oxen . . 70 60
V213 6 s. Villlage and elephant . . 70 60
Nos. V209/13 were issued together, se-tenant, forming a composite design.

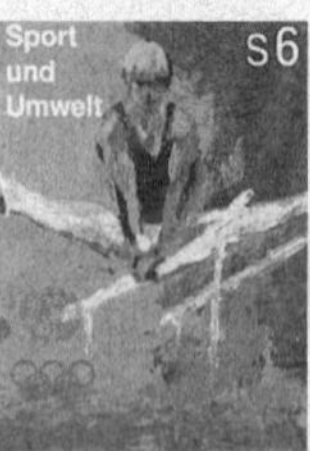

V **206** Gymnastics

1996. Sport and the Environment. Multicoloured.
V214 6 s. Type V **206** 70 60
V215 7 s. Hurdling 80 65

V **208** Dove and Butterflies

1996. "A Plea for Peace". Winners of China Youth Design Competition. Multicoloured.
V217 7 s. Type V **208** 80 65
V218 10 s. Children and flowers in dove . . . . 1·10 90

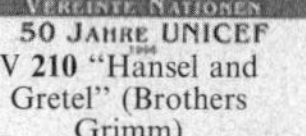

V **210** "Hansel and Gretel" (Brothers Grimm)
V **212** Red Phoenix

1996. 50th Anniv of U.N.I.C.E.F. Children's Stories.
V219 5 s. 50 Type V **210** 65 55
V220 8 s. "How Maui Stole Fire from the Gods" (Pacific Islands myth) 95 80

1997. Details of "Phoenixes flying Down" by Sagenji Yoshida. Multicoloured.
V221 5 s. Type V **212** 60 50
V222 6 s. Green phoenix 70 60

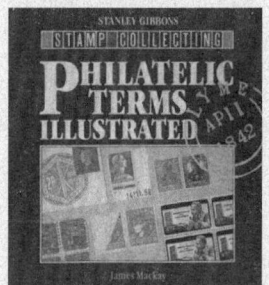

UNITED STATES OF AMERICA

Pt. 22

A Federal Republic in N. America, consisting of 50 states and one federal district.

100 cents = 1 dollar

PRICES. On the issues before 1890 the gum is rarely complete and the unused prices quoted are for stamps with part original gum.

1 Franklin (after drawings by James B. Longacre) **2** Washington (after painting by Stuart)

1847. Imperf.

1	**1**	5 c. brown	£3750	£350
2	**2**	10 c. black	£14000	£1100

The 5 c. blue and 10 c. orange both imperf come from miniature sheets isssued in 1947 to commemorate the Centenary Philatelic Exhibition, New York.

3 Franklin (after bust by Caffieri) **4** Washington (after bust by Houdon) **5** Jefferson (after painting by Stuart)

6 Washington **7** Washington **8** Washington (after paintings by Stuart)

9 Franklin (after bust by Caffieri) **10** Washington (after Trumbull painting)

1851. Imperf.

11	**3**	1 c. blue	£250	55·00
13a	**4**	3 c. red	90·00	4·25
14	**5**	5 c. brown	£6500	£650
16	**6**	10 c. green	£1300	£150
19	**7**	12 c. black	£1700	£170

1857. Perf.

26	**3**	1 c. blue	75·00	14·00
28	**4**	3 c. red	35·00	1·50
33	**5**	5 c. brown	£325	£120
39	**6**	10 c. green	£120	32·00
40c	**7**	12 c. black	£180	60·00
41	**8**	24 c. lilac	£375	£140
42	**9**	30 c. orange	£550	£200
43	**10**	90 c. blue	£850	£2750

11 Franklin **12** Washington **13** Jefferson

14 Washington **15** Washington **16** Washington

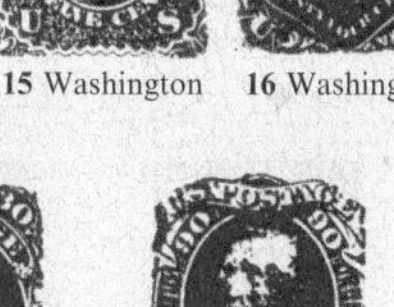

17 Franklin **18** Washington

19 Andrew Jackson (after miniature by J. W. Dodge) **20** Lincoln (from a photograph)

1861.

60b	**11**	1 c. blue	90·00	11·00
69	**19**	2 c. black	£110	16·00
62	**12**	3 c. red	45·00	60
63b	**13**	5 c. yellow	£3750	£275
72		5 c. brown	£250	38·00
64a	**14**	10 c. green	£190	18·00
65	**15**	12 c. black	£375	38·00
73	**20**	15 c. black	£375	50·00
66c	**16**	24 c. blue	£2750	£200
74		24 c. lilac	£200	32·00
74b		24 c. grey	£200	32·00
67	**17**	30 c. orange	£375	48·00
68a	**18**	90 c. blue	£1000	£170

21 Franklin (after Houdon bust) **22** Post Rider **23** Steam Locomotive

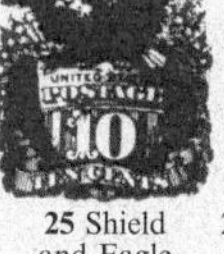

24 Washington (after Stuart) **25** Shield and Eagle **26** Paddle-steamer "Adriatic" (after C. Parsons)

27 Landing of Columbus (after Vanderlyn) **28** Declaration of Independence (after Trumbull) **30** Lincoln (from a photograph)

1869.

114	**21**	1 c. brown	£160	45·00
115	**22**	2 c. brown	£130	18·00
116	**23**	3 c. blue	£140	4·25
117	**24**	6 c. blue	£550	60·00
118	**25**	10 c. orange	£650	60·00
119	**26**	12 c. green	£550	65·00
121	**27**	15 c. blue and brown	£700	95·00
122	**28**	24 c. purple and green	£1700	£325
123	**25**	30 c. red and blue	£1800	£150
124	**30**	90 c. black and red	£5500	£900

31 Franklin **32** Jackson **33** Washington

34 Lincoln **35** Stanton **36** Jefferson

37 Henry Clay **38** Daniel Webster **39** General Winfield Scott

40 Alexander Hamilton **41** Commodore Perry **42** General Zachary Taylor (from a daguerreotype)

1870.

207	**31**	1 c. blue	26·00	30
148	**32**	2 c. brown	50·00	2·50
185		2 c. red	45·00	70
208	**33**	3 c. green	32·00	10
219		3 c. red	32·00	27·00
161	**34**	6 c. red	£150	50
151	**35**	7 c. red	£250	35·00
210	**36**	10 c. brown	60·00	1·50
153	**37**	12 c. purple	£400	42·00
191	**38**	15 c. orange	£120	11·00
155	**39**	24 c. violet	£450	55·00
192	**40**	30 c. black	£350	21·00
222		30 c. brown	£275	55·00
193	**41**	90 c. red	£800	£110
223		90 c. violet	£600	£110

1875.

181	**42**	5 c. blue	£140	4·75

43 Garfield (from a photograph) **44** Washington (after bust by Houdon) **45** Jackson (after bust by Powers)

46 Franklin **47** Franklin

1882.

217	**46**	1 c. blue	45·00	40
213	**44**	2 c. brown	23·00	10
218		2 c. green	17·00	10
214	**45**	4 c. green	£120	4·50
220		4 c. red	£120	7·50
211	**43**	5 c. brown	90·00	2·50
221		5 c. blue	£110	3·50

1890. No triangles in upper corners.

224	**47**	1 c. blue (Franklin)	14·00	10
225a	–	2 c. red (Washington)	12·00	10
226	–	3 c. violet (Jackson)	40·00	3·00
227	–	4 c. sepia (Lincoln)	38·00	1·00
228	–	5 c. brown (Grant)	40·00	1·00
229	–	6 c. red (Garfield)	42·00	11·00
230	–	8 c. purple (Sherman)	26·00	5·50
231	–	10 c. green (Webster)	70·00	1·00
232	–	15 c. blue (Clay)	£120	10·00
233	–	30 c. black (Jefferson)	£180	14·00
234	–	90 c. orange (Perry)	£300	70·00

58 Columbus in Sight of Land **83** Jefferson

1893. Columbian Exposition, Chicago.

235	**58**	1 c. blue	17·00	15
236	–	2 c. purple	15·00	10
237	–	3 c. green	38·00	10·00
238	–	4 c. blue	50·00	4·00
239	–	5 c. brown	60·00	4·50
240	–	6 c. violet	40·00	15·00
241	–	8 c. red	30·00	7·50
242	–	10 c. sepia	85·00	4·25
243	–	15 c. green	£130	38·00
244	–	30 c. orange	£190	50·00
245	–	50 c. slate	£250	75·00
246	–	$1 red	£750	£400
247	–	$2 lake	£900	£325
248	–	$3 green	£1900	£700
249a	–	$4 red	£2750	£1000
250	–	$5 black	£2750	£1100

DESIGNS: 2 c. Landing of Columbus; 3 c. "Santa Maria", flagship of Columbus; 4 c. Fleet of Columbus; 5 c. Columbus soliciting aid of Isabella; 6 c. Columbus welcomed at Barcelona, Ferdinand (left) and Balboa (right); 8 c. Columbus restored to favour; 10 c. Columbus presenting natives; 15 c. Columbus announcing his discovery; 30 c. Columbus at La Rabida; 50 c. Recall of Columbus; $1 Isabella pledging her jewels; $2 Columbus in chains; $3 Columbus describing his third voyage; $4 Isabella and Columbus; $5 Columbus, America and Liberty.

1894. Triangles in upper corners as T **83**. Same portraits as issue of 1890 except dollar values.

267	–	1 c. blue	3·50	10
283	–	1 c. green	6·00	10
270	–	2 c. red	2·75	10
271	–	3 c. violet	22·00	60
285	–	4 c. brown	20·00	40
273	–	5 c. brown	22·00	90
286	–	5 c. blue	22·00	30
274	–	6 c. brown	48·00	2·00
287a	–	6 c. purple	28·00	1·00
275	–	8 c. brown	25·00	60
276	–	10 c. green	35·00	60
289	–	10 c. brown	70·00	1·00
277	–	15 c. blue	£120	4·50
290	–	15 c. green	85·00	3·50
278	**83**	50 c. orange	£160	12·00
279	–	$1 black (Perry)	£350	40·00
281a	–	$2 blue (Madison)	£650	£190
282	–	$5 green (Marshall)	£1400	£300

88 Father Marquette on the Mississippi **97** "City of Alpena" (Great Lakes steamer)

1898. Trans-Mississippi Exposition, Omaha.

291	**88**	1 c. green	18·00	2·75
292	–	2 c. red	17·00	70
293	–	4 c. orange	90·00	13·00
294	–	5 c. blue	75·00	10·00
295	–	8 c. purple	£120	21·00
296	–	10 c. violet	£140	12·00
297	–	50 c. green	£550	60·00
298	–	$1 black	£1400	£375
299	–	$2 brown	£2000	£700

DESIGNS: 2 c. Farming in the West; 4 c. Indian hunting American bison; 5 c. Fremont on Rocky Mountains; 8 c. Troops guarding emigrant train; 10 c. Hardships of emigration; 50 c. Western mining prospector; $1 Western cattle in storm; $2 Bridge over Mississippi at St. Louis and paddle-steamer "Grey Eagle".

1901. Pan-American Exhibition, Buffalo. Inscr "COMMEMORATIVE SERIES, 1901."

300	**97**	1 c. black and green	15·00	2·75
301	–	2 c. black and red	15·00	75
302	–	4 c. black and brown	65·00	10·00
303	–	5 c. black and blue	85·00	13·00
304	–	8 c. black and brown	£100	50·00
305	–	10 c. black and brown	£160	20·00

DESIGNS: 2 c. "Empire State Express"; 4 c. Automobile; 5 c. Railway bridge below Niagara Falls; 8 c. Canal locks at Sault Sainte Marie; 10 c. "Saint Paul" (liner).

103 Franklin **104** Washington **105** Jackson

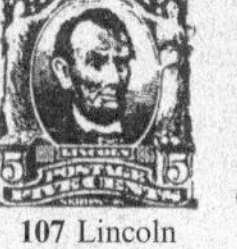

106 Grant **107** Lincoln **108** Garfield

109 Martha Washington **110** Webster **111** Harrison

112 Clay **113** Jefferson **114** Farragut

115 Madison **116** Marshall

1902. Inscr "SERIES 1902". 1, 4 and 5 c. perf or imperf.

306	**103**	1 c. green	6·00	10
307	**104**	2 c. red	7·00	10
308	**105**	3 c. violet	35·00	1·75
309	**106**	4 c. brown	35·00	70
310	**107**	5 c. blue	40·00	45
311	**108**	6 c. lake	42·00	1·40
312	**109**	8 c. violet	24·00	5·00
313	**110**	10 c. brown	50·00	70
314	**111**	13 c. purple	24·00	5·00
315	**112**	15 c. olive	95·00	3·25
316	**113**	50 c. orange	£250	14·00
317	**114**	$1 black	£550	32·00
485	**115**	$2 blue	£375	32·00
486	**116**	$5 green	£300	35·00

117 Washington (after Stuart) **118** Robert R. Livingston (after Stuart)

1903. Perf or imperf.

326	**117**	2 c. red	3·50	10

1904. International Exposition, St. Louis, and Louisiana Purchase. Inscr "COMMEMORATIVE SERIES OF 1904".

330	**118**	1 c. green	20·00	2·75
331	–	2 c. red	18·00	80
332	–	2 c. violet	65·00	22·00
333	–	5 c. blue	75·00	12·00
334	–	10 c. brown	£130	18·00

DESIGNS: 2 c. Thomas Jefferson; 3 c. James Monroe (after Vanderlyn); 5 c. William McKinley; 10 c. Map of Louisiana Purchase.

123 Capt. John Smith, Pocahontas and Powhatan (after painting)

1907. Jamestown Exposition.

335	**123**	1 c. green	12·00	2·75
336	–	2 c. red	15·00	1·75
337	–	5 c. blue	65·00	17·00

DESIGN: 2 c. Founding of Jamestown, 1607; 5 c. Princess Pocahontas.

126 Franklin **127** **128** Washington (after Houdon bust)

1908. 1 to 5 c. perf or imperf.

338	**126**	1 c. green	4·00	10
505	**128**	1 c. green	25	10
339	**127**	2 c. red	3·75	10
506	**128**	2 c. red	20	10
537		3 c. violet	65	10
510		4 c. brown	10·00	10
503		5 c. blue	3·50	70
513		6 c. orange	11·00	15
514		7 c. black	22·00	85
344		8 c. green	23·00	1·75
345		10 c. yellow	45·00	1·00
346		13 c. green	25·00	16·00
347		15 c. blue	40·00	3·50
348		50 c. violet	£200	9·50
349		$1 black	£325	48·00

129 Lincoln (detail of statue by Saint Gaudens in Grant Park, Chicago)

1909. Birth Centenary of Abraham Lincoln. Perf or imperf.

374	**129**	2 c. red	3·75	1·50

130 Wm. H. Seward **131** "Clermont" and "Half Moon" on Hudson River

1909. Alaska–Yukon–Pacific Exposition. Perf or imperf.

377	**130**	2 c. red	6·50	1·00

1909. Hudson–Fulton Celebration. Perf or imperf.

379	**131**	2 c. red	11·00	3·25

133 Franklin (after Caffieri bust) **138**

1912.

515	**133**	8 c. olive	11·00	55
516		9 c. pink	13·00	1·50
517		10 c. yellow	15·00	10
518		11 c. green	8·00	2·50
519		12 c. brown	8·00	30
520		13 c. green	10·00	5·50
521		15 c. grey	3·00	70
522		20 c. blue	40·00	15
523		30 c. orange	30·00	55
524		50 c. lilac	70·00	40
525		$1 black	65·00	1·00
526	**138**	$2 black and orange	£650	£170
527		$2 black and red	£275	23·00
528		$5 black and green	£300	22·00

134 Balboa **135** Panama Canal (after model of Pedro Miguel Locks)

1913. Panama–Pacific Exposition. Inscr "SAN FRANCISCO 1915".

423	**134**	1 c. green	11·00	1·00
424	**135**	2 c. red	12·00	30
425	–	5 c. blue	60·00	6·00
426	–	10 c. yellow	£170	10·00

DESIGNS: 5 c. Golden Gate, San Francisco; 10 c. Discovery of San Francisco Bay (after painting by Mathew).

A **139** Curtiss JN-4 "Jenny" **139** Liberty and Allies' Flags

1918. Air.

A546	A **139**	6 c. orange	70·00	26·00
A547		16 c. green	£100	32·00
A548		24 c. blue and red	£100	35·00

1919. Victory

546	**139**	3 c. violet	6·00	2·50

140 The "Mayflower"

1920. Tercentenary of Landing of Pilgrim Fathers. Inscr as in T **140**.

556	**140**	1 c. green	3·75	2·00
557	–	2 c. red	6·50	1·25
558	–	5 c. blue	32·00	10·00

DESIGNS: 2 c. Landing of the Pilgrims (after drawing by White); 5 c. Signing the Compact.

144 Franklin **157** Indian Chief **158** Statue of Liberty

159 Golden Gate **165** America

1922. Perf or imperf (1 c., $1\frac{1}{2}$ c. 2 c).

559	–	$\frac{1}{2}$ c. brown (Hale)	15	10
632	**144**	1 c. green	15	10
603	–	$1\frac{1}{2}$ c. brown (Harding)	50	10
634	–	2 c. red (Washington)	15	10
636a	–	3 c. violet (Lincoln)	20	10
637	–	4 c. brown (Martha Washington)	2·75	10
608	–	5 c. bl (T. Roosevelt)	1·00	10
639	–	6 c. orange (Garfield)	2·25	10
640	–	7 c. black (McKinley)	2·25	10
641	–	8 c. green (Grant)	2·25	10
642	–	9 c. pink (Jefferson)	2·25	10
610	–	10 c. orange (Monroe)	3·00	10
571a	–	11 c. blue (Hayes)	1·50	15
571b	–	11 c. green (Hayes)	1·40	35
693	–	12 c. violet (Cleveland)	5·00	10
694	–	13 c. green (B. Harrison)	1·75	15
695	**157**	14 c. blue	3·00	40
696	**158**	15 c. grey	8·00	10
698	**159**	20 c. red	9·00	10
699	–	25 c. green (Niagara)	8·50	10
700	–	30 c. brown (American bison)	13·00	10
701	–	50 c. lilac (Arlington Amphitheatre and Unknown Soldier's Tomb)	38·00	10
579	–	$1 brown (Lincoln Memorial)	45·00	20
580	–	$2 blue (Capitol, Washington)	£100	5·50
581	**165**	$5 blue and red	£225	8·00

The 25 c. to $2 are horiz designs as T **159**, the remainder vert as T **144**

A **166** Airplane Radiator and Propeller A **168** De Havilland D.H.4M "Liberty"

1923. Air.

A614	A **166**	8 c. green	30·00	14·00
A615	–	16 c. blue	95·00	32·00
A616	A **168**	24 c. red	£110	28·00

DESIGN: 16 c. Air mail service insignia.

166 Harding **167** "Nieu Nederland" (emigrant ship)

1923. President Harding Memorial.

614	**166**	2 c. black	70	10

1924. Huguenot–Walloon Tercentenary.

618	**167**	1 c. green	3·25	3·00
619	–	2 c. red	7·00	2·00
620	–	5 c. blue	24·00	14·00

DESIGNS: 2 c. Landing at Fort Orange; 5 c. Ribault Memorial, Mayport, Florida.

170 Washington at Cambridge **173** Sloop "Restaurationen"

1925. 150th Anniv of Battle of Lexington and Concord.

621	**170**	1 c. green	3·00	3·00
622	–	2 c. red	5·50	3·75
623	–	5 c. blue	22·00	13·00

DESIGNS: 2 c. Battle of Lexington-Concord; 5 c. Statue of "Minute Man".

1925. Norse-American Centennial. Dated "1825 1925".

624	**173**	2 c. black and red	4·00	2·50
625	–	5 c. black and blue	18·00	16·00

DESIGN: 5 c. "Raven" (replica Viking longship).

176 Wilson

1925.

697	**176**	17 c. black	4·00	25

A **177** Relief Map of U.S.A.

1926. Air.

A628	A **177**	10 c. blue	3·00	20
A629		15 c. brown	3·25	2·00
A630		20 c. green	9·00	1·25

177 Liberty Bell

1926. 150th Anniv of Independence and Sesquicentennial Exhibition.

628	**177**	2 c. red	2·75	45

178 Ericsson Memorial (after statue by J. E. Fraser in Washington, D.C.) **179** Alexander Hamilton's Battery (after painting by E. F. Ward)

1926. John Ericsson Commemoration.

629	**178**	5 c. violet	5·00	2·50

1926. 150th Anniv of Battle of White Plains.

644	**179**	2 c. red	1·50	1·25

A **180** "Spirit of St. Louis"

1927. Air. Lindbergh's Transatlantic Flight.

A646	A **180**	10 c. blue	8·50	1·25

181 Green Mountain Boy **182** Surrender of Gen. Burgoyne (after painting by Trumbull)

1927. 150th Anniv of Independence of Vermont and Battle of Bennington.

646	**181**	2 c. red	1·25	80

1927. 150th Anniv of Burgoyne Campaign.

647	**182**	2 c. red	3·00	2·00

183 Washington at Valley Forge (after engraving by J. C. McRae) A **184** Air Beacon, Sherman Hill, Rocky Mountains

1928. 150th Anniv of Valley Forge.

648	**183**	2 c. red	70	35

1928. Air.

A649	A **184**	5 c. blue and red	4·00	30

1928. 150th Anniv of Discovery of Hawaii. Optd **HAWAII 1778-1928**.

649	2 c. red (No. 634)	3·25	4·00
650	5 c. blue (No. 608)	12·00	15·00

1928. 150th Anniv of Battle of Monmouth. Optd **MOLLY PITCHER**.

651	2 c. red (No. 634)	1·00	1·00

186 Wright Flyer I

1928. Civil Aeronautics Conference and 25th Anniv of Wright Brothers' First Flight.

652	**186**	2 c. red	1·25	90
653	–	5 c. blue	6·00	2·75

DESIGN: 5 c. Globe and Ryan B-5 Brougham airplane.

188 George Rogers Clark at Vincennes (from painting by F. C. Yohn)

1929. 150th Anniv of Surrender of Fort Sackville.

654	**188**	2 c. black and red	75	60

1929. Stamps of 1922 optd. (a) **Kans.**

655	**144**	1 c. green	1·75	2·00
656	**166**	$1\frac{1}{2}$ c. brown	2·50	3·25
657	–	2 c. red	3·00	65
658	–	3 c. violet	13·00	12·00
659	–	4 c. brown	15·00	7·00
660	–	5 c. blue	11·00	8·50
661	–	6 c. orange	24·00	17·00
662	–	7 c. black	22·00	25·00
663	–	8 c. olive	65·00	60·00
664	–	9 c. red	11·00	10·00
665	–	10 c. yellow	19·00	10·00

(b) **Nebr.**

666	**144**	1 c. green	2·00	1·75
667	**166**	$1\frac{1}{2}$ c. brown	2·25	2·75
668	–	2 c. red	1·60	70
669	–	3 c. violet	11·00	9·00
670	–	4 c. brown	17·00	14·00
671	–	5 c. blue	15·00	13·00
672	–	6 c. orange	35·00	25·00
673	–	7 c. black	19·00	16·00
674	–	8 c. olive	25·00	22·00
675	–	9 c. red	30·00	24·00
676	–	10 c. yellow	90·00	16·00

191 Edison's Original Lamp **192** Maj.-Gen. Sullivan

1929. 50th Anniv of Edison's First Electric Lamp.
678 **191** 2 c. red 60 20

1929. 150th Anniv of Maj.-Gen. Sullivan's Western Campaign.
680 **192** 2 c. red 55 50

193 Gen. Wayne Memorial in Fallen Timbers Park, by E.W. Laville

194 Ohio River Lock No. 5, Monongahela R.

1929. 135th Anniv of Battle of Fallen Timbers.
681 **193** 2 c. red 75 75

1929. Completion of Ohio River Canalisation.
682 **194** 2 c. red 55 55

A **195** Air Mail Pilot's Badge

1930. Air.
A684 A **195** 5 c. violet . . . . . . 5·50 25
A685 6 c. orange . . . . . 2·25 10
A686 8 c. green . . . . . . 2·25 15

195 Seal of the Colony

196 Governor and Indian

1930. Massachusetts Bay Colony Tercentenary.
683 **195** 2 c. red 50 40

1930. 250th Anniv of Original Settlement near Charleston.
684 **196** 2 c. red . . . . 1·00 1·10

A **197** Over the Atlantic

1930. Air. "Graf Zeppelin" Europe–Pan-American Flight.
A687 A **197** 65 c. green £300 £225
A688 – $1.30 brown £650 £425
A689 – $2.60 blue £1000 £650
DESIGNS: $1.30, Between continents; $2.60, Over the globe.

197 Harding

199 George Washington (after statue by F. Vittor in Braddock, Pa.)

1930.
685 **197** $1\frac{1}{2}$ c. brown 30 10
686 – 4 c. brown 80 10
DESIGN: 4 c. Taft.

1930. 175th Anniv of Battle of Braddock's Field.
689 **199** 2 c. red 80 90

200 Gen. Wilhelm von Steuben (from medallion by Karl Dautert)

201 Gen. Casimir Pulaski (from etching by H. B. Hall)

1930. Birth Bicentenary of Gen. von Steuben.
690 **200** 2 c. red 50 50

1931. 150th Death Anniv of Gen. Pulaski.
691 **201** 2 c. red 30 15

202 Red Cross Nurse (from poster "The World's Greatest Mother")

203 Rochambeau, Washington, De Grasse (Washington after painting by Trumbull, others from old engravings)

1931. 50th Anniv of American Red Cross Society.
702 **202** 2 c. black and red 15 10

1931. 150th Anniv of Surrender of Cornwallis at Yorktown.
703 **203** 2 c. black and red 30 25

204 George Washington **205**

1932. Birth Bicentenary of George Washington. Portraits dated "1732 1932".
704 **204** $\frac{1}{2}$ c. sepia 10 10
705 **205** 1 c. green 10 10
706 – $1\frac{1}{2}$ c. brown 50 10
707 – 2 c. red 10 10
708 – 3 c. violet 70 10
709 – 4 c. brown 40 10
710 – 5 c. blue . . . . 1·75 10
711 – 6 c. orange . . . . 3·25 10
712 – 7 c. black 50 15
713 – 8 c. olive . . . . 3·25 70
714 – 9 c. red . . . . 3·00 10
715 – 10 c. yellow . . . . . . 11·00 10
For 3 c. as No. 707, see No. 720.

216 Skiing

217 Tree-planting

1932. Winter Olympic Games, Lake Placid.
716 **216** 2 c. red 60 20

1932. 60th Anniv of Establishment of Arbor Day.
717 **217** 2 c. red 15 10

218 Sprinter

219 Discus Thrower

221 Wm. Penn

1932. Summer Olympic Games, Los Angeles.
718 **218** 3 c. violet . . . . 1·25 10
719 **219** 5 c. blue . . . . 2·25 30

1932. As No. 707, but without date.
720 3 c. violet 20 10

1932. 250th Anniv of Penn's Arrival in America.
723 **221** 3 c. violet 30 20

222 Webster

223 Gen. Oglethorpe

224 Washington's H.Q

1932. 150th Birth Anniv of Daniel Webster.
724 **222** 3 c. violet 35 30

1933. Bicentenary of Founding of Georgia.
725 **223** 3 c. violet 30 15

1933. 150th Anniv of Proclamation of Peace after War of Independence.
726 **224** 3 c. violet 15 10

225 Fort Dearbon (after painting by Dwight Benton)

226 Federal Building

1933. "Centenary of Progress" International Exhibition, Chicago.
727 **225** 1 c. green 15 10
728 **226** 3 c. violet 15 10

227 Agriculture, Commerce and Industry

1933. National Recovery Act.
729 **227** 3 c. violet 10 10

A **230** Chicago Federal Building, "Graf Zeppelin" and Friedrichshafen Hanger

1933. Air. "Graf Zeppelin" Chicago Flight.
A732 A **230** 50 c. green . . . . . £100 75·00

230 Routes of various Admiral Byrd Flights

1933. Byrd Antarctic Expedition.
752 **230** 3 c. blue 45 50

231 Gen. Kosciuszko (from statue in Lafayette Park, Washington)

233 The "Ark" and the "Dove" (from drawing by E. Tunis)

1933. 150th Anniv of Naturalization of Kosciusko.
733 **231** 5 c. blue 50 25

1934. Maryland Tercentenary.
735 **233** 3 c. red 20 15

234 "Portrait of my Mother" by Whistler

1934. Mothers' Day. Perf or imperf.
736 **234** 3 c. violet 10 10

235 Nicolet's Landing at Green Bay (after painting by E. W. Deming)

1934. Tercentenary of Wisconsin.
738 **235** 3 c. violet 15 10

236 "El Capitan", Yosemite

237 Grand Canyon

1934. National Parks. Perf or imperf.
739 **236** 1 c. green 15 10
740 **237** 2 c. red 20 10
741 – 3 c. violet 25 10
742 – 4 c. brown 50 40
743 – 5 c. blue . . . . 1·00 70
744 – 6 c. blue . . . . 1·50 1·10
745 – 7 c. black 75 85
762 – 8 c. green . . . . 1·75 2·25
747 – 9 c. red . . . . 1·75 60
748 – 10 c. grey . . . . 3·50 90
DESIGNS—VERT: 5 c. "Old Faithful" geyser, Yellowstone; 8 c. Great White Throne, Zion; 10 c. Mount le Conte, Smoky Mountain. HORIZ: 3 c. Mirror Lake, Mt Rainier; 4 c. Cliff dwellings, Mesa Verde; 6 c. Crater Lake and Wizard Is; 7 c. Great Head, Acadia; 9 c. Mt Rockwell and Two Medicine Lake Glacier.

248 The Charter Oak

1935. Connecticut Tercentenary.
771 **248** 3 c. purple 10 10

249 Exhibition Grounds, Point Loma and San Diego Bay

1935. California Pacific Int Exn, San Diego.
772 **249** 3 c. violet 10 10

250 Boulder Dam, Nevada

251 Seal of Michigan

1935. Dedication of Boulder Dam.
773 **250** 3 c. violet 15 10

1935. Michigan Centenary.
774 **251** 3 c. violet 10 10

A **253** Martin M-130 Flying Boat

1935. Air. Trans-Pacific Air Mail.
A775 – 20 c. green . . . . . 11·00 1·50
A776 A **253** 25 c. blue . . . . . 2·00 75
A777 – 50 c. red . . . . . . 12·00 2·25
Nos. A775 and A777 are as Type A **253** but without the date.

252 S. Houston, S. F. Austin, and the Alamo

253 Roger Williams (from statue in Roger Williams Park, Providence, R. I.)

1936. Centenary of Declaration of Texan Independence.
775 **252** 3 c. violet 10 10

1936. Rhode Island Tercentenary.
776 **253** 3 c. violet 10 10

255 First Settlement, Old State House and Capitol

1936. Centenary of Arkansas.
778 **255** 3 c. violet 10 10

256 Map of Old Oregon Territory

257 Susan B. Anthony (detail from statue by Adelaide Johnson in Capitol)

1936. Centenary of Oregon.
779 **256** 3 c. violet 15 10

1936. 16th Anniv of Women's Suffrage.
780 **257** 3 c. purple 10 10

258 Washington and Greene, Mt. Vernon in background

263 Jones, Barry and Battle of Flamborough Head

1936. Army and Navy Heroes. (a) Army.

781 **258** 1 c. green 10 10
782 – 2 c. red 10 10
783 – 3 c. purple 20 10
784 – 4 c. blue 40 15
785 – 5 c. blue 70 15

DESIGNS: 2 c. Jackson, Scott and the Hermitage; 3 c. Sherman, Grant and Sheridan; 4 c. Lee, Jackson and Stratford Hall; 5 c. West Point Military Acadamy.

(b) Navy.

786 **263** 1 c. green 15 10
787 – 2 c. red 15 10
788 – 3 c. purple 25 10
789 – 4 c. blue 40 15
790 – 5 c. blue 70 15

DESIGNS: 2 c. Decatur, MacDonough and U.S.S. "United States"; 3 c. Farragut, Porter and U.S.S. "Hartford"; 4 c. Sampson, Dewey and Schley; 5 c. Seal of Naval Academy and cadets.

268 Cutler, Putnam and Map of N. W. Territory
269 Virginia Dare

1937. 150th Anniv of Enactment of North West Territory Ordinance.

791 **268** 3 c. violet 15 10

1937. 350th Birth Anniv of Virginia Dare.

792 **269** 5 c. blue 15 15

271 Signing the Constitution (after painting by J. B. Stearns)

1937. 150th Anniv of U.S. Constitution.

794 **271** 3 c. mauve 10 10

272 Statue to Kamehameha I, Honolulu

273 Mt. McKinley, Alaska

274 Fortaleza Castle, Puerto Rico

275 Charlotte Amalie (St. Thomas), Virgin Islands

1937. Territorial Issue.

795 **272** 3 c. violet 10 10
796 **273** 3 c. violet 10 10
797 **274** 3 c. violet 10 10
798 **275** 3 c. mauve 10 10

276 Benjamin Franklin

A 308 American Bald Eagle and Shield

1938. Presidential Series.

799 **276** $\frac{1}{2}$ c. orange 10 10
800 – 1 c. green 10 10
801 – $1\frac{1}{2}$ c. brown 10 10
802 – 2 c. red 10 10
803 – 3 c. violet 10 10
804 – 4 c. purple 50 10
805 – $4\frac{1}{2}$ c. grey 15 10
806 – 5 c. blue 20 10
807 – 6 c. red 30 10
808 – 7 c. brown 35 10
809 – 8 c. green 50 10
810 – 9 c. pink 50 10
811 – 10 c. red 35 10
812 – 11 c. blue 60 10
813 – 12 c. mauve . . . . 1·10 10
814 – 13 c. green . . . . 1·50 10
815 – 14 c. blue 80 10
816 – 15 c. slate 55 10
817 – 16 c. black . . . . 1·00 35
818 – 17 c. red . . . . 1·00 15
819 – 18 c. purple . . . . 1·60 10
820 – 19 c. mauve . . . . 1·25 50
821 – 20 c. green 70 10
822 – 21 c. blue . . . . 1·75 15
823 – 22 c. red . . . . 1·00 50
824 – 24 c. black . . . . 3·00 15
825 – 25 c. mauve 70 10
826 – 30 c. blue . . . . 4·25 10
827 – 50 c. lilac . . . . 6·50 10
828 – \$1 black and purple . . . 7·50 10
830 – \$2 black and green . . . 20·00 3·50
831 – \$5 black and red . . . . 90·00 3·00

DESIGNS: 1 c. Washington; $1\frac{1}{2}$ c. Martha Washington; 2 c. John Adams; 3 c. Jefferson; 4 c. Madison; $4\frac{1}{2}$ c. White House; 5 c. James Monroe; 6 c. John Quincy Adams; 7 c. Jackson; 8 c. Martin van Buren; 9 c. Wm. Henry Harrison; 10 c. John Tyler; 11 c. James K. Polk; 12 c. Zachary Taylor; 13 c. Millard Fillmore; 14 c. Franklin Pierce; 15 c. James Buchanan; 16 c. Lincoln; 17 c. Johnson; 18 c. Grant; 19 c. Rutherford B. Hayes; 20 c. James A. Garfield; 21 c. Chester A. Arthur; 22 c. Grover Cleveland; 24 c. Benjamin Harrison; 25 c. William McKinley; 30 c. Theodore Roosevelt; 50 c. Taft; \$1 Woodrow Wilson; \$2 Harding; \$5 Coolidge.

1938. Air.

A845 A **308** 6 c. red and blue . . 60 10

308 Colonial Court House

1938. 150th Anniv of Ratification of U.S. Constitution.

845 **308** 3 c. violet 15 10

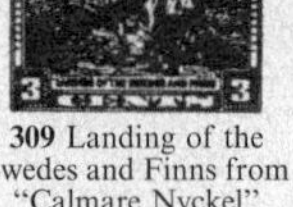
309 Landing of the Swedes and Finns from "Calmare Nyckel" (after S. Arthurs)

310 Colonization of the West (from statue by G. Borglum at Marietta, Ohio)

1938. Tercentenary of Scandinavian Settlement in America.

846 **309** 3 c. mauve 15 10

1938. Northwest Territory Sesquicentennial.

847 **310** 3 c. violet 15 10

311 Old Capitol Building, Iowa

312 Tower of the Sun

1938. Iowa Territory Centennial.

848 **311** 3 c. violet 15 10

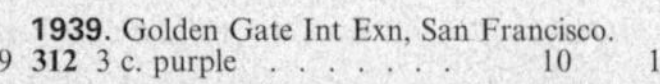

1939. Golden Gate Int Exn, San Francisco.

849 **312** 3 c. purple 10 10

313 Trylon and Perisphere

314 Inauguration of Washington

1939. New York World's Fair.

850 **313** 3 c. violet 10 10

1939. 150th Anniv of Election of Washington as First President.

851 **314** 3 c. purple 20 10

A 315 Winged Globe

1939. Air.

A852 A **315** 30 c. blue . . . . . . 10·00 70

315 Baseball

1939. Baseball Centenary.

852 **315** 3 c. violet 45 10

316 T. Roosevelt Goethals and "Andrea F. Luckenbach" in Gaillard Cut

317 Stephen Daye Press (from sketch by G. F. Trenholm)

1939. 25th Anniv of Opening of Panama Canal.

853 **316** 3 c. purple 25 10

1939. Tercent of Printing in Colonial America.

854 **317** 3 c. violet 10 10

318 Washington, Montana, N. and S. Dakota

319 Washington Irving

324 Henry W. Longfellow

329 Horace Mann

334 John James Audubon

339 Stephen Collins Foster

344 Gilbert Charles Stuart

349 Eli Whitney

1939. 50th Anniv of Statehood of Washington, Montana and N. and S. Dakota.

855 **318** 3 c. mauve 15 10

1940. Famous Americans. (a) Authors.

856 **319** 1 c. green 10 10
857 – 2 c. red 10 10
858 – 3 c. purple 10 10
859 – 5 c. blue 35 25
860 – 10 c. brown . . . . 1·90 1·40

PORTRAITS: 2 c. J. Fenimore Cooper; 3 c. Ralph Waldo Emerson; 5 c. Louisa May Alcott; 10 c. Samuel L. Clemens ("Mark Twain).

(b) Poets.

861 **324** 1 c. green 10 10
862 – 2 c. red 10 10
863 – 3 c. purple 10 10
864 – 5 c. blue 35 25
865 – 10 c. brown . . . . 2·00 1·75

PORTRAITS: 2 c. John Greenleaf Whittier; 3 c. James Russell Lowell; 5 c. Walt Whitman; 10 c. James Whitcomb Riley.

(c) Educationlists.

866 **329** 1 c. green 10 10
867 – 2 c. red 10 10
868 – 3 c. purple 20 10
869 – 5 c. blue 45 25
870 – 10 c. brown . . . . 1·75 1·40

PORTRAITS: 2 c. Mark Hopkins; 3 c. Charles W. Eliot; 5 c. Frances E. Willard; 10 c. Booker T. Washington.

(d) Scientists.

871 **334** 1 c. green 10 10
872 – 2 c. red 10 10
873 – 3 c. purple 10 10
874 – 5 c. blue 30 25
875 – 10 c. brown . . . . 1·10 1·00

PORTRAITS: 2 c. Dr. Crawford W. Long; 3 c. Luther Burbank; 5 c. Dr. Walter Reed; 10 c. Jane Addams.

(e) Composers.

876 **339** 1 c. green 10 10
877 – 2 c. red 15 10
878 – 3 c. purple 15 10
879 – 5 c. blue 50 25
880 – 10 c. brown . . . . 4·50 1·25

PORTRAITS: 2 c. John Philip Sousa; 3 c. Victor Herbert; 5 c. Edward A. MacDowell; 10 c. Ethelbert Nevin.

(f) Artists.

881 **344** 1 c. green 10 10
882 – 2 c. red 10 10
883 – 3 c. purple 10 10
884 – 5 c. blue 50 25
885 – 10 c. brown . . . . 1·75 1·40

PORTRAITS: 2 c. James A. McNeill Whistler; 3 c. Augustus Saint-Gaudens; 5 c. Daniel Chester French; 10 c. Frederic Remington.

(g) Inventors.

886 **349** 1 c. green 10 10
887 – 2 c. red 10 10
888 – 3 c. purple 15 10
889 – 5 c. blue 85 30
890 – 10 c. brown . . . . 11·00 2·00

PORTRAITS: 2 c. Samuel F. B. Morse; 3 c. Cyrus Hall McCormick; 5 c. Elias Howe; 10 c. Alexander Graham Bell.

354 "Pony Express"

355 "The Three Graces" (after Botticelli's "Spring")

1940. 80th Anniv of Inauguration of Pony Express.

891 **354** 3 c. red 30 10

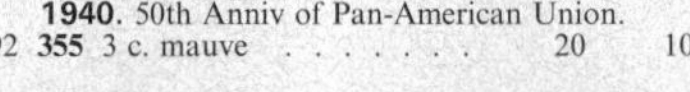

1940. 50th Anniv of Pan-American Union.

892 **355** 3 c. mauve 20 10

356 State Capitol, Boise

357 Wyoming State Seal

1940. 50th Anniv of Idaho.

893 **356** 3 c. violet 20 10

1940. 50th Anniv of Wyoming.

894 **357** 3 c. purple 20 10

358 Coronado and His Captains (after painting by Gerald Cassidy)

360 Anti-aircraft Gun

1940. 400th Anniv of Coronado Expedition.
895 **358** 3 c. violet 20 10

1940. National Defence.
896 – 1 c. green 10 10
897 **360** 2 c. red 10 10
898 – 3 c. violet 10 10
DESIGNS: 1 c. Statue of Liberty; 3 c. Hand holding torch.

362 Emancipation Monument (from statue by Thomas Ball, Lincoln Park, Washington)

363 State Capitol Building, Montpelier

1940. 75th Anniv of Abolition of Slavery.
899 **362** 3 c. violet 20 10

1941. 150th Anniv of Vermont.
900 **363** 3 c. violet 20 10

A **364** Mail Plane

1941. Air.
A901 A **364** 6 c. red 15 10
A902 8 c. green 30 10
A903 10 c. violet 1·25 15
A904 15 c. red 3·00 10
A905 20 c. green 2·00 20
A906 30 c. blue 2·25 15
A907 50 c. orange 10·00 3·00

364 Daniel Boone and Companions viewing Kentucky (from mural by Gilbert White in State Capitol, Frankfort)

365 Symbolical of Victory

1942. 150th Anniv of Kentucky.
901 **364** 3 c. violet 15 10

1942. Independence Day.
902 **365** 3 c. violet 10 10

366 Lincoln and Sun Yat-sen

367 Allegory of Victory

1942. Chinese War Effort.
903 **366** 5 c. blue 30 20

1943. Allied Nations.
904 **367** 2 c. red 10 10

368 Liberty holding Torch of Freedom and Enlightenment

369 Flag of Poland

1943. Four Freedoms.
905 **368** 1 c. green 10 10

1943. Flags of Oppressed Nations. Frames in violet, flags in national colours.
906 5 c. Type **369** 20 10
907 5 c. Czechoslovakia 25 10
908 5 c. Norway 15 10
909 5 c. Luxembourg 15 10
910 5 c. Netherlands 15 10
911 5 c. Belgium 15 10
912 5 c. France 20 10
913 5 c. Greece 60 25
914 5 c. Yugoslavia 45 15
915 5 c. Albania 35 15
916 5 c. Austria 30 15
917 5 c. Denmark 40 15
918 5 c. Korea 25 15

382 "Golden Spike Ceremony" (painting, John McQuarrie)

1944. 75th Anniv of First Transcontinental Railway.
919 **382** 3 c. violet 35 10

383 Paddle-steamer "Savannah"

1944. 125th Anniv of Transatlantic Crossing of "Savannah."
920 **383** 3 c. violet 10 10

384 "What Hath God Wrought"

1944. Centenary of First Telegraph Message.
921 **384** 3 c. mauve 10 10

385 View of Corregidor

1944. Defence of Corregidor.
922 **385** 3 c. violet 15 10

386 Open-air Cinema

1944. 50th Anniv of Motion Pictures.
923 **386** 3 c. violet 10 10

387 Gates of St. Augustine, State Seal and Capitol

1945. Centenary of Statehood of Florida.
924 **387** 3 c. purple 10 10

388 "Toward United Nations"

1945. San Francisco Conference.
925 **388** 5 c. blue 10 10

389 Franklin D. Roosevelt and Hyde Park

393 Raising U.S.A. Flag at Iwo Jima

1945. Pres. Roosevelt Commemoration. Inscr "1882 1945".
926 **389** 1 c. green 10 10
927 – 2 c. red 10 10
928 – 3 c. violet 10 10
929 – 5 c. blue 15 10
DESIGNS: 2 c. "Little White House", Warm Springs, Georgia; 3 c. "White House", Washington; 5 c. Western Hemisphere and Four Freedoms.

1945. U.S. Marines.
930 **393** 3 c. green 10 10

394 U.S. Troops marching through Paris

1945. U.S. Army.
931 **394** 3 c. olive 10 10

395 U.S. Sailors

1945. U.S. Navy.
932 **395** 3 c. blue 10 10

396 "Arthur Middleton" (supply ship) and Coastguard Landing Craft)

397 Alfred E. Smith

1945. U.S. Coastguard.
933 **396** 3 c. green 10 10

1945. Alfred E. Smith (Governor of New York) Commemoration.
934 **397** 3 c. violet 10 10

398 Flags of U.S.A. and Texas

1945. Centenary of Texas Statehood.
935 **398** 3 c. blue 10 10

399 "Liberty" type Freighter unloading Cargo

400 Honourable Discharge Emblem

1946. U.S. Mercantile Marine.
936 **399** 3 c. green 10 10

1946. Honourable Discharged Veterans of Second World War.
937 **400** 3 c. violet 10 10

401 Andrew Jackson, John Sevier and Tennessee State Capitol

1946. 150th Anniv of Tennessee Statehood.
938 **401** 3 c. violet 10 10

402 Iowa State Flag and Map

1946. Centenary of Iowa Statehood.
939 **402** 3 c. blue 10 10

403 Smithsonian Institution

1946. Centenary of Smithsonian Institution.
940 **403** 3 c. purple 10 10

A **404** Douglas DC-4

1946. Air.
A941 A **404** 5 c. red 15 10

404 Entry into Santa Fe (after painting by Kenneth M. Chapman)

405 Thomas A. Edison

1946. Centenary of Entry of Stephen Watts Kearny Expedition into Santa Fe.
941 **404** 3 c. purple 10 10

1947. Birth Cent of Thomas Edison (scientist).
942 **405** 3 c. violet 10 10

A **406** Douglas DC-4

406 Joseph Pulitzer (from portrait by J. S. Sargent)

1947. Air.
A943 A **406** 5 c. red 10 10
A944 6 c. red 15 10

1947. Birth Centenary of Joseph Pulitzer (journalist and newspaper publisher).
943 **406** 3 c. violet 10 10

407 Washington, Franklin and Evolution of Postal Transport

1947. U.S. Postage Stamp Centenary.
944 **407** 3 c. blue 15 10

409 "The Doctor" (after painting by Sir Luke Fildes)

1947. Medical Profession.
946 **409** 3 c. purple 10 10

410 Pioneer Caravan

1947. Centenary of Utah.
947 **410** 3 c. violet 10 10

A **411** Pan-American Union Building, Washington

1947. Air.
A948 A **411** 10 c. black 25 10
A949 – 15 c. green 30 10
A950 – 25 c. blue 75 10
DESIGNS: 15 c. Statue of Liberty and New York City; 25 c. San Fransisco–Oakland Bay Suspension Bridge.

411 U.S.S. "Constitution"

412 Great Blue Heron and Map of Florida

1947. 150th Anniv of Launching of Frigate U.S.S. "Constitution" ("Old Ironsides").
948 **411** 3 c. green 15 10

1947. Dedication of Everglades National Park Florida.
949 **412** 3 c. green 30 10

413 George Washington Carver

414 Sutter's Mill, Coloma

1948. 5th Death Anniv of George Washington Carver (scientist).
950 **413** 3 c. violet 10 10

1948. Cent of Discovery of Gold in California.
951 **414** 3 c. violet 10 10

415 Gov. Winthrop Sargent, Map and Seal of Mississippi Territory (from portrait by Gilbert Stuart)

1948. 150th Anniv of Mississippi Territory.
952 **415** 3 c. purple 10 10

416 Four Chaplains and Liner "Dorchester"

1948. 5th Death Anniv of George Fox, Clark Poling, John Washington and Alexander Goode (who gave up life-jackets).
953 **416** 3 c. black 10 10

417 Scroll and State Capitol, Madison

1948. Centenary of Statehood of Wisconsin.
954 **417** 3 c. violet 10 10

418 Pioneer and Covered Wagon

1948. Centenary of Swedish Pioneers in Middle West.
955 **418** 5 c. blue 15 10

419 Elizabeth Stanton, Carrie C. Catt, and Lucretia Mott

A **420** Map of New York, Ring and Planes (from Poster by G. A. Lorimer)

1948. Progress of American Women.
956 **419** 3 c. violet 10 10

1948. Air. Golden Anniv of New York City Council.
A957 **A 420** 5 c. red 15 10

420 William Allen White

421 Niagara Railway Suspension Bridge (from print by H. Peters)

1948. Honouring W. A. White (editor and author).
957 **420** 3 c. purple 10 10

1948. Centenary of Friendship between United States and Canada.
958 **421** 3 c. blue 15 10

422 Francis Scott Key

1948. Honouring F. S. Key (author of "Star Spangled Banner").
959 **422** 3 c. red 10 10

423 Boy and Girl Students

1948. Salute to Youth.
960 **423** 3 c. blue 10 10

424 John McLoughlin, Jason Lee and Covered Wagon

425 Harlan Fiske Stone

1948. Oregon Territory Centennial.
961 **424** 3 c. red 10 10

1948. Honouring Chief Justice H. F. Stone.
962 **425** 3 c. purple 10 10

426 Palomar Mountain Observatory

427 Clara Barton and Cross

1948. Dedication of Palomar Observatory.
963 **426** 3 c. blue 15 10

1948. Honouring Clara Barton (founder of American Red Cross).
964 **427** 3 c. red 10 10

428 Light Brahma Rooster

1948. Centenary of American Poultry Industry.
965 **428** 3 c. brown 10 10

429 Star and Palm Branch

430 Fort Kearny and Pioneers (Pioneer group from sculpture on Nebraska State Capitol)

1948. Honouring Bereaved Mothers.
966 **429** 3 c. yellow 10 10

1948. Centenary of Fort Kearny, Nebraska.
967 **430** 3 c. violet 10 10

431 Peter Stuyvesant and Fire Engines (from painting in Library of Congress)

1948. Tercentenary of Volunteer Firemen.
968 **431** 3 c. red 10 10

432 Indian Seals and Map of Oklahoma

1948. Centenary of Five Civilized Indian Tribes of Oklahoma.
969 **432** 3 c. brown 10 10

433 Statue of Capt. William Owen "Bucky" O'Neill, Prescott, Arizona (S. H. Borglum)

1948. 50th Anniv of Organization of Rough Riders.
970 **433** 3 c. purple 10 10

434 Juliette Gordon Low

435 Will Rogers

1948. Honouring Juliette Gordon Low (founder of U.S.A. Girl Scouts).
971 **434** 3 c. green 15 10

1948. Honouring Will Rogers (political commentator).
972 **435** 3 c. purple 10 10

436 Rocket Testing

437 Moina Michael and Poppies

1948. Centenary of Fort Bliss.
973 **436** 3 c. red 10 10

1948. Honouring Moina Michael (founder of Memorial Poppy).
974 **437** 3 c. red 10 10

438 Abraham Lincoln (from statue by D. C. French at Lincoln, Neb.)

439 Torch and Emblem

1948. 85th Anniv of Gettysburg Address.
975 **438** 3 c. blue 10 10

1948. Centenary of American Turners' Society.
976 **439** 3 c. red 10 10

440 Joel Chandler Harris

441 Pioneer and Red River Ox Cart

1948. Birth Centenary of J. C. Harris (author).
977 **440** 3c. purple 10 10

1949. Cent of Territorial Status of Minnesota.
978 **441** 3 c. green 10 10

442 Washington, Lee and University Building

1949. Bicentenary of Washington and Lee University, Lexington, Virginia.
979 **442** 3 c. blue 10 10

443 Puerto Rican, Cogwheel and Ballot Box

1949. 1st Gubernatorial Election in Puerto Rico.
980 **443** 3 c. green 10 10

A **444** Wings, Seal, Carlyle House and Gadsby's Tavern

1949. Air. Bicentenary of Alexandria, Virginia.
A981 **A 444** 6 c. red 15 10

444 Map, "Het Vergulde Vsanker" and Shield

1949. Tercentenary of Annapolis, Maryland.
981 **444** 3 c. green 10 10

445 Young and Old Soldiers

446 Edgar Allan Poe

1949. Final National Encampment of the Grand Army of the Republic.
982 **445** 3 c. red 10 10
For similar stamp see No. 995.

1949. Death Centenary of Edgar Allan Poe (poet and author).
983 **446** 3 c. purple 10 10

A **447** U.P.U Monument, Berne and P.O. Department, Washington

1949. Air. 75th Anniv of U.P.U.
A984 **A 447** 10 c. violet 20 25
A985 – 15 c. blue 30 35
A986 – 25 c. red 40 45
DESIGNS: 15 c. Globe and birds; 25 c. Globe and Boeing 377 Stratocruiser.

A **450** Wright Brothers and Flyer I

1949. Air. 46th Anniv of Wright Brothers' First Flight.
A987 **A 450** 6 c. purple 20 10

447 Symbolic of Investments

448 Samuel Gompers

1950. 75th Anniv of American Bankers' Assn.
984 **447** 3 c. green 10 10

1950. Birth Centenary of Samuel Gompers (labour leader).
985 **448** 3 c. purple 10 10

449 Statue of Freedom (by Crawford) on Capitol Dome

450 The White House

1950. National Capital Sesquicentennial.
986 **449** 3 c. blue 10 10
987 **450** 3 c. green 10 10
988 – 3 c. violet 10 10
989 – 3 c. purple 10 10
DESIGNS—HORIZ: No. 988 U.S. Supreme Court building; No. 989 Capitol, Washington.

453 "Casey" Jones and Railway Locomotives

1950. Honouring Railway Engineers.
990 **453** 3 c. purple 10 10

454 Kansas City in 1850 and 1950

1950. Centenary of Kansas City.
991 **454** 3 c. violet 10 10

455 Scouts and Badge

1950. American Boy Scouts.
992 **455** 3 c. brown 15 10

456 First Capitol and W. H. Harrison

1950. Sesquicentennial of Indiana.
993 **456** 3 c. blue 10 10

457 Pioneers

1950. Centenary of California.
994 **457** 3 c. yellow 10 10

1951. Final Reunion of United Confederate Veterans. As T **445**, but initials at left and in hat badge changed to "UCV".
995 **445** 3 c. grey 10 10

458 Log Cabin

1951. Centenary of Nevada.
996 **458** 3 c. olive 10 10

459 Cadillac Disembarking

1951. 250th Anniv of Landing of Cadillac at Detroit.
997 **459** 3 c. blue 10 10

460 Mount of the Holy Cross, State Seal and Capitol

1951. 75th Anniv of Colorado.
998 **460** 3 c. violet 10 10

461 Emblem and Chemical Plant

1951. 75th Anniv of American Chemical Society.
999 **461** 3 c. purple 10 10

462 Washington at Brooklyn

1951. 175th Anniv of Battle of Brooklyn.
1000 **462** 3 c. violet 10 10

463 Betsy Ross and Flag

1952. Birth Bicentenary of Betsy Ross (maker of First American flag).
1001 **463** 3 c. red 10 10

464 Emblem and Young Club Members

1952. 50th Anniv of 4-H Clubs.
1002 **464** 3 c. green 10 10

465 Rail Transport

1952. 125th Anniv of Baltimore and Ohio Railway.
1003 **465** 3 c. blue 15 10

466 Cars of 1902 and 1952

467 "Torch of Freedom"

1952. 50th Anniv of American Automobile Assn.
1004 **466** 3 c. blue 10 10

1952. 3rd Anniv of N.A.T.O.
1005 **467** 3 c. violet 10 10

A 467 Diamond Head, Oahu, Honolulu

1952. Air.
A1005 A **467** 80 c. purple . . . . 7·50 1·00

468 Grand Coulee Dam

1952. 50th Anniv of Columbia Basin Reclamation.
1006 **468** 3 c. green 15 10

469 Lafayette and Flags

1952. 175th Anniv of Lafayette's Arrival in America.
1007 **469** 3 c. blue 10 10

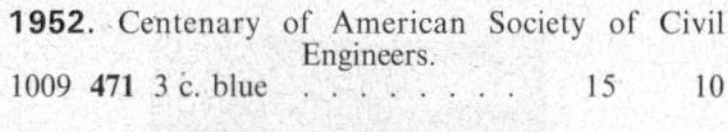

470 Mt. Rushmore National Memorial

471 Bridges in 1852 and 1952

1952. 25th Anniv of Mt Rushmore National Memorial.
1008 **470** 3 c. green 15 10

1952. Centenary of American Society of Civil Engineers.
1009 **471** 3 c. blue 15 10

472 Women in Uniform

1952. Women's Services Commemoration.
1010 **472** 3 c. blue 10 10

473 Gutenberg and Elector of Mainz (after Edward Laning)

1952. 500th Anniv of Printing of First Book from Movable Type.
1011 **473** 3 c. violet 10 10

474 Newspaperboy and Torch of Free Enterprise

1952. Newspaperboys Commemoration.
1012 **474** 3 c. violet 10 10

475 Red Cross and Globe

1952. International Red Cross.
1013 **475** 3 c. blue and red 10 10

476 Guardsman and amphibious Landing

477 Map and Seal of Ohio

1953. National Guard.
1014 **476** 3 c. blue 10 10

1953. 150th Anniv of Ohio.
1015 **477** 3 c. sepia 10 10

478 Seal of Washington Territory and Settlers

1953. Centenary of Washington Territory.
1016 **478** 3 c. green 10 10

479 Monroe, Livingston and Marbois signing Transfer (from sculpture plaque by Karl Bitter)

1953. 150th Anniv of Louisiana Purchase.
1017 **479** 3 c. purple 10 10

A 480 Wright Flyer I and Boeing 377 Stratocruiser

1953. Air. 50th Anniv of Aviation.
A1018 A **480** 6 c. red 15 15

480 Commodore Perry and U.S.S. "Susquehanna" and "Mississippi" in Tokyo Bay

1953. Centenary of Opening of Japan to Foreign Trade.
1018 **480** 5 c. turquoise 15 15

481 "Wisdom", "Justice and Divine Inspiration" and "Truth"

1953. 75th Anniv of American Bar Association.
1019 **481** 3 c. violet 10 10

482 "Sagamore Hill"

1953. Opening of Theodore Roosevelt's Home.
1020 **482** 3 c. green 10 10

483 Young Farmer and Landscape

1953. 25th Anniv of "Future Farmers of America".
1021 **483** 3 c. blue 10 10

484 Truck and Distant City

1953. 50th Anniv of Trucking Industry.
1022 **484** 3 c. violet 10 10

485 Gen. Patton and Tanks in Action

1953. Gen. George Patton and U.S. Armoured Forces.
1023 **485** 3 c. violet 15 10

486 New York in 1653 and 1953

1953. Tercent of Foundation of New York City.
1024 **486** 3 c. purple 10 10

487 Pioneer Family

1953. Centenary of Gadsden Purchase.
1025 **487** 3 c. chestnut 10 10

488 Low Memorial Library

1954. Bicentenary of Columbia University.
1026 **488** 3 c. blue 10 10

490 Washington (after Stuart) **492** Mount Vernon **501** Statue of Liberty

1954. Liberty Issue.

1027	–	½ c. red	10	10
1028	**490**	1 c. green	10	10
1029	–	1¼ c. turquoise	10	10
1030	**492**	1½ c. lake	10	10
1031	–	2 c. red	10	10
1032	–	2½ c. blue	10	10
1033	**501**	3 c. violet	10	10
1034	–	4 c. mauve	10	10
1035	–	4½ c. green	20	10
1036	–	5 c. blue	10	10
1037	–	6 c. red	30	10
1038	–	7 c. red	30	10
1039	**501**	8 c. red and blue	30	10
1040	–	8 c. red and blue	30	10
1041	–	8 c. brown	30	10
1042	–	9 c. purple	40	10
1043	–	10 c. red	20	10
1044	–	11 c. blue and red . . .	30	10
1045	–	12 c. red	45	10
1046	–	15 c. red	75	10
1047	–	20 c. blue	50	10
1059	–	25 c. turquoise	40	20
1049	–	30 c. black	1·25	10
1050	–	40 c. lake	1·75	10
1051	–	50 c. violet	1·75	10
1052	–	$1 violet	6·00	10
1053	–	$5 black	70·00	3·50

DESIGNS — As Type **490**: ½ c. Benjamin Franklin; 2 c. Jefferson; 4 c. Lincoln; 5 c. Monroe; 6 c. Theodore Roosevelt; 7 c. Woodrow Wilson; 8 c. (No. 1040), As Type **501** but torch flame below "P"; 8 c. (No. 1041), Gen. John J. Pershing; 11 c. As No. 1040; 12 c. Benjamin Harrison; 15 c. John Jay; 25 c. Paul Revere; 30 c. Robert E. Lee; 40 c. John Marshall; 50 c. Susan B. Anthony; $1 Patrick Henry; $5 Alexander Hamilton. As Type **492** — VERT: 2½ c. Bunker Hill Monument and Massachusetts flag. HORIZ: 1¼ c. Palace of the Governors, Santa Fe; 4½ c. The Hermitage; 9 c. The Alamo; 10 c. Independence Hall; 20 c. Monticello, Thomas Jefferson's home.

516 "The Sower" and Mitchell Pass (from statue on Capitol, Lincoln, Neb)

1954. Centenary of Nebraska Territory.
1062 **516** 3 c. violet 10 10

517 Pioneers and Cornfield **518** George Eastman

1954. Centenary of Kansas Territory.
1063 **517** 3 c. salmon 10 10

1954. Birth Centenary of Eastman (inventor).
1064 **518** 3 c. purple 10 10

519 Landing on Riverbank, Missouri **A 520** American Bald Eagle in Flight

1954. 150th Anniv of Lewis and Clark Expedition.
1065 **519** 3 c. purple 10 10

1954. Air.
A1066 A **520** 4 c. blue 15 10
A1067 5 c. red 15 10

520 "Peale in his Museum" (self-portrait) **521** Open Book and Symbols of Subjects taught

1955. 150th Anniv of Pennsylvania Academy of Fine Arts.
1066 **520** 3 c. purple 10 10

1955. Centenary of First Land-Grant Colleges.
1067 **521** 3 c. green 10 10

522 Torch, Globe and Rotary Emblem

1955. 50th Anniv of Rotary International.
1068 **522** 8 c. blue 15 10

523 Marine, Coastguard, Soldier, Sailor, Airman

1955. Armed Forces Reserve.
1069 **523** 3 c. purple 10 10

524 "The Old Man of the Mountains" **525** The Great Lakes and "Altadoc" (freighter)

1955. 150th Anniv of Discovery of "The Old Man of the Mountains" (New Hampshire landmark).
1070 **524** 3 c. turquoise 15 10

1955. Soo Locks Centenary.
1071 **525** 3 c. blue 15 10

526

1955. "Atoms for Peace".
1072 **526** 3 c. blue 10 10

527 Plan of Fort, Ethan Allen and Artillery **528** Mellon (after Edward Birley)

1955. Bicentenary of Fort Ticonderoga.
1073 **527** 3 c. brown 10 10

1955. Birth Centenary of Andrew W. Mellon (philanthropist).
1074 **528** 3 c. red 10 10

529 Benjamin Franklin (after painting by Benjamin West) **530** Log Cabin

1956. 250th Birth Anniv of Franklin.
1075 **529** 3 c. red 10 10

1956. Birth Centenary of Booker T. Washington.
1076 **530** 3 c. blue 10 10

532 New York Coliseum and Columbus Monument

1956. 5th International Philatelic Exn, New York.
1078 **532** 3 c. violet 10 10

533 Common Turkey **536** H. W. Wiley

1956. Wild Life Conservation.
1079 **533** 3 c. purple 30 10
1080 – 3 c. sepia 25 10
1081 – 3 c. green 20 10
DESIGNS: No. 1080, Pronghorns; No. 1081, King salmon.

1956. 50th Anniv of Pure Food and Drug Laws.
1082 **536** 3 c. green 10 10

537 Wheatland **538** Mosaic by L. M. Winter, A.F.L-C.I.O. Headquarters

1956. Home of James Buchanan.
1083 **537** 3 c. sepia 10 10

1956. Labour Day.
1084 **538** 3 c. blue 10 10

539 Nassau Hall (contemporary engraving by Dawkins) **540** Devils Tower

1956. Bicentenary of Nassau Hall.
1085 **539** 3 c. black on orange . . . 10 10

1956. 50th Anniv of Devils Tower National Monument.
1086 **540** 3 c. violet 10 10

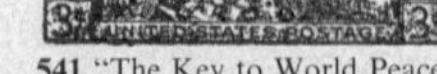

541 "The Key to World Peace"

1956. Children's Friendship.
1087 **541** 3 c. blue 10 10

542 Alexander Hamilton and Federal Hall, New York **543** Women, Children and Shield

1957. Birth Bicentenary of Alexander Hamilton.
1088 **542** 3 c. red 10 10

1957. Infantile Paralysis Relief Campaign.
1089 **543** 3 c. mauve 10 10

544 Survey Flag and Coastguard Vessels "Pathfinder", "Explorer" and "Surveyor"

1957. 150th Anniv of Coast and Geodetic Survey.
1090 **544** 3 c. blue 10 10

545 Ancient and Modern Capitals **546** Eagle and Ladle

1957. Cent of American Institute of Architects.
1091 **545** 3 c. mauve 10 10

1957. Centenary of American Steel Industry.
1092 **546** 3 c. blue 10 10

547 Festival Emblem and Aircraft Carrier U.S.S. "Forrestal"

1957. Jamestown Festival and Int Naval Review.
1093 **547** 3 c. green 15 10

548 Arrow piercing Atomic Symbol

1957. 50th Anniv of Oklahoma Statehood.
1094 **548** 3 c. blue 10 10

549 Teacher with Pupils

1957. Teachers of America Commemoration.
1095 **549** 3 c. red 10 10

550 U.S. Flag

1957. Flag Issue.
1096 **550** 4 c. red and blue 10 10

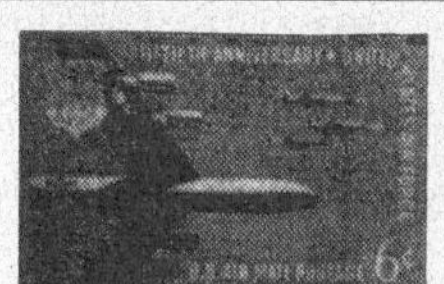
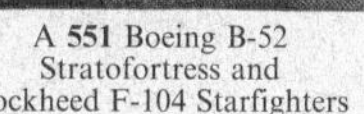

A **551** Boeing B-52 Stratofortress and Lockheed F-104 Starfighters

551 "Virginia of Sagadahock" and Arms of Maine

1957. Air. 50th Anniv of U.S. Air Force.
A1097 A **551** 6 c. blue 15 10

1957. 350th Anniv of American Shipbuilding.
1097 **551** 3 c. violet 10 10

552 Pres. Magsaysay of the Philippines (medallion)

553 Marquis de Lafayette (portrait by Court in Versailles Museum)

1953. Pres. Magsaysay Commemoration.
1098 **552** 8 c. ochre, blue and red . 15 10

1957. Birth Bicentenary of Marquis de Lafayette.
1099 **553** 3 c. red 10 10

554 Whooping Cranes

555 "Religious Freedom"

1957. Wild Life Conservation.
1100 **554** 3 c. blue, orange & green 30 10

1957. Tercentenary of Flushing Remonstrance.
1101 **555** 3 c. black 10 10

556 "Abundance"

557 U.S. Pavilion

1958. Gardening and Horticulture Commem.
1102 **556** 3 c. green 10 10

1958. Brussels International Exhibition.
1103 **557** 3 c. purple 10 10

558 James Monroe (portrait by Stuart)

559 Lake in Minnesota

1958. Birth Bicentenary of Pres. James Monroe.
1104 **558** 3 c. violet 10 10

1958. Centenary of Minnesota Statehood.
1105 **559** 3 c. green 10 10

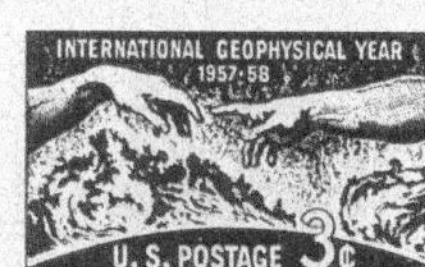

560 Sun's Surface and Hands (after Michelangelo's "The Creation of Adam")

1958. I.G.Y.
1106 **560** 3 c. red and black . . . 15 10

561 Gunston Hall (after drawing by Rene Clarke)

562 Mackinac Bridge

1958. Bicentenary of Gunston Hall, Virginia (home of George Mason, patriot).
1107 **561** 3 c. green 10 10

1958. Mackinac Bridge Commemoration.
1108 **562** 3 c. turquoise 10 10

563 Simon Bolivar (after painting by Ricardo Arcevedo-Bernal)

A **564** Silhouette of Jet Airliner

1958. Bolivar Commemoration.
1109 **563** 4 c. ochre 10 10
1110 8 c. brown, blue & red . 15 10
See also Nos. 1116/17, 1124/5, 1135/6, 1146/7, 1158/9, 1164/5, 1167/8 and 1173/4.

1958. Air.
A1111 A **564** 7 c. blue 15 10
A1112 7 c. red 15 10

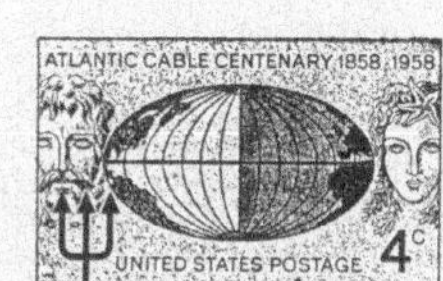

564 Globe, Neptune and Mermaid

1958. Centenary of Inaug of Atlantic Cable.
1111 **564** 4 c. purple 10 10

565 Abraham Lincoln (from painting by G. Healy)

570 Hand with Quill Pen and Printing Press

1958. 150th Birth Anniv of Lincoln.
1112 **565** 1 c. green 10 10
1113 – 3 c. red 15 10
1114 – 4 c. brown 15 10
1115 – 4 c. blue 15 10
DESIGNS: No. 1113, Bust of Lincoln; No. 1114, Addressing Electorate; No. 1115, Lincoln Statue, Washington.

1958. Kossuth Commemoration. Medallion portrait as T **563**.
1116 4 c. green 10 10
1117 8 c. brown, blue and red . . 15 10

1958. Freedom of the Press.
1118 **570** 4 c. black 10 10

571 Mail Coach under Attack

572 Noah Webster (engraving by G. Parker after painting by James Herring)

1958. Overland Mail Centenary.
1119 **571** 4 c. red 10 10

1958. Birth Bicentenary of Noah Webster (lexicographer).
1120 **572** 4 c. red 10 10

573 Forest Pines

574 British Forces occupying Fort Duquesne (from etching by T.B. Smith)

1958. Forest Conservation.
1121 **573** 4 c. yellow, green & brn . 10 10

1958. Bicentenary of Fort Duquesne.
1122 **574** 4 c. blue 10 10

A **575** Stars on Alaskan Map

1959. Air. Alaska Statehood.
A1123 A **575** 7 c. blue 25 10

575 Covered Wagon and Mt. Hood

577 N.A.T.O. Emblem

1959. Centenary of Oregon Statehood.
1123 **575** 4 c. green 10 10

1959. San Martin Commem. Medallion portrait as T **563**.
1124 4 c. blue 10 10
1125 8 c. ochre, red and blue . . . 15 10

1959. 10th Anniv of N.A.T.O.
1126 **577** 4 c. blue 10 10

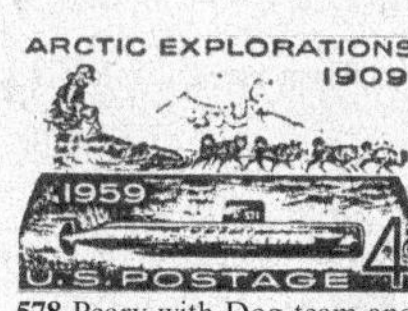

578 Peary with Dog-team and Submarine U.S.S. "Nautilus"

1959. Arctic Explorations by Robert Peary (50th anniv of reaching North Pole) and U.S.S. "Nautilus".
1127 **578** 4 c. blue 10 10

579

1959. World Peace through World Trade.
1128 **579** 8 c. red 15 10

580 Discovery of Silver at Mt. Davidson, Nevada (from a print)

1959. Cent of Discovery of Silver in Nevada.
1129 **580** 4 c. black 10 10

581 Maple Leaf linked with American Eagle

1959. Opening of St. Lawrence Seaway.
1130 **581** 4 c. blue and red 10 10

582 New U.S. Flag (with 49 stars)

1959. Inauguration of New United States Flag.
1131 **582** 4 c. red, blue & orange . 15 10

A **583** Balloon "Jupiter"

A **584** Hawaiian Warrior, Map and Star

1959. Air. Centenary of Balloon "Jupiter's" Mail-carrying Flight.
A1132 A **583** 7 c. red and blue . . 20 10

1959. Air. Hawaii Statehood.
A1133 A **584** 7 c. red 20 10

583 "The Good Earth"

584 Oil Derrick

1959. Soil Conservation.
1132 **583** 4 c. green, brown and blue 10 10

1959. Centenary of First Oil-well at Titusville, Pennsylvania.
1133 **584** 4 c. brown 10 10

A **585** Runner with Olympic Torch

585 "Happy Children with Healthy Teeth"

1959. Air. 3rd Pan-American Games, Chicago.
A1134 A **585** 10 c. red and blue . 30 30

1959. Dental Health. Cent of American Dental Assn.
1134 **585** 4 c. green 10 10

1959. Ernst Reuter Commem. Medallion portrait as T **563**.
1135 4 c. grey 10 10
1136 8 c. ochre, red and blue . . . 20 10

A **588** Statue of Liberty

587 Dr. E. McDowell (from painting)

1959. Air.
A1137 – 10 c. black & green . 1·75 70
A1138 – 13 c. black and red . 40 10
A1139 A **588** 15 c. blk & orge (A) 35 10
A1140 15 c. blk & orge (B) 30 10
A1141 – 25 c. black & brown 50 10
DESIGNS: 10 c., 13 c. Liberty Bell; 15 c. Statue has double frame-line (A) or single frame-line (B); 25 c. Abraham Lincoln.

1959. 150th Anniv of First Recorded Successful Abdominal Operation.
1137 **587** 4 c. purple 10 10

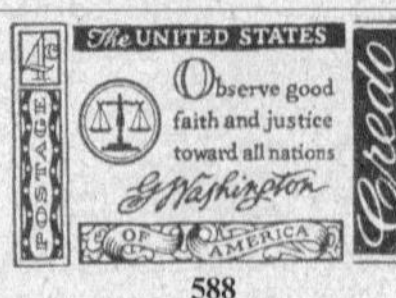

588

1960. "American Credo" series.
1138 **588** 4 c. red and blue 15 10
1139 – 4 c. green and bistre . . 15 10
1140 – 4 c. red and grey 15 10
1141 – 4 c. blue and red 15 10
1142 – 4 c. green and purple . . 20 10
1143 – 4 c. brown and green . . 20 10
INSCRIPTIONS: No. 1139, "Fear to do ill, and you need fear Nought else" (Franklin); No. 1140, "I have sworn . . . Hostility against every form of TYRANNY over the mind of man" (Jefferson); No. 1141, "And this be our Motto in GOD is our TRUST" (Francis Scott Key); No. 1142, "Those who Deny freedom to others Deserve it not for Themselves" (Lincoln); No. 1143, "Give me LIBERTY or give me DEATH" (P. Henry).

594 Scout Saluting **595** Olympic Rings and Snow Crystal

1960. 50th Anniv of American Boy Scout Movement.
1144 **594** 4 c. ochre, red & blue . . 10 10

1960. Winter Olympic Games.
1145 **595** 4 c. blue 10 10

1960. Thomas Masaryk Commem. Medallion portrait as T **563**.
1146 4 c. blue 10 10
1147 8 c. ochre, red and blue . . . 20 10

597 "Towards the Light"

1960. World Refuge Year.
1148 **597** 4 c. black 10 10

598 "Irrigation" **599** S.E.A.T.O. Emblem

1960. Water Conservation Campaign.
1149 **598** 4 c. green, brown & blue 10 10

1960. S.E.A.T.O. Conference.
1150 **599** 4 c. blue 10 10

600 Mother and Child **601** New U.S. Flag (with 50 stars)

1960. American Womanhood Commemoration.
1151 **600** 4 c. violet 10 10

1960. New United States Flag (50 stars).
1152 **601** 4 c. red and blue 10 10

602 Pony Express

1960. Centenary of Pony Express.
1153 **602** 4 c. brown 10 10

603 Cripple operating Press **604** Congress Seal

1960. Employment of the Handicapped Campaign.
1154 **603** 4 c. blue 10 10

1960. 5th World Forestry Congress, Seattle.
1155 **604** 4 c. green 10 10

605 Dolores Bell (Mexico) **606** Washington Monument and Cherry Blossom

1960. 150th Anniv of Mexican Independence.
1156 **605** 4 c. red and green . . . 10 10

1960. Centenary of U.S.–Japan Treaty.
1157 **606** 4 c. red and turquoise . . 10 10

1960. Jan Paderewski Commem. Medallion portrait as T **563**.
1158 4 c. blue 10 10
1159 8 c. ochre, red and blue . . 20 10

608 Robert A. Taft **609** Steering Wheel, Motor Transport and Globes

1960. Robert A. Taft Memorial Issue.
1160 **608** 4 c. violet 10 10

1960. "Wheels of Freedom" (Motor Industry).
1161 **609** 4 c. blue 10 10

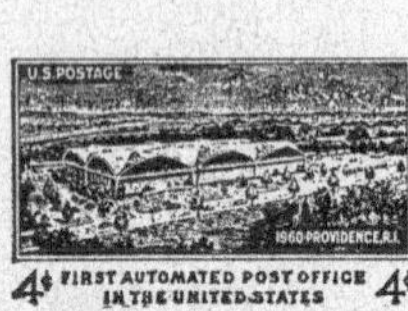

610 Boy **611** New P.O. Building

1960. Cent of Boys' Clubs of America Movement.
1162 **610** 4 c. red, black & indigo 10 10

1960. Inauguration of 1st U.S. Automated P.O., Providence, Rhode Island.
1163 **611** 4 c. blue and red 15 10

1960. Marshal Mannerheim Commem. Medallion portrait as T **563**.
1164 4 c. blue 10 10
1165 8 c. ochre, red and blue . . 20 10

613 Camp Fire Girls Emblem **615** George

1960. 50th Anniv of Camp Fire Girls Movement.
1166 **613** 4 c. rd and blue 10 10

1960. Garibaldi Commem. Medallion portrait as T **563**.
1167 4 c. green 10 10
1168 8 c. ochre, red and blue . . 15 10

1960. Senator Walter F. George Memorial Issue.
1169 **615** 4 c. violet 10 10

616 Andrew Carnegie **617** Dulles

1960. Andrew Carnegie.
1170 **616** 4 c. red 10 10

1960. John Foster Dulles Memorial Issue.
1171 **617** 4 c. violet 10 10

618 "Echo I" Communications Satellite

1960. "Communications for Peace".
1172 **618** 4 c. violet 20 10

1961. Mahatma Gandhi Commem. Medallion portrait as T **563**.
1173 4 c. red on orange 20 10
1174 8 c. ochre, red and blue . . . 35 10

620 Trail Boss and Prairie **621** Horace Greeley (from steel engraving by A. H. Ritchie)

1961. Range Conservation.
1175 **620** 4 c. black, orange & bl . 15 10

1961. Horace Greeley (editor).
1176 **621** 4 c. violet 10 10

622 Sea Coast Gun

1961. Civil War Centennial. Battles.
1177 **622** 4 c. green 20 10
1178 – 4 c. black on pink 20 10
1179 – 5 c. indigo and blue . . . 20 10
1180 – 5 c. black and red 20 10
1181 – 5 c. black and blue . . . 30 10
DESIGNS—HORIZ: No. 1178, Rifleman (Shiloh); No. 1179, Armed combat (Gettysburg); No. 1180, Artillery crew (Wilderness). VERT: No. 1181, Soldier and rifles (Appomattox).

627 Sunflower and Pioneers

1961. Centenary of Kansas Statehood.
1182 **627** 4 c. red, green and brown on yellow 10 10

628 Senator G. W. Norris

1961. Birth Centenary of George W. Norris.
1183 **628** 4 c. green 10 10

629 Curtiss A-1 Seaplane, 1911 (Navy's first Plane)

1961. 50th Anniv of U.S. Naval Aviation.
1184 **629** 4 c. blue 10 10

630 "Balanced Judgement" **631** "The Smoke Signal" (after Remington)

1961. 150th Anniv of Workmen's Compensation Law.
1185 **630** 4 c. blue 10 10

1961. Birth Centenary of Frederic Remington (painter).
1186 **631** 4 c. multicoloured . . . 10 10

632 Dr. Sun Yat-sen **633** Basketball

1961. 50th Anniv of Republic of China.
1187 **632** 4 c. blue 10 10

1961. Birth Centenary of Dr. James A. Naismith (inventor of basketball).
1188 **633** 4 c. brown 15 10

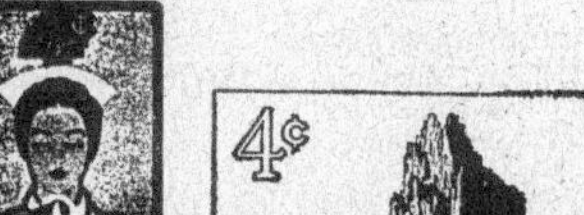

634 Nurse lighting Candle of Dedication **635** Ship Rock. New Mexico

1961. Nursing.
1189 **634** 4 c. multicoloured . . . 10 10

1962. 50th Anniv of Statehood of New Mexico.
1190 **635** 4 c. lake, ochre & turq . 10 10

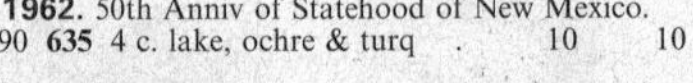

636 Saguaro Cactus and Flowers **637** "U.S. Man in Space"

1962. 50th Anniv of Arizona Statehood.
1191 **636** 4 c. blue, green and red . 10 10

1962. Project Mercury. Colonel John Glenn's Space Flight.
1192 **637** 4 c. blue and yellow . . 10 10

638 U.S. and Campaign Emblems

1962. Malaria Eradication.
1193 **638** 4 c. ochre and blue . . . 10 10

639 C. E. Hughes **640** Space Needle and Monorail

1962. Birth Centenary of Chief Justice Hughes.
1194 **639** 4 c. black on buff . . . 10 10

1962. "Century 21" Exn ("World's Fair"), Seattle.
1195 **640** 4 c. blue and red 10 10

641 Mississippi Sternwheel Steamer

1962. 150th Anniv of Lousiana Statehood.
1196 **641** 4 c. myrtle, red & blue . 10 10

642 Settlers' Homestead

1962. Centenary of Homestead Act.
1197 **642** 4 c. grey 10 10

643 Girl Scout and Flag

1962. 50th Anniv of U.S. Girl Scouts.
1198 **643** 4 c. red 10 10

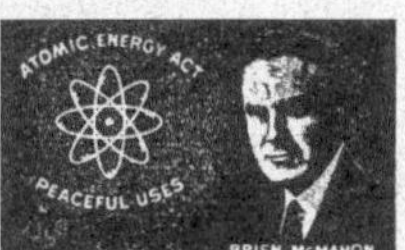

644 Senator McMahon and Atomic Symbol

1962. Brien McMahon.
1199 **644** 4 c. violet 10 10

645 "Transfer of Skill" **646** Sam Rayburn

1962. 25th Anniv of National Apprenticeship Act.
1200 **645** 4 c. black on olive . . . 10 10

1962. Sam Rayburn (Speaker of House of Representatives) Commemoration.
1201 **646** 4 c. brown and blue . . . 10 10

647 Dag Hammarskjold and U.N. Headquarters **648** Christmas Laurel Wreath

1962. Hammarskjold.
1202 **647** 4 c. brown, yell & black . 10 10
1203 4 c. brown, yellow & blk 10 10
No. 1203 has the yellow colour inverted and comes from a special printing made after a few examples had been discovered.

1962. Christmas.
1204 **648** 4 c. green and red . . . 10 10

649 "Lamp of Learning" and Map

1962. Higher Education.
1205 **649** 4 c. black and green . . 10 10

651 Washington (after Houdon) **A 652** Capitol, Washington and Douglas DC-8

1962.
1206 – 1 c. green 10 10
1207 **651** 5 c. blue 10 10
DESIGN: 1 c. Andrew Jackson.

1962. Air.
A1210 **A 652** 8 c. red 30 10

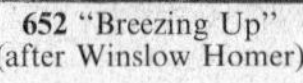

652 "Breezing Up" (after Winslow Homer) **653** U.S. Flag and White House

1962. Winslow Homer.
1210 **652** 4 c. multicoloured . . . 10 10

1963.
1211 **653** 5 c. red and blue 15 10

654 Charter and Quill

1963. 300th Anniv of Carolina Charter.
1212 **654** 5 c. sepia and red . . . 10 10

A 655 P.M.G. Montgomery Blair, Letters and Globe (after portrait by Thomas Sully) **655** "Food for Peace"

1963. Air. Centenary of Paris Postal Conferences.
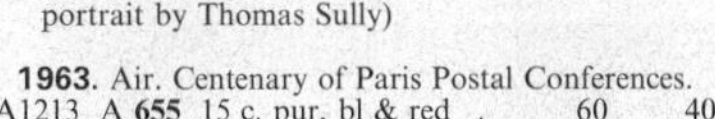
A1213 **A 655** 15 c. pur, bl & red . 60 40

1963. Freedom from Hunger.
1213 **655** 5 c. brown, green & red 10 10

656 Map and State Capitol, Charleston **A 657** American Bald Eagle

1963. Centenary of West Virginia Statehood.
1214 **656** 5 c. red, black & green . 10 10

1963. Air.
A1215 **A 657** 6 c. red 30 10

657 Broken Link **A 658** Amelia Earhart and Lockheed "Electra"

1963. Centenary of Emancipation Proclamation.
1215 **657** 5 c. black, blue & red . 20 10

1963. Air. Amelia Earhart Commemoration.
A1216 **A 658** 8 c. purple and red . 25 10

658 Torch of Progress **659** Cordell Hull

1963. "Alliance for Progress".
1216 **658** 5 c. green and blue . . . 10 10

1963. Cordell Hull Commemoration.
1217 **659** 5 c. turquoise 10 10

660 Eleanor Roosevelt

1963. Eleanor Roosevelt Commemoration.
1218 **660** 5 c. violet 10 10

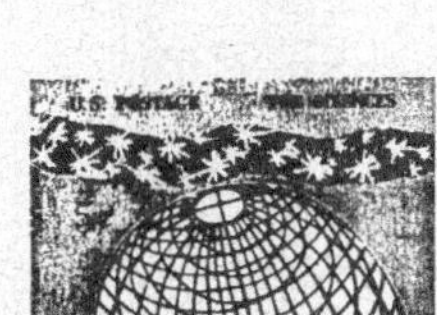

661 "The Sciences" **662** City Mail Postman

1963. Centenary of National Academy of Science.
1219 **661** 5 c. black, red & blue . . 10 10

1963. Cent of City Mail Delivery.
1220 **662** 5 c. black and turquoise . 10 10

663 Red Cross Flag and S.S."Morning Light" **664** Christmas Tree

1963. Red Cross Centenary.
1221 **663** 5 c. black and red 10 10

1963. Christmas.
1222 **664** 5 c. black, blue and red . 10 10

665 "Columbia Jays" (print) (actually Collie's Magpie-jays) **666** Sam Houston (from lithograph by F. Davignon)

1963. John James Audubon Commemoration.
1223 **665** 5 c. multicoloured 30 10
See also No. A1304.

1964. Sam Houston Commemoration.
1224 **666** 5 c. black 20 10

667 "Jerked Down"

1964. Birth Centenary of C. M. Russell (artist).
1225 **667** 5 c. multicoloured 20 10

668 Mall with Unisphere and "The Rocket Thrower" (after De Lue) **669** John Muir (naturalist) and Forest

1964. New York World's Fair.
1226 **668** 5 c. turquoise 10 10

1964. John Muir Commemoration.
1227 **669** 5 c. brown, emer & grn . 10 10

670 Pres. Kennedy and "Eternal Flame" **671** Philip Carteret at Elizabethtown (1664) (after painting in Union County Courthouse)

1964. President Kennedy Memorial Issue.
1228 **670** 5 c. blue on grey 10 10

1964. Tercentenary of New Jersey.
1229 **671** 5 c. blue 10 10

672 Virginia City in 19th Century **673** U.S. Flag

1964. Centenary of Nevada Statehood.
1230 **672** 5 c. multicoloured . . . 10 10

1964. "Register and Vote" Campaign.
1231 **673** 5 c. red and blue 10 10

674 Shakespeare **675** Drs. William and Charles Mayo (after J. E. Fraser)

1964. 400th Birth Anniv of William Shakespeare.
1232 **674** 5 c. sepia on buff 10 10

1964. Mayo Brothers (founders of Mayo Clinic) Commemoration.
1233 **675** 5 c. green 10 10

A 676 R. H. Goddard, "Atlas" Rocket and Launching Tower

1964. Air. Robert H. Goddard Commem.
A1234 **A 676** 8 c. blue, red & yell 60 10

676 Lute, Horn and Music Score

1964. American Music.
1234 **676** 5 c. black, red and blue on light blue 10 10

677 Sampler

1964. "Homemakers" Commemoration.
1235 **677** 5 c. multicoloured . . . 10 10

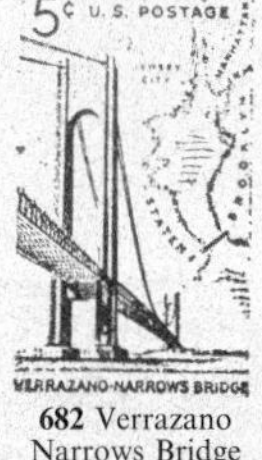

678 Holly **682** Verrazano Narrows Bridge

1964. Christmas. Each red, green and black.
1236 5 c. Type **678** 30 10
1237 5 c. Mistletoe 30 10
1238 5 c. Poinsettia 30 10
1239 5 c. Pine cone 30 10

1964. Opening of Verrazano-Narrows Bridge, New York.
1240 **682** 5 c. green 10 10

683 "Abstract Art" (from lithograph by S. Davis)

1964. "To the Fine Arts".
1241 **683** 5 c. red, black and blue . 15 10

684 Radio Waves **685** General Jackson leading Troops into Battle

1964. Amateur Radio.
1242 **684** 5 c. purple 10 10

1965. 150th Anniv of Battle of New Orleans.
1243 **685** 5 c. red, blue and black . 15 10

686 Discus-thrower (Washington statue) **687** Microscope and Stethoscope

1965. Centenary of Sokol Physical Fitness Organization in the U.S.A.
1244 **686** 5 c. blue and lake 10 10

1965. Crusade Against Cancer.
1245 **687** 5 c. black, violet & red . 10 10

688 Sir Winston Churchill (from photo by Karsh)

1965. Churchill Commemoration.
1246 **688** 5 c. black 10 10

689 Procession of Barons, and King John's Crown

1965. 750th Anniv of Magna Carta.
1247 **689** 5 c. black, yell & violet . 10 10

690 I.C.Y. Emblem **691** "One hundred years of service"

1965. International Co-operation Year.
1248 **690** 5 c. black and blue . . . 10 10

1965. Centenary of Salvation Army.
1249 **691** 5 c. black, red and blue . 15 10

692 Dante **693** Herbert Hoover

1965. 700th Anniv of Dante's Birth.
1250 **692** 5 c. red on flesh 10 10

1965. Hoover Commemoration.
1251 **693** 5 c. red 10 10

694 Robert Fulton (after Houdon) and "Clermont" **695** Spanish Knight and Banners

1965. Birth Bicent of Robert Fulton (inventor).
1252 **694** 5 c. black and blue . . . 10 10

1965. 400th Anniv of Florida Settlement.
1253 **695** 5 c. black, red & yellow . 10 10

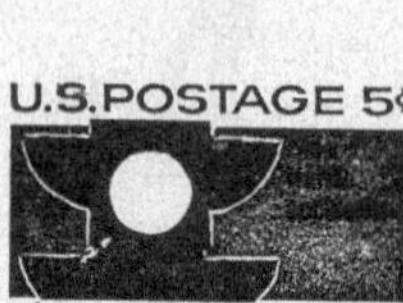

696 Traffic Signal **697** Elizabeth Clarke Copley (from "The Copley Family" by John S. Copley)

1965. Traffic Safety.
1254 **696** 5 c. red, black & green . 10 10

1965. John Singleton Copley.
1255 **697** 5 c. brown, drab & black 10 10

698 Radio "Waves" on World Map (based on Galt projection) **699** Adlai Stevenson (from photo by P. Halsman)

1965. Centenary of I.T.U.
1256 **698** 11 c. red, black & brown 35 15

1965. Stevenson Commemoration.
1257 **699** 5 c. multicoloured . . . 10 10

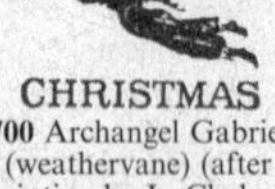

700 Archangel Gabriel (weathervane) (after painting by L. Chabot) **705** Lincoln (after photo by M. Brady)

1965. Christmas.
1258 **700** 5 c. green, ochre & red . 10 10

1965. Prominent Americans (1st series).

1259	–	1 c. green	10	10
1260	–	$1\frac{1}{4}$ c. green	10	15
1261	–	2 c. blue	10	10
1262	–	3 c. violet	10	10
1263	**705**	4 c. black	15	10
1265	–	5 c. blue	10	10
1266	–	6 c. brown	15	10
1282	–	6 c. brown	30	10
1267	–	8 c. violet	20	10
1268	–	10 c. purple	20	10
1269	–	12 c. black	20	10
1270	–	13 c. brown	20	10
1271	–	15 c. red	25	10
1272	–	20 c. green	30	10
1273	–	25 c. red	40	10
1274	–	30 c. purple	60	10
1275	–	40 c. blue	75	10
1276	–	50 c. purple	1·25	10
1283	–	$1 purple	1·50	60
1278	–	$5 black	8·50	1·25

DESIGNS—VERT: 1 c. Thomas Jefferson (after Rembrandt Peale); $1\frac{1}{4}$ c. Albert Gallatin; 2 c. Frank Lloyd Wright and Guggenheim Museum, New York; 5 c. Washington (after Rembrandt Peale); 6 c. (1282) Franklin D. Roosevelt; 8 c. Albert Einstein; 10 c. Andrew Jackson (after T. Sully); 13 c. John F. Kennedy; 15 c. Justice Wendell Holmes; 20 c. George C. Marshall; 25 c. Frederick Douglass; 40 c. Tom Paine (after John W. Jarvis); 50 c. Lucy Stone; $1 Eugene O'Neill; $5 John Bassett Moore. HORIZ: 3 c. Francis Parkman; 6 c. (No. 1266) Franklin D. Roosevelt; 12 c. Henry Ford and Model "T" car; 30 c. John Dewey.

See also Nos. 1383/9.

719 "Migratory Birds"

1966. 50th Anniv of Migratory Bird Treaty.
1286 **719** 5 c. red, blue and black . 10 10

720 Dog **721** Seal, Emblem and Map

1966. Humane Treatment of Animals.
1287 **720** 5 c. black and brown . . 10 10

1966. 150th Anniv of Indiana Statehood.
1288 **721** 5 c. blue, brown and yell . 10 10

722 Lou Jacobs (clown) **723** SIPEX "Letter"

1966. The American Circus.
1289 **722** 5 c. Multicoloured . . . 10 10

1966. 6th Int Philatelic Exn, Washington (SIPEX).
1290 **723** 5 c. multicoloured 10 10

725 "Freedom" opposing "Tyranny" **726** Polish Eagle

1966. 175th Anniv of Bill of Rights.
1292 **725** 5 c. red, indigo and blue . 10 10

1966. Polish Millennium.
1293 **726** 5 c. red 10 10

727 N.P.S. Emblem **728** Marines Past and Present

1966. 50th Anniv of National Park Service.
1294 **727** 5 c. black, green & yell . 10 10

1966. 50th Anniv of Marine Corps Reserve.
1295 **728** 5 c. multicoloured 10 10

729 Women of 1891 and 1966 **730** Johnny Appleseed and Apple

1966. 75th Anniv of General Federation of Women's Clubs.
1296 **729** 5 c. black, pink & blue . 10 10

1966. Johnny Appleseed.
1297 **730** 5 c. black, red & green . 10 10

731 Jefferson Memorial, Washington **732** Map of Great River Road

1966. "Beautification of America" Campaign.
1298 **731** 5 c. black, green & pink 10 10

1966. Opening of Great River Road.
1299 **732** 5 c. red, yellow and blue 10 10

733 Statue of Liberty and U.S. Flag (after photo by B. Noble) **734** "Madonna and Child" (after Memling)

1966. 25th Anniv of U.S. Savings Bond Programme and Tribute to U.S. Servicemen.
1300 **733** 5 c. multicoloured . . . 10 10

1966. Christmas.
1301 **734** 5 c. multicoloured . . . 10 10

735 "The Boating Party' (after Mary Cassatt) A **736** Tlingit Totem, Southern Alaska

1966. Mary Cassatt.
1302 **735** 5 c. multicoloured . . . 10 10

1967. Air. Centenary of Alaska Purchase.
A1303 A **736** 8 c. brown 30 15

736 Recruiting Poster A **737** "Columbia Jays" by Audubon

1967. Centenary of National Grange (farmers' organization).
1303 **736** 5 c. multicoloured . . . 10 10

1967. Air.
A1304 A **737** 20 c. multicoloured . 1·60 10

See also No. 1223.

737 Canadian Landscape

1967. Canadian Centennial.
1304 **737** 5 c. multicoloured . . . 10 10

738 Canal Barge

1967. 150th Anniv of Erie Canal.
1305 **738** 5 c. multicoloured . . . 10 10

739 Peace Dove Emblem

1967. "Search for Peace" (Lions Int essay theme).
1306 **739** 5 c. black, red and blue . 10 10

740 H. D. Thoreau

742 Radio Tower and "Waves"

741 Hereford Bull

1967. 150th Birth Anniv of Henry Thoreau (writer).
1307 **740** 5 c. black, red & green . 15 10

1967. Centenary of Nebraska Statehood.
1308 **741** 5 c. multicoloured . . . 10 10

1967. "Voice of America". 25th Anniv of Radio Branch of United States Information Agency.
1309 **742** 5 c. black, red and blue . 15 10

743 Davy Crockett and Pine

1967. Davy Crockett Commemoration.
1310 **743** 5 c. black, green & yell . 10 10

744 Astronaut in Space

746 "Planned City"

1967. U.S. Space Achievements. Multicoloured.
1311 5 c. Type **744** 40 15
1312 5 c. "Gemini 4" over Earth . 40 15

Nos. 1311/2 were issued together se-tenant, forming a composite design.

1967. Urban Planning.
1313 **746** 5 c. ultramarine, blk & bl 10 10

747 Arms of Finland

748 "The Biglin Brothers racing" (Eakins)

1967. 50th Anniv of Finnish Independence.
1314 **747** 5 c. blue 10 10

1967. Thomas Eakins.
1315 **748** 5 c. multicoloured . . . 15 10

749 "Madonna and Child with Angels" (Memling)

750 Magnolia

1967. Christmas.
1316 **749** 5 c. multicoloured . . . 10 10

1967. 150th Anniv of Mississippi Statehood.
1317 **750** 5 c. brown, green and turquoise 10 10

A 751 "Fifty Stars"

751 U.S. Flag and The White House

1968. Air.
A1318 A **751** 10 c. red 25 5

1968. Flag Issue.
1318 **751** 6 c. multicoloured . . . 20 10
1320 8 c. multicoloured . . . 25 10

752 Homestead and Cornfield

753 Map of the Americas

1968. 150th Anniv of Illinois Statehood.
1323 **752** 6 c. multicoloured . . . 15 10

1968. "HemisFair'68" Exn, San Antonio.
1324 **753** 6 c. blue, pink & white . 15 10

754 Eagle with Pennant (after late 19th-century wood carving)

1968. "Airlift".
1325 **754** $1 brown, blue & buff . 2·75 1·25

No. 1325 was issued primarily for a special reduced-rate parcels service to forces personnel overseas and in Alaska, Hawaii and Puerto Rico.

755 Boys and Girls

756 Policeman with Small Boy

A 756 Curtiss JN-4 "Jenny"

1968. Youth Programme of Elks Benevolent Society.
1326 **755** 6 c. blue and red 15 10

1968. Air. 50th Anniv of Scheduled Airmail Services.
A1327 A **756** 10 c. blk, red & bl . 30 10

1968. "Law and Order".
1328 **756** 6 c. blue, red & black . . 15 10

757 Eagle Weathervane

758 Fort Moultrie, 1776

1968. "Register and Vote".
1329 **757** 6 c. yellow, orge & blk . 15 10

1968. Historic Flags.
1330 **758** 6 c. blue 45 20
1331 – 6 c. red and blue 45 20
1332 – 6 c. green and blue . . . 45 20
1333 – 6 c. red and blue 45 20
1334 – 6 c. blue, yellow & red . . 45 20
1335 – 6 c. red and blue 45 20
1336 – 6 c. blue, red & green . . 45 20
1337 – 6 c. red and blue 45 20
1338 – 6 c. blue, red & yellow . . 45 20
1339 – 6 c. red, yellow & blue . . 45 20

FLAGS: No. 1331, U.S. (Fort McHenry), 1795–1818; 1332, Washington's Cruisers, 1775; 1333, Bennington, 1777; 1334, Rhode Island, 1775; 1335, First Stars and Stripes, 1777; 1336, Bunker Hill, 1775; 1337, Grand Union, 1776; 1338, Philadelphia Light Horse, 1775; 1339, First Navy Jack, 1775.

768 Walt Disney (after portrait by P. E. Wenzel)

769 Father Jacques Marquette (explorer) with Jolliet and Indians Canoeing

1968. Walt Disney Commemoration.
1340 **768** 6 c. multicoloured 25 10

1968. Marquette Commemoration.
1341 **769** 6 c. multicoloured 15 10

770 Rifle, Tomahawk, Powder-horn and Knife

1968. Daniel Boone Commemoration.
1342 **770** 6 c. multicoloured 15 10

771 Ship's Wheel and River Tanker

1968. Arkansas River Navigation Project.
1343 **771** 6 c. black, blue & lt blue . 15 10

772 "Leif Erikson" (statue by Stirling Calder, Reykjavik, Iceland)

773 Pioneers racing to Cherokee Strip

1968. Leif Erikson Commemoration.
1344 **772** 6 c. sepia and brown . . 15 10

1968. 75th Anniv of Opening of Cherokee Strip to Settlers.
1345 **773** 6 c. brown 15 10

774 "Battle of Bunker's Hill (detail) (after John Trumbull)

775 Wood Ducks

1968. John Trumbull.
1346 **774** 6 c. multicoloured . . . 20 10

1968. Waterfowl Conservation.
1347 **775** 6 c. multicoloured . . . 30 10

776 "The Annunciation" (Jan van Eyck)

777 "Chief Joseph" (after C. Hall)

1968. Christmas.
1348 **776** 6 c. multicoloured . . . 15 10

1968. "The American Indian".
1349 **777** 6 c. multicoloured . . . 30 10

A 778 "U.S.A." and Jet Aircraft

1968. Air.
A1350 A **778** 20 c. red, blue & blk 60 10
A1351 21 c. blue, red & blk 55 10

778 Capitol and Flowers ("Cities")

1969. "Beautification of America" Campaign.
1352 **778** 6 c. multicoloured . . . 40 10
1353 – 6 c. multicoloured . . . 40 10
1354 – 6 c. multicoloured . . . 40 10
1355 – 6 c. multicoloured . . . 40 10

DESIGNS: No. 1353, Potomac River and flowers ("Parks"); 1354, Motorway and flowers ("Highways"); 1355, Road and trees ("Streets").

782 "Eagle" (U.S. Seal)

783 "July Fourth"

1969. 50th Anniv of American Legion.
1356 **782** 6 c. black, blue and red . 15 10

1969. Grandma Moses (Mrs. A. M. R. Moses).
1357 **783** 6 c. multicoloured . . . 15 10

784 Earth and Moon's Surface (from an astronaut's photograph)

785 W. C. Handy (statue, Memphis)

1969. Moon Flight of "Apollo 8".
1358 **784** 6 c. ochre, blue and black 20 10

1969. Handy (composer) Commemoration.
1359 **785** 6 c. mauve, blue and violet . . 20 10

786 Belfry, Carmel Mission

787 Powell exploring Colorado River

1969. Bicentenary of California.
1360 **786** 6 c. multicoloured . . . 15 10

1969. John Wesley Powell (geologist). Centenary of Colorado River Exploration.
1361 **787** 6 c. multicoloured . . . 15 10

788 Camellia and Common Flicker

1969. 150th Anniv of Alabama Statehood.
1362 **788** 6 c. multicoloured . . . 30 10

791 Ocotillo

1969. 11th International Botanical Congress, Seattle. Multicoloured.
1363 6 c. Douglas Fir 50 10
1364 6 c. Lady's slipper 50 10
1365 6 c. Type **791** 50 10
1366 6 c. Franklinia 50 10

A **793** Astronaut setting foot on Moon

1969. Air. 1st Man on the Moon.
A1367 A **793** 10 c. multicoloured . . 15 10

793 Daniel Webster and Dartmouth Hall

794 Striker

1969. 150th Anniv of Dartmouth College Legal Case.
1368 **793** 6 c. green 15 10

1969. Centenary of Professional Baseball.
1369 **794** 6 c. multicoloured . . . 45 10

795 Footballer and Coach

1969. Centenary of Intercollegiate Football.
1370 **795** 6 c. green and red . . . 25 10

796 Dwight D. Eisenhower (from photograph by B. Noble)

1969. Eisenhower Commemoration.
1371 **796** 6 c. black, blue & lake . . 20 10

797 "Winter Sunday in Norway, Maine" (unknown artist)

1969. Christmas.
1372 **797** 6 c. multicoloured . . . 15 10

798 Rehabilitated Child

800 "Old Models" (William Harnett)

1969. Rehabilitation of the Handicapped.
1373 **798** 6 c. multicoloured . . . 15 10
No. 1373 also commemorates the 50th anniv of the National Society for Crippled Children and Adults.

1969. William M. Harnett.
1376 **800** 6 c. multicoloured . . . 10 10

804 Prehistoric Creatures (from mural by R. Zallinger in Yale's Peabody Museum)

1970. Natural History. Centenary of American Natural History Museum. Multicoloured.
1377 6 c. American bald eagle . . 30 10
1378 6 c. African elephant herd . 30 10
1379 6 c. Haida ceremonial canoe 20 10
1380 6 c. Type **804** 20 10

805 "The Lighthouse at Two Lights" (painting by Edward Hopper in Metropolitan Museum of Art, New York)

1970. Maine Statehood Sesquicentennial.
1381 **805** 6 c. multicoloured . . . 30 10

806 American Bison

1970. Wildlife Conservation.
1382 **806** 6 c. black on brown . . 15 10

807 Dwight D. Eisenhower

809 Benjamin Franklin

1970. Prominent Americans (2nd series).
1383 **807** 6 c. blue 10 10
1384 **809** 7 c. blue 10 10
1392 **807** 8 c. maroon 30 10
1390 8 c. black, blue & red . 10 10
1386 – 14 c. black 30 10
1387 – 16 c. brown 30 10
1388 – 18 c. violet 45 10
1389 – 21 c. green 50 10
DESIGNS: VERT: 14 c. F. H. La Guardia; 16 c. Ernest T. Pyle; 18 c. Dr. Elizabeth Blackwell; 21 c. Amadeo P. Giannini (after painting by J. Kozlowski).

822 Edgar Lee Masters

823 Suffragettes, 1920, and Woman operating Voting Machine

1970. Edgar Lee Masters (poet) Commem.
1401 **822** 6 c. black and bistre . . . 15 10

1970. 50th Anniv of Women's Suffrage.
1402 **823** 6 c. blue 15 10

824 Symbols of South Carolina

1970. 300th Anniv of South Carolina.
1403 **824** 6 c. multicoloured 15 10

825 Stone Mountain Memorial

1970. Dedication of Stone Mountain Confederate Memorial.
1404 **825** 6 c. black 15 10

826 Fort Snelling and Keel Boat

1970. 150th Anniv of Fort Snelling, Minnesota.
1405 **826** 6 c. multicoloured 15 10

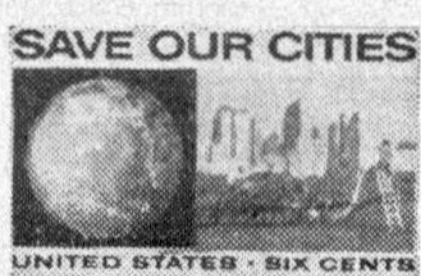

828 City Park

1970. Prevention of Pollution.
1406 6 c. Wheat 45 10
1407 6 c. Type **828** 45 10
1408 6 c. Blue-gill 45 10
1409 6 c. Western gull 60 10

832 Toy Locomotive (after drawing by C. Hemming)

1970. Christmas. Multicoloured.
1410 6 c. "The Nativity" (L. Lotto) (vert) 15 10
1411 6 c. Type **832** 65 10
1412 6 c. Toy horse on wheels . . 40 10
1413 6 c. Mechanised tricycle . . 40 10
1414 6 c. Doll's pram 40 10
Nos. 1412/14 are taken from "Golden Age of Toys" by Fondin and Remise.

836 "U.N." and Emblem

1970. 25th Anniv of U.N.O.
1415 **836** 6 c. red, blue and black . 15 10

837 "Mayflower" and Pilgrims

838 Disabled American Veterans Emblem

1970. 350th Anniv of Landing of the Pilgrim Fathers in America.
1416 **837** 6 c. multicoloured . . . 20 10

1970. 50th Anniv of Disabled American Veterans Organization, and Armed Forces Commemoration.
1417 **838** 6 c. multicoloured . . . 20 10
1418 – 6 c. black, blue and red . 20 10
DESIGN: No. 1418, Inscriptions—"Prisoners of War", "Missing and Killed in Action".

840 Ewe and Lamb

841 General Douglas MacArthur

1970. 450th Anniv of Introduction of Sheep into North America.
1419 **840** 6 c. multicoloured . . . 15 10

1971. 91st Birth Anniv of General Douglas MacArthur.
1420 **841** 6 c. black, blue and red . 15 10

842 "Giving Blood Saves Lives"

1971. Salute to Blood Donors.
1421 **842** 6 c. deep blue, red & blue 15 10

A **844** Jet Aircraft

A **845** Winged Letter

1971. Air.
A1422 – 9 c. red 25 25
A1423 A **844** 11 c. red 35 10
A1424 A **845** 13 c. red 30 10
DESIGN—HORIZ: 9 c. Delta-wing plane.

846 "Settlers and Indians" (after mural "Independence and the Opening of the West" by Thomas H. Benton)

1971. 150th Anniv of Missouri Statehood.
1427 **846** 8 c. multicoloured . . . 25 10

847 Trout

1971. Wildlife Conservation. Multicoloured.
1428 8 c. Type **847** 30 10
1429 8 c. Alligator 30 10
1430 8 c. Polar bear and cubs . . 30 15
1431 8 c. Californian condor . . . 30 10

851 Antarctic Map Emblem

852 Postal Service Emblem

1971. 10th Anniv of Antarctic Treaty.
1432 **851** 8 c. blue and red 20 10

1971. Reorganization of U.S. Post Office as U.S. Postal Service.
1433 **852** 8 c. multicoloured . . . 15 10

853 Bicentennial Emblem — A **854** Head of Statue of Liberty

1971. American Revolution Bicentennial. Bicentennial Commisssion Emblem.
1434 **853** 8 c. multicoloured . . . 25 10

1971. Air.
A1435 A **854** 17 c. blue, red & grn 55 10

855 "The Wake of the Ferry" (John Sloan)

1971. Birth Centenary of John Sloan (artist).
1436 **855** 8 c. multicoloured . . . 15 10

856 Landing Module on Moon — **858** Emily Dickinson

1971. Decade of U.S. Space Achievements. Multicoloured.
1437 8 c. Type **856** 15 10
1438 8 c. Astronauts in lunar rover 15 10
Nos. 1437/8 were issued together se-tenant, forming a composite design.

1971. 85th Death Anniv of Emily Dickinson (poet).
1439 **858** 8 c. mult on green . . . 15 10

859 Watch-tower, El Morro, San Juan — **860** Drug Victim

1971. 450th Anniv of San Juan, Puerto Rico.
1440 **859** 8 c. multicoloured . . . 15 10

1971. Drug Abuse Prevention Week.
1441 **860** 8 c. black, lt blue & bl . 25 10

861 Hands reaching to "CARE" — **866** "Adoration of the Shepherds" (Giorgione)

862 Decatur House, Washington D.C.

1971. 25th Anniv of "CARE" (Co-operative for American Relief Everywhere).
1442 **861** 8 c. multicoloured . . . 20 10

1971. Historic Preservation.
1443 **862** 8 c. blk & flesh on cream 20 10
1444 – 8 c. blk & flesh on cream 20 10
1445 – 8 c. blk & flesh on cream 25 10
1446 – 8 c. blk & flesh on cream 20 10
DESIGNS: No. 1444, Whaling ship, "Charles W. Morgan", Mystic, Conn; No. 1445, San Francisco cable-car; No. 1446, San Xavier del Bac Mission, Tucson, Arizona.

1971. Christmas. Multicoloured.
1447 8 c. Type **866** 25 10
1448 8 c. "Partridge in a Pear Tree" 30 10

868 Sidney Lanier — **869** Peace Corps Poster (D. Battle)

1972. 90th Death Anniv (1971) of Sidney Lanier (poet).
1449 **868** 8 c. black, brown & bl . 20 10

1972. Peace Corps.
1450 **869** 8 c. red, lt blue & blue . 15 10

870/873 Cape Hatteras National Seashore

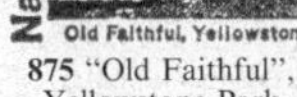

875 "Old Faithful", Yellowstone Park — A **877** Statue and Temple, City of Refuge, Hawaii

1972. Centenary of National Parks.
1451 **870** 2 c. multicoloured (postage) 15 10
1452 **871** 2 c. multicoloured . 15 10
1453 **872** 2 c. multicoloured . 20 10
1454 **873** 2 c. multicoloured . 20 10
1455 – 6 c. multicoloured . 20 10
1456 **875** 8 c. multicoloured . 30 10
1457 – 15 c. multicoloured . 50 45
A1458 A **877** 11 c. mult (air) . . . 35 10
DESIGNS—HORIZ: (As Type A **877**). 6 c. Theatre at night, Wolf Trap Farm, Virginia; 15 c. Mt. McKinley, Alaska.

878 American Family — **879** Glassblower

1972. Family Planning.
1459 **878** 8 c. multicoloured . . . 20 10

1972. Bicentenary of American Revolution. American Colonial Craftsmen.
1460 **879** 8 c. brown on yellow . . 20 10
1461 – 8 c. brown on yellow . . 20 10
1462 – 8 c. brown on yellow . . 20 10
1463 – 8 c. brown on yellow . . 20 10
DESIGNS: No. 1461, Silversmith; No. 1462, Wigmaker; No. 1463, Hatter.

883 Cycling

1972. Olympic Games, Munich and Sapporo, Japan. Multicoloured.
1464 6 c. Type **883** (postage) . . . 20 15
1465 8 c. Bobsleighing 25 10
1466 15 c. Running 40 40
A1467 11 c. Skiing (air) 35 15

887 Classroom Blackboard

1972. 75th Anniv of Parent Teacher Association.
1468 **887** 8 c. black and yellow . . 15 10

888 Northern Fur Seals

1972. Wildlife Conservation. Multicoloured.
1469 8 c. Type **888** 20 10
1470 8 c. Common cardinal (bird) 30 10
1471 8 c. Brown pelicans 30 10
1472 8 c. American bighorn 20 10

892 19th-century Country Post Office and Store

1972. Centenary of Mail Order Business.
1473 **892** 8 c. multicoloured 15 10

893 "Quest for Health" — **894** "Tom Sawyer" (N. Rockwell)

1972. 75th Anniv of American Osteopaths.
1474 **893** 8 c. multicoloured 15 10

1972. "The Adventures of Tom Sawyer" by Mark Twain.
1475 **894** 8 c. multicoloured 25 10

895 "Angels" (detail, "Mary, Queen of Heaven" by Master of the St. Lucy Legend) — **897** Pharmaceutical Equipment

1972. Christmas. Multicoloured.
1476 8 c. Type **895** 20 10
1477 8 c. Santa Claus 20 10

1972. 120th Anniv of American Pharmaceutical Association.
1478 **897** 8 c. multicoloured 25 10

898 Five Cent Stamp of 1847 under Magnifier

1972. 125th Anniv of 1st U.S. Stamp, and Stamp Collecting Promotion.
1479 **898** 8 c. brown, black & grn . 15 10

899 "LOVE"

1973. Greetings Stamp.
1480 **899** 8 c. red, green and blue . . 15 10

900 Pamphleteers with Press

1973. American Revolution Bicentennial. Colonial Communications.
1481 **900** 8 c. green, blue and red . 25 10
1482 – 8 c. black, red and blue . 25 10
1483 – 8 c. multicoloured . . . 25 10
1484 – 8 c. multicoloured . . . 25 10
DESIGNS: No. 1482, Posting a broadside; 1483, Post-rider; 1484, Drummer.

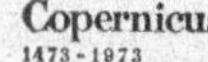

904 George Gershwin (composer) and Scene from "Porgy and Bess" — **908** Nicolas Copernicus (after 18th-cent engraving)

1973. American Arts Commemoration. Mult.
1485 8 c. Type **904** 25 10
1486 8 c. Robinson Jeffers (poet) and people of Carmel 25 10
1487 8 c. Henry Tanner (painter) and palette 25 10
1488 8c. Willa Cather (novelist) and pioneer family 25 10

1973. 500th Birth Anniv of Copernicus (astronomer).
1489 **908** 8 c. black and yellow . . 15 10

909 Counter Clerk — **919** Harry S. Truman

1973. Postal Service Employees. Multicoloured.
1490 8 c. Type **909** 15 10
1491 8 c. Collecting mail 15 10
1492 8 c. Sorting on conveyor belt 15 10
1493 8 c. Sorting parcels 15 10
1494 8 c. Cancelling letters 15 10
1495 8 c. Sorting letters by hand . 15 10
1496 8 c. Coding desks 15 10
1497 8 c. Loading mail-van . . . 15 10
1498 8 c. City postman 15 10
1499 8 c. Rural postman 15 10

1973. Pres. Harry Truman Commemoration.
1500 **919** 8 c. black, red and blue . . 15 10

920/923 Boston Tea Party. (Illustration reduced. Actual size 77 × 47 mm)

1973. American Revolution Bicentennial. The Boston Tea Party.
1501 **920** 8 c. multicoloured . . . 15 10
1502 **921** 8 c. multicoloured . . . 15 10
1503 **922** 8 c. multicoloured . . . 15 10
1504 **923** 8 c. multicoloured . . . 15 10

924 Marconi's Spark Coil and Gap (1901)

1973. Progress in Electronics. Multicoloured.

1505 6 c. Type **924** (postage) . . 20 15
1506 8 c. Modern transistor circuit 25 10
1507 15 c. Early microphone and radio speaker, radio and T.V. camera tubes 45 40
A1508 11 c. DeForest audions (1915) (air) 35 15

928 Lyndon B. Johnson (from painting by Elizabeth Shoumatoff)

929 Angus and Longhorn Cattle (painting by F. C. Murphy)

1973. Pres. Lyndon B. Johnson Commem.

1509 **928** 8 c. multicoloured . . . 20 10

1973. "Rural America" Centenaries.

1510 8 c. Type **929** 20 10
1511 10 c. Institute marquee . . . 40 10
1512 10 c. Steam train crossing wheatfield 40 10

CENTENARIES: No. 1510, Introduction of Aberdeen Angus cattle into United States; 1511, Foundation of Chautauqua Institution (adult education organization); 1512, Introduction of hard winter wheat into Kansas.

932 "Small Cowper Madonna" (Raphael)

933 Christmas Tree in Needlepoint

1973. Christmas.

1513 **932** 8 c. multicoloured . . . 20 10
1514 **933** 8 c. multicoloured . . . 20 10

934 U.S. Flags of 1777 and 1973

935 Jefferson Memorial

936 "Mail Transport" (from poster by R. McDougall)

937 Liberty Bell

1973.

1519 **937** 6.3 c. red 20 20
1515 **934** 10 c. red and blue 20 10
1516 **935** 10 c. blue 30 10
1517 **936** 10 c. multicoloured . . . 20 10

A **938** Statue of Liberty

1974. Air.

A1521 A **938** 18 c. blk, red & bl . 70 40
A1522 – 26 c. blk, bl & red . 80 10

DESIGN: 26 c. Mt. Rushmore National Memorial.

940 "VFW" and Emblem

941 Robert Frost

1974. 75th Anniv of Veterans of Foreign Wars Organization.

1523 **940** 10 c. red and blue . . . 20 10

1974. Birth Centenary of Robert Frost (poet).

1524 **941** 10 c. black 15 10

942 "Cosmic Jumper" and "Smiling Sage" ("Preserve the Environment" theme)

1974. "Expo 74" World Fair, Spokane.

1525 **942** 10 c. multicoloured . . 15 10

943 Horse-racing

1974. Centenary of Kentucky Derby.

1526 **943** 10 c. multicoloured . . 20 10

944 "Skylab" in Orbit

1974. "Skylab" Space Project.

1527 **944** 10 c. multicoloured . . 25 10

945 "Michelangelo" (detail from "School of Athens" by Raphael)

1974. Centenary of U.P.U. Multicoloured.

1528 10 c. Type **945** 15 10
1529 10 c. "Five Feminine Virtues" (Hokusai) 15 10
1530 10 c. "Old Scraps" (J. F. Peto) 15 10
1531 10 c. "The Lovely Reader" (J. Liotard) 15 10
1532 10 c. "The Lady Writing Letter" (G. Terborch) 15 10
1533 10 c. "Inkwell and Quill" (detail from "Young Boy with Top" by J. Chardin) 15 10
1534 10 c. "Mrs. John Douglas" (T. Gainsborough) 15 10
1535 10 c. "Don Antonio Noriega" (F. Goya) 15 10

955 Amethyst

957 Covered Wagon at Fort Harrod

1974. Mineral Heritage. Multicoloured.

1536 10 c. Petrified wood 25 10
1537 10 c. Tourmaline 25 10
1538 10 c. Type **955** 25 10
1539 10 c. Rhodochrosite 25 10

1974. Bicentenary of Fort Harrod, First Settlement in Kentucky.

1540 **957** 10 c. multicoloured . . . 25 10

959 "We ask but for peace..." (First Continental Congress)

962 Slogan, Molecules and Petrol Drops

1974. American Revolution Bicentennial. First Continental Congress.

1541 – 10 c. blue and red 25 10
1542 **959** 10 c. grey, blue and red . 25 10
1543 – 10 c. grey, red and blue . 25 10
1544 – 10 c. red and blue 25 10

DESIGNS: No. 1541, Carpenters' Hall, Philadelphia; 1543, "Deriving their just powers . . ." (Declaration of Independence); 1544, Independence Hall, Philadelphia.

1974. Energy Conservation.

1545 **962** 10 c. multicoloured . . . 20 10

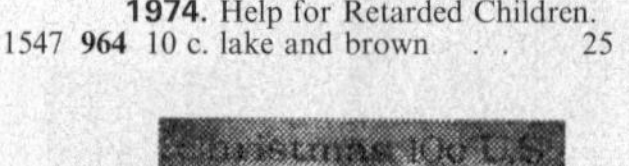

963 "The Headless Horseman"

964 Child clasping Hand

1974. Washington Irving's "Legend of Sleepy Hollow".

1546 **963** 10 c. multicoloured . . . 20 10

1974. Help for Retarded Children.

1547 **964** 10 c. lake and brown . . 25 10

966 "The Road — Winter" (from a Currier and Ives print, drawn by O. Knirsch)

1974. Christmas. Multicoloured.

1548 10 c. "Angel" (detail, Perussis altarpiece) (vert) 20 10
1549 10 c. Type **966** 20 10
1550 10 c. Dove weathervane, Mount Vernon 20 10

No. 1550 has self-adhesive gum.

968 "Benjamin West" (self-portrait)

969 "Pioneer" Spacecraft passing Jupiter

1975. Benjamin West (painter) Commem.

1551 **968** 10 c. multicoloured . . . 15 10

1975. U.S. Unmanned Space Missions. Mult.

1552 10 c. Type **969** 30 10
1553 10 c. "Mariner 10", Venus and Mercury 30 10

971 Overlapping Circles

1975. Collective Bargaining in Labour Relations.

1554 **971** 10 c. multicoloured . . . 15 10

972 Sybil Ludington on Horseback

1975. American Revolution Bicentennial. Contributors to the Cause.

1555 **972** 8 c. multicoloured . . . 20 20
1556 – 10 c. multicoloured . . . 25 10
1557 – 10 c. multicoloured . . . 25 10
1558 – 18 c. multicoloured . . . 50 60

DESIGNS: No. 1556, Salem Poor loading musket; 1557, Haym Salomon writing in ledger; 1558, Peter Francisco carrying cannon.

976 "Lexington" (from painting "Birth of Liberty" by H. Sandham)

977 Paul Laurence Dunbar (poet)

1975. American Revolution Bicentennial. Battles of Lexington and Concord.

1559 **976** 10 c. multicoloured . . . 25 10

1975. Dunbar Commemoration.

1560 **977** 10 c. multicoloured . . . 20 10

978 D. W. Griffith (film producer)

1975. Griffith Commemoration.

1561 **978** 10 c. multicoloured . . . 25 10

979 "Bunker Hill, 1775", (John Trumbull)

980 Marine with Musket

1975. Bicentenary of American Revolution. Battle of Bunker Hill.

1562 **979** 10 c. multicoloured . . . 25 10

1975. American Revolution Bicentennial. U.S. Military Services. Multicoloured.

1563 10 c. Type **980** 25 10
1564 10 c. Militiaman with musket 25 10
1565 10 c. Soldier with flintlock . 25 10
1566 10 c. Sailor with grappling-iron 25 10

984 Docking Manoeuvre

1975. "Apollo-Soyuz" Space Test Project. Mult.

1567 10 c. Type **984** 20 10
1568 10 c. Spacecraft docked . . . 20 10

986 "Worldwide Equality"

1975. International Women's Year.

1569 **986** 10 c. multicoloured . . . 20 10

987 Stagecoach and Modern Lorry

1975. Bicentenary of Postal Services. Mult.

1571 10 c. Type **987** 20 10
1572 10 c. Early steam and modern diesel locomotives 20 10
1573 10 c. Curtiss JN-4 "Jenny" and Boeing 747-100 aircraft . . 20 10
1574 10 c. Telecommunications satellite 20 10

991 Law Book, Gavel and Globe

1975. "World Peace through Law".

1575 **991** 10 c. brown, blue & grn . 20 10

992 Coins and Engine-turned Motif

1975. "Banking and Commerce".

1576 **992** 10 c. multicoloured . . . 20 10

1577 – 10 c. multicoloured . . . 20 10

DESIGN: No. 1577, As Type **992**, but design reversed with different coins.

994 "Madonna and Child" (Ghirlandaio)

995 "Christmas Card" (from early design by Louis Prang)

1975. Christmas.

1578 **994** (10 c.) multicoloured . . 20 10

1579 **995** (10 c.) multicoloured . . 20 10

Nos. 1578/9 were each sold at 10 c. Because of an imminent increase in the postage rates the two designs were issued without face values.

1002 Early Printing Press

1020 Flag over Independence Hall

1975.

1580 – 1 c. deep blue on grey . 10 10

1581 – 2 c. red on cream . . . 10 10

1582 – 3 c. olive on green . . 10 10

1597b – 3.1 c. lake on yellow . 15 10

1598 – 3.5 c. lilac on yellow . 15 10

1582a – 4 c. red on cream . . . 10 10

1599 – 7.7 c. brown on yellow 30 15

1600 – 7.9 c. red on yellow . . 30 15

1601 – 8.4 c. blue on yellow . 30 15

1583 – 9 c. green on grey . . 25 10

1584 – 9 c. green 30 10

1585 – 10 c. purple on grey . . 15 10

1585a **1002** 11 c. orange on grey . 20 10

1585b – 12 c. brown on cream . 20 10

1586 – 13 c. brown on cream . 20 10

1595 – 13 c. multicoloured . . 40 10

1596 – 15 c. blue, red & blk . 45 10

1605 – 16 c. blue 50 15

1589 – 24 c. red on blue . . . 70 10

1589a – 28 c. brown on blue . . 75 10

1590 – 29 c. blue on light bl . 90 30

1591 – 30 c. green on turq . . 55 10

1592 – 50 c. black, red & brn . 70 10

1593 – $1 multicoloured . . . 1·50 10

1594 – $2 multicoloured . . . 3·00 20

1594a – $5 multicoloured . . . 8·00 1·25

DESIGNS: 1 c. Inkwell and quill; 2 c. Speaker's stand; 3 c. Ballot box; 3.1 c. Guitar; 3.5 c. Weaver violins; 4 c. Books, spectacles and bookmark; 7.7 c. Saxhorns; 7.9 c. Drum; 8.4 c. Grand piano; 9 c. (both) Dome of Capitol; 10 c. "Contemplation of Justice" (statue, J. E. Fraser); 12 c. Statue of Liberty torch; 13 c. (No. 1586) Liberty Bell; 13 c. (No. 1595) Eagle and shield; 15 c. Fort McHenry flag; 16 c. Statue of Liberty; 24 c. Old North Church, Boston; 28 c. Fort Nisqually, Washington; 29 c. Sandy Hook Lighthouse, N.J; 30 c. Morris Township School; 50 c. Iron "Betty" lamp; $1 Rush lamp and candle holder; $2 Kerosene lamp; $5 Railway conductor's lantern.

1975.

1606 **1020** 13 c. red and blue . . 40 10

1606c – 13 c. red and blue . . 35 10

DESIGN: No. 1606c, Flag over Capitol, Washington.

MORE DETAILED LISTS

are given in the Stanley Gibbons Catalogues referred to in the country headings. For lists of current volumes see introduction

1021 Drummer Boy (after A. M. Willard)

1024

1976. American Revolution Bicentennial. "The Spirit of '76". Multicoloured.

1607 13 c. Type **1021** 20 10

1608 13 c. Old drummer 20 10

1609 13 c. Fifer 20 10

Nos. 1607/9 were issued together, se-tenant, forming a composite design.

1976. Air.

A1610 **1024** 25 c. black, bl & red . 50 10

A1611 – 31 c. black, bl & red . 55 10

DESIGN: 31 c. As 25 c. but with background of U.S. flag.

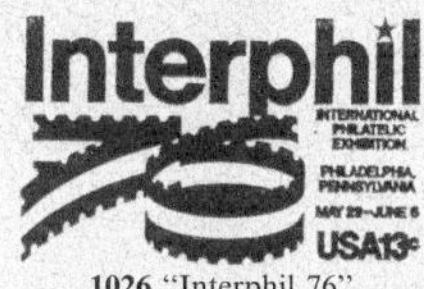

1026 "Interphil 76"

1976. "Interphil 76" International Stamp Exhibition, Philadelphia.

1612 **1026** 13 c. red and blue . . . 35 10

1027 Delaware Flag

1976. Bicentenary of American Revolution. State Flags. Multicoloured.

1613 13 c. Type **1027** 30 20

1614 13 c. Pennsylvania 30 20

1615 13 c. New Jersey 30 20

1616 13 c. Georgia 30 20

1617 13 c. Connecticut 30 20

1618 13 c. Massachusetts 30 20

1619 13 c. Maryland 30 20

1620 13 c. South Carolina 30 20

1621 13 c. New Hampshire . . . 30 20

1622 13 c. Virginia 30 20

1623 13 c. New York 30 20

1624 13 c. North Carolina 30 20

1625 13 c. Rhode Island 30 20

1626 13 c. Vermont 30 20

1627 13 c. Kentucky 30 20

1628 13 c. Tennessee 30 20

1629 13 c. Ohio 30 20

1630 13 c. Louisiana 30 20

1631 13 c. Indiana 30 20

1632 13 c. Mississippi 30 20

1633 13 c. Illinois 30 20

1634 13 c. Alabama 30 20

1635 13 c. Maine 30 20

1636 13 c. Missouri 30 20

1637 13 c. Arkansas 30 20

1638 13 c. Michigan 30 20

1639 13 c. Florida 30 20

1640 13 c. Texas 30 20

1641 13 c. Iowa 30 20

1642 13 c. Wisconsin 30 20

1643 13 c. California 30 20

1644 13 c. Minnesota 30 20

1645 13 c. Oregon 30 20

1646 13 c. Kansas 30 20

1647 13 c. West Virginia 30 20

1648 13 c. Nevada 30 20

1649 13 c. Nebraska 35 20

1650 13 c. Colorado 30 20

1651 13 c. North Dakota 30 20

1652 13 c. South Dakota 30 20

1653 13 c. Montana 30 20

1654 13 c. Washington 30 20

1655 13 c. Idaho 30 20

1656 13 c. Wyoming 30 20

1657 13 c. Utah 30 20

1658 13 c. Oklahoma 30 20

1659 13 c. New Mexico 30 20

1660 13 c. Arizona 30 20

1661 13 c. Alaska 30 20

1662 13 c. Hawaii 30 20

1028 Bell's Telephone

1976. Telephone Centenary.

1663 **1028** 13 c. violet, black and red on brown 25 10

1029 Stout Air Pullman and Laird Swallow Biplane

1976. Commercial Aviation.

1664 **1029** 13 c. multicoloured . . . 20 10

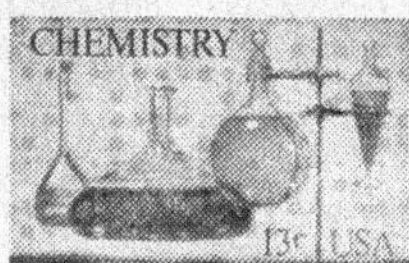

1030 Laboratory Equipment

1976. Centenary of American Chemical Society.

1665 **1030** 13 c. multicoloured . . . 20 10

1035 Benjamin Franklin and 1776 Map of North America

1040 Diving

1036/1039 "Signing the Declaration of Independence" (John Turnbull) (½-size illustration)

1976. American Revolution Bicentennial.

1667 **1035** 13 c. multicoloured . . . 20 10

1976. American Revolution Bicentennial.

1668 **1036** 13 c. multicoloured . . . 30 10

1669 **1037** 13 c. multicoloured . . . 30 10

1670 **1038** 13 c. multicoloured . . . 30 10

1671 **1039** 13 c. multicoloured . . . 30 10

Nos. 1668/71 were issued together, se-tenant, forming the composite design illustrated.

1976. Olympic Games, Innsbruck and Montreal. Multicoloured.

1672 13 c. Type **1040** 25 10

1673 13 c. Skiing 25 10

1674 13 c. Running 25 10

1675 13 c. Skating 25 10

Adolph S. Ochs
PUBLISHER
13c USA

1044 Clara Maass

1045 A. S. Ochs

1976. Birth Centenary of Clara Maass (martyr to yellow fever).

1676 **1044** 13 c. multicoloured . . . 20 10

1976. Adolph S. Ochs (publisher of "New York Times") Commemoration.

1677 **1045** 13 c. black 20 10

1046 "Winter Pastime" (N. Currier)

1976. Christmas.

1678 13 c. Type **1046** 20 10

1679 13 c. "Nativity" (John S. Copley) 20 10

1048 "Washington at Princeton" (Peale)

1050 Zia Pot

13

1049 Early Gramophone

1977. American Revolution Bicentennial.

1680 **1048** 13 c. multicoloured . . 20 10

1977. Centenary of Sound Recording.

1681 **1049** 13 c. multicoloured . . 20 10

1977. American Folk Art, Pueblo Art.

1682 13 c. Type **1050** 20 10

1683 13 c. San Ildefonso pot . . . 20 10

1684 13 c. Hopi pot 20 10

1685 13 c. Acoma pot 20 10

1054 "Spirit of St. Louis"

1977. 50th Anniv of Lindbergh's Transatlantic Flight.

1686 **1054** 13 c. multicoloured . . 20 10

1055 Columbine and Rocky Mountains

1056 American Swallowtail

1977. Centenary (1976) of Colorado Statehood.

1687 **1055** 13 c. multicoloured . . 20 10

1977. Butterflies. Multicoloured.

1688 13 c. Type **1056** 20 10

1689 13 c. Checkerspot 20 10

1690 13 c. Dogface 20 10

1691 13 c. Falcate orange-tip . . . 20 10

1060 Marquis de Lafayette

1977. American Revolution Bicentennial. Bicentenary of Lafayette's Landing on Coast of South Carolina.

1692 **1060** 13 c. black, blue & red . 20 10

1061 Seamstress

1977. American Revolution Bicentenary. "Skilled Hands for Independence". Multicoloured.

1693 13 c. Type **1061** 20 10

1694 13 c. Blacksmith 20 10

1695 13 c. Wheelwright 20 10

1696 13 c. Leatherworker 20 10

1065 Peace Bridge and Dove

1977. 50th Anniv of Opening of Peace Bridge.

1697 **1065** 13 c. blue 20 10

1066 "Herkimer at Oriskany" (F. Yohn)

1977. American Revolution Bicentennial. Bicentenary of Battle of Oriskany.

1698 **1066** 13 c. multicoloured . . 20 10

1067 Farmhouses, El Pueblo

1977. Bicentenary of First Civil Settlement in Alta California.

1699 **1067** 13 c. multicoloured . . 20 10

1068 Members of the Continental Congress

1977. Bicentenary of Drafting of the Articles of Constitution.

1700 **1068** 13 c. brown and red . . 20 10

1069 "Vitaphone" Projector and Sound Equipment

1977. 50th Anniv of Talking Pictures.

1701 **1069** 13 c. multicoloured . . 30 10

1070 "Surrender of Burgoyne at Saratoga" (J. Trumbull)

1977. American Revolution Bicentennial. Surrender of General Burgoyne.

1702 **1070** 13 c. multicoloured . . 20 10

1071 "Conservation" **1073** Washington at Valley Forge (after Leyendecker)

1977. Energy Conservation and Development.

1703 **1071** 13 c. multicoloured . . 20 10

1704 – 13 c. multicoloured . . 20 10

DESIGN: No. 1704, "Development".

1977. Christmas.

1705 **1073** 13 c. multicoloured . . 20 10

1706 – 13 c. multicoloured . . 20 10

DESIGN: No. 1706, Rural mailbox.

1075 Carl Sandburg

USA13c

1076 Indian Head Penny

1978. Birth Centenary of Carl Sandburg (poet and biographer).

1707 **1075** 13 c. black and brown . 20 10

1978.

1708 **1076** 13 c. brown & bl on buff 20 10

1077 Captain James Cook (after Nathaniel Dance) **1079** Harriet Tubman and Slaves

1978. Bicentenary of Capt. Cook's Visits to Hawaii and Alaska.

1709 **1077** 13 c. blue 40 10

1710 – 13 c. green 40 10

DESIGNS—HORIZ: No. 1710, H.M.S. "Resolution" and H.M.S. "Discovery" at Hawaii (after John Webber).

1978. Black Heritage. Harriet Tubman (organizer of slave "underground railway").

1711 **1079** 13 c. multicoloured . . 20 10

1082 Quilt Design

1978. American Folk Art. Quilts.

1712 – 13 c. brown and grey . 20 10

1713 – 13 c. red and grey . . . 20 10

1714 **1082** 13 c. multicoloured . . 20 10

1715 – 13 c. multicoloured . . 20 10

DESIGNS: No. 1712, Chequered; 1713, Dotted; 1715, Striped.

1084 Ballet

1978. American Dance.

1716 **1084** 13 c. blue, mve & blk . 20 10

1717 – 13 c. orange, red & blk 20 10

1718 – 13 c. green, yell & blk . 20 10

1719 – 13 c. blue, ultram & blk 20 10

DESIGNS: No. 1717, Theatre; 1718, Folk dance; 1719, Modern.

1088 "Louis XVI and Benjamin Franklin" (statuette, C.G. Sauvage) **1089** Dr. Papanicolaou

1978. Bicentenary of French Alliance.

1720 **1088** 13 c. black, blue & red 25 10

1978. Dr. George Papanicolaou (developer of Pap (cancer detection) test) Commemoration.

1721 **1089** 13 c. brown 20 10

1090 American Eagle

1091 Jimmie Rodgers

1978. No value expressed.

1722 **1090** (15 c.) orange 20 10

For "B" stamp see No. 1843, for "C" stamp Nos 1909/10 and for "D" stamp Nos. 2137/8.

1978. Performing Arts and Artists. Jimmie Rodgers, "Father of Country Music".

1725 **1091** 13 c. multicoloured . . . 30 10

1093 Camera and Accessories **1094** George M. Cohan

1978. Photography.

1727 **1093** 15 c. multicoloured . . . 20 10

1978. Performing Arts. Birth Centenary of George M. Cohan (actor and playwright).

1728 **1094** 15 c. multicoloured . . . 20 10

1095 "Red Masterpiece" and "Medallion" Roses **1096** "Viking 1" Lander scooping Soil from Mars

1978. Roses.

1729 **1095** 15 c. red, orange & grn . 50 10

1978. 2nd Anniv of "Viking 1" Landing on Mars.

1730 **1096** 15 c. multicoloured . . . 20 10

1097 Great Grey Owl **1101** Wright Brothers and Flyer I

1978. Wildlife Conservation. American Owls. Multicoloured.

1731 15 c. Type **1097** 50 10

1732 15 c. Saw-whet owl 50 10

1733 15 c. Barred owl 50 10

1734 15 c. Great horned owl . . . 50 10

1978. Air. 75th Anniv of First Powered Flight. Multicoloured.

A1735 31 c. Type **1101** 75 10

A1736 31 c. Flyer I and Wright Brothers (in bowler hats) 75 10

1103 White Pine **1107** "Madonna and Child with Cherubim" (Andrea della Robbia)

1978. American Trees. Multicoloured.

1737 15 c. Type **1103** 30 10

1738 15 c. Giant sequoia 30 10

1739 15 c. Grey birch 30 10

1740 15 c. White oak 30 10

1978. Christmas. Multicoloured.

1741 15 c. Type **1107** 20 10

1742 15 c. Child on rocking horse . 20 10

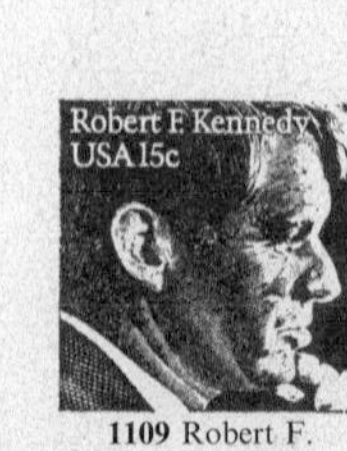
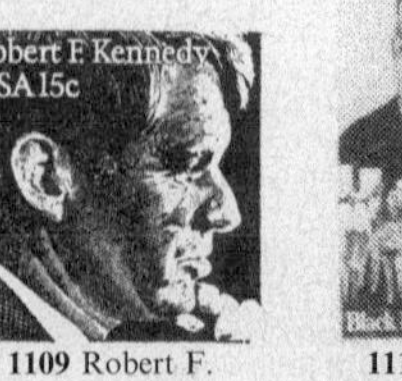

1109 Robert F. Kennedy **1110** Martin Luther King

1979. Robert F. Kennedy Commemoration.

1743 **1109** 15 c. blue 20 10

1979. Black Heritage. Martin Luther King (Civil Rights leader).

1744 **1110** 15 c. multicoloured . . 20 10

1111 Children of Different Races **1112** John Steinbeck

1979. International Year of the Child.

1745 **1111** 15 c. red 20 10

1979. Literary Arts. John Steinbeck (novelist).

1746 **1112** 15 c. blue 20 10

1113 Einstein **1114** Chanute and Glider

1979. Birth Cent of Albert Einstein (physicist).

1747 **1113** 15 c. brown 20 10

1979. Air. Aviation Pioneers. Octave Chanute. Multicoloured.

A1748 21 c. Type **1114** 75 10

A1749 21 c. Chanute and glider (different) 75 10

1116 Coffee Pot **1120** Virginia Rotunda (Thomas Jefferson)

1979. American Folk Art. Pennsylvania Toleware. Multicoloured.

1750 15 c. Type **1116** 20 10

1751 15 c. Tea caddy 20 10

1752 15 c. Sugar bowl with lid . . 20 10

1753 15 c. Coffee pot with gooseneck spout 20 10

1979. American Architecture. Each black and red.

1754 15 c. Type **1120** 20 10

1755 15 c. Baltimore Cathedral (Benjamin Latrobe) . . . 20 10

1756 15 c. Boston State House (Charles Bulfinch) 20 10

1757 15 c. Philadelphia Exchange (William Strickland) . . . 20 10

1124 Persistent Trillium

1128 Guide Dog

1979. Endangered Flora. Multicoloured.

1758 15 c. Type **1124** 20 10

1759 15 c. Hawaiian wild broadbean 20 10

1760 15 c. Contra costa wallflower 20 10

1761 15 c. Antioch dunes evening primrose 20 10

1979. 50th Anniv of First U.S. Guide Dog Programme.

1762 **1128** 15 c. multicoloured . . 30 10

1129 Child with Medal

1130 Throwing the Javelin (Decathlon)

1979. Special Olympic Games for the Handicapped.
1763 **1129** 15 c. multicoloured . . 20 10

1979. Olympic Games, Moscow (1980). Multicoloured.
1764 10 c. Type **1130** (postage) . 15 10
1765 15 c. Running (horiz) . . . 20 10
1766 15 c. Swimming (horiz) . . 20 10
1767 15 c. Rowing (horiz) 20 10
1768 15 c. Show jumping (horiz) . 20 10
A1769 31 c. High jumping (horiz) (air) 50 55

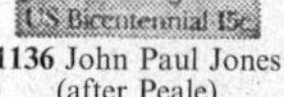

1136 John Paul Jones (after Peale)
1137 "Rest on the Flight to Egypt" (G. David)

1979. American Revolution Bicentennial. John Paul Jones (naval commander).
1770 **1136** 15 c. multicoloured . . 20 10

1979. Christmas. Multicoloured.
1771 15 c. Type **1137** 20 10
1772 15 c. Santa Claus tree ornament 20 10

1139 Will Rogers
1140 Vietnam Service Medal Ribbon

1979. Performing Arts and Artists. Will Rogers (cowboy philosopher).
1773 **1139** 15 c. multicoloured . . 20 10

1979. Vietnam Veterans.
1774 **1140** 15 c. multicoloured . . 20 10

1141 Wiley Post
1143 W. C. Fields

1979. Air. Aviation Pioneers. Wiley Post. Mult.
A1775 25 c. Type **1141** . . . . . 1·50 40
A1776 25 c. Wiley Post and airplane "Winnie Mae" . . . . . 1·50 40

1980. Performing Arts and Artists. W. C. Fields (comedian).
1777 **1143** 15 c. multicoloured . . 20 10

1144 Speed Skating
1148 Robertson Windmill, Williamsburg, Va

1980. Winter Olympic Games, Lake Placid. Mult.
1778 15 c. Type **1144** 20 10
1779 15 c. Downhill skiing 20 10
1780 15 c. Ski jumping 20 10
1781 15 c. Ice hockey 20 10

1980. Windmills.
1782 **1148** 15 c. brown on yellow . 45 10
1783 – 15 c. brown on yellow . 45 10
1784 – 15 c. brown on yellow . 45 10
1785 – 15 c. brown on yellow . 45 10
1786 – 15 c. brown on yellow . 45 10
DESIGNS: No. 1783, Replica of old windmill, Portsmouth, R.I; 1784, Cape Cod windmill, Eastham, Mass; 1785, Dutch mill, Fabyan Park Forest Preserve, Ill; 1786, Southwestern windmill, Texas.

1153 Benjamin Banneker

1980. Black Heritage. Benjamin Banneker (astronomer and mathematician).
1787 **1153** 15 c. multicoloured . . 20 10

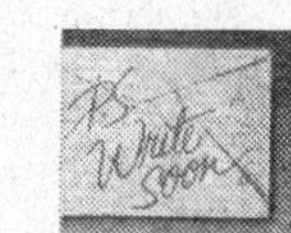

1154 Photograph and Envelope
1157 "P.S. Write Soon"

1980. National Letter Writing Week.
1788 **1154** 15 c. multicoloured . . 20 10
1789 **1157** 15 c. multicoloured (purple background) 20 10
1790 – 15 c. multicoloured . . 20 10
1791 **1157** 15 c. multicoloured (green background) 20 10
1792 – 15 c. multicoloured . . 20 10
1793 **1157** 15 c. blue, blk & red . 20 10
DESIGNS—As T **1154**: No. 1790, Flowers and envelope; 1792, Capitol and envelope.

1158 Frances Perkins
1159 Dolley Madison (after Stuart)

1980. Frances Perkins (first woman Cabinet member) Commemoration.
1794 **1158** 15 c. blue 20 10

1980.
1795 **1159** 15 c. dp brown & brn . 20 10

1160 Emily Bissell
1161 Helen Keller and Anne Sullivan

1980. Emily Bissell (crusader against tuberculosis) Commemoration.
1796 **1160** 15 c. black and red . . 25 10

1980. Birth Centenary of Helen Keller.
1797 **1161** 15 c. multicoloured . . 20 10

1162 Veterans Administration Emblem
1163 Statue of Gen. Galvez, Mobile

1980. 50th Anniv of Veterans Administration.
1798 **1162** 15 c. red and blue . . . 20 10

1980. General Bernardo de Galvez (leader of Spanish forces in Louisiana during American Revolution) Commemoration.
1799 **1163** 15 c. multicoloured . . 20 10

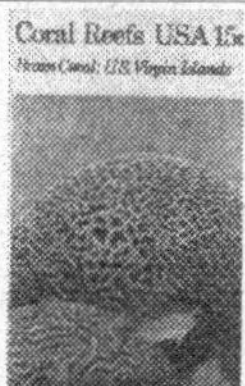

1164 Brain Corals
1168 American Bald Eagle

1980. Coral Reefs. Multicoloured.
1800 15 c. Type **1164** 20 10
1801 15 c. Elkhorn coral 20 10
1802 15 c. Chalice coral 20 10
1803 15 c. Finger coral 20 10

1980. Organized Labour.
1804 **1168** 15 c. multicoloured . . . 30 10

1169 Edith Wharton
1170 "Homage to the Square: Glow" (J. Albers)

1980. Literary Arts. Edith Wharton (novelist).
1805 **1169** 15 c. violet 20 10

1980. American Education.
1806 **1170** 15 c. multicoloured . . . 20 10

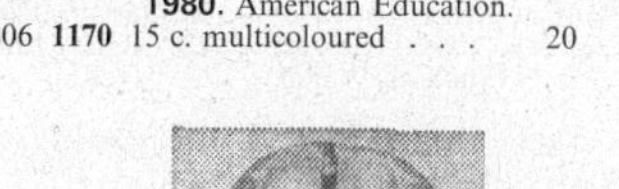

1171 Heiltsuk, Bella Bella

1980. American Folk Art, Indian Masks. Mult.
1807 15 c. Type **1171** 20 10
1808 15 c. Chilkat Tlingit 20 10
1809 15 c. Tlingit 20 10
1810 15 c. Bella Coola 20 10

1175 Smithsonian Institution, Washington (James Renwick)
1179 Philip Mazzei

1980. American Architecture.
1811 **1175** 15 c. black and red . . . 20 10
1812 – 15 c. black and red . . . 20 10
1813 – 15 c. black and red . . . 20 10
1814 – 15 c. black and red . . . 20 10
DESIGNS: No. 1812, Trinity Church, Boston (Henry Hobson Richardson); 1813, Penn Academy, Philadelphia, (Frank Furness); 1814, Lyndhurst, Tarrytown, New York (Alexander Jackson Davis).

1980. Air. Philip Mazzei (patriot) Commem.
A1815 **1179** 40 c. multicoloured . . 50 15

1180 "Madonna and Child" (Epiphany Window, Washington Cathedral)
1181 Antique Toys

1980. Christmas.
1816 **1180** 15 c. multicoloured . . . 20 10
1817 **1181** 15 c. multicoloured . . . 20 10

1191 Sequoyah (Cherokee scholar) (after C. B. Wilson)
1203 Blanche Stuart Scott

1980. Great Americans. With "c" after face value.
1818 – 1 c. black 10 10
1819 – 2 c. black 10 10
1820 – 3 c. green 10 10
1821 – 4 c. violet 10 10
1822 – 5 c. red 10 10
1823 – 10 c. blue 25 10
1824 – 13 c. red 30 10
1825 – 17 c. green 30 10
1826 – 18 c. blue 40 10
1827 **1191** 19 c. brown 40 10
1828 – 20 c. purple 30 10
1829 – 20 c. green 45 10
1830 – 20 c. black 45 10
1831 – 30 c. green 40 10
1832 – 35 c. black 60 10
1833 – 37 c. blue 50 10
1834 – 40 c. green 70 10
DESIGNS: 1 c. Dorothea Dix (social pioneer); 2 c. Igor Stravinsky (composer); 3 c. Henry Clay (politician); 4 c. Carl Schurz (reformer); 5 c. Pearl Buck (author) (after F. Elliot); 10 c. Richard Russell (politician); 13 c. Crazy Horse (Sioux chief) (after K. Ziolkowski); 17 c. Rachel Carson (scientist); 18 c. George Mason (patriot); 20 c. (1828), Ralph Bunche (U.N. Secretariat member); 20 c. (1829), Thomas H. Gallaudet (educator of the deaf); 20 c. (1830), Pres. Harry S. Truman; 30 c. Frank C. Laubach (literacy educator); 35 c. Charles R. Drew (surgeon); 37 c. Robert Millikan (physicist); 40 c. Lillian M. Gilbreth (engineer).
For similar designs without "c", see Nos. 2108/42.

1980. Air. Aviation Pioneers. Multicoloured.
A1839 28 c. Type **1203** 55 15
A1840 35 c. Glenn Curtiss 60 15

1205 Everett Dirksen
1206 Whitney Moore Young

1981. Senator Everett Dirksen Commemoration.
1841 **1205** 15 c. grey 20 10

1981. Black Heritage. Whitney Moore Young (civil rights leader).
1842 **1206** 15 c. multicoloured . . 20 10

1981. Non-denominational "B" stamp. As T **1090**.
1843 (18 c.) lilac 50 10

1207 Rose

1981. Flowers. Multicoloured.
1846 18 c. Type **1207** 25 10
1847 18 c. Camellia 25 10
1848 18 c. Dahlia 25 10
1849 18 c. Lily 25 10

1211 ". . . for amber waves of grain"
USA
1212 Stars

1981.
1851 **1212** 6 c. blue and red . . . 90 15
1850 **1211** 18 c. brown, red and bl 30 10
1852 – 18 c. lilac, red and blue 35 10
1853 – 18 c. brown, blue & red 55 10
DESIGNS—As T **1211**: No. 1852, ". . . for purple mountain majesties"; 1853, ". . . from sea to shining sea".

1215 Nurse and Child **1216** Money Box

1981. Centenary of American Red Cross.
1854 **1215** 18 c. multicoloured . . 25 10

1981. 150th Anniv of First Savings and Loans Association.
1855 **1216** 18 c. multicoloured . . 25 10

1217 American Bighorn **1238** Detroit Electric Auto, 1917

1981. Wildlife.
1856 **1217** 18 c. brown 60 10
1857 – 18 c. brown 60 10
1858 – 18 c. brown 60 10
1859 – 18 c. brown 60 10
1860 – 18 c. brown 60 10
1861 – 18 c. brown 60 10
1862 – 18 c. brown 60 10
1863 – 18 c. brown 60 10
1864 – 18 c. brown 60 10
1865 – 18 c. brown 60 10
DESIGNS: No. 1857, Puma; 1858, Common seal; 1859, American bison; 1860, Brown bear; 1861, Polar bear; 1862, Red deer; 1863, Elk; 1864, White-tailed deer; 1865, Pronghorn.

1981. Transport. With "c" after face value.
1866 – 1 c. violet 10 10
1867 – 2 c. black 10 10
1868 – 3 c. green 10 10
1869 – 4 c. brown 10 10
1870 – 5 c. green 10 10
1871 – 5.2 c. red 15 10
1872 – 5.9 c. blue 10 10
1873 – 7.4 c. brown 25 10
1874 – 9.3 c. red 30 10
1875 – 10.9 c. mauve 50 10
1876a – 11 c. red 15 10
1877 **1238** 17 c. blue 20 10
1878 – 18 c. brown 40 10
1879 – 20 c. red 45 10
DESIGNS: 1 c. Omnibus, 1880s; 2 c. Locomotive, 1870s; 3 c. Handcar, 1880s; 4 c. Concord stage-coach, 1890s; 5 c. Pope motor-cycle, 1913; 5.2 c. Sleigh, 1880s; 5.9 c. Bicycle, 1870s; 7.4 c. Baby buggy, 1880s; 9.3 c. Mail wagon, 1880s; 10.9 c. Hansom cab, 1890s; 11 c. Railway caboose, 1890s; 18 c. Surrey, 1890s; 20 c. Amoskeag fire pumper, 1860s.
For similar designs without "c", see Nos. 2150/74 and 2480/96.

1247 Exploring the Moon ("Apollo" mission) **1255** Joseph Wharton (founder of Wharton School)

1981. Space Achievements.
1886 **1247** 18 c. multicoloured . . 30 10
1887 – 18 c. multicoloured . . 30 10
1888 – 18 c. multicoloured . . 30 10
1889 – 18 c. multicoloured . . 30 10
1890 – 18 c. multicoloured . . 30 10
1891 – 18 c. multicoloured . . 30 10
1892 – 18 c. multicoloured . . 30 10
1893 – 18 c. multicoloured . . 30 10
DESIGNS: No. 1887, Space Shuttle loosing boosters; 1888, Space Shuttle performing experiment; 1889, Understanding the Sun ("Skylab"); 1890, Probing the Planets ("Pioneer II"); 1891, Space Shuttle launch; 1892, Space Shuttle landing; 1893, Comprehending the Universe (space telescope).
Nos. 1886/93 were issued together in se-tenant blocks of eight, each block forming a composite design.

1981. Cent of Professional Management Education.
1894 **1255** 18 c. blue and black . . 25 10

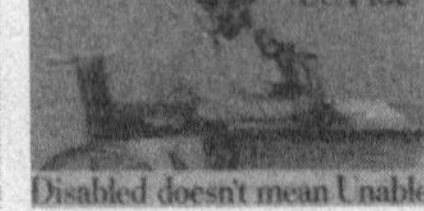

1256 Great Blue Heron **1260** Disabled Man using Microscope

1981. Wildlife Habitats.
1895 **1256** 18 c. multicoloured . . 50 20
1896 – 18 c. multicoloured . . 50 20
1897 – 18 c. multicoloured . . 50 20
1898 – 18 c. multicoloured . . 50 20
DESIGNS: No. 1896, American badger; 1897, Brown bear; 1898, Ruffed grouse.

1981. International Year of Disabled Persons.
1899 **1260** 18 c. multicoloured . . 25 10

1261 Edna St. Vincent Millay **1262** "Alcoholism. You can beat it!"

1981. Edna St. Vincent Millay (poet) Commem.
1900 **1261** 18 c. multicoloured . . 25 10

1981. Anti-alcoholism Campaign.
1901 **1262** 18 c. blue and black . . 25 10

1263 New York University Library (Stanford White) **1267** Bobby Jones (golfer)

1981. American Architecture (3rd series).
1902 **1263** 18 c. black & brown . 25 10
1903 – 18 c. black & brown . 25 10
1904 – 18 c. black & brown . 25 10
1905 – 18 c. black & brown . 25 10
DESIGNS: No. 1903, Biltmore House, Asheville, North Carolina (Richard Morris Hunt); 1904, Palace of Arts, San Francisco (Bernard Maybeck); 1905, Bank, Owatonna, Minnesota (Louis Sullivan).

1981. American Sports Personalities.
1906 **1267** 18 c. green 50 10
1907 – 18 c. red 50 10
DESIGN: No. 1907, Babe Zaharias (golfer and athlete).

1269 "Coming through the Rye"

1981. Frederic Remington (sculptor) Commemoration.
1908 **1269** 18 c. brown, green and light brown 40 10

1981. Non-denominational "C" stamp. As T **1090** but inscribed "Domestic Mail".
1909 (20 c.) brown (19 × 22 mm) . 40 10
1910 (20 c.) brown (15 × 18½ mm) 45 10

1271 James Hoban and White House

1981. 150th Death Anniv of James Hoban (architect).
1912 **1271** 18 c. multicoloured . . 40 20
1913 20 c. multicoloured . . 40 10

1272 Map of Yorktown Peninsula **1274** "Madonna and Child" (Botticelli)

1981. Bicentenary of Battles of Yorktown and Virginia Capes. Multicoloured.
1914 18 c. Type **1272** 35 10
1915 18 c. French ships blocking Chesapeake Bay 35 10

1981. Christmas. No value expressed. Mult.
1916 (20 c.) Type **1274** 25 10
1917 (20 c.) Teddy bear on sleigh 25 10

1276 John Hanson **1277** Barrel Cactus

1981. John Hanson (American revolutionary leader) Commemoration.
1918 **1276** 20 c. multicoloured . . . 35 10

1981. Desert Plants. Multicoloured.
1919 20 c. Type **1277** 50 10
1920 20 c. Agave (horiz) 50 10
1921 20 c. Saguaro 50 10
1922 20 c. Beavertail cactus (horiz) 50 10

1281 Flag over Supreme Court **1282** American Bighorn

1981.
1923 **1281** 20 c. black, red & blue . 35 10

1982.
1926 **1282** 20 c. blue 40 10

1283 Franklin D. Roosevelt

1982. Birth Centenary of President Franklin D. Roosevelt.
1927 **1283** 20 c. blue 30 10

1284 Flowers spelling "Love" **1285** George Washington

1982. Greetings Stamp.
1928 **1284** 20 c. multicoloured . . . 30 10

1982. 250th Birth Anniv of George Washington.
1929 **1285** 20 c. multicoloured . . . 30 10

1286 Common Flicker (inscr "Yellow-hammer") and Camellia (Alabama) **1287** Stripes in National Colours

1982. State Birds and Flowers. Multicoloured.
1930 20 c. Type **1286** 65 20
1931 20 c. Willow grouse (inscr "Ptarmigan") and forget-me-not (Alaska) 65 20
1932 20 c. Cactus wren and saguaro cactus blossom (Arizona) . 65 20
1933 20 c. Northern mockingbird and apple blossom (Arkansas) . 65 20
1934 20 c. California quail and California poppy (California) 65 20
1935 20 c. Lark bunting and Rocky Mountain columbine (Colorado) 65 20
1936 20 c. American robin and mountain laurel (Connecticut) 65 20
1937 20 c. Blue hen chicken and peach blossom (Delaware) . 65 20
1938 20 c. Northern mockingbird and orange blossom (Florida) 65 20
1939 20 c. Brown thrasher and Cherokee rose (Georgia) . . 65 20

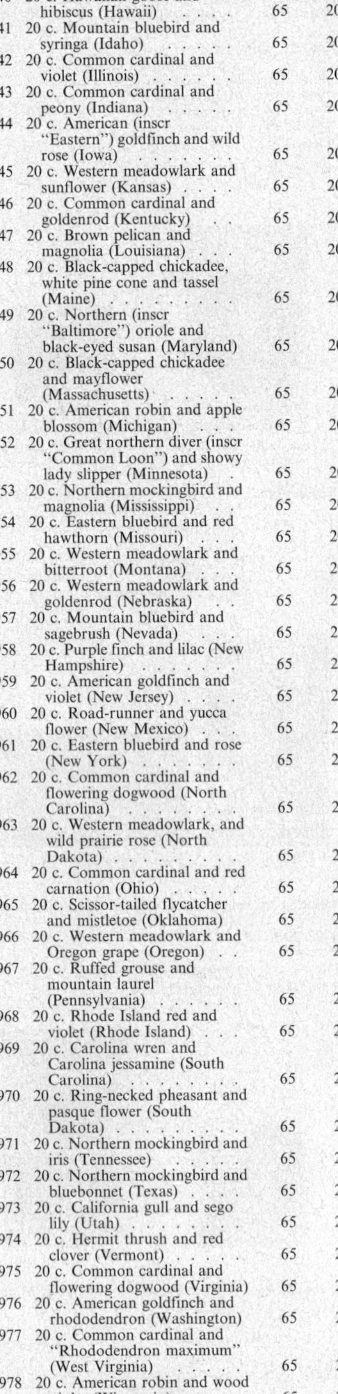

1940 20 c. Hawaiian goose and hibiscus (Hawaii) 65 20
1941 20 c. Mountain bluebird and syringa (Idaho) 65 20
1942 20 c. Common cardinal and violet (Illinois) 65 20
1943 20 c. Common cardinal and peony (Indiana) 65 20
1944 20 c. American (inscr "Eastern") goldfinch and wild rose (Iowa) 65 20
1945 20 c. Western meadowlark and sunflower (Kansas) 65 20
1946 20 c. Common cardinal and goldenrod (Kentucky) . . 65 20
1947 20 c. Brown pelican and magnolia (Louisiana) . . . 65 20
1948 20 c. Black-capped chickadee, white pine cone and tassel (Maine) 65 20
1949 20 c. Northern (inscr "Baltimore") oriole and black-eyed susan (Maryland) 65 20
1950 20 c. Black-capped chickadee and mayflower (Massachusetts) 65 20
1951 20 c. American robin and apple blossom (Michigan) . . . 65 20
1952 20 c. Great northern diver (inscr "Common Loon") and showy lady slipper (Minnesota) . . 65 20
1953 20 c. Northern mockingbird and magnolia (Mississippi) . . 65 20
1954 20 c. Eastern bluebird and red hawthorn (Missouri) . . . 65 20
1955 20 c. Western meadowlark and bitterroot (Montana) . . . 65 20
1956 20 c. Western meadowlark and goldenrod (Nebraska) . . 65 20
1957 20 c. Mountain bluebird and sagebrush (Nevada) . . . 65 20
1958 20 c. Purple finch and lilac (New Hampshire) 65 20
1959 20 c. American goldfinch and violet (New Jersey) 65 20
1960 20 c. Road-runner and yucca flower (New Mexico) . . . 65 20
1961 20 c. Eastern bluebird and rose (New York) 65 20
1962 20 c. Common cardinal and flowering dogwood (North Carolina) 65 20
1963 20 c. Western meadowlark, and wild prairie rose (North Dakota) 65 20
1964 20 c. Common cardinal and red carnation (Ohio) 65 20
1965 20 c. Scissor-tailed flycatcher and mistletoe (Oklahoma) 65 20
1966 20 c. Western meadowlark and Oregon grape (Oregon) . . 65 20
1967 20 c. Ruffed grouse and mountain laurel (Pennsylvania) 65 20
1968 20 c. Rhode Island red and violet (Rhode Island) . . . 65 20
1969 20 c. Carolina wren and Carolina jessamine (South Carolina) 65 20
1970 20 c. Ring-necked pheasant and pasque flower (South Dakota) 65 20
1971 20 c. Northern mockingbird and iris (Tennessee) 65 20
1972 20 c. Northern mockingbird and bluebonnet (Texas) 65 20
1973 20 c. California gull and sego lily (Utah) 65 20
1974 20 c. Hermit thrush and red clover (Vermont) 65 20
1975 20 c. Common cardinal and flowering dogwood (Virginia) 65 20
1976 20 c. American goldfinch and rhododendron (Washington) 65 20
1977 20 c. Common cardinal and "Rhododendron maximum" (West Virginia) 65 20
1978 20 c. American robin and wood violet (Wisconsin) 65 20
1979 20 c. Western meadowlark and Indian paint bush (Wyoming) 65 20

1982. Bicentenary of U.S.A.–Netherlands Diplomatic Relations.
1980 **1287** 20 c. red, blue & black . 30 10

1288 Library of Congress **1289** Garment Tag

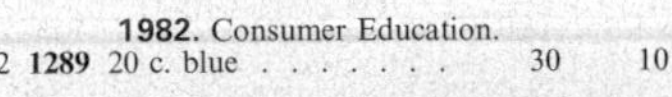

1982. Library of Congress.
1981 **1288** 20 c. black and red . . 30 10

1982. Consumer Education.
1982 **1289** 20 c. blue 30 10

1290 Solar Energy **1294** Frontispiece from "Ragged Dick"

1982. Knoxville World's Fair.
1983 **1290** 20 c. multicoloured . . 40 10
1984 – 20 c. multicoloured . . 40 10
1985 – 20 c. blue, light blue and black 40 10
1986 – 20 c. blue, black and brown 40 10
DESIGNS: No. 1984, Synthetic fuels; 1985, Breeder reactor; 1986, Fossil fuels.

1982. 150th Birth Anniv of Horatio Alger (novelist).
1987 **1294** 20 c. black and red on buff 30 10

1295 Family Group **1296** John, Ethel and Lionel Barrymore

1982. Ageing Together.
1988 **1295** 20 c. red 30 10

1982. Performing Arts and Artists. The Barrymores (theatrical family).
1989 **1296** 20 c. multicoloured . . 30 10

1297 Dr. Mary Walker **1298** Maple Leaf and Rose

1982. Dr. Mary Walker (army surgeon) Commemoration.
1990 **1297** 20 c. multicoloured . . 30 10

1982. 50th Anniv of International Peace Garden (on U.S.A.–Canada border).
1991 **1298** 20 c. multicoloured . . 30 10

1299 Typographic Design **1300** Jackie Robinson

1982. America's Libraries.
1992 **1299** 20 c. red and black . . 30 10

1982. Black Heritage, Jackie Robinson (baseball player).
1993 **1300** 20 c. multicoloured . . 95 10

1301 Touro Synagogue

1982. Touro Synagogue, Newport, Rhode Island.
1994 **1301** 20 c. multicoloured . . 40 10

1302 Open Air Theatre

1982. Wolf Trap Farm Park, Vienna, Virginia.
1995 **1302** 20 c. multicoloured . . 35 10

1303 Fallingwater, Mill Run, Pennsylvania (Frank Lloyd Wright)

1982. American Architecture.
1996 **1303** 20 c. black & brown . 50 10
1997 – 20 c. black & brown . 50 10
1998 – 20 c. black & brown . 50 10
1999 – 20 c. black & brown . 50 10
DESIGNS: No. 1997, Illinois Institute of Technology, Chicago (Mies van der Rohe); 1998, Gropius House, Lincoln, Massachusetts (Walter Gropius); 1999, Dulles Airport, Washington D.C. (Eero Saarinen).

1307 St. Francis and Doves

1982. 800th Birth Anniv of St. Francis of Assisi.
2000 **1307** 20 c. multicoloured . . 30 10

1308 Ponce de Leon and Map of Florida **1309** "Madonna and Child" (Tiepolo)

1982. Ponce de Leon (explorer) Commemoration.
2001 **1308** 20 c. multicoloured . . 30 10

1982. Christmas. Multicoloured.
2002 20 c. Type **1309** 25 10
2003 20 c. Building a snowman (horiz) 35 10
2004 20 c. Sledging (horiz) . . . 35 10
2005 20 c. Decorating a Christmas tree (horiz) 35 10
2006 20 c. Skating (horiz) 35 10

1314 Puppy and Kitten **1316** Industrial Complex

1982.
2007 **1314** 13 c. multicoloured . . 20 10

1983. Science and Industry.
2015 **1316** 20 c. multicoloured . . 30 10

1317 Benjamin Franklin and Great Seal of Sweden

1983. Bicentenary of Sweden–U.S.A. Treaty of Amity and Commerce.
2016 **1317** 20 c. indigo, brown and black 30 10

1319/1320 Hot Air Ballooning

1983. Bicentenary of Manned Flight. Mult.
2017 20 c. "Intrepid", 1861 (vert) 35 10
2018 20 c. Type **1319** 35 10
2019 20 c. Type **1320** 35 10
2020 20 c. "Explorer II", 1935 (vert) 35 10

1322 C.C.C. Workers repairing Trail

1983. 50th Anniv of Civilian Conservation Corps.
2021 **1322** 20 c. multicoloured . . . 30 10

1323 Shot Putting **1327** Joseph Priestley (after G. Stuart)

1983. Air. Olympic Games, Los Angeles (1984) (1st issue). Multicoloured.
A2022 40 c. Type **1323** 60 25
A2023 40 c. Gymnastics 60 25
A2024 40 c. Swimming 60 25
A2025 40 c. Weightlifting 60 25
See also Nos. A2034/7, 2040/3, A2058/61 and 2079/82.

1983. 250th Birth Anniv of Joseph Priestley (discoverer of oxygen).
2026 **1327** 20 c. multicoloured . . . 30 10

1328 Reaching Hands

1983. Voluntary Work.
2027 **1328** 20 c. black and red . . . 30 10

1329 "Concord"

1983. 300th Anniv of First German Settlers in America.
2028 **1329** 20 c. brown 40 10

1330 Joggers and Electrocardiograph Trace

1983. Physical Fitness.
2029 **1330** 20 c. multicoloured . . . 30 10

1331 Brooklyn Bridge

1983. Centenary of Brooklyn Bridge.
2030 **1331** 20 c. blue 40 10

1332 Norris Hydro-electric Dam

1983. 50th Anniv of Tennessee Valley Authority.
2031 **1332** 20 c. multicoloured . . . 30 10

1333 Army, Air Force and Navy Medals of Honour **1334** Scott Joplin

1983. Medal of Honour.
2032 **1333** 20 c. multicoloured . . . 30 10

1983. Black Heritage. Scott Joplin (ragtime composer).
2033 **1334** 20 c. multicoloured . . . 35 10

1335 Gymnastics **1339** Babe Ruth

1983. Air. Olympic Games, Los Angeles (1984) (2nd issue). Multicoloured.
A2034 28 c. Type **1335** 60 15
A2035 28 c. Hurdling 60 15
A2036 28 c. Basketball 60 15
A2037 28 c. Football 60 15

1983. American Sports Personalities. Babe Ruth (baseball player).
2038 **1339** 20 c. blue . . . . 1·00 10

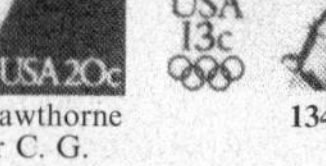

1340 Hawthorne (after C. G. Thompson) **1341** Discus

1983. Literary Arts. Nathaniel Hawthorne (writer).
2039 **1340** 20 c. multicoloured . . 30 10

1983. Olympic Games, Los Angeles (1984) (3rd issue). Multicoloured.
2040 13 c. Type **1341** 25 10
2041 13 c. High jump 25 10
2042 13 c. Archery 25 10
2043 13 c. Boxing 25 10

1345 American Bald Eagle and Moon

1983.
2044 **1345** $9.35 multicoloured . . 17·00 7·00

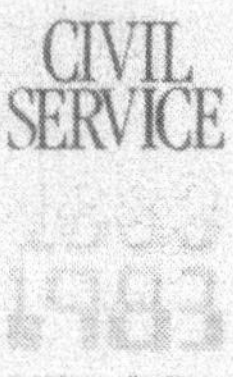

1346 Signing the Treaty of Paris (after Benjamin West) **1347** Text in Early and Modern Type

1983. Bicentenary of Treaty of Paris.
2045 **1346** 20 c. multicoloured . . 35 10

1983. Centenary of Civil Service.
2046 **1347** 20 c. stone, red & black 30 10

1348 Part of Proscenium and Modern Facade

1983. Centenary of Metropolitan Opera, New York.
2047 **1348** 20 c. yellow & purple . 40 10

1349 Charles Steinmetz and Graph

1983. American Inventors.
2048 **1349** 20 c. pink and black . . 35 10
2049 – 20 c. pink and black . . 35 10
2050 – 20 c. pink and black . . 35 10
2051 – 20 c. pink and black . . 35 10
DESIGNS: No. 2049, Edwin Armstrong and frequency modulator; 2050, Nikola Tesla and induction motor; 2051, Philo T. Farnsworth and television camera.

1353 "John Mason" Streetcar, New York, 1832

1983. Streetcars. Multicoloured.
2052 20 c. Type **1353** 45 15
2053 20 c. Early electric streetcar, Montgomery, 1886 . . . . 45 15
2054 20 c. "Bobtail" horsecar, Sulphur Rock, 1926 . . . 45 15
2055 20 c. St. Charles Streetcar, New Orleans, 1923 . . . . . . 45 15

1357 "Madonna and Child" (Raphael)
1358 Santa Claus

1983. Christmas.
2056 **1357** 20 c. multicoloured . . 25 10
2057 **1358** 20 c. multicoloured . . 25 10

1359 Fencing

1983. Air. Olympic Games, Los Angeles (1984) (4th issue). Multicoloured.
A2058 35 c. Type **1359** 60 20
A2059 35 c. Cycling 60 20
A2060 35 c. Volleyball 60 20
A2061 35 c. Pole vault 60 20

1363 Martin Luther
1364 Reindeer and Pipeline

1983. 500th Birth Anniv of Martin Luther.
2062 **1363** 20 c. multicoloured . . 30 10

1984. 25th Anniv of Alaska Statehood.
2063 **1364** 20 c. multicoloured . . 30 10

1365 Ice Dancing
1369 Column and "$" Sign

1984. Winter Olympic Games, Sarajevo. Mult.
2064 20 c. Type **1365** 50 10
2065 20 c. Downhill skiing 50 10
2066 20 c. Cross-country skiing . . 50 10
2067 20 c. Ice hockey 50 10

1984. 50th Anniv of Federal Deposit Insurance Corporation.
2068 **1369** 20 c. multicoloured . . 30 10

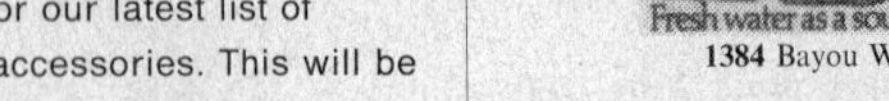

1370 "Love"
1371 Carter G. Woodson

1984. Greetings Stamp.
2069 **1370** 20 c. multicoloured . . 30 10

1984. Black Heritage. Carter G. Woodson (historian).
2070 **1371** 20 c. multicoloured . . 30 10

1372 Hand holding Plant
1373 Coin and "$" Sign

1984. 50th Anniv of Soil and Water Conservation Movement.
2071 **1372** 20 c. multicoloured . . 30 10

1984. 50th Anniv of Credit Union Act.
2072 **1373** 20 c. multicoloured . . 30 10

1374 Wild Pink

1984. Orchids. Multicoloured.
2073 20 c. Type **1374** 50 10
2074 20 c. Yellow lady's slipper . . 50 10
2075 20 c. Spreading pogonia . . 50 10
2076 20 c. Pacific calypso 50 10

1378 Eastern Polynesian Canoe and American Golden Plover

1984. 25th Anniv of Hawaii Statehood.
2077 **1378** 20 c. multicoloured . . 50 10

1379 Silhouettes of Lincoln and Washington
1380 Diving

1984. 50th Anniv of National Archives.
2078 **1379** 20 c. black, ol & red . 30 10

1984. Olympic Games, Los Angeles (5th issue). Multicoloured.
2079 20 c. Type **1380** 35 10
2080 20 c. Long jump 35 10
2081 20 c. Wrestling 35 10
2082 20 c. Canoeing 35 10

1384 Bayou Wildlife

1984. Louisiana World Exposition, New Orleans.
2083 **1384** 20 c. multicoloured . . 40 10

1385 Laboratory Equipment

1984. Health Research.
2084 **1385** 20 c. multicoloured . . . 30 10

1386 Fairbanks in Film Roles
1387 Jim Thorpe

1984. Performing Arts and Artists. Douglas Fairbanks (film actor).
2085 **1386** 20 c. multicoloured . . . 40 10

1984. American Sports Personalities. Jim Thorpe (athlete, footballer and baseball player).
2086 **1387** 20 c. brown 40 10

1388 John McCormack
1389 St. Lawrence Seaway

1984. Performing Arts and Artists. John McCormack (singer).
2087 **1388** 20 c. multicoloured . . . 50 10

1984. 25th Anniv of St. Lawrence Seaway.
2088 **1389** 20 c. multicoloured . . . 30 10

1390 "Mallards dropping In" (Jay Norwood Darling)

1984. 50th Anniv of Migratory Bird Hunting and Conservation Stamp Act.
2089 **1390** 20 c. blue 50 10

1391 "Elizabeth"
1392 Melville (after J. O. Eaton)

1984. Explorers. 400th Anniv of First Raleigh Expedition to Roanoke Island, North Carolina.
2090 **1391** 20 c. multicoloured . . . 40 10

1984. Literary Arts. Herman Melville (novelist).
2091 **1392** 20 c. green 30 10

1393 Horace Moses
1394 Smokey Bear and American Black Bear Cub clinging to burnt Tree

1984. Horace Moses (founder of Junior Achievement (training organization) Commemoration.
2092 **1393** 20 c. orange & black . . 30 10

1984. Smokey Bear (symbol of forest fire prevention campaign).
2093 **1394** 20 c. multicoloured . . . 30 10

1395 Clemente and Flag of Puerto Rico
1396 Beagle and Boston Terrier

1984. American Sports Personalities. Roberto Clemente (baseball player).
2094 **1395** 20 c. multicoloured . . 75 10

1984. Centenary of American Kennel Club. Multicoloured.
2095 20 c. Type **1396** 50 10
2096 20 c. Chesapeake Bay retriever and cocker spaniel . . 50 10
2097 20 c. Alaskan malamute and collie 50 10
2098 20 c. Black and Tan coonhound and American foxhound . 50 10

1400 McGruff (campaign character)
1401 "Family Unity"

1984. National Crime Prevention Month.
2099 **1400** 20 c. multicoloured . . 30 10

1984. National Stamp Collecting Month.
2100 **1401** 20 c. black, red and blue 30 10

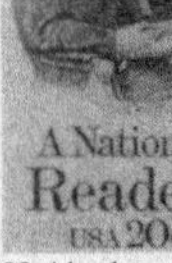

1402 Eleanor Roosevelt
1403 Abraham Lincoln reading to his Son, Tad

1984. Eleanor Roosevelt Commemoration.
2101 **1402** 20 c. blue 30 10

1984. "Nation of Readers".
2102 **1403** 20 c. brown and red . . 30 10

1404 "Madonna and Child (Fra Filippo Lippi)
1406 Uniformed Group and Flag

1984. Christmas.
2103 20 c. Type **1404** 25 10
2104 20 c. Santa Claus 25 10

1984. Hispanic Americans.
2105 **1406** 20 c. multicoloured . . 30 10

1407 Memorial (Maya Ying Lin)

1984. Vietnam Veterans Memorial, Washington, D.C.
2106 **1407** 20 c. black, green and deep green 30 10

1408 Kern

1409 Margaret Mitchell (writer)

1985. Performing Arts and Artists. Birth Centenary of Jerome Kern (composer).
2107 1408 22 c. multicoloured . . 30 10

1985. Great Americans. Without "c" after face value.

2108	1409	1 c. brown	10	10
2109	–	2 c. blue	10	10
2110	–	3 c. blue	10	10
2111	–	4 c. blue	10	10
2112	–	5 c. green	10	10
2113	–	6 c. red	10	10
2114	–	7 c. red	10	10
2115	–	8 c. brown	10	10
2116	–	9 c. green	10	10
2117	–	10 c. red	15	10
2118	–	11 c. blue	15	10
2119	–	14 c. green	20	10
2120	–	14 c. red	20	10
2121	–	15 c. purple	25	10
2122	–	17 c. green	25	10
2123	–	21 c. purple	30	10
2124	–	22 c. blue	30	10
2125	–	23 c. violet	30	10
2126	–	25 c. blue	30	10
2127	–	28 c. green	40	10
2128	–	39 c. mauve	45	10
2129	–	45 c. blue	70	10
2130ab	–	50 c. brown	65	10
2131	–	56 c red	80	10
2132	–	65 c. blue	85	10
2133	–	$1 green	1·40	10
2134	–	$1 blue	1·25	10
2135	–	$2 violet	2·50	10
2136	–	$5 brown	7·25	1·50

DESIGNS: 2 c. Mary Lyon (educator); 3 c. Paul Dudley White (cardiologist); 4 c. Father Flanagan (founder of Boys Town); 5 c. Hugo L. Black (Supreme Court Justice); 6 c. Walter Lippmann (journalist); 7 c. Abraham Baldwin (politician); 8 c. General Henry Knox; 9 c. Sylvanus Thayer (military educator) (after R. Weir); 10 c. Red Cloud (Oglala Sioux chief); 11 c. Alden Partridge (educationist); 14 c. (2119) Sinclair Lewis (writer) (after S. Melik); 14 c. (2120) Julia Ward Howe (author of "Battle Hymn of the Republic") (after J. Elliott); 15 c. Buffalo Bill Cody (showman); 17 c. Belva Ann Lockwood (women's rights campaigner); 21 c. Chester Carlson (inventor of photocopying); 22 c. J. J. Audubon (ornithologist); 23 c. Mary Cassatt (artist); 25 c. Jack London (writer); 28 c. Sitting Bull (Hunkpapa Sioux chief); 39 c. Grenville Clark (peace activist); 45 c. Dr. Harvey Cushing (neurosurgeon); 50 c. Admiral Chester W. Nimitz; 56 c. John Harvard (philanthropist) (after D. C. French); 65 c. Gen. Henry Harley "Hap" Arnold; $1 (2133) Bernard Revel (scholar); $1 (2134) Johns Hopkins (medical pioneer); $2 William Jennings Bryan (politician); $5 Bret Harte (writer).

1985. Non-denominational "D" stamp. As T 1090 but inscribed "Domestic Mail".
2137 (22 c.) green (18 × 21 mm) . . 30 10
2138 (22 c.) green (15 × 18 mm) . . 60 10

1438 Alfred V. Verville

1985. Air. Aviation Pioneers.
A2142 33 c. Type 1438 . . . . . 45 15
A2143 39 c. Lawrence and Elmer Sperry 50 15

1440 Loading Mail into Martin M-130 Flying Boat

1441 Mary McLeod Bethune

1985. Air. 50th Anniv of First Transpacific Airmail Flight.
A2144 1440 44 c. multicoloured . . 55 15

1985. Black Heritage. Mary McLeod Bethune (social activist).
2145 1441 22 c. multicoloured . . 40 10

1442 Lesser Scaup ("Broadbill") Decoy, 1890 (Ben Holmes)

1446 Omnibus, 1880s

1985. American Folk Art. Duck Decoys. Multicoloured.
2146 22 c. Type 1442 . . . . . . 45 10
2147 22 c. Mallard decoy, 1900 (Percy Grant) 45 10
2148 22 c. Canvasback decoy, 1929 (Bob McGraw) 45 10
2149 22 c. Redhead decoy, 1925 (Keyes Chadwick) 45 10

1985. Transport. Without "c" after face value.

2150	1446	1 c. violet	10	10
2151	–	2 c. black	10	10
2152	–	3 c. purple	10	10
2153	–	3.4 c. green	10	10
2154	–	4.9 c. black	10	10
2155	–	5 c. black	10	10
2156	–	5.3 black	10	10
2157	–	5.5 c. red	10	10
2158	–	6 c. brown	10	10
2159	–	7.1 c. red	10	10
2160	–	7.6 c. brown	10	10
2161	–	8.3 c. green	10	10
2162	–	8.4 c. purple	10	10
2163	–	8.5 c. green	10	10
2163a	–	10 c. blue	15	10
2164	–	10.1 c. grey	20	10
2165	–	11 c. black	15	10
2166	–	12 c. blue	15	10
2167	–	12.5 c. green	15	10
2167b	–	13 c. black	15	10
2168	–	13.2 c. green	20	10
2169	–	14 c. blue	20	10
2170	–	15 c. violet	25	10
2170b	–	16.7 c. red	25	10
2171	–	17 c. blue	25	10
2172	–	17.5 c. violet	25	10
2172b	–	20 c. purple	25	10
2172c	–	20.5 c. red	25	10
2172d	–	21 c. green	25	10
2173	–	24.1 c. blue	35	10
2174	–	25 c. brown	35	10

DESIGNS: 2 c. Locomotive, 1870s; 3 c. Conestoga wagon, 1800s; 3.4 c. School bus, 1920s; 4.9 c. Buckboard, 1880s; 5 c. Milk wagon, 1900s; 5.3 c. Lift, 1900s; 5.5 c. Star Route truck, 1910s; 6 c. Tricycle, 1880s; 7.1 c. Tractor, 1920s; 7.6 c. Carreta, 1770s; 8.3 c. "McKean" ambulance, 1860s; 8.4 c. Wheelchair, 1920s; 8.5 c. Tow truck, 1920s; 10 c. Canal barge, 1880s; 10.1 c. Oil wagon, 1890s; 11 c. Stutz "Bearcat", 1933; 12 c. Stanley "Steamer", 1909; 12.5 c. Pushcart, 1880s; 13 c. Police patrol wagon, 1880s; 13.2 c. Coal wagon, 1870s; 14 c. Iceboat, 1880s; 15 c. Tug, 1900s; 16.7 c. Popcorn wagon, 1902; 17 c. Dog sledge, 1920s; 17.5 c. Marmon "Wasp", 1911; 20 c. Cable car, 1880s; 20.5 c. Ahrens-Fox fire engine, 1900s; 21 c. Railway mail van, 1920s; 24.1 c. Pope tandem, 1890s; 25 c. Bread wagon, 1880s.

The 5.3, 7.6, 8.4, 13, 13.2, 16.7, 21 and 24.1 c. were only issued with precancelled inscription of the type of service in red and the 20.5 c. in black. Prices in the unused column are for stamps with full gum.

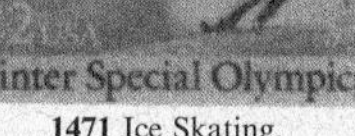
1471 Ice Skating, Skiing and Emblem

1472 Flag over Capitol, Washington

1985. Winter Special Olympic Games, Park City, Utah.
2175 1471 22 c. multicoloured . . 40 10

1985.
2176 1472 22 c. black, red and blue 30 10
2178 – 22 c. black, red and blue 40 10
DESIGNS—40 × 22 mm: No. 2178, Flag over Capitol, Washington, and inscription "Of the People By the People For the People".

1474 Frilled Dogwinkle

1479 Coloured Lines and "Love"

1985. Sea Shells.
2179 1474 22 c. red and black . . 55 10
2180 – 22 c. red, purple and black 55 10
2181 – 22 c. red and black . . 55 10
2182 – 22 c. purple and black . . 55 10
2183 – 22 c. red, purple and black 55 10
DESIGNS: No. 2180, Reticulated helmet; 2181, New England neptune; 2182, Calico scallop; 2183, Lightning whelk.

1985. Greetings Stamp.
2184 1479 22 c. multicoloured . . . 35 10

1480 American Bald Eagle and Moon

1985.
2185 1480 $10.75 multicoloured . . 15·00 12·00

1481 Electricity Pole and Rural Landscape

1985. 50th Anniv of Rural Electrification Administration.
2186 1481 22 c. multicoloured . . . 40 10

1482 1 c. Franklin Stamp, 1870

1483 Abigail Adams

1985. "Ameripex 86" International Stamp Exhibition, Chicago.
2187 1482 22 c. multicoloured . . . 40 10

1985. Abigail Adams (wife of Pres. John Adams and writer) Commemoration.
2188 1483 22 c. multicoloured . . . 35 10

1484 Bartholdi (after J. Frappa) and Statue of Liberty)

1985. Frederic Auguste Bartholdi (sculptor of Statue of Liberty) Commemoration.
2189 1484 22 c. multicoloured . . . 35 10

1485 Troops in Mountain Pass

1985. Korean War Veterans.
2190 1485 22 c. green and red . . . 55 10

1486 Disabled and Needy People

1985. 50th Anniv of Social Security Act.
2191 1486 22 c. blue and deep blue 55 10

1487 Junipero Serra and Mission San Gabriel

1985. Air. Death Bicentenary (1984) of Father Junipero Serra (missionary).
A2192 1487 44 c. multicoloured . . 75 20

1488 "Battle of the Marne" (Harvey Dunn)

1985. World War I Veterans.
2193 1488 22 c. green and red . . 50 10

1489 Quarter Horse

1493 Alphabet, Spectacles, Quill and Apple

1985. Horses. Multicoloured.
2194 22 c. Type 1489 . . . . . . 70 10
2195 22 c. Morgan horse 70 10
2196 22 c. Saddlebred horse . . . 70 10
2197 22 c. Appaloosa 70 10

1985. Public Education.
2198 1493 22 c. multicoloured . . 35 10

1494 Y.M.C.A. Youth Camping (centenary)

1985. International Youth Year. Multicoloured.
2199 22 c. Type 1494 . . . . . . 40 10
2200 22 c. Boy Scouts of America (75th anniv) 40 10
2201 22 c. Big Brothers and Big Sisters 40 10
2202 22 c. Camp Fire Inc. (75th anniv) 40 10

1498 Hungry Faces

1499 Envelopes

1985. "Help End Hunger".
2203 1498 22 c. multicoloured . . 35 10

1985.
2204 1499 21.1 c. multicoloured . 50 10
No. 2204 exists both with and without precancel "ZIP+4".

1500 "Genoa Madonna" (Luca della Robbia)

1502 George Washington (after Stuart) and Washington Monument

1985. Christmas.
2205 1500 22 c. multicoloured . . 35 10
2206 – 22 c. red, green and black 35 10
DESIGN—HORIZ: No. 2206, Poinsettias.

1985.
2207 1502 18 c. multicoloured . . 35 10
No. 2207 exist both with and without precancel "PRESORTED FIRST-CLASS".

1503 Old State House, Little Rock

1986. 150th Anniv of Arkansas State.
2208 1503 22 c. multicoloured . . 40 10

1504 Sheet of Stamps, Handstamp and Magnifying Glass

1508 Puppy

1986. "Ameripex 86" International Stamp Exhibition, Chicago. Stamp Collecting. Multicoloured.
2209 22 c. Type **1504** 55 10
2210 22 c. Boy holding stamp in tweezers 55 10
2211 22 c. Mounted stamps and 3 c. U.S. stamp under glass 55 10
2212 22 c. "Ameripex" miniature sheet on cover and handstamp 55 10

1986. Greetings Stamp.
2213 **1508** 22 c. multicoloured 40 10

1509 Sojourner Truth
1510 Texan Flag and Santa Anna's Spur

1986. Black Heritage. Sojourner Truth (human rights activist).
2214 **1509** 22 c. multicoloured 40 10

1986. 150th Anniv of Battle of San Jacinto.
2215 **1510** 22 c. red, blue & black 40 10

1511 Muskellunge

1986. Fishes. Multicoloured.
2216 22 c. Type **1511** 60 10
2217 22 c. Atlantic cod 60 10
2218 22 c. Largemouth bass 60 10
2219 22 c. Bluefin tuna 60 10
2220 22 c. Catfish 60 10

1516 Modern Hospital
1517 Ellington

1986. Public Hospitals. 250th Anniv of Bellevue Hospital Centre, New York.
2221 **1516** 22 c. multicoloured 40 10

1986. Performing Arts and Artists. Duke Ellington (jazz musician).
2222 **1517** 22 c. multicoloured 40 10

1519 Elisha Kent Kane and Polar Brig "Advance"
1523 Head of Statue

1986. Polar Explorers. Multicoloured.
2224 22 c. Type **1519** 60 10
2225 22 c. Adolphus W. Greely 60 10
2226 22 c. Vilhjalmur Stefansson 60 10
2227 22 c. Robert E. Peary and Matthew Henson 60 10

1986. Centenary of Statue of Liberty.
2228 **1523** 22 c. blue and red 40 10

1524 Blanket Designs **1525**

1526 Blanket Designs **1527**

1986. American Folk Art. Navajo Blankets.
2229 **1524** 22 c. multicoloured 40 10
2230 **1525** 22 c. multicoloured 40 10
2231 **1526** 22 c. multicoloured 40 10
2232 **1527** 22 c. multicoloured 40 10

1528 T. S. Eliot
1529 Highlander Figure (tobacconist)

1986. Literary Arts. Thomas Stearns Eliot (poet).
2233 **1528** 22 c. red 35 10

1986. American Folk Art. Carved Wooden Figures. Multicoloured.
2234 22 c. Type **1529** 45 10
2235 22 c. Ship's figurehead 45 10
2236 22 c. Nautical figure (nautical instrument maker) 45 10
2237 22 c. Indian (cigar store) 45 10

1533 "Madonna" (Il Perugino)
1535 White Pine and Lake Huron

1986. Christmas. Multicoloured.
2238 22 c. Type **1533** 35 10
2239 22 c. Winter village 35 10

1987. 150th Anniv of Michigan Statehood.
2240 **1535** 22 c. multicoloured 35 10

1536 Stylized Runner
1537 Heart

1986. 10th Pan-American Games, Indianapolis.
2241 **1536** 22 c. multicoloured 35 10

1987. Greetings Stamp.
2242 **1537** 22 c. multicoloured 30 10

1538 Du Sable
1539 Caruso as Duke of Mantua in "Rigoletto"

1987. Black Heritage. Jean Baptiste Pointe du Sable (founder of Chicago).
2243 **1538** 22 c. multicoloured 30 10

1987. Performing Arts and Artists. Enrico Caruso (operatic tenor).
2244 **1539** 22 c. multicoloured 40 10

1540 Badges

1987 75th Anniv of Girl Scouts of America.
2245 **1540** 22 c. multicoloured 30 10

1541 "Congratulations!"

1987. Greetings Stamps. Multicoloured.
2246 22 c. Type **1541** 50 10
2247 22 c. "Get Well!" (18 × 33 mm) 50 10
2248 22 c. "Thank You!" (18 × 33 mm) 50 10
2249 22 c. "Love You, Dad!" 50 10
2250 22 c. "Best Wishes!" (18 × 21 mm) 50 10
2251 22 c. "Happy Birthday!" (18 × 21 mm) 50 10
2252 22 c. "Love You, Mother!" 50 10
2253 22 c. "Keep in Touch!" (18 × 21 mm) 50 10

1549 Ethnic Faces
1550 Flag and Fireworks

1987. Centenary of United Way Volunteer Organization.
2254 **1549** 22 c. multicoloured 30 10

1987.
2255 **1550** 22 c. multicoloured 30 10

1551 Barn Swallows
1552 State Seal

1987. "Capex '87" International Stamp Exhibition, Toronto. North American Wildlife. Multicoloured.
2256 22 c. Type **1551** 55 10
2257 22 c. Monarch butterflies on field thistle 45 10
2258 22 c. Bighorn sheep 45 10
2259 22 c. Broad-tailed hummingbird on Colorado columbine 55 10
2260 22 c. Rabbit and red clover 45 10
2261 22 c. Osprey 55 10
2262 22 c. Mountain lion 45 10
2263 22 c. Luna moth on trumpet honeysuckle 45 10
2264 22 c. Mule deer 45 10
2265 22 c. Grey squirrel on red oak 45 10
2266 22 c. Armadillo and Texas prickly pear 45 10
2267 22 c. Eastern chipmunk and European white birch 45 10
2268 22 c. Moose 45 10
2269 22 c. Black bear 45 10
2270 22 c. Tiger swallowtail butterflies on orange milkweed 45 10
2271 22 c. Bobwhite and purple coneflower 55 10
2272 22 c. Ringtail and Cape marigold 45 10
2273 22 c. Red-winged blackbird on common cattail 55 10
2274 22 c. American lobster 45 10
2275 22 c. Black-tailed hare and beavertail 45 10
2276 22 c. Scarlet tanager and American basswood 55 10
2277 22 c. Woodchuck and dandelion 45 10
2278 22 c. Roseate spoonbill and red mangrove 55 10
2279 22 c. American bald eagle 55 10
2280 22 c. Alaskan brown bear 45 10
2281 22 c. Iiwi on "Ohia lehua" 55 10
2282 22 c. Badger 45 10
2283 22 c. Pronghorns 45 10
2284 22 c. River otter 45 10
2285 22 c. Ladybird on rose 45 10
2286 22 c. Beaver, maple and quaking aspen 45 10
2287 22 c. White-tailed deer 45 10
2288 22 c. Blue jays on Table Mountain pine 55 10
2289 22 c. Pikas 45 10
2290 22 c. Bison 45 10
2291 22 c. Snowy egret 55 10
2292 22 c. Grey wolf 45 10
2293 22 c. Mountain goat 45 10
2294 22 c. Deer mouse 45 10
2295 22 c. Black-tailed prairie dog 45 10
2296 22 c. Box turtle and Virginia creeper 45 10
2297 22 c. Wolverine 45 10
2298 22 c. American elk 45 10
2299 22 c. California sea-lion 45 10
2300 22 c. Northern mockingbird on royal poinciana 55 10
2301 22 c. Racoon 45 10
2302 22 c. Bobcat 45 10
2303 22 c. Black-footed ferret 45 10
2304 22 c. Canada goose 55 10
2305 22 c. Red fox and red maple 45 10

1987. Bicentenary of Delaware Statehood.
2306 **1552** 22 c. multicoloured 30 10

1553 Arabesque from Door, Dar Batha Palace, Fez
1554 Faulkner (after M. L. Goldsborough)

1987. Bicentenary of Diplomatic Relations with Morocco.
2307 **1553** 22 c. red and black 30 10

1987. Literary Arts. 25th Death Anniv of William Faulkner (novelist).
2308 **1554** 22 c. green 30 10

1555 Squash Blossoms (Ruth Maxwell)

1556 Floral Design (Mary McPeek)

1557 Floral Design (Leslie Saari)

1558 Dogwood Blossoms (Trenna Ruffner)

1987. American Folk Art. Lacemaking.
2309 **1555** 22 c. white, blue and ultramarine 40 10
2310 **1556** 22 c. white, blue and ultramarine 40 10
2311 **1557** 22 c. white, blue and ultramarine 40 10
2312 **1558** 22 c. white, blue and ultramarine 40 10

1559 Independence Hall

1987. Bicentenary of Pennsylvania Statehood.
2313 **1559** 22 c. multicoloured 30 10

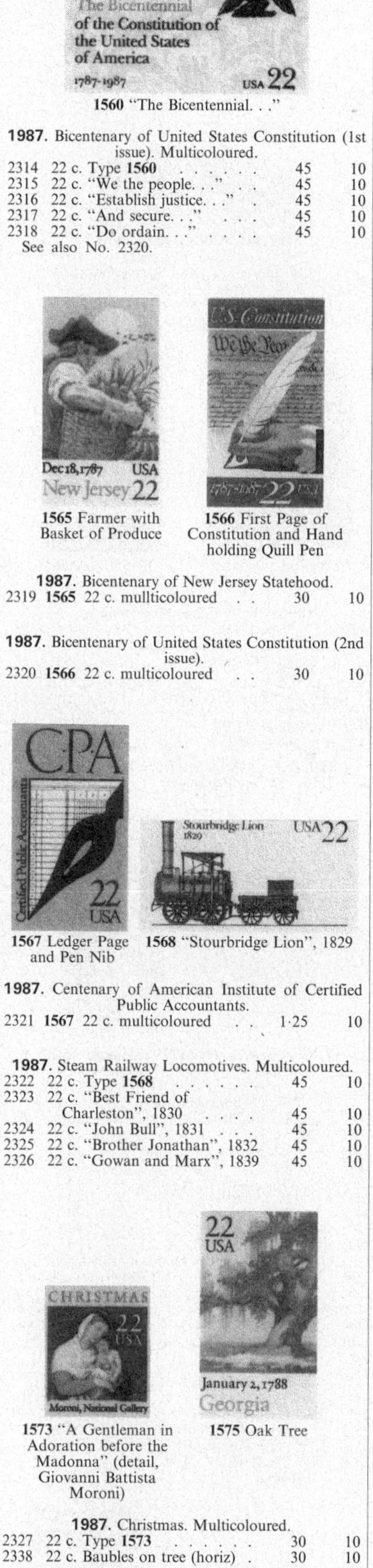

1560 "The Bicentennial. . ."

1987. Bicentenary of United States Constitution (1st issue). Multicoloured.

2314 22 c. Type **1560** 45 10
2315 22 c. "We the people. . ." . . 45 10
2316 22 c. "Establish justice. . ." . 45 10
2317 22 c. "And secure. . ." . . . 45 10
2318 22 c. "Do ordain. . ." 45 10
See also No. 2320.

1565 Farmer with Basket of Produce
1566 First Page of Constitution and Hand holding Quill Pen

1987. Bicentenary of New Jersey Statehood.
2319 **1565** 22 c. mullticoloured . . 30 10

1987. Bicentenary of United States Constitution (2nd issue).
2320 **1566** 22 c. multicoloured . . 30 10

1567 Ledger Page and Pen Nib
1568 "Stourbridge Lion", 1829

1987. Centenary of American Institute of Certified Public Accountants.
2321 **1567** 22 c. multicoloured . . 1·25 10

1987. Steam Railway Locomotives. Multicoloured.
2322 22 c. Type **1568** 45 10
2323 22 c. "Best Friend of Charleston", 1830 . . . . 45 10
2324 22 c. "John Bull", 1831 . . . 45 10
2325 22 c. "Brother Jonathan", 1832 45 10
2326 22 c. "Gowan and Marx", 1839 45 10

1573 "A Gentleman in Adoration before the Madonna" (detail, Giovanni Battista Moroni)
1575 Oak Tree

1987. Christmas. Multicoloured.
2327 22 c. Type **1573** 30 10
2338 22 c. Baubles on tree (horiz) . 30 10

1988. Bicentenary of Georgia Statehood.
2329 **1575** 22 c. multicoloured . . 30 10

1576 "Charles W. Morgan" and Mystic Town
1577 Slalom

1988. Bicentenary of Connecticut Statehood.
2330 **1576** 22 c. multicoloured . . 30 10

1988. Winter Olympic Games, Calgary.
2331 **1577** 22 c. multicoloured . . 30 10

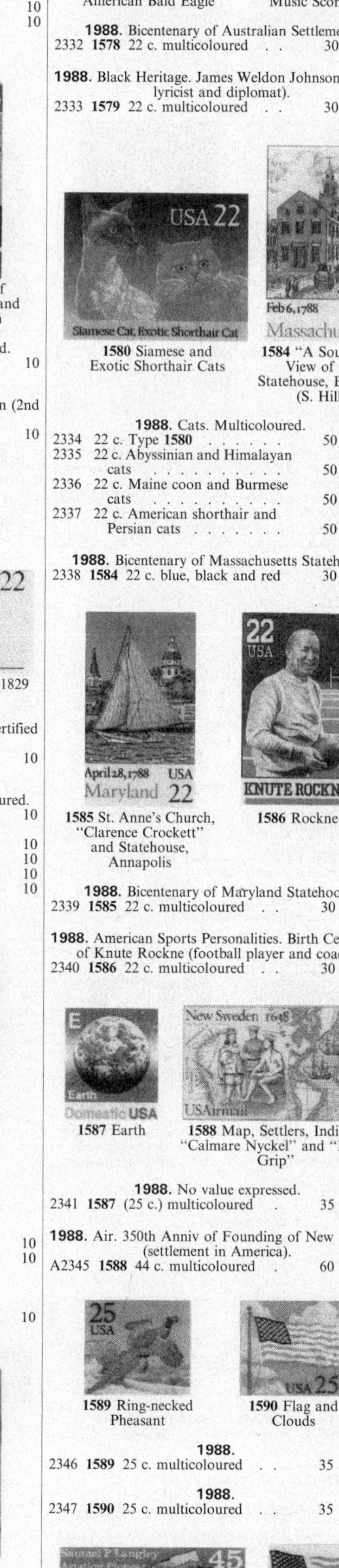

1578 Koala and American Bald Eagle
1579 Johnson and Music Score

1988. Bicentenary of Australian Settlement.
2332 **1578** 22 c. multicoloured . . 30 10

1988. Black Heritage. James Weldon Johnson (writer, lyricist and diplomat).
2333 **1579** 22 c. multicoloured . . 30 10

1580 Siamese and Exotic Shorthair Cats
1584 "A Southwest View of the Statehouse, Boston" (S. Hill)

1988. Cats. Multicoloured.
2334 22 c. Type **1580** 50 10
2335 22 c. Abyssinian and Himalayan cats 50 10
2336 22 c. Maine coon and Burmese cats 50 10
2337 22 c. American shorthair and Persian cats 50 10

1988. Bicentenary of Massachusetts Statehood.
2338 **1584** 22 c. blue, black and red 30 10

1585 St. Anne's Church, "Clarence Crockett" and Statehouse, Annapolis
1586 Rockne

1988. Bicentenary of Maryland Statehood.
2339 **1585** 22 c. multicoloured . . 30 10

1988. American Sports Personalities. Birth Centenary of Knute Rockne (football player and coach).
2340 **1586** 22 c. multicoloured . . 30 10

1587 Earth
1588 Map, Settlers, Indians, "Calmare Nyckel" and "Fagel Grip"

1988. No value expressed.
2341 **1587** (25 c.) multicoloured . 35 10

1988. Air. 350th Anniv of Founding of New Sweden (settlement in America).
A2345 **1588** 44 c. multicoloured . 60 20

1589 Ring-necked Pheasant
1590 Flag and Clouds

1988.
2346 **1589** 25 c. multicoloured . . 35 10

1988.
2347 **1590** 25 c. multicoloured . . 35 10

1591 "Aerodrome No.5" and Langley
1593 Flag over Half Dome, Yosemite National Park

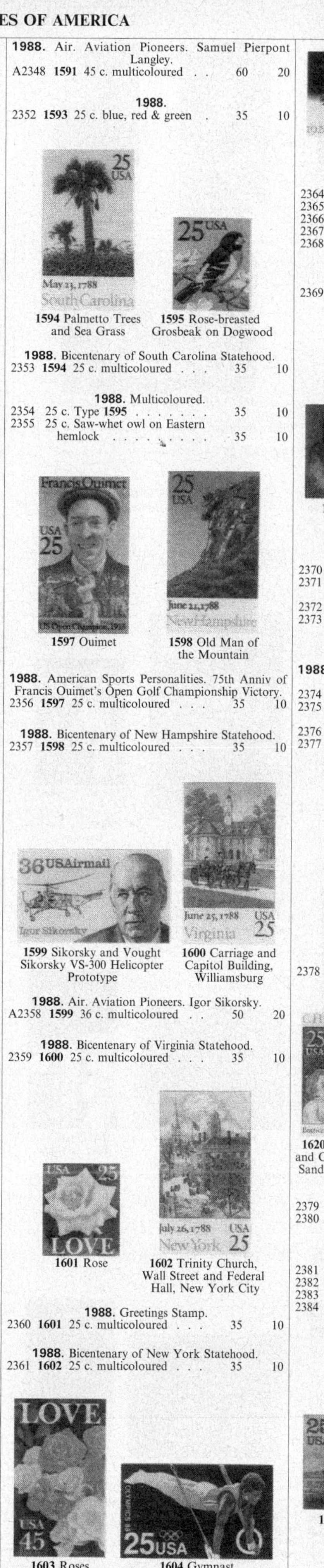

1988. Air. Aviation Pioneers. Samuel Pierpont Langley.
A2348 **1591** 45 c. multicoloured . . 60 20

1988.
2352 **1593** 25 c. blue, red & green . 35 10

1594 Palmetto Trees and Sea Grass
1595 Rose-breasted Grosbeak on Dogwood

1988. Bicentenary of South Carolina Statehood.
2353 **1594** 25 c. multicoloured . . . 35 10

1988. Multicoloured.
2354 25 c. Type **1595** 35 10
2355 25 c. Saw-whet owl on Eastern hemlock 35 10

1597 Ouimet
1598 Old Man of the Mountain

1988. American Sports Personalities. 75th Anniv of Francis Ouimet's Open Golf Championship Victory.
2356 **1597** 25 c. multicoloured . . . 35 10

1988. Bicentenary of New Hampshire Statehood.
2357 **1598** 25 c. multicoloured . . . 35 10

1599 Sikorsky and Vought Sikorsky VS-300 Helicopter Prototype
1600 Carriage and Capitol Building, Williamsburg

1988. Air. Aviation Pioneers. Igor Sikorsky.
A2358 **1599** 36 c. multicoloured . . 50 20

1988. Bicentenary of Virginia Statehood.
2359 **1600** 25 c. multicoloured . . . 35 10

1601 Rose
1602 Trinity Church, Wall Street and Federal Hall, New York City

1988. Greetings Stamp.
2360 **1601** 25 c. multicoloured . . . 35 10

1988. Bicentenary of New York Statehood.
2361 **1602** 25 c. multicoloured . . . 35 10

1603 Roses
1604 Gymnast

1988. Greetings Stamp.
2362 **1603** 45 c. multicoloured . . . 60 20

1988. Olympic Games, Seoul.
2363 **1604** 25 c. multicoloured . . . 35 10

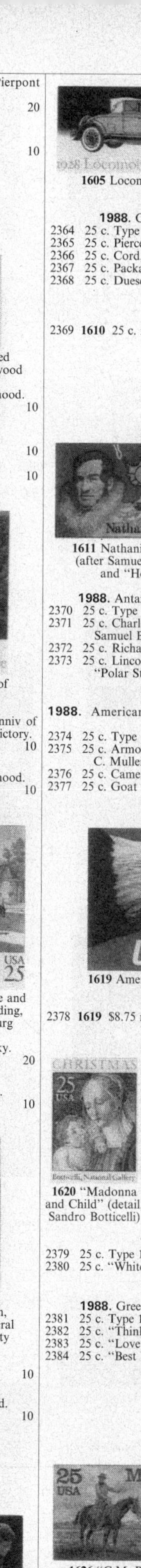
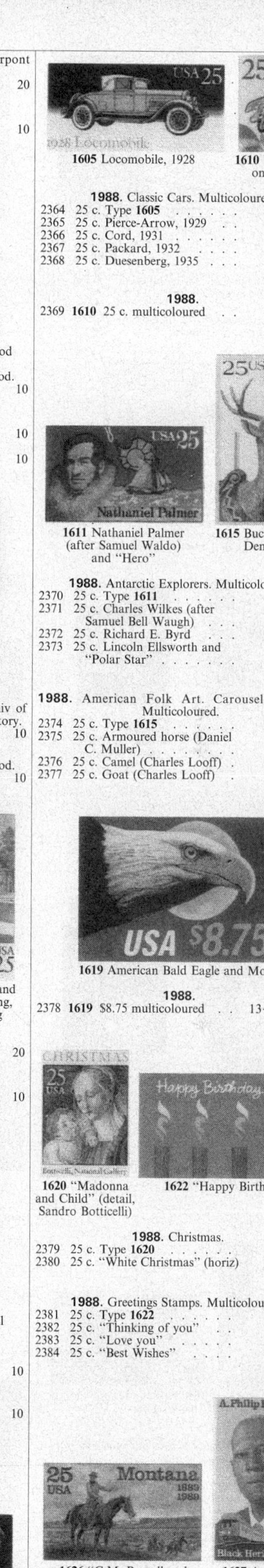

1605 Locomobile, 1928
1610 Honey Bee on Clover

1988. Classic Cars. Multicoloured.
2364 25 c. Type **1605** 40 10
2365 25 c. Pierce-Arrow, 1929 . . 40 10
2366 25 c. Cord, 1931 . . . . . . 40 10
2367 25 c. Packard, 1932 . . . . 40 10
2368 25 c. Duesenberg, 1935 . . . 40 10

1988.
2369 **1610** 25 c. multicoloured . . 35 10

1611 Nathaniel Palmer (after Samuel Waldo) and "Hero"
1615 Buck (Gustav Dentzel)

1988. Antarctic Explorers. Multicoloured.
2370 25 c. Type **1611** 50 10
2371 25 c. Charles Wilkes (after Samuel Bell Waugh) . . . 50 10
2372 25 c. Richard E. Byrd . . . 50 10
2373 25 c. Lincoln Ellsworth and "Polar Star" 50 10

1988. American Folk Art. Carousel Animals. Multicoloured.
2374 25 c. Type **1615** 45 10
2375 25 c. Armoured horse (Daniel C. Muller) 45 10
2376 25 c. Camel (Charles Looff) . 45 10
2377 25 c. Goat (Charles Looff) . 45 10

1619 American Bald Eagle and Moon

1988.
2378 **1619** $8.75 multicoloured . . 13·00 10·00

1620 "Madonna and Child" (detail, Sandro Botticelli)
1622 "Happy Birthday"

1988. Christmas.
2379 25 c. Type **1620** 35 10
2380 25 c. "White Christmas" (horiz) 35 10

1988. Greetings Stamps. Multicoloured.
2381 25 c. Type **1622** 45 10
2382 25 c. "Thinking of you" . . 45 10
2383 25 c. "Love you" 45 10
2384 25 c. "Best Wishes" 45 10

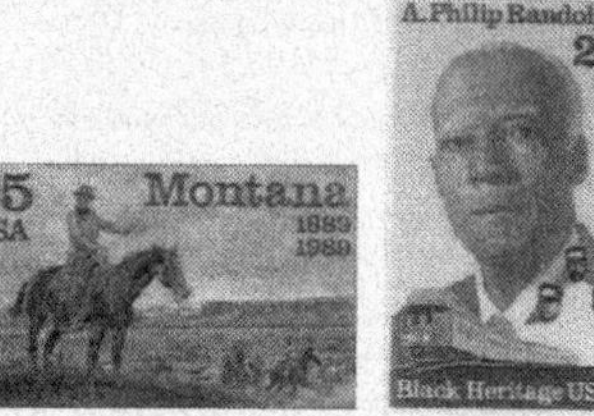

1626 "C.M. Russell and Friends" (Charles M. Russell)
1627 A. Philip Randolph

1989. Centenary of Montana Statehood.
2385 **1626** 25 c. multicoloured . . 40 10

1989. Black Heritage. A. Philip Randolph (trade union activist).
2386 **1627** 25 c. multicoloured . . 30 10

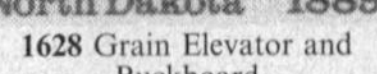

1628 Grain Elevator and Buckboard

1629 Mt. Rainer and Canoe on Reflection Lake

1989. Centenary of North Dakota Statehood.
2387 **1628** 25 c. multicoloured . . 30 10

1989. Centenary of Washington Statehood.
2388 **1629** 25 c. multicoloured . . 30 10

1630 "Experiment", 1788–90

1989. Paddle-steamers. Multicoloured.

2389	25 c. Type **1630**	45	10
2390	25 c. "Phoenix", 1809	45	10
2391	25 c. "New Orleans", 1812	45	10
2392	25 c. "Washington", 1816	45	10
2393	25 c. "Walk in the Water", 1818	45	10

1635 Cancelled 1869 90 c. Lincoln Stamp

1636 Toscanini

1989. "World Stamp Expo'89" International Stamp Exhibition, Washington D.C.
2394 **1635** 25 c. red, black & brown 30 10

1989. Performing Arts and Artists. Arturo Toscanini (conductor).
2395 **1636** 25 c. multicoloured . . 40 10

1637 "Car of History" Clock (Carlo Franzoni)

1638 Eagle and Shield over Vice-President's Chair

1989. Bicentenary of House of Representatives.
2396 **1637** 25 c. multicoloured . . 30 10

1989. Bicentenary of Senate.
2397 **1638** 25 c. multicoloured . . 30 10

1639 George Washington (statue, J. Q. A. Ward)

1640 Pasque Flowers, Pioneer Woman and House

1989. Bicentenary of Executive Branch.
2398 **1639** 25 c. multicoloured . . 30 10

1989. Centenary of South Dakota Statehood.
2399 **1640** 25 c. multicoloured . . 30 10

1641 Gehrig

1643 Hemingway

1642 Liberty, Equality and Fraternity

1989. American Sports Personalities. Lou Gehrig (baseball player).
2400 **1641** 25 c. multicoloured . . 45 10

1989. Air. Bicentenary of French Revolution.
A2401 **1642** 45 c. multicoloured . 60 20

1989. Literary Arts. Ernest Hemingway (novelist).
2402 **1643** 25 c. multicoloured . . 30 10

1644 Astronauts planting Flag on Moon

1645 Dogwood Blossoms

1989. 20th Anniv of First Manned Moon Landing
2403 **1644** $2.40 multicoloured . . 3·00 2·00

1989. Bicentenary of North Carolina Statehood.
2404 **1645** 25 c. multicoloured . . 30 10

1646 Letter Carriers

1647 Eagle and Flag as Shield

1989. Centenary of National Association of Letter Carriers.
2405 **1646** 25 c. multicoloured . . 30 10

1989. Bicentenary of Bill of Rights.
2406 **1647** 25 c. black, red & blue 30 10

1648 Tyrannosaurus Rex

1652 Mimbres Ritual Figure

1989. Prehistoric Animals. Multicoloured.

2407	25 c. Type **1648**	60	10
2408	25 c. Pteranodon	60	10
2409	25 c. Stegosaurus	60	10
2410	25 c. Brontosaurus	60	10

1989. America. Pre-Columbian Carvings. Mult.

2411	25 c. Type **1652** (postage)	30	10
A2412	45 c. Calusa "Key Marco cat" (air)	55	20

1654 "Dream of St. Catherine of Alexandria" (detail, Ludovico Carracci)

1656 Eagle and Shield

1989. Christmas. Multicoloured.

2413	25 c. Type **1654**	40	10
2415	25 c. Gifts on sleigh (horiz)	30	10

1989. Self-adhesive. Imperf.
2416 **1656** 25 c. multicoloured . . . 30 10

1658 Western Stagecoach 1663 Hypersonic Airliner

1989. 20th U.P.U. Congress, Washington D.C. (1st issue). Classic Mail Transport. Multicoloured.

2418	25 c. Type **1658**	45	10
2419	25 c. "Chesapeake" (Mississippi river steamer)	45	10
2420	25 c. Curtiss JN-4 "Jenny" biplane	45	10
2421	25 c. Motor car	45	10

See also Nos. A2423/6.

1989. Air. 20th Universal Postal Union Congress, Washington D.C. (2nd issue). Mail Transport of the Future. Multicoloured.

A2423	45 c. Type **1663**	80	20
A2424	45 c. Hovercar	80	20
A2425	45 c. Rover vehicle delivering mail to space colony	80	20
A2426	45 c. Space shuttle delivering mail to space station	80	20

1668 Mountain Bluebird

1669 Lovebirds

1990. Centenary of Idaho Statehood.
2428 **1668** 25 c. multicoloured . . . 40 10

1990. Greetings Stamp.
2429 **1669** 25 c. multicoloured . . . 40 10

1670 Ida Wells

1671 John Marshall

1990. Black Heritage. Ida B. Wells (civil rights activist).
2431 **1670** 25 c. multicoloured . . . 30 10

1990. Bicentenary of Supreme Court.
2432 **1671** 25 c. multicoloured . . . 30 10

1672 Beach Umbrella

1677 Luis Munoz Marin

1990.
2433 **1672** 15 c. multicoloured . . . 25 10

1990. Great Americans.

2438	**1677**	5 c. red	10	10
2445	–	20 c. red	25	10
2448	–	29 c. blue	40	10
2449	–	29 c. black	40	10
2450	–	32 c. brown	40	15
2451	–	32 c. green	40	15
2452	–	35 c. black	45	10
2454	–	40 c. blue	55	10
2455	–	46 c. red	60	20
2457	–	52 c. lilac	70	10
2458	–	55 c. green	70	25
2462	–	75 c. red	1·00	15
2463	–	78 c. violet	1·00	35

DESIGNS: 20 c. Virginia Agpar; 29 c. (2448) Earl Warren; 29 c. (2449) Thomas Jefferson (President, 1801–09); 32 c. (2450) Milton S. Hershey; 32 c. (2451) Cal Farley; 35 c. Dennis Chavez; 40 c. Lt-Gen. Claire Chennault; 46 c. Ruth Benedict; 52 c. Hubert Humphrey (Vice-president, 1965–69); 55 c. Dr. Alice Hamilton; 75 c. Wendell Wilkie; 78 c. Alice Paul.

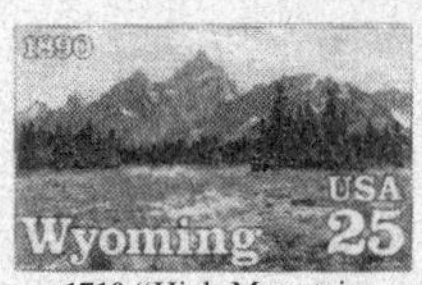

1710 "High Mountain Meadows" (Conrad Schwiering)

1990. Centenary of Wyoming Statehood.
2471 **1710** 25 c. multicoloured . . 40 10

1711 Judy Garland ("The Wizard of Oz")

1715 Marianne Moore

1990. Classic Films. Multicoloured.

2472	25 c. Type **1711**	50	10
2473	25 c. Clark Gable and Vivien Leigh ("Gone with the Wind")	50	10
2474	25 c. Gary Cooper ("Beau Geste")	50	10
2475	25 c. John Wayne ("Stagecoach")	50	10

1990. Literary Arts. Marianne Moore (poet).
2476 **1715** 25 c. multicoloured . . 40 10

1720 Circus Wagon, 1900s

1755 Admiralty Head, Nugent Sound

1990. Transport.

2480	–	4 c. purple	10	10
2481	**1720**	5 c. red	10	10
2504	–	5 c. brown	10	10
2643	–	5 c. red	10	10
2507	–	10 c. green	15	15
2487	–	20 c. green	25	10
2489	–	23 c. blue	30	10
2491	–	32 c. blue	40	15
2496	–	$1 blue and red	1·25	35

DESIGNS; 4 c. Richard Dudgeon steam carriage, 1866; 5 c. (Noss. 2504, 2643) Birch bark canoe, 1800s; 10 c. Tractor trailer, 1930s; 20 c. Cog railway, 1870s; 23 c. Lunch wagon, 1890s; 32 c. Ferryboat, 1900s; $1 Benoist Type XIV flying boat.

For Type **1720** with face value expressed as "5c", see No. 3002.

1990. Lighthouses. Multicoloured.

2516	25 c. Type **1755**	50	10
2517	25 c. Cape Hatteras	50	10
2518	25 c. West Quoddy Head	50	10
2519	25 c. American Shoals	50	10
2520	25 c. Sandy Hook, New York Harbour	50	10

1760 Stars and Stripes

1761 Slater Mill

1990. Self-adhesive. Imperf.
2521 **1760** 25 c. red and blue . . . 35 10

1990. Bicentenary of Rhode Island Statehood.
2522 **1761** 25 c. multicoloured . . 35 10

1763 Bobcat

1990. Wildlife.
2524 **1763** $2 multicoloured . . . 2·75 85

1769 Jesse Owens

1990. American Olympic Medal Winners. Multicoloured.
2530 25 c. Type **1769** 35 10
2531 25 c. Ray Ewry 35 10
2532 25 c. Hazel Wightman . . . 35 10
2533 25 c. Eddie Eagan 35 10
2534 25 c. Helene Madison 35 10

1774 Assiniboine

1990. American Folk Art. Indian Headdresses. Multicoloured.
2535 25 c. Type **1774** 35 10
2536 25 c. Cheyenne 35 10
2537 25 c. Comanche 35 10
2538 25 c. Flathead 35 10
2539 25 c. Shoshone 35 10

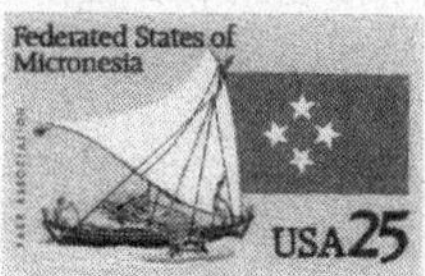

1779 Micronesian Outrigger Canoe and Flag

1990. 4th Anniv of Ratification of Marshall Islands and Micronesia Compacts of Free Association. Multicoloured.
2540 25 c. Type **1779** 35 10
2541 25 c. Marshallese stick chart, outrigger canoe and flag . 35 10

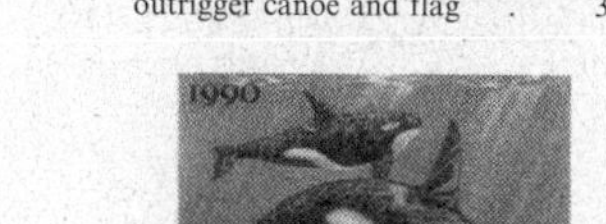

1781 Killer Whales

1990. Marine Mammals. Multicoloured.
2542 25 c. Type **1781** 35 10
2543 25 c. Northern sea lions . . . 35 10
2544 25 c. Sea otter 35 10
2545 25 c. Common dolphin . . . 35 10

1785 Grand Canyon

1990. America. Natural World. Multicoloured.
2546 25 c. Type **1785** (postage) . . 35 10
A2547 45 c. Tropical island coastline (air) 60 15

1787 Eisenhower and Soldiers

1788 "Madonna and Child" (Antonello da Messina)

1990. Birth Centenary of Dwight David Eisenhower (President, 1953–61).
2548 **1787** 25 c. multicoloured . . 35 10

1990. Christmas. Multicoloured.
2549 25 c. Type **1788** 35 10
2551 25 c. Christmas tree 35 10

1790 Tulip

This U.S. stamp, along with 25¢ of additional U.S. postage, is equivalent to the 'F' stamp rate

1791

1991. No value expressed.
2552 **1790** (29 c.) multicoloured . . 40 10

1991. No value expressed. Make-up Rate stamp.
2556 **1791** (4 c.) red and brown . . 10 10

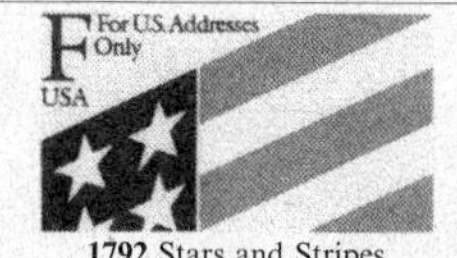

1792 Stars and Stripes

1991. No value expressed. Self-adhesive. Imperf.
2557 **1792** (29 c.) red, blue & black 40 15

1794 Federal Palace, Berne, and Capitol, Washington

1795 Farm

1991. 700th Anniv of Swiss Confederation.
2559 **1794** 50 c. multicoloured . . 65 15

1991. Bicentenary of Vermont Statehood.
2560 **1795** 29 c. multicoloured . . 40 10

1796 Fawn

1797 Flag over Mt. Rushmore

1991.
2561 **1796** 19 c. multicoloured . . 25 10

1991.
2562 **1797** 29 c. red, brown & blk 40 10

1798 Tulip

1799 Wood Duck

1991.
2563 **1798** 29 c. multicoloured . . 40 10

1991. (a) Inscriptions in black.
2565 **1799** 29 c. multicoloured . . 40 15

(b) Inscriptions in red.
2566 **1799** 29 c. multicoloured . . 40 15

1800 Flag and Olympic Rings

1801 Quimby and Bleriot XI

1991.
2567 **1800** 29 c. multicoloured . . 40 10

1991. Air. Aviation Pioneers. Harriet Quimby (first American woman pilot).
A2568 **1801** 50 c. multicoloured . 65 15

1802 American Bald Eagle

1803 Heart-shaped Globe

1991. 50th Anniv of "E Series" Defence Bonds.
2569 **1802** 29 c. multicoloured . . 40 15

1991. Greetings Stamps. Multicoloured.
2570 29 c. Type **1803** 40 10
2572 52 c. Fischer's lovebirds (21 × 35 mm) 70 20

1805 Hot-air Balloon

1806 Piper and Piper J-3 Cub

1991.
2573 **1805** 19 c. multicoloured . . 25 10

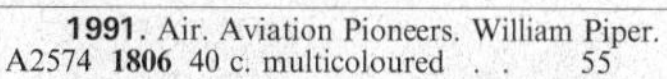
1991. Air. Aviation Pioneers. William Piper.
A2574 **1806** 40 c. multicoloured . . 55 15

1807 Saroyan

1808 Flags on Parade

1991. Literary Arts. 10th Death Anniv of William Saroyan (dramatist and novelist).
2575 **1807** 29 c. multicoloured . . . 40 10

1991. 125th Anniv of Memorial Day.
2576 **1808** 29 c. multicoloured . . . 40 10

1809 Royal Wulff

1814 Porter and Score

1991. Fishing Flies. Multicoloured.
2577 29 c. Type **1809** 40 10
2578 29 c. Jock Scott 40 10
2579 29 c. Apte tarpon fly 40 10
2580 29 c. Lefty's deceiver 40 10
2581 29 c. Muddler minnow . . . 40 10

1991. Performing Arts and Artists. Birth Centenary of Cole Porter (composer).
2582 **1814** 29 c. multicoloured . . . 40 10

1815 American Bald Eagle

1991. U.S. Olympic Festival.
2583 **1815** $9.95 multicoloured . . . 13·00 4·00

1816 U.S.S. "Glacier" (ice-breaker) near Palmer Station

1817 American Kestrel

1991. Air. 30th Anniv of Antarctic Treaty.
A2584 **1816** 50 c. multicoloured . . 65 20

1991. Birds. Multicoloured.
2585 1 c. Type **1817** 10 10
2586 3 c. Eastern bluebird 10 10
2590 30 c. Common cardinal . . . 40 15
For Nos. 2585/6 and 2 c. but with face value expressed as "1c" etc see No. 3019 etc.

1823 Liberty Torch

1824 South-West Asia Service Medal

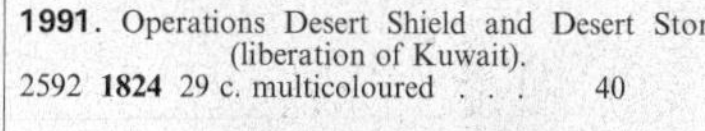
1991. Self-adhesive. Imperf.
2591 **1823** 29 c. green, gold & blk . 40 10

1991. Operations Desert Shield and Desert Storm (liberation of Kuwait).
2592 **1824** 29 c. multicoloured . . . 40 10

1825 American Bald Eagle

1991.
2595 **1825** $2.90 multicoloured . . 3·75 1·90

1826 Pole Vaulting

1831 Rowing Boat

1991. Olympic Games, Barcelona (1992). Mult.
2596 29 c. Type **1826** 40 10
2597 29 c. Throwing the discus . . 40 10
2598 29 c. Running 40 10
2599 29 c. Throwing the javelin . 40 10
2600 29 c. Hurdling 40 10

1991.
2601 **1831** 19 c. multicoloured . . 25 10

1832 Coins and Banknotes

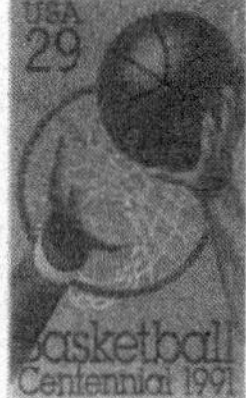

1833 Shot at Goal

1991. Centenary Convention of American Numismatic Association.
2602 **1832** 29 c. multicoloured . . 40 10

1991. Centenary of Basketball.
2604 **1833** 29 c. multicoloured . . 40 10

1834 Stan Laurel and Oliver Hardy

1991.
2605 **1834** 29 c. black, violet & red 40 10
2606 – 29 c. black, red & violet 40 10
2607 – 29 c. black, red & violet 40 10
2608 – 29 c. black, violet & red 40 10
2609 – 29 c. black, red & violet 40 10
DESIGNS: No. 2606, Edgar Bergen and Charlie McCarthy; 2607, Jack Benny; 2608, Fanny Brice; 2609, Bud Abbott and Lou Costello.

1839 American Bald Eagle

1991.
2610 **1839** $14 multicoloured . . . 18·00 5·50

1840 Burma Road Convoy

1991. 50th Anniv of America's Entry into Second World War. Multicoloured.
2611 29 c. Type **1840** 40 15
2612 29 c. America's first peacetime draft 40 15
2613 29 c. Lend-Lease Act 40 15
2614 29 c. Roosevelt and Churchill (Atlantic Charter) 40 15
2615 29 c. Munitions factory . . . 40 15
2616 29 c. Sinking of "Reuben James" (destroyer) 40 15
2617 29 c. Gas mask (Civil Defence) 40 15
2618 29 c. Delivery of "Patrick Henry" (first "Liberty" freighter) 40 15
2619 29 c. U.S.S. "West Virginia" and U.S.S. "Tennessee" ablaze, Pearl Harbor . . . 40 15
2620 29 c. U.S. Declaration of War on Japan 40 15

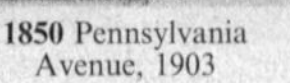

1850 Pennsylvania Avenue, 1903

1851 Matzeliger

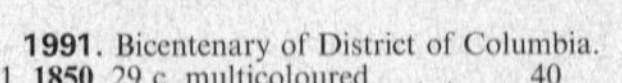

1991. Bicentenary of District of Columbia.
2621 **1850** 29 c. multicoloured . . 40 10

1991. Black Heritage. Jan Ernst Matzeliger (inventor of shoe lasting machine).
2622 **1851** 29 c. multicoloured . . 40 10

1852 Flag

1853 Postal Service Emblem and Olympic Rings

1991.
2623 **1852** 23 c. blue, red & black . 30 30

1991.
2624 **1853** $1 multicoloured . . . 1·25 35

1854 "Mariner 10" and Mercury

1991. Space Exploration. Multicoloured.
2625 29 c. Type **1854** 40 10
2626 29 c. Venus and "Mariner 2" . . 40 10
2627 29 c. Earth and "Landsat" . . 40 10
2628 29 c. Moon and Lunar Orbiter . 40 10
2629 29 c. "Viking" Orbiter and Mars 40 10
2630 29 c. Jupiter and "Pioneer 11" . 40 10
2631 29 c. "Voyager 2" and Saturn . 40 10
2632 29 c. Uranus and "Voyager 2" . 40 10
2633 29 c. Neptune and "Voyager 2" . 40 10
2634 29 c. Pluto 40 10

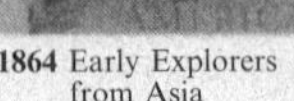

1864 Early Explorers from Asia

1865 "Madonna and Child with Donor" (detail, Antoniazzo Romano)

1991. Air. America. Voyages of Discovery.
A2635 **1864** 50 c. multicoloured . . 65 15

1991. Christmas. No value expressed. Mult.
2636 (29 c.) Type **1865** 40 10
2637 (29 c.) Santa Claus in chimney (horiz) 40 10
2639 (29 c.) Santa Claus checking list (horiz) 40 10
2640 (29 c.) Santa Clause leaving by chimney (horiz) 40 10
2642 (29 c.) Santa Claus on sleigh (horiz) 40 10

1871 Eagle and Shield

1872 Ice Hockey

1991. Inscr "Bulk Rate USA".
2644 **1871** (10 c.) multicoloured . . 15 15
For design T **1871** but inscribed "USA Bulk Rate" see Nos. 2801/2.

1992. Winter Olympic Games, Albertville. Multicoloured.
2645 29 c. Type **1872** 40 10
2646 29 c. Figure skating 40 10
2647 29 c. Speed skating 40 10
2648 29 c. Skiing 40 10
2649 29 c. Two-man bobsleigh . . . 40 10

1877 1869 15 c. Columbus Stamp

1878 Du Bois

1992. "World Columbian Stamp Expo'92", Chicago.
2650 **1877** 29 c. multicoloured . . 40 10

1992. Black Heritage. William Edward Burghardt Du Bois (founder of Niagara Movement (precursor of National Association for Advancement of Coloured People).
2651 **1878** 29 c. multicoloured . . 40 10

1879 Heart in Envelope

1880 Catcher and Baserunner

1992. Greetings Stamp.
2652 **1879** 29 c. multicoloured . . 40 10

1992. Addition of Baseball to Olympic Games.
2654 **1880** 29 c. multicoloured . . 40 10

1881 Flag over White House

1882 Seeking Queen Isabella's Support

1992. Bicentenary of White House.
2655 **1881** 29 c. red and blue . . . 40 10

1992. 500th Anniv of Discovery of America by Columbus. Multicoloured.
2656 29 c. Type **1882** 40 15
2657 29 c. Crossing the Atlantic . . 40 15
2658 29 c. Approaching land . . 40 15
2659 29 c. Coming ashore 40 15

1886 Exchange Facade and Trading Floor

1893 Russian Cosmonaut and Space Shuttle

1992. Bicentenary of New York Stock Exchange.
2660 **1886** 29 c. green, black & red . 40 10

1992. International Space Year. Multicoloured.
2662 29 c. Type **1893** 40 10
2663 29 c. American astronaut and "Mir" space station . . . 40 10
2664 29 c. "Apollo" and "Vostok" spacecraft and Sputnik . . 40 10
2665 29 c. "Soyuz", "Mercury" and "Gemini" spacecraft . . . 40 10

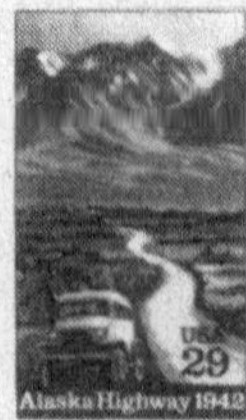

1897 Army Lorry using New Highway

1898 My Old Kentucky Home State Park, Bardstown

1992. 50th Anniv of Alaska Highway.
2666 **1897** 29 c. multicoloured . . 40 10

1992. Bicentenary of Kentucky Statehood.
2667 **1898** 29 c. multicoloured . . 40 10

1899 Football

1904 Ruby-throated Hummingbird

1992. Olympic Games, Barcelona. Multicoloured.
2668 29 c. Type **1899** 40 10
2669 29 c. Gymnastics 40 10
2670 29 c. Volleyball 40 10
2671 29 c. Boxing 40 10
2672 29 c. Swimming 40 10

1992. Hummingbirds. Multicoloured.
2673 29 c. Type **1904** 40 10
2674 29 c. Broad-billed hummingbird 40 10
2675 29 c. Costa's hummingbird . 40 10
2676 29 c. Rufous hummingbird . 40 10
2677 29 c. Calliope hummingbird . 40 10

1909 Flag in "USA"

1910 Indian Paintbrush

1992. Presorted First Class stamp.
2678 **1909** 23 c. multicoloured . . . 30 30

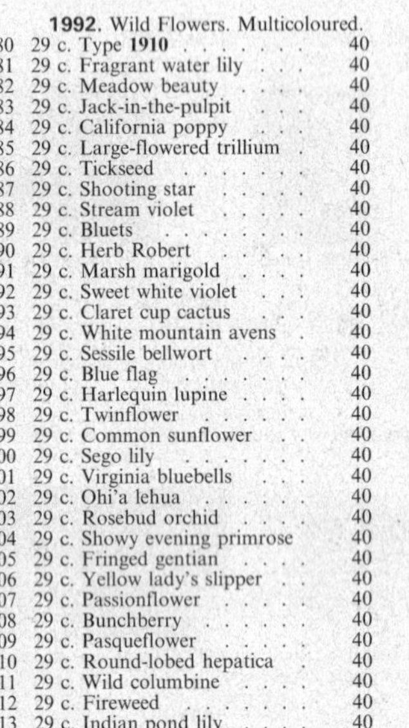

1992. Wild Flowers. Multicoloured.
2680 29 c. Type **1910** 40 10
2681 29 c. Fragrant water lily . . . 40 10
2682 29 c. Meadow beauty 40 10
2683 29 c. Jack-in-the-pulpit . . . 40 10
2684 29 c. California poppy . . . 40 10
2685 29 c. Large-flowered trillium . 40 10
2686 29 c. Tickseed 40 10
2687 29 c. Shooting star 40 10
2688 29 c. Stream violet 40 10
2689 29 c. Bluets 40 10
2690 29 c. Herb Robert 40 10
2691 29 c. Marsh marigold 40 10
2692 29 c. Sweet white violet . . . 40 10
2693 29 c. Claret cup cactus . . . 40 10
2694 29 c. White mountain avens . 40 10
2695 29 c. Sessile bellwort 40 10
2696 29 c. Blue flag 40 10
2697 29 c. Harlequin lupine 40 10
2698 29 c. Twinflower 40 10
2699 29 c. Common sunflower . . . 40 10
2700 29 c. Sego lily 40 10
2701 29 c. Virginia bluebells . . . 40 10
2702 29 c. Ohi'a lehua 40 10
2703 29 c. Rosebud orchid 40 10
2704 29 c. Showy evening primrose 40 10
2705 29 c. Fringed gentian 40 10
2706 29 c. Yellow lady's slipper . . 40 10
2707 29 c. Passionflower 40 10
2708 29 c. Bunchberry 40 10
2709 29 c. Pasqueflower 40 10
2710 29 c. Round-lobed hepatica . 40 10
2711 29 c. Wild columbine 40 10
2712 29 c. Fireweed 40 10
2713 29 c. Indian pond lily 40 10
2714 29 c. Turk's cap lily 40 10
2715 29 c. Dutchman's breeches . . 40 10
2716 29 c. Trumpet honeysuckle . . 40 10
2717 29 c. Jacob's ladder 40 10
2718 29 c. Plains prickly pear . . . 40 10
2719 29 c. Moss campion 40 10
2720 29 c. Bearberry 40 10
2721 29 c. Mexican hat 40 10
2722 29 c. Harebell 40 10
2723 29 c. Desert five spot 40 10
2724 29 c. Smooth Solomon's seal . 40 10
2725 29 c. Red maids 40 10
2726 29 c. Yellow skunk cabbage . 40 10
2727 29 c. Rue anemone 40 10
2728 29 c. Standing cypress 40 10
2729 29 c. Wild flax 40 10

1911 Doolittle Raid on Tokyo

1921 Dorothy Parker

1992. United States Participation in Second World War. Multicoloured.
2730 29 c. Type **1911** 40 15
2731 29 c. Ration stamps 40 15
2732 29 c. Douglas SBD-3 Dauntless on aircraft carrier (Battle of Coral Sea) 40 15
2733 29 c. Japanese occupation of Corregidor 40 15
2734 29 c. Japanese invasion of Aleutian Islands 40 15

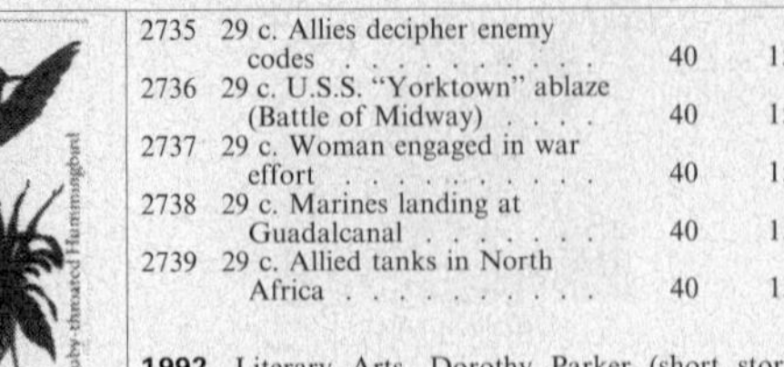

2735 29 c. Allies decipher enemy codes 40 15
2736 29 c. U.S.S. "Yorktown" ablaze (Battle of Midway) 40 15
2737 29 c. Woman engaged in war effort 40 15
2738 29 c. Marines landing at Guadalcanal 40 15
2739 29 c. Allied tanks in North Africa 40 15

1992. Literary Arts. Dorothy Parker (short story writer, poet and critic).
2740 **1921** 29 c. multicoloured . . 40 10

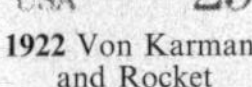

1922 Von Karman and Rocket

1923 Flag and "I pledge allegiance..."

1992. Theodore von Karman (space pioneer).
2741 **1922** 29 c. multicoloured . . 40 10

1992. Centenary of Pledge of Allegiance.
2742 **1923** 29 c. multicoloured (value in black) 40 10
2788 29 c. multicoloured (value in red) 40 10

1924 Azurite

1928 Eagle and Shield

1992. Minerals. Multicoloured.
2743 29 c. Type **1924** 40 10
2744 29 c. Copper 40 10
2745 29 c. Variscite 40 10
2746 29 c. Wulfenite 40 10

1992. Self-adhesive. Imperf.
2747 **1928** 29 c. multicoloured (inscr in red) 40 15
2748 29 c. multicoloured (inscr in green) 40 15
2749 29 c. multicoloured (inscr in brown) 40 15

1929 Spanish Galleon, Map and Cabrillo

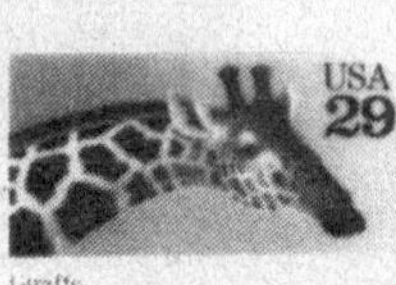

1930 Giraffe

1992. 450th Anniv of Discovery of California by Juan Rodriguez Cabrillo.
2750 **1929** 29 c. multicoloured . . 40 15

1992. Wild Animals. Multicoloured.
2751 29 c. Type **1930** 40 10
2752 29 c. Giant panda 40 10
2753 29 c. Greater flamingo 40 10
2754 29 c. King penguins 40 10
2755 29 c. White Bengal tiger . . . 40 10

1935 "Madonna and Child with Saints" (Giovanni Bellini)

1940 Pumpkinseed Sunfish

1992. Christmas. Multicoloured.
2756 29 c. Type **1935** 40 10
2757 29 c. Wheeled racing horse (horiz) 40 10
2758 29 c. Locomotive (horiz) . . 40 10
2759 29 c. Steam engine (horiz) . . 40 10
2760 29 c. Steamer (horiz) 40 10
No. 2758 also comes imperf and self-adhesive.

1992.
2766 **1940** 45 c. multicoloured . . . 60 10

1941 Rooster

1992. New Year.
2768 **1941** 29 c. multicoloured . . 40 10

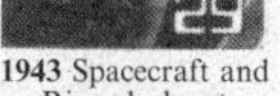

1942 Elvis Presley 1943 Spacecraft and Ringed-planet

1993. Elvis Presley (rock singer and actor).
2769 **1942** 29 c. multicoloured . . 40 10
For similar design but inscr "ELVIS PRESLEY" see Type **1987**.

1993. Space Fantasy. Multicoloured.

2770	29 c. Type **1943**	40	10
2771	29 c. Space capsules	40	10
2772	29 c. Astronauts	40	10
2773	29 c. Spaceship	40	10
2774	29 c. Spacecraft and planet	40	10

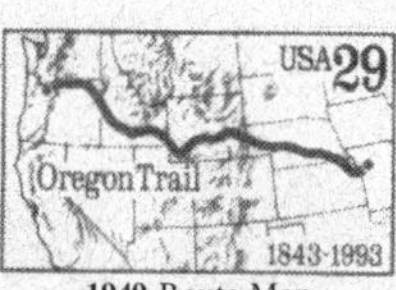

1948 Julian 1949 Route Map

1993. Black Heritage. Percy Lavon Julian (research chemist).
2775 **1948** 29 c. multicoloured . . 40 10

1993. 150th Anniv of Oregon Trail.
2776 **1949** 29 c. multicoloured . . 40 10

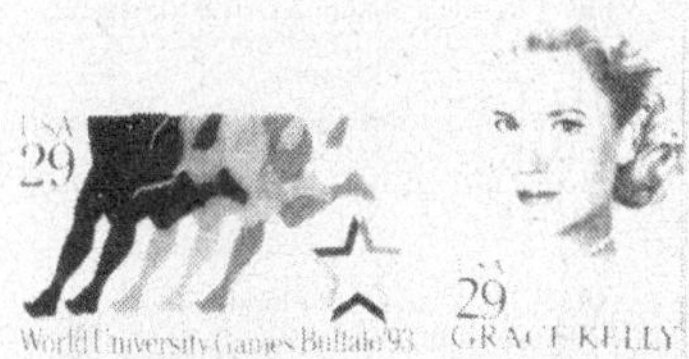

1950 Athletes 1951 Princess Grace

1993. World University Games, Buffalo.
2777 **1950** 29 c. multicoloured . . 40 10

1993. 10th Death Anniv of Princess Grace of Monaco (former Grace Kelly).
2778 **1951** 29 c. blue 40 10

1952 "Oklahoma"

1993. Broadway Musicals. Multicoloured. (a) No frame. Size 36 × 28 mm.
2779 29 c. Type **1952** 40 10

(b) With frame. Size 35 × 27 mm.

2780	29 c. "Show Boat"	40	10
2781	29 c. "Porgy and Bess"	40	10
2782	29 c. Type **1952**	40	10
2783	29 c. "My Fair Lady"	40	10

1956 Clown

1993. Bicentenary of First Circus Performance in America. Multicoloured.

2784	29 c. Type **1956**	40	10
2785	29 c. Ringmaster	40	10
2786	29 c. Trapeze artiste	40	10
2787	29 c. Elephant	40	10

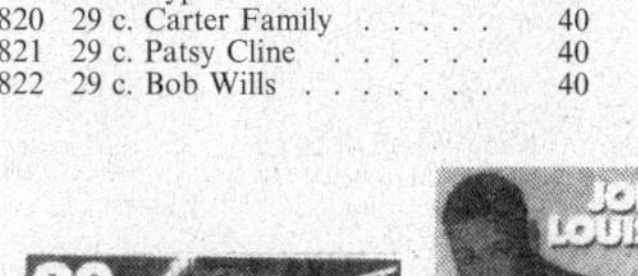

1960 Pioneers racing to Cherokee Strip 1961 Acheson

1993. Centenary of Cherokee Strip Land Run.
2789 **1960** 29 c. multicoloured . . 40 10

1993. Birth Centenary of Dean Acheson (Secretary of State, 1949–53).
2790 **1961** 29 c. green 40 10

1962 Steeplechase 1966 Hyacinths

1993. Equestrian Sports. Multicoloured.

2791	29 c. Type **1962**	40	10
2792	29 c. Thoroughbred racing	40	10
2793	29 c. Harness racing	40	10
2794	29 c. Polo	40	10

1993. Garden Flowers. Multicoloured.

2796	29 c. Type **1966**	40	10
2797	29 c. Daffodils	40	10
2798	29 c. Tulips	40	10
2799	29 c. Irises	40	10
2800	29 c. Lilac	40	10

1971 Eagle and Shield 1972 Atlantic Convoy

1993. Coil stamps. Inscr "USA Bulk Rate". Multicoloured, colours of eagle given.
2801 **1971** (10 c.) yellow & brown 10 10
2802 (10 c.) gold & brown . 10 10
No. 2802 exists with both ordinary gum and self-adhesive gum.
For design as Type **1971** but inscr "Bulk Rate USA" see No. 2644.

1993. United States Participation in Second World War. Multicoloured.

2803	29 c. Type **1972**	40	10
2804	29 c. Treating the wounded	40	10
2805	29 c. Allied attack on Sicily	40	10
2806	29 c. Consolidated B-24 Liberators bombing Ploesti refineries	40	10
2807	29 c. G.I.s with mail from home	40	10
2808	29 c. Allied invasion of Italy	40	10
2809	29 c. War Savings stamps and bonds	40	10
2810	29 c. Willie and Joe (cartoon characters)	40	10
2811	29 c. Gold Star emblem	40	10
2812	29 c. Marine assault on Tarawa, Gilbert Islands	40	10

1982 Futuristic Space Shuttle

1993.
2813 **1982** $2.90 multicoloured . . 3·75 1·50

1983 Hank Williams

1993. Country Music. Multicoloured. (a) No frame.

2815	29 c. Type **1983**	40	10
2816	29 c. Patsy Cline	40	10
2817	29 c. Carter Family	40	10
2818	29 c. Bob Wills	40	10

(b) With frame.

2819	29 c. Type **1983**	40	10
2820	29 c. Carter Family	40	10
2821	29 c. Patsy Cline	40	10
2822	29 c. Bob Wills	40	10

1987 Elvis Presley 1994 Louis

1993. Rock and Rhythm and Blues Music. Multicoloured. (a) No frame.

2823	29 c. Type **1987**	40	10
2824	29 c. Buddy Holly	40	10
2825	29 c. Ritchie Valens	40	10
2826	29 c. Bill Haley	40	10
2827	29 c. Dinah Washington	40	10
2828	29 c. Otis Redding	40	10
2829	29 c. Clyde McPhatter	40	10

(b) With frame.

2830	29 c. Type **1987**	40	10
2831	29 c. Bill Haley	40	10
2832	29 c. Clyde McPhatter	40	10
2833	29 c. Ritchie Valens	40	10
2834	29 c. Otis Redding	40	10
2835	29 c. Buddy Holly	40	10
2836	29 c. Dinah Washington	40	10

1993. Joe Louis (boxer).
2837 **1994** 29 c. multicoloured . . . 40 10

1995 Red Squirrel 1996 Benjamin Franklin, Liberty Hall, Philadelphia, Post Rider and Printing Press

1993. Self-adhesive. Imperf.
2838 **1995** 29 c. multicoloured . . . 40 10

1993. Inauguration of National Postal Museum, Washington. Multicoloured.

2840	29 c. Type **1996**	40	10
2841	29 c. Pony Express rider, Civil War soldier and stagecoach	40	10
2842	29 c. Curtiss JN-4 "Jenny" biplane, pilot, railway mail carriage and mail truck	40	10
2843	29 c. Gold rush miner's letter and stamps	40	10

2000 Rose 2001 Mother signing "I Love You"

1993. Self-adhesive. (a) Pink rose. Imperf (29 c.) or roul (32 c.).
2844 **2000** 29 c. multicoloured . . . 40 10
3031 32 c. multicoloured . . . 40 15

(b) Yellow rose. Roul.
3262 **2000** 32 c. multicoloured . . . 40 15

1993. Deaf Communication. Multicoloured.
2845 29 c. Type **2001** 40 10
2846 29 c. "I Love You" in sign language 40 10

2003 African Violet

1993.
2847 **2003** 29 c. multicoloured . . . 40 10

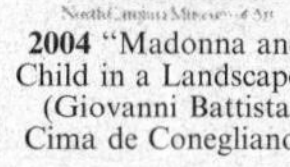

2004 "Madonna and Child in a Landscape" (Giovanni Battista Cima de Conegliano) 2005 Snowman

1993. Christmas. (a) Type **2004**.
2848 29 c. multicoloured 40 10

(b) As T **2005**. Multicoloured. Perf or imperf (self-adhesive).

2849	29 c. Type **2005**	40	10
2850	29 c. Toy soldier	40	10
2851	29 c. Jack-in-the-box	40	10
2852	29 c. Reindeer	40	10

All designs come in more than one version which differ slightly in size.

2009 "Rebecca of Sunnybrook Farm" (Kate Douglas Wiggin)

1993. Classic Children's Books. Multicoloured.

2863	29 c. Type **2009**	40	10
2864	29 c. "Little House on the Prairie" (Laura Ingalls Wilder)	40	10
2865	29 c. "The Adventures of Huckleberry Finn" (Mark Twain)	40	10
2866	29 c. "Little Women" (Louisa May Alcott)	40	10

2013 Latte Stones and Flag 2014 Pine Cone

1993. 15th Anniv of Commonwealth of Northern Mariana Islands.
2867 **2013** 29 c. multicoloured . . 40 10

1993. Self-adhesive. Imperf.
2868 **2014** 29 c. red, green & black 40 10

2015 Caravels off Puerto Rico 2016 Emblem

1993. 500th Anniv of Columbus's Landing at Puerto Rico.
2869 **2015** 29 c. multicoloured . . 40 10

1993. World AIDS Day.
2870 **2016** 29 c. red and black . . 40 10

2017 Skiing 2022 Murrow

1994. Winter Olympic Games. Lillehammer. Multicoloured.

2872	29 c. Type **2017**	40	10
2873	29 c. Luge	40	10
2874	29 c. Ice dancing	40	10
2875	29 c. Cross-country skiing	40	10
2876	29 c. Ice hockey	40	10

1994. 29th Death Anniv of Edward Murrow (radio and television journalist).
2877 **2022** 29 c. brown 40 10

2023 Heart-shaped Sun 2024 Davis

1994. Greetings Stamp. Self-adhesive. Imperf.
2878 **2023** 29 c. multicoloured . . 40 10

1994. Black Heritage. Dr. Allison Davis (educationist).
2879 **2024** 29 c. sepia and brown . 40 10

2025 American Bald Eagle
2026 Pekingese

1994. Self-adhesive. Imperf.
2880 **2025** 29 c. multicoloured . . 40 10

1994. New Year.
2881 **2026** 29 c. multicoloured . . 40 10

2027 Dove on Heart-shaped Bouquet of Roses
2029 Troopers on Western Frontier

1994. Greetings Stamps. Multicoloured.
2882 29 c. Type **2027** (18 × 25 mm) 40 10
2916 29 c. Type **2027** (20 × 27 mm) 40 10
2883 52 c. Doves on flower arrangement 70 25

1994. "Buffalo Soldiers" (U.S. Army black regiments).
2884 **2029** 29 c. multicoloured . . 40 10

2030 Rudolph Valentino
2040 Lilies

1994. Silent Screen Stars.
2885 **2030** 29 c. black, vio & red . 40 10
2886 – 29 c. black, vio & red . 40 10
2887 – 29 c. black, red & vio . 40 10
2888 – 29 c. black, red & vio . 40 10
2889 – 29 c. black, vio & red . 40 10
2890 – 29 c. black, red & vio . 40 10
2891 – 29 c. black, vio & red . 40 10
2892 – 29 c. black, vio & red . 40 10
2893 – 29 c. black, red & vio . 40 10
2894 – 29 c. black, red & vio . 40 10
DESIGNS: No. 2886, Clara Bow; 2887, Charlie Chaplin; 2888, Lon Chaney; 2889, John Gilbert; 2890, Zasu Pitts; 2891, Harold Lloyd; 2892, Keystone Cops; 2893, Theda Bara; 2894, Buster Keaton.

1994. Garden Flowers. Multicoloured.
2895 29 c. Type **2040** 40 10
2896 29 c. Zinnias 40 10
2897 29 c. Gladioli 40 10
2898 29 c. Marigolds 40 10
2899 29 c. Roses 40 10

2045 Surrender at Saratoga (after John Trumbull)
2046 U.S.A. Player kicking Ball

1994.
2900 **2045** $1 blue . . . . 1·25 45

1994. World Cup Football Championship, U.S.A. Multicoloured.
2902 29 c. Type **2046** 35 10
2903 40 c. Controlling the ball . . 50 20
2904 50 c. Heading the ball . . . 60 20

2050 Liberating New Guinea
2060 Statue of Liberty

1994. United States Participation in Second World War. Multicoloured.
2906 29 c. Type **2050** 35 10
2907 29 c. P-51 escorting B-17 bombers 35 10
2908 29 c. Normandy Landings . . 35 10
2909 29 c. Glider and paratroops 35 10
2910 29 c. Submarine crew . . . 35 10
2911 29 c. Liberating Rome . . . 35 10
2912 29 c. Troops clearing Saipan bunkers 35 10
2913 29 c. Red Ball Express truck 35 10
2914 29 c. Battleship (Battle of Leyte Gulf) 35 10
2915 29 c. Battle of the Bulge . . 35 10

1994. Self-adhesive. Imperf.
2917 **2060** 29 c. multicoloured . . 35 10

2061 "Triple Self-portrait"

1994. Birth Centenary of Norman Rockwell (illustrator).
2919 **2061** 29 c. multicoloured . . 35 10

2063 Astronauts planting Flag on Moon

1994. 25th Anniv of First Manned Moon Landing.
2921 **2063** $9.95 multicoloured . . 12·50 4·25

2065 Hudson's "General", 1855

1994. Locomotives. Multicoloured.
2923 29 c. Type **2065** 35 10
2924 29 c. McQueen's "Jupiter", 1868 . . . . 35 10
2925 29 c. Eddy's No. 242, 1874 . 35 10
2926 29 c. Ely's No. 10, 1881 . . 35 10
2927 29 c. Buchanan's No. 999, 1893 35 10

2070 Meany
2072 Al Jolson

2071 Presidents Washington and Jackson

1994. Birth Centenary of George Meany (trades unionist).
2928 **2070** 29 c. blue 35 10

1994.
2929 **2071** $5 green . . . . . . 6·25 2·10

1994. Popular Music. Multicoloured.
2930 29 c. Type **2072** 35 10
2931 29 c. Bing Crosby 35 10
2932 29 c. Ethel Waters 35 10
2933 29 c. Nat "King" Cole . . . 35 10
2934 29 c. Ethel Merman 35 10

2077 "Male Type (eastern seaboard)"
2078 Bessie Smith

1994. Literary Arts. Birth Centenary of James Thurber (writer and cartoonist).
2935 **2077** 29 c. multicoloured . . . 35 10

1994. Jazz and Blues Music. Multicoloured.
2936 29 c. Type **2078** 35 10
2937 29 c. Muddy Waters 35 10
2938 29 c. Billie Holiday 35 10
2939 29 c. Robert Johnson 35 10
2940 29 c. Jimmy Rushing 35 10
2941 29 c. "Ma" Rainey 35 10
2942 29 c. Mildred Bailey 35 10
2943 29 c. Howlin' Wolf 35 10

2086/9 Sea Life (½-size illustration)

1994. Wonders of the Seas.
2944 **2086** 29 c. multicoloured . . . 35 10
2945 **2087** 29 c. multicoloured . . . 35 10
2946 **2088** 29 c. multicoloured . . . 35 10
2947 **2089** 29 c. multicoloured . . . 35 10
Nos. 2944/7 were issued together, se-tenant, forming the composite design illustrated.

2090 Black-necked Crane
2092 Home on the Range

1994. Cranes. Multicoloured.
2948 29 c. Type **2090** 35 10
2949 29 c. Whooping crane 35 10

1994. Legends of the West. Multicoloured.
2950 29 c. Type **2092** 35 10
2951 29 c. Buffalo Bill 35 10
2952 29 c. Jim Bridger 35 10
2953 29 c. Annie Oakley 35 10
2954 29 c. Native American culture 35 10
2955 29 c. Chief Joseph 35 10
2956 29 c. Bill Pickett 35 10
2957 29 c. Bat Masterson 35 10
2958 29 c. John Fremont 35 10
2959 29 c. Wyatt Earp 35 10
2960 29 c. Nellie Cashman 35 10
2961 29 c. Charles Goodnight . . . 35 10
2962 29 c. Geronimo 35 10
2963 29 c. Kit Carson 35 10
2964 29 c. Wild Bill Hickok . . . 35 10
2965 29 c. Western wildlife . . . 35 10
2966 29 c. Jim Beckwourth 35 10
2967 29 c. Bill Tilghman 35 10
2968 29 c. Sacagawea 35 10
2969 29 c. Overland mail 35 10
Each stamp is inscribed on the back, under the gum, with a brief history of the subject depicted.

2097 "Virgin and Child" (Elisabetta Sirani)
2100 Common Cardinal

1994. Christmas. Multicoloured. (a) Perf.
2970 29 c. Type **2097** 35 10
2972 29 c. Stocking 35 10

(b) Self-adhesive. Imperf.
2973 29 c. Santa Claus 35 10
2974 29 c. Type **2100** 35 10
Nos. 2972/3 are as Type **2097** in size.

2102 Dove with Olive Branch
2103 Old Glory

1994. Make-up Rate stamp. No value expressed.
2976 **2102** (3 c.) blue, brown and red 10 10

1994. With service indicator.
(a) Nonprofit Presort. Green background.
2978 **2103** (5 c.) multicoloured . . 10 10

(b) Postcard rate. Yellow background.
2979 **2103** (20 c.) multicoloured (black "G") 25 10
2980 (20 c.) multicoloured (red "G") 25 10

(c) First-Class Presort. Blue background.
2981 **2103** (25 c.) multicoloured . 35 15

2104 Old Glory
2106 Boar

1994. No value expressed. Perf (2982, 2984); perf or imperf (self-adhesive) (2986).
2982 **2104** (32 c.) multicoloured (red "G") 40 15
2984 (32 c.) multicoloured (blue "G") 40 15
2986 (32 c.) multicoloured (black "G") 40 15

1994. New Year.
2991 **2106** 29 c. multicoloured . . 40 15

2107 Cherub (detail from "Sistine Madonna" by Raphael)
2108 Alligator

1995. Greetings Stamp. No value expressed.
(a) Size 20 × 26 mm.
2992 **2107** (32 c.) multicoloured . . 40 15

(b) Size 18 × 22 mm. Self-adhesive. Imperf.
2993 **2107** (32 c.) multicoloured . 40 15
For Type **2107** but with face value "32", see No. 3020.

1995. 150th Anniv of Florida Statehood.
2994 **2108** 32 c. multicoloured . . 40 15

2109 Butte
2110 Front of Motor Car

1995. Non-profit Organizations Stamp. Ordinary or self-adhesive gum.
2995 **2109** (5 c.) orange, blue and yellow 10 10

1995. Bulk Rate Stamp. Ordinary or self-adhesive gum.
2996 **2110** (10 c.) vermilion, black and red 10 10

2111 Motor Car Tail Fin
2112 Juke Box
2113 Flag over Field

1995. First Class Postcard Stamp. Ordinary or self-adhesive gum.
2997 **2111** (15 c.) multicoloured . 20 10

1995. Presorted First Class Stamp. Ordinary or self-adhesive gum.
2999 **2112** (25 c.) multicoloured . 35 15

1995. Self-adhesive. Imperf.
3001 **2113** 32 c. multicoloured . . 40 15

1995. Circus Wagon. As No. 2481 but value expressed as "5c".
3002 **1720** 5 c. red 10 10

2115 Flag over Porch

2116 Globe in Bath (Christy Millard)

1995. Perf or imperf (self-adhesive).

3003	**2115**	32 c. multicoloured	40	15

1995. 25th Anniv of Earth Day. Multicoloured.

3009	32 c. Type **2116**	40	15
3010	32 c. Solar energy (Jennifer Michalove)	40	15
3011	32 c. Youth planting tree (Brian Hailes)	40	15
3012	32 c. Family cleaning up beach (Melody Kiper)	40	15

2120 Nixon

2121 Bessie Coleman

1995. 1st Death Anniv of Richard Nixon (President, 1968–74).

3013	**2120**	32 c. multicoloured	40	15

1995. Birds. Value expressed as "1c" etc. Mult.

3019	1 c. (as T **1817**)	10	10
3153	2 c. Eastern bluebird	10	10
3154	3 c. (as No. 2586)	10	10

1995. Black Heritage. Bessie Coleman (aviator).

3014	**2121**	32 c. black and red	40	15

2125 Cherub

1995. Greetings Stamps. Details from "Sistine Madonna" by Raphael. Ordinary gum (3020/1) or self-adhesive (3156, 3023). Perf (3020/1, 3156) or imperf (3023).

3020	**2107**	32 c. multicoloured (20 × 26 mm)	40	15
3156		32 c. multicoloured (18 × 22 mm)	45	15
3021	**2125**	55 c. multicoloured (27 × 21 mm)	70	25
3023		55 c. multicoloured (21 × 19 mm)	70	25

2126 Golf

1995. Sports. Multicoloured.

3024	32 c. Type **2126**	40	15
3025	32 c. Volleyball	40	15
3026	32 c. Baseball	40	15
3027	32 c. Bowls	40	15
3028	32 c. Tennis	40	15

2131 Flag and Identification Tags

2132 Marilyn Monroe

1995. Memorial Day.

3029	**2131**	32 c. multicoloured	40	15

1995. Legends of Hollywood.

3030	**2132**	32 c. multicoloured	40	15

2133 Blue Jay

2134 Horseman carrying Flag

1995. Ordinary or self-adhesive gum.

3032	**2133**	20 c. multicoloured	25	10

1995. 150th Anniv of Texas Statehood.

3033	**2134**	32 c. multicoloured	40	15

2135 Split Rock, Lake Superior

2140 "Challenger" (space shuttle)

1995. Great Lakes Lighthouses. Multicoloured.

3034	32 c. Type **2135**	40	15
3035	32 c. St. Joseph, Lake Michigan	40	15
3036	32 c. Spectacle Reef, Lake Huron	40	15
3037	32 c. Marblehead, Lake Erie	40	15
3038	32 c. Thirty Mile Point, Lake Ontario	40	15

1995.

3039	**2140**	$3 multicoloured	4·00	1·40

2141 Emblem

2142 U.S.S. "Monitor" and C.S.S. "Virginia" (ironclads) in Battle

1995. 50th Anniv of U.N.O.

3040	**2141**	32 c. blue	40	15

1995. 130th Anniv of End of American Civil War. Multicoloured.

3041	32 c. Type **2142**	40	15
3042	32 c. Gen. Robert E. Lee (Confederate)	40	15
3043	32 c. Clara Barton (Union nurse)	40	15
3044	32 c. Gen. Ulysses S. Grant (Union)	40	15
3045	32 c. Battle of Shiloh	40	15
3046	32 c. Jefferson Davis (Confederate President)	40	15
3047	32 c. Vice-Admiral David Farragut (Union)	40	15
3048	32 c. Frederick Douglass (journalist and diplomat)	40	15
3049	32 c. Rear-Admiral Raphael Semmes (Confederate)	40	15
3050	32 c. Abraham Lincoln (U.S. President, 1861–65)	40	15
3051	32 c. Harriet Tubman (black rights campaigner)	40	15
3052	32 c. Brig.-Gen. Stand Watie (Confederate)	40	15
3053	32 c. Gen. Joseph Johnston (Confederate)	40	15
3054	32 c. Major-Gen. Winfield Hancock (Union)	40	15
3055	32 c. Mary Chesnut (Confederate diarist)	40	15
3056	32 c. Battle of Chancellorsville	40	15
3057	32 c. Major-Gen. William Sherman (Union)	40	15
3058	32 c. Phoebe Pember (Confederate nurse)	40	15
3059	32 c. Lt.-Gen. Thomas "Stonewall" Jackson (Confederate)	40	15
3060	32 c. Battle of Gettysburg	40	15

Each stamp is inscribed on the back, under the gum, with a brief history of the subject depicted.

2147 Peaches

1995. Multicoloured. Ordinary or self-adhesive gum.

3061	32 c. Type **2147**	40	15
3062	32 c. Pear	40	15

2149 King Horse, 1910 (Stein and Goldstein)

2150 Indian Pony, 1905 (Daniel Muller)

2151 Armoured Horse, 1912 (Stein and Goldstein)

2152 Lillie Belle, 1917 (C. W. Parker Co)

1995. Carousel Horses.

3067	**2149**	32 c. multicoloured	40	15
3068	**2150**	32 c. multicoloured	40	15
3069	**2151**	32 c. multicoloured	40	15
3070	**2152**	32 c. multicoloured	40	15

2153 Launch of Space Shuttle "Endeavour"

1995.

3071	**2153**	$10.75 multicoloured	14·00	4·75

2154 1913 and 1976 Women's Rights Marches

1995. 75th Anniv of Ratification of 19th Amendment (giving women the right to vote).

3072	**2154**	32 c. multicoloured	40	15

2155 Coleman Hawkins

1995. Jazz Musicians. Multicoloured. (a) With value in white.

3073	32 c. Louis Armstrong	40	15

(b) With value in black.

3074	32 c. Type **2155**	40	15
3075	32 c. Louis Armstrong	40	15
3076	32 c. James P. Johnson	40	15
3077	32 c. Jelly Roll Morton	40	15
3078	32 c. Charlie Parker	40	15
3079	32 c. Eubie Blake	40	15
3080	32 c. Charles Mingus	40	15
3081	32 c. Thelonious Monk	40	15
3082	32 c. John Coltrane	40	15
3083	32 c. Erroll Garner	40	15

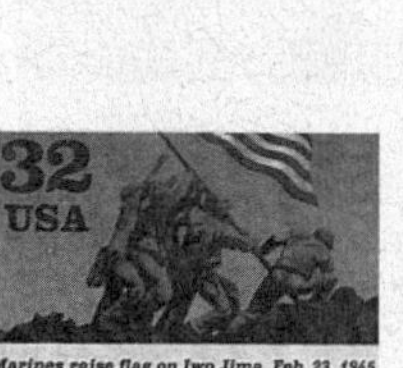

2165 Marines raising Flag on Iwo Jima

2175 Asters

1995. United States Participation in Second World War. Multicoloured.

3084	32 c. Type **2165**	40	15
3085	32 c. Liberation of Manila	40	15
3086	32 c. Troops advancing on Okinawa	40	15
3087	32 c. Bridge across Elbe River	40	15
3088	32 c. Liberation of concentration camp survivors	40	15
3089	32 c. German Surrender at Reims	40	15
3090	32 c. Refugees	40	15
3091	32 c. President Truman announcing Japanese surrender	40	15
3092	32 c. News of victory reaches America	40	15
3093	32 c. Honouring returned service personnel	40	15

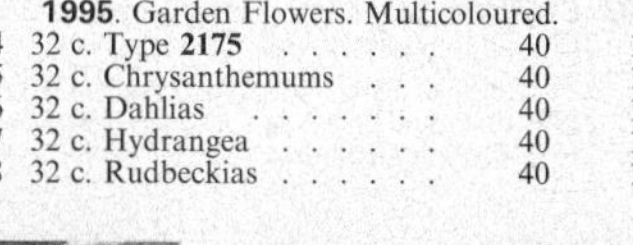

1995. Garden Flowers. Multicoloured.

3094	32 c. Type **2175**	40	15
3095	32 c. Chrysanthemums	40	15
3096	32 c. Dahlias	40	15
3097	32 c. Hydrangea	40	15
3098	32 c. Rudbeckias	40	15

2180 Rickenbacker

2181 Fishes, Shell and Palau Flag

1995. Aviation Pioneers. Eddie Rickenbacker (fighter pilot).

3099	**2180**	60 c. multicoloured	80	30

1995. 1st Anniv of Independence of Palau.

3100	**2181**	32 c. multicoloured	40	15

2182 Santa Claus on Rooftop

2186 The Yellow Kid

1995. Christmas (1st issue). Victorian Designs from writing tablet (2182) or postcards (others). Ordinary or self-adhesive gum.

3101	32 c. Type **2182**	40	15
3102	32 c. Boy holding jumping jack	40	15
3103	32 c. Boy holding tree	40	15
3104	32 c. Santa Claus making toy sleigh	40	15

See also Nos. 3135/9.

1995. Centenary of Comic Strips. Multicoloured.

3113	32 c. Type **2186**	40	15
3114	32 c. Katzenjammer Kids	40	15
3115	32 c. Little Nemo in Slumberland	40	15
3116	32 c. Bringing Up Father	40	15
3117	32 c. Krazy Kat	40	15
3118	32 c. Rube Goldberg's Inventions	40	15
3119	32 c. Toonerville Folks	40	15
3120	32 c. Gasoline Alley	40	15
3121	32 c. Barney Google	40	15
3122	32 c. Little Orphan Annie	40	15
3123	32 c. Popeye	40	15
3124	32 c. Blondie	40	15
3125	32 c. Dick Tracy	40	15
3126	32 c. Alley Oop	40	15
3127	32 c. Nancy	40	15
3128	32 c. Flash Gordon	40	15
3129	32 c. Li'l Abner	40	15
3130	32 c. Terry and the Pirates	40	15
3131	32 c. Prince Valiant	40	15
3132	32 c. Brenda Starr, Reporter	40	15

Each stamp is inscribed on the back, under the gum, with a brief history of the subject depicted.

2187 "Swift" (racing sloop) and Academy Chapel

1995. 150th Anniv of Naval Academy, Annapolis.

3133	**2187**	32 c. multicoloured	40	15

2188 Williams and Streetcar

1995. Literary Arts. Tennessee Williams (dramatist).

3134	**2188**	32 c. multicoloured	40	15

2189 "Enthroned Madonna and Child" (Giotto)

2190 Midnight Angel (after Ellen Clapsaddle)

2191 Children Sledding

2192 Polk

1995. Christmas (2nd issue). (a) Ordinary gum. Perf.
3135 **2189** 32 c. multicoloured . . 40 15

(b) Self-adhesive. Roul (3137) or imperf (3139).
3137 **2190** 32 c. multicoloured . . 40 15
3139 **2191** 32 c. multicoloured . . 40 15

1995. Birth Bicentenary of James K. Polk (President 1844–49).
3140 **2192** 32 c. brown 40 15

2193 Columbia Battery-powered Car, 1898

2198 Delicate Arch, Arches National Park

1996. Veteran Cars. Multicoloured.
3141 32 c. Type **2193** 40 15
3142 32 c. Winton Car, 1899 . . . 40 15
3143 32 c. White Steam-powered Car, 1901 . . . . 40 15
3144 32 c. Duryea Car, 1893 . . . 40 15
3145 32 c. Haynes Car, 1894 . . . 40 15

1996. Centenary of Utah Statehood.
3146 **2198** 32 c. multicoloured . . 40 15

2199 Crocus

2206 Just

1996. Garden Flowers. Multicoloured.
3147 32 c. Type **2199** 40 15
3148 32 c. Winter aconites 40 15
3149 32 c. Pansies 40 15
3150 32 c. Snowdrops 40 15
3151 32 c. Anemones 40 15

1996. Black Heritage. Ernest Just (marine biologist).
3157 **2206** 32 c. multicoloured . . 40 15

2207 The Castle (first Smithsonian building)

1996. 150th Anniv of Smithsonian Institution.
3158 **2207** 32 c. multicoloured . . 40 15

2208 Rat

1996. New Year.
3159 **2208** 32 c. multicoloured . . 40 15

2209 Frederic Ives (halftone process)

2213 Face, Map and Compass

1996. Pioneers of Communication. Multicoloured.
3160 32 c. Type **2209** 40 15
3161 32 c. William Dickson (motion pictures) 40 15
3162 32 c. Eadweard Muybridge (photography) 40 15
3163 32 c. Ottmar Mergenthaler (linotype) 40 15

1996. 50th Anniv of Fulbright Scholarships (international educational exchange programme).
3164 **2213** 32 c. multicoloured . . 40 15

2214 Jacqueline Cochran

2215 Mountains

1996. Aviation Pioneers. Jacqueline Cochran (first woman to fly faster than speed of sound).
3165 **2214** 50 c. multicoloured . . 60 20

1996. Non-profit Organizations. No value expressed. Ordinary or self-adhesive gum.
3166 **2215** (5 c.) multicoloured . . 10 10

2216 Runners

2217 Decathlon

1996. 100th Boston Marathon.
3168 **2216** 32 c. multicoloured . . 40 15

1996. Olympic Games, Atlanta. Multicoloured.
3169 32 c. Type **2217** 40 15
3170 32 c. Men's canoeing 40 15
3171 32 c. Women's running . . . 40 15
3172 32 c. Women's diving . . . 40 15
3173 32 c. Men's cycling 40 15
3174 32 c. Freestyle wrestling . . 40 15
3175 32 c. Women's gymnastics . . 40 15
3176 32 c. Women's sailboarding . 40 15
3177 32 c. Men's putting the shot 40 15
3178 32 c. Women's football . . . 40 15
3179 32 c. Beach volleyball . . . 40 15
3180 32 c. Men's rowing 40 15
3181 32 c. Men's sprinting 40 15
3182 32 c. Women's swimming . . 40 15
3183 32 c. Women's softball . . . 40 15
3184 32 c. Men's hurdling 40 15
3185 32 c. Men's swimming . . . 40 15
3186 32 c. Men's gymnastics . . . 40 15
3187 32 c. Show jumping 40 15
3188 32 c. Men's basketball . . . 40 15

2218 "Red Poppy"

2219 Tennessee State Capitol

1996. 10th Death Anniv of Georgia O'Keeffe (painter).
3193 **2218** 32 c. multicoloured . . 40 15

1996. Bicentenary of Tennessee. Ordinary or self-adhesive gum.
3194 **2219** 32 c. multicoloured . . 40 15

2220 Fancy Dance

2225 Mastodon

1996. Traditional Amerindian Dances.
3196 32 c. Type **2220** 40 15
3197 32 c. Butterfly dance 40 15
3198 32 c. Traditional dance . . . 40 15
3199 32 c. Raven dance 40 15
3200 32 c. Hoop dance 40 15

1996. Prehistoric Animals.
3201 32 c. Type **2225** 40 15
3202 32 c. Sabre-tooth tiger 40 15
3203 32 c. Eohippus 40 15
3204 32 c. Woolly mammoth . . . 40 15

2229 Woman and Ribbon

2230 James Dean

1996. Breast Cancer Awareness Campaign.
3205 **2229** 32 c. multicoloured . . . 40 15

1996. Legends of Hollywood.
3211 **2230** 32 c. multicoloured . . . 40 15

2231 Mighty Casey

2235 "The Discus Thrower" (Miron)

1996. Folk Heroes. Multicoloured.
3212 32 c. Type **2231** 40 15
3213 32 c. Paul Bunyan 40 15
3214 32 c. John Henry 40 15
3215 32 c. Pecos Bill 40 15

1996. Centenary of Modern Olympic Games.
3216 **2235** 32 c. brown 40 15

2236 "Young Corn" (Grant Wood)

2237 Early Postal Carrier and Horse-drawn Mail Wagon

1996. 150th Anniv of Iowa Statehood. Ordinary or self-adhesive gum.
3217 **2236** 32 c. multicoloured . . . 40 15

1996. Centenary of Free Rural Postal Deliveries.
3221 **2237** 32 c. multicoloured . . . 40 15

2238 "Robert E. Lee"

1996. 19th-century Paddle-steamers. Self-adhesive.
3222 32 c. Type **2238** 40 15
3223 32 c. "Sylvan Dell" 40 15
3224 32 c. "Far West" 40 15
3225 32 c. "Rebecca Everingham" . 40 15
3226 32 c. "Bailey Gatzert" 40 15

2243 Count Basie

1996. Big Band Leaders (3227/30) and Songwriters (3231/4). Multicoloured.
3227 32 c. Type **2243** 40 15
3228 32 c. Tommy and Jimmy Dorsey 40 15
3229 32 c. Glenn Miller 40 15
3230 32 c. Benny Goodman . . . 40 15
3231 32 c. Harold Arlen 40 15
3232 32 c. Johnny Mercer 40 15
3233 32 c. Dorothy Fields 40 15
3234 32 c. Hoagy Carmichael . . . 40 15

2251 Fitzgerald

1996. Birth Centenary of Francis Scott Fitzgerald (writer).
3235 **2251** 23 c. multicoloured . . . 30 10

2252 Black-footed Ferret

1996. Endangered Species. Multicoloured.
3236 32 c. Type **2252** 40 15
3237 32 c. Thick-billed parrot . . . 40 15
3238 32 c. Hawaiian monk seal . . 40 15
3239 32 c. American crocodile . . 40 15
3240 32 c. Ocelot 40 15
3241 32 c. Schaus swallowtail . . 40 15
3242 32 c. Wyoming toad 40 15
3243 32 c. Brown pelican 40 15
3244 32 c. California condor . . . 40 15
3245 32 c. Gila trout 40 15
3246 32 c. San Francisco garter snake 40 15
3247 32 c. Woodland caribou . . 40 15
3248 32 c. Florida panther 40 15
3249 32 c. Piping plover 40 15
3250 32 c. Florida manatee . . . 40 15

2253 Circuit Boards covering Brain

1996. Computer Technology. 50th Anniv of ENIAC (Army computer system).
3251 **2253** 32 c. multicoloured . . 40 15

2254 Family at Fireside

2258 Ice Skaters

1996. Christmas (1st issue). Multicoloured. Ordinary or self-adhesive gum (3252/5), self-adhesive (3260).
3252 32 c. Type **2254** 40 15
3253 32 c. Decorating Christmas tree 40 15
3254 32 c. Santa Claus in chimney and child sleeping 40 15
3255 32 c. Mother and child carrying gifts 40 15
3260 32 c. Type **2258** 40 15
See also No. 3263.

2259 Lighted Candles

2260 Madonna and Child (detail from "Adoration of the Shepherds", Paolo de Matteis)

1996. Festival of Hanukkah. Self-adhesive.
3261 **2259** 32 c. multicoloured . . 40 15

1996. Christmas (2nd issue). Ordinary or self-adhesive gum.
3263 **2260** 32 c. multicoloured . . 40 15

2262 Ox

1997. New Year.
3266 **2262** 32 c. multicoloured . . 40 15

CERTIFIED MAIL

C 524 Postman

1955.

C1070	C 524	15 c. red	35	25

NEWSPAPER STAMPS

N 21 Washington (½-size illustration)

1865. 5 c. with coloured or white border.

N78a	N 21	5 c. blue	22·00	18·00
N80	–	10 c. green	25·00	
N81	–	25 c. red	48·00	

DESIGNS: 10 c. Franklin; 20 c. Lincoln.

N 42 "Freedom"

N 87 "Freedom"

1875. Different Frames.

N252	N 42	1 c. black	5·50	3·00
N291	N 87	1 c. black	2·25	1·75
N228	N 42	2 c. black	4·00	3·00
N292	N 87	2 c. black	2·50	1·25
N229	N 42	3 c. black	5·00	3·25
N230		4 c. black	5·50	3·25
N293	N 87	5 c. black	4·00	3·00
N231	N 42	6 c. black	10·00	7·00
N232		8 c. black	10·00	7·00
N185		9 c. black	42·00	38·00
N233		10 c. black	10·00	6·00
N294	N 87	10 c. black	2·50	1·75
N253	A	12 c. red	19·00	8·50
N254		24 c. red	22·00	10·00
N295		25 c. red	5·50	5·50
N255		36 c. red	30·00	12·00
N256		48 c. red	42·00	20·00
N296		50 c. red	6·50	8·00
N191		60 c. red	55·00	30·00
N258		72 c. red	70·00	32·00
N240		84 c. red	£120	60·00
N241		96 c. red	75·00	42·00
N242	–	$1.92 brown	60·00	38·00
N297	–	$2 red	7·50	11·00
N243	–	$3 red	60·00	38·00
N298	–	$5 blue	13·00	18·00
N244	–	$6 blue	£110	65·00
N245	–	$9 orange	75·00	42·00
N299	–	$10 green	12·00	18·00
N246	–	$12 green	£110	55·00
N300	–	$20 black	13·00	19·00
N247	–	$24 purple	£140	75·00
N248	–	$36 red	£180	90·00
N249	–	$48 brown	£225	£120
N301	–	$50 red	16·00	22·00
N250	–	$60 violet	£225	£120
N302	–	$100 violet	18·00	27·00

DESIGNS: A, Astraea or "Justice"; $1.92, Ceres; $2, $3 "Victory"; $5, $6 Clio; $9 Minerva; $10, $12 Vesta; $20, $24 "Peace"; $36, $50 "Commerce"; $48 Hebe; $60, $100 Minnehaha.

OFFICIAL STAMPS

For list of stamps used on correspondence from individual Government Departments, between 1873 and 1879, see the Stanley Gibbons Part 22 (U.S.A.) Catalogue.

O 1315 Eagle

O 1438

O 1588

1983.

O2008	O 1315	1 c. blue, red and black	10	10
O2009		4 c. blue, red and black	10	15
O2010		13 c. blue, red and black	15	45
O2011		14 c. blue, red and black	25	50
O2012		17 c. blue, red and black	25	30
O2015		20 c. blue, red and black	1·75	65
O2016		22 c. blue, red and black	55	50
O2013		$1 blue, red and black	1·50	70
O2014		$5 blue, red and black	6·00	4·00

1985. No value expressed. (a) Inscr "Postal Card Rate D".

O2140	O 1438	(14 c.) blue, red and black	3·00	70

(b) Inscr "Domestic Letter Rate D".

O2141	–	(22 c.) blue, red and black	3·00	70

1988. No value expressed.

O2344	O 1588	(25 c.) blue, black and red	35	15

O 1592 O 1793 O 2122

1988.

O2348	O 1592	1 c. blue, blk & red	10	10
O2349		4 c. blue, blk & red	10	10
O2350		10 c. blue, black and red	10	10
O2354		15 c. blue, black and red	25	10
O2351		19 c. blue, black and red	25	35
O2355		20 c. blue, black and red	30	10
O2352		23 c. blue, black and red	30	15
O2356		25 c. blue, black and red	35	10
O2357		29 c. blue, black and red	40	15
O2353		$1 blue, blk & red	1·25	25

The 10 c. and $1 have an additional inscription ("USA1993" repeated several times) above the face value.

1991. Value expressed as "F".

O2558	O 1793	(29 c.) blue, black and red	40	15

1994. Value expressed as "G".

O2990	O 1793	(32 c.) blue, black and red	40	15

1995.

O3015	O 2122	1 c. blue, black and red	10	10
O3016		20 c. blue, black and red	25	10
O3017		23 c. blue, black and red	30	10
O3018		32 c. blue, black and red	40	15

No. O3015 has the face value expressed as "1 c." The line above the face value consists of "USA" and the year date repeated several times.

PARCEL POST STAMPS

P 134 Post Office Clerk

1912.

P423	P 134	1 c. red	2·75	80
P424	–	2 c. red	2·75	50
P425	–	3 c. red	11·00	4·50
P426	–	4 c. red	20·00	1·50
P427	–	5 c. red	35·00	1·25
P428	–	10 c. red	40·00	1·50
P429	–	15 c. red	50·00	7·00
P430	–	20 c. red	85·00	13·00
P431	–	25 c. red	75·00	4·25
P432	–	50 c. red	£180	28·00
P433	–	75 c. red	50·00	20·00
P434	–	$1 red	£250	16·00

DESIGNS: 2 c. City carrier; 3 c. Railway postal clerk; 4 c. Rural carrier; 5 c. Steam mail train; 10 c. "Kronprinz Wilhelm" (liner) and mail tender; 15 c. Automobile service; 20c. Wright Type A biplane carrying mail; 25 c. Manufacturing (Pullman works); 50 c. Dairying; 75 c. Harvesting; $1 Fruit growing.

PARCEL POST POSTAGE DUE STAMPS

PD 134

1912.

PD423	PD 134	1 c. green	6·50	2·50
PD424		2 c. green	50·00	12·00
PD425		5 c. green	8·00	2·50
PD426		10 c. green	£120	28·00
PD427		25 c. green	55·00	2·75

POSTAGE DUE STAMPS

D 43

D 87

1879.

D207	D 43	1 c. brown	18·00	3·50
D222		2 c. brown	28·00	1·50
D209		3 c. brown	16·00	1·75
D224		5 c. brown	£180	7·50
D225		10 c. brown	£160	4·50
D226		30 c. brown	75·00	16·00
D213		50 c. brown	£170	26·00

1891.

D235	D 43	1 c. red	8·50	35
D236		2 c. red	11·00	30
D237		3 c. red	24·00	2·50
D238		5 c. red	26·00	2·50
D239		10 c. red	48·00	6·50
D240		30 c. red	£180	60·00
D241		50 c. red	£200	65·00

1894.

D529	D 87	½ c. red	40	10
D530		1 c. red	1·25	10
D531		2 c. red	1·00	10
D532		3 c. red	6·00	10
D533		5 c. red	6·00	10
D534a		10 c. red	9·00	10
D535a		30 c. red	38·00	30
D536		50 c. red	60·00	10

D 201 D 202 D 581

1931.

D702	D 201	½ c. red	75	10
D703		1 c. red	15	10
D704		2 c. red	20	10
D705		3 c. red	25	10
D706		5 c. red	35	10
D707		10 c. red	1·10	10
D708		30 c. red	8·00	10
D709		50 c. red	8·50	10
D699a	D 202	$1 red	22·00	10
D700a		$5 red	32·00	15

1959. Centres in black.

D1130	D 581	½ c. red	1·25	1·25
D1131		1 c. red	15	10
D1132		2 c. red	15	10
D1133		3 c. red	15	10
D1134		4 c. red	15	10
D1135		5 c. red	15	10
D1136		6 c. red	15	10
D1137		7 c. red	15	10
D1138		8 c. red	15	10
D1139		10 c. red	15	10
D1140		11 c. red	25	15
D1141		13 c. red	30	25
D1142		17 c. red	30	25
D1143		30 c. red	50	10
D1144		50 c. red	75	10
D1145		$1 red	1·60	10
D1146		$5 red	7·50	15

In the dollar values the numerals are double-lined and vertical.

REGISTERED LETTER STAMP

R 133 American Bald Eagle

1911.

R404	R 133	10 c. blue	75·00	3·00

SPECIAL DELIVERY AIR STAMPS

AE 247 Great Seal of U.S.A.

1934.

AE750	AE 247	16 c. blue	60	70
AE751		16 c. blue and red	40	15

SPECIAL DELIVERY STAMPS

E 46 Messenger Running

1885. Inscr "AT A SPECIAL DELIVERY OFFICE".

E217	E 46	10 c. blue	£160	20·00

1888. As Type E 46, but inscr "AT ANY POST OFFICE".

E283	E 46	10 c. blue	90·00	1·75
E251		10 c. orange	£110	8·50

E 117 Messenger on Bicycle

1917.

E529	E 117	10 c. blue	11·00	15

E 129 Hat of Mercury and Olive-branch

E 143 Delivery by Motor Cycle

1908.

E374	E 129	10 c. green	48·00	20·00

1922.

E648	E 143	10 c. blue	60	10
E648a		10 c. violet	60	10
E649		13 c. blue	45	10
E650		15 c. orange	65	10
E651		17 c. yellow	3·00	2·75

E 144 Delivery by Van

1925.

E652	E 144	20 c. black	1·50	10

E 520 Delivery by Hand

1954.

E1066	E 520	20 c. blue	60	10
E1067		30 c. lake	70	10

E 799 Arrows

1969.

E1374	E 799	45 c. red and blue	1·40	15
E1375		60 c. blue and red	1·40	10

SPECIAL HANDLING STAMPS

SH 173

1925.

SH624	SH 173	10 c. green	1·00	80
SH625		15 c. green	1·10	80
SH626		20 c. green	1·50	25
SH628		25 c. green	16·00	6·00

UNITED STATES POSTAL AGENCY IN SHANGHAI Pt. 17

These stamps were valid for use on mail despatched from the U.S. Postal Agency in Shanghai to addresses in the United States. This agency was closed 31st December 1922.

100 cents = 1 dollar (Chinese)

1919. United States stamps of 1908–12 surch **SHANGHAI CHINA** and new value.

1	**128**	2 c. on 1 c. green	14·00	16·00
17		2 Cts. on 1 c. green	75·00	80·00
2		4 c. on 2 c. pink	14·00	17·00
18		4 Cts. on 2 c. red	75·00	75·00
3		6 c. on 3 c. violet	28·00	40·00
4		8 c. on 4 c. brown	32·00	42·00
5		10 c. on 5 c. blue	38·00	45·00
6		12 c. on 6 c. orange	48·00	60·00
7		14 c. on 7 c. black	50·00	65·00
8	**133**	16 c. on 8 c. olive	40·00	45·00
9		18 c. on 9 c. orange	40·00	45·00
10		20 c. on 10 c. yellow	38·00	40·00
11a		24 c. on 12 c. red	40·00	50·00
12		30 c. on 15 c. grey	55·00	60·00
13		40 c. on 20 c. blue	85·00	95·00
14		60 c. on 30 c. red	80·00	95·00
15		$1 on 50 c. lilac	£500	£400
16		$2 on $1 black	£325	£325

UPPER SENEGAL AND NIGER Pt. 6

A French Colony in W. Africa, E. of Senegal, formerly called Senegambia and Niger, and became part of French Sudan in 1920.

100 centimes = 1 franc

1906. "Faidherbe", "Palms" and "Balay" key-types inscr "HT-SENEGAL-NIGER" in blue (10, 40 c., 5 f.) or red (others).

35	I	1 c. grey	50	60
36		2 c. brown	50	65
37		4 c. brown on blue	70	70
38		5 c. green	2·50	1·25
39		10 c. red	2·50	95
40		15 c. violet	3·25	2·25
41	J	20 c. black on blue	1·00	2·25
42		25 c. blue	6·50	4·50
43		30 c. brown on pink	2·75	4·00
44		35 c. black on yellow	2·50	1·75
45		40 c. red on blue	4·00	4·00
46		45 c. brown on green	4·75	5·25
47		50 c. violet	4·50	4·00
48		75 c. green on orange	5·00	5·50
49	K	1 f. black on blue	10·00	10·00
50		2 f. blue on red	30·00	30·00
51		5 f. red on yellow	50·00	60·00

7 Touareg

1914.

59	**7**	1 c. violet and purple	10	25
60		2 c. purple and grey	10	25
61		4 c. blue and black	10	25
62		5 c. green and light green	10	25
63		10 c. carmine and red	10	90
64		15 c. yellow and brown	25	60
65		20 c. black and purple	30	70
66		25 c. blue and ultramarine	40	80
67		30 c. chocolate and brown	40	80
68		35 c. violet and red	30	1·00
69		40 c. red and grey	80	85
70		45 c. brown and blue	30	65
71		50 c. green and black	50	75
72		75 c. brown and yellow	40	85
73		1 f. purple and brown	1·40	1·75
74		2 f. blue and green	60	1·40
75		5 f. black and violet	6·75	4·75

1915. Red Cross. Surch **5c** and red cross.

76	**7**	10 c. + 5 c. carmine and red	50	55

POSTAGE DUE STAMPS

1906. "Natives" key-type inscr "HT-SENEGAL-NIGER".

D52	L	5 c. green and red	1·25	1·25
D53		10 c. purple and blue	3·75	3·00
D54		15 c. blue & red on blue	5·50	4·75
D55		20 c. black & red on yell	6·00	3·25
D56		50 c. violet and red	15·00	11·00
D57		60 c. black & red on buff	9·75	9·00
D58		1 f. black & red on flesh	25·00	18·00

1915. "Figures" key-type inscr "HT. SENEGAL-NIGER".

D77	M	5 c. green	60	70
D78		10 c. red	60	70
D79		15 c. grey	65	70
D80		20 c. brown	65	70
D81		30 c. blue	1·25	1·50
D82		50 c. black	1·00	1·25
D83		60 c. orange	3·00	3·25
D84		1 f. violet	2·25	3·00

For later issues see **FRENCH SUDAN**.

UPPER SILESIA Pt. 7

Stamps issued during a plebiscite held in 1921 to decide the future of the district. After the plebiscite it was divided between Germany and Poland.

100 pfenning = 1 mark

1

9 Coal-mine in Silesia

1920.

1	**1**	2½ pf. grey	35	50
2		3 pf. brown	30	65
3		5 pf. green	15	25
4		10 pf. brown	15	30
5		15 pf. violet	15	25
6		20 pf. blue	15	25
7		50 pf. purple	3·50	4·75
8		1 m. pink	3·50	7·50
9		5 m. orange	3·50	8·00

1920. Surch.

10	**1**	5 pf. on 15 pf. violet	6·50	18·00
12		5 pf. on 20 pf. blue	10	15
14		10 pf. on 20 pf. blue	10	10
17		50 pf. on 5 m. orange	10·00	22·00

1920.

19	**9**	2½ pf. grey	15	10
20		3 pf. purple	20	10
21		5 pf. green	10	10
22		10 pf. red	10	10
23		15 pf. violet	10	10
24		20 pf. blue	10	10
25		25 pf. brown	15	10
26		30 pf. yellow	10	10
27		40 pf. green	10	10

Same design, but larger.

28	**9**	50 pf. grey	10	10
29		60 pf. blue	20	15
30		75 pf. green	60	40
31		80 pf. purple	50	40
32		1 m. mauve	30	15
33		2 m. brown	30	30
34		3 m. violet	50	30
35		5 m. orange	1·10	85

1921. Optd **Plebiscite 20 mars 1921.**

36	**9**	10 pf. red	2·00	6·00
37		15 pf. violet	2·00	6·00
38		20 pf. blue	2·00	9·00
39		25 pf. brown	5·00	15·00
40		30 pf. yellow	5·00	15·00
41		40 pf. green	5·00	15·00
42		50 pf. grey	5·00	18·00
43		60 pf. blue	6·00	15·00
44		75 pf. green	6·00	18·00
45		80 pf. purple	7·00	26·00
46		1 m. mauve	12·00	45·00

1922. Type **9** in new colours and surch.

47	**9**	4 m. on 60 pf. green	60	1·00
48		10 m. on 75 pf. red	90	2·50
49		20 m. on 80 pf. orange	5·00	10·00

OFFICIAL STAMPS

1920. Stamps of Germany optd **C.I.H.S.** within a circle.

(a) Stamps of 1902 and 1916.

O 1	**24**	2 pf. grey	—	£900
O 2		2½ pf. grey	£1500	£500
O 3	**10**	3 pf. brown	—	£600
O 4		5 pf. green	£800	£400
O 5	**24**	7½ pf. orange	£1400	£700
O 6	**10**	10 pf. red	£500	£225
O 7	**24**	15 pf. violet	£550	£190
O 8	**10**	20 pf. blue	£550	£225
O 9		25 pf. black and red on yellow	—	£900
O10		30 pf. black and orange on pink	£900	£225
O11	**24**	35 pf. brown	£900	£200
O12	**10**	40 pf. black and red	£600	£200
O13		50 pf. black and purple on pink	£600	£200
O14		60 pf. purple	£800	£200
O15		75 pf. black and green	£500	£200
O16		80 pf. black and red on red	—	£750
O17	**12**	1 m. red	£1500	£500
O18	**13**	2 m. blue	—	£750

(b) War Charity. Nos. 105/6.

O19	**10**	10 + 5 pf. red		
O20	**24**	15 + 5 pf. violet		

(c) National Assembly at Weimar. Nos. 107/10.

O21	**26**	10 pf. red	£650	£650
O22	**27**	15 pf. blue and brown	—	£650
O23	**28**	25 pf. red and green	—	£650
O24		30 pf. red and purple	£650	£650

1920. Official stamps of Germany optd **C.G.H.S.**

(a) As Types O **31** and O **32** (with figures "21").

O25		5 pf. green	15	25
O26		10 pf. red	15	25
O27		15 pf. brown	15	25
O28		20 pf. blue	15	25
O29		30 pf. orange on buff	15	25
O30		50 pf. violet on buff	30	50
O31		1 m. red on buff	4·25	7·00

(b) As Types O **31** and O **32** but without figures.

O32		5 pf. green	55	1·75
O33		10 pf red	10	10
O34		15 pf. purple	10	10
O35		20 pf. blue	10	10
O36		30 pf. orange on buff	10	10
O37		40 pf. red	10	10
O38		50 pf. violet on buff	10	10
O39		60 pf. brown	10	10
O40		1 m. red on buff	10	10
O41		1 m. 25 blue on yellow	10	10
O43		2 m. blue	10	20
O44		5 m. brown on yellow	10	20

UPPER VOLTA Pt. 6; Pt 14

Formerly part of Upper Senegal and Niger, Upper Volta was created a separate colony in 1919. In 1932 it was divided among French Sudan, Ivory Coast and Niger but was reconstituted as a separate territory in 1947 from when it used the stamps of French West Africa.

In 1958 it became an autonomous republic within the French Community and attained full independence in 1960.

In 1984 the name of the state was changed to Burkina Faso.

100 centimes = 1 franc

1920. Stamps of Upper Senegal and Niger optd **HAUTE-VOLTA**.

1	**7**	1 c. violet and purple	10	30
2		2 c. purple and grey	10	30
3		4 c. blue and black	10	30
4		5 c. green and light green	30	65
18		5 c. chocolate and brown	10	30
5		10 c. carmine and red	35	65
19		10 c. green and light green	15	30
20		10 c. blue and mauve	25	55
6		15 c. yellow and brown	35	65
7		20 c. black and purple	50	1·00
8		25 c. blue and ultramarine	60	1·00
21		25 c. green and black	45	75
9		30 c. chocolate and brown	1·10	1·50
22		30 c. carmine and red	40	80
23		30 c. red and violet	40	80
23a		30 c. turquoise and green	40	80
10		35 c. violet and red	45	95
11		40 c. red and grey	45	1·00
12		45 c. brown and blue	35	85
13		50 c. green and black	1·50	3·00
24		50 c. blue & ultramarine	20	45
25		50 c. blue and orange	35	80
26		60 c. red	20	40
26a		65 c. blue and brown	65	1·25
14		75 c. brown and yellow	70	1·50
15		1 f. purple and brown	70	1·25
16		2 f. blue and green	90	1·75
17		5 f. black and violet	2·00	3·00

1922. Surch in figures and bars.

27	**7**	0,01 on 15 c. yellow & brn	45	1·00
28		0,20 on 15 c. yellow & brn	45	1·00
29		0,05 on 15 c. yellow & brn	45	1·00
30		25 c. on 2 f. blue and green	50	1·00
31		25 c. on 5 f. black and vio	50	1·00
32		60 on 75 c. violet on pink	35	75
33		65 on 45 c. brown and blue	50	1·00
34		85 on 45 c. brown and yellow	70	1·40
35		90 c. on 75 c. pink and red	90	1·75
36		1 f. 25 on 1 f. lt blue & blue	45	1·00
37		1 f. 50 on 1 f. ultram & bl	1·25	2·00
37a		3 f. on 5 f. brown and pink	1·75	2·75
38		10 f. on 5 f. pink and green	7·75	10·00
39		20 f. on 5 f. violet & brown	10·00	15·00

3 Hausa Man

5 Hausa Warrior

1928.

40	**3**	1 c. blue and green	10	35
41		2 c. brown and mauve	10	35
42		4 c. black and yellow	15	35
43		5 c. indigo and blue	20	40
44		10 c. blue and pink	50	1·00
45		15 c. brown and blue	95	1·50
46		20 c. brown and green	95	1·50
47	–	25 c. brown and yellow	1·00	1·40
48	–	30 c. deep green and green	1·00	1·60
49	–	40 c. black and pink	1·00	1·90
50	–	45 c. brown and blue	1·25	2·00
51	–	50 c. black and green	1·25	1·40
52	–	65 c. indigo and blue	1·50	2·00
53	–	75 c. black and mauve	[illegible]	[illegible]
54	–	90 c. red and mauve	1·25	2·00
55	**5**	1 f. brown and green	1·10	1·90
56		1 f. 10 blue and mauve	1·25	1·90
57		1 f. 50 blue	1·90	3·00
58		2 f. black and blue	2·00	3·00
59		3 f. brown and yellow	2·25	3·50
60		5 f. brown and mauve	2·25	3·50
61		10 f. black and green	8·25	12·00
62		20 f. black and pink	14·00	18·00

DESIGN—VERT: 25 c. to 90 c. Hausa woman.

1931. "Colonial Exhibition" key-types inscr "HAUTE-VOLTA".

63	E	40 c. green and black	1·75	3·00
64	F	50 c. mauve and black	1·75	3·00
65	G	90 c. red and black	1·75	3·00
66	B	1 f. 50 blue and black	2·75	4·25

6 President Coulibaly

7 Antelope Mask

1959. 1st Anniv of Republic.

67	**6**	25 f. purple and black	30	20

1960. Animal Masks.

68	**7**	30 c. violet and red	10	10
69		40 c. purple and ochre	10	10
70		50 c. olive and turquoise	10	10
71	–	1 f. black, brown and red	10	10
72	–	2 f. multicoloured	10	10
73	–	4 f. black, violet and blue	10	10
74	–	5 f. red, brown and bistre	15	10
75	–	6 f. purple and turquoise	15	10
76	–	8 f. brown and red	20	15
77	–	10 f. purple and green	25	20
78	–	15 f. blue, brown and red	35	25
79	–	20 f. green and blue	40	30
80	–	25 f. purple, green and blue	50	30
81	–	30 f. black, brown & turq	65	30
82	–	40 f. black, red and blue	90	40
83	–	50 f. brown, green & mauve	1·10	45
84	–	60 f. blue and brown	1·50	45
85	–	85 f. blue and turquoise	2·25	60

MASKS: 1 f. to 4 f. Wart-hog; 5 f. to 8 f. Monkey; 10 f. to 20 f. Buffalo; 25 f. Antelope; 30 f. to 50 f. Elephant; 60 f., 85 f. Secretary bird.

8 President Yameogo

1960.

86	**8**	25 f. purple and grey	50	25

1960. 10th Anniv of African Technical Co-operation Commission. As T **4** of Malagasy Republic.

87		25 f. indigo and blue	50	40

1960. 1st Anniv of Conseil de l'Entente. As T **9** of Niger.

88		25 f. multicoloured	65	40

9

1960. Proclamation of Independence.

89	**9**	25 f. brown, red and black	55	40

10 Holste Broussard Airplane and Map

1961. Air.

90	**10**	100 f. blue, green and red	1·90	80
91	–	200 f. brown, red and green	4·75	1·40
92	–	500 f. multicoloured	11·00	5·00

DESIGNS: 200 f. Scene at Ouagadougou Airport; 500 f. Aerial view of Champs Elysees, Ouagadougou.

11 W.M.O. Emblem, Sun and Meteorological Instruments

1961. 1st World Meteorological Day.

93	**11**	25 f. red, blue and black	55	35

12 Arms of Republic

1961. Independence Festival.
94 **12** 25 f. multicoloured 45 30

1962. Air. "Air Afrique" Airline. As T **42** of Mauritania.
95 25 f. mauve, green and purple . 55 30

13 W.M.O. Emblem, Weather Station and Crops

1962. World Meteorological Day.
96 **13** 25 f. blue, green and black . 55 40

1962. Malaria Eradication. As T **43** of Mauritania.
97 25 f. +5 f. red 70 70

14 Nurse and Hospital

1962. Establishment of Red Cross in Upper Volta.
98 **14** 25 f. brown, blue and red . . 60 40

15 African Buffalo at Water-hole

1962. Hunting and Tourism.
99 **15** 5 f. green, blue and sepia . 35 20
100 – 10 f. green, yellow & brn . 45 35
101 – 15 f. green, yellow & brn . 1·10 60
102 – 25 f. green, blue & mauve . 1·10 60
103 – 50 f. green, blue & mauve . 1·60 1·40
104 – 85 f. green, blue & brown . 3·75 2·40
DESIGNS—VERT: 15 f. Waterbuck; 85 f. Kob. HORIZ: 10 f. Lion and lioness; 25 f. Arly Camp; 50 f. Diapaga Camp.

1962. Abidjan Games, 1961. As T **13** of Niger Republic. Multicoloured.
105 20 f. Football 45 30
106 25 f. Cycling 65 35
107 85 f. Boating . . . . 1·40 70

1962. 1st Anniv of Union of African and Malagasy States. As T **45** of Mauritania.
108 30 f. multicoloured . . . . . 1·10 75

16 Flag and U.N. Emblem

1962. Air. 2nd Anniv of Admission to U.N.
109 **16** 50 f. multicoloured 65 35
110 100 f. multicoloured . . . 1·40 65

17 G.P.O., Ouagadougou

1962. Air. Opening of Ouagadougou P.O.
111 **17** 100 f. multicoloured . . . . 1·40 60

1963. Freedom from Hunger. As T **51** of Mauritania.
112 25 f. +5 f. blue, brn & myrtle 70 70

18 Rainfall Map 19 Basketball

1963. World Meteorological Day.
113 **18** 70 c. multicoloured . . . 85 55

1963. Dakar Games. Centres in black and red.
114 **19** 20 f. violet 35 20
115 – 25 f. ochre (Discus) . . . 45 20
116 – 50 f. blue (Judo) 90 40

20 "Argyreia nervosa"

1963. Flowers. Multicoloured.
117 50 c. "Hibiscus rosa sinensis" 10 10
118 1 f. "Oldenlandia grandiflora" 10 10
119 1 f. 50 "Portulaca grandiflora" 10 10
120 2 f. "Nicotiana tabacum" . . 10 10
121 4 f. "Ipomaea stolonifera" . . 15 10
122 5 f. "Striga senegalensis" . . 15 10
123 6 f. "Vigna" 20 10
124 8 f. "Lepidagathis heudelotiana" 30 20
125 10 f. "Euphorbia splendens" . 30 15
126 15 f. "Hippeastrum equestre" 40 30
127 25 f. Type **20** 55 30
128 30 f. "Quisqualis indica" . . 70 35
129 40 f. "Nymphea lotus" . . . 1·25 50
130 50 f. "Plumeria alba" . . . . 1·40 55
131 60 f. "Crotalaria retusa" . . 1·75 80
132 85 f. "Hibiscus esculentus" . 2·40 1·10
The 50 c. to 10 f. are vert.

21 Douglas DC-8 in Flight

1963. Air. 1st Jet-flight, Ouagadougou–Paris.
133 **21** 200 f. multicoloured . . . 4·25 1·25

1963. Air. African and Malagasy Posts and Telecommunications Union. As T **56** of Mauritania.
134 85 f. multicoloured . . . . . 1·25 60

22 Centenary Emblem and Globe 24 "Declaration universelle. . ."

1963. Red Cross Centenary.
135 **22** 25 f. multicoloured 90 65

1963. Air. 1st Anniv of "Air Afrique". Surch **AIR AFRIQUE 19-11-63 50F.**
136 **21** 50 f. on 200 f. multicoloured 1·10 65

1963. 15th Anniv of Declaration of Human Rights.
137 **24** 25 f. multicoloured 60 40

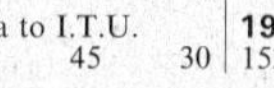

25 "Europafrique" 26 "Telecommunications"

1964. Air. "Europafrique".
138 **25** 50 f. multicoloured . . . . 1·25 70

1964. Admission of Upper Volta to I.T.U.
139 **26** 25 f. multicoloured 45 30

27 Rameses II, Abu Simbel 28 Barograph, Landscape and W.M.O. Emblem

1964. Air. Nubian Monuments Preservation.
140 **27** 25 f. purple and green . . . 65 45
141 100 f. brown and blue . . . 2·25 1·75

1964. World Meteorological Day.
142 **28** 50 f. mauve, blue & green . 85 55

29 Dove and Letters

1964. 1st Anniv of Admission to U.P.U.
143 **29** 25 f. sepia and blue 45 30
144 – 60 f. sepia and orange . . . 90 65
DESIGN: 60 f. Jet airliner and letters.

30 Head of Athlete (bronze) 31 Symbols of Solar Research

1964. Air. Olympic Games, Tokyo.
145 **30** 15 f. green, red and sepia . 35 15
146 – 25 f. green, red and sepia . 50 20
147 – 85 f. green, red and brown . 1·10 70
148 – 100 f. chocolate, red & brn . 1·60 85
DESIGNS: 25 f. Seated athlete (bronze); 85 f. "Victorious athlete" (bronze); 100 f. Venus de Milo.

1964. International Quiet Sun Years.
149 **31** 30 f. red, ochre and green . 60 40

32 Grey Woodpecker 33 President Kennedy

1964. Air.
150 **32** 250 f. multicoloured . . . . 16·00 4·50

1964. French, African and Malagasy Co-operation. As T **68** of Mauritania.
151 70 f. brown, red and blue . . . 1·00 55

1964. Air. Pres. Kennedy Commemoration.
152 **33** 100 f. multicoloured . . . . 1·60 1·10

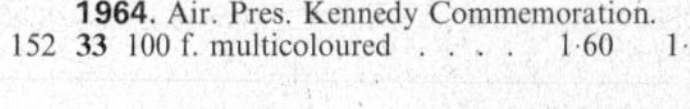

34 Independence Hotel 35 Pygmy Sunbird

1964. Opening of Independence Hotel, Ouagadougou.
153 **34** 25 f. multicoloured . . . . 1·75 65

1965. Birds. Multicoloured.
154 10 f. Type **35** (postage) . . . 1·90 65
155 15 f. Olive-bellied sunbird . . 2·10 85
156 20 f. Splendid sunbird . . . . 3·75 1·25
157 500 f. Abyssinian roller (27 × 48 mm) (air) . . . . 42·00 13·00

36 Sun and Emblems

1965. Air. World Meterological Day.
158 **36** 50 f. multicoloured 85 35

37 Grand Cascade, Banfora

1965. Banfora Waterfalls.
159 – 5 f. brown, blue and green 15 10
160 **37** 25 f. blue, green and red . 55 20
DESIGN—VERT: 5 f. Comoe Cascade.

38 Hughes Telegraph and Modern Telephone

1965. Air. I.T.U. Centenary.
161 **38** 100 f. red, green & turq . . 1·90 85

39 I.C.Y. Emblem

1965. Air. International Co-operation Year.
162 **39** 25 f. multicoloured 45 20
163 100 f. multicoloured . . . 1·25 50

40 Football, Boots and Net 42 "Early Bird" Satellite in Orbit

41 Sacred Alligator of Sabou

1965. 1st African Games, Brazzaville.
164 **40** 15 f. green, red and purple 30 20
165 – 25 f. purple, orange & blue 40 25
166 – 70 f. red and green . . . . 1·00 55
DESIGNS: 25 f. Boxing-gloves and ring; 70 f. Tennis-racquets, ball and net.

1965. Air. Fauna.
167 **41** 60 f. green, turq & brown . 2·25 65
168 – 85 f. brown, bistre & green 2·75 85
DESIGN—VERT: 85 f. Lion.

1965. Air. Space Telecommuncations.
169 **42** 30 f. red, brown and blue . 55 30

43 Lincoln 45 Dromedary

44 President Yameogo

1965. Death Centenary of Abraham Lincoln.
170 **43** 50 f. multicoloured 65 40

1965. Pres. Yameogo.
171 **44** 25 f. multicoloured 45 20

1966. Insects and Fauna. Multicoloured.
172 1 f. "Nemopistha imperatrix" (vert) 10 10
173 2 f. Python (vert) 10 10
174 3 f. "Sphodromantis lineola" . 10 10
175 4 f. "Staurocleis magnifica occidentalis" 15 10
176 5 f. Warthog (vert) 20 10
177 6 f. "Pandinus imperator" . . 20 10
178 8 f. Savanna monkey (vert) . . 35 15
179 10 f. Type **45** 35 20
180 15 f. Leopard (vert) 65 25
181 20 f. African buffalo 90 30
182 25 f. Pygmy hippopotamus (vert) 1·00 35
183 30 f. Agama (lizard) 70 35
184 45 f. Viper (vert) . . . . . . 1·40 40
185 50 f. Chameleon (vert) . . . 1·75 55
186 60 f. "Ugada limbata" (vert) . 2·25 80
187 85 f. African elephant . . . . 2·40 1·00

The 1, 3, 4, 6 and 60 f. are insects, the remainder are fauna.

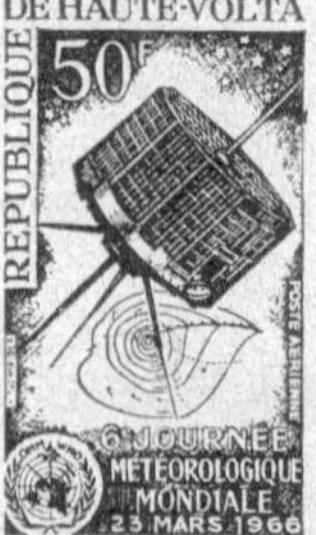

46 Communications Satellite
47 Ritual Mask

1966. Air. World Meteorological Day.
188 **46** 50 f. black, lake and blue . 55 30

1966. World Festival of Negro Arts, Dakar. Multicoloured.
189 20 f. Type **47** 40 15
190 25 f. Plumed head-dress . . . 45 20
191 60 f. Dancer . . . . 1·10 40

48 Bobo-Dioulasso Mosque

1966. Religious Buildings. Multicoloured.
192 25 f. Type **48** 45 30
193 25 f. Po Church 45 30

49 Satellite "FR 1" and Ouagadougou Tracking Station

1966. Air. Inauguration of Ouagadougou Tracking Station.
194 **49** 250 f. lake, brown and blue 4·00 1·90

50 W.H.O. Building

1966. Air. Inauguration of W.H.O. Headquarters, Geneva.
195 **50** 100 f. black, blue & yellow 1·60 70

51 Nurse and Red Cross on Globe
52 Scouts by Campfire

1966. Red Cross.
196 **51** 25 f. multicoloured 55 30

1966. Scouting.
197 **52** 10 f. multicoloured 35 15
198 – 15 f. black, brown & buff . 35 15

DESIGN: 15 f. Scouts on cliff.

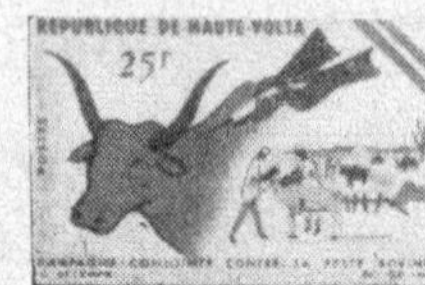

53 Inoculating Cattle

1966. Prevention of Cattle Plague Campaign.
199 **53** 25 f. black, yellow & blue . 85 45

1966. Air. Inaug of DC-8F Air Services. As T **87** of Mauritania.
200 25 f. olive, black and brown . 55 35

54 Ploughing with Donkey

1966. Rural Education (25 f.) and 3rd Anniv of Kamboince Centre (30 f.). Multicoloured.
201 25 f. Type **54** 40 20
202 30 f. "Rotation of crops", Kamboince Centre 45 20

55 Sir Winston Churchill

1966. Air. Churchill Commemoration.
203 **55** 100 f. green and red . . . 1·60 65

56 Pope Paul and Dove over U.N. General Assembly Building

1966. Air. Pope Paul's Peace Appeal before U.N.
204 **56** 100 f. violet and blue . . . 1·60 65

57 U.N.E.S.C.O. Emblem

1966. 20th Anniv of U.N.E.S.C.O. and U.N.I.C.E.F.
205 **57** 50 f. red, blue and black . 65 40
206 – 50 f. violet, purple and red 65 40

DESIGN: No. 206, U.N.I.C.E.F. emblem and child-care theme.

58 Arms of Upper Volta
59 Man and Woman holding Emblems

1967.
207 **58** 30 f. multicoloured 55 15

1967. Europafrique.
208 **59** 60 f. multicoloured 90 40

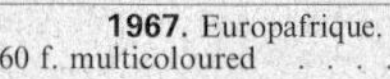

60 Acclaiming Lions Emblem

1967. Air. 50th Anniv of Lions International.
209 **60** 100 f. ultram, bl & brn . . 1·60 65

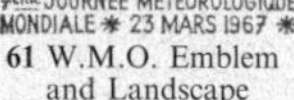

61 W.M.O. Emblem and Landscape
62 "Diamant" Rocket

1967. Air. World Meteorological Day.
210 **61** 50 f. green, turq & blue . . 85 40

1967. Air. French Space Achievements.
211 **62** 5 f. green, orange and blue . 15 10
212 – 20 f. lilac, purple and blue . 40 15
213 – 30 f. green, blue and red . . 55 20
214 – 100 f. green, violet & pur . 1·40 60

DESIGNS—HORIZ: 20 f. "FR-1" satellite; 100 f. "D1-D" satellite. VERT: 30 f. "D1-C" satellite.

63 Dr. Schweitzer and Organ Pipes
64 Scout waving Hat

1967. Air. 2nd Death Anniv of Dr Albert Schweitzer.
215 **63** 250 f. black and purple . . 4·00 1·90

1967. World Scout Jamboree, Idaho. Mult.
216 5 f. Type **64** (postage) 35 10
217 20 f. Scouts' handclasp 80 45
218 100 f. Jamboree emblem and world map (48 × 27 mm) (air) 1·40 65

65 "Virgin and Child" (by 15th-century master)
67 Postman on Cycle

66 Bank Book and Coins

1967. Air. Religious Paintings. Multicoloured.
219 30 f. Type **65** 50 30
220 50 f. "The Deposition of Christ" (Dirk Bouts) 85 40
221 100 f. "Christ giving Blessing" (Bellini) . . . . 1·40 80
222 250 f. "The Evangelists" (Jordaens) . . . . 4·00 1·90

See also Nos. 237/40.

1967. National Savings Bank.
223 **66** 30 f. green, brown & orge . 45 20

1967. Air. 5th Anniv of U.A.M.P.T. As T **101** of Mauritania.
224 100 f. green, lake and blue . . 1·40 55

1967. Stamp Day.
225 **67** 30 f. brown, green & blue . 65 45

1967. 5th Anniv of West African Monetary Union. As T **103** of Mauritania.
226 30 f. violet and blue 30 15

68 "The Two Alps"
69 Human Rights Emblem

1967. Winter Olympic Games, Grenoble (1968).
227 – 15 f. green, blue & brown . 40 30
228 **68** 50 f. blue and green . . . 70 40
229 – 100 f. green, blue and red . 1·60 1·00

DESIGNS—HORIZ: 15 f. St. Nizier-du-Moucherotte; 100 f. Cable-car, Villard-de-Lans.

1968. Human Rights Year.
230 **69** 20 f. red, gold and blue . . 40 15
231 30 f. red, gold and green . . 45 20

70 Student and School

1968. National School of Administration.
232 **70** 30 f. blue, turquoise & brn 45 20

71 Sud Aviation Caravelle "Ouagadougou"

1968. Air.
233 **71** 500 f. black, blue & purple 9·00 4·50

72 W.M.O. Emblem, Sun and Cloud-burst

1968. Air. World Meteorological Day.
234 **72** 50 f. blue, red and green . 85 35

73 Human Figures and W.H.O. Emblem

1968. 20th Anniv of W.H.O.
235 **73** 30 f. indigo, red and blue . 45 20
236 50 f. blue, brown & green . 65 35

1968. Air. Paintings. Old Masters in the Louvre. Multicoloured. As T **65**.
237 20 f. "Still Life" (Gauguin) (36 × 50 mm) 35 30
238 60 f. "Anne of Cleves" (Holbein the Younger) (36 × 50 mm) . 65 50
239 90 f. "The Pawnbroker and His Wife" (Quentin Metsys) (38 × 40 mm) . . . . 1·00 70
240 200 f. "The Cart" (Le Nain) (50 × 37 mm) . . . . . . 2·40 1·60

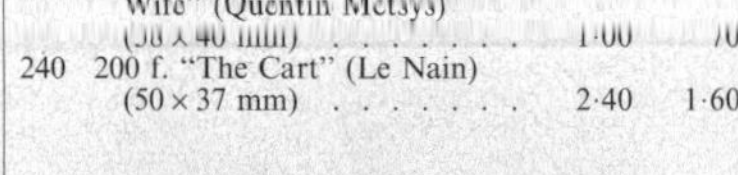

74 "Europafrique"

1968. Air. "Europafrique".
241 **74** 50 f. red, black and ochre . 70 35

75 Telephone Exchange

1968. Inauguration of Automatic Telephone Exchange, Bobo-Dioulasso.
242 **75** 30 f. multicoloured 55 30

76 Colima Acrobat with Bells

1968. Air. Olympic Games, Mexico.
243 **76** 10 f. brown, yellow & red . 35 20
244 – 30 f. blue, red and green . 50 30
245 – 60 f. lake, brown and blue . 1·10 45
246 – 100 f. lake, blue and green . 1·40 70
DESIGNS—VERT: 30 f. Pelota-player (Veracruz); 60 f. Javelin-thrower (Colima). HORIZ: 100 f. Athlete with cape (Jalisco).
The designs represent early Mexican statuary.

77 Weaving

1968. Handicrafts.
247 – 5 f. black, purple and brown (postage) 20 10
248 **77** 30 f. brown, orange and mauve 50 20
249 – 100 f. purple, red and yellow (air) . . . . 1·40 65
250 – 150 f. black, blue & brown 2·25 1·00
DESIGNS—As Type **77**: 5 f. Metal-work; 48 × 27 mm: 100 f. Pottery; 150 f. Basket-making.

1968. Air. "Philexafrique" Stamp Exn, Abidjan (Ivory Coast, 1969) (1st issue). As T **113a** of Mauritania. Multicoloured.
251 100 f. "Too Late" or "The Letter" (A. Cambon) . . . 2·50 2·25
See also No. 256.

78 Mahatma Gandhi **79** "Grain for the World"

1968. Air. "Workers for Peace".
252 **78** 100 f. black, yellow & grn . 1·40 80
253 – 100 f. black, light green and green . . . . 1·40 80
DESIGNS: No. 253, Albert Luthuli.

1969. World Food Programme.
255 **79** 30 f. purple, slate and blue 45 20

1969. Air. "Philexafrique" Stamp Exn, Abidjan (Ivory Coast) (2nd issue). As T **114a** of Mauritania. Multicoloured.
256 50 f. Dancers of Tengrela and stamp of 1928. . . . . . . 2·50 2·25

80 Loom and I.L.O. Emblem

1969. 50th Anniv of I.L.O.
257 **80** 30 f. blue, lake and green . 50 30

81 Cattle and Labourer

1969. Air. World Meteorological Day.
258 **81** 100 f. brown, blue & grn . 2·50 1·40

82 "Lions" Emblem within Eye

1969. Air. 12th Congress of 403 District, Lions International, Ouagadougou.
259 **82** 250 f. multicoloured . . . 2·75 1·40

83 Blood Donor

1969. 50th Anniv of League of Red Cross Societies.
260 **83** 30 f. black, red and blue . 60 40

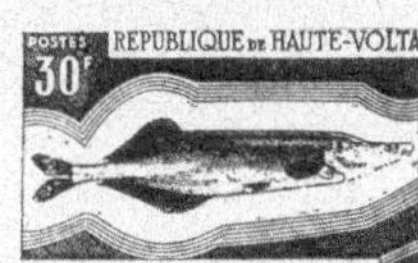

84 "Mormyrops curviceps"

1969. Fishes.
261 – 20 f. buff, brown and blue (postage) 80 35
262 – 25 f. purple, brown and bl 80 35
263 **84** 30 f. black and olive . . . 1·10 50
264 – 55 f. olive, yellow & green 1·40 65
265 – 85 f. blue, mauve & brown 2·50 1·40
266 – 100 f. blue, yellow and purple (air) . . . . 1·60 85
267 – 150 f. blue, black and red . 2·50 1·10
DESIGNS: 20 f. "Nannocharax gobioides"; 25 f. "Hemigrammocharax polli"; 55 f. "Alestes luteus"; 85 f. "Micralestes voltae". LARGER 48 × 27 mm: 100 f. "Phenacogrammus pabrensis"; 150 f. "Synodontis arnoulti".

85 Astronaut and Moon

1969. Air. Moon Flight of "Apollo 8". Embossed on gold foil.
268 **85** 1,000 f. gold . . . . . . 18·00

1969. Air. 1st Man on the Moon. No. 214 optd **L'HOMME SUR LA LUNE JUILLET 1969** and "Apollo 11".
269 100 f. green, violet and purple 3·25 3·25

1969. Air. Birth Bicent of Napoleon Bonaparte. As T **114b** of Mauritania. Multicoloured.
270 50 f. "Bonaparte crossing the Great St. Bernard" (J. L. David) . . . . 1·60 80
271 150 f. "First Presentation of the Legion of Honour" (Debret) 5·00 2·00
272 250 f. "Napoleon before Madrid" (C. Vernet) . . . 6·75 3·25

1969. 5th Anniv of African Development Bank.
273 30 f. brown, emerald and green 35 15

88 Millet **89** Stylised Tree

1969. Agricultural Produce.
274 **88** 15 f. brown, green and yellow (postage) 45 20
275 – 30 f. blue and mauve . . . 55 35
276 – 100 f. brown & violet (air) 1·40 40
277 – 200 f. green and red . . . 2·50 80
DESIGNS: 30 f. Cotton; LARGER 48 × 27mm: 100 f. Ground-nuts; 200 f. Rice.

1969. Air. Europafrique.
278 **89** 100 f. multicoloured . . . 90 55

1969. 10th Anniv of Aerial Navigation Security Agency for Africa and Madagascar (A.S.E.C.N.A.). As T **94a** of Niger.
279 100 f. brown . . . . 1·25 75

90 "Niadale" **91** Lenin

1970. Figurines and Masks in National Museum.
280 **90** 10 f. brown, orge and red . 20 10
281 – 30 f. brown, blue and violet 40 20
282 – 45 f. brown, blue & green . 70 30
283 – 80 f. brown, pur, & violet . 1·25 60
DESIGNS: 30 f. "Niaga"; 45 f. "Iliu bara"; 80 f. "Karan Weeba".

1970. Air. Birth Centenary of Lenin.
284 **91** 20 f. brown and ochre . . . 35 20
285 – 100 f. red, blue and green . 1·25 80
DESIGN—HORIZ: 100 f. "Lenin addressing workers" (A. Serov).

92 African Huts and City Buildings **93** Cauris Dancers

1970. Linked Cities' Day.
286 **92** 30 f. brown, blue and red . 50 30

1970. Upper Volta Dances. Multicoloured.
287 5 f. Mask of Nebwa Gnomo dance (horiz) 20 15
288 8 f. Type **93** 30 15
289 20 f. Gourmantches dancers . 40 15
290 30 f. Larlle dancers (horiz) . . 50 20

94 "Pupils", Sun and Emblem of Education Year

1970. Int Education Year. Multicoloured.
291 40 f. Type **94** 40 20
292 90 f. Visual aids and emblem . 95 45

95 New U.P.U. Headquarters Building, U.P.U. Monument and Abraham Lincoln

1970. New U.P.U. Headquarters Building.
293 **95** 30 f. grey, red and brown . 50 20
294 60 f. purple, green & brn . 85 35

96 Footballers and Cup

1970. Air. World Cup Football Championships, Mexico.
295 **96** 40 f. lake, green & brown . 45 30
296 – 100 f. brown, purple & grn . 1·10 55
DESIGN: 100 f. Goalkeeper saving ball, Globe and footballers.

97 Franklin D. Roosevelt **98** Naval Construction

1970. Air. 25th Anniv of Roosevelt's Death.
297 **97** 10 f. brown, black & grn . 20 20
298 – 200 f. red, violet and grey . 1·60 80
DESIGN—HORIZ: 200 f. Roosevelt with his stamp collection.

1970. Hanover Fair.
299 **98** 15 f. multicoloured 50 35
300 – 45 f. green, blue and black 60 35
301 – 80 f. purple, brown & blk . 1·40 50
DESIGNS: 45 f. Test-tubes and retorts ("Chemistry"); 80 f. Power transmission lines and pylons ("Electro-techniques").

99 Inoculating Cattle

1970. National Veterinary School.
302 **99** 30 f. multicoloured 55 35

100 "Manchurian Cranes and Seashore" and Expo Monorail Coach **101** Nurse attending Patient

1970. Air. World Fair "EXPO 70" Osaka, Japan.
303 50 f. Type **100** 55 35
304 150 f. "Geisha", rocket and satellite . . . . 1·40 80

1970. Upper Volta Red Cross.
305 **101** 30 f. brown, red & green . 60 35

102 "Nurse and Child" (F. Hals) **103** U.N. Emblem and Dove

1970. "Europafrique". Multicoloured.
306 25 f. Type **102** 50 20
307 30 f. "Courtyard in Delft" (Hoogh) 60 35
308 150 f. "Christina of Denmark" (Holbein) . . . . 2·25 90
309 250 f. "Hofburg Courtyard, Innsbruck" (Durer) . . . . 4·00 1·40

1970. Air. 25th Anniv of U.N.O.
310 **103** 60 f. ultram, blue & grn . 65 30
311 – 250 f. violet, brn & grn . 2·75 1·10
DESIGNS—HORIZ: 250 f. U.N. emblem and two doves.

104 Front of Car

1970. Paris Motor Show.
312 **104** 25 f. green, lake & brown 90 35
313 – 40 f. blue, purple & green 1·10 55
DESIGN: 40 f. Old and new cars.

105 "Holy Family"

1970. Christmas.
314 **105** 300 f. silver . . . . 6·75
315 1000 f. gold . . . . 18·00

106 Centre Buildings

1970. Inauguration of Austro-Voltaic Centre.
316 **106** 50 f. orange, green & red . 55 30

107 Arms and Stork

1970. 10th Anniv of Independence.
317 **107** 30 f. multicoloured (postage) 45 20
318 – 500 f. blk, red and gold (air) 5·50
DESIGN—27 × 37 mm: 500 f. Family and flag. No. 318 is embossed on gold foil.

108 U.N. "Key" and Split Globe

1970. 10th Anniv of U.N. Declaration on Colonies.
319 **108** 40 f. red, blue and brown . 60 35
320 – 50 f. multicoloured . . . 55 30
DESIGN: 50 f. Two maps of Africa showing former colonies.

109 Pres. Nasser

111 Heads of Different Races

110 Beingolo Hunting Horn

1971. Air. Pres. Nasser Commemoration.
321 **109** 100 f. multicoloured . . . 90 40

1971. Musical Instruments.
322 **110** 5 f. brown, red and blue . 20 15
323 – 15 f. brown, red & green . 35 20
324 – 20 f. red, grey and blue . 65 20
325 – 25 f. drab, green and red . 80 40
INSTRUMENTS—VERT: 15 f. Mossi "guitar"; 20 f. Gurunssi "flutes". HORIZ: 25 f. Lunga "drum".

1971. Racial Equality Year.
326 **111** 50 f. brown, red & turq . 55 30

112 "The Purple Herons" (Egypt, 1354)

1971. Air. Muslim Miniatures. Multicoloured.
327 100 f. Type **112** . . . . . . 1·10 55
328 250 f. Page from the Koran (Egypt c. 1368–88) (vert) . . 2·75 1·25

113 Telephone and Hemispheres

1971. World Telecommunications Day.
329 **113** 50 f. violet, grey & brown 60 30

114 Olympic Rings and Events

1971. Air. "Pre-Olympic Year".
330 **114** 150 f. red, violet and bl . 2·25 1·10

115 Cutting Cane and Sugar Factory, Banfora

117 Scout and Pagodas

116 "Gonimbrasia hecate"

1971. Local Industries. Multicoloured.
331 10 f. Type **115** 20 10
332 35 f. Cotton-plant and textiles ("Voltex" project) 35 20

1971. Butterflies. Multicoloured.
333 1 f. Type **116** 10 10
334 2 f. "Hamanumida daedalus" 10 10
335 3 f. "Ophideres materna" . . 20 10
336 5 f. "Danaus chrysippus" . . 45 20
337 40 f. "Hypolimnas misippus" 2·25 1·10
338 45 f. "Danaus petiverana" . . 3·25 1·40

1971. Air. 13th World Scout Jamboree, Asagari (Japan).
339 **117** 45 f. multicoloured . . . 65 35

118 Actor with Fan

119 African with Seed-packet

1971. "Philatokyo" Stamp Exn, Tokyo. Mult.
340 25 f. Type **118** 35 20
341 40 f. Actor within mask . . . 50 25

1971. National Seed-protection Campaign. Multicoloured.
342 35 f. Grading seeds (horiz) . 40 20
343 75 f. Type **119** 60 30
344 100 f. Harvesting crops (horiz) 60 35

1971. 10th Anniv of Volta Red Cross. Surch **Xe ANNIVERSAIRE** and new value.
345 **101** 100 f. on 30 f. brown, red and purple . . . . . 1·25 65

121 Teacher and Class

122 Soldier and Tractors

1971. "Women's Access to Education". Multicoloured.
346 35 f. Type **121** 45 20
347 50 f. Family learning alphabet 60 35

1971. Dakiri Project. Military Aid for Agriculture. Multicoloured.
348 15 f. Type **122** 45 15
349 40 f. Soldiers harvesting (horiz) 65 40

123 General De Gaulle and Map

1971. Air. De Gaulle Commemoration.
350 **123** 40 f. multicoloured 55 55
351 – 500 f. gold and green . . . 10·50 9·50
DESIGN—VERT (30 × 40 mm): 500 f. De Gaulle. No. 351 is embossed on gold foil.

1971. Air. 10th Anniv of African and Malagasy Posts and Telecommunications Union. As T **139a** of Mauritania. Multicoloured.
352 100 f. U.A.M.P.T.H.Q. and Mossi dancer . . . . 1·10 50

124 "Simulium damnosum" and Preventive Measures

1971. Regional Anti-Onchocerciasis Campaign.
353 **124** 40 f. multicoloured 55 35

125 Pres. Lamizana

126 Children acclaiming Emblem

1971.
354 **125** 35 f. multicoloured 30 20

1971. 25th Anniv of U.N.I.C.E.F.
355 **126** 45 f. multicoloured 50 35

127 Peulh Straw Hut

1971. Traditional Housing (1st series). Mult.
356 10 f. Type **127** 15 10
357 20 f. Gourounsi house 30 15
358 35 f. Mossi huts 45 30
See also Nos. 370/2.

128 Town Halls of Bobo-Dioulasso and Chalons-sur-Marne, France

1971. "Twin Cities" Co-operation.
359 **128** 40 f. multicoloured 65 40

129 Ice-hockey

130 Running

1972. Air. Winter Olympic Games, Sapporo, Japan.
360 **129** 150 f. purple, blue and red 1·90 1·00

1972. Air. U.N.E.S.C.O. "Save Venice" Campaign. As T **145** of Senegal. Multicoloured.
361 100 f. "La Musica" (P. Longhi) (vert) . . . . 1·90 1·00
362 150 f. "Panorama da Ponte della Marina" (detail-Caffi) (horiz) 2·75 1·25

1972. Air. Olympic Games, Munich.
363 **130** 65 f. brown, blue and green 60 45
364 – 200 f. brown and blue . . 1·90 1·25
DESIGN: 200 f. Throwing the discus.

131 Louis Armstrong

1972. Famous Negro Musicians. Multicoloured.
366 45 f. Type **131** (postage) . . . 1·25 65
367 500 f. Jimmy Smith (air) . . . 6·75 4·50

132 Globe and Emblems

1972. World Red Cross Day.
368 **132** 40 f. multicoloured (postage) 55 40
369 100 f. multicoloured (air) . 1·10 45

133 Bobo House

134 Hair Style

1972. Traditional Housing (2nd series). Mult.
370 45 f. Type **133** 55 30
371 50 f. Dagari house 65 35
372 90 f. Interior of Bango house (horiz) . . . . 1·25 50

1972. Upper Volta Hair Styles.
373 **134** 25 f. multicoloured . . . 35 15
374 – 35 f. multicoloured . . . 50 20
375 – 75 f. multicoloured . . . 1·10 45
DESIGNS: 35, 75 f. Similar hair styles.

135 "Teaching"

1972. 2nd National Development Plan.
376 **135** 10 f. mauve, green and turquoise (postage) . . 10 10
377 – 15 f. brown, orge & grn . 20 15
378 – 20 f. brown, grn & blue . 30 15
379 – 35 f. brown, blue & grn . 50 20
380 – 40 f. brown, green & pur . 55 30
381 – 85 f. black, red & bl (air) 70 50
DESIGNS: 15 f. Doctor and patient ("Health"); 20 f. Factory and silos ("Industry"); 35 f. Cattle ("Cattle-raising"); 40 f. Rice-planting ("Agriculture"); 85 f. Road-making machine ("Infrastructure").

1972. 10th Anniv of West African Monetary Union. As T **149** of Mauritania.
382 40 f. grey, blue and mauve . . 45 20

136 Lottery Building

1972. 5th Anniv of National Lottery.
383 **136** 35 f. multicoloured . . . 50 20

137 Presidents Pompidou and Lamizana

1972. Air. Visit of Pres. Pompidou to Upper Volta.
384 **137** 40 f. multicoloured . . . 1·60 1·60
385 – 250 f. multicoloured . . . 6·00 6·00
DESIGN: 250 f. As T **137** but frame differs and portraits are embossed on gold.

138 Mary Peters (pentathlon)

1972. Air. Gold Medal-winners, Olympic Games, Munich. Multicoloured.
386 40 f. Type **138** 35 15
387 65 f. Ragno-Lonzi (fencing) . 55 20
388 85 f. Touritcheva (gymnastics) 80 30
389 200 f. Maury (sailing) . . . . 1·60 65
390 300 f. Meyfarth (high-jumping) 2·75 1·10

139 Donkeys

1972. Animals. Multicoloured.
392 5 f. Type **139** 10 10
393 10 f. Spur-winged geese . . . 60 15
394 30 f. Goat 55 20
395 50 f. Bull 80 30
396 65 f. Dromedaries . . . . . . 1·10 40

140 "The Nativity" (Della Notte)

1972. Air. Christmas. Religious Paintings. Multicoloured.
397 100 f. Type **140** . . . . . . 1·10 65
398 200 f. "The Adoration of the Magi" (Durer) . . . . . . 2·25 1·60

141 Mossi Hair-style and Village

1973. Air.
399 **141** 5 f. multicoloured 10 10
400 40 f. multicoloured . . . 55 20

1973. 25th Anniv of W.H.O. No. 353 surch **O.M.S. 25 Anniversaire** and value.
401 **124** 45 f. on 40 f. multicoloured 50 30

1973. African and Malagasy Posts and Telecommunications Union. As T **155** of Mauritania.
402 100 f. purple, red and yellow . 1·00 55

1974. 15th Anniv of Council of Accord. As T **184** of Niger.
403 40 f. multicoloured 30 20

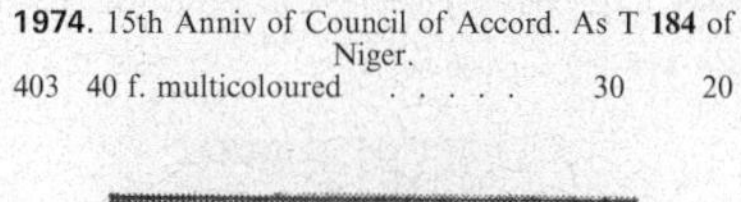

143 Map and Harvester

1974. Kou Valley Project.
404 **143** 35 f. multicoloured . . . 55 35

144 Woman, Globe and I.W.Y. Emblem

1975. International Women's Year.
405 **144** 65 f. multicoloured . . . 65 45

145 Mgr. Joanny Thevenoud and Cathedral

1975. 75th Anniv of Evangelization of Upper Volta.
406 **145** 55 f. black, brn and grn . 65 35
407 – 65 f. black, brn and red . 80 45
DESIGN: 65 f. Father Guillaume Templier and Cathedral.

146 Farmer's Hat, Hoe and Emblem   147 Diseased People

1975. Development of the Volta Valleys.
408 **146** 15 f. multicoloured . . . 15 10
409 50 f. multicoloured . . . 50 25

1976. Campaign against Onchocerciasis (round-worm).
410 **147** 75 f. mauve, orge & grn . 85 35
411 250 f. sepia, orge and brown 2·50 1·10

148 Globe and Emblem

1976. Non-aligned Countries' Summit Conference, Colombo, Sri Lanka. Multicoloured.
412 55 f. Type **148** 45 20
413 100 f. Globe, dove and emblem 90 50

149 Washington at Trenton

1976. "Interphil '76" International Stamp Exhibition, Philadelphia. Multicoloured.
414 60 f. Type **149** (postage) . . . 55 15
415 90 f. Seat of Government, Pennsylvania 80 20
416 100 f. Siege of Yorktown (air) 80 30
417 200 f. Battle of Cape St. Vincent 1·60 60
418 300 f. Peter Francisco's act of bravery . . . . 2·40 80

150 U.P.U. and U.N. Emblems

1976. 25th Anniv of U.N. Postal Administration.
420 **150** 200 f. blue, bronze & red 1·60 90

151 Tenkodogo Commune   152 Bronze Statuette

1977. Arms. Multicoloured.
421 10 f. Type **151** 15 10
422 20 f. Ouagadougou 20 10
423 55 f. Type **151** 55 20
424 100 f. As 20 f. 70 35

1977.
425 **152** 55 f. multicoloured 45 20
426 – 65 f. multicoloured 45 20
DESIGN: 65 f. Bronze statuette of woman with bowl.

153 Samo Granary   154 Gouin Basket

1977. Millet Granaries. Multicoloured.
427 5 f. Type **153** 10 10
428 35 f. Boromo 30 20
429 45 f. Banfora 45 20
430 55 f. Mossi 55 30

1977. Local Handicrafts. Baskets and Bags. Multicoloured.
431 30 f. Type **154** 20 15
432 40 f. Bissa 40 20
433 60 f. Lobi 60 25
434 70 f. Mossi 65 30

155 "Crinum ornatum"   156 General De Gaulle

1977. Fruits and Flowers. Multicoloured.
435 2 f. "Cordia myxa" 10 10
436 3 f. "Opilia celtidifolia" . . . 15 10
437 15 f. Type **155** 20 10
438 25 f. "Haemanthus multiflorus" 20 10
439 50 f. "Hannoa undulata" . . . 10 10
440 90 f. "Cochlospermum planchonii" . . . . 1·00 40
441 125 f. "Clitoria ternatea" . . . 1·10 50
442 150 f. "Cassia alata" . . . . . 1·40 90
443 175 f. "Nauclea latifolia" (horiz) 1·60 1·00
444 300 f. "Bombax costatum" (horiz) . . . . 2·50 1·40
445 400 f. "Eulophia cucullata" . . 4·25 1·40

1977. Personalities. Multicoloured.
446 100 f. Type **156** . . . . . . 1·60 50
447 200 f. King Baudouin . . . . 1·60 50

157 Queen Elizabeth II

1977. Silver Jubilee of Queen Elizabeth II. Multicoloured.
448 200 f. Type **157** . . . . . . 1·60 50
449 300 f. Queen Elizabeth II taking salute at Trooping the Colour 2·25 60

158 Cars on "Road" of Banknotes

1977. 10th Anniv of National Lottery.
451 **158** 55 f. multicoloured . . . 55 40

159 Selma Lagerlof and Bean Geese

1977. Nobel Prize Winners. Multicoloured.
452 55 f. Type **159** (Literature, 1909) 90 20
453 65 f. Guglielmo Marconi and early transmitter (Physics, 1909) 45 20
454 125 f. Bertrand Russell, laurel, book and dove (Literature, 1950) 95 30
455 200 f. L. C. Pauling, formula and atomic explosion (Chemistry, 1954) . . . . 1·40 50
456 300 f. Robert Koch, slide and X-ray plate (Medicine, 1905) 2·40 70

160 "The Three Graces"

1977. 400th Birth Anniv of Rubens.
458 55 f. "Heads of Four Negroes" (horiz) 40 10
459 65 f. Type **160** 50 15
460 85 f. "Bathsheba at the Fountain" 50 20
461 150 f. "The Drunken Silenus" 12·5 45
462 200 f. "The Story of Maria de Medici" (detail) . . . . . . 1·60 55
463 300 f. "The Story of Maria de Medici" (different detail) . 2·50 70

161 Lenin

1977. 60th Anniv of Russian Revolution. Multicoloured.
465 10 f. Type **161** 15 10
466 85 f. Lenin Monument and Kremlin 65 40
467 200 f. Lenin with children (horiz) 1·90 1·10
468 500 f. Lenin and Pres. Brezhnev (horiz) . . . . 4·50 2·25

162 Stadium and Brazil 5 cr. 80 Stamp of 1950

1978. World Cup Football Championship, Argentina. Multicoloured.
469 55 f. Type **162** 35 10
470 65 f. Brazil 1969 Pele stamp . 45 15
471 125 f. G.B. 1966 England winners stamp 90 30
472 200 f. Chile 1962 World Cup stamp . . . . 1·40 45
473 300 f. Switzerland 1954 World Cup stamp . . . . 2·00 65

163 Jean Mermoz

1978. Aviation History. Multicoloured.
475 65 f. Type **163** 60 20
476 75 f. Anthony Fokker 65 30
477 85 f. Wiley Post 75 35
478 90 f. Otto Lilienthal (vert) . . 85 35
479 100 f. Concorde . . . . 1·10 40

164 "Crateva religiosa" **165** Microwave Antennae

1978. Trees of Upper Volta. Multicoloured.
481 55 f. Type **164** 55 35
482 75 f. "Ficus sp" 65 45

1978. World Telecommunications Day.
483 **165** 65 f. multicoloured . . . 55 40

166 Bobo Fetish Portals

1978. Sacred Objects. Multicoloured.
484 55 f. Type **166** 55 30
485 65 f. Mossi fetish 65 40

167 U.P.U. Emblem over Globe

1978. Air. Centenary of Paris Postal Congress.
486 **167** 350 f. multicoloured . . . 2·75 1·60

168 Capt. Cook and H.M.S. "Endeavour"

1978. 250th Birth Anniv of Captain James Cook. Multicoloured.
487 65 f. Type **168** . . . . 1·00 40
488 85 f. Death of Captain Cook . 55 15
489 250 f. Cook and navigation instruments . . . . 1·60 55
490 350 f. Cook and H.M.S. "Resolution" . . . . 3·50 2·25

169 Yury Gagarin and Spacecraft

1978. "Conquest of Space". Multicoloured.
491 50 f. Type **169** 40 20
492 60 f. Jules Verne, "Apollo 11" badge and Neil Armstrong in space-suit 45 20
493 100 f. Montgolfier medallion and balloon, Bleriot XI and Concorde 85 40

170 I.A.Y. Emblem

1978. Air. Anti-Apartheid Year.
494 **170** 100 f. multicoloured . . . 80 45

1978. 25th Anniv of Coronation of Queen Elizabeth II. Nos. 448/9 optd **ANNIVERSAIRE DU COURONNEMENT 1953-1978**.
495 **157** 200 f. multicoloured . . . 1·40 90
496 – 300 f. multicoloured . . . 2·25 1·40

1978. Air. "Philexafrique" Stamp Exhibition, Libreville (Gabon), and Int Stamp Fair, Essen, West Germany (1st series). As T **262** of Niger. Multicoloured.
498 100 f. Common kingfisher and Hanover 1850 1 ggr. stamp 1·50 1·25
499 100 f. Hippopotamus and 1964 250 f. Grey woodpecker stamp 1·50 1·25
See also Nos. 518/9.

172 "Trent Castle"

1978. 450th Death Anniv of Albrecht Durer. Multicoloured.
500 65 f. Type **172** 55 15
501 150 f. "Virgin and Child" (vert) 1·10 35
502 250 f. "Saints George and Eustace" (vert) . . . . . . 1·90 60
503 350 f. "H. Holzschuher" (vert) 2·75 90

173 Horus **174** Jules Verne

1978. Air. U.N.E.S.C.O. Campaign: "Save the Philae Temples". Multicoloured.
504 200 f. Type **173** . . . . 1·40 65
505 300 f. Stylised falcon . . . . 2·00 1·00

1978. 150th Birth Anniv of Jules Verne (author).
506 **174** 20 f. purple, blue & green 1·60 90

175 Human Rights Flame

1978. 30th Anniv of Declaration of Human Rights.
507 **175** 55 f. multicoloured . . . 50 30

1979. World Cup Football Championship Winners. Nos. 469/73 optd.
508 **162** 55 f. multicoloured . . . 45 25
509 – 65 f. multicoloured . . . 50 30
510 – 125 f. multicoloured . . . 95 55
511 – 200 f. multicoloured . . . 1·40 85
512 – 300 f. multicoloured . . . 2·10 1·10

OPTS.: 55 f. **VAINQUEURS 1950 URUGUAY 1978 ARGENTINE**; 65 f. **VAINQUEURS 1970; BRESIL 1978 ARGENTINE**; 125 f. **VAINQUEURS 1966 GRANDE BRETAGNE 1978 ARGENTINE**; 200 f. **VAINQUEURS 1962 BRESIL 1978 ARGENTINE**; 300 f. **VAINQUEURS 1954 ALLEMAGNE (RFA) 1978 ARGENTINE**.

177 Radio Station **179** Wave Pattern and Human Figures

178 Children listening to Story

1979. 10th Anniv of Posts and Telecommunications Organization. Multicoloured.
514 55 f. Type **177** 40 20
515 65 f. Loading mail aboard Beech A100 King Air monoplane . . 50 30

1979. International Year of the Child.
516 **178** 75 f. multicoloured 85 45

1979. World Telecommunications Day.
517 **179** 70 f. multicoloured 55 35

180 Basket Weaving and Upper Volta 50 c. Stamp of 1963

1979. "Philexafrique" Exhibition, Libreville, Gabon (2nd series). Multicoloured.
518 100 f. Type **180** . . . . 1·60 1·40
519 100 f. Concorde, van, shouting man and U.P.U. emblem . . 1·60 1·40

181 "Synodontis voltae" **183** Kob

182 Steam Train

1979. Freshwater Fish. Multicoloured.
520 20 f. Type **181** 35 20
521 50 f. "Micralestes comoensis" 1·00 45
522 85 f. "Silurus" . . . . 1·40 70

1979. Death Centenary of Sir Rowland Hill. Multicoloured.
523 65 f. Type **182** 55 15
524 165 f. Diesel train . . . . . 1·40 40
525 200 f. Diesel train (different) . 1·60 50
526 300 f. French high-speed train . 2·75 60

1979. Endangered Animals. Multicoloured.
528 30 f. Type **183** 20 10
529 40 f. Roan antelope 35 10
530 60 f. Caracal 65 10
531 100 f. African elephant . . . 1·00 35
532 175 f. Hartebeest . . . . . . 1·60 45
533 250 f. Leopard . . . . 2·50 55

184 Teacher and Class

1979. World Literacy Day. Multicoloured.
534 55 f. Farmer reading book (vert) 45 35
535 250 f. Type **184** . . . . 2·00 1·25

185 Telecommunications

1979. 3rd World Telecommunications Exhibition, Geneva.
536 **185** 200 f. multicoloured . . . 1·40 70

186 King Vulture **187** Airport

1979. Protected Birds. Multicoloured.
537 5 f. Type **186** 25 10
538 10 f. Hoopoe 25 10
539 15 f. Ruppell's griffon 30 15
540 25 f. Intermediate egret . . . 45 20
541 35 f. Ostrich 70 25
542 45 f. Crowned crane 85 30
543 125 f. Cassin's hawk eagle . . 1·90 1·10

1979. 20th Anniv of A.S.E.C.N.A. (Air Navigation Security Agency).
544 **187** 65 f. multicoloured . . . 60 40

188 Headquarters Building

1979. Opening of West African Savings Bank Building, Dakar, Senegal.
545 **188** 55 f. multicoloured . . . 50 30

189 Jamot, Map and Tsetse Fly

1979. Birth Centenary of Eugene Jamot (discoverer of cure for sleeping sickness).
546 **189** 55 f. multicoloured . . . 85 45

190 Stamp under Magnifying Glass

1980. Stamp Day.

547 **190** 55 f. multicoloured . . . 50 25

191 Electric Locomotives **192** Pope John Paul II

1980. 25th Anniv of World Locomotive Speed Record.

548 **191** 75 f. multicoloured . . . 1·00 45
549 100 f. multicoloured . . . 1·50 65

1980. Papal Visit. Multicoloured.

550 55 f. Pres. Lamizana, Pope and Cardinal Pau Zoungrana (horiz) . . . 85 35
551 100 f. Type **192** . . . 1·40 85

193 Telephone **194** Mountains and Statue

1980. World Telecommunications Day.

552 **193** 50 f. multicoloured . . . 40 20

1980. Solar Energy. Multicoloured.

553 65 f. Sun and Earth . . . 50 20
554 100 f. Type **194** . . . 80 40

195 Downhill Skiing (L. Stock)

1980. Winter Olympic Games Winners. Mult.

555 65 f. Type **195** . . . 45 15
556 100 f. Women's downhill skiing (A. Moser-Proell) . . . 65 20
557 200 f. Figure skating (A. Poetzsch) . . . 1·40 35
558 350 f. Slalom (I. Stenmark) (vert) 2·25 60

196 Map of Europe and Africa **197** Hand pushing back Sand Dune

1980. Europafrique.

560 **196** 100 f. red, black & green . 90 45

1980. Operation "Green Sahara". Multicoloured.

561 50 f. Type **197** . . . 50 20
562 55 f. Hands planting saplings . 60 35

198 Cyclists

1980. Air. Olympic Games, Moscow. Cycling.

563 **198** 65 f. multicoloured . . . 55 15
564 – 150 f. multicoloured (vert) 1·10 40
565 – 250 f. multicoloured . . . 1·90 55
566 – 350 f. multicoloured . . . 2·75 90

DESIGNS: 150 f. to 350 f. Different cyclists.

199 Installation of Chief

1980. National History. Multicoloured.

568 30 f. Type **199** . . . 35 15
569 55 f. Moro Naba, Emperor of Mossis . . . 55 30
570 65 f. Princess Guimbe Ouattara (vert) . . . 60 30

200 Gourounsi Mask **201** Tractor, Cattle and Grain (Agriculture)

1980. World Tourism Conference, Manila.

571 **200** f. 65 f. multicoloured . . 55 30

1980. 5th Anniv of West African Economic Council. Multicoloured.

572 55 f. Type **201** . . . 35 15
573 65 f. "Communications" . . . 40 30
574 75 f. Dam and highway . . . 45 30
575 100 f. "Industry" . . . 80 40

1980. Air. Olympic Winners. Nos. 563/6 optd.

576 **198** 65 f. multicoloured . . . 30 25
577 – 150 f. multicoloured . . . 75 50
578 – 250 f. multicoloured . . . 1·25 90
579 – 350 f. multicoloured . . . 1·60 1·00

OVERPRINTS: 65 f. **SOUKHOROUCHENKOV (URSS)**; 150 f. **"HESSLICH (RDA)"**; 250 f. **"LANG (POL)"**; 350 f. **"DILL-BUNDI (SUISSE)"**.

203 Coat of Arms and Map

1980. 20th Anniv of Independence.

581 **203** 500 f. multicoloured . . . 4·25 2·50

204 "Sistine Madonna" (detail) **205** "Scarabaeus sacer"

1980. Christmas. Multicoloured.

582 60 f. Type **204** . . . 45 15
583 150 f. "Virgin de l'Impannata" 1·10 40
584 250 f. "Alba Madonna" . . . 1·75 55

1980. 5th Anniv of African Post and Telecommunications. As T **292** of Niger.

585 55 f. multicoloured. . . . 50 30

1981. Insects. Multicoloured.

586 5 f. Type **205** . . . 10 10
587 10 f. "Gryllus campestris" . . 10 10
588 15 f. Termites . . . 15 10
589 20 f. "Mantis religiosa" (vert) 25 10
590 55 f. "Nyctaon pyri" . . . 75 25
591 65 f. "Locusta migratorius" (vert) . . . 85 35

MINIMUM PRICE

The minimum price quoted is 10p which represents a handling charge rather than a basis for valuing common stamps. For further notes about prices, see introductory pages.

206 Bobo Mask, Hounde **207** College Emblem

1981. Masks. Multicoloured.

592 45 f. Type **206** . . . 40 15
593 55 f. Bwa mask . . . 45 20
594 85 f. Kouroumba mask . . . 60 35
595 105 f. Gourounsi mask . . . 80 40

1981. 25th Anniv of Notre-Dame College, Kologh'naba.

596 **207** 55 f. multicoloured . . . 45 20

208 Von Stephan and U.P.U. Emblem

1981. 150th Birth Anniv of Heinrich von Stephan (founder of U.P.U.).

597 **208** 65 f. multicoloured . . . 60 35

209 Ribbons forming Caduceus, I.T.U. and W.H.O. Emblems **210** Diesel Railcar

1981. World Telecommunications Day.

598 **209** 90 f. multicoloured . . . 60 35

1981. Abidjan–Niger Railway. Multicoloured.

599 25 f. Type **210** . . . 30 15
600 30 f. Diesel train "La Gazelle" 45 20
601 40 f. Diesel locomotive "Le Belier" . . . 55 35

211 Group of Trees

1981. Tree Month.

602 **211** 70 f. multicoloured . . . 70 40

212 Nurse and Doctor with Medical Equipment **213** Handicapped Sculptor

1981. 25th Anniv of Upper Volta Red Cross.

603 **212** 70 f. multicoloured . . . 60 40

1981. International Year of Disabled People.

604 **213** 70 f. multicoloured . . . 60 35

214 Koudougou

1981. Landscapes. Multicoloured.

605 35 f. Type **214** . . . 30 15
606 45 f. Toma . . . 40 20
607 85 f. Volta Noire . . . 65 30

215 Agricultural Scenes within Map

1981. World Food Day.

608 **215** 90 f. multicoloured . . . 70 45

216 Topi

1981. Wildlife Protection. Multicoloured.

609 5 f. Type **216** . . . 10 10
610 15 f. Waterbuck . . . 15 15
611 40 f. Roan antelopes . . . 35 20
612 60 f. Dorcas gazelle . . . 60 35
613 70 f. African elephant . . . 1·00 55

217 Campaign Emblem **219** Donkey

218 Papaya

1981. Anti-Apartheid Campaign.

614 **217** 90 f. red . . . 60 35

1981. Fruit and Vegetables. Multicoloured.

615 20 f. Type **218** . . . 15 10
616 35 f. Fruit and vegetables . . 30 15
617 75 f. Mangoes (vert) . . . 50 30
618 90 f. Melons . . . 60 35

1981. Stock Breeding. Multicoloured.

619 10 f. Type **219** . . . 10 10
620 25 f. Pig . . . 20 10
621 70 f. Cow . . . 55 20
622 90 f. Helmet guineafowl (vert) 1·50 65
623 250 f. Rabbit . . . 1·75 90

220 Women carrying Rice **221** Father and Son

1981. 10th Anniv of West African Rice Development Association.

625 **220** 90 f. multicoloured . . . 90 45

1982. 20th Anniv of World Food Programme.

626 **221** 50 f. multicoloured . . . 40 15

222 Morhonaba Palace, Ouagadougou

1982. Traditional Houses. Multicoloured.

627 30 f. Type **222** . . . 20 10
628 70 f. Bobo . . . 50 20
629 100 f. Gourounsi . . . 70 30
630 200 f. Peulh . . . 1·40 60
631 250 f. Dagari . . . 1·60 65

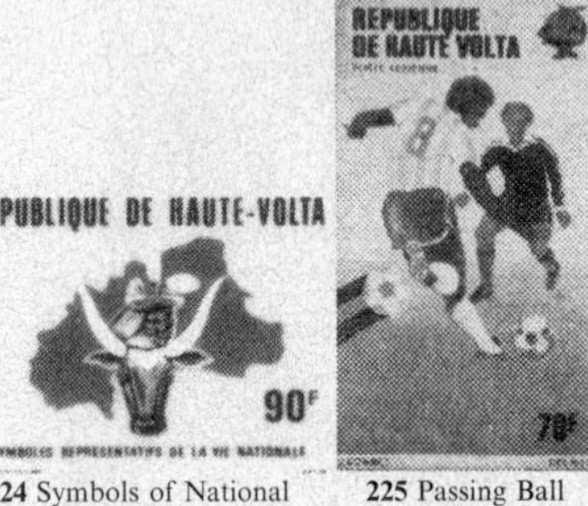

223 Hexagonal Pattern

1982. World Telecommunications Day.
632 **223** 90 f. multicoloured . . . 85 40

224 Symbols of National Life **225** Passing Ball

1982. National Life.
633 **224** 90 f. multicoloured . . . 60 30

1982. Air. World Cup Football Championship, Spain. Multicoloured.
634 70 f. Type **225** 50 15
635 90 f. Tackle 60 30
636 150 f. Running with ball . . . 1·10 40
637 300 f. Receiving ball . . . . . 2·00 85

226 Water Lily **227** Symbols of Communication on Map of Africa

1982. Flowers. Multicoloured.
639 25 f. Type **226** 15 10
640 40 f. Kapoka 35 10
641 70 f. Frangipani 60 35
642 90 f. "Cochlospermum planchonii" 80 45
643 100 f. Cotton 90 45

1982. African Post and Telecommunications Union.
644 **227** 70 f. multicoloured . . . 45 15
645 90 f. multicoloured . . . 65 35

228 Children holding Torch

1982. 25th Anniv of Cultural Aid Fund.
646 **228** 70 f. multicoloured . . . 50 30

229 Hairstyle

1983.
647 **229** 90 f. multicoloured . . . 65 30
648 120 f. multicoloured . . . 90 35
649 170 f. multicoloured . . . 1·25 50

230 Audience watching Film

1983. 8th Film Festival, Ouagadougou. Mult.
650 90 f. Type **230** 85 55
651 500 f. Dumarou Ganda . . . 4·25 2·50

231 Joseph Montgolfier and First Demonstration of Hot-air Balloon, 1783

1983. Bicentenary of Manned Flight. Mult.
652 15 f. Type **231** (postage) . . . 10 10
653 25 f. Jean-Francois Pilatre de Rozier and first manned flight, 1783 . . . . 15 10
654 70 f. Jacques Charles and hydrogen balloon "The Globe", 1783 . . . . 50 10
655 90 f. John Jeffries and first Channel crossing, 1785 . . 65 20
656 100 f. Wilhelmine Reichardt and ascent on a horse, 1798 (air) 85 30
657 250 f. Salomon Andree and Spitzbergen–Expedition, 1897 1·60 55

232 Campaign Emblem and River **233** Man reading Letter

1983. International Drinking Water Decade. Mult.
659 60 f. Type **232** 45 20
660 70 f. Woman carrying water . 55 35

1983. World Communications Year. Multicoloured.
661 30 f. Type **233** 20 15
662 35 f. Type **233** 30 15
663 90 f. Canoe and Boeing 727 airliner 40 20
664 90 f. Woman on telephone . 65 35

234 Space Shuttle "Challenger"

1983. Air. World Events. Multicoloured.
665 90 f. Type **234** 60 20
666 120 f. World Cup football final 85 30
667 300 f. World Cup football final (different) . . . . 1·90 60
668 450 f. Royal wedding . . . . 2·50 85

235 "Synodontis gambiensis"

1983. Fishery Resources. Multicoloured.
670 20 f. Type **235** 15 15
671 30 f. "Palmatochromis guntheri" 35 15
672 40 f. Line fishing (vert) . . . 35 15
673 50 f. Net fishing 40 15
674 75 f. Trap fishing 55 20

236 Soling Class Yacht

1983. Air. Pre-Olympic Year. Multicoloured.
675 90 f. Type **236** 65 20
676 120 f. Type 470 yacht . . . . 1·00 30
677 300 f. Windsurfing . . . . . . 2·25 60
678 400 f. Windsurfing (different) . . 2·75 85

237 Planting a Sapling

1983. Campaign for Control of the Desert. Multicoloured.
680 10 f. Type **237** 15 10
681 50 f. Plantation 40 10
682 100 f. Control of forest fires . 90 35
683 150 f. Woman cooking . . . . 1·40 60
684 200 f. Control of timber trade (vert) . . . . 1·60 90

238 Arms of Upper Volta

1983. 25th Anniv of Republic. Multicoloured.
685 90 f. Type **238** 55 30
686 500 f. Family with flag . . . . 3·25 1·40

239 "Self-portrait" (Picasso)

1983. Celebrities' Anniversaries. Multicoloured.
687 120 f. Type **239** . . . . 1·40 35
688 185 f. "Self-portrait with a Palette" (Manet (1832–1883)) 1·40 45
689 300 f. Fresco detail (Raphael (1483–1520)) (horiz) . . . . 2·25 60
690 350 f. Fresco detail (Raphael) (different) (horiz) . . . . 2·50 85
691 500 f. J. W. Goethe (1749–1832) (portrait by Georg Oswald) . 3·50 1·10

240 "Adoration of the Shepherds" **242** Handball

1983. Air. Christmas. Multicoloured.
692 120 f. Type **240** 85 30
693 350 f. "Virgin of the Garland" 2·40 65
694 500 f. "Adoration of the Magi" 3·00 1·00

1984. Air. Olympic Games, Los Angeles. Multicoloured.
695 90 f. Type **242** 55 20
696 120 f. Volleyball 80 30
697 150 f. Handball (horiz) . . . . 1·10 35
698 250 f. Basketball (horiz) . . . 1·60 50
699 300 f. Football (horiz) . . . . 2·00 65

243 Greater Flamingo

1984. Air. Birds. Multicoloured.
701 90 f. Type **243** . . . . 1·10 40
702 185 f. Kori bustard (vert) . . 1·90 1·00
703 200 f. Red-billed oxpecker (vert) 2·00 1·10
704 300 f. Southern ground hornbill 2·75 1·75

244 Pres. Houari Boumedienne of Algeria

1984. Air. Celebrities. Multicoloured.
705 5 f. Type **244** 10 10
706 125 f. Gottlieb Daimler (automobile designer) and car 90 30
707 250 f. Louis Bleriot (aviator) and Bleriot XI airplane . . . . 1·60 50
708 300 f. Pres. Abraham Lincoln of U.S.A. and White House . 2·25 55
709 400 f. Henry Dunant (founder of Red Cross), red cross and battle of Solferino . . . . . 2·75 70
710 450 f. Auguste Piccard and bathyscape "Trieste" . . . 3·00 1·40
711 500 f. Robert Baden-Powell (founder of Boy Scout movement) and scouts . . . 3·25 95
712 600 f. Anatole Karpov, 1978 world chess champion . . . 3·75 1·10

245 Seedling and Clasped Hands within Circle of Flags **246** "Polystictus leoninus"

1984. 25th Anniv of Council of Unity.
714 **245** 90 f. multicoloured . . . 65 30
715 100 f. multicoloured . . . 80 35

1984. Fungi and Flowers. Multicoloured.
716 25 f. Type **246** (postage) . . . 40 20
717 185 f. "Pterocarpus lucens" . 1·60 60
718 200 f. "Phlebopus colossus sudanicus" . . . . 3·25 1·25
719 250 f. "Cosmos suplhureus" . 2·25 85
720 300 f. "Trametes versicolour" (air) . . . . 4·50 1·40
721 400 f. "Ganoderma lucidum" 5·50 1·75

247 Cheetah with Cubs

1984. Protected Animals. Multicoloured.
723 15 f. Type **247** (postage) . . . 10 10
724 35 f. Two cheetahs 30 10
725 90 f. Cheetah 65 20
726 120 f. Cheetah with cubs (different) 90 35
727 300 f. Baboons (air) . . . . . 2·25 55
728 400 f. Marabou stork and African white-backed vulture 3·50 85

248 "CC2400 ch"

1984. Transport. Multicoloured. (a) Locomotives.

730		40 f. Type **248**	30	10
731		100 f. Steam locomotive No. 1806	75	30
732		145 f. "Livingstone"	1·25	50
733		450 f. Pacific class "C51" steam locomotive	3·25	1·60
		(b) Ships.		
734		20 f. "Maiden Queen"	15	10
735		60 ff. "Scawfell"	45	15
736		120 f. "Harbinger"	90	35
737		400 f. "True Briton"	3·00	1·25

For later issues see **BURKINA FASO**.

OFFICIAL STAMPS

O 18 African Elephant

1963.

O112	O 18	1 f. sepia and brown	10	10
O113		5 f. sepia and green	15	15
O114		10 f. sepia and violet	20	20
O115		15 f. sepia & orange	25	25
O116		25 f. sepia and purple	35	35
O117		50 f. sepia and green	65	65
O118		60 f. sepia and red	75	75
O119		85 f. sepia and myrtle	1·25	1·25
O120		100 f. sepia and blue	1·50	1·50
O121		200 f. sepia and mve	2·75	2·75

POSTAGE DUE STAMPS

1920. Postage Due stamps of Upper Senegal and Niger, "Figures" Key-type, optd **HAUTE-VOLTA**.

D18	M	5 c. green	25	50
D19		10 c. red	25	50
D20		15 c. grey	25	50
D21		20 c. brown	30	60
D22		30 c. blue	45	90
D23		50 c. black	70	1·40
D24		60 c. orange	65	1·40
D25		1 f. violet	90	1·90

1927. Surch.

D40	M	2 f. on 1 f. mauve	2·25	3·50
D41		3 f. on 1 f. brown	2·50	3·75

1928. "Figures" key-type inscr "HAUTE-VOLTA".

D63	M	5 c. green	35	75
D64		10 c. red	35	75
D65		15 c. grey	50	95
D66		20 c. brown	50	95
D67		30 c. blue	65	1·25
D68		50 c. black	1·75	3·00
D69		60 c. orange	2·25	4·00
D70		1 f. violet	3·50	6·50
D71		2 f. purple	6·75	10·00
D72		3 f. brown	7·50	11·00

D 13 Red-fronted Gazelle

1962. Figures of value in black.

D 95	D 13	1 f. blue	10	10
D 96		2 f. orange	10	10
D 97		5 f. blue	15	15
D 98		10 f. purple	30	30
D 99		20 f. green	55	55
D100		50 f. red	1·40	1·40

APPENDIX

The following stamps have either been issued in excess of postal needs or have not been available to the public in reasonable quantities at face value. Such stamps may later be given full listing if there is evidence of regular postal use.

1973.

Gold Medal Winners, Munich Olympic Games (2nd series). Air 50, 60, 90, 150, 350 f.

Christmas 1972. Paintings of the Madonna and Child. Air 50, 75, 100, 125, 150 f.

Moon Mission of "Apollo 17". Air 50, 65, 100, 150, 200 f.

Gold Medal Winners, Munich Olympic Games (3rd series). Air 35, 45, 75, 250, 400 f.

Exploration of the Moon. Air 50, 65, 100, 150, 200 f.

Wild Animals. Air 100, 150, 200, 250, 500 f.

10th Anniv of Organization of African Unity. Air 45 f.

Europafrique. European Paintings. Air 50, 65, 100, 150, 200 f.

Historic Railway Locomotives, French Railway Museum, Mulhouse. Air 10, 40, 50, 150, 250 f.

Upper Volta Boy Scouts. Postage 20 f.; Air 40, 75, 150, 200 f.

Pan-African Drought Relief. Surch on values of 1973 Europafrique issue. Air 100 f. on 65 f., 200 f. on 150 f.

10th Death Anniv of President John Kennedy. Rockets. Postage 5, 10, 30 f.; Air 200, 300 f.

50th Anniv of International Police Organization (Interpol). 50, 65, 70, 150 f.

Tourism. Postage 35, 40 f.; Air 100 f.

Religious Buildings. Postage 35, 40 f.; Air 200 f.

Folk-dancers. Postage 35, 40 f.; Air 100, 225 f.

Famous Men. 5, 10, 20, 25, 30, 50, 60, 75, 100, 175, 200, 250 f.

1974.

World Cup Football Championship, Munich (1st issue). Postage 5, 40 f.; Air 75, 100, 250 f.

Pres. De Gaulle Commemoration. Postage 35, 40, 60 f.; Air 300 f.

World Cup Football Championship (2nd issue). Postage 10, 20, 50 f.; Air 150, 300 f.

Centenary of Universal Postal Union. Postage 35, 40, 85 f.; Air 100, 200, 300 f.

World Cup Football Championship (3rd issue). Previous Finals. Postage 10, 25, 50 f.; Air 150, 200, 250 f.

Centenary of Berne Convention. 1974 U.P.U. issue optd. Postage 35, 40, 85 f., Air 100, 200, 300 f.

Bouquets of Flowers. Postage 5, 10, 30, 50 f.; Air 300 f.

1975.

Birth Centenary of Sir Winston Churchill. 50, 75, 100, 125, 300 f.

Bicentenary of American Revolution (1st issue). 35, 40, 75, 100, 200, 300 f.

Railway Locomotives. Postage 15, 25, 50 f.; Air 100, 200 f.

Vintage and Veteran Cars. Postage 10, 30, 35 f.; Air 150, 200 f.

Bicent of American Revolution (2nd issue). Postage 30, 40, 50 f.; Air 200, 300 f.

Birth Cent of Dr Albert Schweitzer. Postage 5, 15 f.; Air 150, 175, 200 f.

"Apollo–Soyuz" Joint Space Test Project. Postage 40, 50 f.; Air 100, 200, 300 f.

Paintings by Picasso. Postage 50, 60, 90 f.; Air 150, 350 f.

"Expo '75" Exhibition, Okinawa, Japan. Postage 15, 25, 45, 50, 60 f.; Air 150 f.

Winter Olympic Games, Innsbruck. Postage 35, 45, 85 f.; Air 100, 200 f.

1976.

Olympic Games, Montreal (1st issue). "Pre-Olympic Year" (1975). Postage 40, 50, 100 f.; Air 125, 150 f.

Olympic Games, Montreal (2nd issue). Postage 30, 55, 75 f.; Air 150, 200 f.

Zeppelin Airships. Postage 10, 40, 50 f.; Air 100, 200, 300 f.

"Viking" Space Flight. Postage 30, 55, 75 f.; Air 200, 300 f.

1977.

Olympic Games Medal Winners, 1976 Olympic Games issue optd. Postage 30, 55, 75 f.; Air 150, 200 f.

1983.

Bicentenary of Manned Flight. Air 1500 f.

UPPER YAFA — Pt. 19

A Sultanate of South Arabia, formerly part of the Western Aden Protectorate. Independent from September to December 1967 and then part of the People's Democratic Republic of Yemen.

1000 fils = 1 dinar

1 Flag and Map

1967.

UY 1	1	5 f. multicoloured (post)	15	15
UY 2		10 f. multicoloured	15	15
UY 3		20 f. multicoloured	20	20
UY 4		25 f. multicoloured	25	20
UY 5		40 f. multicoloured	40	25
UY 6		50 f. multicoloured	50	30
UY 7	–	75 f. multicoloured (air)	65	50
UY 8	–	100 f. multicoloured	85	60
UY 9	–	250 f. multicoloured	2·00	2·00
UY10	–	500 f. multicoloured	3·50	3·50

DESIGNS: UY 7/10, Arms of Sultanate.

APPENDIX

The following stamps have either been issued in excess of postal needs or have not been available to the public in reasonable quantities at face value. Such stamps may later be given full listing if there is evidence of regular postal use.

1967.

Olympic Games, Mexico (1968). Postage 15, 25, 50, 75 f.; Air 150 f.

Sculptures. Postage 10, 30, 60, 75 f.; Air 150 f.

Paintings from the Louvre. Postage 50 f.; Air 100, 150, 200, 250 f.

World Cup Football Championship, England (1966). Postage 5, 10, 50 f.; Air 100 f.

Paintings by Old Masters. Postage 10, 15, 20, 25, 30, 40, 50, 60, 75 f.; Air 150 f.

Human Rights Year and 5th Death Anniv of J. F. Kennedy. Postage 5, 10, 50, 75 f.; Air 125 f.

Persian Miniatures. 10, 20, 30, 40, 50 f.

Ballet Paintings. 20, 30, 40, 50, 60 f.

Portraits by Old Masters. Postage 25, 50, 75 f.; Air 100, 125, 150, 175, 200, 225, 250 f.

Winter Olympic Games, Grenoble (1968). 1967 World Cup issue optd. Postage 5 f. × 2, 10 f. × 2, 50 f. × 2; Air 100 f. × 2.

20th Anniv of UNICEF. Paintings. Postage 50, 75 f.; Air 100, 125, 250 f.

Flower Paintings. Postage 5, 10, 50 f.; Air 100, 150 f.

URUGUAY — Pt. 20

A republic in S. America, bordering on the Atlantic Ocean, independent since 1828.

1856. 120 centavos = 1 real.
1859. 1000 milesimos = 100 centesimos = 1 peso.

1

1856. Imperf.

1	1	60 c. blue	£190	
2		80 c. green	£170	
3		1 r. red	£150	

3 4

1858. Imperf.

5	3	120 c. blue	£130	£120
6		180 c. green	38·00	55·00
7		240 c. red	38·00	£225

1859. Imperf.

15	4	60 c. purple	15·00	13·50
16		80 c. yellow	£130	25·00
17		100 c. red	38·00	29·00
18		120 c. blue	25·00	9·50
12		180 c. green	9·50	11·50
13		240 c. red	35·00	35·00

6 8 9

1864. Imperf.

20a	6	6 c. red	5·75	3·75
21		8 c. green	9·75	9·75
22		10 c. yellow	13·50	9·25
23		12 c. blue	5·75	4·50

1866. Surch in figures. Imperf.

24	6	5 c. on 12 c. blue	9·50	19·00
25		10 c. on 8 c. green	9·50	25·00
26		15 c. on 10 c. yellow	11·50	29·00
27a		20 c. on 6 c. red	13·50	29·00

1866. Imperf.

28	8	1 c. black	95	1·50
29	9	5 c. blue	1·50	85
30		10 c. green	5·50	2·25
31		15 c. yellow	9·25	3·75
32		20 c. red	11·00	3·75

1866. Perf.

37	8	1 c. black	2·25	2·25
33	9	5 c. blue	2·00	35
34		10 c. green	3·75	35
35		15 c. yellow	2·00	1·40
36		20 c. red	4·50	1·10

10 11

1877. Roul. Various frames.

42	10	1 c. brown	25	20
43	11	5 c. green	30	15
44	10	10 c. red	40	15
45		20 c. bistre	60	25
46		50 c. black	3·00	1·10
47		1 p. blue	17·00	5·50

15 J. Suarez 16

1881. Perf.

60a	15	7 c. blue	75	90

1882.

62	16	1 c. green	40	40
63	–	2 c. red	35	35

The central device on the 2 c. is a mountain.

18 Arms

20 Gen. Maximo Santos

21 General Artigas

26

1883.

66	18	1 c. green	50	30
67		2 c. red	60	40
68	20	5 c. blue	75	60
69	21	10 c. brown	1·10	75

1883. Optd **1883 Provisorio**. Roul.

75	11	5 c. green	50	40

1884. Optd **PROVISORIO 1884** or surch **1 CENTESIMO** also.

76	10	1 c. on 10 c. red	15	15
77	–	2 c. red (No. 63)	50	50

1884.

79	26	5 c. blue	1·00	50

28 29

31 Gen. Artigas

32 M. Santos 33 34

1884. Roul.

100	28	1 c. green	20	20
83a		1 c. grey	40	30
101	29	2 c. red	20	25
85a	28	5 c. blue	1·00	15
86		5 c. lilac	25	10
87	31	7 c. brown	95	60
103		7 c. orange	60	40
88	32	10 c. brown	20	20
89	33	20 c. mauve	75	30
105		20 c. brown	75	40
90	34	25 c. lilac	1·40	50
106		25 c. red	1·10	60

35 36

1887. Roul.

99 **35** 10 c. mauve 70 40

1888. Roul.

104 **36** 10 c. violet 25 25

1889. Optd **Provisorio**. Roul.

114 **28** 5 c. lilac 15 15

38 39 40

41 42 43

44 Figure of Justice 45 Mercury 46

1889. Perf.

115 **38** 1 c. green 40 20
116 **39** 2 c. red 20 25
117 **40** 5 c. blue 20 15
118 **41** 7 c. brown 60 25
119 **42** 10 c. green . . . . 1·50 25
120 **43** 20 c. orange . . . . 1·10 30
121 **44** 20 c. brown . . . . 2·00 40
122 **45** 50 c. blue . . . . 3·50 1·10
123 **46** 1 p. violet . . . . 8·50 2·00

See also Nos. 142/52, 220, 222 224 and 236/7.

1891. Optd **Provisorio 1891**. Roul.

133 **28** 5 c. lilac 10 10

1892. Optd **Provisorio 1892** or surch also in words.

135 **28** 1 c. green 40 40
137 **43** 1 c. on 20 c. orange 15 10
136 **41** 5 c. on 7 c. brown 15 30

50 51 52

53 54 55

1892. Perf.

138 **50** 1 c. green 20 15
139 **51** 2 c. red 25 20
140 **52** 5 c. blue 20 15
141 **53** 10 c. orange 90 40

1894.

142 **38** 1 c. blue 20 25
143 **39** 2 c. brown 25 25
144 **40** 5 c. red 50 20
145 **41** 7 c. green . . . . 2·75 1·10
146 **42** 10 c. orange . . . . 1·50 30
147 **43** 20 c. brown . . . . 2·75 75
148 **44** 25 c. red . . . . 3·50 1·50
149 **45** 50 c. purple . . . . 6·25 2·25
150 **46** 1 p. blue . . . . 11·00 3·00
151 **54** 2 p. red . . . . 11·50 7·00
152 **55** 3 p.purple . . . . 11·50 7·00

56 Gaucho 57 Solis Theatre 58 Steam Locomotive

59 Bull's Head 60 Ceres 61 Steamer "Elbe"

62 Amazon 63 Mercury

64 65 Montevideo Fortress

66 Montevideo Cathedral

1895.

153 **56** 1 c. bistre 20 20
154 **57** 2 c. blue 20 20
155 **58** 5 c. red 20 20
156 **59** 7 c. green . . . . 3·75 1·00
157 **60** 10 c. brown 85 30
158 **61** 20 c. black and green . . . 6·00 55
159 **62** 25 c. black and brown . . 2·75 60
160 **63** 50 c. black and blue . . . 3·50 1·50
161 **64** 1 p. black and brown . . . 5·50 2·00
162 **65** 2 p. green and violet . . . 11·50 7·75
163 **66** 3 p. blue and red . . . . 11·50 6·25

For further stamps in these types, see Nos. 183/93 and 221.

67 J. Suarez 68 J. Suarez Monument 72

1896. Unveiling of President Joaquin Suarez Monument.

177 **67** 1 c. black and red 20 15
178 **68** 5 c. black and blue 25 20
179 – 10 c. black and lake . . . 45 25

DESIGN: 10 c. Larger stamp showing whole Suarez Monument.

1897. Optd **PROVISORIO 1897**.

180 **67** 1 c. black and red 30 30
181 **68** 5 c. black and blue 40 30
182 – 10 c. black and lake . . . 50 50

1897.

183 **56** 1 c. blue 20 15
184 **57** 2 c. purple 30 20
185 **58** 5 c. green 30 15
186 **59** 7 c. orange . . . . 1·75 60
187 **72** 10 c. red 85 35
188 **61** 20 c. black and mauve . . 5·50 40
189 **62** 25 c. blue and red . . . . 1·50 35
190 **63** 50 c. brown and green . . 2·75 70
191 **64** 1 p. blue and brown . . . 4·50 1·40
192 **65** 2 p. red and yellow . . . . 4·50 65
193 **66** 3 p. red and lilac . . . . 4·25 1·10

See also No. 223.

1897. End of Civil War. Optd with palm leaf and **PAZ 1897**.

197 **56** 1 c. blue 40 30
198 **57** 2 c. purple 55 55
199 **58** 5 c. green 85 75
200 **72** 10 c. red . . . . 1·40 1·40

1898. Surch **PROVISIONAL ½ CENTESIMO**.

209 **38** ½ c. on 1 c. blue 15 15
210 **56** ½ c. on 1 c. bistre 15 15
211 **67** ½ c. on 1 c. black and red . 15 15
212 **57** ½ c. on 2 c. blue 15 15
213 **68** ½ c. on 5 c. black & blue . 20 15
214 **59** ½ c. on 7 c. green 20 15

75 Liberty 76 Monument to Gen. Artigas

1898.

215 **75** 5 m. red 20 20
216 5 m. violet 25 25

1899.

217 **76** 5 m. blue 25 15
218 5 m. orange 25 15
220 **39** 2 c. orange 20 20
221a **58** 5 c. blue . . . . 1·50 15
222 **41** 7 c. red . . . . 2·25 1·10
223 **72** 10 c. purple 30 25
224 **43** 20 c. blue . . . . 1·10 20

1900. No. 182 surch **1900 5 CENTESIMOS** and bar.

229 5 c. on 10 c. black and lake . . 25 15

78 79 80

81 82

1900.

230 **78** 1 c. green 30 15
231a **79** 2 c. red 10 15
232b **80** 5 c. blue 60 15
233 **81** 7 c. brown 85 30
234 **82** 10 c. lilac 45 20
236 **45** 50 c. red . . . . 3·50 35
237 **46** 1 p. green . . . . 11·00 75

85 General Artigas 86

87 88

89 90

91

1904.

251 **85** 5 m. yellow 30 15
252 **86** 1 c. green 50 15
253a **87** 2 c. orange 20 15
254b **88** 5 c. blue 40 10
255 **89** 10 c. lilac 40 20
256 **90** 20 c. green . . . . 1·40 40
257 **91** 25 c. bistre . . . . 1·50 10

1904. End of the Civil War. Optd **Paz-1904**.

258 **86** 1 c. green 35 30
259 **87** 2 c. orange 40 35
260 **88** 5 c. blue . . . . 1·00 50

95 96

1906.

268 **95** 5 c. blue 50 15

1906.

269 **96** 5 c. blue 20 10
270 7 c. brown 40 25
271 50 c. red . . . . 2·25 40

98 Cruiser "Montevideo" and Cadet Ship "Diez-y-Ocho de Julio"

1908. 83rd Anniv of Revolt of the "Immortal 33" under Levalleja. Roul.

279 **98** 1 c. green and red . . . . 1·10 85
280 2 c. green . . . . 1·10 85
281 5 c. green and orange . . . 1·10 85

99 Montevideo Port

1909. Opening of the Port of Montevideo.

282 **99** 2 c. black and brown . . . 1·50 80
283 5 c. black and red . . . . 1·50 80

1909. Surch **Provisorio** and value.

284 **82** 8 c. on 10 c. violet 40 30
285 **44** 23 c. on 25 c. brown . . . 75 30

103 Centaur

1910. Centenary of 1810 Argentine Revolution.

286 **103** 2 c. red 30 20
287 5 c. blue 30 20

1910. Surch **PROVISORIO 5 MILESIMOS** (or **CENTESIMOS**) **1910**.

294 **78** 5 m. on 1 c. green . . . 10 20
295 **45** 5 c. on 50 c. red 15 30
296 **96** 5 c. on 50 c. red 40 30

107 Artigas 108

1910.

297 **107** 5 m. purple 15 10
298 1 c. green 15 10
299 2 c. red 20 10
324 2 c. pink 25 10
319 4 c. yellow 30 10
300 5 c. blue 20 10
301 8 c. black 40 15
327 8 c. blue 25 10
302 20 c. brown 70 20
303 **108** 23 c. blue . . . . 1·10 25
330 50 c. orange . . . . . . 1·50 60
331 1 p. red . . . . 4·50 40

109 114 Liberty offering Peace to Uruguay

1911. 1st Pan-American Postal Congress.

306 **109** 5 c. black and red 35 25

1911. Centenary of Battle of Las Piedras. Surch **ARTIGAS**, value and **1811-1911**.

314 **81** 2 c. on 7 c. brown 35 25
315 5 c. on 7 c. brown 35 20

1913. Centenary of 1813 Conference. Optd **CENTENARIO DE LAS INSTRUCCIONES DEL ANO XIII.**

332	**107**	2 c. brown	30	40
333		4 c. yellow	30	40
334		5 c. blue	30	40

1918. Promulgation of New Constitution.

347	**114**	2 c. brown and green	35	25
348		5 c. blue and brown	35	25

115 Montevideo Harbour **116** Statue of Liberty, New York **118** J. E. Rodo

1919.

349	**115**	5 m. grey and violet	15	10
350		1 c. grey and green	20	10
351		2 c. grey and red	20	10
352		4 c. grey and orange	50	10
353		5 c. grey and blue	60	10
354		8 c. brown and blue	70	20
355		20 c. grey and brown	2·50	35
356		23 c. brown and green	3·50	70
357		50 c. blue and brown	4·00	3·25
358		1 p. blue and red	9·50	2·75

1919. Peace Commemoration.

359	**116**	2 c. brown and red	20	10
360		4 c. brown and orange	30	10
361		5 c. brown and blue	35	10
362		8 c. blue and brown	50	20
363		20 c. black and bistre	1·40	40
364		23 c. black and green	2·00	70

1920. Honouring J. E. Rodo (writer).

372	**118**	2 c. black and lake	35	45
373		4 c. blue and orange	40	30
374		5 c. brown and blue	50	35

1921. Air. Optd with airplane and **CORREO AEREO.**

377	**44**	25 c. brown	2·10	1·50

120 Mercury **122** Damaso A. Larranaga

1921.

378	**120**	5 m. mauve	30	10
410		5 m. black	20	10
380		1 c. green	30	10
411a		1 c. violet	25	10
411		1 c. mauve	25	10
412		2 c. orange	35	10
412a		2 c. red	40	10
384		3 c. green	40	20
385		4 c. yellow	25	10
386		5 c. blue	25	10
413		5 c. brown	40	10
414		8 c. red	55	50
388		12 c. blue	1·10	50
389		36 c. olive	4·50	1·50

1921. 150th Birth Anniv of D. A. Larranaga.

390	**122**	5 c. slate	75	55

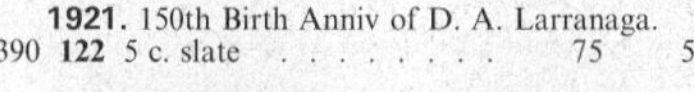

127 Artigas Monument **128** Chilian Lapwing

1923. Unveiling of Monument to Artigas.

418	**127**	2 c. brown and red	30	10
419		5 c. brown and violet	30	10
420		12 c. brown and blue	40	20

1923. Various sizes.

450	**128**	5 m. grey	15	10
422		1 c. yellow	10	15
451		1 c. pink	25	15
477		1 c. purple	50	20
528		1 c. violet	10	20
423		2 c. mauve	10	15
529		2 c. red	10	20
453		3 c. green	35	15
454		5 c. blue	25	10
455		8 c. red	35	15
456		10 c. green	25	10
457		12 c. blue	40	15
458		15 c. mauve	30	15
459		20 c. brown	70	15
429		36 c. green	1·50	65
460		36 c. red	2·25	55
430		50 c. orange	3·00	1·00
461		50 c. olive	3·00	75
431		1 p. red	12·50	7·75
462		1 p. buff	4·75	1·75
432		2 p. green	12·50	7·75
463		2 p. lilac	9·50	5·00

130 **131** Biplane

1923. Centenary of Battle of Sarandi.

433	**130**	2 c. green	35	25
434		5 c. red	35	25
435		12 c. blue	35	25

1924. Air.

436	**131**	6 c. blue	75	85
437		10 c. red	1·10	1·25
438		20 c. green	2·00	2·00

134 "Victory" of Samothrace

1924. Uruguayan Football Victory in Olympic Games.

464	**134**	2 c. red	8·50	6·25
465		5 c. purple	8·50	6·25
466		12 c. blue	8·50	6·25

135 Landing of Lavalleja

1925. Centenary of Rising against Brazilian Rule.

467	**135**	2 c. grey and red	60	70
468		5 c. grey and mauve	60	70
469		12 c. grey and blue	60	70

136 Parliament House **137** White-necked Heron

1925. Inauguration of Parliament House.

470	**136**	5 c. black and violet	60	40
471		12 c. black and blue	60	40

1925. Air. Centenary of Assembly of Florida. (a) Inscr "MONTEVIDEO".

472	**137**	14 c. black and blue	15·00	7·75

(b) Inscr "FLORIDA".

473	**137**	14 c. black and blue	15·00	7·75

138 Gen. F. Rivera **139** Gaucho Cavalryman at Rincon

1925. Centenary of Battle of Rincon.

474	**138**	5 c. pink (postage)	40	30
475	**139**	45 c. green (air)	—	4·50

140 Battle of Sarandi

1925. Centenary of Battle of Sarandi.

482	**140**	2 c. green	60	55
483		5 c. mauve	60	55
484		12 c. blue	75	60

141 Albatross **145** New G.P.O., Montevideo

1926. Air. Imperf.

495	**141**	6 c. blue	70	70
496		10 c. red	95	95
497		20 c. green	1·40	1·40
498		25 c. violet	1·40	1·40

See also Nos. 569/80.

1927. Philatelic Exhibition, Montevideo. Imperf.

534	**145**	2 c. green	2·00	2·00
535		5 c. red	2·00	2·00
536		8 c. blue	2·00	2·00

1928. Opening of San Carlos–Rocha Railway. Surch **Inauguracion Ferrocarril SAN CARLOS a ROCHA 14/1/928** and value.

537	**128**	2 c. on 12 c. blue	85	85
538		5 c. on 12 c. blue	85	85
539		10 c. on 12 c. blue	85	85
540		15 c. on 12 c. blue	85	85

147 Gen. F. Rivera (after M. Bucasso)

1928. Centenary of Conquest of Las Misiones.

541	**147**	5 c. red	30	15

148 Artigas **149** Artigas Statue, Paysandu

1928.

542	**148**	5 m. black	10	10
762		5 m. brown	10	10
868		5 m. orange	10	10
543		1 c. violet	10	10
544		1 c. purple	10	10
869		1 c. blue	10	10
687		15 m. black	25	15
545		2 c. green	10	10
764		2 c. brown	10	10
870		2 c. red	10	10
546		3 c. bistre	20	10
871		3 c. green	10	10
548		5 c. red	15	10
549		5 c. olive	15	10
766		5 c. blue	15	10
767		5 c. turquoise	30	10
872		5 c. violet	10	10
550		7 c. red	15	10
551		8 c. blue	20	10
552		8 c. brown	20	10
553		10 c. orange	30	15
768		12 c. blue	30	10
556		15 c. blue	45	10
557		17 c. violet	40	15
558		20 c. brown	55	15
757		20 c. buff	70	35
770		20 c. red	40	30
771		20 c. violet	35	10
560		24 c. red	70	40
561		24 c. yellow	40	35
562		36 c. olive	70	40
563		50 c. grey	1·75	95
564		50 c. black	2·25	85
772		50 c. sepia	1·10	45
566		1 p. green	4·00	1·50
567	**149**	2 p. brown and blue	5·00	2·75
568		3 p. black and red	6·25	6·25

1928. Air. Re-issue of T **141**. Perf.

634	**141**	4 c. brown	1·50	1·50
569		10 c. green	75	70
570		20 c. orange	1·10	85
571		30 c. blue	1·10	85
572		38 c. green	1·75	1·50
573		40 c. yellow	2·10	2·00
574		50 c. violet	2·25	2·25
575		76 c. orange	4·25	4·25
576		1 p. red	3·50	3·50
577		1 p. 14 blue	10·00	8·75
578		1 p. 52 yellow	15·00	15·00
579		1 p. 90 violet	18·00	17·00
580		3 p. 80 red	50·00	45·00

150 Goal Posts **151** General Garzon

1928. Uruguayan Football Victories in 1924 and 1928 Olympic Games.

581	**150**	2 c. purple	4·50	3·75
582		5 c. red	4·50	3·75
583		8 c. blue	4·50	3·75

1928. Unveiling of Monument to Gen. Garzon. Imperf.

584	**151**	2 c. red	75	75
585		5 c. green	75	75
586		8 c. blue	75	75

154 Artigas **156** Pegasus

1929.

759	**154**	1 p. brown	3·00	1·40
596		2 p. green	5·00	2·75
597		2 p. red	11·00	7·75
760		2 p. blue	5·75	5·50
598		3 p. blue	7·00	5·00
761		3 p. black	8·75	7·00
600		4 p. violet	11·00	8·50
601		4 p. green	11·00	7·75
602		5 p. red	13·50	11·00
603		5 p. orange	11·00	7·75
604		10 p. blue	38·00	35·00
605		10 p. red	38·00	35·00

1929. Air. Size $34\frac{1}{2} \times 23\frac{1}{2}$ mm.

617	**156**	1 c. mauve	25	25
659		1 c. blue	25	25
618		2 c. yellow	25	25
660		2 c. olive	25	25
619		4 c. blue	45	40
661		4 c. lake	45	40
620		6 c. violet	25	40
662		6 c. brown	25	40
621		8 c. orange	1·10	1·10
663		8 c. grey	1·25	1·10
664		8 c. green	35	30
622		16 c. blue	1·10	75
665		16 c. red	1·10	1·10
623		24 c. purple	95	95
666		24 c. violet	1·25	1·10
624		30 c. brown	1·10	1·10
667		30 c. green	60	30
625		40 c. brown	2·00	2·00
668		40 c. orange	2·00	1·75
626		60 c. blue	1·75	1·25
669		60 c. green	3·00	2·25
670		60 c. red	95	60
627		80 c. blue	3·00	3·00
671		80 c. green	5·00	4·00
628		90 c. blue	3·00	2·10
672		90 c. olive	5·00	4·00
629		1 p. red	2·25	2·00
630		1 p. 20 olive	7·00	7·00
673		1 p. 20 red	11·00	9·25
631		1 p. 50 purple	7·00	5·50
674		1 p. 50 sepia	3·75	3·50
632		3 p. red	11·50	11·00
675		3 p. blue	7·75	7·75
633		4 p. 50 black	20·00	18·00
676		4 p. 50 lilac	14·00	12·50
677		10 p. blue	7·00	5·50

For stamps as Type **156**, but smaller, see Nos. 725/44.

157 Rio Negro Bridge **159** "Peace"

1930. Independence Centenary.

639	**157**	5 m. black	20	15
640	–	1 c. sepia	20	15
641	**159**	2 c. lake	20	15
642	–	3 c. green	25	20
643	–	5 c. blue	25	20
644	–	8 c. red	35	20
645	–	10 c. violet	25	35
646	–	15 c. green	30	25
647	–	20 c. blue	1·40	70
648	–	24 c. lake	60	30
649	–	50 c. red	3·25	1·75
650	–	1 p. black	3·00	1·50
651	–	2 p. blue	7·00	4·50
652	–	3 p. red	10·00	7·00
653	–	4 p. orange	11·50	8·50
654	–	5 p. lilac	17·00	10·00

DESIGNS—HORIZ: 1 c. Gaucho horse-breaker; 5 c. Head of Liberty and Uruguayan flag; 10 c. "Artigas", from picture by Blanes; 15 c. Seascape; 20 c. Montevideo harbour, 1830; 24 c. Head of Liberty and Arms of Uruguay; 50 c. Montevideo Harbour, 1930. VERT: 3 c. Montevideo; 8 c. Allegorical figure with torch; 1 p. to 5 p. Artigas Monument.

161 — 163 J. Zorrilla de San Martin

1930. Fund for Old People.

655	**161**	1 c.+1 c. violet	20	15
656		2 c.+2 c. green	25	25
657		5 c.+5 c. red	30	30
658		8 c.+8 c. blue	30	30

1932.

679	**163**	$1\frac{1}{2}$ c. purple	20	10
680		3 c. green	30	10
681		7 c. blue	35	10
682		12 c. blue	30	35
683		1 p. brown	9·25	6·25

1932. Surch.

684	**161**	$1\frac{1}{2}$ c. on 2 c.+2 c. green	25	15

167 J. Zorrilla de San Martin — 168 Flag of the Race

1933. Various portraits.

689	–	15 m. red (Lavalleja)	15	10
690	–	3 c. green (Rivera)	10	10
691	**167**	7 c. grey	15	10

1933. 441st Anniv of Columbus' Departure from Palos.

692	**168**	3 c. green	15	20
693		5 c. pink	20	25
694		7 c. blue	20	20
695		8 c. red	60	30
696		12 c. blue	25	25
697		17 c. violet	75	40
698		20 c. brown	1·50	95
699		24 c. bistre	2·00	95
700		36 c. red	2·25	1·10
701		50 c. brown	2·75	1·40
702		1 p. brown	7·75	3·50

169 Sower — 170 Map and Albatross

1933. Opening of the 3rd National Assembly.

703	**169**	3 c. green	20	15
704		5 c. violet	35	25
705		7 c. blue	30	20
706		8 c. red	40	40
707		12 c. blue	75	45

1933. 7th Pan-American Conference, Montevideo.

708	**170**	3 c. green, brown & blk	1·10	1·10
709		7 c. blue, black & brown	60	45
710		12 c. blue, red and grey	95	75
711		17 c. red, blue and grey	2·10	2·10
712		20 c. yellow, green & blue	2·25	2·25
713		36 c. red, yellow & black	3·00	3·00

1934. Air. Closure of the 7th Pan-American Conference. Optd **SERVICIO POSTAL AEREO 1-1-34** in circle.

714	**170**	17 c. red, blue and grey	7·75	6·25
715		36 c. red, yellow & black	7·25	6·25

172

1934. 1st Anniv of Third Republic.

716	**172**	3 c. green	25	35
717		7 c. red	25	35
718		12 c. blue	60	30
719		17 c. brown and pink	75	70
720		20 c. yellow and grey	95	75
721		36 c. violet and green	95	95
722		50 c. grey and blue	2·50	2·00
723		1 p. red and mauve	6·25	4·00

1935. Air. As T **156**, but size $31\frac{1}{2} \times 21\frac{1}{2}$ mm.

725		15 c. yellow	95	75
726		22 c. red	60	50
727		30 c. purple	95	75
728		37 c. purple	50	40
729		40 c. red	75	50
730		47 c. red	1·50	1·40
731		50 c. blue	50	50
732		52 c. blue	1·50	1·40
733		57 c. blue	75	70
734		62 c. green	70	50
735		87 c. green	2·10	1·75
736		1 p. olive	1·40	85
737		1 p. 12 brown	1·40	85
738		1 p. 20 brown	4·50	3·75
739		1 p. 27 brown	4·50	3·75
740		1 p. 62 red	3·00	3·00
741		2 p. lake	5·00	4·50
742		2 p. 12 grey	5·00	4·50
743		3 p. blue	4·50	4·50
744		5 p. orange	16·00	16·00

173 Friendship of Uruguay and Brazil — 174 Florencio Sanchez

1935. Visit of President Vargas of Brazil.

747	**173**	5 m. brown	50	30
748		15 m. black	25	25
749		3 c. green	30	25
750		7 c. orange	35	20
751		12 c. blue	75	50
752		50 c. brown	2·00	1·50

1935. 25th Death Anniv of F. Sanchez (dramatist).

753	**174**	3 c. green	15	10
754		7 c. brown	20	10
755		12 c. blue	55	35

176 Rio Negro Dam — 178 Artigas

1937.

780	**176**	1 c. violet (postage)	30	10
781		10 c. blue	20	10
782		15 c. red	75	50
783		1 p. brown	3·00	1·10
793		8 c. green (air)	35	35
794		20 c. green	75	50
785		35 c. brown	2·10	2·00
786		62 c. green	25	20
787		68 c. orange	60	40
788		68 c. brown	50	20
789		75 c. violet	2·10	60
790		1 p. red	75	55
791		1 p. 38 red	7·00	6·25
792		3 p. blue	3·75	75

1939. (a) Plain background.

806	**178**	5 m. orange	10	10
807		1 c. blue	10	10
808		2 c. violet	10	10
809		5 c. brown	15	10
810		8 c. red	20	10
811		10 c. green	35	10
812		15 c. blue	40	30
813		1 p. brown	1·25	30
1008		1 p. purple	1·25	30
814		2 p. lilac	3·00	1·25
815		4 p. orange	3·75	1·50
816		5 p. red	5·25	2·50

Nos. 806/12 are size 16×19 mm. No. 1008 is 18×22 mm. and Nos. 813/6 are $24 \times 29\frac{1}{2}$ mm.

(b) Lined background. (i) Size 17×22 mm.

835	**178**	5 m. orange	10	10
848		5 m. black	10	10
849		5 m. blue	10	10
836		1 c. blue	10	10
837		1 c. purple	10	10
838		2 c. violet	10	10
839		2 c. orange	15	10
840a		2 c. brown	10	10
1152		2 c. grey	10	10
841		3 c. green	15	10
842		5 c. brown	15	10
843b		7 c. blue	10	10
844		8 c. red	25	10
845		10 c. green	15	10
851		10 c. brown	25	10
852		12 c. blue	25	10
853		20 c. mauve	70	15
846		50 c. bistre	3·00	60
847		50 c. green	2·10	75
1153		50 c. brown	10	10

(ii) Size $23\frac{1}{2} \times 29\frac{1}{2}$ mm.

1024	**178**	2 p. brown	3·50	1·50

180 Airplane over "La Carreta" (sculpture, Jose Bellini)

1939. Air.

817	**180**	20 c. blue	30	25
818		20 c. violet	20	25
820		35 c. red	25	20
821		50 c. orange	25	20
822		75 c. pink	30	15
823		1 p. blue	85	10
824		1 p. 38 violet	1·50	60
825		1 p. 38 orange	1·40	1·25
826a		2 p. blue	2·25	45
827		5 p. lilac	3·00	60
828		5 p. green	3·75	1·50
829		10 p. red	23·00	15·00

181 Congress of Montevideo

1939. 50th Anniv of 1st International Juridical Congress, Montevideo.

830	**181**	1 c. red	20	10
831		2 c. green	25	20
832		5 c. red	25	20
833		12 c. blue	30	35
834		50 c. violet	1·10	75

183 Juan Manuel Blanes (artist) — 185 Francisco Acuna de Figueroa

1941. 40th Death Anniv of Blanes.

855	**183**	5 m. brown	20	10
856		1 c. brown	20	10
857		2 c. green	20	10
858		5 c. red	50	10
859		12 c. blue	60	45
860		50 c. violet	2·75	2·10

1942. 80th Death Anniv of Figueroa (author of words of National Anthem).

863	**185**	1 c. brown	15	15
864		2 c. green	15	15
865		5 c. red	30	15
866		12 c. blue	60	40
867		50 c. violet	1·75	1·50

1943. Surch **Valor $ 0.005**.

873	**178**	5 m. on 1 c. blue		

187 — 189 Clio

1943.

874	**187**	1 c. on 2 c. brown	10	10
875		2 c. on 2 c. brown	15	10

1943. Centenary of Historical and Geographical Institute. Montevideo.

878	**189**	5 m. violet	20	10
879		1 c. blue	20	10
880		2 c. red	35	15
881		5 c. brown	35	20

191 — 192 Emblems of Y.M.C.A.

1944. 75th Anniv of Founding of Swiss Colony.

889	**191**	1 c. on 3 c. green	10	10
890		5 c. on 7 c. brown	20	10
891		10 c. on 12 c. blue	40	25

1944. Centenary of Young Men's Christian Assn.

892	**192**	5 c. blue	10	10

1944. Air. Air stamps of 1935, Nos. 730, etc, surch.

893		40 c. on 47 c. red	25	40
894		40 c. on 57 c. blue	30	25
895		74 c. on 1 p. 12 brown	30	25
896		79 c. on 87 c. green	1·10	75
897		79 c. on 1 p. 27 brown	1·50	1·25
898		1 p. 20 on 1 p. 62 red	85	60
899		1 p. 43 on 2 p. 12 grey	1·10	75

194 Legislative Palace

1945. Air.

900	**194**	2 p. blue	1·75	70

195 Book — 198 Statue

1945. Birth Centenary of Jose Pedro Varela (writer).

901	**195**	5 m. green	15	10
902	–	1 c. brown (Varela)	15	10
903	–	2 c. red (Statue)	15	10
904a	**198**	5 c. blue	15	10

Nos. 902/3 are vert.

205 Eduardo Acevedo (statesman) — 200 Jose Pedro Varela (writer)

1945.

905	–	5 m. violet	10	10
911	–	1 c. brown	10	10
912	**205**	2 c. purple	10	10
945	–	3 c. green	10	10
906	**200**	5 c. red	15	10
907	–	10 c. blue	25	15
946	–	20 c. brown and green	55	30

PORTRAITS: 5 m. Santiago Vazquez (statesman); 1 c. Sylvestre Blanco (statesman); 3 c. Bruno Mauricio de Zabala (founder of Montevideo); 10 c. Jose Ellauri (President, 1873–75); 20 c. Col. Luis de Larrobla (first Postmaster).

206 Full-rigged Ship "La Eolo"

1945. Air.

913	**206**	8 c. green	1·75	35

1945. Air. Victory. Surch figure as "Victory of Samothrace", **1945** and new value. No. 908 optd **VICTORIA** also.

914	**180**	14 c. on 50 c. orange	35	30
915		23 c. on 50 c. orange	40	35
916		23 c. on 1 p. 38 orange	50	40
908	**156**	44 c. on 75 c. brown	70	40
917	**180**	1 p. on 1 p. 38 orange	2·00	1·10

1946. Inaug of Rio Negro Hydro-electric Power Plant. Optd **INAUGURACION DICIEMBRE, 1945**, No. 918 also surch **CORREO 20 CENTS**.

918	**176**	20 c. on 68 c. brown (postage)	80	35
919		62 c. green (air)	50	45

1946. As T **187**. (a) Postage. Optd **CORREOS** and Caduceus.

920	**187**	5 m. orange	10	10
921		2 c. brown	10	10
922		3 c. green	10	10
923		5 c. blue	10	10
924		10 c. brown	15	10
925		20 c. green	50	15
926		50 c. brown	1·10	60
927		3 p. red	4·25	2·25

(b) Air. Optd **SERVICIO AEREO** and an airplane.

928	**187**	8 c. red	10	10
929		50 c. brown	40	25
930		1 p. blue	50	30
931		2 p. olive	2·25	1·10
932		3 p. red	2·25	1·10
933		5 p. red	4·50	3·00

217 Douglas DC-4 — 215 National Airport

1947. Air.

947	**217**	3 c. brown	10	10
948		8 c. red	15	10
949		10 c. black	10	10
950		10 c. red	10	10
951		14 c. blue	25	15
952		15 c. brown	15	10
953		20 c. purple	15	15
954		21 c. lilac	20	15
955		23 c. green	25	20
956		27 c. green	20	10
957		31 c. brown	30	15
958		36 c. blue	20	10
959		36 c. black	20	15
960		50 c. turquoise	35	25
961		50 c. blue	45	20
962		62 c. blue	40	25
963		65 c. red	40	25
964		84 c. orange	55	40
941	**215**	1 p. brown and red	95	20
965	**217**	1 p. 08 plum	65	45
966		2 p. blue	1·10	40

942 **215** 3 p. brown and blue . . . 1·75 95
967 **217** 3 p. orange . . . . 1·25 50
943 **215** 5 p. brown and green . . 3·75 2·00
968 **217** 5 p. green . . . . 2·50 1·10
969 5 p. grey . . . . 1·50 75
944 **215** 10 p. brown and purple . 4·00 3·00
970 **217** 10 p. green . . . . 6·25 3·50

1947. As T **187** but surch in figures above shield and wavy lines.
976 2 c. on 5 c. blue 10 10
977 3 c. on 5 c. blue 10 10

219 "Ariel" **221** Bas-reliefs

1948. Unveiling of Monument to J. E. Rodo (writer).
978 **219** 1 c. brown and olive . . . 10 10
979 – 2 c. brown and violet . . 10 10
980 **221** 3 c. brown and green . . 15 10
981 5 c. brown and mauve . . 20 10
982 10 c. brown and red . . . 20 10
983 12 c. brown and blue . . 25 15
984 **219** 20 c. brown and purple . 55 35
985 – 50 c. brown and red . . . 1·50 70
DESIGN: 2, 50 c. Bust of J. E. Rodo.
The 5 c. and 12 c. are as Type **221** but inscr "UN GRAN AMOR ES EL ALMA MISMA DE QUIEN AMA".

1948. Air. As T **187**, optd **AVIACION** and airplane.
986 12 c. blue 20 10
987 24 c. green 35 15
988 36 c. grey 50 25

223 Paysandu **225** River Santa Lucia Bridge

1948. Industrial and Agricultural Exhibitions, Paysandu.
989 **223** 3 c. green 15 10
990 – 7 c. blue 20 10
DESIGN—HORIZ: 7 c. Livestock, sower and arms of Paysandu.

1948. Uruguayan–Brazilian Friendship.
991 **225** 10 c. blue 30 15
992 50 c. green . . . . 1·25 50

226 Ploughing

1949. 4th American Labour Conference.
993 **226** 3 c. green 15 10
994 – 7 c. blue 20 10
DESIGN—HORIZ: 7 c. Horseman herding cattle.

227 Medical Faculty

1949. Air. Centenary of Montevideo University.
995 – 15 c. red 10 10
996 **227** 27 c. brown 15 10
997 – 31 c. blue 25 10
998 – 36 c. green 30 10
DESIGNS: 15 c. Architectural faculty; 31 c. Engineering faculty; 36 c. View of University.

228 Cannon and Buildings **229** Kicking Football

1950. Bicentenary of Cordon (district of Montevideo).
1003 **228** 1 c. mauve 10 10
1004 3 c. green 10 10
1005 7 c. blue 15 10

1951. 4th World Football Championship.
1006 **229** 3 c. green 50 15
1007 7 c. blue 75 35

230 Gen. Artigas

231 Emigration from Eastern Provinces

1952. Death Cent of Artigas. Dated "1950".
1009 **230** 5 m. blue 10 10
1010 – 1 c. black and blue . . . 10 10
1011 – 2 c. brown and violet . . 10 10
1012 **231** 3 c. sepia and green . . 10 10
1013 – 5 c. black and orange . 15 10
1014 **231** 7 c. black and olive . . 15 10
1015 – 8 c. black and red . . . 25 10
1016 – 10 c. red, blue & brown 25 10
1017 – 14 c. blue 30 10
1018 – 20 c. red, blue & yellow 45 20
1019 – 50 c. olive and brown . 80 35
1020 – 1 p. olive and blue . . . 1·75 70
DESIGNS (all show Artigas except 10 c. and 20 c.)—As Type **230**: 1 c. at Las Huerfanas; 2 c. at Battle of Las Piedras; 5 c. in Cerrito; 14 c. at Ciudadela; 20 c. Arms; 50 c. in Paraguay; 1 p. Bust. As Type **231**: 7 c. Dictating instructions; 8 c. in Congress; 10 c. Flag.

232 Boeing 377 Stratocruiser over Mail Coach **234** Franklin D. Roosevelt

1952. 75th Anniv of U.P.U. (1949).
1021 **232** 3 c. green 10 10
1022 7 c. black 15 10
1023 12 c. blue 20 10

1953. 5th Postal Congress of the Americas and Spain.
1025 **234** 3 c. green 10 10
1026 7 c. blue 15 10
1027 12 c. brown 25 15

235 Ceibo (National Flower) **236** Ombu Tree

237 Parliament House **239** Exhibition Entrance

1954.
1028 **235** 5 m. multicoloured . . . 10 10
1029 – 1 c. black and red . . . 10 10
1030 **236** 2 c. green and brown . . 10 10
1031 – 3 c. multicoloured . . . 10 10
1032 **237** 5 c. brown and lilac . . 10 10
1033 – 7 c. green and brown . . 10 10
1034 – 8 c. blue and red 20 10
1035 **236** 10 c. green and orange . 20 10
1036 – 12 c. sepia and blue . . 15 10
1037 – 14 c. black and purple . 20 10
1038 **235** 20 c. multicoloured . . . 25 10
1039 – 50 c. multicoloured . . . 55 20
1040 **237** 1 p. brown and red . . . 95 30
1041 – 2 p. sepia and red . . . 2·00 80
1042 – 3 p. green and lilac . . 2·10 60
1043 – 4 p. blue and brown . . 5·50 2·50
1044 **236** 5 p. green and blue . . 5·00 2·00
DESIGNS—As T **235**: 3 c., 50 c. Passion flower. As T **236**—HORIZ: 1 c., 14 c. Gaucho breaking-in horse. VERT: 7 c., 3 p. Montevideo Citadel. As T **237**—VERT: 8 c., 4 p. Isla de Lobos lighthouse and southern sealions. HORIZ: 12 c., 2 p. Outer Gateway of Montevideo, 1836.

1956. 1st National Production Exhibition.
1050 **239** 3 c. green (postage) . . . 10 10
1051 7 c. blue 10 10
1052 – 20 c. blue (air) 30 20
1053 – 31 c. green 35 30
1054 – 36 c. red 60 35
DESIGN—HORIZ: Nos. 1052/4, Exhibition symbol and two airliners.

241 Uruguay's First Stamp and "Diligencia"

1956. Air. Centenary of First Uruguay Stamps. Stamp in blue.
1055 **241** 20 c. green and yellow . . 35 20
1056 31 c. brown and blue . . 40 25
1057 36 c. red and pink 50 35

242 Pres. Jose Batlle y Ordonez **248** High Diver

1956. Birth Centenary of Jose Batlle y Ordonez (President, 1903–07 and 1911–15).
1058 **242** 3 c. red (postage) 10 10
1059 – 7 c. sepia 10 10
1060 – 10 c. mauve (air) 10 10
1061 **242** 20 c. slate 15 10
1062 – 31 c. brown 20 15
1063 – 36 c. green 30 20
PORTRAIT OF PRESIDENT—VERT: 7 c. Wearing overcoat; 10 c. Similar to Type **242**; 36 c. Profile, facing right. HORIZ: 31 c. Seated at desk.

1957. Surch **5** or **10 Cts.**
1071 **242** 5 c. on 3 c. red 10 10
1072 – 10 c. on 7 c. sepia (No. 1059) 10 10

1958. 14th S. American Swimming Championships, Montevideo. Inscr as in T **248**.
1073 **248** 5 c. green 15 10
1074 – 10 c. blue 35 15
DESIGN—HORIZ: 10 c. Diving.

249 Dr. E. Acevedo **250** Flags

1958. Birth Centenary of Dr. Eduardo Acevedo (lawyer).
1075 **249** 5 c. black and green . . . 10 10
1076 10 c. black and blue . . . 15 10

1958. Air. Day of the Americas.
1077 **250** 23 c. black and blue . . . 15 15
1078 34 c. black and green . . . 20 15
1079 44 c. black and mauve . . 35 20

251 Baygorria Dam **252** "Flame of Freedom"

1958. Inauguration of Baygorria Hydro-Electric Power Station.
1080 **251** 5 c. black and green . . . 10 10
1081 10 c. black and brown . . 10 10
1082 – 1 p. black and blue . . . 40 15
1083 – 2 p. black and mauve . . 60 35
DESIGN: 1, 2 p. Aerial view of dam.

1958. Air. 10th Anniv of Declaration of Human Rights.
1084 **252** 23 c. black and blue . . . 15 10
1085 34 c. black and green . . 20 15
1086 44 c. black and red . . . 35 25

1958. Nos. 1028, 1031 and 1033 surch with Caduceus and value.
1087 5 c. on 3 c. multicoloured . . 10 10
1088 10 c. on 7 c. green and brn . 10 10
1089 20 c. on 5 m. multicoloured . 15 10

254 Statue on Capt. Boiso Lanza Monument

1959. Air. Centres in black.
1090 **254** 3 c. brown 10 10
1091 8 c. mauve 10 10
1092 38 c. black 10 10
1093 50 c. yellow 15 10
1094 60 c. violet 15 10
1095 90 c. olive 20 15
1096 1 p. blue 30 15
1097 2 p. orange 70 50
1098 3 p. green 85 50
1099 5 p. purple . . . . 1·10 85
1100 10 p. red . . . . 3·75 2·50
See also Type **266**.

255 Santos-Dumont and his Biplane "14 bis"

1959. Air. Santos-Dumont Commemoration.
1101 **255** 31 c. multicoloured . . . 15 15
1102 36 c. multicoloured . . . 15 15

257 "Tourism in Uruguay" **258** Gabriela Mistral (poet)

1959. Air. Tourist Publicity and 50th Anniv of Punta del Este.
1103 **257** 10 c. blue and ochre . . 10 10
1104 – 38 c. buff and green . . 15 10
1105 – 60 c. buff and violet . . 25 15
1106 **257** 90 c. green and red . . . 30 20
1107 – 1 p. 05 buff and blue . . 35 25
DESIGN: 38, 60 c., 1 p. 05, Beach and compass.

1959. 2nd Death Anniv of Gabriela Mistral.
1108 **258** 5 c. green 10 10
1109 10 c. blue 10 10
1110 20 c. red 15 10

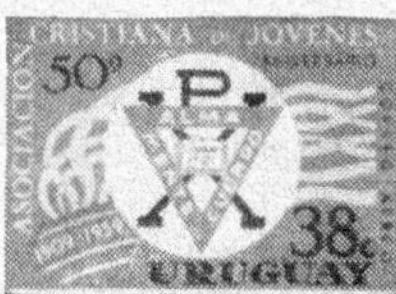

259 Dr. Vaz Ferreira **260** Emblem of Y.M.C.A.

1959. Honouring Dr. Carlos Vaz Ferreira (philosopher).
1111 **259** 5 c. black and blue . . . 10 10
1112 10 c. black and ochre . . 10 10
1113 20 c. black and red . . . 10 10
1114 50 c. black and violet . . 25 10
1115 1 p. black and green . . 40 20

1959. Air. 50th Anniv of Y.M.C.A. in Uruguay.
1116 **260** 38 c. blk, grey and green 25 25
1117 50 c. blk, grey and blue . 30 20
1118 60 c. black, grey and red 35 35

261 Boy and Dam **262** Artigas and Washington

1959. National Recovery.

1119 **261** 5 c. + 10 c. green and orange (postage) 10 10
1120 10 c. + 10 c. blue & orge 10 10
1121 1 p. + 10 c. violet & orge 40 30
1122 38 c. + 10 c. brown and orange (air) 20 20
1123 60 c. + 10 c. green & orge 30 30

1960. Air. Visit of President Eisenhower.

1124 **262** 38 c. black and red 15 15
1125 50 c. black and blue 20 15
1126 60 c. black and green 25 15

1960. Air. Surch with Caduceus and **20 c.**

1128 **217** 20 c. on 27 c. green 10 10

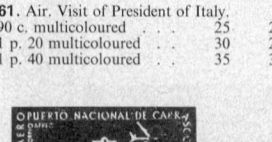

265 Martinez **266** Statue on Lanza Monument

1960. Birth Centenary of Dr. Martin C. Martinez.

1129 **265** 3 c. black and purple 10 10
1130 5 c. black and violet 10 10
1131 10 c. black and blue 10 10
1132 20 c. black and brown 10 10
1133 1 p. black and grey 25 10
1134 2 p. black and orange 55 15
1135 3 p. black and olive 85 30
1136 4 p. black and brown 1·10 65
1137 5 p. black and red 1·25 70

1960. Air.

1138 **266** 3 c. black and lilac 10 10
1139 20 c. black and red 10 10
1140 38 c. black and blue 10 10
1141 50 c. black and buff 10 10
1142 60 c. black and green 15 10
1143 90 c. black and red 25 15
1144 1 p. black and grey 30 15
1145 2 p. black and green 45 25
1146 3 p. black and purple 40 20
1147 5 p. black and salmon 60 40
1148 10 p. black and yellow 1·10 65
1149 20 p. black and blue 2·50 1·25

267 Refugees **268** Scene of Revolution

1960. World Refugee Year.

1150 – 10 c. blk & bl (postage) 10 10
1151 **267** 60 c. black & mve (air) 20 20

DESIGN: 10 c. "Uprooted tree".

1960. 150th Anniv of Argentine May Revolution.

1154 **268** 5 c. black & bl (postage) 10 10
1155 10 c. brown and blue 10 10
1156 38 c. olive & blue (air) 15 10
1157 59 c. red and blue 15 15
1158 60 c. violet and blue 25 15

269 Pres. M. Oribe **270** Pres. Gronchi

1961. 104th Death Anniv of Manuel Oribe (President, 1835–38).

1159 **269** 10 c. black and blue 10 10
1160 20 c. black and brown 10 10
1161 40 c. black and green 15 10

1961. Air. Visit of President of Italy.

1162 **270** 90 c. multicoloured 25 20
1163 1 p. 20 multicoloured 30 25
1164 1 p. 40 multicoloured 35 30

271 Carrasco Airport Building

1961. Air. Carrasco National Airport.

1165 **271** 1 p. grey and violet 20 20
1166 2 p. grey and olive 45 10
1167 3 p. grey and yellow 35 35
1168 4 p. grey and purple 55 20
1169 5 p. grey and turquoise 60 30
1170 10 p. grey and blue 1·10 45
1171 20 p. grey and red 2·00 1·25

272 "Charging Horsmen" (by C. M. Herrera) **273** Welfare, Justice and Education

1961. 150th Anniv of February 28th Revolution.

1172 **272** 20 c. black and blue 15 10
1173 40 c. black and green 25 10

1961. Latin-American Economic Commission Conference, Punta del Este. (a) Postage. Centres in bistre.

1174 **273** 2 c. violet 10 10
1175 5 c. orange 10 10
1176 10 c. red 10 10
1177 20 c. green 10 10
1178 50 c. lilac 10 10
1179 1 p. blue 25 15
1180 2 p. yellow 55 35
1181 3 p. grey 55 35
1182 4 p. blue 85 45
1183 5 p. brown 95 60

(b) Air. Centres in black.

1184 **273** 20 c. orange 10 10
1185 45 c. green 15 10
1186 50 c. purple 15 10
1187 90 c. violet 20 15
1188 1 p. red 25 20
1189 1 p. 40 lilac 35 25
1190 2 p. ochre 20 25
1191 3 p. blue 30 35
1192 4 p. yellow 40 50
1193 5 p. blue 55 40
1194 10 p. green 1·10 70
1195 20 p. mauve 2·00 1·50

274 Gen. Rivera **275** Symbols of Swiss Settlers

1962. Honouring Gen. Fructuoso Rivera (1st President, 1830–35).

1196 **274** 10 c. black and red 10 10
1197 20 c. black and ochre 10 10
1198 40 c. black and green 15 10

1962. Centenary of First Swiss Settlers.

1199 **275** 10 c. red, black and blue (postage) 10 10
1200 20 c. red, black & green 10 10
1201 – 90 c. black, red and orange (air) 20 20
1202 – 1 p. 40 black, red & bl 30 30

DESIGN—HORIZ: 90 c., 1 p. 40, Wheatsheaf, harvester and Swiss flag.

276 B. P. Berro **277** Red-crested Cardinal

1962. Bernardo Prudencio Berro (President, 1860–64).

1203 **276** 10 c. black and blue 10 10
1204 20 c. black and brown 10 10

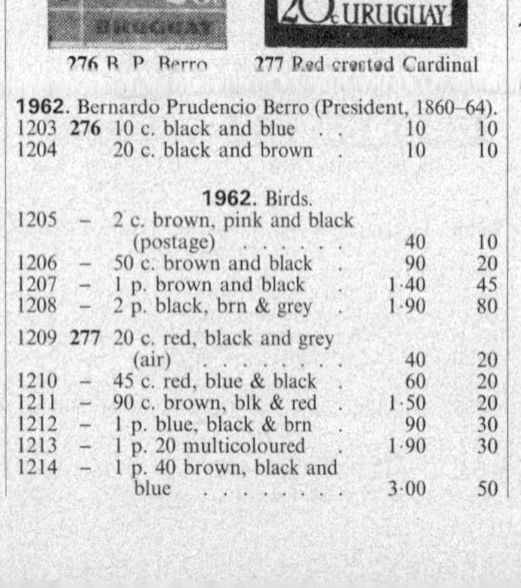

1962. Birds.

1205 – 2 c. brown, pink and black (postage) 40 10
1206 – 50 c. brown and black 90 20
1207 – 1 p. brown and black 1·40 45
1208 – 2 p. black, brn & grey 1·90 80
1209 **277** 20 c. red, black and grey (air) 40 20
1210 – 45 c. red, blue & black 60 20
1211 – 90 c. brown, blk & red 1·50 20
1212 – 1 p. blue, black & brn 90 30
1213 – 1 p. 20 multicoloured 1·90 30
1214 – 1 p. 40 brown, black and blue 3·00 50
1215 – 2 p. yellow, black & brn 1·90 50
1216 – 3 p. black, yellow & brn 3·00 75
1217 – 5 p. black, blue & grn 4·50 1·10
1218 – 10 p. multicoloured 7·50 2·25
1219 – 20 p. orange, black and grey 17·00 7·50

BIRDS—HORIZ: 2 c. Rufous-bellied thrush 45 c. Diademed tanager; 50 c. Rufous hornero; 1 p. (1207), Chalk-browed mockingbird; 1 p. (1212), Common cowbird; 1 p. 20, Great kiskadee; 2 p. (1208), Rufous-collared sparrow; 2 p. (1215), Yellow cardinal; 3 p. Hooded siskin; 5 p. Sayaca tanager; 10 p. Blue and yellow tanager; 20 p. Scarlet-headed blackbird. VERT: 90 c. Vermilion flycatcher; 1 p. 40, Fork-tailed flycatcher.

Nos. 1208, 1210, 1212 and 1215 have no frame; Nos. 1206 and 1214 have a thin frame line; the others are as Type **277**.

278 D. A. Larranaga

1963. 85th Death Anniv of Damaso Antonio Larranaga (founder of National Library).

1220 **278** 20 c. sepia and turquoise 10 10
1221 40 c. sepia and drab 10 10

279 U.P.A.E. Emblem

1963. 50th Anniv of Postal Union of the Americas and Spain.

1222 **279** 20 c. blue & black (postage) 10 10
1223 45 c. green & black (air) 10 10
1224 90 c. red and black 20 15

280 Campaign Emblem **281** Anchors

1963. Freedom from Hunger.

1225 **280** 10 c. yell & grn (postage) 10 10
1226 20 c. yellow and brown 10 10
1227 90 c. yellow & red (air) 20 15
1228 1 p. 40 yellow & violet 25 20

1963. World Voyage of "Alferez Campora".

1229 **281** 10 c. vio & orge (postage) 10 10
1230 20 c. grey and red 10 10
1231 – 90 c. green & orge (air) 20 10
1232 – 1 p. 40 blue and yellow 30 25

DESIGN: 90 c., 1 p. 40, Sailing ship "Alferez Campora".

282 Large Intestine Congress Emblem

1963. 1st Uruguayan Proctological Congress, Punta del Este.

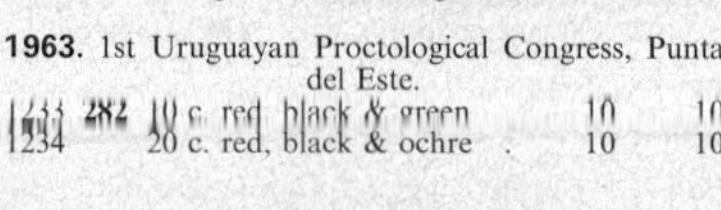

1233 **282** 10 c. red, black & green 10 10
1234 20 c. red, black & ochre 10 10

283 Centenary Emblem

1964. Red Cross Centenary.

1235 **283** 20 c. red and blue 10 10
1236 40 c. red and grey 15 10

284 L. A. de Herrera

1964. 5th Death Anniv of Luis A. de Herrera (statesman).

1237 **284** 20 c. black, green & blue 10 10
1238 40 c. black, lt blue and blue 10 10
1239 80 c. black, yell & blue 15 10
1240 1 p. black, lilac & blue 15 10
1241 2 p. black, slate & blue 25 20

285 Pres. De Gaulle

1964. Air. Visit of President of France. Multicoloured.

1242 1 p. 50 Type **285** 40 15
1243 2 p. 40 Flags of France and Uruguay 50 40

286 Reliefs from Abu Simbel

1964. Nubian Monuments Preservation. Multicoloured.

1244 20 c. Type **286** (postage) 10 10
1245 1 p. 30 Sphinx, Sebua (air) 30 15
1246 2 p. Rameses II, Abu Simbel 65 30

Nos. 1245/6 are vert.

292 Arms **288** Pres. Kennedy

1965. Air.

1261 **292** 20 p. multicoloured 1·25 70
1248 – 50 p. blue, yell & grey 3·75 3·00

DESIGN—HORIZ (38 × 27 mm) 50 p. National flag.

1965. Pres. Kennedy Commemoration. Frame and laurel in gold.

1249 **288** 20 c. blk & grn (postage) 10 10
1250 40 c. black and brown 10 10
1251 1 p. 50 blk & lilac (air) 20 10
1252 2 p. 40 black and blue 30 15

289 "Tete-beche" Pair of Uruguayan 8 c. Stamps of 1864

290 6 c. "Arms-type" of 1964

1965. 1st River Plate Stamp Exn, Montevideo. (a) Postage. T **289**.

1253 40 c. green and black 10 10

(b) Air. As T **290** showing Arms-type stamps of 1864 (values in brackets).

1254 1 p. black and blue (12 c.) 10 10
1255 1 p. black & orange (T **290**) 10 10
1256 1 p. black and green (8 c.) 10 10
1257 1 p. black and bistre (10 c.) 10 10
1258 1 p. black and red (6 c.) 10 10

Nos. 1254/8 were issued together in sheets of 10 (5 × 2), each design arranged in a vertical pair with "URUGUAY" either at top or bottom.

291 B. Nardone

1965. 1st Death Anniv of Benito Nardone (statesman).
1259 **291** 20 c. black and green . . 10 10
1260 – 40 c. black and green . . 10 10
DESIGN—VERT: 40 c. Portrait as Type **291**, but Nardone with microphone.

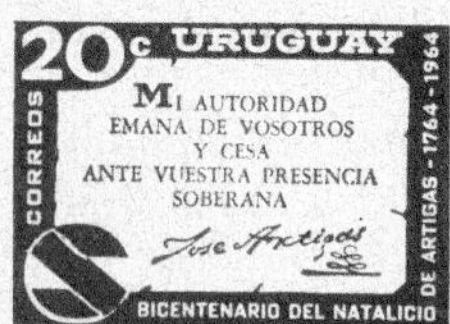

293 Part of Artigas' Speech before the 1813 Congress

1965. Birth Bicent (1964) of Gen. Jose Artigas.
1262 **293** 20 c. red, blue and yellow (postage) 10 10
1263 – 40 c. olive, black & blue . 10 10
1264 – 80 c. multicoloured . . . 10 10
1265 – 1 p. multicoloured (air) . 10 10
1266 – 1 p. 50 multicoloured . . 15 15
1267 **293** 2 p. 40 multicoloured . . 25 20
DESIGNS—HORIZ: 40 c. Bust of Artigas; 80 c. Artigas and his army flag; 1 p. 50, Bust, flag and exodus of his followers to Argentina. VERT: 1 p. Artigas' statue.

295 Football

1965. Olympic Games, Tokyo (1964).
1269 **295** 20 c. orange, black and green (postage) 10 10
1270 – 40 c. olive, black & brown 10 10
1271 – 80 c. red, black & drab . 10 10
1272 – 1 p. green, black & blue . 10 10
1273 – 1 p. grey, blk & red (air) 10 10
1274 – 1 p. 50 blue, black & grn 15 15
1275 – 2 p. blue, black and red . 15 15
1276 – 2 p. 40 orange, blk & bl . 20 15
1277 – 3 p. yellow, black & lilac 25 20
1278 – 20 p. pink, blue & indigo 70 50
DESIGNS: 40 c. Basketball; 80 c. Cycling; 1 p. (No. 1272) Swimming; 1 p. (No. 1273) Boxing; 1 p. 50, Running; 2 p. Fencing; 2 p. 40, Sculling; 3 p. Pistol-shooting; 20 p. Olympic "Rings".

1965. Surch with Caduceus and value.
1280 **178** 10 c. on 7 c. blue 10 10

1966. 50th Anniv of Uruguay Architects' Assn. Surch **CINCUENTENARIO Sociedad Arquitectos del Uruguay** and value.
1281 **261** 4 c. on 5 c. + 10 c. green and orange 10 10

298 I.T.U. Emblem and Satellite

1966. Air. Centenary of I.T.U.
1282 **298** 1 p. deep bl, red & blue . 15 10

299 Sir Winston Churchill

1966. Churchill Commemoration.
1283 **299** 40 c. brown, red and blue (postage) 10 10
1284 – 2 p. brn, red & gold (air) 20 10
DESIGN—VERT: 2 p. Churchill—full-face portrait and signed quotation.

300 Arms and View of Rio de Janeiro

1966. 400th Anniv of Rio de Janeiro.
1285 **300** 40 c. grn & brn (postage) 10 10
1286 80 c. red & brown (air) . 10 10

301 I.C.Y. Emblem

1966. Air. I.C.Y.
1287 **301** 1 p. black and green . . 15 10

302 Army Engineer

304 Pres. Shazar

1966. 50th Anniv of Army Engineers.
1288 **302** 20 c. multicoloured . . 15 10

1966. Air. Visit of President of Israel.
1291 **304** 7 p. multicoloured . . . 40 30

305 Crested Screamer

306 Jules Rimet Cup, Ball and Globe

1966. Air.
1292 **305** 100 p. multicoloured . . 4·50 2·50

1966. Air. World Cup Football Championships.
1293 **306** 10 p. yellow and violet . 50 30

307 Hereford Bull

308 L. Batlle Berres (1947–51 and 1955–56)

1966. Air. Cattle-breeding.
1294 **307** 4 p. brown, chest & sepia 15 10
1295 – 6 p. black, grn & turq . 25 10
1296 – 10 p. mauve, grn & turq 35 20
1297 – 15 p. black, red & orge . 30 30
1298 – 20 p. brown, yell & grey 50 40
1299 – 30 p. brown & yellow . 75 55
1300 – 50 p. brown, grey & grn 1·25 85
DESIGNS (Cattle breeds): 6 p. Dutch; 10 p. Shorthorn; 15 p. Aberdeen Angus; 20 p. Norman; 30 p. Jersey; 50 p. Charolais.

1966. Former Uruguayan Presidents.
1301 **308** 20 c. black and red . . . 10 10
1302 – 20 c. black and blue . . 10 10
1303 – 20 c. brown and blue . . 10 10
PRESIDENTS: No. 1302, Daniel Fernandez Crespo (1963–64); 1303, Dr. Washington Beltran (1965–66).

309 Gutenberg Press

310 Capt. Boiso Lanza

1966. 50th Anniv of State Printing Works.
1304 **309** 20 c. sepia, green & brn 10 10

1966. Air. Honouring Boiso Lanza (pioneer military aviator).
1305 **310** 25 c. black, bl & ultram 75 55

311 Fireman

313 General J. A. Lavalleja

1966. 50th Anniv of Firemen's Corps.
1306 **311** 20 c. black and red . . . 25 15

1966. 2nd River Plate Stamp Exn, Montevideo. (a) Postage. No. 1253 optd **Segunda Muestra y Jornadas Rioplatenses**, etc.
1307 **187** 40 c. green and black . . 10 10

(b) Air. Nos. 1254/8 optd **CENTENARIO DEL SELLO ESCUDITO RESELLADO**, etc.
1308 1 p. blue 10 10
1309 1 p. orange 10 10
1310 1 p. green 10 10
1311 1 p. bistre 10 10
1312 1 p. red 10 10
Nos. 1308/12 commemorate the centenary of Uruguay's first surcharged stamps.

1966. Heroes of War of Independence.
1313 **313** 20 c. brown, red & blue . 10 10
1314 – 20 c. blue, black & grey . 10 10
1315 – 20 c. black and blue . . . 10 10
DESIGNS—VERT: No. 1314, Gen. L. Gomez. HORIZ: 1315, Gen. A. Saravia on horseback.

1966. Air. 40th Anniv of Uruguayan Philatelic Club. No. 1036 surch **40 ANIVERSARIO Club Filatelico del Uruguay $ 1.00 aereo**.
1316 1 p. on 12 p. sepia and blue . 10 10

315 Dante

316 Sunflower

1966. Air. 700th Birth Anniv (1965) of Dante (writer).
1317 **315** 50 c. blown and sepia . . 10 10

1967. 20th Anniv of Young Farmers' Movement.
1318 **316** 40 c. sepia, yellow & brn . 10 10

317 Planetarium

1967. 10th Anniv of Montevideo Planetarium.
1319 **317** 40 c. blk & mve (postage) 15 10
1320 – 5 p. black and blue (air) . 35 15
DESIGN: 5 p. Planetarium projector.

318 Pres. Makarios

319 Dr. Schweitzer

1967. Air. Visit of President of Cyprus.
1321 **318** 6 p. 60 black & mauve . 20 15

1967. Air. Schweitzer Commemoration.
1322 **319** 6 p. multicoloured . . . 20 15

320 Corriedale Ram

322 Church, San Carlos

321 Uruguayan Flag and Globe

1967. Air. Uruguayan Sheep-breeding.
1323 **320** 3 p. black, bistre & red . 10 10
1324 – 4 p. black, bistre & grn . 15 10
1325 – 5 p. black, bistre & blue 20 10
1326 – 10 p. black, bis & yell . 35 30
DESIGNS (sheep breeds): 4 p. "Ideal"; 5 p. Romney Marsh; 10 p. Australian merino.

1967. Air. Heads of State Meeting, Punta del Este.
1327 **321** 10 p. gold, blue & black 25 20

1967. Bicentenary of San Carlos.
1328 **322** 40 c. black, red & blue . 10 10

323 E. Acevedo (lawyer and statesman)

325 Ansina

324 "Numeral" Stamps of 1866

1967. Eduardo Acevedo Commemoration.
1329 **323** 20 c. brown and green . 10 10
1330 40 c. green and orange . 10 10

1967. Air. Centenary of "Numeral" Stamps of 1866.
1331 **324** 3 p. blue, green & blk . 20 10
1332 – 6 p. ochre, red & black . 35 15
DESIGN: 6 p. As T **324**, but depicting 15 c. and 20 c. stamps of 1866.

1967. Air. Honouring Ansina (servant of Gen. Artigas).
1334 **325** 2 p. red, blue and black . 10 10

326 Douglas DC-4 over Runway

327 Making Basket

1967. Air. 30th Anniv of PLUNA Airline.
1335 **326** 10 p. multicoloured . . . 35 25

1967. Air. World Basketball Championships, Montevideo. Multicoloured.
1336 5 p. Type **327** 20 10
1337 5 p. Running 20 10
1338 5 p. Holding 20 10
1339 5 p. Pivot 20 10
1340 5 p. Dribbling 20 10

1967. Air. Nos. 1210 and 1223 surch with new value in figures only.
1343 – 5 p. 90 on 45 c. red, blue and black 45 15
1344 **279** 5 p. 90 on 45 c. green and black 20 15

330 "Don Quixote and Sancho Panza" (after Denry Torres)

1967. Air. 420th Birth Anniv of Cervantes (writer).
1345 **330** 8 p. brown and bistre . . 25 15

331 Arms of Carmelo **332** J. E. Rodo

1967. 150th Anniv of Founding of Carmelo.
1346 **331** 40 c. deep blue, ochre and blue 10 10

1967. 50th Death Anniv of Jose E. Rodo (writer). Multicoloured.
1347 1 p. Type **332** 10 10
1348 2 p. Portrait and sculpture . 10 10
The 2 p. is horiz.

333 S. Rodriguez (founder), Steam Locomotive and Diesel Railcar **334** Child and Map of Americas

1967. Centenary of 1st National Railway in Uruguay.
1349 **333** 2 p. brown and ochre . . 30 10

1967. 40th Anniv of Inter-American Children's Institute.
1350 **334** 1 p. red and violet . . . 15 10

1967. No. 1033 surch **1.00 PESO** and Caduceus.
1351 1 p. on 7 c. green & brown . 10 10

336 Primitive Club **337** Level Crossing and Traffic Sign

1967. Air. Archaeological Discoveries. Each black and grey.
1352 15 p. Type **336** 10 10
1353 20 p. Lance-head 20 10
1354 30 p. Axe-head 45 15
1355 50 p. Sculptured "bird of El Polonio" 60 25
1356 75 p. Cooking pot 60 40
1357 100 p. Sculptured "bird" of Balizas (horiz) 85 35
1358 150 p. Bolas . . . . 1·10 40
1359 200 p. Arrow-heads . . . . . . 1·50 85

1967. Air. Pan American Highways Congress.
1360 **337** 4 p. black, yellow & red . . 10 10

338 Lions Emblem and Map **339** Boy Scout

1967. Air. 50th Anniv of Lions International.
1361 **338** 5 p. violet, yellow & grn . 15 10

1968. Air. Lord Baden-Powell Commemoration.
1362 **339** 9 p. brown & orange . . 15 10

340 Cocoi Heron **341** Sun, Transport and U.N. Emblem

1968. Birds.
1363 – 1 p. brown and buff . . 25 10
1364 **340** 2 p. black and green . . 30 10
1365 – 3 p. purple, blk & orge . 35 10
1366 – 4 p. black and brown . 75 25
1367 – 4 p. black and orange . 75 25
1368 – 5 p. black, yell & brn . 90 30
1369 – 10 p. violet and black . 1·60 50
BIRDS—VERT: 1 p. Great horned owl; 4 p. (No. 1367), Black-tailed stilt. HORIZ: 3 p. Brown-hooded gull; 4 p. (No. 1366), White-faced whistling duck; 5 p. Wattled jacana; 10 p. Snowy egret.

1968. Air. International Tourist Year (1967).
1370 **341** 10 p. multicoloured . . 40 15

342 Presidents of Uruguay and Brazil, and Concord Bridge **343** Footballer

1968. Opening of Concord Bridge between Uruguay and Brazil.
1371 **342** 6 p. brown 15 10

1968. Penarol Club's Victory in Intercontinental Soccer Championships.
1372 **343** 1 p. black and lemon . . 15 10

344 St. John Bosco

1968. 75th Anniv of "Don Bosco Workshops".
1373 **344** 2 p. black and brown . 10 10

345 Octopus

1968. Air. Uruguayan Marine Fauna.
1374 **345** 15 p. black, blue and turquoise 30 15
1375 – 20 p. brown, blue & grn 25 15
1376 – 25 p. multicoloured . . 30 20
1377 – 30 p. black, green & blue 35 25
1378 – 50 p. salmon, blue and green 95 40
DESIGNS—HORIZ: 20 p. Mackerel; 25 p. "Dorado". VERT: 30 p. "Surubi"; 50 p. Short-finned squid.

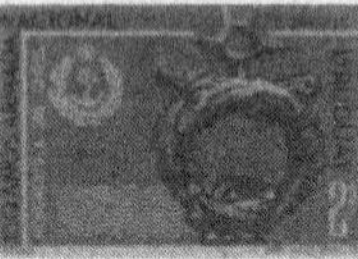
346 Sailors' Monument, Montevideo

1968. 150th Anniv of Uruguayan Navy.
1379 **346** 2 p. black and green (postage) 10 10
1380 – 6 p. black and green . . 10 10
1381 – 12 p. black and blue . . 35 15
1382 – 4 p. blk, red & bl (air) . 10 10
1383 – 6 p. multicoloured . . . 10 10
1384 – 10 p. red, yellow & blue 15 10
1385 – 20 p. black and blue . . 65 15
DESIGNS—HORIZ: 4 p. Tailplane (Naval Air Force); 6 p. (No. 1383), Naval Arms; 12 p. Screw gunboat "Suarez"; 20 p. Artigas's privateer "Isabel". VERT: 6 p. (No. 1380), Buoy and lighthouse; 10 p. Mast-head and signal flags.

347 President Gestido

1968. 1st Death Anniv of President Oscar D. Gestido.
1386 **347** 6 p. brown, red & blue . 10 10

348 Sculling

1969. Air. Olympic Games, Mexico.
1387 **348** 30 p. black, brown & bl 30 20
1388 – 50 p. black, brown & yell 45 30
1389 – 100 p. black, brn & grn . 75 50
DESIGNS: 50 p. Running; 100 p. Football.

349 Cogwheel, Ear of Wheat and Two Heads

1969. 25th Anniv of Uruguay Trades University.
1390 **349** 2 p. black and red 10 10

350 Cycling

1969. World Cycling Championships, Montevideo (1968).
1391 **350** 6 p. blue, orange and green (postage) 20 10
1392 – 20 p. multicoloured (air) . 30 15
DESIGN—VERT: 20 p. Cyclist and globe.

351 EFIMEX "Stamp" on Easel

1969. Air. "EFIMEX" Stamp Exhibition, Mexico City (1968).
1393 **351** 20 p. red, green & blue . 20 15

353 Gymnasts and Emblem **354** Presi. Baltasar Brum

1969. 75th Anniv of "L'Avenir" Gymnastics Club.
1395 **353** 6 p. black and red 15 10

1969. 36th Death Anniv of Baltasar Brum (President, 1919–23).
1396 **354** 6 p. black and red 15 10

356 Sun and Fair Emblem (Actual size 72 × 23 mm)

1969. 2nd World Industrial Fair, Montevideo.
1399 **356** 2 p. multicoloured . . . 15 10

357 Emblem, Quill and Book **358** Modern Diesel Locomotive

1969. Air. 10th Latin-American Notaries' Congress, Montevideo.
1400 **357** 30 p. black, orge & grn . 35 25

1969. Centenary of Uruguayan Railways.
1401 **358** 6 p. black, red & blue . 20 25
1402 – 6 p. black, red & blue . . 30 25
DESIGN: No. 1402 Early locomotive and diesel train.

360 Automobile Club Badge **362** I.L.O. Emblem

361 Belloni and "Combat" (monument). (Actual size 72 × 23 mm)

1969. Air. 50th Anniv of Uruguay Automobile Club.
1404 **360** 10 p. blue and red . . . 15 10

1969. 4th Death Anniv of Jose Belloni (sculptor).
1405 **361** 6 p. grn, black & gold . 10 10

1969. Air. 50th Anniv of I.L.O.
1406 **362** 30 p. turquoise & black . 30 20

363 Training Centre Emblem **364** Exhibition Emblem

1969. 25th Anniv (1967) of Reserve Officers' Training Centre.
1407 **363** 1 p. lemon and blue . . 10 10
1408 – 2 p. brown and blue . . 15 10
DESIGN: 2 p. Reservist in uniform and civilian dress.

1969. Air. "ABUEXPO 69" Philatelic Exhibition, Sao Paulo, Brazil.
1409 **364** 20 p. yellow, blue & grn 25 10

365 Rotary Emblem and Hemispheres **366** Dr. Morquio and Child

1969. Air. South American Regional Rotary Conference, and 50th Anniv of Rotary Club, Montevideo.
1410 **365** 20 p. gold, ultram & blue 40 10

1969. Air. Birth Cent (1967) of Dr. Luis Morquio (pediatrician).
1411 **366** 20 p. brown and red . . 20 10

1969. Air. New Year. No. 1345 surch **FELIZ ANO 1970** and value.
1412 **330** 6 p. on 8 p. brown & bis 10 10

368 Pres. Tomas Berreta **369** Mahatma Gandhi

1969. 22nd Death Anniv of Dr. Tomas Berreta (President, 1947).
1413 **368** 6 p. red and black . . . 15 10

1970. Air. Birth Cent (1969) of Mahatma Gandhi.
1414 **369** 100 p. brown, ochre & blue 85 85

370 Teju Lizard **371** Dr. E. C. Ciganda

1970. Air. Fauna.
1415 – 20 p. black, grn & pur . 70 15
1416 **370** 30 p. black, grn & yell . 40 20
1417 – 50 p. black, brn & yell . 40 35
1418 – 100 p. brown, bistre and orange 60 55
1419 – 150 p. brown & green . 95 80
1420 – 200 p. black, brn & red . 1·25 1·25
1421 – 250 p. black, bl & grey . 1·50 1·50
DESIGNS—VERT: 20 p. Greater rhea. HORIZ: 50 p. Capybara; 100 p. Mulita armadillo; 150 p. Puma; 200 p. Coypu; 250 p. South American fur seal.

1970. Air. Birth Centenary of Evaristo C. Ciganda (pioneer of teachers' pensions law).
1422 **371** 6 p. brown and green . . 10 10

372 Garibaldi **373** Bank Emblem

1970. Air. Centenary of Garibaldi's Participation in Defence of Uruguay against Brazil and Argentina.
1423 **372** 20 p. mauve and pink . . 15 10

1970. 11th Inter-American Development Bank Governors' Meeting, Punta del Este.
1424 **373** 10 p. blue and gold . . . 15 10

374 Stylised Tree **375** Footballer and Emblem

1970. 2nd National Forestry Exhibition.
1425 **374** 2 p. black, green & red . 10 10

1970. Air. World Cup Football Championships, Mexico.
1426 **375** 50 p. multicoloured . . . 55 30

376 Artigas' House, Sauce **377** "U.N."

1970. 120th Death Anniv of Artigas.
1427 **376** 15 p. black, blue & red . 15 10

1970. Air. 25th Anniv of United Nations.
1428 **377** 32 p. blue, gold and light blue 25 15

378 Sun, Sea and Map

1970. Tourist Publicity.
1429 **378** 5 p. blue 10 10

379 Eisenhower and U.S. Flag

1970. Air. 1st Death Anniv of Dwight D. Eisenhower (American soldier and statesman).
1430 **379** 30 p. blue, red and grey . 30 15

380 First Man on the Moon

1970. Air. 1st Anniv of Moon Landing from "Apollo 11".
1431 **380** 200 p. multicoloured . . 1·50 1·50

381 Mt. Fuji

1970. "EXPO 70" World Fair, Osaka, Japan. Each with EXPO emblem and arms of Uruguay.
1432 **381** 25 p. blue, green & yell . 25 15
1433 – 25 p. blue, orange & grn 25 15
1434 – 25 p. blue, yellow & vio 25 15
1435 – 25 p. blue, violet & orge 25 15
DESIGNS: No. 1433, Geishas; 1434, Tower of the Sun; 1435, Youth totem.

382 Flag of 1825

1970. Air. 145th Anniv of Revolt of the "Immortal 33" under Levalleja.
1436 **382** 500 p. black, red & blue 3·50 3·50

383 Rheumatology Congress Emblem **384** Street Scene

1970. Air. 5th Pan-American Rheumatology Congress, Punta del Este.
1437 **383** 30 p. deep blue, blue and yellow 30 15

1970. 290th Anniv of Colonia del Sacramento (1st European settlement in Uruguay).
1439 **384** 5 p. multicoloured . . . 10 10

385 "Mother and Son" (statue, E. Prati) **386** Flags of Member Countries

1970. "Homage to Mothers".
1440 **385** 10 p. black and green . 15 10

1970. Air. 10th Anniv of Founding of Latin-American Association for Free Trade by the Montevideo Treaty.
1441 **386** 22 p. multicoloured . . 30 15

387 "Stamp" Emblem **389** Dr. Alfonso Espinola

388 "Playing Ring-o-Roses" (Ana Gaye)

1970. "URUEXPO 70" Stamp Exn, Montevideo.
1442 **387** 15 p. violet, blue & brn . 15 10

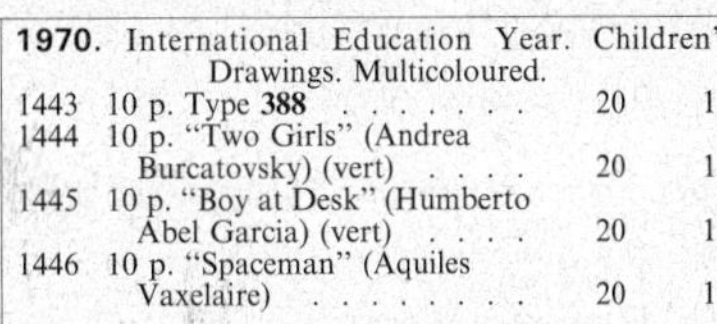

1970. International Education Year. Children's Drawings. Multicoloured.
1443 10 p. Type **388** 20 15
1444 10 p. "Two Girls" (Andrea Burcatovsky) (vert) 20 15
1445 10 p. "Boy at Desk" (Humberto Abel Garcia) (vert) 20 15
1446 10 p. "Spaceman" (Aquiles Vaxelaire) 20 15

1971. 125th Birth Anniv (1970) of Dr. Alfonso Espinola (physician and philanthropist).
1447 **389** 5 p. black and orange . . 15 10

391 "Stamps" and Poster (⅔-size illustration)

1971. "EFU 71" Stamp Exn, Montevideo.
1449 **391** 15 p. multicoloured 20 10

392 5 c. Coin of 1840 (obverse) **393** Dr. Domingo Arena (from caricature by A. Sifredi)

1971. Numismatics Day.
1450 **392** 25 p. black, brown & bl . 40 30
1451 – 25 p. black, brown & bl . 40 30
DESIGN: No. 1451, Reverse of coin showing "Sun" emblem.

1971. Birth Centenary (1970) of Arena (lawyer and statesman).
1452 **393** 5 p. lake 10 10

394 Opening Bars of Anthem **395** Dr. Jose Arias

1971. National Anthem Commemoration.
1453 **394** 15 p. black, blue & gold . 40 25

1971. 1st Death Anniv of Dr Jose Arias (statesman).
1454 **395** 5 p. brown 15 10

396 "Yellow Fever" (J. M. Blanes)

1971. Air. 70th Death Anniv of Juan Blanes (artist).
1455 **396** 50 p. multicoloured . . . 30 30

397 Eduardo Fabini

1971. 21st Death Anniv of Eduardo Fabini (composer).
1456 **397** 5 p. black and red 40 10

398 "Two Races"

1971. Air. Racial Equality Year.
1457 **398** 27 p. black, pink & gold 30 15

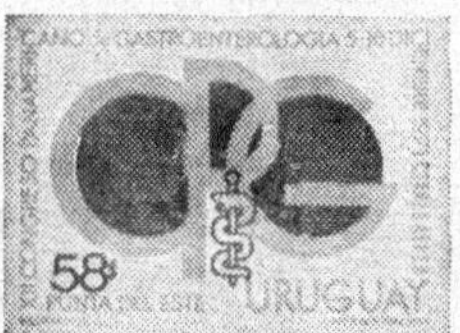

399 Congress Emblem

1971. Air. 12th Pan-American Gastro-enterological Congress, Punta del Este.
1458 **399** 58 p. orange, blk & grn . 55 35

400 J. E. Rodo and U.P.A.E. Emblem

1971. Birth Centenary of Jose E. Rodo (writer and first delegate to U.P.A.E).
1459 **400** 15 p. black and blue . . 20 15

401 Old Water-cart and Tap

1971. Centenary of Montevideo's Water Supply.
1460 **401** 5 p. multicoloured . . . 15 10

402 Sheep and Roll of Cloth

1971. Wool Production.
1461 **402** 5 p. green, grey & lt grn 10 10
1462 – 15 p. grey, violet & blue 20 10
DESIGN: 15 p. Sheep, and loading bales of cloth.

403 Dr. Jose Elorza and Sheep

1971. 12th Death Anniv of Dr. Jose Elorza (sheep-breeder).
1463 **403** 5 p. black, green & bl . . 15 10

404 Creole Horse

1971. Uruguayan Horse-breeding.
1464 **404** 5 p. black, blue and orge 20 10

405 Bull, Sheep and Ears of Corn

1971. Cent of Uruguayan Rural Association.
1465 **405** 20 p. multicoloured . . . 30 15

406 Police Emblem

1971. Honouring Police Heroes.
1466 **406** 10 p. blue, black & grey . 25 10
1467 – 20 p. multicoloured . . . 45 15
DESIGN: 20 p. Policeman and flag.

407 1896 10 Peso Banknote (obverse)

1971. 75th Anniv of Uruguayan State Bank.
1468 **407** 25 p. green, blk & gold . 30 25
1469 – 25 p. green, blk & gold . 30 25
DESIGN: No. 1469 Reverse of banknote showing rural scene.

408 Labourer and Arms

1971. 150th Anniv of Town of Durazno.
1470 **408** 20 p. multicoloured . . . 25 10

409 Shield and Laurel (⅔-size illustration)

1971. Uruguay's Victory in Liberators' Cup Football Championships.
1471 **409** 10 p. gold, red and blue . 20 10

411 Voter and Ballot-box

1971. General Election.
1473 **411** 10 p. black and blue . . 10 10
1474 – 20 p. black and blue . . 25 15
DESIGN—HORIZ: 20 p. Voters in line.

412 C.I.M.E. Emblem and Globe

1971. Air. 20th Anniv of Inter-Governmental Committee for European Migration (C.I.M.E.).
1475 **412** 30 p. multicoloured . . . 35 25

413 Exhibition Emblem and Map of Uruguay

414 Juan Lindolfo Cuestas (1897–1903)

1971. "EXPO LITORAL" Industrial Exhibition, Paysandu.
1476 **413** 20 p. purple and blue . 35 15

1971. Uruguayan Presidents. Each brown and blue.
1477 10 p. Type **414** 10 10
1478 10 p. J. Herrara y Obes (1890–94) 10 10
1479 10 p. Claudio Williman (1907–11) 10 10
1480 10 p. Jose Serrato (1923–27) 10 10
1481 10 p. Andres Martinez Trueba (1951–55) 10 10

415 Llama Emblem

417 Olympic Symbols

1971. Air. "EXFILIMA" Stamp Exn, Lima, Peru.
1482 **415** 37 p. multicoloured . . 35 30

1972. Air. Olympic Games, Munich (1st issue).
1484 **417** 50 p. black, red & yellow 20 10
1485 – 100 p. multicoloured . . 40 30
1486 – 500 p. grey, red & blue . 1·10 1·10
DESIGNS: 100 p. Athlete and torch; 500 p. Discus-thrower.
See also Nos. 1493/4.

418 Chemical Jar

419 Bartolome Hidalgo

1972. Air. 50th Anniv of Discovery of Insulin.
1487 **418** 27 p. multicoloured . . 20 10

1972. 150th Death Anniv (1973) of Bartolome Hidalgo (Gaucho poet).
1488 **419** 5 p. black, red & brown 20 10

420 "Flagship"

421 "Face" on Beethoven Score

1972. Air. American Stamp Day.
1489 **420** 37 p. multicoloured . . 25 15

1972. 12th Eastern Uruguay Choral Festival.
1491 **421** 20 p. black, green & pur 25 10

422 Dove supporting Wounded Bird (after Maria Mullin)

424 Columbus Monument, Colon

423 Footballer and 1928 Gold Medal

1972. Dionisio Diaz (9 year-old hero) Commemoration.
1492 **422** 10 p. multicoloured . . . 15 10

1972. Air. Olympic Games, Munich. Mult.
1493 100 p. Type **423** 40 30
1494 300 p. Olympic flag (vert) . . 70 75

1972. Cent of Colon (suburb of Montevideo).
1495 **424** 20 p. black, blue & red . 10 10

1972. Uruguay's Victory in Intercontinental Football Cup Championships. No. 1471 surch **COPA INTER CONTINENTAL 1971**, football cup and **50**.
1496 **409** 50 p. on 10 p. gold, red and blue 35 30

426 Sapling and Spade

428 U.N.C.T.A.D. Emblem

427 Cross of Remembrance

1972. Tree Planting Campaign.
1497 **426** 20 p. black, myrtle & grn 15 10

1972. Air. 2nd Death Anniv of Dan Mitrione (U.S. police instructor assassinated by terrorists in Uruguay).
1498 **427** 37 p. violet and gold . . 15 10

1972. Air. 3rd United Nations Conference on Trade and Development (U.N.C.T.A.D.), Santiago, Chile.
1499 **428** 30 p. multicoloured . . . 15 10

429 Brazilian "Bull's-Eye" Stamp of 1843

1972. Air. "EXFILBRA 72" Stamp Exhibition, Rio de Janeiro.
1500 **429** 50 p. multicoloured . . . 20 10

430 Compass Rose and Map of South America

431 "Birds' Nests in Tree"

1972. Air. Campaign for Extension of Territorial Waters to 200 Mile Limit.
1501 **430** 37 p. multicoloured . . . 15 10

1972. National Building Project for Communal Dwellings.
1502 **431** 10 p. multicoloured . . . 10 10

432 Amethyst

1972. Uruguayan Mineralogy. Rocks and Gems.
1503 **432** 5 p. multicoloured . . . 15 10
1504 – 9 p. multicoloured . . . 20 10
1505 – 15 p. green, brown & blk 35 15
DESIGNS: 9 p. Agate; 15 p. Chalcedony.

433 "The Three Holy Kings" (R. Barradas)

1972 Air. Christmas.
1506 **433** 20 p. multicoloured . . . 20 15

435 Infantry Uniform of 1830

436 Red Cross over Map

1972. Military Uniforms. Multicoloured.
1509 10 p. Type **435** 15 10
1510 20 p. Artigas cavalry regiment uniform 30 15

1972. 75th Anniv of Uruguayan Red Cross.
1511 **436** 30 p. multicoloured . . . 30 10

438 Open Book

439 General Jose Artigas

1972. 25th Anniv of Full Civil Rights for Uruguayan Women.
1513 **438** 10 p. gold, blue & lt blue 10 10

1972.
1514 **439** 5 p. yellow 10 10
1515 10 p. brown 10 10
1516 15 p. green 10 10
1517 20 p. lilac 10 10
1518 30 p. blue 20 10
1519 40 p. orange 20 10
1520 50 p. red 15 10
1521 75 p. green 25 15
1522 100 p. green 30 15
1523 150 p. brown 15 25
1524 200 p. blue 25 30
1525 250 p. violet 30 35
1526 500 p. grey 60 75
1527 1000 p. blue . . . . . . 1·10 1·10

440 Cup and Ear of Wheat on Map

441 E. Fernandez and J. P. Varela (founders)

1973. 30th Anniv of Inter-american Institute for Agricultural Sciences.
1531 **440** 30 p. black, yell & red . . 15 10

1973. Centenary (1968) of Friends of Popular Education Society.
1532 **441** 10 p. black, green & brn 10 10

442 Columbus and Map

1973. American Tourist Year.
1533 **442** 50 p. purple 20 15

443 Carlos Ramirez

1973. Eminent Uruguayan Jurists. Each black, brown and bistre.

1534 10 p. Type **443** 10 10
1535 10 p. Justino Jimenez de Arechaga 10 10
1536 10 p. Juan Ramirez 10 10
1537 10 p. Justino E. Jimenez de Arechaga 10 10

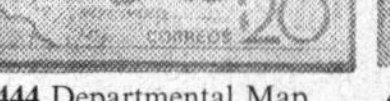

444 Departmental Map **447** Priest, Indians and Soriano Church

446 Francisco de los Santos and Artigas

1973. Uruguayan Departments.

1538 **444** 20 p. multicoloured . . . 30 15
See also No. 1844.

1973. Francisco de los Santos (courier) Commem.

1540 **446** 20 p. emerald, black and green 20 10

1973. Villa Santo Domingo Soriano (first Spanish Settlement in Uruguay) Commemoration.

1541 **447** 20 p. black, violet & blue 15 10

448 "SOYP" and Fish

1973. Inauguration of 1st Fishery Station of Oceanographic and Fishery Service (S.O.Y.P.).

1542 **448** 100 p. multicoloured . . 35 15

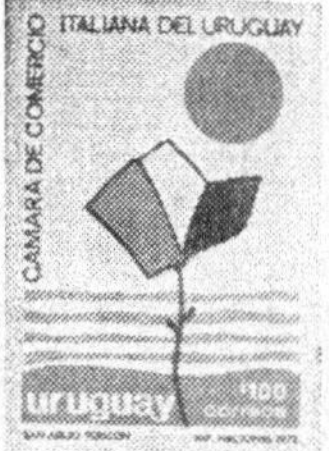

449 Flower and Sun **451** Luis A. de Herrera

1973. Italian Chamber of Commerce in Uruguay.

1543 **449** 100 p. multicoloured . . 25 15

1973. Birth Centenary of Luis A. de Herrera (conservative leader).

1545 **451** 50 p. brown, sepia & grey 20 10

452 Festival Emblem

1973. "Festival of Nations", Montevideo.

1546 **452** 50 p. multicoloured . . . 20 10

453 Artery and Heart within "Arm" **454** "Madonna (R. Barradas)

1973. 3rd Pan-American Voluntary Blood Donors' Congress.

1547 **453** 50 p. black, red & pink . 20 10

1973. Christmas.

1548 **454** 50 p. black, yell & grn . 15 10

455 Copernicus ($\frac{2}{3}$-size illustration)

1973. 500th Birth Anniv of Nicholas Copernicus (astronomer).

1549 **455** 50 p. multicoloured . . 15 10

456 Hands in Prayer, and Andes **457** O.E.A. Emblem and Map

1973. Rescue of Survivors from Andes Air-crash.

1550 **456** 50 p. green, blue & blk . 15 10
1551 – 75 p. multicoloured . . 20 15
DESIGN: 75 p. Flower with broken stem, and Christ of the Andes statue.

1974. 25th Anniv of Organization of American States (O.E.A).

1552 **457** 250 p. multicoloured . . 40 50

458 Games' Emblem

1974. 1st International Scout Games, Montevideo.

1553 **458** 250 p. multicoloured . . 40 50

459 Hector Sedes and Motor-car **462** "The Three Gauchos"

1974. Hector Sedes (motor-racing driver) Commemoration.

1554 **459** 50 p. brown, black & grn 15 10

1974. Centenary of Antonio Lussich's Poem "Los Tres Gauchos".

1560 **462** 50 p. multicoloured . . 15 10

463 Rifle, Target and Swiss Flag

1974. Centenary of Swiss Rifle Club, Nueva Helvecia.

1561 **463** 100 p. multicoloured . . 30 15

464 Compass Rose on Map **465** Emblem and Stadium

1974. Military Geographical Service.

1562 **464** 50 p. black, emerald & grn 15 10

1974. World Cup Football Championships, Munich. Multicoloured.

1563 50 p. Type **465** 15 10
1564 75 p. Emblem and footballer (horiz) 20 15
1565 1000 p. Emblem and footballer (different) (horiz) . . . . . 11·00 7·50

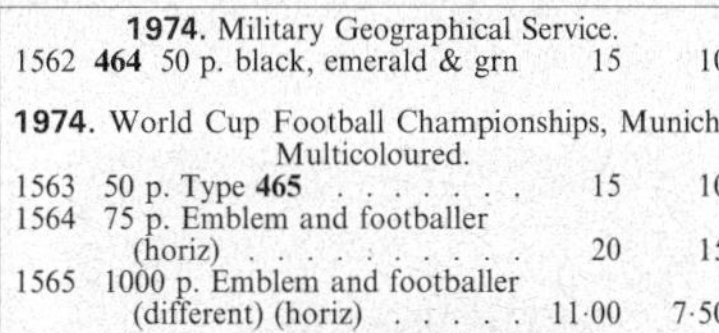

466 Old and New School Buildings, and Founders

1974. Centenary of Osimani-Llerena Technical School, Salto.

1566 **466** 75 p. black and brown . . 20 15

467 Carlos Gardel **468** "Ball and Net"

1974. 39th Death Anniv of Carlos Gardel (singer).

1567 **467** 100 p. multicoloured . . 35 15

1974. 1st Women's World Cup Volleyball Championships.

1568 **468** 200 p. purple, yell & blk . 45 25

469 "Protect Your Heart" **470** Vidal and Statue

1974. Uruguayan "Pro Cardias" Heart Foundation.

1569 **469** 75 p. red, yellow & green 20 15

1974. Bicentenary (1973) of Founding of San Jose by Eusebio Vidal.

1570 **470** 75 p. blue and light blue . 15 10
No. 1570 is incorrectly inscr "1873–1973".

471 Artigas Monument **472** W.P.Y. Emblem

1974. Dedication of Artigas Monument, Buenos Aires, Argentine Republic.

1571 **471** 75 p. multicoloured . . . 15 10

1974. Air. World Population Year.

1572 **472** 500 p. red, black and grey 55 70

473 Montevideo Citadel Gateway and Emblem **474** Mast and Radio Waves

1974. Air. Events of 1974.

1573 **473** 200 p. multicoloured . . 55 40
1574 300 p. multicoloured . . 70 60

1974. 50th Anniv of Broadcasting in Uruguay.

1575 **474** 100 p. multicoloured . . 20 10

475 "Sheet of Stamps" and "URUEXPO 74" Emblem

1974. 10th Anniv of "Circulo Filatelico" Journal of Montevideo Stamp Club.

1576 **475** 100 p. blue, red & blk . 20 10

476 Envelopes and Emblem

1974. Centenary of Universal Postal Union.

1577 **476** 100 p. multicoloured . . 10 10
1578 – 200 p. black, gold & lilac 20 10
DESIGN—VERT: 200 p. U.P.U. emblem on envelope, laurel and globe.

477 Mexican Official Stamp of 1884 and Arms

1974. Air. "EXFILMEX" Interamerican Philatelic Exhibition, Mexico City.

1579 **477** 200 p. multicoloured . . 20 10

478 Artigas Monument

1974. Dedication of Artigas Monument. Ventura Hill, Minas.

1580 **478** 100 p. multicoloured . . 10 10

479 Early Map of Montevideo

1974. 250th Anniv of Montevideo's Fortifications.

1581 **479** 300 p. brown, red & grn 50 20

480 Naval Vessel in Dry-dock and Badge

1974. Centenary of Montevideo Naval Arsenal.

1582 **480** 200 p. multicoloured . . 40 30

481 Balloon

1974. History of Aviation. Multicoloured.
1583 100 p. Type **481** 25 15
1584 100 p. Farman H.F.III biplanes 25 15
1585 100 p. Castaibert's Morane Saulnier Type I 25 15
1586 100 p. Bleriot XI 25 15
1587 150 p. Military and civil pilots' "wings" 35 20
1588 150 p. Nieuport 17 biplane . 35 20
1589 150 p. Breguet Bidon biplane 35 20
1590 150 p. Caproni Ca 5 biplane . 35 20

482 Pan de Azucar Mountain and Cross

1974. Centenary of Pan de Azucar (town).
1591 **482** 150 p. multicoloured . . 25 20

483 Adoration of the Kings

1974. Christmas. Multicoloured.
1592 100 p. Type **483** (postage) . . 10 10
1593 150 p. Kings with Gifts . . . 15 10
1594 240 p. Kings following the Star (air) 20 15

484 Rowers, Fireworks and Nike of Samothrace Statue

1975. Centenary of Montevideo Rowing Club.
1596 **484** 150 p. multicoloured . . 15 10

485 "Treaty of Purificacion, 1817" (J. Zorrilla de San Martin)

1975. Recognition of Artigas Government by Great Britain in Treaty of Purificacion, 1817.
1597 **485** 100 p. multicoloured . . . 10 10

486 Spanish 6 c. Stamp of 1850, and National Colours

1975. Air. "ESPANA 75" Stamp Exhibition, Madrid.
1598 **486** 400 p. multicoloured . . 35 20

487 Rose

1975. Bicentenary of Rosario.
1600 **487** 150 p. multicoloured . . 20 10

488 "The Oath of the Thirty-three" (J. M. Blanes)

1975. 150th Anniv of 1825 Liberation Movement.
1601 **488** 150 p. multicoloured . . 20 10

489 Michelangelo's Motif for Floor of Capitol, Rome

1975. Air. 500th Birth Anniv of Michelangelo.
1602 **489** 1 p. multicoloured . . . 60 50

490 Columbus and Caravel

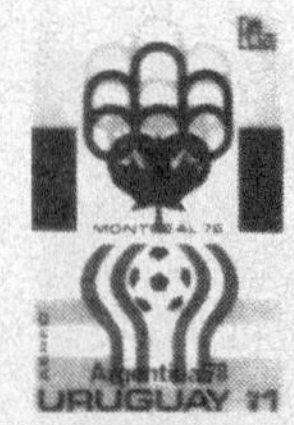

492 Emblem of Montreal Olympics (1976) and World Cup Football Championship Finals (Argentina, 1978)

491 Sun and 4 p. 50 Air Stamp of 1929

1975. Spanish–American Stamp Day.
1603 **490** 1 p. multicoloured . . . 1·00 60

1975. Air. Uruguayan Stamp Day.
1604 **491** 1 p. blk, yell and grey . 2·00 70

1975. Air. "Exfilmo-Espamer 75" Stamp Exhibition, Montevideo. Multicoloured.
1605 1 p. Type **492** 40 60
1606 1 p. "Independence" (U.S. and Uruguayan flags) 40 60
1607 1 p. Emblems of U.P.U. and Spanish–American Postal Union 40 60

493 Jose Artigas and J. Francisco de Larrobla

1975. 150th Anniv of Independence.
1608 **493** 50 c. multicoloured . . 40 35

494 Col. L. Oliveira and Fortress

1975. 150th Anniv of Capture of Santa Teresa Fortress.
1609 **494** 10 c. multicoloured . . . 20 10

495 Battle Scene from Painting by D. Hequet

1975. 150th Anniv of Battle of Rincon.
1610 **495** 15 c. black and gold . . . 20 10
See also Nos. 1620/1.

496 Florencio Sanchez

1975. Birth Cent of Florencio Sanchez (dramatist). Multicoloured.
1611 20 c. Type **496** 30 10
1612 20 c. "En Familia" 30 10
1613 20 c. "Barranca Abajo" . . . 30 10
1614 20 c. "Mi Hijo el Doctor" . . 30 10
1615 20 c. "Camilita" 30 10
Nos. 1612/15 show scenes from plays and are horiz 38 × 26 mm.

1975. Surch in revalued currency.
1616 **439** 10 c. on 20 p. lilac . . . 10 10
1617 15 c. on 40 p. orange . . 10 10
1618 50 c. on 50 p. red . . . 35 20
1619 1 p. on 1000 p. blue . . . 40 40

1975. 150th Anniv of Artigas' Exile and Battle of Sarandi. As T **495**. Multicoloured.
1620 15 c. Artigas' house, Ibiray (Paraguay) 20 10
1621 25 c. Battle scene 40 20

498 Maria E. Vaz Ferreira (poetess)

1975. Birth Centenaries.
1622 **498** 15 c. black, yellow & pur 20 10
1623 – 15 c. black, orge & pur . 20 10
DESIGN: No. 1623, Julio Herrera y Reissig (poet).

499 "Virgin and Child" (stained-glass window) **500** Colonel L. Latorre

1975. Christmas. Multicoloured.
1624 20 c. Type **499** 35 15
1625 30 c. "Virgin and Child" (different) 50 30
1626 60 c. "Fireworks" (horiz) . . 40 40

1975. 59th Death Anniv of Col. Lorenzo Latorre (President, 1876–80).
1627 **500** 15 c. multicoloured . . . 15 10

501 "Ariel", Stars and Book

1976. 75th Anniv of Publication of "Ariel" by Jose Rodo.
1628 **501** 15 c. multicoloured . . . 15 10

502 "Oncidium bifolium" (orchid)

1976. Air. Multicoloured.
1629 50 c. Type **502** 45 20
1630 50 c. Geoffroy's cat 45 20

503 "Water Sports" **504** Telephone Receiver

1976. 23rd South American Swimming, Diving and Water-polo Championships, Maldonado.
1631 **503** 30 c. multicoloured . . . 20 15

1976. Telephone Centenary.
1632 **504** 83 c. multicoloured . . . 30 25

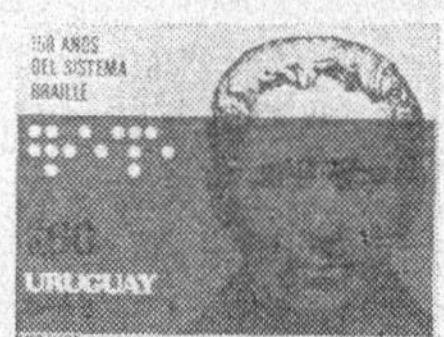

505 Dornier Wal Flying Boat "Plus Ultra" **506** Dornier Wal Flying Boat and Airliner rising around Hour-glass

1976. 50th Anniv of "Plus Ultra" Spain–South America Flight.
1633 **505** 63 c. multicoloured . . . 60 25

1976. 50th Anniv of Lufthansa Airline.
1634 **506** 83 c. multicoloured . . . 55 35

507 Louis Braille and word "Braille"

1976. 150th Anniv of Braille System for the Blind.
1635 **507** 60 c. black and brown . 40 25

508 Signing of Declaration of Independence

1976. Bicentenary of American Revolution.
1636 **508** 1 p. 50 multicoloured . . 1·25 95

509 "Candombe" (Pedro Figari)

1976. 150th Anniv of Abolition of Slavery.
1637 **509** 30 c. multicoloured . . . 15 10

510 Rivera Monument — 511 Chilian Lapwing

1976. Dedication of General Rivera Monument.
1638 **510** 5 p. on 10 p. mult . . . 2·00 95

1976.

1639	**511**	1 c. violet	30	10
1640	–	5 c. green	10	10
1641	–	15 c. red	15	10
1642	–	20 c. black	10	10
1643	–	30 c. grey	15	10
1644	–	45 c. blue	10	10
1645	–	50 c. green	25	10
1646	–	1 p. brown	45	10
1646b	–	1 p. yellow	25	10
1647	–	1 p. 75 green	35	10
1648	–	1 p. 95 grey	40	10
1649	–	2 p. green	90	70
1649a	–	2 p. mauve	35	10
1650	–	2 p. 65 violet	45	15
1651	–	5 p. blue	2·00	2·00
1651a	–	10 p. brown	3·25	2·00

DESIGNS—VERT: 5 c. Passion flower; 15 c. National flower; 20 c. Indian lance-head; 30 c. Indian statue; 45 c., 1 p. (No. 1646b), 1 p. 75, 1 p. 95, 2 p. (both), 2 p. 65, 5, 10 p., Artigas; 1 p. (No. 1646), "At Dawn" (J. M. Blanes). HORIZ: 50 c. "Branding Cattle" (J. M. Blanes).

513 Office Building and Reverse of First Uruguayan Coin of 1840

1976. 150th Anniv of State Accounting Office.
1652 **513** 30 c. black, brown & bl . 25 15

514 Hand-pump within Flames — 516 Championship Emblem

515 Uruguay 60 c. Stamp of 1856 and "Commemorative Postmark"

1976. Centenary of Fire Service.
1653 **514** 20 c. black and red . . . 15 10

1976. 50th Anniv of Uruguay Philatelic Club.
1654 **515** 30 c. red, blue & bistre . 15 10

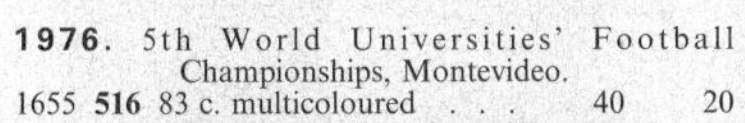
1976. 5th World Universities' Football Championships, Montevideo.
1655 **516** 83 c. multicoloured . . . 40 20

517 Human Eye and Spectrum

1976. Prevention of Blindness.
1656 **517** 20 c. multicoloured . . 25 10

518 Map of Montevideo

1976. 250th Anniv of Montevideo. Multicoloured.

1657	30 c. Type **518**	15	10
1658	45 c. Montevideo panorama. 1842	20	10
1659	70 c. First settlers, 1726	35	15
1660	80 c. Montevideo coin (vert)	40	20
1661	1 p. 15 Montevideo's first arms (vert)	55	30

519 "VARIG" Emblem

1977. 50th Anniv of VARIG Airline.
1662 **519** 80 c. multicoloured . . 50 40

520 Artigas Mausoleum

1977. Mausoleum of General Jose Artigas.
1663 **520** 45 c. multicoloured . . 30 10

521 Arch on Map

1977. Cent of Salesian Education in Uruguay.
1664 **521** 45 c. multicoloured . . 30 10

522 Globe and Emblems — 523 Children

1977. Air. 150th Anniv of Uruguayan Postal Services.
1665 **522** 8 p. multicoloured . . . 2·75 2·50

1977. 50th Anniv of Inter-American Children's Institute.
1667 **523** 45 c. multicoloured . . 30 10

524 "Windmills" — 525 Sun on "Stamp" and Stripes of Uruguayan Flag

1977. Hispanidad Day.
1668 **524** 70 c. red, yellow & blk . 35 15

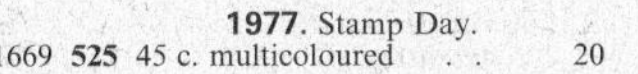
1977. Stamp Day.
1669 **525** 45 c. multicoloured . . 20 10

527 Globe and Aircraft

1977. 30th Anniv of International Civil Aviation Organization.
1670 **527** 45 c. mutlicoloured . . . 15 10

528 "The Holy Family"

1977. Christmas.
1671 **528** 45 c. multicoloured . . . 15 10
1672 – 70 c. red, yellow & blk . 20 10
DESIGN—HORIZ: (45×26 mm): 70 c. "Santa Claus".

529 Arms, Map and Products — 530 Postman clearing Mail-box

1977. Rio Negro Department.
1673 **529** 45 c. multicoloured . . . 15 10

1977. 150th Anniv of National Mail Service. Multicoloured.

1674	50 c. Type **530**	15	10
1675	50 c. Loading mail-van	15	10
1676	50 c. Post Office counter, Montevideo G.P.O.	15	10
1677	50 c. Post-boxes area	15	10
1678	50 c. Sorting mail	15	10
1679	50 c. Postal sorters	15	10
1680	50 c. Postmen sorting "walks"	15	10
1681	50 c. Postman on rounds	15	10
1682	50 c. Postmen on motor-scooters	15	10
1683	50 c. Postal counter, Carrasco Airport	15	10

531 Edison's First "Phonograph"

1977. Centenary of Sound Recording.
1684 **531** 50 c. purple and yellow . 15 10

532 "R" and Spectrum

1977. World Rheumatism Year.
1685 **532** 50 c. multicoloured . . . 15 10

533 Emblem, Diploma, Sword and Flag

1978. 50th Anniv of Military College.
1686 **533** 50 c. multicoloured . . . 15 10

534 Arms and Map — 537 "Wandering Angels" (detail)

1978. Department of Artigas.
1687 **534** 45 c. multicoloured . . . 30 10

1978. Air. "Riccione" and "Europhil 78" Stamp Exhibitions, Italy and Urphila Stamp Exhibition, Uruguay. Optd **EUROPA 1978 ITALIA Riccione 78 urphila 78**.
1689 **522** 8 p. multicoloured . . . 3·00 2·50

1978. National Artists. Luis A. Solari. Multicoloured.

1690	1 p. 50 Type **537**	30	20
1691	1 p. 50 "Wandering Angels" (horiz 38×30 mm)	30	20
1692	1 p. 50 "Wandering Angels" (detail)	30	20

538 Bernardo O'Higgins

1978. Birth Bicentenary of Bernardo O'Higgins (national hero of Chile).
1693 **538** 1 p. multicoloured . . . 25 10

539 Telephone Dials and "Antel" Emblem

1978. Telephone Automatisation.
1694 **539** 50 c. multicoloured . . . 10 10

540 San Martin and Army of the Andes Monument (J. M. Ferrari) — 541 Spanish Tiles

1978. Birth Bicentenary of General Jose de San Martin.
1695 **540** 1 p. multicoloured . . . 25 10

1978. Hispanidad.
1696 **541** 1 p. blue, yellow & blk . 25 10

542 Corners of "Stamps"

1978. Stamp Day.
1697 **542** 50 c. multicoloured . . . 10 10

543 Boeing 727 in Flight — 545 Flag Monument, Montevideo

544 Angel blowing Trumpet

1978. PLUNA Airline Inaugural Boeing 727 Flight.
1698 **543** 50 c. multicoloured . . . 15 10

1978. Christmas.
1699 **544** 50 c. green, orge & blk . 10 10
1700 1 p. blue, red and black . 20 10

1978. Homage to the National Flag.
1701 **545** 1 p. multicoloured . . . 25 10

546 Horacio Quiroga **547** Arms and Map of Paysandu

1978. Birth Centenary of Horacio Quiroga (playwright).
1702 **546** 1 p. black, yellow & red . 25 10

1979. Department of Paysandu.
1703 **547** 45 c. multicoloured . . . 10 10

548 Olympic Rings and Ciudadela

1979. Olympic Games, Moscow (1980) and Winter Olympics, Lake Placid (1980). Multicoloured.
1704 5 p. Type **548** 90 85
1705 7 p. Lake Placid emblem . . 1·10 1·25
See also Nos. 1728/9.

549 Arms and Map of Salto **550** Artilleryman, 1830

1979. Department of Salto.
1706 **549** 45 c. multicoloured . . . 10 10

1979. Uruguayan Military Uniforms. Mult.
1707 5 p. Type **550** 85 85
1708 5 p. Sapper, 1837 . . . . . . 85 85

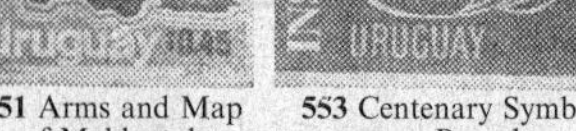

551 Arms and Map of Maldonado **553** Centenary Symbol and Branch

552 Salto Grande Dam

1979. Department of Maldonado.
1709 **551** 45 c. multicoloured . . 10 10

1979. Salto Grande Dam.
1710 **552** 2 p. multicoloured . . . 50 15

1979. Centenary of Crandon Uruguayan–American High School.
1711 **553** 1 p. blue and violet . . 20 10

554 Kites

1979. International Year of the Child (1st issue).
1712 **554** 2 p. multicoloured . . . 35 15
See also Nos. 1715, 1718 amd 1720.

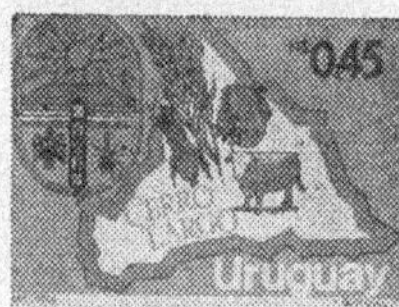

555 Arms and Map of Cerro Largo

1979. Department of Cerro Largo.
1713 **555** 45 c. multicoloured . . 10 10

556 Arms and Map of Trienta y Tres **557** Cinderella

1979. Department of Trienta y Tres.
1714 **556** 50 c. multicoloured . . 10 10

1979. International Year of the Child (2nd issue).
1715 **557** 2 p. multicoloured . . . 35 20

558 National Coat of Arms

1979. 150th Anniv of First National Coat of Arms.
1716 **558** 8 p. multicoloured . . . 1·10 1·10

559 U.P.U. Emblem and Arrow

1979. 18th U.P.U. Congress, Rio de Janeiro.
1717 **559** 5 p. multicoloured . . . 85 50

560 "Chico Carlo" (Juana de Ibarbourou) **561** Drawing by J. M. Torres-Garcia

1979. International Year of the Child (3rd issue).
1718 **560** 1 p. multicoloured . . . 20 10

1979. 31st Death Anniv of Joaquin Torres-Garcia (artist).
1719 **561** 10 p. yellow and black . 1·40 1·25

562 Madonna and Child

1979. Christmas and International Year of the Child (4th issue).
1720 **562** 10 p. multicoloured . . . 1·40 1·25

563 Arms and Map of Durazno

1979. Department of Durazno.
1721 **563** 50 c. multicoloured . . . 15 10

564 Dish Aerial and Sun

1979. 3rd World Telecommunications Exposition, Geneva.
1722 **564** 10 p. black, yell & lavender 95 80

565 Caravel

1979. Hispanidad Day.
1723 **565** 10 p. multicoloured . . . 1·75 85

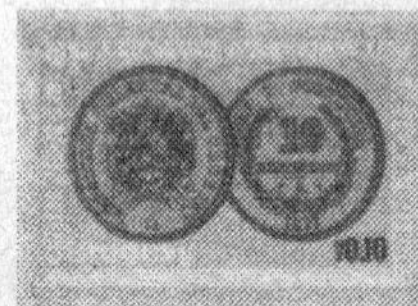

566 10 c. Coin of 1877

1979. Centenary of 1st Silver Coinage. Multicoloured.
1724 **566** 10 c. silver, black & green 10 10
1725 – 20 c. silver, black & green 10 10
1726 – 50 c. silver, black & blue . 10 10
1727 – 1 p. silver, black & blue . 20 10
DESIGNS: 20 c. 1877 20 c. coin; 50 c. 1877 50 c. coin; 1 p. 1877 1 p. coin.

1980. Events. Multicoloured.
1728 3 p. Type **548** 60 25
1729 3 p. As No. 1705 . . . . . . 60 25
1730 5 p. Olympic rings 90 40
1731 5 p. "Uruguay 79" stamp exhibition emblem 90 40
1732 7 p. Chessboard and rook (23rd Chess Olympiad, Buenos Aires, 1978) . . . . 1·25 55
1733 7 p. Detail from Greek vase (Olympic Games) . . . . . 1·25 55
1734 10 p. Detail from Greek vase (different) . . . . 1·75 80

568 Thomas Edison and Lamp

1980. Centenary of Electric Light.
1736 **568** 2 p. multicoloured . . . 40 20

569 Arms of Colonia **571** Association Emblem

1980. Colonia.
1737 **569** 50 c. multicoloured . . . 15 10

1980. 50th Anniv of Uruguayan Printers' Association.
1739 **571** 1 p. yellow, mauve & bl . 20 15

572 Geometric Design **573** Zorilla de San Martin and Page of "La Leyenda Patria"

1980. Stamp Day.
1740 **572** 1 p. multicoloured . . . 20 10

1980. "La Leyenda Patria".
1741 **573** 1 p. multicoloured . . . 20 10

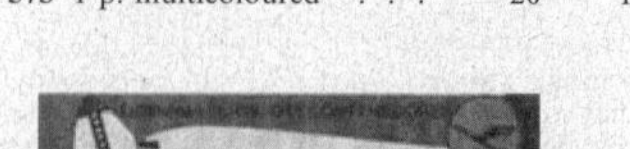

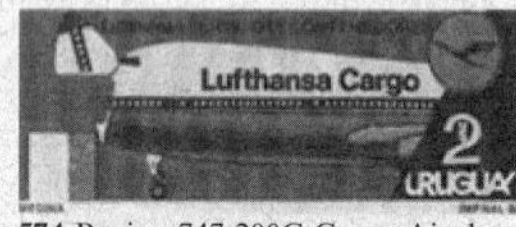

574 Boeing 747-200C Cargo Airplane

1980. Inauguration of Lufthansa Cargo Container Service.
1742 **574** 2 p. multicoloured . . . 40 20

575 Conference Emblem and Flags

1980. 8th World Hereford Conference, Punta del Este, and Livestock Exhibition, Prado, Montevideo.
1743 **575** 2 p. multicoloured . . . 40 20

576 Lions Emblem and Map of South America

1980. 9th Latin-American Lions Forum.
1744 **576** 1 p. multicoloured . . . 20 10

579 Rotary Emblem and Globe **580** Hand stubbing out Cigarette

1980. 75th Anniv of Rotary International.
1747 **579** 5 p. multicoloured . . . 85 70

1980. World Health Day. Anti-smoking Campaign.
1748 **580** 1 p. pink, black and grn 20 10

581 Jose Artigas **582** Angel blowing Trumpet

1980.

1749 **581** 10 c. blue 10 10
1750 20 c. orange 10 10
1751 50 c. red 10 10
1752 60 c. yellow 10 10
1753 1 p. grey 15 15
1754 2 p. brown 35 15
1755 3 p. green 55 30
1756 4 p. blue 65 40
1757 5 p. green 30 10
1757a 6 p. orange 10 10
1758 7 p. purple 95 70
1759 10 p. blue 50 25
1760 12 p. black 20 10
1761 15 p. 50 green 25 15
1762 20 p. purple . . . . . . 1·00 85
1763 30 p. brown . . . . . . 1·25 1·25
1764 50 p. blue . . . . 2·00 2·00

1980. Christmas.
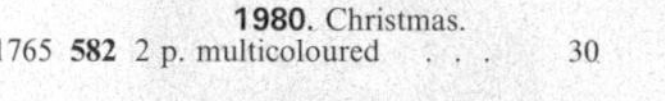
1765 **582** 2 p. multicoloured . . . 30 15

583 Title Page of Constitution

1980. 150th Anniv of Constitution.
1766 **583** 4 p. blue and gold . . . 70 35

584 Montevideo Football Stadium **585** Conquistador

1980. Gold Cup Football Championship, Montevideo.
1767 **584** 5 p. multicoloured . . . 50 35
1768 – 5 p. yellow, black & red . 50 35
1769 – 10 p. multicoloured . . . 1·10 1·10
DESIGNS—As T **584**. No. 1768, Gold cup. 25×79 mm: No. 1769, Mascot and flags of participating countries.

1981. Hispanidad Day.
1771 **585** 2 p. multicoloured . . . 35 15

586 U.P.U. Emblem **587** Alexander von Humboldt

1981. Centenary of U.P.U. Membership.
1772 **586** 2 p. multicoloured . . . 35 15

1981. 122nd Death Anniv of Alexander von Humboldt (naturalist).
1773 **587** 2 p. multicoloured . . . 40 15

588 Trophy and Open Book

1981. International Education Exhibition and Congress, Montevideo.
1774 **588** 2 p. green, blk & lilac . 35 15

589 Flags and Trophy **590** Musical Notes over Map of the Americas

1981. Uruguayan Victory in Gold Cup Football Championship.
1775 **589** 2 p. multicoloured . . . 40 15
1776 5 p. multicoloured . . . 60 35

1981. 40th Anniv of Inter-american Institute of Musicology.
1777 **590** 2 p. multicoloured . . . 40 15

591 Boeing 707

1981. Inaugural Flight to Madrid of Pluna Airline.
1778 **591** 2 p. multicoloured . . . 40 15
1779 5 p. multicoloured . . . 60 40
1780 10 p. multicoloured . . 1·25 70
Nos 1778/80 are inscribed "BOEING 737".

592 Cavalryman of Gen. Manuel Oribe, 1843

1981. Army Day. Multicoloured.
1781 2 p. Type **592** 40 15
1782 2 p. Infantry of Montevideo, 1843 . . . . 40 15

593 Conference Emblem on Suitcase

1981. World Tourism Conference, Manila (1980).
1783 **593** 2 p. multicoloured . . . 35 15

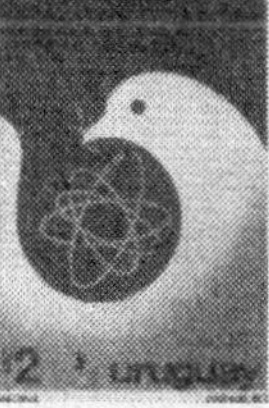
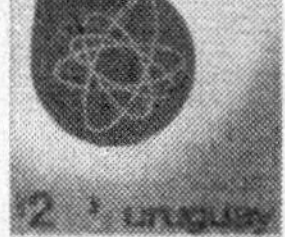

594 Peace Dove and Atomic Emblem **595** Footballer

1981. 25th Anniv of National Atomic Energy Commission.
1784 **594** 2 p. multicoloured . . . 35 15

1981. Europe–South America Football Cup.
1785 **595** 2 p. multicoloured . . . 40 15

596 Arms and Map of Rocha **597** Carved Stone Tablets

1981. Department of Rocha.
1786 **596** 2 p. multicoloured . . . 40 15

1981. Salto Grande Archaeological Rescue Excavations.
1787 **597** 2 p. multicoloured . . . 40 15

598 Artigas Monument, Minas **599** A.N.C.A.P. Anniversary Emblem

1981. 10th Lavalleja Week.
1788 **598** 4 p. multicoloured . . . 70 35

1981. 50th Anniv of National Administration for Combustible Fuels, Alcohol and Portland Cement.
1789 **599** 2 p. multicoloured . . . 35 15

600 I.Y.D.P. Emblem

1981. International Year of Disabled Persons.
1790 **600** 2 p. deep blue, red and blue 35 15

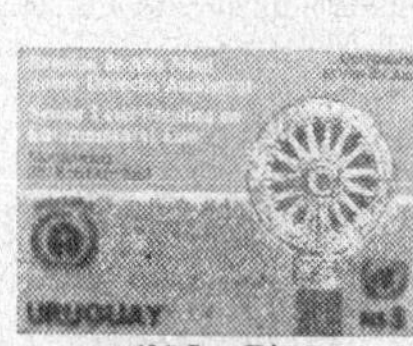

601 Sun Disc

1981. Senior Level Meeting on Environmental Law, Montevideo.
1791 **601** 5 p. multicoloured . . . 60 35

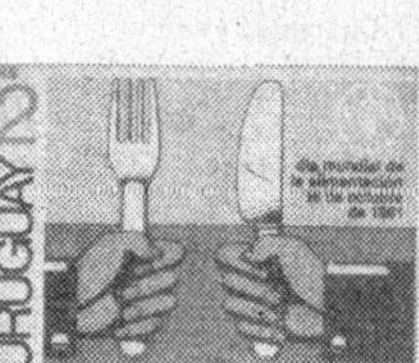

602 Hands holding Knife and Fork **603** Theodolite and Measuring Rod on Map of Uruguay

1981. World Food Day.
1792 **602** 2 p. multicoloured . . . 40 15

1981. 150th Anniv of Topographic Survey.
1793 **603** 2 p. multicoloured . . . 40 15

604 Bank of Uruguay

1981. 85th Anniv of Bank of Uruguay.
1794 **604** 2 p. multicoloured . . . 40 15

605 Palmar Dam

1981. Palmar Central Hydro-electric Project.
1795 **605** 2 p. multicoloured . . . 40 15

606 Father Christmas **607** Joaquin Suarez

1981. Christmas.
1796 **606** 2 p. multicoloured . . . 40 15

1982. Birth Bicentenary of Joaquin Suarez.
1797 **607** 5 p. multicoloured . . . 60 35

608 Lockheed Super Constellation and Route Map

1982. 25th Anniv of 1st Germany–Uruguay Lufthansa Flight. Multicoloured.
1798 3 p. Type **608** 50 30
1799 7 p. Boeing 747-200 and route map 90 70

609 American Air Forces Co-operation Emblem **610** Private, Florida Battalion, 1865

1982. 22nd American Air Forces' Commanders Conference.
1800 **609** 10 p. multicoloured . . . 1·25 80

1982. Army Day. Multicoloured.
1801 3 p. Type **610** 55 20
1802 3 p. Captain of Artillery, 1872 55 20

611 Face and Satellite in Outer Space **612** Pinocchio

1982. Peaceful Uses of Outer Space Conference, Vienna.
1803 **611** 3 p. multicoloured . . . 75 40

1982. Centenary of Publication of Carlo Collodi's "Pinocchio".
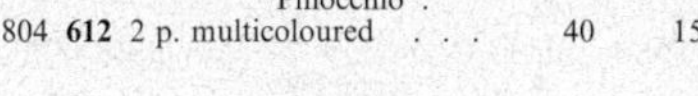
1804 **612** 2 p. multicoloured . . . 40 15

613 Arms of Flores

1982. Department of Flores.
1805 **613** 2 p. multicoloured . . . 40 15

614 Zorrilla de San Martin

1982. 50th Death Anniv of Juan Zorrilla de San Martin (writer).
1806 **614** 3 p. multicoloured . . . 60 35

615 Cadet Schooner "Capitan Miranda" (after J. Rivera)

1982. 165th Anniv of Navy.
1807 **615** 3 p. multicoloured . . . 75 20

616 Figures reading Book **617** Scales of Justice

1982. National Literacy Campaign.
1808 **616** 3 p. blue, deep blue and yellow 25 10

1982. Stamp Day.
1809 **617** 3 p. green 30 15
1810 – 3 p. red 30 15
DESIGN: No. 1810, Volcano.

618 Star, Family and Symbols of Economic Progress

1982. Christmas.
1811 **618** 3 p. multicoloured . . . 30 15

619 Fabini

1983. Birth Centenary of Edouardo Fabini (composer).
1812 **619** 3 p. deep brown & brown 30 15

620 2nd Cavalry Regiment, 1885 **621** "Santa Maria" on Globe

1983. Army Day. Multicoloured.
1813 3 p. Type **620** 40 15
1814 3 p. Military College, 1885 . 40 15

1983. Visit of King and Queen of Spain. Multicoloured.
1815 3 p. Type **621** . . . . 1·50 30
1816 7 p. Royal couple and Uruguayan and Spanish flags (44 × 31 mm) 80 40

622 Headquarters Building **623** Exhibition Emblem

1983. Inauguration of Postal Union of the Americas and Spain H.Q., Montevideo.
1817 **622** 3 p. black, blue & brn . 30 15

1983. "Brasiliana 83" International Stamp Exhibition, Rio de Janeiro.
1818 **623** 3 p. multicoloured . . . 30 15

624 Space Shuttle "Columbia"

1983. 1st Flight of Space Shuttle "Columbia".
1819 **624** 7 p. multicoloured . . . 65 30

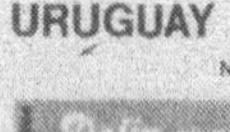

625 "Delin 1900" Car

1983. 1st Imported Car.
1820 **625** 3 p. blue and black . . 30 15

626 Goethe and Scene from "Faust"

1983. 150th Death Anniv (1982) of Johann Wolfgang von Goethe (writer).
1821 **626** 7 p. blue and black . . 65 30

627 "Moonlit Landscape" **628** Statue of Lavelleja

1983. 6th Death Anniv of Jose Cuneo (artist).
1822 **627** 3 p. multicoloured . . . 30 15

1983. Bicentenary of Minas City.
1823 **628** 3 p. multicoloured . . . 30 15

629 W.C.Y. Emblem

1983. World Communications Year.
1824 **629** 3 p. multicoloured . . . 20 10

630 Garibaldi

1983. Death Centenary (1982) of Guiseppe Garibaldi (Italian revolutionary).
1825 **630** 7 p. multicoloured . . . 50 30

631 "Graf Zeppelin"

1983. Zeppelin Flight over Montevideo (1934).
1826 **631** 7 p. black, blue & mauve 90 35

632 Footballers, World Cup and Italian Team Badge

1983. Italy's Victory in World Cup Football Championship (1982).
1827 **632** 7 p. multicoloured . . . 65 30

633 Virgin, Child and Star

1983. Christmas.
1828 **633** 4 p. 50 multicoloured . . 25 10

634 "50" on Telephone Dial

1984. 50th Anniv of Automatic Telephone Dialling.
1829 **634** 4 p. 50 multicoloured . . 25 10

635 Leandro Gomez **636** Emblem, Map, Flag and Tanker

1984. General Leandro Gomez Commemoration.
1830 **635** 4 p. 50 blue, light blue and black 25 10

1984. 25th Anniv (1983) of International Maritime Organization.
1831 **636** 4 p. 50 multicoloured . . 50 15

637 Flags and Emblem **638** Map of Uruguay and Bank Emblem

1984. American Women's Day.
1832 **637** 4 p. 50 multicoloured . . 25 10

1984. 25th Annual Meeting of Governors of International Development Bank, Punta del Este.
1833 **638** 10 p. blue, gold & black 55 20

639 Simon Bolivar

1984. Birth Bicentenary (1983) of Simon Bolivar.
1834 **639** 4 p. 50 lt brown & brown 25 10

640 Club Emblem and Radio Waves **641** Monument

1984. 50th Anniv (1983) of Uruguay Radio Club.
1835 **640** 7 p. multicoloured . . . 40 20

1984. 1930 World Cup Football Championship Monument.
1836 **641** 4 p. 50 multicoloured . . 25 10

642 National Emblem within "200"

1984. Bicentenary (1983) of San Jose de Mayo.
1837 **642** 4 p. 50 multicoloured . . 25 10

643 Emblem

1984. 50th Anniv of Tourist Organization.
1838 **643** 4 p. 50 gold, violet and blue 25 10

644 Artillery Uniform, 1895 **645** Artigas on Horseback

1984. Army Day. Multicoloured.
1839 4 p. 50 Type **644** 25 15
1840 4 p. 50 2nd Battalion Cazadores uniform, 1894 . . . . . . 25 15

1984.
1841 **645** 4 p. 50 black and blue . 25 15
1842 8 p. 50 brown and blue . 45 25

646 Trophy

1984. Penarol Athletic Club. Winners of European–South American Football Cup, 1982.
1843 **646** 4 p. 50 black, yellow and deep yellow 25 10

1984. Uruguayan Departments.
1844 **444** 4 p. 50 multicoloured . . 25 10

647 Child holding Flower and "50 ANOS"

1984. 50th Anniv of Children's Council.
1845 **647** 4 p. 50 multicoloured . . 25 10

648 Christmas Tree with Candles

649 Pelota Player and Flags

1984. Christmas.
1846 **648** 6 p. multicoloured . . . 30 10

1985. 1st Junior Pelota World Championship.
1847 **649** 4 p. 50 multicoloured . . 25 10

650 Bruno Mauricio de Zabala

652 Carlos Gardel

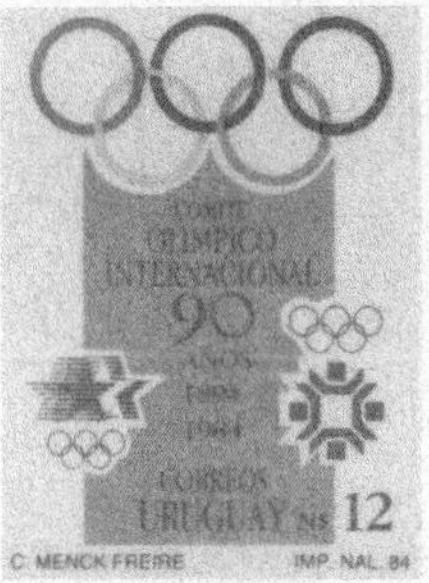
651 Emblems of Los Angeles and Sarajevo Games and Olympic Rings

1985. 300th Birth Anniv (1983) of Don Bruno Mauricio de Zabala (Governor of Buenos Aires and founder of Montevideo).
1848 **650** 4 p. 50 multicoloured . . 25 10

1985. 90th Anniv of International Olympic Committee.
1849 **651** 12 p. multicoloured . . . 45 25

1985. 50th Death Anniv of Carlos Gardel (entertainer).
1850 **652** 6 p. grey, blue and brown 25 10

653 Emblem and Flags of Member States

1985. 25th Anniv of American Air Forces' Co-operation System.
1851 **653** 12 p. multicoloured . . 20 10

654 Icarus

1985. 40th Anniv of I.C.A.O.
1852 **654** 4 p. 50 deep blue, green and blue 10 10

655 Stylised Factory and "50"

656 Cross and Clasped Hands

1985. 50th Anniv of FUNSA Tyre Factory.
1853 **655** 6 p. multicoloured . . . 10 10

1985. Centenary of Catholic Workers Circle.
1854 **656** 6 p. multicoloured . . . 10 10

657 I.Y.Y. Emblem

659 Books forming "8"

658 Peace Dove and Sun

1985. International Youth Year.
1855 **657** 12 p. red and black . . 20 10

1985. "Return to Democracy".
1856 **658** 20 p. blue, yellow and violet 30 15

1985. 8th International Book Exhibition.
1857 **659** 20 p. multicoloured . . 30 15

660 Emblem

661 Map and Arms

1985. Centenary of Military School.
1858 **660** 10 p. multicoloured . . 20 10

1985. Centenary of Flores Department.
1859 **661** 6 p. multicoloured . . . 10 10

662 Father Christmas

1985. Christmas.
1860 **662** 10 p. multicoloured . . 20 10
1861 22 p. multicoloured . . 35 20

663 Monument to Isabel the Catholic

1985. Hispanidad Day.
1862 **663** 12 p. black, red and brown 15 10

664 Emblem and Meeting Logo

1986. 3rd Inter-American Agriculture Co-operation Institute Meeting.
1863 **664** 12 p. yellow, red & black 20 10

665 Emblem and Flag

1986. World Post Day.
1864 **665** 15 p 50 multicoloured . . 25 10

666 Map and Symbolic House

1986. 6th Population and 4th Housing Census (1985).
1865 **666** 10 p. black, blue and yellow 20 10

667 Emblem

1986. 50th Anniv (1985) of Conaprole Milk and Cattle Co-operative.
1866 **667** 10 p. gold, blue and light blue 20 10

668 U.N. Emblem and Population Diagram

1986. 40th Anniv (1985) of U.N.O.
1867 **668** 20 p. multicoloured . . . 30 15

669 Emblem

670 Manuel Oribe

1986. 50th Anniv (1985) of National Brokers and Auctioneers Association.
1868 **669** 10 p. black, deep blue and blue 15 10

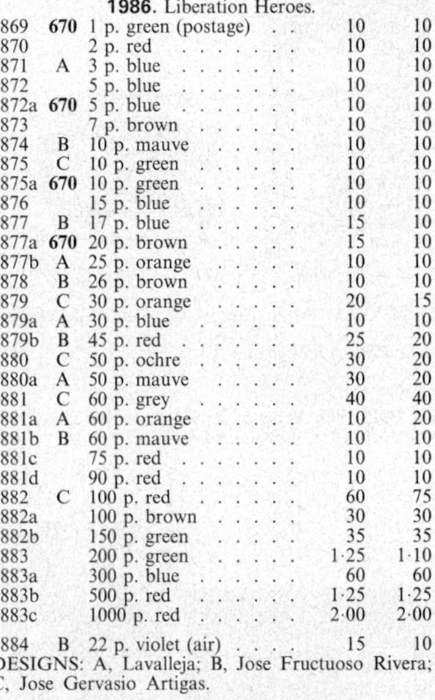

1986. Liberation Heroes.

1869	**670**	1 p. green (postage) . .	10	10
1870		2 p. red	10	10
1871	A	3 p. blue	10	10
1872		5 p. blue	10	10
1872a	**670**	5 p. blue	10	10
1873		7 p. brown	10	10
1874	B	10 p. mauve	10	10
1875	C	10 p. green	10	10
1875a	**670**	10 p. green	10	10
1876		15 p. blue	10	10
1877	B	17 p. blue	15	10
1877a	**670**	20 p. brown	15	10
1877b	A	25 p. orange	10	10
1878	B	26 p. brown	10	10
1879	C	30 p. orange	20	15
1879a	A	30 p. blue	10	10
1879b	B	45 p. red	25	20
1880	C	50 p. ochre	30	20
1880a	A	50 p. mauve	30	20
1881	C	60 p. grey	40	40
1881a	A	60 p. orange	10	10
1881b	B	60 p. mauve	10	10
1881c		75 p. red	10	10
1881d		90 p. red	10	10
1882	C	100 p. red	60	75
1882a		100 p. brown	30	30
1882b		150 p. green	35	35
1883		200 p. green	1·25	1·10
1883a		300 p. blue	60	60
1883b		500 p. red	1·25	1·25
1883c		1000 p. red	2·00	2·00
1884	B	22 p. violet (air)	15	10

DESIGNS: A, Lavalleja; B, Jose Fructuoso Rivera; C, Jose Gervasio Artigas.

671 Mosaic in National Colours

1986. Italian Chamber of Commerce in Uruguay.
1885 **671** 20 p. multicoloured . . . 20 10

672 Armenian Flag and Monument

673 Emblem and Footballer

1986. 71st Anniv of Armenian Genocide.
1886 **672** 10 p. black, red & blue . 10 10

1986. World Cup Football Championship, Mexico.
1887 **673** 20 p. multicoloured . . . 20 15

674 Newspaper Page

675 Alan Garcia

1986. Centenary of "El Dia".
1888 **674** 10 p. gold, black & red . 10 10

1986. Visit of President of Peru.
1889 **675** 20 p. brown, red & blue 15 15

676 Map, Gen. Sucre and Simon Bolivar

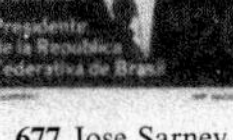
677 Jose Sarney

1986. Visit of Pres. Jaime Lusinchi of Venezuela.
1890 **676** 20 p. multicoloured . . . 15 15

1986. Visit of President of Brazil.
1891 **677** 20 p. multicoloured . . . 15 15

678 Michelini

679 Menorah and "50"

1986. 10th Death Anniv of Zelmar Michelini (senator).
1892 **678** 10 p. blue and red . . . 10 10

1986. 50th Anniv of B'nai B'rith in Uruguay.
1893 **679** 10 p. brown, gold & red . 10 10

680 Handshake across "GATT"

681 Dr. Raul Alfonsin

1986. General Agreement on Tariffs and Trade Assembly, Punta del Este.
1894 **680** 10 p. multicoloured . . . 10 10

1986. Visit of President of Argentina.
1895 **681** 20 p. orange, black & bl . 15 15

682 Fishes in Sea

1986. Quality Exports. Multicoloured.
1896 20 p. Type **682** 15 15
1897 20 p. Lambs 15 15

683 Flags and Dr. Blanco

684 Dr. Pertini

1986. Visit of Dr. Salvador Jorge Blanco, President of Dominican Republic.
1898 **683** 20 p. multicoloured . . . 15 15

1986. Visit of Dr. Sandro Pertini, President of Italy.
1899 **684** 20 p. yellow and green . 15 15

685 Douglas DC-10 and DC-3 Aircraft and Flags

1986. 40th Anniv of First Scheduled Spain–Uruguay Flight.
1900 **685** 20 p. multicoloured . . . 45 15

686 Statue of Sts. Philip and John and Montevideo Cathedral

1987. Hispanidad Day.
1901 **686** 10 p. red and black . . . 10 10

687 Emblem

688 Ruiz

1987. 50th Anniv (1986) of Juventus Catholic Cultural Organization.
1902 **687** 10 p. yellow, black and blue 10 10

1987. 10th Death Anniv (1986) of Hector Gutierrez Ruiz (Chamber of Deputies member).
1903 **688** 10 p. brown and red . . 10 10

689 Emblem

690 "Arrowhead" of Flying Doves

1987. International Science and Technology Symposium, Montevideo and Punta del Este (1986).
1904 **689** 20 p. multicoloured . . 15 15

1987. Visit of Pope John Paul II.
1905 **690** 50 p. orange and grey . 35 45

691 Dr. Arias and Emblem

692 "70" and Menorah

1987. Birth Centenary of Dr. Jose F. Arias (founder of Uruguay Trades University).
1906 **691** 10 p. multicoloured . . 10 10

1987. 70th Anniv of Uruguayan Jewish Community.
1907 **692** 10 p. blue, orange & blk 10 10

693 De Havilland Dragon Fly

1987. 50th Anniv (1986) of Pluna National Airline. Multicoloured.
1908 10 p. Type **693** 10 10
1909 20 p. Douglas DC-3 . . . . 15 10
1910 25 p. Vickers Viscount 810 . 15 15
1911 30 p. Boeing 707 . . . . . 20 15

694 Artigas Antarctic Base

1987.
1912 **694** 20 p. multicoloured . . 15 15

695 Sun, Symbolic House and "75"

1987. 75th Anniv of Uruguayan Mortgage Bank.
1913 **695** 26 p. multicoloured . . 20 15

696 Dairy Products

697 "Holy Family"

1987. Uruguayan Quality Exports. Multicoloured.
1914 51 p. Type **696** 35 20
1915 51 p. Map and cattle 35 20

1987. Christmas. Stained Glass Windows. Multicoloured.
1916 17 p. Type **697** 15 10
1917 66 p. "Angels" 45 55

698 Pres. Duarte

699 Airplane and Globe forming "60"

1988. Visit of Pres. Jose Napoleon Duarte of El Salvador.
1918 **698** 20 p. blue and yellow . . 15 15

1988. 60th Anniv (1987) of VARIG (airline).
1919 **699** 66 p. blue, yellow & blk . 45 50

700 Emblem and Globe

1988. International Peace Year (1986).
1920 **700** 10 p. multicoloured . . . 10 10

701 Flags and Beret

702 Farman "Shorthorn" within Airplane Wing

1988. 75th Anniv (1987) of Basque Immigration.
1921 **701** 66 p. multicoloured . . . 45 45

1988. 75th Anniv of Air Force.
1922 **702** 17 p. multicoloured . . . 20 10

703 Lantern and "75"

1988. 75th Anniv (1987) of UTE (hydro-electric dam programme).
1923 **703** 17 p. multicoloured . . . 15 10
1924 – 17 p. black, blue & grn . 15 10
1925 – 51 p. black and blue . . . 35 20
1926 – 51 p. black, blue & red . 35 20
1927 – 66 p. blue, black & yell . 45 25
DESIGNS: No. 1924, Baygorria Dam; 1925, Dr. Gabriel Terra Dam; 1926, Constitucion Dam; 1927, Map showing dam sites on River Negro.

704 Flag and Globe

1988. 75th Anniv (1986) of Postal Union of the Americas and Spain.
1928 **704** 66 p. multicoloured . . . 45 45

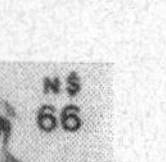
705 Menorah in "40"

1988. 40th Anniv of Israel.
1929 **705** 66 p. blue and black . . 45 45

706 Airmail Envelope and Postman

1988. "Post, Messenger of Peace".
1930 **706** 66 p. multicoloured . . . 45 45

707 Emblem on Map

1988. 60th Anniv of Inter-American Institute for the Child.
1931 **707** 30 p. lt green, grn & blk 20 15

708 Matos Rodriguez

1988. Gerardo H. Matos Rodriguez (composer) Commemoration.
1932 **708** 17 p. black and violet . . 15 10
1933 – 51 p. brown on lt brown 35 20
DESIGN: 51 p. Matos Rodriguez and score of "La Cumparsita".

709 Col. Pablo Banales (founder)

711 Citrus Fruits

710 Route Map and "Capitan Miranda"

1988. Centenary (1987) of Fire Service. Mult.
1934 17 p. Type **709** 15 10
1935 26 p. Fireman, 1900 . . . . 20 15
1936 34 p. Emblem (horiz) 20 15
1937 51 p. Merryweather fire engine, 1907 (horiz) 35 20
1938 66 p. 8-man hand pump, 1888 (horiz) 45 25
1939 100 p. Magirus mechanical ladder, 1921 (44 × 25 mm) . 70 40

1988. 1st World Voyage of "Capitan Miranda".
1940 **710** 30 p. multicoloured . . . 50 20

1988. Exports. Multicoloured.
1941 30 p. Type **711** 20 15
1942 45 p. Rice 35 20
1943 55 p. Shoes 40 20
1944 55 p. Clothes 40 20

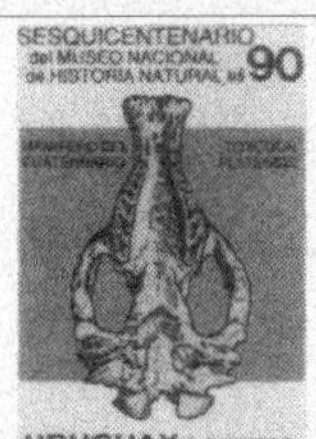

712 "Toxodon platensis" (mammal bone) 713 Bird posting Letter

1988. 150th Anniv of National Natural History Museum, Montevideo.
1945 – 30 p. brown, yell & blk . 50 20
1946 **712** 90 p. brown, blue & blk . 65 60
DESIGN: 30 p. "Usnea densirostra" (moss).

1988. Postal Officers' Day. Unissued stamp surch.
1947 **713** 30 p. on 10 p. + 5 p. yellow, black and blue 10 10

714 Abstract

1988. 150th Anniv (1986) of Battle of Carpinteria.
1948 **714** 30 p. multicoloured . . . 10 10

715 Virgin and Child **716** "Self-portrait" (Joaquin Torres Garcia)

1988. Christmas.
1949 **715** 115 p. multicoloured . . 55 55

1988. Uruguayan Painters. Multicoloured.
1950 115 p. Type **716** 50 50
1951 115 p. Poster for Pedro Figari exhibition, Montevideo . . 50 50
1952 115 p. "Squares and Rectangles LXXVIII" (Jose P. Costigliolo) 50 50
1953 115 p. "Manolita Pina, 1920" (Joaquin Torres Garcia) . . 50 50

717 "Santa Maria"

1989. Hispanidad Day.
1954 **717** 90 p. multicoloured . . . 40 40
1955 115 p. multicoloured . . 50 50

718 Emblem

1989. Cent of Armenian Organization Hnchakian.
1956 **718** 210 p. blue, yellow & red 40 35

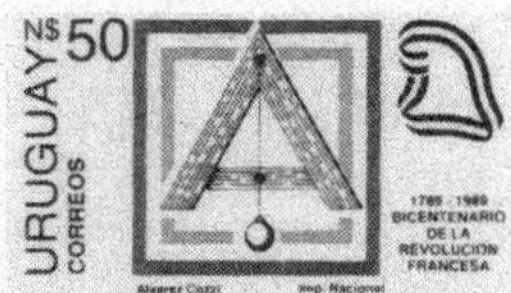

719 Plumb Line suspended on Frame

1989. Bicentenary of French Revolution. Each black, red and blue.
1957 50 p. Type **719** 10 10
1958 50 p. Tree of Liberty 10 10
1959 210 p. Eye in centre of sunburst 40 35
1960 210 p. "Liberty", "Equality", "Fraternity" around phrygian cap 40 35

720 Map

1989. "Use the Post Code". Each black and red.
1961 50 p. Type **720** 10 10
1962 210 p. Map showing numbered zones (vert) 40 35

721 Map, Cow, Factory and Baby **722** "Tiradentes"

1989. 3rd Pan-American Milk Congress.
1963 **721** 170 p. dp blue & blue . 30 25

1989. Birth Bicentenary of Joaquin Jose da Silver Xavier.
1964 **722** 170 p. multicoloured . . 30 25

723 Emblem and Flag

1989. Interparliamentary Union Centenary Conference, London.
1965 **723** 210 p. red, blue & black 40 35

724 F.A.O. Emblem, Map and Fruit Slices

1989. 8th Intergovernmental Group on Citrus Fruits Meeting.
1966 **724** 180 p. multicoloured . . 30 25

725 Flower, Hand and Emblem

1989. U.N. Decade for Disabled People. Mult.
1967 50 p. Type **725** 10 10
1968 210 p. Disabled people and emblem 40 35

726 Nacurutu Artefact **727** Virgin of the Thirty Three

1989. America. Pre-Columbian Culture.
1969 **726** 60 p. multicoloured . . . 10 10
1970 180 p. multicoloured . . 30 25

1989. Christmas. Multicoloured.
1971 70 p. Type **727** 10 10
1972 210 p. "Adoration of the Animals" (Barradas) (horiz) 15 15

728 Old and Modern Buildings

1989. Bicentenary of Pando.
1973 **728** 60 p. multicoloured . . . 10 10

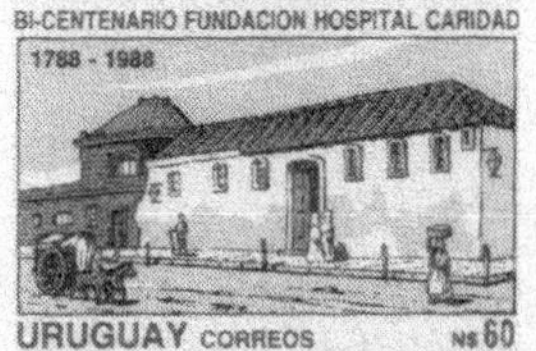

729 Hospital Building

1990. Bicentenary of Charity Hospital.
1974 **729** 60 p. flesh, black & brown 10 10

730 Map and Arms of Soriano **731** Luisa Luisi

1990. Departments. Multicoloured.
1975 70 p. Type **730** 10 10
1976 70 p. Florida (vert) 10 10
1977 90 p. San Jose (vert) 10 10
1978 90 p. Canelones 10 10
1979 90 p. Lavalleja (vert) 10 10
1980 90 p. Rivera 10 10

1990. Writers. Multicoloured.
1981 60 p. Type **731** 10 10
1982 60 p. Javier de Viana 10 10
1983 75 p. J. Zorilla de San Martin 10 10
1984 75 p. Dekmira Agustini . . . 10 10
1985 170 p. Julio Casal 45 45
1986 170 p. Alfonsina Storni . . . 45 45
1987 210 p. Juana de Ibarbourou . . 55 55
1988 210 p. Carlos Roxlo 55 55

732 Mercedes Church **733** Ear of Wheat and Tractor

1990. Bicentenary of Mercedes.
1989 **732** 70 p. multicoloured . . . 10 10

1990. 10th Anniv of International Agricultural Fund.
1990 **733** 210 p. multicoloured . . 55 55

734 Glass and Smashed Car

1990. Road Safety. Multicoloured.
1991 70 p. Type **734** 70 70
1992 70 p. Traffic waiting at red light 70 70
1993 70 p. Road signs 70 70
1994 70 p. Children crossing road at green light 70 70

735 Sculpture of Artigas **736** Woman

1990. Artigas Day.
1995 **735** 60 p. blue and red . . . 10 10

1990. International Women's Day.
1996 **736** 70 p. multicoloured . . . 10 10

737 Gonzalo Ramirez **738** Microphone and Radio Mast

1990. Centenary of 1st International Juridical Congress, Montevideo.
1997 **737** 60 p. black, yell & mve . 55 55
1998 – 60 p. black, blue & mve . 55 55
1999 – 60 p. multicoloured . . . 55 55
2000 – 60 p. multicoloured . . . 55 55
DESIGNS: No. 1998, Ildefonso Garcia; 1999, Flags and left half of 50th anniversary memorial; 2000, Flags and right half of memorial.

1990. The Media. Multicoloured.
2001 70 p. Type **738** 70 70
2002 70 p. Newpaper vendor . . . 70 70
2003 70 p. Television screen, camera and aerial 70 70
2004 70 p. Books and type 70 70

739 Burning Trees **741** "Nativity" (Juan B. Maino)

740 American Deer

1990. Fire Prevention.
2005 **739** 70 p. black, yell & red . 70 70

1990. America. The Natural World. Mult.
2006 120 p. Type **740** 10 10
2007 360 p. "Peltophorum dubium" (vert) 85 85

1990. Christmas.
2008 **741** 170 p. multicoloured . . 40 40
2009 830 p. multicoloured . . 2·00 2·00

742 Carlos Federico Saez

1990. Artists. Multicoloured.
2010 90 p. Type **742** 10 10
2011 90 p. Pedro Blanes Viale . . 10 10
2012 210 p. Edmundo Prati . . . 55 55
2013 210 p. Jose L. Zorrilla de San Martin 55 55

743 Mechanical Digger

1991. 75th Anniv of Army Engineers Division.
2014 **743** 170 p. multicoloured . . 40 40

744 Drum and Masks

1991. Carnival.
2015 **744** 170 p. multicoloured . . 40 40

745 Campaign Emblem

1991. Campaign against Aids.
2016 **745** 170 p. multicoloured . . 40 40
2017 830 p. multicoloured . . 2·00 2·00

746 Anniversary Emblem

1991. Centenary of Organization of American States.
2018 **746** 830 p. yellow, blue & blk 2·00 2·00

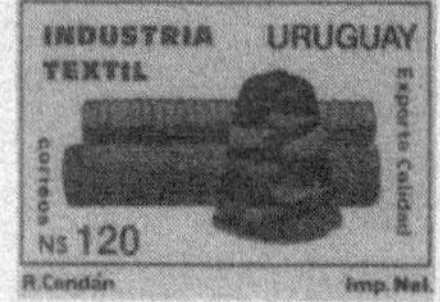

747 Textiles

1991. Uruguayan Quality Exports. Multicoloured.
2019 120 p. Type **747** 10 10
2020 120 p. Clothes (vert) 10 10
2021 400 p. Semi-precious stones and granite 55 60

748 Flint Axe and Stone Monument

1991. Education. Multicoloured.
2022 120 p. Type **748** 10 10
2023 120 p. Wheel and pyramids . 10 10
2024 330 p. Printing press and diagram of planetary orbits 45 45
2025 330 p. Space probe and computer diagram 45 45

749 Sword piercing Crab

1991. Anti-Cancer Day.
2026 **749** 360 p. red and black . . 45 45

750 College Arms 751 College Building

1991. Centenary of Holy Family College.
2027 **750** 360 p. multicoloured . . 45 45

1991. Centenary of Immaculate Heart of Mary College.
2028 **751** 1370 p. multicoloured . 1·60 1·60

752 Emblem

1991. 7th Pan-American Maccabiah Games.
2029 **752** 1490 p. multicoloured . 1·75 1·75

753 World Map and Dornier Wal Flying Boat "Plus Ultra"

1991. "Espamer '91" Spain–Latin America Stamp Exhibition, Buenos Aires.
2030 **753** 1510 p. multicoloured . 2·00 2·00

754 "Oath of the Constitution" (P. Blanes Viale)

1991. 1830 Constitution.
2031 **754** 360 p. multicoloured . . 45 45

755 Gateway, Sacramento 756 "William Tell" (statue) and Flags

1991.
2032 **755** 360 p. brown & yellow . 45 45
2033 – 540 p. grey and blue . . 65 65
2034 **755** 600 p. brown, yell & blk 55 55
2035 – 825 p. grey, blue & blk . 75 75
2036 – 1510 p. brown & green . 2·00 2·00
2037 – 2500 p. brn, grn & blk . 2·00 2·00
DESIGNS: 540, 825 p. First locomotive, 1869; 1510, 2500 p. Horse-drawn tram.
For 800 p. as Type **755** see No. 2103.

1991. 700th Anniv of Swiss Confederation.
2038 **756** 1510 p. multicoloured . 2·50 2·50

757 Yacht 758 Emblem

1991. Whitbread Regatta.
2040 **757** 1510 p. multicoloured . . 1·75 1·75

1991. 50th Anniv of Uruguayan Society of Actors.
2041 **758** 450 p. black and red . . 50 50

759 Camera and Photograph

1991. 150th Anniv of First Photograph in Rio de la Plata.
2042 **759** 1370 p. multicoloured . . 1·50 1·50

760 Anniversary Emblem

1991. 25th Anniv of CREA (livestock organization).
2043 **760** 450 p. multicoloured . . 50 50

761 Margarita Xirgu

1991. 22nd Death Anniv of Margarita Xirgu (actress).
2044 **761** 360 p. brown, light brown and yellow 40 40

762 "General Rivera" (gunboat)

1991. Centre for Study of Naval and Maritime History. Multicoloured.
2045 450 p. Type **762** 45 45
2046 450 p. "Salto" (coastguard patrol boat) 45 45
2047 1570 p. "Uruguay" (cruiser) . 1·60 1·60
2048 1570 p. "Pte. Oribe" (tanker) 1·60 1·60

763 "Rio de la Plata, 1602" (woodcut)

1991. America. Voyages of Discovery.
2049 **763** 450 p. brown and yellow . 50 50
2050 – 1740 p. green and brown 1·90 1·90
DESIGN—HORIZ: 1740 p. Amerigo Vespucci.

764 "The Tree is the Fountain of Life"

1991. World Food Day.
2051 **764** 1740 p. multicoloured . . 1·75 1·75

765 "The Table" (Zoma Baitler)

1991.
2052 **765** 360 p. multicoloured . . 40 40

766 Gladiator, 1902

1991. Old Cars. Multicoloured.
2053 360 p. Type **766** 40 40
2054 1370 p. E.M.F., 1909 . . . . 1·50 1·50
2055 1490 p. Renault, 1912 . . . 1·50 1·50
2056 1510 p. Clement-Bayard, 1903 (vert) . . . . 1·75 1·75

767 Emblem 768 Club Badge and Trophy

1991. 60th General Assembly of Interpol, Punta del Este.
2057 **767** 1740 p. multicoloured . . 1·75 1·75

1991. National Football Club, Winners of World Cup Football Cup, 1988, and the Toyota Cup. Multicoloured.
2058 450 p. Type **768** 50 50
2059 450 p. Trophies on football pitch (horiz) 50 50

769 School and Pupils

1991. Centenary of Maria Auxiliadora Institute.
2060 **769** 450 p. blue, black & red 50 50

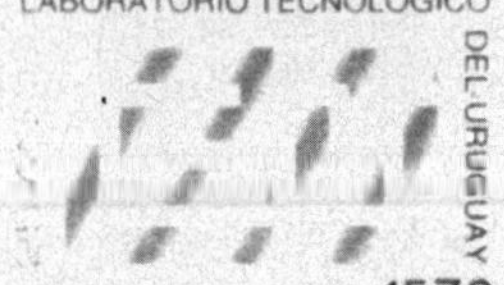

770 "LATU"

1991. 25th Anniv of Uruguay Technological Laboratory.
2061 **770** 1570 p. blue & deep blue 1·50 1·50

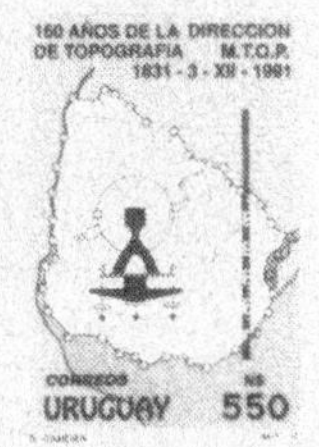

771 Emblem and Couple **772** Theodolite and Measuring Rod on Map of Uruguay

1991. World AIDS Day.
2062 **771** 550 p. black, yellow & bl 55 55
2063 2040 p. black, lilac & grn 2·00 2·00

1991. 160th Anniv of Topographic Survey.
2064 **772** 550 p. multicoloured . . 55 55

773 Angel

1991. Christmas. Multicoloured.
2065 550 p. Type **773** 55 55
2066 2040 p. "Adoration of the Angels" . . . . 1·90 1·90

774 Anibal Troilo

1992. Musicians.
2067 **774** 450 p. black, mauve & bl 40 40
2068 – 450 p. black, orge & red . 40 40
2069 – 450 p. black, light green and green 40 40
2070 – 450 p. black, blue & mve 40 40
DESIGNS: No. 2068, Francisco Canaro; 2069, Pintin Castellanos; 2070, Juan de Dios Filiberto.

775 Worker and Factory Building

1992. Quality Exports.
2071 **775** 120 p. multicoloured . . 15 15

776 Pres. Aylwin **777** Trophy

1992. Visit of President Patricio Aylwin of Chile.
2072 **776** 550 p. multicoloured . . 50 50

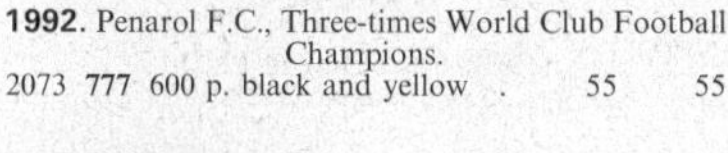

1992. Penarol F.C., Three-times World Club Football Champions.
2073 **777** 600 p. black and yellow . 55 55

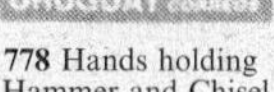

778 Hands holding Hammer and Chisel **779** No Smoking Emblem

1992. 120th Anniv of La Paz.
2075 **778** 550 p. multicoloured . . 50 50

1992. World No Smoking Day.
2076 **779** 2500 p. red, black & brn 2·00 2·00

780 Heart and Emblems

1992. World Health Day. "Health in Rhythm with the Heart".
2077 **780** 2500 p. ultramarine, blue and red . . . . 2·10 2·10

781 Map of South America and Food Products

1992. Mercosur (South American economic organization).
2078 **781** 2500 p. multicoloured . 2·10 2·10

782 Stamp

1992. "Olymphilex 92" International Olympic Stamps Exhibition, Barcelona.
2079 **782** 2900 p. multicoloured . 2·25 2·25

783 Emblems

1992. 22nd Latin American–Caribbean Regional Conference of Food and Agricultural Organization.
2080 **783** 2500 p. multicoloured . 1·75 1·75

784 Children with Basket of Food

1992. International Nutrition Conference, Rome.
2081 **784** 2900 p. multicoloured . 2·10 2·10

785 Vallejo

1992. Birth Centenary of Cesar Vallejo (painter and poet).
2082 **785** 2500 p. brown & lt brown 1·75 1·75

786 Monument and Route Map **787** Ruins of Sacramento and Lighthouse

1992. Centenary of Christopher Columbus Monument, Durazno.
2083 **786** 700 p. black, blue & grn . 50 50

1992. 500th Anniv of Discovery of America by Columbus.
2084 **787** 700 p. multicoloured . . 50 50

788 Caravel **789** Emblem

1992. America. 500th Anniv of Discovery of America by Columbus. Multicoloured.
2085 700 p. Type **788** 50 50
2086 2900 p. Globe showing Americas and old map (horiz) 2·10 2·10

1992. Centenary of Christopher Columbus Philanthropic Society.
2087 **789** 700 p. black, mauve and magenta 50 50

790 Emblem

1992. 500th Anniv of Presence of Jews in America.
2088 **790** 2900 p. multicoloured . . 2·10 2·10

791 Arms

1992. 50th Anniv of Jose Pedro Varela Teachers' College.
2089 **791** 700 p. multicoloured . . 50 50

792 Cambadu Building **793** Emblem

1992. Centenary of Chamber of Wholesale and Retail Traders.
2090 **792** 700 p. grey, black & red . 50 50

1992. 50th Anniv of Lebanon Club of Uruguay.
2091 **793** 2900 p. multicoloured . . 2·10 2·10

794 Nativity **796** Immigrant

1992. Christmas. Multicoloured.
2092 800 p. Type **794** 55 55
2093 3200 p. Star . . . . 2·10 2·10

1992. 22nd Latin American and Carribean Lions Clubs Forum.
2094 **795** 2700 p. multicoloured . . 1·75 1·75

1992. Immigrants Day.
2095 **796** 800 p. green and black . 55 55

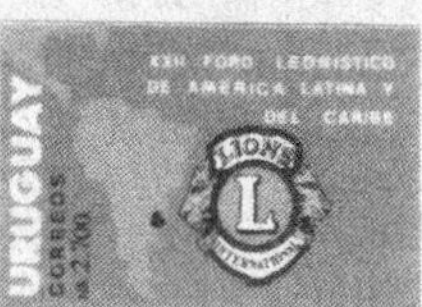

795 Map and Emblem

797 Oribe **799** Anniversary Emblem

798 Anniversary Emblem

1992. Birth Bicentenary of Manuel Oribe (Liberation hero). Multicoloured.
2096 800 p. Type **797** 55 55
2097 800 p. Oribe (founder) and Eastern University (horiz) . 55 55

1992. 90th Anniv of Pan-American Health Organization.
2098 **798** 3200 p. multicoloured . . 2·10 2·10

1992. 50th Anniv of Jose H. Molaguero S.A.
2099 **799** 800 p. brown and stone . 55 55

800 Satellite and Map

1992. 70th Anniv of ANDEBU (association of broadcasting stations).
2100 **800** 2700 p. multicoloured . . 1·75 1·75

801 Emblem and Shanty Town

1992. 30th Anniv of Caritas Uruguaya.
2101 **801** 3200 p. multicoloured . . 2·00 2·00

802 Gonzalez Pecotche (founder) and Emblem

1992. 60th Anniv of Logosofia.
2102 **802** 800 p. yellow and blue . 55 55

1993. Size 35 × 24 mm.
2103 **755** 800 p. olive and green . 30 15

Currency Reform
1 (new) peso = 1000 (old) pesos

803 Wilson Ferreira Aldunate **804** Post Car

1993.
2104 **803** 80 c. red, black and grey 30 15

1993.
2105 **804** 1 p. blue and yellow 40 20

805 Graph and Personal Computer

1993. Centenary of Economic Sciences and Accountancy College.
2106 **805** 1 p. multicoloured 40 20

807 Magirus Deutz Fire Engine, 1958 **808** Earth

1993. 50th Anniv of National Fire Service.
2108 **807** 1 p. multicoloured 40 20

1993. 15th Congress of Postal Union of the Americas, Spain and Portugal.
2109 **808** 3 p. 50 multicoloured 1·25 60

809 Schooner and Pedro Campbell (first Navy General)

1993. 175th Anniv (1992) of Uruguayan Navy.
2110 **809** 1 p. multicoloured 20 10

810 Emblem

1993. 25th Anniv of International University Circles.
2111 **810** 1 p. multicoloured 20 10

811 Hupmobile, 1910

1993. 75th Anniv of Uruguay Automobile Club.
2112 **811** 3 p. 50 multicoloured 70 35

813 Bird **814** Armadillo

1993. No value expressed.
2114 **813** (1 p. 20) blue and azure 25 15
2115 (1 p. 40) emerald and green 30 15
2147 (1 p. 60) red and pink 35 20
2148 (1 p. 80) brown and pink 30 15
2186 (2 p.) grey 35 20
2207 (2 p. 30) violet 35 20
These were sold at the current inland letter rate.

1993.
2116 **814** 1 p. 20 brown and green 25 15

815 Village and Soldier

1993. Uruguayan Battalion of Peace-keeping Force in Cambodia.
2117 **815** 1 p. multicoloured 20 10

816 Dish Aerials and Studio

1993. 30th Anniv of National Television Channel 5.
2118 **816** 1 p. 20 multicoloured 25 15

817 "The Tree of Life" (detail, Pablo Serrano)

1993. 60th Anniv of Anda.
2119 **817** 1 p. 20 multicoloured 25 15

818 Arms and Officers

1993. 50th Anniv of Juan Carlos Gomez Folle National Police School.
2120 **818** 1 p. 20 multicoloured 25 15

819 Graphics

1993. 75th Anniv of "Diario El Pais" (newspaper).
2121 **819** 1 p. 20 multicoloured 25 15

820 Broad-nosed Caiman

1993. America. Endangered Animals. Multicoloured.
2122 1 p. 20 Type **820** 25 15
2123 3 p. 50 Burrowing owl (vert) 70 35

821 Power Lines supplying Illuminated Building

1993. 14th Latin-American Conference on Rural Electrification.
2124 **821** 3 p. 50 multicoloured 70 35

822 Emblem **823** Red-legged Seriema

1993. 150th Anniv of B'nai B'rith (Jewish cultural and social organization).
2125 **822** 3 p. 70 multicoloured 75 40

1993. Natural World.
2126 **823** 20 c. brown and pink 10 10
2127 – 30 c. yellow and violet 10 10
2128 – 50 c. brown and pink 10 10
DESIGNS—VERT: 30 c. Saffron-cowled blackbird. HORIZ: 50 c. Two-toed anteater.

825 Crucifix, Mother Francisca and Nuns with Sick People **826** Amerindian

1993. Beatification of Mother Francisca Rubatto.
2130 **825** 1 p. 20 multicoloured 25 15

1993. International Year of Indigenous Peoples.
2131 **826** 3 p. 50 multicoloured 70 35

827 Emblem on Map

1993. 75th Anniv of Montevideo Rotary Club.
2132 **827** 3 p. 50 blue and gold 70 35

829 Phoenician Cargo Ship (carving)

1993. 50th Anniv of Independence of Lebanon.
2134 **829** 3 p. 70 brown, deep brown and green 75 40

830 Haedo **831** Ribbon

1993. Eduardo Victor Haedo.
2135 **830** 1 p. 20 multicoloured 25 15

1993. Anti-AIDS Campaign.
2136 **831** 1 p. 40 multicoloured 30 15

832 Adoration of the Wise Men **833** Adult with Chick and Eggs

1993. Christmas. Multicoloured.
2137 1 p. 40 Type **832** 30 15
2138 4 p. Adoration of the Shepherds 80 40

1993. The Greater Rhea. Multicoloured.
2139 20 c. Type **833** 10 10
2140 20 c. Adults sitting and standing 10 10
2141 50 c. Close-up of head 10 10
2142 50 c. Adults feeding 10 10

834 Child's view of life (Alejandro Cuende) **835** Emblem

1994. Children's Rights Day.
2143 **834** 1 p. 40 multicoloured 30 15

1994. National Postal Directorate.
2144 **835** 1 p. 40 blue and yellow 30 15

836 Torch Carrier

1994. 5th World Sports Congress, Punta del Este.
2145 **836** 4 p. multicoloured 80 40

837 Frigate

1994. 17th Inter-American Naval Conference.
2146 **837** 3 p. 70 multicoloured 75 40

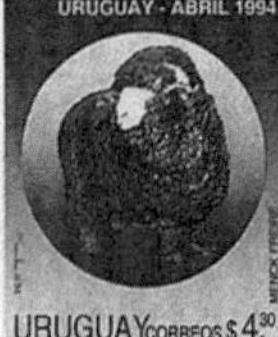

838 Emblem **839** Sheep

1994. 7th Iberian–American Youth Organization Conference.
2149 **838** 3 p. 90 multicoloured 70 35

1994. 4th International Merino Sheep Conference.
2150 **839** 4 p. 30 multicoloured 75 40

840 Anniversary Emblem **844** Dove flying from Ballot Box

843 Estable

1994. 75th Anniv of I.L.O.
2151 **840** 4 p. 30 multicoloured 75 40

1994. Birth Centenary of Clemente Estable (biologist).
2154 **843** 1 p. 60 green and black 30 15

1994. 75th Anniv of Electoral Court.
2155 **844** 1 p. 60 multicoloured 30 15

845 Hand pulling Worm from Dog's Mouth

1994. National Commission on Eradication of Tapeworms.
2156 **845** 1 p. 60 multicoloured . . 30 15

847 First Co-operative Headquarters, Rochdale, England

1994. 150th Anniv of Co-operative Movement.
2158 **847** 4 p. 30 multicoloured . . 75 40

848 National Flags on Plugs

1994. 30th Anniv of Commission for Regional Integration of Electricity.
2159 **848** 1 p. 60 multicoloured . . 30 15

849 Astronaut standing on Moon

1994. 25th Anniv of First Manned Moon Landing.
2160 **849** 3 p. multicoloured . . . 55 30

850 Family

1994. International Year of the Family.
2161 **850** 4 p. 80 multicoloured . . 85 45

851 Fr. Pierre (founder)

854 Swimmer

856 Saravia

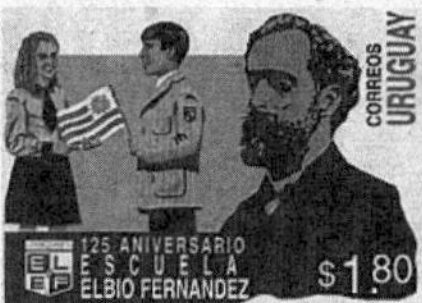
855 Fernandez and Pupils with National Flag

852 Pillar-box

1994. 45th Anniv of Emmaus Movement (social welfare organization).
2162 **851** 4 p. 80 multicoloured . . 85 45

1994. 150th Anniv of Neighbourhood Pillar-boxes.
2163 **852** 50 c. yellow and green . 10 10
2164 1 p. yellow and brown . 15 10
2165 1 p. 80 yellow and blue . 30 15
2166 2 p. 60 yellow and brown 40 20
2168 7 p. 50 yellow and violet 1·10 55

853 "The Man of Lugano"

1994. 50th Death Anniv of Goffredo Sommavilla (painter).
2169 **853** 4 p. 80 multicoloured . . 85 45

1994. Centenary of International Olympic Committee.
2170 **854** 4 p. 80 multicoloured . 85 45

1994. 125th Anniv of Elbio Fernandez School.
2171 **855** 1 p. 80 multicoloured . 30 15

1994. 90th Death Anniv of Gen. Aparicio Saravia.
2172 **856** 1 p. 80 blue, turquoise and deep blue 30 15

857 Statuette

858 Town Plan

1994. 65th Anniv of General Association of Uruguayan Writers.
2173 **857** 1 p. 80 multicoloured . 30 15

1994. 6th Latin American Town Planning Congress.
2174 **858** 4 p. 80 multicoloured . 85 45

860 Mail Coach

1994. America. Postal Transport. Multicoloured.
2176 1 p. 80 Type **860** 30 15
2177 4 p. 80 "Eolo" (paddle-steamer) 85 45

861 Plan

1994. 1st International Seminar on Provision of Roads in Uruguay, Punte del Este.
2178 **861** 2 p. multicoloured . . . 35 20

863 Computer Terminal and Reporter

1994. 50th Anniv of Uruguay Press Association.
2180 **863** 2 p. multicoloured . . . 35 20

864 Statuette

1994. 50th Anniv of Uruguay Marketing Association.
2181 **864** 2 p. multicoloured . . . 35 20

866 Dove over Latin America

1994. 25th Anniv of Latin American Movement "Long Live the People".
2183 **866** 4 p. 30 multicoloured . . 75 40

867 Draw Balls

1994. 55th Anniv of Lottery.
2184 **867** 2 p. multicoloured . . . 35 20

868 Footballers

869 Tree

1994. 85th Anniv of Young Men's Christian Association.
2185 **868** 2 p. multicoloured . . . 35 20

1994. Christmas. Multicoloured.
2187 2 p. Type **869** 35 20
2188 5 p. 50 Star over village . . . 1·00 50

870 Emblem and Venue

1994. 4th Assembly of Latin American and Caribbean Organization of Higher Fiscal Entities, Montevideo.
2189 **870** 5 p. 50 multicoloured . . 1·00 50

871 Cross and Crescent on Globe

1994. 75th Anniv of International Federation of Red Cross and Red Crescent Societies.
2190 **871** 5 p. multicoloured . . . 90 45

872 Chuy Post Office

1995.
2191 **872** 20 c. green 10 10
2195 10 p. brown . . . . . . 1·50 75

873 CANT 18 Flying Boat

1995. 70th Anniv of Naval Aviation.
2198 **873** 2 p. multicoloured . . . 30 15

874 Swimming Park

1995. 20th Anniv of World Tourism Organization. Multicoloured.
2199 5 p. Type **874** 75 40
2200 5 p. Deer and greater rhea . 75 40
2201 5 p. Ranch 75 40
2202 5 p. Beach resort 75 40

875 Lifeboat

1995. 17th World Lifeguards' Conference.
2203 **875** 5 p. multicoloured . . . 75 40

876 Globe and Emblem forming "90"

1995. 90th Anniv of Rotary International.
2204 **876** 5 p. ultramarine, blue and gold 75 40

877 Anniversary Emblem and Airplane

1995. 50th Anniv of International Civil Aviation Organization.
2205 **877** 5 p. ultramarine, orange and blue 75 40

878 Mascagni and Set from "Cavalleria Rusticana" (opera)

1995. 50th Death Anniv of Piero Mascagni (composer).
2206 **878** 5 p. multicoloured . . . 75 40

879 Cimarron

1995.
2208 **879** 2 p. 30 multicoloured . 35 20

881 Paysandu Players

882 Orange incorporating Globe

1995. America Cup Football Championship, Uruguay. Multicoloured.
2210 2 p. 30 Type **881** 35 20
2211 2 p. 30 Rivera players . . . 35 20
2212 2 p. 30 Ball in net 35 20
2213 2 p. 30 Montevideo players . 35 20
2214 2 p. 30 Maldonado players . 35 20
Nos. 2210/14 were issued together, se-tenant, forming a composite design of a match.

1995. 50th Anniv of F.A.O.
2215 **882** 5 p. 50 multicoloured . 80 40

883 U.N. Soldier and Detail of World Map

1995. Participation in United Nations Peace-keeping Forces.
2216 **883** 2 p. 30 multicoloured . 35 20

884 Italian National Colours on Map of Italy

1995. Visit of President Scalfaro of Italy.
2217 **884** 5 p. 50 multicoloured . 80 40

885 People walking Hand in Hand towards Gateway

887 Postal Symbol

1995. Latin-American Integration Day.
2218 **885** 5 p. multicoloured . . . 75 40

1995. No Value Expressed.
2220 **887** (2 p. 60) yellow and green 40 20
2222 (3 p. 20) pink and red 45 25
2223 (3 p. 50) brown & purple 50 25

888 Carlos Gardel (entertainer)

1995.
2226 **888** 5 p. 50 multicoloured . 80 40

889 "Notocactus roseinflorus"

890 Varela

1995. Flowers. Multicoloured.
2227 3 p. Type **889** 45 25
2228 3 p. "Verbena chamaedryfolia" 45 25
2229 3 p. "Bauhinia candicans" . . 45 25
2230 3 p. "Tillandsia aeranthos" . 45 25
2231 3 p. "Eichhornia crassipes" . 45 25

1995. 150th Birth Anniv of Jose Verela (educationalist).
2232 **890** 2 p. 60 multicoloured . 40 20

891 Monument

892 "Dicksonia sellowiana"

1995. Holocaust Monument, Pueblo Judio.
2233 **891** 6 p. multicoloured . . . 90 45

1995. America. Environmental Protection. Multicoloured.
2234 3 p. Type **892** 45 25
2235 6 p. Maned wolf (horiz) . . 90 45

894 Anniversary Emblem over Globe

1995. 50th Anniv of U.N.O.
2237 **894** 6 p. multicoloured . . 90 45

895 Beyer & Peacock, 1876

1995. Steam Railway Locomotives. Multicoloured.
2238 3 p. Type **895** 45 25
2239 3 p. Criollo, 1895 . . . . . 45 25
2240 3 p. Beyer & Peacock, 1910 . 45 25

896 Brigantine (privateer of Artigas)

1995. 178th Anniv of Naval Service. Multicoloured.
2241 3 p. Type **896** 45 25
2242 3 p. "Montevideo" (training frigate) 45 25
2243 3 p. "Pte. Rivera" (tanker) . 45 25

897 Crib

900 Rosa Luna (dancer)

898 Lumiere Brothers and Film Reel

1995. Christmas. Multicoloured.
2244 2 p. 90 Type **897** 45 25
2245 6 p. 50 Beam of light and rose window 95 50

1995. Centenary of Motion Pictures.
2246 **898** 6 p. violet, deep mauve and mauve 90 45

1996. Carnival. Multicoloured.
2248 2 p. 90 Type **900** 45 25
2249 2 p. 90 Santiago Luz (clarinettist) 45 25
2250 2 p. 90 Pepino (clown) . . . 45 25

901 Cantegril Country Club

1996. Golf. Multicoloured.
2251 2 p. 90 Type **901** 45 25
2252 2 p. 90 Cerro Golf Club . . 45 25
2253 2 p. 90 Fay Crocker and trophy 45 25
2254 2 p. 90 Lago Golf Club . . 45 25
2255 2 p. 90 Uruguay Golf Club . 45 25

902 Solis Theatre

1996. Montevideo, Latin American Cultural Capital.
2256 **902** 2 p. 90 multicoloured . . 45 25

904 Zitarrosa

1996. 60th Birth Anniv of Alfredo Zitarrosa (musician).
2258 **904** 3 p. multicoloured . . . 45 25

906 Skeletons

1996. Archaeological Congress.
2260 **906** 3 p. 20 multicoloured . . 45 25

907 "Glyptodon claripes"

1996. Prehistoric Animals. Multicoloured.
2261 3 p. 20 Type **907** 45 25
2262 3 p. 20 "Macrauchenia patachonica" 45 25
2263 3 p. 20 "Toxodon platensis" . 45 25
2264 3 p. 20 "Glossotherium robostum" 45 25
2265 3 p. 20 "Titanosaurus" . . . 45 25

908 People-Houses

1996. Population and Housing Censuses.
2266 **908** 3 p. 20 multicoloured . . 45 25

909 Dion-Buton Double-deck Bus, 1912

1996. Old Vehicles. Multicoloured.
2267 3 p. 20 Type **909** 45 25
2268 3 p. 20 Ford Model "A" patrol car, 1928 . . . . 45 25
2269 3 p. 20 Raleigh bicycle, 1940 . 45 25
2270 3 p. 20 Magirus fire-engine, 1976 . . . . 45 25
2271 3 p. 20 Hotchkiss ambulance, 1917 . . . . 45 25

911 Children and Globe holding Hands (Soraya Campanella)

1996. "Care for Our Planet: Everyone's Mission".
2273 **911** 3 p. 20 multicoloured . . 45 25

912 New Postal Administration Emblem

914 "Nuestra Senora de la Encina" (caravel), 1726

1996. Postal Emblems.
2274 **912** 7 p. yellow and blue . . 1·00 50

1996. Sailing Ships. Multicoloured.
2276 3 p. 20 Type **914** 45 25
2277 3 p. 20 "San Francisco" (ship of the line), 1729 . . . 45 25
2278 3 p. 20 Etienne Moreau's fleet, 1720 . . . . 45 25
2279 3 p. 20 "Atrevida" (corvette), 1789–94 . . . . 45 25
2280 3 p. 20 "Nuestra Senora de la Luz" (brig), 1752 . . . . 45 25

915 "Flores Landscape" (Carmelo de Arzadun)

1996.
2281 **915** 3 p. 50 multicoloured . 50 25

916 Old Jewish Quarter

1996. 80th Anniv of Jewish Community in Uruguay.
2282 **916** 7 p. 50 red, yellow and purple . . . . 1·10 55

917 Dr. Victor Bertullo (veterinary researcher)

1996. Scientists. Multicoloured.
2283 3 p. 50 Type **917** 50 25
2284 3 p. 50 Tomas Beno Hirschfeld (chemical engineer) (horiz) 50 25
2285 3 p. 50 Enrique Legrand (astronomer and physicist) 50 25
2286 3 p. 50 Dr. Miguel C. Rubino (veterinary researcher) (horiz) 50 25

919 Aristotle (philosopher)

1996. Scientists. Multicoloured.
2288 7 p. 50 Type **919** . . . . . . 1·10 55
2289 7 p. 50 Sir Isaac Newton (mathematician) . . . . . 1·10 55
2290 7 p. 50 Albert Einstein (physicist) . . . . 1·10 55

920 500 Peso Note

1996. Centenary of Republica Oriental Bank. Multicoloured.
2291 3 p. 50 Type **920** 50 25
2292 3 p. 50 Ten peso note . . . 50 25

921 Narbona Chapel

1996. National Heritage Day. Multicoloured.
2293 3 p. 50 Type **921** 50 25
2294 3 p. 50 Map of Gorriti Island showing sites of Spanish fortifications 50 25

922 "125" and Emblem

1996. 125th Anniv of Uruguay Rural Association.
2295 **922** 3 p. 50 multicoloured . 50 25

924 Angel Rodriguez (South American boxing champion, 1917)

1996. Sports Personalities. Multicoloured.
2297 3 p. 50 Type **924** 50 25
2298 3 p. 50 Leandro Noli (winner of first Uruguayan cycling race, 1939) 50 25
2299 3 p. 50 Eduardo G. Risso (Olympic rowing medallist, 1948) 50 25
2300 3 p. 50 Estrella Puente (South American javelin champion, 1949) 50 25
2301 3 p. 50 Oscar Moglia (Olympic basketball medallist, 1956) . 50 25

925 Gaucho

1996. America. Traditional Costumes. Multicoloured.
2302 3 p. 50 Type **925** 50 25
2303 3 p. 50 Countrywoman . . . 50 25

927 Satellite

1996. 3rd Space Conference of the Americas.
2305 **927** 3 p. 50 multicoloured . 50 25

928 "Football Match" (Julio Suarez)

1996. Centenary of Comics. Museum of Humour and Anecdotes, Minas.
2306 **928** 4 p. multicoloured . . . 60 30

HAVE YOU READ THE NOTES AT THE BEGINNING OF THIS CATALOGUE?
These often provide the answers to the enquiries we receive.

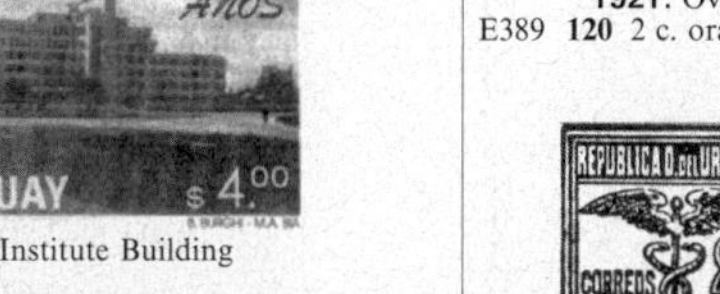
929 Institute Building

1996. Centenary of Hygiene Institute.
2307 **929** 4 p. multicoloured . . 60 30

930 De Azara

1996. 175th Death Anniv of Felix de Azara (naturalist).
2308 **930** 4 p. multicoloured . . 60 30

931 Angels blowing Trumpets over Globe

1996. Centenary of Seventh Day Adventist Church in Uruguay.
2309 **931** 3 p. 50 multicoloured . 50 25

EXPRESS MAIL STAMPS

1921. Overprinted **MENSAJERIAS**.
E389 **120** 2 c. orange 50 20

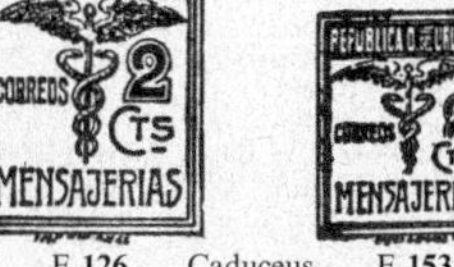
E 126 Caduceus E 153

1923.
E415 E **126** 2 c. red 30 10
E416 2 c. blue 30 10

1928.
E591 E **153** 2 c. black on green . 15 10
E635a 2 c. green 15 10
E636 2 c. blue 15 10
E637 2 c. pink 15 10
E638 2 c. brown 10 10

1957. Surch **$0.05.**
E1065 E **153** 5 c. on 2 c. brown . . 15 10

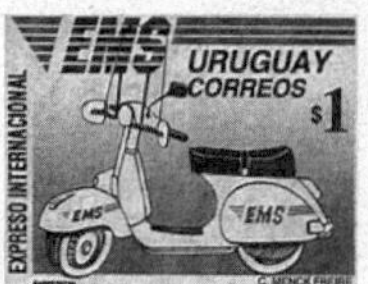
E 859 Motor Scooter

E 913

1994. International Service.
E2170 E **859** 1 p. orange and blue . 20 15

1996.
E2275 E **913** 8 p. yellow and blue . 1·25 65

LATE FEE STAMPS

L 175

1936.
L774 L **175** 3 c. green 10 10
L775 5 c. violet 15 10
L776 6 c. green 15 10
L777 7 c. brown 20 10
L778 8 c. red 40 25
L779 12 c. blue 60 50

NEWSPAPER STAMPS

1922. Optd **PRENSA** (= Printed Matter) or surch also.
N519 **128** 3 c. olive (imperf) 40 25
N447 **118** 3 c. on 2 c. black and lake (perf) 40 35
N403 **120** 3 c. on 4 c. yellow (perf) 20 30
N448 **118** 6 c. on 4 c. blue and orange (perf) 40 35
N449 9 c. on 5 c. brown and blue (perf) 40 35
N520 **128** 9 c. on 10 c. green (imperf) 45 35
N521 15 c. mauve (imperf) . . 60 40

OFFICIAL STAMPS

1880. Optd **OFICIAL**. Perf.
O51 **9** 15 c. yellow . . . . 2·00 2·00

1880. Optd **OFICIAL**. Roul.
O48 **10** 1 c. brown . . . . 1·10 1·10
O49 **11** 5 c. green 45 45
O61 **15** 7 c. blue (perf) . . . . . . 1·50 1·50
O50 **10** 10 c. red 70 70
O52 20 c. bistre 95 95
O53 50 c. black . . . . 6·25 6·25
O55 1 p. blue . . . . 6·25 6·25

1883. Optd **OFICIAL**.
O64 **16** 1 c. green . . . . 2·00 2·00
O65 – 2 c. red (No. 63) . . . . . . 3·75 3·00

1883. Optd **OFICIAL**.
O70 **18** 1 c. green . . . . 11·50 11·50
O71 2 c. red . . . . 3·70 3·75
O72 **20** 5 c. blue . . . . 1·10 85
O73 **21** 10 c. brown . . . . 2·75 1·40

1884. Optd **FRANCO** in frame.
O74 **18** 1 c. green . . . . 13·50 11·50

1884. Optd **OFICIAL**.
O80 **10** 1 c. on 10 c. (No. 76) . . . 80 80
O81 – 2 c. red (No. 77) . . . . . 2·25 2·25
O82 **26** 5 c. blue 95 70

1884. Optd **OFICIAL**. Roul.
O 91a **28** 1 c. grey . . . . 3·75 2·00
O 91 1 c. green 75 45
O 92 **29** 2 c. red 45 30
O 93a **28** 5 c. blue . . . . 1·25 1·40
O 94 5 c. lilac . . . . 1·50 1·25
O 95 **31** 7 c. brown . . . . 1·10 65
O110 7 c. orange . . . . 1·10 75
O 96 **32** 10 c. brown 60 35
O111 **36** 10 c. violet . . . . 5·75 3·00
O 97 **33** 20 c. mauve . . . . 1·10 65
O112 20 c. brown . . . . 5·75 2·25
O 98 **34** 25 c. lilac . . . . 1·10 75
O113 25 c. red . . . . 5·75 2·25

1890. Optd **OFICIAL**. Perf.
O124 **38** 1 c. green 40 20
O125 **39** 2 c. red 40 20
O126 **40** 5 c. blue 75 80
O127 **41** 7 c. brown 60 60
O128 **42** 10 c. green 60 50
O129 **43** 20 c. orange 60 50
O130 **44** 25 c. brown 60 50
O131 **45** 50 c. blue . . . . 2·75 2·75
O132 **46** 1 p. violet . . . . 3·00 2·75

1891. Optd **OFICIAL**.
O134 **28** 5 c. lilac (No. 133) . . . 75 75

1895. Optd **OFICIAL**.
O164 **38** 1 c. blue 85 85
O165 **39** 2 c. brown . . . . 1·10 1·10
O166 **40** 5 c. red . . . . 1·50 1·50
O167 **45** 50 c. purple . . . . . . 3·00 3·00

1895. Optd **OFICIAL**.
O168 **56** 1 c. bistre 20 20
O169 **57** 2 c. blue 20 20
O170 **58** 5 c. red 40 25
O171 **59** 7 c. green 40 40
O172 **60** 10 c. brown 40 40
O173 **61** 20 c. black and green . . 1·25 60
O174 **62** 25 c. black and brown . 60 60
O175 **63** 50 c. black and blue . . 55 55
O176 **64** 1 p. black and brown . . 2·75 2·75

1897. Nos. 180/2 optd **OFICIAL**.
O194 **67** 1 c. black and red . . . 60 60
O195 **68** 5 c. black and blue . . . 70 60
O196 – 10 c. black and lake . . 95 75

1897. Optd **OFICIAL**.
O201 **56** 1 c. blue 35 30
O202 **57** 2 c. purple 60 55
O203 **58** 5 c. green 60 35
O204 **72** 10 c. red . . . . 2·00 1·10
O205 **61** 20 c. black and mauve . 5·50 2·00
O206 **62** 25 c. blue and red . . . 2·25 1·10
O207 **63** 50 c. brown and green . 3·00 1·10
O208 **64** 1 p. blue and brown . . 4·50 3·00

1899. Optd **OFICIAL**.
O226 **39** 2 c. orange 50 25
O227a **58** 5 c. blue 60 50
O228 **72** 10 c. purple 95 95
O243 **43** 20 c. blue . . . . 3·00 2·25

1901. Optd **OFICIAL**.
O238 **78** 1 c. green 20 25
O239 **79** 2 c. red 25 25
O240 **80** 5 c. blue 25 30
O241 **81** 7 c. brown 30 30
O242 **82** 10 c. lilac 35 35
O245 **46** 1 p. green . . . . 3·75 3·00

1904. Optd **OFICIAL**.
O272 **86** 1 c. green 20 15
O262 **87** 2 c. orange 20 20
O263 **88** 5 c. blue 20 20
O275 **89** 10 c. lilac 20 15
O276 **90** 20 c. green . . . . 1·10 70
O277 **91** 25 c. bistre 75 35

1907. Optd **OFICIAL**.
O273 **96** 5 c. blue 20 15
O274 7 c. brown 20 15
O278 50 c. red 45 40

1910. Optd **OFICIAL 1910**.
O288 **79** 2 c. red . . . . 3·75 2·25
O289 **80** 5 c. blue . . . . 2·25 2·00
O290 **82** 10 c. lilac . . . . 1·10 70
O291 **43** 20 c. green . . . . 1·10 70
O292 **44** 25 c. brown . . . . 2·00 1·40
O293 **96** 50 c. red . . . . 2·50 1·40

O 110

1911.
O307 O **110** 2 c. brown 25 25
O308 5 c. blue 25 20
O309 8 c. slate 25 20
O310 20 c. brown 40 30
O311 23 c. red 60 40
O312 50 c. orange 75 45
O313 1 p. red . . . . . 2·00 70

1915. Optd **Oficial**.
O340 **107** 2 c. pink 40 45
O341 5 c. blue 40 45
O342 8 c. blue 40 45
O343 20 c. brown 85 35
O344 **108** 23 c. blue . . . . 2·25 2·00
O345 50 c. orange . . . . . . 3·75 2·00
O346 1 p. red . . . . 4·50 2·00

1919. Optd **Oficial**.
O365 **115** 2 c. grey and red . . . 60 30
O366 5 c. grey and blue . . . 70 25
O367 8 c. brown and blue . . 70 25
O368 20 c. grey and brown . 1·40 45
O369 23 c. brown & green . . 1·40 45
O370 50 c. blue and brown . 2·00 95
O371 1 p. blue and red . . . 5·00 1·50

1924. Optd **OFICIAL** in frame. (a) Perf.
O439 **128** 2 c. mauve 40 15
O440 5 c. blue 40 15
O593 8 c. red 95 25
O594 10 c. green . . . . . . 1·40 25
O441 12 c. blue 25 15
O442 20 c. brown 25 25
O443 36 c. green 95 70
O444 50 c. orange . . . . . . 2·10 1·50
O445 1 p. red . . . . 3·50 2·75
O446 2 p. green . . . . . . 6·25 5·00

(b) Imperf.

No.	Type	Description	Unused	Used
O499	**128**	2 c. mauve	45	10
O500		5 c. blue	40	15
O501		8 c. red	45	20
O502		12 c. blue	60	20
O503		20 c. brown	95	40
O504		36 c. pink	2·00	60

PARCEL POST STAMPS

P 123 P 144

1922. (a) Inscr "EXTERIOR".

No.	Type	Description	Unused	Used
P391	**P 123**	5 c. green on buff	20	10
P516		5 c. black on yellow	30	10
P392		10 c. green on blue	35	10
P517		10 c. black on blue	40	10
P393		20 c. green on rose	1·10	50
P518		20 c. black on pink	85	15
P394		30 c. green on green	1·10	20
P395		50 c. green on blue	2·00	30
P396		1 p. green on orange	2·75	70

(b) Inscr "INTERIOR".

No.	Type	Description	Unused	Used
P397	**P 123**	5 c. green on buff	25	10
P512		5 c. black on yellow	30	10
P398		10 c. green on blue	25	10
P513		10 c. black on blue	35	10
P399		20 c. green on pink	50	25
P514		20 c. black on pink	45	15
P400		30 c. green on green	85	25
P515		30 c. black on green	85	25
P401		50 c. green on blue	1·10	30
P402		1 p. green on orange	3·00	60

1927.

No.	Type	Description	Unused	Used
P522	**P 144**	1 c. blue	10	10
P606		1 c. violet	10	10
P523		2 c. green	10	10
P524		4 c. violet	15	10
P609a		5 c. red	15	10
P526		10 c. brown	30	10
P527		20 c. orange	40	20

P 152 P 155 P 177 Sea and Rail Transport

1928.

No.	Type	Description	Unused	Used
P587	**P 152**	5 c. black on yellow	10	10
P588		10 c. black on blue	15	10
P589		20 c. black on red	35	10
P590		30 c. black on green	55	10

1929. Agricultural parcels.

No.	Type	Description	Unused	Used
P610	**P 155**	10 c. orange	30	20
P611		15 c. blue	30	20
P612		20 c. brown	45	30
P613		25 c. red	50	35
P614		50 c. grey	95	45
P615		75 c. violet	3·75	3·75
P616		1 p. olive	2·75	1·40

1938.

No.	Type	Description	Unused	Used
P 971	**P 177**	5 c. orange	10	35
P 801		10 c. red	40	25
P 972		10 c. purple	15	10
P1066		10 c. green	20	40
P 973		20 c. red	35	35
P1067		20 c. blue	25	30
P 974		30 c. blue	40	10
P1068		30 c. purple	55	20
P1069		50 c. green	85	30
P 805		1 p. red	1·40	10
P 975		1 p. blue	20	20
P1070		1 p. green	70	90

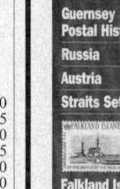

P 188 P 204 University

1943.

No.	Type	Description	Unused	Used
P876	**P 188**	1 c. red	10	10
P877		2 c. green	10	10

1944. Optd ANO 1943.

No.	Type	Description	Unused	Used
P882	**P 155**	10 c. orange	20	10
P883		15 c. blue	20	20
P884		20 c. brown	30	20
P885		25 c. red	50	30
P886		50 c. grey	70	50
P887		75 c. violet	1·40	95
P888		1 p. olive	1·75	1·40

1945.

No.	Type	Description	Unused	Used
P 909	A	1 c. green	10	10
P 999	**P 204**	1 c. red	10	10
P 910		2 c. violet	10	10
P1000	A	2 c. blue	10	10
P1047	B	5 c. grey	35	10
P1045		5 c. brown	10	10
P1001	A	10 c. turqoise	10	10
P1002		10 c. olive	10	10
P1048	C	20 c. yellow	10	10
P1049		20 c. brown	15	10
P1046	D	1 p. blue	1·50	1·10
P1290		1 p. brown	10	10

DESIGNS—HORIZ: A, Bank. VERT: B, Custom House; C. Solis Theatre; D. Montevideo Railway Station.

P 211 Custom House **P 212** Mail Coach (Guillermo Rodriguez)

1946.

No.	Type	Description	Unused	Used
P934	**P 211**	5 c. blue & brown	15	10

1946.

No.	Type	Description	Unused	Used
P935	**P 212**	5 p. brown & red	7·00	2·25

1946. Armorial type as T **187** obliterated by arrow-head device. (a) Optd **IMPUESTO** and **ENCOMIENDAS**.

No.	Type	Description	Unused	Used
P936		1 c. mauve	10	10
P937		2 c. brown	10	10
P938		5 c. blue	10	10

(b) Optd **ENCOMIENDAS** only.

No.	Type	Description	Unused	Used
P939		1 p. blue	75	20
P940		5 p. red	2·50	95

1957. No. P1047 surch **$0.30.**

No.	Type	Description	Unused	Used
P1064		30 c. on 5 c. grey	20	10

P 263 National Printing Works

1960.

No.	Type	Description	Unused	Used
P1127	**P 263**	30 c. green	10	10

1965. Surch with Caduceus and **$5.00 ENCOMIENDAS**.

No.	Type	Description	Unused	Used
P1268	**217**	5 p. on 84 c. orange	30	15

1966. No. 1092 surch with Caduceus **ENCOMIENDAS** and value.

No.	Type	Description	Unused	Used
P1289	**254**	1 p. on 38 c. black	10	10

P 355 Sud Aviation Caravelle and Motor-coach

1969.

No.	Type	Description	Unused	Used
P1397	**P 355**	10 p. blk, red & grn	15	10
P1398	–	20 p. yell, blk & bl	30	20

DESIGN: 20 p. Side views of Sud Aviation Caravelle and motor-coach.

1971. No. 1121 surch **Encomiendas $0.60.**

No.	Type	Description	Unused	Used
P1448	**261**	60 c. on 1 p. + 10 c. violet and orange	45	30

1971. No. 1380 surch **IMPUESTOS A ECOMIENDAS**, diesal-engine and value.

No.	Type	Description	Unused	Used
P1472		60 c. on 6 p. black & green	30	25

1972. Nos. 1401/2 surch **IMPUESTO A ENCOMIENDAS**, emblem and value.

No.	Type	Description	Unused	Used
P1507	**358**	1 p. on 6 p. black, red and blue	40	25
P1508	–	1 p. on 6 p. black, red and blue	40	25

P 460 Parcels and Arrows

1974.

No.	Type	Description	Unused	Used
P1555	**P 460**	75 p. multicoloured	15	10

P 461 Mail-van

1974. Old-time Mail Transport.

No.	Type	Description	Unused	Used
P1556	**P 461**	100 p. multicoloured	30	20
P1557	–	150 p. multicoloured	1·25	1·25
P1558	–	300 p. blk, bl & orge	75	50
P1559	–	500 p. multicoloured	1·25	70

DESIGNS: 150 p. Steam locomotive; 300 p. Paddle-steamer; 500 p. Monoplane.

POSTAGE DUE STAMPS

D 84

1902.

No.	Type	Description	Unused	Used
D795	**D 84**	1 c. green	10	10
D405		2 c. red	25	15
D796		2 c. brown	10	10
D491		3 c. brown	35	25
D797		3 c. red	10	10
D798		4 c. violet	10	10
D799		5 c. blue	10	10
D746		5 c. red	35	20
D494		6 c. brown	40	30
D800		8 c. red	15	10
D249		10 c. blue	45	35
D409a		10 c. green	30	15
D250		20 c. orange	85	45

1904. Surch **PROVISORIO UN cent'mo.**

No.	Type	Description	Unused	Used
D267	**D 84**	1 c. on 10 c. blue	45	45

UZBEKISTAN Pt. 10

Formerly a constituent republic of the Soviet Union, Uzbekistan became independent in 1991.

1992. 100 kopeks = 1 rouble.
1994 (June). Sum (temporary coupon currency).
1994 (Sept). 100 tyin = 1 sum.

1 Princess Nadira (from portrait by S. Khasanov)

2 "Melitaea acreina" (butterfly)

1992. Birth Bicentenary of Princess Nadira (Uzbek poetess).
1 **1** 20 k. multicoloured . . . . 1·00 1·00

1992. Nature Protection.
2 **2** 1 r. multicoloured 50 50

3 National Flag and Kukeldash Mosque, Tashkent

1992. 1st Anniv of Independence.
3 **3** 1 r. multicoloured . . . . .

4 Kutlug-Murad-inak Mosque, Khiva

1992. Uzbek Architecture.
4 **4** 50 k. multicoloured 50 50

5 Mosque, Registan Square, Samarkand

1992. Award of Aga Khan Prize for Architecture to Samarkand.
5 **5** 10 r. multicoloured . . . . . 1·50 1·50

6 Copper Water Pot, Kokand, and Sculptured Relief

1992. Uzbek Handicrafts.
6 **6** 50 k. multicoloured 25 25

7 Plate-tailed Gecko

ЎЗБЕКИСТОН 15-00
(8)

1993. Animals. Multicoloured.
7 1 r. Type **7** 10 10
8 2 r. Cobra 10 10
9 2 r. Muskrat (vert) 10 10
10 3 r. Osprey (vert) 15 15
11 5 r. Penduline tit (vert) 35 35
12 10 r. Forest dormouse (vert) . . 70 70
13 15 r. Desert monitor . . . . . 1·25 1·25

1993. Stamps of Russia surch as T **8**.
15 2 r. on 1 k. brown (No. 5940) . 10 10
16 8 r. on 4 k. red (No. 4672) . . 20 20
17 15 r. on 2 k. mauve (No. 4670) 40 40
18 15 r. on 2 k. brown (No. 6073) 40 40
19 15 r. on 3 k. green (No. 5941) . 40 40
20 15 r. on 4 k. red (No. 4672) . . 40 40
21 15 r. on 4 k. blue (No. 6075) . 40 40
22 15 r. on 5 k. red (No. 6076) . 40 40
23 15 r. on 6 k. blue (No. 4673) . 40 40
24 15 r. on 7 k. blue (No. 6077) . 40 40
25 15 r. on 10 k. brown (No. 6078) 40 40
26 15 r. on 15 k. blue (No. 6081) 40 40
27 20 r. on 4 k. red (No. 4672) . 50 50
28 30 r. on 3 k. red (No. 4671) . 60 60
29 100 r. on 1 k. green (No. 4533) 1·25 1·25
30 500 r. on 1 k. green (No. 4533) 5·00 5·00

9 Arms and Flag

10 "Colchicum kesselringii"

1993.
31 **9** 8 r. multicoloured 10 10
32 15 r. multicoloured 20 20
33 50 r. mult (19 × 27 mm) . . 55 55
34 100 r. multicoloured . . . . 1·10 1·10

1993. Flowers. Multicoloured.
35 20 r. Type **10** 25 25
36 20 r. "Dianthus uzbekistanicus" 25 25
37 25 r. "Crocus alatavicus" . . . 35 35
38 25 r. "Salvia bucharica" . . . 35 35
39 30 r. "Tulipa kaufmanniana" . 45 45
40 30 r. "Tulipa greigii" 45 45

12 Arms

13 Bakhouddin Nakshband Mosque, Bukhara

1994.
43 **12** 75 s. red 35 35
See also Nos. 58/60.

1994. 675th Birth Anniv of Sheikh Bakhouddin Nakshband.
44 **13** 100 s. multicoloured 65 65

14 Statue of Tamerlane, Tashkent

15 Ulugh Beg Mosque, Samarkand

1994.
45 **14** 20 t. multicoloured 25 25

1994. 600th Birth Anniv of Ulugh Beg (central Asian ruler).
46 30 t. Type **15** 10 10
47 35 t. Ulugh Beg Mosque, Bukhara 15 15
48 40 t. Astronomical equipment 20 20
49 45 t. Statue, Tashkent 25 25

ЎЗБЕКИСТОН 200 сўм
(16)

ЎЗБЕКИСТОН 2·00
(17)

1995. Stamps of Russia surch. (a) With T **16** in coupon currency.
51 200 s. on 2 k. brown (No. 6073) 50 50
52 200 s. on 2 k. brown (imperf) (No. 6073) 50 50
53 200 s. on 4 k. blue (No. 6075) 50 50
54 200 s. on 5 k. blue (No. 5061) 50 50
55 200 s. on 15 k. blue (No. 6081) 50 50

(b) With T **17** in permanent currency.
56 2 s. on 1 k. green (No. 4533) . 50 50
57 2 s. on 3 k. turquoise (No. 5941) 50 50

1995. As T **12** but value expressed as "1.00" etc. (a) Size 14 × 22 mm.
58 1 s. green 20 20

(b) Size 22 × 33 mm.
59 3 s. red 45 45
60 6 s. blue 75 75

VATHY Pt. 6

A town on the island of Samos, where there was a French Post Office which closed in 1914.

25 centimes = 1 piastre

1893. Stamps of France optd **Vathy** or surch also.
82 **10** 5 c. green . . . . 3·25 4·25
84 10 c. black and lilac . . . . 6·75 6·75
86 15 c. blue . . . . 6·75 6·75
87 1 pi. on 25 c. black on pink . 5·50 6·25
88 2 pi. on 50 c. pink . . . . . 16·00 17·00
89 4 pi. on 1 f. green . . . . . 18·00 11·50
90 8 pi. on 2 f. brown on blue . 50·00 45·00
91 20 pi. on 5 f. mauve . . . . 70·00 65·00

VATICAN CITY Pt. 8

A small area in Rome under the independent sovereignty of the Pope since 1929.

100 centesimi = 1 lira

1 Papal Tiara and St. Peter's Keys

2 Pope Pius XI

4

1929.
1 **1** 5 c. brown on pink 15 30
2 10 c. green on green 20 35
3 20 c. violet on lilac 80 55
4 25 c. blue on blue 80 50
5 30 c. black on yellow 85 60
6 50 c. black on orange . . . . 1·25 60
7 75 c. red on grey . . . . . . 1·75 1·40
8 **2** 80 c. red . . . . 1·50 45
9 1 l. 25 blue . . . . 1·75 75
10 2 l. brown . . . . 6·00 2·25
11 2 l. 50 red . . . . 5·00 2·25
12 5 l. green . . . . 6·50 12·00
13 10 l. black . . . . 10·00 18·00

1931. Surch **C. 25** and bars.
14 **1** 25 c. on 30 c. black on yell . . 1·75 80

1933. "Holy Year" (1933–1934).
15 **4** 25 c.+ 10 c. green . . . . . 4·25 5·50
16 75 c.+ 15 c. red . . . . . . 6·50 12·00
17 80 c.+ 20 c. brown . . . . . 22·00 16·00
18 1 l. 25 + 25 c. blue . . . . . 6·00 12·00
The 80 c. and 1 l. 25 have inscriptions and frame differently arranged.

6 Arms of Pope Pius XI

9 Pope Pius XI

1933.
19 **6** 5 c. red 10 10
20 – 10 c. black and brown . . . 10 10
21 – $12\frac{1}{2}$ c. black and green . . . 10 10
22 – 20 c. black and orange . . . 10 10
23 – 25 c. black and green . . . 10 10
24 – 30 c. brown and black . . . 10 10
25 – 50 c. brown and purple . . . 10 10
26 – 75 c. brown and red 10 10
27 – 80 c. brown and pink 10 10
28 **9** 1 l. black and violet . . . . 4·00 1·00
29 1 l. 25 black and blue . . . 12·00 4·00
30 2 l. black and brown . . . . 18·00 14·00
31 2 l. 75 black and purple . . . 20·00 24·00
32 – 5 l. green and brown 20 35
33 – 10 l. green and blue 25 45
34 – 20 l. green and black 30 60
DESIGNS—As Type **6**: 10 c. to 25 c. Wing of Vatican Palace; 30 c. to 80 c. Vatican Gardens and Dome of St. Peter's. As Type **9**: 5 l. to 20 l. St. Peter's Basilica.

1934. Surch.
35 **2** 40 c. on 80 c. red . . . . . 1·75 1·50
36 1 l. 30 on 1 l. 25 blue . . . 70·00 24·00
37 2 l. 05 on 2 l. brown . . . . £140 5·00
38 2 l. 55 on 2 l. 50 red . . . . 70·00 £125
39 3 l. 05 on 5 l. green £250 £275
40 3 l. 70 on 10 l. black £225 £350

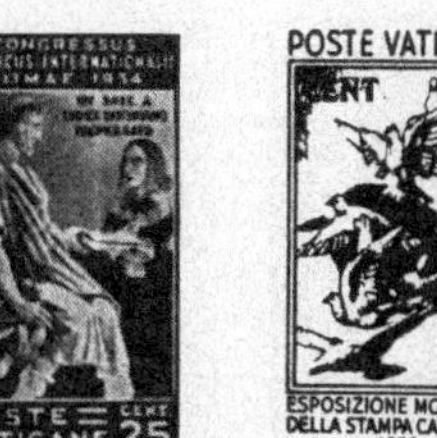
13 Tribonian presenting Pandects to Justinian

15 Doves and Bell

1935. International Juridical Congress, Rome. Frescoes by Raphael.
41 **13** 5 c. orange 20 40
42 10 c. violet 20 40
43 25 c. green . . . . 2·00 3·50
44 – 75 c. red . . . . 24·00 18·00
45 – 80 c. brown . . . . 18·00 17·00
46 – 1 l. 25 blue . . . . 20·00 12·00
DESIGN: 75 c. to 1 l. 25, Pope Julius II (wrongly inscribed as representing Pope Gregory IX).

1936. Catholic Press Exhibition, Rome.
47 **15** 5 c. green 25 60
48 – 10 c. black 25 60
49 – 25 c. green . . . . 20·00 5·00
50 **15** 50 c. purple 25 60
51 – 75 c. red . . . . 20·00 20·00
52 – 80 c. brown . . . . 50 1·75
53 – 1 l. 25 blue . . . . 60 2·00
54 – 5 l. brown . . . . 60 6·00
DESIGNS: 10, 75 c. Church and Bible; 25, 80 c. St. John Bosco; 1 l. 25, 5 l. St. Francis of Sales.

16 Statue of St. Peter

17 Ascension of Elijah

1938. Air.
55 **16** 25 c. brown 10 10
56 – 50 c. green 10 10
57 **17** 75 c. red 15 15
58 – 80 c. blue 20 30
59 **16** 1 l. violet 30 40
60 – 2 l. blue 50 50
61 **17** 5 l. black . . . . 1·10 1·50
62 – 10 l. purple . . . . 1·10 1·75
DESIGNS: 50 c., 2 l. Dove with olive branch and St. Peter's Square; 80 c., 10 l. Transportation of the Holy House.

18 Crypt of Basilica of St. Cecilia

20 Coronation

1938. International Christian Archaeological Congress. Inscr "CONGRESSVS INTERNAT. ARCHAEOLOGIAE CHRIST".
63 **18** 5 c. brown 20 15
64 10 c. red 20 20
65 25 c. green 20 20
66 – 75 c. red . . . . 5·00 7·00
67 – 80 c. violet . . . . 12·00 14·00
68 – 1 l. 25 blue . . . . 14·00 12·00
DESIGN: 75, 80 c. and 1 l. 25, Basilica of Saints Nereus and Achilles in the Catacombs of Domitilla.

1939. Death of Pope Pius XI. Optd **SEDE VACANTE MCMXXXIX.**
69 **1** 5 c. brown on pink . . . . 20·00 3·00
70 10 c. green on green 20 20
71 20 c. violet on lilac 20 20
72 25 c. blue on blue . . . . . 40 3·00
73 30 c. black on yellow 40 20
74 50 c. black on orange 20 20
75 75 c. red on grey 40 20

1939. Coronation of Pope Pius XII.
76 **20** 25 c. green 85 30
77 75 c. red 15 30
78 80 c. violet . . . . 1·90 2·50
79 1 l. 25 blue 15 30

21 Arms of Pope Pius XII

22 Pope Pius XII

1940. 1st Anniv of Coronation of Pope Pius XII.
80 **21** 5 c. red 10 10
99 5 c. grey 10 10
100 30 c. brown 10 10
101 50 c. green 10 10
81 **22** 1 l. black and violet 15 10
102 – 1 l. black and brown . . . 10 10
82 – 1 l. 25 black and blue . . . 15 10
103 – 1 l. 50 black and red . . . 10 15
83 **22** 2 l. black and brown . . . . 50 1·00
104 – 2 l. 50 black and blue . . . 10 15
84 – 2 l. 75 black and purple . . 50 1·25
105 **22** 5 l. black and lilac 15 20
106 20 l. black and green . . . 25 35
DESIGN: 1 l. (No. 102), 1 l. 25, 1 l. 50, 2 l. 50, and 2 l. 75, as Type **22** but with portrait of Pope facing left.

23

24 Consecration of Archbishop Pacelli

1942. Prisoners of War Relief Fund (1st series). Inscr "MCMXLII".

85 **23** 25 c. green 10 15
86 80 c. brown 10 15
87 1 l. 25 blue 10 15

See also Nos. 92/4 and 107/9.

1943. Pope's Episcopal Silver Jubilee.

88 **24** 25 c. turquoise and green . . 10 10
89 80 c. chocolate and brown . 10 20
90 1 l. 25 blue & ultramarine . 10 20
91 5 l. blue and black 15 40

1944. Prisoners of War Relief Fund (2nd series). Inscr "MCMXLIII".

92 **23** 25 c. green 10 10
93 80 c. brown 10 15
94 1 l. 25 blue 10 25

25 Raphael

27 St. Ignatius of Loyola

1944. 4th Centenary of Pontifical Academy of the Virtuosi of the Pantheon.

95 **25** 25 c. olive and green 10 10
96 – 80 c. violet and lilac . . . 20 20
97 – 1 l. 25 blue and violet . . . 20 20
98 – 10 l. bistre and yellow . . . 40 1·50

PORTRAITS: 80 c. Antonio da Sangallo (architect); 1 l. 25, Carlo Maratti (painter) (after Francesco Maratta); 10 l. Antonio Canova (sculptor, self-portrait).

1945. Prisoners of War Relief Fund (3rd series). Inscr "MCMXLIV".

107 **23** 1 l. green 10 15
108 3 l. red 10 15
109 5 l. blue 10 15

1946. Surch in figures between bars.

110 **21** 20 c. on 5 c. grey 10 10
111 25 c. on 30 c. brown 10 10
112 1 l. on 50 c. green 10 10
113 – 1 l. 50 on 1 l. black and brown (No. 102) 10 10
114 – 3 l. on 1 l. 50 black and red (No. 103) 15 15
115 – 5 l. on 2 l. 50 black and blue (No. 104) 25 20
116 **22** 10 l. on 5 l. black & lilac . 1·25 55
117 30 l. on 20 l. black & green 3·75 1·60

1946. 400th Anniv of Inauguration of Council of Trent.

118 – 5 c. brown and bistre . . . 15 15
119 – 25 c. brown and violet . . . 15 15
120 – 50 c. sepia and brown . . . 15 15
121 **27** 75 c. brown and black . . . 15 15
122 – 1 l. brown and purple . . . 15 15
123 – 1 l. 50 brown and red . . . 15 15
124 – 2 l. brown and green . . . 15 15
125 – 2 l. 50 brown and blue . . . 15 15
126 – 3 l. brown and red 15 15
127 – 4 l. brown and bistre . . . 15 15
128 – 5 l. brown and blue 15 15
129 – 10 l. brown and red 15 15

DESIGNS: 5 c. Trent Cathedral; 25 c. St. Angela Merici; 50 c. St. Anthony Maria Zaccaria; 1 l. St. Cajetan of Thiene; 1 l. 50, St. John Fisher, Bishop of Rochester; 2 l. Cristoforo Madrussi, Bishop of Trent; 2 l. 50, Reginald Pole, Archbishop of Canterbury; 3 l. Marcello Cervini; 4 l. Giovanni Maria Del Monte; 5 l. Emperor Charles V; 10 l. Pope Paul III Farnese.

28 Dove with Olive Branch over St. Peter's Forecourt

29 Barn Swallows circling Spire of St. Peter's Basilica

1947. Air.

130 **28** 1 l. red 15 10
131 – 4 l. brown 15 10
132 **28** 5 l. blue 15 10
133 **29** 15 l. violet . . . . 1·10 75
134 – 25 l. green . . . . 3·50 1·40
135 **29** 50 l. black . . . . 5·00 2·25
136 100 l. orange . . . . . . 19·00 4·25

DESIGN–As Type **28**: 4 l., 25 l. Transportation of the Holy House.

30 "Raphael accompanying Tobias" (after Botticelli)

1948. Air.

137 **30** 250 l. black . . . . 14·00 3·00
138 500 l. blue £300 £225

31 St. Agnes's Basilica

32 Pope Pius XII

1949.

139 **31** 1 l. brown 10 10
140 – 3 l. violet 10 10
141 – 5 l. orange 10 10
142 – 8 l. green 15 15
143 – 13 l. green . . . . 2·25 2·25
144 – 16 l. grey 25 25
145 – 25 l. red . . . . 4·50 55
146 – 35 l. mauve . . . . 20·00 9·00
147 – 40 l. blue 25 15
148 **32** 100 l. black . . . . 3·50 3·50

DESIGNS (Basilicas)—VERT: 3 l. St. Clement; 5 l. St. Praxedes; 8 l. St. Mary in Cosmedin. HORIZ: 13 l. Holy Cross; 16 l. St. Sebastian; 25 l. St. Laurence's; 35 l. St. Paul's; 40 l. Sta. Maria Maggiore.

33 Angels over Globe

1949. Air. 75th Anniv of U.P.U.

149 **33** 300 l. blue . . . . 18·00 8·00
150 1000 l. green . . . . . . 70·00 48·00

34 "I Will Give You the Keys of the Kingdom"

35 Guards Marching

1949. "Holy Year".

151 **34** 5 l. brown and lt brown . 10 10
152 – 6 l. brown and black . . . 10 10
153 – 8 l. green and blue . . . 50 50
154 – 10 l. blue and green . . . 10 10
155 **34** 20 l. brown and green . . 80 30
156 – 25 l. blue and brown . . . 45 30
157 – 30 l. purple and green . . 1·40 1·00
158 – 60 l. red and brown . . . 1·25 1·00

DESIGNS: 6, 25 l. Four Basilicas; 8, 30 l. Pope Boniface VIII; 10, 60 l. Pope Pius XII opening the Holy Door.

1950. Centenary of Papal Guard.

159 **35** 25 l. brown . . . . 3·00 3·25
160 35 l. green . . . . 3·00 3·25
161 55 l. brown . . . . 1·90 3·25

36 Pope Proclaiming Dogma

37 Pope Pius X

1951. Proclamation of Dogma of the Assumption.

162 **36** 25 l. purple 60 60
163 – 55 l. blue . . . . 3·75 8·50

DESIGN: 55 l. Angels over St. Peter's.

1951. Beatification of Pope Pius X.

164 **37** 6 l. gold and violet 10 15
165 10 l. gold and green 15 15
166 – 60 l. gold and blue . . . . 5·00 5·00
167 – 115 l. gold and brown . . . 14·00 12·00

DESIGN: 60, 115 l. Pope looking left.

38 Final Session of Council (fresco)

1951. 1500th Anniv of Council of Chalcedon.

168 **38** 5 l. grey 15 15
169 – 25 l. red . . . . 2·75 1·40
170 **38** 35 l. red . . . . 3·25 3·00
171 – 60 l. blue . . . . 12·00 11·00
172 **38** 100 l. brown . . . . 30·00 22·00

DESIGN: 25, 60 l. "Pope Leo I meeting Attila" (Raphael).

39 Gratian 41 Mail Coach and First Stamp

1951. Air. 800th Anniv of Decree of Gratian.

173 **39** 300 l. purple £170 £140
174 500 l. blue . . . . 22·00 12·00

1952. No. 143 surch **L. 12** and bars.

175 – 12 l. on 13 l. green . . . . . 1·25 1·00

1952. Centenary of First Papal States' Stamp.

176 **41** 50 l. black & blue on cream 3·25 4·00

42 St. Maria Goretti

43 St. Peter and Inscription

1953. 50th Anniv of Martyrdom of St. Maria Goretti.

177 **42** 15 l. violet and brown . . . 3·75 2·50
178 25 l. brown and red . . . 2·75 2·50

1953. St. Peter's Basilica. Medallions in black.

179 **43** 3 l. red 10 10
180 – 5 l. grey 10 10
181 – 10 l. green 10 10
182 – 12 l. brown 10 10
183 – 20 l. violet 25 15
184 – 25 l. brown 10 10
185 – 35 l. red 10 10
186 – 45 l. brown 25 20
187 – 60 l. blue 10 10
188 – 65 l. red 30 15
189 – 100 l. purple 10 10

DESIGNS: 5 l. Pius XII and Roman sepulchre; 10 l. St. Peter's tomb; 12 l. St. Sylvester I and Constantine's basilica (previous building); 20 l. Julius II and Bramante's design; 25 l. Paul III and apse; 35 l. Sixtus V and cupola; 45 l. Paul V and facade; 60 l. Urban VIII and baldaquin; 65 l. Alexander VII and colonnade; 100 l. Pius VI and sacristy.

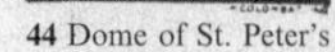

44 Dome of St. Peter's

45 St. Clare of Assisi (after Giotto)

1953. Air.

190 **44** 500 l. brown & dp brown . 18·00 6·00
190a 500 l. green & turquoise . 6·00 4·50
191 1000 l. blue and dp blue . 50·00 12·00
191a 1000 l. red and lake . . . 65 85

1953. 700th Death Anniv of St. Clare (founder of Poor Clares Order).

192 **45** 25 l. dp brown, brown & bl 1·75 75
193 35 l. brown, lt brown & red 10·00 10·00

46 "St. Bernard" (after Lippi)

47 Lombard's Episcopal Seal

1953. 800th Death Anniv of St. Bernard of Clairvaux.

194 **46** 20 l. purple and green . . 65 75
195 60 l. green and blue . . . 6·50 6·00

1953. 800th Anniv of "Libri Sententiarum" (theological treatise by Peter Lombard, Bishop of Paris).

196 **47** 100 l. yellow, blue and red 23·00 15·00

48 Pope Pius XI and Vatican City

1954. 25th Anniv of Lateran Treaty.

197 **48** 25 l. red, brown and blue . 1·25 90
198 60 l. blue, grey and brown 2·75 2·25

49 Pope Pius XII

1954. Marian Year and Centenary of Dogma of the Immaculate Conception.

199 – 3 l. violet 10 10
200 **49** 4 l. red 10 10
201 – 6 l. red 10 10
202 **49** 12 l. green . . . . 1·00 1·00
203 – 20 l. brown 75 65
204 **49** 35 l. blue . . . . 1·75 1·50

DESIGN: 3, 6, 20 l. Pope Pius IX facing right with different inscr and dates "1854–1954".

50 St. Pius X

51 Basilica of St. Francis of Assisi

1954. Canonization of Pope Pius X.

205 **50** 10 l. yellow, red & brown . 15 10
206 25 l. yellow, red and violet 2·50 2·00
207 35 l. yellow, red and black 3·75 3·00

1954. Bicentenary of Elevation of Basilica of St. Francis of Assisi to Papal Chapel.

208 **51** 20 l. black and cream . . . 2·00 1·00
209 35 l. brown and cream . . 1·50 1·50

52 "St. Augustine" (after Botticelli)

53 Madonna of Ostra Brama, Vilna

1954. 1600th Birth Anniv of St. Augustine.

210 **52** 35 l. green 75 60
211 50 l. brown . . . . 1·50 1·25

1954. Termination of Marian Year.

212 **53** 20 l. multicoloured 75 75
213 35 l. multicoloured . . . . 6·00 6·00
214 60 l. multicoloured . . . . 10·00 9·00

54 St. Boniface and Fulda Cathedral

55 "Pope Sixtus II and St. Lawrence" (fresco, Niccolina Chapel)

1955. 1200th Anniv of Martyrdom of St. Boniface.

215	**54**	10 l. green	10	10
216		35 l. violet	65	55
217		60 l. green	90	70

1955. 500th Death Anniv of Fra Giovanni da Fiesole, "Fra Angelico" (painter).

218	**55**	50 l. red and blue	3·75	2·25
219		100 l. blue and flesh	2·50	2·25

56 Pope Nicholas V

57 St. Bartholomew

1955. 5th Death Centenary of Pope Nicholas V.

220	**56**	20 l. brown and blue	20	15
221		35 l. brown and pink	35	30
222		60 l. brown and green	70	65

1955. 900th Death Anniv of St. Bartholomew the Young.

223	**57**	10 l. black and brown	10	10
224		25 l. black and red	35	30
225		100 l. black and green	2·00	1·75

58 "Annunciation" (Melozzo da Forli)

59 Corporal of the Guard

1956. Air.

226	**58**	5 l. black	10	10
227	A	10 l. green	10	10
228	B	15 l. orange	10	10
229	**58**	25 l. red	10	10
230	A	35 l. red	35	35
231	B	50 l. brown	10	10
232	**58**	60 l. blue	2·00	2·25
233	A	100 l. brown	10	10
234	B	300 l. violet	60	70

PAINTINGS: A, "Annunciation" (P. Cavallini); B, "Annunciation" (Leonardo da Vinci).

1956. 450th Anniv of Swiss Guard.

235	–	4 l. red	10	10
236	**59**	6 l. orange	10	10
237	–	10 l. blue	10	10
238	–	35 l. brown	45	50
239	**59**	50 l. violet	65	65
240	–	60 l. green	95	95

DESIGNS: 4, 35 l. Captain Roust; 10, 60 l. Two drummers.

60 St. Rita

61 St. Ignatius presenting Jesuit Constitution to Pope Paul III

1956. 5th Death Centenary of St. Rita at Cascia.

241	**60**	10 l. grey	10	10
242		25 l. brown	50	50
243		35 l. blue	40	40

1956. 4th Death Cent of St. Ignatius of Loyola.

244	**61**	35 l. brown	45	45
245		60 l. grey	80	80

62 St. John of Capistrano

63 Madonna and Child

1956. 5th Death Centenary of St. John of Capistrano.

246	**62**	25 l. green and black	1·75	1·75
247		35 l. brown and purple	65	65

1956. "Black Madonna" of Czestochowa Commemoration.

248	**63**	35 l. black and blue	30	30
249		60 l. blue and green	30	30
250		100 l. purple and brown	60	60

64 St. Domenico Savio

65 Cardinal D. Capranica (founder) and Capranica College

1957. Death Centenary of St. Domenico Savio.

251	**64**	4 l. brown	10	10
252	–	6 l. red	10	10
253	**64**	25 l. green	20	20
254	–	60 l. blue	1·00	1·00

DESIGN: 6, 60 l. St. Domenico Savio and St. John Bosco.

1957. 5th Centenary of Capranica College.

255	**65**	5 l. red	10	10
256	–	10 l. brown	10	10
257	**65**	35 l. grey	15	15
258	–	100 l. blue	50	50

DESIGNS: 10, 100 l. Pope Pius XII and plaque.

66 Pontifical Academy of Science

1957. 20th Anniv of the Pontifical Academy of Science.

259	**66**	35 l. green and blue	40	40
260		60 l. blue and brown	50	50

67 Mariazell Basilica

68 Apparition of the Virgin Mary

1957. 8th Centenary of Mariazell Basilica.

261	**67**	5 l. green	10	10
262	–	15 l. black	10	10
263	**67**	60 l. blue	85	85
264	–	100 l. violet	1·10	1·10

DESIGN: 15, 100 l. Statue of the Virgin of Mariazell within Sanctuary.

1958. Centenary of Apparition of the Virgin Mary at Lourdes.

265	**68**	5 l. blue	10	10
266	–	10 l. green	10	10
267	–	15 l. brown	10	10
268	**68**	25 l. red	10	10
269	–	35 l. brown	10	10
270	–	100 l. violet	10	10

DESIGNS: 10, 35 l. Invalid at Lourdes; 15, 100 l. St. Bernadette.

69 "Civitas Dei" ("City of God" at Exhibition)

70 Pope Clement XIII (from sculpture by A. Canova)

1958. Brussels International Exhibition.

271	–	35 l. purple	25	25
272	**69**	60 l. red	55	55
273		100 l. violet	2·00	2·00
274	–	300 l. blue	1·10	1·75

DESIGN: 35, 300 l. Pope Pius XII.

1958. Birth Bicentenary of Antonio Canova (sculptor).

275	**70**	5 l. brown	10	10
276	–	10 l. red	10	10
277	–	35 l. green	35	25
278	–	100 l. blue	1·25	1·25

SCULPTURES: 10 l. Pope Clement XIV; 35 l. Pope Pius VI; 100 l. Pope Pius VII.

71 St. Peter's Keys

1958. "Vacant See".

279	**71**	15 l. brown on yellow	1·40	1·40
280		25 l. brown	10	10
281		60 l. brown on lilac	10	10

72 Pope John XXIII

1959. Coronation of Pope John XXIII. Inscr "IV-XI MCMLVIII".

282	**72**	25 l. multicoloured	10	10
283	–	35 l. multicoloured	10	10
284	**72**	60 l. multicoloured	10	10
285	–	100 l. multicoloured	10	10

DESIGN: 35, 100 l. Arms of Pope John XXIII.

73 St. Lawrence

74 Pope Pius XI

1959. 1700th Death Annivs (15 to 100 l in 1958) of Martyrs under Valerian.

286	**73**	15 l. brown, yellow & red	10	10
287	–	25 l. brown, yellow & lilac	15	15
288	–	50 l. multicoloured	30	30
289	–	60 l. brown, yellow & green	25	25
290	–	100 l. brown, yell & purple	25	25
291	–	300 l. sepia and brown	40	40

PORTRAITS: 25 l. Pope Sixtus II; 50 l. St. Agapitus; 60 l. St. Filisissimus; 100 l. St. Cyprian; 300 l. St. Fructuosus.

1959. 30th Anniv of Lateran Treaty.

292	**74**	30 l. brown	10	10
293		100 l. blue	20	15

75 Radio Mast

76 Obelisk and St. John Lateran Basilica

1959. 2nd Anniv of St. Maria di Galeria Radio Station Vatican City.

294	**75**	25 l. pink, yellow & black	10	10
295		60 l. yellow, red and blue	25	25

1959. Air. Roman Obelisks.

296	**76**	5 l. violet	10	10
297	–	10 l. green	10	10
298	–	15 l. brown	10	10
299	–	25 l. green	10	10
300	–	35 l. blue	10	10
301	**76**	50 l. green	15	15
302	–	60 l. red	15	15
303	–	100 l. blue	20	20
304	–	200 l. brown	25	25
305	–	500 l. brown	50	50

DESIGNS: 10, 60 l. Obelisk and Church of Sta. Maria Maggiore; 15, 100 l. Vatican Obelisk and Apostolic Palace; 25, 200 l. Obelisk and Churches of St. Mary in Montesanto and St. Mary of the Miracles, Piazza del Popolo; 35, 500 l. Sallustian Obelisk and Trinita dei Monti Church.

77 St. Casimir, Vilna Palace and Cathedral

1959. 500th Birth Anniv of St. Casimir (patron saint of Lithuania).

306	**77**	50 l. brown	15	15
307		100 l. green	20	20

78 "Christ Adored by the Magi" (after Raphael)

1959. Christmas.

308	**78**	15 l. black	10	10
309		25 l. red	10	10
310		60 l. blue	20	20

79 "St. Antoninus" (after Dupre)

80 Transept of St. John Lateran Basilica

1960. 500th Death Anniv of St. Antoninus of Florence.

311	**79**	15 l. blue	10	10
312	–	25 l. green	10	10
313	**79**	60 l. brown	25	25
314	–	110 l. purple	45	45

DESIGN: 25, 110 l. "St. Antoninus preaching sermon" (after Portigiani).

1960. Roman Diocesan Synod.

315	**80**	15 l. brown	10	10
316		60 l. black	20	20

81 "The Flight into Egypt" (after Beato Angelico)

82 Cardinal Sarto (Pius X) leaving Venice for Conclave in Rome

1960. World Refugee Year.

317	**81**	5 l. green	10	10
318	–	10 l. brown	10	10
319	–	25 l. red	15	15
320	**81**	60 l. violet	25	25
321	–	100 l. blue	90	1·00
322	–	300 l. green	65	70

DESIGNS: 10, 100 l. "St. Peter giving Alms" (Masaccio); 25, 300 l. "Madonna of Mercy" (Piero della Francesca).

1960. 1st Anniv of Transfer of Relics of Pope Pius X from Rome to Venice.

323	**82**	15 l. brown	20	10
324	–	35 l. red	55	65
325	–	60 l. green	1·25	1·40

DESIGNS: 35 l. Pope John XXIII kneeling before relics of Pope Pius X; 60 l. Relics in procession across St. Mark's Square, Venice.

83 "Feeding the Hungry"

1960. "Corporal Works of Mercy". Della Robbia paintings. Centres in brown.

326	**83**	5 l. brown	10	10
327	–	10 l. green	10	10
328	–	15 l. black	10	10
329	–	20 l. red	10	10

330 – 30 l. violet 10 10
331 – 35 l. brown 10 10
332 – 40 l. orange 10 10
333 – 70 l. stone 10 10
DESIGNS: 10 l. "Giving drinks to the thirsty"; 15 l. "Clothing the naked"; 20 l. "Sheltering the homeless"; 30 l. "Visiting the sick"; 35 l. "Visiting the imprisoned"; 40 l. "Burying the dead"; 70 l. Pope John XXIII between "Faith" and "Charity".

84 "The Nativity" after Gerard Honthorst (Gherardo delle Notte)

85 St. Vincent de Paul

1960. Christmas.
334 **84** 10 l. black and green 10 10
335 15 l. dp brown & brown 10 10
336 70 l. blue and turqoise 20 20

1960. Death Tercentenaries of St. Vincent de Paul and St. Louise de Marillac.
337 **85** 40 l. violet 30 30
338 – 70 l. black 30 30
339 – 100 l. brown 40 40
DESIGNS: 70 l. St. Louise de Marillac; 100 l. St. Vincent giving child to care of St. Louise.

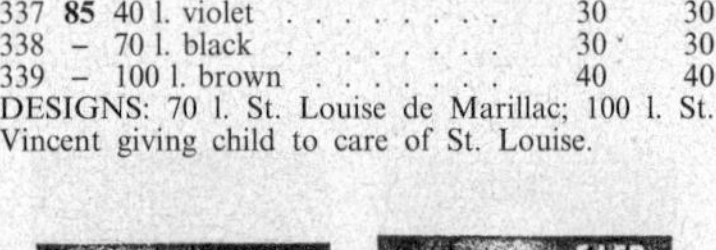

86 St. Meinrad

87 "Pope Leo I meeting Attila" (Algardi)

1961. 11th Death Centenary of St. Meinrad.
340 **86** 30 l. black 35 35
341 – 40 l. lilac 60 80
342 – 100 l. brown 1·40 1·50
DESIGNS—VERT: 40 l. The "Black Madonna", Einsiedeln Abbey. HORIZ: 100 l. Einsiedeln Abbey, Switzerland.

1961. 15th Death Centenary of Pope Leo I.
343 **87** 15 l. red 15 10
344 70 l. green 50 40
345 300 l. brown 1·10 1·25

88 Route of St. Paul's Journey to Rome

1961. 1900th Anniv of St. Paul's Arrival in Rome.
346 **88** 10 l. green 10 10
347 – 15 l. black and brown 10 10
348 – 20 l. black and red 15 15
349 **88** 30 l. blue 15 20
350 – 75 l. black and brown 35 45
351 – 200 l. black and blue 80 1·10
DESIGNS: 15, 75 l. St. Paul's arrival in Rome (after sculpture by Maraini); 20, 200 l. Basilica of St. Paul-outside-the-Walls, Rome.

89 "L'Osservatore Romano", 1861 and 1961

1961. Centenary of "L'Osservatore Romano" (Vatican newspaper).
352 **89** 40 l. black and brown 25 20
353 – 70 l. black and blue 50 50
354 – 250 l. black and yellow 1·10 1·10
DESIGNS: 70 l. "L'Osservatore Romano" offices; 250 l. Printing machine.

90 St. Patrick (ancient sculpture)

1961. 15th Death Centenary of St. Patrick.
355 **90** 10 l. green and buff 10 10
356 – 15 l. brown and blue 10 10
357 **90** 40 l. green and yellow 15 15
358 – 150 l. brown and blue 40 50
DESIGN: 15, 150 l. St. Patrick's Sanctuary, Lough Derg.

91 Arms of Roncalli Family

92 "The Nativity"

1961. Pope John XXIII's 80th Birthday.
359 **91** 10 l. brown and black 10 10
360 – 25 l. green and brown 10 10
361 – 30 l. violet and blue 10 10
362 – 40 l. blue and violet 10 10
363 – 70 l. brown and grey 15 15
364 – 115 l. black and brown 30 30
DESIGNS: 25 l. Church of St. Mary, Sotto il Monte; 30 l. Church of St. Mary, Monte Santo; 40 l. Church of Saints Ambrose and Charles, Rome; 70 l. St. Peter's Chair, Vatican Basilica; 115 l. Pope John XXIII.

1961. Christmas. Centres multicoloured.
365 **92** 15 l. green 10 10
366 40 l. black 10 10
367 70 l. purple 15 15

93 "Annunciation" (after F. Valle)

94 "Land Reclamation" Medal of 1588

1962. Air.
368 **93** 1000 l. brown 1·00 1·00
369 1500 l. blue 1·50 1·50

1962. Malaria Eradication.
370 **94** 15 l. violet 10 10
371 – 40 l. red 10 10
372 **94** 70 l. brown 15 15
373 – 300 l. green 35 35
DESIGN: 40, 300 l. Map of Pontine Marshes reclamation project (at time of Pope Pius VI).

95 "The Good Shepherd" (statue, Lateran Museum)

96 St. Catherine (after Il Sodoma (Bazzi))

1962. Religious Vocations.
374 **95** 10 l. black and violet 10 10
375 – 15 l. brown and blue 10 10
376 **95** 70 l. black and green 20 20
377 – 115 l. brown and red 1·10 1·10
378 **95** 200 l. black and brown 90 1·10
DESIGN: 15, 115 l. Wheatfield ready for harvest.

1962. 5th Centenary of St. Catherine of Siena's Canonization.
379 **96** 15 l. brown 10 10
380 60 l. violet 30 30
381 100 l. blue 30 35

97 Paulina M. Jaricot

98 St. Peter and St. Paul (from graffito on child's tomb)

1962. Death Centenary of Paulina M. Jaricot (founder of Society for the Propagation of the Faith). Multicoloured centres.
382 **97** 10 l. lilac 10 10
383 50 l. green 20 20
384 150 l. grey 35 35

1962. 6th International Christian Archaeology Congress, Ravenna.
385 **98** 20 l. brown and violet 10 10
386 – 40 l. green and brown 10 10
387 **98** 70 l. brown and turquoise 10 10
388 – 100 l. green and red 15 15
DESIGN: 40, 100 l. "The Passion" (from bas relief on tomb in Domitilla cemetery, near Rome).

99 "Faith" (after Raphael)

100 "The Nativity"

1962. Ecumenical Council.
389 **99** 5 l. brown and blue 10 10
390 – 10 l. brown and green 10 10
391 – 15 l. brown and red 10 10
392 – 25 l. grey and red 10 10
393 – 30 l. black and mauve 10 10
394 – 40 l. brown and red 10 10
395 – 60 l. brown and green 10 10
396 – 115 l. red 10 10
DESIGNS—Divine Virtues: 10 l. "Hope"; 15 l. "Charity" (both after Raphael); 25 l. Arms of Pope John XXIII and symbols of Evangelists (frontispiece of "Humanae Salutis" by Arrigo Bravi); 30 l. Central Nave, St. Peter's (council venue); 40 l. Pope John XXIII; 60 l. "St. Peter" (bronze in Vatican Basilica); 115 l. The Holy Ghost in form of dove.

1962. Christmas. Centres multicoloured.
397 **100** 10 l. grey 10 10
398 15 l. drab 10 10
399 90 l. green 15 15

101 "Miracle of the Loaves and Fishes" (after Murillo)

102 Pope John XXIII

1963. Freedom from Hunger.
400 **101** 15 l. sepia and brown 10 10
401 – 40 l. green and red 10 10
402 **101** 100 l. brown and blue 10 10
403 – 200 l. green and turquoise 10 10
DESIGN: 40, 200 l. "Miracle of the Fishes" (after Raphael).

1963. Award of Balzan Peace Prize to Pope John XXIII.
404 **102** 15 l. brown 10 10
405 160 l. black 20 20

103 St. Peter's Keys

104 Pope Paul VI

1963. "Vacant See".
406 **103** 10 l. brown 10 10
407 40 l. brown on yellow 10 10
408 100 l. brown on violet 10 10

1963. Coronation of Pope Paul VI.
409 **104** 15 l. black 10 10
410 – 40 l. red 10 10
411 **104** 115 l. brown 15 15
412 – 200 l. grey 15 15
DESIGN: 40, 200 l. Arms of Pope Paul VI.

105 "The Nativity" (African terracotta statuette)

106 St. Cyril

1963. Christmas.
413 **105** 10 l. brown & lt brown 10 10
414 40 l. brown and blue 10 10
415 100 l. brown and green 10 10

1963. 1100th Anniv of Conversion of Slavs by Saints Cyril and Methodius.
416 **106** 30 l. purple 10 10
417 – 70 l. brown 10 10
418 – 150 l. purple 15 15
DESIGNS: 70 l. Map of Moravia; 150 l. St. Methodius.

107 Pope Paul VI

108 St. Peter, Pharaoh's Tomb, Wadi-es-Sebua

1964. Pope Paul's Visit to the Holy Land.
419 **107** 15 l. black 10 10
420 – 25 l. red 10 10
421 – 70 l. sepia 10 10
422 – 160 l. blue 15 15
DESIGNS: 25 l. Church of the Nativity, Bethlehem; 70 l. Church of the Holy Sepulchre, Jerusalem; 160 l. Well of the Virgin Mary, Nazareth.

1964. Nubian Monuments Preservation.
423 **108** 10 l. brown and blue 10 10
424 – 20 l. multicoloured 10 10
425 **108** 70 l. brown & lt brown 10 10
426 – 200 l. multicoloured 15 15
DESIGN: 20, 200 l. Philae Temple.

109 Pope Paul VI

110 Michelangelo

1964. Vatican City's Participation in New York World's Fair.
427 **109** 15 l. blue 10 10
428 – 50 l. brown 10 10
429 **109** 100 l. blue 10 10
430 – 250 l. brown 20 20
DESIGNS: 50 l. Michelangelo's "Pieta"; 250 l. Detail of Madonna's head from "Pieta".

1964. 400th Death Anniv of Michelangelo. Paintings in the Sistine Chapel.
431 **110** 10 l. black 10 10
432 – 25 l. purple 10 10
433 – 30 l. green 10 10
434 – 40 l. violet 10 10
435 – 150 l. green 10 10
PAINTINGS: 25 l. Prophet Isaiah; 30 l. Delphic Sibyl; 10 l. Prophet Jeremiah, 150 l. Prophet Joel.

111 "The Good Samaritan" (after Emilio Greco)

1964. Red Cross Centenary (1963). Cross in red.
436 **111** 10 l. brown 10 10
437 30 l. blue 10 10
438 300 l. brown 30 30

112 "Christmas Scene" (after Kimiko Koseki) **114** Pope Paul at prayer

113 Cues's Birthplace

1964. Christmas.

439	**112**	10 l. multicoloured	10	10
440		15 l. multicoloured	10	10
441		135 l. multicoloured	10	10

1964. 500th Death Anniv of Nicholas Cues (Cardinal Cusanus).

442	**113**	40 l. green	10	10
443	–	200 l. red	20	20

DESIGN: 200 l. Cardinal Cusanus's sepulchre, St. Peter's (relief by A. Bregno).

1964. Pope Paul's Visit to India.

444	**114**	15 l. purple	10	10
445	–	25 l. green	10	10
446	–	60 l. brown	10	10
447	–	200 l. purple	20	20

DESIGN—HORIZ: 25 l. Public altar, "The Oval", Bombay; 60 l. "Gateway to India", Bombay. VERT: 200 l. Pope Paul walking across map of India.

115 Sts. Mbaga Tuzinde, Carolus Lwanga and Kizito **116** Dante (after Raphael)

1965. Ugandan Martyrs.

448	–	15 l. turquoise	10	10
449	**115**	20 l. brown	10	10
450	–	30 l. blue	10	10
451	–	75 l. black	10	10
452	–	100 l. red	10	10
453	–	160 l. violet	10	10

DESIGNS: 15 l. St. Joseph Mukasa and six other martyrs; 30 l. Sts. Matthias Mulumba, Noe Mawagalli and Lucas Banabakintu; 75 l. Sts. Gonzaga Gonza, Athanasius Bazzekuketta, Pontianus Ngondwe and Bruno Serunkuma; 100 l. Sts. Anatolius Kiriggwajjo, Andreas Kaggwa and Adulphus Mukasa; 160 l. Sts. Mukasa Kiriwananvu and Gyavira.

1965. 700th Anniv of Dante's Birth.

454	**116**	10 l. brown & light brown	10	10
455	–	40 l. brown and red	10	10
456	–	70 l. brown and green	15	15
457	–	200 l. brown and blue	20	20

DESIGNS—After drawings by Botticelli: 40 l. "Inferno"; 70 l. "Purgatory"; 200 l. "Paradise".

117 St. Benedict (after Perugino) **118** Pope Paul

1965. Declaration of St. Benedict as Patron Saint of Europe.

458	**117**	40 l. brown	10	10
459	–	300 l. green	25	25

DESIGN: 300 l. Montecassino Abbey.

1965. Pope Paul's Visit to the U.N., New York.

460	**118**	20 l. brown	10	10
461	–	30 l. blue	10	10
462	–	150 l. green	10	10
463	**118**	300 l. purple	20	20

DESIGN: 30, 150 l. U.N.O. Headquarters, New York.

119 "The Nativity" (Peruvian setting) **120** Pope Paul

1965. Christmas.

464	**119**	20 l. red	10	10
465		40 l. brown	10	10
466		200 l. green	15	15

1966.

467	**120**	5 l. brown	10	10
468	–	10 l. violet	10	10
469	–	15 l. brown	10	10
470	–	20 l. green	10	10
471	–	30 l. brown	10	10
472	–	40 l. turquoise	10	10
473	–	55 l. blue	10	10
474	–	75 l. purple	10	10
475	–	90 l. mauve	10	10
476	–	130 l. green	10	10

DESIGNS (SCULPTURES): 10 l. "Music"; 15 l. "Science"; 20 l. "Painting"; 30 l. "Sculpture"; 40 l. "Building"; 55 l. "Carpentry"; 75 l. "Agriculture"; 90 l. "Metallurgy"; 130 l. "Learning".

121 Queen Dabrowka and King Mieszko I

1966. Poland's Christian Millennium.

477	**121**	15 l. black	10	10
478	–	25 l. violet	10	10
479	–	40 l. red	10	10
480	–	50 l. red	10	10
481	–	150 l. grey	10	10
482	–	220 l. brown	15	15

DESIGNS: 25 l. St. Adalbert (Wojciech) and Wroclaw and Gniezno Cathedrals; 40 l. St. Stanislas, Skalka Cathedral and Wawel Royal Palace, Cracow; 50 l. Queen Jadwiga (Hedwig); Ostra Brama Gate with Mater Misericordiae, Wilno, and Jagellon University Library, Cracow; 150 l. "Black Madonna", Jasna Gora Monastery (Czestochowa) and St. John's Cathedral, Warsaw; 220 l. Pope Paul VI greeting Poles.

122 Pope John XXIII and St. Peter's, Rome

1966. 4th Anniv of Opening of Ecumenical Council.

483	**122**	10 l. black and red	10	10
484	–	15 l. green and brown	10	10
485	–	55 l. mauve and brown	10	10
486	–	90 l. black and green	10	10
487	–	100 l. yellow and green	10	10
488	–	130 l. sepia and brown	10	10

DESIGNS: 15 l. Book of Prayer, St. Peter's; 55 l. Mass; 90 l. Pope Paul with Patriarch Athenagoras; 100 l. Episcopal ring; 130 l. Pope Paul at closing ceremony (12.10.65).

123 "The Nativity" (after sculpture by Scorzelli) **124** Jetliner over St. Peter's

1966. Christmas.

489	**123**	20 l. purple	10	10
490		55 l. green	10	10
491		225 l. brown	15	15

1967. Air.

492	**124**	20 l. violet	10	10
493	–	40 l. lilac and pink	10	10
494	–	90 l. blue and grey	10	10
495	**124**	100 l. black and red	10	10
496	–	200 l. lilac and grey	15	10
497	–	500 l. brown & light brown	45	35

DESIGNS: 40, 200 l. Radio mast and St. Gabriel's statue; 90, 500 l. Aerial view of St. Peter's.

125 St. Peter **126** "The Three Shepherd Children" (sculpture)

1967. 1900th Anniv of Martyrdom of Saints Peter and Paul. Multicoloured.

498	15 l. Type **125**	10	10
499	20 l. St. Paul	10	10
500	55 l. The two Saints	10	10
501	90 l. Bernini's baldachin, St. Peter's	10	10
502	220 l. Arnolfo di Cambio's tabernacle, St. Paul's Basilica	20	20

1967. 50th Anniv of Fatima Apparitions. Multicoloured.

503	30 l. Type **126**	10	10
504	50 l. Basilica of Fatima	10	10
505	200 l. Pope Paul VI praying before Virgin's statue at Fatima	20	20

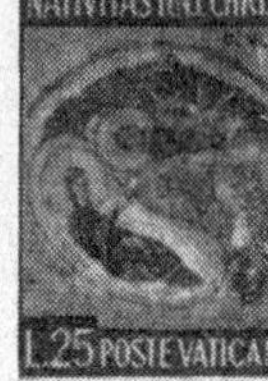

127 Congress Emblem **128** "The Nativity" (Byzantine carving)

1967. 3rd World Apostolic Laity Congress, Rome.

506	**127**	40 l. red	15	15
507		130 l. blue	15	15

1967. Christmas.

508	**128**	25 l. multicoloured	10	10
509		55 l. multicoloured	10	10
510		180 l. multicoloured	15	15

129 "Angel Gabriel" (detail from "The Annunciation" by Fra Angelico) **130** Pope Paul VI

1968. Air.

511	**129**	1000 l. red on cream	70	80
512		1500 l. black on cream	1·10	1·10

1968. Pope Paul's Visit to Colombia.

513	**130**	25 l. brown and black	10	10
514	–	55 l. brown, grey & black	10	10
515	–	220 l. brown, blue & black	20	20

DESIGNS: 55 l. Monstrance (Raphael's "Disputa"); 220 l. Map of South America.

131 "The Holy Child of Prague" **132** "The Resurrection" (Fra Angelico)

1968. Christmas.

516	**131**	20 l. purple and red	10	10
517		50 l. violet and lilac	10	10
518		250 l. blue and light blue	20	20

1969. Easter.

519	**132**	20 l. red and buff	10	10
520		90 l. green and buff	10	10
521		180 l. blue and buff	15	15

133 Colonnade **134** Pope with Young Africans

1969. Europa.

522	**133**	50 l. brown and grey	10	10
523		90 l. brown and red	15	15
524		130 l. brown and green	15	15

1969. Pope Paul's Visit to Uganda.

525	**134**	25 l. brown and ochre	10	10
526	–	55 l. brown and red	10	10
527	–	250 l. multicoloured	20	20

DESIGNS: 55 l. Pope with African bishops; 250 l. Map of Africa and olive branch.

135 Pope Pius IX **136** "Expo 70" Emblem

1969. Centenary of St. Peter's Circle Society.

528	**135**	30 l. brown	10	10
529	–	50 l. grey	10	10
530	–	220 l. purple	20	20

DESIGNS: 50 l. Monogram of Society; 220 l. Pope Paul VI.

1970. "Expo 70" World's Fair, Osaka. Mult.

531	25 l. Type **136**	10	10
532	40 l. Osaka Castle	10	10
533	55 l. "Madonna and Child" (Domoto)	10	10
534	90 l. Vatican pavilion	10	10
535	110 l. Mt. Fuji	10	10

137 Commemorative Medal of Pius IX

1970. Centenary of 1st Vatican Council.

536	**137**	20 l. brown and orange	10	10
537	–	50 l. multicoloured	10	10
538	–	180 l. purple and red	15	15

DESIGNS: 50 l. Arms of Pius IX; 180 l. Council souvenir medal.

138 "Christ" (Simone Martini)

1970. 50th Anniv of Pope Paul's Ordination as Priest. Multicoloured.

539	15 l. Type **138**	10	10
540	25 l. "Christ" (R. v. d. Weyden)	10	10
541	50 l. "Christ" (Durer)	10	10
542	90 l. "Christ" (El Greco)	10	10
543	180 l. Pope Paul VI	15	15

139 "Adam" (Michelangelo) **140** Pope Paul VI

1970. 25th Anniv of United Nations.
544 20 l. Type **139** 10 10
545 90 l. "Eve" (Michelangelo) . . 10 10
546 220 l. Olive branch 20 20

1970. Pope Paul's Visit to Asia and Oceania. Multicoloured.
547 25 l. Type **140** 10 10
548 55 l. "Holy Child of Cebu" (Philippines) 10 10
549 100 l. "Madonna and Child", Darwin Cathedral (G. Hamori) 10 10
550 130 l. Manila Cathedral . . . 10 10
551 220 l. Sydney Cathedral . . . 15 15

141 "Angel with Lectern"

142 "Madonna and Child" (F. Gnissi)

1971. Racial Equality Year. Multicoloured.
552 20 l. Type **141** 10 10
553 40 l. "Christ Crucified, and Doves" 10 10
554 50 l. Type **141** 10 10
555 130 l. As 40 l. 10 10

1971. Easter. Religious Paintings. Multicoloured.
556 25 l. Type **142** 10 10
557 40 l. "Madonna and Child" ("Sassetta", S. di Giovanni) 10 10
558 55 l. "Madonna and Child" (C. Crivelli) 10 10
559 90 l. "Madonna and Child" (C. Maratta) 10 10
560 180 l. "The Holy Family" (G. Ceracchini) 15 15

143 "St. Dominic Guzman" (Sienese School)

1971. 800th Birth Anniv of St. Dominic Guzman (founder of Preaching Friars Order). Mult.
561 25 l. Type **143** 10 10
562 55 l. Portrait by Fra Angelico 10 10
563 90 l. Portrait by Titian 10 10
564 180 l. Portrait by El Greco . . 15 15

144 "St. Matthew"

1971. Air.
565 **144** 200 l. black and green . . 15 25
566 – 300 l. black and brown . . 25 35
567 – 500 l. black and pink . . 60 65
568 – 1000 l. black and mauve . 80 75
DESIGNS: "The Four Evangelists" (ceiling frescoes by Fra Angelico in the Niccolina Chapel, Vatican City): 300 l. "St. Mark"; 500 l. "St. Luke"; 1000 l. "St. John".

145 "St. Stephen" (from chasuble, Szekesfehervar Church, Hungary)

146 Bramante's Design for Cupola, St. Peter's

1971. Millennium of St. Stephen, King of Hungary.
569 **145** 50 l. multicoloured 10 10
570 – 180 l. black and yellow . . 15 15
DESIGN: 180 l. "Madonna, Patroness of Hungary", (sculpture, circa 1511).

1972. Bramante Celebrations.
571 **146** 25 l. black and yellow . . 10 10
572 – 90 l. black and yellow . . 10 10
573 – 130 l. black and yellow . . 15 15
DESIGNS: 90 l. Donato Bramante (architect) from medal; 130 l. Spiral staircase, Innocent VIII's Belvedere, Vatican.

147 "St. Mark at Sea" (mosaic)

1972. U.N.E.S.C.O. "Save Venice" Campaign. Multicoloured.
574 25 l. Type **147** 30 30
575 50 l. Venice (top left-hand section) 15 15
576 50 l. Venice (top right-hand section) 15 15
577 50 l. Venice (bottom left-hand section) 15 15
578 50 l. Venice (bottom right-hand section) 15 15
579 180 l. St. Mark's Basilica . . . 1·00 1·00
Nos. 575/8 are smaller 39×28 mm and were issued together, se-tenant, forming a composite design of a 1581 fresco showing a panoramic map of Venice.

148 Gospel of St. Mark (from codex "Biblia dell'Aracoeli")

1972. International Book Year. Illuminated Manuscripts. Multicoloured.
581 30 l. Type **148** 10 10
582 50 l. Gospel of St. Luke ("Biblia dell'Aracoeli") 10 10
583 90 l. 2nd Epistle of St. John (Bologna codex) 10 10
584 100 l. Revelation of St. John (Bologna codex) 10 10
585 130 l. Epistle of St. Paul to the Romans (Italian codex) . . 15 15

149 Luigi Orione (founder of "Caritas")

1972. Birth Centenaries. Multicoloured.
586 50 l. Type **149** 10 10
587 180 l. Lorenzo Perosi (composer) 25 30

150 Cardinal Bassarione (Roselli fresco, Sistine Chapel)

151 Congress Emblem

1972. 500th Death Anniv of Cardinal Bassarione.
588 – 40 l. green 10 10
589 **150** 90 l. red 10 10
590 – 130 l. black 15 15
DESIGNS: 40 l. "Reading of Bull of Union" (relief); 130 l. Arms of Cardinal Bassarione.

1973. Int Eucharistic Congress. Melbourne. Mult.
591 25 l. Type **151** 10 10
592 75 l. Michelangelo's "Pieta" . 10 10
593 300 l. Melbourne Cathedral . 20 20

152 St. Theresa's Birthplace

153 Torun (birthplace)

1973. Birth Centenary of St. Theresa of Lisieux.
594 **152** 25 l. black and red . . . 10 10
595 – 55 l. black and yellow . . 10 10
596 – 220 l. black and blue . . 15 15
DESIGNS: 55 l. St. Theresa; 220 l. Basilica of Lisieux.

1973. 500th Birth Anniv of Copernicus.
597 **153** 20 l. green 10 10
598 – 50 l. brown 10 10
599 **153** 100 l. purple 15 15
600 – 130 l. blue 15 20
DESIGN: 50, 130 l. Copernicus.

154 "St. Wenceslas"

1973. Millenary of Prague Diocese. Mult.
601 20 l. Type **154** 10 10
602 90 l. Arms of Prague Diocese . 10 10
603 150 l. Tower of Prague Cathedral 15 15
604 220 l. "St. Adalbert" 25 25

155 Church of St. Hripsime

156 "Angel" (porch of St. Mark's, Venice)

1973. 800th Death Anniv of St. Narsete Shnorali (Armenian patriarch).
605 **155** 25 l. brown and ochre . . 10 10
606 – 90 l. black and lilac . . . 10 10
607 – 180 l. purple and green . . 20 20
DESIGNS: 90 l. Armenian "khatchkar" (stone stele) inscribed "Victory"; 180 l. St. Narsete Shnorali.

1974. Air.
608 **156** 2500 l. multicoloured . . . 2·00 2·00

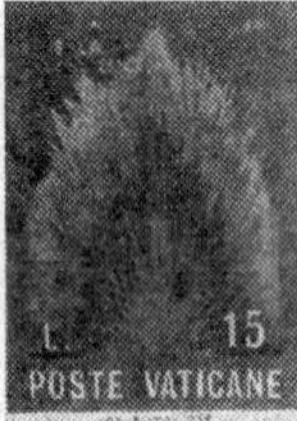

157 "And there was Light"

159 Pupils

158 Noah's Ark and Dove

1974. International Book Year (1973). "The Bible". Biblical Texts. Multicoloured.
609 15 l. Type **157** 10 10
610 25 l. "Noah entrusts himself to God" (horiz) 10 10
611 50 l. "The Annunciation" . . . 10 10
612 90 l. "The Nativity" 10 10
613 180 l. "The Lord feeds His People" (horiz) 15 15

1974. Centenary of U.P.U. Mosaics. Multicoloured.
614 50 l. Type **158** 10 10
615 90 l. Sheep in landscape . . . 20 20

1974. 700th Death Anniv of St. Thomas Aquinas (founder of Fra Angelico School). "The School of St. Thomas" (painting, St. Mark's Convent, Florence). Each brown and gold.
616 50 l. Type **159** 10 10
617 90 l. St. Thomas and pupils (24×40 mm) 15 15
618 220 l. Pupils (different) . . . 20 20
Nos. 616/18 were issued together, se-tenant, forming a composite design.

160 "Civita" (medieval quarter), Bagnoregio

161 Christus Victor

1974. 700th Death Anniv of St. Bonaventura of Bagnoregio. Wood-carvings. Multicoloured.
619 40 l. Type **160** 10 10
620 90 l. "Tree of Life" (13th-century motif) 10 10
621 220 l. "St. Bonaventura (B. Gozzoli) 15 15

1974. Holy Year (1975). Multicoloured.
622 10 l. Type **161** 10 10
623 25 l. Christ 10 10
624 30 l. Christ (different) 10 10
625 40 l. Cross and dove 10 10
626 50 l. Christ enthroned 10 10
627 55 l. St. Peter 10 10
628 90 l. St. Paul 10 10
629 100 l. St. Peter 10 10
630 130 l. St. Paul 10 10
631 220 l. Arms of Pope Paul VI . 20 20
632 250 l. Pope Paul VI giving blessing 20 20

162 Fountain, St. Peter's Square

1975. European Architectural Heritage Year. Fountains.
633 **162** 20 l. black and brown . . 10 10
634 – 40 l. black and lilac . . . 10 10
635 – 50 l. black and pink . . . 10 10
636 – 90 l. black and green . . 10 10
637 – 100 l. black and green . . 10 10
638 – 200 l. black and blue . . 15 15
FOUNTAINS: 40 l. Piazza St. Martha; 50 l. Del Forno; 90 l. Belvedere courtyard; 100 l. Academy of Sciences; 200 l. Galley fountain.

163 "Pentecost" (El Greco)

164 "Miracle of Loaves and Fishes" (gilt glass)

1975. Pentecost.
639 **163** 300 l. orange and red . . 30 30

1975. 9th International Christian Archaeological Congress. 4th-century Art. Multicoloured.
640 30 l. Type **164** 10 10
641 150 l. Christ (painting) . . . 10 10
642 200 l. Raising of Lazarus (gilt glass) 20 20

165 Pope Sixtus IV investing Bartolomeo Sacchi as First Librarian (fresco)

1975. 500th Anniv of Apostolic Library.
643 **165** 70 l. red and violet . . . 10 10
644 – 100 l. green & light green 10 10
645 – 250 l. red and blue . . . 25 25
DESIGNS—VERT: 100 l. Pope Sixtus IV (codex). HORIZ: 250 l. Pope Sixtus IV visiting library (fresco).

MINIMUM PRICE

The minimum price quoted is 10p which represents a handling charge rather than a basis for valuing common stamps. For further notes about prices, see introductory pages.

166 Passionists' House, Argentario
167 Detail from Painting

1975. Death Bicentenary of St. Paul of the Cross (founder of Passionist religious order). Mult.

646 50 l. Type **166** 10 10
647 150 l. "St. Paul" (D. della Porta) (26 × 31 mm) 15 15
648 300 l. Basilica of Saints John and Paul 30 30

1975. International Women's Year. Painting by Fra Angelico. Multicoloured.

649 100 l. Type **167** 15 15
650 200 l. Detail from painting (different) 25 25

168 "The Last Judgement" (detail)
170 Eucharist Ear of Wheat and Globe

169 "Madonna in Glory with the Child Jesus and Six Saints" (detail)

1976. Air.

651 **168** 500 l. brown and blue . . 1·00 1·00
652 – 1000 l. brown and blue . . 1·10 1·00
653 – 2500 l. brown and blue . . 1·50 1·50

DESIGNS: 1000 l., 2500 l. Different motifs from Michelangelo's "The Last Judgement".

1976. 400th Death Anniv of Titian. Details from "The Madonna in Glory with the Child Jesus and Six Saints".

654 **169** 100 l. red 20 20
655 – 300 l. red 30 30

1976. 41st Int Eucharist Congress, Philadelphia.

656 **170** 150 l. multicoloured . . . 15 15
657 – 200 l. gold and blue . . . 20 20
658 – 400 l. gold and green . . . 30 30

DESIGNS: 200 l. Eucharist within protective hands; 400 l. Adoration of the Eucharist.

171 "Transfiguration" (detail)

1976. Details of Raphael's "Transfiguration". Multicoloured.

659 30 l. Type **171** ("Moses") . . 10 10
660 40 l. "Christ Transfigured" . . 10 10
661 50 l. "Prophet Elijah" 10 10
662 100 l. "Two Apostles" 10 10
663 150 l. "The Relatives" 15 15
664 200 l. "Landscape" 20 20

172 St. John's Tower and Fountain

1976. Architecture.

665 **172** 50 l. brown and lilac . . 10 10
666 – 100 l. sepia and brown . . 10 10
667 – 120 l. black and green . . 10 10
668 – 180 l. black and grey . . 20 20
669 – 250 l. brown and stone . 25 25
670 – 300 l. purple 30 30

DESIGNS: 100 l. Fountain of the Sacrament; 120 l. Fountain at entrance to Gardens; 180 l. Cupola of St. Peter's and Sacristy Basilica; 250 l. Borgia Tower, Sistine Chapel and Via della Fondamenta; 300 l. Apostolic Palace, Courtyard of St. Damasius.

173 "Canticles of Brother Sun" (detail)

1977. 750th Death Anniv of St. Francis of Assisi. Details from "Canticles of Brother Sun" by D. Cambellotti. Multicoloured.

671 50 l. Type **173** ("The Lord's Creatures") 10 10
672 70 l. "Brother Sun" 10 10
673 100 l. "Sister Moon and Stars" 10 10
674 130 l. "Sister Water" 10 15
675 170 l. "Praise in Infirmities and Tribulations" 15 20
676 200 l. "Praise for Bodily Death" 20 20

174 Detail from Fresco
175 "Death of the Virgin"

1977. 600th Anniv of Return of Pope Gregory from Avignon. Fresco by G. Vasari. Multicoloured.

677 170 l. Type **174** 20 25
678 350 l. Detail from fresco (different) 40 40

1977. Festival of Assumption. Miniatures from Apostolic Library. Multicoloured.

679 200 l. Type **175** 25 25
680 400 l. "Assumption of Virgin into Heaven" 40 45

176 "God of the Nile"

1977. Classical Sculpture in Vatican Museums (1st series). Statues. Multicoloured.

681 50 l. Type **176** 10 10
682 120 l. "Pericles" 10 10
683 130 l. "Husband and Wife with joined Hands" 15 15
684 150 l. "Belvedere Apollo" . . 15 15
685 170 l. "Laocoon" 15 15
686 350 l. "Belvedere Torso" . . 20 30

See also Nos. 687/92.

177 "Creation of the Human Race"

1977. Classical Sculpture in Vatican Museums (2nd series). Paleo-Christian Sarcophagi Carvings. Multicoloured.

687 50 l. Type **177** 10 10
688 70 l. "Three Youths in the Fiery Furnace" 10 10
689 100 l. "Adoration of the Magi" 10 10
690 130 l. "Christ raising Lazarus from the Dead" 15 15
691 200 l. "The Good Shepherd" 25 25
692 400 l. "Resurrection" 40 40

178 "Madonna with the Parrot" (detail)
180 Arms of Pope Pius IX

179 "The Face of Christ"

1977. 400th Birth Anniv of Rubens.

693 **178** 350 l. multicoloured . . . 40 40

1978. 80th Birthday of Pope Paul VI. Mult.

694 350 l. Type **179** 35 35
695 400 l. "Pope Paul VI" (drawing by L. B. Barriviera) 40 40

1978. Death Cent of Pope Pius IX. Multicoloured.

696 130 l. Type **180** 10 10
697 170 l. Seal of Pius IX 15 15
698 200 l. Portrait of Pius IX . . . 25 25

181 Microwave Antenna and Radio Vatican Emblem
182 St. Peter's Keys

1978. Air. 10th World Telecommunications Day.

699 **181** 1000 l. multicoloured . . . 80 60
700 2000 l. multicoloured . . . 1·75 1·50
701 3000 l. multicoloured . . . 2·50 2·00

1978. "Vacant See".

702 **182** 120 l. blue and violet . . . 15 15
703 150 l. pink and violet . . . 15 15
704 250 l. yellow and violet . . 20 20

183 St. Peter's Keys
184 Pope John Paul I on Throne

1978. "Vacant See".

705 **183** 120 l. yellow, blue & blk . 15 20
706 200 l. yellow, red & blk . . 15 20
707 250 l. multicoloured . . . 20 30

1978. Pope John Paul I Commem. Mult.

708 70 l. Type **184** 10 10
709 120 l. The Pope smiling . . . 15 15
710 250 l. The Pope in Vatican Gardens 20 20
711 350 l. The Pope giving blessing (horiz) 30 30

185 Arms of Pope John Paul II
186 The Martyrdom (14th-century Latin codex)

1979. Inauguration of Pontificate of Pope John Paul II. Multicoloured.

712 170 l. Type **185** 20 20
713 250 l. The Pope giving his blessing 25 25
714 400 l. "Christ handing the keys to St. Peter" (relief, A. Buonvicino) 45 45

1979. 900th Death Anniv of St. Stanislaus. Multicoloured.

715 120 l. Type **186** 15 15
716 150 l. St. Stanislaus appears to the people (14th century Latin codex) 15 15
717 250 l. Gold reliquary 25 25
718 500 l. Cracow Cathedral . . . 40 40

187 Meteorograph

1979. Death Centenary of Angelo Secchi (astronomer). Multicoloured.

719 180 l. Type **187** 20 20
720 220 l. Spectroscope 25 25
721 300 l. Telescope 30 30

188 St. Basil and Vignette "Handing Monastic Laws to a Hermit"
189 Aerial View of Vatican City

1979. 160th Death Anniv of St. Basil the Great. Multicoloured.

722 150 l. Type **188** 15 15
723 520 l. St. Basil and vignette "Caring for the Sick" . . . 45 55

1979. 50th Anniv of Vatican City State.

724 **189** 50 l. brown, black & pink 10 10
725 – 70 l. multicoloured . . . 10 10
726 – 120 l. multicoloured . . . 15 15
727 – 150 l. multicoloured . . . 15 15
728 – 170 l. multicoloured . . . 20 20
729 – 250 l. multicoloured . . . 30 30
730 – 450 l. multicoloured . . . 55 65

DESIGNS—POPES AND ARMS: 70 l. Pius XI; 120 l. Pius XII; 150 l. John XXIII; 170 l. Paul VI; 250 l. John Paul I; 450 l. John Paul II.

190 Child in Swaddling Clothes (relief, Foundling Hospital, Florence)

1979. International Year of the Child. Sculptures by Della Robbia.

731 **190** 50 l. multicoloured . . . 10 10
732 – 120 l. multicoloured . . . 20 20
733 – 200 l. multicoloured . . . 25 25
734 – 350 l. multicoloured . . . 40 45

DESIGNS: 120 l. to 350 l. Similar sculptures.

191 Abbot Desiderius offering Codices to St. Benedict

1980. 1500th Birth Anniv of St. Benedict of Nursia (founder of Benedictine Order). Multicoloured.

735 80 l. Type **191** 10 10
736 100 l. St. Benedict composing rules of the Order 10 10
737 150 l. Page of St. Benedict's Rules 15 15
738 220 l. Death of St. Benedict . 20 20
739 450 l. Montecassino Abbey (after Paul Bril) 40 40

192 Hands reaching out to Pope and Arms of Santo Domingo

1980. Air. Pope John Paul II's Journeys (1st series). Different coats of arms.
740 **192** 200 l. multicoloured . . . 25 25
741 – 300 l. multicoloured . . . 35 35
742 – 500 l. violet, red & black . 60 60
743 – 1000 l. multicoloured . . 1·25 90
744 – 1500 l. multicoloured . . . 1·75 1·40
745 – 2000 l. red, blue & black . 2·25 2·00
746 – 3000 l. black, red & blue . 3·50 3·00
COATS OF ARMS: 300 l. Mexico; 500 l. Poland; 1000 l. Ireland; 1500 l. United States; 2000 l. United Nations; 3000 l. Pope John Paul II, Archbishop Dimitrios and arms of Turkey.
See also Nos. 768/78, 814/25, 862/9, 886/93, 912/16, 940/4, 963/6, 992/6, 1019/22, 1049/51, 1076/80, 1113/14 and 1136/41.

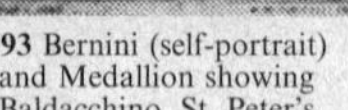
193 Bernini (self-portrait) and Medallion showing Baldacchino, St. Peter's

194 St. Albertus on Mission of Peace

1980. 300th Death Anniv of Gian Lorenzo Bernini (artist and architect). Multicoloured.
747 80 l. Type **193** 10 10
748 170 l. Bernini and medallion showing his plan for St. Peter's 15 15
749 250 l. Bernini, medallion of bronze chair and group "Doctors of the Church", St. Peter's 25 25
750 350 l. Bernini and medallion of Apostolic Palace stairway . 35 35

1980. 700th Death Anniv of St. Albertus Magnus. Multicoloured.
751 300 l. Type **194** 35 35
752 400 l. St. Albertus as Bishop . 45 45

195 Communion of the Saints

1980. Feast of All Saints. Multicoloured.
753 250 l. Type **195** 30 30
754 500 l. Christ and saints . . . 55 55

196 Marconi, Pope Pius XI and Radio Emblem

1981. 50th Anniv of Vatican Radio. Mult.
755 100 l. Type **196** 10 10
756 150 l. Microphone 15 15
757 200 l. Antenna of Santa Maria di Galeria Radio Centre and statue of Archangel Gabriel 20 20
758 600 l. Pope John Paul II . . . 65 65

197 Virgil and his Writing-desk

1981. Death Bimillenary of Virgil (Roman poet). Multicoloured.
759 350 l. Type **197** 40 50
760 600 l. As Type **197** but inscr "P. VERGILI MARONIS AENEIDOS LIBRI" . . . 65 65

198 Congress Emblem and Apparition of Virgin to St. Bernadette

199 Jan van Ruusbroec writing Treatise

1981. 42nd International Eucharistic Congress, Lourdes. Multicoloured.
761 80 l. Congress emblem . . . 10 10
762 150 l. Type **198** 20 20
763 200 l. Emblem and pilgrims going to Lourdes 25 25
764 500 l. Emblem and Bishop with faithful venerating Virgin . 55 55

1981. 600th Death Anniv of Jan van Ruusbroec (Flemish mystic). Multicoloured.
765 200 l. Type **199** 25 25
766 300 l. Ruusbroec 35 35

200 Turin Shroud and I.Y.D.P. Emblem

201 Arms of John Paul II

1981. International Year of Disabled Persons.
767 **200** 600 l. multicoloured . . . 60 60

1981. Pope John Paul II's Journeys (2nd series). Multicoloured.
768 50 l. Type **201** 10 10
769 100 l. Crucifix and map of Africa 10 10
770 120 l. Hands holding crucifix 15 15
771 150 l. Pope performing baptism 15 15
772 200 l. Pope embracing African bishop 20 20
773 250 l. Pope blessing sick man 30 30
774 300 l. Notre-Dame Cathedral, Paris 35 35
775 400 l. Pope addressing U.N.E.S.C.O., Paris . . . 45 45
776 600 l. "Christ of the Andes", Rio de Janeiro 70 70
777 700 l. Cologne Cathedral . . 80 80
778 900 l. Pope giving blessing . . 1·00 1·00

202 Agnes handing Church to Grand Master of the Crosiers of the Red Star

203 "Pueri Cantores" (left panel)

1982. 700th Death Anniv of Blessed Agnes of Prague. Multicoloured.
779 700 l. Type **202** 75 75
780 900 l. Agnes receiving letter from St. Clare 95 95

1982. 500th Death Anniv of Luca della Robbia (sculptor).
781 **203** 1000 l. green and blue . . 1·00 1·00
782 – 1000 l. multicoloured . . 1·00 1·00
783 – 1000 l. green and blue . . 1·00 1·00
DESIGNS—As T **203**: No. 783, "Pueri Cantores" (right panel). 44 × 36 mm: No. 782, "Virgin Mary in Prayer".

204 Virgin Mary and St. Joseph clothe St. Theresa

205 Examining Globe

1982. 400th Death Anniv of St. Theresa of Avila.
784 **204** 200 l. orange, grey and red 25 25
785 – 600 l. grey, orange and blue 65 65
786 – 1000 l. grey, orange and mauve . . . . 1·00 1·00
DESIGNS: 600 l. Ecstasy of St. Theresa; 1000 l. St. Theresa writing "The Interior Castle".

1982. 400th Anniv of Gregorian Calendar. Details from Pope Gregory XIII's tomb.
787 **205** 200 l. green 25 25
788 – 300 l. black 35 35
789 – 700 l. mauve 75 75
DESIGNS: 300 l. Presenting proposals to Pope Gregory XIII; 700 l. Kneeling figures.

206 "Nativity" (Veit Stoss)

1982. Christmas.
791 **206** 300 l. stone, brn & gold . 35 35
792 – 450 l. lilac, purple & silver 50 50
DESIGN: 450 l. "Nativity with Pope John Paul II" (Enrico Manfrini).

207 Crucifixion

209 "Theology"

1983. Holy Year. Multicoloured.
793 300 l. Type **207** 35 35
794 350 l. Christ the Redeemer . . 40 40
795 400 l. Pope bringing message of redemption to world 45 45
796 2000 l. Dove of the Holy Spirit passing through Holy Door . 2·25 2·25

1983. 500th Birth Anniv of Raphael (artist).
798 **209** 50 l. blue & ultramarine . 10 10
799 – 400 l. purple and mauve . 45 45
800 – 500 l. brown & chestnut . 55 55
801 – 1200 l. green & turquoise . 1·25 1·25
DESIGNS—Allegories on the Segnatura Room ceiling: 400 l. "Poetry"; 500 l. "Justice"; 1200 l. "Philosophy".

210 "Moses explaining the Law to the People" (Luca Signorelli)

1983. Air. World Communications Year. Multicoloured.
804 2000 l. Type **210** . . . . . . 2·50 2·00
805 5000 l. "St. Paul preaching in Athens" (Raphael) . . . . . 5·50 4·75

211 Mendel and Hybrid Experiment

212 St. Casimir and Vilna Cathedral and Castle

1984. Death Centenary of Gregor Johann Mendel (geneticist).
806 **211** 450 l. multicoloured . . . 65 65
807 1500 l. multicoloured . . . 1·75 1·75

1984. 500th Death Anniv of St. Casimir (patron saint of Lithuania).
808 **212** 550 l. multicoloured . . . 75 75
809 1200 l. multicoloured . . . 1·75 1·75

213 Pontifical Academy of Sciences

1984. Cultural and Scientific Institutions.
810 **213** 150 l. yellow and brown . 25 25
811 – 450 l. multicoloured . . . 55 55
812 – 550 l. yellow and violet . 65 65
813 – 1500 l. yellow and blue . 1·75 1·75
DESIGNS: 450 l. Seals and document from Vatican Secret Archives; 550 l. Entrance to Vatican Apostolic Library; 1500 l. Vatican Observatory, Castelgandolfo.

214 Pope in Karachi

215 Damascus and Sepulchre of Sts. Marcellinus and Peter

1984. Pope John Paul II's Journeys (3rd series). Multicoloured.
814 50 l. Type **214** 10 10
815 100 l. Pope and image of Our Lady of Penafrancia, Philippines 10 10
816 150 l. Pope with crucifix (Guam) 20 10
817 250 l. Pope and Tokyo Cathedral 50 30
818 300 l. Pope at Anchorage, Alaska 30 20
819 400 l. Crucifix, crowd and map of Africa 40 15
820 450 l. Pope and image of Our Lady of Fatima (Portugal) . 45 15
821 550 l. Pope, Archbishop of Westminster and Canterbury Cathedral . . . . 1·25 90
822 1000 l. Pope and image of Our Lady of Lujan (Argentina) . 2·00 1·25
823 1500 l. Pope, Lake Leman and Geneva . . . . 3·00 2·00
824 2500 l. Pope and Mount Titano (San Marino) . . . . 5·00 3·00
825 4000 l. Pope and Santiago de Compostela Cathedral (Spain) 8·00 3·75

1984. 1600th Death Anniv of Pope St. Damasus. Multicoloured.
826 200 l. Type **215** 30 30
827 500 l. Damasus and epigraph from St. Januarius's tomb . 90 90
828 2000 l. Damasus and basilica ruins . . . . 3·00 3·00

216 More (after Holbein) and Map

217 St. Methodius holding Religious Paintings

1985. 450th Death Anniv of Saint Thomas More. Multicoloured.
829 250 l. Type **216** 45 45
830 400 l. St. Thomas More and title page of "Utopia" 85 85
831 2000 l. St. Thomas More and title page of "Life of Thomas More" by Domenico Regi . 3·50 3·50

1985. 1100th Death Anniv of Saint Methodius. Multicoloured.
832 500 l. Type **217** 75 75
833 600 l. Saints Cyril and Methodius with Pope Clement I's body 1·00 1·00
834 1700 l. Saints Benedict, Cyril and Methodius . . . . 2·50 2·50

218 Cross on Map of Africa

219 Eagle (from Door, St. Paul's Basilica, Rome)

1985. 43rd International Eucharistic Congress, Nairobi. Multicoloured.
835 100 l. Type **218** 15 15
836 400 l. Assembly of bishops . . 45 45
837 600 l. Chalice 65 65
838 2300 l. Family gazing at cross 2·75 2·75

1985. 900th Death Anniv of Pope Gregory VII. Multicoloured.
839 150 l. Type **219** 30 30
840 450 l. Pope Gregory VII . . . 75 75
841 2500 l. Pope Gregory's former sarcophagus (horiz) . . . . 4·00 4·00

220 Mosaic Map of Italy and Symbol of Holy See

1985. Ratification of Modification of 1929 Lateran Concordat.
842 **220** 400 l. multicoloured . . . 60 60

221 Carriage **222** "Nation shall not Lift up Sword against Nation. . ."

1985. "Italia '85" Int Stamp Exn, Rome.
843 **221** 450 l. red and blue 65 65
844 – 1500 l. blue and mauve . . 2·10 2·10
DESIGN: 1500 l. Carriage (different).

1986. International Peace Year. Multicoloured.
846 50 l. Type **222** 10 10
847 350 l. Messenger's feet ("How beautiful. . .are the feet. . .") 50 50
848 450 l. Profiles and olive branch ("Blessed are the peace-makers. . .") 80 80
849 650 l. Dove and sun ("Glory to God in the highest. . .") . . 1·00 1·00
850 2000 l. Pope's hand releasing dove over rainbow ("Peace is a value with no frontiers. . .") 3·00 3·00

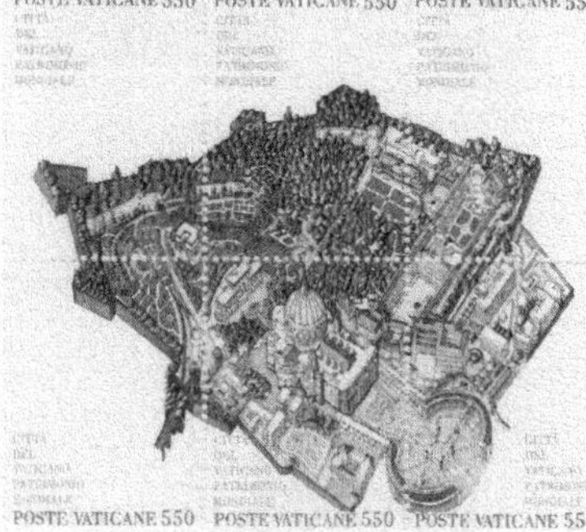

223/228 Vatican City (actual size 89 × 80 mm)

1986. World Heritage. Vatican City. Mult.
851 **223** 550 l. multicoloured . . . 1·00 1·00
852 **224** 550 l. multicoloured . . . 1·00 1·00
853 **225** 550 l. multicoloured . . . 1·00 1·00
854 **226** 550 l. multicoloured . . . 1·00 1·00
855 **227** 550 l. multicoloured . . . 1·00 1·00
856 **228** 550 l. multicoloured . . . 1·00 1·00
Nos. 851/6 were printed together, se-tenant, forming the composite design illustrated.

229 St. Camillus saving Invalid from Flood (after Pierre Subleyras) **230** "The Philosophers"

1986. Centenary of Proclamation of St. Camillus de Lellis and St. John of God as Patron Saints of Hospitals and the Sick.
857 **229** 700 l. green, violet & red . 1·00 1·00
858 – 700 l. blue, green & red . . 1·00 1·00
859 – 2000 l. multicoloured . . . 3·50 3·50
DESIGNS: No. 858, St. John supporting the sick (after Gomez Moreno); 859, Emblems of Ministers of the Sick and Brothers Hospitallers, and Pope John Paul II talking to patient.

1986. 50th Anniv of Pontifical Academy of Sciences. Details from fresco "School of Athens" by Raphael. Multicoloured.
860 1500 l. Type **230** . . . . . . 2·50 2·50
861 2500 l. "The Scientists" . . . 3·75 3·75

231 Pope and Young People (Central America) **232** "St. Augustine reading St. Paul's Epistles" (fresco, Benozzo Gozzoli)

1986. Air. Pope John Paul II's Journeys (4th series). Multicoloured.
862 350 l. Type **231** 60 60
863 450 l. Pope in prayer, Warsaw Cathedral and Our Lady of Czestochowa (Poland) . . . 75 75
864 700 l. Pope kneeling and crowd at Lourdes (France) . . . . . 1·10 1·10
865 1000 l. Sanctuary of Mariazell and St. Stephen's Cathedral, Vienna (Austria) . . . . . 1·60 1·40
866 1500 l. Pope and representatives of nations visited (Alaska, Asia and Pacific Islands) . . . 2·50 2·00
867 2000 l. Image of St. Nicholas of Flue, Basilica of Einsiedeln and Pope (Switzerland) . . 3·25 2·50
868 2500 l. Crosses, Notre Dame Cathedral, Quebec, and Pope (Canada) . . . . 3·75 3·00
869 5000 l. Pope, bishop and young people with cross (Spain, Dominican Republic and Puerto Rico) . . . . 7·50 6·00

1987. 1600th Anniv of Conversion and Baptism of St. Augustine. Multicoloured.
870 300 l. Type **232** 55 50
871 400 l. "Baptism of St. Augustine" (Bartolomeo di Gentile) . . 70 70
872 500 l. "Ecstasy of St. Augustine" (fresco, Benozzo Gozzoli) . 80 80
873 2200 l. "Dispute of the Sacrament" (detail of fresco, Raphael) . . . . 3·75 3·75

233 Statue of Christ, Lithuanian Chapel, Vatican Crypt **234** Chapter of Riga Church Seal

1987. 600th Anniv of Conversion to Christianity of Lithuania. Multicoloured.
874 200 l. Type **233** 45 45
875 700 l. Statue of Virgin Mary with body of Christ and two angels 1·25 1·25
876 3000 l. Lithuanian shrine . . . 4·25 4·25

1987. 800th Anniv of Conversion to Christianity of Latvia. Multicoloured.
877 700 l. Type **234** . . . . 1·00 1·00
878 2400 l. Basilica of the Assumption, Aglona . . . 3·75 3·75

235 Judge **236** Stamp Room and 1929 5 c. Stamp

1987. "Olymphilex '87" Olympic Stamps Exhibition, Rome. Figures from Caracalla Baths floor mosaic. Multicoloured.
879 400 l. Type **235** 70 70
880 500 l. Runner 80 80
881 600 l. Discus-thrower . . . . 1·00 1·00
882 2000 l. Athlete . . . . 3·50 3·50

1987. Inauguration of Philatelic and Numismatic Museum. Multicoloured.
884 400 l. Type **236** 60 60
885 3500 l. Coin room and reverse of 1000 l. 1986 coin . . . . . . 5·00 5·00

1987. Pope John Paul II's Journeys (5th series). As T **231**. Multicoloured.
886 50 l. Youths, Pope and Machu Picchu (Venezuela, Ecuador, Peru, Trinidad and Tobago) 20 20
887 250 l. Antwerp Cathedral, smoke stacks and Pope (Netherlands, Luxembourg and Belgium) . 50 50
888 400 l. People, buildings and Pope (Togo, Ivory Coast, Cameroun, Central African Republic, Zaire, Kenya and Morocco) 90 90
889 500 l. Pope holding Cross and youths (Liechtenstein) . . . 1·10 1·10
890 600 l. Pope, Indians and Delhi Mosque (India) . . . . . . 1·50 1·50
891 700 l. Pope, people, ceramic and Bogota Cathedral (Colombia and St. Lucia) . . . . 1·60 1·60
892 2500 l. Pope, Cure d'Ars and Lyon Cathedral (France) . . 6·00 6·00
893 4000 l. Hands releasing dove and symbols of countries visited (Bangladesh, Singapore, Fiji, New Zealand, Australia and Seychelles) . . . . 9·00 9·00

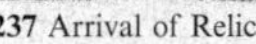

237 Arrival of Relics **238** Children and Sister of Institute of the Daughters of Mary Help of Christians

1987. 900th Anniv of Transfer of St. Nicholas's Relics from Myra to Bari. Multicoloured.
894 500 l. Type **237** . . . . 1·00 1·00
895 700 l. St. Nicholas giving purses of gold to save from dishonour the three daughters of a poor man . . . . 1·50 1·50
896 3000 l. St. Nicholas saving a ship 8·75 8·75

1988. Death Centenary of St. John Bosco (founder of Salesian Brothers). Multicoloured.
897 500 l. Type **238** 75 75
898 1000 l. Bosco and children . . 1·25 1·25
899 2000 l. Children and Salesian lay brother . . . . 2·50 2·50
Nos. 897/9 were printed together, se-tenant, forming a composite design.

239 The Annunciation **240** Prince Vladimir the Great (15th-century icon)

1988. Marian Year. Multicoloured.
900 50 l. Type **239** 10 10
901 300 l. Nativity 40 40
902 500 l. Pentecost 65 65
903 750 l. The Assumption 85 85
904 1000 l. Mother of the Church . 1·25 1·25
905 2400 l. Refuge of Sinners . . . 3·00 3·00

1988. Millenary of Conversion to Christianity of Rus of Kiev. Multicoloured.
906 450 l. Type **240** 65 65
907 650 l. St. Sophia's Cathedral, Kiev . . . . 1·00 1·00
908 2500 l. "Mother of God in Prayer" (mosaic, St. Sophia's Cathedral) . . . . 3·50 3·50

241 "Marriage at Cana" (detail) **242** Angel with Olive Branch

1988. 400th Death Anniv of Paolo Veronese (painter).
909 **241** 550 l. blue and red . . . 90 90
910 – 650 l. multicoloured . . . 1·25 1·25
911 – 3000 l. red and brown . . 3·25 3·25
DESIGNS—HORIZ: 650 l. "Self-portrait". VERT: 3000 l. "Marriage at Cana" (different detail).

1988. Air. Pope John Paul II's Journeys (6th series). As T **231**. Multicoloured.
912 450 l. Hands releasing dove, St. Peter's, Rome, Santiago Cathedral and Sanctuary of Our Lady, Lujan (Uruguay, Chile and Argentina) . . . 75 75
913 650 l. Pope in act of blessing, Speyer Cathedral and youths (German Federal Republic) 95 95
914 1000 l. Hands releasing dove, Gdansk altar and intertwined flowers and thorns (Poland) 1·40 1·40
915 2500 l. Skyscrapers and Pope blessing youths (U.S.A.) . . 3·50 3·50
916 5000 l. Hands releasing dove, tepee at Fort Simpson and American Indians (Canada) 6·00 6·00

1988. Christmas. Multicoloured.
917 50 l. Type **242** 10 10
918 400 l. Angel holding olive branch in both hands 50 50
919 500 l. Angel with olive branch (flying from right) 70 70
920 550 l. Shepherds 75 75
921 850 l. Nativity . . . . 1·00 1·00
922 1500 l. Wise Men . . . . . . 1·75 1·75

244 The Annunciation **245** Yellow-bibbed Lory

1989. 600th Anniv of Feast of Visitation of Virgin Mary. Illuminated Initials. Multicoloured.
925 550 l. Type **244** 80 80
926 750 l. Virgin Mary and St. Elizabeth 95 95
927 2500 l. Virgin Mary and St. Elizabeth with Jesus and John the Baptist as babies . . . 3·25 3·25

1989. Birds featured in "Histoire Naturelle des Oiseaux" by Eleazar Albin. Multicoloured.
928 100 l. Type **245** 20 20
929 150 l. Green woodpecker . . 25 25
930 200 l. Goldcrest ("Crested wren") and winter ("Common") wren 35 35
931 350 l. Common kingfisher . . 50 50
932 500 l. Common cardinal ("red Groas Beak of Virginia" . . 70 70
933 700 l. Bullfinch . . . . 1·00 1·00
934 1500 l. Lapwing ("Lapwing Plover") . . . . 2·50 2·50
935 3000 l. Green-winged ("French") teal . . . . 5·00 5·00

246 Broken Bread (Congress emblem) **247** Pope's Arms, Map of South America and Pope

1989. 44th International Eucharistic Congress, Seoul.
936 **246** 550 l. red and green . . . 65 65
937 – 850 l. multicoloured . . . 1·10 1·10
938 – 1000 l. multicoloured . . 1·25 1·25
939 – 2500 l. green, pink and violet 3·00 3·00
DESIGNS: 850 l. Cross; 1000 l. Cross and fishes; 2500 l. Small cross on wafer.

1989. Pope John Paul II's Journeys (7th series). Multicoloured.
940 50 l. Type **247** 15 15
941 550 l. Austria 75 75
942 800 l. Southern Africa . . . . 1·25 1·25
943 1000 l. France . . . . 1·50 1·50
944 4000 l. Italy . . . . 5·00 5·00

248 Basilica of the Assumption, Baltimore **249** Vision of Ursulines on Mystical Stair

1989. Bicentenary of 1st Catholic Diocese in U.S.A. Each agate and brown.

945 450 l. Type **248** 60 60
946 1350 l. John Carroll (first Archbishop of Baltimore) . 1·75 1·75
947 2400 l. Cathedral of Mary Our Queen, Baltimore (after Martin Barry) . . . . 3·50 3·50

1990. 450th Death Anniv of St. Angela Merici (founder of Company of St. Ursula). Mult.

948 700 l. Type **249** 90 90
949 800 l. St. Angela teaching Ursulines . . . . 1·25 1·25
950 2800 l. Ursulines . . . . . . 4·25 4·25

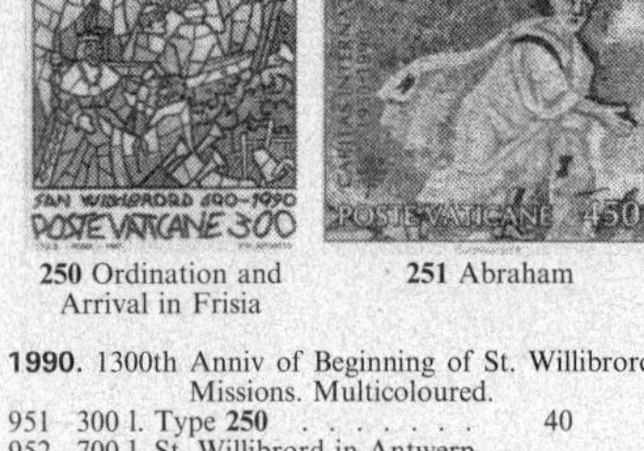

250 Ordination and Arrival in Frisia **251** Abraham

1990. 1300th Anniv of Beginning of St. Willibrord's Missions. Multicoloured.

951 300 l. Type **250** 40 40
952 700 l. St. Willibrord in Antwerp, creation as bishop by Pope Sergius I and gift of part of Echternach by Abbess of Euren 90 90
953 3000 l. Gift of Echternach by King Pepin and St. Willibrord's death . . . . . 4·00 4·00

1990. 40th Anniv of Caritas Internationalis. Details of mosaic from Basilica of Sta. Maria Maggiore, Rome. Multicoloured.

954 450 l. Type **251** 60 60
955 650 l. Three visitors 80 80
956 800 l. Sarah making bread . . 95 95
957 2000 l. Visitors seated at Abraham's table . . . . . . 2·75 2·75

252 Fishermen on Lake Peking **253** Pope and African Landscape

1990. 300th Anniv of Peking–Nanking Diocese. Details of two enamelled bronze vases given by Peking Apostolic Delegate to Pope Pius IX. Multicoloured.

959 500 l. Type **252** 65 65
960 750 l. Church of the Immaculate Conception (first Peking church, 1650) . . . . 1·00 1·00
961 1500 l. Lake Peking . . . . . 2·00 2·00
962 2000 l. Church of the Redeemer, Peking, 1703 . . . . 2·75 2·75

1990. Air. Pope John Paul II's Journeys (8th series). Multicoloured.

963 500 l. Type **253** 70 70
964 1000 l. Northern European landscape (Scandinavia) . . 1·25 1·25
965 3000 l. Cathedral (Santiago de Compostela, Spain) . . . . 3·75 3·75
966 5000 l. Oriental landscape (Korea, Indonesia and Mauritius) . . . . 6·25 6·25

254 Choir of Angels

1990. Christmas. Details of painting by Sebastiano Mainardi. Multicoloured.

967 50 l. Type **254** 20 20
968 200 l. St. Joseph 30 30
969 650 l. Holy Child 80 80
970 750 l. Virgin Mary 95 95
971 2500 l. "Nativity" (complete picture) (vert) . . . . 3·25 3·25

255 "Eleazar" (left half)

1991. Restoration of Sistine Chapel. Details of Lunettes of the Ancestors of Christ by Michelangelo. Multicoloured.

972 50 l. Type **255** 15 15
973 100 l. "Eleazar" (right half) . 15 15
974 150 l. "Jacob" (left half) . . 15 15
975 250 l. "Jacob" (right half) . . 30 30
976 350 l. "Josiah" (left half) . . 45 45
977 400 l. "Josiah" (right half) . . 55 55
978 500 l. "Asa" (left half) . . . 60 60
979 650 l. "Asa" (right half) . . . 80 80
980 800 l. "Zerubbabel" (left half) 1·00 1·00
981 1000 l. "Zerubbabel" (right half) 1·40 1·40
982 2000 l. "Azor" (left half) . . 2·50 2·50
983 3000 l. "Azor" (right half) . . 3·75 3·75

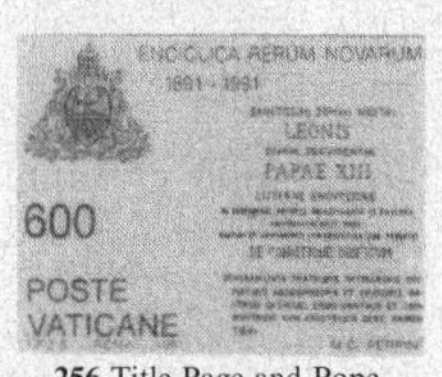

256 Title Page and Pope Leo XIII's Arms

1991. Centenary of "Rerum Novarum" (encyclical on workers' rights).

984 **256** 600 l. blue and green . . 85 85
985 – 750 l. green and brown . 1·00 1·00
986 – 3500 l. purple and black . 4·75 4·75

DESIGNS: 750 l. Allegory of Church, workers and employers (from Leo XIII's 15th Anniv medal, 1892); 3500 l. Profile of Pope Leo XIII (from same medal).

257 Astrograph (astronomical camera) **258** "Apparition of Virgin Mary" (Biagio Puccini)

1991. Centenary of Vatican Observatory. Mult.

987 750 l. Type **257** 90 90
988 1000 l. Castelgandolfo observatory (horiz) . . . . 1·40 1·40
989 3000 l. Vatican Observatory telescope, Mount Graham, Tucson, U.S.A. . . . . . . 4·25 4·25

1991. 600th Anniv of Canonisation of St. Bridget (founder of Order of the Holy Saviour). Multicoloured.

990 1500 l. Type **258** . . . . . . 2·00 2·00
991 2000 l. "Revelation of Christ" (Biagio Puccini) . . . . . 2·75 2·75

259 Cathedral of the Immaculate Conception, Ouagadougou **260** Colonnade of St. Peter's Cathedral, Rome

1991. Pope John Paul II's Journeys (9th series). Multicoloured.

992 200 l. Type **259** (Cape Verde, Guinea-Bissau, Mali, Burkina Faso and Chad) 30 30
993 550 l. St. Vitus's Cathedral, Prague (Czechoslovakia) . 70 70
994 750 l. Basilica of Our Lady of Guadaloupe (Mexico and Curacao) 95 95
995 1500 l. Ta'Pinu Sanctuary, Gozo (Malta) . . . . 2·00 2·00
996 3500 l. Cathedral of Christ the King, Giteca (Tanzania, Burundi, Rwanda and Ivory Coast) . . . . 5·00 5·00

1991. Synod of Bishops' Special Assembly for Europe. Each black and brown.

997 300 l. Type **260** 45 45
998 500 l. St. Peter's Cathedral and square 70 70
999 4000 l. Apostolic Palace and colonnade . . . . 6·00 6·00

Nos. 997/9 were issued together, se-tenant, forming a composite design.

261 Christopher Columbus **262** "Our Lady of Childbirth"

1992. 500th Anniv of Discovery of America by Columbus. Multicoloured.

1000 500 l. Type **261** 70 70
1001 600 l. St. Pedro Claver . . . 80 80
1002 850 l. "Virgin of the Catholic Kings" . . . . 1·25 1·25
1003 1000 l. Bortolome de las Casas 1·50 1·50
1004 2000 l. Junipero Serra . . . . 3·00 3·00

1992. 500th Death Anniv of Piero della Francesca (painter). Multicoloured.

1006 300 l. Type **262** 35 35
1007 750 l. "Our Lady of Childbirth" (detail) 85 85
1008 1000 l. "The Resurrection" . 1·25 1·25
1009 3000 l. "The Resurrection" (detail) . . . . 3·75 3·75

263 St. Giuseppe comforting the Sick **264** Maize

1992. 150th Death Anniv of St. Giuseppe Benedetto Cottolengo. Multicoloured.

1010 650 l. Type **263** 70 70
1011 850 l. St. Giuseppe holding Piccolo Casa della Divina Provvidenza (infirmary), Turin 90 90

1992. Plants of the New World. Illustrations from the 18th-century "Phytanthoza Iconographia". Multicoloured.

1012 850 l. Type **264** . . . . 1·00 1·00
1013 850 l. Tomatoes ("Solanum pomiferum") . . . . 1·00 1·00
1014 850 l. Cactus ("Opuntia") . . 1·00 1·00
1015 850 l. Cacao ("Cacaos, Cacavifera") . . . . 1·00 1·00
1016 850 l. Peppers ("Solanum tuberosum") . . . . 1·00 1·00
1017 850 l. Pineapple ("Ananas sagitae") . . . . 1·00 1·00

265 Our Lady of Guadalupe, Crucifix and Mitres **266** Pope, Dove and Map of Europe

1992. 4th Latin American Episcopal Conference, Santo Domingo.

1018 **265** 700 l. gold, emerald and green . . . . 1·25 1·25

1992. Air. Pope John Paul II's Journeys (10th series). Multicoloured.

1019 500 l. Type **266** (Portugal) . . 60 60
1020 1000 l. Map of Europe highlighting Poland . . . . 1·10 1·10
1021 4000 l. Our Lady of Czestochowa and map highlighting Poland and Hungary . . . . 4·25 4·25
1022 6000 l. Map of South America highlighting Brazil . . . . 6·50 6·50

267 "The Annunciation" **268** "St. Francis healing the Man from Ilerda" (fresco by Giotto in Upper Church, Assisi)

1992. Christmas. Mosaics in Church of Sta. Maria Maggiore, Rome. Multicoloured.

1023 600 l. Type **267** 70 70
1024 700 l. "Nativity" 80 80
1025 1000 l. "Adoration of the Kings" . . . . 1·25 1·25
1026 1500 l. "Presentation in the Temple" . . . . 1·75 1·75

1993. "Peace in Europe" Prayer Meeting, Assisi.

1027 **268** 1000 l. multicoloured . . 1·25 1·25

269 Dome of St. Peter's Cathedral **270** "The Sacrifice of Isaac"

1993. Architectural Treasures of Rome and the Vatican. Multicoloured.

1028 200 l. Type **269** 20 20
1029 300 l. St. John Lateran's Basilica 30 30
1030 350 l. Basilica of Sta. Maria Maggiore 30 30
1031 500 l. St. Paul's Basilica . . . 45 45
1032 600 l. Apostolic Palace, Vatican 50 50
1033 700 l. Apostolic Palace, Lateran 60 60
1034 850 l. Papal Palace, Castelgandolfo 80 80
1035 1000 l. Chancery Palace . . 1·00 1·00
1036 2000 l. Palace of Propagation of the Faith . . . . 2·00 2·00
1037 3000 l. San Calisto Palace . . 3·00 3·00

1993. Ascension Day. Multicoloured.

1038 200 l. Type **270** 20 20
1039 750 l. Jesus handing New Law to St. Peter 80 80
1040 3000 l. Christ watching servant washing Pilate's hands . . 2·75 2·75

Nos. 1038/40 were issued together, se-tenant, forming a composite design of the bas-relief "Traditio Legis" from 4th-century sarcophagus.

271 Cross and Grape Vines **273** St. John, Cross, Fish and Moldava River

272 "Crucifixion" (Felice Casorati)

1993. 45th Int Eucharistic Congress, Seville. Mult.

1041 500 l. Type **271** 50 50
1042 700 l. Cross and hands offering broken bread 70 70
1043 1500 l. Hands holding chalice 1·50 1·50
1044 2500 l. Cross, banner and ears of wheat . . . . 2·40 2·40

1993. Europa. Contemporary Art. Multicoloured.

1045 750 l. Type **272** 75 75
1046 850 l. "Rouen Cathedral" (Maurice Utrillo) . . . 85 85

1993. 600th Death Anniv of St. John of Nepomuk (patron saint of Bohemia). Multicoloured.

1047 1000 l. Type **273** . . . . . . 1·00 1·00
1048 2000 l. Charles Bridge, Prague 2·00 2·00

274 Pope praying

1993. Pope John Paul II's Journeys (11th series). Multicoloured.
1049 600 l. Type **274** (Senegal, Gambia and Guinea) . . . 50 50
1050 1000 l. Pope with Pastoral Staff (Angola and St. Thomas and Prince Islands) 90 90
1051 5000 l. Pope with hands clasped in prayer (Dominican Republic) . . . . 4·50 4·50

275 "Madonna of Solothurn" (detail)

1993. 450th Death Anniv of Hans Holbein the Younger (artist). Multicoloured.
1052 700 l. Type **275** 65 65
1053 1000 l. "Madonna of Solothurn" . . . . 1·00 1·00
1054 1500 l. "Self-portrait" . . . . 1·50 1·50

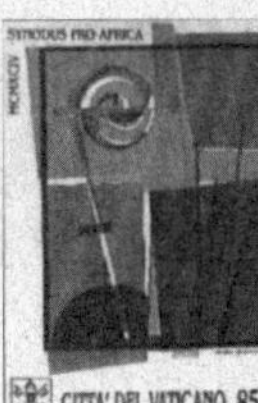

276 "Creation of the Planets" (left detail) **277** Crosier and Dome

1994. Completion of Restoration of Sistine Chapel. Multicoloured.
1055 350 l. Type **276** 50 50
1056 350 l. God creating planets (right detail) 50 50
1057 500 l. Adam (left detail, "The Creation of Adam") . . . 70 70
1058 500 l. God (right detail) . . . 70 70
1059 1000 l. Adam and Eve taking forbidden fruit (left detail, "The Original Sin") . . . 1·40 1·40
1060 1000 l. Angel casting out Adam and Eve from the Garden (right detail) . . . . 1·40 1·40
1061 2000 l. People climbing from swollen river (left detail, "The Flood") . . . . 2·75 2·75
1062 2000 l. Floodwaters surrounding temporary shelter (right detail) . . . . 2·75 2·75
Stamps of the same value were issued together, se-tenant, each pair forming a composite design.

1994. Special Assembly for Africa of Synod of Bishops. Multicoloured.
1064 850 l. Type **277** 80 80
1065 1000 l. Crucifix, dome of St. Peter's and African scene (horiz) . . . . 1·10 1·10

278 God creating Man and Woman **280** Bishop Euphrasius and Archdeacon Claudius

279 Timeline of Knowledge from Wheel to Atom

1994. Int Year of the Family. Mult.
1066 400 l. Type **278** 40 40
1067 750 l. Family 70 70
1068 1000 l. Parents teaching son . 95 95
1069 2000 l. Youth helping elderly couple . . . . 1·90 1·90

1994. Europa. Discoveries. Multicoloured.
1070 750 l. Type **279** 80 80
1071 850 l. Galileo, solar system and scientific apparatus 90 90

1994. 13th International Congress on Christian Archaeology, Split and Porec, Croatia. Mosaics from Euphrasian Basilica, Porec. Multicoloured.
1072 700 l. Type **280** 70 70
1073 1500 l. Madonna and Child with two angels . . . . 1·40 1·40
1074 3000 l. Jesus Christ between Apostles St. Peter and St. Paul . . . . 3·00 3·00

281 Route Map, Mongolian Village and Giovanni da Montecorvino

1994. 700th Anniv of Evangelization of China.
1075 **281** 1000 l. multicoloured . . 95 95

282 Houses, Mahdi's Mausoleum, Omdurman, and St. Mary's Basilica, Lodonga (Benin, Uganda and Sudan)

1994. Pope John Paul II's Journeys (12th series).
1076 **282** 600 l. brown, green & red 55 55
1077 – 700 l. violet, brown & grn 70 70
1078 – 1000 l. brown, blue & vio 95 95
1079 – 2000 l. black, blue & red 1·75 1·75
1080 – 3000 l. blue, violet & brn 2·75 2·75
DESIGNS: 700 l. St. Mary's Church, Apollonia, Mosque and statue of Skanderbeg, Tirana (Albania); 1000 l. Church of the Saint, Huelva Region, and The Giralda, Real Maestranza and Golden Tower, Seville (Spain); 2000 l. Skyscrapers and St. Thomas's Theological Seminary, Denver, "El Castillo" (pyramid), Kulkulkan, Jamaican girl and Mexican boy (Jamaica, Mexico and United States); 3000 l. Tallin, "Hymn to Liberty" (monument), Riga, and Tower, Cathedral Square, Vilnius (Lithuania, Latvia and Estonia).

283 Holy Family

1994. Christmas. Details of "Nativity" by Tintoretto. Multicoloured.
1081 700 l. Type **283** 70 70
1082 1000 l. Upper half of painting (45 × 28 mm) 95 95
1083 1000 l. Lower half of painting (45 × 28 mm) 95 95
Nos. 1082/3 were issued together, se-tenant, forming a composite design of the complete painting.

284 Angel with Chalice (Melozzo da Forli) (St. Mark's) **286** Fountain of the Triton (Bernini), Vatican Gardens

285 Hands and Broken Chains

1995. 700th Anniv of Shrine of the Holy House, Loreto. Details from the vaults of sacristies. Multicoloured.
1084 600 l. Type **284** 60 60
1085 700 l. Angel with lamb (Melozzo) (Sacristy of St. Mark) 70 70
1086 1500 l. Angel with lute (Luca Signorelli) (St. John's) . . 1·40 1·40
1087 2500 l. Angel (Signorelli) (St. John's) . . . . 2·40 2·40

1995. Europa. Peace and Freedom. Multicoloured.
1089 750 l. Type **285** 65 65
1090 850 l. Globe, olive wreath, dove and handclasp 75 75

1995. European Nature Conservation Year. Multicoloured.
1091 200 l. Type **286** 20 20
1092 300 l. Avenue of roses, Castelgandolfo 30 30
1093 400 l. Statue of Apollo, Vatican Gardens 35 35
1094 550 l. Ruins of Domitian's Villa, Castelgandolfo 50 50
1095 750 l. Box elder, Vatican Gardens 70 70
1096 1500 l. Belvedere Gardens, Castelgandolfo . . . . . . 1·40 1·40
1097 2000 l. Eagle fountain, Vatican Gardens . . . . 1·75 1·75
1098 3000 l. Avenue of cypresses, Castelgandolfo . . . . . . 2·75 2·75

287 Guglielmo Marconi and Transmitter

1995. One Hundred Years of Radio. Multicoloured.
1099 850 l. Type **287** . . . . 1·00 1·00
1100 1000 l. Archangel Gabriel, Pope John Paul II with microphone and Vatican broadcasting station . . . . 1·25 1·25

288 St. Antony of Padua (statue by Donatello) **289** Dove and Hearts

1995. Saints' Anniversaries.
1101 **288** 500 l. brown and green . 40 40
1102 – 750 l. green and violet . . 60 60
1103 – 3000 l. blue and purple . 2·40 2·40
DESIGNS: 500 l. Type **288** (800th birth anniv); 750 l. St. John of God (founder of Order of Hospitallers, 500th birth anniv) (sculpture, Filippo Valle); 3000 l. St. Philip Neri (founder of Friars of the Oratory, 400th death anniv) (sculpture, Giovanni Battista Maini).

1995. 50th Anniv of U.N.O. Multicoloured.
1104 550 l. Type **289** 45 45
1105 750 l. Human faces 60 60
1106 850 l. Doves 65 65
1107 1250 l. Symbolic lymph system . . . . 1·00 1·00
1108 2000 l. People gazing at "explosion" of flowers . . 1·60 1·60

290 "The Annunciation" (Johannes of Ienzenstein) **291** Pope, Statue of Virgin Mary and Zagreb Cathedral

1995. Holy Year 2000 (1st issue). Illustrations from illuminated manuscripts in Vatican Apostolic Library. Multicoloured.
1109 400 l. Type **290** 30 30
1110 850 l. "Nativity" (from King Matthias I Corvinus's breviary) 65 65
1111 1250 l. "Flight into Egypt" (from Book of Hours) . . . 1·00 1·00
1112 2000 l. "Jesus among the Teachers" (Pietro Lombardo) . . . . 1·60 1·60
See also Nos. 1132/5.

1995. Pope John Paul II's Journeys (13th series). Multicoloured.
1113 1000 l. Type **291** (Croatia) . . 80 80
1114 2000 l. Pope, Genoa Lantern, Orvieto Cathedral and Valley of the Temples, Agrigento (Italy) . . . . 1·60 1·60

INDEX

Countries can be quickly located by referring to the index at the end of this volume.

292 Marco Polo receiving Golden Book from the Great Khan

1996. 700th Anniv of Marco Polo's Return from China. Multicoloured.
1115 350 l. Type **292** 30 30
1116 850 l. The Great Khan giving alms to poor, Cambaluc . 65 65
1117 1250 l. Marco Polo delivering Pope Gregory X's letter to the Great Khan . . . . 1·00 1·00
1118 2500 l. Marco Polo in Persia listening to Nativity story . 2·00 2·00

293 Angel with Crosses **294** Gianna Molla (surgeon)

1996. Anniversaries. Multicoloured.
1120 1250 l. Type **293** (400th Anniv of Union of Brest-Litovsk . 1·00 1·00
1121 2000 l. Latin and Byzantine mitres and Tree of Life (350th Anniv of Union of Uzhorod) 1·60 1·60

1996. Europa. Famous Women.
1122 **294** 750 l. blue 60 60
1123 – 850 l. brown 65 65
DESIGN: 850 l. Edith Stein (Carmelite nun).

295 "Sun and Steel" **297** "Baptism of Jesus"

296 Wawel Cathedral

1996. Cent of Modern Olympic Games. Mult.
1124 1250 l. Type **295** . . . . . . 1·00 1·00
1125 1250 l. "Solar Plexus" . . . 1·00 1·00
1126 1250 l. Hand and golden beams . . . . 1·00 1·00
1127 1250 l. "Speculum Aevi" (athlete and shadow) . . . 1·00 1·00
1128 1250 l. Hercules . . . . 1·00 1·00

1996. 50th Anniv of Ordination of Karol Wojtyla (Pope John Paul II) at Wawel Cathedral, Crakow, Poland. Multicoloured.
1129 500 l. Type **296** 40 40
1130 750 l. Pope John Paul II . . 60 40
1131 1250 l. St. John Lateran's Basilica in Rome (seat of Bishop of Eternal City) . . 1·00 1·00

1996. Holy Year 2000 (2nd issue). Illustrations from 13th-century illuminated New Testament in Vatican Apostolic Library. Multicoloured.
1132 550 l. Type **297** 45 45
1133 850 l. "Temptation in the Desert" 65 65
1134 1500 l. "Cure of a Leper" . . 1·50 1·50
1135 2500 l. "Jesus the Teacher" . 2·00 2·00

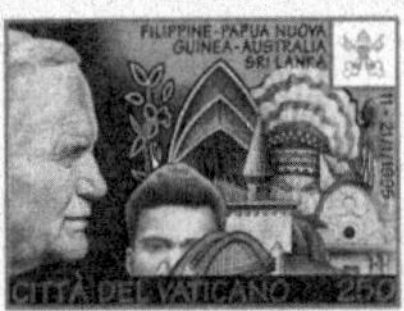

298 Philippines, Papua New Guinea, Australia and Sri Lanka

1996. Pope John Paul II's Journeys (14th series).
1136 **298** 250 l. blue and black . 20 20
1137 – 500 l. green and black . 40 40
1138 – 750 l. green and black . 60 60
1139 – 1000 l. brown and black 80 80

1140	–	2000 l. grey and black .	1·60	1·60
1141	–	5000 l. pink and black .	4·00	4·00

DESIGNS: 500 l. Czech Republic and Poland; 750 l. Belgium; 1000 l. Slovakia; 2000 l. Cameroun, South Africa and Kenya; 5000 l. United States of America and United Nations Headquarters.

299 "Nativity" (Murillo)

1996. Christmas.

1142	**299**	750 l. multicoloured . .	60	60

300 Pope St. Celestine V

1996. Saints' Anniversaries. Multicoloured.

1143	1250 l. Type **300** (700th death)	1·00	1·00
1144	1250 l. St. Alfonso Maria de' Liguori (founder of Redemptorists Order) (300th birth)	1·00	1·00

EXPRESS LETTER STAMPS

E 3

1929.

E14	E **3**	2 l. red	13·00	10·00
E15		2 l. 50 blue	9·00	12·00

E **12** Vatican City

1933.

E 35	E **12**	2 l. brown and red . .	30	35
E 36		2 l. 50 brown and blue	30	55
E107		3 l. 50 blue and red . .	35	55
E108		5 l. green and blue . .	40	85

1945. Surch in figures over bars.

E118	E **12**	6 l. on 3 l. 50 blue & red	2·75	1·50
E119		12 l. on 5 l. grn & blue	2·75	1·50

E **28** Matthew Giberti, Bishop of Verona

1946. 400th Anniv of Council of Trent.

E130	E **28**	6 l. brown and green .	15	15
E131	–	12 l. sepia & brown . .	25	25

DESIGN: 12 l. Cardinal Gaspare Contarini, Bishop of Belluno.

1949. As Nos. 139/48 (Basilicas), but inscr "ESPRESSO".

E149	40 l. grey	8·00	2·50
E150	80 l. brown	24·00	15·00

DESIGNS—HORIZ: 40 l. St. Peter's; 80 l. St. John's.

1953. Designs as Nos. 179/89, but inscr "ESPRESSO".

E190	50 l. brown and turquoise .	20	15
E191	85 l. brown and orange . . .	40	25

DESIGNS: 50 l. St. Peter and tomb; 85 l. Pius XII and sepulchre.

1960. Designs as Nos. 326/33 (Works of Mercy), but inscr "ESPRESSO". Centres in brown.

E334	75 l. red	10	10
E335	100 l. blue	10	10

DESIGN: 75, 100 l. Arms of Pope John XXIII between "Justice" and "Hope".

1966. Designs as Nos. 467/76, but inscr "ESPRESSO".

E477	–	150 l. brown	10	10
E478	**120**	180 l. brown	15	15

DESIGN: 150 l. Arms of Pope Paul VI.

PARCEL POST STAMPS

1931. Optd **PER PACCHI**.

P15	**1**	5 c. brown on pink	25	40
P16		10 c. green on green . . .	25	40
P17		20 c. violet on lilac	1·50	2·75
P18		25 c. blue on blue	7·00	4·75
P19		30 c. black on yellow . . .	7·50	4·75
P20		50 c. black on orange . . .	8·00	4·75
P21		75 c. red on grey	1·00	4·75
P22	**2**	80 c. red	65	4·75
P23		1 l. 25 blue	75	4·75
P24		2 l. brown	60	4·75
P25		2 l. 50 red	60	4·75
P26		5 l. green	60	4·75
P27		10 l. black	60	4·75

PARCEL POST EXPRESS STAMPS

1931. Optd **PER PACCHI**.

PE15	E **3**	2 l. red	1·00	4·75
PE16		2 l. 50 blue	1·00	4·75

POSTAGE DUE STAMPS

1931. Optd **SEGNATASSE** and cross or surch also.

D15	**1**	5 c. brown on pink	20	60
D16		10 c. green on green . . .	20	60
D17		20 c. violet on lilac	1·25	2·25
D18		40 c. on 30 c. blk on yell .	1·40	5·50
D19	**2**	60 c. on 2 l. brown	30·00	24·00
D20		1 l. 10 on 2 l. 50 red . . .	4·75	18·00

D **26** D **49** State Arms

1945. Coloured network shown in brackets.

D107	D **26**	5 c. black (yellow) . .	10	10
D108		20 c. black (violet) . .	10	10
D109		80 c. black (red) . . .	10	10
D110		1 l. black (green) . .	10	10
D111		2 l. black (blue) . . .	10	15
D112		5 l. black (grey) . . .	10	15

1954. Coloured network shown in brackets.

D199	D **49**	4 l. black (red) . . .	10	10
D200		6 l. black (green) . .	20	20
D201		10 l. black (yellow) .	10	10
D202		20 l. black (blue) . .	40	40
D203		50 l. black (brown) .	10	10
D204		70 l. black (brown) .	10	10

D **130**

1968.

D513	D **130**	10 l. black on grey .	10	10
D514		20 l. black on blue .	10	10
D515		50 l. black on pink .	10	10
D516		60 l. black on grn .	10	10
D517		100 l. black on buff .	10	10
D518		180 black on mauve	10	10

VEGLIA Pt. 8

During the period of D'Annunzio's Italian Regency of Carnaro (Fiume), separate issues were made for the island of Veglia (now Krk).

100 centesimi = 1 lira

1920. Nos. 148, etc of Fiume optd **VEGLIA**.
1 5 c. green 2·50 2·50
2 10 c. red 4·50 4·50
3 20 c. bistre 7·50 7·50
4 25 c. blue 7·50 7·50
5 50 on 20 c. bistre 7·50 7·50
6 55 on 5 c. green 7·50 7·50

EXPRESS LETTER STAMPS

1920. Nos. E163/4 of Fiume optd **VEGLIA**.
E7 30 c. on 20 c. bistre 42·00 35·00
E8 50 on 5 c. green 32·00 35·00

VENEZIA GIULIA AND ISTRIA Pt. 3

Formerly part of Italy. Stamps issued during Allied occupation, 1945-47. The Peace Treaty of 1947 established the Free Territory of Trieste (q.v.) and gave the rest of the territory to Yugoslavia.
For stamps of Austria overprinted Venezia Giulia see AUSTRIAN TERRITORIES ACQUIRED BY ITALY in Volume 1..

100 centesimi = 1 lira

A. YUGOSLAV OCCUPATION PROVISIONAL ISSUES

Issue for Trieste.

1945. Stamps of Italian Social Republic 1944, surch **1.V.1945 TRIESTE TRST**, five-pointed star and value
4 – 20 c.+ 1 l. on 5 c. brown (No. 106) 10 30
5 13 + 1 l. on 25 c. green 10 30
6 – + 1 l. on 30 c. brown (No. 110) 10 30
7 – + 1 l. on 50 c. violet (No. 111) 10 30
8 – + 1 l. on 1 l. violet (No. 113) 10 30
9 – + 2 l. on 1 l. 25 blue (No. 114) 10 30
2 12 2 + 2 l. on 25 c. green 10 15
10 – + 2 l. on 3 l. green (No. 115) 10 30
11 – 5 + 5 l. on 1 l. violet (No. 113) 10 30
12 – 10 + 10 l. on 30 c. brown (No. 110) 70 1·10
13 – 20 + 20 l. on 5 c. brown (No. 106) 3·00 3·00

Issue for Istria.

In 1945 various stamps of Italy were overprinted "ISTRA" and further surcharged for use in Istria and Pola but they were not issued. However, four of these were further surcharged and issued later.

1945. Stamps of Italy (No. 14) or Italian Social Republic (others) surch **ISTRA** with new value and bars obliterating old surch.
14 99 4 l. on 2 l. on 1 l. (No. 249) violet 80 1·00
15 – 6 l. on 1,50 l. on 75 c. (No. 112) red 2·25 2·75
16 – 10 l. on 0,10 l. on 5 c. (No. 106) brown 10·00 12·00
17 103 20 l. on 1 l. on 50 c. (No. 247) violet 3·25 3·50

Issue for Fiume.

1945. Stamps of Italian Social Republic 1944, surch **3-V-1945 FIUME RIJEKA**, five-pointed star over rising sun and new value.
18 12 2 l. on 25 c. green 10 30
20 – 4 l. on 1 l. vio (No. 113) 10 30
21 – 5 l. on 10 c. brn (No. 107) 10 30
22 – 6 l. on 10 c. brn (No. 107) 10 30
23 13 10 l. on 25 c. green 15 30
24 – 16 l. on 75 c. red (No. 112) 8·00 9·00
25 E 16 20 l. on 1 l. 25 c. green 40 75

B. ALLIED MILITARY GOVERNMENT

1945. Stamps of Italy optd **A.M.G. V.G.** in two lines.

(a) Imperial Series.
26 – 10 c. brown (No. 241) 20 15
27 – 10 c. brown (No. 633) 20 15
28 99 20 c. red (No. 243) 20 30
29 20 c. red (No. 640) 20 15
31 – 60 c. red (No. 636) 20 15
32 103 60 c. green (No. 641) 20 15
33 99 1 l. violet (No. 637) 25 15
34 – 2 l. red (No. 638) 30 15
35 98 5 l. red (No. 645) 45 25
36 – 10 l. violet (No. 646) 60 70
37 99 20 l. green (No. 257) 1·40 1·90

(b) Stamps of 1945–48.
38 – 25 c. blue (No. 649) 20 20
39 – 2 l. brown (No. 656) 40 40
40 – 3 l. red (No. 657) 30 15
41 – 4 l. red (No. 658) 45 30
42 195 6 l. violet (No. 660) 1·25 1·40
43 – 20 l. purple (No. 665) 22·00 1·00
44 196 25 l. green (No. 666) 2·75 3·50
45 50 l. purple (No. 668) 3·00 4·25
46 197 100 l. red (No. 669) 12·00 16·00

1945. Air stamps of Italy, optd as above.
47 110 50 c. brown (No. 271) 15 25
48 198 1 l. grey (No. 670) 25 35
49 – 2 l. blue (No. 671) 25 35
50 – 5 l. green (No. 673) 1·50 1·75
51 198 10 l. red (No. 674) 1·50 1·75
52 – 25 l. blue (No. 675) 1·50 1·75
53 – 25 l. brown (No. 676) 10·00 14·00
54 198 50 l. green (No. 677) 2·00 3·25

EXPRESS LETTER STAMPS

1946. Express Letter Stamps of Italy optd **A.M.G. V.G.** in two lines.
E55 – 10 l. blue (No. E680) 2·25 3·00
E56 E 200 30 l. vio (No. E683) 6·00 8·00

C. YUGOSLAV MILITARY GOVERNMENT

6 Grapes

7 Roman Amphitheatre, Pula and Istrian Fishing Vessel

8 Tunny

1945. Inscr "ISTRA SLOVENSKO PRIMORJE — ISTRIA LITTORALE SLOVENO".
74 6 0.25 l. green 30 10
58 – 0.50 l. brown 10 10
59 – 1 l. red 10 10
76 – 1 l. green 10 10
77 – 1.50 l. green 10 10
61 – 2 l. green 10 10
100 – 3 l. red 15 10
62 7 4 l. blue 10 10
79 4 l. red 10 10
80 – 5 l. black 10 10
101 7 6 l. blue 20 15
81 – 10 l. brown 20 10
65 8 20 l. purple 3·00 2·25
82 20 l. blue 2·50 30
66 – 30 l. mauve 3·25 1·50

DESIGNS—As Type **6**: 0.50 l. Donkey and view; 1 l. Rebuilding damaged homes; 1.50 l. Olive branch; 2, 3 l. Duino Castle near Trieste. As Type **7**: 5 l. Birthplace of Vladimir Gortan, Piran; 10 l. Ploughing. As Type **8**: 30 l. Viaduct over the Solkan.

1946. Nos. 82 and 66 surch.
96 8 1 on 20 l. blue 60 15
97 – 2 on 30 l. mauve 2·00 2·25

1947. As Nos. 514 and O540 of Yugoslavia with colours changed, surch **VOJNA UPRAVA JUGOSLAVENSKE ARMIJE** and new value.
102 1 l. on 9 d. pink 10 10
103 1.50 l. on 0.50 d. blue 10 10
104 2 l. on 9 d. pink 10 10
105 3 l. on 0.50 d. blue 10 10
106 5 l. on 9 d. pink 10 10
107 6 l. on 0.50 d. blue 10 10
108 10 l. on 9 d. pink 30 10
109 15 l. on 0.50 d. blue 40 10
110 35 l. on 9 d. pink 40 10
111 50 l. on 0.50 d. blue 50 20

POSTAGE DUE STAMPS

1945. Stamps of 1945 surch **PORTO** and value in Lit.
D72 8 0.50 on 20 l. purple 30 20
D67 6 1 l. on 0.25 l. green 1·50 60
D73 – 2 l. on 30 l. mauve 50 50
D68 – 4 l. on 0.50 l. brown 30 15
D69 – 8 l. on 0.50 l. brown 30 15
D70 – 10 l. on 0.50 l. brown 4·00 2·00
D71 – 20 l. on 0.50 l. brown 6·00 3·00

1946. Stamps of 1945 surch **PORTO** and value expressed in Lira.
D90 6 1 l. on 0.25 l. green 80 1·00
D84 – 1 l. on 1 l. green (No. 76) 15 10
D91 6 2 l. on 0.25 l. green 1·10 1·25
D85 – 2 l. on 1 l. green (No. 76) 15 10
D92 6 4 l. on 0.25 l. green 1·10 1·00
D86 – 4 l. on 1 l. green (No. 76) 20 15
D93 8 10 l. on 20 l. blue 1·25 1·25
D87 – 10 l. on 30 l. mauve (No. 66) 50 1·50
D94 8 20 l. on 20 l. blue 5·00 6·00
D88 – 20 l. on 30 l. mauve (No. 66) 4·00 2·75
D95 8 30 l. on 20 l. blue 8·00 12·00
D89 – 30 l. on 30 l. mauve (No. 66) 4·00 2·75

1947. No. D528 of Yugoslavia with colour changed and surch **Vojna Uprava Jugoslavenske Armije** and value.
D112 1 l. on 1 d. green 10 10
D113 2 l. on 1 d. green 10 10
D114 6 l. on 1 d. green 10 10
D115 10 l. on 1 d. green 10 10
D116 30 l. on 1 d. green 10 15

VENEZUELA Pt. 20

A republic in the N. of S. America, independent since 1811.

1859. 100 centavos = 8 reales = 1 peso.
1879. 100 centesimos = 1 venezolano.
1880. 100 centimos = 1 bolivar.

1 2 3

1859. Imperf.
7 1 ½ r. orange 6·75 2·50
8 1 r. blue 11·50 7·25
3 2 r. red 27·00 10·50

1862. Imperf.
13 2 ½ c. green 11·50 65·00
14 ½ c. lilac 19·00 £130
15 1 c. brown 27·00 £140

1863. Imperf.
16 3 ½ c. red 32·00 55·00
17a 1 c. grey 38·00 65·00
21 ½ r. yellow 2·50 1·50
19 1 r. blue 19·00 8·25
20 2 r. green 15·00 13·50

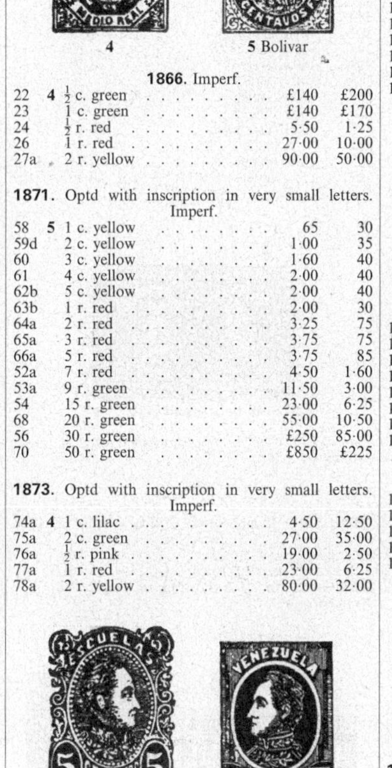
4 5 Bolivar

1866. Imperf.
22 4 ½ c. green £140 £200
23 1 c. green £140 £170
24 ½ r. red 5·50 1·25
26 1 r. red 27·00 10·00
27a 2 r. yellow 90·00 50·00

1871. Optd with inscription in very small letters. Imperf.
58 5 1 c. yellow 65 30
59d 2 c. yellow 1·00 35
60 3 c. yellow 1·60 40
61 4 c. yellow 2·00 40
62b 5 c. yellow 2·00 40
63b 1 r. red 2·00 30
64a 2 r. red 3·25 75
65a 3 r. red 3·75 75
66a 5 r. red 3·75 85
52a 7 r. red 4·50 1·60
53a 9 r. green 11·50 3·00
54 15 r. green 23·00 6·25
68 20 r. green 55·00 10·50
56 30 r. green £250 85·00
70 50 r. green £850 £225

1873. Optd with inscription in very small letters. Imperf.
74a 4 1 c. lilac 4·50 12·50
75a 2 c. green 27·00 35·00
76a ½ r. pink 19·00 2·50
77a 1 r. red 23·00 6·25
78a 2 r. yellow 80·00 32·00

7 Bolivar

8 Bolivar

1879. New Currency. Optd with inscription in small letters. Imperf.
83 7 1 c. yellow 2·00 15
84 5 c. yellow 3·00 30
85 10 c. blue 4·25 40
86 30 c. blue 5·25 1·00
87 50 c. blue 6·25 1·00
88 90 c. blue 25·00 5·25
89 1 v. red 55·00 7·25
90 3 v. red 90·00 29·00
91 5 v. red £160 55·00

1880. New Currency. Without opt. Perf.
92 7 5 c. yellow 1·00 15
93 10 c. yellow 1·60 15
94 25 c. yellow 1·50 20
95 50 c. yellow 3·00 25
96 1 b. blue 7·25 60
97 2 b. blue 11·50 70
98 5 b. blue 27·00 60
99 10 b. red £140 45·00
100 20 b. red £850 £140
101 25 b. red £3500 £425

1880.
107 8 5 c. blue 6·25 3·25
108 10 c. red 10·50 6·25
109 25 c. yellow 6·25 3·25
110 50 c. brown 32·00 17·00
106 1 b. green 50·00 25·00

9 Bolivar

10 Bolivar

1882. Various frames. Perf or roul.
111 9 5 c. green 10 10
112 10 c. brown 10 10
113 25 c. orange 10 10
114 50 c. blue 15 10
115 1 b. red 20 10
116 3 b. violet 20 10
117 10 b. brown 40 50
118 20 b. purple 55 55

1882. Various frames. Perf or roul.
119 10 5 c. blue 20 10
120 10 c. brown 20 10
121 25 c. brown 40 20
122 50 c. green 1·25 25
123 1 b. violet 2·10 70

1892. Surch **RESOLUCION DE 10 DE OCTUBRE DE 1892** and value in circle.
134 9 25 c. on 5 c. green 8·25 5·00
138 10 25 c. on 5 c. blue 25·00 25·00
135 9 25 c. on 10 c. brown 8·25 5·00
139 10 25 c. on 10 c. brown 10·00 10·00
136 9 1 b. on 25 c. orange 10·50 5·75
140 10 1 b. on 25 c. brown 10·00 10·00
137 9 1 b. on 50 c. blue 14·50 5·75
141 10 1 b. on 50 c. green 11·50 11·50

1893. Optd with coat of arms and diagonal shading.
142 9 5 c. green 10 10
150 10 5 c. blue 20 10
143 9 10 c. brown 10 10
151 10 10 c. brown 55 65
144 9 25 c. orange 10 10
152 10 25 c. brown 35 25
145 9 50 c. blue 10 10
153 10 50 c. green 50 20
146 9 1 b. red 55 20
154 10 1 b. violet 1·25 50
147 9 3 b. violet 50 35
148 10 b. brown 1·50 1·25
149 20 b. purple 1·25 1·25

13 Bolivar 14 Bolivar

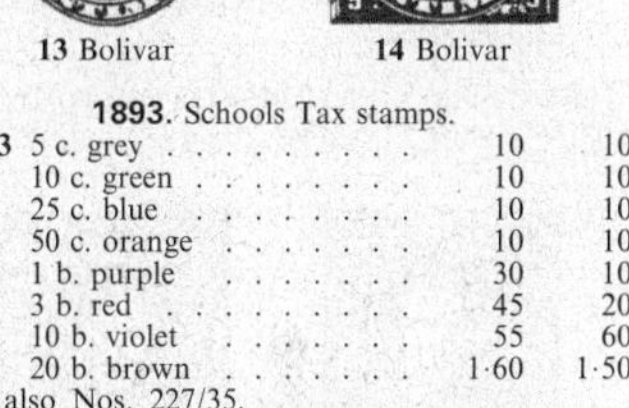

1893. Schools Tax stamps.
155 13 5 c. grey 10 10
156 10 c. green 10 10
157 25 c. blue 10 10
158 50 c. orange 10 10
159 1 b. purple 30 10
160 3 b. red 45 20
161 10 b. violet 55 60
162 20 b. brown 1·60 1·50
See also Nos. 227/35.

1893.
163 14 5 c. brown 60 10
164 10 c. blue 2·10 65
165 25 c. mauve 10·00 20
166 50 c. purple 2·10 20
167 1 b. green 2·75 65

15 Landing of Columbus

1893. Columbian Exposition, Chicago, and 400th Anniv of Discovery of America by Columbus.
168 15 25 c. purple 6·75 40

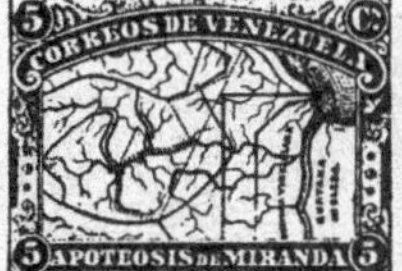
16 Map of Venezuela

18 Bolivar

1896. 80th Death Anniv of Gen. Miranda.
169 16 5 c. green 2·10 1·60
170 10 c. blue 2·10 1·60
171 25 c. yellow 2·50 3·25
172 50 c. red 32·00 17·00
173 1 b. mauve 25·00 17·00

1899.
179 18 5 c. green 65 15
180 10 c. red 85 15
181 25 c. blue 1·00 50
182 50 c. black 1·25 60
183 50 c. orange 1·00 30
184 1 b. green 21·00 10·50
185 2 b. yellow £250 £160

(21) "R.T.M." = Ramon Tellos Mendoza, Minister of Interior

(23)

1900. Stamps of 1893 optd with T **21**.
191 13 5 c. grey 10 10
192 10 c. green 10 10
193 25 c. blue 10 10
194 50 c. orange 10 10
195 1 b. purple 20 10
196 3 b. red 30 10
197 10 b. violet 65 40
198 20 b. brown 4·25 4·25

1900. Stamps of 1899 optd with T **21**.

199 **18** 5 c. green 60 30
200 10 c. red 60 35
201 25 c. blue 4·25 60
202 50 c. black 2·10 50
203 1 b. green 85 40
204 2 b. yellow 1·50 1·00

1900. Stamps of 1893 optd **1900**. Colours changed.

206 **13** 5 c. orange 10 10
207 10 c. blue 10 10
208 25 c. purple 10 10
209 50 c. green 60 10
210 1 b. black 4·75 55
211 3 b. brown 1·25 60
212 10 b. red 5·00 1·40
213 20 b. violet 10·00 2·75

1900. Stamps of 1899 optd **1900**.

214 **18** 5 c. green £120 £120
215 10 c. red £120 £120
216 25 c. blue £250 £120
217 50 c. orange 15·00 85
218 1 b. black 85 60

1900. Stamps of 1899 optd with T **23**.

219 **18** 5 c. green 4·25 50
220 10 c. red 3·25 55
221 25 c. blue 4·25 50

1901. Re-issue of T **13** in new colours.

227 **13** 5 c. orange 10 10
228 10 c. red 10 10
229 10 c. blue 10 10
231 50 c. green 15 15
232 1 b. black 2·25 55
233 3 b. brown 20 10
234 10 b. red 35 25
235 20 b. violet 80 50

1902. Stamp of 1901 optd **1901**.

236 **13** 1 b. black 45 30

1904. No. 231 surch **CORREOS Vale B 0,05 1904**.

310 **13** 5 c. on 50 c. green 40 55

38 General Sucre **39** Bolivar

1904.

311 **38** 5 c. green 40 15
312 10 c. red 25 15
313 15 c. violet 45 30
314 25 c. blue 3·25 30
315 50 c. red 45 40
316 1 b. red 50 40

1904.

317 **39** 5 c. green 10 10
318 10 c. grey 10 10
319 25 c. red 10 10
320 50 c. yellow 10 10
321 1 b. red 1·90 25
322 3 b. blue 35 15
323 10 b. violet 45 25
324 20 b. red 1·10 35

41 President Castro **42** Liberty

1905. 6th Anniv of General Castro's Revolt.

330 **41** 5 c. red 2·10 2·10
331a 10 c. blue 3·25 2·75
332a 25 c. yellow 1·00 1·00

1910. Independence Centenary.

333 **42** 25 c. blue 8·25 45

43 F. de Miranda **44**

1911. Portraits as T **43**.

340 **43** 5 c. green 25 15
341 10 c. red 35 10
342 – 15 c. grey (Urdaneta) 3·25 20
343 – 25 c. blue (Urdaneta) 1·60 25
344 – 50 c. violet (Bolivar) 2·10 25
339 – 1 b. orange (Bolivar) 2·10 1·00

1911. Portraits as T **44**.

345 – 5 c. blue (Vargas) 10 10
346 – 10 c. yellow (Avila) 10 10
347 – 25 c. grey (Sanz) 10 10
348 **44** 50 c. red (Blanco) 10 10
349 – 1 b. green (Bello) 10 10
350 – 2 b. brown (Sanabria) 55 35
351 – 3 b. violet (Paez) 55 25
352 – 10 b. purple (Sucre) 1·10 50
353 – 20 b. blue (Bolivar) 1·10 70

46 Bolivar **47** Bolivar

1914.

359 **46** 5 c. green 20·00 25
360 10 c. red 18·00 40
361 25 c. blue 3·25 20

1915. Various Frames.

362a **47** 5 c. green 2·75 25
379 5 c. brown 55 10
570 7½ c. green 60 35
571 10 c. red 2·10 30
380 10 c. green 20 10
381 15 c. olive 1·25 50
382 15 c. brown 30 10
383 25 c. blue 1·25 10
384 25 c. red 20 10
368 40 c. green 14·50 6·25
385 40 c. blue 55 20
369 50 c. violet 3·75 40
386 50 c. blue 55 20
371 75 c. turquoise 38·00 12·50
387 1 b. black 55 25
388 3 b. orange 8·25 2·75
389 5 b. violet 10·00 5·50

See also Nos. 414/5.

48 Bolivar and Sucre

1924. Centenary of Battle of Ayacucho.

390 **48** 25 c. blue 1·90 35

1926. Fiscal stamps surch **CORREOS VALE 1926** and value.

392 0,05 b. on 1 b. olive 40 35
393 0,25 b. on 5 c. brown 40 40

DESIGNS: No. 392, Portrait of Sucre; No. 393, Numeral.

50 General J. V. Gomez and Ciudad Bolivar **51** Biplane and Venezuela

1928. 25th Anniv of Capture of Ciudad Bolivar and Peace in Venezuela.

394 **50** 10 c. green 1·10 55

1930. Air.

395 **51** 5 c. brown 15 10
575 5 c. green 30 10
396 10 c. yellow 15 10
576 10 c. ornge 1·10 55
577 12½ c. purple 50 30
397 15 c. grey 15 10
578 15 c. blue 70 15
398 25 c. violet 15 10
579 25 c. brown 2·40 65
399 40 c. green 15 10
581 70 c. red 17·00 5·25
400 75 c. red 45 15
401 1 b. blue 55 15
402 1 b. 20 green 50 35
403 1 b. 70 blue 70 40
404 1 b. 90 green 75 50
405 2 b. 10 blue 1·25 40
406 2 b. 30 red 1·25 50
407 2 b. 50 blue 1·25 50
408 3 b. 70 green 1·25 45
409 10 b. purple 3·25 1·10
410 20 b. green 5·50 2·50

See also Nos. 426/49.

52 Simon Bolivar **53**

1930. Death Centenary of Bolivar.

411 **52** 5 c. yellow 60 40
412 10 c. blue 60 30
413 25 c. red 60 30

1932. Stamps of 1915 on paper printed with pattern as T **53**.

414 **47** 5 c. violet 40 10
415 7½ c. green 50 40
416 10 c. green 25 10
417 15 c. yellow 65 25
418 22½ c. red 1·60 35
419 25 c. red 55 10
420 37½ c. blue 2·10 1·00
421 40 c. blue 2·10 30
422 50 c. olive 2·10 40
423 1 b. blue 2·75 45
424 3 b. brown 21·00 8·25
425 5 b. brown 27·00 11·00

1932. Air. Air stamps as 1930 on paper printed with pattern as T **53**.

426 **51** 5 c. brown 40 10
427 10 c. yellow 40 10
428 15 c. grey 40 10
429 25 c. blue 55 10
430 40 c. green 50 10
431 70 c. red 65 10
432 75 c. orange 70 25
433 1 b. slate 85 10
434 1 b. 20 green 1·50 60
435 1 b. 70 brown 3·00 40
436 1 b. 80 blue 1·50 30
437 1 b. 90 green 3·50 2·50
438 1 b. 95 blue 4·25 2·10
439 2 b. brown 3·00 1·75
440 2 b. 10 blue 6·25 4·25
441 2 b. 30 red 3·00 1·60
442 2 b. 50 blue 3·50 1·00
443 3 b. violet 3·50 60
444 3 b. 70 green 5·00 4·25
445 4 b. orange 3·50 1·00
446 5 b. black 5·00 1·60
447 8 b. red 9·75 3·25
448 10 b. violet 20·00 5·25
449 20 b. green 42·00 15·00

54 Arms of Bolivar

1933. 150th Birth Anniv of Bolivar.

450 **54** 25 c. red 1·60 1·25

1934. Surch **1933** and figures of value and old value blocked out.

451 **47** 7½ on 10 c. green (380) 55 30
453 22½ on 25 c. red (384) 1·10 60
452 22½ on 25 c. red (419) 1·00 1·00
454 37½ on 40 c. blue (385) 1·25 60

1937. Air. Air stamps of 1932 surch **1937 VALE POR** and new value.

455 **51** 5 c. on 1 b. 70 brown 8·00 4·50
456 10 c. on 3 b. 70 green 8·00 4·50
457 15 c. on 4 b. orange 3·50 2·25
458 25 c. on 5 b. black 3·50 2·25
459 1 b. on 8 b. red 2·75 2·25
460 2 b. on 2 b. 10 blue 21·00 15·00

1937. Surch **1937 VALE POR** and value.

461 **47** 25 c. on 40 c. (No. 421) 4·25 55

59 Nurse and Child **60** Ploughing

61 "Flight" **64** Caribbean Coast

1937. (a) Postage.

463 **59** 5 c. violet 35 25
464 – 10 c. green 80 25
465 – 15 c. brown 65 35
466 **59** 25 c. red 65 40
467 – 50 c. green 4·25 2·75
468 **60** 3 b. red 7·25 5·00
469 **59** 5 b. brown 15·00 10·00

DESIGNS—VERT: 10 c. Sailing barges on Orinoco; 15 c. Women gathering cocoa-beans. HORIZ: 50 c. Rounding up cattle.

(b) Air.

470 **61** 5 c. brown 35 35
471 – 10 c. orange 20 10
472 – 15 c. black 40 35
473 **64** 25 c. violet 50 35
474 – 40 c. green 70 40
475 **61** 70 c. red 70 35
476 – 75 c. bistre 1·60 65
477 **61** 1 b. grey 1·00 45
478 – 1 b. 20 green 4·25 1·90
479 **61** 1 b. 80 blue 2·10 90
480 – 1 b. 95 blue 6·25 3·75
481 **64** 2 b. brown 2·50 1·50
482 2 b. 50 blue 7·50 4·75
483 – 3 b. lilac 4·25 2·25
484 **64** 3 b. 70 red 6·00 5·00
485 – 10 b. purple 16·00 6·50
486 **61** 20 b. black 17·00 11·50

DESIGNS—HORIZ: 10, 40 c., 1 b. 20, 3 b. Puerto Cabello; 15, 75 c., 1 b. 95, 10 b. Caracas.

65 "Venezuela" welcoming La Guaira **67** Bolivar

1937. Acquisition of La Guaira Harbour.

487 **65** 25 c. blue (postage) 85 55
488 – 70 c. green (air) 2·25 80
489 – 1 b. 80 blue 4·00 1·50

DESIGN: 70 c., 1 b. 80, Statue of Bolivar and La Guaira Harbour.

1937. Red Cross Fund.

490 **67** 5 c. green 75 50

1937. Stamps of 1937 optd **RESELLADO 1937-1938**.

491 **59** 5 c. violet (postage) 3·00 1·60
492 – 10 c. green 1·40 65
493 **59** 25 c. red 60 55
494 **60** 3 b. red £120 60·00
495 – 10 c. orange (air) 85 55
496 **64** 25 c. violet 1·60 75
497 – 40 c. green 1·60 1·10
498 **61** 70 c. red 1·00 75
499 1 b. grey 1·60 1·10
500 – 1 b. 20 green 20·00 12·50
501 **61** 1 b. 80 blue 3·50 85
502 – 1 b. 95 blue 6·50 3·75
503 **64** 2 b. brown 42·00 19·00
504 2 b. 50 blue 42·00 15·00
505 – 3 b. lilac 20·00 7·75
506 – 10 b. purple 60·00 32·00
507 **61** 20 b. black 55·00 30·00

69 Gathering Coffee Beans **72** La Guaira

1938. (a) Postage. As T **69**.

508 **69** 5 c. green 40 15
509 A 10 c. red 40 15
510 B 15 c. violet 85 25
544 15 c. green 55 30
511 A 25 c. blue 40 15
546 37½ c. blue 1·60 55
513 B 40 c. sepia 12·50 3·25
547 40 c. black 10·50 3·25
514 **69** 50 c. olive 17·00 3·25
548 50 c. violet 5·75 55
515 A 1 b. brown 6·75 3·25
516 **69** 3 b. orange 60·00 22·00
517 B 5 b. black 7·25 3·25
750 5 b. orange 27·00 13·50
751 5 b. brown 9·25 3·50

DESIGNS: A, Bolivar; B, G.P.O., Caracas.

(b) Air. As T **72**.

550 **72** 5 c. gren 65 40
551 C 10 c. red 20 10
552 **72** 12½ c. violet 35 30
520 D 15 c. violet 2·00 75
553 15 c. blue 60 10
521 **72** 25 c. blue 2·00 75
554 25 c. brown 25 10
555 D 30 c. violet 1·40 20
522 C 40 c. violet 2·25 85
556 40 c. brown 1·60 20
557 **72** 45 c. green 65 20
558 C 50 c. blue 75 10
523 D 70 c. red 60 40
524 **72** 75 c. brown 4·50 1·25
559 75 c. green 90 25
560 D 90 c. red 65 20
525 C 1 b. green 4·50 1·75
561 1 b. violet 75 20
526 D 1 b. 20 orange 13·00 4·25
562 1 b. 20 green 1·40 60

527 72 1 b. 80 blue 1·40 35
528 C 1 b. 90 black 3·25 2·10
529 D 1 b. 95 blue 2·75 1·90
530 72 2 b. green 29·00 10·00
563 2 b. red 1·10 50
531 C 2 b. 50 brown 29·00 12·00
564 2 b. 50 orange 7·25 2·10
565 D 3 b. green 3·25 1·25
533 72 3 b. 70 black 4·75 3·50
566 D 5 b. red 4·75 1·25
771 5 b. green 3·50 1·60
534 C 10 b. purple 14·50 1·75
773 10 b. yellow 4·50 1·75
535 D 20 b. orange 40·00 19·00
DESIGNS: C, National Pantheon; D, Oil Wells.

1938. Surch **VALE BS. 0,40 1938.**
536 59 40 c. on 5 b. brown 5·75 2·50

1938. Air. Postage stamps surch **1938 VALE CINCO** (or other value) **CENTIMOS.**
537 61 5 c. on 1 b. 80 blue 70 50
538 64 10 c. on 2 b. 50 blue 2·10 60
539 15 c. on 2 b. brown 1·00 60
540 – 25 c. on 40 c. green (No. 474) 1·10 70
541 64 40 c. on 3 b. 70 red 2·25 1·25

77 Teresa Carreno

78 Allegory of Labour and Statue of Bolivar

1938. Repatriation of Ashes of Teresa Carreno (concert pianist).
567 77 25 c. blue 3·25 55

1938. Labour Day.
568 78 25 c. blue 3·75 55

80 **81** Monuments at Carabobo

82 Gen. J. I. Paz Castillo

1938. Air. Independence Issue.
583 – 20 c. brown 25 35
584 80 30 c. violet 35 35
585 81 45 c. blue 55 25
586 – 50 c. blue 45 25
587 81 70 c. red 8·25 4·50
588 80 90 c. orange 75 30
589 81 1 b. 35 black 90 45
590 – 1 b. 40 slate 3·75 1·50
591 80 2 b. 25 green 1·90 1·00
DESIGN: 20, 50 c., 1 b. 40, Airplane over Sucre Monument.

1939. 80th Anniv of Venezuelan Posts.
592 82 10 c. red 1·50 55

83 View of Ojeda

84 Dr. Cristobal Mendoza

1939. Founding of Ojeda.
593 83 25 c. blue 5·50 40

1939. Centenary of Death of Dr. Mendoza.
594 84 5 c. green 25 30
595 10 c. red 25 30
596 15 c. violet 65 40
597 25 c. blue 55 30
598 37½ c. blue 10·00 5·00
599 50 c. olive 10·00 3·25
600 1 b. brown 4·25 2·75

85 Diego B. Urbaneja

86 Bolivar and Carabobo Monument

1940. Independence Issue.
601 85 5 c. green (postage) 50 15
602 7½ c. green 40 25
603 15 c. olive 55 25
604 37½ c. blue 85 40
605 40 c. blue 60 30
745 40 c. mauve 30 25
746 40 c. orange 30 25
606 50 c. violet 3·25 85
607 1 b. brown 1·60 55
748 1 b. blue 1·00 25
608 3 b. red 5·00 2·00
749 3 b. grey 2·10 55
609 86 15 c. blue (air) 25 15
610 20 c. olive 20 10
611 25 c. brown 1·40 35
612 40 c. brown 1·00 15
613 1 b. lilac 2·25 25
614 2 b. red 4·25 35

87 Foundation of Greater Colombia

1940. Air. 50th Anniv of Pan-American Union.
615 87 15 c. brown 60 30

88 Battle of Carabobo

89 "The Crossing of the Andes" (after Salas)

1940. 150th Birth Anniv of Gen. Paez.
616 88 25 c. blue 3·75 55

1940. Death Centenary of Gen. Santander.
617 89 25 c. blue 3·75 55

90 Monument and Urn

91 Statue of Bolivar at Caracas

1940. 110th Anniv of Death of Simon Bolivar. (a) Postage.
738 90 5 c. green 10 10
739 5 c. blue 15 10
619 – 10 c. pink 30 10
620 – 15 c. green 40 15
741 – 15 c. red 30 10
621 – 20 c. blue 70 10
622 – 25 c. blue 40 10
742 – 25 c. violet 25 10
623 – 30 c. mauve 1·00 25
743 – 30 c. black 50 35
744 – 30 c. purple 1·00 15
624 – 37½ c. blue 2·10 70
625 – 50 c. violet 1·25 50
747 – 50 c. green 55 25
DESIGNS—VERT: 15 c. Bolivar's baptism; 25 c. Simon Bolivar on horseback. HORIZ: 10 c. Bolivar's bed; 20 c. House where Bolivar was born; 30 c. Courtyard and Bolivar's baptismal font; 37½ c. Courtyard of house where Bolivar was born; 50 c. "Rebellion of 1812".

(b) Air.
626 91 5 c. green 10 10
752 5 c. orange 10 10
627 10 c. red 10 10
753 10 c. green 10 10
628 12½ c. violet 45 35
754 12½ c. brown 25 45
629 15 c. blue 25 10
755 15 c. grey 15 10
630 20 c. brown 35 10
756 20 c. violet 20 10
631 25 c. brown 25 10
757 25 c. green 15 10
632 30 c. violet 25 10
758 30 c. blue 20 10
633 40 c. brown 35 10
759 40 c. green 35 10
634 45 c. green 50 10
760 45 c. red 30 15
635 50 c. blue 50 10
761 50 c. claret 30 15
636 70 c. pink 1·00 35
762 70 c. red 55 30
637 75 c. olive 4·25 75
763 75 c. orange 2·75 1·60
764 75 c. violet 30 15
638 90 c. orange 65 35
765 90 c. black 45 40
639 1 b. mauve 35 10
766 1 b. blue 35 20
640 1 b. 20 green 1·40 35
767 1 b. 20 brown 65 45
641 1 b. 35 black 5·50 2·50
642 2 b. red 1·10 20
643 3 b. black 1·60 35
768 3 b. brown 6·75 2·50
769 3 b. blue 1·00 35
644 4 b. black 1·40 35
645 5 b. brown 11·00 4·00

1941. No. 622 surch **HABILITADO 1941 VALE BS.0.20.**
646 20 c. on 25 c. blue 40 15

1941. Optd **HABILITADO 1940.**
647 59 5 c. violet 1·25 50
648 – 10 c. green (No. 464) 1·25 35

94 Bolivar's Funeral

95 Condor

1941. Centenary of Arrival of Bolivar's Ashes at Caracas and Liberator's Monument Fund.
649 94 20 c. + 5 c. blue (postage) 3·25 35
650 95 15 c. + 10 c. brown (air) 1·10 45
651 30 c. + 5 c. violet 1·10 60

96 Symbolical of Industry

97 Caracas Cathedral

100 National and Red Cross Flags

1942. National Industrial Exhibition.
652 96 10 c. red 60 25

1943.
653 97 10 c. red 40 15
740 10 c. orange 10 10

1943. Surch **Habilitado Vale Bs. 0.20.**
654 59 20 c. on 25 c. red 15·00 15·00
655 65 20 c. on 25 c. blue 42·00 32·00
656 77 20 c. on 25 c. blue 8·25 8·25
657 78 20 c. on 25 c. blue 8·25 8·25

1943. Optd **Resellado 1943.**
658 59 5 c. violet 7·50 4·25
659 – 10 c. green (No. 464) 5·00 3·50
660 – 50 c. green (No. 467) 4·00 2·10
661 60 3 b. red 25·00 9·25

1943. Air. Optd **Resellado 1943.**
662 – 10 c. orange (No. 471) 85 55
663 64 25 c. violet 85 60
664 – 40 c. green (No. 474) 1·00 60
665 61 70 c. red 85 60
666 – 70 c. green (No. 488) 1·00 60
667 – 75 c. bistre (No. 476) 1·10 75
668 61 1 b. grey 1·10 75
669 – 1 b. 20 green (No. 478) 1·60 90
670 61 1 b. 80 blue 1·50 75
671 – 1 b. 80 blue (No. 489) 2·10 1·00
672 – 1 b. 95 blue (No. 480) 2·25 1·10
673 64 2 b. brown 2·25 1·90
674 2 b. 50 blue 2·75 1·90
675 – 3 b. lilac (No. 483) 3·25 2·10
676 64 3 b. 70 red 38·00 27·00
677 – 10 b. purple (No. 485) 14·00 8·25
678 61 20 b. black 22·00 17·00

1944. Air. 80th Anniv of Int Red Cross and 37th Anniv of Adherence of Venezuela.
680 100 5 c. green 10 10
681 10 c. mauve 15 10
682 20 c. blue 15 10
683 30 c. blue 35 10
684 40 c. brown 50 15
685 45 c. green 90 35
686 90 c. orange 85 30
687 1 b. black 1·25 25

101 Baseball Players

103 Charles Howarth

1944. Air. 7th World Amateur Baseball Championship Games, Caracas. Optd **AEREO.**
688 101 5 c. brown 35 25
689 10 c. green 40 25
690 20 c. blue 50 35
691 30 c. red 40 50
692 45 c. purple 1·00 45
693 90 c. orange 1·90 90
694 1 b. grey 2·10 90
695 1 b. 20 green 6·25 4·75
696 1 b. 80 yellow 8·25 6·50

1944. Air. No. 590, surch **Habilitado 1944 VALE Bs.0.30.**
697 30 c. on 1 b. 40 c. slate 35 35

1944. Air. Cent of Rochdale Co-operative Society.
698 103 5 c. black 25 15
699 10 c. violet 25 15
700 20 c. brown 50 30
701 30 c. green 35 35
702 1 b. 20 brown 1·60 1·50
703 1 b. 80 blue 3·00 1·90
704 3 b. 70 red 3·75 3·00

104 Antonio Jose de Sucre

105 Antonio Jose de Sucre and Douglas DC-4

1945. 150th Anniv of Birth of Gen. Sucre.
705 104 5 c. yellow (postage) 75 35
706 10 c. blue 1·00 70
707 20 c. red 1·25 70
708 105 5 c. orange (air) 20 15
709 10 c. purple 25 20
710 20 c. black 35 25
711 30 c. green 55 40
712 40 c. olive 55 35
713 45 c. brown 70 35
714 90 c. brown 1·25 45
715 1 b. mauve 90 35
716 1 b. 20 black 2·10 1·90
717 2 b. yellow 3·00 1·50

106 Andres Bello

107 Gen. Rafael Urdaneta

1946. 80th Death Anniv of A. Bello (educationalist).
718 106 20 c. blue (postage) 55 35
719 30 c. green (air) 40 30

1946. Death Centenary of Gen. R. Urdaneta.
720 107 20 c. blue (postage) 55 35
721 30 c. green (air) 40 30

108 Allegory of Republic

110 Western Hemisphere and Anti-tuberculosis Inst, Maracaibo

1946. 1st Anniv of Revolution.
722 108 20 c. blue (postage) 55 35
723 – 15 c. blue (air) 20 30
724 – 20 c. bistre 25 30
725 – 30 c. violet 30 25
726 – 1 b. red 2·10 1·50
Nos. 723/6 are as Type 108, but vert.

1947. 12th Pan-American Health Conf, Caracas.
727 110 20 c. yell & blue (postage) 50 35
728 – 15 c. yellow & blue (air) 35 25
729 – 20 c. yellow and brown 35 40
730 – 30 c. yellow and violet 35 25
731 – 1 b. yellow and red 2·50 2·10
Nos. 728/31 are as Type 110 but vert.

1947. Surch **J.R.G. CORREOS Vale Bs. 0.15 1946.**
732 85 15 c. on 1 b. brown 55 35

1947. Air. Surch **J.R.G. AEREO Vale Bs.**, new value, and **1946.**
733 47 10 c. on 22½ c. red (No. 418) 20 10
734 – 15 c. on 25 c. blue (No. 622) 45 15
735 91 20 c. on 50 c. blue 40 25
736 85 70 c. on 1 b. brown 50 35
737 – 20 b. on 20 b. orange (No. 535) 18·00 9·50

1947. Nos. 743 and 624 surch **CORREOS Vale Bs.**, new value, and **1947.** (a) Postage.
776 5 c. on 30 c. black 25 10
777 5 c. on 37½ c. blue 30 10
(b) Air. No. 621 with **AEREO** instead of **CORREOS.**
778 5 c. on 20 c. blue 40 10
779 10 c. on 20 c. blue 40 10

116 **117**
Freighter "Republica de Venezuela" and Ship's Wheel

1948. 1st Anniv of Greater Colombia Merchant Marine. Frame size $37\frac{1}{2} \times 22\frac{1}{2}$ mm or $22\frac{1}{2} \times 37\frac{1}{2}$ mm. Inscr "AMERICAN BANK NOTE COMPANY" at foot.

780 **116** 5 c. blue (postage) 20 10
781 $7\frac{1}{2}$ c. red 70 35
782 10 c. red 55 10
783 15 c. grey 75 15
784 20 c. sepia 40 10
785 25 c. violet 75 20
786 30 c. yellow . . . . 4·75 1·90
787 $37\frac{1}{2}$ c. brown . . . . 2·00 1·40
788 40 c. olive . . . . 3·00 1·75
789 50 c. mauve 85 25
790 1 b. green . . . . 2·00 50

791 **117** 5 c. brown (air) 10 10
792 10 c. green 10 10
793 15 c. buff 15 10
794 20 c. purple 20 10
794 25 c. grey 25 10
796 30 c. olive 35 15
797 45 c. blue 60 25
798 50 c. black 80 35
799 70 c. orange . . . . 1·75 35
800 75 c. blue . . . . 3·00 45
801 90 c. red . . . . 1·75 1·00
802 1 b. violet . . . . 2·00 70
803 2 b. slate . . . . 2·25 1·00
804 3 b. green . . . . 8·50 3·25
805 4 b. blue . . . . 4·00 3·25
806 5 b. red . . . . 17·00 5·50

For stamps as T **116/17** in larger size and inscribed "COURVOISIER S.A." at foot, see Nos. 1012/7.

118 Arms of Venezuela

1948. New Constitution Promulgation.

807 **118** 5 c. blue . . . . 1·00 55
808 10 c. red . . . . 1·25 60

120 Santos Michelena **121**

1949. 110th Anniv of 1st International Postal Convention, Bogota.

810 **120** 5 c. blue (postage) 25 15
811 10 c. red 25 15
812 20 c. sepia . . . . 1·00 35
813 1 b. green . . . . 3·25 1·60

814 **121** 5 c. brown (air) 20 15
815 10 c. grey 25 15
816 15 c. orange 30 15
817 25 c. green 60 30
818 30 c. purple 60 30
819 1 b. violet . . . . 3·00 1·25

122 **123**
Columbus, Indian, "Santa Maria" and Map

1949. 450th Anniv of Columbus's Discovery of America.

820 **122** 5 c. blue (postage) 75 15
821 10 c. red . . . . 3·50 60
822 20 c. sepia . . . . 4·75 90
823 1 b. green . . . . 10·00 3·25

824 **123** 5 c. brown (air) 70 10
825 10 c. grey 75 25
826 15 c. orange . . . . 1·40 30
827 25 c. green . . . . 2·50 65
828 30 c. mauve . . . . 3·50 90
829 1 b. violet . . . . 14·00 2·75

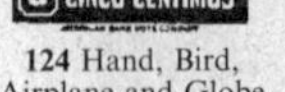

124 Hand, Bird, Airplane and Globe **125** Francisco de Miranda

126 Declaration of Independence

1950. Air. 75th Anniv of U.P.U.

830 **124** 5 c. lake 20 10
831 10 c. green 10 10
832 15 c. brown 20 10
833 25 c. grey 25 40
834 30 c. olive 35 20
835 50 c. black 25 25
836 60 c. blue 75 35
837 90 c. red . . . . 1·00 45
838 1 b. violet . . . . 1·10 30

1950. Birth Bicentenary of Miranda.

839 **125** 5 c. blue (postage) . . . 25 10
840 10 c. green 30 10
841 20 c. brown 60 25
842 1 b. red . . . . 2·75 1·25

843 **126** 5 c. red (air) 35 15
844 10 c. brown 35 15
845 15 c. violet 30 35
846 30 c. blue 45 25
847 1 b. green . . . . 2·50 1·10

127 Tabebuia (National Tree) **128** Map and Statistics

1950. Air. Protection of Flora. Centres in yellow.

848 **127** 5 c. brown 35 20
849 10 c. green 25 10
850 15 c. mauve 35 15
851 25 c. green . . . . 2·50 1·00
852 30 c. orange . . . . 2·75 1·40
853 50 c. grey . . . . 1·50 35
854 60 c. blue . . . . 2·50 65
855 90 c. red . . . . 4·50 1·40
856 1 b. violet . . . . 5·50 1·60

1950. Census of the Americas.

857 **128** 5 c. blue (postage) . . . 20 10
858 10 c. grey 20 10
859 15 c. sepia 30 10
860 25 c. green 25 15
861 30 c. red 35 25
862 50 c. violet 65 25
863 1 b. brown . . . . 1·60 85

864 **128** 5 c. grey (air) 15 10
865 10 c. green 10 10
866 15 c. olive 30 15
867 25 c. black 25 25
868 30 c. orange 35 20
869 50 c. brown 25 25
870 60 c. blue 25 35
871 90 c. red 90 35
872 1 b. violet . . . . 1·50 1·10

129 Alonso de Ojeda **131**

1950. 450th Anniv of Discovery of Lake Maracaibo.

873 **129** 5 c. blue (postage) . . . 25 15
874 10 c. red 35 15
875 15 c. grey 40 20
876 20 c. blue . . . . 1·00 40
877 1 b. green . . . . 4·25 2·10

878 5 c. brown (air) 25 10
879 10 c. red 35 15
880 15 c. sepia 45 20
881 25 c. purple 45 40
882 30 c. orange 90 35
883 1 b. green . . . . 3·75 1·90

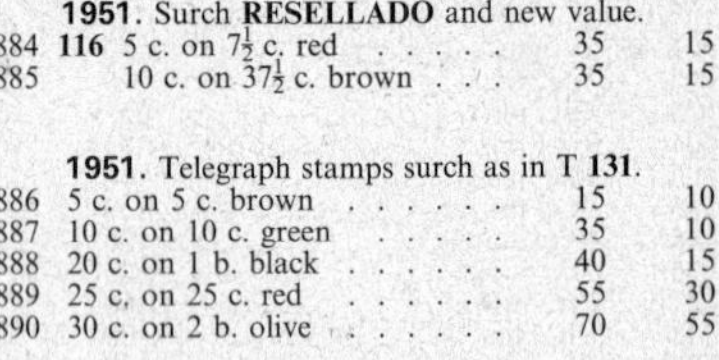

1951. Surch **RESELLADO** and new value.

884 **116** 5 c. on $7\frac{1}{2}$ c. red 35 15
885 10 c. on $37\frac{1}{2}$ c. brown . . . 35 15

1951. Telegraph stamps surch as in T **131**.

886 5 c. on 5 c. brown 15 10
887 10 c. on 10 c. green 35 10
888 20 c. on 1 b. black 40 15
889 25 c. on 25 c. red 55 30
890 30 c. on 2 b. olive 70 55

132 Arms of Caracas and View **133** Statue of Bolivar, New York

1951. Arms issue. Federal District of Caracas.

891 **132** 5 c. green (postage) . . . 30 10
892 10 c. red 40 10
893 15 c. brown . . . . 1·00 25
894 20 c. blue . . . . 2·10 25
895 25 c. brown . . . . 3·00 55
896 30 c. blue . . . . 2·75 60
897 35 c. violet . . . . 27·00 16·00

898 5 c. turquoise (air) 40 15
899 $7\frac{1}{2}$ c. green . . . . 1·60 60
900 10 c. red 25 25
901 15 c. brown . . . . 3·75 40
902 20 c. blue . . . . 2·50 40
903 30 c. blue . . . . 4·25 85
904 45 c. purple . . . . 2·50 55
905 60 c. green . . . . 8·25 1·00
906 90 c. red . . . . 5·00 4·25

See also Nos. 922/37, 938/53, 954/69, 970/85, 991/1006, 1018/33, 1034/49, 1050/65, 1066/81, 1082/97, 1098/113, 1137/52, 1153/68, 1169/84, 1185/1200, 1201/16, 1217/32, 1258/73, 1274/89, 1290/1305, 1306/21, 1322/37, and 1338/53.

1951. Transfer of Statue of Bolivar to Central Park, New York.

907 **133** 5 c. green (postage) . . . 35 10
908 10 c. red 35 25
909 20 c. blue 35 25
910 30 c. grey 45 40
911 40 c. green 60 40
912 50 c. brown . . . . 1·25 45
913 1 b. black . . . . 4·00 2·10

914 5 c. violet (air) 40 15
915 10 c. green 25 15
916 20 c. grey 25 15
917 25 c. olive 30 20
918 30 c. red 35 25
919 40 c. brown 35 25
920 50 c. slate . . . . 1·10 45
921 70 c. orange . . . . 1·90 1·10

134 Arms of Venezuela and Bolivar Statue **138** Isabella the Catholic

1951. Arms issue. National Arms of Venezuela.

922 **134** 5 c. green (postage) . . . 25 10
923 10 c. red 35 10
924 15 c. brown . . . . 1·90 35
925 20 c. blue . . . . 1·90 45
926 25 c. brown . . . . 3·00 70
927 30 c. blue . . . . 3·00 70
928 35 c. violet . . . . 17·00 12·50

929 5 c. turquoise (air) 25 10
930 $7\frac{1}{2}$ c. green 70 55
931 10 c. red 35 15
932 15 c. brown . . . . 1·60 55
933 20 c. blue . . . . 2·25 40
934 30 c. blue . . . . 4·25 90
935 45 c. purple . . . . 1·90 35
936 60 c. green . . . . 9·25 1·90
937 90 c. red . . . . 5·75 4·25

1951. Arms issue. State of Tachira. As T **132** showing Arms of Tachira and agricultural products.

938 5 c. green (postage) 25 10
939 10 c. red 30 25
940 15 c. brown 60 20
941 20 c. blue . . . . 1·50 35
942 50 c. orange . . . . 90·00 11·50
943 1 b. green . . . . 1·50 55
944 5 b. purple . . . . 3·75 2·10

945 5 c. turquoise (air) 15 15
946 10 c. red 25 10
947 15 c. brown 55 25
948 30 c. blue . . . . 7·50 90
949 60 c. green . . . . 5·75 90
950 1 b. 20 lake . . . . 5·75 4·25
951 3 b. green . . . . 1·50 75
952 5 b. purple . . . . 3·25 1·60
953 10 b. violet . . . . 4·75 3·25

1951. Arms issue. State of Zulia. As T **132** showing Arms of Zulia and Oil Well.

954 5 c. green (postage) 25 10
955 10 c. red 25 10
956 15 c. brown 55 25
957 20 c. blue 70 35
958 50 c. orange . . . . 4·25 3·00
959 1 b. green . . . . 1·50 55
960 5 b. purple . . . . 3·00 2·10

961 5 c. turquoise (air) 30 15
962 10 c. red 15 10
963 15 c. brown 35 35
964 30 c. blue . . . . 2·50 1·00
965 60 c. green . . . . 1·40 35
966 1 b. 20 lake . . . . 5·75 4·25
967 3 b. green . . . . 1·50 65
968 5 b. purple . . . . 2·50 1·60
969 10 b. violet . . . . 4·25 3·25

1951. Arms issue. State of Carabobo. As T **132** showing Arms of Carabobo and agricultural produce.

970 5 c. green (postage) 15 10
971 10 c. red 15 10
972 15 c. brown 20 20
973 20 c. blue 30 30
974 25 c. brown 35 35
975 30 c. blue 70 30
976 35 c. violet . . . . 2·75 2·25

977 5 c. turquoise (air) 10 10
978 $7\frac{1}{2}$ c. green 25 25
979 10 c. red 15 10
980 15 c. brown 20 20
981 20 c. blue 30 30
982 30 c. blue . . . . 1·00 35
983 45 c. purple 45 40
984 60 c. green 90 45
985 90 c. red . . . . 2·50 1·50

1951. Air. 500th Birth Anniv of Isabella the Catholic.

986 **138** 5 c. green and light green 25 15
987 10 c. red and yellow . . . 25 15
988 20 c. blue and grey . . . 45 25
989 30 c. blue and grey . . . 45 20

1951. Arms issue. State of Anzoategui. As T **132** showing Arms of Anzoategui and globe.

991 5 c. green (postage) 15 10
992 10 c. red 20 10
993 15 c. brown 55 25
994 20 c. blue 90 30
995 40 c. orange . . . . 1·90 90
996 45 c. purple . . . . 5·50 3·00
997 3 b. blue . . . . 2·10 1·00

998 5 c. turquoise (air) 25 10
999 10 c. red 20 10
1000 15 c. brown 25 25
1001 25 c. black 35 15
1002 30 c. blue 90 65
1003 50 c. orange 90 35
1004 60 c. green . . . . 1·40 20
1005 1 b. violet . . . . 1·60 65
1006 2 b. violet . . . . 3·00 1·50

140 National Stadium **147** Juan de Villegas

1951. Air. 3rd Bolivarian Games, Caracas.

1007 **140** 5 c. green 55 25
1008 10 c. red 60 25
1009 20 c. brown 70 35
1010 30 c. blue 90 45

1951. As Nos. 780/806 but frame size $38 \times 23\frac{1}{2}$ mm or $23\frac{1}{2} \times 38$ mm. Inscr "COURVOISIER S.A." at foot.

1012 **116** 5 c. green (postage) . . . 55 10
1013 10 c. red 90 10
1014 15 c. slate . . . . 3·00 10

1015 **117** 5 c. brown (air) 75 10
1016 10 c. brown . . . . 1·10 10
1017 15 c. olive . . . . 1·50 10

1952. Arms issue. State of Aragua. As T **132** showing Arms of Aragua and Stylised Farm.

1018 5 c. green (postage) 20 10
1019 10 c. red 15 10
1020 15 c. brown 35 10
1021 20 c. blue 30 30
1022 25 c. brown 75 40
1023 30 c. blue 75 35
1024 35 c. violet . . . . 4·25 3·00

1025 5 c. turquoise (air) 35 15
1026 $7\frac{1}{2}$ c. green 25 60
1027 10 c. red 15 10
1028 15 c. brown 85 40
1029 20 c. blue 45 40
1030 30 c. blue . . . . 1·40 25
1031 45 c. purple . . . . 1·10 40
1032 60 c. green . . . . 2·25 35
1033 90 c. red . . . . 11·50 6·75

1952. Arms issue. State of Bolivar. As T **132** showing Arms of Bolivar and Iron Foundry.

1034 5 c. green (postage) 15 10
1035 10 c. red 25 10
1036 15 c. brown 25 20
1037 20 c. blue 55 30
1038 40 c. orange . . . . 2·10 70
1039 45 c. purple . . . . 5·50 3·75
1040 3 b. blue . . . . 2·50 1·60

1041 5 c. turquoise (air) 2·50 25
1042 10 c. red 15 10
1043 15 c. brown 30 15
1044 25 c. black 25 10
1045 30 c. blue 1·50 75
1046 50 c. red 1·00 35
1047 60 c. green 1·90 45
1048 1 b. violet 1·50 35
1049 2 b. violet 3·00 1·50

1952. Arms issue. State of Lara. As T **132** showing Arms of Lara and Sisal Industry.
1050 5 c. green (postage) 25 10
1051 10 c. red 25 10
1052 15 c. brown 20 30
1053 20 c. blue 50 35
1054 25 c. brown 60 45
1055 30 c. blue 1·00 35
1056 35 c. violet 4·25 3·00
1057 5 c. turquoise (air) 35 15
1058 7½ c. green 25 25
1059 10 c. red 15 10
1060 15 c. brown 55 20
1061 20 c. blue 75 30
1062 30 c. blue 1·90 35
1063 45 c. purple 75 30
1064 60 c. green 1·90 55
1065 90 c. red 11·00 8·25

1952. Arms issue. State of Miranda. As T **132** showing Arms of Miranda and Agricultural Products.
1066 5 c. green (postage) 20 10
1067 10 c. red 25 10
1068 15 c. brown 35 20
1069 20 c. blue 40 30
1070 25 c. brown 55 40
1071 30 c. blue 90 40
1072 35 c. violet 5·50 3·75
1073 5 c. turquoise (air) 35 10
1074 7½ c. green 45 25
1075 10 c. red 15 10
1076 15 c. brown 35 30
1077 20 c. blue 55 40
1078 30 c. blue 90 35
1079 45 c. purple 75 30
1080 60 c. green 1·90 55
1081 90 c. red 10·00 6·75

1952. Arms issue. State of Sucre. As T **132** showing Arms of Sucre, Palms and Seascape
1082 5 c. green (postage) 25 10
1083 10 c. red 25 10
1084 15 c. brown 60 20
1085 20 c. blue 60 15
1086 40 c. orange 2·10 55
1087 45 c. purple 7·50 4·50
1088 3 b. blue 1·90 1·25
1089 5 c. turquoise (air) 25 15
1090 10 c. red 25 10
1091 15 c. brown 30 20
1092 25 c. black 7·00 25
1093 30 c. blue 2·25 70
1094 50 c. red 1·00 35
1095 60 c. green 1·40 55
1096 1 b. violet 1·60 40
1097 2 b. violet 3·75 1·90

1952. Arms issue. State of Trujillo. As T **132** showing Arms of Trujillo and Stylised Coffee Plant.
1098 5 c. green (postage) 15 10
1099 10 c. red 25 10
1100 15 c. brown 75 25
1101 20 c. blue 75 35
1102 50 c. orange 4·25 2·50
1103 1 b. green 1·00 45
1104 5 b. purple 2·50 1·60
1105 5 c. turquoise (air) 3·75 30
1106 10 c. red 15 10
1107 15 c. brown 90 15
1108 30 c. blue 4·25 90
1109 60 c. green 3·25 85
1110 1 b. 20 lake 3·00 2·00
1111 3 b. green 1·40 85
1112 5 b. purple 3·00 1·50
1113 10 b. violet 5·00 3·25

1952. 4th Centenary of Barquisimeto.
1114 **147** 5 c. green (postage) 35 10
1115 10 c. red 35 10
1116 20 c. slate 55 35
1117 40 c. orange 2·50 1·25
1118 50 c. brown 1·40 65
1119 1 b. violet 2·50 85
1120 5 c. turquoise (air) 30 10
1121 10 c. red 15 10
1122 20 c. blue 25 10
1123 25 c. black 35 25
1124 30 c. blue 45 20
1125 40 c. orange 2·50 1·25
1126 50 c. bronze 85 35
1127 1 b. purple 3·25 1·60

148 Our Lady of Coromoto

157 G.P.O., Caracas

1952. 300th Anniv of Apparition of Our Lady of Coromoto.
1128 **148** 1 b. red (17×26½ mm) 4·25 65
1129 1 b. red (26½×41 mm) 3·00 65
1130 1 b. red (36×65 mm) 1·40 55

1952. National Objective Exn. Telegraph stamps as T **131** surch **Correos Exposicion Objetiva Nacional 1948-1952** and new value.
1131 5 c. on 25 c. red 35 10
1132 10 c. on 1 b. black 35 10

1952. Telegraph stamps as T **131** surch **CORREOS HABILITADO 1952** and new value.
1133 20 c. on 25 c. red 45 15
1134 30 c. on 2 b. olive 1·60 1·00
1135 40 c. on 1 b. black 60 50
1136 50 c. on 3 b. orange 2·10 1·25

1953. Arms issue. State of Merida. As T **132** showing Arms of Merida and Church.
1137 5 c. green (postage) 15 10
1138 10 c. red 15 10
1139 15 c. brown 20 25
1140 20 c. blue 55 25
1141 50 c. orange 2·50 1·00
1142 1 b. green 65 45
1143 5 b. purple 2·50 1·40
1144 5 c. turquoise (air) 20 15
1145 10 c. red 20 10
1146 15 c. brown 35 15
1147 30 c. blue 3·00 65
1148 60 c. green 1·40 35
1149 1 b. 20 lake 2·50 1·60
1150 3 b. green 1·40 65
1151 5 b. purple 3·00 1·60
1152 10 b. violet 4·25 2·75

1953. Arms issue. State of Monagas. As T **132** showing Arms of Monagas and Horses.
1153 5 c. green (postage) 15 10
1154 10 c. red 20 10
1155 15 c. brown 25 25
1156 20 c. blue 35 35
1157 40 c. orange 1·60 60
1158 45 c. purple 5·25 3·00
1159 3 b. blue 2·10 1·60
1160 5 c. turquoise (air) 20 15
1161 10 c. red 15 10
1162 15 c. brown 35 20
1163 25 c. black 25 15
1164 30 c. blue 2·50 75
1165 50 c. red 90 35
1166 60 c. green 1·10 35
1167 1 b. violet 1·60 45
1168 2 b. violet 2·25 1·40

1953. Arms issue. State of Portuguesa. As T **132** showing Arms of Portuguesa and Woodland.
1169 5 c. green (postage) 15 10
1170 10 c. red 15 10
1171 15 c. brown 20 20
1172 20 c. blue 45 20
1173 50 c. orange 2·25 1·50
1174 1 b. green 60 25
1175 5 b. purple 2·50 1·60
1176 5 c. turquoise (air) 90 40
1177 10 c. red 35 10
1178 15 c. brown 40 25
1179 30 c. blue 3·00 1·25
1180 60 c. green 2·10 40
1181 1 b. 20 lake 5·25 3·00
1182 3 b. green 1·60 85
1183 5 b. purple 3·00 1·60
1184 10 b. violet 4·50 3·75

1953. Arms issue. Federal Territory of Delta Amacuro. As T **132** showing Arms of Delta Amacuro and map.
1185 5 c. green (postage) 15 10
1186 10 c. red 20 10
1187 15 c. brown 25 15
1188 20 c. blue 40 25
1189 40 c. orange 1·40 85
1190 45 c. purple 6·25 3·75
1191 3 b. blue 1·60 1·25
1192 5 c. turquoise (air) 25 10
1193 10 c. red 15 10
1194 15 c. brown 35 25
1195 25 c. black 55 40
1196 30 c. blue 1·90 55
1197 50 c. red 90 40
1198 60 c. green 1·50 40
1199 1 b. violet 1·90 60
1200 2 b. violet 3·00 2·25

1953. Arms issue. State of Falcon. As T **132** showing Arms of Falcon and Stylised Oil Refinery.
1201 5 c. green (postage) 15 10
1202 10 c. red 20 10
1203 15 c. brown 35 15
1204 20 c. blue 35 20
1205 50 c. orange 1·60 85
1206 1 b. green 1·00 65
1207 5 b. purple 3·00 1·60
1208 5 c. turquoise (air) 40 30
1209 10 c. red 15 10
1210 15 c. brown 35 25
1211 30 c. blue 3·00 75
1212 60 c. green 2·25 75
1213 1 b. 20 lake 3·00 2·50
1214 3 b. green 3·00 1·60
1215 5 b. purple 5·00 3·25
1216 10 b. violet 5·00 3·75

1953. Arms issue. State of Guarico. As T **132** showing Arms of Guarico and Factory.
1217 5 c. green (postage) 15 10
1218 10 c. red 15 10
1219 15 c. brown 30 25
1220 20 c. blue 35 30
1221 40 c. orange 1·60 1·10
1222 45 c. purple 3·75 2·25
1223 3 b. blue 1·60 1·00
1224 5 c. turquoise (air) 25 10
1225 10 c. red 35 10
1226 15 c. brown 35 20
1227 25 c. black 55 25
1228 30 c. blue 2·10 85
1229 50 c. red 1·00 50
1230 60 c. green 1·25 55
1231 1 b. violet 2·10 55
1232 2 b. violet 3·00 1·60

1953. Inscr "EE. UU. DE VENEZUELA".
1233 **157** 5 c. green (postage) 15 10
1234 7½ c. green 30 20
1235 10 c. red 35 10
1236 15 c. black 30 10
1237 20 c. blue 40 15
1238 25 c. mauve 30 10
1239 30 c. blue 1·60 25
1240 35 c. mauve 70 25
1241 40 c. orange 1·00 35
1242 45 c. violet 1·60 55
1243 50 c. orange 1·00 35
1244 5 c. orange (air) 10 10
1245 7½ c. green 20 20
1246 15 c. purple 15 10
1247 20 c. slate 20 10
1248 25 c. sepia 30 10
1249 30 c. brown 1·60 85
1250 40 c. red 30 15
1251 45 c. purple 30 15
1252 50 c. red 45 10
1253 60 c. red 1·60 1·00
1254 70 c. myrtle 90 45
1255 75 c. blue 3·25 65
1256 90 c. brown 75 35
1257 1 b. violet 75 35
See also Nos. 1365/82.

1953. Arms issue. State of Cojedes. As T **132** showing Arms of Cojedes and Cattle.
1258 5 c. green (postage) 15 10
1259 10 c. red 25 10
1260 15 c. brown 25 10
1261 20 c. blue 30 15
1262 25 c. brown 75 35
1263 30 c. blue 1·10 35
1264 35 c. violet 1·50 90
1265 5 c. turquoise (air) 2·10 45
1266 7½ c. green 55 50
1267 10 c. red 20 10
1268 15 c. brown 35 15
1269 20 c. blue 40 20
1270 30 c. blue 2·75 40
1271 45 c. purple 1·00 35
1272 60 c. green 2·10 35
1273 90 c. red 2·50 1·50

1954. Arms issue. Federal Territory of Amazonas. As T **132** showing Arms of Amazonas and Orchid.
1274 5 c. green (postage) 40 10
1275 10 c. red 40 10
1276 15 c. brown 90 20
1277 20 c. blue 2·50 40
1278 40 c. orange 3·00 90
1279 45 c. purple 4·50 2·25
1280 3 b. blue 6·75 2·50
1281 5 c. turquoise (air) 70 10
1282 10 c. red 40 10
1283 15 c. brown 70 25
1284 25 c. black 1·50 25
1285 30 c. blue 3·75 35
1286 50 c. red 3·00 60
1287 60 c. green 3·75 60
1288 1 b. violet 14·50 2·10
1289 2 b. violet 5·75 2·50

1954. Arms issue. State of Apure. As T **132** showing Arms of Apure, Horse and Bird.
1290 5 c. green (postage) 15 10
1291 10 c. red 15 10
1292 15 c. brown 25 20
1293 20 c. blue 1·50 25
1294 50 c. orange 1·90 1·50
1295 1 b. green 60 55
1296 5 b. purple 3·75 2·10
1297 5 c. turquoise (air) 35 15
1298 10 c. red 15 10
1299 15 c. brown 35 20
1300 30 c. blue 1·60 65
1301 60 c. green 1·60 35
1302 1 b. 20 lake 2·50 1·60
1303 3 b. green 1·60 65
1304 5 b. purple 3·00 1·40
1305 10 b. violet 4·25 3·00

1954. Arms issue. State of Barinas. As T **132** showing Arms of Barinas, Cow and Horse.
1306 5 c. green (postage) 15 10
1307 10 c. red 15 10
1308 15 c. brown 20 20
1309 20 c. blue 1·50 35
1310 50 c. orange 1·60 1·00
1311 1 b. green 45 35
1312 5 b. purple 3·75 1·90
1313 5 c. turquoise (air) 35 15
1314 10 c. red 15 10
1315 15 c. brown 60 25
1316 30 c. blue 2·10 85
1317 60 c. green 2·10 40
1318 1 b. 20 lake 3·00 1·60
1319 3 b. green 1·90 85
1320 5 b. purple 3·00 1·00
1321 10 b. violet 4·50 3·25

1954. Arms issue. State of Nueva Esparta. As T **132** showing Arms of Nueva Esparta and Fishes.
1322 5 c. green (postage) 15 10
1323 10 c. red 15 10
1324 15 c. brown 35 25
1325 20 c. blue 40 15
1326 40 c. orange 1·90 70
1327 45 c. purple 4·50 2·75
1328 3 b. blue 2·10 1·50
1329 5 c. turquoise (air) 30 15
1330 10 c. red 20 10
1331 15 c. brown 55 20
1332 25 c. black 90 35
1333 30 c. blue 1·90 40
1334 50 c. red 1·90 40
1335 60 c. green 1·90 40
1336 1 b. violet 2·75 60
1337 2 b. violet 3·75 1·90

1954. Arms issue. State of Yaracuy. As T **132** showing Arms of Yaracuy and Tropical Foliage.
1338 5 c. green (postage) 30 10
1339 10 c. red 15 10
1340 15 c. brown 25 20
1341 20 c. blue 35 30
1342 25 c. brown 55 40
1343 30 c. blue 60 30
1344 35 c. violet 1·50 90
1345 5 c. turquoise (air) 35 20
1346 7½ c. green 5·00 5·00
1347 10 c. red 20 10
1348 15 c. brown 55 15
1349 20 c. blue 70 15
1350 30 c. blue 1·50 40
1351 45 c. purple 1·00 40
1352 60 c. green 1·00 40
1353 90 c. red 3·00 2·10

164 Simon Rodriguez

165 Bolivar and 1824 Edict

1954. Air. Death Cent of Rodriguez (Bolivar's tutor).
1354 **164** 5 c. turquoise 35 10
1355 10 c. red 50 10
1356 20 c. blue 35 10
1357 45 c. purple 55 35
1358 65 c. green 1·90 85

1954. Air. 10th Pan-American Conf, Caracas.
1359 **165** 15 c. black and brown 15 10
1360 25 c. brown and grey 45 15
1361 40 c. brown and orange 35 15
1362 65 c. black and blue 90 45
1363 80 c. brown and red 75 35
1364 1 b. violet and mauve 1·50 30

1954. As T **157** but inscr "REPUBLICA DE VENEZUELA".
1365 5 c. green (postage) 15 10
1366 10 c. red 15 10
1367 15 c. black 30 10
1368 20 c. blue 35 10
1369 30 c. blue 55 50
1370 35 c. mauve 55 20
1371 40 c. orange 85 30
1372 45 c. violet 1·00 40
1373 5 c. yellow (air) 15 10
1374 10 c. bistre 15 10
1375 15 c. purple 20 10
1376 20 c. slate 35 10
1377 30 c. brown 35 10
1378 40 c. red 60 30
1379 45 c. purple 60 40
1380 70 c. green 1·60 70
1381 75 c. blue 1·00 40
1382 90 c. brown 55 30

166

167

1955. 400th Anniv of Valencia Del Rey.
1383 **166** 5 c. green (postage) 25 10
1384 20 c. blue 50 10
1385 25 c. brown 55 10
1386 50 c. orange 85 35
1387 5 c. turquoise (air) 10 10
1388 10 c. red 15 10
1389 20 c. blue 25 10
1390 25 c. black 25 10
1391 40 c. violet 35 35
1392 50 c. red 35 35
1393 60 c. olive 75 35

1955. 1st Postal Convention, Caracas.
1394 **167** 5 c. green (postage) 25 10
1395 20 c. blue 80 10
1396 25 c. lake 65 10
1397 50 c. orange 85 10
1398 5 c. yellow (air) 15 10
1399 15 c. brown 35 10
1400 25 c. black 35 10
1401 40 c. red 35 20
1402 50 c. orange 35 25
1403 60 c. red 75 50

168 O'Leary College, Barinas

1956. Air. Public Works.
1404 **168** 5 c. yellow 15 10
1405 10 c. sepia 15 10
1406 15 c. brown 20 10
1407 A 20 c. blue 20 10
1408 25 c. black 25 10
1409 30 c. brown 25 15

1410 B 40 c. red 30 20
1411 45 c. brown 20 15
1412 50 c. orange 35 15
1413 C 60 c. olive 35 25
1414 65 c. blue 60 35
1415 **168** 70 c. green 60 25
1416 C 75 c. blue 65 30
1417 A 80 c. red 75 35
1418 B 1 b. purple 45 20
1419 C 2 b. red 90 60
DESIGNS—HORIZ: A, University Hospital, Caracas; B, Caracas–La Guaira Highway; C, Simon Bolivar Centre.

169

170

1956. 1st American Book Festival, Caracas.
1420 **169** 5 c. turquoise and green (postage) 10 10
1421 10 c. purple and red . . 10 10
1422 20 c. blue and ultram . . 25 10
1423 25 c. grey and green . . 35 15
1424 30 c. blue & light blue . . 35 15
1425 40 c. sepia and brown . . 50 25
1426 50 c. brown and red . . 55 35
1427 1 b. slate and violet . . . 85 40

1428 **170** 5 c. brown & orge (air) . . 10 10
1429 10 c. sepia and brown . . 15 10
1430 20 c. blue and turquoise . . 15 10
1431 25 c. slate and violet . . 35 10
1432 40 c. purple and red . . 50 15
1433 45 c. brn and chocolate . . 35 15
1434 60 c. grey and olive . . . 75 35

171 Tamanaco Hotel, Caracas

172 Simon Bolivar

1957. Tamanaco Hotel, Caracas Commem.
1435 **171** 5 c. green (postage) . . . 10 10
1436 10 c. red 10 10
1437 15 c. black 40 10
1438 20 c. blue 25 10
1439 25 c. purple 25 10
1440 30 c. blue 45 35
1441 35 c. lilac 25 15
1442 40 c. orange 35 25
1443 45 c. purple 45 35
1444 50 c. yellow 60 25
1445 1 b. myrtle 85 35

1446 5 c. yellow (air) 10 10
1447 10 c. brown 10 10
1448 15 c. brown 15 10
1449 20 c. slate 30 10
1450 25 c. brown 25 10
1451 30 c. blue 15 20
1452 40 c. red 20 15
1453 45 c. brown 25 15
1454 50 c. orange 25 20
1455 60 c. green 45 25
1456 65 c. orange . . . . . . 1·25 60
1457 70 c. black 65 30
1458 75 c. turquoise 75 35
1459 1 b. purple 75 35
1460 2 b. black . . . . . . 1·25 45

1957. 150th Anniv of Oath of Monte Sacro and 125th Anniv of Death of Bolivar.
1461 **172** 5 c. green (postage) . . . 10 10
1462 10 c. red 15 10
1463 20 c. blue 50 15
1464 25 c. red 50 15
1465 30 c. blue 40 15
1466 40 c. orange 60 25
1467 50 c. yellow 85 40

1468 5 c. orange (air) 15 10
1469 10 c. brown 20 10
1470 20 c. blue 45 20
1471 25 c. purple 50 25
1472 40 c. red 45 20
1473 45 c. purple 55 35
1474 65 c. brown 90 35

173 G.P.O., Caracas

174 Arms of Santiago de Merida

1958.
1475 **173** 5 c. green (postage) . . . 10 10
1476 10 c. red 10 10
1477 15 c. grey 10 10
1478 20 c. blue 20 10
1479 25 c. yellow 20 10
1480 **173** 30 c. grey 25 10
1481 35 c. purple 30 10
1482 40 c. red 50 15
1483 45 c. violet . . . . . . 1·00 70
1484 50 c. yellow 45 15
1485 1 b. olive 60 50

1486 5 c. yellow (air) 10 10
1487 10 c. brown 10 10
1488 15 c. brown 10 10
1489 20 c. blue 10 10
1490 25 c. grey 20 10
1491 30 c. blue 20 10
1492 35 c. olive 30 10
1493 40 c. green 30 10
1494 50 c. red 30 10
1495 55 c. olive 45 20
1496 60 c. mauve 15 20
1497 65 c. red 20 20
1498 70 c. green 55 25
1499 75 c. brown 80 20
1500 80 c. brown 80 35
1501 85 c. red . . . . . . 1·00 50
1502 90 c. violet 30 35
1503 95 c. purple 90 50
1504 1 b. mauve 35 35
1505 1 b. 20 brown . . . . . 4·50 3·00

1958. 400th Anniv of Santiago de Merida de los Caballeros.
1506 **174** 5 c. green (postage) . . 10 10
1507 10 c. red 10 10
1508 15 c. grey 10 10
1509 20 c. blue 20 10
1510 25 c. purple 35 10
1511 30 c. violet 35 15
1512 35 c. violet 40 15
1513 40 c. orange 50 35
1514 45 c. purple 25 15
1515 50 c. yellow 45 35
1516 1 b. grey . . . . . . 1·25 45

1517 5 c. ochre (air) 10 10
1518 10 c. brown 10 10
1519 15 c. brown 15 10
1520 20 c. blue 15 10
1521 25 c. olive 40 15
1522 30 c. blue 35 10
1523 40 c. red 50 15
1524 45 c. purple 50 20
1525 50 c. orange 35 35
1526 60 c. olive 50 25
1527 65 c. brown 90 35
1528 70 c. black 55 50
1529 75 c. blue . . . . . . 1·00 55
1530 80 c. violet 65 50
1531 90 c. green 65 30
1532 1 b. lilac 75 35

175 G.P.O., Caracas

176 Arms of Trujillo and Bolivar Monument

1958.
1533 **175** 5 c. green (postage) . . 35 10
1534 10 c. red 50 10
1535 15 c. black 40 10

1536 5 c. yellow (air) 35 10
1537 10 c. brown 50 10
1538 15 c. brown 40 10

1958. 400th Anniv of Trujillo.
1539 **176** 5 c. green (postage) . . 10 10
1540 10 c. red 10 10
1541 15 c. grey 10 10
1542 20 c. blue 15 10
1543 25 c. mauve 35 20
1544 30 c. blue 50 15
1545 35 c. lilac 55 25
1546 45 c. purple 40 35
1547 50 c. yellow 40 25
1548 1 b. olive . . . . . . 1·00 55

1549 5 c. buff (air) 10 10
1550 10 c. brown 10 10
1551 15 c. brown 25 10
1552 20 c. blue 30 15
1553 25 c. grey 40 20
1554 30 c. blue 40 20
1555 40 c. green 25 25
1556 50 c. orange 25 30
1557 60 c. mauve 35 40
1558 65 c. red . . . . . . 1·10 55
1559 1 b. violet 75 25

177 Caracas Stadium

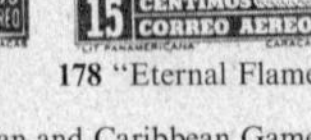

178 "Eternal Flame"

1959. 8th Central American and Caribbean Games.
1560 **177** 5 c. green (postage) . . 25 10
1561 10 c. mauve 25 10
1562 20 c. blue 35 35
1563 30 c. blue 45 40
1564 50 c. lilac 65 35
1565 **178** 5 c. yellow (air) 15 10
1566 10 c. brown 35 15
1567 15 c. orange 40 20
1568 30 c. slate 35 40
1569 50 c. green 45 50

179 Venezuelan ½ Real Stamp of 1859, Gen. J. I. Paz Castillo and Postman

180 Alexander von Humboldt

1959. Cent of First Venezuelan Postage Stamps.
1570 **179** 25 c. ochre (postage) . . 25 15
1571 – 50 c. blue 45 35
1572 – 1 b. red 85 35

1573 **179** 25 c. ochre (air) 25 15
1574 – 50 c. blue 35 35
1575 – 1 b. red 75 35
DESIGNS: 50 c. (2), 1 real stamp of 1859, Don Jacinto Gutierrez and postman on mule; 1 b. (2), 2 reales stamp of 1859, Don Miguel Herrera, and steam mail train and Douglas DC-6 airliner.

1960. Death Centenary of Von Humboldt (naturalist).
1576 **180** 5 c. olive & grn (postage) 35 10
1577 30 c. violet and blue . . . 85 20
1578 40 c. brown and orange . 1·00 50

1579 5 c. brown & bistre (air) . 35 10
1580 20 c. turquoise and blue . 85 20
1581 40 c. bronze and olive . . 1·10 50

181 Bolivar Peak, Merida

1960. Tourist issue.
1582 **181** 5 c. green & emerald (postage) 85 85
1583 – 15 c. grey and purple . . 2·25 2·25
1584 – 35 c. purple & light purple . . . . . . 1·90 1·90

1585 **181** 30 c. blue and deep blue (air) . . . . . . 1·75 1·60
1586 – 50 c. brown and orange . 1·75 1·60
1587 – 65 c. brown and orange . 1·75 1·60
DESIGNS: 15, 50 c. Caroni Falls, Bolivar; 35, 65 c. Cuacharo Caves, Monagas.

182 National Pantheon, Caracas

183 A. Eloy Blanco

1960. Pantheon in olive.
1588 **182** 5 c. green (postage) . . . 10 10
1589 20 c. blue 50 15
1590 25 c. olive 70 20
1591 30 c. grey 85 25
1592 40 c. brown . . . . . . 1·25 50
1593 45 c. violet . . . . . . 1·25 50

1594 5 c. bistre (air) 10 10
1595 10 c. brown 25 10
1596 15 c. brown 35 10
1597 20 c. blue 50 15
1598 25 c. grey . . . . . . 1·10 35
1599 30 c. violet . . . . . . 1·25 55
1600 40 c. green 50 15
1601 45 c. violet 75 20
1602 60 c. mauve 75 40
1603 65 c. red 75 40
1604 70 c. grey 90 35
1605 75 c. blue . . . . . . 1·90 60
1606 80 c. blue . . . . . . 1·60 50
1607 1 b. 20 yellow . . . . . 1·90 70

1960. 5th Death Anniv of Blanco (poet). Portrait in black.
1608 **183** 5 c. green (postage) . . 15 10
1609 30 c. grey 35 15
1610 50 c. yellow 60 30

1611 20 c. blue (air) 35 15
1612 75 c. turquoise . . . . . 1·00 40
1613 90 c. violet . . . . . . 1·00 40

184 1808 Newspaper and Caracas, 1958

185 A. Codazzi

1960. 150th Anniv of "Gazeta de Caracas". Centres in black.
1614 **184** 10 c. red (postage) . . . 35 15
1615 20 c. blue 45 20
1616 35 c. violet 85 70

1617 5 c. yellow (air) . . . . 1·50 65
1618 15 c. brown . . . . . . 1·00 35
1619 65 c. orange . . . . . . 1·25 60

1960. Death Centenary of Codazzi (geographer).
1620 **185** 5 c. deep green and light green (postage) 10 10
1621 15 c. black and grey . . 45 15
1622 20 c. blue & light blue . . 40 15
1623 45 c. purple and lilac . . 45 30

1624 5 c. brown & orge (air) . . 10 10
1625 10 c. sepia and brown . . 15 10
1626 25 c. black and grey . . 35 10
1627 30 c. deep blue & blue . . 45 15
1628 50 c. brown and lt brown . 70 30
1629 70 c. black and brown . . 1·25 45

186 Declaration of Independence

1960. 150th Anniv of Independence. Centres multicoloured.
1630 **186** 5 c. green (postage) . . . 50 10
1631 20 c. blue . . . . . . 1·00 30
1632 30 c. blue . . . . . . 1·00 40

1633 50 c. orange (air) 80 30
1634 75 c. turquoise . . . . . 1·00 35
1635 90 c. violet . . . . . . 1·25 40

187 Drilling for Oil

188 L. Caceres de Arismendi

1960. Oil Industry.
1636 **187** 5 c. myrtle & turquoise (postage) . . . . . . 1·40 70
1637 10 c. brown and red . . 70 25
1638 15 c. mauve and purple . 85 30

1639 – 30 c. indigo & blue (air) . 50 20
1640 – 40 c. olive and green . . 85 35
1641 – 50 c. brown & orange . . 1·00 40
DESIGN: Nos. 1639/41, Oil refinery.

1960. 94th Death Anniv of Luisa Caceres de Arismendi. Centres multicoloured.
1642 **188** 20 c. blue (postage) . . . 1·00 30
1643 25 c. yellow 85 30
1644 30 c. blue . . . . . . 1·10 40

1645 5 c. bistre (air) 80 30
1646 10 c. brown . . . . . . 1·00 45
1647 60 c. red . . . . . . 1·90 55

189 Gen. J. A. Anzoategui

190 Gen. A. J. de Sucre

1960. 140th Death Anniv of Gen. Anzoategui.
1648 **189** 5 c. olive & grn (postage) 20 10
1649 15 c. purple and brown . 40 10
1650 20 c. deep blue & blue . 45 15

1651 25 c. brown & grey (air) . 40 20
1652 40 c. olive and yellow . . 40 20
1653 45 c. purple and mauve . 60 30

1960. 130th Death Anniv of Gen. A. J. de Sucre.
1654 **190** 10 c. mult (postage) . . 35 15
1655 15 c. multicoloured . . . 40 20
1656 20 c. multicoloured . . . 60 30

1657 25 c. multicoloured (air) . 60 30
1658 30 c. multicoloured . . . 85 40
1659 50 c. multicoloured . . . 1·25 60

191 Skyscraper

192 "Population and Farming"

1961. National Census. Skyscraper in orange.
1660 **191** 5 c. green 10 10
1661 10 c. red 10 10
1662 15 c. grey 10 10
1663 20 c. blue 15 10
1664 25 c. brown 25 15
1665 30 c. blue 25 10
1666 35 c. purple 35 15
1667 40 c. brown 50 25
1668 45 c. violet 70 35
1669 50 c. yellow 50 20

1961. Air. 9th Population Census and 3rd Farming Census. Animal's head and inscr in black.
1670 **192** 5 c. yellow 10 10
1671 10 c. brown 10 10
1672 15 c. orange 10 10
1673 20 c. blue 15 10
1674 25 c. grey 20 10
1675 30 c. blue 25 10
1676 40 c. green 35 15
1677 45 c. violet 35 20
1678 50 c. orange 40 25
1679 60 c. mauve 50 25
1680 65 c. red 45 35
1681 70 c. grey 65 25
1682 75 c. turquoise 60 40
1683 80 c. violet 60 35
1684 90 c. violet 90 35

193 R. M. Baralt

195 Arms of San Cristobal

1961. Death Centenary of R. M. Baralt (writer).
1685 **193** 5 c. turq & grn (postage) 10 10
1686 15 c. brown and grey . . 25 10
1687 35 c. violet and mauve . 40 15

1688 25 c. sepia & grey (air) 45 30
1689 30 c. violet and blue . . 55 35
1690 40 c. bronze and green . 65 35

1961. Air. 4th Centenary of San Cristobal. Arms in red, yellow and blue.
1692 **195** 5 c. sepia and orange . . 10 10
1693 55 c. black and green . . 45 25

196 Yellow-crowned Amazon

197 J. J. Aguerrevere (first College President)

1961. Birds. Multicoloured.
1694 30 c. Type **196** (postage) . 1·50 45
1695 40 c. Snowy egret . . . . . 1·75 45
1696 50 c. Scarlet ibis . . . . . 4·00 90

1697 5 c. Troupial (air) . . . . . 2·75 1·25
1698 10 c. Guianan cock of the rock 1·50 65
1699 15 c. Tropical mockingbird . 1·75 70

1961. Engineering College Centenary.
1700 **197** 25 c. blue 15 10

198 Battle Scene

1961. 140th Anniv of Battle of Carabobo. Centres multicoloured.
1702 **198** 5 c. green (postage) . . . 10 10
1703 40 c. brown 70 30

1704 – 50 c. blue (air) 70 15
1705 – 1 b. 05 orange . . . . . 1·10 60
1706 – 1 b. 50 mauve . . . . . 1·60 60
1707 – 1 b. 90 violet . . . . . 1·90 85
1708 – 2 b. sepia . . . . 2·10 85
1709 – 3 b. blue . . . . 2·75 1·00
DESIGN: 50 c. to 3 b. Cavalry charge.

199 Cardinal's Arms

200 Archbishop Blanco

1962. Air. Elevation to Cardinal of Jose Humberto Quintero.
1710 **199** 5 c. mauve 10 10

1962. Air. 4th Anniv of Archbishop Blanco's Pastoral Letter.
1712 **200** 75 c. mauve 70 30

201 "Oncidium papilio Lindl"

1962. Orchids. Multicoloured.
1713 5 c. Type **201** (postage) . . . 10 10
1714 10 c. "Caularthron bilamellatum (Rchb. f.) R.E. Schultes" 15 10
1715 20 c. "Stanhopea Wardii Lodd. ex Lindl" 40 10
1716 25 c. "Catasetum pileatum Rchb. f." 35 10
1717 30 c. "Masdevallia tovarensis Rchb. f." 40 15
1718 35 c. "Epidendrum Stamfordianum Batem" (horiz) 45 25
1719 50 c. "Epidendrum atropurpureum Willd" . . 55 35
1720 3 b. "Oncidium falcipetalum Lindl." . . . . 3·00 1·60

1721 5 c. "Oncidium volvox Rchb. f." (air) 10 10
1722 20 c. "Cycnoches chlorochilon Kl." 20 10
1723 25 c. "Cattleya Gaskelliana Rchb. f. var. alba" 30 15
1724 30 c. "Epidendrum difforme Jacq." (horiz) 20 15
1725 40 c. "Catasetum callosum Lindl" (horiz) 30 20
1726 50 c. "Oncidium bicolor Lindl" 35 30
1727 1 b. "Brassavola nodosa Lindl" (horiz) 60 25
1728 1 b. 05 "Epidendrum lividum Lindl" . . . . 1·60 85
1729 1 b. 50 "Schomburgkia undulata Lindl" . . . . . 1·90 90
1730 2 b. "Oncidium zebrinum Rchb. f." . . . . 2·25 1·40

202 Signing of Independence

1962. 150th Anniv of Declaration of Independence. Multicoloured centres; frame colours given.
1731 **202** 5 c. green (postage) . . 15 10
1732 20 c. blue 35 15
1733 25 c. orange 55 30

1734 55 c. green (air) 45 20
1735 1 b. 05 mauve . . . . . 1·50 60
1736 1 b. 50 violet . . . . . 1·25 55

1962. Air. Bicentenary of Upata. Surch **BICENTENARIO DE UPATA 1762–1962 RESELLADO AEREO VALOR Bs 2,00.**
1739 **173** 2 b. on 1 b. olive . . . 1·60 75

204 Putting the Shot

1962. 1st National Games, Caracas, 1961.
1740 **204** 5 c. green (postage) . . 10 10
1741 – 10 c. mauve 15 10
1742 – 25 c. blue 30 15
1744 – 40 c. grey (air) 40 25
1745 – 75 c. brown 60 35
1746 – 85 c. red . . . . 1·40 55
SPORTS: 10 c. Football; 25 c. Swimming; 40 c. Cycling; 75 c. Baseball; 85 c. Gymnastics.

Each value is arranged in blocks of 4 within the sheet, with the top corners of each stamp converging to the centre of the block.

205 Vermilion Cardinal

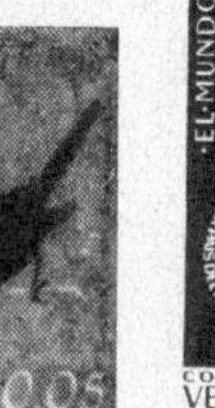

206 Campaign Emblem and Map

1962. Birds. Multicoloured.
1748 5 c. Type **205** (postage) . . . 25 10
1749 10 c. Great kiskadee 50 10
1750 20 c. Glossy-black thrush . . 1·10 25
1751 25 c. Collared trogons . . . . 1·40 35
1752 30 c. Swallow tanager . . . . 1·90 40
1753 40 c. Long-tailed sylph . . . 2·50 60
1754 3 b. Black-necked stilts . . . 13·50 5·75

1755 5 c. American kestrel (air) . . 50 15
1756 20 c. Red-billed whistling duck (horiz) . . . . 1·25 25
1757 25 c. Amazon kingfisher . . . 1·40 35
1758 30 c. Rufous-vented chachalaca 1·75 40
1759 50 c. Oriole blackbird . . . . 2·75 65
1760 55 c. Pauraque . . . . 5·00 1·10
1761 2 b. 30 Red-crowned woodpecker . . . . 13·50 5·00
1762 2 b. 50 White-faced quail dove 13·50 4·50

1962. Malaria Eradication.
1763 **206** 50 c. brn & blk (postage) 40 20
1764 – 30 c. green & black (air) . 35 20
DESIGN: As T **206** but size 26 × 36 mm.

207 Collared Peccary

208 Fisherman

1963. Venezuelan Wild Life. Multicoloured.
1766 5 c. White-tailed deer (postage) 10 10
1767 10 c. Type **207** 10 10
1768 35 c. Widow monkey 25 10
1769 50 c. Giant otter 35 25
1770 1 b. Puma . . . . 1·60 85
1771 3 b. Capybara . . . . 3·25 1·60

1772 5 c. Spectacled bear (vert) (air) 20 10
1773 40 c. Paca 60 25
1774 50 c. Pale-throated sloth . . . 80 35
1775 55 c. Giant anteater . . . . . 1·00 40
1776 1 b. 50 Brazilian tapir . . . . 2·75 1·60
1777 2 b. Jaguar . . . . 4·25 2·10

1963. Freedom from Hunger.
1778 **208** 25 c. bl on pink (postage) 20 15
1779 – 40 c. red on green (air) . 50 25
1780 – 75 c. sepia on yellow . . 30 40
DESIGNS: 40 c. Farmer with lambs; 75 c. Harvester.

209 Bocono Cathedral

211 Flag

210 St. Peter's Basilica, Vatican City

1963. 400th Anniv of Bocono.
1781 **209** 50 c. mult on buff (postage) 45 20
1782 – 1 b. mult on buff (air) . . 1·25 40
DESIGNS: 1 b. Bocono Arms.

1963. Ecumenical Council, Vatican City.
1783 **210** 35 c. brn & bl (postage) . 35 15
1784 45 c. brown and green . 35 20

1785 – 80 c. multicoloured (air) 85 35
1786 – 90 c. multicoloured . . . 85 40
DESIGN: 80, 90 c. Arms of Vatican City and Venezuela.

1963. National Flag and Arms Centenary. Mult.
1787 30 c. Type **211** (postage) . . 20 15
1788 70 c. Venezuela Arms (vert) (air) 85 50

212 Maracaibo Bridge

213 Arms, Map and Guardsman

1963. Opening of Higher Bridge, Lake Maracaibo.
1789 **212** 30 c. brn & bl (postage) . 55 10
1790 35 c. brown and green . 65 20
1791 80 c. brown and green . 1·25 40

1792 – 90 c. ochre, brown and green (air) . . . . . . 1·00 50
1793 – 95 c. ochre, brown & bl . 1·00 55
1794 – 1 b. ochre, brown & blue 95 50
DESIGN—HORIZ: 90 c. to 1 b. Aerial view of bridge and mainland.

1963. 25th Anniv of National Guard.
1795 **213** 50 c. green, red & blue on cream (postage) . . . 40 20
1796 1 b. blue and red on cream (air) . . . . 1·25 70

214 Dag Hammarskjold and Atlantic Map

1963. 1st Death Anniv (1962) of Dag Hammarskjold (U.N. Secretary-General, 1953–61).
1797 **214** 25 c. indigo & bl (postage) 20 15
1798 55 c. green & turquoise . 75 35

1799 80 c. blue and dp blue (air) 75 45
1800 90 c. violet and blue . . 1·00 60

215 Dr. L. Razetti (medallion)

216 Dr. F. A. Risquez (Venezuelan Red Cross President, 1922–23)

1963. Birth Centenary (1962) of Dr. Luis Razetti (founder of University School of Medicine and of Vargas Hospital).
1802 **215** 35 c. brown, ochre and blue (postage) 35 20
1803 45 c. brn, ochre & mve . 50 20

1804 – 95 c. blue & mauve (air) 90 60
1805 – 1 b. 05 sepia and green . 1·25 70
DESIGN: 95 c., 1 b. 05, Portrait of Dr. Razetti.

1963. Red Cross Centenary. Multicoloured.
1806 15 c. Type **216** (postage) . . 15 10
1807 20 c. Dr. Carlos J. Bello (President of Venezuelan Red Cross, 1928–31) 20 10
1808 40 c. Sir Vincent K. Barrington (first President of Venezuelan Red Cross) (air) 40 35
1809 75 c. Nurse and child 70 50
All designs show centenary emblem.

217 Labourer

218 Pedro Gual

1964. Centenary of Venezuelan Ministry of Works and National Industries Exhibition, Caracas. Multicoloured.
1810 5 c. Type **217** (postage) . . . 10 10
1811 10 c. Petrol industry 20 10
1812 15 c. Building construction . 25 10
1813 30 c. Road and rail transport 25 35
1814 40 c. Agricultural machine . 60 25
1815 5 c. Loading ship (air) . . . 10 10
1816 10 c. Tractor and maize . . . 10 10
1817 15 c. Type **217** 15 10
1818 20 c. Petrol industry 20 10
1819 50 c. Building construction . 60 30

1964. Death Cent (1962) of Pedro Gual (statesman).
1820 **218** 40 c. olive (postage) . . . 40 20
1821 50 c. brown 45 25
1822 75 c. turquoise (air) . . . 60 25
1823 1 b. mauve 70 30

219 Dr. C. Arvelo

1964. Death Cent (1962) of Carlos Arvelo (physician).
1824 **219** 1 b. black and blue . . . 1·00 40

220 Blast Furnace

1964. Inaug of Orinoco Steel Works. Mult.
1825 20 c. Type **220** (postage) . . 25 10
1826 50 c. Type **220** 50 20
1827 80 c. Cauldron and map (air) 85 35
1828 1 b. As 80 c. . . . . 1·10 40
The 80 c. and 1 b. are vert.

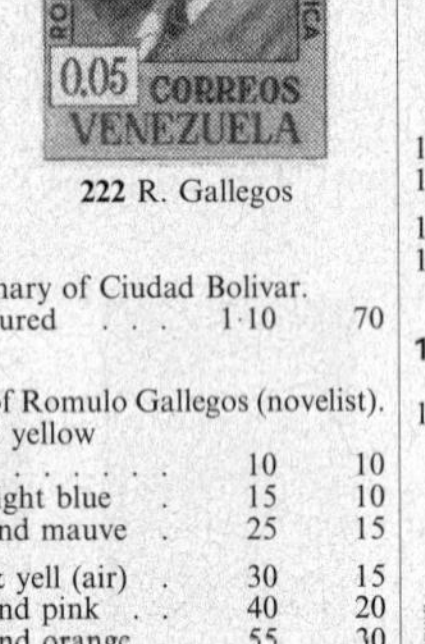

221 Arms of Ciudad Bolivar

222 R. Gallegos

1964. Air. Bicentenary of Ciudad Bolivar.
1829 **221** 1 b. multicoloured . . . 1·10 70

1964. 80th Birth Anniv of Romulo Gallegos (novelist).
1830 **222** 5 c. green and yellow (postage) 10 10
1831 10 c. blue & light blue . 15 10
1832 15 c. purple and mauve . 25 15
1833 – 30 c. brown & yell (air) . 30 15
1834 – 40 c. purple and pink . . 40 20
1835 – 50 c. brown and orange . 55 30
DESIGN: Nos. 1833/5, Gallegos and book.

223 Angel Falls (Bolivar State)

224 Eleanor Roosevelt

1964. Tourist Publicity. Inscr "Conozca a Venezuela Primera" ("See Venezuela First"). Multicoloured.
1836 5 c. Type **223** 10 10
1837 10 c. Tropical landscape (Sucre) 15 10
1838 15 c. Rocks, San Juan (Guarico) 20 10
1839 30 c. Fishermen casting nets (Anzoategui) 40 15
1840 40 c. Mountaineering (Merida) 60 15

1964. Air. 15th Anniv (1963) of Declaration of Human Rights.
1841 **224** 1 b. orange and violet . . 70 40

1965. Various stamps surch **RESELLADO VALOR** and new value. (a) Postage.
1842 5 c. on 1 b. (No. 1485) . . . 50 10
1843 10 c. on 45 c. (1668) . . . 15 10
1844 15 c. on 55 c. (1798) . . . 15 10
1845 20 c. on 3 b. (1754) . . . . 1·00 15
1846 25 c. on 45 c. (1623) . . . 20 15
1847 25 c. on 3 b. (1720) 25 15
1848 25 c. on 1 b. (1770) 35 15
1849 25 c. on 3 b. (1771) 20 15
1850 30 c. on 1 b. (1516) 25 15
1851 40 c. on 1 b. (1824) 70 20
1852 60 c. on 80 c. (1791) 85 35

(b) Air.
1853 5 c. on 55 c. (1495) 10 10
1854 5 c. on 70 c. (1498) 10 10
1855 5 c. on 80 c. (1500) 15 10
1856 5 c. on 85 c. (1501) 10 10
1857 5 c. on 90 c. (1502) 10 10
1858 5 c. on 95 c. (1503) 10 10
1859 5 c. on 1 b. (1796) 50 35
1860 10 c. on 3 b. (804) 15 10
1861 10 c. on 4 b. (805) 70 35
1862 10 c. on 70 c. (1681) . . . 35 15
1863 10 c. on 90 c. (1684) . . . 25 10
1864 10 c. on 1 b. 05 (1705) . . . 50 25
1865 10 c. on 1 b. 90 (1707) . . . 25 15
1866 10 c. on 2 b. (1708) 35 15
1867 10 c. on 3 b. (1709) 35 15
1868 10 c. on 80 c. (1785) . . . 15 10
1869 10 c. on 90 c. (1786) . . . 15 10
1870 15 c. on 3 b. (769) 35 15
1871 15 c. on 90 c. (1613) . . . 25 10
1872 15 c. on 80 c. (1799) . . . 25 10
1873 15 c. on 90 c. (1800) . . . 25 10
1874 15 c. on 1 b. (1829) 35 15
1875 20 c. on 2 b. (1460) 40 15
1876 20 c. on 55 c. (1693) . . . 30 10
1877 20 c. on 55 c. (1760) . . . 1·50 25
1878 20 c. on 2 b. 30 (1761) . . . 1·00 15
1879 20 c. on 2 b. 50 (1762) . . . 1·50 25
1880 20 c. on 70 c. (1788) . . . 50 35
1881 25 c. on 70 c. (1629) . . . 55 30
1882 25 c. on 1 b. 05 (1728) . . . 35 15
1883 25 c. on 1 b. 50 (1729) . . . 35 15
1884 25 c. on 2 b. (1730) 50 25
1885 25 c. on 1 b. 50 (1776) . . . 50 15
1886 25 c. on 2 b. (1777) 50 25
1887 25 c. on 95 c. (1804) . . . 45 25
1888 25 c. on 1 b. 05 (1805) . . . 50 25
1889 30 c. on 1 b. (1782) 70 35
1890 40 c. on 1 b. 05 (1736) . . . 50 25
1891 50 c. on 65 c. (1603) . . . 25 15
1892 50 c. on 1 b. 20 (1607) . . . 70 35
1893 50 c. on 1 b. (1841) 35 15
1894 60 c. on 90 c. (1792) . . . 70 25
1895 60 c. on 95 c. (1793) . . . 75 35
1896 75 c. on 85 c. (1746) . . . 75 40

(c) Revenue stamps additionally optd **CORREOS**.
1897 5 c. on 5 c. green 10 10
1898 5 c. on 20 c. brown 10 10
1899 10 c. on 10 c. bistre 10 10
1900 15 c. on 40 c. green 10 10
1901 20 c. on 3 b. blue 35 15
1902 25 c. on 5 b. blue 70 35
1903 25 c. on 5 b. blue 35 15
1904 60 c. on 3 b. blue 60 40

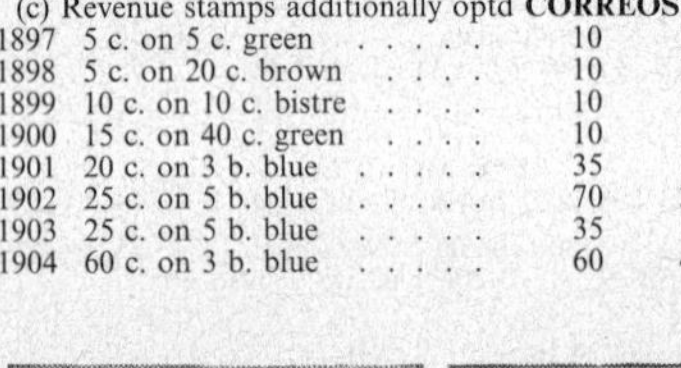

226 Pres. Kennedy and Alliance Emblem

227 Federation Emblem

1965. "Alliance for Progress".
1905 **226** 20 c. black (postage) . . 35 15
1906 40 c. violet 50 20
1907 60 c. turquoise (air) . . 70 30
1908 80 c. brown 85 35

1965. Air. 20th Anniv of Venezuelan Medical Federation.
1909 **227** 65 c. red and black . . . 1·00 45

228 Venezuelan Pavilion

229 Andres Bello

1965. Air. New York World's Fair.
1910 **228** 1 b. multicoloured . . . 65 35

1965. Air. Death Cent of Andres Bello (poet).
1911 **229** 80 c. brown & orange . 75 60

230 Restrepo's Map, 1827

1965. Guyana Claim. Multicoloured.
1912 5 c. Codazzi's map, 1840 (vert) (postage) 10 10
1913 15 c. Type **230** 30 10
1914 40 c. L. de Surville's map, 1778 55 15
1915 25 c. Cruz Cano's map, 1775 (air) 40 15
1916 40 c. (50 c.) Map stamp of 1896 (vert) 55 15
1917 75 c. Foreign Relations Ministry map 75 35

231 I.T.U. Emblem, Satellite, and Aerials of 1865 and 1965

1965. Air. I.T.U. Centenary.
1919 **231** 75 c. black and green . . 70 30

232 Bolivar and Part of Letter

233 Children on "Magic Carpet" and "Three Kings"

1965. Air. 150th Anniv of Bolivar's Letter from Jamaica.
1920 **232** 75 c. black and blue . . . 60 30

1965. Air. Children's (Christmas) Festival.
1921 **233** 70 c. blue and yellow . . 80 55

234 Father F. Toro

235 Sir Winston Churchill

1965. Air. Death Cent of Father Fermin Toro.
1922 **234** 1 b. black and orange . . 60 30

1965. Air. Churchill Commemoration.
1923 **235** 1 b. black and lilac . . . 90 40

236 I.C.Y. Emblem

237 Emblem and Map

1965. Air. International Co-operation Year.
1924 **236** 85 c. violet and gold . . . 1·00 40

1965. Air. 75th Anniv of Organization of American States.
1925 **237** 50 c. gold, black & blue . 85 35

238 "Eurytides protesilaus"

239 Farms of 1936 and 1966

1966. Butterflies. Multicoloured.
1926 20 c. Type **238** (postage) . . . 40 15
1927 30 c. "Morpho peleides" . . . 55 20
1928 50 c. "Papilio zagreus" . . . 80 30
1929 65 c. "Anaea marthesia" (air) 1·00 40
1930 85 c. "Anaea clytemnestra" . 1·60 55
1931 1 b. "Caligo atreus" . . . . . 2·10 60

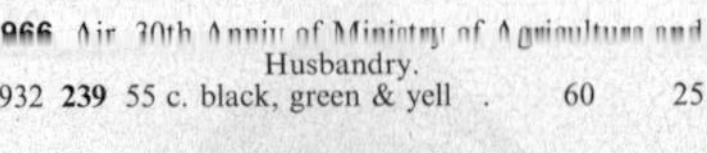

1966. Air. 30th Anniv of Ministry of Agriculture and Husbandry.
1932 **239** 55 c. black, green & yell . 60 25

240 19th-century Sailing Packet crossing Atlantic

1966. Bicentenary of Maritime Mail.
1933 **240** 60 c. black, blue & brown 1·50 50

241 Sebucan Dance

1966. "Popular Dances". Multicoloured.
1934 5 c. Type **241** (postage) . . . 10 10
1935 10 c. Candlemas 20 10
1936 15 c. Chichamaya 30 10
1937 20 c. Carite 40 15
1938 25 c. "Round Drum" 60 25
1939 35 c. Devil Dance, Feast of Corpus Christi 65 35
1940 40 c. Tamunanque (air) . . . 50 35
1941 50 c. Parranda de San Pedro 60 40
1942 60 c. Las Turas 35 25
1943 70 c. Joropo 85 55
1944 80 c. Chimbanguele 90 35
1945 90 c. "The Shepherds" . . . 1·10 50

242 Title Page

1966. Air. 150th Death Anniv (1964) of Jose Lamas (composer).
1946 **242** 55 c. black, bistre & grn 60 30
1947 95 c. black, bistre & mve 60 40

243 A. Michelena (self-portrait)

244 Lincoln

1966. Birth Centenary (1963) of Arturo Michelena (painter). Multicoloured.
1948 95 c. sepia and cream (Type **243**) (postage) 85 35
1949 1 b. "Pentesilea" (battle scene) 75 35
1950 1 b. 05 "La Vara Rota" ("The Red Cloak") 85 35
1951 95 c. "Escena de Circo" ("Circus Scene") (air) . . 60 35
1952 1 b. "Miranda in La Carraca" 75 35
1953 1 b. 05 "Carlota Corday" . . 85 35
Nos. 1949/53 are horiz.

1966. Air. Death Cent (1965) of Abraham Lincoln.
1954 **244** 1 b. black and drab . . 70 55

245 Construction Worker

246 Dr. Hernandez

1966. 2nd O.E.A. Labour Ministers Conference.
1955 **245** 10 c. black and yellow . 10 10
1956 20 c. black and turquoise 20 10
1957 – 30 c. violet and blue . '15 15
1958 – 35 c. olive and yellow . . 25 15
1959 – 50 c. purple and pink . . 40 20
1960 – 65 c. purple and red . . 60 30
DESIGNS: 30, 65 c. Labour Monument; 35 c. Machinist; 50 c. Car assembly line.

1966. Air. Birth Centenary (1964) of Dr. Jose Hernandez (physician).
1961 **246** 1 b. deep blue & blue . . 1·00 45

247 Dr. M. Dagnino (founder) and Hospital

1966. Air. Centenary of Chiquinquira Hospital, Maracaibo.
1962 **247** 1 b. deep green & green . 1·00 40

248 Marbled Cichlid

249 R. Arevalo Gonzalez

1966. Fishes. Multicoloured.
1963 15 c. Type **248** (postage) . . 15 10
1964 25 c. Eye spot cichlid 25 15
1965 45 c. Piranha 70 30
1966 75 c. Head-standing fish (vert) (air) 90 50
1967 90 c. Swordtail characin . . . 90 50
1968 1 b. Butterfly dwarf cichlid . 90 50

1966. Air. Birth Centenary of Rafael Arevalo Gonzalez.
1969 **249** 75 c. black and yellow . 65 35

250 Simon Bolivar, 1816 (after anonymous artist)

251 "Justice"

1966. Air. Bolivar Commemoration.
1970 **250** 5 c. multicoloured . . . 10 10
1971 10 c. multicoloured . . . 10 10
1972 20 c. multicoloured . . . 10 10
1973 – 25 c. multicoloured . . . 15 10
1974 – 30 c. multicoloured . . . 20 10
1975 – 35 c. multicoloured . . . 15 10
1976 – 40 c. multicoloured . . . 30 15
1977 – 50 c. multicoloured . . . 30 15
1978 – 60 c. multicoloured . . . 30 15
1979 – 80 c. multicoloured . . . 60 30
1980 – 1 b. 20 multicoloured . . 80 60
1981 – 4 b. multicoloured . . . 3·00 1·90

BOLIVAR PORTRAITS: 25, 30, 35 c. After paintings by Jose Gil de Castro, 1825; 40, 50, 60 c. Anonymous artist, 1825; 80 c., 1 b. 20., 4 b. Anonymous artist, circa 1829.

1966. Air. 50th Anniv of Political and Social Sciences Academy.
1982 **251** 50 c. purple and lilac . . 55 25

252 Nativity

253 Globe and Communications Emblems

1966. Christmas.
1983 **252** 65 c. black and violet . . 50 25

1966. 30th Anniv of Venezuelan Communications Ministry.
1984 **253** 45 c. multicoloured . . . 40 20

254 Angostura Bridge

1967. Air. Opening of Angostura Bridge, Orinoco River.
1985 **254** 40 c. multicoloured . . . 35 20

255 Ruben Dario (poet)

256 University Building and Arms

1967. Birth Centenary of Ruben Dario.
1986 **255** 70 c. indigo and blue . . 85 35

1967. 75th Anniv of Zulia University.
1987 **256** 80 c. black, red & gold . 85 35

257 Venzuelan Pavilion

1967. Air. World Fair, Montreal.
1988 **257** 1 b. multicoloured . . . 60 30

258 Cacique Guaicaipuro (statue)

259 Francisco Esteban Gomez

1967. Air. 400th Anniv of Caracas. Multicoloured.
1989 10 c. Palace of the Academies (horiz) 10 10
1990 15 c. Type **258** 10 10
1991 45 c. Capt. F. Fajardo . . . 35 15
1992 50 c. St. Teresa's Church . . 35 15
1993 55 c. Diego de Losada (founder) 45 20
1994 60 c. Constellations over Caracas (horiz) 50 25
1995 65 c. Arms of Caracas . . . 55 30
1996 70 c. Federal Legislative Building (horiz) 55 25
1997 75 c. University City (horiz) 70 30
1998 85 c. El Pulpo road junction (horiz) 70 35
1999 90 c. Map of Caracas (horiz) 75 35
2000 1 b. Plaza Mayor, Caracas c. 1800 (horiz) 85 45
2001 2 b. Avenida Libertador (horiz) 2·00 65

1967. Air. 150th Anniv of Battle of Matasiete.
2003 **259** 90 c. multicoloured . . 70 35

260 J. V. Gonzalez

261 Child with Toy Windmill

1967. Air. Death Centenary of Juan Gonzalez (journalist).
2016 **260** 80 c. black and yellow . 55 30

1967. Air. Children's Festival.
2017 **261** 45 c. multicoloured . . 40 20
2018 75 c. multicoloured . . 60 25
2019 90 c. multicoloured . . 70 35

262 "The Madonna of the Rosary" (Lochner)

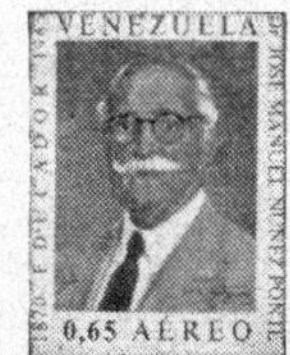

263 Dr. J. M. Nunez Ponte (educator)

1967. Air. Christmas.
2020 **262** 1 b. multicoloured . . . 80 40

1968. Air. 3rd Death Anniv of Dr. Jose Manuel Nunez Ponte.
2021 **263** 65 c. multicoloured . . 35 25

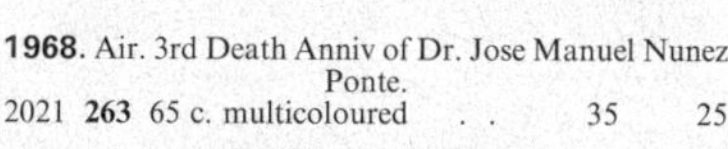

264 General Miranda and Printing Press

1968. Air. 150th Death Anniv of General Francisco de Miranda. Multicoloured.
2022 20 c. Type **264** 20 10
2023 35 c. Portrait and Houses of Parliament, London 35 15
2024 45 c. Portrait and Arc de Triomphe, Paris 55 30
2025 70 c. Portrait (vert) 65 25
2026 80 c. Bust and Venezuelan flags (vert) 80 45

265 Title Page and Printing Press

266 "Spodoptera frugiperda"

1968. 150th Anniv of Newspaper "Correo del Orinoco".
2027 **265** 1 b. 50 multicoloured . . 1·25 50

1968. Insects. Multicoloured.
2028 20 c. Type **266** (postage) . . . 50 20
2029 75 c. "Anthonomus grandis" . 60 30
2030 90 c. "Manduca sexta" . . . 80 40
2031 5 c. "Atta sextens" (air) . . . 15 10
2032 15 c. "Aeneolamia varia" . . 35 15
2033 20 c. "Systena sp." 50 20

The 20 (air), 75 and 90 c. are horiz.

267 Keys

268 Pistol-shooting

1968. Air. 30th Anniv of Office of Controller-General.
2034 **267** 95 c. multicoloured . . . 65 30

1968. Air. Olympic Games, Mexico. Mult.
2035 5 c. Type **268** 10 10
2036 15 c. Running (horiz) 25 10
2037 30 c. Fencing (horiz) 35 20
2038 75 c. Boxing (horiz) 75 35
2039 5 b. Sailing . . . . 3·75 1·40

269 Guayana Sub-station

270 "The Holy Family" (F. J. de Lerma)

1968. Rural Electrification. Multicoloured.
2040 15 c. Type **269** 15 10
2041 45 c. Encantado Dam 40 20
2042 50 c. Macagua Dam 55 20
2043 80 c. Guri Dam 85 40

The 45 and 50 c. are horiz.

1968. Air. Christmas.
2044 **270** 40 c. multicoloured . . . 35 15

271 House and Savings Bank

272 Children and Star

1968. National Savings System.
2045 **271** 45 c. multicoloured . . . 30 20

1968. Air. Children's Festival.
2046 **272** 80 c. orange and violet . 55 25

273 Planting a Tree

1968. Conservation of Natural Resources. Multicoloured designs each incorporating central motif as in T **273**.
2047 15 c. Type **273** (postage) . . 10 10
2048 20 c. Plantation 15 10
2049 30 c. Waterfall 30 15
2050 45 c. Logs 35 15
2051 55 c. Cultivated land 70 35
2052 75 c. Bonito (fish) 50 25
2053 15 c. Marbled wood quails (air) 80 15
2054 20 c. Scarlet ibis, jabiru, great blue heron and red-billed whistling duck 90 15
2055 30 c. Wood-carving 25 10
2056 90 c. Brown trout 75 35
2057 95 c. Mountain highway . . 1·25 55
2058 1 b. Red-eyed vireo and common cowbird (young) . 2·00 50

The 15 c. (both), 20 c. (air), 30 c. (both) and 55 c. are vert, the remainder are horiz.

274 Colorada Beach, Sucre

1969. Tourism. Multicoloured.
2059 15 c. Type **274** (postage) . . 15 10
2060 45 c. San Francisco de Yare Church, Miranda 50 15
2061 90 c. Houses on stilts, Zulia . 75 55
2062 15 c. Desert landscape, Falcon (air) 20 10
2063 30 c. Humboldt Hotel, Caracas 25 15
2064 40 c. Mountain cable-car, Merida 45 25

275 Bolivar addressing Congress

1969. 150th Anniv of Angostura Congress.
2066 **275** 45 c. multicoloured . . . 40 20

276 Dr. Martin Luther King

278 "On the Balcony" (C. Rojas)

277 "Tabebuia pentaphylla"

1969. 1st Death Anniv of Martin Luther King (American Civil Rights leader).
2067 **276** 1 b. multicoloured . . . 50 25

1969. Nature Conservation. Trees. Multicoloured.
2068 50 c. Type **277** (postage) . . 50 20
2069 65 c. "Erythrina poeppigiana" 70 30
2070 90 c. "Platymiscium sp." . . 1·00 50
2071 5 c. "Cassia grandis" (air) . 10 10
2072 20 c. "Triplaris caracasana" . 25 10
2073 25 c. "Samanea saman" . . 35 15

1969. Paintings by Cristobal Rojas. Multicoloured.
2074 25 c. Type **278** 20 15
2075 35 c. "The Pheasant" 35 20
2076 45 c. "The Christening" . . . 55 30
2077 50 c. "The Empty Place" . . 70 35
2078 60 c. "The Tavern" 85 40
2079 1 b. "The Arm" (27 × 55 mm) 1·25 70

Nos. 2075/2078 are horiz.

279 I.L.O. Emblem

1969. 50th Anniv of I.L.O.
2080 **279** 2 b. 50 black and brown . . . 1·75 1·10

280 Charter and Arms of Guayana

1969. Industrial Development. Multicoloured.
2081 45 c. Type **280** 45 20
2082 1 b. SIDOR steel-works . . . 65 30

281 Arcade, Casa del Balcon

1969. 400th Anniv of Carora. Multicoloured.
2083 20 c. Type **281** 15 10
2084 25 c. Ruins of La Pastora Church 25 15
2085 55 c. Chapel of the Cross . . 60 30
2086 65 c. Museum and library building 70 35

282 "Alexander von Humboldt" (J. Stieler)

283 A. Alfinger, A. Pacheco and P. Maldonado (founders)

1969. Air. Birth Bicent of Alexander von Humboldt (German naturalist).
2087 **282** 50 c. multicoloured . . . 50 20

1969. Air. 400th Anniv of Maracaibo. Mult.
2088 20 c. Type **283** 20 15
2089 25 c. Map of Maracaibo, 1562 25 15
2090 40 c. City coat-of-arms . . . 30 20
2091 70 c. University Hospital . . 60 35
2092 75 c. Cacique Mara Monument 70 40
2093 1 b. Baralt Plaza 80 50
Nos. 2089/92 are vert.

284 "Bolivar's Wedding" (T. Salas)

1969. "Bolivar in Spain".
2094 **284** 10 c. multicoloured . . . 10 10
2095 – 15 c. black and red . . . 20 10
2096 – 35 c. multicoloured . . . 35 15
DESIGNS—VERT: 15 c. "Bolivar as a Student" (artist unknown); 35 c. Bolivar's statue, Madrid.

285 Astronauts and Moon Landing

1969. Air. 1st Man on the Moon.
2098 **285** 90 c. multicoloured . . . 1·00 45

286 "Virgin of the Rosary" (17th-cent Venetian School)

1969. Air. Christmas. Multicoloured.
2100 75 c. Type **286** 60 25
2101 80 c. "The Holy Family" (Landaeta School, Caracas, 18th cent) 65 30

287 "Children and Birds"

1969. Children's Day. Multicoloured.
2102 5 c. Type **287** 10 10
2103 45 c. "Children's Camp" . . 55 30

288 Map of Greater Colombia

1969. 150th Anniv of Greater Colombia Federation.
2104 **288** 45 c. multicoloured . . 50 20

289 San Antonio Church, Clarines

1970. Architecture of the Colonial Era. Mult.
2105 10 c. Type **289** 10 10
2106 30 c. Church of the Conception, Caroni 25 15
2107 40 c. San Miguel Church, Burbusay 50 25
2108 45 c. San Antonio Church, Maturin 70 35
2109 75 c. San Nicolas Church, Moruy 85 40
2110 1 b. Coro Cathedral . . . . 1·00 50

290 Seven Hills of Valera

291 "Simon Bolivar" (M. N. Bate)

1970. 150th Anniv of Valera.
2112 **290** 95 c. multicoloured . . 65 30

1970. Air. Portraits of Bolivar. Stamps in brown on buff; inscriptions in green; colours of country name and value given below.
2113 **291** 15 c. brown 15 10
2114 45 c. blue 35 15
2115 55 c. orange 50 25
2116 – 65 c. brown 50 25
2117 – 70 c. blue 55 35
2118 – 75 c. orange 45 40
2119 – 85 c. brown 60 45
2120 – 90 c. blue 65 25
2121 – 95 c. orange 75 25
2122 – 1 b. brown 75 25
2123 – 1 b. 50 blue 90 55
2124 – 2 b. orange . . . . . . 1·90 90
PORTRAITS BY: 65, 70, 75 c. F. Roulin; 85, 90, 95 c. J. M. Espinoza (1828); 1, 1 b. 50, 2 b. J. M. Espinoza (1830).

292 Gen. A. Guzman Blanco and Dr. M. J. Sanabria

1970. Air. Centenary of Free Compulsory Education in Venezuela.
2125 **292** 75 c. black, green & brn . 50 30

293 Map of Venezuela

1970. States of Venezuela. Maps and Arms of the various States. Multicoloured.
2126 5 c. Federal District (postage) 10 10
2127 15 c. Monagas 15 10
2128 20 c. Nueva Esparta 20 10
2129 25 c. Portuguesa (vert) . . . 25 10
2130 45 c. Sucre 35 15
2131 55 c. Tachira (vert) 20 20
2132 65 c. Trujillo 30 25
2133 75 c. Yaracuy 45 35
2134 85 c. Zulia (vert) 60 35
2135 90 c. Amazonas Federal Territory (vert) 90 40
2136 1 b. Federal Island Dependencies . . . . 1·10 45
2137 5 c. Type **293** (air) 10 10
2138 15 c. Apure 20 10
2139 20 c. Aragua 25 10
2140 20 c. Anzoategui 25 10
2141 25 c. Barinas 25 10
2142 25 c. Bolivar 25 10
2143 45 c. Carabobo 55 20
2144 55 c. Cojedes (vert) 60 25
2145 65 c. Falcon 65 25
2146 75 c. Guarico 60 30
2147 85 c. Lara 95 35
2148 90 c. Merida (vert) 95 40
2149 1 b. Miranda 95 50
2150 2 b. Delta Amacuro Federal Territory . . . . 2·00 80

294 "Monochaetum humboldtianum"

295 "The Battle of Boyaca" (M. Tovar y Tovar)

1970. Flowers of Venezuela. Multicoloured.
2151 20 c. Type **294** (postage) . . . 30 10
2152 25 c. "Symbolanthus vasculosus" 60 15
2153 45 c. "Cavendishia splendens" 80 35
2154 1 b. "Befaria glauca" . . . . 1·10 50
2155 20 c. "Epidendrum secundum (air) 25 10
2156 25 c. "Oyedaea verbesinoides" 35 15
2157 45 c. "Heliconia villosa" . . . 80 35
2158 1 b. "Macleania nitida" . . . 1·10 50

1970. 150th Anniv (1969) of Battle of Boyaca.
2159 **295** 30 c. multicoloured . . . 35 15

296 Archiepiscopal Cross

297 "Caracciolo Parra Olmedo" (T. Salas)

1970. Religious Art. Multicoloured.
2160 35 c. Type **296** 35 15
2161 40 c. "Our Lady of the Valley" 45 25
2162 60 c. "Our Lady of Belen de San Mateo" 65 35
2163 90 c. "The Virgin of Chiquinquira" 75 50
2164 1 b. "Our Lady of Socorro de Valencia" . . . . 1·00 55

1970. Air. 150th Birth Anniv of Caracciola Parra Olmedo (lawyer).
2166 **297** 20 c. multicoloured . . . 25 10

298 National Flags and Exhibition Emblem

299 "Guardian Angel" (J. P. Lopez)

1970. "EXFILCA 70" Philatelic Exhibition, Caracas. Multicoloured.
2167 20 c. Type **298** 20 10
2168 25 c. 1871 1 c. stamp and emblem (horiz) 30 15
2169 70 c. 1930 2 b. 50 air stamp and emblem 50 30

1970. Christmas.
2171 **299** 45 c. multicoloured . . . 35 15

300 Caudron G-3 Biplane and Dassault Mirage III

1970. 50th Anniv of Venezuelan Air Force.
2172 **300** 5 c. multicoloured . . . 20 10

301 People in Question Mark

1971. National Census.
2173 **301** 30 c. black, green and red (postage) 60 30
2174 – 70 c. multicoloured (air) 65 45
DESIGN: 70 c. National flag and "pin-men".

302 Battle Scene

1971. 150th Anniv of Battle of Carabobo.
2175 **302** 2 b. multicoloured . . . 1·10 80

303 "Cattleya percivaliana"

304 Adoration of the Child

1971. Air. Venezuelan Orchids. Multicoloured.
2176 20 c. Type **303** 25 15
2177 25 c. Cattleya gaskelliana (horiz) 30 20
2178 75 c. "Cattleya mossiae" . . 60 40
2179 90 c. "Cattleya violacea o superba" (horiz) 65 35
2180 1 b. "Cattleya lawrenceana" (horiz) 80 40

1971. Christmas. Multicoloured.
2181 25 c. Type **304** 25 15
2182 25 c. Madonna and Child . . 25 15

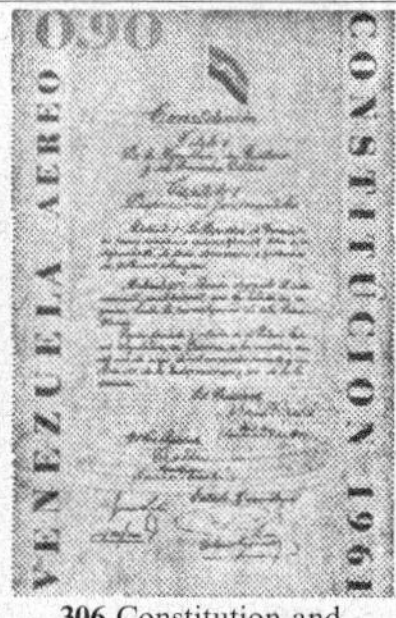

305 Dr. Luis D. Beauperthuy **306** Constitution and Government Building

1971. Death Centenary of Luis P. Beauperthuy (scientist).

2183 **305** 1 b. multicoloured . . . 70 30

1971. Air. 10th Anniv of 1961 Constitution.

2184 **306** 90 c. multicoloured . . . 80 35

307 Heart-shaped Globe **308** Arms of Venezuela and National Flags

1972. World Heart Month.

2185 **307** 1 b. black, red and blue . . 60 40

1972. "Venezuela in the Americas". Mult.

2186 3 b. Type **308** . . . . 1·90 85
2187 4 b. Venezuelan flag . . . . 2·25 1·40
2188 5 b. National anthem . . . . 2·75 1·60
2189 10 b. "Araguaney" (national tree) . . . . 5·50 2·50
2190 15 b. Map of the Americas . 8·25 3·25

309 Tower Blocks

1972. Central Park Housing Project. Mult.

2191 30 c. Type **309** 25 15
2192 30 c. View from ground level 25 15
2193 30 c. Aerial view 25 15

310 Mahatma Gandhi

1972. Birth Centenary (1969) of Mahatma Gandhi.

2194 **310** 60 c. multicoloured . . . 50 35

311 Children making Music

1972. Christmas. Multicoloured.

2195 30 c. Type **311** 25 15
2196 30 c. Children roller-skating . 25 15

Nos. 2195/6 were issued together, se-tenant, forming a composite design.

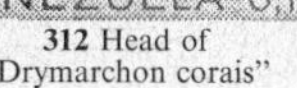

312 Head of "Drymarchon corais" **313** Planetary System

1972. Snakes. Multicoloured.

2197 10 c. Type **312** 10 10
2198 15 c. "Spilotes pullatus" . . 15 10
2199 25 c. "Bothrops venezuelensis" 40 15
2200 30 c. "Micrurus dumerili carinicaudus" 50 20
2201 60 c. "Crotalus vegrandis" . 50 35
2202 1 b. Boa constrictor 75 50

1973. 500th Birth Anniv of Copernicus (astronomer). Multicoloured.

2203 5 c. Type **313** 10 10
2204 10 c. Copernicus 20 10
2205 15 c. Book—"De Revolutionibus rbium Coelestium" 25 10

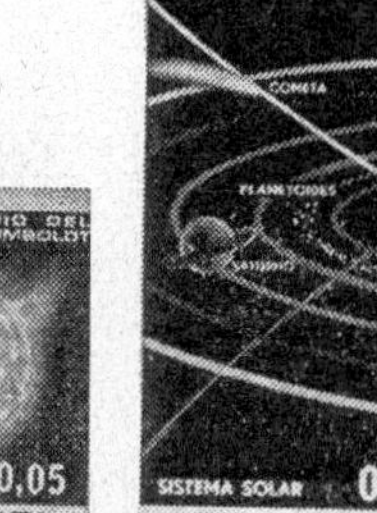

314 The Sun **315** Part of Solar System (left-hand)

1973. 10th Anniv of Humboldt Planetarium. Multicoloured. (a) As Type **314**.

2206 5 c. Type **314** 10 10
2207 5 c. Earth 10 10
2208 20 c. Mars 35 10
2209 20 c. Saturn 25 10
2210 30 c. Asteroids 30 15
2211 40 c. Neptune 35 20
2212 50 c. Venus 50 35
2213 60 c. Jupiter 60 40
2214 75 c. Uranus 75 50
2215 90 c. Pluto 90 40
2216 90 c. Moon . . . . 1·00 70
2217 1 b. Mercury . . . . 1·25 60

(b) As Type **315**.

2218 10 c. Type **315** 30 10
2219 15 c. Solar System (centre) . 40 10
2220 15 c. Solar System (right-hand) 40 10

Nos. 2218/20 form a composite design of the Solar System.

316 O.A.S. Emblem and Map

1973. 25th Anniv of Organization of American States.

2221 **316** 60 c. multicoloured . . 50 20

317 General Paez in Uniform **319** Bishop Ramos de Lora

318 Admiral Padilla, Gen. Montilla and Gen. Manrique

1973. Death Centenary of General Jose A. Paez.

2222 **317** 10 c. multicoloured . . . 10 10
2223 – 30 c. gold, black & red . 25 15
2224 – 50 c. black, ultramarine and blue 50 25
2225 – 1 b. multicoloured . . . 75 50
2226 – 2 b. multicoloured . . . 1·25 75

DESIGNS—VERT: 30 c. Paez and horse (old engraving); 50 c. Gen. Paez in civilian dress; 1 b. Street of the Lancers, Puerto Cabello. HORIZ: 2 b. "The Charge at Centauro".

1973. 150th Anniv of Naval Battle of Maracaibo. Multicoloured.

2227 50 c. Type **318** 40 20
2228 1 b. "Battle of Maracaibo" (M. F. Rincon) 60 40
2229 2 b. Plan of opposing fleets . . 1·10 60

1973. 250th Birth Anniv (1972) of Bishop Ramos de Lora.

2230 **319** 75 c. gold and brown . . 45 20

320 Ship, Jet Airliner and Map **322** General Paez Dam

321 Waterfall and Map

1973. Margarita Island Free Zone.

2231 **320** 5 c. multicoloured 15 10

1973. Completion of Golden Highway. Multicoloured.

2232 5 c. Type **321** 10 10
2233 10 c. Map and scarlet macaw 1·00 20
2234 20 c. Map and Santa Elena Church, Uairen 25 10
2235 50 c. Map and ancient mountain sanctuary 65 25
2236 60 c. As 50 c. 65 25
2237 90 c. Map and Santa Teresita church, Cabanayen 85 35
2238 1 b. Map and flags of Venezuela and Brazil 90 40

1973. Completion of General Paez Dam, Merida.

2239 **322** 30 c. multicoloured 30 10

323 Child on Slide

1973. Children's Festival. Multicoloured.

2240 10 c. Type **323** 25 15
2241 10 c. Fairy tale animals . . . 25 15
2242 10 c. "Paginas Para Imaginar" (children's book) 25 15
2243 10 c. Holidaymakers leaving airliner 25 15

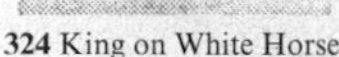

324 King on White Horse **326** Vase and Lace ("Handicrafts")

325 Regional Map

1973. Christmas. Multicoloured.

2244 30 c. Type **324** 25 10
2245 30 c. Two Kings 25 10

1973. Regional Development.

2246 **325** 25 c. multicoloured . . . 30 10

1973. Venezuelan Industrial Development Commission. Multicoloured.

2247 15 c. Type **326** 15 10
2248 35 c. Industrial estate ("Construction") 35 10
2249 45 c. Cogwheels and chimney ("Small and medium industries") 50 20

327 Map and Revellers

1974. 10th Anniv of Carupano Carnival.

2250 **327** 5 c. multicoloured . . . 10 10

328 Congress Emblem

1974. 9th Venezuelan Engineering Congress, Maracaibo.

2251 **328** 50 c. multicoloured . . . 50 15

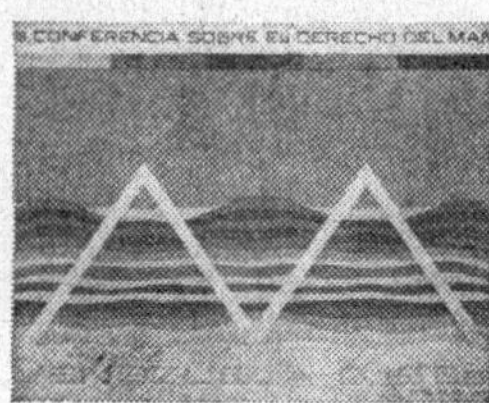

329 "Law of the Sea" Emblem

1974. 3rd Law of the Sea Conference, Caracas. Multicoloured.

2252 15 c. Type **329** 10 10
2253 35 c. Fish in sea-weed . . . 20 10
2254 75 c. Sea-bed scene 50 25
2255 80 c. Underwater grotto . . 55 35

330 Pupil and New School

1974. "Pay Your Taxes" Campaign.

2256 **330** 5 c. multicoloured . . . 10 10
2257 10 c. multicoloured . . . 10 10
2258 15 c. multicoloured . . . 10 10
2259 20 c. multicoloured . . . 10 10
2260 A 25 c. multicoloured . . . 15 10
2261 30 c. multicoloured . . . 40 20
2262 35 c. multicoloured . . . 20 10
2263 40 c. multicoloured . . . 35 15
2264 B 45 c. multicoloured . . . 35 15
2265 50 c. multicoloured . . . 35 15
2266 55 c. multicoloured . . . 55 30
2267 60 c. multicoloured . . . 45 20
2268 C 65 c. multicoloured . . . 1·00 50
2269 70 c. multicoloured . . . 50 20
2270 75 c. multicoloured . . . 50 25
2271 80 c. multicoloured . . . 50 25
2272 D 85 c. multicoloured . . . 50 25
2273 90 c. multicoloured . . . 70 25
2274 95 c. multicoloured . . . 1·00 70
2275 1 b. multicoloured . . . 70 35

DESIGNS: A, Suburban housing project; B, City centre motorway; C, Sports stadium; D, Surgical team in operating theatre.

331 "Bolivar at Junin" (A. H. Tovar)

1974. 150th Anniv of Battle of Junin.

2276 **331** 2 b. multicoloured . . . 1·25 70

332 World Map

1974. Centenary of U.P.U. Multicoloured.

2277 45 c. Type **332** 35 15
2278 50 c. Mounted courier, sailing packet, modern liner and jet airliner 40 20

333 Rufino Blanco-Fombona and Books
334 Children on Paper Dart

1974. Birth Centenary of Rufino Blanco-Fombona (writer).

2279 **333** 10 c. multicoloured . . . 10 10
2280 – 30 c. multicoloured . . . 20 10
2281 – 45 c. multicoloured . . . 30 15
2282 – 90 c. multicoloured . . . 50 25

DESIGNS: Nos. 2280/2, Portraits of Rufino Blanco-Fombona against a background of books similar to Type **333**.

1974. Children's Festival.

2283 **334** 70 c. multicoloured . . . 40 20

335 Marshal Sucre
336 "Shepherd"

1974. 150th Anniv of Battle of Ayacucho. Multicoloured.

2284 30 c. Type **335** 20 10
2285 50 c. South American flags on globe 30 25
2286 1 b. Map showing battle sites 55 35
2287 2 b. "Battle of Ayacucho" ($43\frac{1}{2}\times22$ mm) . . . . . . 1·00 70

1974. Christmas. Details from "The Adoration of the Shepherds" (J. B. Mayno). Multicoloured.

2288 30 c. Type **336** 25 15
2289 30 c. "Holy Family" 25 15

Nos. 2288/9 were issued se-tenant, forming a composite design.

337 Road Construction, 1905, and El Ciempies Junction, 1972

1974. Centenary of Ministry of Public Works. Multicoloured.

2290 5 c. Type **337** 10 10
2291 20 c. J. Munoz Tebar (first Minister of Public Works) . 25 10
2292 25 c. Bridges on Caracas–La Guaira Road, 1912 and 1953 30 10
2293 40 c. Views of Caracas, 1874 and 1974 . . . . 30 15
2294 70 c. Tucacas Railway Station, 1911, and projected Caracas terminal 70 20
2295 80 c. Anatomical Institute, 1911, and Social Security Hospital, 1969 . . . . . . 85 30
2296 85 c. Quininari River bridge, 1904, and Orinoco River bridge, 1967 . . . . 1·00 35
2297 1 b. As 20 c. . . . . 1·40 50

338 Women in Profile
340 The Nativity

339 Emblem and "Tents"

1975. International Women's Year.

2298 **338** 90 c. multicoloured . . 50 30

1975. 14th World Scout Jamboree.

2299 **339** 20 c. multicoloured . . 15 10
2300 80 c. multicoloured . . 55 25

1975. Christmas. Multicoloured.

2301 30 c. Type **340** 20 10
2302 30 c. "The Shepherds" . . . 20 10

Nos. 2301/2 were issued se-tenant, forming a composite design.

341 Red Cross Nurse
342 Altar

1975. Venezuelan Red Cross.

2303 **341** 30 c. + 15 c. multicoloured 35 20
2304 50 c. + 25 c. multicoloured 50 30

1976. Centenary of National Pantheon.

2305 **342** 30 c. grey and blue . . . 15 10
2306 – 1 b. 05 brown and red . 50 25

DESIGN: 1 b. 05, Pantheon building.

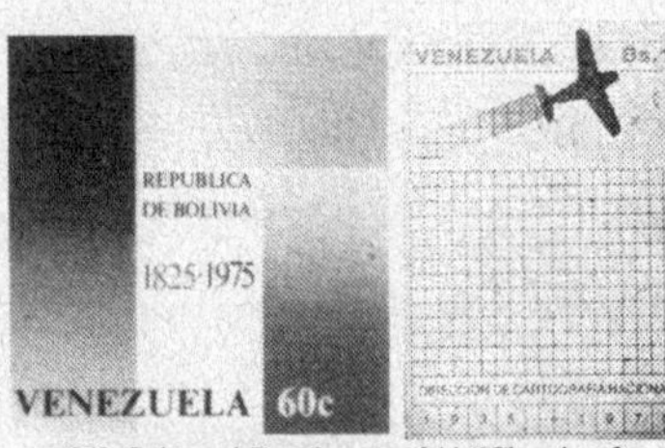

343 Coloured Panels
344 "Charting from Aircraft"

1976. 150th Anniv of Bolivian Independence (1975).

2307 **343** 60 c. multicoloured . . 25 15

1976. 40th Anniv of National Cartographic Institute (1975).

2308 **344** 1 b. black and blue . . 50 20

345 Signature of General Jose Felix Ribas

1976. Birth Bicentenary of General Jose Ribas. Multicoloured.

2309 **345** 40 c. green and red . . . 25 10
2310 – 55 c. multicoloured . . . 35 15

DESIGN—HORIZ: (40 × 30 mm): 55 c. General Jose Felix Ribas.

346 "Musicians of Chacao School" (A. Barrios)

1976. Birth Bicentenary (1975) of Jose Angel Lamas (composer).

2311 **346** 75 c. multicoloured . . 45 25
2312 – 1 b. 25 red, grey and buff 65 35

DESIGN—40 × 28 mm: 1 b. 25, Lamas' colophon.

347 "Bolivar" (J. M. Espinoza)
348 Maze symbolising Opportunity

1976.

2313 **347** 5 c. turquoise 10 10
2314 10 c. red 10 10
2315 15 c. brown 10 10
2316 20 c. black 10 10
2317 25 c. orange 10 10
2613 25 c. red 10 10
2318 30 c. blue 10 10
2319 45 c. lilac 15 10
2320 50 c. orange 20 10
2614 50 c. blue 10 10
2321 65 c. blue 25 10
2615 75 c. mauve 10 10
2322 1 b. red 35 15
2616 1 b. orange 10 10
2323 2 b. grey 70 35
2617 2 b. yellow 15 10
2324 3 b. blue 65 50
2618 3 b. green 10 10
2325 4 b. orange 85 45
2619 4 b. brown 15 10
2620 5 b. red 15 10
2327 10 b. lilac . . . . 2·25 1·10
2621 10 b. yellow 65 15
2328 15 b. blue . . . . 3·50 1·60
2622 15 b. purple . . . . . . 1·00 15
2329 20 b. red . . . . 4·50 2·25
2623 20 b. blue . . . . 1·40 65
2329a 25 b. blue . . . . 4·50 2·25
2623a 25 b. bistre . . . . . . 1·60 85
2329b 30 b. blue . . . . 5·50 2·75
2623b 30 b. lilac . . . . 2·00 1·00
2329c 50 b. purple . . . . . . 8·75 4·50
2623c 50 b. red . . . . 3·50 1·60

Nos. 2323/9 are larger, 27 × 33 mm.

1976. 250th Anniv of Central University.

2330 **348** 30 c. multicoloured . . . 15 10
2331 – 50 c. black, orge & yell . 25 15
2332 – 90 c. yellow and black . . 50 30

DESIGNS: 50 c. University building; 90 c. Faculty symbols.

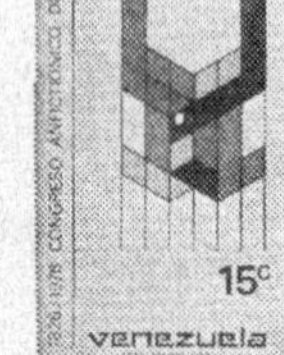

349 C. A. Fernadez de Leoni (founder)
350 "Unity" Emblem

1976. Children's Foundation. Multicoloured.

2333 30 c. + 15 c. Type **349** 25 20
2334 50 c. + 25 c. Children in "home" (31 × 44 mm) 45 30

1976. 150th Anniv of Panama Amphictyonic Congress.

2335 **350** 15 c. multicoloured . . . 10 10
2336 – 45 c. multicoloured . . . 25 10
2337 – 1 b. 25 multicoloured . . 55 30

DESIGN: 45 c., 1 b. 25, As Type **275**, but with different "Unity" emblems.

351 George Washington

1976. Bicentenary of American Revolution.

2338 **351** 1 b. black and brown . . 55 35
2339 – 1 b. black and green . . . 55 55
2340 – 1 b. black and purple . . 55 35
2341 – 1 b. black and blue . . . 55 35
2342 – 1 b. black and brown . . 55 35

DESIGNS: No. 2339, Thomas Jefferson; No. 2340, Abraham Lincoln; No. 2341, Franklin D. Roosevelt; No. 2342, John F. Kennedy.

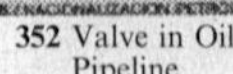

352 Valve in Oil Pipeline
353 "The Nativity" (B. Rivas)

1976. Oil Nationalization.

2343 **352** 10 c. multicoloured . . . 10 10
2344 – 30 c. multicoloured . . . 15 10
2345 – 35 c. multicoloured . . . 20 10
2346 – 40 c. multicoloured . . . 20 10
2347 – 55 c. multicoloured . . . 30 15
2348 – 90 c. multicoloured . . . 55 25

DESIGNS: 30 c. to 90 c. Various computer drawings of valves and pipelines.

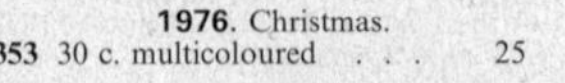

1976. Christmas.

2349 **353** 30 c. multicoloured . . . 25 10

354 Patient
355 Declaration Emblem

1976. Anti-tuberculosis Society Fund.

2350 **354** 10 c. + 5 c. multicoloured 15 15
2351 30 c. + 10 c. multicoloured 20 20

1976. 10th Anniv of Bogota Declaration.

2352 **355** 60 c. black and yellow . 30 15

356 Arms of Barinas

1977. 400th Anniv of Barinas.

2353 **356** 50 c. multicoloured . . . 30 15

357 "Christ Crucified"
358 Coro Settlement

1977. 400th Anniv (1976) of La Grita.

2354 **357** 30 c. multicoloured . . . 15 10

1977. 450th Anniv of Coro.

2355 **358** 1 b. multicoloured . . . 35 15

359 I.P.C.T.T. Emblem and Stylised Dove

1977. 9th Inter-American Postal and Telecommunications Staff Congress, Caracas.

2356 **359** 85 c. multicoloured . . . 35 15

360 Cable Links to Domestic Equipment
361 "VENEZUELA" and Value as Rolled Steel

1977. Inauguration of "Columbus" Submarine Cable.

2357 **360** 95 c. grey, blue & green . 35 15

1977. 1st Anniv of Nationalization and Exploitation of Steel.

2358 **361** 30 c. black and yellow . 15 10
2359 – 50 c. black and orange . 25 10
2360 – 80 c. black and grey . . 35 15
2361 – 1 b. 05 black and red . . 40 20
2362 – 1 b. 25 black & yellow . 45 20
2363 – 1 b. 50 black and grey . 65 25

DESIGNS: 50 c. to 1 b. 50, Similar to Type **361** but each differently arranged.

362 J. P. Duarte
363 "The Holy Family"

1977. Death Cent (1976) of Juan Pablo Duarte.

2364 **362** 75 c. black and mauve . 30 15

1977. Christmas.

2365 **363** 30 c. multicoloured . . . 15 10

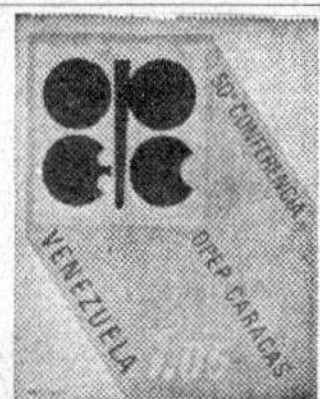
364 O.P.E.C. Emblem

1977. 50th O.P.E.C. Conference, Caracas.
2366 **364** 1 b. 05 black and blue . 50 15

365 Cyclists Racing

1978. World Cycling Championships, San Cristobal, Tachira. Multicoloured.
2367 5 c. Type **365** 10 10
2368 1 b. 25 Cyclist racing 65 20

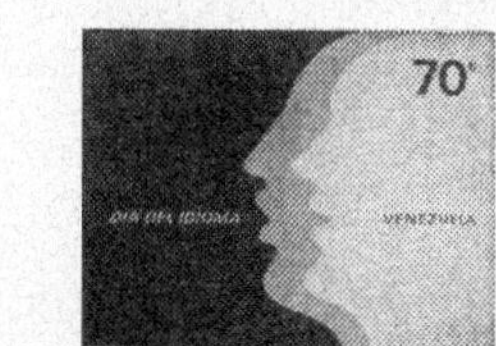

366 Heads in Profile

1978. Language Day.
2369 **366** 70 c. black, grey & mve . 25 15

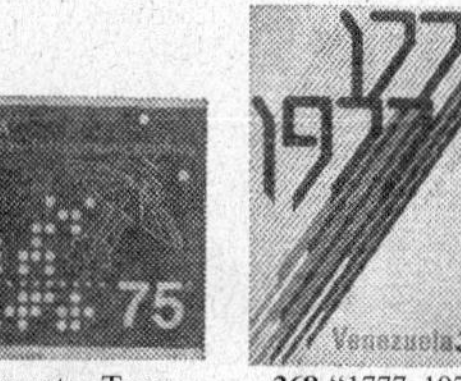

367 Computer Tape and Satellite **368** "1777–1977"

1978. 10th World Telecommunications Day.
2370 **367** 75 c. blue 30 20

1978. Bicentenary of Venezuelan Unification. Multicoloured.
2381 30 c. Type **368** 10 10
2382 1 b. Computer print of Goya's "Carlos III" 40 15

369 Bolivar in Nurse Hipolita's Arms

1978. Birth Bicent (1983) of Simon Bolivar (1st issue).
2383 **369** 30 c. black, brown & grn 15 10
2384 – 1 b. black, brown & bl . 40 25
DESIGN: 1 b. Juan Vicente Bolivar (father).
See also Nos. 2399/40, 2408/9, 2422/3, 2431/2, 2467/8, 2480/1, 2483/4, 2494/5, 2498/9, 2518/19 and 2521/2.

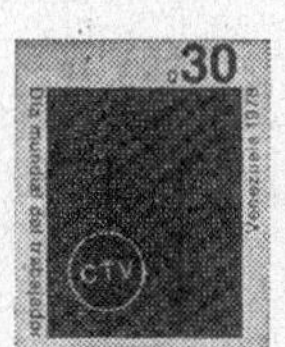

370 "T" ("Trabajadors") **371** Medical Abstract

1978. Workers' Day.
2385 **370** 30 c. red and black . . . 10 10
2386 – 30 c. blue and black . . 10 10
2387 – 30 c. yellow, blue & blk . 10 10
2388 – 30 c. red, blue & black . 10 10
2389 – 30 c. red and black . . . 10 10
2390 – 95 c. black and red . . . 30 15
2391 – 95 c. grey and blue . . . 30 15
2392 – 95 c. black and red . . . 30 15
2393 – 95 c. blue and black . . 30 15
2394 – 95 c. multicoloured . . . 30 15
DESIGNS: Nos. 2386/94 based on the letter "T", also inscribed "CTV".

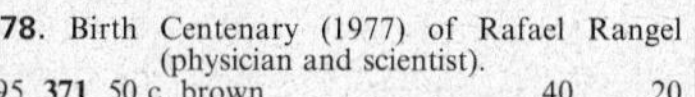
1978. Birth Centenary (1977) of Rafael Rangel (physician and scientist).
2395 **371** 50 c. brown 40 20

372 Drill Head and Map of Tachira Oilfield

1978. Centenary of Venezuelan Oil Industry. Multicoloured.
2396 30 c. Type **372** 15 10
2397 1 b. 05 Letter "P" as pipeline 50 20

373 Christmas Star **375** Dam holding back Water

374 "P T"

1978. Christmas.
2398 **373** 30 c. multicoloured . . 15 10

1978. Birth Bicentenary (1983) of Simon Bolivar (2nd issue). As T **369**.
2399 30 c. black, brown & pur . . 10 10
2400 1 b. black, grey and red . . 30 15
DESIGNS: 30 c. Bolivar at 25 (after M. N. Bate); 1 b. Simon Rodriguez (Bolivar's tutor).

1979. Creation of Postal and Telegraph Institute.
2402 **374** 75 c. blk, & red on cream 25 15

1979. 10th Anniv of Guri Dam.
2403 **375** 2 b. silver, grey & black 70 30

376 "General San Martin" (E. J. Maury)

1979. Birth Bicentenary of General Jose de San Martin. Multicoloured.
2404 40 c. Type **376** 15 10
2405 60 c. Portrait by Mercedes San Martin 25 10
2406 70 c. San Martin Monument, Guayaquil 30 15
2407 75 c. San Martin's signature 35 20

1979. Birth Bicentenary (1983) of Simon Bolivar (3rd series). As T **369**.
2408 30 c. black, violet and red . 10 10
2409 1 b. black, orange and red . 30 15
DESIGNS: 30 c. Alexandre Sabes Petion (President of Haiti); 1 b. Bolivar's signature.

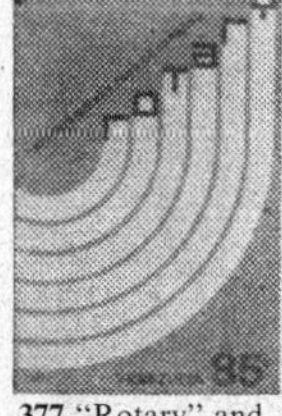

377 "Rotary" and Curves **378** Statue of Virgin working Miracles, 1654

1979. 50th Anniv of Rotary Club of Caracas.
2411 **377** 85 c. black and gold . . 25 15

1979. 25th Anniv of Canonization of Virgin of Coromoto.
2412 **378** 55 c. black and red . . . 20 10

379 Miranda, London Residence and Arms

1979. Acquisition by Venezuela of Francisco de Miranda's House in London.
2413 **379** 50 c. multicoloured . . 20 10

380 O'Leary and Maps

1979. 125th Death Anniv of Daniel O'Leary (publisher of Bolivar's memoirs).
2414 **380** 30 c. multicoloured . . . 10 10

381 Boy with Nest **382** Candle

2979. International Year of the Child.
2415 **381** 70 c. black and blue . . . 25 15
2416 – 80 c. multicoloured . . . 30 15
DESIGN: 80 c. Boys playing in sea.

1979. Christmas.
2417 **382** 30 c. multicoloured . . . 10 10

383 Caudron G-3 Biplane

1979. "Exfilve 79" National Stamp Exhibition and 59th Anniv of Air Force. Multicoloured.
2418 75 c. Type **383** 35 20
2419 75 c. Stearman Kaydett biplane 35 20
2420 75 c. Bell Iroquois helicopter . 35 20
2421 75 c. Dassault Mirage IIIC jet fighter 55 20

1979. Birth Bicentenary (1983) of Simon Bolivar (4th series). As T **369**.
2422 30 c. black, red and turq . . 10 10
2423 1 b. black, blue and red . . 30 15
DESIGNS: 30 c. Bolivar; 1 b. Slave.

384 Emblem and World Map

1979. Introduction of New Emblem for Postal and Telegraph Institute.
2425 **384** 75 c. multicoloured . . . 25 15

385 Queen Victoria and Hill

1980. Death Centenary of Sir Rowland Hill (1979).
2426 **385** 55 c. multicoloured . . . 20 10

386 Augusto Pi Suner

1980. Birth Centenary (1979) of Dr. Augusto Pi Suner (physiologist).
2427 **386** 80 c. multicoloured . . . 30 15

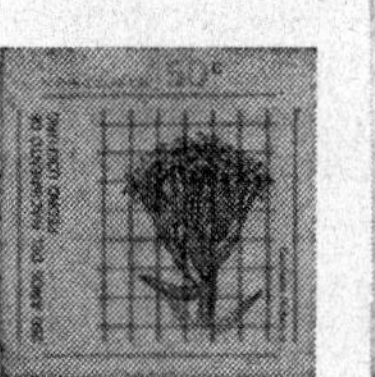

387 "Cotyledon hispanica" **388** Lovera (self-portrait)

1980. 250th Birth Anniv of Pedro Loefling (Swedish botanist).
2428 **387** 50 c. multicoloured . . . 20 10

1980. Birth Bicentenary (1978) of Juan Lovera (artist).
2429 **388** 60 c. blue and red . . . 20 10
2430 75 c. violet and orange . 25 15

1980. Birth Bicentenary (1983) of Simon Bolivar (5th issue). As T **369**.
2431 30 c. black, green & purple . 10 10
2432 1 b. black, dp brown & brown 30 15
DESIGNS: 30 c. Signing document; 1 b. Congress House, Angostura.

389 "Self-portrait with Children" (detail) **390** Bernardo O'Higgins

1980. 25th Death Anniv (1979) of Armando Reveron (artist). Multicoloured.
2434 50 c. Type **389** 20 10
2435 65 c. "Self-portrait" (26 × 41 mm) 35 20

1980. 204th Birth Anniv of Bernardo O'Higgins.
2436 **390** 85 c. black, red & blue . 50 25

391 Frigate "Mariscal Sucre"

1980. Venezuelan Navy. Multicoloured.
2437 1 b. 50 Type **391** . . . . . 1·00 40
2438 1 b. 50 Submarine "Picua" . 1·00 40
2439 1 b. 50 Naval School . . . . 1·00 40
2440 1 b. 50 Cadet barque "Simon Bolivar" (33 × 52 mm) . . 1·00 40

392 Figures supporting O.P.E.C. Emblem

1980. 20th Anniv of Organization of Petroleum Exporting Countries. Multicoloured.
2441 1 b. 50 Type **392** 50 25
2442 1 b. 50 O.P.E.C. emblem and globe 50 25

393 "The Death of Bolivar" (Antonio Herrera Toro)

1980. 150th Death Anniv of Simon Bolivar.
2443 **393** 2 b. multicoloured . . . 70 30

394 Antonio Jose de Sucre **395** "The Adoration of the Shepherds" (Rubens)

1980. 150th Death Anniv of Marshal Antonio Jose de Sucre.
2444 **394** 2 b. multicoloured . . . 70 30

1980. Christmas.
2445 **395** 1 b. multicoloured . . . 20 10

396 Helen Keller's Initials in Braille and Print

1981. Birth Centenary (1980) of Helen Keller.
2446 **396** 1 b. 50 grey, orge & blk . 40 15

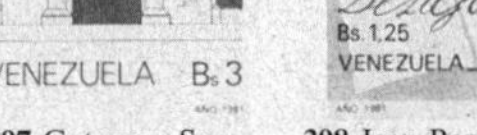
397 Gateway, San Felipe
398 Jean Baptiste de la Salle (founder)

1981. 250th Anniv of San Felipe.
2447 **397** 3 b. blue, grey and red . 70 35

1981. 300th Anniv (1980) of Brothers of Christian Schools.
2448 **398** 1 b. 25 silver, red & black 30 15

399 Municipal Theatre

1981. Centenary of Caracas Municipal Theatre.
2449 **399** 1 b. 25, pink, blk & lilac 30 15

400 U.P.U. Emblem, Map of Venezuela and Envelope
401 People on Map

1981. Centenary of Admission to Universal Postal Union.
2450 **400** 2 b. multicoloured . . . 50 20

1981. 11th National Population and Housing Census.
2451 **401** 1 b. lilac, violet, and blk . 30 15

402 Games Emblem
404 Musicians

403 "Penny-farthing" Bicycle

1981. 9th Bolivarian Games, Barquismeto.
2452 **402** 95 c. multicoloured . . . 30 15

1981. Transport History (1st series). Mult.
2453 1 b. Type **403** 35 20
2454 1 b. 05 Steam locomotive, 1926 90 60
2455 1 b. 25 Buick car, 1937 . . . 40 25
2456 1 b. 50 Horse-drawn cab . . 50 25
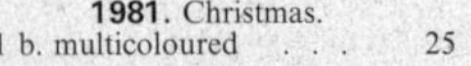
See also Nos. 2490/3 and 2514/7.

1981. Christmas.
2457 **404** 1 b. multicoloured . . . 25 10

405 Mt. Autana
407 "Landscape"

406 Calligraphic Script and Arms

1982. 50th Anniv of Venezuelan Natural Sciences Society. Multicoloured.
2458 1 b. Type **405** 30 20
2459 1 b. 50 Sarisarinama 50 20
2460 2 b. Guacharo Cave 40 35

1982. 20th Anniv of Constitution.
2461 **406** 1 b. 85 gold and black . 40 25

1982. 20th Anniv of Agricultural Reform.
2462 **407** 3 b. multicoloured . . . 70 40

408 Jules Verne
410 Rose

409 Bars of National Anthem

1982. Jules Verne (writer) Commemoration.
2463 **408** 1 b. deep blue and blue . 30 15

1982. Centenary of National Anthem (1981).
2464 **409** 1 b. multicoloured . . . 30 15

1982. 1300th Anniv of Bulgarian State.
2465 **410** 65 c. multicoloured . . 20 10

411 Flags
412 Cecilio Acosta

1982. 6th National Plan.
2466 **411** 2 b. multicoloured . . . 35 15

1982. Birth Bicentenary (1983) of Simon Bolivar (6th issue). As T **369**.
2467 30 c. black, brown and orange 10 10
2468 1 b. black, brown and green 25 15
DESIGNS: 30 c. Col. Rondon; 1 b. General Anzoategui.

1982. Death Centenary (1981) of Cecilio Acosta (statesman).
2469 **412** 3 b. black, blue and violet 35 25

413 "Fourcroya humboldtiana"

1982. Flora and Fauna. Multicoloured.
2471 1 b. 05 Type **413** 35 15
2472 2 b. 55 Turtle ("Podocnemis expansa") 85 30
2473 2 b. 75 "Oyedaea verbesinoides" 90 35
2474 3 b. Oilbird . . . . 2·75 85

414 Andres Bello and Initials

1982. Birth Bicentenary of Andres Bello (1981).
2475 **414** 1 b. 05 light blue, blue and black 25 15
2476 2 b. 55 yellow, violet and black 45 30
2477 2 b. 75 blue, deep blue and black 50 35
2478 3 b. olive, deep olive and black 55 40

415 "Nativity"
416 Bermudez

1982. Christmas.
2479 **415** 1 b. multicoloured . . . 20 10

1982. Birth Bicentenary (1983) of Simon Bolivar (7th issue). As T **369**.
2480 30 c. black, grey and red . . 10 10
2481 1 b. black, grey and red . . . 25 15
DESIGNS: 30 c. Carabobo Monument; 1 b. Gen. Jose Antonio Paez.

1982. Birth Bicentenary (1983) of Simon Bolivar (8th issue). As T **369**.
2483 30 c. black, blue & dp blue . 10 10
2484 1 b. black, violet and red . . 25 15
DESIGNS: 30 c. Commemorative plaque to the meeting at Guayaquil; 1 b. Bolivar and San Martin (detail of monument).

1982. Birth Bicentenary of General Jose Francisco Bermudez (statesman).
2486 **416** 3 b. multicoloured . . . 35 30

417 Briceno

1982. Birth Bicentenary of Antonio Nicolas Briceno (liberation hero).
2487 **417** 3 b. multicoloured . . . 35 30

418 Rejoicing Crowd and Flag

1983. 25th Anniv of 1958 Reforms.
2488 **418** 3 b. multicoloured . . . 35 30

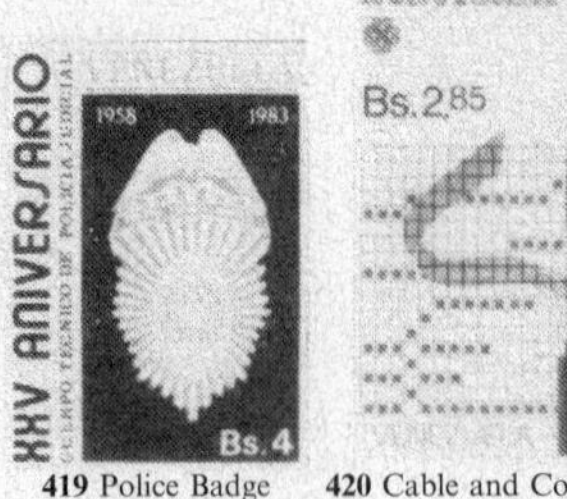
419 Police Badge
420 Cable and Computer Circuitboard

1983. 25th Anniv of Judicial Police Technical Department.
2489 **419** 4 b. red and green 40 30

1983. Transport History (2nd series). As T **403**. Multicoloured.
2490 75 c. Lincoln touring car, 1923 20 10
2491 80 c. Steam locomotive No. 129, 1889 . . . . 1·50 90
2492 85 c. Willys truck, 1927 . . . 25 10
2493 95 c. Cleveland motorcycle, 1920 . . . . 25 10

1983. Birth Bicentenary of Simon Bolivar (9th issue). As T **369**.
2494 30 c. black, red and blue . . 10 10
2495 1 b. black, gold and blue . . 25 15
DESIGNS: 30 c. Gen. Antonio Sucre; 1 b. Sword hilt.

1983. World Communications Year.
2497 **420** 2 b. 85 multicoloured . . 25 30

1983. Birth Bicentenary of Simon Bolivar (10th issue). As T **369**.
2498 30 c. multicoloured 10 10
2499 1 b. black, yellow and blue . 25 15
DESIGNS: 30 c. Flags; 1 b. "Ascent of Potosi".

421 Map of the Americas
422 Power Pylon

1983. 9th Pan-American Games, Caracas. Multicoloured.
2501 2 b. Type **421** 30 20
2502 2 b. Swimming 30 20
2503 2 b. 70 Cycling 15 30
2504 2 b. 70 Fencing 15 30
2505 2 b. 85 Weightlifting 20 15
2506 2 b. 85 Running 20 15

1983. 25th Anniv of State Electricity Authority.
2508 **422** 3 b. blue, silver and red . 70 30

423 Nativity

1983. Christmas.
2509 **423** 1 b. multicoloured . . . 10 10

424 Erecting a Tent

1983. 75th Anniv (1982) of Scout Movement. Multicoloured.
2510 2 b. 25 Type **424** 30 15
2511 2 b. 55 Nature watch 30 15
2512 2 b. 75 Mountaineering . . . 35 15
2513 3 b. Camp at night 35 15

1983. Transport History (3rd series). Caracas Underground Railway. As T **403**. Multicoloured.
2514 55 c. black, orange & silver . 30 10
2515 75 c. black, yellow & silver . 45 15
2516 95 c. black, green and silver . 55 20
2517 2 b. black, blue and silver . . 1·25 45
DESIGNS: 55 c. Central computer building; 75 c. Maintenance bay; 95 c. Train on elevated section; 2 b. Train at Cano Amarillo station.

1984. Birth Bicentenary of Simon Bolivar (11th issue). As T **369**.
2518 30 c. black, red and brown . 10 10
2519 1 b. black, green and blue . 10 10
DESIGNS: 30 c. Open volume of "Opere de Raimondo Montecuccoli"; 1 b. Dr. Jose Maria Vargas (President, 1835–36).

1984. Birth Bicentenary of Simon Bolivar (12th issue). As T **369**.
2521 30 c. black, red and lilac . . 10 10
2522 1 b. black, green & orange . 10 10
DESIGNS: 30 c. Pedro Gual (President, 1859 and 1861); 1 b. Jose Faustino Sanchez Carrion.

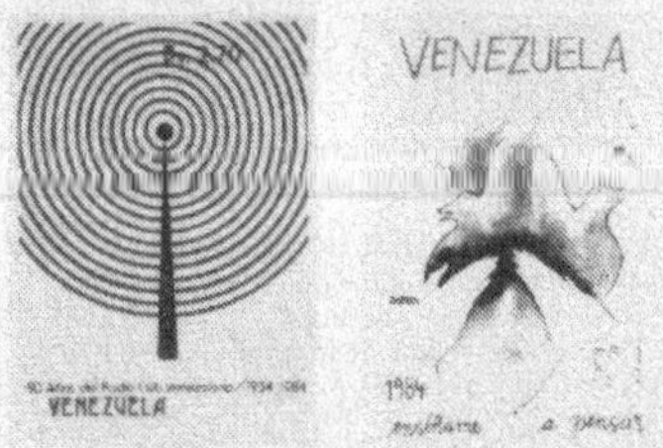
425 Radio Mast and Waves
426 Doves and Hands covering Eyes

1984. 50th Anniv of Venezuela Radio Club.
2524 **425** 2 b. 70 multicoloured . . 35 15

1984. "Intelligentsia for Peace". Multicoloured.
2525 1 b. Type **426** 10 10
2526 2 b. 70 Profile head 30 15
2527 2 b. 85 Profile head, flower and hexagonal nut 35 15

427 Romulo Gallegos 428 Emblem and Digital Eight

1984. Birth Centenary of Romulo Gallegos (writer and President, 1948). Multicoloured.
2528 **427** 1 b. 70 multicoloured . . 25 15
2529 – 1 b. 70 multicoloured . . 25 15
2530 – 1 b. 70 green, grey and black 25 15
2531 – 1 b. 70 deep green, green and black 25 15
DESIGNS: Nos. 2529/31, Different portraits of Gallegos.

1984. 18th Pan-American Union of Engineering Associations Convention.
2532 **428** 2 b. 55 buff and blue . . 35 15

429 "Nativity" (Maria Candelaria de Ramirez)

1984. Christmas.
2533 **429** 1 b. multicoloured . . . 10 10

430 Pope and "Virgin of Coromoto"

1985. Visit of Pope John Paul II (1st issue).
2534 **430** 1 b. multicoloured . . . 20 10
See also Nos. 2628/33.

431 Cross, Hand holding Candle and Agricultural Scene

1985. Bicentenary of Valle de la Pascua City.
2535 **431** 1 b. 50 multicoloured . . 20 10

432 St. Vincent de Paul

1985. Centenary of Venezuelan Society of St. Vincent de Paul.
2536 **432** 1 b. brown, yellow & red 15 10

433 Text and "SELA"

1985. 10th Anniv of Latin American Economic System.
2537 **433** 4 b. black and red . . . 70 35

434 "Divine Shepherdess" **435** Map and Emblem

1985. 2000th Birth Anniv of Virgin Mary. Multicoloured.
2538 1 b. Type **434** 20 15
2539 1 b. "Virgin of Chiquinquira" 20 15
2540 1 b. "Virgin of Coromoto" . 20 15
2541 1 b. "Virgin of the Valley" . 20 15
2542 1 b. "Virgin of Perpetual Succour" 20 15
2543 1 b. "Virgin of Peace" . . . 20 15
2544 1 b. "Virgin of the Immaculate Conception" 20 15
2545 1 b. "Virgin of Solitude" . . 20 15
2546 1 b. "Virgin of Consolation" 20 15
2547 1 b. "Virgin of the Snow" . 20 15

1985. 25th Anniv of Organization of Petroleum Exporting Countries.
2548 **435** 6 b. black, blue and light blue 70 35

436 Dr Briceno-Iragorry

1985. 27th Death Anniv of Dr. Mario Briceno-Iragorry (politician).
2549 **436** 1 b. 25 silver and red . . 15 10

437 Museum

1985. 10th Anniv (1983) of Museum of Modern Art, Caracas.
2550 **437** 3 b. multicoloured . . . 35 20

438 Emblem and Dove as Hand

1985. 40th Anniv of U.N.O.
2551 **438** 10 b. blue and red . . . 1·10 60

439 Rainbow and Emblem

1985. International Youth Year.
2552 **439** 1 b. 50 multicoloured . 20 10

440 Shepherds and Camels

1985. Christmas. Multicoloured.
2553 2 b. Type **440** 25 10
2554 2 b. Holy Family and the Three Kings 25 10
Nos. 2553/4 were printed together, se-tenant, forming a composite design of the Nativity.

441 Petroleos de Venezuela Emblem

1985. 10th Anniv of National Petrochemical Industry.
2555 **441** 1 b. blue and black . . . 15 10
2556 – 1 b. multicoloured . . . 15 10
2557 – 2 b. multicoloured . . . 25 15
2558 – 2 b. multicoloured . . . 25 15
2559 – 3 b. multicoloured . . . 35 20
2560 – 3 b. multicoloured . . . 80 30
2561 – 4 b. multicoloured . . . 50 25
2562 – 4 b. multicoloured . . . 50 25
2563 – 5 b. multicoloured . . . 60 30
2564 – 5 b. multicoloured . . . 60 30
DESIGNS: No. 2556, Refinery and Isla S. A. emblem; 2557, Bariven oil terminal; 2558, Pequiven storage tank; 2559, Corpoven drilling site; 2560, Support vessel, oil rig and Maraven emblem; 2561, Meneven refinery; 2562, Intervep scientist; 2563, "Nodding Donkey"; 2564, Lagoven refinery.

442 Five Reales Silver Coin, 1873 **443** Drago

1985. Coins with Portrait of Simon Bolivar. Multicoloured.
2565 2 b. Type **442** 25 15
2566 2 b. 70 Five bolivares gold coin, 1886 . . . . 30 15
2567 3 b. Birth bicentenary gold proof coin, 1983 . . . . . 35 20

1985. 125th Birth Anniv (1984) of Dr. Luis Maria Drago (Argentine politician).
2568 **443** 2 b. 70 black, orge & red 30 15

444 Guayana City

1985. 25th Anniv of Guayana Development Corporation. Multicoloured.
2569 2 b. Type **444** 25 15
2570 3 b. Orinoco steel mill . . . 35 20
2571 5 b. Raul Leoni-Guri dam . . 60 35

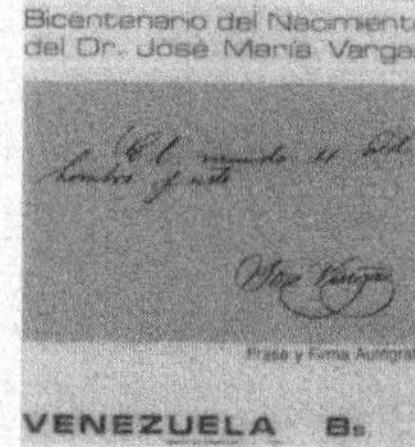

445 Signature

1985. Birth Bicentenary of Dr. Jose Maria Vargas (President, 1835–36). Multicoloured.
2572 3 b. Type **445** 30 15
2573 3 b. "Vargas" (Martin Tovar y Tovar) (vert) 30 15
2574 3 b. Statue at Palace of Academies (vert) 30 15
2575 3 b. "Exfilbo '86" National Stamp Exhibition emblem and flags 30 15
2576 3 b. Facade of Vargas Hospital, Caracas 30 15
2577 3 b. Title page of Vargas's "Manual and Compendium of Surgery" (vert) 30 15
2578 3 b. "Vargas" (Alirio Palacios) (vert) 30 15
2579 3 b. "Gesneria vargasii" (flower) 30 15
2580 3 b. Portraits of Vargas and Bolivar on Sixth Venezuelan Congress of Medical Sciences medal 30 15
2581 3 b. "Vargas" (anonymous) (vert) 30 15

446 Francisco Miranda

1986. Bicentenary (1981) of Francisco Miranda's Work for Latin American Liberation.
2583 **446** 1 b. 05 multicoloured . . 10 10

447 Children painting Wall **448** Lorries and Processing Plant

1986. Foundation for Educational Buildings and Equipment. Multicoloured.
2584 3 b. Type **447** 25 15
2585 5 b. Boys at woodwork class 35 15

1986. 45th Anniv of Venezuelan Dairy Industry Corporation. Multicoloured.
2586 2 b. 55 Type **448** 20 15
2587 2 b. 70 Map and milk containers 25 15
2588 3 b. 70 Processing plant Machiques, Edo Zulia (horiz) 35 15

449 Emblem

1986. 25th Anniv of VIASA (airline). Mult.
2589 3 b. Type **449** 35 20
2590 3 b. Douglas DC-8 in flight . 35 20
2591 3 b. Douglas DC-8 on ground 35 20
2592 3 b. Boeing 747 flying out to sea 35 20
2593 3 b. Tail fins of Douglas DC-10s 35 20
2594 3 b. 25 Hemispheres 35 20
2595 3 b. 25 Douglas DC-10 flying through cloud 35 20
2596 3 b. 25 Douglas DC-8 and DC-10 on ground 35 20
2507 3 b. 25 Douglas DC-9 flying over mountains 35 20
2598 3 b. 25 Manned flight deck . 35 20

450 Giant Armadillo

1986. Flora and Fauna. Dated "1983". Mult.
2599 70 c. Type **450** 10 10
2600 85 c. "Espeletia angustifolia" 10 10
2601 2 b. 70 Orinoco crocodile . . 20 10
2602 3 b. Mountain rose 20 10

451 Romulo Betancourt **452** Library Entrance

1986. 5th Death Anniv of Romulo Betancourt (President, 1959–64). Each black, deep brown and brown.
2603 2 b. Type **451** 20 10
2604 2 b. 70 Betancourt in armchair 20 10
2605 2 b. 70 Betancourt and inscription 20 10
2606 2 b. 70 Betancourt wearing sash 20 10
2607 2 b. 70 Betancourt working . 20 10
2608 3 b. As No. 2606 . . . . . 25 15
2609 3 b. As No. 2607 . . . . . 25 15
2610 3 b. As No. 2605 . . . . . 25 15
2611 3 b. Type **451** 25 15
2612 3 b. As No. 2604 . . . . . 25 15

1986. 40th Anniv of Re-opening of Zulia University. Each grey, black and blue.
2624 2 b. 70 Type **452** 20 10
2625 2 b. 70 University building . 20 10

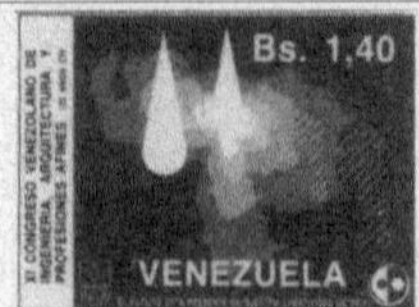

453 Map and Droplets

1986. 11th Venezuelan Engineers, Architects and Affiliated Professions Congress.
2626 **453** 1 b. 40 blue, blk & yell . . 25 15
2627 1 b. 55 multicoloured . . 25 15

454 Pope and Andes **455** "United Families" (Vianny Hernandez)

1986. Visit of Pope John Paul II (1985) (2nd issue). Multicoloured.
2628 1 b. Type **454** 10 10
2629 1 b. Pope and Maracaibo bridge 15 10
2630 3 b. Pope kissing ground . . 25 15
2631 3 b. Pope and "Virgin of Coromoto" 25 15
2632 4 b. Pope holding crucifix, Caracas 35 15
2633 5 b. 25 Pope and waterfall . 40 20

1986. 20th Anniv of Childrens' Paintings. Multicoloured.
2634 2 b. 55 Type **455** 20 10
2635 2 b. 55 "Love and Peace" (Yuraima L. Jimenez) . . . 20 10
2636 2 b. 55 "Woodland Animals" (Maria Valentina Arias) . . 20 10
2637 2 b. 55 "Noah's Ark" (Andreina Acero) 20 10
2638 2 b. 55 "House on Hillside" (Yenelsa) 20 10
2639 2 b. 70 "Flowers on Table" (Yenny Jimenez) 20 10
2640 2 b. 70 "Peace Lover" (Ramon Briceno) 20 10
2641 2 b. 70 "Children for World Peace" (Blanca Yesenia Hernandez) 20 10
2642 2 b. 70 "Lighthouse and Cable Railway" (Julio V. Hernandez) 20 10
2643 2 b. 70 "Flowers of a Thousand Colours" (with butterfly) (Maryolin Rodriguez Ortega) 20 10

456 Three Kings

1986. Christmas. Crib figures modelled by Eliecer Alvarez. Multicoloured.
2644 2 b. Type **456** 15 10
2645 2 b. Nativity 15 10
Nos. 2644/5 were printed together, se-tenant, forming a composite design.

457 Treating Accident Victim

1986. 17th Anniv of Caracas City Police. Multicoloured.
2646 2 b. 70 Type **457** 20 10
2647 2 b. 70 On duty at sporting event 20 10
2648 2 b. 70 Computer identification bar code 20 10
2649 2 b. 70 Cadets on parade . . 20 10
2650 2 b. 70 Motor cycle police . . 20 10

458 Prehispanic Musical Instrument

1987. Native Art. Multicoloured.
2651 2 b. Type **458** 15 10
2652 2 b. Woven fabric 15 10
2653 3 b. Prehispanic ceramic bottle 25 15
2654 3 b. Basket design 25 15

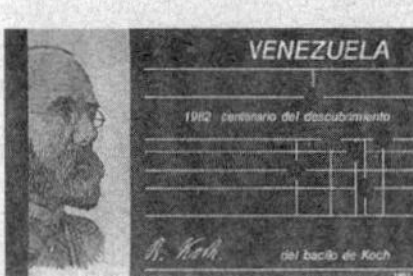

459 Robert Koch (discoverer) and Bacillus Symbol

1987. Centenary (1982) of Discovery of Tubercle Bacillus.
2655 **459** 2 b. 55 multicoloured . 20 10

460 "Entry of Jesus into Jerusalem" (Antonio Herrera Toro)

1987. Holy Week. Multicoloured.
2656 2 b. Type **460** 15 10
2657 2 b. "Christ at the Pillar" (statue, Jose Francisco Rodriguez) 15 10
2658 2 b. "Jesus of Nazareth" (wood carving, School of Seville) 15 10
2659 2 b. "Descent from the Cross" (Jose Rivadefrecha, El Campeche) 15 10
2660 2 b. "Virgin of Solitude" (sculpture) 15 10
2661 2 b. 25 "The Last Supper" (Arturo Michelena) . . . 15 10
2662 2 b. 25 "Ecce Homo" (sculpture) 15 10
2663 2 b. 25 "The Crucifixion" (sculpture, Gregorio de Leon Quintana) 15 10
2664 2 b. 25 "Holy Sepulchre" (sculpture, Sebastian de Ochoa Montes) 15 10
2665 2 b. 25 "The Resurrection" (attr. Peter Paul Rubens) . 15 10

461 "Bolivar and Bello" (Marisol Escobar) **462** Barquisimeto Hilton Hotel

1987. World Neurochemical Congress. Mult.
2666 3 b. Type **461** 25 15
2667 4 b. 25 Retinal cells 30 15

1987. Tourism Development. Multicoloured.
2668 6 b. Type **462** 35 15
2669 6 b. Lake Hotel Intercontinental, Maracaibo 35 15
2670 6 b. Macuto Sheraton Hotel, Caraballeda 35 15
2671 6 b. Melia Caribe Hotel, Caraballeda 35 15
2672 6 b. Melia Hotel, Puerto la Cruz 55 20
2673 6 b. 50 Pool, Barquisimeto Hilton Hotel 35 15
2674 6 b. 50 Lake Hotel Intercontinental, Maracaibo, at night 35 15
2675 6 b. 50 Macuto Sheraton Hotel, Caraballeda, and marina . 55 20
2676 6 b. 50 Melia Caribe Hotel, Caraballeda (different) . . 35 15
2677 6 b. 50 Melia Hotel, Puerto la Cruz (different) 55 20

463 Amazon Federal Terrritory Map and Ship's Bow

1987. 35th Anniv of National Canals Institute. Multicoloured.
2678 2 b. Type **463** 10 10
2679 4 b. 25 Map of River Orinoco and buoy 25 15

464 Music School, Caracas

1987. Birth Centenary of Vicente Emilio Sojo (composer). Each deep brown and brown.
2680 2 b. Type **464** 15 10
2681 4 b. Conducting choir 25 15
2682 5 b. Score of "Hymn to Bolivar" 30 15
2683 6 b. Standing beside blackboard 40 20
2684 7 b. Sojo and signature . . . 50 25

465 "Simon Bolivar, Academician" (Roca Rey)

1987. 20th Anniv of Simon Bolivar University. Multicoloured.
2685 2 b. Type **465** 10 10
2686 3 b. "Solar Delta" (sculpture, Alejandro Otero) 15 10
2687 4 b. Rector's residence . . . 20 10
2688 5 b. Laser beam 25 15
2689 6 b. Owl sculpture 30 15

466 Motor Vehicles

1987. 10th Anniv of Ministry of Transport and Communications. Multicoloured.
2690 2 b. Type **466** 10 10
2691 2 b. Bulk carrier and crane . 20 10
2692 2 b. Electric local train . . . 10 10
2693 2 b. Envelopes and telegraph key 10 10
2694 2 b. Transmission masts and globe 10 10
2695 2 b. 25 Motorway interchange system 10 10
2696 2 b. 25 Boeing 737 airliner . . 30 15
2697 2 b. 25 Electric mainline train 10 10
2698 2 b. 25 Dish aerial 10 10
2699 2 b. 25 Globe and communications satellite . . 10 10
Nos. 2690/9 were printed together, se-tenant, each horizontal pair forming a composite design.

467 Administration Building, Caracas

1987. 70th Anniv of Venezuelan Navigation Company. Multicoloured.
2700 2 b. Type **467** 10 10
2701 2 b. Containers being loaded . 10 10
2702 3 b. Company emblem on ship's funnel 15 10
2703 3 b. Ship's engine-room . . . 15 10
2704 4 b. "Zulia" (freighter) at sea 40 20
2705 4 b. "Guarico" (freighter) off Venezuelan coast 50 20
2706 5 b. "Cerro Bolivar" (bulk carrier) 55 20
2707 5 b. Ship's bridge 25 15
2708 6 b. Map 30 15
2709 6 b. Containers being loaded onto Ro-Ro ferry 30 15

468 Air-sea Rescue

1987. 50th Anniv of National Guard. Mult.
2710 2 b. Type **468** 35 10
2711 2 b. Traffic patrol 10 10
2712 2 b. Guard on horseback . . 10 10
2713 2 b. Guard with children . . 10 10
2714 2 b. Armed guard on industrial site 10 10
2715 4 b. As No. 2714 . . . . . . 20 10
2716 4 b. As No. 2713 . . . . . . 20 10
2717 4 b. As No. 2712 . . . . . . 20 10
2718 4 b. As No. 2711 . . . . . . 20 10
2719 4 b. Type **468** 60 20

469 "Departure from Puerto Palos" (detail, Jacobo Borges)

1987. 500th Anniv (1992) of Discovery of America by Columbus. Multicoloured.
2720 2 b. Type **469** 10 10
2721 7 b. "Discovery of America" (Tito Salas) 30 15
2722 11 b. 50 "Fr. de las Casas, Protector of the Indians" (detail, Tito Salas) 50 25
2723 12 b. "Trade in Venezuela during the Time of the Conquest" (detail, Tito Salas) 1·00 25
2724 12 b. 50 "Rout of Guaicaipuro" (Jacobo Borges) 55 25

470 "Annunciation" (Juan Pedro Lopez)

1987. Christmas. Multicoloured.
2725 2 b. Type **470** 10 10
2726 3 b. "Nativity" (Jose Francisco Rodriguez) 15 10
2727 5 b. 50 "Adoration of the Kings" (anon) 30 15
2728 6 b. "Flight into Egypt" (Juan Pedro Lopez) 30 15

471 Steel Plant Building

1987. 25th Anniv of Steel Production by National SIDOR Mills.
2729 **471** 2 b. multicoloured . . . 10 10
2730 – 2 b. multicoloured . . . 10 10
2731 – 6 b. multicoloured . . . 30 15
2732 – 6 b. multicoloured . . . 30 15
2733 – 7 b. multicoloured . . . 30 15
2734 – 7 b. multicoloured . . . 30 15
2735 – 11 b. 50 multicoloured . 75 25
2736 – 11 b. 50 multicoloured . 75 25
2737 – 12 b. black 80 25
2738 – 12 b. multicoloured . . . 80 25
DESIGNS: No. 2730, Rolling strip; No. 2731, Walkways and towers of plant; No. 2732, Drawing steel bars; No. 2733, Walkway, towers and buildings; No. 2734, Slab mill; No. 2735, Building and towers; No. 2736, Steel bar production; No. 2737, Company emblem; No. 2738, Anniversary emblem.
Nos. 2729/38 were printed together, se-tenant, Nos. 2729, 2731, 2733 and 2735 forming a composite design of the SIDOR steel plant.

472 Flags

1987. 1st Meeting of Eight Latin-American Presidents of Contadora and Lima Groups, Acapulco.
2739 **472** 6 b. multicoloured . . . 30 15

473 Plastics

1987. 10th Anniv of Petro-Chemical Company of Venezuela. Multicoloured.

2740 2 b. Type **473** 10 10
2741 6 b. Formulae (oil refining) . 30 15
2742 7 b. Leaves (fertilizers) . . . 30 15
2743 11 b. 50 Pipes (installations) . 75 25
2744 12 b. Expansion 80 25

474 St. John Bosco and People on Map

1987. Birth Centenary of St. John Bosco (founder of Salesian Brothers). Multicoloured.

2745 2 b. Type **474** 10 10
2746 3 b. National Temple, Caracas 15 10
2747 4 b. Vocational training . . . 15 10
2748 5 b. Church of Maria Auxiliadora 20 10
2749 6 b. Missionary work 25 15

475 Emblem

1988. 29th Governors' Meeting of Inter-American Development Bank.

2750 **475** 11 b. 50 multicoloured . 60 30

476 Bank Branch

1988. 30th Anniv of Banco Republica. Mult.

2751 2 b. Type **476** 10 10
2752 2 b. Pottery (small business finance) 10 10
2753 2 b. Factory and security guards (industrial finance) 10 10
2754 2 b. Laboratory workers (technology finance) . . . 10 10
2755 2 b. Quay-side scene (exports and imports) 10 10
2756 6 b. Farm workers (agricultural finance) 35 15
2757 6 b. Fishing boat (fisheries finance) 35 15
2758 6 b. Milk production (livestock development) 35 15
2759 6 b. Building site (construction finance) 35 15
2760 6 b. Tourist bus (tourism development) 35 15

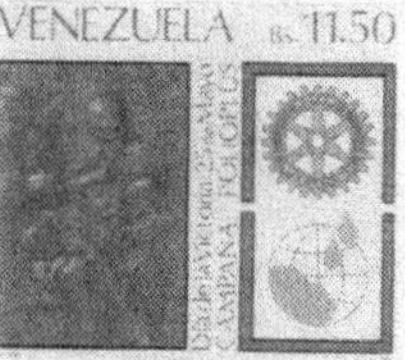

477 "Mother and Children" and Emblems

1988. Rotary International Anti-polio Campaign Victory Day.

2761 **477** 11 b. 50 multicoloured . 65 35

478 Carlos Eduardo Frias (publicist)

1989. 50th Anniv of Publicity Industry. Mult.

2762 4 b. Three profiles of Frias . 30 15
2763 10 b. Type **478** 60 30

479 Smelter **481** Bolivar in Dress Uniform, 1828

480 Red Siskins

1988. 10th Anniv of Venalum (aluminium company).

2764 **479** 2 b. multicoloured . . . 10 10
2765 – 6 b. black 30 15
2766 – 7 b. multicoloured . . . 30 15
2767 – 11 b. 50 multicoloured . 65 35
2768 – 12 b. multicoloured . . 65 35

DESIGNS: 6 b. Plan of electrolytic cell; 7 b. Aluminium pipes; 11 b. 50, Loading ship with aluminium for export; 12 b. Workers playing football.

1988. Endangered Birds. Multicoloured.

2769 2 b. Type **480** 20 10
2770 6 b. Scarlet ibis 55 25
2771 11 b. 50 Harpy eagle . . . . 1·10 45
2772 12 b. Greater flamingoes . . 1·10 45
2773 12 b. 50 Northern helmeted curassow . . . . 1·25 55

1988. Army Day. Multicoloured.

2774 2 b. Type **481** 10 10
2775 2 b. Lieutenant in ceremonial uniform, 1988 . . . . . . 10 10
2776 6 b. Gen. Jose Antonio Paez in dress uniform, 1821 . . . 30 15
2777 6 b. Major-General in No. 1 dress, 1988 . . . . 30 15
2778 7 b. Major-General, 1820 . . 30 15
2779 7 b. Line infantryman, 1820 30 15
2780 11 b. 50 Brigadier-General, 1820 60 30
2781 11 b. 50 Garrison infantryman, 1820 . . . . 60 30
2782 12 b. Artilleryman, 1836 . . 60 30
2783 12 b. Light cavalryman, 1820 60 30

482 Urdaneta (after Salas)

1988. Birth Bicentenary of General Rafael Urdaneta. Multicoloured.

2784 2 b. Sword and scabbard . . 10 10
2785 4 b. 75 "Wedding of the General" (Tito Salas) . . 20 10
2786 6 b. Type **482** 30 15
2787 7 b. "Siege of Valencia" (Tito Salas) 30 15
2788 12 b. "Retreat from San Carlos" (Tito Salas) . . . 65 35

483 Marino (after Martin Tovar y Tovar) **484** Games Emblem

1988. Birth Bicentenary of General Santiago Marino.

2789 **483** 4 b. 75 multicoloured . 20 10

1988. Olympic Games, Seoul.

2790 **484** 12 b. multicoloured . . 60 30

485 "Virgin of Copacabana" (Bolivia)

1988. Marian Year. Multicoloured.

2791 4 b. 75 Type **485** 25 15
2792 4 b. 75 "Virgin of Chiquinquira" (Colombia) . 25 15
2793 4 b. 75 "Virgin of Coromoto" (Venezuela) 25 15
2794 4 b. 75 "Virgin of the Cloud" (Ecuador) 25 15
2795 4 b. 75 "Virgin of Antigua" (Panama) 25 15
2796 6 b. "Virgin of Evangelisation" (Peru) 30 15
2797 6 b. "Virgin of Lujan" (Argentina) 30 15
2798 6 b. "Virgin of Altagracia" (Dominican Republic) . . . 30 15
2799 6 b. "Virgin of Aparecida" (Brazil) 30 15
2800 6 b. "Virgin of Guadelupe" (Mexico) 30 15

486 Bardou Refracting Telescope

1988. Centenary of Juan Manuel Cagigal Observatory. Multicoloured.

2801 2 b. Type **486** 20 10
2802 4 b. 75 Universal "AUZ-27" theodolite 25 15
2803 6 b. Bust of Cagigal 30 15
2804 11 b. 50 Boulton Cupola and night sky over Caracas in September 60 30
2805 12 b. Satellite photographing Hurricane Allen 65 35

487 Keys **488** Commemorative Medal

1988. 50th Anniv of Controller-General's Office.

2806 **487** 10 b. multicoloured . . . 45 25

1988. Cent of National Historical Museum. Mult.

2807 6 b. Type **488** 30 15
2808 6 b. 50 Juan Pablo Rojas Paul (founder) (after Cristobal Rojas) 30 15

489 First Headquarters

1988. Centenary of Electricity Industry. Mult.

2809 2 b. Type **489** 10 10
2810 4 b. 75 "Electrical Plant, 1888" (Jaime Carrillo) 20 15
2811 10 b. Plaza Bolivar, 1888 . . 45 25
2812 11 b. 50 Baralt Theatre, 1888 60 30
2813 12 b. 50 Ramon Laguna Central Thermo-electricity Station . 60 30

490 "Nativity" (Tito Salas, left-hand detail)

1988. Christmas. Multicoloured.

2814 4 b. Type **490** 20 10
2815 6 b. "Christ Child" (anonymous) 30 15
2816 15 b. "Nativity" (Salas, right-hand detail) 65 35

Nos. 2814 and 2816 form a composite design.

491 "Bolivar and Ricardo" (John de Pool)

1989. "The Liberator at Curacao". Multicoloured.

2817 10 b. Type **491** 60 15
2818 10 b. "The Octagon" (John de Pool) 60 15
2819 11 b. "Doctor Mordechay Ricardo" 75 20

Nos. 2817/19 were printed together, se-tenant, Nos. 2817/18 forming a composite design.

492 Cardinal Quintero (Archbishop of Caracas, 1960–80)

1989. 25th Anniv of Convention with Holy See. Multicoloured.

2820 4 b. Type **492** 15 10
2821 4 b. Dr. Raul Leoni (President, 1964–69) 15 10
2822 12 b. Arms of Luciano Storero (Papal Nuncio) 70 20
2823 12 b. Arms of Cardinal Lebrun (Archbishop of Caracas) . 70 20
2824 16 b. Pope Paul VI 90 25

493 "Cacao Harvest" (Tito Salas)

1989. Centenary of Bank of Venezuela. Mult.

2825 4 b. Type **493** 15 10
2826 4 b. "Teaching Sowing Time of Coffee" (Tito Salas) . . . 15 10
2827 4 b. Head Office, Caracas . . 15 10
2828 4 b. Archive of the Liberator, Caracas 15 10
2829 4 b. Tree-planting programme 15 10
2830 4 b. Family planting tree . . 15 10
2831 8 b. Left-hand side of 50 b. banknote 25 15
2832 8 b. Right-hand side of 50 b. bank-note 25 15
2833 8 b. Portrait of Bolivar on left-hand side of 500 b. banknote 25 15
2834 8 b. Right-hand side of 500 b. banknote 25 15

Nos. 2825/34 were printed together, se-tenant, Nos. 2831/2 and 2833/4 forming composite designs.

494 Dish

1989. America. Pre-Columbian Artefacts. Multicoloured.

2835 6 b. Type **494** 20 10
2836 24 b. Figure . . . . 2·00 1·00

495 Shepherds and Sheep

1989. Christmas. Multicoloured.

2837 5 b. As Type **495** but inscr at top 10 10
2838 5 b. Type **495** 10 10
2839 6 b. Angel and shepherds (inscr at top) 15 10

2840 6 b. As No. 2839 but inscr at bottom 15 10
2841 6 b. Nativity (inscr at top) . 15 10
2842 6 b. As No. 2841 but inscr at bottom 15 10
2843 12 b. Shepherds (inscr at top) 70 15
2844 12 b. As No. 2843 but inscr at bottom 70 15
2845 15 b. Adoration of the Magi (inscr at top) 85 15
2846 15 b. As No. 2845 but inscr at bottom 85 45

Nos. 2837/46 were printed together, each horizontal strip forming a composite design.

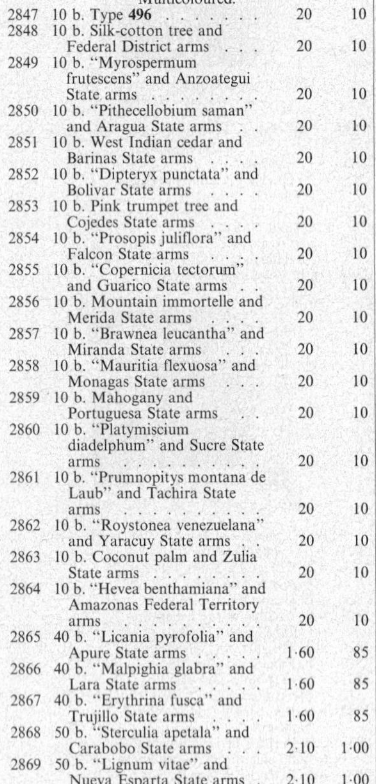

496 Araguaney Tree and State Arms

1990. 20th Anniv of Bank of Venezuela Foundation. Multicoloured.

2847 10 b. Type **496** 20 10
2848 10 b. Silk-cotton tree and Federal District arms . . . 20 10
2849 10 b. "Myrospermum frutescens" and Anzoategui State arms 20 10
2850 10 b. "Pithecellobium saman" and Aragua State arms . . 20 10
2851 10 b. West Indian cedar and Barinas State arms 20 10
2852 10 b. "Dipteryx punctata" and Bolivar State arms 20 10
2853 10 b. Pink trumpet tree and Cojedes State arms 20 10
2854 10 b. "Prosopis juliflora" and Falcon State arms 20 10
2855 10 b. "Copernicia tectorum" and Guarico State arms . . 20 10
2856 10 b. Mountain immortelle and Merida State arms 20 10
2857 10 b. "Brawnea leucantha" and Miranda State arms . . . 20 10
2858 10 b. "Mauritia flexuosa" and Monagas State arms . . . 20 10
2859 10 b. Mahogany and Portuguesa State arms . . 20 10
2860 10 b. "Platymiscium diadelphum" and Sucre State arms 20 10
2861 10 b. "Prumnopitys montana de Laub" and Tachira State arms 20 10
2862 10 b. "Roystonea venezuelana" and Yaracuy State arms . . 20 10
2863 10 b. Coconut palm and Zulia State arms 20 10
2864 10 b. "Hevea benthamiana" and Amazonas Federal Territory arms 20 10
2865 40 b. "Licania pyrofolia" and Apure State arms . . . . . 1·60 85
2866 40 b. "Malpighia glabra" and Lara State arms . . . . . 1·60 85
2867 40 b. "Erythrina fusca" and Trujillo State arms . . . . 1·60 85
2868 50 b. "Sterculia apetala" and Carabobo State arms . . . 2·10 1·00
2869 50 b. "Lignum vitae" and Nueva Esparta State arms . 2·10 1·00
2870 50 b. Mangrove and Amacuro Federal Territory arms . . 2·10 1·00

497 Dr. Francisco Ochoa (founder)

1990. Centenary of Zulia University.

2871 **497** 10 b. black and blue . . 20 10
2872 – 10 b. black and blue . . 20 10
2873 – 15 b. multicoloured . . . 60 15
2874 – 15 b. multicoloured . . . 60 15
2875 – 20 b. multicoloured . . . 85 25

DESIGNS: No. 2872, Dr. Jesus E. Lossada (Rector, 1946–47); 2873, Research into acid soils; 2874, Petroleum research; 2875, Transplant surgery.

498 Santa Capilla, 1943

1990. 50th Anniv of Central Bank. Multicoloured.

2876 10 b. Type **498** 20 10
2877 10 b. Headquarters, 1967 . . 20 10
2878 10 b. Left half of 1940 500 b. note 20 10
2879 10 b. Right half of 1940 500 b. note 20 10
2880 10 b. "Sun of Peru" decoration, 1825 . . . . 20 10
2881 10 b. Medals 20 10
2882 15 b. Peruvian sword, 1825 . 60 15
2883 15 b. Cross, Bucaramanga, 1830 60 15
2884 40 b. Medallion of George Washington, 1826 . . . . 1·60 85
2885 50 b. Gen. O'Leary (enamel portrait) . . . . 2·10 1·00

Nos. 2876/85 were printed together, se-tenant, Nos. 2878/9 forming a composite design.

500 "St. Joseph and the Child" (Juan Pedro Lopez)

501 Lake House, Maracaibo

1990. Christmas. Multicoloured.

2887 10 b. Type **500** 20 10
2888 10 b. "Nativity" (Juan Pedro Lopez) 20 10
2889 10 b. "Return from Egypt" (Matheo Moreno) 20 10
2890 20 b. "Holy Family" (anon) 85 25
2891 20 b. "Nativity" (Juan Pedro Lopez) (different) 85 25

1990. America. The Natural World. Mult.

2892 10 b. Type **501** 20 10
2893 40 b. East Venezuelan shore 1·60 80

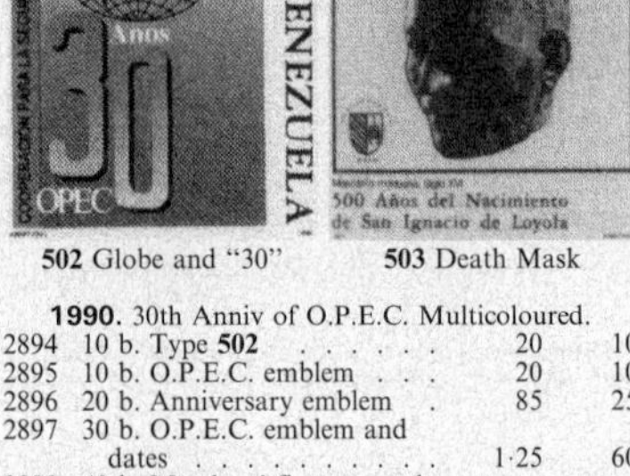

502 Globe and "30"

503 Death Mask

1990. 30th Anniv of O.P.E.C. Multicoloured.

2894 10 b. Type **502** 20 10
2895 10 b. O.P.E.C. emblem . . . 20 10
2896 20 b. Anniversary emblem . 85 25
2897 30 b. O.P.E.C. emblem and dates . . . . 1·25 60
2898 40 b. Members' flags around O.P.E.C. emblem . . . . 1·60 85

1991. 500th Birth Anniv of St. Ignatius de Loyola (founder of Society of Jesus). Multicoloured

2899 12 b. Type **503** 25 15
2900 12 b. St. Ignatius de Loyola College, Caracas 25 15
2901 40 b. Silver statue of Loyola by Francisco de Vergara . . 1·50 75
2902 50 b. "Our Lady of Montserrat" (wooden statue) . . . . . 1·90 95

504 Elisa Elvira Zuloaga (painter and engraver)

1991. 50th Anniv of American–Venezuelan Cultural Centre. Designs showing Centre directors.

2903 **504** 12 b. green and black . 25 15
2904 – 12 b. violet and black . 25 15
2905 – 12 b. red and black . . 25 15
2906 – 40 b. blue and black . . 1·50 80
2907 – 50 b. brown and black . . 1·00 80

DESIGNS: No. 2904, Gloria Stolk (writer); 2905, Caroline Lloyd (composer); 2906, Jules Waldman (linguist and journalist); 2907, William Coles (entrepreneur).

505 "Acineta alticola"

1991. Orchids. Multicoloured.

2908 12 b. Type **505** 25 15
2909 12 b. "Brassavola nodosa" . . 25 15
2910 12 b. "Brachionidium brevicaudatum" 25 15
2911 12 b. "Bifrenaria maguirei" . 25 15
2912 12 b. "Odontoglossum spectatissimum" 25 15
2913 12 b. "Catasetum macrocarpum" 25 15
2914 40 b. "Mendocella jorisiana" 80 40
2915 40 b. "Cochleanthes discolor" 80 40
2916 50 b. "Maxillaria splendens" 1·00 50
2917 50 b. "Pleurothallis dunstervillei" . . . . 1·00 50

506 Voters at Ballot Box

1991. 50th Anniv of Democratic Action Party.

2919 **506** 12 b. multicoloured . . . 25 15
2920 – 12 b. multicoloured . . . 25 15
2921 – 12 b. multicoloured . . . 25 15
2922 – 12 b. black and blue . . . 25 10

DESIGNS: No. 2920, Agrarian reform; 2921, Education; 2922, Nationalization of petroleum industry.

507 Rodrigues Suarez and Terepaima Chieftain

1991. America. Voyages of Discovery. Showing paintings by Pedro Centeno. Multicoloured.

2923 12 b. Type **507** 25 15
2924 40 b. Paramaconi chieftain and Garcia Gonzalez . . . . . 1·90 80

508 Family in House

1991. 25th Anniv of Children's Foundation. Multicoloured.

2925 12 b. Type **508** 20 10
2926 12 b. Children's playground . 20 10
2927 12 b. Fairground 20 10
2928 12 b. Mother and daughter . 20 10
2929 12 b. Boy in hospital 20 10
2930 12 b. Children and tree . . . 20 10
2931 40 b. Girls at home 65 35
2932 40 b. Children in classroom . 65 35
2933 50 b. Children acting in play . 80 40
2934 50 b. Children playing ring-a-ring of roses 80 40

509 "Stable" (Barbaro Rivas)

1991. Christmas. Multicoloured.

2935 10 b. Type **509** 15 10
2936 12 b. "Nativity" (Elisa Morales) 20 10
2937 20 b. "Nativity" (model, Glenda Mendoza) 30 15
2938 25 b. "Shepherds watching flock (Maritza Marin) 40 20
2939 30 b. "Nativity" (Antonia Azuaje) 50 25

1991. Nos. 2613/15 surch **RESELLADO** and value.

2940 **347** 5 b. on 25 c. red 10 10
2941 5 b. on 75 c. mauve . . . 10 10
2942 10 b. on 25 c. red . . . 15 10
2943 10 b. on 75 c. mauve . . 15 10
2944 12 b. on 50 c. blue . . . 20 10
2945 12 b. on 75 c. mauve . . 20 10
2946 20 b. on 50 c. blue . . . 65 15
2947 20 b. on 75 c. mauve . . 65 35
2948 40 b. on 50 c. blue . . . 1·40 65
2949 40 b. on 75 c. mauve . . 1·40 65
2950 **347** 50 b. on 50 c. blue . . . 1·60 85
2951 50 b. on 75 c. mauve . . 1·60 85

512 Columbus's Arms

1991. 500th Anniv (1992) of Discovery of America by Columbus.

2953 **512** 12 b. multicoloured . . . 20 10
2954 – 12 b. black, blue & orge 20 10
2955 – 12 b. multicoloured . . . 20 10
2956 – 40 b. black, brn & orge . 65 35
2957 – 50 b. black and orange . 80 40

DESIGNS: No. 2954, "Santa Maria"; 2955, Juan de la Cosa's map; 2956, Sighting land; 2957, Columbus before King Ferdinand and Queen Isabella the Catholic.

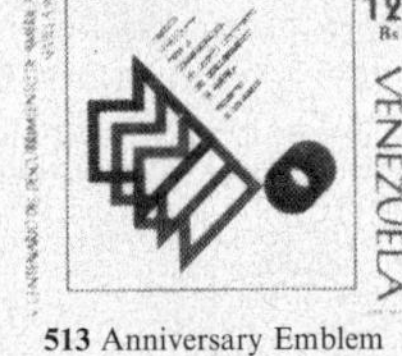

513 Anniversary Emblem

1992. "Expo 92" World's Fair, Seville. 500th Anniv of Discovery of America by Columbus.

2958 **513** 12 b. black, red & blue . 20 10
2959 – 12 b. multicoloured . . . 20 10
2960 – 12 b. multicoloured . . . 20 10
2961 – 12 b. multicoloured . . . 20 10
2962 – 12 b. multicoloured . . . 20 10
2963 – 12 b. multicoloured . . . 20 10
2964 – 40 b. multicoloured . . . 65 35
2965 – 40 b. multicoloured . . . 65 35
2966 – 50 b. multicoloured . . . 80 40
2967 – 50 b. black and brown . . 80 40

DESIGNS: No. 2959, Venezuelan pavilion at "Expo 92"; 2960, Landmarks and map of southern Spain; 2961, Columbus; 2962, "Encounters"; 2963, "0x500 America"; 2964, "Imago-Mundi"; 2965, "The Grand Voyage"; 2966, "Golden Beach"; 2967, Idols.

514 Red-footed Tortoise

1992. Tortoises. Multicoloured.

2969 12 b. Type **514** 20 10
2970 12 b. "Red-footed tortoise ("Geochelone carbonaria") (different) 20 10
2971 12 b. South American river turtle ("Podocnemis expansa") (on land) . . . 20 10
2972 12 b. South American river turtle (swimming) 20 10

515 Native Hut

516 Figure holding Sheaf of Wheat

1992. Electricity Distribution in the South.

2973 **515** 12 b. multicoloured . . . 20 10
2974 – 12 b. black and blue . . . 20 10
2975 – 12 b. multicoloured . . . 20 10
2976 – 40 b. multicoloured . . . 65 35
2977 – 50 b. multicoloured . . . 80 40

DESIGNS: No. 2974, Pylons; 2975, Horses galloping through water; 2976, Engineers working on pylon; 2977, Traditional baskets beside lake.

1992. "Offering to My Race" (Mateo Manaure). Designs showing various "mother" figures. Multicoloured.

2978 12 b. Type **516** 20 10
2979 12 b. Orange figure 20 10
2980 12 b. Yellow figure 20 10
2981 12 b. Pink figure 20 10
2982 40 b. Brown figure 65 35
2983 40 b. Purple and orange figures 65 35
2984 50 b. Three-quarter length figure 80 40
2985 50 b. Head and shoulders . . 80 40

517 Catechism in Venezuela, 1975 **518** "And on the Third Voyage" (Elio Caldera)

1992. Beatification of Josemaria Escriva (founder of Opus Dei).

2986 **517** 18 b. multicoloured . . . 20 10
2987 – 18 b. multicoloured . . . 20 10
2988 – 18 b. multicoloired . . . 20 10
2989 – 18 b. black and yellow . . 20 10
2990 – 18 b. multicoloured . . . 20 10
2991 – 18 b. multicoloured . . . 20 10
2992 – 60 b. multicoloured . . . 70 35
2993 – 60 b. multicoloured . . . 70 35
2994 – 75 b. multicoloured . . . 85 45
2995 – 75 b. multicoloured . . . 85 45

DESIGNS: No. 2987, Celebrating mass; 2988, Jose Escriva and Dolores Albas (parents); 2989, Text and autograph; 2990, With statuette of Madonna and Child; 2991, Commemorative medal; 2992, With Pope Paul VI, 1964; 2993, Writing at desk; Portrait; 2995, Portrait in St. Peter's Square, 17 May 1992.

1992. America. 500th Anniv of Discovery of America by Columbus. Multicoloured.

2996 18 b. Type **518** 20 10
2997 60 b. "Descontextura" (Juan Pablo Nascimiento) 70 35

519 "Adoration of the Shepherds" **520** Simon Bolivar

1992. Christmas. Paintings by Lucio Rivas. Multicoloured.

2998 18 b. Type **519** 20 10
2999 75 b. "Adoration of the Magi" 85 45

1993. Portraits and Monuments.

3001 **520** 1 b. silver 10 10
3002 2 b. blue 10 10
3005 – 5 b. red 10 10
3006 – 10 b. purple 10 10
3007 – 20 b. green 25 15
3008 – 25 b. orange 25 15
3009 – 35 b. green 35 20
3010 – 40 b. blue 40 20
3011 – 50 b. orange . . . . . 1·10 55
3012 – 50 b. mauve 50 25
3013 – 100 b. brown . . . . . 2·25 1·10
3014 – 100 b. blue 95 50
3015 – 200 b. orange . . . . . 1·90 95

DESIGNS: 5 b. National Pantheon, Caracas; 10 b. War of Independence Memorial, Carabobo; 20 b. General Jose Antonio de Paez (President, 1830–35, 1837–43 and 1861–63); 25 b. Luisa Caceres de Arismendi; 35 b. General Ezespiel Zamora (politician); 40 b. Cristobal Mendoza (jurist and provincial governor); 50 b. (3011) National Library; 50 b. (3012) Jose Felix, Ribas (independence fighter); 100 b. (3013), 200. Bolivar (different); 100 b. (3014) General Manuel Piar.

521 "Cattleya percivaliana"

1993. Orchids. Multicoloured.

3016 20 b. Type **521** 25 15
3017 20 b. "Anguloa ruckeri" . . 25 15
3018 20 b. "Chondrorhyncha flaveola" 25 15
3019 20 b. "Stenia pallida" 25 15
3020 20 b. "Zygosepalum lindeniae" 25 15
3021 20 b. "Maxillaria triloris" . . 25 15
3022 80 b. "Stanhopea wardii" . . 90 45
3023 80 b. "Oncidium papilio" . . 90 45
3024 100 b. "Oncidium hastilabium" 1·10 55
3025 100 b. "Sobralia cattleya" . . 1·10 55

522 Woman

1993. 150th Anniv of Tovar Colony, Aragua State. Multicoloured.

3027 24 b. Type **522** 30 15
3028 24 b. Children 30 15
3029 24 b. Catholic church . . . 30 15
3030 24 b. St. Martin of Tours (patron saint) 30 15
3031 24 b. Vegetables and fruit . 30 15
3032 24 b. School 30 15
3033 80 b. House of Augustin Codazzi (founder) 90 45
3034 80 b. House of Alexander Benitz 90 45
3035 100 b. Breidenbach mill . . 1·10 55
3036 100 b. Procession of Jokili (carnival group) . . . . . 1·10 55

VENEZUELA Elige: tabaco o salud Bs.24 SOCIEDAD ANTICANCEROSA

523 Tucacas Steam Locomotive, 1813 **524** Smoker and Non-Smoker

1993. 19th Pan-American Railways Congress. Multicoloured.

3037 24 b. Type **523** 30 15
3038 24 b. Halcon steam locomotive, 1894, on Las Mostazas bridge 30 15
3039 24 b. Maracaibo steam locomotive 30 15
3040 24 b. Tender and carriages in Palo Grande station . . . 30 15
3041 24 b. Fiat diesel locomotive, 1957 . . . . 30 15
3042 24 b. "GP-9-L" diesel locomotive, 1957 . . . . 30 15
3043 80 b. "GP-15-L" diesel locomotive, 1982 . . . . 90 45
3044 80 b. Underground train, Caracas 90 45
3045 100 b. Electric locomotive . 1·10 55
3046 100 b. Carriages . . . . . . 1·10 55

Nos. 3037/46 were issued together, se-tenant, Nos. 3039/40 and 3043/4 forming composite designs.

1993. World No Smoking Day. Each black, blue and red.

3047 24 b. Type **524** 30 15
3048 80 b. No smoking sign . . . 90 45

525 Yellow-shouldered Amazon **526** Yanomami Boys

1993. America. Endangered Animals. Mult.

3049 24 b. Type **525** 35 15
3050 80 b. Scarlet macaw 90 45

1993. Amerindians. Multicoloured.

3051 1 b. Type **526** 10 10
3052 1 b. Yanomami woman preparing casabe 10 10
3053 40 b. Panare children in Katyayinto ceremony . . 50 25
3054 40 b. Taurepan man paddling canoe 50 25
3055 40 b. Piaroa mother holding child 50 25
3056 40 b. Panare man playing nose flute 50 25
3057 40 b. Taurepan woman weaving 50 25
3058 40 b. Masked Piaroa dancers in Warime ceremony 50 25
3059 100 b. Hoti man with blowpipe 1·25 65
3060 100 b. Hoti woman carrying child and fruit . . . . . . 1·25 65

527 Joseph

1993. Christmas. (a) Each cream, brown and black

3062 24 b. Type **527** 30 15
3063 24 b. Madonna and Child . . 30 15
3064 24 b. Shepherd girl, wise man and sheep 30 15
3065 80 b. Wise man and shepherd girl . . . . 1·10 55
3066 100 b. Wise man and shepherd girl . . . . 1·25 65

(b) Each cream, purple and black

3067 24 b. Type **527** 30 15
3068 24 b. As No. 3063 . . . . . 30 15
3069 24 b. As No. 3064 . . . . . 30 15
3070 80 b. As No. 3065 . . . . . 1·10 55
3071 100 b. As No. 3066 . . . . . 1·25 65

Nos. 3062/71 were issued together, se-tenant, each horizontal strip forming a composite design of the Nativity.

528 "Chrysocycnis schlimii"

1994. Orchids. Multicoloured.

3072 35 b. Type **528** 35 20
3073 35 b. "Galeandra minax" . . 35 20
3074 35 b. "Oncidium falcipetalum" 35 20
3075 35 b. "Oncidium lanceanum" 35 20
3076 40 b. "Sobralia violacea" . . 40 20
3077 40 b. "Sobralia infundibuligera" 40 20
3078 80 b. "Mendoncella burkei" . 75 40
3079 80 b. "Phragmipedium caudatum" 75 40
3080 100 b. "Phragmipedium kaieteurum" 95 50
3081 200 b. "Stanhopea grandiflora" 1·90 95

529 Federation Emblem

1994. 50th Anniv of Federation of Chambers of Industry and Commerce.

3083 – 35 b. blue, gold and black 25 15
3084 – 35 b. black and brown . . 25 15
3085 **529** 35 b. blue and black . . . 25 15
3086 80 b. blue and black . . . 60 30
3087 – 80 b. black, brown and blue 60 30
3088 – 80 b. blue, gold and black 60 30

DESIGNS: Nos. 3083, 3088, "50" on text; 3084, 3087, Luis Gonzalo Marturet (first Federation President).

530 State Arms

1994. Judicial Service.

3089 **530** 100 b. multicoloured . . 75 40

531 "Nativity" (School of Jose Lorenzo de Alvarado)

1994. Christmas. Multicoloured.

3090 35 b. Type **531** 25 15
3091 35 b. "Nativity" 25 15
3092 35 b. "Nativity" (School of Jose Lorenzo de Alvarado) . . . 25 15
3093 35 b. Holy Family (inscr "Adoracion de los Pastores") 25 15
3094 35 b. "Nativity" (School of Tocuyo) 25 15
3095 80 b. As No. 3094 . . . . . 60 30
3096 80 b. Type **531** 60 30
3097 80 b. As No. 3091 . . . . . 60 30
3098 80 b. As No. 3092 . . . . . 60 30
3099 80 b. As No. 3093 but inscr "El Nacimiento" 60 30

532 Sucre (anonymous portrait)

1995. Birth Bicentenary of Antonio Jose de Sucre (President of Bolivia, 1825–29). Multicoloured.

3100 25 b. Type **532** 20 10
3101 25 b. Mariana Carcelen y Larrea, Marquesa de Solanda (Sucre's wife) (after Juan Pinto Ortiz) 20 10
3102 35 b. Equestrian statue of Sucre (Turini Verana), Cumana . 25 15
3103 35 b. Base of statue 25 15
3104 40 b. "Battle of Pichincha" (top detail) (Victor Mideros Almeida) 30 15
3105 40 b. "Battle of Pichincha" (bottom detail) 30 15
3106 80 b. "Battle of Ayacucho" (left detail) (Antonio Herrera Toro) 60 30
3107 80 b. "Battle of Ayacucho" (right detail) 60 30
3108 100 b. "Capitulation of Ayacucho" (left detail) (Daniel Hernandez) . . . 75 40
3109 100 b. "Capitulation of Ayacucho" (right detail) . 75 40

Nos. 3100/9 were issued together, se-tenant, the 35, 40, 80 and 100 b. values forming four composite designs.

533 Mobile Post Office

1995. America (1994). Postal Transport. Mult.

3111 35 b. Type **533** 25 15
3112 80 b. Short S.7 Skyvan mail plane 60 30

534 St. John Bosco (founder) and Boy with Salesian

1995. Centenary of Salesian Brothers in Venezuela. Multicoloured.

3113 35 b. Type **534** 25 15
3114 35 b. Boy sitting in street and Virgin and Child 25 15
3115 35 b. Men working machinery 25 15
3116 35 b. Youths working on radio 25 15
3117 35 b. Boys playing baseball . 25 15
3118 35 b. Youths playing basketball 25 15
3119 80 b. Men planting saplings . 60 30
3120 80 b. Youth and boxes of produce 60 30
3121 100 b. Salesian and Amerindian boys 75 40
3122 100 b. Amerindian youth . . 75 40

535 Laboratory Technicians

1995. 50th Anniv of Christian Brothers' La Colina School, Caracas. Multicoloured.

3123 35 b. Type **535** but country inscr at right 25 15
3124 35 b. Young people camping (country inscr at left) . . . 25 15
3125 35 b. Youths playing football (country inscr at right) . . 25 15
3126 35 b. Type **535**. 25 15
3127 35 b. As No. 3124 but country inscr at right 25 15
3128 35 b. As No. 3125 but country inscr at left 25 15
3129 80 b. School building (country inscr at left) 60 30
3130 35 b. As No. 3129 but country inscr at right 60 30
3131 100 b. Jean Baptiste de la Salle (founder of Order) (country inscr at right) 70 40
3132 100 b. As No. 3131 but country inscr at left 70 40

536 "Maxillaria guareimensis"

1995. Orchids. Multicoloured.

3133 35 b. Type **536** 25 15
3134 35 b. "Paphinia lindeniana" . 25 15
3135 35 b. "Coryanthes biflora" . 25 15
3136 35 b. "Catasetum pileatum" . 25 15
3137 35 b. "Mormodes convolutum" 25 15
3138 35 b. "Huntleya lucida" . . . 25 15
3139 50 b. "Catasetum longifolium" 40 20
3140 50 b. "Anguloa clowesii" . . 40 20
3141 80 b. "Maxillaria histrionica" 60 30
3142 80 b. "Sobralia ruckeri" . . . 60 30

537 Anniversary Emblem

1995. 25th Anniv of Andean Pact (international co-operation group).

3144 **537** 80 b. multicoloured . . . 60 30

538 People of Different Races

1995. 50th Anniv of U.N.O. Multicoloured.

3145 50 b. Type **538** 40 20
3146 50 b. U.N. flag 40 20

Nos. 3145/6 were issued together, se-tenant, forming a composite design.

539 Mother Maria

1995. Beatification of Mother Maria de San Jose. Multicoloured.

3147 35 b. Type **539** 25 15
3148 35 b. Pope John Paul II . . . 25 15
3149 35 b. Handing out books to girls 25 15
3150 35 b. Embroidering 25 15
3151 35 b. Statue of Virgin Mary and altar 25 15
3152 35 b. Mother Maria in prayer before altar 25 15
3153 80 b. Mother Maria and three nuns in hospital ward . . . 60 30
3154 80 b. Nun beside hospital beds 60 30
3155 100 b. Nuns with poor children 75 40
3156 100 b. Nun giving alms to beggar 75 40

Nos. 3147/56 were issued together, se-tenant, each horizontal pair forming a composite design.

540 Monagas

1995. Birth Bicentenary of Jose Gregorio Monagas (anti-slavery campaigner and President 1851–55). Multicoloured.

3157 50 b. Type **540** 40 20
3158 50 b. Freed slaves 40 20

Nos. 3157/8 were issued together, se-tenant, forming a composite design.

541 Chirino

1995. Bicentenary of Jose Chirino's Insurrection. Multicoloured.

3159 50 b. Type **541** 40 20
3160 50 b. Insurrectionists 40 20

Nos. 3159/60 were issued together, se-tenant, forming a composite design.

542 Red Cross Workers and Child

1995. Centenary of Venezuelan Red Cross. Multicoloured.

31561 35 b. Type **542** 25 15
3162 35 b. Volunteers carrying injured man on stretcher . 25 15
3163 35 b. Operating theatre . . . 25 15
3164 80 b. Carlos J. Bello Hospital 60 30
3165 100 b. Red Cross flag . . . 75 40

543 River

1995. America. Environmental Protection. Mult.

(a) With thin frame line over face value.

3166 35 b. Type **543** 25 15
3167 80 b. Hillside 60 30

(b) Without thin frame line over face value.

3168 35 b. Type **543** 25 15
3169 80 b. As No. 3162 . . . . . 60 30

544 Ye'kuana Chief

1995. Amerindians (2nd series). Multicoloured.

3170 25 b. Type **544** 20 10
3171 25 b. Ye'kuana woman making manioc cake 20 10
3172 35 b. Guahibo musicians . . 25 15
3173 35 b. Guahibo shaman treating boy 25 15
3174 50 b. Uruak fisherman . . . 40 20
3175 50 b. Uruak woman cooking 40 20
3176 80 b. Warao woman making thread 60 30
3177 80 b. Warao couple transporting belongings in sailing canoe 60 30
3178 100 b. Bari men hunting . . 75 40
3179 100 b. Bari man making fire 75 40

545 Ricardo Zuloaga (pioneer)

1995. Centenary of Electricity in Caracas. Multicoloured.

3181 35 b. Type **545** 25 15
3182 35 b. El Encantado Plant . . 25 15
3183 35 b. Caracas sub-station . . 25 15
3184 35 b. Electric tram 25 15
3185 35 b. Streetlamps outside Congress building 25 15
3186 35 b. Streetlamps, Plaza Bolivar 25 15
3187 80 b. Engineer repairing streetlamp 60 30
3188 80 b. Avila Cross 60 30
3189 100 b. Teresa Carreño Cultural Centre 75 40
3190 100 b. Ricardo Zuloaga power station 75 40

546 The Annunciation

1995. Christmas. Multicoloured.

3191 35 b. Type **546**
3192 35 b. Mary and Joseph turned away from the inn 25 15
3193 35 b. Archangel Gabriel visits shepherds 25 15
3194 35 b. Three wise men bearing gifts 25 15
3195 40 b. Family gathering . . . 30 15
3196 40 b. Children on rollerskates 30 15
3197 40 b. Women and girl preparing food 30 15
3198 40 b. Woman and children preparing food 30 15
3199 100 b. Mary and Joseph holding Child Jesus 75 40
3200 100 b. Box of toys 75 40

Nos. 3191/3200 were issued together, se-tenant, Nos. 3195/6 and 3197/8 forming composite designs.

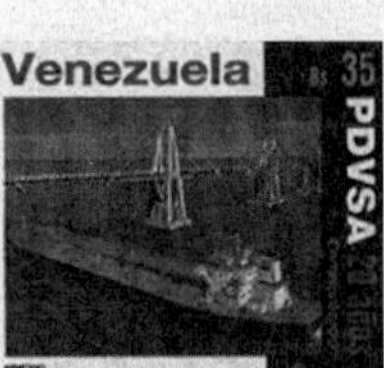

547 Arms

1995. 450th Anniv of El Tocuyo. Multicoloured.

3201 35 b. Type **547** 25 15
3202 35 b. Cutting sugar cane . . . 25 15
3203 35 b. Church of Our Lady of the Immaculate Conception . . 25 15
3204 35 b. "Our Lady of the Immaculate Conception" (statue) 25 15
3205 35 b. Ruins of Santo Domingo Temple 25 15
3206 35 b. Cultural centre 25 15
3207 80 b. Natural vegetation . . . 60 30
3208 80 b. Cactus 60 30
3209 100 b. Sword dance 75 40
3210 100 b. Man playing guitar . . 75 40

Nos. 3201/10 were issued together, se-tenant, Nos. 3209/10 forming a composite design.

548 Oil Tanker

1995. 20th Anniv of PDVSA National Fossil Fuels Association. Multicoloured.

3211 35 b. Type **548** 25 15
3212 35 b. Orimulsion storage tanks 25 15
3213 35 b. Coal 25 15
3214 35 b. Lorry carrying sacks . . 25 15
3215 35 b. Petrol station 25 15
3216 35 b. Gas storage cylinders . 25 15
3217 80 b. Drilling for oil 60 30
3218 80 b. Refinery 60 30
3219 100 b. Emblems ("Lagoven" at top) 75 40
3220 100 b. Emblems ("bitor" at top) 75 40

549 Pope John Paul II with Children

1996. Papal Visit. Multicoloured.

3221 25 b. Type **549** 20 10
3222 25 b. Pope with young couple 20 10
3223 40 b. Pope with family . . . 30 15
3224 40 b. Pope with elderly man . 30 15
3225 50 b. Pope with mother and son 35 20
3226 50 b. Pope with patient . . . 35 20
3227 60 b. Pope with prisoner . . . 45 25
3228 60 b. Pope with workman . . 45 25
3229 100 b. Pope giving speech to workers 75 40
3230 100 b. Pope with priest and nuns 75 40

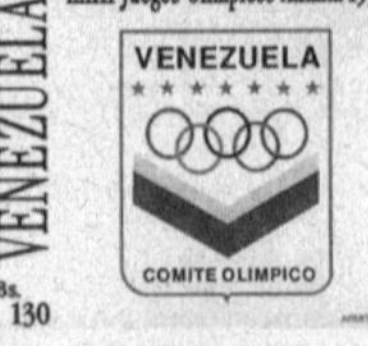

550 "Epidendrum fimbriatum"

1996. Orchids. Multicoloured.

3232 60 b. Type **550** 45 25
3233 60 b. "Myoxanthus reymondii" 45 25
3234 60 b. "Catasetum pileatum" . 45 25
3235 60 b. "Ponthieva maculata" . 45 25
3236 60 b. "Maxillaria triloris" . . 45 25
3237 60 b. "Scaphosepalum breve" 45 25
3238 60 b. "Cleistes rosea" . . . 45 25
3239 60 b. "Maxillaria sophronitis" 45 25
3240 60 b. "Catasetum discolor" . 45 25
3241 60 b. "Oncidium ampliatum" . 45 25

551 National Olympic Committee Emblem

1996. Olympic Games, Atlanta. Multicoloured.

3243 130 b. Type **551** 95 50
3244 130 b. Swimming 95 50
3245 130 b. Boxing 95 50
3246 130 b. Cycling 95 50
3247 130 b. Medal winners on podium 95 50

552 Emblem

1996. 25th Anniv of Liberator Simon Bolivar International Airport, Maiquetia, as Autonomous Company. Multicoloured.

3248 80 b. Type **552** 60 30
3249 80 b. Flight paths into airport 60 30
3250 80 b. La Guaira Aerodrome, 1929 . . . . 60 30
3251 80 b. Maiquetia Airport, 1944 60 30
3252 80 b. Liberator Simon Bolivar Airport, 1972 . . . . . . 60 30
3253 80 b. Airport interior by Carlos Cruz Diez 60 30
3254 80 b. Control tower and airport police 60 30
3255 80 b. Fire tender 60 30
3256 80 b. Airplanes at terminal building 60 30
3257 80 b. Boeing 747 airliner and terminal buildings 60 30

Nos. 3248/57 were issued together, se-tenant, Nos. 3256/7 formning a composite design.

EXPRESS LETTER STAMPS

E 119 E 194

1949.

E809 E **119** 30 c. lake 30 25

1961.

E1691 E **194** 30 c. orange 50 25

OFFICIAL STAMPS

O 17

1898.

O174 O **17** 5 c. black and green . 30 50
O175 10 c. black and red . . 60 65
O176 25 c. black and blue . 85 90
O177 50 c. black and yellow 1·60 1·60
O178 1 b. black and mauve . 1·60 1·50

1899. Surch **1899** and new value.

O187 O **17** 5 c. on 50 c. black and yellow . . . . . . 3·00 2·75
O188 5 c. on 1 b. black and mauve . . . . . . 11·50 10·50
O189 25 c. on 50 c. black and yellow . . . . . . 11·50 10·50
O190 25 c. on 1 b. black and mauve . . . . . . 6·75 6·25

1900. Optd **1900** in upper corners.

MINIMUM PRICE

The minimum price quoted is 10p which represents a handling charge rather than a basis for valuing common stamps. For further notes about prices, see introductory pages.

O222	O **17**	5 c. black and green .	35	35
O223		10 c. black and red . .	45	45
O224		25 c. black and blue .	45	45
O225		50 c. black and yellow	50	50
O226		1 b. black and mauve .	55	55

O **40** With Stars

O **41** Without Stars

1904.

O325	O **40**	5 c. black and green .	25	25
O326		10 c. black and red . .	50	50
O327		25 c. black and blue .	50	50
O328		50 c. black and red . .	2·10	1·90
O329		1 b. black and lake . .	1·00	90

1912.

O354	O **41**	5 c. black and green .	15	25
O355		10 c. black and red . .	15	25
O356		25 c. black and blue .	15	25
O357		50 c. black and violet .	20	35
O358		1 b. black and yellow .	40	35

REGISTRATION STAMPS

R **19** Bolivar

1899.

R186	R **19**	25 c. brown	2·10	1·60

1899. Optd with T **21**.

R205	R **19**	25 c. brown	1·25	1·25

VIETNAM Pt. 21

A. DEMOCRATIC REPUBLIC

The Democratic Republic was proclaimed by the Viet Minh Nationalists on 2 September 1945 and recognised by France on 6 March, 1946, as a free state within the Indo-China Federation. It consisted of Tongking, Annam and Cochin-China.

1945. 100 cents = 1 piastre.
1945. 100 xu = 10 hao = 1 dong.

Stamps of Indo-China overprinted.

VIET-NAM
DAN-CHU CONG-HOA
DOC-LAP
TU-DO HANH-PHUC
BUU-CHINH III
(1)

("DAN-CHU CONG-HOA" = Democratic Republic; "DOC-LAP TU-DO HANH-PHUC = Independence, Freedom, Happiness; "BUU-CHINH" = Postage.)

1945. Independence. Variously optd as T **1** (all with **DOC-LAP TU-DO HANH-PHUC** in opt).

No.	Type	Description	Unused	Used
1	**53**	1 c. brown	40	40
2	–	2 c. mauve (No. 315)	25	25
3	–	3 c. brown (Courbet)	25	25
4	–	4 c. brown (No. 316)	25	25
5	–	5 c. sepia (De Genouilly)	35	35
6	–	6 c. red (No. 304)	35	35
7	–	6 c. red (No. 305)	60	60
8	–	10 c. green (No. 307)	60	60
9	–	10 c. green (No. 322)	40	40
10	–	20 c. red (No. 309)	75	75
11	**64**	40 c. blue	35	35
12	–	$1 green (No. 311)	75	75

Nos. 3 and 5 were not issued without opt and are as Nos. 304 and 305 of Indo-China respectively.

1945. Variously optd as follows:—(a) **VIET-NAM DAN-CHU CONG-HOA**.

No.	Type	Description	Unused	Used
13	**69**	10 c. purple and yellow	1·50	1·25
14	–	15 c. purple (No. 292)	25	25
15	–	30 c. brown (No. 294)	40	40
16	**69**	50 c. red	3·75	3·75
17	–	$1 green (No. 295)	25	25

(b) **VIET-NAM DAN-CHU CONG-HOA BUU-CHINH**.

No.	Type	Description	Unused	Used
18	**53**	3 c. brown	40	40
19	–	4 c. yellow (No. 317)	40	40
20	**53**	6 c. red	40	40
21		10 c. green	75	75
22	–	10 c. green (No. 320)	70	70
23	–	20 c. red (Pavie)	35	35
24	**53**	40 c. blue	50	50
25		40 c. grey	1·25	1·25

No. 23 was not issued without opt and is as No. 320 of Indo-China.

VIET-NAM
DAN-CHU
3$00 CONG-HOA
CUU-DOI
(2)

("CUU-DOI" = Famine Relief.)

1945. Famine Relief. Surch as T **2**.

No.	Type	Description	Unused	Used
26	**70**	"2 $00" on 15 c.+ 60 c. purple	5·00	5·00
27		"3 $00" on 40 c.+ $1.10 c. blue	5·00	5·00

1945. War Wounded. Surch as T **2** but with **Binh-si Binan** (= Fund for War Wounded).

No.	Type	Description	Unused	Used
28	**70**	"5 $00" on 15 c.+ 60 c. purple	7·00	7·00

1945. Surch in new currency and variously optd as before (except Nos. 43/7). (a) **VIET-NAM DAN-CHU CONG-HOA BUU-CHINH**.

No.	Type	Description	Unused	Used
29	**64**	30 x. on 1 c. brown	40	40
30	–	30 x. on 15 c. purple (Garnier)	35	35
31	**67**	50 x. on 1 c. brown	75	75
32	–	60 x. on 1 c. brown (313)	70	70
33	–	1 d. on 5 c. brown (303)	1·50	1·50
34	–	1 d. 60 x. on 10 c. green (319)	40	40
35	**64**	3 d. on 15 c. purple	75	75
36	**67**	3 d. on 15 c. purple	1·00	1·00
37	–	4 d. on 1 c. brown (302)	50	50
38	–	5 d. on 1 c. brown (301)	90	90

(b) **VIET-NAM DAN-CHU CONG-HOA**.

No.	Type	Description	Unused	Used
39	–	1 d. on 5 c. purple (318)	50	50
40	**49**	2 d. on 3 c. brown	7·50	7·50
41	–	2 d. on 10 c. green (321)	75	75
42	**49**	4 d. on 6 c. red	7·50	7·50

(c) Surch only.

No.	Type	Description	Unused	Used
43	**56**	50 x. on 1 c. brown	60	60
44		2 d. on 6 c. red	5·00	5·00
45	**48**	5 d. on 1 c. orange	7·50	7·50
46		10 d. on 6 c. violet	8·75	8·75
47		15 d. on 25 c. blue	8·75	8·75

No. 30 was not issued without opt and is as No. 301 of Indo-China.

OVERPRINT. Nos. 48/55 are all optd **VIET-NAM DAN-CHU CONG-HOA** with varying additional words as noted in headings.

1945. National Defence (**Quoc-Phong**).

No.	Type	Description	Unused	Used
48	**49**	"+ 5 d." on 3 c. brown	1·25	1·50
49		"+ 10 d." on 6 c. red	1·25	1·50

1946. People's Livelihood. (**DAN SINH**).

No.	Type	Description	Unused	Used
50	**57**	"30 xu. + 3 d." on 6 c. red	65	65
51	**55**	"30 xu. + 3 d." on 6 c. red	65	65

1946. Campaign against Illiteracy (**Chong nan mu chu**).

No.	Type	Description	Unused	Used
52	**59**	"+ 4 dong" on 6 c. red	75	75

1946. New Life Movement (**Doi song moi**).

No.	Type	Description	Unused	Used
53	**66**	"+ 4 dong" on 6 c. red	1·50	1·50

1946. Child Welfare (**Bao-Anh**).

No.	Type	Description	Unused	Used
54	–	"+ 2 dong" on 6 c. red (290)	75	75

1946. War Wounded (**Binh si bi nan**).

No.	Type	Description	Unused	Used
55	–	"+ 3 dong" on 20 c. red (293)	1·50	1·25

Definitive issues.

3 Ho Chi Minh

1946.

No.	Type	Description	Unused	Used
56	**3**	1 h. green	40	40
57		3 h. red	40	40
58		9 h. yellow	40	40

1946. National Defence.

No.	Type	Description	Unused	Used
59	**3**	4 + 6 h. blue	75	75
60		6 + 9 h. brown	75	75

The Viet-Minh Government was at war with the French from 19 December 1946, until July 1954, and the stamps issued by the Democratic Republic in this period are listed as North Viet-Nam Nos. N1/13, NO 1/9 and ND 1/4.

B. INDEPENDENT STATE

On 14 June 1949, Vietnam, comprising Tongking, Annam and Cochin-China, became an independent state within the French Union under Emperor Bao-Dai. Until the 1951 issue Indo-Chinese stamps continued in use.

By the Geneva Declaration of 21 July 1954, Vietnam was partitioned near the 17th Parallel, and all authority of Bao-Dai's Government north of that line ended. Later issues are therefore those of SOUTH VIETNAM and NORTH VIETNAM.

100 cents = 1 piastre

4 Bongour Falls, Dalat

1951.

No.	Type	Description	Unused	Used
61	**4**	10 c. bronze	10	10
62	–	20 c. purple	20	10
63	–	30 c. blue	25	10
64	–	50 c. red	50	20
65	**4**	60 c. sepia	25	10
66	–	1 p. brown	25	10
67	–	1 p. 20 brown	1·90	1·25
68	–	2 p. violet	60	20
69	–	3 p. blue	1·90	25
70	**4**	5 p. green	1·40	35
71	–	10 p. red	3·50	65
72	–	15 p. brown	11·50	3·25
73	–	30 p. green	25·00	4·50

DESIGNS—HORIZ: 20 c., 2 p., 10 p. Imperial Palace, Hue; 30 c., 15 p. Small Lake, Hanoi; 50 c., 1 p. Temple of Remembrance, Saigon. VERT: 1 p. 20, 3 p., 30 p. Emperor Bao Dai.

9

1952. Air.

No.	Type	Description	Unused	Used
74	**9**	3 p. 30 green and lake	45	35
75		4 p. yellow and brown	70	25
76		5 p. 10 pink and blue	60	55
77	–	6 p. 30 red and yellow (symbolic of airlines)	75	65

10 Empress Nam Phuong

11 Globe and Lightning

1952.

No.	Type	Description	Unused	Used
78	**10**	30 c. brown, yellow & purple	30	40
79		50 c. brown, yellow & blue	60	40
80		1 p. 50 brown, yell & olive	1·25	40

1952. 1st Anniv of Admission of Vietnam into I.T.U.

No.	Type	Description	Unused	Used
81	**11**	1 p. blue	3·75	1·90

12 Dragon

1952. Air. Day of Wandering Souls.

No.	Type	Description	Unused	Used
82	**12**	40 c. red	1·00	65
83		70 c. green	1·00	65
84		80 c. blue	1·00	65
85		90 c. brown	1·00	80
86	–	3 p. 70 purple	1·40	90

DESIGN—VERT: 3 p. 70, Dragon.

13 U.P.U. Monument, Berne, and Coastline

1952. 1st Anniv of Admission of Vietnam into U.P.U.

No.	Type	Description	Unused	Used
87	**13**	5 p. brown	4·75	1·25

1952. Red Cross. T **10** surch, with red cross and **+50 c.**

No.	Type	Description	Unused	Used
88	**10**	1 p. 50 + 50 c. brown, yellow and blue	4·50	4·50

15 Emperor Bao Dai and Gateway

1952. 40th Birthday of Emperor.

No.	Type	Description	Unused	Used
89	**15**	1 p. 50 purple	2·25	95

16 Sabres and Flag

17 Crown Prince Bao Long

1952. Wounded Soldiers' Relief Fund.

No.	Type	Description	Unused	Used
90	**16**	3 p. 30 + 1 p. 70 lake	1·60	1·60

1959.

No.	Type	Description	Unused	Used
91	**17**	40 c. turquoise	50	50
92		70 c. lake	60	60
93		80 c. sepia	75	75
94	–	90 c. green	1·75	1·75
95	–	20 p. red	3·75	3·75
96	–	50 p. violet	8·00	8·00
97	**17**	100 p. blue	17·00	17·00

PORTRAIT: 90 c. to 50 p. Crown Prince in uniform.

POSTAGE DUE STAMPS

D 10 Dragon

1952.

No.	Type	Description	Unused	Used
D78	**D 10**	10 c. green and red	20	10
D79		20 c. yellow and green	35	10
D80		30 c. orange and violet	35	10
D81		40 c. pink and green	40	15
D82		50 c. grey and lake	70	25
D83		1 p. silver and blue	1·00	35

C. SOUTH VIETNAM

100 cents = 1 piastre

INDEPENDENT STATE
(Within the French Union)

1 Turtle

1955. 1st Anniv of Govt of Ngo Dinh Diem.

No.	Type	Description	Unused	Used
S1	**1**	30 c. purple	75	25
S2		50 c. green	2·75	90
S3		1 p. 50 blue	1·25	40

2 Phoenix

1955. Air.

No.	Type	Description	Unused	Used
S4	**2**	4 p. mauve and violet	1·00	25

3 Refugees

1955. 1st Anniv of Arrival of Refugees from North Vietnam.

No.	Type	Description	Unused	Used
S 5	**3**	70 c. red	65	40
S 6		80 c. purple	1·50	85
S 7		10 p. blue	2·75	1·60
S 8		20 p. brown, orange & vio	5·50	2·25
S 9		35 p. sepia, yellow & blue	11·00	8·75
S10		100 p. purple, orge & grn	25·00	14·50

No. S9 is inscribed "CHIEN-DICH-HUYNE-DE" in margin at foot. See also No. S26.

REPUBLIC
(from 26th October, 1955)

4 G.P.O., Saigon

5 Pres. Ngo Dinh Diem

1956. 5th Anniv of Entry of Vietnam into U.P.U.

No.	Type	Description	Unused	Used
S11	**4**	60 c. green	55	40
S12		90 c. violet	1·75	65
S13		3 p. brown	3·00	90

1956.

No.	Type	Description	Unused	Used
S14	**5**	20 c. brown	10	10
S15		30 c. purple	20	20
S16		50 c. red	10	10
S17		1 p. violet	30	15
S18		1 p. 50 violet	50	15
S19		3 p. sepia	50	15
S20		4 p. blue	70	20
S21		5 p. brown	95	20
S22		10 p. blue	1·25	40
S23		20 p. black	3·25	70
S24		35 p. green	8·50	1·60
S25		100 p. brown	18·00	6·25

1956. No. S9 with bottom marginal inscription obliterated by bar.

No.	Type	Description	Unused	Used
S26	**3**	35 p. sepia, yellow & blue	4·75	3·25

1956. Optd **Cong-thu Buu-dien** (= "Government Postal Building").

No.	Type	Description	Unused	Used
S27	**4**	60 c. green	85	50
S28		90 c. violet	1·50	50
S29		3 p. brown	2·25	75

7 Bamboo

8 Refugee Children

1956. 1st Anniv of Republic.

No.	Type	Description	Unused	Used
S30	**7**	50 c. red	30	10
S31		1 p. 50 purple	65	10
S32		2 p. green	85	10
S33		4 p. blue	2·10	20

1956. United Nations "Operation Brotherhood".

No.	Type	Description	Unused	Used
S34	**8**	1 p. mauve	30	10
S35		2 p. turquoise	40	15
S36		6 p. violet	75	15
S37		35 p. blue	4·25	1·00

9 Hunters on Elephants

10 Ship's Cargo being offloaded at Saigon

1957. 3rd Anniv of Govt of Ngo Dinh Diem.

S38	9	20 c. purple and green	30	10
S39		30 c. red and bistre	40	10
S40	–	90 c. sepia and green	50	20
S41	–	2 p. blue and green	85	25
S42	–	3 p. brown and violet	1·25	40

DESIGN—VERT: 90 c. to 3 p. Mountain hut.

1957. 9th Colombo Plan Conference, Saigon.

S43	10	20 c. purple	15	10
S44		40 c. olive	20	15
S45		50 c. red	35	15
S46		2 p. blue	60	25
S47		3 p. green	90	30

11 Torch and Constitution

12 Youth felling Tree

1957. Inauguration of National Assembly.

S48	11	50 c. salmon, green & blk	10	10
S49		80 c. purple, blue & black	20	10
S50		1 p. red, green and black	25	15
S51		4 p. brown, myrtle & blk	45	20
S52		5 p. olive, turq and black	60	30
S53		10 p. brown, blue and black	1·00	60

1958. Better Living Standards.

S54	12	50 c. green	25	20
S55		1 p. violet	35	20
S56		2 p. blue	45	20
S57		10 p. red	1·10	50

13 Young Girl with Chinese Lantern

14

1958. Children's Festival.

S58	13	30 c. lemon	20	20
S59		50 c. red	20	20
S60		2 p. red	20	20
S61		3 p. green	50	25
S62		4 p. olive	60	25

1958. United Nations Day.

S63	14	1 p. light brown	25	20
S64		2 p. turquoise	35	20
S65		4 p. red	40	20
S66		5 p. purple	90	40

15 U.N.E.S.C.O. Emblem and Building

16 U.N. Emblem and "Torch of Freedom"

1958. Inauguration of U.N.E.S.C.O. Headquarters Building, Paris.

S67	15	50 c. blue	20	20
S68		2 p. red	25	20
S69		3 p. purple	40	20
S70		6 p. violet	70	40

1958. 10th Anniv of Declaration of Human Rights.

S71	16	50 c. blue	30	15
S72		1 p. lake	40	20
S73		2 p. green	60	20
S74		6 p. purple	95	45

MINIMUM PRICE

The minimum price quoted is 10p which represents a handling charge rather than a basis for valuing common stamps. For further notes about prices, see introductory pages.

17 PhuCam Cathedral

18 Saigon Museum

1958.

S75	17	10 c. slate	20	10
S76	–	30 c. green	30	20
S77	18	40 c. green	15	15
S78	–	50 c. green	25	15
S79	–	2 p. blue	40	20
S80	–	4 p. lilac	40	25
S81	18	5 p. red	55	25
S82	17	6 p. brown	65	25

DESIGNS—HORIZ: 30 c., 4 p. Thien Mu Pagoda; 50 c., 2 p. Palace of Independence, Saigon.

19 Trung Sisters (national heroines) on Elephants

1959. Trung Sisters Commemoration.

S83	19	50 c. multicoloured	80	55
S84		2 p. multicoloured	1·25	75
S85		3 p. multicoloured	2·40	1·10
S86		6 p. multicoloured	3·00	1·60

20

21 Diesel Train

1959. Agricultural Reform.

S87	20	70 c. purple	15	10
S88		2 p. green and blue	15	10
S89		3 p. olive	30	10
S90		6 p. red and deep red	65	40

1959. Re-opening of Trans-Vietnam Railway. Centres in green.

S91	21	1 p. violet	50	20
S92		2 p. grey	70	40
S93		3 p. blue	80	30
S94		4 p. lake	1·60	50

22 Tilling the Land

25 Scout climbing Mountain

1959. 4th Anniv of Republic.

S95	22	1 p. brown, green & blue	30	20
S96		2 p. violet, green & orge	30	20
S97		4 p. indigo, blue & bistre	75	35
S98		5 p. brown, olive and light brown	95	50

1959. 1st National Scout Jamboree, Trang Bom.

S 99	25	3 p. green	45	20
S100		4 p. mauve	60	25
S101		8 p. mauve and purple	1·40	50
S102		20 p. dp turq & turq	3·00	1·25

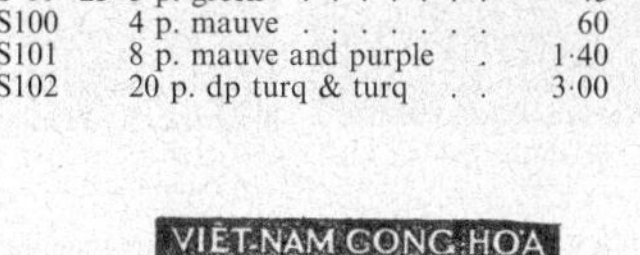

26 "Family Code"

1960. 1st Anniv of Family Code.

S103	26	20 c. green	15	10
S104		30 c. blue	25	15
S105		2 p. red and orange	25	15
S106		6 p. violet and red	60	30

27 Refugee Family in Flight

28 Henri Dunant

1960. World Refugee Year.

S107	27	50 c. mauve	35	10
S108		3 p. green	30	15
S109		4 p. red	70	30
S110		5 p. violet	80	40

1960. Red Cross Day. Cross in red.

S111	28	1 p. blue	45	20
S112		3 p. green	55	25
S113		4 p. red	85	35
S114		6 p. mauve	1·00	55

29 Co-operative Farm

1960. Establishment of Co-operative Rice Farming.

S115	29	50 c. blue	20	15
S116		1 p. green	20	15
S117		3 p. orange	50	25
S118		7 p. mauve	90	25

30 X-ray Camera and Patient

31 Flag and Map

1960. National T.B. Relief Campaign Day.

S119	30	3 p.+ 50 c. green & red	60	60

1960. 5th Anniv of Republic. Flag and map in red and yellow.

S120	31	50 c. turquoise	15	10
S121		1 p. blue	20	10
S122		3 p. violet	35	10
S123		7 p. green	55	25

32 Woman with Rice

1960. F.A.O. Regional Conference, Saigon.

S124	32	2 p. turquoise and green	45	25
S125		4 p. ultramarine and blue	65	40

33 Crane carrying Letter

1960. Air.

S126	33	1 p. green	50	20
S127		4 p. blue and turquoise	75	40
S128		5 p. violet and brown	1·25	65
S129		10 p. mauve	2·25	1·00

34 Farm Tractor

35 Child and Plant

1961. Agricultural Development and Pres. Diem's 60th Birthday.

S130	34	50 c. brown	20	10
S131		70 c. mauve	25	10
S132		80 c. red	25	20
S133		10 p. mauve	80	35

1961. Child Welfare.

S134	35	70 c. blue	20	10
S135		80 c. blue	20	10
S136		4 p. bistre	35	20
S137		7 p. green and turquoise	75	40

36 Pres. Ngo Dinh Diem

37 Young People and Torch

1961. 2nd Term of President.

S138	36	50 c. blue	25	20
S139		1 p. red	40	20
S140		2 p. purple	50	20
S141		4 p. violet	95	35

1961. Sports and Youth.

S142	37	50 c. red	15	10
S143		70 c. mauve	25	10
S144		80 c. mauve and red	35	20
S145		8 p. purple and red	75	35

38 Bridge over Mekong

1961. Inaug of Saigon–Bien Hoa Motor Highway.

S146	38	50 c. green	25	15
S147		1 p. brown	25	15
S148		2 p. blue	35	20
S149		5 p. purple	60	25

39 Alexander of Rhodes

40 Vietnamese with Torch

1961. Death Tercent of Alexander of Rhodes.

S150	39	50 c. red	20	10
S151		1 p. purple	20	10
S152		3 p. bistre	30	10
S153		6 p. green	70	25

1961. Youth Moral Rearmament.

S154	40	50 c. red	15	10
S155		1 p. green	20	10
S156		3 p. red	35	20
S157		8 p. brown and purple	70	25

41 Gateway of Van Mieu Temple, Hanoi

42 Tractor and Cottages

1961. 15th Anniv of U.N.E.S.C.O.

S158	41	1 p. green	25	10
S159		2 p. red	25	20
S160		5 p. olive	50	25

1961. Rural Reform.

S161	42	50 c. green	20	10
S162		1 p. lake and blue	20	20
S163		2 p. brown and green	25	20
S164		10 p. turquoise	70	45

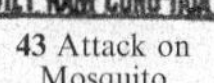

43 Attack on Mosquito

44 Postal Cheque Building, Saigon

1962. Malaria Eradication.

S165	43	50 c. mauve	25	10
S166		1 p. orange	25	15
S167		2 p. green	35	20
S168		6 p. blue	75	25

1962. Inauguration of Postal Cheques Service.

S169	44	70 c. green	25	20
S170		80 c. brown	25	20
S171		4 p. purple	50	20
S172		7 p. red	60	40

45 St. Mary of La Vang **46** Armed Guards and Fortified Village

1962. St. Mary of La Vang Commemoration.

No.	Type	Description		
S173	45	50 c. red and violet	20	10
S174		1 p. blue and brown	25	15
S175		2 p. lake and brown	40	15
S176		8 p. blue and turquoise	90	35

1962. Strategic Villages.

No.	Type	Description		
S177	46	50 c. red	20	10
S178		1 p. bronze	20	15
S179		1 p. 50 purple	35	15
S180		7 p. blue	60	30

47 Gougah Waterfalls, Dalat **48** Trung Sisters Monument

1963. Pres. Ngo Dinh Diem's 62nd Birthday and Spring Festival.

No.	Type	Description		
S181	47	60 c. red	20	15
S182		1 p. blue	35	15

1963. Women's Day.

No.	Type	Description		
S183	48	50 c. green	20	10
S184		1 p. red	25	15
S185		3 p. purple	30	20
S186		8 p. blue	60	40

49 Harvester

1963. Freedom from Hunger.

No.	Type	Description		
S187	49	50 c. red	20	10
S188		1 p. red	25	15
S189		3 p. purple	35	20
S190		5 p. violet	60	35

50 Sword and Fortress **51** Soldier and Emblem

1963. Communal Defence and 9th Anniv of Inaug of Pres. Diem.

No.	Type	Description		
S191	50	30 c. bistre	20	10
S192		50 c. mauve	25	15
S193		3 p. green	45	20
S194		8 p. red	70	35

1963. Republican Combatants.

No.	Type	Description		
S195	51	50 c. red	15	10
S196		1 p. green	20	15
S197		4 p. violet	40	20
S198		5 p. orange	65	45

52 Centenary Emblem and Globe **53** Scales of Justice and Book

1963. Red Cross Centenary. Cross in red.

No.	Type	Description		
S199	52	50 c. blue	25	10
S200		1 p. red	35	20
S201		3 p. orange	45	20
S202		6 p. brown	80	45

1963. 15th Anniv of Declaration of Human Rights.

No.	Type	Description		
S203	53	70 c. orange	20	10
S204		1 p. mauve	25	15
S205		3 p. green	35	15
S206		8 p. ochre	75	35

54 Danhim Hydro-Electric Station

1964. Inauguration of Danhim Hydro-Electric Station.

No.	Type	Description		
S207	54	40 c. red	15	10
S208		1 p. brown	25	15
S209		3 p. violet	35	20
S210		8 p. green	65	35

55 Atomic Reactor

1964. Peaceful Uses of Atomic Energy.

No.	Type	Description		
S211	55	80 c. olive	20	10
S212		1 p. 50 brown	25	20
S213		3 p. brown	45	20
S214		7 p. blue	70	40

56 "Meteorology" **57** "Unification"

1964. World Meteorological Day.

No.	Type	Description		
S215	56	50 c. ochre	20	10
S216		1 p. red	25	20
S217		1 p. 50 lake	35	20
S218		10 p. green	65	40

1964. 10th Anniv of Partition of Vietnam.

No.	Type	Description		
S219	57	30 c. blue and green	15	15
S220		50 c. blue, red & yellow	20	15
S221		1 p. 50 indigo, bl & orge	25	15

58 Hatien Beach

1964.

No.	Type	Description		
S222	58	20 c. blue	20	10
S223		3 p. green	40	15

59 "Support of the People"

1964. 1st Anniv of Revolution of 1 November 1963.

No.	Type	Description		
S224	59	50 c. blue and purple	25	10
S225	–	80 c. brown and lilac	30	20
S226	–	3 p. brown and blue	50	20

DESIGNS—HORIZ: 80 c. Soldier breaking chain. VERT: 3 p. Allegory of Revolution.

60 Temple and Monument, Botanic Gardens, Saigon

1964. Monuments and Views.

No.	Type	Description		
S227	60	50 c. brown, green & bl	20	15
S228	–	1 p. slate and bistre	25	15
S229	–	1 p. 50 green and drab	40	20
S230	–	3 p. red, green & violet	75	25

DESIGNS: 1 p. Tomb of Minh Mang, Hue; 1 p. 50, Phan Thiet waterfront; 3 p. General Le Van Duyet Temple, Gia Dinh.

For 1 p. in smaller size, see No. S352.

61 Face of Bronze Drum

1965. Hung Vuong (legendary founder of Vietnam, 2000 B.C.).

No.	Type	Description		
S231	61	3 p. orange and lake	1·90	65
S232		100 p. violet and purple	12·00	6·50

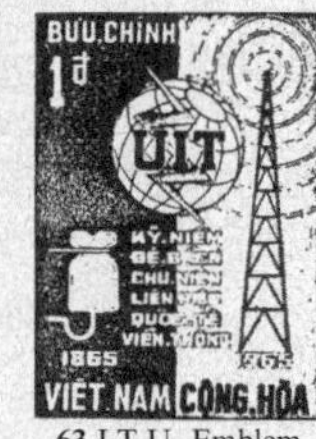

62 Dharmachakra and "Fire of Clemency" **63** I.T.U. Emblem and Symbols

1965. Buddhism.

No.	Type	Description		
S233	62	50 c. red	20	15
S234	–	1 p. 50 orange, blue & deep blue	20	15
S235	–	3 p. deep brown, sepia and brown	40	20

DESIGNS—HORIZ: 1 p. 50, Dharmachakra, lotus and globe. VERT: 3 p. Dharmachakra and flag.

1965. I.T.U. Centenary.

No.	Type	Description		
S236	63	1 p. red and bistre	25	20
S237		3 p. red, mauve & brown	40	20

64 "World Solidarity" **65** Ixora

1965. International Co-operation Year.

No.	Type	Description		
S238	64	50 c. blue and brown	20	15
S239		1 p. sepia and brown	25	15
S240		1 p. 50 red and grey	35	15

1965. Mid-Autumn Festival.

No.	Type	Description		
S241	65	70 c. red, green & dp green	20	15
S242	–	80 c. purple, grn & mve	30	20
S243	–	1 p. yellow, blue and deep blue	50	25
S244	–	1 p. 50 green and olive	60	25
S245	–	3 p. orange and green	80	40

FLOWERS—VERT: 80 c. Orchid; 1 p. Chrysanthemum; 3 p. "Ochna harmandii". HORIZ: 1 p. 50, Nenuphar.

66 Student and University Building

1965. Re-opening of Vietnam University.

No.	Type	Description		
S246	66	50 c. brown	20	15
S247		1 p. green	25	20
S248		3 p. red	40	20
S249		7 p. violet	45	25

67 Young Farmers

1965. 10th Anniv of "4-T" Rural Youth Clubs.

No.	Type	Description		
S250	67	3 p. red and green	50	25
S251	–	4 p. violet, blue & purple	50	25

DESIGN: 4 p. Young farmer and club banner.

68 Basketball **69** Aerial Mast and Equipment

1965. 3rd S.E. Asia Peninsular Games, Kuala Lumpur (Malaysia).

No.	Type	Description		
S252	68	50 c. bistre, brown and red	35	10
S253	–	1 p. red and brown	40	20
S254	–	1 p. 50 green	55	25
S255	–	10 p. lake and purple	1·50	60

DESIGNS: 1 p. Throwing the javelin; 1 p. 50, "Physical Culture" (gymnasts and Olympic Games' symbols); 10 p. Pole-vaulting.

1966. 1st Anniv of Saigon Microwave Station.

No.	Type	Description		
S256	69	3 p. sepia, blue & brown	25	15
S257	–	4 p. purple, red & green	40	20

DESIGN: 4 p. Aerial mast, telephone dial and map.

70 Hook and Hemispheres **71** Help for Refugees

1966. "Free World's Aid to Vietnam".

No.	Type	Description		
S258	70	3 p. red and grey	20	10
S259		4 p. violet and brown	25	15
S260		6 p. blue and green	35	20

1966. Refugee Aid.

No.	Type	Description		
S261	71	3 p. olive, mauve & brn	25	15
S262		7 p. vio, brown & mve	40	20

72 Paper "Soldiers"

1966. Wandering Souls' Festival.

No.	Type	Description		
S263	72	50 c. bistre, brown & red	20	10
S264	–	1 p. 50 red, green & brn	30	15
S265	–	3 p. vermilion, crim & red	50	20
S266	–	5 p. brown, ochre and deep brown	65	25

DESIGNS: 1 p. 50, Obeisance; 3 p. Pool of candles; 5 p. Votive offering.

73 "Violinist"

1966. Ancient Musical Instruments.

No.	Type	Description		
S267	73	1 p. deep brown, mauve and brown	20	10
S268	–	3 p. violet and purple	25	15
S269	–	4 p. brown and red	40	20
S270	–	7 p. deep blue and blue	75	30

DESIGNS: 3 p. "Harpist"; 4 p. Small band; 7 p. "Flautists".

For 3 p. in smaller size, see No. S302.

74 W.H.O. Building

1966. Inaug of W.H.O. Headquarters, Geneva.

No.	Type	Description		
S271	74	50 c. pur, violet & red	20	10
S272	–	1 p. 50 black, blue & lake	25	15
S273	–	8 p. blue, sepia & turq	40	20

DESIGNS—VERT: 1 p. 50, W.H.O. Building and flag; 8 p. U.N. flag and W.H.O. Building.

75 Spade in Hand, and Soldiers

1966. 3rd Anniv of Overthrow of Diem Government.

No.	Type	Description		
S274	75	80 c. brown and bistre	20	10
S275	–	1 p. 50 purple, red & yell	20	15
S276	–	3 p. grn, brown & chest	25	20
S277	–	4 p. lake, black & purple	65	35

DESIGNS—HORIZ: 1 p. 50, Agricultural workers, soldier and flag. VERT: 3 p. Soldier, tractor and labourers; 4 p. Soldier and horseman.

76 U.N.E.S.C.O. Emblem and Tree **77** Cashew Apples

1966. 20th Anniv of U.N.E.S.C.O.

S278 **76** 1 p. brown and lake 20 10

S279 – 3 p. brown, turq & blue 25 20

S280 – 7 p. blue, turquoise & red 65 30

DESIGNS—VERT: 3 p. Globe and laurel sprigs. HORIZ: 7 p. Pagoda.

1967. Exotic Fruits.

S281 **77** 50 c. red, green & blue 30 10

S282 – 1 p. 50 orange, grn & brn 30 15

S283 – 3 p. brown, green & choc 45 20

S284 – 20 p. olive, green & lake 1·50 65

FRUITS—HORIZ: 1 p. 50, Bitter "cucumbers"; 3 p. Cinnamon apples; 20 p. Areca-nuts.

78 Phan Boi Chau

1967. Vietnamese Patriots.

S285 **78** 1 p. purple, brown & red 25 10

S286 – 20 p. black, violet & grn 90 50

DESIGN: 20 p. Phan Chau-Trinh (portrait and making speech).

79 Horse-cab

1967. Life of the People.

S287 – 50 c. ultram, bl & grn 20 10

S288 – 1 p. violet, grn & myrtle 25 10

S289 **79** 3 p. lake and red 30 15

S290 – 8 p. violet and red 50 20

DESIGNS: 50 c. Itinerant merchant; 1 p. Market-place; 8 p. Pastoral activities.

80 Pottery-making

1967. Arts and Crafts. Multicoloured.

S291 50 c. Type **80** 20 10

S292 1 p. 50 Wicker basket and vase 25 20

S293 3 p. Weavers and potters 40 25

S294 35 p. Baskets and pottery 1·75 90

The 3 p. is a horiz design.

81 Wedding Procession

1967. Vietnamese Wedding.

S295 **81** 3 p. red, violet & purple 50 25

82 "Culture"

1967. Foundation of Vietnamese Cultural Institute.

S296 **82** 10 p. multicoloured 50 25

83 "Freedom and Justice"

1967. Democratic Elections. Multicoloured.

S297 4 p. Type **83** 30 20

S298 5 p. Vietnamese and hands casting votes 45 25

S299 30 p. Two Vietnamese with Constitution and flaming torch 1·25 65

84 Lions Emblem and Pagoda

1967. 50th Anniv of Lions International.

S300 **84** 3 p. multicoloured 75 40

85 Class on Globe

1967. World Literacy Day (8 Sept).

S301 **85** 3 p. multicoloured 55 15

1967. Mobile Post Office Inaug. As No. S268 but smaller size 23 × 17 mm.

S302 3 p. violet and purple 12·00 10·00

87 Tractor

1968. Rural Development. Multicoloured.

S303 1 p. Type **87** 30 20

S304 9 p. Bulldozer 35 20

S305 10 p. Workers with wheel-barrow and tractor 50 20

S306 20 p. Building construction 1·00 40

88 W.H.O. Emblem

1968. 20th Anniv of W.H.O.

S307 **88** 10 p. yellow, blk & grn 50 25

89 Flags of Allied Nations

1968. Thanks for International Aid. Mult.

S308 1 p. Handclasp, flags and soldiers 45 10

S309 1 p. 50 S.E.A.T.O. emblem and flags 50 20

S310 3 p. Handclasp and flags 70 25

S311 50 p. Type **89** 3·25 90

92 Farmers, Farm, Factory and Transport

93 Human Rights Emblem

1968. Development of Private Ownership. Multicoloured.

S318 80 c. Type **92** 20 10

S319 2 p. Motor vehicles and labourers 20 10

S320 10 p. Tractor and tri-car 40 20

S321 30 p. Motor vehicles and labourers 1·40 60

1968. Human Rights Year. Multicoloured.

S322 10 p. Type **93** 40 15

S323 16 p. Men of all races acclaiming Human Rights Emblem 55 25

94 Children with U.N.I.C.E.F. "Kite"

1968. U.N.I.C.E.F. Day. Multicoloured.

S324 6 p. Type **94** 45 20

S325 16 p. Mother and child 70 25

95 Diesel Train, Map and Mechanical Loader

97 Peasant Woman

1968. Re-opening of Trans-Vietnam Railway. Multicoloured.

S326 1 p. 50 Type **95** 40 20

S327 3 p. Type **95** 55 20

S328 9 p. Diesel train and permanent-way workers 1·00 30

S329 20 p. As No. S328 2·50 95

1969. Vietnamese Women.

S331 **97** 50 c. violet, ochre & blue 20 10

S332 – 1 p. brown and green 20 15

S333 – 3 p. black, blue & sepia 35 15

S334 – 20 p. multicoloured 70 40

DESIGNS—VERT: 1 p. Tradeswoman; 20 p. "Ladies of fashion". HORIZ: 3 p. Nurse.

98 Soldier and Militiaman

1969. "Open-arms" National Unity Campaign. Multicoloured.

S335 2 p. Type **98** 30 20

S336 50 p. Family welcoming soldier 1·25 50

99 Vietnamese and Scales of Justice

1969. 1st Anniv of New Constitution. Mult.

S337 1 p. Type **99** 25 10

S338 20 p. Voters at polling station 50 35

100 Mobile Post Office Van in Street

1969. Vietnamese Mobile Post Offices System. Multicoloured.

S339 1 p. Type **100** 25 10

S340 3 p. Clerk serving customers 25 15

S341 4 p. Child with letter, and mobile post office 35 20

S342 20 p. Queue at mobile post office, and postmark 60 40

101 Djarai Woman

1969. 2nd Anniv of Ethnic Minorities Statute. Multicoloured.

S343 1 p. Type **101** 45 25

S344 6 p. Mnong-gar woman 1·00 40

S345 50 p. Bahnar man 5·00 1·75

102 "Civilians to Soldiers"

1969. General Mobilisation.

S346 **102** 1 p. 50 multicoloured 15 10

S347 – 3 p. multicoloured 20 10

S348 – 5 p. brown, red & yellow 35 20

S349 – 10 p. multicoloured 40 25

DESIGNS: 3 p. Bayonet practice; 5 p. Recruits arriving at depot; 10 p. Happy conscripts.

103 I.L.O. Emblem and Globe

104 Imperial Palace, Hue

1969. 50th Anniv of I.L.O.

S350 **103** 6 p. black, grey & green 25 10

S351 20 p. black, grey & red 65 25

1970. Reconstruction of Hue.

S352 **104** 1 p. blue and brown 6·50 6·50

105 Asian Golden Weaver and Baya Weaver

1970. Birds of Vietnam. Multicoloured.

S353 2 p. Type **105** 45 20

S354 6 p. Chestnut mannikin 85 40

S355 7 p. Great Indian hornbill 1·25 65

S356 30 p. Tree sparrow 5·75 1·60

106 Ruined House and Family

1970. Aid for Victims of Communist Tet Offensive. Multicoloured.

S357 10 p. Type **106** 40 20

S358 20 p. Refugee family, and First Aid 55 30

107 Man, Woman and Priest in Traditional Costume

1970. Vietnamese Traditional Costumes. Multicoloured.

S359 1 p. Type **107** 25 10

S360 2 p. Seated woman (horiz) 25 10

S361 3 p. Three women with carved lion (horiz) 35 20

S362 100 p. Man and woman (horiz) 3·00 1·75

108 Builders and Pagoda

1970. Reconstruction of Hue. Multicoloured.

S363 6 p. Type **108** 45 25

S364 20 p. Mixing cement 85 40

109 Ploughing Paddyfield

1970. "Land to the Tiller" Agrarian Reform Law.

S365 **109** 6 p. black, green & brn 45 25

110 Scaffolding and New Building

1970. Reconstruction after Tet Offensive. Multicoloured.
S366 8 p. Type **110** 40 20
S367 16 p. Construction workers . 55 25

111 A.P.Y. Symbol

1970. Asian Productivity Year.
S368 **111** 10 p. multicoloured . . . 50 25

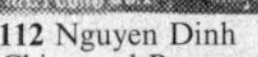
112 Nguyen Dinh Chieu and Poems

113 I.E.Y. Emblem

1970. Nguyen Dinh Chieu (poet) Commem.
S369 **112** 6 p. brown, red & violet 25 20
S370 10 p. brown, red & grn . 50 25

1970. International Education Year.
S371 **113** 10 p. black, yell & brn . 50 20

114 Senate House

115 Two Dancers

1970. 9th Council Meeting and 6th General Assembly of Asian Interparliamentary Union, Saigon. Multicoloured.
S372 6 p. Type **114** 25 20
S373 10 p. House of Representatives 50 20

1971. Vietnamese Traditional Dances.
S374 **115** 2 p. multicoloured . . . 30 10
S375 – 6 p. brown, blue & grn . 45 20
S376 – 7 p. red, blue & brown . 65 25
S377 – 10 p. multicoloured . . . 80 35
DESIGNS—HORIZ: 6 p. Drum dance; 7 p. Drum dancers in various positions. VERT: 10 p. Flower dance.

116 Paddyfield, Peasants and Agrarian Law

1971. 1st Anniv of "Land to the Tiller" Agrarian Reform Law. Multicoloured.
S378 2 p. Type **116** (dated "26.3.1971") 30 20
S378a 2 p. Type **116** (dated "26.3.1970") . . . . . .
S379 3 p. Tractor and Law . . . 30 20
S380 16 p. Peasants ringing Law . 45 25

117 Postal Courier

119 Hog-deer

118 Armed Forces on Map of Vietnam

1971. History of Vietnam Postal Service. Multicoloured.
S381 2 p. Type **117** 35 20
S382 6 p. Mounted courier with banner 75 30

1971. Armed Forces Day.
S383 **118** 3 p. multicoloured . . . 35 25
S384 40 p. multicoloured . . 1·60 70

1971. Vietnamese Fauna. Multicoloured.
S385 9 p. Type **119** 50 20
S386 30 p. Tiger . . . . 1·00 50

120 Rice Harvesters

1971. "The Rice Harvest".
S387 **120** 1 p. multicoloured . . . 25 10
S388 – 30 p. lilac, black & red . 75 25
S389 – 40 p. brown, yell & blue 1·00 45
DESIGNS: 30 p. Threshing and winnowing rice; 40 p. Harvesters in paddyfield.

121 New H.Q. Building

1971. New U.P.U. Headquarters Building, Berne.
S390 **121** 20 p. multicoloured . . 80 40

122 Ca Bong

123 "Local Delivery"

1971. Vietnam Fishes. Multicoloured.
S391 2 p. Type **122** 30 10
S392 10 p. Ca Nau (horiz) . . . 95 20
S393 100 p. Ca Ong Tien (horiz) . 6·75 2·75

1971. Development of Rural Post System. Multicoloured.
S394 5 p. Type **123** 30 15
S395 10 p. Symbolic crane . . . 60 25
S396 20 p. Cycle postman delivering letter 70 25

124 Fishermen in Boat, and Modern Trawler

1972. Vietnamese Fishing Industry. Multicoloured.
S397 4 p. Type **124** 35 25
S398 7 p. Fishermen hauling net . 35 25
S399 50 p. Trawl net . . . . . . 2·00 1·00

125 Emperor Quang Trung

126 Community Workers

1972. Emperor Quang Trung (victor of Dong Da) Commemoration.
S400 **125** 6 p. multicoloured . . . 25 10
S401 20 p. multicoloured . . . 65 30

1972. Community Development Projects.
S403 **126** 3 p. multicoloured . . . 15 10
S404 8 p. multicoloured . . . 25 10

127 Harvesting Rice

1972. Farmers' Day. Multicoloured.
S405 1 p. Type **127** 20 10
S406 10 p. Sowing rice 30 15

128 Boeing 727 over Dalat

1972. 20th Anniv of Viet-Nam Airlines. Mult.
S407 10 p. Type **128** 65 30
S408 10 p. Boeing 727 over Ha Tien 65 30
S409 10 p. Boeing 727 over Hue . 65 30
S410 10 p. Boeing 727 over Saigon 65 30
S411 25 p. Type **128** 95 65
S412 25 p. As No. S408 . . . . . 95 65
S413 25 p. As No. S409 . . . . . 95 65
S414 25 p. As No. S410 . . . . . 95 65

129 Vietnamese Scholar

130 Sentry

1972. Vietnamese Scholars. Multicoloured.
S415 5 p. Type **129** 20 10
S416 20 p. Scholar with pupils . . 45 25
S417 50 p. Scholar with scroll . . . 1·50 50

1972. Civilian Self-defence Force. Multicoloured.
S418 2 p. Type **130** 20 10
S419 6 p. Young volunteer and badge (horiz) 25 20
S420 20 p. Volunteers at rifle practice 50 35

131 Hands supporting Savings Bank

1972. Treasury Bonds Savings Scheme.
S421 **131** 10 p. multicoloured . . . 25 10
S422 25 p. multicoloured . . . 50 20

132 Three Guards with Horse

133 Wounded Soldier

1972. Traditional Vietnamese Frontier Guards. Multicoloured.
S423 10 p. Type **132** 35 20
S424 30 p. Pikeman (vert) 65 35
S425 40 p. Guards on parade . . . 95 50

1972. Vietnamese War Veterans. Multicoloured.
S426 9 p. Type **133** 15 10
S427 16 p. Soldier on crutches . . 40 20
S428 100 p. Veterans' memorial . . 3·00 1·10

134 Soldiers on Tank, and Memorial

1972. Victory at Binh Long. Mulicoloured.
S429 5 p. Type **134** 20 10
S430 10 p. Soldiers on map of An Loc (vert) 90 15

135 "Books for Everyone"

136 "200,000th Returnees"

1972. International Book Year. Multicoloured.
S431 2 p. Type **135** 15 10
S432 4 p. Book Year emblems encircling globe 20 10
S433 5 p. Emblem, books and globe 50 20

1973. 200,000th Returnees under "Open Arms" National Unity Campaign.
S434 **136** 10 p. multicoloured . . . 50 25

137 Soldiers raising Flag

138 Satellite and Globe

1973. Victory at Quang Tri. Multicoloured.
S435 3 p. Type **137** 65 10
S436 10 p. Map and defenders . . 95 20

1973. World Meteorological Day.
S437 **138** 1 p. multicoloured . . . 60 15

139 Programme Emblem and Farm-workers

1973. Five-Year Agricultural Development Programme. Multicoloured.
S438 2 p. Type **139** . . . . 1·50 15
S439 5 p. Ploughing in paddy-field 1·50 15
S439a 10 p. As T **149** but dated "26-03-1973" (34 × 54 mm) 40·00

140 Emblem and H.Q. Paris

1973. 50th Anniv of International Criminal Police Organization (Interpol). Multicoloured.
S440 1 p. Type **140** 10 10
S441 2 p. "INTERPOL 1923 1973" 20 15
S442 25 p. Emblem and view of headquarters (different) . . 1·40 25

141 I.T.U. Emblem

142 Lamp in Hand

1973. World Telecommunications Day.
S443 **141** 1 p. multicoloured . . . 15 15
S444 – 2 p. black and blue . . . 35 15
S445 – 3 p. multicoloured . . . 60 15
DESIGNS: 2 p. Globe; 3 p. I.T.U. emblem in frame.

1973. National Development.
S446 **142** 8 p. multicoloured . . . 30 15
S447 – 10 p. blue, black & brn . 45 15
S448 – 15 p. multicoloured . . 70 15
DESIGNS: 10 p. "Agriculture, Industry and Fisheries"; 15 p. Workers on power pylon.

143 Water Buffaloes

1973. "Year of the Buffalo". Multicoloured.
S449 5 p. Type **143** 50 15
S450 10 p. Water buffalo 75 20

144 Flame Emblem and "Races of the World"

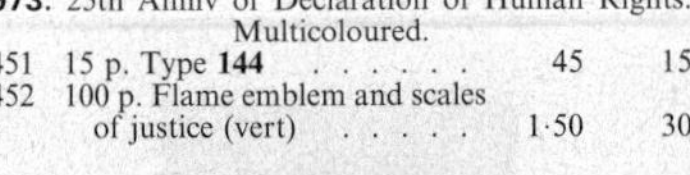
1973. 25th Anniv of Declaration of Human Rights. Multicoloured.
S451 15 p. Type **144** 45 15
S452 100 p. Flame emblem and scales of justice (vert) . . . . . 1·50 30

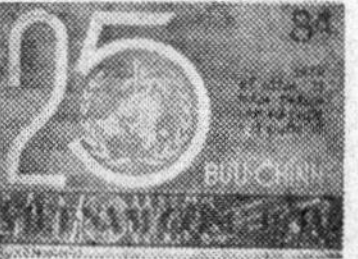
145 Emblem within "25"

1973. 25th Anniv of W.H.O.
S453 **145** 8 p. multicoloured . . . 40 15
S454 – 15 p. blue, red & brown 60 15
DESIGN: 15 p. W.H.O. emblem and inscription.

146 Sampan crossing River

1974. Vietnamese Sampan Women. Multicoloured.
S455 5 p. Type **146** 60 25
S456 10 p. Sampan and passengers 95 25

147 Flags and Soldiers of Allies

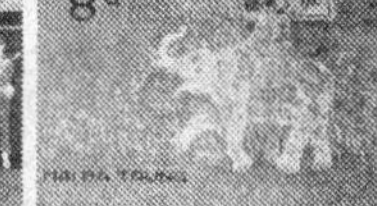
148 Trung Sisters on Elephant

1974. Allies Day. Multicoloured.
S457 8 p. Type **147** 25 15
S458 15 p. Soldiers and flags . . . 60 15
S459 15 p. Allied Nations Monument 60 15
S460 60 p. Raising South Vietnamese flag, and map (vert) . . . 1·75 30

1974. Trung Sisters' Festival.
S461 **148** 8 p. green, yellow & blk . 30 25
S462 15 p. red, yellow & blk . 45 25
S463 80 p. blue, pink & blk . 95 40

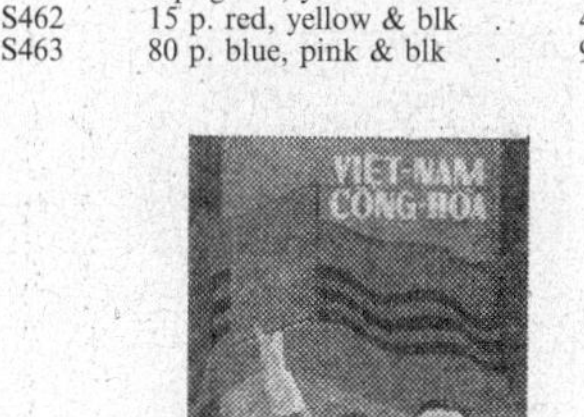

149 Pres. Thieu holding Agrarian Reform Law

1974. Farmers' Day. Multicoloured.
S464 10 p. Type **149** 60 15
S465 20 p. Farm-workers (32 × 22 mm) 35 15
S466 70 p. Girl harvesting rice (22 × 32 mm) 60 35

150 King Hung Vuong

1974. King Hung Vuong (first Vietnamese monarch) Commemoration. Multicoloured.
S467 20 p. Type **150** 40 25
S468 100 p. Banner inscribed "Hung Vuong, National Founder" 1·50 60

151 National Library

152 Allied Nations Memorial, Saigon

1974. New National Library Building. Mult.
S469 10 p. Type **151** 35 20
S470 15 p. Library and Phoenix bas-relief 50 25

1974. Surch.
S470a **142** 10 p. on 8 p. mult . . .
S470b **145** 10 p. on 8 p. mult . . .
S470c **120** 25 p. on 1 p. mult . . .
S470d **140** 25 p. on 1 p. mult . . .
S470e **138** 25 p. on 1 p. mult . . .
S470f **141** 25 p. on 1 p. mult . . .
S470g – 25 p. on 7 p. red, blue and brown (No. S376) . .
S470h **147** 25 p. on 8 p. mult . . .
S470i – 25 p. on 16 p. mult (No. S427) . . . .
S470j – 25 p. on 16 p. mult (No. S380) . . . .

1974. International Aid Day. Multicoloured.
S471 10 p. Type **152** 35 10
S472 20 p. Flags on crane (horiz) . 75 15
S473 60 p. Crate on hoist . . . . 2·50 35

153 "Tourist Attractions"

1974. Tourism. Multicoloured.
S474 5 p. Type **153** 45 15
S475 10 p. Xom Bong Bridge Nhatrang 45 15
S476 15 p. Thien Mu Pagoda, Hue (vert) 80 15

154 "Rhynchostylis gigantea"

1974. Orchids. Multicoloured.
S477 10 p. Type **154** 20 15
S478 20 p. "Cypripedium callosum" (vert) 30 15
S479 200 p. "Dendrobium nobile" 3·25 1·00

155 "International Exchange of Mail"

1974. Centenary of U.P.U. Multicoloured.
S480 20 p. Type **155** 50 20
S481 30 p. "U.P.U. letter" and Hemispheres 90 20
S482 300 p. U.P.U. emblem and Vietnamese girl (vert) . . 3·00 1·25

156 Hien Lam Pavilion, Hue

157 Conference Emblem

1975. Historical Sites. Multicoloured.
S483 25 p. Type **156** 50 10
S484 30 p. Throne Room, Imperial Palace, Hue 60 20
S485 60 p. Tu Duc's Pavilion, Hue 1·10 25

1975. International Conference on Children and National Development, Saigon. Multicoloured.
S486 20 p. Type **157** 35 20
S487 70 p. Vietnamese family (32 × 22 mm) . . . . . . 1·25 25

158 Unicorn Dance

1975. Vietnamese New Year Festival. Mult.
S488 20 p. Type **158** 40 20
S489 30 p. Letting-off fire-crackers (vert) 55 30
S490 100 p. New Year greeting custom (vert) . . . . . . 1·25 60

159 Military Mandarin ("San Hau" play)

1975. "Hat Bo" Vietnamese Traditional Theatre. Multicoloured.
S491 25 p. Type **159** 50 20
S492 40 p. Two characters from "Tam Ha Nam Duong" (vert) 75 35
S493 100 p. Heroine, "Luu Kim Giai Gia Tho Chau" (vert) . . 2·50 1·10

160 Produce for Export and Map

1975. Farmers' Day. Multicoloured.
S494 10 p. Type **160** 25 15
S495 50 p. Ancient and modern irrigation 75 30

MILITARY FRANK STAMPS

MF 29 Soldier and Barracks

1961. No value indicated. Roul.
SMF115 MF 29 (–) yellow, brown, green & black . 5·00 5·00
SMF116 (–) yellow, brown and green . . . 6·00 6·00

POSTAGE DUE STAMPS

D 1 Dragon

1955.
SD 1 D 1 2 p. yellow and mauve . 40 40
SD 2 3 p. turquoise & violet . 45 45
SD 3 5 p. yellow and violet . 75 60
SD 4 10 p. red and green . . 95 70
SD14 – 20 p. green and red . . 2·50 1·60
SD15 – 30 p. yellow and green . 3·75 2·50
SD16 – 50 p. yellow & brown . 8·00 5·75
SD17 – 100 p. yellow & violet . 12·50 10·00

The 20 p. to 100 p. are inscribed "BUU-CHINH" instead of "TIMBRE TAXE".

D 90 Butterfly

D 91 Butterflies

1968.
SD312 D 90 50 c. multicoloured . 55 50
SD313 1 p. multicoloured . . 55 50
SD314 2 p. multicoloured . . 1·00 95
SD315 D 91 3 p. multicoloured . . 1·40 1·25
SD316 5 p. multicoloured . . 2·50 2·40
SD317 10 p. multicoloured . 4·00 3·50

1974. Surch.
SD470k D 91 5 p. on 3 p. mult . . 5·00
SD470l D 90 10 p. on 50 c. mult . 5·00
SD470m 40 p. on 1 p. mult . 5·00
SD470n 60 p. on 2 p. mult . 5·00

D. NATIONAL FRONT FOR THE LIBERATION OF SOUTH VIETNAM

The National Front for the Liberation of South Vietnam was formed by the Communists, known as the Vietcong, in December 1960. With the support of troops from North Vietnam the Vietcong gradually gained control of more and more territory within South Vietnam until the surrender of the last South Vietnamese Republican forces in May 1975 enabled them to take control of the entire country. The following stamps were used in those areas controlled by the National Liberation Front.

1963. 100 xu = 1 dong

The value of the N.L.F. dong fluctuated considerably and was not on parity with the North Vietnamese currency.

1 Vietcong Flag

1963. 3rd Anniv of National Liberation Front.
NLF1 1 20 x. multicoloured (English inscr) . . . . 3·25 2·75
NLF2 20 x. multicoloured (French inscr) . . . . 3·25 2·75
NLF3 20 x. multicoloured (Spanish inscr) . . . . 3·25 2·75

2 Attack on Village

1963. 3rd Anniv of Revolutionary Struggle in South Vietnam. Multicoloured.
NLF4 10 x. Type **2** . . . . 2·50 1·50
NLF5 10 x. Attack on U.S. helicopter . . . . 2·50 1·50

3 Demonstrators with Banner

1964. 4th Anniv of National Liberation Front.
NLF6 10 x. Type **3** . . . . 1·00 1·00
NLF7 20 x. multicoloured . . . . 1·40 1·40
NLF8 30 x. green and blue . . . 3·00 2·25

DESIGNS: 20 x. Harvesting rice; 30 x. Sinking of U.S.S. "Card" (destroyer).

4 Attack on Bien Hoa Airfield

1965. 5th Anniv of National Liberation Front.
NLF 9 4 10 x. multicoloured . . 75 75
NLF10 – 20 x. black, grey & red . 1·10 1·10
NLF11 – 40 x. multicoloured . . 5·25 5·25

DESIGNS: 20 x. Nguyen Van Troi facing firing squad; 40 x. Vietcong flags.

5 Vietcong Soldiers on U.S. Tanks

6 "Guerrilla"

1967. 7th Anniv of National Liberation Front. Multicoloured.
NLF12 20 x. Type **5** 70 60
NLF13 20 x. Vietcong guerrillas (horiz) 70 60
NLF14 30 x. Crowd with banners 1·50 1·50

1968. "The Struggle For Freedom". Paintings. Multicoloured.
NLF15 10 x. Type **6** 70 70
NLF16 20 x. "Jungle Patrol" (horiz) 90 90
NLF17 30 x. "Woman Soldier" . 1·50 1·50
NLF18 40 x. "Towards the Future" (horiz) . . . . 2·25 2·25

7 Casting Votes

1968. 8th Anniv of National Liberation Front. Multicoloured.
NLF19 20 x. Type **7** 35 35
NLF20 20 x. Bazooka crew and burning airplane . . . 35 35
NLF21 30 x. Vietcong flag and crowd (French inscr) . 70 70
NLF22 30 x. Vietcong flag and crowd (English inscr) . 70 70

8 Lenin and Vietcong Flag

1970. Birth Centenary of Lenin.
NLF23 8 20 x. multicoloured . . 30 20
NLF24 30 x. multicoloured . . 35 30
NLF25 50 x. multicoloured . . 50 35
NLF26 2 d. multicoloured . . . 1·90 1·40

9 Ho Chi Minh watering Kainito Plant

10 Vietcong "Lightning Flash"

1970. 80th Birth Anniv of Ho Chi Minh.
NLF27 **9** 20 x. multicoloured . . 30 20
NLF28 30 x. multicoloured . . 35 30
NLF29 50 x. multicoloured . . 50 35
NLF30 2 d. multicoloured . . . 1·60 1·40

1970. 10th Anniv of National Liberation Front.
NLF31 **10** 20 x. multicoloured . . 30 20
NLF32 30 x. multicoloured . . 35 30
NLF33 50 x. multicoloured . . 55 50
NLF34 3 d. multicoloured . . 3·00 2·25

11 Home Guards defending Village

1971. 10th Anniv of People's Liberation Armed Forces. Multicoloured.
NLF35 20 x. Type **11** 65 65
NLF36 30 x. Surrender of U.S. tank 1·00 1·00
NLF37 50 x. Agricultural workers 1·40 1·40
NLF38 1 d. Vietcong ambush . . 2·25 2·25

12 Children in School

13 Harvesting Rice

14 Ho Chi Minh with Vietcong Soldiers

1971. 2nd Anniv of Provisional Government. Life in Liberated Areas. Multicoloured.
NLF39 20 x. Type **12** 20 20
NLF40 30 x. Women sewing Vietcong flag 35 35
NLF41 40 x. Fortifying village . . 1·10 1·10
NLF42 50 x. Medical clinic . . . 1·50 1·50
NLF43 1 d. Harvesting . . . . . 2·25 2·25

1974. 5th Anniv of Provisional Government. Multicoloured.
NLF44 10 d. Type **13** 20 20
NLF45 10 d. Demonstrators with banner 20 20
NLF46 10 d. Schoolchildren . . . 20 20
NLF47 10 d. Women home guards 20 20
NLF48 10 d. Vietcong conference delegate 20 20
NLF49 10 d. Soldiers and tanks . . 20 20
NLF50 10 d. Type **14** 30 30
NLF51 20 d. Type **14** 80 80
For other values as Type **14**, see Nos. NLF57/60.

15 Ho Chi Minh watering Kainito Plant

1975. 85th Birth Anniv of Ho Chi Minh (1st issue).
NLF52 **15** 5 d. multicoloured . . . 20 20
NLF53 10 d. multicoloured . . 25 25
NLF54 30 d. mult (mauve frame) . . . . . . 1·50 1·50
NLF54a 30 d. mult (green frame) 1·50 1·50

1975. 15th Anniv of National Front for Liberation of South Vietnam. As T **14** but 35½ × 26 mm.
NLF55 **14** 15 d. black and green . . 50 50
NLF56 30 d. black and red . . 1·00 1·00
NLF57 60 d. black and blue . 1·50 1·50
NLF58 300 d. black & yellow . 4·50 4·50

1975. 85th Birth Anniv of Ho Chi Minh (2nd issue). As T **284** of North Vietnam, but inscr "MIEN NAM VIET NAM".
NLF59 30 d. multicoloured . . . 60 60
NLF60 60 d. multicoloured . . . 1·10 1·10

1976. Various stamps surch in South Vietnamese currency.
NLF61 – 10 p. on 1 d. multicoloured (NLF38)
NLF62 – 20 p. on 6 x. yellow and red (NLF75) . . . .
NLF63 – 20 p. on 20 x. multicoloured (NLF27)
NLF64 – 20 p. on 40 x. multicoloured (NLF11)
NLF65 **9** 20 p. on 2 d. multicoloured (NLF30)
NLF66 **15** 20 p. on 5 d. multicoloured (NLF52)
NLF67 **14** 20 p. on 10 d. multicoloured (NLF50)
NLF68 **15** 20 p. on 10 d. multicoloured (NLF53)
NLF69 20 p. on 30 d. multicoloured (NLF54)
NLF70 20 p. on 30 d. mult (NLF54a) . . . . .

17 "Cocos nucifera"

1976. Fruits. Multicoloured.
NLF71 20 d. Type **17** 80 80
NLF72 30 d. "Garcinia mangostana" . . . . . 1·25 1·25
NLF73 60 d. "Nargifera indica" . 2·50 2·50

1976. First Elections to Unified National Assembly. As Nos. N858/60 of North Vietnam, but inscr "MIEN NAM VIET NAM".
NLF74 6 x. red and blue (as N858) 20 20
NLF75 6 x. yellow and red (as N859) 20 20
NLF76 12 x. red and green (as N860) 50 50

18 Flag of Provisional Revolutionary Government

1976. 1st Anniv of Liberation of South Vietnam.
NLF77 **18** 30 d. multicoloured . . . 60 50

1976. 1st Session of Unified National Assembly. As Nos. N861/2 of North Vietnam, but inscr "MIEN NAM VIET NAM".
NLF78 6 x. brown, red & yellow 20 20
NLF79 12 x. turquoise, red & yell 40 40

The unified National Assembly proclaimed the reunification of Vietnam on 2 July 1976 and the united country was then known as the Socialist Republic of Vietnam.

E. NORTH VIETNAM

(Vietnam Democratic Republic)

Issues before April 1954 were made in Tongking and Central Annam, in areas under Viet Minh control. From 21 July 1954 French troops withdrew from north of the 17th Parallel and the Ho Chi Minh Government assumed complete control.

1946. 100 cents = 1 dong.
1959. 100 xu = 1 dong.

GUM. All stamps were issued without gum unless otherwise stated.

I. TONGKING

1946. No. 190 of Indo-China optd **V VIET-NAM N DAN-CHU CONG-HOA BUU CHINH**.
N1 25 c. blue . . . . 60·00 60·00

2 Ho Chi Minh

3 Ho Chi Minh and Vietnam Map

1948.
N2a **2** 2 d. brown . . . . 10·00
N3a 5 d. red . . . . 10·00

1951. Imperf or perf.
N4 **3** 100 d. green . . . . 3·00 3·00
N5 100 d. brown . . . . 3·00 3·00
N6 200 d. red . . . . 3·00 3·00

5 Blacksmith

7 Malenkov, Ho Chi Minh, Mao Tse-tung and Flags

1953. Production Campaign.
N11 **5** 100 d. violet . . . . 4·25 1·25
N12 500 d. brown . . . . 8·00 3·75

1954. Friendship Month.
N13 **7** 100 d. red . . . . 18·00 18·00

II. CENTRAL ANNAM

NA 1 Ho Chi Minh

1950. Imperf. (a) Figures of value in white.
NA1 **NA 1** 1 d. violet . . . . . .
NA2 1 d. green . . . . . .
NA3 5 d. green . . . . . .
NA4 15 d. brown . . . . .

(b) Figures coloured.
NA7 **NA 1** 300 d. blue £325 £325
NA8 500 d. red £700 £700

1952. Surch in figures. Imperf. (a) Figures in white.
NA5 **NA 1** 30 d. on 5 d. green . £200 £170
NA6 60 d. on 1 d. violet . £250 £225
NA8a 90 d. on 3 d. red . .

(b) Figures coloured.
NA8b **NA 1** 5 d. on 10 d. mauve .
NA8c 100 d. on 300 d. blue

III. GENERAL ISSUES

8 Malenkov, Ho Chi Minh and Mao Tse-tung

1954.
N14 **8** 50 d. brown and red . . . . 18·00 18·00
N15 100 d. red and yellow . . . 20·00 20·00

9 Battlefield

1954. Dien Bien Phu Victory. Imperf or perf.
N16a **9** 10 d. bistre and red . . . . 10·00 2·50
N17a 50 d. ochre and red . . . . 10·00 2·75
N18d 150 d. blue and brown . . 10·00 4·50
See also No. NO24.

1954. (a) Handstamped thus: **10 dNH**.
N19 **3** 10 d. on 100 d. green . . . 5·00 5·00
N20 10 d. on 100 d. brown . . . 7·00 7·00
N21 20 d. on 200 d. red . . . . 5·00 5·00

(b) Handstamped thus: **10 d.**
N22 **3** 10 d. on 100 d. green . . . 6·00 6·00
N25 10 d. on 100 d. brown . . . 10·00 10·00
N28 20 d. on 200 d. red . . . 10·00 10·00
See also Nos. N46/9.

12 Lake of the Returned Sword, Hanoi

1954. Proclamation of Hanoi as Capital.
N30 **12** 10 d. blue . . . . 3·75 3·75
N31 50 d. green . . . . 3·75 3·75
N32 150 d. red . . . . 7·50 7·50

13 Distribution of Title Deeds

1955. Land Reform.
N33 **13** 5 d. green . . . . 6·00 6·00
N34 10 d. grey . . . . 6·00 6·00
N35 20 d. orange . . . . . . 7·50 7·50
N36 50 d. mauve . . . . . . 18·00 18·00
N37 100 d. brown . . . . . . 28·00 28·00

14 Crowd welcoming Steam Train

1956. Hanoi–China Railway Re-opening.
N38 **14** 100 d. blue . . . . 18·00 18·00
N39 200 d. turquoise . . . . . 18·00 18·00
N40 300 d. violet . . . . . . 32·00 32·00
N41 500 d. brown . . . . . . 40·00 40·00

15 Parade, Ba Dinh Square, Hanoi

1956. Return of Govt to Hanoi.
N42 **15** 1000 d. violet . . . . . . 50·00 38·00
N43 1500 d. blue . . . . . . 75·00 55·00
N44 2000 d. turquoise . . . . 75·00 55·00
N45 3000 d. turquoise . . . . 85·00 80·00

1956. Surch thus: **10 d** in frame.
N46 **3** 10 d. on 100 d. green . . . 14·00 14·00
N48 10 d. on 100 d. brown . . . 16·00 16·00
N49 20 d. on 200 d. red . . . . 12·00 12·00

17 Tran Dang Ninh

1956. 1st Death Anniv of Tran Dang Ninh (patriot).
N50 **17** 5 d. green . . . . 4·00 1·75
N51 10 d. red . . . . 4·00 1·75
N52 20 d. brown . . . . 5·00 2·40
N53 100 d. blue . . . . 5·50 3·00

18 Mac Thi Buoi

1956. 5th Death Anniv of Mac Thi Buoi (guerilla heroine).
N54 **18** 1000 d. red . . . . 12·00 8·00
N55 2000 d. brown . . . . . 19·00 9·25
N56 4000 d. green . . . . . . 30·00 23·00
N57 5000 d. blue . . . . . . 50·00 28·00

19 Bai Thuong Dam

1956. Reconstruction of Bai Thuong Dam.
N58 **19** 100 d. violet and brown . 6·75 6·00
N59 200 d. red and black . . 10·00 6·00
N60a 300 d. red and lake . . . 13·30 11·30

1956. Surch **50 DONG**.
N61 **2** 50 d. on 5 d. red . . . . . 50·00 70·00

21 Cotton Mill

1957. 1st Anniv of Opening of Nam Dinh Mill.
N62 **21** 100 d. brown and red . . . 5·00 5·00
N63 200 d. grey and blue . . . 5·75 5·75
N64 300 d. lt green & green . . 7·50 7·50

22 Pres. Ho Chi Minh 23 Arms of Republic

1957. President's 67th Birthday.
N65 **22** 20 d. green 2·50 1·75
N66 60 d. bistre 2·50 1·75
N67 100 d. blue 3·00 2·75
N68 300 d. brown 5·00 4·00

1957. 12th Anniv of Democratic Republic.
N69 **23** 20 d. green 2·75 2·25
N70 100 d. red 5·75 3·75

24 Congress Emblem

1957. 4th World T.U. Congress, Leipzig.
N71 **24** 300 d. purple 7·50 5·00
See also Nos. NO69/72.

25 Presidents Voroshilov and Ho Chi Minh

1957. 40th Anniv of Russian Revolution.
N72 **25** 100 d. red 6·25 5·00
N73 500 d. brown 8·25 5·50
N74 1000 d. orange 17·00 16·00

26 Open-air Class 27 Girl Gymnast

1958. Education Campaign.
N75 **26** 50 d. blue 4·75 3·75
N76 150 d. red 7·00 5·50
N77 1000 d. brown 16·00 9·00

1958. Physical Education.
N78 **27** 150 d. brown and blue 11·00 9·00
N79 500 d. brown and rose 18·00 14·00

28 29 Congress Emblem

1958. Labour Day.
N80 **28** 50 d. yellow and red 3·25 2·10
N81 150 d. red and yellow 5·00 3·75

1958. 4th International Congress of Democratic Women, Vienna.
N82 **29** 150 d. blue 7·00 5·75

30 Cup, Basket and Lace 31 Hanoi–Saigon Railway Reconstruction

1958. Arts and Crafts Fair, Hanoi.
N83 **30** 150 d. sepia and turq 2·75 1·60
N84 2000 d. black and lilac 9·00 5·25

1958. Re-unification of Vietnam Propaganda.
N85 **31** 50 d. blue 1·40 85
N86 150 d. brown 1·60 1·50

32 Revolution in Hanoi

1958. 13th Anniv of Vietnamese Revolution.
N87 **32** 150 d. red 1·90 1·10
N88 500 d. blue 3·75 1·90

33 Woman Potter

1958. Handicrafts Exhibition.
N89 **33** 150 d. lake and red 1·90 1·60
N90 1000 d. brown & ochre 9·00 3·50

34 Vo Thi Sau and Crowd 35 Tran Hung Dao

1958. 13th Anniv of South Vietnam Resistance Movement.
N91 **34** 50 d. green and buff 2·75 1·40
N92 150 d. red and orange 5·50 1·60

1958. 658th Death Anniv of Tran Hung Dao.
N93 **35** 150 d. grey and blue 1·75 80

36 Hanoi Factories 37 Harvesting Rice

1958. Hanoi Mechanical Engineering Plant.
N94 **36** 150 d. sepia 2·25 95

1958. Mutual Aid Teams.
N95 **37** 150 d. lake 5·25 1·60
N96 500 d. brown 6·50 3·25

38 Temple of Jade, Hanoi 39 Furniture-makers

1958.
N 97 **38** 150 d. green 3·75 1·75
N 98 – 150 d. blue 2·25 55
N 99 – 350 d. brown 3·75 95
N100 **38** 2000 d. green 32·00 9·00
DESIGNS—HORIZ: 150 d. blue, 350 d. Bay of Halong.

1958. Furniture Co-operatives.
N101 **39** 150 d. blue 2·25 60

40 Cam Pha Coal Mines 41 The Trung Sisters

1959.
N102 **40** 150 d. blue 2·00 80

1959. Trung Sisters Commemoration.
N103 **41** 5 x. red and yellow 1·10 50
N104 8 x. deep brown and brown 1·75 65

42 Mother and Child

1959. 10th Anniv of World Peace Movement.
N105 **42** 12 x. violet 1·10 55

43 Xuan Quan Dam

1959. Bac Hung Hai Irrigation Project.
N106 **43** 6 x. yellow, green & vio 3·25 80
N107 12 x. ochre, blue & grey 6·25 1·10

44 Victims in Phu Loi Concentration Camp 45 Radio Mast

1959. The Phu Loi Massacre on 1 December 1958.
N108 **44** 12 x. salmon, olive & blk 1·90 45
N109 20 x. ochre, grey & black 4·00 90

1959. Me Tri Radio Station.
N110 **45** 3 x. green and orange 1·40 35
N111 12 x. sepia and blue 2·25 55

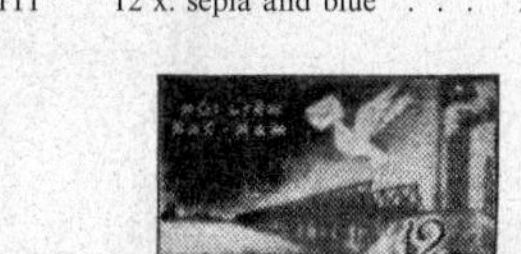

46 Hien Luong Railway Bridge

1959. Vietnam Day.
N112 **46** 12 x. red and black 1·40 65

47 Rifle-shooting

1959. Sports.
N113 **47** 1 x. deep blue and blue 1·60 55
N114 – 6 x. olive and red 2·25 90
N115 – 12 x. red and rose 3·25 1·40
DESIGNS: 6 x. Swimming; 12 x. Wrestling.

48 Balloons 49 Coconuts

1959. 10th Anniv of Chinese People's Republic.
N116 **48** 12 x. red, yellow & grn 95 45

1959. Fruits. Multicoloured.
N117 3 x. Type **49** 1·10 45
N118 12 x. Bananas 2·10 85
N119 30 x. Pineapple 6·00 1·90

50 Convair CV 340

1959. Air.
N120 **50** 20 x. black and blue 10·00 6·25

51 Soldiers 52 Sailing Ship

1959. 15th Anniv of N. Vietnam People's Army.
N121 **51** 12 x. yellow, brown & bl 1·50 75

1959. 30th Anniv of N. Vietnam Workers' Party.
N122 **52** 2 x. multicoloured 1·10 65
N123 12 x. multicoloured 2·25 1·25

53 Girl in "E-De" Costume 54 Women of Vietnam

1960. National Costumes.
N124 **53** 2 x. red, blue & purple 80 35
N125 – 10 x. blue, orange & grn 1·25 45
N126 – 12 x. blue and brown 1·90 70
N127 – 12 x. blue and buff 1·90 70
COSTUMES: No. N125, "Meo"; N126, "Thai"; N127, "Tay".

1960. National Census.
N128 **54** 1 x. green 40 20
N129 – 12 x. brown and red 55 25
DESIGN: 12 x. Workers and factories.

55 Emblem and Women 56 Hung Vuong Temple

1960. 50th Anniv of International Women's Day.
N130 **55** 12 x. multicoloured 75 35

1960. Hung Vuong Anniversary Day.
N131 **56** 12 x. green and buff 6·50 3·75
N132 4 d. brown and blue 65·00 28·00

57 Lenin 58 Ballot Box

1960. 90th Birth Anniv of Lenin.
N133 **57** 5 x. red and blue 55 30
N134 12 x. blue and buff 80 50

1960. 2nd Election of Parliamentary Deputies.
N135 **58** 12 x. multicoloured 65 35

59 Red Cross Nurse 60 Pres. Ho Chi Minh

1960. International Red Cross Commem.
N136 **59** 8 x. blue, red and bistre 65 35
N137 12 x. green, red & grey 1·00 50

1960. President Ho Chi Minh's 70th Birthday.
N138 **60** 4 x. lilac and green 45 30
N139 12 x. purple and rose 85 40
N140 – 12 x. multicoloured 85 40
DESIGN—24½ × 39 mm: No. N140, Ho Chi Minh and children.

61 "New Constitution"

1960. Opening of 2nd National Assembly.
N141 **61** 12 x. sepia and ochre . . 1·50 75

62 Pres. Ho Chi Minh at Microphone

1960. 15th Anniv of Vietnam Democratic Republic.
N142 **62** 4 x. multicoloured . . . 2·50 1·00
N143 12 x. multicoloured . . . 3·75 1·10
N144 – 12 x. deep blue & blue . 3·75 1·10
N145 – 12 x. green and yellow . 3·75 1·10
N146 – 12 x. blue and brown . . 3·75 1·10
DESIGNS: No. N144, Ploughing; N145, Electricity Works, Vietri; N146, Classroom.

63 Workers and Flags

1960. 3rd Vietnam Workers' Party Congress.
N147 **63** 1 x. multicoloured . . . 1·75 70
N148 12 x. multicoloured . . . 2·25 90

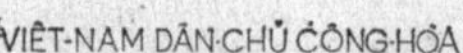

64 Handclasp of Three Races

1960. 15th Anniv of W.F.T.U.
N149 **64** 12 x. black and red . . . 5·75 4·00

65 Dragon

1960. 950th Anniv of Hanoi.
N150 **65** 8 x. yellow, brn & turq 1·75 95
N151 12 x. yellow, brown & bl 3·75 1·40

66 Exhibition Entrance

1960. "Fifteen Years of Republic" Exhibition.
N152 **66** 2 x. grey and red 90 60
N153 12 x. green and red . . . 1·75 85

67 Badge, Dove and Flag

1960. 15th Anniv of World Federation of Democratic Youth.
N154 **67** 12 x. multicoloured . . . 2·50 1·50

68 Emblem of Vietnamese Trade Unions
69 Woman, Globe and Dove

1961. 2nd National Congress of Trade Unions.
N155 **68** 12 x. red, blue & yellow 1·75 70

1961. 3rd National Congress of Women.
N156 **69** 6 x. green and blue . . . 2·40 50
N157 12 x. green & salmon . . 2·40 75

IMPERF STAMPS. Many issues from here onwards also exist imperf.

70 Sambar
71 Ly Tu Trong (revolutionary)

1961. Vietnamese Fauna.
N158 **70** 12 x. buff, black & olive 3·00 1·25
N159 – 20 x. multicoloured . . 4·25 2·50
N160 – 50 x. grey, black & grn 7·50 3·75
N161 – 1 d. black, grey & green 10·00 5·00
DESIGNS: 20 x. Sun bear; 50 x. Indian elephant; 1 d. Crested gibbon.

1961. 3rd Congress of Vietnam Labour Youth Union.
N162 **71** 2 x. olive and blue . . . 90 45
N163 12 x. olive and salmon . 2·10 1·00

72 Bugler and Drummer
73 Disabled Soldier learning to use Crutches

1961. 20th Anniv of Vietnam Youth Pioneers.
N164 **72** 1 x. multicoloured . . . 1·50 75
N165 12 x. multicoloured . . 2·75 1·40

1961. 101st Anniv of Proposal for Int Red Cross.
N166 **73** 6 x. multicoloured . . . 1·90 75
N167 12 x. multicoloured . . 3·50 1·40

74 Nurse weighing Baby

1961. International Children's Day.
N168 **74** 4 x. green, black & red . 1·25 65
N169 12 x. yellow, blk & red . 2·75 1·40

75 Major Yuri Gagarin

1961. World's First Manned Space Flight.
N170 **75** 6 x. red and violet . . . 12·50 5·00
N171 12 x. red and green . . . 12·50 5·00

76
77 Women

1961. Vietnam Reunification Campaign.
N172 **76** 12 x. multicoloured . . . 50 50
N173 2 d. multicoloured . . . . 8·50 4·00

1961. Tripling of Hanoi, Hue and Saigon.
N174 **77** 12 x. multicoloured . . . 2·50 1·60
N175 3 d. brown, myrtle and green . . . . 20·00 11·00

78 Mother and Child
79 Prospecting Team

1961. National Savings Campaign.
N176 **78** 3 x. multicoloured 85 40
N177 12 x. multicoloured . . . 1·50 85

1961. Geological Research.
N178 **79** 2 x. green, blue & purple . 1·50 40
N179 12 x. brown, blk & turq . . 3·00 85

80 Thien Mu Tower, Hue
81 Workers and Rocket

1961. Ancient Towers.
N180 **80** 6 x. brown and chestnut . 75 40
N181 – 10 x. olive and buff . . . 1·50 55
N182 – 12 x. olive and green . . 2·10 65
N183 – 12 x. brown and blue . . 2·10 65
TOWERS: No. N181, Pen Brush, Bac Ninh; N182, Binh Son, Vinh Phuc; N183, Cham, Phan Rang.

1961. 22nd Communist Party Congress, Moscow.
N184 **81** 12 x. red and black . . . 2·00 1·25

82 Major Titov and Rocket

1961. 2nd Manned Space Flight.
N185 **82** 6 x. multicoloured . . . . 2·00 90
N186 12 x. multicoloured . . . 3·50 1·75

83 Freighter at Haiphong

1961. Haiphong Port Commemoration.
N187 **83** 5 x. grey, grn & myrtle . 1·25 60
N188 12 x. brown, light brown and sepia . . . . 3·00 1·25

84 Cymbalist
85 Congress Emblem

1961. 3rd Writers and Artists Congress. Mult.
N189 12 x. Type **84** . . . . 1·25 60
N190 12 x. Flautist . . . . 1·25 90
N191 30 x. Fan dancer . . . . . . 3·50 1·25
N192 50 x. Guitarist . . . . 5·00 2·40

1961. 5th W.F.T.U. Congress, Moscow.
N193 **85** 12 x. mauve and drab . . 60 40

86 Resistance Fighters
87 "Pigs"

1961. 15th Anniv of National Resistance.
N194 **86** 4 x. multicoloured . . . 35 20
N195 12 x. multicoloured . . . 65 35

1962. New Year.
N196 **87** 6 x. multicoloured . . . 1·00 50
N197 – 12 x. multicoloured . . . 2·00 1·00
DESIGN: 12 x. "Poultry".

88 Watering Tree
89 Tea Plant

1962. Tree-planting Festival.
N198 **88** 12 x. multicoloured . . . 1·60 85
N199 40 x. multicoloured . . . 2·50 1·50

1962. Multicoloured.
N200 2 x. Type **89** 75 40
N201 6 x. Aniseed 75 40
N202 12 x. Coffee . . . . 2·75 1·10
N203 12 x. Castor-oil . . . . . . 2·75 1·10
N204 30 x. Lacquer-tree . . . . . 5·75 2·50

90 Gong Dance
91 Hibiscus

1962. Folk-dancing. Multicoloured.
N205 12 x. Type **90** . . . . . . 2·00 60
N206 12 x. Bamboo dance . . . 2·00 60
N207 30 x. Hat dance . . . . . 5·00 60
N208 50 x. Parasol dance . . . 10·00 2·00

1962. Flowers. Multicoloured.
N209 12 x. Type **91** . . . . . . 2·00 75
N210 12 x. Frangipani . . . . . 2·00 75
N211 20 x. Chrysanthemum . . . 3·75 2·10
N212 30 x. Lotus . . . . 6·00 2·75
N213 50 x. Ipomoea . . . . . . 9·00 3·50

92 Kim Lien Flats, Hanoi
93 Workers and Rose

1962. 1st Five-Year Plan (1st issue).
N214 **92** 1 x. blue, black & grey . 40 20
N215 – 3 x. multicoloured . . . 70 30
N216 – 8 x. violet, blk & stone . 1·25 50
DESIGNS: 3 x. State agricultural farm; 8 x. Institute of Hydraulic and Electro-Dynamic Studies.
See also Nos. N245/8, N251/2, N270/1 and N294/6.

1962. 3rd National "Heroes of Labour" Congress.
N217 **93** 12 x. orange, olive & red 1·75 40

94 Dai Lai Lake

1962.
N218 **94** 12 x. turq and brown . . 2·25 85

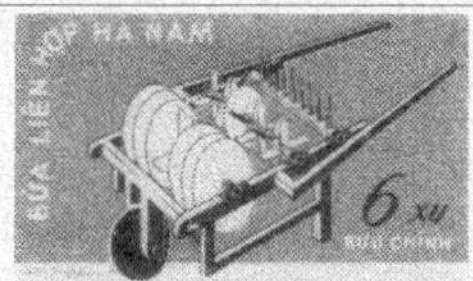
95 "Plough of Perfection"

1962.
N219 **95** 6 x. black & turquoise . . 1·10 40

96 Titov greeting Children

1962. Visit of Major Titov.
N220 **96** 12 x. sepia and blue . . . 85 50
N221 – 20 x. sepia and salmon . 1·75 55
N222 – 30 x. sepia and green . . 3·25 1·10
DESIGNS: 20 x. Pres. Ho Chi Minh pinning medal on Titov; 30 x. Titov in space-suit.

97 Mosquito and Red Cross

1962. Malaria Eradication.
N223 **97** 8 x. red, black & blue . . 1·25 55
N224 12 x. red, black & violet . 1·50 80
N225 20 x. red, black & purple 2·75 1·10

98 Factory and Soldiers

99 Ban Gioc Falls

1962. 8th Anniv of Geneva Vietnamese Agreements.
N226 **98** 12 x. multicoloured . . . 70 35

1962. Vietnamese Scenery.
N227 – 12 x. purple and blue . . 1·10 35
N228 **99** 12 x. sepia & turquoise . 1·10 35
DESIGN—HORIZ: (32½ × 23 mm): No. N227, Ba Be Lake.

99a Weightlifting

1962. Int Military Sports Festival of Socialist States, Prague.
N228a **99a** 12 x. multicoloured . . 60·00 95·00

100 Quang Trung

101 Groundnuts

1962. National Heroes.
N229 **100** 3 x. yellow, brn & grey . 60 25
N230 – 3 x. orange, blk & ochre 50 25
N231 **100** 12 x. yellow, grn & grey 85 35
N232 – 12 x. orge, blk & grey . 85 35
PORTRAIT: Nos. N230, N232, Nguyen Trai.

1962. Multicoloured.
N233 1 x. Type **101** 40 25
N234 4 x. Haricot beans 70 30
N235 6 x. Sweet potatoes 90 35
N236 12 x. Maize . . . . 2·25 80
N237 30 x. Manioc . . . . 5·00 2·00

102 Girl feeding Poultry

1962. Farm Stock-breeding.
N238 **102** 2 x. red, grey & blue . 60 30
N239 – 12 x. ochre, turquoise and blue . . . . 1·75 40
N240 – 12 x. brown, green and deep green . . . . . 1·75 40
N241 – 12 x. buff, mauve and sepia 1·75 40
DESIGNS: No. N239, Woman tending pigs; N240, Herdgirl with oxen; N241, Boy feeding buffalo.

103 Popovich in "Vostok 4"

1962. First "Team" Manned Space Flights.
N242 **103** 12 x. multicoloured . . 1·00 60
N243 – 20 x. ochre, blue & blk 1·75 60
N244 – 30 x. red, blue & black 2·75 1·25
DESIGNS—HORIZ: 20 x. Nikolaev in "Vostok 3". VERT: 30 x. "Vostoks 3 and 4".

104 Teacher and Students

1962. 1st Five-Year Plan (2nd issue). Higher Education and Land Cultivation.
N245 **104** 12 x. black & yellow . 1·00 35
N246 – 12 x. black, brn & buff 2·10 90
DESIGN: No. N246, Tree felling.

105 Guerrilla Fighter

106 Hoang Hoa Tham

1963. 1st Five-Year Plan (3rd issue). National Defence.
N247 **105** 5 x. green and grey . . 75 25
N248 12 x. brown and buff . 1·10 40

1963. 50th Death Anniv of Hoang Hoa Tham (freedom fghter).
N249 **106** 6 x. myrtle and blue . . 60 40
N250 12 x. black and brown . 85 50

107 Workers in Field

108 Karl Marx

1963. 1st Five-Year Plan (4th issue). Agricultural and Chemical Manufacture.
N251 **107** 12 x. multicoloured . . 1·00 60
N252 – 12 x. red, mauve and black 75 40
DESIGN: No. N252, Lam Thao Fertiliser Factory.

1963. 80th Death Anniv of Karl Marx.
N253 **108** 3 x. black and green . . 50 30
N254 12 x. black and drab on pink 75 35

109 Castro and Vietnamese Soldiers

111 Nurse tending Child

110 Doves and Labour Emblem

1963. Vietnamese–Cuban Friendship.
N255 **109** 12 x. multicoloured . . . 75 45

1963. Labour Day.
N256 **110** 12 x. orange, blk & bl . 75 40

1963. Red Cross Centenary.
N257 **111** 12 x. red, black & blue . 1·25 55
N258 – 12 x. red, grey & turq . 1·25 55
N259 – 20 x. red, grey and yellow 2·10 75
DESIGNS: No. N258, Child and syringe inscr "BCG". 25 × 42 mm: 20 x. Centenary emblem.

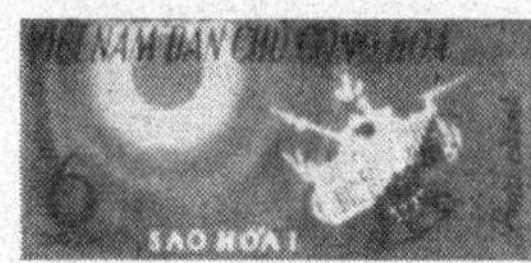
112 "Mars 1" Interplanetary Station

1963. Launching of Soviet Rocket "Mars 1". Multicoloured.
N260 6 x. Type **112** 60 35
N261 12 x. Type **112** 80 45
N262 12 x. "Mars 1" in space (vert) 80 45
N263 20 x. "Mars 1" in space (vert) 2·00 80

113 Carp

1963. Fishing Industry. Multicoloured.
N264 12 x. Type **113** . . . . 4·50 1·60
N265 12 x. Fishes and trawler . . 4·50 1·60

114 Pres. Ho Chi Minh embracing Prof. Nguyen Van Hien of South Vietnam

1963. Campaign for Reunification of Vietnam.
N266 **114** 12 x. black, blue & turq 70 35

115 Globe and "Vostoks 3 and 4"

1963. 1st Anniv of "Team" Manned Space Flights.
N267 **115** 12 x. black, brn & yell . 70 35
N268 – 20 x. black, blue & grn . 1·00 60
N269 – 30 x. black, violet & bl . 1·75 95
DESIGNS: 20 x. Nikolaev and "eagle" motif; 30 x. Popovich and "phoenix" motif.

116 Viet Tri Insecticide Factory

1963. 1st Five-Year Plan (5th issue).
N270 **116** 3 x. buff, brown & blue . 30 25
N271 – 12 x. pink, brown and bistre 65 40
DESIGN: 12 x. Viet Tri chemical factory.

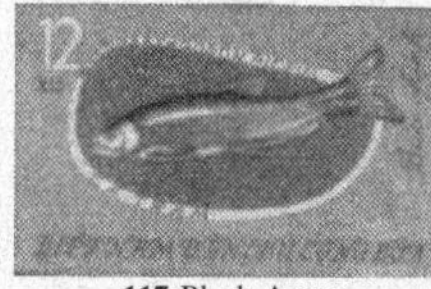
117 Black Amur

1963. Freshwater Fish Culture. Multicoloured.
N272 12 x. Type **117** . . . . . . 1·25 60
N273 12 x. Carp . . . . 1·25 60
N274 12 x. Silver carp . . . . . 1·25 60
N275 20 x. Snakehead . . . . . . 3·00 1·25
N276 30 x. Mozambique mouth-breeder . . . . 4·50 2·75

118 Chinese Francolin

119 Broken Chain and Map

1963. Birds. Multicoloured.
N277 12 x. Type **118** . . . . . . 2·75 1·00
N278 12 x. Chinese jungle mynah 2·75 1·00
N279 12 x. White-breasted kingfisher 2·75 1·00
N280 20 x. Siamese fireback pheasant (horiz) . . . . . 6·50 2·10
N281 30 x. Eastern reef heron . . 10·50 3·25
N282 40 x. Slaty-headed parakeet 14·00 5·00

1963. W.F.T.U. Assembly, Hanoi.
N283 **119** 12 x. multicoloured . . 50 40

120 Football

121 "Rauwolfia verticillata"

1963. "GANEFO" Athletic Games, Jakarta.
N284 **120** 12 x. black, grey & ochre 80 35
N285 – 12 x. black, grey & orge 80 35
N286 – 12 x. black, grey & blue 80 35
N287 – 30 x. black, grey & mag 1·60 75
DESIGNS—VERT: No. N285, Volleyball. HORIZ: No. N286, Swimming; N287, High-jumping.

1963. Medicinal Plants. Multicoloured.
N288 6 x. Type **121** 80 35
N289 12 x. "Chenopodium ambrosioides" 95 35
N290 12 x. "Sophora japonica" . 95 65
N291 12 x. "Fibraurea tinctoria" . 95 65
N292 20 x. "Momordica cochinchinensis" . . . . 4·50 1·10

122 "Solidarity"

123 Pylon

1963. 3rd Anniv of South Vietnam National Liberation Front.
N293 **122** 12 x. blk, brn & ochre . 55 35

1964. 1st Five-Year Plan (6th issue).
N294 – 6 x. black, red & pur . 50 30
N295 – 12 x. multicoloured . . 1·60 50
N296 **123** 12 x. black, grey & orge 1·60 50
DESIGNS—HORIZ: (40 × 22½ mm): 6 x. Tapping cast-iron; No. N295, Thai Ngyuen Iron and Steel Works.

124 Sun, Globe and Dragon

1964. International Quiet Sun Years.
N297 **124** 12 x. orange, blk & grn 40 25
N298 50 x. drab, black & pur 1·50 85

125 Twin Space Flights

1964. Space Flights of Bykovsky and Tereshkova. Multicoloured.
N299 12 x. Type **125** . . . . . . 1·25 35
N300 12 x. Bykovsky and "Vostok 5" . . . . 1·25 35
N301 30 x. Tereshkova and "Vostok 6" . . . . 3·00 1·10

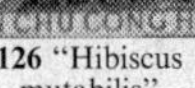

126 "Hibiscus mutabilis"   **127** Rural Costume

1964. Flowers. Multicoloured.
N302 12 x. Type **126** . . . . . . 1·50 40
N303 12 x. "Persica vulgaris" . . 1·50 40
N304 12 x. "Saraca dives" . . . . 1·50 40
N305 12 x. "Passiflora hispida" . 1·50 40
N306 20 x. "Michelia champaca" . 3·75 1·25
N307 30 x. "Camellia amplexicaulis" 5·50 1·75

1964. National Costumes. Multicoloured.
N308 6 x. Type **127** 50 25
N309 12 x. "Ceremonial" . . . . 1·00 35
N310 12 x. "Everyday" . . . . . 1·00 35

128 Artillery

1964. 10th Anniv of Battle of Dien Bien Phu.
N311 **128** 3 x. black and red . . . 40 25
N312 – 6 x. black and blue . . 50 35
N313 – 12 x. black and yellow . 95 40
N314 – 12 x. black and purple . 95 40
DESIGNS: 6 x. Machine-gun post; No. N313, Bomb-disposal; N314, Dien Bien Phu and tractor.

129 Ham Rong Railway Bridge

1964. Inaug of Reconstructed Ham Rong Bridge.
N315 **129** 12 x. multicoloured . . 1·25 50

130 Spotted Deer   **131** Women Fighters, Map, Industrial Scene and Watch-towers

1964. Wild Animals. Multicoloured.
N316 12 x. Type **130** . . . . . . 1·90 60
N317 12 x. Malayan tapir (horiz) . 1·90 60
N318 12 x. Tiger . . . . 1·90 60
N319 20 x. Water buffalo (horiz) . 3·75 1·25
N320 30 x. Sumatran rhinoceros (horiz) . . . . 4·25 1·90
N321 40 x. Banteng (horiz) . . . 5·00 2·50

1964. 10th Anniv of Geneva Agreements on Vietnam.
N322 **131** 12 x. multicoloured . . 65 35
N323 – 12 x. multicoloured . . 65 35
DESIGN—VERT: (23 × 45 mm): No. N323, Map of Vietnam, T.U. emblem and flag, inscr ("NHAN DAN MIEN NAM") etc.

132 Nhu Quynh Pumping Station

1964. Irrigation for Agriculture.
N324 **132** 12 x. slate and black . 75 35

133 Populace Greeting Soldiers

1964. 10th Anniv of Liberation of Hanoi. Multicoloured.
N325 6 x. Type **133** 35 25
N326 12 x. Building construction 70 50

134 Naval Longboat

1964. "National Defence" Games.
N327 **134** 5 x. black, grey & blue 90 35
N328 – 12 x. black, grey & yell 1·90 50
N329 – 12 x. black, brn & bl . 1·90 50
N330 – 12 x. multicoloured . . 1·90 50
DESIGNS—HORIZ: No. N328, Pistol-shooting. VERT: No. N329, Gliding; N330, Parachuting.

135 "Guarcinia mangostana"

1964. Tropical Fruits. Multicoloured.
N331 12 x. Type **135** . . . . . 1·60 45
N332 12 x. "Mangifera indica" . 1·60 45
N333 12 x. "Nephelium litchi" . 1·60 45
N334 20 x. "Anona squamosa" . 2·75 85
N335 50 x. "Citrus medica" . . . 7·50 1·90

136 Conference Building

1964. World Solidarity Conf, Hanoi. Mult.
N336 12 x. Type **136** 75 35
N337 12 x. Soldier greeting workers 75 35
N338 12 x. Clenched fist, ships and Boeing B-52 Stratofortress 75 35

137 Soldiers with Standard

1964. 20th Anniv of Vietnamese People's Army. Multicoloured.
N339 12 x. Type **137** . . . . . 1·00 30
N340 12 x. Coastguards . . . . . 1·00 30
N341 12 x. Frontier guards (vert) 1·00 30

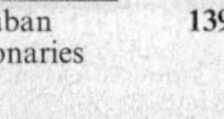

138 Cuban Revolutionaries   **139** Le Hong Phong

140 Party Flag

1965. 6th Anniv of Cuban Republic.
N342 **138** 12 x. black, red & blue 75 35
N343 – 12 x. multicoloured . . 75 35
DESIGN: No. N343, Flags of Cuba and North Vietnam.

1965. 35th Anniv of Vietnamese Workers' Party.
(a) As T **139**. Portraits and inscr purple-brown; background colours given.
N344 **139** 6 x. grey 40 20
N345 – 6 x. bistre 40 20
N346 – 6 x. drab 40 20
N347 – 6 x. brown 40 20
N348 – 6 x. lilac 40 20
DESIGNS: No. N345, Tran Phu; N346, Hoang Van Thu; N347 Hgo Gia Tu; N348 Nguyen van Cu (Party leaders).

(b) As T **140**.
N349 **140** 12 x. yellow, red and mauve 60 30
N350 – 12 x. mauve, yellow and red 60 30
DESIGN: No. N350, Foundryman and guerilla fighter.

141 Women tending Maize   **142** Locomotive and Nguyen Van Troi (patriot)

1965. Populating Mountain Settlements.
N351 **141** 2 x. multicoloured . . . 25 20
N352 3 x. multicoloured . . . 35 25
N353 – 12 x. indigo, orange and blue 60 35
DESIGN: 12 x. Young girls going to school.

1965. Transport Ministers' Congress, Hanoi.
N354 **142** 12 x. blue and red . . . 1·60 50
N355 – 30 x. black and green . . 3·00 1·10
DESIGN: 30 x. As Type **142** but position of locomotive, portrait and value transposed.

143 Cosmonauts Komarov, Feoktistov, Yegorov, and "Voskhod I"

1965. Three-manned Space Flight.
N356 **143** 20 x. violet, green & bl . 1·50 40
N357 – 1 d. violet, red & mauve 5·25 1·50
DESIGN: 1 d. "Voskhod I" and cosmonauts.

144 Lenin with Red Guards   **145** Pres. Ho Chi Minh

1965. Lenin's 95th Birth Anniv.
N358 **144** 8 x. purple and buff . . 50 25
N359 12 x. purple and grey . . 75 30

1965. Pres. Ho Chi Minh's 75th Birthday.
N360 **145** 6 x. violet, yell & grn . . 50 20
N361 12 x. violet, yell & buff . 1·00 25

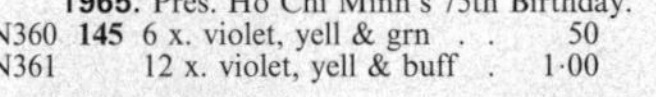

146 Hands clasping Serpent   **147** Two Soldiers advancing

1965. 10th Anniv of Afro-Asian Conf, Bandung.
N362 **146** 12 x. multicoloured . . . 60 30

1965. Trade Union Conference, Hanoi.
N363 **147** 12 x. blue and purple . . 60 25
N364 – 12 x. multicoloured . . . 60 25
N365 – 12 x. red, black & grn . 60 25
DESIGNS—HORIZ: No. N364, Sea battle; N365, "Peoples of the World" on Globe, and soldiers.

148 Yellow-throated Marten

1965. Fauna Protection. Multicoloured.
N366 12 x. Type **148** 80 45
N367 12 x. Owston's palm civet . 1·25 45
N368 12 x. Chinese pangolin . . . 1·25 45
N369 12 x. Francois' monkey (vert) 1·25 45
N370 20 x. Red giant flying squirrel 3·75 1·25
N371 50 x. Lesser slow loris (vert) 6·25 2·25

149 Marx and Lenin   **150** Nguyen Van Troi (patriot)

1965. Postal Ministers Congress, Peking.
N372 **149** 12 x. multicoloured . . 1·00 35

1965. Nguyen Van Troi Commemoration.
N373 **150** 12 x. sepia, brn & grn . 60 25
N374 50 x. sepia, brn & ochre 1·25 70
N375 4 d. sepia and red . . . 8·00 3·75

151 "Rhynchocoris humeralis"   **152** Revolutionaries

1965. Noxious Insects. Multicoloured.
N376 12 x. Type **151** . . . . . . 1·00 45
N377 12 x. "Tessaratoma papillosa" 1·00 45
N378 12 x. "Poeciliocoris latus" . 1·00 45
N379 12 x. "Tosena melanoptera" . 1·00 45
N380 20 x. "Cicada sp." . . . . 3·50 1·60
N381 30 x. "Fulgora candelaria" . 5·00 2·00
Nos. N379/81 are vert 20½ × 38 mm.

1965. 20th Anniv of August Revolution.
N382 **152** 6 x. brown, black & blue 30 20
N383 12 x. black and red . . 65 25

153 Prawn

1965. Marine Life. Multicoloured.
N384 12 x. Type **153** . . . . . . 2·25 60
N385 12 x. Shrimp . . . . 2·25 60
N386 12 x. Swimming crab . . . 2·25 60
N387 12 x. Serrate swimming crab 2·25 60
N388 20 x. Spiny lobster . . . . 4·25 1·90
N389 50 x. Fiddler crab . . . . . 8·75 3·25

154 Air Battle   **155** Foundryman ("Heavy Industries")

1965. "500th U.S. Aircraft Brought Down over North Vietnam".
N390 **154** 12 x. green and lilac . . 5·50 3·75

1965. 20th Anniv of Republic and Completion of 1st Five-Year Plan.
N391 **155** 12 x. black and orange . 50 20
N392 – 12 x. black and green . 50 15
N393 – 12 x. black and purple . 50 15
DESIGNS: No. N392, Irrigation, pylon and power station ("Hydro-electric Power"); N393, Nurse examining child ("Social Medicine").
See also Nos. N417/19.

156 Drummer and Peasants

1965. 35th Anniv of Movement of Nghe An and Ha Tinh Soviet Peasants.

N394 **156** 10 x. multicoloured . . 35 20
N395 12 x. multicoloured . . 65 25

157 Girls and Flags

1965. 16th Anniv of Friendship between China and Vietnam. Multicoloured.

N396 12 x. Type **157** 50 25
N397 12 x. Vietnamese and Chinese girls with flags (vert) . . . 50 25

158 Tsiolkovsky and "Sputnik 1"

1965. Space Flight of "Voskhod 2".

N398 **158** 12 x. blue and purple . . 90 30
N399 – 12 x. ochre and blue . . 90 30
N400 – 50 x. blue and green . . 2·10 90
N401 – 50 x. blue & turquoise . . 2·10 90

DESIGNS: No. N399, Leonov, Belyaev and "Voskhod 2"; N400, Gagarin; N401, Leonov in space.

159 Red Lacewing

1965. Butterflies. Multicoloured.

N402 12 x. Type **159** . . . . . . 2·50 50
N403 12 x. Leopard lacewing . . . 2·50 50
N404 12 x. Blue triangle . . . . . 2·50 50
N405 12 x. Indian purple emperor 2·50 50
N406 20 x. Paris peacock . . . . 7·50 1·75
N407 30 x. Common rose . . . . 10·50 3·00

160 Norman R. Morrison and Demonstrators

161 Birthplace of Nguyen Du (poet)

1965. Homage to Norman R. Morrison (American Quaker who immolated himself).

N408 **160** 12 x. black and red . . 60 30

1965. Nguyen Du Commem. Multicoloured.

N409 12 x. Type **161** 50 25
N410 12 x. Nguyen Du Museum . 50 25
N411 20 x. "Kieu" (volume of poems) . . . . 1·00 35
N412 1 d. Scene from "Kieu" . . 2·10 1·00

162 Pres. Ho Chi Minh

163 Rice-field and Insecticide-sprayer ("Agriculture")

1965. Engels' 145th Birth Anniv. Multicoloured.

N413 12 x. Type **162** 60 25
N414 12 x. Marx 60 25
N415 12 x. Lenin 60 25
N416 50 x. Engels . . . . 1·90 90

1965. Completion of First Five-Year Plan (2nd issue).

N417 **163** 12 x. orange and green 60 25
N418 – 12 x. blue and red . . . 60 25
N419 – 12 x. orange and blue . 60 25

DESIGNS: No. N418, Factory-worker ("Light Industries"); N419, Children at play and students ("Social Education").

164 Soldier and Demonstrators

1965. 5th Anniv of South Vietnam National Liberation Front.

N420 **164** 12 x. violet and lilac . . 60 25

165 Casting Votes

166 "Dendrobium moschatum"

1966. 20th Anniv of 1st Vietnamese General Elections.

N421 **165** 12 x. black and red . . 45 20

1966. Orchids. Multicoloured.

N422 12 x. Type **166** . . . . . . 1·25 40
N423 12 x. "Vanda teres" . . . . 1·25 40
N424 12 x. "Dendrobium crystallinum" . . . . . . 1·25 40
N425 12 x. "Dendrobium nobile" 1·25 40
N426 20 x. "Vandopsis gigantea" 3·00 1·00
N427 30 x. "Dendrobium" . . . 5·75 1·90

167 Child on Rocking-horse

168 "Physignathus cocincinus"

1966. New Year.

N428 **167** 12 x. multicoloured . . 50 20

1966. Protection of Nature—Reptiles. Multicoloured.

N429 12 x. Type **168** . . . . . . 1·00 40
N430 12 x. "Trionyx sinensis" . . 1·00 40
N431 12 x. Gecko (inscr "GEKKO GECKO") . . . . 1·00 40
M432 12 x. "Testudo elongata" . 1·00 40
M433 20 x. "Varanus salvator" . 2·75 1·60
M434 40 x. "Eretmochelys imbricata" . . . . 4·50 1·60

169 Wrestling

170 Ly Tu Trong (revolutionary), Badge and Banner

1966. National Games.

N435 **169** 12 x. multicoloured . . 60 30
N436 – 12 x. multicoloured . . 60 30
N437 – 12 x. multicoloured . . 60 30

GAMES: No. N436, Archery (with crossbow); N437, "Fencing".

1966. 35th Anniv of Labour Youth Union.

N438 **170** 12 x. multicoloured . . 45 20

171 Republic Thunderchief in Flames

1966. "1,000th U.S. Aircraft Brought Down over North Vietnam".

N439 **171** 12 x. multicoloured . . . 4·25 1·90

172 Worker and Rifle 174 Children and Banners

173 Battle Scene on Con Co Island

1966. Labour Day.

N440 **172** 6 x. black, red and salmon 50 25

1966. Defence of Con Co ("Steel Island").

N441 **173** 12 x. multicoloured . . . 50 20

1966. 25th Anniv of Vietnam Youth Pioneers.

N442 **174** 12 x. black and red . . . 50 25

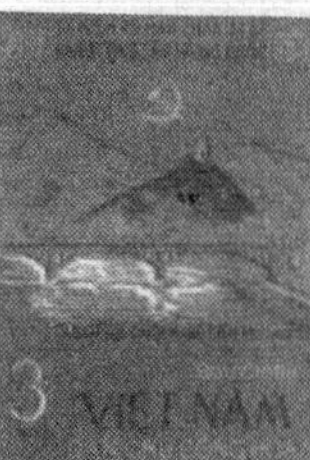

175 View of Dien An (Yenan)

176 "Luna 9" in Space

1966. 45th Anniv of Chinese Communist Party. Multicoloured.

N443 3 x. Type **175** 35 20
N444 12 x. Ho Chi Minh and Mao Tse-tung 60 40

1966. "Luna 9" Space Flight. Multicoloured. Inscr "MAT TRANG 9".

N445 12 x. Type **176** 50 25
N446 50 x. "Luna 9" on Moon . . 2·00 1·00

177 Airplane in Flames

1966. "1,500th U.S. Aircraft Brought Down over North Vietnam".

N447 **177** 12 x. multicoloured . . . 4·50 2·50
N448 12 x. mult (optd **NGAY 14.10.1966**) . . . . . 5·00 3·25

178 Liberation Fighter

1966. Victories of Liberation Army. Inscr "1965–1966".

N449 **178** 1 x. purple 25 15
N450 12 x. multicoloured . . . 50 25
N451 – 12 x. multicoloured . . . 50 25

DESIGN: No. N451, Soldier escorting prisoners-of-war.

See also No. 646.

179 Women from different Regions, and Child

1966. 20th Anniv of Vietnamese Women's Union.

N452 **179** 12 x. black & salmon . 50 25

180 Moluccan Pittas

1966. Birds. Multicoloured.

N453 12 x. Type **180** . . . . . . 1·60 40
N454 12 x. Black-naped orioles . 1·60 40
N455 12 x. Common kingfisher . 1·60 40
N456 12 x. Long-tailed broadbill . 1·60 40
N457 20 x. Hoopoe . . . . 3·50 1·50
N458 30 x. Maroon orioles . . . 6·50 1·90

Nos. N454/5 and N457 are vert.

181 Football

1966. Ganefo Games. Multicoloured.

N459 12 x. Type **181** 50 25
N460 12 x. Rifle-shooting 50 25
N461 30 x. Swimming . . . . . . 1·25 50
N462 30 x. Running . . . . . . 1·25 50

182 Harvesting Rice

1967. Agricultural Production.

N463 **182** 12 x. multicoloured . . 60 25

183 Ho Chi Minh Text and Fighters

1967. Ho Chi Minh's Appeal.

N464 **183** 12 x. purple and red . . 30 20
N465 – 12 x. purple and red . . 45 20

DESIGNS: No. N465, Ho-Chi-Minh text and marchers with banners.

See also Nos. 519/22.

184 Bamboo ("Arundinaria rolleana")

1967. Bamboo. Multicoloured.

N466 12 x. Type **184** 75 25
N467 12 x. "Arundinaria racemosa" 75 25
N468 12 x. "Bambusa bingami" . 75 25
N469 12 x. "Bambusa arundinaceu" 75 25
N470 30 x. "Bambusa nutans" 2·00 1·00
N471 50 x. "Dendrocalamus patellaris" . . . . 3·75 1·75

185 Dhole

1967. Wild Animals. Multicoloured.

No.	Type	Description	Unused	Used
N472		12 x. Type **185**	1·00	40
N473		12 x. Binturong	1·00	40
N474		12 x. Hog-badger	1·00	40
N475		20 x. Large Indian civet	2·00	75
N476		40 x. Bear macaque	3·25	1·25
N477		50 x. Clouded leopard	5·00	1·90

186 Captured Pilot

187 Rocket Launching and Agricultural Scene

1967. "2,000th U.S. Aircraft Brought Down over North Vietnam".

No.	Type	Description	Unused	Used
N478	**186**	6 x. blk & red on pink	1·90	80
N479		12 x. blk & red on grn	1·90	80

1967. Launching of First Chinese Rocket. Multicoloured.

No.	Type	Description	Unused	Used
N480		12 x. Type **187**	60	25
N481		30 x. Rocket launching, and Gate of Heavenly Peace, Peking	1·25	50

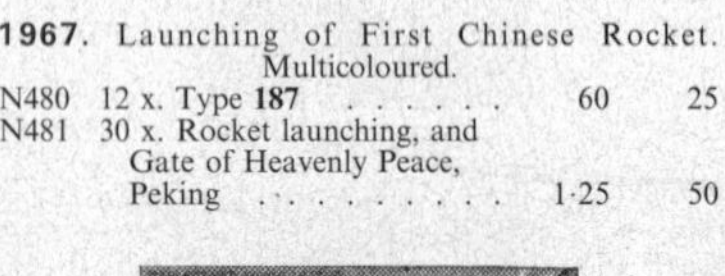

188 Siamese Tiger Fish

1967. Vietnamese Fishes. Multicoloured.

No.	Type	Description	Unused	Used
N482		12 x. Type **188**	65	20
N483		12 x. Spanish mackerel	65	20
N484		12 x. Lizard fish	65	25
N485		20 x. Spangled emperor	1·25	50
N486		30 x. German fish	2·50	75
N487		50 x. Golden-striped snapper	3·75	95

189 Lenin and Revolutionary Soldiers

1967. 50th Anniv of October Revolution. Multicoloured.

No.	Type	Description	Unused	Used
N488		6 x. Type **189**	25	15
N489		12 x. Lenin and revolutionaries	45	20
N490		12 x. Lenin, Marx and Vietnamese soldiers	45	20
N491		20 x. Cruiser "Aurora"	75	40

190 Air Battle

1967. "2,500th U.S. Aircraft Brought Down over North Vietnam".

No.	Type	Description	Unused	Used
N492	**190**	12 x. black, red & grn	4·25	1·25
N493	–	12 x. black, red & blue	4·25	1·25

DESIGN—VERT: No. N493, Boeing B-52 Stratofortress falling in flames.

191 Atomic Symbol and Gate of Heavenly Peace, Peking

1967. 1st Chinese "H"-Bomb Test. Multicoloured.

No.	Type	Description	Unused	Used
N494		12 x. Type **191**	75	30
N495		20 x. Chinese lantern, atomic symbol & dove (30 × 35 mm)	1·10	45

192 Factory Anti-aircraft Unit

1967. Anti-aircraft Defences. Multicoloured.

No.	Type	Description	Unused	Used
N496		12 x. Type **192**	50	25
N497		12 x. Rifle-fire from trenches	50	25
N498		12 x. Seaborne gun-crew	50	25
N499		12 x. Militiawoman with captured U.S. pilot	50	25
N500		20 x. Air battle	95	40
N501		30 x. Military anti-aircraft post	1·75	75

193 Chickens

1968. Domestic Fowl. Multicoloured designs showing cocks and hens.

No.	Type	Description	Unused	Used
N502		12 x. Type **193**	85	40
N503		12 x. Inscr "Ga ri"	85	40
N504		12 x. Inscr "Ga trong thien ri"	85	40
N505		12 x. Inscr "Ga den chanchi"	85	40
N506		20 x. Junglefowl	1·90	60
N507		30 x. Hen	2·25	1·00
N508		40 x. Hen and chicks	2·75	1·25
N509		50 x. Two hens	3·25	1·60

194 Gorky

1968. Birth Centenary of Maxim Gorky.

No.	Type	Description	Unused	Used
N510	**194**	12 x. black & brown	60	30

195 Burning Village

1968. Victories of 1966–67.

No.	Type	Description	Unused	Used
N511	**195**	12 x. brown and red	50	25
N512	–	12 x. brown and red	50	25
N513	–	12 x. brown and red	50	25
N514	–	12 x. brown and red	50	25
N515	–	12 x. black and violet	50	25
N516	–	12 x. black and violet	50	25
N517	–	12 x. black and violet	50	25
N518	–	12 x. black and violet	50	25

DESIGNS: No. N512, Firing mortars; N513, Attacking tanks with rocket-gun; N514, Sniping; N515, Attacking gun-site; N516, Escorting prisoners; N517, Interrogating refugees; N518, Civilians demonstating.

197 Ho Chi Minh Text and Fighters

198 Hong boch Rose

1968. Intensification of Production.

No.	Type	Description	Unused	Used
N519	**197**	6 x. blue on yellow	30	15
N520		12 x. blue	40	20
N521		12 x. purple	40	20
N522		12 x. red	40	20

1968. Roses. Multicoloured.

No.	Type	Description	Unused	Used
N523		12 x. Type **198**	60	25
N524		12 x. Hong canh sap	60	25
N525		12 x. Hong leo	60	25
N526		20 x. Hong vang	1·90	65
N527		30 x. Hong nhung	2·50	80
N528		40 x. Hong canh tim	3·75	1·25

199 Ho Chi Minh and Flag

200 Karl Marx

1968. Ho Chi Minh's New Year Message.

No.	Type	Description	Unused	Used
N529	**199**	12 x. brown and violet	40	20

1968. 150th Birth Anniv of Karl Marx.

No.	Type	Description	Unused	Used
N530	**200**	12 x. black and green	50	25

201 Anti-aircraft Machine-gun Crew

1968. "3,000th U.S. Aircraft Brought Down over North Vietnam". Multicoloured.

No.	Type	Description	Unused	Used
N531		12 x. Type **201**	1·50	65
N532		12 x. Women manning anti-aircraft gun	1·50	65
N533		40 x. Aerial dogfight	3·50	1·40
N534		40 x. Anti-aircraft missile	3·50	1·40

202 Rattan-cane Work

1968. Arts and Crafts. Multicoloured.

No.	Type	Description	Unused	Used
N535		6 x. Type **202**	35	15
N536		12 x. Bamboo work	40	25
N537		12 x. Pottery	40	25
N538		20 x. Ivory carving	80	35
N539		30 x. Lacquer work	1·25	45
N540		40 x. Silverware	1·60	75

203 Quarter-staff Contest

1968. Traditional Sports. Multicoloured.

No.	Type	Description	Unused	Used
N541		12 x. Type **203**	50	20
N542		12 x. Dagger fighting	50	20
N543		12 x. Duel with sabres	50	20
N544		30 x. Unarmed combat	1·25	55
N545		40 x. Scimitar fighting	2·00	70
N546		50 x. Sword and buckler	2·25	95

205 Temple, Khue

1968. Vietnamese Architecture. Multicoloured.

No.	Type	Description	Unused	Used
N548		12 x. Type **205**	30	25
N549		12 x. Bell tower, Keo Pagoda	50	25
N550		20 x. Bridge, Bonze Pagoda (horiz)	70	30
N551		30 x. Mot Cot Pagoda, Hanoi	70	35
N552		40 x. Gateway, Ninh Phuc Pagoda (horiz)	1·25	55
N553		50 x. Tay Phuong Pagoda (horiz)	1·75	60

206 Vietnamese Militia

1968. Cuban–North Vietnamese Friendship. Multicoloured. With gum.

No.	Type	Description	Unused	Used
N554		12 x. Type **206**	35	20
N555		12 x. Cuban revolutionary (vert)	35	20
N556		20 x. "Revolutionary Solidarity" (vert)	80	25

207 "Ploughman with Rifle"

1968. "The War Effort". Paintings. With gum.

No.	Type	Description	Unused	Used
N557	**207**	12 x. black, bl & yell	25	15
N558	–	12 x. multicoloured	25	15
N559	–	30 x. brown, blue and turquoise	85	30
N560	–	40 x. multicoloured	95	35

DESIGNS—HORIZ: No. N558, "Defending the Mines"; N559, "Repairing Railway Track"; N560, "Crashed Aircraft".

208 Nam Ngai shooting down Aircraft

1969. Lunar New Year. Victories of the National Liberation Front. Multicoloured.

No.	Type	Description	Unused	Used
N561		12 x. Type **208**	40	20
N562		12 x. Tay Nguyen throwing grenade	40	20
N563		12 x. Gun crews, Tri Thien	40	20
N564		40 x. Insurgents, Tay Ninh	1·00	40
N565		50 x. Home Guards	1·60	80

209 Loading Timber Lorries

1969. North Vietnamese Timber Industry. Multicoloured.

No.	Type	Description	Unused	Used
N566		6 x. Type **209**	25	15
N567		12 x. Log raft on river	35	20
N568		12 x. Tug towing "log train"	35	20
N569		12 x. Elephant hauling logs	60	20
N570		12 x. Insecticide spraying	35	20
N571		20 x. Buffalo hauling log	1·25	40
N572		30 x. Logs on overhead cable	1·90	75

210 "Young Guerrilla" (Co Tan Long Chau)

1969. "South Vietnam—Land and People". Paintings. Multicoloured.

No.	Type	Description	Unused	Used
N573		12 x. Type **210**	45	30
N574		12 x. "Scout on Patrol" (Co Tan Long Chau)	45	30
N575		20 x. "Woman Guerrilla" (Le Van Chuong) (vert)	70	45
N576		30 x. "Halt at a Relay Station" (Co Tan Long Chau)	70	45
N577		40 x. "After a Skirmish" (Co Tan Long Chau)	1·50	1·10
N578		50 x. "Liberated Hamlet" (Huynh Phuong Dong)	1·90	1·25

211 Woman Soldier, Ben Tre

1969. Victories in Tet Offensive (1968).

No.	Type	Description	Unused	Used
N579	**211**	8 x. black, grn & pink	45	20
N580		12 x. black, emer & green	45	20
N581	–	12 x. multicoloured	45	20
N582	–	12 x. multicoloured	45	20
N583	–	12 x. multicoloured	45	20

DESIGNS—VERT: No. N581, Urban guerilla and attack on U.S. Embassy, Saigon; N582, Two soldiers with flag, Hue; N583, Mortar crew, Khe Sanh.

212 Soldier with Flame-thrower

1969. 15th Anniv of Liberation of Hanoi.

N584 212 12 x. black and red . . 1·10 50
N585 – 12 x. multicoloured . . 1·10 50
DESIGN: No. N585, Children with construction toy.

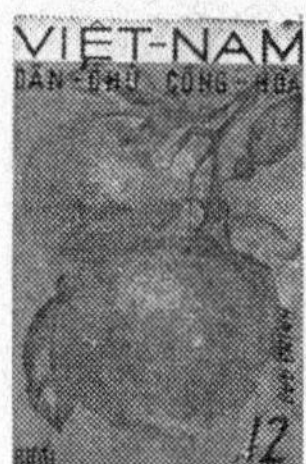

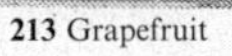
213 Grapefruit 214 Tribunal Emblem and Falling Airplane

1969. Fruits. Multicoloured.

N586 12 x. Type **213** 35 15
N587 12 x. Pawpaw 35 15
N588 20 x. Tangerines 50 20
N589 30 x. Oranges 85 35
N590 40 x. Lychees . . . . 1·40 70
N591 50 x. Persimmons . . . . . . 1·90 1·00
See also Nos. N617/21 and N633/6.

1969. International War Crimes Tribunal, Stockholm and Roskilde.

N592 **214** 12 x. black, red & brown 45 20

215 Ho Chi Minh in 1924

1970. 40th Anniv of Vietnamese Workers' Party. Multicoloured.

N593 12 x. Type **215** 40 20
N594 12 x. Ho Chi Minh in 1969 . 40 20
N595 12 x. Le Hong Phong . . . 40 20
N596 12 x. Tran Phu 40 20
N597 12 x. Nguyne Van Cu . . . 40 20
Nos. N595/7 are smaller than Type **215**, size 40 × 24 mm.

216 Playtime in Nursery School

1970. Children's Activities. Multicoloured.

N598 12 x. Type **216** 30 20
N599 12 x. Playing with toys . . . 30 20
N600 20 x. Watering plants . . . 45 25
N601 20 x. Pasturing buffalo . . . 45 25
N602 30 x. Feeding chickens . . . 60 40
N603 40 x. Making music 80 50
N604 50 x. Flying model airplane . 1·25 75
N605 60 x. Going to school . . . 2·10 95

217 Lenin and Red Flag

1970. Birth Centenary of Lenin.

N606 **217** 12 x. multicoloured . . 30 15
N607 – 1 d. purple, red & yell . 1·90 50
DESIGN: 1 d. Portrait of Lenin.

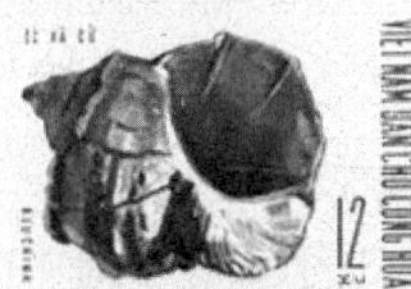

218 Great Green Turban

1970. Sea-shells. Multicoloured.

N608 12 x. Type **218** . . . . . . 1·25 25
N609 12 x. Indian volute . . . . 1·25 25
N610 20 x. Tiger cowrie . . . . 1·60 35
N611 1 d. Trumpet triton . . . . 4·75 1·00

219 Ho Chi Minh in 1930

1970. Ho Chi Minh's 80th Birth Anniv.

N612 **219** 12 x. black, brn & flesh 30 15
N613 – 12 x. black, bl & grn . . 30 15
N614 – 2 d. black, ochre & yell 1·90 1·10
PORTRAITS: No. N613, In 1945 with microphone; N614, In 1969.

220 Vietcong Flag

1970. 1st Anniv of National Liberation Front Provisional Government in South Vietnam.

N616 **220** 12 x. multicoloured . . 40 20

221 Water-melon 222 Power Linesman

1970. Fruits. Multicoloured.

N617 12 x. Type **221** 30 20
N618 12 x. Pumpkin 30 20
N619 20 x. Cucumber 45 25
N620 50 x. Courgette . . . . . . 1·00 45
N621 1 d. Charantais melon . . . 2·00 85

1970. North Vietnamese Industries.

N622 **222** 12 x. blue and red . . . 50 15
N623 – 12 x. red, yellow & bl . 50 15
N624 – 12 x. black, orge & bl . 50 25
N625 – 12 x. yellow, pur & grn 50 25
DESIGNS—VERT: No. N623, Hands winding thread on bobbin ("Textiles"); N624, Stoker and power station ("Electric Power"); N625, Workers and lorry ("More coal for the Fatherland").

223 Peasant Girl with Pigs 225 Chuoi Tieu Bananas

224 Ho Chi Minh proclaiming Republic, 1945

1970. North Vietnamese Agriculture.

N626 **223** 12 x. multicoloured . . 60 25

1970. 25th Anniv of Democratic Republic of Vietnam.

N627 **224** 12 x. black, brn & red . 25 10
N628 – 12 x. deep brown, brown and green 25 10
N629 – 12 x. brn, grey and red 25 10
N630 – 12 x. deep brown, brown and green 25 10
N631 – 20 x. brn, red & bistre . 40 15
N632 – 1 d. brown, drab and chestnut . . . . . 1·40 60
DESIGNS: No. N628, Vo Thi Sau facing firing-squad; N629, Nguyen Van Troi and captors; N630, Phan Dinh Giot attacking pill-box; N631, Nguyen Viet Xuan encouraging troops; N632, Nguyen Van Be attacking tank.

1970. Bananas. Multicoloured.

N633 12 x. Type **225** 35 20
N634 12 x. Chuoi Tay 35 20
N635 50 x. Chuoi Ngu 95 35
N636 1 d. Chuoi Mat . . . . . 1·90 75

226 Flags, and Bayonets in Helmet

1970. Indo-Chinese People's Summit Conference.

N637 **226** 12 x. multicoloured . . . 35 15

227 Engels and Signature

1970. 150th Birth Anniv of Friedrich Engels.

N638 **227** 12 x. black, brn & red . . 35 15
N639 1 d. black, brown & grn 1·10 60

228 "Akistrodon ciatus" 229 Mother and Child with Flag

1970. Snakes. Multicoloured.

N640 12 x. Type **228** 60 20
N641 20 x. "Calliophis macclellandii" 95 40
N642 50 x. "Bungarus faciatus" . . 1·60 55
N643 1 d. "Trimeresurus gramineus" 2·50 95

1970. 10th Anniv of National Front for Liberation of South Vietnam. Multicoloured.

N644 6 x. Type **229** 20 15
N645 12 x. Vietcong flag and torch (horiz) 25 15

1971. Victories of Liberation Army. As No. N449, but value and colours changed.

N646 **178** 2 x. black and orange . . 30 20

232 Satellite in Earth Orbit

1971. 1st Anniv of Launching of Chinese Satellite.

N649 **232** 12 x. multicoloured . . . 50 20
N650 50 x. multicoloured . . . 1·10 30

234 Ho Chi Minh Medal

1971. 81st Birth Anniv of Pres. Ho Chi Minh.

N652 **234** 1 x. multicoloured . . . 10 10
N653 3 x. multicoloured . . . 20 10
N654 10 x. multicoloured . . . 25 10
N655 12 x. multicoloured . . . 35 20

235 Emperor Quang Trung liberating Hanoi

1971. Bicentenary of Tay Son Rising.

N657 **235** 6 x. multicoloured . . . 35 20
N658 12 x. multicoloured . . . 50 25

236 Karl Marx and Music of the "Internationale"

1971. Centenary of Paris Commune.

N659 **236** 12 x. black, red & pink 50 25

237 Hai Thuong Lan Ong

1971. 250th Birth Anniv of Hai Thuong Lan Ong (physician).

N660 **237** 12 x. black, grn & brn . 25 10
N661 50 x. multicoloured . . 50 25

238 "Kapimala" 239 Ho Chi Minh, Banner and Young Workers

1971. Folk Sculptures in Tay Phuong Pagoda. Multicoloured.

N662 12 x. Type **238** 45 20
N663 12 x. "Sangkayasheta" . . . 45 20
N664 12 x. "Vasumitri" 45 20
N665 12 x. "Dhikaca" 45 20
N666 30 x. "Bouddha Nandi" . . 1·50 35
N667 40 x. "Rahulata" . . . . . 1·60 50
N668 50 x. "Sangha Nandi" . . . 1·75 55
N669 1 d. "Cakyamuni" . . . . 2·10 70

1971. 40th Anniv of Ho Chi Minh Working Youth Union.

N670 **239** 12 x. multicoloured . . 30 15

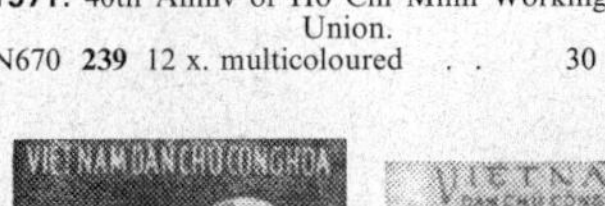

240 "Luna 16" on Moon 241 "Luna 17" landing on Moon

1971. Moon Flight of "Luna 16".

N671 – 12 x. multicoloured . . 40 20
N672 – 12 x. multicoloured . . 40 20
N673 **240** 1 d. brown, bl & turq . 1·75 60
DESIGNS: No. N671, Flight to Moon; N672, Return to Earth.
Nos. N671/2 were issued together horizontally se-tenant, each pair forming a composite design.

1971. Moon Flight of "Luna 17".

N674 **241** 12 x. red, blue & grn . . 40 20
N675 – 12 x. pink, green & myrtle 40 20
N676 – 1 d. pink, brown & grn 1·10 50
DESIGNS—HORIZ: No. N675, "Luna 17" on Moon; N676, "Lunokhod 1" crossing Moon crevasse.

243 "White Tiger"

1971. "The Five Tigers" (folk-art paintings). Multicoloured.
N679 12 x. Type **243** 40 25
N680 12 x. "Yellow Tiger" 40 25
N681 12 x. "Red Tiger" 40 25
N682 40 x. "Green Tiger" . . . . 1·10 35
N683 50 x. "Grey Tiger" . . . . 1·50 50
N684 1 d. "Five Tigers" . . . . . 2·50 95

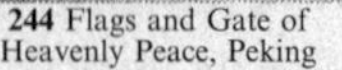

244 Flags and Gate of Heavenly Peace, Peking
245 Mongolian Emblem

1971. 50th Anniv of Chinese Communist Party.
N686 **244** 12 x. multicoloured . . 20 10

1971. 50th Anniv of Mongolian People's Republic.
N687 **245** 12 x. multicoloured . . 30 15

246 Drum Procession

1972. Dong Ho Folk Engravings.
N688 **246** 12 x. pink, brown & blk 40 25
N689 – 12 x. pink and black . . 40 25
N690 – 12 x. multicoloured . . 40 25
N691 – 12 x. multicoloured . . 40 25
N692 – 40 x. multicoloured . . 1·75 40
N693 – 50 x. multicoloured . . 2·10 75
DESIGNS—HORIZ: No. N689, "Traditional Wrestling"; N692, "Wedding of Mice"; N693, "The Toads' School". VERT: No. N690, "Jealous Attack"; N691, "Gathering Coconuts".

247 Workers
248 Planting Rice

1972. 3rd Vietnamese Trade Unions Congress.
N694 **247** 1 x. black and blue . . 25 10
N695 – 12 x. black and orange . 35 20
DESIGN: 12 x. As Type **247**, but design reversed.

1972. 25th Anniv of National Resistance.
N696 **248** 12 x. multicoloured . . 25 15
N697 – 12 x. multicoloured . . 25 15
N698 – 12 x. multicoloured . . 25 15
N699 – 12 x. turq, red & pink . 25 15
DESIGNS: No. N697, Munitions worker; N698, Soldier with flame-thrower; N699, Text of Ho Chi Minh's Appeal.

249 Ho Chi Minh's Birthplace

1972. 82nd Birth Anniv of Ho Chi Minh.
N700 **249** 12 x. black, drab & ochre 25 15
N701 – 12 x. black, grn & pink 25 15
DESIGN: No. N701, Ho Chi Minh's house, Hanoi.

250 Captured Pilot and Falling Airplane
251 Georgi Dimitrov

1972. "3,500th U.S. Aircraft Brought Down over North Vietnam".
N702 **250** 12 x. green and red . . 95 60
N703 12 x. black and red . . 95 60
No. N703 has the inscription, amended to record the actual date on which the 3,500th aircraft was brought down–20.4.1972.

1972. 90th Birth Anniv of Georgi Dimitrov (Bulgarian statesman).
N704 **251** 12 x. brown and green . 25 15
N705 – 12 x. black and pink . 25 15
DESIGN: No. N705, Dimitrov at Leipzig Court, 1933.

252 Falcated Teal
253 Anti-aircraft Gunner

1972. Vietnamese Birds. Multicoloured.
N706 12 x. Type **252** 60 25
N707 12 x. Red-wattled lapwing . 60 25
N708 30 x. Cattle egret 95 30
N709 40 x. Water cock . . . . . 1·25 45
N710 50 x. Purple swamphen . . 2·00 75
N711 1 d. Greater adjutant stork 4·00 1·10

1972. "4,000th U.S. Aircraft Brought Down over North Vietnam".
N712 **253** 12 x. black, mauve and pink 65 25
N713 – 12 x. green, black and red 65 25
DESIGN: No. N713, Anti-aircraft gunner with shell.

254 Umbrella Dance

1972. Tay Nguyen Folk Dances. Multicoloured.
N714 12 x. Type **254** 25 15
N715 12 x. Drum dance 25 15
N716 12 x. Shield dance 25 15
N717 20 x. Horse dance 45 20
N718 30 x. Ka-Dong dance . . . 50 20
N719 40 x. Grinding-rice dance . 70 25
N720 50 x. Gong dance 90 50
N721 1 d. Cham Rong dance . . 1·75 70

255 "Soyuz 11" Spacecraft and "Salyut" Space Laboratory

1972. Space Flight of "Soyuz 11".
N722 **255** 12 x. blue and lilac . . 25 15
N723 – 1 d. brown and flesh . 1·00 45
DESIGN: 1 d. "Soyuz 11" astronauts.

256 Dhole

1973. Wild Animals (1st series). Multicoloured.
N724 12 x. Type **256** 40 20
N725 30 x. Leopard 60 20
N726 50 x. Leopard cat . . . . 1·10 40
N727 1 d. European otter . . . 2·00 50
See also Nos. N736/9.

257 Copernicus and Globe

1973. 500th Birth Anniv of Copernicus (astronomer).
N728 **257** 12 x. black, red & brn . 30 20
N729 – 12 x. black, red & brn . 30 20
N730 – 30 x. black & brown . . 65 25
DESIGNS—HORIZ: 12 x. (No. N729), Copernicus and sun. VERT: 30 x. Copernicus and facsimile signature.

258 "Drummers"

1973. Engravings from Ngoc Lu Bronze Drums. Each yellow and green.
N731 12 x. Type **258** 50 25
N732 12 x. "Pounding rice" . . . 50 25
N733 12 x. "Folk-dancing" . . . 50 25
N734 12 x. "War canoe" 50 25
N735 12 x. "Birds and beasts" . . 50 25

259 Lesser Malay Chevrotain
260 Striated Canegrass Warblers

1973. Wild Animals (2nd series). Multicoloured.
N736 12 x, Type **259** 35 20
N737 30 x. Mainland serow . . . 60 20
N738 50 x. Wild boar . . . . . 1·10 35
N739 1 d. Siberian musk deer . . . 2·00 50

1973. Birds useful to Agriculture. Multicoloured.
N740 12 x. Type **260** 55 30
N741 12 x. Red-whiskered bulbuls 55 30
N742 20 x. Magpie robin 70 35
N743 40 x. White-browed fantails . 1·25 40
N744 50 x. Great tits . . . . . 2·10 70
N745 1 d. Japanese white eyes . . 4·25 1·00

262 "Ready to Learn"

1973. "Three Readies" Youth Movement.
N748 **262** 12 x. brown and green . 20 10
N749 – 12 x. violet and blue . 20 10
N750 – 12 x. green and mauve . 20 10
DESIGNS: No. N749, Soldiers on the march ("Ready to Fight"); N750, Road construction ("Ready to Work").

263 Flags of North Vietnam and North Korea

1973. 25th Anniv of People's Republic of Korea.
N751 **263** 12 x. multicoloured . . . 25 10

264 Dogfight over Hanoi

1973. Victory over U.S. Air Force.
N752 **264** 12 x. multicoloured . . . 25 15
N753 – 12 x. multicoloured . . . 25 15
N754 – 12 x. multicoloured . . . 25 15
N755 – 1 d. black and red . . . 1·[illegible] 55
DESIGNS: No. N753, Boeing B-52 Stratofortress exploding over Haiphong; N754, Anti-aircraft gun; N755, Aircraft wreckage in China Sea.

266 Elephant hauling Logs
267 Dahlia

1974. Vietnamese Elephants. Multicoloured.
N758 12 x. Type **266** 50 20
N759 12 x. War elephant 50 20
N760 40 x. Elephant rolling logs . 1·25 35
N761 50 x. Circus elephant . . . 1·50 45
N762 1 d. Elephant carrying war supplies . . . . 3·25 95

1974. Flowers.
N763 **267** 12 x. red, lake & green . 45 20
N764 – 12 x. red, lake & green . 45 20
N765 – 12 x. yellow, grn & bl . 45 20
N766 – 12 x. multicoloured . . 75 30
N767 – 12 x. multicoloured . . 75 30
FLOWERS: No. N764, Rose; N765, Chrysanthemum; N766, Bach Mi; N767, Dai Doa.

268 Soldier planting Flag
269 Armed Worker and Peasant

1974. 20th Anniv of Victory at Dien Bien Phu.
N768 12 x. Type **268** 20 10
N769 12 x. Victory badge 20 10

1974. "Three Responsibilities" Women's Movement.
N770 **269** 12 x. blue and pink . . 25 10
N771 – 12 x. blue and pink . . 25 10
DESIGN: No. N771, Woman operating loom.

270 Cuc Nau Chrysanthemum
271 "Corchorus capsularis"

1974. Vietnamese Chrysanthemums. Mult.
N772 12 x. Type **270** 30 20
N773 12 x. Cuc Vang 30 20
N774 20 x. Cuc Ngoc Khong Tuoc 55 25
N775 30 x. Cuc Trang 60 30
N776 40 x. Kim Cuc 75 45
N777 50 x. Cuc Hong Mi . . . . 1·10 50
N778 60 x. Cuc Gam . . . . . . 1·40 55
N779 1 d. Cuc Tim . . . . . . 2·50 1·00

1974. Textile Plants.
N780 **271** 12 x. brown, green and olive 50 15
N781 – 12 x. brown, grn & pink 50 15
N782 – 30 x. brown, grn & yell 1·00 35
DESIGNS: No. N781, "Cyperus tojet jormis"; N782, "Morus alba".

272 Nike Statue, Warsaw

1974. 30th Anniv of People's Republic of Poland.
N783 **272** 1 x. pur, pink and red . 25 15
N784 2 x. red, pink and red . 25 15
N785 3 x. brn, pink and red . 25 15
N786 12 x. lt red, pink & red 65 25

273 Flags of China and Vietnam

1974. 25th Anniv of People's Republic of China.
N787 **273** 12 x. multicoloured . . 35 15

274 Handclasp with Vietnamese and East German Flags

1974. 25th Anniv of German Democratic Republic.

N788	274	12 x. multicoloured	35	15

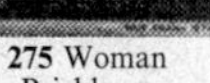

275 Woman Bricklayer

276 Pres. Allende with Chilean Flag

1974. 20th Anniv of Liberation of Hanoi. Multicoloured.

N789		12 x. Type **275**	20	10
N790		12 x. Soldier with child	20	10

1974. 1st Death Annivs of Salvador Allende (President of Chile) and Pablo Neruda (Chilean poet).

N791	276	12 x. blue and red	20	10
N792	–	12 x. blue (Pablo Neruda)	20	10

277 "Rhizostoma"

1974. Marine Life. Multicoloured.

N793	12 x. Type **277**	50	15
N794	12 x. "Loligo"	50	15
N795	30 x. Variously coloured abalone	75	20
N796	40 x. Japanese pearl oyster	1·00	25
N797	50 x. Common cuttlefish	1·60	50
N798	1 d. "Palinurus japonicus"	3·25	1·00

278 Flags of Algeria and Vietnam

279 Albanian Emblem

1974. 20th Anniv of Algerian War of Liberation.

N799	278	12 x. multicoloured	40	15

1974. 30th Anniv of People's Republic of Albania. Multicoloured.

N800	12 x. Type **279**	20	10
N801	12 x. Girls from Albania and North Vietnam	20	10

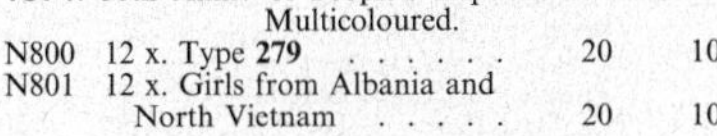

280 Signing of Paris Agreement

1975. 2nd Anniv of Paris Agreement on Vietnam.

N802	280	12 x. blk, grn and emerald	25	20
N803	–	12 x. blk, blue and grey	25	20

DESIGN: No. N803, International Conference in session.

281 Tran Phu

1975. 45th Anniv of Vietnamese Workers' Party.

N804	281	12 x. brown, red & pink	20	10
N805	–	12 x. brown, red & pink	20	10
N806	–	12 x. brown, red & pink	20	10
N807	–	12 x. brown, red & pink	20	10
N808	–	60 x. brown, chestnut and pink	75	35

PORTRAITS—HORIZ: No. N805, Nguyen Van Cu; N806, Le Hong Phong; N807, Ngo Gia Tu. VERT: No. N808, Ho Chi Minh in 1924.

282 "Costus speciosus"

283 "Achras sapota"

1975. Medicinal Plants. Multicoloured.

N809	12 x. Type **282**	30	15
N810	12 x. "Rosa laevigata"	30	15
N811	12 x. "Curcuma zedoaria"	30	15
N812	30 x. "Erythrina indica"	55	20
N813	40 x. "Lilium brownii"	70	25
N814	50 x. "Hibiscus sagittifolius"	75	35
N815	60 x. "Papaver somniferum"	1·10	40
N816	1 d. "Belamcanda chinensis"	2·25	70

1975. Fruits. Multicoloured.

N817	12 x. Type **283**	20	10
N818	12 x. "Persica vulgaris"	20	10
N819	20 x. "Eugenia jambos"	25	15
N820	30 x. "Chrysophyllum cainito"	35	20
N821	40 x. "Lucuma mamosa"	40	20
N822	50 x. "Prunica granitum"	55	20
N823	60 x. "Durio ziberthinus"	75	35
N824	1 d. "Prunus salicina"	1·40	65

284 Ho Chi Minh

285 Ho Chi Minh proclaiming Independence, 1945

1975. 85th Birth Anniv of Ho Chi Minh.

N825	284	12 x. multicoloured	20	15
N826		60 x. multicoloured	45	20

1975. 30th Anniv of Democratic Republic of Vietnam. Multicoloured.

N827	12 x. Type **285**	20	10
N828	12 x. Democratic Republic emblem	20	10
N829	12 x. Democratic Republic flag	20	15

286 "Dermochelys coriacea"

287 Arms of Hungary

1975. Reptiles. Multicoloured.

N831	12 x. Type **286**	35	15
N832	12 x. "Physignathus cocincinus"	35	15
N833	20 x. "Hydrophis brookii"	50	15
N834	30 x. "Platysternum megacephalum"	60	20
N835	40 x. "Leiolepis belliana"	90	20
N836	50 x. "Python molurus"	1·00	35
N837	60 x. "Naja hannah"	1·25	45
N838	1 d. "Draco maculatus"	2·50	55

1975. 30th Anniv of Liberation of Hungary.

N839	287	12 x. multicoloured	35	15

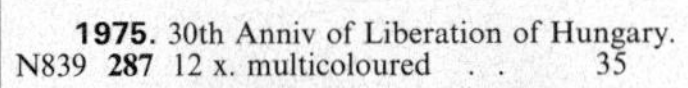

288 "Pathysa antiphates"

1976. Butterflies. Multicoloured.

N840	12 x. Type **288**	50	10
N841	12 x. "Danaus genutia"	50	10
N842	20 x. "Gynautocera papilionaria"	65	15
N843	30 x. "Maenas salaminia"	75	20
N844	40 x. "Papilio machaon"	1·00	20
N845	50 x. "Ixias pyrene"	1·10	30
N846	60 x. "Eusemia vetula"	1·50	50
N847	1 d. "Eriboea hbri"	2·75	65

289 Hoang Thao Orchid

290 Masked Palm Civet

1976. Lunar New Year.

N848	289	6 x. yellow, grn & blue	60	25
N849		12 x. yellow, grn & red	95	25

1976. Wild Animals. Multicoloured.

N850	12 x. Type **290**	25	10
N851	12 x. Belly-banded squirrel	25	10
N852	20 x. Rhesus macaque	30	10
N853	30 x. Chinese porcupine	50	15
N854	40 x. Racoon-dog	60	20
N855	50 x. Asiatic black bear	75	30
N856	60 x. Leopard	1·10	45
N857	1 d. Malayan flying lemur	1·90	65

291 Voters and Map

1976. 1st Elections Unified National Assembly.

N858	291	6 x. red and sepia	25	10
N859	–	6 x. yellow and red	25	10
N860	291	12 x. red and blue	75	20

DESIGN:—35 × 24 mm: No. N859, Map and ballot box.

See also Nos. NLF64/6 of National Front for the Liberation of South Vietnam.

292 Map and Text

1976. 1st Session of Unified National Assembly.

N861	292	6 x. purple, red & yell	25	10
N862		12 x. turquoise, red & yell	60	20
N863	–	12 x. bistre, red & yellow	60	20

DESIGN—VERT (27 × 42 mm): No. N863, Vietnam map and design from Ngoc Lu Drum. No. N862 shows different text from Type **292**.

See also Nos. NLF68/9 of National Front for the Liberation of South Vietnam.

293 "Dendrobium devonianum"

1976. Orchids. Multicoloured.

N864	12 x. Type **293**	25	10
N865	12 x. "Habenaria rhodocheila"	25	10
N866	20 x. "Dendrobium tortile"	40	10
N867	30 x. "Doritis pulcherima"	50	10
N868	40 x. "Dendrobium farmeri"	70	15
N869	50 x. "Dendrobium aggregatum"	80	25
N870	60 x. "Eria pannae"	1·10	45
N871	1 d. "Paphiopedilum concolor"	1·40	55

FRANK STAMPS

F 29

F 42 Invalids in Rice-field

1958. No value indicated.

NF82	F 29	(–) red, yellow and green	10·00	4·50

Issued to war-disabled persons for private correspondence.

1959. No value indicated.

NF105	F 42	(–) brown	3·00	90
NF106		(–) olive and blue	4·50	1·40

Issued to invalids in agriculture for private correspondence

F 230 Invalid's Badge

1971. No value indicated.

NF647	F 230	(–) brown and red	60	25

Issued to disabled ex-servicemen for private correspondence.

F 233 Disabled Soldier with Baby

F 261 "Returning Home"

1971. No value indicated.

NF651	F 233	(—) brown, red and yellow	45	20

1973.

NF746	F 261	12 x. black and red	30	10
NF747	–	12 x. black & blue	30	10

DESIGN—22 × 33 mm: No. NF747, Disabled soldier with drill.

Issued to disabled veterans for private correspondence.

MILITARY FRANK STAMPS

MF 46 Soldier and Steam Train

1959. No value indicated.

NMF112	MF 46	(–) black & grn	6·50	2·25

MF 68 Mounted Frontier Guard

MF 118 Military Medal and Invalid's Badge

1961. No value indicated.

NMF154	MF 68	(–) multicoloured	11·00	5·50

1963.

NMF277	MF 118	12 x. mult	3·50	2·50

For use on disabled soldier's mail.

MF 133 Soldier and Army Badge

MF 150 Soldier in Action

1964. No value indicated.

NMF325	MF 133	(–) green, black and orange	1·90	60

1965. No value indicated.

NMF373	MF 150	(–) black & red	1·75	45
NMF374		(–) black & grn	1·75	45

MF 177 Soldiers and Weapons

1966. No value indicated.

NMF447	MF 177	(–) violet & black	6·50	6·50

MF 189 "Star" Badge of People's Army

MF 204 Soldiers attacking

1967. No value indicated.
NMF488 MF **189** (-) mult 60 30

1968. No value indicated.
NMF519 (-) brown and green . . .
No. NMF519 is similar in design to No. NMF447, but shows more modern equipment and is dated "1967".

1968. No value indicated.
NMF547 MF **204** (-) lilac 65 30

1969. Type MF 177, but undated. No value indicated.
NMF579 MF **177** (-) brown & grn

MF **231** Nguyen Van Be attacking Tank

1971. No value indicated.
NMF648 MF **231** (-) black, red & drab 50 25

MF **242** Nguyen Viet Yuan and Anti-aircraft Gun

1971. No value indicated.
NMF677 MF **242** (-) black, pink and buff . . . 40 20
NMF678 (-) brown & grn 40 20

MF **265** Soldier with Bayonet advancing

1974. No value indicated.
NMF756 MF **265** (-) black, yell and blue . . . 25 10
NMF757 – (-) black, red and brown 25 10
NMF758 MF **265** (-) black, flesh and red . . . 50 20
DESIGN: No. NMF757 Soldier with sub-machine gun, and tanks. No. NMF757 is 40×24 mm; No. NMF758 31×21 mm.

OFFICIAL STAMPS

The values on Official stamps issued 1952 to 1954 are in kilogrammes of rice, the basis of the State's economy.

A. Tongking.

O **6** Rice harvester

1953. Production and Economy Campaign.
NO17 O **6** 0.600 k. red . . . . . 4·50 1·90
NO18 1.000 k. brown . . . . 4·50 3·25
NO19 2.000 k. orange . . . . 7·00 3·75
NO20 5.000 k. slate . . . . . 9·00 7·00

B. Central Annam.

NAO **3** "Family Left Behind"

1952. Issue for Central Annam. Imperf.
NAO 9 NAO **3** 0.050 k. red . . . — £150
NAO10 0.300 k. red . . . — £150
NAO11 0.300 k. violet . . — £150
NAO12 0.600 k. green . . — £150
NAO13 0.600 k. blue . . — £150
NAO14 1000 k. green . . — £250

1954. No. NA5 surch **TEMSU VU 0.k300 THOC**.
NAO15 NA **1** 0.300 k. on 30 d. on 5 d. green . . . £325 £225

1954. Nos. 56/7 of Vietnam Democratic Republic surch in **Kg.** No. NAO17 also optd **LKV** at top and **THOC** below value.
NAO16 **3** 0 kg 05 on 1 h. green . £170
NAO17 0 kg 050 on 3 h. red . £170

1954. Surch **TEMSU VU** and new value. (a) On unsurcharged stamps with coloured (NAO20) or white (others) figures.
NAO20 NA **1** 0,750 k. on 10 d. mauve . . . . .
NAO21 0,800 k. on 1 d. violet
NAO22 0,900 k. on 5 d. green
(b) On stamps with coloured figures, previously surcharged.
NAO23 NA **1** 0,030 k. on 3 d. on 35 d. purple . .
NAO24 0,050 k. on 35 d. on 300 d. blue . . .
NAO25 0,350 k. on 70 d. on 100 d. grey . . .

C. General issues.

1954. Dien-Bien-Phu Victory. As T **9** but value in "KILO". Imperf.
NO24 0.600 k. ochre and sepia . 12·50 7·50

1955. Surch **0 k, 100 THOC**.
NO33 **2** 0.100 k. on 2 d. brown . £150 £120
NO34 0.100 k. on 5 d. red . . . £150 £120

1955. Land Reform. As T **13** but inscr "SU VU".
NO38 40 d. blue . . . . 10·00 5·00
NO39 80 d. red . . . . 15·00 6·25

O **17** Cu Chinh Lan (Tank Destroyer)

1956. Cu Chinh Lan Commemoration.
NO50 O **17** 20 d. green & turq . 2·75 2·75
NO51 80 d. mauve and red 3·50 3·50
NO52 100 d. sepia & drab . 4·00 4·00
NO53 500 d. blue & lt bl . 11·50 11·50
NO54 1000 d. brown & orge 26·00 26·00
NO55 2000 d. purple & grn 40·00 40·00
NO56 3000 d. lake & lilac 75·00 75·00

1957. 4th World T.U. Conference, Leipzig. As T **24** but inscr "SU VU".
NO69 20 d. green . . . . 2·10 1·25
NO70 40 d. blue . . . . 2·50 1·25
NO71 80 d. lake . . . . 3·75 2·25
NO72 100 d. brown . . . . . 4·00 2·75

O **26** Mot Cot Pagoda, Hanoi

O **30** Lathe

1957.
NO75 O **26** 150 d. brown & green 5·50 2·75
NO76 150 d. black & yellow 8·50 4·75

1958. Arts and Crafts Fair, Hanoi.
NO83 O **30** 150 d. black & pink . 1·90 1·40
NO84 200 d. blue & orange 2·75 1·90

O **31** Congress Symbol

1958. 1st World Congress of Young Workers, Prague.
NO85 O **31** 150 d. red and green 2·25 90

O **34** Soldier, Factory and Crops

1958. Military Service.
NO91 O **34** 50 d. blue and purple 1·40 60
NO92 150 d. brown & green 2·25 75
NO93 200 d. red and yellow 2·75 90

O **40** Footballer and Hanoi Stadium

1958. Opening of New Hanoi Stadium.
NO102 O **40** 10 d. lilac and blue . 65 30
NO103 20 d. olive & salmon 1·00 50
NO104 80 d. brown & ochre 1·75 45
NO105 150 d. brown & turq 2·75 85

O **97** Armed Forces on Boat

O **100** Woman with Rice-planter

1962. Miltiary Service.
NO223 O **97** 12 x. multicoloured . 4·25 1·75

1962. Rural Service.
NO229 O **100** 3 x. red 50 20
NO230 6 x. turquoise . . . 75 25
NO231 12 x. olive 95 35

O **176** Postman delivering Letter

1966. Rural Service.
NO445 O **176** 3 x. purple, bistre and lilac 40 25
NO446 – 6 x. purple, bistre and turquoise 65 25
DESIGN: 6 x. As Type O **176** but design reversed.

POSTAGE DUE STAMPS

1952. Handstamped **TT** in diamond frame.
ND33 **3** 100 d. green . . . . . . 40·00 40·00
ND34 100 d. brown . . . . . . 40·00 40·00
ND35 **5** 100 d. violet . . . . . . 50·00 50·00
ND36 **3** 200 d. red . . . . 50·00 50·00

D **13** Letter Scales

D **39**

1955.
ND40 D **13** 50 d. brown & lemon 11·00 8·75

1958.
ND101 D **39** 10 d. red and violet . 70 60
ND102 20 d. green & orange 1·50 90
ND103 100 d. red and slate . 3·00 2·40
ND104 300 d. red and olive . 4·50 3·25

F. SOCIALIST REPUBLIC OF VIETNAM

Following elections in April 1976 a National Assembly representing the whole of Vietnam met in Hanoi on 24 June 1976 and on 2 July proclaimed the reunification of the country as the Socialist Republic of Vietnam, with Hanoi as capital.

100 xu = 1 dong

18 Red Cross and Vietnam Map on Globe

1976. 30th Anniv of Vietnamese Red Cross.
99 **18** 12 x. red, blue and green . . 50 25

20 "Lutjanus sebae"

1976. Marine Fishes. Multicoloured.
102 12 x. Type **20** 25 10
103 12 x. "Dampieria melanotaenia" 25 10
104 20 x. "Therapon theraps" . . 35 10
105 30 x. "Amphiprion bifasciatus" 50 15
106 40 x. "Abudefduf sexfasciatus" 65 15
107 50 x. "Heniochus acuminatus" 75 20
108 60 x. "Amphiprion macrostoma" 95 35
109 1 d. "Symphorus spilurus" . . 1·60 50

22 Party Flag and Map

23 Workers and Flag

1976. 4th Congress of Vietnam Workers' Party (1st issue). Flag in yellow and red, background colours given below.
111 **22** 2 x. blue 10 10
112 3 x. purple 10 10
113 5 x. green 20 10
114 10 x. green 25 10
115 12 x. green 30 10
116 20 x. green 50 20

1976. 4th Congress of Vietnam Workers' Party (2nd issue).
117 **23** 12 x. black, red & yellow . 30 10
118 – 12 x. red, orange & black . 30 10
DESIGN: No. 118, Industry and agriculture.

24 Ho Chi Minh and Map of Vietnam

1976. "Unification of Vietnam".
119 **24** 6 x. multicoloured 20 15
120 12 x. multicoloured 25 15

25 Soldiers seizing Buon Me Thuot

1976. Liberation of South Vietnam. Mult.
121 2 x. Type **25** 20 10
122 3 x. Soldiers on Son Tra peninsula, Da Nang 20 10
123 6 x. Soldiers attacking Presidential Palace, Saigon . 20 10
124 50 x. Type **25** 55 20
125 1 d. As 3 x. 95 45
126 2 d. As 6 x. . . . . 1·75 90

1976. As Nos. N848/9 but inscr "VIET NAM 1976" at foot and background colours changed.
126a **289** 6 x. yellow, grn & orge . 1·60 50
126b 12 x. yellow, light green and green . . . . 1·60 50

26 "Crocothemis servilia" (Ho)

1977. Dragonflies. Multicoloured.
127 12 x. Type **26** 20 10
128 12 x. "Ictinogomphus clavatus" (Bao) 20 10
129 20 x. "Rhinocypha fenestrella" 30 10
130 30 x. "Neurothemis tullia" . . 35 15
131 40 x. "Neurobavis chinensis" . 50 15
132 50 x. "Neurothemis fulvia" . 75 15
133 60 x. "Rhyothemis variegata" 1·00 35
134 1 d. "Rhyothemis fuliginosa" 1·75 45

27 Great Indian Hornbill and Emblem of Protection

28 Thang Long Tower and Bronze Drum

1977. Rare Birds. Multicoloured.

135 12 x. Type **27** 20 10
136 12 x. Tickell's hornbill 20 10
137 20 x. Long-crested hornbill . . 40 15
138 30 x. Wreathed hornbill 50 20
139 40 x. Indian pied hornbill . . 60 30
140 50 x. Black hornbill 85 30
141 60 x. Great Indian hornbill . . 1·10 45
142 1 d. Rufous-necked hornbill . 1·75 60

1977. 1st Anniv of National Assembly General Election.

143 **28** 4 x. multicoloured 15 10
144 – 5 x. multicoloured 15 10
145 – 12 x. bistre, black and green 15 10
146 – 50 x. multicoloured 40 20

DESIGNS: 5 x. Map of Vietnam and drum; 12 x. Lotus flower and drum; 50 x. Vietnamese flag and drum.

29 "Anoplophora bowringii"

30 "Thevetia peruviana"

1977. Beetles. Multicoloured.

147 12 x. Type **29** 15 10
148 12 x. "Anoplophora horsfieldi" 15 10
149 20 x. "Aphrodisium griffithi" . 25 10
150 30 x. Musk beetle 35 15
151 40 x. "Calloplophora tonkinea" 50 20
152 50 x. "Thysia wallacei" . . . 60 25
153 60 x. "Aristobia approximator" 1·00 40
154 1 d. "Batocera rubus" . . . . 1·60 60

1977. Wild Flowers. Multicoloured.

155 12 x. Type **30** 20 10
156 12 x. "Broussonetia papyrifera" 20 10
157 20 x. "Aleurites montana" . . 25 15
158 30 x. "Cerbera manghes" . . . 35 15
159 40 x. "Cassia multijuga" . . . 50 20
160 50 x. "Cassia nodosa" 60 20
161 60 x. "Hibiscus schizopetalus" 85 35
162 1 d. "Lagerstroesnia speciosa" 1·40 55

31 Pink Dahlias (Hoa Dong Tien)

32 Children drawing Map of Vietnam

1977. Cultivated Flowers (1st series). Multicoloured.

163 6 x. Type **31** 15 10
164 6 x. Orange cactus dahlias (Bong tien kep) 15 10
165 12 x. Type **31** 25 10
166 12 x. As No. 164 . . . . . . 25 10

See also Nos. 192/5.

1977. Unification of Vietnam.

167 **32** 4 x. multicoloured 20 15
168 5 x. multicoloured 20 15
169 10 x. multicoloured 30 15
170 12 x. multicoloured 30 15
171 30 x. multicoloured 50 20

33 Goldfish (Dong Nai Hoa)

1977. Goldfish. Multicoloured.

172 12 x. Type **33** 20 15
173 12 x. Hoa nhung 20 15
174 20 x. Tau xanh 35 15
175 30 x. Mat rong 35 15
176 40 x. Cam trang 45 20
177 50 x. Ngu sac 75 25
178 60 x. Dong nai . . . . 1·00 30
179 1 d. Thap cam . . . . 1·75 50

34 Ho Chi Minh and Lenin Banner

35 Hill Myna

1977 60th Anniv of Russian Revolution. Mult.

180 12 x. Type **34** (blue background) 25 10
181 12 x. Type **34** (bistre background) 25 10
182 50 x. Mother holding child with flag 45 20
183 1 d. Workers, banner, Moscow Kremlin and battleship "Aurora" 95 40

1978. Songbirds. Multicoloured.

184 12 x. Type **35** 35 25
185 20 x. Spotted dove 40 30
186 20 x. Hwamei 40 30
187 30 x. Black-headed shrike . . 85 35
188 40 x. Crimson-winged laughing thrush . . . . 1·10 45
189 50 x. Black-throated laughing thrush . . . . 1·75 50
190 60 x. Chinese jungle mynah . 2·40 75
191 1 d. Yersin's laughing thrush 3·25 1·25

1978. Cultivated Flowers (2nd series). As T **31**. Multicoloured.

192 5 x. Sunflower 15 10
193 6 x. Marguerites 15 10
194 10 x. As 5 x. 25 10
195 12 x. As 6 x. 25 10

36 Vietnamese Children

37 Throwing the Discus

1978. International Children's Day.

196 **36** 12 x. multicoloured . . . 35 20

1978. Athletics. Multicoloured.

197 12 x. Type **37** 20 10
198 12 x. Long jumping 20 10
199 20 x. Hurdling 25 10
200 30 x. Throwing the hammer . 45 15
201 40 x. Putting the shot 55 20
202 50 x. Throwing the javelin . . 75 25
203 60 x. Sprinting . . . . 1·10 40
204 1 d. High jumping . . . . . 1·60 55

38 Ho Chi Minh and Workers

39 Ho Chi Minh

1978. 4th Vietnamese Trade Union Congress. Multicoloured.

205 10 x. Trade Union Emblem . 25 10
206 10 x. Type **38** 25 10

1978. 88th Birth Anniv of Ho Chi Minh. Multicoloured.

207 10 x. Type **39** 35 20
208 12 x. Ho Chi Minh Monument (38 × 22 mm) 35 20

40 Young Pioneers' Cultural House, Hanoi

1978. International Children's Day.

209 **40** 10 x. black, flesh and red . 35 20

MINIMUM PRICE

The minimum price quoted is 10p which represents a handling charge rather than a basis for valuing common stamps. For further notes about prices, see introductory pages.

41 Sanakavasa

1978. Sculptures from Tay Phuong Pagoda. Multicoloured.

210 12 x. Type **41** 20 10
211 12 x. Parsva 20 10
212 12 x. Punyasas 20 10
213 20 x. Kumarata 25 10
214 20 x. Nagarjuna 25 10
215 30 x. Yayata 30 15
216 40 x. Cadiep 45 20
217 50 x. Ananda 50 25
218 60 x. Buddhamitra 65 30
219 1 d. Asvaghosa . . . . . . 1·10 50

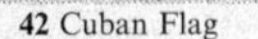
42 Cuban Flag

43 Worker, Peasant, Soldier and Intellectual

1978. 25th Anniv of Cuban Revolution.

220 **42** 6 x. red, black and blue . . 25 10
221 12 x. red, black and blue . . 30 10

1978. 33rd Anniv of Proclamation of Vietnam Democratic Republic.

222 **43** 6 x. red, yellow & mauve . 15 10
223 – 6 x. turquoise, green & bl . 15 10
224 **43** 12 x. red, yellow & mauve . 25 15
225 – 12 x. red and pink 25 15

DESIGN: Nos. 223 and 225, Industrial complex and tractor on field.

44 "Sputnik"

1978. 20 Years of Russian Space Exploration. Multicoloured.

226 12 x. Type **44** 20 10
227 12 x. "Venus 1" 20 10
228 30 x. Space capsules docking 20 15
229 40 x. "Molniya 1" satellite . . 30 20
230 60 x. "Soyuz" 50 25
231 2 d. A. Gubarev and G. Grechko 1·75 75

45 Printed Circuit

47 Chrysanthemum "Cuc Tim"

46 Telephone Dial and Letter

1978. World Telecommunications Day.

232 **45** 12 x. orange and brown . . 25 10
233 – 12 x. brown and orange . . 25 10

DESIGN: No. 233, I.T.U. emblem.

1978. 20th Congress of Socialist Countries' Postal Ministers.

234 **46** 12 x. multicoloured 35 10

1978. Chrysanthemums. Multicoloured.

235 12 x. Type **47** 20 10
236 12 x. "Cuc kim tien" 20 10
237 20 x. "Cuc hong" 25 15
238 30 x. "Cuc van tho" 35 15
239 40 x. "Cuc vang" 35 15
240 50 x. "Cuc thuy tim" 55 25
241 60 x. "Cuc vang mo" 90 35
242 1 d. "Cuc nau do" . . . . . 1·60 50

48 Plesiosaurus

49 Cuban and Vietnamese Flags and Militiawomen

1979. Prehistoric Animals. Multicoloured.

243 12 x. Type **48** 20 10
244 12 x. Brontosaurus 20 10
245 20 x. Iguanodon 25 10
246 30 x. Tyrannosaurus 30 15
247 40 x. Stegosaurus 35 15
248 50 x. Mozasaurus 45 20
249 60 x. Triceratop . . . . . . 1·10 25
250 1 d. Pteranodon . . . . . . 1·60 45

1979. 20th Anniv of Socialist Republic of Cuba.

251 **49** 12 x. multicoloured 30 10

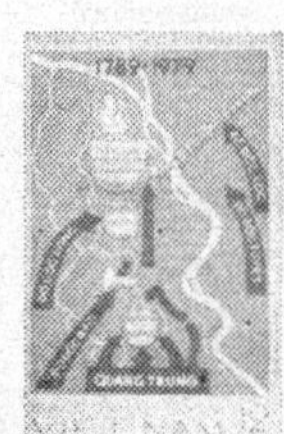
50 Battle Plan

51 Einstein

1979. 190th Anniv of Quang Trung's Victory over the Thanh.

252 **50** 12 x. green, red and blue . 25 10
253 – 12 x. multicoloured 25 10

DESIGN: No. 253, Quang Trung.

1979. Birth Centenary of Albert Einstein (physicist).

254 **51** 12 x. black, brown & blue . 25 10
255 – 60 x. multicoloured 80 30

DESIGN: 60 x. Equation, sun and planets.

52 Ram

53 Emblem

1979. Domestic Animals. Multicoloured.

256 10 x. Type **52** 20 10
257 12 x. Ox 20 10
258 20 x. Ewe and lamb 35 15
259 30 x. White buffalo (vert) . . 45 15
260 40 x. Cow 50 15
261 50 x. Goat 60 20
262 60 x. Buffalo and calf . . . . 1·00 30
263 1 d. Young goat (vert) . . . . 1·75 55

1979. Five Year Plan.

264 **53** 6 x. mauve and light mauve 10 10
265 – 6 x. green and buff 10 10
266 – 6 x. green and purple . . . 10 10
267 – 6 x. orange and green . . . 10 10
268 – 6 x. blue and yellow . . . 10 10
269 **53** 12 x. red and pink 20 10
270 – 12 x. brown and pink . . . 20 10
271 – 12 x. green and yellow . . . 20 10
272 – 12 x. blue and brown . . . 20 10
273 – 12 x. purple and blue . . . 20 10

DESIGNS: Nos. 265, 270, Worker; 266, 271, Peasant and tractor; 267, 272, Soldier; 268, 273, Intellectual.

54 "Philaserdica '79" Emblem

55 Ho Chi Minh and Children

1979. "Philaserdica '79" International Stamp Exhibition, Sofia, Bulgaria.

274 **54** 12 x. blue, brown & orange 25 10
275 30 x. blue, brown and pink 35 10

1979. International Children's Day. Mult.

276 12 x. Type **55** 15 10
277 20 x. Nurse, mother and child 30 10
278 50 x. Children with painting materials and model glider . 45 15
279 1 d. Children of different races 95 35

56 Silver Pheasant **58** Cat (Meo Muop)

57 "Dendrobium heterocacpum"

1979. Ornamental Birds. Multicoloured.

280 12 x. Siamese fireback pheasant ("Lophura diardi") (horiz) . . 20 10
281 12 x. Temminck's tragopan ("Tragopan temminckii") (horiz) 20 10
282 20 x. Ring-necked pheasant (horiz) 30 15
283 30 x. Edwards's pheasant (horiz) 40 20
284 40 x. Type **56** 45 25
285 50 x. Germain's peacock-pheasant 60 35
286 60 x. Rheinhard's pheasant . . 95 40
287 1 d. Green peafowl . . . . . 1·40 60

1979. Orchids. Multicoloured.

288 12 x. Type **57** 20 10
289 12 x. "Cymbidium hybridum" 20 10
290 20 x. "Rhynchostylis gigantea" 25 10
291 30 x. "Dendrobium nobile" . 30 15
292 40 x. "Aerides falcatum" . . . 35 15
293 50 x. "Paphiopedilum callosum" 60 25
294 60 x. "Vanda teres" 95 25
295 1 d. "Dendrobium phalaenopsis" 1·50 45

1979. Cats. Multicoloured.

296 12 x. Type **58** 20 10
297 12 x. Meo Tam The (horiz) . . 20 10
298 20 x. Meo Khoang 25 10
299 30 x. Meo Dom Van (horiz) . 35 15
300 40 x. Meo Muop Dom 40 15
301 50 x. Meo Vang 70 30
302 60 x. Meo Xiem (horiz) . . . 1·00 40
303 1 d. Meo Van Am (horiz) . . 1·90 55

60 Citizens greeting Soldiers

1979. 35th Anniv of Vietnam People's Army.

306 **60** 12 x. brown and green . . 30 20
307 – 12 x. brown and green . . 30 20

DESIGN: No. 307, Soldiers in action.

62 Red and Pink Roses **63** "Nelumbium nuciferum"

1980. Roses. Multicoloured.

311 1 x. Type **62** 15 10
312 2 x. Single pink rose 15 10
313 12 x. Type **62** 30 20
314 12 x. As No. 312 . . . . . . 30 20

1980. Water Flowers. Multicoloured.

315 12 x. Type **63** 15 10
316 12 x. "Nymphala stellata" . . . 15 10
317 20 x. "Ipomola reptans" . . . 20 10
318 30 x. "Nymphoides indicum" . 30 15
319 40 x. "Jussiala repens" 35 15
320 50 x. "Eichhornia crassipes" . 70 25
321 60 x. "Monochoria voginalis" 95 25
322 1 d. "Nelumbo nucifera" . . . 1·50 40

64 Peasants with Banner and Implements as Weapons

1980. 50th Anniv of Vietnamese Communist Party. Multicoloured.

323 12 x. Type **64** 10 10
324 12 x. Ho Chi Minh proclaiming independence 10 10
325 20 x. Soldiers with flag at Dien Bien Phu 25 15
326 20 x. Map of Vietnam and soldiers and tanks storming Palace (Unification of Vietnam) 25 15
327 2 d. Ho Chi Minh, soldier and workers and industrial and agricultural scene . . . . . 1·60 60

65 Lenin

1980. 110th Birth Anniv of Lenin.

328 **65** 6 x. flesh and green . . . 15 10
329 12 x. flesh and purple . . 25 10
330 1 d. flesh and blue 80 35

66 Running **67** Ho Chi Minh in 1924

1980. Olympic Games, Moscow. Multicoloured.

331 12 x. Type **66** 10 10
332 12 x. Hurdles 10 10
333 20 x. Basketball 20 15
334 30 x. Football 30 15
335 40 x. Wrestling 40 15
336 50 x. Gymnastics (horiz) . . 45 20
337 60 x. Swimming (horiz) . . . 65 25
338 1 d. Sailing (horiz) 95 45

1980. President Ho Chi Minh's 90th Birthday.

339 12 x. Type **67** 35 15
340 40 x. Ho Chi Minh as President 50 20

68 Children dancing around Globe **69** Soviet and Vietnamese Cosmonauts

1980. International Children's Day.

341 **68** 5 x. multicoloured 25 15

1980. Soviet–Vietnamese Space Flight. Mult.

342 12 x. Type **69** 10 10
343 12 x. Launch of rocket . . . 10 10
344 20 x. "Soyuz 37" 20 10
345 40 x. "Soyuz-Salyut" space complex 30 15
346 1 d. "Soyuz" re-entering Earth's atmosphere 70 25
347 2 d. Parachute landing . . . 1·40 65

70 "Rhincodon typus"

1980. Fishes. Multicoloured.

349 12 x. Type **70** 15 10
350 12 x. "Galeocerdo cuvier" . . 15 10
351 20 x. "Orectolobus japonicus" 20 10
352 30 x. "Heterodontus zebra" . 30 10
353 40 x. "Dasyatis uarnak" . . . 50 15
354 50 x. "Pristis microdon" . . . 60 20
355 60 x. "Sphyrna lewini" . . . 85 25
356 1 d. "Myliobatis tobijei" . . 1·25 40

71 Ho Chi Minh telephoning **72** Pink Rose (Hong Bach)

1980. Posts and Telecommunications Day. Multicoloured.

357 12 x. Ho Chi Minh reading newspaper "Nhan Dan" . . 20 10
358 12 x. Type **71** 25 10
359 50 x. Kim Dong, "the heroic postman", carrying magpie robin in cage . . . . 1·10 30
360 1 d. Dish aerial . . . . 1·00 35

1980. Flowers.

361 **72** 12 x. pink and green . . . 35 15
362 – 12 x. red and green 35 15
363 – 12 x. mauve and green . . . 35 15

DESIGNS—As Type **72**: No. 362, Red roses (Hong nhung). 15 × 20 mm: No. 363, Camellia.

73 Telephone Switchboard Operator **74** Ho Chi Minh

1980. National Telecommunications Day.

364 12 x. Type **73** 20 10
365 12 x. Diesel train and railway route map 30 10

1980. 35th Anniv of Democratic Republic of Vietnam. Multicoloured.

366 12 x. Type **74** 25 10
367 12 x. Arms of Vietnam (29 × 40 mm) 25 10
368 40 x. Pac Bo cave (29 × 40 mm) 40 15
369 1 d. Source of Lenine (40 × 29 mm) 95 40

75 Vietnamese Arms **76** Nguyen Trai

1980. National Emblems.

370 **75** 6 x. multicoloured 25 10
371 – 12 x. yellow, red and black . 25 10
372 – 12 x. black, orange & yell . 25 10

DESIGNS—VERT: No. 372, National Anthem. HORIZ: No. 371, National flag.

1980. 600th Birth Anniv of Nguyen Trai (national hero).

373 **76** 12 x. yellow and black . . . 20 10
374 – 50 x. black and blue 45 20
375 – 1 d. black and brown . . . 95 40

DESIGNS—HORIZ: 50 x. Three books by Nguyen Trai. VERT: 1 d. Ho Chi Minh reading commemorative stele in Con Son Pagoda.

77 Ho Chi Minh with Women **78** "Biguoniaceae venusta"

1980. 50th Anniv of Vietnamese Women's Union.

376 **77** 12 x. green, blue and lilac . . 25 10
377 – 12 x. blue and lilac 25 10

DESIGN: No. 377, Group of women.

1980. Flowers. Multicoloured.

378 12 x. Type **78** 20 10
379 12 x. "Ipomoea pulchella" . . 20 10
380 20 x. "Petunia hybrida" . . . 30 10
381 30 x. "Trapaeolum majus" . . 40 15
382 40 x. "Thunbergia grandiflora" 45 15
383 50 x. "Anlamanda cathartica" 55 20
384 60 x. "Campsis radicans" . . 80 25
385 1 d. "Bougainvillaea spectabilis" 1·50 45

79 "Symphysodon aequifasciata"

1981. Ornamental Fishes. Multicoloured.

386 12 x. Type **79** 20 10
387 12 x. "Betta splendens" . . . 20 10
388 20 x. "Poecilobrycon eques" . 30 10
389 30 x. "Gyrinocheilus aymonieri" 40 15
390 40 x. "Barbus tetrazona" . . 45 15
391 50 x. "Pterophyllum eimekei" 60 20
392 60 x. "Xiphophorous helleri" . 85 25
393 1 d. "Trichopterus sumatranus" 1·50 50

80 Rocket, Flowers and Flag **82** Green Imperial Pigeon

81 Bear Macaque

1981. 26th U.S.S.R. Communist Party Congress. Multicoloured.

394 20 x. Type **80** 25 10
395 50 x. Young citizens with flag 50 20

1981. Animals of Cue Phuong Forest. Mult.

396 12 x. Type **81** 10 10
397 12 x. Crested gibbons 10 10
398 20 x. Asiatic black bears . . . 20 10
399 30 x. Dhole 40 15
400 40 x. Wild boar 50 15
401 50 x. Sambars 65 25
402 60 x. Leopard 75 25
403 1 d. Tiger . . . . 1·40 40

1981. Turtle Doves. Multicoloured.

404 12 x. Type **82** 25 20
405 12 x. White-bellied wedge-tailed green pigeon (horiz) 25 20
406 20 x. Red turtle dove 30 25
407 30 x. Bar-tailed cuckoo dove . 55 30
408 40 x. Mountain imperial pigeon 75 35
409 50 x. Pin-tailed green pigeon (horiz) . . . . 1·00 40
410 60 x. Emerald dove (horiz) . . 1·25 45
411 1 d. White-bellied pin-tailed green pigeon (horiz) . . . . 2·25 85

83 Yellow-backed Sunbird **85** "Elaeagnus latifolia"

1981. Nectar-sucking Birds. Multicoloured.

412 20 x. Type **83** 35 25
413 20 x. Ruby-cheeked sunbird . 35 25
414 20 x. Black-throated sunbird . 45 30
415 40 x. Mrs. Gould's sunbird . 80 35
416 50 x. Macklot's sunbird . . . 1·00 40
417 50 x. Blue-naped sunbird . . 1·00 40
418 60 x. Van Hasselt's sunbird . 1·10 45
419 1 d. Green-tailed sunbird . . 2·00 70

1981. Fruits. Multicoloured.

422 20 x. Type **85** 20 10
423 20 x. "Fortunella japonica" . 20 10
424 30 x. "Nephelium lappaceum" 35 15
425 40 x. "Averrhoa bilimbi" . . . 40 15
426 50 x. "Ziziphus mauritiana" . 50 20
427 50 x. Strawberries ("Fragaria vesca") 50 20
428 60 x. "Bouea oppositifolia" . . 60 25
429 1 d. "Syzygium aqueum" . . . 1·25 40

86 Girl with Rice Sheaf

87 Ho Chi Minh planting Tree

1981. World Food Day.

430 **86** 30 x. green 25 15
431 50 x. green 30 15
432 – 2 d. orange . . . . 1·10 40

DESIGN: 2 d. F.A.O. emblem and rice.

1981. Tree Planting Festival.

433 **87** 30 x. orange and blue . . . 55 25
434 – 30 x. pink and blue 55 25

DESIGN: No. 434, Family planting tree.

88 European Bison

1981. Animals. Multicoloured.

435 30 x. Type **88** 25 10
436 30 x. Orang-utan 25 10
437 40 x. Hippopotamus 40 20
438 40 x. Red kangaroo 40 20
439 50 x. Giraffe 60 20
440 50 x. Javan rhinoceros 60 20
441 60 x. Common zebra 65 25
442 1 d. Lion . . . . 1·40 45

89 Congress Emblem

1982. 10th World Trade Unions Congress, Havana, Cuba.

443 **89** 50 x. multicoloured 30 15
444 5 d. multicoloured . . . . 3·25 1·10

90 Ho Chi Minh and Party Flag

1982. 5th Vietnamese Communist Party Congress (1st issue). Multicoloured.

445 30 x. Type **90** 50 20
446 30 x. Hammer, sickle and rose 50 20

See also Nos. 455/6.

91 "Thyreus decorus" (carpenter bee)

1982. Bees and Wasps. Multicoloured.

447 20 x. Type **91** 20 10
448 20 x. "Vespa affinis" (wasp) . 20 10
449 30 x. "Eumenes esuriens" (mason wasp) 30 15
450 40 x. "Polistes sp." (wasp) . . 45 20
451 50 x. "Sphex sp." (wasp) . . . 65 25
452 50 x. "Chlorion lobatum" (wasp) 65 25
453 60 x. "Xylocopa sp." (carpenter bee) 75 35
454 1 d. Honey bee . . . . 1·25 50

92 Electricity Worker and Pylon

1982. 5th Vietnamese Communist Party Congress (2nd issue).

455 **92** 30 x. stone, black & mauve 60 25
456 – 50 x. multicoloured . . . 70 25

DESIGN: 50 x. Women harvesting rice.

93 Football

1982. Football Training Movement.

457 **93** 30 x. multicoloured . . . 35 15
458 – 30 x. multicoloured (Two players) 35 15
459 – 40 x. multicoloured . . . 40 20
460 – 40 x. mult (diag striped background) 40 20
461 – 50 x. mult (vert striped background) 45 20
462 – 50 x. mult (horiz striped background) 45 20
463 – 60 x. multicoloured . . . 65 25
464 – 1 d. multicoloured 90 40

DESIGNS: Nos. 458/64, Various football scenes.

94 Militiawoman

1982.

465 **94** 30 x. multicoloured . . . 65 25

See also Nos. MF466/7.

95 Arms of Bulgaria

1982. 1300th Anniv of Bulgarian State.

468 **95** 30 x. pink and red 40 10
469 50 x. stone and red . . . 50 15
470 2 d. orange and red . . . 2·25 75

96 Map of Vietnam and Red Cross

97 Georgi Dimitrov

1982. 35th Anniv of Vietnamese Red Cross.

471 **96** 30 x. red, blue and black . 30 15
472 – 1 d. red, green and black 1·25 50

DESIGN: 1 d. Red Cross.

1982. Birth Centenary of Georgi Dimitrov (Bulgarian statesman).

473 **97** 30 x. orange and black . . 35 15
474 3 d. brown and black . . 2·75 95

98 Rejoicing Women

99 Common Kestrel

1982. 5th National Women's Congress. Mult.

475 12 x. Type **98** 40 15
476 12 x. Congress emblem and three women 40 15

1982. Birds of Prey. Multicoloured.

477 30 x. Type **99** 45 35
478 30 x. Pied falconet 45 35
479 40 x. Black baza 70 40
480 50 x. Black kite 90 45
481 50 x. Lesser fishing eagle . . . 90 45
482 60 x. Fieldens falconet (horiz) 1·00 55
483 1 d. Black-shouldered kite (horiz) 2·25 1·10
484 1 d. Short-toed eagle . . . . . 2·25 1·10

100 Red Dahlia

101 Dribble

1982. Dahlias. Multicoloured.

485 30 x. Type **100** 40 15
486 30 x. Orange dahlia 40 15
487 40 x. Rose dahlia 45 15
488 50 x. Red decorative dahlia . . 60 20
489 50 x. Yellow dahlia 60 20
490 60 x. Red single dahlia 70 25
491 1 d. White dahlia . . . . . . 1·25 50
492 1 d. Pink dahlia . . . . 1·25 50

1982. World Cup Football Championship, Spain. Multicoloured.

493 50 x. Type **101** 50 20
494 50 x. Tackle 50 20
495 50 x. Passing ball 50 20
496 1 d. Heading ball . . . . . . 1·10 40
497 1 d. Goalkeeper saving ball . . 1·10 40
498 2 d. Shooting . . . . 1·90 70

102 Cuban Flag

104 Rabindranath Tagore

103 Ho Chi Minh and Children planting Tree

1982. 20th Anniv of Cuban Victory at Giron.

499 **102** 30 x. multicoloured 45 15

1982. World Environment Day.

500 **103** 30 x. green and black . . . 35 15
501 – 30 x. green and black . . . 35 15

DESIGN: No. 501, U.N. environment emblem and plants.

1982. 120th Birth Anniv (1981) of Rabindranath Tagore (Indian poet).

502 **104** 30 x. orange, brown and black 45 25

105 "Sycanus falleni" (soldier bug)

106 Lenin and Cruiser "Aurora"

1982. Harmful Insects. Multicoloured.

503 30 x. Type **105** 30 10
504 30 x. "Catacanthus incarnatus" (shieldbug) 30 10
505 40 x. "Nezara viridula" (shield-bug) 40 15
506 50 x. "Helcomeria spinosa" (squashbug) 70 20
507 50 c. "Lohita grandis" (fire bug) 70 20
508 60 x. "Chrysocoris stolli" (shieldbug) 75 25
509 1 d. "Tiarodes ostentans" (soldier bug) . . . . 1·25 50
510 1 d. "Pterygamia grayi" (squashbug) . . . . 1·25 50

1982. 65th Anniv of Russian Revolution.

511 **106** 30 x. red and black . . . 40 15
512 – 30 x. red and black . . . 40 15

DESIGN: No. 512, Russian man and woman, Lenin and space station.

108 Swimming

1982. 9th South East Asian Games, New Delhi.

514 **108** 30 x. blue and lilac . . . 40 15
515 – 30 x. blue and mauve . . . 40 15
516 – 1 d. orange and blue . . . 1·10 40
517 – 2 d. green and brown . . 1·90 65

DESIGNS: 30 x. (No. 515) Table tennis; 1 d. Wrestling; 2 d. Rifle shooting.

109 "Samaris cristatus"

1982. Fishes. Soles. Multicoloured.

518 30 x. Type **109** 30 10
519 30 x. "Tephrinectes sinensis" . 30 10
520 40 x. "Psettodes erumei" . . . 45 15
521 40 x. "Zebrias zebra" 45 15
522 50 x. "Pardachirus pavoninus" 65 20
523 50 x. "Cynoglossus puncticeps" 65 20
524 60 x. "Brachirus orientalis" . . 80 35
525 1 d. "Psettina iijimae" . . . . 1·10 45

110 Foundry and Textile Workers

112 Sampan

111 Lenin on Map

1982. "All for the Socialist Fatherland, All for Happiness of the People".

526 **110** 30 x. light blue and blue . 30 10
527 – 30 x. brown and yellow . 30 10
528 – 1 d. brown and green . . 1·10 40
529 – 2 d. pink and purple . . . 2·00 75

DESIGNS: 30 x. Women holding sheaf of wheat and basket of grain; 1 d. Soldiers; 2 d. Nurse with children holding books.

1982. 60th Anniv of U.S.S.R.

530 **111** 30 x. multicolouired . . . 55 20

1983. Boats. Multicoloured.

531 30 x. Type **112** 20 10
532 50 x. Junk with striped sails . 30 10
533 1 d. Houseboats 65 25
534 3 d. Junk 95 30
535 5 d. Sampan with patched sails 1·40 40
536 10 d. Sampan (horiz) . . . . 2·00 95

113 Class "231-300"

1983. Railway Locomotives. Multicoloured.

537 30 x. Type **113** 25 10
538 50 x. Class "230-000" 35 10
539 1 d. Class "140-601" 50 25
540 2 d. Class "241-000" 75 30
541 3 d. Class "141-500" 95 30
542 5 d. Class "150-000" . . . . 1·40 50
543 8 d. Class "40-300" . . . . . 2·25 75

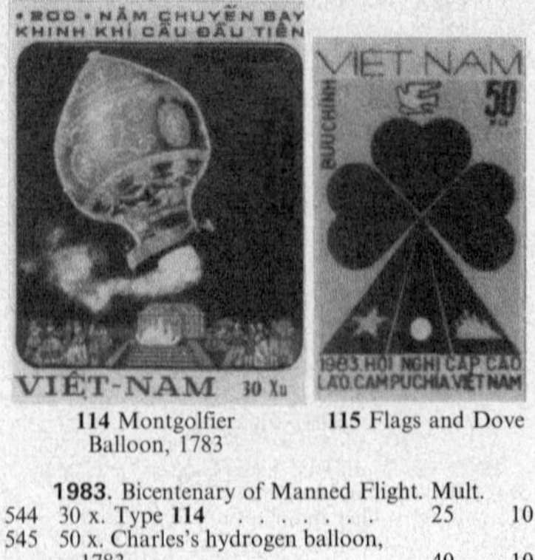

114 Montgolfier Balloon, 1783 **115** Flags and Dove

1983. Bicentenary of Manned Flight. Mult.
544 30 x. Type **114** 25 10
545 50 x. Charles's hydrogen balloon, 1783 40 10
546 1 d. Parseval Sigsfeld kite-type observation balloon, 1898 65 25
547 2 d. Eugene Godard's balloon "L'Aigle", 1864 95 30
548 3 d. Blanchard and Jeffries' balloon, 1785 1·10 30
549 5 d. Nadar's balloon "Le Geant", 1863 1·75 40
550 8 d. Balloon 2·75 70

1983. Laos–Kampuchea–Vietnam Summit Conference.
552 **115** 50 x. red, yellow & blue 35 15
553 5 d. red, blue & yellow 3·50 1·60

116 Robert Koch

1983. Centenary of Discovery of Tubercle Bacillus.
554 **116** 5 d. black, blue & red 3·50 1·60

117 "Teratolepis fasciata"

1983. Reptiles. Multicoloured.
555 30 x. Type **117** 20 10
556 30 x. Jackson's chameleon 20 10
557 50 x. Spiny-tailed agamid 25 15
558 80 x. "Heloderma suspectum" 35 15
559 1 d. "Chamaeleo meileri" 50 20
560 2 d. "Amphibolurus barbatus" 1·00 25
561 5 d. "Chlamydosaurus kingi" 2·00 40
562 10 d. "Phrynosoma coronatum" 4·00 90

118 A. Gubarev and V. Remek

1983. Cosmonauts. Multicoloured.
563 30 x. Type **118** 20 10
564 50 x. P. Klimuk and Miroslaw Hermaszewski 25 10
565 50 x. V. Bykovsky and Sigmund Jahn 25 10
566 1 d. Nikolai Rukavishnikov and Georgi Ivanov 40 15
567 1 d. Bertalan Farkas and V. Kubasov 40 15
568 2 d. V. Gorbatko and Pham Tuan 70 25
569 2 d. Arnaldo Tamayo Mendez and I. Romanenko 70 25
570 5 d. V. Dzhanibekov and Gurragcha 1·40 40
571 8 d. L. Popov and D. Prunariu 1·75 60

119 "Madonna of the Chair" **121** Burmese King and Rook

1983. 500th Birth Anniv of Raphael (artist). Multicoloured.
573 30 x. Type **119** 25 10
574 50 x. "Madonna of the Grand Duke" 40 10
575 1 d. "Sistine Madonna" 50 15
576 2 d. "The Marriage of Mary" 90 30
577 3 d. "The Beautiful Gardener" 1·25 35
578 5 d. "Woman with Veil" 1·75 45
579 8 d. "Self-portrait" 2·25 65

1983. Chess Pieces. Multicoloured.
582 30 x. Type **121** 20 10
583 50 x. 18th-century Delhi king (elephant) 25 10
584 1 d. Lewis knight and bishop 40 15
585 2 d. 8th/9th-century Arabian king (elephant) 80 30
586 3 d. 12th-century European knight 1·25 35
587 5 d. 16th-century Russian rook (sailing boat) 1·75 50
588 8 d. European Chinese-puzzle bishop and rook (fool and elephant) 2·25 75

123 Long Jumping **125** Common Grass Yellow

1983. Olympic Games, Los Angeles (1984). Multicoloured.
591 30 x. Type **123** 20 10
592 50 x. Running 25 10
593 1 d. Javelin throwing 40 15
594 2 d. High jumping (horiz) 70 30
595 3 d. Hurdling (horiz) 1·00 35
596 5 d. Putting the shot 1·40 45
597 8 d. Pole vaulting 1·75 65

1983. Butterflies. Multicoloured.
600 30 x. Type **125** 30 10
601 30 x. Green dragontail ("Leptocircus meges") 30 10
602 40 x. "Nyctalemon patroclus" 40 15
603 40 x. Tailed jay ("Zetides agamemnon") 40 15
604 50 x. Peacock ("Precis almana") 50 20
605 50 x. "Papilio chaon" 50 20
606 60 x. Tufted jungle king 60 25
607 1 d. Leaf buttefly 1·00 40

128 Karl Marx

1983. Death Centenary of Karl Marx.
617 **128** 50 x. black and red 45 25
618 10 d. black and purple 5·00 2·75

129 Postman

1983. World Communications Year. Mult.
619 50 x. Type **129** 25 10
620 2 d. Mail sorting office 75 30
621 8 d. Telephonists 2·00 50
622 10 d. Wireless operator and dish aerial 3·00 75

130 Running, Stadium and Sports Pictograms

1983. National Youth Sports Festival.
624 **130** 30 x. blue and turquoise 65 25
625 1 d. brown and orange 1·60 70

131 Oyster Fungus ("Pleurotus ostreatus") **132** Child with Fish

1983. Fungi. Multicoloured.
626 50 x. Type **131** 60 10
627 50 x. Common ink cap ("Coprinus atramentarius") 60 10
628 50 x. Golden mushroom ("Flammulina velutipes") 60 10
629 50 x. Chanterelle ("Cantharellus cibarius") 60 10
630 1 d. Chinese mushroom 85 15
631 2 d. Red-staining mushroom 1·75 30
632 5 d. Common morel 3·25 70
633 10 d. Caesar's mushroom 7·25 1·40

1983. World Food Day. Multicoloured.
634 50 x. Type **132** 25 10
635 4 d. Family 1·25 45

133 Envelope with I.T.U. Emblem

1983. World Telecommunications Year.
636 **133** 50 x. + 10 x. blue, green & red 95 65
637 – 50 x. + 10 x. red, buff and brown 95 65

DESIGN: No. 637, W.C.Y. emblem and dish aerial.

134 Building Dam

1983. 5th Anniv of U.S.S.R.–Vietnam Co-operation Treaty.
640 **134** 4 d. grey and black 1·90 65

135 Girl with Flowers

1983. 5th Trade Unions Congress.
642 **135** 50 x. blue, orange & blk 20 10
643 – 2 d. black, blue & brown 50 25
644 – 30 d. black, blue & pink 7·50 2·25

DESIGNS: 2, 30 d. Worker and industrial complex.

136 Grey Herons **137** Conference Emblem and Hands

1983. Birds. Multicoloured.
645 50 x. Type **136** 35 25
646 50 x. Painted storks ("Ibis leucocephalus") 35 25
647 50 x. Black storks ("Ciconia nigra") 35 25
648 50 x. Purple herons ("Ardea purpurea") 35 25
649 1 d. Common cranes 50 30
650 2 d. Black-faced spoonbills 1·10 55
651 5 d. Black-crowned night herons 2·25 80
652 10 d. Asian open-bill storks 4·75 1·50

1983. World Peace Conference, Prague.
653 – 50 x. blue, red & yellow 15 10
654 **137** 3 d. green, red & yellow 1·10 45
655 5 d. lilac, red & yellow 1·90 75
656 20 d. blue, red & yellow 7·50 2·50

DESIGN: 50 x. Conference emblem and women.

138 Biathlon

1984. Winter Olympic Games, Sarajevo. Multicoloured.
657 50 x. Type **138** 30 10
658 50 x. Cross-country skiing 30 10
659 1 d. Speed skating 45 15
660 2 d. Bobsleighing 75 30
661 3 d. Ice hockey (horiz) 1·00 35
662 5 d. Ski jumping (horiz) 1·60 45
663 6 d. Slalom (horiz) 1·90 65

139 Marbled Cat

1984. Protected Animals. Multicoloured.
665 50 x. Type **139** 25 10
666 50 x. Leopard 25 10
667 50 x. Tiger 25 10
668 1 d. Common gibbon 50 25
669 1 d. Slow loris 50 25
670 2 d. Indian elephant 1·00 30
671 2 d. Gaur 1·00 30

140 Orchid Tree **141** "Brasse cattleya"

1984. Flowers. Multicoloured.
672 50 x. Type **140** 15 10
673 50 x. "Caesalpinia pulcherrima" 15 10
674 1 d. Golden shower 35 15
675 2 d. Flamboyant 70 25
676 3 d. "Artabotrys uncinatus" 1·00 40
677 5 d. "Corchorus olitorius" 1·75 65
678 8 d. "Bauhinia grandiflora" 2·75 1·00

1984. Orchids. Multicoloured.
680 50 x. Type **141** 25 10
681 50 x. "Cymbidium sp." 25 10
682 1 d. "Cattleya dianx" var. "alba" 40 15
683 2 d. "Cymbidium sp." (different) 70 30
684 3 d. "Cymbidium hybridum" 1·10 35
685 5 d. Phoenix-winged orchids 1·75 45
686 8 d. Yellow queen orchids 2·25 65

1984. Nos. 362 and 373 surch **50xu**.
687 – 50 x. on 12 x. red and green 60 15
688 **76** 50 x. on 12 x. yellow and black 60 15

143 Flying Fish

1984. Deep Sea Fishes. Multicoloured.
688a 30 x. Type **143** 10 10
688b 30 x. Long-horned cow fish ("Ostracion cornutus") 10 10
688c 50 x. Porcupine fish 20 10
688d 80 x. Coral fish 30 10
688e 1 d. Angler fish 40 10
688f 2 d. Fire fish 75 20
688g 5 d. Sun fish 1·90 55
688h 10 d. Grey sting fish 3·75 1·00

146 Ho Chi Minh discussing Battle Plan

1984. 30th Anniv of Battle of Dien Bien Phu. Multicoloured.
691 50 x. Type **146** 25 10
692 50 x. Vietnamese soldiers and truck 25 10
693 1 d. Students carrying provisions 50 15
694 2 d. Pulling field gun up hill . 90 30
695 3 d. Anti-aircraft gun and crashed airplane . . . . . . 1·10 40
696 5 d. Fighting against tanks . . 1·60 50
697 8 d. Vietnamese soldiers with flag on bunker . . . . 2·00 65

148 Blue Gourami

149 Nguyen Duc Canh

1984. Fishes. Multicoloured.
700 50 x. Type **148** 20 10
701 50 x. Zebra fish ("Brachydanio rerio") 20 10
702 1 d. Paradise fish 40 15
703 2 d. Black tetra 75 25
704 3 d. Tetra . . . . 1·25 35
705 5 d. Red-tailed black labeo . . 1·75 45
706 8 d. Siamese fighting fish . . . 2·25 65

1984. 55th Anniv of Vietnamese Trade Union Movement.
707 **149** 50 x. red and black . . . 15 10
708 – 50 x. red and black . . . 15 10
709 – 1 d. multicoloured 35 15
710 – 2 d. multicoloured 70 25
711 – 3 d. multicoloured . . . . 1·25 40
712 – 5 d. multicoloured . . . . 1·90 90
DESIGNS—VERT: No. 708, Founder's house. HORIZ: No. 709, Workers presenting demands to employer; 710, Ho Chi Minh with workers; 711, Factory; 712, Workers, procession and doves.

150 Hon Dua

1984. Coastal Scenes. Multicoloured.
714 50 x. Type **150** 20 10
715 50 x. Hang Con Gai 20 10
716 50 x. Hang Bo Nau 20 10
717 50 x. Nui Yen Ngua 20 10
718 1 d. Hon Ga Choi 40 15
719 1 d. Hon Coc 40 15
720 2 d. Hon Dinh Huong 75 30
721 3 d. Hon Su Tu . . . . 1·10 35
722 5 d. Hon Am . . . . 1·75 50
723 8 d. Nui Bai Tho . . . . . . 2·75 80

151 Styracosaurus

1984. Prehistoric Animals. Multicoloured.
724 50 x. Type **151** 20 10
725 50 x. Diplodocus 20 10
726 1 d. Rhamphorhynchus . . . 40 10
727 1 d. Corythosaurus 40 10
728 2 d. Seymouria 85 25
729 3 d. Allosaurus . . . . 1·25 35
730 5 d. Dimetrodon . . . . 2·10 55
731 8 d. Brachiosaurus . . . . . . 3·25 85

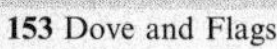
153 Dove and Flags

155 Students and Cultural and Industrial Motifs

1984. Laos–Kampuchea–Vietnam Co-operation.
733 **153** 50 x. red, blue & yellow . 25 10
734 10 d. red, blue & yellow . 3·75 1·25

1984. 5th Anniv of Kampuchea–Vietnam Friendship Treaty. Multicoloured.
736 50 x. Type **155** 15 15
737 3 d. Type **155** 85 25
738 50 d. Kampuchean and Vietnamese dancers . . . . 12·00 2·50

156 Bridge

1984. 30th Anniv of Liberation of Hanoi.
739 **156** 50 x. green and yellow . . 55 20
740 – 1 d. brown and red . . . 1·00 45
741 – 2 d. brown and mauve . . 2·25 75
DESIGNS: 1 d. Gateway; 2 d. Ho Chi Minh mausoleum.

157 Vis-a-vis

159 "Lenin" (V. A. Serov)

1984. Motor Cars. Multicoloured.
743 50 x. Type **157** 20 10
744 50 x. Two-seater 20 10
745 1 d. Tonneau 40 15
746 2 d. Double phaeton 75 25
747 3 d. Landaulet . . . . 1·00 35
748 5 d. Torpedo . . . . 1·75 45
749 6 d. Town coupe . . . . . . 1·90 65

1984. 60th Death Anniv of Lenin. Multicoloured.
751 50 x. Type **159** 20 10
752 1 d. Painting by A. Plotnov of Lenin at meeting 40 15
753 3 d. Painting by K. V. Filatov of Lenin at factory . . . . . 1·25 35
754 5 d. Painting by V. A. Serov of Lenin with three comrades . 2·25 65

160 "Madonna and Child with St. John"

1984. 450th Death Anniv of Correggio (artist). "Madonna and Child" Paintings. Multicoloured.
755 50 x. Type **160** 15 10
756 50 x. Bolognini Madonna . . 15 10
757 1 d. Campori Madonna 25 15
758 2 d. "Virgin adoring the Child" 55 30
759 3 d. "Madonna della Cesta" . 75 35
760 5 d. "Madonna della Scodella" 1·40 45
761 6 d. "Madonna and Child with Angels" . . . . 1·90 50

161 "Keep the Peace" (Le Quoc Loc)

1984. U.N.I.C.E.F. Multicoloured.
763 30 x. Type **161** 15 10
764 50 x. "Sunday" (Nguyen Tien Chung) 20 15
765 1 d. "Baby of the Mining Region" (Tran Van Can) . 30 15
766 3 d. "Little Thuy" (Tran Van Can) (vert) 80 25
767 5 d. "Children at Play" (Nguyen Phan Chanh) . . . . . . 1·75 65
768 10 d. "After Guard Duty" (Nguyen Phan Chanh) (vert) 3·75 1·10

162 Mounted Frontier Guards

163 Water Buffalo

1984. 25th Anniv of Frontier Forces.
769 **162** 50 x. black, blue & brn . . 20 15
770 30 d. black, green & turq . 8·00 2·00

1984.
771 **163** 20 x. brown 10 10
772 – 30 x. red 10 10
773 – 50 x. green 15 10
774 – 50 x. red 15 10
775 – 50 x. mauve 15 10
776 – 50 x. brown 15 10
777 – 1 d. violet 35 15
778 – 1 d. orange 35 15
779 – 1 d. blue 35 15
780 – 1 d. blue 55 15
781 – 2 d. brown 70 25
782 – 2 d. orange 70 25
783 – 2 d. red 70 25
784 – 5 d. mauve . . . . 1·75 65
785 – 10 d. green . . . . 3·50 1·40
DESIGNS: No. 772, Marbled cat; 773, Fighting fish; 774, Cabbage rose; 775, Hibiscus; 776, Lesser panda; 777, "Chrysanthemum sinense"; 778, Tiger; 779, Water lily; 780, Eastern white pelican; 781, Slow loris; 782, Dahlia; 783, Crab-eating macaque; 784, Tokay gecko; 785, Great Indian hornbill.

165 Ho Chi Minh and Troops

984. 40th Anniv of Vietnamese People's Army. Multicoloured.
787 50 x. Type **165** 15 10
788 50 x. Oath-taking ceremony . . 15 10
789 1 d. Soldier with flag and Boeing B-52 Stratofortress bomber on fire 35 15
790 2 d. Civilians building gun emplacement 70 25
791 5 d. Soldiers and tank breaking through gates . . . . 1·00 40
792 5 d. Soldier instructing civilians 1·75 45
793 8 d. Map and soldiers . . . . 2·75 1·00

166 Boy on Buffalo

167 "Echinocereus knippelianus"

1985. New Year. Year of Buffalo.
795 **166** 3 d. purple and pink . . . 1·10 40
796 5 d. brown and orange . . 1·75 65

1985. Flowering Cacti. Multicoloured.
797 50 x. Type **167** 20 10
798 50 x. "Lemaireocereus thurberi" 20 10
799 1 d. "Notocactus haselbergii" . 40 10
800 2 d. "Parodia chrysacanthion" 75 20
801 3 d. "Pelecyphora pseudopectinata" . . . . . 1·10 30
802 5 d. "Rebutia frebrighii" . . . 1·90 50
803 8 d. "Lobivia aurea" . . . . . 2·75 70

168 Nguyen Ai Quoc (Ho Chi Minh)

169 Soldiers with Weapons

1985. 55th Anniv of Vietnam Communist Party.
804 **168** 2 d. grey and red 75 25

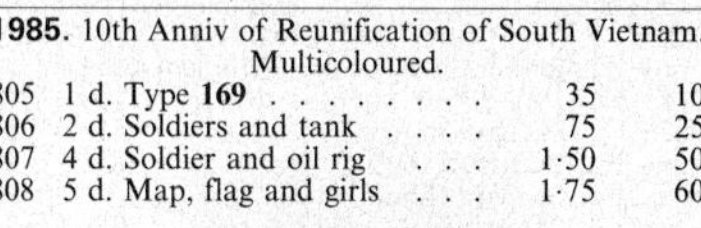
1985. 10th Anniv of Reunification of South Vietnam. Multicoloured.
805 1 d. Type **169** 35 10
806 2 d. Soldiers and tank 75 25
807 4 d. Soldier and oil rig . . . 1·50 50
808 5 d. Map, flag and girls . . . 1·75 60

170 Long Chau Lighthouse

1985. 30th Anniv of Liberation of Haiphong.
810 **170** 2 d. multicoloured 70 30
811 – 5 d. multicoloured . . . . 1·75 80
DESIGN—HORIZ: 5 d. An Duong bridge.

171 Ho Chi Minh and Soldiers

1985. 95th Birth Anniv of Ho Chi Minh (President). Multicoloured.
813 1 d. Type **171** 35 15
814 2 d. Ho Chi Minh reading in cave at Viet Bac 70 25
815 4 d. Portrait (vert) . . . . . 1·40 50
816 5 d. Ho Chi Minh writing in garden of Presidential Palace 1·75 65

172 Soviet Memorial, Berlin-Treptow

173 Globe and People carrying Flags

1985. 40th Anniv of Victory in Europe Day. Multicoloured.
818 1 d. Type **172** 35 15
819 2 d. Soldier and fist breaking swastika 75 25
820 4 d. Hand releasing dove and eagle falling . . . . 1·50 50
821 5 d. Girl releasing doves . . . 1·90 65

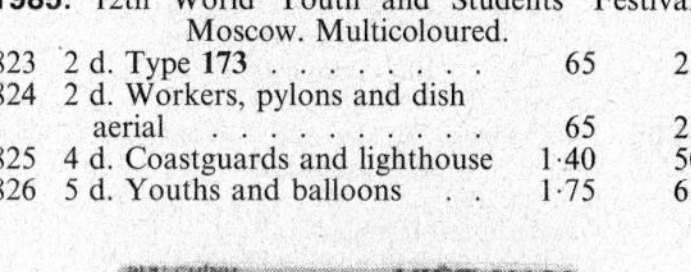
1985. 12th World Youth and Students' Festival, Moscow. Multicoloured.
823 2 d. Type **173** 65 25
824 2 d. Workers, pylons and dish aerial 65 25
825 4 d. Coastguards and lighthouse 1·40 50
826 5 d. Youths and balloons . . 1·75 65

174 Daimler, 1885

1985. Centenary of Motor Cycle. Multicoloured.
828 1 d. Type **174** (wrongly inscr "1895") 30 10
829 1 d. Three-wheeled vehicle, France, 1898 . . . . 30 10
830 2 d. Harley Davidson, U.S.A., 1913 . . . . 60 20
831 2 d. Cleveland, U.S.A., 1918 . 60 20
832 3 d. Simplex, U.S.A., 1935 . . 90 30
833 4 d. Minarelli, Italy, 1984 . . 1·10 40
834 6 d. Honda, Japan, 1984 . . . 1·75 1·10

175 King Penguin

176 "Holothuria monacaria"

1985. "Argentina '85". International Stamp Exhibition, Buenos Aires. Multicoloured.

836 1 d. Type **175** 55 10
837 1 d. Patagonian cavy 55 10
838 2 d. Capybara (horiz) 65 20
839 2 d. Leopard (horiz) 65 20
840 3 d. Lesser rhea 95 30
841 4 d. Giant armadillo (horiz) . 1·25 45
842 6 d. Andean condor (horiz) . . 1·90 65

1985. Marine Life. Multicoloured.

844 3 d. Type **176** . . . . 1·10 30
845 3 d. "Stichopus chloronotus" . 1·10 30
846 3 d. "Luidia maculata" . . . 1·10 30
847 3 d. "Nadoa tuberculata" . . 1·10 30
848 4 d. "Astropyga radiata" . . . 1·40 35
849 4 d. "Linckia laevigata" . . . 1·40 35
850 4 d. "Astropecten scoparius" . 1·40 35

177 Flag and Sickle "40" **178** Globe, Transport and People around Postman

1985. 40th Anniv of Socialist Republic. Mult.

851 2 d. Type **177** 65 20
852 3 d. Doves around globe as heart above handclasp 95 30
853 5 d. Banner . . . . 1·60 50
854 10 d. Ho Chi Minh, flag and laurel branch . . . . 3·25 1·00

1985. 40th Anniv of Postal and Telecommunications Service. Multicoloured.

856 2 d. Type **178** 45 15
857 2 d. Telephonist and telegraph operator 45 15
858 4 d. Wartime deliveries and postwoman Nguyen Thi Nghia 90 30
859 5 d. Dish aerial . . . . 1·10 35

179 Profile of Ho Chi Minh and Policeman

1985. 40th Anniv of People's Police.

860 **179** 10 d. red and black . . . 4·50 1·25

180 Gymnasts

1985. 1st National Sports and Gymnastics Games. Multicoloured.

862 5 d. Type **180** . . . . 1·60 55
863 10 d. Badminton player, gymnast, athlete and swimmer 3·25 1·10

181 Locomotive "Reuth", 1840

1985. 150th Anniv of German Railways. Multicoloured.

864 1 d. Type **181** 30 10
865 1 d. German tank locomotive, 1990 . . . . 30 10
866 2 d. Locomotive "Der Adler", 1835 . . . . 60 20
867 2 d. German passenger locomotive, 1850 . . . . . 60 20
868 3 d. German steam locomotive No. 2024, 1910 . . . . 90 30
869 4 d. German steam tank locomotive, 1920 . . . . . 1·25 40
870 6 d. Bavarian State steam locomotive No. 659, 1890 . 1·75 60

182 Off-shore Rig, Derrick and Helicopter

1985. 30th Anniv of Geological Service.

872 **182** 1 d. blue and purple . . 65 25
873 – 1 d. green and brown . . 65 25

DESIGN: No. 873, Airplane over coastline.

183 Alfa Romeo, 1922

1985. "Italia'85" International Stamp Exhibition, Rome. Motor Cars. Multicoloured.

874 1 d. Type **183** 30 10
875 1 d. Bianchi "Berlina", 1932 . 30 10
876 2 d. Isotta Fraschini, 1928 . . 60 20
877 2 d. Bugatti, 1930 . . . . . . 60 20
878 3 d. Itala, 1912 . . . . 90 30
879 4 d. Lancia "Augusta", 1934 1·25 40
880 6 d. Fiat, 1927 . . . . 1·75 60

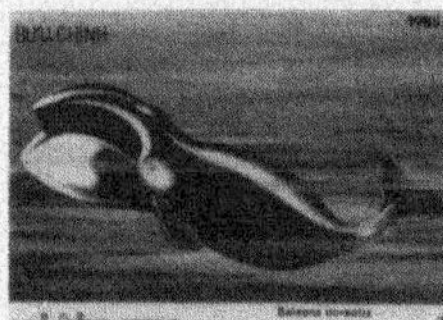

184 Sei Whale

1985. Marine Mammals. Multicoloured.

882 1 d. Type **184** 30 10
883 1 d. Blue whale 30 10
884 2 d. Killer whale 60 20
885 2 d. Common dolphin 60 20
886 3 d. Humpback whale 90 30
887 4 d. Fin whale . . . . 1·25 40
888 6 d. Black right whale . . . . 1·75 60

185 Goalkeeper attempting to save Ball

1985. World Cup Football Championship, Mexico (1986) (1st issue). Multicoloured.

889 1 d. Type **185** 30 10
890 1 d. Scoring goal 30 10
891 2 d. Goalkeeper diving for ball 60 20
892 2 d. Goalkeeper holding ball (vert) 60 20
893 3 d. Goalkeeper preparing to catch ball (vert) 90 30
894 4 d. Punching ball away (vert) 1·25 40
895 6 d. Goalkeeper catching ball (vert) . . . . 1·75 60

See also Nos. 920/6.

186 Laotian Girl and Dove

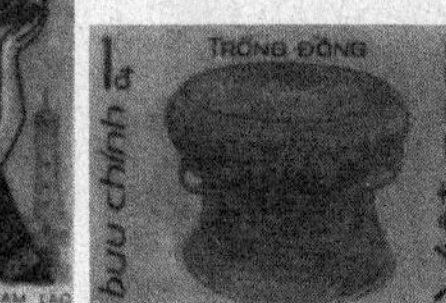

187 Decorated Drum

1985. 10th Anniv of Laos People's Democratic Republic. Multicoloured.

897 1 d. Type **186** 50 20
898 1 d. Laotian girl and arms . . 50 20

1985. Traditional Musical Instruments. Mult.

899 1 d. Type **187** 40 10
900 1 d. Xylophone 40 10
901 2 d. Double-ended drum . . 80 25
902 2 d. Flutes 80 25
903 3 d. Single-stringed instrument 1·25 35
904 4 d. Four-stringed instrument 1·60 45
905 6 d. Double-stringed bowed instrument . . . . 2·40 70

188 Agriculture

189 Hands, Emblem and Dove

1985. 40th Anniv of Independence.

906 10 d. Type **188** 80 20
907 10 d. Industry 80 20
908 20 d. Health care . . . . . . 1·60 40
909 30 d. Education . . . . 2·40 60

1986. 40th Anniv of U.N.O.

910 **189** 1 d. multicoloured 55 20

190 Ho Chi Minh, Map, Line of Voters and Ballot Box

191 Isaac Newton

1986. 40th Anniv of First Assembly Elections.

911 **190** 50 x. mauve and black . . 35 15
912 1 d. orange and black . . 65 25

1986. Appearance of Halley's Comet.

913 2 d. Type **191** 85 25
914 2 d. Edmond Halley 85 25
915 3 d. Launch of "Vega" space probe and flags . . . . . . 1·25 40
916 5 d. Comet and planet . . . . 2·10 65

192 Map of U.S.S.R. and Kremlin Buildings

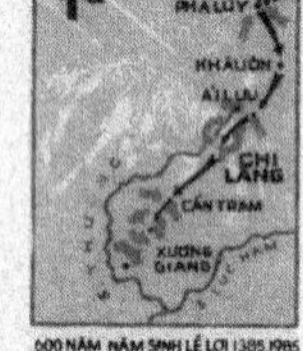

193 Plan of Battle of Chi Lang

1986. 27th Communist Party Congress, Moscow. Multicoloured.

917 50 x. Type **192** 30 15
918 1 d. Lenin on flag and transport, industrial and scientific motifs 65 25

1986. 600th Birth Anniv (1985) of Le Loi (founder of Le Dynasty).

919 **193** 1 d. multicolourerd 65 25

194 Footballer

1986. World Cup Football Championship, Mexico (2nd issue). Multicoloured.

920 1 d. Type **194** 25 10
921 1 d. Two players 25 10
922 2 d. Player heading ball . . . 50 20
923 3 d. Player tackling 75 30
924 3 d. Two players chasing ball . 75 30
925 5 d. Footballer (different) . . . 1·25 40
926 5 d. Two players (different) . . 1·25 40

195 Konstantin Tsiolkovski and "Sputnik 1"

1986. 25th Anniv of 1st Man in Space. Multicoloured.

928 1 d. Type **195** 25 10
929 1 d. Rocket on launch vehicle, Baikanur cosmodrome . . . 25 10
930 2 d. Yuri Gagarin and "Vostok 1" 50 20
931 3 d. Valentina Tereshkova and "Vostok VI" on launch vehicle (vert) 75 30
932 3 d. Cosmonaut Leonov and cosmonaut on space walk . . 70 30
933 5 d. "Soyuz"–"Apollo" link and crews . . . . 1·25 40
934 5 d. "Salyut"–"Soyuz" link and two cosmonauts . . . . . . 1·25 40

196 Thalmann and Flag **197** Flag, Hammer and Globe in Sickle

1986. Birth Centenary of Ernst Thalmann (German Communist leader).

936 **196** 2 d. red and black . . . . 1·10 25

1986. Centenary of May Day.

937 **197** 1 d. red and blue 40 10
938 5 d. red and brown . . . 2·10 55

198 Hawker Hart

1986. "Expo '86" World's Fair, Vancouver. Historic Aircraft. Multicoloured.

939 1 d. Type **198** 25 10
940 1 d. Curtiss JN-4 "Jenny" . . 25 10
941 2 d. PZL P-23 Karas 55 20
942 3 d. Yakovlev Yak-11 . . . . 80 30
943 3 d. Fokker Dr-1 triplane . . 80 30
944 5 d. Boeing P12, 1920 . . . . 1·40 55
945 5 d. Nieuport-Delage 29C1, 1929 1·40 55

199 Ho Chi Minh and People working on Barriers

1986. 40th Anniv of Committee for Protection of Flood Barriers.

946 **199** 1 d. pink and brown . . . 50 20

200 Black and White Cat

1986. Cats. Multicoloured.

947 1 d. Type **200** 30 10
948 1 d. Grey and white cat . . . 30 10
949 2 d. White cat 65 20
950 3 d. Brown-faced cat 95 30
951 3 d. Beige cat 95 30
952 5 d. Black-faced cat (vert) . . 1·60 50
953 5 d. Beige and cream cat . . . 1·60 50

201 Thai Den House

1986. Traditional Architecture. Multicoloured.

954 1 d. Type **201** 35 15
955 1 d. Nung house 35 15
956 2 d. Thai Trang house 70 25
957 3 d. Tay house . . . . 1·00 40
958 3 d. H'mong house . . . . . 1·00 40
959 5 d. Dao house . . . . 1·75 65
960 5 d. Tay Nguyen house (vert) 1·75 65

202 European Bee Eater

203 Plymouth Rock Cock

1986. "Stockholmia 86" International Stamp Exhibition. Birds. Multicoloured.

962 1 d. Type **202** 25 10
963 1 d. Green magpie 25 10
964 2 d. Red-winged shrike babbler 55 20
965 3 d. White-crested laughing thrush 80 30
966 3 d. Long-tailed broadbill (horiz) 80 30
967 5 d. Pied wagtail 1·40 55
968 5 d. Azure-winged magpie (horiz) 1·40 55

1986. Domestic Fowl. Multicoloured.

970 1 d. Type **203** 40 15
971 1 d. Common turkey 40 15
972 2 d. Rhode Island Red cock 75 25
973 2 d. White Plymouth Rock cock 75 25
974 3 d. Rhode Island (inscr "Islan") Red hen 1·10 35
975 3 d. White Leghorn cock 1·10 35
976 3 d. Rhode Island Red cock (different) 1·10 35
977 5 d. Barred Plymouth Rock cock 1·90 65

204 Emblem

1986. 11th World Federation of Trades Unions Congress, Berlin.

978 **204** 1 d. blue and red 50 15

206 Woman-shaped Sword Handle

1986. Historic Bronzes Excavated at Mt. Do. Multicoloured.

980 1 d. Type **206** 35 10
981 1 d. Seated figure with man on back 35 10
982 2 d. Saddle pommel (horiz) 75 25
983 3 d. Shoe-shaped hoe (horiz) 1·10 40
984 3 d. Bowl (horiz) 1·10 40
985 5 d. Vase (horiz) 1·75 60
986 5 d. Pot with lid (horiz) 1·75 60

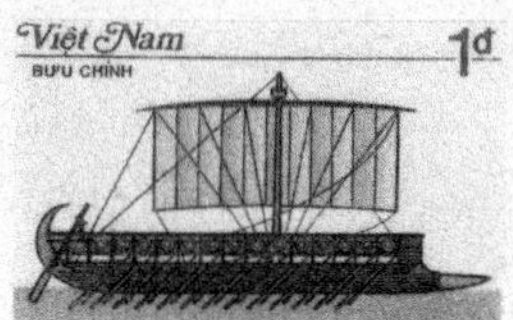

207 Greek Bireme

1986. Sailing Ships. Multicoloured.

988 1 d. Type **207** 25 10
989 1 d. Viking longship 25 10
990 2 d. Medieval kogge (36 × 46 mm) 55 20
991 3 d. Greek cargo galley 80 30
992 3 d. Phoenician war galley with ram 80 30
993 5 d. Ancient Mediterranean cargo ship 1·40 55
994 5 d. Roman trireme 1·40 55

208 Hands cupping Red Cross in Flower

1986. 40th Anniv of Vietnamese Red Cross.

995 **208** 3 d. mauve and blue 1·10 30

209 "Catopsilia scylla"

1986. Butterflies. Multicoloured.

996 1 d. Type **209** 25 10
997 1 d. "Euploea midamus" 25 10
998 2 d. Orange albatross 55 20
999 3 d. Common mormon ("Papilio polytes") 80 30
1000 3 d. African monarch ("Danaus chrysippus") 80 30
1001 5 d. Tawny rajah ("Charaxes polyxena") 1·40 55
1002 5 d. Magpie crow ("Euploea diocletiana") 1·40 55

210 Red Flag and Symbols of Industry and Agriculture

1986. 6th Vietnamese Communist Party Congress. Multicoloured.

1003 1 d. Type **210** 30 10
1004 2 d. Red flag and weapons 65 20
1005 4 d. Red flag and Ho Chi Minh 1·25 40
1006 5 d. Red flag and symbols of peace 1·60 50

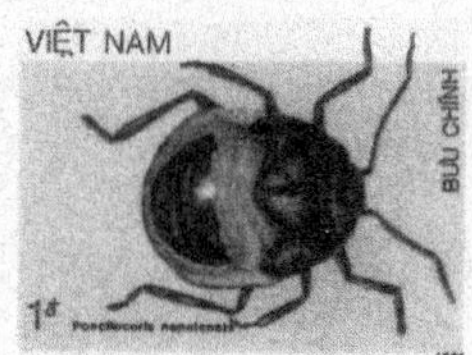

211 "Poecilocoris nepalensis" (shieldbug)

1986. Insects. Multicoloured.

1008 1 d. Type **211** 25 10
1009 1 d. "Bombus americanorum" (bee) 25 10
1010 2 d. "Romalea microptera" (grasshopper) 55 20
1011 3 d. "Chalcocoris rutilans" (shieldbug) 80 30
1012 3 d. "Chrysocoris sellatus" (shieldbug) 80 30
1013 5 d. "Crocisa crucifera" (wasp) 1·40 55
1014 5 d. "Paranthrene palmi" (moth) 1·40 55

212 Dove and Emblem **213** "Ficus glomerata"

1986. International Peace Year.

1016 **212** 1 d. green and black 40 15
1017 3 d. pink and black 1·25 40

1986. Bonsai. Multicoloured.

1018 1 d. Type **213** 35 10
1019 1 d. "Ficus benjamina" 35 10
1020 2 d. "Ulmus tonkinensis" 75 25
1021 3 d. "Persica vulgaris" 1·10 35
1022 3 d. "Strebius asper" 1·10 35
1023 5 d. "Podocarpus macrophyllus" 1·75 60
1024 5 d. "Pinus khasya" 1·75 60

214 Basket

1986. Basketry and Wickerwork. Multicoloured.

1026 1 d. Type **214** 35 10
1027 1 d. Tall basket with lid and handles 35 10
1028 2 d. Stool 75 25
1029 3 d. Handbag 1·10 35
1030 3 d. Dish 1·10 35
1031 5 d. Tall basket for carrying on back 1·75 60
1032 5 d. Square basket with star-shaped foot 1·75 60

215 Soldiers and Women **216** "Fokienia hodginsii"

1986. 40th Anniv of National Resistance.

1034 **215** 2 d. brown and green 80 20

1986. Fruits of Conifers. Multicoloured.

1035 1 d. Type **216** 35 10
1036 1 d. "Amentotaxus yunnanensis" 35 10
1037 2 d. "Pinus kwangtungensis" 70 20
1038 3 d. "Cupressus torulosa" 1·10 35
1039 3 d. "Taxus chinensis" 1·10 35
1040 5 d. "Tsuga yunnanensis" 1·75 55
1041 5 d. "Ducampopinus krempfii" 1·75 55

217 Mother and Calf

1986. Elephants.

1043 1 d. Type **217** 30 10
1044 1 d. Two elephants 30 10
1045 3 d. Elephant (vert) 85 30
1046 3 d. Elephant feeding 85 30
1047 5 d. Working elephant (vert) 1·40 50
1048 5 d. Elephants by water (68 × 27 mm) 1·40 50

218 Girl watering Tree **219** My Chan

1987. New Year. Year of the Cat.

1049 **218** 3 d. brown and mauve 50 25

1987. "Son Tinh-Thuy Tinh" (folktale). Multicoloured.

1050 3 d. Type **219** 1·10 30
1051 3 d. Mountain Genius bearing gift and leading horse 1·10 30
1052 3 d. Elephants carrying materials for flood barrier 1·10 30
1053 3 d. Men working through the night against flood sent by Water Genius 1·10 30
1054 3 d. Men felling trees 1·10 30
1055 3 d. Pounding rice in preparation for festival after storms 1·10 30
1056 3 d. Canoes bringing fruit and grain 1·10 30
1057 3 d. Canoe 1·10 30

Nos. 1050/7 were issued together, se-tenant, forming a composite design.

220 "Nymphaea lotus" **222** Temple, Da Nang

221 Crowd attacking Building (August 1945 Revolution)

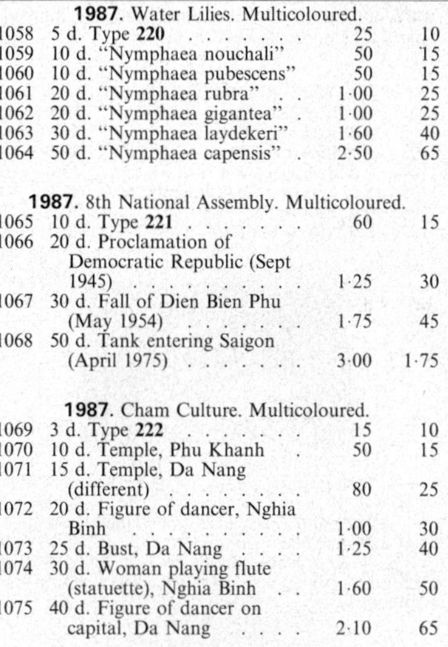

1987. Water Lilies. Multicoloured.

1058 5 d. Type **220** 25 10
1059 10 d. "Nymphaea nouchali" 50 15
1060 10 d. "Nymphaea pubescens" 50 15
1061 20 d. "Nymphaea rubra" 1·00 25
1062 20 d. "Nymphaea gigantea" 1·00 25
1063 30 d. "Nymphaea laydekeri" 1·60 40
1064 50 d. "Nymphaea capensis" 2·50 65

1987. 8th National Assembly. Multicoloured.

1065 10 d. Type **221** 60 15
1066 20 d. Proclamation of Democratic Republic (Sept 1945) 1·25 30
1067 30 d. Fall of Dien Bien Phu (May 1954) 1·75 45
1068 50 d. Tank entering Saigon (April 1975) 3·00 1·75

1987. Cham Culture. Multicoloured.

1069 3 d. Type **222** 15 10
1070 10 d. Temple, Phu Khanh 50 15
1071 15 d. Temple, Da Nang (different) 80 25
1072 20 d. Figure of dancer, Nghia Binh 1·00 30
1073 25 d. Bust, Da Nang 1·25 40
1074 30 d. Woman playing flute (statuette), Nghia Binh 1·60 50
1075 40 d. Figure of dancer on capital, Da Nang 2·10 65

223 Hanoi

1987. Tourism. Multicoloured.

1077 5 d. Type **223** 25 10
1078 10 d. Hai Phong 50 15
1079 15 d. Thien Mu Pagoda, Hue 75 25
1080 20 d. Da Nang 1·00 25
1081 25 d. Nha Trang 1·25 30
1082 30 d. Waterfall, Da Lat 1·50 35
1083 40 d. Ho Chi Minh City 2·00 50

224 Cactus **226** Man from Bana

225 People on Globe

1987. Cacti.

1085 **224** 5 d. multicoloured 15 10
1086 – 10 d. multicoloured 30 15
1087 – 15 d. multicoloured 50 20
1088 – 20 d. multicoloured 65 25
1089 – 25 d. multicoloured 80 30
1090 – 30 d. multicoloured 1·00 35
1091 – 40 d. multicoloured 1·25 40

DESIGNS: 10 to 40 d. Various flowering cacti.

1987. Day of Five Billion Inhabitants of Earth.

1093 **225** 5 d. mauve and blue 65 20

1987. Costumes. Multicoloured.

1094 5 d. Type **226** 25 10
1095 20 d. Woman from Bana 1·00 25
1096 20 d. Woman from Gia Rai 1·00 25
1097 30 d. Man from Gia Rai 1·60 45
1098 30 d. Man from Ede 1·60 45
1099 40 d. Woman from Ede 2·10 55

227 Silhouettes of Soldiers and Disabled Soldier **228** Rose

1987. 40th Anniv of Association of Disabled Soldiers.
1100 **227** 5 d. red and violet . . . 65 20

1987. Roses. Multicoloured.
1101 5 d. Type **228** 15 10
1102 10 d. Red hybrid tea 35 15
1103 15 d. Pink hybrid tea 50 20
1104 20 d. Species rose 70 25
1105 25 d. Species rose (different) . 85 30
1106 30 d. Floribunda . . . . . . 1·00 35
1107 40 d. "Rosa odorata" . . . . 1·40 50

229 Postwoman and Mail Transport

1987. 40th Anniv of Postal Trade Union.
1109 **229** 5 d. black and pink 20 10
1110 – 30 d. black and green . . 1·25 40
DESIGN: 30 d. Linesman, dish aerial and telephonist.

230 Siamese Fighting Fish

1987. Fishes. Multicoloured.
1111 5 d. Type **230** 15 10
1112 10 d. Red-tailed black labeo . 35 10
1113 15 d. Damsel barb 50 15
1114 20 d. Pearl danio 70 20
1115 25 d. Rosy barb 85 25
1116 30 d. Siamese fighting fish (different) . . . . 1·00 30
1117 40 d. "Botia lecontei" . . . . 1·40 45

231 I.Y.S.H. Emblem

1987. International Year of Shelter for the Homeless.
1118 **231** 5 d. black and blue . . . 65 25

233 Crested Gibbons

235 Industrial and Agricultural Symbols

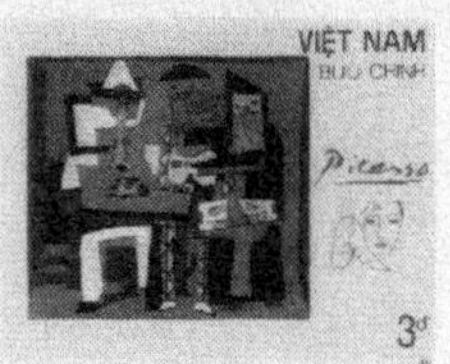
234 "Three Musicians"

1987. Monkeys. Multicoloured.
1120 5 d. Type **233** 15 10
1121 5 d. Variegated langurs . . . 15 10
1122 15 d. Crested gibbon (different) 50 20
1123 40 d. Variegated langur (different) . . . . 1·40 50

1987. Paintings by Picasso. Multicoloured.
1124 3 d. Type **234** 10 10
1125 20 d. Horse-drawn wagon . . 70 20
1126 20 d. Winged horse on shore 70 20
1127 30 d. "Child with Dove" (vert) 1·00 30
1128 30 d. "Gertrude Stein" (vert) 1·00 30
1129 40 d. "Guernica" (44 × 27 mm) 1·40 40

1987. 70th Anniv of Russian Revolution. Mult.
1131 5 d. Type **235** 20 10
1132 20 d. Soviet Memorial, Berlin-Treptow, cruiser "Aurora" and Lenin 70 25
1133 30 d. "70" and symbols of progress . . . . 1·10 35
1134 50 d. Ho Chi Minh and scenes of Vietnamese history . . . 1·75 60

236 Consolidated PBY-5 Catalina Flying Boat

1987. "Hafnia 87" International Stamp Exhibition, Copenhagen. Flying Boats. Multicoloured.
1136 5 d. Type **236** 15 10
1137 10 d. Liore et Olivier LeO 246 35 10
1138 15 d. Dornier Do-18 . . . . 50 15
1139 20 d. Short Sunderland . . . 70 20
1140 25 d. Flying boat, 1923 . . . 85 25
1141 30 d. Chetverikov ARK-3 . 1·00 30
1142 40 d. Cant Z.509 . . . . . 1·40 45

237 Epanouis

1987. Corals. Multicoloured.
1144 5 d. Type **237** 25 10
1145 10 d. Acropora 55 15
1146 15 d. Rhizopsammia 80 25
1147 20 d. Acropora (different) . 1·10 35
1148 25 d. Alcyone . . . . 1·40 40
1149 30 d. Corollum . . . . . . 1·60 50
1150 40 d. Cristatella . . . . . . 2·10 65

238 Doves as Clasped Hands forming Heart

1987. 5th Anniv of Vietnam–Czechoslovak Friendship Treaty. Each blue, yellow and red.
1151 10 d. Type **238** 35 10
1152 50 d. Pagoda on One Pillar (Hanoi), flags and buildings of Prague . . . . 1·75 50

239 Symbols of Industry and Agriculture

1987. Soviet–Vietnam Friendship Treaty.
1153 **239** 5 d. pink, black and orange 15 10
1154 – 50 d. pink, brown and orange . . . . 1·75 55
DESIGN: 50 d. Buildings of Moscow Kremlin and Hanoi.

240 Coloured Circles

1987. Peace.
1155 **240** 10 d. multicoloured . . 90 30

241 Saddle-back Fungus

243 Wrecked Boeing B-52 Stratofortress Bomber and Girl watering Flowers

242 Dove on Open Hands

1987. Fungi. Multicoloured.
1156 5 d. Type **241** 25 10
1157 10 d. Trumpet agaric 55 15
1158 15 d. "Tricholoma terreum" . 80 20
1159 20 d. Golden russula . . . . 1·10 25
1160 25 d. Spindle shank . . . . 1·25 35
1161 30 d. "Cortinarius violaceus" 1·60 40
1162 40 d. Bronze boletus . . . . 2·25 60

1987. 30th Anniv of Africa–Asia Co-operation Committee.
1163 **242** 10 d. blue, black & yell . 40 15
1164 – 30 d. black, brown & yell 1·25 40
DESIGN—VERT: 30 d. Hands and map.

1987. 15th Anniv of U.S. Air Bombardment of Vietnam.
1165 **243** 10 d. black and yellow . . 40 15
1166 – 30 d. black and orange . 1·10 45
DESIGN: 30 d. Young Pioneers and weapons.

244 Woman carrying Bales of Cloth

246 Anniversary Emblem and Dove

245 Junk, Man blowing Horn and Map

1987. 6th Party Congress Decisions.
1167 **244** 5 d. green and brown . . 20 10
1168 – 20 d. orange & brown . . 80 25
1169 – 30 d. violet and blue . . 1·25 45
DESIGNS: 20 d. Tractor driver; 30 d. Loading crate on freighter.

1988. Paracel and Spratley Islands.
1170 **245** 10 d. black, pink & red . 35 15
1171 – 100 d. light brown, black and brown . . . . . . 3·50 1·75
DESIGN: 100 d. Maps showing Paracel Islands.

1988. 125th Anniv of International Red Cross.
1172 **246** 10 d. red, black & blue . 75 25

247 Fleet

1988. 700th Anniv of Battle of Bach Dang River.
1173 **247** 80 d. black, red & pink . 1·25 45
1174 – 200 d. multicoloured . . 3·25 1·10
DESIGN: 200 d. Battle scene.

248 Oil Rig

249 Blue and Yellow Macaw

1988. Oil Industry.
1175 **248** 1000 d. black, blue & red 10·50 2·50

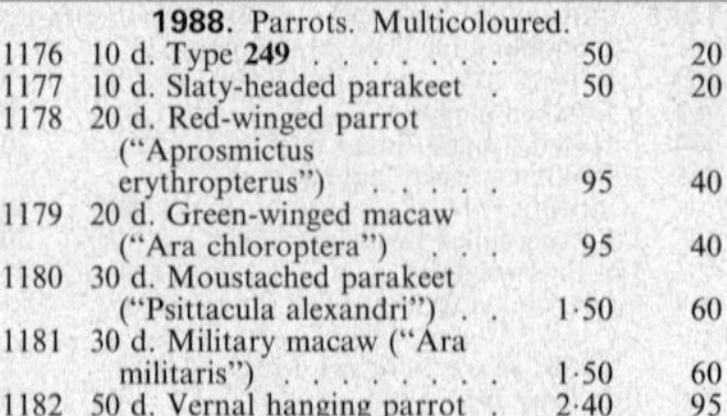

1988. Parrots. Multicoloured.
1176 10 d. Type **249** 50 20
1177 10 d. Slaty-headed parakeet . 50 20
1178 20 d. Red-winged parrot ("Aprosmictus erythropterus") 95 40
1179 20 d. Green-winged macaw ("Ara chloroptera") . . . 95 40
1180 30 d. Moustached parakeet ("Psittacula alexandri") . . 1·50 60
1181 30 d. Military macaw ("Ara militaris") . . . . 1·50 60
1182 50 d. Vernal hanging parrot . 2·40 95

250 Map

251 Child and Syringe

1988. 33rd Council for Mutual Economic Aid Meeting and 10th Anniv of Vietnam's Membership.
1184 **250** 200 d. multicoloured . . 1·25 45
1185 – 300 d. blue and bistre . . 1·90 70
DESIGN: 300 d. COMECON headquarters building, Moscow.

1988. Child Vaccination Campaign.
1186 **251** 60 d. orange, black & bl 90 40

252 Emblem and Building

1988. 30th Anniv of "Peace and Socialism" (magazine).
1187 **252** 20 d. multicoloured . . . 75 30

253 Ton Duc Thang

254 Emblem

1988. Birth Centenary of Pres. Ton Duc Thang.
1188 **253** 150 d. multicoloured . . 1·75 75

1988. 6th Trade Unions Congress. Multicoloured.
1189 50 d. Type **254** 80 40
1190 100 d. "VI" and couple . . . 1·75 75

255 Pointed-scaled Pit Viper

1988. Snakes. Multicoloured.
1191 10 d. Type **255** 35 10
1192 10 d. Pope's pit viper ("Trimeresurus popeorum") 35 10
1193 20 d. Banded krait ("Bungarus fasciatus") 75 25
1194 20 d. Malayan krait ("Bungarus candidus") 75 25
1195 30 d. Coral snake ("Calliophis maclellandi") . . . . . 1·10 35
1196 30 d. Striped beaked snake ("Ancistridon acutus") . . 1·10 35
1197 50 d. King cobra (vert) . . 1·90 55

256 Family (Trieu Khac Tien)

1988. Children's Drawings. Multicoloured.
1198 10 d. Type **256** 35 10
1199 10 d. Couple and house (Phuong Ti) 35 10
1200 20 d. Fishermen (Lam Hoang Thang) 75 25
1201 20 d. Children flying kite (Nguyen Xuan Anh) 75 25
1202 30 d. Couple (Hong Hanh) (vert) 1·10 35
1203 30 d. Animals and girl playing guitar (Quynh May) 1·10 35
1204 50 d. Woman holding dove (Ta Phuong Tra) (vert) 1·90 55

257 Tri An

1988. U.S.S.R.–Vietnam Co-operation. Hydro-electric Power Stations.
1206 **257** 2000 d. blk, orge & red 6·00 4·25
1207 – 3000 d. black, bistre and red 9·00 3·50
DESIGN: 3000 d. Hoa Binh.

258 Kamov Ka-26

1988. Helicopters. Multicoloured.
1208 10 d. Type **258** 35 10
1209 10 d. Boeing-Vertol 234 Commercial Chinook 35 10
1210 20 d. MBB-Bolkow Bo 105 75 25
1211 20 d. Mil Mi-10K 75 25
1212 30 d. Kawasaki-Hughes 369HS 1·10 35
1213 30 d. Bell JetRanger 1·10 35
1214 50 d. Mil Mi-8 1·90 55

259 Gaur

260 Flower and Banners

1988. Mammals. Multicoloured.
1216 10 d. Type **259** 30 10
1217 10 d. Banteng 30 10
1218 20 d. Malayan tapir ("Tapirus indicus") 60 20
1219 20 d. Hog deer ("Axis porcinus") 60 20
1220 30 d. Mainland serow ("Capricornis sumatraensis") 85 30
1221 30 d. Wild boar ("Sus scrofa") 85 30
1222 50 d. Water buffalo 1·50 50

1988. 10th Anniv of U.S.S.R.–Vietnam Friendship.
1224 **260** 50 d. multicoloured 55 25

261 Indian Star Tortoise ("Testudo elegans")

262 Skaters

1988. Turtles and Tortoises.
1225 10 d. Type **261** 35 10
1226 10 d. Three-banded box turtle ("Cuora trifasciata") 35 10
1227 20 d. Big-headed turtle ("Platysternon megacephalum") 75 25
1228 20 d. Hawksbill turtle ("Eretmochelys imbricata") 75 25
1229 30 d. Indian Ocean green turtle ("Chelonia mydas") 1·10 35
1230 30 d. Leatherback turtle ("Dermochelys coriacea") 1·10 35
1231 50 d. Loggerhead turtle ("Caretta caretta") 1·90 55

1988. Ice Skating. Multicoloured.
1233 **262** 10 d. multicoloured 30 10
1234 – 10 d. multicoloured 30 10
1235 – 20 d. multicoloured 60 20
1236 – 20 d. mult (horiz) 60 20
1237 – 30 d. multicoloured 85 30
1238 – 30 d. mult (horiz) 85 30
1239 – 50 d. mult (horiz) 1·50 50
DESIGNS: Nos. 1234/9 Different skating scenes.

263 Bowden "Spacelander"

264 Fidel Castro

1988. Bicycles. Multicoloured.
1241 10 d. Type **263** 35 10
1242 10 d. Rabasa Derbi with red tyres 35 10
1243 20 d. Huffy 70 25
1244 20 d. Rabasa Derbi with black tyres 70 25
1245 30 d. VMX-PL 1·00 35
1246 30 d. Premier 1·00 35
1247 50 d. Columbia RX5 1·75 55

1988. 30th Anniv of Cuban Revolution. Mult.
1248 100 d. Type **264** 40 15
1249 300 d. National flags and Cuban and Vietnamese workers 1·10 45

265 Cosmonauts on Spacecraft Wing

1988. Cosmonauts Day. Multicoloured.
1250 10 d. Type **265** 30 10
1251 10 d. Spacecraft moving across surface of planet 30 10
1252 20 d. Space rocket heading for planet 60 20
1253 20 d. Spacecraft and cosmonauts on planet with Earth in sky 60 20
1254 30 d. Spacecraft hovering over surface 85 30
1255 30 d. "Soyuz"–"Salyut" complex 85 30
1256 50 d. Space "bubble" and rocket 1·50 50

266 Soldier Cone

1988. Sea Shells. Multicoloured.
1258 10 d. Type **266** 35 10
1259 10 d. Silver conch ("Strombus lentiginosus") 35 10
1260 20 d. Common frog shell ("Bursa rana") 70 25
1261 20 d. Tapestry turban ("Turbo petholatus") 70 25
1262 30 d. Red-mouth olive ("Oliva erythrostoma") 1·00 35
1263 30 d. Chambered nautilus ("Nautilus") 1·00 35
1264 50 d. Episcopal mitre 1·75 55
The inscriptions on Nos. 1261 and 1263 have been transposed.

267 Class "VL85" Locomotive, U.S.S.R

1988. Electric Locomotives. Multicoloured.
1266 20 d. Type **267** 60 20
1267 20 d. LRC, Canada 60 20
1268 20 d. Monorail, Japan 60 20
1269 20 d. KIHA 80, Japan 60 20
1270 30 d. Class "DR 1A", U.S.S.R. 90 30
1271 30 d. Class "RC 1" 90 30
1272 50 d. Class "TE-136", U.S.S.R. 1·50 50

268 Gourd

1988. Fruits. Multicoloured.
1274 10 d. Type **268** 35 10
1275 10 d. "Momordica charantia" 35 10
1276 20 d. Pumpkin ("Cucurbita moschata") 70 25
1277 20 d. Eggplant ("Solanum melongena") 70 25
1278 30 d. "Benincasa hispida" 1·00 35
1279 30 d. Luffa gourd 1·00 35
1280 50 d. Tomatoes 1·75 55

269 Soldiers and Field Workers

1989. 10th Anniv of People's Republic of Kampuchea. Multicoloured.
1281 100 d. Type **269** 40 15
1282 500 d. Crowd greeting soldier and mother with child 1·90 70

270 Junk from Quang Nam

1989. Regional Fishing Junks. Multicoloured.
1283 10 d. Type **270** 35 10
1284 10 d. Quang Tri 35 10
1285 20 d. Thua Thien 75 20
1286 20 d. Da Nang 75 20
1287 30 d. Quang Tri (different) 1·10 30
1288 30 d. Da Nang (different) 1·10 30
1289 50 d. Hue 1·90 55

271 Caribbean Buckeye ("Junonia evarete")

1989. "India-89" International Stamp Exhibition, New Delhi (1st issue). Butterflies. Multicoloured.
1290 50 d. Type **271** 30 15
1291 50 d. "Anaea echemus" 30 15
1292 50 d. Great southern white ("Ascia monuste") 30 15
1293 100 d. Red-splashed sulphur ("Phoebis avellaneda") 60 25
1294 100 d. Jamaican orange ("Eurema proterpia") 60 25
1295 200 d. "Papilio palamedes" 1·25 55
1296 300 d. Monarch ("Danaus plexippus") 1·90 80
See also Nos. 1298/1301.

272 Flag and Telecommunications

274 Emblems on Banner

273 Festival

1989. "India-89" International Stamp Exhibition, New Delhi (2nd issue).
1298 **272** 100 d. multicoloured 40 15
1299 – 100 d. multicoloured 40 15
1300 – 300 d. multicoloured 1·10 35
1301 – 600 d. brown, orge & grn 2·25 75
DESIGNS: 100 d. (No. 1299), Oil and electricity industries; 300 d. Government Secretariat and Asokan capital; 600 d. Jawaharlal Nehru (Indian statesman, birth centenary).

1989. Bicentenary of Battle of Dongda.
1302 **273** 100 d. violet and green 40 15
1303 – 1000 d. mauve and pink 4·00 1·40
DESIGN: 1000 d. Battle scene.

1989. Centenary of Interparliamentary Union.
1304 **274** 100 d. multicoloured 50 20
1305 – 200 d. gold, ultramarine and blue 1·00 40
DESIGN: 200 d. "100" on banner.

275 Dachshunds

1989. Dogs. Multicoloured.
1306 50 d. Type **275** 30 10
1307 50 d. Basset hounds 30 10
1308 50 d. Setter (vert) 30 10
1309 100 d. Hunting dog (vert) 65 20
1310 100 d. Basset hounds (66 × 25 mm) 65 20
1311 200 d. Hound (vert) 1·25 40
1312 300 d. Basset hound puppy 1·90 65

276 Footballers

277 Jug

1989. World Cup Football Championship, Italy (1st issue). Multicoloured.
1313 50 d. Type **276** 30 10
1314 50 d. Striker and goalkeeper 30 10
1315 50 d. Goalkeeper 30 10
1316 100 d. Player No. 5 tackling 65 20
1317 100 d. Tackling (vert) 65 20
1318 200 d. Player No. 3 (vert) 1·25 40
1319 300 d. Players heading ball (vert) 1·90 65
See also Nos. 1382/8 and 1482/9.

1989. Pottery. Multicoloured.
1321 50 d. Type **277** 30 10
1322 100 d. Bowl with geometric pattern 65 20
1323 100 d. Round pot with flower decoration 65 20
1324 200 d. Tall pot with animal decoration 1·25 40
1325 300 d. Vase 1·90 65

278 Baby Thanh Giong with Mother

1989. Legend of Thanh Giong. Multicoloured.
1326 50 d. Type **278** 30 10
1327 100 d. Thanh Giong with King's messenger 65 20
1328 100 d. Thanh Giong at head of army 65 20
1329 200 d. Thanh Giong beating out flames 1·25 40
1330 300 d. Thanh Giong riding to heaven 1·90 65

279 "Fuchsia fulgens"

280 Bird carrying Envelope above Dish Aerial

1989. Flowers. Multicoloured.
1331 50 d. Type **279** 35 10
1332 50 d. Bird-of-paradise flower ("Strelitzia reginae") . . . 35 10
1333 100 d. Glory lily ("Gloriosa superba") 70 25
1334 100 d. Orange day lily ("Hemerocallis fulva") . . 70 25
1335 200 d. "Paphiopedilum siamense" . . . . 1·40 45
1336 300 d. "Iris sp." . . . . 2·10 70
On Nos. 1332 and 1335 the inscriptions have been transposed.

1989. Communications.
1337 **280** 100 d. brown 65 25

281 Birds

283 Man and Ox

282 "Return from Varennes"

1989. Bicentenary of French Revolution and "Philexfrance 89" International Stamp Exhibition, Paris. (a) As T **281**. Multicoloured.
1338 100 d. Type **281** 55 20
1339 500 d. "Liberty guiding the People" (detail, Eugene Delacroix) . . . . 2·75 90

(b) As T **282**.
1340 50 d. Type **282** 25 10
1341 50 d. "Revolutionary Court" 25 10
1342 50 d. "Oath of the Tennis Court" (Jacques-Louis David) (vert) 25 10
1343 100 d. "Assassination of Marat" (David) (vert) . . . 55 20
1344 100 d. "Storming the Bastille" (vert) 55 20
1345 200 d. Two children (Pierre-Paul Prud'hon) (vert) . . . . . 1·10 35
1346 300 d. "Slave Trade" (Jean-Leon Gerome) . . . . . . 1·60 55

1989. Rice Cultivation. Multicoloured.
1348 50 d. Type **283** 30 10
1349 100 d. Ploughing with ox . . . 65 20
1350 100 d. Flooding fields 65 20
1351 200 d. Fertilizing . . . . . . 1·25 40
1352 300 d. Harvesting crop . . . 1·90 65

284 Appaloosa

1989. Horses. Multicoloured.
1353 50 d. Type **284** 35 10
1354 50 d. Tennessee walking horse 35 10
1355 50 d. Tersky 35 10
1356 100 d. Kladruber 70 25
1357 100 d. Welsh cob 70 25
1358 200 d. Pinto . . . . 1·40 40
1359 300 d. Pony and bridle (68 × 27 mm) . . . . 2·10 70

285 Brandenburg Gate, Flag and Emblem

1989. 40th Anniv of German Democratic Republic.
1360 **285** 200 d. yellow, blk & mve 65 25

286 Polio Oral Vaccination

1989. Immunization Campaign.
1361 **286** 100 d. brown, blk & red 30 20
1362 – 100 d. pink, blk & grn . 30 20
1363 – 100 d. green, blk & red . 30 20
DESIGNS: No. 1362, Vaccinating pregnant woman; 1363, Health clinic.

287 Horse

1989. Paintings of Horses by Hsu Pei-Hung. Multicoloured.
1364 100 d. Type **287** 10 10
1365 200 d. Two horses galloping 15 10
1366 300 d. Three horses grazing . 25 10
1367 500 d. Horse galloping (horiz) 45 15
1368 800 d. Galloping horse . . . 70 25
1369 1000 d. Two horses under tree 85 30
1370 1500 d. Galloping horse (different) . . . . 1·25 40

288 "Nina", "Pinta" and "Santa Maria" and Mochica Ceramic Figure
($\frac{2}{3}$ - size illustration)

1989. 500th Anniv (1992) of Discovery of America by Columbus (1st issue). Multicoloured.
1372 50 d. Type **288** 20 10
1373 100 d. Columbus and King Ferdinand the Catholic and Peruvian ceramic bottle . 35 10
1374 100 d. Columbus's arrival at Rabida and Mexican decorated vessel 35 10
1375 100 d. Columbus offering gifts (18th-century engraving) and human-shaped jug 35 10
1376 200 d. Early map and Peruvian ceramic 70 25
1377 200 d. Portrait and arms of Columbus and Nazca ceramic 70 25
1378 300 d. Chart by Toscanelli and Chimu vessel . . . . . . 1·10 35
See also Nos. 1545/51 and 1664/8.

289 Storming of Presidential Palace, Saigon, and Ho Chi Minh

1990. 60th Anniv of Vietnamese Communist Party. Multicoloured.
1380 100 d. Type **289** 10 10
1381 500 d. Industry, workers, hammer and sickle and flag 30 10

290 Players

1990. World Cup Football Championship, Italy (2nd issue). Multicoloured.
1382 100 d. Type **290** 10 10
1383 200 d. Argentina player with possession 10 10
1384 300 d. Netherlands and Scotland players 15 10
1385 500 d. Soviet Union player tackling 25 10
1386 1000 d. Scotland and West Germany player 55 20
1387 2000 d. Soviet Union player losing possession . . . . 1·10 35
1388 3000 d. Goalkeeper . . . . 1·60 55

291 Hybrids of Mallard and Local Species

1990. Ducks. Multicoloured.
1390 100 d. Type **291** 40 10
1391 300 d. European mallard . . 45 10
1392 500 d. Mallards 60 15
1393 1000 d. Red-billed pintails . . 90 20
1394 2000 d. White duck preening . 1·10 35
1395 3000 d. African yellow-bills . 2·00 55

292 Mack Truck and Trailer

1990. Trucks. Multicoloured.
1396 100 d. Type **292** 10 10
1397 200 d. Volvo "F89" tipper . . 10 10
1398 300 d. Tatra "915 S1" tipper . 15 10
1399 500 d. Hino "KZ30000" lorry 25 10
1400 1000 d. Italia Iveco 55 20
1401 2000 d. Leyland-Daf "Super Comet" tipper . . . . . . 1·10 35
1402 3000 d. Kamaz "53212" lorry 1·60 55

293 8th/9th-century Viking Longship

1990. Sailing Ships. Multicoloured.
1403 100 d. Type **293** 10 10
1404 500 d. 15th-century caravel . 25 10
1405 1000 d. 15th-century carrack (vert) 50 15
1406 1000 d. 14th/15th-century carrack 50 15
1407 1000 d. 17th-century frigate . 50 15
1408 2000 d. 16th-century galleons and pinnace (vert) . . . . 1·00 35
1409 3000 d. 16th-century galleon . 1·50 50

294 Red-bodied Goldfish

1990. Goldfish.
1411 **294** 100 d. multicoloured . . 10 10
1412 – 300 d. multicoloured . . 15 10
1413 – 500 d. multicoloured . . 25 10
1414 – 1000 d. mult (vert) . . . 45 15
1415 – 2000 d. mult (vert) . . . 95 30
1416 – 3000 d. mult (vert) . . . 1·40 45
DESIGNS: 300 d. to 3000 d. Different goldfish.

295 Gate of Noble Mankind

1990. Hue Temples. Multicoloured.
1417 100 d. Type **295** 35 10
1418 100 d. Lotus pool at tomb of Emperor Tu Duc 35 10
1419 200 d. Southern Gate 70 25
1420 300 d. Thien Pagoda . . . . 1·10 35

296 "Antonia Zarate" (Francisco de Goya)

1990. "Stamp World London 90" International Stamp Exhibition. Multicoloured.
1422 100 d. Type **296** 10 10
1423 200 d. "Girl with Paper Fan" (Auguste Renoir) 10 10
1424 300 d. "Janet Grizel" (John Russell) 15 10
1425 500 d. "Love unfasten's Beauty's Girdle" (Joshua Reynolds) 25 10
1426 1000 d. "Portrait of a Lady" (George Romney) (wrongly inscr "Omney") 55 20
1427 2000 d. "Mme. Ginoux" (Vincent van Gogh) . . . 1·10 35
1428 3000 d. "Lady in Green" (Thomas Gainsborough) 1·60 55

297 Henry Giffard's Steam-powered Dirigible Airship

1990. "Helvetia 90" International Stamp Exhibition, Geneva. Airships. Multicoloured. With or without gum.
1430 100 d. Type **297** 10 10
1431 200 d. Lebaudy-Juillot airship No. 1 "La Jaune" 10 10
1432 300 d. "Graf Zeppelin' . . . 15 10
1433 500 d. R-101 . . . . 25 15
1434 1000 d. "Osoaviakhim" . . . 55 20
1435 2000 d. Tissandier Brothers' airship . . . . 1·10 40
1436 3000 d. U.S. Navy "N" Class airship . . . . 1·60 60
No. 1431 is wrongly inscr "Lebandy".

298 Silver Tabby and White Cat

1990. Cats. Multicoloured.
1438 100 d. Type **298** 10 10
1439 200 d. Black cat (vert) . . . 10 10
1440 300 d. Black and white cat . 15 10
1441 500 d. Brown tabby and white (vert) 30 10
1442 1000 d. Silver tabby 55 20
1443 2000 d. Tortoiseshell and white (vert) . . . . 1·10 35
1444 3000 d. Tortoiseshell tabby and white (vert) . . . . 1·75 60

299 Ho Chi Minh, 1923

300 King Charles Spaniel

1990. Birth Centenary of Ho Chi Minh. Mult.
1446 100 d. Type **299** 10 10
1447 300 d. Ho Chi Minh, 1945 . 15 10
1448 500 d. Dove, hand holding rifle, and Ho Chi Minh 25 10
1449 1000 d. Ho Chi Minh conducting 50 15
1450 2000 d. Ho Chi Minh embracing child . . . . 1·00 35
1451 3000 d. Globe and Ho Chi Minh 1·50 50

1990. "New Zealand 90" International Stamp Exhibition, Auckland. Dogs. Multicoloured.
1453 100 d. Type **300** 10 10
1454 200 d. Spaniel 10 10
1455 300 d. Saluki 15 10
1456 500 d. Dachshund 30 10
1457 1000 d. Dalmatian 55 20
1458 2000 d. Highland terrier . . 1·10 35
1459 3000 d. Boxer . . . . 1·75 60

301 Gorgosaurus

1990. Prehistoric Animals. Multicoloured.

1461 100 d. Type **301** 10 10
1462 500 d. Ceratosaurus 30 10
1463 1000 d. Ankylosaurus 60 20
1464 2000 d. Ankylosaurus (different) . . . . 1·25 40
1465 3000 d. Edaphosaurus . . . 1·90 65

302 High Jumping

1990. 11th Asian Games, Peking. Multicoloured.

1466 100 d. Type **302** 10 10
1467 200 d. Basketball 10 10
1468 300 d. Table tennis 15 10
1469 500 d. Volleyball 25 10
1470 1000 d. Gymnastics 55 20
1471 2000 d. Tennis . . . . 1·10 35
1472 3000 d. Judo . . . . 1·60 55

1990. Tourism. Nos. 626/33 optd **DULICH'90** and emblem.

1474 50 x. Type **131** 10 10
1475 50 x. Common ink cap ("Coprinus atramentarius") 10 10
1476 50 x. Golden mushroom ("Flammulina velutipes") . 10 10
1477 50 x. Chanterelle ("Cantharellus cibarius") 10 10
1478 1 d. Chinese mushroom . . . 20 10
1479 2 d. Red-staining mushroom . 40 15
1480 5 d. Common morel . . . . 1·00 35
1481 10 d. Caesar's mushroom . . 2·10 70

1990. World Cup Football Championship, Italy (3rd series). Nos. 457/64 optd **ITALIA'90** and ball.

1482 **90** 30 x. multicoloured . . . 20 10
1483 – 30 x. mult (No. 458) . . 20 10
1484 – 40 x. mult (No. 459) . . 25 10
1485 – 40 x. mult (No. 460) . . 25 10
1486 – 50 x. mult (No. 461) . . 45 15
1487 – 50 x. mult (No. 462) . . 45 15
1488 – 60 x. multicoloured . . . 55 20
1489 – 1 d. multicoloured . . . 1·25 40

305 "Pyotr Yemtsov" (container ship)

1990. Ships. Multicoloured.

1490 100 d. Type **305** 10 10
1491 300 d. Mexican Lines container ship 15 10
1492 500 d. Liner 25 10
1493 1000 d. "Ben Nevis" (tanker) 55 20
1494 2000 d. Roll-on roll-off ferry 1·10 35
1495 3000 d. Sealink train ferry . . 1·75 60

306 Emblem, Globe and Dove

1990. 45th Anniv of Postal Service. Mult.

1496 100 d. Type **306** 10 10
1497 1000 d. Emblem, dish aerial and globe 55 20

307 Red Flags and Symbols of Construction and Agriculture

308 Thach Sanh collecting Wood

1990. 45th Anniv of Independence. Multicoloured.

1498 100 d. Type **307** 10 10
1499 500 d. Map, storming of Government Palace (1945), siege of Dien Bien Phu and tank entering Presidential Palace, Saigon (1975) . . 25 10
1500 1000 d. Satellite communications ship, dish aerial and "VI" 50 15
1501 3000 d. Hammer and sickle, industrial symbols and couple 1·50 50

1990. Legend of Thach Sanh. Multicoloured.

1503 100 d. Type **308** 10 10
1504 300 d. Ly Thong 15 10
1505 500 d. Thach Sanh fighting fire-breathing snake 25 10
1506 1000 d. Thach Sanh shooting down bird 55 20
1507 2000 d. Thach Sanh in prison 1·10 35
1508 3000 d. Thach Sanh and wife 1·75 60

1990 World Cup Football Championship Results. Nos. 1382/8 optd **1. GERMANY 2. ARGENTINA 3. ITALY**.

1509 **290** 100 d. multicoloured . . 10 10
1510 – 200 d. multicoloured . . 10 10
1511 – 300 d. multicoloured . . 15 10
1512 – 500 d. multicoloured . . 25 10
1513 – 1000 d. multicoloured . 55 20
1514 – 2000 d. multicoloured . 1·10 35
1515 – 3000 d. multicoloured . 1·60 55

1990. Red Cross. Nos. N598/605 optd with red cross and **FOR THE FUTURE GENERATION** in various languages (given in brackets).

1517 12 x. mult (Italian) 20 10
1518 12 x. mult (Chinese) 20 10
1519 20 x. mult (German) 30 10
1520 20 x. mult (Vietnamese) . . 30 10
1521 30 x. mult (English) 45 15
1522 40 x. mult (Russian) 60 20
1523 50 x. mult (French) 75 25
1524 60 x. mult (Spanish) 90 30

311 Soldier

1990. 60th Anniv of Vietnamese Women's Union. Multicoloured.

1525 100 d. Type **311** 10 10
1526 500 d. Women in various occupations 30 10

312 Emblems

1990. 20th Anniv of Asian–Pacific Postal Training Centre, Bangkok.

1527 **312** 150 d. multicoloured . . 20 10

313 Hands holding Forest and City

1990. Preservation of Forests. Multicoloured.

1528 200 d. Type **313** 10 10
1529 1000 d. Forest fire, "S.O.S." and river 55 20

314 Panther Cap

315 Yachting

1991. Poisonous Fungi. Multicoloured.

1530 200 d. Type **314** 15 10
1531 300 d. Death cap 20 10
1532 1000 d. Destroying angel . . 75 20
1533 1500 d. Fly agaric . . . . . 1·10 35
1534 2000 d. "Russula emetica" . . 1·50 50
1535 3000 d. Satan's mushroom . . 2·40 75

1991. Olympic Games, Barcelona (1992). Mult.

1536 200 d. Type **315** 10 10
1537 300 d. Boxing 15 10
1538 400 d. Cycling 20 10
1539 1000 d. High jumping 45 15
1540 2000 d. Show jumping 95 30
1541 3000 d. Judo . . . . 1·40 45
1542 3000 d. Wrestling (horiz) . . 1·40 45

316 Nguyen Binh Khiem

1991. 500th Birth Anniv of Nguyen Binh Khiem (poet).

1544 **316** 200 d. black, brown and ochre 40 25

317 "Marisiliana"

318 Woman in Blue Tunic

1991. 500th Anniv (1992) of Discovery of America by Columbus (2nd issue). Multicoloured.

1545 200 d. Type **317** 10 10
1546 400 d. "Venitien" 15 10
1547 400 d. "Cromster" (vert) . . 15 10
1548 2000 d. "Pinta" 75 25
1549 2000 d. "Nina" 75 25
1550 3000 d. "Howker" (vert) . . 1·10 35
1551 5000 d. "Santa Maria" . . . 1·90 65

1991. Golden Heart Charity.

1553 **318** 200 d. multicoloured . . 10 10
1554 – 500 d. multicoloured . . 10 10
1555 – 1000 d. multicoloured . . 45 15
1556 – 5000 d. multicoloured . . 2·10 70

DESIGNS: 500 d. to 5000 d. Traditional women's costumes.

319 Japanese White-necked Crane

1991. Birds. Multicoloured.

1557 200 d. Type **319** 10 10
1558 300 d. Sarus crane chick (vert) 10 10
1559 400 d. Manchurian crane (vert) 15 10
1560 1000 d. Sarus cranes (adults) (vert) 40 15
1561 2000 d. Black-necked crane (vert) 80 25
1562 3000 d. South African crowned cranes (vert) . . . . 1·25 40
1563 3000 d. Great white crane . . 1·25 40

320 Blacktip Reef Shark

1991. Sharks. Multicoloured.

1564 200 d. Type **320** 10 10
1565 300 d. Grey reef shark . . . 10 10
1566 400 d. Leopard shark 15 10
1567 1000 d. Great hammerhead . . 40 15
1568 2000 d. Whitetip reef shark . 80 25
1569 3000 d. Great white shark . 1·25 40
1570 3000 d. Bull shark . . . . . 1·25 40

321 Lobster

1991. Shellfish. Multicoloured.

1571 200 d. Type **321** 10 10
1572 300 d. "Alpheus bellulus" . . 10 10
1573 400 d. "Periclemenes brevicarpalis" 15 10
1574 1000 d. Lobster (different) . 40 15
1575 2000 d. Lobster (different) . 80 25
1576 3000 d. Lobster (different) . 1·25 40
1577 3000 d. "Astacus sp." . . . 1·25 40

322 "Fusee", 1829

323 Ho Chi Minh, "VII" and Buildings

1991. Early Locomotives. Multicoloured.

1578 400 d. Type **322** 15 10
1579 400 d. Hedley's "Puffing Billy", 1811 . . . . 15 10
1580 500 d. John Stevens locomotive, 1825 (horiz) 20 10
1581 1000 d. Crampton No. 80 locomotive, 1852 (horiz) . 40 15
1582 2000 d. "Locomotion", 1825 (horiz) 80 25
1583 3000 d. "Saint-Lo", 1843 (horiz) 1·25 40
1584 3000 d. "Coutances", 1855 (horiz) . . . . 1·25 40

1991. 7th Vietnamese Communist Party Congress. Multicoloured.

1586 200 d. Type **323** 25 10
1587 300 d. Workers 35 10
1588 400 d. Mother and children . 45 10

324 Pioneers

326 Yellow-banded Poison-arrow Frog

325 Lada

1991. 50th Anniv of Vietnam Youth Pioneers (200 d.) and United Nations Convention on Children's Rights (400 d.). Multicoloured.

1589 200 d. Type **324** 30 10
1590 400 d. Child's face and U.N. emblem 65 20

1991. Rally Cars. Multicoloured.

1591 400 d. Type **325** 15 10
1592 400 d. Nissan 15 10
1593 500 d. Ford Sierra RS Cosworth 20 10
1594 1000 d. Suzuki 40 15
1595 2000 d. Mazda "323" 80 25
1596 3000 d. Peugeot . . . . . . 1·25 40
1597 3000 d. Lancia . . . . 1·25 40

1991. Frogs. Multicoloured.

1599 200 d. Type **326** 10 10
1600 400 d. Edible frog 15 10
1601 500 d. Golden mantella . . . 25 10
1602 1000 d. Dyeing poison-arrow frog 40 15
1603 2000 d. Tree frog 80 25
1604 3000 d. Red-eyed tree frog ("Agalychnis calidryas") . 1·25 40
1605 3000 d. Golden tree frog ("Hyla aurea") . . . . 1·25 40

327 Ho Chi Minh and Party Emblem

328 Speed Skating

1991. 60th Anniv (1990) of Vietnamese Communist Party.

1606 **327** 100 d. red 10 10

1991. Winter Olympic Games, Albertville (1992) (1st issue). Multicoloured.

1607 200 d. Type **328** 10 10
1608 300 d. Freestyle skiing . . . 10 10
1609 400 d. Four-man bobsleighing (horiz) 15 10
1610 1000 d. Biathlon (rifle shooting) (horiz) 40 15
1611 2000 d. Skiing (horiz) 80 25
1612 3000 d. Cross-country skiing . 1·25 40
1613 3000 d. Ice skating . . . . . 1·25 40

See also Nos. 1659/63.

329 "Arsinoitherium zitteli"

1991. Prehistoric Animals. Multicoloured.

1615 200 d. Type **329** 10 10
1616 500 d. "Elephas primigenius" 25 10
1617 1000 d. "Baluchitherium" . . 45 15
1618 2000 d. "Deinotherium giganteum" 90 30
1619 3000 d. "Brontops" . . . . . 1·40 45
1620 3000 d. "Uintatherium" . . . 1·40 45

330 Pawn

1991. Chess. Staunton Pieces.

1621 200 d. Type **330** 10 10
1622 300 d. Knight 15 10
1623 1000 d. Rook 45 15
1624 2000 d. Queen 85 30
1625 3000 d. Bishop . . . . . . 1·40 40
1626 3000 d. King . . . . 1·40 40

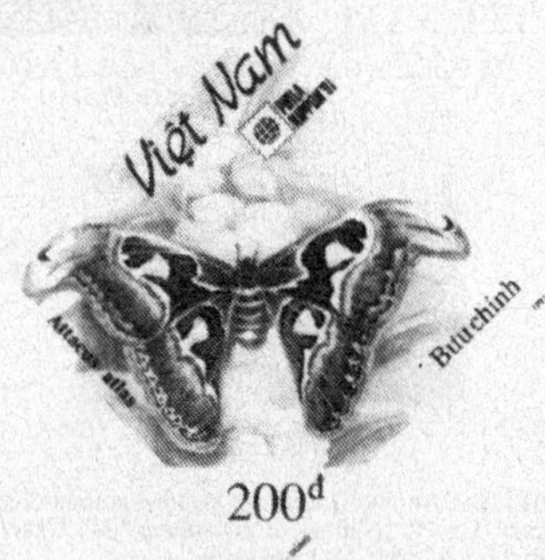

331 Atlas Moth

1991. "Phila Nippon '91" International Stamp Exhibition, Tokyo. Moths and Butterflies. Mult.

1628 200 d. Type **331** 10 10
1629 400 d. Blue morpho 15 10
1630 500 d. Birdwing 20 10
1631 1000 d. Red admiral 40 15
1632 1000 d. "Papilio demetrius" . 40 15
1633 3000 d. "Papilio weiskei" . . 1·25 40
1634 5000 d. Lesser purple emperor 2·00 65

MINIMUM PRICE

The minimum price quoted is 10p which represents a handling charge rather than a basis for valuing common stamps. For further notes about prices, see introductory pages.

332 Means of Communication

333 Eye and Clasped Hands

1991. 25th Anniv of Posts and Telecommunications Research Institute.

1636 **332** 200 d. multicoloured . . 40 20

1991. Golden Heart Charity for Disabled People.

1638 **333** 200 d. blue, lilac & orge 10 10
1639 – 3000 d. violet, blue and turquoise . . . . . . 1·25 40

DESIGN: 3000 d. Tennis player in wheelchair.

334 Gymnastics

1992. Olympic Games, Los Angeles (1984). Mult.

1640 50 x. Type **334** 15 10
1641 50 x. Football (vert) 15 10
1642 1 d. Wrestling 25 10
1643 2 d. Volleyball (vert) 50 15
1644 3 d. Hurdling 75 25
1645 5 d. Basketball (vert) . . . . 1·25 40
1646 8 d. Weightlifting . . . . . 2·00 65

1992. "Expo '92" World's Fair, Seville. Nos. 1372/8 optd **SEVILLA'92** and emblem.

1648 **288** 50 d. multicoloured . . . 25 10
1649 – 100 d. mult (No. 1373) . 50 15
1650 – 100 d. mult (No. 1374) . 50 15
1651 – 100 d. mult (No. 1375) . 50 15
1652 – 200 d. mult (No. 1376) . 95 30
1653 – 200 d. mult (No. 1377) . 95 30
1654 – 300 d. multicoloured . . 1·40 45

336 Chu Van An teaching

1992. 700th Death Anniv of Chu Van An.

1656 **336** 200 d. multicoloured . . 25 15

337 Atomic Symbol, Communications, Industry and Agriculture

1992. Resolutions of 7th Communist Party Congress. Multicoloured.

1657 200 d. Type **337** 10 10
1658 2000 d. Hands clasped and map of Asia 55 20

338 Biathlon

1992. Winter Olympic Games, Albertville (2nd issue). Multicoloured.

1659 200 d. Type **338** 10 10
1660 2000 d. Ice hockey 45 15
1661 4000 d. Skiing (slalom) . . . 85 30
1662 5000 d. Ice skating . . . . . 1·10 35
1663 6000 d. Skiing (downhill) . . 1·25 40

339 Columbus's Fleet

1992. 500th Anniv of Discovery of America by Columbus (3rd issue). Multicoloured.

1664 400 d. Type **339** 10 10
1665 3000 d. "Santa Maria" . . . 60 20
1666 4000 d. Columbus and flag on land 80 25
1667 6000 d. Columbus offering gifts to Amerindians . . . . . . 1·25 40
1668 8000 d. Ship returning home . 1·60 55

340 Tupolev Tu-154M

1992. Aircraft. Multicoloured.

1670 400 d. Type **340** 10 10
1671 500 d. Concorde 10 10
1672 1000 d. Airbus Industrie A-320 20 10
1673 3000 d. Airbus Industrie A340-300 . . . . 65 20
1674 4000 d. De Havilland D.H.C.8 Dash Eight-400 . . . . . . 90 30
1675 5000 d. Boeing 747-200 . . . 1·10 35
1676 6000 d. McDonnell Douglas MD-11CF . . . . 1·25 40

341 Weather System and Forecasting Equipment

342 Archery

1992. International Decade for Natural Disaster Reduction. Multicoloured.

1677 400 d. Type **341** 10 10
1678 4000 d. Man taking flood depth readings 90 30

1992. Olympic Games, Barcelona (2nd issue). Multicoloured.

1679 400 d. Type **342** 10 10
1680 600 d. Volleyball 15 10
1681 1000 d. Wrestling 20 10
1682 3000 d. Fencing 65 20
1683 4000 d. Running 90 30
1684 5000 d. Weightlifting . . . . 1·10 35
1685 6000 d. Hockey . . . . 1·25 40

343 Suzuki "500 F"

1992. Racing Motor Cycles. Multicoloured.

1687 400 d. Type **343** 10 10
1688 500 d. Honda "CBR 600F" . . 10 10
1689 1000 d. Honda "HRC 500F" . 20 10
1690 3000 d. Kawasaki "250F" (vert) 65 20
1691 4000 d. Suzuki "RM 250 F" (vert) 90 30
1692 5000 d. Suzuki "500F" . . . 1·10 35
1693 6000 d. BMW "1000F" . . . 1·25 40

344 Shuttle Launch

346 Footballer

345 Main Entrance

1992. International Space Year. Multicoloured.

1695 400 d. Type **344** 10 10
1696 500 d. Launch of space shuttle "Columbia" 10 10
1697 3000 d. "Columbia" in space (horiz) 65 20
1698 4000 d. Projected shuttle "Hermes" docked at space station (horiz) 85 30
1699 5000 d. "Hermes" in space with solar panel (horiz) . . . . 1·10 35
1700 6000 d. Astronauts repairing Hubble space telescope . . 1·25 40

1992. Centenary of Saigon Post Office.

1701 **345** 200 d. multicoloured . . 40 15

1992. European Cup Football Championship. Multicoloured.

1703 200 d. Type **346** 10 10
1704 2000 d. Goalkeeper 45 15
1705 4000 d. Two players with ball on ground 85 30
1706 5000 d. Two players with ball in air . . . . 1·10 35
1707 6000 d. Three players . . . . 1·25 40

347 "Portrait of a Girl" (Francisco de Zurbaran)

1992. "Expo '92" World's Fair, Seville. Paintings by Spanish Artists. Multicoloured.

1709 400 d. Type **347** 10 10
1710 500 d. "Woman with a Jug" (Bartolome Esteban Murillo) 10 10
1711 1000 d. "Maria Aptrickaia" (Diego Velazquez) 20 10
1712 3000 d. "Holy Family with St. Katharine" (Jose de Ribera) 60 20
1713 4000 d. "Madonna and Child with Sts. Agnes and Thekla" (El Greco) 80 25
1714 5000 d. "Woman with Jug" (Francisco Goya) . . . . 1·00 35
1715 6000 d. "The Naked Maja" (Francisco Goya) (horiz) . 1·25 40

348 Clean Water sustaining Life and Polluted Water

1992. 20th Anniv of United Nations Conference on Environmental Protection. Multicoloured.

1717 200 d. Type **348** 10 10
1718 4000 d. Graph comparing current world development and environmentally sound development 95 30

349 Cu Lao Xanh Lighthouse

350 "Citrus maxima"

1992. "Genova '92" International Thematic Stamp Exhibition. Lighthouses. Multicoloured.

1719 200 d. Type **349** 10 10
1720 3000 d. Can Gio 60 20
1721 5000 d. Vung Tau . . . . . 1·00 35
1722 6000 d. Long Chau . . . . . 1·40 45

1992. Flowers. Multicoloured.

1723 200 d. Type **350** 10 10
1724 2000 d. "Nerium indicum" . 40 15
1725 4000 d. "Ixora coccinea" . . 80 25
1726 5000 d. "Cananga oborata" . 1·00 35
1727 6000 d. "Cassia surattensis" . 1·25 40

351 Australian Pied Imperial Pigeons **353** Memorials and "45"

352 Guinea Pig

1992. Pigeons and Doves. Multicoloured.
1728 200 d. Type **351** 10 10
1729 2000 d. Red-plumed pigeon 40 15
1730 4000 d. Rock dove 80 25
1731 5000 d. Top-knot pigeon 1·00 35
1732 6000 d. Laughing doves (horiz) 1·25 40

1992. Rodents. Multicoloured.
1733 200 d. Type **352** 10 10
1734 500 d. Guinea pigs 10 10
1735 3000 d. Indian crested porcupine 60 20
1736 4000 d. Lesser Egyptian gerbil (vert) 80 25
1737 5000 d. Red giant flying squirrel (vert) 1·00 35
1738 6000 d. Common rabbit (vert) 1·25 40

1992. 45th Anniv of Disabled Soldiers' Day.
1739 **353** 200 d. multicoloured 40 15

354 Stylized Sportsmen

1992. 3rd Phu Dong Games.
1740 **354** 200 d. blue, ultramarine and light blue 40 15

355 Siamese Fighting Fish

1992. Siamese Fighting Fishes.
1741 **355** 200 d. multicoloured 10 10
1742 – 500 d. multicoloured 10 10
1743 – 3000 d. multicoloured 60 20
1744 – 4000 d. multicoloured 80 25
1745 – 5000 d. multicoloured 1·00 35
1746 – 6000 d. multicoloured 1·25 40
DESIGNS: 500 d. to 6000 d. Different Siamese fighting fishes.

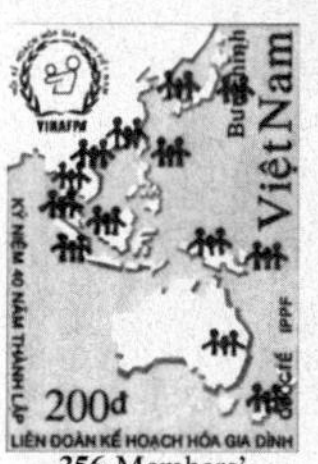

356 Members' Locations on Map **358** Adult protecting Child

357 Trainee Doctors

1992. 40th Anniv of International Planned Parenthood Federation. Multicoloured.
1747 200 d. Type **356** 10 10
1748 4000 d. Emblem on world map (horiz) 95 30

1992. 90th Anniv of Hanoi Medical School. Multicoloured.
1749 200 d. Type **357** 10 10
1750 5000 d. Alexandre Yersin (bacteriologist) and school 1·10 35

1992. SOS Children's Villages. Multicoloured.
1751 200 d. Type **358** 10 10
1752 5000 d. Houses and woman with children 1·10 35

359 Kick Boxing

1993. 17th South-East Asian Games, Singapore.
1753 **359** 200 d. multicoloured 40 15

360 Giant Bee

1993. Bees. Multicoloured.
1754 200 d. Type **360** 10 10
1755 800 d. "Apis koschevnikovi" 15 10
1756 1000 d. "Apis laboriosa" 20 10
1757 2000 d. "Apis cerana japonica" 40 15
1758 5000 d. "Apis cerana cerana" 1·00 35
1759 10000 d. Honey bee (vert) 2·00 65

361 Tam-Cam returning from the River **362** Rooster with Family

1993. Legend of Tam-Cam. Multicoloured.
1760 200 d. Type **361** 10 10
1761 800 d. Apparition of old man by goldfish basin 15 10
1762 1000 d. Tam-Cam with unsold rice at the market 20 10
1763 3000 d. Tam-Cam trying on slipper for Prince 60 20
1764 4000 d. Tam-Cam rising from lotus 80 25
1765 10000 d. The royal couple 2·00 65

1993. New Year. Year of the Cock. Multicoloured.
1766 200 d. Type **362** 10 10
1767 5000 d. Rooster with family (different) 1·10 35

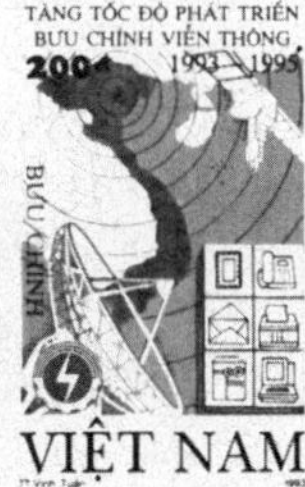

363 "Atractylodes macrocephala" **364** Communications Equipment

1993. Medicinal Plants. Multicoloured.
1768 200 d. Type **363** 10 10
1769 1000 d. Rangoon creeper ("Quisqualis indica") 20 10
1770 1000 d. Japanese honeysuckle ("Lonicera japonica") 20 10
1771 3000 d. "Rehmannia glutinosa" 65 20
1772 12000 d. "Gardenia jasminoides" 2·50 85

1993. "Communication in Service of Life". Multicoloured.
1773 200 d. Type **364** 10 10
1774 2500 d. Fibre-optic cable and map of Hong Kong–Sri Racha submarine cable route 60 20

365 Giant Panda

1993. Mammals. Multicoloured.
1775 200 d. Type **365** 10 10
1776 800 d. Tiger 15 10
1777 1000 d. Indian elephant 20 10
1778 3000 d. Indian rhinoceros 55 20
1779 4000 d. Family of gibbons 75 25
1780 10000 d. Clouded leopard 1·90 65

366 Players, Statue of Liberty and Emblem

1993. World Cup Football Championship, U.S.A. (1994) (1st issue).
1782 **366** 200 d. multicoloured 10 10
1783 – 1500 d. multicoloured 20 10
1784 – 7000 d. multicoloured 1·10 35
DESIGNS: 1500, 7000 d. Different match scenes.
See also Nos. 1865/70.

367 Wheelbarrow

1993. Traditional Transport. Multicoloured.
1785 200 d. Type **367** 10 10
1786 800 d. Buffalo cart 15 10
1787 1000 d. Rickshaw 20 10
1788 2000 d. Rickshaw with passenger 40 15
1789 5000 d. Rickshaw (different) 1·00 35
1790 10000 d. Horse-drawn carriage 2·00 65

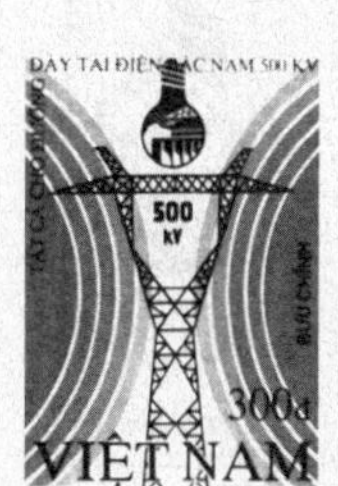

368 Pylon and Lightbulb **369** "Sunflowers" (Vincent van Gogh)

1993. 500kv Electricity Lines.
1791 **368** 300 d. black, orange and red 20 10
1792 400 d. black, blue and orange 25 10

1993. "Polska'93" International Stamp Exhibition, Poznan. Paintings. Multicoloured.
1793 200 d. Type **369** 10 10
1794 1000 d. "Young Woman" (Amedeo Modigliani) 20 10
1795 1000 d. "Couple in Forest" (Henri Rousseau) 20 10
1796 5000 d. "Harlequin with Family" (Pablo Picasso) 90 30
1797 10000 d. "Female Model" (Henri Matisse) (horiz) 1·75 60

370 "Paphiopedilum hirsutissimum"

1993. Centenary of Da Lat. Orchids. Multicoloured.
1799 400 d. Type **370** 10 10
1800 1000 d. "Paphiopedilum gratrixianum" 20 10
1801 1000 d. "Paphiopedilum malipoense" 20 10
1802 12000 d. "Paphiopedilum hennisianum" 2·10 70

371 Wat Phra Sri Rattana Satsadaram, Thailand

1993. Historic Asian Architecture. Multicoloured.
1803 400 d. Type **371** 10 10
1804 800 d. Prambanan Temple, Indonesia 15 10
1805 1000 d. City Hall, Singapore 15 10
1806 2000 d. Angkor Vat, Cambodia (horiz) 30 10
1807 2000 d. Ubudiah Mosque, Kuala Kangsar, Malaysia (horiz) 30 10
1808 6000 d. That Luang, Laos (horiz) 95 30
1809 8000 d. Omar Ali Saifuddin Mosque, Brunei (horiz) 1·25 40

372 Industry and Communications

1993. 7th Trade Union Congress. Multicoloured.
1811 400 d. Type **372** 10 10
1812 5000 d. Doves, atomic symbol, hammer in hand and flowers 90 30

373 "Scylla serrata"

1993. Salt-water Crabs. Multicoloured.
1813 400 d. Type **373** 10 10
1814 800 d. "Portunus sanguinolentus" 15 10
1815 1000 d. "Charybdis bimaculata" 15 10
1816 2000 d. "Paralithodes brevipes" 30 10
1817 5000 d. "Portunus pelagicus" 75 25
1818 10000 d. "Lithodes turritus" 1·50 50

374 Stamps and Globe

1993. Stamp Day. Multicoloured.
1819 400 d. Type **374** 10 10
1820 5000 d. Airmail letter 90 30

375 Player **376** Lo Lo Costume

1994. Tennis.
1821 **375** 400 d. multicoloured 10 10
1822 – 1000 d. multicoloured (male player) 15 10
1823 – 1000 d. multicoloured (female player) 15 10
1824 – 12000 d. multicoloured 2·10 70
DESIGNS: Nos. 1822/4, Different players.

1993. "Bangkok 1993" International Stamp Exhibition.
1825 400 d. Type **376** 10 10
1826 800 d. Thai costume 15 10
1827 1000 d. Dao Do costume 15 10
1828 2000 d. H'mong costume 30 10
1829 5000 d. Kho Mu costume 70 25
1830 10000 d. Kinh costume 1·40 45

377 Dog with Puppies

1994. New Year. Year of the Dog. Multicoloured.

1832 400 d. Type **377** 10 10
1833 6000 d. Dog . . . . 1·10 35

378 Peach

380 Hoi Lim

379 Anatoly Karpov

1994. Flowers of the Four Seasons. Multicoloured.

1834 400 d. Type **378** (spring) . . 15 10
1835 400 d. "Chrysanthemum morifolium" (autumn) . . 15 10
1836 400 d. "Rosa chinensis" (winter) 15 10
1837 15000 d. "Delonix regia" (summer) . . . . 2·10 70

1994. Chess. Multicoloured.

1838 400 d. Type **379** 10 10
1839 1000 d. Gary Kasparov . . . 15 10
1840 2000 d. Robert Fischer . . . 35 10
1841 4000 d. Emanuel Lasker . . . 70 25
1842 10000 d. Jose Raul Capablanca 1·75 60

No. 1840 is wrongly inscribed "Robers".

1994. "Hong Kong '94" Stamp Exhibition. Traditional Festivals. Multicoloured.

1844 400 d. Type **380** 10 10
1845 800 d. Cham 15 10
1846 1000 d. Tay Nguyen 20 10
1847 12000 d. Nam Bo . . . . . 2·10 70

381 Loi Nhuoc

382 Red Gladioli

1994. Operatic Masks. Multicoloured.

1848 400 d. Type **381** 10 10
1849 500 d. Dao Tax Xuan 10 10
1850 2000 d. Ta Ngoc Lan 35 10
1851 3000 d. Ly Khac Minh . . . 55 20
1852 4000 d. Ta On Dinh 75 25
1853 7000 d. Khuong Linh Ta . . 1·25 40

1994. Gladioli. Multicoloured.

1854 400 d. Type **382** 10 10
1855 2000 d. Salmon gladioli . . . 35 10
1856 5000 d. White gladioli . . . 80 25
1857 8000 d. Magenta gladioli . . 1·25 40

383 Painting by Utamaro Kitagawa

1994. Paintings by Japanese Artists. Multicoloured.

1858 400 d. Type **383** (wrongly inscr "Kigatawa") 10 10
1859 500 d. Harunobu Suzuki . . . 10 10
1860 1000 d. Hokusai Katsushika . 15 10
1861 2000 d. Hiroshige 35 10
1862 3000 d. Hokusai Katsushika (different) 50 15
1863 4000 d. Utamaro Kitagawa (different) 65 20
1864 9000 d. Choki Eishosai . . . 1·50 50

384 Footballers

386 Pioneers reading Newspaper

385 Hauling Piece of Equipment

1994. World Cup Football Championship, U.S.A. (2nd issue). Multicoloured.

1865 400 d. Type **384** 10 10
1866 600 d. Running with ball . . 10 10
1867 1000 d. Heading ball 15 10
1868 2000 d. Goalkeeper 35 10
1869 3000 d. Two players chasing ball 50 15
1870 11000 d. Tackling . . . . . 1·90 65

1994. 40th Anniv of Victory at Dien Bien Phu.

1872 **385** 400 d. brown, cinnamon and black 10 10
1873 – 3000 d. ultramarine, blue and black 50 15

DESIGN: 3000 d. Entertaining the troops.

1994. 40th Anniv of "Young Pioneer" (newspaper).

1874 **386** 400 d. red and black . . 30 10

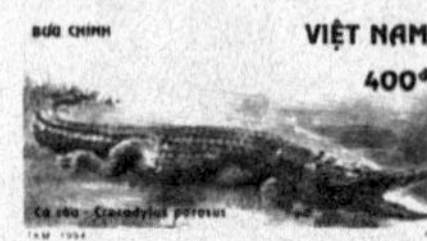

387 Estuarine Crocodile

1994. Reptiles. Multicoloured.

1875 400 d. Type **387** 10 10
1876 600 d. Mississippi alligator . 10 10
1877 2000 d. Nile crocodile . . . 35 10
1878 3000 d. Chinese alligator . . 50 15
1879 4000 d. Paraguay caiman . . 65 20
1880 9000 d. Australian crocodile 1·50 50

388 Alexandre Yersin

389 Pierre de Coubertin (founder)

1994. Centenary of Discovery of Plague Bacillus.

1882 **388** 400 d. multicoloured . . 30 10

1994. Centenary of International Olympic Committee. Multicoloured.

1883 400 d. Anniversary and National Committee emblems and sports pictograms . . 10 10
1884 6000 d. Type **389** . . . . . 1·10 35

390 "Cicindela aurulenta"

1994. Beetles. Multicoloured.

1885 400 d. Type **390** 10 10
1886 1000 d. "Harmonia octomaculata" 15 10
1887 6000 d. "Cicindela tennipes" 1·00 35
1888 7000 d. "Collyris sp." . . . 1·25 40

391 Anniversary Emblem

1994. 120th Anniv of U.P.U. Multicoloured.

1889 400 d. Type **391** 10 10
1890 5000 d. Envelopes forming world map 75 25

392 Curlew

393 "Bambusa blumeana"

1994. "Philakorea 1994" International Stamp Exhibition, Seoul. Sea Birds. Multicoloured.

1892 400 d. Type **392** 10 10
1893 600 d. Wilson's petrel 10 10
1894 1000 d. Great frigate bird . . 15 10
1895 2000 d. Cape gannet 30 10
1896 3000 d. Tufted puffins 50 15
1897 11000 d. Band-tailed gulls . . 1·75 60

1994. "Singpex '94" Stamp Exhibition, Singapore. Bamboos. Multicoloured.

1899 400 d. Type **393** 10 10
1900 1000 d. "Phyllostachys aurea" 15 10
1901 2000 d. "Bambusa vulgaris" . 30 10
1902 4000 d. "Tetragonocalamus quadrangularis" 65 20
1903 10000 d. "Bambusa venticosa" 1·60 55

394 Log Bridge with Handrail

1994. Rudimentary Bridges. Multicoloured.

1904 400 d. Type **394** 10 10
1905 900 d. Interwoven bridge . . 15 10
1906 8000 d. Log bridge on stilts . 1·10 35

395 Girl in Wheelchair and Boy playing

1994. "For Our Children's Future". Multicoloured.

1907 400 d. + 100 d. Type **395** . . 10 10
1908 2000 d. Children dancing around emblem (vert) . . . 40 15

396 Tram with Overhead Conductor

1994. Trams. Multicoloured.

1909 400 d. Type **396** 10 10
1910 900 d. Paris tram 15 10
1911 8000 d. Philadelphia mail tram 1·10 35

397 Civilians greeting Soldiers

1994. 40th Anniv of Liberation of Hanoi. Multicoloured.

1912 400 d. Type **397** 10 10
1913 2000 d. Workers and students and symbols of development 35 10

398 Airplane in Air

1994. 50th Anniv of I.C.A.O. Multicoloured.

1914 400 d. Type **398** 10 10
1915 3000 d. Airplane on ground . 50 15

399 Parade

1994. 50th Anniv of Vietnamese People's Army. Multicoloured.

1916 400 d. Type **399** 10 10
1917 1000 d. Plan of attacks on Saigon 15 10
1918 2000 d. Veteran recounting the past to young girl 35 10
1919 4000 d. Naval anti-aircraft gun crew 70 25

400 Sow with Piglets

401 Osprey ("Pandion haliaetus")

1995. New Year. Year of the Pig. Multicoloured.

1920 400 d. Type **400** 10 10
1921 8000 d. Pig . . . . 1·00 35

1995. Birds.

1922 **401** 400 d. blue 10 10
1923 – 400 d. green 10 10
1924 – 400 d. purple 10 10
1925 – 400 d. orange 10 10
1926 – 5000 d. red 75 25

DESIGNS—HORIZ: No. 1923, Sociable weaver ("Philetarius socius"); 1924, Sharpbill ("Oxyruncus cristatus"); 1925, Golden plover ("Pluvialis apricaria"). VERT: No. 1926, Red-legged seriema ("Cariama cristata").

402 Girls with Bicycle

403 Statue and Building

1995. Women's Costumes. Multicoloured.

1927 400 d. Type **402** 10 10
1928 3000 d. Girl with sheaf of flowers 40 15
1929 5000 d. Girl with traditional hat 65 20

1995. "Vietstampex '95" Stamp Exhibition. F.I.A.P. Executive Committee Meeting.

1930 **403** 5500 d. multicoloured . . 65 20

404 Brown Fish Owl

1995. Owls. Multicoloured.

1931 400 d. Type **404** 10 10
1932 1000 d. Tawny owl 10 10
1933 2000 d. Great grey owl . . . 25 10
1934 5000 d. Spotted wood owl . . 60 20
1935 10000 d. White-faced scops owl 1·25 40

405 Schwarzer Angel Fish

1995. Fishes. Multicoloured.

1937 400 d. Type **405** 10 10
1938 1000 d. Patchy trigger fish . . 10 10
1939 2000 d. Royal angel fish . . 25 10
1940 4000 d. Queen angel fish . . 45 15
1941 5000 d. Queen trigger fish . . 60 20
1942 9000 d. Clown trigger fish . . 1·10 35

406 Throwing the Hammer

407 Lenin

1995. Olympic Games, Atlanta (1996). Multicoloured.

1943 400 d. Type **406** 10 10
1944 3000 d. Cycling 35 10
1945 4000 d. Running 45 15
1946 10000 d. Pole vaulting . . . 1·25 40

1995. 125th Birth Anniv of Lenin.

1948 **407** 400 d. black and red . . 15 10

408 Adult and Young

1995. The Malayan Tapir. Multicoloured. (a) With World Wildlife Fund emblem.

1949 400 d. Type **408** 10 10
1950 1000 d. Standing 15 10
1951 2000 d. Walking 30 10
1952 4000 d. Calling 60 20

Nos. 1949/52 were issued together, se-tenant, forming a composite design.

(b) Without W.W.F. emblem.

1953 4000 d. Standing by trees . . 60 20
1954 4000 d. Eating 60 20
1955 5000 d. Swimming 75 25
1956 6000 d. In water 90 30

Nos. 1953/6 were issued together, se-tenant, forming a composite design.

409 Dove and "50"

1995. 50th Anniv of End of Second World War in Europe.

1957 **409** 400 d. multicoloured . . 20 10

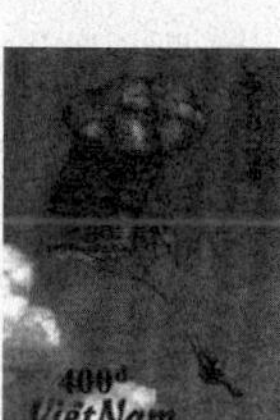

410 Montgolfier's Hot Air Balloon, 1783

411 Parachutist

1995. "Finlandia 95" International Stamp Exhibition, Helsinki. Balloons. Multicoloured.

1958 500 d. Type **410** 15 10
1959 1000 d. Jacques Charles and Marie-Noel Robert's balloon (first untethered flight by manned hydrogen balloon) 20 10
1960 2000 d. Jean-Pierre Blanchard's oared balloon 40 15
1961 3000 d. Jean-Francois Pilatre de Rozier and Jules Romain's balloon over English Channel, 1785 . . . . . . 50 15
1962 4000 d. Free balloon 65 20
1963 5000 d. Captive balloon over Red Square, Moscow, 1890 75 25
1964 7000 d. Auguste Piccard's balloon "F.N.R.S.", 1931 . 1·25 40

1995. Parachuting. Multicoloured.

1965 400 d. Type **411** 10 10
1966 2000 d. Two parachutists . . 40 15
1967 3000 d. Landing 50 15
1968 4000 d. Gathering in the parachute 65 20

Nos. 1965/8 were issued together, se-tenant, forming a composite design.

412 "Rhododendron fleuryi"

1995. Rhododendrons. Multicoloured.

1969 400 d. Type **412** 15 10
1970 1000 d. "Rhododendron sulphoreum" 25 10
1971 2000 d. "Rhododendron sinofalconeri" 50 15
1972 3000 d. "Rhododendron lyi" 65 20
1973 5000 d. "Rhododendron ovatum" 90 30
1974 9000 d. "Rhododendron tanastylum" . . . . 1·60 55

413 Tan and Lang pay Court to Lu's Daughter

1995. "Betel and Areca Nut" (fable). Multicoloured.

1975 400 d. Type **413** 15 10
1976 1000 d. Girl chooses Tan . . 25 10
1977 3000 d. Lang changes into rock 65 20
1978 10000 d. Girl changes in to betel pepper plant and Tan into areca nut palm . . . . . 1·60 55

Nos. 1975/8 were issued together, se-tenant, forming a composite design.

414 Statue of Mother and Child

415 Flags around Emblem

1995. 65th Anniv of Women's Union (400 d.) and World Conference on Women, Peking (3000 d.). Multicoloured.

1979 400 d. Type **414** 15 10
1980 3000 d. Globe and women of different races (horiz) . . 65 20

1995. Admission of Vietnam to Association of South East Asian Nations.

1981 **415** 400 d. multicoloured . 15 10

416 Ho Chi Minh, Dove and Crowd

1995. Anniversaries. Multicoloured.

1982 400 d. Type **416** (65th Anniv of Communist Party of Indo-China) 10 10
1983 400 d. Ho Chi Minh embracing child (105th birth anniv) . 10 10
1984 1000 d. Civic building, road bridge, power lines and oil derrick (40th anniv of evacuaton of French troops from North Vietnam) . . 25 10
1985 1000 d. Ho Chi Minh saluting and building flying flags (20th anniv of end of Vietnam war) 25 10
1986 2000 d. Soldiers and flag (50th anniv of National Liberation Army) 45 15
1987 2000 d. Radio mast, dish aerial, motor cycle couriers and mail van (50th anniv of postal and telecommunications services) 45 15

417 Bust of Hill and Penny Black

1995. Birth Bicentenary of Sir Rowland Hill (instigator of postage stamp).

1988 **417** 4000 d. multicoloured . . 75 25

418 Torch Carriers and Sports Pictograms

1995. National Sports Festival.

1989 **418** 400 d. blue, red and lilac 25 10

419 "Paphiopedilum druryi"

1995. "Singapore'95" International Stamp Exhibition. Orchids. Multicoloured.

1990 400 d. Type **419** 15 10
1991 2000 d. "Dendrobium ochraceum" 40 10
1992 3000 d. "Vanda sp." 50 15
1993 4000 d. "Cattleya sp." 65 20
1994 5000 d. "Paphiopedilum hirsutissimum" 90 30
1995 6000 d. "Christenosia vietnamica" . . . . 1·25 40

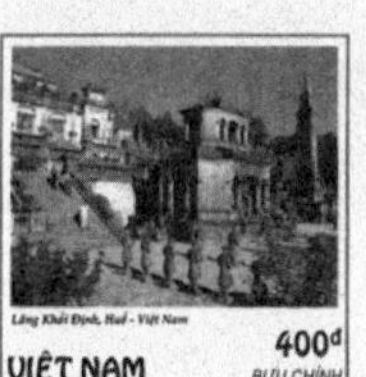

420 Palace, Hue

1995. Asian Cityscapes. Multicoloured.

1997 400 d. Type **420** 15 10
1998 3000 d. Park, Doanh Chau . 50 15
1999 4000 d. Temple, Macao . . . 65 20
2000 5000 d. Kowloon, Hong Kong 90 30
2001 6000 d. Pagoda, Dai Loan . . 1·25 40

421 Dove and Anniversary Emblem

1995. 50th Anniv of U.N.O.

2002 **421** 2000 d. multicoloured . . 40 10

422 Woman with Vase of Flowers (To Ngoc Van)

1995. Paintings. Multicoloured.

2003 400 d. Type **422** 15 10
2004 2000 d. Woman washing hair (Tran Van Can) 55 15
2005 6000 d. Woman and vase of flowers (To Ngoc Van) . . 85 30
2006 8000 d. Two women resting (Tran Van Can) . . . . . 1·10 35

423 Map and Eclipse

1995. Total Eclipse of the Sun.

2007 **423** 400 d. multicoloured . . 15 10

424 Rats carrying Canopy and on Horseback

1996. New Year. Year of the Rat. Multicoloured.

2008 400 d. Type **424** 15 10
2009 8000 d. Rats in and carrying sedan chair . . . . 1·10 35

FRANK STAMPS

F 19 Invalid's Badge

F 158 Children and Disabled Teacher

1976. For use by disabled veterans. Dated "27.7.75". No value indicated.

F100	F **19**	(–) red and blue	50	25
F101	–	(–) green, light green and brown	50	25

DESIGN: No. F101, Disabled veteran in factory.

1984. Disabled and Invalids. No value indicated.

F750	F **158**	(–) brown & ochre	50	25

No value indicated. As T **179**.

F861	(–) Policeman and militia members	50	25

MILITARY FRANK STAMPS

MF 21 Soldier and Map of Vietnam

1976. No value indicated.

MF110	MF **21**	(–) black and red	60	25

MF 59 Pilot

1979. 35th Anniv of Vietnam People's Army. No value indicated.

MF304	MF **59**	(–) purple and pink	35	10
MF305	–	(–) purple and pink	35	10

DESIGN: No. MF305, Badge of People's Army.

MF 61 Tank Driver and Tanks

MF 84 Ho Chi Minh in Naval Uniform

1979. No value indicated.

MF308	MF **61**	(–) black and mauve	30	15
MF309	–	(–) violet and green	30	15
MF310	–	(–) black and red	30	15

DESIGNS: No. MF309, Sailor and ship; MF310, Pilot and jet fighters.

1981. No value indicated.

MF420	MF **84**	(–) pink and blue	25	20
MF421	–	(–) multicoloured	25	20

DESIGN—13 × 17 mm: No. MF421, Factory militiawoman.

1982. Multicoloured. No value indicated.

MF466	(–) Soldier and militiawoman	25	10
MF467	(–) Type **94**	25	10

MF 107 Disabled Soldier

1982. 35th Anniv of Disabled Soldiers' Day. No value indicated.

MF513	MF **107**	(–) mauve and green	50	20

MF 120 Militia

1983. No value indicated.

MF581	MF **120**	(–) multicoloured	60	25

MF 152 Coastal Militia

MF 145 Star and Soldiers on Bunker

1984. 30th Anniv of Battle of Dien Bien Phu. No value indicated.

MF690	MF **145**	(–) yellow, orange and brown	65	20

1984. No value indicated.

MF732	MF **152**	(–) brown, orange and yellow	65	25

MF 164 Soldiers and Emblem

MF 205 Soldier and Woman holding Sheaf of Rice

1984. No value indicated.

MF786	MF **164**	(–) orange, red and black	50	25

1986.

MF979	MF **205**	1 d. brown and black	65	30

MF 232 Armed Forces Personnel and Flag

1987.

MF1119	MF **232**	5 d. red & brown	90	40

WALLIS AND FUTUNA ISLANDS

Pt. 6

A group of French islands in the Pacific Ocean north-east of Fiji. Attached to New Caledonia for administrative purposes in 1888. In 1961 they became a French Overseas Territory.

100 centimes = 1 franc

1920. Stamps of New Caledonia optd **ILES WALLIS et FUTUNA**.

1	**15**	1 c. black on green	25	35
2		2 c. brown	30	40
3		4 c. blue on orange	30	40
4		5 c. green	40	45
18		5 c. blue	40	55
5		10 c. red	50	45
19		10 c. green	50	60
6		15 c. lilac	50	50
7	**16**	20 c. brown	50	60
8		25 c. blue on green	60	60
21		25 c. red on yellow	50	50
9		30 c. brown on orange	70	70
22		30 c. red	50	50
24		30 c. green	1·10	1·10
10		35 c. black on yellow	55	55
11		40 c. red on green	55	55
12		45 c. purple	60	60
13		50 c. red on orange	60	60
25		50 c. blue	70	70
26		50 c. grey	90	90
27		65 c. blue	2·25	2·25
14		75 c. green	1·25	1·25
15	**17**	1 f. blue on green	2·00	2·00
28		1 f. 10 brown	1·60	1·75
16		2 f. red on blue	3·25	3·25
17		5 f. black on orange	5·50	5·50

1922. As last surch.

29	**15**	0,01 on 15 c. lilac	40	50
30		0,02 on 15 c. lilac	40	50
31		0,04 on 15 c. lilac	40	50
32		0,05 on 15 c. lilac	40	50
33	**17**	25 c. on 2 f. red on blue	50	60
34		25 c. on 5 f. black on orge	50	60
35	**16**	65 on 40 c. red on green	60	60
36		85 on 75 c. green	60	60
37		90 on 75 c. red	90	90
38	**17**	1 f. 25 on 1 fr. blue	50	50
39		1 f. 50 on 1 fr. blue on blue	1·75	1·75
40		3 f. on 5 f. mauve	3·50	3·50
41		10 f. on 5 f. green on mve	14·00	14·00
42		20 f. on 5 f. red on yellow	20·00	20·00

1930. Stamps of New Caledonia, some with colours changed, optd **ILES WALLIS et FUTUNA**.

43	**22**	1 c. blue and purple	20	30
44		2 c. green and brown	30	35
45		3 c. blue and red	35	40
46		4 c. green and red	30	35
47		5 c. brown and blue	35	25
48		10 c. brown and lilac	30	40
49		15 c. blue and brown	30	40
50		20 c. brown and red	35	45
51		25 c. brown and green	50	60
52	**23**	30 c. turquoise and green	45	55
53		35 c. green and deep green	55	65
54		40 c. green and red	45	55
55		45 c. red and blue	50	60
56		45 c. green and turquoise	45	55
57		50 c. brown and mauve	45	55
58		55 c. red and blue	1·25	1·25
59		60 c. red and blue	40	50
60		65 c. blue and brown	80	80
61		70 c. brown and mauve	50	60
62		75 c. drab and blue	1·25	1·25
63		80 c. green and purple	50	50
64		85 c. brown and green	2·00	2·00
65		90 c. carmine and red	1·10	1·10
66		90 c. red and brown	45	55
67	**24**	1 f. red and drab	2·00	2·00
68		1 f. carmine and red	85	80
69		1 f. green and red	35	45
70		1 f. 10 brown and green	15·00	15·00
71		1 f. 25 green and brown	1·10	1·25
72		1 f. 25 carmine and red	45	55
73		1 f. 40 red and blue	60	60
74		1 f. 50 blue & ultramarine	45	55
75		1 f. 60 brown and green	65	65
76		1 f. 75 red and blue	6·25	6·25
77		1 f. 75 blue	1·25	1·25
78		2 f. brown and orange	80	80
79		2 f. 25 blue & ultramarine	65	65
80		2 f. 50 brown	65	65
81		3 f. brown and purple	80	80
82		5 f. brown and blue	80	80
83		10 f. brn & mve on pink	1·50	1·50
84		20 f. brown & red on yellow	2·25	2·25

1931. "Colonial Exhibition" key-types.

85	E	40 c. green and black	3·00	3·00
86	F	50 c. mauve and black	3·00	3·00
87	G	90 c. red and black	3·00	3·00
88	H	1 f. 50 blue and black	3·00	3·00

1939. New York World's Fair. As T **28** of Mauritania.

89	1 f. 25 red	1·00	1·00
90	2 f. 25 blue	1·00	1·00

1939. 150th Anniv of French Revolution. As T **29** of Mauritania.

91	45 c. + 25 c. green and black	7·50	7·50
92	70 c. + 30 c. brown and black	7·50	7·50
93	90 c. + 35 c. orange & black	7·50	7·50
94	1 f. 25 c. + 1 f. red and black	7·50	7·50
95	2 f. 25 c. + 2 f. blue & black	7·50	7·50

1941. Adherence to General de Gaulle. Stamps of 1930 optd **France Libre**.

96	**22**	1 c. blue and purple	70	70
97		2 c. green and brown	70	70
97a		3 c. blue and red	60·00	60·00
98		4 c. green and orange	70	70
99		5 c. brown and blue	70	70
100		10 c. brown and lilac	70	70
101		15 c. blue and brown	70	70
102		20 c. brown and red	1·40	1·40
103		25 c. brown and green	1·40	1·40
104	**23**	30 c. green	1·40	1·40
105		35 c. green	70	70
106		40 c. green and red	1·40	1·40
107		45 c. red and blue	1·40	1·40
107a		45 c. green & turquoise	60·00	60·00
108		50 c. brown and mauve	70	70
109		55 c. red and blue	70	70
109a		60 c. red and blue	60·00	60·00
110		65 c. blue and brown	70	70
111		70 c. brown and mauve	70	70
112		75 c. drab and blue	1·40	1·40
113		80 c. green and purple	70	70
114		85 c. brown and green	1·40	1·40
115		90 c. carmine and red	70	70
116	**24**	1 f. carmine and red	1·40	1·40
117		1 f. green and brown	1·40	1·40
118		1 f. blue and deep blue	70	70
119		1 f. blue	70	70
120		2 f. brown and orange	1·40	1·40
121		2 f. 50 brown	£110	£110
122		3 f. brown and purple	70	70
123		3 f. brown and blue	2·75	2·75
124		10 f. brown and mauve on pink	35·00	35·00
125		20 f. brown & red on yell	55·00	55·00

5 Native Ivory Head

1944. Free French Administration.

126	**5**	5 c. brown	15	30
127		10 c. blue	15	30
128		25 c. green	15	20
129		30 c. orange	15	30
130		40 c. green	30	45
131		80 c. purple	35	45
132		1 f. purple	30	40
133		1 f. 50 red	20	30
134		2 f. black	25	35
135		2 f. 50 blue	45	60
136		4 f. violet	40	50
137		5 f. yellow	40	50
138		10 f. brown	85	90
139		20 f. green	1·10	1·25

1944. Mutual Aid and Red Cross Funds. As T **31** of New Caledonia.

140	5 f. + 20 f. orange	1·10	1·10

1945. Surch.

141	**5**	50 c. on 5 c. brown	50	60
142		60 c. on 5 c. brown	50	60
143		70 c. on 5 c. brown	45	55
144		1 f. 20 on 5 c. brown	40	50
145		2 f. 40 on 35 c. green	40	50
146		3 f. on 25 c. green	60	70
147		4 f. 50 on 25 c. green	1·10	1·25
148		15 f. on 2 f. 50 blue	1·10	1·25

1946. Air. Victory. As T **34** of New Caledonia.

149	8 f. violet	50	75

1946. Air. From Chad to the Rhine. As Nos. 300/305 of New Caledonia.

150	5 f. violet	80	90
151	10 f. green	80	90
152	15 f. brown	80	90
153	20 f. blue	1·00	1·25
154	25 f. orange	1·25	1·50
155	50 f. red	1·75	2·00

1949. Air. 75th Anniv of Universal Postal Union. As T **38** of New Caledonia.

156	10 f. multicoloured	4·25	5·00

1949. Air. Nos. 325/6 of New Caledonia, with colours changed, optd **WALLIS ET FUTUNA.**

157	**37**	50 f. red and yellow	4·75	4·75
158	–	100 f. brown and yellow	6·75	7·00

1952. Centenary of Military Medal. As T **40** of New Caledonia.

159	2 f. turquoise, yellow & green	1·90	1·75

1954. Air. 10th Anniv of Liberation. As T **42** of New Caledonia.

160	3 f. brown and deep brown	4·25	4·50

7 Making Tapa (cloth)

9 Trumpet Triton

8 Father Chanel

1955. (a) Postage, as T **7**.
161 – 3 f. purple, mauve & lilac . 75 80
162 **7** 5 f. chocolate, brn & grn . 75 80
163 – 7 f. brown and turquoise . 1·10 1·10
164 – 9 f. deep purple, purple and blue . . . . 1·50 1·50
165 – 17 f. multicoloured . . . . 1·90 1·90
166 – 19 f. green and red . . . . 2·00 2·00

(b) Air, as T **8**.
167 **8** 14 f. blue, green & ind . . 2·00 1·40
168 – 21 f. green, brown & bl . 3·50 2·75
168a – 27 f. green, blue & brn . . 3·50 2·00
169 – 33 f. brown, blue & turq . 5·50 5·00
DESIGNS—HORIZ: 9 f. Wallisian and island view; 7 f. Preparing kava; 17 f. Dancers; 21 f. View of Mata-Utu, Queen Amelia and Mgr. Bataillon; 27 f. Wharf, Mata-Utu; 33 f. Map of Wallis and Futuna Islands and "Stella Matutina" (full-rigged ship). VERT: 19 f. Paddle dance.

1958. Tropical Flora As T **47** of New Caledonia.
170 5 f. multicoloured . . . . . . 2·75 2·00
DESIGN—HORIZ: 5 f. "Montrouziera".

1958. 10th Anniv of Declaration of Human Rights. As T **48** of New Caledonia.
171 17 f. blue and ultramarine . . 3·50 3·50

1962. 5th South Pacific Conference. Pago Pago As T **49d** of New Caledonia.
172 16 f. multicoloured . . . . . 2·75 2·25

1962. Marine Fauna.
173 **9** 25 c. brown and green (postage) 55 55
174 – 1 f. red and green 55 55
175 – 2 f. brown and blue . . . . 1·10 1·10
176 – 4 f. brown and blue . . . . 1·60 1·60
177 – 10 f. multicoloured . . . . 3·50 3·50
178 – 20 f. brown and blue . . . 6·50 6·50
179 – 50 f. brown, bl & pur (air) . 7·75 5·00
180 – 100 f. black, green & pur . 15·00 11·00
DESIGNS—As T **9**: 1 f. Episcopal mitre; 2 f. Bull-mouth helmet; 4 f. Venus comb murex; 10 f. Red-mouth olive; 20 f. Tiger cowrie. 26½ × 48 mm: 50 f. Ventral harp. 48 × 26½ mm: 100 f. Fishing under water for commercial trochus shells.

1962. Air. 1st Trans-Atlantic TV Satellite Link. As T **50** of New Caledonia.
181 12 f. blue, purple and violet . 2·50 2·50

1963. Red Cross Cent. As T **53** of New Caledonia.
182 12 f. red, grey and purple . . 2·50 1·60

1963. 15th Anniv of Declaration of Human Rights. As T **54** of New Caledonia.
183 29 f. ochre and red . . . . . 5·50 4·50

1964. "PHILATEC 1964" Int Stamp Exn, Paris. As T **54c** of New Caledonia.
184 9 f. red, green and deep green 2·50 1·75

10 Throwing the Javelin

11 Inter-island Ferry "Reine Amelia"

1964. Air. Olympic Games. Tokyo.
185 **10** 31 f. purple, red & green . 15·00 10·00

1965.
186 **11** 11 f. multicoloured . . . . 5·00 4·00

1965. Air. Centenary of I.T.U. As T **56** of New Caledonia.
187 50 f. brown, purple and red . 16·00 12·00

1966. Air. Launching of 1st French Satellite. As Nos. 398/9 of New Caledonia.
188 7 f. red, claret & vermilion . . 2·75 2·75
189 10 f. red, claret & vermilion . . 3·50 3·50

1966. Air. Launching of Satellite "D1" As T **56e** of New Caledonia.
190 10 f. red, lake and green . . . 2·50 2·50

12 W.H.O. Building

1966. Air. Inauguration of W.H.O. Headquarters, Geneva.
191 **12** 30 f. red, yellow and blue . 3·00 3·00

13 Art Students

1966. Air. 20th Anniv of U.N.E.S.C.O.
192 **13** 50 f. brown, green & orange 4·50 3·50

14 Athlete and Decorative Pattern

1966. Air. South Pacific Games, Noumea.
193 **14** 32 f. multicoloured . . . . 3·50 2·50
194 – 38 f. green and mauve . . 4·00 3·00
DESIGN: 38 f. Woman with ball, and decorative pattern.

15 Samuel Wallis's Frigate H.M.S. "Dolphin" at Uvea

1967. Air. Bicentenary of Discovery of Wallis Island.
195 **15** 12 f. multicoloured . . . . 5·00 3·50

1968. 20th Anniv of W.H.O. As T **68** of New Caledonia.
196 17 f. purple, orange & green . 4·00 3·50

1968. Human Rights Year. As T **69** of New Caledonia.
197 19 f. brown, mauve & purple 2·50 2·50

1969. Air. 1st Flight of Concorde. As T **75** of New Caledonia.
198 20 f. black and purple . . . . 10·00 6·50

16 Gathering Coconuts

1969. Scenes of Everyday Life. Multicoloured.
199 1 f. Launching outrigger canoe (35 × 22 mm) (postage) . . 80 80
200 20 f. Type **16** (air) . . . . . 1·75 1·00
201 32 f. Horse-riding . . . . . . 3·00 1·50
202 38 f. Wood-carving . . . . . . 3·50 1·90
203 50 f. Fishing . . . . 5·00 3·50
204 100 f. Marketing fruit . . . . 10·00 5·50

1969. 50th Anniv of Int Labour Organization. As T **79** of New Caledonia.
205 9 f. blue, brown and salmon . 2·00 2·00

1970. Inauguration of New U.P.U. Headquarters Building, Berne As T **81** of New Caledonia.
206 21 f. brown, blue and purple . 2·50 2·50

1971. Surch.
207 12 f. on 19 f. (No. 166) (postage) 1·10 1·10
208 21 f. on 33 f. (No. 169) (air) . 3·50 2·75

18 Weightlifting

20 Pacific Island Dwelling

1971. 4th South Pacific Games, Papeete, Tahiti.
209 **18** 24 f. brown, blue and green (postage) . . . . 3·00 2·25
210 – 36 f. blue, olive and red . 3·75 2·75
211 – 48 f. brown, green and lilac (air) . . . . 4·25 2·25
212 – 54 f. red, purple and blue . 4·50 3·50
DESIGNS—As T **18**: 36 f. Basketball. 47 × 27 mm: 48 f. Pole-vaulting; 54 f. Archery.

1971. 1st Death Anniv of General Charles de Gaulle. As Nos. 493/4 of New Caledonia.
213 30 f. black and blue . . . . . 5·00 2·75
214 70 f. black and blue . . . . . 9·00 5·50

1972. Air. 25th Anniv of South Pacific Commission. As T **96** of New Caledonia.
215 44 f. multicoloured . . . . . . 4·50 2·75

1972. Air. South Pacific Arts Festival, Fiji.
216 **20** 60 f. violet, green & red . . 5·50 3·50

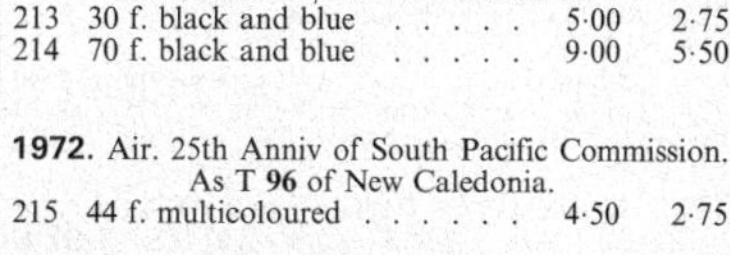

21 Model Pirogue

1972. Sailing Pirogues. Multicoloured.
217 14 f. Type **21** (postage) . . . . 4·00 2·25
218 16 f. Children with model pirogues . . . . 4·00 2·25
219 18 f. Racing pirogue . . . . . 4·50 3·50
220 200 f. Pirogue race (47 × 27 mm) (air) . . . . 25·00 14·00

22 La Perouse and "La Boussole"

1973. Air. Explorers of the Pacific.
221 **22** 22 f. brown, grey and red . 2·40 1·60
222 – 28 f. green, red and blue . 3·00 2·25
223 – 40 f. brown, blue & lt bl . . 5·00 3·50
224 – 72 f. brown, blue & violet . 7·50 4·50
DESIGNS: 28 f. Samuel Wallis and H.M.S. "Dolphin"; 40 f. Dumont d'Urville and "L'Astrolabe"; 72 f. Bougainville and "La Boudeuse.".

23 General De Gaulle

1973. Air. 3rd Death Anniv of General Charles de Gaulle.
225 **23** 107 f. purple and brown . . 9·50 6·00

24 "Plumeria rubra"

1973. Air. Flora of Wallis Islands. Multicoloured.
226 12 f. Type **24** . . . . 1·10 75
227 17 f. "Hibiscus tiliaceus" . . . 1·40 90
228 19 f. "Phaeomeria magnifica" . 1·60 1·00
229 21 f. "Hibiscus rosa sinensis" . 1·60 1·00
230 23 f. "Allamanda cathartica" . 2·00 1·50
231 27 f. "Barringtonia asiatica" . 2·00 2·00
232 39 f. Bouquet in vase . . . . 5·50 3·50

25 Rhinoceros Beetle

1974. Insects Multicoloured.
233 15 f. Type **25** . . . . 1·40 90
234 25 f. "Cosmopolites sordidus" (weevil) . . . . 2·00 1·40
235 35 f. Tropical fruit-piercer . . 2·75 1·60
236 45 f "Pantala flavescens" (darter) 4·50 2·75

26 "Flower Hand" holding Letter

27 "Holy Family" (Kamalielf-Filimoehala)

1974. Air. Centenary of Universal Postal Union.
237 **26** 51 f. purple, brown & grn . 4·50 2·75

1974. Air. Christmas.
238 **27** 150 f. multicoloured . . . 8·50 5·50

28 Tapa Pattern

1975. Air. Tapa Mats. Each brown, gold and yellow.
239 3 f. Type **28** 55 45
240 24 f. "Villagers" . . . . . . 1·60 1·10
241 36 f. "Fishes" . . . . 2·75 1·75
242 80 f. "Fishes and Dancers" . 5·50 4·00

29 Boeing 707 in Flight

30 Volleyball

1975. Air. 1st Regular Air Service to New Caledonia.
243 **29** 100 f. multicoloured . . . 5·00 4·00

1975. Air. 5th South Pacific Games, Guam. Multicoloured.
244 26 f. Type **30** . . . . 1·50 85
245 44 f. Football . . . . 1·75 1·25
246 56 f. Throwing the javelin . . 3·00 2·00
247 105 f. Aqua-diving . . . . . 6·00 4·50

1976. Pres. Pompidou Commemoration. As T **125** of New Caledonia.
248 50 f. grey and blue . . . . . 4·00 2·50

31 Lalolalo Lake, Wallis

1976. Landscapes. Multicoloured.
249 10 f. Type **31** (postage) . . . 80 40
250 29 f. Vasavasa, Futuna (air) . 2·00 1·10
251 41 f. Sigave Bay, Futuna . . . 2·75 1·50
252 68 f. Gahi Bay, Wallis . . . . 4·00 2·50

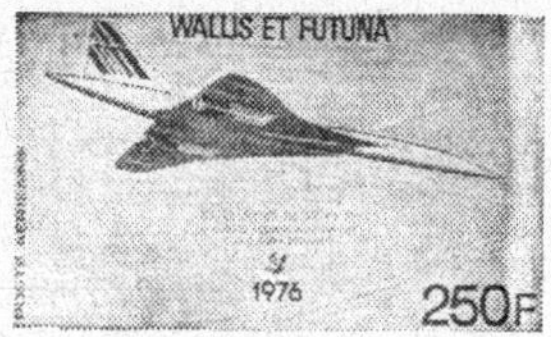

32 Concorde

1976. Air. 1st Commercial Flight of Concorde.
253 **32** 250 f. multicoloured . . . 18·00 11·00

33 Washington and Battle of Yorktown

1976. Bicentenary of American Revolution.

No.	Type	Description	Unused	Used
254	**33**	19 f. green, blue and red .	1·40	90
255	–	47 f. purple, red and blue .	3·00	2·25

DESIGN: 47 f. Lafayette and sea-battle of the Virginia Capes.

34 Throwing the Hammer

1976. Air. Olympic Games, Montreal.

No.	Type	Description	Unused	Used
256	**34**	31 f. purple, blue and red .	2·00	1·50
257	–	39 f. mauve, red & purple .	3·00	2·00

DESIGN: 39 f. High-diving.

35 Admiral Cone

1976. Sea Shells. Multicoloured.

No.	Description	Unused	Used
258	20 f. Type **35**	1·40	1·25
259	23 f. Banded cowrie	1·40	1·25
260	43 f. Tapestry turban	3·00	2·50
261	61 f. Papal mitre	4·50	4·00

36 Father Chanel and Sanctuary Church, Poi

1977. Father Chanel Memorial. Multicoloured.

No.	Description	Unused	Used
262	22 f. Type **36**	1·25	85
263	32 f. Father Chanel and map .	1·60	1·00

36a De Gaulle Memorial

1977. 5th Anniv of General de Gaulle Memorial.

No.	Type	Description	Unused	Used
264	**36a**	100 f. multicoloured . . .	6·00	4·50

37 Tanoa (bowl), Lali (mortar trough) and Ipu (coconut shell)

1977. Handicrafts. Multicoloured.

No.	Description	Unused	Used
265	12 f. Type **37**	65	30
266	25 f. Wallis and Futuna kumetes (bowls) and tuluma (box) .	1·25	60
267	33 f. Milamila (comb), ike (club) and tutua (model outrigger)	1·50	80
268	45 f. Kolo (Futuna clubs) . .	1·60	1·25
269	69 f. Kailao (Wallis and Futuna lances)	2·75	2·00

1977. Air. 1st Commercial Flight of Concorde. Paris–New York. Optd **PARIS NEW-YORK 22.11.77 Ier VOL COMMERCIAL**.

No.	Type	Description	Unused	Used
270	**32**	250 f. multicoloured . . .	13·50	10·00

39 Post Office, Mata-Utu

1977. Building and Monuments. Multicoloured.

No.	Description	Unused	Used
271	27 f. Type **39**	1·40	80
272	50 f. Sia Hospital Mata-Utu .	1·75	1·25
273	57 f. Government Buildings, Mata-Utu	2·00	2·00
274	63 f. St Joseph's Church, Sigave	2·75	2·00
275	120 f. Royal Palace, Mata-Utu	5·00	3·00

1977. Bicentenary of Captain Cook's Discovery of Hawaii. Nos. 254/5 optd **JAMES COOK Bicentenaire de la decouverte des Iles Hawaii 1778–1978.**

No.	Type	Description	Unused	Used
276	**33**	19 f. green, blue and red .	2·50	1·60
277	–	47 f. purple, red & blue .	4·50	2·75

41 "Balistes niger"

1977. Air. Fishes. Multicoloured.

No.	Description	Unused	Used
278	26 f. Type **41**	1·00	55
279	35 f. Anemone fish	1·40	1·75
280	49 f. Emperor angelfish . . .	2·00	1·75
281	51 f. Moorish idol	2·75	2·00

42 Map of Futuna and Alofi

1978. Maps of Wallis and Futuna Islands.

No.	Type	Description	Unused	Used
282	**42**	300 f. turquoise, blue and ultramarine	12·00	9·50
283	–	500 f. brown, blue and ultramarine	16·00	12·75

DESIGN—VERT: 500 f. Map of Wallis Island.

43 Father Bataillon and Churches

1978. Air. Arrival of 1st French Missionaries. Multicoloured.

No.	Description	Unused	Used
284	60 f. Type **43**	2·00	1·50
285	72 f. Monsgr. Pompallier and map	2·50	2·00

44 I.T.U. Emblem and Antennae

1978. Air. World Telecommunications Day.

No.	Type	Description	Unused	Used
286	**44**	66 f. multicoloured	2·50	1·60

45 "Triomphant" (destroyer)

1978. Free French Pacific Naval Force, 1940–1944. Multicoloured.

No.	Description	Unused	Used
287	150 f. Type **45**	7·25	5·00
288	200 f. "Cap des Palmes" and "Chevreuil" (patrol boats) .	10·00	6·50
289	280 f. "Savorgnan de Brazza" (destroyer)	14·00	10·00

46 "Solanum seaforthianum" **47** Eastern Reef Heron

1978. Tropical Flowers. Multicoloured.

No.	Description	Unused	Used
290	16 f. Type **46**	80	40
291	24 f. "Cassia alata"	90	55
292	29 f. "Gloriosa superba" . .	1·50	80
293	36 f. "Hymenocallis littoralis" .	2·00	1·10

1978. Ocean Birds. Multicoloured.

No.	Description	Unused	Used
294	17 f. Type **47**	70	40
295	18 f. Red-footed booby	70	40
296	28 f. Brown booby	1·50	85
297	35 f. White tern	2·00	1·25

48 Costumed Carpet-sellers

1978. Costumes and Traditions. Multicoloured.

No.	Description	Unused	Used
298	53 f. Type **48**	1·75	1·10
299	55 f. "Festival of God" procession	2·25	1·50
300	59 f. Guards of honour	2·75	1·50

49 Nativity Scene

1978. Air. Christmas.

No.	Type	Description	Unused	Used
301	**49**	160 f. multicoloured	5·50	3·50

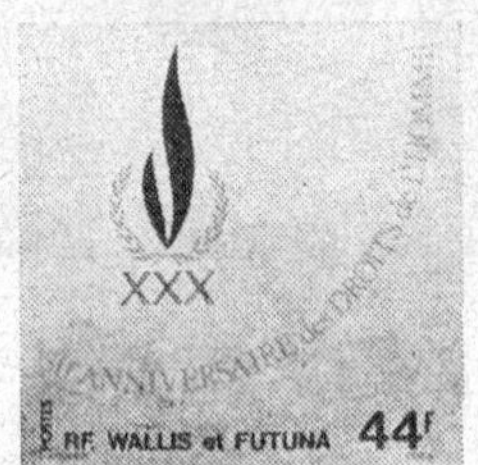

50 Human Rights Emblem

1978. 30th Anniv of Declaration of Human Rights.

No.	Type	Description	Unused	Used
302	**50**	44 f. multicoloured	1·50	1·00
303		56 f. multicoloured	2·00	1·50

51 Pope Paul VI

1979. Air. Popes. Multicoloured.

No.	Description	Unused	Used
304	37 f. Type **51**	1·40	1·00
305	41 f. Pope John-Paul I	1·60	1·40
306	105 f. St Peter's, Rome, and Popes Paul VI and John-Paul I (horiz)	4·00	2·50

52 Britten Norman Islander

1979. Air. Inter-Island Communications (1st series). Multicoloured.

No.	Description	Unused	Used
307	46 f. Type **52**	1·40	90
308	68 f. Freighter "Moana II" . .	1·75	1·40
309	80 f. Hihifo Airport	2·50	1·60

See also Nos. 349/51.

53 Fishing Boat

1979. Tagging Bonito Fish. Multicoloured.

No.	Description	Unused	Used
310	10 f. Type **53**	40	30
311	30 f. Weighing bonito	90	55
312	34 f. Young fishes	1·00	75
313	38 f. Tagging bonito	1·40	85
314	40 f. Angling for bonito . . .	1·50	1·10
315	48 f. Bonito fish	2·00	1·60

54 Boy with Model Outrigger Canoe

1979. International Year of the Child. Multicoloured.

No.	Description	Unused	Used
317	52 f. Type **54**	1·50	95
318	58 f. Girl on horseback . . .	1·75	1·00

55 "Bombax ellipticum"

1979. Flowering and Fruiting Trees. Mult.

No.	Description	Unused	Used
319	50 f. Type **55**	1·25	90
320	64 f. "Callophyllum inophyllum"	2·10	1·00
321	76 f. "Pandanus odoratissimus"	2·75	1·75

56 French 1876 5 c Stamp and "Eole" Meteorological Satellite

1979. Air. Death Centenary of Sir Rowland Hill.

No.	Type	Description	Unused	Used
322	**56**	5 f. multicoloured	55	30
323	–	70 f. multicoloured	1·75	1·10
324	–	90 f. black and red	2·50	1·50
325	–	100 f. brown, yellow & bl .	2·75	2·00

DESIGNS—VERT: 70 f. Hibiscus and Wallis and Futuna 1920 1 f. stamp. HORIZ: 90 f. Sir Rowland Hill and Great Britain Penny Black; 100 f. "Birds" (Kano School) and Japan 1872 ½ stamp.

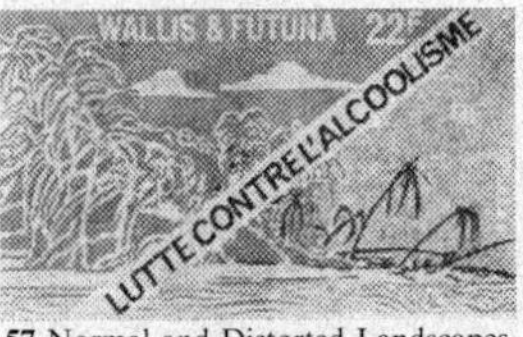

57 Normal and Distorted Landscapes

1979. Anti-alcoholism Campaign.

No.	Type	Description	Unused	Used
326	**57**	22 f. multicoloured	1·10	90

58 Heads looking at Cross of Lorraine

1979. Air. 39th Anniv of 18 June Appeal by General de Gaulle.

No.	Type	Description	Unused	Used
327	**58**	33 f. red, blue and grey . .	1·40	1·00

59 "Crinum moorei" 60 Map of Islands and French Arms

1979. Flowers (1st series) Multicoloured.

328	20 f. Type **59**	50	30
329	42 f. Passion flower	1·50	90
330	62 f. "Canna indica"	2·00	1·40

See also Nos. 392/4.

1979. Air. Presidential Visit.

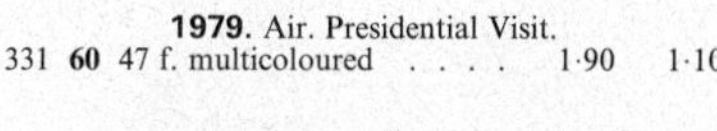

331	**60**	47 f. multicoloured	1·90	1·10

61 Cook and Death Scene, Hawaii

1979. Air. Death Bicentenary of Captain Cook.

332	**61**	130 f. grey, blue & brown	4·00	2·75

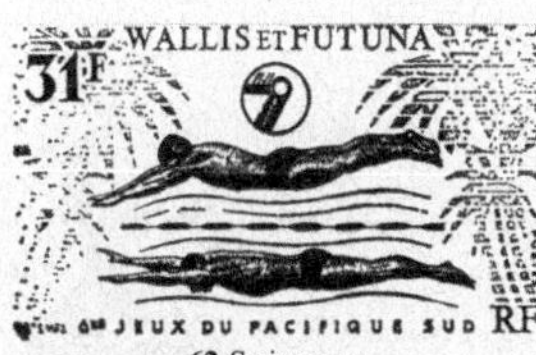

62 Swimmers

1979. Sixth South Pacific Games, Fiji.

333	**62**	31 f. olive, red and green	1·50	80
334	–	39 f. brown, turq & grn	2·00	1·00

DESIGN: 39 f. High-jumper.

63 Garlands

1979. Necklaces. Multicoloured.

335	110 f. Type **63**	2·50	2·00
336	140 f. Coral necklaces	4·50	2·50

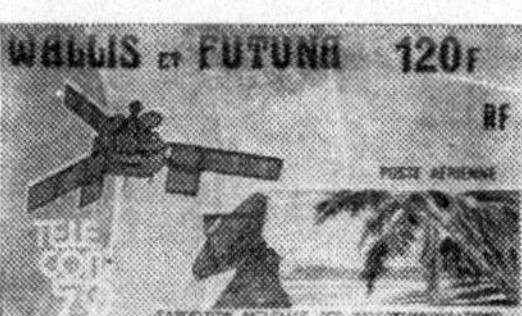

64 Satellite and Dish Aerial

1979. Air. 3rd World Telecommunications Exhibition, Geneva.

337	**64**	120 f. multicoloured	3·50	2·50

65 Detail of Painting by Mme. Sutita

1979. Works of Local Artists. Multicoloured.

338	27 f. Painting by Mme Sutita (detail) (different)	1·00	90
339	65 f. Painting by M. A. Pilioko (detail) (vert)	1·75	1·40
340	78 f. Type **65**	2·50	1·75

66 Squilla

1979. South Pacific Fauna. Multicoloured.

341	15 f. Type **66**	50	30
342	23 f. Spanish dancer	60	50
343	25 f. Cat's-tongue thorny oyster	1·00	65
344	43 f. Sea fan	1·25	65
345	45 f. Starfish	1·40	80
346	63 f. Fluted giant clam	2·50	1·75

67 "Virgin of the Crescent Moon" (detail, Durer)

1979. Air. Christmas.

347	**67**	180 f. black and red	5·50	4·00

See also No. 554.

68 Concorde, Map and Rotary Emblem

1980. Air. 75th Anniv of Rotary International.

348	**68**	86 f. multicoloured	3·50	2·50

1980. Inter-Island Communications (2nd series). As Nos. 307/9.

349	1 f. Type **52**	15	15
350	3 f. As No. 308	15	15
351	5 f. As No. 309	25	15

69 Radio Station

71 Rochambeau and Soldiers

70 "Jesus laid in the Tomb" (Maurice Denis)

1980. 1st Anniv of Radio Station FR3.

352	**69**	47 f. multicoloured	1·50	1·00

1980. Easter.

353	**70**	25 f. multicoloured	1·10	65

1980. Air. Bicentenary of Rochambeau's Landing at Newport, Rhode Island.

354	**71**	102 f. sepia, blue & brown	3·50	2·75

72 Flags and Island

1980. Air. National Day.

355	**72**	71 f. multicoloured	1·75	1·00

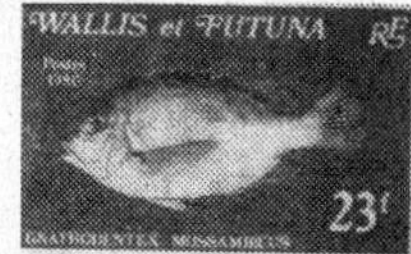

73 "Gnathodentex mossambicus"

1980. Fishes. Multicoloured.

356	23 f. Type **73**	70	40
357	27 f. Blue-spotted snapper	85	55
358	32 f. Ruby snapper	1·25	90
359	51 f. Rock cod	1·75	1·25
360	59 f. Flame snapper	2·50	2·00

74 Mermoz and "Arc en Ciel"

1980. Air. 50th Anniv of 1st South Atlantic Airmail Flight.

361	**74**	122 f. blue, dp blue & red	3·50	2·50

1980. "Sydpex 80" International Stamp Exhibition, Sydney. No. 315 surch **50F SYDPEX 80 29 Septembre**.

362	50 f. on 48 f. multicoloured	2·00	2·10

76 Fleming and Penicillin Slide

1980. Air. 25th Death Anniv of Alexander Fleming (discoverer of penicillin).

363	**76**	101 f. blue, brown & red	2·50	1·75

77 Charles de Gaulle

1980. Air. 10th Death Anniv of Charles de Gaulle (French statesman).

364	**77**	200 f. green and brown	5·50	4·00

78 "The Virgin, Child and St. Catherine" (Lorenzo Lotto)

1980. Air. Christmas.

365	**78**	150 f. multicoloured	3·50	2·50

79 Alan Shepard and "Freedom 7"

1981. Air. 20th Anniv of First Men in Space. Multicoloured.

366	37 f. Type **79**	1·00	65
367	44 f. Yury Gagarin and "Vostok I"	1·25	90

80 Ribbons and I.T.U. and W.H.O. Emblems forming Caduceus and Satellite

1981. World Telecommunications Day.

368	**80**	49 f. multicoloured	1·25	90

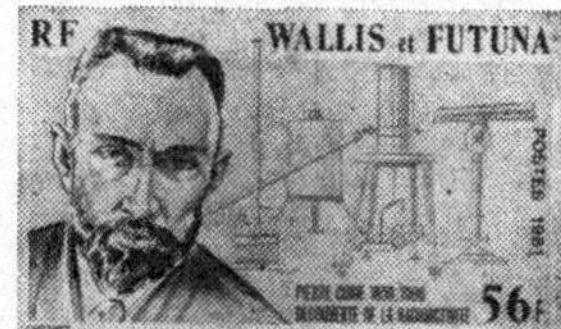

81 Curie and Laboratory Equipment

1981. 75th Death Anniv of Pierre Curie (physicist and discoverer of radium).

369	**81**	56 f. multicoloured	1·40	1·00

82 Coral 84 Section of Globe

83 Doctor inoculating Child

1981. Undersea Fauna. Multicoloured.

370	28 f. Type **82**	85	60
371	30 f. Blue-green algae	85	60
372	31 f. "Ceratium vultur" (dinoflagellate)	1·00	65
373	35 f. "Amphiprion frenatus" (fish)	1·10	65
374	40 f. Textile cone	1·25	90
375	55 f. Feather-star (echinoderm)	1·75	1·00

1981. 60th Anniv of 1st B.C.G. Anti-tuberculosis Inoculation.

376	**83**	27 f. multicoloured	75	50

1981. International Year of Disabled Persons.

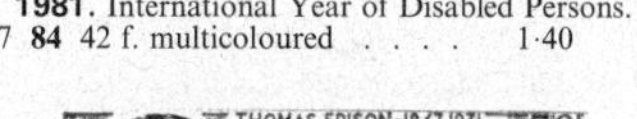

377	**84**	42 f. multicoloured	1·40	75

85 Edison and Phonograph

1981. 50th Death Anniv of Thomas Edison (inventor).

378	**85**	59 f. black, blue and red	1·40	1·00

1981. No. 341 surch **5F.**

379	5 f. on 15 f. multicoloured	30	20

87 Battle Scene 88 "Vase of Flowers" (Cezanne)

1981. Bicentenary of Battle of Virginia Capes.

380	–	66 f. purple, blue and slate	1·40	1·10
381	**87**	74 f. green, violet and light green	2·00	1·10

DESIGN: 66 f. Admiral Francois de Grasse and battle scene.

1981. Air. 75th Death Anniv of Paul Cezanne and Birth Centenary of Pablo Picasso (artists).
382 53 f. Type **88** . . . . 1·50 1·00
383 135 f. "Harlequin leaning" (Picasso) . . . . 3·50 2·25

89 Football

1981. Air. World Cup Football Championship, Spain (1982).
384 **89** 120 f. brown, black & green 2·50 2·00
385 120 f. brown, mauve and green . . . . 2·50 2·00

90 Patrol Boat "La Dieppoise"

1981. Surveillance of 200-mile zone. Mult.
386 60 f. Type **90** . . . . 1·40 1·00
387 85 f. Frigate "Protet" . . . . 2·00 1·50

91 Crib

1981. Air. Christmas.
388 **91** 180 f. multicoloured . . . 4·00 2·75

92 "Pilioko Aloi" (tapestry) **93** Dr Robert Koch at Microscope

1982. Air.
389 **92** 100 f. multicoloured . . . 2·25 1·75

1982. Centenary of Discovery of Tubercle Bacillus.
390 **93** 45 f. multicoloured . . . . 1·10 90

94 "Fishing Boats at Collioure"

1982. Air. Death Centenary of Georges Braque (painter).
391 **94** 300 f. multicoloured . . . 6·50 4·50

1982. Flowers (2nd series). Multicoloured.
392 1 f. As Type **59** 10 10
393 2 f. As No. 329 . . . . 15 10
394 3 f. As No. 330 . . . . 15 10

95 1930 Stamp

1982. "Philexfrance" International Stamp Exhibition, Paris.
395 **95** 140 f. violet, blue and red . 2·50 1·75

96 "Acanthe phippium"

1982. Orchids. Multicoloured.
396 34 f. Type **96** 80 55
397 68 f. "Acanthe phippium" (different) . . . . 1·75 1·25
398 70 f. "Spathoglottis pacifica" 2·00 1·25
399 83 f. "Mussaenda raiateensis" 2·50 1·75

97 Lord Baden-Powell

1982. 125th Birth Anniv of Lord Baden-Powell (founder of Boy Scout Movement).
400 **97** 80 f. multicoloured . . . . 2·00 1·25

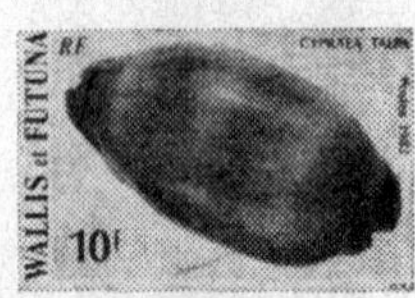

98 Mole Cowrie

1982. Sea Shells (1st series). Multicoloured.
401 10 f. Type **98** 20 15
402 15 f. Pacific deer cowrie . . . 30 15
403 25 f. Eyed cowrie 40 30
404 27 f. Closely-related carnelian cowrie 55 40
405 40 f. All-red map cowrie . . 80 55
406 50 f. Tiger cowrie . . . . . . 1·10 80
See also Nos. 428/33, 440/5, 459/64, 481/6 and 510/15.

99 Santos-Dumont, Airship "Ballon No. 14" and Biplane "14 bis"

1982. Air. 50th Death Anniv of Alberto Santos-Dumont (aviation pioneer).
407 **99** 95 f. brown, green and blue 2·25 1·40

1982. Air. World Cup Football Championship Result. No. 384 optd **ITALIE VAINQUEUR 1982**.
408 **89** 120 f. brown, black and green 2·75 2·00

101 Beach

1982. Air. Overseas Week.
409 **101** 105 f. multicoloured . . . 2·25 1·75

102 Coral

1982. Marine Life. Multicoloured.
410 32 f. Type **102** 65 45
411 35 f. Starfish 75 45
412 46 f. Spanish dancer . . . . 1·00 75
413 63 f. Cat's-tongue thorny oyster 1·40 1·10

103 Hands reaching towards Eye **104** St Theresa of Avila

1982. Air. Blind Day.
414 **103** 130 f. blue, scarlet & red . 2·25 2·00

1982. 400th Death Anniv of St. Theresa of Avila.
415 **104** 31 f. brown, green and deep brown 80 55
See also No. 447.

105 "Adoration of the Virgin" (Correggio)

1982. Air. Christmas.
416 **105** 170 f. multicoloured . . . 3·50 2·50

106 Wallis Meeting House

1983.
417 **106** 19 f. multicoloured 55 30

107 Eiffel and Eiffel Tower under Construction

1983. 60th Death Anniv of Gustave Eiffel (engineer).
418 **107** 97 f. purple, red and green 2·00 1·60

108 Windsurfing **110** Vincenzo Lunardi's Balloon, 1784

109 Island Scene and U.P.U. Emblem

1983. Air.
419 **108** 270 f. multicoloured . . . 5·50 3·25

1983. Air. World U.P.U. Day.
420 **109** 100 f. multicoloured . . . 2·25 1·40

1983. Air. Bicentenary of Manned Flight.
421 **110** 205 f. multicoloured . . . 4·25 2·75

111 "Cat"

1983. Air. 15th Death Anniv of Foujita (painter).
422 **111** 102 f. multicoloured . . . 2·25 1·40

112 Thai Goddess **113** Javelin-thrower

1983. "Bangkok 1983" International Stamp Exn.
423 **112** 92 f. red, black and blue . 1·75 1·10

1983. Air. Olympic Games, Los Angeles (1984) (1st issue).
424 **113** 250 f. brown, grn & yell . 4·50 3·50
See also No. 438.

114 Nobel

1983. Air. 150th Birth Anniv of Alfred Nobel (inventor of dynamite and founder of Nobel Prizes).
425 **114** 150 f. red and green . . . 3·00 2·00

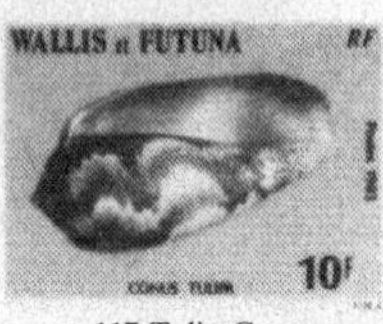

115 Satellite, Dish Aerial and W.C.Y. Emblem **117** Tulip Cone

116 Niepce and Early Photograph

1983. World Communications Year.
426 **115** 20 f. multicoloured . . . 45 35

1983. Air. Death Centenary of Nicephore Niepce (pioneer of photography).
427 **116** 75 f. purple and green . . 1·90 1·10

1983. Sea Shells (2nd series). Multicoloured.
428 10 f. Type **117** 40 15
429 17 f. Captain cone 45 20
430 21 f. Virgin cone 45 20
431 39 f. Calf cone 75 20
432 52 f. Marble cone . . . . . . 1·00 80
433 65 f. Leopard cone . . . . . 1·40 1·00

118 "Triumph of Galatea"

1983. Air. 500th Birth Anniv of Raphael (artist).
434 **118** 167 f. multicoloured . . . 3·25 2·50

119 Pandanus Tree

1983. Air.
435 **119** 137 f. multicoloured . . . 2·75 1·75

120 "Madonna and Pope Sixtus" (Raphael)

1983. Air. Christmas.
436 **120** 200 f. multicoloured . . . 4·25 2·75

121 Frigate "Commandant Bory"

1984. Air.
437 **121** 67 f. multicoloured . . . 1·50 1·00

122 Weightlifting

1984. Air. Olympic Games, Los Angeles (2nd issue).
438 **122** 85 f. multicoloured . . . 2·00 1·40

123 Frangipani

1984. Air.
439 **123** 130 f. multicoloured . . . 2·75 1·75

1984. Sea Shells (3rd series). As T **117**. Mult.
440 22 f. Silver conch 40 30
441 25 f. Chiragra spider conch . . 40 30
442 35 f. Samar conch 75 40
443 43 f. Scorpion conch . . . . . 1·10 65
444 49 f. Diana conch . . . . . . 1·40 90
445 76 f. Orange spider conch . . 1·90 1·40

124 "Deposition of Christ" (Alele Chapel)

1984. Air. Easter.
446 **124** 190 f. multicoloured . . . 3·50 2·50

1984. "Espana 84" International Stamp Exhibition, Madrid. As T **104** but with "Espana 84" emblem.
447 70 f. sepia, green and brown . 1·50 1·10

125 Diderot and Title Page of Encyclopedia **126** Killer Whale

1984. Death Bicent of Denis Diderot (encyclopedist).
448 **125** 100 f. brown and blue . . 2·00 1·40

1984. Nature Protection.
449 **126** 90 f. multicoloured . . . 2·00 1·40

127 Painting **128** Tiki

1984. Air. 95th Birth Anniv of Jean Cocteau (artist).
450 **127** 150 f. multicoloured . . . 3·00 2·25

1984. Air. Soane Hoatau Sculpture.
451 **128** 175 f. multicoloured . . . 3·25 2·50

129 "Alice" **130** "Pilioko Aloi" (tapestry)

1984. Air. Birth Centenary of Amedeo Modigliani (painter).
452 **129** 140 f. multicoloured . . . 3·00 2·00

1984. Air. "Ausipex 84" International Stamp Exhibition, Melbourne.
453 **130** 180 f. multicoloured . . . 3·50 2·25

131 "Local Dances" (Jean Michon)

1984. Air.
454 **131** 110 f. multicoloured . . . 2·50 1·75

132 Altar, Mount Lulu Chapel

1984. Air.
455 **132** 52 f. multicoloured . . . . 1·10 75

133 Islanders wearing Leis

1985. 4th Pacific Arts Festival.
456 **133** 160 f. multicoloured . . . 3·00 2·25

134 Common Spider Conch and Virgin and Child

1984. Air. Christmas.
457 **134** 260 f. multicoloured . . . 5·00 2·75

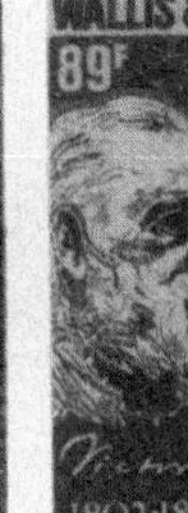

135 Lapita Pottery **136** Victor Hugo

1985. Archaeological Expedition, 1983
458 **135** 53 f. multicoloured . . . . 1·00 55

1985. Sea Shells (4th series). As T **117**. Multicoloured.
459 2 f. Chambered nautilus . . . 10 10
460 3 f. Adusta murex 10 10
461 41 f. Vibex bonnet 75 45
462 47 f. Flag cone . . . . 1·00 65
463 56 f. True harp . . . . 1·10 75
464 71 f. Ramese murex . . . . . 1·60 1·00

1985. Death Centenary of Victor Hugo (writer).
465 **136** 89 f. deep blue, blue and red 2·00 1·25

137 "Pilioko Aloi" (tapestry)

1985. Air.
466 **137** 500 f. multicoloured . . . 8·50 5·50

138 Flying Fox **139** Children

1985.
467 **138** 38 f. multicoloured . . . . 1·00 55

1985. International Youth Year.
468 **139** 64 f. multicoloured . . . . 1·25 80

140 "The Post Office"

1985. Air. 30th Death Anniv of Maurice Utrillo (artist).
469 **140** 200 f. multicoloured . . . 3·50 2·25

141 Hands and U.N. Emblem

1985. 40th Anniv of U.N.O.
470 **141** 49 f. green, blue & red . . 1·00 65

142 Sailing Canoe

1985. Air.
471 **142** 350 f. multicoloured . . . 6·00 3·25

143 Ronsard, Organist and Muse of Poetry

1985. 400th Death Anniv of Pierre de Ronsard (poet).
472 **143** 170 f. brown, deep brown and blue . . . . 3·50 2·25

144 Landing Ship "Jacques Cartier" **145** "Portrait of Young Woman" (Patrice Nielly)

1985. Air.
473 **144** 51 f. deep blue, blue and turquoise . . . . 1·00 65

1985. Air.
474 **145** 245 f. multicoloured . . . 4·25 2·25

146 Schweitzer, African Boy and Cathedral Organ

1985. 20th Death Anniv of Dr. Albert Schweitzer (missionary).
475 **146** 50 f. black, purple & brown 1·00 65

INDEX

Countries can be quickly located by referring to the index at the end of this volume.

147 "Virgin and Child" (Jean Michon)

1985. Air. Christmas.

476 **147** 330 f. multicoloured . . . 6·00 4·00

148 Bread-fruit

1986. Food and Agriculture Organization.

477 **148** 39 f. multicoloured . . . 90 55

149 Flamboyant Flower

1986.

478 **149** 38 f. multicoloured . . . 90 55

150 Comet and "Giotto" Space Probe

1986. Air. Appearance of Halley's Comet.

479 **150** 100 f. multicoloured . . . 2·00 1·40

151 Vianney praying

1986. Air. Birth Bicentenary of Cure d'Ars.

480 **151** 200 f. light brown, brown and black . . . 4·00 2·50

1986. Sea Shells (5th series). As T **117**. Mult.

481 4 f. Giant spider conch . . . 10 10
482 5 f. Trumpet triton . . . 10 10
483 10 f. Red-mouth olive . . . 20 15
484 18 f. Common distorsio . . . 30 20
485 25 f. Episcopal mitre . . . 55 35
486 107 f. Distant cone . . . 2·00 1·40

152 Players and Boy with Football

1986. World Cup Football Championship, Mexico.

487 **152** 95 f. multicoloured . . . 2·00 1·25

153 Willem Schouten and "Eendracht"

1986. 370th Anniv of Discovery of Horn Islands. Each purple, green and blue.

488 8 f. Type **153** . . . 20 15
489 9 f. Jacob le Maire and "Hoorn" . . . 20 15
490 155 f. Map of Futuna and Alofi Islands . . . 3·00 2·50

154 Watt and Steam Engine

1986. 250th Birth Anniv of James Watt (inventor).

491 **154** 74 f. red and black . . . 1·50 1·10

155 Queen Amelia

1986. Air. Centenary of Request for Protectorate and 25th Anniv of French Overseas Territory Status. Each purple, red and blue.

492 90 f. Type **155** . . . 1·75 1·75
493 137 f. Law of 1961 bestowing Overseas Territory status . . . 2·50 2·50

156 Patrol Boat "La Lorientaise"

1986. Naval Ships.

494 **156** 6 f. red, purple and blue . . . 15 10
495 – 7 f. violet, orange & red . . . 15 10
496 – 120 f. turquoise, red & bl . . . 2·25 1·60

DESIGNS: 7 f. Frigate "Commandant Blaison"; 120 f. Frigate "Balny".

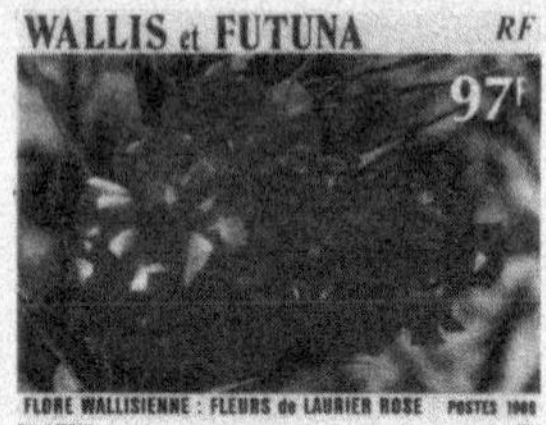

157 Oleander

1986.

497 **157** 97 f. multicoloured . . . 2·00 1·40

158 U.P.U. Emblem and Dove carrying Envelope

1986. Air. World Post Day.

498 **158** 270 f. multicoloured . . . 5·00 3·50

159 New York, Statue and Paris

1986. Air. Centenary of Statue of Liberty.

499 **159** 205 f. multicoloured . . . 4·00 2·50

160 "Virgin and Child" (Botticelli)

1986. Christmas.

500 **160** 250 f. multicoloured . . . 4·50 3·00

161 "Papilio montrouzieri"

162 Father Chanel and Basilica

1987. Butterflies. Multicoloured.

501 2 f. Type **161** . . . 30 20
502 42 f. Caper white . . . 75 45
503 46 f. "Delias ellipsis" . . . 90 55
504 50 f. "Danaus pumila" . . . 1·00 65
505 52 f. "Lutbrodes cleotas" . . . 1·00 65
506 59 f. Meadow argus . . . 1·40 90

1987. Air. 1st Anniv of Poi Basilica.

507 **162** 230 f. multicoloured . . . 4·50 2·50

163 "Telstar", Globe and Pleumeur-Bodou

1987. Air. World Communications Day. 25th Anniv of Launch of "Telstar" Communications Satellite.

508 **163** 200 f. blue, black and red . . . 3·50 2·00

164 Wrestlers

1987. World Wrestling Championships, Clermont-Ferrand.

509 **164** 97 f. multicoloured . . . 1·90 1·25

1987. Sea Shells (6th series). As T **117**. Mult.

510 3 f. Common hairy triton . . . 15 10
511 4 f. Textile cone . . . 15 10
512 28 f. Humpback cowrie . . . 55 35
513 44 f. Giant frog shell . . . 90 55
514 48 f. Turtle cowrie . . . 1·00 65
515 78 f. Bull-mouth helmet . . . 1·60 1·10

165 Piccard, Stratosphere Balloon "F.N.R.S." and Bathyscaphe

167 Bust of Girl

1987. Air. 25th Death Anniv of Auguste Piccard (physicist).

516 **165** 135 f. deep blue, blue and green . . . 2·50 1·60

1987. "Olymphilex 87" Olympic Stamps Exhibition, Rome. No 509 optd **OLYMPHILEX '87 ROME** and Olympic rings.

517 **164** 97 f. multicoloured . . . 1·90 1·25

1987. 70th Death Anniv of Auguste Rodin (sculptor).

518 **167** 150 f. purple . . . 2·75 1·75

See also No. 557.

168 Letters between Globes and Postbird

1987. World Post Day.

519 **168** 116 f. blue, deep blue and yellow . . . 2·25 1·40

169 Spotbill Duck

1987. Birds. Multicoloured.

520 6 f. Type **169** . . . 10 10
521 19 f. American golden plover . . . 35 20
522 47 f. Friendly quail dove . . . 90 55
523 56 f. Turnstone . . . 1·00 65
524 64 f. Banded rail . . . 1·25 65
525 68 f. Bar-tailed godwit . . . 1·40 90

170 Mgr. Bataillon, French Frigate and Islands

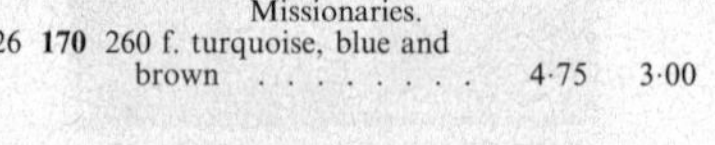

1987. Air. 150th Anniv of Arrival of First Missionaries.

526 **170** 260 f. turquoise, blue and brown . . . 4·75 3·00

171 Nativity Scene

1987. Air. Christmas.

527 **171** 300 f. multicoloured . . . 5·50 3·50

172 Carco and Parisian Scenes

1988. 30th Death Anniv of Francis Carco (writer).

528 **172** 40 f. multicoloured . . . 80 45

173 Morane Saulnier Type I and Garros

1988. Air. 70th Death Anniv of Roland Garros (aviator).
529 **173** 600 f. deep blue, brown and blue . . . . 10·50 6·75

174 La Perouse, "L'Astrolabe" and "La Boussole"

1988. Bicentenary of Disappearance of La Perouse's Expedition.
530 **174** 70 f. green, blue & brown 1·50 90

175 "Self-portrait wearing Lace Jabot"

1988. Air. Death Bicentenary of Maurice Quentin de la Tour (painter).
531 **175** 500 f. multicoloured . . . 9·00 6·00

176 Arrows and Dish Aerial

1988. Air. World Telecommunications Day.
532 **176** 100 f. multicoloured . . . 1·75 1·25

177 Map and Bishop with Crosier

1988. Air. South Pacific Episcopal Conference.
533 **177** 90 f. multicoloured . . . 1·75 1·10

178 Nurse, Child and Anniversary Emblem

1988. 125th Anniv of International Red Cross.
534 **178** 30 f. black, green & red . 60 45

179 Throwing the Javelin

1988. Olympic Games, Seoul. Each brown, red and blue.
535 11 f. Type **179** 35 20
536 20 f. Volleyball 45 35
537 60 f. Windsurfing . . . . . . 1·25 1·00
538 80 f. Yachting . . . . 1·60 1·40

180 Envelopes forming Map

1988. World Post Day.
539 **180** 17 f. yellow, blue & black 40 20

181 Becquerel

1988. Birth Bicentenary of Antoine Cesar Becquerel (physicist).
540 **181** 18 f. black and blue . . . 40 20

182 Nativity Scene

1988. Air. Christmas.
541 **182** 400 f. multicoloured . . . 7·25 4·50

183 "Amiral Charner" (frigate)

1989. International Maritime Organization.
542 **183** 26 f. multicoloured . . . 75 45

184 Renior and Scene from "The Great Illusion"

1989. 10th Death Anniv of Jean Renoir (film director).
543 **184** 24 f. brown, mauve & orge 50 35

185 Royal Throne (Aselo Kulimoetoke) **186** Map

1989. Air.
544 **185** 700 f. multicoloured . . . 12·00 7·25

1989. Futuna Hydro-electric Power Station.
545 **186** 25 f. multicoloured . . . 50 35

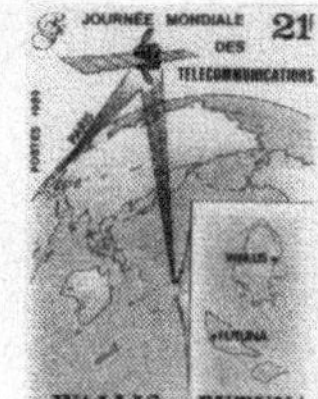
188 Satellite above Earth

1989. International Telecommunications Day.
546 **188** 21 f. multicoloured 45 35

189 Mural (H. Tailhade)

1989.
547 **189** 22 f. multicoloured 45 35

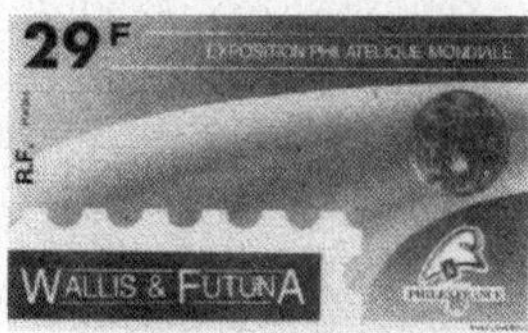
190 Globe and Emblem

1989. "Philexfrance '89" International Stamp Exhibition Paris (548) and Bicentenary of Declaration of Rights of Man and South Pacific Youth Meeting (549). Multicoloured.
548 29 f. Type **190** (postage) . . . 50 35
549 900 f. Sportsmen (air) . . . . 14·50 11·50

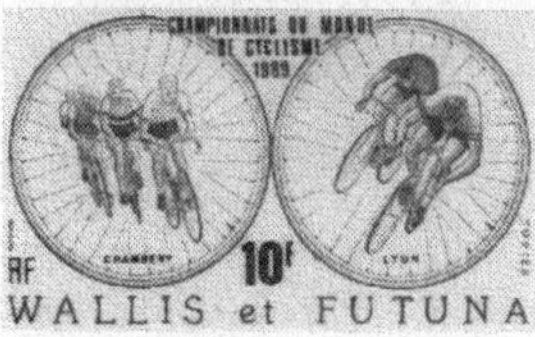
191 Cyclists

1989. World Cycling Championships, France.
551 **191** 10 f. black, brown & grn . 30 15

192 Envelopes around Globe of Flags

1989. World Post Day.
552 **192** 27 f. multicoloured 50 35

193 Landscape

1989.
553 **193** 23 f. multicoloured 75 60

1989. Air. Christmas. As No. 347 but date, value and colour changed.
554 **67** 800 f. mauve . . . . 14·00 9·00

194 "Star of Bethlehem"

1990.
555 **194** 44 f. multicoloured 80 55

195 Tortoise Fossil

1990.
556 **195** 48 f. multicoloured . . . 80 55

1990. 150th Birth Anniv of Auguste Rodin (sculptor). As No. 518 but value and colour changed.
557 **167** 200 f. blue . . . . 4·00 2·25

197 Footballers

1990. World Cup Football Championship, Italy.
558 **197** 59 f. multicoloured . . . 1·10 80

198 Orchids

1990. Mothers' Day.
559 **198** 78 f. multicoloured . . . 1·60 1·10

199 "Avion III", Airbus Industrie A310 and Clement Ader

1990. Air. Cent of First Heavier-than-Air Flight and 1st Anniv of Wallis–Tahiti Air Link.
560 **199** 56 f. brown, mauve & red 1·10 65

200 Red-tailed Tropic Bird

1990. Multicoloured.
561 300 f. Type **200** . . . . 5·50 3·25
562 600 f. South Pacific islet . . . 11·50 6·75

201 "Moana II" (inter-island freighter)

1990. Ships.
563 **201** 40 f. brown, green & blue 90 60
564 – 50 f. brown, blue & green 1·10 80
DESIGN: 50 f. "Moana III" (container ship) at jetty.

202 Traditional Dwellings

1990.
565 **202** 28 f. multicoloured . . . 55 35

203 Doves and Globe

204 Outrigger Canoe

1990. Stamp Day.
566 **203** 97 f. multicoloured . . . 1·90 1·40

1990.
567 **204** 46 f. multicoloured . . . 1·25 65

205 De Gaulle

1990. Air. Birth Centenary of Charles de Gaulle (French statesman).
568 **205** 1000 f. multicoloured . . 17·00 10·00

206 Palm Trees

1990. "Best Wishes".
569 **206** 100 f. multicoloured . . . 1·90 1·40

207 Patrol Boat "La Glorieuse"

1991.
570 **207** 52 f. blue, green and red . 1·50 85
See also No. 578.

208 Warrior

1991. Tradition.
571 7 f. Breadfruit gatherer . . . 10 10
572 54 f. Taro planter . . . . . 1·00 55
573 63 f. Spear fisherman . . . 1·10 65
574 72 f. Type **208** . . . . . 1·25 65
575 90 f. Kailao dancer . . . . 1·60 80

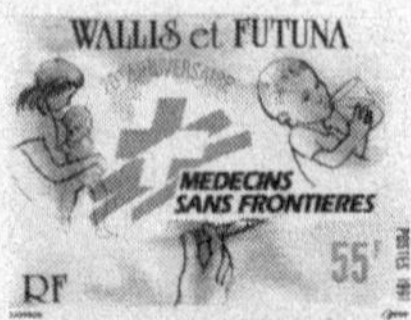
209 Aspects of Health Care

1991. 20th Anniv of Medecins sans Frontieres (medical charity).
577 **209** 55 f. multicoloured . . . 1·00 65

1991. Patrol Boat "La Moqueuse". As T **207**.
578 42 f. black, blue and red . . . 1·25 65

210 Chanel and Reliquary

1991. Air. 150th Death Anniv of Father Chanel (missionary).
579 **210** 235 f. multicoloured . . . 4·50 2·75

211 Players through the Ages ($\frac{1}{2}$-size illustration)

1991. Air. Centenary of French Open Tennis Championships.
580 **211** 250 f. black, orange & grn 4·75 2·75

212 Map and Microlight

1991. Microlight Aircraft Flying in Wallis and Futuna.
581 **212** 85 f. multicoloured . . . 1·75 1·10

213 "Portrait of Jean"

1991. 150th Birth Anniv of Pierre Auguste Renior (painter). Perf or imperf (self-adhesive).
582 **213** 400 f. multicoloured . . . 7·25 4·00

214 Map

1991. 30th Anniv of French Overseas Territory Status.
584 **214** 102 f. multicoloured . . . 1·60 1·10

215 Islanders in Festive Dress and Angel

1991. Feast of the Assumption.
585 **215** 30 f. multicoloured . . . 55 35

216 Mozart and Scene from "The Marriage of Figaro"

1991. Air. Death Bicentenary of Wolfgang Amadeus Mozart (composer).
586 **216** 500 f. blue, lilac and red . 8·25 4·50

217 Imprisoned Figure

1991. 30th Anniv of Amnesty International.
587 **217** 140 f. yellow, violet & blue 2·75 1·40

218 House and Generator

1991. 50th Anniv of Central Economic Co-operation Bank.
588 **218** 10 f. multicoloured 15 10

219 "Allamanda cathartica"

1991. Flowers. Multicoloured.
589 1 f. Type **219** 10 10
590 4 f. "Hibiscus rosa sinensis" (vert) 10 10
591 80 f. Water lily . . . . 1·40 90

220 Santa Claus on Beach

1991. Christmas.
592 **220** 60 f. multicoloured . . . . 1·00 55

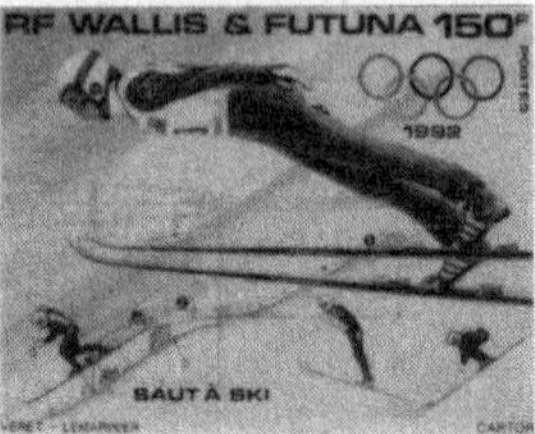
221 Ski Jumping

1992. Winter Olympic Games, Albertville.
593 **221** 150 f. multicoloured . . . 2·75 1·60

222 Map, Plants and Dassault Breguet Mystere Falcon 20

1992. "Escadrille 9S' Maritime Surveillance Service.
594 **222** 48 f. multicoloured 90 45

223 Canadian 1938 $1 and Wallis & Futuna 1920 2 f. Stamps ($\frac{1}{2}$ size illustration)

1992. "Canada 92" International Youth Philatelic Exhibition, Montreal.
595 **223** 35 f. black, red and violet . 45 30

224 Throwing the Javelin

1992. Olympic Games, Barcelona.
596 **224** 106 f. indigo, blue & grn . 1·60 95

225 Spanish 1975 4 p. Stamp and Wallis Post Office

1992. "Granada 92" International Stamp Exhibition.
597 **225** 100 f. black, blue & purple 1·40 85

226 Columbus's Fleet, Pavilion and Seville

1992. "Expo 92" World's Fair, Seville.
598 **226** 200 f. green, blue & orange 2·75 2·10

227 Saddleback Butterfly Fish

1992. Butterfly and Angel Fishes, Multicoloured.
599 21 f. Type **227** 25 20
600 22 f. Threadfin butterfly fish . 30 20
601 23 f. Horned coachman . . . 30 20
602 24 f. Royal angelfish 30 20
603 25 f. Spectacled angelfish . . 30 20
604 26 f. One spot butterfly fish . 35 25

228 Columbus and Map

1992. Air. "World Columbian Stamp Expo 92", Chicago.
605 **228** 100 f. multicoloured . . . 1·25 80
See also No. 612.

229 Three Spearmen

1992. Wallis Islands. Multicoloured.
606 70 f. Type **229** 90 55
607 70 f. Two spearmen and palm trees 90 55
608 70 f. Pirogues 90 55
609 70 f. Two fishermen and palm trees 90 55
610 70 f. Three fishermen and palm trees 90 55
Nos. 606/10 were issued together, se-tenant, forming a composite design.

1992. Air. "Genova '92" International Thematic Stamp Exhibition. As T **228** but with different Exhibition emblem.
612 800 f. multicoloured . . . . . 10·00 6·25

230 Victorious Marianne

1992. Air. Bicentenary of Year One of First French Republic.
613 **230** 350 f. black, blue and red 4·50 2·75

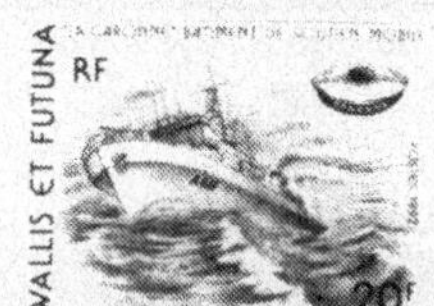

231 "La Garonne" (supply vessel)

1992.
614 **231** 20 f. multicoloured . . . 25 15

232 "L'Idylle d'Ixelles"

1992. 75th Death Anniv of Auguste Rodin (sculptor).
615 **232** 300 f. black and mauve . 3·75 2·40

233 "Mirabilis jalapa"

1992.
616 **233** 200 f. multicoloured . . . 2·50 1·60

234 Dassault Breguet Gardian, Frigate and Native Canoes

1993. French Naval Forces in the Pacific.
617 **234** 130 f. multicoloured . . . 1·75 1·25

235 Abstract (J. E. Korda)

1993. School Art.
618 **235** 56 f. multicoloured . . . 1·60 1·00
See also Nos. 635/6.

236 Banded Rail

1993. Birds. Multicoloured.
619 50 f. Type **236** 65 40
620 60 f. Purple swamphen 75 50
621 110 f. Grey's fruit dove . . . 1·40 85

237 Building Facade

1993. Air. Bicentenary of the Louvre, Paris.
622 **237** 315 f. ultramarine, red and blue . . . . 4·00 2·50

238 Copernicus and Planetary Model

1993. Air. "Polska 93" International Stamp Exhibition, Poznan. 450th Death Anniv of Nicolas Copernicus (astronomer).
623 **238** 600 f. red, brown and crimson . . . . 7·75 4·75

239 Hibiscus

1993. Mothers' Day. Multicoloured.
624 95 f. Type **239** . . . . . . 1·25 75
625 120 f. Bouquet of stephanotis 1·50 95

240 Sailfin Surgeon Fish

1993. Fishes. Multicoloured.
626 27 f. Spinefoot 35 25
627 35 f. Type **240** 45 30
628 45 f. Flag-tailed surgeon fish . 60 40
629 53 f. Fox-face 70 45

241 D'Entrecasteaux and Flagship

1993. Death Bicentenary of Bruni d'Entrecasteaux (explorer).
630 **241** 170 f. red, blue & black . 2·25 1·40

242 Symbols of Taiwan

1993. "Taipei '93" International Stamp Exhibition.
631 **242** 435 f. multicoloured . . . 5·50 3·25

243 Tepa Church, Wallis Island

1993. Churches. Multicoloured.
632 30 f. Type **243** 40 25
633 30 f. Vilamalia Church, Futuna Island 40 25

244 "La Marseillaise"

1993. Air. Bicentenary of Year Two of First French Republic.
634 **244** 400 f. red, blue & black . . 5·00 3·00

1993. School Art. As T **235**.
635 28 f. blue, black and grey . . . 35 25
636 52 f. multicoloured 65 40
DESIGNS—HORIZ: 28 f. Palm trees (T. Tuhimutu). VERT: 52 f. People (M. Hakula).

245 Nativity

1993. Christmas.
637 **245** 80 f. multicoloured . . . . 1·00 60

246 "Wallis Landscape" (P. Legris)

1994. Air.
638 **246** 400 f. multicoloured . . . 5·00 3·00

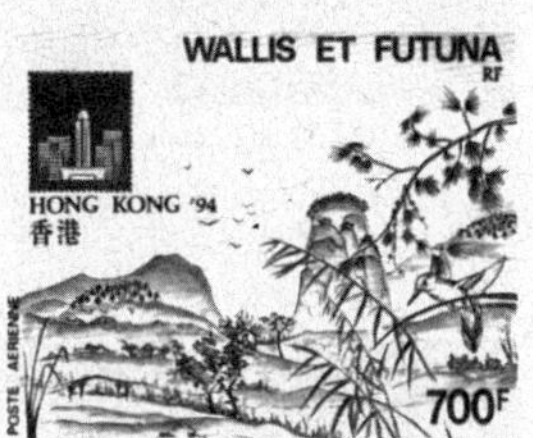

247 Landscape and Emblem

1994. Air. "Hong Kong '94" International Stamp Exhibition.
639 **247** 700 f. multicoloured . . . 9·00 5·50

248 Emblem

1994. Traditional Crafts Show, Wallis and Futuna.
640 **248** 80 f. multicoloured . . . . 1·10 70

249 Manning the Barricades

1994. 50th Anniv of Liberation of Paris.
641 **249** 110 f. black, red and blue . 1·60 1·00

250 Pacific Islands on Globe

1994. Air. South Pacific Geographical Days.
642 **250** 85 f. multicoloured . . . 1·25 75

251 Earth Station

1994. Satellite Communications.
643 **251** 10 f. multicoloured . . . 15 10

252 Goalkeeper saving Ball

1994. World Cup Football Championship, U.S.A.
644 **252** 105 f. multicoloured . . . 1·50 90

253 Uvean Princesses, 1903

1994.
645 **253** 90 f. black, red and blue . 1·25 75

254 Seaplane

1994. Microlight Aircraft.
646 **254** 5 f. multicoloured 10 10

255 Four Suits

1994. Bridge.
647 **255** 40 f. multicoloured . . . 55 35

256 Dahlia **257** Trees and Coconuts

1994. Air. 1st European Stamp Salon, Flower Gardens, Paris.
648 **256** 300 f. multicoloured . . . 4·25 2·75

1994. The Coconut.
649 **257** 36 f. multicoloured . . . 50 30

258 Saint-Exupery and Aircraft

1994. Air. 50th Death Anniv of Antoine de Saint-Exupery (author and pilot).
650 **258** 800 f. olive, green and blue 11·50 7·00

259 Blue-crowned Lories

1994. Parrots of Futuna.
651 **259** 62 f. multicoloured . . . 90 55

260 Lodge Emblem and Symbols of Freemasonry

1994. Centenary of Grand Lodge of France.
652 **260** 250 f. brown, turquoise and blue . . . . 3·50 2·10

261 Polynesian Baby

1994. Air. Christmas.
653 **261** 150 f. multicoloured . . . 2·10 1·25

262 Preparing Traditional Meal (after P. Legris)

1995.
654 **262** 80 f. multicoloured . . . 1·10 70

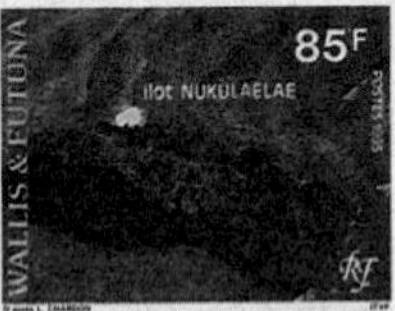

263 Nukulaelae

1995. Aerial Views of Lagoon Islets. Multicoloured.
655 85 f. Type **263** . . . . . . 1·20 70
656 90 f. Nukufetau (vert) . . . . 1·25 75
657 100 f. Nukufotu and Nukuloa 1·40 85

264 Pasteur

1995. Air. Death Centenary of Louis Pasteur (chemist).
658 **264** 350 f. multicoloured . . . 5·00 3·00

265 Outrigger Canoes (emblem of district)

266 Emblem

1995. Mua District.
659 **265** 35 f. multicoloured . . . 50 30

1995. University of the Pacific Teacher Training Institute.
660 **266** 115 f. multicoloured . . . 1·60 1·00

267 Coconuts

1995. Air.
661 **267** 200 f. multicoloured . . . 2·75 1·75

268 U.N. Helmet and Blitzed and Rebuilt Cities
(½-size illustration)

1995. 50th Anniv of Signing of U.N. Charter.
662 **268** 55 f. multicoloured . . . 80 50

269 Young People

1995. Air. 10th Anniv of International Youth Year.
663 **269** 450 f. multicoloured . . . 6·50 4·00

270 Javelin Thrower

1995. 10th South Pacific Games, Tahiti.
664 **270** 70 f. multicoloured . . . 1·00 60

271 City Skyline

1995. Air. "Singapore'95" Int Stamp Exn.
665 **271** 500 f. multicoloured . . . 7·25 4·50

272 Lumiere Brothers and Film
(½-size illustration)

1995. Air. Centenary of Motion Pictures.
666 **272** 600 f. multicoloured . . . 8·50 5·25

273 Breadfruit

1995. Shrubs. Multicoloured.
667 20 f. Type **273** 30 20
668 60 f. Tarot 85 55
669 65 f. Kava 95 60
See also Nos. 675/6.

274 De Gaulle

1995. Air. 25th Death Anniv of Charles de Gaulle (French statesman).
670 **274** 315 f. black, red and blue . 4·50 2·75

275 Human Activities

276 Three Generations

1995. Tapa (bark of paper-mulberry tree) Designs. Multicoloured.
671 25 f. Type **275** 35 25
672 26 f. Marine life (horiz) . . . 35 25

1995. Island Mothers.
673 **276** 80 f. multicoloured . . . . 1·10 70

277 Golf Course

1995. Golfing on Wallis.
674 **277** 95 f. multicoloured . . . . 1·40 85

1996. Tuberous Plants. As T **273**. Multicoloured.
675 28 f. Taro ("Mahoa") 35 25
676 52 f. Yam ("Ufi") 70 45

278 Pirogue

1996. Air. World Polynesian Pirogue Championships, Noumea.
677 **278** 240 f. multicoloured . . . 3·25 2·00

279 Emblems

280 "Cananga odorata"

1996. Air. Sisia College, Futuna.
678 **279** 235 f. multicoloured . . . 3·25 2·00

1996. Flowers. Multicoloured.
679 27 f. Type **280** 35 25
680 45 f. Hibiscus 60 40

281 Trees reflected in Water

1996. Swamplands.
681 **281** 53 f. multicoloured . . . 70 45

282 Chessmen and Board

1996. Chess in Wallis and Futuna.
682 **282** 110 f. multicoloured . . . 1·50 90

283 Guglielmo Marconi (inventor) and Radio Equipment

1996. Air. Centenary of Radio-telegraphy.
683 **283** 550 f. brown, blue and orange . . . . 7·25 4·50

284 Stadium and Sportsmen

1996. Air. Centenary of Modern Olympic Games.
684 **284** 1000 f. blue . . . . 13·50 8·25

285 Caladium

1996. Flowers. Multicoloured.
685 30 f. Type **285** 40 25
686 48 f. Caladium (different) . . 65 40

286 Woman with Stamps in Hair

1996. Air. 50th Autumn Stamp Fair.
687 **286** 175 f. multicoloured . . . 2·40 1·50

MINIMUM PRICE

The minimum price quoted is 10p which represents a handling charge rather than a basis for valuing common stamps. For further notes about prices, see introductory pages.

287 Map and Perroton

1996. Francoise Perroton (first woman missionary to Wallis) Commemoration.

688	**287**	50 f. multicoloured . . .	65	40

288 Distressed Woman with Children and Drunken Man

1996. Air. Campaign against Alcohol Abuse.

689	**288**	260 f. multicoloured . . .	3·50	2·10

289 Children and Emblem

1996. 50th Anniv of U.N.I.C.E.F.

690	**289**	25 f. multicoloured . . .	35	25

POSTAGE DUE STAMPS

1920. Postage Due Stamps of New Caledonia optd **ILES WALLIS et FUTUNA.**

D18	D **18**	5 c. blue	60	70
D19		10 c. brown on buff . .	60	70
D20		15 c. green	60	70
D21		20 c. black on yellow .	70	80
D22		30 c. red	70	80
D23		50 c. blue on cream . .	1·00	1·25
D24		60 c. green on blue . .	1·40	1·50
D25		1 f. green on cream . .	1·75	1·75

1927. As Postage Due stamp of New Caledonia, but colour changed, surch.

D43	D **18**	2 f. on 1 f. mauve . . .	6·50	7·00
D44		3 f. on 1 f. brown . . .	6·50	7·00

1930. Postage Due stamps of New Caledonia optd **ILES WALLIS et FUTUNA.**

D85	D **25**	2 c. brown and blue . .	20	30
D86		4 c. green and red . . .	25	35
D87		5 c. blue and red . . .	25	35
D88		10 c. blue and purple .	25	35
D89		15 c. red and green . .	30	40
D90		20 c. brown & purple .	30	45
D91		25 c. blue and brown .	30	45
D92		30 c. brown & green . .	60	75
D93		50 c. red and brown . .	40	50
D94		60 c. red and mauve . .	1·00	1·25
D95		1 f. green and blue . .	75	85
D96		2 f. brown and red . .	75	90
D97		3 f. brown and mauve .	75	90

1943. Nos. D85/97 optd **FRANCE LIBRE.**

D126	D **25**	2 c. brown and blue .	18·00	25·00
D127		4 c. green and red . .	18·00	25·00
D128		5 c. blue and red . . .	18·00	25·00
D129		10 c. blue & purple . .	18·00	25·00
D130		15 c. red and green . .	18·00	25·00
D131		20 c. brown & purple .	18·00	25·00
D132		25 c. blue and brown .	18·00	25·00
D133		30 c. brown & green .	18·00	25·00
D134		50 c. red and brown .	18·00	25·00
D135		60 c. red and mauve .	18·00	25·00
D136		1 f. green and blue . .	20·00	27·00
D137		2 f. brown and red . .	20·00	27·00
D138		3 f. brown and mauve	20·00	27·00

D 18 Moorish Idol

1963. Fishes.

D182	D **18**	1 f. black, yellow & bl	65	65
D183	–	3 f. red, green & blue .	1·00	1·00
D184	–	5 f. orange, blk & bl .	1·60	1·60

DESIGNS—HORIZ: 3 f. Green wrasse; 5 f. Orange anemone fish.

WENDEN Pt. 10

Formerly part of W. Russia but later became part of Latvia. Issued stamps for use within the district until 1903.

100 kopeks = 1 rouble

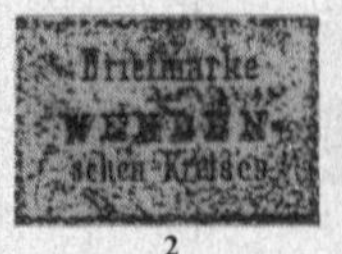

2

3

1863. Inscr "Briefmarke des WENDEN-schen Kreises". Imperf.

1	2	2 k. black and red	£180	£225

1863. Inscr "Packenmarke des WENDEN-schen Kreises". Imperf.

2	3	4 k. black and green	£120	£200

6

7

8

1863. Imperf.

6	6	2 k. green and red	20·00	24·00

1864. As T 6, but with horse in central oval. Imperf.

5		2 k. green and red	60·00	£120

1871. Imperf.

7	7	2 k. green and red	15·00	18·00

1872. Perf.

8	8	2 k. red and green	20·00	27·00

9 Arms of Wenden 10

1875.

9	9	2 k. green and red	5·00	7·00

1878.

10	10	2 k. green and red	5·00	9·00
11		2 k. red, brown and green	5·00	9·00
13		2 k. green, black and red	6·00	15·00

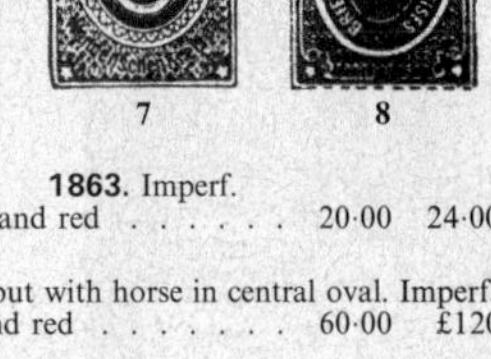

11 Castle of Wenden

1901.

14	11	2 k. brown and green	4·00	10·00
15		2 k. red and green	4·00	10·00
16		2 k. purple and green	4·00	10·00

WEST IRIAN Pt. 21

The following stamps superseded Nos. 1/19 of West New Guinea, after the former Dutch territory became part of Indonesia. From 1971 Indonesian stamps have been used.

100 cents or sen = 1 rupiah

1963. Stamps of Indonesia optd **IRIAN BARAT**, or surch also.

1	–	1 s. on 70 s. red (No. 724)	10	15
2	–	2 s. on 90 s. grn (No. 727)	10	15
3	–	5 s. grey (No. 830)	10	15
4	–	6 s. on 20 s. bistre (No. 833)	10	15
5	–	7 s. on 50 s. blue (No. 835)	10	15
6	–	10 s. brown (No. 831)	10	15
7	–	15 s. purple (No. 832)	10	15
8	134	25 s. green	10	20
9	–	30 s. on 75 s. red (No. 836)	10	20
10	–	40 s. on 1 r. 15 red (No. 837)	10	20
11	99	1 r. mauve	20	35
12		2 r. green	25	45
13		3 r. blue	50	65
14		5 r. brown	80	1·10

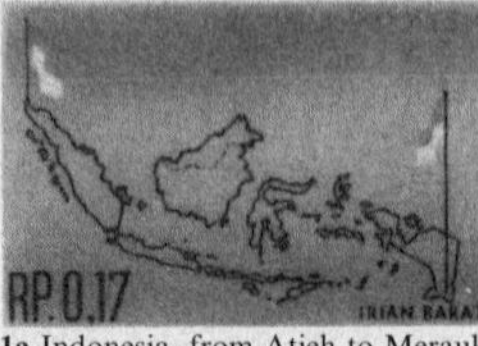

1a Indonesia, from Atjeh to Merauke

1963. Acquisition of West Irian.

21	1a	12 s. orange, red and blk	10	15
22		17 s. orange, red and blk	10	15
23	–	20 s. blue, green & purple	10	15
24	–	50 s. blue, green & purple	10	15
25	–	60 s. brown, yellow & grn	75	35
26	–	75 s. brown, yellow & grn	95	40

DESIGNS: 20, 50 s. Parachutist; 60, 75 s. Greater bird of paradise.

2 "Maniltoa gemmipara"

4 Mother and Child Figurine

3 Map of Indonesia

1968. Flora and Fauna.

27	2	5 s. purple and green	25	25
28	–	15 s. violet and green	25	25
29	–	30 s. green and orange	25	25
30	–	40 s. violet and yellow	35	35
31	–	50 s. black and purple	85	50
32	–	75 s. black and blue	1·40	65
33	–	1 r. black and brown	1·10	80
34	–	3 r. black and green	2·40	1·60
35	–	5 r. multicoloured	1·10	1·25
36	–	10 r. multicoloured	2·25	1·90

DESIGNS: 15 s. "Dendrobium lancifolium"; 30 s. "Gardenia gjellerupii"; 40 s. "Maniltoa gemmipara" (blossom); 50 s. Common phalanger; 75 s. One-wattled cassowary; 1 r. Common forest wallaby 3 r. Blue crowned pigeons; 5 r. Black-capped lory; 10 r. Greater bird of paradise.

1968. West Irian People's Pledge of 9 May 1964.

43	3	10 s. gold and blue	65	25
44		25 s. gold and red	95	40

1970. West Irian Woodcarvings. Multicoloured.

45		5 s. Type 4	10	15
46		6 s. Carved shield	10	15
47		7 s. Man and serpents	10	15
48		10 s. Drum	10	15
49		25 s. Seated warrior	15	20
50		30 s. "Female" drum	20	20
51		50 s. Bamboo vessel	20	20
52		75 s. Seated man and tree	20	20
53		1 r. Decorated shield	25	35
54		2 r. Seated figure	25	35

Nos. 45/54 are inscr "I.B." ("Irian Barat").

POSTAGE DUE STAMPS

1963. Postage Due Stamps as Type D **100** of Indonesia optd **IRIAN BARAT**.

D15		1 s. slate	10	25
D16		5 s. olive	10	25
D17		10 s. turquoise	10	25
D18		25 s. slate	10	25
D19		40 s. orange	10	50
D20		100 s. brown	15	95

1968. As Type D **100** of Indonesia, but with coloured network background incorporating "1968" optd **IRIAN BARAT.**

D37		1 s. blue and green	10	25
D38		5 s. green and pink	10	25
D39		10 s. red and grey	10	25
D40		25 s. green and yellow	10	25
D41		40 s. purple and green	20	50
D42		100 s. red and olive	35	95

WEST NEW GUINEA Pt. 4

U.N. Administration of former Netherlands New Guinea from 1 Oct 1962 to 30 April 1963, when it became known as West Irian and became part of Indonesia.

100 cents = 1 gulden

1962. "United Nations Temporary Executive Authority". Stamps of Netherlands New Guinea optd **UNTEA**.

1	5	1 c. yellow and red	1·10	1·25
21	–	2 c. orange	1·10	1·40
3	5	5 c. yellow and brown	1·10	1·40
4	–	7 c. pur, bl & brn (No. 60)	1·50	1·60
5	–	10 c. brown & bl (No. 27)	1·10	1·40
6	–	12 c. pur, bl & grn (No. 61)	1·60	1·90
7	–	15 c. brown & yell (No. 28)	1·60	1·90
8	–	17 c. pur, bl & blk (No. 62)	1·60	1·60
9	–	20 c. brown & grn (No. 29)	1·60	1·60
10	6	25 c. red	2·75	2·75
11		30 c. blue	2·75	2·75
12		40 c. orange	2·75	2·75
13		45 c. green	3·25	4·00
14		55 c. turquoise	3·25	4·00
34		80 c. grey	21·00	18·00
16		85 c. brown	8·50	8·00
17		1 g. purple	8·50	7·50
18	–	2 g. brown (No. 20)	25·00	20·00
19	–	5 g. green (No. 21)	20·00	17·00

For later issues see **WEST IRIAN**.

WEST UKRAINE Pt. 10

Before the 1914/18 War this district, known as E. Galicia was part of Austria. It achieved temporary independence after the war when stamps were issued. In June 1919 it became part of Poland but was transferred to the Ukraine in 1945.

100 heller = 1 krone

(5)

1919. Stamps of Austria 1916 optd with T **5**.

70	49	3 h. violet	30
71		5 h. green	30
72		6 h. orange	30
73		10 h. red	30
74		12 h. blue	30
75	60	15 h. red	30
76		20 h. green	30
77		25 h. blue	30
78		30 h. violet	30
79	51	40 h. olive	40
80		50 h. green	40
81		60 h. blue	40
82		80 h. brown	50
83		90 h. purple	50
84		1 k. red on yellow	55
85	52	2 k. blue	65
86		3 k. red	90
87		4 k. green	5·00
88		10 k. violet	6·50

For other issues which were mainly of a local character, see Part 10 (Russia) of the standard catalogue.

WURTTEMBERG Pt. 7

Formerly an independent kingdom, Wurttemberg became part of the German Empire in 1902.

1851. 60 kreuzer = 1 gulden.
1875. 100 pfennige = 1 mark.

1

2

1851. Imperf.

1	1	1 k. black on buff	£600	90·00
3		3 k. black on yellow	£200	3·00
5		6 k. black on green	£900	26·00
7		9 k. black on pink	£4000	24·00
9		18 k. black on lilac	£950	£600

1857. Imperf.

10	2	1 k. brown	£375	55·00
24		3 k. orange	£200	3·25
15		6 k. green	£450	45·00
17		9 k. red	£750	38·00
19		18 k. blue	£1400	£950
85		70 k. purple	£1400	£3000

1859. Perf.

45	2	1 k. brown	£300	£225
40		3 k. yellow	55·00	19·00
41		6 k. green	£225	45·00
42		9 k. red	£650	£140
43		9 k. purple	£750	£190
44		18 k. blue	£900	£900

1863. Perf or roul.

60	2	1 k. green	32·00	5·50
63		3 k. pink	25·00	1·40
54		6 k. blue	£110	35·00
66		7 k. blue	£800	£130
57		9 k. brown	£190	42·00
59		18 k. orange	£900	£325

3

4

1869. Roul or perf (1 k.); perf (others).

72	3	1 k. green	20·00	1·60
74		2 k. orange	£140	£100
77		3 k. pink	10·00	70
78		7 k. blue	55·00	16·00
80		9 k. bistre	70·00	35·00
82		14 k. yellow	70·00	40·00

1875. New Currency.

123	4	2 pf. grey	2·00	1·00
89		3 pf. green	12·00	1·60
124		3 pf. brown	80	10
91		5 pf. mauve	6·50	30
127		5 pf. green	1·75	10
93		10 pf. red	1·00	10
95		20 pf. blue	1·00	10
97		25 pf. brown	70·00	8·50
130		25 pf. orange	3·00	1·00
151		30 pf. black and orange	4·00	4·50
152		40 pf. black and red	4·50	7·00
99		50 pf. grey	£500	27·00
101		50 pf. green	45·00	3·75
132		50 pf. brown	3·00	1·00
102		2 m. yellow	£650	£225
103		2 m. red on orange	£1700	£120
121		2 m. black and orange	8·00	12·00
122		5 m. black and blue	45·00	£130

For issues of 1947–49 see Germany (French Zone).

MUNICIPAL SERVICE STAMPS

M 5

1875.

M147	M 5	2 pf. grey	1·25	1·00
M169		2½ pf. grey	50	20
M170		3 pf. brown	50	20
M104		5 pf. mauve	25·00	1·75
M171		5 pf. green	50	20
M172		7½ pf. orange	50	20
M173		10 pf. red	50	20
M261		10 pf. orange	15	25
M174		15 pf. brown	2·75	20
M262		15 pf. violet	15	25
M176		20 pf. blue	1·00	20
M263		20 pf. green	15	25
M177		25 pf. orange	70	20
M178		25 pf. black & brown	1·00	20
M179		35 pf. brown	3·50	85
M264		40 pf. red	15	25
M265		50 pf. purple	30	25
M266		60 pf. green	50	25
M267		1 m. 25 green	30	25
M268		2 m. grey	35	25
M269		3 m. brown	35	25

1906. Centenary of Establishment of Kingdom. Optd **1806–1906** under crown.

M153	M 5	2 pf. grey	40·00	7·50
M154		3 pf. brown	14·00	7·50
M155		5 pf. green	3·75	2·00
M156		10 pf. pink	3·75	2·50
M157		25 pf. orange	50·00	7·50

1916. Surch **25 Pf.**

M199	M 5	25 pf. on 25 pf. orange	3·00	65

M 9

M 14

1916. Jubilee of King Wilhelm II.

M202	M 9	2½ pf. grey	3·75	1·60
M203		7½ pf. red	3·00	1·60
M204		10 pf. red	3·00	1·60
M205		15 pf. bistre	3·00	1·60
M206		20 pf. blue	3·00	1·60
M207		25 pf. grey	8·00	1·60
M208		50 pf. brown	14·00	1·60

1919. Surch **2.**

M219	M 5	2 on 2½ pf. grey	1·10	20

1919. Optd **Volksstaat Wurttemberg.**

M222	M 5	2½ pf. grey	20	60
M223		3 pf. brown	12·00	1·25
M224		5 pf. green	20	30
M225		7½ pf. orange	50	60
M226		10 pf. pink	20	30
M227		15 pf. purple	20	30
M228		20 pf. blue	20	30
M229		25 pf. black & brown	20	60
M230		35 pf. brown	4·50	1·25
M231		50 pf. purple	5·50	1·00

1920.

M245	M 14	10 pf. purple	2·00	2·25
M246		15 pf. brown	2·00	2·25
M247		20 pf. blue	2·00	2·25
M248		30 pf. green	3·00	2·25
M249		50 pf. yellow	3·00	2·25
M250		75 pf. bistre	6·50	2·25

1922. Surch in Marks.

M270	M 5	5 m. on 10 pf. orange	15	35
M271		10 m. on 15 pf. violet	10	35
M272		12 m. on 40 pf. red	25	35
M273		20 m. on 10 pf. orange	20	35
M274		25 m. on 20 pf. green	10	35
M275		40 m. on 20 pf. green	30	35
M276		50 m. on 60 pf. green	15	35
M277		60 m. on 1 m. 25 grn	15	35
M278		100 m. on 40 pf. red	15	35
M279		200 m. on 2 m. grey	15	35
M280		300 m. on 50 pf. pur	20	35
M281		400 m. on 3 m. brown	20	35
M282		1000 m. on 60 pf. green	20	35
M283		2000 m. on 1 m. 25 grn	20	35

1923. Surch with new value (T = Tausend (thousand); M = Million; Md = Milliard).

M284	M 5	5 T. on 10 pf. orange	20	30
M285		20 T. on 40 pf. red	20	3·50
M286		50 T. on 15 pf. violet	1·25	30
M287		75 T. on 2 m. grey	6·00	30
M288		100 T. on 20 pf. green	20	6·50
M289		250 T. on 3 m. brown	20	30
M290		1 M. on 60 pf. green	2·50	30
M291		2 M. on 50 pf. purple	20	30
M292		5 M. on 1 m. 25 green	30	30
M293		4 Md. on 50 pf. purple	7·00	30
M294		10 Md. on 3 m. brown	2·50	30

1923. Surch in figure only, representing gold pfennige.

M295	M 5	3 pf. on 25 pf. orange	40	30
M296		5 pf. on 25 pf. orange	40	30
M297		10 pf. on 25 pf. orange	40	30
M298		20 pf. on 25 pf. orange	40	30
M299		50 pf. on 25 pf. orange	2·00	30

OFFICIAL STAMPS

O 5 O 10 King Wilhelm II

1881.

O181	O 5	2 pf. grey	40	20
O182		2½ pf. grey	45	20
O108		3 pf. green	5·00	2·75
O183		3 pf. brown	40	20
O112		5 pf. mauve	3·25	60
O184		5 pf. green	40	20
O185		7½ pf. orange	45	20
O186		10 pf. pink	40	20
O187		15 pf. brown	45	20
O188		15 pf. purple	90	20
O189		20 pf. blue	40	20
O117		25 pf. brown	12·00	3·75
O191		25 pf. orange	40	20
O192		25 pf. black & brown	35	20
O193		30 pf. black & orange	40	20
O194		35 pf. brown	1·60	2·40
O195		40 pf. black and red	40	20
O119		50 pf. green	22·00	4·50
O141		50 pf. brown	£180	£1200
O196		50 pf. purple	40	20
O120		1 m. yellow	90·00	£190
O197		1 m. violet	3·00	20
O198		1 m. black and grey	5·50	40

1906. Centenary of Establishment of Kingdom. Optd **1806–1906** under crown.

O158	O 5	2 pf. grey	32·00	12·00
O159		3 pf. brown	6·00	25
O160		5 pf. green	4·50	25
O161		10 pf. pink	4·50	25
O162		20 pf. blue	4·50	25
O163		25 pf. orange	12·00	10·00
O164		30 pf. black & orange	12·00	10·00
O165		40 pf. black and red	35·00	12·00
O166		50 pf. purple	35·00	12·00
O167		1 m. violet	75·00	12·00

1916. Surch.

O200	O 5	25 pf. on 25 pf. orange	3·50	80
O201		50 pf. on 50 pf. purple	3·50	80

1916. Jubilee of King Wilhelm II.

O209	O 10	2½ pf. grey	3·75	1·00
O210		7½ pf. red	2·50	1·00
O211		10 pf. red	2·50	1·00
O212		15 pf. bistre	2·50	1·00
O213		20 pf. blue	2·50	1·00
O214		25 pf. grey	3·75	1·50
O215		30 pf. green	3·75	1·50
O216		40 pf. purple	5·50	1·50
O217		50 pf. brown	7·50	1·50
O218		1 m. mauve	7·50	2·00

1919. Surch in figures only.

O220	O 5	2 on 2½ pf. grey	1·10	60
O221		75 on 3 pf. brn (O183)	2·25	60

1919. Optd **Volksstaat Wurttemberg**.

O232	O 5	2½ pf. grey	35	20
O233		3 pf. brown	10·00	60
O234		5 pf. green	20	20
O235		7½ pf. orange	35	20
O236		10 pf. pink	20	20
O237		15 pf. purple	20	20
O238		20 pf. blue	35	20
O239		25 pf. black & brown	35	20
O240		30 pf. black & orange	75	20
O241		35 pf. brown	35	20
O242		40 pf. black and red	60	20
O243		50 pf. purple	70	40
O244		1m. black and green	1·00	40

O 16 Ulm

1920.

O251	–	10 pf. purple	1·50	1·60
O252	O 16	15 pf. brown	1·50	1·60
O253	–	20 pf. blue	1·50	1·60
O254	–	30 pf. green	1·50	1·60
O255	–	50 pf. yellow	1·50	1·60
O256	O 16	75 pf. bistre	2·25	1·60
O257	–	1 m. red	2·25	1·60
O258	–	1 m. 25 violet	2·25	1·60
O259	–	2 m. 50 blue	3·75	1·60
O260	–	3 m. green	3·75	1·60

VIEWS: 10, 50 pf., 2 m. 50, 3 m. Stuttgart; 20 pf., 1 m. Tubingen; 30 pf., 1 m. 25, Ellwangen.

YEMEN Pt. 19

A Republic in S.W. Arabia, ruled as a kingdom and imamate until 1962. From 1962 stamps were issued concurrently by the Republican Government and the Royalists. The latter are listed after the Republican issues.

In 1990 the Yemen Arab Republic and Yemen People's Democratic Republic united (see YEMEN REPUBLIC (combined)).

1926. 40 bogaches = 1 imadi.
1964. 40 bogaches = 1 rial.
1975. 100 fils = 1 riyal.

KINGDOM

1 (2½ b.)

1926. Imperf or perf.

1	1	2½ b. black on white	38·00	38·00
2		2½ b. black on orange	38·00	38·00
3		5 b. black on white	38·00	38·00

2

3

1930.

10	2	½ b. yellow	25	25
11		1 b. green	25	15
5		2 b. green	65	50
12		2 b. brown	40	25
13		3 b. lilac	40	25
14		4 b. red	75	40
15		5 b. grey	90	65
16	3	6 b. blue	1·25	90
17		8 b. purple	1·50	1·00
18		10 b. brown	1·90	1·25
19		20 b. green	6·25	4·50
9		1 i. blue and brown	18·00	11·50
20		1 i. green and purple	16·00	11·00

4 Flags of Saudi Arabia, Yemen and Iraq

7

6 8

1939. 2nd Anniv of Arab Alliance.

21	4	4 b. blue and red	1·75	75
22		6 b. ultramarine and blue	1·00	1·00
23		10 b. blue and brown	1·40	1·40
24		14 b. blue and green	2·50	2·50
25		20 b. blue and green	3·75	3·75
26		1 i. blue and purple	7·50	7·50

1939. Surch with T **6**.

27	2	4 b. on ½ b. yellow	7·50	3·25
65		4 b. on 1 b. green	2·50	1·25
66		4 b. on 2 b. brown	9·00	3·75
67		4 b. on 3 b. lilac	2·50	1·25
68		4 b. on 5 b. grey	2·50	1·25

1940.

28	7	½ b. blue and orange	25	25
29		1 b. red and green	25	25
30		2 b. violet and bistre	40	25
31		3 b. blue and mauve	40	25
32		4 b. green and red	40	25
33		5 b. bistre and green	50	25
34	8	6 b. orange and blue	65	25
35		8 b. blue and purple	65	40
36		10 b. green and orange	75	55
37		14 b. violet and green	1·00	90
38		18 b. black and green	1·90	1·50
39		20 b. purple and green	2·50	1·90
40		1 i. red, green and purple	6·25	3·75

The 5 b. (for which there had originally been no postal use) was released in 1957 to serve as 4 b., without surcharge.

9

10

1942.

41	9	1 b. green and orange	25	20
42		2 b. green and orange	30	20
43		4 b. green and orange	40	30
44		6 b. blue and orange	50	35
45		8 b. blue and orange	85	50
46		10 b. blue and orange	1·10	65
47		12 b. blue and orange	1·40	1·00
48		20 b. blue and orange	2·75	1·75

Although inscribed "TAXE A PERCEVOIR" these stamps were only used for ordinary postage purposes as there is no postage due system in Yemen.

1945. Surch with T **6**.

49a	7	4 b. on ½ b. blue & orange	2·50	1·00
50		4 b. on 1 b. red and green	2·50	1·25
51a		4 b. on 2 b. violet & bistre	1·75	1·10
52a		4 b. on 3 b. blue & mauve	2·00	1·25
53		4 b. on 5 b. bistre and green	2·50	1·25

1949. Inauguration of Yemeni Hospital.

54	10	4 b. black and green	1·25	90
55		6 b. pink and green	1·90	1·50
56		10 b. blue and green	2·50	2·00
57		14 b. olive and green	4·50	3·25

11 Coffee Plant

12 Douglas DC-4 Airliner over Sana'a

1947.

58	11	½ b. brown (postage)	10	10
59		1 b. purple	25	20
60		2 b. violet	45	40
61	–	4 b. red	45	40
62	–	5 b. blue	40	40
62a	11	6 b. green	75	60
63	12	10 b. blue (air)	5·50	5·50
64		20 b. green	7·50	7·50

DESIGN—VERT: 4 b., 5 b. Palace, Sana'a.

The 5 b. was put on sale in 1957 to serve as 4 b., without surcharge.

1949. Surch as T **6** (size varies).

68a	11	4 b. on ½ b. brown	2·00	1·40
69a		4 b. on 1 b. purple	1·90	1·40
70b		4 b. on 2 b. blue	2·25	70

13 View of Sana'a Parade Ground

15 Palace of the Rock, Wadi Dhahr

14 Flag and View of Sana'a and Hodeida

1951. (a) Postage.

71	13	1 b. brown	15	15
72		2 b. brown	15	15
73		3 b. mauve	25	15
74	–	5 b. red and blue	35	15
75	–	6 b. red and purple	45	20
76	–	8 b. green and blue	45	20
77	–	10 b. purple	60	30
78	–	14 b. green	90	35
79	–	20 b. red	1·75	60
80	–	1 i. violet	2·75	1·50

DESIGNS—HORIZ: 5 b. Yemeni flag; 10 b. Mosque, Sana'a; 14 b. Walled city of Sana'a; 20 b., 1 i. Taiz and citadel. VERT: 6 b. Eagle and Yemeni flag; 8 b. Coffee plant.

(b) Air. With airplane.

81		6 b. blue	1·75	1·40
82		8 b. brown	2·50	1·75
83		10 b. green	5·00	3·75
84		12 b. blue	3·25	2·50
85		16 b. purple	3·25	2·50
86		20 b. orange	5·00	3·75
87		1 i. red	13·00	8·00

DESIGNS—HORIZ: 6 b., 8 b. Sana'a; 10 b. Trees; 16 b. Taiz Palace. VERT: 12 b. Palace of the Rock, Wadi Dhahr; 20 b. Crowd of people; 1 i. Landscape.

The 5 b. postage stamp was released in 1956 to serve as 4 b. without surcharge and it was again put on sale as 8 b. in 1957. The 6 b. and 8 b. air stamps were released in 1957 to serve as ordinary postage stamps.

1952. 4th Anniv of Accession of King Ahmed. Flag in red. Perf or imperf.

88	14	1 i. blk & lake (postage)	18·00	18·00
89		1 i. blue & brown (air)	15·00	15·00

1952. 4th Anniv of Victory. As T **14** but inscr "COMMEMORATION OF VICTORY". Flag in red. Perf or imperf.

90		30 b. green and red (postage)	12·00	12·00
91		30 b. blue and green (air)	12·00	12·00

1952. Surch as T **6**.

91	13	4 b. on 1 b. brown	2·00	1·75
92		4 b. on 2 b. brown	1·25	1·25
93		4 b. on 3 b. mauve	2·00	1·75

1952. Sky in blue. Perf or imperf.

94	15	12 b. green & brn (postage)	6·00	6·00
95	–	20 b. brown and red	9·50	9·50
96	15	12 b. brown & green (air)	10·00	10·00
97	–	20 b. brown and blue	9·00	9·00

DESIGN: 20 b. (2), Walls of Ibb.

1953. Surch as T **6**.

98	9	4 b. on 1 b. green & orange	4·50	3·75
99		4 b. on 2 b. green & orange	4·50	3·75

16

16a Bab al-Yemen Gate, Sana'a

1953.

100	16	4 b. orange (postage)	45	20
101		6 b. blue	65	40
102		8 b. green	90	50
103		10 b. red (air)	45	30
104		12 b. blue	60	45
105		20 b. brown	1·00	65

1956. Unissued official stamps issued for ordinary postal use without surch.

105a	16a	1 b. brown	40	25
105b		5 b. blue	40	25
105c		10 b. blue	70	50

The 1 and 5 b. were each sold for use as 4 b. and the 10 b. as 10 b. for inland registered post.

1957. Arab Postal Union. As T **96a** of Syria but inscr "YEMEN" at top and inscriptions in English.

106		4 b. brown	1·00	85
107		6 b. green	1·25	1·00
108		16 b. violet	1·60	1·25

1959. 1st Anniv of Proclamation of United Arab States (U.A.R. and Yemen). As T **139a** of Syria.

109		1 b. black and red (postage)	20	20
110		2 b. black and green	30	30
111		4 b. red and green	40	35
112		6 b. black and orange (air)	40	35
113		10 b. black and red	70	45
114		16 b. red and violet	80	50

1959. Arab Telecommunications Union. As T **138a** of Syria.

115		4 b. red	50	50

1959. Inauguration of Automatic Telephone, Sana'a. Optd **AUTOMATIC TELEPHONE INAUGURATION SANAA MARCH 1959** in English and Arabic.

116 **3** 6 b. blue . . . . 1·90 1·25
117 8 b. red . . . . 2·00 2·00
118 10 b. brown . . . . 2·50 2·50
119 20 b. green . . . . 5·00 5·00
120 1 i. green and red . . . . . 7·50 7·50

1960. Air. Optd with Douglas DC-4 airliner and **AIR MAIL 1959** in English and Arabic.

121 **3** 6 b. blue . . . . 2·00 2·00
122 10 b. brown . . . . 3·50 3·50

1960. Inaug of Arab League Centre, Cairo. As T **154a** of Syria but with different arms.

123 4 b. black and green 30 25

IMPERF STAMPS. From this point many issues also exist imperf. This applies also to Republican and Royalist issues.

1960. World Refugee Year. As T **155a** of Syria.

124 4 b. brown 50 50
125 6 b. green 75 75

19 Olympic Torch

1960. Olympic Games, Rome.

126 **19** 2 b. red and black 15 15
127 4 b. yellow and black . . . 25 25
128 6 b. orange and black . . . 45 45
129 8 b. green and brown . . . 70 70
130 20 b. orange and violet . . 1·10 90

20 U.N. Emblem

1961. 15th Anniv of U.N.O.

131 **20** 1 b. violet 15 15
132 2 b. green 15 15
133 3 b. blue 15 15
134 4 b. blue 25 25
135 6 b. purple 60 60
136 14 b. red . . . . 1·00 70
137 20 b. brown . . . . 2·25 1·90

21 Hodeida Port and Freighter

1961. Inauguration of Hodeida Port.

138 **21** 4 b. multicoloured 50 40
139 6 b. multicoloured 95 75
140 16 b. multicoloured . . . . 1·90 1·90

22 Alabaster Death-mask **23** Imam's Palace, Sana'a

1961. Statues of Marib.

141 1 b. black & orange (postage) 15 15
142 2 b. black and violet 20 15
143 4 b. black and brown 20 15
144 8 b. black and mauve 25 15
145 10 b. black and yellow 45 20
146 12 b. black and blue 60 45
147 20 b. black and grey 70 60
148 1 i. black and green . . . . . 1·50 1·10

149 6 b. black and green (air) . . 15 15
150 16 b. black and blue . . . . . 2·50 1·50

DESIGNS: 1 b. Type **22**; 2 b. Horned head (8th-century B.C. frieze, Temple of the Moon God); 4 b. Bronze head of Himyaritic emperor of 1st or 2nd century; 6 b. "Throne of Bilqis" (8th-century B.C. limestone columns, Moon God Temple); 8 b. Bronze figure of Himyaritic Emperor Dhamar Ali, 2nd or 3rd century; 10 b. Alabaster statuette of 2nd or 3rd-century child; 12 b. Entrance to Moon God Temple; 16 b. Control tower and spillway, Marib dam; 20 b. 1st-century alabaster relief of boy with dagger riding legendary monster, Moon God Temple; 1 i. 1st-century alabaster relief of woman with grapes, Moon God Temple.

1961. Yemeni Buildings.

151 4 b. blk, grn & turq (postage) 20 15
152 8 b. black, green and mauve . 40 30
153 10 b. black, green and orange 45 40

154 6 b. black, grn & blue (air) . 25 25
155 16 b. black, green and pink . 1·75 2·00

DESIGNS—VERT: 4 b. Type **23**; 10 b. Palace of the Rock, Wadi Dhahr; 16 b. Palace of the Rock (different view). HORIZ: 6 b. Bab al-Yemen Gate, Sana'a; 8 b. Imam's Palace, Sana'a (different view).

24 Hodeida–Sana'a Highway.

1961. Inaug of Hodeida–Sana'a Highway.

156 **24** 4 b. multicoloured 40 25
157 6 b. multicoloured 55 35
158 10 b. multicoloured . . . 90 45

25 Nubian Temple

1962. U.N.E.S.C.O. Campaign for Preservation of Nubian Monuments.

159 **25** 4 b. brown 65 45
160 6 b. green . . . . 1·50 1·00

1962. Arab League Week. As T **76** of Libya.

161 4 b. green 30 25
162 6 b. blue 40 35

26 Nurse weighing Child **26a** Campaign Emblem

1962. Maternity and Child Centre. Multicoloured.

163 2 b. Putting child to bed . . 25 25
164 4 b. Type **26** 30 30
165 6 b. Taking child's temperature 35 35
166 10 b. Weighing baby 55 45

1962. Malaria Eradication.

167 **26a** 4 b. orange and black . . 25 15
168 – 6 b. green and brown . . 55 40

DESIGN: 6 b. As T **26a** but with laurel and inscription around emblem.

1962. 17th Anniv of U.N.O. Nos. 131/7 optd **1945–1962** in English and Arabic with bars over old dates.

169 **20** 1 b. violet 45 45
170 2 b. green 45 45
171 3 b. blue 45 45
172 4 b. blue 45 45
173 6 b. purple 45 45
174 14 b. red 45 45
175 20 b. brown . . . . 2·25 2·25

REPUBLIC

Y.A.R. 27.9.1962

(28)

1963. Various issues optd as T **28**. (a) Nos. 141/50.

176 1 b. black & orange (postage) 15 15
177 2 b. black and violet 15 15
178 4 b. black and brown 40 40
179 8 b. black and mauve 65 65
180 10 b. black and yellow . . . 1·25 1·25
181 12 b. black and blue . . . . 1·25 1·25
182 20 b. black and grey . . . . 1·60 1·60
183 1 i. black and green . . . . 5·00 5·00

184 6 b. black & turquoise (air) . 70 70
185 16 b. black and blue . . . . 1·90 1·90

(b) Nos. 151/5.

186 4 b. black, grn & turq (post) 40 40
187 8 b. black, green and mauve 1·00 1·00
188 10 b. black, green & orange . 1·60 1·60

189 6 b. blk, green & blue (air) . 75 75
190 16 b. black, green and pink . 2·50 2·50

(c) Nos. 163/6.

191 2 b. multicoloured 40 40
192 4 b. multicoloured 40 40
193 6 b. multicoloured 50 50
194 10 b. multicoloured . . . . 1·90 1·90

29 "Torch of Freedom"

1963. "Proclamation of Republic".

195 – 4 b. brown & mauve (postage) 50 50
196 – 6 b. red and blue 75 75

197 – 8 b. black & purple (air) . . 95 95
198 **29** 10 b. red and violet . . . . 1·60 1·60
199 – 16 b. red and green . . . . 1·90 1·90

DESIGNS—VERT: 4 b. Soldier with flag; 6 b. Tank and flag; 8 b. Bayonet and torch. HORIZ: 16 b. Flag and torch.

29a Cow and Emblem

1963. Freedom from Hunger.

200 **29a** 4 b. brown and red 65 50
201 – 6 b. yellow and violet . . . 75 70

DESIGN: 6 b. Corn-cob and ear of wheat.

Y.A.R. 27-9-1962

(30)

Y. A. R. 27. 9. 1962

(31)

1963. Various issues optd. (a) With T **30**. On Nos. 161/2.

202 4 b. green . . . . 2·00 2·00
203 6 b. blue . . . . 4·25 4·25

(b) With T **31**.

207 **2** 5 b. grey 95 95
204 **3** 6 b. blue . . . . 1·25 1·25
208 8 b. purple . . . . 1·25 1·25
205 10 b. brown . . . . 1·90 1·90
210 20 b. green . . . . 2·25 2·25
206 1 i. blue and brown . . . . 5·50 5·50
211 1 i. green and purple . . . 5·50 5·50

(c) As T **31** but with lowest line of inscription at top.

212 **10** 6 b. pink and green . . . . 1·75 1·75
213 10 b. blue and green . . . . 3·00 3·00
214 14 b. olive and green . . . . 5·00 5·00

(d) As T **31** but with lowest line of inscription omitted and bar at top. On Nos. 167/8.

215 4 b. orange and black . . . . 2·25 2·25
216 6 b. green and brown . . . . 3·00 3·00

Y. A. R 27. 9. 1962

(32)

(e) With T **32**. (i) On Nos. 139/40.

217 **21** 6 b. multicoloured . . . . 1·25 1·25
218 16 b. multicoloured . . . . 2·00 2·00

(ii) On Nos. 157/8.

219 **24** 6 b. multicoloured . . . . 1·25 1·25
220 10 b. multicoloured . . . . 1·90 1·90

(f) As T **32** but with only one bar over old inscription. (i) Nos. 126/8.

221 **19** 2 b. red and black . . . . . 6·25 6·25
222 4 b. yellow and black . . . 6·25 6·25
223 6 b. orange and black . . . 6·25 6·25

(ii) Nos. 159/60.

224 **25** 4 b. brown . . . . 8·25 8·25
225 6 b. green . . . . 10·50 10·50

AIR MAIL Y.A.R.

(34)

35 Flag and Laurel Sprig

(g) Air. With T **34**.

226 **4** 6 b. ultramarine and blue . . 1·00 1·00
227 10 b. blue and brown . . . 1·25 1·25
228 14 b. blue and green . . . . 1·60 1·60
229 20 b. blue and green . . . . 2·50 2·50
230 1 i. blue and purple . . . . 5·00 5·00

1963. 1st Anniv of Revolution.

231 – 2 b. red, green and black . . 40 25
232 – 4 b. red, black and green . . 50 40
233 **35** 6 b. red, black and green . . 1·00 65

DESIGNS—HORIZ: 4 b. Flag, torch and broken chain. VERT: 2 b. Flag, torch and candle.

36 Hands reaching for Centenary Emblem **38** Globe and Scales of Justice

37

1963. Red Cross Centenary. Crescent red; inscription black.

234 **36** $\frac{1}{4}$ b. blue 40 25
235 $\frac{1}{3}$ b. brown 65 40
236 $\frac{1}{2}$ b. grey 65 40
237 – 4 b. lilac 90 50
238 – 8 b. stone . . . . 1·25 1·00
239 – 20 b. green . . . . 3·25 2·50

DESIGN: 4 b. to 20 b. Centenary emblem.

1963. Air. "Honouring Astronauts". T **37** and similar designs showing rockets, etc.

240 **37** $\frac{1}{4}$ b. multicoloured 65 65
241 – $\frac{1}{3}$ b. multicoloured 65 65
242 – $\frac{1}{2}$ b. multicoloured 65 65
243 – 4 b. multicoloured . . . . 1·25 1·25
244 – 20 b. multicoloured . . . . 6·25 5·00

1963. 15th Anniv of Declaration of Human Rights.

245 – 4 b. black, orange & lilac . 40 40
246 **38** 6 b. black, green & turq . . 50 50

DESIGN: 4 b. As Type **38** but differently arranged.

39 Darts

1964. Olympic Games, Tokyo (1st issue).

247 $\frac{1}{4}$ b. green, brown and orange (postage) 10 10
248 $\frac{1}{3}$ b. brown, blue and violet . . 10 10
249 $\frac{1}{2}$ b. brown, blue and mauve . 10 10
250 1 b. brown, green and blue . . 40 25
251 $1\frac{1}{2}$ b. red, brown and grey . . 50 25

252 4 b. brown, black & bl (air) . 50 35
253 20 b. blue, dp blue & brown . 1·40 1·25
254 1 r. red, brown and green . . 4·50 3·50

DESIGNS—HORIZ: $\frac{1}{4}$ b. Type **39**; $\frac{1}{3}$ b. Table tennis; 4 b. Horse-racing; 20 b. Pole vaulting. VERT: $\frac{1}{2}$ b. Running; 1 b. Volleyball; $1\frac{1}{2}$ b. Football; 1 r. Basketball. All designs include the Olympic "Rings" symbol.

See also Nos. 272/80.

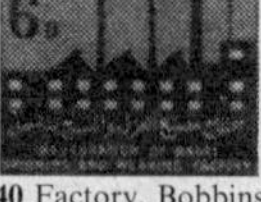

40 Factory, Bobbins and Cloth **42** Boeing 707 on Runway

1964. Inauguration of Bagel Spinning and Weaving Factory.

255 – 2 b. blue & yellow (postage) 25 15
256 – 4 b. blue and yellow . . . 40 25
257 **40** 6 b. green and brown . . . 65 30

258 – 16 b. orange , blue and grey (air) . . . . 1·60 1·25

DESIGNS—VERT: 2 b. Factory, bobbins and cloth (different); 4 b. Loom. HORIZ: 16 b. Factory and lengths of cloth.

1964. Air. President Kennedy Memorial Issue. Nos. 240/2 optd **JOHN F. KENNEDY 1917 1963** in English and Arabic and with portrait and laurel.

259 **37** $\frac{1}{4}$ b. multicoloured 85 85
260 – $\frac{1}{3}$ b. multicoloured 85 85
261 – $\frac{1}{2}$ b. multicoloured 85 85

1964. Inauguration of Hodeida Airport.

262 **42** 4 b. yellow and blue . . . 40 25
263 – 6 b. green and blue 45 35
264 – 10 b. blue, yellow & dp bl 60 45

DESIGNS: 6 b. Control tower and Boeing 707 on runway; 10 b. Control tower, Boeing 707 and ship.

43 New York, Boeing 707 and Sana'a

1964. New York World's Fair.

265 **43** $\frac{1}{4}$ b. brn, bl & grn (postage) 20 10
266 – $\frac{1}{3}$ b. black, red & green . . 30 10
267 – $\frac{1}{2}$ b. green, red & blue . . . 40 20
268 **43** 1 b. indigo, blue & green . 50 25
269 – 4 b. blue, red & green . . . 90 55

270 – 16 b. brn, red & blue (air) . 1·90 1·25
271 **43** 20 b. purple, blue & green . 2·50 1·60

DESIGNS: $\frac{1}{3}$ b., 4 b. Flag, Empire State Building, New York, and Mosque, Sana'a; $\frac{1}{2}$ b., 16 b. Statue of Liberty, New York, liner and Harbour, Hodeida.

44 Globe and Flags **45** Scout hoisting Flag

1964. Olympic Games, Tokyo (2nd issue). Multicoloured.

272 $\frac{1}{4}$ b. Type **44** (postage) 10 10
273 $\frac{1}{3}$ b. Olympic Torch 15 10
274 $\frac{1}{2}$ b. Discus-thrower 25 15
275 1 b. Yemeni flag 25 15
276 $1\frac{1}{2}$ b. Swimming (horiz) . . . 45 30

277 4 b. Swimming (horiz) (air) . . 50 40
278 6 b. Olympic Torch 75 55
279 12 b. Type **44** . . . . 1·60 1·00
280 20 b. Discus-thrower . . . . . 3·00 1·75

1964. Yemeni Scouts. Multicoloured.

281 $\frac{1}{4}$ b. Type **45** (postage) 10 10
282 $\frac{1}{3}$ b. Scout badge and scouts guarding camp 10 10
283 $\frac{1}{2}$ b. Bugler 10 10
284 1 b. As No. 282 . . . . 25 15
285 $1\frac{1}{2}$ b. Scouts by camp-fire . . . 40 20

286 4 b. Type **45** (air) 40 20
287 6 b. As No. 282 . . . . 45 25
288 16 b. Bugler . . . . 1·25 75
289 20 b. Scouts by camp-fire . . . 1·90 1·25

46 Hamadryas Baboons **47** Gentian

1964. Animals.

290 **46** $\frac{1}{4}$ b. brn & lilac (postage) . 10 10
291 – $\frac{1}{3}$ b. brown and blue 10 10
292 – $\frac{1}{2}$ b. brown and orange . . 20 10
293 – 1 b. brown and blue . . . 30 15
294 – $1\frac{1}{2}$ b. brown and blue . . . 50 20

295 – 4 b. red and green (air) . . 65 30
296 – 12 b. brown and buff . . . 1·90 95
297 – 20 b. brown and blue . . . 3·75 1·75

ANIMALS: $\frac{1}{2}$ Arab horses; $\frac{1}{2}$, 12 b. Bullock; 1, 20 b. Lion and lioness; $1\frac{1}{2}$, 4 b. Mountain gazelles.

1964. Flowers. Multicoloured.

298 $\frac{1}{4}$ b. Type **47** (postage) 10 10
299 $\frac{1}{3}$ b. Lily 10 10
300 $\frac{1}{2}$ b. Poinsettia 20 15
301 1 b. Rose 30 15
302 $1\frac{1}{2}$ b. Viburnum 45 20

303 4 b. Rose (air) 65 30
304 12 b. Poinsettia . . . . 1·90 95
305 20 b. Viburnum . . . . 3·75 1·90

48 Boeing 707 and Hawker Siddeley Comet 4 Airliners over Mountains **49** A.P.U. Emblem

1964. Inauguration of Sana'a Int Airport.

306 **48** 1 b. brn & blue (postage) . 10 10
307 – 2 b. brown and blue . . . 15 10
308 – 4 b. brown and blue . . . 25 15
309 **48** 8 b. brown and blue . . . 60 35

310 – 6 b. brown & blue (air) . . 50 45

DESIGNS: 2 b., 4 b. Boeing 707 and Vickers Viscount 800 airliners over runway; 6 b. Hawker Siddeley Comet 4 airliners in flight and on ground.

1964. 10th Anniv of Arab Postal Union's Permanent Office, Cairo.

311 **49** 4 b. black, red and orange (postage) 65 65

312 6 b. black, green and turquoise (air) 75 75

50 Flags and Dove **51** Flaming Torch

1964. 2nd Arab Summit Conference.

313 **50** 4 b. green 45 40
314 – 6 b. brown 75 60

DESIGN: 6 b. Arms within conference emblem and map.

1964. 2nd Anniv of Revolution.

315 **51** 2 b. brown and blue . . . 25 15
316 – 4 b. green and yellow . . . 35 25
317 – 6 b. pink, red and green . 65 35

DESIGNS: 4 b. Yemeni soldier; 6 b. Candles on map.

52 Western Reef Herons **52a** Dagger on Deir Yassin, Palestine

1965. Birds. Multicoloured.

318 $\frac{1}{4}$ b. Type **52** (postage) 20 10
319 $\frac{1}{2}$ b. Arabian chukar (inscr "Arabian red-legged partridge") 45 10
320 $\frac{3}{4}$ b. Eagle owl (vert) 45 10
321 1 b. Hammerkop 70 15
322 $1\frac{1}{2}$ b. Yemeni linnets 75 25
323 4 b. Hoopoes . . . . 2·00 70

324 6 b. Violet starlings (air) . . 1·25 40
325 8 b. Waldrapp (inscr "Bald ibis") (vert) . . . . 2·25 80
326 12 b. Arabian woodpecker (vert) 4·00 1·60
327 20 b. Bateleur (vert) . . . . 5·50 2·25
328 1 r. Yellow-bellied ("Bruce's") green pigeon . . . . . 9·00 4·00

1965. Deir Yassin Massacre.

329 **52a** 4 b. purple and blue (postage) 65 40

330 6 b. red and orange (air) . 75 45

53 I.T.U. Emblem and Symbols

1965. I.T.U. Centenary.

331 – 4 b. red and blue 50 40
332 **53** 6 b. green and red 75 40

DESIGN—VERT: 4 b. As Type **53** but rearranged.

53a Lamp and Burning Library

1965. Burning of Algiers Library.

333 **53a** 4 b. green, red & black (postage) 60 35

334 6 b. blue, red and deep red (air) 60 35

54 Tractor and Agricultural Produce **55** I.C.Y. and U.N. Emblems

1965. 3rd Anniv of Revolution.

335 **54** 4 b. blue and yellow 50 40
336 – 6 b. blue and yellow 75 50

DESIGN: 6 b. Tractor and landscape.

1965. International Co-operation Year.

337 **55** 4 b. green and orange . . . 65 35
338 – 6 b. brown and blue 90 50

DESIGN: 6 b. U.N. Headquarters and General Assembly Building, New York.

56 Pres. Kennedy, Map and Rocket-launching

1965. Pres. Kennedy Commem. Designs each include portrait of Pres. Kennedy. Multicoloured.

339 $\frac{1}{4}$ b. Type **56** (postage) 20 10
340 $\frac{1}{4}$ b. Rocket gantries 20 10
341 $\frac{1}{4}$ b. Rocket 20 10
342 $\frac{1}{3}$ b. Type **56** 20 10
343 $\frac{1}{2}$ b. Rocket 20 10
344 4 b. Capsule and U.S. flag . . 60 50

345 8 b. Capsule in ocean (air) . . 1·25 95
346 12 b. Rocket gantries . . . . . 2·50 1·60

57 Belyaev and Rocket

1965. Space Achievements. Multicoloured.

347 $\frac{1}{4}$ b. Type **57** (postage) 15 10
348 $\frac{1}{4}$ b. Leonov and rocket 15 10
349 $\frac{1}{4}$ b. Scott and capsule 15 10
350 $\frac{1}{3}$ b. Carpenter and rocket gantry 15 10
351 $\frac{1}{2}$ b. Scott and capsule 15 10

352 4 b. Leonov and rocket (air) . 90 90
353 8 b. Type **57** . . . . 1·60 1·60
354 16 b. Carpenter and rocket gantry . . . . 2·50 2·50

1966. Anti T.B. Campaign. Nos. 200/1 optd **Tuberculous Campaign 1965** in English and Arabic.

356 4 b. brown and red 60 50
357 6 b. yellow and violet . . . . 1·25 1·00

59 Torch Signalling

1966. Telecommunications.

359 **59** $\frac{1}{4}$ b. black & red (postage) . 15 10
360 – $\frac{1}{4}$ b. black and blue 15 10
361 – $\frac{1}{4}$ b. black and brown . . . 15 10
362 – $\frac{1}{3}$ b. black and red 15 10
363 – $\frac{1}{2}$ b. black and blue 15 10

364 – 4 b. black & green (air) . . 50 40
365 – 6 b. black and brown . . . 75 50
366 – 20 b. black and blue . . . . 3·75 2·75

DESIGNS: No. 360, Morse telegraphy; 361, Early telephone; 362, Wireless telegraphy; 363, Television; 364, Radar; 365, Telex; 366, "Early Bird" Satellite.

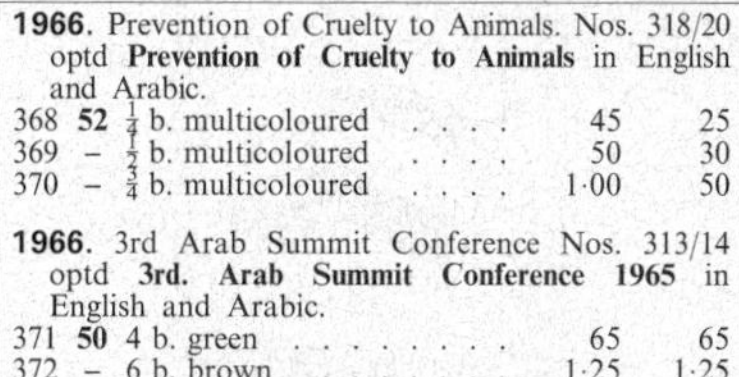

1966. Prevention of Cruelty to Animals. Nos. 318/20 optd **Prevention of Cruelty to Animals** in English and Arabic.

368 **52** $\frac{1}{4}$ b. multicoloured 45 25
369 – $\frac{1}{2}$ b. multicoloured 50 30
370 – $\frac{3}{4}$ b. multicoloured . . . . 1·00 50

1966. 3rd Arab Summit Conference Nos. 313/14 optd **3rd. Arab Summit Conference 1965** in English and Arabic.

371 **50** 4 b. green 65 65
372 – 6 b. brown . . . . 1·25 1·25

62 Pres. Kennedy and Globe

1966. "Builders of World Peace". (a) Postage. Size $39 \times 28\frac{1}{2}$ mm.

374 **62** $\frac{1}{4}$ b. brown 20 15
375 – $\frac{1}{4}$ b. green 20 15
376 – $\frac{1}{4}$ b. blue 20 15
377 – $\frac{1}{3}$ b. brown 20 15
378 – $\frac{1}{2}$ b. purple 25 15
379 **62** 4 b. purple 50 30

(b) Air. Size 51×38 mm.

381 – 6 b. brown and green . . . 95 60
382 – 10 b. brown and blue . . . 1·10 95
383 – 12 b. brown and mauve . . 2·10 1·25

PORTRAITS: Nos. 375, 377, Dag Hammarskjold; 376, 378, Nehru; 381, Mohammed Abdul Chalek Hassuna; 382, U. Thant; 383, Pope Paul VI.

63 Red Junglefowl

1986. Animals and Insects. Multicoloured. (a) Postage.

385 $\frac{1}{4}$ b. Type **63** 25 10
386 $\frac{1}{4}$ b. Brown hare 25 10
387 $\frac{1}{4}$ b. Pony 25 10
388 $\frac{1}{3}$ b. Cat 25 10
389 $\frac{1}{2}$ b. Sheep and lamb 25 10
390 4 b. Dromedary 65 45

(b) Air. Butterflies.

391 6 b. Red admiral . . . . . . 3·00 90
392 8 b. Swallowtail . . . . 3·50 1·10
393 10 b. Garden tiger moth . . . 4·00 1·25
394 16 b. Mocker swallowtail . . 5·50 1·75

1966. Space Flight of "Luna 9". Nos. 347/54 optd **LUNA IX 3 February 1966** in English and Arabic and space-craft.

396 **57** $\frac{1}{4}$ b. multicoloured (postage) 20 15
397 – $\frac{1}{4}$ b. multicoloured 20 15
398 – $\frac{1}{4}$ b. multicoloured 20 15
399 – $\frac{1}{3}$ b. multicoloured 20 15
400 – $\frac{1}{2}$ b. multicoloured 20 15

401 – 4 b. multicoloured (air) . . 45 30
402 **57** 8 b. multicoloured 85 60
403 – 16 b. multicoloured . . . . 1·90 1·50

65 Jules Rimet Cup **66** Traffic Signals

1966. World Cup Football Championships, England.

405 **65** $\frac{1}{4}$ b. multicoloured (postage) 20 15
406 – $\frac{1}{4}$ b. multicoloured 20 15
407 – $\frac{1}{4}$ b. multicoloured 20 15
408 – $\frac{1}{3}$ b. multicoloured 20 15
409 – $\frac{1}{2}$ b. multicoloured 20 15

410 – 4 b. multicoloured (air) . . 50 45
411 – 5 b. multicoloured 75 65
412 – 20 b. multicoloured . . . . 1·90 1·60

DESIGNS: No. 406/11, Footballers in play (all different); 412, World Cup emblem.

1966. Traffic Day.

414 **66** 4 b. red, emerald & green . 95 65
415 6 b. red, emerald & green . 1·60 95

1966. Space Flight of "Surveyor 1". Nos. 347/51 surch with space-craft and **SURVEYOR 1 2 June 1966** and new value in English and Arabic.

417 **57** 1 b. on $\frac{1}{4}$ b. multicoloured . 65 65
418 – 1 b. on $\frac{1}{4}$ b. multicoloured . 65 65
419 – 1 b. on $\frac{1}{4}$ b. multicoloured . 65 65
420 – 3 b. on $\frac{1}{3}$ b. multicoloured . 1·25 1·25
421 – 4 b. on $\frac{1}{2}$ b. multicoloured . 1·90 1·90

68 Yemeni Flag

1966. 4th Anniv of Revolution.

422 **68** 2 b. black, red and green . 25 15
423 – 4 b. multicoloured 50 25
424 – 6 b. multicoloured 80 40

DESIGNS—VERT (25×42 mm): 4 b. Automatic weapon; 6 b. "Agriculture and Industry".

1966. "World Fair, Sana'a, 1965". Nos. 265/71 optd **1965 SANA'A** in English and Arabic.

425 **43** $\frac{1}{4}$ b. brn, bl & grn (postage) 20 15
426 – $\frac{1}{3}$ b. black, red and green . 20 15
427 – $\frac{1}{2}$ b. green, red and blue . . 20 15
428 **43** 1 b. indigo, blue & green . 35 25
429 – 4 b. blue, red and green . . 50 50

430 – 16 b. brown, red & bl (air) 2·50 2·50
431 **43** 20 b. purple, blue & green . 3·75 3·25

70 Galen, Helianthus and W.H.O. Building

1966. Inauguration of W.H.O. Headquarters, Geneva. Designs incorporating W.H.O. Building. Mult.

433 $\frac{1}{4}$ b. Type **70** (postage) 30 20
434 $\frac{1}{4}$ b. Hippocrates and ipomoeas 30 20
435 $\frac{1}{4}$ b. Ibn Sina (Avicenna) and peonies 30 30

436 4 b. Type **70** (air) 65 30
437 8 b. As No. 434 . . . . 1·25 65
438 16 b. As No. 435 . . . . . . 2·50 1·25

71 Space-craft Launching

1966. Space Flight of "Gemini 6" and "7". Multicoloured.

440 $\frac{1}{4}$ b. Type **71** (postage) 20 15
441 $\frac{1}{4}$ b. Astronauts 20 15
442 $\frac{1}{4}$ b. "Gemini" space-craft (horiz) 20 15
443 $\frac{1}{3}$ b. "Gemini 6" and "7" (horiz) 20 15
444 $\frac{1}{2}$ b. Recovery operations at sea 20 15
445 2 b. As $\frac{1}{3}$ b. 30 20

446 8 b. As $\frac{1}{2}$ b. (air) . . . . 1·00 75
447 12 b. "Gemini 6" and "7" link (horiz) . . . . 1·50 75

1966. Space Flight of "Gemini 9". Nos. 440/7 optd **GEMINI IX CERNAN–STAFFORD JUNE 3-1966** in English and Arabic.

449 **71** $\frac{1}{4}$ b. multicoloured (postage) 15 15
450 – $\frac{1}{4}$ b. multicoloured 15 15
451 – $\frac{1}{4}$ b. multicoloured 15 15
452 – $\frac{1}{3}$ b. multicoloured 15 15
453 – $\frac{1}{2}$ b. multicoloured 15 15
454 – 2 b. multicoloured 40 25

455 8 b. multicoloured (air) . . 1·40 1·00
456 12 b. multicoloured . . . . 1·50 1·00

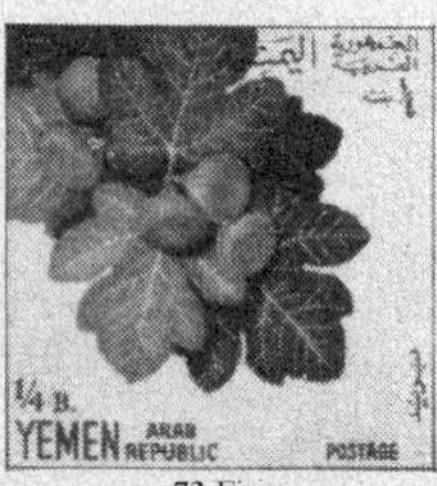

73 Figs

1967. Fruits. Multicoloured.

458 $\frac{1}{4}$ b. Type **73** (postage) 15 10
459 $\frac{1}{2}$ b. Quinces 15 10
460 $\frac{1}{4}$ b. Grapes 15 10
461 $\frac{1}{3}$ b. Dates 15 10
462 $\frac{1}{2}$ b. Apricots 15 15
463 2 b. Quinces 50 25
464 4 b. Oranges . . . . 1·25 65

465 6 b. Bananas (air) . . . . . 1·25 65
466 8 b. Type **73** . . . . 1·50 85
467 10 b. Grapes . . . . 2·25 1·00

1967. Arab League Day. As T **328** of Egypt.

471 4 b. brown and violet 50 40
472 6 b. brown and violet . . . . 1·00 80
473 8 b. brown and violet . . . . 1·40 1·25
474 20 b. brown and green . . . 2·00 1·40
475 40 b. black and green . . . . 5·00 4·00

73a Women in Factory

1967. Labour Day.

475a **73a** 2 b. blue and violet . . 40 35
475b 4 b. green and red . . . 80 70
475c 6 b. purple and green . 1·25 90
475d 8 b. green and blue . . 1·50 90

74 Ploughing and Sunset

1967.

476 **74** 1 b. multicoloured 15 15
477 2 b. multicoloured 20 15
478 4 b. multicoloured 35 15
479 6 b. multicoloured 45 15
480 8 b. multicoloured 75 15
481 10 b. multicoloured . . . 1·25 30
482 12 b. multicoloured . . . 1·50 50
483 16 b. multicoloured . . . 1·75 65
484 20 b. multicoloured . . . 2·75 1·10
485 40 b. multicoloured . . . 5·00 2·50

75 Pres. Al-Salal and Soldiers

1968. 6th Anniv of Revolution. Multicoloured.

486 2 b. Type **75** 25 25
487 4 b. Yemen Arab Republic flag 35 35
488 6 b. Pres. Abdullah al-Salal (vert) 75 75

76 Map of Yemen and Dove

1969. 7th Anniv of Revolution. Multicoloured.

490 2 b. Type **76** 20 20
491 4 b. Government building (horiz) 30 30
492 6 b. Yemeni workers (horiz) . 75 75

77 "Lenin addressing Crowd"

1970. Air. Birth Centenary of Lenin. Mult.

494 6 b. Type **77** . . . . 1·25 95
495 10 b. "Lenin with Arab Delegates" . . . . 2·50 1·60

78 Arab League Flag, Arms and Map

1970. 25th Anniv of Arab League.

496 **78** 5 b. purple, green & orange 30 30
497 7 b. brown, green & blue . 65 65
498 16 b. blue, green and olive . 1·60 1·60

1971. Various 1968 issues listed in Appendix surch.

499a 40 b. on 10 b. black, red and green on gold foil (Yemen Red Crescent issue) . . . . 5·00 5·00
499b 60 b. on 15 b. multicoloured on gold foil (Olympics—Chariot Racing issue) . . . . . . 6·25 6·25
499c 80 b. on 10 b. multicoloured on gold foil (Int Human Rights and U Thant issue) . . . . 8·75 8·75

79 Yemeni Castle

1971. 8th Anniv (1970) of Revolution. Mult.

500 5 b. Type **79** (postage) . . . . 1·25 60

501 7 b. Yemeni workers and soldier (air) . . . . 1·50 70
502 16 b. Clasped hands, flag and torch . . . . 1·75 90

1971. Air. Proclamation of first Permanent Constitution. No. 502 optd **PROCLAMATION OF THE INSTITUTION 1/11/1390 H. 28/12/ 1970 C.** in English and Arabic.

504 16 b. multicoloured . . . . . 4·00 3·25

81 U.N. Emblems and Globe

1971. 25th Anniv (1970) of U.N.O.

505 **81** 5 b. purple, green and olive 50 35
506 7 b. indigo, green and blue 75 50

82 View of Sana'a

1972. 9th Anniv (1971) of Revolution.

508 7 b. Type **82** 95 95
509 18 b. Military parade . . . . . 1·90 1·90
510 24 b. Mosque, Sana'a . . . . 3·50 3·50

83 A.P.U. Emblem and Flags

1972. 25th Anniv (1971) of Founding of Arab Postal Union at Sofar Conference.

512 **83** 3 b. multicoloured 50 50
513 7 b. multicoloured 75 75
514 10 b. multicoloured . . . . 1·25 1·25

84 Arms and Flags **85** Skeleton and Emblem

1972. 10th Anniv of Revolution.

516 **84** 7 b. mult (postage) 75 75
517 10 b. multicoloured . . . . 1·10 1·10

518 21 b. multicoloured (air) . 3·00 3·00

1972. 25th Anniv of W.H.O.

519 **85** 2 b. multicoloured 50 40
520 21 b. multicoloured . . . . 2·00 1·50
521 37 b. multicoloured . . . . 3·75 3·00

86 Dome of the Rock, Jerusalem

1973. 2nd Anniv of Burning of Al-Aqsa Mosque, Jerusalem.

522 **86** 7 b. multicoloured (postage) 65 50
523 18 b. multicoloured . . . . 2·50 2·00

524 24 b. multicoloured (air) . 2·50 1·90

87 Arab Child with Book

1973. 25th Anniv (1971) of U.N.I.C.E.F.

526 **87** 7 b. multicoloured (postage) 65 50
527 10 b. multicoloured . . . . 1·25 1·00

528 18 b. multicoloured (air) . 1·50 1·25

88 Modern Office Building

1973. Air. 11th Anniv of Revolution.

530 **88** 7 b. red and green 40 40
531 – 10 b. orange and green . . . 55 55
532 – 18 b. violet and green . . . 1·25 1·25

DESIGNS: 10 b. Factory; 18 b. Flats.

89 U.P.U. Emblem **90** Yemeni Town and Emblem

1974. Centenary of U.P.U.

533 **89** 10 b. red, black and blue . 30 30
534 30 b. red, black & green . 95 95
535 40 b. red, black & stone . 1·60 1·60

1975. 10th Anniv of F.A.O. World Food Programme.

536 **90** 10 b. multicoloured 65 65
537 30 b. multicoloured . . . . 1·60 1·60
538 63 b. multicoloured . . . . 2·75 2·75

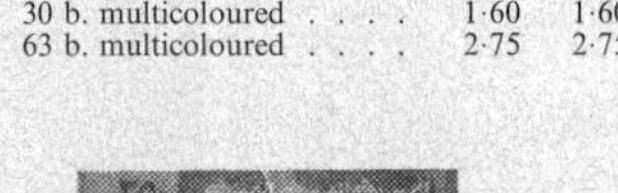

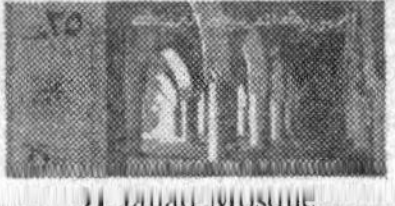
91 Jahad Mosque

1975. 12th Anniv (1974) of Revolution. Mult.

539 25 f. Type **91** 65 50
540 75 f. Althawra Hospital . . . 1·90 1·40

1975. Various stamps surch.

541 **84** 75 f. on 7 b. mult (postage) 1·25 1·40
542 **86** 75 f. on 7 b. multicoloured 1·25 95
542b **85** 75 f. on 21 b. multicoloured 1·40 1·40
542c **89** 160 f. on 40 b. red, black and stone . . . . 2·50 2·50
543 **86** 278 f. on 7 b. multicoloured 5·00 4·25

544 **87** 75 f. on 18 b. mult (air) . 1·25 95
544a **84** 75 f. on 21 b. multicoloured 1·50 1·50
545 **88** 90 f. on 7 b. red and grn . 1·60 1·25
546 – 120 f. on 18 b. violet and green (No. 532) . . . . 2·25 1·90

93 Early and Modern Telephones

94 Coffee Beans

1976. Telephone Centenary.

547 **93** 25 f. black and purple 40 40
548 75 f. black and green 1·25 90
549 160 f. black and brown 2·10 1·90

1976.

551 **94** 1 f. multicoloured 10 15
552 3 f. multicoloured 10 15
553 5 f. multicoloured 10 10
554 10 f. multicoloured 15 10
555 25 f. multicoloured 25 25
556 50 f. multicoloured 55 55
557 75 f. multicoloured 1·00 75
558 1 r. multicoloured 1·40 1·00
559 1 r. 50 multicoloured 2·50 1·90
560 2 r. multicoloured 3·75 2·50
561 5 r. multicoloured 8·75 6·25

Nos. 558/61 are larger 22 × 30 mm.

95 Industrial Scaffolding

96 Emblem of National Institute of Public Administration

1976. 2nd Anniv of Reformation Movement. Multicoloured.

562 75 f. Type **95** 1·25 1·25
563 135 f. Hand holding pick 1·90 1·90

1976. 14th Anniv of Revolution. Mult.

565 25 f. Type **96** 40 40
566 75 f. Yemeni family (Housing and population census) 1·25 1·25
567 160 f. Shield emblem (Sana'a University) 2·25 2·25

97 President Ibrahim M. al-Hamdi

1977. 1st Anniv of Assassination of Pres. Ibrahim al-Hamdi.

569 **97** 25 f. green and black 30 25
570 75 f. brown and black 95 75
571 160 f. blue and black 1·90 1·50

98 Sa'ada and Sana'a

1978. 15th Anniv (1977) of Revolution. Mult.

573 25 f. Type **98** 35 25
574 75 f. Television and transmitter 90 60
575 160 f. Type **98** 1·90 1·50

99 A.P.U. Emblem

100 Dish Aerial

1978. 25th Anniv of Arab Postal Union.

577 **99** 25 f. multicoloured 65 50
578 60 f. multicoloured 1·60 1·00

1978. 3rd Anniv of Correction Movement. Multicoloured.

580 25 f. Type **100** 35 25
581 75 f. Operating a computer 90 50

101 View of Sana'a

1979. 30th Anniv (1977) of I.C.A.O.

583 **101** 75 f. multicoloured 1·25 45
584 135 f. multicoloured 2·25 1·25

102 Koran on Map of World

1979. The Arabs.

586 **102** 25 f. multicoloured 40 25
587 75 f. multicoloured 1·10 75

103 Viewers and Video-screen

104 Dome of the Rock, Jerusalem

1980. World Telecommunications Day (1979). Multicoloured.

589 75 f. Type **103** 1·25 65
590 135 f. As No. 589 but horiz 2·10 1·25

1980. Palestinian Welfare.

592 **104** 5 f. multicoloured 25 10
593 10 f. multicoloured 40 10

105 Girl and Chaffinch

1980. Int Year of the Child (1979). Mult.

594 25 f. Type **105** (postage) 1·40 30
595 50 f. Girl and great tit 1·75 65
596 75 f. Child and butterfly 1·90 1·00
597 80 f. Girl and bullfinch (air) 2·50 1·10
598 100 f. Child and butterfly 2·50 1·10
599 150 f. Child and butterfly 3·75 1·50

Each stamp shows a different variety of bird or butterfly.

106 Scoring a Goal (Austria v. Spain)

1980. World Cup Football Championship, Argentina (1978). Multicoloured.

601 25 f. Type **106** (postage) 45 45
602 30 f. Tunisia v. Mexico 50 40
603 35 f. Netherlands v. Iran 65 45
604 50 f. Brazil v. Sweden 95 65
605 60 f. Peru v. Scotland (air) 1·25 70
606 75 f. Italy v. France 1·60 85
607 80 f. Argentina v. Hungary 1·75 1·00
608 100 f. West Germany v. Poland 2·25 1·40

107 Scout Fishing

1980. World Scout Jamboree. Multicoloured.

610 25 f. Type **107** (postage) 50 25
611 35 f. Scouts and Concorde Supersonic airliner 1·10 45
612 40 f. Parade and scout on horseback 95 45
613 50 f. Scouts with telescope 1·25 55
614 60 f. Parade and cyclist (air) 1·60 65
615 75 f. Poppy and fencer 1·90 90
616 120 f. Scouts catching butterflies 3·00 1·25

108 Match Scene and Flag of Poland

1980. World Cup Football Championship Quarter Finalists. Match Scenes and Flags. Multicoloured.

617 25 f. Type **108** (postage) 45 45
618 30 f. Peru 50 35
619 35 f. Brazil 65 45
620 50 f. Austria 95 65
621 60 f. Italy (air) 1·25 65
622 75 f. Netherlands 1·50 75
623 80 f. West Germany 1·75 95
624 100 f. Argentina (winners) 2·25 1·40

109 Kaaba, Mecca

1980. Pilgrimage to Mecca. Multicoloured.

625 25 f. Type **109** 10 10
626 75 f. Type **109** 35 25
627 160 f. Pilgrims around the Kaaba 75 45

110 Government Buildings, Sana'a

1980. 18th Anniv of Revolution. Multicoloured.

629 25 f. Arm and cogwheel encircling flower and factories (vert) 10 10
630 75 f. Type **110** 60 50

111 Al-Rawdha Mosque

1980. 1400th Anniv of Hegira. Multicoloured.

632 25 f. Type **111** 15 10
633 75 f. Al-Aqsa Mosque 45 25
634 100 f. Al-Nabawi Mosque 70 35
635 160 f. Al-Haram Mosque 1·25 60

HAVE YOU READ THE NOTES AT THE BEGINNING OF THIS CATALOGUE?
These often provide the answers to the enquiries we receive.

112 Figure clothed in Palestinian Flag

1980. Int Day of Solidarity with Palestinian People.

637 **112** 25 f. multicoloured 15 10
638 75 f. multicoloured 60 40

113 Al-Aamiriya Mosque

1981. 9th Arab Archaeological Conf. Mult.

639 75 f. Type **113** 60 35
640 125 f. Al-Hadi Mosque 70 50

114 Tower and Ramparts

1981. World Tourism Conf, Manila. Mult.

642 25 f. Type **114** 15 10
643 75 f. Mosque and houses 45 25
644 100 f. Columns (horiz) 50 30
645 135 f. Bridge 60 40
646 160 f. View of Sana'a (horiz) 90 50

115 Hill and U.P.U. Emblem

1981. Sir Roland Hill Commemoration. Mult.

648 25 f. Type **115** (postage) 90 50
649 30 f. U.P.U. and A.P.U. emblems and Y.A.R. 4 b. stamp of 1963 1·00 60
650 50 f. Hill, magnifying glass and stamps 1·50 90
651 75 f. Hill and jet airliner circling globe (air) 2·50 1·50
652 100 f. Hill, album and hand holding stamp with tweezers 3·25 1·90
653 150 f. Air letter, jet airliner and Y.A.R. 160 f. stamp of 1976 5·00 3·00

1981. Nos. 551/5 surch.

654 **94** 125 f. on 1 f. multicoloured 1·90 1·25
655 150 f. on 3 f. multicoloured 2·25 1·90
656 325 f. on 5 f. multicoloured 4·50 3·00
657 350 f. on 10 f. multicoloured 5·00 3·00
658 375 f. on 25 f. multicoloured 5·00 3·00

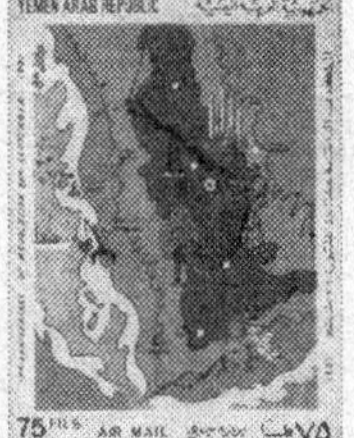

117 Map of Yemen

1982. Air. 19th Anniv (1981) of Revolution. Multicoloured.

659 75 f. Type **117** 75 40
660 125 f. Yemenis looking towards map within sun 1·10 60
661 325 f. Sun, fist, dove with flags for wings and industrial scene 3·25 2·10
662 400 f. Air display 4·25 2·50

118 Al-Hasan ibn Ahmed al-Hamadani

1982. Air. Birth Millenary of Al-Hasan ibn Ahmed al-Hamadani (philosopher).

664 **118** 125 f. multicoloured 1·25 65
665 325 f. multicoloured 3·25 1·60

119 Common Rabbits

1982. World Food Day. Multicoloured.

667 25 f. Type **119** 95 40
668 50 f. Cock and hens 1·90 90
669 60 f. Turkeys 2·25 1·10
670 75 f. Sheep 2·75 1·40
671 100 f. Cow and calf 3·75 1·60
672 125 f. Red deer 4·00 1·90

120 Gymnast

1982. Air. Olympic Games, Moscow (1980). Multicoloured.

674 25 f. Type **120** 95 40
675 50 f. Pole vault 1·75 75
676 60 f. Throwing the javelin 2·25 90
677 75 f. Runner 2·75 1·10
678 100 f. Basketball 3·75 1·60
679 125 f. Football 4·00 1·90

121 Otto Lilienthal's Monoplane Glider and Satellite

1982. Air. Progress in Air Transport. Multicoloured.

681 25 f. Type **121** 1·00 40
682 50 f. Alberto Santos-Dumont's biplane "14 bis" 1·50 55
683 60 f. Biplane and satellite 1·90 60
684 75 f. Early airplane and satellite 2·25 75
685 100 f. De Havilland D.H.60G biplane Gipsy Moth and satellite 2·50 1·10
686 125 f. Fokker F.VIIa/3m airplane and satellite 3·50 1·50

122 Crocuses and Nurse pushing Wheelchair

1982. Air. International Year of Disabled Persons (1981). Multicoloured.

688 25 f. Type **122** 1·00 40
689 50 f. Bowl of roses and nurse pushing wheelchair 1·25 70
690 60 f. Bowl of pasque flowers and nurse pushing wheelchair 1·50 90
691 75 f. Mixed flower arrangement and nurse pushing wheelchair 2·50 1·40
692 100 f. Bowl of lilies and nurse pushing wheelchair 3·25 1·75
693 125 f. Bowl of gladioli and nurse pushing wheelchair 4·00 1·90

123 Aerials and Satellite circling Globe

1982. Air. Telecommunications Progress. Multicoloured.

695 25 f. Modern radio communications 50 25
696 50 f. Type **123** 75 40
697 60 f. Radio masts, watch and dish aerials 90 60
698 75 f. Dish aerials and landscape 1·10 75
699 100 f. Dish aerials, satellites and morse transmitter 1·40 90
700 125 f. Aerials, jet airliner and globe 1·75 1·40

124 Oranges, "TB" and Cross of Lorraine

1982. Air. Centenary of Discovery of Tubercle Bacillus. Multicoloured.

702 25 f. Type **124** 55 20
703 50 f. Blossom, pears, cross of Lorraine and Robert Koch 85 35
704 60 f. Pomegranates, flowers and cross of Lorraine 1·00 50
705 75 f. Roses, grapes and bacillus 1·65 65
706 100 f. Cherries, blossom and microscope 1·60 70
707 125 f. Lemons, cross of Lorraine and microscope 2·00 1·00

125 Tackling

1982. Air. World Cup Football Championship, Spain. Multicoloured.

709 25 f. Type **125** 45 15
710 50 f. Marking the opposition 65 25
711 60 f. Players with ball 95 35
712 75 f. Scoring a goal 1·00 55
713 100 f. Dribbling 1·40 70
714 125 f. Intercepting the ball 1·60 90

126 Map, Boy with Flag, Tents and Dome of the Rock

1982. Air. Palestinian Children's Day. Multicoloured.

716 75 f. Type **126** 1·50 70
717 125 f. As Type **126** but girl with flag 2·40 1·40
718 325 f. As Type **126** but boy and girl 5·00 2·75

127 Map under Grid and Airplane

1982. Air. 30th Anniv of Arab Postal Union. Multicoloured.

720 75 f. Type **127** 1·00 55
721 125 f. Map under grid and ship 1·50 85
722 325 f. Map under grid and emblem 4·50 1·75

128 Passengers and Airliners

1983. 20th Anniv of Yemen Airways.

724 **128** 75 f. multicoloured 1·10 70
725 125 f. multicoloured 2·00 1·10
726 325 f. multicoloured 4·50 2·50

129 Man with Donkey and Foal

1983. Traditional Costumes. Multicoloured.

727 50 f. Type **129** (postage) 2·10 1·10
728 50 f. Woman in embroidered veil carrying jug on head 2·10 1·10
729 50 f. Shepherds in country 2·10 1·10
730 50 f. Man walking through city and shepherds 2·10 1·10
731 75 f. Women at well (horiz) (air) 3·00 1·60
732 75 f. Woman sitting by shore (horiz) 3·00 1·60
733 75 f. Man ploughing with camel (horiz) 3·00 1·60
734 75 f. Man reading (horiz) 3·00 1·60

130 Map of Yemen

1983. 20th Anniv (1982) of Revolution. Mult.

736 100 f. Houses, airliner, telephone and dish aerial 1·50 85
737 150 f. Literacy campaign emblem 2·10 1·10
738 325 f. Tree and houses 4·50 2·50
739 400 f. Type **130** 7·00 3·25

131 Emblem, Satellite, Dish Aerial and Telephone on Flag

1983. World Communications Year.

741 **131** 150 f. multicoloured 2·40 1·40
742 325 f. multicoloured 5·25 3·00

132 Man at Window and Men planting Tree

1984. 21st Anniv (1983) of Revolution. Mult.

744 100 f. Type **132** 1·90 85
745 150 f. Fist and bust 2·10 1·25
746 325 f. Sun, tank and open gates 4·75 2·40

133 Woman in Bombed Street

134 Profiles and Clasped Hands as Doves

1984. "Israeli Aggression against Lebanon".

748 **133** 150 f. multicoloured 2·40 1·25
749 325 f. multicoloured 5·50 3·00

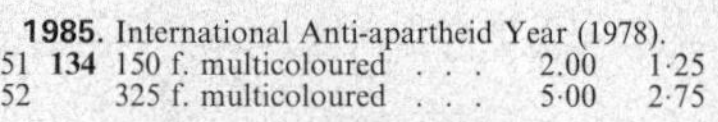

1985. International Anti-apartheid Year (1978).

751 **134** 150 f. multicoloured 2.00 1·25
752 325 f. multicoloured 5·00 2·75

135 Winged Figure and Globe

1985. 40th Anniv of I.C.A.O.

754 **135** 25 f. multicoloured 35 15
755 50 f. multicoloured 75 25
756 150 f. multicoloured 1·75 80
757 325 f. multicoloured 4·25 1·75

136 Monument of Unknown Soldier

1985. 22nd Anniv (1984) of Revolution. Mult.

759 50 f. Type **136** 85 40
760 150 f. Reconstruction of Marem Dam 2·40 1·50
761 325 f. Althawrah Sports Stadium 4·75 2·75

137 Wrestling

1985. Air. Olympic Games, Los Angeles (1984). Multicoloured.

763 20 f. Type **137** 30 20
764 30 f. Boxing 40 25
765 40 f. Running 55 40
766 60 f. Hurdling 65 50
767 150 f. Pole vaulting 1·40 85
768 325 f. Throwing the javelin 3·25 1·90

138 Emblem and Satellite over Globe

1986. 1st Anniv of "Arabsat" Communications Satellite.

770 **138** 150 f. multicoloured 2·50 1·40
771 325 f. multicoloured 5·25 2·75

139 Dish Aerial and Cables

1986. 120th Anniv of World Telecommunications.

773 **139** 150 f. multicoloured 2·50 1·40
774 325 f. multicoloured 5·25 2·75

140 Emblem

1986. 2nd Anniv of General People's Conference.
776 **140** 150 f. multicoloured . . . 2·00 1·40
777 325 f. multicoloured . . . 4·00 2·75

141 Emblem and Sana'a 142 Emblem and Dove

1986. 15th Islamic Foreign Ministers Conference, Sana'a (1984).
779 **141** 150 f. multicoloured . . . 2·00 1·40
780 325 f. multicoloured . . . 4·00 2·75

1986. 40th Anniv of U.N.O.
782 **142** 150 f. multicoloured . . . 2·00 1·40
783 325 f. multicoloured . . . 4·00 2·75

143 Members' Flags, Map and Emblem

1986. 39th Anniv (1984) of Arab League.
785 **143** 150 f. multicoloured . . . 2·00 1·40
786 325 f. multicoloured . . . 4·00 2·75

144 Anniversary Emblem

1987. 25th Anniv of Revolution.
787 **144** 100 f. multicoloured . . . 75 25
788 150 f. multicoloured . . . 1·10 60
789 425 f. multicoloured . . . 3·25 2·00
790 450 f. multicoloured . . . 3·50 2·10

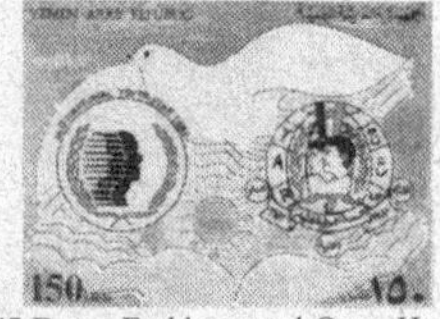

145 Dove, Emblems and Open Hands

1987. International Youth Year (1985).
792 **145** 150 f. multicoloured . . . 1·50 75
793 425 f. multicoloured . . . 4·50 2·40

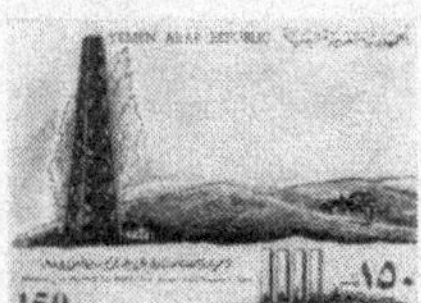

146 Burning Oil

1987. 3rd Anniv of Discovery of Oil in Yemen Arab Republic. Multicoloured.
795 150 f. Type **146** . . . . 1·50 70
796 425 f. Oil derrick and refinery 4·50 2·40

147 Numbers and Emblem

1987. General Population and Housing Census (1986).
798 **147** 150 f. multicoloured . . . 1·50 75
799 425 f. multicoloured . . . 4·50 3·50

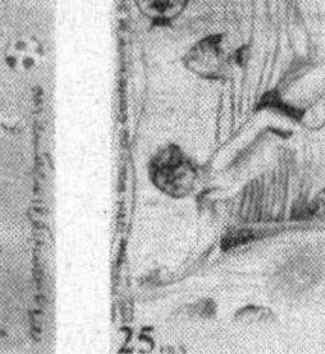

148 Footballers and Pique (mascot) 149 Skin Diving

1988. World Cup Football Championship, Mexico (1986). Multicoloured.
801 100 f. Type **148** . . . . 1·00 50
802 150 f. Goalkeeper saving ball 1·50 75
803 425 f. Players and Pique (horiz) 4·25 2·10

1988. 17th Scout Conference, Sana'a. Scout Activities. Multicoloured.
805 25 f. Type **149** 20 10
806 30 f. Table tennis 30 15
807 40 f. Tennis 25 20
808 50 f. Game with flag 55 25
809 60 f. Volleyball 65 35
810 100 f. Tug-of-war . . . . . . 1·25 55
811 150 f. Basketball . . . . . . 1·75 85
812 425 f. Archery . . . . 4·75 2·50

150 Old City

1988. Int Campaign for Preservation of Old Sana'a.
814 **150** 25 f. multicoloured . . . 30 10
815 50 f. multicoloured . . . 50 25
816 100 f. multicoloured . . . 1·10 55
817 150 f. multicoloured . . . 1·75 85
818 425 f. multicoloured . . . 4·50 2·40

151 Horseman

1988. 800th Anniv (1987) of Battle of Hattin.
820 **151** 150 f. multicoloured . . . 2·50 1·25
821 425 f. multicoloured . . . 7·50 3·75

152 Building, Dish Aerial, Telephone and Emblem

1988. Arab Telecommunications Day (1987).
823 **152** 100 f. multicoloured . . . 1·25 60
824 150 f. multicoloured . . . 2·00 1·00
825 425 f. multicoloured . . . 5·75 2·75

153 Torch and Symbols of Development

1989. 26th Anniv (1988) of Revolution. Mult.
827 300 f. Type **153** . . . . 1·25 50
828 375 f. Type **153** . . . . 1·75 70
829 850 f. Flag, Koran and symbols of agriculture and industry (vert) . . . . 3·75 1·50
830 900 f. As No. 829 . . . . . . 4·00 1·60

154 Old and New Cities and Crowd

1989. 25th Anniv of 14th October Revolution. Multicoloured.
831 300 f. Type **154** . . . . 1·25 50
832 375 f. Type **154** . . . . 1·75 70
833 850 f. City street and crowd (vert) 3·75 1·50
834 900 f. As No. 833 (vert) . . . 4·00 1·60

155 Sports

1989. Olympic Games, Seoul (1988). Mult.
835 300 f. Type **155** . . . . 1·50 50
836 375 f. Football . . . . 1·90 70
837 850 f. Football and judo (vert) 4·25 1·50
838 900 f. Emblem and torch bearer 4·50 1·60

156 Flag, Couple and Fist

1989. Palestinian "Intifida" Movement. Multicoloured.
840 300 f. Type **156** . . . . 1·25 50
841 375 f. Soldier raising flag (vert) 1·75 70
842 850 f. Dome of the Rock, youths and burning tyres . . . . . 3·75 1·50
843 900 f. Crowd of youths (vert) . 4·00 1·60

157 Emblem

1990. 1st Anniv of Arab Co-operation Council.
845 **157** 300 f. multicoloured . . . 1·25 50
846 375 f. multicoloured . . . 1·75 70
847 850 f. multicoloured . . . 3·75 1·50
848 900 f. multicoloured . . . 4·00 1·60

158 Loading Tanker 159 Emblem

1990. 1st Shipment of Oil. Multicoloured.
850 300 f. Type **158** . . . . 1·25 50
851 375 f. Type **158** . . . . 1·75 70
852 850 f. Pipeline around globe and tanker . . . . 3·75 1·50
853 900 f. As No. 852 . . . . . . 4·00 1·60

1990. 10th Anniv (1989) of Arab Board for Medical Specializations.
855 **159** 300 f. multicoloured . . . 1·00 50
856 375 f. multicoloured . . . 1·25 60
857 850 f. multicoloured . . . 2·75 1·25
858 900 f. multicoloured . . . 3·00 1·50

160 Woman feeding Baby

1990. Immunization Campaign. Multicoloured.
860 300 f. Type **160** . . . . 1·25 50
861 375 f. Type **160** . . . . 1·75 70
862 850 f. Nurse weighing baby (horiz) . . . . 3·75 1·50
863 900 f. As No. 862 . . . . . . 4·00 1·60

For further issues see **YEMEN REPUBLIC (combined).**

POSTAGE DUE STAMPS

1964. Designs as Nos. 291, 295/6 (Animals), but inscr "POSTAGE DUE".
D298 4 b. brown and green . . . . 1·90 65
D299 12 b. brown and orange . . 3·75 1·90
D300 20 b. black and violet . . . 7·00 2·50
DESIGNS: 4 b. Mountain gazelles; 12 b. Bullock; 20 b. Arab horses.

1964. Designs as Nos. 303/5, but inscr "POSTAGE DUE". Multicoloured.
D306 4 b. Roses . . . . 1·60 65
D307 12 b. Poinsettia . . . . . . 4·00 1·25
D308 20 b. Viburnum . . . . . . 7·00 2·50

1966. Nos. 324/8 optd **POSTAGE DUE** in English and Arabic.
D371 6 b. multicoloured . . . . . 2·25 1·50
D372 8 b. multicoloured . . . . . 2·50 1·90
D373 12 b. multicoloured . . . . 3·50 2·40
D374 20 b. multicoloured . . . . 5·75 4·25
D375 1 r. multicoloured . . . . . 12·50 8·75

1966. Designs as Nos. 410/12 (Football), but inscr "POSTAGE DUE".
D414 4 b. multicoloured . . . . . 1·25 95
D415 5 b. multicoloured . . . . . 2·50 1·60
D416 20 b. multicoloured . . . . 5·75 3·75

1967. Designs as Nos. 465/7, but inscr "POSTAGE DUE" instead of "AIR MAIL". Multicoloured.
D468 – 6 b. Bananas . . . . . . 1·90 1·25
D469 **73** 8 b. Figs . . . . 3·00 1·90
D470 – 10 b. Grapes . . . . . . 4·50 2·50

ROYALIST CIVIL WAR ISSUES

Fighting continued between the Royalists and Republicans until 1970. In 1970 Saudi Arabia recognised the Republican government as the rulers of Yemen, and the royalist position crumbled.

1962. Various issues optd. (i) Optd **FREE YEMEN FIGHTS FOR GOD, IMAM, COUNTRY** in English and Arabic.
R1 **19** 2 b. red and black . . . . 3·00 3·00
R3 4 b. yellow and black . . . 3·00 3·00

(ii) Optd **FREE YEMEN FIGHTS FOR GOD, IMAM & COUNTRY** in English and Arabic.

(a) Nos. 156/8.
R5 **24** 4 b. multicoloured . . . . 3·00 3·00
R6 6 b. multicoloured . . . . 3·75 3·75
R7 10 b. multicoloured . . . . 5·75 5·75

(b) Nos. 159/60.
R8 **25** 4 b. brown . . . . 25·00 25·00
R9 6 b. green . . . . 25·00 25·00

(c) Nos. 161/2.
R10 4 b. green . . . . 3·75 3·75
R11 6 b. blue . . . . 3·75 3·75

(d) Nos. 167/8.
R12 4 b. orange and black . . . . 3·75 3·75
R13 6 b. green and brown . . . . 3·75 3·75

(e) Nos. 126/30.
R14 **19** 2 b. red and black . . .
R15 4 b. yellow and black . . .
R16 6 b. orange and black . .
R17 8 b. green and brown . .
R18 20 b. orange and violet
Set of 5 . . . . £130 £130

(f) Nos. 169/75.
R19 **20** 1 b. violet 95 95
R20 2 b. green 95 95
R21 3 b. blue . . . . 1·25 1·25
R22 4 b. blue . . . . 1·90 1·90
R23 6 b. purple . . . . 3·25 3·25
R24 14 b. red . . . . 5·75 5·75
R25 20 b. brown . . . . 8·25 8·25

R 6 Five Ears of Wheat

1963. Air. Freedom from Hunger.
R26 R **6** 4 b. red, green & stone . 75 75
R27 6 b. red, green & blue . 75 75

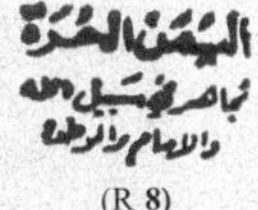

(R 7) (R 8)

1963. Captured Y.A.R. stamps variously optd. (a) No. 195 optd with Type R **7**.
R28 4 b. brown and mauve . . . 45·00 50·00

(b) No. 196 optd with Type R **7** plus first line of Arabic inscr repeated at foot.
R29 6 b. red and blue . . . . . . 45·00 50·00

(c) No. 196 optd with Types R 7 and R **8**.
R30 6 b. red and blue . . . . . . 55·00 65·00

1963. Surch in figures with stars over old value, for use on circulars.
R31 R **6** 1 b. on 4 b. red, green and stone . . . . 90 1·00
R32 2 b. on 6 b. red, green and blue . . . . 90 1·00

R 10 Red Cross Field Post

1963. Red Cross Cent. Flags in red; inscr in black.

R33 R **10** $\frac{1}{8}$ b. violet (postage) . . 50 50
R34 $\frac{1}{4}$ b. mauve 50 50
R35 $\frac{1}{2}$ b. brown 65 65
R36 4 b. green 90 90
R37 6 b. blue (air) . . . . . . 2·50 2·50

R 11

1963. Consular Fee stamp optd **YEMEN** in English and "POSTAGE 1383" (Moslem Year) in Arabic with bar over old inscr, as in Type R **11**.

R38 R **11** 10 b. black and red . . 75·00 75·00

R **12** Troops in Action

1964. Air. "The Patriotic War". Flags and emblem in red.

R39 R **12** $\frac{1}{2}$ b. green 50 55
R40 1 b. black 65 70
R41 2 b. purple 65 75
R42 4 b. green 80 90
R43 6 b. blue . . . . 1·90 2·10

1964. Air. Surch **AIR MAIL**, red cross, **1963–64 HONOURING BRITISH RED CROSS SURGICAL TEAM** and value and Arabic equivalent.

R44 R **12** 10 b. on 4 b. green . . . 4·25 4·25
R45 18 b. on $\frac{1}{2}$ b. green . . . 6·00 6·00

1964. Air. Surch **AIR MAIL** and value in English and Arabic and airplane motif.

R46 R **10** 10 b. on $\frac{1}{8}$ b. violet . . . 3·50 3·50
R47 18 b. on $\frac{1}{4}$ b. mauve . . 5·50 5·50
R48 28 b. on $\frac{1}{2}$ b. brown . . 8·50 8·50

1964. Air. Surch **4 REVALUED** in English and Arabic with dotted frameline around stamp.

R49 R **12** 4 b. on $\frac{1}{2}$ b. green . . . 9·00 9·00
R50 4 b. on 1 b. black . . . 9·00 9·00
R51 4 b. on 2 b. purple . . . 9·00 9·00

R **16** Olympic Flame and "Rings"

1964. Olympic Games, Tokyo.

R52 R **16** 2 b. blue (postage) . . . 60 60
R53 4 b. violet 80 80
R54 6 b. brown (air) . . . . 1·25 1·25

R **17** Rocket

1964. Astronauts.

R55 R **17** 2 b. orange, violet and black (postage) . . . 1·90 1·90
R56 4 b. brown, blue and black 3·75 3·75
R57 6 b. yellow & blk (air) . 5·00 5·00

R **18** (Actual size 80 × 26 mm)

1964. Consular Fee stamps optd across a pair as in Type R **18**.

R58 R **18** 10 b. (5 b. + 5 b.) purple

Owing to a shortage of 10 b. postage stamps, 5 b. Consular Fee stamps were optd across pairs with **YEMEN** in English and "POSTAGE 1383" (Moslem Year) in Arabic, in frame, together with the Ministry of Communications' Royal Arms seal and a bar over old inscription at foot.

1965. Air. British Yemen Relief Committee. Nos. R 46/8 additionally optd **HONOURING BRITISH YEMEN RELIEF COMMITTEE 1963 1965** in English and Arabic.

R59 R **10** 10 b. on $\frac{1}{8}$ b. violet . . 2·50 2·50
R60 18 b. on $\frac{1}{4}$ b. mauve . . 5·00 5·00
R61 28 b. on $\frac{1}{2}$ b. brown . . 7·50 7·50

R **20** Seif-al-Islam Ali

1965. Prince Seif-al-Islam Ali Commemoration.

R62 R **20** 4 b. grey and red . . . 1·90 1·90

R **21** Kennedy as Young Man

1965. Pres. Kennedy Commemoration.

R63 R **21** $\frac{1}{8}$ b. black, mauve and gold (postage) 25 25
R64 – $\frac{1}{4}$ b. vio, turq & gold . 25 25
R65 – $\frac{1}{2}$ b. brn, blue & gold . 25 25
R66 – 4 b. brown, yell & gold 1·25 1·25
R67 – 6 b. black, green and gold (air) . . . . 1·75 1·75

DESIGNS (Kennedy): $\frac{1}{4}$ b. As naval officer; $\frac{1}{2}$ b. Sailing with Mrs. Kennedy; 4 b. In rocking-chair; 6 b. Full face portrait.

1965. Churchill Commemoration (1st issue). No. R62, with colours changed, optd **IN MEMORY OF SIR WINSTON CHURCHILL 1874–1965** in English and Arabic.

R68 R **20** 4 b. blue and red . . . 9·50 9·50

R **23** Satellite and Emblems

1965. I.T.U. Centenary.

R69 R **23** 2 b. yellow, violet and black (postage) . . . 2·50 2·50
R70 4 b. red, blue and blk . 3·75 3·75
R71 6 b. green, violet and black (air) . . . . 5·00 5·00

R **24** Hammerkop

1965. Birds. Multicoloured.

R72 $\frac{1}{8}$ b. Type R **24** (postage) . . 90 60
R73 $\frac{1}{4}$ b. Yemeni linnet . . . . . 1·00 60
R74 $\frac{1}{2}$ b. Hoopoe . . . . 1·25 60
R75 4 b. Arabian woodpecker . 2·50 1·90
R76 6 b. Violet starling (air) . . . 6·25 2·50

R **25** Sir Winston Churchill and St. Paul's Cathedral

1965. Churchill Commem (2nd issue). Mult.

R77 $\frac{1}{8}$ b. Type R **25** 20 15
R78 $\frac{1}{4}$ b. Churchill and Houses of Parliament 20 15
R79 $\frac{1}{2}$ b. Full-face portrait 20 15
R80 1 b. Type R **25** 35 25
R81 2 b. Churchill and Houses of Parliament 60 50
R82 4 b. Full-face portrait . . . . 1·25 1·00

R **26** Iman Al-Badr

1965.

R83 R **26** 1 b. black & blue (post) 35 35
R83a 1$\frac{1}{2}$ b. black and green . 25 25
R84 – 2 b. red and green . . 1·25 1·25
R85 R **26** 4 b. black and purple . 1·75 1·75
R86 – 6 b. red & violet (air) . 2·50 2·50
R87 – 18 b. red and brown . 4·25 4·25
R88 – 24 b. red and blue . . 7·00 7·00

DESIGNS—VERT: 2 b., 18 b. Royal arms. HORIZ: 6 b., 24 b. Flag.

1965. Space Flight of "Mariner 4". Nos. R55/7 optd **MARINER 4** in English and Arabic.

R89 R **17** 2 b. orange, violet and black (postage) . . . 60 60
R90 4 b. brown, blue & blk . 1·75 1·75
R91 6 b. yell and black (air) . 2·25 2·25

R **28** I.C.Y. Emblem, King Faisal of Saudi Arabia and Iman Al-Badr

1965. International Co-operation Year.

R92 R **28** 2 b. blue and brown (postage) . . . . . . 1·25 95
R93 4 b. red and green . . . 2·50 1·90
R94 6 b. brown & blue (air) . 3·75 2·50

1965. Space Flight of "Gemini 5". Nos. R69/71 optd **'GEMINI-V' GORDON COOPER & CHARLES CONRAD AUGUST 21-29, 1965** and space capsule.

R95 R **23** 2 b. yellow, violet and black (postage) . . . 1·90 1·50
R96 4 b. red, blue and black 3·75 3·00
R97 6 b. green, violet and black (air) . . . . 6·25 6·25

R **30** Black Persian

1965. Cats. Multicoloured.

R99 $\frac{1}{8}$ b. Type R **30** 40 25
R100 $\frac{1}{4}$ b. Tortoise-shell 40 25
R101 $\frac{1}{2}$ b. Seal point Siamese . . . 50 30
R102 1 b. Silver tabby Persian . . 75 45
R103 2 b. Cream Persian . . . . . 1·50 95
R104 4 b. Red tabby . . . . . . 3·50 1·90

Nos. R102/4 are vert.

R **31** Red Saxifrage

1965. Flowers. Multicoloured.

R106 $\frac{1}{8}$ b. Verbena (vert) 35 20
R107 $\frac{1}{4}$ b. Dianthus (vert) 35 25
R108 $\frac{1}{2}$ b. Dahlia (vert) 65 40
R109 1 b. Nasturtium 75 45
R110 2 b. Type R **31** . . . . . . 1·50 65
R111 4 b. Wild rose . . . . . . 2·75 1·25

R **32** Flag and Globe

1965. Pope Paul's Visit to U.N. Organization.

R113 R **32** 2 b. red, black & grn . 1·90 1·25
R114 4 b. red, black & vio . 3·25 2·50
R115 6 b. red, black & blue . 4·50 3·25

R **33** Moon Landing

1965. Space Achievements. Multicoloured. (a) Postage. (i) Size as Type R **33**.

R117 $\frac{1}{8}$ b. Type R **33** 25 25
R118 $\frac{1}{4}$ b. Astronauts on Moon . . 30 30
R119 $\frac{1}{2}$ b. Pres. Kennedy and Cape Kennedy (vert) 40 40

(ii) Size 48 × 28 mm.

R120 4 b. Belyaev and Leonov in space . . . . 2·75 2·25

(b) Air. Size 48 × 28 mm.

R121 6 b. White and Mcdivitt in space . . . . 3·75 2·50

R **34** Football and Gold Medal

1965. Winners of Olympic Games, Tokyo (1964). Each design showing a sport with a gold medal. Multicoloured.

R123 $\frac{1}{8}$ b. Type R **34** (postage) . . 20 10
R124 $\frac{1}{4}$ b. Running 20 10
R125 $\frac{1}{2}$ b. Throwing the discuss . 50 25
R126 2 b. Judo . . . . 1·10 75
R127 4 b. Wrestling . . . . 2·25 1·25
R128 6 b. Horse-jumping (air) . . 4·50 3·25

R **35** Arms

R **36** Nehru

1966. Air. Size varies. Imperf.

R130 R **35** 10 b. red on white . .
R131 10 b. violet on white .
R132 10 b. red on yellow .
R133 10 b. violet on orange
R134 10 b. violet on mauve

These handstamps were also applied directly to envelopes and aerogrammes.

1966. Builders of World Peace (1st series). Portraits in gold and black; inscr in black.

R136 R **36** $\frac{1}{8}$ b. green 25 15
R137 – $\frac{1}{4}$ b. brown 25 15
R138 – $\frac{1}{2}$ b. grey 50 35
R139 – 1 b. blue . . . . . . 1·25 65
R140 – 4 b. green . . . . . 2·75 2·50

DESIGNS: $\frac{1}{4}$ b. Dag Hammarskjold; $\frac{1}{2}$ b. Pope John XXIII; 1 b. Sir Winston Churchill; 4 b. Pres. Kennedy.

See also Nos. R146/51.

1966. Nos. R63/5 and R67 surch with new values in English and Arabic.

R142 **R 21** 4 b. on ⅛ b. black, mauve and gold (postage) . 35 35
R143 – 8 b. on ¼ b. violet, turquoise and gold . 70 70
R144 – 10 b. on ½ b. brown, blue and gold 75 75
R145 – 1 r. on 6 b. black, green and gold (air) . . . 2·50 2·50

1966. Builders of World Peace (2nd series). As Type **R 36**. Portraits in black and gold; inscr in black.

R146 ⅛ b. yellow 10 10
R147 ¼ b. pink 10 10
R148 ½ b. mauve 25 25
R149 1 b. blue 25 25
R150 1 b. green 25 25
R151 4 b. green 90 90

PORTRAITS: ⅛ b. Pres. Lubke; ¼ b. Pres. De Gaulle; ½ b. Pope Paul VI; 1 b. (R149) Pres. Johnson; 1 b. (R150) King Faisal of Saudi Arabia; 4 b. U. Thant.

1966. Newspaper Stamps. Optd **PERIODICALS** in English and Arabic in frame.

(a) Similar to Nos. R26/7, but imperf.

R153 **R 6** 4 b. red, grn & stone . . 12·00
R154 6 b. red, green & blue . 12·00

(b) Unissued 1963 Red Cross Centenary issue (Nos. R26/7 surch).

R155 **R 6** 1 b. on 4 b. red, green and stone . . . . 16·00
R156 2 b. on 6 b. red, green and blue . . . . 25·00

1966. Air. Olympic Games Preparation, Mexico (1968). Nos. R123/5 in new colours surch **AIR MAIL OLYMPIC GAMES PREPARATION MEXICO 1968** and new value in English and Arabic with aircraft and flag.

R158 **R 34** 12 b. on ⅛ b. mult . . 5·00 5·00
R159 – 28 b. on ¼ b. mult . . 6·00 6·00
R160 – 34 b. on ½ b. mult . . 7·50 7·50

R 40 Yemeni Cannon

1966. Shaharah Fortress. Frame and stars in red.

R162 **R 40** ½ b. bistre (postage) . . 65 65
R163 – 1 b. grey . . . . 1·00 1·00
R164 – 1½ b. blue . . . . . . 1·25 1·25
R165 – 2 b. brown . . . . . . 1·50 1·50
R166 – 4 b. green . . . . . . 2·50 2·50
R167 – 6 b. violet (air) . . . . 4·00 4·00
R168 – 10 b. black . . . . . . 5·25 5·25

DESIGNS—VERT: 1 b. Bombed Mosque; 2 b. Victory Gate; 4 b. Yemeni cannon (different); 10 b. Bombed houses. HORIZ: 1½ b. Shaharah Fortress; 6 b. Yemeni cannon (different).

1966. Nos. R33/5 surch **4B REVALUED** in English and Arabic within border of stars. Flags red; inscr in black.

R170 **R 10** 4 b. on ⅛ b. violet . . . 30·00 30·00
R171 4 b. on ¼ b. mauve . . 30·00 30·00
R172 4 b. on ½ b. brown . . 30·00 30·00

R 42 President Kennedy

1967. 3rd Anniv of Pres. Kennedy's Death and Inauguration of Arlington Grave.

R173 **R 42** 12 b. multicoloured . . 1·90 1·90
E174 28 b. multicoloured . . 3·75 3·75
E175 34 b. multicoloured . . 5·50 5·50

1967. England's Victory in World Cup Football Championship (1966). Nos. R123/8 optd **WORLD CHAMPIONSHIP-CUP ENGLAND 1966** in English and Arabic, **ENGLAND WINNER** in English only and World Cup emblem.

R177 **R 34** ⅛ b. mult (postage) . . 25 25
R178 – ¼ b. multicoloured . . 25 25
R179 – ½ b. multicoloured . . 25 25
R180 – 2 b. multicoloured . . 2·00 1·90
R181 – 4 b. multicoloured . . 3·50 3·25
R182 – 6 b. multicoloured (air) 4·00 2·50

1967. Surch **4B REVALUED** in English and Arabic within border of stars. (a) Nos. R123/5.

R183 **R 34** 4 b. on ⅛ b. mult . . .
R184 – 4 b. on ¼ b. mult . . .
R185 – 4 b. on ½ b. mult . . .

(b) Nos. R177/9.

R186 **R 34** 4 b. on ⅛ b. mult . . .
R187 – 4 b. on ¼ b. mult . . .
R188 – 4 b. on ½ b. mult . . .

R 44 Bazooka

1967. Freedom Fighters. Designs showing Freedom Fighters with various weapons. Multicoloured.

R189 4 b. Type **R 44** 90 50
R190 4 b. Fighter in fez with rifle 90 50
R191 4 b. Bare-headed man with rifle 90 50
R192 4 b. Fighters holding bazooka and round 90 50
R193 4 b. Anti-aircraft gun . . . 90 50
R194 4 b. Heavy machine-gun . . 90 50
R195 4 b. Light machine-gun . . 90 50
R196 4 b. Fighter with bazooka on mount and rifle 90 50

R 45 Rembrandt — Self-portrait

1967. "AMPHILEX" Stamp Exhibition, Amsterdam. Rembrandt Paintings. Mult. (a) Borders in gold.

R198 2 b. "An Elderly Man as St. Paul" 10 10
R199 4 b. Type **R 45** 10 10
R200 6 b. "Portrait of Jacob Trip" 15 15
R201 10 b. "An Old Man in an Armchair" 25 15
R202 12 b. Self-portrait (different) 45 20
R203 20 b. "A Woman Bathing" 50 25

(b) Borders in silver.

R205 2 b. As No. R198 . . . . . 20 20
R206 4 b. Type **R 45** 35 35
R207 6 b. As No. R200 . . . . 40 40
R208 10 b. As No. R201 . . . . 60 50
R209 12 b. As No. R202 . . . . 90 55
R210 20 b. As No. R203 . . . . 1·50 65

1967. Pres. Kennedy's 50th Birth Anniv. Nos. R173/5 optd **50th. ann. 29 MAY** in English only.

R212 **R 42** 12 b. multicoloured . 1·60 1·60
R213 28 b. multicoloured . 3·50 3·50
R214 34 b. multicoloured . 4·50 4·50

R 47 Trigger Fish

1967. Red Sea Fish. Multicoloured.

R216 ⅛ b. Type **R 47** (postage) . . 90 25
R217 ¼ b. Rudder fish 90 25
R218 ½ b. Butterfly fish 90 25
R219 1 b. Grouper . . . . 1·10 25
R220 4 b. Dragon fish . . . . . 1·25 25
R221 6 b. Dark clown fish . . . 1·75 25
R222 10 b. Violet-hued berycid . 2·75 25
R224 12 b. As No. R222 (air) . . 90 10
R225 14 b. Cuckoo wrasse . . . 1·25 10
R226 16 b. Deepwater squirrel fish 1·60 15
R227 18 b. As No. R221 . . . . 1·75 20
R228 24 b. As No. R220 . . . . 2·00 30
R229 34 b. As No. R219 . . . . 2·50 45

Nos. R216/22 are Type **R 47**; Nos. R224/9 are larger, size 58 × 42 mm.

R 48 "The Gipsy Girl" (Frans Hals)

1967. Air. Famous Paintings. Multicoloured.

R230 8 b. Type **R 48** 20 15
R231 10 b. "The Zouave" (Van Gogh) 25 15
R232 12 b. Self-portrait (Rubens) . 25 15
R233 14 b. "Boys Eating Melon" (Murilio) 40 20
R234 16 b. "The Knight's Dream" (Raphael) 50 20
R235 20 b. "St. George and the Dragon" (Ucello) (horiz) . 60 25

1967. "For Poison Gas Victims". Surch **FOR POISON GAS VICTIMS** and surcharge in English and Arabic, with skull and crossbones within frame.

R236 **R 40** ½ b. + 1 b. (No. R162) (postage) . . . . .
R237 – 1 b. + 1 b. (R163) . .
R238 – 1½ b. + 1 b. (R164) . .
R239 – 2 b. + 1 b. (R84) . . .
R240 – 2 b. + 1 b. (R126) . . .
R241 – 2 b. + 1 b. (R165) . . .
R242 **R 20** 4 b. + 2 b. (R62) . . .
R243 – 4 b. + 2 b. (R66) . . .
R244 **R 20** 4 b. + 2 b. (R68) . . .
R245 **R 26** 4 b. + 2 b. (R85) . . .
R246 **R 34** 4 b. + 2 b. (R93) . . .
R247 – 4 b. + 2 b. (R127) . .
R248 – 4 b. + 2 b. (R166) . .
R249 – 6 b. + 3 b. (R86) (air)
R250 – 6 b. + 3 b. (R128) . .
R251 – 6 b. + 3 b. (R167) . .
R252 **R 35** 10 b. + 5 b. (R130) . .
R253 – 10 b. + 5 b. (R168) . .
R254 **R 32** 12 b. + 6 b. (R158) . .
R255 – 18 b. + 9 b. (R87) . .
R256 **R 12** 24 b. + 12 b. red and blue (imperf, size 57 × 36 mm) . . .
R257 – 24 b. + 12 b. (R88) . .
R258 – 28 b. + 14 b. (R159) . .
R259 – 34 b. + 17 b. (R160) .

The amount of surcharge was 50 per cent of the face value of each stamp (except Nos. R236/8 where the surcharge was 1 b. each). Some higher values have two handstamps, which, when added together, make up the 50 per cent.

1967. Jordan Relief Fund. Surch **JORDAN RELIEF FUND** and value in English and Arabic with Crown. (a) No. R66 (Kennedy).

R261 – 4 b. + 2 b. brown, yellow and gold . . . . . . 3·00 3·00

(b) Nos. R75/6 (Birds).

R262 – 4 b. + 2 b. mult (postage) 1·00 1·00
R263 – 6 b. + 3 b. mult (air) . . . 1·75 1·75

(c) Nos. R92/4 (I.C.Y.).

R265 **R 34** 2 b. + 1 b. blue and brown (postage) . . 60 60
R266 4 b. + 2 b. red and green 60 60
R267 6 b. + 3 b. brown and blue (air) 60 60

(d) Nos. R102/4 (Cats).

R269 – 1 b. + 1 b. multicoloured . 1·00 1·00
R270 – 2 b. + 1 b. multicoloured . 1·00 1·00
R271 – 4 b. + 2 b. multicoloured . 1·00 1·00

(e) R109/11 (Flowers).

R273 – 1 b. + 1 b. multicoloured 1·00 1·00
R274 **R 30** 2 b. + 1 b. multicoloured 1·00 1·00
R275 – 4 b. + 2 b. multicoloured 1·00 1·00

(f) Nos. R136/40 (Builders of World Peace).

R277 **R 36** ⅛ b. + 1 b. gold, black and green 30 30
R278 – ¼ b. + 1 b. gold, black and brown 30 30
R279 – ½ b. + 1 b. gold, black and grey 30 30
R280 – 1 b. + 1 b. gold, black and blue 50 50
R281 – 4 b. + 2 b. gold, black and green . . . . . 1·75 1·75

(g) Nos. R146/51 (Builders of World Peace).

R283 – ⅛ b. + 1 b. gold, black and yellow 30 30
R284 – ¼ b. + 1 b. gold, black and pink 30 30
R285 – ½ b. + 1 b. gold, black and mauve 30 30
R286 – 1 b. + 1 b. gold, black and blue 50 50
R287 – 1 b. + 1 b. gold, black and green 50 50
R288 – 4 b. + 2 b. gold, black and green 75 75

HAVE YOU READ THE NOTES AT THE BEGINNING OF THIS CATALOGUE?

These often provide the answers to the enquiries we receive.

R 51 "The Pharmacy"

1967. Air. Paintings. Multicoloured. (a) Asiatic Paintings.

R290 ⅛ b. "Mountains and Forests" (Wang Hwei) 10 10
R291 ¼ b. "Tiger" (Sim Sajoug) . 10 10
R292 ½ b. "Mountain Views" (Tong K'itch'ang) 10 10
R293 ¾ b. "Rama Lakshama and Shiva" (Indian 16th century) 10 10
R294 1 b. "Ladies" (T. Kiyomitsu) 10 10

(b) Arab Paintings.

R295 1½ b. "Bayad plays the Oud and sings" 15 10
R296 2 b. Type **R 51** 20 10
R297 3 b. "Dioscorides and a Student" 20 10
R298 4 b. "The Scribe" 25 20
R299 6 b. "Abu Zayd asks to be taken over by boat" . . . 50 25

The ⅛, 1½, 2 and 6 b. are horiz and the remainder vert.

R 52 Bugler

1967. World Scout Jamboree, Idaho. Mult.

R301 ¼ b. Type **R 52** (postage) . . 10 10
R302 ½ b. Campfire 10 10
R303 4 b. Type **R 52** 25 10
R304 6 b. As ½ b. 35 15
R305 ⅛ b. Scout badge and Yemeni flag (air) 10 10
R306 10 b. As ⅛ b. 35 15
R307 20 b. Scout and satellite . . 70 20

1967. Jordan Refugees Relief Fund. Surch **JORDAN REFUGEES RELIEF FUND** and value in English and Arabic, and Refugee Emblem. (a) Nos. R52/4 (Olympic Games).

R309 **R 16** 2 b. + 2 b. bl (postage) 50 50
R310 4 b. + 4 b. violet . . 70 70
R311 6 d. + 6 d. brown (air) 1·25 1·25

(b) Nos. R55/7 (Astronauts).

R313 **R 17** 2 b. + 2 b. brown, violet & black (postage) . 50 50
R314 4 b. + 4 b. brown, blue and black 70 70
R315 6 b. + 6 b. yellow and black (air) . . . . . 1·25 1·25

(c) Nos. R63/7 (Kennedy).

R317 **R 21** ⅛ b. + ⅛ b. black, mauve and gold (postage) . 20 20
R318 – ¼ b. + ¼ b. violet, turquoise & gold . . 20 20
R319 – ½ b. + ½ b. brown, blue & gold 20 20
R320 – 4 b. + 4 b. brown, yellow and gold . . . . . 2·00 2·00
R321 – 6 b. + 6 b. black, green and gold (air) . . . 3·00 3·00

(d) No. R68 (Churchill opt).

R323 **R 20** 4 b. + 4 b. bl & red . 12·00 12·00

(e) R69/71 (I.T.U.).

R324 **R 23** 2 b. + 2 b. yell, violet and black (postage) 40 40
R325 4 b. + 4 b. red, blue and black 70 70
R326 6 b. + 6 b. grn, violet and black (air) . . . 2·50 2·50

(f) R77/82 (Churchill).

R328 **R 25** ⅛ b. + ⅛ b. multicoloured 10 10
R329 – ¼ b. + ¼ b. multicoloured 10 10
R330 – ½ b. + ½ b. multicoloured 15 15
R331 **R 25** 1 b. + 1 b. multicoloured 25 20
R332 – 2 b. + 2 b. multicoloured 40 30
R333 – 4 b. + 4 b. multicoloured 60 40

R 54 Vaquero

1967. Olympic Games, Mexico (1968). Multicoloured.

R335 ⅛ b. Type **R 54** (postage) . . 10 10
R336 ¼ b. Fishermen on Lake Patzcuaro 10 10
R337 ½ b. Football (vert) 10 10

R338	4 b. Avenida de la Reforma, Mexico City	10	10
R339	8 b. Fine Arts Theatre, Mexico City	30	10
R340	12 b. Mayan ruins (air)	40	10
R341	16 b. Type R **54**	50	10
R342	20 b. As ¼ b.	3·00	90

R 55 Battle Scene

1967. Moorish Art in Spain. Multicoloured.

R344	2 b. Moor slaying knight (horiz) (postage)	10	10
R345	4 b. Arab kings of Granada (horiz)	15	10
R346	6 b. Diagram of chess game (from King Alfonso X's "Book of Chess, Dice and Tablings") (horiz)	50	10
R347	10 b. Type R **55**	60	10
R348	12 b. Moors with prisoners	80	10
R349	20 b. Meeting of Moor and Christian (air)	2·00	10
R350	22 b. Bullfight	2·00	10
R351	24 b. Lute players	2·75	15

APPENDIX

The following stamps have either been issued in excess of postal needs or have not been available to the public in reasonable quantities at face value. Such stamps may later be given full listing if there is evidence of regular postal use.

REPUBLIC

1967.

5th Anniv of Revolution Nos. 476/81 optd in Arabic 1, 2, 4, 6, 8, 10 b.

Paintings by Flemish Masters. Postage ¼, ⅓, ½ b.; Air 3, 6 b.

Paintings by Florentine Masters. Postage ¼, ⅓, ½ b.; Air 3, 6 b.

Paintings by Spanish Masters. Postage ¼, ⅓, ½ b.; Air 3, 6 b.

Winter Olympic Games, Grenoble (1968) (1st issue). Embossed on gold foil. Air 5, 10, 15, 50 b.

Winter Olympic Games, Grenoble (1968) (2nd issue). Sports ¼, ⅓, ½, 3, 6 b.

Chancellor Adenauer Commemoration (1st issue). Embossed on gold foil. Air 50 b.

1968.

Yemen Red Crescent. Embossed on gold foil. Air 5, 10, 15, 50 b.

Paintings by Gauguin. Postage ¼, ¼, ⅓, ⅓, ½, ½ b.; Air 3, 3, 6, 6 b.

Paintings by Van Gogh. Postage ¼, ¼, ⅓, ⅓, ½, ½ b.; Air 3, 3, 6, 6 b.

Paintings by Rubens. Postage ¼, ¼, ⅓, ⅓, ½, ½ b.; Air 3, 3, 6, 6 b.

Provisionals. Various 1930/31 values optd "Y.A.R." and date in English and Arabic. ½, 1, 1, 2, 2, 3, 4, 4, 5, 6, 6, 10, 10, 20 b., 1, 1 i.

Gold Medal Winners. Winter Olympic Games, Grenoble (1st issue). 1967 Winter Olympic Games (1st issue) optd with names of various winners. Air 50 b. × 4.

1st Death Anniv of Vladimir Komarov (Russian cosmonaut). Air 5, 10, 15, 50 b.

International Human Rights Year and U Thant Commemoration. Embossed on gold foil. Air 5, 10, 15, 50 b.

Chancellor Adenauer Commemoration (2nd issue). Air 5, 10, 15 b.

Refugee Relief. Adenauer (2nd issue) optd in Arabic only. Air 5, 10, 15, 50 b.

Olympic Games, Mexico (1st issue). Chariot-racing. Embossed on gold foil. Air 5, 10, 15, 50 b.

Paintings of Horses. Postage ¼, ⅓, ½ b.; Air 3, 6 b.

Paintings by Raphael. Postage ¼, ⅓, ½ b.; Air 3, 6 b.

Paintings by Rembrandt. Postage ¼, ⅓, ½ b.; Air 3, 6 b.

Dr. Martin Luther King Commemoration (1st issue). Human Rights issue optd. Air 50 b.

Gold Medal Winners. Winter Olympic Games, Grenoble (2nd issue). Postage ¼, ⅓, ½, 2 b.; Air 3, 4 b.

Olympic Games, Mexico (2nd issue). Greek and Mexican Folklore. Postage ¼, ⅓, ½, 2 b.; Air 3, 4 b.

Gold Medal Winners, Olympic Games, Mexico (1st issue). Mexico Olympics (1st issue) optd with names of various winners. Air 50 b. × 4.

Gold Medal Winners Olympic Games, Mexico (2nd issue). Postage ¼, ⅓, ½, 2 b.; Air 3, 4 b.

Dr. Martin Luther King Commemoration (2nd issue). Embossed on gold foil. 16 b.

Emblems of Winter Olympic Games. Postage ¼, ⅓, ½, 2 b.; Air 3, 4 b.

Emblems of Olympic Games. Postage ¼, ⅓, ½, 2 b.; Air 3, 4 b.

Dag Hammarskjold and Kennedy Brothers Commemoration. ½, 2, 6, 14 b.

Dr. Christian Barnard's Heart Transplant Operations. ¼, ¾, 8, 10 b.

Dr. Martin Luther King Commemoration (3rd issue). 1, 4, 12, 16 b.

John and Robert Kennedy Commemoration. Embossed on gold foil. 10 b.

1969.

Paintings from the Louvre, Paris. Postage ¼, ⅓, ½, 2 b.; Air 3, 4 b.

1st Death Anniv of Yury Gagarin (Russian cosmonaut). Optd on 1968 Komarov issue. Air 50 b.

Paintings from the Uffizi Gallery, Florence. Postage ¼, ⅓, ½, 2 b.; Air 3, 4 b.

Paintings from the Prado, Madrid. Postage ¼, ⅓, ½, 2 b.; Air 3, 4 b.

Birth Bicentenary of Napoleon (1st issue). Embossed on gold foil. Air 4 b.

Space Exploration (1st series). Inscr "DISCOVERIES OF UNIVERSE". Postage ¼, ¼, ⅓, ⅓ b.; Air 3, 6, 10 b.

Space Exploration (2nd series). Inscr "FLIGHTS TO THE PLANETS". Postage ¼, ¼, ⅓, ⅓ b.; Air 2, 4, 22 b.

First Man on the Moon. Embossed on gold foil. Air 10 b.

50th Anniv of International Labour Organization. Postage 1, 2, 3, 4 b.; Air 6, 8, 10 b.

Space Exploration (3rd series). Inscr "MAN IN SPACE". Postage ¼, ¼, ⅓, ⅓ b.; Air 3, 6, 10 b.

Birth Bicentenary of Napoleon (2nd issue). Postage ¼, ⅓, ½, ¾ b.; Air 4, 8, 10 b.

Space Exploration (4th series). "Apollo" Moon Flights. Postage ¼, ¼, ⅓, ⅓ b.; Air 2, 4, 22 b.

Winter Olympic Games, Sapporo (1972) Preparation. Optd on 1967 Grenoble Winter Olympics issue. Air 50 b.

Olympic Games, Munich (1972) Preparation. Optd on 1968 Mexico Olympics issue. Air 50 b.

Paintings from the National Gallery, Washington. Postage ¼, ⅓, ½, 2 b.: Air 3, 4 b.

Paintings from the National Gallery, London. Postage ¼, ⅓, ½, 2 b.: Air 3, 4 b.

French Monarchs and Statesmen. Postage 1¾, 2, 2¼, 2½ b.: Air 3½, 5, 6 b.

1970.

Tutankhamun Exhibition, Paris. Postage ¼, ⅓, ½, 2 b.; Air 3, 4 b.

Siamese Sculptures. Postage ¼, ⅓, ½, 2 b.; Air 3, 4 b.

"EXPO 70" World Fair, Osaka, Japan (1st issue). Japanese Paintings. Postage ¼, ⅓, ½, 2 b.; Air 3, 4 b.

EXPO 70" World Fair, Osaka, Japan (2nd issue). Japanese Puppets. Postage ¼, ⅓, ½, 2 b.; Air 3, 4 b.

World Cup Football Championship, Mexico (1st issue). Views and Maps. Postage 1¾, 2, 2¼, 2½ b.; Air 3½, 5, 6, 7, 8 b.

World Cup Football Championship, Mexico (2nd issue). Jules Rimet. Embossed on gold foil. Air 10 b.

"United Europe". Postage 1⅓, 1¾, 2¼, 2½, 5 b.; Air 7, 8, 10 b.

25th Anniv of Victory in Second World War. Gen. de Gaulle. Embossed on gold foil. Air 6 b.

Moon Mission of "Apollo 12". Postage 1, 1¼, 1⅓, 1½ b.; Air 4, 4½, 7 b.

World Cup Football Championship, Mexico (3rd issue). Teams. Postage ¼, ⅓, ½, ¾ b.; Air 4, 4½ b.

World Cup Football Championship, Mexico (4th issue). Beckenbauer and Pele. Embossed on gold foil. Air 10 b.

World Cup Football Championship, Mexico (5th issue). Footballers and Mexican Antiquities. Postage 1, 1¼, 1⅓, 1½ b.; Air 3, 10 b.

Interplanetary Space Travel. Postage 1¾, 2, 2¼, 2½ b.; Air 5, 8, 10, 22 b.

Inaug of New U.P.U. Headquarters Building, Berne. Postage ⅓, 1¼, 1½, 2 b.; Air 3½, 4½, 6 b.

"Philympia 70" Stamp Exhibition, London. Postage ¼, ½, ¾, 1, 3 b.; Air 4 b.

8th Anniv of Revolution. Flowers. ¼ b. × 5.

Olympic Games, Munich (1972) (1st issue). Buildings. Postage 1, 1¾, 2½, 3, 3½ b.; Air 8, 10 b.

Olympic Games, Munich (2nd issue). Statue. Embossed on gold foil. Air 6 b.

25th Anniv of United Nations. Human Rights Year issue of 1968 optd. Air 50 b.

Winter Olympic Games, Sapporo (1st issue). Buildings and Emblem. Postage 1½, 2½, 4½, 5, 7 b.; Air 8, 10 b.

Winter Olympic Games, Sapporo (2nd issue). Snow Sculpture. Embossed on gold foil. Air 40 b.

General Charles de Gaulle Commemoration. 1970 25th Anniv of Victory issue optd. Air 6 b.

German Gold Medal Winners in Olympic Games. Postage ¼, ¼, ⅓, ⅓ b. Air 6 b.

1971.

Pres. Gamal Nasser of Egypt Commemoration. Postage ¼ b. × 4, ½ b. × 2; Air 1, 2, 5, 7, 10, 16 b.

International Sporting Events. Postage ¼, ⅓, ½, 2 b.; Air 3, 4 b.

Olympic Games, Munich (3rd issue). Theatre Productions. Postage ½, 1¼, 1¾, 2¼, 4½ b.; Air 5, 6 b.

Moon Mission of "Apollo 14" 1969 Moon Landing issue optd. Air 10 b.

Olympic Games, Munich (4th issue). Paintings from the Pinakothek. Postage ¼, ⅓, ¾, 1½, 2 b.; Air 4, 7 b.

Chinese Paintings. Postage ¼, ⅓, ½, 2 b.; Air 3, 4 b.

Winter Olympic Games, Sapporo (3rd issue). Winter Sports and Japanese Works of Art. Postage ¼, ½, 1, 1⅓, 2 b.; Air 3, 4 b.

Winter Olympic Games, Sapporo (4th issue). Japanese Skier. Embossed on gold foil. Air 8 b.

Launching of Soviet "Salyut" Space Station. Interplanetary issue of 1970 optd. Air 22 b.

Olympic Games, Munich (5th issue). Sports and Sculptures. Postage ⅛, 1, 1⅓, 1¾, 2¼ b.; Air 4½, 7, 10 b.

Olympic Games, Munich (6th issue). Gold Medals. Embossed on gold foil. Air 8 b.

Exploration of Outer Space. Postage ¼, ⅓, ½, ¾ b.; Air 3, 3½, 6 b.

Birth Bicentenary of Beethoven. Postage ¼ × 4, ½ b. × 2; Air 1, 2, 5, 7, 10 b.

Indian Paintings. Postage ¼, ⅓, ½, 2 b.; Air 3, 4 b.

Olympic Games, Munich (7th issue). Sailing Events at Kiel. Postage ¼, ½, 1¼, 2, 3 b.; Air 4 b.

Winter Olympic Games, Sapporo (5th issue). Sports. Postage ⅓, ¾, 1¼, 1¾, 2¼ b.; Air 3½, 6 b.

Winter Olympic Games, Sapporo (6th issue). Slalom Skier. Embossed on gold foil. Air 10 b.

Persian Miniatures. Postage ¼, ⅓, ½, 2 b.; Air 3, 4 b.

Olympic Games, Munich (8th issue). Sports. Postage ¾, 1½, 2½, 3½, 5 b.; Air 6, 8 b.

Olympic Games, Munich (9th issue). Discus-thrower. Embossed on gold foil. Air 10 b.

Italian Gold Medal Winners in Olympic Games. Postage ¼ b. × 2, ⅓ b. × 2; Air 22 b.

1972.

French Gold Medal Winners in Olympic Games. Postage 2, 3 b.; Air 4, 10 b.

Works of Art. Postage 1, 1¼, 1⅓, 1½ b.; Air 3, 4½, 7 b.

ROYALIST ISSUES

1967.

Visit of Queen of Sheba to Solomon. ⅛, ¼, ½, 4, 6, 20, 24 b.

Arab Horses. ⅛, ¼, ½, 4, 10 b.

1968.

Winter Olympic Games, Grenoble (1st issue). Nos. R216/29 optd. Postage ⅛, ¼, ½, 1, 4, 6, 10 b.; Air 12, 14, 16, 24, 34 b.

Butterflies. Air 16, 20, 40 b.

Postage Due. Butterflies and Horse. 4, 16, 20 b.

Winter Olympic Games, Grenoble (2nd issue). Sports. Postage 1, 2, 3, 4, 6 b.; Air 10, 12, 18, 24, 28 b.

Gold Medal Winners, Grenoble Winter Olympics. Winter Olympic Games, Grenoble (2nd issue) optd with names of various medal winners. Postage 1, 2, 3, 4, 6 b.; Air 10, 12, 18, 24, 28 b.

20th Anniv of UNESCO. ½, 1, 1½, 2, 3, 4, 6, 10 b.

Mothers' Day. Paintings. Postage 2, 4, 6 b.; Air 24, 28, 34 b.

Olympic Games, Mexico (1st issue). Sports. Postage 1, 2, 3, 4, 6 b.; Air 10, 12, 18, 24, 28 b.

UNESCO. "Save Florence" Campaign. Paintings. Postage 2, 4, 6 b.; Air 10, 12, 18 b.

UNESCO. "Save Venice" Campaign. Paintings. ½, 1, 1½, 24 b.; Air 28, 34 b.

Olympic Games, Mexico (2nd issue). Athletes and Flags. 4 b. × 11.

Winter Olympic Games since 1924. Competitors and Flags. Postage. 1, 2, 3, 4, 6 b.; Air 10, 12, 18, 24, 28 b.

International Human Rights Year. 2 b. × 4, 4 b. × 4, 6 b. × 4.

Paintings by European and American Artists. Postage 1, 2, 3, 4, 6, 10 b.; Air 12, 18, 24, 28 b.

Coronation of Shah of Iran. Postage 1, 2, 3, 4 b.; Air 24, 28 b.

International Philately. Postage 1, 2, 3, 4, 6 b.; Air 10, 12, 18, 24, 28 b.

World Racial Peace. Postage 4, 6, 18 b.; Air 10 b.

Children's Day. Paintings. Postage 1, 2, 3, 4 b.; Air 6, 10, 12, 18, 24, 28 b.

Gold Medal Winners, Mexico Olympic Games (1st issue). Mexico Olympics (1st issue) optd with names of various medal winners. Postage 1, 2, 3, 4, 6 b.; Air 10, 12, 18, 24, 28 b.

Gold Medal Winners, Mexico Olympics (2nd issue). Athletes and Medals. Air 12, 18, 24, 28, 34 b.

Gold Medal Winners, Mexico Olympics (3rd issue). Embossed on gold foil. 28 b.

"EFIMEX 68" Stamp Exhibition, Mexico City. Air 12, 18, 24, 28, 34 b.

1969.

Motor-racing Drivers. Postage 1, 2, 3, 4, 6 b.; Air 10, 12, 18, 24, 28 b.

Space Flight of "Apollo 7". 4, 8, 12, 24, 28 b.

Space Flight of "Apollo 8" (1st issue). 4, 6, 10, 18, 34 b.

Space Flight of "Apollo 8" (2nd issue). Embossed on gold foil. 28 b.

5th Anniv of Imam's Meeting with Pope Paul VI at Jerusalem (1st issue). Scenes from Pope's Visit. ⅛, ¼, ¼, 1, 1½, 2, 3, 4, 5, 6 b.

5th Anniv of Imam's Meeting with Pope Paul VI at Jerusalem (2nd issue). Paintings of the Life of Christ. Postage 1, 2, 3, 4, 5, 6, 7, 8, 9, 10 b.; Air 11, 12, 13, 14, 15, 16, 17, 18, 19, 20, 21, 22, 23, 24, 25, 26, 27, 28, 29, 30 b.

5th Anniv of Imam's Meeting with Pope Paul VI at Jerusalem (3rd issue). Abraham's Tomb, Hebron. 4 b.

Paintings by Rembrandt (1st series). Postage 1, 2, 4 b.; Air 6, 12 b., 1 i.

Paintings by Rembrandt (2nd series). Embossed on gold foil. 20 b.

Paintings by European Artists. Postage ½, 1½, 3, 5 b.; Air 10, 18, 24, 28, 34 b.

"Apollo" Moon Programme. Postage 1, 2, 3, 4, 5 b.; Air 6, 7, 8, 9, 10, 11, 12, 13, 14, 15 b.

Moon Flight of "Apollo 10". Postage 2, 4, 6 b.; Air 8, 10, 12, 18, 24, 28, 34 b.

Olympic Games, Munich (1972). Athletes and Olympic Rings. Postage 1, 2, 4, 5, 6 b.; Air 10, 12, 18, 24, 34 b.

World Wildlife Conservation. Postage ½ b. × 2 1 b. × 2, 2 b. × 2, 4 b. × 2, 6 b. × 2; Air 8 b. × 2, 10 b. × 2, 18 b. × 2.

First Man on the Moon (1st issue). Air 6, 10, 12, 18 b.

First Man on the Moon (2nd issue). Air 6, 10, 12, 18, 24 b.

First Man on the Moon (3rd issue). Embossed on gold foil. 24 b. × 2.

First Man on the Moon (4th issue). Embossed on gold foil. 28 b.

First Man on the Moon (5th issue). Air 10, 12 18, 24 b.

Palestine Holy Places. Postage 4 b. × 4, 6 b. × 10; Air 12 b. × 8.

Famous Men. Postage 4 b. × 4, 6 b. × 10; Air 12 b. × 2.

History of Space Exploration. Air 6 b. × 27.

Olympic Sports. Postage 1, 2, 4, 5, 6 b.; Air 10, 12, 18, 24, 34 b.

World Cup Football Championship, Mexico. Air 12 b. × 8.

Christmas. Ikons. Postage ½, 1, 1½, 2, 4, 5, 6 b.; Air 10, 12, 18, 24, 28, 34 b.

Burning of Al-Aqsa Mosque, Jerusalem. Postage 4 b. + 2 b., 6 b. + 3 b.; Air 10 b. + 5 b.

1970.

Brazil's Victory in World Cup Football Championship, Mexico. 1969 World Cup issue optd. Air 12 b. × 3.

Dogs. Postage 2, 4, 6 b.; Air 8, 12 b.

Paintings of Horses. Postage 2, 4, 6 b.; Air 8, 12 b.

We close the Appendix with stamps believed to have been issued prior to July 1970, when first Saudi Arabia and then the United Kingdom recognised the Republican government in Yemen.

YEMEN PEOPLE'S DEMOCRATIC REPUBLIC — Pt. 19

The former People's Republic of Southern Yemen was known by the above title from 30 November 1970.

In 1990 it united with Yemen Arab Republic (see YEMEN REPUBLIC (combined)).

1000 fils = 1 dinar

22 Temple of Isis, Philae, Egypt

1971. Preservation of Philae Temples Campaign.

65	**22**	5 f. multicoloured	10	10
66		35 f. multicoloured	50	30
67		65 f. multicoloured	1·25	80

23 Symbols of Constitution

1971. Introduction of First Constitution.

68	**23**	10 f. multicoloured	10	10
69		15 f. multicoloured	25	20
70		35 f. multicoloured	50	35
71		50 f. multicoloured	65	50

24 Heads of Three Races and Flame

1971. Racial Equality Year.

72 **24** 20 f. multicoloured 20 20
73 35 f. multicoloured 40 40
74 75 f. multicoloured 70 70

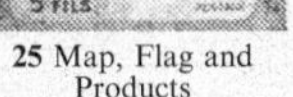

25 Map, Flag and Products — 26 Hand holding Sub-machine Gun, and Map

1971.

75 **25** 5 f. multicoloured 10 10
76 10 f. multicoloured 10 10
77 15 f. multicoloured 15 10
78 20 f. multicoloured 15 10
79 25 f. multicoloured 20 10
80 35 f. multicoloured 25 15
81 40 f. multicoloured 35 15
82 50 f. multicoloured 50 35
82a 60 f. multicoloured 1·00 40
83 65 f. multicoloured 65 45
84 80 f. multicoloured 75 60
84a 90 f. multicoloured 1·10 50
84b – 110 f. multicoloured 1·50 65
85 – 125 f. multicoloured 1·25 1·10
86 – 250 f. multicoloured 2·25 1·50
87 – 500 f. multicoloured 4·50 3·00
88 – 1 d. multicoloured 9·75 6·25

DESIGN 42 × 25 mm: Nos. 84b/8, "Dam-al-Khawain" tree, Socotra.

1971. 6th Anniv of Revolutionary Activity in Arabian Gulf Area. Multicoloured.

89 15 f. Type **26** 20 15
90 45 f. Girl guerrilla and emblem (horiz) 50 40
91 50 f. Guerrilla on the march 85 55

27 Hands supporting Cogwheel — 29 Gamal Nasser

28 Eagle and Flags

1971. 2nd Anniv of "Corrective Move" in Revolutionary Government. Multicoloured.

92 15 f. Type **27** 15 10
93 25 f. Torch and revolutionary emblems 30 25
94 65 f. Salt-works and windmill 75 50

1971. 9th Anniv of 26th September Revolution. Multicoloured.

95 10 f. Type **28** 10 10
96 40 f. Flag on "United Jemen" 50 40

1971. 1st Death Anniv of Gamal Nasser (Egyptian statesman).

97 **29** 65 f. multicoloured 65 50

30 "Children of the World" — 31 Domestic Pigeons

1971. 25th Anniv of U.N.I.C.E.F.

98 **30** 15 f. black, red & orange 10 10
99 40 f. black, purple & blue 30 25
100 50 f. black, red and green 50 45

1971. Birds.

101 **31** 5 f. black, purple & blue 20 15
102 – 40 f. multicoloured 90 50
103 – 65 f. black, red and green 2·10 80
104 – 100 f. multicoloured 3·50 1·40

DESIGNS: 40 f. Arabian chukar (inscr "Partridge"); 65 f. Helmet guineafowl and Arabian chukar (inscr "Partridge"); 100 f. Black kite (inscr "Glede").

32 Dhow-building

1972. Dhow-building in Aden. Multicoloured.

105 25 f. Type **32** 50 25
106 80 f. Dhow at sea (vert) 1·50 1·00

33 Singer with Oud (lute), and Band

1972. Folk Dances. Multicoloured.

107 10 f. Type **33** 15 10
108 25 f. Yemeni girls dancing 40 20
109 40 f. Dancing teams 75 40
110 80 f. Festival dance 1·25 85

34 Palestinian Guerrilla and Barbed-wire

1972. Palestine Day.

111 **34** 5 f. multicoloured 15 10
112 20 f. multicoloured 40 20
113 65 f. multicoloured 90 65

35 Police Colour Party

1972. Police Day. Multicoloured.

114 25 f. Type **35** 35 25
115 80 f. Girls of People's Militia on parade 1·60 1·00

36 Start of Cycle Race

1972. Arab Youth Week. Multicoloured.

117 10 f. Type **36** 30 10
118 15 f. Girls on parade 30 10
119 40 f. Guides and scouts 65 40
120 80 f. Acrobatic team (vert) 1·25 75

37 Turtle

1972. Marine Life. Multicoloured.

121 15 f. Type **37** 55 20
122 40 f. Sailfish 65 50
123 65 f. Kingfish 95 70
124 125 f. Lobster 2·25 1·40

HAVE YOU READ THE NOTES AT THE BEGINNING OF THIS CATALOGUE?
These often provide the answers to the enquiries we receive.

38 Book Year Emblem

1972. International Book Year.

125 **38** 40 f. multicoloured 50 40
126 65 f. multicoloured 75 60

39 Farmworkers and Field

1972. Agriculture Day.

127 **39** 10 f. multicoloured 15 10
128 25 f. multicoloured 40 25
129 40 f. multicoloured 75 50

40 Soldiers advancing

1972. 5th Anniv of Independence. Multicoloured.

130 5 f. Type **40** 15 10
131 20 f. Soldier and town 40 25
132 65 f. Vignettes of Yemeni life (vert) 75 60

41 Population Graph

1973. Population Census.

134 **41** 25 f. emerald, red & green 35 20
135 40 f. lt blue, mauve and blue 65 35

42 W.H.O. Emblem within "25" — 43 Taweela Tanks, Aden

1973. 25th Anniv of W.H.O. Multicoloured.

136 5 f. Type **42** 10 10
137 25 f. W.H.O. emblem on globe (horiz) 25 20
138 125 f. "25" and W.H.O. emblem (horiz) 1·50 1·25

1973. Tourism. Multicoloured.

139 20 f. Type **43** 25 15
140 25 f. Shibam Town (horiz) 40 25
141 40 f. Elephant Bay, Aden (horiz) 65 50
142 100 f. Al-Mohdar Mosque, Tarim (horiz) 1·25 95

44 Modern Apartments and Slum Clearance

1973. Nationalization of Buildings (1972). Multicoloured.

143 20 f. Type **44** 25 15
144 80 f. Street scene (vert) 1·00 75

45 Women's Corps on Parade

1973. People's Army. Multicoloured.

145 10 f. Type **45** 15 10
146 20 f. Soldiers marching 25 15
147 40 f. Naval contingent 65 45
148 80 f. Column of tanks 1·50 90

46 Quayside Crane

1973. 10th Anniv of World Food Programme. Multicoloured.

149 20 f. Type **46** 25 10
150 80 f. Granary workers 1·00 75

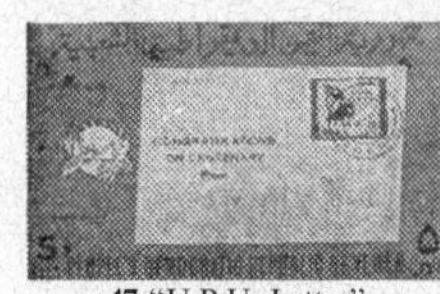

47 "U.P.U. Letter"

1974. Centenary of U.P.U. Multicoloured.

151 5 f. Type **47** 10 10
152 20 f. "100" formed of people and U.P.U. emblems 25 20
153 40 f. U.P.U. emblem and Yemeni flag (vert) 50 35
154 125 f. Map of People's Republic (vert) 1·00 80

48 Irrigation Canal

1974. Agricultural Progress. Multicoloured.

155 10 f. Type **48** 15 15
156 20 f. Bulldozers clearing land 25 15
157 100 f. Tractors with harrows 90 60

49 Lathe Operator — 50

1975. Industrial Progress. Multicoloured.

158 10 f. Type **49** 15 10
159 40 f. Workers in clothing factory 55 40
160 80 f. Women textile workers (horiz) 85 60

1975. Women's Costumes.

161 **50** 5 f. brown and black 15 10
162 – 10 f. violet and black 15 10
163 – 15 f. green and black 20 15
164 – 25 f. purple and black 30 20
165 – 40 f. blue and black 60 45
166 – 50 f. brown and black 90 60

DESIGNS: Nos. 162/6 show different costumes.

51 Women in Factory

1975. International Women's Year.

167 **51** 40 f. black and brown 50 35
168 50 f. black and green 65 50

52

53 Lunar Launch

1976. Yemeni Football.

169 **52** 5 f. multicoloured 10 10
170 – 40 f. multicoloured 50 35
171 – 80 f. multicoloured 95 75

DESIGNS: Nos. 170/1 show footballers in different positions.

1976. Russian Space Exploration. Multicoloured.

172 10 f. Type **53** 10 10
173 15 f. V. A. Shatalov (cosmonaut) 15 10
174 40 f. Luna vehicle (horiz) . . . 65 35
175 65 f. Valentina Tereshkova and rocket . . . . 1·00 60

54 Members of Presidential Council

1977. 1st Anniv of Unification Congress. Multicoloured.

176 25 f. Type **54** 25 15
177 35 f. Text of document 35 30
178 65 f. Girls of People's Militia . 65 45
179 95 f. Aerial view of textile factory 95 55

55 Traffic Policeman and Woman Trainee

1977. Traffic Change to Right.

180 **55** 25 f. black and red 35 25
181 60 f. black and yellow . . . 90 65
182 75 f. black and green . . . 1·25 90
183 110 f. black and blue . . . 2·50 1·40

56 A.P.U. Emblem within Flags of Member States

1977. 25th Anniv of Arab Postal Union.

184 **56** 20 f. multicoloured 25 15
185 60 f. multicoloured 60 50
186 70 f. multicoloured 75 60
187 90 f. multicoloured 90 65

57 Festive Volute

58 Dove of Peace and Flag

1977. Cowries. Multicoloured.

188 60 f. Type **57** 60 25
189 90 f. Pringle's marginella (horiz) 95 35
190 110 f. Clay cone (horiz) . . . 1·25 60
191 180 f. Broderip's cowrie (horiz) 2·25 1·25

1977. 10th Anniv of Independence. Multicoloured.

192 5 f. Type **58** 10 10
193 20 f. Man with broken manacle 15 10
194 90 f. Oil pipeline 50 25
195 110 f. "Pillar of Freedom" . . 80 30

59 Dome of the Rock, Jerusalem

1978. Palestinian Welfare.

196 **59** 5 f. multicoloured 25 10

For smaller design with value at top right, see No. 264.

60 Almarfaa (drum)

1978. Musical Instruments. Multicoloured.

197 35 f. Type **60** 25 10
198 60 f. Almizmar (pipes) . . . 60 25
199 90 f. Alqnboos (fiddle) . . . 1·00 35
200 110 f. Simsimiya (lyre) . . . 1·25 50

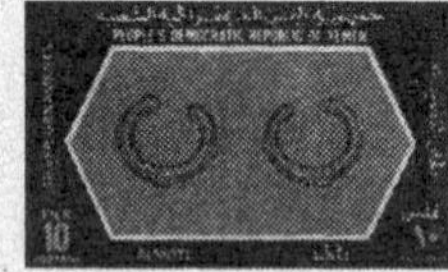
61 Almotl (armbands)

1978. Silver Ornaments. Multicoloured.

201 10 f. Type **61** 10 10
202 15 f. Aloodhad (ring) 15 10
203 20 f. Al Hizam (necklace) . . . 20 10
204 60 f. Alhoogaalah (bangle) . 40 20
205 90 f. Al Muk-Hala (perfume flask) 75 40
206 110 f. Al Janbiya (dagger) . . 95 50

62 Palm Tree Emblem

63 "V" for Vanguard and Cogwheel

1978. 11th World Youth Festival, Cuba. Multicoloured.

207 5 f. Type **62** 10 10
208 60 f. Global emblem 40 20
209 90 f. Flower emblem 60 30
210 110 f. Girl, youth and emblems 85 45

1978. 1st Conference of Vanguard Party.

211 **63** 5 f. multicoloured 10 10
212 20 f. multicoloured 15 10
213 60 f. multicoloured 25 25
214 180 f. multicoloured . . . 90 50

64 Calligraphic Emblem, Symbols of Peace and Freedom

1978. 15th Anniv of 14 October Revolution. Mult.

215 10 f. Type **64** 10 10
216 35 f. Emblems of growth (vert) 20 10
217 60 f. Candle and figure "15" (vert) 35 20
218 110 f. Revolutionaries and figure "15" (vert) 65 50

65 Map of Yemen, Child with Olive-branch and Dove

66 "Agricultural Progress"

1979. International Year of the Child.

219 **65** 15 f. multicoloured 15 10
220 20 f. multicoloured 15 10
221 60 f. multicoloured 35 15
222 90 f. multicoloured 65 40

1979. 10th Anniv of "Corrective Move" in Revolutionary Government. Multicoloured.

223 20 f. Type **66** 10 10
224 35 f. "Industrial Progress" . . 15 10
225 60 f. Students 35 15
226 90 f. Woman with star and doves 60 40

67 Sir Rowland Hill and Yemeni Costume Stamp of 1970

1979. Death Cent of Sir Rowland Hill. Mult.

227 90 f. Type **67** 20 15
228 110 f. Yemeni camel stamp of 1970 . . . . 35 20

68 World Map, Koran and Symbols of Arab Achievements

1979. The Arabs.

230 **68** 60 f. multicoloured 45 20

69 Emblem of Yemeni Socialist Party

70 "Cassia adenensis"

1979. 1st Anniv of Yemeni Socialist Party.

231 **69** 60 f. multicoloured 45 20

1979. Flowers (1st series). Multicoloured.

232 20 f. Type **70** 10 10
233 90 f. "Nerium oleander" . . . 50 40
234 110 f. "Calligonum comosum" 95 45
235 180 f. "Adenium obesum" . . 1·25 65

See also Nos. 265/8.

71 Ayatollah Khomeini and Crowd

73 Woman Basket-making

72 "Dido"

1980. 1st Anniv of Iranian Revolution.

236 **71** 60 f. multicoloured 90 75

1980. Screw Steamers. Multicoloured.

237 110 f. Type **72** 65 50
238 180 f. "Anglia" . . . . 1·00 95
239 250 f. "India" . . . . 1·50 1·25

1980. "London 1980". Handicrafts. Mult.

240 60 f. Type **73** 35 20
241 90 f. Making a hubble-bubble pipe 50 25
242 110 f. Man at loom 70 40
243 250 f. Boy making clay pot . 1·25 75

74 Skink

1980. Reptiles. Multicoloured.

244 20 f. Type **74** 20 10
245 35 f. Mole viper 25 15
246 110 f. Gecko . . . . 1·00 40
247 180 f. Cobra . . . . 1·60 65

75 Misha the Bear (Olympic Mascot)

77 Lenin

76 Farming

1980. Olympic Games, Moscow.

248 **75** 110 f. multicoloured . . . 65 30

1980. 10th Anniv of Peasants' Uprising. Multicoloured.

249 50 f. Type **76** 30 15
250 90 f. Peasants 45 25
251 110 f. Corn sickle and fist . . 65 30

1980. 110th Birth Anniv of Lenin.

252 **77** 35 f. multicoloured 25 15

78 Douglas DC-3

1981. Democratic Yemen Airlines. Multicoloured.

253 60 f. Type **78** 50 35
254 90 f. Boeing 707 . . . . 95 55
255 250 f. De Havilland D.H.C.7 Dash Seven . . . . 2·10 1·25

79 Map, Dish Aerial and Satellite

80 "Conocarpus lancifolius"

1981. Ras Boradli Satellite Station.

256 **79** 60 f. multicoloured 60 25

1981. Trees. Multicoloured.

257 90 f. Type **80** 60 25
258 180 f. "Ficus vasta" . . . . . 1·25 65
259 250 f. "Maerua crassifolia" . 1·90 1·00

81 Council Building, Citizens and Flag

1981. 10th Anniv of Supreme People's Council.
260 **81** 180 f. multicoloured . . . . 1·10 50

82 Sand Fox

1981. Wildlife Conservation. Multicoloured.
261 50 f. Type **82** 25 20
262 90 f. Leopard 70 40
263 250 f. Ibex . . . . 1·25 1·00

1981. Palestinian Welfare. As T **59**, but smaller, 25 × 27 mm, and value at top right.
264 5 f. multicoloured 25 10

1981. Flowers (2nd series). As T **70**. Mult.
265 50 f. "Tephrosia apollinea" . . 40 25
266 90 f. "Citrullus colocynthis" . . 75 40
267 110 f. "Aloe squarrosa" . . . 1·10 40
268 250 f. "Lawsonia inermis" . . 2·25 1·25

83 Blind People Basket-weaving and Typing

1982. International Year of Disabled Persons.
269 **83** 50 f. multicoloured 15 10
270 100 f. multicoloured . . . 35 20
271 150 f. multicoloured . . . 50 40

84 Microscope Slides and Lungs

1982. Centenary of Discovery of Tubercle Bacillus.
272 **84** 50 f. black, orange and red 65 25

85 A.P.U. Emblem and Map within Heart

1982. 30th Anniv of Arab Postal Union.
273 **85** 100 f. red, black and blue . 90 40

86 Footballers

1982. World Cup Football Championship, Spain. Multicoloured.
274 50 f. Type **86** 40 25
275 100 f. Match scene 75 50
276 150 f. Players and shield . . . 1·25 75
277 200 f. Player and flags . . . . 1·75 1·00

87 Emblems and Flags of Russia and Yemen

1982. 60th Anniv of U.S.S.R.
279 **87** 50 f. multicoloured 40 20

1982. World Cup Football Championship Result. Nos. 274/7 optd **WORLD CUP WINNERS 1982 1st ITALY 2nd W-GERMANY 3rd POLAND 4th FRANCE** and player holding trophy.
280 50 f. Type **86** 40 25
281 100 f. Match scene 75 55
282 150 f. Players and shield . . . 1·25 90
283 200 f. Player and flags . . . 1·75 1·10

89 Yasser Arafat

1983. Palestinian Solidarity. Multicoloured.
285 50 f. Type **89** 65 40
286 100 f. Yasser Arafat and Dome of the Rock . . . . 1·40 55

1983. "Tembal 83" Stamp Exhibition, Basel. No. 248 optd **TEMBAL 83 MAY 21st-29th, 1983** and emblem.
288 **75** 110 f. multicoloured . . . 3·25 1·25

91 Man with Letter, Postal Barge and Postman

1983. World Communications Year.
289 **91** 50 f. black and blue . . . 50 35
290 – 100 f. black and red . . . 1·00 45
291 – 150 f. black, green and olive 1·60 75
292 – 200 f. multicoloured . . . 1·90 80
DESIGNS: 100 f. Postman, stage coach and morse code equipment; 150 f. Motor coach and telephones; 200 f. Transmitter, airplane, satellite, television, envelope and dish aerial.

92 "The Poor Family"

1983. 10th Death Anniv of Picasso (artist). Multicoloured.
294 50 f. Type **92** 60 35
295 100 f. "Woman with Crow" . . 1·00 70

93 Show Jumping

1983. Olympic Games, Los Angeles (1st issue). Equestrian Events. Multicoloured.
297 25 f. Type **93** 65 65
298 50 f. Show jumping (different) 1·10 50
299 100 f. Horse crossing water (Three-day event) . . . . . 1·75 1·00
See also Nos. 316/18.

94 "P 8" Steam Locomotive, 1905

1983. Railway Locomotives. Multicoloured.
301 25 f. Type **94** 75 25
302 50 f. Class "880" steam locomotive, 1915 . . . . . 1·25 55
303 100 f. Class "Gt 2 × 4/4" locomotive, 1923 . . . . . 2·10 1·10

95 Liner "Europa"

1983. Ships. Multicoloured.
305 50 f. Type **95** 80 50
306 100 f. Liner "World Discoverer" 1·75 90

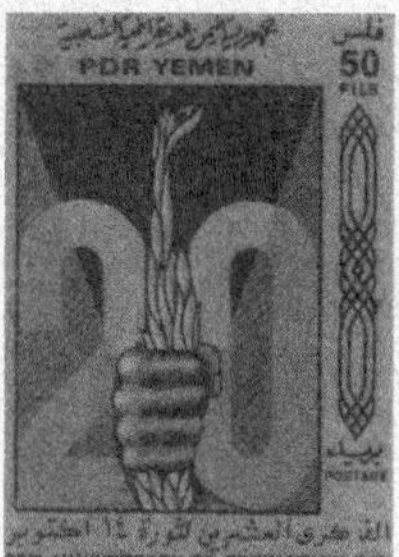

96 "20" and Hand holding Sheaf of Corn

1983. 20th Anniv of Revolution. Multicoloured.
308 50 f. Type **96** 65 35
309 100 f. Flag, man with gun and "XX" . . . . 1·40 65

97 Pierre Testu-Brissy's Balloon, 1798

1983. Bicentenary of Manned Flight. Mult.
310 50 f. Type **97** 50 25
311 100 f. Unmanned Montgolfier balloon, 1783 . . . . 1·10 50

98 Skiing

1983. Winter Olympic Games, Sarajevo. Multicoloured.
313 50 f. Type **98** 65 35
314 100 f. Bobsleigh . . . . 1·00 50

99 Fencing

1984. Olympic Games, Los Angeles (2nd issue). Multicoloured.
316 25 f. Type **99** 25 15
317 50 f. Fencing (different) . . . 50 25
318 100 f. Fencing (different) . . . 85 50

100 "Soyuz 10"–"Salyut 1" Link-up, 1971

1984. Space. Multicoloured.
320 15 f. Type **100** 15 15
321 20 f. "Apollo 8" and Moon, 1968 20 15
322 50 f. "Apollo 11" and first man on Moon, 1969 . . . . . . 50 35
323 100 f. "Soyuz"–"Apollo" link-up, 1975 . . . . 85 65

1984. Nos. 83 and 84b surch.
325 **25** 50 f. on 65 f. multicoloured 65 40
326 – 100 f. on 110 f. multicoloured 1·40 65

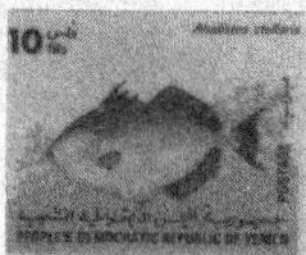

102 "Abalistes stellaris"

1984. Fishes. Multicoloured.
327 10 f. Type **102** 10 10
328 15 f. "Caranx speciocus" . . 10 10
329 20 f. "Pomadasys maculatus" 10 10
330 35 f. "Chaetodon fasciatus" . 15 10
331 35 f. Imperial angelfish . . . 25 10
332 50 f. "Rastrelliger kanagurta" 35 15
333 100 f. Wavyback skipjack . . 70 25
334 150 f. Longfin butterfly fish . 1·10 50
335 200 f. Blue moon angelfish . . 1·60 65
336 250 f. "Pterois russelli" . . . 2·00 1·10
337 400 f. "Argyrops spinifer" . . 3·25 1·60
338 500 f. "Dasyatis uarnak" . . . 4·00 2·00
339 1 d. "Epinephelus chlorostigma" 8·75 4·75
340 2 d. "Drepane longimana" . . 18·00 9·50

1984. Olympic Winners, Sarajevo. No. 314 optd **WINNERS B Lehmann-B. Musiol (DDR)**.
341 100 f. multicoloured . . . . . 5·00 4·25

104 Women writing **105** Victory Parade, Red Square

1985. National Literacy Campaign. Mult.
343 50 f. Type **104** 95 50
344 100 f. Pen held in manacled fist 1·90 75

1985. 40th Anniv of End of Second World War.
345 **105** 100 f. multicoloured . . . . 1·00 40

106 Flag within Emblem **107** Modern Buildings

1985. 12th World Youth and Students' Festival, Moscow. Multicoloured.
346 50 f. Type **106** 95 50
347 100 f. Hand holding emblem as placard . . . . 1·90 75

1985. U.N.E.S.C.O. World Heritage Site. Shibam City. Multicoloured.
348 50 f. Type **107** 95 60
349 50 f. View of city 95 60
350 100 f. Screen . . . . 1·90 95
351 100 f. Gate (vert) . . . . 1·90 95

108 Industrial Symbols **109** Mother feeding Child

1985. Third Yemeni Socialist Party General Congress. Multicoloured.
352 25 f. Type **108** 50 25
353 50 f. Crane loading ship . . . 75 40
354 100 f. Combine harvesters . . 1·60 70

1985. U.N.I.C.E.F. Child Survival Campaign. Multicoloured.
355 50 f. Type **109** 95 60
356 50 f. Immunization 95 60
357 100 f. Breastfeeding . . . . . 1·90 95
358 100 f. Oral rehydration therapy 1·90 95

110 Wheat and Al-Mohdar Mosque, Tarim — **111** Lenin addressing Crowd in Red Square

1986. World Food Day. 40th Anniv (1985) of F.A.O. Multicoloured.

No.	Description		
359	20 f. Type **110**	60	20
360	180 f. Palm trees	2·50	1·10

1986. 27th Russian Communist Party Congress. Multicoloured.

No.	Description		
361	**111** 75 f. multicoloured	95	45
362	250 f. multicoloured	2·50	1·25

112 Bride in Yashmak

113 Ali Ahmed N. Antar

1986. Brides and Bridegrooms of Yemen. Mult.

No.	Description		
363	50 f. Type **112**	60	25
364	50 f. Bride with striped shawl	60	25
365	50 f. Bride with long dressed hair	60	25
366	100 f. Bridegroom in modern jacket with knife	1·25	50
367	100 f. Bridegroom in traditional clothes with gun	1·25	50
368	100 f. Bride in modern dress	1·25	50

1986. "Party and Homeland Martyrs". Mult.

No.	Description		
369	75 f. Type **113**	65	35
370	75 f. Saleh Musleh Kasim	65	35
371	75 f. Ali Shayaa Hadi	65	35
372	75 f. Abdul Fattah Ismail	65	35

114 Immunizing Pregnant Woman against Tetanus

1987. U.N.I.C.E.F. Immunization Campaign. Multicoloured.

No.	Description		
373	20 f. Type **114**	25	10
374	75 f. Immunizing baby	75	40
375	140 f. Nurse giving oral poliomyelitis vaccine to baby	1·25	65
376	150 f. Pregnant woman and children carrying syringes	1·50	75

115 Party Emblem and Worker

116 Lenin and Soldier

1987. Yemeni Socialist Party General Conference.

No.	Description		
377	**115** 75 f. multicoloured	65	25
378	150 f. multicoloured	1·25	65

1987. 70th Anniv of Russian October Revolution.

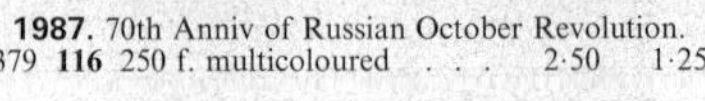

No.	Description		
379	**116** 250 f. multicoloured	2·50	1·25

117 Steps to King's Court

1987. Shabwa Remains. Multicoloured.

No.	Description		
380	25 f. Type **117**	25	10
381	75 f. Royal Palace	70	35
382	140 f. Winged lion, King's Court (vert)	1·25	65
383	150 f. Inscribed bronze plaque (vert)	1·60	75

118 Students and College Buildings

1987. 20th Anniv of Independence. Mult.

No.	Description		
384	25 f. Type **118**	25	10
385	75 f. Family and housing	75	35
386	140 f. Workers, oil derrick and power station	1·40	65
387	150 f. Party headquarters and members	1·40	65

119 Tank and Liberty Monument, Sana'a

1988. 25th Anniv (1987) of 26th September Revolution in Yemen.

No.	Description		
388	**119** 75 f. multicoloured	65	25

120 Tap, Boy and Rainbow (safe water)

121 Weightlifting

1988. World Health Day. 40th Anniv of W.H.O. Multicoloured.

No.	Description		
389	40 f. Type **120**	30	20
390	75 f. Child with globe as head breaking cigarette (No Smoking day)	60	30
391	140 f. Nurse immunizing baby (immunization campaign)	1·25	50
392	250 f. Red Crescent worker instructing group (Health for all)	1·90	90

1988. Olympic Games, Seoul. Multicoloured.

No.	Description		
393	40 f. Type **121**	35	20
394	75 f. Running	65	35
395	140 f. Boxing	1·25	70
396	150 f. Football	1·50	95

122 Crowd and Flag

123 Yellow-bellied Green Pigeon

1988. 25th Anniv of 14 October Revolution.

No.	Description		
397	**122** 25 f. black and red	25	15
398	– 75 f. multicoloured	70	30
399	– 300 f. multicoloured	2·50	1·25

DESIGNS—HORIZ: 75 f. Radfan mountains and revolutionary. VERT: 300 f. Anniversary emblem.

1988. Birds. Multicoloured.

No.	Description		
400	40 f. Type **123**	40	20
401	50 f. Lilac-breasted roller (vert)	60	40
402	75 f. Hoopoe (vert)	90	50
403	250 f. Houbara bustard	2·50	1·40

124 Incense Burner

125 Shipping entering Old Harbour

1988. Traditional Crafts. Multicoloured.

No.	Description		
404	25 f. Type **124**	20	20
405	70 f. Mashjub (rack used when impregnating dresses with incense)	70	30
406	150 f. Cosmetic basket made of palm fibre with cowrie shell decoration	1·25	80
407	250 f. Woman making palm fibre basket	2·25	1·25

1988. Centenary of Port of Aden. Mult.

No.	Description		
408	75 f. Type **125**	95	40
409	300 f. Section of new harbour project	2·75	1·40

126 Old City

1988. International Campaign for Preservation of Old Sana'a. Multicoloured.

No.	Description		
410	75 f. Type **126**	65	50
411	250 f. City (different)	2·25	1·00

127 Sand Cat Kitten

1989. Endangered Animals. Multicoloured.

No.	Description		
412	20 f. Type **127**	20	10
413	25 f. Adult sand cat	20	10
414	50 f. Fennec fox cub	40	20
415	75 f. Adult fennec fox	50	25

128 Symbols of War in Star

129 Ismail

1989. 20th Anniv of "Corrective Move" in Revolutionary Government. Multicoloured.

No.	Description		
416	25 f. Type **128**	20	10
417	35 f. Industrial symbols in hook	25	15
418	40 f. Agricultural symbols	35	15

1989. 50th Birth Anniv of Adbul Fattah Ismail (founder of People's Socialist Party).

No.	Description		
419	**129** 75 f. multicoloured	50	25
420	150 f. multicoloured	1·00	50

130 "Children at Play" (Abeer Anwer)

131 Sana'a and Fighters

1989. 15th Anniv of Ali Anter Pioneer Organization. Multicoloured.

No.	Description		
421	10 f. Type **130**	10	10
422	25 f. Girl pioneer	20	10
423	75 f. Pioneers parading at Khormaksar (horiz)	50	40

1989. 22nd Anniv of Siege of Sana'a.

No.	Description		
424	**131** 150 f. multicoloured	1·25	65

132 Taj Mahal and Nehru — **133** Coffee Plant

1989. Birth Centenary of Jawaharal Nehru (Indian statesman).

No.	Description		
425	**132** 250 f. black and brown	1·90	90

1989. Centenary of Interparliamentary Union.

No.	Description		
426	**133** 300 f. multicoloured	2·50	1·25

134 Seera Rock, Aden, Birds and Arc de Triomphe, Paris

1989. Bicentenary of French Revolution.

No.	Description		
427	**134** 250 f. multicoloured	2·25	1·25

135 U.S.A. v Belgium (Uruguay, 1930)

1990. World Cup Football Championship, Italy. Matches from previous championships. Mult.

No.	Description		
428	5 f. Type **135**	10	10
429	10 f. Switzerland v Netherlands (Italy, 1934)	10	10
430	20 f. Italy v France (France, 1938)	15	10
431	35 f. Sweden v Spain (Brazil, 1950)	20	10
432	50 f. West Germany v Austria (Switzerland, 1954)	30	15
433	60 f. Brazil v England (Sweden, 1958)	40	20
434	500 f. U.S.S.R. v Uruguay (Chile, 1962)	2·75	1·00

YEMEN REPUBLIC (combined)

Pt. 19

A draft joint constitution was ratified by the parliaments of Yemen Arab Republic and the Yemen People's Democratic Republic on 21 May 1990 and the unification of the two countries was declared the following day.

The currencies of both the previous republics have legal validity throughout Yemen.

100 fils = 1 rial (North Yemen)
1000 fils = 1 dinar (South Yemen)

1 Scouts supporting Globe

1990. 60th Anniv of Arab Scout Movement. Multicoloured.

No.	Description		
1	300 f. Type **1**	1·00	50
2	375 f. Type **1**	1·25	60
3	850 f. Oil derrick, scouts with flag, anniversary emblem and tower	2·75	1·25
4	900 f. As No. 3	3·00	1·50

Nos. 1/4 are inscribed "YEMEN ARAB REPUBLIC".

2 Pintail — **3** City Rooftops

1990. Ducks. Multicoloured.

No.	Description		
6	10 f. Type **2**	10	10
7	20 f. European wigeon	10	10
8	25 f. Ruddy shelduck	15	10
9	40 f. Gadwall	20	10
10	75 f. Common shelduck	35	15
11	150 f. Common shoveler pair	75	30
12	600 f. Green-winged teal	3·00	1·25

1990. 40th Anniv of U.N. Development Programme.

No.	Description		
14	**3** 150 f. multicoloured	75	35

4 "Dirphia multicolor"

5 Protembolotherium

1990. Moths and Butterflies. Multicoloured.

15 5 f. Type **4** 10 10
16 20 f. "Automeris io" 10 10
17 25 f. Swallowtail 15 10
18 40 f. Bhutan glory 20 10
19 55 f. Silver king shoemaker 25 10
20 75 f. Tiger moth 35 15
21 700 f. "Attacus edwardsii" (moth) 3·50 1·40

1990. Prehistoric Animals. Multicoloured.

23 5 f. Type **5** 10 10
24 10 f. Diatryma 10 10
25 35 f. Mammoth (horiz) 15 10
26 40 f. Edaphosaurus (horiz) 15 10
27 55 f. Dimorphodon (horiz) 25 10
28 75 f. Phororhacos (horiz) 35 15
29 700 f. Ichthyosaurus (wrongly inscr "Ichtyosaurus") 3·75 1·50

6 Abyssinian Kitten **7** "Boletus aestivalis"

1990. Cats. Multicoloured.

31 5 f. Type **6** 10 10
32 15 f. Blue longhair 10 10
33 35 f. Siamese 15 10
34 55 f. Burmese 30 15
35 60 f. Sealpoint colourpoint 30 15
36 150 f. Red British shorthair 80 30
37 600 f. Leopard cat 3·00 1·25

1991. Fungi. Multicoloured.

39 50 f. Type **7** 40 15
40 60 f. Butter mushroom 50 15
41 80 f. Beefsteak morel 55 20
42 100 f. Brown birch bolete 80 25
43 130 f. Fly agaric 1·00 35
44 200 f. Flaky-stemmed witches' mushroom 1·60 55
45 300 f. Red cap 2·40 80

8 State Arms **9** Shaking Hands

1991. 1st Anniv of Yemen Republic. Mult.

47 300 f. Type **8** 60 25
48 375 f. Type **8** 75 30
49 850 f. Hand holding flag, map and sun 1·60 65
50 900 f. As No. 49 1·75 70

1991. Signing of Unity Agreement (in November 1989) Commemoration. Multicoloured.

52 225 f. Type **9** 45 15
53 300 f. Hand holding flag over map 60 25
54 375 f. As No. 53 75 30
55 650 f. Type **9** 1·25 50
56 850 f. As No. 53 1·60 65

10 Cigarettes and Skull on Globe

1991. World Anti-smoking Day. Multicoloured.

58 225 f. Type **10** 45 15
59 300 f. Skull smoking and man 60 25
60 375 f. As No. 59 75 30
61 650 f. Type **10** 1·25 50
62 850 f. As No. 59 1·60 65

11 Emblem

1991. 45th Anniv of U.N.O.

64 **11** 5 r. multicoloured 1·00 40
65 8 r. multicoloured 1·60 65
66 10 r. multicoloured 2·00 80
67 12 r. multicoloured 2·40 95

1993. Various stamps surch. (a) Stamps of Yemen Arab Republic. (i) Postage.

69 **94** 5 r. on 75 f. multicoloured 85 35
70 **144** 8 r. on 425 f. multicoloured 1·40 55
71 **150** 8 r. on 425 f. multicoloured 1·40 55
72 – 10 r. on 900 f. mult (No. 830) 1·75 70
73 – 10 r. on 900 f. mult (No. 834) 1·75 70
74 – 10 r. on 900 f. mult (No. 838) 1·75 70
75 – 10 r. on 900 f. mult (No. 843) 1·75 70
76 **157** 10 r. on 900 f. multicoloured 1·75 70
77 – 10 r. on 900 f. mult (No. 853) 1·75 70
78 **159** 10 r. on 900 f. multicoloured 1·75 70
79 – 10 r. on 900 f. mult (No. 863) 1·75 70
80 – 12 r. on 850 f. mult (No. 829) 2·00 80
81 – 12 r. on 850 f. mult (No. 833) 2·00 80
82 – 12 r. on 850 f. mult (No. 837) 2·00 80
83 – 12 r. on 850 f. mult (No. 842) 2·00 80
84 **157** 12 r. on 850 f. multicoloured 2·00 80
85 – 12 r. on 850 f. mult (No. 852) 2·00 80
86 **159** 12 r. on 850 f. multicoloured 2·00 80

(ii) Air. Additionally optd **AIR MAIL** (except for No. 87).

87 **118** 3 r. on 125 f. multicoloured 60 25
88 – 3 r. on 125 f. mult (No. 672) 60 25
89 – 3 r. on 125 f. mult (No. 679) 60 25
90 – 3 r. on 125 f. mult (No. 686) 60 25
91 – 3 r. on 125 f. mult (No. 700) 60 25
92 – 3 r. on 125 f. mult (No. 707) 60 25
93 – 5 r. on 75 f. mult (No. 670) 85 35
94 – 5 r. on 75 f. mult (No. 677) 85 35
95 – 5 r. on 75 f. mult (No. 684) 80 35
96 – 5 r. on 75 f. mult (No. 691) 80 35
97 – 5 r. on 75 f. mult (No. 698) 80 35
98 – 5 r. on 75 f. mult (No. 705) 80 35
99 **145** 8 r. on 425 f. multicoloured 1·40 55
100 – 8 r. on 425 f. mult (No. 796) 1·40 55
101 **147** 8 r. on 425 f. multicoloured 1·40 55
102 – 8 r. on 425 f. mult (No. 803) 1·40 55
103 – 8 r. on 425 f. mult (No. 812) 1·40 55
104 **151** 8 r. on 425 f. multicoloured 1·40 55
105 **152** 8 r. on 425 f. multicoloured 1·40 55
106 – 12 r. on 850 f. mult (No. 862) 2·00 80

(b) Stamps of Yemen Republic (combined).

107 – 10 r. on 900 f. mult (No. 4) 1·75 70
108 – 10 r. on 900 f. mult (No. 50) 1·75 70
109 – 12 r. on 850 f. mult (No. 3) 2·00 80
110 – 12 r. on 850 f. mult (No. 49) 2·00 80
111 – 12 r. on 850 f. mult (No. 56) 2·00 80
112 – 12 r. on 850 f. mult (No. 62) 2·00 80
113 – 50 r. on 150 f. mult (No. 11) 10·50 4·25
114 **3** 50 r. on 150 f. multicoloured 10·50 4·25
115 **10** 50 r. on 225 f. multicoloured
116 **8** 50 r. on 375 f. multicoloured 10·50 4·25
117 – 50 r. on 375 f. mult (No. 54) 10·50 4·25
118 – 50 r. on 375 f. mult (No. 60) 10·50 4·25
119 **8** 100 r. on 300 f. mult 21·00 8·25
120 – 100 r. on 300 f. mult (No. 53)
121 – 100 r. on 300 f. mult (No. 59)

(c) Stamps of Yemen People's Democratic Republic. (i) In Western and Arabic figures.

122 – 8 r. on 110 f. mult (No. 84b) 1.50 60
123 – 8 r. on 110 f. mult (No. 200) 1·50 60
124 – 8 r. on 110 f. mult (No. 206) 1·50 60
125 – 8 r. on 110 f. mult (No. 218) 1·50 60
126 – 8 r. on 110 f. mult (No. 234) 1·50 60
127 **72** 8 r. on 110 f. multicoloured 1·50 60
128 – 8 r. on 110 f. mult (No. 246) 1·50 60
129 – 8 r. on 110 f. mult (No. 267) 1·50 60
130 – 50 r. on 500 f. multicoloured (No. 434)
131 **133** 100 r. on 300 f. mult 21·00 8·25
132 – 100 r. on 2 d. mult (No. 340) 21·00 8·25
133 **25** 200 r. on 5 f. multicoloured 42·00 17·00
134 **135** 200 r. on 5 f. multicoloured
135 **127** 200 r. on 20 f. multicoloured 42·00 17·00
136 – 200 r. on 20 f. mult (No. 430)
137 – 200 r. on 75 f. mult (No. 423) 42·00 17·00
138 **132** 200 r. on 250 f. black and brown 42·00 17·00

(ii) Surch **R.** and Arabic figures.

139 **100** 200 r. on 15 f. multicoloured 42·00 17·00
140 – 200 r. on 15 f. mult (No. 328) 42·00 17·00
141 – 200 r. on 20 f. mult (No. 321) 42·00 17·00
142 – 200 r. on 20 f. mult (No. 329) 42·00 17·00

15 Sana'a **16** Player dribbling Ball

1994. 4th Anniv of Yemen Republic.

143 – 3 r. multicoloured 55 25
144 – 5 r. multicoloured 95 40
145 **15** 8 r. multicoloured 1·50 60
146 – 20 r. multicoloured 3·75 1·50

DESIGNS: Nos. 143/4, 146, Different views of the principal building in Type **15**.

1994. World Cup Football Championship, U.S.A. Multicoloured.

148 2 r. Type **16** 40 15
149 6 r. Dribbling (different) 1·10 45
150 10 r. Goalkeeper catching ball (horiz) 1·90 75
151 12 r. Player heading ball 2·25 90

17 Arabian Leopard **18** Hand holding Seedling

1995. World Environmental Protection Day. Multicoloured.

153 15 r. Type **17** 40 15
154 20 r. Caracal lynx 55 25
155 30 r. Guineafowl (horiz) 80 35

1995. 50th Anniv of F.A.O. Multicoloured.

157 10 r. Type **18** 25 10
158 25 r. Hand holding seeds 65 30
159 30 r. Hand holding fish 80 35

19 Old Sana'a **20** Kashmim

1995. 50th Anniv of U.N.O. Multicoloured.

161 10 r. Type **19** 25 10
162 20 r. Different viewpoint of scene on 10 r 55 25
163 25 r. Rampart walk (horiz) 65 30

1995. Naseem Hamed Kashmim (boxer). Mult.

165 10 r. Kashmim with Lonsdale Belt 25 10
166 20 r. Type **20** 55 25
167 25 r. Scene from boxing match (horiz) 65 30
168 30 r. Kashmim raising arm in triumph 80 35

22 Wrestling **23** Popular Heritage Museum, Seiyoan

1996. Olympic Games, Atlanta, U.S.A. Multicoloured.

171 20 r. Type **22** 20 10
172 50 r. High jumping (horiz) 50 20
173 60 r. Running 60 25
174 70 r. Gymnastics 65 30
175 100 r. Judo 95 40

1996. Heritage Sites. Multicoloured.

177 10 r. Type **23** 10 10
178 15 r. Rock Palace, Wadi Dhahr (vert) 15 10
179 20 r. Old Sana'a city 20 10
180 30 r. Al-Mohdhar minaret, Tarim (vert) 30 15
181 40 r. As 15 r. 40 20
182 50 r. As 30 r. 50 20
183 60 r. As 15 r. 60 25
184 70 r. As 10 r. 65 30
185 100 r. As 20 r. 95 40
186 150 r. As 30 r. 1·40 60
187 200 r. As 20 r. 1·90 80
188 250 r. As 10 r. 2·40 1·00
189 300 r. As 30 r. 3·00 1·25
190 500 r. As 15 r. 4·75 1·90

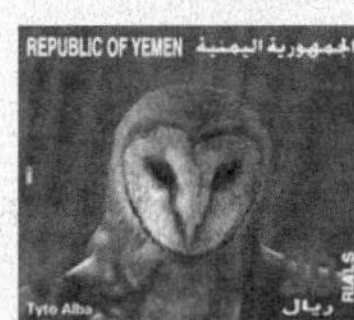

24 Barn Owl

1996. Birds. Multicoloured.

191 20 r. Type **24** 20 10
192 50 r. Philby's rock partridge 50 20
193 60 r. Lammergeier 60 25
194 70 r. Arabian chukar 65 30
195 100 r. Houbara bustard 95 40

25 "Parodia maasii" **26** Girls reading

1996. Multicoloured. (a) Rare Plants.

197 20 r. Type **25** 20 10
198 50 r. "Notocatus cristata" 50 20
199 60 r. "Adenium obesum socotranum" 60 25
200 70 r. Dragon's blood tree 65 30
201 100 r. "Mammillaria erythrosperma" 95 40

(b) Fishes.

203 20 r. Pennant coral-fish 20 10
204 50 r. Maori wrasse 50 20
205 60 r. Tang 60 25
206 70 r. Imperial butterfly fish 65 30
207 100 r. Angelfish 95 40

1996. 50th Anniv of U.N.I.C.E.F. Multicoloured.

209 20 r. Type **26** 20 10
210 50 r. Girls playing 50 20
211 60 r. Mother and child 60 25
212 70 r. Mother with three children 65 30

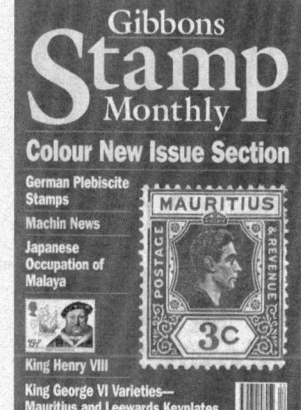

YUGOSLAVIA Pt. 3

The kingdom of the Serbs, Croats and Slovenes, in S.E. Europe, established after the 1914-18 war and comprising Serbia, Montenegro, Bosnia, Herzegovina and parts of pre-war Hungary.

From 1945 it was a Federal Republic comprising six republics. In 1991 four of these republics seceded, from when the Federation consisted of the Republics of Montenegro and Serbia and the two autonomous provinces of Kosovo and Vojvodina.

A. KINGDOM OF THE SERBS, CROATS AND SLOVENES

I. ISSUES FOR BOSNIA AND HERZEGOVINA

100 heller = 1 kruna

1918. 1910 commem stamps of Bosnia (with date labels) optd **DRZAVA S.H.S. 1918 1918 Bosna i Hercegovina** or the same in Cyrillic characters or surch also.

1 3 h. olive (No. 345) . . . . . . 50 1·00
2 5 h. green 30 45
3 10 h. red 30 45
4 20 h. sepia 30 45
5 25 h. blue 30 45
6 30 h. green 30 45
7 40 h. orange 30 45
8 45 h. red 30 45
9 50 h. purple 20 25
10 60 h. on 50 h. purple 15 25
11 80 h. on 6 h. brown 10 75
12 90 h. on 35 h. green 10 20
13 2 k. green 20 50
14 3 k. on 3 h. olive . . . . 1·50 1·00
15 4 k. on 1 k. lake . . . . 3·00 3·00
16 10 k. on 2 h. violet . . . . . . 7·50 3·75

1918. Newspaper Express stamps of Bosnia. 5 h. optd as last and **HELERA** and 2 h. the same but in Cyrillic.

17 N **35** 2 h. red . . . . 2·50 4·00
18 5 h. green . . . . 1·75 2·00

These were issued for use as ordinary postage stamps.

1918 Bosnian War Invalids Fund stamps optd **DRAVA S.H.S. Bosna Hercegovina** or the same in Cyrillic characters.

19 **31** 5 h. (+2 h.) green £130 £160
20 – 10 h. (+2 h.) red . . . . . 85·00 £140
21 – 10 h. (+2 h.) blue . . . . . 75 3·75
22 **31** 15 h. (+2 h.) brown . . . . 1·25 3·25

6a

(7)

1918. Newspaper stamps of Bosnia of 1913 (as T **6a**) surch. Imperf.

50 **6a** 2 on 6 h. mauve £120 £150
51 2 on 10 h. red . . . . 60·00 90·00
52 2 on 20 h. green . . . . . . 7·50 15·00
23 3 on 2 h. blue 10 20
24 5 on 6 h. mauve 10 20

Most of these were used for ordinary postage purposes.

1919. Perf.

25 **6a** 2 h. blue 10 25
26 6 h. mauve . . . . 75 1·25
27 10 h. red 25 25
28 20 h. green 20 25

The above were issued for use as ordinary postage stamps.

These stamps imperforate were issued as Newspaper stamps for Bosnia q.v.

1919. Types of Bosnia optd with T **7** or similar type with wording **KRALJEVSTVO S.H.S.**, or surch also.

29 **25** 3 h. lake . . . . 10 1·10
30 5 h. green 10 10
31 10 on 6 h. black 10 10
32 **26** 20 on 35 h. green 10 15
33 **25** 25 h. blue 10 15
34 30 h. red 75 25
35 **26** 45 h. brown 10 25
36 **33** 45 on 80 h. brown 10 10
37 **26** 50 h. blue . . . . 40·00 50·00
38 50 h. on 72 h. blue 10 10
39 60 h. purple 10 25
40 **33** 80 h. brown 10 25
41 90 h. purple 10 25
42 – 2 k. green (No. 200) 15 25
43 **26** 3 k. red on green 25 50
44 **34** 4 k. red on green . . . . . 1·00 1·50
45 **26** 5 k. lilac on grey . . . . . 2·40 1·75
46 **34** 10 k. violet on grey . . . . . 2·40 3·00

1919. War Victims' Fund. Stamps of Bosnia of 1906 surch **KRALJEVSTVO Srba. Hrvata i Slovenaca** or same in Cyrillic characters and new value.

47 – 10 x. + 10 x. on 40 h. orange (No. 196) . . . . 1·25 2·25
48 – 20 x. + 10 x. on 20 h. sepia (No. 192) . . . . 65 1·50
49 **5** 45 x. + 15 x. on 1 k. lake . . . 3·75 6·00

II. ISSUES FOR CROATIA

100 filir (heller) = 1 kruna (krone)

The provisional issues on Hungarian stamps were sold in Yugoslavia "heller" and "krone" currency, but as this is not expressed on the stamps (except for Nos. 69/73) we have retained the Hungarian descriptions to facilitate reference to the original stamps.

1918. Various issues of Hungary optd **HRVATSKA SHS** and bar or wheel.

"Turul" issue of 1900.

53 **7** 6 f. olive . . . . 75 1·25
54 50 f. lake on blue . . . . . 1·00 1·90

"Harvesters" and "Parliament" issues of 1916.

55 **18** 2 f. brown 10 15
56 3 f. red 10 10
57 5 f. green 10 10
58 6 f. green 10 10
59 10 f. red . . . . 6·00 4·50
60 15 f. violet (No. 244) . . . 45·00 60·00
61 15 f. violet (No. 251) . . . 10 10
62 20 f. brown 10 10
63 25 f. blue 10 20
64 35 f. brown 10 10
65 40 f. olive 15 30
66 **19** 50 f. purple 10 10
67 75 f. blue 10 10
68 80 f. green 10 20
69 1 k. lake 10 10
70 2 k. brown 10 10
71 3 k. grey and violet 20 30
72 5 k. brown . . . . 1·00 1·25
73 10 k. lilac and brown . . . 7·50 9·00

The kroner values are overprinted **KRUNA** or **KRUNE** also.

"Charles" and "Zita" issue of 1918.

74 **27** 10 f. red 10 15
75 20 f. brown 10 15
76 25 f. blue 10 40
77 **28** 40 f. olive 10 15

1918. Stamps of Hungary optd **HRVATSKA SHS. ZF. ZA NAROD. VIJECE.**

War Charity issue of 1916.

78 **20** 10+2 f. red 20 30
79 – 15+2 f. violet 10 25
80 **22** 40+2 f. lake 10 25

Coronation issue of 1916.

81 **23** 10 f. mauve . . . . 22·00 55·00
82 – 15 f. red . . . . 22·00 55·00

20 "Freedom of Croatia"

1918. Freeing of the Yugoslavs.

83 **20** 10 h. lake . . . . 2·40 2·50
84 20 h. violet . . . . 2·40 4·25
85 25 h. blue . . . . 6·00 7·50
86 45 h. black . . . . 35·00 40·00

21 Angel of Peace

22 Sailor with Standard and Falcon

23 Falcon ("Liberty")

1919.

87 **21** 2 h. brown 10 25
88 3 h. mauve 10 30
89 5 h. green 10 10
90 **22** 10 h. red 10 10
91 20 h. brown 10 10
92 25 h. blue 10 10
93 45 h. olive 10 10
94 **23** 1 k. red 15 15
95 – 3 k. purple 75 65
96 – 5 k. brown 75 55

DESIGN: 3, 5 k. as Type **5** but light background behind falcon.

III. ISSUES FOR SLOVENIA

1919. 100 vinar (heller) = 1 kruna (krone)
1920. 100 paras = 1 dinar

25 Chainbreakers **26**

27 "Yugoslavia" with Three Falcons

28 Angel of Peace

29 King Peter I

1919. Perf or rouletted.

97a **25** 3 v. violet 10 10
127 3 v. purple 10 10
98a 5 v. green 15 10
99b 10 v. red 20 10
100 15 v. blue 10 10
101 **26** 20 v. brown 30 10
102 25 v. blue 25 10
103 30 v. pink 25 10
111 30 v. red 25 10
104a 40 v. yellow 25 10
122 **27** 50 v. green 15 10
113b 60 v. violet 60 25
114b **28** 1 k. red 35 20
120 2 k. blue 35 15
126 **29** 5 k. red 35 15
139a 10 k. blue . . . . 2·00 55
105 15 k. green . . . . 5·25 12·50
106 20 k. purple . . . . 1·00 1·40

31 Chainbreaker

32 "Yugoslavia" with Three Falcons

34 King Peter I

1920. Perf (2 d. to 10 d.) or roul.

150 **31** 5 p. olive 15 10
151 10 p. green 10 10
152 15 p. brown 10 10
153 20 p. red 40 25
154 25 p. brown 40 10
155 **32** 40 p. violet 10 15
156 45 p. yellow 10 15
157 50 p. blue 10 10
158 60 p. brown 10 10
159 **34** 1 d. brown 10 10
160 – 2 d. black 10 10
161 **34** 4 d. slate 20 20
162 – 6 d. olive 10 65
163 – 10 d. brown 20 50

The 2, 6 and 10 d. are as Type **34** but larger.

1920. Carinthian Plebiscite. Newspaper stamps of Yugoslavia of 1919 surch **KGCA** and new value. Imperf.

163a N **30** 5 p. on 4 v. grey 10 15
163b 15 p. on 4 v. grey . . . 10 15
163c 25 p. on 4 v. grey . . . 10 20
163d 45 p. on 2 v. grey . . . 15 40
163e 50 p. on 2 v. grey . . . 10 25
163f 2 d. on 2 v. grey . . . . 90 3·50

These stamps were sold at three times face value on aid of the Plebiscite Propaganda Fund.

IV. ISSUES FOR THE WHOLE KINGDOM

100 paras = 1 dinar

35 King Alexander when Prince

37 Kosovo Maiden, 1389

1921. Inscr "KRALJEVSTVO" at foot.

164 **35** 2 p. brown 10 10
165 5 p. green 10 10
166 10 p. red 10 10
167 15 p. purple 10 10
168 20 p. black 10 10
169 25 p. blue 10 10
170 50 p. olive 10 10
171 60 p. red 20 10
172 75 p. violet 10 10
173 – 1 d. orange 20 10
174 – 2 d. olive 40 10
175 – 4 d. green 90 10
176 – 5 d. red . . . . 2·50 15
177 – 10 d. brown . . . . 5·50 50

DESIGN: 1 d. to 10 d. as Type **35**, but portrait of King Peter I.

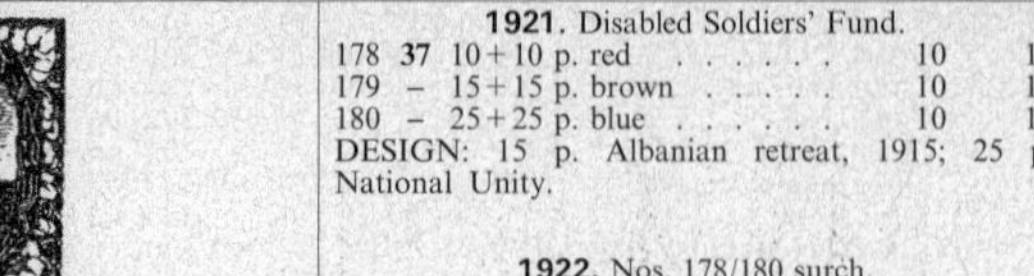

1921. Disabled Soldiers' Fund.

178 **37** 10+10 p. red 10 10
179 – 15+15 p. brown 10 10
180 – 25+25 p. blue 10 15

DESIGN: 15 p. Albanian retreat, 1915; 25 p. National Unity.

1922. Nos. 178/180 surch.

181 1 d. on 10 p. red 10 10
183 1 d. on 15 p. brown 10 10
182 1 d. on 25 p. blue 20 10
184 3 d. on 15 p. brown 25 10
186 8 d. on 15 p. brown . . . . . 1·00 25
187 20 d. on 15 p. brown . . . . 9·00 75
188 30 d. on 15 p. brown . . . . 12·50 2·25

1923. As T **35**, but inscr "KRALJEVINA" at foot.

189 **35** 1 d. brown . . . . 1·25 10
190 5 d. red . . . . 6·50 30
191 8 d. purple . . . . 7·50 30
192 20 d. green . . . . 30·00 75
193 30 d. orange . . . . 90·00 2·50

1924. Nos. 171 and 191 surch.

195 **35** 20 p. on 60 p. red 25 10
196 5 d. on 8 d. purple . . . . 8·00 65

44 King Alexander **46**

1924.

197 **44** 20 p. black 10 10
198 50 p. brown 10 10
199 1 d. red 10 10
200 2 d. green 30 10
201 3 d. blue 30 10
202 5 d. brown . . . . 3·00 10
203 – 10 d. violet . . . . 15·00 10
204 – 15 d. olive . . . . 10·50 20
205 – 20 d. orange . . . . . . 10·50 20
206 – 30 d. green . . . . 7·50 1·25

The 10 d. to 30 d. have the head in a square panel.

1925. Surch.

207 **44** 25 p. on 3 d. blue 15 10
208 50 p. on 3 d. blue 15 10

1926.

209 **46** 25 p. green 10 10
210 50 p. sepia 10 10
211 1 d. red 20 10
212 2 d. black 20 10
213 3 d. blue 35 10
214 4 d. orange 70 10
215 5 d. violet . . . . 1·40 10
216 8 d. brown . . . . 4·50 10
217 10 d. olive . . . . 2·50 10
218 15 d. brown . . . . 12·00 10
219 20 d. purple . . . . 15·00 15
220 30 d. yellow . . . . 75·00 50

1926. Danube Flood Fund. Surch.

221 **46** 25 p.+0.25 green 10 10
222 50 p.+0.50 sepia 10 10
223 1 d. +0.50 red 20 10
224 2 d.+0.50 black 40 10
225 3 d.+0.50 blue 25 15
226 4 d.+0.50 orange 40 10
227 5 d.+0.50 violet 60 10
228 8 d.+0.50 brown 90 40
229 10 d.+1.00 olive . . . . . 3·00 15
230 15 d.+1.00 brown . . . . . 6·50 50
231 20 d.+1.00 purple . . . . 5·00 40
232 30 d.+1.00 yellow . . . . 22·00 1·25

1928. Nos. 223/32 optd **XXXX** over previous surch.

233 **46** 1 d. red 50 10
234 2 d. black 75 10
235 3 d. blue . . . . 1·40 25
236 4 d. orange . . . . 2·75 30
237 5 d. violet . . . . 2·00 15
238 8 d. brown . . . . 9·00 50
239 **46** 10 d. olive . . . . 18·00 15
240 15 d. brown . . . . 90·00 1·90
241 20 d. purple . . . . 55·00 1·90
242 30 d. yellow . . . . £120 11·50

B. KINGDOM OF YUGOSLAVIA

100 paras = 1 dinar

49 Duvno Cathedral

1929. Millenary of Croatian Kingdom (1925).

243 **49** 50 p.+50 p. olive 30 25
244 – 1 d.+50 p. red 70 35
245 – 3 d.+1 d. blue . . . . . 1·25 65

DESIGNS—As Type **49**: 3 d. King Tomislav. HORIZ (34×23 mm): 1 d. Kings Tomislav and Alexander I.

52 Dobropolje **53** Serbian War Memorial, Paris

1931. Serbian War Memorial (Paris) Fund.
246 **52** 50 p. + 50 p. green 10 10
247 **53** 1 d. + 50 p. red 10 15
248 – 3 d. + 1 d. blue 15 25
DESIGN—As Type **52**: 3 d. Kajmaktchalan.

55 King Alexander **57** Rowing "four" on Lake Bled

1931.
249 **55** 25 p. black 15 10
250 50 p. green 15 10
262 75 p. green 25 10
251 1 d. red 15 10
263 1 d. 50 red 50 10
263b 1 d. 75 red 1·00 45
252 3 d. blue 1·00 10
263c 3 d. 50 blue 1·25 15
253 4 d. orange 3·75 10
254 5 d. violet 4·50 10
255 10 d. olive 12·00 10
256 15 d. brown 11·00 10
257 20 d. purple 22·00 15
258 30 d. red 13·50 55

1931. Optd **KRALJEVINA JUGOSLAVIJA** and also in Cyrillic characters.
259 **49** 50 p.+50 p. olive 10 10
260 – 1 d.+50 p. red 10 10
261 – 3 d.+1 d. blue 35 20

1932. European Rowing Championship. Inscr ending "EUROPE 1932".
264 – 75 p.+50 p. green 65 1·00
265 **57** 1 d.+½ d. red 1·00 1·25
266 – 1½ d.+½ d. red 1·00 1·25
267 – 3 d.+1 d. blue 1·75 2·50
268 – 4 d.+1 d. blue and orange 5·25 12·00
269 – 5 d.+1 d. lilac and violet 5·25 10·00
DESIGNS—HORIZ: 75 p. Single sculler on Danube at Smederevo; 1½ d. Rowing "eight" on Danube at Belgrade; 3 d. Rowing "pair" at Split harbour. VERT: 4 d. Rowing "pair" on river and Zagreb Cathedral; 5 d. Prince Peter.

1933. 11th Int Pen Club Congress Dubrovnik. As T **25** with additional value and "XI. int. kongres Pen-Klubova u Dubrovniku 1933" below in Roman or Cyrillic characters.
270 **55** 50 p.+25 p. black 3·75 7·00
271 75 p.+25 p. green 3·75 7·00
272 1 d. 50+50 p. red 3·75 7·00
273 3 d.+1 d. blue 3·75 7·00
274 4 d.+1 d. green 3·75 7·00
275 5 d.+1 d. yellow 3·75 7·00

60 Crown Prince Peter in "Sokol" Uniform **62**

1933. "Sokol" Meeting, Ljubljana.
276 **60** 75 p.+ 25 p. green 25 30
277 1½ d.+ ½ d. red 25 30

1933. Optd **JUGOSLAVIJA** in Roman and Cyrillic characters. (a) Postage.
278 **46** 25 p. green 15 10
279 50 p. sepia 15 10
280 1 d. red 50 10
281 2 d. black 55 15
282 3 d. blue 1·90 10
283 4 d. orange 1·00 10
284 5 d. violet 1·90 10
285 8 d. brown 4·75 1·25
286 10 d. olive 9·25 10
287 15 d. brown 14·00 1·40
288 20 d. purple 24·00 50
289 30 d. yellow 23·00 50

(b) Charity stamps. Nos. 221/3.
290 **46** 25 p.+0.25 green 35 25
291 50 p.+0.50 sepia 35 15
292 1 d.+0.50 red 1·40 45

1933. Obligatory Tax. Red Cross.
293 **62** 50 p. red and blue 15 10

63 Osprey over R. Bosna **64** Athlete and Falcon (from sculpture by Krsinic)

1934. 20th Anniv of "Sokol" Games, Sarajevo.
294 **63** 75 p.+25 p. green 7·25 4·50
295 1 d. 50+50 p. red 8·00 5·25
296 1 d. 75+25 p. brown 20·00 7·00

1934. 60th Anniv of Croat "Sokol" Games, Zagreb.
297 **64** 75 p.+25 p. green 2·50 2·50
298 1 d. 50+50 p. red 3·75 5·00
299 1 d. 75+25 p. brown 10·00 6·00

65 Dubrovnik **69** Mostar Bridge

1934. Air.
300 **65** 50 p. purple 15 20
301 – 1 d. green 15 20
302 – 2 d. red 35 25
303 – 3 d. blue 1·25 40
304 **69** 10 d. orange 2·25 2·00
DESIGNS: 1 d. Lake of Bled; 2 d. Waterfall at Jajce; 3 d. Oplenats.

1934. King Alexander Mourning issue. With black margins.
305 **55** 25 p. black (postage) 10 10
306 50 p. green 10 10
307 75 p. green 10 10
308 1 d. red 10 10
309 1 d. 50 red 10 10
310 1 d. 75 red 10 10
311 3 d. blue 10 10
312 3 d. 50 p. blue 30 10
313 4 d. orange 30 10
314 5 d. violet 40 10
315 10 d. olive 2·10 10
316 15 d. brown 4·00 15
317 20 d. purple 7·00 15
318 30 d. red 4·00 40
319 – 3 d. blue (No. 303) (air) 3·75 2·00

70 King Peter II **71** King Alexander

1935.
320 **70** 25 p. black 10 10
321 50 p. orange 10 10
322 75 p. green 15 10
323 1 d. brown 15 10
324 1 d. 50 red 15 10
325 1 d. 75 red 30 10
325a 2 d. red 15 10
326 3 d. orange 15 10
327 3 d. 50 blue 50 10
328 4 d. green 1·10 10
329 4 d. blue 30 10
330 10 d. violet 90 10
331 15 d. brown 90 10
332 20 d. blue 2·75 25
333 30 d. pink 2·25 25

1935. 1st Anniv of King Alexander's Assassination.
334 **71** 75 p. green 20 25
335 1 d. 50 red 20 25
336 1 d. 75 brown 25 50
337 3 d. 50 blue 1·60 2·10
338 7 d. 50 red 1·00 2·10

72 **73** Queen Marie

1935. Winter Relief Fund.
339 **72** 1 d. 50+1 d. brown 1·00 1·75
340 3 d. 50+1 d. 50 blue 2·10 2·75

1936. Child Welfare.
341 **73** 75 p. + 25 p. green 45 40
342 1 d. 50 + 50 p. red 45 40
343 1 d. 75 + 75 p. brown 1·10 75
344 3 d. 50 + 1 d. blue 1·60 1·10

74 Nicola Tesla

1936. 80th Birthday of Dr. Tesla (physicist).
345 **74** 75 p. brown and green 15 20
346 1 d. 75 black and blue 25 25

75 Prince Paul **76** Dr. V. Georgevitch

1936. Red Cross Fund.
347 **75** 75 p. + 50 p. green 10 30
348 1 d. 50 + 50 p. red 15 40

1936. Obligatory Tax. Jubilee of Serbian Red Cross.
349 **76** 50 p. brown 15 10

77 Princess Tomislav and Andrew **78** Oplenats

1937. Child Welfare. T **77** and similar horiz portrait.
350 – 25 p. + 25 p. brown 15 25
351 – 75 p. + 75 p. orange 35 50
352 **77** 1 d. 50 + 1 d. orange 65 50
353 2 d. + 1 d. purple 75 75

1937. Little Entente.
354 **78** 3 d. green 75 20
355 4 d. blue 75 30

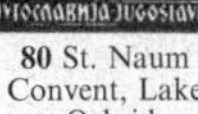

80 St. Naum Convent, Lake Ochrid **83** Arms of Yugoslavia, Greece, Rumania and Turkey

1937. Air.
360 **80** 50 p. brown 15 10
361 – 1 d. green 15 10
362 – 2 d. blue 15 10
363 – 2 d. 50 red 25 15
364 **80** 5 d. violet 30 20
365 – 10 d. red 50 25
366 – 20 d. green 75 65
367 – 30 d. blue 1·40 1·10
DESIGNS—VERT: 1, 10 d. Rab (Arbe) Harbour. HORIZ: 2, 20 d. Sarajevo; 2 d. 50, 30 d. Laibach (Ljubljana).

1937. Balkan Entente.
368 **83** 3 d. green 55 15
369 4 d. blue 80 50

84 **85**

1938. Child Welfare.
370 **84** 50 p. + 50 p. brown 20 30
371 **85** 1 d. + 1 d. green 20 30
372 **84** 1 d. 50 + 1 d. 50 red 45 60
373 **85** 2 d. + 2 d. mauve 1·00 1·00

86 Searchlight Display and Parachute Tower **87** Entrance to Demir Kapija Cliff

1938. Int Aeronautical Exhibition, Belgrade, and Yugoslav Air Club Fund.
374 **86** 1 d.+50 p. green 30 60
375 1 d. 50 +1 d. red 1·00 75
376 2 d.+1 d. mauve 2·25 1·50
377 3 d.+1 d. blue 2·75 2·25

1938. Railway Employees' Hospital Fund.
378 **87** 1 d.+1 d. green 40 45
379 – 1 d. 50+1 d. 50 red 1·10 95
380 – 2 d.+2 d. mauve 2·00 2·10
381 – 3 d.+3 d. blue 2·40 2·40
DESIGNS—HORIZ: 1 d. 50, Demir Kapija Hospital. VERT: 2 d. Runner carrying torch; 3 d. King Alexander.

90 Hurdling

1938. 9th Balkan Games.
382 – 50 p.+50 p. orange 75 1·00
383 **90** 1 d.+1 d. green 1·50 1·50
384 – 1 d. 50+1 d. 50 mauve 2·25 2·00
385 – 2 d.+2 d. blue 3·00 3·00
DESIGNS—HORIZ: 1 d. 50, Pole-vaulting. VERT: 50 p. Runner; 2 d. Putting the shot.

91 Maiden of Kosovo (after P. Jovanovic)

1938. Red Cross.
386 **91** 50 p. multicoloured 15 10
386a 50 p. red and blue 20 10

1938. Child Welfare. Optd **SALVATE PARVULOS**.
387 **84** 50 p.+50 p. brown 30 30
388 **85** 1 d.+1 d. green 30 50
389 **84** 1 d. 50+1 d. 50 red 60 85
390 **85** 2 d.+2 d. mauve 1·25 2·00

93 Mail Carrier

1939. Postal Centenary and Railway Benevolent Association Fund.
391 – 50 p.+50 p. orange and brown 50 75
392 **93** 1 d.+1 d. green and black 50 75
393 – 1 d. 50 +1 d. 50 red 2·75 1·25
394 – 2 d.+2 d. purple & violet 1·40 2·75
395 – 4 d.+4 d. blue 2·25 4·50
DESIGNS: 50 p. Mounted postmen; 1 d. 50, Mail train; 2 d. Mail coach; 4 d. Lockheed 10 Electra mail plane.

94 Meal-time **95** Milosh Obilich

1939 Child Welfare.
396 **94** 1 d.+1 d. green 40 75
397 – 1 d. 50 +1 d. 50 red and brown 2·00 3·50
398 – 2 d.+2 d. mauve & brown 1·25 2·40
399 – 4 d.+4 d. blue 2·40 4·75
DESIGNS—HORIZ: 2 d. Young carpenter. VERT: 1 d. 50, Children playing on sands; 4 d. Children whispering.

1939. 550th Anniv of Battle of Kosovo.
400 – 1 d.+1 d. green 1·00 1·25
401 **95** 1 d. 50+1 d. 50 red 1·00 1·25
DESIGN: 1 d. King Lazar.

96 Motor Cycle and Sidecar **97** Cadet Barquentine "Jadran"

1939. 1st International Motor Races, Belgrade. Inscr "I. MEDUNARODNE AUTO I MOTO", etc.

No.	Type	Description	Mint	Used
402	96	50 p. + 50 p. orange and brown	1·10	85
403	–	1 d. + 1 d. green and black	1·40	1·25
404	–	1 d. 50 + 1 d. 50 red	2·00	2·00
405	–	2 d. + 2 d. blue	3·00	3·00

DESIGNS—HORIZ: 1, 2 d. Racing cars. VERT: 1 d. 50, Motor cycle.

1939. King Peter's Birthday and Adriatic Guard Fund. Inscr "ZA JADRANSKU STRAZU".

No.	Type	Description	Mint	Used
406	97	50 p. + 50 p. red	65	60
407	–	1 d. + 50 p. green	85	60
408	–	1 d. 50 + 1 d. red	1·50	1·25
409	–	2 d. + 1 d. 50 blue	2·40	2·00

DESIGNS: 1 d. Liner "King Alexander"; 1 d. 50, Freighter "Triglav"; 2 d. Destroyer "Dubrovnik".

98 Unknown Warrior's Tomb, Avala

99 King Peter II

1939. 5th Death Anniv of King Alexander. War Invalids' Fund.

No.	Type	Description	Mint	Used
410	98	1 d. + 50 p. green	1·10	1·25
411		1 d. 50 + 1 d. red	1·10	1·25
412		2 d. + 1 d. 50 purple	1·60	1·60
413		3 d. + 2 d. blue	2·50	2·50

1939.

No.	Type	Description	Mint	Used
414	99	25 p. black	15	10
415		50 p. orange	15	10
416		1 d. green	15	10
417		1 d. 50 red	15	10
418		2 d. mauve	15	10
419		3 d. brown	20	10
420		4 d. blue	20	10
420a		5 d. blue	20	20
420b		5 d. 50 violet	50	10
421		6 d. blue	90	10
422		8 d. brown	90	10
423		12 d. violet	1·90	10
424		16 d. purple	2·00	20
425		20 d. blue	2·00	20
426		30 d. pink	6·00	35

100 Postman delivering Letters

101 Arrival of Thorval

1940. Belgrade Postal Employees' Fund. Inscr "ZA DOM P.T.T. ZVAN. I SLUZ".

No.	Type	Description	Mint	Used
427	100	50 p. + 50 p. orge & brn	50	1·10
428	–	1 d. + 1 d. green & black	50	1·10
429	–	1 d. 50 + 1 d. 50 red & brown	1·00	2·40
430	–	2 d. + 2 d. mauve & purple	5·00	3·75
431	–	4 d. + 4 d. blue and grey	3·75	6·00

DESIGNS—VERT: 1 d. Postman collecting letters; 4 d. Telegraph linesman. HORIZ: 1 d. 50, Mail-van; 2 d. Mail-train.

1940. Zagreb Postal Employees' Fund. Inscr "ZA DOM P.T.T. CINOV U ZAGREBU".

No.	Type	Description	Mint	Used
432	101	50 p. + 50 p. orange & brown	50	1·10
433	–	1 d. + 1 d. green	35	40
434	–	1 d. 50 + 1 d. 50 red	55	75
435	–	2 d. + 2 d. red	1·00	1·25
436	–	4 d. + 2 d. blue	1·50	1·75

DESIGNS—25½ × 37½ mm: 1 d. King Tomislav enthroned; 1 d. 50, Death of Matthew Gubac. 37 × 27 mm: 2 d. Radich Brothers. 34 × 25 mm: 4 d. Divisional map of Yugoslavia.

102 Winter Games

1940. Child Welfare. Inscr "ZA NASU DECU".

No.	Type	Description	Mint	Used
437	102	50 p. + 50 p. orange and brown	20	25
438	–	1 d. + 1 d. green	20	30
439	102	1 d. 50 + 1 d. 50 red and brown	50	60
440	–	2 d. + 2 d. mauve	1·25	1·40

DESIGN—VERT: 1, 2 d. Children at seaside (Summer games).

103 Arms of Yugoslavia, Greece, Rumania and Turkey

104 Zagreb Cathedral and Junkers Ju 86

1940. Balkan Entente. Inscr "JUGOSLAVIJA" alternately at top in Cyrillic (I) or Roman (II) throughout the sheet.

No.	Type	Description	I. Mint	I. Used	II. Mint	II. Used
441	103	3 d. blue	90	55	90	55
442		4 d. blue	90	55	90	55

1940. Air.

No.	Type	Description	Mint	Used
443	104	40 d. green	1·25	2·00
444	–	50 d. blue	1·75	2·50

DESIGN: 50 d. Suspension Bridge at Belgrade and Fokker F.VIIa/3m.

105 Obod, Scene of early Press, 1493

1940. 5th Centenary of Invention of Printing Press by Johannes Gutenberg.

No.	Type	Description	Mint	Used
445	105	5 d. 50 green	1·50	3·50

1940. Anti-T.B. Fund. Nos. 364/7 surch.

No.	Type	Description	Mint	Used
446	80	50 p. + 50 p. on 5 d. violet	20	35
447	–	1 d. + 1 d. on 10 d. red	20	35
448	–	1 d. 50 + 1 d. 50 on 20 d. green	80	1·10
449	–	2 d. + 2 d. on 30 d. blue	1·25	2·10

107 St. Peter's Cemetery, Ljubljana

109 Kamenita Gate, Zagreb

1941. Ljubljana War Veterans' Fund.

No.	Type	Description	Mint	Used
450	107	50 p. + 50 p. green	20	25
451	–	1 d. + 1 d. red	20	25
452	–	1 d. 50 + 1 d. 50 green	80	75
453	–	2 d. + 2 d. lilac and blue	1·25	2·10

DESIGNS—HORIZ: 2 d. War Memorial, Brezje. VERT: 1 d. National costumes; 1 d. 50, Memorial Chapel, Kajmakcalan.

1941. Philatelic Exhibitions. (a) 2nd Croatian Philatelic Exhibition, Zagreb.

No.	Type	Description	Mint	Used
454	109	1 d. 50 + 1 d. 50 brown	50	1·50
455	–	4 d. + 3 d. black	50	1·50

(b) 1st Philatelic Exhibition, Slav Brod.

No.	Type	Description	Mint	Used
456	109	1 d. 50 + 1 d. 50 black	7·50	18
457	–	4 d. + 3 d. brown	7·50	18·00

DESIGN: 4 d. (2) Old Cathedral, Zagreb.

NOTE. From 1941 until 1945 Yugoslavia ceased to exist as a stamp-issuing entity, except for the following series, Nos 468/81, which were issued by the exiled government for the use of the Yugoslav Merchant Navy working with the Allies.

110 King Peter II

112 Vodnik

1943. 2nd Anniv of Overthrow of Regency and King Peter's Assumption of Power.

No.	Type	Description	Mint	Used
468	110	2 d. blue	15	15
469		3 d. grey	15	20
470		5 d. red	20	35
471		10 d. black	30	70

1943. Red Cross Fund. Surch **CRVENI KRST + 12.50**.

No.	Type	Description	Mint	Used
472	110	2 d. + 12 d. 50 blue	70	1·25
473		3 d. + 12 d. 50 grey	70	1·25
474		5 d. + 12 d. 50 red	70	1·25
475		10 d. + 12 d. 50 black	70	1·25

1943. 25th Anniv of Formation of Yugoslavia. 19th-century Patriots and Writers.

No.	Type	Description	Mint	Used
476	112	1 d. black and red	10	
477	–	2 d. black and green	15	
478	–	3 d. blue and blue	15	
479	–	4 d. black and violet	40	
480	–	5 d. brown and purple	40	
481	–	10 d. deep brown and brown	1·10	

PORTRAITS: 2 d. Njegos; 3 d. Gaj; 4 d. Karadzic; 5 d. Strosmajer; 10 k. Karageorge.

C. DEMOCRATIC FEDERATION OF YUGOSLAVIA

I. REGIONAL ISSUES

Bosnia and Herzegovina

Currency: Croatian Kunas

1945: Mostar Issue. Stamps of Croatia surch **Demokratska Federativna Jugoslavija** and value.

(a) Pictorial Stamps of 1941–43.

No.	Type	Description	Mint	Used
R 1		10 k. on 25 b. red	35	35
R 2		10 k. on 50 b. green	20	20
R 3		10 k. on 2 k. red	25	25
R 4		10 k. on 3 k. 50 brown	60	60
R 5		40 k. on 1 k. green	20	20
R 6		50 k. on 4 k. blue	3·00	3·00
R 7		50 k. on 5 k. blue	16·00	16·00
R 8		50 k. on 6 k. green	3·00	3·00
R 9		50 k. on 7 k. red	90·00	90·00
R10		50 k. on 8 k. brown	£110	£110
R11		50 k. on 10 k. violet	60	60

(b) Famous Croats issue of 1943.

No.	Type	Description	Mint	Used
R12		30 k. on 1 k. blue	25	25
R13		30 k. on 12 k. 50 purple	20	20

(c) Boskovic issue of 1943.

No.	Type	Description	Mint	Used
R14	28	30 k. on 3 k. 50 blue	25	25
R15		30 k. on 12 k. 50 purple	1·50	1·50

(d) War Victims Charity Tax stamps of 1944.

No.	Type	Description	Mint	Used
R16	34	20 k. on 1 k. green	15	15
R17	35	20 k. on 2 k. red	25	25
R18		20 k. on 5 k. green	25	25
R19		20 k. on 10 k. blue	25	25
R20		20 k. on 20 k. brown	70	70

Croatia

Currency: Kunas

DEMOKRATSKA FEDERATIVNA ★ 20 KUNA JUGOSLAVIJA

(R 2)

1945. Split issue. Stamps of Croatia 1941–43 surch as Type R **2**.

No.	Type	Description	Mint	Used
R21		10 k. on 25 b. red	10	10
R22		10 k. on 50 b. green	10	10
R23		10 k. on 75 b. green	10	10
R24		10 k. on 1 k. green	10	10
R25		20 k. on 2 k. red	10	10
R26		20 k. on 3 k. brown	15	15
R27		20 k. on 3 k. 50 brown	10	10
R28		20 k. on 4 k. blue	10	10
R29		20 k. on 5 k. blue	15	15
R30		20 k. on 6 k. green	8·50	8·50
R31		30 k. on 7 k. red	10	10
R32		30 k. on 8 k. brown	9·25	9·25
R33		30 k. on 10 k. violet	10	10
R34		30 k. on 12 k. 50 black	10	10
R35		40 k. on 20 k. brown	15	15
R36		40 k. on 30 k. brown	20	20
R37		50 k. on 50 k. green	15	15

1945. Zagreb issue. Stamps of Croatia, 1941–43, surch **DEMOKRATISKA FEDERATIVNA JUGOSLAVIJA KN,** value and star.

No.	Type	Description	Mint	Used
R38		20 k. on 5 k. blue	15	15
R39		40 k. on 1 k. green	10	10
R40		60 k. on 3 k. 50 brown	10	10
R41		80 k. on 2 k. red	10	10
R42		160 k. on 50 b. green	15	15
R43		200 k. on 12 k. 50 black	20	20
R44		400 k. on 25 b. red	20	20

Montenegro

Currency: Italian Lire.

Демократска ★ Федеративна Југославија

(R 4)

1945. Cetinje issue. Stamps of Italian Occupation surch with Type R **4**. (a) National Poem Issue of 1943.

No.	Type	Description	Mint	Used
R50		1 l. on 10 c. green	65	80
R51		2 l. on 25 c. green	40	50
R52		3 l. on 50 c. mauve	40	50
R53		5 l. on 1 l. 25 blue	40	50
R54		10 l. on 15 c. brown	80	1·00
R55		15 l. on 20 c. orange	80	1·00
R56		20 l. on 2 l. green	80	1·00

(b) Air stamps of 1943, for use as ordinary postage stamps.

No.	Type	Description	Mint	Used
R57		3 l. on 50 c. brown	3·00	3·00
R58		6 l. on 1 l. blue	3·00	3·00
R59		10 l. on 2 l. red	3·00	3·00
R60		20 l. on 5 l. green	3·00	3·00

Serbia

Currency: Hungarian Filler

1944. Senta issue. Various stamps of Hungary optd with a large star, **8.X.1944** and "Yugoslavia" in Cyrillic characters.

No.	Type	Description	Mint	Used
R63		1 f. grey	6·25	4·75
R64		2 f. red	6·25	4·75
R65		3 f. blue	6·25	4·75
R66		4 f. brown	6·25	4·75
R67		5 f. red	6·25	4·75
R68		8 f. green	6·25	4·75
R69		10 f. brown	£120	£120
R70		24 f. brown	£150	£150
R71		24 f. purple	9·25	9·25
R72		30 f. red	£120	£120

Slovenia

Currencies: Italian (Ljubljana)
German (Maribor)
Hungarian (Murska Sobota)

(R 5)

1945. Ljubljana issue. Pictorial stamps of German Occupation, 1945, optd as Type R **5**.

No.	Type	Description	Mint	Used
R74		5 c. brown	10	10
R75		10 c. orange	10	10
R76		20 c. brown	10	10
R77		25 c. green	10	10
R78		50 c. violet	10	10
R79		75 c. red	40	40
R80		1 l. green	15	10
R81		1 l. 25 blue	25	20
R82		1 l. 50 green	10	10
R83		2 l. blue	20	15
R84		2 l. 50 brown	10	10
R85		3 l. mauve	35	25
R86		5 l. brown	40	35
R87		10 l. green	30	35
R88		20 l. blue	3·00	3·00
R89		30 l. red	20·00	20·00

1945. Maribor issue. Hitler stamps of Germany, 1941–44, optd **SLOVENIJA 9.5.1945 JUGOSLAVIJA** and star.

No.	Type	Description	Mint	Used
R 90	173	1 pf. grey	2·75	2·75
R 91		3 pf. brown	25	25
R 92		4 pf. grey	2·00	2·00
R 93		5 pf. green	1·75	1·75
R 94		6 pf. violet	25	15
R 95		8 pf. red	50	50
R 96		10 pf. brown (No. 775)	1·75	1·75
R 97		12 pf. red (No. 776)	15	15
R 98		15 pf. brown	3·75	3·75
R 99		20 pf. blue	2·50	2·50
R100		24 pf. brown	2·00	2·00
R101		25 pf. blue	6·00	6·00
R102		30 pf. green	50	50
R103		40 pf. mauve	50	50
R104	225	42 pf. green	40	40
R105	173	50 pf. green	1·25	1·25
R106		60 pf. brown	50	50
R107		80 pf. blue	1·00	1·00

1945. Murska Sobota issue. Various stamps of Hungary optd as Nos. R90/107.

No.	Type	Description	Mint	Used
R108		1 f. grey	5·00	5·00
R109		4 f. brown	35	35
R110		5 f. red	4·50	4·50
R111		10 f. brown	35	35
R112		18 f. black	35	35
R113		20 f. brown	35	35
R114		30 f. red	35	35
R115		30 f. red	35	35
R116		50 f. blue	7·50	7·50
R117		70 f. brown	7·50	7·50
R118		80 f. brown	42·00	42·00
R119		1 p. green	6·25	6·25

II. GENERAL ISSUES

100 paras = 1 dinar

(113)

1944. Stamps of Serbia, 1942, surch as T **113**.

No.	Type	Description	Mint	Used
482	–	3 d. + 2 d. pink (No. 64)	10	20
485	–	4 d. + 21 d. blue (No. 65)	10	20
483	–	7 d. + 3 d. green (No. 66)	10	20

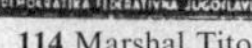

114 Marshal Tito

115 Chapel at Prohor Pcinjski

1945.

491 **114** 25 p. green 35 15
492 50 p. green 35 10
493 1 d. red . . . . 4·50 40
494 2 d. red 35 10
495 4 d. blue 75 10
487 5 d. green 10 10
496 6 d. violet 80 10
497 9 d. brown . . . . 1·40 20
488 10 d. red 10 10
498 20 d. yellow . . . . 5·00 1·40
489 25 d. violet 15 15
490 30 d. blue 25 15

1945. 1st Anniv of Anti-Fascist Chamber of Deputies, Macedonia.

499 **115** 2 d. red 70 25

116 Partisans

1945. Red Cross Fund.

500 **116** 1 d.+4 d. blue 90 80
501 – 2 d.+6 d. red 90 80
DESIGN—VERT: 2 d.+6 d. Child's head.

119 Partisans **120** Marshal Tito

1945. Partisans.

502 **119** 50 p. brown 10 10
503 1 d. green 15 10
504 – 1 d. 50 brown 20 10
505 **120** 2 d. red 15 10
506 – 2 d. 50 red 60 10
507 – 3 d. brown . . . . 1·00 10
508 – 3 d. red 60 10
509 **120** 4 d. blue 30 10
510 – 5 d. green . . . . 1·00 10
511 – 5 d. blue . . . . 1·75 10
512 – 6 d. black 60 10
513 – 8 d. yellow 65 10
514 – 9 d. mauve 55 10
515 – 12 d. blue . . . . 1·00 10
516 **119** 16 d. blue . . . . 1·00 10
517 – 20 d. red . . . . 2·25 20
DESIGNS—As Type **119**: 1 d. 50, 12, 20 d. Riflemen. VERT: 3, 5 d. Town of Jajce inscr "29-XI-1943". HORIZ: 2 d. 50, 6, 8, 9 d. Girl with flag.

122 Russian and Yugoslav Flags

1945. 1st Anniv of Liberation of Belgrade.

518 **122** 2 d. +5 d. multicoloured. 70 40

124 "Industry and Agriculture" **126**

1945. Meeting of the Constituent Assembly. Inscr in Cyrillic at top and Roman characters at foot (I) or vice-versa (II).

			I.		II.	
519	**124**	2 d. red	3·00	3·00	3·00	3·00
520		4 d. blue	3·00	3·00	3·00	3·00
521		6 d. green	3·00	3·00	3·00	3·00
522		9 d. orange . . .	3·00	3·00	3·00	3·00
523		16 d. blue	3·00	3·00	3·00	3·00
524		20 d. brown . . .	3·00	3·00	3·00	3·00

D. FEDERAL PEOPLE'S REPUBLIC

100 paras = 1 dinar

1946. Type of 1945 (Girl with flag), surch.

525 2 d. 50 on 6 d. red 60 10
526 8 d. on 9 d. orange . . . . . 1·00 10

1946 1st Anniv of Victory over Fascism. Star in red.

527 **126** 1 d. 50 orange 40 50
528 2 d. 50 red 60 70
529 5 d. blue . . . . 1·75 1·50

127 Symbolic of Communications **128** Railway Construction

1946. Postal Congress.

530 **127** 1 d. 50+1 d. green . . . 4·50 4·50
531 2 d. 50+1 d. 50 red . . . 4·50 4·50
532 5 d.+2 d. blue . . . . . 4·50 4·50
533 8 d.+3 d. 50 brown . . . 4·50 4·50

1946. Volunteer Workers' Railway Reconstruction Fund.

534 **128** 50 p.+50 p. brown, red and blue . . . . 3·50 2·00
535 1 d. 50+1 d. green, blue and red . . . . 3·50 1·75
536 2 d. 50+2 d. lilac, red and blue . . . . 3·50 1·75
537 5 d.+3 d. grey, red and bl 3·50 2·25

129 Svetozar Markovic **130** Theatre in Sofia

1946. Birth Centenary of S. Markovic (socialist writer).

538 **129** 1 d. 50 green 75 40
539 2 d. 50 purple 75 45

1948. Slav Congress.

540 **130** ½ d. brown 10 10
541 – 1 d. green 10 10
542 – 1½ d. red 15 10
543 – 2½ d. orange 20 10
544 – 5 d. blue 75 60
DESIGNS—HORIZ: 1 d. Charles Bridge and Hradcany, Prague. VERT: 1½ d. Sigismund Monument, Warsaw; 2½ d. Victory Monument, Belgrade; 5 d. Kremlin Tower, Moscow.

131 Roofless Houses **132** Ilyushin Il-4 DB-3 over Kalimegdan Terrace, Belgrade

1947. Obligatory Tax. Red Cross.

545 **131** 50 p. brown 15 10

1947. Air. Inscr in Cyrillic at top and Roman characters at foot (I) or vice versa (II).

			I.		II.	
546	**132**	50 p. olive & lake	15	15	15	15
547	–	1 d. red & olive	25	20	25	20
548	**132**	2 d. blue & blk	40	25	40	25
549	–	5 d. grn & grey	45	30	45	30
550	–	10 d. brn & sep	55	40	55	40
551	**132**	20 d. blue & ol	1·00	65	1·00	65

DESIGN: 1, 5, 20 d. Ilyushin Il-4 DB-3 over Dubrovnik.

133 "Wreath of Mountains" **134** P. P. Njegos

1947. Centenary of Publication of "Wreath of Mountains".

552 **133** 1½ d. black and green . . 15 10
553 **134** 2 d. 50 red and buff . . . 20 15
554 **133** 5 d. black and blue . . . 35 20

135 Girl Athlete, Star and Flags **137** Gymnast

1947. Federal Sports Meeting.

555 – 1 d. 50 brown 15 10
556 **135** 2 d. 50 red 20 15
557 – 4 d. blue 50 40
DESIGNS—VERT: 1 d. 50, Physical training groups. HORIZ: 4 d. Parade of athletes.

1947. Balkan Games.

558 **137** 1 d. 50+50 p. green . . . 15 10
559 2 d. 50+50 p. red 30 20
560 4 d.+50 p. blue 40 35

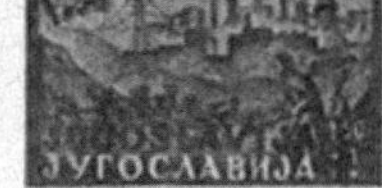

138 Star and Map of Julian Province **139** Railway Construction

1947. Annexation of Julian Province to Yugoslavia.

561 **138** 2 d. 50 red and blue . . . 15 10
562 5 d. brown and green . . . 15 10

1947. Juvenile Labour Organizations' Relief Fund.

563 **139** 1 d.+50 p. orange 30 15
564 1 d. 50+1 d. green 35 25
565 2 d. 50+1 d. 50 red . . . 60 30
566 5 d.+2 d. blue . . . . . . 1·25 70

140 Music Book and Fiddle **141** Vuk Karadzic (poet)

1947. Centenary of Serbian Literature.

567 **140** 1 d. 50 green 10 10
568 **141** 2 d. 50 red 15 15
569 **140** 5 d. blue 20 20

142 "B.C.G. Vaccine defeating Tuberculosis" **143** "Illness and Recovery"

144 "Fight against Tuberculosis" **145** Map of Yugoslavia and Symbols of Industry and Agriculture

1948. Anti-T.B. Fund.

570 **142** 1 d. 50+1 d. green & red . 10 10
571 **143** 2 d. 50+2 d. green & red . 15 15
572 **144** 5 d.+3 d. blue and red . . 25 20

1948. International Fair, Zagreb.

573 **145** 1 d. 50 green, blue and red 10 10
574 2 d. 50 purple, blue and red 10 10
575 5 d. indigo, blue and red 15 10

146 Flag-bearers **147** Djura Danicic

1948. 5th Yugoslav Communist Party Congress, Belgrade.

576 **146** 2 d. green 20 15
577b 3 d. red and lake 20 15
578a 10 d. blue 45 45

1948. 80th Anniv of Yugoslav Academy.

579 **147** 1 d. 50+50 p. green . . . 15 15
580 – 2 d. 50+1 d. red 25 15
581 – 4 d.+2 d. blue 35 30
PORTRAITS: 2 d. 50, Franjo Racki; 4 d. Josip J. Strosmajer.

148 Danube Bridge and "Krajina" (former royal yacht)

1948. Danube Conference.

582 **148** 2 d. green . . . . 2·50 2·50
583 3 d. red . . . . 3·75 3·75
584 5 d. blue . . . . 4·50 4·50
585 10 d. brown . . . . . . 8·50 8·50

149 Kosir **150** Kosir and his Birthplace

1948. 80th Death Anniv of Laurence Kosir ("idealogical creator of first postage stamp").

586 **149** 3 d. purple (postage) . . . 15 10
587 5 d. blue 15 15
588 10 d. orange 20 10
589 12 d. green 35 25
590 **150** 15 d. mauve (air) 90 45

151 Putting the Shot **152** **153** Arms of Montenegro

1948. Projected Balkan Games.

591 **151** 2 d.+1 d. green 30 20
592 – 3 d.+1 d. red 30 20
593 – 5 d.+2 d. blue 50 40
DESIGNS: 3 d. Girl hurdler; 5 d. Pole-vaulting.

1948. Obligatory Tax. Red Cross.

594 **152** 50 p. red and blue 15 10

1948. 5th Anniv of Republic.

595 – 3 d. blue (Serbia) 40 30
596 – 3 d. red (Croatia) 40 30
597 – 3 d. orange (Slovenia) . . 40 30
598 – 3 d. green (Bosnia and Herzegovina) 40 30
599 – 3 d. mauve (Macedonia) . 40 30
600 **153** 3 d. black 40 30
601 – 10 d. red (Yugoslavia) . . 2·00 2·00
No. 601 is larger 24½×34½ mm.

154 F. Presern **155** Ski-jump, Planica

1949. Death Centenary of Franc Presern (author).

602 **154** 3 d. blue 20 15
603 5 d. orange 25 20
604 10 d. sepia . . . . 1·50 35

1949. Ski-jumping Competition, Planica.

605 **155** 3 d. blue 20 12
606 – 12 d. slate (Ski-jumper) . 1·25 65

156 Soldiers **158** Globe, Letters and Forms of Transport

1949. 5th Anniv of Liberation of Macedonia.

(a) Postage

607 **156** 3 d. red 50 40
608 – 5 d. blue . . . . 1·25 65
608a – 12 d. brown . . . . . . 2·75 2·50
DESIGNS: 5 d. Industrial and agricultural workers; 12 d. Arms and flags of Yugoslavia and Macedonia.

(b) Air. Optd with Lisunov Li-2 airplane and **AVIONSKA POSTA**.

609 **156** 3 d. red . . . . 2·50 2·50
610 – 5 d. blue (No. 608) . . . 2·50 2·50
610a – 12 d. brown (No. 608a) . 2·50 2·50

1949. 75th Anniv of U.P.U.

611 **158** 3 d. red . . . . 2·75 2·75
612 – 5 d. blue 45 45
613 **158** 12 d. brown. 45 45
DESIGN—HORIZ: 5 d. Airplane, train and mail coach.

1949. Surch with bold figures and bars.

614 O **130** 3 d. on 8 d. brown . . 40 10
615 3 d. on 12 d. violet . . 50 15

160 Nurse and Child

1949. Obligatory Tax. Red Cross.

616	160	50 p. brown and red	15	10

ФНР ЈУГОСЛАВИЈА

≡ D3 FNR JUGOSLAVIJA (161)

F N R D10 ≡ JUGOSLAVIJA (162)

1949. Surch with T **161** or **162**.

617	–	3 d. on 8 d. yellow (No. 513)	50	10
618	–	10 d. on 20 d. red (No. 517)	65	10

FNR JUGOSLAVIJA (163)

ФНР

F N R (164)

F N R JUGOSLAVIJA (165)

1949. Optd with T **163** on 2 d., **164** on 3 d. and 5 d., or **165** on others.

619	119	50 p. olive	10	10
620		1 d. green	10	10
621		1 d. orange	30	10
622	120	2 d. red	15	10
623		2 d. green	30	10
624	–	3 d. red (No. 508)	15	10
625	–	3 d. pink	30	10
626	–	5 d. blue (No. 511)	40	20
627	–	5 d. blue	50	10
628	–	12 d. violet (No. 515)	35	10
629	119	16 d. blue	1·25	40
630		20 d. red	85	15

166 Steam Locomotive of 1849

167 Surveying

1949. Centenary of National Railways.

631	166	2 d. green	1·25	35
632	–	3 d. red	1·25	35
633	–	5 d. blue	5·00	65
633a	–	10 d. orange	23·00	8·00

DESIGNS: 3 d. Modern steam locomotive; 5 d. Diesel train; 10 d. Electric locomotive.

1950. Completion of Belgrade–Zagreb Road.

634	167	2 d. green	40	15
635	–	3 d. pink	25	15
636	–	5 d. blue	1·00	70

DESIGNS: 3 d. Map, road and car; 5 d. Youth, road and flag.

168 Marshal Tito

169 Child Eating

1950. May Day.

637	168	3 d. red	2·10	40
638		5 d. blue	2·10	40
639		10 d. brown	35·00	21·00
640		12 d. black	2·10	2·00

1950. Child Welfare.

641	169	3 d. red	35	10

170 Launching Model Glider

171 Chessboard and Bishop

1950. 3rd Aeronautical Meeting.

642	170	2 d. green	80	90
643	–	3 d. red	85	90
644	–	5 d. violet	2·10	90
645	–	10 d. brown	2·25	2·10
646	–	20 d. blue	15·00	15·00

DESIGNS—VERT: 3 d. Glider in flight; 5 d. Parachutists landing; 10 d. Woman pilot; 20 d. Glider on water.

1950. 9th Chess Olympiad, Dubrovnik.

647	171	2 d. red	90	40
648	–	3 d. bistre, sepia and drab	90	30
649	–	5 d. multicoloured	1·75	50
650	–	10 d. multicoloured	2·40	1·25
651	–	20 d. yellow and blue	30·00	20·00

DESIGNS—VERT: 3 d. Rook and flags; 5 d. Chessboard showing position in 1924 Capablanca v. Lasker game, pieces and globe; 10 d. Chequered globe and map; 20 d. Knights and flags.

172 Girl Harvester

173 Train and Map

1950.

652	–	50 p. brown	10	10
653	–	1 d. green	20	10
705	–	1 d. grey	20	10
654	172	2 d. orange	20	10
718		2 d. red	3·00	15
655	–	3 d. red	20	10
656	–	5 d. blue	1·25	10
719	–	5 d. orange	1·40	15
657	–	7 d. grey	1·25	10
720	–	8 d. blue	4·50	25
658	–	10 d. brown	1·50	10
721	–	10 d. green	7·50	15
722	–	12 d. purple	45·00	25
723	–	15 d. red	18·00	10
660	–	16 d. blue	3·50	15
723a	–	17 d. purple	6·00	20
661	–	20 d. olive	3·50	15
710	–	20 d. purple	7·50	10
711a	172	25 d. bistre	13·50	10
662	–	30 d. brown	9·00	35
712	–	30 d. blue	1·75	10
713	–	35 d. brown	2·50	10
662a	–	50 d. violet	45·00	16·00
714	–	50 d. green	2·00	10
715	–	75 d. violet	3·00	10
716	–	100 d. sepia	10·50	20

DESIGNS—VERT: 50, 100 d. Metallurgy; 1 d. Electrical supply engineer; 3, 35 d. Man and woman with wheelbarrow; 5 d. Fishing; 7, 8 d. Mining; 10 d. Apple-picking; 12, 75 d. Lumbering; 14, 15, 16 d. Picking sunflowers; 17, 20 d. Woman and farm animals; 30 d. Girl printer; 50 d. Dockers unloading cargo.

1950. Zagreb Exhibition.

663	173	3 d. red	1·25	50

174 Girl in National Costume

175 Galleon

1950. Obligatory Tax. Red Cross

664	174	50 p. green and red	15	10

1950. Navy Day.

665	175	2 d. purple	30	15
666	–	3 d. brown	30	10
667	–	5 d. green	1·40	10
668	–	10 d. blue	80	15
669	–	12 d. grey	1·90	50
670	–	20 d. red	4·25	2·00

DESIGNS: 3 d. Partisan patrol boat; 5 d. Freighter discharging cargo; 10 d. "Zagreb" (freighter) and globe; 12 d. Yachts; 20 d. Sailor, gun and "Golesnica" (torpedo boat).

176 Patriots of 1941

177 Stane-Rozman

1951. 10th Anniv of Revolt against Pact with Axis.

671	176	3 d. lake and red	3·75	2·25

1951. 10th Anniv of Partisan Rising in Slovenia.

672	177	3 d. brown	50	25
673	–	5 d. blue (Boy courier)	75	35

178 Children Painting

1951. International Children's Day.

674	178	3 d. red	1·10	25

179 "Iron Gates", Danube

181 Z. Jovanovic

1951. Air.

675	179	1 d. orange	15	10
676	–	2 d. green	25	10
677	–	3 d. red	25	10
677a	–	5 d. brown	30	10
678	–	6 d. blue	4·50	4·50
679	–	10 d. brown	50	10
680	–	20 d. grey	75	10
681	–	30 d. red	2·50	10
682	–	50 d. violet	3·75	10
683	–	100 d. grey	60·00	5·00
683a	–	100 d. green	1·40	15
683b	–	200 d. red	1·75	25
683c	–	500 d. blue	7·00	1·25

DESIGNS: (all show airplane)—As T **179**: 2, 5 d. Plitvice Cascades; 3, 100 d. (green) Gozd-Martuljak (mountain village); 6, 200 d. Old Bridge, Mostar; 10 d. Ohrid; 20 d. Kotor Bay; 30 d. Dubrovnik; 50 d. Bled. 40×27 mm: 100 d. (grey), 500 d. Belgrade.

1951. Air. Zagreb Philatelic Exhibition. No. 678 in new colour optd **ZEFIZ 1951**.

684		6 d. green	90	70

1951. 10th Anniv of Serbian Insurrection.

685	181	3 d. brown	75	40
686	–	5 d. blue	1·10	65

DESIGN—HORIZ: 5 d. Armed insurgents.

183 Mt. Kopaonik

184 S. Kovacevic

1951. Air. International Mountaineering Assn Meeting, Bled. Inscr "UIAA-1951".

687	183	3 d. mauve	1·60	1·60
688	–	5 d. blue	1·60	1·60
689	–	20 d. green	95·00	65·00

DESIGNS: 5 d. Mt. Triglav; 20 d. Mt. Kalnik.

1951. 10th Anniv of Montenegrin Insurrection.

690	184	3 d. red	1·00	75
691	–	5 d. blue	1·75	1·00

DESIGN—HORIZ: 5 d. Partisan and mountains.

185 M. Oreskovic Statue

186 S. Solaj

1951. 10th Anniv of Croatian Insurrection.

692	185	3 d. red	75	35
693	–	5 d. green	1·25	65

DESIGN—VERT: 5 d. Statue: "Transport of a Wounded Man".

1951. 10th Anniv of Insurrection of Bosnia and Herzegovina.

694	186	3 d. red	90	40
695	–	5 d. blue	1·25	65

DESIGN—VERT: 5 d. Group of insurgents.

187 Parachutists Landing

189 P. Trubar (author)

1951. Air. 1st World Parachute Jumping Championship, Bled.

696	187	6 d. lake	5·00	2·00

As No. 682 in new colour optd **I SVETSKO TAKMICENJE PADOBRANACA 1951.**

697		50 d. blue	80·00	45·00

1951. Cultural Anniversaries.

698	189	10 d. black	40	25
699	–	12 d. orange	40	25
700	–	20 d. violet	5·75	4·75

PORTRAITS: 12 d. M Marulic (poet); 20 d. Tsar Stefan Dusan.

190 National Products

191 Hoisting the Flag

1951. Zagreb International Fair.

701	190	3 p. yellow, red & blue	1·10	35

1951. Obligatory Tax. Red Cross.

702	191	50 p. blue and red	15	10

192 M. Acev

193 P. P. Njegos

1951. 10th Anniv of Macedonian Insurrection.

703	192	3 d. mauve	75	40
704	–	5 d. violet	1·75	55

DESIGN—HORIZ: 5 d. War Victims' Monument, Skopje.

1951. Death Centenary of Njegos (poet).

724	193	15 d. purple	1·75	55

194 Soldier and Badge

195 Marshal Tito

1951. Army Day.

725	194	15 d. red (postage)	60	10
726	195	150 d. blue (air)	15·00	9·00

196 Marshal Tito

197

1952. Marshal Tito's 60th Birthday.

727	196	15 d. brown	1·00	1·00
728	197	28 d. lake	1·75	1·75
729	–	50 d. green	45·00	42·00

DESIGN—As T **196**: 50 d. Statue of Marshal Tito.

198

199 Gymnastics

1952. Children's Week.

730	198	15 d. red	7·50	40

1952 15th Olympic Games, Helsinki. Inscr "XV OLIMPIJADA 1952".

731	199	5 d. brown on buff	40	25
732	–	10 d. brown on yellow	40	25
733	–	15 d. brown on pink	90	30
734	–	28 d. brown on flesh	1·25	90
735	–	50 d. green on green	6·00	3·00
736	–	100 d. brown on mauve	60·00	23·00

DESIGNS: 10 d. Running; 15 d. Swimming; 28 d. Boxing; 50 d. Basketball; 100 d. Football.

200 "Fishing Boat" (from relief by Krsinic) **200a** Belgrade (XVI Cent)

1952. Navy Day. Views. Inscr "1952".
737 – 15 d. purple . . . . 1·75 60
738 **200** 28 d. brown . . . . 3·25 90
739 – 50 d. black . . . . 23·00 19·00
DESIGNS: 15 d. Split, Dalmatia; 50 d. Sveti Stefan, Montenegro.

1952. Philatelic Exhibition, Belgrade.
739a **200a** 15 d. purple . . . . . . 9·00 9·00
No. 739a was only sold at the Exhibition at 35 d. (20 d. entrance fee).

201 **202** Workers in Procession (from fresco by S. Pengov)

1952. Obligatory Tax. Red Cross.
740 **201** 50 p. red, grey & black . . 30 10

1952. 6th Yugoslavia Communist Party Congress.
741 **202** 15 d. brown . . . . 1·50 1·10
742 15 d. turquoise . . . . . 1·50 1·10
743 15 d. brown . . . . 1·50 1·10
744 15 d. blue . . . . 1·50 1·10

203 N. Tesla **204** Fresco, Sopocani Monastery

1953. 10th Death Anniv of Tesla (inventor).
745 **203** 15 d. lake . . . . 1·25 15
746 30 d. blue . . . . 4·00 40

1953. United Nations Commemoration.
747 **204** 15 d. green . . . . 1·50 60
748 – 30 d. blue . . . . 3·00 60
749 – 50 d. lake . . . . 18·00 4·75
DESIGNS—VERT: 30 d. Fresco, St. Panteleimon Church, Nerezim, Skopje; 50 d. Fresco, St. Dimitri Church, Pec.

205

1953. Adriatic Car and Motor-cycle Rally.
750 **205** 15 d. lake and pink 25 10
751 – 30 d. deep blue and blue . 70 10
752 – 50 d. brown and yellow . 1·60 10
753 – 70 d. green & turquoise . 5·00 80
DESIGNS—HORIZ: 30 d. Motor-cyclist and coastline; 50 d. Racing car and flags; 70 d. Saloon car descending mountain roadway.

206 Marshal Tito **207**

1953. Marshal Tito Commemoration.
754 **206** 50 d. violet . . . . 9·00 1·25

1953. 38th Esperanto Congress, Zagreb.
755 **207** 15 d. grn & blk (postage) . 4·50 1·50
756 300 d. green & blue (air) . £300 £275

208 "Insurrection" (from painting by B. Lazevski) **209**

1953. 50th Anniv of Macedonian Insurrection.
757 **208** 15 d. purple . . . . . . 1·00 75
758 – 30 d. green . . . . 3·25 2·00
DESIGN: 30 d. N. Karev (revolutionary).

1953. 10th Anniv of Liberation of Istria and Slovene Coast.
759 **209** 15 d. green . . . . 12·50 1·75

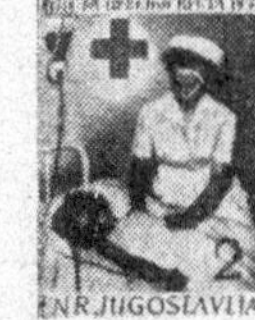

210 B. Radicevic **211** Blood-transfusion

1953. Death Centenary of Radicevic (poet).
760 **210** 15 d. purple . . . . . . 6·00 1·00

1953. Obligatory Tax. Red Cross.
761 **211** 2 d. red and purple . . . 35 35

212 Jajce **213** European Souslik

1953. 10th Anniv of 1st Republican Legislative Assembly.
762 **212** 15 d. green . . . . 1·50 45
763 – 30 d. red . . . . 2·00 1·00
764 – 50 d. sepia . . . . 11·50 9·00
DESIGNS: 30 d. Assembly Building; 50 d. Marshal Tito addressing assembly.

1954. Animals.
765 **213** 2 d. slate, buff and green 20 10
766 – 5 d. brown and green . . 35 15
767 – 10 d. brown and slate . . 60 25
768 – 15 d. brown and blue . . 80 30
769 – 17 d. sepia and purple . . 1·40 30
770 – 25 d. yellow, blue & vio . 2·50 30
771 – 30 d. sepia and blue . . . 5·00 35
772 – 35 d. black and brown . . 6·00 90
773 – 50 d. brown and bronze . 15·00 1·75
774 – 65 d. black and lake . . . 21·00 12·00
775 – 70 d. brown and turq . . 18·00 12·00
776 – 100 d. black and blue . . 60·00 32·00
DESIGNS—HORIZ: 5 d. Lynx; 10 d. Red deer; 15 d. Brown bear; 17 d. Chamois; 25 d. Eastern white pelican. VERT: 30 d. Lammergeier; 35 d. "Procerus gigas" (black beetle); 50 d. "Callimenius microgaster" (grasshopper); 65 d. Black Dalmatian lizard; 70 d. Blind cave-dwelling salamander; 100 d. Trout.

214 Ljubljana (XVII Cent)

1954. Philatelic Exhibition, Ljubljana.
777 **214** 15 d. brown, grn & blk . 15·00 11·00
No. 777 was only sold at the Exhibition at 35 d. (20 d. entrance fee).

215 Cannon, 1804

1954. 150th Anniv of Serbian Insurrection. Multicoloured.
778 15 d. Serbian flag . . . . . . 1·25 40
779 30 d. Type **215** . . . . . . 2·00 75
780 50 d. Seal of insurgents' council 3·75 90
781 70 d. Karageorge . . . . . . 35·00 10·00

215a **216**

1954. Children's Week.
781a **215a** 2 d. red 35 60

1954. Obligatory Tax. Red Cross.
782 **216** 2 d. red and green 20 10

217 V. Lisinski (composer) **218** "A Midsummer Night's Dream" (Shakespeare)

1954. Cultural Anniversaries.
783 **217** 15 d. green . . . . 3·00 45
784 – 30 d. brown . . . . 2·25 1·00
785 – 50 d. purple . . . . 2·50 1·60
786 – 70 d. blue . . . . 5·00 3·00
787 – 100 d. violet . . . . . . 22·00 18·00
PORTRAITS—VERT: 30 d. A. Kacic-Miosic (writer); 50 d. J. Vega (mathematician); 70 d. Z. J. Jovanovic (poet); 100 d. F. Visnjic (poet and musician).
See also Nos. 975/80.

1955. Dubrovnik Festival.
788 – 15 d. lake . . . . 1·00 35
789 **218** 30 d. blue . . . . 3·50 1·10
DESIGN—VERT: 15 d. Scene from "Robinja" by Hanibal Lucic.

219 **220**

1955. 1st Int Exn of Engraving, Ljubljana.
790 **219** 15 d. brown and green on grey . . . . 3·75 75

1955. 2nd World Congress of the Deaf and Dumb.
791 **220** 15 d. lake . . . . 1·90 35

221 Hops **222** Laughing Girl

1955. Vert floral designs as T **221**.
792 5 d. green & brown (T **221**) . . 15 10
793 10 d. purple, green & buff . . 15 10
794 15 d. multicoloured 20 10
795 17 d. buff, green and lake . . 30 15
796 25 d. yellow, green and blue . 30 15
797 30 d. multicoloured 70 45
798 50 d. red, green and brown . . 3·75 1·75
799 70 d. orange, green and brown 5·00 3·00
800 100 d. multicoloured . . . . . 26·00 15·00
FLOWERS: 10 d. Tobacco; 15 d. Poppy; 17 d. Linden; 25 d. Camomile; 30 d. Sage; 50 d. Wild rose; 70 d. Gentian; 100 d. Adonis.

1955. Obligatory Tax. Children's Week.
801 **222** 2 d. red 15 10

223 Peace Monument, U.N. Building, New York (A. Augustincic) **224** Red Cross Nurse

1955. 10th Anniv of United Nations.
802 **223** 30 d. black and blue . . . 1·40 55

1955. Obligatory Tax. Red Cross.
803 **224** 2 d. grey and red 20 10

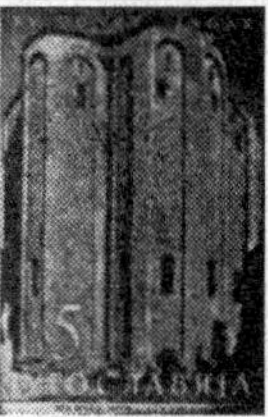

225 Woman and Dove **226** St. Donat's Church, Zadar

1955. 10th Anniv of Republic.
804 **225** 15 d. violet 40 20

1956. Yugoslav Art.
805 **226** 5 d. grey 40 10
806 – 10 d. myrtle 40 10
807 – 15 d. brown 45 10
808 – 20 d. lake 45 15
809 – 25 d. sepia 55 15
810 – 30 d. red 55 20
811 – 35 d. olive . . . . 1·10 30
812 – 40 d. lake . . . . 2·00 40
813 – 50 d. brown . . . . 5·00 30
814 – 70 d. green . . . . 12·00 7·50
815 – 100 d. purple . . . . . . 32·00 18·00
816 – 200 d. blue . . . . 48·00 30·00
DESIGNS—VERT: 10 d. Bas-relief of Croat King, Diocletian Palace, Split; 15 d. Church portal, Studenica, Serbia; 20 d. Master Radovan's portal, Trogir Cathedral; 25 d. Fresco, Sopocani, Serbia; 30 d. Monument, Radimije, Herzegovina; 50 d. Detail from Bozidarevic Triptych, Dubrovnik; 70 d. Carved figure, Belec Church, Croatia; 100 d. Self-portrait of R. Jakopic; 200 d. Peace Monument by A. Augustinic, New York. HORIZ: 35 d. Heads from Cathedral cornice, Sibenik, Dalmatia; 40 d. Frieze, Kotor Cathedral, Montenegro.

227 Zagreb through the Centuries **228** Houses ruined by Avalanche

1956. Yugoslav Int Philatelic Exn, Zagreb.
817 **227** 15 d. brown, orange and black (postage) 30 15
818 30 d. blue, red and black (air) 1·50 55

1956. Obligatory Tax. Red Cross.
819 **228** 2 d. sepia and red 15 10

229 "Technical Education" **230** Induction Motor

1956. Air. 10th Anniv of Technical Education.
820 **229** 30 d. red and black . . . 1·25 90

1956. Birth Centenary of Tesla (inventor).
821 **230** 10 d. olive 15 10
822 – 15 d. brown 40 10
823 – 30 d. blue 70 15
824 – 50 d. purple . . . . 2·25 40
DESIGNS: 15 d. Transformer; 30 d. "Telekomanda" (invention); 50 d. Portrait.

231 Sea-horse **232**

1956. Adriatic Sea Creatures. Multicoloured.
825 10 d. Type **231** 15 10
826 15 d. Common paper nautilus 15 10
827 20 d. Rock lobster 20 10
828 25 d. "Sea prince" 30 10
829 30 d. Perch 40 10
830 35 d. Red mullet 80 15
831 50 d. Scorpion fish . . . . 3·25 75
832 70 d. Wrasse . . . . 4·75 1·25
833 100 d. Dory . . . . 14·00 3·50

1956. Obligatory Tax. Children's Week.
834 **232** 2 d. green 15 10

233 Running 234

1956. Olympic Games. Figures, values and country name in ochre.

835	**233**	10 d. red	10	10
836	–	15 d. blue (Canoeing)	10	10
837	–	20 d. blue (Skiing)	20	10
838	–	30 d. green (Swimming)	30	10
839	–	35 d. sepia (Football)	45	10
840	–	50 d. green (Water-polo)	1·25	15
841	–	70 d. purple (Table-tennis)	3·75	1·25
842	–	100 d. red (Shooting)	6·50	2·50

1957. Obligatory Tax. Red Cross.

843	**234**	2 d. red, black and blue	15	10

235 Centaury **236** Factory in Worker's Hand

1957. Flowers. Multicoloured.

844	10 d. Type **235**	10	10
845	15 d. Belladonna	15	10
846	20 d. Autumn crocus	15	10
847	25 d. Marsh-mallow	20	10
848	30 d. Valerian	25	15
849	35 d. Woolly foxglove	50	15
850	50 d. Fern	1·50	40
851	70 d. Green-winged orchid	3·00	75
852	100 d. Pyrethrum	16·00	9·00

1957. 1st Congress of Workers' Councils, Belgrade.

853	**236**	15 d. lake	40	10
854		30 d. blue	85	25

237 Gymnastics

1957. 2nd Gymnastics Festival, Zagreb. Vert designs as T **237**.

855	**237**	10 d. olive and black	25	10
856	–	15 d. brown and black	25	10
857	–	30 d. blue and black	65	10
858	–	50 d. brown and black	2·00	1·50

239 Musician and Dancers of Slovenia **240** Children

1957. Yugoslav Costumes (1st series).

860	–	10 d. multicoloured	20	10
861	–	15 d. multicoloured	30	10
862	–	30 d. multicoloured	30	10
863	–	50 d. green, brn & buff	1·00	2·00
864	–	70 d. black, brn & buff	1·25	35
865	**239**	100 d. multicoloured	6·00	2·50

DESIGNS—HORIZ: 10 d. Montenegrin musician, man and woman; 15 d. Macedonian dancers; 30 d. Croatian shepherdess and shepherd boys. VERT: 50 d. Serbian peasants; 70 d. Bosnian villagers.
See also Nos. 1020/5.

1957. Obligatory Tax. Children's Week.

866	**240**	2 d. slate and red	15	10

241 Revolutionaries **242** S. Gregorcic (poet)

1957. 40th Anniv of Russian Revolution.

867	**241**	15 d. red and ochre	40	20

1957. Cultural Anniversaries.

868	**242**	15 d. sepia	30	10
869	–	30 d. blue	40	10
870	–	50 d. brown	90	10
871	–	70 d. violet	8·50	2·25
872	–	100 d. green	14·00	13·00

PORTRAITS—VERT: 30 d. A. Linhart (dramatist); 50 d. O. Kucera (physicist); 70 d. S. Mokranjac (composer); 100 d. J. Popovic (writer).

244 **245** Fresco of Sopocani Monastery

1958. 7th Yugoslav Communist Party Congress.

877	**244**	15 d. purple	20	10

1958. Obligatory Tax. Red Cross.

878	**245**	2 d. multicoloured	20	10

246 Mallard **247** Pigeon

1958. Yugoslav Game Birds. Birds in natural colours. Background colours given below.

879	**246**	10 d. brown	10	10
880	–	15 d. mauve (Capercaillie)	15	10
881	–	20 d. blue (Ring-necked pheasant)	30	10
882	–	25 d. green (Common coot)	35	10
883	–	30 d. turquoise (Water rail)	55	15
884	–	35 d. bistre (Great bustard)	65	15
885	–	50 d. purple (Rock partridge)	2·75	65
886	–	70 d. blue (Woodcock)	4·75	1·50
887	–	100 d. brown & black (Common crane)	10·50	3·50

The 25, 30, 50 and 100 d. values are vert.

1958. Opening of Postal Museum, Belgrade.

888	**247**	15 d. black	20	15

248 Battle Flag **249** Pomet, hero of Drzic's comedy "Dundo Maroje", and ancient fountain at Dubrovnik

1958. 15th Anniv of Battle of Sutjeska River.

889	**248**	15 d. lake	25	10

1958. 450th Birth Anniv of Marin Drzic (writer).

890	**249**	15 d. brown and black	40	15

243 Steel Plant, Sisak **250** Children at Play

1958.

891	–	2 d. green	10	10
892	–	5 d. red	15	10
983	–	5 d. orange	30	10
893	–	8 d. purple	25	10
984	–	8 d. violet	30	10
894	**243**	10 d. green	15	10
985	–	10 d. brown	30	10
896	–	15 d. red	30	10
986	–	15 d. green	35	10
898	–	17 d. purple	15	10
899	–	20 d. red	75	10
987	–	20 d. blue	45	10
987a	–	20 d. green	45	10
900	–	25 d. grey	35	10
988	–	25 d. red	30	10
901	–	30 d. blue	30	10
989	–	30 d. brown	4·50	10
989a	–	30 d. red	75	10
902	–	35 d. red	30	10
903	–	40 d. red	35	10
904	–	40 d. blue	1·75	10
990	–	40 d. purple	40	10
905	–	50 d. blue	35	10
991	–	50 d. blue	75	10
906	–	55 d. red	3·00	10
992	–	65 d. green	20	10
907	–	70 d. red	1·00	10
908	–	80 d. red	7·00	10
909	–	100 d. green	9·00	10
993	–	100 d. green	3·00	10
994	–	150 d. red	1·00	15
910	–	200 d. brown	3·25	15
995	–	200 d. blue	70	10
996	–	300 d. green	1·75	30
911	–	500 d. blue	6·00	35
997	–	500 d. violet	1·60	10
998	–	1000 d. brown	3·00	15
999	–	2000 d. purple	7·50	40

DESIGNS—VERT: 2, 100 d. (993) Oil derricks, Nafta; 5 d. Shipbuilding; 8, 17 d. Timber industry, cable railway; 15 (896), 20 d. Jablanica Dam; 15 (986), 25 d. (900) Ljubljana–Zagreb motor road; 25 d. (988) Cable industry; 30 d. "Litostroj" turbine factory, Ljubljana; 35, 40 d. (990) Coke plant, Lukavac; 50 d. (991) Iron foundry, Zenica; 65 d. Furnace, Sovojno. HORIZ: 40 (903/4), 150 d. Hotel Titograd; 50 (905), 55, 200 d. (995) Skopje; 70, 80, 300 d. Sarajevo railway station and obelisk; 100 (909), 500 d. (997) Bridge, Ljubljana; 200 (910), 1000 d. Theatre, Zagreb; 500 (911), 2000 d. Parliament House, Belgrade.
See also Nos. 1194/1204.

1958. Obligatory Tax. Children's Week.

912	**250**	2 d. black, olive & yellow	15	10

251 Ship with Oceanographic Equipment **252** "Human Rights"

1958. I.G.Y.

913	**251**	15 d. purple (postage)	55	15
914	–	300 d. blue (air)	7·50	2·25

DESIGN: 300 d. Moon and earth with orbital tracks of artificial satellites.

1958. 10th Anniv of Declaration of Human Rights.

915	**252**	30 d. green	65	45

253 Old City, Dubrovnik **254** Communist Party Emblem and Red Flags

1959. Tourist Publicity (1st series). Views.

916	**253**	10 d. yellow and red	10	10
917	–	10 d. blue and green	10	10
918	–	15 d. violet and blue	10	10
919	–	15 d. green and blue	10	10
920	–	20 d. green and brown	15	10
921	–	20 d. green and turquoise	15	10
922	–	30 d. violet and buff	1·00	10
923	–	30 d. green and blue	1·00	10
924	–	70 d. black and turquoise	3·00	1·00

DESIGNS: No. 917, Bled; 918, Postojna grottoes; 919, Ohrid; 920, Plitvice Lakes; 921, Opatija; 922, Split; 923, Sveti Stefan; 924, Belgrade.
See also Nos. 1033/41, 1080/5 and 1165/70.

1959. 40th Anniv of Yugoslav Communist Party.

925	**254**	20 d. multicoloured	15	10

255 "Family Assistance" **256** Dubrovnik (XV Cent)

1959 Obligatory Tax. Red Cross.

926	**255**	2 d. blue and red	15	10

1959. Philatelic Exhibition, Dubrovnik ("JUFIZ IV").

927	**256**	20 d. myrtle, green and blue	75	65

257 Lavender **258** Tug-of-War

1959. Medicinal Plants.

928	**257**	10 d. violet, green & bl	10	10
929	–	15 d. multicoloured	10	10
930	–	20 d. purple, green & bis	10	10
931	**257**	25 d. lilac, green & olive	20	10
932	–	30 d. green, blue & pink	25	15
933	–	35 d. blue, green & brn	50	15
934	–	50 d. yellow, grn & brn	2·00	40
935	–	70 d. multicoloured	3·00	75
936	–	100 d. grey, green & brn	5·00	2·00

FLOWERS: 15 d. Black alder; 20 d. Scopolia; 25 d. Monk's-head; 30 d. Bilberry; 35 d. Juniper; 50 d. Cowslip; 70 d. Pomegranate; 100 d. Thorn-apple.

1959. "Partisan" Physical Culture Festival, Belgrade.

937	**258**	10 d. black and ochre	10	10
938	–	15 d. blue and sepia	10	10
939	–	20 d. violet and brown	10	10
940	–	35 d. purple and grey	15	10
941	–	40 d. violet and grey	20	10
942	–	55 d. green and brown	35	10
943	–	80 d. olive and slate	75	40
944	–	100 d. violet and ochre	2·25	75

DESIGNS—HORIZ: 15 d. High-vaulting and running; 20 d. Gymnasium exercise; 35 d. Female exercises with hoops; 40 d. Sailors' exercises; 55 d. Handball and basketball; 80 d. Swimming and diving. VERT: 100 d. "Partisan" Association insignia.

259 Fair Emblem **260**

1959. Zagreb International Fair.

945	**259**	20 d. black and blue	45	15

1959. Obligatory Tax. Children's Tax.

946	**260**	2 d. slate and yellow	15	10

261 Athletes **262** "Reconstruction" (sculpture by L. Dolinar)

1960. Olympic Games.

947	**261**	15 d. yellow, buff and violet	10	10
948	–	20 d. drab, lav and blue	10	10
949	–	30 d. bl, stone & ultram	15	10
950	–	35 d. grey, brn & purple	15	10
951	–	40 d. drab, green and bronze	20	10
952	–	55 d. blue, drab & green	35	15
953	–	80 d. ochre, grey & red	50	25
954	–	100 d. ochre, drab and violet	60	30

DESIGNS: 20 d. Swimming; 30 d. Skiing; 35 d. Graeco-Roman wrestling; 40 d. Cycling; 55 d. Yachting; 80 d. Horse-riding; 100 d. Fencing.
Nos. 948, 950, 952 and 954 are inscr in Cyrillic characters.

1960. Obligatory Tax. Red Cross.

955	**262**	2 d. blue and red	15	10

1960. Yugoslav Forest Mammals. As T **213**. Animals in natural colours. Background colours given.

956	15 d. blue (West European hedgehog)	10	10
957	20 d. olive (Eurasian red squirrel)	15	10
958	25 d. turq (Pine marten)	15	10
959	30 d. olive (Brown hare)	20	10
960	35 d. brown (Red fox)	25	10
961	40 d. lake (Eurasian badger)	30	10
962	55 d. blue (Wolf)	45	20
963	80 d. violet (Roe deer)	70	20
964	100 d. red (Wild boar)	1·25	90

263 Lenin **264** Accelerator

1960. 90th Birth Anniv of Lenin.

965	**263**	20 d. grey and green	15	10

1960. Nuclear Energy Exhibition, Belgrade.

966	**264**	15 d. green	10	10
967	–	20 d. red	10	10
968	–	40 d. blue	20	15

DESIGNS: 20 d. Neutron generator; 40 d. Nuclear reactor.

265 Young Girl

266 Serbian National Theatre. Novi Sad (Centenary)

1960. Obligatory Tax. Children's Week.
969 **265** 2 d. red 15 10

1960. Jubilee Anniversaries.
970 **266** 15 d. black 10 10
971 – 20 d. sepia 10 10
972 – 40 d. blue 10 10
973 – 55 d. purple 15 10
974 – 80 d. green 15 10
DESIGNS: 20 d. Part of "Illyrian Renaissance" (allegorical figure), after V. Bukovac (cent of Croat National Theatre, Zagreb); 40 d. Edvard Rusijan and Bleriot XI airplane (50th anniv of 1st flight in Yugoslavia); 55 d. Symbolic hand holding fruit (15th anniv of Republic); 80 d. Symbol of nuclear energy (15th anniv of U.N.O.).

1960. Cultural Annivs. Portraits as T **217**.
975 15 d. green 10 10
976 20 d. brown 10 10
977 40 d. bistre 15 10
978 55 d. red 20 10
979 80 d. blue 40 10
980 100 d. turquoise 40 15
PORTRAITS: 15 d. I. Cankar (writer); 20 d. S. S. Kranjcevic (poet); 40 d. P. Jovanovic (painter); 55 d. D. Jaksic (writer); 80 d. M. Pupin (physician); 100 d. R. Boskovic (astronomer).

268 "Blood Transfusion"

269 "Atomic Energy"

1961. Obligatory Tax. Red Cross. Perf or imperf.
981 **268** 2 d. multicoloured 15 10

1961. Int Nuclear Electronic Conference, Belgrade.
982 **269** 25 d. red and grey 15 10

1961. Medicinal Plants. As T **257**. Multicoloured.
1000 10 d. Yellow foxglove 10 10
1001 15 d. Marjoram 10 10
1002 20 d. Hyssop 10 10
1003 25 d. White thorn 10 10
1004 40 d. Rose mallow 15 10
1005 50 d. Soapwort 15 10
1006 60 d. Clary-sage 25 10
1007 80 d. Blackthorn 40 10
1008 100 d. Marigold 90 40
See also Nos. 1074/9.

271 Stevan Filipovic (statue by V. Bakic)

273 St. Clement (14th-century wood-carving)

272

1961. 20th Anniv of Yugoslav Insurrection. Inscriptions in gold.
1009 **271** 15 d. brown and red . . 10 10
1010 – 20 d. yellow and sepia . . 10 10
1011 – 25 d. green and turq . . 10 10
1012 – 60 d. violet and blue . . 15 10
1013 – 100 d. indigo and blue . . 30 20
DESIGNS: 20 d. Insurrection Monument, Bosansko Grahovo (relief by S. Stojanovic); 25 d. Executed Inhabitants Monument, Kragujevac (by A Grzetic); 60 d. Nova Gradiska Victory monument (by A. Augustincic); 100 d. Marshal Tito (Revolution Monument, Titovo Uzice, statue by Krsinic).

1961. Non-Aligned Countries Conf, Belgrade.
1014 **272** 25 d. sepia (postage) . . 10 10
1015 – 50 d. green 20 10

1016 **272** 250 d. purple (air) . . . 1·00 50
1017 – 500 d. blue . . . . . . 2·50 1·25
DESIGN: 50, 500 d. National Assembly Building, Belgrade.

1961. 12th International Congress of Byzantine Studies, Ohrid.
1018 **273** 25 d. sepia and olive . . 20 10

274 Bird with Flower in Beak

275 L. Vukalovic (revolutionary leader)

1961. Obligatory Tax. Children's Week.
1019 **274** 2 d. orange and violet . 15 10

1961. Yugoslav Costumes (2nd series). As T **239**. Inscr "1941–1961".
1020 15 d. multicoloured 15 10
1021 25 d. black, red and brown . 15 10
1022 30 d. sepia, red and brown . 25 10
1023 50 d. multicoloured 35 10
1024 65 d. multicoloured 45 10
1025 100 d. multicoloured . . . . 1·60 50
DESIGNS-HORIZ: Costumes of: 15 d. Serbia; 25 d. Montenegro; 30 d. Bosnia and Herzegovina; 50 d. Macedonia; 65 d. Croatia; 100 d. Slovenia.

1961. Centenary of Herzegovina Insurrection.
1026 **275** 25 d. black 15 10

276 Hands holding Flower and Rifle

277 Miladinovci Brothers

1961. 20th Anniv of Yugoslav Partisan Army.
1027 **276** 25 d. blue and red . . . 20 10

1961. Centenary of Macedonian National Songs by brothers Miladinovci.
1028 **277** 25 d. purple and buff . . 20 10

278 "Mother's Play" (after P. Krsinic)

279 Mosquito

1962. 15th Anniv of U.N.I.C.E.F.
1029 **278** 50 d. black on buff . . 15 10

1962. Malaria Eradication.
1030 **279** 50 d. black on blue . . 15 10

280 Goddess Isis (from Temple at Kalabscha)

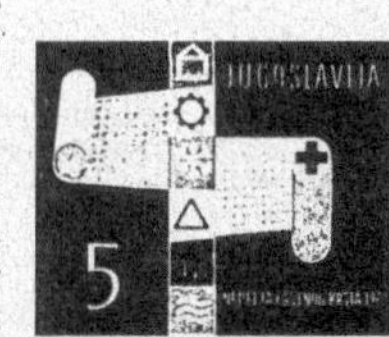

281 Bandages and Symbols

1962. 15th Anniv of U.N.E.S.C.O.
1031 **280** 25 d. green on cream . . 10 10
1032 – 50 d. brown on buff . . 20 10
DESIGN: 50 d. Rameses II (Nubian monument) and U.N.E.S.C.O. emblem.

1962. Tourist Publicity (2nd series). Views as T **253**. Inscr "1941–1961".
1033 15 d. olive and blue 15 10
1034 15 d. orange and turquoise . . 15 10
1035 25 d. brown and blue . . . 20 10
1036 25 d. blue and light blue . . 20 10
1037 30 d. blue and brown . . . 30 10
1038 30 d. blue and purple . . . 50 10
1039 50 d. turq and bistre . . . 1·25 10
1040 50 d. blue and bistre . . . 1·25 10
1041 100 d. grey and green . . . 5·00 60
VIEWS: No. 1033, Portoroz; 1034, Jajce; 1035, Zadar; 1036, Popova Sapka; 1037, Hvar; 1038, Kotor Bay; 1039, Djerdap; 1040, Rab; 1041, Zagreb.

1962. Obligatory Tax. Red Cross.
1042 **281** 5 d. red, brown & grey . 15 10

282 Marshal Tito (after sculpture by A. Augustincic)

283 Pole-vaulting

1962. Marshal Tito's 70th Birthday.
1043 **282** 25 d. turquoise 10 10
1044 – 50 d. brown 20 10
1045 **282** 100 d. blue 65 20
1046 – 200 d. myrtle . . . . . 1·50 75
DESIGN: 50, 200 d. As Type **282** but profile view of bust.

1962. Yugoslav Amphibians and Reptiles. As T **213**. Inscr "1962". Animals in natural colours. Background colours given.
1047 15 d. green (Crested newt) . . 15 10
1048 20 d. violet (Spotted salamander) 15 10
1049 25 d. brown (Yellow-bellied toad) 15 10
1050 30 d. blue (Marsh frog) . . . 15 10
1051 50 d. brown (Pond tortoise) . 20 10
1052 65 d. green (Wall lizard) . . 25 10
1053 100 d. black (Green lizard) . 40 25
1054 150 d. brn (Leopard snake) . 1·00 50
1055 200 d. red (Common viper) . 2·25 1·10

1962. 7th European Athletic Championships, Belgrade. Sportsmen in black.
1056 **283** 15 d. blue 10 10
1057 – 25 d. purple 10 10
1058 – 30 d. green 10 10
1059 – 50 d. red 10 10
1060 – 65 d. blue 15 10
1061 – 100 d. turquoise 25 15
1062 – 150 d. orange 35 20
1063 – 200 d. brown 65 40
DESIGNS—HORIZ: 25 d. Throwing the discus; 50 d. Throwing the javelin; 100 d. Start of sprint; 200 d. High jumping. VERT: 30 d. Running; 65 d. Putting the shot; 150 d. Hurdling.

284 "Physical Culture"

285 "Bathing the Newborn Child" (Decani Monastery)

1962. Children's Week.
1064 **284** 25 d. black and red . . . 15 10

1962. Yugoslav Art. Multicoloured.
1065 25 d. Situla of Vace (detail from bronze vessel) (horiz) . . . 10 10
1066 30 d. Golden Mask of Trebiniste (5th-cent burial mask) (horiz) 10 10
1067 50 d. The God Kairos (Trogir Monastery) 15 10
1068 65 d. Pigeons of Nerezi (detail from series of frescoes, "The Visitation", Nerezi Church, Skopje) 25 20
1069 100 d. Type **285** 55 30
1070 150 d. Icon of Ohrid (detail from 14th-cent icon, "The Annunciation") (horiz) . . 1·10 75
See also Nos. 1098/1103.

286 Ear of Wheat and Parched Earth

287 Dr. A. Mohorovicic (meteorologist)

1963. Freedom from Hunger.
1071 **286** 50 d. purple on stone . . 20 10

1963. World Meteorological Day.
1072 **287** 50 d. blue on grey 20 10

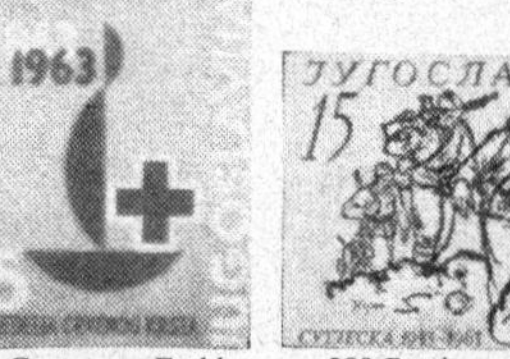

288 Centenary Emblem

289 Partisans in File

1963. Obligatory Tax. Red Cross Centenary and Red Cross Week.
1073 **288** 5 d. red, grey and ochre . 20 10

1963. Medicinal Plants. As T **257** but dated "1963". Flowers in natural colours. Colours of backgrounds, panels and inscr given.
1074 15 d. dp green, green & blk . 15 10
1075 25 d. cobalt, blue & violet . 15 10
1076 30 d. grey and blue 15 10
1077 50 d. light brown & brown . 20 10
1078 65 d. light brown & brown . 40 15
1079 100 d. slate and deep slate . 1·40 40
FLOWERS: 15 d. Lily of the valley; 25 d. Iris; 30 d. Bistort; 50 d. Henbane; 65 d. St. John's wort; 100 d. Caraway.

1963. Tourist Publicity (3rd series). Views as T **253**. Inscr "1963". Multicoloured.
1080 15 d. Pula 10 10
1081 25 d. Vrnjacka Banja 10 10
1082 30 d. Crikvenica 10 10
1083 50 d. Korcula 15 10
1084 65 d. Durmitor 15 15
1085 100 d. Ljubljana 90 25

1963. 20th Anniv of Battle of Sutjeska River.
1086 **289** 15 d. green and drab . . 10 10
1087 – 25 d. green 10 10
1088 – 50 d. violet and pale brn 20 10
DESIGNS—VERT: 25 d. Sutjeska Gorge. HORIZ: 50 d. Partisans in battle.
See also No. 1125.

290 Gymnast on "Horse"

291 "Mother"

1963. 5th European Cup Gymnastic Championships.
1089 **290** 25 d. green and black . . 10 10
1090 – 50 d. blue and black . . 15 15
1091 – 100 d. brown and black . 50 45
DESIGNS—Gymnast: 50 d. on parallel bars; 100 d. exercising with rings.

1963. Sculptures by Ivan Mestrovic.
1092 **291** 25 d. bistre on brown . . 10 10
1093 – 50 d. blue on black . . 15 10
1094 – 65 d. green on blue . . . 50 30
1095 – 100 d. black on grey . . 65 50
SCULPTURES: 50 d. "Reminiscence" (nude female figure); 65 d. "Kraljevic Marko" (head); 100 d. "Indian on horseback".

292 Children with Toys

293 Soldier and Emblem

1963. Children's Week.
1096 **292** 25 d. multicoloured . . . 25 10

1963. 20th Anniv of Yugoslav Democratic Federation.
1097 **293** 25 d. red, green and drab 15 10

1963 Yugoslav Art. Designs as T **285**. Inscr "1963". Multicoloured.
1098 25 d. "Man", relief on Radimlje tombstone (13th-15th cents) 10 10
1099 30 d. Detail of relief on door of Split Cathedral, after A. Buvina (13th-cent) 10 10
1100 50 d. Detail of fresco in Beram Church (15th-cent) 15 10
1101 65 d. Archangel Michael from plaque in Dominican Monastery, Dubrovnik (15th-cent) 20 15
1102 100 d. Figure of man on Baroque fountain, by F. Robba, Ljubljana (18th-cent) 25 15
1103 150 d. Archbishop Eufraise, detail of mosaic in Porec Basilica (6th-cent) 70 70
The 30 and 50 d. are horiz.

294 D. Obradovic (writer)

295 Parachute

1963. Cultural Celebrities.
1104 **294** 25 d. black on buff . . . 10 10
1105 – 30 d. black on blue . . . 10 10
1106 – 50 d. black on cream . . 15 10
1107 – 65 d. black on lilac . . . 25 20
1108 – 100 d. black on pink . . 40 35
PORTRAITS: 30 d. V. S. Karadzic (language reformer); 50 d. F. Miklosic (philologist); 65 d. L. Gaj (writer); 100 d. P. P. Njegos (poet).
See also Nos. 1174/9.

1964. Obligatory Tax. Red Cross Week and 20th Anniv of Yugoslav Red Cross.
1109 **295** 5 d. red, purple & blue . 15 10

296 "Inachis io" **297** Fireman saving Child

1964. Butterflies. Multicoloured.
1110 25 d. Type **296** 10 10
1111 30 d. "Nymphalis antiopa" . 10 10
1112 40 d. "Daphnis nerii" 10 10
1113 50 d. "Parnassius apollo" . . 15 10
1114 150 d. "Nyctaon pyri" . . . 45 25
1115 200 d. "Papilio machaon" . . 65 35

1964. Centenary of Voluntary Fire Brigade
1116 **297** 25 d. sepia and red . . . 20 10

298 Running **299** "Reconstruction"

1964. Olympic Games, Tokyo.
1117 **298** 25 d. yellow, blk & grey . 10 10
1118 – 30 d. violet, blk & grey . 10 10
1119 – 40 d. green, blk & grey . 10 10
1120 – 50 d. multicoloured . . 15 10
1121 – 150 d. multicoloured . . 20 15
1122 – 200 d. blue, black & grey 30 25
DESIGNS: 30 d. Boxing; 40 d. Rowing; 50 d. Basketball; 150 d. Football; 200 d. Water-polo.

1964. 1st Anniv of Skopje Earthquake.
1123 **299** 25 d. brown 15 10
1124 – 50 d. blue 20 10
DESIGN: 50 d. "International Aid" (U.N. flag over town).

1964. 20th Anniv of Occupation of Vis Island. As T **289** but inscr "VIS 1944–1964" at foot.
1125 25 d. red and grey 15 10

300 Costumes of Kosovo-Metohija (Serbia) **301** F. Engels

1964. Yugoslav Costumes (3rd series). As T **300**. Multicoloured.
1126 25 d. Type **300** 10 10
1127 30 d. Slovenia 15 10
1128 40 d. Bosnia and Herzegovina 15 10
1129 50 d. Hrvatska (Croatia) . . 15 10
1130 150 d. Macedonia 65 25
1131 200 d. Crna Gora (Montenegro) 85 40

1964. Centenary of "First International".
1132 **301** 25 d. black on cream . . 10 10
1133 – 50 d. black on lilac . . 15 10
DESIGN: 50 d. Karl Marx.

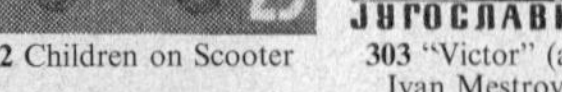

302 Children on Scooter **303** "Victor" (after Ivan Mestrovic)

1964. Children's Week.
1134 **302** 25 d. green, black & red . 20 10

1964. 20th Anniv of Liberation of Belgrade.
1135 **303** 25 d. black and green on pink 10 10

304 Initial of Hilander's Gospel (13th cent) **305** "Hand of Equality"

1964. Yugoslav Art. Inscr "1964". Multicoloured.
1136 25 d. Type **304** 10 10
1137 30 d. Initial of Miroslav's gospel (12th cent) 10 10
1138 40 d. Detail from Cetinje octateuch (15th cent) . . . 10 10
1139 50 d. Miniature from Trogir's gospel (13th cent) 10 10
1140 150 d. Miniature from Hrvoe's missal (15th cent) 30 10
1141 200 d. Miniature from Herman Priory, Bistrica (14th cent) (horiz) 55 40

1964. 8th Yugoslav Communist League Congress. Multicoloured.
1142 25 d. Type **305** 10 10
1143 50 d. Dove and factory ("Peace and Socialism") 10 10
1144 100 d. Industrial plant ("Socialism") 25 20

306 Table-tennis Player **307** Children around Red Cross

1965. World Table-tennis Championship, Ljubljana.
1145 **306** 50 d. multicoloured . . 15 10
1146 – 150 d. multicoloured . . 35 20
DESIGN: 150 d. As Type **306** but design arranged in reverse.

1965. Obligatory Tax. Red Cross Week.
1147 **307** 5 d. red and brown . . 10 10

308 Titograd **309** Young Partisan (after D. Andrejevic-Kun)

1965. 20th Anniv of Liberation. Yugoslav Capitals.
1148 **308** 25 d. purple 10 10
1149 – 30 d. brown 10 10
1150 – 40 d. violet 10 10
1151 – 50 d. green 10 10
1152 – 150 d. violet 25 10
1153 – 200 d. blue 50 45
CAPITALS: 30 d. Skopje; 40 d. Sarajevo; 50 d. Ljubljana; 150 d. Zagreb; 200 d. Belgrade.

1965. "Twenty Years of Freedom" Pioneer Games.
1154 **309** 25 d. blk & brn on buff 15 10

310 T.V. Tower, Avala (Belgrade) **311** Yarrow

1965. Centenary of I.T.U.
1155 **310** 50 d. blue 15 10

1965. Inauguration of Djerdap Hydro-Electric Project. As Nos. 3271/2 of Rumania.
1156 – 25 d. (30 b.) green & grey 15 10
1157 – 50 d. (55 b.) red & grey . 30 10
DESIGN: 25 d. Djerdap Gorge; 50 d. Djerdap Dam.
Nos. 1156/7 were issued simultaneously in Rumania.

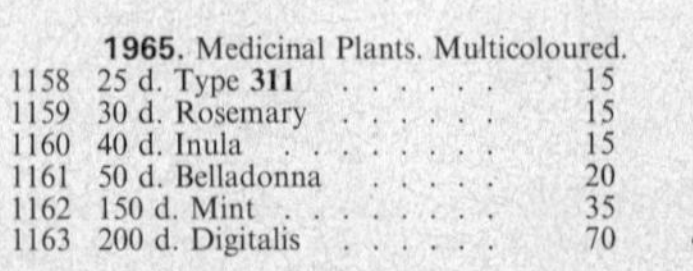

1965. Medicinal Plants. Multicoloured.
1158 25 d. Type **311** 15 10
1159 30 d. Rosemary 15 10
1160 40 d. Inula 15 10
1161 50 d. Belladonna 20 10
1162 150 d. Mint 35 15
1163 200 d. Digitalis 70 40

312 I.C.Y. Emblem **313** Sibenik

1965. International Co-operation Year.
1164 **312** 50 d. violet, indigo and blue 15 10

1965. Tourist Publicity (4th series). Multicoloured.
1165 25 d. Rogaska Slatina 10 10
1166 30 d. Type **313** 10 10
1167 40 d. Prespa Lake 10 10
1168 50 d. Prizren 10 10
1169 150 d. Skadar Lake 25 10
1170 200 d. Sarajevo 40 40

314 Cat **316** Marshal Tito

1965. Children's Week.
1171 **314** 30 d. lake and yellow . . 40 10

1965. Nos. 984 and 988 surch.
1172 5 d. on 8 d. violet 40 10
1173 50 d. on 25 d. red 40 10

1965. Cultural Celebrities. Portraits as T **294**.
1174 30 d. red on pink 10 10
1175 50 d. slate on blue 10 10
1176 60 d. sepia on brown 10 10
1177 85 d. indigo on blue 15 10
1178 200 d. olive on pale olive . . 15 15
1179 500 d. mauve on purple . . . 35 30
PORTRAITS: 30 d. B. Nusic (author and dramatist); 50 d. A. G. Matos (poet); 60 d. I. Mazuranic (author); 85 d. F. Levstik; 200 d. J. Pancic (botanist); 500 d. D. Tucovic (politician).

(Currency revalued. 100 paras = 1 dinar = 100 old dinars)

1966.
1180 **316** 20 p. green 25 10
1181 30 p. red 45 10

317 Jumping (Balkan Games, Sarajevo) **318** "T", 15th-cent Psalter

1966. Sports Events.
1182 **317** 30 p. red 10 10
1183 – 50 p. violet 10 10
1184 – 1 d. green 10 10
1185 – 3 d. brown 20 15
1186 – 5 d. blue 45 35
DESIGNS AND EVENTS: 50 p. Ice-hockey and 3 d. Ice-hockey sticks and puck (World Ice-hockey Championships, Jesenice, Ljubljana and Zagreb); 1 d. Rowing and 5 d. Oars (World Rowing Championships, Bled).

1966. Yugoslav Art. Manuscript initials. Multicoloured.
1187 30 p. Type **318** 10 10
1188 50 p. "V", 14th-cent Divos gospel 10 10
1189 60 p. "R", 12th-cent Libri moralium of Gregory I . . 10 10
1190 85 p. "P", 12th-cent Miroslav gospel 15 15
1191 2 d. "B", 13th-cent Radomir gospel 25 15
1192 5 d. "F", 11th-cent passional 45 30

319 Red Cross Emblem

320 Beam Aerial on Globe

1966. Obligatory Tax. Red Cross Week.
1193 **319** 5 p. multicoloured . . . 10 10

1966. As Nos. 983, etc, but values expressed "0.05" etc, colours changed and new values.
1194 5 p. orange 10 10
1195 10 p. brown 10 10
1196 15 p. blue 20 10
1197 20 p. green 25 10
1198 30 p. red 75 10
1199 40 p. purple 30 10
1200 50 p. blue 30 10
1201 60 p. brown 30 10
1202 65 p. green 30 10
1203 85 p. purple 40 10
1204 1 d. olive 65 10
NEW VALUES: 60 p. as No. 988, 85 p. as No. 984.

1966. International Amateur Radio Union Regional Conference, Opatija.
1205 **320** 85 p. blue 15 10

321 "Lucanus cervus" **322** Serbian 1 para Stamp of 1866

1966. Insects. Multicoloured.
1206 30 p. Type **321** 10 10
1207 50 p. "Cetonia aurata" . . . 10 10
1208 60 p. "Meloe violaceus" . . 10 10
1209 85 p. "Coccinella septempunctata" 15 10
1210 2 d. "Rosalia alpina" 25 15
1211 5 d. "Dytiscus marginalis" . 55 25

1966. Serbian Stamp Centenary.
1212 **322** 30 p. green, lake & brn . 10 10
1213 – 50 p. lake, bistre & ochre 10 10
1214 – 60 p. orange and green . 10 10
1215 – 85 p. red and blue . . . 15 15
1216 – 2 d. bl, bronze & green . 45 25
DESIGNS—(Serbian Stamps of 1866): 50 p.—2 p.; 60 p.—10 p.; 85 p.—20 p.; 2 d.—40 p.

323 Rebels on Shield **324** Strossmayer and Racki (founders)

1966. 25th Anniv of Yugoslav Insurrection.
1218 **323** 20 p. brown, gold & grn 10 10
1219 30 p. mauve, gold & buff 10 10
1220 85 p. blue, gold and stone 10 10
1221 2 d. violet, gold & blue . 15 15

1966. Centenary of Yugoslav Academy.
1222 **324** 30 p. black and drab . . 15 10

325 Old Bridge, Mostar **325a** Medieval View of Sibenik

1966. 400th Anniv of Old Bridge, Mostar.
1223 **325** 30 p. purple 75 10

1966. 900th Anniv of Sibenik.
1224 **325a** 30 p. purple 20 10

326 "The Girl in Pigtails" **327** U.N.E.S.C.O. Emblem

1966. Children's Week.
1225 **326** 30 p. multicoloured . . . 50 10

1966. 20th Anniv of U.N.E.S.C.O.
1226 **327** 85 p. blue 20 10

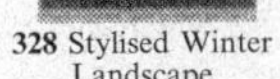

328 Stylised Winter Landscape
329 Dinar of Durad I Balsic

1966. Christmas.
1227 **328** 15 p. yellow and blue . . 10 10
1228 – 20 p. yellow and blue . . 10 10
1229 – 30 p. yellow and green . . 10 10
DESIGNS: 20 p. Father Christmas; 30 p. Stylised Christmas tree.
See also Nos. 1236/8.

1966. Yugoslav Art. Designs showing different coins.
1230 **329** 30 p. multicoloured . . . 10 10
1231 – 50 p. multicoloured . . . 10 10
1232 – 60 p. multicoloured . . . 10 10
1233 – 85 p. multicoloured . . . 10 10
1234 – 2 d. multicoloured . . . 30 15
1235 – 5 d. multicoloured . . . 70 30
MEDIEVAL COINS (Dinars of): 50 p. King Stefan Tomasevic; 60 p. Durad Brankovic; 85 p. Ljubljana; 2 d. Split; 5 d. Emperor Stefan Dusan.

1966. New Year. As Nos. 1227/9 but colours changed.
1236 15 p. gold, blue and indigo . 15 15
1237 20 p. gold, red and pink . . 15 15
1238 30 p. gold, myrtle and green . 15 15

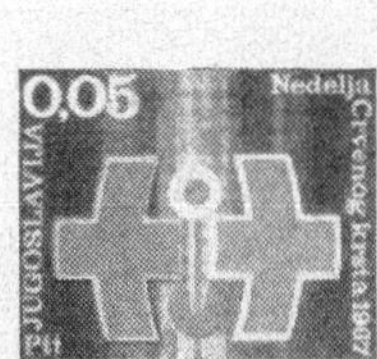

330 Flower between Red Crosses
331 "Arnica montana"

1967. Obligatory Tax. Red Cross Week.
1239 **330** 5 p. red, green and blue . 10 10

1967. Medicinal Plants. Multicoloured.
1240 30 p. Type **331** 10 10
1241 50 p. "Linum usitatissimum" 10 10
1242 85 p. "Nerium oleander" . . 10 10
1243 1 d. 20 "Gentiana cruciata" . 15 10
1244 3 d. "Laurus nobil" 30 15
1245 5 d. "Peganum harmais" . . 65 40

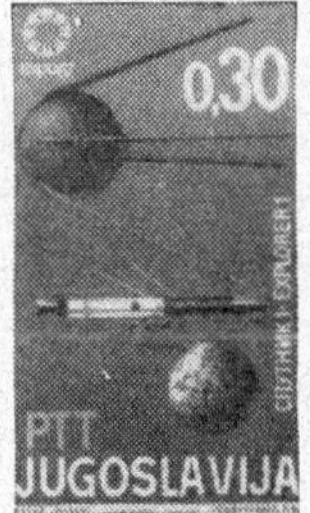

332 President Tito
333 "Sputnik I" and "Explorer I"

1967. Pres. Tito's 75th Birthday. (a) Size as T **332**.
1256 **332** 5 p. orange 15 10
1257 10 p. brown 15 10
1258 15 p. violet 15 10
1259 20 p. green 15 10
1260 20 p. blue . . . . . . 1·50 10
1261 25 p. red 15 10
1262a 30 p. red . . . . . . 1·50 10
1263 30 p. myrtle 30 10
1264 40 p. black 15 10
1265 50 p. turquoise . . . . . 2·00 10
1266a 50 p. red 30 10
1267 60 p. purple 15 10
1268 70 p. sepia 40 10
1269 75 p. green 50 10
1270 80 p. brown . . . . . . 2·25 10
1270a 80 p. red 45 10
1271 85 p. blue 50 10
1272 90 p. brown 35 10
1273 1 d. lake 25 15
1274 1 d. 20 blue 75 10
1274a 1 d. 20 green 70 10
1275 1 d. 25 blue 55 10
1276 1 d. 50 green 50 10

(b) Size 20 × 30 mm.
1277 **332** 2 d. sepia . . . . . . 1·50 10
1278 2 d. 50 green . . . . . 1·50 10
1279 5 d. purple . . . . . . 1·25 20
1280 10 d. purple . . . . . . 3·00 35
1281 20 d. green . . . . . . 2·75 40

1967. World Fair, Montreal. Space Achievements. Multicoloured.
1282 30 p. Type **333** 10 10
1283 50 p. "Tiros", "Telstar" and "Molyna" 10 10
1284 85 p. "Luna 9" and lunar orbiter 10 10
1285 1 d. 20 "Mariner 4" and "Venus 3" 15 10
1286 3 d. "Vostok I" and Gemini-Agena space vehicle . . . 15 15
1287 5 d. Leonov in space 50 50

334 St. Tripun's Church, Kotor

1967. International Tourist Year.
1288 **334** 30 p. green and blue . . 10 10
1289 – 50 p. violet and brown . 10 10
1290 – 85 p. purple and blue . 10 10
1291 – 1 d. 20 brown & purple 15 10
1292 – 3 d. olive and brown . . 40 10
1293 – 5 d. brown and olive . . 60 55
DESIGNS: 50 p. Town Hall, Maribor; 85 p. Trogir Cathedral; 1 d. 20, Fortress gate, Nis; 3 d. Bridge, Visegrad; 5 d. Ancient bath, Skopje.

335 Bobwhite
336 Congress Emblem

1967. International Hunting and Fishing Exhibition and Fair, Novi Sad. Multicoloured.
1294 30 p. Type **335** 40 10
1295 50 p. Pike 15 10
1296 1 d. 20 Red deer 25 10
1297 5 d. Peregrine falcon . . . . 2·25 55

1967. International Astronautical Federation Congress, Belgrade.
1298 **336** 85 p. gold light blue and blue 15 10

337 Old Theatre Building
338 "Winter Landscape" (A. Becirovic)

1967. Centenary of Slovene National Theatre, Ljubljana.
1299 **337** 30 p. brown and green . 15 10

1967. Children's Week.
1300 **338** 30 p. multicoloured . . 50 10

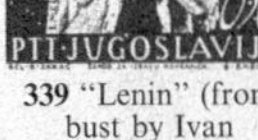

339 "Lenin" (from bust by Ivan Mestrovic)
340 Four-leaved Clover

1967. 50th Anniv of October Revolution.
1301 **339** 30 p. violet 10 10
1302 85 p. brown 15 10

1967. New Year. Inscr "1968".
1304 **340** 20 p. gold, blue & grn . 10 10
1305 – 30 p. gold, violet and yellow 10 10
1306 – 50 p. gold, red and lilac 10 10
DESIGNS: 30 p. Sweep with ladder; 50 p. Horseshoe and flower.
See also Nos. 1347/9.

341 "The Young Sultana" (V. Bukovac)

1967. Yugoslav Paintings (1st series). Multicoloured.
1307 85 p. "The Watchtower" (D. Jaksic) 10 10
1308 1 d. Type **341** 15 10
1309 2 d. "At Home" (J. Petkovsek) 20 15
1310 3 d. "The Cock-fight" (P. Jovanovic) 30 25
1311 5 d. "Summer" (I. Kobilca) . 50 40
The 85 p. and 5 d. are vert.
See also Nos. 1337/41, 1399/1404. 1438/43, 1495/1500, 1535/40, 1570/5, 1616/19, 1750/5 and 1793/8.

342 Ski-jumping

1968. Winter Olympic Games, Grenoble.
1312 **342** 50 p. purple and blue . . 10 10
1313 – 1 d. olive and brown . . 10 10
1314 – 2 d. lake and black . . . 15 10
1315 – 5 d. blue and olive . . . 50 40
DESIGNS: 1 d. Figure-skating (pairs); 2 d. Downhill skiing; 5 d. Ice-hockey.

343 "The Madonna and Child" (St. George's Church, Prizren)
344 Honeycomb on Red Cross

1968. Medieval Icons. Multicoloured.
1316 50 p. Type **343** 10 10
1317 1 d. "The Annunciation" (Ohrid Museum) 15 10
1318 1 d. 50 "St. Sava and St. Simeon" (Belgrade Museum) 20 10
1319 2 d. "The Descent" (Ohrid Museum) 30 20
1320 3 d. "The Crucifixion" (St. Clement's Church, Ohrid) 35 25
1321 5 d. "The Madonna and Child" (Gospe od zvonika Church, Split) 75 75

1968. Obligatory Tax. Red Cross Week.
1322 **344** 5 p. multicoloured . . . 10 10

345 Bullfinch
346 Running (Women's 800 metres)

1968. Song Birds. Multicoloured.
1323 50 p. Type **345** 15 10
1324 1 d. Goldfinch 15 10
1325 1 d. 50 Chaffinch 30 10
1326 2 d. Greenfinch 40 15
1327 3 d. Red crossbill 80 15
1328 5 d. Hawfinch . . . . . . 1·25 50

1968. Olympic Games, Mexico.
1329 **346** 50 p. pur & brn on cream 10 10
1330 – 1 d. olive & turq on grn . 10 10
1331 – 1 d. 50 sep & bl on flesh 15 10
1332 – 2 d. grn & bistre on cream 15 10
1333 – 3 d. indigo & violet on blue 15 10
1334 – 5 d. pur & grn on mauve 35 40
DESIGNS: 1 d. Basketball; 1 d. 50, Gymnastics; 2 d. Sculling; 3 d. Water-polo; 5 d. Wrestling.

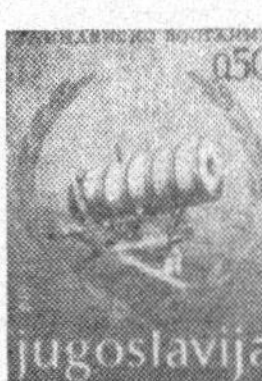

347 Rebel Cannon
348 "Mother and Children" (fresco in Hrastovlje Church, Slovenia)

1968. 65th Anniv of Ilinden Uprising.
1335 **347** 50 p. brown and gold . . 15 10

1968. 25th Anniv of Partisan Occupation of Istria and Slovenian Littoral.
1336 **348** 50 p. multicoloured . . . 10 10

349 "Lake of Klansko" (M. Pernhart)

1968. Yugoslav Paintings (2nd series). 19th-cent Landscapes. Multicoloured.
1337 1 d. Type **349** 10 10
1338 1 d. 50 "Bavarian Landscape" (M. Popovic) 15 10
1339 2 d. "Gateway, Zadar" (F. Quiquerez) 25 10
1340 3 d. "Triglav from Bohinj" (A. Karinger) 35 20
1341 5 d. "Studenica Monastery" (D. Krstic) 85 90

350 A. Santic
351 "Promenade" (Marina Cudov)

1968. Birth Centenary of Aleksa Santic (poet).
1342 **350** 50 p. blue 10 10

1968. Children's Week.
1343 **351** 50 p. multicoloured . . . 15 10

352 Karl Marx (after sculpture by N. Mitric)
353 Aztec Emblem and Olympic Rings

1968. 150th Birth Anniv of Karl Marx.
1344 **352** 50 p. red 10 10

1968. Obligatory Tax. Olympic Games Fund.
1345 **353** 10 p. multicoloured . . . 10 10

354 Old Theatre and View of Kalemegdan
355 Hassan Brkic

1968. Centenary of Serbian National Theatre, Belgrade.
1346 **354** 50 p. bistre and green . . 10 10

1968. New Year. Designs as Nos. 1304/6 but colours changed and inscr "1969".
1347 20 p. gold, blue and lilac . . 10 10
1348 30 p. gold, violet and green . 10 10
1349 50 p. gold, red and yellow . 10 10

1968. Yugoslav National Heroes.
1350 **355** 50 p. violet 10 10
1351 – 75 p. black 15 10
1352 – 1 d. 25 brown 15 10
1353 – 2 d. blue 20 10
1354 – 2 d. 50 green 25 15
1355 – 5 d. lake 60 60
PORTRAITS: 75 p. I. Milutinovic; 1 d. 25, R. Koncar; 2 d. K. Josifovski; 2 d. 50, T. Tomsic; 5 d. M. Pijade.

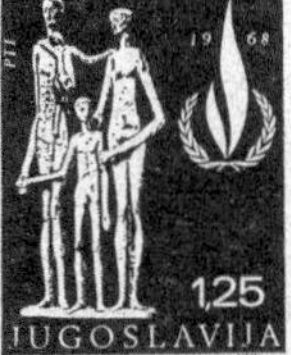

356 "Family" (sculpture by J. Soldatovic) and Human Rights Emblem
357 I.L.O. Emblem

1968. Human Rights Year.
1357 **356** 1 d. 25 blue 10 10

1969. 50th Anniv of I.L.O.
1358 **357** 1 d. 25 black and red . . 10 10

358 Dove on Hammer and Sickle Emblem
359 "St. Nikita" (Manasija Monastery)

1969. 50th Anniv of Yugoslav Communist Party.
1359 **358** 50 p. red and black . . . 10 10
1360 – 75 p. black and ochre . . 10 10
1361 – 1 d. 25 black and red . . 15 10
DESIGNS: 75 p. "Tito" and star (wall graffiti); 1 d. 25, Five-pointed crystal formation.

1969. Medieval Frescoes in Yugoslav Monasteries. Multicoloured.
1363 50 p. Type **359** 10 10
1364 75 p. "Jesus and the Apostles" (Sopocani) 10 10
1365 1 d. 25 "The Crucifixion" (Studenica) 15 10
1366 2 d. "Cana Wedding Feast" (Kalenic) 20 10
1367 3 d. "Angel guarding Tomb" (Mileseva) 20 10
1368 5 d. "Mourning over Christ" (Nerezi) 90 90

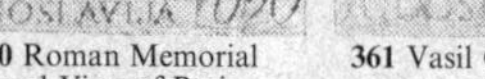

360 Roman Memorial and View of Ptuj
361 Vasil Glavinov

1969. 1900th Anniv of Ptuj (Poetovio) (Slovene town).
1369 **360** 50 p. brown 10 10

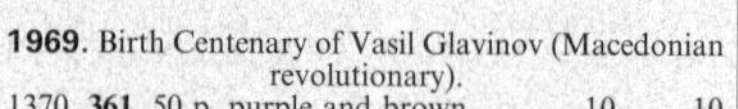

1969. Birth Centenary of Vasil Glavinov (Macedonian revolutionary).
1370 **361** 50 p. purple and brown . 10 10

362 Globe between Hands
363 Single Peony

1969. Obligatory Tax. Red Cross Week.
1371 **362** 20 p. black, red and deep red 10 10

1969. Flowers. Multicoloured.
1372 50 p. Type **363** 10 10
1373 75 p. Coltsfoot 15 10
1374 1 d. 25 Primrose 15 10
1375 2 d. Christmas rose 25 10
1376 2 d. 50 Violet 30 10
1377 5 d. Pasque flower 85 75

364 "Eber" (V. Ivankovic)

1969. Dubrovnik Summer Festival. Sailing Ships. Multicoloured.
1378 50 p. Type **364** 10 10
1379 1 d. 25 "Tare in Storm" (Franasovic) 15 10
1380 1 d. 50 "Brig Sela" (Ivankovic) 25 10
1381 2 d. 50 "16th-century Dubrovnik Galleon" . . . 30 20
1382 3 d. 25 "Frigate Madre Mimbelli" (A. Roux) . . . 60 25
1383 5 d. "Shipwreck" (16th-century icon) . . . . 1·40 1·25

365 Games' Emblem
366 Bosnian Mountain Horse

1969. 9th World Deaf and Dumb Games, Belgrade.
1384 **365** 1 d. 25 lilac and red . . 20 10

1969. 50th Anniv of Veterinary Faculty, Zagreb. Multicoloured.
1385 75 p. Type **366** 15 10
1386 1 d. 25 Lipizzaner horse . . 15 10
1387 3 d. 25 Ljutomer trotter . . 40 10
1388 5 d. Yugoslav half-breed . . 85 75

367 Children and Chicks
368 Arms of Belgrade

1969. Children's Week.
1389 **367** 50 p. multicoloured . . 15 10

1969. 25th Anniv of Yugoslav Liberation. Arms of Regional Capitals. Multicoloured.
1390 50 p. Type **368** 15 10
1391 50 p. Skopje 15 10
1392 50 p. Titograd (Podgorica) . 15 10
1393 50 p. Sarajevo 15 10
1394 50 p. Zagreb 15 10
1395 50 p. Ljubljana 15 10

369 Dr. Josip Smodlaka
370 Torch, Globe and Olympic Rings

1969. Birth Centenary of Dr. Josip Smodlaka (politician).
1397 **369** 50 p. blue 10 10

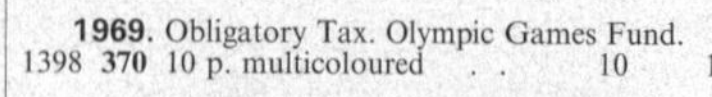

1969. Obligatory Tax. Olympic Games Fund.
1398 **370** 10 p. multicoloured . . 10 10

371 "Gipsy Girl" (N. Martinoski)

1969. Yugoslav Nude Paintings. Mult.
1399 50 p. Type **371** 15 10
1400 1 d. 25 "Girl in Red Armchair" (S. Sumanovic) 20 10
1401 1 d. 50 "Girl Brushing Hair" (M. Tartaglia) 25 10
1402 2 d. 50 "Olympia" (M. Kraljevic) (horiz) . . 40 20
1403 3 d. 25 "The Bather" (J. Bijelic) 70 40
1404 5 d. "Woman on a Couch" (M. Sternen) (horiz) . . . 1·50 1·50

372 University Building

1969. 50th Anniv of Ljubljana University.
1405 **372** 50 p. green 10 10

373 University Seal
374 Colonnade

1969. 300th Anniv of Zagreb University.
1406 **373** 50 p. gold, purple & blue 10 10

1969. Europa.
1407 **374** 1 d. 25 brown & green . . 3·00 3·00
1408 3 d. 25 blue, grey & purple 9·00 9·00

375 Jovan Cvijic (geographer)
376 "Punishment of Dirka" (4th-cent mosaic)

1970. Famous Yugoslavs.
1409 **375** 50 p. purple 10 10
1410 – 1 d. 25 black 15 10
1411 – 1 d. 50 purple 15 10
1412 – 2 d. 50 olive 15 15
1413 – 3 d. 25 brown 25 15
1414 – 5 d. blue 30 40
CELEBRITIES: 1 d. 25, Dr. A. Stampar (hygienist); 1 d. 50, J. Krcovski (author); 2 d. 50, M. Miljanov (soldier); 3 d. 25, V. Pelagic (socialist revolutionary); 5 d. O. Zupancic (poet).

1970. Mosaics. Multicoloured.
1415 50 p. Type **376** 10 10
1416 1 d. 25 "Cerberus" (5th-cent) (horiz) 15 10
1417 1 d. 50 "Angel of Annunciation" (6th-cent) . 15 10
1418 2 d. 50 "Hunters" (4th-cent) . 25 10
1419 3 d. 25 "Bull beside Cherries" (5th-cent) (horiz) 35 15
1420 5 d. "Virgin and Child Enthroned" (6th-cent) . . . 90 90

377 Lenin (after sculpture by S. Stojanovic)
378 Trying for Goal

1970. Birth Centenary of Lenin.
1421 **377** 50 p. lake 10 10
1422 – 1 d. 25 blue 15 10
DESIGN: 1 d. 25, As Type **377**, but showing left side of Lenin's bust.

1970. 6th World Basketball Championships.
1423 **378** 1 d. 25 red 15 10

379 Red Cross Trefoil

1970. Obligatory Tax. Red Cross Week.
1424 **379** 20 p. multicoloured . . . 10 10

380 "Flaming Sun"

1970. Europa.
1425 **380** 1 d. 25 deep blue, turquoise and blue 15 10
1426 3 d. 25 brown, vio & pur 35 40

381 Istrian Short-haired Hound
382 Olympic Flag

1970. Yugoslav Dogs. Multicoloured.
1427 50 p. Type **381** 10 10
1428 1 d. 25 Yugoslav tricolour hound 15 10
1429 1 d. 50 Istrian hard-haired hound 15 10
1430 2 d. 50 Balkan hound . . . 25 15
1431 3 d. 25 Dalmatian 40 15
1432 5 d. Shara mountain dog . . 1·00 1·00

1970. Obligatory Tax. Olympic Games Fund.
1433 **382** 10 p. multicoloured . . . 10 10

383 Telegraph Key
384 "Bird in Meadow"

1970. Montenegro Telegraph Centenary.
1434 **383** 50 p. gold, black & brn . 10 10

1970. Children's Week.
1435 **384** 50 p. multicoloured . . . 15 10

385 "Gymnast"
386 "Hand Holding Dove" (Makoto)

1970. 17th World Gymnastic Championships, Ljubljana.
1436 **385** 1 d. 25 blue and purple . 15 10

1970. 25th Anniv of United Nations.
1437 **386** 1 d. 25 multicoloured . . 15 10

1970. Yugoslav Paintings. Baroque Period. Designs as T **341**. Multicoloured.
1438 50 p. "The Ascension" (T. Kracun) 10 10
1439 75 p. "Abraham's Sacrifice" (F. Benkovic) 10 10
1440 1 d. 25 "The Holy Family" (F. Jelovsek) 15 10
1441 2 d. 50 "Jacob's Dream" (H. Zefarovic) 25 15
1442 3 d. 25 "Christ's Baptism" (Serbian village artist) . . 35 15
1443 5 d. 75 "Coronation of the Virgin" (T. Kokolja) . . . 75 75

388 Rusty-leaved Alpenrose

1970. Nature Conservation Year. Multicoloured.
1444 1 d. 25 Type **388** . . . . . . 1·00 1·00
1445 3 d. 25 Lammergeier . . . . 13·00 7·50

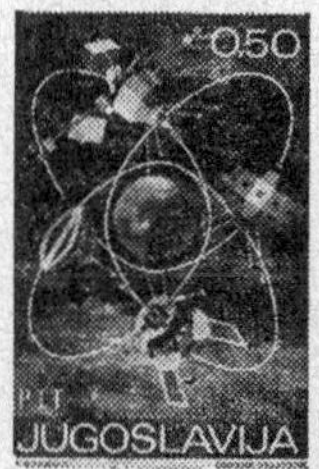

389 F. Supilo
390 Different Nations' Satellites ("International Co-operation")

1971. Birth Cent of Frano Supilo (politician).

No.	Type	Description	Mint	Used
1446	**389**	50 p. brown and buff	10	10

1971. Space Exploration. Multicoloured.

No.	Type	Description	Mint	Used
1447		50 p. Type **390**	15	10
1448		75 p. Telecommunications satellite	15	10
1449		1 d. 25 Unmanned Moon flights	20	10
1450		2 d. 50 Exploration of Mars and Venus (horiz)	35	15
1451		3 d. 25 Space-station (horiz)	50	30
1452		5 d. 75 Astronauts on the Moon (horiz)	1·75	1·75

391 "Proclamation of the Commune" (A. Daudenarde, after A. Lamy)

1971. Centenary of Paris Commune.

No.	Type	Description	Mint	Used
1453	**391**	1 d. 25 brown & orange	15	10

392 Red Cross Ribbon

1971. Obligatory Tax. Red Cross Week.

No.	Type	Description	Mint	Used
1454	**392**	20 p. multicoloured	10	10

393 Europa Chain

1971. Europa.

No.	Type	Description	Mint	Used
1455	**393**	1 d. 50 multicoloured	15	10
1456		4 d. pink, purple & mve	55	55

394 Congress Emblem (A. Pajvancic)

1971. 20th Anniv of Yugoslav "Self-Managers" Movement.

No.	Type	Description	Mint	Used
1457	**394**	50 p. red, black & gold	15	10
1458	–	1 d. 25 red, black & gold	60	60

DESIGN: 1 d. 25, "Self-Managers" emblem (designed by M. Miodragovic).

395 Common Mallow **396** Olympic "Spiral" and Rings

1971. Flowers. Multicoloured.

No.	Type	Description	Mint	Used
1459		50 p. Type **395**	15	10
1460		1 d. 50 Buckthorn	15	10
1461		2 d. Water-lily	20	10
1462		2 d. 50 Wild poppy	40	10
1463		4 d. Wild chicory	50	15
1464		6 d. Bladder-herb	90	70

1971. Obligatory Tax. Olympic Games Fund.

No.	Type	Description	Mint	Used
1465	**396**	10 p. black, purple & blue	10	10

397 Krk, Dalmatia **398** "Prince Lazar Hrebeljanovic" (from fresco, Lazarica Church)

1971. Tourism.

No.	Type	Description	Mint	Used
1641	–	5 p. orange	10	10
1642	–	10 p. brown	10	10
1468	–	20 p. lilac	15	10
1644	–	25 p. red	20	10
1469	**397**	30 p. green	55	10
1645		30 p. olive	10	10
1646	–	35 p. red	15	10
1647	–	40 p. olive	10	10
1473	–	50 p. red	1·00	15
1474	–	50 p. green	20	10
1650	–	60 p. purple	10	10
1476	–	75 p. green	50	10
1652	–	75 p. purple	20	10
1477	–	80 p. red	1·10	10
1478	–	1 d. red	2·25	30
1656	–	1 d. lilac	15	10
1657	–	1 d. green	15	10
1479	–	1 d. 20 green	1·40	15
1480	–	1 d. 25 blue	65	15
1481	–	1 d. 50 blue	30	10
1660	–	1 d. 50 red	20	10
1482	–	2 d. turquoise	60	10
1661	–	2 d. 10 green	25	10
1483	–	2 d. 50 violet	60	15
1662a	–	2 d. 50 red	20	10
1663	–	2 d. 50 blue	20	10
1664a	–	3 d. grey	10	10
1665	–	3 d. 20 blue	45	10
1666	–	3 d. 40 green	20	10
1667	–	3 d. 50 red	20	10
1668a	–	4 d. red	10	10
1669	–	4 d. 90 blue	35	10
1670	–	5 d. green	10	10
1671	–	5 d. 60 olive	25	10
1672	–	6 d. brown	10	10
1673a	–	6 d. 10 green	20	10
1674	–	8 d. grey	30	10
1675a	–	8 d. 80 grey	25	10
1676	–	10 d. purple	20	10
1677	–	16 d. 50 blue	25	10
1678	–	26 d. blue	30	10
1679	–	38 d. mauve	50	10
1680	–	70 d. blue	45	10

DESIGNS: 5 p. Krusevo, Macedonia; 10 p. Gradacac; 20 p., 75 p. Bohinj, Slovenia; 25 p. Budva; 35 p. Omis, Dalmatia; 40 p. Pec; 50 p. (1473/4), Krusevac, Serbia; 60 p. Logarska valley; 75 p. (1652), Rijeka; 80 p. Piran; 1 d. (1478), Bitola, Macedonia; 1 d. (1656/7), 16 d. 50, Ohrid; 1 d. 20, 4 d. Pocitelj; 1 d. 25, 1 d. 50 (1481), 8 d. 80, Herceg Novi; 1 d. 50 (1660), Bihac; 2 d. Novi Sad; 2 d. 10, 6 d. 10, Hvar; 2 d. 50 (1483), Rijeka Crnojevica, Montenegro; 2 d. 50 (1662a/3), Kragujevac; 3 d., 3 d. 20, Skofja Loka; 3 d. 40, Vranje; 3 d. 50, Vrsac; 4 d. 90, Perast; 5 d. Osijek; 5 d. 60, Travnik; 6 d. Kikinda; 8 d. Dubrovnik; 10 d. Sarajevo; 26 d. Korcula; 38 d. Maribor; 70 d. Zagreb.

1971. 600th Anniv of City of Krusevac.

No.	Type	Description	Mint	Used
1487	**398**	50 p. multicoloured	10	10

399 "Satyr" **400** "Children in Balloon"

1971. Bronze Archaeological Discoveries. Multicoloured.

No.	Type	Description	Mint	Used
1488		50 p. Head of Emperor Constantine	10	10
1489		1 d. 50 "Boy with Fish" (statuette)	10	10
1490		2 d. "Hercules" (statuette)	15	10
1491		2 d. 50 Type **399**	30	10
1492		4 d. "Goddess Aphrodite" (head)	40	15
1493		6 d. "Citizen of Emona" (statue)	70	70

1971. Children's Week and 25th Anniv of U.N.I.C.E.F.

No.	Type	Description	Mint	Used
1494	**400**	50 p. multicoloured	25	10

1971. Yugoslav Portraits. As T **371**. Multicoloured.

No.	Type	Description	Mint	Used
1495		50 p. "Girl in Serbian Dress" (K. Ivanovic)	10	10
1496		1 d. 50 "Ivanisevic the Merchant" (A. Bocaric)	15	10
1497		2 d. "Anne Kresic" (V. Karas)	15	10
1498		2 d. 50 "Pavla Jagodica" (K. Danil)	20	10
1499		4 d. "Louise Pasjakova" (M. Stroj)	30	15
1500		6 d. "Old Man at Ljubljana" (M. Langus)	90	75

402 "Postal Codes" **403** Dame Gruev

1971. Introduction of Postal Codes.

No.	Type	Description	Mint	Used
1501	**402**	450 p. multicoloured	10	10

1971. Birth Centenary of Dame Gruev (Macedonian revolutionary).

No.	Type	Description	Mint	Used
1502	**403**	50 p. blue	10	10

404 Speed-skating

1972. Winter Olympic Games, Sapporo, Japan. Multicoloured.

No.	Type	Description	Mint	Used
1503		1 d. 25 Type **404**	60	45
1504		6 d. Slalom-skiing	2·00	2·25

405 First Page of Statute **406** Ski-jump, Planica

1972. 700th Anniv of Dubrovnik Law Statutes.

No.	Type	Description	Mint	Used
1505	**405**	1 d. 25 multicoloured	15	10

1972. 1st World Ski-jumping Championships, Planica.

No.	Type	Description	Mint	Used
1506	**406**	1 d. 25 multicoloured	20	10

407 Water-polo **408** Red Cross and Hemispheres

1972. Olympic Games, Munich. Multicoloured.

No.	Type	Description	Mint	Used
1507		50 p. Type **407**	10	10
1508		1 d. 25 Basketball	10	10
1509		2 d. 50 Swimming	15	10
1510		3 d. 25 Boxing	20	10
1511		5 d. Running	30	15
1512		6 d. 50 Sailing	60	55

1972. Obligatory Tax. Red Cross Week.

No.	Type	Description	Mint	Used
1513	**408**	20 p. multicoloured	10	10

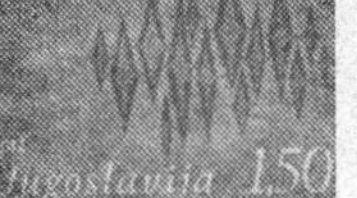

409 "Communications" **410** Wallcreeper

1972. Europa.

No.	Type	Description	Mint	Used
1514	**409**	1 d. 50 multicoloured	25	20
1515		5 d. multicoloured	1·10	1·00

1972. Birds. Multicoloured.

No.	Type	Description	Mint	Used
1516		50 p. Type **410**	20	10
1517		1 d. 25 Little bustard	20	10
1518		2 d. 50 Chough	35	15
1519		3 d. 25 White spoonbill	85	20
1520		5 d. Eagle owl	1·50	20
1521		6 d. 50 Rock ptarmigan	3·50	95

411 President Tito **412** Communications Tower, Olympic Rings and 1972 Games' Emblem

1972. President Tito's 80th Birthday.

No.	Type	Description	Mint	Used
1522	**411**	50 d. brown and buff	15	10
1523		1 d. 25 blue and grey	50	25

1972. Obligatory Tax. Olympic Games Fund.

No.	Type	Description	Mint	Used
1525	**412**	10 p. multicoloured	10	10

413 Locomotive No. 1 "King of Serbia", 1882

1972. 50th Anniv of International Railway Union. Multicoloured.

No.	Type	Description	Mint	Used
1526		1 d. 50 Type **413**	20	10
1527		5 d. Modern "Bo-Bo" electric locomotive	80	40

414 Glider in Flight **415** Pawn

1972. 13th World Gliding Championships, Vrsac.

No.	Type	Description	Mint	Used
1528	**414**	2 d. black, blue & gold	20	15

1972. 20th Chess Olympiad, Skopje.

No.	Type	Description	Mint	Used
1529	**415**	1 d. 50 brown, vio & pur	35	15
1530	–	6 d. black, blue & dp bl	80	75

DESIGN: 6 d. Stylised king and queen on board.

416 "Child on Horse" (B. Zlatec) **417** G. Delcev

1972. Children's Week.

No.	Type	Description	Mint	Used
1531	**416**	80 p. multicoloured	15	10

1972. Birth Centenary of Goca Delcev (Macedonian revolutionary).

No.	Type	Description	Mint	Used
1532	**417**	80 p. black and green	10	10

418 Father Martica

1972. 150th Birth Anniv of Father Grge Martica (politician).

No.	Type	Description	Mint	Used
1533	**418**	80 p. black, green and red	10	10

419 National Library

1972. 140th Anniv of and Re-opening of National Library, Belgrade.

No.	Type	Description	Mint	Used
1534	**419**	50 p. brown	10	10

420 "Fruit Dish and Broken Majolica Vase" (M. Tenkovic)

1972. Yugoslav Art. Still Life. Mult.

No.	Type	Description	Mint	Used
1535		50 p. Type **420**	10	10
1536		1 d. 25 "Mandoline and Book" (J. Petkovsec) (vert)	10	10
1537		2 d. 50 "Basket with Grapes" (K. Jovanovic)	20	10
1538		3 d. 25 "Water-melon" (K. Danil)	35	15
1539		5 d. "In a Stable" (N. Masic) (vert)	45	20
1540		6 d. 50 "Scrap-books" (C. Medovic)	1·00	1·00

421 Battle of Stubica

1973. 500th Anniv of Slovenian Peasant Risings and 400th Anniv of Croatian–Slovenian Rebellion. Multicoloured.
1541 2 d. Type **421** 20 10
1542 6 d. Battle of Krsko . . . . 1·25 75

422 R. Domanovic

424 "Novi Sad" (P. Demetrovic)

423 Skofja Loka

1973. Birth Centenary of Radoje Domanovic (Serbian satirist).
1543 **422** 80 p. brown and drab . . 25 10

1973. Millenary of Skofja Loka.
1544 **423** 80 p. brown 20 10

1973. Old Engravings of Yugoslav Towns. Each black and gold.
1545 50 p. Type **424** 10 10
1546 1 d. 25 "Zagreb" (J. Szeman) 10 10
1547 2 d. 50 "Kotor" (P. Montier) 15 10
1548 3 d. 25 "Belgrade" (Mancini) 20 15
1549 5 d. "Split" (L. F. Cassas) . . 30 15
1550 6 d. 50 "Kranj" (M. Merian) 60 45

425 Table-tennis Bat and Ball

1973. 32nd World Table-tennis Championships, Sarajevo.
1551 **425** 2 d. multicoloured . . . 30 10

426 Red Cross Emblem

427 Europa "Posthorn"

1973. Obligatory Tax. Red Cross Week.
1552 **426** 20 p. multicoloured . . . 10 10

1973. Europa.
1553 **427** 2 d. lilac, green & blue . . 15 10
1554 5 d. 50 pink, green & purple 1·40 1·25

428 "Aristolochia clematatis"

429 Globe and Olympic Rings

1973. Flora. Medicinal Plants. Multicoloured.
1555 80 p. Type **428** 15 10
1556 2 d. "Echinops ritro" 20 10
1557 3 d. "Olea europaea" 30 10
1558 4 d. "Corydalis cava" 45 15
1559 5 d. "Viscum album" 65 20
1560 6 d. "Symphytum officinale" 2·00 2·00

1973. Obligatory Tax. Olympic Games Fund.
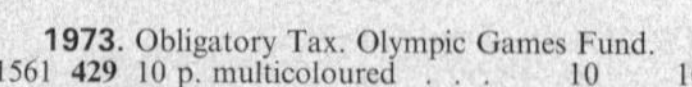
1561 **429** 10 p. multicoloured . . . 10 10

430 A. Jansa and Bee

431 Aquatic Symbol

1973. Death Bicentenary of Anton Jansa (apiculturist).
1562 **430** 80 p. black 10 10

1973. 1st World Aquatic Championships, Belgrade.
1563 **431** 2 d. multicoloured . . . 20 10

432 "Children on Boat"

433 Posthorn

1973. Children's Week.
1564 **432** 80 p. multicoloured . . 25 10

1973.
1565 **433** 30 p. brown 15 10
1565a 50 p. blue 15 10
1566 80 p. red 15 10
1566a 1 d. green 15 10
1567 1 d. 20 red 15 10
1567a 1 d. 50 red 15 10

434 J. Dalmatinac (from sculpture by I. Mestrovic)

435 "N. Petrovic" (self-portrait)

1973. 500th Death Anniv of Juraj Dalmatinac (sculptor and architect).
1568 **434** 80 p. olive and green . . 10 10

1973. Birth Centenary of Nadezda Petrovic (painter).
1569 **435** 2 d. multicoloured . . . 20 15

436 "The Plaster Head" (M. Celebonovic)

1973. Yugoslav Art. Interiors. Mult.
1570 80 p. Type **436** 10 10
1571 2 d. "St. Duja Church" (E. Vidovic) 10 10
1572 3 d. "Slovenian Housewife" (M. Tartaglia) 15 10
1573 4 d. "Dedicated to Karas"—painter at easel (M. Stancic) 30 15
1574 5 d. "My Studio" (M Konjovic) 50 15
1575 6 d. "Tavern in Stara Loka" (F. Slana) 70 60

437 D. Dudic

438 "M" for "Metrication"

1973. National Heroes. (a) Each black.
1576 80 p. Type **437** 10 10
1577 80 p. S. Pindzur 10 10
1578 80 p. B. Kidric 10 10
1579 80 p. R. Dakic 10 10

(b) Each red.
1580 2 d. J. Mazar-Sosa 15 15
1581 2 d. Z. Zrenjanin 15 15
1582 2 d. E. Duraku 15 15
1583 2 d. I. Lola Ribar 15 15

1974. Centenary of Introduction of Metric System in Yugoslavia.
1584 **438** 80 p. multicoloured . . . 10 10

439 Skater

440 Satjeska Monument

1974. European Figure-skating Championships, Zagreb.
1585 **439** 2 d. multicoloured . . . 40 20

1974. Monuments.
1586 – 3 d. green 75 10
1587 – 4 d. 50 brown . . . . . 1·25 10
1588 – 5 d. violet . . . . . . 1·25 10
1589 **440** 10 d. green . . . . . . 1·50 20
1590 – 20 d. purple . . . . . . 1·75 20
1591 – 50 d. blue . . . . . . 4·00 90
DESIGNS—VERT: 3 d. Ljubljana; 4 d. 50, Kozara; 5 d. Belcista. HORIZ: 20 d. Podgaric; 50 d. Kragujevac.

441 Mailcoach

1974. Centenary of Universal Postal Union.
1592 **441** 80 p. black, yellow and buff 10 10
1593 – 2 d. black, red and rose . 10 10
1594 – 8 d. black, blue and pale blue 40 45
DESIGNS: 2 d. U.P.U. H.Q. Building; 8 d. Boeing 707 airliner.

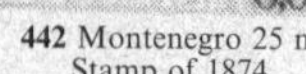
442 Montenegro 25 n. Stamp of 1874

443 President Tito

1974. Montenegro Stamp Centenary. Mult.
1595 80 p. Montenegrin 2 n. stamp of 1874 . . . . 15 10
1596 6 d. Type **442** 35 35

1974.
1597 **443** 50 p. green 15 10
1598 80 p. red 20 10
1599 1 d. 20 green 25 10
1600 2 d. blue 30 10

444 Lenin

445 Red Cross Emblems

1974. 50th Death Anniv of Lenin.
1601 **444** 2 d. black and silver . . . 15 10

1974. Obligatory Tax. Red Cross Week.
1602 **445** 20 p. multicoloured . . . 10 10

446 "Dwarf" (Lepenski settlement, c. 4950 B.C.)

447 Great Tit

1974. Europa. Sculptures. Multicoloured.
1603 2 d. Type **446** 15 15
1604 6 d. "Widow and Child" (I. Mestrovic) . . . . 1·00 1·25

1974. Youth Day. Multicoloured.
1605 80 p. Type **447** 70 15
1606 2 d. Roses 50 15
1607 6 d. "Pieris brassicae" (butterfly) . . . . 2·00 1·10

448 Congress Poster

449 Olympic Rings and Stadium

1974. 10th Yugoslav League of Communists' Congress, Belgrade.
1608 **448** 80 p. multicoloured . . . 10 10
1609 2 d. multicoloured . . . 15 10
1610 6 d. multicoloured . . . 35 30

1974. Obligatory Tax. Olympic Games Fund.
1611 **449** 10 p. multicoloured . . . 10 10

450 Dish Aerial, Ivanjica

451 World Cup

1974. Inauguration of Satellite Communications Station, Ivanjica.
1612 **450** 80 p. blue 20 10
1613 – 6 d. lilac . . . . 1·25 70
DESIGN: 6 d. "Intelstat 4" in orbit.

1974. World Cup Football Championships, West Germany.
1614 **451** 4 d. 50 multicoloured . . 70 50

452 Edelweiss and Klek Mountain

1974. Centenary of Croatian Mountaineers' Society.
1615 **452** 2 d. multicoloured . . . 15 10

453 "Children's Dance" (J. Knjazovic)

1974. Paintings. Multicoloured.
1616 80 p. Type **453** 10 10
1617 2 d. "Crucified Rooster" (I. Generalic) (vert) 15 15
1618 5 d. "Laundresses" (I. Lackovic) (vert) 35 20
1619 8 d. "Dance" (J. Brasic) . . 1·10 1·25

454 "Rooster and Flower" (K. Milinojsin)

1974. Children's Week and 6th "Joy of Europe" meeting, Belgrade. Children's Paintings. Mult.
1620 1 d. 20 Type **454** 15 10
1621 3 d. 20 "Girl and Boy" (E. Medrzecka) (vert) . . . 25 10
1622 5 d. "Cat and Kitten" (J. Anastasijevic) 70 40

455 Interior of Library

1974. Bicentenary of National and University Library.
1623 **455** 1 d. 20 black 10 10

456 "White Peonies" (P. Dobrovic)

458 Dove and Map of Europe

457 Title Page of Volume I

1974. Floral Paintings. Multicoloured.

1624	80 p. Type **456**	10	10
1625	2 d. "Carnations" (V. Gecan)	15	15
1626	3 d. "Flowers" (M. Konjovic)	15	15
1627	4 d. "White Vase" (S. Sumanovic)	35	20
1628	5 d. "Branching Larkspurs" (S. Kregar)	40	20
1629	8 d. "Roses" (P. Lubarda)	70	50

1975. 150th Anniv of "Matica Srpska" Annals.

1630	**457** 1 d. 20 blk, brn and green	10	10

1975. 2nd European Security and Co-operation Conference, Belgrade.

1631	**458** 3 d. 20 multicoloured	20	10
1632	8 d. multicoloured	90	65

459 Gold-plated Bronze Ear-ring (14th–15th-century), Alisici, Bosnia

460 "S. Markovic" (sculpture by S. Bodnarov)

1975. Archaeological Discoveries. Multicoloured.

1633	1 d. 20 Type **459**	10	10
1634	2 d. 10 Silver bracelet (19th-century), Kosovo	10	10
1635	3 d. 20 Gold-plated silver buckle (18th-century), Bitola	15	10
1636	5 d. Gold-plated ring (14th-century), Novi Sad	30	10
1637	6 d. Silver necklace (17th-century), Kosovo	45	15
1638	8 d. Gold-plated bronze bracelet (18th-century), Bitola	75	70

1975. Death Centenary of Svetozar Markovic (writer and statesman).

1639	**460** 1 d. 20 blue	10	10

461 "Fettered" (sculpture by F. Krsinic)

1975. International Women's Year.

1640	**461** 3 d. 20 brown and gold	15	15

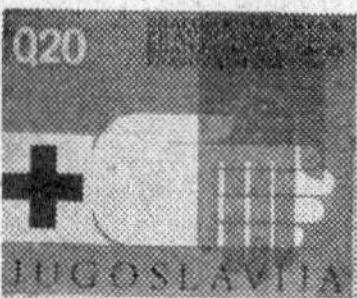

462 Red Cross and Hands

1975. Obligatory Tax. Red Cross Week.

1681	**462** 20 p. multicoloured	10	10

463 "Still Life with Eggs" (M. Pijade)

1975. Europa. Paintings. Multicoloured.

1682	3 d. 20 Type **463**	15	15
1683	8 d. "The Three Graces" (I. Radovic)	50	50

464 "Liberation Monument" (Dzamonja)

465 Garland-flower

1975. 30th Anniv of Liberation.

1684	**464** 3 d. 20 multicoloured	15	10

1975. National Youth Day. Flowers. Mult.

1685	1 d. 20 Type **465**	15	10
1686	2 d. 10 Touch-me-not	15	10
1687	3 d. 20 Rose-mallow	20	10
1688	5 d. Mourning widow	40	10
1689	6 d. Crocus	50	15
1690	8 d. Rose-bay	75	50

466 Games Emblem

467 Canoeing

1975. Obligatory Tax. Olympic Games Fund.

1691	**466** 10 p. multicoloured	10	10

1975. World Canoeing Championships, Macedonia.

1692	**467** 3 d. 20 multicoloured	20	10

468 "Herzegovinian Insurgents in Ambush"

1975. Centenary of Bosnian-Herzegovinian Uprising.

1693	**468** 1 d. 20 multicoloured	15	10

469 "Skopje Earthquake"

470 S. M. Ljubisa

1975. Obligatory Tax. Solidarity Week.

1694	**469** 30 p. black, grey & bl	10	10

See also Nos. 1885 and 1933.

1975. Writers.

1695	**470** 1 d. 20 black and red	10	10
1696	– 2 d. 10 black and grn	15	10
1697	– 3 d. 20 black and brown	15	10
1698	– 5 d. black and orange	20	10
1699	– 6 d. black and green	20	10
1700	– 8 d. black and blue	35	50

PORTRAITS: 2 d. 10, I. Prijatelj; 3 d. 20, J. Ignjatovic; 5 d. D. Jarnevic; 6 d. S. Corivic; 8 d. I. Brlic-Mazuranic.

471 "Young Lion" (A. Savic)

1975. Children's Week and 7th "Joy of Europa" meeting, Belgrade. Children's Paintings. Mult.

1701	3 d. 20 Type **471**	20	10
1702	6 d. "Baby in Pram"	90	50

472 Peace Dove within "EUROPA"

1975. European Security and Co-operation Conference, Helsinki.

1703	**472** 3 d. 20 multicoloured	15	10
1704	8 d. multicoloured	50	30

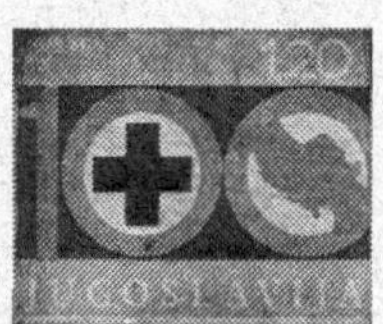

473 Red Cross and Map within "100"

1975. Centenary of Red Cross. Multicoloured.

1705	1 d. 20 Type **473**	15	10
1706	8 d. Red Cross and people	50	25

474 "Folk Kitchen" (D. Andrejevic-Kun)

1975. Republic Day. Paintings. Multicoloured.

1707	1 d. 20 Type **474**	10	10
1708	2 d. 10 "On the Doorstep" (V. Grdan)	10	10
1709	3 d. 20 "The Drunken Coach-load" (M. Detoni) (horiz)	15	10
1710	5 d. "Lunch" (T. Kralj) (horiz)	20	10
1711	6 d. "Waterwheel" (L. Licenoski)	30	15
1712	8 d. "Justice" (K. Hegedusic)	55	60

475 Diocletian's Palace, Split (3rd-century)

1975. European Architectural Heritage Year.

1713	**475** 1 d. 20 brown	15	10
1714	– 3 d. 20 black	15	10
1715	– 8 d. blue	50	50

DESIGNS—VERT: 3 d. 20, House of Ohrid (19th-century). HORIZ: 8 d. Gracanica Monastery, Kosovo (14th-century).

476 Ski-jumping

1976. Winter Olympic Games, Innsbruck.

1716	**476** 3 d. 20 blue	15	10
1717	– 8 d. lake	55	50

DESIGN: 8 d. Figure-skating.

477 Red Flag

1976. Centenary of "Red Flag" Insurrection (workers' demonstration), Kragujevac.

1718	**477** 1 d. 20 multicoloured	15	10

478 S. Miletic

479 B. Stankovic

1976. 150th Birth Anniv of Svetozar Miletic (politician).

1719	**478** 1 d. 20 green and grey	15	10

1976. Birth Cent of Boran Stankovic (writer).

1720	**479** 1 d. 20 red, brown and yellow	15	10

480 "King Matthias" (sculpture J. Pogorelec)

1976. Europa. Handicrafts. Multicoloured.

1721	3 d. 20 Type **480**	10	10
1722	8 d. Base of beaker	40	40

481 I. Cankar

1976. Birth Centenary of Ivan Cankar (Slovenian writer).

1723	**481** 1 d. 20 purple, brown and pink	10	10

482 Stylized Figure

1976. Obligatory Tax. Red Cross Week.

1724	**482** 20 p. multicoloured	60	60

483 Train crossing Viaduct

1976. Inauguration of Belgrade–Bar Railway.

1725	**483** 3 d. 20 brown	25	15
1726	– 8 d. blue	65	45

DESIGN: 8 d. Train crossing bridge.

484 "Anax Imperator"

485 V. Nazor

1976. Youth Day. Freshwater Fauna. Multicoloured.

1727	1 d. 20 Type **484**	10	10
1728	2 d. 10 River snail	10	10
1729	3 d. 20 Rudd	15	10
1730	5 d. Common frog	30	10
1731	6 d. Ferruginous duck	1·50	20
1732	8 d. Muskrat	60	60

1976. Birth Centenary of Vladimir Nazor (writer).

1733	**485** 1 d. 20 blue and lilac	10	10

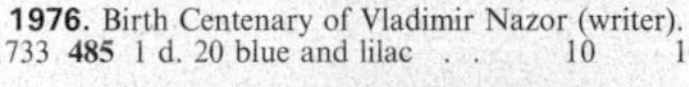

486 "Battle of Vucji Dol" (from "Eagle" journal of 1876)

1976. Centenary of Montenegrin Liberation Wars.

1734	**486** 1 d. 20 multicoloured	10	10

487 Jug, Aleksandrova, Serbia

1976. Ancient Pottery. Multicoloured.

1735	1 d. 20 Type **487**	10	10
1736	2 d. 10 Pitcher, Ptuj, Slovenia	10	10
1737	3 d. 20 Coffee-pot, Visnjica, Sarajevo	15	10

1738 5 d. Pitcher, Backi Breg, Vojvodina 30 15
1739 6 d. Goblet, Vranestice, Macedonia 40 15
1740 8 d. Jug, Prizren, Kosovo . . 75 50

488 N. Tesla Monument and Niagara Falls

1976. 120th Birth Anniv of Nikola Tesla (scientist).
1741 **488** 5 d. blue and green . . . 25 10

489 Long-jumping

1976. Olympic Games, Montreal.
1742 **489** 1 d. 20 purple 10 10
1743 – 3 d. 20 brown 15 10
1744 – 5 d. brown 20 10
1745 – 8 d. blue 40 35
DESIGNS: 3 d. 20, Handball; 5 d. Shooting; 8 d. Rowing.

490 Stadium and Olympic Rings **491** Globe

1976. Obligatory Tax. Olympic Games Fund.
1746 **490** 10 p. blue 10 10

1976. 5th Non-aligned Nations' Summit Conf, Colombo.
1747 **491** 4 d. 90 multicoloured . . 20 10

492 "Navy Day" (N. Mitar)

1976. Children's Week. 8th "Joy of Europe" meeting, Belgrade. Children's Paintings. Multicoloured.
1748 4 d. 90 Type **492** 15 10
1749 8 d. "Children's Trains" (W. Gulbrandsen) 50 40

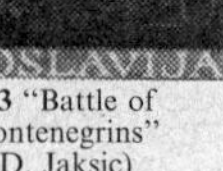

493 "Battle of Montenegrins" (D. Jaksic) **495** "Prota Mateja Nenadovic" (U. Knezevic)

1976. Paintings. Historical events. Mult.
1750 1 d. 20 Type **493** 10 10
1751 2 d. 10 "Nikola Subic Zrinjski at Siget" (O. Ivekovic) . . 15 10
1752 3 d. 20 "Herzegovinian Fugitives" (U. Predic) (horiz) 20 10
1753 5 d. "The Razlovic Uprising" (B. Lazeski) (horiz) 25 15
1754 6 d. "Enthronement of the Slovenian Duke, Gosposvetsko Field" (A. G. Kos) (horiz) 40 20
1755 8 d. "Breach of the Solun Front" (V. Stanojevic) (horiz) 50 45

1976. No. 1203 surch.
1756 1 d. on 85 p. plum 15 10

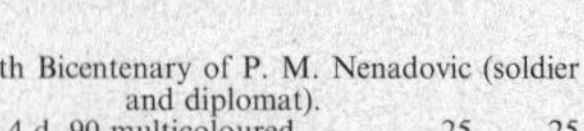

1977. Birth Bicentenary of P. M. Nenadovic (soldier and diplomat).
1757 **495** 4 d. 90 multicoloured . . 25 25

496 R. Zinzifov **497** Phlox

1977. Death Centenary of Rajko Zinzifov (writer).
1758 **496** 1 d. 50 brown & sepia . 10 10

1977. Flowers. Multicoloured.
1759 1 d. 50 Type **497** 10 10
1760 3 d. 40 Tiger-lily 20 10
1761 4 d. 90 Dicentra 25 10
1762 6 d. Zinnia 30 15
1763 8 d. Marigold 40 15
1764 10 d. Horseshoe geranium . 65 60

498 Institute Building **499** Alojz Kraigher

1977. 150th Anniv of Croatian Music Institute.
1765 **498** 4 d. 90 blue & brown . 20 10

1977. Birth Centenary of Alojz Kraigher (author).
1766 **499** 1 d. 50 brown and buff . 10 10

500 "Boka Kotorske" (Milo Milunovic)

1977. Europa. Landscapes. Multicoloured.
1767 4 d. 90 Type **500** 15 10
1768 10 d. "Zagorje in November" (Ljubo Babic) 40 40

501 Figure and Emblems

1977. Obligatory Tax. Red Cross Week.
1769 **501** 20 p. red and brown . . 1·75 70
1770 50 p. red and green . . 50 20
1771 1 d. red and blue . . . 25 10

502 "President Tito" (O. Mujadzic) **503** Alpine Scene

1977. 85th Birthday of President Tito.
1772 **502** 1 d. 50 brown, olive and gold 10 10
1773 4 d. 90 brown, pink and gold 20 15
1774 8 d. brn, olive and gold 50 45

1977. International Environment Protection Day. Multicoloured.
1775 4 d. 90 Type **503** 20 10
1776 10 d. Plitvice waterfall and red-breasted fly-catcher . . . 2·25 55

504 Petar Kocic

1977. Birth Centenary of Petar Kocic (writer).
1777 **504** 1 d. 50 mauve & green . 10 10

505 Dove and Map of Europe

1977. European Security and Co-operation Conference, Belgrade (1st issue).
1778 **505** 4 d. 90 multicoloured . . 30 15
1779 10 d. multicoloured . . . 1·50 1·50
See also Nos. 1784/5.

506 Tree **507** "Bather" (M. Franci)

1977. Obligatory Tax. Anti-tuberculosis Week.
1780 **506** 50 p. multicoloured . . . 3·00 3·00
1781 1 d. multicoloured . . . 45 45

1977. Children's Week and 9th "Joy of Europe" meeting, Belgrade. Children's Paintings. Mult.
1782 4 d. 90 Type **507** 20 10
1783 10 d. "One Fruit into Pail — the other into Mouth" (T. Ilinskaja) 70 50

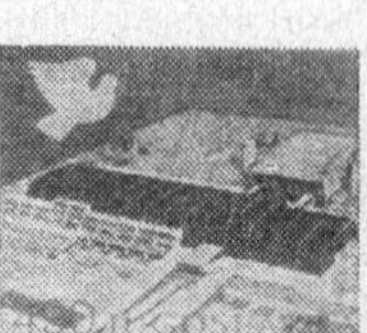

508 Congress Building, Belgrade **509** Exhibition Emblem

1977. European Security and Co-operation Conference, Belgrade (2nd issue).
1784 **508** 4 d. 90 grey, blue & gold 25 15
1785 10 d. red, rose and gold . 1·50 1·50

1977. "Balkanphila 6" Stamp Exhibition, Belgrade.
1786 **509** 4 d. 90 multicoloured . . 15 10

510 Double Flute

1977. Musical Instruments in Ethnographical Museum, Belgrade.
1787 **510** 1 d. 50 brown & yellow . 10 10
1788 – 3 d. 40 brown & green . . 20 10
1789 – 4 d. 90 yellow & brown . 25 10
1790 – 6 d. brown and blue . . . 30 15
1791 – 8 d. brown and orange . 50 25
1792 – 10 d. brown and green . . 65 55
DESIGN: 3 d. 40, Tamburitza; 4 d. 90, Fiddle; 6 d. Lijerica; 8 d. Bagpipe; 10 d. Pan's flute.

511 Ivan Vavpotic **512** Globe and Olympic Rings

1977. Self-portraits. Multicoloured.
1793 1 d. 50 Type **511** 10 10
1794 3 d. 40 Mihailo Vukotic . . . 15 10
1795 4 d. 90 Kosta Hakman . . . 20 10
1796 6 d. Miroslav Kraljevic . . . 25 15
1797 8 d. Nikola Martinovski . . . 35 20
1798 10 d. Milena Paviovic-Barili . 60 65

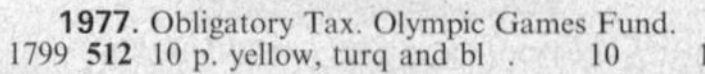

1977. Obligatory Tax. Olympic Games Fund.
1799 **512** 10 p. yellow, turq and bl . 10 10

513 "Ceremony of Testaccio" (miniature from Officum Virginis) **514** Pre-stamp Letter (Bavaniste-Kubin)

1978. 400th Death Anniv of Julije Klovic (Croat miniaturist). Multicoloured.
1800 4 d. 90 Type **513** 20 10
1801 10 d. "Portrait of Klovic" (El Greco) 50 35

1978. Post Office Museum Exhibits. Mult.
1802 1 d. 50 Type **514** 10 10
1803 3 d. 40 19th-century mail box 15 10
1804 4 d. 90 Ericsson induction table telephone 20 10
1805 10 d. Morse's first electro-magnetic telegraph set . . 40 40

515 Battle of Pirot

1978. Centenary of Serbo-Turkish War.
1806 **515** 1 d. 50 multicoloured . . 90 45

516 S-49A Trainer

1978. Aeronautical Day.
1807 **516** 1 d. 50 pink, brown and orange 10 10
1808 – 3 d. 40 blue, black and slate 15 10
1809 – 4 d. 90 black & brown . 30 10
1810 – 10 d. yellow, brn & grn . 55 50
DESIGNS: 3 d. 40, SOKO Gabeb 3 jet trainer; 4 d. 90, UTVA 75 elementary trainer; 10 d. Jurom Orao jet fighter.

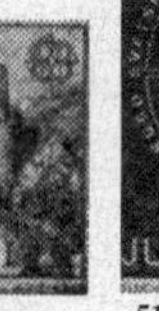

517 Golubac **518** Boxing Glove on Glove

1978. Europa. Multicoloured.
1811 4 d. 90 Type **517** 20 15
1812 10 d. St. Naum Monastery . . 1·00 1·00

1978. 2nd World Amateur Boxing Championship, Belgrade.
1813 **518** 4 d. 90 brown, blue and deep blue 20 10

519 Symbols of Red Crescent, Red Cross and Red Lion **520** "Apis mellifera"

1978. Obligatory Tax. Red Cross Week. No. 1814 surch.
1814 **519** 20 p. on 1 d. blue & red 30 10
1815 1 d. blue and red 10 10

1978. Bees. Multicoloured.
1816 1 d. 50 Type **520** 10 10
1817 3 d. 40 "Halictus scabiosae" 25 10
1818 4 d. 90 "Xylocopa violacea" 40 15
1819 10 d. "Bombus terrestris" . . 85 65

521 Filip Filipovic and Radovan Dragovic

1978. Birth Centenaries of F. Filipovic and R. Dragovic (socialist movement leaders).
1820 **521** 1 d. 50 green and red . . 10 10

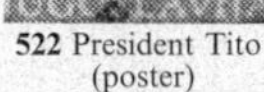

522 President Tito (poster)

524 Conference Emblem over Belgrade

1978. 11th Communist League Congress. Mult.
1821 2 d. Type **522** 10 10
1822 4 d. 90 Hammer and sickle (poster) 25 10

1978. Various stamps surch.
1829 – 35 p. on 10 p. brown (No. 1642) 15 10
1830 **332** 60 p. on 85 p. blue (No. 1271) 15 10
1831 **443** 80 p. on 1 d. 20 green (No. 1599) 15 10
1832 – 2 d. on 1 d. green (No. 1657) 15 10
1833 – 3 d. 40 on 2 d. 10 green (No. 1662) 20 10

1978. Conference of Foreign Ministers of Non-aligned Countries.
1834 **524** 4 d. 90 blue and lt blue . 10 10

525 Championship Emblem

526 North Face, Mount Triglav

1978. 14th Kayak and Canoe "Still Water" World Championships, Belgrade.
1835 **525** 4 d. 90 black, blue and light blue 20 10

1978. Bicent of First Ascent of Mount Triglav.
1836 **526** 2 d. multicoloured . . . 15 10

527 Hand holding Flame

528 Black Lake, Durmitor

1978. Obligatory Tax. Anti-tuberculosis Week.
1837 **527** 1 d. multicoloured . . . 20 10

1978. Protection of the Environment. Multicoloured.
1838 4 d. 90 Type **528** 25 10
1839 10 d. River Tara 60 40

529 Olympic Rings on Map of World

1978. Obligatory Tax. Olympic Games Fund.
1840 **529** 30 p. multicoloured . . . 10 10

530 Star Map

1978. 29th International Astronautical Federation Congress, Dubrovnik.
1841 **530** 4 d. 90 multicoloured . . 20 10

531 "People in Forest" (I. Balen)

1978. Children's Week and 10th "Joy of Europe" Meeting, Belgrade. Multicoloured.
1842 4 d. 90 Type **531** 20 10
1843 10 d. "Family round a Pond" (V. Christel) 70 40

532 Seal

1978. Centenary of Kresna Uprising.
1844 **532** 2 d. black, brown and gold 15 10

533 Old College Building

1978. Bicentenary of Teachers' Training College, Sombor.
1845 **533** 2 d. brown, yell & gold . 15 10

534 Red Cross

1978. Centenary of Croatian Red Cross.
1846 **534** 2 d. red, blue & black . 15 10

535 Metallic Sculpture "XXII" (D. Dzamonja)

1978. Modern Sculpture.
1847 **535** 2 d. black, brown & sil . 10 10
1848 – 3 d. 40 blue, grey and silver 15 10
1849 – 4 d. 90 olive, brown and silver 15 10
1850 – 10 d. brown, buff and silver 40 45
DESIGNS—VERT: 3 d. 40, "Circulation in Space I" (V. Bakic); 4 d. 90, "Tectonic Octopod" (O. Jevric). HORIZ: 10 d. "The Tree of Life" (D. Trsar).

536 "Crossing the Neretva" (I. Mujezinovic)

537 "People from the Seine" (Marijan Detoni)

1978. 35th Anniv of Battle of Neretva.
1851 **536** 2 d. multicoloured . . . 15 10

1978. Republic Day. Graphic Art.
1852 **537** 2 d. black, stone and gold 10 10
1853 – 3 d. 40 black, grey and gold 15 10
1854 – 4 d. 90 black, yellow and gold 15 10
1855 – 6 d. black, flesh and gold 20 15
1856 – 10 d. black, flesh and gold 35 40
DESIGNS 3 d. 40, "Labourers" (Maksim Sedej); 4 d. 90, "Felling of Trees" (Daniel Ozmo); 6 d. "At a Meal" (Pivo Karamatijevic); 10 d. "They are not afraid, even at a most loathsome crime" (Djordje Andrejevic Kun).

538 Eurasian Red Squirrel

539 Masthead

1978. New Year. Multicoloured.
1857 1 d. 50 Type **538** 15 10
1858 1 d. 50 Larch 15 10
1859 2 d. Red deer 15 10
1860 2 d. Sycamore 15 10
1861 3 d. 40 Rock partridge (pink background) 85 15
1861a 3 d. 40 Rock partridge (green background) 85 25
1862 3 d. 40 Alder (pink background) 25 10
1862a 3 d. 40 Alder (green background) 40 15
1863 4 d. 90 Capercaillie (green background) 95 15
1863a 4 d. 90 Capercaillie (yellow background) 95 25
1864 4 d. 90 Oak (green background) 30 10
1864a 4 d. 90 Oak (yellow background) 55 25

1979. 75th Anniv of "Politika" Newspaper.
1865 **539** 2 d. black and gold . . . 15 10

540 Flags

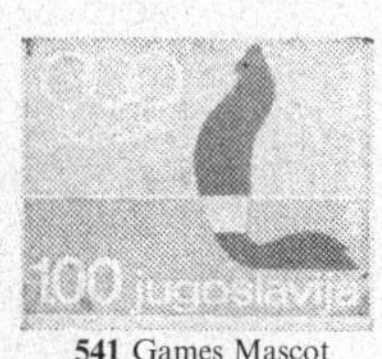

541 Games Mascot

1979. 10th Anniv of Self-Managers' Meeting.
1866 **540** 2 d. multicoloured . . . 15 10

1979. Obligatory Tax. Mediterranean Games Fund.
1867 **541** 1 d. blue and deep blue . 15 10
See also No. 1886.

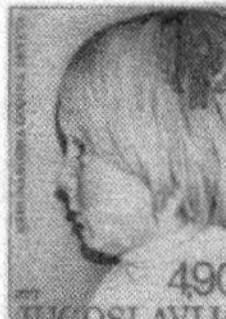

542 Child

543 Sabre, Mace and Enamluk (box holding Koranic texts)

1979. International Year of the Child.
1868 **542** 4 d. 90 blue and gold . . 40 30

1979. Ancient Weapons from Ethnographic Museum, Belgrade. Multicoloured.
1869 2 d. Type **543** 10 10
1870 3 d. 40 Pistol and ammunition stick 15 10
1871 4 d. 90 Carbine and powder-horn 25 10
1872 10 d. Rifle and cartridge-pouch 55 45

544 Hammer and Sickle on Star

545 Kiril-Meotdij University

1979. 60th Anniv of Yugoslav Communist Party and League for Communist Youth.
1873 **544** 2 d. multicoloured . . . 10 10
1874 4 d. 90 multicoloured . . 25 15

1979. 30th Anniv of Kiril-Metodij University.
1875 **545** 2 d. brown, buff and pink 10 10

546 "Panorama of Belgrade" (C. Goebel)

1979. Europa. Multicoloured.
1876 4 d. 90 Type **546** 15 15
1877 10 d. Postilion and view of Ljubljana (after Jan van der Heyden) 40 40

547 Stylized Bird

1979. Obligatory Tax. Red Cross Week.
1878 **547** 1 d. turq, blue and red . 15 10

548 "Cicerbita alpina"

549 Milutin Milankovic (after Paja Jovanovic)

1979. Alpine Flowers. Multicoloured.
1879 2 d. Type **548** 10 10
1880 3 d. 40 "Anemone narcissiflora" 15 10
1881 4 d. 90 "Astragalus sempervirens" 30 15
1882 10 d. "Trifolium alpinum" . 60 40

1979. Birth Centenary of Milutin Milankovic (scientist).
1883 **549** 4 d. 90 multicoloured . . 20 10

550 Kosta Abrasevic

551 Rowing Crew

1979. Birth Centenary of Kosta Abrasevic (poet).
1884 **550** 2 d. grey, pink & black . 10 10

1979. Obligatory Tax. Solidarity Week. As T **469** but inscribed "1.-7.VI".
1885 30 p. black, grey and blue . 15 10

1979. Obligatory Tax. Mediterranean Games Fund. As No. 1867 but colour changed.
1886 **541** 1 d. blue & deep blue . . 10 10

1979. 9th World Rowing Championships. Bled.
1887 **551** 4 d. 90 multicoloured . . 30 10

552 Games Emblem

553 Girl playing Hopscotch

1979. 8th Mediterranean Games. Multicoloured.
1888 2 d. Type **552** 10 10
1889 4 d. 90 Mascot and emblem . 20 10
1890 10 d. Map and flags of participating countries . . 45 40

1979. Obligatory Tax. Anti-tuberculosis Week.
1891 **553** 1 d. multicoloured . . . 10 10

554 Arms of Zagreb, 1499

555 Lake Palic

1979. 450th Anniv of Zagreb Postal Service.
1892 **554** 2 d. grey and red 15 10

1979. Environmental Protection. Multicoloured.
1893 4 d. 90 Type **555** 20 10
1894 10 d. Lake in Prokletije range . 55 30

556 Emblems

1979. Meeting of International Bank for Reconstruction and Development and of International Monetary Fund.
1895 **556** 4 d. 90 multicoloured . . 20 10
1896 10 d. multicoloured . . . 40 30

557 Street in Winter (Mirjana Markovic)

1979. 11th "Joy of Europe" Meeting, Belgrade. Children's Paintings. Multicoloured.

1897 4 d. 90 Type **557** 20 10
1898 10 d. House and garden (Jacques An) 65 45

558 Milhailo Pupin 559 Olympic Rings

1979. 125th Birth Anniv of Milhailo Pupin (scientist).

1899 **558** 4 d. 90 brown, light blue and blue 20 10

1979. Obligatory Tax. Olympic Games Fund.

1900 **559** 30 p. red and blue . . . 10 10

560 Marko Cepenkov 561 Pristina University

1979. 150th Anniv of Marko Cepenkov (author and folklorist).

1901 **560** 2 d. brown, green and olive 15 10

1979. 10th Anniv of Pristina University.

1902 **561** 2 d. multicoloured . . . 10 10

562 Lion on Column (Trogir Cathedral) 563 Sarajevo University

1979. Romanesque Sculpture. Multicoloured.

1903 2 d. Type **562** 10 10
1904 3 d. 40 Apostle (detail of choir stall, Split Cathedral) . . . 15 10
1905 4 d. 90 Window (Church of the Ascension, Decani) 20 10
1906 6 d. Detail of Buvina door (Split Cathedral) 30 15
1907 10 d. Virgin and Child (West door, Church of the Virgin, Studenica) 40 40

1979. 30th Anniv of Sarajevo University.

1908 **563** 2 d. black, brown & grey 10 10

564 Djakovic and Hecimovic

1979. 50th Death Anniv of Djuro Djakovic and Nikola Hecimovic (leaders of socialist movement).

1909 **564** 2 d. multicoloured . . . 10 10

565 Paddle Steamer "Serbia"

1979. Danube Conference. Multicoloured.

1910 4 d. 90 Paddle steamer "Deligrad" 75 50
1911 10 d. Type **565** . . . . 1·50 1·00

566 Milton Manaki 567 Edvard Kardelj

1980. Birth Centenary of Milton Manaki (first Balkan film maker).

1912 **566** 2 d. purple and ochre . 15 10

1980. 70th Birth Anniv of Edvard Kardelj (revolutionary).

1913 **567** 2 d. multicoloured . . . 10 10

1980. Renaming of Ploce as Kardeljevo. No. 1913 optd **PLOCE-1980-KARDELJEVO**.

1914 **567** 2 d. multicoloured . . . 15 15

569 Speed Skating

1980. Winter Olympic Games, Lake Placid. Multicoloured.

1915 4 d. 90 Type **569** 15 10
1916 10 d. Skiing 75 70

570 Belgrade University

1980. 75th Anniv of Belgrade University.

1917 **570** 2 d. multicoloured . . . 10 10

571 Fencing

1980. Olympic Games, Moscow. Multicoloured.

1918 2 d. Type **571** 10 10
1919 3 d. 40 Cycling 15 10
1920 4 d. 90 Hockey 20 10
1921 10 d. Archery 40 40

572 President Tito (relief by Antun Augustincic) 573 Pres. Tito

1980. Europa. Multicoloured.

1922 4 d. 90 Type **572** 15 10
1923 13 d. Portrait of Tito by Djordje Prudnikov . . . . 1·75 1·75

1980. Death of President Tito. Portraits by Bozidar Jakac.

1924 **573** 2 d. 50 purple 15 10
1925 – 4 d. 90 black 30 20

DESIGN: 4 d. 90, Different portrait of President Tito.

574 Sculpture of S. Kovacevic 575 Sava Kovacevic

1980. Obligatory Tax. Red Cross Week.

1926 **574** 1 d. multicoloured . . . 15 10

1980. 75th Birth Anniv of Sava Kovacevic (partisan).

1927 **575** 2 d. brown, orge & yell . 10 10

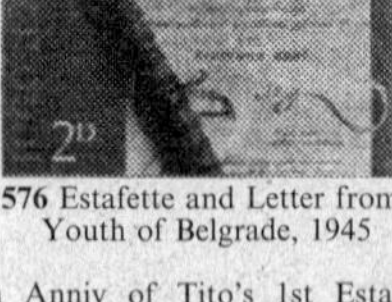

576 Estafette and Letter from Youth of Belgrade, 1945

1980. 35th Anniv of Tito's 1st Estafette (youth celebration of Tito's birthday).

1928 **576** 2 d. multicoloured 15 10

577 Flying Gurnard 578 Decius Trajan (249–51)

1980. Adriatic Sea Fauna. Multicoloured.

1929 2 d. Type **577** 15 10
1930 3 d. 40 Turtle 25 15
1931 4 d. 90 Little tern 90 15
1932 10 d. Common dolphin . . . 45 40

1980. Obligatory Tax. Solidarity Week. As No. 1885.

1933 **469** 1 d. black, grey and blue . 15 10

1980. Roman Emperors on Coins. Multicoloured.

1934 2 d. Type **578** 15 10
1935 3 d. 40 Aurelian (270–75) . . 20 10
1936 4 d. 90 Probus (276–82) . . . 30 15
1937 10 d. Diocletian (284–305) . . 55 40

1980. Nos. 1660 and 1652 surch.

1938 2 d. 50 on 1 d. 50 red 15 10
1939 5 d. on 75 p. purple 40 10

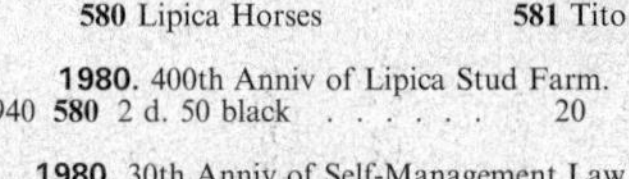

580 Lipica Horses 581 Tito

1980. 400th Anniv of Lipica Stud Farm.

1940 **580** 2 d. 50 black 20 10

1980. 30th Anniv of Self-Management Law.

1941 **581** 2 d. deep red and red . . 10 10

582 Novi Sad University 583 Mljet

1980. 20th Anniv Novi Sad University.

1942 **582** 2 d. 50 green 10 10

1980. Protection of the Environment. Mult.

1943 4 d. 90 Type **583** 25 10
1944 13 d. Galicica, Ohrid 65 50

584 Pyrrhotine 585 Lake

1980. Crystals. Multicoloured.

1945 2 d. 50 Type **584** 10 10
1946 3 d. 40 Dolomite 15 10
1947 4 d. 90 Sphalerite 25 15
1948 13 d. Wulfenite 50 40

1980. Obligatory Tax. Anti-Tuberculosis Week.

1949 **585** 1 d. multicoloured . . . 15 10

586 Kotor

1980. 21st Session of U.N.E.S.C.O. General Conference, Belgrade.

1950 **586** 4 d. 90 blue, gold, and deep blue 20 10

587 "Children with Balloons" (Gabrijela Radojevic) 588 Olympic Flag and Globe

1980. 12th "Joy of Europe" Meeting, Belgrade. Multicoloured.

1951 4 d. 90 Type **587** 20 10
1952 13 d. "Face" (Renata Pisarcikova) 65 40

1980. Obligatory Tax. Olympic Games Fund.

1953 **588** 50 p. multicoloured . . . 10 10

589 Dove and Madrid

1980. European Security and Co-operation Conference, Madrid.

1954 **589** 4 d. 90 green and deep green 20 15
1955 13 d. bistre and brown . 40 40

590 Flag of Bosnia and Herzegovina Socialist Republic

1980. Flags of Yugoslav Socialist Republics and of Federal Republic.

1956 **590** 2 d. 50 multicoloured . . 10 10
1957 – 2 d. 50 multicoloured . . 10 10
1958 – 2 d. 50 multicoloured . . 10 10
1959 – 2 d. 50 multicoloured . . 10 10
1960 – 2 d. 50 multicoloured . . 10 10
1961 – 2 d. 50 red, gold and grey 10 10
1962 – 2 d. 50 multicoloured . . 10 10
1963 – 2 d. 50 multicoloured . . 10 10

DESIGNS: No. 1957, Montenegro; 1958, Croatia; 1959, Yugoslavia (inscr in Roman alphabet); 1960, Yugoslavia (inscr in Cyrillic alphabet); 1961, Macedonia; 1962, Slovenia; 1963, Serbia.

591 "Complaint" (Milos Vuskovic) 593 Ivan Ribar

592 Sports Complex, Novi Sad

1980. Paintings. Multicoloured.

1964 2 d. 50 "Woman in a Straw Hat" (Stojan Aralica) (horiz) 10 10
1965 3 d. 40 "Atelier No. 1" (Gabrijel Stupica) (horiz) 15 10
1966 4 d. 90 "To the Glory of Sutjeska Fighters" (detail Ismet Mujezinovic) (horiz) 20 10
1967 8 d. "Serenity" (Marino Tartaglia) 35 15
1968 13 d. Type **591** 50 45

1980. Obligatory Tax. World Table Tennis Championships, Novi Sad.

1969 **592** 1 d. green, yellow & bl . . 15 10

1981. Birth Centenary of Ivan Ribar (politician).

1970 **593** 2 d. 50 black and red . . 10 10

594 "Cementusa" Hand Bomb

1981. Partisan Arms in Belgrade Military Museum.
1971 **594** 3 d. 50 black and red . . 15 10
1972 – 5 d. 60 black and green . . 25 10
1973 – 8 d. black and brown . . 30 10
1974 – 13 d. black and purple . . 45 35
DESIGNS: 5 d. 60, "Partizanka" rifle; 8 d. Cannon; 13 d. Tank.

595 Virgin of Eleousa Monastery

1981. 900th Anniv of Virgin of Eleousa Monastery, Veljusa, Macedonia.
1975 **595** 3 d. 50 grey, brown and blue 15 10

596 Table Tennis

1981. "SPENS '81" World Table Tennis Championships, Novi Sad.
1976 **596** 8 d. multicoloured . . . 30 15

597 "Lamp"

598 "Herzegovinian Wedding" (detail)

1981. Obligatory Tax. Red Cross Week.
1977 **597** 1 d. multicoloured . . . 10 10

1981. Europa. Paintings by Nikola Arsenovic. Multicoloured.
1978 8 d. Type **598** 25 10
1979 13 d. "Witnesses at a Wedding" 50 30

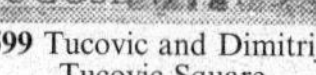

599 Tucovic and Dimitrije Tucovic Square

600 Tito (after Milivoje Unkovic)

1981. Birth Centenary of Dimitrije Tucovic (socialist leader).
1980 **599** 3 d. 50 blue and red . . 15 10

1981. 89th Birth Anniv of Tito.
1981 **600** 3 d. 50 multicoloured . . 35 15

601 Sunflower

602 Congress Emblem

1981. Cultivated Plants. Multicoloured.
1982 3 d. 50 Type **601** 15 10
1983 5 d. 60 Hop 20 15
1984 8 d. Corn 30 15
1985 13 d. Wheat 60 35

1981. 3rd Congress of Self-managers.
1986 **602** 3 d. 50 multicoloured . . 15 10

603 Djordje Petrov

604 Star

1981. 60th Death Anniv of Djordje Petrov (politician).
1987 **603** 3 d. 50 yellow and red . . 15 10

1981. 40th Anniv of Yugoslav Insurrection.
1988 **604** 3 d. 50 yellow and red . 15 10
1989 8 d. orange and red . . . 25 15

605 Apple and Target

1981. Obligatory Tax. "Spet 81" European Shooting Championships, Titograd.
1991 **605** 1 d. blue, red & orange . 3·00 3·00

1981. Nos. 1666 and 1669 surch.
1992 3 d. 50 on 3 d. 40 green . . 25 10
1993 5 d. on 4 d. 90 blue 25 10

606 Varazdin (18th-century illustration)

1981. 800th Anniv of Varazdin.
1994 **606** 3 d. 50 yellow and blue . 15 10

607 Parliament Building, Belgrade

608 "Flower"

1981. 20th Anniv of 1st Non-aligned Countries Conference, Belgrade.
1995 **607** 8 d. blue and red . . . 25 10

1981. Obligatory Tax. Anti-tuberculosis Week.
1996 **608** 1 d. red, yellow & blue . 15 10

609 Printing Press and Serbian Newspaper

1981. 150th Anniv of First Serbian Printing House.
1997 **609** 3 d. 50 pink and blue . 15 10

610 Fran Levstik

1981. 150th Birth Anniv of Fran Levstik (writer).
1998 **610** 3 d. 50 grey and red . . 15 10

611 "Village Scene" (Saso Arsovski)

1981. 13th "Joy of Europe" Meeting, Belgrade. Multicoloured.
1999 8 d. Type **611** 20 10
2000 13 d. "Skiers" (Aino Jokinen) 55 45

612 Pusher "Karlovac"

1981. 125th Anniv of European Danube Commission. Multicoloured.
2001 8 d. Type **612** 50 25
2002 13 d. Sip Canal . . . . . . 1·25 70

613 Postal Savings Bank Emblem

614 Emblem

1981. 60th Anniv of Postal Savings Bank.
2003 **613** 3 d. 50 red and yellow . . 15 10

1982. World Intellectual Property Organization Conference.
2004 **614** 8 d. red and gold 25 15

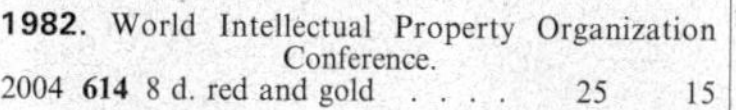

615 Forsythia and Rugovo Ravine

616 August Senoa

1981. Protection of Nature. Multicoloured.
2005 8 d. Type **615** 25 10
2006 13 d. Lynx and Prokletije . . 60 40

1981. Death Centenary of August Senoa (writer).
2007 **616** 3 d. 50 purple and brown 15 10

617 "Still Life with Fish" (Jovan Bijelic)

1981. Paintings of Animals. Multicoloured.
2008 3 d. 50 Type **617** 15 10
2009 5 d. 60 "Raven" (Milo Milunovic) 50 10
2010 8 d. "Bird on Blue Background" (Marko Celebonovic) . . . 75 10
2011 10 d. "Horses" (Peter Lubarda) 40 15
2012 13 d. "Sheep" (Nikola Masic) 40 35

618 Mosa Pijade (politician)

1982. 40th Anniv of Foca Regulations.
2013 **618** 3 d. 50 blue and mauve . 15 10

619 Mastheads

620 Cetinje

1982. 60th Anniv of "Borba" (newspaper).
2014 **619** 3 d. 50 black and red . . 15 10

1982. 500th Anniv of City of Cetinje.
2015 **620** 3 d. 50 brown and black . 15 10

621 Visin's Ship "Splendido"

1982. Europa. Multicoloured.
2016 8 d. Capt. Ivo Visin (first Yugoslav to sail round world) and naval chart 25 15
2017 15 d. Type **621** 80 25

622 Clasped Hands

624 House Sparrow (male)

1982. Obligatory Tax. Red Cross Week.
2018 **622** 1 d. black and red . . . 10 10

1982. Multicoloured.
2020 3 d. 50 Type **624** 40 10
2021 5 d. 60 House sparrow (female) 45 15
2022 8 d. Spanish sparrow (female) 70 25
2023 15 d. Tree sparrow (male) . . 1·75 40

625 "Tito" (after Dragan Dosen)

627 Jaksic (self-portrait)

626 Poster (Dobrilo Nikolic)

1982. 90th Birth Anniv of Tito.
2024 **625** 3 d. 50 multicoloured . . 15 10

1982. 12th Communist League Congress, Belgrade.
2025 **626** 3 d. 50 brn, orge & red . . 15 10
2026 8 d. light grey, grey and red 25 15

1982. 150th Birth Anniv of Dura Jaksic (writer and painter).
2028 **627** 3 d. 50 multicoloured . . 15 10

628 Kayaks

1982. Sports Championships.
2029 **628** 8 d. light blue and blue . 25 15
2030 – 8 d. light green and green 25 15
2031 – 8 d. pink and red . . . 25 15
DESIGNS AND EVENTS: No. 2029, Type **628** (World Kayak and Canoe Still Water Championships, Belgrade); 2030, Weightlifting (36th World Weightlifting Championships, Ljubljana); 2031, Gymnastics (6th World Gymnastic Cup, Zagreb).

629 Ivan Zajc

630 Breguet 19 and Potez 25 Biplanes

1982. 150th Birth Anniv of Ivan Zajc (composer).
2032 **629** 4 d. orange & brown 15 10

1982. 40th Anniv of Air Force, Anti-aircraft Defence and Navy.
2033 **630** 4 d. black and blue . . . 20 10
2034 – 6 d. 10 multicoloured . . 30 10
2035 – 8 d. 80 black and green . 50 15
2036 – 15 d. multicoloured . . . 90 30
DESIGNS: 6 d. 10, SOKO G-4 Super Galeb jet trainer; 8 d. 80, National Liberation Army armed tug; 15 d. "Rade Koncar" (missile gunboat).

631 Tara National Park and Pine Cones

1982. Nature Protection. Multicoloured.
2037 8 d. 80 Type **631** 25 15
2038 15 d. Kornati National Park and Mediterranean monk seal 50 40

632 Dr. Robert Koch

1982. Obligatory Tax. Anti-tuberculosis Week.
2039 **632** 1 d. orange, blk & red . 10 10

633 "Traffic" (Tibo Bozo)

1982. 14th "Joy of Europe" Meeting, Belgrade. Children's Drawings. Multicoloured.
2040 8 d. 80 Type **633** 25 15
2041 15 d. "In the Bath" (Heiko Jakel) 50 35

634 Small Onofrio Fountain, Dubrovnik

1982. 16th World Federation of Travel Agents' Associations Congress, Dubrovnik.
2042 **634** 8 d. 80 multicoloured . . 25 15

635 Herceg Novi (from old engraving)

1982. 600th Anniv of Herceg Novi.
2043 **635** 4 d. multicoloured . . . 15 10

636 Bridge, Miljacka

1982. Winter Olympic Games, Sarajevo. Each black, light blue and blue.
2044 4 d. Type **636** 25 15
2045 6 d. 10 Mosque tower and cable cars, Sarajevo 30 20
2046 8 d. 80 Evangelical Church, Sarajevo 40 25
2047 15 d. Old Street, Sarajevo . . 55 40

637 Bihac

1982. 40th Anniv of Avnoj-a (anti-fascist council) Session, Bihac.
2048 **637** 4 d. brown and orange . . 15 10

638 "Prophet on Golden Background" (Joze Ciuha)

639 Predic (self-portrait)

1982. Modern Art. Multicoloured.
2049 4 d. Type **638** 15 10
2050 6 d. 10 "Journey to the West" (Andrej Jemec) 20 10
2051 8 d. 80 "Black Comb with Red Band" (Riko Debenjak) . 25 15
2052 10 d. "Manuscript" (Janez Bernik) (horiz) 30 20
2053 15 d. "Display Case" (Adriana Maraz) (horiz) 50 35

1982. 125th Birth Anniv of Uros Predic (painter).
2054 **639** 4 d. orange and brn . . 15 10

641 Pioneer Badge

644 Lead Pitcher (16th century)

1982. 40th Anniv of Pioneer League.
2056 **641** 4 d. brown, silver and red 15 10

1983. Nos. 1663 and 1667 surch.
2057 30 p. on 2 d. 50 blue . . . 10 10
2055a 50 p. on 2 d. 50 blue . . . 10 10
2058 60 p. on 2 d. 50 blue . . . 10 10
2059a 1 d. on 3 d. 50 red 10 10
2060 2 d. on 2 d. 50 red 10 10

1983. Museum Exhibits.
2061 **644** 4 d. black, bistre and silver 10 10
2062 – 6 d. 10 black, brown and silver 15 10
2063 – 8 d. 80 gold, purple and grey 20 15
2064 – 15 d. gold, purple and grey 40 25
DESIGNS: 6 d. 10, Silver-plated tin jar (18th century); 8 d. 80, Silver-gilt dish (16th century); 15 d. Bronze mortar (15th century).

645 Jalovec Mountain Peak and Edelweiss

646 Ericsson Wall Telephone and War Ministry, Belgrade

1983. 90th Anniv of Slovenian Mountaineering Society.
2065 **645** 4 d. blue, light blue and deep blue 10 10

1983. Centenary of Telephone in Serbia.
2066 **646** 3 d. brown and blue . . 10 10

647 I.M.O. Emblem and Freighters

1983. 25th Anniv of International Maritime Organization.
2067 **647** 8 d. 80 multicoloured . 35 15

648 Field Mushroom

1983. Edible Mushrooms. Multicoloured.
2068 4 d. Type **648** 20 10
2069 6 d. 10 Morel 35 10
2070 8 d. 80 Cep 55 15
2071 15 d. Chanterelle . . . . . 1·10 30

649 Series "401" Steam Locomotive

650 Monument, Landovica

1983. 110th Anniv of Rijeka Railway.
2072 **649** 4 d. grey and red . . . 20 10
2073 – 23 d. 70 on 8 d. 80 red and grey 60 30
DESIGN: 23 d. 70, Series "442" electric locomotive. No. 2073 was only issued surcharged.

1983. 40th Death Anniv of Boro Vukmorivic and Ramiz Sadiku (revolutionaries).
2074 **650** 4 d. grey and violet . . 10 10

651 Nobel Prize Medal and Manuscript of "Travnik Chronicle" by Andric

1983. Europa. Multicoloured.
2075 8 d. 80 Type **651** 20 15
2076 20 d. Ivo Andric (author and Nobel Prize winner) and bridge over the Drina . . . 50 40

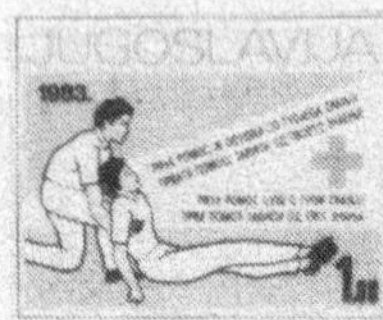
652 First Aid

1983. Obligatory Tax. Red Cross Week.
2077 **652** 1 d. deep brown, brown and red 15 10
2078 2 d. deep brown, brown and red 15 10

653 Combine Harvester

654 "Assault" (Pivo Karamatijevic)

1983. 50th International Agriculture Fair. Novi Sad.
2079 **653** 4 d. green and purple . . 10 10

1983. 40th Anniv of Battle of Sutjeska.
2080 **654** 3 d. pink and brown . . 10 10

655 Tito (after Bozidar Jakac) and Parliament Building

656 Delahaye Postbus, 1903

1983. 30th Anniv of Tito's Election to Presidency.
2081 **655** 4 d. brown and green . . 10 10

1983. 80th Anniv of Postbus Service in Montenegro.
2082 **656** 4 d. black and brown . . 10 10
2083 – 16 d. 50 brown & black . 40 25
DESIGN: 16 d. 50, Road used by first postbus.

657 Statue by V. Bakic, Valjevo

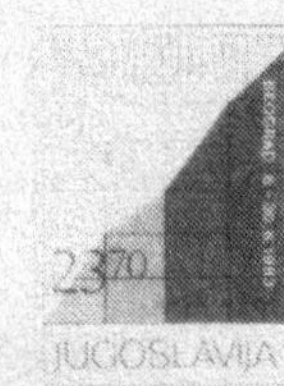
658 Graph

1983. Monuments.
2084 **657** 100 d. orange and blue . 1·25 50
2085 – 200 d. orange and green . 2·50 50
DESIGN—HORIZ: 200 d. Triumphal Arch, Titograd.

1983. 6th U.N. Conference for Trade and Development Session, Belgrade.
2086 **658** 23 d. 70 multicoloured . 50 30

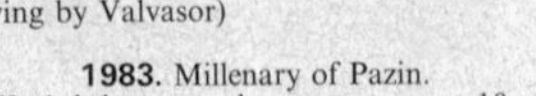
659 Pazin (after engraving by Valvasor)

660 Skopje

1983. Millenary of Pazin.
2087 **659** 4 d. brown and green . . 10 10

1983. 20th Anniv of Skopje Earthquake.
2088 **660** 23 d. 70 red 50 30

661 "The Victor"

662 Gentian and Kupaonik National Park

1983. Birth Cent of Ivan Mestrovic (sculptor).
2089 **661** 6 d. deep brown, brown and blue 15 10

1983. Nature Protection. Multicoloured.
2090 16 d. 50 Type **662** 40 25
2091 23 d. 70 Chamois and Sutjeska National Park 50 30

663 Apple

664 "Newly Weds" (Vesna Paunkovic)

1983. Obligatory Tax. Anti-tuberculosis Week.
2092 **663** 1 d. red, black & turq . 10 10
2093 2 d. red, black & turq . 15 10

1983. 15th "Joy of Europe" Meeting, Belgrade. Children's Drawings.
2094 **664** 16 d. 50 yellow, black and red 40 25
2095 – 23 d. 70 multicoloured . 50 30
DESIGN: 23 d. 70, "Andres and his Mother" (Marta Lopez-Ibor).

665 School and Seal

666 Monument by Antun Augustincic

1983. 150th Anniv of Kragujevac Grammar School.
2096 **665** 5 d. brown and blue . . 10 10

1983. Centenary of Timocka Buna Uprising.
2097 **666** 5 d. blue and purple . . 10 10

667 Skier and Games Emblem

668 Zmaj and "Neven" Periodical

1983. Obligatory Tax. Winter Olympic Games, Sarajevo.
2098 **667** 2 d. blue and deep blue . 15 10

1983. 150th Birth Anniv of Jovan Jovanovic Zmaj (poet and editor).
2099 **668** 5 d. red and green . . . 10 10

669 Ski Jump, Malo Polje, Mt. Igman

1983. Winter Olympic Games, Sarajevo (1st issue).
2100 **669** 4 d. black, green & brn . 10 10
2101 – 4 d. dp blue, bl & brn . 10 10
2102 – 16 d. 50 lilac, deep brown and brown 35 20
2103 – 16 d. 50 green, bl & brn 35 30
2104 – 23 d. 70 deep brown, green and brown 45 30
2105 – 23 d. 70 black, green and brown 45 30
DESIGNS: No. 2101, Women's slalom run, Mt Jahorina; 2102, Bob-sleigh and luge run, Mt. Trebevic; 2103, Men's alpine downhill ski run, Mt. Bjelasnica; 2104, Olympic Hall (for ice hockey and figure skating), Zetra; 2105, Speed skating rink, Zetra.

670 "The Peasant Wedding" (Brueghel the Younger)

671 Jajce

1983. Paintings. Multicoloured.

2107 4 d. Type **670** 10 10
2108 16 d. 50 "Susanna and the Elders" (Master of "The Prodigal Son") 35 20
2109 16 d. 50 "The Allegory of Wisdom and Strength" (Veronese) 35 20
2110 23 d. 70 "The Virgin Mary from Salamanca" (Robert Campin) 45 30
2111 23 d. 70 "St. Anne with the Madonna and Jesus" (Durer) 45 30

1983. 40th Anniv of 2nd Avnoj-a (anti-fascist council) Session, Jajce.

2112 **671** 5 d. red and blue 10 10

672 Drawing by Hasukic Sabina

673 Koco Racin

1983. World Communications Year.

2114 **672** 23 d. 70 multicoloured . 40 25

1983. 75th Birth Anniv of Koco Racin (writer).

2115 **673** 5 d. blue and brown . . 10 10

674 First Issue of "Politika"

675 Veljko Petrovic

1984. 80th Anniv of "Politika" (daily newspaper).

2116 **674** 5 d. black and red . . . 10 10

1984. Birth Centenary of Veljko Petrovic (writer).

2117 **675** 5 d. brown, orange and grey 10 10

676 Giant Slalom

1984. Winter Olympic Games, Sarajevo (2nd issue). Multicoloured.

2118 4 d. Type **676** 10 10
2119 4 d. Biathlon 10 10
2120 5 d. Slalom 10 10
2121 5 d. Bobsleigh 10 10
2122 16 d. 50 Speed skating . . . 25 15
2123 16 d. 50 Ice hockey 25 15
2124 23 d. 70 Ski jumping 35 20
2125 23 d. 70 Downhill skiing . . 35 20

677 Marija Bursac

678 Bond and Banknote

1984. Women's Day. National Heroines. Each grey, blue and black.

2127 5 d. Type **677** 10 10
2128 5 d. Jelena Cetkovic 10 10
2129 5 d. Nada Dimic 10 10
2130 5 d. Elpida Karamandi . . . 10 10
2131 5 d. Toncka Cec Olga 10 10
2132 5 d. Spasenija Babovic Cana . 10 10
2133 5 d. Jovanka Radivojevic Kica 10 10
2134 5 d. Sonja Marinkovic . . . 10 10

1984. 40th Anniv of Slovenian Monetary Institute.

2135 **678** 5 d. blue and red 10 10

679 Belgrade Central Station and Steam Mail Train, 1884

680 Jure Franko and Silver Medal

1984. Centenary of Serbian Railway.

2136 **679** 5 d. brown and deep brown 10 10

1984. 1st Yugoslav Winter Olympics Medal.

2137 **680** 23 d. 70 multicoloured . 35 20

681 Bridge

682 Globe as Jigsaw Pieces

1984. Europa. 25th Anniv of European Post and Telecommunications Conference.

2138 **681** 23 d. 70 multicoloured . 35 20
2139 50 d. multicoloured . . 75 40

1984. Obligatory Tax. Red Cross Week.

2140 **682** 1 d. multicoloured . . . 10 10
2141 2 d. multicoloured . . . 15 10
2142 4 d. multicoloured . . . 30 15
2143 5 d. multicoloured . . . 35 25

683 Basketball

1984. Olympic Games, Los Angeles. Multicoloured.

2144 5 d. Type **683** 10 10
2145 16 d. 50 Diving 25 15
2146 23 d. 70 Equestrian 35 20
2147 50 d. Running 70 40

684 Tito (after Bozidar Jakac)

685 "Skopje Earthquake"

1984. 40th Anniv of Failure of German Attack on National Liberation Movement's Headquarters at Drvar.

2148 **684** 5 d. brown and light brown 10 10

1984. Obligatory Tax. Solidarity Week.

2149 **685** 1 d. 50 blue and red . .

686 Mt. Biokovo Natural Park and "Centaurea gloriosa"

1984. Nature Protection. Multicoloured.

2150 26 d. Type **686** 40 25
2151 40 d. Pekel Cave and "Anophthalmus schmidti" 60 35

687 Great Black-backed Gull

1984. Birds. Multicoloured.

2152 4 d. Type **687** 20 10
2153 5 d. Black-headed gull . . . 20 10
2154 16 d. 50 Herring gull . . . 55 20
2155 40 d. Common tern . . . . 1·25 45

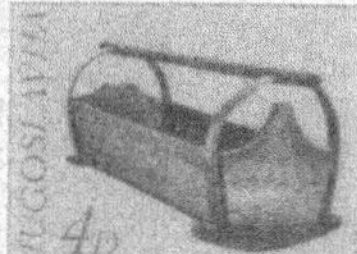

688 Cradle from Bihac, Bosnia and Herzegovina

1984. Museum Exhibits. Cradles.

2156 **688** 4 d. green 10 10
2157 – 5 d. purple and red . . . 10 10
2158 – 26 d. light brown and brown 35 20
2159 – 40 d. ochre and orange . 60 40

DESIGNS: Cradles from—5 d. Montenegro; 26 d. Macedonia; 40 d. Rasina, Serbia.

689 Red Cross and Leaves

691 "National Costume" (Erika Sarcevic)

690 Olive Trees, Mirovica

1984. Obligatory Tax. Anti-tuberculosis Week.

2160 **689** 1 d. multicoloured . . . 10 10
2161 2 d. multicoloured . . . 10 10
2162 2 d. 50 multicoloured . . 10 10
2163 4 d. multicoloured . . . 20 10
2164 5 d. multicoloured . . . 25 15

1984.

2165 **690** 5 d. multicoloured . . . 10 10

1984. 16th "Joy of Europe" Meeting, Belgrade. Children's Paintings. Multicoloured.

2166 26 d. Type **691** 35 20
2167 40 d. "Girl pushing bear in buggy" (Eva Gug) 60 40

692 Virovitica (17th-century engraving)

1984. 750th Anniv of Virovitica.

2168 **692** 5 d. orange and black . . 10 10

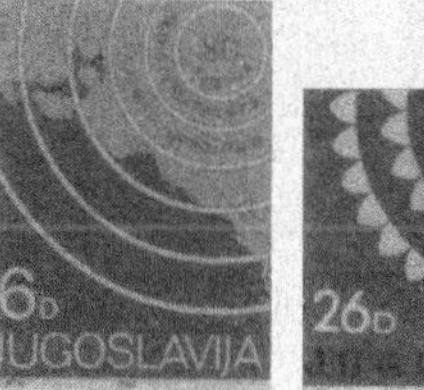

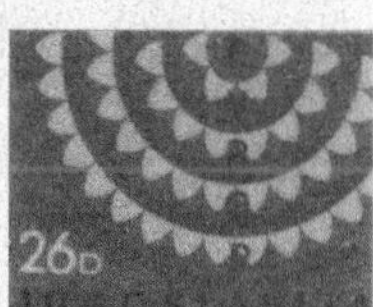

693 Map and Radio Waves

694 "Flower"

1984. 80th Anniv of Radio-Telegraphic Service in Montenegro.

2169 **693** 6 d. blue and green . . . 15 10

1984. Veterans' Conference on Security, Disarmament and Co-operation in Europe, Belgrade.

2170 **694** 26 d. pink, black and violet 90 90
2171 40 d. green, black and blue 90 90

695 City Arms and "40"

696 Milojevic and Music Score

1984. 40th Anniv of Liberation of Belgrade.

2172 **695** 6 d. red, silver and blue . 15 10

1984. Birth Centenary of Miloje Milojevic (composer).

2173 **696** 6 d. lilac and green . . . 15 10

697 Issues of 1944 and 1984

1984. 40th Anniv of "Nova Makedoniya" (newspaper).

2174 **697** 6 d. blue and red 15 10

698 Boxing

1984. Yugoslav Olympic Games Medal Winners. Each blue and red.

2175 26 d. Type **698** 35 20
2176 26 d. Wrestling 35 20
2177 26 d. Canoeing 35 20
2178 26 d. Handball 35 20
2179 26 d. Football 35 20
2180 26 d. Basketball 35 20
2181 26 d. Water polo 35 20
2182 26 d. Rowing 35 20

699 "Madame Tatichek" (Ferdinand Waldmuller)

1984. Paintings. Multicoloured.

2183 6 d. Type **699** 15 10
2184 26 d. "The Bathers" (Pierre-Auguste Renoir) 35 20
2185 26 d. "At the Window" (Henri Matisse) 35 20
2186 38 d. "The Tahitians" (Paul Gauguin) (horiz) 40 25
2187 40 d. "The Ballerinas" (Edgar Degas) (horiz) 60 40

1984. Nos. 1675a, 1668a and 2088 surch.

2188a 2 d. on 8 d. 80 grey 10 10
2189 6 d. on 4 d. red 10 10
2190 20 d. on 23 d. 70 red . . . 25 10

701 "Aturia aturi" (cephalopod)

1985. Museum Exhibits. Fossils.

2191 **701** 5 d. purple and blue . . 10 10
2192 – 6 d. brown and light brown 10 10
2193 – 33 d. brown and yellow . 40 25
2194 – 60 d. brown & orange . 65 45

DESIGNS: 6 d. "Pachyophis woodwardi" (snake); 33 d. "Chaetodon hoeferi" (fish); 60 d. Skull of Neanderthal man.

702 Hopovo Church

703 Three Herons in Flight

1985. 40th Anniv of Organized Protection of Yugoslav Cultural Monuments.

2195 **702** 6 d. red, yellow & grn . . 10 10

1985. 50th Anniv of Planica Ski-jump.

2196 **703** 6 d. multicoloured . . . 90 30

704 Lammergeier and Douglas DC-10 over Mountains

705 Osprey

1985. Air. Multicoloured.
2197 500 d. Type **704** . . . . . . 5·00 2·00
2199 1000 d. Red-rumped swallow and airplane at airport . . 10·00 4·50

1985. Nature Protection. Birds. Multicoloured.
2202 42 d. Type **705** . . . . 1·90 60
2203 60 d. Hoopoe . . . . 2·40 90

706 Three Herons in Flight

707 "St. Methodius" (detail "Seven Slav Saints", St. Naum's Church Ohrid)

1985. Obligatory Tax. 50th Anniv of Planica Ski-jump.
2204 **706** 2 d. blue and green . . . 10 10

1985. 1100th Death Anniv of Saint Methodius, Archbishop of Moravia.
2205 **707** 10 d. multicoloured . . . 1·10 60

708 Handshake

1985. Tenth Anniv of Osimo Agreements between Yugoslavia and Italy.
2206 **708** 6 d. blue and deep blue . 10 10

709 Flute, Darabukka and Josip Slavenski (composer)

1985. Europa. Multicoloured.
2207 60 d. Type **709** 60 60
2208 80 d. Score of "Balkanophonia" (Slavenski) 60 60

710 Red Cross and Faces

711 Vujic (after Dimitrije Auramovic)

1985. Obligatory Tax. Red Cross Week.
2209 **710** 1 d. violet and red . . . 10 10
2210 2 d. violet and red . . . 10 10
2211 3 d. violet and red . . . 10 10
2212 4 d. violet and red . . . 15 10

1985. 150th Anniv of Joakim Vujic Theatre, Kragujevac.
2213 **711** 10 d. multicoloured . . . 15 10

712 Order of Liberty

1985. 40th Anniv of V.E. (Victory in Europe) Day. Multicoloured.
2214 10 d. Type **712** 15 10
2215 10 d. Order of National Liberation 15 10

713 Franjo Kluz and Rudi Cajavec (pilots) and Potez 25 Biplane

714 Tito (after Bozidar Jakac)

1985. Air Force Day.
2216 **713** 10 d. blue, purple & brn 30 10

1985. 93rd Birth Anniv of Tito.
2217 **714** 10 d. multicoloured . . 45 10

715 Red Cross and "Skopje Earthquake"

716 Villa, Map of Islands and Arms

1985. Obligatory Tax. Solidarity Week. (a) As Nos. 1885 and 1933.
2218 2 d. 50 black, grey and bl . 10 10
2219 3 d. black, grey and blue . . 10 10

(b) Type **715**.
2220 **715** 3 d. blue and red . . . 60 60
See also Nos. 2315/16, 2460 and 2532.

1985. Centenary of Tourism in Cres-Losinj Region.
2221 **716** 10 d. multicoloured . . 15 10

717 U.N. Emblem and Rainbow

718 Regatta Emblem

1985. 40th Anniv of U.N.O.
2222 **717** 70 d. multicoloured . . 35 35

1985. 30th Anniv of International European Danubian Regatta.
2223 **718** 70 d. multicoloured . . 35 35

719 Aerial View of Yacht

720 Model Airplane

1985. Nautical Tourism. Multicoloured.
2225 8 d. Type **719** 10 10
2226 10 d. Windsurfing 15 10
2227 50 d. Yacht in sunset . . . 55 30
2228 70 d. Yacht by coastline . . 75 45

1985. World Free Flight Aeromodels Championships, Livno.
2229 **720** 70 d. multicoloured . . 80 35

721 Emblem and Text

722 Boy with Football

1985. Obligatory Tax. 20th European Shooting Championships, Osijek.
2230 **721** 3 d. blue 10 10

1985. Obligatory Tax. Anti-tuberculosis Week.
2231 **722** 2 d. black, orge & red . 10 10
2232 3 d. black, orge & red . 10 10
2233 4 d. black, orge & red . 10 10
2234 5 d. black, orge & red . 15 10

723 "Corallina officinalis" and Seahorses

725 Selling Vegetables from Cart (Branka Lukic)

724 Federation Emblem

1985. Marine Flora. Multicoloured.
2235 8 d. Type **723** 10 10
2236 10 d. "Desmarestia viridis" . 10 10
2237 50 d. Bladder wrack seaweed . 45 25
2238 70 d. "Padina pavonia" . . . 1·00 75

1985. 73rd International Stomatologists Federation Congress, Belgrade.
2239 **724** 70 d. multicoloured . . . 60 35

1985. 17th "Joy of Europe" Meeting, Belgrade. Children's Paintings. Multicoloured.
2240 50 d. Type **725** 40 20
2241 70 d. "Children playing" (Suzanne Straathof) 90 90

726 Detail of Theatre Facade

1985. 125th Anniv of Croatian National Theatre, Zagreb.
2242 **726** 10 d. multicoloured . . . 10 10

727 Miladin Popovic

728 State Arms

1985. 75th Birth Anniv and 40th Death Anniv of Miladin Popovic (Communist Party worker).
2243 **727** 10 d. brown & orange . . 10 10

1985. 40th Anniv of Federal Republic.
2244 **728** 10 d. multicoloured . . . 10 10

729 "Royal Procession" (Iromie Wijewardena)

1985. Paintings. Multicoloured.
2246 8 d. Type **729** 10 10
2247 10 d. "Return from Hunting" (Mama Cangare) 10 10
2248 50 d. "Drum of Coca" (Agnes Ovando Sanz de Franck) . 35 20
2249 50 d. "The Cock" (Mariano Rodriguez) (vert) 35 20
2250 70 d. "Three Women" (Quamrul Hassan) (vert) . . 80 80

1985. Nos. 1641, 1644, 1646, 1671, 1672 and 1677/9 surch.
2251 1 d. on 25 p. red 60 10
2252 2 d. on 5 p. orange 35 10
2253 3 d. on 35 p. red 10 10
2254 4 d. on 5 d. 60 olive 10 10
2255 8 d. on 6 d. brown 10 10
2256 20 d. on 26 d. blue 15 10
2257 50 d. on 16 d. 50 blue . . . 60 15
2258 70 d. on 38 d. mauve . . . 90 20

731 Zagreb Exhibition Hall

1986.
2259 **731** 100 d. violet and yellow . 40 40

732 Patrol Car

1986. 40th Anniv of Yugoslav Automobile Association. Multicoloured.
2260 10 d. Type **732** 10 10
2261 70 d. Emergency first aid helicopter . . . . 1·25 75

733 Wildlife on River Bank

734 Church of the Virgin

1986. Nature Protection. River Tara. Mult.
2262 100 d. Type **733** . . . . . 3·00 60
2263 150 d. Bridge over river . . . 90 90

1986. 800th Anniv of Studenica Monastery.
2264 **734** 10 d. red, green & blue . 60 30

735 Postman on Motor Cycle

736 Player and Ball in Goal

1986. Postal Services.
2265 **735** 20 d. purple 10 10
2266 – 30 d. brown 10 10
2267 – 40 d. red 10 10
2268 – 50 d. violet 10 10
2269 – 60 d. green 10 10
2273 – 93 d. blue 10 10
2275 – 100 d. purple 10 10
2276 – 106 d. red 10 10
2277 – 106 d. brown 10 10
2277a – 120 d. green 10 10
2277b – 140 d. red 10 10
2277c – 170 d. green 10 10
2278 – 200 d. blue 10 10
2278c – 220 d. brown 10 10
2278d – 300 d. red 10 10
2280 – 500 d. blue and brown . 15 10
2281 – 500 d. blue and yellow . 15 10
2282 **735** 800 d. blue 10 10
2284 – 1000 d. violet & green . 30 10
2284b – 2000 d. green & orange 10 10
2285 – 5000 d. blue and red . . 1·50 40
2285b – 10000 d. violet & orange 30 20
2285c – 20000 d. brown & green 65 35

DESIGNS—VERT: 30, 10000 d. Postman giving letters to man; 60 d. Posting letters; 93 d. Envelope and leaflet; 106 d. (No. 2276) Woman working at computer and woman filling envelope; 106 d. (No. 2277) Woman working at computer; 120 d. Woman with Valentine card; 140 d. Woman working at computer; 170, 300 d. Flower and postbox; 220 d. Mail coach and cover; 500 d. Postal sorter; 1000 d. Woman using public telephone; 5000 d. Posthorn, globe and bird with stamp. HORIZ: 40 d. Forklift truck; 50, 20000 d. Train; 200 d. Freighter; 2000 d. Telephone card, tokens and handset. 20 × 18 mm: 100 d. Postman and van.

See also Nos. 2586/99.

1986. World Cup Football Championships, Mexico. Multicoloured.
2286 70 d. Type **736** 60 60
2287 150 d. Players and ball in goal 60 60

737 St. Clement and Model of Ohrid (fresco, Church of St. Spas)

1986. 1100th Anniv of Arrival of St. Clement of Ohrid in Macedonia.
2288 **737** 10 d. multicoloured . . . 1·00 60

1986. No. 1674 surch.
2289 5 d. on 8 d. grey 10 10

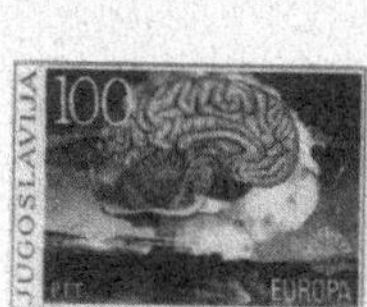

739 Human Brain as Nuclear Cloud

740 Judo

1986. Europa. Multicoloured.

2290 100 d. Type **739** 50 30
2291 200 d. Injured deer on road . 90 50

1988. European Men's Judo Championships, Belgrade.

2292 **740** 70 d. brown, pink & bl . 30 20

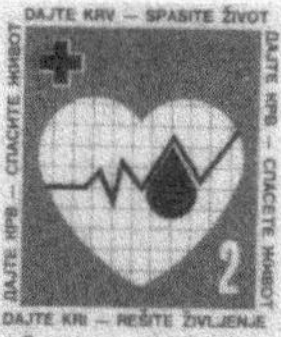

741 Graph and Blood Drop within Heart

742 Costume of Slovenia

1986. Obligatory Tax. Red Cross Week.

2293 **741** 2 d. black, blue and red . 10 10
2294 3 d. black, blue and red . 10 10
2295 4 d. black, blue and red . 10 10
2296 5 d. black, blue and red . 10 10
2297 11 d. black, bl and red . 10 10
2298 20 d. black, bl and red . 15 10

1986. Yugoslav Costumes. Multicoloured.

2299 50 d. Type **742** 25 15
2300 50 d. Vojvodina (woman with red apron) 25 15
2301 50 d. Croatia (man in embroidered trousers) . . . 25 15
2302 50 d. Macedonia (woman hand spinning) 25 15
2303 50 d. Serbia (woman in bolero) 25 15
2304 50 d. Montenegro (man with rifle) 25 15
2305 50 d. Kosovo (woman carrying basket) 25 15
2306 50 d. Bosnia and Herzegovina (man carrying bag on back) 25 15

743 Sailing Boats

Jugoslavija 10

744 Tito (after Safet Zec)

1986. "Flying Dutchman" Class European Sailing Championships, Moscenicka Draga. Multicoloured.

2307 50 d. Type **743** 25 15
2308 80 d. Sailing boats (different) 35 25

1986. 94th Birth Anniv of Tito.

2310 **744** 10 d. multicoloured . . . 10 10

745 "Eudia pavonia"

746 "Skopje Earthquake"

1986. Butterflies and Moths. Multicoloured.

2311 10 d. Type **745** 10 10
2312 20 d. "Inachis io" 15 10
2313 50 d. "Parnassius apollo" . . 20 20
2314 100 d. "Apatura iris" 25 35

1986. Obligatory Tax. Solidarity Week. (a) As No. 2200.

2315 **715** 10 d. blue and red . . . 10 10

(b) As Type **715** but inscr "Solidarity Week" in four languages.

2316 10 d. blue and red 10 10

(c) Type **746**.

2317 **746** 10 d. lilac and red . . . 10 10

747 Bosancica Manuscript

1986. Museum Exhibits. Ancient Manuscripts. Multicoloured.

2319 10 d. Type **747** 10 10
2320 20 d. Leontije's Gospel . . . 10 10
2321 50 d. Astrological writing, Mesopotamia 25 15
2322 100 d. Hagada (ritual book), Spain 50 30

748 Congress Poster (B. Dobanovacki)

1986. 13th Communist League Conference, Belgrade.

2323 **748** 10 d. black and red . . 10 10
2324 – 20 d. black and red . . 10 10

DESIGN: 20 d. Another part of the Congress poster.

749 Trubar and Title Page of "Abecedari"

1986. 400th Death Anniv of Primoz Trubar (founder of Slovenian literary language and religious reformer).

2326 **749** 20 d. multicoloured . . 45 25

750 Emblem

751 Dancers

1986. 125th Anniv of Serbian National Theatre, Novi Sad.

2327 **750** 40 d. multicoloured . . 20 10

1986. Rugovo Dance.

2328 **751** 40 d. multicoloured . . 20 10

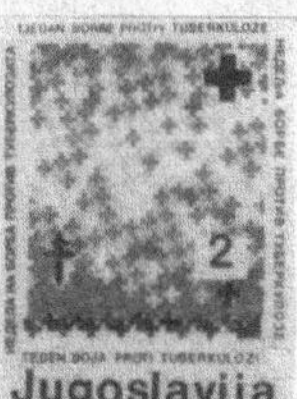

753 Crosses forming Earth and Sky

1986. Obligatory Tax. Anti-tuberculosis Week.

2330 **753** 2 d. multicoloured . . . 10 10
2331 5 d. multicoloured . . . 10 10
2332 6 d. multicoloured . . . 10 10
2333 7 d. multicoloured . . . 15 10
2334 8 d. multicoloured . . . 15 10
2335 10 d. multicoloured . . 15 10
2336 11 d. multicoloured . . 20 15
2337 14 d. multicoloured . . 20 15
2338 20 d. multicoloured . . 20 15

754 Volleyball

755 "Bird and Child running on Globe" (Tanja Faletic)

1986. "Universiade '87" University Games, Zagreb. Multicoloured.

2339 30 d. Type **754** 10 10
2340 40 d. Canoeing 15 10
2341 100 d. Gymnastics 40 25
2342 150 d. Fencing 60 35

1986. 18th "Joy of Europe" Meeting, Belgrade. Children's Paintings. Multicoloured.

2343 100 d. Type **755** 40 25
2344 150 d. "City of the Future" (Johanna Kraus) 60 35

756 Diagram of Rotary Selector and Bled

1986. 50th Anniv of Automatic Telephone Exchange Network.

2345 **756** 40 d. multicoloured . . . 15 10

757 Criminal in Stocking Mask

758 Brigade Member addressing Crowd (after D. Andrejevic-Kun)

1986. 55th Interpol General Assembly Session, Belgrade.

2346 **757** 150 d. multicoloured . . 60 35

1986. 50th Anniv of Formation of International Brigades in Spain.

2347 **758** 40 d. brown, gold and orange 15 10

759 Academy

1986. Centenary of Serbian Academy of Arts and Sciences.

2348 **759** 40 d. multicoloured . . . 15 10

760 People riding on Doves (Branislav Barnak)

1986. International Peace Year.

2349 **760** 150 d. multicoloured . . 65 35

761 "Portrait" (Bernard Buffet)

762 European Otter

1986. Paintings in Museum of Contemporary Arts, Skopje. Multicoloured.

2350 30 d. "Still Life" (Frantisek Muzika) 10 10
2351 40 d. "Disturbance" (detail, Rafael Canogar)(horiz) . . 15 10
2352 100 d. Type **761** 40 25
2353 100 d. "IOL" (Victor Vasarely) 40 25
2354 150 d. "Woman's Head" (Pablo Picasso) 60 35

1987. Protected Animals. Multicoloured.

2355 30 d. Type **762** 10 10
2356 40 d. Goat 15 10
2357 100 d. Red deer 40 25
2358 150 d. Brown bear 60 35

763 Boskovic, Brera Observatory and Solar Eclipse

764 Mountains, Woodlands and Animal Feeder

1987. Death Bicentenary of Ruder Boskovic (astronomer).

2359 **763** 150 d. multicoloured . . 60 35

1987. Nature Protection. Triglav National Park. Multicoloured.

2360 150 d. Type **764** 90 90
2361 400 d. Mountains, woodland and glacial lake 90 90

765 Potez 29-4 Biplane

1987. 60th Anniv of Civil Aviation in Yugoslavia. Multicoloured.

2362 150 d. Type **765** 75 40
2363 400 d. Douglas DC-10 . . . 1·75 1·00

766 Mateja Svet

1987. Yugoslav Medals at World Alpine Skiing Championships, Crans Montana.

2364 **766** 200 d. multicoloured . . 50 50

767 Kole Nedelkovski

1987. 75th Birth Anniv of Kole Nedelkovski (poet and revolutionary).

2365 **767** 40 d. multicoloured . . . 15 10

768 Battle Flags and Gusle

1987. 125th Anniv of Liberation Wars of Montenegro.

2366 **768** 40 d. multicoloured . . . 15 10

769 "Founding the Party at Cebine, 1937" (Anton Gojmir Kos)

1987. 50th Anniv of Slovenian Communist Party.

2367 **769** 40 d. multicoloured . . . 15 10

770 Tito Bridge (Ilija Stojadinovic)

771 Children of Different Races in Flower

1987. Europa. Architecture. Multicoloured.
2368 200 d. Type **770** . . . . . . 1·75 60
2369 400 d. Bridges over River Ljubljanica (Joze Plecnik) . 85 75

1987. Obligatory Tax. Red Cross Week.
2370 **771** 2 d. multicoloured . . . 10 10
2371 4 d. multicoloured . . . 10 10
2372 5 d. multicoloured . . . 10 10
2373 6 d. multicoloured . . . 10 10
2374 7 d. multicoloured . . . 10 10
2375 8 d. multicoloured . . . 10 10
2376 10 d. multicoloured . . . 10 10
2377 11 d. multicoloured . . . 10 10
2378 12 d. multicoloured . . . 10 10
2379 14 d. multicoloured . . . 10 10
2380 17 d. multicoloured . . . 10 10
2381 20 d. multicoloured . . . 10 10

772 Almonds **773** "Josip Broz Tito" (Mosa Pijade)

1987. Fruit. Multicoloured.
2382 60 d. Type **772** 10 10
2383 150 d. Pears 15 10
2384 200 d. Apples 45 35
2385 400 d. Plums 75 75

1987. 95th Birth Anniv of Tito.
2386 **773** 60 d. multicoloured . . . 10 10

774 "Skopje Earthquake" **776** Mail Coach in Zrenjanin

775 Bust of Karadzic (Petar Ubavkic), Trsic (birthplace) and Vienna

1987. Obligatory Tax. Solidarity Week.
2387 **774** 30 d. multicoloured . . . 10 10

1987. Birth Bicentenary of Vuk Stefanovic Karadzic (linguist and historian). Multicoloured.
2388 60 d. Type **775** 10 10
2389 200 d. Serbian alphabet and Karadzic (portrait by Uros Knezevic) 20 10

1987. 250th Anniv of Postal Services in Zrenjanin.
2390 **776** 60 d. multicoloured . . . 10 10

777 Emblem and Mascot **778** Hurdling

1987. Obligatory Tax. "Universiade '87" University Games, Zagreb.
2391 **777** 20 d. blue and green . . 10 10

1987. "Universiade '87" University Games, Zagreb. Multicoloured.
2392 60 d. Type **778** 10 10
2393 150 d. Basketball 15 10
2394 200 d. Gymnastics 20 10
2395 400 d. Swimming 75 75

779 Canadair CL-215 Amphibian spraying Forest Fire **780** Monument, Anindol Park

1987. Fire Fighting. Multicoloured.
2396 60 d. Type **779** 20 10
2397 200 d. Fire-fighting tug . . . 20 10

1987. 50th Anniv of Croatian Communist Party.
2398 **780** 60 d. multicoloured . . 10 10

781 School and Foundation Document **782** Crosses and Children's Head

1987. 150th Anniv of Sabac High School.
2399 **781** 80 d. brown, orange and blue 10 10

1987. Obligatory Tax. Anti-tuberculosis Week.
2400 **782** 2 d. multicoloured . . . 10 10
2401 4 d. multicoloured . . . 10 10
2402 6 d. multicoloured . . . 10 10
2403 8 d. multicoloured . . . 10 10
2404 10 d. multicoloured . . 10 10
2405 12 d. multicoloured . . 10 10
2406 14 d. multicoloured . . 10 10
2407 20 d. multicoloured . . 10 10
2408 25 d. multicoloured . . 10 10
2409 40 d. multicoloured . . 10 10

783 Emblem, Map and Flowers

1987. "Balkanphila XI" International Stamp Exhibition, Novi Sad.
2410 **783** 250 d. multicoloured . . 20 10

1987. No. 2269 surch **80**.
2412 80 d. on 60 d. green 10 10

785 "Children playing amongst Trees" (Bedic Aranka) **786** Arslanagica Bridge, Trebinje

1987. 19th "Joy of Europe" Meeting. Mult.
2413 250 d. Type **785** 60 60
2414 400 d. "Child and scarecrow in orchard" (Ingeborg Schaffer) 60 60

1987. Bridges. Multicoloured.
2415 80 d. Type **786** 10 10
2416 250 d. Terzija Bridge, Djakovica 20 10

787 Tug in Canal **788** SPRAM Emblem

1987. 600th Anniv of Titov Vrbas.
2417 **787** 80 d. multicoloured . . . 15 10

1987. Obligatory Tax.
2418 **788** 20 d. blue 10 10

789 Eclipse, Telescope and Old Observatory Building

1987. Centenary of Astronomocal and Meteorological Observatory, Belgrade.
2419 **789** 80 d. multicoloured . . 10 10

790 "St. Luke the Evangelist" (Raffaello Santi)

1987. Paintings in Mimara Museum, Zagreb. Multicoloured.
2420 80 d. Type **790** 10 10
2421 200 d. "Infanta Maria Theresa" (Diego Velazquez) 20 10
2422 250 d. "Nicolaes Rubens" (Peter Paul Rubens) 20 10
2423 400 d. "Louise Laure Sennegon" (Camille Corot) 35 20

791 Bull Fighting (Grmec)

1987. Museum Exhibits. Folk Games. Multicoloured.
2424 80 d. Type **791** 10 10
2425 200 d. Sword used in Ljuvicevo Horse Games 20 10
2426 250 d. Crown worn at Moresca Games (Korcula) 20 10
2427 400 d. Sinj Iron Ring 60 60

792 Foundation Document, View of Town and Arms

1988. 700th Anniv of Vinodolski.
2428 **792** 100 d. multicoloured . . 10 10

793 Skier **794** Cub

1988. 25th Anniv of Golden Fox Skiing Competition, Maribor.
2429 **793** 350 d. multicoloured . . 30 15

1988. Protected Wildlife. Brown Bear. Multicoloured.
2430 70 d. Type **794** 10 10
2431 80 d. Bears among branches . 10 10
2432 200 d. Adult bear 20 10
2433 350 d. Adult stalking prey . . 30 15

795 Slalom Skier **797** Basketball

1988. Winter Olympic Games, Calgary. Multicoloured.
2434 350 d. Type **795** 60 55
2435 1200 d. Ice hockey 60 55

1988. Olympic Games, Seoul. Multicoloured.
2437 106 d. Type **797** 10 10
2438 450 d. High jumping 35 20
2439 500 d. Gymnastics 40 25
2440 1200 d. Boxing . . . . 1·00 55

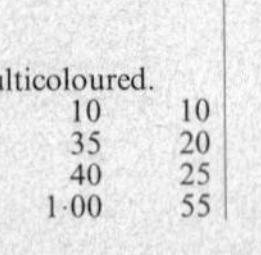

798 White Carnations **799** "INTELSAT V-A", Globe and Dish Aerials, Ivanjica

1988. Obligatory Tax. Anti-cancer Campaign. Multicoloured.
2442 4 d. Type **798** 10 10
2443 8 d. Red flowers 10 10
2444 12 d. Red roses 10 10

1988. Europa. Transport and Communications. Multicoloured.
2445 450 d. Type **799** 15 10
2446 1200 d. Woman using mobile telephone and methods of transport 40 25

800 Great Top Shell **801** Anniversary Emblem

1988. Molluscs. Multicoloured.
2447 106 d. Type **800** 50 50
2448 550 d. St. James's scallop . . 50 50
2449 600 d. Giant tun 55 50
2450 1000 d. "Argonauta cygnus" (wrongly inscr "argo") . . 65 50

1988. Obligatory Tax. 125th Anniv of Red Cross.
2451 **801** 4 d. blue, red and grey . 10 10
2452 8 d. blue, red and grey . 10 10
2453 10 d. blue, red and grey . 10 10
2454 12 d. blue, red and grey . 10 10
2455 20 d. blue, red and grey . 10 10
2456 30 d. blue, red and grey . 10 10
2457 50 d. blue, red and grey . 10 10

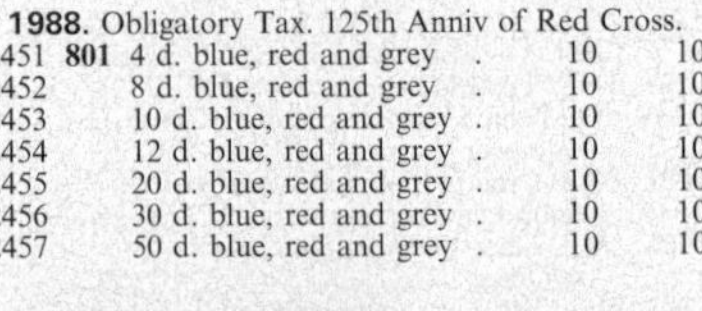

802 Josip Broz Tito **803** "Skopje Earthquake"

1988. 60th Anniv of Trial of Tito.
2458 **802** 106 d. brown and black . 10 10

1988. Obligatory Tax. Solidarity Week. (a) Type **803**.
2459 **803** 50 d. grey, brown & red 10 10

(b) As No. 2220 but value changed.
2460 **715** 50 d. blue and red . . . 10 10

(c) No. 2387 surch.
2461 **774** 50 d. on 30 d. mult . . . 10 10

1988. Nos. 2273 and 2277 surch.
2462 120 d. on 93 d. blue 10 10
2463 140 d. on 106 d. brown . . . 10 10

806 First Lyceum Building **807** Krleza

1988. 150th Anniv of Belgrade University.
2464 **806** 106 d. multicoloured . . 10 10

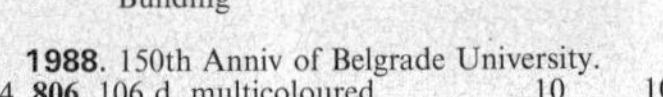

1988. Obligatory Tax. Culture Fund. 95th Birth Anniv of M. Krleza (writer).
2465 **807** 30 d. brown & orange . 10 10

808 "Phelypaea boissieri" **809** Globe and Flags

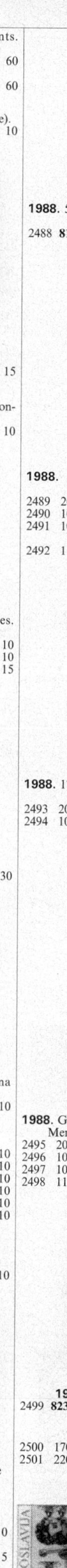
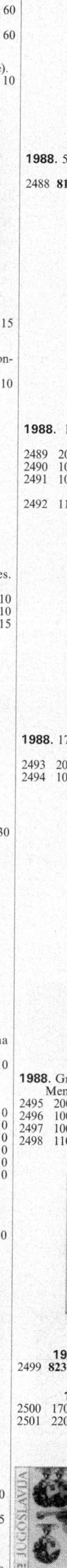

1988. Nature Protection Macedonian Plants. Multicoloured.
2466 600 d. Type **808** 60 60
2467 1000 d. "Campanula formanekiana" 60 60

1988. Centenary of Esperanto (invented language).
2468 **809** 600 d. blue and green . . 20 10

810 Shipping on the Danube
811 Globe as Ball in Basket

1988. 40th Anniv of Danube Conference.
2469 **810** 1000 d. multicoloured . . 30 15

1988. 13th European Junior Basketball Championships, Tito Vrbas and Srbobran.
2471 **811** 600 d. multicoloured . . 20 10

812 Horse Racing

1988. 125th Anniv of Belgrade Horse Races. Multicoloured.
2472 140 d. Type **812** 10 10
2473 600 d. Show-jumping event . 20 10
2474 1000 d. Trotting race 30 15

813 Douglas DC-10 and Globe

1988. Air.
2475 **813** 2000 d. multicoloured . . 80 30

814 Museum and Bosnian Bellflower
815 Flame and Hand

1988. Centenary of Bosnia amd Herzegovina Museum, Sarajevo.
2476 **814** 140 d. multicoloured . . 10 10

1988. Obligatory Tax. Anti-tuberculosis Week.
2477 **815** 4 d. multicoloured . . . 10 10
2478 8 d. multicoloured . . . 10 10
2479 12 d. multicoloured . . . 10 10
2480 20 d. multicoloured . . . 10 10
2481 50 d. multicoloured . . . 10 10
2482 70 d. multicoloured . . . 10 10

1988. Obligatory Tax. No. 2039 surch **1988 12**.
2483 **632** 12 d. on 1 d. orange, black and red 10 10

817 Arm and Crab's Claw (Anti-cancer)
818 "Daughter of the Artist" (Peter Ranosovic)

1988. Health Campaigns. Multicoloured.
2484 140 d. Type **817** 10 10
2485 1000 d. Screaming mouth in splash of blood (Anti-AIDS) 30 15

1988. 20th "Joy of Europe" Meeting. Mult.
2486 1000 d. Type **818** 60 60
2487 1100 d. "Girl wuth Straw Hat" (Pierre-Auguste Renoir) . . 60 60

819 1701 Arms and Present Emblem

1988. 50th Anniv of Slovenian Academy of Arts and Sciences.
2488 **819** 200 d. multicoloured . . 10 10

820 Galicnik Wedding

1988. Museum Exhibits. Traditional Crafts and Customs. Multicoloured.
2489 200 d. Type **820** 10 10
2490 1000 d. Weapons from Bokelji 30 15
2491 1000 d. Vojvodina embroidery (horiz) 30 15
2492 1100 d. People wearing masks, Kurenti (horiz) 35 20

821 Title Page of "Gorski Vijenac" and Njegos (after J. Boss)

1988. 175th Birth Anniv of Prince-Bishop Petar II of Montenegro. Multicoloured.
2493 200 d. Type **821** 10 10
2494 1000 d. Njegos Mausoleum, Lovcen and Njegos in bishop's robes (after Josip Tominc) 30 15

822 "Girl with Lyre"

1988. Greek Terracotta Figures from Josip Broz Tito Memorial Centre Collection. Multicoloured.
2495 200 d. Type **822** 10 10
2496 1000 d. "Girl on a stone" . 30 15
2497 1000 d. "Eros and Psyche" . 30 15
2498 1100 d. "Girl by the Stele" . 35 20

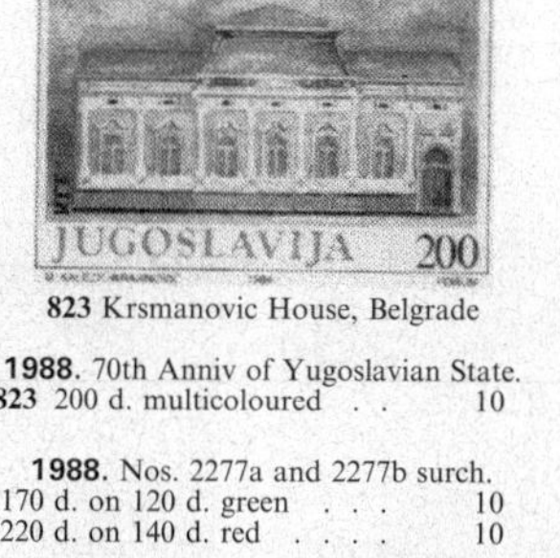

823 Krsmanovic House, Belgrade

1988. 70th Anniv of Yugoslavian State.
2499 **823** 200 d. multicoloured . . 10 10

1988. Nos. 2277a and 2277b surch.
2500 170 d. on 120 d. green . . . 10 10
2501 220 d. on 140 d. red 10 10

825 Pistol shooting

826 Gundulic and Dubrovnik

1988. Yugoslavian Medals at Olympic Games. Multicoloured.
2502 500 d. Type **825** (2 gold, 1 bronze) 15 10
2503 500 d. Handball (bronze) . . 15 10
2504 500 d. Table tennis (silver and bronze) 15 10
2505 500 d. Wrestling (silver) . . . 15 10
2506 500 d. Rowing (bronze) . . . 15 10
2507 500 d. Basketball (2 silver) . . 15 10
2508 500 d. Waterpolo (gold) . . . 15 10
2509 500 d. Boxing (bronze) . . . 15 10

1989. 400th Birth Anniv of Ivan Gundulic (poet).
2510 **826** 220 d. multicoloured . . 10 10

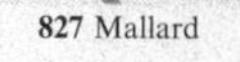

827 Mallard
828 Valvasor and Wagensperg Castle

1989. Wild Ducks. Multicoloured.
2511 300 d. Type **827** 15 10
2512 2100 d. Green-winged teal . . 1·00 40
2513 2200 d. Pintail . . . . 1·10 45
2514 2200 d. Common shoveler . . 1·10 45

1989. 300th Anniv of Publishing of "The Glory of the Duchy of Kranjska" by Johann Weickhard Valvasor.
2515 **828** 300 d. multicoloured . . 10 10

829 "Bulbocodium vernum"

832 Competitor

830 Envelopes and Dish Aerial

1989. Flowers. Multicoloured.
2516 300 d. Type **829** 10 10
2517 2100 d. White water-lily . . . 65 35
2518 2200 d. "Fritillaria degeniana" (vert) 70 40
2519 3000 d. "Orchis simia" (vert) . 90 45

1989. Air.
2520 **830** 10000 d. blue, mauve and yellow . . . . 1·50 90
2521 – 20000 d. orange, violet and red . . . . 1·40 1·40
DESIGN: 20000 d. Map and satellite.

1989. No. 1657 surch **100 d**.
2522 100 d. on 1 d. green 10 10

1989. 6th World Air Gun Championships, Sarajevo.
2523 **832** 3000 d. multicoloured . . 40 40

833 Girl looking through Magic Cube

834 Anniversary Emblem

1989. Europa. Children's Games and Toys. Multicoloured.
2524 3000 d. Type **833** 90 75
2525 6000 d. Boy playing with marbles and paper boats . . 90 90

1989. Obligatory Tax. 125th Anniv of Red Cross Movement (1988).
2526 **834** 20 d. blue, silver and red . 10 10
2527 80 d. blue, silver and red . 10 10
2528 150 d. bl, silver and red . 10 10
2529 160 d. bl, silver and red . 10 10

835 Tito

836 "Skopje Earthquake"

1989. 70th Anniv of Yugoslavian Communist Party.
2530 **835** 300 d. multicoloured . . 10 10

1989. Obligatory Tax. Solidarity Week. (a) Type **836**.
2531 **836** 250 d. silver and red . . 10 10

(b) As T **715**.
2532 **715** 400 d. blue and red . . . 10 10

837 Pole Vaulting
838 Racers

1989. 15th European Trophy Athletic Clubs Championship, Belgrade.
2533 **837** 4000 d. multicoloured . . 15 10

1989. Motor Cycle Grand Prix, Rijeka. Mult.
2534 500 d. Type **838** 10 10
2535 4000 d. Racers (different) . . 15 10

839 Flags of Netherlands, Italy, USSR and Spain and Ball

1989. 26th European Men's Basketball Championship, Zagreb. Multicoloured.
2537 2000 d. Type **839** 10 10
2538 2000 d. Flags of France, Yugoslavia, Greece and Bulgaria and ball 10 10

840 Ancient Greek Galleys

1989. Sailing Ships. Multicoloured.
2539 1000 d. Type **840** 15 10
2540 1000 d. Roman warships . . 15 10
2541 1000 d. 13th-century Crusader nefs 15 10
2542 1000 d. 16th-century Dubrovnik navas 15 10
2543 1000 d. 17th-century French warships 15 10
2544 1000 d. 18th-century ships of the line 15 10

841 "Battle of Kosovo" (lithograph, Adam Stefanovic)

1989. 600th Anniv of Battle of Kosovo.
2546 **841** 500 d. multicoloured . . 10 10

842 Danilovgrad

1989. Centenary of First Reading Room at Danilovgrad.
2547 **842** 500 d. multicoloured . . 10 10

1989. No. 2278c surch **700**.
2548 700 d. on 220 d. brown . . . 10 10

1989. Nos. 2266 and 2277c surch.
2549 400 d. on 30 d. brown . . . 10 10
2550 700 d. on 170 d. green . . . 10 10

845 Stone Tablet, Detail of Charter and Mule Train

1989. 800th Anniv of Kulin Ban Charter (granting free trade to Dubrovnik).
2551 **845** 500 d. multicoloured . . 10 10

846 Rowers

847 Houses of Parliament, London

1989. World Rowing Championship, Bled.
2552 **846** 10000 d. multicoloured . 30 15

1989. Centenary of Interparliamentary Union.
2553 10000 d. Type **847** 30 15
2554 10000 d. Notre Dame Cathedral, Paris 30 15

848 Belgrade and Cairo

849 Emblem

1989. 9th Non-aligned Conference, Belgrade. Multicoloured.
2555 10000 d. Type **848** 30 15
2556 10000 d. Lusaka and Algiers . . 30 15
2557 10000 d. Colombo and Havana . 30 15
2558 10000 d. New Delhi and Harare . 30 15

1989. Obligatory Tax. USAOJ-A Conference, Bihac.
2560 **849** 400 d. blue and red . . . 10 10

850 Brezovica-Jazinac Lake, Kosovo

851 Crosses as Basket of Flowers

1989. Nature Protection. Multicoloured.
2561 8000 d. Type **850** 25 15
2562 10000 d. Mirusa Canyon, Kosovo 30 15

1989. Obligatory Tax. Anti-tuberculosis Week.
2563 **851** 20 d. red and black . . . 10 10
2564 200 d. red and black . . 10 10
2565 250 d. red and black . . 10 10
2566 400 d. red and black . . 10 10
2567 650 d. red and black . . 10 10

852 "Child with Lamb" (Jovan Popovic)

853 Men Fighting

1989. 21st "Joy of Europe" Meeting. Mult.
2568 10000 d. Type **852** 30 15
2569 10000 d. "Girl feeding Dog" (Aelbert Cuyp) 30 15

1989. 300th Anniv of Karpos Insurrection.
2570 **853** 1200 d. multicoloured . 10 10

854 Cancelled 100 d. Stamp, Quill and Seal

1989. Stamp Day.
2571 **854** 1200 d. multicoloured . 10 10

855 Packsaddle Maker

1989. Museum Exhibits. Traditional Crafts. Multicoloured.
2572 1200 d. Type **855** 10 10
2573 14000 d. Cooper 45 25
2574 15000 d. Wine maker . . . 50 25
2575 30000 d. Weaver 95 50

856 Aerospatiale/Aeritalia ATR 42, Arrows and Map

857 "Apostle Mathias"

1989. Air.
2576 **856** 50000 d. blue & orange . 1·60 80

1989. Frescoes by Iohannes de Kastua from Holy Trinity Church, Hrastovlje, Slovenia. Multicoloured.
2577 2100 d. Type **857** 10 10
2578 21000 d. "St. Barbara" . . . 35 35
2579 30000 d. "Creation of the Universe, the Fourth Day" (horiz) 60 50
2580 50000 d. "Creation of the Universe, the Fifth Day" (horiz) 90 80

858 Barn Swallow, Envelope and Flower

860 Colour Spectrum entering Star

1989.
2581 **858** 100000 d. green & orge . 1·75 1·50

1989. No. 1680 surch.
2582 700 d. on 70 d. blue 10 10

1990. 14th Extraordinary Congress of League of Communists of Yugoslavia.
2583 **860** 10000 d. multicoloured . 30 15
2584 – 50000 d. multicoloured . 40 40
DESIGN: 50000 d. Hammer and sickle on V.D.U. screen.

1990. Postal Services. As T **735** but in revised currency
2586 10 p. violet and green 10 10
2587 20 p. red and yellow 10 10
2588 30 p. green and orange . . . 10 10
2589 40 p. green and purple . . . 10 10
2590 50 p. green and violet . . . 10 10
2591 60 p. mauve and red 10 10
2595 1 d. blue and purple 10 10
2596 2 d. blue and red 20 10
2597 3 d. blue and red 30 15
2599 5 d. ultramarine and blue . . 50 25
2603 10 d. blue and red . . . . . 1·50 60
2605 20 d. red and orange . . . . 1·10 55
DESIGNS—VERT: 10 p. Man posting letters; 20 p. Postal sorter; 30 p. Postman giving letters to man; 40 p., 20 d. Woman telephoning; 50 p. Posthorn, globe and bird; 60 p. Telephone card, tokens and handset; 3 d. Post-box; 5 d. Aerospatiale/Aeritalia ATR 42 airplane, letters and map; 10 d. Barn swallow, flower and envelope. HORIZ: 1 d. Train; 2 d. Freighter.

861 Gloved Hand holding Lighted Cigarette

1990. Anti-smoking Campaign.
2610 **861** 10 d. multicoloured . . . 1·00 85

862 Northern Pike

1990. Endangered Fishes. Multicoloured.
2611 1 d. Type **862** 10 10
2612 5 d. European catfish 50 25
2613 10 d. Burbot . . . . 1·00 85
2614 15 d. River perch . . . . . . 1·50 1·25

863 Zabljak Fortress, Printed Page and Arms

1990. 500th Anniv of Enthronement of Djuradj Crnojevic.
2615 **863** 50 p. multicoloured . . . 10 10

864 Telegraphist and V.D.U. Screen

1990. 125th Anniv of I.T.U.
2616 **864** 6 d. 50 multicoloured . . 65 35

865 Footballers

866 Skopje Posts and Telecommunications Centre

1990. World Cup Football Championship, Italy.
2617 – 6 d. 50 multicoloured . . . 65 30
2618 **865** 10 d. multicoloured . . . 1·00 50
DESIGN: 6 d. 50, Footballers (different).

1990. Europa. Post Office Buildings. Mult.
2619 6 d. 50 Type **866** 65 30
2620 10 d. Belgrade Telephone Exchange . . . . 1·00 50

867 Chicago Water Tower and Carnation

868 Record, Notes and Pen

1990. Centenary of Labour Day.
2621 **867** 6 d. 50 multicoloured . . 65 30

1990. Eurovision Song Contest, Zagreb. Mult.
2622 6 d. 50 Type **868** 65 30
2623 10 d. Conductor and Score of "Te Deum" . . . . 1·00 50

869 Cross and Leaves

870 Large Yellow Flowers

1990. Obligatory Tax. Red Cross Week.
2624 **869** 10 p. red and green . . . 10 10
2625 20 p. red and green . . . 10 10
2626 30 p. red and green . . . 10 10
(b) 45th Anniv of Macedonian Red Cross. Flower Paintings by Zivko A. Popovski. Multicoloured.
2627 20 p. Type **870** 10 10
2628 20 p. Arrangement of small yellow flowers 10 10
2629 20 p. Anniversary emblem . 10 10
See also Nos. 2636/7.

871 Server

873 Tito (bronze, Antun Augustincic)

1990. Yugoslav Open Tennis Championship, Umag. Multicoloured.
2630 6 d. 50 Type **871** 65 30
2631 10 d. Receiver . . . . 1·00 50

1990. No. 2282 surch **0,50**.
2632 **735** 50 p. on 800 d. blue . . 10 10

1990. 98th Birth Anniv of Tito.
2633 **873** 50 p. multicoloured . . . 10 10

874 "Tartar Post Riders" (Carl Goebel)

1990. 150th Anniv of Public Postal Service in Serbia.
2634 **874** 50 p. multicoloured . . . 10 10

875 "Skopje Earthquake" **876**

1990. Obligatory Tax. Solidarity Week.
2635 **875** 20 p. brown, red & silver 10 10
2636 – 20 p. multicoloured . . . 10 10
2637 – 20 p. multicoloured . . . 10 10
2638 **876** 20 p. blue and red . . . 10 10
2639 **715** 30 p. blue and red . . . 10 10
DESIGNS—As T **870**: No. 2636, Mauve flowers; 2637, Red and yellow flowers.

877 Fantail

878 Idrija Town

1990. Pigeons. Multicoloured.
2640 50 p. Type **877** 10 10
2641 5 d. Serbian high flier . . . 50 25
2642 6 d. 50 Carrier pigeon (vert) . 65 30
2643 10 d. Pouter (vert) . . . . . 1·00 50

1990. 500th Anniversaries of Idrija Town (2644) and Mercury Mine (2645). Multicoloured.
2644 50 p. Type **878** 10 10
2645 6 d. 50 Mine 65 30

879 Newspaper Offices, Museum and Mastheads — **881** Runners leaving Blocks

1990. 50th Anniv of "Vjesnik" (newspaper).
2646 **879** 60 p. multicoloured . . . 10 10

1990. Nos. 2587 and 2588 surch.
2647 50 p. on 20 p. red & yellow . 10 10
2648 1 d. on 30 p. green & orange 10 10

1990. European Athletics Championships, Split. Multicoloured.
2649 1 d. Type **881** 10 10
2650 6 d. 50 Runners' feet 65 30

882 Nurse and Sun — **883** Flowers in Vase and Birds

1990. Obligatory Tax. Anti-tuberculosis Week.
2652 **882** 20 p. yellow, blue & red . 10 10
2653 25 p. yellow, blue & red . 10 10
2654 50 p. yellow, blue & red . 10 10
2655 **883** 50 p. brown, red & grey . 10 10

884 "Pec Patriachate" (D. Cudov)

1990. 300th Anniv of Great Migration of Serbs. Multicoloured.
2656 1 d. Type **884** 10 10
2657 6 d. 50 "Migration of Serbs" (Paja Jovanovic) 65 30

1990. No. 2589 surch **2**.
2658 2 d. on 40 p. green & pur . . 20 10

887 "Little Sisters" (Ivana Kobilca) — **888** Chess Pieces

1990. 22nd "Joy of Europe" Meeting. Mult.
2660 6 d. 50 Type **887** 65 30
2661 10 d. "Willem III of Orange as a child" (Adriaen Hanneman) (vert) . . . . 1·00 50

1990. 29th Chess Olympiad, Novi Sad. Mult.
2662 1 d. Type **888** 10 10
2663 5 d. Rook, bishop, knight and chessboard 50 25
2664 6 d. 50 Knights, queen, king, pawn and chessboard 65 30
2665 10 d. Chess pieces and symbols 1·00 50

889 "St. Vlaho and Ragusa" (detail of triptych, Nikola Bozidarevic) and Penny Black

1990. Stamp Day.
2667 **889** 2 d. multicoloured . . . 20 10

890 Vransko Lake

1990. Nature Protection. Multicoloured.
2668 6 d. 50 Type **890** 65 30
2669 10 d. Griffon vulture . . . . 2·25 60

891 "King Milutin" and Notre Dame Monastery, Ljeviska

1990. Monastery Frescoes. Multicoloured.
2670 2 d. Type **891** 20 10
2671 5 d. "St. Sava" and Mileseva Monastery 50 25
2672 6 d. 50 "St. Elias" and Moraca Monastery 65 30
2673 10 d. "Jesus Christ" and Sopocani Monastery . . . . 1·00 50

892 Milanovic and Kringa (birthplace)

1990. Birth Centenary of Dr. Bozo Milanovic (politician).
2674 **892** 2 d. multicoloured . . . 20 10

893 Bringing Mary into the Temple — **894** Lapwing

1990. Iconostasis of St. Jovan Bigorski Monastery. Multicoloured.
2675 2 d. Type **893** 20 10
2676 5 d. Nativity 50 25
2677 6 d. Flight into Egypt (horiz) 65 30
2678 10 d. Entry into Jerusalem (horiz) . . . . 1·00 50

1991. Protected Birds. Multicoloured.
2679 2 d. Type **894** 25 10
2680 5 d. Woodchat shrike . . . 60 25
2681 6 d. 50 Common crane . . . 75 30
2682 10 d. Goosander . . . . . . 1·25 50

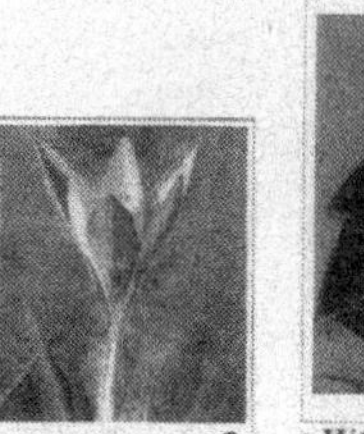

895 "Crocus kosaninii" — **896** Bishop Josip Juraj Strossmayer (founder) (after Vlaho Bukovac)

1991. Crocuses. Multicoloured.
2683 2 d. Type **895** 20 10
2684 6 d. "Crocus scardicus" . . 60 30
2685 7 d. 50 "Crocus rujanensis" 75 35
2686 15 d. "Crocus adamii" . . . 1·50 75

1991. 125th Anniv of Yugoslav Academy of Arts and Sciences.
2687 **896** 2 d. multicoloured . . . 20 10

897 Mozart (after P. A. Lorenzoni) — **898** Edvard Rusijan (Slovenian pioneer)

1991. Death Bicentenary of Wolfgang Amadeus Mozart (composer).
2688 **897** 7 d. 50 multicoloured . . 75 35

1991. Centenary of First Heavier-than-Air Flight by Lilienthal. Multicoloured.
2689 7 d. 50 Type **898** 75 35
2690 15 d. Otto Lilienthal . . . . 1·50 75

899 Route of Climb and Cesen

1991. 1st Anniv of Tomo Cesen's Ascent of South Face of Lhotse Peak.
2691 **899** 7 d. 50 multicoloured . . 75 35

900 Satellite and Earth

1991. Europa. Europe in Space. Multicoloured.
2692 7 d. 50 Type **900** 75 35
2693 15 d. Telecommunications . . 1·50 75

901 Figures — **902** Red Cross and Rays

1991. Obligatory Tax. Red Cross Week.
2694 **901** 60 p. multicoloured . . . 10 10
2695 1 d. 20 multicoloured . . 10 10
2696 1 d. 50 multicoloured . . 15 10
2697 – 1 d. 70 multicoloured . . 10 10
2698 **902** 1 d. 70 multicoloured . . 10 10
2699 – 1 d. 70 multicoloured . . 10 10
2700 – 1 d. 70 multicoloured . . 10 10
2701 – 1 d. 70 multicoloured . . 10 10
DESIGNS—29 × 24mm: No. 2697, similar to T **901** but differently inscribed. As T **902**: No. 2699, Pink flowers; 2700, Children on globe; 2701, Yellow flowers.

903 Miraculous Icon of St. Mary of Trsat (14th-century) — **904** River Steamer

1991. 700th Anniv of Franciscan Monastery, Rijeka.
2702 **903** 3 d. 50 multicoloured . . 20 10

1991. Community of Danubian Regions Conference, Belgrade. Multicoloured.
2703 7 d. 50 Type **904** 70 25
2704 15 d. River at sunset . . . . 1·40 50

905 Woman with Horse

1991. Obligatory Tax. Solidarity Week.
2706 **876** 2 d. green and orange . 10 10
2707 – 2 d. brown, red & gold . 10 10
2708 **905** 2 d. brown, red & gold . 10 10
2709 – 2 d. brown, red & gold . 10 10
2710 – 2 d. brown, red & gold . 10 10
2711 **715** 2 d. 20 blue and red . . 10 10
DESIGNS—As T **905**: No. 2707, "Skopje Earthquake"; 2709, Woman and tree; 2710, Woman holding cockerel.

906 "Karawanke Pass" (17th-century engraving, J. Valvasor)

1991. Karawanke Road Tunnel. Multicoloured.
2712 4 d. 50 Type **906** 25 15
2713 11 d. Tunnel entrance . . . 60 35

907 Balls and Baskets — **908** Order of the Partisan Star

1991. Centenary of Basketball. Multicoloured.
2714 11 d. Type **907** 60 35
2715 15 d. Aerial view of baskets . 80 50

1991. 50th Anniversaries of Yugoslav Insurrection and National Army. Multicoloured.
2716 4 d. 50 Type **908** 25 15
2717 11 d. Order for Bravery . . . 60 35

909 Ujevic — **910** Score and Gallus

1991. Birth Centenary of Tin Ujevic (writer).
2718 **909** 4 d. 50 multicoloured . . 25 15

1991. 400th Death Anniv of Jacobus Gallus (composer).
2719 **910** 11 d. multicoloured . . . 60 35

911 Savudrija, 1818

1991. Lighthouses of the Adriatic and the Danube. Multicoloured.
2720 10 d. Type **911** 50 30
2721 10 d. Sveti Ivan na Pucini, 1853 50 30
2722 10 d. Porer, 1833 . . . . . . 50 30
2723 10 d. Stoncica, 1865 . . . . 50 30
2724 10 d. Olipa, 1842 . . . . . . 50 30
2725 10 d. Glavat, 1884 . . . . . 50 30
2726 10 d. Veli Rat, 1849 . . . . 50 30
2727 10 d. Vir, 1881 . . . . 50 30
2728 10 d. Tajerske Sestrice, 1876 50 30
2729 10 d. Razanj, 1875 . . . . . 50 30
2730 10 d. Derdap, Danube . . . 50 30
2731 10 d. Tamis, Danube 50 30

912 "Sremski Karlovci School" (Ljubica Sokic)

1991. Bicent of Sremski Karlovci High School.
2732 **912** 4 d. 50 multicoloured . . 25 15

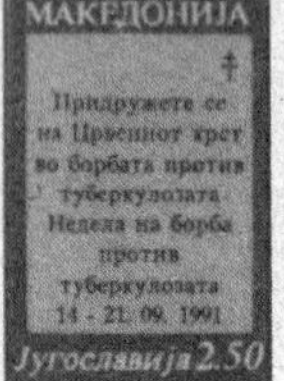

913 Girl 914 Inscription

1991. Obligatory Tax. Anti-tuberculosis Week.
2733 **913** 1 d. 20 blue, red & yellow 10 10
2734 2 d. 50 blue, red & yellow 15 10
2735 **914** 2 d. 50 black, yell & mve 15 10
2736 – 2 d. 50 multicoloured . . 15 10
2737 – 2 d. 50 multicoloured . . 15 10
2738 – 2 d. 50 blk, yell & mve . 15 10
DESIGNS—As T **914**: No. 2736, Doctor; 2737, Children; 2738, Girls with birds and flowers.

915 Mayfly 916 Town Hall (stained glass)

1991. Nature Protection. Multicoloured.
2739 11 d. Type **915** 60 35
2740 15 d. Pygmy cormorants . . 1·25 40

1991. 600th Anniv of Subotica.
2741 **916** 4 d. 50 multicoloured . . 25 15

917 Honey Bees and Congress Emblem 918 "Little Dubravka" (Jovan Bijelic)

1991. "Apimondia" 33rd International Bee Keeping Congress, Split.
2742 **917** 11 d. multicoloured . . . 60 35

1991. 23rd "Joy of Europe" Meeting. Mult.
2743 5 d. Type **918** 25 15
2744 30 d. "Little Girl with a Cat" (Mary Cassatt) . . . . . . 1·60 95

919 Statue of Prince Michael Obrenovich and Serbian 1866 1 p. Newspaper Stamp

1991. Stamp Day.
2745 **919** 4 d. 50 multicoloured . . 25 15

920 Battle of Vucji. Flag and Medal for Military Valour 921 Angel carrying Sun (Andrija Raicevic) (17th century)

1991. Cetinje Museum Exhibits, Montenegrin Flags and Medals. Multicoloured.
2746 20 d. Type **920** . . . . . . 1·10 65
2747 30 d. Battle of Grahovo flag and medal . . . . 1·60 95
2748 40 d. State flag and Medal for bravery . . . . 2·10 1·25
2749 50 d. Court flag and Petrovic dynasty commemorative medal . . . . 2·60 1·60

1991. Illustrations from Ancient Manuscripts. Multicoloured.
2750 20 d. Type **921** . . . . . . 1·10 65
2751 30 d. "April" (Celnica Gospel) (14th century) . . . . . . 1·60 95
2752 40 d. "Annunciation" (Trogir Evangeliarum) (13th century) 2·10 1·25
2753 50 d. Mary Magdalene in initial V (Miroslav Gospel) (12th century) . . . . 2·60 1·60

1991. Nos. 2591 and 2586 surch.
2754 5 d. on 60 p. mauve and red 25 15
2755 10 d. on 10 p. violet & grn . 50 30

923 Delcev 924 Trophies and Club Emblem

1992. 120th Birth Anniv of Goce Delcev (revolutionary).
2756 **923** 5 d. multicoloured . . . 25 15

1992. Victories of Red Star Club, Belgrade, in European and World Football Championships.
2757 **924** 17 d. multicoloured . . 90 55

925 Luge

1992. Winter Olympic Games, Albertville. Multicoloured.
2758 80 d. Type **925** . . . . . . 4·00 2·40
2759 100 d. Acrobatic skiing . . . 5·25 3·25

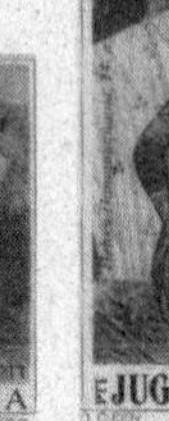

926 European Hare 927 "Mary feeding Jesus" (fresco, Pec Patriarchate)

1992. Protected Animals. Multicoloured.
2760 50 d. Type **926** . . . . . . 2·50 1·50
2761 60 d. Siberian flying squirrels 3·00 1·75
2762 80 d. Forest dormouse . . . 4·00 2·50
2763 100 d. Common hamsters . . 5·25 3·25

1992. United Nations Children's Fund Breastfeeding Campaign.
2764 **927** 80 d. multicoloured . . 4·00 2·50

928 Skier

1992. Centenary of Skiing in Montenegro.
2765 **928** 8 d. multicoloured . . . 40 25

929 Fountain, Belgrade 930 "Titanic"

1992.
2766 **929** 50 d. violet . . . . 2·50 1·50
2767 – 100 d. deep green and green . . . . 5·00 3·00
DESIGN: 100 d. Fountain, Kalemegdan Fortress, Belgrade.
See also Nos. 2825/32 and 2888/9.

1992. 80th Anniv of Sinking of "Titanic".
2783 **930** 150 d. multicoloured . . 8·00 4·75

931 La Barqueta Bridge and Seville (engraving)

1992. "Expo '92" World's Fair, Seville.
2784 **931** 150 d. multicoloured . . 8·00 4·75

932 Christopher Columbus

1992. Europa. 500th Anniv of Discovery of America by Columbus. Multicoloured.
2785 300 d. Type **932** 95 60
2786 500 d. Columbus's fleet . . . 1·25 75

934 Water Polo 935 Players' Legs

1992. Olympic Games, Barcelona. Multicoloured.
2791 500 d. Type **934** . . . . . . 1·25 75
2792 500 d. Shooting . . . . 1·25 75
2793 500 d. Tennis . . . . 1·25 75
2794 500 d. Handball . . . . 1·25 75

1992. European Football Championship, Sweden. Multicoloured.
2795 1000 d. Type **935** 75 45
2796 1000 d. Players 75 45

936 Red Tabby

1992. Domestic Cats. Multicoloured.
2797 1000 d. Type **936** . . . . . . 1·50 90
2798 1000 d. White Persian . . . . 1·50 90
2799 1000 d. Blue and white British shorthair . . . . 1·50 90
2800 1000 d. Red-point colourpoint longhair . . . . 1·50 90

937 JDZ 162, 1880

1992. Steam Locomotives. Multicoloured.
2801 1000 d. Type **937** . . . . . . 1·75 1·10
2802 1000 d. JDZ 151, 1885 . . . . 1·75 1·10
2803 1000 d. JDZ 73, 1913 . . . . 1·75 1·10
2804 1000 d. JDZ 83, 1929 . . . . 1·75 1·10
2805 1000 d. JDZ 16, 1936 . . . . 1·75 1·10
2806 1000 d. Private train of Prince Nicolas, 1909 . . . . 1·75 1·10

Currency reform.
10 (old) dinars = 1 (new) dinar.

1992. Various stamps surch.
2807 2 d. on 30 p. green and orange (No. 2588) 10 10
2808 5 d. on 20 p. red and yellow (No. 2587) 10 10
2809 5 d. on 40 p. green and purple (No. 2589) 10 10
2810 10 d. on 50 p. green and violet (No. 2590) 10 10
2811 10 d. on 5 d. ultramarine and blue (No. 2599) 10 10
2812 20 d. on 1 d. blue and purple (No. 2595) 10 10
2813 20 d. on 5 d. blue, green and yellow (as No. 2599) . . . 10 10
2814 50 d. on 2 d. blue and red (No. 2596) 20 15
2815 100 d. on 3 d. blue and red (No. 2597) 40 25
No. 2813 was not issued without surcharge.

939 Fischer (champion, 1972–75) 941 "Ballerina" (Edgar Degas)

940 Old Telephone and Buildings in Novi Sad, Subotica and Zrenjanin

1992. Unofficial Chess Re-match between Former World Champions Robert Fischer and Boris Spassky. Multicoloured.
2816 500 d. Type **939** . . . . . . 1·50 90
2817 500 d. Spassky (1969–72) . . 1·50 90

1992. Centenary of Telephone Service in Vojvodina.
2818 **940** 10 d. multicoloured . . 20 15

1992. 24th "Joy of Europe" Meeting. Paintings. Multicoloured.
2819 500 d. Type **941** . . . . . . 1·75 1·10
2820 500 d. Youth (V. Knezevic) . 1·75 1·10

942 Montenegro 1874 25 n. Stamp and Musician

1992. Stamp Day.
2821 **942** 50 d. multicoloured . . 25 15

943 Capercaillie, Durmitor Mountains 944 Book and Emblem

1992. Nature Protection. Multicoloured.
2822 500 d. Type **943** . . . . . . 1·50 90
2823 500 d. Eastern white pelican ("Pelecanus onocrotalus"), Skadar Sea . . . . 1·50 90

1992. Centenary of Serbian Literary Association.
2824 **944** 100 d. multicoloured . . 35 20

1992. As T **929**.
2825 5 d. brown and green 10 10
2826 50 d. blue and azure 10 10
2827 100 d. lilac and pink 10 10
2828 300 d. brown and chestnut . 10 10
2829 500 d. green and flesh . . . 10 10
2830 3000 d. orange 35 20
2831 5000 d. purple and yellow . . 40 25
2832 500000 d. violet and blue . . 90 55
DESIGNS: 5 d. 14th-century relief; 50 d. As No. 2767; 100 d. Type **929**; 300 d. Fountain, Kalemegdan Fortress, Belgrade; 500 d. Fountain, Sremski Korlovci; 3000 d. Fountain, Studenica; 5000 d. Fountain, Oplentsu; 500000 d. Thermal baths, Vrnjacka Banja.

945 Brvnara Summer Pasture Hut, Zlatibor

946 Sun over Able-bodied and Disabled People

1992. Museum Exhibits. Traditional Houses. Multicoloured.

No.	Description	Unused	Used
2833	500 d. Type **945**	75	45
2834	500 d. House, Morava	75	45
2835	500 d. House, Metokhija	75	45
2836	500 d. Farmhouse, Vojvodina	75	45

1992. Obligatory Tax. Disabled Persons' Week.

No.	Description	Unused	Used
2837	**946** 13 d. yellow and blue	20	10

947 St. Simeon Nemanja with Model of Church of the Blessed Virgin, Studenica (mosaic)

1992. Mosaics and Icons. Multicoloured.

No.	Description	Unused	Used
2838	500 d. Type **947**	75	45
2839	500 d. Prince Lazarevic with model of Ravanica Monastery (mosaic)	75	45
2840	500 d. St. Petka (icon) and St. Petka's Church, Belgrade (horiz)	75	45
2841	500 d. St. Vasilii Ostronoski (icon) and Monastery, Montenegro (horiz)	75	45

948 Bleriot XI (monoplane)

949 Detail of Fresco, Sirmium

1992. 80th Anniv of Aviation in Yugoslavia.

No.	Description	Unused	Used
2842	**948** 500 d. multicoloured	90	55

1993. 1700th Anniv of Formation of the Tetrarchy (Diocletian's reform of government of Roman Empire).

No.	Description	Unused	Used
2843	**949** 1500 d. multicoloured	70	40

950 Museum and Medal

1993. Centenary of Cetinje State Museum.

No.	Description	Unused	Used
2844	**950** 2500 d. multicoloured	65	40

951 Baltic Sturgeon

952 Charter and 1868 10 p. Coin

1993. Marine Animals. Multicoloured.

No.	Description	Unused	Used
2845	10000 d. Type **951**	60	35
2846	10000 d. Large-scaled scorpion fish	60	35
2847	10000 d. Broadbill swordfish	60	35
2848	10000 d. Bottle-nosed dolphin	60	35

1993. 125th Anniv of Reintroduction of Serbian Coins (2849) and 120th Anniv of the Dinar (2850). Multicoloured.

No.	Description	Unused	Used
2849	10000 d. Type **952**	60	35
2850	10000 d. 5 d. banknote and 1879 5 d. coin	60	35

953 Milos Crnjanski (writer)

954 Girl holding Flowers, and Bird (M. Markovski)

1993. Celebrities. Multicoloured.

No.	Description	Unused	Used
2851	40000 d. Type **953**	1·00	60
2852	40000 d. Nicola Tesla (physicist)	1·00	60
2853	40000 d. Mikhailo Petrovic (mathematician)	1·00	60
2854	40000 d. Aleksa Santic (poet)	1·00	60

1993. Children for Peace. Multicoloured.

No.	Description	Unused	Used
2855	50000 d. Type **954**	1·25	75
2856	50000 d. Birds flying above children (J. Rugovac)	1·25	75

955 Illuminated Letter from Miroslav Gospel

956 "Nude with Mirror" (M. Milunovic)

1993. No value expressed.

No.	Description	Unused	Used
2857	**955** A (3000 d.) red	25	15

1993. Europa. Contemporary Art. Multicoloured.

No.	Description	Unused	Used
2858	95000 d. Type **956**	1·50	90
2859	95000 d. "Composition" (M. P. Barili)	1·50	90

957

958 Map of Europe and Envelopes

1993. Obligatory Tax. Red Cross Week.

No.	Description	Unused	Used
2860	**957** 350 d. black and red	10	10
2861	1000 d. black and red	20	10

No. 2860 was for use in Montenegro and No. 2861 for Serbia.

1993.

No.	Description	Unused	Used
2862	**958** 50000 d. silver and blue	80	50
2863	– 100000 d. blue and red	1·25	75

DESIGN: 100000 d. Airplane.

960 Sutorina

1993. Fortresses. Multicoloured.

No.	Description	Unused	Used
2865	900000 d. Type **960**	75	45
2866	900000 d. Kalemegdan, Belgrade	75	45
2867	900000 d. Medun	75	45
2868	900000 d. Petrovaradin	75	45
2869	900000 d. Bar	75	45
2870	900000 d. Golubac	75	45

961 Marguerites and Roses

1993. Flower Arrangements. Multicoloured.

No.	Description	Unused	Used
2871	1000000 d. Type **961**	75	45
2872	1000000 d. Roses and gerbera	75	45
2873	1000000 d. Roses and lilies	75	45
2874	1000000 d. Rose, carnations and stephanotis	75	45

962 Generating Plant, Street Lamp and Town

1993. Centenary of Electrification of Serbia.

No.	Description	Unused	Used
2875	**962** 2500000 d. multicoloured	30	20

963 Jays

1993. Nature Protection. Fruska Highlands. Multicoloured.

No.	Description	Unused	Used
2876	300,000,000 d. Type **963**	1·25	75
2877	300,000,000 d. Golden oriole	1·25	75

Currency reform.
1000000 (old) dinars = 1 (new) dinar.

1993. Various stamps surch.

No.	Description	Unused	Used
2878	10 d. on 100000 d. blue and red (No. 2863)	10	10
2879	50 d. on 5 d. brown and green (No. 2825)	10	10
2880	100 d. on 5000 d. purple and yellow (No. 2831)	10	10
2881	500 d. on 50 d. blue and azure (No. 2826)	10	10
2882	1000 d. on 3000 d. orange (No. 2830)	15	10
2883	10000 d. on 300 d. brown and chestnut (No. 2828)	25	15

965 River Freighters

1993. The Danube, "River of Co-operation". Multicoloured.

No.	Description	Unused	Used
2884	15000 d. Type **965**	1·10	65
2885	15000 d. Passenger ferry	1·10	65

966 Jagodina Cancellation and Market

968 "Boy with Cat" (Sava Sumanovci)

1993. Stamp Day. 150th Anniv of Jagodina Postal Service.

No.	Description	Unused	Used
2887	**966** 12000 d. multicoloured	55	35

1993. Thermal Baths. As T **929**.

No.	Description	Unused	Used
2888	10000 d. blue and violet	10	10
2889	100000 d. brown and red	10	10

DESIGNS: 10000 d. As No. 2832; 100000 d. Bukovacka Banja.

1993. Unissued stamp as No. 2825 surch **50 000**.

No.	Description	Unused	Used
2890	50000 d. on 50 d. on 5 d. stone, brown and green	25	15

1993. 25th "Joy of Europe" Meeting. Multicoloured.

No.	Description	Unused	Used
2891	2000000 d. Type **968**	1·10	65
2892	2000000 d. "Circus Rider" (Georges Rouault)	1·10	65

969 "Madonna and Child" (from Bogorodica Ljeviska)

970 Summer Pasture Hut, Savardak

1993. Icons. Multicoloured.

No.	Description	Unused	Used
2893	400,000,000 d. Type **969**	75	45
2894	400,000,000 d. "Christ entering Jerusalem" (from Oplenac)	75	45
2895	400,000,000 d. "Birth of Christ" (from Studenica)	75	45
2896	400,000,000 d. "The Annunciation" (from Mileseva)	75	45

Currency reform.
1,000,000,000, (old) dinars = 1 (new) dinar.

1993. Museum Exhibits. Traditional Buildings. Multicoloured.

No.	Description	Unused	Used
2897	50 d. Type **970**	80	50
2898	50 d. "Crmnicka" house, Bar	80	50
2899	50 d. Watchtower, Chardak (vert)	80	50
2900	50 d. Coast house, Primorsten (vert)	80	50

971 Illuminated Page

972 Egyptian Vultures

1994. 500th Anniv of Printing of "Oktoukh" (book). Multicoloured.

No.	Description	Unused	Used
2901	1000 d. Type **971**	50	30
2902	1000 d. Illustration of church and saints	50	30

Currency reform.
13,000,000 (old) dinars = 1 new dinar.

1994. Birds. Multicoloured.

No.	Description	Unused	Used
2903	80 p. Type **972**	80	50
2904	80 p. Saker falcons ("Falco cherrug")	80	50
2905	80 p. Long-legged buzzards ("Buteo rufinus")	80	50
2906	80 p. Lesser kestrels ("Falco naumanni")	80	50

973 Mimosa

974 Illumination from "Miroslav Gospel" and Museum

1994. International Mimosa Festival, Herceg Novi.

No.	Description	Unused	Used
2907	**973** 80 p. multicoloured	80	50

1994. 150th Anniv of National Museum (2908) and 125th Anniv of National Theatre (2909), Belgrade. Multicoloured.

No.	Description	Unused	Used
2908	80 p. Type **974**	80	50
2909	80 p. Prince Milos Obrenovic and theatre	80	50

975 Speed Skating

976 Caudron C-61 and Route Map

1994. Winter Olympic Games, Lillehammer, Norway. Multicoloured.

No.	Description	Unused	Used
2910	60 p. Type **975**	65	40
2911	60 p. Olympic rings and flame	65	40
2912	60 p. Skiing	65	40

1994. Europa. 71st Anniv of First Paris–Belgrade–Bucharest–Istanbul Regular Night Flight. Multicoloured.

No.	Description	Unused	Used
2913	60 p. Type **976**	65	40
2914	1 d. 80 Caudron C-61, Belgrade and route map	1·40	85

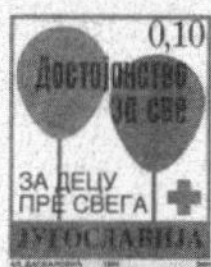

977 Balloons

1994. Obligatory Tax. Red Cross Week.

No.	Description	Unused	Used
2915	**977** 10 p. red, black and blue	10	10

978 "The Burning of St. Sava"

1994. 400th Anniv of Burning of St. Sava's Relics.
2916 **978** 60 p. multicoloured . . 65 40

979 Jubilant Players **980** Basset Hound

1994. World Cup Football Championship, U.S.A. Multicoloured.
2917 60 p. Type **979** 65 40
2918 1 d. Goalkeeper and players on ground . . . . 1·10 65

1994. Dogs. Multicoloured.
2919 60 p. Type **980** 65 40
2920 60 p. Maltese terrier 65 40
2921 60 p. Welsh terrier 65 40
2922 1 d. Husky . . . . 1·10 65

1994. Nos. 2888/9 surch.
2923 10 p. on 100000 d. brown and red 10 10
2924 50 p. on 10000 d. blue and violet 45 25

982 Bell and Globe **983** Crna Gora National Park

1994. Assembly of Eastern Orthodox Nations.
2925 **982** 60 p. multicoloured . . 65 40

1994. Protection of Environment in Montenegro.
2926 **983** 50 p. multicoloured . . 50 30

984 Moraca **985** St. Arsenius and Sremski

1994. Churches.
2927 **984** 1 p. violet and brown . 10 10
2928 – 5 p. blue and brown . . 10 10
2929 – 10 p. green and red . . 10 10
2930 – 20 p. purple and claret . 10 10
2931 – 20 p. black and red . . 10 10
2932 – 50 p. purple and violet . 10 10
2933 – 1 d. red and blue . . . 15 10
2935 – 5 d. violet and blue . . 20 10
2936 – 10 d. red and orange . . 30 20
2938 – 20 d. turquoise and blue 45 30

DESIGNS: 5 p. Gracanica; 10 p. Ostrog Monastery; 20 p. (2930/1) Lazarica; 50 p. Studenica; 1 d. Sopocani; 5 d. Ljeviska; 10 d. Zica; 20 d. Decani.

1994. Bicentenary of St. Arsenius Seminary, Sremski Karlovci.
2940 **985** 50 p. multicoloured . . 50 30

986 Syringe

1994. Obligatory Tax. Anti-tuberculosis Week.
2941 **986** 10 p. black, yellow and red 10 10

987 River Bojana **988** Painting by U. Knezevic

1994. Nature Protection. Multicoloured.
2942 1 d. Type **987** . . . . . . 1·00 60
2943 1 d. 50 Lake Biograd . . . . 1·25 75

1994. 26th "Joy of Europe" Meeting.
2944 **988** 1 d. multicoloured . . . 1·00 60

989 "Revenge" (English galleon) **990** Aerospatiale ATR 42 Mail Plane, Mail Coach and Letter

1994. Ships in Bottles. Multicoloured.
2945 50 p. Type **989** 55 35
2946 50 p. 17th-century yacht . . 55 35
2947 50 p. "Santa Maria" (Columbus's flagship) . . 55 35
2948 50 p. 15th-century nau . . . 55 35
2949 50 p. "Mayflower" (Pilgrim Fathers' ship) 55 35
2950 50 p. 14th-century caravel . 55 35

1994. Stamp Day.
2951 **990** 50 p. multicoloured . . 55 35

991 Tombstone **992** "Madonna and Child" (T. I. Cesljar)

1994. Museum Exhibits. Illustrated Tombstones. Multicoloured.
2952 50 p. Type **991** 55 35
2953 50 p. Double stone and railing 55 35
2954 50 p. Two stones 55 35
2955 50 p. Cemetery 55 35

1994. Paintings. Multicoloured.
2956 60 p. Type **992** 65 40
2957 60 p. "Adoration of the Three Wise Men" (N. Neshkovic) 65 40
2958 60 p. "The Annunciation" (D. Bacevic) 65 40
2959 60 p. "St. John baptizing Christ" (T. Krachun) . . 65 40

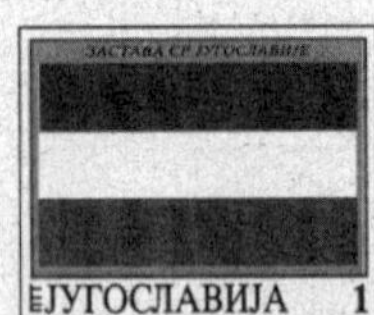
993 National Flag

1995. Multicoloured.
2960 1 d. Type **993** 25 15
2961 1 d. National arms 25 15

994 Wilhelm Steinitz (1886–94)

1995. Chess (1st series). Chessmen or World Champions. Multicoloured.
2962 60 p. Type **994** 15 10
2963 60 p. Pieces 15 10
2964 60 p. Emanuel Lasker (1894–1921) 15 10
2965 60 p. Black knight 15 10
2966 60 p. Pawns, king and knight 15 10
2967 60 p. Jose Raul Capablanca (1921–27) 15 10
2968 60 p. Rook, bishop, queen and pawns 15 10
2969 60 p. Aleksandr Alekhine (1927–35 and 1937–46) . . 15 10

See also Nos. 2988/95 and 3021/9.

995 Emblem

1995. 50th Anniv of Red Star Sports Club, Belgrade.
2970 **995** 60 p. red, blue and gold 15 10

996 Fire Salamander **997** Sportsman and Emblem

1995. Amphibians. Multicoloured.
2971 60 p. Type **996** 15 10
2972 60 p. Alpine newt ("Triturus alpestris") 15 10
2973 60 p. Stream frog ("Rana graeca") 15 10
2974 60 p. Eastern spadefoot ("Pelobates syriacus balcanicus") 15 10

1995. 75th Anniv of Radnicki Sports Club, Belgrade.
2975 **997** 60 p. multicoloured . . . 15 10

998 Eagle over Mountainside **999** Globes

1995. Europa. Peace and Freedom. Multicoloured.
2976 60 p. Type **998** 15 10
2977 1 d. 90 Child with tricycle and elderly couple on park bench (horiz) 50 30

1995. Obligatory Tax. Red Cross Week.
2978 **999** 10 p. yellow, blue and red 10 10

1000 Dove with Black Bird in Beak **1001** Station Concourse and Train

1995. 50th Anniv of End of Second World War.
2979 **1000** 60 p. multicoloured . . . 15 10

1995. Opening of Vukov Monument Underground Railway Station, Belgrade.
2980 **1001** 60 p. multicoloured . . . 15 10

1002 Leaves and Flowers

1995. "Draba bertiscea". Multicoloured.
2981 60 p. Type **1002** 15 10
2982 60 p. Clumps of leaves and flowers 15 10
2983 60 p. Plant growing on mountainside 15 10
2984 60 p. Plant and tree branch . 15 10

1003 Shore Lark, Rtanj

1995. Nature Protection. Multicoloured.
2985 60 p. Type **1003** 15 10
2986 1 d. 90 Blasius's horseshoe bat, Lazareva Reka Canyon . . 50 30

1004 Slovakian Village Gathering (Zuzka Medvedova)

1995.
2987 **1004** 60 p. multicoloured . . 15 10

1995. Chess (2nd series). Chessmen or World Champions. As T **994**. Multicoloured.
2988 60 p. Max Euwe (1935–37) . 15 10
2989 60 p. Pawn and chessboard and pieces 15 10
2990 60 p. Mikhail Botvinnik (1948–57, 1958–60 and 1961–63) . 15 10
2991 60 p. Queen and chessboard and pieces 15 10
2992 60 p. Board and white bishop and knight 15 10
2993 60 p. Vasily Smyslov (1957–58) 15 10
2994 60 p. Rook, knight, queen and board 15 10
2995 60 p. Mikhail Tal (1960–61) . 15 10

1005 Wilhelm Rontgen (discoverer of X-rays) **1006** Player on Globe

1995. Obligatory Tax. Anti-tuberculosis Week.
2996 **1005** 10 p. red and blue . . . 10 10

1995. Centenary of Volleyball.
2997 **1006** 90 p. multicoloured . . 25 15

1007 Church **1008** Coronation of King Peter II

1995. 800th Anniv of St. Luke's Church, Kotor.
2998 **1007** 80 p. multicoloured . . 20 10

1995. Centenary of Motion Pictures. Each brown and orange.
2999 1 d. 10 Type **1008** 30 20
3000 2 d. 20 Auguste and Louis Lumiere (cine camera pioneers) 60 35

1009 Club Emblem **1010** Golden Gate Bridge, San Francisco

1995. 50th Anniv of Partisan Army Sports Club.
3001 **1009** 80 p. multicoloured . . 20 10

1995. 50th Anniv of U.N.O.
3002 **1010** 1 d. 10 multicoloured . . 30 20

1011 Post Office, Seal and Letter **1012** "Flower Seller" (Milos Tenkovic)

1995. Stamp Day.
3003 **1011** 1 d. 10 multicoloured . 30 20

1995. 27th "Joy of Europe" Meeting. Multicoloured.
3004 1 d. 10 Type **1012** 30 20
3005 2 d. 20 "Child at Table" (Pierre Bonnard) 60 35

1014 Saric No. 1 **1015** "Birth of Christ" (D. Milojevic)

1995. Museum Exhibits. Aircraft. Multicoloured.

3007	1 d. 10 Type **1014**	30	20
3008	1 d. 10 Douglas DC-3	30	20
3009	2 d. 20 Fizir FN biplane	60	35
3010	2 d. 20 Sud Aviation Caravelle jetliner	60	35

1995. Paintings. Multicoloured.

3011	1 d. 10 Type **1015**	30	20
3012	1 d. 10 "Flight into Egypt" (Z. Halupova) (horiz)	30	20
3013	2 d. 20 "Sunday" (M. Rasic)	60	35
3014	2 d. 20 "Traditional Christmas Festival" (J. Brasic) (horiz)	60	35

1016 Battle Scene **1017** Painting

1996. 70th Anniv of Battle of Mojkovac.

3015	**1016**	1 d. 10 multicoloured	30	20

1996. Birth Centenary of Save Sumanovic (painter).

3016	**1017**	1 d. 10 multicoloured	30	20

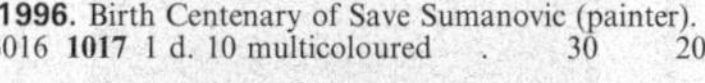

1018 "Pyrgomorphela serbica"

1996. Protected Insects. Multicoloured.

3017	1 d. 10 Type **1018**	30	20
3018	1 d. 10 Red wood ant ("Formica rufa")	30	20
3019	2 d. 20 Searcher ("Calosoma sycophanta")	60	35
3020	2 d. 20 Owl-fly ("Ascalaphus macaronius")	60	35

1996. Chess (3rd series). Chessmen and Timepieces or World Champions. As T **994**. Multicoloured.

3021	1 d. 50 Gigran Vartanovich Petrosian (1963–69)	40	25
3022	1 d. 50 Queen, knight and portable sundial	40	25
3023	1 d. 50 Boris Vasilevich Spassky (1969–72)	40	25
3024	1 d. 50 Competition clock, chessboard and pieces	40	25
3025	1 d. 50 Garry Kimovich Kasparov (1985–93)	40	25
3026	1 d. 50 Chessboard, pieces and hourglass	40	25
3027	1 d. 50 Robert Fischer (1972–75)	40	25
3028	1 d. 50 Chesspieces, clocks and chessboard	40	25
3029	1 d. 50 Anatoly Yevgenievich Karpov (1975–85 and 1993–)	40	25

1019 Discus Throwers

1996. Centenary of Modern Olympic Games. Multicoloured.

3030	1 d. 50 Type **1019**	40	25
3031	2 d. 50 Ancient Greek and modern athletes	65	40

1020 Athletics

1996. Olympic Games, Atlanta. Multicoloured.

3032	1 d. 50 Type **1020**	40	25
3033	1 d. 50 Basketball	40	25
3034	1 d. 50 Handball	40	25
3035	1 d. 50 Shooting	40	25
3036	1 d. 50 Volleyball	40	25
3037	1 d. 50 Water polo	40	25

1021 Postman, Railway Mail Van and Arms of Royal Serbian Post **1022** Isidora Sekulic

1996. Stamp Day.

3039	**1021**	1 d. 50 multicoloured	40	25

1996. Europa. Famous Women Writers. Multicoloured.

3040	2 d. 50 Type **1022**	65	40
3041	5 d. Desanka Maksimovic	1·25	75

1023 Dr. Vladan Djordjevic (founder)

1996. 120th Anniv of Serbian Red Cross.

3042	**1023**	1 d. 50 multicoloured	40	25

1025 Columns, Caryatid and Diagrams of Proportion **1026** White Spoonbill

1996. 150th Anniv of Architecture Education in Serbia.

3044	**1025**	1 d. 50 light blue, deep blue and blue	40	25

1996. Nature Protection. Multicoloured.

3045	2 d. 50 Type **1026**	65	40
3046	5 d. Glossy ibis	1·25	75

1027 Prince Petar I Petrovic (Battle of Martinici)

1996. Battle Bicentenaries. Multicoloured.

3047	1 d. 50 Type **1027**	40	25
3048	2 d. 50 "Prince's Guard" (Theodore Valerio) (Battle of Kruse) (vert)	65	40

1028 Waiting for the Off

1996. Ljubicevo Race Meeting. Multicoloured.

3049	1 d. 50 Type **1028**	40	25
3050	2 d. 50 Horses racing	65	40

1029 Palm Cockatoo

1996. 60th Anniv of Belgrade Zoo. Multicoloured.

3051	1 d. 50 Type **1029**	40	25
3052	1 d. 50 Common zebra	40	25
3053	2 d. 50 Maroon-breasted crowned pigeon	65	40
3054	2 d. 50 Tiger	65	40

1031 Fantasy Scene

1996. 28th "Joy of Europe" Meeting. Multicoloured.

3056	1 d. 50 Type **1031**	40	25
3057	2 d. 50 Toucan	65	40

1032 Basketball (silver) **1033** Coins, Banknotes and Credit Card

1996. Olympic Games Medal Winners. Multicoloured.

3058	2 d. 50 Type **1032**	65	40
3059	2 d. 50 Small-bore rifle shooting (gold)	65	40
3060	2 d. 50 Air-rifle shooting (bronze)	65	40
3061	2 d. 50 Volleyball (bronze)	65	40

1996. 75th Anniv of Post Office Savings Bank.

3062	**1033**	1 d. 50 multicoloured	40	25

1034 Footballer **1035** Mother and Child (statuette)

1996. Centenary of Football in Serbia.

3063	**1034**	1 d. 50 multicoloured	40	25

1996. Museum Exhibits. Archaeological Finds. Multicoloured.

3064	1 d. 50 Type **1035**	40	25
3065	1 d. 50 Tombstone depicting Genius, god of autumn	40	25
3066	2 d. 50 Marble head of woman	65	40
3067	2 d. 50 Statuette of red-headed goddess	65	40

1036 "The Annunciation" (icon) (Nikola Neskovic)

1996. Icons from Serbian Orthodox Church Museum, Belgrade. Multicoloured.

3068	1 d. 50 Type **1036**	40	25
3069	1 d. 50 "Madonna and Child"	40	25
3070	2 d. 50 "Nativity"	65	40
3071	2 d. 50 "Entry of Christ into Jerusalem" (Stanoje Popovic)	65	40

EXPRESS LETTER STAMP

CROATIA

1918. Express Letter stamp of Hungary optd **HRVATSKA SHS ZURNO**.

E84	**E 18**	2 f. olive and red	10	15

NEWSPAPER STAMPS

CROATIA

1918. Newspaper stamp of Hungary optd **HRVATSKA SHS**.

N83	**N 9**	2 f. orange	10	15

N 25

1919. Imperf.

N97	**N 25**	2 h. yellow	10	75

SLOVENIA

N 30 Cherub with Newspapers

1919. Imperf.

N150	**N 30**	2 v. grey	10	15
N155		2 v. blue	10	10
N151		4 v. grey	10	25
N156		4 v. blue	10	15
N152		6 v. grey	3·00	3·75
N157		6 v. blue	2·50	3·00
N153		10 v. grey	10	15
N158		10 v. blue	10	10
N154		30 v. grey	10	25

(N 35) (N 36)

1920. Surch as Type N **35** (2 to 6 p.) or Type N **36** (10 p. and 30 p.).

N164	**N 30**	2 p. on 2 v. grey	30	65
N169		2 p. on 2 v. blue	10	10
N165		4 p. on 2 v. grey	30	65
N170		4 p. on 2 v. blue	10	10
N166		6 p. on 2 v. grey	45	65
N171		6 p. on 2 v. blue	10	10
N167		10 p. on 2 v. grey	65	75
N172		10 p. on 2 v. blue	15	40
N168		30 p. on 2 v. grey	65	1·00
N173		30 p. on 2 v. blue	20	50

OFFICIAL STAMPS

O 130

1946.

O540	**O 130**	50 p. orange	15	10
O541		1 d. green	15	10
O542		1 d. 50 olive	30	10
O543		2 d. 50 red	30	10
O544		4 d. brown	60	10
O545		5 d. blue	80	10
O546		8 d. brown	1·10	15
O547		12 d. violet	1·40	30

POSTAGE DUE STAMPS

BOSNIA AND HERZEGOVINA

ДРЖАВА С.Х.С.
БОСНА И
ХЕРЦЕГОВИНА

хелера

(D 5)

КРАЉЕВСТВО
СРБА, ХРВАТА
И СЛОВЕНАЦА

ПОРТО

5 X

(D 13)

1918. Postage Due Stamps of Bosnia optd as Type D5 or **DRZAVA S.H.S. BOSNA I HERCEGOVINA HELERA.**

D19	**D 35**	2 h. red	10	10
D20		4 h. red	30	50
D21		5 h. red	10	10
D22		6 h. red	50	35
D23		10 h. red	10	10
D24		15 h. red	5·25	5·25
D25		20 h. red	10	10
D26		25 h. red	35	35
D27		30 h. red	35	35
D28		40 h. red	15	15
D29		50 h. red	70	70
D30		1 k. blue	35	35
D31		3 k. blue	25	25

1919. "Eagle" type of Bosnia surch as Type D **13** or **KRALJEVSTVO SRBA, HRVATA I SLOVENACA PORTO** and value.

D50	**2**	2 h. on 35 h. blue	25	15
D51		5 h. on 45 h. blue	45	75
D52		10 h. on 10 h. red	10	10
D53		15 h. on 40 h. orange	25	30
D54		20 h. on 5 h. green	10	10
D55		25 h. on 20 h. pink	20	25
D56		30 h. on 30 h. brown	20	25
D57		1 k. on 50 h. purple	10	35
D58		3 k. on 25 h. blue	25	35

КРАЉЕВСТВО
СРБА, ХРВАТА
И СЛОВЕНАЦА
40

40 хелера 40

(D 14)

1919. Postage Due stamps of Bosnia with surch or optd as Type D **14** or **KRALJEVSTVO SRBA HRVATA SLOVENACA** and value.

D59	D **4**	40 h. on 6 h. black, red and yellow	10	10
D60		50 h. on 8 h. black, red and yellow	10	10
D61		200 h. black, red & grn	6·25	5·25
D62		4 k. on 7 h. black, red and yellow	20	35

CROATIA

1919. Postage Due stamps of Hungary, with figures in red (except 50 f. in black), optd **HRVATSKA SHS**.

D85	D **9**	1 f. green (No. D190)	22·00	28·00
D86		2 f. green	90	90
D87		10 f. green	65	65
D88		12 f. green	85·00	95·00
D89		15 f. green	50	50
D90		20 f. green	50	50
D91		30 f. green	1·60	1·60
D92		50 f. green (No. D177)	25·00	30·00

SLOVENIA

D 30

1919.

D150	D **30**	5 v. red	10	10
D151		10 v. red	10	10
D152		20 v. red	10	10
D153		50 v. red	10	10
D154		1 k. blue	25	25
D155		5 k. blue	45	25
D156		10 k. blue	80	65

(D 35)

(D 36)

1920. Stamps of 1919 issue surch as Types D **35** or D **36**.

D164	**25**	5 p. on 15 v. blue	10	10
D165		10 p. on 15 v. blue	50	40
D166		20 p. on 15 v. blue	15	10
D167		50 p. on 15 v. blue	10	10
D168	**26**	1 d. on 30 v. pink (or red)	15	15
D169		3 d. on 30 v. pink (or red)	30	15
D170		8 d. on 30 v. pink (or red)	75	45

GENERAL ISSUES

D 39 King Alexander I when Prince

D 40

1921.

D182	D **39**	10 on 5 p. green	15	10
D183		30 on 5 p. green	20	10

1921.

D184	D **40**	10 p. red	10	10
D185		30 p. green	15	10
D197		50 p. violet	10	10
D187		1 d. brown	10	10
D188		2 d. blue	20	10
D189		5 d. orange	1·60	10
D190		10 d. brown	7·50	25
D191		25 d. pink	30·00	1·00
D192		50 d. green	30·00	1·50

There are two issues in this type, differing in the lettering, etc.

1939. Surcharged 10.

D233	D **40**	10 on 25 d. pink	3·75	25
D234		10 on 50 d. green	3·75	25

D 56

(D 62)

1931.

D259	D **56**	50 p. violet	10	10
D260		1 d. red	10	10
D261		2 d. blue	10	10
D262		5 d. orange	10	10
D263		10 d. brown	20	10

1933. Optd with Type D **62**.

D293a	D **40**	50 p. violet	15	10
D294a		1 d. brown	15	10
D295b		2 d. blue	30	10
D296		5 d. orange	90	35
D297a		10 d. brown	3·50	10

1933. Red Cross. As T **62** but inscr "PORTO" in Latin and Cyrillic characters.

D298	**62**	50 p. red and green	25	10

DEMOCRATIC FEDERATION OF YUGOSLAVIA

(a) REGIONAL ISSUES

CROATIA

1945. Zagreb issue. Croatian Postage Due stamps of 1942 surch **DEMOKRATSKA FEDERATIVNA JUGOSLAVIJA**, value and star.

RD45	D **15**	40 k. on 50 b. brown and blue	10	10
RD46		60 k. on 1 k. brown and blue	10	10
RD47		80 k. on 2 k. brown and blue	10	10
RD48		100 k. on 5 k. brown and blue	15	15
RD49		200 k. on 6 k. brown and blue	20	20

MONTENEGRO

1945. Cetinje issue. National Poem issue of Italian Occupation surch as Type R **4**, with "PORTO" in addition.

RD61	10 l. on 5 c. violet	62·00	£225
RD62	20 l. on 5 l. red on brown	90·00	85·00

SERBIA

1944. Senta issue. No. D684 of Hungary optd with a large star, **8.X.1944** and "Yugoslavia" in Cyrillic characters and surch in addition.

RD73	D **115**	10 (f.) on 2 f. brn	45·00	45·00

(b) GENERAL ISSUES

D 114

D 115

D 126

1944. Postage Due stamps of Serbia optd in Cyrillic characters, as Type D **114**.

D487	10 d. red	30	50
D488	20 d. blue	30	50

1945. (a) Value in black.

D489	D **115**	2 d. brown	10	10
D490		3 d. violet	10	10
D491		5 d. green	10	10
D492		7 d. brown	10	10
D493		10 d. lilac	15	10
D494		20 d. blue	20	10
D495		30 d. green	35	15
D496		40 d. red	40	20

(b) Value in colour.

D497	D **115**	1 d. green	10	10
D498		1 d. 50 blue	10	10
D499		2 d. red	15	10
D500		3 d. brown	30	10
D501		4 d. violet	40	20

1946.

D 527	D **126**	50 p. orange	10	10
D 528		1 d. orange	10	10
D 724		1 d. brown	25	10
D 529		2 d. blue	10	10
D 725		2 d. green	25	10
D 530		3 d. green	15	10
D 531		5 d. violet	15	10
D 726		5 d. blue	40	10
D 532		7 d. red	65	10
D 533		10 d. pink	1·00	20
D 727		10 d. red	1·60	10
D 534		20 d. lake	2·25	45
D1030		20 d. violet	2·40	10
D1031		30 d. orange	5·25	10
D1032		50 d. blue	26·00	40
D1033		100 d. purple	10·50	95

1947. Red Cross. As No. 545, but with "PORTO" added. Colour changed.

D546	**131**	50 p. green and red	30	10

1948. Red Cross. As No. 594, but inscr "PORTO".

D595	**152**	50 p. red and green	25	10

1949. Red Cross. As T **160** but inscr "PORTO".

D617	**160**	50 p. purple and red	40	10

ФНР ЈУГОСЛАВИЈА

FNR JUGOSLAVIJA

(D 168)

D 175 Map

1950. Optd with Type D **168**.

D637	D **115**	1 d. 50 blue	10	10
D638		3 d. brown	10	10
D639		4 d. violet	20	15

1950. Red Cross.

D665	D **175**	50 p. brown & red	30	10

1951. Red Cross. Inscr "PORTO".

D703	**191**	50 p. green and red	30	10

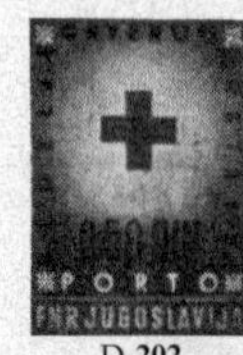

D 202

D 251 Child with Toy

1952. Red Cross.

D741	D **202**	50 p. red and grey	30	10

1953. Red Cross. Inscr "PORTO".

D762	**211**	2 d. red and brown	50	10

1954. Red Cross. Inscr "PORTO".

D783	**216**	2 d. red and lilac	45	10

1955. Children's Week. Inscr "PORTO".

D802	**222**	2 d. green	35	10

1955. Red Cross. Inscr "PORTO".

D804	**224**	2 d. brown, deep red & red	50	10

1956. Red Cross. Inscr "PORTO".

D820	**228**	2 d. green and red	35	10

1956. Children's Week. Inscr "PORTO".

D835	**232**	2 d. green and red	30	10

1957. Red Cross. Inscr "PORTO".

D844	**234**	2 d. red, black and grey	35	10

1957. Children's Week. Inscr "PORTO".

D867	**240**	2 d. brown and blue	30	10

1958. Red Cross. Inscr "PORTO".

D879	**245**	2 d. multicoloured	50	10

1958. Children's Week.

D913	D **251**	2 d. black and blue	40	10

1959. Red Cross. Inscr "PORTO".

D927	**255**	2 d. orange and red	30	10

1959. Children's Week. As T **260**. Inscr "PORTO".

D947	2 d. purple and yellow	25	10

DESIGN: Tree, cockerel and ears of wheat.

1960. Red Cross. Inscr "PORTO".

D956	**262**	2 d. purple and red	25	10

1960. Children's Week. As T **265**. Inscr "PORTO".

D970	2 d. blue (Young boy)	20	10

1961. Red Cross. Inscr "PORTO". Perf or imperf.

D982	**268**	2 d. multicoloured	25	10

1961. Children's Week. Inscr "PORTO".

D1020	**274**	2 d. green and sepia	20	10

1962. Red Cross. Inscr "PORTO".

D1043	**281**	5 d. red, brown and blue	20	10

1963. Red Cross Cent. and Week. Inscr "PORTO".

D1074	**288**	5 d. red, purple and orange	30	10

REGISTERED LETTER STAMPS

R 959 Hands holding Envelope

1993. No value expressed.

R 2864	R**959**	R (11000 d.) blue	15	10

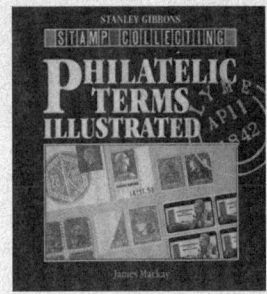

YUNNANFU Pt. 17

Yunnanfu (formerly Yunnansen), the chief city of the Chinese province of Yunnan, had an Indo-Chinese Post Office from 1900 to 1922.

1901. 100 centimes = 1 franc.
1918. 100 cents = 1 piastre.

Stamps of Indo-China surcharged.

1903. "Tablet" key-type surch with value in Chinese and **YUNNANSEN**.

1 D 1 c. black and red on blue 3·75 3·00
2 2 c. brown and blue on buff 3·00 3·00
3 4 c. brown and blue on grey 3·00 3·00
4 5 c. green and red 3·00 2·75
5 10 c. red and blue 3·00 2·75
6 15 c. grey and red 3·75 2·00
7 20 c. red and blue on green 4·50 3·50
8 25 c. blue and red 3·00 3·25
9 30 c. brown and blue on drab 4·75 3·50
10 40 c. red and blue on yellow 45·00 27·00
11 50 c. red and blue on pink £200 £200
12 50 c. brown and red on blue £100 £100
13 75 c. brown and red on orange 30·00 27·00
14 1 f. green and red 32·00 30·00
15 5 f. mauve and blue on lilac 70·00 65·00

1906. Surch **Yunnan-Fou** and value in Chinese.

16 8 1 c. green 1·40 1·40
17 2 c. purple on yellow 1·40 1·40
18 4 c. mauve on blue 1·75 1·60
19 5 c. green 1·90 1·90
20 10 c. pink 1·90 1·90
21 15 c. brown on blue 3·75 3·75
22 20 c. red on green 2·25 2·25
23 25 c. blue 2·75 2·50
24 30 c. brown on cream 2·25 2·25
25 35 c. black on yellow 3·75 3·75
26 40 c. black on grey 2·75 2·75
27 50 c. brown on cream 3·75 3·75
28 D 75 c. brown on orange 27·00 27·00
29 8 1 f. green 12·50 12·50
30 2 f. brown on yellow 12·50 12·50
31 D 5 f. mauve on lilac 45·00 45·00
32 8 10 f. red on green 50·00 50·00

1908. Native types surch **YUNNANFOU** and value in Chinese.

33 10 1 c. black and brown 45 50
34 2 c. black and brown 45 55
35 4 c. black and blue 45 55
36 5 c. black and green 60 60
37 10 c. black and red 45 50
38 15 c. black and violet 2·50 1·75
39 11 20 c. black and violet 2·75 2·25
40 25 c. black and blue 2·75 2·25
41 30 c. black and brown 2·50 2·75
42 35 c. black and green 3·75 3·00
43 40 c. black and brown 4·00 4·00
44 50 c. black and red 4·00 4·00
45 12 75 c. black and orange 4·75 4·00
46 1 f. black and red 7·50 6·25
47 2 f. black and green 13·50 12·00
48 5 f. black and blue 32·00 27·00
49 10 f. black and violet 60·00 60·00

1919. As last, surch in addition with value in figures and words.

50 10 $\frac{2}{5}$ c. on 1 c. black & brown 45 40
51 $\frac{4}{5}$ c. on 2 c. black & brown 55 55
52 $1\frac{3}{5}$ c. on 4 c. black and blue 65 60
53 2 c. on 5 c. black and green 55 55
54 4 c. on 10 c. black and red 60 50
55 6 c. on 15 c. black and violet 60 45
56 11 8 c. on 20 c. black & violet 85 70
57 10 c. on 25 c. black & blue 1·10 95
58 12 c. on 30 c. black & brown 95 85
59 14 c. on 35 c. black & grn 1·90 1·60
60 16 c. on 40 c. black & brn 2·00 1·60
61 20 c. on 50 c. black & red 1·10 1·10
62 12 30 c. on 75 c. black & orge 2·00 2·00
63 40 c. on 1 f. black and red 2·50 2·25
64 80 c. on 2 f. black & green 3·25 3·25
65 2 p. on 5 f. black and blue 23·00 23·00
66 4 p. on 10 f. black & violet 8·00 7·50

ZAIRE Pt. 14

In 1971 the Congo Republic (Kinshasa), formerly Belgian Congo, changed its name to Zaire.

100 sengi = 1(li) kuta; 100 (ma) kuta = 1 zaire

176 Nurse tending Child

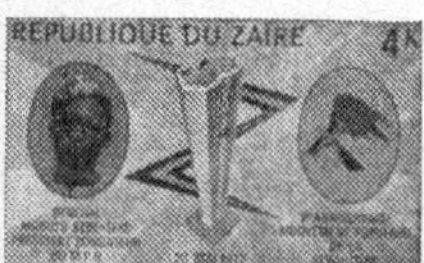

177 Pres. Mobutu, Memorial and Emblem

1971. 25th Anniv of U.N.I.C.E.F. Multicoloured.

788 4 k. Type **176** 30 20
789 14 k. Zaire Republic on map of Africa 85 55
790 17 k. Child in African village 1·10 90

1972. 5th Anniv of Revolution.

791 177 4 k. multicoloured 3·25 2·75
792 14 k. multicoloured 3·25 2·75
793 22 k. multicoloured 4·50 3·25

177a Arms

177b Pres. Mobutu

1972.

794 177a 10 s. orange and black 10 10
795 40 s. blue and black 10 10
796 50 s. yellow and black 10 10
797 177b 1 k. multicoloured 10 10
798 2 k. multicoloured 10 10
799 3 k. multicoloured 10 10
800 4 k. multicoloured 10 10
801 5 k. multicoloured 15 10
802 6 k. multicoloured 15 10
803 8 k. multicoloured 20 15
804 9 k. multicoloured 30 15
805 10 k. multicoloured 35 15
806 14 k. multicoloured 45 20
807 17 k. multicoloured 50 35
808 20 k. multicoloured 65 40
809 50 k. multicoloured 1·75 85
810 100 k. multicoloured 3·50 2·00

178 Inga Dam

1973. Inga Dam. Completion of 1st Stage.

811 178 0.04 z. multicoloured 10 10
812 0.14 z. multicoloured 45 35
813 0.18 z. multicoloured 80 45

1973. As T **177b**, but face values in Zaires.

814 0.01 z. multicoloured 10 10
815 0.02 z. multicoloured 10 10
816 0.03 z. multicoloured 10 10
817 0.04 z. multicoloured 10 10
818 0.10 z. multicoloured 45 20
819 0.14 z. multicoloured 80 35

179 Africa on World Map

1973. 3rd International Fair, Kinshasa.

820 179 0.04 z. multicoloured 15 10
821 0.07 z. multicoloured 30 15
822 0.18 z. multicoloured 80 45

180 Emblem on Hand

1973. 50th Anniv of Criminal Police Organisation (Interpol).

823 180 0.06 z. multicoloured 35 20
824 0.14 z. multicoloured 80 35

181 Leopard with Football on Globe

1974. World Cup Football Championships, Munich.

825 181 1 k. multicoloured 10 10
826 2 k. multicoloured 10 10
827 3 k. multicoloured 15 10
828 4 k. multicoloured 20 10
829 5 k. multicoloured 30 10
830 14 k. multicoloured 1·40 55

182 Muhamed Ali and George Foreman

185 Waterfall

1974. World Heavyweight Boxing Title Fight, Kinshasa.

831 182 1 k. multicoloured 10 10
832 4 k. multicoloured 15 10
833 6 k. multicoloured 20 10
834 14 k. multicoloured 55 30
835 20 k. multicoloured 90 40

1975. World Heavyweight Boxing Title Fight, Kinshasa. As T **182** optd with amended date **25-9-74.**

836 182 0.01 z. multicoloured 10 10
837 0.04 z. multicoloured 10 10
838 0.06 z. multicoloured 20 10
839 0.14 z. multicoloured 45 15
840 0.20 z. multicoloured 80 30

Nos. 836/40 differ from Type **182** by having the face values expressed as decimals of the zaire. Both dates are in fact incorrect as the fight was held on 30 October, 1974.

1975. 12th U.I.C.N. General Assembly, Kinshasa.

858 185 1 k. multicoloured 10 10
859 2 k. multicoloured 10 10
860 3 k. multicoloured 20 10
861 4 k. multicoloured 30 10
862 5 k. multicoloured 40 10

186 Okapis

1975. 50th Anniv of Virunga National Park.

863 186 1 k. multicoloured 10 10
864 2 k. multicoloured 20 10
865 3 k. multicoloured 35 10
866 4 k. multicoloured 45 10
867 5 k. multicoloured 55 10

187 Woman Judge with Barristers

1975. International Women's Year.

868 187 1 k. multicoloured 10 10
869 2 k. multicoloured 10 10
870 4 k. multicoloured 20 10
871 14 k. multicoloured 65 20

188 Sozacom Building

189 Pende Statuette

1976. 10th Anniv of "New Regime". Mult.

872 1 k. Type **188** 10 10
873 2 k. Siderna Maluku Industrial Complex (horiz) 10 10
874 3 k. Flour mill, Matadi 10 10
875 4 k. Women parachutists (horiz) 20 10
876 8 k. Pres. Mobutu with Mao Tse-Tung 35 10
877 10 k. Soldiers clearing vegetation along the Salongo (horiz) 45 20
878 14 k. Pres. Mobutu addressing U.N. General Assembly, 4 October 1973 (horiz) 65 30
879 15 k. Rejoicing crowd (horiz) 80 20

1977. Masks and Statuettes. Multicoloured.

880 2 z. Type **189** 10 10
881 4 z. Type **189** 10 10
882 5 z. Tshokwe mask 10 10
883 7 z. As 5 k. 15 10
884 10 z. Suku mask 20 10
885 14 z. As 10 k. 35 15
886 15 z. Kongo statuette 40 15
887 18 z. As 15 k. 45 30
888 20 z. Kuba mask 65 35
889 25 z. As 20 k. 80 45

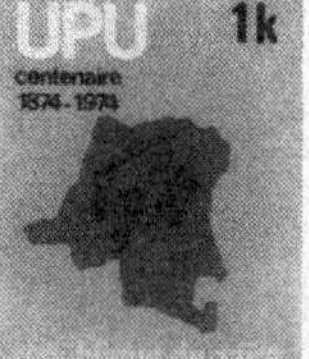

190 U.P.U. Emblem on Map

192 "Pantodon buchholzi"

1977. Centenary of Universal Postal Union.

890 190 1 k. multicoloured 10 10
891 4 k. multicoloured 20 10
892 7 k. multicoloured 50 35
893 50 k. multicoloured 4·25 2·25

1977. Various stamps of Congo (Kinshasa) and Zaire, surch **REPUBLIQUE DU ZAIRE** or with new value only (No. 904).

894 158 1 k. on 10 s. red & black 10 10
895 152 2 k. on 9.6 k. blk on red 10 10
896 158 5 k. on 30 s. grn & blk 10 10
897 173 10 k. on 10 s. mult 35 10
898 158 10 k. on 15 s. blue & blk 15 10
899 – 20 k. on 9.6 k. mult (No. 673) 35 15
900 167 25 k. on 10 s. mult 65 30
901 174 30 k. on 12 s. mult 65 35
902 159 40 k. on 9.6 k. mult 1·00 50
903 168 48 k. on 10 s. mult 1·10 55
904 158 100 k. on 40 s. blue & blk 2·40 95

1978. Fishes. Multicoloured.

905 30 s. Type **192** 10 10
906 70 s. "Aphyosemion striatum" 10 10
907 5 k. "Ctenopoma fasciolatum" 10 10
908 8 k. "Malapterurus" 20 10
909 10 k. "Hemichromis bimaculatus" 35 10
910 30 k. "Marcusenius isidori" 55 40
911 40 k. "Synodontis nigriventris" 90 50
912 48 k. "Julidochromis ornatus" 1·10 65
913 100 k. "Nothobranchius brieni" 2·75 1·25

193 Argentina v. France

194 Mama Mobutu

1978. World Cup Football Championship, Argentina. Multicoloured.

915 1 k. Type **193** 10 10
916 3 k. Austria v Brazil 10 10
917 7 k. Scotland v Iran 10 10
918 9 k. Netherlands v Peru 10 10
919 10 k. Hungary v Italy 15 10
920 20 k. West Germany v Mexico 35 20
921 50 k. Tunisia v Poland 85 45
922 100 k. Spain v Sweden 1·90 1·00

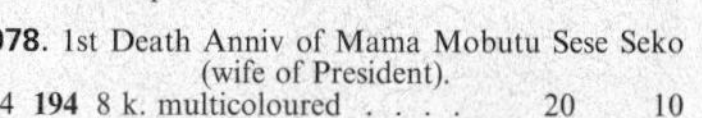

1978. 1st Death Anniv of Mama Mobutu Sese Seko (wife of President).

924 194 8 k. multicoloured 20 10

197 Da Vinci, Lilienthal and Flying Machines

1978. History of Aviation. Multicoloured.

927 30 s. Type **197** 10 10
928 70 s. Wright Type A and Santos-Dumont's "14 bis" 10 10
929 1 k. Farman F 60 Goliath and Bleriot XI 10 10
930 5 k. Junkers G.38ce "Deutschland" and "Spirit of St. Louis" 10 10
931 8 k. Macchi Castoldi MC-72 seaplane and Sikorsky S-42B flying boat 15 15
932 10 k. Boeing 707 and Fokker F.VIIb/3m 30 20
933 50 k. "Apollo XI" space capsule and Concorde 1·10 55
934 75 k. Sikorsky S-61N helicopter and Douglas DC 10 1·40 90

198 President Mobutu

199 "Phylloporus ampliporus"

1978.

936 198 2 k. multicoloured 10 10
937 5 k. multicoloured 10 10
938 6 k. multicoloured 10 10
939 8 k. multicoloured 10 10
940 10 k. multicoloured 10 10
941 25 k. multicoloured 10 10
942 48 k. multicoloured 35 15
942a 50 k. multicoloured 20 10
943 1 z. multicoloured 80 30
943a 2 z. multicoloured 65 35
943b 5 z. multicoloured 1·50 85

1979. Mushrooms. Multicoloured.

944 30 s. Type **199** 10 10
945 5 k. "Engleromyces goetzei" 15 10
946 8 k. "Scutellinia virungae" 25 10
947 10 k. "Pycnoporus sanguineus" 30 10
948 30 k. "Cantharellus miniatescens" 90 25
949 40 k. "Lactarius phlebonemus" 1·40 30
950 48 k. "Phallus indusiatus" 2·25 40
951 100 k. "Ramaria moelleriana" 3·50 80

200 Ntore Dancer

1979. Zaire River Expedition. Multicoloured.

952 1 k. Type **200** 10 10
953 3 k. Regal sunbird 75 25
954 4 k. African elephant 10 10
955 10 k. Diamond, cotton boll and tobacco 10 10
956 14 k. Hand holding flaming torch 15 10
957 17 k. Lion and water lily 20 15
958 25 k. Inzia Falls 30 15
959 50 k. Wagenia fisherman 55 35

201 President Mobutu and Flag

1979. 5th Anniv (1970) of 2nd Republic.

961 **201** 3 z. gold, red and blue 22·00

203 Globe and Drummer **204** Boy with Drum

1979. 6th International Fair, Kinshasa.

963 **203** 1 k. multicoloured 10 10
964 9 k. multicoloured 10 10
965 90 k. multicoloured 65 30
966 100 k. multicoloured 80 35

1979. International Year of the Child. Mult.

968 5 k. Type **204** 10 10
969 10 k. Girl 10 10
970 20 k. Boy 20 10
971 50 k. Laughing boy 40 20
972 100 k. Two children 85 35
973 300 k. Mother and child 3·00 1·60

205 Desk standing on Globe

1979. 50th Anniv of International Bureau of Education.

975 **205** 10 k. multicoloured 15 10

207 "Puffing Billy", England

1980. Locomotives. Multicoloured.

977 50 s. Type **207** 15 15
978 1 k. 50 Buddicom No. 33, France 15 15
979 5 k. "Elephant", Belgium 25 25
980 8 k. No. 601, Zaire 25 25
981 50 k. "Slieve Gullion", Ireland 50 50
982 75 k. "Black Elephant", Germany 95 95
983 2 z. Type "1-15", Zaire 2·75 2·75
984 5 z. "Golden State", U.S.A. 6·75 6·75

208 Sir Rowland Hill and Congo 5 f. Stamp, 1886

1980. Death Cent of Sir Rowland Hill. Mult.

986 2 k. Type **208** 10 10
987 4 k. Congo 10 f. stamp, 1887 10 10
988 10 k. Congo 1 f. African elephant stamp, 1884 10 10
989 20 k. Belgian Congo overprinted 3 f. 50 stamp, 1909 15 10
990 40 k. Belgian Congo 10 f. African Elephant stamp, 1925 20 10
991 150 k. Belgian Congo 1 f. 50+1 f. 50 Chimpanzees stamp, 1939 85 40
992 200 k. Belgian Congo 1 f. 75 Leopard stamp, 1942 1·25 60
993 250 k. Belgian Congo 2 f. 50 Railway stamp, 1948 2·50 2·50

209 Einstein

1980. Birth Centenary of Albert Einstein (physicist).

995 **209** 40 s. brown, black & mve 10 10
996 2 k. brown, blk & grn 10 10
997 4 k. brown, blk & yell 10 10
998 15 k. brown, blk, & bl 15 10
999 50 k. brown, blk & red 35 20
1000 300 k. brown, blk & lilac 2·00 1·00

210 Booth Memorial Medical Centre, Flushing, New York

1980. Centenary of Salvation Army in the United States. Multicoloured.

1002 50 s. Type **210** 10 10
1003 4 k. 50 Arrival of Railton in America 10 10
1004 10 k. Mobile dispensary, Musina, Zaire 10 10
1005 20 k. General Evangeline Booth and salvationist holding child (vert) 10 10
1006 40 k. Army band 20 15
1007 75 k. Mobile clinic in bush, Zaire 45 20
1008 1 z. 50 Canteen serving firefighters 90 40
1009 2 z. American unit marching with flags (vert) 1·40 55

212 Musical Instrument

1980. 75th Anniv of Rotary International. Mult.

1013 50 k. Drawing of mother and child (Kamba) 30 15
1014 100 k. Type **212** 55 30
1015 500 k. Statuette (Liyolo) (vert) 2·00 1·40

213 "Chaetodon collaris"

1980. Tropical Fishes Multicoloured.

1017 1 k. Type **213** 10 10
1018 5 k. "Zebrasoma veliferum" 10 10
1019 10 k. "Euxiphipops xanthometapon" 10 10
1020 20 k. "Pomacanthus annularis" 10 10
1021 50 k. "Centropyge loriculus" 15 10
1022 150 k. "Oxymonacanthus longirostris" 50 30
1023 200 k. "Balistoides niger" 1·40 65
1024 250 k. "Rhinecanthus aculeatus" 1·25 60

214 Belgium 40 c. Congo Independence Stamp, 1960 and "Phibelza"

1980. "Phibelza" Belgian-Zaire Stamp Exhibition, Kinshasa. Multicoloured.

1026 1 z. Type **214** 40 30
1027 1 z. Congo 20 f. Independence stamp, 1960 40 30
1028 2 z. Belgium 10 f. + 5 f. Zoo stamp, 1968 85 55
1029 2 z. Congo 40 c. Birds stamp, 1963 85 40
1030 3 z. Belgium 10 f. + 5 f. Brussels stamp, 1971 1·25 85
1031 3 z. Zaire 22 k. stamp, 1972 1·25 85
1032 4 z. Belgium 25 f. + 10 f. stamp, 1980 1·60 1·10
1033 4 z. Congo 24 f. stamp, 1966 1·60 1·10

Nos. 1026/33 exist in two versions with the exhibition logo either at the right or the left of the design. Prices are the same for either version.

1980. 20th Anniv of Independence. Various stamps optd **20e Anniversaire - Independance - 1960–1980.**

1034 **207** 50 s. "Puffing Billy" 10 10
1035 – 1 k. 50 Locomotive "Buddicom" No. 33 (No. 978) 25 25
1036 – 10 k. Boeing 707 and Fokker F.VIIb/3m (No. 932) 10 10
1037 – 50 k. "Slieve Gullion" (No. 981) 25 25
1038 – 75 k. Sikorsky S-61N helicopter and Douglas DC-10 (No. 934) 35 15
1039 **203** 100 k. Globe and drummer 45 25
1040 – 1 z. on 5 z. on 100 k. Two children (No. 972) 45 25
1041 – 250 k. Rowland Hill and railway stamp of 1948 (No. 993) 2·25 2·25
1042 – 5 z. on 100 k. Two children (No. 972) 2·75 1·25

216 Leopold I and 1851 Map of Africa

1980. 150th Anniv of Belgian Independence.

1043 **216** 10 k. green and blue 10 10
1044 – 75 k. brown and blue 45 20
1045 – 100 k. violet and blue 45 20
1046 – 145 k. blue & deep blue 1·60 50
1047 – 270 k. red and blue 1·60 85

DESIGNS: 75 k. Leopold II and Stanley's expedition; 100 k. Albert I and colonial troops of 1914–18 war; 145 k. Leopold III and African animals; 270 k. Baudouin I and visit to Zaire of King Baudouin and Queen Fabiola.

217 Angels appearing to Shepherds

1980. Christmas. Multicoloured.

1048 10 k. Type **217** 10 10
1049 75 k. Flight into Egypt 35 20
1050 80 k. Three Kings 45 20
1051 145 k. In the stable 80 45

218 Girl dancing to Cello

1981. Norman Rockwell Paintings. Multicoloured.

1053 10 k. Type **218** 10 10
1054 20 k. Couple with saluting boy scout 10 10
1055 50 k. Sorter reading mail 20 10
1056 80 k. Cupid whispering in youth's ear 35 15
1057 100 k. Signing Declaration of Independence 50 20
1058 125 k. Boy looking through telescope held by sailor 80 25
1059 175 k. Boy in armchair playing trumpet 1·00 40
1060 200 k. Weakling exercising with dumb bells 1·10 50

219 Pope John-Paul II and Pres. Mobutu **220** Footballers

1981. Papal Visit. Multicoloured.

1061 5 k. Pope kneeling at shrine (horiz) 10 10
1062 10 k. Pres. Mobutu greeting Pope (horiz) 10 10
1063 50 k. Type **219** 20 10
1064 100 k. Pope talking to child (horiz) 65 35
1065 500 k. Pope leading prayers 2·75 1·25
1066 800 k. Pope making speech (horiz) 4·00 2·00

1981. World Cup Football Championship, Spain (1982).

1067 **220** 2 k. multicoloured 10 10
1068 – 10 k. multicoloured 10 10
1069 – 25 k. multicoloured 10 10
1070 – 90 k. multicoloured 35 15
1071 – 2 z. multicoloured 65 35
1072 – 3 z. multicoloured 1·25 55
1073 – 6 z. multicoloured 2·40 1·10
1074 – 8 z. multicoloured 3·25 1·60

DESIGN: Nos. 1068/74, Similar football scenes.

221 Archer in Wheelchair

1981. International Year of Disabled People. Multicoloured.

1076 2 k. Type **221** 10 10
1077 5 k. Ear and sound wave 10 10
1078 10 k. One-legged person with crutch 10 10
1079 18 k. Glasses, Braille and white cane 10 10
1080 50 k. Crippled legs 20 10
1081 150 k. Sign language 45 20
1082 500 k. Hand and model showing joints 1·60 90
1083 800 k. Dove shedding feathers 2·50 1·60

222 Children performing Carols **224** Red Cross Helicopters

1981. Christmas. Multicoloured.

1084	25 k. Type **222**	10	10
1085	1 z. Boy lighting candle	35	15
1086	1 z. 50 Boy praying	45	20
1087	3 z. Girl with presents	95	45
1088	5 z. Children admiring baby	1·75	85

1982. Telecommunications and Health. Mult.

1091	1 k. Type **224**	10	10
1092	25 k. Doctor and telephone	10	10
1093	90 k. Antenna and map	20	15
1094	1 z. Patient	35	15
1095	1 z. 70 Teleprinter	45	20
1096	3 z. Nurse and television	90	35
1097	4 z. 50 Tape recorder	1·60	85
1098	5 z. Babies and walkie-talkie	1·75	85

225 U.P.U. Emblem

1982. 20th Anniv (1981) of African Postal Union.

1099 **225**	1 z. green and gold	45	20

226 El Salvador v. Hungary

1982. World Cup Championship, Spain. Multicoloured.

1100	2 k. Type **226**	10	10
1101	8 k. Cameroun v Peru	10	10
1102	25 k. Brazil v Russia	10	10
1103	50 k. Kuwait v Czechoslovakia	10	10
1104	90 k. Yugoslavia v Northern Ireland	30	15
1105	1 z. Austria v Chile	35	15
1106	1 z. 45 France v England	45	15
1107	1 z. 70 West Germany v Algeria	55	35
1108	3 z. Spain v Honduras	1·00	50
1109	3 z. 50 Belgium v Argentina	1·10	60
1110	5 z. Scotland v New Zealand	1·60	85
1111	6 z. Italy v Poland	2·00	95

228 Hands reaching towards Zaire

1982. Ninth French and African Heads of State Conference, Kinshasa.

1113 **228**	75 k. multicoloured	20	10
1114	90 k. multicoloured	30	15
1115	1 z. multicoloured	35	15
1116	1 z. 50 multicoloured	45	20
1117	3 z. multicoloured	95	50
1118	5 z. multicoloured	1·60	85
1119	8 z. multicoloured	2·50	1·10

229 Lions

1982. Virunga National Park. Multicoloured.

1120	1 z. Type **229**	35	20
1121	1 z. 70 African buffalo	55	35
1122	3 z. 50 African elephant	1·10	65
1123	6 z. 50 Topi	2·00	1·00
1124	8 z. Hippopotamus	2·75	1·40
1125	10 z. Savanna monkey	4·00	1·60
1126	10 z. Leopard	4·00	1·60

230 Scout Camp

233 Malachite

231 Red-billed Quelea

1982. 75th Anniv of Boy Scout Movement. Multicoloured.

1127	90 k. Type **230**	30	15
1128	1 z. 70 Camp-fire	55	25
1129	3 z. Scout	95	45
1130	5 z. Scout carrying injured person	1·75	85
1131	8 z. Scout signalling with flags	2·75	1·10

1982. Birds. Multicoloured.

1133	25 k. Type **231**	25	15
1134	50 k. African pygmy kingfisher	35	20
1135	90 k. Knysna turaco	60	25
1136	1 z. 50 Three-banded plover	1·00	45
1137	1 z. 70 Temminck's courser	1·10	50
1138	2 z. Bennett's woodpecker	1·40	65
1139	3 z. Little grebe	1·75	75
1140	3 z. 50 Lizard buzzard (vert)	2·25	1·00
1141	5 z. Black crake	3·00	1·40
1142	8 z. White-headed vulture (vert)	5·00	2·40

1983. Malachite. Multicoloured.

1144	2 k. Type **233**	10	10
1145	45 k. Quartz (horiz)	20	10
1146	75 k. Gold (horiz)	35	10
1144	1 z. Uranium and pitch-blende (horiz)	45	15
1148	1 z. 50 Bournonite	55	30
1149	3 z. Cassiterite (horiz)	1·10	50
1150	6 z. Dioptase	2·25	95
1151	8 z. Cuprite	3·25	1·40

234 Dr. Koch and Microscope

1983. Centenary (1982) of Discovery of Tubercle Bacillus.

1153 **234**	80 k. multicoloured	20	15
1154	1 z. 20 multicoloured	35	20
1155	3 z. 60 multicoloured	1·10	55
1156	9 z. 60 multicoloured	2·75	1·40

235 "Zaire Diplomat" (Lufwa Mawidi)

1983. Kinshasa Monuments. Multicoloured.

1157	50 k. Type **235**	15	10
1158	1 z. "Echo of Zaire" (Lufwa Mawidi) (horiz)	25	15
1159	1 z. 50 "Messengers" (Liyolo Limbe Mpuanga)	40	20
1160	3 z. "Shield of Revolution" (Liyolo Limbe Mpuanga)	85	20
1161	5 z. "Weeping Woman" (Wuma Mbambila) (horiz)	1·40	85
1162	10 z. "The Militant" (Liyolo Limbe Mpuanaga)	2·50	1·25

236 Satellite over Globe

1983. I.T.U. Delegates' Conference, Nairobi. Multicoloured.

1163	2 k. Type **236**	10	10
1164	4 k. Dish aerial	10	10
1165	25 k. Dish aerial (different)	10	10
1166	1 z. 20 Satellite and microwave antenna	45	15
1167	2 z. 05 Satellite	65	30
1168	3 z. 60 Satellite and microwave antenna (different)	1·10	45
1169	6 z. Map of Zaire	1·60	70
1170	8 z. Satellite (different)	2·40	1·40

238 Giant Eland

1984. Garamba National Park. Multicoloured.

1172	10 k. Type **238**	10	10
1173	15 k. Tawny eagles	90	30
1174	3 z. Servals	20	10
1175	10 z. White rhinoceros	80	35
1176	15 z. Lions	1·00	55
1177	37 z. 50 Warthogs	2·75	1·10
1178	40 z. Kori bustards	5·00	2·00
1179	40 z. South African crowned cranes and game lodge	5·00	2·00

239 Visual Display Unit and Ferry

1984. World Communications Year. Multicoloured.

1180	10 k. Type **239**	10	10
1181	15 k. Communications satellite	10	10
1182	8 z. 50 Radio telephone	45	30
1183	10 z. Satellite and aerial	55	35
1184	15 z. Video camera	1·25	55
1185	37 z. 50 Satellite and dish antenna	2·75	1·25
1186	80 z. Switchboard operator	5·50	2·75

240 "Hypericum revolutum"

241 Basketball

1984. Flowers. Multicoloured.

1187	10 k. Type **240**	10	10
1188	15 k. "Borreria dibrachiata"	10	10
1189	3 z. "Disa erubescens"	20	10
1190	8 z. 50 "Scaevola plumieri"	55	35
1191	10 z. "Clerodendron thompsonii"	80	35
1192	15 z. "Thumbergia erecta"	1·10	65
1193	37 z. 50 "Impatiens niamniamesis"	2·75	1·60
1194	100 z. "Canarina eminii"	7·75	3·25

1984. Olympic Games, Los Angeles. Multicoloured.

1195	2 z. Type **241**	15	10
1196	3 z. Equestrian	20	10
1197	10 z. Running	70	35
1198	15 z. Long jump	1·10	55
1199	20 z. Football	1·60	80

242 Montgolfier Balloon, 1783

243 Okapi feeding

1984. Bicentenary of Manned Flight. Mult.

1201	10 k. Type **242**	10	10
1202	15 k. Charles's hydrogen balloon, 1783	10	10
1203	3 z. Montgolfier balloon "Le Gustave", 1784	15	10
1204	5 z. Santos-Dumont's airship "Ballon No. 3", 1899	30	15
1205	10 z. Piccard's stratosphere balloon "F.N.R.S.", 1931	70	40
1206	15 z. Airship "Hindenburg"	1·10	60
1207	37 z. 50 Balloon "Double Eagle II", 1978	2·50	1·40
1208	80 z. Hot-air balloons	6·00	3·00

1984. Wildlife Protection. Okapi. Multicoloured.

1209	2 z. Type **243**	15	10
1210	3 z. Okapi resting	30	10
1211	8 z. Okapi and foal	65	35
1212	10 z. Okapi crossing stream	85	35

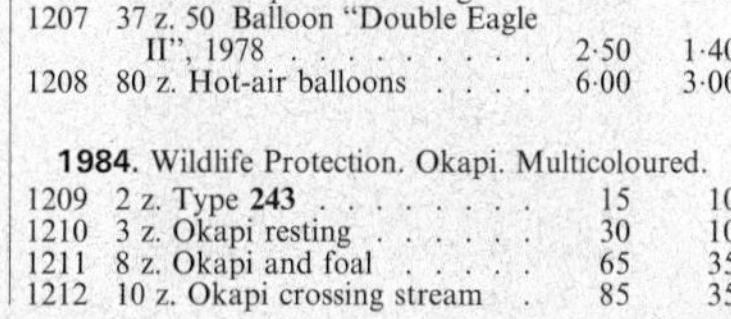

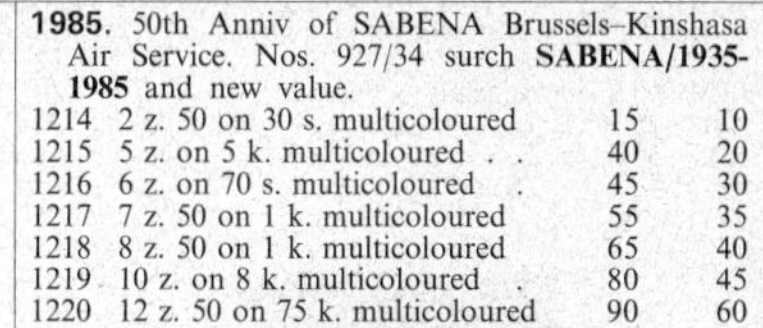

1985. 50th Anniv of SABENA Brussels–Kinshasa Air Service. Nos. 927/34 surch **SABENA/1935-1985** and new value.

1214	2 z. 50 on 30 s. multicoloured	15	10
1215	5 z. on 5 k. multicoloured	40	20
1216	6 z. on 70 s. multicoloured	45	30
1217	7 z. 50 on 1 k. multicoloured	55	35
1218	8 z. 50 on 1 k. multicoloured	65	40
1219	10 z. on 8 k. multicoloured	80	45
1220	12 z. 50 on 75 k. multicoloured	90	60
1221	30 z. on 50 k. multicoloured	2·25	1·25

245 Swimming

1985. "Olymphilex '85" Olympic Stamps Exhibition, Lausanne. Multicoloured.

1223	1 z. Type **245**	10	10
1224	2 z. Football (vert)	15	10
1225	3 z. Boxing	20	10
1226	4 z. Basketball (vert)	30	15
1227	5 z. Show jumping	35	20
1228	10 z. Volleyball (vert)	70	45
1229	15 z. Running	1·00	65
1230	30 z. Cycling (vert)	2·25	1·25

1985. Second Papal Visit. Nos. 1061/5 surch **AOUT 1985**.

1231	2 z. on 5 k. multicoloured	15	10
1232	3 z. on 10 k. mult	20	15
1233	5 z. 50 multicoloured	45	20
1234	10 z. on 100 k. mult	90	50
1235	15 z. on 500 k. mult	1·40	65
1236	40 z. on 800 k. mult	3·00	1·40

247 Great Egrets

1985. Birth Bicentenary of John J. Audubon (ornithologist). Multicoloured.

1238	5 z. Type **247**	55	25
1239	10 z. Common scoter	1·10	50
1240	15 z. Black-crowned night heron	1·90	75
1241	25 z. Surf scoter	3·75	1·60

248 National Flag and "25" on Flag

249 U.N. and Zaire Flags

1985. 25th Anniv of Independence.

1242 **248**	5 z. multicoloured	20	10
1243	10 z. multicoloured	45	20
1244	15 z. multicoloured	65	35
1245	20 z. multicoloured	90	40

1985. 40th Anniv of U.N.O. and 25th Anniv of Zaire Membership. Multicoloured.

1247	10 z. Type **249**	45	30
1248	50 z. U.N. building and emblem	2·25	1·10

1985. International Youth Year. Nos. 1127/31 optd **1985** and I.Y.Y. emblem and surch also.

1249	3 z. on 3 z. multicoloured	10	10
1250	5 z. on 5 z. multicoloured	20	10
1251	7 z. on 90 k. multicoloured	35	15
1252	10 z. on 90 k. multicoloured	45	15
1253	15 z. on 1 z. 70 multicoloured	55	25
1254	20 z. on 8 z. multicoloured	1·10	45
1255	50 z. on 90 k. multicoloured	2·75	1·00

252 "Kokolo" (pusher tug)

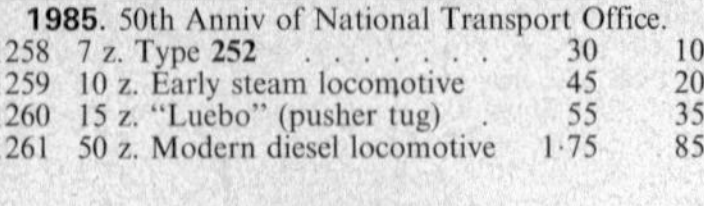

1985. 50th Anniv of National Transport Office.

No.	Type	Description	Mint	Used
1258		7 z. Type **252**	30	10
1259		10 z. Early steam locomotive	45	20
1260		15 z. "Luebo" (pusher tug)	55	35
1261		50 z. Modern diesel locomotive	1·75	85

253 Pope John Paul II

1985. Beatification of Sister Anuarite Nengapeta. Multicoloured.

No.	Type	Description	Mint	Used
1262		10 z. Type **253**	45	20
1263		15 z. Sister Anuarite	65	35
1264		25 z. Pope and Sister Anuarite (horiz)	1·10	55

254 Map and 1886 25 c. Stamp

1988. Centenary of 1st Congo Free State Stamp.

No.	Type	Description	Mint	Used
1266	**254**	25 z. blue, grey and deep blue	1·10	55

255 Congo Free State 1898 10 f. stamp

1988. "Cenzapost" Stamp Centenary Exhibition. Multicoloured.

No.	Type	Description	Mint	Used
1267		7 z. Type **255**	30	10
1268		15 z. Belgian Congo 1939 1 f. 25 + 1 f. 25 stamp	55	30
1269		20 z. Belgian Congo 1942 50 f. stamp (vert)	65	30
1270		25 z. Zaire 1982 8 k. stamp	80	35
1271		40 z. Zaire 1984 37 z. 50 stamp (vert)	1·40	65

256 African Egg Eater

1987. Reptiles. Multicoloured.

No.	Type	Description	Mint	Used
1273		2 z. Type **256**	10	10
1274		5 z. Rainbow lizard	10	10
1275		10 z. Royal python	20	10
1276		15 z. Cape chameleon	45	15
1277		25 z. Green mamba	65	30
1278		50 z. Black-necked cobra	1·25	55

257 "Virgin and Child with Angels" (from Cortone triptych)

1987. Christmas. Paintings by Fr. Angelico. Multicoloured.

No.	Type	Description	Mint	Used
1279		50 z. Type **257**	65	35
1280		100 z. "St. Catherine and St. Peter adoring the Child"	1·40	65
1281		120 z. "Virgin and Child of the Angels and Four Saints" (detail, Fiesole Retable)	1·60	80
1282		180 z. "Virgin and Child and Six Saints" (detail, Annalena Retable)	2·50	1·10

1990. Various stamps surch.

No.	Type	Description	Mint	Used
1283	–	20 z. on 20 k. mult (No. 920)	20	10
1284	**236**	40 z. on 2 k. mult	45	30
1285	–	40 z. on 4 k. mult (1164)	45	30
1286	**218**	40 z. on 10 k. mult	45	30
1287	**231**	40 z. on 25 k. mult	45	30
1288	–	40 z. on 25 k. mult (1165)	45	30
1289	–	40 z. on 50 k. mult (1055)	45	30
1290	–	40 z. on 50 k. mult (1134)	45	30
1291	**235**	40 z. on 50 k. mult	45	30
1292	**228**	40 z. on 75 k. mult	45	30
1293	–	40 z. on 80 k. mult (1056)	45	30
1294	–	40 z. on 90 k. mult (1093)	45	30
1295	**228**	40 z. on 90 k. mult	45	30
1296	–	40 z. on 90 k. mult (1135)	45	30
1297	**236**	80 z. on 2 k. mult	90	35
1298	–	80 z. on 4 k. mult (1164)	95	55
1299	**218**	80 z. on 10 k. mult	95	55
1300	**231**	80 z. on 25 k. mult	90	35
1301	–	80 z. on 25 k. mult (1165)	95	55
1302	–	80 z. on 50 k. mult (1134)	95	55
1303	**235**	80 z. on 50 k. mult	90	35
1304	**228**	80 z. on 75 k. mult	90	35
1305	–	80 z. on 80 k. mult (1056)	95	55
1306	–	80 z. on 90 k. mult (1093)	90	35
1307	**228**	80 z. on 90 k. mult	95	55
1308	–	80 z. on 90 k. mult (1135)	95	55
1309	**209**	100 z. on 40 s. brown, black and mauve	1·10	45
1311	**220**	100 z. on 2 k. mult	1·10	45
1312	**221**	100 z. on 2 k. mult	1·10	45
1313	**226**	100 z. on 2 k. mult	1·10	45
1314	**209**	100 z. on 4 k. brown, black and yellow	1·10	55
1315	–	100 z. on 5 k. mult (930)	1·10	45
1316	–	100 z. on 5 k. mult (1061)	1·10	45
1317	–	100 z. on 5 k. mult (1077)	1·10	55
1318	–	100 z. on 8 k. mult (908)	1·10	45
1319	–	100 z. on 8 k. mult (931)	1·10	55
1320	–	100 z. on 8 k. mult (946)	1·10	45
1322	–	100 z. on 10 k. mult (947)	1·10	55
1323	–	100 z. on 10 k. mult (969)	1·10	45
1324	–	100 z. on 10 k. mult (1036)	1·10	55
1325	**217**	100 z. on 10 k. mult	1·10	55
1326	–	100 z. on 10 k. mult (1062)	1·10	55
1327	–	100 z. on 10 k. mult (1068)	1·10	55
1328	**209**	100 z. on 15 k. brown, black and blue	1·10	55
1329	–	100 z. on 18 k. mult (1079)	1·10	55
1330	–	100 z. on 20 k. mult (970)	1·10	55
1331	–	100 z. on 20 k. mult (1020)	1·10	45
1332	**177**	100 z. on 22 k. mult	1·10	45
1333	–	100 z. on 25 k. mult (1069)	1·10	55
1335	–	100 z. on 48 k. mult (912)	1·10	55
1336	–	100 z. on 48 k. mult (950)	1·10	55
1337	–	100 z. on 50 k. mult (1013)	1·10	45
1338	–	100 z. on 50 k. mult (1080)	1·10	55
1339	–	100 z. on 50 k. mult (1103)	1·10	55
1340	–	100 z. on 75 k. mult (1038)	1·10	45
1341	–	100 z. on 75 k. mult (1049)	1·10	45
1342	**203**	100 z. on 90 k. mult	1·10	45
1343	–	100 z. on 80 k. mult (1050)	1·10	55
1344	**234**	100 z. on 80 k. mult	1·10	45
1345	–	100 z. on 90 k. mult (1070)	1·10	55
1346	–	100 z. on 90 k. mult (1104)	1·10	55
1348	**233**	300 z. on 2 k. mult	3·50	1·60
1349	–	300 z. on 8 k. mult (980)	3·50	1·60
1350	**216**	300 z. on 10 k. green and blue	3·50	1·60
1351	–	300 z. on 14 k. mult (789)	3·50	1·60
1352	**159**	300 z. on 17 k. mult (807)	3·50	1·60
1353	–	300 z. on 20 k. mult (989)	3·50	1·60
1354	–	300 z. on 45 k. mult (1145)	3·50	1·60
1355	–	300 z. on 75 k. brown and blue (1044)	3·50	1·60
1356	–	300 z. on 75 k. mult (1146)	3·50	2·00
1357	**198**	500 z. on 8 k. multicoloured	6·00	3·25
1358		500 z. on 10 k. mult	6·00	2·75
1359		500 z. on 25 k. mult	6·00	2·75
1360		500 z. on 48 k. mult	6·25	2·75

259 "Sida" forming Owl's Face

1990. Anti-AIDS Campaign. Multicoloured.

No.	Type	Description	Mint	Used
1361		30 z. Type **259**	50	20
1362		40 z. Skeleton firing arrow through "SIDA"	60	35
1363		80 z. Leopard	1·10	80

260 Administration Building

1990. 50th Anniv of Regideso (development organization). Multicoloured.

No.	Type	Description	Mint	Used
1365		40 z. Type **260**	55	35
1366		50 z. Modern factory	65	45
1367		75 z. Old water treatment plant	1·00	65
1368		120 z. Communal water tap	1·40	80

261 Maps of France and Zaire and Birds

1990. Bicentenary of French Revolution. Mult.

No.	Type	Description	Mint	Used
1369		40 z. Type **261**	55	35
1370		50 z. Article 1 of Declaration of Rights of Man and the Citizen within outline of person	65	45
1371		100 z. Crowd	1·25	65
1372		120 z. Globe	1·40	80

262 Stairs of Venus, Mount Hoyo

1990. Tourist Sites. Multicoloured.

No.	Type	Description	Mint	Used
1373		40 z. Type **262**	45	20
1374		60 z. Scenic road to village	65	35
1375		100 z. Lake Kivu	1·25	55
1376		120 z. Niyara Gongo volcano	1·60	25

1991. Various stamps surch.

No.	Type	Description	Mint	Used
1379	–	1000 z. on 100 k. mult (1064)	15	15
1380	–	1000 z. on 1 z. mult (1105)	15	15
1381	**214**	1000 z. on 1 z. mult (1026)	15	15
1383	–	1000 z. on 1 z. mult (1027)	15	15
1385	–	2000 z. on 100 k. violet and blue (1045)	30	30
1386	–	2000 z. on 1 z. mult (1147)	30	30
1387	**228**	2500 z. on 1 z. mult	40	40
1388	**225**	3000 z. on 1 z. green and gold	45	45
1389	–	4000 z. on 1 z. mult (1158)	60	60
1390	–	5000 z. on 1 z. mult (1158)	75	75
1391	**228**	10000 z. on 1 z. mult	1·50	1·50
1392	**225**	15000 z. on 1 z. green and gold	2·25	2·25

Nos. 1381 and 1383 exist in two versions with the exhibition logo either at the right or left of the design.

1992. Various stamps surch.

No.	Type	Description	Mint	Used
1393	–	50,000 z. on 125 k. multicoloured (1058)	10	10
1394	–	100,000 z. on 1 z. 20 multicoloured (1166)	10	10
1395	**234**	150,000 z. on 1 z. 20 multicoloured	10	10
1396	–	200,000 z. on 145 k. blue and indigo (1046)	15	10
1397	**234**	250,000 z. on 1 z. 20 multicoloured	20	15
1398	–	300,000 z. on 1 z. 20 multicoloured (1166)	25	20
1399	**234**	500,000 z. on 1 z. 20 multicoloured	35	25

1993. Various stamps surch. (a) Nos. 944/51.

No.	Type	Description	Mint	Used
1400	**199**	500,000 z. on 30 s. multicoloured	10	10
1401	–	500,000 z. on 5 k. multicoloured	10	10
1402	–	750,000 z. on 8 k. multicoloured	15	10
1403	–	750,000 z. on 10 k. multicoloured	15	10
1404	–	1,000,000 z. on 30 k. multicoloured	20	15
1405	–	1,000,000 z. on 40 k. multicoloured	20	15
1406	–	5,000,000 z. on 48 k. multicoloured	95	60
1407	–	10,000,000 z. on 100 k. multicoloured	1·90	1·10

(b) Nos. 1262/4.

No.	Type	Description	Mint	Used
1408	**253**	3,000,000 z. on 10 z. multicoloured	55	35
1409	–	5,000,000 z. on 15 z. multicoloured	95	60
1410	–	10,000,000 z. on 25 z. multicoloured	1·90	1·10

BOGUS SURCHARGES. Surcharges with commemorative inscriptions on Nos. 1365/8 for the inauguration of a pumping station and on Nos. 1373/6 for the sixth anniversary of the National Tourism Office are bogus.

Currency Reform
1 (new) zaire = 3000000 (old) zaire

268 Eland and Calf

1993. 50th Anniv of Garamba National Park. Multicoloured.

No.	Type	Description	Mint	Used
1412		30 k. Type **268**	10	10
1413		50 k. African elephants	10	10
1414		1 z. 50 Giant elands	20	10
1415		2 z. 50 Two white rhinoceros	30	20
1416		5 z. Bongo	60	35

1993. Various stamps surch. (a) Nos. 1201/8.

No.	Type	Description	Mint	Used
1417	**242**	30 k. on 10 k. multicoloured	15	10
1418	–	50 k. on 15 k. multicoloured	35	20
1419	–	1 z. 50 on 3 z. multicoloured	65	40
1420	–	2 z. 50 on 5 z. multicoloured	90	55
1421	–	3 z. 50 on 10 z. multicoloured	1·25	75
1422	–	5 z. on 15 z. multicoloured	1·75	1·10
1423	–	7 z. 50 on 37 z. 50 multicoloured	2·50	1·50
1424	–	10 z. on 80 z. multicoloured	3·50	2·10

(b) Nos. 1043/7.

No.	Type	Description	Mint	Used
1425	**216**	30 k. on 10 k. green and blue	25	15
1426	–	50 k. on 75 k. brown and blue	40	25
1427	–	1 z. 50 on 100 k. violet and blue	1·25	75
1428	–	3 k. 50 on 145 k. blue and deep blue	1·75	1·10
1429	–	5 z. on 270 k. red and blue	2·00	1·25

(c) Nos. 1238/41.

No.	Type	Description	Mint	Used
1430	**247**	50 k. on 5 z. multicoloured	40	25
1431	–	1 z. 50 on 10 z. multicoloured	1·25	75
1432	–	3 z. 50 on 15 z. multicoloured	1·75	1·10
1433	–	5 z. on 25 z. multicoloured	2·00	1·25

1994. Various stamps surch.

No.	Type	Description	Mint	Used
1434	–	20 z. on 3 z. multicoloured (No. 1139)	10	10
1435	–	40 z. on 270 k. red and blue (No. 1047)	10	10
1436	–	50 z. on 3 z. multicoloured (No. 1174)	15	10
1437	–	75 z. on 3 z. multicoloured (No. 1196)	20	10
1438	–	100 z. on 2 z. 05 multicoloured (No. 1167)	35	20
1439	–	150 z. on 1 z. 70 multicoloured (No. 1121)	40	25
1440	–	200 z. on 50 k. multicoloured (No. 1413)	50	30
1441	–	250 z. on 1 z. 50 multicoloured (No. 1136)	55	35
1442	**234**	300 z. on 3 z. 60 multicoloured	65	40
1443	–	500 z. on 3 z. 60 multicoloured (No. 1168)	90	55

OFFICIAL STAMPS

1975. Optd **SP**.

No.	Type	Description	Mint	Used
O841	**172**	10 s. orange & black	10	10
O842		40 s. blue and black	10	10
O843		50 s. yellow and black	10	10
O844	**177b**	1 k. multicoloured	10	10
O845		2 k. multicoloured	10	10
O846		3 k. multicoloured	10	10
O847		4 k. multicoloured	15	10
O848		5 k. multicoloured	20	10
O849		6 k. multicoloured	20	10
O850		8 k. multicoloured	35	15
O851		9 k. multicoloured	35	20
O852		10 k. multicoloured	45	20
O853		14 k. multicoloured	55	25
O854		17 k. multicoloured	80	45
O855		20 k. multicoloured	1·00	50
O856		50 k. multicoloured	2·50	1·00
O857		100 k. multicoloured	6·75	2·75

ZAMBEZIA Pt. 9

Formerly administered by the Zambezia Co. This district of Portuguese E. Africa was later known as Quelimane and is now part of Mozambique.

1000 reis = 1 milreis

1894. "Figures" key-type inscr "ZAMBEZIA".

No.	Type	Description	Mint	Used
1	R	5 r. orange	15	15
3		10 r. mauve	20	20
4		15 r. brown	25	25
5		20 r. lilac	25	25
12		25 r. green	40	30
13		50 r. blue	40	30
14		75 r. pink	90	90
15		80 r. green	75	60
8		100 r. brown on buff	70	60
16		150 r. red on pink	90	75
17		200 r. blue on blue	90	80
18		300 r. blue on brown	1·75	1·50

1898. "King Carlos" key-type inscr "ZAMBEZIA". Name and value in red (500 r.) or black (others).

20	S	$2\frac{1}{2}$ r. grey	20	15
21		5 r. red	20	15
22		10 r. green	20	15
23		15 r. brown	45	40
55		15 r. green	65	55
24		20 r. lilac	40	35
25		25 r. green	40	35
56		25 r. red	45	35
26		50 r. blue	50	40
57		50 r. brown	1·10	90
58		65 r. blue	2·75	2·25
27		75 r. pink	2·75	2·00
59		75 r. purple	1·25	1·00
28		80 r. mauve	1·75	1·50
29		100 r. blue on blue	80	75
60		115 r. brown on pink	3·75	2·75
61		130 r. brown on yellow	3·75	2·75
30		150 r. brown on yellow	1·75	1·40
31		200 r. purple on pink	1·75	1·40
32		300 r. blue on pink	2·10	1·50
62		400 r. blue on cream	4·00	3·25
33		500 r. black on blue	3·00	2·50
34		700 r. mauve on yellow	3·50	3·00

1902. Surch.

63	S	50 r. on 65 r. blue	2·00	1·25
35	R	65 r. on 10 r. mauve	2·10	1·75
36		65 r. on 15 r. brown	2·10	1·75
37		65 r. on 20 r. lilac	2·10	1·75
38		65 r. on 300 r. blue on brn	2·10	1·75
40		115 r. on 5 r. orange	2·10	1·75
41		115 r. on 25 r. green	2·10	1·75
42		115 r. on 80 r. green	2·10	1·75
46	V	130 r. on $2\frac{1}{2}$ r. brown	2·10	1·75
43	R	130 r. on 75 r. pink	2·10	1·75
45		130 r. on 150 r. red on pink	1·75	1·50
47		400 r. on 50 r. blue	80	70
49		400 r. on 100 r. brn on buff	80	70
50		400 r. on 200 r. blue on blue	80	70

1902. 1898 issue optd **PROVISORIO**.

51	S	15 r. brown	75	60
52		25 r. green	75	60
53		50 r. blue	75	60
54		75 r. pink	2·10	1·50

1911. 1898 issue optd **REPUBLICA**.

64	S	$2\frac{1}{2}$ r. grey	10	10
65		5 r. red	10	10
66		10 r. green	15	15
67		15 r. green	15	15
68		20 r. lilac	20	10
69		25 r. red	45	20
108		25 r. green	4·00	3·00
70		50 r. brown	15	15
71		75 r. purple	40	30
72		100 r. blue on blue	40	30
73		115 r. brown on pink	45	35
74		130 r. brown on yellow	45	35
75		200 r. purple on pink	45	35
76		400 r. blue on cream	75	60
77		500 r. black on blue	75	60
78		700 r. mauve on yellow	75	60
		50 r. blue		

1914. Provisionals of 1902 optd **REPUBLICA**.

94	S	50 r. blue (No. 53)	25	20
95		50 r. on 65 r. blue	1·00	85
81		75 c. pink (No. 54)	50	45
96	R	115 r. on 5 r. orange	25	20
97		115 r. on 25 r. green	25	20
98		115 r. on 80 r. green	25	20
99	V	130 r. on $2\frac{1}{2}$ r. brown	25	20
100	R	130 r. on 75 r. pink	25	20
102		130 r. on 150 r. red on pink	25	20
90		400 r. on 50 r. blue	85	75
92		400 r. on 100 r. brn on buff	90	75
93		400 r. on 200 r. blue on blue	90	75

NEWSPAPER STAMP

1893. "Newspaper" key-type inscr "ZAMBEZIA".

N1	V	$2\frac{1}{2}$ r. brown	20	15

ADDENDA AND CORRIGENDA

LIECHTENSTEIN

AMENDMENT. Change Nos. 1116 (5 f. Vaduz Castle) to 1128 and 1117/35 to 1130/48.

Add to Nos. 1115 etc (Scenes):

1116	20 r. Planken	15	10
1123	1 f. 30 Triesen	1·10	85
1125	1 f. 70 Schaanwald	1·50	1·10

365 "Poltava"

366 St. Matthew

1996. 43rd Death Anniv of Eugen Zotow (painter). Multicoloured.

1142	70 r. Type **365**	60	60
1143	1 f. 10 "Three Bathers in a Berlin Park"	95	95
1144	1 f. 40 "Vaduz"	1·25	1·25

1996. Christmas. Illustrations from Illuminated Manuscript "Liber Viventium Fabariensis". Multicoloured.

1145	70 r. Type **366**	60	60
1146	90 r. Emblems of St. Mark	75	75
1147	1 f. 10 Emblems of St. Luke	95	95
1148	1 f. 80 Emblems of St. John	1·50	1·50

367 Schubert

368 The Wild Gnomes

1997. Birth Bicentenary of Franz Schubert (composer).

1149	**367**	70 r. multicoloured	60	60

1997. Europa. Tales and Legends. Multicoloured.

1150	90 r. Type **368**	75	75
1151	1 f. 10 Man, pumpkin and rabbit (The Foal of Planken)	95	95

NOTE. The first supplement containing new issues not in this catalogue or Addenda appeared in the September 1997 number of *Gibbons Stamp Monthly*.

INDEX

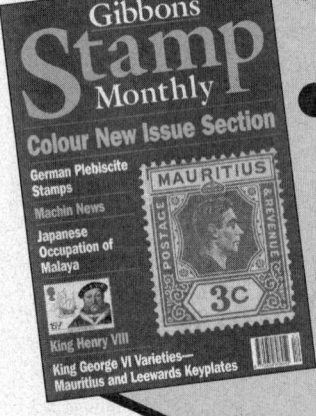

ATTLEBOROUGH

The evolution of a town

PHILIP BUJAK

'. . . the small market town of Attleborough which, apart from the church of St Mary, has little of interest.'

(Geographica Guide – East Anglia p.57)

Cover: An aerial view of the centre of the town. The current geography and architecture overlays many centuries of history (Derek A Edwards – Norfolk Archaeological Unit)

Dedication

To my father Jan Felix Bujak
Born Wejhorowo, Poland 1919
Died Attleborough, Norfolk 1983

Attleborough High Street c1905.

Published by Poppyland Publishing, North Walsham, Norfolk
Designed by Top Floor Design
Printed by Printing Services (Norwich) Ltd

First Edition published 1990
ISBN 0 946148 45 7

Contents

Introduction

There are a number of reasons why I decided to write this history of the town of Attleborough. I believe it essential that we all have a sense of belonging to somewhere and that we should therefore try to understand as much as we can about our heritage. In my profession as a schoolteacher I try to sow the seeds of curiosity and a thirst for knowledge amongst pupils to encourage them to question and enquire. In the same way, it is my hope that those townspeople who read this work will want to carry the process a stage further. It has not been my aim therefore to provide all the answers, indeed a great deal more research waits to be done, perhaps by someone now reading this introduction. Nor have I attempted to produce a wholly academic work. This book is intended for the use of those of whom it is written, namely the community of Attleborough.

At times I have thought it prudent to place events in the town against the background of national history more for information rather than as a diversion and hopefully fill in some of the blank spaces in our knowledge of the past.

Another motivating force was the quotation on the title page. Any book that can dismiss a whole town and its community so completely is clearly bereft of true knowledge. Attleborough has had a rich if perhaps unspectacular history that revolves around more than just the rood screen in St Mary's church – impressive though it is. It is my hope that a great deal more about the history of this town will now be apparent both to those whose homes are in Attleborough and to those who pass through.

I am indebted to a great many individuals and institutions for their support and advice in the preparation of this book and I list them in no order of priority and thank them all for their valuable help:

The Rev John Aves, vicar of St Mary's parish church; Mrs P Berdos of Atleboro Public Library, Mass, USA; Norfolk Geneological Society; Mr Derek Edwards and Mr John Wymer of Norfolk Archaeological Unit; Miss Barbara Green and the staff at Norwich Castle Museum; Dr John Pound; Library staff at the University of East Anglia; Mr R Plumbley; Mr Pat Ramm; Mr E J Moore; Canon Ivo Webb; Mr W D Gardiner; Mrs K Norman; Mr Howard Dover, Computer Studies Department, Langley School; Miss F Foster; Mrs P E and Mr E J Bujak, and lastly, Mr and Mrs P J R Stibbons.

My greatest thanks go to my wife for her patience and help over the many hours of her family life given up to produce this book.

P E Bujak
July 1990

View over the Bannister Bridge, north from the town in 1912. The bridge is now covered by a flyover for the A11 bypass and the fields have been built on.

The Setting

Norfolk is an area packed full of variety. In its geography, culture and landscape the discerning eye can record a sometimes subtle, sometimes drastic change in scenery, architecture, land use and even dialect of various parts of the county. It is often said that Norfolk people are some of the most provincial and introverted in the whole country, that they are Norfolk first and English second. But for those who know the county and its people well, there is yet another deeper dimension to the Norfolk character, that of an internal sub-division of the county making a north Norfolk resident almost a foreigner to a citizen of the south of the county. But why should this be so and how has it affected the development of one particular community, that of the town of Attleborough?

Undoubtedly the geology of the county plays an important part. Norfolk is not flat. Low, by comparison to other parts of the kingdom perhaps, but there are parts of north Norfolk that strain the best car engines, forcing them down a gear or even two. In the same way the whole county is not given over to arable farming, as one might imagine by looking at a map of the physical relief of Norfolk. The rich variety of geological regions present in Norfolk has played a large part in determining the character and development of its people.

The area that contains the present day expanding town of Attleborough is one predominantly composed of boulder clay, the northern tip of a wide band of such material extending as far south as Essex. To the west is Breckland and to the east Norwich and the rivers and waters of the Norfolk Broads.

Breckland is composed of light sandy soils and considerable expanses of heathland and forests. Sparsely populated, apart from the town of Thetford, Breckland has the air of a timeless landscape. Low flatland covered with varieties of heather, gorse and ferns punctuated with large tracts of forests of pines and conifers characterise this area. Ancient man did occupy Breckland, as the flint mines of Grimes Graves and the numerous man-made stone implements testify, but the nature of the landscape was not suited to larger scale colonisation. Instead Breckland became an area easy to travel through using the many ancient pathways of which the Icknield Way, running down from the north Norfolk coast, is one.

Just a few miles north east and the soil becomes heavier and the countryside gradually changes to a more undulating landscape, heavily farmed and broken by hedgerows and streams. The nature of the soil in this area has given rise to a vastly different pattern of land use and population distribution from that of nearby Breckland. The fields have a fertility that has been exploited by man for thousands of years and caused them to study carefully the features of the land in order to begin settlement in the most advantageous position. Attleborough itself lies exactly in the area where Breckland fades into the boulder clay plateau that extends across a large part of Norfolk.

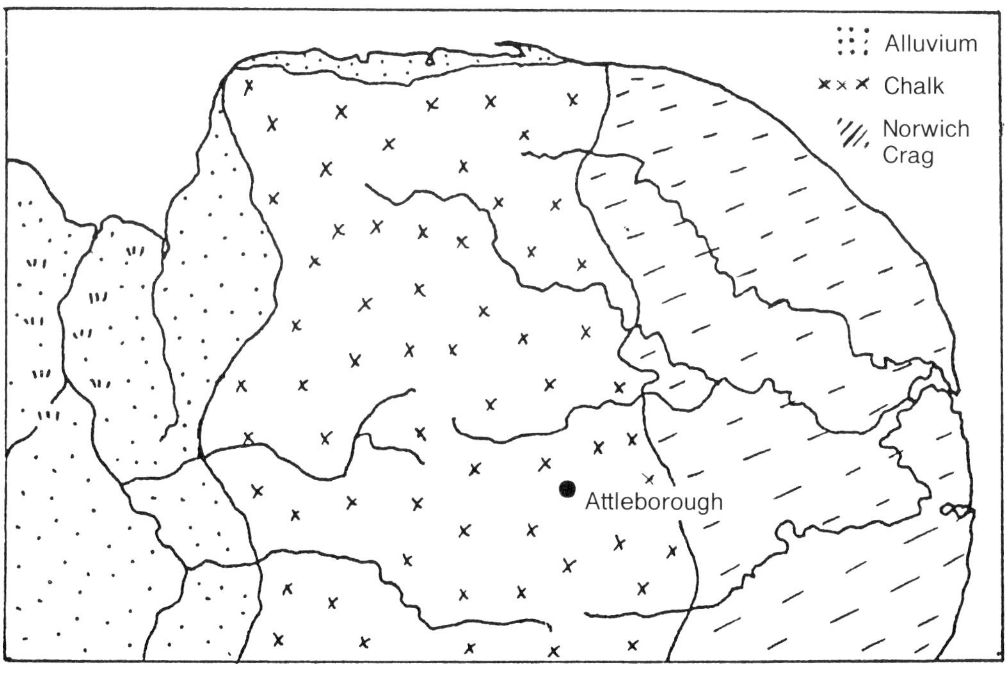

The basic geology of Norfolk and position of Attleborough.

First Human Activity in the area

Stone Age

The oldest human relics found in Norfolk generally date from the New Stone Age when the first rudimentary farming and hunting began. Scattered throughout Norfolk knapped and rolled flints appear in varying concentrations and give some clues to the prehistoric land use of certain areas, though evidence of more permanent settlement is naturally far more scarce.

As far as the prehistoric occupation of the Attleborough area is concerned, the majority of finds have come to light at various times over the last two centuries.

The earliest officially recorded find is that of a polished flint axehead found to the south of the town, near the parish boundary with Old Buckenham, by Mr H Beever in 1822. (NCM 9140) In 1823 and again in 1850 a selection of Neolithic ridged flakes came to light along with a succession of flint arrowheads and axes. Again these later finds were to the south of the town and partially on the estate of the then Sir Thomas Beever near Quidenham. (NCM 9086–91) Around 1942 Captain Gaymer, a member of the locally prominent Gaymer family, discovered a polished Neolithic flint axe (NCM 9123) although it was partially broken. The latest and perhaps one of the most important complete flint hand-axes was discovered in 1988 near Crowshall Bridge just to the north west of the present day town. Belonging to the Paleolithic period, this find is typical of those associated with the first half of the Last Glaciation some 80,000–50,000 years ago, when Europe was inhabited by Neanderthal Man. This is the only hand-axe so far found in the Attleborough area and provides further evidence of hunting, probably of a tribal nature.

Evidence of more permanent occupation is too small to be able to draw any firm conclusions. A large chipped flint axe ploughhead was discovered to the east of the town in an area known locally as Swangey Fen. This item is attributed more to the Late New Stone Age and is illustrative of crude cultivation of the surface soils.

It is of course possible that many of the worked flints had their origins some 20 miles away at the extensive New Stone Age flint mines of Grimes Graves near Thetford. The several hundred pit shafts and interconnecting tunnels illustrate the importance attached to this particular material and the surplus quantities produced would probably have been traded over a wide area.

Bronze Age

The next major step in the history of civilisation brings us to the Bronze Age, c2000–700 BC, and although closer in time to our own there is rather less material to study than that of the preceeding millenium.

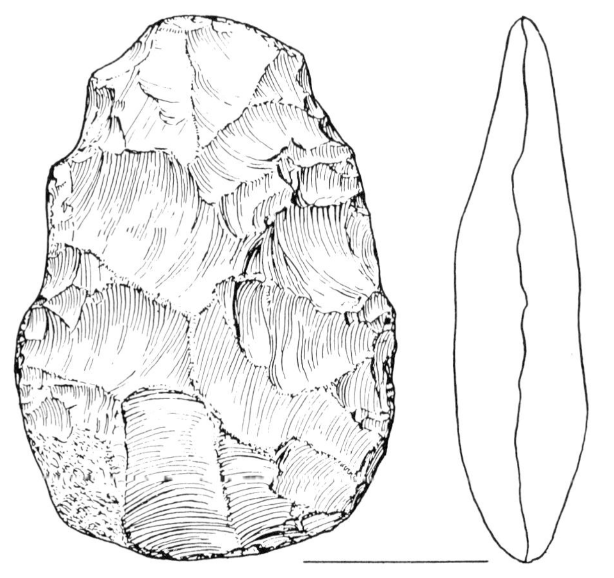

Paleolithic flint hand axe found by Mr E C Amos in 1988 (Courtesy John Wymer, Norfolk Archaeological Unit).

What finds there have been are fascinating in their workmanship and state of preservation. The skills necessary to shape the Middle Bronze Age palstave axe found to the north of Attleborough Hall in 1953 are impressive and yet belong to a time commonly thought of as being primitive.

The state of preservation and the bevelled edged design are similar to other palstave axes found close to the town, which are held by the Ashmoleum and Spalding Museums. (NCM 9092 and 9093.) In 1965 another bronze palstave axe was discovered, this time in the circumference of the present day town in Dodd's Lane. (NCM 9141) Although this one was quite badly pitted, taken together with the collection of other Bronze Age items found near the town it is very likely that habitation on some scale in this vicinity must have existed during the Bronze Age period. Bronze Age hoards have been found in many other parts of Norfolk. Along with the numerous round burial barrows of the period found in Eaton, Salthouse and Rushford, they indicate widespread occupation of Norfolk in the Bronze Age.

Plan and section of the Bronze Age palstave axe found by Mr Roger Rout in 1965 (NCM 9141 Courtesy Norfolk Museums Service)

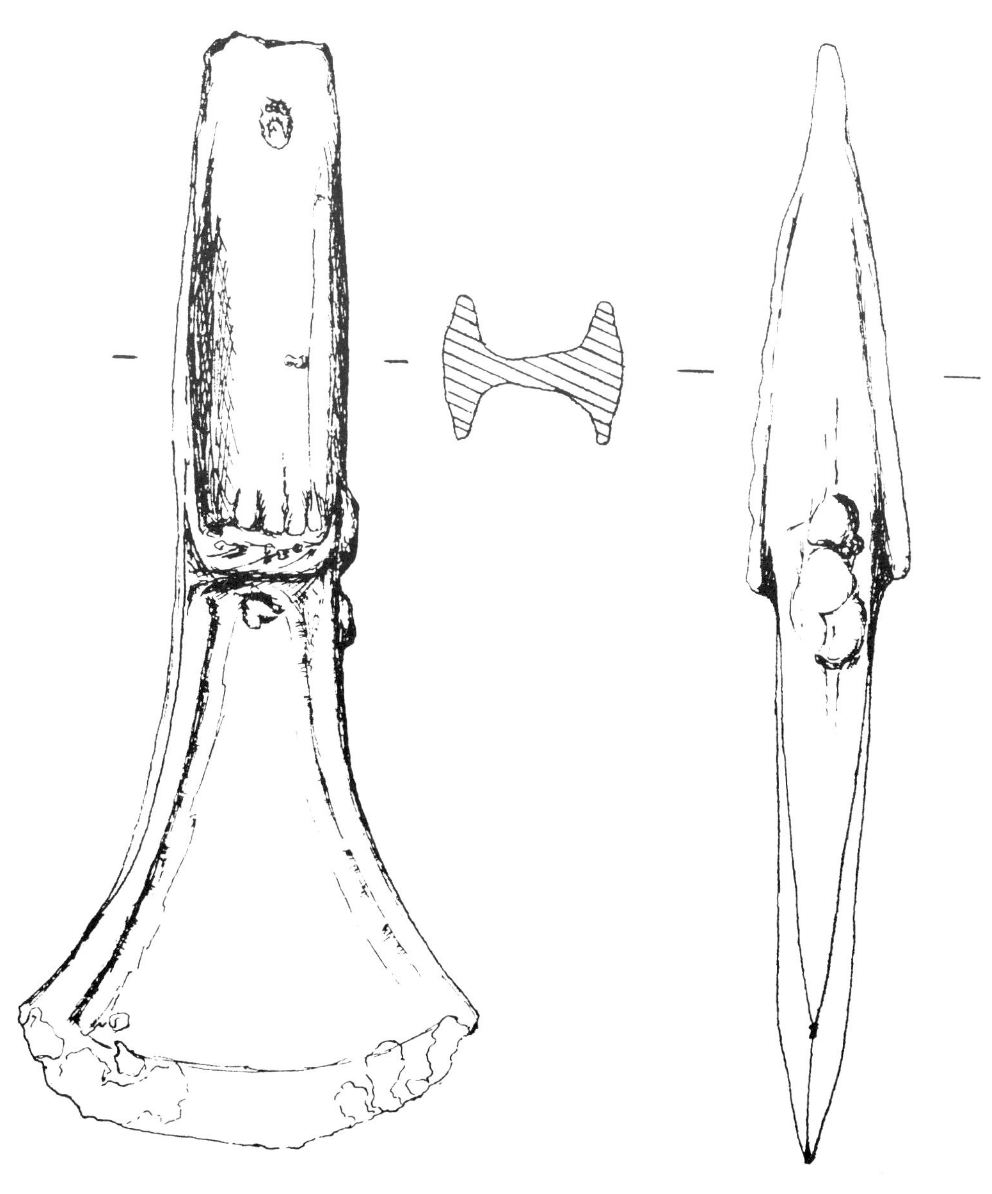

First Settlement

The Iron Age

Flint and bronze remained the staple materials in the period before the first Roman invasion of 43AD. Although iron gradually became the main metal used for weapons and tools it could not easily replace the more malleable bronze, or gold for finer pieces such as personal jewellery. Unfortunately, little evidence of occupation exists for the area apart from a quantity of iron age pottery found in a sand pit ('Pointers Pit') in 1928; the collection was roughly illustrated and donated to the Castle Museum by its finder, Mr H Apling. (NCM 9142) It is probable that the vicinity of Attleborough was by now inhabited in some way, it being the most probable route into Norfolk from the south-west and having access to water, good soils and most likely a plentiful supply of wood from large tracts of forest.

The Roman Occupation of Norfolk

To the Romans in 50BC "the spine chilling sea and the Britons at the very end of the earth" presented something of a mystery. A tribal system had evolved to a stage where one could associate tribes with certain areas. For the eastern region, north of the Thames and south of the Wash, it was the Iceni tribe that provided the major influence.

The Iceni did not dominate what later became known as East Anglia but they did control Norfolk and as such would have had widespread contact with their new Roman masters. Tribal organisation, current research suggests, was quite advanced. They were also wealthy, as the rich hoards of artefacts from Snettisham and Ringstead testify. More gold torques and bracelets have been found in Norfolk than in all the rest of Britain.

Whether they fitted Julius Caesar's general description of the Britons (the collective name for the tribes) we can only guess. He saw them as "...covering themselves with woad which produces a blue dye. They wear their hair long and shave every part of their body except the upper lip."

Norfolk was well colonised by the Romans between the 1st and 4th centuries AD for a variety of reasons. It was relatively easy to reach from the south, especially from the large garrison at Camulodonum (Colchester); being mainly flat and already traversed by ancient pathways internal communication was already good; the abundance of navigable waterways to the east of the region would facilitate trade across the North Sea. After Boudicca's revolt of 60AD a strong Roman presence in the area was essential to maintain order.

Part of the Roman pewter hoard (NCM 9188 – Courtesy Norfolk Museums Service)

Thus it was that a significant number of Roman country houses were built in Norfolk. Either side of the Peddars Way, stretching from north to south across the county, proved popular because of the fertile soils.

Whilst little physical evidence of Roman buildings remains, because of the lack of good building stone in the county, the Attleborough area has slowly yielded its own contribution to the Roman period. In 1963 what was described as "..an important archaeological discovery" was made when a mechanical digger revealed nine items of Roman pewter plate as well as a quantity of pottery. They were dated to the second half of the 4th century AD and would have formed part of a well-to-do farmer's tableware. Other similar items have been found which indicate Roman occupation and therefore probably attempts to continue to clear the forests and cultivate the area surrounding Breckland by Roman settlers.

These include Roman bricks (NCM 9095) and pottery recorded by Mr R D Clover in 1965 and the traces of a Roman road running parallel to the main A11 trunk road. One further item associated with this period was a coin of the Emperor Constantine II (NCM 9094) which was found in 1957 but has since disappeared. Though the lack of a Roman building in the vicinity undermines any attempt to establish the extent of Roman occupation of the area close to the present day town, there is enough evidence to suggest that occupation did exist.

The Saxon period

Sometimes referred to as the Romano-British period, it is possible to begin to establish that the 'Attleborough' of the post Roman period had a growing influence over the surrounding territory. Certainly the low-lying lands of eastern Britannia became a popular route for the flow of Saxon tribes such as the Angles and widescale settlement was superimposed on the scattered Romano-British population. Soon the Kingdoms of the North Folk and South Folk became established units in the Saxon amalgam of new territorial regions.

There are a number of strands that make it likely that Attleborough emerged as a community of some size and influence at sometime during the 5th to 7th centuries AD. The Thetford monk John Brame relates that the town was founded by Atlinge, king of the province, to oppose Rond King of Thetford, in one of the many minor civil and tribal wars of the period. Atlinge is supposed to have fortified the town with a ditch and a wall complete with four gates and four towers. Evidence to support this writing does not exist though the considerable linear earthwork close to the south of the town, Bunns Bank, has often been suggested as the source of the 'burgh' of Attleburgh and therefore part of the late Saxon system of earthen defensive banks known as burghs.

Apart from Brame we have a perhaps more reliable analysis of the origins of the town's name in Thomas Amyot's article. Here the reader is led through the mists and uncertainty surrounding the kings of the East Angles and their influence over the region as well as being advised that Brame's writings are 'worthless'. Amyot exposes what he sees as mistaken spelling by Brame to reveal that Atlinge was in fact Athla who, according to Galfridus de Fontibus was the founder of 'the Ancient and royal town of Attleburgh in Norfolk'. Amyot is therefore in no doubt that Attleburgh was the seat of a member of an early Saxon royal family. He goes further in suggesting that the town may well have been founded by an Aetheling, a Saxon of distinguished rank. Amyot's judgements are made in the light of his consideration not only of John Brame but also Blomefield's 18th century 11 volume 'History of Norfolk'. Here too we find other explanations of the origins of the town's name. According to Blomefield the name Attleborough is merely a corruption of "At-le-burgh" or "at-the-fort (burgh)". Blomefield's conclusions are neither as exciting or likely as Amyot's conjecture and very likely rest on the assumption that the aforementioned earthwork to the south of the town was in fact part of a Saxon burgh.

Bunns Bank

Very close to the south of the present day town lies a 1700 metre earthwork that runs east-west across the B-road to Old Buckenham. As with the name of the town, so too various theories have been put forward as to the age and purpose of this bank.

The fact that it is to be found in an area known as 'Burgh Common' should not however be taken as substantive proof that this earthwork owes its construction to the Saxon period of English history. Evidence that the bank has pre-conquest origins is both scanty and inconclusive as shown in recent studies of the available material by the author in 1985 and 1987.[1]

Harrod's assertion that it was a form of tribal boundary (Bunde Bank) of the Saxon period is countered by claims that it was in fact a post-Domesday deer park boundary. The park was probably for hunting purposes in early medieval Norfolk. Both arguments have their merits and demerits but what is certain is that whenever the bank was built the occupants of the settlement we now know as Attleborough would have played a large part in its erection.

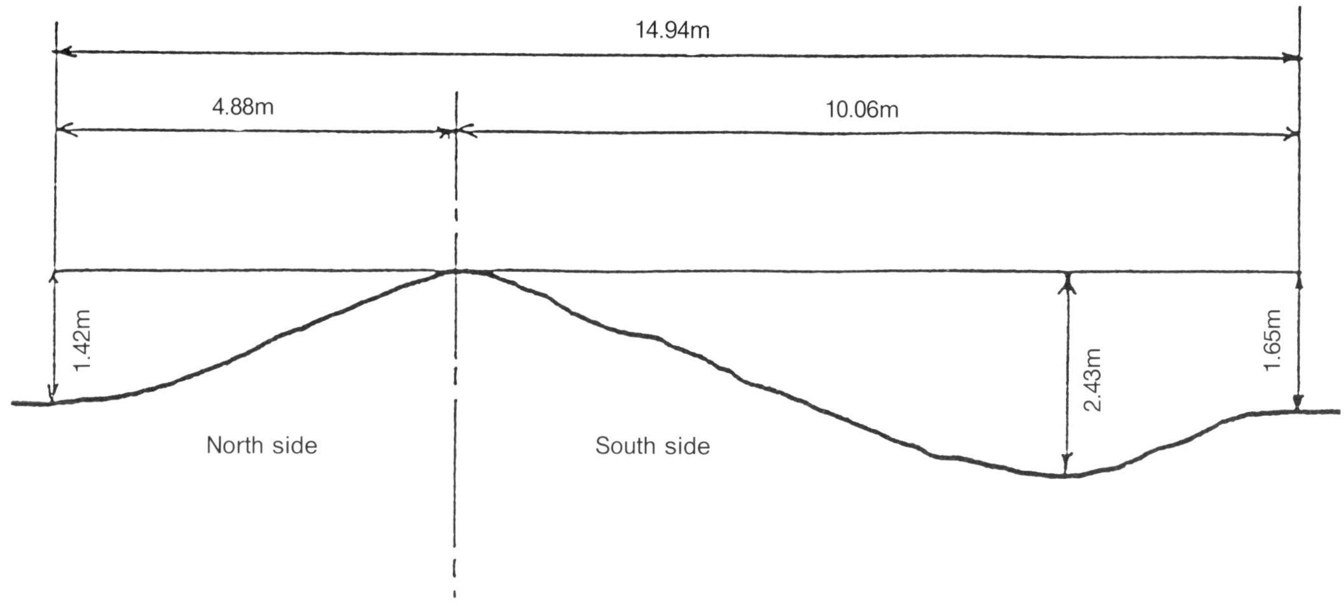

Cross section through the north-eastern end of Bunns Bank in a survey of 1986

In places the bank and ditch are over 15 metres wide and some two metres high. It is an impressive structure even today. Allowing for weathering processes, such as surface run-off and gravitational soil creep, that will have substantially reduced the original dimensions we must assume that the Bank was a major enterprise for the local population and unlikely to have been constructed for deer hunting purposes.

This does raise the question of whether the bank is very much older than we may imagine, but it has undoubtedly served as stimulus to the idea that Attleborough did have an influential status in the pre-medieval period. According to William White, writing in the 19th century, Attleborough was a place of great consequence during the Saxon era. He states that it was the seat of both Offa and Edmund, Kings of the East Angles, who fortified it against the 9th and 10th century incursions of the Danes with Bunns Bank remaining as evidence of this. Certainly Blomefield suggests that local dignatories in the reign of Henry II (1154–1189) lived "atte-the-dyke".

What other evidence is there to suggest a substantial Saxon presence at Attleborough? A variety of middle Saxon pottery sherds have been located close to the town and also a rare Saxon silver ring was located in 1848 during the construction of the local railway (NCM 9098). Inscribed with the words 'Ethaldric' and 'Baldric', it is in remarkably good condition and helps to provide substance to the picture emerging of the town in the pre-conquest period.

Saxon period silver ring (NCM 9098) inscribed 'Ethaldric Baldric' (Courtesy Norfolk Museums Service)

Attleborough's place in Domesday England

The effects of the Norman conquest of Anglo-Saxon Britain are only now being fully understood. Certainly Norman rule manifested itself in the provinces in a number of ways. The Christian religion received a stimulus from the new rulers in that many more churches were planned and built, the square-towered Norman designs dominating their smaller and less imposing Saxon counterparts. The Norman desire for efficiency and control not only gave England a greater cohesiveness as a single kingdom but its legacy has given us an enriched source of evidence of the history of the period after the Dark Ages.

The area around Attleborough – Atleburc in Domesday – was divided up into manorial units over a period of time after the Conquest. The Domesday survey was launched in 1085[2] by King William I to ascertain the taxable revenue of his newly-won kingdom and was eventually composed of two returns known as Little Domesday and Great Domesday. The Eastern circuit was covered in the Little Domesday book and its headings were picked out in red to give it a more formal appearance. Though the contents of the survey went rapidly out of date the two volumes were widely used for administrative purposes for many centuries. As proof of ancient landholding rights it is unequalled.

The Domesday survey illustrates a kingdom composed of 35 counties with an estimated total value of £73,000 and a population of somewhere in the region of four million. The king himself held about 17% of the total land, the bishops and abbots about 26% and the two hundred or so tenants in chief held about 54% between them.

Individual holdings varied enormously in size from about a dozen leading Barons controlling a quarter of all England down to the remnants of the once proud Saxon aristocracy whose holdings were vastly reduced.

At the time of the survey there were three manors for the Attleborough area; Plassing, Attleborough Mortimer and Baconsthorpe. The first lay to the south and east of the town in what is today known as the parish of Besthorpe and derived its name from 'plashes' or marshy places. Later it is referred to as Plassett or Plassing Hall.

The first manor of Atleburc, which became known as Attleborough Mortimer, and contained within it the church and main part of the town, we find held by; *'Thorkell with 2 carucates of land before 1066* (probably assessed during the reign of Edward the Confessor). *Always six villeins and five smallholders (borders). Twenty-four acres of meadow. Pannage* (woodland) *for 60 hogs. Always i plough in Lordship; two men's ploughs; there could be one plough. Now ½ mill; ½ fishery. Also 17 Freemen, 47 acres of land; meadow 8 acres; woodland,12 pigs; always three ploughs. Then one cob* (cart horse)*; always two head of cattle. Then 6 pigs, now 4.*

Value then and later 40/–, now 60/–. The whole has 2 leagues in length and one league in width. Whoever holds there tax of 34½d.'

The Plasset manor lay to the south east of the town and contained part of Besthorpe and was held by;

'Thorold before 1066 (again probably assessed as recently as the reign of the Confessor), *2 carucates of land and 3 acres. Always 6 villagers; and 5 smallholders. Then i slave, now 3. Meadow 23 acres. Always i plough in Lordship; 2 mens ploughs; woodland, 60 pigs; 2 thirds of a mill; ½ a fishery. Then 2 cobs, now i; always one cow. Then 6 pigs, now 5; 8 sheep. Also 21 freemen, 80 acres of land; meadow 12 acres; woodland 8 pigs. Then and later 2 ploughs, now three.*

Value then and later 40/– now 60.'

The third major manorial holding is that which later became known as Baconsthorpe, Crowshall or Copsy. It lay to the north of the present town.

Statistical Summary of Information Contained in Domesday for the 3 manors of the Attleborough area formed by 1087.

All measures of land approximate.

	Baconsthorpe	Mortimer	Plassing
Ploughland (Carucate = 200 acres)	2 + 1½	2	2
Meadow	16 + 12 + 6	24 + 8	23 + 12
Pannage (woodland for ? Hogs)	Pannage for 48 Hogs	Pannage for 72 Hogs	Pannage for 60 Hogs
Villeins (Hold own land of 0.3 acres)	8	6	6
Freemen	5 (with 1½ carucates!)	–	–
Borders	3 (with 12 acres meadow)	5	5
Socmen	20 (4 plough teams 6 meadows)	17 (with 47 acres and 8 meadows)	21 (with 80 acres + 12 meadows)
Total ploughs	10 (where is all the land for these ploughs?)	3	3
Serfs	–	–	–
Cows	8	–	1
Cart Horses	2	1	1
Hogs	28 (Pannage for 48)	– (Pannage for 72)	5
Sheep	38	–	–
Mills, Fisheries etc.	–	½ Fishery	½ Fishery
Goats	26	–	Smaller due to presence of Old Buckenham Castle to the South?

Placing Attleborough in the Domesday Context/
– Safe to say road was already there, route from Norwich to London.
– Mound where church is = natural, therefore roads ran around it. Perhaps cleared for erection of church by Mortimers?
– to North East – Wymondham, to South West Thetford, to South Old Buckenham.

Notes: 1) A carucate = between 60 and 180 acres, dependingon soil
2) Pannage = Woodland suitable for Hogs to forage in
3) Population figures represent male inhabitants only. No reference is made to the number of females or children present in each manor.

'In Atleburc Alfred holds two carucates of land for a Manor. Always 8 villeins and 16 acres of meadow; and always 2 plough teams for a manor. Always 8 villeins and 16 acres of meadow; and always 2 plough teams in the demesne and 1 plough team amongst the tenants. Pannage for 40 hogs. And twenty socmen with ½ carucate of land; meadow 6 acres; always 4 ploughs. Also 5 freemen, 1½ carucates of land. 3 smallholders. Meadow 12 acres, always 3 ploughs. Woodland, 8 pigs. Always 2 cobs. Then 6 head of cattle now 8. Then 20 pigs now 28. Then 20 sheep now 28. Always 26 goats. Value then 60/– now £4.'

Attleborough Hall clearly showing the fortified stone walls and moat. The main access road approaches from the south (Derek A Edwards – Norfolk Archaeological Unit)

Observations

One of the most striking elements of this survey of the manors in the Attleborough area for 1087 is the generally equitable distribution of resources especially land. Each manor has a minimum of 2 carucates (approximately equal to 400 hectares in present day terms) of suitable farming land and the plough teams with which to farm this were considerable.

In most respects it is the manor of Baconsthorpe that is best endowed. In ploughs and animal stock it outnumbers its neighbours and is even able to allocate an extra 1½ carucates of land to its five freemen. These considerable advantages suggest that this manor had been well established by its Anglo-Saxon inhabitants and became the property of a fortunate Norman lord.

Although we cannot be certain of the demarcation lines of the three manors we can make assumptions based on current place-name evidence and a little guesswork. This would indicate that Baconsthorpe lay northwards from the town, as did Mortimer, because in the 13th century it was closely associated with Attleborough wood – the few traces which still remain can also be found to the north of the town where we also find Oaks Common, Wood Farm and Cock Robin Common today.[3]

Plassing on the other hand was located in the Besthorpe area to the south of the town and according to Domesday shared a fishery with Mortimer which would in all likelihood be on the tributary of the Thet which winds to the north of the town centre as it stands today.

It is probable that the routines, customs and practices of Norman feudalism became established with relative ease in these manors. Resistance would have been futile and the administrative ability of the new Norman lords would have brought a fresh and possibly more productive approach. The intricate workings of the feudal system are well researched and the population would have soon realised that fulfilling one's obligations to their respective lords was essential to their survival, as indeed it was for their lords in relation to the greater tenants and the King himself.

Pinpointing what might have been the centre of the Saxon settlement is still not easy, even with the information we have from Domesday. There is evidence that there was a church, apart from the claim in the church guide for Saxon foundations under the floor. Certainly the valley formed by the stream is overlooked to north and south by two low bluffs and the road and stream ran between them. The church was built on the southern side while to the north, overlooking both stream, valley and church, was the site of Mortimer's manor house. If we place faith in material claiming the early importance of Attleborough then it is very likely that a Saxon church already existed and formed the focus of the small settlement when the Normans arrived.

The male population for the year 1087 can be assessed as being not much over 100 from this survey. This excludes the Lord's retinue of men at arms, if he had any, servants and so on. Sexual equality had not yet entered the minds of the average Norman knight and we are therefore also deprived of numbers of women and children. Life expectancy, family size and names are beyond our reach until the parish records of the 16th century, but it is still possible to build a picture of this newly-won land with its small congregation of thatch and wooden houses scattered around a well-used road and stream and a small church. The population was small and confined to farming an area within large tracts of forest, especially to the north of the settlement. The forest no doubt contained wild animals now long extinct.

Attleborough after Domesday was linked to London, albeit in a small way, and the relationship between central government and the provinces was to grow from this time onwards. This helps us in future centuries chart the further development of the community.

The Early Modern Town 1549–1638

1549–1613

The wide ranging and fundamental desire for increased knowledge in the early modern period is reflected in the more abundant documentary records that gradually emerge after c1500. Much of the initiative for breaking away from the 'medieval' character of England came from Henry VII who, at his death, had partially reformed the machinery of government and created a more stable economic and social environment in which trade and progress could hopefully develop hand in hand.

Although the concept of a centralised administrative bureaucracy was still in its infancy, most Tudor monarchs initiated and supported legislative programmes that improved London's knowledge of the state of the nation. But superimposing an ever enquiring and interfering centralised bureaucracy on the provinces was never going to be a straight forward task. The fiercely independent nature of many counties made them suspicious of and resistant to the growth of central government. Attleborough demonstrated that they were prepared to go to extreme measures to do what they felt was right. The events of Kett's rebellion help us to understand better the townspeople and their problems before we venture into a more detailed analysis of their lives provided by the unique parish records.

Kett's Rebellion Summer 1549

'We desire liberty and an equal use of all things. This we will have otherwise these tumults and our lives shall only be ended together.'
(From *The Rebels Complaint* in *Neville's Norfolk Furies.*)

One of the key social and political events associated with the mid-Tudor period, for Norfolk in particular, was the rebellion against the 13-year-old son of Henry VIII, Edward VI, who later died of consumption at the age of 17. The Tudor state was not designed for rebellion as evidence of grievance. Rebellion was treason. In this light Henry VIII had dealt with the Pilgrimage of Grace in 1539 and so too would the rebellion in Norfolk be erased. But what did Attleborough have to do with the dramatic events of the summer of 1549? To put it as simply as possible it was the townsmen together with their compatriots in nearby villages who began the revolt in the first place.

The economic mismanagement of central government, firstly by the later executed Edward Seymour, Duke of Somerset, and closely followed (though not to the block) by John Dudley, Duke of Northumberland, combined to produce a miserable scene for the ordinary people. The new practice of enclosing traditionally common land was for many the last straw. Every town and village had an area of common land, and some had more than one common field or heath. In most cases the legal origins of ownership were uncertain and derived from a very early time when everyone knew what was and what was not common land. When John Green, Lord of Wilby Manor, decided to enclose part of the commons of Attleborough and nearby Hargham a fury and anger against the landowning classes was unleashed. On 20th June 1549 local men tore down Lord Green's fences and hedges in the first physical manifestation of open defiance. This would have ended here had it not been for events in neighbouring Wymondham. News travelled up the main Norwich road to Wymondham Abbey where an unusually large gathering was commemorating the martyrdom of Thomas a'Becket. Robert Kett, a local landowner himself, latched onto the actions of the men from Attleborough to rapidly head a band of hundreds that met under a locally famous oak tree, or trees as it would have been at that time.

By 27th August the forces of central government had moved into action and between two and three thousand of Kett's followers were killed at the battle of 'Dussingdale', an area to the north of Norwich. Whether any men from Attleborough were with Kett at this time it is of course impossible to say, but by 9th September Kett was imprisoned in the Tower of London. He was returned to his native county where he was drawn and hung at Norwich Castle on December 7th. His loyal brother William met the same grisly death reserved for traitors, although his hanging place was the wall of the great west tower of Wymondham Abbey. The symbolism of using two of the most imposing buildings of that time, one secular and one religious, would not have been lost on the local populations.[4]

The parish church and the community

What type of town community was it that witnessed the dramatic events of 1549? By the 16th century the manor had ceased to be the main administrative, economic and social unit of the nation and had been replaced by around 11,000 parishes of greatly varying sizes. This was the lowest link in an ecclesiastical chain of command that had at its apex the Pope in Rome itself. The interdependancy of the political structure with its religious counterpart was already well established, but the power and authority of the Church received an enormous boost with the Henrisian reformation. The break with Rome and the concommitant desire for power over a new and reliable Church of England was combined in the person of Thomas Cromwell who went on to instigate many measures in the religious life of the parish, many of which are evident today.

The parish priest was a focal point in the local community. It was through him that central government exercised control at the most basic level. The church wardens, overseers and other local officials worked closely with the priest who in turn was the lowest cog in the machine that ran up through the deanery, archdeaconry and the provincial diocese of the church structure. For the common people the priest represented an amalgam of forces. As a religious figure he was the image of a god whom they, almost without exception, both trusted and feared to guide them through their often short lives. At the same time the priest was also the representative of temporal power and of the King's law. With the monumental changes of the Reformation years from 1529 to 1536 these two powers became more closely linked as Henry VIII became head of both church and state.

Oak and iron bound almsbox from the interior of St Mary's church

The church of St Mary of Norman cruciform style. It was at one time listed as the Church of the Assumption

St Mary's Church

A church was built in the Norman Period and part of the lower tower remains today. The erection of the south chapel by Sir William Mortimer in 1297, sometimes known as Mortimer's Chapel but formerly called that of the Holy Cross, is the first documented source relating to the church although, as mentioned earlier, it probably occupies the site of a Saxon religious building. The church is dedicated to the Assumption of the Blessed Virgin and has a Collegiate form of structure. St Mary's also boasts a large square tower (that once had a spire), an equally impressive nave with aisles, and a porch to the south side of the church. The outward appearance of the church today differs !ittle in structure from how it would have appeared in the 16th century. By the standards of the time this was an imposing building designed to give the same impressions of authority and power to the common people that the Norman castles had done 400 years previously. The interior of the church is equally worthy of note, particularly the rood screen that shields the altar. The screen is the only one of its type in Norfolk. It stretches completely across nave and aisles, and is 52 feet long and 19 feet high. Built around 1475 by a member of the Ratcliffe family, it is without doubt worthy of its continual praise, and would have focused the attention of the congregation in the 16th century as it still does today.

The College

Another building in the town associated with this period is that often known as The College. The original building was erected by a descendant of Sir William Mortimer, namely Sir Robert de Mortimer. The College or Chantry began its life as a bequest in Sir Robert's will dated 1387 when he left 2,000 marks for the building which was to house a Master and a small number of monks. As his only son had died he also made his three daughters, now his heiresses, promise that each of their husbands would also contribute 1,000 marks to complete the building. The Master held his position for life and ensured that services were held regularly for the soul of Sir Robert and his wife. The building was erected a few hundred yards to the north-west of the churchyard.

Neither the church nor the college remained unscathed by the reformation.

From 1538 a bible was to be placed in every church, the priest was to preach at least once every four months and, most importantly for the local historian, a register of births, marriages and deaths was to be instituted and kept by the priest – one of the minority who could read and write. Few religious buildings escaped unscathed from the Reformation years. In 1540–41, with the monastic dissolution well under way, the chancel and nave to the east of the tower were destroyed by Robert Earl of Sussex. This section of the church was that used by the college begun by Sir Robert Mortimer. The marble memorial stones and brasses were removed from St Mary's and are supposed to have ended up decorating Sir Robert's manor house. The remnants of that building can still be seen on the exterior east wall of the tower of St Mary's prior to moving to the south-west of the churchyard. Apart from the painting out of many of the biblical scenes on the walls, the interior of the church remained undamaged as far as can be ascertained.

As for the separate college, the whole and its possessions were also granted to the Earl of Sussex, then holder of the manor of Attleborough Mortimer, and like the chapel received rough treatment.

The church and its associated institutions therefore played a significant part in the life of the community and continued to do so despite the ravages of the tumultuous years of the Henrisian reformation.

The Parish Registers

It is no longer fashionable in the school curriculum to dwell on the mid-Tudor and early Stuart periods of English history. But those of us who do may be fortunate to discover a variety of unexplored material to help us rebuild the history of this exciting period.

According to Volume XII of the Norfolk and Norwich Genealogical Society (1980) the deposit of the Attleborough registers was the largest and most complete transcript that they had received at that time. Indeed, Volume XII was by far the largest set of parish registers to have been published by the society and contains most of the information from the 24 folders of Attleborough records. Although substantial the registers are not quite complete. None survive from the earliest period, that is from 1538, but some exist from 1552 which is six years earlier than the Elizabethan instruction of 1558, that copying of registers onto stronger vellum rather than paper should begin with the registers from 1558. Some individual leaves for the 17th century are missing and four boxes of records were removed from the church in 1948 and did not survive their storage in a stable. Nevertheless, the rest of the material was painstakingly transcribed by Mr E W Sanderson and covers the church registers from 1552 through to the late 19th century.

The registers survive as follows:

Register 1:	Baptisms, marriages and deaths 1551 to 1652
Register 2:	Baptisms and marriages 1653 to 1698 Burials 1653 to 1696
Register 3:	Baptisms and burials 1683 to 1782 Marriages 1683 to 1753
Register 4:	Marriages 1754 to 1812
Register 5:	Baptisms and burials 1783 to 1812
Register 6:	Burials 1813 to 1847
Register 7:	Marriages 1813 to 1837
Register 8:	Baptisms 1813 to 1841

The Parochial Registers and Records Measure of 1978 governs the custody of parish registers and they can only be kept in the possession of the parish providing they have the necessary storage facilities. Economics dictate that most parish records are therefore stored in central archival repositories and it is in the Norwich Records Office that the original Attleborough registers may be consulted.[5]

The majority of registers of this type tend to be a straightforward chronological listing of the relevant information. For the period 1552 to 1613 the various rectors of the Greater and Lesser Parts of the parish kept to this pattern faithfully. There is, however, one outstanding set of Attleborough registers and they are for the period of the incumbency of John Forbie, from 1613 until 1638. As with any other rector, John Forbie noted down in careful detail each service that he was asked to perform, but in his case he also included in his registers a wide variety of 'jottings' and notations normally outside the traditional pattern of the village records. To those of us trying to rebuild a fragment of the town's past these jottings are an invaluable bonus, together with the statistical information contained in the registers.

Demographic Trends 1552-1613

The parish registers record 1,510 baptisms for this period. Taking into account that statistics for six years are missing, this gives an annual baptismal rate of very nearly 27. Naturally there are limitations as to how valuable this figure is and how accurate a reflection of the actual birth rate it is. The birth rate was certainly higher but infant mortality was also high and therefore many newborn children would not have survived to be baptised. Also, how common was baptism and therefore what percentage of the newborn population are we actually witnessing? The death rate for the same period can be estimated in terms of the 1,165 recorded burials which averages out over the 51 years of available material for 1551–1613 at 22 p.a.

On this evidence alone one could estimate a 6% growth rate for the population of the town. It is a well documented fact that a growing population was a feature of the period 1500 to 1600. Although geographically the rates vary, the national population may have risen by as much as 40%. The burden of poverty and the problems of vagrancy therefore increased substantially, placing reform of poor relief at the forefront of late Elizabethan legislation.[6]

Thatched Cottage, Connaught Road, of mid–16th century construction using timber, wattle and daub on a brick plinth (Courtesy Mr and Mrs J Smith)

Plague

The registers yield other information worthy of note. Plague was still as unpredictable in its frequency and ferocity in the 16th century as it had been throughout the medieval period. Poor harvests too could carry off large numbers but tended to have a longer term impact on population figures, which makes this latter interpretation of the following material unlikely. The average burial rate of 22 in Attleborough is punctuated by an exceedingly bad run in the years 1555–1559 when the annual average climbed to 55, and over 80 burials are recorded in 1555 alone. Without this five year period the actual annual burial rate would be reduced to around 19, further increasing the town's population. An even closer look reveals that the rector, John Williamson, recorded 14 burials in August and 19 in September 1555 alone, including the son and daughter of William Dayling, both daughters of Robert Burstone, and the wife and son of John Stephenson. Clearly some Attleborough families were decimated by the events of 1555, whatever their cause.

Also in 1555 we have evidence of what may be the first licensing of the Griffin public house in the town as recorded in the Patent Rolls:

'May 7th 1555. License for ten years to James de Venesia Pezalochia of the city of London, vintener, to keep a tavern or taverns for the sale of wine or retail or in gross in any county; with effect from Michaelmas following the Act Edward VI.'

'May 7th 1555. The like for ten years to Anne Gryffin of Atleburgh, Co.Norfolk, widow with the like effect.' (1&2 Philip & Mary Pt.14).

Although there is no mention of the event in the parish registers Attleborough, in common with many towns of the time suffered a 'great fire' in 1559. The extent of the blaze is unknown and no trace of it has yet been discovered. That it followed the years of high mortality which we have already examined must have increased the dismay of the townspeople.

Other entries, rare for their causes of death being noted down, come in December 1585, when William Ruggles was 'slayn in ye Parke with a pece of timber', and then, in 1605, when two girls fatally poisoned themselves, deliberately or not we cannot tell. In the same year Richard Deane cut his own throat. In 1607 we find that Henry Davy hanged himself, and in the same year Alice Freman murdered herself. Troubled times indeed, but perhaps the most striking feature of all the limited incidental information included in the burial registers prior to that of John Forbie is the incidence of 'strangers' in need of burial by the town rector.

Vagrancy

Unstable economic conditions, the increasing rate of enclosure and a rising population, without an increase in employment opportunities, caused Elizabethan England many problems.

Collectively called vagrants, tens of thousands of people moved from town to town in search of work or shelter. Often they did not make it to their destination but died on the way or sought permanent refuge in the large forests as robbers and the like. The problem of what to do with the poor and vagrants was not a new one. The 1391 Statute of Mortmain allowed certain tithes (a one tenth tax usually paid to the church) to be allocated to support the poor. But by 1494 attitudes had hardened and vagrants were to be whipped, lose their ears and even be hung. Henry VIII supported his own legislation of branding proven vagrants on the cheek, but punitive measures were not going to solve the problem as it existed in the late 16th century. In 1572 the first parish overseers were created and a rate was to be levied on each parish making them responsible for their own poor. These measures were not changed in any substantial way until the national reform of the Poor Laws by Lord Grey's Whig ministry of 1834.

In Norfolk evidence of the scale of the problem in late Tudor and early Stuart Norwich has been exhaustively researched by John Pound. In 1570 for example a census of over 2,300 poor men, women and children was carried out. Over 25% were over sixty and some in their eighties and nineties. The established myth is that few people lived to old age. However this Norwich material is not alone. Current archaeological excavations in London have shown that even our medieval ancestors could and often did live to an older age than we have come to believe.

There were also twice as many women as men and nearly 300 of those recorded had migrated to the city from other parts of Norfolk and Suffolk. Another 44 had arrived from as far away as Yorkshire and Lancashire.[7]

Although Attleborough has no equivalent census the registers do show a significant level of unattached and unknown people being buried in the town. Bearing in mind the location of Attleborough on the main road to Norwich it is reasonable to assume that many of these were migrating vagrants themselves, as entries for the second of our periods go on to show.

1613-1638

With the arrival of John Forbie as rector in 1613 for the Greater part and 1629 for the Lesser part (the parish having at one time been divided between the manorial units) the registers enter a new era of information for the researcher. To what end he added his own notes we can only speculate, but is it possible that here was a man recognising the potential use such records may have for posterity? As the Genealogical Society's introduction states 'his incumbancy is filled with jottings well outside the scope one expects to find in such a register.' For us these jottings provide an amazing insight into the personalities and experiences of an early 16th century town.

Like any new broom he began his ministry by reorganising his home, the parsonage:

'I altered the Kitchinge from three rooms into one; made the wyndowes & other rooms there. I built anew the butterie there out of the haul and so made chambers for servants where before the house had none. I built up the parlor, the chimnie, and stayer there; and all the wyndowes about the house. And glased all the wyndowes...I built up the p'ting wall next the Griiffen barnyard...All this cost about two hundred marke.' Johannes Forbie, 1614.

The life of the community and the influence of the church on it were indistinguishable. It is likely that Attleborough was no different from any other rural community of the Stuart period in its daily life and social structure. In stark contrast to the vagrancy examined earlier, the town was also blessed with men of property and wealth.

Easter 1628

'There was a new Cumunion Cupp made for the use of the Church before the old Cupp. So now there are two such cuppes & chalices for the use and Administracon of the Holy Sacrement and Comunion. Thomas Greene gave towards it of free guift 10s., Richard Hynds being sick 5s., Stephen Trapett a gift by his will 10s...'

1636

'There was given to the church of Atleburgh & for the devout use of the Comunion table there, the hie Alter by one Mrs Marie Greene wife of one William Greene there sonne of Gilbert Greene who had given to this church before a pulpit cloath & a flagon for the Comunion Wyne.'

Such charitable gifts to the church from the more wealthy citizens of the town show a depth of attachment and its significance in their daily lives. But charitable acts were not only directed at helping the church and although the person in the following example was not, as far as we can tell, a resident of Attleborough, he was buried there and therefore the works of Phillipp Coullier deserve mention in these pages.

December 24 1625

'Phillipp Coullier a yeoman Dwellinge in Wyndham of land & livinge about a hundred pownds a yeere died 1625. He was verie charitablie mynded and cloathed every yeere at Christmas longe before his death Twentie poore children with all things from the head to the foot: Meaning so (?) that he would cloath them all (?) inthe towne in (?) yeere: He did also feast them whom he did then cloath att the same Christmas: And brought them that daye to the Church and gave God all the thanks. There were certon poore houses burnt downe in a great fire in that towne: And he built them all upp agayne for the benefitt of the towne and poore.'

Within the pages of the registers kept by John Forbie it is possible to meet a number of his congregation. Some of them receive an emotional tribute from him in the pages of the burial registers.

In 1619 he was forced to bury one of his own daughters:
'Frances, my sweet child, and daughter of Mr John Forbie, Clerke and Parson of the Rectorie of the two p'ts of this Church was buried 23 January. Beinge of age one yeere & 3 quarters and was of much knowledge for her age.'

In April 1623 John Forbie officiated at the burial of Joane Allen:
'She died on Easter daye morninge about 3 a clock and so in a blessed tyme went as to meet Christ our Saviour risinge. There was a verie great Congregacon of people att her buriall. The Church could not contain nor receive them. Her husband bestowed (?) all the poore people that came which were very many and made a great banquett for all the others att the Signe of the Griffen which might content all.'

Death was never far away from any community in this period and this is further underlined when in January 1624 John Forbie has to bury his second daughter Ann:
'And so was the first fruit in Gods Kingdom in this yeere. She was two yeere old & about 14 weeks and was of much knowledge & forwardness & towardness for her age: And yt did uppon a vomitinge continueinge uppon her for about 12 howers together which could not be (?). There was such a general Agew in this beinge: but few died of yt: yett many young children died.'

One of the longest monologues written in respect of the burial of a member of the town's community came in 1630:
'Prudence eld dau of William Spoorle a virgine mayd of 23 yeers of age of comely feature & good behaviour and who had bene the good duid of her fathers house about 11 or 12 yeers he beinge a wyddower all that tyme. She was of much modestie, sobrietrie, myld and meek and gentle of speech, beloved by all: bot hautie minded, nor hie conceited of herself: not desiros to heare evil of anyone or speake it: of a faire affecon & (?) likinge to be att her owne house without any resortinge much into companie abroad. Decent (?) & comely in her Apparelinge herself but without pride. She was never idle but (?) workinge of somethinge for herself or her fathers house: And had so made upp for herselfe much good head lynnen & other varieties of Apparelinge. She might seeme thus to prepare to for many yeers and longe life, but she otherwise intende yt: for she desired uppon her deathto have much of her Aparell & lynninge to be bestowed amonge her fellow virgines in the towne (& such) had bene with her watchinge in her tyme of sickness & yt was so given amongst them as she appoynted. She seemed also in her life rather to expect death for she had a Box full of pennies & halfe pennies about 200 which she appoynted to be given att her buriall amonge the poore & were so bestowed & much more by her father, there beinge about 300 poore people att her buriall....She had a show of consumption & she fell sicke about the myd. of June ..unto the tyme of her death which was 7 weeks.'

This narrative on Prudence Spoorle goes on to describe in equal length a funeral at which her coffin was carried on the shoulders of her 'fellow virgines' and the route was strewn with 'herbes and flowers'. Clearly Prudence was held in great esteem by a large number of the townsfolk being 'an example of goodness in life & death for all others.'

There are also many references in the burial registers to some of the causes of death.

1616: 'John Mallett who by amyss (mistake) hanged himself in the Griffen Barne yard.'

1634: 'John Howes a younge man and hopefull hanged himself in his Barne.'

1635: 'Phillipp Harold early in a morninge was found in his owne yard drowned.'

Perhaps the most informative passage referring to the causes of death in the town comes early in the Spring of 1635 when what clearly seems to be a description of an outbreak of plague is written in the records. Like the year 1555, 1634 was equally disastrous for the town's population.

'In one yeere since Januarie 1634 all these died & many of them of a strange burninge Agew which made them senceless: And so died within 10 or 12 dayes: And yett more recovered, then died. Yt was expected to be infectios & so partly was: but many visited one another without danger.'

As well as these embellishments to the normal function of the registers as a statistical record, John Forbie also recorded what can only be described as news items during his ministry.

1615 '*...the 10th daye of June, Wymdham was burnt beinge sett on fyre by Rouges comynge on that purpose to the towne: & were there the man & the woman destroyed.' (Perhaps an instance of local rivalry between the young men of neighbouring villages?)*

1622 *'In the month of March in this yeere 1622 went forth the Royall and Noble Prince Charles with the Marques (billman) & sune after Duke of Buckingham unto Spayne with a few others accompaninge them in their journey by Land. And they returned agayne into England landed att Portsmouth the 5th of October 1623 beinge Sunday.'*

'In this yeere 1623 and month of November begane a Parliament. Wherin yt was agreed by the Kinge Maj'tie that any further Treaties for the match of the Prince with Spayne should be broken off. And warre declared for the restoringe of the Court Palatinate & his Heire to the Palatinate.'

'Kinge James our gratious, peacable and most learned Prince in all Europe died att Theobalds March 27 (1625) & this yeere havinge then reigned 22 yeers in England & 3 dayes.'

And lastly we have an early 16th century weather report:
1625 *'There had bene 2 or 3 winters before this yeere fludde of waters: But there was (in) this yeere in June on St.Barnabie even suche a fall of rayne & water that the like was not sene longe before: the waters were so deepe att (Gres..ine) bridge in this Comen by the Parke & in the Parke, that the Two bridges were carried awaye. And this somer continuinge a strange cold & wett somer, as the last was strange and drie somer.'*

Clearly the information that John Forbie chose to include in his Parish Registers is exceptional. Through their pages one is able to get to know some of the inhabitants of the town at that time far more intimately than would normally be possible from such a source. At the same time the material provides a valuable source of information concerning wealth and property, causes and attitudes to death, as well as developing topics normally beyond the reach of research.

Atleboro, Massachusetts, USA

Perhaps the final legacy of the registers of John Forbie worthy of mention in this chapter is that concerning early emigration to New England on the east coast of America.

That there was large scale migration to the new lands across the Atlantic Ocean is not in dispute. From East Anglia alone 'Norfolk', 'Norwich' and many other place-names reappear as towns and cities of New England. Many of them were founded by the adventurous settlers from various parts of England who made their way there during the early 16th century. Attleborough too has its opposite number to be found in the state of Massachusetts, although this one is named Atleboro.

In the Atleboro Public Library one can consult a book entitled 'A sketch of the History of Atleboro' by John Daggett which states on page 770:
'Atleboro derived its name without doubt from the town of Attleborough in Norfolk County, England. Some of our early inhabitants emigrated to this country from that region, settling at first in several different places, but finally a few of them are known to have come to Rehoboth, and, afterwards becoming interested in the purchase and settlement of this territory, there is every reason to suppose that when it became a town they selected and bestowed the name in remembrance of their native place...One Thomas Doggett came to this country from Attleborough, England, and he is supposed to be the brother of John, the first ancestor of the Daggetts of Massachusetts and Connecticut. A John Sutton with his wife and four children also came from that place.'

It is an interesting and stimulating thought that some of the same members of John Forbies congregation whom he knew well may have left the town and emigrated to the New World. Certainly he makes reference to such an event in 1639:
'John Adcocke, who had dwelt longe in this towne & for a discontent (as was thought) for a daughter whom he loved dearly that with her husband & children one Payne a man & would needs shipp him out with many others factious people into New England Anno 1639.'

As far as the registers can be used to identify which families may have emigrated there is no trace of any Thomas Doggett as mentioned in the earlier text. The task of identification in the Baptism records is made easier by the fact that Thomas Doggett was examined for a certificate to emigrate to New England in May 1637 at which time he was 30 years old. No Doggetts or Daggetts appear anywhere in the Parish records which must throw some considerable doubt on the veracity of the aforementioned book.

In the case of John Sutton, however, the situation is different. On 27th October 1629 John Forbie recorded the baptism of one Judith Sutton, daughter of John Sutton. There seems to be no trace of the other three children mentioned in the work by John Daggett nor for that matter any future mention of John or his family. It is therefore quite likely that this is the same John Sutton who emigrated to New England sometime in the 1630s.

The Developing Town 1678-1900

Within this period it is possible to identify a number of interesting developments concerned with the social and economic history of the town. The 18th century progressed at a quicker pace in terms of economic expansion and social change and in Attleborough this manifested itself in an enlarged infrastructure of services, wider employment and better communications.

Carriers and Turnpikes

Attleborough benefited from its location on an ancient arterial highway linking Norfolk to the rest of England. This route passed through the centre of the town and brought not only up-to-date news of events on horseback but also extra revenue from the coaches and their occupants. The Griffen Inn dates from the mid17th century and was enlarged during the 18th century. This timber-framed building with rendered brick walls and pantiled roof was a central part of the early 17th century life of the community. As transport increased its role became largely that of a coaching inn. As at other inns in the town, carriers (haulage contractors using wagons) made regular stops collecting passengers and a wide variety of goods for transportation throughout the county and, indeed, the country. That traffic was regularly using the Griffen Inn in the early 17th century is testified by the death of a much loved carrier to London, John Webster, who had frequently stopped at the Griffen. He carried 'people from Norwich to London' and his demise was recorded sorrowfully in the parish records.

The carriage entrance to the right of the Griffen still exists with a sitting room over the top and would have had stables, hay lofts and rooms in abundance for the travellers to and from Norwich. It was at the Griffen that a notorious fire broke out in 1762. By all accounts this could have been checked had the cries of a local boy been believed. The history of the Griffen Inn is an integral part of the heritage of the town and various landlords have recognised the importance of the building and tried to preserve its place in the community.

Not long after the fire it seems that the Market Cross in the centre of the town was pulled down and not replaced, unlike that at Wymondham which still survives as a most interesting and valuable reminder of the function of the market place in the local community.

Along with the need for a coaching inn went that for a good roadway. Prior to the widespread use of tarmacadam, rural stretches of road were often muddy and rutted and virtually impassable at certain times of the year. It is not surprising therefore that in 1675 what may well be the first of the Turnpike roads was built between Attleborough and Wymondham. A gift of £200 was given by Sir Edward Riches (born at Thetford in 1594 and a member of the legal profession) for the repair and upkeep of the road. This was noted by Act of Parliament (7th and 8th, William and Mary). This generous deed was commemorated by a square stone pillar situated on the main road near the town

The pillar was renovated in 1888 and inscribed:

'This pillar was erected by the order of the session of the Peace of Norfolk as a gratefull rememberance of the charity of Sir. Edwin Rich, Kt. who freely gave ye sume of Two Hundred pounds towards ye repair of ye highway between Wymondham and Attleburgh, A.D.1675. (Edwin Rich mentioned on the pillar is taken to be the Edward Riches named in contemporary documents).

The pillar erected to Sir Edwin Rich, dated 1675, located on the Norwich side of the old A11 trunk road.

Noverint universi per presentes nos Margaretam Nerford [illegible] vid. [illegible] Margaretam Nerford et [illegible] Nerford [illegible] Attleburgh in Comitat Norff [illegible] teneri et firmiter obligari Venerabili viro Henrico [illegible] Legum Doctori [illegible] Archidiaconatus Norff officiali [illegible] in [illegible] bone et legalis monete Anglie solvend eidem [illegible] aut suo certo attornato executoribus administratoribus vel assignatis suis ad quam quidem solucionem bene et fideliter faciend obligamus nos [illegible] heredes executores et administratores nostros firmiter per presentes sigillis nostris sigillat Dat [illegible] die mensis July Anno Regni Domini nostri Caroli Secundi nunc Regis Anglie &c [illegible] Anno Domini 1683

The condicion of this obligation is such that whereas Henry Nerford late of Attleburgh Clark being in good & perfect minde & memory did make & declare his last will & testament [illegible] in writing & of the same did make & appoint William Heath his kinsman sole executor who hath come before his ordinary & voluntarily & expressed refused to take upon him the execution of the same will And whereas therefore the Administration of all & singular the goods rights credits & chattles with the will annexed of the said Henry Nerford deceased is committed and granted unto the within bounden Margaret Nerford widdow legatarie now that the sd Margaret Nerford doe make or cause to be made a true & perfect Inventory of all & singular the goods rights credits & chattles of the said deceased & the same soe made doe exhibit or cause to be exhibited into the office of Registry kept for the Archdeaconry of Norff upon or before the first day of August 1683 And alsoe y said Margaret Nerford widdow well & truly paie or cause to be paid all such debts as the said deceased ought at the time of his death & all & singular such guifts legacies and bequests as are given & bequeathed in the last will & testament of the said deceased at such dayes time or times to such person or persons as are specified named & declared in the same will according to the true meaning thereof so farr as the said goods will reach & extend And alsoe doe well & truly [illegible] the last will & testament of the said deceased according to the true intent & meaning of y said testator And further that the said Margaret Nerford widow doe make & yeeld up a just true & perfect account of in & upon the said goods & administration when she shall be thereunto lawfully called then this obligation to be void or else to be in force &c

Signum [illegible]

Margaret Nerford

Sealed & Delivered in y presence of
Wm. [illegible]
Will: Heath
Will: Jarvis

Margaret Nerford

[illegible] Nerford

Educational Charity and Bequests to the Poor 1678-1760

The ministry of the Rev Henry Nerford was probably as varied as that of his predecessor, yet the parish records kept by him revert to the normal statistical pattern. This does not mean that the Rev Nerford is left out of the story of the town. In his will of December 1678 he bequeathed in trust a total of eight acres of land in Baconsthorpe Street (no longer in existence but probably lead out of the town to the north). The profits of farming this land were to be paid twice yearly at Lady Day and Michaelmas to a schoolmaster, who was to be a University graduate, in return for the teaching of grammar, reading and writing to six poor children of the town without any charge. At a time when even the most elementary forms of education were scarce, save that given by the Rector himself, this would have been of considerable help to a small number of children.

His was not the only charitable bequest to the poor. Andrew Reeder left two acres of land in his will of 1655, the income from which was to be distributed annually to the eight most aged, impotent and poor people every first Sunday in Lent. In 1845 it came to about £6. Also, in 1760, Sir Francis Bickly left the College Close of some five acres to the relief of the poor each Christmas; the rent from this bequest amounting to £8 by 1845.

Architectural remains

Evidence about how the shape and structure of the town developed during the 18th and 19th centuries can be assessed through the town's buildings.

Thanks to Section 54 of the Town and Country Planning Act of 1971 lists of buildings of special architectural or historic interest have been compiled. In the case of Attleborough this listing illustrates many whole or parts of buildings that were constructed from the mid–11th century church up to the end of the 19th century.

The land immediately surrounding the churchyard was the common building area, and especially that situated

A basic town plan showing the location of some of the buildings of architectural and historical importance.

11th century
1. St Mary's church

16th century
2. Attleborough Hall
3. Thatched Cottage

17th century
4. Griffin Hotel
5. Cyprus House (c1700)
6. The Crown PH

18th century
7. Two cottages (late 18th century)
8. King's Antiques
9. Bush Antiques
10. White House
11. The Doric

19th century
12. Attleborough Lodge (c1840)
13. Baptist Chapel (c1841)
14. Ironmongers
15. Bank Cottage
16. The Corn Hall (c 1860)
17. Site of Wesleyan Chapel

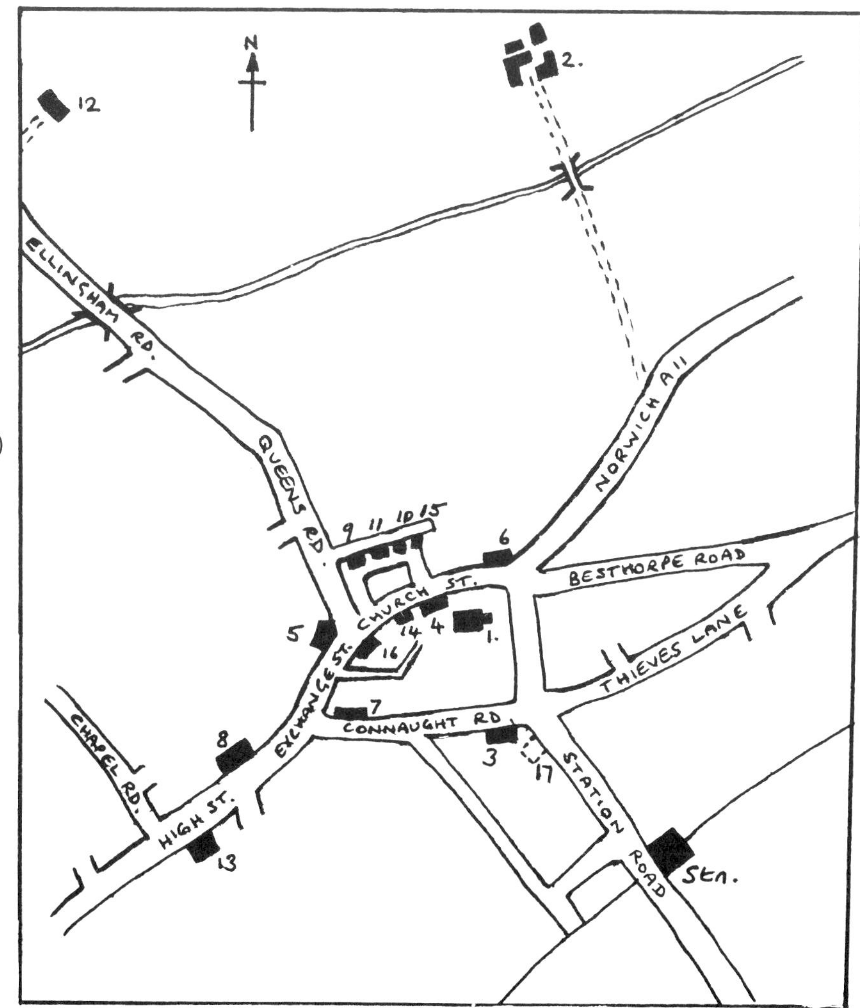

The will of Rev Henry Nerford, signed and sealed by Margarat, Margaret and Sarah Nerford. Note the three different styles in the writing of 'Nerford' (Norfolk Record Office) (left).

The Crimean War Memorial, at the junction of Connaught and Station Roads, complete with lamp holders

to the north of the church where the main road ran. By the mid–19th century Attleborough could boast a wide selection of buildings that enriched the visible heritage of the town. To the 11th century church had been added the 12th century College House. To the north of the town much of the site of the manor of Attleborough Mortimer had been built in the 16th century and this was joined in the same period by the large thatched cottage built to the south of the church. Victorian period buildings were added to this 17th and 18th century selection, and a variety of styles are apparent today.

Inevitably there have been casualties. Of the 19th century Wesleyan Chapel on Station Road there is no trace. A more tragic and recent example was the 1972 demolition of College House, to make way for part of the town centre development programme.[8] That this site was of enormous importance to the heritage of the town is not in doubt, but the fact that it also occupied an area of high land value stood against it when development plans were drawn up.

Perhaps the major phase of town centre redevelopment came in the late 1980s. Demolition erased buildings that belonged to the heritage of the town in order to provide more and better facilities for the inhabitants. Thankfully, as was pointed out by local historian Mr Eustace Partridge in 1989, their replacements have been tastefully designed to blend with what is a rich mixture of building styles.[9]

The prejudices and procedures of planners are quite often a mystery to the mortal who simply has to rely on common sense for his reaction to a new building. Let us hope that contemporary planners consider not just the present but the future and preserve the visible remains of the town's heritage even though it may well prevent 'progress'.

Apart from buildings Attleborough also has a number of other interesting items worthy of note. A good example is the monument that stands at the junction of Station Road and Connaught Road, dedicated to the battles of the Crimean War (1852–1855). A costly, and at times embarassing conflict, it is rare to find in any town a monument dedicated to this war. Standing well over 15 feet in height, it was lucky to survive being hit in 1983 by one of the thousands of cars that passed it every day. It has been restored more than once and bears on its four sides the names of famous battles associated with the Crimea – Balaclava, Inkerman, Alma and Sebastopol – together with the inscription 'Peace 1856'.

The acorn-crowned water pump on Queens Square, complete with inscribed stone tablet recording its erection in celebration of Queen Victoria's jubilee

The most noticeable monument in town is the water pump which, together with Queen's Square itself, was erected in celebration of Queen Victoria's Diamond Jubilee in 1897. At one time it would have been vital to the community, before there was piped water. It is really a 'tree pump', carved from a single tree trunk that has been bored through and clamped around with iron brackets or 'dogs'. Older residents used to claim that water from the pump was far purer than any other. Topped by an acorn motif it still stands, though it has not been used since the 1930s.

The Poor and Poor Law Relief

The Poor Laws introduced in the Elizabethan period to try to control the depths and extent of poverty rested on the basis that each parish was responsible for the maintenance of its own poor. Through a method often known as 'outdoor relief' ratepayers in each parish were further taxed to provide a small payment to the poor. Definitions of who was poor and unemployed were vague, and the sick, elderly and lazy were all grouped together as in need of poor relief. It is not surprising therefore that the poor law was not only inefficient but also out of control by the time the national population had reached over ten million by the 1830s. The reforms of the 1834 Poor Law Amendment Act were therefore far reaching. At the time they were welcomed by the ratepayers but hated by the genuinely unemployed. In essence parishes were to group together into Unions and provide a workhouse which was to be the only place where 'relief' could be received. With outdoor relief abolished conditions inside the workhouses were deliberately made unpleasant to discourage attendance. Twelve parishes were joined in the Wayland Union, namely; Attleborough, Besthorpe, Great Ellingham, Hargham, Hockham, Illington, Larling, Roudham, Rockland All Saints, Rockland St Andrew, Shropham and Snetterton.

At the 1841 census there was a total of 36 persons listed as residing in the workhouse which, according to White's Directory, was at Rockland All Saints, although what is now the Wayland Hospital is still the old workhouse to many of the older residents of Attleborough who can remember the poor walking through the streets up to this building in the 1930's.

After a potted history of the town White goes on to tell us that a Baptist Chapel was built in 1833 at a cost of £1,000, together with a Wesleyan Chapel in the same year (below). No trace of the Wesleyan Chapel remains as it was demolished to make way for a doctor's surgery, which in its turn has also been demolished! However, it is possible to see the appearance of the chapel in the form of an old postcard.

The year 1841 not only heralded the second prime ministerial period of Sir Robert Peel at the head of the newly recognised Conservative Party, but also the founding of the first National School in Attleborough. At a cost of £700 about 70 boys and 80 girls attended and would therefore hopefully, as far as the National Society were concerned, not fall into the hands of the non-conformists. The non-conformists provided their own schools for the education of the poor through the British and Foreign Bible Society. The National School also reaped the benefit of the proceeds of the Nerford land which by 1845 had grown to 10 acres and the rents of which were directed to the support of the school.

The Wesleyan Chapel on Station Road, now demolished

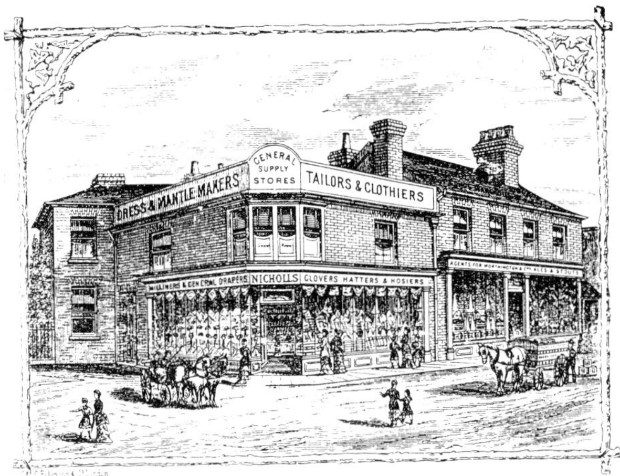

A late 19th century engraving of Nicholls drapers, next to an off-licence of unknown identity, both in Exchange Street

The Town, its Trades and Occupations, c1845-1900

In 1845 William White published his 'History, Gazetteer, and Directory of Norfolk'. By analysing the individual Hundreds, Parishes and Boroughs he provides the researcher with a most accurate and valuable primary source. Much of what he says is reproduced elsewhere, notably in that other 19th century masterpiece of statistical and historical research, Blomefield's 'History of Norfolk'.

Attleborough came under the administrative auspices of the Shropham Hundred, which in turn derived its importance from the manorial influence of the castle of Old Buckenham. On page 410 of White's survey we find that the 'improving town of Attleborough' heads the breakdown of the 21 parishes that went to make up this Hundred.

The Corn Exchange, later a cinema, now an electrical warehouse for A W Myhill & Son, in Exchange Street

The first national census of 1801 listed the population of Attleborough as 1,333. By 1845 Attleborough certainly dominated the surrounding parishes with a population of very nearly 2,000 and an acreage of some 5,200 and was a growing centre of trade and commerce. Attleborough had held the right to hold a market and fair since the 16th century. What is now known as Queen's Square was at one time 'market hill' and in all likelihood the place where travelling fairs and the exchange of goods took place.

By the 19th century local trade had grown to the extent that a Corn Exchange was built in 1863 in the High Street. Built in the neo-classical style so typical of many public buildings in the Victorian period, it was owned by a company of local farmers and run by an employed agent. The grain would be graded, priced and displayed for purchase and then dispatched to breweries, bakeries and the like. Over the doorway to what is now a warehousing unit for Myhills Electricals, can still be seen the sheaves of corn that symbolised its original role. A chequered career was to follow, more of which will be revealed in a later chapter.

With the advent of the census it becomes possible for the local historian to identify, albeit quite crudely, the extent and type of occupations in the local community. Misleading generalisations are commonplace as occupations are often grouped together and tradesmen commonly offered a range of services. Nevertheless, this can be a guide to the wealth of a community and also, to a certain degree, the range of services available, especially when compared to other similar communities.

In the personal research provided by William White in 1845 one can feel more confident of a realistic impression of the extent of services in the town at this time.

Occupation	No. evident in 1845
Auctioneer	2
Academies (teachers)	6
Attorneys	5
Bakers	3
Blacksmiths	3
Boot and Shoe makers	6
Butchers	4
Corn Millers	3
Farmers	33
Grocers and Drapers	4
Joiners	2
Plumbers, Painters, Glaziers	2
Saddlers	2
Surgeons	2
Tailors	4
Watchmakers	2

These figures support the fact that the town was at the centre of a rural community farming the majority of the

5,247 acres attributed by White as belonging to the Attleborough parish. The total annual value of this landholding he estimated at £9,604. Trade in agricultural produce at the Corn Hall would have provided a regular influx of custom, confirming Attleborough's market town status in the 19th century.

Corn milling, baking and smithying would also have owed their existence largely to farming. It is important to note that the figures quoted in White, although they are supported by the names of those involved in the professions, are likely to be those of employers only; the actual number of people would have been larger. In support of the labour force it was essential to have enough inns or taverns, and Attleborough did not fail its inhabitants in this respect.

Apart from The Griffen, which has to be by far the oldest hostelry in the town, Attleborough in 1845 boasted:

The Angel licensed by James Lovick
The Bear licensed by Robert Ebbage
The Cock licensed by Samuel Peck
The Crown licensed by William Green
The White Horse licensed by William Gayford

Of these The Griffen, The Bear and The Cock still ply their trade, complemented by the London Tavern and Royal Hotel. The Crown was closed after a long career as both a tavern and depot for carriers to Norwich and Thetford. It was sold to Norfolk County Council for use as a Youth Centre in 1972. The Angel, virtually opposite the Griffen in Church Street, grew into a popular hotel. This was especially the case on market days in the late 19th century. After standing derelict for some time it was converted into a building society branch in the 1980s.

The Norwich to Brandon Railway

Part of the White survey of Attleborough mentions communication services available at that time. The Post Office was at a Mr Samuel Caley's and mail left the town for London at 6.30 in the evening and for Norwich at 7.30 each morning. There were also mail carts travelling to Hingham, Buckenham and other villages at 9.00 each morning. This quite extensive system of postal communication was supported by a string of 'Coaches, Vans &c.' which left for Norwich, London, Thetford and Cambridge. William White expected that these would soon be put out of business by the arrival of the railway in the summer of 1845. The railway certainly provided another option for employment and increased the service that Attleborough provided for the surrounding communities. In 1896 the building of the Gaymers cider-making plant, just to the south of the railway, was another opportunity for the employment prospects of the local labour force and Gaymers soon became established as the largest employer in the town. Prior to this Gaymers had been making cider at their plant in Banham since at least the 1700s, and in all likelihood much earlier than that. The building of the factory began a new era in security of employment for men and women of the town, still the case today.

The Griffin Hotel – Mid 17th century and 18th century timber framed, brick and rendered with pantile roof in a T-plan. Note the carriage entrance to the right.

Patriotism, Pride and Sacrifice 1900-1918

Apart from finding work locally in agriculture or a trade there were few exciting careers open to the young energetic men typical of any community. For some the lure of the life serving Queen and Country was very attractive. The Victorian British Empire already had a number of young Attleborough men in uniform before the world conflagration that began in 1914.

Yet again Attleborough is fortunate to have a chronicler from whom the historian can draw detailed information that would otherwise have been lost. In this instance it is a book written after 1918 by Major J H Kennedy, a local recruiting officer and resident of the town. His work in producing a comprehensive memorial to the sacrifices made in the Great War is of enormous value.[10]

One of the most useful sections of Major Kennedy's book tells of the previous service of all those who fought and not, as is so often the case, just those who were killed in action. From this we can deduce, quite surprisingly in fact, that a number of men from the town were serving with the Royal Navy well before 1914.

Frederick Beck (Petty Officer) first enlisted 4/4/1894, served on board HMS Sandfly (later killed in action).

Arthur Blaxhall (Able Seaman) enlisted 10/10/1877, served RNR (Discharged 1915).

Albert G Clarke (Chief Steward) enlisted 1906, served on board HMS Baccante, Lancaster, Essex, Lord Nelson and many more.

It was, however, the Norfolk Regiment that was the natural destination for any local lad aiming to join the forces. Here again a surprising number of young Attleborough men were already serving with the colours as regular soldiers well before the Great War began. Some had seen action in South Africa during the Boer Wars (1899–1901), for example:

Sergeant Major Benjamin Dickerson who had enlisted in the 2/4th Norfolks in 1891 and served in South Africa as part of his total of 21 years service that ended with his demobilisation in 1917. Another townsman who served in action against the Boers and survived was Private Thomas Fincham who enlisted in the 1st Yorkshires and was posted straight away to South Africa.

The Royal Visit, October 1909

As if to stimulate and monitor the level of patriotic feeling present in the country, King Edward VII paid a brief visit to Attleborough on October 25th 1909. The population swelled on that day when thousands turned out to see the King. According to contemporary newspaper reports the King was visiting the Earl of Albermarle at his home at Quidenham and decided to pay an unofficial visit to Attleborough. The King was photographed walking calmly through the streets and onto Queen's Square in suit and bowler hat. He stayed with the Earl and Countess for one night and then travelled to Norwich where he made the first royal visit to that city since Charles II in 1671.

Looking north-east along Church Street c1910, showing the Angel Hotel to the left and the Griffin Inn to the right

June to August, 1914

Many writers have recorded how the summer of 1914 was hot and somewhat sultry. Attleborough went about its normal routine with great activity as the Gaymers cider factory dealt with the fruits of summer. At the end of July many of the townspeople prepared for their annual Bank Holiday trips, perhaps to friends or to the coast at Yarmouth. Some of the better read residents of the town may have remembered that June 28th had been the day that the heir to the throne of the Austro-Hungarian Empire, Archduke Franz Ferdinand, had been assassinated, along with his wife Sophie, in the obscure capital of Bosnia, a small nation situated in the Balkans. Not that this event seemed to have any relevance to the holidays about to begin in Attleborough in England. That is until a meeting was held on Queen's Square in the centre of the town on July 31st – over a month after the assassination.

As the meeting in Attleborough finished listening to the first speaker, on the Irish situation, another mounted the platform to announce that he wondered if the towns-people were aware that at any moment Europe could be plunged into war. After an explanation of the unfolding of events since June 28th and the realisation that Germany was about to declare war on both France and Russia in defence of Austria, the gravity of the situation became apparent. Within five days Germany had carried out those threatened actions and also invaded Belgium as part of the famous Schlieffen plan designed to eliminate France within six weeks. Therefore, on August 4th, Britain, acting to uphold her 1839 Treaty committment to Belgium, had to declare war on Germany.

The Initial Response to War

Although one can be sure that reactions to the fact that Britain was at war with Germany varied within the town, the overriding sentiment was one of patriotic pride. There was no shortage of volunteers ready to leave work and families to join up before it was all over. Indeed there were already over 30 men from the town serving in the pre1914 armed forces.

Between August 1914 and January 1915, 145 men from the town enlisted for active service. Some men re-enlisted, such as Sgt Major Benjamin Dickerson and Private P J Forster. Private Forster had already served with the colours for 11 years and yet re-enlisted on 5th August 1914 clearly he allowed little discussion with his family over this issue.

Within a few weeks Private Forster was fighting on the river Aisne in Flanders as part of a hard-pressed British Expeditionary Force that was desperately trying to check the massive German advance through Belgium. Eight weeks into the war and Private Forster had been seriously wounded in the heavy fighting as the BEF was pushed steadily back to the Marne. The fall of Paris seemed close. Private Forster was one of the first men to be returned to England to receive treatment for his wounds, and tragically he was also one of the first to die of his wounds in this country, as a contemporary newspaper report tells:

A HERO OF THE 1st NORFOLKS
ATTLEBOROUGH MAN'S FUNERAL
Military Honours At Brighton

'The funeral of Private Philip James Forster, of the 1st Norfolk Regiment, who died at the 2nd Eastern General Hospital, Brighton, last Thursday from wounds received during the fierce fighting at the Aisne, took place with full military honours at the Extra Mural Cemetery, Brighton, on Monday.

The deceased soldier had only arrived home with 130 wounded the previous Monday, and he was constantly visited by a Norfolk lady living in Brighton. He was suffering from a bullet wound in the eye, that had caused a slight fracture of the skull, and although an operation was performed, he succumbed to his injuries on the Thursday. He was one of the four soldier sons of Mrs Forster, of Miller's Square, Attleborough, who received the news of Private Forster's serious condition exactly seven weeks from the day she said good bye to him when the regiment left Norwich to join the First Expeditionary Force bound for the seat of war.

The funeral was solemnised in conjunction with that of a comrade in arms of the Highland Light Infantry and was a very impressive event. The bodies of the two soldiers were conveyed on gun carriages drawn by a gun team supplied by the Cadet Battalion of the St Peter's and St Nicholas Church Lads Brigade. The bearers were drawn from the Ambulance Corps of the RAMC under the command of Major Booth CC who, with Lt Walker and Lt Ross, marched in the long procession to the cemetery. The Band of the Royal Field Artillery (T) headed the cortege, and performed Chopin's "Funeral March" and Handel's "Death March from Saul". Thousands of sympathetic spectators gathered all along the route from the hospital to the cemetery, where the Rev.Canon Hoskyns, Vicar of Brighton, performed the last sad rite, and the two soldiers were buried side by side. As the coffins, of polished elm, with handsome brass fittings were lowered into their last resting place a firing party of the 6th Cyclist Battalion, Royal Sussex Regiment (Hove), fired the farewell volleys over the grave, and the "Last Post" was sounded by Bugler Virgo, RAMC.

The chief mourners at Private Forster's funeral were his mother, four sisters, and two brothers, his nephew, Mr Fred Halstead, and his brother in law, Mr Fred Smith. Lovely floral tributes were sent by his mother and sorrowing family, and from members of the Parkinsville Club, Belton, Durham, while Mr and Mrs Russell Coggs, late of Watton sent a wreath inscribed "In memory of a brave East Anglian." '[11]

The death of Private Forster was the first of many that the town of Attleborough was to experience. By November 1918 a total of 96 men from Attleborough were to be posted as killed or missing in action, including Private Sydney Percy Forster and Private Charles Forster, brothers of the aforementioned Philip.

The August 1914 volunteers from Attleborough, with Sgt Dickerson on the right, lined up on the Station platform prior to embarking for Norwich. (Courtesy Mrs K Norman)

The town's recruiting office was opened on August 12th with the aim of attracting as many young men to the colours as possible. The regular British Army of the time was small and supplemented by Territorial (reserve) units most of whom were immediately posted to France. The majority of Attleborough men would be trained for Lord Kitchener's new army that was hastily being constructed. As a result many would not see fighting until well into 1915 or, fatally for some, until 1916 when they would be thrown into the battles of the Somme.

The leaving of the largest group of Attleborough men was recorded by the local press and they received a salutory send off by Mr William Gaymer, the town's largest employer, from Attleborough station.

What inspired these young men to volunteer so readily is perhaps not so difficult for us to understand today. One only has to remember the emotions stirred by the Falklands conflict in 1982 to see that valour is often a foolhardy sentiment, blind to the realities of war. The catalogue of slaughter and survival of all the Attleborough men that served is recorded for posterity in Major Kennedy's book, which is therefore a rare piece of contemporary research for which future generations can be grateful.

The Town at War

The Auxiliary Hospital

The first flushes of excitement and fear within the town were translated into action very quickly. On August 8th the Town Hall was lent, free of charge, as a temporary hospital. It was expected that casualties would arrive any day and it was the ladies of the local Red Cross Society, founded in Attleborough in 1911, that made the first preparations and staffed the 16-bed Auxiliary Hospital. It was not until November that the first wounded arrived after a long journey from Flanders via London and the Norfolk and Norwich Hospital. The Hospital developed into the focus of the town's main wartime experience. Most of the soldiers came from units with no connections with Norfolk, but for the home community these sick and wounded represented what little they knew of the western front. The hospital regularly received supplies of locally donated vegetables, cakes, tobacco and even the odd brace of pheasants.

In June 1915 the Hospital was enlarged to 22 beds and around it grew an active social life. The Christmas of 1914–15, the one that the war was supposed to be over by, saw a carol service held for the troops at the hospital. In August 1915 the staff and patients were joined by similar auxiliary hospitals in the area in a sports afternoon held in the grounds of Old Buckenham Hall. Patients came and went, some cured and some unfortunately not, but the dedication of the local ladies who administered and cared for the hospital remained until April 1917 when the War Office opened the Wayland Infirmary, two miles north of the town. This had over 100 beds and the auxiliary hospital was no longer needed and was closed in November 1917. In the three years that it had functioned it had treated 656 patients and provided a valuable place of convalescence, and three of the staff had been mentioned in dispatches. The population of the town had also contributed financially to its upkeep by donating a total of £782.6s3d It was Mrs Kennedy, wife of the Major, who as Commandant received the news of closure with sadness and frustration, especially as the excuse given was that the existing building was not 'structurally suitable for a hospital'. The fact that it stood up for many years after gave lie to this. By April 1919 the Wayland Infirmary had treated 997 further casualties of war, a testament to the consistently high casualty lists in the later part of the war.

Recruiting

There were many other ways in which the town tried to contribute to the war effort. Invasion was always talked about, especially after the rumour that the Kaiser planned to make Norwich his headquarters if he succeeded in landing on the east coast. Major Kennedy tells us that he had a force of 35 men ready within days of the outbreak of war. These men busied themselves guarding roads at night and checking telegraph wires for sabotage.

In 1915 Norfolk was divided into sections for recruiting purposes and Attleborough became the Headquarters of the largest of these. Major Kennedy was appointed Recruiting Officer for this district and used his home, Attleborough Lodge, about a mile to the north of the town as his recruiting office until the Autumn of 1916, when a new ministerial department was set up, to be known as the Ministry of National Service. The War Office had lost its commander, Lord Kitchener, who was drowned on board the torpedoed HMS Hampshire in June 1916, and a lot of credibility, as the enormous losses on the Somme filtered through to the families at home. Major Kennedy now moved his office to the Royal Hotel and staffed it with 27 clerks. The drain on manpower by this date had been heavy. The introduction of the Compulsory Service Bill and the Military Service Act were attempts to call up even more than the 5,041,000 already recruited. By late 1916 all men between the ages of 18 and 41 were called up. Attleborough, with a pre-war population of 2,500, had seen 400 men leave to fight and it is difficult to imagine where more could come from, but find them they did. The Johnson Brothers printing firm which backed onto the Drill Hall had to close when all its employees were called up.

The casualty list had grown lengthy for Attleborough even before the battle of the Somme began on July 1st 1916. The BEF had ceased to exist as 95% were dead, wounded or missing by mid-1915. Along with Pte Forster, Sgt Fisher of the 1st Northamptonshire Regt had been wounded on the Aisne. Pte F E Crummett of the 7th Norfolks was killed in October 1915 when Attleborough men found themselves fighting in the hell hole that was Gallipoli. War Office telegrams went out to the families of Sgt John Dye and Pte Albert Shaw, both killed in action at Gallipoli on 12th August. Only three days later another Attleborough man, Pte Charles Lincoln, was drowned when HMS Royal Edward sank in the Dardanelles. Pte Albert Shaw's brother, Robert, was also killed at Gallipoli three weeks later on September 7th while serving with the 4th Norfolks – they had both enlisted on the same day on August 15th 1914. It was not uncommon for families to be seen crying in the street. These scenes are hard for us to imagine today but one can only feel great pity for mothers such as Mrs Forster who saw three of her sons march off to war only to have three War Office telegrams delivered to her door.

Towards the End

1916 was not only important for the wholesale slaughter of the Somme battles led by Field Marshall Haig, but also because it heralded the arrival of what came to be known as 'total war'. A Zeppelin roaming the skies above East Anglia was admittedly a rare but nonetheless frightening sight. As early as December 1915 a lighting order had been issued restricting the traffic of vehicles on the roads at night unless they had both a pass and shaded lamps. January 1916 saw Swaffham bombed, and also Dereham where five people were killed. On May 31st a Zeppelin arrived over Attleborough, dropped its bombs in fields and left without causing any casualties. This was the first but not the last recorded bombing of the town.

In other ways too the town came ever closer to the realities of war. During 1917 severe shortages of flour, sugar and many other foodstuffs heightened the desire to get the war over with. The strain on the morale and patriotic spirit of the community clearly comes through in the pages of Major Kennedy's book. With the introduction of rationing in August 1917 came the beginning of hoarding and the black market although, not surprisingly, there are few details to relate here.

There were those whose resolve was not so easily dented. The collection and passing of clothing and smaller items useful in the hospitals and front lines was organised through the Norwich War Hospital Supply Depot and from Attleborough came a total of 18,434 items collected by the ladies of the Attleborough branch.

By 1918 the war had to end. The supply of manpower was not inexhaustable. Gaymer's Cider works had provided 105 men, and women were now tending the equipment. Although the war struggled on as though it did not want to finish until the last possible moment, when the end did come events unfolded quickly. Although Major Kennedy's impression from afar of the German Army as being 'utterly vanquished and hopelessly disorganised' betrays an acute lack of understanding of the realities of their defeat, it was nevertheless what he and every other citizen hoped was the truth.

The last Attleborough man to be killed in the Great War was Pte H R Rudd who was killed by an explosion on the western front one week before the fighting ended on November 11th 1918. Two more men were to die later, one of his wounds and the other in Turkish captivity.

Demobilisation of the armed forces was to be a lengthy process and it was many months before the last men returned to their families. For Attleborough the reality was that the town had provided 550 men and 11 women to the war effort (one fifth of the total population) and of these 96 were listed as killed or missing in action. If records of bravery are measured in terms of medals for gallantry then Attleborough can feel proud that its offspring served their country well. A total of 9 Military Medals and 4 Military Crosses were awarded to men from the town, including posthumous awards to Pte H Stephenson, who died of wounds in April 1917, and Cpl W Sturman, who died a prisoner of war ten days before the war ended.

It was to take many years before the full horrors of the Great War became known and accepted. The cost in terms of human lives was so unimaginable. Many men were never to return to their home soil but end up buried 'in some corner of a foreign field'. The dead of Attleborough were no exception and as in thousands of communities the length and breadth of England there was a deep sense of loss that was to be almost impossible to overcome as the millions of bereaved families would very likely never see the graves of their loved ones. With the unveiling of the focus of national mourning, the Cenotaph in Whitehall, came the realisation that it was not enough and so a myriad of village, town and city memorials were erected to give each community a more accessible focus for their grief. In Attleborough the town memorial was dedicated amidst a huge gathering on June 27th 1920. Gaymers Cider placed their own plaque to the eight men from their works who never returned. The town memorial contains the names of a lost generation whose sacrifice cut short their contribution to the development of their community.

A view along Queens Road, looking towards the War Memorial (above)

The June 1920 dedication of the town War Memorial (below)

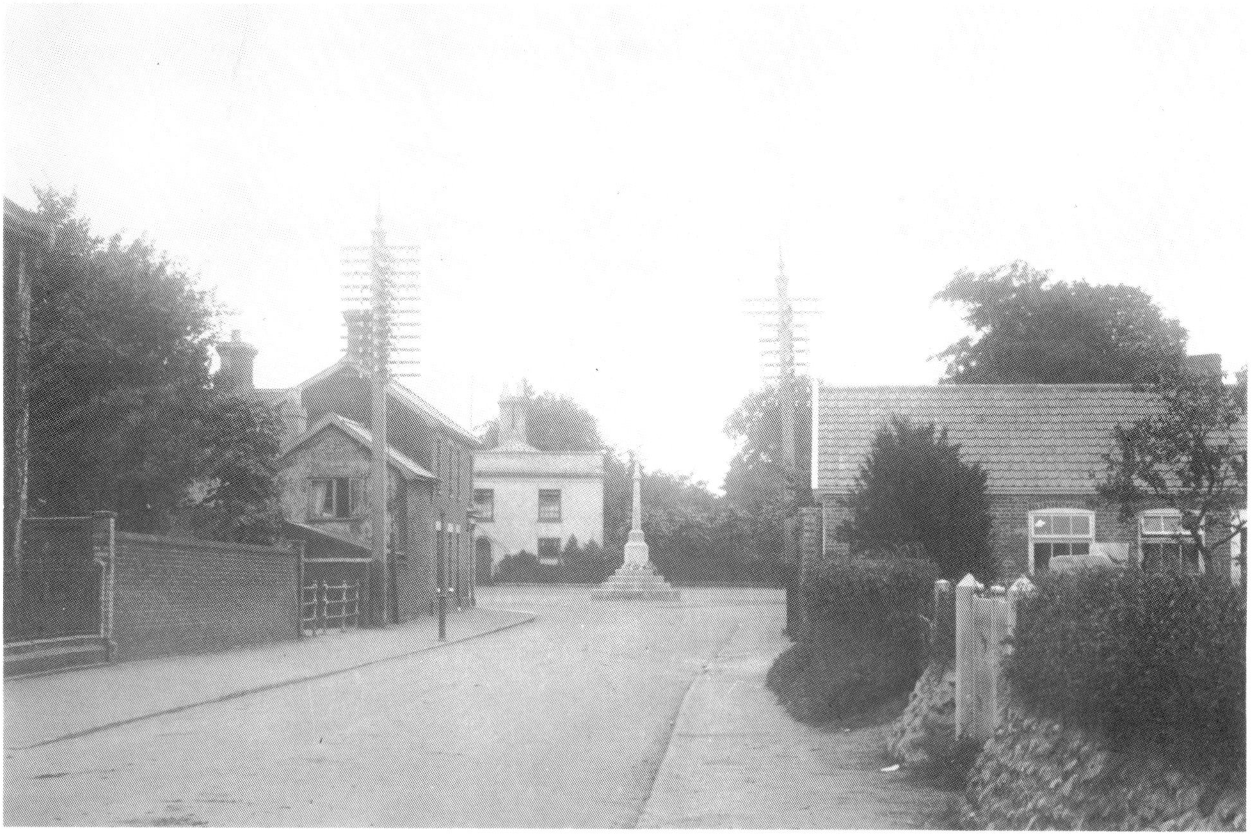

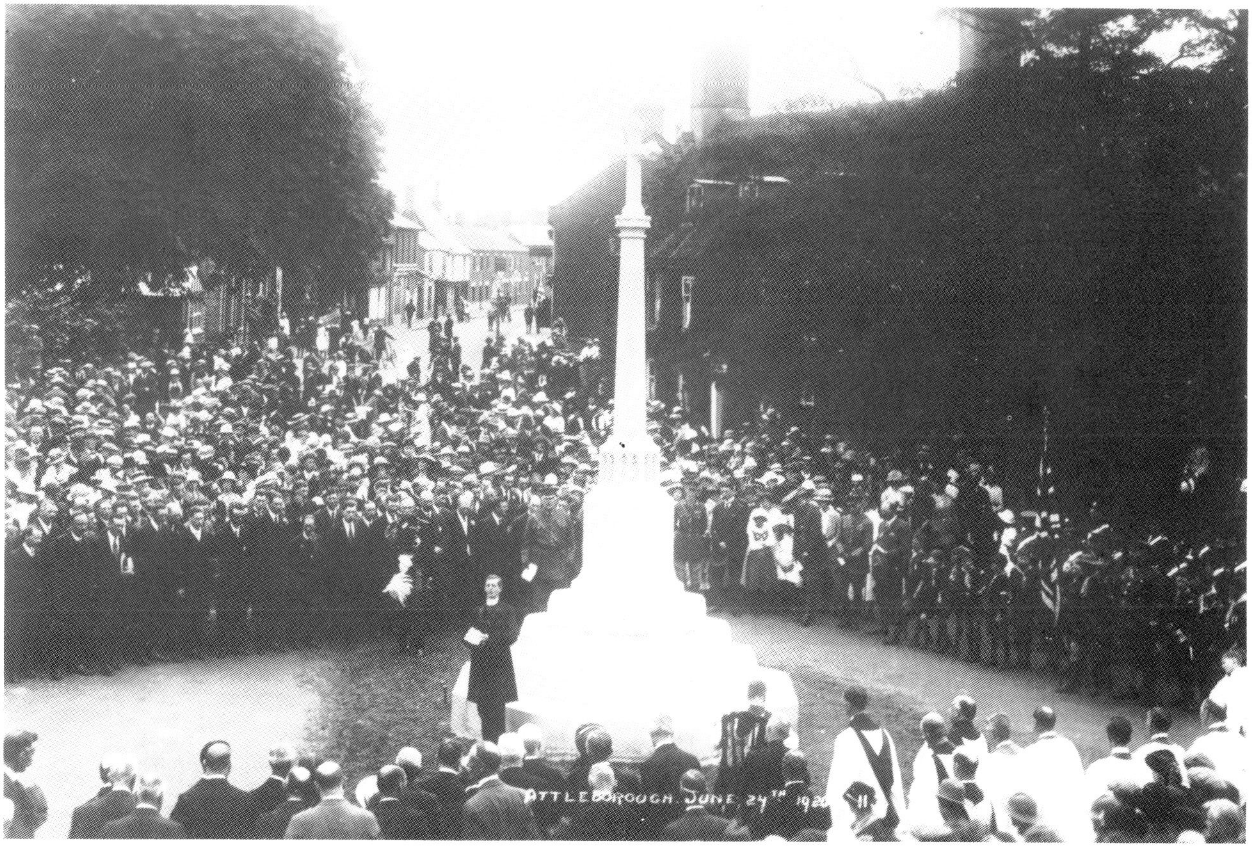
ATTLEBOROUGH. JUNE 24TH
11

Depression and War

Mr Frederick Foster and Mr Billy Allen at the Stone Pits to the north-west of the town in the 1920s. Later, waste and ammunition from nearby American airfields were dumped here

1920–1942

The 1920s saw continuing growth of the town as a market centre. Market day was on a Thursday and consisted of a spread of stalls along the pavements of Church Street, and a congregation of stands selling fish, fresh meat and an abundance of local wares in an open area next to the then Angel Hotel, opposite the Griffen Inn. Naturally hundreds flocked to the market and brought a great deal of trade to the Angel which became a most successful and respectable establishment in the 1930s, with a large staff, dining rooms and large kitchens. Early each morning it was possible to see young housemaids dressed in their familiar black and white uniforms busily polishing the large red doorsteps and shining the brass handles marking out the Angel as a completely different establishment to its rival across the street. The employment prospects for women were as limited as they had been before the war. Admittedly, the labour shortage of the war years had given the role of women in British society a new definition but these new values were a long way short of being established. It was still very much a case of the Victorian attitude towards women and work. Any family of status could not dream of allowing the wife or mother to go out to work. But for millions of others it was a case of necessity in order to feed the family. Work opportunities for women largely revolved around domestic jobs in large establishments, such as the Angel Hotel, or employment in one of the shops in the town.

It was the turkey sales that made the town a thriving market centre in the 1930s. Turkey farming had become a most profitable venture and Messrs Salter and Simpson, Auctioneers, sold thousands of turkeys each year on Michaelmas day. This aspect of the town's past is enshrined, not just on the town sign to be found on Queens Square, but also in the badge of Attleborough High School.

Local employment still largely revolved around the Gaymers cider works and a number of those demobilised after 1918 found work there and, more importantly for those with large families, it was largely stable employment. The work could be hard and the hours long and in recognition of this it was the custom to 'test' the cider over lunch breaks, which on very hot days could result in a very happy but sleepy workforce! Cider was a popular drink in the pubs too and was cheaper and quicker than beer in achieving the required result. Fights were not uncommon and many stories existed relating to unsavoury incidents amongst the townsmen, often late at night and on Queens Square – a natural boxing ring.

A view of Queens Road in the 1920s (above).

This view of the horsepond in the 1920s shows both watering hole and a variety of contemporary advertising on the wall of Smith's Motor Repair shop (below).

'Hollywood' Arrives in Attleborough

The public houses were not the only forms of entertainment in 1920s Attleborough. As if indicative of the oncoming depression the Corn Hall was sold to become one of the early 'picture houses' or cinemas. With the arrival of mechanised transport increasing amounts of

corn were transported direct to purchasers or to Norwich to fetch higher prices, making the Corn Hall obsolete.

The first silent films were shown by Mr and Mrs Yates, the latter famous for her attempts to stop the local boys from throwing monkey nut shells around the cinema (these being the only refreshment available then). No cinema could operate without a resident pianist at an upright iron-frame piano, expert in tempo and tension to provide the necessary atmosphere for the films. There are still those alive today who found watching Mr 'Fiddler' Wright get up steam underneath the stage during a good Gene Autrey western more entertaining than the film itself! Mr Wright owned a sweetshop on Church Street and also played the organ at Hingham church.

Mr John Bracey recalls his first visit to the Attleborough cinema in 1933;

'As a boy I spent a number of my summer holidays out of the metropolis of Norwich with a Mr Potter, a farmer and widower at Wattlefield. In 1933 he had a young housekeeper named Winnie who lived at Wicklewood. Mr Potter was a very benevolent old gentleman and he decided on one summer evening to treat me and his housekeeper to a film show at the nearest picture house at Attleborough.

'The horse and trap was duly assembled and we set off only to arrive late. We fumbled our way through the darkness trying to keep as quiet as possible as we were led to our precise seats and I being a 'city slicker' pulled the tip up seat down straight away and got comfortable. Unfortunately the whole experience was new to Winnie. A few minutes into the film there began murmurs from behind and muffled grunts "Sit down" and "We can't see!" I turned to my right to see what was going on only to notice Winnie sitting perched uncomfortably on the top of the seat unaware that it folded down. She was already engrossed in the film!'

For those in the Wayland workhouse in the 1930s free tickets were provided for films on a Saturday morning and two by two these poor people were route-marched the two miles or so, some in very poor or no shoes at all, to the cinema.

It was a tremendous treat to be able to go to the cinema and throughout the 1930s demand remained high, especially as the 'talkies' began to arrive. 'If I had a talking picture of you' was the first 'talkie' to be shown at the town's cinema. There was great excitement to see this film and a full house had to pay an expensive 6d instead of the normal 2d to watch it.

In the late 1930s the cinema was bought by Walter Bostock, a circus owner, as one of a string of cinemas all over England. But it was to be the early 1940s that were the heyday of the cinema, as we shall see.

The Depression Years

For the majority of the population making money was hard and saving money was a luxury reserved for a privileged few. Payment was usually in cash on a weekly basis and the gold sovereign was the major symbol of financial success. In July 1919 Lloyds Bank opened their Attleborough branch in a wooden army hut just off Station Road next to what was then the town hall, and in 1924 moved to its present site next to the Corn Hall in Exchange Street.

It was to take some months for the full impact of the world decline in trade, sparked off by the American stock market crash of October 1929, to affect the rural domestic economy. But when it came the experience was to mark itself indelibly on those who went through it. It is still possible to question those who were children at the time of the depression and they recall a period of great poverty and hardship, especially for the labouring classes. Some aspects of life in Attleborough at that time reflect this poverty.

A view of London Road in the 1930s showing the present methodist chapel on the left.

Children whose worn-out shoes could not be replaced went barefoot or relied on their parents to repair them with old leather cut from belts, or packed the insides with newspaper. An increasingly common form of footwear was the wooden clog, carved out of solid wood and heavy and hard on the feet, but better than nothing. For those who could afford the proper repairs there was Cockings in Church Street, who had been repairing shoes since 1890. Otherwise, hob-nails could be nailed to the soles of boots, or even small steel horseshoes to the heels. Naturally the boys had more hobnails to carry in their shoes than the young ladies. School life could become a miserable ordeal for those with little on their feet. The post war boom in family size meant that often five or more children had to be clothed and fed and the optimism of the 1920s was not fulfilled by the 1930s.[12]

For those out of work the situation was even more serious. The system of means testing by which the father and/or mother had to go before a tribunal to plead poverty was both slow and, most of all, degrading, yet this was the only way to get any sort of financial help. A father of 6 children for instance could expect to receive 30/– (£1.50) for his family for one week, if he was lucky. Not surprisingly many chose to pretend that they were not below the poverty line and starvation visited many families in the 1930s. One resident recalled two men who cycled to Yarmouth in search of work but failed, and other men who were out of work for at least two years.

Just to the north of the town, in an area known as Crowes Hall, were the local stone pits purchased at a cost of £900 by Mr David Barnard. The flint used for roads was no longer needed due to the increased use of tarmacadam, but walls still provided a livelihood. Pitt stone can still be seen fronting a number of houses in the town, especially on Queens Road. The rest was sold all over the county. The massive stones were dug up by hand using picks or 'eight time' forks and sledge hammers, leaving huge craters which the men bathed in during the hot summer weather. It was literally a back breaking job and specially made eyeglasses were essential to stop flint splinters, of which there were many, slicing your eyes.

The home was, for the majority, a simple and crowded place. Central heating was part of science fiction and the fireplace was where much of the activity took place. It was at one time the only form of heat in the house, as well as heating the aluminium kettle strung above it and the evening stew or pudding beside it. To depart from the fire meant shivering cold at most times of the year. Food had to go a long way. Water was plentiful, therefore so was soup, or in other words a stock cube in a large pot. Puddings were popular and economical. A resourceful mother could make a pudding out of almost anything, such as onions or the cheapest cuts of meat. A sheeps head stew could feed the family, with some vegetables if they could be found. Clothes too had to last far longer than children today would expect. Fashion was a luxury reserved for a few, indeed one tailor in Church Street offered a glass of wine with the purchase of any suit such was the gratitude for the sale! The elbows on jumpers and cardigans would be sewn up and the repair sewn up again if necessary, while fixed shirt collars would be turned when worn out. For the ladies legs there were as yet few nylons in the country and long socks or nothing at all was the order of the day.

Well into the 1930s lighting was by oil lamp and no household was without one. Then came the building of the Gas Works at the top of Queens Road (since demolished, although the Gas Keepers house is still there). Gradually gas came to be piped into homes but it was to be a slow process.

A photograph of the no doubt talented Attleborough school netball team in 1930. From left to right – Back Row: Mabel Chapman, Frances Foster, Miss Nora Greenacre, Dina Gooch, Dorothy Myhill. Front Row: Eileen Corly, Ethel Bugg, Ruby Eaves.

War Again 1939-1945

As if to illustrate that life was to go on as normal in Attleborough, during 1939 the old Post Office was sold. It became the Doric Restaurant on Queens Square. The present building in Exchange Street was opened in that year.

Unlike the Great War, this time the community had plenty of time to monitor the unfolding of events in Europe. From 1936 it was disturbing to see Fascism grow into an untameable monster and there had hardly been a year without an international crisis of one sort or another. September 1938 had seen barrage balloons going up in London and trenches being dug at strategic points, but the action of the Prime Minister, Neville Chamberlain, turned this dangerous situation around and secured what he hoped would be 'peace in our time'. Unfortunately for the fate of millions he was wrong and on the morning of September 3rd 1939 many Attleborough people must have sat beside their radio sets to hear him break the news that Britain was once more at war with Germany.

In contrast to 1914 there was no great rush of volunteers to join the forces before it was all over. Instead the initial fears of bombing raids and invasion gave way to the disconcerting 'Phoney War', lasting from the fall of Poland in September 1939 to the attack on France in May 1940.

In Attleborough a number of preparations were made towards the town's war efforts. A Drill Hall was set up in one of the terraced houses in Queens Road and a uniformed sentry was posted outside every night for the next four years. The 'hall' was also used as the recruiting office and there was always a Union Jack flying over the building. A number of buildings in the town were used to house units of the Army in transit. The Bear public house gave up its clubroom for the use of troops staying in the town. Another temporary barracks was the back room of the London Tavern. Here the sound of hobnailed boots thudding up and down the staircases became accepted by the regular drinkers. A bicycle shed at the back of the pub became the cookhouse and the troops did not have far to go for evening refreshments.

The substantial gardens of the Rectory (situated on Surrogate Street at this time) extended westwards along Connaught Road as none of the present housing existed then. They were utilised by the army and were soon covered with tents and wooden huts. The Church Hall, a prefabricated building marking the end of the rectory lands along Connaught Road, was not taken over but became used for all manner of events during the war. Wartime weddings, dances and school activities were held there, including classes for evacuee children living with families in the town.

The present Wayland Rural District Council offices were at that time a substantial private house which became the centre for ration card distribution. Emergency cards were also available here to those on a short stay in the town. Orange juice and cod liver oil could also be obtained for babies.

In so many other ways the life of the town changed quickly as if the experiences of the Great War had been a practice for total war now much closer to home. The town's children attended school (now the Infant School on the Norwich Road) in the mornings only, while the evacuee children had their lessons in the afternoon – no escape for them! Some children could then go off in the afternoons to help in farm work while others helped to collect waste paper in wheel barrows for use in the war effort. The increased number of children made it necessary to use the church hall for some lessons, and cloakrooms at the school were converted into classrooms.

The legendary Beaverbrook 'pots and pans for victory' appeal had two effects on Attleborough. Though the metal items collected were of very little use to the military, it did have the required effect of drawing the town closer together in the nation's darkest hour. At the same time almost every set of iron railings disappeared to be recycled into Spitfire parts, or so they thought. Not even the field artillery gun that stood on Queens Square as a reminder of the Great War, was safe and was taken away never to return. More seriously, for the children, war took away their sweet supply. Four gobstoppers for 1d from Mr Secker on Queens Square was a thing of the past and not until the arrival of the Americans in 1942 did things start to pick up on the sweet, and many other, fronts. Cigarettes, like so many goods, were scarce. Familiar names like Black Cat, Navy Cut, De Riske Minor and, most popular of all, Woodbines, were available from the right places at the right time.

The threat of aerial bombardment was very real and the town had its own ARP unit based at Evergreen Lodge at the town end of Queens Road. Complete with whistle, gas mask and helmet it fell to the wardens to train the population into safe habits of lighting at night. Car lamps were blacked out, save for a little slit, and to compensate roadside trees had two or three white lines painted round them. Air raid shelters of the cheap

Anderson type spread quickly, though initially they were used as another garden shed rather than a refuge from bombing. Discussions about whether it was preferable to dig in the shelter underground or leave it on the surface were rife – the fear of being buried alive meant that a lot were left on the surface. A main shelter was erected on Queens Square with a supposed capacity of 250 and was designed for those at work and unable to reach their homes before a raid.

Mr and Mrs Baxter were usually to be found on duty each day sitting in an office whose large front window had a sign saying 'Stirrup Pump, Ladder, Ropes' which were available if a raid occurred. The wardens on duty in the streets always wore blue overcoats and helmets with a white 'W' painted on the front and a large shining whistle around their necks. At night the warden was supported by a pair of fire-watchers on each street and the police, all of whom shouted 'Put that light out' at some time during the evening. A fine of 25/– was payable by those who broke the blackout repeatedly or deliberately. One would have thought movement at night was difficult with no lighting allowed but not so. To the north-east of the town at Deopham Green was an army searchlight unit who lit up the sky with horizontal cross beams each evening, casting a dim glow over the town which made it just possible to see one's way home. Between September 1939 and the attack on France in May 1940 fear of immediate invasion or attack from German planes was very real and the searchlights were on every night, as they were during the Blitz on Britain's cities which began later in 1940.

The transportation system did not go unaffected. Apart from posters in the town asking 'Is your journey really necessary' the trains and buses were usually crammed to capacity. Most porter's jobs at railway stations were now held by women. Over ten female staff ran the station at Attleborough, which was becoming a very busy staging point for troops on their way in and out of Norfolk, even before the arrival of the American forces in 1942. The coal fires in the wooden floored waiting rooms saw many a tearful farewell between soldier and sweetheart on Attleborough station.

Air raid warnings became more frequent, especially during 1940–41, and in one raid on the town the Gaymers plant was machine-gunned. The empty cartridge cases from the machine guns of the ME110 fell throughout the town. Though there were no casualties the war seemed very close. A number of Attleborough men were serving with the 'forgotten' 14th Army in the Far East, of which Norfolk Regiment units were part. Thus it was that, with the fall of the 'impregnable' fortress of Singapore on February 15th 1942, into a miserable and fatal captivity went a number of Attleborough men. The gloom was only lightened by the news that America had at last entered the war on the Allied side. Before too long the vast resources of that nation began making their way into the heartland of England.

A 1930s postcard of High Street

The American Experience 1942–1945

The young men of a typical B17 aircrew pictured beside their 'St Louis Woman' from the 452nd Bomb Group and Deopham Green (Courtesy Mr P Ramm)

East Anglia was chosen to be the base area of the American Eighth Army Air Force. One of the first signs of change was the arrival in Norfolk of large numbers of labourers, many of them Irish, who worked for John Laing Builders, the main contractors for Taylor Woodrow. Work began to construct the airfields that would be home for the massive B–17 Flying Fortresses and the B–24 Liberators. The work went on seven days a week and it was compulsory for the local inhabitants to house workers if they had the room.

By this time the Blitz had arrived with a vengeance on Norwich and once again the Wayland Hospital became a refuge for evacuated wounded. At times during 1942 special Red Cross buses arrived almost daily bringing Norwich civilians, wounded in air raids, from the Norfolk and Norwich Hospital. Ambulances were in critically short supply and at times horses and carts were used, with straw being laid on the poorer parts of the roads by local farmers to ease the ride for those en route to the hospital.

With the imminent arrival of the American forces there was a significant increase in security. Along roads leading to the airfields in the Attleborough area barricades were built, consisting of two large concrete blocks in the centre of the road. They were manned by smartly dressed soldiers to whom it was something of a pleasure for many of the young girls of the town to show their identity cards. Pill boxes were constructed from thick reinforced concrete. To the left of the main cemetery gates on Queens Road one such bunker was built with arcs of fire towards and away from the town. At the back of this area was an old dumping ground for the rubbish and waste produced by the community. Two soldiers manned the check points day and night shouting their familiar commands and checking the identity cards that had to be produced if one was to proceed.

The first Americans rode through the town on the back of trucks in long convoys on their way to the two main stations in the immediate vicinity. Station 142 was at Deopham Green, two miles north-east of the town, while Station 144 was situated at Old Buckenham, four miles south of Attleborough. Towards the end of 1942 the bombers began to arrive at their new homes. The low grinding groan of the four-engined monsters was a noise that was to become part of every-day life.

It did not take long for the routines on the fields to become part of the daily life of the civilian community. The vastness of the airfields and their ancillary buildings, combined with the thousands of personnel stationed there and the regularity of their raids on Germany, brought the town of Attleborough firmly into contact with the war. Memories are still fresh. The town knew the sound of the plane engines warming up in the evening, the noise of take off and the endless circling in the skies as the squadrons congregated before setting off, the low rumble of the returning aircraft early in the morning and the meaning of the coloured flares fired from the cockpits. In the early morning mist it was possible to see planes circling the fields for what seemed like hours waiting their turn to land, while their comrades who had fired red flares tried to land ahead of them carrying wounded or dead aircrew. For the injured on board their destination once on the ground varied. The Wayland Emergency Hospital held beds for such casualties, but most wounded flying crew went to the specially built hospital at Morley (now Wymondham College). The dead were taken daily via Exchange

A young Mr Pat Ramm, complete with air crew hat, with members of the 735th Bomb Squadron, part of the 453rd Bomb Group stationed at Old Buckenham airfield (Courtesy Mr P Ramm)

Three distinguished USAAF officers at the opening of either the Anglo Club in Attleborough or the Red Cross Club at Old Buckenham airfield. From the left: Sgts Ralph Mclure, Angelo Fermo and J Kelly, together with General Timberlake (Commander 2nd Air Division), Col Potts (Commander 453rd Bomb Group) and Major James Stewart, Operations Officer of the 453rd (Courtesy Mr P Ramm)

Street in the town to the Cambridge Hospital. On one occasion a lorry carrying five German prisoners-of-war skidded on a road just outside the town and they too ended up at Cambridge.

The townsfolk, and especially the young girls, also knew when the flyers and their ground crew had a chance to relax and head for the town. An active social life developed although, contrary to popular myth, there were no fish and chip shops open in wartime Attleborough to tempt the Americans. Instead it was off to the ever popular cinema, or perhaps to one of the dances at the town hall on Station Road.

The Heyday of the Cinema

Films came to the cinema in Attleborough straight from Norwich. They were on a circuit with other cinemas and left Attleborough for Wymondham, then on to Watton. The feature films were usually shown from Monday to Wednesday, then a new film until Sunday. Each evening the cinema would have long queues of khaki-clad American servicemen, some with their new girlfriends on their arms, waiting to get in. The car park was never full of cars – there were not that many around – but it was regularly filled with rows of large steel khaki American service motor cycles that had been driven from the airfields. It would take too long to list all the films that passed through the Attleborough cinema during the dark wartime years but some of us may remember the emotions and romance of such films as

'Sunday, Monday or Always' or 'The Bells Of Saint Mary's' starring Bing Crosby and Ingrid Bergman.

'Farewell My Lovely' with Dick Powell,

'Piccadilly Incident' and 'Spring in Park Lane' both starring Anna Neagle and Michael Wilding.

'Millions Like Us' about the RAF, and the classic 'Mrs Miniver'

Along with these came the escapism of the Hollywood musicals with Fred Astaire. 'Cover Girl', starring Rita Hayworth, was a natural hit with the American troops as her picture was painted on the fuselage of many a bomber!

It was not uncommon for the film to break down and with a packed house of American aircrew this was not to be recommended. The torn celluloid was repaired as quickly as possible and whistles and cat calls then died down. So popular was the cinema that the film programme was posted up four weeks in advance giving many in the town, especially the young, something quite special to look forward to in those days of danger and uncertainty.

The young were not ignored either. Their time was the Saturday Matinee. Admission was 4d (2p) and the programme ran from 2–4pm. The serial was the most popular, and the westerns the favourite. Gene Autrey and Roy Rogers gave a ray of optimism to every child that saw them.

For the usherettes the wages were low, but there was the compensation of meeting packed houses of GIs, and jobs in the cinema were highly sought. For those over 18 the wages were 18/– (90p) per week and those between 16 and 18 received 12/6d (62p) a week. The hours were long with just time for a cup of tea or a quick meal between performances, but with the clocks forward two hours it was never a dark walk home after the excitement ended each evening.

Apart from the cinema there was the local dance as relaxation. The YMCA prefabricated building which later became the first town hall was taken over as a club for the American forces. Local girls worked as hostesses, providing they had written references, and the dances always took place on Thursday evenings. A

Top right: A B17 Fortress from Deopham Green in flight, with bomb doors open and vapour trails from the four engines (Courtesy Mr P Ramm)

Lord and Lady Ironside with Col Potts and the hostess from the Red Cross Club, Old Buckenham Airfield.

American Servicemen at the Red Cross Club, Old Buckenham Airfield

The Headquarters Building at Old Buckenham Airfield, complete with well-kept garden, bicycle racks and the invaluable jeep, still standing at the present entrance opposite Bunns Bank (Courtesy Mr P Ramm)

radiogram played music by the romantic Victor Sylvester and his Ballroom Orchestra. 'I'll See You Again' was the traditional closing number at 10.30pm, the notes ringing down the surrounding streets each Thursday as the troops and local girls departed for another week. Later on Glenn Miller, Joe Loss, Tommy Dorsey and Harry James made their impact, along with the infamous 'jitterbugging' which made the caretaker so concerned about his wooden floor. The 'NO JITTERBUGGING' notices were put up, and promptly ignored.

The hall also saw its share of wartime weddings and some local girls returned to the States with their new-found loves after the war. The Americans are fondly remembered, not just for their clean-cut image and smart uniforms, but also for their love of life and the hope and dynamism that they brought to the town. Their passing must not be forgotten but recorded as an important and precious part of the heritage of the town.

A view of the Old Buckenham Airfield taken from an incoming B24. Note the bomb shelters close to each of the billets and workshops and the variety of activities on this busy airfield. Most, but not all, of these hangars and huts have now disappeared – as has the concrete control tower. (Courtesy Mr. P. Ramm.)

Epilogue

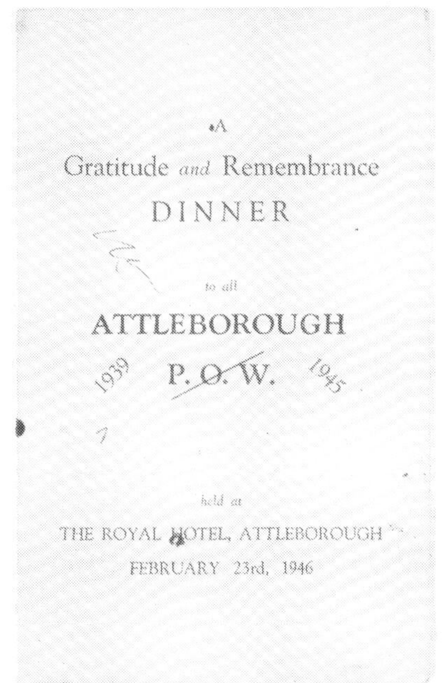

A
Gratitude *and* Remembrance
DINNER
to all
ATTLEBOROUGH
1939 P.O.W. 1945
held at
THE ROYAL HOTEL, ATTLEBOROUGH
FEBRUARY 23rd, 1946

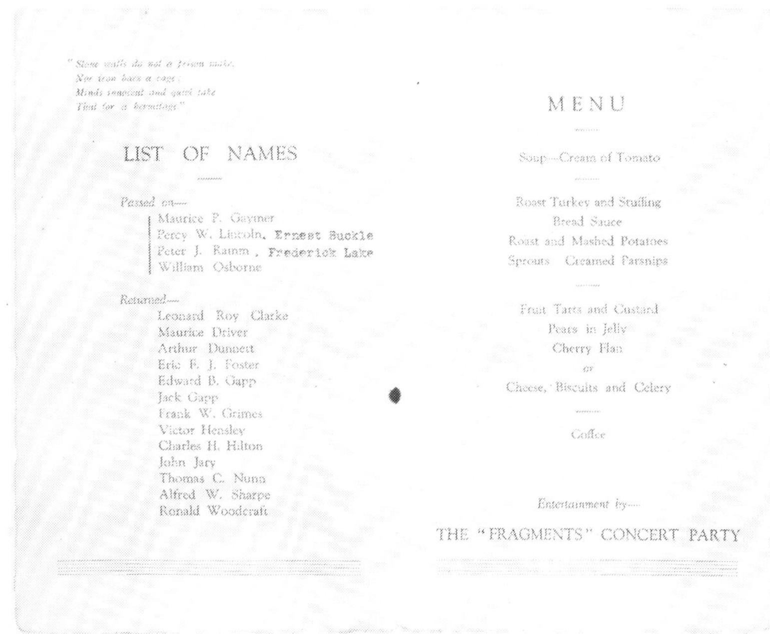

"Stone walls do not a prison make,
Nor iron bars a cage;
Minds innocent and quiet take
That for a hermitage."

LIST OF NAMES

Passed on—
Maurice P. Gaymer
Percy W. Lincoln, Ernest Buckle
Peter J. Ramm, Frederick Lake
William Osborne

Returned—
Leonard Roy Clarke
Maurice Driver
Arthur Dunnett
Eric F. J. Foster
Edward B. Gapp
Jack Gapp
Frank W. Grimes
Victor Hensley
Charles H. Hilton
John Jary
Thomas C. Nunn
Alfred W. Sharpe
Ronald Woodcraft

MENU

Soup—Cream of Tomato

Roast Turkey and Stuffing
Bread Sauce
Roast and Mashed Potatoes
Sprouts Creamed Parsnips

Fruit Tarts and Custard
Pears in Jelly
Cherry Flan
or
Cheese, Biscuits and Celery

Coffee

Entertainment by—
THE "FRAGMENTS" CONCERT PARTY

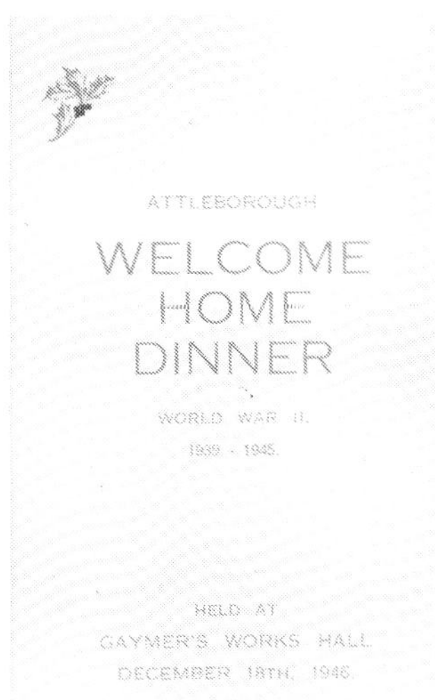

ATTLEBOROUGH
WELCOME HOME DINNER
WORLD WAR II.
1939 - 1945
HELD AT
GAYMER'S WORKS HALL
DECEMBER 18TH, 1946

"Far and far our homes are set round the Seven Seas;
Woe for us if we forget, we who hold by these!"

Toast List

1. THE FALLEN
2. H.M. THE KING
3. RETURNED EX-SERVICE MEMBERS OF ATTLEBOROUGH
   Proposer - Mr. T. H. [illegible]
   Response - Mr. J. R. Woods
4. HIS MAJESTY'S FORCES
   Proposer - Mr. W. Chapman Gaymer
   Response - Major H. W. Wilby, R.M. (Retd.)

Menu

SOUP - OXTAIL
COLD ROAST TURKEY AND HAM
SAUSAGES
BOILED AND BAKED POTATOES
BRUSSELS SPROUTS
CHRISTMAS PUDDING
RUM SAUCE
MINCE PIES
OR
CHEESE

Catering by Langfords, Norwich

Two original programmes for dinners at the end of the Second World War, held at the Royal Hotel and Gaymers Cider Works respectively

The end of World War II did not begin a new and drastically different life for Attleborough. The return to a peacetime environment was as routine as in thousands of other English towns and took just as long. Rationing continued for two years after 1945 to underline the difficulties that this country was to face in re-establishing itself as a force on the new international stage.

Some of the townsmen did not return home but lay in military cemeteries in foreign lands. It is the War Graves Commission that now bears the responsibilty for preserving the memory of the sacrifice made by men from the town. A total of 24 Attleborough men lost their lives fighting in the Second World War, and Raymond Maurice Perfect was killed in the Korean War (1950–53). The town has tried to remember those who never returned. As early as 1946 two dinners were held to pay tribute to the men who had fought for King and country. In February 1946 a 'Gratitude and Remembrance Dinner' was held at the Royal Hotel commemorating those who had been prisoners of war and, in December of the same year, a 'Welcome Home Dinner' was held at the Gaymer's works. After toasts and tributes to the town's fallen the guests were entertained by the 'Sharps and Flats' including 'Hylda (Tilly) Gray with a song and a smile'.

Structurally the town changed little during the 1950s and there were no great leaps in population growth. The 1960s were very different. The 'overspill' programme and new town development brought many thousands of new families into south Norfolk and it was only a matter of time before Attleborough had to make some challenging decisions for the future. New development zones were designated and the first estate programmes began with the building of the council-owned Cyprus Estate to the north west of the town centre. This first step has since been complemented by many other new private estate housing schemes such as Fairfields and Ollands, mainly built in the 1970s.

The traditional traffic route along the A11 trunk road became a bottle neck as it ran southwards two-ways through Church Street, along High Street and out onto the London Road. Thus it was that in the 1970s a one-way system was opened that channelled traffic quite sensibly around the natural ring road surrounding the church. The volume of road traffic continued to increase making even this change obsolete, so that the Attleborough bypass was opened in 1984.

To support such an enlarged population the support services have also grown and the list of those now available is endless.

The education system was radically changed with the opening of the then Secondary Modern School, now Attleborough High School, on the Norwich Road in 1963. At that time the school had a capacity of 300. This has since risen to 600 and is supported by a Middle School opened on the Besthorpe Road.

For many years the town's medical service was provided by a small number of GPs, namely Dr John Rogers, Dr Hamilton, Dr Bruce and Dr Goodwill. Their contribution to the life and well-being of the town spanned many years and their successors tend to the needs of an ever-growing and demanding population from a new health centre built recently in the town.

Many of the recent changes have been the most drastic and Attleborough has changed from a town community where everybody just about knew everybody else, to an extended one of communities within a community. The Church is most active and continues to play a central part in the life of Attleborough, offering a never changing focus of stability and security of which the town can be very proud. It was once common to see the town characters on the streets. Alas they are now mostly gone and were a last link with the Attleborough of earlier times. They deserve a book on their own to draw together all their stories and relate all their experiences. They were perhaps the last generation that expected to grow up and die in their home town. With them was embodied a great deal of what is perhaps missing in our society today.

As for the future, Attleborough will undoubtedly continue to find new areas into which the expanding community can move. One may only hope that the succeeding generations will retain some sense of belonging and contribute to the betterment of their community with an understanding, partially at least, of how it has evolved to its present form.

A 1990 view of Exchange Street looking south-west

References

1. P E Bujak *Bunns Bank: Observations on a Linear Earthwork* NRC Vol 36; P E Bujak *Bunns Bank* NARG News Vol 49 pp21–25

2. According to Barlow the occasion of the Survey was the confusion in 1085 when William tried to find quarters for mercenary troops. F Barlow *The Feudal Kingdoms of England 1042–1216* pp98–99 (Longman 1979)

3. C Barringer *The Commons of Attleborough* NRC 31 1984 pp6–9

4. Adrian Hoare *In Search of Robert Kett*

5. For more information on sources for local history see P Riden *Record Sources for Local History Research*

6. John Pound *Poverty and Vagrancy in Tudor England* pp5–6 (Longman 1977)

7. Ibid pp27–28

8. Article in The Journal October 20th 1972

9. The Link parish magazine November 1989

10. See also *Norfolk and Suffolk in the Great War* Chapter 4 pp47–61 P E Bujak (Gliddon Books 1989)

11. Pte Forster was a relative of the author

12. Cockings has recently been demolished to make way for further shop development in Church Street

Bibliography

T Hugh Bryant – *Churches of Norfolk* (1913)

Blomefields *History of Norfolk Vol 1*

Frank Barlow – *The Feudal Kingdom of England, 10421216* (Longman 1979)

Philippa Brown (Ed) *Domesday Survey* Norfolk Edition (Philimore 1984)

John Campbell-Kease – *A Companion to Local History Research* (Alphabooks 1989)

Peter Daniel and Michael Hopkinson – *The Geography of Settlement* (Oliver and Boyd 1982)

Eilbert Ekwall – *The Concise Oxford Dictionary of English Placenames* 4th Edn (Clarendon 1970)

Henry Harrod – *Gleanings amongst the Castles and Priories of Norfolk* (1857)

B A Holderness – *Pre-Industrial England* (J M Dent & Sons Ltd 1976)

W G Hoskins *Fieldwork in Local History* (Book Club Associates 1983)

M R James – *Suffolk and Norfolk* (J M Dent & Sons Ltd 1930)

Norfolk Roll of Honour 1914–1918 (1920)

John Pound *Poverty and Vagrancy in Tudor England* (Longman 1977)

P Riden – *Record Sources for Local History* (Batsford 1987)

Christopher Taylor – *Village and Farmstead*

E A Wrigley – *An Introduction to English Demography* (1966)

London Road circa 1920.

Index